Baker's Biographical Dictionary of Twentieth-Century Classical Musicians

Baker's Biographical Dictionary of Twentieth-Century Classical Musicians

NICOLAS SLONIMSKY

Edited by
LAURA KUHN

Associate Editor
DENNIS McINTIRE

SCHIRMER BOOKS
An Imprint of Simon & Schuster Macmillan
NEW YORK

Prentice Hall International
LONDON • MEXICO CITY • NEW DELHI • SINGAPORE • SYDNEY • TORONTO

Schirmer Books
An Imprint of Simon & Schuster Macmillan
1633 Broadway
New York, NY 10019

Library of Congress Catalog Number: 96-6515

Printed in the United States of America

Printing number:

1 2 3 4 5 6 7 8 9 10

Library of Congress Cataloging-in-Publication Data

Slonimsky, Nicolas, 1894–1995

Baker's biographical dictionary of twentieth-century classical musicians / Nicolas Slonimsky ; edited by Laura Kuhn ; associate editor, Dennis McIntire.

p. cm.

ISBN 0–02–871271–4 (alk. paper)

1. Music—20th century—Bio-bibliography—Dictionaries. I. Kuhn, Laura Diane. II. McIntire, Dennis. III. Title.

ML105.S612 1997

780'.92'2—dc21

[B] 96-6515
CIP
MN

This paper meets the requirements of ANSI/NISO Z39.48-1992 (Permanence of Paper).

Preface

The American composer John Cage once asked Arragon, the historian, how history was written. "You have to invent it," he replied. Nowhere is the truth of this statement more clearly in evidence than a biographical dictionary, where a collection of individuals, bound tightly together between two covers of a book, is made to define an era. Giving some room to some, more room to others, ignoring the rest—displaying in both what is included and what is not both the ignorance and the prescience of its compilers. Nicolas Slonimsky, whose ignorance and prescience gave shape and value to previous editions of *Baker's Biographical Dictionary of Musicians*, knew this well. *His* history was written not only in what he did and did not include, but in the length of his entries, in their tone, their completeness, and the seriousness (or not) with which they were treated.

Slonimsky's career as editor of *Baker's Biographical Dictionary of Musicians* was launched with a fifth edition in 1958; he produced a total of four editions in his lifetime, the last in 1991, just five years shy of his 100th birthday. He liked to say that lexicography was a happenstance profession for him, but he certainly was no stranger to publishing. Beginning in 1937 he produced a handful of highly original works, including *Music Since 1900* (1937; supplement, 1986; 5th edition, 1994), *The Music of Latin America* (1945), *The Road to Music* (1947), and *A Thing or Two About Music* (1948). He also compiled the now infamous *Lexicon of Musical Invective* (1952), a random collection of perjorative reviews of musical masterpieces, and the quirky *Thesaurus of Scales and Melodic Patterns* (1947), an inventory of all conceivable (and inconceivable) tonal combinations, which aroused the interest of a variety of jazz and rock players, including Frank Zappa, who became a supportive friend. My contributions to Slonimsky's work, spanning the years 1982 to 1994, were various: in the beginning, massive amounts of research, typing, and proofreading; in the end, full-charge editorial direction and original writing. Our work together, serious but always with a spirit of play, resulted most prominently in the eighth edition of *Baker's Biographical Dictionary of Musicians* (1991) and both the intervening supplement to (1986) and fifth edition of *Music Since 1900* (1994). But I was also given the arduous task of transferring his long-in-progress autobiography to word processor, and, once complete, the more pleasurable job of "first-cut" editing. The book recounts, in both fact and fiction, the story of one of the most original figures in the history of 20th-century music: irreverant, idiosyncratic, inventive, full of an almost childlike wonder, and at times as engaging as Slonimsky himself. While his text is only modestly probing, Slonimsky's original choice for its title, *Failed Wunderkind: A Rueful Autopsy*, reveals something about the quality of his reflection. Unfortunately, owing to the jittery nature of its publishers, it appeared, in 1988, under the more benign title, *Perfect Pitch*.

I say unfortunately because the pitch, if you will, of Slonimsky's life was anything but perfect, as his history attests. But that history is frequently told, in his autobiography as in the musicologically sound *Baker's Biographical Dictionary of Musicians*, with a sly, almost silly humor, becoming a hallmark of the notorious Slonimsky "style." No one but Slonimsky could get away with the things he did! Take simply his daunting linguistic command—his proficiency with the polysyllabic, the alliterative, the anachronistic, the mundane and the arcane—which is all the more impressive in light of his early struggles with English upon his own tongue-tied landing in America after the Russian Revolution. For a time, he'd pridefully confide, the librettos to Gilbert and Sullivan operettas were his only teacher. How delighted he was, decades later, to see us running for dictionaries, suggesting, perhaps, that his command was the result of not only a lifelong, inordinate ambition to succeed, but an equally lifelong and somewhat adolescent tendency to show off. A test of the fundamental intelligence of his visitors was often in the area of *their* command: Can you distinguish between "lay" and "lie" in a household sentence? Can you spell "accommodate?" "Millennium?" Where was Guido d'Arras born? Incorrect answers (the norm) inevitably elicited a lecture on etymological logic so lucid in its detail that the same mistake could never be made again. *His* command is seen in its fullest splendor in his neologisms, which, once begun, could run remarkably rampant. In the present edition, these may be found throughout the "Glossary of Terms," borrowed intact from his *Music Since 1900*, but for a particularly full-tilt example, see SESQUIPEDALIAN MACROPOLYSYLLABIFICATION!

Slonimsky's obsessions with the personal habits of musicians, and especially those he considered full-blown eccentricities, could enliven his biographies: the sweeping mysticism of Sorabji, the mystifying superstitions of Horowitz, Rossini, and Schoenberg, Karajan's intermittent vegetarianism, the glorious illogic of Cage's Zen. He was equally intrigued by notably "eccentric" compositions, and especially those exalting the baser aspects of human anatomy. The lyrics to Frank Zappa's *Penis Dimension*, with the soloist bemoaning the diminutive size of his member, were a source of unmitigated joy. A postcard reproduction of cellist Charlotte Moorman's topless performance of Nam June Paik's *Opéra Sextronique* was always prominently displayed, and he carefully coveted his own personal copy of Charles Amirkhanian's *Mooga Pook*, a "tetraphallic symphony" in charmingly graphic notation, which he kept reverently stored, under brown paper wrapping, in a rickety filing cabinet. *This* was taken out, with great solemnity, for only the most impressionable of visitors.

Slonimsky also illogically skirted touchy issues (homosexuality, Nazi collusion, graft) while not skirting others (homosexuality, Nazi collusion, graft), seemingly without discretion or cause. Sometimes the results were disastrous. For the alacrity with which he spoke of such subjects, with or without the corroboration of adequate facts, led, on occasion, to an outraged reply from one or another of his victims. While protests were usually founded, it may surprise the loudest among them to learn that Slonimsky was not only mortified by their distress, but also greatly surprised.

For, as he himself put it, he also had the nose of a beagle, which usually went a long way in softening his bite. He turned this nose not only to the grosser, grander facts of musical biography—people and works, in impeccable breadth and detail—but to matters of musical minutiae as well. Any number of examples could be cited, but perhaps the sweetest concerns the confusion about the weather at Mozart's funeral: Was it or was it not a stormy day in Vienna in December 1791 when Mozart was buried? Slonimsky suspected not, and he became determined to prove it, which he did, in the end, with a simple inquiry to the Vienna Weather Bureau, which had maintained its records for more than two centuries. With what he called a "malicious sense of gratification," Slonimsky put the matter to rest by authoritatively reporting that "the temperature on that day was well above freezing and that a gentle Zephyr wind blew from the West. No snowballs. No frigid weather which frightened away Mozart's friends. No melodrama, except the tragedy of Mozart's death so young." Yes, his was an absolutely dogged pursuit of facts, in some cases, as in his search for details about the elusive fate of Walter Dahms, an obscure German author of musical biographies, extending over years. A titbit of interest to (maybe) ten music enthusiasts the world over (many of whom were backstage contributors to his books) could make his week.

During the last years of his life, as the 8th edition of *Baker's Biographical Dictionary of Musicians* was nearing its close, Slonimsky was in particularly hot pursuit of centenarians or near-centenarians, whom he collectively referred to as likely "stiffs." Was this an expression of anxiety about his own looming mortality? Perhaps. But his macabre interest in illness of all kinds (and especially depression, alcoholism, and dementia) seems to have been an almost lifelong obsession. The facts of a death, indeed the minutest details of a death, liberally litter his tomes. And suicides were *always* carefully noted. But how long would *he* last? As Slonimsky neared the incredible age of 100, padding about his West Los Angeles home in stockinged feet, tinkering with writing, stroking his cat, amusing his guests, he waged a personal competition with George Burns, whose roguish lifestyle, to the end, was a source of extreme vicarious pleasure.

Slonimsky died on December 25, 1995, making the eighth edition of *Baker's Biographical Dictionary of Musicians* his last. By this time, the work had grown to over 2,000 pages, some two and a half million words, and it was literally bursting its seams. All the while, new musicians, representing a wide variety of musical periods and styles, blithely continued to emerge. For this reason, a series of specialized *Baker's* volumes, representing particularized musical periods and styles, is planned, each providing more comprehensive coverage; the standard, complete *Baker's Biographical Dictionary of Musicians*, with its concise overview of individuals collectively representing *all* periods and styles, will of course continue to be published. While this plan will take about a decade to complete, we offer the present volume, *Baker's Biographical Dictionary of 20th-Century Classical Musicians*, as a first step. The 20th century was the natural choice for the first of these specialized editions, being a period particularly dear to Slonimsky's heart. But by pressing as it does on into the 21st, addressing in its detail the myriad changes in music that ensue, this first specialized edition begins to move outside the areas of his greatest command. For Slonimsky was, to the end, a man squarely situated in the early years of the century, as evidenced by his editions. His essays on Igor Stravinsky, Arnold Schoenberg, Henry Cowell, Edgar Varèse, Charles Ives, and other early beacons whose works Slonimsky unfailingly championed, are lucid, indeed prescient, in ways only possible from an inside track. But his biases, belying his ignorance, were also apparent. He was frequently dismissive of late mixed media forms, shortsighted about women, the popular, and the ethnic, even baffled by computers. Developments squarely situated in the end-of-the-century musical world did not always resonate in his beginning-of-the-century musical heart.

This is not to say, of course, that the present volume rights all the wrongs, or doesn't create a few of its own. For, overall, lexicography is lexicography, and Slonimsky's challenges continue to be our own. "Stiffs" dying out of order, indeed. Were that the only obstacle. What this edition does and doesn't do, *its* strengths and weaknesses, surely speaks of the ignorance and prescience of *its* compilers. Its limitations can be quickly surmised: entries contained in these pages are restricted to contemporary, classical musicians only, with complete works lists and carefully selected bibliographies. As in previous editions of *Baker's*, a determined effort has been made to provide as many first performance dates as possible, and especially for large, significant (and potentially significant) works. Pop and jazz artists, idiosyncratically covered at best in previous editions of *Baker's*, have been excised, set aside for more complete coverage in future, specialized editions. The same is true for non-Western musics and musicians: hence the clear, intentional Western bias of the present edition. Abbreviations are, in most cases, the obvious ones, although a list of those in use is provided.

This book has relied heavily upon Slonimsky's work. But it also would not have been possible without the tireless and meticulous assistance of many, many others, chief among them the inimitable Dennis McIntire, whose inclination toward dogged pursuit rivals Slonimsky's at its best. Without McIntire, the present volume (as well as numerous previous volumes, with Slonimsky at the helm) would be much slimmer than it is. And there are others—some in official capacities, some simply close, communicative friends—too many, in fact, to thank personally. All have been relegated to the heartfelt list of acknowledgements that follows.

This book is, of course, dedicated to Nicolas Slonimsky.

Laura Kuhn
Phoenix, Arizona
December 1996

Abbreviations

A.B.	Bachelor of Arts
ABC	American Broadcasting Company
A.M.	Master of Arts
ASCAP	American Society of Composers, Authors, and Publishers
assn./Assn.	association/Association
assoc.	associate
aug.	augmented
B.A.	Bachelor of Arts
BBC	British Broadcasting Corporation
B.M.	Bachelor of Music
CBC	Canadian Broadcasting Corporation
CBS	Columbia Broadcasting System
cons./Cons.	conservatory/Conservatory
dept./Dept.	department/Department
diss.	dissertation
D.M.A.	Doctor of Musical Arts
ed(s).	edit(ed), editor(s), edition(s)
enl.	enlarged
IRCAM	Institut de Recherche et de Coordination Acoustique/Musique
ISCM	International Society for Contemporary Music
inst./Inst.	institute/Institute
M.A.	Master of Arts
M.M.	Master of Music
MS(S)	manuscript(s)
Mus.B.	Bachelor of Music
Mus.D.	Doctor of Music
Mus.M.	Master of Music
NAACP	National Association for the Advancement of Colored People
NBC	National Broadcasting Company
n.d.	no date
NEA	National Endowment for the Arts
NHK	Japan Broadcasting Company

Abbreviations

no(s).	number(s)
N.Y.	New York
op(p).	opus
orch./Orch.	orchestra/Orchestra
p(p).	page(s)
PBS	Public Broadcasting Service
perf.	performance
Ph.D.	Doctor of Philosophy
phil./Phil.	philharmonic/Philharmonic
posth.	posthumously
prof.	professor
publ.	publish(ed)
RAI	Radiotelevisione Italiana
rev.	revised
RIAS	Radio in the American Sector
S.	San, Santo, Santa
Ss.	Santi, Sante
St(e).	Saint(e)
sym(s).	symphony (-ies)
tr.	translate(d), translation
univ./Univ.	university/University
vol(s).	volume(s)
WDR	Westdeutscher Rundfunk (West German Radio)

Acknowledgements

Charles Amirkhanian, Artistic Director, The Djerassi Foundation, Woodside, Calif.
Professor Juozas Antanavicius, Vice Rector, Lithuanian Conservatory, Vilnius
ASCAP (American Society of Composers, Authors, and Publishers), N.Y.
Paul Attinello, San Francisco
Maria Bánkúti, Promotion, Editio Musica Budapest
Douglas J. Beck, Manager of Publicity, ICM Artists, Ltd., N.Y.
Stig Berg, Librarian, Kungliga Biblioteket, Sveriges Nationalbibliotek, Stockholm
Biblioteca Nacional, Rio de Janeiro
Dr. Carol June Bradley, State University of New York at Buffalo
Buma/Stemra, Amsterdam
John G. Clem, Edinburg, Va.
Columbia Artists Management, Inc., N.Y.
Ronald A. Crutcher, Vice President of Academic Affairs and Dean of the Conservatory, Cleveland Institute of Music
David Cummings, Editor, *The Hutchinson Encyclopedia of Music* and *The International Who's Who in Music and Musicians' Directory*
Czech Music Information Centre, Prague
Kenneth DeKay, Esperance, N.Y.
Thea Dispeker, Inc., N.Y.
Donemus, Amsterdam
Stephen W. Ellis, Glenview, Ill.
Michael Fling, The Music Library, Indiana University, Bloomington
William Flowers, London
Richard Freed, Rockville, Md.
Dr. Robert Freeman, Director, Eastman School of Music, Rochester, N.Y.
Rina Gordon, Academic Advisor, Jerusalem Rubin Academy of Music and Dance
Dr. Anne Gray, Editor, *The Popular Guide to Classical Music* and *The Popular Guide to Women in Classical Music*
Thorunn Gudmundsdóttir, Iceland Music Information Centre, Reykjavík
Dominique Hausfater, Department of Music, Bibliothèque Nationale, Paris
Mieko Hirano, Chief, International Cooperation Division, National Diet Library, Tokyo
John Holzaepfel, Atkinson, Wisc.

IMG Artists, N.Y.
Indianapolis-Marion County Public Library, Central Library, Dan Gann, Head, Arts Division
Indianapolis Symphony Orchestra
Intermusica Artists' Management, Ltd., London
Heidi I. Irgens, Brentwood, Md.
Ralph N. Jackson, Senior Director, Concert Music Relations, BMI (Broadcast Music, Inc.), N.Y.
Dr. János Kárpáti, Franz Liszt Academy of Music, Budapest
Michael Kennedy, O.B.E., Music Critic, *The Sunday Telegraph*, London, and Editor, *The Oxford Dictionary of Music*
Dr. Michael Keyton, Dallas
Paul Landau, Director, Israel Music Institute, Tel Aviv
Lars Mahinske, Editorial Division, *Encyclopaedia Britannica*
Miriam Martínez, Subdirector, Public Services, Biblioteca Nacional José Marti, Havana
Karen McFarlane, Director, Karen McFarlane Artists, Inc., Cleveland
Ernst Meier, Head of Music Service, SUISA (Schweizerische Gesellschaft für die Rechte der Urheber musikalischer Werke), Zürich
Dr. Kurt Oehl, General Editor, *Brockhaus Riemann Musik Lexikon*
Alain Pâris, Editor, French edition, *Baker's Biographical Dictionary of Musicians*, and Editor, *Dictionnaire des Interprètes*
Anthea Parker, Reference Librarian, Australian Music Centre, Ltd., Sydney
C.F. Peters Corporation, N.Y.
Larry Polansky, Dartmouth College, Lebanon, N.H.
Svend Ravnkilde, Danish Music Information Centre, Copenhagen
Anne Ricotti, Comitato Nazionale Italiano Musica, Rome
Curt A. Roesler, Dramaturg, Deutsche Oper, Berlin
Klaus G. Roy, Cleveland
Jan Olof Rudén, Swedish Music Information Center, Stockholm
Karen E. Rygh, Librarian, Norwegian Music Information Centre, Oslo
Leena Salakari, Information Services Coordinator, Finnish Music Information Centre, Helsinki
Dr. Arthur Sabatini, Arizona State University West, Phoenix
Shaw Concerts, Inc., N.Y.
Kimiko Shimbo, Secretary General, Japan Federation of Composers, Tokyo
Slovak Music Information Centre, Bratislava
Kerala J. Snyder, Professor of Musicology, Eastman School of Music, Rochester, N.Y.
Sociedad Argentina de Autores y Compositores de Música, Buenos Aires
Southern African Music Rights Organization, Ltd., Johannesburg
Jeffrey S. Sposato, Watertown, Mass.
Samuel Sprince, Wollaston, Mass.
George Sturm, Executive Director, Music Associates of America, Englewood, N.J.
Jonathan Tichler, Press Department, Metropolitan Opera, N.Y.
Helen Turner, Terry Harrison Artists Management, London
Lissa Twomey, Servicing and Publicity Department, Harrison/Parrott, Ltd., London
Van Walsum Management, Ltd., London
Bálint András Varga, Universal Edition, Vienna
Dr. Marion Verhaalen, Milwaukee
Eszter Vida, Director, Music Information Centre, Hungarian Music Council, Budapest
Bendt Viinholt Nielsen, Danish Music Information Centre, Copenhagen
Peter Watchorn, Cambridge, Mass.
Dr. Charles H. Webb, Dean, School of Music, Indiana University, Bloomington
Arlene B. Woehl, Professor of Music, Holy Names College, Oakland, Calif.

Aaltonen, Erkki (actually, **Erik Verner**), Finnish violinist, violist, conductor, and composer; b. Hämeenlinna, Aug. 17, 1910. He studied violin at the Helsinki Cons., composition privately with Väinö Raitio and Selim Palmgren, and conducting at the Sibelius Academy in Helsinki (diploma, 1947). He played in the Helsinki Phil. (1936–66) and was director of the Kullervo Choir (1956–63). From 1966 to 1973 he was music director in Kemi, where he also was director of the Music College (1967–73).

WORKS: DRAMATIC: Ballet music; film scores. **ORCH.:** *Hämeenlinna,* rhapsody (1945); 5 syms. (1947; *Hiroshima,* 1949; *Popular,* 1952; 1959; 1964); 2 piano concertos (1948, 1954); *Folk Music* (1953–60); Violin Concerto (1966). **CHAMBER:** 5 string quartets; piano pieces. **VOCAL:** Choral pieces; songs.

Aarne, Els, Estonian composer and teacher; b. Makeyevka, Ukraine, March 30, 1917. She studied piano with Lemba at the Tallinn Cons. in Estonia and composition with Arthur Kapp. From 1944 to 1974 she taught at the Tallinn Cons.

WORKS: ORCH.: Piano Concerto (1945); 2 syms. (1961, 1966); Double Bass Concerto (1968); 3 cello concertos (1974, 1980, 1987). **CHAMBER:** Wind Quintet (1965); *Nocturne* for Cello and Piano (1970); 2 cello sonatas (1979, 1985). **VOCAL:** *Fatherland,* cantata for Chorus and Orch. (1939); *Sing, Free People,* cantata (1949); numerous songs.

Aav, Evald, Estonian composer; b. Reval, Feb. 22, 1900; d. there (Tallinn), March 21, 1939. He studied composition in Reval with Arthur Kapp. He wrote mostly vocal music to words in the Estonian language. In 1928 he composed the first national Estonian opera, *The Vikings* (Tallinn, Sept. 8, 1928). He also wrote a Sym. (1939) and a tone poem, *Life.* As a composer, he followed the model of Tchaikovsky.

Aavik, Juhan, Estonian conductor, pedagogue, and composer; b. Holstre, near Reval, Jan. 29, 1884; d. Stockholm, Nov. 26, 1982. He studied at the St. Petersburg Cons. After conducting in Tartu (1911–23), he was a prof. and director of the Reval (Tallinn) Cons. (1925–44) before settling in Sweden. He publ. a history of Estonian music (4 vols., Stockholm, 1965–69).

WORKS: OPERA: *Autumn Dream* (1939). **ORCH.:** 2 syms. (1946, 1948); Violin Concerto (1945); 2 cello concertos (1945, 1949); Double Bass Concerto (1950). **VOCAL:** *Requiem* (1959); choruses; songs. **OTHER:** Chamber music.

Abbado, Claudio, outstanding Italian conductor, brother of **Marcello Abbado**; b. Milan, June 26, 1933. He received his early training in music from his father, a professional violinist; then enrolled in the Milan Cons., graduating in 1955 in piano. He also received instruction in conducting from Votto and took piano lessons in Salzburg with Friedrich Gulda (1955). From 1956 to 1958 he attended the conducting classes of Hans Swarowsky at the Vienna Academy of Music, spending the summers working with Carlo Zecchi and Alceo Galliera at the Accademia Musicale Chigiana in Siena. In 1958 he made his conducting debut in Trieste; he also won the Koussevitzky conducting prize at the Berkshire Music Center in Tanglewood, and, in 1963, was 1 of 3 winners of the Mitropoulos Competition in N.Y. He made his American conducting debut with the N.Y. Phil. on April 7, 1963. In 1965 he appeared as a sym. conductor at La Scala in Milan; he also began conducting the Vienna Phil., leading it in Salzburg, in Vienna, and on tour. He joined the opera at La Scala in 1967, and, in 1972, became principal guest conductor of the London Sym. Orch. In 1972–73 he took the Vienna Phil. to Japan and China; in 1974, conducted concerts in Russia with the La Scala company; in 1976, led appearances in the U.S. with both the Vienna Phil. and the La Scala company, which had its American debut during the celebrations of the Bicentennial. In 1978 he founded the European Community Youth Orch.; from 1981 he was principal conductor of the Chamber Orch. of Europe, which was composed of the former's members. In 1979 he was appointed principal conductor of the London Sym. Orch., and in 1982 he was named principal guest conductor of the Chicago Sym. Orch., which post he held until 1986. He founded La Filarmonica della Scala in Milan in 1982. From 1983 to 1988 he was music director of the London Sym. Orch. From 1986 to 1991 he was chief conductor of the Vienna State Opera. In 1989 he was elected Karajan's successor with the Berlin Phil. However, unlike the aristocratic and domineering Karajan, who had held the title of chief conductor-for-life of the Berlin Phil., the more democratically-inclined Abbado asked for a regular contract as artistic director. In 1994 he also became artistic director of the Salzburg Easter Festival. Abbado's conducting engagements have taken him all over the globe. A fine technician, he is capable of producing distinguished performances of works from both the Classical era and the cosmopolitan avant-garde. Among his honors are the Mozart Medal of the Mozart-Gemeinde of Vienna (1973), the Golden Nicolai Medal of the Vienna Phil. (1980), the Gran Croce of his homeland (1984), and the Mahler Medal of Vienna (1985); in 1986 he was made a member of the Légion d'honneur of France.

Abbado, Marcello, Italian pianist and composer, brother of **Claudio Abbado**; b. Milan, Oct. 7, 1926. He studied at the Milan Cons. with Gavazzeni (piano) and Ghedini (composition), graduating in 1947. In 1951 he was appointed instructor at the Venice Cons.; in 1958 he became director of the Liceo Musicale in Piacenza; in 1966 he was appointed director of the Rossini Cons. in Pesaro; in 1972 he became director of the Milan Cons. He wrote a cantata, *Ciapo* (1945); *Lento e Rondo* for Violin and Piano (1949); *Costruzioni* for 5 Small Orchs. (1964); Double Concerto for Violin, Piano, and 2 Chamber Orchs. (1967); *Quadruple Concerto* for Piano, Violin, Viola, Cello, and Orch. (1969); Double Concerto for Flute, Guitar and Orch. (1995); 3 string quartets (1947, 1953, 1969); piano pieces.

Abe, Kōmei, Japanese composer and teacher; b. Hiroshima, Sept. 1, 1911. He studied cello at the Tokyo Academy of Music (graduated, 1933), where he also took postgraduate courses with Pringsheim (composition, 1933–36) and Rosenstock (conducting, 1935–39). He then was a prof. at the Elizabeth Music College at Kyoto, and subsequently at the Kyoto Municipal Univ. of Arts (1953–77). In his compositions, he demonstrated an assured command of traditional forms.

WORKS: ORCH.: *Theme and Variations* (1935; Tokyo, Feb. 8, 1936); *Kleine Suite* (1936; Tokyo, Feb. 27, 1937); Cello Concerto (Tokyo, March 31, 1942); Piano Concerto (1945; Tokyo, March 27, 1947); 2 syms.: No. 1 (Tokyo, May 9, 1957) and No. 2 (Tokyo, Oct. 10, 1960); *Serenade* (Tokyo, Oct. 7, 1963); *Sinfonietta* (1964; Tokyo, Jan. 14, 1965); *Piccola Sinfonia* for Strings (1984). **CHAMBER:** 16 string quartets (1934, 1937, 1939, 1941, 1946, 1948, 1950, 1952, 1955, 1978, 1982, 1987, 1989, 1990, 1992, 1994); 2 flute sonatas (1942, 1949); Clarinet Quintet (1942); *Divertimento* for Saxophone and Piano (1951; also for Orch., 1953); *Divertimento* for 9 Instruments (1954); Sextet for Flute, Clarinet, Violin, Viola, Cello, and Piano (1964); *Variations on a Subject by Grieg* for 4 Trumpets, 4 Horns, 3 Trombones, and Tuba (1972); piano music. **OTHER:** Choral music; songs; film music.

Abejo, Rosalina, Filipino pianist and composer; b. Tagoloan, Oriental Misamis, July 13, 1922; d. Fremont, Calif., June 5, 1991. She studied at the Philippine Women's Univ. (M.M., 1957); then went to Cincinnati, where she studied composition with Felix Labunski; she later took courses with Wayne Barlow at the Eastman School of Music in Rochester, N.Y. She joined the Order of the Virgin Mary, and was the first nun to conduct a sym. orch. An exceptionally prolific composer, she wrote a number of sacred works, among them *Thanatopsis* for Orch. (1956) and *The Trilogy of Man* for Orch. (1971), and also several secular works on political themes, including a symphonic poem entitled *Guerrilla*, dedicated to President Marcos of the Philippines (1971). Other works include a Guitar Concerto, a Marimba Concerto, diverse chamber music pieces, piano compositions, and song cycles. She also publ. several teaching manuals.

Abell, Arthur M., American music critic; b. Norwich, Conn., April 6, 1868; d. Hastings-on-Hudson, N.Y., Feb. 8, 1958. He studied in Weimar with Carl Halíř (violin), Wilhelm Saal (piano), and Fritz Hartmann (theory). He remained in Europe (1890–1918) as a correspondent for the *Musical Courier* and other publications. He knew Brahms, and also was a friend of Richard Strauss, Max Bruch, Joseph Joachim, and other celebrated musicians. In 1955 he publ. a book of memoirs, *Talks with Great Composers*.

Abendroth, Hermann, prominent German conductor and pedagogue; b. Frankfurt am Main, Jan. 19, 1883; d. Jena, May 29, 1956. He studied in Munich with Wirzel-Langenham (piano), Mottl (conducting), and Thuille (composition). In 1903–04 he conducted the Munich Orchestral Soc. In 1905 he went to Lübeck as a sym. conductor (until 1911), and also conducted the City Theater (1907–11). After serving as music director in Essen (1911–15), he was appointed music director of the Gürzenich Orch. and director of the Cons. in Cologne in 1915. In 1918 he was made Cologne's Generalmusikdirektor. In 1933 the Nazi government removed him from his positions, but in 1934 he was appointed music director of the Leipzig Gewandhaus Orch., succeeding Bruno Walter, who had been removed as a Jew. Abendroth also served as a prof. at the Leipzig Cons. With the collapse of the Nazi regime in 1945, he remained in the Eastern sector of Germany as music director of the Weimar National Theater. In 1946 he was made Generalmusikdirektor there. In 1949 he became chief conductor of the Leipzig Radio Sym. Orch., and then of the (East) Berlin Radio Sym. Orch. in 1953. Abendroth's willingness to serve the Nazi and East German Communist regimes made him suspect in some circles but there was no denying his distinction as an interpreter of the Austro-German masters.

Abert, Anna Amalie, distinguished German musicologist, daughter of **Hermann Abert**; b. Halle, Sept. 19, 1906; d. Kiel, Jan. 4, 1996. She studied musicology with her father, with Blume, and with Sachs at the Univ. of Berlin (Ph.D., 1934, with the diss. *Die stilistischen Voraussetzungen der "Cantiones sacrae" von Heinrich Schütz*); she then joined the staff of the Univ. of Kiel, where she completed her Habilitation in 1943 with *Claudio Monteverdi und das musikalische Drama* (publ. in Lippstadt, 1954); in 1950 she became a prof. there, and also a research fellow in 1962; she retired in 1971. From 1949 to 1958 she was an ed. of *Die Musik in Geschichte und Gegenwart*. She contributed important articles to the *Mozart-Jahrbuch*; her writings also include *Christoph Willibald Gluck* (Munich, 1959); *Die Opern Mozarts* (Wolfenbüttel, 1970; Eng. tr. in *The New Oxford History of Music*, vol. VII, London, 1973); *Richard Strauss: Die Opern* (Velber, 1972).

BIBL.: K. Hortschansky, ed., *Opernstudien: A.A. A. zum 65. Geburtstag* (Tutzing, 1975).

Abert, Hermann, eminent German musicologist, father of **Anna Amalie Abert**; b. Stuttgart, March 25, 1871; d. there, Aug. 13, 1927. He studied with his father, Johann Joseph Abert (b. Kochowitz, Sept. 20, 1832; d. Stuttgart, April 1, 1915); then with Bellermann, Fleischer, and Friedlaender in Berlin; he received his Ph.D. from the Univ. of Berlin in 1897 with the diss. *Die Lehre vom Ethos in der griechischen Musik* (publ. in Leipzig, 1899); completed his Habilitation in 1902 at the Univ. of Halle with *Die ästhetischen Grundsätze der mittelalterlichen Melodiebildung* (publ. in Halle, 1902); was named honorary prof. there in 1909 and lecturer in 1911. In 1920 he became prof. at the Univ. of Leipzig and, in 1923, at the Univ. of Berlin. He was one of the outstanding scholars of his time, noted for his wide-ranging musicological interests. Among his important writings, his exhaustively rewritten and revised ed. of Jahn's biography of Mozart is still valuable; it was publ. as *Wolfgang Amadeus Mozart: Neu bearbeitete und erweitert Ausgabe von Otto Jahns "Mozart"* (2 vols., Leipzig, 1919–21; further rev. by his daughter and publ. in 1955–56). Other books include *Robert Schumann* (Berlin, 1903; 4th ed., 1920); *Die Musikanschauung* *des Mittelalters und ihre Grundlagen* (Halle, 1905); *Niccolo Jommelli als Opernkomponist* (Halle, 1908); *Goethe und die Musik* (Engelhorn, 1922); he also wrote a biography of his father (Leipzig, 1916). His collected writings were posthumously ed. by F. Blume as *Gesammelte Schriften und Vorträge* (Halle, 1929).

BIBL.: F. Blume, ed., *Gedenkschrift für H. A. von seinen Schulern* (Halle, 1928); H. Brockhaus, *H. A.s Konzeption der musikalischen Historiographie* (Habilitationsschrift, Humboldt Univ. of Berlin, 1966); A. Abert, "H. A.s Weg zur Musikwissenschaft," in *Musa—Mens—Musici: Im Gedenken an Walther Vetter* (Leipzig, 1969).

Abraham, Gerald (Ernest Heal), eminent English musicologist; b. Newport, Isle of Wight, March 9, 1904; d. Midhurst, March 18, 1988. A man of many and varied interests, he studied philology and mastered the Russian language. He was active with the BBC (1935–47) and served as ed. of the *Monthly Musical Record* (1945–60); after being the first prof. of music at the Univ. of Liverpool (1947–62), he returned to the BBC as assistant controller of music (1962–74). In 1974 he was made a Commander of the Order of the British Empire. He publ. *Borodin: The Composer and His Music* (1927; 2nd ed., 1935); *This Modern Stuff* (1933; 2nd ed., rev., 1952, as *This Modern Music*; 3rd ed., 1955); *Studies in Russian Music* (1935; 2nd ed., 1969); *Masters of Russian Music* (with M. Calvocoressi, 1936; 2nd ed., rev., 1958); *A Hundred Years of Music* (1938; 4th ed., rev., 1974); *Chopin's Musical Style* (1939); *On Russian Music* (1939); *Beethoven's Second-period Quartets* (1942); *Eight Soviet Composers* (1943); *Tchaikovsky* (1944); *Rimsky-Korsakov: A Short Biography* (1945); *Design in Music* (1949); *Slavonic and Romantic Music* (1968); *The Tradition of Western Music* (1974); *The Concise Oxford History of Music* (1979); *Essays on Russian and East European Music* (1985). He also ed. Calvocoressi's *Mussorgsky* (1946; 2nd ed., rev., 1974) and symposiums on Tchaikovsky (1945), Schubert (1946; 2nd ed., 1952), Sibelius (1947; 2nd ed., 1952), Grieg (1948; 2nd ed., 1952), Schumann (1952), and Handel (1954). For *The New Oxford History of Music*, he ed. vol. III, *Ars Nova and the Renaissance 1300–1540* (with A. Hughes, 1960), vol. IV, *The Age of Humanism 1540–1630* (1968), vol. VIII, *The Age of Beethoven* (1982), and vol. IX, *Romanticism 1830–1890* (1990).

Abraham, Paul (originally, **Pál Ábrahám**), Hungarian composer; b. Apatin, Nov. 2, 1892; d. Hamburg, May 6, 1960. He studied in Budapest, and began his career as a composer of serious scores. Turning his attention to lighter music, he became conductor and composer at the Fővárosi Operettszinház in 1927. He scored his greatest success with the operetta *Viktória* (Budapest, Feb. 21, 1930), which subsequently was performed widely abroad. Other works of merit included the operettas *Die Blume von Hawaii* (Leipzig, July 24, 1931) and *Ball im Savoy* (Berlin, Dec. 23, 1932), and his film score for *Die Privat-sekretärin* (1931). With the rise of the Nazi regime, Abraham left Europe and settled in the U.S. in 1938, where he made ends meet as a pianist. He eventually settled in Hamburg, ill and largely forgotten. All the same, several of his works continued to be revived long after his death.

WORKS: MUSIC THEATER: *Zenebona* (Budapest, March 2, 1928); *Az utolsó Verebély lány* (Budapest, Oct. 13, 1928); *Szeretem a feleségem* (Budapest, June 15, 1929); *Viktória* (Budapest, Feb. 21, 1930; also known as *Viktoria und ihr Husar*); *Die Blume von Hawaii* (Leipzig, July 24, 1931); *Ball im Savoy* (Berlin, Dec. 23, 1932); *Märchen im Grand-Hotel* (Vienna, March 29, 1934); *Viki* (Budapest, Jan. 26, 1935); *Történnek még csodák* (Budapest, April 20, 1935); *Dschainah, das Mädchen aus dem Tanzhaus* (Vienna, Dec. 20, 1935); *3:1 a szerelem javára* (Budapest, Dec. 18, 1936); *Roxy und ihr Wunderteam* (Vienna, March 25, 1937); *Júlia* (Budapest, Dec. 23, 1937); *Fehér hattyú* (Budapest, Dec. 23, 1938).

BIBL.: G. Sebestyén, *P. A.: Aus dem Leben eines Operettenkomponisten* (Vienna, 1987).

Abrahamsen, Hans, Danish composer; b. Copenhagen, Dec. 23, 1952. He studied horn, theory, and music history at the Royal Danish Cons. of Music in Copenhagen (1969–71), then composition at the Jutland Academy of Music in Århus with Gudmundsen-Holmgreen and Nørgård. His music presents an effective blend of folkloric Scandinavian elements and modernistic devices often veering off into atonal melos, vitalized by polyrhythmic dynamic contrasts.

WORKS: ORCH.: *Skum* (Foam; 1970); Sym. in C (1972); 2 numbered syms. (1974, 1982); *Stratifications* (1973–75); *Nacht und Trompeten* (1981; Berlin, March 25, 1982); *Märchenbilder* for 14 Players (1984; London, Feb. 7, 1985); Cello Concerto (1987). **CHAMBER:** *Fantasy Pieces after Hans-Jorgen Nielsen* for Flute, Horn, Cello, and Piano (1969; rev. 1976); *October* for Piano, left hand (1969; rev. 1976); *Herbst* for Tenor, Flute, Guitar, and Cello (1970–72; rev. 1977); *Round and In Between* for Brass Quintet (1972); 2 woodwind quintets: No. 1, *Landscapes* (1972) and No. 2, *Walden* (1978); *Nocturnes*, 4 pieces for Flute and Piano (1972); *Flowersongs* for 3 Flutes (1973); *Scraps* for Cello and Piano (1973); 2 string quartets: No. 1, *10 Preludes* (1973) and No. 2 (1981); *Flush* for Saxophone (1974; rev. 1979); *Songs of Denmark* for Soprano and 5 Instruments (1974; rev. 1976); *Double* for Flute and Guitar (1975); *Winternacht* for 7 Instruments (1976–79); *Canzone* for Accordion (1978); *Aria* for Soprano and 4 Instruments (1979); *Geduldspiel* for 10 Instruments (1980); *6 Pieces* for Violin, Horn, and Piano (1984); *10 Studies* for Piano (1983–87). **VOCAL:** *Universe Birds* for 10 Sopranos (1973).

Ábrányi, Emil, Hungarian conductor and composer; b. Budapest, Sept. 22, 1882; d. there, Feb. 11, 1970. His grandfather was the pianist, composer, and writer on music Kornél Ábrányi (b. Szentgyörgy-Ábrányi, Oct. 15, 1822; d. Budapest, Dec. 20, 1903). He studied composition with Koessler at the Royal Academy of Music in Budapest and conducting with Nikisch in Leipzig. After conducting in Cologne (1904–07) and Hannover (1907–11), he returned to Budapest as conductor at the Royal Opera; also was director of the municipal theater (1921–26). He wrote the operas *A ködkirály* (The King of the Mist; Budapest, 1902); *Monna Vanna* (Budapest, March 2, 1907); *Paolo e Francesca* (Budapest, Jan. 13, 1912); *Don Quijote* (Budapest, Nov. 30, 1917); *Ave Maria* (Budapest, 1922); *Az éneklő dervis* (Singing Dervishes; 1935); *Liliomos herceg* (The Prince with the Lillies; 1938); *Bizánc* (Byzantium; 1942); *Éva boszorkány* (Sorceress Eve; 1944); *Balatoni rege* (The Tale of Balaton; 1945); *A Tamás templom karnagya* (The Cantor of St. Thomas Church; 1947).

Abravanel, Maurice, distinguished Greek-born American conductor of Spanish-Portuguese Sephardic descent; b. Saloniki, Jan. 6, 1903; d. Salt Lake City, Sept. 22, 1993. He attended the univs. of Lausanne (1919–21) and Zürich (1921–22) before studying composition in Berlin with Kurt Weill. In 1924 he made his conducting debut in Berlin, and then conducted widely in Germany until he was compelled to go to Paris by the advent of the Nazis in 1933. After touring Australia (1934–36), he made his Metropolitan Opera debut in N.Y. conducting *Samson et Dalila* on Dec. 26, 1936, remaining on its roster until 1938; then conducted on Broadway. In 1940–41 he was a conductor at the Chicago Opera. In 1947 he became music director of the Utah Sym. Orch. in Salt Lake City, which, by the time of his retirement in 1979, he had molded into one of the finest U.S. orchs. He also served as artistic director of the Music Academy of the West in Santa Barbara from 1954 to 1980. From 1982 he was active at the Tanglewood Music Center. On his 90th birthday on Jan. 6, 1993, the Utah Sym. Orch.'s concert hall was renamed in his honor.

BIBL.: L. Durham, *A.!* (Salt Lake City, 1989).

Abreu (Rebello), Sergio (b. Rio de Janeiro, June 5, 1948) and **Eduardo** (b. Rio de Janeiro, Sept. 19, 1949), sibling Brazilian guitarists. They first studied with their grandfather, Antonio Rebello, and then with Adolfina Raitzin Tavora; they began their career in 1963 with concerts throughout South America, making their European debut in London in 1968, and their U.S. debut in N.Y. in 1970; they later toured extensively all over the world.

Absil, Jean, eminent Belgian composer and pedagogue; b. Bonsecours, Oct. 23, 1893; d. Brussels, Feb. 2, 1974. He studied organ and composition at the Brussels Cons., and later took lessons in advanced composition with Paul Gilson. He won the Prix Agniez for his first Sym. (1921); in 1922 he won a 2nd Prix de Rome for the cantata *La Guerre*; he also received the Prix Rubens in 1934. His first Piano Concerto was commissioned by the 1938 Concours Ysaÿe in Brussels as the compulsory work for the 12 finalists in the contest eventually won by Emil Gilels. He was music director of the Academy of Etterbeek in Brussels (1922–64), taught at the Brussels Cons. (1930–59), and was one of the founders of the Revue Internationale de Musique. Absil evolved an individual style, characterized by rhythmic variety, free tonality, and compact counterpoint.

WORKS: DRAMATIC: *Peau d'âne*, lyrical poem (1937); *Ulysse et les sirènes*, radio play (1939); *Fansou ou Le Chapeau chinois*, musical comedy (1944); *Le Miracle de Pan*, ballet (1949); *Pierre Breughel l'Ancien*, radio play (1950); *Épouvantail*, ballet (1950); *Les Voix de la mer*, opera (1951; Brussels, March 26, 1954); *Les Météores*, ballet (1951). **ORCH.:** 5 syms. (1920, 1936, 1943, 1969, 1970); *La Mort de Tintagiles*, symphonic poem (1923–26); *Rapsodie flamande* (1928; also for Wind Ensemble); *Berceuse* for Small Orch. and Cello or Saxophone (1932); 2 violin concertos (1933, 1964); *Petite suite* for Small Orch. (1935; also for Wind Ensemble); 3 piano concertos (1937, 1967, 1973); *Rapsodie No. 2* (1938); *Hommage à Lekeu* (1939); Cello Concertino (1940); *Sérénade* (1940); *Variations symphoniques* (1942); Viola Concerto (1942); *Rapsodie roumaine* for Violin and Orch. (1943); *Concerto grosso* for Wind Quintet and Orch. (1944); *Jeanne d'Arc*, symphonic poem (1945); *Rites*, triptych for Wind Ensemble (1952); *Rapsodie brésilienne* (1953); *Mythologie*, suite (1954); *Croquis sportifs* for Wind Ensemble (1954); *Divertimento* for Saxophone Quartet and Chamber Orch. (1955); *Introduction et Valses* (1955); *Legend* for Wind Ensemble (1956); *Suite*, after Romanian folklore (1956); *Suite bucolique* for Strings (1957); *Fantaisie concertante* for Violin and Orch. or Piano (1959); *Danses bulgares* (1959; also for Wind Quintet or Piano); *Rapsodie bulgare* (1960); *2 Danses rituelles* for Small Orch. (1960); *Triptyque* for Small Orch. (1960); *Fantaisie-humoresque* for Clarinet and Strings or Piano (1962); *Rapsodie No. 6* for Horn and Orch. or Piano (1963); Viola Concertino (1964); *Nymphes et faunes* for Wind Orch. (1966); *Allegro brillante* for Piano and Orch. (1967); *Fantaisie-caprice* for Saxophone and Strings (1971); Guitar Concerto (1971); *Ballade* for Saxophone, Piano, and Small Orch. (1971); *Déités*, suite (1973). **CHAMBER:** 4 string quartets (1929, 1934, 1935, 1941); 2 piano trios (1931, 1972); 2 string trios (1935, 1939); *Fantaisie rapsodique* for 4 Cellos (1936); Cello Quartet (1937); Quartet for Saxophones (1937); Piano Quartet (1938); *Fantaisie* for Piano Quartet (1939); *Concert à cinq* for Flute, Violin, Viola, Cello, and Harp (1939); 2 suites for Cello and Piano (1942, 1968); *Chaconne* for Violin (1949); *3 Contes* for Trumpet and Piano (1951); Suite for Trombone and Piano (1952); *Sonatine en duo* for Violin and Viola (1962); Saxophone Sonata (1963); *3 Pièces* for Organ (1965); Quartet for Clarinets (1967); Sonata for Solo Violin (1967); *Croquis pour un carnaval* for 4 Clarinets and Harp (1968); *Suite mystique* for 4 Flutes (1969); Violin Sonata (1970); *Esquisses* for Wind Quartet (1971); *Images stellaires* for Violin and Cello (1973); also numerous guitar pieces. **PIANO:** *3 Impromptus* (1932); 3 sonatinas (1937, 1939, 1965); *3 Marines* (1939); *Bagatelles* (1944); *2 Grand Suites* (1944, 1962); *Sketches on the 7 Capital Sins* (1954); *Variations* (1956); *Chess Game*, suite (1957); *Passacaglia* (1959); *Rapsodie No. 5* for 2 Pianos (1959); *Humoresques* (1965); *Ballade* (1966); *Asymétries* for 2 Pianos (1968); *Alternances* (1968); *Féeries* (1971); *Poésie et vélocité*, 20 pieces (1972). **VOCAL:** *La Guerre*, cantata (1922); *Philatélie*, chamber cantata (1940); *Les Bénédictions*, cantata (1941); *Les Chants du mort*, cantata for Vocal Quartet and Small Orch. (1941); *Le Zodiaque* for Chorus, Piano, and Orch. (1949); *Phantasmes* for Contralto, Saxophone, Piano, and Percussion (1950); *Le Cirque volant*, cantata (1953); *Petites polyphonies* for 2 Voices and Orch. (1966); *À cloche-pied* for Children's Chorus and Orch. (1968).

BIBL.: R. de Guide, *J. A.: Vie et oeuvre* (Tournai, 1965).

Accardo, Salvatore, outstanding Italian violinist and conductor; b. Turin, Sept. 26, 1941. He studied with Luigi d'Ambrosio at the Conservatorio S. Pietro a Majella in Naples and with Yvonne Astruc at the Accademia Musicale Chigiana in Siena. He won the Vercelli (1955), Geneva (1956), and Paganini (Genoa, 1958) competitions, then pursued a remarkable career, appearing both as soloist with major orchs. of the world and as recitalist. He was also active in later years as a conductor. In 1993 he was appointed music director of the Teatro San Carlo in Naples. He publ. *L'arte del violino* (ed. by M. Delogu; Milan, 1987). As a violin virtuoso, Accardo excels in a vast repertoire; in addition to the standard literature, he performs many rarely heard works, including those by Paganini. His playing is marked by a fidelity to the classical school of violin playing, in which virtuosity is subordinated to stylistic propriety.

Achron, Isidor, Lithuanian-born American pianist, teacher, and composer, brother of **Joseph Achron**; b. Warsaw, Nov. 24, 1892; d. N.Y., May 12, 1948. He studied with Essipova (piano), Liadov (composition), and Steinberg (orchestration) at the St. Petersburg Cons. In 1922 he settled in the U.S., becoming a naturalized American citizen in 1928. After serving as accompanist to Heifetz (1922–33), he pursued a career as a soloist with orchs. and as a recitalist. His compositions, all in the moderate Romantic manner prevalent of his time, included 2 pianos concertos (No. 1, N.Y., Dec. 9, 1937, composer soloist, and No. 2, 1942), a *Suite Grotesque* for Orch. (St. Louis, Jan. 30, 1942), and numerous works for Piano and Violin.

Achron, Joseph, Lithuanian-born American violinist and composer, brother of **Isidor Achron**; b. Łozdzieje, Russian Poland, May 13, 1886; d. Los Angeles, April 29, 1943. He studied violin in Warsaw and made his debut there at age 7; then was a pupil of Auer (violin) and Liadov (composition) at the St. Petersburg Cons. (1898–1904), where he also later studied theory and composition (1907). After a sojourn in Palestine (1924–25), he settled in the U.S. and became a naturalized American citizen in 1928. In 1934 he went to Hollywood, where he was active as a violinist and composer. His early works are marked by characteristic Russian harmonies with a distinctly Romantic aura; later he developed an idiom based on structural principles employing atonal and polytonal devices. In his *Golem Suite* for Chamber Orch. (1932), the last section is the exact retrograde movement of the first sections, which symbolizes the undoing of the monster Golem.

WORKS: ORCH.: *Hazan* for Cello and Orch. (1912); 3 violin concertos: No. 1 (Boston, Jan. 24, 1927, composer soloist), No. 2 (Los Angeles, Dec. 19, 1936, composer soloist), and No. 3 (Los Angeles, March 31, 1939, composer soloist); *Golem Suite* for Chamber Orch. (1932); Piano Concerto (1941). **CHAMBER:** *4 tableaux fantastiques* for Violin and Piano (1907); *Chromatic String Quartet* (1907); 2 violin sonatas (1910, 1918); *Hebrew Melody* for Violin and Piano (1911); *2 Hebrew Pieces* for Violin and Piano (1912); *Suite bizarre* for Violin and Piano (1916); *Elegy* for String Quartet (1927); Sextet for Flute, Oboe, Clarinet, Bassoon, Horn, and Trumpet (1938). **OTHER:** Piano pieces; choral works; film music.

BIBL.: P. Moddel, *J. A.* (Tel Aviv, 1966).

Achucarro, Joaquín, Spanish pianist; b. Bilbao, Nov. 1, 1936. He began to play the piano as a child in Bilbao, where he studied at the Cons.; he made his public debut in Bilbao at the age of 12; then took courses at the Madrid Cons. At 17, he won 1st prize in the Viotti Competition in Vercelli, Italy; he subsequently continued studies with Gieseking, Magaloff, Seidlhofer, and Kabos. In 1959 he won 1st prize in the Liverpool International Pianoforte Competition, which marked the beginning of a successful career.

Acker, Dieter, German composer and pedagogue; b. Sibiu, Romania (of German parents), Nov. 3, 1940. He studied piano, organ, and theory with Franz Dressler in Sibiu (1950–58), then composition with Toduţă at the Cluj Cons. (1959–64), where he subsequently served on the faculty (1964–69). He then settled in West Germany and taught at the Robert Schumann Cons. in Düsseldorf (1969–72); he joined the faculty at the Munich Hochschule für Musik in 1972, where he was a prof. of composition from 1976.

WORKS: ORCH.: *Texturae* (1970); *Quodlibet II* for Chamber Orch. (1975); 3 syms.: No. 1, *Lebensläufe* (1977–78), No. 2, *Sinfonia concertante* (1982), and No. 3 (1992); Bassoon Concerto (1979–80); Violin Concerto (1981); Concerto for Strings (1984); Piano Concerto (1984); *Musik* for Strings and Harp (1987); *Ballad* for Violin and Orch. (1989); *Musik* for Oboe and Strings (1989); *Musik* for 2 Horns and Strings (1989); 2 sinfonia concertantes (1991, 1991); *Musik* for Viola, Harp, and Strings (1992). **CHAMBER:** 3 string trios (1963, 1983, 1987); 5 string quartets (1964; 1965–66; 1966–68; 1971–75; 1990); Clarinet Quintet (1973); *Nachstücke* for Winds (1978); *Mörike Sonata* for Cello and Piano (1978); *Serenata Notturna* for Wind Quintet (1983); String Sextet (1983); *Rilke Sonata* for Violin and Piano (1983); *Eichendorff Sonata* for Clarinet and Piano (1983); piano trios nos. 2 (1984) and 3 (1992); *Kammerspiel* for 12 Solo Instruments (1985); Viola Sonata (1985); Harp Quartet (1986); 2 piano quartets (1986, 1986); Quartet for Oboe, Violin, Viola, and Cello (1988); Trio for 2 Flutes and Piano (1988); Octet for Clarinet, Horn, Bassoon, 2 Violins, Viola, Cello, and Double Bass (1989); Trio for Trumpet, Trombone, and Piano (1990); *Sinfonia brevis* for 10 Brass Instruments (1993); also piano pieces; organ music. **VOCAL:** Choral pieces; songs.

Ackerman, William, successful American composer, guitarist, and entrepreneur; b. in Germany, Nov. 16, 1949. He was orphaned and subsequently adopted at the age of 9 by a Stanford Univ. (Palo Alto, Calif.) prof.; soon began playing guitar, eventually mastering folk, classical, and rock styles. He studied at Stanford Univ., dropping out just before graduation to become a carpenter; as an avocation, he composed guitar pieces for theater productions. He eventually invested $300 to make a record, initiating a business that grew in 13 years to become the $3,000,000 Windham Hill Records Corp. He is among the most important businessmen and also one of the best composers in the "New Age" style, which was created and popularized by his record company, and which generally involves folk and modal elements performed by guitar, piano, or electronics. His company also produces recordings of jazz and folk music and children's stories, in addition to videos. Among his most popular recordings are *Passage* (1981), *Past Light* (1983), *Conferring with the Moon* (1986), and *Imaginary Roads* (1988).

Ackermann, Otto, admired Romanian-born Swiss conductor; b. Bucharest, Oct. 18, 1909; d. Wabern, near Bern, March 9, 1960. After attending the Bucharest Cons. (1920–25), he studied with Prüwer, Szell, and Valeska Burgstaller at the Berlin Hochschule für Musik (1926–28). He was active at the Royal Opera in Bucharest (1925–26) and at the Düsseldorf Opera (1928–32) before becoming chief conductor of the Brno Opera in 1932, and then of the Bern Opera in 1935. After conducting at the Theater an der Wien in Vienna (1947–53), he served as Generalmusikdirektor of the Cologne Opera (1953–58); subsequently conducted at the Zürich Opera. Ackermann distinguished himself as an interpreter of the standard operatic and symphonic repertory. He also had a special affinity for the operettas of the Viennese Strauss family and of Lehár.

Ackté (real name, **Achté), Aino,** Finnish soprano; b. Helsinki, April 23, 1876; d. Nummela, Aug. 8, 1944. She studied first with her mother, the soprano Emmy Strömer-Achté (1850–1924), and then with Duvernoy, Girodet, and P. Vidal at the Paris Cons. On Oct. 8, 1897, she made her operatic debut as Marguerite at the Paris Opéra, which role she also chose for her Metropolitan Opera debut in N.Y. on Feb. 20, 1904; sang there until 1905. On Jan. 16, 1907, she made her first appearance at London's Covent Garden as Elsa; on Dec. 8, 1910, she sang Salome in the first British perf. of Strauss's opera there, which led the satisfied composer to invite her to repeat her success in Dresden and Paris. In later years, Ackté pursued her career in Finland. In 1938–39 she was director of the Finnish National Opera in Helsinki. Her other notable roles included Elisabeth, Senta, Juliette, Ophélie, Gilda, and Nedda. She publ. *Minnen och fantasier* (Stockholm, 1916), *Muistojeni kirja* (The Book of My Recollections; Helsinki, 1925), and *Taiteeni taipaleelta* (My Life as an Artist; Helsinki, 1935).

Adam, Claus, Austrian-born American cellist, pedagogue, and composer; b. Sumatra, Dutch East Indies (of Austrian parents), Nov. 5, 1917; d. N.Y., July 4, 1983. His father was an ethnologist. After studies at the Salzburg Mozarteum, he went to N.Y. in 1929 and became a naturalized American citizen in 1935. He studied cello with Stoffnegen, Dounis, and Feuermann, conducting with Barzin, and composition with Blatt. After playing in the National Orchestral Assn. in N.Y. (1935–40), he was first cellist in the Minneapolis Sym. Orch. (1940–43). Following composition lessons with Wolpe, he was a cellist with WOR Radio in N.Y. (1946–48) and the New Music Quartet (1948–55). From 1955 to 1974 he was a member of the Juilliard String Quartet. He also taught at the Juilliard School of Music (1955–83) and the Mannes College of Music (1974–83) in N.Y., numbering among his students Stephen Kates, who premiered his Cello Concerto, and Joel Krosnick, who eventually replaced him in the Juilliard String Quartet. In 1976 he was composer-in-residence at the American Academy in Rome. Adam's career as a composer was overshadowed by his success as a cellist and pedagogue. His works, marked by pragmatic modernism free from doctrinaire adherence to any particular technique, included a Cello Concerto (1972–73; Cincinnati, Oct. 26, 1973); *Concerto Variations* for Orch. (1976; N.Y., April 5, 1977); 2 string quartets (1948, 1975); Piano Sonata (N.Y., May 2, 1948); String Trio (1967); *Herbstgesang* for Soprano and Piano, after Trakl (1969); *Fantasy* for Cello (1980); and *Toccato and Elegie* for String Quartet (1983; from an unfinished 3rd string quartet).

Ádám, Jenő, Hungarian conductor, pedagogue, and composer; b. Szigetszentmiklós, Dec. 12, 1896; d. Budapest, May 15, 1982. He studied organ and theory at the Budapest Teacher Training College (1911–15), composition with Kodály at the Budapest Academy of Music (1920–25), and conducting with Weingartner in Basel (1933–35). He was conductor of the orch. (1929–39) and the choir (1929–54) at the Budapest Academy of Music, where he also was a teacher (1939–59). In 1955 he was made a Merited Artist by the Hungarian government and in 1957 was awarded the Kossuth Prize. Among his writings were textbooks on singing (with Kodály) and *A muzsikáról* (On Music; Budapest, 1954). His compositions, written in a Romantic style, are notable for their utilization of Hungarian folk tunes, particularly in his operas, i.e. his *Magyar karácsony* (Hungarian Christmas; 1930; Budapest, Dec. 22, 1931) and *Mária Veronika* (1934–35; Budapest, Oct. 27, 1938). He also composed *Dominica*, orch. suite (1926); 2 string quartets (1925, 1931); Cello Sonata (1926); many vocal pieces with orch.; choral works; folksong arrangements.

Adam, Theo, distinguished German bass-baritone; b. Dresden, Aug. 1, 1926. As a boy, he sang in the Dresdner Kreuzchor; studied voice in his native city with Rudolf Dittrich (1946–49). On Dec. 25, 1949, he made his operatic debut as the Hermit in *Der Freischütz* at the Dresden State Opera, and in 1952 made his first appearance at the Bayreuth Festival, quickly rising to prominence as one of the leading Wagnerian heroic bass-baritones of his time. He was a principal member of the Berlin

State Opera from 1953, and made guest appearances at London's Covent Garden, the Vienna State Opera, the Paris Opéra, the Salzburg Festivals, the San Francisco Opera, and the Chicago Lyric Opera. On Feb. 7, 1969, he made his debut at the Metropolitan Opera in N.Y. as Hans Sachs. In addition to his Wagnerian roles, he also sang in operas by Mozart, Verdi, and R. Strauss with notable success; he appeared in various contemporary works as well, creating the leading roles in Cerha's *Baal* (1981) and Berio's *Un Re in ascolto* (1984). In 1979 he was made an Austrian Kammersänger. He publ. *Seht, hier ist Tinte, Feder, Papier . . .* (1980) and *Die hundertste Rolle, oder, Ich mache einen neuen Adam* (1987).

Adamis, Michael, Greek composer of ultramodern music; b. Piraeus, May 19, 1929. While studying theology at the Univ. of Athens (1948–54), he took music courses at the Athens Cons. (1947–51) and courses on Byzantine music and harmony at Piraeus Cons. (1951–56); also studied composition with Papaioannou at the Hellikon Cons. in Athens (1956–59), followed by advanced studies in electronic music and Byzantine musical paleography at Brandeis Univ. in Waltham, Mass. (1962–65). His works are derived from a universal spectrum of musical techniques and sonorous resources: dodecaphonic, electronic, liturgical, neo-Baroque, and choreographic.

WORKS: ORCH.: *Liturgikon Concerto* for Oboe, Clarinet, Bassoon, and Strings (1955); *Variations* for Strings (1958); *Sinfonia da camera* for Flute, Clarinet, Horn, Trumpet, Percussion, Piano, and Strings (1960–61). **CHAMBER:** *2 Pieces* for Violin and Piano (1958); *Suite in ritmo antico* for Piano (1959); *Duo* for Violin and Piano (1961); *3 Pieces* for Double Bass and Piano (1962); *Anakyklesis* for Flute, Oboe, Celesta, Violin, and Cello (1964); *Perspective* for Flute, Piccolo, and Percussion (1965). **VOCAL:** *Apocalypse (6th Seal)* for Chorus, Narrator, Piano, and Tape (1967); *Byzantine Passion* for 6 Soloists, Chorus, and Percussion (1967); *Genesis* for Choruses, Narrator, Tape, Painting, Projection, and Dance (1968); *Lamentation* for 2 Chanters, 2 Drone Chanters, Percussion, and Tape (1970); *Tetelestai* for Narrator, Choruses, Tape, and Bells (1971); *Iketirion* for Women's Chorus, Percussion, and Tape (1971); *Kratima* for Narrator, Oboe, Tuba, and Tape (1971); *The Fiery Furnace* for Chanters' Chorus and 3 Children (1972; based on a 15th-century MS that is the only extant specimen of Byzantine liturgical drama); *Orestes* for Baritone, Percussion, and Tape (1972); *Photonymon* for Narrator, Chorus, and Percussion (1973). **OTHER:** Numerous tape pieces and works for Tape and Voice; electronic stage music for plays by Aeschylus, Euripides, Shakespeare, and others; etc.

Adamowski, Joseph (actually, **Josef**), Polish-American cellist, brother of **Timothée Adamowski**; b. Warsaw, July 4, 1862; d. Cambridge, Mass., May 8, 1930. He studied at the Warsaw Cons. (1873–77) with Goebelt, and at the Moscow Cons. with Fitzenhagen; also attended Tchaikovsky's classes there. He gave concerts from 1883 to 1889 in Warsaw. From 1889 to 1907 he played in the Boston Sym. Orch. In 1896 he married the pianist Antoinette Szumowska. With his wife and brother, he formed the Adamowski Trio.

Adamowski, Timothée, Polish-American violinist, conductor, teacher, and composer, brother of **Joseph Adamowski**; b. Warsaw, March 24, 1857; d. Boston, April 18, 1943. He was a pupil of Katski and Roguski at the Warsaw Cons. (graduated, 1874) before completing his studies at the Paris Cons. In 1879 he made his first tour of the U.S., and then was a violinist in the Boston Sym. Orch. (1884–86; 1889–1907) and conductor of its summer pops concerts (1890–94; 1900–1907). In 1888 he founded the Adamowski String Quartet. With his brother Joseph and his sister-in-law Antoinette Szumowska, he organized the Adamowski Trio in 1896. From 1908 to 1933 he taught violin at the New England Cons. of Music in Boston. He composed works for violin and piano, and songs.

Adams, John (Coolidge), prominent American composer; b. Worcester, Mass., Feb. 15, 1947. He spent the tender years of his life in the healthy atmosphere of Vermont and New Hampshire; his father taught him clarinet, and he later took clarinet lessons with Felix Viscuglia, a member of the Boston Sym. Orch. He subsequently entered Harvard College, receiving his B.A. (magna cum laude) in 1969 and his M.A. in music composition in 1971. At Harvard, his principal teacher was Leon Kirchner; he also studied composition with David Del Tredici and had some sessions with Sessions. While still in college, he conducted the Bach Soc. Orch. and was a substitute clarinetist with the Boston Sym. Orch. and the Boston Opera Co. In 1969 he played the solo part in Piston's Clarinet Concerto at Carnegie Hall in N.Y. In 1971 he moved to San Francisco, where he found a congenial environment for his activities as a conductor and composer. He was head of the composition dept. at the San Francisco Cons. (1971–81). In 1978 he became adviser on new music to the San Francisco Sym. and subsequently was its composer-in-residence (1982–85). In 1982 he was awarded a Guggenheim fellowship. From 1988 to 1990 he held the title of creative adviser to the St. Paul (Minn.) Chamber Orch. In his compositions, Adams reveals himself as an apostle of the idea that a maximum effect can be achieved with a minimum of means, a notion usually described by the somewhat inaccurate term "minimalism," wherein a composer postulates harmonic and melodic austerity with audacious repetitiveness, withal electing to use the simplest time-honored units of the musical structure, to wit, major triads in the fundamental positions, with the tonic in the bass. Adams is a modernist among minimalists, for he allows for a constant flow of divergent tonalities in his works while also exploiting such elementary harmonic progressions as the serenely cadential alternations of the tonic and the dominant, achieving a desired effect. Typical of such works are his *Harmonium* for Chorus and Orch. (1980) and the grandiose popular score, *Grand Pianola Music* (1981–82). Many of his works have been performed by leading U.S. orchs. His topical opera *Nixon in China* (1987) brought him international attention. In 1995 he received the Grawemeyer Award of the Univ. of Louisville for his Violin Concerto (1993).

WORKS: OPERAS: *Nixon in China* (Houston, Oct. 22, 1987); *The Death of Klinghoffer* (Brussels, March 19, 1991); *I Was Looking at the Ceiling and Then I Saw the Sky*, song play (Berkeley, Calif., May 11, 1995). **ORCH.:** *Common Tones in Simple Time* (1979); *Harmonium* for Chorus and Orch., after John Donne and Emily Dickinson (1980; San Francisco, April 15, 1981); *Grand Pianola Music* for 2 Sopranos, 2 Pianos, and Small Orch. (1981–82; San Francisco, Feb. 20, 1982); *Shaker Loops* for Strings (1983; also for String Septet, 1978); *Harmonielehre* (1984–85; San Francisco, March 21, 1985); *Fearful Symmetries* (N.Y., Oct. 29, 1988); *The Wound-Dresser* for Baritone and Chamber Orch. (1988–89; St. Paul, Minn., Feb. 24, 1989); *Eros Piano* for Piano and Chamber Orch. (1989); *El Dorado* (San Francisco, Nov. 11, 1991); Violin Concerto (1993; Minneapolis, Jan. 19, 1994). **CHAMBER:** Piano Quintet (1970); *American Standard* for Unspecified Ensemble (1973); *Grounding* for 3 Voices, Instruments, and Electronics (1975); *Shaker Loops* for String Septet (1978; also for String Orch., 1983); Chamber Sym. (1992; The Hague, Jan. 17, 1993); *John's Box of Alleged Dances* for String Quartet and Foot-controlled Sampler (Escondido, Calif., 1994). **PIANO:** *Ragamarole* (1973); *China Gates* (1977); *Phrygian Gates* (1977). **TAPE:** *Onyx* (1976).

Adams, Suzanne, American soprano; b. Cambridge, Mass., Nov. 28, 1872; d. London, Feb. 5, 1953. She studied with Bouhy and Mathilde Marchesi in Paris, where she made her operatic debut as Gounod's Juliette at the Opéra on Jan. 9, 1895; remained on its roster until 1898. On May 10, 1898, she made her first appearance at London's Covent Garden as Juliette and sang there until 1904; on Nov. 8, 1898, she sang Juliette again in her Metropolitan Opera debut during the company's visit to Chicago, and then again for her formal debut with the company in N.Y. on Jan. 4, 1899. She remained on its roster until 1903, but also was active as an oratorio singer in the U.S. and Europe. After the death of her husband, the cellist Leo Stein, in

1904, she retired from the operatic stage but appeared in vaudeville in London before settling there as a voice teacher. Her best roles, in addition to the ubiquitous Juliette, were Donna Elvira, Marguerite de Valois, and Micaëla.

Adaskin, Murray, Canadian composer and teacher; b. Toronto, March 28, 1906. He studied violin in Toronto with his brother Harry Adaskin and with Luigi von Kunits, in N.Y. with Kathleen Parlow, and in Paris with Marcel Chailley. Returning to Toronto, he was a violinist in the Sym. Orch. there (1923–36). He then pursued training in composition with Weinzweig (1944–48), with Milhaud at the Aspen (Colo.) Music School (summers, 1949–50; 1953), and with Charles Jones in California (1949–51). In 1952 he became head of the music dept. at the Univ. of Saskatchewan, where he also was composer-in-residence from 1966 until his retirement in 1972. From 1957 to 1960 he was conductor of the Saskatoon Sym. Orch. In 1973 he settled in Victoria, where he continued to be active as a teacher and composer. In 1931 he married **Frances James**. In 1981 he was made a member of the Order of Canada. Adaskin's output followed along neo-Classical lines with occasional infusions of folk elements; in some of his works, he utilized serial techniques.

WORKS: OPERAS: *Grant, Warden of the Plains* (1966; Winnipeg, July 18, 1967); *The Travelling Musicians* (1983). **ORCH.:** Suite (1948; CBC, Toronto, June 22, 1949); 3 marches (1950, 1953, 1981); 2 syms.: *Ballet Symphony* (1951; Toronto, March 26, 1952) and *Algonquin Symphony* (1958; Toronto, May 3, 1959); *Coronation Overture* (CBC, Toronto, June 2, 1953); *Serenade Concertante* (1954); *Saskatchewan Legend* (Saskatoon, Sept. 27, 1959); Bassoon Concerto (1960; Vancouver, Feb. 5, 1961); *Capriccio* for Piano and Orch. (1961); *Rondino* (1964); *Diversion* (1969); *Qalala and Nilaula of the North* for Small Orch. (CBC, Winnipeg, July 1, 1969); *Fanfare* (1970); *There Is My People Sleeping* (1970; CBC, Toronto, March 1971); *Divertimento No. 4* for 2 Trumpets and Orch. (1970), *No. 5* for 2 Guitars and Chamber Orch. (1980), and *No. 6* for Percussion and Orch. (1984); *Essay* for Strings (1972); *Nootka Ritual* (1974); *In Praise of Canadian Painting in the Thirties* for Strings (1975); *Adagio* for Cello and Orch. (1975); *3 Tunes* for Strings (1976); *Dance Concertante* (1983); *T'filat shalom* for Violin and Orch. (1986; also for Violin and Piano); *In Memoriam Frances James Adaskin* for Chamber Orch. (1988); *Concerto for Orchestra* (1990). **BAND:** *Night Is No Longer Summer Soft* (1970); *Divertimento No. 8* (1986). **CHAMBER:** Violin Sonata (1946); *Canzona and Rondo* for Violin and Piano (1949); *Sonatine Baroque* for Solo Violin (1952); *Divertimento No. 1* for 2 Violins and Piano (1956), *No. 2* for Violin and Harp (1964), *No. 3* for Violin, Horn, and Bassoon (1965), and *No. 7* for 2 Cellos and Piano (1985); *Introduction and Rondo* for Piano Quartet (1957); *Rondino* for 9 Instruments (1961); 2 string quartets (1961, 1994); *Cassenti Concertante* for Oboe, Clarinet, Bassoon, Violin, and Piano (1963); *Quiet Song* for Violin and Piano (1963); Trio for Flute, Cello, and Piano (1970); *2 Portraits* for Violin and Piano (1973); 2 woodwind quintets (1974, 1993); *Music* for Brass Quintet (1977); Quintet for Bassoon and String Quartet (1977); *Nocturne* for Clarinet and Piano (1978); Cello Sonata (1981); *Vocalize* for Clarinet (1988), Viola (1990), and Flute (1990); also piano pieces. **OTHER:** Vocal music.

BIBL.: G. Lazarevich, *The Musical World of Frances James and M. A.* (Toronto, 1987).

Addinsell, Richard (Stewart), English composer; b. London, Jan. 13, 1904; d. there, Nov. 14, 1977. He studied law at Hertford College, Oxford, and music at the Royal College of Music in London, in Berlin, and in Vienna. He wrote various scores for the theater, films, and radio; among his best film scores were *Fire Over England* (1937), *Goodbye Mr. Chips* (1939), *Dangerous Moonlight* (1941; contains a movement for piano and orch. which became immensely popular as the *Warsaw Concerto*), *Blithe Spirit* (1945), and *A Tale of Two Cities* (1958).

Addison, Adele, black American soprano; b. N.Y., July 24, 1925. She studied at Westminster Choir College, Princeton, and the Berkshire Music Center at Tanglewood, and also took lessons with Povla Frijsh. She made her N.Y. debut at Town Hall in 1952, then sang with the New England Opera and the N.Y. City Opera; she made numerous appearances with major American orchs. Her extensive repertoire included works extending from the Baroque era to the 20th century.

Addison, John (Mervyn), English composer; b. Chobham, Surrey, March 16, 1920. He studied at the Royal College of Music in London. Although he wrote several orch. and chamber works, he composed mainly for the theater, films, and television. Among his many film scores, particularly effective in films with epic subjects and with understated humor, were *Tom Jones* (1963; Academy Award), *Torn Curtain* (1966), *The Charge of the Light Brigade* (1968), *Sleuth* (1972), *The Seven Per Cent Solution* (1976), and *Strange Invaders* (1983).

Adkins, Cecil (Dale), American musicologist; b. Red Oak, Iowa, Jan. 30, 1932. He studied at the Univ. of Omaha (B.F.A., 1953), the Univ. of South Dakota (M.M., 1959), and the Univ. of Iowa (Ph.D., 1963, with the diss. *The Theory and Practice of the Monochord*). After teaching at Mount Mercy College in Cedar Rapids, Iowa (1960–63), he was prof. of music at North Texas State Univ. in Denton (from 1963). He served as chairman of the International Musicological Soc.'s Center for Musicological Works in Progress (from 1969) and president of the American Musical Instrument Soc. (1987–91). In addition to contributing numerous articles to reference books and journals, he ed. the valuable *Doctoral Dissertations in Musicology* (5th ed., Philadelphia, 1971; 7th ed., 1984, with A. Dickinson; first cumulative ed., 1990, with A. Dickinson); he also publ. *A Trumpet by Any Other Name: A History of the Trumpet Marine* (with A. Dickinson; Buren, 1987).

Adler, Clarence, American pianist; b. Cincinnati, March 10, 1886; d. N.Y., Dec. 24, 1969. He studied at the Cincinnati College of Music (1898–1904); then in Berlin with Godowsky (1905–09). He toured in Europe as a pianist in the Hekking Trio. Returning to America in 1913, he settled in N.Y.; made his American debut with the N.Y. Sym. Orch. (Feb. 8, 1914). In 1941 he broadcast all of Mozart's piano concertos. He publ. an album of piano pieces, as well as arrangements of works by Dvořák and Franck. His son, Richard Adler (b. N.Y., Aug. 3, 1921), was a composer of popular music.

Adler, F. Charles, American conductor; b. London, July 2, 1889; d. Vienna, Feb. 16, 1959. He studied piano with August Halm, theory with Beer-Walbrunn, and conducting with Mahler. He was assistant to Felix Mottl at the Royal Opera in Munich (1908–11); in 1913 he became 1st conductor of the Municipal Opera in Düsseldorf; conducted sym. concerts in Europe (1919–33). He was owner of Edition Adler in Berlin until 1933, when he went to America. In 1937 he founded the Saratoga Springs Music Festivals in N.Y.

Adler, Guido, eminent Austrian musicologist; b. Eibenschütz, Moravia, Nov. 1, 1855; d. Vienna, Feb. 15, 1941. He studied at the Vienna Cons. under Bruckner and Dessoff; entered the Univ. of Vienna in 1874 and founded, in cooperation with Felix Mottl and K. Wolf, the academical Wagner Soc.; took the degree of Dr.Jur. in 1878, and, in 1880, that of Ph.D. (diss., *Die historischen Grundklassen der christlich-abendlandischen Musik bis 1600*); in 1882 he completed his Habilitation with *Studie zur Geschichte der Harmonie* (publ. in Vienna, 1881). With Chrysander and Spitta he founded, in 1884, the *Vierteljahrsschrift für Musikwissenschaft.* In 1885 he was appointed prof. of music history at the German Univ. at Prague. In 1892 he was elected president of the Central Committee of the Internationale Ausstellung für Musik und Theater. In 1895 he succeeded Hanslick as prof. of music history at the Univ. of Vienna, retiring in 1927. He was also ed. of the monumental collection Denkmäler der Tonkunst in Österreich from its inception (the

1st vol. appeared in 1894) until 1938 (83 vols. in all). He contributed many articles to music periodicals.

WRITINGS: *Richard Wagner: Vorlesungen* (Leipzig, 1904); *Joseph Haydn* (Vienna and Leipzig, 1909); *Der Stil in der Musik* (Leipzig, 1911; 2nd ed., 1929); *Gustav Mahler* (Vienna, 1916); *Methode der Musikgeschichte* (Leipzig, 1919); ed. *Handbuch der Musikgeschichte* (Frankfurt am Main, 1924; 2nd ed., rev., 1930); *Wollen und Wirken: Aus dem Leben eines Musikhistorikers* (Vienna, 1935).

BIBL.: *Studien zur Musikgeschichte: Festschrift für G. A.* (Vienna, 1930); C. Engel, "G. A. in Retrospect," *Musical Quarterly* (July 1941); R. Heinz, "G. A.'s Musikhistorik als historistisches Dokument," in W. Wiora, ed., *Die Ausbreitung des Historismus über die Musik* (Regensburg, 1969); E. Reilly, *Gustav Mahler und G. A.* (Vienna, 1978).

Adler, Kurt, Czech-American conductor; b. Neuhaus, Bohemia, March 1, 1907; d. Butler, N.J., Sept. 21, 1977. He studied musicology with Guido Adler and Robert Lach at the Univ. of Vienna. After serving as assistant conductor of the Berlin State Opera (1927–29) and the German Theater in Prague (1929–32), he was conductor of the Kiev Opera (1933–35) and the Stalingrad Phil. (1935–37). In 1938 he settled in the U.S. He was assistant conductor (1943–45), chorus master (1945–73), and a conductor (1951–68) at the Metropolitan Opera in N.Y. He publ. *The Art of Accompanying and Coaching* (Minneapolis, 1965) and *Phonetics and Diction in Singing* (Minneapolis, 1967).

Adler, Kurt Herbert, notable Austrian-American conductor and operatic administrator; b. Vienna, April 2, 1905; d. Ross, Calif., Feb. 9, 1988. He studied at the Vienna Academy of Music and the Univ. of Vienna. He made his debut as a conductor at the Max Reinhardt Theater in Vienna in 1925, and subsequently conducted at the Volksoper there, as well as in Germany, Italy, and Czechoslovakia. He served as assistant to Toscanini at the Salzburg Festival in 1936. As the dark cloud of Nazidom descended upon central Europe, Adler moved to the U.S., and from 1938 to 1943 was on the staff of the Chicago Opera; he subsequently was appointed choirmaster (1943), artistic director (1953), and general director (1956) of the San Francisco Opera. After his retirement in 1981, he was made general director emeritus. Under his direction, the San Francisco Opera prospered greatly, advancing to the foremost ranks of American opera theaters. In 1980 he was awarded an honorary knighthood by Queen Elizabeth II of England.

BIBL.: K. Lockhart, ed., *The A. Years* (San Francisco, 1981).

Adler, Larry (actually, **Lawrence Cecil**), virtuoso American harmonica player; b. Baltimore, Feb. 10, 1914. He took up the harmonica as a youth, winning the Maryland Harmonica Championship at age 13; his first stage appearance occurred in N.Y. the following year. After attending Baltimore City College, he played in various venues; in 1939 he made his debut as a concert soloist with the Sydney (Australia) Sym. Orch. In 1940, determined to read music, he took lessons with Toch. In subsequent years, he performed with the dancer Paul Draper. In 1949 both Adler and Draper were accused of Communist sympathies and were blacklisted. After they lost a libel case against their attacker, Adler made his home in London. From 1959 he again performed in the U.S. He commissioned works for his instrument from many composers, including Vaughan Williams, Rodrigo, and Milhaud. He composed some film scores and other works. His autobiography was publ. as *It Ain't Necessarily So* (London, 1984).

Adler, Peter Herman, Czech-American conductor; b. Gablonz, Bohemia, Dec. 2, 1899; d. Ridgefield, Conn., Oct. 2, 1990. He studied with Fidelio Finke, Vitěszlav Novák, and Alexander von Zemlinsky at the Prague Cons. After conducting opera in Bremen (1929–32) and sym. concerts in Kiev (1933–36), he settled in the U.S. and appeared as a guest conductor. From 1949 to 1959 he was music director of the NBC-TV Opera in N.Y., and then of the Baltimore Sym. Orch. (1959–68). In 1969 he helped found the NET (National Educational Television) Opera in N.Y., with which he appeared as a conductor. On Sept. 22, 1972, he made his Metropolitan Opera debut in N.Y. conducting *Un ballo in maschera.* He was director of the American Opera Center at the Juilliard School in N.Y. (1973–81).

Adler, Samuel (Hans), German-born American composer, conductor, and pedagogue; b. Mannheim, March 4, 1928. His father was a cantor and composer, and his mother an amateur pianist. Adler began violin study as a child with Albert Levy; in 1939 the family emigrated to the U.S. After composition lessons with Herbert Fromm in Boston (1941–46), he studied with Hugo Norden (composition) and Karl Geiringer (musicology) at Boston Univ. (B.M., 1948) before pursuing composition training with Piston, Randall Thompson, and Irving Fine at Harvard Univ. (M.A., 1950); also attended the classes of Copland (composition) and Koussevitzky (conducting) at the Berkshire Music Center in Tanglewood (summers, 1949–50). In 1950 he joined the U.S. Army, and was founder-conductor of the 7th Army Sym. Orch., for which he received the Army Medal of Honor. Upon his discharge, he went to Dallas as music director of Temple Emanu-El (1953–56) and of the Lyric Theater (1954–58). From 1957 to 1966 he was prof. of composition at North Texas State Univ. in Denton. He was prof. of composition (1966–94) and chairman of the music dept. (1973–94) at the Eastman School of Music in Rochester, N.Y. Adler received many honors and awards, including the ASCAP-Deems Taylor Award (1983) for his book *The Study of Orchestration.* In 1984–85 he held a Guggenheim fellowship. In 1990 he received an award from the American Academy and Inst. of Arts and Letters. In his compositions, he has followed a path of midstream modernism, in which densely interwoven contrapuntal lines support the basically tonal harmonic complex, with a frequent incidence of tangential atonal episodes. Much of his music is inspired by the liturgical cantilena of traditional Jewish music; oriental inflections also occur.

WORKS: DRAMATIC: *The Outcasts of Poker Flat*, opera (1959; Denton, Texas, June 8, 1962); *The Wrestler*, sacred opera (1971; Dallas, May 1972); *The Lodge of Shadows*, music drama for Baritone, Dancers, and Orch. (1973; Fort Worth, Texas, May 3, 1988); *The Disappointment*, reconstruction of an early American ballad opera of 1767 (1974; Washington, D.C., Nov. 1976); *The Waking*, celebration for Dancers, Chorus, and Orch. (1978; Louisville, April 1979). **ORCH.:** 6 syms: No. 1 (Dallas, Dec. 7, 1953), No. 2 (1957; Dallas, Feb. 12, 1958), No. 3, *Diptych* (1960; rev. 1980–81), No. 4, *Geometrics* (1967; Dallas, May 1970), No. 5, *We Are the Echoes*, for Mezzo-soprano and Orch. (Fort Worth, Texas, Nov. 10, 1975), and No. 6 (1985); 3 concertinos (1954, 1976, 1993); *Toccata* (1954); *Summer Stock*, overture (1955); *The Feast of Lights* (1955); *Jubilee* (1958) *Rhapsody* for Violin and Orch. (1961); *Song and Dance* for Viola and Orch. (1961); *4 Early American Folk Songs* for Strings (1962); *Elegy* for Strings (1962); *Requiescat in Pace*, in memory of President John F. Kennedy (1963); *City by the Lake* (1968); Organ Concerto (1970); *Concerto for Orchestra* (1971); *Sinfonietta* (1971); *A Little Bit . . .* for Strings (1976); Flute Concerto (1977); *Joi, Amor, Cortezia* for Chamber Orch. (1982); Piano Concerto (1983; Washington, D.C., Jan. 3, 1985); *In Just Spring*, overture (1984); Saxophone Quartet Concerto (1985; Leeuwarden, June 25, 1986); *The Fixed Desire of the Human Heart* (Geneva, July 5, 1988); *Beyond the Land* (1988; Oklahoma City, March 10, 1990); *Shadow Dances* (1990); *To Celebrate a Miracle* (1991); Wind Quintet Concerto (1991; Mannheim, June 1, 1992); *Celebration*, for the 100th anniversary of the Cincinnati Sym. Orch. (1993). **BAND:** *Southwestern Sketches* (1961); *Festive Prelude* (1965); Concerto (1968); *A Little Night and Day Music* (1976); *An American Duo* (1981); *Merrymakers* (1982); *Ultralight*, fanfare (1990). **WIND ENSEMBLE:** *Double Visions* (1987). **BRASS:** *Concert Piece* for Brass Choir (1946); *Praeludium* for Brass Choir (1947); *Divertimento* for Brass Choir (1948); *5 Vignettes* for Trombone Choir (1968); *Brass Fragments* for Brass Choir

(1970); *Histrionics* for Brass Choir and Percussion (1971); *Trumpet Triptych* for 7 Trumpets (1979). **CHAMBER:** 8 string quartets (1945; 1950; 1953, rev. 1964; 1963; 1969; 1975; 1981; 1990); Horn Sonata (1948); 4 violin sonatas (1948, 1956, 1965, 1989); 2 piano trios (1964, 1978); Sonata for Solo Cello (1966); *7 Epigrams* for Wind Sextet (1966); *Quintalogues* for Flute, Oboe, Clarinet, Bassoon, and Percussion (1968); *Canto I* for Trumpet (1970), *II* for Bass Trombone (1970), *III* for Violin (1976), *IV* for Saxophone (1975), *V* for Soprano, Flute, Cello, and 3 Percussionists (1968), *VI* for Double Bass (1971), *VII* for Tuba (1972), *VIII* for Piano (1973), *IX* for Timpani and Roto Toms (1976), *X* for Cello (1979), *XI* for Horn (1984), and *XII* for Bassoon (1989); *Xenia* for Organ and Percussion (1971); *4 Dialogues* for Euphonium and Percussion (1974); *Aeolus, King of the Winds* for Clarinet and Piano Trio (1978); *Line Drawings* for Saxophone Quartet (1979); Sonata for Solo Flute (1981); *Gottschalkiana* for Brass Quintet (1982); Viola Sonata (1984); Oboe Sonata (1985); *Double Portrait* for Violin and Piano (1985); Sonata for Solo Guitar (1985); *Acrostics* for Flute, Oboe, Clarinet, Violin, Cello, and Harpsichord (1986); *Herinnering* for String Quartet (1987); *Pasiphae* for Piano and Percussion (1987); Clarinet Sonata (1989); *Close Encounters* for Violin and Cello (1989); *Sounding* for Alto Saxophone and Piano (1989); *Triolet* for Flute, Viola, and Harp (1989); *Ports of Call* for 2 Violins and Guitar (1992); *Into the Radiant Boundaries of Light* for Viola and Guitar (1993). **KEYBOARD: PIANO:** *Sonata breve* (1963); *Gradus* (3 books, 1979); Sonatina (1979); Duo Sonata for 2 Pianos (1983). **ORGAN:** 2 meditations (1955, 1964); *Toccata, Recitation, and Postlude* (1959); *Epistrophe*, sonata (1990). **VOCAL:** *Miscellany* for Mezzo-soprano, English Horn, and String Quartet (1956); *The Vision of Isaiah* for Bass, Chorus, and Orch. (1962); *B'shaaray tefilah*, sabbath service for Bass, Chorus, and Organ or Orch. (1963); *Behold Your God*, Christmas cantata for Soloists, Chorus, Winds, and Percussion (1966); *The Binding*, oratorio for Chorus and Orch. (1967); *From Out of Bondage* for Soloists, Chorus, Brass Quintet, Percussion, and Organ (1968); *Lament* for Baritone and Chamber Orch. (1968); *A Whole Bunch of Fun*, secular cantata for Mezzo-soprano or Baritone, 3 Choruses, and Orch. (1969); *Begin My Muse* for Men's Chorus and Percussion Ensemble (1969); *We Believe*, ecumenical mass for Mixed Voices and 8 Instruments (1974); *A Falling of Saints* for Tenor, Baritone, Chorus, and Orch. (1977); *Snow Tracks* for High Voice and Wind Ensemble (1981); *The Flames of Freedom* for Chorus and Piano (1982); *Choose Life*, oratorio for Mezzo-soprano, Tenor, Chorus, and Orch. (1986); *High Flight* for Chorus and Chamber Orch. (1986); *'Round the Globe*, folk song suite for Treble Voices and Piano or Orch. (1986); *Stars in the Dust*, cantata for Soloists, Chorus, and Orch. (1988); *Any Human to Another*, cantata for Chorus, Piano, and Orch. (1989); *Ever Since Babylon*, cantata for Soloists, Chorus, and Orch. (1991; Chicago, March 8, 1992); *Reconciliation* for Soprano, Flute, Clarinet, Violin, Cello, and Piano (1992); *Time in Tempest Everywhere* for Soprano, Oboe, Piano, and Orch. (1994; Cleveland, May 1, 1995).

WRITINGS: *Anthology for the Teaching of Choral Conducting* (N.Y., 1971; 2nd ed., 1985, as *Choral Conducting: An Anthology*); *Singing and Hearing* (N.Y., 1979); *The Study of Orchestration* (N.Y., 1982; 2nd ed., 1989).

Adni, Daniel, Israeli pianist; b. Haifa, Dec. 6, 1951. He began his training in Haifa, where he made his debut when he was 12; then studied with Perlemuter at the Paris Cons. (1968–69; won 3 premiers prix) and with Anda in Zürich (1970). In 1970 he made his London debut; after winning N.Y.'s Young Concert Artists International Auditions (1976) and Phillip M. Faucett prize (1981), he toured throughout the world, becoming best known for his performances of the Romantic repertoire.

Adolphus, Milton, productive American composer; b. N.Y., Jan. 27, 1913; d. Hyannis, Mass., Aug. 16, 1988. In 1935 he moved to Philadelphia, where he took composition lessons with Scalero; in 1938 he relocated to Harrisburg, where he took a job in the Dept. of Labor and Industry of the Commonwealth of Pennsylvania. Although he never practiced music vocationally, he became extremely prolific, including among his compositions 13 syms. and 31 string quartets. Some of his works show a measure of sophisticated humor, exemplified by his *Bitter Suite* for Oboe, 4 Clarinets, and Strings (1955) and *Petits fours* for Cello and Piano (1960). In 1980 he wrote a Percussion Concerto.

Adomián, Lan, Russian-born Mexican composer; b. near Mogilev, April 29, 1905; d. Mexico City, May 9, 1979. He emigrated to the U.S. in 1923, and studied at the Peabody Cons. of Music in Baltimore (1924–26) and at the Curtis Inst. of Music in Philadelphia (1926–28), where his teachers were Bailly (viola) and R.O. Morris (composition). He moved to N.Y. in 1928, where he conducted working-class choruses and bands. In 1936 he joined the Abraham Lincoln Brigade and went to Spain to fight on the Republican side during the Spanish Civil War. Upon his return to America, he wrote music for documentary films. In 1952 his radical politics made it prudent for him to leave the U.S. He moved to Mexico and became a naturalized citizen. Adomián was uncommonly prolific as a composer. Among his voluminous works are 8 syms.; an opera, *La Macherata* (1969–72); a dramatic scene, *Auschwitz*, for Baritone and Instruments (1970); and choruses and songs.

BIBL.: *La voluntad de crear* (2 vols., Mexico City, 1980, 1981; vol. 2 contains a complete list of works).

Adorno (real name, **Wiesengrund**), **Theodor,** significant German social philosopher, music sociologist, and composer; b. Frankfurt am Main, Sept. 11, 1903; d. Visp, Switzerland, Aug. 6, 1969. He studied with Sekles (composition) and Eduard Jung (piano) at the Hoch Cons. in Frankfurt am Main; also took courses in philosophy, sociology, psychology, and musicology at the Univ. of Frankfurt am Main (Ph.D., 1925). Following further training with Alban Berg (composition) and Steuermann (piano) in Vienna, he completed his Habilitation at the Univ. of Frankfurt am Main (1931). From 1928 to 1931 he ed. the journal *Anbruch*, and also was Privatdozent at the Univ. of Frankfurt am Main until being dismissed by the Nazis in 1933. In 1934 he went to Oxford, and in 1938 to N.Y., where he joined the Institut für Sozialforschung; also was music director of the Princeton Radio Research Project (until 1940). After living in Los Angeles (from 1941), he returned to Frankfurt am Main (1949); in 1950 he became an honorary prof. and in 1956 a prof. of philosophy and sociology at the Univ. there. Adorno exercised a deep influence on the trends in musical philosophy and general aesthetics, applying the sociological tenets of Karl Marx and the psychoanalytic techniques of Sigmund Freud. In his speculative writings, he introduced the concept of "cultural industry," embracing all types of music, from dodecaphonic to jazz. His compositions, mainly vocal, were reflective of modern trends.

WRITINGS (all publ. in Frankfurt am Main unless otherwise given)**:** *Philosophie der neuen Musik* (Tübingen, 1949; 3rd ed., 1967; Eng. tr., 1973); *Versuch über Wagner* (Berlin, 1952; 2nd ed., 1964; Eng. tr., 1991); *Prismen: Kulturkritik und Gesellschaft* (1955; Eng. tr., 1967; 3rd Ger. ed., 1969); *Dissonanzen: Musik in der verwalteten Welt* (Göttingen, 1956; 3rd ed., aug., 1963); *Klangfiguren: Musikalische Schriften I* (Berlin, 1959); *Mahler: Eine musikalische Physiognomik* (1960; 2nd ed., 1963; Eng. tr., 1992); *Einleitung in die Musiksoziologie: Zwölf theoretische Vorlesungen* (1962; 2nd ed., 1968; Eng. tr., 1976); *Der getreue Korrepetitor: Lehrschriften zur musikalischen Praxis* (1963); *Quasi una fantasia: Musikalische Schriften II* (1963; Eng. tr., 1992); *Moments musicaux: Neu gedruckte Aufsätze 1928 bis 1962* (1964); *Ohne Leitbild: Parva aesthetica* (1967; 2nd ed., 1968); *Berg: Der Meister des kleinsten Übergangs* (Vienna, 1968; Eng. tr., 1991); *Impromptus: Zeite Folge neu gedruckter musikalischer Aufsätze* (1968). A complete ed. of his writings in 20 vols. commenced publication in Frankfurt am Main in 1970.

WORKS: 6 Short Pieces for Orch. (1925–29); *Kinderjahr*, 6 pieces for Small Orch., after Schumann's op. 68 (1941); 6 Studies for String Quartet (1920); String Quartet (1921); String Trio (1921–22); 2 Pieces for String Quartet (1925–26); *Variations* for Violin (1946); String Trio (1946); also piano music, including *Die böhmischen Terzen* (1945); 2 Songs for Voice and Orch (1932–33); many songs with piano; choral pieces.

BIBL.: M. Horkheimer, ed., *T.W. A. zum 60. Geburtstag* (Frankfurt am Main, 1963); H. Schweppenhäuser, ed., *T.W. A. zum Gedächtnis* (Frankfurt am Main, 1971); K. Oppens et al., *Über T.W. A.* (Frankfurt am Main, 1971); W. Gramer, *Musik und Verstehen: Eine Studie zur Musikästhetik T.W. A.* (Mainz, 1976); O. Kolleritsch, ed., *A. und die Musik* (Graz, 1979); B. Lindner and W. Ludke, eds., *Materialien zur ästhetischen Theorie T.W. A.s: Konstruktion der Moderne* (Frankfurt am Main, 1980); M. Jay, *A.* (London, 1984); S. Schibli, *Der Komponist T.W. A.: Vorläufige Anmerkungen zu einem noch nicht überschaubaren Thema* (Frankfurt am Main, 1988); T. Müller, *Die Musiksoziologie T.W. A.s: Ein Model ihrer Interpretation am Beispiel Alban Bergs* (Frankfurt am Main, 1990); R. Klein, *Solidarität mit Metaphysik?: Ein Versuch über die musikphilosophische Problematik der Wagner-Kritik T.W. A.s* (Würzburg, 1991); M. Paddison, *A.'s Aesthetics of Music* (Cambridge, 1993).

Adrio, Adam, distinguished German musicologist; b. Essen, April 4, 1901; d. Ritten, Bozen, Sept. 18, 1973. He studied with Abert, Schering, and Blume at the Univ. of Berlin (Ph.D., 1934, with the diss. *Die Anfänge des geistlichen Konzerts*; publ. in Berlin, 1935), where he also taught (1932–45). After completing his Habilitation at the Free Univ. in Berlin (1949), he was a reader (1951–53) and a prof. (1953–67) of musicology there. Adrio was an authority on Protestant church music, contributing many articles to *Die Musik in Geschichte und Gegenwart* and to music journals; also ed. the works of Johann Hermann Schein.

Agnew, Roy (Ewing), Australian composer and pianist; b. Sydney, Aug. 23, 1893; d. there, Nov. 12, 1944. He went to London and studied with Gerrard Williams (1923–28); gave concerts in England (1931–34). He then returned to Australia, where he became director of Australian Radio (1938–43); also taught at the Sydney Cons. Among his compositions are *Breaking of the Drought* for Mezzo-soprano and Orch. (1928), as well as many piano works, including *Dance of the Wild Men* (1920), *Fantasia Sonata* (1927), *Sonata Poem* (1935), *Sonata Ballade* (1936), and *Sonata Legend "Capricornia"* (1940).

Agosti, Guido, Italian pianist and teacher; b. Forlì, Aug. 11, 1901; d. Milan, June 2, 1989. He studied piano with Busoni at the Bologna Cons. He began his professional career as a pianist in 1921; subsequently taught piano at the Venice Cons. (1933–40) and at the Rome Cons. (1941–45). In 1947 he was appointed prof. of piano at the Accademia Musicale Chigiana in Siena; subsequently went abroad in 1963 and taught at Weimar until 1970, when he joined the faculty of the Sibelius Academy in Helsinki; eventually he returned to Italy. Agosti also wrote some acceptable pieces for solo piano.

Agostini, Mezio, Italian composer, pianist, conductor, and pedagogue; b. Fano, Aug. 12, 1875; d. there, April 22, 1944. He studied with Carlo Pedrotti at the Liceo Rossini in Pesaro (1885–92), where he subsequently was a prof. of harmony (1900–09); was then director of the Liceo Benedetto Marcello in Venice (1909–40). He was active as an opera conductor in Venice and other Italian cities, and gave chamber music concerts as a pianist. His *Trio* won 1st prize at the international competition in Paris in 1904. He wrote the operas *Iovo e Maria* (1896); *Il Cavaliere del Sogno* (Fano, Feb. 24, 1897); *La penna d'Airone* (1896); *Alcibiade* (1902); *America* (also entitled *Hail Columbia*, 1904); *L'ombra* (1907); *L'agnello del sogno* (1928); *La Figlio del navarca* (Fano, Sept. 3, 1938). He also wrote a Sym., 4 orch. suites, a Piano Concerto, 2 string quartets, 2 piano trios, a Cello Sonata, a Violin Sonata, the cantata *A Rossini*, numerous piano pieces, and songs.

Aguirre, Julián, Argentine composer; b. Buenos Aires, Jan. 28, 1868; d. there, Aug. 13, 1924. He was taken to Spain as a child, and studied at the Madrid Cons. In 1887 he returned to Buenos Aires. His best known works are piano miniatures in the form of stylized Argentine dances and songs. His *Huella, Canción argentiana* (1917) and *Gato* (1918) were orchestrated by Ansermet, who conducted them in Buenos Aires (April 6, 1930). The *Huella* was also arranged for violin and piano by Jascha Heifetz. Other compositions include *Atahualpa*, incidental music (Buenos Aires, Nov. 5, 1897); *Preambulo, Triste y Gato* for Orch. (Buenos Aires, Nov. 5, 1910); *Belkiss*, orch. suite (1910); *De mi pais*, orch. suite (Buenos Aires, Oct. 27, 1916); chamber music; numerous piano pieces; choral works; songs.

BIBL.: J. Giacobbe, *J. A.* (Buenos Aires, 1945); C. García Muñoz, *J. A.* (Buenos Aires, 1970); idem, "J. A. (1868–1924)," *Revista del Instituto de Investigación Musicológica Carlos Vega*, VII (Benos Aires, 1986).

Ahern, David (Anthony), Australian composer; b. Sydney, Nov. 2, 1947; d. there, Jan. 30, 1988. After training with Butterley and Meale, he took courses with Stockhausen in Cologne and with Cardew in London, exploring the outer regions of the art of hypermusical speculations. Returning to Sydney, he became active in avant-garde circles; introduced scores by contemporary Australian, American, and other composers with his own ensemble AZ Music during the 1960s and 1970s. Thereafter, he was estranged from the Australian music scene. His early works are rigidly serial, but after 1965 he began employing random theatrical effects. Among his compositions were orch. pieces, chamber music, and electronic scores.

Ahlersmeyer, Mathieu, German baritone; b. Cologne, June 29, 1896; d. Garmisch-Partenkirchen, July 23, 1979. He studied voice in Cologne. He made his operatic debut in Mönchen as Wolfram (1929); then sang with the Kroll Opera in Berlin (1930–31) and at the Hamburg State Opera (1931–33). He was subsequently on the staff of the Dresden State Opera, and again with the Hamburg State Opera (1946–61); also sang in Berlin, Vienna, Milan, and London until his retirement in 1973. He created the role of the Barber in Strauss's *Die schweigsame Frau* (Dresden, June 24, 1935).

Ahlgrimm, Isolde, eminent Austrian fortepianist, harpsichordist, and pedagogue; b. Vienna, July 31, 1914; d. there, Oct. 11, 1995. In 1921 she entered the Vienna Academy of Music, graduating in 1932 in the piano class of Viktor Ebenstein; completed her studies in the master classes there of Emil von Sauer and Franz Schmidt (1932–34). In 1935 she attracted notice at the Hamburg International Music Festival. After making her recital debut as a fortepianist in 1937, she taught herself to play the harpsichord and subsequently concentrated on both instruments. From 1937 to 1956 she was active with the Concerte für Kenner und Liebhaber in Vienna; was also first prof. of harpsichord at the Vienna Academy of Music (1945–49). After teaching at the Salzburg Mozarteum (1958–62), she made her first visit to the U.S. in 1962 at the Oberlin (Ohio) College Cons. of Music; then was a prof. at the Vienna Hochschule für Musik (1964–84). Ahlgrimm did much to further the cause of period instrument performances of music from the Baroque and Classical eras.

Ahlin, Čvetka, Yugoslav mezzo-soprano; b. Ljubljana, Sept. 28, 1928; d. Hamburg, June 30, 1985. She studied at the Ljubljana Academy of Music. In 1952 she made her operatic debut at the Ljubljana Opera; after winning 1st prize at the Munich Competition (1954), she was a member of the Hamburg State Opera (1955–74); also was a guest artist in various European opera centers. From 1974 she taught at the Lübeck Hochschule für Musik. Among her best roles were Orpheus, Amneris, Azucena, and Marina.

Ahlstrom, David, American composer; b. Lancaster, N.Y., Feb. 22, 1927; d. San Francisco, Aug. 23, 1992. He studied composition with Henry Cowell and Bernard Rogers; became interested in Asian philosophy and had instruction from Haridas Chaudhuri. He obtained a Ph.D. in composition from the Eastman

School of Music in Rochester, N.Y., in 1961; then taught theory at Northwestern Univ. (1961–62), Southern Methodist Univ. in Dallas (1962–67), and Eastern Illinois Univ. in Charleston (1967–76). In 1976 he moved to San Francisco, and became active in the production of new American stage music. Among his own works, the most significant is his opera *America, I Love You*, to a libretto by e.e. cummings (San Francisco, June 25, 1983, composer conducting); other operas were *Doctor Faustus Lights the Lights*, after Gertrude Stein (San Francisco, Oct. 29, 1982), and *3 Sisters Who Are Not Sisters*, also after Stein (San Francisco, Sept. 17, 1982). He also wrote several syms. and clarinet sonatas, and a number of theater works employing electronic sound and dance.

Ahnsjö, Claes-H(åkan), noted Swedish tenor; b. Stockholm Aug. 1, 1942. He studied with Erik Saeden, Askel Schiøtz, and Max Lorenz in Stockholm. In 1969 he made his operatic debut as Tamino at the Royal Theater in Stockholm; from 1969 he also sang at the Drottningholm Court Theater. In 1973 he became a member of the Bavarian State Opera in Munich, where he was made a Kammersänger in 1977. His guest engagements took him to the major operatic and concert centers of Europe, the U.S., and Japan. His operatic repertoire includes roles by Haydn, Mozart, Rossini, Verdi, and Wagner; also appeared as a soloist with orchs. and as a recitalist.

Aho, Kalevi, prominent Finnish composer, pedagogue, and writer on music; b. Forssa, March 9, 1949. He was a student of Rautavaara at the Sibelius Academy in Helsinki (composition diploma, 1971) and of Boris Blacher at the Staatliche Hochschule für Musik and Darstellende Kunst in Berlin (1971–72). From 1974 to 1988 he lectured on musicology at the Univ. of Helsinki, and then was acting prof. of composition at the Sibelius Academy (1988–93). He has written numerous articles on music for various publications. Among his honors are the Leonie Sonning Prize of Denmark (1974) and the Henrik Steffens Prize of Germany (1990). After composing in a neo-Classical vein, he embraced a more modern idiom. In his later works, his style became refreshingly varied, ranging from the traditional to the postmodern.

WORKS: DRAMATIC: *Avain* (The Key), dramatic monologue for Singer and Chamber Orch. (1978–79; Helsinki, Sept. 4, 1979); *Hyönteiselämää* (Insect Life), opera (1985–87). **ORCH.:** 9 syms.: No. 1 (1969; Helsinki, Feb. 18, 1971), No. 2 (1970; Helsinki, April 17, 1973), No. 3, *Sinfonia concertante No. 1*, for Violin and Orch. (1971–73; Helsinki, Feb. 20, 1975), No. 4 (1972–73; Helsinki, March 12, 1974), No. 5 (1975–76; Helsinki, April 19, 1977), No. 6 (1979–80; Helsinki, Feb. 13, 1980), No. 7, *Hyönteissinfonia* (Insect Symphony; Helsinki, Oct. 26, 1988), No. 8 for Organ and Orch. (1993; Lahti, Aug. 4, 1994), and No. 9, *Sinfonia concertante No. 2*, for Trombone and Orch. (1993–94; Helsinki, Sept. 2, 1994); 2 chamber syms. for Strings: No. 1 (Helsinki, Aug. 22, 1976) and No. 2 (1991–92; Kokkola, Feb. 9, 1992); Violin Concerto (1981; Helsinki, Sept. 29, 1982); *Hiljaisuus* (Silence; Finnish Radio, Dec. 23, 1982; first public perf., Helsinki, Oct. 9, 1985); Cello Concerto (1983–84; Helsinki, Sept. 1, 1984); *Fanfare for YS* for Brass Ensemble (Helsinki, April 18, 1986); Piano Concerto (1988–89; Helsinki, Aug. 29, 1990); *Paloheimo Fanfare* (Lahti, Aug. 31, 1989); *Pergamon* for 4 Instrumental Groups, 4 Reciters, and Electric Organ for the 350th anniversary of the Univ. of Helsinki (Helsinki, Sept. 9, 1990). **CHAMBER:** 3 string quartets: No. 1 (suppressed), No. 2 (Helsinki, Nov. 18, 1970), and No. 3 (Helsinki, Oct. 6, 1971); Quintet for Oboe and String Quartet (1973; Jyväskylä, July 2, 1974); Sonata for Solo Violin (1973; Helsinki, April 17, 1978); *Prelude, Toccata, and Postlude* for Cello and Piano (1974; Helsinki, Feb. 14, 1977); *Solo I* for Violin (1975; Kaustinen, Jan. 26, 1986) and *III* for Flute (1990–91; Helsinki, April 14, 1991); Quintet for Flute, Oboe, Violin, Viola, and Cello (1977; Helsinki, March 24, 1983); Quintet for Bassoon and String Quartet (1977; Helsinki, Jan. 16, 1978); Quartet for Flute, Alto Saxophone, Guitar, and Percussion (Amsterdam, Oct. 1, 1982); Oboe Sonata (1984–85; Helsinki, March 26, 1985); 2 sonatas for Solo Accordion: No. 1 (1984; Kuhmo, July 29, 1989) and No. 2 (1990; Ikaalinen, June 8, 1991); *3 Melodies* for 1 to 4 Kanteles (1984; Kaustinen, June 1985); *Inventions* for Oboe and Cello (1986); *Quartetto piccolo* for 3 Violins and Cello or String Quartet (1989); *Nuppu* for Flute and Piano (Helsinki, Dec. 8, 1991); *Halla* for Violin and Piano (1992; Kuhmo, July 27, 1994); *Epilogue* for Trombone and Organ (1994); Quintet for Alto Saxophone, Bassoon, Viola, Cello, and Double Bass (Lahti, Dec. 7, 1994). **KEYBOARD: PIANO:** Sonata (Helsinki, Sept. 6, 1980); *2 Easy Piano Pieces for Children* (1983); *Solo II* (1985; Helsinki, Feb. 27, 1986); Sonatine (1993). **ORGAN:** *Ludus Solemnis* (1978); *In memoriam* (1980); *3 Interludes* (1993; arr. from the Sym. No. 8; Copenhagen, March 1994). **VOCAL:** *Jäähyväiset Arkadialle* for Voice and Piano (1971); *Lasimaalaus* (Stained Glass) for Women's Chorus (Forssa, May 16, 1975); *Kolme laulua elämästä* (3 Songs about Life) for Tenor and Piano (1977); *Hiljaisuus* (Silence) for Chorus (1978; Helsinki, April 23, 1986); *Sheherazade* for Chorus (1978; Tampere, June 2, 1979); *Kyynikon paratiisi* (A Cynic's Paradise) for Tenor and Chamber Ensemble (Tampere, April 30, 1991; also for Tenor and Piano); *Hyvät ystävät* (Dear Friends) for Baritone and Orch. (Helsinki, Oct. 17, 1992); *Veet välkkyy taas* (The Waters Shimmer Once More) for Men's Chorus (Espoo, May 17, 1992); *Mysteerio* for Women's Chorus (Forssa, Nov. 20, 1994). **OTHER:** Various orchestrations and arrangements.

Ahrens, Joseph (Johannes Clemens), German organist, teacher, and composer; b. Sommersell, Westphalia, April 17, 1904. He displayed an early talent for improvisation on the organ; after studying with Middelschulte, he was appointed an organist at St. Hedwigs-Kathedrale in Berlin; later he was prof. of Catholic church music at the Berlin Hochschule für Musik. In 1968 he received a silver pontifical medal from the Vatican for his accomplishments in sacred music. Ahrens was the author of the study *Die Formprinzipien des Gregorianischen Chorals, und mein Orgelstil* (Heidelberg, 1978). He composed almost exclusively for organ and chorus, maintaining the strict form of the Gregorian chorale within the framework of complex polyphony, and applying advanced melodic and harmonic formulas, including the 12-tone technique. Among his works are *Missa choralis* (1945); *Missa dorica* (1946); *Missa gotica* (1948); *Missa hymnica* (1948); *Missa Salvatoris* (1949); *Missa pro unitate* (1963); *Missa dodekaphonica* (1966); *Passion of St. Matthew* (1950); *Passion of St. John* (1961); *Fantasie und Ricercare* for Organ (1967).

Ahronovich, Yuri (Mikhailovich), Russian-born Israeli conductor; b. Leningrad, May 13, 1932. He studied with Kurt Sanderling and Nathan Rachlin at the Leningrad Cons. (graduated, 1954). After serving as music director of the Saratov Phil. (1956–57) and the Yaroslavl Sym. Orch. (1957–64), he was chief conductor of the Moscow Radio Sym. Orch. (1964–72). He then emigrated to Israel and became a naturalized citizen. He was music director of the Gürzenich Orch. in Cologne (1975–86) and chief conductor of the Stockholm Phil. (1982–87).

Aitken, Hugh, American composer and teacher; b. N.Y., Sept. 7, 1924. He received his primary training at home; his father was an accomplished violinist, and his paternal grandmother was a pianist. He took clarinet lessons and also enrolled in a chemistry class at N.Y. Univ. From 1943 to 1945 he served as a navigator in the U.S. Army Air Corps. Returning from World War II, he entered the Juilliard School of Music in N.Y. as a student in composition of Bernard Wagenaar, Vincent Persichetti, and Robert Ward (M.S., 1950); in 1960 he joined the faculty there, and in 1970 became a prof. of music at William Paterson College of N.J. in Wayne. In his music he professes moral dedication to Classical ideals, regarding deviation from the natural melodic flow and harmonic euphony as unjustifiable tonicide.

WORKS: DRAMATIC: *Fables*, chamber opera (1975); *Felipe*, opera (1981). **ORCH.:** Chamber Concerto for Piano, Winds, Brass, and String Quintet (1947; rev. 1977); *Toccata* (1950);

Piano Concerto (1953); *Short Suite* for Strings (1954); *Partita I* (1957), *II* (1959), *III* (1964), and *IV* (1964); *7 Pieces* for Chamber Orch. (1957); *Serenade* for Chamber Orch. (1958); *Partita* for Strings and Piano (1960); *Partita* for String Quartet and Orch. (1964); *Rameau Remembered* for Flute, 2 Oboes, Bassoon, and Strings (1980); *In Praise of Ockeghem* for Strings (1981); 3 violin concertos (1984, 1988, 1992); *Happy Birthday* for the 40th anniversary of the Aspen (Colo.) Music Festival (1988); *Songdance* (1992); band music. **CHAMBER:** *Short Suite* for Wind Quintet and Piano (1948); String Trio (1951); Suite for Clarinet (1955); *Partita* for 6 Instruments (1956); Quintet for Oboe and Strings (1957); *8 Studies* for Wind Quintet (1958); *Partita* for Violin (1958); Quartet for Clarinet and Strings (1959); *Trombone Music* (1961); Suite for Bass (1961); *Montages* for Bassoon (1962); *Serenade* for Oboe and String Trio (1965); Trios for 11 Players (1970); *Trumpet!* (1974); *Oboe Music* (1975); *Tromba* for Trumpet and String Quartet (1976); *Johannes* for 5 Renaissance Instruments (1977); *For the Violin* (1978); *For the Cello* (1980); *Op. 95 Revisited* for String Quartet (1980); *Flute Music* (1981); *5 Short Pieces* for 3 Clarinets (1982); Trio for Flute, Clarinet, and Cello (1984); Concertino for Contrabass and String Trio (1984); *Music for the Horn* (1985); Duo for Cello and Piano (1989); *Études and Interludes* for 3 Percussionists (1993); piano pieces; organ music. **VOCAL:** *The Revelation of St. John the Divine* for Soloists, Chorus, and Orch. (1953–90); 10 cantatas (1958–94); *2 Tales from Grimm* for Narrator, Flute, Oboe, String Trio, and Piano (1991); choruses.

Aitken, Robert (Morris), Canadian flutist, pedagogue, and composer; b. Kentville, Nova Scotia, Aug. 28, 1939. He studied flute with Nicholas Fiore at the Royal Cons. of Music of Toronto (1955–59); concurrently received lessons in composition from Barbara Pentland at the Univ. of British Columbia; then studied electronic music with Myron Schaeffer and composition with John Weinzweig at the Univ. of Toronto (B.Mus., 1961; M.Mus., 1964); also flute with Marcel Moyse in Europe and in Marlboro, Vt., Jean-Pierre Rampal in Paris and Nice, Gazzelloni in Rome, André Jaunet in Zürich, and Hubert Barwahser in Amsterdam. In 1958–59 he was principal flutist in the Vancouver Sym. Orch.; then was 2nd flutist in the CBC Sym. Orch. (1960–64). After serving as co-principal flutist in the Toronto Sym. (1965–70), Aitken devoted himself to a concert career. He also was artistic director of the New Music Concerts in Toronto (from 1971) and of the advanced studies in music program at the Banff Centre School of Fine Arts (1985–89). He taught at the Royal Cons. of Music of Toronto (1957–64; 1965–68), the Univ. of Toronto (1960–64; 1965–78), the Banff Centre School of Fine Arts (1977–89), and the Staatliche Hochschule für Musik in Freiburg im Breisgau (from 1988).

WORKS: *Rhapsody* for Orch. (1961); Quartet for Flute, Oboe, Viola, and Double Bass (1961); *Music* for Flute and Electronic Tape (1963); *Noësis* for Electronic Tape (1963); Concerto for 12 Solo Instruments (1964); *Spectra* for 4 Chamber Groups (1969); *Kebyar* for Flute, Clarinet, 2 Double Basses, Percussion, and Tape (1971); *Shadows I: Nekuia* for Orch. (1971), *II: Lalitá* for Flute, 3 Cellos, 2 Percussionists, and 2 Harps (1972), and *III: Nira* for Violin, Flute, Oboe, Viola, Double Bass, Piano, and Harpsichord (1974–88); *Spiral* for Orch., with Amplified Flute, Oboe, Clarinet, and Bassoon (1975); *Icicle* for Flute (1977); *Plainsong* for Flute (1977); *Folia* for Woodwind Quintet (1980); *Monody* for Chorus (1983).

Aitken, Webster, American pianist and teacher; b. Los Angeles, June 17, 1908; d. Santa Fe, N.Mex., May 11, 1981. He studied piano in Europe with Artur Schnabel and Emil von Sauer. In 1929 he made his professional debut in Vienna. Returning to America, he gave a concert in N.Y. (Nov. 17, 1935); in 1938 he presented a series of recitals in N.Y. in programs featuring all of Schubert's piano works. He subsequently devoted himself mainly to teaching.

Ajmone-Marsan, Guido, Italian-born American conductor; b. Turin, March 24, 1947. He was taken to the U.S. as a child and became a naturalized American citizen in 1962. He studied clarinet and conducting at the Eastman School of Music in Rochester, N.Y. (B.A., 1968); continued his studies in Salzburg, Venice, and Siena. He took a course in conducting with Franco Ferrara at the Accademia di Santa Cecilia in Rome (1968–71). His conducting career received its decisive impetus in 1973, when he won 1st prize in the Solti Competition in Chicago; subsequently he appeared as a guest conductor with the Chicago, Philadelphia, and Cleveland orchs., and with various orchs. abroad. He was music director of Arnhem's Het Gelders Orch. (1982–86), music advisor and principal conductor of the Orch. of Illinois in Chicago (1982–87), and Generalmusikdirektor of the Essen City Theater (1986–90).

Akimenko (real name, **Yakimenko**), **Fyodor (Stepanovich),** Russian composer; b. Kharkov, Feb. 20, 1876; d. Paris, Jan. 3, 1945. He studied with Balakirev at the Court Chapel in St. Petersburg (1886–90), then with Liadov and Rimsky-Korsakov at the St. Petersburg Cons. (1895–1900). He was the first composition teacher of Stravinsky, whom he taught privately. After the Russian Revolution, he emigrated to Paris. He wrote mostly for piano in the manner of the Russian lyric school. His compositions also include an opera, *The Fairy of the Snows* (1914); a concert overture (St. Petersburg, Nov. 20, 1899); an orch. fantasy (St. Petersburg, Oct. 28, 1900); *Petite ballade* for Clarinet and Piano; *Pastorale* for Oboe and Piano; Piano Trio; Violin Sonata; Cello Sonata; 2 Sonata-Fantasias for Piano; numerous character pieces for piano; and songs.

Akiyama, Kazuyoshi, Japanese conductor; b. Tokyo, Jan. 2, 1941. He was a student of Hideo Saito at the Toho School of Music in Tokyo. In 1964 he made his conducting debut with the Tokyo Sym. Orch. and that same year he was made its music director, a post he retained for 30 years. From 1972 to 1985 he was resident conductor and music director of the Vancouver (British Columbia) Sym. Orch., and concurrently served as music director of the American Sym. Orch. in N.Y. from 1973 to 1978. From 1985 to 1993 he was music director of the Syracuse (N.Y.) Sym. Orch. He also was music advisor and principal conductor of the Sapporo Sym. Orch. from 1988.

Akses, Necil Kâzim, Turkish composer and pedagogue; b. Constantinople, May 6, 1908. He studied at the Constantinople Cons.; in 1926 he went to Vienna, where he had instruction with Joseph Marx; subsequently moved to Prague and took lessons with Alois Hába and Josef Suk (1931–34). Returning to Turkey in 1935, he was appointed to the Teachers College in Ankara; he also attended classes of Paul Hindemith, who was teaching in Ankara at the time. In 1936 Akses became a composition teacher at the Ankara State Cons.; in 1958 he was made a prof. there. His music incorporates elements of Turkish folk songs, but the contrapuntal and harmonic formulation is entirely modern.

WORKS: OPERAS: *Mete* (1933); *Bayönder* (Ankara, Dec. 27, 1934). **ORCH.:** *Ankara Castle*, tone poem (Ankara, Oct. 22, 1942); *Poem* for Cello and Orch. (Ankara, June 29, 1946); *Ballade* (Ankara, April 14, 1948); Sym. (1966). **CHAMBER:** *Allegro feroce* for Saxophone and Piano (1931); Flute Sonata (1939); piano pieces.

Akutagawa, Yasushi, noted Japanese composer and conductor; b. Tokyo, July 12, 1925; d. there, Jan. 31, 1989. He received training in piano, conducting, and composition (from Hashimoto and Ifukube) at the Tokyo Academy of Music (1943–49). In subsequent years, he devoted himself mainly to composition while making occasional appearances as a conductor. He was president of the Japanese Federation of Composers (1980–89) and the Japanese Performing Rights Soc. (1981–89). His orch. music was widely disseminated outside his homeland. His father was the famous Japanese author of *Rashomon*.

WORKS: DRAMATIC: OPERA: *Kurai Kagami* (Dark Mirror; Tokyo, March 27, 1960; rev. ver. as *Orpheus in Hiroshima*,

NHK-TV, Aug. 27, 1967). **BALLETS:** *The Dream of the Lake* (Tokyo, Nov. 6, 1950); *Paradise Lost* (Tokyo, March 17, 1951); *Kappa* (July 21, 1957); *Spider's Web* (Tokyo, March 17, 1969); also film scores. **ORCH.:** *Prelude* (1947); *3 Symphonic Movements* (Tokyo, Sept. 26, 1948); *Music* (1950); *Triptyque* for Strings (1953); Sinfonia (1953); *Divertimento* (1955); *Symphony for Children: Twin Stars* for Narrator and Orch. (1957); *Ellora Symphony* (1958); *Negative Picture* for Strings (1966); *Ostinato Sinfonica* (Tokyo, May 25, 1967); *Concerto Ostinato* for Cello and Orch. (Tokyo, Dec. 16, 1969); *Ballata Ostinata* (1970); *Rhapsody* (Tokyo, Oct. 4, 1971); *River of Poipa and Tree of Poipa* for Narrator and Orch. (1979); *La Princesse de la Lune* (1982); *Sounds* for Organ and Orch. (1986). **CHAMBER:** *Music for Strings* for Double String Quartet and Double Bass (1962). **VOCAL:** *Hymn for the 21st Century* for Chorus, Brass, and Orch. (1983); *Inochi* for Chorus and Orch. (1988).

Alain, Jehan (Ariste), gifted French organist and composer, brother of **Marie-Claire** and **Olivier Alain**; b. St. Germain-en-Laye, Feb. 3, 1911; d. Petits-Puis, near Saumur, June 20, 1940. He studied organ with his father and piano with Augustin Pierson; then entered the Paris Cons. (1927), where he studied composition with Dukas and Roger-Ducasse (premier prix for harmony and fugue, 1934) and organ with Dupré (premier prix, 1939). He was organist at St. Nicolas Cathedral in Maisons-Lafitte, near Paris (1935–39). His death at 29, while leading a motorcycle patrol in the early months of World War II, was a great loss to French music. In addition to many works for organ and piano, he wrote choral pieces, chamber music, and songs. His works for organ have proved to be the most enduring; among the most frequently performed are *Fantaisies* Nos. 1 and 2 (1934, 1936) and *Litanies* (1937).

BIBL.: B. Gavoty, *J. A., musicien français (1911–1940)* (Paris, 1945); M.-C. Alain, "L'OEuvre d'orgue de J. A.," *L'organo*, VI (1968); J. Welch, "Chronological Dating of the Organ Works of J. A.," *Music—the A.G.O.-R.C.C.O. Magazine* (July 1978).

Alain, Marie-Claire, renowned French organist and pedagogue, sister of **Jehan (Ariste)** and **Olivier Alain**; b. St. Germain-en-Laye, Aug. 10, 1926. She was a pupil of Duruflé (harmony), Plé-Caussade (counterpoint and fugue), and Dupré (organ) at the Paris Cons. At age 11 she made her debut in St. Germain-en-Laye; in 1950, made her formal debut in Paris, the same year she won the Geneva International Competition. In subsequent years, she made frequent tours of Europe; in 1961, made her first tour of the U.S. She lectured at the Haarlem Summer Academy of Organists in the Netherlands (1956–72); also gave master classes around the world. Her exhaustive repertory includes works by the Baroque masters as well as contemporary scores.

Alain, Olivier, French pianist, musicologist, and composer, brother of **Jehan (Ariste)** and **Marie-Claire Alain**; b. St. Germain-en-Laye, Aug. 3, 1918; d. Paris, Feb. 28, 1994. He studied organ and piano in his youth; then took courses in composition with Aubin and Messiaen at the Paris Cons. From 1950 to 1964 he served as director of the Cons. in St. Germain-en-Laye; in 1961 he was appointed to the faculty of the École César Franck in Paris. He composed an oratorio, *Chant funèbre sur les morts en montagne* (1950); also motets and pieces for organ and piano. He publ. the manual *L'Harmonie* (Paris, 1965) and the monograph *Bach* (Paris, 1970).

Alaleona, Domenico, Italian music theorist and composer; b. Montegiorgio, Nov. 16, 1881; d. there, Dec. 28, 1928. He studied organ and clarinet in his native town; in 1901, went to Rome, where he studied piano with Sgambati, organ with Renzi, and theory with De Sanctis at the Accademia di Santa Cecilia; was then active as a choral conductor in Leghorn and Rome; in 1911, obtained the post of prof. of musical aesthetics at the Accademia di Santa Cecilia. He wrote an opera, *Mirra* (1912; Rome, March 31, 1920); a Requiem; *Sinfonia italiana*; *12 Canzoni italiane*; and *4 Laudi italiane* for various Instrumental Groups; a cycle of 18 songs, *Melodie Pascoliane*; etc. However, his importance lies in his theoretical writings. His valuable book *Studi sulla storia dell'oratorio musicale in Italia* (Turin, 1908), once a standard, was reprinted in Milan (1945) as *Storia dell'oratorio musicale in Italia*. A believer in musical progress, Alaleona contributed several original ideas to the theory of modern music, notably in his article "L'armonia modernissima," *Rivista Musicale Italiana*, XVIII (1911); he also originated the term "dodecafonia."

BIBL.: G. Cardi, *D. A.: Musicista e musicologo* (Ascoli Piceno, 1957).

Alarie, Pierrette (Marguerite), Canadian soprano and teacher; b. Montreal, Nov. 9, 1921. She studied voice and acting with Jeanne Maubourg and Albert Roberval. After appearing on radio as an actress and singer of popular music, she continued vocal training with Salvator Issaurel (1938–43) and as a scholarship student with Elisabeth Schumann at the Curtis Inst. of Music in Philadelphia (1943–46). In 1943 she made her debut as Mozart's Barbarina in Montreal. She won the Metropolitan Opera Auditions of the Air in 1945, and on Dec. 8 of that year made her debut with the company in N.Y. as Verdi's Oscar; remained on its roster until 1947. In subsequent years, she appeared frequently in opera and in concert with her husband, **Léopold Simoneau**, whom she married in 1946. In addition to her festival appearances in Aix-en-Provence, Edinburgh, Glyndebourne, Vienna, and Munich, she sang opera in Montreal, Toronto, Vancouver, San Francisco, Philadelphia, N.Y., and New Orleans, becoming particularly well known for her performances of works by Mozart and of works from the French repertoire. In 1966 she retired from the operatic stage and in 1970 made her farewell appearance as a concert singer. After teaching and staging opera in California (1972–82), she went to Victoria, British Columbia, where she was founder-director with her husband of the Canada Opera Piccola. In 1967 she was made an Officer of the Order of Canada. In 1990 the French government made her a Chevalière of the Ordre des arts et des lettres de France.

BIBL.: R. Maheu, *P. A., Léopold Simoneau: Deux voix, un art* (Montreal, 1988).

Albanese, Licia, noted Italian-born American soprano; b. Bari, July 22, 1909. She studied with Emanuel de Rosa in Bari and Giuseppina Baldassare-Tedeschi in Milan. In 1934 she made an unexpected operatic debut at Milan's Teatro Lirico when she was called in to substitute as Cio-Cio-San for the 2nd act of *Madama Butterfly*. In 1935 she made her first appearance at Milan's La Scala as Puccini's Lauretta, and subsequently sang there with distinction in such roles as Mimi and Micaëla. In 1937 she made her debut at London's Covent Garden as Liù. On Feb. 9, 1940, she made her first appearance at the Metropolitan Opera in N.Y. as Cio-Cio-San, and remained on its roster as one of its most admired artists until 1963. In 1964 she rejoined its roster and sang with it until her farewell appearance as Mimi in a concert performance at the Newport (R.I.) Opera Festival on July 12, 1966. During her years at the Metropolitan Opera, she was greatly admired for her portrayals in operas by Puccini. She also excelled as Mozart's Countess, Susanna, Adriana Lecouvreur, Desdemona, Massenet's Manon, and Violetta. In 1945 she became a naturalized American citizen. In 1995 she was awarded the Medal of Arts by President Clinton.

d'Albert, Eugen (actually **Eugène Francis Charles**), Scottish-born German pianist and composer; b. Glasgow, April 10, 1864; d. Riga, March 3, 1932. His father, Charles Louis Napoléon d'Albert (b. Nienstetten, near Hamburg, Feb. 25, 1809; d. London, May 26, 1886), was a dancing master who wrote popular music; it was from him that Albert received his early instruction in music. At the age of 10, he entered the National Training School in London, where he studied piano with Pauer and theory with Stainer, Prout, and Arthur Sullivan. He made extraordinary progress as both a pianist and a composer, and after several appearances at the Popular Concerts, was the soloist in Schumann's Concerto at the Crystal Palace in London (Feb. 5, 1881). On Oct. 24, 1881, when only 17, he played his own piano concerto at one of Hans Richter's concerts, arousing great enthusiasm; the press compared him to Mozart and Mendelssohn. He received a Mendelssohn fellowship and went to Vienna; later he studied with Liszt, who was greatly impressed by his technique and often referred to him as "the young Tausig." In 1895 d'Albert was appointed conductor at Weimar; in 1907 he became director of the Hochschule für Musik in Berlin. In the wake of his success, he repudiated his English birth, adopting German citizenship, and made repeated statements derogatory to English culture and even to his former English teachers; he further changed his first name from Eugène to its German form, Eugen. During World War I, he was vocal in his enmity toward England, which led in turn to an understandable repugnance among British musicians to accept his music. Despite a brilliant beginning, d'Albert did not fulfill his early promise; his musical idiom oscillates between the Italian melodic style and German contrapuntal writings, and fails to achieve originality; his operas and other works were rarely revived. A considerable corpus of his autograph MSS, including 11 of his operas (although not *Tiefland*), was acquired in 1963 by the Library of Congress in Washington, D.C. D'Albert's personal life was a stormy one. He was married 6 times; his first wife (1892–95) was **Teresa Carreño**; his 2nd was the singer Hermine Finck. D'Albert composed industriously. He publ. 2 pianos concertos; Cello Concerto; overtures: *Hyperion* and *Esther*, Sym. (1886); Orch. Suite (1924); Piano Sonata; Piano Suite; 2 string quartets; *Der Mensch und das Leben* for Chorus and Orch.; 4 piano pieces (*Waltz, Scherzo, Intermezzo, Ballade*); minor piano pieces and songs. Of his 20 operas, the most successful were *Tiefland* (Prague, Nov. 15, 1903) and *Die toten Augen* (Dresden, March 5, 1916). His other operas were: *Der Rubin* (Karlsruhe, Oct. 12, 1893); *Ghismonda* (Dresden, Nov. 28, 1895); *Gernot* (Mannheim, April 11, 1897); *Die Arbreise* (Frankfurt am Main, Oct. 20, 1898); *Der Improvisator* (Berlin, Feb. 20, 1902); *Flauto solo* (Prague, Nov. 12, 1905); *Tragaldabas* or *Der geborgte Ehemann* (Hamburg, Dec. 3, 1907); *Izeÿl* (Hamburg, Nov. 6, 1909); *Die verschenkte Frau* (Vienna, Feb. 6, 1912); *Liebesketten* (Vienna, Nov. 12, 1912); *Der Stier von Olivera* (Leipzig, March 10, 1918); *Revolutionshochzeit* (Leipzig, Oct. 26, 1919); *Scirocco* (Darmstadt, May 18, 1921); *Mareike von Nymwegen* (Hamburg, Oct. 31, 1923); *Der Golem* (Frankfurt am Main, Nov. 14, 1926); *Die schwarze Orchidee* (Leipzig, Dec. 1, 1928); *Mister Wu* (unfinished; completed by Leo Blech; Dresden, Sept. 29, 1932).

BIBL.: W. Raupp, *E. d'A.: Ein Künstler- und Menschenschicksal* (Leipzig, 1930); H. Heisig, *D.'A.s Opernschaffen* (diss., Univ. of Leipzig, 1942).

Albert, Karel, Belgian composer; b. Antwerp, April 16, 1901; d. Liedekerke, May 23, 1987. He was a student of Jong at the Royal Flemish Cons. in Antwerp. From 1933 to 1961 he was active with the Belgian Radio. He publ. *De evolutie van de muziek van de Oudheid tot aan Beethoven aan de hand van fonoplaten* (Brussels, 1947).

WORKS: DRAMATIC: OPERA BUFFA: *Europa ontvoerd* (1950). **BALLETS:** *De toverlantaarn* (1942); *Tornooi* (1953). **ORCH.:** Chamber Sym. (1932); *Pieta* (1933); *Wilde jacht* (1933); *Ananke*, overture (1934); *Lentewandeling* (1935); *Humoresque* (1936); *Het Land* (1937); *Impulsions* (1939); 4 syms. (1941, 1943, 1945, 1966); *Suite flamande* (1947); *De Nacht* (1956); Suite (1958); *Dansende beeldekens* (1959); *3 Constructions* for Strings (1959); *In the Beginning Was the Word* for Baritone and Orch. (1962); *Sinfonietta* (1968). **CHAMBER:** 2 string quartets (1929, 1941); Trio for Oboe, Clarinet, and Bassoon (1930); Quintet for Flute, Oboe, Violin, Viola, and Cello (1954); *Étude* for Alto and Wind Quintet (1958); Quartet for 4 Saxophones (1960); Brass Quartet (1964).

Albert, Stephen (Joel), distinguished American composer and teacher; b. N.Y., Feb. 6, 1941; d. in an automobile accident in Truro, Mass., Dec. 27, 1992. He studied piano, horn, and trumpet in his youth. He received training in composition from Elie Siegmeister in Great Neck, N.Y. (1956–58), from Milhaud at the Aspen (Colo.) School of Music (summer, 1958), and from Bernard Rogers at the Eastman School of Music in Rochester, N.Y. (1958–60). After studies with Karl-Birger Blomdahl in Stockholm, he pursued training with Castaldo at the Philadelphia Musical Academy (B.M., 1962) and with George Rochberg at the Univ. of Pa. (1963). He received 2 Rome Prizes (1965, 1966) and 2 Guggenheim fellowships (1967–68; 1978–79). In 1967–68 he held a Ford Foundation grant as composer-in-residence of the Lima, Ohio, public schools and community orch. He taught at the Philadelphia Musical Academy (1968–70), Stanford Univ. (1970–71), Smith College (1974–76), Boston Univ. (1981–84), and the Juilliard School in N.Y. (1988–92). In 1985 he was awarded the Pulitzer Prize in Music for his first sym., *RiverRun*. From 1985 to 1988 he was composer-in-residence of the Seattle Sym. Orch., and later of the Bowdoin (Maine) Summer Music Festival (1991–92). As a composer, Albert breathed life into traditional forms; his works are marked by expert craftsmanship, intensity, passion, and lyricism.

WORKS: ORCH.: *Bacchae Prologue* (1967); *Leaves from the Golden Notebook* (1970; Chicago, Dec. 2, 1971); *Voices Within* (Tanglewood, Aug. 14, 1975); 2 syms.: No. 1, *RiverRun* (1983–84; Washington, D.C., Jan. 17, 1985) and No. 2 (1992; N.Y., Nov. 10, 1994); *In Concordiam* for Violin and Orch. (Pittsburgh, Dec. 19, 1986; rev. 1988); *Anthem and Processionals* (Seattle, March 7, 1988); Cello Concerto (Baltimore, May 31, 1990); *Tapioca Pudding* (Baltimore, April 18, 1991); *Wind Canticle* for Clarinet and Orch. (Philadelphia, Oct. 17, 1991). **CHAMBER:** *Illuminations* for 2 Pianos, Brass, Harps, and Percussion (1962); *Imitations (after Bartók)* for String Quartet (1963); *Cathedral Music/Concerto for 4 Quartets* for 2 Amplified Flutes and 2 Amplified Cellos, of 2 Horns, Trumpet, and Trombone, of 2 Percussion, Amplified Harp, and Amplified Guitar, and of Electric Organ, Electric Piano, and 2 Pianos (1971–72); *Tribute* for Violin and Piano (Washington, D.C., Oct. 28, 1988). **VOCAL:** *Supernatural Songs* for Soprano and Orch. (1964); *Wedding Songs* for Soprano and Piano (1964); *Bacchae Canticles* for Narrator, Chorus, and Orch. (Lima, Ohio, May 1968); *Wolf Time* for Soprano, Orch., and Amplified Instruments (1968–69; Seattle, Dec. 3, 1970); *To Wake the Dead* for Soprano, Flute, Clarinet, Harmonium, Piano, Violin, and Cello (Geneseo, N.Y., Nov. 28, 1978); *Into Eclipse* for Tenor and 13 Instrumentalists (1981; Washington, D.C., March 7, 1982; also for Tenor and Orch., Seattle, Sept. 8, 1986); *TreeStone* for Soprano, Tenor, and 12 Instrumentalists (1983–84; N.Y., Jan. 16, 1985; also for Soprano, Tenor, and Orch., N.Y., May 13, 1989); *Flower of the Mountain* for Soprano and Orch. (1985; N.Y., May 17, 1986); *The Stone Harp* for Tenor, Timpani, and Harp (N.Y., Feb. 18, 1988; withdrawn; rev. for Soprano or Tenor, Percussion, Harp, 2 Violas, and 2 Cellos, N.Y., March 7, 1989); *Distant Hills* for Soprano, Tenor, and 11 Instrumentalists (1989; N.Y., April 27, 1990; also for Soprano, Tenor, and Orch., N.Y., Feb. 8, 1992); *Sun's Heat* for Tenor and 11 Instrumentalists (1989; N.Y., April 27, 1990; also for Tenor and Orch., N.Y., Feb. 8, 1992); *Rilke Song* for Soprano, Flute, Clarinet, Violin, Cello, and Piano (N.Y., March 7, 1991); *Ecce Puer* for Soprano, Oboe, Horn, and Piano (Philadelphia, April 11, 1992).

BIBL.: M. Humphrey, *S. A.* (N.Y., 1993).

Albertsen, Per Hjort, Norwegian organist and composer; b. Trondheim, July 27, 1919. He studied organ at the Oslo Cons., graduating in 1946; took lessons in composition with Sven Erik Tarp in Copenhagen, Ralph Downes in London, and Hanns Jelinek in Vienna. He was an organist in Trondheim (1947–68); then lectured in the music dept. of the univ. there (1968–72). Much of his music has been written for performance in schools.

WORKS: SCHOOL OPERA: *Russicola* (1956). **ORCH.:** Flute Concertino (1948); *Symphonic Prelude* (1951); *Gunnerus Suite* for Strings (1952); *Little Suite* for Strings (1955); *Presentation*, overture (1958); *Notturno e Danza* (1960); *Concerto piccolo* for

Violin or Clarinet and Amateur Strings (1961); Concerto for Piano and School Orch. (1969); *Tordenskioldiana* (1972). **CHAMBER:** Clarinet Sonatina (1950); *4 Religious Folksongs* for Violin, Cello, and Organ (1974); Suite for String Quartet (1984); Violin Sonatine (1985); piano pieces; organ music. **VOCAL:** 2 folk ballads: *Villemann og Magnill* for Soprano, Baritone, Men's Chorus, and Orch. (1951); *Bendik og Årolilja* for Tenor, Chorus, and Piano (1943; orch. 1979).

Albrecht, Alexander, Slovak composer, conductor, and pedagogue; b. Arad, Hungary, Aug. 12, 1885; d. Bratislava, July 30, 1958. He was a student at the Budapest Academy of Music (1904–08) of Koessler (composition), Thomán and Bartók (piano), Szandtner (conducting), and Popper (chamber music), and then in Vienna of Dittrich (organ). After settling in Bratislava, he was active as a conductor and served as director of the church music soc. (1921–52); also was director of the music school. His early works were composed in a late Romantic vein but he later pursued more adventuresome paths.

WORKS: ORCH.: *Scherzo: Humoreske* (1907); *Dornröschen*, symphonic poem (1921); *Symphony in 1 Movement* (1929); *Tobias Wunderlich: Túžby a spomienky* (Desires and Memories), symphonic poem (1935); *Variations* for Trumpet and Orch. (1946; also for Trumpet and Piano); *Scherzo* for Strings (1949; also for String Quartet). **CHAMBER:** Piano Trio (1907); String Quintet (1908); Piano Quintet (1913); String Quartet (1918); Sonatine for 11 Instruments (1925); *Quintetto frammento* for Winds and Piano (1929); Trio for 2 Violins and Viola (1943); *Präludium und Fuge* for Viola and Cello (1950); *Die Nacht* for Cello and Piano (1950); Suite Concertante for Viola and Piano (1952); *Weihnachten* for String Quartet (1956); 6 Pieces for String Trio (1957); piano pieces, including a Sonata (1905) and a Suite (1924); organ music. **VOCAL:** *Mass* (1902); *Drei Gedichte aus dem Marienleben* for Soprano, Chorus, and Orch. (1928); *Cantate Domino* for Chorus and Orch. (1938); *Šuhajko*, cantata on Slovakian Folk Songs for Chorus and Orch. (1950); choruses; songs.

BIBL.: F. Klinda, *A. A.* (Bratislava, 1959).

Albrecht, Gerd, German conductor, son of **Hans Albrecht**; b. Essen, July 19, 1935. He studied conducting with Brückner-Rüggeberg at the Hamburg Hochschule für Musik and musicology at the univs. of Kiel and Hamburg. After winning the Besançon (1957) and Hilversum (1958) conducting competitions, he conducted at the Württemberg State Theater in Stuttgart (1958–61). He was 1st conductor in Mainz (1961–63), and then Generalmusikdirektor in Lübeck (1963–66) and Kassel (1966–72). From 1972 to 1979 he was chief conductor of the Deutsche Oper in West Berlin and of the Tonhalle Orch. in Zürich from 1975 to 1980. From 1976 he was a guest conductor at the Vienna State Opera. In 1981 he made his U.S. debut conducting the U.S. premiere of Reimann's *Lear* at the San Francisco Opera. In 1986 he made his first appearance as a sym. conductor in the U.S. when he led a guest engagement with the Houston Sym. Orch. He served as chief conductor of the Hamburg State Opera and the Phil. State Orch. from 1988. From 1994 to 1996 he was chief conductor of the Czech Phil. in Prague. He publ. the book *Wie eine Opernaufführung zustande kommt* (Zürich, 1988).

Albrecht, Hans, German musicologist, father of **Gerd Albrecht**; b. Magdeburg, March 31, 1902; d. Kiel, Jan. 20, 1961. He studied at the Essen Cons., the Univ. of Münster, and with Wolf, Abert, Sachs, and Hornbostel at the Univ. of Berlin (Ph.D., 1925, with the diss. *Die Aufführungspraxis der italienischen Musik des 14. Jahrhunderts*; completed his Habilitation there, 1942, with his *Caspar Othmayr: Leben und Werk*, publ. in Kassel, 1950). He taught at the Essen Cons. (1925–37). In 1939 he joined the Staatliche Institut für Deutsche Musikforschung in Berlin, where he was a prof. (from 1940) and its director (from 1941). In 1947 he became director of the Landesinstitut für Musikforschung in Kiel; also taught at the Univ. of Kiel, where he became a prof. in 1955. He was ed. of *Die Musikforschung* (1948–60) and *Acta Musicologica* (1957–60).

BIBL.: W. Brennecke and H. Haase, eds., *H. A. in Memoriam* (Kassel, 1962).

Albrecht, Otto Edwin, eminent American musicologist; b. Philadelphia, July 8, 1899; d. there, July 6, 1984. He studied at the Univ. of Pa. (A.B., 1921; M.A., 1925; Ph.D., 1931, with the diss. *Four Latin Plays of St. Nicholas from the 12th Century Fleury Play-book*; publ. in Philadelphia and London, 1935), where he was an instructor in French (1923–38) and curator of its Music Library (from 1937); from 1938 he was also a lecturer in its music dept. He retired in 1970 and was made emeritus prof. of music.

WRITINGS: *A Census of Autograph Music Manuscripts of European Composers in American Libraries* (Philadelphia, 1953); *The Mary Flagler Cary Music Collection* (N.Y., 1970).

BIBL.: J. Hill, ed., *Studies in Musicology in Honor of O.E. A.* (Kassel, 1977; Clifton, N.J., 1980).

Albright, William (Hugh), American composer, pianist, organist, and teacher; b. Gary, Ind., Oct. 20, 1944. He studied piano with Rosetta Goodkind and theory with Hugh Aitken at the Juilliard Preparatory Dept. in N.Y. (1959–62); then took courses in composition with Finney and Bassett at the Univ. of Mich. in Ann Arbor; also studied organ with Marilyn Mason there (1963–70). He also received training from Rochberg, and at the Paris Cons. from Olivier Messiaen (1968); also took private lessons with Max Deutsch. In 1970 he joined the faculty of the Univ. of Mich., where he was a prof. of music from 1982; also served as assoc. director of its Electronic Music Studio. He received Guggenheim fellowships in 1976 and 1987; was composer-in-residence at the American Academy in Rome in 1979. In his compositions, Albright pursues quaquaversal methods of experimental music, using varied techniques according to need. He also made a concert career as a pianist and organist in ragtime, jazz, and contemporary music.

WORKS: MULTIMEDIA AND DRAMATIC: *Tic* for Soloist, 2 Jazz-rock Improvisation Ensembles, Tape, and Film (1967); *Beulahland Rag* for Narrator, Jazz Quartet, Improvisation Ensemble, Tape, Film, and Slides (1967–69); *Cross of Gold*, music theater for Actors, Chorus, Saxophone, Trombone, Double Bass, Percussion, and Electric Organ (1975); *Full Moon in March*, 5 songs and incidental music to a play by Yeats (1978; Ann Arbor, Jan. 13, 1979). **ORCH.:** *Alliance*, suite (1967–70); *Night Procession* for Chamber Orch. (1972); *Gothic Suite* for Organ, Strings, and Percussion (1973); *Heater* for Saxophone and Symphonic Band (1977); *Bacchanal* for Organ and Orch. (Lincoln, Nebr., Nov. 16, 1981); *Chasm: Symphonic Fragment* (1988); Concerto for Harpsichord and Strings (1991). **CHAMBER:** *Foils* for Winds and Percussion (1963); *Frescoes* for Wind Quartet (1964); *Salvos* for 7 Instruments (1964); *Caroms* for 8 Instruments (1966); *Amerithon* for Variable Ensemble (1966–67); *Marginal Worlds* for Ensemble (1969); *Danse Macabre* for Violin, Cello, Flute, Clarinet, and Piano (1971); *Take That* for 4 Drummers (1972); *Stipendium Peccati* for Organ, Piano, and Percussion (1973); *7 Deadly Sins* for Optional Narrator, Flute, Clarinet, String Quartet, and Piano (1974); *Introduction, Passacaglia, and Rondo Capriccioso* for Tack Piano and Winds (1974); *Dream and Dance* for Organ and Percussion (1974); *Doo-Dah* for 3 Alto Saxophones (1975); *Peace Pipe* for 2 Bassoons (1976); *Saints Preserve Us* for Clarinet (1976); *Jericho, Battle Music* for Trumpet and Organ (1976); *Shadows* for Guitar (1977); *Halo* for Organ and Metal Percussion Instruments (1978); *4 Fancies* for Harpsichord (1979); *Romance* for Horn and Organ (1981); *Enigma Syncopations* for Flute, Organ, Double Bass, and Percussion (1982); *Brass Tacks*, rag march for Brass Quintet (1983); Saxophone Sonata (1984); *Canon in D (Berimbau!)* for Contrabass and Harpsichord (1984); *3 New Chestnuts* for 2 Harpsichords or Harpsichord and Tape (1986); Clarinet Quintet (1987); *Abiding Passions* for Woodwind Quintet (1988); *The Great Amen* for Flute and Piano

(1992); *Pit Band* for Alto Saxophone, Bass Clarinet, and Piano (1993); *Fantasy-Études* for Saxophone Quartet (1993–94); *Rustles of Spring, 1994* for Flute, Alto Saxophone, Violin, Cello, and Piano (1994). **KEYBOARD: PIANO:** *9 Pieces* (1962); *Pianoàgogo* (1965–66); *3 Original Rags* (1967–68); *Grand Sonata in Rag* (1968); *3 Novelty Rags* (1969); *Dream Rags* (1970); *Sweet Sixteenths* (1975); *5 Chromatic Dances* (1976); *Sphaera* (1985); *Stoptime for George* for George Rochberg's 70th birthday (1987); *The Machine Age: A Set of Short Piano Pieces for Our Time* (1988); *New Leaves* (1991); *Ragtime Lullabye* (1991). **ORGAN:** *Juba* (1965); *3 Organbooks: I* (1967), *II*, with Tape (1971), and *III*, subtitled *12 Études* (1977–78); *King of Instruments*, "Parade of Music and Verse" with Narrator (1978); *De spiritum* (1980–81); *That Sinking Feeling* (1982); *In Memoriam* (1983); *1732: In Memoriam Johannes Albrecht*, "program sonata" (1984); *Carillon-Bombarde* (1985); *Chasm*, with optional "echo" instrument or tape (1985); Sym. with Percussion or Tape (1986); *Whistler Nocturnes* (1989); *Flights of Fancy* (1982). **CHORAL:** *Mass in D* for Chorus, Organ, Percussion, and Congregation (1974); *Chichester Mass* for Chorus (1974); *Pax in Terra* for Soprano, Tenor, and Chorus (1981); *David's Songs* for Chorus (1982); *A Song to David*, oratorio (Minneapolis, Nov. 1, 1983); *Take Up the Song* for Soprano, Chorus, and Piano (1986); *Antigone's Reply* for Chorus and Piano (1987); *Deum de Deo* for Chorus and Organ (1989); *Dona Nobis Pacem* for Chorus and Piano (1992).

Alcaide, Tomáz (de Aquino Carmelo), Portuguese tenor; b. Estremoz, Feb. 16, 1901; d. Lisbon, Nov. 9, 1967. He studied at the Univ. of Coimbra; took voice lessons in Lisbon, and later in Milan. In 1925 he made his operatic debut at the Teatro Carcano in Milan as Wilhelm Meister in *Mignon*. He subsequently sang principal roles in Italian and French operas at La Scala in Milan, the Paris Opéra, the Vienna State Opera, the Salzburg Festival, and the Rome Opera; also made concert tours of Europe and the U.S. After his retirement from the stage in 1948, he settled in Lisbon. He wrote an autobiography, *Um cantor no palco e na vida* (Lisbon, 1961).

Alcantara, Theo, Spanish conductor; b. Cuenca, April 16, 1941. He studied at the Madrid Cons.; then took courses in conducting at the Mozarteum in Salzburg. He began his career as a conductor with the Frankfurt am Main Opera Orch. (1964–66); then went to the U.S., where he served as director of orchs. at the Univ. of Mich. in Ann Arbor (1968–73), and then as music director of the Grand Rapids Sym. Orch. (1973–78). From 1978 to 1989 he was music director of the Phoenix Sym. Orch.; he was also artistic director of the Music Academy of the West in Santa Barbara from 1981 to 1984. In 1987 he became principal conductor of the Pittsburgh Opera.

Alda, Frances (real name, **Frances Jeanne Davies**), New Zealand-born American soprano; b. Christchurch, May 31, 1883; d. Venice, Sept. 18, 1952. She studied with Marchesi in Paris, and made her operatic debut as Manon at the Opéra-Comique there (April 15, 1904). She later sang in Brussels, London, Milan, Warsaw, and Buenos Aires. Her debut at the Metropolitan Opera was on Dec. 7, 1908 (opposite Caruso in *Rigoletto*); she made her farewell appearance there, on Dec. 28, 1929, in *Manon Lescaut*. She also made numerous recital tours in the U.S. Her principal roles included Louise, Mimi, Manon, Marguerite, Juliette, Gilda, Violetta, and Aida. She married **Giulio Gatti-Casazza** on April 3, 1910; they divorced in 1928; she married Ray Vir Den in 1941. In 1939 she became a naturalized American citizen. She wrote an autobiography, *Men, Women and Tenors* (Boston, 1937).

Aldenhoff, Bernd, German tenor; b. Duisburg, June 14, 1908; d. Munich, Oct. 8, 1959. He studied in Cologne, where he began his operatic career; then sang at the Düsseldorf Opera (1938–44), the Dresden State Opera (1944–52), the Bayreuth Festivals (1951–52; 1957), and the Bavarian State Opera in Munich (1952–59). On Feb. 25, 1955, he made his Metropolitan Opera debut in N.Y. as Tannhäuser. He was best known as a Wagnerian.

Aldrich, Putnam (Calder), American harpsichordist and pedagogue; b. South Swansea, Mass., July 14, 1904; d. Cannes, France, April 18, 1975. He studied at Yale Univ. (B.A., 1926); then took piano lessons with Tobias Matthay in London (1926–27) and harpsichord lessons with Wanda Landowska in Paris (1929–33); then completed his education at Harvard Univ. (M.A., 1936; Ph.D., 1942). He toured as a harpsichordist; also taught at the Univ. of Texas (1942–44), Western Reserve Univ. (1946–48), Mills College (1948–50), and Stanford Univ. (1950–69). He publ. an important treatise, *Ornamentation in J.S. Bach's Organ Works* (N.Y., 1950), as part of a much larger and very valuable work on Baroque ornamentation, originally submitted as his doctoral diss. at Harvard; the work still awaits publication. He also publ. *Rhythm in Seventeenth-century Italian Monody* (London, 1965).

Aldrich, Richard, American music critic; b. Providence, July 31, 1863; d. Rome, June 2, 1937. He studied with Paine at Harvard Univ. (graduated, 1885), then was music critic of the *Providence Journal* (1885–89) and the *Evening Star* (1889–91). From 1891 to 1901 he was assistant to H.E. Krehbiel on the *N.Y. Tribune*, then was music ed. of the *N.Y. Times* (1902–23). A selection of his articles from the *Times* was publ. in *Musical Discourse* (1928) and in *Concert Life in New York, 1902–1923* (1941). He also wrote *Guide to Parsifal* (1904) and *Guide to the Ring of the Nibelung* (1905). His critical writings were urbane and witty; while liberal-minded in regard to milder types of modern music, he vehemently opposed extreme trends.

Alemshah, Kourkene, Armenian composer; b. Yerevan, May 22, 1907; d. Detroit, Dec. 14, 1947. He studied in Milan with Pizzetti (1924–30). In 1931 he settled in Paris. His music was strongly permeated with Armenian melos, and the settings were impressionistic. A memorial festival of his music was presented in Paris on Feb. 19, 1950. Among his compositions were the symphonic poems *Légende* (Paris, June 19, 1932) and *La Bataille d'Avarayr* (Paris, June 2, 1934); also *Danses populaires armeniennes* for Orch. (Paris, June 2, 1934). Alemshah died during an American tour, which he undertook as a choral conductor.

Aler, John, American tenor; b. Baltimore, Oct. 4, 1949. He studied with Rilla Mervine and Raymond McGuire at the Catholic Univ. of America in Washington, D.C. (M.M., 1972), with Oren Brown at the American Opera Center at the Juilliard School in N.Y. (1972–76), with Marlene Malas, and at the Berkshire Music Center at Tanglewood. In 1977 he made his operatic debut as Ernesto at the American Opera Center, the same year he won 1st prizes for men and for the interpretation of French art song at the Concours International de Chant in Paris. In 1979 he made his European operatic debut as Belmonte at the Théâtre Royal de la Monnaie in Brussels. He made his first appearance at London's Covent Garden as Ferrando in 1986. In 1988 he made his debut at the Salzburg Festival as Don Ottavio. He also sang in many other operatic centers and pursued a career as a concert and oratorio singer.

Alessandrescu, Alfred, eminent Romanian composer and conductor; b. Bucharest, Aug. 14, 1893; d. there, Feb. 18, 1959. He studied piano and theory at the Bucharest Cons. with Kiriac and Castaldi (1903–11); then went to Paris, where he took composition courses with d'Indy at the Schola Cantorum and with Paul Vidal at the Cons. (1913–14). Returning to Bucharest, he was active as a pianist. In 1921 he was appointed conductor of the Romanian Opera in Bucharest, retaining this post until his death; also conducted the Bucharest Phil. (1926–40) and was artistic director of the Bucharest Radio (1933–59); was piano accompanist to Georges Enesco, Jacques Thibaud et al. Among his compositions were *Amurg de toamnă* (The Twilight of Autumn) for String Orch. (1910); *Didona*, symphonic poem (1911); *Fantezie română* for Orch. (1913); Violin Sonata (1914);

Acteon, symphonic poem (Bucharest, Dec. 20, 1915); *Pièce pour quatuor à cordes* (1921); songs.

BIBL.: V. Tomescu, *A. A.* (Bucharest, 1962).

d'Alessandro, Raffaele, Swiss pianist, organist, and composer; b. St. Gallen, March 17, 1911; d. Lausanne, March 17, 1959. He studied music with Victor Schlatter and Willi Schuh in Zürich; then went to Paris, where he studied composition with Boulanger and organ with Dupré. In 1940 he returned to Switzerland and settled in Lausanne, where he became active as a pianist, organist, and composer.

WORKS: BALLET: *Isla persa* (1952). **ORCH.:** 3 piano concertos (1939, 1945, 1951); *Rumba sinfonica* (1940); *Conga contrapuntique* (1941); Violin Concerto (1941); Flute Concerto (1943); 2 syms. (1948, 1953); Bassoon Concerto (1955); Oboe Concerto (1958). **CHAMBER:** 2 violin sonatas (1936, 1953); Cello Sonata (1937); Piano Trio (1940); Flute Sonata (1943); 2 string quartets (1947, 1952); Oboe Sonata (1949); Sonatina for Solo Oboe (1953); Sonatina for Clarinet and Piano (1953); Bassoon Sonata (1957); Sonata for Flute, Viola, and Piano (1958). **PIANO:** Sonatina for left hand alone (1939); 24 Preludes (1940); Sonatina for 2 Pianos (1943); 12 études (1952); *Contes drolatiques* (1952); *6 Klavierstücke* for left hand alone (1958). **OTHER:** Many pieces for organ; choruses; several songs with orch., organ, or piano.

Alessandro, Victor (Nicholas), American conductor; b. Waco, Texas, Nov. 27, 1915; d. San Antonio, Nov. 27, 1976. He received training in horn with his father. After studying composition with Howard Hanson and Bernard Rogers at the Eastman School of Music in Rochester, N.Y. (Mus. B., 1937), he pursued training at the Salzburg Mozarteum (1937) and with Pizzetti at the Accademia di Santa Cecilia in Rome (1938). From 1938 to 1951 he was conductor of the Oklahoma Sym. Orch. He was conductor of the San Antonio Sym. Orch. from 1951 until his death.

Alexander, Haim, German-born Israeli composer and teacher; b. Berlin, Aug. 9, 1915. He studied piano at the Stern Cons. in Berlin. In 1936 he emigrated to Palestine and took courses in piano and composition with Irma and Stefan Wolpe at the Palestine Cons. (graduated, 1945). He completed his training in Freiburg im Breisgau. From 1945 he was active as a teacher, and later served on the faculties of the Rubin Academy of Music in Jerusalem (1972–82) and the Univ. of Tel Aviv (1972–82). Alexander's works encompass both traditional and avant-garde idioms.

WORKS: ORCH.: *6 Israeli Dances* (1956; also for Piano, 1950); *Morasha* (Heritage), suite for Chamber Orch. (1980); Concerto for Piano and Chamber Orch. (1982). **CHAMBER:** *Metamorphoses* for Violin (1968); *See My Love* for Trombone (1969); *Nabut* for 9 Players (1971); *Yemenite Dance* for Oboe and Piano (1974); *Hassidic Tunes* for 2 Oboes (1975); *Variations on a Hassidic Niggun* for Oboe (1975); *A Tunisian Wedding Song* for 2 Flutes (1977). **PIANO:** *6 Israeli Dances* (1950; also for Orch., 1956); *Sonata brevis* for 2 Pianos (1959); *Soundfigures* (1965); *Patterns* (1973); *3 Pieces in Black and White* (1974); *Metamorphoses on a Theme by Mozart* (1990). **VOCAL:** *Journey Into the Present* for Narrator and Orch. (1971); *Ba'olam*, 7 songs for Mezzo-soprano or Baritone and 7 Instruments (1976); *Song of Faith* for Chorus and Orch. (1977–78); *Mein Blaues Klavier* for 8 Singers and Percussion (1990); *Questions and Answers* for Soprano, Flute, and Piano (1993–94); choruses; other songs.

Alexander, John, American tenor; b. Meridian, Miss., Oct. 21, 1923; d. there, Dec. 8, 1990. He studied at the Cincinnati Cons. of Music, making his operatic debut in Cincinnati in 1952. In 1957 he sang at the N.Y. City Opera; made his Metropolitan Opera debut in N.Y. as Ferrando in *Così fan tutte* on Dec. 19, 1961. He also appeared with the Vienna State Opera (1968) and the Royal Opera at Covent Garden in London (1970). In 1974 he joined the faculty of the Univ. of Cincinnati-College Cons. of Music. He became particularly adept in lyric tenor roles; also gained success as a concert artist.

Alexander, Josef, American composer; b. Boston, May 15, 1907; d. N.Y., Feb. 28, 1992. He studied piano at the New England Cons. of Music in Boston (graduated, 1925; postgraduate diploma, 1926), with Piston (composition) and Edward B. Hill (orchestration) at Harvard Univ. (B.A., 1938; M.A., 1941), with Boulanger in Paris (1939), and with Copland (composition) and Koussevitzky (conducting) at the Berkshire Music Center in Tanglewood (1940). He taught at Brooklyn College of the City Univ. of N.Y. (1943–77). In his works, Alexander adopted a facile laissez-faire idiom marked by a pleasurable admixture of euphonious dissonances.

WORKS: ORCH.: Piano Concerto (1938; Boston, June 8, 1940); *The Ancient Mariner*, symphonic poem (1938; Boston, June 8, 1940); *Doina* (1940); *A New England Overture* (St. Louis, Feb. 12, 1943); *Williamsburg Suite* (N.Y., Aug. 19, 1944); *Dithyrambe* (1947); *Epitaphs* (1947; N.Y., March 8, 1951); 4 syms.: No. 1, *Clockwork* (1948; N.Y., Nov. 28, 1949), No. 2 (1954), No. 3 (1961; N.Y., April 27, 1970), and No. 4 (1968); *Andante and Allegro* for Strings (1952; St. Louis, Feb. 20, 1953); Duo Concertante for Trombone, Percussion, and Strings (1959); *Quiet Music* for Strings (1965); *Trinity* for Brass and Percussion (1976). **CHAMBER:** String Quartet (1940); Piano Quintet (1942); Piano Trio (1944); Wind Quintet (1949); Piano Quartet (1952); Violin Sonata (1953); Cello Sonata (1953); Flute Sonata (1954); Clarinet Sonata (1957); Trombone Sonata (1959); Brass Trio (1971); Horn Sonata (1979); *Of Masks and Mirrors* for Cello, Soprano Saxophone, Piano, and Percussion (1981); *Escapades* for Marimba (1988); also hundreds of solo piano pieces. **VOCAL:** *Canticle of Night* for Mezzo-soprano or Baritone and Orch. (1959); *Gitanjali* for Soprano, Harpsichord, and Percussion (1973); *Symphonic Odes* for Men's Chorus and Orch. (1975); song cycles.

Alexander, Roberta, admired black American soprano; b. Lynchburg, Va., March 3, 1949. She was reared in a musical family; studied at the Univ. of Mich. in Ann Arbor (1969–71; M.Mus., 1971) and with Herman Woltman at the Royal Cons. of Music at The Hague. She appeared as Pamina at the Houston Grand Opera in 1980, as Daphne in Santa Fe (1981), and as Elettra in *Idomeneo* in Zürich (1982). Following a tour of Europe, she made a successful debut at the Metropolitan Opera in N.Y. as Zerlina on Nov. 3, 1983; later sang Bess in *Porgy and Bess* and the title role in Janáček's *Jenůfa*, a role she repeated at her Glyndebourne Festival debut in 1989. In 1984 she made her first appearance at the Aix-en-Provence Festival in Mozart's *La finta giardiniera*. She made her debut in Vienna as Cleopatra in Handel's *Giulio Cesare* at the Theater an der Wien in 1985. In 1986 she was a soloist with the Vienna Phil. at the Salzburg Festival and in 1988 she appeared with the English Chamber Orch. at the London Promenade Concerts. In 1995 she appeared as Vitellia at the Glyndebourne Festival. Among her other operatic roles are Mozart's Fiordiligi, Donna Elvira, Ilia, and the Countess, Offenbach's Antonia, Verdi's Luisa Miller, and Massenet's Manon and Thaïs.

Alexandra, Liana, Romanian composer; b. Bucharest, May 27, 1947. She studied at the Porumbescu Academy of Music in Bucharest (1965–71) and in Darmstadt; subsequently lectured in orchestration and analysis at the Bucharest Academy of Music. She won many honors for her compositions, including the Weber Prize (Dresden, 1979), 1st prize from the Gaudeamus Foundation (Netherlands, 1980), and the Romanian State Prize (1980).

WORKS: OPERA: *The Snow Queen*, children's opera (1979); *Labyrinth* (1987). **ORCH.:** 5 syms. (1971; *Hymns*, 1978; *Diacronies*, 1981; 1984; 1986); *Valences* (1973); *Resonances* for Piano and Orch. (1973); Clarinet Concerto (1974); *Music for 5 Soloists* (Clarinet and Piano Quartet) and Orch. (1975); Concerto for Flute, Viola, and Chamber Orch. (1980). **CHAMBER:** *Music* for Clarinet, Harp, and Percussion (1972); Sonata for Solo

Flute (1973); *Lyric Sequence* for Clarinet, Trumpet, and Piano (1974); *Collages* for Brass Quintet (1977); *2 Incantations*: No. 1 for Mezzo-soprano, Flute, Percussion, and Harpsichord (1978) and No. 2 for Clarinet and Piano Quartet (1978); *5 Consonances*: No. 1 for 4 Trombones (1978), No. 2 for Clarinet and Piano (1979), No. 3 for Organ (1979), No. 4 for Clarinet and Tape (1980), and No. 5 for Organ (1980). **VOCAL:** 4 cantatas (1971, 1977, 1977, 1978); 2 Sequences for Soprano and Chamber Orch. (1976).

Alexandrov, Alexander, Russian composer; b. Plakhino, April 13, 1883; d. Berlin, July 8, 1946. He studied with Rimsky-Korsakov and Glazunov at the St. Petersburg Cons. (1899–1901) and later at the Moscow Cons. with Vasilenko (1909–13). In 1928 he organized the Red Army Ensemble, which he conducted on numerous tours in Russia and abroad. His song *Hymn of the Bolshevik Party*, with a new set of words, was proclaimed the Soviet national anthem on March 15, 1944. He died while on a concert tour.

Alexandrov, Anatoli, eminent Russian pianist, teacher, and composer; b. Moscow, May 25, 1888; d. there, April 16, 1982. He studied with Taneyev at the Moscow Cons. (1907–10); also studied composition there with Vasilenko and piano with Igumnov, graduating in 1916; subsequently was a prof. there (from 1923). He composed mainly for piano, including 14 sonatas (1914–71). In his style of composition, he followed the main lines of Rachmaninoff and Scriabin. Other works include 2 operas, *Bela* (Moscow, Dec. 10, 1946) and *Wild Bara* (Moscow, March 2, 1957); 4 string quartets (1914–53); *Classical Suite* for Orch. (1926); *Dithyramb* for Double Bass and Piano (1959); Sym. No. 1 (1965); several song cycles; and incidental music for plays.

Alexanian, Diran, noted Armenian cellist and pedagogue; b. Constantinople, 1881; d. Chamonix, July 27, 1954. While studying with Grützmacher, he had the honor of playing chamber music with Brahms and Joachim; commenced his career as a virtuoso at age 17. In 1901 he went to Paris, where he later taught at the École Normale de Musique (1921–37); then settled in the U.S. Among his outstanding students were Maurice Eisenberg and Antonio Janigro. With Casals, he wrote the treatise *Traité théorique et pratique du violoncelle* (1922); also prepared a critical ed. of the Bach solo cello suites (1929).

Alexeev, Dmitri, talented Russian pianist; b. Moscow, Aug. 10, 1947. He entered Moscow's Central Music School at the age of 6; then studied with Bashkirov in Moscow, winning 2nd prize at the Long-Thibaud Competition in Paris (1969) and becoming the first Russian pianist to win 1st prize at the Leeds Competition (1975); subsequently gave recitals in Europe, Japan, and Australia. He made his American debut as a soloist with the Chicago Sym. Orch. in 1976, and in 1978 appeared at Carnegie Hall in N.Y. He further played duo-piano recitals with his wife, Tatiana Sarkissova. As a soloist, he is notable in the Romantic piano repertoire.

Alfano, Franco, eminent Italian composer and teacher; b. Posilippo, March 8, 1875; d. San Remo, Oct. 27, 1954. He studied composition with Serrao in Naples, and with Jadassohn and Sitt in Leipzig. From the beginning of his musical career, Alfano was interested in opera. His first stage work, *Miranda*, was written when he was barely 20; another opera, *La fonte di Enchir*, followed (Breslau, Nov. 8, 1898). In 1899 he went to Paris and became fascinated by light theater music. While in Paris he wrote *Napoli*, a ballet in the folk manner, which was staged at the Folies-Bérgères (Jan. 28, 1901), proving so successful that it ran for 160 successive performances. Returning to Italy, he began work on an opera based on Tolstoy's novel *Resurrection*. It was premiered as *Risurrezione* in Turin (Nov. 4, 1904) with sensational acclaim; the American premiere (Chicago, Dec. 31, 1925) was equally successful; there were also numerous performances in Germany and France. The opera was widely praised for its dramatic power and melodic richness in the best tradition of realistic Italian opera. Alfano continued to compose industriously for another half-century, but his later operas failed to equal his earlier successes. Among these later works are *Il Principe Zilah* (Genoa, Feb. 3, 1909); *L'ombra di Don Giovanni* (La Scala, April 3, 1914); *La leggenda di Sakuntala* (Bologna, Dec. 10, 1921; score destroyed during World War II; recomposed as *Sakuntala*, 1952); *Madonna Imperia*, lyric comedy (Turin, May 5, 1927); *L'Ultimo Lord* (Naples, April 19, 1930); *Cyrano de Bergerac* (Rome, Jan. 22, 1936); *Il Dottor Antonio* (Rome, April 30, 1949). Alfano also wrote 3 syms. (1909, 1932, 1934), 3 string quartets, a Violin Sonata, a Cello Sonata, and a ballet, *Vesuvius* (1938; a symphonic poem was drawn from it in 1946). He completed Puccini's last opera, *Turandot*, adding the last scene. His *Hymn to Bolivar* for Chorus and Orch., written for the centennial of Bolivar's death, was performed in Caracas, Venezuela, on Dec. 22, 1930. He was director of the Liceo Musicale in Bologna (1918–23) and of the Turin Cons. (1923–39), superintendent of the Teatro Massimo in Palermo (1940–42), and acting director of the Rossini Cons. in Pesaro (1947–50).

BIBL.: G. Gatti, "F. A.," *Musicisti moderni d'Italia e di fuori* (Bologna, 1920; also in the *Musical Times*, March 1921); G. Cesari, "La leggenda di Sakuntala di F. A.," *Rivista Musicale Italiana*, XXVIII (1921); A. della Corte, *Ritratto di F. A.* (Turin, 1935).

Alford, Kenneth J. See **Ricketts, Frederick J.**

Alfvén, Hugo (Emil), eminent Swedish composer and choral conductor; b. Stockholm, May 1, 1872; d. Falun, May 8, 1960. He was a student of Johan Lindberg (violin) and Aron Bergenson (harmony) at the Stockholm Cons. (1887–90); during this period, he also pursued training in painting with Otto Hesselbom and Oscar Törnå. From 1890 to 1897 he was a violinist in the Royal Opera Orch. in Stockholm. He also studied violin with Lars Zetterquist and composition with Johan Lindegren (1891–7). In 1896, 1897, and 1899 he held the composer's scholarship of the Royal Academy of Music, which allowed him to travel abroad, including a sojourn in Brussels to study violin with César Thomson (1897–98). From 1900 to 1903 he was a Jenny Lind scholar, which enabled him to study in various European cities, including Dresden with Hermann Kutzschbach, where he also received training in conducting (1901–02). From 1910 to 1939 he served as Director Musices of the Univ. of Uppsala. He also was conductor of the Orphei Drängar (1910–47), the Uppsala studentkars allmänna sangförening (1919–31; 1934–38), and the Svenska sangarförbundet (1921–43). In 1908 he was made a member of the Royal Academy of Music. He was awarded an honorary doctorate by the Univ. of Uppsala in 1917. His vivid autobiography was publ. in 4 vols. in Stockholm as *Första satsen: Ungdomsminnen* (1946), *Tempo furioso: Vandringsår* (1948), *I dur och moll: Från Uppsalaåren* (1949), and *Final* (1952). Alfvén's early training in painting is reflected in his adoption as a composer of a carefully crafted but colorful late Romantic idiom. He won distinction as a composer of orch. music and choral works. His folksong settings for chorus were particularly successful in Sweden. Outside his homeland, he remains best known for his popular first Swedish rhapsody for orch., *Midsommarvaka* (Midsummer Vigil; 1903).

WORKS: DRAMATIC: *Bergakungen* (The Mountain King), pantomime drama (1916–23; Stockholm, Feb. 7, 1923); *Gustav II Adolf*, incidental music (Stockholm, Nov. 6, 1932); *Den förlorade sonen* (The Prodigal Son), ballet (Stockholm, April 27, 1957). **ORCH.:** 5 syms.: No. 1 (1896–97; Stockholm, Feb. 9, 1897; rev. 1903–04; Stockholm, May 10, 1904), No. 2 (1897–98; Stockholm, May 2, 1899), No. 3 (1905; Göteborg, Dec. 3, 1906), No. 4, *Från havsbandet* (From the Outermost Skerries; 1918–19; Stockholm, Nov. 4, 1919), and No. 5 (1942–52; 1st complete perf., Stockholm, April 30, 1952); 3 Swedish rhapsodies: No. 1, *Midsommarvaka* (Midsummer Vigil; 1903; Stockholm, May 10, 1904), No. 2, *Uppsala-rhapsodi: Akademisk festouverture* (Uppsala, May 23, 1907), and No. 3, *Dala-rhapsodien* (1931; Stockholm, April 27, 1932); *En skärgårdssägen* (A Legend of the

Skerries), symphonic poem (1904; Stockholm, March 31, 1905); *Festpel* (1907; Stockholm, Feb. 18, 1908); *Drapa*, in memory of King Oscar II (Stockholm, May 16, 1908); *Bröllopsmarsch* (Wedding March; 1909); *Fest-ouverture* for Military Band (1909); *Elegie (Vid Emil Sjögrens bår* [Elegie: At Emil Sjögren's Funeral], tone poem (Stockholm, Oct. 18, 1918); *Hjalmar Brantings sorgmarsch* (Hjalmar Branting's Funeral March) for Wind Orch. (1924; Stockholm, March 1, 1925); *Synnöve Solbakken*, suite (Stockholm, Oct. 22, 1934); *Festmarsch för orkester till Stockholmsutställningengs öppnande 1930* (1930); *Fest-ouverture* (Malmö, Sept. 24, 1944); *En bygdesaga* (A District Fairy Tale), suite (1944). **CHAMBER:** Violin Sonata (Stockholm, March 20, 1896); *Elegi* for Horn or Cello and Organ (1897); *Serenade* for Violin and Piano (c.1902); *Serenade på Mammas födelsedag* (Serenade on Mother's Birthday) for Flute, Clarinet, Violin, and Piano (1902); *Andante religioso* for Celesta, Harp, and String Quartet (1913; also for String Orch.); *Roslagspolketta* for Violin and Piano (1956); piano pieces, including 3 *Skärgårdsbilder* (Pictures from the Skerries; 1901–02). **VOCAL:** Cantatas: *Vid sekelskiftet: Nyårskantaten* for Soloist, Chorus, and Orch. (1899; Stockholm, Jan. 1, 1900); *Uppenbarelsekantat* for Bass or Baritone, Chorus, and Orch. (Saltsjöbaden, May 18, 1913); *Kantat vid Baltiska utställningens i Malmö öppnande* for Baritone, Chorus, and Orch. (Malmö, May 15, 1914); *Kantat vid Uppsala läns Kungl. Hushållningssallskaps 100-årsjubileum 1915* for Chorus and Orch. (Uppsala, Dec. 1, 1915); *Kantat vid Reformationsfesten i Uppsala 1917* for Baritone, Chorus, and Orch. (Uppsala, Oct. 31, 1917); *Kantat vid Vårldspostunionens halvesekelsjubileum 1924* for Baritone, Chorus, and Orch. (Stockholm, Aug. 16, 1924); *Kantat vid Uppsala universitets 450-årsjubileum* for Alto, Baritone, Chorus, and Orch. (Uppsala, Sept. 15, 1927); *Kantat vid Svenska Röda korsets högtidssammankomst 2 maj 1930* for Alto, Chorus, and Orch. (Stockholm, May 2, 1930); *Kantat vid Sveriges Riksdags 500-års minnesfest 1935* for Baritone, Chorus, and Orch. (Stockholm, May 28, 1935); other works include *Herrens bön* for Soprano, Alto, Baritone, Chorus, and Orch. (1899–1901; Stockholm, Dec. 2, 1902); many men's choruses, including *Frihetssång* (1900), *Gustaf Frödings jordafärd* (1911), *Sverges flagga* (1916), and *Gryning vid havet* (1933); numerous folk song arrangements.

BIBL.: S. Svensson, *H. A. Som människa och konstnär* (Uppsala, 1946); P. Lindfors, *H. A. berättar* (Stockholm, 1966); J. Rudén, *H. A.: Kompositioner/Musical Works: Käll-och Verkförteckning/Thematic Index* (Stockholm, 1972); special issue of *Musikrevy*, XXVI/2 (1972); L. Hedwall, *H. A.: En svensk tonsättares liv och verk* (Stockholm, 1973); idem, *H. A.: Ein bildbiografi* (Tierp, 1990).

Ali Akbar Khan, Indian instrumentalist; b. Shibpore, Bengal, April 14, 1922. He studied dhrupad, dhamar, khayal, and sarod with his father and pakhawaj and tabla with his uncle. He founded the Ali Akbar College of Music in Calcutta in 1956; toured widely in Europe, America, and Japan as a virtuoso; held the post of court musician in Jodhpur. He has written a number of new rāgas. Several of his students achieved prominence as Indian instrumentalists in their own right.

Allanbrook, Douglas, American composer and teacher; b. Melrose, Mass., April 1, 1921. He studied with Boulanger at the Longy School of Music in Cambridge, with Piston at Harvard College (B.A., magna cum laude, 1948), and again with Boulanger in Paris. During World War II, he served in the infantry in Italy, receiving a Bronze Star Medal. In 1950 he received a Fulbright fellowship to study harpsichord and early keyboard music with Ruggero Gerlin in Naples; returning to the U.S. in 1952, he taught at St. John's College in Annapolis.

WORKS: OPERAS: *Ethan Frome* (1952); *Nightmare Abbey* (1960). **ORCH.:** 7 syms., including Nos. 1 (1958), 3, *Orchestral Landscapes* (1966), 5 for Brass Quintet and Orch. (1977), 6, *Heroic Attitudes* (1968), and 7, *Music from the Country* (1979); Concerto for Harpsichord and Small Orch. (1957); Violin Concerto (1959); *Serenade* for Piano and Orch. (1982). **CHAMBER:** 2 piano sonatas (1948, 1949); other piano pieces, including *5 Transcendental Studies* (1980) and *5 Night Pieces* (1986). **VOCAL:** *Ash Wednesday* for Soprano, Chorus, and Orch. (1947); *Te Deum* (1948); *Songs to Shakespeare Sonnets* for Medium Voice and Orch. (1951); *3 Noble Love Songs* for Baritone and Orch. (1960); *The 7 Last Words* for Mezzo-soprano, Baritone, Chorus, and Orch. (1970).

Alldahl, Per-Gunnar, Swedish composer; b. Solna, Oct. 11, 1943. He studied organ and composition at the Stockholm Musikhögskolan (1968–71); later joined its staff as an instructor. In his music, he pursues the twin goals of total freedom of realization and strict observance of minuscule tonal data.

WORKS: *Nulla ars . . .* for String Orch. (1966; Helsinki, Feb. 24, 1967); *Biceps* for Chamber Orch. and Tape (1968–69; Swedish Radio, Dec. 7, 1969); *Music* for Cello (1968); *Light Music* for 5 Flutes, Hammond Organ, and Vibraphone (1968); *Play* for Orch. (Bollnäs, April 4, 1970); *Ad lib* for Any Instruments (1971; originally for Bass Clarinet, Trombone, and Cello); *Bruspolska* for Nyckelharps (1972); *Stämma blod* for Chorus and Percussion (1972); *Unisona* for Alto Voice, Flute, Trombone, Double Bass, and Vibraphone (1972); *Från när och fjärran* for Jazz Quartet (1973); *Mot värk* for Chorus and Percussion (1973; sequel to *Stämma blod*); *Knaver-lik* for Nyckelharp and String Orch. (1974); *. . . ljudens dikt sjunger i venden . . .* for Narrator, Chorus, and Small Orch. (1974); *Till flöjten, ordern och kärleken* for Chorus and Chamber Ensemble (1980); *Var och en av oss* for Chorus and Organ (1986).

Alldis, John, English choral conductor; b. London, Aug. 10, 1929. He was educated at King's College, Cambridge. In 1962 he joined the faculty of the Guildhall School of Music in London; founded the John Alldis Choir, which soon achieved prominence. Later he conducted the London Sym. Orch. Chorus (1966–69), the London Phil. Orch. Chorus (1969–82), the Danish Radio Chorus in Copenhagen (1972–77), and the Groupe Vocal de France (1978–83).

Allen, Betty, black American mezzo-soprano, teacher, and administrator; b. Campbell, Ohio, March 17, 1930. She attended Wilberforce Univ. (1944–46), the Hartford School of Music (1950–53), and the Berkshire Music Center in Tanglewood; among her mentors were Sarah Peck More, Zinka Milanov, and Paul Ulanowsky. She made her N.Y. City Opera debut as Queenie in *Showboat* (1954). She made her N.Y. recital debut in 1958. After making her U.S. operatic debut in San Francisco in 1966, she sang with other U.S. opera companies, including the Metropolitan Opera in N.Y. (debut as Commère in *Four Saints in Three Acts* during the company's visit to the Manhattan Forum, Feb. 20, 1973) and the N.Y. City Opera (1973–75); also toured as a concert singer. She taught at the North Carolina School of the Arts in Winston-Salem (1978–87), was executive director (1979–92) and president (1992) of the Harlem School of the Arts, and gave master classes at the Curtis Inst. of Music in Philadelphia (from 1987).

Allen, Sir Hugh (Percy), eminent English organist and music educator; b. Reading, Dec. 23, 1869; d. Oxford, Feb. 20, 1946. He studied with F. Read in Reading, and at Christ's College, Cambridge, as an organ scholar, and at the Univ. of Oxford (Mus.Doc., 1898). At the age of 11, he acted as church organist in Reading. Thereafter he was an organist at various churches and cathedrals until the turn of the century. He was organist at New College, Oxford (1901–18), and later (1908–18) director of music at Univ. College in Reading. In 1918 he became prof. of music at Oxford, and, in the same year, director of the Royal College of Music in London, from which he resigned in 1937. He was knighted in 1920. In 1935 he was made a Knight of the Grand Cross of the Royal Victorian Order. For many years, he conducted the London and the Oxford Bach choirs. Allen was an ardent promoter of British music.

BIBL.: C. Bailey, *H.P. A.* (London, 1948).

Allen, Paul Hastings, American composer; b. Hyde Park, Mass., Nov. 28, 1883; d. Boston, Sept. 28, 1952. He studied at

Harvard Univ. (A.B., 1903); then went to Italy. During World War I, he was in the American diplomatic service in Italy; returning to the U.S. in 1920, he settled in Boston. He learned to play virtually all the orch. instruments as well as piano, and acquired fluent knowledge of Italian, German, and French, as well as a smattering of Russian. His vocal music reflected the Italian techniques in operatic composition, while his instrumental works were written largely in a Romantic vein. He wrote much chamber music for unusual combinations, including a Quartet for 2 Clarinets, Basset Horn, and Bass Clarinet. Among his operas are *Il filtro* (Genoa, Oct. 26, 1912), *Milda* (Venice, June 14, 1913), *L'ultimo dei Mohicani* (Florence, Feb. 24, 1916), *Cleopatra* (1921), and *La piccola Figaro* (1931); also composed *Pilgrim Symphony* (1910; received the Paderewski prize); piano pieces; choral works; songs.

Allen, Thomas (Boaz), notable English baritone; b. Seaham, Sept. 10, 1944. He studied organ and voice at the Royal College of Music in London (1964–68). After singing in the Glyndebourne Festival Chorus (1968–69), he made his operatic debut as Rossini's Figaro at the Welsh National Opera in Cardiff in 1969, where he sang until 1972. In 1971 he made his first appearance at London's Covent Garden as Donald in *Billy Budd*, and quickly established himself there as a leading member of the company. He also sang at the Glyndebourne (from 1973) and Aldeburgh (from 1974) festivals. On Nov. 5, 1981, he made his Metropolitan Opera debut in N.Y. as Papageno. In 1986 he sang the title role in Busoni's *Doktor Faust* in its first stage mounting in England with the English National Opera in London. He made his debut at Milan's La Scala as Don Giovanni in 1987. In 1990 he sang for the first time at the Chicago Lyric Opera as Rossini's Figaro. In 1993 he sang Count Almaviva at the Salzburg Festival. From 1994 he was the Prince Consort Prof. at the Royal College of Music. He publ. *Foreign Parts: A Singer's Journal* (North Pomfret, 1994). In 1989 Allen was made a Commander of the Order of the British Empire.

Allende (-Sarón), (Pedro) Humberto, eminent Chilean composer and pedagogue; b. Santiago, June 29, 1885; d. there, Aug. 16, 1959. He studied violin and theory at the National Cons. in Santiago (1889–1908); then taught in public schools there. In 1918 he visited France and Spain; in 1928 he served as Chilean delegate to the Congress of Popular Arts in Prague, under the auspices of the League of Nations; in 1929 he took part in the Festival of Ibero-American Music in Barcelona. Returning to Santiago, he taught composition at the National Cons. (1930–50). He received the National Arts Prize in appreciation of his work in musical ethnology. His music is marked with an exquisite sense of authentic Chilean folk song, while the purely formal structure follows the impressionistic manner akin to that of Debussy, Ravel, and Granados. His symphonic poem, *La voz de las calles* (1921), incorporates street cries of Chilean cities.

WORKS: ORCH.: Sym. (1910); *Escenas campesinas chilenas* (1913); Cello Concerto (1915); *La voz de las calles*, symphonic poem (Santiago, May 20, 1921); *La despedida* for 2 Sopranos, Contralto, and Orch. (Santiago, May 7, 1934); Violin Concerto (Santiago, Dec. 4, 1942); Piano Concerto (1945). **CHAMBER:** String Quartet (1945). **PIANO:** 3 sonatas (1906–15); *12 tonadas de carácter popular chileno* (1918–22; also for Orch.). **OTHER:** Songs.

BIBL.: N. Slonimsky, "H. A., First Modernist of Chile," *Musical America* (Aug. 1942); special issue of *Revista Musical Chilena* (Sept. 1945).

Allers, Franz, Czech-born American conductor; b. Karlsbad, Aug. 6, 1905; d. Las Vegas, Jan. 26, 1995. He studied violin at the Prague Cons., violin, piano, conducting, and composition at the Berlin Hochschule für Musik (diploma, 1926), and musicology at the Univ. of Berlin (1926). After playing in the Berlin Phil. (1924–26), he conducted at the Wuppertal Theater (1926–33), in Ústí nad Labem (1933–38), and with the Ballet Russe de Monte Carlo. He then settled in the U.S. and became a naturalized American citizen. He was active as a guest conductor with various orchs. and on Broadway. On Oct. 13, 1957, he made his N.Y. City Opera debut conducting *Die Fledermaus*, which score he also chose for his Metropolitan Opera debut in N.Y. on Nov. 30, 1963. He conducted at the Metropolitan until 1969; returned for the 1970–72 seasons and again in 1975–76. He was chief conductor of the Gärtnerplatz State Theater in Munich (1973–76).

Allin, Norman, English bass and teacher; b. Ashton-under-Lyne, Nov. 19, 1884; d. Hereford, Oct. 27, 1973. He studied at the Royal Manchester College of Music (1906–10). He made his operatic debut with the Beecham Opera Co. in London in 1916. In 1922 he became a director and leading bass of the British National Opera Co. in London, remaining with it until 1929; from 1942 to 1949 he was a member of the Carl Rosa Opera Co. He led vocal classes at the Royal Academy of Music in London (1935–60) and the Royal Manchester College of Music (1938–42). In 1958 he was made a Commander of the Order of the British Empire.

Almeida, Antonio (Jacques) de, French conductor of Portuguese-American descent; b. Paris, Jan. 20, 1928. He studied with Alberto Ginastera in Buenos Aires, attended the Mass. Inst. of Technology, received training in theory from Paul Hindemith at Yale Univ. (B.Mus., 1949), and took courses in conducting with Koussevitzky and Bernstein at the Berkshire Music Center in Tanglewood. After serving as a conductor with the Portuguese Radio in Lisbon (1957–60), he was principal conductor of the Stuttgart Phil. (1960–64). He was the principal guest conductor of the Houston Sym. Orch. (1969–71), and then music director of the Nice Phil. (1976–78). In 1993 he became music director of the Moscow Sym. Orch. As a guest conductor, Almeida appeared with many of the world's major orchs. and opera houses; he also was active in researching and ed. the works of Offenbach.

Almeida, Laurindo, lyrical Brazilian-born American guitarist and composer; b. São Paulo, Sept. 2, 1917; d. Van Nuys, Calif., July 26, 1995. He studied at the Escola Nacional de Música in Rio de Janeiro. After appearing on the radio and leading his own orch., he settled in the U.S. in 1947 and became a naturalized American citizen in 1961. He was soloist with Stan Kenton's orch. (1947–50); then appeared as a soloist with sym. orchs. and as a recitalist; also composed for films. In 1971 he married the soprano Deltra Eamon, with whom he appeared in recitals.

Alnar, Hasan Ferit, Turkish conductor, teacher, and composer; b. Constantinople, March 11, 1906; d. Ankara, July 27, 1978. He learned to play Turkish instruments as a child; studied with Joseph Marx (composition) and Kabasta (conducting) in Vienna (1927–32). He taught composition at the Instanbul Cons. (1937–46); was chief conductor of the Phil. (1946–53) and Opera (1954–60) in Ankara. From his earliest studies, Alnar was fascinated with indigenous Turkish percussion instruments and many of his compositions are marked with native colorations; among his works are *Turkish Suite* (1930) and *Istanbul Suite* (1937–38) for Orch., a Cello Concerto (1943), a Concerto for Kanun (Turkish psaltery) and Orch. (1951), a String Quartet (1933), and a Piano Trio (1967).

Alpaerts, Flor, Belgian composer, conductor, and music educator, father of **Jef Alpaerts**; b. Antwerp, Sept. 12, 1876; d. there, Oct. 5, 1954. He studied composition with Benoit and Blockx and violin at the Flemish Cons. in Antwerp; in 1903 he joined its staff, serving as its director from 1934 to 1941. He conducted the local orch. at the Zoological Gardens (1919–51). His music is marked by an intense feeling for the modalities of Flemish folk songs. His 5-vol. treatise *Muzieklezen en Zingen* was for many years the official textbook in all Flemish music institutions.

WORKS: DRAMATIC: OPERA: *Shylock* (Antwerp, Nov. 22, 1913); incidental music. **ORCH.:** 7 symphonic poems: *Psyche* (1900); *Herleving* (1903); *Cyrus* (1905); *Pallieter* (1921); *Thijl*

Uilenspiegel (1927); *Avondindruk* (1928); *Zomeridyll* (1928); *Poème symphonique* for Flute and Orch. (1903); *Karakterstuk* for Trumpet and Strings (1904); *Bosspeling* (1904); *Salomé danse* (1907); *Vlaamse Idylle* (1920); *Romanza* for Violin and Small Orch. (1928); *James Ensor Suite* (1929); 2 suites for Small Orch. (1932); *Humor* (1936); *Serenade* for Cello and Orch. (1936); *Small Suite* for Strings (1947); Violin Concerto (1948); *Capriccio* (1953). **CHAMBER:** *2 Pieces* for Piano Trio (1906); *Avondmuziek* for 8 Woodwinds (1915); 4 string quartets (1943, 1944, 1945, 1950); *3 petites pièces* for Violin and Piano (1944); *4 Bagatelles* for String Quartet (1953). **OTHER:** Choral works and songs.

Alpaerts, Jef, Belgian conductor and teacher, son of **Flor Alpaerts**; b. Antwerp, July 17, 1904; d. there, Jan. 15, 1973. He received his primary education at the Royal Flemish Cons. in Antwerp; then went to Paris, where he studied piano with Isidor Philipp and with Cortot, and composition with d'Indy at the Schola Cantorum. Returning to Belgium in 1936, he was appointed to the faculty of the Royal Flemish Cons.; retired in 1969. In 1938 he inaugurated the Collegium Musicum Antverpiense for performances of early music.

Alpenheim, Ilse von, Austrian pianist; b. Innsbruck, Feb. 11, 1927. She studied with Franz Ledwinka and Winfried Wolf at the Salzburg Mozarteum; then appeared in recital and chamber music concerts; toured Europe, Japan, Australia, and the U.S. as a soloist; played with the Cleveland Orch., Philadelphia Orch., National Sym. Orch. of Washington, D.C., Detroit Sym. Orch., and Boston Sym. Orch. She was a sensitive interpreter of Haydn, Mozart, and Schubert. In 1969 she married **Antal Doráti**.

Alsina, Carlos Roqué, Argentine composer; b. Buenos Aires, Feb. 19, 1941. He studied theory with various local teachers; was active with the modern society Agrupación de Nueva Música in Buenos Aires (1959–64); from 1964 to 1966 he worked in Berlin on a Ford Foundation grant; there he took instruction with Luciano Berio, who inculcated him in the arcana of ultramodern compositional techniques. From 1966 to 1968 he lived in Buffalo, where he taught at the State Univ. of N.Y.; in 1969 he founded, along with Vinko Globokar, Jean-Pierre Drouet, and Michel Portal, the improvisatory group New Phonic Art, which toured Europe. His music is of a functional nature, peculiar to the cosmopolitan avant-garde; it presents a colorful synthesis of quaquaversal idioms, ranging from stark, cloistered dissonance to overt, triadic formalism. Aleatory techniques are in evidence in his improvisatory performances.

WORKS: DRAMATIC: *Texts 1967*, theater piece for Soprano, Flute, Trombone, Violin, Cello, Double Bass, Percussion, and Piano (1967); *Fusion*, choreographic music for Dancer, 2 Pianos, and 2 Percussionists (1974); *Encore*, musical spectacle (1976); *La Muraille*, opera (Avignon, July 28, 1981); *Del Tango*, azione scenica (1982). **ORCH.:** *3 Pieces* for Strings (1964); *Symptom* (1969); *Dispersion 1969* for Chamber Orch. (1969); *Überwindung* for 4 Instrumental Soloists and Orch. (Donaueschingen, Oct. 18, 1970); *Omnipotenz* for Chamber Orch. (1971); *Schichten I* for Chamber Orch. (1971) and *II* for Chamber Ensemble (1972); *Approach* for Piano, Percussion, and Orch. (1972; West Berlin, March 14, 1973); *Thema II* for Percussion and Strings (1974–75; Royan, March 26, 1975); *Stücke* (Royan, April 4, 1977); *Señales* for Piano and Chamber Orch. (La Rochelle, July 3, 1977); *Decisions* for Chamber Orch. (1977); *Études* for Orch. and Tape (Metz, Nov. 17, 1979); 2 syms.: No. 1, *Prima sinfonia*, for Flute, Soprano, Cello, and Orch. (1983) and No. 2 (1992); Piano Concerto (Paris, Nov. 16, 1985); *Suite indirecte* (1989); *Fantasie* for Clarinet and Orch. (1991). **CHAMBER:** *Quinteto de Maderas* for Wind Quintet (1961); *Funktionen* for Flute, Clarinet, Bassoon, Trumpet, Violin, Cello, Piano, and 2 Percussionists (1965); *Consecuenza* for Trombone (1966); *Auftrag* for 9 Players (1966); *Trio 1967* for Cello, Trombone, and Percussion (1967); *Rendez-vous* for 4 Players (1970); *Unity* for Clarinet and Cello (1973); *A Letter* for Wind Quintet (1973); *Étude* for Zarb (1973); *Thema* for Percussion (1974); *Hinterland* for Piano, Percussion, and Tape (1982); *Voie avec vox* for String Quartet (1984); *Deux Phases* for 7 Instruments (1987); *Éloignements* for 6 Percussionists (1990); *Passages* for Flute, Clarinet, Violin, Cello, and Piano (1990). **VOCAL:** *Requiem y aleluya* for Soprano, 5 Instruments, and Percussion (1960); *Oratorio* for 3 Soloists, 4 Actors, and 3 Small Instrumental Ensembles (1964); *Text* for Chorus, Trombone, and 3 Percussion Instruments (1966); *Consecuenza II* for Voice (1971); Cantata for Tenor, Chorus, and Orch. (Radio France, April 22, 1977); *Harmonies* for Children's Chorus, 2 Lectors, Narrator, 4 Soloists, Tape, and Orch. (Paris Radio, Dec. 22, 1979); *Pénombres* for Chorus, Children's Chorus, and Orch. (1994).

Alsop, Marin, American conductor; b. N.Y., Oct. 16, 1956. She pursued her musical training at the Juilliard School in N.Y. (B.M., 1977; M.M., 1978). During the summers of 1988 and 1989, she held the Leonard Bernstein Conducting Fellowship at the Tanglewood Music Center, where she was a student of Bernstein, Ozawa, and Gustav Meier; in 1989 she became the first woman to receive the Koussevitzky conducting prize there, and that same year she was a prizewinner in the Stokowski conducting competition in N.Y. In 1984 she became founder-artistic director of her own N.Y.-based orch., Concordia, with which she presented a varied repertoire of not only standard and contemporary works, but also jazz. She was also active as a jazz violinist, and was founder-director of her own swing band, String Fever. She served as music director of the Eugene (Oreg.) Sym. Orch. (1989–96), the Long Island Phil. (1990–96), the Cabrillo Music Festival (from 1992), and the Oregon Festival of American Music (from 1992), as well as principal conductor of the Colorado Sym. Orch. in Denver (from 1993). She also held the 1st Creative Conductor's Chair with the St. Louis Sym. Orch. from 1996.

Altenburg, Detlef, German musicologist; b. Bad Hersfeld, Jan. 9, 1947. He was educated at the Univ. of Cologne (Ph.D., 1973, with the diss. *Untersuchungen zur Geschichte der Trompete im Zeitalter der Clarinblaskunst (1500–1800)*; publ. in Regensburg, 1973; Habilitationsschrift, 1980, *Studien zum Musikdenken und zu den Reformplänen von Franz Liszt*). From 1983 he was a prof. at the Univ.-Gesamthochschule-Paderborn in Detmold. From 1986 to 1989 he was an ed. for *Die Musikforschung*. An authority on Liszt, he served as ed. of the new critical edition of Liszt's writings (9 vols., Wiesbaden, 1989 et seq.). In 1990 he became president of the Franz-Liszt-Gesellschaft in Weimar, and was ed. of its *Liszt-Jahrbuch* from 1992. Among his other writings are *Zum Repertoire der Hoftrompeter im 17. und 18. Jahrhundert* (Tutzing, 1976), *Eine Theorie der Musik der Zukunft: Zur Funktion des Programms im symphonischen Werk Franz Liszts* (Graz, 1977), and *Die Projekte der Liszt-Forschung* (with G. Winkler; Eisenstadt, 1991).

Altenburger, Christian, German violinist; b. Heidelberg, Sept. 5, 1957. He began to study violin with his father; at the age of 7, he made his first public appearance; subsequently enrolled at the Vienna Academy of Music, graduating at 16; then went to the U.S. as a scholarship student at the Juilliard School in N.Y., where he studied with Dorothy DeLay (graduated, 1978). In 1976 he made his professional debut in a recital at the Musikverein in Vienna; then appeared as soloist with the Berlin Phil., Vienna Phil., Concertgebouw Orch. of Amsterdam, London Sym. Orch., Chicago Sym. Orch., and other orchs.

Althouse, Paul (Shearer), American tenor and teacher; b. Reading, Pa., Dec. 2, 1889; d. N.Y., Feb. 6, 1954. He studied with Oscar Saenger. He made his operatic debut as Dimitri in the American premiere of *Boris Godunov* at the Metropolitan Opera on March 19, 1913; continued on its roster until 1920, and joined it again in 1923; sang Wagnerian roles as a Heldentenor at the Metropolitan from 1934 to 1940; also toured in Europe, Australia, and New Zealand as a concert singer; subsequently was chiefly active as a vocal teacher in N.Y. Among his most prominent students were Eleanor Steber and Richard Tucker.

Altman, Ludwig, German-American organist and composer; b. Breslau, Sept. 2, 1910; d. San Francisco, Nov. 27, 1990. He studied with Arthur Schmitz and Peter Epstein at the Univ. of Breslau, with Hans Joachim Moser, Arnold Schering, Johannes Wolf, and Friedrich Blume at the Berlin-Spandau School for Church Music (1929–33), and organ with Arthur Zubke. After serving as organist of Berlin's Neue Synagoge (1933–36), he emigrated to the U.S. and concentraed his career in San Francisco, where he was organist and choral director at Temple Emanu-El (from 1937), organist of the San Francisco Sym. (1940–73), and municipal organist of San Francisco (from 1952); also toured widely as a recitalist. His extensive repertory ranged from the Baroque masters to scores by contemporary composers. He wrote much sacred music and many solo organ pieces.

BIBL.: E. Glaser and C. Crawford, *L. A.: A Well-Tempered Musician's Unfinished Journey Through Life* (Berkeley, 1990).

Altmann, Wilhelm, German music scholar; b. Adelnau, near Posen, April 4, 1862; d. Hildesheim, March 25, 1951. He studied philology and government in Marburg and Berlin (Ph.D., 1885). He served as librarian in Greifswald (1889–1900). In 1900 he was appointed a librarian of the Prussian Library in Berlin; in 1915 he became director of the music dept., retiring in 1927. In 1906 he founded, in cooperation with Breitkopf & Härtel, the Deutsche Musiksammlung at the Berlin Library. Altmann compiled a number of valuable bibliographical works, among them *Chronik des Berliner Phil. Orchesters* (1902); *Richard Wagners Briefe* (1905; a list of 3,143 letters with brief synopses); *Wagners Briefwechsel mit seinen Verlegern* (2 vols., 1911); *Kammermusik-Literatur-Verzeichnis,* a list of chamber music publ. since 1841 (1910; 6th ed., rev., 1945); and *Max-Reger-Katalog* (1917, 1923). He also ed. Paul Frank's *Tonkünstler-Lexikon* (1926, 1927, 1936, 1949). Furthermore, he publ. bibliographies of books on instruments and made arrangements of classical works.

Altmeyer, Jeannine (Theresa), American soprano; b. La Habra, Calif., May 2, 1948. She received instruction from Marshall Singher and Lotte Lehmann in Santa Barbara, California; later took courses at the Salzburg Mozarteum. She made her operatic debut as the Heavenly Voice in *Don Carlos* at the Metropolitan Opera (N.Y., Sept. 25, 1971); then sang Freia in *Das Rheingold* at the Chicago Lyric Opera (1972), in Salzburg (1973), and at London's Covent Garden (1975). From 1975 to 1979 she was a member of the Württemberg State Theater in Stuttgart; subsequently appeared in Bayreuth (1979), Paris (1987), Zürich (1989), and Milan (1990). She is notably successful in Wagnerian roles, including Elisabeth, Gutrune, Eva, Brünnhilde, Elsa, and Sieglinde.

Altmeyer, Theo(dor David), German tenor; b. Eschweiler, March 16, 1931. He was educated in Cologne. In 1956 he joined the Berlin Städtische Oper, remaining on its roster until 1960; then became a member of the Hannover Opera; later appeared at the Stuttgart Opera and the Vienna State Opera; also toured North America. In 1974 he joined the faculty of the Hochschule für Musik in Hannover; continued to appear in opera and concerts.

Altschuler, Modest, Russian-born American cellist and conductor; b. Mogilev, Feb. 15, 1873; d. Los Angeles, Sept. 12, 1963. He studied cello at the Warsaw Cons. as a child; then went to Moscow, where he took courses in composition with Arensky and Taneyev and in piano and conducting with Safonov at the Cons., graduating in 1890. After touring Russia as a cellist, he emigrated to America, and in 1903 organized in N.Y. the Russian Sym. Soc. He conducted its first concert on Jan. 7, 1904; for some 12 years the concerts of this organization became an important cultural medium for performances of Russian music in America. One of Altschuler's notable accomplishments was the premiere of Scriabin's *Le Poème de l'extase,* which he gave in N.Y. on Dec. 10, 1908, in advance of its Russian performance. At the same concert, Mischa Elman made his American debut as a concert violinist. Altschuler also conducted the first American performance of Scriabin's *Prométhée* (N.Y., March 20, 1915), at which he made an unsuccessful attempt to include the part of *Luce,* a color organ prescribed by Scriabin in the score. Among other Russian composers whose works Altschuler presented for the first time in America were Rachmaninoff, Liadov, Vasilenko, and Ippolitov-Ivanov. Altschuler eventually retired to Los Angeles. He wrote an autobiography which remains unpubl.

Alva, Luigi (real name, **Luis Ernesto Alva Talledo**), noted Peruvian tenor; b. Lima, April 10, 1927. He was a pupil of Rosa Morales in Lima, where he made his operatic debut as Beppe in 1950. He then completed his training at the La Scala opera school in Milan. In 1954 he made his European operatic debut as Alfredo at Milan's Teatro Nuovo, and then sang Paolino in *Il matrimonio segreto* at the opening of Milan's La Piccola Scala in 1955; his La Scala debut followed as Count Almaviva in 1956. In 1957 he sang at the Salzburg Festival, in 1960 at London's Covent Garden (debut as Count Almaviva), and in 1961 at the Chicago Lyric Opera. On March 6, 1964, he made his Metropolitan Opera debut in N.Y. as Fenton; remained on its roster until 1966, and again for the 1967–69, 1971–72, and 1973–75 seasons. In subsequent years, he continued to make appearances in Europe until his retirement in 1989. He served as artistic director of the Fundación Pro Arte Lírica in Lima from 1982. Alva was particularly esteemed for his roles in Mozart's operas, but he also won success for his Italian roles from the early 19th century repertory.

Alvarez (de Rocafuerte), Marguerite d', English contralto of Peruvian descent; b. Liverpool, c.1886; d. Alassio, Oct. 18, 1953. She made her first public appearance at a London diplomatic reception when she was 16. After training in Brussels, she made her operatic debut in 1904 as Dalila in Rouen; in 1909 she made her U.S. debut with Hammerstein's company in N.Y. as Fidès; in 1911 she appeared at the London Opera House as the Queen in *Hérodiade* and later sang at London's Covent Garden, in Chicago, and in Boston. In her later years, she devoted herself mainly to a concert career, retiring in 1939. Her autobiography was publ. as *Forsaken Altars* (London, 1954; U.S. ed. as *All the Bright Dreams,* N.Y., 1956).

Alvary, Lorenzo, Hungarian-born American bass; b. Debrecen, Feb. 20, 1909. He studied law at the univs. of Geneva (B.L., 1930) and Budapest (LL.M., 1932) and voice in Milan and Berlin. In 1934 he made his operatic debut at the Budapest Royal Opera, and then sang at the Vienna State Opera in 1937. In 1938 he emigrated to the U.S., becoming a naturalized American citizen in 1944. In 1939 he made his U.S. debut as the Police Commissioner in *Der Rosenkavalier* at the San Francisco Opera, where he returned regularly until 1977. On Nov. 26, 1942, he made his Metropolitan Opera debut in N.Y. as Zuñiga, remaining on its roster until 1961; appeared there again (1962–72, 1977–78).

Alwin, Karl (real name, **Alwin Oskar Pinkus**), German conductor; b. Königsberg, April 15, 1891; d. Mexico City, Oct. 15, 1945. He studied composition in Berlin with Humperdinck and Hugo Kaun; then conducted in Halle (1913), Posen (1914), Düsseldorf (1915–17), and Hamburg (1917–20). From 1920 to 1938 he was a conductor at the Vienna State Opera. He left Austria in 1938, after the Anschluss, and went to Mexico, where he conducted opera from 1941 until his death. From 1920 to 1936 he was married to **Elisabeth Schumann**.

Alwyn, Kenneth, English conductor; b. Croydon, July 28, 1925. He received his musical training at the Royal Academy of Music in London; then conducted ballet at the Sadler's Wells Theatre; was an assistant conductor at the Royal Ballet (1957–61) and from 1961 a conductor at the Western Theatre Ballet; he served as its music director from 1967 to 1969. He was also active in broadcasting and films; was a conductor with the BBC Concert Orch. from 1968; in 1969 he became principal conductor of the BBC Northern Ireland Orch.

Alwyn, William, English composer; b. Northampton, Nov. 7, 1905; d. Southwold, Sept. 11, 1985. He studied with McEwen at the Royal Academy of Music in London (1920–23), where he subsequently taught (1926–56), although he had failed to graduate; was also active as a poet, translator, and painter. In 1978 he was made a Commander of the Order of the British Empire. Although Alwyn wrote a significant number of concert and stage works, he was particularly facile when writing for films.

WORKS: OPERAS: *Juan, or The Libertine* (1965–71); *Miss Julie* (1970–73; BBC, July 16, 1977); over 60 film scores. **ORCH.:** 5 syms. (1949, 1953, 1956, 1959, 1973); 3 concerti grossi (1942, 1950, 1964); Oboe Concerto (1951); *The Magic Island* (1952); *Lyra Angelica,* concerto for Harp and Strings (1954); *Autumn Legend* for English Horn and Strings (1955); *6 Elizabethan Dances* (1957); *Derby Day* (1960); 2 sinfoniettas (1970, 1976). **CHAMBER:** 2 string quartets (1955, 1976); String Trio (1962); Clarinet Sonata (1963); *Naiades,* sonata for Flute and Harp (1971); piano pieces. **VOCAL:** Song cycles.

Åm, Magnar, Norwegian composer; b. Trondheim, April 9, 1952. He studied organ at the Bergen Cons. and received lessons in composition from Lidholm at the Stockholm Musikhögskolan (1971–72). He was awarded a State Guaranteed Income for Artists and devoted himself to composition. In his output, Åm has generally pursued a freely tonal style. While preferring traditional forms, his experimental bent has led him to explore the realm of electro-acoustics.

WORKS: ORCH.: *Song* for Brass and Percussion (1974); *Study on a Norwegian Hymn* for Strings (1977); *ajar* for Double Bass and Orch. (1981); *my planet, my soul,* sym. (1982); *right through all this* (1985); *The Oblique One,* march for Symphonic Band (1985); *can tell you a mile off* for Symphonic Band (1988); *if we lift as one* (1988); *timeless energy* (1991); *Naked Tones* for Symphonic Band (1993). **CHAMBER:** *2 Movements* for String Quartet (1970); *Lyrikk* for 2 Horns and Hardanger Fiddle (1971); *Intermezzo* for 3 Woodwinds (1976); Sonata for Flute, Guitar, and Cello (1976); *Dance* for Harp, Guitar, and Harpsichord (1977); *in nude,* octet for Clarinet, Bassoon, Horn, 2 Violins, Viola, Cello, and Double Bass (1977); *Du, bli her* (You Stay Here!) for Viola and Cello (1979); *sing, pain* for Viola, 2 Cellos, Percussion, and Piano (1979); *like a leaf on the river* for Guitar (1983); *pas de deux* for Violin and Cello (1984); *still* for Flute and Harp (1985); *Freetonal Conversation* for Violin, Cello, and Piano (1986); *hovering depths* for Double Bass (1986); *air . . . of breath have you come, to breath shall you be* for Double Bass and Tape (1987); *summen . . . ,* canon for 4 Trumpets (1990). **VOCAL:** *Prayer* for Soprano, Chorus, and String Orch. (1972); *Mot dag* (Dawn Is Breaking), oratorio for Chorus and Orch. (1972); *point zero,* version A for Soprano, Chorus, Children's Chorus, and Orch. (1978–83), version B for Soprano, Chorus, Congregation, Organ, and Orch. (1978–83), and version C for Soprano, Chorus, Congregation, and Organ (1982); *trollsenga* for Narrator and Saxophone or Flute or Percussion (1980); *Agamemnon,* choral drama for Soprano, Women's Chorus, and 2 Clarinets (1981); *wings* for 3 Choruses and 5 Instruments (1981); *A Caged-Bird's Dream (Music for Closed Eyes)* for Chorus, Violin, 2 Percussion, Piano, and Slides (1982); *Omen* for Reciter, Violin, Horn, and Upright Piano (1983–89); *till we grow out of ourselves* for Soprano, Chorus, Children's Chorus, Narrator, and Organ (1983); *conqilia* for Narrator, Violin, Horn, and Piano (1984); *a miracle and a tear* for Chorus (1987); *fritt fram* for Soprano, Flute, Clarinet, Violin, Cello, Percussion, and Piano (1987); *grain of sand seeks oyster* for Soprano, Flute, Clarinet, Guitar, Violin, and Double Bass (1987); *a new-born child* for Chorus, Flute, Percussion, Marimba, and Harp (1988); *and let the boat slip quietly out* for Voice and Orch. (1989); *Pilgrimsmusikk* for Nidaros Cathedral for Boy Soprano, Tenor, Children's Chorus, Mixed Chorus, and Chamber Orch. (1990); *. . . og livet,* oratorio for 2 Narrators, Soprano and Tenor Voices, Children's Chorus, Mixed Chorus, and Chamber Orch. (1990); *effata* for Soprano, Men's Voices, and Organ (1991); *quiet ruby* for Chorus (1992); *Is it Like this Among Humans, Too?* for Alto, Chorus, Flute, Synthesizer, Piano, and Percussion (1992). **OTHER:** *water music,* electro-acoustic piece (1984); *pa en stol,* visual concert for Clarinet, Trumpet, Percussion, Piano, Mime, and Audience (1989); *Tonebath,* music experience (1989); *Voyage,* music experience (1993).

Amacher, Maryanne, American composer, performer, sound architect, and mixed-media artist; b. Kates, Pa., Feb. 25, 1943. She studied with Rochberg at the Univ. of Pa. (B.F.A., 1964) and with Stockhausen; then became involved in computer science at the univs. of Pa. and Illinois, the Mass. Inst. of Technology, and Radcliffe College. In 1967 she initiated the City-Links series, sound-displacement experiments in which she transmitted, via microphone installations, the sounds of distant locations to her own studio or performance space; then developed theories about the psychoacoustical effects of sound on daily life patterns, which have informed all subsequent work. Since 1980 she has been developing a form of music theater utilizing the "virtual environment" (3D simulated reality), to which the Vivarium Group at M.I.T. is similarly directed. Her *Music for Sound-joined Rooms,* in which various architectural features of a building are used as sound structures, are complex mixed-media works incorporating video, 3D graphics, projected images, lighting, furniture, sculpture, photography, and texts. Her *Fake Ears* is programmable software that means to enhance the capabilities of the human ear. Because of the extreme technological sophistication of her work, public access is limited; live performances are rare.

WORKS: *City-Links,* mixed media (1967–79); *Lecture on the Weather* (1975; in collaboration with John Cage); *Remainder,* dance music (1976); *Close Up* (for Cage's *Empty Words;* 1979); *Music for Sound-joined Rooms,* mixed media (1980–82); *Sound House,* Mini-Sound Series (1985); *The Music Rooms,* Mini-Sound Series (1987); other electronic and mixed-media scores.

BIBL.: T. Johnson, "M. A.: Acoustics Joins Electronics," *Village Voice* (Dec. 15, 1975); L. Durner, "M. A.: Architect of Aural Design," *Ear Magazine,* XIII, no. 10 (Feb. 1989).

Amaducci, Bruno, Swiss conductor; b. Lugano, Jan. 5, 1925. He studied at the École Normale de Musique in Paris and at the Milan Cons.; then toured widely as an opera and sym. conductor in Europe, and also appeared in North America. On Oct. 5, 1967, he made his Metropolitan Opera debut in N.Y. conducting *Falstaff.* He became closely associated with the Orch. della Radiotelevisione della Svizzera Italiana in Lugano, where he was active as a conductor and later as chief of music programming. He publ. *Music of the Five Composers of the Puccini Dynasty* (1973).

Amar, Licco, Hungarian violinist and teacher; b. Budapest, Dec. 4, 1891; d. Freiburg im Breisgau, July 19, 1959. He studied with Emil Bare at the Royal Academy of Music in Budapest and with Henri Marteau at the Berlin Hochschule für Musik in Berlin; in 1912, joined the Marteau Quartet as 2nd violinist. He subsequently was concertmaster of the Berlin Phil. (1915–20) and at the National Theater in Mannheim (1920–23). In 1921 he organized the Amar Quartet, with Hindemith as violist, Walter Caspar as 2nd violinist, and Maurits Frank as cellist. In 1933 he was compelled to leave Germany; in 1935 he was engaged as a prof. at the Ankara Cons. In 1957 he returned to Germany and taught at the Hochschule für Musik in Freiburg im Breisgau.

Amara (real name, **Armaganian**), **Lucine,** American soprano of Armenian descent; b. Hartford, Conn., March 1, 1927. She studied violin; began her vocal training in San Francisco after her parents moved west. She made her operatic debut at the Metropolitan Opera in N.Y. on Nov. 6, 1950, as the Heavenly Voice in Verdi's *Don Carlos.* Although criticized for a lack of celestial quality in that part, she made progress in her career. In 1954 she sang at the Glyndebourne Festival, and at the Vienna

State Opera in 1960. She made a world tour in 1968, which included several appearances in Russia. She also made a cameo film appearance, as the female interest in *The Great Caruso* (1951), opposite Mario Lanza.

Amato, Pasquale, remarkable Italian baritone; b. Naples, March 21, 1878; d. N.Y., Aug. 12, 1942. He studied at the Naples Cons. (1896–99). In 1900 he made his operatic debut as Germont at the Teatro Bellini in Naples, and then sang in other Italian music centers. In 1904 he sang Amonasro at his debut at London's Covent Garden. In 1907–08 he appeared at Milan's La Scala. On Nov. 20, 1908, he made his Metropolitan Opera debut in N.Y. as Germont, and quickly established himself as one of its principal members, remaining on its roster until 1918 and returning there from 1919 to 1921, excelling in all the major Italian roles as well as several French and German. On Dec. 10, 1910, he created the role of Jack Rance in *La fanciulla del West* there. After his retirement, he taught voice in N.Y. In 1933 he came out of retirement to celebrate the 25th anniversary of his Metropolitan Opera debut with a gala appearance at N.Y.'s Hippodrome. Amato's extraordinary vocal prowess was equalled by his dramatic versatility, which ran the gamut from serious to comic roles.

Ambros, Vladimír, Czech composer; b. Prostějov, Moravia, Sept. 18, 1890; d. there, May 12, 1956. He studied at the Brünn Organ School (1908–10) and at the Frankfurt am Main Cons., later becoming active as a conductor with the Carl Rosa Opera Co. in England. After World War I, he returned to Prostějov. His works include the operas *Ukradené štěstí* (Stolen Happiness; 1924) and *Maryla* (1951); 3 syms. (1941; 1944; 1946–51); Symphonietta (1938); a cantata, *Veliký navrat* (Grand Return; 1951); chamber music; songs.

BIBL.: V. Gregor, *V. A.* (Prostějov, 1969).

Ambrosius, Hermann, German composer; b. Hamburg, July 25, 1897; d. Engen am Hegau, Oct. 25, 1983. He studied at the Univ. of Leipzig; later took private lessons in composition with Pfitzner. In 1925 he joined the faculty of the Leipzig Cons.; eventually settled in Engen am Hegau. A prolific composer, he wrote 12 syms. (1920–63); 3 piano concertos (1926–52); 2 cello concertos (1928–38); 2 guitar concertos (1953–62); an orch. suite, *Iskusstvo* (Art), inspired by Russian paintings; and an astonishing number of pieces for accordion; also pieces for Trautonium. His fecundity was noted in an admiring Festschrift, ed. by F. Hirtler, publ. on his 70th birthday.

Ameling, Elly (actually, **Elisabeth Sara**), outstanding Dutch soprano; b. Rotterdam, Feb. 8, 1934. After studies in Rotterdam and The Hague, she completed her training with Bernac in Paris; won the 's-Hertogenbosch (1956) and Geneva (1958) competitions, then made her formal recital debut in Amsterdam (1961). Subsequent appearances with the Concertgebouw Orch. in Amsterdam and the Rotterdam Phil. secured her reputation. In 1966 she made her London debut and in 1968 her N.Y. debut; her first appearance in opera was as Ilia in *Idomeneo* with the Netherlands Opera in Amsterdam in 1973, but she chose to concentrate upon a career as a concert artist. She gained renown for her appearances with major European orchs. and for her lieder recitals. In 1971 she was made a Knight of the Order of Oranje Nassau by the Dutch government. She established the Elly Ameling Lied Prize to be awarded at the 's-Hertogenbosch competition. Her remarkable career came to a close with a series of farewell recitals in 1995.

Amellér, André (Charles Gabriel), French composer; b. Arnaville, Jan. 2, 1912; d. Garenne-Colombes, near Paris, May 14, 1990. He studied composition with Roger-Ducasse and Gaubert at the Paris Cons.; also violin and double bass. From 1953 to 1981 he was director of the Dijon Cons. He wrote operas: *La Lance de Fingal* (1947); *Sampiero Corso, Monsieur Personne* (1957); *Cyrnos* (Nancy, April 6, 1962); ballets: *La Coupe de sang* (1950) and *Oiseaux du vieux Paris* (1967); Cello Concerto (1946); *Jeux de table* for Saxophone and Piano (1955); *Terre secrète*, 6 poems for Voice and Orch. (1956); *Airs hétérogènes* for Wind Ensemble (1966); *Hétérodoxes* for 2 Flutes, 2 Trumpets, String Quartet, and String Orch. (1969); *Suite Florentine* for Cello (1986); *Uranie* for Flute and Piano (1986); Duo Concertant for Double Basses (1987).

Ameln, Konrad, German musicologist and choral conductor; b. Neuss am Rhein, July 6, 1899; d. Lüdenscheid, Sept. 1, 1994. He studied at the Univ. of Göttingen (1919–21) and with Gurlitt at the Univ. of Freiburg im Breisgau (Ph.D., 1924, with the diss. *Beiträge zur Geschichte der Melodien "Innsbruck, ich muss dich lassen" und "Ach Gott, von Himmel sieh darein"*). After serving as a music consultant to the Central Office for General Librarianship in Leipzig (1926–28), he taught Protestant church music at the Univ. of Münster (1930–39). He also was founder-director of the Lüdenscheider Musikvereinigung (1935–73). He taught at the Landeskirchenmusikschulen in Hannover (1947–48) and the Rhineland (1949–57). With C. Mahrenholz and W. Thomas, he was ed. of the valuable *Handbuch der deutschen evangelische Kirchenmusik* (Göttingen, 1932 et seq.). Ameln was the author of the studies *Leonhard Lechner* (Lüdenscheid, 1957) and *The Roots of German Hymnody of the Reformation Era* (St. Louis, 1964).

BIBL.: G. Schuhmacher, ed., *Traditionen und Reformen in der Kirchenmusik: Festschrift für K. A. zum 75. Geburtstag* (Kassel, 1974).

Amengual (-Astaburuaga), René, Chilean composer; b. Santiago, Sept. 2, 1911; d. there, Aug. 2, 1954. He studied with Allende at the National Cons. in Santiago. His compositions are few, and mostly in small forms, showing influences of the modern French school. Among his works are a Piano Sonatina (1938); *Introduction and Allegro* for 2 Pianos (1939); Piano Concerto (Santiago, June 30, 1942); and *El Vaso* for Voice and Chamber Orch. (Santiago, Aug. 25, 1944).

Amfitheatrof, Daniele (Alexandrovich), Russian-born American composer and conductor; b. St. Petersburg, Oct. 29, 1901; d. Rome, June 7, 1983. He was a son of a famous Russian journalist. He studied composition with Wihtol and Shcherbachov at the St. Petersburg Cons., with Křička in Prague, and with Respighi at the Conservatorio di Santa Cecilia in Rome (diploma, 1924); also organ at Rome's Pontifical Academy of Sacred Music. After conducting in Italy and Europe, he went to the U.S. in 1937 and became a naturalized American citizen in 1944. Amfitheatrof was assoc. conductor of the Minneapolis Sym. Orch. (1937–38), and then went to Hollywood in 1939, where he wrote over 50 film scores until 1965; then settled in Italy. His works followed in the exuberant Romantic tradition espoused by Respighi. Among his orchestral compositions are *Poema del mare* (1925), *Miracolo della rosa* (1927), *Panorama americano* (1933), and a Piano Concerto (1937–46); he also composed a Requiem (1960) and much chamber music.

Amirkhanian, Charles (Benjamin), American avant-garde composer, influential radio producer, and arts administrator of Armenian descent; b. Fresno, Calif., Jan. 19, 1945. He studied English literature at Calif. State Univ. at Fresno (B.A., 1967), interdisciplinary creative arts at San Francisco State College (M.A., 1969), and electronic music and sound recording at Mills College (M.F.A., 1980). In his early percussion compositions, he experimented with the potentialities of sound phenomena independent of traditional musical content; his *Composition No. 1* is a solo for an acoustically amplified Ratchet (1965), and his *Symphony I* (1965) is scored for 12 Players and 200-odd non-musical objects, ranging from pitchpipes to pitchforks. In collaboration with the painter Ted Greer, he developed a radical system of notation in which visual images are transduced by performers into sound events. Representative of this intermedia genre are *Micah, the Prophet*, cantata for 4 Intoning Males, 2 Accordions, 2 Drummers, and 2 Painters (1965), and, particularly, *Mooga Pook*, a tetraphallic action for Dancers, realistically notated on graph paper (San Francisco, Dec. 12, 1967). He also evolved the art of "text-sound composition," in which the voice, percussively intoning and articulating decontextualized words and phrases, is featured; to this category belong *Words* (1969), *Oratora konkurso rezulto: Auturo de la Jaro*, an Esperanto recitation (1970), *If In Is* (1971), *Spoffy Nene* (1971), *Just* (1972), *Heavy Aspirations* (1973), *Seatbelt Seatbelt* (1973), *MUGIC* (1973), *Muchrooms* (1974), *Beemsterboer* (1975), *Mahogany Ballpark* (1976), and *Dutiful Ducks* (1977). His compositions since the early 1980s make extensive use of sampled ambient sounds created and manipulated by a Synclavier digital synthesizer; among these are *Gold and Spirit* (for the Los Angeles Summer Olympics; 1984), *The Real Perpetuum Mobile* (on the occasion of N. Slonimsky's 90th birthday; Los Angeles, April 27, 1984), *Metropolis San Francisco* (for WDR/Köln Studio 3 Hörspiel; 1985–86), *Walking Tune* (a tribute to Percy Grainger; 1986–87), *Pas de voix* ("Portrait of Samuel Beckett"; 1987), *Politics as Usual* (incorporating sounds of gongs in the collections of Lou Harrison and Toni Marcus, mixed with sounds of talking parrots, crunching apples, and revolving ice cubes; 1988), *Im Frühling* (1990), and *Loudspeakers* (utilizing materials from a 1984 interview with Morton Feldman; 1990). Amirkhanian served as music director at the radio station KPFA in Berkeley, California (1969–92), for which he was awarded the American Music Center's annual Letter of Distinction (1984) and the ASCAP-Deems Taylor Award (1989). He was also producer and host of the "Speaking of Music" interview series at San Francisco's Exploratorium Science Museum (1983–92) and cofounding director of the "Composer-to-Composer" Festival in Telluride, Colo. (1988–91). In 1992 he became executive director of the Djerassi Resident Artists Program in Woodside, California, and program director of "Other Minds" in San Francisco.

BIBL.: P. Kresh, "An Art between Speech & Music," *N.Y. Times* (April 3, 1983); K. Burch, ed., *The Guests Go in to Supper* (Oakland, Calif., 1986); S. Cahill, "C. A.," *Ear Magazine* (July 1989).

Amirov, Fikret Dzhamil, Azerbaijani composer; b. Gyandzha, Nov. 22, 1922; d. Baku, Feb. 20, 1984. He received early music instruction from his father, a singer and guitarist; he then studied composition at the Azerbaijan Cons., graduating in 1948. His compositions reflect the melorhythmic patterns of popular Azerbaijani music, marked by characteristic oriental inflections, while retaining a classical format and development, particularly in variation form. Among his works are the operas *Ulduz* (1948) and *Sevil* (Baku, Dec. 25, 1953); a symphonic poem, *To the Memory of the Heroes of the Great National War* (1944); Double Concerto for Violin, Piano, and Orch. (1948); *The Pledge of the Korean Guerrilla Fighter* for Voice and Orch. (1951); several symphonic suites based on the national modes ("mugamas"), of which *Shur* (1948) is the best known. He also wrote a Piano Concerto on Arab themes (1957; in collaboration with Nazirova); *Azerbaijan Capriccio* for Orch. (1961); *Symphonic Dances* (1963); *Arabian Nights*, ballet (1979).

BIBL.: D. Danilov, *F. A.* (Baku, 1958).

Ammann, Benno, Swiss composer; b. Gersau, June 14, 1904; d. Rome, March 14, 1986. He studied with Karg-Elert, Grabner, and Reuter at the Leipzig Cons. (1925) and with Honegger, Milhaud, and Albert Rousseau in Paris (1934–35); later he attended courses in electronic music conducted by Eimert and Meyer-Eppler in Darmstadt (from 1952). He was active at the Studio R7 in Rome (1969–71), the Inst. of Sonology at the Univ. of Ghent (1971–73), and the Columbia-Princeton Electronic Music Center in N.Y. (1977–78). In his works, Ammann embraced a variety of contemporary means of expression.

WORKS: BALLETS: *Zweimal Besuch* (1960); *Waterplants* (1974). **ORCH.:** *Vision pastorale* (1954); *Tre Modi* for 2 String Orchs. or Strings and Tape (1962); *Triodon*, 3 pieces for Strings (1963); *Gradations* for Chamber Orch. (1973). **CHAMBER:** *Successions* for Flute (1963); *Syntexte* for Flute, Harp, and Percussion (1966); *IV Phonemata* for Cello (1967); *12 Phases* for Guitar and Tape (1970); *Spatial Forms* for 2 String Quartets (1972); *Mouvements* for Harp and Tape (1976); *The Gnome's Memory* for Tuba and Tape (1979); *Riflessi per quattro* for 4 Clarinets (1981); *Lieto per Liuto* for Lute (1983); *Incontri* for 24 Trumpets in 4 Groups (1984). **VOCAL:** *Flucht aus der Tiefe*, cantata for Baritone, 3 Choruses, and Percussion Orch. (1960); *Sumerian Song* for Soprano, 6 Percussion, and Orch. (1971); *Ti Porteranno* for Soprano, Flute, Cello, Trombone, and Percussion (1974); *Tre Canti* for Baritone, 2 Clarinets, and Harp (1983); choral pieces; other songs. **ELECTRONIC:** *Breath of the Desert* (1974); *Splendeurs Nocturnes* (1974–79); *Poemetto* (1977); *Mutazione* (1978); *Wandering strophe* (1979).

Amoyal, Pierre, French violinist and teacher; b. Paris, June 22, 1949. He studied at the Paris Cons.; won the Ginette Neveu prize in 1963, the Paganini prize in 1964, and the Enesco prize in 1970; took sporadic lessons with Jascha Heifetz in Los Angeles (1966–71). He was soloist with the Orchestre de Paris, the BBC Sym. Orch. of London, the Hallé Orch. of Manchester, and the Berlin Phil.; also toured in Russia, Japan, and South Africa. In the U.S., he was a soloist with the Boston Sym. Orch., the Cleveland Orch., the Detroit Sym. Orch., and the Houston Sym. Orch. From 1977 he was a member of the faculty of the Paris Cons.

Amram, David (Werner, III), American horn player, conductor, and and composer; b. Philadelphia, Nov. 17, 1930. He studied horn at the Oberlin (Ohio) College Cons. of Music (1948) and pursued his education at George Washington Univ. (B.A. in history, 1952); after playing horn in the National Sym. Orch. in Washington, D.C. (1951–52) and the 7th Army Sym. Orch. in Europe, he completed his training with Mitropoulos, Giannini, and Schuller at the Manhattan School of Music (1955) and privately with Charles Mills. He first gained recognition as a composer for theater, films, and television; in 1966–67, was the first composer-in-residence of the N.Y. Phil. He also was active in jazz settings and as a conductor. His autobiography was publ. as *Vibrations: The Adventures and Musical Times of David Amram* (N.Y., 1968).

WORKS: DRAMATIC: OPERAS: *The Final Ingredient* (ABC-TV, April 11, 1965); *Twelfth Night* (1965–68; Lake George, N.Y., Aug. 1, 1968); incidental music; film scores. **ORCH.:** *Autobiography* for Strings (1959); *Shakespearean Concerto* for Oboe, 2 Horns, and Strings (N.Y., May 8, 1960); *King Lear Variations* for Woodwinds, Brass, Percussion, and Piano (1965; N.Y., March 23, 1967); Horn Concerto (1966); Triple Concerto for Woodwinds, Brass, Jazz Quintets, and Orch. (1970; N.Y., Jan. 10, 1971); Bassoon Concerto (1971; Washington, D.C., March 21, 1972); *Elegy* for Violin and Orch. (1971); *The Trail of Beauty* for Mezzo-soprano, Oboe, and Orch. (Philadelphia, March 3, 1977); Violin Concerto (1980; St. Louis, May 2, 1981); *Ode to Lord Buckley*, saxophone concerto (Portland, Maine, March 17, 1981); *Overture: Honor Song* for Cello and Orch. (N.Y., July 3, 1983); *Across the Wide Missouri: A Musical Tribute to Harry S. Truman* (Kansas City, Mo., May 10, 1984); *Travels* for Trumpet and Orch. (N.Y., March 26, 1985); *American Dance Suite* (Omaha, Oct. 18, 1986); *A Little Rebellion: Thomas Jefferson* for Narrator and Orch. (Washington, D.C., Oct. 22, 1995, E.G. Marshall narrator, composer conducting). **CHAMBER:** Trio for Saxophone, Horn, and Bassoon (1958); Violin Sonata (1960); String Quartet (1961); Sonata for Solo Violin (1964); Wind Quintet (1968); *Native American Portraits* for Violin, Piano, and Percussion (1976); *Landscapes* for Percussion Quartet (1980). **VOCAL:** *The American Bell*, cantata (Philadelphia, July 4, 1962); *A Year in Our Land*, cantata (1964); *Let Us Remember*, cantata (1965); *3 Songs for America* for Baritone and String Quintet (1969); *Journals of Kerouac* for Voice and Chamber Orch. (N.Y., Oct. 28, 1995).

Amy, Gilbert, French conductor, music educator, and composer; b. Paris, Aug. 29, 1936. He studied composition with Milhaud and Messiaen and piano with Loriod at the Paris Cons.; also received instruction in counterpoint and fugue from Plé-Caussade in Paris and attended Darmstadt summer courses in new music given by Boulez. In 1962 he began his conducting career; was director of the Domaine Musical in Paris (1967–73) and founder-conductor of the Nouvel Orchestre Philharmonique de Radio France in Paris (1976–81). After teaching briefly at Yale Univ. (1982), he returned to France and became director of the Lyons Cons. (1984). His early compositions reflect the influence of Boulez; after experimenting with doctrinaire serial procedures, he adopted greater freedom in his later works.

WORKS: ORCH.: *Mouvements* (1958); *Diaphonies* (1962); *Antiphonies* for 2 Orchs. (1963); *Triade* (1965); *Trajectoires* for Violin and Orch. (1966); *Chant* (1968–69; rev. 1980); *Jeux et formes* for Oboe and Chamber Orch. (1971); *Refrains* (1972); *7 Sites* for 14 Instruments (1975); *Écho XIII* for 13 Instruments (1976); *Adagio et stretto* (1977–78); *Orchestrahl* (1985). **CHAMBER:** *Variations* for Flute, Clarinet, Cello, and Piano (1956); *Inventions* for Flute, Vibraphone or Marimbaphone, Harp, and Piano or Celesta (1959–61); *Alpha-beth* for Wind Sextet (1963–64); *Cycle* for Percussion Sextet (1964–66); *Relais* for Brass Quintet (1969); *Quasi scherzando* for Cello (1981); *3 Interludes* for Violin and Percussion (1984); *En trio* for Clarinet, Violin, and Piano (1985–86); *5/16* for Flute and Optional Percussion (1986); *Posaunen* for 4 Trombones (1987); *Mèmoire* for Cello and Piano (1989); String Quartet No. 1 (1992). **KEYBOARD: PIANO:** Sonata (1957–60); *Épigrammes* (1961; rev. 1967); *Cahiers d'Épigrammes* (1964); *Obliques I* (1987), *II* (1987), and *III* (1989). **ORGAN:** *7 Bagatelles* (1975); *Quasi una toccata* (1981). **VOCAL:** *Oeil de fumée* for Soprano and Piano (1955; orchestrated, 1957); *Cette étoile enseigne à s'incliner* for Men's Chorus and Instruments (1970); *. . . d'un désastre obscur* for Mezzo-soprano and Clarinet (1970); *D'un espace déployé* for Soprano, 2 Pianos, and 2 Orch. Groups (1972–76); *Sonata pian'e forte* for Soprano, Mezzo-soprano, and 12 Instruments (1974); *Après ". . . d'un désastre obscur"* for Mezzo-soprano and Small Ensemble (1976); *Messe* for Soprano, Alto, Tenor, Bass, Children's Chorus ad libitum, Chorus, and Orch. (1982–83); *Écrits sur toiles* for Reciter and Small Ensemble (1983); *Choros* for Countertenor, Tenor, Bass-baritone, Chorus, and Orch. (1989).

Ančerl, Karel, eminent Czech conductor; b. Tučapy, April 11, 1908; d. Toronto, July 3, 1973. He studied at the Prague Cons. (1925–29) with Šourek (percussion) and with Křička and Alois Hába (composition); under Hába's tutelage, he composed a *Suite for Quarter Tone Piano* (1928) and *Music* for String Orch. in quarter tones (1928–29); he also studied conducting with Scherchen in Strasbourg, serving as his assistant in Königsberg (1929–31), and with Talich in Prague (1933–34). In 1933 he became music director of the Prague Radio Orch. As a Jew, he was removed from his post after the Nazi occupation of his homeland in 1939, and in 1942 was deported to the Jewish ghetto camp in Theresienstadt, where he played chamber music as a violist and conducted a camp orch. On Sept. 13, 1944, he conducted the premiere of Pavel Haas's Theresienstadt-composed *Study* for String Orch. In late 1944, Ančerl was transported to the Auschwitz concentration camp, where his entire family was put to death. After his liberation in 1945, he resumed his post with the Prague Radio Orch. and was cofounder of the 5th of May Opera in Prague. In 1950 Ančerl became chief conductor of the Czech Phil. in Prague. In spite of political constraints under the Communist regime, he restored the orch. to world renown, leading it in distinguished tours of Europe, North America, Australia, and Japan. In 1966 he was made a People's Artist by the Czech government. In mid-Aug. 1968 Ančerl was unexpectedly called to Tanglewood, Mass., to conduct the Boston Sym. Orch. as a last-minute replacement for an ailing Charles Munch, and thus was abroad when Soviet bloc troops invaded his homeland on Aug. 20–21. Ančerl refused to return to Czechoslovakia and gave up his post as chief conductor of the Czech Phil. In 1969 he became music director of the Toronto Sym., a post he retained until his death. During much of his Toronto tenure, he was plagued by ill health, due largely to lingering conditions resulting from his Nazi internment. He died at the age of 65. After the Czech Communist regime was swept from power by the Velvet Revolution in 1989, plans were made to return Ančerl's remains to a free Czech Republic. On May 12, 1993, his remains were interred with appropriate ceremony at Prague's Vyšehrad cemetery and a bust of the conductor by the sculptor Jan Kodet was dedicated in his memory. Ančerl was held in great esteem for his idiomatic interpretations of the music of his homeland. He also demonstrated remarkable insight into masterworks of the 20th century.

BIBL.: K. Šrom, *K. A.* (Prague and Bratislava, 1968); J. Karas, *Music in Terezín, 1941–1945* (N.Y., 1985).

Anda, Géza, eminent Hungarian-born Swiss pianist, conductor, and pedagogue; b. Budapest, Nov. 19, 1921; d. Zürich, June 13, 1976. He studied with Dohnányi at the Franz Liszt Academy of Music in Budapest. In 1938 he made his debut in Budapest. After receiving the Liszt Prize in 1940, he attracted notice as a soloist with Furtwängler and the Berlin Phil. in 1941. In 1942 he settled in Zürich, and in 1955 became a naturalized Swiss citizen. Following the close of World War II in 1945, he pursued a notable career as a soloist with the world's leading orchs. and as a recitalist. In later years, he took up conducting and became active as a pedagogue. Anda was one of the finest interpreters of Mozart, appearing on occasion as both soloist and conductor in Mozart's piano concertos. He also was esteemed for his performances of Beethoven, Liszt, Brahms, and Bartók.

BIBL.: H.-C. Schmidt, *G. A.: "Sechzehntel sind auch Musik!": Dokumente seines Lebens* (Zürich, 1991).

Anderberg, Carl-Olof, Swedish pianist, conductor, and composer; b. Stockholm, March 13, 1914; d. Malmö, Jan. 4, 1972. He studied piano with Olof Wibergh in Stockholm, and took courses in composition there and in Copenhagen, Paris, and London (1936–38), as well as in Vienna and Salzburg; he also studied conducting in Salzburg at the Mozarteum with Paumgartner, Walter, and Weingartner. In 1934 he made his debut as a pianist in Malmö as soloist in his own, youthful Concertino for Piano and Chamber Orch. He was active as a theater conductor, and also served as founder-conductor of the Malmö Chamber Orch. (1946–50). From 1956 he was active in his own music studio in Malmö. He publ. the vol. *Hän mot en ljudkonst* (Towards a New Sound Art; Malmö, 1961). Anderberg was a leading figure in Swedish avant-garde music circles. He developed an individual serial style which incorporated both aleatory techniques and improvisation.

WORKS: OPERA: *Episode*, chamber opera (1952). **ORCH.:** *Music I* (1947) and *II* (1948) for Chamber Orch.; Sym. (1948); *Cyclus Stellarum I* (1949) and *II* (1957) for Strings; *Teater*, suite (1958); *Transfers* (1960); *Acroama I* and *II* (1965–66); Piano Concerto (Malmö, March 18, 1969); *Concerto for a Ballet* for Piano, Winds, Percussion, and Double Basses (1969–70; Swedish Radio, March 4, 1972); *Orkesterspel I* and *II* (Orchestral Game; 1969–70). **CHAMBER:** *3 estampies* for Piano, Percussion, and Violins (1953); 2 string quartets (1955, 1957); Cello Sonata (1956); *4 Serious Caprices* for Clarinet and Piano (1956); *Duo I* for Flute and Piano (1958), and *II* and *III* for Violin and Piano (1968); *Triad* for Violin (1959); *Variationer över Variationer* for Clarinet, Bassoon, Violin, Cello, and Harp (1959); *Hexafoni* for 6 Instruments (1963); *Execution I* for Clarinet, Piano, and Percussion (1963); *Music* for Piano, Winds, and Tape (1970). **PIANO:** 3 sonatas (1950, 1952, 1956); *Klangskap* (Soundscape) *I* (1968). **VOCAL:** *Fyra legeringar* (4 Alloys) for Soprano and 5 Instruments (1958); *Höstens Hökar* for Narrator and 5 Instruments (1959); *Di Mi Se Mai* for Soprano, Narrator, and Orch. (1963); *Strändernas svall* (The Surge of the Seaside), cantata for Soprano, Baritone, Narrator, and Instrumental Ensemble (1963–64); *Dubbelspel* (Double Play) for Soprano, Baritone, Clarinet, Cello, Piano, and Tape (1971); songs.

Anders, Peter, distinguished German tenor; b. Essen, July 1, 1908; d. in an automobile accident in Hamburg, Sept. 10, 1954.

He was a pupil of Grenzebach and Mysz-Gemeiner in Berlin, making his debut there in *La belle Hélène* (1931). After singing in Heidelberg (1932), Darmstadt (1933–35), Cologne (1935–36), Hannover (1937–38), and Munich (1938–40), he was a principal member of the Berlin State Opera (1940–48) and the Hamburg State Opera (1948–54). In 1950 he made his British debut as Bacchus at the Edinburgh Festival; in 1951, appeared as Walther von Stolzing at London's Covent Garden. Anders was one of the finest German tenors of his generation. He excelled in operas by Mozart, Wagner, and Verdi; he also was a noted lieder artist.

BIBL.: F. Pauli, *P. A.* (Berlin, 1963).

Andersen, Karl August, Norwegian composer and cellist; b. Christiania, Sept. 29, 1903; d. there (Oslo), Aug. 15, 1970. He studied cello and composition in Christiania and later cello with Hugo Becker and composition with Hermann Grabner in Berlin (1921–22); then became a cellist in the Oslo Phil. (1924). He composed in a neo-Classical style.

WORKS: 3 string quartets, including No. 1 (1934) and No. 3 (1961–67); Sym. for Chamber Orch. (1936); Suite for Orch. (1937); Trio for Flute, Clarinet, and Cello (1939); *Vårdagen* for Men's Chorus (1942); *Allegro festivo e solenne Norwegese* (Festforspill) for Orch. (1950); *Variations over Theme and Rhythm* for Wind Quintet (1966).

Andersen, Karsten, Norwegian conductor; b. Christiania, Feb. 16, 1920. He was trained in Norway and Italy. He began his career as a violinist. In 1945 he was named music director of the Stavanger Sym. Orch.; concurrently was music director of the Stavanger Radio Ensemble. In 1965 he became music director of the Bergen Harmonien Soc., leading the concerts of the Bergen Sym. Orch. until 1985. He was a founder of the noted Bergen Music Festival. From 1973 to 1980 he also was chief conductor of the Iceland Sym. Orch. in Reykjavík. In 1985 he became prof. of conducting at the Norwegian State Academy of Music in Oslo.

Anderson, Beth (actually, **Barbara Elizabeth**), inventive American composer and performance artist; b. Lexington, Ky., Jan. 3, 1950. After piano studies at the Univ. of Kentucky (1966–68), she continued piano training at the Univ. of Calif. at Davis, where she also took courses in composition with Larry Austin, John Cage, and Richard Swift (B.A., 1971). Following further training in piano (M.F.A., 1973) and in composition (M.A., 1974) with Robert Ashley and Terry Riley at Mills College in Oakland, California, she attended N.Y. Univ. (1977–78). She was coeditor and publ. of *Ear Magazine* (1973–79); also taught at the College of New Rochelle in N.Y. (1978–86). As a composer, she has pursued a diagonal tangent upon her own highly original path. Her resources are manifold, passing through a wide spectrum of sound, sight, and motion in specially designed multimedia productions. She espouses text-sound composition, and also applies collage techniques. Anderson is also a professional astrologer who's made an earnest attempt to connect ideas of harmony with cosmic consciousness, extrasensory perception, and numerology.

WORKS: DRAMATIC: *Queen Christina*, opera (Oakland, Calif., Dec. 1, 1973); *Soap Tuning*, theater piece (1976); *Zen Piece*, theater piece (1976); *Nirvana Manor*, musical (1981); *Elizabeth Rex*, musical (1983); *The Fat Opera*, musical comedy (N.Y., April 22, 1991). **MULTIMEDIA:** *Morning View and Maiden Spring* for Tape, Speaker, Slides, and Light (1978). **ORCH.:** *Revelation* (1981); *Revel* (1985). **CHAMBER:** *Music for Charlemagne Palestine* for String Quartet (1973); *The Praying Mantis and the Bluebird* for Flute and Piano (1979); *Dream* or *Trio: Dream* for Piano, Flute, and Cello (1980); *Little Trio* for Flute, Viola, and Guitar (1984); *Pennyroyal Swale* for String Quartet (1985); *Rosemary Swale* for String Quartet (1986); piano pieces. **VOCAL:** *Joan*, oratorio (Aptos, Calif., Aug. 22, 1974); song cycles; solo songs; chants. **OTHER:** Tape pieces; text-sound compositions, including the opera *Riot Rot* (1984).

Anderson, Emily, Irish musicologist; b. Galway, March 17, 1891; d. London, Oct. 26, 1962. She went to Germany for her education, and attended the univs. of Berlin and Marburg. Returning to England, she was employed in the British Foreign Office while pursuing her interest in music history and biography as an avocation. Of value are her translations of the correspondence of Mozart and Beethoven as publ. in *Letters of Mozart and His Family* (3 vols., London, 1938; 2nd ed., rev., 1966 by A. Hyatt King and M. Carolan; 3rd ed., rev., 1985 by S. Sadie and F. Smart) and *The Letters of Beethoven* (3 vols., London, 1961).

Anderson, June, admired American soprano; b. Boston, Dec. 30, 1952. She received singing lessons as a child and at age 14 made her first appearance in opera in a production of Toch's *Die Prinzessin auf der Erbse.* In 1970 she was the youngest finalist in the Metropolitan Opera National Auditions. After taking her B.A. in French literature at Yale Univ. in 1974, she pursued vocal training in N.Y. with Robert Leonard. In 1976 she attracted favorable notice as soloist in Mozart's Mass in C minor, K.427, with the N.Y. Choral Soc., and then sang at the Chicago Lyric Opera in 1977. On Oct. 26, 1978, she made her debut at the N.Y. City Opera as the Queen of the Night, and continued to appear there until 1982 when she made her European debut as Semiramide in Rome. In 1983 she scored a major success in N.Y. when she sang Semiramide in a concert performance at Carnegie Hall. In 1984 she was tapped to sing the soundtrack for the Queen of the Night for the film version of *Amadeus.* She made her first appearance at the Paris Opéra as Isabelle in *Robert le diable* in 1985; in 1986 she won accolades at her debut at Milan's La Scala as Amina, and later that year sang for the first time at London's Covent Garden as Lucia. In 1988 she appeared with the Opera Orch. of N.Y. as Beatrice di Tenda with fine success. On Nov. 30, 1989, she made her Metropolitan Opera debut in N.Y. as Gilda to critical acclaim. Her debut at N.Y.'s Carnegie Hall followed on Dec. 12, 1991. In 1993 she was heard as Bellini's Elvira at the San Francisco Opera. In subsequent years, Anderson sang with major U.S. and European opera houses; she also was active as a concert singer.

Anderson, Laurie, imaginative American performance artist and composer; b. Chicago, June 5, 1947. She received violin lessons before studying art history at Barnard College (B.A., 1969) and sculpture at Columbia Univ. (M.F.A., 1972); then trained with the painter Sol Lewitt. From 1973 to 1975 she taught art history at City College of the City Univ. of N.Y. In 1983 she held a Guggenheim fellowship. Renouncing the tradition of conventional modernism, she set for herself a goal of uniting all arts as they once existed in ancient theatrical practice; in doing so, she made use of all available modern techniques, from topical pop to electronics, even making her own body a part of the instrumental combination, playbacking with herself on magnetic tape and projecting images on a screen. In her performances, she combines speech, song, and bodily exertions; she also uses a variety of instrumentations, including a homemade violin activated by a luminous bow made of electronic tape. She has become particularly famous for her multimedia cyberpunk projections, extending the principles of cybernetics to deliberately commonplace movements, behavior, and language. Her programmed compositions are mostly improvisations in which she alters her natural voice electronically, making use of vocal glissando, crooning, panting, and heavy aspiration. Her satirical piece *New York Social Life* uses oriental drum effects; another piece, *Time to Go*, scored for guitar, violin, and organ, portrays the repeated exhortation of a museum guard to visitors to leave at closing time. In 1976 she gave a successful exhibition of psychomusicurgy at the Berlin Akademie der Kunst. In 1981 her song *O Superman (for Massenet)* became a genuine hit. In 1983 she produced her grandiose collage epic, simply entitled *United States*, on themes of travel, politics, money, and love. Her book *United States* was publ. in N.Y. in 1984. On Oct. 3, 1989, she presented a large-scale solo work, *Empty Places*, at the Brooklyn Academy of Music.

BIBL: J. Kardon, ed., *L. A.: Works from 1969 to 1983* (Philadelphia, 1983).

Anderson, Leroy, American composer and arranger; b. Cambridge, Mass., June 29, 1908; d. Woodbury, Conn., May 18, 1975. He began his music training at the New England Cons. of Music in Boston when he was 11; later studied harmony with Walter Spalding, counterpoint with Edward Ballantine, canon and fugue with Heilman, and orchestration with Hill and Piston at Harvard Univ. (B.A., 1929; M.A., 1930); subsequently, took courses in German and Scandinavian languages there (1930–34) and was director of the univ. band (1931–35). He eventually became notably successful as a composer and arranger of light music for orch. From 1946 to 1950 he was an orchestrator and arranger for the Boston Pops. Between 1954 and 1974 he appeared as a conductor of his own works with various North American orchs. In 1988 he was elected a posthumous member of the Songwriters Hall of Fame. Anderson's output revealed an inventive melodic and rhythmic bent, which proved immediately appealing.

WORKS: MUSICAL: *Goldilocks* (N.Y., Oct. 11, 1958). **ORCH.:** (Many of the following works were also arranged for Strings and/or Band): *Harvard Fantasy* (1936; rev. as *A Harvard Festival,* 1969); *Jazz Legato* (1938); *Jazz Pizzicato* (1938); *Promenade* (1945); *The Syncopated Clock* (1945); *Chicken Reel* (1946); *Fiddle Faddle* (1947); *Serenata* (1947); *The Irish Suite* (1947, 1949); *Sleigh Ride* (1948); *A Trumpeter's Lullaby* (1949); *The Typewriter* (1950); *The Waltzing Cat* (1950); *Belle of the Ball* (1951); *Blue Tango* (1951); *Horse and Buggy* (1951); *The Penny Whistle Song* (1951); *Plink, Plank, Plunk!* (1951); Piano Concerto (Chicago, July 18, 1953); *Bugler's Holiday* (1954); *Forgotten Dreams* (1954); *Sandpaper Ballet* (1954); *Scottish Suite* (1954); *Suite of Carols* (1954); *Lady in Waiting,* ballet music (1959); *Arietta* (1962); *Balladette* (1962); *The Captains and the Kings* (1962); *Home Stretch* (1962); *Lullaby of the Drums* (1970); *March of the 2 Left Feet* (1970); *Waltz Around the Scale* (1970).

Anderson, Marian, celebrated black American contralto, aunt of **James (Anderson) DePreist**; b. Philadelphia, Feb. 17, 1897; d. Portland, Oreg., April 8, 1993. She gained experience as a member of the Union Baptist Church choir in Philadelphia. After studies with Giuseppe Boghetti, she pursued vocal training with Frank La Forge in N.Y. In 1925 she won 1st prize in the N.Y. Phil. competition, which led to her appearance as soloist with it at the Lewisohn Stadium on Aug. 27 of that same year. In 1929 she sang at N.Y.'s Carnegie Hall, and then made her European debut at London's Wigmore Hall in 1930. She subsequently toured Europe, with increasing success. Her first appearance at N.Y.'s Town Hall on Nov. 30, 1935, proved a notable turning point in her U.S. career, and she thereafter toured throughout the country. In spite of her success, she became the center of national attention in 1939 when the Daughters of the American Revolution denied her the right to give a concert at Constitution Hall in Washington, D.C., citing the organization's long-standing rules of racial segregation. The ensuing controversy led to widespread support for Anderson, who subsequently appeared in concert at the Lincoln Memorial in Washington, D.C. (April 9, 1939). Her success was enormous and secured her reputation as one of America's outstanding musicians. In later years, she toured not only in the U.S. and Europe, but worldwide. On Jan. 7, 1955, she became the first black singer to appear at the Metropolitan Opera in N.Y. when she made her debut as Ulrica. She then continued her concert career until retiring in 1965. Her autobiography appeared as *My Lord, What a Morning* (N.Y., 1956). Anderson received numerous honors from governments and institutions of higher learning, among them the U.S. Medal of Freedom (1963), a gold medal from the U.S. Congress (1977), and the National Medal of Arts (1986).

BIBL.: K. Vehanen, *M. A.* (N.Y., 1941); J. Sims, *M. A.: An Annotated Bibliography and Discography* (Westport, Conn., 1981); C. Patterson, *M. A.* (N.Y., 1988); A. Tedards, *M. A.* (N.Y., 1988).

Anderson, (Evelyn) Ruth, American flutist and composer; b. Kalispell, Mont., March 21, 1928. She studied flute (B.A., 1949) and composition (M.A., 1951) at the Univ. of Washington in Seattle; then electronic music and composition with Ussachevsky and Kim at Columbia and Princeton Univs.; also studied composition privately with Boulanger and Milhaud and flute with John Wummer and Jean-Pierre Rampal. She was active as an orch. player and as an orchestrator for Broadway and television before becoming a teacher at Hunter College of the City Univ. of N.Y. (1966), where she designed and installed its electronic music studio (1968–70).

WORKS: MIXEDMEDIA: *Centering* for Dancer, 4 Performers, and Live Electronics (1979). **TEXT PIECES:** *Naming* (1975); *A Long Sound* (1976); *Sound Portraits I-II* (1977); *Silent Sound* (1978); *Greetings from the Right Hemisphere* (1979); *Communications* (1980). **TAPE:** *The Pregnant Dream* (1968); *ES II* (1969); *DUMP,* collage (1970); *3 Studies* (1970); *3 Pieces* (1970–71); *So What,* Nos. 1 and 2 (1971); *SUM (State of the Union Message),* collage (1973); *Conversations* (1974); *Points* (1974); *Dress Rehearsal* (1976); *I Come Out of Your Sleep* (1979). **SOUND SCULPTURES:** *Sound Environment* (1975); *Time and Tempo* (1984).

Anderson, T(homas) J(efferson, Jr.), black American composer and teacher; b. Coatesville, Pa., Aug. 17, 1928. He studied at West Virginia State College (B.Mus., 1950) and at Pa. State Univ. (M.Ed., 1951) before pursuing training in composition with Scott Huston at the Univ. of Cincinnati College-Cons. of Music (1954), Philip Bezanson and Richard Hervig at the Univ. of Iowa (Ph.D., 1958), and Darius Milhaud at the Aspen (Colo.) School of Music (summer, 1964). He was prof. of music and chairman of the dept. at Langston (Okla.) Univ. (1958–63), and prof. of music at Tenn. State Univ. (1963–69). From 1969 to 1971 he was composer-in-residence of the Atlanta Sym. Orch. From 1972 to 1990 he was prof. of music at Tufts Univ., and also chairman of the dept. (1972–80). In 1988–89 he held a Guggenheim fellowship. Anderson played a major role in the revival of Scott Joplin's music. He arranged Joplin's opera *Treemonisha* for its first complete performance (Atlanta, Jan. 28, 1972). Anderson's own works are audaciously modern, while preserving a deeply felt lyricism. His harmonies are taut and intense without abandoning the basic tonal frame. His contrapuntal usages suggest folklike ensembles, but he freely varies his techniques according to the character of each particular piece.

WORKS: DRAMATIC: *The Shell Fairy,* operetta (1976–77); *Re-Creation* for 3 Readers, Dancer, and Instrumentalists (1978); *Soldier Boy, Soldier,* opera (Bloomington, Ind., Oct. 23, 1982); *Thomas Jefferson's Orbiting Minstrels and Contraband,* a "21st Century celebration of 19th Century form" for Dancer, Soprano, String Quartet, Woodwind Quintet, Jazz Sextet, Computer, Visuals, and Keyboard Synthesizer (1984; DeKalb, Ill., Feb. 12, 1986); *Walker,* chamber opera (1992; Boston, Dec. 9, 1993). **ORCH.:** *Pyknon Overture* (1958); *Introduction and Allegro* (1959); *New Dances* (1960); *Classical Symphony* (1961); *6 Pieces* for Clarinet and Chamber Orch. (1962); *Symphony in 3 Movements,* in memory of President John F. Kennedy (Oklahoma City, April 10, 1964); *Squares: An Essay for Orchestra* (1965); Chamber Sym. (1968; Nashville, Tenn., Nov. 24, 1969); *Intervals* (1970–71); *Messages: A Creole Fantasy* (1979; Atlanta, May 3, 1980); Concerto for 2 Violins and Chamber Orch. (Chicago, May 29, 1988); *Remembrances,* chamber concerto (Cleveland, Oct. 30, 1988); *Bahia, Bahia* for Chamber Orch. (1990). **BAND:** *Trio Concertante* for Clarinet, Trumpet, Trombone, and Band (1960); *Rotations* (1967); *In Memoriam Zach Walker* (1968); *Fanfare* for Trumpet and 4 Mini-bands (1976). **CHAMBER:** String Quartet (1958); *5 Bagatelles* for Oboe, Violin, and Harpsichord (1963); *5 Études and a Fancy* for Woodwind Quintet (1964); *Connections, a Fantasy* for String Quintet (1966); *Transitions* for Chamber Ensemble (1971); *Swing Set* for Clarinet and

Piano (1972); *5 Easy Pieces* for Violin, Piano, and Jew's Harp (1974); *Minstrel Man* for Bass Trombone and Percussionist (1978); *Variations on a Theme by Alban Berg* for Viola and Piano (1977); *Vocalise* for Violin and Harp (1980); *Inaugural Piece* for 3 Trumpets and 3 Trombones (1982); *Intermezzi* for Clarinet, Alto Saxophone, and Piano (1983; also as solo pieces for each of these instruments); *Sunstar* for Trumpet and Cassette Recorder (1984); *Bridging and Branching* for Flute and Double Bass (1986); *Ivesiana* for Violin, Cello, and Piano (1988); *What Ever Happened to the Big Bands?* for Alto Saxophone, Trumpet, and Trombone (1991); *Spirit Songs* for Cello and Piano (1993). **KEYBOARD: PIANO:** *5 Portraitures of 2 People* for Piano, 4-hands (1965); *Watermelon* (1971); *Street Song* (1977); *Play Me Something* (1979); *Call and Response* (1982); *Passacaglia and Blues* (1990). **ORGAN:** *In Memoriam: Graham Wootton* (1985). **VOCAL:** *Personals*, cantata for Chorus, Narrator, and Brass Septet (1966); *Variations on a Theme by M.B. Tolson*, cantata for Soprano and 6 Instruments (1969); *This House* for Men's Glee Club and 4 Chromatic Pitch Pipes (1971); *Block Songs* for Soprano, Children's Toys, Chromatic Pitch Pipe, and Jack-in-the-Box (1972); *Beyond Silence* for Tenor and 5 Instruments (1973); *Im Memoriam Malcolm X* for Voice and Orch. (N.Y., April 7, 1974); *Horizons '76* for Soprano and Orch. (1975; Chicago, June 11, 1978); *Spirituals* for Tenor, Narrator, Chorus, Children's Chorus, Jazz Quartet, and Orch. (1979; Atlanta, Jan. 19, 1982); *Jonestown* for Chorus and Piano (1982; Boston, May 6, 1984); *Thomas Jefferson's Minstrels* for Baritone, Men's Glee Club, and Jazz Band (1982; Medford, Mass., April 15, 1983); *What Time is It?* for Boy's Chorus and Jazz Orch. (N.Y., Dec. 1, 1986); *Songs of Illumination* for Soprano, Tenor, and Piano (Medford, Mass., April 27, 1990); *Ancestral Voices* for Bass and Piano (Strasbourg, Sept. 21, 1990); *Dear John, Dear Coltrane* for Chorus and Piano (Minneapolis, Dec. 4, 1990); *Egyptian Diary* for Soprano and 2 Percussionists (1991; Chicago, April 26, 1992); *Here in the Flesh*, hymn for Congregation and Piano (Charlotte, N.C., June 28, 1993).

Andrašovan, Tibor, Slovak composer and conductor; b. Slovenská Lupča, April 3, 1917. He studied with Suchoň, A. Moyzes, A. Kafendová, and others at the Bratislava Cons., later serving as artistic director of the Slovak Folk Artistic Ensemble (1955–58; 1969–74). He received many awards, including Merited Artist (1971). He was active in unifying folk elements with concert music and in promoting Slovak stage works. His opera *Gelo the Joker* (1957) was the first Slovak comic opera.

WORKS: DRAMATIC: *Orpheus and Euridice*, ballet (1948); *The Song of Peace*, ballet (1949); *Gelo the Joker*, opera (1957); *The Quadrille*, operetta (1960); *The White Disease*, music drama (1967); *The Gamekeeper's Wife*, opera (1973–74); *The King of Fools*, musical (1982); *The Festival of Solstice*, ballet (1985); incidental music; film scores. **ORCH.:** *Little Goral Overture* (1961); *Robber's Overture* (1963); *Dukla: The Gate of Freedom*, overture (1975); Concerto for Harpsichord and Strings (1977). **CHAMBER:** String Quartet, *Folklorica* (1976). **VOCAL:** *Tokajik*, cantata for Soprano, Chorus, and Orch. (1975); several song cycles. **OTHER:** Pieces for Folklore Ensembles.

André, Franz, Belgian conductor; b. Brussels, June 10, 1893; d. there, Jan. 20, 1975. He studied violin with César Thomson at the Brussels Cons., and conducting with Weingartner in Berlin. He was mobilized at the advent of World War I, and spent the years 1914–18 on the crucial front in the trenches at Ypres. After the war, he taught violin; was on the faculty of the Brussels Cons. from 1920 to 1944. In 1935 he organized the Belgian Radio Sym. Orch. in Brussels, which he led until 1958. He trained the orch. in difficult modern works which he insisted on reading *à livre ouvert* at rehearsals; he cultivated, especially, the works of modern French and Belgian composers, and also conducted several orch. scores by Schoenberg.

André, Maurice, famous French trumpeter and pedagogue; b. Alès, May 21, 1933. After working as a coal miner in his youth (1947–51), during which time he took up the trumpet, he pursued formal studies with Barthélémy at the Paris Cons., receiving the Prix d'Honneur. He was 1st trumpeter in the Lamoureux Orch. (1953–60), the Orchestre Philharmonique de l'ORTF (1953–62), and the orch. of the Opéra-Comique (1962–67) in Paris. In 1954 he made his formal debut as a soloist in Paris; then won the Geneva (1955) and Munich (1963) international competitions. From 1967 he pursued an international career as a trumpet virtuoso. He also taught at the Paris Cons. (1967–78) and gave master classes at home and abroad. His exhaustive repertory ranged from works from the Baroque era to contemporary scores. Among composers who wrote works especially for him were Blacher, Jolivet, and Landowski.

Andreae, Marc (Edouard), Swiss conductor, grandson of **Volkmar Andreae**; b. Zürich, Nov. 8, 1939. He studied piano and conducting at the Zürich Cons. (graduated, 1962), composition with Boulanger in Paris (1962–63), and conducting with Ferrara at the Accademia di Santa Cecilia in Rome and at the Accademia Musicale Chigiana in Siena (1964–68). He was conductor of the Orchestre Pro Arte in Zürich (1960–62). After winning 1st prize in the national Swiss competition there in 1966, he was assistant to Peter Maag (1967–68). From 1969 to 1990 he was chief conductor of the Orch. della Radiotelevisione della Svizzera Italiana in Lugano.

Andreae, Volkmar, distinguished Swiss conductor, pedagogue, and composer, grandfather of **Marc (Edouard) Andreae**; b. Bern, July 5, 1879; d. Zürich, June 18, 1962. He studied with Karl Munzinger in Bern and with Wüllner at the Cologne Cons. (1897–1900). After serving as répétiteur at the Munich Court Opera (1900–1902), he settled in Zürich and was conductor of its mixed chorus (1902–49) and men's chorus (1904–19); was chief conductor of the Tonhalle Orch. (1906–49) and director of the Zürich Cons. (1914–41). He championed the works of Bruckner, Strauss, Reger, Mahler, and Debussy. In his own compositions, he reflected post-Romantic tendencies.

WORKS: OPERAS: *Ratcliff* (Duisburg, May 25, 1914); *Abenteuer des Casanova* (Dresden, June 17, 1924). **ORCH.:** 2 syms. (n.d.; Zürich, Nov. 3, 1919); *Rhapsody* for Violin and Orch. (1920); *Musik* (Zürich, Nov. 12, 1929); Violin Concerto (1940); Oboe Concertino (1942). **CHAMBER:** 2 piano trios (1901, 1908); Violin Sonata (1903); 2 string quartets (1905, 1922); String Trio (1919); *Divertimento* for Flute and String Trio (1945); piano pieces. **VOCAL:** Various works for Soloists, Chorus, and Orch., choruses, and songs.

BIBL.: F. Seiler, *Dr. V. A. . . . zum Jubiläum seiner 25-jährigen Tätigkeit* (Zürich, 1931); M. Engeler and E. Lichtenhahn, eds., *Briefe an V. A.: Ein halbes Jahrhundert Züricher Musikleben, 1902–1959* (Zürich, 1986).

Andreis, Josip, eminent Croatian music historian; b. Split, March 19, 1909; d. Zagreb, Jan. 16, 1982. He received training in Romance languages at the univs. of Zagreb and Rome (graduated, 1931); also had private instruction in composition and attended the Zagreb Academy of Music, where he subsequently served on its faculty as prof. of music history and head of the musicology dept. (1945–72). He was ed. of the journal *Muzičke novine* (1950–51). His *Historija muzike* (3 vols., Zagreb, 1951–54; 2nd ed., rev., 1966) is the standard history of music in Serbo-Croat. He was general ed. of the *Muzička enciklopedija* (2 vols., Zagreb, 1958, 1963), the pioneering publ. of its kind in Yugoslavia. He was founder-ed. of the musicological annual *Arti musices* (1969–70). Andreis's contribution to the study of Croatian music history remains of great value.

WRITINGS: *Povijest glazbe* (History of Music; Zagreb, 1942); *Uvod u glazbenu estetiku* (Introduction to the Aesthetics of Music; Zagreb, 1944); *Hector Berlioz* (Zagreb, 1946); *Historija muzike* (3 vols., Zagreb, 1951–54; 2nd ed., rev., 1966); with S. Zlatić, *Yugoslav Music* (Belgrade, 1959); *Vječni Orfej* (Eternal Orpheus; Zagreb, 1968); *Music in Croatia* (Zagreb, 1974).

Andrésen, Ivar, Norwegian bass; b. Christiania, July 27, 1896; d. Stockholm, Nov. 25, 1940. He studied at the Royal Opera School in Stockholm. He made his operatic debut in Stockholm in 1919 as the King in *Aida*. From 1925 to 1934 he was a member of the Dresden State Opera, and also appeared at the Bayreuth Festivals (1927–36) and at London's Covent Garden (1928–31). On Nov. 1, 1930, he made his Metropolitan Opera debut in N.Y. as Daland, continuing on its roster until 1932. From 1934 to 1936 he sang at the Berlin State Opera, and in 1935 appeared at the Glyndebourne Festival. His success in Germany led to his being made a Kammersänger. Although principally known as a Wagnerian, he also sang such roles as Sarastro and Osmin to great effect.

Andricu, Mihail (Gheorghe), Romanian pianist, teacher, and composer; b. Bucharest, Jan. 3, 1895; d. there, Feb. 4, 1974. He studied at the Bucharest Cons. (1903–09), later serving on its faculty (1926–59). He was also active as piano accompanist to Georges Enesco.

WORKS: BALLETS: *Cenuşăreasa* (Cinderella; 1929); *Taina* (The Secret; 1932; Bucharest, Feb. 8, 1936); *Luceăfarul* (The Morning Star; Bucharest, Sept. 24, 1951). **ORCH.:** *Poem* for Piano and Orch. (1923); 8 suites (1924–67); *3 Symphonic Pictures* (1925); 3 chamber syms. (1927, 1961, 1965); *Serenade* (1928); 2 sets of *3 Symphonic Sketches* (1936, 1951); *Fantezie* for Piano and Orch. (1940); 11 syms. (1944; 1947; 1950; 1954; 1955; 1957; 1958; 1960; 1962; 1968; *In Memoriam*, 1970); 13 sinfoniettas (1945–72); *3 Symphonic Pieces* (1950); *Rapsodie* (1952); Violin Concerto (1960); Cello Concerto (1961); *6 Portraits* (1969); *Evocation* (1971); *Miniatures and Images* (1971). **CHAMBER:** *4 Novelettes* for Piano Quartet (1925); Octet (1928); String Quartet (1931); Sextet (1932); 2 quintets (1938, 1956); Violin Sonata (1941); *3 Pieces* for Piano and Winds (1964). **OTHER:** Piano pieces; choral works; songs.

Andriessen, Hendrik (Franciscus), eminent Dutch organist, pedagogue, and composer, brother of **Willem (Christiaan Nicolaas)** and father of **Jurriaan** and **Louis (Joseph) Andriessen**; b. Haarlem, Sept. 17, 1892; d. Heemstede, April 12, 1981. He studied music with his brother; then took piano and organ lessons with Louis Robert and J.B. de Pauw; studied composition with Bernard Zweers at the Amsterdam Cons. (1914–16); subsequently taught harmony there (1926–34). He succeeded his father as organist at St. Joseph's Church in Haarlem (1913–34); was then organist at Utrecht Cathedral (1934–49). He was director of the Royal Cons. of Music in The Hague (1949–57) and special prof. at the Catholic Univ. in Nijmegen (1952–63). His music is Romantically inspired; some of his instrumental works make use of modern devices, including melodic atonality and triadic polytonality. He was particularly esteemed for his revival of the authentic modalities of Gregorian chant; his choral works present a remarkable confluence of old usages with modern technical procedures.

WORKS: OPERAS: *Philomela* (Holland Festival, June 23, 1950; *De Spiegel uit Venetië* (The Mirror from Venice; 1964; Dutch TV, Oct. 5, 1967). **ORCH.:** 4 syms. (1930, 1937, 1946, 1954); *Variations and Fugue on a Theme of Kuhnau* for Strings (1935); *Capriccio* (1941); *Variations on a Theme of Couperin* for Flute, Harp, and Strings (1944); *Ballet Suite* (1947); *Ricercare* (1949); *Wilhemus van Nassouwe*, rhapsody (1950); Organ Concerto (1950); *Symphonic Étude* (The Hague, Oct. 15, 1952); *Libertas venit*, rhapsody (1954); *Mascherata*, fantasy (1962); *Symphonie concertante* (1962); Violin Concerto (1968–69); Concertino for Oboe and Strings (1969–70); *Concertino* for Cello and Orch. (1970); *Chromatic Variations* for Flute, Oboe, Violin, Cello, and Strings (1970); *Canzone* (1971); *Chantecler*, overture (1972). **CHAMBER:** Cello Sonata (1926); Violin Sonata (1932); *3 Inventions* for Violin and Cello (1937); Piano Trio (1939); Suite for Violin and Piano (1950); Sonata for Solo Cello (1951); Suite for Brass Quintet (1951); Wind Quintet (1951); *Ballade* for Oboe and Piano (1952); *Theme and Variations* for Flute, Oboe, and Piano (1953); 3 string quartets (1957, 1961, 1969); *Pezzo festoso* for Organ, 2 Trumpets, and 2 Trombones (1962); *Canzonetta* for Harpsichord (1963); *Canzone*, Trio No. 2 for Flute, Oboe, and Piano (1965); Viola Sonata (1967); *Concert spirituel* for Flute, Oboe, Violin, and Cello (1967); *Haydn Variations* for English Horn and Piano (1968); Clarinet Sonata (1971); *Choral varié* for 3 Trumpets and 3 Trombones (1973). **KEYBOARD: PIANO:** 2 sonatas (1934, 1966); *Pavane* (1937); *Serenade* (1950). **ORGAN:** 4 chorales (1913, c.1918, 1920, 1952); Toccata (1917); *Fête-Dieu* (1918); *Sonata de Chiesa* (1927); Passacaglia (1929); *Sinfonia* (1940); *Intermezzi* (1943); *Theme and Variations* (1949); 4 Studies (1953). **VOCAL:** *Missa Simplex* for Chorus (1927); *Missa Sponsa Christi* for Men's Chorus and Organ (1933); *Missa Christus Rex* for Double Chorus and Organ (1938); 2 Madrigals for Chorus and Strings (1940); *Te Deum Laudamus I* for Chorus and Organ or Orch. (1943–46), and *II* for Chorus and Orch. (1968); *De Zee en het land* (Declamatorium) for Chorus, Speaker, and Orch. (1953); *Veni Creator* for Chorus and Orch. (1960); *Psalm IX* for Chorus, Tenor, and Orch. (1968); *Lux Jocunda* for Chorus, Tenor, and Orch. (1968); *Carmen Saeculare (Horatius)* for Chorus, Soprano, Tenor, Winds, Harpsichord, and Double Bass (1968). **SOLO SONG CYCLES** (most with Organ or Orch.): *L'Aube spirituelle* (1916); *L'Invitation au voyage* (1918); *Magna res est amor* (1919); *L'Attente mystique* (1920); *Miroir de peine* (1923); *Cantique spirituel* (1924); *La Vièrge à midi* (1966).

BIBL.: A. de Jager, P. Op de Coul, and L. Samama, eds., *Duizend kleuren van muziek: Leven en werk van H. A.* (Zutphen, 1992)

Andriessen, Jurriaan, Dutch composer, son of **Hendrik (Franciscus)**, brother of **Louis (Joseph)**, and nephew of **Willem (Christiaan Nicolaas) Andriessen**; b. Haarlem, Nov. 15, 1925. After training in theory from his father, he studied conducting with Willem van Otterloo at the Utrecht Cons. (graduated, 1947); following studies in Paris, he was a composition student of Copland at the Berkshire Music Center in Tanglewood (summers, 1949–50). His television opera *Kalchas* (Dutch TV, June 28, 1959) was the first such score to be produced in the Netherlands.

WORKS: DRAMATIC: *Kalchas*, television opera (Dutch TV, June 28, 1959); *Het Zwarte Blondje* (The Black Blonde), opera buffa (1964); incidental music to many plays. **ORCH.:** Piano Concertino (1943); *Symphonietta concertante* for 4 Trumpets and Orch. (1947); Piano Concerto (1948); 5 syms.: No. 1, *Berkshire Symphonies* (1949; perf. as the ballet *Jones Beach*, N.Y., March 12, 1950), No. 2 for Wind Orch. (1962), No. 3, *Symphonyen fan Fryslân* (1963), No. 4, *Aves* (The Birds), for Chorus and Orch. (1963), and No. 5, *Time Spirit*, for Clarinet, Pop Group, 6 Dancers, and Orch. (1970); Flute Concerto (1951); *Cymbeline*, overture (1954); *Inno della Tecnica* (1957); *Ritratto di una citta (Ouverture Den Haag)* (1957); *Thai*, symphonic rhapsody on jazz tunes by King Bhumibol Adulyadej of Thailand (1960); *Concerto Rotterdam* for Jazz Combo and Orch. (1966); *Contra-bande* for Sousaphone and Orch. (1967); *Omaggio a Sweelinck* for Harpsichord and 24 Strings (1968); *Trelleborg Concerto* for Harpsichord and 3 Orch. Groups (1969); *Antifona dell'Aja* (1969); *Pasticcio-Finale* for Orch., Dixieland Band, and Tape (1974); *Monomania e policromia* (1984); *Serenade* for Chamber Orch. (1988); Violin Concerto (1991–92). **CHAMBER:** *Hommage à Milhaud* for 11 Instruments (1945; also for Flute and String Quartet, 1948); Violin Sonata (1946); *Octet Divertissement* for Winds (1948); *Rouw past Electra* (Mourning Becomes Electra), suite for 11 Winds and Percussion (1954); 5 trios: No. 1 for Flute, Oboe, and Piano (1955), No. 2 for Flute, Viola, and Piano (1955), No. 3 for 3 Recorders (1957), No. 4 for Flute, Oboe, and Bassoon (1957), and No. 5, *Sonata da camera*, for Flute, Viola, and Guitar (1959); *L'incontro di Cesare e Cleopatra*, sextet for Winds and Piano (1956); Concertino for Bassoon and Winds (1962); *Respiration*, suite for Double Wind Quintet (1962); *Movimenti I* for Trumpet, Horn, Trombone, Strings, and Timpani (1965), *II* for Oboe, Clarinet, Bassoon, Strings, and Percussion (1972), and *III* for Violin, Viola, Cello, Winds, and Percussion (1974); Trio for Clarinet, Cello, and Piano (1965); *Antifono e Fusione* for Wind Quintet, Brass Quartet, and Timpani (1966); *In pompa magna* for Brass and Percussion (1966); *Quartetto buffo* for Clarinet and String Trio (1974); *The Cave* for Cello, 12 Winds, 4 Keyboard Instruments, and Electronics (1976); Clarinet Quartet (1984); String Trio (1988); Bassoon Sonata (1990); *Divertimento* for 2 Oboes and English Horn (1990); Quartet for Flute, Violin, Viola, and Cello (1992). **OTHER:** Piano pieces and vocal music.

Andriessen, Louis (Joseph), Dutch composer and teacher, son of **Hendrik (Franciscus)**, brother of **Jurriaan**, and nephew of **Willem (Christiaan Nicolaas) Andriessen**; b. Utrecht, June 6, 1939. He first studied with his father and with Kees van Baaren at the Royal Cons. of Music in The Hague (1957–62); then took lessons with Berio in Milan (1962–63). In 1978 he became a prof. of composition at the Royal Cons. of Music at The Hague. His works are conceived in an advanced idiom.

WORKS: Flute Sonata (1956); *Séries* for 2 Pianos (1958); *Percosse* for Flute, Trumpet, Bassoon, and Percussion (1958); *Nocturnes* for Soprano and Chamber Orch. (1959); *Aanloop en sprongen* for Flute, Oboe, and Clarinet (1961); *Ittrospezione I* for 2 Pianos (1961), *II* for Orch. (1963), and *III* for 2 Pianos and Chamber Ensemble or Saxophone (1964); *A Flower Song I* for Violin (1963), *II* for Oboe (1963), and *III* for Cello (1964); *Sweet* for Recorder or Flute (1964); *Double* for Clarinet and Piano (1965); *Paintings* for Recorder or Flute and Piano (1965); *Souvenirs d'enfance* for Piano and Tape (1966); *Anachronie*, to the memory of Charles Ives, *I* for Orch. (1965–66; Rotterdam, Jan. 18, 1968) and *II* for Oboe, 4 Horns, Piano, Harp, and String Orch. (1969); *Contra-tempus* for 23 Musicians (1968); *Reconstructie*, anti-imperialist collective opera (1968–69; Holland Festival, June 29, 1969; in collaboration with Reinbert de Leeuw, Misha Mengelberg, Peter Schat, and Jan van Vlijmen); *Hoe het is* (What It's Like) for Live-Electronic Improvisers and 52 Strings (Rotterdam, Sept. 14, 1970); *Spektakel* (Uproar) for 16 Winds, 6 Percussionists, and Electronic Instruments (1970); *The 9 Symphonies of Beethoven* for Promenade Orch. and Ice Cream Bell (1970); *De Volharding* (The Persistence) for Piano and Winds (1972); *De Statt* (The State) for 4 Women's Voices and 27 Instruments (1972–76); *On Jimmy Yancey* for Chamber Ensemble (1973); *Il Principe*, for Choruses, Winds, Piano, and Bass Guitar, after Machiavelli (1974); *Symphonieen der Nederlanden* for Brass Band (1974); *Workers' Union*, symphonic movement for any loud-speaking group of Instruments (1975); *Hoketus* for 2 Panpipes, 2 Pianos, and Electronics (1977); *Orpheus*, theater piece (1977); Sym. for Open Strings (1978); *De tijd* (Time) for Chorus and Orch. (1981); *De snelheid* (Velocity) for Orch. (1983; San Francisco, Jan. 11, 1984); *De Stijl* for Orch. (1985); *Double Track* for Harpsichord, Piano, Glockenspiel, and Celesta (1986); *De Lijn* for 3 Flutes (1986); *De Materie*, opera (1989); *Nietzsche redet* for Reciter, Woodwinds, 2 Pianos, and Strings (1989); *Widow/Song Lines* for Saxophone Orch. (1990); *Facing Death* for String Quartet (1991); *6 Moods* for Saxophone Ensemble (1993); Trumpet Sonata (1994).

Andriessen, Willem (Christiaan Nicolaas), Dutch pianist, teacher, and composer, brother of **Hendrik (Franciscus)** and uncle of **Jurriaan** and **Louis (Joseph) Andriessen**; b. Haarlem, Oct. 25, 1887; d. Amsterdam, March 29, 1964. He studied piano and composition at the Amsterdam Cons. (1903–08); taught piano at The Hague Cons. (1910–17) and at the Rotterdam Cons.; from 1937 to 1953 he was director of the Amsterdam Cons. He was a professional pianist of a high caliber. He wrote a Piano Concerto (1908); *3 Songs* for Voice and Orch. (1911); *Hei, 't was de Mei*, scherzo for Orch. (1912); Piano Sonata (1938); Piano Sonatina (1945).

Andsnes, Leif Ove, Norwegian pianist; b. Stavanger, April 7, 1970. He took up the piano when he was only 5, and at age 16 he entered the Bergen Cons. of Music, where he pursued training with Jiří Hlinka. At 17, he made his formal debut in Oslo and was awarded the Hindemith Prize of Frankfurt am Main. In 1988 he won the Levin Prize of Bergen and the Norwegian Music Critics Prize of Oslo. He made his British debut as soloist with Jansons and the Oslo Phil. at the Edinburgh Festival in 1989, and subsequently was engaged by leading European orchs. In 1990 he won the Grieg Prize of Bergen and made his U.S. debut as soloist with Järvi and the Cleveland Orch. at the Blossom Music Festival. He subsequently appeared as a soloist with major North American orchs., including those of Los Angeles, Detroit, San Francisco, St. Louis, Chicago, Toronto, Montreal, and Baltimore. In 1992 he made his first appearance at the London Promenade Concerts as soloist with the BBC Phil. of Manchester. His recital engagements have taken him to London, Munich, Paris, Amsterdam, Berlin, N.Y., and Washington, D.C.

d'Angeli, Andrea, Italian composer and writer on music; b. Padua, Nov. 9, 1868; d. S. Michele, near Verona, Oct. 28, 1940. He studied at the Univ. of Padua; then was an instructor at the Liceo Rossini in Pesaro. He wrote the operas *L'Innocente; Il Negromante; Al Ridotto di Venezia; Fiori e Colombi; Maurizio e Lazzaro*; also a number of libretti. He publ. monographs on Verdi (Milan, 1924) and Benedetto Marcello (Milan, 1930), and numerous essays on music for *La Cronaca Musicale*, of which he was ed. (1907–14).

d'Angelo, Louis, Italian-born American baritone; b. Naples, May 6, 1888; d. Jersey City, N.J., Aug. 9, 1958. He was taken to the U.S. as a child, and was first apprenticed as a glove cutter in Gloversville, N.Y.; then sang in a local church choir. He went to N.Y. City at the age of 18, studied at the College of Music, and appeared in vaudeville; he made his Metropolitan Opera debut as Wagner in *Faust* (Nov. 17, 1917), and remained on its roster until 1946. He had some 130 operatic roles in his repertoire.

Angerer, Paul, Austrian conductor, teacher, and composer; b. Vienna, May 16, 1927. He received violin and piano lessons as a child; later he studied violin, piano, and composition at the Vienna Academy of Music. He was made a violist in the Vienna Sym. Orch. (1947), Zürich's Tonhalle Orch. (1948), and Geneva's l'Orchestre de la Suisse Romande (1949); then was 1st violist of the Vienna Sym. Orch. (1953–57). After serving as director and chief conductor of the Vienna Chamber Orch. (1956–63), he was 1st conductor at the Bonn Stadttheater (1964–66); then was music director of the Ulm Theater (1966–68), chief conductor of the Salzburg Landestheater (1967–72), and director of the South West German Chamber Orch. in Pforzheim (1971–82). In 1982 he founded the Concilium Musicum of Vienna for the performance of 17th and 18th century music on original instruments. From 1982 to 1992 he taught at the Vienna Hochschule für Musik. In 1977 he was made an Austrian Prof. Among his other honors were the Austrian State Prize (1956), the Theodor Körner Prize (1958), and the culture prizes of the city of Vienna (1983) and the State of Niederösterreich (1987).

WORKS: DRAMATIC: *Das verräterische Herz*, pantomime and ballet (1956); *Die Passkontrolle*, television opera (1958); *Hotel Comedie*, musical (1970). **ORCH.:** *Musica ad pulsum et impulsum* for Strings and Percussion (1955); *Musica fera* (1956); *Concerto pour la jeunesse* (1956); *Étude* for Violin and Chamber Orch. (1956); *Gloriatio* for Double Bass and Chamber Orch. (1957); Concerto for Piano and Strings (1962); Viola Concerto (1962); *Ire in orbem* for Strings (1975); *Luctus et gaudium* for Trumpet and Strings (1977). **CHAMBER:** *Musik* for Viola (1948); Quartet for Oboe, Horn, Viola, and Cello (1951); Trio for Recorder, Viola d'Amore, and Lute (1953); *Musica exanimata* for Cello and Piano (1954); Quintet for Flute, Oboe, Clarinet, Horn, and Bassoon (1956); *Chanson gaillarde* for Oboe, Cello, and Harpsichord (1963); *Cogitatio* for 9 Instruments (1964); *Musica articolata* for 13 Winds (1970); *Oblectatio vespertina* for Flute and Harp (1970); Quartet for Recorder, Viola da Gamba, Guitar, and Percussion (1971); *Syngrapha* for Violin, Viola, and Cello (1975); *Exercitium canonicum*, 4 pieces for 2 Violins (1980); *Obolus* for 6 Oboes (1983–84); *Hilasatio* for Viola d'Amore, Flute, Violin, and Double Bass (1987); organ and harpsichord pieces. **VOCAL:** *Missa Seitenstettensis* (1987–88).

Angermüller, Rudolph (Kurt), German musicologist, editor, and music librarian; b. Bielefeld, Sept. 2, 1940. He studied at the Försterling Cons. in Bielefeld and pursued training in musicology in Mainz, Münster, and at the Univ. of Salzburg (Ph.D., 1970, with the diss. *Antonio Salieri: Sein Leben und seine weltlichen Werke unter besonderer Berücksichtigung seiner "grossen" Opern*; publ. in 3 vols., Munich, 1971–74), where he joined its musicological inst. in 1968. He served as chief ed. of the Neue Mozart-Ausgabe (from 1972), and was librarian (from 1972), chief of the research dept. (from 1981), and general secretary (from 1988) of the International Mozarteum Foundation in Salzburg.

WRITINGS: *Untersuchungen zur Geschichte des Carmen-Stoffes* (1967); *W.A. Mozarts Musikalische Umwelt in Paris (1777–78): Eine Dokumentation* (1982); *"Auf Ehre und Credit": Die Finanzen des W.A. Mozart* (1983); with O. Schneider, *Mozart-Bibliographie, 1981–1985: Mit Nachträgen zur Mozart-Bibliographie bis 1980* (1987); *Vom Kaiser zum Sklaven: Personen in Mozarts Opern: Mit bibliographischen Notizen über die Mozart-Sänger der Uraufführungen und Mozarts Librettisten* (1989); with J. Senigl, *Mozart-Bibliographie, 1986–1991: Mit Nachträgen zur Mozart-Bibliographie bis 1985* (1992); *Der Salzburger Mozart-Denkmal: Eine Dokumentation (bis 1845) zut 150-Jahre-Enthüllungsgeier* (Salzburg, 1992).

Anglès, Higini, eminent Catalonian musicologist; b. Maspujols, Jan. 1, 1888; d. Rome, Dec. 8, 1969. He studied theology and philosophy at the Seminario de Tarràgona (ordained, 1912); then pursued music training with José Cogul (harmony), Vicente de Gilbert (harmony, counterpoint, fugue, and organ), Barberá (composition and folksong), and Pedrell (musicology and music history) in Barcelona (1913–19). In 1917 he became head of the music dept. of the Biblioteca de Catalunya in Barcelona. In 1923–24 he completed his studies with W. Gurlitt at the Univ. of Freiburg im Breisgau and F. Ludwig at the Univ. of Göttingen. From 1927 to 1936 he was prof. of music history at the Barcelona Cons. In 1943 he became director of the Instituto Español de Musicologia. In 1947 he was made director of the Pontifical Inst. of Sacred Music in Rome. He was an authority on Spanish music of the Middle Ages and the Renaissance; he publ. *Cantigas del Rei N'Anfos el Savi* (Barcelona, 1927), *Historia de la música española* (Barcelona, 1935), *La música a Catalunya fins al segle XIII* (Barcelona, 1935), *La música española desde la edad media hasta nuestros dias* (Barcelona, 1941), *L'opera di Morales e lo sviluppo della polifonia sacra spangola nel 1500* (Rome, 1954), and *Studio musicologia* (Rome, 1959). He ed. *El Códex Musical de Las Huelgas* (1927–31) and the works of J. Pujol (1927–32) and J. Cabanilles (1927–56). In 1941 he initiated the series Monumentos de la música española, which publ. *La música en la corte de los Reyes Católicos* (1941–51) and the works of Morales (1952–69), Victoria (1965–69), and Cabezón (1966).

Anhalt, István, Hungarian-born Canadian composer and teacher; b. Budapest, April 12, 1919. He studied composition with Kodály at the Budapest Academy of Music (1937–41); then received training in composition from Boulanger, in conducting from Fourestier, and in piano from S. Stravinsky in Paris (1946–49). In 1949 he went to Montreal and joined the faculty of McGill Univ., where he was founder-director of its electronic music studio (1964–71); in 1969 he also was Slee Prof. at the State Univ. of N.Y. in Buffalo. From 1971 to 1981 he was head of the music dept. at Queen's Univ. in Kingston, Ontario, where he was made prof. emeritus in 1984. In 1982 he was awarded an honorary D.Mus. from McGill Univ. He publ. *Alternative Voices: Essays on Contemporary Vocal and Choral Composition* (Toronto, 1984). In a number of his works, he utilizes synthetic sounds.

WORKS: MUSIC THEATER AND MULTIMEDIA: *Arc en ciel*, ballet "in 3 nights" for 2 Pianos (1951); *Foci* for Amplified Soprano, Instrumental Ensemble, and Electronics (1969); *La Tourangelle* for 3 Sopranos, Tenor, Bass, Instrumental Ensemble, and Tapes (1972–74; Toronto, July 17, 1975); *Thisness*, duodrama for Mezzo-soprano and Piano (1985; Vancouver, Jan. 19, 1986); *Winthrop* for Solo Voices, Chorus, Boy's Chorus, and Orch. (Kitchener, Sept. 6, 1986); *Traces (Tikkun)*, drama for Baritone and Orch. (1994). **ORCH.:** *Concerto in stilo di Handel* for 2 Oboes, 2 Horns, and Strings (1946); *Interludium* for Strings, Piano, and Timpani (1950); *Funeral Music* (1951); Sym. (1954–58); *Symphony of Modules* (1967); *Simulacrum* (Ottawa, Oct. 1987); *Sparkskraps* (1988); *Sonance-Resonance: Welche Töne?* (Toronto, Sept. 13, 1989). **CHAMBER:** Piano Trio (1953); Violin Sonata (1954); *Doors . . . Shadows (Glenn Gould in Memory)* for String Quartet (Toronto, Sept. 24, 1992). **PIANO:** Sonata (1951); *Fantasia* (1954). **VOCAL:** *The Bell Man* for Chorus, 2 Bells, and Organ (1954; rev. 1980); *Cento: Cantata Urbana* for 12 Speakers and Tape (1968); *Foci* for Soprano, Chamber Ensemble, and Tape (1969); choruses; songs. **ELECTRO-ACOUSTIC:** *Sine Nomine I* (1959) and *II* (1959); *Birds and Bells* (1960); *On the Beach* (1961).

Anievas, Agustin, American pianist and teacher; b. N.Y., June 11, 1934. He commenced piano lessons at age 4 with his mother; following appearances as a child pianist, he pursued formal training with Steuermann, Samaroff, and Marcus at N.Y.'s Juilliard School of Music. In 1952 he made his formal debut as soloist with the Little Orch. Soc. of N.Y.; after winning the Concert Artists Guild Award in 1959 and capturing 1st prize in the Mitropoulos Competition in 1961, he toured widely; served as prof. of piano at Brooklyn College of the City Univ. of N.Y. (from 1974).

Anosov, Nikolai, Russian conductor and pedagogue, father of **Gennadi Rozhdestvensky**; b. Borisoglebsk, Feb. 18, 1900; d. Moscow, Dec. 2, 1962. He conducted orchs. in Rostov-na-Donu (1937–38) and Baku (1938–39); studied piano and composition at the Moscow Cons. (graduated 1943), where he later joined the faculty. He appeared as a guest conductor in Germany, Hungary, Poland, and China; was noted for reviving operas by Bortniansky and Fomin. He wrote a textbook on reading orch. scores, and composed a few works, including a Concertino for Piano and Orch. and a Quartet for Woodwinds. He was married to the soprano Natalia Rozhdestvenskaya; their son Gennadi assumed his mother's name.

Anrooy (properly, **Anrooij**), **Peter van,** Dutch conductor and composer; b. Zalt-Bommel, Oct. 13, 1879; d. The Hague, Dec. 31, 1954. He studied with Johan Wagenaar in Utrecht; in 1899 he went to Moscow, where he studied violin and conducting with Willem Kes and Taneyev. He played the violin in the orchs. of Glasgow and Zürich (1902); then was active as a conductor in Groningen (1905) and Arnhem (1910); in 1917 he became conductor of the Residentie Orch. in The Hague, retiring in 1935. He wrote an orch. rhapsody on Dutch themes, *Piet Hein* (1901), a *Ballade* for Violin and Orch. (1902), and several chamber pieces.

Ansermet, Ernest (Alexandre), celebrated Swiss conductor; b. Vevey, Nov. 11, 1883; d. Geneva, Feb. 20, 1969. He studied mathematics at the Univ. of Lausanne and at the Paris Sorbonne, and received music training from Gédalge in Paris and from Denéréaz, Barblan, and Ernest Bloch in Geneva. In 1910 he made his conducting debut in Montreux, where he subsequently conducted sym. concerts. In 1915 he settled in Geneva as a conductor. From 1915 to 1923 he also conducted Diaghilev's Ballets Russes, which he took on tours of Europe and North and South America. During this period, Ansermet attracted favorable notice as the conductor of the premieres of several works by Stravinsky, Ravel, Falla, and Prokofiev. In 1918 he founded l'Orchestre de la Suisse Romande in Geneva, which he led as chief conductor for nearly 50 years. He added luster to his reputation through appearances as a guest conductor with the world's leading orchs. In 1946 he made his debut at the Glyndebourne Festival conducting the premiere of Britten's *The Rape of Lucretia*; subsequently appeared with various major U.S. orchs., and made his belated Metropolitan Opera debut in N.Y. conducting *Pelléas et Mélisande* on Nov. 30, 1952.

Ansermet acquired a distinguished reputation as an interpreter of Debussy, Stravinsky, Ravel, Prokofiev, and Bartók. While he conducted the works of various other 20th-century composers, his sympathies did not extend to Schoenberg or his disciples; indeed, Ansermet disdained the 12-tone system and other avant-garde techniques. Among his writings were *Le Geste du chef d'orchestre* (1943), *Les Fondements de la musique dans la conscience humaine* (2 vols., 1961), *Entretiens sur la musique* (with J.-C. Piguet; 1963), and *Les compositeurs et leurs oeuvres* (ed. by J.-C. Piguet; 1989).

BIBL.: *E. A.: 1883–1969* (Lausanne, 1983); F. Hundry, *E. A.: Pionnier de la Musique* (1983).

Ansseau, Fernand, Belgian tenor; b. Boussu-Bois, March 6, 1890; d. Brussels, May 1, 1972. He was a pupil of Demest in Brussels. In 1913 he made his operatic debut as Jean in *Hérodiade* in Dijon; in 1918 he sang in Brussels. In 1919 he made his first appearance at London's Covent Garden; after singing at the Paris Opéra-Comique (1920–21), he was a member of the Chicago Civic Opera (1923–28). In later years, he sang in France and Belgium, retiring in 1939; then taught voice in Brussels.

Antheil, George (actually, **Georg Carl Johann**), remarkable American composer; b. Trenton, N.J., July 8, 1900; d. N.Y., Feb. 12, 1959. He began piano lessons at age 6; after studying theory and composition with Constantin Sternberg in Philadelphia (1916–19), he pursued composition lessons with Ernest Bloch in N.Y. (1919–21). Defying the dictates of flickering musical conservatism, Antheil wrote piano pieces under such provocative titles as *Airplane Sonata, Sonata Sauvage, Jazz Sonata,* and *Mechanisms.* In 1922 he went to Europe and toured successfully as a pianist, giving a number of concerts featuring his own compositions. While living in Berlin (1922–23), he met Stravinsky, who greatly influenced him. In 1923 he went to Paris and entered the circle of Joyce, Pound, Yeats, Satie, and the violinist Olga Rudge, with whom he performed his 3 violin sonatas. Hailed as a genius, he soon became the self-styled *enfant terrible* of modern music. He became naively infatuated with the world of the modern machine, winning extraordinary success with his *Ballet mécanique* for Percussion Ensemble, including electric bells, propellers, and siren (Paris, June 19, 1926). His Piano Concerto (Paris, March 12, 1927) paled in comparison, so Antheil returned to N.Y to introduce his *Ballet mécanique* to U.S. audiences at Carnegie Hall (April 10, 1927), which precipitated an uproar both in the audience and in the press. Abandoning attempts to shock the public by extravaganza, he turned to opera. However, his *Transatlantic* (Frankfurt am Main, May 25, 1930) and *Helen Retires* (N.Y., Feb. 28, 1934) met with little success. In 1936 he went to Hollywood as a film composer. He also pursued various sidelines, including penning a syndicated lonely-hearts column and patenting a radio-guided torpedo with the actress Hedy Lamarr (patent No. 2,292,387, June 10, 1941, for an invention relating to a "secret communication system involving the use of carrier waves of different frequencies, especially useful in the remote control of dirigible craft, such as torpedoes;" it is not known whether the Antheil-Lamarr device was ever used in naval warfare). While continuing to write film music, Antheil pursued serious composition. Among his most important later scores were the 4th (1942) and 5th (1947–48) syms., the opera *Volpone* (1949–52), and the ballet *Capital of the World* (1952). His colorful autobiography was publ. as *Bad Boy of Music* (N.Y., 1945). He was married to Elizabeth ("Boski") Markus, a niece of the Austrian dramatist and novelist Arthur Schnitzler, who died in 1978. Antheil was the subject of a monograph by Ezra Pound entitled *Antheil and the Treatise on Harmony with Supplementary Notes* (Paris, 1924; 2nd ed., Chicago, 1927), which, however, had little bearing on Antheil and even less on harmony.

WORKS: DRAMATIC: OPERAS: *Transatlantic* (1927–28; Frankfurt am Main, May 25, 1930); *Helen Retires* (1930–31; N.Y., Feb. 28, 1934); *Volpone* (1949–52; Los Angeles, Jan. 9, 1953); *The Brothers* (Denver, July 28, 1954); *Venus in Africa* (1954; Denver, May 24, 1957); *The Wish* (1954; Louisville, April 2, 1955). **OPERA-BALLET:** *Flight (Ivan the Terrible)* (1927–30; arr. as *Crucifixion Juan Miro* for String Orch., 1927; not extant). **BALLETS:** *Dance in Four Parts* (c.1933–34; N.Y., Nov. 11, 1934; not extant; based on *La femme 100 têtes*); *Eyes of Gutne* (c.1934; not extant); *The Seasons* (c.1934; not extant); *Dreams* (1934–35; N.Y., March 5, 1935); *Serenade* (N.Y., June 9, 1934; not extant; orchestrated from Tchaikovsky); *Transcendance* (Bryn Mawr, Pa., Feb. 7, 1935; not extant; orchestrated from Liszt); *Course* (1935; not extant); *The Cave Within* (c.1948; not extant); *Capital of the World* (1952; telecast, Dec. 6, 1953). **FILM MUSIC:** *The Plainsman* (1936); *Angels Over Broadway* (1940); *Specter of the Rose* (1946); *Knock on Any Door* (1949); *The Juggler* (1952); *Not as a Stranger* (1955); *The Pride and the Passion* (1957). Also music for plays, radio, and television. **ORCH.:** 2 piano concertos: No. 1 (1922) and No. 2 (1926; Paris, March 12, 1927); Symphonie No. 1, *Zingareska* (1920–22; Berlin, Nov. 21, 1922; rev. 1923); *Ballet mécanique* (1923–25; Paris, June 19, 1926; rev. 1952–53); *A Jazz Symphony* (1925; rev. 1955); *Symphony en fa* (1925–26; Paris, June 19, 1926); Suite (1926); *Capriccio* (1930); Sym. No. 2 (1931–38; rev. 1943); *Morceau (The Creole)* (1932); Sym. No. 3, *American* (1936–39; rev. 1946); Sym. No. 4, *1942* (1942; N.Y., Feb. 13, 1944); *Water-Music for 4th-of-July-Evening* for Strings (1942–43); *Decatur et Algiers* (1943); *Over the Plains* (1945); Sym. No. 5, *Tragic* (1945–46); Violin Concerto (1946); *Autumn Song* (1947); another Sym. No. 5, *Joyous* (1947–48; Philadelphia, Dec. 21, 1948); Sym. No. 6 (1947–48; San Francisco, Feb. 10, 1949; rev. 1949–50); *American Dance Suite No. 1* (1948); *McKonkeys Ferry Overture* (1948); *Serenade* for Strings (1948) and for Chamber Orch. (1949); *Tom Sawyer* (1949); *Accordion Dance* (1951); *Nocturne in Skyrockets* (1951). **CHAMBER:** Sym. for 5 Instruments (1922–23; 2nd ver., 1923); 4 violin sonatas (1923; 1923; 1924; 1947–48); 3 string quartets (1924, 2nd ver., 1925; 1927, rev. 1943; 1948); Concertino for Flute, Bassoon, and Piano (1930); *6 Little Pieces* for String Quartet (1931); *Concert* for Chamber Ensemble (1932); Sonatina for Violin and Cello or Piano (1932); Violin Sonatina (1945); Flute Sonata (1951); Trumpet Sonata (1951); *Bohemian Grove at Night* for 5 Instruments (1952). **PIANO:** *Airplane Sonata,* Sonata No. 2 (1921); *Sonata Sauvage,* Sonata No. 1 (c.1922); *Death of Machines,* Sonata No. 3 (1923); *Jazz Sonata,* Sonata No. 4 (c.1922); Sonata No. 5 (1923); Sonata (1923); *Woman Sonata,* Sonata No. 6 (c.1923; not extant); *The Perfect Modernist* (c.1923; not extant); *Mechanisms* (c.1923; not extant); *Habañera, Tarantelle, Serenata* for 2 Pianos (1924); *Sonatina für Radio* (1929); *La femme 100 têtes* (1933); *La vie Parisienne* (1939); *The Ben Hecht Valses* (1943); Sonatas Nos. 3 (1947), 4 (1948), and 5 (1950). **VOCAL:** *8 Fragments from Shelley* for Chorus and Piano (1951; 3 mvts. orchestrated, 1951); *Cabeza de vaca,* cantata for Chorus (1955–56; orch. by E. Gold, 1959; CBS-TV, June 10, 1962); songs.

BIBL.: E. Pound, *A. and the Treatise on Harmony with Supplementary Notes* (Paris, 1924; 2nd ed., 1927); A. Copland, "G. A.," *League of Composers Review,* II/1 (1925); R. Thompson, "American Composer: V: G. A.," *Modern Music,* VIII/4 (1931); D. Friede, *The Mechanical Angel: His Adventures and Enterprises in the Glittering 1920's* (N.Y., 1948); W. Hoffa, "Ezra Pound and G. A.: Vorticist Music and the *Cantos,*" *American Literature,* XLIV/1 (1972); L. Whitesitt, *The Life and Music of G. A., 1900–1959* (Ann Arbor, 1983).

Anthony, James R(aymond), American musicologist; b. Providence, R.I., Feb. 18, 1922. He studied at Columbia Univ. (B.S., 1946; M.A., 1948), the Univ. of Paris (diploma, 1951), and the Univ. of Southern Calif. in Los Angeles (Ph.D., 1964, with the diss. *The Opera-ballets of André Campra: A Study of the First Period French Opera-ballet*); taught at the Univ. of Montana (1948–50) and the Univ. of Arizona (from 1952). He publ. the study *French Baroque Music from Beaujoyeul to Rameau* (London, 1973; 2nd ed., rev., 1978); also contributed articles to *The New Grove Dictionary of Music and Musicians* (1980).

BIBL.: J. Heyer, ed., *Jean-Baptist Lully and the Music of the French Baroque: Essays in Honour of J. A.* (Cambridge, 1988).

Antill, John (Henry), Australian composer; b. Sydney, April 8, 1904; d. there, Dec. 29, 1986. He studied with Alfred Hill at the New South Wales State Conservatorium of Music in Sydney; from 1934 to 1971 he worked for the Australian Broadcasting Commission (later Corp.). In 1971 he received the Order of the British Empire, and in 1981 was made a Companion of the Order of St. Michael and St. George.

WORKS: DRAMATIC: OPERAS: *Endymion* (1922; Sydney, July 22, 1953); *The Music Critic* (1953); *The First Christmas* (ABC, Dec. 25, 1969). **BALLETS:** *Corroboree* (c.1935–46; Sydney, July 3, 1950; rev. 1960); *Wakooka* (1957); *Black Opal* (1961); *Snowy* (1961); *Paean to the Spirit of Man* (1968). Also film scores. **ORCH.:** *Variations* (1953); *Symphony of a City* (1959); *Music for a Royal Pageant* (1962); Harmonica Concerto (1964); *The Unknown Land* (1968). **VOCAL:** *The Song of Hagar*, oratorio (1958); songs.

Antoine, Georges, Belgian composer; b. Liège, April 28, 1892; d. Bruges, Nov. 15, 1918. He was a student of Sylvain Dupuis at the Liège Cons. (1902–13). In 1914 he joined the Belgian army. He died at an extremely young age of an ailment acquired during his military service in World War I. Among his few works are a Violin Sonata (1912–15); Piano Concerto (1914); *Vendanges* for Voice and Orch. (1914); Piano Quartet (1916); *Veillée d'armes*, symphonic poem (1918); songs.

BIBL.: M. Paquot, *G. A.* (Brussels, 1935).

Antonicelli, Giuseppe, Italian conductor; b. Castrovillari, Dec. 29, 1897; d. Trieste, March 10, 1980. He studied in Turin, where he began his career as a répétiteur at the Teatro Regio. After conducting at Milan's La Scala (1934–37), he served as artistic director of the Teatro Giuseppe Verdi in Trieste (1937–45). On Nov. 10, 1947, he made his Metropolitan Opera debut in N.Y. conducting *Un ballo in maschera*, remaining on its roster until 1950; then served once more as artistic director of the Teatro Giuseppe Verdi in Trieste (1951–68). His wife was **Franca Somigli**.

Antonini, Alfredo, Italian-American conductor and composer; b. Milan, May 31, 1901; d. Clearwater, Fla., Nov. 3, 1983. After studying at the Milan Cons., he emigrated to the U.S. in 1929. From 1941 he was active as a conductor and composer with CBS in N.Y.; also was conductor of the Tampa Phil. (1957–68).

Antoniou, Theodore, Greek-American composer, conductor, and teacher; b. Athens, Feb. 10, 1935. He studied in Athens at the National Cons. (violin and voice, 1947–58), with Manolis Kalomiris (composition), and at the Hellenic Cons. (composition and orchestration with Yannis Papaioannou, 1958–61); continued his training in Munich with Günter Bialas and Mennerich (composition and conducting) at the Hochschule für Musik (1961–65), and with Riedl at the Siemens Studio for Electronic Music; also attended courses on new music in Darmstadt (summers, 1963–66). Returning to Athens, he became director and chief conductor of the sym. orch. in 1967 and founder-director of the Group for New Music. In 1968 he was in Berlin under the auspices of the Deutscher Akademischer Austauschdienst. He was composer-in-residence at the Berkshire Music Center at Tanglewood (summer, 1969), Stanford Univ. (1969–70), and the Univ. of Utah in Salt Lake City (1970–72). From 1970 to 1979 he was prof. of composition and director of the New Music Group of the Philadelphia College of the Performing Arts; concurrently was conductor of the Philadelphia Musical Academy Sym. Orch. (1971–75). From 1979 he was prof. of composition at Boston Univ. Antoniou's early music is remarkably compendious in its integration of quaquaversal layers of sound; folk elements in Greek modalities are also in evidence, and many titles have Greek philosophic or literary connotations. His later style developed to embrace a modified serialism.

WORKS: DRAMATIC: *Noh-Musik*, music theater (1964); *Klytemnestra*, sound-action for Actresses, Ballet, Orch., and Tape (1967; Kassel, June 4, 1968); *Kassandra*, sound-action for Dancers, Actors, Chorus, Orch., Tape, Lights, and Projections (1969; Barcelona, Nov. 14, 1970); *Protest I* for Actors and Tape (1970) and *II* for Medium Voice, Actors, Tape, and Synthesizer (Athens, Sept. 26, 1971); *Chorochronos I* for Baritone, Narrator, Instruments, Film, Slides, and Lighting (Philadelphia, May 11, 1973); *Circle of Accusation*, ballet (1975); *Periander*, mixed-media opera (1977–79); *Bacchae*, ballet (1980); *The Magic World*, ballet (1984); incidental music to many plays; film scores. **ORCH.:** Concerto for Clarinet, Trumpet, Violin, and Orch. (1959); Overture (1961); Concertino for Piano, Strings, and Percussion (Athens, Dec. 16, 1962); *Antithesen* (1962; Hannover, Jan. 20, 1966); *Jeux* for Cello and Strings (1963; Hannover, Jan. 28, 1965; as a ballet, Munich, Sept. 20, 1974); *Mikrographien* (1964; Kassel, March 4, 1968); Violin Concerto (Athens, Aug. 16, 1965); *Kinesis ABCD* for 2 String Groups (Athens, July 13, 1966); *Op Ouverture* for Orch. and Tape (1966); *Events I* for Violin, Piano, and Orch. (1967–68; Hagen, June 10, 1968), *II* for Orch. and Tape (Tanglewood, July 30, 1969), and *III* for Orch. and Tape (Barcelona, Oct. 8, 1969); *Threnos* for Wind Orch., Piano, Percussion, and Double Bass (Tampa, Nov. 19, 1972); *Fluxus I* (1974–75; Basel, Dec. 17, 1979) and *II* for Piano and Chamber Orch. (1975; Philadelphia, April 4, 1976); Double Concerto for 2 Percussionists and Orch. (1977; Philadelphia, April 26, 1978); *The GBYSO Music* (1982); *Skolion* (1986); Concerto for Tambura and Chamber Orch. (1988); *Paean* (1989). **CHAMBER:** String Quartet (1960); Trio for Flute, Viola, and Cello (1961); Sonata for Solo Violin (1961); Concertino for Piano, 9 Winds, Percussion, and Tape (1963); *Quartetto giocoso* for Oboe, Violin, Cello, and Piano (1965); *Lyrics* for Violin and Piano (1967); *Katharsis* for Flute, Ensemble, Tape, and Lights (1968); *5 Likes* for Oboe (1969); *Cheironomiës* for Variable Instruments (1971); *Synthesis* for Oboe, Electric Organ, Percussion, Double Bass, and 4 Synthesizers (1971); *Paratasis I* for Percussion and Tape (1977) and *II* for Percussion, Ensemble, and Tape (1977); *DO Quintet* for 2 Trumpets, Horn, Trombone, and Tuba (1978); Octet (1986); *Ertnos* for Ensemble (1986–87); *Dexiotechnikā Idiómela* for Ensemble (1989); *Commos* for Cello and Piano (1989); piano pieces. **VOCAL:** *Melos* for Mezzo-soprano, Baritone, and Orch. (1962); *Epilogue* for Mezzo-soprano, Speaker, and Instruments (1963); *Kontakion* for Soloists, Chorus, and Strings (1965); *Climate of Absence* for Baritone and Chamber Orch. (1968); *Moirologhia for Jani Christou* for Baritone and Piano (1970; also for Baritone, Piano, and Other Instruments); *Nenikikamen* (We Are Victorious) for Speaker, Mezzo-soprano, Baritone, Chorus, and Orch. (1971); *Chorochronos II* for Baritone, Speaker, and Chamber Orch. (1973) and *III* for Bass, Piano, Percussion, and Tape (1974–75); *Die weisse Rose* for Speaker, Baritone, Choruses, and Orch. (1974–75); *Circle of Thanatos and Genesis* for Tenor, Speaker, Chorus, and Orch. (1977–78); *Die Revolution der Toten: Antiliturgy* for Soloists, Chorus, and Orch. (1981); *Epigrams* for Soprano and Chamber Orch. (1981); *Prometheus* for Baritone, Speaker, Chorus, and Orch. (1983); *Oneiro Mega* for Soprano, Tenor, Speaker, and Chamber Orch. (1984); *Crete: The Great Dream* for Speaker, Soprano, Tenor, and Chamber Ensemble (1984); *For Ernst* for Soprano and Chamber Ensemble (1985); *Oraseis Opsonde* for Speaker, Chorus, and Orch. (1988).

Antunes, Jorge, Brazilian composer and teacher; b. Rio de Janeiro, April 23, 1942. He enrolled at the National School of Music at the Univ. of Brazil in Rio de Janeiro in 1960 to study violin; then pursued training in composition and conducting there (from 1964) with Henrique Morelembaum, José Siqueira, and Eleazar de Carvalho; also took courses in physics at the Univ. and studied composition with Guerra Peixe at Rio de Janeiro's Pró-Arte. In 1969–70 he held a postgraduate scholarship at the Torcuato Di Tella Inst. in Buenos Aires and studied with Ginastera, Luis de Pablo, Eric Salzman, Francisco Kröpfl, and Gerardo Gandini. Following research under König and Greta Vermeulen at the Inst. of Sonology at the Univ. of Utrecht (1970), he went to Paris to work with the Groupe de Recherches Musicales de l'ORTF (1971–73) and to study with

Daniel Charles at the Sorbonne (Ph.D. in music aesthetics, 1977, with the diss. *Son Nouveau, Nouvelle Notation*). Antunes's avant-garde convictions prompted him to pursue experimental byways while he was still a student at the Univ. of Brazil when he founded the Chromo-Music Research Studio. In 1967 he organized the music research center and became a prof. of electro-acoustic music at the Villa-Lobos Inst. in Rio de Janeiro. In 1973 he became a teacher of composition at the Univ. of Brasilia, where he later served as prof. of composition and acoustics. He also oversaw its electronic music studio and founded the experimental music group GeMUnB. In 1972 he won Rio de Janeiro's National Composition Competition, and in 1983 its Funarte Prize. In 1991 he was awarded the Vitae Prize of São Paulo.

WORKS: DRAMATIC: *Vivaldia MCMLXXV*, chamber opera buffa (1975); *Qorpo Santo*, opera (1983); *Olga*, opera (1987–93); *The Single-tone King*, children's mini chamber opera (1991). **ORCH.:** *Seresta pra Juvenil* for Strings (1966); *Acusmorfose* (1968); *Tartinia MCMLXX* for Violin and Orch. (1970); *Isomerism* for Chamber Orch. (1970); *Poetica* (1971); *Idiosynchronie* for Chamber Orch. and Electronics (1972); *Scryabinia MCMLXXII* for Piano, Lights, and Chamber Orch. (1972); *Concerto para um Mês de Sol* for Amplified Cello and Orch. (1974); *Concerto para um Mês de Neblina* for Violin and Orch. (1992–93). **CHAMBER:** *Insubstituivel Segunda* for Cello and Tape (1967); *Invocation en Defense de la Machine* for 4 Percussionists and Tape (1968); *Tres Comportamentos* for Violin, Cello, and Piano (1969); *Bartókollagia MCMLXX* for String Quartet (1970); *Tartinia MCMLXX* for Violin and Piano (1970); *Music for 8 Persons Playing Things* (1970–71); *Colludwiguia MXMLXXI* for String Quartet (1971); *Flautatualf* for Flute (1972); *Intervertige* for String Quartet, Wind Quintet, 2 Percussionists, and Electronics (1974); *Vortices* for Wind Quintet (1975); *Tres Impressões Cancioneirigenas* for Flute, Viola, and Cello (1976); *Sighs* for Guitar (1976): *Canto Esthereofonico* for 7 Instruments and Tape (1978); *Microformobiles III: Re-tornos* for Violin and Piano (1982); *Dramatic Polimaniquexixe* for Clarinet, Cello, and Piano (1984); *Modinha pour Mindinha* for 7 Violas (1985); *Serie Enfants* for Violin and Tape (1987); *Lecture* for Bass Clarinet (1990); *Amerika 500* for Flute, Bass Clarinet, Percussion, Piano, Viola, and Cello (1992). **VOCAL:** *Missa Populorum Progressio* for Chorus and Tape (1967); *Acusmorfose 1970* for 2 Narrators, 2 Choruses, and 2 Orchs. (1969); *Concertatio I* for Vocal Trio, Orch., and Tape (1969); *Proudhonia* for Chorus and Tape (1972); *Catastrophe Ultra-violette* for Chorus, Orch., and Tapes (1974); *Elegie Violette pour Monseigneur Romero* for 2 Child Soloists, Children's Chorus, Piano, and Chamber Orch. (1980); *Arbres de Lasar* for Chorus (1988); *Quatre Petites Pièces de Peuple* for Chorus (1991). **OTHER:** *Microformobiles II* for Flute, Clarinet, Viola, Cello, Percussion, Baritone, and the Public (1972); *Source* for Mezzo-soprano, Flute, Viola, Cello, Piano, Synthesizer, and Tape (1974); *Coreto* for Flute, Clarinet, Horn, Viola, Cello, Piano, and 3 Amateur Actors (1975); *Source vers SP* for Dancer, Synthesizer, Flute, Oboe, Mezzo-soprano, Piano, Horn, Viola, Cello, Tape, Amplification, and Lights (1975); *Sinfonia das Diretas* for Orch., Declamation, Choruses, and Tape (1984).

Anzaghi, Davide, Italian composer; b. Milan, Nov. 29, 1936. He studied piano, conducting, and composition (with Maggioni) at the Milan Cons., graduating in 1957; then took courses in composition with Ghedini and Donatoni in Venice. He subsequently taught at the Milan Cons.

WORKS: ORCH.: *Riturgia* (Venice, Sept. 15, 1972); *Limbale* (Bologna, Nov. 10, 1973); *Ausa* (1973; La Rochelle, France, July 5, 1974); *Egophonie* (1974; Milan, Feb. 3, 1975); *Aur'ore* for Chorus and Orch. (1975–76; Milan, Feb. 4, 1977); *Ermosonio* (1978; Milan, Nov. 30, 1979); *Anco* (1984; Milan, March 30, 1985); 3 piano concertos: No. 1 (1987–88; Milan, March 30, 1989), No. 2 (1990–91), and No. 3 (1993); *Concerto breve* for Clarinet and Orch. (1990–91); Violin Concerto (1992). **CHAMBER:** *Limine* for String Trio (1971); *Aulografia* for Flute (1975); *In-Chiostro* for 2 Violins and Viola (1975; rev. 1982); *Alena* for 10 Wind Instruments (1976); *Remota* for 7 Players (1977); *Alia* for Bass Clarinet and Piano (1980); *Oiseau triste* for Piccolo and Piano (1980); *Soavodia* for Clarinet and Piano (1980); *Làbia* for String Quartet (1982); *Ricrío*, brass octet (1982); *Soliludio* for Flute, Clarinet, Violin, Cello, and Piano (1982); *Mitofania* for Flute, Clarinet, Violin, Cello, Piano, and Percussion (1983); *For Four* for String Quartet (1983); *Elan* for 9 Instruments (1984); *Pri-ter* for String Quartet (1985); *Apogèo* for 5 Instruments (1987); *Tremes* for Viola (1988); *Viol-Once-All* for Cello (1988); *Settimino* for Clarinet, Horn, Bassoon, Piano, Violin, Viola, and Cello (1992). **PIANO:** *Segni* (1968); *Ritografia* (1971); *Revenants*, 8 prelude-variations (1981).

Apel, Willi, eminent German-American musicologist; b. Konitz, Oct. 10, 1893; d. Bloomington, Ind., March 14, 1988. He studied mathematics at the univs. of Bonn and Munich (1912–14), and then of Berlin (1918–21), where he returned in 1936 to take his Ph.D. with the diss. *Accidentien und Tonalität in den Musikdenkmälern des 15. und 16. Jahrhunderts* (publ. in Berlin, 1936; 2nd ed., aug., 1972). After emigrating to the U.S., he taught at Harvard Univ. (1938–42); from 1950 to 1964 he was a prof. of music at Indiana Univ. in Bloomington, where he continued to lecture as prof. emeritus until 1970. In 1971 he was made an honorary member of the American Musicological Soc. He was founding ed. of the Corpus of Early Keyboard Music and contributed 10 vols. to the series. Apel was an authority on 14th-century music, the history of instrumental music, and Latin chant. He acknowledged his lack of interest in either opera or modern developments in music; he was a musical purist who regarded the developments of musical composition after the era of Bach as of passing significance to music history.

WRITINGS: *Die Fuge* (Berlin, 1932); ed. *Musik aus früher Zeit für Klavier* (2 vols., Mainz, 1934); *The Notation of Polyphonic Music, 900–1600* (Cambridge, Mass., 1942; 5th ed., rev., 1961; Ger. tr., rev., 1970); ed. *The Harvard Dictionary of Music* (Cambridge, Mass, 1944; 2nd ed., rev. and enl., 1969); ed. with A. Davison, *Historical Anthology of Music* (Cambridge, Mass.; Vol. I, 1946; 2nd ed., rev., 1950; Vol. II, 1950); *Masters of the Keyboard* (Cambridge, Mass., 1947); *Gregorian Chant* (Bloomington, Ind., 1958); *Geschichte der Orgel- und Klaviermusik bis 1700* (Kassel, 1967; Eng. tr., rev., 1972); *Die italienische Violinmusik im 17. Jahrhundert* (Wiesbaden, 1983; Eng. tr., 1990); *Medieval Music: Collected Articles and Reviews* (Stuttgart, 1986); with R. Schechner, *By Means of Performance: Intercultural Studies of Theatre and Ritual* (Cambridge, 1990).

BIBL.: H. Tischler, ed., *Essays in Musicology: A Birthday Offering for W. A.* (Bloomington, Ind., 1968).

Aperghis, Georges, innovative Greek composer; b. Athens, Dec. 23, 1945. After studies with Yannis Papaioannou in Athens, he settled in Paris in 1963 and completed his training with Xenakis, who initiated him into the mysteries of ultramodern techniques involving such arcana as musical indeterminacy and audiovisual coordinates in spatial projection. He was founder-director of the Atelier Théâter et Musique (1976–91), an experimental workshop for theater, music, and language. From 1992 he pursued his career in Nanterre. Aperghis has followed an avant-garde path as a composer, and has produced numerous theater pieces.

WORKS: DRAMATIC: OPERAS: *Pandaemonium* (1973); *Jacques le Fataliste* (1974); *Histoires de loup* (1976); *Je vous dis que je suis mort* (1978); *Liebestod* (1981); *L'écharpe rouge* (1984); numerous music theater pieces. **ORCH.:** *Contrepoint* (1967); *Libretto* (1968); *Symplexis* for 22 Jazz Soloists and Orch. (1970); *Die Wände haben Ohren* (1972); Overture (1973); *Declamations* (1990). **CHAMBER:** *Antistixis A* for 3 String Quartets (1964–65); *Contrepoint* for 3 String Quartets, Piano, Trombone, and Percussion (1968); Quartet for 4 Double Basses (1970); Quartet for 4 Percussionists (1970); *Parenthèses* for Chamber Ensemble (1977); *Ilios* for 10 Instruments (1978); *Triangle carré* for String Quartet and Percussion Trio (1989). **VOCAL:** *Vesper*, oratorio

(1970); *Les lauriers sont coupés* for Voice and Chamber Ensemble (1975); *Un musée de l'homme*, oratorio (1980); *Tingel-Tangel* for Voice, Accordion, and Percussion (1990); *Ritournelles* for 2 Baritones and 9 Instruments (1992).

ApIvor, Denis, Irish-born English composer of Welsh descent; b. Collinstown, April 14, 1916. He studied at the Univ. of Wales (1933–34) and Univ. College, London (1934–39), and received training in composition from Patrick Hadley and Rawsthorne in London (1937–39). He contributed articles to several books and music journals; ed. works by and wrote articles on Bernard van Dieren; also was active as a translator. In his compositions, ApIvor adopted a fairly advanced technique of composition while adhering to tradition in formal design.

WORKS: DRAMATIC: OPERAS: *She Stoops to Conquer*, after Goldsmith (1943–47; rev. 1976–77); *Yerma*, after García Lorca (1955–58); *Ubu roi*, after Jarry (1965–66); *Bouvard and Pecuchet*, after Flaubert (1970). **BALLETS:** *The Goodman of Paris* (1951); *A Mirror for Witches* (1951); *Blood Wedding* (1953); *Saudades* (1954); *Corporal Jan* (1967); *Glide the Dark Door Wide* (1977). **ORCH.:** Piano Concerto (1948); Concerto for Violin and 15 Instruments (1950); 5 syms. (1952; 1963; 1978–79; 1985; 1991); Guitar Concertino (1953); *Overtones*, after Paul Klee's paintings (1961–62); *String Abstract*, later renamed Triple Concerto for String Trio and String Orch. (1967); *Tarot* for Chamber Orch. (1968); *Neumes* (1969); *The Tremulous Silence* for Guitar and Chamber Orch. (1972); Violin Concerto (1975); Cello Concerto (1976–77); *Fantasy Concertante* for Horn and Orch. (1980). **CHAMBER:** Violin Sonata (1944–45); *Concertante* for Clarinet, Piano, and Percussion (1944–45); Wind Quintet (1960); 3 string quartets (1964; 1976; 1989–90); *Crystals* for Percussion, Hammond Organ, Guitar, and Double Bass (1964–65); *Exotics Theater* for Chamber Ensemble (1972); *Psycho-pieces* for Clarinet and Piano (1973); *Studies for Wind*, 1 each for Flute, Oboe, Clarinet, Bassoon, Horn, Trumpet, and Trombone (1974); Clarinet Quintet (1975); *Duo Concertante* for Horn and Piano (1981); *Vista* for Double Wind Quintet (1983); *Cinquefoil*, trio for Violin, Flute, and Guitar (1984); *Pieces of 5* for Saxophone (1992); Saxophone Sonatina (1992); Violin Sonatina (1992); *In the Landscape of Spring*, septet (1993). **VOCAL:** *The Hollow Men*, canata after T.S. Eliot (1939; BBC, London, Feb. 21, 1950); Cantata, after Dylan Thomas (1960); *Resonance of the Southern Flora* for Wordless Chorus and Orch. (1972); *Fern Hill* for Tenor and 11 Instruments, after Dylan Thomas (1973); *Bats* for Tenor, Piccolo, Violin, and Percussion (1979); *7 Songs* for Chorus and Small Orch. (1983); *Love's Season* for Voice and String Quintet or Piano (1983); *Majestatas dei Ultra Stellas* for Chorus and Small Orch. or Piano (1986); *T.S. Eliot Songs* for Voice and Piano (1994); other songs. **OTHER:** Piano pieces, organ music, and arrangements of works by other composers.

Aponte-Ledée, Rafael, Puerto Rican composer and teacher; b. Guayama, Oct. 15, 1938. He studied composition at the Madrid Cons. (1957–63), where he completed his training with Cristóbal Halffter (1963–64); then took courses with Ginastera at the Latin American Center of Advanced Musical Studies at the Di Tella Inst. in Buenos Aires (1965–66). Returning to Puerto Rico, he founded in San Juan, with the collaboration of Francis Schwartz, the Fluxus group for the promotion of new music (1967); taught composition and theory at the Univ. of Puerto Rico (1968–74) and at the Puerto Rico Cons. (from 1968). His music is highly advanced, employing nearly every conceivable technique of the cosmopolitan avant-garde.

WORKS: *Tema y 6 Diferencias* for Piano (1963; rev. 1986); *Dialogantes 1* for Flute and Violin (1965) and *2* for 3 Flutes, 3 Trombones, and 3 Clarinets (1968); *Elejía* for 13 Strings (1965; also for 50 Strings, 1967); *Presagio de Pájaros muertos* for Narrator and Tape (1966); *Impulsos: In memoriam Julia de Burgos* for Orch. (1967); *Epíthasis* for 3 Oboes, 2 Trombones, Double Bass, and 3 Percussionists (1967); *La ventana abierta* for 3 Mezzo-sopranos, 3 Flutes, Clarinet, Trumpet, 2 Percussionists, Celesta, Piano, Violin, Cello, and Double Bass (1968; also for 3 Mezzo-sopranos, Flutes, Clarinet, 2 Trumpets, Horn, 2 Percussionists, Guitar, Piano, and 2 String Quartets, 1969); *Streptomicyne* for Soprano, Flute, Clarinet, Trumpet, and Piano (1970); *SSSSSS²* for Double Bass, 3 Flutes, Trumpet, and Percussion (1971); *Volúmenes* for Piano (1971); *Elvira en sombras* for Piano and Orch. (1973); *Estravagario, In memoriam Salvador Allende* for Orch. and Tape (1973); *Cuídese de los angeles que caen*, musique concrète (1974); *Los huevos de Pandora* for Clarinet and Tape (1974); *El palacio en sombras* for Orch. without Violins and Cellos (1977); *Estas sombras* for Prepared Piano (1978); *A flor de piel* for 2 Sopranos and Orch. (1980); *Asiento en el Paraíso* for Clarinet, Violin, Cello, and Piano (1984); *Dos cuentos* for Orch. (1986); Cantata for Soli and Orch. (1986); *3 Bagatelles* for Guitar (1987); *Azaleas* for Clarinet (1988); *La muchacha de la bragas de oro* for Orch. (1989); *Canción de albada y Epitafio* for Orch. (1991).

Apostel, Hans Erich (Heinrich), German-born Austrian composer and teacher; b. Karlsruhe, Jan. 22, 1901; d. Vienna, Nov. 30, 1972. He studied in Karlsruhe before settling in Vienna in 1921, where he completed his training with Schoenberg and Alban Berg. He was an ed. at Universal Edition and in that capacity prepared for publication the posthumous works of Berg. He was also active as a teacher. Among his honors were the grand prizes of Vienna (1948) and the Republic of Austria (1957). His works were written in an atonal expressionist style until 1957 when he embraced strict serialism. He also experimented in Klangfarben effects, and applied audible overtones in his piano pieces by holding down the keys without actually striking them.

WORKS: ORCH.: *Adagio* for Strings, 2 Harps, Celesta, and Piano (1937); *Variationen über ein Thema von Joseph Haydn* (1949; Zurich, May 10, 1951); *Ballade* (1955); *Variations on 3 Folk Songs* for Small Orch. (1956); *Rondo ritmico* (1957); Piano Concerto (1958; Venice, Sept. 24, 1959); *5 Austrian Miniatures* (1959); Kammersymphonie (1965–67; Vienna, June 4, 1968); *Epitaph* for Strings (1969); *Haydn-Variationen, Teil II: Paralipomena dodekaphonica* (1969–70; Donawitz, Oct. 29, 1970); *Passacaglia* (2nd mvt. of an unfinished *Concerto for Orchestra*, 1972; London, July 10, 1974). **CHAMBER:** 2 string quartets (1935, 1956); Quartet for Flute, Clarinet, Horn, and Bassoon (1947–49); sonatinas for Solo Flute (1951), Clarinet (1951), Bassoon (1951), Oboe (1964), and Horn (1964); *5 Bagatelles* for Flute, Clarinet, and Bassoon (1952); *Intrada* for Brass and Percussion (1954); *Studie* for Flute, Violin, and Guitar (1958; rev. 1964); *6 épigrammes* for String Quartet (1962); Cello Sonata (1962); *Kleine Kammerkonzert* for Flute, Viola, and Guitar (1964); *Fischerhaus-Serenade* for 4 Winds, 3 Brasses, and String Quartet (1971); *12 Stücke für 12 Musici* for 4 Winds, 3 Brasses, and 5 Strings (1972). **PIANO:** Sonata (1929); *Sonatina ritmica* (1934); *Kubiniana*, 10 pieces (1945–50); *Suite concise*, 7 pieces (1955); *Fantasie* (1959). **VOCAL:** *Requiem* for Chorus and Orch., after Rilke (1933; Vienna Radio, May 3, 1958); *5 Lieder* for Low Voice and Orch., after Hölderlin (1939–40); *3 Lieder* for Low Woman's Voice, 4 Violins, 2 Cellos, and Double Bass, after Trakl, (1951); *5 Lieder* for Medium Voice, Flute, Clarinet, and Bassoon (1953); *Ode* for Alto and Chorus (1962).

Appeldoorn, Dina, Dutch composer; b. Rotterdam, Feb. 26, 1884; d. The Hague, Dec. 4, 1938. She was the composer of several works in the Romantic style, including 2 symphonic poems, *Noordzee* and *Volkfeest*; also wrote chamber music and songs.

Appia, Edmond, Italian-Swiss violinist and conductor; b. Turin, May 7, 1894; d. Geneva, Feb. 12, 1961. He studied violin with Marteau at the Geneva Cons., in Paris with Capet, and at the Brussels Cons., obtaining the premier prix in 1920; toured Europe (1920–35); taught violin in Geneva and Lausanne. In 1935 he became a conductor of Radiodiffusion Suisse in Lausanne; in 1938 he was appointed conductor of the Geneva Radio Orch.

Applebaum, Edward, American composer; b. Los Angeles, Sept. 28, 1937. He had piano lessons in his youth; later studied composition with Henri Lazarof and Lukas Foss at the Univ. of Calif. at Los Angeles (Ph.D., 1966). In 1969 he was composer-in-residence of the Oakland Sym. Orch.; in 1971, became a prof. of theory and composition at the Univ. of Calif. at Santa Barbara. From 1985 to 1987 he was composer-in-residence of the Santa Barbara Sym. Orch., and then of the Music Academy of the West in Santa Barbara (1988). In 1989 he became prof. of composition and director of the new-music ensemble at Florida State Univ. in Tallahassee. He served as dean (1991–92) and as prof. of music (1991–94) at Edith Cowan Univ. in Perth, Australia.

WORKS: Piano Sonata (1965); String Trio (1966); Concerto for Viola and Chamber Orch. (1967); *Montages* for Clarinet, Cello, and Piano (1968); *Shantih* for Cello and Piano (1969); 4 syms.: No. 1 (1970), No. 2 (St. Louis, Oct. 6, 1983), No. 3 (1989), and No. 4 (1995); *Foci* for Viola and Piano (1971); *The Face in the Cameo* for Clarinet and Piano (1973); *The Frieze of Life*, chamber opera (1974); *To Remember*, trio for Clarinet, Cello, and Piano (1976); *The Garden* for Soprano, Chamber Ensemble, and Tape (1979); *Prelude* for String Quartet (1984); *And with, and to* for Men's Chorus (1984); *The Princess in the Garden* for String Orch. (1985); *Dreams and Voyage*, piano concerto (1986); *Night Waltz*, guitar concerto (1987); *The Waltz in 2* for Narrator and Orch. (1988); *Whispers of Yesterday* for Woodwind Quintet (1988); *Song of the Sparrows*, oratorio for Soloists, Narrator, Choruses, and Orch. (1988).

Applebaum, Louis, Canadian composer, administrator, and conductor; b. Toronto, April 3, 1918. He studied in Toronto at the Cons. of Music and at the Univ., his principal mentors being Boris Berlin in piano and Healey Willan, Leo Smith, and Sir Ernest MacMillan in theory; he then pursued training in composition in N.Y. as a scholarship student of Roy Harris and Bernard Wagenaar (1940–41). Returning to Canada, he served as music director of the National Film Board (1942–48), for which he composed scores for some 250 films (1942–60). He also served as music director of World Today films in N.Y. (1946–49). From 1955 to 1960 he oversaw the musical activities at the Stratford (Ontario) Festival, for which he composed much incidental music. He served as president of Group Four productions, makers of television documentaries and programs, from 1960 to 1966. From 1971 to 1980 he was executive director of the Ontario Arts Council. From 1980 to 1982 he was chairman of the Federal Cultural Policy Review Committee. He was interim artistic director of the Guelph Spring Festival in 1988–89, and also president of the Composers, Authors, and Publishers Assn. of Canada from 1988 to 1990, and its successor, the Soc. of Composers, Authors, and Music Publishers of Canada, from 1990 to 1992. In 1977 he was made an Officer of the Order of Canada. Applebaum's long association with films and stage productions resulted in a particularly assured command in the composing of dramatic scores.

WORKS: DRAMATIC: *Suite of Miniature Dances*, ballet (1953); *Legend of the North*, ballet (1957); *Ride a Pink Horse*, musical comedy (1959); *Homage*, ballet (1969); *The Legend of Sleepy Hollow*, ballet (1991); *So You Think You're Mozart?*, musical play (1991); incidental music for over 50 plays; film scores; innumerable scores for radio and television. **ORCH.:** *East by North* (1947); *Revival Meeting and Finale* from *Barbara Allen* (1964); *Dialogue with Footnotes* for Big Jazz Band and Orch. (1984); *Celebration York* for Band (1985); *High Spirits* for Band (1986). **CHAMBER:** *Touch Wood* for Piano (1969); *Essay* for Flute (1973); *Keep Moving* for Piano (1973); *4 Dances in a Nineteenth Century Style* for Brass Quintet (1987). **VOCAL:** *Cry of the Prophet* for Baritone and Piano (1951; rev. 1952); *A Folio of Shakespearean Songs* for Medium Voice and Piano (1954–87); *Inunit*, 5 episodes for Voice and Orch. (1977); *Of Love and High Times* for Soprano, Chorus, Flute, Horn, and Percussion (1981); *The Harper of the Stones* for Narrator and Chamber Ensemble (1987). **OTHER:** Many fanfares and ceremonial pieces.

Appledorn, Mary Jeanne van. See **van Appledorn, Mary Jeanne.**

Appleton, Jon (Howard), American composer and teacher; b. Los Angeles, Jan. 4, 1939. He studied at Reed College (B.A., 1961), with Imbrie in Berkeley, California (1961–62), with Homer Keller at the Univ. of Oregon (M.A., 1965), with William Mitchell at Columbia Univ., and with Ussachevsky and Davidovsky at the Columbia-Princeton Electronic Music Center (1965–66); held Guggenheim and Fulbright fellowships (1970). He taught at Oakland Univ. in Rochester, Mich. (1966–67) and at Dartmouth College (from 1967), where he founded the Bregman Electronic Music Center; also helped to develop the Dartmouth Digital Synthesizer and the Synclavier, a polyphonic digital synthesizer. In 1992 he was composer-in-residence of the Montalvo Foundation in Saratoga, California, and in 1993 resident composer of the Rockefeller Foundation Study and Conference Center in Bellagio, Italy. He wrote many articles on electronic music; with R. Perera, ed. *The Development and Practice of Electronic Music* (1975). He also publ. *Twenty-First Century Musical Instruments: Hardware and Software* (Brooklyn, 1989).

WORKS: ORCH.: *After "Nude Descending a Staircase"* (1965). **CHAMBER:** *2 Movements* for Woodwind Quintet (1963); *6 Movements* for Woodwind Quintet (1964); *4 Explorations* for Violin and Piano (1964); *4 Inventions* for 2 Flutes (1965); *Winesburg, Ohio* for Flute, Clarinet, Violin, Cello, and Piano (1972); String Quartet (1976). **VOCAL:** *This Is America* for Chorus (1976); *Sonaria* for 4 Voices and Live Electronics (1978); *The Lament of Kamuela* for 4 Voices, Live Electronics, Rock Band, String Quartet, Shamisen, Slides, Film, and Video (1983); *Le Dernier Voyage* for Narrator, Children's Chorus, and Synclavier (1988); *Tres Canciones Cubanas* for Voice and Piano (1991); *Canciones Latinas* for Voice and Piano (1992); *Our Voyage to America* for Chorus (1992); *HOPI: La Naissance du désert* for Children's Chorus and Orch. (1993). **OTHER:** Many electronic and electro-acoustic pieces, including *Chef d'oeuvre* (1967); *Times Square Times 10* (1969); *Stereopticon* (1972); *Zoetrope* (1974); *In deserto* (1977); *Nukuoro* (1979); *Sashasonjon* (1981); *Oskuldens Dröm* (1983); *Brush Canyon* (1986); *Homenaje à Milanés* (1987); *Sudden Death* (1989); *Dima Dobralsa Domoy* (1993); *Duobatoni* (1994).

Aragall (y Garriga), Giacomo (actually, **Jaime**), Spanish tenor; b. Barcelona, June 6, 1939. He was a pupil of Francesco Puig in Barcelona and of Vladimiro Badiali in Milan. In 1963 he won the Verdi Competition in Busseto, sang Gastone in *Jérusalem* in Venice, and appeared as Mascagni's Fritz at Milan's La Scala. In 1966 he made his London debut at Covent Garden as the Duke of Mantua and his Vienna State Opera debut as Rodolfo. On Sept. 19, 1968, he made his Metropolitan Opera debut in N.Y. as the Duke of Mantua. He also sang in Rome, Berlin, Hamburg, Chicago, San Francisco, and other opera centers. In 1992 he sang in the gala ceremonies for the Olympic Games in Barcelona. Among his other roles were Edgardo, Alfredo, and Cavardossi.

Araiza, (José) Francisco, Mexican tenor; b. Mexico City, Oct. 4, 1950. He was a student of Irma Gonzales at the Univ. of Mexico City, where he sang in its choir. He made his concert debut in Mexico City in 1969, where he subsequently appeared for the first time in opera in 1970 as Jaquino. Following additional training with Richard Holm and Erik Werba in Munich, he was a member of the Karlsruhe (1974–77) and Zürich (from 1977) operas. He appeared as a guest artist in Munich, Paris, Vienna, Salzburg, Bayreuth, San Francisco, Chicago, and other opera centers. On March 12, 1984, he made his Metropolitan Opera debut in N.Y. as Belmonte. He scored remarkable success as Lohengrin in Venice in 1990 and as Walther von Stolzing at the Metropolitan Opera in 1993. He also had fine success as a concert and lieder artist. Among his other distinguished operatic roles were Tamino, Ferrando, Gounod's Faust, Massenet's Des Grieux, Alfredo, and Rodolfo.

Arakishvili, Dmitri, Russian conductor, teacher, and composer; b. Vladikavkaz, Feb. 23, 1873; d. Tbilisi, Aug. 13, 1953. He studied composition at the Moscow Phil. Inst. with Ilyinsky and also took private lessons with Gretchaninov. At the same time, he studied archaeology and ethnic sciences. In 1901 he became a member of the Musical Ethnographic Commission at the Univ. of Moscow. In 1906 he took part in the organization of the Moscow People's Cons., which offered free music lessons to impecunious students. He was ed. of the Moscow publication *Music and Life* (1908–12). In 1918 he moved to Tiflis, where he was active as a teacher and conductor. He composed one of the earliest national Georgian operas, *The Legend of Shota Rustaveli* (Tiflis, Feb. 5, 1919); a comic opera, *Dinara* (1926); 3 syms. (1934, 1942, 1951); *Hymn of the New East* for Orch. (1933); and film music. However, his best compositions are some 80 art songs composed in a lyrico-dramatic manner reflecting Georgian modalities.

Arangi-Lombardi, Giannina, Italian soprano; b. Marigliano, near Naples, June 20, 1891; d. Milan, July 9, 1951. She studied with Beniamino Carelli at the Cons. di S. Pietro a Majella in Naples. She made her operatic debut as a mezzo-soprano in 1920 at the Teatro Costanzi in Rome as Lola in *Cavalleria rusticana*. After further training from Adelina Sthele in Milan, she sang soprano roles from 1923; appeared at La Scala in Milan (1924–30). In 1928 she accompanied Melba on an Australian tour; also sang in South America. After retiring from the stage, she taught voice at the Milan Cons. (1937–47) and, later, in Ankara. She was at her best in the lyrico-dramatic roles of the Italian repertoire.

d'Arányi, Jelly (in full, **Jelly Eva Arányi de Hunyadvar**), Hungarian-English violinist, grandniece of Joseph Joachim and sister of **Adila Fachiri**; b. Budapest, May 30, 1893; d. Florence, March 30, 1966. She studied violin with Hubay in Budapest and Grunfeld in Vienna. After giving concerts in Europe, she settled in England in 1913. She made her U.S. debut in a solo recital in N.Y. on Nov. 26, 1927; made her 2nd American tour in 1932. She frequently appeared in joint recitals with Myra Hess. A pioneer in modern music, she gave first performances of many new works. Bartók's 1st Violin Sonata, Ravel's *Tzigane*, and Vaughan Williams's *Concerto accademico* for Violin and Orch. are dedicated to her. She attracted considerable attention in 1937 when she proclaimed that Schumann's spirit appeared to her during a seance and revealed the secret of his unpubl. Violin Concerto; but Schumann's ghost spoke ungrammatical German, which aroused suspicion concerning the authenticity of the phenomenon; besides, it had long been known that the MS of the concerto was preserved at the Berlin State Library; the first performance of the piece was eventually given in Germany by another violinist. D'Arányi was given a chance, however, to perform it with the BBC Sym. Orch. in London on Feb. 16, 1938.

BIBL.: J. Macleod, *The Sisters d'A.* (London, 1969).

Arapov, Boris (Alexandrovich), eminent Russian composer and pedagogue; b. St. Petersburg, Sept. 12, 1905; d. there, Jan. 27, 1992. He was a scion of an intellectual family; his grandfather was a lawyer; his father was a naturalist. He spent his childhood in Poltava, where he received his early musical training; in 1921 the family returned to St. Petersburg (now renamed Petrograd); he studied composition with Shcherbachev at the Cons. there, graduating in 1930; was then appointed to its faculty as an instructor (1930) and later prof. (1940). Among his pupils were many Soviet composers of stature, including Dmitri Tolstoy, Falik, Uspensky, Banshchikov, Knaifel, and Sergei Slonimsky. The years 1941–44 Arapov spent in Tashkent, in Uzbekistan, where the entire faculty of the Leningrad Cons. was evacuated during the siege of Leningrad. There he studied indigenous folklore, and wrote an Uzbeki opera, *Khodja Nasreddin*. After the siege was lifted, Arapov returned to Leningrad, resumed his pedagogical duties, and continued to compose. In 1955–56 he was in China, where he wrote several works on Chinese themes. In 1959 he visited Korea, and composed a sym. using the pentatonic Korean modes. During the years 1950–73, he also traveled in Europe. Arapov's compositions represent to perfection the evolutionary character of Soviet music, taking their source in the Russian traditions of the previous centuries, making ample use of ethnic materials of the constituent regions of the immense territory of the U.S.S.R., and integrating the native homophonic melorhythms in an increasingly complex tapestry of colorful fabrics, richly ornamented with occasional application of such modern devices as dodecaphonic melodic structures. However, Arapov was also able to produce a virtuoso display of instrumental techniques for piano and other instruments.

WORKS: DRAMATIC: OPERAS: *Khodja Nasreddin*, on Uzbeki motifs (Tashkent, April 1944); *Frigate Victory*, after Pushkin's novella *The Moor of Peter the Great* (radio premiere, Leningrad, Oct. 12, 1959); *Rain*, after Somerset Maugham (concert perf., Leningrad, April 25, 1968). **BALLET:** *The Picture of Dorian Gray* (1971; concert perf., Leningrad, April 20, 1973). Also film scores. **ORCH.:** *Fugato* (Leningrad, Feb. 2, 1928); *Tadzhikistan Suite* (1938; Leningrad, Feb. 13, 1939); 6 syms.: No. 1 (1947), No. 2 (1959; Leningrad, Oct. 2, 1960), No. 3 (1962; Leningrad, March 20, 1963), No. 4 for Narrator, 2 Soloists, 2 Mixed Choruses, and Orch. (1975; Leningrad, June 29, 1977), No. 5 (1981; Leningrad, Nov. 1, 1982), and No. 6 for Soloists, Chorus, and Orch. (1983; Leningrad, Sept. 14, 1985); *Russian Suite* (Leningrad, March 11, 1950); Violin Concerto (1964; Leningrad, April 18, 1965); *Concerto for Orchestra* (Leningrad, April 1969); Concerto for Violin, Piano, Percussion, and Chamber Orch., in memory of Stravinsky (1973; Copenhagen, Feb. 21, 1974); *4 Preludes and Fugues by J.S. Bach* for Chamber Orch. (1986); symphonic poem (1987). **CHAMBER:** Sonata for Solo Violin (1930); *3 Pieces on Mongolian Themes* for Clarinet, Violin, and Piano (1943); Violin Sonata (1978); Quintet for Oboe, Horn, Harp, Viola, and Cello (1979); Horn Sonata (1981); Cello Sonata (1985); *Decimet* for 10 Instruments (1986). **PIANO:** *Variations* (1929); *Humoresque* (1938); 6 Pieces on Chinese themes (1955); *Étude-Scherzo* (1969); 4 sonatas (1970, 1976, 1988, 1990); 3 Pieces (1976). **VOCAL:** Vocal symphonic cycle for Tenor, Baritone, and Orch. (1937; Leningrad, Dec. 27, 1940); *Dzhelal Eddin*, oratorio (Tashkent, Dec. 26, 1944); *Songs of Protest*, suite for Bass and Jazz Orch. (radio premiere, Feb. 12, 1940); *4 Songs* to texts by Alexander Blok (1948); *Monologue* for Baritone, Trumpet, Percussion, and Piano (1969); *Sonnets of Petrarca*, song cycle for Mezzo-soprano and Piano (1975); *4 Seasons of a Year* for Soprano, Tenor, and Instruments (1977); *2 Monologues* for Voice and Piano, after Boris Pasternak (1979); Vocal Cycle for Mezzo-soprano and Instruments, after Russian poets (1988).

BIBL.: A. Kenigsberg, *B.A. A.* (Moscow and Leningrad, 1965); L. Danke, *B. A.* (Leningrad, 1980).

Arbós, Enrique Fernández, notable Spanish violinist, conductor, pedagogue, and composer; b. Madrid, Dec. 24, 1863; d. San Sebastián, June 2, 1939. He received training in violin from Monasterio in Madrid, Vieuxtemps in Brussels, and Joachim in Berlin. In 1886–87 he was concertmaster of the Berlin Phil. He also made successful concert tours of Europe. Returning to Madrid in 1888, he taught at the Cons. In 1889 he was concertmaster of the Glasgow Sym. Orch. From 1894 to 1916 he was a prof. at the Royal College of Music in London. In 1903–04 he was concertmaster of the Boston Sym. Orch. From 1904 to 1936 he was conductor of the Madrid Sym. Orch.; also appeared as a guest conductor in the U.S. (1928–31), and then in Europe. He composed the comic opera *El centro de la tierra* (Madrid, Dec. 22, 1895) and several chamber music pieces. Arbós was a brilliant orchestrator. His arrangement of music from Albéniz's *Iberia* became very popular.

BIBL.: V. Espinós Moltó, *El Maestro A.* (Madrid, 1942).

Archer (originally, **Balestreri**), **Violet,** Canadian composer and teacher; b. Montreal, April 24, 1913. She studied with Shearwood-Stubington (piano; Teacher's Licentiate, 1934) and Weatherseed (organ) at the McGill Cons., and composition with Champagne and Douglas Clarke at McGill Univ. (B.Mus., 1936).

After receiving her assoc. diploma from the Royal Canadian College of Organists (1938), she studied composition with Bartók in N.Y. (1942) and with Donovan and Hindemith at Yale Univ. (B.Mus., 1948; M.Mus., 1949). Later she pursued studies in electronic music at the Royal Cons. of Music of Toronto (1968) and at Goldsmith's College, Univ. of London (1973). From 1940 to 1947 she was percussionist in the Montreal Women's Sym. Orch.; from 1943 to 1947 she taught at the McGill Cons. After serving as percussionist of the New Haven (Conn.) Sym. Orch. (1947–49), she was composer-in-residence at North Texas State College in Denton (1950–53). From 1953 to 1961 she taught at the Univ. of Okla. She was assoc. prof. (1962–70) and then prof. (1970–78) at the Univ. of Alberta, where she also served as head of the theory and composition dept. (1962–78). In 1983 she was made a Member of the Order of Canada. In 1993 her 80th birthday was celebrated with a festival of her music under the auspices of the Univ. of Alberta and the CBC. Hindemith's influence is paramount in many of her works; also prevalent is the use of folk elements. Overall, her music is structurally strong, polyphonically disciplined, and generally kept within organized tonality, with occasional dodecaphonic episodes.

WORKS: OPERAS: *Sganarelle* (1973; Edmonton, Feb. 5, 1974); *The Meal* (1983; Edmonton, Oct. 19, 1985). **ORCH.:** *Poem* (1940); *Scherzo Sinfonico* (1940); *Fantasia Concertante* for Flute, Oboe, Clarinet, and Strings (1941); *Britannia—A Joyful Overture* (1941); *Fantasy* for Clarinet and Strings (1942); *Fantasy on a Ground* (1946; rev. 1956); Sym. (1946); Clarinet Concertino (1946; rev. 1956); *Fanfare and Passacaglia* (1949); Piano Concerto (1956); *Divertimento* (1957); Violin Concerto (1959); *3 Sketches* (1961); *Prelude-Incantation* (1964); *Sinfonietta* (1968); Sinfonia (1969); *Little Suite* for Strings (1970); *Divertimento* for Piano and Strings (1985); *Evocations* for 2 Pianos and Orch. (1987); *Improvisation on a Name* for Chamber Orch. (1987); *4 Dialogues* for Classical Guitar and Chamber Orch. (1990). **CHAMBER:** 3 string quartets (1940, 1949, 1981); Sonata for Flute, Clarinet, and Piano (1944); Quartet for Flute, Oboe, Clarinet, and Bassoon (1944); *Fantasy* for Violin and Piano (1946); *Divertimento No. 1* for Oboe, Clarinet, and Bassoon (1949) and *No. 2* for Oboe, Violin, and Cello (1957); *Fantasy in the Form of a Passacaglia* for Chamber Ensemble (1951); 2 string trios (1953, 1961); 2 piano trios (1954, 1957); *Prelude and Allegro* for Violin and Piano (1954); Cello Sonata (1956); Violin Sonata (1956); *Divertimento* for Brass Quintet (1963); *Introduction, Dance, and Finale* for Trumpet, Horn, Trombone, Tuba, Harp or Piano, and Percussion (1963); Horn Sonata (1965); Clarinet Sonata (1970); Suite for 4 Violins (1971); Alto Saxophone Sonata (1972); Oboe Sonata (1973); *Little Suite* for Trumpet and Piano (1975); Sonata for Viola, Cello, and Piano (1976); Suite for Flute (1976); Oboe Sonatina (1977); Bassoon Sonatina (1978); Clarinet Sonatina (1978); *Divertimento* for Saxophone Quartet (1979); Bassoon Sonata (1980); Sonata for Solo Cello (1981); *12 Miniatures* for Violin and Piano (1982); *Celebration* for Brass Quintet (1983); *Ikpakhuag* for Violin, Cello, and Piano (1984); *I va vari* for Brass Quintet (1985); *Moods* for Clarinet and Alto Saxophone (1985); *6 Miniatures* for String Bass and Piano (1986); *4 Miniatures* for Classical Accordion (1988); *3 Essays* for Saxophone (1988); *Improvisation* for Snare Drum (1990); *Prelude and Dance* for Timpani (1990); *One Fifth on Four* for Xylophone, Celesta, Piano, Clarinet, and Piano (1991). **KEYBOARD: PIANO:** *3 Scenes* (1945); 2 sonatas (1945, rev. 1957; 1979); 3 sonatinas (1945, 1946, 1973); *6 Preludes* (1947); *3 Sketches* for 2 Pianos (1947); Suite (1947); *Theme and Variations on Là'Haut* (1952); *10 Folk Songs* for Piano, 4-hands (1953); *Rondo* (1955); *11 Short Pieces* (1960); *Theme and Variations* (1963); *Improvisations* (1968); *Lydian Mood and a Quiet Chat* (1971); *4 Bagatelles* (1977); *4 Contrapuntal Moods* (1978); *Here and Now* (1980); *4 Vignettes* for Piano, 4-hands (1984); *Dancing on the Seashore* (1991). **ORGAN:** Sonatina (1944); *2 Chorale Preludes* (1948); *Chorale Improvisation on O Worship the King* (1967); *Prelude and Fantasy on Winchester New* (1978); *Festive Fantasy* (1979); *Improvisation on Veni Creator* (1984); *Variations on Aberystwyth* (1984). **VOCAL:** Liturgical pieces for Chorus and Organ; secular choruses and songs. **ELECTRONIC:** *Episodes* (1973).

BIBL.: L. Hartig, *V. A.: A Bio-Bibliography* (N.Y., 1991).

Ardévol, José, Cuban composer; b. Barcelona, March 13, 1911; d. Havana, Jan. 7, 1981. He studied with his father, conductor of an orch. in Barcelona; at the age of 19, he went to Havana, where he organized a chamber group; he also ed. the magazine *La Música.* He became active in musical politics after the revolution of 1959, and served in various capacities in Cuba and elsewhere; was appointed national director for music, a post he held until 1965. Several of his works have distinct revolutionary connotations, including *Cantos de la revolución* (1962); *Por Viet-Nam,* to words by Fidel Castro (1966); *Cantata Ché comandante* (glorifying the revolutionary role of Ché Guevara, 1968); and *Cantata Lenin* (1970). He also wrote a Concerto for 3 Pianos and Orch. (1938); 3 syms. (1943, 1945, 1946); *Tríptico de Santiago* for Orch. (Cologne, May 25, 1953); *Música para pequeña orquestra* (Washington, D.C., April 19, 1958); several string quartets; numerous piano pieces; and songs.

Arel, Bülent, Turkish-born American composer; b. Constantinople, April 23, 1918; d. Stony Brook, N.Y., Nov. 24, 1990. He studied composition with Necil Kâzim Akses, piano with Ferhunde Erkin, conducting with Ernst Praetorius, and 20th-century music with Edward Zuckmayer at the Ankara State Cons. (1940–47); then took courses in sound engineering in Paris (1951). He taught in Ankara at the State Cons. and at the Teachers College (1947–59); was also a sound engineer and director of Western music programming at the Ankara Radio (1951–59). In 1959 he went to the U.S. on a Rockefeller research grant and worked at the Columbia-Princeton Electronic Music Center until 1963; was also an instructor in electronic music at Yale Univ. (1961–62). After again working at the Ankara Radio (1963–65), he returned to teach at Yale Univ. (1965–70) and Columbia Univ. (1970–71). He was prof. of music and director of the electronic music studio at the State Univ. of N.Y. at Stony Brook from 1971 to 1989. In 1973 he became a naturalized American citizen. In his early works, Arel explored Turkish folk songs; he then wrote pieces alternatively in a neo-Classical and impressionistic manner while experimenting with serial techniques, eventually turning to electronic composition.

WORKS: Piano Concerto (1946); *Suite intime* for Orch. (1949); *Masques* for Winds and Strings (1949); 2 syms. (1951, 1952); *6 Bagatelles* for Strings (1958); *Short Piece* for Orch. (1967); electronic pieces: *Short Study* (1960); *Fragment* (1960); *Electronic Music No. 1* (1960); *Stereo Electronic Music I* (1960) and *II* (1970); *Impressions of Wall Street* (1961); *Music for a Sacred Service* (1961); *Capriccio for T.V.* (1969); dance scores: *Mimiana I* (1968), *II* (1969), and *III* (1973).

Aretz (de Ramón y Rivera), Isabel, Argentine-born Venezuelan folklorist and composer; b. Buenos Aires, April 13, 1909. She studied piano and composition at the National Cons. of Music in Buenos Aires; subsequently dedicated herself to research in Argentine folklore at the Museo de Ciencias Naturales de Buenos Aires (1938–44); she received her Ph.D. in musicology in 1967 at the Argentine Catholic Univ. in Buenos Aires with the diss. *Música tradicional argentina: La Rioja.* She served as an assoc. member of the Instituto Argentino de Musicología (1938–50); then was the first prof. of ethnomusicology at the Escuela Nacional de Danzas de Argentina (1950–52). In 1953 she settled in Caracas, Venezuela, as a research fellow in ethnomusicology and folklore at the Instituto Nacional de Folklore de Venezuela; in 1965 she became director of the folklore dept. of the Instituto Nacional de Cultura y Bellas Artes, and, in 1970, of the Instituto Interamericano de Etnomusicología y Folklore. As a composer, Aretz's music reflects interest in folk music and contemporary European trends.

WRITINGS: *Música tradicional argentina: Tucumán, historia y folklore* (Buenos Aires, 1946); *El folklore musical argentino* (Buenos Aires, 1953); *Manual de folklore venezolano*

(Caracas, 1957; 3rd ed., 1972); *Cantos navidenos en el folklore venezolano* (Caracas, 1962); *Instrumentos musicales de Venezuela* (Cumaná, 1967); *La artesania en Venezuela* (Caracas, 1967); *El traje en Venezuela* (Caracas, 1972); *El tamunangue* (Barquisimeto, 1976).

Argenta (Maza), Atáulfo, Spanish conductor; b. Castro Urdiales, Santander, Nov. 19, 1913; d. Los Molinos, near Madrid, Jan. 21, 1958. He enrolled at the Madrid Cons. at the age of 13 and studied piano, violin, and composition; after winning the Premio Extraordinario for piano and the Nilsson prize, he continued his training in Belgium and took conducting lessons with Carl Schuricht in Germany. From 1939 he conducted in Spain; in 1945, became chief conductor of the Orquesta Nacional de España in Madrid; also appeared as a guest conductor in Europe and South America. In addition to his idiomatic performances of Spanish music, Argenta displayed a flair for Russian and French scores.

BIBL.: A. Fernandez-Cid, *A. A.* (Madrid, 1958).

Argenta (real name, **Herbison**), **Nancy,** Canadian soprano; b. Nelson, British Columbia, Jan. 17, 1957. She spent her early years in the settlement of Argenta, from which she later took her professional name. She was a student of Jacob Hamm in Vancouver and of Martin Chambers at the Univ. of Western Ontario. In 1980 she won 1st prize in the S.C. Eckhardt-Gramatté Competition. After further training with Jacqueline Richard in Düsseldorf (1980–81), she settled in London and completed her studies with Vera Rosza. In 1983 she attracted critical attention as La Chasseuresse in Rameau's *Hippolyte et Aricie* at the Aix-en-Provence Festival. As a gifted exponent of the early music repertoire, she was engaged by many of the leading early music groups and by the principal music festivals; in 1989 she appeared as soloist with the English Concert in N.Y. and also made her Wigmore Hall recital debut in London. In 1990 she sang Rossane in the North American premiere of Handel's *Floridante* in Toronto. Among her other esteemed roles are Monteverdi's Poppea and Orfeo, Purcell's Dido and King Arthur, Handel's Astreia, and Mozart's Barbarina and Susanna. Her concert repertoire is expansive, ranging from the Baroque era to contemporary scores.

Argento, Dominick, greatly talented American composer; b. York, Pa., Oct. 27, 1927. He taught himself piano, theory, and harmony before pursuing formal training. In 1947 he enrolled at the Peabody Cons. of Music in Baltimore, where he took courses with Nicolas Nabokov and Hugo Weisgall, graduating in 1951 with a B.A. degree. He then went to Italy on a Fulbright fellowship and studied piano with Pietro Scarpini and composition with Luigi Dallapiccola at the Florence Cons. Upon returning to the U.S., he attended classes of Cowell in composition at the Peabody Cons. of Music, taking his M.M. degree in 1954; eager to pursue his studies further, he entered the Eastman School of Music in Rochester, N.Y., where his teachers were Howard Hanson, Bernard Rogers, and Hovhaness; in 1957 he received his doctorate in music there. In 1957 he was awarded a Guggenheim fellowship, which enabled him to go once more to Florence and work on his opera *Colonel Jonathan the Saint*; in 1964 he obtained his 2nd Guggenheim fellowship. In 1958 he was appointed to the music faculty of the Univ. of Minnesota in Minneapolis; in 1964 he became a founder of the Center Opera in Minnesota, later renamed the Minnesota Opera. The connection gave Argento an opportunity to present his operas under his own supervision. In 1975 he received the Pulitzer Prize in Music for his song cycle *From the Diary of Virginia Woolf.* In 1980 he was elected a member of the American Academy and Inst. of Arts and Letters. In the pantheon of American composers, Argento occupies a distinct individual category, outside any certifiable modernistic trend or technical idiom. He writes melodious music in a harmonious treatment, so deliberate in intent that even his apologists profess embarrassment at its unimpeded flow; there is also a perceptible ancestral strain in the bel canto style of his Italianate opera scores; most important, audiences, and an increasing number of sophisticated critics, profess their admiration for his unusual songfulness. All the same, an analysis of Argento's productions reveals the presence of acerbic harmonies and artfully acidulated melismas.

WORKS: DRAMATIC: OPERAS: *The Boor* (Rochester, N.Y., May 6, 1957); *Colonel Jonathan the Saint* (1958–61; Denver, Dec. 31, 1971); *Christopher Sly* (1962–63; Minneapolis, May 31, 1963); *The Masque of Angels* (1963; Minneapolis, Jan. 9, 1964); *The Shoemaker's Holiday* (Minneapolis, June 1, 1967); *Postcard from Morocco* (Minneapolis, Oct. 14, 1971); *The Voyage of Edgar Allan Poe* (1975–76; St. Paul, April 24, 1976); *Miss Havisham's Fire* (1977–78; N.Y., March 22, 1979); *Casanova's Homecoming* (1980–84; St. Paul, April 12, 1985); *The Aspern Papers* (Dallas, Nov. 19, 1988); *The Dream of Valentino* (1993; Washington, D.C., Jan. 15, 1994). **MONODRAMAS:** *A Water Bird Talk* (1974; N.Y., May 19, 1977); *Miss Havisham's Wedding Night* (1980; Minneapolis, May 1, 1981). **BALLETS:** *The Resurrection of Don Juan* (1955; Rochester, N.Y., May 5, 1956); *Royal Invitation, or Homage to the Queen of Tonga* (St. Paul, March 22, 1964). **INCIDENTAL MUSIC:** To Shaw's *St. Joan* (1964); Molière's *Volpone* (1964); O'Neill's *S.S. Glencairn* (1966); Aeschylus's *Oresteia* (1967). **ORCH.:** *Ode to the West Wind*, concerto for Soprano and Orch. (1956; Rochester, N.Y., April 20, 1957); *Variations for Orchestra: The Mask of Night* (1965; Minneapolis, Jan. 26, 1966); *Bravo Mozart!*, "imaginary biography" for Violin, Oboe, Horn, and Orch. (Minneapolis, July 3, 1969); *A Ring of Time, Preludes and Pageants* for Orch. and Bells (Minneapolis, Oct. 5, 1972); *In Praise of Music* (1977); *Fire Variations* (1981); *Le Tombeau d'Edgar Poe* (1985; Baltimore, Feb. 27, 1986); *Capriccio: Rossini in Paris* for Clarinet and Orch. (St. Louis, May 16, 1986). **CHAMBER:** *Divertimento* for Piano and Strings (1954); String Quartet (1956). **VOCAL:** *Songs about Spring*, 5 songs for Soprano and Piano or Chamber Orch. (1954); *6 Elizabethan Songs* for High Voice and Piano (1958; also for Baroque Ensemble); *The Revelation of St. John the Divine* for Tenor, Men's Chorus, Brass, and Percussion (1966); *A Nation of Cowslips* for Chorus (1968); *Letters from Composers*, 7 songs for Tenor and Guitar (1968); *Tria carmina paschalia*, Easter cantata for Women's Voices, Harp, and Guitar (1970); *To Be Sung upon the Water*, song cycle for High Voice, Clarinet, and Piano (1972); *Jonah and the Whale*, oratorio for Tenor, Bass, Narrator, Chorus, and Small Ensemble (1973; Minneapolis, March 11, 1974); *From the Diary of Virginia Woolf*, song cycle for Mezzo-soprano and Piano (1974; Minneapolis, Jan. 5, 1975); *Peter Quince at the Clavier*, sonatina for Chorus and Piano (1979); *I Hate and I Love*, song cycle for Chorus and Percussion (1981); *The Andrér Expedition*, song cycle for Baritone and Piano (1982); *Casa Guidi*, 5 songs for Mezzo-soprano and Orch. (1983); *Te Deum* for Chorus and Orch. (1987; Buffalo, March 4, 1988).

Argerich, Martha, outstanding Argentine pianist; b. Buenos Aires, June 5, 1941. She made her first public appearance at the age of 5; after studies with Vincenzo Scaramuzza, she made her debut in Buenos Aires at age 8; later, pursued training with Gulda in Vienna and with Magaloff and Madeleine Lipatti in Geneva; also received lessons from Michelangeli. At the age of 16, she captured 1st prizes in both the Geneva and Busoni competitions; then won the Chopin Competition in Warsaw (1965). She pursued a notable career as a virtuoso, appearing with the leading orchs. of the world, as a recitalist, and as a chamber music artist. Her formidable repertoire ranges from Liszt and Chopin to Ravel and Prokofiev. She was married to **Charles Dutoit** and, later, to **Stephen Kovacevich**.

Arizaga, Rodolfo (Bernardo), Argentine composer; b. Buenos Aires, July 11, 1926; d. there, May 12, 1985. He studied philosophy at the Univ. of Buenos Aires and composition with Luis Gianneo; then went to Paris, where he took lessons with Boulanger and Messiaen. Beginning with folkloric composition of the traditional Latin American type, he traversed the entire gamut of modern techniques, including 12-tone structures and aleatory composition, and applied these diverse methods liberally according to need and intention. Arizaga also publ. the monographs *Manuel de Falla* (Buenos Aires, 1961) and *Juan José Castro* (Buenos Aires, 1963), and ed. the *Enciclopedia de la música argentina* (Buenos Aires, 1971). With P. Camps, he wrote *Historia de la música en la Argentina* (Buenos Aires, 1990).

WORKS: *Prometeo 45*, opera (1958); *Sonata breve* for Ondes Martenot and Piano (1958); Piano Concerto (1963); *Tientos para Santa María* for Orch. (1965); *Música para Christóbal Colón* for Orch. (1966); *Diferenzas del tercer tiento* for Organ (1966); 2 string quartets (1968, 1969); various vocal works and piano pieces.

Arkhipova, Irina (Konstantinovna), outstanding Russian mezzo-soprano; b. Moscow, Dec. 2, 1925. She attended vocal classes at the Moscow Architectural Inst., graduating in 1948; then continued vocal training with Leonid Savransky at the Moscow Cons., graduating in 1953. She sang with the Sverdlovsk Opera (1954–56); then made her debut as Carmen at Moscow's Bolshoi Theater (1956), where she quickly rose to prominence; traveled with it outside Russia, garnering praise for her appearances at Milan's La Scala (1965) and at the Montreal EXPO (1967). She appeared as Amneris at the San Francisco Opera in 1972 and as Azucena at London's Covent Garden in 1975. In 1992 she sang the Countess in *The Queen of Spades* with the Kirov Opera of St. Petersburg during its visit to the Metropolitan Opera in N.Y. In 1966 she was made a People's Artist of the U.S.S.R. She excelled particularly in the Russian repertoire, but also distinguished herself in French and Italian music.

Arkor, André d', Belgian tenor; b. Tilleur, near Liège, Feb. 23, 1901; d. Brussels, Dec. 19, 1971. He studied with Malherbe and Seguin at the Liège Cons. He made his operatic debut in 1925 as Gérard in *Lakmé* at the Liège Théâtre Royal; then sang in Ghent and Lyons; in 1930 he joined the Théâtre de la Monnaie in Brussels, where he remained as a leading tenor until 1945; from 1945 to 1965 he was director of the Liège Théâtre Royal. He was particularly esteemed as a Mozartean.

Arlt, Wulf (Friedrich), German musicologist; b. Breslau, March 5, 1938. He studied musicology at the Univ. of Cologne; then received his Ph.D. in 1966 from the Univ. of Basel with the diss. *Ein Festoffizium des Mittelalters aus Beauvais in seiner liturgischen Bedeutung* (publ. in Cologne, 1970); subsequently completed his Habilitation there in 1970 with his *Praxis und Lehre der "Ars subtilior": Studien zur Geschichte der Notation im Spätmittelalter.* He joined the faculty of the Univ. of Basel as a lecturer in 1965; became a prof. there in 1972. In 1971 he also became director of the Schola Cantorum Basiliensis. Arlt devoted his critical capacities to elucidating the problems of music in the Middle Ages, and contributed important articles on the subject to music journals. He also publ. *Italien als produktive Erfahrung franko-flämischer Musiker im 15. Jahrhundert* (1993) and *Lo Bozolari: Ein Klerikerfest des MA aus Le Puy* (1995).

Arma, Paul (real name, **Imre Weisshaus**), Hungarian-born French composer; b. Budapest, Oct. 22, 1904; d. Paris, Nov. 28, 1987. From 1921 to 1924 he attended classes of Bartók at the Budapest Academy of Music, then went to N.Y., where he became associated with radical political and musical groups and contributed highly complex pieces to Cowell's publication *New Music Quarterly*. A composer of empiric persuasion, he explored quaquaversal paths of modern techniques in contrasting sonorities. In 1930 he went to Paris and worked under the pseudonym Paul Arma. In 1947 he publ. in Paris a modernistically planned *Nouveau dictionnaire de musique.* Typical of his modernistic techniques, reflected in the titles of some of his works, are Concerto for String Quartet and Orch. (1947); Violin Sonata (1949); *31 instantanés* for Woodwind, Percussion, Celesta, Xylophone, and Piano (1951); *Polydiaphonie* for Orch. (1962); *Structures variées* for Orch. (1964); *Prismes sonores* for Orch. (1966); *6 transparences* for Oboe and String Orch. (1968); *Résonances* for Orch. (1971); *6 Convergences* for Orch. (1978); *Silences and Emergences* for String Quartet (1979); *Deux Regards* for Violin and Piano (1982); *Deux Images* for Cello and Piano (1982); numerous experimental pieces for various instrumental combinations.

Armin, Georg (actually, **Herrmann**), German singer and pedagogue; b. Braunschweig, Nov. 10, 1871; d. Karlslunde Strand, Denmark, Feb. 16, 1963. He studied architecture; then turned to singing. He settled in Berlin as a voice teacher; from 1925 to 1942 he ed. the periodical *Der Stimmwart.* His home in Berlin was destroyed in an air raid during World War II; in 1949 he settled in Denmark. He publ. several papers on vocal production, among them *Das Stauprinzip* (1905) and *Von der Urkraft der Stimme* (1921).

BIBL.: J. Berntsen, *Ein Meister der Stimmbildungskunst* (Leipzig, 1936).

Armstrong, Karan, American soprano; b. Horne, Mont., Dec. 14, 1941. She studied at Concordia College in Moorhead, Minn. (B.A., 1963). In 1969 she won both the San Francisco Opera and Metropolitan Opera auditions; then appeared with the N.Y. City Opera, Baltimore Opera, Houston Opera, Seattle Opera, and others. In 1976 she made her European debut as Salome with the Strasbourg Opera; in 1979 she sang Elsa at the Bayreuth Festival, and returned there in subsequent seasons. She made her debut at Covent Garden in London as Lulu in Berg's opera in 1981. She also appeared with the Vienna State Opera, Bavarian State Opera in Munich, Paris Opéra, and Hamburg State Opera. Her finest roles include Violetta, Tosca, Mimi, Alice Ford, Countess Almaviva, and Eva. She married **Götz Friedrich**.

Armstrong, Richard, English conductor; b. Leicester, Jan. 7, 1943. He studied at Corpus Christi College, Cambridge. In 1966 he joined the staff of the Royal Opera House, Covent Garden, London; in 1968 he became assistant conductor of the Welsh National Opera, Cardiff; from 1973 to 1986 he was its music director; also appeared as a guest conductor. In 1993 he became music director of Glasgow's Scottish Opera and chief conductor of the new National Orch. of Scotland. That same year he was made a Commander of the Order of the British Empire.

Armstrong, Sheila, English soprano; b. Ashington, Northumberland, Aug. 13, 1942. She was educated at the Royal Academy of Music in London, winning the 1965 Kathleen Ferrier Memorial Scholarship. She made her operatic debut as Despina at the Sadler's Wells Theatre in London in 1965; then sang at the Glyndebourne Festival from 1966 and at the Royal Opera House, Covent Garden, London from 1973. She was also active as an oratorio singer. She retired in 1993.

Arndt, Günther, German choral conductor; b. Berlin-Charlottenburg, April 1, 1907; d. Berlin, Dec. 25, 1976. He was educated at the Akademie für Schul- und Kirchenmusik in Berlin; also studied musicology at the Univ. of Berlin; then was engaged as lecturer at the Volkshochschule in Berlin (1932–40). After the end of World War II in 1945, he headed the chamber music dept. of the Berlin Radio RIAS; also conducted the Berlin Motet Choir (1950–60) and the RIAS Chamber Choir (1955–72); served as deputy head of music for the RIAS (1964–72). He gained distinction as a conductor of an extensive choral repertoire.

Arndt-Ober, Margarethe, German mezzo-soprano; b. Berlin, April 15, 1885; d. Bad Sachsa, March 24, 1971. She studied in Berlin with Benno Stolzenberg and later with Arthur Arndt, who became her husband. In 1906 she made her operatic debut as Azucena in Frankfurt an der Oder; in 1907, joined the Berlin Royal Opera. On Nov. 21, 1913, she made her Metropolitan Opera debut in N.Y. as Ortrud, remaining on its roster until 1917; then was interned until the end of World War I. In 1919 she became a member of the Berlin State Opera, where she sang until the end of World War II.

Arnell, Richard (Anthony Sayer), English composer and teacher; b. London, Sept. 15, 1917. He studied with John Ireland at the Royal College of Music in London (1935–39). In 1939 he went to America; when Winston Churchill had a reception at Columbia Univ. in 1946, Arnell wrote *Prelude and Flourish* for Brass Instruments, performed at the occasion. In 1948 Arnell returned to London and taught at Trinity College of Music until 1964. From 1975 to 1988 he was music director of the International Film School. His music is festive without pomposity, and very English.

WORKS: DRAMATIC: OPERAS: *Love in Transit* (London, Feb. 27, 1958); *The Petrified Princess* (London, May 5, 1959); *Moonflowers* (Kent, July 23, 1959); *Combat Zone* (Hempstead, N.Y., April 27, 1969). **BALLETS:** *Harlequin in April* (London, May 8, 1951); *The Great Detective* (1953). **ORCH.:** 7 syms.; *The New Age*, overture (N.Y., Jan. 13, 1941); *Quasi variazioni* (N.Y., March 15, 1942); Violin Concerto (N.Y., April 22, 1946); 2 piano concertos (1946, 1966); *Abstract Forms*, suite for Strings (Bath, June 2, 1951); *Lord Byron*, symphonic portrait (London, Nov. 19, 1952). **CHAMBER:** 6 string quartets; piano pieces.

Arnestad, Finn (Oluf Bjerke), Norwegian composer and music critic; b. Christiania, Sept. 23, 1915. He studied violin and piano in Oslo and, briefly, composition with Brustad; in 1952 he studied African and oriental folk music in Paris; after returning to Oslo, he was active as a music critic. His music is influenced by French Impressionism, with tangential use of dodecaphony.

WORKS: ORCH.: *Constellation*, intermezzo (1948); *Conversation*, concert intermezzo for Piano and Orch. (1950); *Meditation*, intermezzo (1952); *I.N.R.I.*, 2 concert suites from a symphonic mystery play (1952–55); Violin Concerto (1957); *Aria appassionata* (1962); *Cavatina cambiata* (1965; orig. titled *Dopplersonance*); *Overture* (1970); *Væsletjennet* for Norwegian Recorder and Orch. (1970; based on a 1938 piano piece); *Toccata* (1972); *Arabesque* (1975); Piano Concerto (1976); *Mouvement concertant*, concert piece for Double Bass and Orch. (1978). **CHAMBER:** String Quartet (1947); Sextet for Flute, Clarinet, Bassoon, Violin, Cello, and Piano (1959); Quintet for Flute and Strings (1962); *Suite in Old Dance Rhythms* for Flute, Oboe, Harpsichord, and Strings (1966); Trombone Sonata (1971); Sonata for Solo Violin (1980); Sonata for Solo Double Bass (1980). **PIANO:** 2 sonatas (1967; *Ritagliata*, 1967); *Tango*, 3-part canon (1981). **VOCAL:** *Missa Brevis* for Chorus and 6 Instruments (1951); *Amen* for Chorus (1959); *Smeden og Bageren* (The Blacksmith and the Baker) for Baritone, Flute, Oboe, Harpsichord, and Strings (1966).

Arnič, Blaž, Slovenian composer and teacher; b. Luče, Jan. 31, 1901; d. Ljubljana, Feb. 1, 1970. He studied organ and theory at the Ljubljana Cons. (1925–29) and at the New Vienna Cons. (1929–32). In 1945 he was appointed prof. at the Ljubljana Academy of Music. Most of his music is of programmatic content; all of his syms. bear descriptive titles, and much of the melodic and rhythmic material of his music reflects the folk motifs of Slovenia.

WORKS: ORCH.: Organ Concerto (1931); *Symphonic Rhapsody* (1933); 2 symphonic poems: *Memento mori* (1934) and *Witch Dance* (1951); 7 syms.: *Resurrection* (1935), *Reverie* (1940), *The Whirlwind of War* (1941), *Pioneer* (1948), *Symphony of Labor* (1950), *In the Fatherland's Soul* (1951), and *War and Peace* (1960); 3 violin concertos (1953, 1953, 1966); Cello Concerto (1960); Clarinet Concerto (1963); Viola Concerto (1967). **OTHER:** Chamber music; piano pieces; songs.

Arnold, Byron, American composer and teacher; b. Vancouver, Wash., Aug. 15, 1901; d. Oscoda, Mich., Dec. 25, 1971. He studied composition with Bernard Rogers and Howard Hanson at the Eastman School of Music in Rochester, N.Y. Upon graduation, he filled various teaching posts in Alabama and elsewhere. He created a certain stir in musical circles by writing a symphonic suite entitled *5 Incapacitated Preludes*, each portraying a serious neurological ailment affecting sight, hearing, and muscular structures; in the deaf prelude the players are instructed to make an outward pretense at playing, blowing, and soundless drumbeating. It was performed in Rochester, N.Y., on April 19, 1937. He also wrote *3 Fantasticisms* for Orch. Among his normal contributions is his *Folksongs of Alabama* (1950).

Arnold, Denis (Midgley), distinguished English musicologist; b. Sheffield, Dec. 15, 1926; d. Budapest, April 28, 1986. He was educated at the Univ. of Sheffield (B.A., 1947; B.Mus., 1948; M.A., 1950). From 1951 to 1960 he was a lecturer and from 1960 to 1964 a reader in music at Queen's Univ., Belfast; in 1964 he was made senior lecturer at the Univ. of Hull; in 1969 he became prof. of music at the Univ. of Nottingham; from 1975 he was Heather Prof. of Music at the Univ. of Oxford. From 1976 to 1980 he was joint ed. of *Music & Letters*. From 1979 to 1983 he was president of the Royal Musical Assn. In 1983 he was made a Commander of the Order of the British Empire. He was regarded as one of the foremost authorities on Italian music of the Renaissance and the early Baroque period.

WRITINGS: *Monteverdi* (London, 1963; 3rd ed., rev., 1990 by T. Carter); *Marenzio* (London, 1965); *Monteverdi Madrigals* (London, 1967); ed. with N. Fortune, *The Monteverdi Companion* (London, 1968; 2nd ed., rev., 1985, as *The New Monteverdi Companion*); ed. with N. Fortune, *The Beethoven Companion* (London, 1971); *Giovanni Gabrieli* (London, 1974); *Giovanni Gabrieli and the Music of the Venetian High Renaissance* (Oxford, 1979); *Monteverdi Church Music* (London, 1982); ed. *The New Oxford Companion to Music* (2 vols., Oxford, 1983); *Bach* (Oxford, 1984); with E. Arnold, *The Oratorio in Venice* (London, 1986).

BIBL.: Special issue of the *Journal of the Royal Musical Association*, 113/2 (1988).

Arnold, Sir Malcolm (Henry), prolific and versatile English composer; b. Northampton, Oct. 21, 1921. He studied trumpet with Ernest Hall and composition with Gordon Jacob at the Royal College of Music in London (1938–41). He played trumpet in the London Phil. (1941–42), serving as its first trumpeter (1946–48); also played trumpet in the BBC Sym. Orch. in London (1945). He then devoted himself chiefly to composition, developing a melodious and harmonious style of writing that possessed the quality of immediate appeal to the general public while avoiding obvious banality; many of his works reveal modalities common to English folk songs, often invested in acridly pleasing harmonies. His experience as a trumpeter and conductor of popular concerts provided a secure feeling for propulsive rhythms and brilliant sonorities. He had a particular knack for composing effective film music. In his sound track for *The Bridge on the River Kwai*, he popularized the rollicking march *Colonel Bogey*, originally composed by Kenneth Alford in 1914. In 1970 Arnold was made a Commander of the Order of the British Empire, and in 1993 he was knighted.

WORKS: DRAMATIC: OPERAS: *The Dancing Master* (1951); *The Open Window* (London, Dec. 14, 1956). **BALLETS:** *Homage to the Queen* (London, June 2, 1953); *Rinaldo and Armida* (1954); *Sweeney Todd* (1958); *Electra* (1963). **OTHER STAGE WORKS:** *Song of Simeon*, nativity play (1958); *The Turtle Drum*, children's spectacle (1967). **FILM MUSIC:** *The Captain's Paradise* (1953); *I Am a Camera* (1955); *Trapeze* (1956); *Island in the Sun* (1957); *The Bridge on the River Kwai* (1957); *Inn of the Sixth Happiness* (1958); *Roots of Heaven* (1958); *Nine Hours to Rama* (1962); *The Chalk Garden* (1963); *David Copperfield* (1969). **ORCH.:** Sym. for Strings (1946); 9 numbered syms.: No. 1 (Cheltenham, July 6, 1951), No. 2 (Bournemouth, May 25, 1953), No. 3 (1954–57; London, Dec. 2, 1957), No. 4 (London, Nov. 2, 1960), No. 5 (Cheltenham, 1961), No. 6 (1967; Sheffield, June 28, 1968), No. 7 (1973; London, May 1974), No. 8 (N.Y., May 5, 1979), and No. 9 (1987); solo concertos: 2 for Horn (1945, 1956); 2 for Clarinet (1948, 1974); 1 for Piano Duet (1951); 1 for Oboe (1952); 2 for Flute (1954, 1972); 1 for Harmonica (London, Aug. 14, 1954); 1 for Organ (1954); 1 for Guitar (1958); 1 for 2 Violins (1962); 1 for 2 Pianos, 3-hands (1969); 1 for Viola (1970); 1 for Trumpet (1981); 1 for Recorder (1988);

1 for Cello (London, March 9, 1989); 10 overtures: *Beckus the Dandipratt* (1943); *Festival Overture* (1946); *The Smoke* (1948); *A Sussex Overture* (1951); *Tam O'Shanter* (1955); *A Grand, Grand Overture* for 3 Vacuum Cleaners, 1 Floor Polisher, 4 Rifles, and Orch. (London, Nov. 13, 1956); *Commonwealth Christmas Overture* (1957); *Peterloo* (1968); *Anniversary Overture* (1968); *The Fair Field* (1972); *Larch Trees*, tone poem (1943); *Serenade* for Small Orch. (1950); *8 English Dances* in 2 sets (1950–51); *The Sound Barrier*, rhapsody (1952); 3 sinfoniettas (1954, 1958, 1964); *2 Little Suites* (1955, 1962); *Serenade* for Guitar and Strings (1955); *4 Scottish Dances* (1957); *4 Cornish Dances* (1966); Concerto for 28 Players (1970); *Fantasy* for Audience and Orch. (1970); *A Flourish* (1973); *Fantasy* for Brass Band (1974); *Philharmonic Concerto* (1977); Sym. for Brass Instruments (1979); *Manx Suite* (1990). **CHAMBER:** Trio for Flute, Viola, and Bassoon (1943); *3 Shanties* for Wind Quintet (1944); Duo for Flute and Viola (1945); 2 violin sonatas (1947, 1953); Viola Sonata (1947); Flute Sonatina (1948); 2 string quartets (1949, 1976); Oboe Sonatina (1951); Clarinet Sonatina (1951); Recorder Sonatina (1953); Piano Trio (1955); Oboe Quartet (1957); *Toy Symphony* for 12 Toy Instruments, Piano, and String Quartet (1957); 2 brass quintets (1961, 1988); 5 pieces for Violin and Piano (1965); 9 solo fantasies: for Bassoon, Clarinet, Horn, Flute, Oboe, Trumpet, Trombone, Tuba, and Guitar (1966–70); *Trevelyan Suite* for Wind Instruments (1968); *Fantasy* for Recorder and String Quartet (1991); piano pieces. **VOCAL:** Choral pieces; songs.

BIBL.: A. Poulton, *M. A.: A Catalogue of His Music* (London, 1986); H. Cole, *M. A.: An Introduction to His Music* (London and Boston, 1989); P. Burton-Page, *Philharmonic Concerto: The Life and Music of M. A.* (London, 1994).

Arnold, Maurice (real name, **Maurice Arnold Strothotte**), American conductor, teacher, and composer; b. St. Louis, Jan. 19, 1865; d. N.Y., Oct. 23, 1937. He studied in Cincinnati, then in Germany with several teachers, including Bruch. The performance of his orch. work *American Plantation Dances* (N.Y., 1894) aroused the interest of Dvořák, because of the Negro melodies used in it, and he engaged Arnold to teach at the National Cons. of Music of America in N.Y., of which Dvořák was then head. Arnold subsequently was active as a conductor of light opera, and as a violin teacher. He wrote a comic opera, *The Merry Benedicts* (Brooklyn, 1896); a grand opera, *Cleopatra*; a Sym.; a cantata, *The Wild Chase*; *Minstrel Serenade* for Violin and Piano; and a Fugue for Piano, 8-hands.

Arnoldson, Sigrid, Swedish soprano; b. Stockholm, March 20, 1861; d. there, Feb. 7, 1943. She was the daughter of the celebrated tenor Oscar Arnoldson (1830–81). She studied voice with Maurice Strakosch and Désirée Artôt. She made her professional debut in Prague in 1885; in 1886 she was a guest artist in Moscow, and in 1887 appeared in London; subsequently sang in Paris, Nice, and Rome. In 1888 she was engaged as a regular member at Covent Garden in London. On Nov. 29, 1893, she made her debut at the Metropolitan Opera in N.Y. as Gounod's Baucis, remaining on its roster for one season. In 1910 she was elected a member of the Royal Swedish Academy of Music in Stockholm; in 1922 she was in Vienna as a singing teacher; later also taught voice in Berlin. On June 16, 1888, she married the Austrian impresario Alfred Fischhof, a nephew of Maurice Strakosch.

Aronowitz, Cecil (Solomon), South African-born English violist and teacher of Russian-Lithuanian descent; b. King William's Town, March 4, 1916; d. Ipswich, Sept. 7, 1978. He studied at the Royal College of Music in London, where his principal teachers were Vaughan Williams and Jacob (composition) and Rivarde (violin). He turned to the viola later in life, and served as first violist in the Boyd Neel Orch., the Goldsborough (later English) Chamber Orch., and the London Mozart Players; also was a member of the Melos Ensemble and the Pro Arte Piano Quartet. He was a prof. of viola at the Royal College of Music (1948–75), head of the string school at the Royal Northern College of Music in Manchester (1975–77), and director of string studies at the Snape Maltings School (1977–78).

Arrau, Claudio, celebrated Chilean-born American pianist; b. Chillán, Feb. 6, 1903; d. Mürzzuschlag, Austria, June 9, 1991. He received early training from his mother, and made his first public appearance in Chillán when he was only 5; at age 6, he played in Santiago. After instruction from Bindo Paoli, he received a scholarship from the Chilean government in 1910 to pursue studies in Berlin, where he was a pupil of Martin Krause at the Stern Cons. (1913–18). On Dec. 10, 1914, he made his Berlin debut in a recital, then attracted considerable attention through tours of Germany and Scandinavia. In 1918 he made his first tour of Europe. In 1921 he performed in South America and in 1922 in London. In the 1923–24 season, he played in the U.S. but, failing to elicit much of a response from audiences and critics, he pursued his career in Europe; also taught at the Stern Cons. (1924–40). In 1927 he won the Grand Prix International des Pianistes in Geneva, and from 1935 he consolidated his European reputation by giving a series of acclaimed cycles of the keyboard works of Bach, Mozart, Beethoven, and others. In 1940 he left war-ravaged Europe for Santiago, where he opened a piano school. In 1941 he made a highly successful tour of the U.S., where he settled. In subsequent years, he appeared with all the major U.S. orchs. and gave countless recitals. Following the end of World War II in 1945, he pursued an eminent international career and established himself as one of the premier masters of the piano. In 1978 he gave up his Chilean citizenship in protest against the military regime in his homeland; in 1979, he became a naturalized American citizen. All the same, he remained a revered figure in Chile and in 1983 was awarded the Chilean National Arts Prize. In 1984 he toured the land of his birth to enormous acclaim after an absence of 17 years. He died in Austria while preparing for a recital at the new Brahms museum in Mürzzuschlag. Arrau was a dedicated master of the keyboard and a authoritative interpreter of Beethoven; he also gave distinguished performances of Mozart, Chopin, Schumann, Liszt, and Brahms, among others. In his playing, he combined a Classical purity and precision of style with a rhapsodic éclat.

BIBL.: J. Horowitz, *Conversations with A.* (N.Y., 1982); I. Harden, *C. A.: Ein Interpretenporträt* (Frankfurt am Main, 1983); H. Kupferberg, "C. A.," *Musical America* (March 1988); S. Dorantes Guzmán, *A.: El gran artista latinoamericano* (Xalapa, 1991).

Arrieu, Claude, French composer; b. Paris, Nov. 30, 1903; d. there, March 7, 1990. She studied piano with Marguerite Long and took courses in composition at the Paris Cons. with Dukas, G. Caussade, Roger-Ducasse, and N. Gallon, graduating with a premier prix in 1932. In 1949 she received the Prix Italia. She was notably successful as a composer for the theater.

WORKS: DRAMATIC: *Noël* musical (1934; Strasbourg, Jan. 29, 1950); *Cadet Roussel*, comic opera (1938–39; Marseilles, Oct. 2, 1953); *Les Amours de Don Perlimplin et Belisa dans son jardin*, opera (1947; Tours, March 1, 1980); *Fête galante*, ballet (1947); *Les Deux Rendez-vouz*, comic opera (1948; Radio France, June 22, 1951); *La Princesse de Babylone*, comic opera (1953–55; Rheims, March 4, 1960); *La Cabine téléphonique*, radiophonic sketch (1958; Paris, March 15, 1959); *Cymbeline*, opera (1958–63); *La Statue*, ballet (1968); *Un clavier pour un autre*, comic opera (1969–70; Avignon, April 3, 1971). **ORCH.:** Piano Concerto (1932); Concerto for 2 Pianos and Orch. (1934); *Partita* (1934); 2 violin concertos (1938, 1949); *Petite suite* (1945); Flute Concerto (1946); Suite for Strings (1959); *Suite funambulesque* (1961); Concerto for Wind Quintet and Strings (1962); Concerto for Trumpet and Strings (1965); *Variations classiques* for Strings (1970). **CHAMBER:** String Trio (1936); Sonatine for 2 Violins (1937); Sonatine for Flute and Piano (1943); Violin Sonata (1948); Wind Quintet (1955); Trio for Piano, Violin, and Cello (1957). **VOCAL:** *Cantate sur sept* *poèmes d'amour en guerre* for Soprano, Baritone, and Orch. (1946); *Mystère de noël*, oratorio for Soloists, Chorus, and Orch. (1951); choruses.

Arrigo, Girolamo, Italian composer; b. Palermo, April 2, 1930. He studied at the Palermo Cons., and later in Rome and Paris. His works are mostly in small forms, and virtually all with programmatic connotations. The most important among them are *3 occasioni* for Soprano and 32 Instruments (1958); *Quarta occasione* for 7 Voices, Horn, Viola, Mandolin, Guitar, and Celesta (1959); *Fluxus* for 9 Instruments (1959); *Episodi* for Soprano and Flute, to texts by ancient Greek poets (1963); *Shadows* for Orch. (1965); *Infrarosso* for 16 Instruments (1967). He also wrote a "collage opera," *Orden* (1969), consisting of several not necessarily related numbers, to texts in French, Italian, and Spanish, and an "epopée musicale," *Addio Garibaldi* (Paris, Oct. 10, 1972).

Arriola, Pepito (actually, **José Rodriguez**), Spanish *wunderkind* of the piano; b. Betanzos, Feb. 28, 1896; d. Barcelona, Oct. 24, 1954. Even dismissing tales of his incredible precocity (he was reported as playing in public at the age of 6), the fact remains that he made successful European tours as a child prodigy in programs of adult difficulty. He also composed piano pieces in a Spanish manner. However, as happens in so many pathetic cases of premature development, poor Arriola lost his glamour as soon as he had to drop his baby pet name Pepito, doff his velvet pants, and dress in grown-up clothes. He ceased to attract attention and lingered for the remainder of his life in utter obscurity and abject poverty.

Arro, Elmar, Estonian musicologist; b. Riga, July 2, 1899; d. Vienna, Dec. 14, 1985. He studied musicology at the Univ. of Vienna, where he received his Ph.D. in 1928 with the diss. *Über das Musikleben in Estland im 19. Jahrhundert*. In 1933 he joined the faculty of the German Luther Academy in Dorpat; in 1939 he went to Germany and taught at the Univ. of Heidelberg (from 1955) and the Univ. of Kiel (from 1968). He was instrumental in helping to found the Ost-Europa Institut (later the J.G. Herder Forschungsstelle für Musikgeschichte). After settling in Vienna, he founded the journal *Musica slavica*. Arro was an authority on the music of Russia and the Baltic nations. In addition to his important articles in journals, he publ. *Geschichte der estnischen Musik* (Dorpat, 1933), ed. with others *Muzïka sovetskoy Estonii* (Tallinn, 1956), and was founder-ed. of *Musik des Ostens* (1962 et seq.).

Arroyo, Martina, esteemed American soprano of Hispanic and black descent; b. N.Y., Feb. 2, 1936. Her principal teacher was Marinka Gurewich, but she also studied with Turnau at Hunter College of the City Univ. of N.Y. (B.A., 1956). In 1958 she won the Metropolitan Opera Auditions of the Air and made her professional operatic debut in N.Y. in the U.S. premiere of Pizzetti's *Assassinio nella cattedrale*. On March 14, 1959, she made her debut with the Metropolitan Opera as the Celestial Voice in *Don Carlos*; she subsequently sang minor roles there until 1963 when she went to Europe, where she appeared in major roles in Vienna, Düsseldorf, Berlin, and Frankfurt am Main. From 1963 to 1968 she sang in Zürich. On Feb. 6, 1965, she scored a remarkable success at the Metropolitan Opera when she substituted for Birgit Nilsson as Aida. In subsequent years, she sang major roles there, and also appeared at London's Covent Garden (from 1968) and the Paris Opéra (from 1973). In 1989 she retired from the operatic stage. She taught at the Indiana Univ. School of Music in Bloomington from 1993. Arroyo was especially admired in Verdi spinto roles, but she also acquitted herself well as Donna Anna, Liù, Santuzza, and Cio-Cio San. She also proved herself technically equal to the complex soprano parts in the works of such avant-garde composers as Varèse, Dallapiccola, and Stockhausen.

Artyomov, Viacheslav (Petrovich), Russian composer; b. Moscow, June 29, 1940. He studied composition with Pirumov at the Moscow Music School (1958–62) and then at the Moscow Cons. with Sidelnikov, graduating in 1968. Together with Gubaidulina and Suslin, he formed the folk-instrument improvisatory group Astrea in 1975. In his compositions, he applies euphonious dissonances over the basic lines of simulated Russian folk modalities, with asymmetrical rhythms in spasmodically lyric melos.

WORKS: String Quartet (1960); 3 pieces for String Quartet (1960); Piano Concerto (1961); *Chamber Suite* for Wind Quintet (1966); 2 clarinet sonatas (1966, 1971); *Northern Songs* for Mezzo-soprano, Percussion, and Piano (1966); *Jubilee Overture* (1967); *Concerto 13* for Instrumental and Vocal Ensemble (1967); Violin Concerto (1968); *Tempo constante* for Orch. (1970); Accordion Concerto (1971); *Variations* for Flute and Piano (1974); *Capriccio for 1975* for Soprano Saxophone, Baritone Saxophone, and Vibraphone (1975); *Totem* for Percussion Ensemble (1976); *Recitations* for Various Solo Instruments (1976–80); *Elegiac Symphony* for 2 Violins, Percussion, and Strings (1977); *Awakening* for 2 Violins (1978); *The Road to Olympus* for Orch. (1978; Moscow, Oct. 11, 1979); *Invocations* for Soprano and Percussion (1979–80); *Sola Fide*, ballet (1985–87); *Requiem* for Soloists, Chorus, and Orch. (1985–88); *Ave Maria* for Soprano, Chorus, and Orch. (1989).

Artzt, Alice (Josephine), American guitarist; b. Philadelphia, March 16, 1943. She first studied piano and flute, turning to the classical guitar when she was 13 and later studying with Ida Presti and Alexandre Lagoya in France and with Julian Bream in England; also took courses with Lang and Luening at Columbia Univ. (B.A., 1967), and studied composition with Milhaud. She made her formal debut in London in 1969, and subsequently toured throughout the world; she was also active as a teacher, serving on the faculties of the Mannes College of Music in N.Y. (1966–69) and Trenton (N.J.) State College (1977–80).

Arundell, Dennis (Drew), English actor, singer, opera producer, writer on music, and composer; b. London, July 22, 1898; d. there, Dec. 10, 1988. He studied at Tonbridge and with Rootham, Henry Moule, and Stanford at St. John's College, Cambridge. Although he made appearances as an actor and singer, he was particularly noted as an opera producer in Cambridge (from 1922) and at the Sadler's Wells Theatre in London (from 1946). In 1974 he became a teacher at the Royal Northern College of Music in Manchester. In 1978 he was made a Member of the Order of the British Empire. Among his compositions were the operas *Ghost of Abel* and *A Midsummer Night's Dream* (1927). He publ. the vols. *Henry Purcell* (London, 1927), *The Critic at the Opera* (London, 1957), and *The Story of Sadler's Wells* (London, 1965; 2nd ed., 1977).

Arutiunian, Alexander, Armenian composer; b. Yerevan, Sept. 23, 1920. He studied piano and composition at the local cons.; later went to Moscow, where he took a course in composition with Litinsky; then pursued his career in Armenia. In his works, he utilizes authentic folk-song inflections of Armenian popular music; his *Cantata of the Fatherland* on native themes (1948) achieved considerable success. Other important works are his Piano Concerto (1941); Trumpet Concerto (1950); Piano Concertino (1951); Sym. (1957); *Chronicle of the Armenian People*, symphonic poem (1961); Horn Concerto (1962); Concerto for 5 Wind Instruments and Orch. (1964); *Sayat-Nova*, opera (1967); *Ode to Lenin* (1967); *Hymn to Brotherhood* (1970); *My Armenia*, cycle for Chorus (1971); chamber music.

Asafiev, Boris (Vladimirovich), prominent Russian musicologist and composer; b. St. Petersburg, July 29, 1884; d. Moscow, Jan. 27, 1949. He took courses in history and philology at the Univ. of St. Petersburg (graduated, 1908), and in orchestration with Rimsky-Korsakov and in composition with Liadov at the St. Petersburg Cons. (graduated, 1910). In 1914 he began writing music criticism under the pseudonym Igor Glebov. In 1917 he helped to found the music dept. of the Petrograd Inst. of the History of the Arts, becoming director of its music history dept. in 1920. From 1924 to 1928 he was ed. of the journal *Novaya*

Muzyka. From 1925 to 1943 he was prof. of history, theory, and composition at the Leningrad Cons. In 1943 he went to Moscow as a prof. and director of the research section of the Cons., and as a senior research fellow at the Inst. for the History of the Arts. In 1948 he was made chairman of the Union of Soviet Composers. Asafiev was an influential writer on music. Among his works are *Russkaya poeziya v russkoy muzïke* (Russian Poetry in Russian Music; Petrograd, 1921; 2nd ed., rev., 1922); *Instrumental'noye tvorchestvo Chaykovskovo* (Tchaikovsky's Instrumental Works; Petrograd, 1922); *Pyotr Il'ich Chaykovsky: Evo zhizn' i tvorchestvo* (Piotr Ilyich Tchaikovsky: Life and Works; Petrograd, 1922); *Simfonicheskiye etyudï* (Symphonic Studies; Petrograd, 1922; 2nd ed., 1968); *Kniga o Stravinskom* (A Book About Stravinsky; Leningrad, 1929); *Muzïkal'naya forma kak protsess* (Music Form as a Process; 2 vols., Moscow, 1930, 1947; 3rd ed., 1971); *Russkaya muzïka ot nachala XIX stoletiya* (Russian Music from the Beginning of the XIX Century; Moscow, 1930; 2nd ed., 1968, by E. Orlova as *Russkaya muzïka: XIX i nachala XX veka* [Russian Music: The XIX and Early XX Centuries]); *Kompozitorï pervoy polovinï XIX veka: Russkaya klassicheskaya muzïka* (Composers of the First Half of the XIX Century: Russian Classical Music; Moscow, 1945); *Glinka* (Moscow, 1947; 2nd ed., 1950); *Kriticheskiye stat'i, ocherki i retsenzii* (Critical Articles, Essays and Reviews; Moscow, 1967); *Ob opere: Izbranniye stat'i* (Collected Opera Criticism; Leningrad, 1976). As a composer, Asafiev was much less significant. Among his numerous compositions were 11 operas; 28 ballets; 5 syms.: No. 1, *Pamyati Lermontova* (In Memory of Lermontov; 1938), No. 2, *Iz epokh krestyanskikh vosstaniy* (From the Age of the Peasant Uprisings; 1938), No. 3, *Rodina* (Homeland; 1938–42), No. 4, *Privetstvennaya* (Welcome; 1938–42), and No. 5, *Vremena goda* (The Seasons; 1942; unfinished); chamber music; piano pieces; songs.

BIBL: A. Ossovsky, *B.V. A.: Sovetskaya muzïka* (Moscow, 1945); D. Kabalevsky, ed., *Pamyati akademika B.a V.a A.a* (In Memory of the Academician B.V. A.; Moscow, 1951); idem, *B.V. A.— Igor Glebov* (Moscow, 1954); E. Orlova, *B.V. A.: Put' issledovatel'ya i publitsista* (B.V. A.'s Development as a Researcher and Writer; Leningrad, 1964); J. Jiránek, *Asafajevova teorie intonance: Jeji geneze a vyznam* (A.'s Intonation Theory: Its Origins and Significance; Prague, 1967).

Aschaffenburg, Walter, German-born American composer and teacher; b. Essen, May 20, 1927. He went to the U.S. at the age of 11 and in 1944 became a naturalized American citizen. He studied composition with Robert Doellner at the Hartt School of Music in Hartford, Conn. (1945), Elwell at the Oberlin (Ohio) College Cons. of Music (B.A., 1951), Rogers at the Eastman School of Music in Rochester, N.Y. (M.A., 1952), and Dallapiccola in Florence (1956). In 1952 he joined the faculty of the Oberlin College Cons. of Music, serving as chairman of its theory dept. (1968–73). In 1971 he was made a prof. of composition and theory, and in 1983 chairman of the composition dept., positions he held until his retirement in 1987. In 1955–56 and 1973–74 he held Guggenheim fellowships. While Aschaffenburg has employed the 12-tone system in some of his works, his scores are often embued with a meticulous expressivity.

WORKS: DRAMATIC: *The Flies*, incidental music to Sartre's play (1953); *Bartleby*, opera (1956–62; Oberlin, Nov. 12, 1964). **ORCH.:** *Oedipus Rex*, overture (1951); *Ozymandias* (Rochester, N.Y., April 22, 1952); *Elegy* for Strings (1961); *3 Dances* (1966–67); Oboe Concerto (1985; Oberlin, Jan. 25, 1987). **CHAMBER:** Trio for Piano, Violin, and Cello (1950–51); *Divertimento* for Trumpet, Horn, and Trombone (1951); *Chaconne* for Brass Ensemble (1952); Cello Sonata (1953); Sonata for Solo Violin (1954); String Quartet (1955); *Festive Music* for Winds (1963); Wind Quintet (1967); *Proem* for Brass and Percussion (1968–69); *fan-FARE for HErmAN Melville* for 2 Trumpets and Trombone (1969); *Blossom Music Center Fanfare* for 2 Trumpets and 2 Horns (1970); Duo for Violin and Cello (1971); *A Slight Music* for Clarinet, Bassoon, and Tuba (1975); Concertino for Violin, 10 Winds, and Contrabass (1979–81); *Festive Fanfare and Hymn* for Brass and Percussion (1983); *. . . from South Mountain* for Brass Quintet (1987); *Coalescence* for Oboe and Cello (1989); *Parings*, 4 pieces for Clarinet and Piano (1992–93). **PIANO:** Sonatina (1953–54); *Conversations*, 6 pieces (1973); *Carousel*, 24 little pieces (1980); Sonata for Fortepiano or Piano (1990). **VOCAL:** *The 23rd Psalm* for Tenor, Chorus, Oboe, and Organ (1963); *3 Shakespeare Sonnets* for Tenor and Piano (1966–67); *Libertatem Appellant* for Tenor, Baritone, and Orch. (1974–76); *Laughing Time* for Chorus and Clown (1983).

Ascher, Leo, Austrian composer; b. Vienna, Aug. 17, 1880; d. N.Y., Feb. 25, 1942. He received training in law and music. The success of his first operetta, *Vergeltsgott* or *Der Bettlerklub* (Vienna, Oct. 14, 1905), encouraged him to devote himself to composing for the theater. His first major work, *Die arme Lori* (Vienna, March 12, 1909), was followed by his first notable success, *Hoheit tanzt Walzer* (Vienna, Feb. 24, 1912); then followied the highly successful scores *Was tut man nicht alles aus Liebe* (Vienna, Dec. 17, 1914), *Botschafterin Leni* (Vienna, Feb. 19, 1915), *Der Soldat der Marie* (Berlin, Sept. 2, 1916), *Egon und seine Frauen* (Berlin, Aug. 25, 1917), and *Bruder Leichtsinn* (Vienna, Dec. 28, 1917). Among his later works were *Der Künstlerpreis* (Vienna, Oct. 1, 1919), *Was Mädchen träumen* (Vienna, Dec. 6, 1919), *Princessin Friedl* (Berlin, May 14, 1920), *Zwölf Uhr Nachts!* (Vienna, Nov. 12, 1920), *Baronesschen Sarah* (Berlin, Dec. 25, 1920), *Ein Jahr ohne Liebe* (Berlin, Jan. 12, 1923), *Sonja* (Vienna, March 6, 1925), *Das Amorettenhaus* (Hamburg, Jan. 1926), *Ich hab' dich Lieb . . .* (Vienna, April 16, 1926), *Ninon am Scheideweg* (Berlin, Dec. 27, 1926), *Frühling in Wienerwald* (Vienna, April 17, 1930), and *Bravo Peggy!* (Leipzig, March 27, 1932). He also composed film scores for *Purpur und Waschblau* (1931) and *Mein Leopold* (1932). His last stage work was *Um ein bisschen Liebe* (Vienna, June 5, 1936). With the Anschluss in 1938, Ascher emigrated to the U.S.

Ascone, Vicente, Uruguayan composer of Italian descent; b. Siderno, Aug. 16, 1897; d. Montevideo, March 5, 1979. He was taken to Uruguay as a child, where he studied trumpet and composition. Most of his music is rooted in Uruguayan folk songs, while stylistically he followed traditional Italian formulas. He wrote 5 operas, including *Paraná Gauzú*, based on an Indian subject, which was premiered in Montevideo on July 25, 1931. He further wrote 3 syms. (1945, 1955, 1959); *Sobre el Río Uruguay*, symphonic poem (1946); *Politonal* for Piano and Orch. (1967); Trumpet Concerto (1969); Violin Concerto (1970); numerous songs.

Ashforth, Alden (Banning), American composer, teacher, and writer on music; b. N.Y., May 13, 1933. He studied at Oberlin (Ohio) College (A.B., 1958) and composition with Joseph Wood and Richard Hoffmann at its Cons. (Mus.B., 1958); subsequently took courses with Sessions, Milton Babbitt, and Earl Kim at Princeton Univ. (M.F.A., 1960; Ph.D., 1971). He taught at Princeton Univ. (1961), Oberlin College (1961–65), N.Y. Univ. (1965–66), the City College of the City Univ. of N.Y. (1966–67), and the Univ. of Calif. at Los Angeles (from 1967). He was active as a jazz researcher and as a recorder/producer of many jazz recordings; also contributed articles to the *Annual Review of Jazz Studies* and to *The New Grove Dictionary of Jazz*.

WORKS: DRAMATIC: *The Quintessential Zymurgistic Waffle*, musical comedy (1975; in collaboration with P. Reale). **ORCH.:** *Variations* (1958). **CHAMBER:** Piano Sonata (1955); Sonata for Flute and Harpsichord (1956); *Fantasy-Variations* for Violin and Piano (1959); *Episodes*, chamber concerto for 8 Instruments (1962–68); *Pas seul* for Flute (1974); *The Flowers of Orcus (Intavolatura)* for Guitar (1976); *St. Bride's Suite* for Harpsichord (1983); other piano pieces. **VOCAL:** *The Unquiet Heart* for Soprano, and Chamber Orch. or Piano (1959–68); choral pieces; songs. **ELECTRONIC:** *Cycles* (1965); *Mixed Brew* (1968); *Byzantia: 2 Journeys after Yeats* for Organ and Tape (1971–73).

Ashkenazy, Vladimir (Davidovich), greatly gifted Russian-born Icelandic pianist and conductor; b. Gorki, July 6, 1937. His parents were professional pianists and taught him to play at an early age; subsequently he took formal lessons with Anaida Sumbatian at the Central Music School in Moscow (from 1945), and in 1955 entered the class of Oborin at the Moscow Cons. (graduated, 1963). In 1955 he won 2nd prize at the Chopin Competition in Warsaw. A great turning point in his career was reached when in 1956, at the age of 19, he won 1st prize in the Queen Elisabeth of Belgium Competition in Brussels; in 1958 he made his first tour of the U.S.; in 1962 he and John Ogdon were both awarded 1st prizes in the Tchaikovsky Competition in Moscow. In 1961 he married a young pianist, Sofia Johannsdottir of Iceland, who was studying in Moscow at the time. In 1963 they went to England while retaining their common Soviet citizenship. In 1968 they moved to Reykjavík, and in 1972 Ashkenazy became a naturalized Icelandic citizen. He was also drawn into conducting, and in 1981 was appointed principal guest conductor of the Philharmonia Orch. of London. From 1987 to 1994 he was music director of the Royal Phil. in London; was also principal guest conductor of the Cleveland Orch. (1987–94) and chief conductor of the (West) Berlin Radio Sym. Orch. (from 1989), and of its successor, the Deutsches Symphonie Orchester Berlin (from 1994). With J. Parrott, he brought out the book *A.: Beyond Frontiers* (London, 1984). As a piano virtuoso, Ashkenazy has gained an international reputation for his penetrating insight and superlative technique; his mastery extends from Haydn to the contemporary era. As a conductor, he has demonstrated particular affinity for the 19th- and 20th-century repertoire. He has prepared and conducted his own effective orchestration of Mussorgsky's *Pictures at an Exhibition*.

Ashley, Robert (Reynolds), pioneering American composer, performer, director, and writer; b. Ann Arbor, Mich., March 28, 1930. He studied theory at the Univ. of Mich. (B.Mus., 1952) and piano and composition with Wallingford Riegger at the Manhattan School of Music in N.Y. (M.Mus., 1954); then returned to the Univ. of Mich. for further composition study with Ross Lee Finney, Leslie Bassett, and Roberto Gerhard (1957–60), where he also took courses in psychoacoustics and cultural speech patterns at its Speech Research Laboratories and was employed as a research assistant (1960–61) in acoustics at its Architectural Research Laboratory. He was active with Milton Cohen's Space Theater (1957–64), the ONCE Festival and ONCE Group (1958–69), and the Sonic Arts Union (1966–76), touring widely with them in the U.S. and Europe; also served as director of the Center for Contemporary Music at Mills College in Oakland, California (1970–81). As the first opera composer of the post-proscenium age, Ashley is one of the most influential and highly acclaimed artists in the 20th-century avant-garde music and experimental performance tradition. He has produced several hundred music and music-theater compositions for live performance as well as audio and video recordings and broadcast television series, which have been performed the throughout the world. In his compositions from the mid-1970s, often experimental, technologically-driven, and collaborative, he has developed a complex, episodic treatment of his materials, marked by striking imagery, textual multiplicity, and a graceful and highly individualized integration of speech and song. Ashley has also provided music for the dance companies of Douglas Dunn (*Idea from the Church*, 1978), Steve Paxton (*The Park* and *The Backyard*, 1978), Trisha Brown (*Son of Gone Fishin'*, 1983), and Merce Cunningham (*Problems in the Flying Saucer*, 1988). In 1995 he was commissioned by the Florida Grand Opera, Miami-Dade Community College, and the South Florida Composers Alliance to do a new opera based on the lives of the *balseros* (the Cuban "rafters"), to be premiered in 1997. He was married first to the artist Mary Ashley, with whom he collaborated; then to Mimi Johnson, director of Performing Artservices in N.Y. Ashley is one of four featured composers (with Cage, Glass, and Anderson) in Peter Greenaway's video series, *Four American Composers*. His *Perfect Lives* was published, in book form, in 1991.

WORKS: OPERAS: *The Wolfman* for Amplified Voice and *The Wolfman Tape* (1964); *That Morning Thing* for 5 Principal Voices, 8 Dancers, Women's Chorus, and Tape, in 4 parts: *Four Ways, Frogs, Purposeful Lady Slow Afternoon,* and *She Was A Visitor* (1967; Ann Arbor, Feb. 8, 1968); *Music with Roots in the Aether*, television opera for Voices and Electronics (Paris, 1976); *Title Withdrawn*, television opera for Voices and Electronics (Paris, 1976; from *Music with Roots in the Aether*); *What She Thinks*, television opera for Voices and Electronics (1976; from *Music with Roots in the Aether*); *Perfect Lives (Private Parts)*, television opera for Voices, Piano, and Electronic Orch. (1978–80), in 7 parts: *The Backyard, The Bank, The Bar, The Church, The Living Room, The Park,* and *The Supermarket*); *Music Word Fire And I Would Do It Again Coo Coo: The Lessons*, television opera for Voices, Piano, and Electronic Orch. (1981); *Atalanta (Acts of God)*, television opera for Voice, Chorus, and Instruments (Paris, 1982; concert version as *Atalanta (Acts of God), aka Songs from Atalanta* for Voice, Chorus, and Instruments, 1982); *Tap Dancing in the Sand* for Voice (1982); *Atalanta Strategy*, television opera (N.Y., 1984); *Now Eleanor's Idea*, tetralogy: *I: Improvement (Don Leaves Linda)* (1984–85), *II: Foreign Experiences* (1994), *III: el/Aficionado* (1987), and *Now Eleanor's Idea* (1993); *Yellow Man with Heart with Wings* for Voice and Tape (1990); *Love is a Good Example* for Voice (1994); *When Famous Last Words Fail You* for Voice (1994); *Yes, But is it Edible?* for Voice (1994). **ELECTRONIC MUSIC THEATER:** *# + Heat* (1961); *Public Opinion Descends Upon the Demonstrators* (1961; Ann Arbor, Feb. 18, 1962); *Boxing* (1963; Detroit, April 9, 1964); *Combination Wedding and Funeral* (1964; N.Y., May 9, 1965); *Interludes for the Space Theater* (1964; Cleveland, May 4, 1965); *Kitty Hawk (An Antigravity Piece)* (1964; St. Louis, March 21, 1965); *The Lecture Series* (1964; N.Y., May 9, 1965; in collaboration with M. Ashley); *The Wolfman Motorcity Revue* (1964; Newport Beach, Calif., Jan. 11, 1969); *Morton Feldman Says* (1965); *Orange Dessert* (1965; Ann Arbor, April 9, 1966); *Night Train* (1966; Waltham, Mass., Jan. 7, 1967; in collaboration with M. Ashley); *Unmarked Interchange* (Ann Arbor, Sept. 17, 1965); *The Trial of Anne Opie Wehrer and Unknown Accomplices for Crimes Against Humanity* (Sheboygan, Wis., April 30, 1968); *Fancy Free or It's There* (1970; Ann Arbor, April 1971); *Illusion Models* (1970); *It's There* (Brussels, April 1970); *Night Sport* (L'Aquila, Italy, April 1973); *Over the Telephone* (N.Y., March 1975). **INSTRUMENTAL:** *Piano Sonata (Christopher Columbus Crosses to the New World in the Niña, the Pinta, and the Santa Maria Using Only Dead Reckoning and a Crude Astrolabe)* (1959; rev. 1979); *Maneuvres for Small Hands* for Piano (1961); *Fives* for 2 Pianos, 2 Percussion, and String Quartet (1962); *Details* for 2 Pianos (1962); *In Memoriam . . . Crazy Horse* for 20 or More Wind, String, or Sustaining Instruments (1963); *In Memoriam . . . Esteban Gomez* for 4 Instrumentalists (1963); *In Memoriam . . . John Smith* for 3 Instrumentalists (1963); *In Memoriam . . . Kit Carson* for 8-part Ensemble (1963); *Trios (White on White)* for Any Sustaining Instruments, Gongs, and Voice (1963); *The Entrance* for Electric Organ (1965); *Waiting Room* for Wind or String Quartet (1965; rev. 1978); *Revised, Finally, for Gordon Mumma* for Pairs of Bell-like Instruments (1973); *Odalisque* for Voice, Chorus, and 24 Instruments (1973); *Basic 10* for Snare Drum (1988); *Superior Seven* for Flute, Chorus, and Instruments (1988); *Outcome Inevitable* for Chamber Orch. of 8 or More (1991); *Van Cao's Meditation* for Piano (1991); *Tract* for Voice and String Trio or 2 Keyboards (1992). **WITH ELECTRONICS:** *Something* for Clarinet, Pianos and Tape (1961); *Complete with Heat* for Instruments and Tape (1962); *In Sara, Mencken, Christ and Beethoven There Were Men and Women* for Voice and Electronics (1972); *String Quartet Describing the Motions of Large Real Bodies* for String Quartet and Electronics (1972); *How Can*

I Tell The Difference? for Violin or Viola, Electronics, and Tape (1974); *Automatic Writing* for Voices, Keyboards, and Electronics (1979). **TAPE:** *The Fourth of July* (1960); *Big Danger in Five Parts* (1962); *Detroit Divided* (1962); *Heat* (1962); *The Wolfman Tape* (1964); *Untitled Mixes* for Jazz Trio and Tape (1965); *Interiors Without Flash* (1979); *Factory Preset* (1993). **FILM:** (in collaboration with G. Manupelli unless otherwise given): *The Image in Time* (1957); *Bottleman* (1960); *The House* (1961); *Jenny and the Poet* (1964); *My May* (1965); *Overdrive* (1967); *Dr. Chicago* (in 4 parts: *Dr. Chicago, Dr. Chicago Goes to Sweden, Ride, Dr. Chicago, Ride,* and *Cry Dr. Chicago*; 1968–70); *Portraits, Self-Portraits and Still Lifes* (1969); *Battery Davis* (1970; in collaboration with P. Makanna). **VIDEO:** *The Great Northern Automobile Presence* (1975); *What She Thinks* (1976). **TELEVISION:** *Music Word Fire* (N.Y., Channel 13/WNET, 1981).

BIBL.: N. Osterreich, "Music with Roots in the Aether," *Perspectives of New Music,* 16/1 (1977); C. Gagne and T. Caras, "R. A.," in *Soundpieces: Interviews with American Composers* (Metuchen, N.J., 1982); J. Rockwell, "Post-Cageian Experimentation and New Kinds of Collaboration: R. A.," *All-American Music: Composition in the Late Twentieth Century* (N.Y., 1983); T. DeLio, *Circumscribing the Open Universe: Essays on Cage, Feldman, Wolff, A. and Lucier* (Washington, D.C., 1984).

Ashrafi, Mukhtar, Russian composer; b. Bukhara, June 11, 1912; d. Tashkent, Dec. 15, 1975. He studied at the Moscow Cons. (1934–37) and later at the Leningrad Cons. (1941–43). As the war situation led to a siege of Leningrad, he was evacuated to Tashkent. Since he never acquired comprehensive technique of composition, his operas were orchestrated by his teacher at the Moscow Cons., Vasilenkov; 2 were premiered in Tashkent: *Buran* (June 12, 1939) and *The Grand Canal* (Jan. 12, 1941). He further wrote several ballets and 2 syms. on patriotic themes, several orch. suites on central Asian themes, and a number of songs.

Asia, Daniel, American composer and teacher; b. Seattle, June 27, 1953. He was a student of Stephen Albert at Smith College and of Druckman, Weisberg, and Penderecki at the Yale School of Music (M.M., 1977). He taught at the Oberlin (Ohio) College Cons. of Music (1981–86) and lectured at London's City Univ. In 1988 he became head of the composition dept. at the Univ. of Arizona in Tucson. He also served as composer-in-residence of the Phoenix Sym. Orch. from 1991. His music belies a variety of American influences, ranging from Copland and Bernstein to John Adams and Druckman.

WORKS: ORCH.: 4 syms.: No. 1 (1987; Seattle, Feb. 19, 1990), No. 2, *Celebration Symphony, In Memory of Leonard Bernstein* (1989–90; Tucson, April 30, 1992), No. 3 (1991–2; Phoenix, May 6, 1992), and No. 4 (1993–94); *Black Light* (1990; N.Y., Oct. 13, 1991); *At the Far Edge* (1991); Piano Concerto (1994; Grand Rapids, Feb. 10, 1995). **CHAMBER:** *Piano Set I* (1976) and *II* (1977); *Dream Sequence I* for Amplified Trombone (1976) and *II* for Flute (1989); String Quartet No. 1 (1976–77); *Sand I* for Flute, Horn, and Double Bass (1977); *Live Images* for 4 Woodwinds (1978); *Rivalries* for Chamber Ensemble (1980); *Scherzo Sonata* for Piano (1978); Piano Quartet (1989). **VOCAL:** *Sand II* for Mezzo- soprano and Chamber Orch. (1978); *Ossabaw Island Dream* for Mezzo-soprano and Chamber Orch. (1982); *Celebration* for Baritone, Chorus, Brass Quintet, and Organ (1988).

Askenase, Stefan, Polish-born Belgian pianist and pedagogue; b. Lemberg, July 10, 1896; d. Bonn, Oct. 18, 1985. He studied with Theodor Pollak in Lemberg and Emil von Sauer at the Vienna Academy of Music. In 1919 he made his debut in Vienna, and subsequently toured throughout the world. He also taught at the Rotterdam Cons. (1937–40) and the Brussels Cons. (1954–61). In 1950 he became a naturalized Belgian citizen. Askenase distinguished himself as an interpreter of Chopin. He publ. the vol. *Wie Meister üben I* (Zürich, 1966).

Asriel, André, Austrian composer; b. Vienna, Feb. 22, 1922. He was enrolled in the Vienna Academy of Music at the age of 13; in 1938, went to England, where he took courses at the Royal College of Music in London. In 1946 he went to East Berlin and studied piano and composition at the Hochschule für Musik; also had lessons with Eisler at the Academy of the Arts. In 1951 he was appointed instructor at the newly founded Deutsche Hochschule für Musik; from 1967 to 1984 he was a prof. there. He wrote a number of songs on socialist themes, among them *Freundschaft, Einheit, Frieden,* and *Das neue Deutschland*; he further composed music for film documentaries; also became interested in jazz as a type of American folk music. He wrote a cycle of choral pieces to texts from Aesop's fables. Among his purely instrumental works are *4 Inventions* for Trumpet, Trombone, and Orch. (1963) and *Serenade* for 9 Instruments (1969). He also publ. *Jazz Analysen und Aspekte* (Berlin, 1966; 4th ed., 1984).

Aston, Peter (George), English conductor, teacher, and composer; b. Birmingham, Oct. 5, 1938. He studied composition and conducting at the Birmingham School of Music before completing his education at the Univ. of York (Ph.D., 1970, with the diss. *George Jeffreys and the English Baroque*). From 1958 to 1965 he was director of the Tudor Consort, and then of the English Baroque Ensemble (1968–70); subsequently was conductor of the Aldeburgh Festival Singers (1975–88). He lectured at the Univ. of York (1964–72), where he then was senior lecturer in music (1972–74); subsequently served as prof. and head of music at the Univ. of East Anglia (from 1974), where he also was dean of the School of Fine Arts and Music (1981–84). He ed. the complete works of George Jeffreys, and publ. the vols. *Sound and Silence* (1970), *The Music of York Minster* (1972), and *Music Theory in Practice* (3 vols., 1992–93). He composed mainly sacred and secular vocal music, including *5 Songs of Crazy Jane* for Soprano (1963); *3 Shakespeare Songs* for Soprano and Chorus (1964); *My Dancing Day,* cantata for Soprano, Tenor, Flute, Clarinet, and String Quartet (1966); *Sacrapant, the Sorcerer,* children's opera (1967); *Haec Dies,* Resurrection cantata for Chorus and Organ (1972); *Carmen Luminis,* cantata for Small Chorus and Wind Quintet (1975); *The True Glory* for Chorus and Orch. or Organ (1976); *A Song of the Lord, thy Keeper* for Chorus, String Orch., Piano, and Percussion (1983); *From the Book of Thel,* threnody for 5 Solo Voices or Small Chorus (1983); *A Mass for All Saints* for Chorus and Organ (1987); *Great Is the Lord* for Chorus and Organ (1988); also orch. pieces and chamber works.

Åstrand, (Karl) Hans (Vilhelm), Swedish music historian and lexicographer; b. Bredaryd, Feb. 5, 1925. He studied organ, double bass, and cello; also took courses in Romance languages at the Univ. of Lund (Licentiate, 1958). He was music critic of the Malmö newspaper *Kvällsposten* (from 1950), founder-director of the Chamber Choir '53 (1953–62), and founder (1960) and director (1965–71) of the Ars Nova Soc. for New Music. From 1963 to 1971 he taught music history at the Malmö National School of Drama, and then was music critic of Stockholm's *Veckojournalen* (from 1976). He served as ed. in chief of the fundamental Swedish musical encyclopedia, *Sohlmans musik-lexikon* (5 vols., Stockholm, 1975–79). He was a board member (from 1966) and perpetual secretary (from 1973) of the Royal Swedish Academy of Music in Stockholm. In 1983 he was made a prof. and in 1985 received an honorary doctorate at the Univ. of Lund. Åstrand also contributed various articles on musicological and general music subjects to many books and journals.

BIBL.: B. van Boer, Jr., ed., *Gustav III and the Swedish Stage: Opera, Theatre and Other Foibles: Essays in Honor of H. A.* (Lewiston, Queenston, and Lampeter, 1993).

Asuar, José Vicente, Chilean composer; b. Santiago, July 20, 1933. He studied electrical engineering and music, first in Santiago and later in Berlin. From 1963 to 1965 he was prof. of acoustics and contemporary music at the Santiago National Cons.; from 1965 to 1968 he led a studio for electronic music in Caracas; he composed and performed there a multimedia work, *Imagen de Caracas*, employing synchronized projectors of 8 films plus chorus and orch.; from 1968 to 1972 he directed a course in sound technology at the Univ. of Chile. He composed mostly for electronic tape.

Atanasov, Georgi, Bulgarian composer and bandmaster; b. Plovdiv, May 18, 1881; d. Fasano, Italy, Nov. 17, 1931. He went to Italy in 1901, and took lessons in composition with Mascagni at the Pesaro Cons. Returning to Bulgaria, he became active as a military bandmaster, as well as a composer. He wrote 2 of the earliest operas on national Bulgarian subjects, *Borislav* (Sofia, March 4, 1911) and *Gergana* (Sofia, June 19, 1917); other operas were *Zapustialata vodenitza* (The Abandoned Mill; Sofia, March 31, 1923), *Altzek*, and *Tzveta*; he also wrote 2 children's operas, *The Sick Teacher* and *About Birds*.

BIBL.: I. Sagaev, *Maestro G. A.* (Sofia, 1961).

Atanasov, Nikola, Bulgarian conductor, teacher, and composer; b. Kyustendil, Oct. 25, 1886; d. Sofia, Sept. 30, 1969. He studied with F. Dugan at the Croatian Cons. in Zagreb; after teaching music in Stara-Zagora (1913–22), he was active in Sofia as a conductor (1923–48), and also as a prof. (from 1929) and director (1934–37) of the Cons. In 1912 he wrote the first Bulgarian sym.; composed two more syms. (1922, 1950), as well as 2 overtures, *Christo Botev* (1928) and *Forest Murmurs* (1931); also chamber music; piano pieces; songs.

BIBL.: P. Londev, *N. A.* (Sofia, 1963).

Atherton, David, English conductor; b. Blackpool, Jan. 3, 1944. He was educated at the Univ. of Cambridge, and in London at the Royal Academy of Music and the Guildhall School of Music. In 1967 he founded the London Sinfonietta, serving as its music director until 1973. From 1968 to 1980 he was resident conductor at London's Covent Garden. He was principal conductor and artistic advisor of the Royal Liverpool Phil. (1980–83), and then was its principal guest conductor (1983–86). From 1981 to 1987 he served as music director of the San Diego Sym. Orch. He was principal guest conductor of the BBC Sym. Orch. in London (1985–90), and also was music director of the Hong Kong Phil. (from 1989) and again of the London Sinfonietta (1989–91).

Atkins, Sir Ivor (Algernon), English organist, conductor, and composer; b. Llandaff, Nov. 29, 1869; d. Worcester, Nov. 26, 1953. He studied in Truro and Hereford. From 1897 to 1950 he served as organist at Worcester Cathedral, and also was conductor of the Three Choirs Festivals for more than 50 years. He was knighted in 1921. Atkins championed the music of Elgar and was active as an ed. of the music of Bach. His own output consisted of choral music.

Atlantov, Vladimir (Andreievich), distinguished Russian tenor and baritone; b. Leningrad, Feb. 19, 1939. He studied with Bolotina at the Leningrad Cons., taking the Glinka Prize in 1962 and graduating in 1963. After making his formal operatic debut at Leningrad's Kirov Theater in 1963, he was a student artist at Milan's La Scala (1963–65). He was a medalist at the Tchaikovsky Competition in Moscow in 1966, and in competitions in Montreal and Sofia in 1967. In 1967 he became a member of the Bolshoi Theater in Moscow, with which he later toured with notable success to Milan, N.Y., Paris, and Vienna. From 1977 he also sang baritone roles. In 1987 he made his debut at London's Covent Garden as Otello, one of his most famous roles. In 1990 he sang for the first time with an American opera company when he appeared as Canio with the San Francisco Opera. He also toured extensively as a concert artist. In addition to the Russian repertoire, Atlantov is esteemed for his portrayals of Don José, Cavardossi, Alfredo, Radames, Posa, and Siegmund.

Atlas, Allan W(arren), American musicologist; b. N.Y., Feb. 19, 1943. He was educated at Hunter College (B.A., 1964) and N.Y. Univ. (M.A., 1966; Ph.D., 1971, with the diss. *The Cappella Giulia Chansonnier and the Dissemination of the Franco-Netherlandish Chanson in Italy, c.1460–c.1520*). In 1971 he was appointed to the faculty of Brooklyn College. He contributed numerous articles to *The New Grove Dictionary of Music and Musicians* (1980); ed. *The Cappella Giulia Chansonnier: Rome, Biblioteca Apostolica Vaticana, C.G.XIII.27* (2 vols., N.Y., 1975–76), *Papers Read at the Dufay Quincentenary Conference, Brooklyn College, December 6–7, 1974* (Brooklyn, 1976), *Robert Morton: The Collected Works* (N.Y., 1981), *Aedvardus of Ortona: Missa Sine nomine* (Newton Abbot, 1985), and *Music in the Classic Period: Essays in Honor of Barry S. Brook* (N.Y., 1985). He wrote the important study *Music at the Aragonese Court of Naples* (Cambridge, 1985).

Atlas, Dalia (née **Sternberg**), Israeli conductor; b. Haifa, Nov. 14, 1933. After piano training at the Rubin Academy of Music in Jerusalem (graduated, 1952), she studied conducting with various mentors abroad, including Ferrara, Celibidache, Swarowsky, and Boulez. She was the first woman to obtain prizes in the Cantelli (Novara, 1963), Mitropoulos (N.Y., 1964), and Royal Liverpool Phil. (1964) conducting competitions; she later received the Eugene Ormandy Award (Philadelphia, 1980). In the meantime, she launched her career in her homeland by founding the Israel Pro-Musica Orch. After joining the faculty of the Technion Inst. of Technology in Haifa, she founded its sym. orch. and choir; later founded the Atlas Camerata, a chamber orch., which she conducted on a world tour in 1991. As a guest conductor, she appeared with major orchs. in Europe, the U.S., and Australia.

Atterberg, Kurt (Magnus), eminent Swedish composer; b. Göteborg, Dec. 12, 1887; d. Stockholm, Feb. 15, 1974. He studied engineering and was employed in the wireless service; then took courses in composition at the Stockholm Cons. with Hallén, and in Berlin with Schillings (1910–12). In 1913 he was appointed conductor at the Drama Theater in Stockholm, holding this post until 1922; in 1919 he began writing music criticism and continued to contribute to Stockholm newspapers until 1957; concurrently he was also employed at the Swedish patent office (1912–68) and served as secretary of the Royal Swedish Academy of Music in Stockholm (1940–53). He was one of the founders of the Soc. of Swedish Composers in 1924, and was on its board until 1947. During all this time, he continued to compose with inexhaustible energy, producing works in all genres: operas, ballets, syms., concertos, choruses, and chamber music, all with preordained precision of form and technique. It is ironic that his music remained hermetically sealed within the confines of Sweden, rarely if ever performed beyond its borders. Atterberg's name attracted unexpected attention when he was declared winner of the ill-conceived Schubert Centennial Contest organized in 1928 by the Columbia Phonograph Co., with the declared intention to finish Schubert's *Unfinished Symphony*. The entire venture was severely criticized in musical circles as an attempt to derive commercial advantage under the guise of an homage to a great composer. Rumors spread that Atterberg had deliberately imitated the style of composition of some members of the jury (Glazunov, Alfano, Nielsen) in order to ingratiate himself with them so as to secure the prize, but Atterberg denied any such suggestion, pointing out that he knew the names only of those in the jury from the Nordic zone, whereas the international membership comprised 10 national zones. Furthermore, the sym. he had submitted was written in a far more advanced style than Atterberg's previous symphonic works and was certainly much more modern than any music by the jury members, using as it did such procedures as polytonality. There can be no doubt, however, that Atterberg was a master technician of his craft, and that his music had a powerful appeal. That it never gained a wider audience can be ascribed only to an unfathomable accident of world culture.

WORKS: DRAMATIC: OPERAS (all first perf. in Stockholm): *Härvard Harpolekare* (Härvard the Potter; 1915–17; Sept. 29, 1919; rev. as *Harvard der Harfner* and perf. in German at Chemnitz, 1936; a later ver. with new 3rd act perf. in Linz, June

14, 1952); *Bäckahästen* (1923–24; Jan. 23, 1925); *Fanal* (1929–32; Jan. 27, 1934); *Aladdin* (1936–41; March 18, 1941); *Stormen*, after Shakespeare's *Tempest* (1946–47; Sept. 19, 1948). **BALLETS:** *Per Svinaherde* (Peter the Swineherd; 1914–15); *De fåvitska jungfrurna*, ballet-pantomime (The Wise and Foolish Virgins; Paris, Nov. 18, 1920). **ORCH.:** 9 numbered syms.: No. 1 (1909–11; Stockholm, Jan. 10, 1912), No. 2 (1911–13; Stockholm, Feb. 11, 1912), No. 3 (1914–16; Stockholm, Nov. 28, 1916), No. 4, *Sinfonia piccola* (1918; Stockholm, March 27, 1919), No. 5, *Sinfonia funèbre* (1919–22; Stockholm, Jan. 6, 1923), No. 6 (1927–28; Stockholm, Oct. 15, 1928), No. 7, *Sinfonia romantica* (1942; Frankfurt am Main, Feb. 14, 1943), No. 8 (1944; Helsinki, Feb. 9, 1945), and No. 9, *Sinfonia visionaria*, for Mezzo-soprano, Baritone, Chorus, and Orch. (1955–56; Helsinki, Feb. 26, 1957); also a Sinfonia for Strings (1952–53); 9 suites, among them No. 3, for Violin, Viola, and Strings (1917), No. 4, *Turandot* (1921), No. 5, *Suite barocco* (1922), and No. 8, *Suite pastorale* (1931); *Rhapsody* for Piano and Orch. (1909); Violin Concerto (1913; Göteborg, Feb. 11, 1914); Cello Concerto (1917–22; Berlin, Jan. 6, 1923); 2 Suites for the play *Stormen*, after Shakespeare's *Tempest*: No. 1 (1921; rev. 1962–63) and No. 2 (1964–65); *Rondeau retrospectif* (1926); Horn Concerto (1926; Stockholm, March 20, 1927); Piano Concerto (1927–35; Stockholm, Jan. 12, 1936); *Älven* (The River), symphonic poem (1929–30); *Varmlandsrhapsodie* for Selma Langerlöf's 75th birthday (Swedish Radio, Nov. 20, 1933); *Ballad and Passacaglia* (1936); *Rondeau caractéristique* (1939–40); *Indian Tunes* (1950); *Ballad utan ord* (Ballad without Words; 1957–58); Concerto for Violin, Cello or Viola, and Orch. (1959–60; ver. with String Orch., 1963); *Vittorioso* (1962); *Adagio amoroso* for Flute and Strings (1967). **CHAMBER:** 2 string quartets (1915, 1937); Cello Sonata (1925); Piano Quintet (1927); *Variations and Fugue* for String Quartet (1943); *Trio concertante* for Violin, Cello, and Harp (1959–60; rev. 1965). **VOCAL:** *Requiem* (1913); *Järnbäraland*, cantata (1919).

Atzmon (real name, **Groszberger**), **Moshe,** Hungarian-born Israeli conductor; b. Budapest, July 30, 1931. He was taken to Palestine in 1944, where he attended the Tel Aviv Academy of Music (1958–62); then pursued conducting studies at the Guildhall School of Music in London. In 1964 he won 1st prize in the Liverpool conducting competition, and then appeared as a guest conductor with various British orchs. He was chief conductor of the Sydney (Australia) Sym. Orch. (1969–71), the North German Radio Sym. Orch. in Hamburg (1972–76), the Basel Sym. Orch. (1972–77), and the Tokyo Metropolitan Sym. Orch. (1978–82). With Giuseppe Patane, he served as co-principal conductor of the American Sym. Orch. in N.Y. (1982–84); then was chief conductor of the Nagoya Phil. in Japan (1986–92). From 1991 he was Generalmusikdirektor of the Dortmund Opera.

Aubert, Louis-François-Marie, French composer; b. Paramé, Ille-et-Vilaine, Feb. 19, 1877; d. Paris, Jan. 9, 1968. Of precocious talent, he entered the Paris Cons. as a child, and studied piano with Diémer, theory with Lavignac, and advanced composition with Fauré; also sang in church choirs. His song *Rimes tendres* was publ. when he was 19. His *Fantaisie* for Piano and Orch. was performed in Paris by the Colonne Orch. with Diémer as soloist (Nov. 17, 1901). His *Suite brève* for 2 Pianos was presented at the Paris Exposition in 1900; an orch. version of it was performed for the first time in Paris on April 27, 1916. Aubert's major work was an operatic fairy tale, *La Forêt bleue* (Geneva, Jan. 7, 1913); a Russian production was given in Boston on March 8, 1913, attracting considerable attention. The Paris production of *La Forêt bleue*, delayed by World War I, took place on June 10, 1924, at the Opéra-Comique. Aubert's style was largely determined by the impressionistic currents of the early 20th century; like Debussy and Ravel, he was attracted by the music of Spain and wrote several pieces in the Spanish idiom, of which the symphonic poem *Habanera* (Paris, March 22, 1919) was particularly successful. The list of Aubert's works further includes: *La Légende du sang* for Narrator, Chorus, and Orch. (1902); 3 ballets: *La Momie* (1903); *Chrysothémis* (1904); *La Nuit ensorcélée* (1922); *6 poèmes arabes* for Voice and Orch. (1907); *Crépuscules d'automne*, song cycle (Paris, Feb. 20, 1909); *Nuit mauresque* for Voice and Orch. (1911); *Sillages*, 3 piano pieces (1913); *Dryade* for Orch. (1921); *Caprice* for Violin and Orch. (1925); *Feuilles d'images*, symphonic suite (Paris, March 7, 1931); *Saisons* for Chorus and Orch. (1937); *Offrande aux victimes de la guerre* for Orch. (1947); *Le Tombeau de Châteaubriand* for Orch. (1948); *Cinéma*, ballet (1953); *Improvisation* for 2 Guitars (1960); Piano Quintet; songs; etc.

BIBL.: L. Vuillemin, *L. A. et son oeuvre* (Paris, 1921); M. Landowski and G. Morançon, *L. A.* (Paris, 1967).

Aubin, Tony (Louis Alexandre), French composer, conductor, and pedagogue; b. Paris, Dec. 8, 1907; d. there, Sept. 21, 1981. He studied at the Paris Cons. with Samuel-Rousseau, Noël Gallon, and Dukas; in 1930 he won the 1st Grand Prix de Rome. Upon his return to Paris from Rome, he studied conducting with Gaubert, and later was in charge of the music division at the Paris Radio until the collapse of France in 1940; from 1945 to 1960 he served as conductor with the French Radio; concurrently he taught at the Paris Cons. In 1968 he was elected a member of the Académie des Beaux-Arts. A pragmatic composer, Aubin cultivated an eclectic idiom calculated to impress professionals and please common music-lovers.

WORKS: 2 syms. (*Symphonie romantique*, 1934–36; 1944); *Jeanne d'Arc à Orléans*, oratorio (1942); *La Chasse du chevalier Pecopim*, symphonic scherzo (1945); *Suite éolienne* for Clarinet, Flute, and Strings (1958); *Concertinetto dell'amicizia* for Flute and Piano (1964); *Concertinetto* for Violin and Piano (1964); *Brughiera* for Bassoon and Piano (1966); *Goya*, opera (1970).

Auda, Antoine, French-Belgian organist and music scholar; b. St. Julien-en-Jarez, Loire, Oct. 28, 1879; d. Brussels, Aug. 19, 1964. He studied music at Marseilles; then established himself at Liège as an organist. He publ. important studies on the musical history of the region: *Etienne de Liège* (1923) and *La Musique et les musiciens de l'ancien pays de Liège* (1930); also valuable theoretical works: *Les Modes et les tons* (1931) and *Les Gammes musicales* (1947).

Auer, Leopold, celebrated Hungarian violinist and pedagogue, great-uncle of **György (Sándor) Ligeti**; b. Veszprém, June 7, 1845; d. Loschwitz, near Dresden, July 15, 1930. He studied with Ridley Kohne at the Budapest Cons.; after making his debut in the Mendelssohn Concerto in Budapest, he continued his training with Jacob Dont in Vienna and then with Joachim in Hannover (1861–63). He was concertmaster in Düsseldorf (1864–66) and Hamburg (1866–68). In 1868 he was called to St. Petersburg as soloist in the Imperial Orch., and prof. of violin at the newly-founded Cons. He became one of the most famous violin teachers in Russia; among his pupils were Elman, Zimbalist, and Heifetz. Tchaikovsky originally dedicated his Violin Concerto to him, but was offended when Auer suggested some revisions and changed the dedication to Brodsky. Nevertheless, the Concerto became Auer's favorite work, and he made it a *pièce de résistance* for all his pupils. He was active as a teacher in London (1906–11), Dresden (1912–14), and Norway (1915–17). In the summer of 1917 he left Russia, never to return. On March 23, 1918, he played a concert in N.Y.; settling permanently in America, he devoted himself mainly to teaching, first at the Inst. of Musical Art in N.Y. (from 1926) and then at the Curtis Inst. of Music in Philadelphia (from 1928). He publ. the manuals *Violin Playing as I Teach It* (N.Y., 1921) and *Violin Master Works and Their Interpretation* (1925), and an autobiography, *My Long Life in Music* (1923). Auer's performances were marked by an assured technique, exemplary taste, and nobility of expression.

Auer, Max, Austrian writer on music; b. Vöcklabruck, May 6, 1880; d. Vienna, Sept. 24, 1962. He studied in Vienna; later taught in provincial public schools in Austria. He was one of the foremost authorities on Bruckner. He publ. *Anton Bruckner: Sein Leben und Werk* (Vienna, 1923) and *Anton Bruckner* *als Kirchenmusiker* (Regensburg, 1927); completed vols. 2–4 (1928, 1932, 1937) of Göllerich's monumental biography, *Anton Bruckner: Ein Lebens- und Schaffensbild.*

Auger, Arleen (Joyce), esteemed American soprano; b. Los Angeles, Sept. 13, 1939; d. Amsterdam, June 10, 1993. She majored in education at Calif. State Univ. in Long Beach (B.A., 1963); then studied voice with Ralph Errolle in Chicago. She made her European operatic debut as the Queen of the Night in *Die Zauberflöte* at the Vienna State Opera (1967), remaining on its roster until 1974; also chose that role for her N.Y. City Opera debut (March 16, 1969). She appeared with the conductor Helmuth Rilling on a tour of Japan in 1974, and subsequently gained prominence through a major series of recordings of the music of Bach under his direction; also devoted increasing attention to a concert career. On Oct. 2, 1978, she made her Metropolitan Opera debut in N.Y. as Marzelline in *Fidelio*, and, in 1984, made a notably successful N.Y. recital debut. Her appearance in the title role of Handel's *Alcina* in London (1985) and Los Angeles (1986) elicited further critical accolades. In 1986 she was chosen to sing at the royal wedding of Prince Andrew and Sarah Ferguson in London. During the 1986–87 season, she made an extensive concert tour of the U.S. and Europe. In 1992 her career was tragically ended when she was stricken with a fatal brain tumor.

Auriacombe, Louis, French conductor; b. Pau, Feb. 22, 1917; d. Toulouse, March 12, 1982. He studied in Pau, took courses in violin, singing, and harmony at the Toulouse Cons., and received training in conducting from Igor Markevitch in Salzburg. He was founder-conductor of the Toulouse Chamber Orch. (1953–71), which he led in performances of early and 20th-century scores.

Auric, Georges, notable French composer; b. Lodève, Hérault, Feb. 15, 1899; d. Paris, July 23, 1983. He first studied music at the Montpellier Cons.; then went to Paris, where he was a student of Caussade at the Cons. and of d'Indy and Roussel at the Schola Cantorum. While still in his early youth (1911–15), he wrote something like 300 songs and piano pieces; at 18, he composed a ballet, *Les Noces de Gamache.* At 20, he completed a comic opera, *La Reine de coeur*, however, he was dissatisfied with this early effort and destroyed the MS. In the aftermath of continental disillusion following World War I, he became a proponent of the anti-Romantic movement in France, with the apostles of this age of disenchantment, Erik Satie and Jean Cocteau, preaching the new values of urban culture, with modern America as a model. Satie urged young composers to produce "auditory pleasure without demanding disproportionate attention from the listener," while Cocteau elevated artistic ugliness to an aesthetic ideal. Under Satie's aegis, Auric joined several French composers of his generation in a group described as *Les Nouveaux Jeunes*, which later became known as *Les Six* (the other 5 were Milhaud, Honegger, Poulenc, Durey, and Tailleferre). Auric soon established an important connection with the impresario Serge Diaghilev, who commissioned him to write a number of ballets for his Paris company; Auric's facile yet felicitous manner of composing, with mock-Romantic connotations, fit perfectly into Diaghilev's scheme; particularly successful were Auric's early ballets, *Les Fâcheux* (1924) and *Les Matelots* (1925). He also wrote music for films, of which *Á nous la liberté* (1932) achieved popular success as a symphonic suite. Auric's familiarity with the theater earned him important administrative posts; from 1962 to 1968 he acted as general administrator of both the Grand Opéra and the Opéra-Comique in Paris. From 1954 to 1977 he served as president of the French Union of Composers and Authors. In 1962 he was elected to the membership of the Académie des Beaux-Arts. He publ. his memoirs as *Quand j'étais là* (Paris, 1979).

WORKS: BALLETS: *Les Mariés de la Tour Eiffel* (Paris, June 15, 1921; in collaboration with Milhaud and 4 other members of *Les Six*); *Les Fâcheux* (Monte Carlo, Jan. 19, 1924); *Les Matelots* (Paris, June 17, 1925); *La Pastorale* (Paris, May 26, 1926); *Les Enchantements d'Alcine* (Paris, May 21, 1929); *Les Imaginaires* (Paris, May 31, 1934); *Le Peintre et son modèle* (Paris, Nov. 16, 1949); *Phèdre* (Paris, May 23, 1950); *La Pierre enchantée* (Paris, June 23, 1950); *Chemin de lumière* (Munich, March 27, 1952); *Coup de feu* (Paris, May 7, 1952); *La Chambre* (1955); *Le Bal des voleurs* (1960); *Eurydice* (1963). **FILM SCORES:** *Le Sang d'un poète* (1930); *A nous la liberté* (1931); *Les Mystères de Paris* (1936); *L'Éternal Retour* (1943); *Le Bossu* (1944); *Torrents* (1946); *La Belle et la bête* (1946); *Symphonie pastorale* (1946); *L'Aigle à deux têtes* (1947); *Les Parents terribles* (1949); *Orphée* (1950); *Moulin Rouge* (1952); *Le Salaire de la peur* (1953); *Notre-Dame de Paris* (1956); *Gervaise* (1956); *Bonjour, tristesse* (1957); *Les Sorcières de Salem* (1957); *Christine* (1958); *Aimez-vous Brahms?* (1960); *La Grande Vadrouille* (1966). **ORCH.:** *Ouverture* (1938); *La Seine au matin* (1938); *L'Hommage à Marguerite Long* (1956); *Suite symphonique* (1960). **CHAMBER:** Piano Sonata (1932); Violin Sonata (1937); *Partita* for 2 Pianos (1958); Flute Sonata (1964).

BIBL.: A. Goléa, *G. A.* (Paris, 1958); J. Roy, *Le groupe des six: Poulenc, Milhaud, Honegger, A., Tailleferre, Durey* (Paris, 1994).

Aus der Ohe, Adele, German pianist; b. Hannover, Dec. 11, 1864; d. Berlin, Dec. 7, 1937. She studied with Kullak in Berlin and then with Liszt (1877–84). She played throughout Europe; made her U.S. debut as soloist in Liszt's 1st Piano Concerto (N.Y., Dec. 23, 1886), and continued to appear in the U.S. until 1906. She was soloist in Tchaikovsky's 1st Piano Concerto under the composer's direction at his last concert (St. Petersburg, Oct. 28, 1893).

Austin, Ernest, English composer, brother of **Frederic Austin**; b. London, Dec. 31, 1874; d. Wallington, Surrey, July 24, 1947. He had no formal musical education; began to compose at the age of 33 after a business career. His compositions, therefore, acquired an experimental air; he was particularly interested in a modern treatment of old English tunes. He publ. a book, *The Fairyland of Music* (1922).

WORKS: *The Vicar of Bray* for String Orch. (1910); *Hymn of Apollo* for Chorus and Orch. (Leeds, 1918); *Stella Mary Dances* (London, 1918); *Ode on a Grecian Urn*, after Keats (1922); 14 sonatinas on English folk songs for children; a cycle of organ works in 12 parts (inspired by Bunyan's *Pilgrim's Progress*); chamber music and songs.

Austin, Frederic, English baritone and composer, brother of **Ernest Austin**; b. London, March 30, 1872; d. there, April 10, 1952. He studied with Charles Lunn. After working as an organist and music teacher in Liverpool, he appeared as a singer in London in 1902. In 1908 he made his debut at London's Covent Garden as Gunther in the English-language mounting of the *Ring* cycle. He subsequently was principal baritone of the Beecham Opera Co. In 1920 he prepared a new version of *The Beggar's Opera* for London, in which he scored notable success in the role of Peachum. He then brought out a new edition of its sequel, *Polly* (London, Dec. 30, 1922). After serving as artistic director of the British National Opera Co. in London (1924–29), he devoted himself to teaching voice. Among his other compositions were a Sym., a symphonic poem, and choral music.

Austin, Henry Richter, English-American organist, music publisher, and editor; b. London, May 17, 1882; d. Marblehead, Mass., May 13, 1961. He was organist at the English Royal Church in Berlin (1904–06); settled in the U.S.; held positions as a church organist in and around Boston until 1948. He conducted experiments with the acoustical characteristics of non-tempered scales and devised a keyboard, Novaton, comprised of 16 keys (8 white, 8 black) providing the true 7th partial tone. He became president of the Arthur P. Schmidt Co. in 1954, after many years with the firm; after his death, the firm was bought out by Summy-Birchard, Inc., of Evanston, Ill.

Austin, John Turnell, English-American organ builder; b. Podington, Bedfordshire, May 16, 1869; d. Hartford, Conn., Sept.

17, 1948. He emigrated to the U.S. in 1889 and entered the employ of Ferrand & Votey in Detroit, where he experimented with his "universal wind-chest" system; in 1893 he joined Clough & Warren there, where he utilized his new system. In 1899 he settled in Hartford and founded his own firm, which he headed until his retirement in 1937 when it was reorganized as Austin Organs, Inc. Austin organs have been installed in many U.S. churches and concert halls.

Austin, Larry (Don), American composer and teacher; b. Duncan, Okla., Sept. 12, 1930. He was a student of Violet Archer at the Univ. of North Texas in Denton (B.M.E., 1951; M.M., 1952). After studies with Darius Milhaud at Mills College in Oakland, California (summer, 1955), he pursued graduate training with Andrew Imbrie at the Univ. of Calif. at Berkeley (1955–58). He later studied electronic music at the San Francisco Tape Music Center (1965–66), and computer music at Stanford Univ. (summer, 1969) and the Mass. Inst. of Technology (summer, 1978). In 1958 he joined the faculty of the Univ. of Calif. at Davis, where he was director of its bands (1958–72), founder and co-director of its New Music Ensemble (1963–68), and a prof. (1970–72). In 1966 he also helped to found the unique and invaluable avant-garde music journal *Source*, which he ed. until it suspended publication with its 13th issue in 1971. From 1972 to 1978 Austin was a prof. at the Univ. of South Florida in Tampa, where he was chairman of the music dept. (1972–73) and founder-director of the Systems Complex for the Studio and Performing Arts (1972–78). In 1978 he became a prof. at the Univ. of North Texas, where he was director of the electronic music center (1981–82) and founder-director of the Center for Experimental Music and Intermedia (1982–91). He was co-founder and president of the Consortium to Distribute Computer Music (from 1986) and president of the International Computer Music Assn. (1990–94). With T. Clark, he publ. the textbook *Learning to Compose: Modes, Materials, and Models of Musical Invention* (Dubuque, 1989). Most of Austin's compositions are for mixed media, in which theatrical, acoustical, and dynamic elements are wholly integrated. In order to attain a maximum impact with a minimum of anarchy, he introduced the concept of coordinated improvisation, which he termed "open style." In his later works, he made innovative uses of computer technologies.

WORKS: *Piano Variations* (1960); *Fantasy on a Theme by Berg* for Jazz Band (1960); Suite for Massed Bands (1961); *Triptych* for Chorus and String Quartet (1961); *Improvisations* for Jazz Soloists and Orch. (1961); *A Broken Consort* for Flute, Clarinet, Trumpet, Horn, Piano, Bass, and Drum Set (1962); *Collage* for Several Instruments (1963); *Music for Richard II* for Shakespeare's play (1963); *In Memoriam JFK* for Concert Band (1964); *Agape*, celebration for Priests, Musicians, Actors, Dancers, Celebrants, Films, Ritual, Sculpture, and Tapes (1970); *Walter* for Viola, Viola d'amore, Tape, and Films (1970–71); *Agape Set*, suite for Jazz Band (1971); *Quartet 3*, electronic music on tape (1971); *Prelude and Postlude to Plastic Surgery* for Keyboards, Film, and Tape (1971); *Quartet 4*, electronic music on tape (1971); *Primal Hybrid*, electronic music on tape (1972); *Quadrants: Event/Complex No. 1* for Symphonic Wind Ensemble (1972), *No. 2* for Chorus and Tape (1972), *Nos. 3–7* for Violin, Piano, Cello, Clarinet, Flute, and Tape (1973), *No. 8* for Viola and Tape (1973), *No. 9* for Percussion and Tape (1974), *No. 10* for Trombone and Tape (1976), and *No. 11* for Contrabass and Tape (1977); *Tableaux Vivants* for 4 to 6 Musicians, Tape, and Slides (1973; rev. 1981); *1976*, text-sound piece on tape (1973); *Life Plus Prelude* for Percussion Ensemble, based on Ives's unfinished *Universe Symphony* (1974–84); *A Universe Symphony: The Earth, Life Pulse, and Heavens*, symphonic fantasy for Multiple Orchs., based on Ives's unfinished *Universe Symphony* (1974–93); *Phoenix*, computer music on tape (1974); *1st Fantasy on Ives's Universe Symphony—The Earth* for Narrator, Double Brass Quintet, and Tape (1975); *2nd Fantasy on Ives's Universe Symphony—The Heavens* for Clarinet, Viola, Keyboards, Percussion, and Tape (1976); *Maroon Bells* for Voice, Piano, and Tape (1976); *Organ Mass* (1977); *Phantasmagoria: Fantasies on Ives's Universe Symphony* for Narrator, Orch., Digital Synthesizer, and Tape (1977; rev. 1981); *Catalogo Sonoro—Narcisso* for Viola and Tape (1978); *Catalogo Gesto—Timbro* for Percussionist and Dancer (1978); *Catalogo Voce*, mini-opera for Bass-baritone, Tape, and Slides (1979); *Protoforms: Hybrid Musics* for 3 Sopranos and Real-time Computer Music System (1980); *Ceremony* for Organ and Voice (1980); *Protoforms*, fractals for Computer Band (1980); *Protoforms*, fractals for Cello Choir and Computer Band (1981); *Canadian Coastlines*, canonic fractals for Musicians and Computer Band (1981); *Euphonia: A Tale of the Future*, opera for Soloists, Chorus, Chamber Orch., Digital Synthesizer, and Tape (1981–82); *art is self-alteration is Cage is . . .*, uni-word omniostic for String Bass Quartet (1982); *Beachcombers* for 4 Musicians and Tape (1983); *Sonata Concertante* for Piano and Computer Music on Tape (1983–84); *Ludus Fractalis*, video piece (1984); *Clarini!* for 20 Trumpets (1985); *Montage: Theme and Variations* for Violin and Computer Music on Tape (1985); *Sinfonia Concertante: A Mozartean Episode* for Chamber Orch. and Computer Music Narrative (1986); *Concertante Cibernetica*, interactions for Performer and Synclavier (1987); *Euphonia 2344*, intermezzo for Voices and Computer Music on Tape (1988); *Snare Drum Cycles* for Snare Dum (1989); *Transmission 2: The Great Excursion* for Chorus, Computer Music Ensemble, and Recorded Dialogue (1989–90); *SoundPoemSet: Pauline Oliveros/Jerry Hunt/Morton Subotnick/David Tudor*, computer music on tape (1991); *La Barbara: The Name/The Sounds/The Music* for Voice and Computer Music (1991); *Accidents 2*, sound projections for Piano and Computer Music (1992); *¡Rompido!—Music for Dance and Sculpture* for Percussionist and Computer Music on Tape (1993).

BIBL.: "To Arms . . . Be Uncommon: L. A. Interviews L. A.," *Ear Magazine* (June 1984).

Austin, William W(eaver), American musicologist; b. Lawton, Okla., Jan. 18, 1920. He studied at Harvard Univ., obtaining his Ph.D. in 1951 with the diss. *Harmonic Rhythm in Twentieth-Century Music*. In 1947 he was appointed to the faculty of Cornell Univ., retiring in 1990. In 1961–62 he held a Guggenheim fellowship.

WRITINGS: *Music in the 20th Century from Debussy through Stravinsky* (N.Y., 1966); *"Susanna," "Jeanie" and "The Old Folks at Home": The Songs of Stephen C. Foster from His Time to Ours* (N.Y., 1975; 2nd ed., 1987); ed. *New Looks at Italian Opera: Essays in Honor of Donald J. Grout* (Ithaca, N.Y., 1968); tr. *Musikästhetik* by Carl Dahlhaus into Eng. as *Esthetics of Music* (Cambridge, 1982).

Austral (real name, **Wilson), Florence,** Australian soprano; b. Richmond, near Melbourne, April 26, 1892; d. Newcastle, New South Wales, May 15, 1968. She studied at the Melbourne Cons. (1914–18). She made her operatic debut as Brünnhilde at Covent Garden in London, under the auspices of the newly formed British National Opera Co. (May 16, 1922); later she sang the roles of Isolde and Aida. She toured the U.S. between 1925 and 1931 with her husband, the flutist John Amadeo.

Autori, Franco, Italian-born American conductor; b. Naples, Nov. 29, 1903; d. Tulsa, Oct. 16, 1990. After study in Italy, he emigrated to the U.S. in 1928 and became a naturalized American citizen in 1936. He conducted at the Chicago Civic Opera (1928–32) and the Dallas Sym. Orch. summer series (1932–34). After serving as a staff conductor with the Federal Music Project in N.Y. (1934–37), he was conductor of the Buffalo Phil. (1936–45), assoc. conductor of the N.Y. Phil. (1949–59), and conductor of the Tulsa Phil. (1961–71).

Avdeyeva, Larissa (Ivanovna), prominent Russian mezzo-soprano; b. Moscow, June 21, 1925. She studied at the Stanislavsky Opera Studio in Moscow. In 1947 she joined the Stanislavsky Music Theater there; in 1952 she became a member of Moscow's Bolshoi Theater, where she distinguished herself as an outstanding interpreter in operas by Tchaikovsky, Borodin, Mussorgsky, and Rimsky-Korsakov; she also made tours of Europe, the U.S., and Japan. She was made a People's Artist of the R.S.F.S.R. in 1964. She married **Evgeny Svetlanov**.

Avenary, Hanoch (real name, **Herbert Loewenstein**), Israeli musicologist; b. Danzig, May 25, 1908. He studied musicology and other subjects at the univs. of Leipzig, Munich, and Frankfurt am Main; then received his Ph.D. in 1931 from the Univ. of Königsberg with the diss. *Wort und Ton bei Oswald von Wolkenstein* (publ. in Königsberg, 1932). He went to Palestine in 1936 and was active as a publisher of Jewish art books. He also served in the Israeli air force. In 1965 he joined the faculty of Hebrew Univ. in Jerusalem, where he remained until 1972; from 1966 he was also a lecturer at the Univ. of Tel Aviv. His books include *Studies in the Hebrew, Syrian and Greek Liturgical Recitative* (Tel Aviv, 1963); *Hebrew Hymn Tunes: Rise and Development of a Musical Tradition* (Tel Aviv, 1971); *The Ashkenazi Tradition of Biblical Chant between 1500 and 1900* (Tel Aviv, 1978); *Encounters of East and West in Music* (Tel Aviv, 1979); *Kantor Salamon Sulzer und seine Zeit: Eine Dokumentation* (Sigmaringen, 1985).

BIBL.: *Essays in Honor of H. A.* (vol. 10 of *Orbis Musicae*, Tel Aviv, 1991).

Avidom (real name, **Kalkstein**), **Menahem,** prominent Polish-born Israeli composer and administrator; b. Stanislawow, Jan. 6, 1908; d. Herzliya, Aug. 5, 1995. He emigrated to Palestine in 1925. After taking courses in art and science at the American Univ. in Beirut (B.A., 1928), he went to Paris to study with Rabaud at the Cons. (1928–31). Following a sojourn in Alexandria, Egypt (1931–35), he settled in Tel Aviv as a teacher. From 1945 to 1952 he was secretary-general of the Israel Phil. He was director-general of ACUM (Soc. of Authors, Composers, and Music Publishers) of Israel from 1955 to 1980. From 1958 to 1972 he also was chairman of the Israel Composers League, of which he was elected honorary chairman for life in 1982. In 1961 he received the Israel State Prize for his opera *Alexandra*. In 1982 ACUM awarded him its prize for his life's work. In his extensive output, Avidom ranged widely stylistically. While he utilized folk modalities of the Middle East, he also embraced dodecaphony.

WORKS: DRAMATIC: *Alexandra*, opera (1952; Tel Aviv, Aug. 15, 1959); *In Every Generation*, opera (1955); *The Crook*, comic opera (1966–67; Tel Aviv, April 22, 1967); *The Farewell*, radiophonic opera (1969; broadcast Nov. 1971); *The Pearl and the Coral*, ballet (1972); *The Emperor's New Clothes*, comic opera (1976); *Yodfat's Cave*, musical drama (1977); *The Cave of Jotapata*, dramatic scene (1977); *The End of King Og*, children's opera (1979); *The 1st Sin*, satirical opera (1980). **ORCH.:** *Polyphonic Suite* for Strings (1938); 10 syms.: No. 1, *A Folk Symphony* (1946), No. 2, *David* (1948; Tel Aviv, Dec. 1, 1949), No. 3, *Mediterranean Sinfonietta* (1951), No. 4 (1955), No. 5, *The Song of Eilät*, for Voice and Orch. (1956–57), No. 6 (1960), No. 7, *Philharmonic* (1961), No. 8, *Festival Sinfonietta* (Jerusalem, July 27, 1966), No. 9, *Symphonie variée*, for Chamber Orch. (1968), and No. 10, *Sinfonia brevis* (1980); Concerto for Flute and Strings (1946); *Music* for Strings (1949); Violin Concertino (1953); *Jubilee Suite* (1959); *Triptyque symphonique* (1966); *Spring*, overture (1972); *Movements* for Strings (1979; also for String Quartet); *Ballet Suite for Youth* for Chamber Orch. (1985); *Prelude* for Youth Orch. (1989). **CHAMBER:** 2 woodwind quartets (1937, 1984); 3 string quartets (1953, 1960, 1991); *Enigma* for 5 Winds, Piano, and Percussion (1962); Brass Quartet (1963); *Monothema*, sonatina for String Quartet (1982); Woodwind Quintet (1983); Sonata for Solo Viola (1984); *Bachiana (B.A.C.H.)* for Brass Quintet (1985); *Triologue*, trio-passacaglia for Piano, Viola, and Cello (1985); Trio for Oboe, Piano, and Cello (1986); *Triptyque* for Flute, Horn, and Piano (1988); Clarinet Sonata (1988); *A Tre* for Piano, Viola, and Clarinet (1990); *Pour la Clarinette* (1994). **PIANO:** 2 sonatinas (1939, 1945); *12 Changing Preludes* (1965); *6 Inventions on the Name of Artur Rubinstein* (1973); *Piece on the Name of SCHOEnBerG* (1974); *Once Upon a Time . . .*, 5 tales (1977); Duo Sonatina for Piano, 4-hands (1982); *Triptique* (1984); *6 epigrams* (1985–87). **VOCAL:** *5 Psalms* for Mezzo-soprano or Alto, 2 Clarinets, and Percussion ad libitum (1976); *12 Hills*, cantata (1976); *Beyond*, cantata for Voice and Instruments (1977); *Peace Upon All*, cantata for Baritone and Chamber Orch. (1994); choruses; songs.

Avni, Tzvi (Jacob), German-born Israeli composer, teacher, and writer on music; b. Saarbrücken, Sept. 2, 1927. He emigrated to Palestine in 1935; studied with Abel Ehrlich and Mordecai Seter at the Tel Aviv Academy of Music (diploma, 1958), and also received private instruction in orchestration from Paul Ben-Haim. He was a student of Copland and Lukas Foss at the Berkshire Music Center in Tanglewood (summer, 1963), later pursuing studies in electronic music with Ussachevsky and in music librarianship at Columbia Univ. (1963–64). He also studied with Myron Schaeffer at the Univ. of Toronto (1964). He was director of the AMLI Central Music Library in Tel Aviv (1961–75), served as ed. of the journal *Gitit* (1966–80), was director of the electronic music studio (from 1971) and a prof. (from 1976) at the Rubin Academy of Music in Jerusalem, and was chairman of the Israel League of Composers (1978–80) and of the music committee of the National Council for Culture and Art (1983–87). In 1986 he was awarded the ACUM Prize for his life's work. In many of his mature compositions, Avni utilized advanced techniques; he later pursued neo-tonal writing.

WORKS: DRAMATIC: Ballets; incidental music. **ORCH.:** *Prayer* for Strings (1961; rev. 1969); *Meditations on a Drama* for Chamber Orch. (1965); *Holiday Metaphors* (1970); *By the Rivers of Babylon* for Chamber Orch. (1971; also for Full Orch., 1972); *In This Cape of Death* for Chamber Orch. (1974); *2 Psalms* for Oboe and Strings (1975; also for Oboe and String Quartet); *Michtam of David* for Harp and Strings (1975–78; also for Harp and String Quartet); *2 Movements from Sinfonia Sacra* (1977); *Programme Music* (1980); *Mizmor* for Santur or Xylophone and Orch. (1982); *Metamorphoses on a Bach Chorale* (1985); *Kaddish* for Cello and Strings (1987); *Mashav*, concertino for Xylophone, Strings or Winds, and Percussion (1988); *Desert Scenes*, sym. (1990). **CHAMBER:** Wind Quintet (1959); *Summer Strings* for String Quartet (1962); *2 Pieces* for 4 Clarinets (1965); *Elegy* for Cello (1967); *5 Pantomimes* for 8 Players (1968); *De Profundis*, 2nd string quartet (1969); *Lyric Episodes* for Oboe and Tape (1972); *Beyond the Curtain* for Piano Quartet (1979); *Tandu* for 2 Flutes (1982); Saxophone Quartet (1990); *Vitrage* for Harp (1990); *Fagotti Fugati* for 2 Bassoons (1991); *Variations on a Sephardic Tune* for Recorder Ensemble (1992). **PIANO:** *Capriccio* (1955; rev. 1975); 3 sonatas (1961; *Epitaph*, 1979; *On the Verge of Time*, 1983); *Triptych* (1994). **VOCAL:** *Collage* for Voice, Flute, Percussion, and Tape (1967); *Jerusalem of the Heavens* for Baritone, Chorus, and Orch. (1968); *The Destruction of the Temple* for Chorus and Orch. (1968); *Synchromotrask* for Woman's Voice, Tape, and a Door (1976); *A Monk Observes a Skull* for Mezzo-soprano, Cello, and Tape (1981); *Deep Calleth Unto Deep*, Psalm-cantata for Soprano, Chorus, and Orch. or Organ (1988–89); many choral pieces and songs. **ELECTRONIC:** *Vocalise* (1964).

Avshalomov, Aaron, Russian-born American composer, father of **Jacob (David) Avshalomov**; b. Nikolayevsk, Siberia, Nov. 11, 1894; d. N.Y., April 26, 1965. He studied at the Zürich Cons. In 1914 he went to China, where he wrote a number of works on Chinese subjects, making use of authentic Chinese themes. On April 24, 1925, he conducted the first performance in Beijing of his first opera, on a Chinese subject, *Kuan Yin*; his 2nd opera, also on a Chinese subject, *The Great Wall*, was staged in Shanghai on Nov. 26, 1945, as were *The Soul of the Ch'in*, ballet (May 21, 1933); *Incense Shadows*, pantomime (March 13, 1935); Piano Concerto (Jan. 19, 1936); Violin Concerto (Jan. 16, 1938); 1st Sym. (March 17, 1940, composer conducting); and *Buddha and the 5 Planetary Deities*, choreographic tableau (April 18, 1942). In 1947 Avshalomov went to America, where he continued to compose works in large forms, among them his 2nd (Cincinnati, Dec. 30, 1949), 3rd (1950), and 4th (1951) Syms.

Avshalomov, Jacob (David), Russian-born American conductor, teacher, and composer, son of **Aaron Avshalomov**; b. Tsingtao, China, March 28, 1919. His father was Russian and his mother American. He studied with his father before emigrating to the U.S. with his mother in 1937. After studies with Ernst Toch in Los Angeles, he went to Portland, Oreg., in 1938 and pursued his training with Lucia and Jacques Gershkovitch. He also played percussion and cello under the latter's direction in the Portland Junior Sym. After attending Reed College (1939–41), he completed his studies with Rogers at the Eastman School of Music in Rochester, N.Y. (1941–43; B.M., M.A.). During World War II, he served in the U.S. Army and in 1944 became a naturalized American citizen. From 1946 to 1954 he taught at Columbia Univ. In 1952 he held a Guggenheim fellowship. In 1953 he was awarded the N.Y. Music Critics Circle Award for his choral work *Tom o' Bedlam*. In 1954 he became conductor of the Portland (Oreg.) Junior Sym., which was renamed the Portland Junior Phil. in 1978. Avshalomov conducted it for 40 years, retiring in 1994. During his tenure, he trained numerous students in the rigors of orchestral playing and led them on 6 international tours. He publ. *Music is Where You Make It* (2 vols., 1959, 1979) and *The Concerts Reviewed: 65 Years of the Portland Youth Philharmonic* (1991). His music reflects the many cultures to which he was exposed; while his forms are cohesive, his materials are multifarious, with tense chromatic harmonies and quasi-oriental inflections.

WORKS: ORCH.: *The Taking of T'ung Kuan* (1943; rev. ver., Detroit, Nov. 20, 1953); *Slow Dance* (1945); *Sinfonietta* (1946; N.Y., Nov. 29, 1949); *Evocations* for Clarinet and Chamber Orch. (1947; Saratoga Springs, N.Y., Aug. 17, 1950); *The Plywood Age* (Portland, Oreg., June 20, 1955); *Phases of the Great Land* (1959); 3 syms.: No. 1, *The Oregon* (1959–61), No. 2, *Glorious the Assembled Fires*, for Chorus and Orch. (1985), and No. 3, *Symphony of Songs*, for the 70th anniversary of the Portland Youth Phil. (1993; Portland, Oreg., Feb. 26, 1994); *Raptures* (1975); *Open Sesame!* (1985); *Up at Timberline* for Contrabass, Winds, and Brasses (1986). **CHAMBER:** Viola Sonatina (1947); *Quodlibet Montagna* for Brass Sextet (1975). **VOCAL:** *Prophecy* for Cantor, Chorus, and Organ (1948); *How Long, O Lord*, cantata (1948–49); *Tom o' Bedlam* for Chorus (N.Y., Dec. 15, 1953); *Psalm 100* for Chorus and Winds (1956); *Inscriptions for the City of Brass* for Narrator, Chorus, and Orch., after the Arabian Nights (1956); *City Upon the Hill* for Narrator, Chorus, Orch., and "liberty bell" (1965); *The 13 Clocks* for 2 Storytellers and Orch. (1973); *Praises from the Corners of the Earth* for Chorus and Orch. (1976); *The Most Triumphant Bird* for Chorus, Piano, and Viola Concertante (1985); *Songs from the Goliards* for Chorus and Cello Concertante (1992); *Songs in Season* for Chorus, Piano, and Contrabass Concertante (1993).

BIBL.: W. Bergsma, "The Music of J. A.," *American Composers Alliance Bulletin*, III/3 (1956); E. Encell, *J. A.'s Works for Chorus and Orchestra: Aspects of Style* (diss., Univ. of Wash., 1983).

Ax, Emanuel, outstanding Polish-born American pianist; b. Lwów, June 8, 1949. He began to play the violin at age 6; soon took up the piano and studied with his father, who was a coach at the Lwów Opera House. The family moved to Warsaw when he was 8, and then to Winnipeg, Canada, when he was 10; in 1961 they settled in N.Y., where he enrolled at the Juilliard School of Music as a student of Mieczyslaw Munz; he also received a bachelor's degree in French from Columbia Univ. in 1970. He made a concert tour of South America in 1969. Ax became a naturalized American citizen in 1970. He competed at the Chopin (1970) and Queen Elisabeth (1972) competitions, placing 7th in both; in 1971, won 3rd place in the Vianna da Motta Competition in Lisbon; then made his N.Y. debut at Alice Tully Hall on March 12, 1973. A long-awaited victory came in 1974, when he won first place in the Artur Rubinstein International Piano Master Competition in Tel Aviv; among its awards was a contract for an American concert tour; there followed numerous appearances throughout the U.S. and Europe. Ax was awarded the Avery Fisher Prize in 1979. In addition to his fine interpretations of the standard repertoire, he has also distinguished himself as a champion of contemporary music.

Axman, Emil, Czech composer; b. Rataje, June 3, 1887; d. Prague, Jan. 25, 1949. He studied musicology with Nejedlý and Hostinský at the Univ. of Prague (Ph.D., 1912, with the diss. *Moravské opery ve století 18.* [18th Century Moravian Operas]; publ. in *Časopis moravského musea*, 1912), and received private training in composition with Novák (1908–10) and Ostrčil (1920). In 1913 he became keeper of the music archives at the National Museum in Prague. He was the author of *Morava v české hudbě 19. století* (Moravian and Czech Music of the 19th Century; Prague, 1920). His music was of a highly lyrical nature.

WORKS: ORCH.: 2 symphonic poems: *Sorrows and Hopes* (1919–20) and *A Bright Sky* (1921–22); 6 syms.: No. 1, *Tragic* (1925–26), No. 2, *Giocosa* (1926–27; Frankfurt am Main, July 3, 1927), No. 3, *Spring* (1928), No. 4, *Eroica* (1932), No. 5, *Dithyrambic* (1936), and No. 6, *Patriotic* (1942); *From the Beskids* for Chamber Orch. (1934); Violin Concerto (1936); Piano Concerto (1939); Cello Concerto (1940); Double Concerto for Violin, Cello, and Orch. (1944); *Suite in the Form of Variations* (1948). **CHAMBER:** Violin Sonata (1923); 4 string quartets (1924, 1925, 1929, 1946); Cello Sonata (1924); Piano Trio (1924–25); Wind Quintet (1938); Suite for String Quartet (1940); *Divertimento* for Nonet (1944); *3 Moravian Dances* for Nonet (1944); *Variations* for String Quartet (1944). **PIANO:** 3 sonatas (*Appassionata*, 1922; *To the Memory of a Great Man*, 1922; 1924); *Sonatina charakeristicka* (1922); *Moravia Sings* (1925; also for Orch., 1935). **VOCAL:** Cantatas, including *My Mother* (1926) and *The Cemetery of Sobotka* (1933); choruses; song cycles.

BIBL.: L. Hovorka, *Sborová tvorba A.ova* (Prague, 1940); F. Pala, *E. A.* (Prague, 1951).

Ayala Pérez, Daniel, Mexican conductor and composer; b. Abalá, Yucatán, July 21, 1906; d. Veracruz, June 20, 1975. He went to Mérida, Yucatán, to study music; entered the National Cons. in Mexico City in 1927; studied violin with Ezequiel Sierra and Revueltas, and composition with Ponce, Huízar, and Carrillo. He played in nightclubs in Mexico City; in 1931, became a violinist with the Orquesta Sinfónica de México; in 1934, together with Moncayo, Contreras, and Galindo, formed the Grupo de los Cuatro (Group of the 4). He became conductor of the Banda de Policía in Mérida in 1940 and in 1942 founded the Mérida Sym. Orch.; was director of the Yucatán Cons. (from 1944) and the Veracruz School of Music (from 1955). His music, inspired by ancestral melos of the Mayan civilization and legends, is cast in pentatonic modes and possesses a vigorous rhythmic pulse.

WORKS: BALLETS: *El Hombré Maya* (as a symphonic suite, Mexico City, Nov. 21, 1940); *La gruta diabólica* (1940). **ORCH.:** *Tribú* (Mexico City, Oct. 18, 1935); *Paisaje* (Landscape; 1935; Mexico City, June 2, 1936); *Panoramas de México* (1936; Dallas, Dec. 1, 1940); *Mi viaje a Norte America* (1947). **PIANO:** *Radiograma* (1931). **VOCAL:** *4 Canciones* for Voice and Piano (1932); *Uchben X'Coholte* (Ancient Cemetery) for Soprano and Chamber Orch. (Mexico City, Oct. 13, 1933; ballet ver., Mexico City, March 6, 1936); *El grillo* (Cricket) for Soprano, Clarinet, Violin, Timbrel, and Piano (1933); *U Kayil Chaac*, an incantation for rain, for Soprano, Mexican Percussion Instruments, and Chamber Orch. (1934); *Brigadier de Choque* for Chorus and Percussion (1935); *Suite infantil* for Soprano and Chamber Orch. (1937); *Los Yaquis y los Seris*, 2 suites for Voice, Chamber Ensemble, and Mexican Percussion Instruments (1938; Mérida, July 31, 1942).

Ayestarán, Lauro, Uruguayan musicologist; b. Montevideo, July 9, 1913; d. there, July 22, 1966. He studied voice and music history and became an instructor of choral music in municipal schools in Montevideo. He is the author of the important monograph *Domenico Zipoli, El gran compositor y organista romano en el Rio de la Plata* (Montevideo, 1941); also wrote *El folklore musical Uruguayo* (Montevideo, 1967).

Ayres, Frederic (real name, **Frederick Ayres Johnson**), American composer; b. Binghamton, N.Y., March 17, 1876; d. Colorado Springs, Nov. 23, 1926. He studied with Edgar S. Kelley (1897–1901) and Arthur Foote (1899). His works include an overture, *From the Plains*; 2 string quartets; 2 piano trios; 2 violin sonatas; a Cello Sonata; and numerous songs. In his later music, he showed a tendency toward impressionism and used moderately complex harmonic combinations.

BIBL.: W. Upton, "Frederick A.," *Musical Quarterly* (Jan. 1932).

Azkué (Aberasturi), Resurrección María de, Spanish composer and musicologist; b. Lequeitio, Aug. 5, 1864; d. Bilbao, Nov. 9, 1951. He studied theology in Spain, then went to Paris and studied music at the Schola Cantorum. He wrote 2 operas to Basque texts: *Ortzuri* (Bilbao, 1911) and *Urlo* (Bilbao, 1913); an oratorio, *Daniel*; a *Te Deum*; and several zarzuelas. He publ. a valuable collection, *Cancionero popular Vasco* (11 vols.), and *Literatura popular del País Vasco* (4 vols., the last containing musical examples).

Aznavour, Charles (real name, **Varenagh Aznavurian**), French chansonnier; b. Paris, May 22, 1924. A son of an Armenian baritone from Tiflis, he received early music training at home; acted in Paris variety shows at the age of 5; learned to play the guitar. He made several American tours as a nightclub entertainer with a valuable French accent; also acted in films. He composed a great number of songs, of the genre of "tristesse chansons" and frustration ballads, among them the popular *On ne sait jamais, Comme des étrangers*, and *Ce jour tant attendu*. His operetta *Monsieur Carnaval* was performed in Paris on Dec. 17, 1965. He wrote an autobiography, *Aznavour par Aznavour* (Paris, 1970; Eng. tr., 1972).

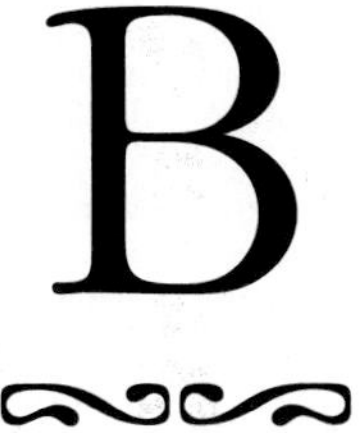

Baaren, Kees van, important Dutch composer and pedagogue; b. Enschede, Oct. 22, 1906; d. Oegstgeest, Sept. 2, 1970. He studied with F.E. Koch at the Berlin Hochschule für Musik and with Willem Pijper in Rotterdam. He was the director of the Amsterdam Academy of Music (1948–53), the Utrecht Cons. (1953–57), and the Royal Cons. of Music in The Hague (1958–70). Baaren was a major influence on many of the leading Dutch composers of the post-World War II avant-garde. After composing along traditional lines, he embraced a serial path à la Pijper and Anton von Webern in 1947.

WORKS: ORCH.: Piano Concertino (1934); Suite for School Orch. (1951); *Sinfonia* (1956–57); *Variations* (1959); Piano Concerto (1964); *Musica* (Rotterdam, May 18, 1966; rev. 1968). **CHAMBER:** 2 string quartets (1932–33; *Sovraposizioni I,* 1962); Trio for Flute, Clarinet, and Bassoon (1936); Septet for Flute, Oboe, Clarinet, Bassoon, Horn, Violin, and Double Bass (1952); *Sovraposizioni II,* wind quintet (1963); *Musica* for Flute (1965). **KEYBOARD: PIANO:** Sonatina (1948). **ORGAN:** *Musica* (1968–69). **CARILLON:** *Musica* for 72 Carillons (1964); *Musica* for 47 Carillons (1964; rev. 1969). **VOCAL:** *The Hollow Men* for Chorus and Orch. (1948); choruses.

BIBL.: J. Hill, *The Music of K. v.B.* (diss., Univ. of North Carolina, 1970).

Babadzhanian, Arno, Armenian pianist and composer; b. Yerevan, Jan. 22, 1921; d. Moscow, Nov. 15, 1983. He studied at the Yerevan Cons.; after graduation in 1947, he went to Moscow, where he took courses in piano with Igumnov at the Cons. and in composition with Litinsky at the Armenian Culture Center; graduated from both in 1948. In 1950 he joined the piano faculty at the Yerevan Cons. His music is derived from the folk-song patterns of Armenia, continuing the line cultivated by Khachaturian, with emphasis on rhythmic coloration in a characteristic quasi-oriental manner. His most ambitious works are a Violin Concerto (1949) and a Cello Concerto (1962); he also wrote *Heroic Ballad* for Piano and Orch. (1950), 2 string quartets (1942, 1947), Piano Trio (1952), Violin Sonata (1959), and a number of popular ballads under such appealing titles as *The Song of 1st Love* and *Make a Wish.*

Babayev, Andrei, Russian composer; b. Azerbaijan, Dec. 27, 1923; d. Moscow, Oct. 21, 1964. He studied in Baku; played native instruments; then entered the Baku Cons., where he was a student in composition of Gadzhibekov and Karayev, graduating in 1950; later took advanced courses with Shaporin at the Moscow Cons. His music is inspired mainly by Armenian folk melodies; he also arranged songs of Central Asia and India; some of his original songs (*I Met a Girl, Lovely Eyes,* etc.) acquired popularity. Other compositions include *Eagles' Bastion,* opera (1957); *October,* cantata (1947); Sym. (1950); *Indian Fantasy* for Orch. (1958); pieces for native instruments.

Babbitt, Milton (Byron), prominent American composer, teacher, and theorist; b. Philadelphia, May 10, 1916. He received early music training in Jackson, Miss., at the same time revealing an acute flair for mathematical reasoning; this double faculty was to determine the formulation of his musical theories. In 1931 he entered the Univ. of Pa. as a mathematics student, but then pursued training in music with Marion Bauer and Philip James at N.Y. Univ. (B.A., 1935); after private lessons with Sessions, he pursued studies with that mentor at Princeton Univ. (M.F.A., 1942). In 1938 he joined the faculty of Princeton Univ. as a music teacher; after teaching mathematics there (1942–45), he again taught music there from 1948; in 1966 he became William Shubael Conant Prof. there; also served as director of the Columbia-Princeton Electronic Music Center (from 1959). In 1984 he retired as prof. emeritus at Princeton Univ. He also taught at N.Y.'s Juilliard School (from 1973) and at various other venues in the U.S. and Europe. In 1949 and 1964 he received the N.Y. Music Critics' Circle awards. In 1960–61 he held a Guggenheim fellowship. He was elected a member of the National Inst. of Arts and Letters in 1965, and of the American Academy of Arts and Letters in 1986, receiving its Gold Medal in Music in 1988. In 1974 he became a fellow of the American Academy of Arts and Sciences. In 1982 he was awarded a Pulitzer Prize Special Citation for "his life's work as a distinguished and seminal American composer." From 1986 to 1991 he was a MacArthur fellow. In 1992 Princeton Univ. awarded him his Ph.D. for a diss. he had written as a student there but which had been rejected. A new review of his diss. prompted Princeton to award him his Ph.D., noting that the diss. had been so advanced for its time that it could not be properly evaluated. Taking as the point of departure Schoenberg's advanced compositional methods, Babbitt extended the serial principle to embrace 12 different note values, 12 different time intervals between instrumental entities, 12 different dynamic levels, and 12 different instrumental timbres. In order to describe the potential combinations of the basic 4 aspects of the tone row, he introduced the term "combinatoriality," with symmetric parts of a tone row designated as "derivations." Babbitt's scientific theories have profoundly influenced the musical thinking of young American composers. His paper "Twelve-Tone Invariants as Compositional Determinants," publ. in the *Musical Quarterly* of April 1960, gives a resume of his system of total serialism. The serial application of rhythmic values is expounded in Babbitt's paper "Twelve-Tone Rhythmic Structure and the Electronic Medium," publ. in *Perspectives of New Music* (Fall 1962). For a general exposition of his views on music, see S. Dembski and J. Straus, eds., *Milton Babbitt: Words about Music (The Madison Lectures)* (Madison, Wisc., 1987).

WORKS: MUSIC THEATER: *Fabulous Voyage* (1946). **ORCH.:** *Relata I* (1965; Cleveland, March 3, 1966) and *II* (1968; N.Y., Jan. 16, 1969); *Ars combinatoria* for Small Orch. (Bloomington, Ind., July 16, 1981); Piano Concerto (1985; N.Y., Jan. 19, 1986); *Transfigured Notes* for Strings (1986). **CHAMBER:** *Composition* for 4 Instruments (1948); *Composition* for 12 Instruments (1948; rev. 1954); 6 string quartets (1948, withdrawn; 1954; 1969–70; 1970; 1982; 1993); Wind Quartet (1953); *All Set* for 8 Instruments (1957); *Sextets* for Violin and Piano (1966); *Arie de capo* for 6 Instruments (1973–74); *Paraphrases* for 11 Instruments (1979); *Groupwise* for 7 Instruments (1983); *4 Play* for Clarinet, Violin, Cello, and Piano (1984); *Whirled Series* for Saxophone and Piano (1987); *The Crowded Air* for 11 Instruments (1988); *Consortini* for 5 Instruments (1989); *Play It Again, Sam* for Viola (1989); *Soli e Duettini* for 2 Guitars (1989); *None But the Lonely Flute* for Flute (1991); *Septet, But Equal* for 3 Clarinets, String Trio, and Piano (1992); *Counterparts* for Brass Quintet (1992); *Around the Horn* for Horn (1993); *Fanfare for All* for Brass Quintet (1993); *Triad* for Clarinet, Viola, and Piano (1994). **PIANO:** *3 Compositions* (1947); *Partitions* (1957); *Postpartitions* (1966); *Tableaux* (1972); *My Complements to Roger* (1978); *Canonical Form* (1983); *Lagniappe* (1985); *Emblems (Ars Emblemantica)* (1989); *Envoi* for Piano, 4-hands (1990); *Preludes, Interludes, Postlude* (1991); *Tutte Le Corde* (1994). **VOCAL:** *Du*, song cycle for Soprano and Piano (1951); *Composition* for Tenor and 6 Instruments (1960); *4 Canons* for Women's Chorus (1968); *A Solo Requiem* for Soprano and 2 Pianos (1976–77); *More Phonemena* for 12 Voices (1978); *An Elizabethan Sextette* for 6 Women's Voices (1979); *The Head of the Bed* for Soprano and 4 Instruments (1982); *4 Cavalier Settings* for Tenor and Guitar (1991); *Mehr "Du"* for Soprano, Viola, and Piano (1991); *Quatrains* for Soprano and 2 Clarinets (1993); *No Longer Very Clear* for Soprano and 4 Instruments (1994). **OTHER:** *Composition* for Synthesizer and Tape (1961); *Vision and Prayer* for Soprano and Tape (1961); *Ensembles* for Synthesizer and Tape (1962–64); *Philomel* for Soprano and Tape (1964); *Correspondences* for String Orch. and Tape (1967); *Occasional Variations* for Tape (1971); Concerti for Violin, Small Orch., and Tape (1974–76); *Phonemena* for Soprano and Tape (1975); *Reflections* for Piano and Tape (1975); *Images* for Saxophone and Tape (1979).

BIBL.: A. Mead, *An Introduction to the Music of M. B.* (Princeton, N.J., 1993).

Babin, Victor, Russian-born American pianist, teacher, and composer; b. Moscow, Dec. 13, 1908; d. Cleveland, March 1, 1972. He studied at the Riga Cons. (graduated, 1927) and with Artur Schnabel (piano) and Franz Schreker (composition) at the Berlin Hochschule für Musik. In 1933 he married **Vitya Vronsky**, with whom he toured extensively as a duo pianist. In 1937 they emigrated to the U.S. and Babin became a naturalized American citizen in 1944. He continued to tour widely with his wife from 1945, and also served as pianist of the Festival Quartet (1954–62). He taught at the Aspen (Colo.) Music School, where he was its director (1951–54), at the Berkshire Music Center in Tanglewood, at the Cleveland Inst. of Music, where he was its director (1961–72), and at Case Western Reserve Univ. His output, in a post-Romantic style, includes 2 concertos for 2 Pianos and Orch., orch. pieces, chamber music, songs, and pieces for Piano and Duo Piano.

Babitz, Sol, American violinist and writer on music; b. N.Y., Oct. 11, 1911; d. Los Angeles, Feb. 18, 1982. In 1932 he went to Berlin, where he studied violin with Carl Flesch and composition with Juon; also took a course in musicology with Curt Sachs. In 1933 he proceeded to Paris and continued violin instruction with Marcel Chailley. Shortly afterward he returned to the U.S., and was a violinist in the Los Angeles Phil. (1933–37). From 1942 to 1961 he played violin in studio orchs. in Hollywood. He publ. *Principles of Extensions in Violin Fingering* (N.Y., 1947); *The Violin: Views and Reviews* (Urbana, Ill., 1959); *The Great Baroque Hoax: A Guide to Baroque Performance for Musicians and Connoisseurs* (Los Angeles, 1970); *Vocal De-Wagnerization and Other Matters* (with G. Pont; Los Angeles, 1973).

Bacarisse, Salvador, Spanish composer; b. Madrid, Sept. 12, 1898; d. Paris, Aug. 5, 1963. He studied at the Madrid Cons. with Conrado del Campo; received the Premio Nacional de Música in 1923, 1930, and 1934. During the Spanish Civil War, he was active in the music section of the loyalist army; after its defeat in 1939, he settled in Paris. He wrote the operas *Charlot* (1933), *El Tesoro de Boabdil* (1958), and *Fuenteovejuna* (1962); the symphonic poem *La tragedia de Doña Ajada* (1929); the ballet *Corrida de feria* (1930); 3 piano concertos (1933, 1957, 1958); *Tres movimientos concertantes* for String Trio and Orch. (1934); a cantata, *Por la paz y felicidad de las naciones* (1950); Concerto for Guitar and Orch. (Paris, Oct. 22, 1953); 3 string quartets; piano pieces; songs.

BIBL.: C. Heine, *S. B. (1898–1963): Die Kriterien seines Stils während der Schaffenszeit in Spanien (bis 1939)* (Frankfurt am Main, 1993).

Baccaloni, Salvatore, noted Italian bass; b. Rome, April 14, 1900; d. N.Y., Dec. 31, 1969. He began his training at the Sistine Chapel choir school at the Vatican, and then studied with Giuseppe Kaschmann. In 1922 he made his operatic debut as Rossini's Bartolo at the Teatro Adriano in Rome; from 1926 to 1940 he sang at Milan's La Scala, where he was esteemed in buffo roles. In 1928 he made his debut at London's Covent Garden as Puccini's Timur, and in 1930 his U.S. debut at the Chicago Civic Opera as Verdi's Melitone. From 1931 to 1941 he appeared at the Teatro Colón in Buenos Aires, and from 1936 to 1939 at the Glyndebourne Festivals. On Dec. 3, 1940, he made his first appearance with the Metropolitan Opera as Mozart's Bartolo during the company's visit to Philadelphia; then sang for the first time on the Metropolitan stage in N.Y. in the same role on Dec. 7, 1940, and subsequently was its leading buffo artist until 1962; his farewell appearance with the company was as Rossini's Bartolo in Brookville, N.Y., on Aug. 8, 1965. Baccaloni was the foremost comic bass of his generation. Among his memorable roles were Don Pasquale, Osmin, Leporello, Dulcamara, Varlaam, and Gianni Schicchi.

Bacewicz, Grażyna, notable Polish composer and violinist; b. Łódź, Feb. 5, 1909; d. Warsaw, Jan. 17, 1969. She learned to play the violin in her youth in Łódź, and began to compose at age 13. She then was a student of Józef Jarzębski (violin), Józef

Turczýnski (piano), and Sikorski (composition) at the Warsaw Cons., graduating in 1932. She also studied philosophy at the Univ. of Warsaw. A scholarship from Paderewski enabled her to study violin with André Touret and composition with Boulanger at the École Normale de Musique in Paris (1932–33). After teaching at the Łódź Cons. (1933–34), she returned to Paris to study violin with Flesch. In 1935 she received honorable mention at the 1st Wieniawski violin competition in Warsaw, and then played in the Polish Radio Sym. Orch. there (1936–38). From 1945 to 1955 she was active as a concert violinist. From 1966 until her death, she taught at the Warsaw State College of Music. In 1949 she won the Warsaw Prize, and in 1950 and 1952 the National Prize for composition. Bacewicz's large catalog of works generally adhered to neo-Classical principles. After the rise of the new Polish school of composition, she pursued more adventuresome paths.

WORKS: DRAMATIC: *Z chłopa król* (The Peasant King), ballet (1953); *Przygoda króla Artura* (The Adventures of King Arthur), radio comic opera (1959); *Esik w Ostendzie* (Esik in Ostend), ballet (1964); *Pożądanie* (Desire), ballet (1968); incidental music. **ORCH.:** Suite for Strings (1931); *Sinfonietta* (1932); *3 Caricatures* (1932); *Convoi de Joie* (1933); 7 violin concertos (1937, 1945, 1948, 1951, 1954, 1957, 1965); 2 unnumbered syms. (1938; Sym. for Strings, 1946); 4 numbered syms. (1942–45; 1951; 1952; 1953); Overture (1943); *Introduction and Caprice* (1947); Concerto for Strings (1948); Piano Concerto (1949); *Polish Rhapsody* for Violin and Orch. (1949); 2 cello concertos (1951, 1963); *Polish Overture* (1954); *Partita* (1955); *Symphonic Variations* (1957); *Music* for Strings, Trumpets, and Percussion (1958); *Pensieri Notturni* for Chamber Orch. (1961); *Concerto for Orchestra* (1962); *Musica Sinfonica in Tre Movimenti* (1965); *Divertimento* for Strings (1965); Concerto for 2 Pianos and Orch. (1966); *Contradizione* for Chamber Orch. (1966); *In una Parte* (1967); Viola Concerto (1968). **CHAMBER:** Double Fugue for String Quartet (1928); 2 unnumbered sonatas for Solo Violin (1929, 1932); 2 numbered sonatas for Solo Violin (1941, 1958); 1 unnumbered violin sonata (1929); 5 numbered violin sonatas (*Sonata da camera*, 1945; 1946; 1947; 1949; 1951); 2 unnumbered string quartets (1930, 1931); 7 numbered string quartets (1938, 1943, 1947, 1951, 1955, 1960, 1965); Wind Quintet (1932); Trio for Oboe, Violin, and Cello (1935); Suite for 2 Violins (1949); Trio for Oboe, Clarinet, and Bassoon (1948); Quartet for 4 Violins (1949); 2 piano quintets (1952, 1965); Quartet for 4 Cellos (1964); *Incrustations* for Horn and Chamber Ensemble (1965); Trio for Oboe, Harp, and Percussion (1965); etc. **KEYBOARD: PIANO:** 6 sonatas (1930, 1935, 1938, 1942, 1949, 1953); 2 sonatinas (1933, 1955); *10 Études* (1956); many other pieces. **ORGAN:** *Esquisse* (1966). **VOCAL:** *De Profundis*, cantata for Soloists, Chorus, and Orch. (1932); *3 Songs* for Tenor and Orch. (1938); *Olympic Cantata* for Chorus and Orch. (1948); *Acropolis*, cantata for Chorus and Orch. (1964); other songs.

BIBL.: S. Kisielewski, *G. B. i jej czasy* (G. B. and Her Times; Kraków, 1963); J. Rosen, *G. B.: Her Life and Works* (Los Angeles, 1984); S. Shafer, *The Contribution of G. B. (1909–1969) to Polish Music* (Lewiston, N.Y., 1992).

Bach, Jan (Morris), American composer and teacher; b. Forrest, Ill., Dec. 11, 1937. He pursued composition studies with Gaburo and Kelly at the Univ. of Illinois (B.M., 1959; D.M.A., 1971); also took courses with Copland (becoming co-winner of the Koussevitzky prize at the Berkshire Music Center in Tanglewood, 1961), Gerhard, and Musgrave. From 1966 he taught theory and composition at Northern Illinois Univ. in De Kalb. In his compositions, Bach effectively combines traditional and contemporary elements in an accessible style.

WORKS: DRAMATIC: *The System*, opera (1973; N.Y., March 5, 1974); *The Student from Salamanca*, opera (1979; N.Y., Oct. 9, 1980); *Romeo and Juliet*, incidental music (1984). **ORCH.:** *Toccata* (1959); *Burgundy Variations* (1968); Piano Concerto (1975; Chicago, July 8, 1981); *Gala Fanfare* (1979); *Sprint* (1982; Greenwich, Conn., March 26, 1983); Horn Concerto (Chicago, June 4, 1983); *Escapade* (1984); *Alla Breve*, fanfare-overture (1984); *Dompes and Jompes* for Strings (London, April 17, 1986); Harp Concerto (1986; Indianapolis, Feb. 6, 1987); Concerto for Trumpet and Wind Ensemble (1987); *Estampie* (1988); Euphonium Concerto (1990); Steel Drum Concerto (1994). **BAND OR WIND:** *Dionysia* for Symphonic Band (1964); *Recitative and March* for Viola and Wind Ensemble (1966); *The Eve of St. Agnes* for Wind Ensemble (1976); *Praetorius Suite* for Concert Band (1977). **CHAMBER:** String Trio (1956); *Divertimento* for Oboe and Bassoon (1956); Quartet for Strings (1957); Clarinet Sonata (1957); Quintet for Oboe and Strings (1958); *Partita* for Flute, Harpsichord, and Cello (1958); *Rondelle* for Alto Flute, Violin, Horn or Bassoon, and Piano (1961); *4 2-Bit Contraptions* for Flute and Horn (1964); *Skizzen* for Woodwind Quintet (1967); *Turkish Music* for Multi-percussion Solo (1967); *Woodwork* for Percussion Quartet (1970); *Laudes* for Brass Quintet (1971); *Eisteddfod* for Flute, Viola, and Harp (1972); *My Very 1st Solo* for Alto Saxophone and Electric Piano (1974); *Canon and Caccia* for 5 Horns (1977); *Concert Variations* for Euphonium and Piano (1977); Quintet for Tuba and Strings (1978); *Lowlands* for Contrabass and Piano (1981); *French Suite* for Horn (1982); *Helix* for Alto Saxophone, Flute, Clarinet, Bassoon, Horn, Trumpet, Trombone, and 2 Percussionists (1983); *New Egyptian Fanfare* for 3 Trumpets and 3 Percussionists (1983); *8 Duetudes* for Flute and Bassoon (1983) *Gypsy Rock* for String Quartet (1984); *Little Suite* for Harp (1984); *Lazy Blues* for 5 Bassoons (1985); *Triptych* for Brass Quintet (1989); *Anachronisms* for String Quartet (1991). **PIANO:** *3 Bagatelles* (1963; rev. 1971). **VOCAL:** *3 Shakespearean Songs* for Chorus (1960: *Exhortation* for Chorus and Piano (1961; rev. 1964); *A Lyke-wake Dirge* for Chorus or Quartet (1962); *Dirge for a Minstrel* for Chorus (1969); *3 Choral Dances* for Women's Chorus (1969); *Spectra* for Soprano, Baritone, Chorus, and Orch. (1971); *3 Sonnets on Woman* for Tenor and Harpsichord (1972); *My Wilderness* for Chorus (1974); *The Oregon Trail* for Tenor, Baritone, Chorus, and Orch. (1975); *Hair Today* for Chorus (1977); *The Happy Prince* for Narrator, Violin, and Chamber Orch. (1978); *Laudate Dominum* for Chorus, Children's Chorus, and Organ (1981); *5 Sylvan Songs* for Baritone and String Quartet (1981); *A Solemn Music* for Chorus (1987); *We Have But Faith* for Chorus and Organ (1988); *With Trumpet and Drum* for 16 Solo Voices and Piano (1991); *People of Note* for Voices and Instruments (1993).

Bachauer, Gina, eminent Greek-born English pianist of Austrian descent; b. Athens, May 21, 1913; d. there, Aug. 22, 1976. She showed her aptitude as a pianist at age 5; entered the Athens Cons., where her teacher was Waldemar Freeman. She then went to Paris, where she took lessons with Cortot at the École Normale de Musique. In 1933 she won the Medal of Honor at the Vienna International Competition; between 1933 and 1935 she received occasional instructions from Rachmaninoff in France and Switzerland; in 1935 she made her professional debut with the Athens Sym. Orch. under the direction of Mitropoulos; she was also piano soloist in Paris in 1937 with Monteux. During World War II she lived in Alexandria, Egypt, and played several hundred concerts for the Allied Forces in the Middle East. On Jan. 21, 1946, she made her London debut with the New London Orch. under the direction of Alec Sherman, who became her 2nd husband. Her first American appearance took place in N.Y. on Oct. 15, 1950. Only 35 people attended this concert, but she received unanimous acclaim from the critics, and her career was assured. The uncommon vigor of her technique suggested comparisons with Teresa Carreño; her repertoire ranged from Mozart to Stravinsky; in both standard and modern works, she displayed impeccable taste. She died of a heart attack in Athens on the day she was to appear as soloist with the National Sym. Orch. of Washington, D.C., at the Athens Festival. In 1976 the Gina Bachauer International Piano Competition was founded in Salt Lake City.

Bachelet, Alfred, French composer; b. Paris, Feb. 26, 1864; d. Nancy, Feb. 10, 1944. He studied at the Paris Cons.; received the Grand Prix de Rome for his cantata, *Cléopâtre* (1890). From his earliest works, Bachelet devoted himself mainly to opera. In his youth, he was influenced by Wagnerian ideas, but later adopted a more national French style. During World War I, he conducted at the Paris Opéra; in 1919 he became director of the Nancy Cons.; in 1939 he was elected a member of the Académie des Beaux Arts.

WORKS: Lyric dramas: *Scémo* (Paris, May 6, 1914) and *Un Jardin sur l'Oronte* (Paris, Nov. 3, 1932); *Quand la cloche sonnera*, music drama (Paris, Nov. 6, 1922); ballets: *La Fête chez la Pouplinière* and *Castor et Pollux* by Rameau (adapted and rewritten); orch. works with voices: *L'Amour des Ondines, Joie, Le Songe de la Sulamith, Noël; Surya* for Tenor, Chorus, and Orch. (1940); *Ballade* for Violin and Orch.; songs.

Bachmann, Alberto Abraham, Swiss-born French violinist and composer; b. Geneva, March 20, 1875; d. Neuilly-sur-Seine, Nov. 24, 1963. He studied violin at the Lille Cons., then took courses in succession with Ysaÿe, César Thomson, Hubay, and Brodsky. He was in the U.S. from 1916 to 1926; then lived near Paris. He composed 3 violin concertos (the last of which is called *American Concerto*); 12 improvisations for solo violin; about 250 various pieces and as many transcriptions for violin. He publ. *Le Violon* (1906); *Les Grands Violonistes du passé* (1913); *Gymnastique à l'usage des violonistes* (1914); *L'École du violoniste* (in 4 parts); and *Encyclopedia of the Violin* (N.Y., 1925).

Bäck, Sven-Erik, significant Swedish composer; b. Stockholm, Sept. 16, 1919; d. there, Jan. 10, 1994. He studied violin at the Stockholm Musikhögskolan (1938–43); also had training in composition from Rosenberg in Stockholm (1940–45) before pursuing studies in early music with Ina Lohr and Wenzinger at the Basel Schola Cantorum (1948–50); later had advanced composition studies with Petrassi in Rome (1951–52). He played violin in the Kyndel (1940–44) and Barkel (1944–53) string quartets, as well as in the Lilla Chamber Orch. (1943–48). After conducting the "Chamber Orch. '53" (1953–57), he was director of the Swedish Radio music school at Edsberg Castle outside Stockholm (from 1959). In 1961 he was elected to membership in the Royal Academy of Music in Stockholm. In his compositions, Bäck experimented with serialism and, later, electronic sound. His liturgical works are particularly notable.

WORKS: DRAMATIC: OPERAS: *Tranfjädrarna* (The Twilight Crane), a symbolist subject from Japanese Noh drama (1956; Swedish Radio, Feb. 28, 1957; 1st stage perf., Stockholm, Feb. 19, 1958); *Ett spel om Maria, Jesu Moder* (A Play about Mary, Mother of Jesus; Swedish Radio, April 4, 1958); *Gästabudet* (The Feast; Stockholm, Nov. 12, 1958); *Fågeln* (The Birds; 1960; Swedish Radio, Feb. 14, 1961). **BALLETS:** *Ikaros* (Stockholm, May 1963); *Movements* (Swedish TV, Feb. 27, 1966); *Kattresan* (Cat's Journey; 1969); *Mur och Port* (Wall and Gate; 1970; Stockholm, Jan. 17, 1971); *Genom Jorden, Genom Havet* (Through the Earth, Through the Sea; 1971–72; Stockholm, June 17, 1972). **ORCH.:** *Sinfonia per archi* (1951); *Sinfonia da camera* (1954); *Fantasy on Dies sind die Heiligen Zehn Gebot* (1954; rev. 1957); Violin Concerto (1957); *A Game around a Game* for Piano, Celesta, Percussion, and Strings (Donaueschingen, Oct. 17, 1959); *Arkitektur 60* for 2 Wind Orchs., Piano, Double Bass, and Percussion (1960); *Intrada* for Small Orch. (Stockholm, April 26, 1964); *Arkitektur 65* for 2 Wind Orchs., Piano, Double Bass, and Percussion (1965); Cello Concerto (1965); *O Altitudo II* (1966; also for Organ as *Altitudo I*); *Ruoli per orchestra* (1968); *Aperio* for 3 Orch. Groups and Tape (1973); *Ciklos*, concerto for Piano, Strings, and Percussion (1975); *Sumerki*, serenade for Strings (1976–77); *4 Motets* (1978; also for Strings); *3 Dialogue Motets* for Cello and Strings (1984); *Ekvator* for Orch. and Tape (1988); *Pro Musica Vitae*, concerto for Strings (1989). **CHAMBER:** 4 string quartets (1945, 1947, 1962, 1981); String Quintet (1948); *Préambule pour Pierre* for String Quartet (1949); Sonata for Solo Flute (1949); *Nocturne* for 3 Recorders, Percussion, Lute, Viola da Gamba, and Violin (1953); Trio for Violin, Cello, and Double Bass (1954); *Nature morte* for Viola, Bassoon, and Percussion (1955); Sonata for 2 Cellos (1957); *Favola* for Clarinet, Percussion, and Piano (1962); *Postludium* for Flute, Piano, and Percussion (1967); *Sentire* for Flute, Cello, and Piano (1969); Trio for Violin, Viola, and Cello (1970); *Decet* for Wind Quintet, String Quartet, and Double Bass (1973); *Fa-Ce* for Bassoon and Harpsichord or Piano (1975); *Signos* for 6 Percussion (1979); *Trio in 1 Movement* for Piano, Violin, and Cello (1984); *3 consorts* for 2 Trumpets and 3 Trombones (1993). **PIANO:** *Expansive Preludes* (1949); *Sonata alla ricercare* (1950); *Danssuit* for 2 Pianos (1951); *Impromptu* (1957); *Tollo I* for Piano Duet (1974) and *II* for 2 Pianos and Microphones (1975); *Sonata in 2 Movements and Epilogue* (1980). **VOCAL:** *Ur Johannes* for 3 Voices and Organ ad libitum (1944); *Ur Johannes 9* for Voices and Organ (1947); *Svanesang* for Chamber Chorus, Flute, Viola, and Timpani (1947); *Gladje i Gud*, cantata for Soloist, Voices, and Organ (1948); *Dithyramb* for Woman's Voice, Unison Chorus, and Chamber Orch. (1949); *Sinfonia sacra* for Voices and Orch. (1953); *Uppbrottets massa* for Soloist, Unison Voices, Organ, and Percussion (1967); *Neither Nor* for Soprano, Piano, and Percussion (1971); *Där fanns en brunn* for Chorus, Flute, Clarinet, Cello, Percussion, and Piano or Organ (1973); *Just da de langsta skuggorna . . .* for 4 Singers and 10 Instruments (1974); *Naktergalen och Hoken* for Chorus, String Orch., Piano, and Percussion (1975); *Te Deum* for Chorus, Brass, and Organ (1980); *Annus Solaris* for 2 Sopranos and Tape (1980); various choral pieces.

Backers, Cor, Dutch pianist, conductor, music historian, and composer; b. Rotterdam, June 5, 1910. He studied piano with Dirk Schäfer and composition at the Rotterdam Cons. He gave piano recitals in the Netherlands; also traveled through Europe and East Africa; conducted the chamber choir Haags Kamerkoor (1950–60), specializing in forgotten masterpieces of the past. He publ. a valuable compendium, *Nederlandse componisten van 1400 tot op onze tijd* (The Hague, 1941; 2nd ed., enl., 1948), which details the evolution of music in the Netherlands, with particular emphasis on modern Dutch music; he also publ. monographs on Handel, Puccini, Gershwin, and others. He composed mostly for voices and organ; among his works are a "declamatorio," *Joost de Decker*, for Narrator and Piano; Piano Sonata (1935); *6 Goethe-Lieder* for Chorus (1969); *Missa Sancta* for Soloists, Chorus, and Organ (1973–74); *Te Deum Laudamus* for Chorus and Organ or Orch. (1973–75).

Backhaus, Wilhelm, eminent German-born Swiss pianist and pedagogue; b. Leipzig, March 26, 1884; d. Villach, Austria, July 5, 1969. He studied with Reckendorf in Leipzig (1891–99), making his debut there at the age of 8. After studying briefly with d'Albert in Frankfurt am Main (1899), he began his career with a major tour in 1900, aquiring a fine reputation in Europe as both a pianist and a teacher. He made his U.S. debut on Jan. 5, 1912, as soloist in Beethoven's 5th Piano Concerto with Walter Damrosch and the N.Y. Sym. Orch. In 1930 he settled in Lugano, where he continued to teach, and became a naturalized Swiss citizen. Following World War II, he resumed his concert tours; made his last appearance in the U.S. at a recital in N.Y. in 1962, at the age of 78, displaying undiminished vigor as a virtuoso. He died while visiting Austria for a concert engagement. He was particularly distinguished in his interpretations of Beethoven and Brahms.

BIBL.: F. Herzog, *W. B.* (Berlin, 1935); A. Eichmann, *W. B.* (Ghent, 1957; Eng. tr., 1958).

Bacon, Ernst, remarkable American composer; b. Chicago, May 26, 1898; d. Orinda, Calif., March 16, 1990. He studied theory at Northwestern Univ. with P.C. Lutkin (1915–18), and later at the Univ. of Chicago with Arne Oldberg and T. Otterstroem (1919–20); also took private piano lessons in Chicago with Alexander Raab (1916–21). In 1924 he went to Vienna, where he took private composition lessons with Karl Weigl and Franz Schmidt. Returning to America, he studied composition with

Ernest Bloch in San Francisco, and conducting with Eugene Goossens in Rochester, N.Y.; completed his education at the Univ. of Calif. (M.A., 1935). From 1934 to 1937 he was supervisor of the Federal Music Project in San Francisco; simultaneously deployed numerous related activities, as a conductor and a music critic. He was on the faculty of Converse College in South Carolina (1938–45) and Syracuse Univ. (1945–63). In 1939 and 1942 he held Guggenheim fellowships. He also engaged in literary pursuits—wrote poetry and publ. a book of aphorisms—and espoused radical politics. A musician of exceptional inventive powers, he publ. a brochure, *Our Musical Idiom* (Chicago, 1917), when he was 19; in it he outlines the new resources of musical composition. He later publ. *Words on Music* (1960) and *Notes on the Piano* (1963). In some of his piano works, he evolved a beguiling technique of mirror reflection between right and left hands, exact as to the intervals, with white and black keys in 1 hand reflected respectively by white and black keys in the other. However, Bacon is generally regarded as primarily a composer of lyric songs.

WORKS: DRAMATIC: *Take Your Choice* (San Francisco, 1936; in collaboration with P. Mathias and R. Stoll); *A Tree on the Plains*, musical play (Spartanburg, S.C., May 2, 1942); *A Drumlin Legend*, folk opera (N.Y., May 4, 1949); *Dr. Franklin*, musical play (1976). **BALLETS:** *Jehovah and the Ark* (1968–70); *The Parliament of Fowls* (1975). **ORCH.:** *Fantasy and Fugue* (1926); *Symphonic Fugue* for Piano and Strings (1932); 4 syms.: No. 1 for Piano and Orch. (1932; San Francisco, Jan. 5, 1934), No. 2 (1937; Chicago, Feb. 5, 1940), No. 3, *Great River*, for Narrator and Orch. (1956), and No. 4 (1963); *Bearwall* for Piano and Strings (1936); *Country Roads, Unpaved* (1936); *Ford's Theater* (1946); *From these States* (1951); *Fables* for Narrator and Orch. (1953); Concerto grosso (1957); *Elegy* for Oboe and Strings (1957); *Erie Waters* (1961); 2 piano concertos: No. 1, *Riolama* (1963) and No. 2 (1982); *Over the Waters*, overture (1976). **CHAMBER:** Piano Quintet (1946); Cello Sonata (1946); Quintet for String Quartet and Double Bass (1950); *Peterborough*, suite for Viola and Piano (1961–82); *A Life*, suite for Cello and Piano (1966–81); *Tumbleweeds* for Violin and Piano (1979); Piano Trio (1981); Violin Sonata (1982); Viola Sonata (1987); piano pieces. **VOCAL:** Cantatas: *On Ecclesiastes* (1936); *The Lord Star* (1950); *By Blue Ontario* (1958); *Nature* (1968–70); *The Last Envocation*, Requiem for Bass, Chorus, and Orch. after Whitman, Dickinson et al. (1968–71); numerous songs; arrangements.

Bacquier, Gabriel (-Augustin-Raymond-Théodore-Louis), noted French baritone; b. Béziers, May 17, 1924. He studied at the Paris Cons., winning 3 premiers prix. In 1950 he made his debut in Landowski's *Le Fou* in Nice with José Beckman's Compagnie Lyrique, and remained with the company until 1952; then sang at the Théâtre Royal de la Monnaie in Brussels (1953–56). He was a member of the Opéra-Comique (1956–58) and the Opéra (from 1958) in Paris. In 1962 he made his U.S. debut as the High Priest in *Samson et Dalila* in Chicago; in 1964 he first appeared at London's Covent Garden; on Oct. 17, 1964, he made his Metropolitan Opera debut in N.Y. as the aforementioned High Priest, and continued to sing there until 1982. In 1987 he became a teacher at the Paris Cons. He was made a Chevalier of the Légion d'honneur in 1975. He was equally at home in both dramatic and comic roles, numbering among his most esteemed portrayals Leporello, Dr. Bartolo, Dulcamara, Boccanegra, Falstaff, Golaud, and Scarpia.

Badea, Christian, Romanian-born American conductor; b. Bucharest, Dec. 10, 1947. He studied violin and composition at the Bucharest Cons.; subsequently took courses in Brussels, in Salzburg, and at the Juilliard School in N.Y. He conducted at the Spoleto Festival of Two Worlds in Charleston, S.C., and Spoleto, Italy; served as music director of the Savannah (Ga.) Sym. Orch. (1977–84) and the Columbus (Ohio) Sym. Orch. (1983–91).

Baden, (Peter) Conrad (Krohn), Norwegian organist, teacher, and composer; b. Drammen, Aug. 31, 1908; d. Oslo, June 11, 1989. He began his training with the Drammen organist Daniel Hanssen in 1926; after pursuing organ studies at the Oslo Cons. (graduated, 1931), he received composition instruction in Leipzig (1931–32), with Honegger and Rivier in Paris (1951–52), and in Vienna (1965). He served as a church organist in Drammen (1928–61) and Oslo (1961–75); taught at the Oslo Cons. (1948–73) and the Oslo Academy of Music (1973–78). His neo-Romanticism eventually gave way to a more modern style of composition.

WORKS: ORCH.: 6 syms. (1952; 1958; *Sinfonia Piccola*, 1959; 1970; *Sinfonia Voluntatis*, 1976; *Sinfonia Espressiva*, 1980); *Divertimento* (1951); *Gioia*, overture (1951); Concertino for Clarinet and Strings (1953); *Pastorale and Fugue* for Chamber Orch. (1957); *Eventyr-Suite* (Fairy Tale Suite; 1960); *Variazioni* (1963); *Fantasia Breve* (1965); *Concerto for Orchestra* (1968); *Intrada Sinfonica* (1969); Viola Concerto (1973); Piano Concerto (1979); Concerto for Bassoon and Strings (1981); *Rondo* (1983); *Pastorale* for Chamber Orch. (1983). **CHAMBER:** Violin Sonata (c.1942); 3 string quartets (1944, 1946, 1961); 2 trios for Flute, Oboe, and Clarinet (1957, 1964); 2 woodwind quintets (1963, 1982); Sonata for Solo Flute (1958); *Divertimento* for Flute, Oboe, and Clarinet (1964); *Hymnus* for Alto Voice, Flute, Oboe, and Viola (1966); *Mini-Trio* for Flute, Clarinet, and Bassoon (1977); Flute Sonata (1984); piano pieces; organ music. **CHORAL:** Mass for Soloists, Chorus, and Orch. (1949); cantatas for Skien's 600th (1958), Strömsö Church's 300th (1966–67), and Dröbak Church's 200th (1973) anniversaries; *Mennesket* (The Human Being), cantata (1971).

Badescu, Dinu (Constantin), Romanian tenor; b. Craiova, Oct. 17, 1904. He studied in Bucharest. He made his operatic debut as a baritone in 1931 in Cluj as Germont, returning later that year to make his tenor debut as Lionel in *Martha*. He was a leading member of the Bucharest Opera (1936–61); also sang at the Vienna Volksoper (1941–44) and at the Vienna State Opera (from 1948); he was highly successful as a guest artist with the Bolshoi Theater in Moscow, in Leningrad, Budapest, Prague, etc., making a specialty of lyrico-dramatic roles in Verdi's operas.

Badia, Conchita (Conxita), noted Spanish soprano; b. Barcelona, Nov. 14, 1897; d. there, May 2, 1975. She studied piano and voice with Granados; also had lessons with Casals and Manuel de Falla. She made her debut in Barcelona as a concert singer in 1913 in the first performance of *Canciónes amatorias* by Granados, with the composer as piano accompanist. She subsequently devoted herself to concert appearances, excelling as an interpreter of Spanish and Latin American music; often appeared in performances with Casals and his orch. in Barcelona. In later years she taught voice in Barcelona, where her most famous pupil was Montserrat Caballé.

BIBL.: J. Alavedra, *Conxita B.: Una vida d'artista* (Barcelona, 1975).

Badings, Henk (Hendrik Herman), eminent Dutch composer and pedagogue; b. Bandung, Dutch East Indies, Jan. 17, 1907; d. Maarheeze, June 26, 1987. He was orphaned at an early age and taken to the Netherlands; studied mining engineering at the Delft Polytechnic Univ. before taking up composition without formal training; an early sym. was premiered by Mengelberg and the Concertgebouw Orch. in Amsterdam (July 6, 1930). After composition lessons with Willem Pijper (1930–31), he taught at the Rotterdam Cons. (1934–37), the Amsterdam Lyceum (1937–41), and the Royal Cons. of Music at The Hague (1941–45). In 1945 he was barred from professional activities as a cultural collaborator during the Nazi occupation of his homeland, but in 1947 was permitted to resume his career. From 1961 to 1977 he taught at the Univ. of Utrecht musicological inst.; also was a prof. of composition at the Stuttgart Hochschule für Musik (1966–72). Badings began his career as a composer in the Romantic vein. In his melodic foundation, he often employed the scale of alternating major and minor seconds. From 1950 he experimented with electronic sound and also adapted some of his works to the scale of 31 melodic divisions devised by the Dutch physicist Adriaan Fokker.

WORKS: OPERAS: *De Nachtwacht* (The Night Watch; 1942; Antwerp, May 13, 1950); *Liebesränke* (Love's Ruses; 1944–45; Hilversum, Jan. 6, 1948); *Orestes*, radio opera (Florence, Sept. 24, 1954); *Asterion*, radio opera (Johannesburg, April 11, 1958); *Salto mortale*, television chamber opera (Dutch TV, Eindhoven, June 19, 1959; 1st opera to be accompanied solely by electronic sound); *Martin Korda, D.P.* (Amsterdam, June 15, 1960). **BALLETS FOR INSTRUMENTS:** *Balletto Grottesco* for 2 Pianos (1939); *Orpheus und Eurydike* for Soloists, Chorus, and Orch. (Amsterdam, April 17, 1941); *Balletto Serioso* for Orch. or 2 Pianos (1955); *Balletto Notturno* for 2 Pianos (1975). **BALLETS FOR ELECTRONIC SOUND:** *Kain und Abel* (The Hague, June 21, 1958; 1st all-electronic sound ballet); *Evolutions* (Hannover, Sept. 28, 1958); *Der sechste Tag* (Innsbruck, Nov. 7, 1959); *Jungle* (Amsterdam, 1959); *The Woman of Andras* (Hannover, April 14, 1960); *Marionetten* (Salzburg, 1961). **ORCH.:** 4 violin concertos (1928; 1933–35; 1944; 1947); 1 unnumbered sym. (Amsterdam, July 6, 1930); 14 numbered syms.: No. 1 for 16 Solo Instruments (1932; Hilversum, March 19, 1959), No. 2 (Amsterdam, Oct. 5, 1932), No. 3 (1934; Amsterdam, May 2, 1935), No. 4 (1943; Rotterdam, Oct. 13, 1947), No. 5 (Amsterdam, Dec. 7, 1949), No. 6, *Psalm*, for Chorus and Orch. (Haarlem, June 25, 1953), No. 7, *Louisville* (1954; Louisville, Ky., Feb. 26, 1955), No. 8, *Hannover* (1956; Vancouver, Jan. 11, 1957), No. 9 for Strings (1959; Amsterdam, Dec. 17, 1960), No. 10 (1961; Rotterdam, Jan. 29, 1962), No. 11, *Sinfonia Giocosa* (Eindhoven, Oct. 26, 1964), No. 12, *Symphonische klangfiguren* (The Hague, Nov. 20, 1964), No. 13 for Wind Orch. (Pittsburgh, June 29, 1967), and No. 14, *Symphonische Triptiek* (Ghent, Sept. 4, 1968); 2 cello concertos (1930, 1939); 2 piano concertos (1939; *Atlantic Dances*, 1955); Saxophone Concerto (1951–52); 2 organ concertos (1952, 1966); 2 concertos for 2 Violins and Orch. (1954, 1969); 2 flute concertos (1956, 1963); Concerto for Bassoon, Double Bassoon, and Wind Orch. (1964); Concerto for 2 Pianos and Orch. (1964); Concerto for Viola and Strings (1965); *Pittsburgh Concerto* for Clarinet, Brass, Percussion, and Tape (1965); Concerto for Violin, Viola, and Orch. (1965); Concerto for 3 Horns, Wind Orch., and Tape (1970); *American Folk Song Suite*, concerto for English Horn and Wind Orch. (1975); *Azioni musicali* (1980); Triple Concerto No. 3 for Flute, Oboe, Clarinet, and Orch. (1981); *Concerto for Orchestra* (1982); Quadruple Concerto for 4 Saxophones and Orch. (1984); *Serenade* for Strings (1985). **CHAMBER:** 6 quintets: No. 1 for Flute, Piano, and String Trio (1928), No. 2 for Wind Quintet (1929), No. 3 for Harp, Flute, and String Trio (1936), No. 4 for Wind Quintet (1948), No. 5 for Piano Quintet (1952), and No. 6 for Clarinet, Violin, Cello, Guitar, and Harp (1986); 2 cello sonatas (1929, 1934); 6 string quartets (1931, 1936, 1944, 1966, 1980, 1984); 5 violin sonatas (1933; 1939; 1952; 1931, rescored 1966; 1984); 9 trios for Various Instrumental Combinations (1934–62); 3 sonatas for Solo Violin (1940, 1951, 1951); 2 sonatas for Solo Cello (1941, 1951); Sonata for Solo Harp (1944); Viola Sonata (1951); much piano music, including 6 sonatas (1934, 1941, 1944, 1945, 1945, 1947); organ pieces. **VOCAL:** Oratorios: *Apocalypse* (1948; Rotterdam, Nov. 25, 1959) and *Jonah* (Adelaide, Sept. 30, 1963); *St. Mark Passion* (1971; Rotterdam, May 18, 1992); *Missa antiphonica* (1985); cantatas; choral pieces.

BIBL.: J. Wouters, "H. B.," *Sonorum Speculum*, 32 (1967); R. de Beer, "An odour of taboo: H. B., 1907–1987," *Key Notes*, 24 (1987); P. Klemme, *Catalog of the Works of H. B., 1907–87* (Warren, Mich., 1993).

Badini, Ernesto, Italian baritone; b. San Colombano al Lambro, Sept. 14, 1876; d. Milan, July 6, 1937. He studied at the Milan Cons. and with Cesari. In 1895 he made his operatic debut as Rossini's Figaro in San Colombano al Lambro; sang in many regional opera houses of Italy. In 1913 Toscanini chose him for the Verdi centennial celebrations in Parma, then invited him to Milan's La Scala, where he created Puccini's Gianni Schicchi (1922); remained on its roster until 1931. He also appeared at Rome's Teatro Costanzi (1921) and London's Covent Garden (debut as Gianni Schicchi, 1924). In addition to buffo roles, Badini also sang a number of contemporary roles.

Badinski, Nicolai, Bulgarian-born German violinist, teacher, and composer; b. Sofia, Dec. 19, 1937. He studied at the Bulgarian State Cons. in Sofia (diploma, 1961), then pursued master classes in composition at the (East) Berlin Academy of Arts (1967–70) and at the Accademia Musicale Chigiana in Siena (1975–76); also worked with Ligeti, Stockhausen, Xenakis, and Kagel in Darmstadt (summers 1974–78). He settled in West Germany, becoming a naturalized citizen in 1980. In 1979 he received the Trieste Prize, in 1981 a Prix de Rome, and in 1982 a Prix de Paris. In his music, he follows practical modernistic trends, avoiding extreme applications of experimental techniques.

WORKS: 3 syms. (1967, 1978, 1981); 3 violin concertos (1971, 1972, 1972); Viola Concerto (1975); Harpsichord Concerto (1977); *Homage to Stravinsky* for String Orch. (1979); *Klavieriada* for Piano and Orch. (1981); 3 string quartets (1965, 1973, 1978); Wind Quintet (1969); *The Ruins under Sofia*, octet (1972); *Silenzio disturbato* for Sextet (1976); *Imaginable Trio* for Computer (1980); *Wiederspiegelungen der Weisheit* for Soloists, Chorus, and Orch. (1984); *6 Capricci* for Baritone and Piano (1991); numerous pieces of electronic music, including *Rotation*, in memory of a Soviet cosmonaut, for Electronic Sound (1974); *Musik mit Papier* and *Luftmusik* for Electronics (1980–81); *Traumvisionen* for Electronic Sound (1982).

Badura-Skoda (real name, **Badura**), **Paul,** eminent Austrian pianist, music editor, and pedagogue; b. Vienna, Oct. 6, 1927. He was brought up by his stepfather, Skoda, whose name he adopted professionally. He studied science as well as music; graduated from the Vienna Cons. in 1948 as a piano pupil of Edwin Fischer. A scholarly musician, he won several prizes for excellence. He had a successful career as a concert pianist; gave recitals in Europe; made his N.Y. debut on Jan. 10, 1953. From 1966 until 1971 he was artist-in-residence at the Univ. of Wisc. On Sept. 19, 1951, he married Eva Halfar (b. Munich, Jan. 15, 1929), who collaborated with him on his various eds. He publ. *Mozart-Interpretation* (with his wife; Vienna, 1957; Eng. tr., 1962, as *Interpreting Mozart on the Keyboard*; also in Japanese, Tokyo, 1963); *Die Klaviersonaten von Ludwig van Beethoven* (with J. Demus; Wiesbaden, 1970); *Bach-Interpretation: Die Klavierwerke Johann Sebastian Bachs* (Laaber, 1990; Eng. tr., 1992, as *Interpreting Bach at the Keyboard*); also contributed valuable articles on Chopin, Schubert, and others to German music journals.

Baervoets, Raymond, Belgian composer; b. Brussels, Nov. 6, 1930; d. Rome, Aug. 19, 1989. He studied with Absil, Bourguignon, and Barbier at the Brussels Cons., and then with Defossez at the Accademia di Santa Cecilia in Rome (1961–62). His music followed along classical lines, with contents evolving in an ultra-chromatic coloristic idiom with occasional use of quarter tones.

WORKS: BALLETS: *Métamorphose* (1963); *La Chasse fantastique* (Antwerp, Sept. 28, 1968). **ORCH.:** *Mouvement symphonique* (1955); *Elégie et Passacaille* (1956); Concerto for Guitar and Chamber Orch. (1958); Violin Concerto (1961); *Composizione* (1962); *Notturno* for Chamber Orch. (1971); *Immagini* for Chamber Orch. (1976); *Memoria* (1975–76); Piano Concerto (1981); *Douze épisodes pour "La Métamorphose" de Kafka* (1986). **CHAMBER:** *Impromptu* for Trombone and Piano (1958); *Étude* for String Quartet (1961); *Musica Notturna* for Harpsichord, Violin, Cello, and Flute (1969); Quartet for Flute, Clarinet, Violin, and Piano (1974); piano pieces. **OTHER:** Vocal works, including *Les Dents de la terre* for Narrator, Soloists, Chorus, and 2 Orchs. (1968).

Baeyens, August, Belgian composer; b. Antwerp, June 5, 1895; d. there, July 17, 1966. He studied at the Royal Flemish Cons. in Antwerp. From 1911 he was a violist in Belgian orchs., and later served as director of the Royal Flemish Opera in Antwerp (1944–48; 1953–58). Despite his intimate association with the Flemish currents in the music of Belgium, he turned away from the dominant national direction and wrote music in a distinctly expressionistic style, rooted in a quasi-atonal chromaticism.

WORKS: DRAMATIC: *De Dode Dichter*, ballet (1920); *De Liefde en de Kakatoes*, a "grotesque" (1928); *Coriolanus*, radio opera (1941); *De Ring van Gyges*, opera (1943); *De Triomferende Min*, opera (1948). **ORCH.:** *Entrata* (1917); *Niobé* (1918); 8 syms. (1923, 1939, 1949, 1952, 1954, 1955, 1958, 1961); *4 Small Pieces* (1923); *Arlequin* (1924); *Cyclops* (1925); *Sinfonia Breve* (1928); *Arkadia*, chamber sym. (1951); *Notturno* (1953); Viola Concerto (1956); Trumpet Concerto (1959); Horn Concerto (1960); *Rhapsodie* for Clarinet and Orch. (1966). **CHAMBER:** 6 string quartets (1922, 1925, 1927, 1949, 1951, 1962); Wind Quintet (1950); Concertino for Oboe, Clarinet, and Bassoon (1951); *Piranesi Suite* for Flute and Cello (1951); Violin Sonata (1952). **PIANO:** Sonata (1930). **VOCAL:** *Lofzang aan de haven*, cantata (1929); *Barabbas* for Narrator and Orch. (1949); songs.

Baggiani, Guido, Italian composer; b. Naples, March 4, 1932. He studied composition at the Accademia di Santa Cecilia in Rome; then attended courses given by Stockhausen in Cologne, which were crucial for his further development. In Rome he organized a group for propagandizing contemporary music with the meaningful name of Nuova Consonanza. In 1970 he was appointed prof. of composition at the Pesaro Cons. In 1972 he formed a group with the curious Italian-American name Gruppo Team Roma for performances of electronic music. His principal works are *Mimesi* for Strings and Woodwinds (1967); *Metafora* for Solo Strings (1968); *UBU-ng* for Soprano, Piano, Vibraphone, Electric Guitar, and 6 Chinese Gongs (1970); *Twins* for Piano and Magnetic Tape (1971); *Memoria* for Chamber Orch. and 2 Magnetic Tapes (1972); *Accordo Presunto* for 2 Instrumental Groups and Electronic Media (1973); *ContriAzione* for 2 Orchs. (1975); *Double* for Chamber Ensemble (1977); *Il crudo e il cotto* for 4 Women's Voices, 2 Flutes, 2 Clarinets, and Electronic Media (1982).

Bahner, Gert, German conductor; b. Neuwiese, March 26, 1930. He was educated at the Leipzig Hochschule für Musik. In 1957 he made his debut at the Berlin Komische Oper; from 1958 to 1962 he was music director in Potsdam; then Generalmusikdirektor of Karl-Marx-Stadt (1962–65). In 1965 he became first conductor of the Berlin Komische Oper; in 1969 its music director. In 1973 he became music director of the Leipzig Opera. In 1983 he settled in (East) Berlin as an opera conductor; also taught at the Hochschule für Musik.

Bahr-Mildenburg (actually, **Bellschau-Mildenburg**), **Anna (von),** famous Austrian soprano; b. Vienna, Nov. 29, 1872; d. there, Jan. 27, 1947. She was a pupil of Rosa Papier in Vienna and Bernhard Pollini, director of the Hamburg Opera, who engaged her to make her operatic debut there as Brünnhilde in *Die Walküre* on Sept. 12, 1895. In 1897 she appeared as Kundry at the Bayreuth Festival, and subsequently sang there with distinction until 1914. From 1898 to 1917 she was a leading member of the Vienna Court Opera, where she continued to make guest appearances until 1921. In 1906, 1910, and 1913 she sang at London's Covent Garden. She was a prof. at the Munich Academy of Music (from 1921) and stage director at the Bavarian State Opera in Munich (1921–26). In 1930 she made her farewell operatic apperance as Klytemnestra in Augsburg. In 1909 she married the playwright Hermann Bahr, with whom she wrote *Bayreuth und das Wagner Theater* (Leipzig, 1910; Eng. tr., 1912); she also publ. her memoirs (Vienna and Berlin, 1921) and *Darstellung der Werke Richard Wagner aus dem Geiste der Dichtung und Musik* (Leipzig, 1936). She was one of the foremost Wagnerians of her day.

BIBL.: P. Stefan, *A. B.-M.* (Vienna, 1922).

Bailey, Norman (Stanley), English baritone; b. Birmingham, March 23, 1933. He received a B.Mus. degree from Rhodes Univ. in South Africa; then studied at the Vienna Academy of Music, his principal teachers there being Julius Patzak, Adolf Vogel, and Josef Witt. He made his operatic debut with the Vienna Chamber Opera in 1959 in *Cambiale di matrimonio*; was then a member of the Linz Landestheater (1960–63), the Wuppertal Opera (1963–64), the Deutsche Oper am Rhein in Düsseldorf (1964–67), and the Sadler's Wells Opera in London (1967–71). In 1969 he made his first appearance at London's Covent Garden, and that same year his debut at Bayreuth as Hans Sachs. On Oct. 23, 1976, he made his Metropolitan Opera debut in N.Y. as Hans Sachs. In 1977 he was made a Commander of the Order of the British Empire. He was particularly noted for his performances in Wagner's operas. In 1985 he married **Kristine Ciesinski**.

Baillie, Dame Isobel (Isabella), esteemed Scottish soprano; b. Hawick, Roxburghshire, March 9, 1895; d. Manchester, Sept. 24, 1983. She was a pupil of Sadler Fogg in Manchester and of Guglielmo Somma in Milan. In 1921 she made her concert debut in Manchester, and thereafter made numerous appearances as an oratorio and lieder artist in England. In 1933 she sang for the first time in the U.S. She taught at the Royal College of Music in London (1955–57), Cornell Univ. in Ithaca, N.Y. (1960–61), and the Manchester School of Music (from 1970). In 1951 she was made a Commander of the Order of the British Empire; in 1978 she was made a Dame Commander of the Order of the British Empire. She sang in hundreds of performances of *Messiah*, and was also noted for her championship of works by Elgar, Vaughan Williams, and Howells. Her autobiography was aptly titled *Never Sing Louder Than Lovely* (London, 1982).

Bailly, Louis, French violist and pedagogue; b. Valenciennes, June 13, 1882; d. Cowansville, Quebec, Nov. 21, 1974. He studied violin and viola at the Paris Cons., graduating with 1st prize in 1899; was subsequently the violist in the Capet, Flonzaley (1917–24), Elman, and Curtis quartets; served as head of the viola and chamber music dept. at the Curtis Inst. of Music in Philadelphia; in 1954 he went to Canada and taught in Montreal.

Bain, Wilfred, American music educator and administrator; b. Shawville, Quebec, Jan. 20, 1908. He was educated at Houghton College (A.B., 1929) and York Univ. (M.A., 1936; Ed.D., 1938). He was head of the music dept. at Central College, S.C. (1929–30); then of voice and choral music at Houghton College (1931–38). He was dean of music at North Texas State Univ. (1938–47). In 1947 he was appointed dean of the Indiana Univ. School of Music in Bloomington; he retired in 1973.

Bainbridge, Simon (Jeremy), English composer and conductor; b. London, Aug. 30, 1952. He learned to play the recorder and clarinet as a child, later studying composition with John Lambert at the Royal College of Music in London (1969–72) and with Schuller at the Berkshire Music Center in Tanglewood (summers 1973–74). Subsequently he was active as a conductor.

WORKS: *Heterophony* for Orch. (1970); *Spirogyra* for 7 Instruments (1971; rev. and used in *3 Pieces* for Chamber Ensembles, 1982); Wind Quintet (1971); String Quartet (1972); *Flugal* for 10 Instruments (1973; rev. and used in *3 Pieces* for Chamber Ensembles, 1982); Wind Quartet (1974); *People of the Dawn* for 3 Clarinets, Soprano Saxophone, Piano or Celesta, Percussion, and Soprano (1975); Viola Concerto (1976); *Landscapes and Magic Words* for Soprano and Ensemble (1981); *Voicing* for Ensemble (1982); *Devil's Punchbowl* for Chamber Orch., Children, and Instrumental Ensemble (1987); *Trace*, dance score for Instrumental Ensemble and Electronics (1987); *Metamorphosis* for 13 Instruments (Amsterdam, June 6, 1988); String Sextet (1988); *Cantus contra cantum* for Orch. (1989; rev. 1990); *A Song from Michelangelo* for Soprano and Ensemble (1989); Double Concerto for Oboe, Clarinet, and Chamber Orch. (1990); *Marimolin Inventions* for Violin and Marimba

(1990); *Caliban Fragments and Aria* for Mezzo-soprano and Ensemble (1991); *A Song from Tagore* for Children's Voices and Ensemble (1991); *Mobile* for English Horn and Piano (1991); Clarinet Quintet (1992–93).

Baines, Anthony, respected English organologist; b. London, Oct. 6, 1912. He studied at the Royal College of Music in London. After playing bassoon in the London Phil. (1935–39; 1946–48) and working as a conductor, he concentrated on organology. In 1946 he helped to found the Galpin Soc., serving as ed. of its journal (1955–63; 1971–83). In 1970 he joined the faculty of the Univ. of Oxford as a lecturer on music and as curator of the Bate Collection of Historical Instruments. He retired in 1981.

WRITINGS: *Woodwind Instruments and Their History* (London, 1957; 3rd ed., rev., 1967); *Bagpipes* (Oxford, 1960); ed. *Musical Instruments through the Ages* (Baltimore, 1961; 2nd ed., rev., 1976); *European and American Musical Instruments* (London, 1966); *Brass Instruments: Their History and Development* (London, 1976); ed. *The Oxford Companion to Musical Instruments* (Oxford, 1992).

Bainton, Edgar Leslie, English composer and pedagogue; b. London, Feb. 14, 1880; d. Sydney, Australia, Dec. 8, 1956. He studied piano and composition at the Royal College of Music in London with Davies and Stanford. He taught piano and composition at the Cons. of Newcastle upon Tyne from 1901 until 1914, and also was its director (1912–14). The outbreak of World War I found him in Berlin, and he was interned as an enemy alien. After the end of the War, he resumed his pedagogical activities as director of the Newcastle Cons. In 1934 he went to Australia and was director of the State Cons. at Sydney until 1947. As a composer, he followed the tenets of the English national school, writing in broad diatonic expanses with a Romantic élan. His works include 2 operas: *Oithona* (Glastonbury, Aug. 11, 1915) and *The Pearl Tree* (Sydney, May 20, 1944); 3 syms. (1903–56); *Before Sunrise* for Voice, Chorus, and Orch. (1917); *Paracelsus*, symphonic poem (1921); *Concerto-Fantasia* for Piano and Orch. (Carnegie Award, 1917; London, Jan. 26, 1922); chamber music; songs.

BIBL.: H. Bainton, *Remembered on Waking: E.L. B.* (Sydney, 1960).

Baird, Martha, American pianist and music patroness; b. Madera, Calif., March 15, 1895; d. N.Y., Jan. 24, 1971. She studied at the New England Cons. of Music in Boston and with Artur Schnabel in Berlin; appeared as soloist with Beecham in London and Koussevitzky in Boston. In 1957 she married John D. Rockefeller, Jr., and became a benefactress of opera and concert music.

Baird, Tadeusz, prominent Polish composer; b. Grodzisk Mazowiecki, July 26, 1928; d. Warsaw, Sept. 2, 1981. He studied music privately in Łódž with Sikorski and Woytowicz (1943–44); then at the Warsaw Cons. with Rytel and Perkowski (1947–51); had piano lessons with Wituski (1948–51); also studied musicology with Lissa at the Univ. of Warsaw (1948–52). In 1949, together with Krenz and Serocki, he founded a progressive society of composers under the name Group 49. In 1956 he became active in initiating the 1st International Festival of Contemporary Music during the "Warsaw Autumn." In 1977 he was appointed prof. of composition at the Chopin Academy of Music in Warsaw. As a composer, Baird won numerous awards, among them the Fitelberg Competition of 1958, 3 prizes of the Tribune Internationale des Compositeurs in Paris (1959, 1963, 1966), and the Polish State Awards for his 3 syms. (1951, 1964, 1969). He also was awarded the Commander's Cross of the Order of Poland's Revival (1964) and the Order of the Banner of Labor, 2nd and 1st Class (1974, 1981). His early music followed the neo-Romantic modalities characteristic of Polish music; further evolution was marked by complex structures in the manner of dynamic expressionism, with occasional applications of serialism.

WORKS: OPERA: *Jutro* (Tomorrow; 1964–66). **ORCH.:** Sinfonietta (1949); 3 syms. (1950; *Sinfonia quasi una fantasia*, 1952; 1969); *Overture in Old Style* (1950); *Colas Breugnon*, suite for Flute and Strings (1951); *Overture giocosa* (1952); *Concerto for Orchestra* (1953); *Cassazione* (1956); *4 Essays* (1958); *Espressioni varianti* for Violin and Orch. (1958–59); *Variations without a Theme* (1961–62); *Epiphany Music* (1963); *4 Dialogues* for Oboe and Chamber Orch. (1966); *4 Novelettes* for Chamber Orch. (Hanover, N.H., July 16, 1967); *Sinfonia breve* (1968); *Psychodrama* (1971–72); Oboe Concerto (Warsaw, Sept. 23, 1973); Elegy (1973); *Concerto lugubre* for Viola and Orch. (1974–75; Nuremberg, May 21, 1976); Double Concerto for Cello, Harp, and Orch. (1976); *Scenes* for Cello, Harp, and Orch. (1976); *Canzona* (1980). **CHAMBER:** *4 Preludes* for Bassoon and Piano (1954); *Divertimento* for Flute, Oboe, Clarinet, and Bassoon (1956); String Quartet (1957); *Play* for String Quartet (1971); *Variations in Rondo Form* for String Quartet (1978). **VOCAL:** *Lyrical Suite*, 4 songs for Soprano and Orch. (1953); *4 Love Sonnets*, after Shakespeare, for Baritone and Chamber Ensemble (1956; also for Baritone, Strings, and Harpsichord, 1969); *Exhortations* on old Hebrew texts for Narrator, Chorus, and Orch. (1959–60); *Erotyki* (Love Songs), cycle of 6 songs for Soprano and Orch. (1961); *Study* for 28 Mixed Voices, 6 Percussion Players, and Piano (1967); *4 songs* for Mezzo-soprano and Chamber Orch. (1966); *5 Songs* for Mezzo-soprano and Chamber Orch. (1968); *Goethe-Briefe*, cantata (1970; Dresden, June 6, 1971); *Voices from Afar*, 3 songs for Baritone and Orch. (1981).

BIBL.: T. Zielinski, *T. B.* (Kraków, 1966).

Bairstow, Sir Edward (Cuthbert), English organist, pedagogue, and composer; b. Huddersfield, Aug. 22, 1874; d. York, May 1, 1946. He studied organ and theory at the Univ. of Durham (Mus.B., 1894; Mus.D., 1901); was organist at Wigan (1899–1906), at Leeds (1906–13), and at York Minster (1913–46); also was prof. of music at the Univ. of Durham (from 1929). In 1932 he was knighted. He composed church music, anthems, part-songs, and an organ sonata (1937). He publ. *Counterpoint and Harmony* (1937) and *The Evolution of Musical Form* (1943).

BIBL.: E. Bradbury, "Sir E. B.: A Birthday Tribute," *Musical Times* (Aug. 1944).

Bajoras, Feliksas, Lithuanian composer; b. Alytus, Oct. 7, 1934. He studied violin and composition at the Lithuanian Cons. in Vilnius (1957–63). In his compositions, he employs the melorhythmic features of Lithuanian folklore in a modern harmonic dressing.

WORKS: ORCH.: 3 syms.: No. 1 (1964; rev. 1968–70), No. 2, *Stalactites*, for Strings (1970), and No. 3 (1972; rev. 1976); *Intermezzo and Postlude* for Chamber Orch. (1964); *Suite of Verbs* for Chamber Orch. (1966); *Prelude and Toccata* for Strings (1966); *Legends*, symphonic poem (1969); *Mourning Music* for Wind Orch. (1972); *Rondo* (1976). **CHAMBER:** Violin Sonatina (1961); *Variations* for Double Bass and String Quartet (1968); *4 Pieces* for String Quartet (1968); *Cycle of 15 Pieces* for Violin and Piano (1973); 2 string quartets (1974, 1975); Suite for Septet (1975); Violin Sonata (1979). **PIANO:** *3 Pieces* (1958); *Variations* (1959); *Variations on a Folk Theme* (1971).

Bakala, Břetislav, Czech conductor and composer; b. Fryšták, Feb. 12, 1897; d. Brno, April 1, 1958. He studied with Kurz (piano), Neumann (conducting), and Janáček (composition) at the Brno Cons. He was chief conductor of the Opera (1929–31), the Radio Sym. Orch. (1937–56), and the State Phil. (1956–58) in Brno, where he also taught conducting at the Janáček Academy of Music (1951–58). Bakala championed the music of Janáček. His own works include a *Scherzo* for Orch. (1923), a *Fantasie* for String Quartet, choruses, and songs.

Bakaleinikov, Vladimir, Russian-American violist, conductor, pedagogue, and composer; b. Moscow, Oct. 12, 1885; d. Pittsburgh, Nov. 5, 1953. He studied violin with Michael Press; graduated from the Moscow Cons. in 1907; subsequently played viola in the Grand Duke of Mecklenburg Quartet (1910–20), taught at the St. Petersburg Cons. (1913–20), and conducted opera at the Musicalnaya Drama in St. Petersburg (1914–16). Returning to Moscow, he taught at the Cons. (1920–24); was in charge of the opera branch of the Moscow Art Theater (1920–27). He went to America in 1927; was assistant conductor of the Cincinnati Sym. Orch. until 1937, and then was assoc. conductor of the Pittsburgh Sym. Orch. (1940–41). Among his pupils was Lorin Maazel. He wrote a Viola Concerto (1937) and a suite of oriental dances for Orch.; publ. several arrangements of works by Bach and Beethoven; also *Elementary Rules of Conducting* (1937) and *The Instruments of the Band and Orchestra* (N.Y., 1940).

Bake, Arnold Adriaan, Dutch music scholar; b. Hilversum, May 19, 1899; d. London, Oct. 8, 1963. He studied oriental languages at the Univ. of Leiden; received his Ph.D. in 1930 from the Univ. of Utrecht with the diss. *Bytrage tot de Kennis der Voor-Indische musiek* (publ. in Paris, 1930). He subsequently went to India, where he studied Indian music and languages at Tagore's school in Santiniketan; he also served as music adviser to the All India Radio in Delhi and as director of European music of the Calcutta Radio. In 1937 he was made a corresponding member of the American Musicological Soc. In 1948 he went to London, where he became a lecturer on Sanskrit and Indian music at the School of Oriental and African Studies. His interests also included Indian philosophy, tribal music, and dance.

Baker, Claude, American composer and teacher; b. Lenoir, N.C., April 12, 1948. He received training in theory and composition at East Carolina Univ. in Greenville, N.C. (B.M., 1970), and then pursued studies in composition principally with Adler and Benson at the Eastman School of Music in Rochester, N.Y. (M.M., 1973; D.M.A., 1975). He was an instructor in theory and composition at the Univ. of Georgia (1974–76), and then a prof. of those subjects at the Univ. of Louisville (1976–88); in 1985, was also a visiting prof. of composition at the Eastman School of Music. In 1988 he became a prof. at the Indiana Univ. School of Music in Bloomington. He also served as composer-in-residence of the St. Louis Sym. Orch. from 1991. Baker composed a number of eclectic instrumental scores, both tonal and atonal. With his *Awaking the Winds* for Orch. (1991–93), he turned to a more freely chromatic style of expression.

WORKS: ORCH.: Concertino for 3 Quintets, Piano, and Percussion (1969–70; Greensboro, N.C., July 20, 1970); *Strophes* for Strings (1971–72); *Capriccio* for Concert Band or Wind Ensemble (1974; Rochester, N.Y., Feb. 6, 1976); *Speculum Musicae, Pars II* (Greensboro, N.C., July 22, 1976); *Caractères* for Bass Trombone and Wind Ensemble (1975–76; Athens, Ga., March 12, 1976; rev. 1977; Louisville, Feb. 19, 1978); *The Glass Bead Game* (1982; Louisville, Feb. 11, 1983); *3 Pieces* for 5 Timpani, 5 Roto-toms, and Orch. (1989; Rochester, N.Y., Dec. 8, 1990; also for 5 Timpani, 5 Roto-toms, and Wind Ensemble, 1990; Kansas City, Mo., Feb. 21, 1991); *Awaking the Winds* (1991–93; St. Louis, May 14, 1993; also for Chamber Orch., Cleveland, Jan. 23, 1994); *Blow Out . . .* (St. Louis, Oct. 1, 1994); *Whispers and Echoes: 4 Night Pieces* (1994–95; St. Louis, Oct. 26, 1995). **CHAMBER:** *Invention* for Flute and Clarinet (1968); String Quartet No. 1 (1968–69); *3 Bagatelles* for 2 Horns and 2 Trombones (1969); *2 Pieces* for Violin and Cello (1970); *Canzonet* for Tuba (1972); *Jeu de cartes* for Wind Quartet, 4 Tape Recorders, and Card Dealer (1974; Athens, Ga., Jan. 23, 1975); *Speculum Musicae* for String Quartet, Wind Quartet, Brass Trio, Piano, and Percussion (1974–75; Rochester, N.Y., Feb. 23, 1975); *Banchetto Musicale* for Clarinet, Violin, Piano, and Percussion (1977–78; Manchester, Vt., July 29, 1978); *Elegy* for Violin (1978–79; N.Y., Dec. 17, 1979); *Divertissement* for Clarinet, Violin, Cello, and Piano (1979–80; Louisville, April 12, 1981); *Omaggi e Fantasie* for Tuba and Piano (1980–81; rev. 1987; Athens, Ga., Feb. 8, 1988; also for Double Bass and Piano, 1984; Rochester, N.Y., Nov. 20, 1985); *4 Nachtszenen* for Harp (1985; Bowling Green, Ohio, Oct. 24, 1987; rev. version, Paris, July 11, 1990); *Fantasy Variations* for String Quartet (Troy, N.Y., Aug. 15, 1986); *Tableaux Funèbres* for Piano and String Quartet (1987–88; Louisville, March 20, 1988). **VOCAL:** *3 Songs on Poems by Kenneth Patchen* for Soprano and Chamber Ensemble (Rochester, N.Y., April 14, 1971); *How Tyll Got His Name Ulenspiegel* for Narrator and Horn (Rochester, N.Y., April 28, 1971); *Rest, Heart of the Tired World* for Soprano and Orch. (1972–73; Rochester, N.Y., April 24, 1974); *4 Songs on Poems by Kenneth Patchen* for Soprano and Orch. (1973; rev. 1975; Granada, July 3, 1976).

Baker, David (Nathaniel), black American jazz instrumentalist, teacher, and composer; b. Indianapolis, Dec. 21, 1931. He was educated at Indiana Univ. (B.M.Ed., 1953; M.M.Ed., 1954); also studied theory privately with Heiden, Schuller, Orrego-Salas, William Russo, and George Russell. He subsequently taught music in small colleges and public schools; in 1966 he became chairman of the dept. of jazz studies at Indiana Univ. As a jazz performer, he played the trombone with Stan Kenton, Lionel Hampton, and Quincy Jones. His own compositions fuse jazz improvisation with ultramodern devices, including serial procedures. He has written many articles on jazz; among his books are *Jazz Improvisation: A Comprehensive Method of Study for All Players* (1969) and *Techniques of Improvisation* (1971); with L. Belt and H. Hudson, he ed. *The Black Composer Speaks* (1978); also ed. *New Perspectives on Jazz* (Washington, D.C., 1991).

WORKS: ORCH.: *Reflections* for Orch. and Jazz Ensemble (1969); Concerto for Violin and Jazz Band (1969; Bloomington, Ind., April 5, 1970); Concerto for Flute, Jazz Ensemble, and String Quartet (1971); Concerto for Double Bass, Jazz Ensemble, String Quartet, and Solo Violin (1972); Concerto for Trombone, Jazz Band, and Chamber Orch. (1972); *Kosbro* (1973; rev. 1975); *Levels*, concerto for Double Bass, Jazz Band, Flute Quartet, Horn Quartet, and String Quartet (1973); *Le Chat qui pêche* for Orch., Jazz Quartet, and Soprano (1974); *2 Improvisations* for Orch. and Jazz Combo (1974); Concerto for Tuba, Jazz Band, Percussion, Chorus, Dancers, Slide Projections, and Tape Recorders (1975); Concerto for Cello and Chamber Orch. (1975–76); Concerto for 2 Pianos, Jazz Band, Chamber Orch., and Percussion (1976); Clarinet Concerto (1985); *Concert Piece* for Trombone and Strings (Bloomington, Ind., Nov. 3, 1991). **CHAMBER:** String Quartet No. 1 (1962); Viola Sonata (1966); *Ballade* for Horn, Saxophone, and Cello (1967); Violin Sonata (1967); *Salute to Beethoven* for Piccolo, Wind Quintet, Flute Choir, Jazz Ensemble, and Tape (1970); Sonata for Brass Quintet and Piano (1970); Sonata for Piano and String Quintet (1971); Sonata for Tuba and String Quartet (1971); Sonata for Viola, Guitar, and Double Bass (1973); Cello Sonata (1973); Sonata for Violin and Cello (1974); Suite for Violin (1975); *Contrasts* for Piano Trio (1976); *Ethnic Variations on a Theme of Paganini* for Violin and Piano (1976); *Roots* for Piano Trio (1976); *Fantasy* for Alto Saxophone, 4 Cellos, and Percussion (1977); *Shapes* for Percussion Ensemble (1977); *Concerto for Fours* for Flute, Cello, Tuba, Double Bass, 4 Tubas, 4 Double Basses, and 4 Percussion (1980); *Singers of Songs, Weavers of Dreams* for Cello and Percussion (1980); Sonata for Violin, Cello, and 4 Flutes (1980); *Dedication* for Soprano Saxophone, Double Bass, and String Quartet (1981); *Blues* for Violin Ensemble and Piano (1985); *Calypso* for Violin Ensemble and Piano (1985); *En rouge et noir* for Flute, Piano, Double Bass, and Drums (1985); Suite for Horn, Trumpet, Saxophone, and Rhythm Section (1985); Quintet for Jazz Violin and String Quartet (1987; Washington, D.C., March 13, 1988); Duo for Clarinet and Cello (Indianapolis, Oct. 25, 1988); *Impressions* for 2 Cellos (Bloomington, Ind., Sept. 8, 1989); piano pieces; numerous other works for jazz ensembles of various instruments. **VOCAL:** *Lutheran Mass* for Chorus and Jazz Septet (1967); *The Beatitudes* for Chorus, Soloists, Narrator, Jazz Ensemble, String Orch., and Dancers (1968); *Black America: To the Memory of Martin Luther King*, jazz cantata (1968); *Catholic Mass for Peace* for Chorus and Jazz Ensemble (1969); *A Song of Mankind* for

Chorus, Orch., Jazz Ensemble, Rock Band, Lights, and Sound Effects (1970); *Songs of the Night* for Soprano, String Quartet, and Piano (1972); *Give and Take* for Soprano and Chamber Ensemble (1975).

Baker, Dame Janet (Abbott), celebrated English mezzo-soprano; b. Hatfield, Yorkshire, Aug. 21, 1933. Her parents were music-lovers and she grew up in an artistic atmosphere. She was a student of Hélène Isepp and Meriel St. Clair in London. She began her career singing in the Leeds Phil. Choir, with which she made her debut as a soloist in Haydn's *Lord Nelson Mass* in 1953. In 1955 she became a member of the Ambrosian Singers. In 1956 she won 2nd prize in the Kathleen Ferrier Competition, making her operatic debut as Roza in Smetana's *The Secret* with the Univ. of Oxford Opera Club. In 1959 she was awarded the Queen's Prize and began to sing major roles with the Handel Opera Soc. From 1962 she also appeared at the Aldeburgh Festival. In 1964 she toured Russia as Lucretia with the English Opera Group. In 1966 she made her debut at London's Covent Garden as Hermia in Britten's *A Midsummer Night's Dream*, her U.S. debut as soloist in Mahler's *Das Lied von der Erde* with the San Francisco Sym., and her N.Y. recital debut. In 1967 she appeared as Dorabella with Glasgow's Scottish Opera, returning there as Berlioz's Dido in 1969, Strauss's Octavian in 1971 and Composer in 1975, and Gluck's Orfeo in 1979. In 1970 she sang Diana in *La Calisto* at Glyndebourne, returning there as Penelope in *Il ritorno d'Ulisse in patria* in 1972. On May 16, 1971, she created the role of Kate in Britten's *Owen Wingrave* on BBC-TV, a role she sang again at the work's premiere staging at Covent Garden in 1973. In 1971 she appeared as Monteverdi's Poppea with the Sadler's Wells Opera in London, returning there as Donizetti's Mary Stuart in 1973 and with its successor, the English National Opera, as Massenet's Charlotte in 1977. She sang in concert with Abbado and the London Sym. Orch. at the Salzburg Festival in 1973. In 1982 she retired from the operatic stage singing Gluck's Orfeo at Glyndebourne, although as late as 1989 she appeared in a concert performance of the role in N.Y. From 1983 to 1991 she was president of the Scottish Academy of Music and Drama in Glasgow. She was chancellor of the Univ. of York from 1991. She publ. the autobiographical vol. *Full Circle* (London, 1982). In 1970 she was made a Commander of the Order of the British Empire. She was made a Dame Commander of the Order of the British Empire in 1976. In 1990 she was awarded the Gold Medal of the Royal Phil. Soc. of London, and in 1994 she was made a Companion of Honour. Baker was one of the outstanding singers of her era. In addition to her expansive operatic repertoire, she won great renown as a concert artist in a repertoire of Lieder, English and French songs, and oratorio. She was especially distinguished in her performances of Schubert, Schumann, and Mahler.

BIBL: A. Blyth, *J. B.* (London, 1973).

Baker, Julius, American flutist and teacher; b. Cleveland, Sept. 23, 1915. He studied at the Eastman School of Music in Rochester, N.Y., and with William Kincaid at the Curtis Inst. of Music in Philadelphia. He played in the Cleveland Orch. (1937–41); then was 1st flutist of the Pittsburgh Sym. Orch. (1941–43), the CBS Sym. Orch. in N.Y. (1943–51), the Chicago Sym. Orch. (1951–53), and the N.Y. Phil. (1965–83); also taught at the Juilliard School of Music in N.Y. (from 1954), the Curtis Inst. of Music (from 1980), and at Carnegie-Mellon Univ. in Pittsburgh (from 1991).

Baker, Michael (Conway), American-born Canadian composer; b. West Palm Beach, Fla., March 13, 1937. He moved to Canada in 1958; studied at the London (Ontario) College of Music (assoc. degree, 1959), with Coulthard and Weisgarber at the Univ. of British Columbia (B.M., 1966), at Western Washington Univ. (M.A., 1971), and with Berkeley in London (1974–75). He subsequently taught film music at the Univ. of British Columbia and devoted himself to composition. His works follow along tonal lines with effective utilization of contemporary techniques.

WORKS: BALLET: *The Letter* (1974). **MUSIC THEATER:** *Washington Square* (1978). **ORCH.:** *Counterplay* for Viola and Strings (1971; also for Viola and Piano); *Okanagan Landscapes* for Piano and Orch. (1972); *Contours* for Double Bass, Harpsichord, and Strings (1973); *A Gabriel Fauré: In Memoriam* (1973); Concerto for Flute and Strings (1974); *Point No Point* for Viola and String Orch. (1975); Concerto for Piano and Chamber Orch. (1976); *Duo Concertante* for Violin, Viola, and Strings (London, Aug. 19, 1976); *A Struggle for Dominion* for Piano and Orch. (Vancouver, Sept. 26, 1976); Sym. No. 1 (1977); *Baroque Diversions* for Chamber Orch. (Mannheim, Oct. 18, 1981); *Evocations* for Flute, String Trio, and Orch. (1981; Winnipeg, Feb. 3, 1982); *Rita Joe*, tone poem (1983); *Chanson joyeuse* (1987); *Through the Lion's Gate* (1989); *Capriccio* for Clarinet and Orch. (1991). **CHAMBER:** *Ballade* for Cello and Piano (1961); Flute Sonata (1963); *5 Epigrams* for Woodwind Trio (1965); Wind Quintet (1965); Piano Quartet (1966); *Scherzo* for Trumpet and Organ (1967); String Quartet (1969); *Concert Piece* for Organ, Piano, and Timpani (1969–70); Piano Trio (1972); *Elegy* for Flute and Organ (1972); *Music for 6 Players* for Flute, Oboe, Harpsichord, and String Trio (1973); *Combinations* for Double Bass and Harpsichord (1974); *En rapport* for 2 Guitars (1974); *4 Views from a Nursery Tune* for Violin, Horn, and Piano (1975); *Dance Sequences* for Cello (1975); *Mirage* for Trumpet, Horn, and Organ (1981); *Red on White* for Flute and String Trio (1981); Duo for Flute and Bassoon (1981); *Intermezzo* for Flute and Harp (1988). **KEYBOARD: PIANO:** *Capriccio* for 2 Pianos (1964); 4 pieces (1973); Sonata (1975); *Theme for Jane* (1981); *Rainforest Suite* (1987); also organ music. **VOCAL:** *Dialogues* for Baritone, Chorus, and Orch. (1971); *7 Wonders*, song cycle for Voice and Piano (1983); *Street Scenes* for Men's Chorus and Piano (1985); *Capriccio* for Solo Voices, Instruments, and Orch. (1986).

Baker, Theodore, American writer on music; b. N.Y., June 3, 1851; d. Dresden, Oct. 13, 1934. As a young man, he was trained for business pursuits; in 1874 he decided to devote himself to the study of music; he studied with Oskar Paul at the Univ. of Leipzig, where he received his Ph.D. in 1882 with the diss. *Über die Musik der nordamerikanischen Wilden*, the first serious study of American Indian music. He lived in Germany until 1890; then returned to the U.S., and became literary ed. and tr. for the publishing house of G. Schirmer, Inc. (1892); he retired in 1926 and went back to Germany. In 1895 he publ. *A Dictionary of Musical Terms*, which went through more than 25 printings and sold over a million copies; another valuable work was *A Pronouncing Pocket Manual of Musical Terms* (1905). He also issued *The Musician's Calendar and Birthday Book* (1915–17). In 1900 G. Schirmer, Inc., publ. *Baker's Biographical Dictionary of Musicians*, which became Baker's imperishable monument; a 2nd ed. was publ. in 1905; the 3rd ed., rev. and enl. by Alfred Remy, was issued in 1919; the 4th ed. appeared in 1940 under the general editorship of Carl Engel. A supplement in 1949 was compiled by Nicolas Slonimsky, who undertook in 1958 a completely revised 5th ed. of the dictionary and compiled the supplements of 1965 and 1971. In 1978 Slonimsky edited the 6th ed., in 1984 the 7th ed., and in 1992 the 8th ed.

Baklanov (real name, **Bakkis), Georgy (Andreievich),** esteemed Latvian baritone; b. Riga, Jan. 17, 1881; d. Basel, Dec. 6, 1938. He studied at the Kiev Cons. and with Vanya in Milan. In 1903 he made his operatic debut in Kiev as A. Rubinstein's Demon; after singing at Moscow's Bolshoi Theater and in St. Petersburg (1905–09), he appeared throughout Europe. On Nov. 8, 1909, he made his U.S. debut as Barnaba in *La Gioconda* in the first performance at the Boston Opera House, where he sang with notable success until 1911 and again from 1915 to 1917. On Feb. 16, 1910, he made his only appearance with the Metropolitan Opera as Rigoletto during the company's visit to Baltimore. From 1917 to 1926 he was a member of the Chicago Opera. He later was a principal artist of the Russian Opera Co. of N.Y. In addition to Rigoletto, Baklanov was also highly praised for his portrayals of Prince Igor, Boris Godunov, Méphistophélès, and Scarpia.

Balada, Leonardo, Spanish composer and teacher; b. Barcelona, Sept. 22, 1933. He was early on apprenticed to his father's tailoring shop in Barcelona, but after piano training at the Cons. there, he went to N.Y. and pursued studies at the N.Y. College of Music (1956–57), the Juilliard School of Music (1958–60), and the Mannes College of Music (1961–62). His principal mentors in composition were Copland, Tansman, and Vincent Persichetti. He also studied conducting in Paris with Igor Markevitch. He eked out a living by working at odd jobs in the garment district in N.Y.; subsequently he obtained a teaching position at the United Nations International School (1963–70), and then joined the faculty of Carnegie-Mellon Univ. in Pittsburgh in 1970, where he served as a prof. from 1975. In his works, Balada has utilized both constructionist and expressionist elements.

WORKS: OPERAS: *Hangman, Hangman!* (Barcelona, Oct. 10, 1982); *Zapata!* (1982); *Cristóbal Colón* (1987; Barcelona, Sept. 24, 1989); *Death of Columbus* (1994). **ORCH.:** *Musica tranquila* for Strings (1960); Piano Concerto (1964); Guitar Concerto (1965; Madrid, Oct. 21, 1967); *Guernica* (1966; New Orleans, April 25, 1967); 4 syms: No. 1, *Sinfonia en negro,* homage to Martin Luther King, Jr. (1968; Madrid, June 21, 1969), No. 2, *Cumbres,* for Band (Pittsburgh, April 18, 1971), No. 3, *Steel Symphony* (1972; Pittsburgh, Jan. 12, 1973), and No. 4, *Lausanne,* for Chamber Orch. (Lausanne, Dec. 7, 1992); Bandoneon Concerto (1970); *Persistences,* sinfonia concertante for Guitar and Orch. (1972; Madrid, Jan. 9, 1987); *Auroris* (1973; Madrid, Jan. 25, 1974); *Ponce de León* for Narrator and Orch. (New Orleans, Oct. 9, 1973); Concerto for Piano, Winds, and Percussion (Pittsburgh, April 15, 1974); *Homage to Casals* (1975; Pittsburgh, May 7, 1976); *Homage to Sarasate* (1975; Pittsburgh, May 7, 1976); Concerto for 4 Guitars and Orch. (1976; Barcelona, Dec. 17, 1977); *3 Anecdotes,* concertino for Castanets or Wood Percussion and Chamber Orch. (1977; 1st perf. with wood percussion, Pittsburgh, Nov. 8, 1978, and with castanets, Santander, Aug. 28, 1980); *Sardana* (1979; Pittsburgh, Oct. 21, 1982); *Quasi un pasodoble* (1981; N.Y., Nov. 24, 1982); Violin Concerto (N.Y., Nov. 11, 1982); *Fantasias sonoras* (Pittsburgh, Oct. 4, 1987); *Zapata: Images* (1987); *Alegrias* for Flute and Strings (1988); *Music* for Flute and Strings (1988; also for Flute and String Quartet); *Divertimento* for Strings (Girona, Spain, Aug. 14, 1991); *Columbus: Images* (1991; Madrid, Jan. 10, 1992); *Celebration* (Barcelona, Nov. 19, 1992); *Music (Lament from the Cradle of the Earth)* for Oboe and Orch. (Pittsburgh, Nov. 5, 1993); *Shadows* (1994; Cincinnati, March 31, 1995); *Morning Music* for Flute and Chamber Orch. (1994; Pittsburgh, March 12, 1995). **BAND:** *Quasi Adelita* for Symphonic Wind Ensemble (1981; Washington, Pa., May 14, 1982); *Song and Dance* for Wind Ensemble (1992; Pittsburgh, Feb. 18, 1994); *Union of the Oceans* (Aviles, Spain, Sept. 29, 1993). **CHAMBER:** Violin Sonata (1960); Concerto for Cello and 9 Players (1962); *Geometrias No. 1* for Flute, Oboe, Clarinet, Bassoon, Trumpet, and Percussion (1966) and *No. 2* for String Quartet (1967); *Cuatris* for Instrumental Ensemble (1969); *Mosaico* for Brass Quintet (1970); *Tresis* for Flute, Guitar, and Cello (1973); *Apuntes* for Guitar Quartet (1974); Sonata for 10 Winds (1980); *Music* for Flute and String Quintet (1988; also for Flute and String Orch.); *Diary of Dreams* for Piano, Violin, and Cello (1995); guitar music; piano pieces. **VOCAL:** *Maria Sabina* for Narrators, Chorus, and Orch. (1969); *Las moradas* for Chorus and Instrumental Ensemble (1970); *No-Res,* cantata (1974); *Torquemada,* cantata (1980); *En la era* for Voice and Piano (1989); *Thunderous Scenes,* cantata for Soloists, Chorus, and Orch. (Alicante, Spain, Sept. 24, 1992).

Balakauskas, Osvaldas, Lithuanian composer; b. Ukmerge, Dec. 19, 1937. He graduated from the Vilnius State Pedagogical Inst. in 1961; in 1969 he took composition courses from Liatoshinsky at the Kiev Cons. In his music, he adopts a colorful manner, often sharply modernistic in melodic curvature, rhythmic angularity, and harmonic heterophony, while retaining the generic classical definitions of form.

WORKS: ORCH.: Piano Concertino (1966); *Rhapsody* (1967); *Ludus modorum,* cello concerto (1972); Sym. (1973); Suite for Strings (1973); *The Mountain Sonata,* sym. for Piano and Orch. (1975); *Ad astra* (1976). **CHAMBER:** *Dance Suite* for Violin and Piano (1964); *Variations* for Flute, Oboe, and Bassoon (1965); Suite for Cello and Violin (1965); *Auletika* for Flute and Oboe (1966); *Extrema* for Piccolo, English Horn, Bass Clarinet, Double Bassoon, Trumpet, Xylophone, and Harp (1966); *Aerophonia* for Wind Quintet (1968); Violin Sonata (1969); *Quartetto concertante* for Flute, Violin, Cello, and Piano (1970); 2 string quartets (1971, 1971); *Les Musiques* for Cello and Wind Quintet (1972); Violin Sonatina (1972); *Impresonata* for Flute and Piano (1974); *Suite of the Globe* for Violin and Piano (1974); *Retrospectives* for Cello and Piano (1974); *9 Sources* for Oboe and Harpsichord (1974); *Like a Touch of a Sea Wave,* 3 pieces for Violin and Piano (1975); *A Tree and a Bird,* viola sonata (1976). **KEYBOARD: PIANO:** *3 Caprices* (1964); *Cascades* (1967); *Studi sonori* for 2 Pianos (1971). **ORGAN:** Sonata (1973).

Balanchine, George (real name, **Georgi Melitonovich Balanchivadze**), celebrated Russian-American choreographer, son of **Meliton (Antonovich)** and brother of **Andrei (Melitonovich) Balanchivadze**; b. St. Petersburg, Jan. 22, 1904; d. N.Y., April 30, 1983. He attended the Imperial Theater School in St. Petersburg, where he learned the rudiments of classical dance. He also took piano lessons at the Petrograd Cons., and acquired a certain ability to read scores. In 1924 he undertook a tour through Germany and England; then joined Diaghilev's Ballets Russes in Paris, for which he created a number of works. In 1933, at the invitation of Lincoln Kirstein, he went to N.Y.; together they formed the School of American Ballet, which opened on Jan. 2, 1934. In 1935 it was incorporated as the American Ballet, with Balanchine as its chief choreographer. The group was renamed the Ballet Soc. in 1946, and in 1948 it was reorganized as the N.Y. City Ballet, and became part of the City Center. In 1962 Balanchine made a tour of Russia with this company. He was distinguished for his modern productions, with music by Stravinsky, Ives, and other contemporary composers. In 1983 he received the Presidential Medal of Freedom. Early in that year he was hospitalized with an ailment diagnosed as "progressive cerebral disintegration." As a gesture of devotion, he was named director emeritus of the N.Y. City Ballet, but had to abandon all active work, and soon died of pneumonia. Balanchine adored women; he used to say, "Ballet is woman." He was married 5 times, each time to a dancer: the first was Tamara Geva, whom he married in Russia when he was 18 and she was 15; his second wife was Alexandra Danilova, whom he married in 1927; his third and most famous wife was Vera Zorina, whom he married in 1938; then followed Maria Tallchief, and, finally, Tanaquil LeClercq, from whom he was divorced in 1969. In his long life as a choreographer, Balanchine created nearly 200 ballets to musical scores ranging from the Baroque to the avant-garde; he once said: "Music must be seen, and dance must be heard."

BIBL.: G. and F. Mason, *B.'s Complete Stories of the Great Ballets* (Garden City, N.Y., 1954); B. Taper, *B.* (N.Y. 1963); H. Koegler, *B. und das moderne Ballet* (Hannover, 1964); L. Kirstein, *The New York City Ballet* (N.Y., 1973); *Choreography by G. B.: A Catalogue of Works* (N.Y., 1983).

Balanchivadze, Andrei (Melitonovich), Russian composer, son of **Meliton (Antonovich) Balanchivadze** and brother of **George Balanchine**; b. St. Petersburg, June 1, 1906. He studied with his father; then entered the Tiflis Cons., where he took courses in piano, and in composition with Ippolitov-Ivanov. In 1935 he joined its staff, and in 1962 became chairman of the composition dept.; numerous Georgian composers studied under him. In his music, he makes use of Georgian folk motifs in a tasteful harmonic framework characteristic of the Russian national school. Among his works is the first Georgian ballet, *The Heart of the Mountains* (1936); another ballet, *Mtsyri* (Tbilisi, 1964). Other works include 3 syms. (1944, 1959, 1984); a symphonic poem, *The Ocean* (1952); 4 piano concertos (1944, 1946, 1952, 1968); choruses and songs.

BIBL.: G. Ordzhonikidze, *A. B.* (Tbilisi, 1967).

Balanchivadze, Meliton (Antonovich), noted Russian composer, father of **George Balanchine** and **Andrei (Melitonovich) Balanchivadze**; b. Banodzha, Dec. 24, 1862; d. Kutaisi, Nov. 21, 1937. He was educated in the ecclesiastical seminary in Tiflis, where he sang in a chorus. In 1880 he became a member of the local opera theater; in 1882 he organized a chorus and arranged Georgian folk songs. In 1889 he went to St. Petersburg, where he took voice lessons, and in 1891 entered Rimsky-Korsakov's class in composition. In 1895 he organized a series of choral concerts of Georgian music. After the Revolution he returned to Georgia, where he continued his work of ethnic research. He composed a national Georgian opera, *Tamara the Treacherous* (1897), and a number of songs in the manner of Georgian folk music.

BIBL.: P. Khuchua, *M. B.* (Tbilisi, 1964).

Balasanian, Sergei, Tadzhik composer; b. Ashkhabad, Aug. 26, 1902; d. Moscow, June 3, 1982. He studied at the Moscow Cons., graduating with a degree in music history in 1935. From 1936 to 1943 he was mainly active in Tadzhikistan; then was in charge of radio programming there. In 1948 he joined the faculty of the Moscow Cons.; was chairman of the composition dept. (1962–71). He was one of the founders of the national school of composition in Tadzhikistan; in his works, he made use of native folk motifs, in ingenious harmonic coloration.

WORKS: DRAMATIC: OPERAS: *The Revolt of Vose* (1939; rev. 1959); *The Blacksmith Kova* (1941); *Bakhtyor and Nisso* (1954). **BALLETS:** *Leyly and Medzhnun* (1947); *Shakuntala* (1963). **ORCH.:** 4 symphonic suites on Central Asian folk motifs; *Armenian Rhapsody* (1944); *The Islands of Indonesia* (1960). **OTHER:** Numerous choruses, songs, and instrumental pieces.

Balassa, Sándor, Hungarian composer; b. Budapest, Jan. 20, 1935. He studied choral conducting at the Béla Bartók Music Secondary School (1952–56) and composition with Szervánszky at the Budapest Academy of Music (graduated, 1965). From 1964 to 1980 he was a music producer for the Hungarian Radio; then taught at the Budapest Academy of Music. In 1972 he was awarded the Erkel Prize, in 1983 the Kossuth Prize, and in 1988 the Bartók-Pásztory Award. In 1983 he was made a Merited Artist by the Hungarian government and was named an Outstanding Artist in 1989.

WORKS: OPERAS: *Az ajtón kívül* (The Man Outside; 1973–76); *A harmadik bolygó* (The Third Planet; 1986–87). **ORCH.:** Violin Concerto (1964); *Iris* (1971); *Lupercalia*, concerto in memory of Stravinsky for Woodwinds and Brass (1972); *Tabulae* for Chamber Orch. (1972); *Glarusi ének* (Chant of Glarus; 1978); *Az örök ifjúság szigete* (The Island of Everlasting Youth), overture (1979); *Hivások és kiáltások* (Calls and Cries; 1981; Boston, Oct. 21, 1982); *Egy álmodozó naplója* (A Daydreamer's Diary; 1983); *Három fantázia* (3 Fantasies; 1984); *Szőlőcske és halacska* (Little Grape and Little Fish; 1987). **CHAMBER:** *Dimensioni* for Flute and Viola (1966); Wind Quintet (1966); Quartet for Percussion (1969); Trio for Violin, Viola, and Harp (1970); *Xenia* for Chamber Ensemble (1970); *Intermezzo* for Flute and Piano (1971); *The Last Shepherd* for Cello (1978); Quintetto d'ottoni (1979); *Hatja viragai* (Flowers of Hajta) for Cimbalom (1984). **VOCAL:** *Zenith* for Alto and Orch. (1967); *Antinomia* for Soprano, Clarinet, and Cello (1968); *Requiem Kassák Lajosért* (Requiem for Lajos Kassák) for Soprano, Tenor, Baritone, Chorus, and Orch. (1969); *Cantata Y* for Soprano and Orch. (1970); *Kyrie* for Chorus (1982); *Bánatomtól szabadulnék* for Women's Chorus (1988).

Baldwin, Dalton, American pianist; b. Summit, N.J., Dec. 19, 1931. He studied at the Juilliard School of Music in N.Y. and at the Oberlin (Ohio) College Cons. of Music; later pursued training with Boulanger and Madeleine Lipatti in Paris, and also received invaluable coaching from Sibelius, Poulenc, and others. He acquired a fine reputation as a discerning accompanist to such eminent singers as Gérard Souzay, Elly Ameling, Marilyn Horne, and Jessye Norman; also gave master classes in the art of accompaniment in the U.S. and abroad.

Bales, Richard (Henry Horner), American conductor and composer; b. Alexandria, Va., Feb. 3, 1915. He studied at the Eastman School of Music in Rochester, N.Y. (Mus.B., 1936), at the Juilliard Graduate School in N.Y. (1938–41), and with Koussevitzky at the Berkshire Music Center in Tanglewood (summer, 1940). In 1935 he made his conducting debut with the National Sym. Orch. in Washington, D.C.; then was conductor of the Virginia-North Carolina Sym. Orch. (1936–38). In 1942 he became the first music director of the National Gallery of Art in Washington, D.C., and in 1943 founded the National Gallery Orch., which he conducted until his retirement in 1985. He also was music director of the Washington, D.C., Cathedral Choral Soc. (1945–46). In 1960 he received the Alice M. Ditson Award. During his long tenure at the National Gallery of Art, he introduced numerous works by American composers, both old and new.

WORKS: ORCH.: *Music* for Strings (1940); *From Washington's Time* for Strings (1941); *National Gallery Suites: I* (1943), *II* (1944), *III* (1957), and *IV* (1965); *Theme and Variations* for Strings (1944); *Music of the American Revolution*, Suite No. 2 for Strings (1952); *Stony Brook Suite* for Strings (1968); *Fitzwilliam Suite* for Strings (1972); *The Spirit of Engineering*, suite (1984). **CHAMBER:** *Sarcasms* for Violin, Viola, and Cello (1937); String Quartet (1944); *Reverie and Virginia Reels* for Violin and Piano (1989). **OTHER:** Piano pieces, including the suite *To Elmira with Love* (1972; orchestrated, 1983), *Diary Pages* for 2 Pianos (1978), and *Aaronesque* (for Aaron Copland's 80th birthday; 1980); various vocal scores, choral pieces, and songs; also film scores and many transcriptions and arrangements.

Balfoort, Dirk Jacobus, Dutch musicologist; b. Utrecht, July 19, 1886; d. The Hague, Nov. 11, 1964. He studied with Evert Cornelis; played violin in various German orchs.; then held teaching posts in the Netherlands; also organized concerts of early music by Dutch composers. He publ. *De Hollandsche vioolmakers* (Amsterdam, 1931); *Het Muziekleven in Nederland in de 17e en 18e eeuw* (Amsterdam, 1938); a monograph on Stradivarius (Amsterdam, 1945; also in Ger. and Eng.); etc.

Balkwill, Bryan (Havell), English conductor; b. London, July 2, 1922. He was educated at the Royal Academy of Music in London. He was an assistant conductor of the New London Opera Co. (1947–48) and assoc. conductor of the International Ballet Co. (1948–49); then was music director of the London Festival Ballet (1950–52) and of Opera for All (1953–63); also conducted at the Glyndebourne Festivals (1950–58), and in London at Covent Garden (from 1953) and at the Sadler's Wells Opera (from 1957). From 1959 to 1965 he was resident conductor at the Royal Opera, Covent Garden; then was music director of the Welsh National Opera in Cardiff (1963–67) and of the Sadler's Wells Opera (1966–69). He served as a prof. of music at the Indiana Univ. School of Music in Bloomington from 1978 to 1992.

Ball, Michael, English composer; b. Manchester, Nov. 10, 1946. He began composing at an early age, writing a children's opera when he was 11; in 1964 he entered the Royal College of Music in London, where he studied with Herbert Howells, Humphrey Searle, and John Lambert, and was awarded all of its major composition prizes; then completed his training with Donatoni in Siena (summers, 1972–73), where he also attended the master classes of Luciano Berio and György Ligeti.

WORKS: DRAMATIC: *The Belly Bag*, chamber opera (1992). **ORCH.:** *Resurrection Symphonies* (1982; Manchester, May 23, 1984); *Frontier!* for Brass Band (1984); *Omaggio* for Wind Band (1986); Concerto for Organ, Brass, Percussion, and Strings (1987); *Danses vitales: Danses macabres* (1987); *Farnesong* for Chamber Orch. (1990); *Midsummer Music* for Brass Band (1991); *Chaucer's Tunes* for Wind Band (1993); Concerto for Saxophone and Wind Band (1994). **CHAMBER:** *The Piper at the Gates of Dawn* for Recorder and Tape (1983); *Music for an Island* for 2 Guitars (1989); *Serenade for Seikilos* for Saxophone Quartet (1991). **PIANO:** *Miriam's Music* (1991). **VOCAL:** *Sainte*

Marye Virgine, motet for Chorus (1977–79); *A Hymn to God My God* for 16 Solo Voices (1983–84); *Pageant* for Chorus, Winds, and Brass (1984–85); *Lindisfarne Fragments*, song cycle for Baritone and Piano (1988); *The Pentecost Castle* for Chorus (1988); *Nocturnes* for Chorus, 2 Pianos, and 2 Percussion (1990).

Ballantine, Edward, American composer and teacher; b. Oberlin, Ohio, Aug. 6, 1886; d. Oak Bluffs, Mass., July 2, 1971. He studied with Walter Spalding at Harvard Univ., graduating with highest honors in 1907; took piano courses with Artur Schnabel and Rudolph Ganz in Berlin (1907–09). In 1912 he was appointed instructor at Harvard, becoming assistant prof. in 1926, and assoc. prof. in 1932; he retired in 1947. His first publ. work was a musical play, *The Lotos Eaters* (1907); 3 of his orch. pieces were performed by the Boston Sym. Orch.: *Prelude to The Delectable Forest* (Dec. 10, 1914), *The Eve of St. Agnes* (Jan. 19, 1917), and *From the Garden of Hellas* (Feb. 9, 1923); and one, *By a Lake in Russia*, by the Boston Pops (June 27, 1922). He also wrote a Violin Sonata and songs. His most striking work is a set of piano variations on *Mary Had a Little Lamb* (1924) in the styles of 10 composers; a 2nd series of variations on the same tune (1943) includes stylizations of Stravinsky, Gershwin, and others.

Ballard, Louis W(ayne), preeminent native American composer and music educator; b. Devil's Promenade, Quapaw Indian Reservation, Okla., July 8, 1931. He is of distinguished Quapaw-Cherokee descent and was given the name Honganózhe (Grand Eagle). In his youth, he is immersed in native American music but also received piano lessons at the local Baptist mission school. He later pursued an intensive study of the musics of various native American tribes. He studied at the Univ. of Okla., and then at the Univ. of Tulsa, where he took B.M., B.M.E., and M.M. degrees. He also studied with Milhaud and Castelnuovo-Tedesco. From 1962 to 1969 he was an administrator with the Inst. of American Indian Arts in Santa Fe. From 1969 to 1979 he was in charge of the music curriculum of the U.S. Bureau of Indian Affairs school system. He also was chairman of minority concerns in music education for the state of New Mexico from 1976 to 1982. He publ. *My Music Reaches to the Sky* (1973) and *Music of North American Indians* (1975). In some of his compositions, he has used the name Joe Miami. In his music, Ballard combines native American elements with advanced Western compositional techniques.

WORKS: DRAMATIC: *Jijogweh, the Witch-water Gull*, ballet (1962); *Koshare*, ballet (1965; Barcelona, May 17, 1966); *The 4 Moons*, ballet commemorating the 60th anniversary of the statehood of Oklahoma (Tulsa, Oct. 28, 1967); *Sacred Ground*, film score (1975); *The Maid of the Mist and the Thunderbeings*, dance piece (Buffalo, Oct. 18, 1991; symphonic suite, Aptos, Calif., Aug. 8, 1993); *Moontide*, opera (1994). **ORCH.:** *Fantasy Aborigine No. 1: Sipapu* (1963; Santa Fe, April 12, 1964), *No. 2: Tsiyako* (Seattle, Oct. 10, 1976), *No. 3: Kokopelli* (Flagstaff, April 5, 1977), *No. 4: Xactce'oyan-Companion of Talking God* (N.Y., Nov. 15, 1982), and *No. 5: Naniwaya* (1988; Tulsa, Sept. 21, 1989); *Scenes from Indian Life* (1964; Rochester, N.Y., May 2, 1968); *Why the Duck Has a Short Tail* for Narrator and Orch. (Tempe, Ariz., May 8, 1969); *Devil's Promenade* (Tulsa, May 22, 1973); *Incident at Wounded Knee* for Chamber Orch., dramatizing the rebellion of the Sioux Indians at the locality known as Wounded Knee in South Dakota (Warsaw, Oct. 24, 1974); *Siouxiana* for Wind Ensemble (Grand Forks, N.D., Jan. 28, 1974); *Ishi: America's Last Civilized Man* (Aptos, Calif., Aug. 24, 1975); *Wamus-77* for Band (Washington, D.C., Nov. 24, 1977); *Nighthawk Keetowah Dances*, suite for Concert Band (Chicago, April 5, 1978); *Ocotillo Festival Overture* for Concert Band (Tempe, Ariz., March 11, 1979); *The Maid of the Mist and the Thunderbeings*, suite (Aptos, Calif., Aug. 8, 1993; also as a dance piece, Buffalo, Oct. 18, 1991); *The Indian Feast Day* (1994; San Jose, Calif., Jan. 6, 1995). **CHAMBER:** Trio for Violin, Viola, and Cello (1959); *Percussion Ego* for 3 Percussion (1963); *Rhapsody* for 4 Bassoons (1963); *Ritmo Indio* for Wind Quintet (Santa Fe, March 8, 1969); *Cacega Ayuwipi* for Chamber Ensemble (Santa Fe, July 28, 1970); *Katcina Dances*, cello-piano suite (Santa Fe, July 28, 1970); *Desert Trilogy* for Octet (Lubbock, Texas, Oct. 28, 1971); *Rio Grande Sonata* for Violin and Piano (Santa Fe, May 15, 1976); *Music for the Earth and the Sky* for Chamber Ensemble (Saarbrücken, May 31, 1986); *Bellum Atramentum*, trio for Oboe, Violin, and Cello (1988; Santa Fe, May 21, 1989); *Capientur a Nullo*, trio for Violin, Cello, and Double Bass (1988); *The Lonely Sentinel* for Wind Sextet (1993). **PIANO:** *4 American Indian Piano Preludes* (1963); *City of Silver: Buenos Aires* (1980); *City of Fire: Los Alamos* (N.Y., Oct. 20, 1984); *City of Light: Paris* (1986; N.Y., Feb. 15, 1987). **VOCAL:** *Espiritu de Santiago* for Chorus, Flute, Piano, and Guitar (1963); *The Gods Will Hear*, cantata for Chorus and Orch. (Liberty, Mo., May 12, 1964); *Mojave Bird Dance Song* for Chorus and Percussion (1970); *Portrait of Will Rogers*, cantata for Narrator, Chorus, and Orch. (Liberty, Mo., April 3, 1972); *Thus Spake Abraham*, cantata for Soloists, Chorus, and Piano (1976; Buenos Aires, Aug. 23, 1980); *Dialogue Differentia* for Mezzo-soprano, Tenor, Baritone, and Orch. (Bonn, June 1, 1989); *Live On, Heart of My Nation*, cantata for Narrator, Soloists, Chorus, and Orch. (McAlester, Okla., April 1, 1990).

Ballif, Claude (André François), French composer and pedagogue; b. Paris, May 22, 1924. After training at the Bordeaux Cons. (1942–48), he took courses with Tony Aubin, Noël Gallon, and Messiaen at the Paris Cons. (1948–51); he then studied with Blacher and Rufer at the Berlin Hochschule für Musik (1953–55), and also attended Scherchen's classes in Darmstadt. He was associated with the French Radio and Television in Paris (1959–63), and then was a prof. there at the École Normal de Musique (1963–65); after serving as a prof. at the Rheims Cons. (1964–71), he was prof. of analysis (1971–90) and assoc. prof. of composition (1982–90) at the Paris Cons.; he subsequently was prof. of composition at the Sevran Cons. (from 1990). In 1984 he was made a Commander des Arts et des Lettres. As a composer, Ballif has followed an independent course, developing a system he describes as metatonality, notable for its avoidance of the extremes of diatonicism and chromaticism.

WRITINGS (all publ. in Paris): *Introduction à la métatonalité* (1956); *Berlioz* (1968); *Voyage de mon oreille* (1979); *Économie musicale—Souhaits entre symboles* (1988).

WORKS: OPERAS: *Dracoula* (1982; rev. 1983; Paris, Sept. 19, 1984); *Il suffit d'un peu d'air* (1990; Montreal, Dec. 11, 1991). **ORCH.:** *Lovecraft* (1955); *Voyage de mon oreille* (1957); *Fantasio* (1957; rev. 1976); *A Cor et à cri* (1962); *Ceci et cela* (1965); *Cinquième Imaginaire* for Chamber Orch. (1968; rev. 1978); *Sixième Imaginaire* for Chamber String Orch. (1974); *Ivre, moi, immobile* for Clarinet and Orch. (1976); *Haut les Rêves* for Violin and Small Orch. (1984); *Le Jouet du jeu* for Oboe and Chamber Orch. (1988). **CHAMBER:** 4 quintets (1952, 1954, 1958, 1960); 5 string quartets (1955, 1958, 1959, 1987, 1989); Violin Sonata (1957); Flute Sonata (1958); 15 works entitled *Solfeggietto* for Various Solo Instruments (1961–88); *Le Taille-Lyre* for 7 Instruments (1990); also 5 piano sonatas (1957–60); 4 organ sonatas (1956). **VOCAL:** *Quatre Antiennes à la Sainte Vierge* for 6 Soloists and Orch. (1952–53); *La Vie du monde qui vient: Première symphonie mystique*, requiem for 8 Soloists, 6 Choruses, and Orch. (1953–55; rev. 1972); *Les Battements du coeur de Jésus* for Double Chorus, Trumpet, and Trombone (1971); *Un Coup de dés* for Chorus, 6 Instruments, and Tape (1980); *Le Livre du Seigneur* for Baritone, 3 Choruses, and Orch. (1985–88).

BIBL.: M. Tosi, *C. B.* (Bezières, 1991).

Ballista, Antonio, Italian pianist and teacher; b. Milan, March 30, 1936. He studied piano and composition at the Milan Cons., graduating in 1955. He subsequently pursued a successful career as a soloist; was particularly noted for his discerning performances of avant-garde music; he also appeared in duo recitals with the pianist Bruno Canino. Ballista was a prof. at the Milan Cons. from 1974.

Ballou, Esther (Williamson), American composer, pianist, and teacher; b. Elmira, N.Y., July 17, 1915; d. Chichester, England, March 12, 1973. She studied composition with Otto Luening at Bennington (Vt.) College (graduated, 1937); after further training at Mills College in Oakland, California (1938), she studied composition with Bernard Wagenaar at the Juilliard School of Music in N.Y. (graduated, 1943); also received private instruction from Wallingford Riegger. She made many tours of the U.S. as a pianist with dance companies; taught at the American Univ. in Washington, D.C. (1959–73). In 1963, her *Capriccio* for Violin and Piano was the first score by an American woman composer to be played at the White House in Washington, D.C. Her works generally followed along Classical lines.

WORKS: ORCH.: Suite for Chamber Orch. (1939); *Intermezzo* (1943); *Blues* (1944); 2 piano concertos (1945, 1964), *Prelude and Allegro* for Piano and Strings (1951); Concertino for Oboe and Strings (1953); *Adagio* for Bassoon and Strings (1960); *Im memoriam* for Oboe and Strings (1960); Guitar Concerto (1964); *Konzertstück* for Viola and Orch. (1969). **CHAMBER:** *Impertinence* for Clarinet and Piano (1936); *In Blues Tempo* for Clarinet and Piano (1937); *Nocturne* for String Quartet (1937); *War Lyrics* for Piano, Trumpet, and Percussion (1940); *Christmas Variations* for Oboe and Harpsichord (1954); Piano Trio (1955; rev. 1957); *Divertimento* for String Quartet (1958); Violin Sonata (1959); *A Passing Word* for Flute, Cello, Piano, and Oboe (1960); *Capriccio* for Violin and Piano (1963); *Dialogues* for Oboe and Guitar (1966; rev. 1969); *Prism* for String Trio (1969); *Romanzo* for Violin and Piano (1969). **PIANO:** *Dance Suite* (1937); 2 sonatas for 2 Pianos (1943, 1958); *Beguine* for Piano, 8-Hands (1950; also for 2 Pianos, 1957, and for Orch., 1960); Sonata (1955). **OTHER:** Organ music, choral pieces, and songs.

BIBL.: R. Ringenwald, *The Music of E.W. B.: An Analytical Study* (thesis, American Univ., 1960); J. Heintze, *E.W. B.: A Bio-Bibliography* (Westport, Conn., 1987).

Balmer, Luc, Swiss conductor and composer; b. Munich, July 13, 1898. He was the son of the painter Wilhelm Balmer. Following training with Hans Huber, Ernst Lévy, and Egon Petri at the Basel Cons. (1915–19), he attended Busoni's master class in composition at the Prussian Academy of Arts in Berlin (1921–22). He conducted the Kursaal in Lucerne (1928–32) and at the Zürich Opera (1932–35). Settling in Bern, he conducted at the Opera (1932–35), and then was conductor of the Orch. Assn. (1935–41) and the Music Soc. (1941–64); he also was on the staff of the Bern Radio (1938–68). In 1969 he was awarded the music prize of the City of Bern, and in 1986 the music prize of the Canton of Bern. His compositions, notable for their ludic craftsmanship, were in an accessible style.

WORKS: OPERA: *Die drei gefoppten Ehemänner* (1967–68). **ORCH.:** Piano Concertino (1956); Cello Concertino (1967); *Symphonische Suite* for Strings (1977); *Concerto grosso* for 2 Cellos and Strings (1977). **CHAMBER:** 3 string quartets (1931, 1961, 1972); *Kleine Suite* for 2 Flutes (1968); *Etuden* for Cello and Piano (1969); Suite for Cello and Piano (1975); *Feierabend-Trio* for Violin, Cello, and Piano (1978); *Divertimento Clarinettistico* for Clarinet and Piano (1979); *Eichendorff-Quintett* for 2 Violins, Viola, Cello, and Double Bass (1980). **ORGAN:** *6 Choral-Vorspiele* (1978). **VOCAL:** *Sonette del Petrarca* for Chorus, Men's Voices, and Orch. or Organ (1930); Mass for Chorus and Orch. (1970); *25. Psalm Davids* for Soprano, Baritone, and String Orch. (1971); *Drei geistliche Lieder* for Tenor and Organ or Orch. (1971); Cantata for Choruses, Orch., and Piano, 4-hands (1982); *4 Psalmen* for Soprano, Baritone, Trumpet, and Organ (1984).

Balogh, Ernö, Hungarian-American pianist and teacher; b. Budapest, April 4, 1897; d. Mitchellville, Md., June 2, 1989. He played in public as an infant; later entered the Royal Academy of Music in Budapest as a pupil of Béla Bartók in piano and Zoltan Kodály in theory. In 1924 he emigrated to the U.S. where he taught and performed. From 1947–60 he was a member of the artists' faculty of Peabody Cons.. He composed some amiable instrumental pieces of brief dimensions, including *Caprice antique* and *Arabesque*, which were performed by Fritz Kreisler.

Baloković, Zlatko, Croatian violinist; b. Zagreb, March 21, 1895; d. Venice, March 29, 1965. He studied at the Zagreb Cons. as a child, then in Vienna with Sevčik. He appeared as a soloist all over the world, including Australia, where he received a state prize. He gave the first performance of John Alden Carpenter's Violin Concerto with the Chicago Sym. Orch. on Nov. 18, 1937. He then divided his activities between America and Europe.

Balsam, Artur, Polish-born American pianist and pedagogue; b. Warsaw, Feb. 8, 1906; d. N.Y., Sept. 1, 1994. He studied in Łódź, making his debut there at the age of 12; then enrolled at the Berlin Hochschule für Musik; in 1930 he obtained the prestigious Mendelssohn Prize; in 1932 he made a U.S. tour with Yehudi Menuhin. With the advent of the anti-Semitic Nazi regime in 1933, he settled in America, where he became a superlative accompanist to celebrated artists; he also played much chamber music and gave occasional solo recitals. He served on the faculties of the Eastman School of Music in Rochester, N.Y., Boston Univ., and the Manhattan School of Music.

Balsys, Eduardas, Lithuanian composer and teacher; b. Nikolayev, Dec. 20, 1919; d. Druskininkai, Nov. 3, 1984. He studied composition with Račiunas at the Lithuanian Cons. in Vilnius, graduating in 1950; then took music courses at the Leningrad Cons. (1953). In 1953 he joined the faculty of the Lithuanian Cons.; in 1960 he was appointed chairman of the composition dept. In his music, he adhered to classical forms but made experimental use of certain modern techniques, including dodecaphonic progressions.

WORKS: DRAMATIC: *Eglė žalčių karalienė* (Egle, Queen of Grass Snakes), ballet (Vilnius, 1960; orch. suite, 1961; 4 fragments for Violin and Piano, 1963); *The Journey to Tilže*, opera (1980). **ORCH.:** *Vilnius*, sym. (1950); *Heroic Poem* (1953); 2 violin concertos (1954, 1958); *Folk Dance Suite* (1958); *Dramatic Frescoes* for Violin, Piano, and Orch. (1965); *Symphony-Concerto* for Organ, Percussion, and Orch. (1977); *Sea Reflections* for Strings (1981); *Portraits* (1983). **CHAMBER:** Piano Sonata (1947); *Variations* for Piano (1948); String Quartet (1953); Concerto for Solo Violin (1984). **VOCAL:** 3 cantatas: *Song for My Land* for Chorus and Orch. (1962), *Saulę nešantis* (He Who Carries the Sun) for High Voice, Chorus, Organ, and Percussion (1972), and *Glory to Lenin* for Mixed Chorus, Men's Chorus, and Children's Chorus (1976); *Nelieskite mėlyno gaublio* (Don't Touch the Blue Globe), oratorio for Soloists, Children's Chorus, 2 Pianos, Double Bass, and Percussion (1969).

Baltsa, Agnes, prominent Greek mezzo-soprano; b. Lefkas, Nov. 19, 1944. She was educated in Athens, Munich, and Frankfurt am Main. In 1968 she made her debut at the Frankfurt Opera, remaining there until 1972; also sang at the Deutsche Oper in West Berlin from 1970. In 1971 she made her U.S. debut as Carmen in Houston. In 1976 she made her debut at the Vienna State Opera; in 1977 she sang at Salzburg. On Dec. 13, 1979, she made her debut with the Metropolitan Opera in N.Y. as Octavian. Subsequent engagements took her to many of the world's major operatic centers. Among her best roles were Dorabella, Rosina, Orpheus, Berlioz's Dido, Bellini's Romeo, and Strauss's Composer. She also had a fine career as a concert artist.

BIBL.: C. Baumann, *A. B.: Eine Bildmonographie* (Zürich, 1986).

Bal y Gay, Jesús, Spanish composer and musicologist; b. Lugo, June 23, 1905. He studied in Madrid. After the outbreak of the Spanish Civil War he went to England, and eventually to Mexico, where he was on the staff of the Instituto Nacional de Bellas Artes (1949–65). He publ. a number of valuable essays on

Spanish music, among them *Tientos ensayos de estética musical* (Mexico City, 1960), which traces the development of the Ricercare in Spain. He composed some symphonic and chamber music.

Bamberger, Carl, Austrian-born American conductor and pedagogue; b. Vienna, Feb. 21, 1902; d. N.Y., July 18, 1987. He attended the Univ. of Vienna; received training in piano and theory from Schenker and in cello from Buxbaum. He was conductor of the Gdańsk (1924–27) and Darmstadt (1927–31) operas, and then conducted in Russia. In 1937 he settled in N.Y. and became a naturalized American citizen; taught at the Mannes College of Music (1938–75) and was active as a conductor mainly in N.Y. He publ. the manual *The Conductor's Art* (N.Y., 1965).

Bamboschek, Giuseppe, Italian-American conductor; b. Trieste, June 12, 1890; d. N.Y., June 24, 1969. He studied at the Trieste Cons., graduating in 1907. In 1913 he went to the U.S. as accompanist for Pasquale Amato; in 1918 he joined the staff at the Metropolitan Opera in N.Y., specializing in the Italian repertoire. After 1929 he was active mainly as a conductor for radio and films.

Bamert, Matthias, Swiss conductor and composer; b. Ersigen, July 5, 1942. He studied in Bern, Zürich, Darmstadt, Salzburg, and Paris, his principal composition teachers being Rivier and Boulez. He was 1st oboist of the Salzburg Mozarteum Orch. (1965–69); then was assistant conductor to Stokowski with the American Sym. Orch. of N.Y. (1970–71). He received the 1st George Szell Memorial Award, joining the conducting staff of the Cleveland Orch. in 1971. From 1977 to 1983 he was music director of the Swiss Radio Orch. in Basel; then was principal guest conductor of the Scottish National Orch. in Glasgow (1985–90). In 1992 he became director of the Lucerne Music Festival and in 1993 music director of the London Mozart Players.

WORKS: Concertino for English Horn, Piano, and String Orch. (1966); *Septuria Lunaris* for Orch. (1970); *Rheology* for String Orch. (1970); *Mantrajana* for Orch. (1971); *Once Upon an Orchestra* for Narrator, 12 Dancers, and Orch. (1975); *Ol-Okun* for String Orch. (1976); *Keepsake* for Orch. (1979); *Circus Parade* for Narrator and Orch. (1979); *Snapshots* for Orch. (1989).

Bampton, Rose (Elizabeth), American soprano; b. Cleveland, Nov. 28, 1909. She studied with Queena Mario at the Curtis Inst. of Music in Philadelphia; also took academic courses at Drake Univ. in Des Moines, Iowa, where she obtained a doctorate of fine arts. She sang as a contralto with the Philadelphia Opera (1929–32), then changed to mezzo-soprano and finally to soprano, so that she could sing the roles of both Amneris and Aida. She made her debut at the Metropolitan Opera in N.Y. on Nov. 28, 1932, as Laura in *La Gioconda*, and continued on its staff until 1945 and again from 1947 to 1950. She made annual appearances at the Teatro Colón in Buenos Aires from 1942 to 1948; then returned to N.Y., where she taught voice at the Manhattan School of Music (1962–82) and at the Juilliard School (from 1974). She was married to **Wilfrid Pelletier**.

Bandrowska-Turska, Eva, Polish soprano; b. Kraków, May 20, 1897; d. Warsaw, June 25, 1979. She studied with her uncle, Alexander Bandrowski-Sas (b. Lubaczów, April 22, 1860; d. Kraków, May 28, 1913), a noted tenor; then took further instruction with Helena Zboinska-Ruszkowska. She made her debut as a concert singer in 1919, and subsequently appeared in opera; in later years she gained distinction as a solo singer, excelling particularly as a congenial interpreter of the songs of Debussy, Ravel, Roussel, and Szymanowski.

BIBL.: Z. Bieske, *E. B.-T.: Wspomnienia artystki* (Warsaw, 1989).

Bank, Jacques, Dutch composer; b. Borne, April 18, 1943. He studied with Jos Kunst and Ton de Leeuw at the Amsterdam Cons., graduating in 1974. Apart from his musical activities, he taught English in Amsterdam schools.

WORKS: *Blind Boy Fuller I* for Recorder, Piano, and Optional Voice, being a recording of *Thousand Women Blues*, sung by Blind Boy Fuller in 1940 in Chicago (1966); *The Memoirs of a Cyclist* for 2 Recorders (1967–70); *Emcée* for Voices (1969); *Put Me on My Bike I* for Baritone, Recorder, and Chorus (1971); *Fan It* for Orch. (1973); *Song of Sitting Bull* for Recorder Player possessing a Baritone Voice and Organ (1974); *Monk's Blues* for Piano, 14 Voices, and 12 Winds (1974); *Die Ouwe* (The Old One) for Bass Recorder, Bass Clarinet, and Piano (1975); *Thomas* for the recorded Voice of poet Dylan Thomas reading his *Lament*, and 19 Instruments (1975); *Pathétique* for Orch. (1976); *Lied* for Countertenor or Mezzo-soprano, Clavichord or Harpsichord, 2 Percussion Players, 2 Violins, Viola, and Cello (1976); *Mezmerized* for Mezzo-soprano or Tenor, 3 Trumpets, 3 Percussion Players, and Piano (1977); *Alexandre's Concerto* for Piano and Orch. (1978); *Muziek voor een slaapstad* for Chorus and Orch. (1979); *Recorders*, concerto for Recorder, Strings, and Percussion (1981); *Coda* for Chorus and Orch. (1983); *Requiem voor een levende* for Narrator, Chorus, and Chamber Ensemble (1985); *Een Tanthologie*, opera (1986–87); *Episodes de la vie d'un artiste* for Soloists, Boy's Chorus, Mixed Chorus, and Orch. (1992–93; Rotterdam, June 11, 1994).

Banks, Don(ald Oscar), Australian composer; b. Melbourne, Oct. 25, 1923; d. Sydney, Sept. 5, 1980. He took piano lessons as a child and played in dance bands as a youth; served in the Australian Army (1941–46). After World War II, he studied composition with Nickson and Le Gallienne at the Melbourne Cons. (1947–49); went to England, where he studied composition privately in London with Mátyás Seiber (1950–52), then in Florence with Luigi Dallapiccola (1952–53). He remained in England and worked as an arranger and composer of film and television music; was music director of Goldsmiths' College of the Univ. of London (1965–70). In 1971 he returned to Australia and was head of composition and electronic music at the Canberra School of Music (1974–78), and then of composition at the Sydney Conservatorium (1978–80). In 1980 he was made a member of the Order of Australia. In some of his works, he applied serial methods, modified so as not to destroy the sense of tonality; he also made effective use of electronics.

WORKS: ORCH.: *4 Pieces* (1953; London, June 1, 1954); *Episode* for Chamber Orch. (1958); *Elizabethan Miniatures* for Lute, Viola da Gamba, and Strings (1962); *Divisions* (Cheltenham, July 12, 1965); Horn Concerto (1965; London, Feb. 27, 1966); *Assemblies* (Melbourne, Dec. 3, 1966); Violin Concerto (London, Aug. 12, 1966); *Intersections* for Orch. and Tape (1969; London, Jan. 1970); *Meeting Place* for Chamber Orch., Jazz Group, and 2 Synthesizers (London, June 15, 1970); *Nexus* for Jazz Quintet and Orch. (1970; Kassel, April 8, 1971); *Music* for Wind Band (1971); *Prospects* (1974); *Trilogy* (1977). **CHAMBER:** *Duo* for Violin and Cello (1951–52); *Divertimento* for Flute and String Trio (1951–52); Violin Sonata (1953); *Sonata da Camera*, in memory of Seiber, for 8 Instruments (1961); *Equation I* for 12 Players (1963), *II* for 12 Players (1969), and *III* for Chamber Group, Jazz Quartet, and Synthesizers (1972); Trio for Violin, Horn, and Piano (1962); *Sequence* for Cello (1967); *Prelude, Night Piece and Blues for 2* for Clarinet and Piano (1968); *4 Pieces* for String Quartet (1971); *Take 8* for String Quartet and Jazz Quartet (1973); String Quartet (1976); *4 x 2* for Clarinet(s) and Tape (1977). **PIANO:** *Pezzo dramatico* (1956); *Commentary* for Piano and Tape (1971). **VOCAL:** *5 North Country Folk Songs* for Voice and String Orch. or Piano (1953–54); *Psalm 70* for Voice and Chamber Orch. (1954); *Settings from Roget* for Voice and Jazz Quartet (1966); *Tirade*, triptych for Soprano, Harp, Piano, and 3 Percussionists (1968); *Findings Keepings* for Chorus and Percussion (1969); *Limbo*, cantata for 3 Singers, 8 Instruments, and 2-channel Tape (1971); *Benedictus* for Voices, Jazz Quartet, 5 Synthesizers, Fender Electric Piano, and Tape (1976).

Banshchikov, Gennadi, Russian composer; b. Kazan, Nov. 9, 1943. He studied composition with Balasanian at the Moscow Cons. (1961–64) and with Arapov at the Leningrad Cons. (1965–66); in 1973 he was appointed to the faculty of the

Leningrad Cons. In his works he adopts a fairly progressive, even aggressive, modern idiom, making occasional use of serial techniques.

WORKS: DRAMATIC: *The Legend Remained*, radio opera for children (1967); *Lyubov and Silin*, chamber opera (1968); *The Stolen Sun*, television opera (1969); *Vestris*, ballet (1969); *Opera about How Ivan Ivanovich Quarreled with Ivan Nikiforovich*, comic opera (1971); *The Death of Cornet Klauzov*, opera (1976). **ORCH.:** *Triade* (1962); 5 cello concertos: No. 1 (1962), No. 2 (1963), No. 3 for Cello Solo (1965), No. 4, *Duodecimet*, for Cello and 11 Instruments (1966), and No. 5 (1970); Piano Concerto (1963; rev. 1978); Trumpet Concertino (1963); 2 syms.: No. 1 (1967) and No. 2 for Strings (1977). **CHAMBER:** *4 Impressions* for Cello and Piano (1963; rev. 1978); *Small Duet* for Violin and Piano (1965); *4 Pieces* for Clarinet and Piano (1968); Cello Sonata (1970); Trio-Sonata for Violin, Viola, and Cello (1972); Clarinet Sonata (1972); Flute Sonata (1975); Accordion Sonata (1977). **PIANO:** *Concert Allegro* (1963); *Syllogisms* (1964); 3 sonatas (1968, 1973, 1974). **VOCAL:** Song cycle for Soprano and Piano (1962); 3 cantatas: *Architects* for Bass, Men's Chorus, and Orch. (1964); *To the Memory of García Lorca* for Chorus and Chamber Orch. (1965); *Ashes in the Palms*, chamber cantata (1978).

Bantock, Sir Granville, eminent English composer; b. London, Aug. 7, 1868; d. there, Oct. 16, 1946. He studied at the Royal Academy of Music in London, graduating in 1892; was the first holder of the Macfarren Scholarship. His earliest works were presented at the Academy concerts: an Egyptian ballet suite, *Rameses II*; an overture, *The Fire Worshippers*; and a short opera, *Caedmar*, later presented at London's Crystal Palace (Oct. 18, 1893). He then engaged in varied activities; he was founder and ed. of the *New Quarterly Musical Review* (1893–96); toured as a musical comedy conductor (1894–95); organized and conducted concerts devoted to works by young British composers; conducted a military band and later a full orch. at New Brighton (1897–1901). At the same time, he was engaged in teaching; in 1907 he succeeded Elgar as prof. of music at the Univ. of Birmingham, a post he retained until 1934, when he became chairman of the board of Trinity College of Music. He was knighted in 1930. As a composer, Bantock was attracted to exotic subjects with mystical overtones; his interests were cosmopolitan and embraced all civilizations, with a particular predilection for the Celtic and oriental cultures; however, his music was set in Western terms. He was a strong believer in the programmatic significance of musical images, and most of his works bear titles relating to literature, mythology, or legend. Yet he was a typically British composer in the treatment of his materials. His works are brilliantly scored and effective in performance, but few of them have been retained in the repertoire.

WORKS: 3 Celtic operas: *Caedmar* (1892), *The Pearl of Iran* (1894), and *The Seal-Woman* (Birmingham, Sept. 27, 1924); ballets: *Egypt* (1892), *Lalla Rookh* (1902), and *The Great God Pan* (1902); 5 tone poems: *Thalaba the Destroyer* (1900), *Dante* (1901; rev. 1910), *Fifine at the Fair* (1901), *Hudibras* (1902), and *The Witch of Atlas* (1902); overture: *The Pierrot of the Minute* (1908); *Hebridean Symphony* (Glasgow, Jan. 17, 1916); *Pagan Symphony* (1923–28); *Celtic Symphony* for Strings and 6 Harps (1940); *2 Heroic Ballads* (1944); *The Funeral* (1946); choral works with Orch.: *The Time Spirit* (1902); *Sea Wanderers* (1906); *Omar Khayyám* (1906–09); *The Pilgrim's Progress* (1928); *Prometheus Unbound* (1936); numerous works for Unaccompanied Chorus, among them 3 "choral syms.": *Atalanta in Calydon* (1911), *Vanity of Vanities* (1913), and *A Pageant of Human Life* (1913); also *The Golden Journey to Samarkand* (1922); choral suites; children's songs; works for brass band, cello, and orch. and for voice and orch.; 2 string quartets; 3 violin sonatas; viola sonatas; cello sonatas; several sets of piano pieces: *Songs of the East* (6 cycles of 6 songs each); several sets of *Songs from the Chinese Poets*; sets of Celtic songs; etc.

BIBL.: H. Anderton, *G. B.* (London, 1915); H. Antcliffe, "A Brief Survey of the Works of G. B.," *Musical Quarterly* (July 1918); P. Pirie, "B. and His Generation," *Musical Times* (Aug. 1968); M. Bantock, *G. B.: A Personal Portrait* (London, 1972).

Bär, Olaf, prominent German baritone; b. Dresden, Dec 19, 1957. He sang in the Kreuzchor (1966–75) and studied at the Hochschule für Musik in Dresden. In 1982 he won 1st prize in the Dvořák vocal competition in Karlovy Vary, and, in 1983, 1st prize in the vocal competition sponsored by the East German opera houses and the Walter Grüner lieder competition in London. In 1981 he made his operatic debut in Dresden, and from 1985 to 1991 he was a principal member of the State Opera there. He made his British debut in a recital at London's Wigmore Hall in 1983, returning to London in 1985 to make his British operatic debut as Strauss's Harlekin at Covent Garden. In 1986 he appeared as Ariadne at the Aix-en-Provence Festival, and as Papageno at the Vienna State Opera and at La Scala in Milan. On March 19, 1987, he made his U.S. debut as Christ in Bach's *St. Matthew Passion* with Solti and the Chicago Sym. Orch., and that same year sang the role of the Count in *Capriccio* at the Glyndebourne Festival. On April 18, 1991, he made his N.Y. recital debut at Alice Tully Hall. In addition to his roles in operas by Mozart and Strauss, he has won distinction as a concert and lieder artist.

Bar-Illan, David (Jacob), Israeli pianist; b. Haifa, Feb. 7, 1930. He first studied piano in his native city; then continued studies at the Juilliard School of Music and the Mannes College of Music in N.Y. In 1946 he made his formal debut as a soloist with the Palestine Broadcasting Service Orch.; then made his first appearance with the N.Y. Phil. in 1960; in subsequent seasons he appeared with all of the major orchs. of the U.S.; also played with many orchs. of Europe. From 1980 he taught at the Mannes College of Music. He is best known as an interpreter of works from the Classical and Romantic periods.

Barab, Seymour, American cellist and composer; b. Chicago, Jan. 9, 1921. He studied with Persichetti, Wolpe, Varèse, and Harrison. He played in the Indianapolis Sym. Orch., the Cleveland Orch., the CBS Sym. Orch., the Portland (Oreg.) Sym. Orch., the San Francisco Sym., the ABC Sym. Orch., and the Brooklyn Philharmonia; also played in the Galimir String Quartet, the N.Y. Pro Musica, the N.Y. Trio, the New Music Quartet, and the Composers Quartet; served on the faculties of Black Mountain College, Rutgers, the State Univ. of N.J., and the New England Cons. of Music in Boston. As a cellist, Barab commissioned and premiered scores by several American composers. His own large output includes 3 full-length operas: *Phillips Marshall, Mortals*, and *A Piece of String*; 25 one-act operas; Concerto Grosso for Orch.; *Tales of Rhyme and Reason* for Orch.; Cello Concerto; Concertino for Alto Saxophone and Orch.; Wind Quintet; Quartet for Saxophones; 4 string quartets; 5 piano trios; Trio for Flute, Viola, and Harp; choral works; numerous songs.

Baranović, Krešimir, Croatian conductor, pedagogue, and composer; b. Šibenik, July 25, 1894; d. Belgrade, Sept. 17, 1975. He studied piano, theory, and composition in Zagreb and in Vienna. He was subsequently a theater conductor in Zagreb (1915–27); then traveled with Anna Pavlova's ballet group (1927–28). Returning to Yugoslavia, he was director of the Zagreb Opera (1929–40); then served as a prof. at the Belgrade Academy of Music (1946–61); was also conductor of the Belgrade Phil. (1952–61). A prolific composer, he was successful mostly in music for the theater.

WORKS: DRAMATIC: COMIC OPERAS: *Striženo-Košeno* (Clipped and Mowed; Zagreb, May 4, 1932); *Nevjesta od Cetingrada* (The Bride from Cetingrad; Belgrade, May 12, 1951). **BALLETS:** *Licitarsko srce* (The Gingerbread Heart; 1924); *Kineska priča* (Chinese Tale; Belgrade, April 30, 1955). **ORCH.:** *Pjesma guslara* (Song of the Minstrel; Zagreb, Jan. 25, 1947). **VOCAL:** *Pan* for Narrator, Voices, and Orch. (Belgrade, March 10, 1958); *Oblaci* (The Clouds) for Mezzo-soprano and Orch. (Belgrade, Oct. 31, 1964).

Barati, George (real name, **György Baráti**), Hungarian-born American cellist, conductor, and composer; b. Györ, April 3, 1913; d. San Jose, Calif., June 22, 1996. After initial training at the Györ Music School (graduated, 1932), he studied at the Franz Liszt Academy of Music in Budapest (graduated, 1935; teacher's diploma, 1937; artist diploma, 1938); he also was a member of the Budapest Concert Orch. (1933–36) and 1st cellist of the Budapest Sym. Orch. and Municipal Opera orch. (1936–38). In 1939 he emigrated to the U.S., becoming a naturalized American citizen in 1944; he studied composition with Georges Couvreur and Henri Switten at Westminster Choir College in Princeton, N.J. (1938–39), and with Sessions at Princeton Univ. (1939–43). He played cello in the Pro Ideale (later Westminster) String Quartet (1936–39), then taught at Princeton Univ. (1939–43). He also conducted the Princeton Ensemble and Choral Union (1941–43) and the Alexandria (La.) Military Sym. Orch. (1944–46). He was a cellist in the San Francisco Sym. Orch. and the California String Quartet (1946–50); he also was music director of the Barati Chamber Orch. of San Francisco (1948–52). From 1950 to 1968 he was music director of the Honolulu Sym. Orch. and Opera, leaving to become executive director of the Montalvo Center for the Arts and conductor of the Montalvo Chamber Orch. in Saratoga, California (1968–78). From 1971 to 1980 he was music director of the Santa Cruz County Sym. Orch. in Aptos, California; he then was music director of the Barati Ensemble (1989–92). In 1991 the George Barati Archive was opened at the Univ. of Calif. at Santa Cruz Library. In 1959 he received the Naumburg Award, in 1962 the Alice M. Ditson Award, and in 1965–66 a Guggenheim fellowship. As a composer, Barati wrote fine music in a modern European tradition. During his stay in Hawaii, he studied native melodic and rhythmic patterns of exotic South Sea islands, and these found reflection in some of his works of the period.

WORKS: DRAMATIC: OPERA: *Noelani* (1968). **BALLET:** *The Love of Don Perlimplin* (1947). **INCIDENTAL MUSIC:** *Thirty Pieces of Silver* for Narrator and Chamber Orch. (1951). **FILM SCORES:** *The Ugly Duckling* (1981; arr. as a suite for Narrator and Chamber Orch. or Band, 1982–83); *What Do 2 Rights Make?* (1983). **ORCH.:** *Fever Dreams* (1938); *2 Symphonic Movements* (1941); *Lamentoso* (1943); *Scherzo* (1946); *Configuration* (1947); Chamber Concerto for Flute, Oboe, Clarinet, Bassoon, and Strings (1952); *Tribute* (1952); Cello Concerto (1953; rev. 1957); *The Dragon and the Phoenix* (1960); Sym. (1963); *Polarization* (1965); *Baroque Quartet Concerto* for Flute, Oboe, Harpsichord, Double Bass, and Orch. (1968); *Festival Hula* (1968); *Vaudeville* (1968); Piano Concerto (1973); Guitar Concerto (1976; rev. 1982); *Branches of Time* for 2 Pianos and Orch. (1981); *Confluence* (1982); Violin Concerto (1986); *Serenata Capricciosa* for Chamber Orch. (1990); *Chant of Darkness* (1993); *Seachange* (1993); *Chant of Light* (1995). **CHAMBER:** 3 string quartets (1944, 1961, 1991); Woodwind Quintet (1954); Violin Sonata (1956); Quintet for Oboe and Strings (1961); Harpsichord Quartet for Flute, Oboe, Harpsichord, and Double Bass (1964); Octet for Flute, Oboe, Double Bass, Harpsichord, and String Quartet (1966); *Lumberjack* for Trombone and Piano (1969; rev. 1992); *Hawaiian Forests* for 7 Instruments (1971; rev. 1989); Trio for Flute, Violin, and Guitar (1976; rev. 1979); Triptych for Flute, Oboe, Viola, and Piano (1983); Woodwind Trio (1984); *. . . And the Shadows Were Filled with Light* for 9 Instruments (1984); *Spring Serenade* for Flute, Viola, and Cello (1987); *Trio Profundo* for Viola, Cello, and Contrabass (1988; rev. 1990); Trio for Clarinet, Violin, and Cello (1988); *Dialogue* for Flute and Piano (1990); *Aquinas Suite* for 3 Unspecified Instruments (1991); *Second Edition,* "encore" for String Quartet (1991); *Spring Rain* for Clarinet and Guitar (1993); piano pieces.

Barbe, Helmut, German organist and composer; b. Halle, Dec. 28, 1927. He studied theory in Berlin with Ernst Pepping and choral conducting with Gottfried Grote; was active as a church organist and conductor in Berlin. In 1952 he became Kantor at St. Nikolai Church in Spandau; in 1955 he was appointed a member of the faculty of the Berlin Kirchenmusikschule. In 1973 he was named Landeskirchenmusikdirektor. In his works, he adopted a modified dodecaphony. He composed mostly sacred choral works and various organ pieces; also wrote a Violin Concerto (1966) and *Hovs Hallar* for Organ, 12 Solo Strings, and Percussion (1970).

Barbeau, (Charles) Marius, eminent Canadian anthropologist, ethnologist, and folklorist; b. Ste.-Marie-de-Beauce, Quebec, March 5, 1883; d. Ottawa, Feb. 27, 1969. He studied music with his mother; after taking courses in the humanities at the Collège de Ste.-Anne-de-la-Procatière and in law at Laval Univ., he won a Rhodes scholarship in 1907 and pursued training in anthropology, archeology, and ethnology at Oriel College, Oxford (graduated with a B.S. degree and a diploma in anthropology, 1910); also took courses at the Sorbonne and the École d'anthropologie in Paris. In 1911 he became anthropologist and ethnologist at the Museum Branch of the Geological Survey of Canada; after it became the National Museum in 1927, he remained with it until 1948; also taught at the Univ. of Ottawa (1942) and at Laval Univ. (1942–45), where he subsequently served as prof. agrégé. He was founder-director of the Canadian Folk Music Soc. (1956–63). Barbeau collected more than 6,000 melodies and 13,000 texts of French-Canadian folk songs, as well as many thousands of Canadian Indian melodies. He publ. 30 books and 10 song anthologies, some in collaboration with others. Among his most important writings were "Chants populaires du Canada," *Journal of American Folklore* (with E. Massicotte; 1919); *Folk-songs of French Canada* (with E. Sapir; New Brunswick, 1925); *Folk-songs of Old Quebec* (Ottawa, 1935); *Where Ancient France Lingers* (Toronto, 1936); *Modalité dans nos mélodies populaire* (Ottawa, 1944); *Jongleur Songs of Old Quebec* (Toronto, 1962).

BIBL.: I. Katz, "M. B., 1883–1969," *Journal of the Society for Ethnomusicology* (Jan. 1970).

Barber, Samuel, outstanding American composer of superlative gifts; b. West Chester, Pa., March 9, 1910; d. N.Y., Jan. 23, 1981. He was the nephew of **Louise Homer** and her husband **Sidney Homer**, who encouraged him in his musical inclination. At the age of 6, he began piano lessons, and later had some cello lessons. He was only 10 when he tried his hand at composing a short opera, *The Rose Tree.* At 12, he gained practical experience as organist at Westminster Presbyterian Church. Even before graduating from high school at age 16, he entered the first class at the newly organized Curtis Inst. of Music in Philadelphia when he was 14, where he was a pupil of George Boyle and Isabelle Vengerova (piano), Rosario Scalero (composition), and Fritz Reiner (conducting). He also took voice lessons with Emilio de Gogorza and gave recitals as a baritone at the Curtis Inst., where he graduated in 1934. He then went to Vienna to pursue vocal training with John Braun, and also appeared in public as a singer there. In the meantime, his interest in composing grew apace. In 1928 his Violin Sonata won the Bearns Prize of Columbia Univ. It was followed by such enduring scores as his *Serenade* for String Quartet (1928), *Dover Beach* for Voice and String Quartet (1931), and the Cello Sonata (1932). In 1933 he won the Bearns Prize again for his overture to *The School for Scandal,* which was favorably received at its premiere by the Philadelphia Orch. on Aug. 30 of that year. Then followed the successful premiere of his *Music for a Scene from Shelley* by the N.Y. Phil. on March 24, 1935, under Werner Janssen's direction. Thanks to a Pultizer Traveling Scholarship and a Rome Prize, Barber pursued composition at the American Academy in Rome in 1935 and 1936. During his sojourn there, he wrote his 1st Sym., which was premiered under Molinari's direction on Dec. 13, 1936. He also wrote his String Quartet in 1936. Rodzinski conducted Barber's 1st Sym. at the Salzburg Festival on July 25, 1937, the first score by an American composer to be played there. Toscanini conducted the premiere of Barber's (1st) *Essay for Orchestra* with the NBC Sym. Orch. in N.Y. on Nov. 5, 1938. On the same program, he also conducted the *Adagio* for Strings, a transcription of the 2nd movement of the String Quartet, which was destined to become Barber's most celebrated work, an epitome of his lyrical and Romantic bent. From 1939 to 1942 he directed the Madrigal Chorus at the Curtis Inst. His most notable work of this period was his Violin Concerto, which was first performed by Albert Spalding with Ormandy and the Philadelphia Orch. on Feb. 7, 1941. With his friend Gian Carlo Menotti, he purchased a house ("Capricorn") in Mount Kisco, N.Y., which was to remain the center of his activities until 1973. In 1942 he was conscripted into the U.S. Army and the following year was assigned to the Army Air Force, which commissioned his 2nd Sym. Called "Flight Symphony," it included an electronic instrument producing sound in imitation of radio signals. Koussevitzky conducted its premiere with the Boston Sym. Orch. on March 3, 1944. After his discharge from military service in 1945, Barber revised the score; it was first performed by the Philadelphia Orch. on Jan. 21, 1949. Still dissatisfied with the work, he destroyed the MS except for the 2nd movement, which he revised as *Night Flight*, which was first performed by Szell and the Cleveland Orch. on Oct. 8, 1964. Barber's Cello Concerto (1945), which was introduced by Raya Garbousova with Koussevitzy conducting the Boston Sym. Orch. on April 5, 1946 won the N.Y. Music Critics' Circle Award that same year. For Martha Graham, he composed the ballet *Medea* (N.Y., May 10, 1946), which was revised as *The Cave of the Heart* (N.Y., Feb. 27, 1947). He made an orch. suite from the ballet (Philadelphia, Dec. 5, 1947) and the orch. piece, *Medea's Meditation and Dance of Vengeance* (N.Y., Feb. 2, 1956). One of Barber's most distinguished scores, *Knoxville: Summer of 1915* for High Voice and Orch., after James Agee, was first performed by Eleanor Steber with Koussevitzky conducting the Boston Sym. Orch. on April 9, 1948. His remarkable Piano Sonata, premiered by Horowitz in Havana on Dec. 9, 1949, amply utilized contemporary resources, including 12-tone writing. For Menotti's Festival of 2 Worlds, Barber composed the 1-act opera *A Hand of Bridge*, scored for 4 Soloists and Chamber Orch., which was performed on June 17, 1959, in Spoleto, Italy. Barber composed his first opera, *Vanessa* (1956–57), to a libretto by Menotti. It was successfuly premiered at the Metropolitan Opera in N.Y. on Jan. 15, 1958, and was awarded the Pulitzer Prize in Music. It was followed by his strikingly brilliant Piano Concerto, which was first performed by John Browning with Leinsdorf conducting the Boston Sym. Orch. at the opening week of N.Y.'s Lincoln Center for the Performing Arts on Sept. 24, 1962. Barber was awarded his 2nd Pulitzer Prize in Music for this work. A commission from the Metropolitan Opera spurred Barber on to compose his most ambitious work for the stage, the 3-act opera *Antony and Cleopatra*. With Zeffirelli as librettist, producer, director, and designer, it was premiered at the opening of the new Metropolitan Opera House in N.Y. on Sept. 16, 1966. Unfortunately, the production, with its complicated and problematic paraphernalia and overinflated staging, eclipsed serious evaluation of the music, and the opera received vitriolic reviews. Barber revised the score with a revamped libretto by Menotti; the new version was given a more favorable reception at its first performance by N.Y.'s Opera Theater of the Juilliard School on Feb. 6, 1975, and subsequent performances at Spoleto and Chicago.

During the final years of his life, Barber wrote almost exclusively vocal music, including the cycle *Despite and Still*, for Leontyne Price, and the cantata *The Lovers*, from the poetry of Neruda. In 1945, 1947, and 1949 he held Guggenheim fellowships. He was elected to the National Inst. of Arts and Letters in 1941 and to the American Academy of Arts and Letters in 1958. Barber was one of the most distinguished American composers of the 20th century. He excelled primarily as a melodist, being remarkably sensitive in his handling of vocally shaped patterns. Although the harmonic structures of his music remained fundamentally tonal, he made free use of chromatic techniques, verging on atonality and polytonality, while his mastery of modern counterpoint enabled him to write canons and fugues in effective neo-Baroque sequences. His orchestration was opulent without being turgid, and his treatment of solo instruments was unfailingly congenial to their nature even though requiring a virtuoso technique.

WORKS: DRAMATIC: OPERAS: *Vanessa* (1956–57; N.Y., Jan. 15, 1958, Mitropoulos conducting; rev. 1964); *A Hand of Bridge* (Spoleto, June 17, 1959); *Antony and Cleopatra* (N.Y., Sept. 16, 1966, Schippers conducting; rev. 1974; N.Y., Feb. 6, 1975, Conlon conducting). **BALLETS:** *Medea* or *Serpent Heart* (N.Y., May 10, 1946; rev. as *The Cave of the Heart*, N.Y., Feb. 27, 1947; as a ballet suite, Philadelphia, Dec. 5, 1947, Ormandy conducting; as *Medea's Meditation and Dance of Vengeance* for Orch., 1955; N.Y., Feb. 2, 1956, Mitropoulos conducting); *Souvenirs* (1952; N.Y., Nov. 15, 1955; as a ballet suite, 1952; Chicago, Nov. 12, 1953, Reiner conducting; also for Solo Piano or Piano, 4-hands). **ORCH.:** *Serenade* for String Quartet (1928; also for String Orch.); *The School for Scandal* overture (1931–32; Philadelphia, Aug. 30, 1933, Smallens conducting); *Music for a Scene from Shelley* (1933; N.Y., March 24, 1935, Janssen conducting); 2 syms.: No. 1 (Rome, Dec. 13, 1936, Molinari conducting; rev. 1942) and No. 2 (Boston, March 3, 1944, Koussevitzky conducting; rev. version, Philadelphia, Jan. 21, 1949, Ormandy conducting; 2nd movement rev. as *Night Flight*, Cleveland, Oct. 8, 1964, Szell conducting); *Adagio* for Strings (arranged from the 2nd movement of the String Quartet, 1936; N.Y., NBC, Nov. 5, 1938, Toscanini conducting); (3) *Essay*(s): No. 1 (1937; N.Y., NBC, Nov. 5, 1938, Toscanini conducting), No. 2 (N.Y., April 16, 1942, Walter conducting), and No. 3 (N.Y., Sept. 14, 1978, Mehta conducting); Violin Concerto (1939; Philadelphia, Feb. 7, 1941, Spalding soloist, Ormandy conducting); *Funeral March* (1943); *Commando March* for Band (Atlantic City, May 23, 1943, composer conducting; also for Orch., Boston, Oct. 29, 1943, Koussevitzky conducting); *Capricorn Concerto* for Flute, Oboe, Trumpet, and Strings (N.Y., Oct. 8, 1944, Saidenberg conducting); Cello Concerto (1945; Boston, April 5, 1946, Garbousova soloist, Koussevitzky conducting); *Horizon* (c.1945; June 17, 1945, San Francisco, Kurtz conducting); *Adventure* for Flute, Clarinet, Horn, Harp, and Exotic Instruments (CBS-TV, Nov. 28, 1954); *Toccata festiva* for Organ and Orch. (Philadelphia, Sept. 30, 1960, Callaway soloist, Ormandy conducting); *Die natalie*, choral preludes for Christmas (Boston, Dec. 22, 1960, Munch conducting); Piano Concerto (N.Y., Sept. 24, 1962, Browning soloist, Leinsdorf conducting); *Fadograph of a Yestern Scene* (Pittsburgh, Sept. 11, 1971, Steinberg conducting); *Canzonetta* for Oboe and Strings (orchestrated by C. Turner, 1977–78; N.Y., Dec. 17, 1981, H. Gomberg soloist, Mehta conducting). **CHAMBER:** *Serenade* for String Quartet (1928; Philadelphia, May 5, 1930, Swastika Quartet; also for String Orch.); Violin Sonata (Philadelphia, Dec. 10, 1928, Gilbert violinist, composer pianist; not extant); Cello Sonata (1932; N.Y., March 5, 1933, Cole cellist, composer pianist); String Quartet (Rome, Dec. 14, 1936, Pro Art Quartet; 2nd movement arranged as the *Adagio* for Strings, 1936); *Commemorative March* for Violin, Cello, and Piano (n.d.); *Summer Music* for Wind Quintet (1955; Detroit, March 20, 1956); *Canzone (Elegy)* for Flute or Violin and Piano (1962; transcription of the 2nd movement of the Piano Concerto); *Mutations from Bach* for 4 Horns, 3 Trumpets, 3 Trombones, and Tuba or Timpani (1967; N.Y., Oct. 7, 1968). **KEYBOARD: PIANO:** (2) *Interludes* (Philadelphia, May 12, 1932, composer pianist); (4) *Excursions* (1942–44; 1st complete perf., N.Y., Dec. 22, 1948, Behrend pianist); Sonata (Havana, Dec. 9, 1949, Horowitz pianist); *Souvenirs* (1952; also for Piano, 4-hands, and as a ballet); *Nocturne: Homage to John Field* (San Diego, Oct. 1959, Browning pianist); *Ballade* (Fort Worth, Sept. 11, 1977, Steven de Groote, pianist). **ORGAN:** *Wondrous Love: Variations on a Shape Note Hymn* (Grosse Pointe, Mich., Oct. 19, 1958, Roeckelein organist). **VOCAL:** 3 Songs for Voice and Piano, Op. 2: *The Daisies, With rue my heart is laden, Bessie Bobtail* (1927–34; London, June 25, 1935, Bampton singer, Westmoreland pianist); 3 Songs for Voice and Piano, Op. 10 (after Joyce): *Rain has fallen, Sleep now; I hear an army* (1935–37; nos. 1 and 2, Rome, April 22, 1936, composer singer and pianist; no. 3 also for Voice and Orch., CBS, May 5, 1945, Tourel soloist, composer conducting); 4 Songs for Voice and Piano, Op. 13: *A Nun Takes the Veil, Secrets of the Old, Sure on this shining night, Nocturne* (1937–40; New York, April 4, 1941, Troxell singer, Bossart pianist; nos. 3 and 4 also arr.

for Voice and Orch., CBS, May 5, 1945, Tourel soloist, composer conducting); *Dover Beach* for Medium Voice and String Quartet (1931; N.Y., March 5, 1933, Bampton singer, N.Y. Art Quartet); *The Virgin Martyrs* for Women's Voices (1935; CBS, April 17, 1939, composer conducting); *Let Down the Bars, O Death* for Chorus (1936); *God's Grandeur* for Double Chorus (Shippensburg, Pa., Jan. 31, 1938, Westminster Choir); *A Stopwatch and an Ordnance Map* for Men's Voices, Brass Ensemble, and Timpani (1st perf. without brass, Philadelphia, April 23, 1940, composer conducting; 1st perf. with brass, N.Y., Dec. 17, 1945, Shaw conducting); *Reincarnations* for Chorus (1940); *Monks and Raisins* for Medium Voice and Piano (1943; also for Medium Voice and Orch., CBS, May 5, 1945, Tourel soloist, composer conducting); Nuvoletta for High Voice and Piano (1947); *Knoxville: Summer of 1915* for Voice and Orch. (1947; Boston, April 9, 1948, Steber soloist, Koussevitzky conducting; rev. version for Voice and Chamber Orch., Washington, D.C., April 1, 1950); (5) *Mélodies Passagères* for Voice and Piano (1950–51; 1st complete perf., Paris, Feb. 1952, Bernac singer, Poulenc pianist); (10) *Hermit Songs* for Voice and Piano (1952–53; Washington, D.C., Oct. 30, 1953, Price singer, composer pianist); *Prayers of Kierkegaard* for Soprano, Chorus, and Orch. (Boston, Dec. 3, 1954, Price soloist, Munch conducting); *Andromache's Farewell* for Soprano and Orch. (1962; N.Y., April 4, 1963, Arroyo soloist, Schippers conducting); *Easter Chorale* for Chorus, Brass Sextet, Timpani, and Organ ad libitum (Washington, D.C., May 7, 1964); *Agnus Dei* for Chorus and Piano or Organ ad libitum (1967; arranged from the 2nd movement of the String Quartet, 1936); *Despite and Still*, song cycle for High or Medium Voice and Piano (N.Y., April 27, 1969, Price singer, Garvey pianist); *The Lovers* for Baritone, Chorus, and Orch. (Philadelpha, Sept. 22, 1971, Krause soloist, Ormandy conducting); 3 Songs for Voice and Piano, Op. 45 (1972; New York, April 30, 1974, Fischer-Dieskau singer, Wadsworth pianist).

BIBL.: N. Broder, *S. B.* (N.Y., 1954); R. Friedewald, *A Formal and Stylistic Analysis of the Published Music of S. B.* (diss., Univ. of Iowa, 1957); L. Wathen, *Dissonance Treatment in the Instrumental Music of S. B.* (diss., Northwestern Univ., 1960); S. Carter, *The Piano Music of S. B.* (diss., Texas Tech Univ., 1980); H. Gleason and W. Becker, "S. B.," *20th-century American Composers* (2nd ed., rev., Bloomington, Ind., 1981); A. Kozinn, "S. B.: The Last Interview and the Legacy," *High Fidelity* (June-July 1981); D. Hennessee, *S. B.: A Bio-Bibliography* (Westport, Conn., 1985); J. Kreiling, *The Songs of S. B.: A Study in Literary Taste and Text-Setting* (Ann Arbor, Mich., 1987); B. Heyman, *S. B.: The Composer and His Music* (Oxford, 1992); P. Wittke, *S. B.: An Improvisatory Portrait* (N.Y., 1994; includes works list by N. Ryan).

Barbier, René (Auguste-Ernest), Belgian composer and teacher; b. Namur, July 12, 1890; d. Brussels, Dec. 24, 1981. He studied with Gilson at the Brussels Cons. and with Dupuis at the Liège Cons. He taught at the Liège Cons. (1920–49) and at the Brussels Cons. (1949–55); concurrently was director of the Namur Cons. (1923–63). In 1923 he received the Belgian Royal Academy Prize for his symphonic poem *Les Génies du sommeil*, and in 1968 he was elected to membership in the Academy.

WORKS: DRAMATIC: OPERAS: *Yvette* (1910); *La Fête du vieux Tilleul* (1912). **BALLET:** *Les Pierres magiques* (1957). **ORCH.:** *Pièce symphonique* for Trumpet and Orch. (1918); 2 piano concertos (1922, 1934); *Les Génies du sommeil*, symphonic poem (1923); *Les Éléments: Suite Platonicienne* (1935); *Poème* for Cello and Orch. (1936); *Fantaisie concertante* for Violin and Orch. (1937); Cello Concerto (1938); *Poco adagio et Allegro brillante* for Clarinet and Orch. (1940); *Diptyque* (1941); *La Musique de perdition*, symphonic poem (1947); *Introduction (Fanfare) et 3 Esquisses symphoniques* (1956); *Pièce concertante* for Violin or Saxophone and Orch. (1958); Guitar Concerto (1960); *3 mouvements symphoniques* for Strings (1962); *Tableau symphonique* (1963); Horn Concerto (1964); *Introduction et Allegro symphonique* (1967); Concerto for Organ, Strings, and Percussion (1967); *Ouverture concertante* (1969); Concertino for 2 Guitars and Strings (1971). **CHAMBER:** Violin Sonata (1914); Piano Quintet (1915); Viola Sonata (1916); Piano Trio (1919); String Quartet (1939); Quartet for 4 Horns (1956); Quartet for 4 Saxophones (1961); Trio for Flute, Cello, and Piano (1971). **VOCAL:** Oratorios and other works.

Barbieri, Fedora, Italian mezzo-soprano; b. Trieste, June 4, 1920. She studied in Trieste with Luigi Toffolo and in Milan with Giulia Tess. She made her professional debut as Fidalma in Cimarosa's *Il matrimonio segreto* at Florence's Teatro Comunale in 1940; in 1942 she made her first appearance at Milan's La Scala as Meg Page; in 1950 she first sang at London's Covent Garden as a member of the visiting La Scala company, and returned to Covent Garden as a guest artist in 1957–58 and 1964. From 1947 she sang at the Teatro Colón in Buenos Aires. On Nov. 6, 1950, she made her Metropolitan Opera debut in N.Y. as Eboli, remaining on its roster until 1954, and again for the 1956–57, 1967–68, 1971–72, and 1974–77 seasons. Her large repertory included over 80 roles, both standard and modern, among them Adalgisa, Carmen, Amneris, Santuzza, and Azucena.

Barbirolli, Lady Evelyn (née **Rothwell**), English oboist and teacher; b. Wallingford, Jan. 24, 1911. She was a student of Goossens at the Royal College of Music in London. She played in the Covent Garden Touring Orch. (1931–32), the Scottish Orch. in Glasgow (1933–36), the Glyndebourne Opera orch. (1934–39), and the London Sym. Orch. (1935–39). Upon her marriage to **John Barbirolli** in 1939, she pursued a career as a soloist and recitalist. From 1971 to 1987 she was a prof. of oboe at the Royal Academy of Music in London. In addition to preparing many editions and arrangements of oboe music, she publ. the books *Oboe Technique* (1953; 3rd ed., 1987) and *The Oboist's Companion* (3 vols.). In 1984 she was made an Officer of the Order of the British Empire.

BIBL.: H. Atkins and P. Cotes, *The B.s: A Musical Marriage* (London, 1983).

Barbirolli, Sir John (actually, **Giovanni Battista**), eminent English conductor of Italian-French descent; b. London, Dec. 2, 1899; d. there, July 29, 1970. He studied cello; received a scholarship to London's Trinity College of Music in 1910 and another to London's Royal Academy of Music, graduating in 1916; he made his first appearance as a cellist at the age of 12, on Dec. 16, 1911, at the Queen's Hall in London. In 1916 he became a member of the Queen's Hall Orch. In 1923 he joined the International String Quartet and toured with it. In 1924 he organized a chamber orch. in Chelsea, which he conducted for several years; was a conductor with the British National Opera Co. (1926–29). He gained recognition on Dec. 12, 1927, when he successfully substituted for Beecham at a concert of the London Sym. Orch. In 1928 he was a guest conductor at London's Covent Garden, and a regular conductor there from 1929 to 1933; in 1933 he was named conductor of the Scottish Orch., Glasgow, and the Leeds Sym. Orch. He made his American debut with the N.Y. Phil. on Nov. 5, 1936, and was engaged as its permanent conductor in 1937. However, he failed to impress the N.Y. critics, and in 1943 he returned to England, where he was named conductor of the Hallé Orch. of Manchester. In 1958 he was appointed its conductor-in-chief. Renewing his American career, he served as conductor of the Houston Sym. Orch. (1961–67), while continuing his tenancy of the Hallé Orch., from which he finally retired in 1968 with the title of Conductor Laureate for Life. He was knighted in 1949 and made a Companion of Honour in 1969. A commemorative postage stamp with his portrait was issued by the Post Office of Great Britain on Sept. 1, 1980. Barbirolli was distinguished primarily in the Romantic repertoire; his interpretations were marked by nobility, expressive power, and brilliance. He had a fine pragmatic sense of shaping the music according to its inward style, without projecting his own personality upon it. However, this very objectivity tempered his success with American audiences, accustomed to charismatic flamboyance. He had a special affinity for English music, and performed many works of Elgar, Delius, and Britten. He conducted the first performances of the 7th and 8th syms. by

Vaughan Williams; also made transcriptions for string orch. and horns of 5 pieces from the Fitzwilliam Virginal Book (perf. by him under the title *Elizabethan Suite* in Los Angeles, Dec. 4, 1941). For his 2nd wife, **Lady Evelyn Barbirolli**, he composed an Oboe Concerto on themes by Pergolesi.

BIBL.: C. Rigby, *J. B.* (Altrincham, 1948); M. Kennedy, *Hallé Orchestra* (Manchester, 1968; rev. ed., 1976); idem, *B., Conductor Laureate* (London, 1971); C. Reid, *J. B.* (London, 1971); H. Atkins and P. Cotes, *The B.s: A Musical Marriage* (London, 1983).

Barblan, Guglielmo, eminent Italian musicologist; b. Siena, May 27, 1906; d. Milan, March 24, 1978. He first studied jurisprudence, then entered the Rome Cons. as a cello student of Forino and Becker; also took courses in theory at the Bolzano Cons. and attended lectures on musicology by Liuzzi in Rome and Sandberger in Munich. He served as a music critic for *La Provincia di Bolzano* (1932–50), and concurrently lectured on music history at the Bolzano Cons. (1932–49). In 1949 he became head librarian of the Milan Cons.; in 1965 he was appointed prof. of music history there; also taught at the Univ. of Milan from 1961. Barblan's principal contribution as a music scholar was in the field of Italian music history. In addition to his books, he ed. works by Bonporti and Cambini.

WRITINGS: *Un musicista trentino: F.A. Bonporti* (Florence, 1940); *Musiche e strumenti musicali dell'Africa orientale italiana* (Naples, 1941); *L'opera di Donizetti nell'età romantica* (Bergamo, 1948); ed. with A. Della Corte, *Mozart in Italia: I viaggi e le lettere* (Milan, 1956); *Guida al "Clavicembalo ben temperato" di J.S. Bach* (Milan, 1961); with C. Gallico and G. Pannain, *Claudio Monteverdi nel quarto centenario della nascita* (Turin, 1967); ed. *Conservatorio di musica G. Verdi, Milano; Catalogo della biblioteca* (Florence, 1972); with B. Zanolini, *Gaetano Donizetti: Vita e opera di un musicista romantico* (Bergamo, 1983).

Barblan, Otto, Swiss organist, conductor, teacher, and composer; b. Scanfs, March 22, 1860; d. Geneva, Dec. 19, 1943. He studied at the Stuttgart Cons. (1878–84); made his debut as an organist at Augsburg (1885); taught at Chur (1885–87); then became organist at the Cathedral of Geneva, prof. at the Cons., and conductor of the Société de Chant Sacre (1887). He wrote an *Ode patriotique* (1896); a *Festspiel* (Chur, May 28, 1899) commemorating the 400th anniversary of the battle of Calven, and containing the chorus *Terre des monts*, which attained great popularity, placing it next to the national anthem as a patriotic song; *Post tenebras lux*, cantata for the Calvin jubilee (1909); String Quartet; *Variations and Triple Fugue on B-A-C-H*; *Passion According to St. Luke* (Geneva, April 9, 1919).

BIBL.: E. Perini, *O. B.* (Zürich, 1960).

Barbosa-Lima, Carlos, Brazilian guitarist; b. São Paulo, Dec. 17, 1944. He began guitar study when he was 7; made his debut in São Paulo at 12. His principal teachers were Isaias Savio in Brazil and Andrés Segovia in Spain. In 1967 he made his first tour of the U.S.; also gave concerts in South America, Europe, and Israel, with notable success. He commissioned works for guitar from Ginastera, Balada, and Mignone; also made effective transcriptions of works by Bach, Handel, and other masters. He combined his concert career with teaching; was a member of the faculty at the Manhattan School of Music.

Barbour, J(ames) Murray, American musicologist; b. Chambersburg, Pa., March 31, 1897; d. Homestead, Pa., Jan. 4, 1970. He studied at Dickinson College (M.A., 1920) and Temple Univ. (Mus.B., 1924), then with Otto Kinkeldey at Cornell Univ. where, in 1932, he received the first doctorate in musicology awarded by a U.S. univ. with the diss. *Equal Temperament: Its History from Ramis (1482) to Rameau (1737)*; subsequently received a 2nd Ph.D. in music from the Univ. of Toronto in 1936. He taught English at Ithaca College (1932–39); then was a teacher at Michigan State College (later Univ.), where he was a prof. (1954–64). He contributed learned essays to music journals; also publ. *Tuning and Temperament: A Historical Survey* (East Lansing, 1951; 2nd ed., 1953), *The Church Music of William Billings* (East Lansing, 1960), and *Trumpets, Horns and Music* (East Lansing, 1964). Among his compositions are a *Requiem* and some chamber pieces.

Barce, Ramón, Spanish composer and music critic; b. Madrid, March 16, 1928. He studied languages at the Univ. of Madrid but was mainly autodidact in music; then was active with new music groups and as a music critic. He composed theater, orch., chamber, and vocal pieces in a modern idiom.

BIBL.: A. Medina, *R. B. en la vanguardia musical española* (Oviedo, 1983).

Bárdos, Lajos, Hungarian choral conductor, musicologist, and composer; b. Budapest, Oct. 1, 1899; d. there, Nov. 18, 1986. He studied composition with Siklós and Kodály at the Budapest Academy of Music, where he then taught (1928–67); also conducted Budapest's Cecilia Chorus (1926–41), Palestrina Chorus (1929–33), Budapest Chorus (1941–47), and St. Matyas Choir (1942–62). He publ. books on Liszt (1968, 1976), Bartók (1970, 1971), Stravinsky (1971), and Kodály (1972). Among his compositions were choral and chamber pieces.

Barenboim, Daniel, greatly talented Israeli pianist and conductor; b. Buenos Aires, Nov. 15, 1942. He began music training with his parents, making his public debut as a pianist in Buenos Aires when he was only 7. During the summers of 1954 and 1955, he studied piano with Edwin Fischer, conducting with Igor Markevitch, and chamber music with Enrico Mainardi at the Salzburg Mozarteum. He also pursued training in theory with Boulanger in Paris (1954–56), was one of the youngest students to receive a diploma from the Accademia di Santa Cecilia in Rome (1956), and took a conducting course with Carlo Zecchi at the Accademia Musicale Chigiana in Siena. In 1955 he made his debut as a soloist with orch. in Paris, and then made his British debut in Bournemouth. In Jan. 1956 he made his first appearance in London as soloist with Krips and the Royal Phil. He made his U.S. debut as soloist in Prokofiev's 1st Piano Concerto with Stokowski and the Sym. of the Air at N.Y.'s Carnegie Hall on Jan. 20, 1957. Later that year he made his first appearance as a conductor in Haifa. On Jan. 17, 1958, he made his U.S. recital debut in N.Y. In 1960 he played cycles of all the Beethoven piano sonatas in Israel and South America, and later in London (1967, 1970) and N.Y. (1970). From 1965 he was active as a soloist and conductor with the English Chamber Orch. in London. In 1967 he married **Jacqueline DuPré**, with whom he subsequently appeared in numerous concerts until she was tragically stricken with multiple sclerosis in 1973 and was compelled to abandon her career. In 1967 he conducted the Israel Phil. on a tour of the U.S., returning thereafter to appear as a guest conductor with various orchs. He also appeared as a guest conductor throughout Europe. He made his operatic debut in 1973 conducting *Don Giovanni* at the Edinburgh Festival. In 1975 he became music director of the Orchestre de Paris, a position he held until 1989. In 1981 he made his first appearance at the Bayreuth Festival conducting *Tristan und Isolde.* In 1988 he was named artistic director of the new Opéra de la Bastille in Paris by the French minister of culture. However, following the French presidential election, a new minister of culture was appointed and disagreements over artistic policy and remuneration led to Barenboim's abrupt dismissal in Jan. 1989. That same month he was appointed music director of the Chicago Sym. Orch., succeeding Solti. During the 1989–91 seasons, he served as its music director-designate before fully assuming his duties as music director for the orch.'s 100th anniversary season in 1991–92. In 1993 he also became Generalmusikdirektor of the Berlin State Opera. His autobiography appeared as *A Life in Music* (1991). From the earliest years of his professional career as a pianist, Barenboim has been held in the highest esteem. Particularly notable have been his performances of Bach, Mozart, Beethoven, Chopin, and Brahms. In addition to his distinguished appearances as a recitalist and chamber music artist, he has won great admiration as an accompanist. Barenboim's career as a conductor has been less remarkable. While he has maintained an extensive repertoire, he has been most successful with scores from the Romantic and late Romantic eras. He has also championed contemporary works, conducting premieres by such composers as Boulez and Corigliano.

Barere, Simon, virtuoso Russian pianist; b. Odessa, Sept. 1, 1896; d. N.Y., April 2, 1951. He began formal piano study at age 11, and entered the St. Petersburg Cons. as a pupil of Anna Essipova; after her death in 1914, he continued his studies there with Felix Blumenfeld, graduating with the Rubinstein Prize in 1919. Following extensive tours, he went to Berlin in 1929. In 1934 he made his London debut and in 1938 his N.Y. debut. During World War II, he lived in Stockholm; after the War, he resumed touring. On April 2, 1951, he was soloist in Grieg's Piano Concerto with Ormandy and the Philadelphia Orch. at N.Y.'s Carnegie Hall. During the performance, he was fatally stricken with a cerebral hemorrhage. In spite of extensive efforts to save him, he died backstage within minutes. Barere was a master keyboard artist who excelled in the Romantic repertory.

Barilli, Bruno, Italian writer on music and composer; b. Fano, Dec. 14, 1880; d. Rome, April 15, 1952. He studied in Parma and later in Munich. His collections of essays were publ. under the titles *Il sorcio nel violino* (Milan, 1926) and *Il paese del melodramma* (Lanciano, 1929). He wrote 2 operas, *Medusa* (1910; Bergamo, Sept. 11, 1938) and *Emiral* (Rome, March 11, 1924).

BIBL.: E. Falqui, ed., *Opere di B. B.* (Florence, 1963).

Barjansky, Alexander, Russian cellist; b. Odessa, Dec. 16, 1883; d. Brussels, Jan. 6, 1961. He left Russia before World War I and lived in Germany and Italy. He distinguished himself by giving performances of new works for cello, among them *Schelomo* by Ernest Bloch, which he played under Bloch's direction in Rome on Jan. 22, 1933; he also gave the premiere of the Cello Concerto by Delius on Jan. 31, 1921, in London. His wife publ. a book of recollections about him under the title *Portraits and Backgrounds* (London, 1940).

Bark, Jan (Helge Guttorm), Swedish trombonist and composer; b. Harnosand, April 19, 1934. He was first a jazz trombonist; then studied at the Stockholm Musikhögskolan, taking courses in composition with Lars-Erik Larsson and Karl Birgir Blomdahl; was initiated into ultramodern music by Györgi Ligeti in Stockholm; made an American trip in 1962 and worked with avant-garde groups at the Tape Music Center in San Francisco; in 1964 he traveled to the Far East to study oriental music. Returning to Sweden, he joined the radio and television center of the Swedish Broadcasting Service. He was cofounder with Folke Rabe of the Culture Quartet, which explored the potentialities of modern trombone playing. Many of his pieces are of a theatrical, almost exhibitionistic, nature, often with a healthy radical tinge.

WORKS: Piano Sonata (1957); 2 string quartets (1959, 1962); *Metakronismer* for Orch. (1960; Oslo, March 4, 1961); 2 works for the Culture Quartet, in collaboration with Folke Rabe: *Bolos* (1962) and *Polonaise* (1965); *Lamento* for Percussion, Piano, and Double Basses (1962); *Boca Chica* for Chamber Ensemble (1962); *Pyknos* for Orch. (1962); *Eko* for News Broadcaster and 5 Tape Recorders (1962); *Missa Bassa* for Small Orch. with 7 Conductors, 6 of whom also sing (1964; Swedish Radio, April 1, 1967); *Nota* for "choreographic" Chorus (1964); *Ost-Funk* for 8 Jazz Musicians (1964); *Mansbot* for Men's Chorus and 12 Guitars (1964); *Tredjedels Signeri* for 3 Hammond Organs (1967); *Bar*, electronic music (1967); *Light Music* for Chorus (1968); *Lyndon Bunk Johnson*, a "poster" work, composed collectively (1968); *Irk-Ork 1970* for Chamber Ensemble (1970); *Het Jacht von het vliegende Joachim* for Trombone, Cello, and Piano (1971); *Memoria in memoria* for Chamber Group (1974); *Utspel* for Band (1976); *Malumma* for Tuba and Band (1984); *Concerto for Orchestra* (1985); various theater pieces and film music.

Barkauskas, Vytautas (Pranas Marius), outstanding Lithuanian composer; b. Kaunas, March 25, 1931. He studied piano at the Vilnius College of Music while also studying mathematics at the Pedagogical Inst. there (1949–53); then took composition classes with Račiunas and orchestration classes with Balsys at the Lithuanian State Cons. (1953–59); in 1961 he joined its faculty. He wrote several cantatas following the compositional tenets of socialist realism; in his instrumental compositions, he makes use of more advanced cosmopolitan techniques, including serialism and aleatory improvisation.

WORKS: DRAMATIC: *Conflict*, "choreographic scene" for 3 Performers (1965); *Legend about Love*, opera (Vilnius, March 29, 1975). **ORCH.:** *Tone Poem* for Piano and Orch. (1960); 5 syms. (1962, 1971, 1979, 1984, 1986); *Choreographic Miniatures* (1965); Concertino for 4 Chamber Groups (1966); *Expressivistic Structures* for Chamber Orch. (1967); *Paraphrase* for Chamber Orch. (1967); *3 Aspects* (1969); *Overture a priori* (1976); *Toccamento*, concerto for Chamber Orch. (1978); Concerto for Viola and Chamber Orch. (1981); *The Sun*, symphonic picture (1983); Concerto piccolo for Chamber Orch. (1988); Piano Concerto (1992); *Konzertstück* (1992). **CHAMBER:** Piano Trio (1958); *Partita* for Violin (1967); *Intimate Composition* for Oboe and 12 Strings (1968); *Contrast Music* for Flute, Cello, and Percussion (1969); *Pro memoria* for Flute, Bass Clarinet, Piano or Harpsichord, and 5 Percussion (1970); *Monologue* for Oboe (1970); 2 string quartets (1972, 1983); 3 violin sonatas: No. 1, *Sonata Subita* (1976), No. 2, *Dialogue* (1978), and No. 3 (1984); Sextet for 2 Violins, Viola, Cello, Double Bass, and Piano (1985); Double Bass Sonata (1987); *Nino* for 2 Violins, Viola, Cello, Double Bass, and Piano (1990); Trio for Clarinet, Violin, and Piano (1990); *Lare* for Clarinet and Piano (1991); Concert Suite for Cello and Piano (1993); *Intimate Music* for Flute and Percussion (1993); *Trio à deux* for Violin, Viola, and Cello (1995). **KEYBOARD: PIANO:** *Poetry*, cycle (1964); *Variations* for 2 Pianos (1967); *Sonate pathétique* (1969); *5 Pictures of Vytukas* for Piano, 4-hands (1971); *Legend about Čiurlionis* (1972); *Elegy and Fantastical Toccata* (1972); *Prelude and Fugue* for 2 Pianos (1974); *Polyphonic Suite* (1979); *3 Concert Études* (1981); *Winter 1982* for Piano, 4-hands (1982); Sonata for 2 Pianos and 3 Performers (1984); *Le poème du coeur* (1984); *Sunday Music* for 2 Pianos and 4 Performers (1985); *13 Pieces* (1986); *Vision* (1988); *The Second Legend of Čiurlionis* (1988); *Divertimento* for Piano, 6-hands (1993); *The Third Legend of Čiurlionis* (1993). **ORGAN:** *Gloria Urbi* (1972); *Zodiac*, polyphonic cycle (1980); *The Rebirth of Hope* (1989). **VOCAL:** *Pathetic Thoughts* for Chorus (1962); *Word about Revolution*, cantata-poem for Narrator, Men's Chorus, and Orch. (1967); *La vostra nominanza e color d'erba* for Chamber Chorus and String Quintet (1971); *Prelude and Fugue* for Chorus (1974); *Salute Your Land*, oratorio-mystery for 4 Soloists, Women's Chorus, and Orch. (1976); *Open Window*, 5 sketches for Mezzo-soprano and 5 Instruments (1978); *We Both*, cantata for Soprano, Bass, Chorus, and 5 Instruments (1986); *Hope*, oratorio (1988).

Barkel, Charles, Swedish violinist and conductor; b. Stugun, Feb. 6, 1898; d. Stockholm, March 7, 1973. He studied at the Stockholm Cons. and the Copenhagen Cons.; then took lessons in Berlin with Flesch; concurrently played in several Swedish orchs. In 1921 he joined the Stockholm Concert Soc. Orch. He founded his own string quartet in 1928; from 1942 to 1954 he was conductor of the Uppsala Concert Soc. Orch. From 1926 to 1965 he taught violin in Stockholm.

Barkin, Elaine R(adoff), American composer and writer on music; b. N.Y., Dec. 15, 1932. She studied with Karol Rathaus at Queens College of the City Univ. of N.Y. (B.A., 1954), with Irving Fine at Brandeis Univ. (M.F.A., 1956), and Boris Blacher at the Berlin Hochschule für Musik (1957); completed her studies with Berger and Shapero at Brandeis Univ. (Ph.D., 1974). She taught at various colleges, finally joining the faculty of the Univ. of Calif. at Los Angeles in 1974. She was an ed. of the journal *Perspectives of New Music* (1963–85). In her early works, she utilized serial techniques, later delving into what she described as "group interactive autonomous alternative music-making culture."

WORKS: String Quartet (1969); *Plus ça change* for String Orch. and Percussion (1971); *Prim Cycles* for Flute, Clarinet, Violin, and Cello (1972); *Inward and Outward Bound* for 13 Instruments (1975); *Ebb Tide* for 2 Vibraphones (1977); *De amore*, chamber mini-opera (1980); *Quilt Piece*, graphic score for 7 Instruments (1984); *Rhapsodies* for Flutes and Clarinet (1986); *[Be]coming Together Apart* for Violin and Marimba (1987); *Encore* for Javanese Gamelan Ensemble (1988); *Legong Dreams* for Oboe (1990); *Social Contracts*, theater piece (1990); *Exploring the Rigors of in Between* for Flute, Horn, Violin, Viola, and Cello (1991); *Kotekan Jam* for Gamelan (1991); *Gamélange* for Harp and Gamelan Band (1992).

Barlow, David (Frederick), English composer; b. Rothwell, May 20, 1927; d. Newcastle upon Tyne, June 9, 1975. He studied at Emmanuel College, Cambridge, with Jacob at the Royal College of Music in London, and with Boulanger in Fontainebleau; was on the faculty of King's College, Newcastle upon Tyne (from 1951). After writing in a late Romantic style, he developed a lyrical serial mode of expression (from 1963).

WORKS: DRAMATIC: *David and Bathsheba*, church opera (1969); *The Selfish Giant*, children's opera (1974–75); *Judas Iscariot*, church opera (1974–75). **ORCH.:** 3 Pieces for Strings (1948–51); 2 syms. (1949–50;1956–59); *Pastorale and Variations* (1960); *Microcosm* for Strings (1963); *Variations* for Cello and Orch. (1969); Sinfonietta concertante for Clarinet and Orch. (1972); *Fantasy* (1972). **CHAMBER:** Violin Sonata (1956); Oboe Quartet (1963); String Trio (1964); String Quartet (1967–69); String Quintet (1970); *In memoriam Igor Stravinsky* for Flute, Clarinet, and String Quartet (1972); Brass Quintet (1972); also piano and organ pieces. **VOCAL:** Choral music and pieces for solo voice.

Barlow, Fred, French composer of English and Alsatian descent; b. Mulhouse, Oct. 2, 1881; d. Boulogne, Jan. 3, 1951. He studied in Paris with Jean Huré and his cousin, Charles Koechlin.

WORKS: DRAMATIC: MUSICAL COMEDY: *Sylvie* (1919–21; Paris, March 2, 1923). **OPERETTA:** *Mam'zelle Prudhomme* (Monte Carlo, Dec. 22, 1932). **BALLETS:** *Gladys, ou La légère incartade* (1915–16; Mulhouse, Jan. 7, 1956); *Polichinelle et Colombine* (1926–27); *La grande Jatte* (1936–38; Paris, July 12, 1950). **CHAMBER:** *Juventa*, violin sonata (1909); *La basilique*, cello sonata (1910–11; rev. 1938–39); *Quatuor des saisons* (1946–47; also for String Orch. and Timpani as *Sinfonietta des saisons*, 1948); also piano music, including a Sonata (1940). **VOCAL:** Songs.

Barlow, Harold, American writer on music and composer; b. Boston, May 15, 1915; d. Manhasset, N.Y., Feb. 15, 1993. He studied violin at Boston Univ. (B.M., 1937), and later played in various orchs.; also led a U.S. Army band. He compiled 2 valuable reference works, for which he designed an original method of indexing melodic themes by letters plus accidentals: *A Dictionary of Musical Themes* (N.Y., 1948) and *A Dictionary of Vocal Themes* (N.Y., 1950), both with S. Morgenstern. He also composed popular songs.

Barlow, Howard, American conductor; b. Plain City, Ohio, May 1, 1892; d. Bethel, Conn., Jan. 31, 1972. He studied at the Univ. of Colorado and at Columbia Univ. He conducted the American National Orch., N.Y. (1923–25), and at the Neighborhood Playhouse there (1925–27); was conductor of the CBS Sym. Orch. (1927–43), with which he presented numerous new works.

Barlow, Samuel L(atham) M(itchell), American composer; b. N.Y., June 1, 1892; d. Wyndmoor, Pa., Sept. 19, 1982. He studied at Harvard Univ. (B.A., 1914), with Goetschius and Franklin Robinson in N.Y., with Philipp (piano) in Paris, and with Respighi (orchestration) in Rome (1923). He was active in various N.Y. music, civic, and liberal organizations, and also taught. His autobiography appeared as *The Astonished Muse* (N.Y., 1961).

WORKS: DRAMATIC: OPERAS: *Mon ami Pierrot* (1934; Paris, Jan. 11, 1935); *Amanda* (1936). **BALLET:** *Ballo sardo* (1928). **ORCH.:** *Vocalise* (1926); *Alba*, symphonic poem (1927); Piano Concerto (1930; Rochester, N.Y., Jan. 23, 1931); *Circus Overture* (1930); *Babar*, symphonic concerto with slides (1935); *Biedermeier Waltzes* (1935); *Sousa ad Parnassum* (1939). **CHAMBER:** *Ballad, Scherzo* for String Quartet (1933); *Conversation with Chekov*, piano trio (1940); piano pieces. **VOCAL:** Choruses and songs.

Barlow, Wayne (Brewster), American composer, pedagogue, organist, and choirmaster; b. Elyria, Ohio, Sept. 6, 1912. He studied with Bernard Rogers and Howard Hanson at the Eastman School of Music in Rochester, N.Y. (B.M., 1934; M.M., 1935; Ph.D., 1937); also took courses from Schoenberg at the Univ. of Southern Calif. in Los Angeles (1935) and later pursued training in electronic music with Schaeffer at the Univ. of Toronto (1963–64) and postdoctoral research at the univs. of Brussels, Ghent, and Utrecht (1964–65). From 1937 to 1978 he taught at the Eastman School of Music, where he also was director of graduate studies (1955–57; 1973–78), chairman of its composition dept., and director of the electronic music studio (1968–73). He served as organist and choirmaster at St. Thomas Episcopal Church (1946–76) and at Christ Episcopal Church (1976–78) in Rochester. He was the author of *Foundations of Music* (N.Y., 1953). In his compositions, Barlow followed a varied stylistic path which was basically tonal with free 12-tone development.

WORKS: BALLETS: *False Faces* (1935); *3 Moods for Dancing* (1940). **ORCH.:** *De Profundis* (1934); 2 sinfoniettas (1936, 1950); *The Winter's Passed* for Oboe and Strings (1938); *Lyrical Pieces* for Clarinet and Strings (1943); *Nocturne* for Chamber Orch. (1946); *Rondo Overture* (1947); *Lento and Allegro* (1955); *Night Song* (1958); *Rota* for Chamber Orch. (1959); *Images* for Harp and Orch. (1961); *Sinfonia da camera* for Chamber Orch. (1962); *Vistas* (1963); Concerto for Saxophone and Band (1970); *Hampton Beach*, overture (1971); *Soundscapes* for Tape and Orch. (1972); *Divertissement* for Flute and Chamber Orch. (1980); *Frontiers* for Band (1982). **CHAMBER:** *Prelude, Air, and Variations* for Bassoon, Piano, and String Quartet (1949); Piano Quintet (1951); *Tryptych* for String Quartet (1953); *Intrada, Fugue, and Postlude* for Brass (1959); Trio for Oboe, Viola, and Piano (1964); *Elegy* for Viola and Piano (1967; also for Viola and Orch.); *Duo* for Harp and Tape (1969); *Vocalise and Canon* for Tuba and Piano (1976); *Intermezzo* for Viola and Harp (1980); *Sonatine for 4* for Flute, Clarinet, Cello, and Harp (1984). **KEYBOARD: PIANO:** Sonata (1948); *Dynamisms* for 2 Pianos (1967). **ORGAN:** *Hymn Voluntaries for the Church Year* (4 vols., 1963–81); *4 Chorale Voluntaries* (1979–80). **VOCAL:** *Zion in Exile*, cantata (1937); *Songs from the Silence of Amor* for Soprano and Orch. (1939); *The 23rd Psalm* for Chorus and Organ or Orch. (1944); Mass for Chorus and Orch. (1951); *Poems for Music* for Soprano and Orch. (1958); *Missa Sancti Thomae* for Chorus and Organ (1959); *We All Believe in One True God* for Chorus, Brass Quartet, and Organ (1965); *Wait for the Promise of the Father*, cantata (1968); *Voices of Darkness* for Reader, Piano, Percussion, and Tape (1974); *Voices of Faith* for Reader, Soprano, Chorus, and Orch. (1975); *Out of the Cradle Endlessly Rocking* for Tenor, Chorus, Clarinet, Viola, Piano, and Tape (1978); *The 7 Seals* for Soloists, Chorus, and Orch. (1991). **TAPE:** *Study in Electronic Sound* (1965); *Moonflight* (1970); *Soundprints in Concrete* (1975).

Barnes, Edward Shippen, American organist and composer; b. Seabright, N.J., Sept. 14, 1887; d. Idyllwild, Calif., Feb. 14, 1958. He was a student of Horatio Parker and David Stanley Smith at Yale Univ., and studied organ with Harry B. Jepson there. He was organist at St. Stephen's Episcopal Church in Philadelphia and later at the First Presbyterian Church in Santa Monica, California, retiring in 1954. He wrote 2 organ syms., much sacred music, and several books of organ arrangements for schools.

Barnes, Milton, Canadian conductor and composer; b. Toronto, Dec. 16, 1931. He studied composition with John Weinzweig; conducting with Victor Feldbrill, Boyd Neel, and Walter Susskind; and piano with Samuel Dolin at the Royal Cons. of Music of Toronto (1952–55). Then he pursued further training in conducting at the Accademia Musicale Chigiana in Siena, at the Berkshire Music Center at Tanglewood, and with Swarowsky at the Vienna Academy of Music (graduated, 1961). He began his career as a jazz drummer and guitarist; during his student days, he composed many dramatic scores for productions at the Univ. of Toronto. He was music director and composer at the Crest Theatre (1961–63), and founder-conductor of the Toronto Repertory Orch. (1964–73); he also was conductor of the St. Catharines (Ontario) Sym. Orch. and Chorus (1964–73) and of the Niagara Falls (N.Y.) Phil. and Chorus (1965–73), and was composer and conductor-in-residence of the Toronto Dance Theatre (1968–73). An eclectic composer, he has utilized classical, jazz, and popular styles.

WORKS: MULTIMEDIA: *Amber Garden,* ballet suite (1972); *The Spiral Stairs* for 7 Instruments (1973); *The Dybbuk,* masque for dancing for Tenor and 6 Instruments (1977); film and television scores. **ORCH.:** *Invocations* (1962); 2 syms.: No. 1 (1964) and No. 2 for String Orch. (1976); *Pinocchio,* symphonic poem (1966); *Variations* for Clarinet and Orch. (1968); *Classical Concerto* for Piano and Orch. (1973); *Shebetim,* tableau for Strings (1974); Concerto for Violin and Strings (1975); Chamber Concerto for Wind Quintet and Strings (1976); Viola Concerto (1977); Concerto No. 1 for Flute and Strings (1978); *Serenade* for String Quartet and String Orch. (1979); *Follies Overture* (1983); Double Concerto for 2 Guitars and Strings (1986; Toronto, Nov. 18, 1987); *The Odyssey: A Symphonic Tale* (1990); *Song of the Bow,* concerto for String Bass and Orch. (1991). **CHAMBER:** *Burletta* for String Quartet (1957–58); Flute Sonata (1965); *Concerto Grosso* for Flute, Clarinet, Violin, Cello, and 2 Pianos (1973); String Quartet No. 2, *Scenes from Jewish Life* (1978); *Annexus* for 5 Percussionists (1981); *Papageno Variations* for String Bass and Piano (1988). **OTHER:** Solo vocal works; *Thespis,* cantata (1956; rev. 1973); choruses.

Barnett, Alice (Ray), American composer; b. Lewiston, Ill., May 26, 1886; d. San Diego, Aug. 28, 1975. She studied in Chicago with Rudolph Ganz and Felix Borowski at the Musical College (B.M., 1906), with Heniot Lévy and Adolf Weidig at the American Cons., and with Wilhelm Middleschulte; completed her training in Berlin with Hugo Kaun (1909–10). In 1917 she settled in San Diego, where she taught music at the High School (until 1926) and was active in various musical organizations. She wrote a Piano Trio (1920) and violin solos (1924), but was at her finest as a composer of art songs, of which she publ. 49 (1906–32).

Barnett, Bonnie, American singer and composer; b. Chicago, May 2, 1947. She studied at the Univ. of Ill. (B.S., 1968) and with Kenneth Gaburo, Pauline Oliveros, and Robert Erickson at the Univ. of Calif. at San Diego (M.A., 1972). She then moved to San Francisco, where she developed the *TUNNEL HUM Project,* a series of participatory vocal events taking place in acoustically interesting environments. A conducive tonality is established by a group of instrumentalists (E-flat major is used often); the participating hummers then improvise on that tonality, following a written process score. Since 1981 Barnett has produced 29 *Hums* in a variety of contexts, including 2 satellite-linked live national radio broadcasts (1983, 1984), a Houston subterranean shopping mall (1986), and *Auto Hum,* a live radio broadcast for car-commuter participation throughout Southern California (1985). Her intent is to re-create the participatory pleasures of group vocalizations as a means of "tuning the world"; her *Global Hum,* part of the "Music and Peace" event sponsored by the World Phil. Orch. in Montreal, sent live singers in San Francisco worldwide through satellite broadcast. She was the recipient of a 1983 grant from NPR and a 1984 NEA grant. Since 1986 she has lived in Los Angeles, where she teaches privately and co-hosts the KPFK-radio program "Imaginary Landscape." She is currently developing a more elaborate *Global Hum* and, eventually, an *Intergalactic Hum.*

WRITINGS: "Aspects of Vocal Multiphonics," *Interface, Journal of New Music Research* (Amsterdam, 1977); "Live Radio Art," *Whole Earth Review* (Sausalito, Calif., Winter 1987).

Barnett, John (Manley), American conductor; b. N.Y., Sept. 3, 1917. He studied piano, violin, and trumpet; took courses at Teachers College of Columbia Univ., the Manhattan School of Music, and the Salzburg Mozarteum (1936); received training in conducting from Bruno Walter, Weingartner, Enesco, and Malko. He was assistant conductor of the National Orchestral Assn. in N.Y. (1937–41), and also a conductor with the WPA Federal Music Project there (1939–42), serving concurrently as conductor of the Stamford (Conn.) Sym. Orch. From 1946 to 1956 he was assoc. conductor of the Los Angeles Phil., and from 1956 to 1958 its assoc. music director. In 1947 he organized the Phoenix (Ariz.) Sym. Orch., conducting it until 1949. He later served as music director of the Hollywood Bowl (1953–57) and of the Los Angeles Guild Opera Co. (1954–79). From 1958 to 1972 he was music director of the National Orchestral Assn. in N.Y.; from 1961 to 1971 he held the post of music director of the Phil. Sym. Orch. of Westchester, N.Y. From 1972 to 1978 he served as artistic consultant to the NEA. From 1979 to 1985 he was music director of the Puerto Rico Sym. Orch. in Santurce.

Barolsky, Michael, Lithuanian-born German-Israeli composer; b. Vilnius, July 19, 1947. He studied piano, theory, and ethnology; in 1965 he took lessons in composition with Lutoslawski in Warsaw; in 1968 he went to Moscow and studied privately with Denisov and Schnittke. From 1969 to 1971 he was music adviser at the Lithuanian Radio. In 1971 he emigrated to Germany. In 1972 he attended seminars with Ligeti, Kagel, and Stockhausen in Darmstadt; in 1974 he went to Israel, and taught at the Pedagogic Inst. in Tel Aviv. In 1977 he settled in Cologne on a stipend of the Deutsche Akademie; also worked on electronic music with Humpert. In his compositions, he devotes himself totally to contemporary means of expression, astutely applying the full resources of electronic music.

WORKS: Violin Sonata (1964); String Trio (1964); Woodwind Quartet (1965); *Recitative and Melody* for Flute, Cello, and Piano (1966); Concertino for Violin, Trumpet, Trombone, Piano, and Percussion (1967); *Basso Ostinato* for Cello (1967); *Telefonoballade,* cantata for Baritone, 6 Narrators, and Chamber Ensemble (1969); *Exodus* for Orch. (1970); *Scriptus,* after Kafka's letters, for Baritone, Mime, and Chamber Ensemble (1972); *Dakar* for Percussion, Piano, and Electronics (1972); *Photogenesis I, II, III,* and *IV,* respectively for Harpsichord, Brass Quintet, Bass Flute, and Percussion (1973); *Melos* for Mezzo-soprano, Cello, Piano, Electric Organ, Percussion, and Synthesizer (1975); *Sublimatio* for Flute, Cello, 2 Pianos, Percussion, and Tape (1975); *Cries and Whispers* for Chamber Ensemble and Electronics (1975; Chicago, Jan. 24, 1976); *Blue Eye, Brown Eye,* opera (Tel Aviv, July 29, 1976); *Apocalypse,* song cycle with Electronic Tape (1976); *Iris* for Flute, Oboe, Clarinet, Violin, Cello, and Piano (1976); *Pranah* for Violin and Electronic Tape (1976); *Sternengesang* for Chamber Orch. (1977); *The Book of Emanations* for Orch. (1978); *Ein Stück aus der Nacht* for Actor and Electronics (1978); *Tonus* for Quadraphonic Synthesizer (1979); *Cinderella* for Cello and Piano (1981); *Seelenkalender* for Mezzo-soprano and Piano (1982); *The Book of Changes* for Piano (1983); *Stück-Mund-Stück* for Trombone, Computer Sounds, and Video Tape (1983); *Piccolostück* for Piccolo and Computer Sounds (1983); *Rainbow Music* for 6 Recorders (Bonn, Feb. 12, 1984); *Trioirtrio* for Violin, Cello, and Piano (1984); Cello Concerto (1985); *Computer Time* for Violin, Cello, and Piano (1988); Cello Concerto (1985); *Computer Time* for Violin, Cello, and Piano (1988).

Baron, Maurice, French-American composer and conductor; b. Lille, Jan. 1, 1889; d. Oyster Bay, N.Y., Sept. 5, 1964. He studied music in France; emigrated to America, where he became a theater conductor. He publ. several hundred pieces of light music under his own name and the whimsical noms de plume **Francis Delille** (i.e., "de Lille," a native of Lille) and **Morris Aborn** (anagram of Baron); also used the name of his wife, **Alice Tremblay**. Among his more ambitious works was *Ode to Democracy* for Narrator, Chorus, and Orch. (N.Y., Jan. 23, 1949).

Baron, Samuel, American flutist, conductor, and teacher; b. N.Y., April 27, 1925. He studied at Brooklyn College; was a pupil in flute of Georges Barrère and Arthur Lora and in conducting of Edgar Schenkman at the Juilliard School of Music in N.Y. (1942–48). He was founder-conductor of the N.Y. Brass Ensemble in 1948; also was founding member and played in the N.Y. Woodwind Quintet (1946–69; again from 1980) and other chamber groups; was a member (from 1965) and music director (from 1980) of the Bach Aria Group. He taught at the Yale Univ. School of Music (1965–67), the State Univ. of N.Y. at Stony Brook (from 1966), the Mannes College of Music (1969–72), and the Juilliard School (from 1974). He publ. *Chamber Music for Winds* (N.Y., 1969).

Barraine, Elsa, French composer; b. Paris, Feb. 13, 1910. Her father was a cellist, her mother a singer. She studied at the Paris Cons. with Paul Dukas, Jean Gallon, and George Caussade; received the 2nd Prix de Rome in 1928. She composed 3 syms. (1931, 1938, 1947) and a curiously realistic symphonic poem, *Pogromes* (referring to the Nazi persecutions of Jews; Paris, March 11, 1939). Other works include stage scores; *Suite astrologique* for Orch. (1947); *Atmosphère* for Oboe and 10 Instruments, on Hindu rhythms (1967); *Musique rituelle* for Organ, Gongs, and Xylorimba (1968); other chamber music; choral works and songs.

Barraqué, Jean, French composer of theosophic aspirations; b. Paris, Jan. 17, 1928; d. there, Aug. 17, 1973. He studied at the Paris Cons. with Jean Langlais and privately with Olivier Messiaen, a kindred spirit, but eschewed the latter's persistent Catholicism, let alone the Franciscan ornithophilia. Rather, Barraqué's grandiosity of musical ideals followed Scriabin's dreams of uniting all arts and all religions in an ultimate proclamation of universal faith. He had the advantage of using ultra-modern technical resources, particularly electronics, to create his world sym., which was to be in 13 connected parts. But, as in Scriabin's *Mysterium*, the project remained in fragments. The work that first attracted attention was Barraqué's expansive Piano Sonata No. 1 (1950–52), cast in Lisztian dimensions and dialectic assumptions. This was followed by another significant work of philosophic intent, *Séquence* for Soprano, Piano, Harp, Violin, Cello, and Percussion (1950–55). Of equal force were *Le Temps restitué* for Voice, Chorus, and Orch. (1956–68); *Au delà du hasard* for Voices, 4 Instrumental Groups, Vibraphone, and Clarinet (1959); Concerto for 6 Instrumental Groups, Vibraphone, and Clarinet (1962–68); and *Chant après chant* for Voice, Percussion, and Piano (1965–66). All these works were to constitute a preamble to his magnum opus, *Mort de Virgile*, inspired by a philosophical vol. of that title by Hermann Broch; the text refers to the Roman poet Virgil, traveling to the end of the universe. This work was to be composed for varying complexes of instruments, ranging from piano solo and string quartet to choral ensembles and to the ultimate climax, entitled *Discours*, scored for 11 voices and 130 instruments. In Barraqué's music, melodies and rhythms function as asymptotes converging on the verticals of harmony, with the tonal reference never totally absent. For further elucidation, a book by André Hodeir, *La Musique depuis Debussy* (Paris, 1961), is useful, if the reader detracts the extremities of the author's enthusiasm.

BIBL.: Special issue of *Entretemps*, no. 5 (1987).

Barraud, Henry, French composer; b. Bordeaux, April 23, 1900. He received training in harmony and counterpoint in Bordeaux, and then was a pupil of Dukas (composition), Caussade (fugue), and Aubert (composition and orchestration) at the Paris Cons. (1926–27). In 1937 he was director of music for the Paris International Exposition. He served as head of music (1944–48) and director of the national program (1948–65) of Radiodiffusion Française. He publ. *Berlioz* (Paris, 1955; 3rd ed., 1979), *La France et la musique occidentale* (Paris, 1956), *Pour comprendre les musiques d'aujord'hui* (Paris, 1968), and *Les cinq grands opéras* (Paris, 1972).

WORKS: DRAMATIC: OPERAS: *La Farce du maître Pathelin* (1938; Paris, June 24, 1948); *Numance* (1950–52; Paris, April 15, 1955; rev. 1970; arranged as the *Symphonie de Numance*, Baden-Baden, Dec. 3, 1950); *Lavinia*, comic opera (1959; Aix-en-Provence, July 20, 1961); *Le roi Gordogne* (1979); *Tête d'or* (1980). **BALLETS:** *Le diable à la kermesse* (1943); *L'astrologue dans le puits* (1948). **ORCH.:** *Poème* (1933); *Concerto da camera* (1934); Piano Concerto (1939; N.Y., Dec. 5, 1946); *Offrande à une ombre* (1942); *Images pour un poète maudit* (1954); Sym. for Strings (1955); Sym. No. 3 (1957; Boston, March 7, 1958); *Rapsodie cartésienne* (1959); Flute Concerto (1962); *Rapsodie dionysienne* (1962); *Divertimento* (1962); Symphonie concertante for Trumpet and Orch. (1966); *Trois études* (1967); *Une saison en enfer* (1968–69); Concerto for Strings (1971). **CHAMBER:** Trio for Oboe, Clarinet, and Bassoon (1935); String Trio (1936; rev. 1943); String Quartet (1940); Concertino for Piano, Flute, Clarinet, Bassoon, and Horn (1954); Saxophone Quartet (1972); piano pieces. **VOCAL:** *Le feu* for Chorus and Orch. (1937); *Le mystère des Saints Innocents* for Solo Voices, Chorus, and Orch. (1946–47); *Te Deum* for Chorus and 16 Winds (1955); *Pange lingua* for Soprano, Baritone, Chorus, and Orch. (1964); *La divina comédie* for 5 Solo Voices and Orch. (1972).

Barrère, Georges, outstanding French-born American flutist and pedagogue; b. Bordeaux, Oct. 31, 1876; d. Kingston, N.Y., June 14, 1944. He was a student of Joseph-Henri Altès and Paul Taffanel at the Paris Cons. (1889–95), graduating with a premier prix. In 1895 he organized the Société Moderne des Instruments à Vent in Paris, with which he presented more than 80 new compositions; he also was 1st flutist in the Colonne orch. and the Opéra orch. (1897–1905). He then emigrated to the U.S. in 1905, becoming a naturalized American citizen in 1937. From 1905 to 1928 he was 1st flutist in the N.Y. Sym. Orch.; he also organized the Barrère Ensemble of Wind Instruments in 1910, which became the Barrère Little Sym. in 1914; also founded the Trio de Lutèce in 1914 and the Barrère-Britt-Salzedo Trio in 1932. He taught at N.Y.'s Inst. of Musical Art (1905–30) and Juilliard School of Music (from 1931). Barrère gave premieres of several scores, including Varèse's *Density 21.5* (N.Y., Feb. 16, 1936). He also composed.

BIBL.: G. Barrère, *G. B.* (N.Y., 1929); *The Platinum Flute and G. B.* (N.Y., 1935).

Barrientos, Maria, celebrated Spanish soprano; b. Barcelona, March 10, 1884; d. Ciboure, France, Aug. 8, 1946. She entered the Barcelona Cons. at age 6, where she received training in piano, violin, and composition before graduating at 12; then studied voice with Francesco Bonet. In 1898 she made her operatic debut as Inèz in *L'Africaine*; while still a youth, she appeared in Rome, Berlin, Leipzig, Milan, and other European music centers. On Jan. 31, 1916, she made her Metropolitan Opera debut in N.Y. as Lucia, continuing to sing there until 1920. She then devoted most of her time to concert engagements; she also taught in Buenos Aires (1939–45). In her heyday, Barrientos was acclaimed as one of the finest coloratura sopranos. Among her notable roles were Rosina, Gilda, Amina, Lakmé, Norina, and the Queen of Shemakha.

Barrios Fernandez, Angel, Spanish composer; b. Granada, Jan. 4, 1882; d. Madrid, Nov. 27, 1964. Of a musical family (his father was a guitarist), he studied violin and played in bands as a child. He later studied theory with Conrado del Campo in Madrid and with Gédalge in Paris. At the same time, he perfected his guitar playing; formed a trio, Iberia, and traveled in Europe playing Spanish popular music. In collaboration with Conrado del Campo, he wrote a successful operetta, *El Avapiés* (Madrid, 1919), and several zarzuelas: *La Suerte, La Romeria,*

Seguidilla gitana, Castigo de Dios, En Nombre del Rey, and *Lola se va a los puertos*; also numerous overtures and other orch. pieces based on popular Spanish motifs.

Barron, Louis, American composer; b. Minneapolis, April 23, 1920; d. Los Angeles, Nov. 1, 1989. He studied at the Univ. of Minnesota. In 1947 he married Bebe (née Charlotte Wind) Barron (b. Minneapolis, June 16, 1927), who studied political science and also took theory lessons with Riegger and Cowell in N.Y. (1947). In 1948 the couple founded an electro-acoustic music studio in N.Y., one of the first of its kind. They gained wide recognition with their electronic score for the film *Forbidden Planet* (1956). They were divorced in 1970 but continued to collaborate on various works. Among their other electronic scores for films are *Bells of Atlantis* (1952), *Miramagic* (1954), *Jazz of Lights* (1956), *Bridges* (1959), *Crystal Growing* (1959), *The Computer Age* (1968), *More than Human* (1974), and *Cannabis* (1975).

Barroso Neto, Joaquim Antonio, Brazilian composer and teacher; b. Rio de Janeiro, Jan. 30, 1881; d. there, Sept. 1, 1941. He studied with Braga, Nepomuceno, and others; appeared as a pianist in public at an early age; his compositions, in a mildly Romantic manner, are mostly for piano. He enjoyed a fine reputation as a teacher.

BIBL.: T. Gomes, *B.N.* (Rio de Janeiro, 1939).

Barrows, John, American horn player; b. Glendale, Calif., Feb. 12, 1913; d. Madison, Wis., Jan. 11, 1974. His first instrument was the cello. He studied horn at the Eastman School of Music in Rochester, N.Y. (1930–32), theory and orchestration at San Diego State Teachers College (1933–34), and composition (with Donovan and Smith) and cello at Yale Univ. (1934–38). He played horn with the Minneapolis Sym. Orch. (1938–42), the N.Y. City Opera orch. (1946–49), the N.Y. City Ballet orch. (1952–55), and the Casals Festival orch. in Puerto Rico (1958–61). Barrows was a member of the N.Y. Woodwind Quintet (1952–61); toured Europe with the Marlboro Festival Orch. He taught horn at Yale Univ. (1957–61), N.Y. Univ. (1958–61), and the Univ. of Wisc. (1961–74). He composed 2 string quartets, a String Trio, and a Wind Quintet, and made arrangements for band.

Barry, Gerald (Anthony), Irish composer; b. County Clare, April 28, 1952. He studied at Univ. College, Dublin (B.Mus., 1973; M.A., 1975); also studied composition with Peter Schat and organ with Piet Kee in Amsterdam, and with Stockhausen and Kagel at the Cologne Hochschule für Musik (1975–80), and received some guidance from Cerha in Vienna (1977). After a brief stint as a lecturer at Univ. College, Cork (1982–86), he concentrated on composing.

WORKS: *Things That Gain by Being Painted* for Soprano, Speaker, Cello, and Piano (1977); *Ein Klavier Konzert* for Piano and Orch. (1978); *Décolletage* for Soprano and Actress (1979); __________ Ensemble (1979); Ø for 2 Pianos (1979); *Sleeping Beauty* for 2 Performers and Bass Drum (1980); *Unkrautgarten*, ballet (1980); *The Intelligence Park*, opera (1981–87); *Sweet Cork* for Soprano, Bass, Recorder, Viol, and Harpsichord (1985); *Of Queens' Gardens* for Chamber Orch. (Dublin, Sept. 29, 1986); *Sweet Punishment* for Brass Quintet (1987); *Chevaux-de-frise* for Orch. (London, Aug. 15, 1988); Oboe Quartet (1988); *Diner* for Orch. (Belfast, Aug. 5, 1988); *Reflections on Guinness* for Orch. (1988); *Children Aged 10–17* for Orch. (1989); *Bob* for 2 Clarinets, Violin, Cello, Piano, and Marimba (1989); *Hard D* for Orch. (1992); Sextet (1992); *The Triumph of Beauty and Deceit*, television opera (1992–93).

Barry, Jerome, American baritone; b. Boston, Nov. 16, 1939. He studied voice and linguistics; in 1963, received his master's degree in languages from Tufts Univ., and acquired fluency in 8 European languages and in Hebrew. He studied voice privately with Pierre Bernac, Jennie Tourel, and Luigi Ricci. He began his professional career in Italy; gave a great many concerts in Israel; returning to the U.S., he developed activities in many fields, as a lecturer and a singer; settled in Washington, D.C., where he organized the Washington Music Ensemble.

Barshai, Rudolf (Borisovich), Russian conductor; b. Labinskaya, near Krasnodar, Sept. 28, 1924. He studied violin at the Moscow Cons. with Lev Zeitlin and viola with Borisovsky, graduating in 1948; also studied conducting with Ilya Musin in Leningrad. He began his career as a violist, touring throughout Russia; also played in the Borodin and Tchaikovsky string quartets. In 1955 he organized the Moscow Chamber Orch., which became extremely successful; many Soviet composers wrote works for it. In 1976 he emigrated to Israel, and led the Israel Chamber Orch. in Tel Aviv until 1981. He also appeared as a guest conductor in Europe, the U.S., and Japan. From 1982 to 1988 he was principal conductor and artistic adviser of the Bournemouth Sym. Orch.; also was music director of the Vancouver (B.C.) Sym. Orch. (1985–87) and principal guest conductor of the Orchestre National de France in Paris (from 1987).

Barsova (real name, **Vladimirova**), **Valeria,** Russian soprano; b. Astrakhan, June 13, 1892; d. Sochi, Dec. 13, 1967. She studied voice with Umberto Mazetti at the Moscow Cons., graduating in 1919; from 1920 to 1948 she was on the staff of the Bolshoi Theater in Moscow. She distinguished herself mainly in the Russian repertoire, but also sang Violetta and Gilda. Her silvery coloratura enabled her to sing such demanding roles as Lakmé. From 1950 to 1953 she taught at the Moscow Cons. She gave solo recitals in Russia and abroad, including England and Germany.

BIBL.: G. Polyanovsky, *V.V. B.* (Moscow and Leningrad, 1941).

Barstow, Dame Josephine (Clare), noted English soprano; b. Sheffield, Sept. 27, 1940. She studied at the Univ. of Birmingham (B.A. in English), the London Opera Centre, and with Eva Turner and Andrew Field. In 1964 she made her operatic debut as Mimi with Opera for All. In 1967 she made her first appearance at the Sadler's Wells Opera in London as Cherubino, and sang with its successor, the English National Opera, from 1974; also sang with the Welsh National Opera from 1968. In 1969 she joined London's Covent Garden, where she created the roles of Denise in *The Knot Garden* (1970), the Young Woman in *We Come to the River* (1976), and Gayle in *The Ice Break* (1977). On March 28, 1977, she made her Metropolitan Opera debut in N.Y. as Musetta. In 1983 she appeared as Gutrune in the *Ring* at Bayreuth. In 1986 she made her first appearance at the Salzburg Festival creating the role of Benigna in Penderecki's *Die schwarze Maske*. Her appearances in the title role of *Gloriana* with Opera North in Leeds in 1993 and at Covent Garden in 1994 won her critical accolades. In 1985 she was made a Commander of the Order of the British Empire and in 1995 a Dame Commander of the Order of the British Empire. Barstow is a versatile singer whose repertoire ranges from traditional to contemporary roles.

Bárta, Lubor, Czech composer; b. Lubná, Aug. 8, 1928; d. Prague, Nov. 5, 1972. He studied with Řídký at the Prague Academy of Musical Arts (1948–52). His music presents an effective amalgam of modernistic procedures, influenced by Bartók in its rhythms, by Stravinsky in its meters, and by Hindemith in its neo-Classical harmonies.

WORKS: ORCH.: 2 violin concertos (1952, 1970); 3 syms. (1955; *The Bitter Summer*, 1969; 1972); Concerto for Chamber Orch. (1956); Viola Concerto (1957); *Dramatic Suite* (1958); Piano Concerto (1958–59); *From East Bohemia*, symphonic suite (1961); *Concertante Overture* (1964); *Ludi* for 8 Winds and String Orch. (1964); *Musica Romantica* for Strings (1971). **CHAMBER:** 2 violin sonatas (1949, 1959); 2 wind quintets (*Divertimento*, 1949; 1969); 3 string quartets (1950, 1957, 1967); Piano Trio (1955); Trombone Sonatina (1956); Clarinet Sonata (1958); *Ballad and Burlesque* for Cello and Piano (1963); Concertino for Trombone and Piano (1964); Sonata for Solo Guitar (1965); *4 Pieces* for Violin and Guitar (1966); Flute Sonata (1966); *Fragments* for Clarinet and Piano (1967); *Amoroso* for

Horn and Piano (1970); Cello Sonata (1971). **KEYBOARD: PIANO:** *Variations* (1948); 3 sonatas (1956, 1961, 1971). **HARPSICHORD:** Sonata (1967). **VOCAL:** 2 cantatas: *Komsomol* (1951) and *Song of the New Age* (1962); songs.

Bartels, Wolfgang von, German composer; b. Hamburg, July 21, 1883; d. Munich, April 19, 1938. He studied with Beer-Walbrunn in Munich and with Gédalge in Paris; then became a music critic in Munich. His early works show impressionist influences; later he adopted an eclectic style. Among his compositions were 2 melodramas: *The Little Dream,* after Galsworthy (Manchester, 1911) and *Li-I-Lan* (Kassel, 1918); also several song cycles; Violin Concerto; Viola Concerto.

Barth, Hans, German-born American pianist, pedagogue, and composer; b. Leipzig, June 25, 1897; d. Jacksonville, Fla., Dec. 8, 1956. When still a child, he studied on scholarship at the Leipzig Cons. with Carl Reinecke. In 1907 he was taken to the U.S. and in 1908 he made his N.Y. recital debut. In 1912 he became a naturalized American citizen. His meeting with Busoni inspired him to experiment with new scales; with George Weitz, he perfected a portable quarter tone piano (1928). He toured the U.S. and Europe playing piano, quarter tone piano, and harpsichord. He served as director of the Inst. of Musical Art in Yonkers and of the National School for Musical Culture in N.Y.; also taught at the Mannes School in N.Y. and at the Jacksonville (Fla.) College of Music (from 1948).

WORKS: OPERETTA: *Miragia* (1938). **ORCH.:** Piano Concerto (1928); Concerto for Quarter Tone Piano and Quarter Tone Strings (1930); Concerto for Quarter Tone Piano and Strings (Philadelphia, March 28, 1930, composer soloist, Stokowski conducting); *Drama Symphony* (1940); *Prince of Peace,* sym. (1940); *10 Études* for Quarter Tone Piano and Orch. (1942–44). **CHAMBER:** Quintet for Quarter Tone Piano and Strings (1930); Suite for Brass, Timpani, and Quarter Tone Strings (1930). **PIANO:** 2 sonatas (1929, 1932); 2 suites (1938, 1941). **VOCAL:** Numerous songs.

Bartha, Dénes, eminent Hungarian musicologist; b. Budapest, Oct. 2, 1908; d. near there, Sept. 7, 1993. He studied at the Univ. of Berlin with Abert, Blume, Hornbostel, Sachs, Schering, and Wolf (Ph.D., 1930, with the diss. *Benedictus Ducis und Appenzeller*; publ. in Wolfenbüttel, 1930). Returning to Budapest, he was a librarian in the music division of the Hungarian National Museum (1930–42), a lecturer (1930–47) and prof. (from 1947) at the Franz Liszt Academy of Music, and a Privatdozent at the Univ. (from 1935). After serving as ed. of *Magyar zénei szemle* (1941–44), he was co-ed. of *Zénei szemle* (1947–49), *Zenetudományi tanulmányok* (1953–61), and *Studia musicologica* (1961–93). He was a visiting prof. at Smith College (1964); Harvard Univ. (summers, 1964–65); Cornell Univ. (1965–66); the Univ. of Pittsburgh (1966–67), where he subsequently was the Andrew W. Mellon Prof. (1969–79); and the Univ. of Wash. in Seattle (1980–81). In 1963 he received the Dent Medal of England, and in 1982 the Ehrenkreuz für Kunst und Wissenschaft of Austria. In 1982 he was made a corresponding member of the American Musicological Soc., and in 1990 of the Hungarian Academy of Sciences.

WRITINGS (all published in Budapest unless otherwise given): *Das Musiklehrbuch einer ungarischen Klosterschule aus 1490* (1934); *Lehrbuch der Musikgeschichte* (1935); *Franz Liszt* (Leipzig, 1936); *Beethoven* (1939); with Z. Kodály, *Die ungarische Musik* (1943); *Anthologie der Musikgeschichte* (1948); *J.S. Bach* (1956; 2nd ed., 1960); *Beethoven kilenc szimfóniája* (1956; 5th ed., rev., 1975); with L. Somfai, *Haydn als Opernkapellmeister* (1960); ed. *J. Haydn: Gesammelte Briefe und Aufzeichnungen* (Kassel, 1965); ed. *Zénei Lexikon* (2nd ed., 3 vols., 1965–66).

Bartholomée, Pierre, Belgian conductor and composer; b. Brussels, Aug. 5, 1937. He studied with Louel, Souffrian, and Stekke at the Royal Cons. in Brussels (1952–57) and privately with Pousseur and Boulez. In 1962 he founded in Brussels an instrumental ensemble, Groupe Musiques Nouvelles, which he conducted until 1977. He also was prof. of analysis at the Royal Cons. in Brussels (from 1972). In 1977 he became music director of the Liège Orch., which post he retained when it became the Orchestre Philharmonique de Liège in 1980, and then the Orchestre Philharmonique de Liège et de la Communauté française de Belgique in 1983.

WORKS: *Chanson* for Cello (1964); *Cantate aux Alentours* for Voices, Instruments, and Live Electronics (1966); *La Ténèbre souveraine* for Soloists, Double Chorus, and Orch. (1967); *Tombeau de Marin* for Violin, 2 Viole da Gamba, and Harpsichord (1967); *Premier alentour* for Flute and 2 Viole da Gamba (1967); *Catalogue* for 4 Harps (1968); *Deuxième alentour: "Cueillir"* for Mezzo-soprano, Piano, and Percussion (1969); *Harmonique* for Orch. (1970); *Fancy I* for Harp and *II* for Instrumental Group (1974–75; can be played together under the title *Sonata quasi una fantasia*); *Trois pôles entrelacés* for 7 Instruments (1985); *Adieu* for Clarinet and Piano (1987); *Rumeur* for Orch. (1989).

Bartlett, Ethel, English pianist; b. Epping Forest, June 6, 1896; d. Los Angeles, April 17, 1978. She studied with Matthay; specialized as a piano duet player with her husband, **Rae Robertson**; made annual tours in Europe and the U.S.

Barto, Tzimon, (real name, **John Barto Smith, Jr.**), American pianist, conductor, and composer; b. Eustis, Fla., Jan. 2, 1963. He was 5 when he began piano studies with his grandmother. After attending the Brevard Music Center (1978–79), he studied at the Tanglewood Inst., where he was named the most outstanding conducting student (1980); then pursued piano training with Adele Marcus at the Juilliard School in N.Y. (1981–84). In 1983 he captured 1st prize in the Gina Bachauer piano competition in Salt Lake City. In 1985 he made his formal debut as a pianist at the Spoleto Festival of Two Worlds, and subsequently was engaged as a soloist with leading orchs. and as a recitalist in principal music centers; also was active as a guest conductor. While his repertoire ranges from Bach to jazz, he has become particularly known for his performances of the 19th and 20th century piano literature.

Bartók, Béla (Viktor János), great Hungarian composer; b. Nagyszentmiklós, March 25, 1881; d. N.Y., Sept. 26, 1945. His father was a school headmaster; his mother was a proficient pianist, from whom and he received his first piano lessons. He began playing the piano in public at the age of 11. In 1894 the family moved to Pressburg, where he took piano lessons with László Erkel, son of the famous Hungarian opera composer; he also studied harmony with Anton Hyrtl. In 1899 he enrolled at the Royal Academy of Music in Budapest, where he studied piano with István Thomán and composition with Hans Koessler; he graduated in 1903. His earliest compositions reveal the combined influence of Liszt, Brahms, and Richard Strauss; however, he soon became interested in exploring the resources of national folk music, which included not only Hungarian melorhythms but also elements of other ethnic strains in his native Transylvania, including Romanian and Slovak. He formed a cultural friendship with Zoltan Kodály, and together they traveled through the land collecting folk songs, which they publ. in 1906. In 1907 Bartók succeeded Thomán as prof. of piano at the Royal Academy of Music. His interest in folk-song research led him to tour North Africa in 1913. In 1919 he served as a member of the musical directorate of the short-lived Hungarian Democratic Republic with Dohnányi and Kodály; was also deputy director of the Academy of Music. Bartók was a brilliant pianist whose repertoire extended from Scarlatti to Szymanowski, as well as his own works; he also gave concerts playing works for 2 pianos with his 2nd wife, **Ditta Pásztory**. In his own compositions, he soon began to feel the fascination of tonal colors and impressionistic harmonies as cultivated by Debussy and other modern French composers. The basic texture of his music remained true to tonality, which he expanded to chromatic polymodal structures and unremittingly dissonant chordal combinations; in his piano works, he exploited the extreme registers of the keyboard, often in the form of tone clusters to simulate pitchless drumbeats. He made use of strong asymmetrical rhythmic figures suggesting the modalities of Slavic folk music, a usage that imparted a somewhat acrid coloring to his music. The melodic line of his works sometimes veered toward atonality in its chromatic involutions; in some instances, he employed melodic figures comprising the 12 different notes of the chromatic scale; however, he never adopted the integral techniques of the 12-tone method.

Bartók toured the U.S. as a pianist from Dec. 1927 to Feb. 1928; also gave concerts in the Soviet Union in 1929. He resigned his position at the Budapest Academy of Music in 1934, but continued his ethnomusicological research as a member of the Hungarian Academy of Sciences, where he was engaged in the preparation of the monumental Corpus Musicae Popularis Hungaricae. With the outbreak of World War II, Bartók decided to leave Europe; in the fall of 1940 he went to the U.S., where he remained until his death from polycythemia. In 1940 he received an honorary Ph.D. from Columbia Univ.; he also undertook folk-song research there as a visiting assistant in music (1941–42). His last completed score, the *Concerto for Orchestra*, commissioned by Koussevitzky, proved to be his most popular work. His 3rd Piano Concerto was virtually completed at the time of his death, except for the last 17 bars, which were arranged and orchestrated by his pupil Tibor Serly.

Throughout his life, and particularly during his last years in the U.S., Bartók experienced constant financial difficulties, and complained bitterly of his inability to support himself and his family. Actually, he was apt to exaggerate his pecuniary troubles, which were largely due to his uncompromising character. He arrived in America in favorable circumstances; his traveling expenses were paid by the American patroness Elizabeth Sprague Coolidge, who also engaged him to play at her festival at the Library of Congress in Washington, D.C., for a generous fee. Bartók was offered the opportunity to give a summer course in composition at a midwestern college on advantageous terms, when he was still well enough to undertake such a task, but he proposed to teach piano instead, and the deal collapsed. Ironically, performances and recordings of his music increased enormously after his death, and the value of his estate reached a great sum of money. Posthumous honors were not lacking: Hungary issued a series of stamps with Bartók's image; a street in Budapest was named for him; the centenary of his birth was celebrated throughout the world by concerts and festivals devoted to his works. Forty-three years after his death, his remains were removed from the Ferncliff Cemetery in Hartsdale, N.Y., and taken to Budapest for a state funeral on July 7, 1988.

Far from being a cerebral purveyor of abstract musical designs, Bartók was an ardent student of folkways, seeking the roots of meters, rhythms, and modalities in the spontaneous songs and dances of the people. Indeed, he regarded his analytical studies of popular melodies as his most important contribution. Even during the last years of his life, already weakened by illness, he applied himself assiduously to the arrangement of Serbo-Croatian folk melodies of Yugoslavia from recordings placed in his possession. He was similarly interested in the natural musical expression of children; he firmly believed that children are capable of absorbing modalities and asymmetrical rhythmic structures with greater ease than adults trained in the rigid disciplines of established music schools. His remarkable collection of piano pieces entitled, significantly, *Mikrokosmos*, was intended as a method to initiate beginners into the world of unfamiliar tonal and rhythmic combinations; in this he provided a parallel means of instruction to the Kodály method of schooling.

WORKS: DRAMATIC: *A kékszakállú herceg vará* (Duke Bluebeard's Castle), opera in 1 act, op. 11 (1911; rev. 1912, 1918; Budapest, May 24, 1918, Egisto Tango conducting; U.S. premiere, N.Y., Oct. 2, 1952); *A fából faragott királyfi* (The Wooden Prince), ballet in 1 act, op. 13 (1914–16; Budapest, May 12, 1917, Egisto Tango conducting; orch. suite, 1924; Budapest, Nov. 23, 1931; rev. 1932); *A czodálatos mandarin* (The Miraculous Mandarin), pantomime in 1 act, op. 19 (1918–19; Cologne, Nov. 27, 1926; orch. suite, 1924; rev. 1927; Budapest, Oct. 15, 1928, Ernst von Dohnanyi conducting).

ORCH.: *Scherzo* (only scored movement of a projected sym. in E-flat major, 1902; Budapest, Feb. 29, 1904); *Kossuth*, symphonic poem (1903; Budapest, Jan. 13, 1904); *Rhapsody* for Piano and Orch., op. 1 (1904; Paris, Aug. 1905, composer soloist); *Scherzo* for Piano and Orch., op. 2 (1904; Budapest, Sept. 28, 1961); 2 suites: No. 1, op. 3 (1905; movements 1, 3–5 perf. in Vienna, Nov. 29, 1905; 1st complete perf., Budapest, March 1, 1909; rev. 1920) and No. 2 for Small Orch., op. 4 (1905–07; 1st perf. of 2nd movement, Scherzo, only; Berlin, Jan. 2, 1909; 1st complete perf., Budapest, Nov. 22, 1909; rev. 1920, 1943; transcribed for 2 Pianos, 1941); *2 Portraits*, op. 5 (No. 1, 1907–08; No. 2, 1911; No. 1, Budapest, Feb. 12, 1911; 1st complete perf., Budapest, April 20, 1916); Violin Concerto No. 1 (1907–08; score discovered in 1958; Basel, May 30, 1958, Schneeberger soloist, Paul Sacher conducting); *2 Pictures (Deux Images)*, op. 10 (1910; Budapest, Feb. 25, 1913); *4 Pieces*, op. 12 (1912; orchestrated 1921; Budapest, Jan. 9, 1922); *Dance Suite* (Budapest, Nov. 19, 1923); 3 piano concertos: No. 1 (1926; Frankfurt am Main, July 1, 1927, composer soloist, Furtwängler conducting), No. 2 (1930–31; Frankfurt am Main, Jan. 23, 1933, composer soloist, Rosbaud conducting), and No. 3 (1945; last 17 measures composed by Tibor Serly; Philadelphia, Feb. 8, 1946, Sándor soloist, Ormandy conducting); *Rhapsody* No. 1 for Violin and Orch. (1928; also versions for Violin or Cello, and Piano; Königsberg, Nov. 1, 1929, Szigeti soloist, Scherchen conducting); *Rhapsody* No. 2 for Violin and Orch. (1928; also for Violin and Piano; Budapest, Nov. 25, 1929, Székely soloist, E. Dohnányi conducting); *Music for Strings, Percussion, and Celesta*, one of Bartók's most often played works (1936; Basel, Jan. 21, 1937, Paul Sacher conducting); Violin Concerto No. 2 (1937–38; Amsterdam, March 23, 1939, Székely soloist, Mengelberg conducting); *Divertimento* for String Orch. (1939; Basel, June 11, 1940); Concerto for 2 Pianos and Orch. (1940; orchestration of Sonata for 2 Pianos and Percussion; London, Nov. 14, 1942); *Concerto for Orchestra* (commissioned by Koussevitzky, 1943; perf. under his direction, Boston, Dec. 1, 1944); Viola Concerto (1945; left unfinished in sketches; reconstructed and orchestrated by Tibor Serly, 1947–49; Minneapolis, Dec. 2, 1949, Primrose soloist, Doráti conducting; also arranged by Serly for Cello and Orch.); various orch. transcriptions of Romanian and Hungarian folk and peasant dances, orig. for piano.

CHAMBER: 3 unnumbered violin sonatas: C minor, op. 5 (1895), A major, op. 17 (1897), and E minor (1903); Piano Quartet in C minor, op. 20 (1898); an unnumbered String Quartet in F major (1898); Duo for 2 Violins (1902); *Albumblatt* for Violin and Piano (1902); Piano Quintet (1904; Vienna, Nov. 21, 1904); 6 numbered string quartets: No. 1, op. 7 (1908; Budapest, March 19, 1910), No. 2, op. 17 (1915–17; Budapest, March 3, 1918), No. 3 (1927; London, Feb. 19, 1929), No. 4 (1928; Budapest, March 20, 1929), No. 5 (1934; Washington, D.C., April 8, 1935), and No. 6 (1939; N.Y., Jan. 20, 1941); 2 numbered violin sonatas: No. 1 (1921; Vienna, Feb. 8, 1922) and No. 2 (1922; Berlin, Feb. 7, 1923); *Rhapsody* No. 1 for Violin and Piano (1928; Budapest, Nov. 22, 1929, Szigeti violinist, composer pianist; also versions for Cello and Piano, and Violin and Orch.); *Rhapsody* No. 2 for Violin and Piano (Amsterdam, Nov. 19, 1928; rev. 1944; also a version for Violin and Orch.); *44 Duos* for 2 Violins (1931); Sonata for 2 Pianos and Percussion (1937; Basel, Jan. 16, 1938, composer and his wife, Ditta Bartók, soloists; also for Orch. as Concerto for 2 Pianos and Orch.); *Contrasts* for Violin, Clarinet, and Piano (1938; N.Y., Jan. 9, 1939); *Caprichos*, ballet based on the music of *Contrasts* (N.Y., Jan. 29, 1950); Sonata for Solo Violin (1944; N.Y., Nov. 26, 1944, Menuhin soloist).

PIANO: *Rhapsody*, op. 1 (1904; Pressburg, Nov. 4, 1906; composer soloist); *14 Bagatelles*, op. 6 (Berlin, June 29, 1908); *10 Easy Pieces* (1908); *2 Elegies*, op. 8b (1908–09; Budapest, April 21, 1919, composer soloist); *For Children* (orig. 85 easy pieces in 4 vols., 1908–09; rev., 1945, reducing the number to 79, divided into 2 vols.); *7 Sketches*, op. 9 (1908–10; rev. 1945); *4 Dirges* (1910); *3 Burlesques* (1908–11); *Allegro barbaro* (1911); *6 Romanian Folk Dances* (1909–15); *Romanian Christmas Carols, or Colinde* (1915); Sonatina (1915); *Suite*, op. 14 (1916; Budapest, April 21, 1919, composer soloist); *15 Hungarian Peasant Songs* (1914–18); *3 Etudes*, op. 18 (1918); *8 Improvisations on Hungarian Peasant Songs* (1920; Budapest, Feb. 27, 1921, composer soloist); Sonata (Budapest, Dec. 8, 1926, composer soloist); *Out of Doors* (1926); 9 Little Pieces (Budapest, Dec. 8, 1926, composer soloist); *3 Rondos on Folk Tunes* (No. 1, 1916; Nos. 2 and 3, 1927); *Petite Suite* (1936); *Mikrokosmos* (153 pieces, 1926–39); *7 Pieces from Mikrokosmos* for 2 Pianos (c.1939); Suite for 2 Pianos (1941; transcription from Suite No. 2, for Small Orch., op. 4).

VOCAL: *20 Hungarian Folksongs* for Voice and Piano (1st 10 by Bartók, 2nd 10 by Kodály; 1906; rev. 1938); *8 Hungarian Folksongs* for Voice and Piano (1907–17); *3 Village Scenes* for Women's Voices and Chamber Orch. (1926; N.Y., Feb. 1, 1927; a transcription of 3 of *5 Village Scenes* for Voice and Piano, 1924; Budapest, Dec. 8, 1926); *20 Hungarian Folksongs* for Voice and Piano (4 vols., 1929); *Cantata Profana* for Tenor, Baritone, Chorus, and Orch. (1930; BBC, London, May 25, 1934); 27 Choruses for Women's or Children's Voices (1935); numerous settings of various folk songs.

WRITINGS: *Cântece poporale româneşti din comitatul Bihor (Ungaria)/Chansons populaires roumaines du département Bihar (Hongrie)* (Bucharest, 1913; rev. ed. in Eng. as incorporated in B. Suchoff, ed., *Rumanian Folk Music*, The Hague, vols. I–III, 1967); with Z. Kodály, *Erdélyi magyarság népdalok* (Transylvanian Folk Songs; Budapest, 1923); "Die Volksmusik der Rumänen von Maramureş," *Sammelbände für vergleichende Musikwissenschaft*, IV (Munich, 1923; in Eng. as incorporated in B. Suchoff, ed., *Rumanian Folk Music*, The Hague, vol. V, 1975); *A magyar népdal* (Budapest, 1924; Ger. tr. as *Das ungarische Volkslied*, Berlin, 1925; Eng. tr. as *Hungarian Folk Music*, London, 1931; enl. ed., with valuable addenda, as *The Hungarian Folk Song*, ed. by B. Suchoff, Albany, N.Y., 1981); *Népzenenk és a szomszéd népek népzenéje* (Our Folk Music and the Folk Music of Neighboring Peoples; Budapest, 1934; Ger. tr. as *Die Volksmusik der Magyaren und der benachbarten Völker*, Berlin, 1935; French tr. as "La Musique populaire des Hongrois et des peuples voisins," *Archivum Europae Centro Orientalis*, II; Budapest, 1936); *Die Melodien der rumänischen Colinde (Weihnachtslieder)* (Vienna, 1935; Eng. tr. in B. Suchoff, ed., *Rumanian Folk Music*, The Hague, vol. IV, 1975); *Miért és hogyan gyűjtsünk népzenét* (Why and How Do We Collect Folk Music?, Budapest, 1936; French tr. as *Pourquoi et comment recueille-t-on la musique populaire?*, Geneva, 1948); with A. Lord, *Serbo-Croatian Folk Songs* (N.Y., 1951; reprinted in B. Suchoff, ed., *Yugoslav Folk Music*, vol. I, Albany, N.Y., 1978); also articles in various musical magazines, among them "Hungarian Peasant Music," *Musical Quarterly* (July 1933).

The N.Y. Bartók Archive publ. an ed. of Bartók's writings in English trs. in its Studies in Musicology series. The following vols., under the editorship of Benjamin Suchoff, were publ.: *Rumanian Folk Music* (The Hague, vols. I–III, 1967; vols. IV–V, 1975); *Turkish Folk Music from Asia Minor* (Princeton, 1976); *Béla Bartók's Essays* (selected essays; London and N.Y., 1976); *Yugoslav Folk Music* (4 vols., Albany, N.Y., 1978); *The Hungarian Folk Song* (Albany, N.Y., 1981).

BIBL.: An extensive literature in many languages exists concerning various aspects of Bartók's life and music; in addition to the writings listed below, see the journal *Documenta Bartókiana* (Budapest, 1964–70; 1977–). *Musikblätter des Anbruch*, III/5 (Vienna, 1921); *Zénei Szemle*, VIII (Budapest, 1928); A. Révész, *Bartók Béla utja* (Budapest, 1936); D. Dille, *B. B.* (Antwerp, 1939); H. Pleasants and T. Serly, "B.'s Historic Contribution," *Modern Music*, XVII (1940); G. Abraham, "The B. of the Quartets," *Music & Letters* (Oct. 1945); M. Seiber, *The String Quartets of B. B.* (London, 1945); J. Demény, *B.* (Budapest, 1946); B. Kiss, *Bartók Béla müvészete* (Cluj, 1946); D. Dille, *B. B.* (Brussels, 1947); G. Láng, *B. élete és müvei* (Budapest, 1947); J. Deményi, ed., *Bartók Béla levelek* (Budapest, 3 vols., 1948, 1951, and 1955; 2nd ed., 1976; Ger. tr., 1960; 2nd ed., 1973; Eng. tr., 1971); J. Demény, *B. élete és müvei* (Budapest, 1948); A. Molnár, *B. müvészete* (Budapest, 1948); M. Babbitt, "The String Quartets of B.," *Musical Quarterly* (July 1949); "B. B., A Memorial Review," *Tempo*, 13–14 (1949–50); S. Moreux, *B. B., Sa vie, ses oeuvres, son langage* (Paris, 1949; Ger. tr., Zürich, 1950; Eng. tr., London, 1953); C. Mason, "B. B. and Folksong," *Music Review*, XI (1950); B. Rondi, *B.* (Rome, 1950); *Új Zenei Szemle*, I/4 (Budapest, 1950); *Musik der Zeit*, III (Bonn, 1953); H. Stevens, *The Life and Music of B. B.* (N.Y., 1953; 2nd ed., rev., 1964; 3rd ed., rev. 1993, by M. Gillies); *Revue Musicale*, 244 (1955); P. Csobádi, *B.* (Budapest, 1955); E. Lendvai, *B. stilusa* (Budapest, 1955); F. Bónis, *B. élete képekben* (Budapest, 1956; 4th ed., 1980; Ger. tr., 1964; French tr., 1964; Eng. tr., 1964, as *B. B.: His Life in Pictures*); B. Suchoff, *Guide to B.'s Mikrokosmos* (London, 1957; 3rd ed., N.Y., 1982); B. Szabolcsi, ed., *B., Sa vie et son oeuvre* (Budapest, 1956; 2nd ed., 1968; Ger. tr., 1957; enl. ed., 1972); J. Szegő, *Bartók Béla a népdalkutató* (Bucharest, 1956); R. Traimer, *B. B.s Kompositionstechnik, dargestellt an seinen sechs Streichquartetten* (Regensburg, 1956); K. Kristóf, *Beszélgetések B. Bélaval* (Budapest, 1957); A. Fassett, *The Naked Face of Genius; B. B.'s American Years* (Boston, 1958; reprint as *B. B.; The American Years*, N.Y., 1970); R. Petzoldt, *B. B., Sein Leben in Bildern* (Leipzig, 1958); W. Reich, *B. B.; Eigene Schriften und Erinnerungen der Freunde* (Basel and Stuttgart, 1958); J. Ujfalussy, ed., *B. breviárium; Levelek, írások, dokumentumok* (Budapest, 1958; 2nd ed., rev., 1974); J. Uhde, *B. B.* (Berlin, 1959); J. Demény, ed., *Ausgewählte Briefe* (Budapest, 1960; Eng. tr., London, 1971); A. Forte, "B.'s 'Serial' Composition," *Musical Quarterly* (April 1960); L. Lesznai, *B. B.: Sein Leben, seine Werke* (Leipzig, 1961; Eng. tr., 1973, as *B.*); B. Szabolcsi, *B. B.: Leben und Werk* (Leipzig, 1961; 2nd ed., 1968); G. Kroó, *B. szinpadi müvei* (Budapest, 1962); V. Bator, *The B. B. Archives: History and Catalogue* (N.Y., 1963); P. Citron, *B.* (Paris, 1963); Z. Pálová-Vrbova, *B. B.: Život a dilo* (Prague, 1963); E. Lendvai, *B. dramaturgiája* (Budapest, 1964); W. Rudziński, *Warsztat kompozytorski Béli Bartóka* (Kraków, 1964); E. Helm, *B. B. in Selbstzeugnissen und Bilddokumenten* (Hamburg, 1965); J. Ujfalussy, *Bartók Béla* (Budapest, 1965; 3rd ed., 1976; Eng. tr., Boston, 1972; Russian tr., 1971; Ger. tr., 1973); J. Kárpáti, *B. vonósnégyesei* (Budapest, 1967; rev. ed. as *B. kamarazenéje*, 1976; Eng. tr., 1975; enl. ed. as *B.'s Chamber Music*, 1993); A. Szőllősy, ed., *B. összegyüjtött irásai I* (Budapest, 1967); *Sesja Bartókowska* (Warsaw, 1967); J. Demény, *Bartók Béla a zongoraművész* (Budapest, 1968; 2nd ed., 1973); H. Heinsheimer, *Best Regards to Aida* (includes material on B.'s American travels; N.Y., 1968); I. Martynov, *B. B.* (Moscow, 1968); I. Nestyev, *B. B.* (Moscow, 1969); J. Szegő, *Bartók Béla élete* (Budapest, 1969); F. Weselowski, ed., *Sesja Bartókowska* (Lodz, 1969); T. Zielínski, *B.* (Kraków, 1969; Ger. tr., Zürich, 1973); *B. B.: A Complete Catalogue of His Published Works* (London, 1970); V. Čižik, *B.s Briefe in die Slowakei* (Bratislava, 1971); E. Kraus, "Bibliographie und Diskographie: B. B.," *Musik und Bildung* (Oct. 1971); G. Kroó, *B. kalauz* (Budapest, 1971; Eng. tr., 1974; Ger. tr., 1974); T. Hundt, *B.'s Satztechnik in den Klavierwerken* (Regensburg, 1971); E. Lendvai, *B. költöi világa* (Budapest, 1971); idem, *B. B.: An Analysis of His Music* (London, 1971); *International Musicological Conference in Commemoration of B. B.: Budapest 1971*; P. Petersen, *Die Tonalität im Instrumentalschaffen von B. B.* (Hamburg, 1971); F. Bónis, *Bartók Béla élete képekben és dokumentumokban* (Budapest, 1972; Ger. tr., 1972; Eng. tr., 1972, as *B. B.: His Life in Pictures and Documents*); D. Dille, *Thematisches Verzeichnis der Jugendwerke B. B.s 1890–1904* (Budapest, 1974); H. Fladt, *Zur Problematik traditioneller Formtypen dargestellt an Sonatensatzen in den Streichquartetten B. B.s* (Munich, 1974); F. László, ed., *B.-dolgozatok* (Bucharest, 1974); J. McCabe, *B. Orchestral Music* (London, 1974); T. Crow, ed., *B. Studies* (Detroit, 1976); B. Suchoff, "B. in America," *Musical Times* (Feb. 1976); G. Perle, "The String

Quartets of B. B.," in *A Musical Offering: Essays in Honor of Martin Bernstein* (N.Y., 1977); E. Lendvai, *B. and Kodály* (4 vols., Budapest, 1978–80); F. László, *Bartók Béla: Tanulmányok és tanúságok* (Bucharest, 1980); P. Autexier, ed., *B. B.: Musique de la vie* (Paris, 1981); B. Bartók, Jr., *Apám életének krónikája* (Budapest, 1981); idem, *Bartók Béla családi levelei* (Budapest, 1981); T. Tallián, *Bartók Béla* (Budapest, 1981); Y. Queffélec, *B. B.* (Paris, 1981); B. Bartók, Jr., *Bartók Béla műhelyében* (Budapest, 1982); H. Milne, *B.: His Life and Times* (Tunbridge Wells, 1982); S. Walsh, *B.'s Chamber Music* (London, 1982); E. Lendvai, *The Workshop of B. and Kodály* (Budapest, 1983); E. Antokoletz, *The Music of B. B.* (Berkeley, Los Angeles, and London, 1984); P. Griffiths, *B.* (London, 1984); D. Locke, "Numerical Aspects of B.'s String Quartets," *Musical Times* (June 1987); G. Ránki, ed., *B. and Kodály Revisited* (Budapest, 1987); E. Antokoletz, *B. B.: A Guide to Research* (N.Y., 1988); M. Gillies and A. Gombocz, "The 'Colinda' Fiasco: B. and Oxford University Press," *Music & Letters* (Oct. 1988); J. Platthy, *B.: A Critical Biography* (Santa Claus, Ind., 1988); D. Yeomans, *B. for Piano: A Survey of His Solo Literature* (Bloomington, Ind., 1988); M. Gillies, *B. in Britain: A Guided Tour* (Oxford, 1989); L. Somfai, "B. and the Paper Studies: The Case of String Quartet No. 4," *Hungarian Music Quarterly*, vol. 1, No. 1 (1989); D. Dille, *B. B.: Regard sur le passé* (Louvain-la-Neuve, 1990); M. Gilles, *B. Remembered* (London and Boston, 1990); R. Cohn, "B.'s Octatonic Strategies: A Motivic Approach," *Journal of the American Musicological Society* (Summer 1991); N. John, ed., *The Stage Works of B. B.* (London and Riverrun, N.Y., 1991); P. Wilson, *The Music of B. B.* (New Haven, 1992); J. de Waard, *B.* (Haarlem, 1993); B. Suchoff, *B.: The Concerto for Orchestra: Understanding B.'s World* (N.Y., 1995); L. Somfai, *B. B.: Composition, Concepts, and Autograph Sources* (Berkeley, 1996).

Bartoletti, Bruno, noted Italian conductor; b. Sesto Fiorentino, June 10, 1926. He studied flute at the Florence Cons., and then received training in piano and composition while serving as a flutist in the orch. of the Florence Teatro Comunale. In 1949 he became an assistant conductor there, making his formal debut conducting *Rigoletto* in 1953. In 1954 he made his debut as a sym. conductor at the Maggio Musicale Fiorentino, where he later was director (1957–64). On Oct. 23, 1956, he made his U.S. debut at the Chicago Lyric Opera conducting *Il Trovatore*, and then served as its resident conductor until 1963. With Pino Donati, he was its co-artistic director from 1964 to 1975, and then its sole artistic director from 1975. He also was artistic director of the Rome Opera (1965–69), and later artistic advisor (1986–87) and artistic director (1987–92) of the Florence Teatro Comunale. As a guest conductor, he appeared throughout Europe, the U.S., and South America, becoming especially admired for his idiomatic readings of the Italian operatic repertoire; also conducted various French and Russian operas with success.

Bartoli, Cecilia, outstanding Italian mezzo-soprano; b. Rome, June 4, 1966. She began vocal training at a very early age with her mother; at the age of 9, sang the off-stage role of the shepherd in *Tosca*. After studying trombone at the Accademia di Santa Cecilia in Rome, she pursued a vocal career, attracting favorable attention when she was 19 on an Italian television special with Ricciarelli and Nucci. Her formal stage debut followed in Verona in 1987. She then received valuable coaching from Karajan and Barenboim. On July 17, 1990, she made her U.S. debut as soloist at the Mostly Mozart Festival in N.Y. During the 1990–91 season, she made successful debuts with the Opéra de la Bastille in Paris as Cherubino, at La Scala in Milan as Isolier in *Le Comte Ory*, at the Maggio Musicale Fiorentino as Dorabella, and at the Teatro Liceo in Barcelona as Rosina. In 1992 she performed admirably as Cherubino and Dorabella in concert performances with Barenboim and the Chicago Sym. Orch.; also appeared as Despina at the Salzburg Festival. On April 23, 1993, she made a sensational U.S. operatic stage debut with the Houston Grand Opera as Rosina. She made her first appearance at the John F. Kennedy Center for the Performing Arts in Washington, D.C., on March 25, 1994. On Sept. 29, 1994, she regaled audiences at the opening of the 1994–95 season of N.Y.'s Carnegie Hall when she appeared as soloist with Marriner and the Academy of St. Martin-in-the-Fields. The event was later telecast to the nation over PBS. The matchless combination of her vocal perfection and extraordinary dramatic gifts have made Bartoli one of the most heralded singers of her day. Among her other acclaimed operatic roles are Concepción, Bellini's Romeo, Massenet's Charlotte, and Offenbach's Hélène. In addition to opera, she pursues a remarkably successful concert career.

Bartolozzi, Bruno, Italian violinist and composer; b. Florence, June 8, 1911; d. Fiesole, Dec. 12, 1980. After studying violin at the Cherubini Cons. in Florence (1926–30), he was active as a violinist from 1941 to 1965 in the orch. of the Maggio Musicale Fiorentino; turned to composition quite late in life; took courses with Fragapane at the Cherubini Cons. (1946–49); in 1964 he was appointed to its faculty. In his music, he followed the modified dodecaphonic techniques as promulgated by Dallapiccola, including triadic constructions. He wrote *New Sounds for Woodwind* (in Eng.; London, 1967; 2nd ed., rev., 1982), demonstrating the possibility of producing simultaneously several pitches on a single woodwind instrument.

WORKS: ORCH.: *Concerto for Orchestra* (1952; Rome, Jan. 18, 1956); *Divertimento* for Chamber Orch. (1953); 2 violin concertos: No. 1 for Violin, Strings, and Harpsichord (San Francisco, Dec. 2, 1957) and No. 2 (1979); *Concertazioni* for Bassoon, Strings, and Percussion (1963; Rome, March 6, 1965); *Memorie* for 3 Guitars and Orch. (1975; Florence, Oct. 7, 1977); *Risonanze* for 18 Instruments and Percussion (1978). **CHAMBER:** *Serenata* for Violin and Guitar (1952); *3 Pieces* for Guitar (1952); *Musica a 5* for Bassoon, Trumpet, Guitar, Violin, and Viola (1953); *Variazioni* for Violin (1957); 2 string quartets (1960, 1979); *Concertazioni* for Oboe, Viola, Guitar, Double Bass, and Percussion (1965); *Andamenti* for Viola (1967); *Collage* for Oboe (1968); *The Hollow Man* for Any Woodwind (1968); *Concertazioni a quattro* for Flute, Oboe, Clarinet, and Bassoon (1969); *Collage* for Bassoon (1969); *Sinaulodia* for 4 Flutes (1969); *Cantilena* for Flute (1970); *Musica per Piero* for 2 Violas (1971); *Auser* for Oboe and Guitar (1973); *Collage* for Clarinet (1973); *Concertazioni* for Clarinet, Horn, Trumpet, Trombone, Guitar, Viola, Cello, Double Bass, and Percussion (1973); *Repitu* for Flute, Viola, Guitar, and Percussion (1975); *Per Olga* for Flute (1976); *The Solitary* for English Horn and Percussion (1976); *Adles* for Guitar (1977); *Atma* for 3 Groups of Solo Instruments (1978). **VOCAL:** *Sentimento del sogno* for Soprano and Orch. (1952); *Immagine* for Soprano and 17 Instruments (1959); *Tres recuerdos del cielo* for Soprano and 10 Instruments (1967; Vienna, Sept. 11, 1968).

Bartoš, František, Czech music critic, editor, and composer; b. Brněnec, June 13, 1905; d. Prague, May 21, 1973. He was a pupil of Jírák and Křička (1921–25) and attended the master classes of Foerster (1925–28) at the Prague Cons. He was active as a music critic and served as co-ed. of Prague's *Tempo* (1935–38; 1946–48). Among his books were *Smetana ve vzpomínkách a dopisech* (Smetana in Reminiscences and Letters; Prague, 1939; 9th ed., 1954; Ger. tr., 1954; Eng. tr., 1955) and *Bedřich Smetana* (Prague, 1940).

WORKS: DRAMATIC: *Jaro* (Spring), melodrama (1925); music for plays and films. **ORCH.:** Suite (1928); *Rozhlasová hudba* (Radio Music; 1936). **CHAMBER:** String Sextet (1926); 2 string quartets (1928; 1933–35); *Scherzo* for Wind Quintet (1932); *Měšťák šlechticem* (Le bourgeois gentilhomme) for Wind Quintet (1934); Duo for Violin and Viola (1937); *Polka rusticana* for Wind Trio (1952); piano pieces. **VOCAL:** Choral works, songs, and folksong arrangements.

Bartoš, Jan Zdeněk, Czech composer; b. Dvůr Králové nad Labem, June 4, 1908; d. Prague, June 1, 1981. He played the violin as a youth; then took composition lessons with Šín and Křička at the Prague Cons., graduating in 1943. He earned his living playing in dance orchs.; from 1945 to 1956 he was a member of the Music Section of the Ministry of Education and Culture; in 1958 he was appointed teacher of composition at the Prague Cons. In his music, he followed the national traditions of the Czech school.

WORKS: DRAMATIC: OPERAS: *Rýparka* (Ripar's Wife; 1949); *Prokletý zámek* (The Accursed Castle; 1949); *Útok na nebe* (The Attack of Heaven; 1953–54). **OPERETTA:** *Je libo ananas?* (Do You Like Pineapples?; 1956. **BALLETS:** *Hanuman* (1941); *Mirella* (1956); *Král maněže* (King of the Manege; 1963). **ORCH.:** *Song of St. Matthias*, symphonic poem (1945); 7 syms: No. 1 (1949–52), No. 2, *da camera* (1956), No. 3, *Giocosa*, for Strings (1964–65), No. 4, *Concertante*, for Oboe d'Amore and Strings (1968), No. 5 for Wind Orch. (1973–74), No. 6 for Wind Quartet and Strings (1977), and No. 7, *Brevis* (1978); *Intermezzo* (1961); *Concerto da camera* for Oboe and Strings (1963); 2 viola concertos (1963, 1970); *Fantasy* for Flute and Orch. (1964); *Inventions* for Bass Clarinet and Strings (1966); Concerto for Accordion and Strings (1966); Horn Concerto (1967); Concerto for Violin and Strings (1970); Concerto-Sym. for Violin and String Orch. (1973); Fantasy for Organ and Strings (1975); *Concerto per due Boemi* for Bass Clarinet, Piano, and Strings (1975); Concerto for Violin, Viola, and Strings (1976); *Music* for String Quartet and Orch. (1976); *Rhapsody* for Cello and Strings (1979). **CHAMBER:** Cello Sonata (1938); 2 nonets (1939, 1974); 11 string quartets (1940, 1946, 1948, 1951, 1952, 1956, 1960, 1963, 1970, 1971, 1973); *Partita* for Viola (1944); 3 wind quintets (1946–63); Quintet for Flute, Harp, Viola, Cello, and Guitar (1947); 17 divertimentos for various combinations of instruments (1956–79); Trio for Violin, Viola, and Harp (1961); Double-Bass Sonata (1962); *Suite concertante* for Viola, Double Bass, and 9 Wind Instruments (1964); String Trio (1967); 4 piano trios (1968, 1969, 1971, 1979); Sextet for 2 Oboes, English Horn, 2 Bassoons, and Harp (1976); Trombone Sonata (1978); Trio for Viola, Clarinet, and Piano (1980). **PIANO:** 2 sonatas (1953, 1959). **VOCAL:** Cantatas; choruses; songs, including *Sonnets of Prague* for Narrator, Tenor, Harp, and String Orch. (1966).

Bartoš, Josef, Czech writer on music; b. Vysoké Myto, March 4, 1887; d. Prague, Oct. 27, 1952. He studied with Stecker at the Prague Cons., and with Hostinský and Nejedlý at the Univ. of Prague (1905–09); also attended the Sorbonne in Paris. He was active as a teacher and music critic. He publ. valuable monographs on Dvořák (1913), Fibich (1914; new ed., 1941), Foerster (1923), and Ostrčil (1936); also an important work on the National Opera of Prague (1938).

Bary, Alfred (Erwin) von, German tenor; b. La Valetta, Malta, Jan. 18, 1873; d. Munich, Sept. 13, 1926. He studied medicine at the Univ. of Munich (M.D., 1898) and voice with Richard Müller in Leipzig. In 1903 he made his operatic debut as Lohengrin at the Dresden Court Opera, where he sang until 1915; also appeared at the Bayreuth Festivals (1904–14); was a member of the Munich Court Opera (1915–18). Among his best roles were Parsifal, Siegmund, Tristan, and Siegfried.

Barzin, Leon (Eugene), Belgian-born American conductor; b. Brussels, Nov. 27, 1900. He was taken to the U.S. in 1902; became a naturalized American citizen in 1924. His father played viola in the orch. of the Metropolitan Opera in N.Y.; his mother was a ballerina. He studied violin with his father and later in Belgium with Eugène Ysaÿe. In 1919 he became a violist in the N.Y. Phil.; in 1925 he became its 1st violist, retaining his post until 1929, when he was engaged as assistant conductor of the American Orchestral Soc., which was reorganized in 1930 as the National Orchestral Assn., with Barzin as music director; he continued in this capacity until 1958, and again from 1970 to 1976. He was also music director of the Hartford (Conn.) Sym. Orch. (1938–40), the Ballet Soc. (1947–48), and the N.Y. City Ballet (1948–58); from 1958 to 1960 he conducted concerts of the Assoc. des Concerts Pasdeloup in Paris and was at the same time an instructor at the Schola Cantorum there. He received the Order of the Légion d'honneur in 1960. Barzin was particularly successful in training semi-professional and student orchs.; especially with the National Orchestral Assn., he attained remarkable results.

Barzun, Jacques, eminent French-born American historian, educator, and writer on music; b. Creteil, Seine, Nov. 30, 1907. He went to America in 1919; was educated at Columbia Univ. (A.B., 1927; Ph.D., 1932); became a lecturer in history there in 1927, and a full prof. in 1945; he became a naturalized American citizen in 1933. In 1955 he was made dean of the Columbia graduate faculties, then dean of faculties and provost in 1958; he also assumed the chair of Seth Low Prof. of History in 1960; he resigned these posts in 1967; continued to lecture there until 1975. He exercised considerable influence on American higher education by advocating broad reading in various fields rather than narrow specialization. His books concerned with music include *Darwin, Marx, Wagner; Critique of a Heritage* (Boston, 1941; rev. ed., 1958); *Berlioz and the Romantic Century* (an outstanding modern study of his life and works; 2 vols., Boston, 1950; 3rd ed., rev., 1969); ed. *Pleasures of Music* (N.Y., 1951); ed. and tr. *Nouvelles lettres de Berlioz, 1830–1868*; *New Letters of Berlioz, 1830–1868* (N.Y., 1954); publ. a new tr. of Berlioz's *Evenings with the Orchestra* (N.Y., 1956; 2nd ed., 1973); also wrote a survey, *Music in American Life* (N.Y., 1956) and publ. *Critical Questions on Music and Letters, Culture and Biography, 1940–1980* (N.Y., 1982).

BIBL.: D. Weiner and W. Keylor, eds., *From Parnassus: Essays in Honor of J. B.* (N.Y., 1976).

Bashkirov, Dmitri (Alexandrovich), Russian pianist and pedagogue; b. Tiflis, Nov. 1, 1931. He studied in Moscow with Alexander Goldenweiser. In 1955 he won 2nd prize in the Long-Thibaud Competition in Paris; in 1970 he won the International Schumann Competition in Zwickau. In 1957 he became a member of the faculty of the Moscow Cons.; also taught at the Kiev Cons. from 1968. His repertoire is a comprehensive one, ranging from classical to contemporary compositions.

Bashmakov, Leonid, Finnish music educator, composer, and conductor of Russian descent; b. Terijoki, April 4, 1927. He studied composition and conducting at the Sibelius Academy in Helsinki (1947–54). In 1960 he became a theater conductor in Tampere. From 1979 to 1990 he was director of the Tampere Cons.

WORKS: Suite for Marimba and String Quartet (1951); *Fantastic Pictures* for Orch. (1953); 6 syms. (1963; 1965; Sinfonietta, 1971; 1977; 1979; 1982); 2 violin concertos (1966, 1987); 2 violin sonatinas (1968–69); *Canzona I* for Chorus and Orch. (1969) and *II* for Soprano and Orch. (1971); Octet for Piano, Winds, and Brass (1970); Sonata for Percussion (1970); *4 Bagatelles* for Flute and Percussion (1971); *Dialogues* for Organ and Percussion (1971); Overture for Wind Orch. (1971); *Divertimento* for Oboe and Strings (1971); Sonata for Viola, Cello, and Piano (1971); String Quartet (1972); *Fantasia* for 3 Different Flutes, 1 Player (1972); Cello Concerto (1972); Flute Concerto (1973); Organ Concerto (1975); *Tumma*, ballet (1976); *Conversazioni per 2* for Soprano, Violin, and Small Orch. (1978); Wind Quintet (1978); *Crescendo* for Wind Orch. (1980); music for plays and films.

Bashmet, Yuri, outstanding Russian violist; b. Rostov-na-Donu, Jan. 24, 1953. He began his training in Lwów, and then was a student of Borisovski and Druyinine at the Moscow Cons. After winning 2nd prize in the Budapest International Competition in 1975, and 1st prize in the Munich International Competition in 1976, he pursued a career as a viola virtuoso. In addition to engagements as a soloist with the world's foremost orchs., he also toured widely as a recitalist. In 1984 he founded the Moscow Soloists; also taught at the Moscow Cons. Bashmet's authoritative performances have placed him among the foremost masters of his instrument. He has done much to encourage new works for viola by championing scores by Denisov, Schnittke, and Pettersson.

Basilides, Mária, Hungarian contralto; b. Jolsva, Nov. 11, 1886; d. Budapest, Sept. 26, 1946. She was educated at the Royal Academy of Music in Budapest; in 1915 she became a member of the Budapest Opera, remaining on its roster until her death; she also made appearances with the Berlin State Opera, the Dresden State Opera, and the Bavarian State Opera of Munich. She championed the music of Bartók and Kodály as a soloist in recitals and with sym. orchs.

BIBL.: J. Molnár, *Basilides Mária* (Budapest, 1967).

Bašinskas, Justinas, Lithuanian composer and teacher; b. Mažoji Trakiške, Jan. 22, 1923. He was a pupil at the Kaunas Music School (1945–50), then studied composition with Juzeliunas at the Lithuanian State Cons. in Vilnius (1950–55), where he subsequently taught. In 1983 he won the Lithuanian S.S.R. National prize and received the title of Merited Culture Worker. A prolific composer, Bašinkas dedicated himself to optimistic themes, glorifying nature and extolling human friendship in his vocal music, while building tense tonal structures in his instrumental compositions.

WORKS: BALLET: *The Accursed Monks* (1982). **ORCH.:** 8 syms.: No. 1 (1953), No. 2 (1960), No. 3 (1970), No. 4, *The Bells* (1973), No. 5, *Being* (1977), No. 6, *The Lamentations* (1979), No. 7, *In the Whirlpools* (1983), and No. 8, *The Call of the Earth* (1986); Chamber Sym. (1984); 3 Symphonic Dances (1967); Concerto for Flute, Strings, and Percussion (1971). **CHAMBER:** Violin Sonata (1979); String Quartet (1980); Sonata for Solo Viola (1983). **PIANO:** *Variations* (1951); Sonata (1952); Sonata for Piano, 4-hands (1979). **VOCAL: ORATORIO:** *Oak* (1957). **CANTATAS:** *A Tale about Soldier's Bread* (1961); *Requiem* (1969); *Morning* (1974); *Mother's Hands* (1978). **SONG CYCLES:** *After the Storm* (1958); *The Animals in Winter* (1968); *The Autumn* (1969); *The Hour of the Eagle-Owl* (1985). Also choruses; solo songs; arrangements of Lithuanian folk songs.

Basiola, Mario, Italian baritone; b. Annico, July 12, 1892; d. there, Jan. 3, 1965. He was a pupil of Cotogni in Rome. In 1918 he made his operatic debut, and then sang in Barcelona (1920) and Florence (1921) before appearing with the San Carlo Opera Co. in the U.S. (1923–25). On Nov. 11, 1925, he made his Metropolitan Opera debut in N.Y. as Amonasro, remaining on its roster until 1932; he then sang at Milan's La Scala and in Rome (1933–38), and at London's Covent Garden (1939). In 1946 he toured Australia, where he taught until 1951; then settled in Milan as a voice teacher. Among his prominent roles were Rossini's Figaro, Valentin, Iago, Rigoletto, and Scarpia.

Bassett, Leslie (Raymond), distinguished American composer and teacher; b. Hanford, Calif., Jan. 22, 1923. He studied piano; played the trombone in jazz combos; was a trombonist during his military service, playing in the 13th Armored Division Band. He then enrolled in Fresno (Calif.) State College (B.A., 1947); later studied composition with Ross Lee Finney at the Univ. of Mich. (M.M., 1949; D.M., 1956); also took private lessons with Arthur Honegger and Boulanger in Paris in 1950. In 1952 he was appointed to the faculty of the Univ. of Mich.; was made a prof. there in 1965 and was chairman of the composition dept. (1970–85); in 1977 he became the Albert A. Stanley Distinguished Univ. Prof. of Music there, retiring in 1992. He held the American Prix de Rome (1961–63), and received the National Inst. of Arts and Letters Award in 1964. In 1966 he received the Pulitzer Prize in Music for his *Variations* for Orch. He held a Guggenheim fellowship in 1973–74 and again in 1980–81. In 1981 he became a member of the American Academy and Inst. of Arts and Letters. In 1988 he held a Rockefeller Foundation grant for study at its Villa Serbelloni in Bellagio, Italy. In his music, Bassett pursues the ideal of structural logic within the judicial limits of the modern school of composition, with some serial elements discernible in his use of thematic rhythms and motivic periodicity.

WORKS: ORCH.: Suite in G (Fresno, Calif., Dec. 3, 1946); *5 Movements* (1961; Rome, July 5, 1962); *Variations* (Rome, July 6, 1963); *Colloquy* (1968; Fresno, Calif., May 23, 1969); *Forces* (1972; Des Moines, Iowa, May 1, 1973); *Echoes from an Invisible World* (1974–75; Philadelphia, Feb. 27, 1976); Concerto for 2 Pianos and Orch. (1976; Midland, Mich., April 30, 1977); *Concerto lirico* for Trombone and Orch. (1983; Toledo, Ohio, April 6, 1984); *From a Source Evolving* (1985; Midland, Mich., Nov. 1, 1986); *Concerto for Orchestra* (1991; Detroit, Feb. 6, 1992). **BAND AND WIND ENSEMBLES:** *Designs, Images, and Textures* (1964; Ithaca, N.Y., April 28, 1965); *Sounds, Shapes, and Symbols* (1977; Ann Arbor, Mich., March 17, 1978); *Concerto grosso* (1982; Ann Arbor, Mich., Feb. 4, 1983); *Colors and Contours* (1984; Boulder, Colo., March 1, 1985); *Lullaby for Kirsten* (Ann Arbor, Mich., Oct. 4, 1985); *Fantasy* for Clarinet and Wind Ensemble (1986; Ann Arbor, Mich., Oct. 2, 1987). **CHAMBER:** 4 string quartets (1951, 1957, 1962, 1978); Horn Sonata (1952); Trio for Viola, Clarinet, and Piano (1953); Quintet for 2 Violins, Viola, Cello, and Piano (1954); Viola Sonata (1956); Woodwind Quintet (1958); Violin Sonata (1959); Quintet for 2 Violins, Viola, Cello, and Piano (1962); Nonet (1967); *Music* for Alto Saxophone and Piano (1968); Sextet for 2 Violins, 2 Violas, Cello, and Piano (1971); *Sounds Remembered* for Violin and Piano (1972); *Wind Music* for Wind Sextet (1975); Sextet for Flutes, Clarinets, and Strings (1979); Trio for Violin, Clarinet, and Piano (1980); *Concerto da camera* for Trumpet and Chamber Ensemble (1981); *Dialogues* for Oboe and Piano (1987); *Duo-Inventions* for 2 Cellos (1988); *Illuminations* for Flute and Piano (1989); *Arias* for Clarinet and Piano (1992); *Narratives* for Guitar Quartet (1993); *Song and Dance* for Tuba and Piano (1993). **KEYBOARD: PIANO:** *6 Pieces* (1951); *Mobile* (1961); *Elaborations* (1966); (7) *Preludes* (1984); (5) *Configurations* (1987). **ORGAN:** *Voluntaries* (1958); *4 Statements* (1964); *Liturgies* (1980). **VOCAL:** *Easter Triptych* for Tenor and Winds (1958); *For City, Nation, World*, cantata for Chorus, Optional Children, Tenor, 4 Trombones, Organ, and Congregation (1959; Buffalo, Feb. 21, 1960); *Moonrise* for Women's Voices and 10 Instruments (1960); *Eclogue, Encomium, and Evocation* for Women's Voices, Piano, Harp, and 2 Percussion (1962); *Prayers for Divine Service* for Men's Voices and Organ (1965); *Collect* for Soprano and Tape (1969); *Moon Canticle* for Amplified Speaker, Soprano, Chorus, and Cello (1969); *Celebration in Praise of Earth* for Amplified Speaker, Chorus, and Orch. (1970; Berea, Ohio, Oct. 14, 1971); *Time and Beyond* for Baritone, Clarinet, Cello, and Piano (1973); *Pierrot Songs* for Soprano, Flute, Clarinet, Violin, Cello, and Piano (1988); numerous works for Chorus and Organ or Piano; songs. **ELECTRONIC:** *3 Studies in Electronic Sound* (1965); *Triform* (1966).

BIBL.: E. Johnson, *L. B.: A Bio-Bibliography* (Westport, Conn., 1994).

Bassi, Amedeo (Vittorio), Italian tenor; b. Montespertoli, near Florence, July 20, 1874; d. Florence, Jan. 14, 1949. He was a pupil of Pavesi in Florence, where he made his operatic debut in 1897 in Marchetti's *Ruy Blas*; then sang in various Italian opera houses. In 1902 he made his first tour of South America, and in 1908 sang Radames at the opening of the new Teatro Colón in Buenos Aires. On Dec. 19, 1906, he made his U.S. debut in that same role at N.Y.'s Manhattan Opera House, remaining on its roster until 1908. In 1907 he made his first appearance at London's Covent Garden; also made appearances with the Chicago Grand Opera Co. (1910–16). He made his Metropolitan Opera debut in N.Y. on March 2, 1911, as Ramerrez in *La Fanciulla del West*. After singing at Milan's La Scala (1921–26), he retired from the operatic stage and sang widely in concerts. He also taught in Florence. His most famous student was Ferruccio Tagliavini. Bassi was particularly known for his roles in Italian operas, but he also sang such Wagnerian roles as Loge, Siegfried, and Parsifal. He created the roles of Lionello in Mascagni's *Amica* (1905) and Angel Clare in d'Erlanger's *Tess* (1906).

Bastianini, Ettore, Italian baritone; b. Siena, Sept. 24, 1922; d. Sirmione, Jan. 25, 1967. He studied in Florence with Flaminio Contini. In 1945 he made his debut as a bass singing Colline in Ravenna; in 1948 he made his first appearance at Milan's La

Scala as Tiresia in *Oedipus Rex*. Following additional training with Rucciana Bertarini, he turned to baritone roles in 1952. He sang Andrei in the rev. version of *War and Peace* in Florence in 1953. On Dec. 5, 1953, he made his Metropolitan Opera debut in N.Y. as Germont, and was on its roster until 1957 and again 1959–60 and 1964–66. From 1954 he also sang again at La Scala. In 1956 he made his first appearance in Chicago as Riccardo in *I Puritani*. In 1962 he made his debut at London's Covent Garden as Renato. Among his other roles were Rigoletto, Amonasro, Don Carlo, Escamillo, and Scarpia.

BIBL.: M. Boagno and G. Starone, *E. B.: Una voce di bronzo e di velluto* (Parma, 1991).

Bastin, Jules, Belgian bass; b. Pont, Aug. 18, 1933. He studied at the Brussels Cons. In 1960 he became a member of the Théâtre de la Monnaie in Brussels; also appeared in London, Chicago, N.Y., and Toronto. He was best known for his appearances in such French operas as *Le Prophète, Benvenuto Cellini, Pelléas et Mélisande*, and Massenet's *Cendrillon*. In 1979 he took part in the Paris premiere of the 3-act version of Berg's *Lulu*. He also pursued an active concert career.

Bate, Jennifer (Lucy), English organist; b. London, Nov. 11, 1944. She began organ lessons as a youth and made her debut in London in 1957. After studies at the Royal Academy of Music in London (Licentiate, 1959) and at the Univ. of Bristol (B.A., 1966), she began to tour widely. In 1976 she made her U.S. debut in Savannah, Ga. She subsequently pursued an international career as a concert organist. She also gave master classes and composed organ pieces. Her exhaustive repertory ranges from early music to contemporary scores, and includes numerous concertos and surveys of the complete organ works of such diverse masters as Liszt, Franck, and Messiaen.

Bate, Philip (Argall Turner), English music scholar; b. Glasgow, March 26, 1909. He studied clarinet in Aberdeen; then attended classes in general science at the Univ. of Aberdeen (B.Sc., 1932). In 1934 he joined the staff of the BBC in London, and subsequently held various positions there (until 1968). He gathered a valuable collection of wind instruments, which he donated to the Univ. of Oxford. In 1946 he founded the Galpin Soc., serving as its first chairman and, in 1977, its president.

WRITINGS: *The Oboe* (London, 1956; 3rd ed., 1975); *The Trumpet and Trombone* (London, 1966); *The Flute: A Study of Its History, Development and Construction* (London, 1969; 2nd ed., 1975).

Bate, Stanley (Richard), English composer and pianist; b. Plymouth, Dec. 12, 1911; d. (suicide) London, Oct. 19, 1959. He studied composition with Vaughan Williams, Morris, and Jacob and piano with Benjamin at the Royal College of Music in London (1932–36), and then pursued composition training with Boulanger in Paris and Hindemith in Berlin. He toured widely as a pianist. In 1938 he married **Peggy Glanville-Hicks**; they divorced in 1948. He wrote music in a finely structured cosmopolitan manner, making use of modern devices but observing the classical forms and shunning doctrinaire systems.

WORKS: DRAMATIC: BALLETS: *Eros* (1935); *Goyescas* (1937); *Perseus* (1938); *Cap over Mill* (1938); *Highland Fling* (1947); *Troilus and Cressida* (1948); *Dance Variations* (1948); music for plays and films. **ORCH.:** 4 syms., including No. 3 (1940; Cheltenham, July 14, 1954) and No. 4 (London, Nov. 20, 1955); 2 sinfoniettas; 3 piano concertos; 3 violin concertos; Viola Concerto (1946); *Concerto grosso* for Piano and Strings (1952); Harpsichord Concerto (1953); Cello Concerto (1953). **CHAMBER:** Flute Sonata; 2 string quartets; Violin Sonata; Oboe Sonata; 2 piano sonatas and other pieces. **VOCAL:** Songs.

Bates, Leon, black American pianist; b. Philadelphia, Nov. 3, 1949. He began studying piano and violin when he was 6; at 7, gave his first piano recital in Philadelphia. From 1962 to 1967 he was a pupil of Irene Beck at the Philadelphia Settlement Music School; subsequently was a student of Natalie Hinderas at the Esther Boyer College of Music at Temple Univ. in Philadelphia. In 1969 he won the senior student audition of the Philadelphia Orch., and in 1970 he made a highly successful debut with that orch. under Ormandy's direction as soloist in Ravel's G Minor Concerto. In later seasons, he appeared as a soloist with various orchs., as a recitalist, and as a chamber music artist. While blessed with a virtuoso technique, Bates is also capable of the most refined playing. His repertoire is one of great diversity, ranging from the classics to the moderns. He has made a special effort to program works outside the mainstream, including 19th- and 20th-century American scores, jazz, and works by black and women composers. In 1992 he was soloist in the premiere of Hailstorck's 1st Piano Concerto.

Bath, Hubert, English composer and conductor; b. Barnstaple, Nov. 6, 1883; d. Harefield, Middlesex, April 24, 1945. He was a pupil of Beringer (piano) and Corder (composition) at the Royal Academy of Music in London; was active as a conductor of popular orch. and choral concerts.

WORKS: OPERAS: *Spanish Student* (1904); *Young England*, comic opera (Birmingham, 1915); *Bubbles* (Belfast, Nov. 26, 1923); *The Sire de Maletroit's Door* (n.d.); *The 3 Strangers* (n.d.); *Trilby* (n.d.). **ORCH.:** *Midshipman Easy*, overture (1911); *The Visions of Hannele*, symphonic poem (1913; rev. 1920); *African Suite* (n.d.); *Pierrette by the Stream*, suite (n.d.); *Woodland Scenes*, suite (n.d.). **OTHER:** 7 cantatas, chamber music, and songs.

Bathori, Jane (real name, **Jeanne-Marie Berthier**), French mezzo-soprano; b. Paris, June 14, 1877; d. there, Jan. 21, 1970. She studied voice with Émile Engel at the Paris Cons., whom she married in 1908; she also received training in violin and piano there. In 1898 she made her concert debut in Paris and in 1900 her operatic debut in Nantes. She subsequently devoted herself to a concert career, often accompanying herself at the piano in her recitals. She gave first performances of works by Debussy, Ravel, Satie, Milhaud, and others. During World War II, she lived in Buenos Aires. After the War, she returned to Paris, where she taught. She publ. *Conseils sur le chant* (Paris, 1929) and *Sur l'interprétation des mélodies de Claude Debussy* (Paris, 1953).

BIBL.: L. Cuneo-Laurent, *The Performer as Catalyst: The Role of the Singer J. B. (1877–1970) in the Careers of Debussy, Ravel, Les Six, and their Contemporaries in Paris 1904–1926* (diss., N.Y. Univ., 1982).

Báthy, Anna, Hungarian soprano; b. Beregszász, June 13, 1901; d. Budapest, May 20, 1962. She studied voice at the Academy of Music in Budapest. She made her operatic debut at the Municipal Theater in Budapest in 1928 as Elisabeth in *Tannhäuser*; in 1929 she joined the Budapest Opera, where she sang mostly Verdi and Wagner.

BIBL.: V. Somogyi and I. Molnár, *Báthy Anna* (Budapest, 1969).

Bátiz (Campbell), Enrique, Mexican conductor; b. Mexico City, May 4, 1942. He commenced piano lessons at an early age and made his first public appearance when he was only 5; following studies at the Univ. of Mexico (degree, 1959) and Southern Methodist Univ. in Dallas (1960–62), he continued his training at the Juilliard School of Music in N.Y. (1963–65) and undertook postgraduate work at the Warsaw Cons. In 1969 he made his conducting debut in Mexico City, and in 1971 founded the Orquesta Sinfónica del Estado de México, which developed into one of Mexico's leading orchs. From 1983 to 1990 he was artistic director of the Orquesta Filarmónica de la Ciudad de México; he also served (from 1984) as principal guest conductor of the Royal Phil. of London, which he conducted on a major tour of his homeland in 1988. He again served as conductor of the Orquesta Sinfónica del Estado de México from 1990.

Battle, Kathleen (Deanna), outstanding black American soprano; b. Portsmouth, Ohio, Aug. 13, 1948. She studied with Franklin Bens at the Univ. of Cincinnati College-Cons. of Music

(B.Mus., 1970; M.Mus., 1971). After making her professional debut as a soloist in the Brahms *Requiem* at the Spoleto Festival in 1972, she pursued further training with Italo Tajo in Cincinnati. In 1974 she captured 1st prize in the WGN-Illinois Opera Guild Auditions of the Air and in 1975 1st prize in the Young Artists Awards in Washington, D.C. In 1975 she made her formal operatic debut as Rosina with the Michigan Opera Theatre in Detroit, and later that year her first appearance at the N.Y. City Opera as Mozart's Susanna. On Dec. 22, 1977, she made her Metropolitan Opera debut in N.Y. as the Shepherd in *Tannhäuser*, and quickly established herself as one of its most esteemed artists via such roles as Massenet's and Strauss's Sophie, Despina, Blondchen, Zerlina, and Pamina. She also appeared with other major opera houses in the U.S. and Europe, and toured extensively as a soloist with leading orchs. and as a recitalist. On June 17, 1985, she made her Covent Garden debut in London as Zerbinetta. In 1987 she appeared as soloist at the New Year's Day Concert of the Vienna Phil. conducted by Karajan, which was telecast throughout the world. Although Battle's vocal gifts were undeniable, she acquired a reputation as an extremely temperamental artist. In Jan. 1993 she quit the Metropolitan Opera's production of *Der Rosenkavalier* during rehearsal. During rehearsal for her starring role in its revival of *La Fille du Régiment* on Feb. 7, 1994, general manager Joseph Volpe found her behavior so objectionable that he summarily dismissed her from the Metropolitan Opera roster.

Baud-Bovy, Samuel, Swiss music educator; b. Geneva, Nov. 27, 1906; d. there, Nov. 2, 1986. He studied at the Univ. of Geneva; after studying violin with Closset at the Geneva Cons., conducting with Nilius and music history with Adler in Vienna, composition with Dukas and musicology with Pirro in Paris, and conducting with Weingartner in Basel and Scherchen in Geneva, he returned to the Univ. of Geneva to take his doctorat ès lettres in 1936. He was an orch. teacher (1933–73) and a conductor (1942–73) at the Geneva Cons., where he also served as co-principal (1947–57) and principal (1957–70); was also director of studies (from 1931) and an assistant prof. (from 1942) at the Univ. of Geneva. From 1961 to 1963 he was president of the International Soc. for Music Education. He was an authority on Greek folk music, of which he publ. several collections. In addition to many scholarly articles in music journals, he publ. the books *La chanson populaire grecque du Dodécanèse* (Paris, 1936), *Études sur la chanson cleftique* (Athens, 1958), and *Essai sur la chanson populaire grecque* (Athens, 1983).

BIBL.: R. Brandl and E. Konstantinou, eds., *Griechische Musik und Europa: Antike-Byzanz-Volksmusik der Neuzeit: Im Gedenken an S. B.-B.* (Alano, 1988).

Baudo, Serge (Paul), French conductor, nephew of **Paul Tortelier**; b. Marseilles, July 16, 1927. His father was a prof. of oboe at the Paris Cons. He studied conducting with Fourestier and theory with Jean and Noël Gallon at the Paris Cons., winning premiers prix in harmony, percussion, chamber music, and conducting. After serving as conductor of the orch. of Radio Nice (1959–62), he conducted at the Paris Opéra (1962–65). He held the post of 1st conductor of the Orchestre de Paris from 1967 to 1970. On Sept. 16, 1970, he made his Metropolitan Opera debut in N.Y. conducting *Les Contes d'Hoffmann*. He was music director of the Lyons Opéra (1969–71), and then of the Orchestre Philharmonique Rhône-Alpes (later known as the Orchestre National de Lyons) from 1971 to 1987. He was also the founder-artistic director of the Berlioz Festival in Lyons (1979–89).

Baudrier, Yves (Marie), French composer; b. Paris, Feb. 11, 1906; d. there, Nov. 9, 1988. He spent his entire life in Paris. While mainly autodidact as a composer, he studied with the organist of Sacre-Coeur, Georges Loth (1929–33), and received advice from Messiaen (1935) before taking lessons in counterpoint with Daniel-Lesur at the Schola Cantorum. With Messiaen, Jolivet, and Daniel-Lesur, he founded the group Le Jeune France in 1936. He also helped to found the IDHEC (Institut des Hautes Études Cinématographiques), with which he was active from 1945 to 1965. He publ. *L'intelligence et la musique* (Paris, 1950).

WORKS: DRAMATIC: *Treize histoires liées par un fil de flûte*, ballet radiophonique (1967); film scores, including *La Bataille du rail* (1945), *Les Maudits* (1947), *Château de verre* (1950), and *Le Monde de silence* (1955); stage and television music. **ORCH.:** *Le Chant de jeunesse* (1935); *Raz de sein*, symphonic poem (1936); *Le Musicien dans la cité* (1936–37; rev. 1947 and 1964); *Eleonora* for Ondes Martenot and Chamber Orch. (1938); Suite for Strings (1938); *Le Grand Voilier*, symphonic poem (1939); Sym. (1944); *Prélude à quelque sortilèges* (1953); *Partition trouvée dans une bouteille* (1963). **CHAMBER:** *Deux Images* for Flute and Piano (1938); 2 string quartets (1940; *Autour de Mallarmé*, 1961); Suite for Trumpet (1966); piano music. **VOCAL:** *Agnus Dei* for Chorus and Organ (1938); *Cantate de la Pentecôte* for Women's Chorus and Small Orch. (1952; in collaboration with M. Constant and M. Rosenthal); *Credo adjuva Domine . . .* for Chorus and Orch. (1960); many songs.

BIBL.: S. Gut, *Le Groupe Jeune France* (Paris, 1977).

Bauer, Harold, distinguished English-born American pianist and teacher; b. New Malden, Surrey, April 28, 1873; d. Miami, March 12, 1951. He studied violin with his father and Adolf Politzer; from the age of 9, made appearances as a violinist. When he was 19 he appeared as a pianist in London, and then had lessons from Paderewski in Paris, where he played in 1893. After touring Europe, he made his U.S. debut as soloist with the Boston Sym. Orch. in 1900, and subsequently played in major U.S. cities. In 1912 he was awarded the Gold Medal of the Royal Phil. Soc. of London. During World War I, he settled in the U.S. and became a naturalized American citizen. He was founder-director of the Beethoven Assn. of N.Y. (1918–41), an esteemed chamber music society; he also was active as a teacher. He publ. *Harold Bauer, His Book* (N.Y., 1948). Bauer was particularly known as an interpreter of Beethoven, but he was also admired for his performances of Brahms, Franck, Debussy, and Ravel.

Bauer, Marion (Eugenie), American composer, teacher, and writer on music; b. Walla Walla, Wash., Aug. 15, 1887; d. South Hadley, Mass., Aug. 9, 1955. She began her training with her father, an amateur musician. In 1904 she went to N.Y. to study with Huss; after piano lessons with Pugno in Paris (1905), she returned to N.Y. in 1907 to study theory with Eugene Heffley. In 1910 she went to Germany to pursue composition lessons with Rothwell, and then to Paris in 1923 to complete her training with André Gédalge (fugue) and Boulanger (composition). She taught at N.Y. Univ. (1926–51), Chautauqua (from 1928), and the Juilliard School of Music in N.Y. (1940–44). Her music oscillated pleasurably between German Romanticism and Gallic Impressionism.

WRITINGS (all publ. in N.Y.): with E. Peyser, *How Music Grew: From Prehistoric Times to the Present Day* (1925; 2nd ed., rev., 1939); with E. Peyser, *Music Through the Ages: A Narrative for Student and Layman* (1932; 2nd ed., rev., 1946; 3rd ed., rev. and enl., 1967 by E. Rogers as *Music Through the Ages: An Introduction to Music History*); *Twentieth Century Music* (1933; 2nd ed., rev., 1947); *Musical Questions and Quizzes: A Digest of Information About Music* (1941); with E. Peyser, *How Opera Grew: From Ancient Greece to the Present Day* (1956).

WORKS: ORCH.: *Indian Pipes* (1927; orchestrated by M. Bernstein; arr. for Piano, 1928); *Lament on African Themes* for Chamber Orch. (1928); Symphonic Suite for Strings (1940); Piano Concerto, *American Youth* (1943); Sym. (1947–50). **CHAMBER:** *Allegro giocoso* for 11 Instruments (1920); Violin Sonata (1922); String Quartet (1928); Sonata for Viola or Clarinet and Piano (1935); Concertino for Oboe, Clarinet, and String Quartet (1939–43); 2 trio sonatas (1944, 1951); *Aquarelle* for Woodwinds or Chamber Orch. (1948). **PIANO:** *In the Country*

(1913); *From New Hampshire Woods* (1921); *Sun Splendor* (1926); *Dance Sonata* (1932); *2 Aquarelles* (1945). **VOCAL:** Many choruses and songs.

BIBL.: N. Stewart, *The Solo Piano Music of M. B.* (diss., Univ. of Cincinnati, 1990).

Bauer-Theussl, Franz (Ferdinand), Austrian conductor; b. Zillingdorf, Sept. 25, 1928. He was a pupil of Seidlhofer (piano) and Clemens Krauss (conducting) at the Vienna Academy of Music. After making his conducting debut with *Les Contes d'Hoffmann* at the Salzburg Landestheater in 1953, he was assistant conductor at the Salzburg Festivals (1953–57); then was resident conductor of the Vienna Volksoper (from 1957) and conductor of the Netherlands Opera in Amsterdam (1960–64).

Bauld, Alison (Margaret), Australian composer; b. Sydney, May 7, 1944. After training at the National Inst. of Dramatic Art, she studied at the Univ. of Sydney (B.Mus., 1968); then was a scholarship student of Lutyens and Keller, completing her education at the Univ. of York (Ph.D., 1974). She was music director of the Laban Centre for Dance at the Univ. of London (1975–78) and composer-in-residence at the New South Wales State Conservatorium in Sydney (1978). Later she was a part-time instructor at Hollins College in London.

WORKS: *On the Afternoon of the Pigsty* for Female Speaker, Piano, Alto Melodica, and Percussion (1971); *In a Dead Brown Land* for 2 Mime Actors, 2 Speakers, Soprano, Tenor, Chorus, and 5 Instruments (1971); *Humpty Dumpty* for Tenor, Flute, and Guitar (1972); *Pumpkin 2* for 4 Actors and 5 Instruments (London, June 21, 1973); *Egg* for Tenor, Flute, Cello, and Percussion (Snape, June 25, 1973); *Mad Moll* for Soprano (1973); *1 Pearl* for Soprano or Countertenor and String Quartet (Southampton, Nov. 11, 1973; also known as *1 Pearl II* for Soprano, Alto Flute, and String Orch., London, April 30, 1976); *Exiles* for 4 Actors, Tenor, Mezzo-soprano, Chorus, Flute, Alto Melodica, Percussion, and String Quartet (1974; Sydney, May 1975); *Concert* for Pianist and Tape (1st half for mime only, 2nd half for tape only; Sydney, Dec. 1974); *The Busker's Story* for Alto Saxophone, Bassoon, Trumpet, Violin, and Double Bass (Sydney, Sept. 25, 1978); *Richard III* for Voice and String Quartet (BBC, July 4, 1985); *Monday* for Flute (Sydney, Oct. 1, 1985); *Once upon a Time* for 5 Vocal Soloists and Small Chamber Orch. (BBC, Dec. 29, 1986); *Nell*, ballad opera (London, June 1, 1988); *My Own Island* for Clarinet and Piano (1989); *Farewell Already* for String Quartet (1993).

Baum, Kurt, Czech-born American tenor; b. Prague, March 15, 1908; d. N.Y., Dec. 27, 1989. He studied with Garbin in Milan and Scolari in Rome; in 1933, won the Vienna International Competition, then made his operatic debut in the premiere of Zemlinsky's *Der Kreidekreis* in Zürich (Oct. 14, 1933). After singing with the German Theater in Prague (1934–39), he made his U.S. debut as Radames in Chicago in 1939, where he sang until 1941. On Nov. 27, 1941 he made his Metropolitan Opera debut in N.Y. as the Singer in *Der Rosenkavalier*, remaining on its roster until 1962, and again from 1964 to 1966; also made guest appearances at Milan's La Scala (1947–48), the Florence Maggio Musicale (1952), London's Covent Garden (1953), the San Francisco Opera, and in South America.

Baumann, Hermann (Rudolf Konrad), noted German horn player and pedagogue; b. Hamburg, Aug. 1, 1934. He studied in Hamburg; then played 1st horn in Dortmund (1957–61) and with the Stuttgart Radio Sym. Orch. (1961–67); won the International Music Competition in Munich in 1964, and made tours in Germany and abroad. In 1969 he was appointed a prof. at the Staatliche Folkwang Hochschule in Essen, and, in 1980, at the Hochschule für Musik in Stuttgart. After appearing as soloist with the Buffalo Phil. in N.Y. on Jan. 12, 1993, he suffered a stroke.

Baumann, Max Georg, German conductor, teacher, and composer; b. Kronach, Nov. 20, 1917. From 1939 to 1943 he studied composition and conducting at the Berlin Hochschule für Musik, where his teachers included Blacher and Distler; he became a lecturer there in 1946, and a prof. in 1953; was named director of its school music dept. in 1963; also made appearances as a conductor with the Berlin Collegium Musicum. He composed much sacred vocal music, including masses, motets, a cantata, and an oratorio; also a ballet, *Pelléas und Mélisande* (1954).

BIBL.: A. Geck-Böttger and J. Overath, eds., *Te decet hymnus: Festgabe für M. B. zur Vollendung des 75. Lebensjahres* (Sankt Augustin, 1992).

Baumgartner, Paul, Swiss pianist and pedagogue; b. Altstätten, July 21, 1903; d. Locarno, Oct. 19, 1976. He was a student of Paul Müller in St. Gallen, Walter Braunfels in Munich, and Eduard Erdmann in Cologne. He was active as both a soloist and chamber music player. He taught at the Rheinische Musikschule and the Hochschule für Musik in Cologne (1927–35), and then was head of the piano dept. at the Basel Cons. (from 1937); after teaching at the Hannover Hochschule für Musik (1952–61), he was head of piano master classes at the Basel Academy of Music (from 1961).

Baumgartner, Rudolf, Swiss violinist and conductor; b. Zürich, Sept. 14, 1917. He studied at the Univ. and Cons. in Zürich, and then pursued violin training in Paris and Vienna, his principal mentors being Geyer, Flesch, and Schneiderhan. He then performed as a violin soloist and in chamber music ensembles; in 1965 he co-founded (with Schneiderhan) the Festival Strings Lucerne, which he served as director; also was director of the Lucerne Cons. (1960–87) and the Lucerne Festival (1968–80).

Baur, Jürg, esteemed German composer and pedagogue; b. Düsseldorf, Nov. 11, 1918. He was a student of Philipp Jarnach (composition) and Michael Schneider (organ) at the Cologne Cons. (1937–39). During military service in World War II (1939–45), he was taken prisoner-of-war by the Russians; after his release, he returned to Cologne to continue his music training (1946–48); then studied musicology with Fellerer at the Univ. there (1948–51). He also was a lecturer in theory at the Robert Schumann Cons. in Düsseldorf (1946). From 1952 to 1966 he served as choirmaster at the Pauluskirche in Düsseldorf. In 1965 he became director of the Robert Schumann Cons. there, and in 1969 was made a prof. From 1971 to 1991 he was prof. of composition at the Cologne Hochschule für Musik. In 1957 he received the Robert Schumann Prize of the City of Düsseldorf and in 1994 the music prize of the City of Duisburg. In his early works, Baur was much influenced by Bartók and Hindemith. He later pursued a highly personal approach to the utilization of dodecaphony, serialism, and aleatory, which blossomed into an admirably crafted synthesis of styles.

WORKS: ORCH.: Concerto for Strings (1941–48; Bochum, April 11, 1958); Overture (1946–50; Düsseldorf, April 19, 1951); *Partita über "Wie schön leuchtet der Morgenstern"* for Trumpet and Strings (1946–91); *Carmen-Variationen* (1947; Düsseldorf, May 23, 1983); Concerto for Viola and Chamber Orch. (Cologne, April 22, 1951); *Musik* for Strings (1952–53; Duisburg, July 3, 1954); *Sinfonia montana* (1953; Weimar, May 23, 1955)); *Konzertante Musik* for Piano and Orch. (1958; Düsseldorf, Jan. 26, 1959); Concertino for Flute, Oboe, Clarinet, Strings, and Timpani (Wuppertal, Aug. 16, 1959); *Concerto Romano* for Oboe and Orch. (1960; Münster, Feb. 19, 1961); *Romeo und Julia* (1962–63; Düsseldorf, Sept. 19, 1963); *Piccolo mondo* (1963; 1st complete perf., Darmstadt, May 21, 1966); *Lo Specchio I* (1965; Düsseldorf, May 5, 1966) and *II* (1966; Munich, July 9, 1967); *Sinfonischer Prolog* (Münster, Nov. 5, 1966); *Pentagram*, Wind Quintet concerto (Essen, Nov. 25, 1966; rev. 1969; Hannover, Feb. 9, 1970); *Abbreviaturen* for 13 Solo Strings (Zagreb, May 7, 1969); *Concerto Ticino* for Clarinet and Orch. (1970; Düsseldorf, Jan. 7, 1971); *Giorno per giorno*, "in memoriam B.A. Zimmermann" (Aachen, June 2, 1971); *Musik mit Robert Schumann* (Hananover, March 13, 1972); *Vier Por-*

traits for Cello and Orch. (Saarbrücken, Dec. 18, 1972); *Sinfonia breve* (Augsburg, April 8, 1974; rev. 1974; Münster, June 2, 1976); *Triton-Sinfonietta* for Chamber Orch. (1974; Dortmund, Jan. 26, 1975); *Concerto da camera* for Recorder and Chamber Orch. (Essen, May 4, 1975); 2 violin concertos: No. 1, *Ich sag ade* (Bielefeld, June 25, 1976) and No. 2 (Düsseldorf, Nov. 16, 1978); *Sentimento del tempo* for Oboe, Clarinet, Bassoon, and Orch. (Gelsenkirchen, Nov. 24, 1980); *Sinfonische Metamorphosen über Gesualdo* (1981; Bremen, Feb. 1, 1982); 2 syms: No. 1, *Sinfonie einer Stadt (Pathetica)* for the 1,100th anniversary of Duisburg (Duisburg, Sept. 7, 1983) and No. 2, *Aus dem Tagebuch des Alten* (1987; Dortmund, March 14, 1988); *Fresken* for Chamber Orch. (1984; Saarbrücken, Nov. 28, 1985); *Konzertante Fantasie* for Organ and Strings (1984–85; Halle, Jan. 30, 1985); *Sentieri musicale*, sinfonietta (1990; Hannover, April 8, 1991). **CHAMBER:** 2 unnumbered string quartets (1935, 1938); 3 numbered string quartets: No. 1 (1938–46; Düsseldorf, Oct. 19, 1946), No. 2 (1942–46; Düsseldorf, April 30, 1949), and No. 3 (1952; Düsseldorf, April 20, 1954); *Fantasie and Fuge* for String Quartet (1941); Violin Sonata (1943–48; Cologne, May 10, 1950); *Ostinato und Trio* for Flute, Oboe, 2 Clarinets, and 2 Bassoons (1948); *Musik* for Cello and Piano (1950); *Reminiszenzen* for Wind Quintet, "in memoriam Paul Hindemith" (1950–80; Aachen, April 25, 1981); *Fantasie* for Oboe and Piano (1954); *Quintetto sereno* for Flute, Oboe, Clarinet, Horn, and Bassoon (Düsseldorf, May 21, 1958); *Metamorphosen* for Violin, Cello, and Piano (1959–60); *Ballata Romana* for Clarinet and Piano (1960; also for Alto Saxophone and Piano, 1991); *Incontri (Begegnungen)*, 3 pieces for Recorder and Piano (1960; also for Flute and Piano); Sonata for Solo Violin (1961–62; Karlsruhe, Nov. 27, 1963); *Divertimento*, 3 fantasies for Harpsichord and Percussion (1961–62; also for Accordion and Percussion, 1990); *Mutazioni* for Recorder (1962) and for Flute (1962); *Dialoge* for Cello and Piano (1962); *Pezzi uccelli* for Recorder (1964); *3 Fantasien* for Guitar (1964); *Kontraste* for Violin, Viola, and Cello (1964); *6 Bagatellen* for Clarinet or Bass Clarinet (1964); Sonata for Solo Viola (1969; Gelsenkirchen, Feb. 14, 1971); *Movimenti* for Violin, Horn, and Piano (1969–70); *Cinque Impressioni* for String Quartet (1970; Munich, Jan. 20, 1971); *Tre studi per quattro* for Recorder Quartet (1972); *Nonett-Skizzen* for Wind Quintet and String Quartet (1973); *Skizzen* for Flute, Oboe, Clarinet, Horn, and Bassoon (Stuttgart, June 17, 1974); *Moments musicaux* for Violin and Piano (1976); *Kontrapunkte 77* for Flute, English Horn, and Bassoon (Düsseldorf, April 1, 1977); *Echoi: Hirtenrufe und Weisen* for 2 Oboes and English Horn (1980); *Pour rien* for 2 Clarinets, 2 Horns, and 2 Bassoon (1980; Krefeld, Sept. 24, 1982); *Ricordi* for 3 Recorders (1983); *Ritratti* for Percussionists, Celesta, and Bass Instrument (Düsseldorf, June 3, 1984); *Cinque foglie* for Saxophone Quartet (1986; Rottenburg, Feb. 1, 1987); *Quintetto pittoresco* for Wind Quintet (1986; Lüdenscheid, Nov. 11, 1987); *Passacaglia* for 4 Trumpets and 4 Trombones (1989; Düsseldorf, May 20, 1990); *Arabesken, Girlanden, Figuren* for Contrabassoon (1990); *Marginalien über Mozart* for Guitar (1991); *Reflexionen* for Guitar and Organ (1991; also for Guitar and Accordion, 1992); *Petite suite* for Flute Quartet (Düsseldorf, Nov. 17, 1992); *Et respice finem* for String Quartet (Saarbrücken, Oct. 27, 1993); also piano pieces and organ music. **VOCAL:** *Triptychon* for Chorus and Orch. (1948–49); *Im Waldesschatten*, 5 songs for Baritone and Piano (1952; also for Baritone and String Quartet, 1980); *Pfingstmotette: Wer mich liebt* for Baritone and Chorus (1955; Düsseldorf, May 13, 1956); *Vom tiefinnern Sang*, song cycle for Mezzo-soprano and Piano (1957; Düsseldorf, April 25, 1958; also for Mezzo-soprano, Clarinet, and String Quartet, 1989; Bochum, March 12, 1990); *Herb stirb oder singe*, 4 songs for High Voice and Piano (1960; Düsseldorf, June 11, 1961; also for Soprano, Flute, and String Orch., 1964; Baden-Baden, March 29, 1965; also for High Voice, Flute, and String Quartet, Düsseldorf, Sept. 12, 1984); *Mit wechselndem Schlüssel* for Baritone and Piano (1967); *Perché (Warum?)* for Soli, Chorus, and Orch. (1967–68; Düsseldorf, Oct. 24, 1968; also for Soli and Chorus, 1969; Ludwigsburg, Oct. 24, 1970); *Die Blume des Scharon*, 3 lyric motets for Chorus (1979; Aachen, March 12, 1983); other choral pieces and songs.

BIBL.: J. Scholl, ed., *Der Komponist J. B.: Eine Dokumentation* (Düsseldorf, 1993).

Bautista, Julián, Spanish composer; b. Madrid, April 21, 1901; d. Buenos Aires, July 8, 1961. He studied violin with Julio Francés, piano with Pilar Fernández de la Mora, and composition with Conrado del Campo at the Madrid Cons.; then taught there during the Spanish Civil War. After Madrid fell in 1939, Bautista fled to Argentina, where he was on the faculty of the National Cons. of Buenos Aires. His music, delicately colored and rhythmically robust, invariably reflected Spanish folk melodies.

WORKS: *Juerga*, ballet (1921); *Colores*, 6 piano pieces (1922); Sonatina for String Trio (1924); *Obertura para una ópera grotesca* for Orch. (1932); *Tres ciudades* for Voice and Orch. (1937); *4 poemas gallegos* for Voice, Flute, Oboe, Clarinet, Viola, Cello, and Harp (1946); 2 syms. (*Sinfonia breve*, 1956; 1957); 3 string quartets; songs.

Bavicchi, John (Alexander), American conductor, teacher, and composer; b. Boston, April 25, 1922. He studied at the New England Cons. of Music in Boston with Carl McKinley and Francis Judd Cooke (B.M., 1952); then attended Harvard Univ. Graduate School, taking courses in theory with Archibald T. Davison, composition with Piston, and musicology with Otto Gombosi (1952–55). He served in the U.S. Navy during World War II, and saw action in Guadalcanal, Okinawa, and Japan (1943–45). Returning to Boston after the war, he devoted himself to teaching, composing, and conducting; led the Arlington-Belmont Chorale; lectured on music history at the Cambridge Center for Adult Education (1960–73). He also conducted the American Festival Ballet Co. (1962–65) and the Arlington Phil. (1968–82). His music is couched in Classical forms, while presenting a variegated texture of decidedly modernistic invention.

WORKS: ORCH.: Concerto for Clarinet and Strings (1954); Suite No. 1 (1955); *A Concert Overture* (1957); *Fantasy* for Harp and Chamber Orch. (1959); Concertante for Oboe, Bassoon, and Strings (1961); *Caroline's Dance* (1974–75); *Mont Blanc*, overture (1976–77); *Music* for Small Orch. (1981); *Fusions* for Trombone and Orch. (1984–85); *Pyramid* (1986); *Canto I* for String Orch. (1987) and *III* for Concert Band (1991); *Sherbrooke West* (1988) Concerto for Tuba and Concert Band (1988). **CHAMBER:** 10 trios for a variety of instrumental combinations (1950–83); 2 cello sonatas (1953, 1956); 2 sonatas for Solo Clarinet (1956, 1959); Brass Quartet No. 1 (1956); *A Musical Sketchbook* for Flute, or for Flute, Oboe, Clarinet, Bassoon, and Piano (1960); String Quartet (1960); 2 woodwind quintets (1961, 1973); *Music* for Horn and Piano (1980); Concertino for Tuba and Brass Quartet (1984); Flute Sonata (1986); *Triptych* for Multiple Horns (1987); *Canto II* for Clarinet (1990) and *IV* for Flute, Bassoon, Violin, and Piano (1992); Violin Sonatina (1993); piano pieces. **VOCAL:** *4 Songs* for Contralto and Orch. (1952); *3 Psalms* for Soloists, Chorus, 2 Trumpets, and String Orch. (1963); *There is Sweet Music Here* for Soprano and Orch. (1985); *6 Songs to Poems of William Blake* for Soprano, Violin, and Piano (1987); *Songs of Remembrance* for Soloists, Chorus, and Orch. (1990); *Talk to Me* for Chorus and Piano (1992); *Infinite Patience* for Mezzo-soprano, Clarinet, and Piano (1992).

Bax, Sir Arnold (Edward Trevor), outstanding English composer; b. London, Nov. 8, 1883; d. Cork, Ireland, Oct. 3, 1953. He entered the Royal Academy of Music in London in 1900; studied piano with Matthay and composition with Corder there; won the Academy's Gold Medal as a pianist in 1905, the year in which he completed his studies. After a visit to Dresden in 1905, he went to Ireland. Although not ethnically Irish, he became interested in ancient Irish folklore; wrote poetry and prose under the name of Dermot O'Byrne; also found inspiration in Celtic legends for his work as a composer. In 1910 he returned to England. In 1931 he received the Gold Medal of the Royal Phil. Soc. of London; was awarded honorary degrees from the univs. of Oxford (1934) and Durham (1935); was knighted at the Coronation of King George VI in 1937; was made Master of the King's Musick in 1941. Bax was an excellent pianist, but was reluctant to play in public; he also never appeared as a conductor of his own works. He was a prolific composer; his style is rooted in neo-Romanticism, but impressionistic elements are much in evidence in his instrumental compositions; his harmonies are elaborate and rich in chromatic progressions; his contrapuntal fabric is free and emphasizes complete independence of component melodies. In his many settings of folk songs, he succeeded in adapting simple melodies to effective accompaniments in modern harmonies; in his adaptations of early English songs, he successfully re-created the archaic style of the epoch. He recorded the story of his life and travels in his candid autobiography, *Farewell, My Youth* (London, 1943, ed. by L. Foreman, 1992, as *Farewell, My Youth and Other Writings*).

WORKS: DRAMATIC: BALLETS: *King Kojata* (1911); *Between Dusk and Dawn* (1917); *The Frog Skin* (1918). **INCIDENTAL MUSIC:** *The Truth about the Russian Dancers* (1920; rev. 1926); *Golden Eagle* (1945). **FILM MUSIC:** *Malta GC* (1942; orch. suite, 1943); *Oliver Twist* (1948; orch. suite, 1948); *Journey into History* (1952). **ORCH.:** 14 tone poems: *Cathaleen-ni-Hoolihan* for Small Orch. (1903–05); *A Song of Life and Love* (1905); *A Song of War and Victory* (1905); *Eire: Into the Twilight* (1908); *In the Faery Hills* (1909); *Rosc-Catha* (1910); *Christmas Eve on the Mountains* (1911; rev. c.1933); *Nympholept* (1912–15); *The Garden of Fand* (1913–16); *The Happy Forest* (1914–21); *November Woods* (1917); *Tintagel* (1917–19); *The Tale the Pine-trees Knew* (1931); *A Legend* (1944); *Variations: Improvisations* (1904); *A Connemara Revel* (1905); *An Irish Overture* (1906); *Festival Overture* (1911; rev. 1918); *Prelude to Adonais* (1912); *4 Pieces* (also known as *4 Sketches* or *4 Irish Pieces*) (1912–13; rev. 1928); *Spring Fire*, sym. (1913); *Symphonic Scherzo* (arr. from a piano piece; orchestrated 1917; rev. 1933); *Symphonic Variations* for Piano and Orch. (1918); *Russian Suite* (arr. from piano pieces; 1919); *Summer Music* (1917–20; rev. 1932); *Phantasy*, viola concerto (1920); 7 syms: No. 1 (1921; London, Dec. 4, 1922), No. 2 (1924–25; Boston, Dec. 13, 1929), No. 3 (1929; London, March 14, 1930), No. 4 (1930; San Francisco, March 16, 1932), No. 5 (1931; London, Jan. 15, 1934), No. 6 (1934; London, Nov. 21, 1935), and No. 7 (N.Y., June 9, 1939); *Mediterranean* (arr. from a piano piece; 1922); *Cortège* (1925); *Romantic Overture* for Chamber Orch. (1926); *Overture, Elegy and Rondo* (1927); *Northern Ballad* Nos. 1 (1927–31) and 2 (1934); *Prelude for a Solemn Occasion* (1927–33); *3 Pieces* (1928); *Overture to a Picaresque Comedy* (1930); *Winter Legends*, sinfonia concertante for Piano and Orch. (1930); *Sinfonietta* (1932); Cello Concerto (1932); *Rogue's Comedy Overture* (1936); *Overture to Adventure* (1936); *London Pageant* (1937); *Paean* (arr. from a piano piece; 1938); Violin Concerto (1938); *Work in Progress*, overture (1943); *Morning Song: Maytime in Sussex* for Piano and Orch. (c.1946); Concertante for English Horn, Clarinet, Horn, and Orch. (1948); *Variations on the Name Gabriel Fauré* for Harp and Strings (1949; also for Piano); Concertante, concerto for Piano, Left-hand and Orch. (1949); *Coronation March* (1953). **CHAMBER:** 2 unnumbered string quartets (1902, 1903); 3 numbered string quartets (1918, 1925, 1936); *Concert Piece* for Violin or Viola and Piano (1903); *Fantasy* for Violin or Viola and Piano (1904); 2 piano trios (1906, 1946); 2 string quintets (1908, 1933); 3 violin sonatas (1910, rev. 1915, 1920, and 1945; 1915, rev. 1920; 1927); *4 Pieces* for Flute and Piano (1912); 2 piano quintets (1915, 1922); *Legend* for Violin and Piano (1915); *4 Pieces* for Violin and Piano (1915); *Ballad* for Violin and Piano (1916); *Elegiac Trio* for Flute, Viola, and Harp (1916); *Im memoriam* for English Horn, Harp, and String Quartet (1917); *Folk Tale* for Cello and Piano (1918); Harp Quintet (1919); Viola Sonata (1922); Oboe Quintet (1922); Cello Sonata (1923); *Fantasy Sonata* for Viola and Harp (1927); Sonatina for Flute and Harp (1928; arr. as the Concerto for Flute, Oboe, Harp, and String Quartet, 1936); *Legend* for Viola and Piano (1929); Nonet for Flute, Oboe, Clarinet, Harp, String Quartet, and Double Bass (1930); Cello Sonatina (1933); Clarinet Sonata (1934); Octet for Horn, Piano, and String Sextet (1934); *Threnody and Scherzo* for Bassoon, Harp, and String Sextet (1936); *Rhapsodic Ballad* for Cello (1939); *Legend-Sonata* for Cello and Piano (1943). **PIANO:** *Fantasia* for Piano Duo (1900); 3 unnumbered sonatas; 4 numbered sonatas (1910, rev. 1921; 1919; 1926; 1932); *Concert Valse* (1910); *2 Russian Tone Pictures: May Night in the Ukraine* and *Gopak* (1912); *Toccata* (1913); *The Princess's Rose Garden* (1915); *In a Vodka Shop* (1915); *The Maiden with the Daffodil* (1915); *Apple Blossom Time* (1915); *Sleep Head* (1915); *A Mountain Mood* (1915); *Winter Waters* (1915); *Dream in Exile* (1916); *Nereid* (1916); *Moy Mell (The Pleasant Plain: An Irish Tone Poem)* for Piano Duo (1917); *On a May Evening* (1918); *Whirligig* (1919); *The Slave Girl* (1919); *What the Minstrel Told Us* (1919); *Lullaby* (1920); *Burlesque* (1920); *Ceremonial Dance* (1920); *Country-Tune* (1920); *A Hill Tune* (1920); *Mediterranean* (1920); *Paean* (1920); *Serpent Dance* (1920); *Water Music* (1920); *Hardanger* for Piano Duo (1927); *The Poisoned Fountain* for Piano Duo (1928); Duo Sonata (1929); *The Devil that Tempted St Anthony* for Piano Duo (1929); *Red Autumn* for Piano Duo (1931); *O Dame Get Up and Bake Your Pies* (1945). **VOCAL: CHORAL:** *Fatherland* for Tenor, Chorus, and Orch. (1907; rev. 1934); *Enchanted Summer* for 2 Sopranos, Chorus, and Orch. (1910); *Of a Rose I Sing a Song* for Chorus, Harp, Cello, and Double Bass (1920); *Now Is the Time of Christymas* for Men's Voices, Flute, and Piano (1921); *Mater ora Filium* for Chorus (1921); *This Worldes Joie* for Chorus (1922); *The Boar's Head* for Men's Voices (1923); *I Sing of a Maiden that is Makeless* for Chorus (1923); *St. Patrick's Breastplate* for Chorus and Orch. (1923); *To the Name above Every Name* for Soprano, Chorus, and Orch. (1923); *Walsinghame* for Tenor, Chorus, and Orch. (1926); *The Morning Watch* for Chorus and Orch. (1935); *5 Fantasies on Polish Christmas Carols* for Unison Treble Voices and Strings (1942); *5 Greek Folksongs* for Chorus (1944); *To Russia* for Baritone, Chorus, and Orch. (1944); *Nunc dimittis* for Chorus and Organ (1944); *Te Deum* for Chorus and Organ (1944); *Gloria* for Chorus and Organ (1945); *Epithalamium* for Chorus and Organ (1947); *Magnificat* for Chorus and Organ (1948); *What is it Like to be Young and Fair* for Chorus (1953); numerous solo songs, some with orch.

BIBL.: E. Evans, "A. B.," *Musical Quarterly* (April 1923); R. Hull, *A Handbook on A. B.'s Symphonies* (London, 1932); A. Fleischmann, "A. B.," *Recorded Sound* (Jan./April 1968); R. Foreman, "Bibliography of Writings on A. B.," *Current Musicology* 10 (1970); idem, "The Musical Development of A. B.," *Music & Letters* (Jan. 1971); C. Scott-Sutherland, *A. B.* (London, 1973); L. Foreman, *B.: A Composer and His Times* (London, 1983; 2nd ed., 1988).

Bay, Emmanuel, Russian pianist; b. Simferopol, Crimea, Jan. 20, 1891; d. Jerusalem, Dec. 2, 1967. In 1908 Bay enrolled at the St. Petersburg Cons., studying piano with Drosdov; graduated in 1913 with 1st prize. He subsequently took a master class in piano with Godowsky in Vienna. He became mainly known as an excellent accompanist; toured in that capacity with Zimbalist (1922–29) and with Heifetz (1931–51); also was accompanist to Elman, Milstein, Francescatti, Szigeti, Piatigorsky, Peerce, and Traubel.

Bayle, François, French composer and administrator; b. Tamatave, Madagascar, April 27, 1932. Following training in letters and mathematics in Bordeaux (1946–54), he went to Paris to study with Olivier Messiaen and to work with Pierre Schaeffer and the Groupe de Musique Concrète (1958–60); also attended Stockhausen's summer courses in new music in Darmstadt (1959–62). Returning to Paris, he became director of the Groupe de Musique Concrète in 1966, which became the Group de Recherches Musicales in 1968. He also served as director of the Institut National de l'Audiovisuel from 1975. He was the author of *Musique Acousmatique: Propositions . . . positions* (1993). In 1976 he received the Ordre du Mérite, in 1986 he was made a Commandeur des Arts et Lettres, and in 1990 he became a member of the Légion d'honneur. He wrote mainly electronic pieces, many of which are montages, collages, and acoustical barrages; these include *Trois portraits d'un oiseau qui n'existe pas* (1962); *L'Archipel* (1963); *Pluriel* (1963); *Espaces inhabitables* (1967); *Trois rêves d'oiseau* (1972); *Vibrations composées* (1973); *Camera obscura* (1976); *Erosphère* (1978–80); *Les Couleurs de la nuit* (1982); *Son Vitesse-Lumière* (1980–83); *Aéroformes* (1982–84); *Motion-Émotion* (1985–86); *Aêr* (1987); *Théâtre d'ombres* (1988–89); *Fabulae* (1990–91).

Bazelaire, Paul, French cellist, teacher, and composer; b. Sedan, March 4, 1886; d. Paris, Dec. 11, 1958. He graduated from the Paris Cons. as a cellist at the age of 11, with the premier prix; after a concert career, he was prof. of cello at the Paris Cons. (1918–56); founded a unique ensemble of 50 cellos. Among his compositions are *Suite française sur des chants populaires* for Orch.; *Cléopâtre*, symphonic poem (Paris, Jan. 23, 1908); *Suite grecque* for Small Orch. (1910); and *Rapsodie dans le style russe* for Cello and Orch. (Paris, Feb. 2, 1941). He also orchestrated Bach's 6 cello suites and publ. a teaching manual, *Pédagogie du violoncelle.*

Bazelon, Irwin (Allen), American composer; b. Evanston, Ill., June 4, 1922; d. N.Y., Aug. 2, 1995. He studied piano with Irving Harris and Magdalen Messmann, and composition with Leon Stein. After pursuing his education at De Paul Univ. in Chicago (B.A., 1944; M.A., 1945), he studied composition with Hindemith at Yale Univ., Milhaud at Mills College in Oakland, California (1946–48), and Ernest Bloch at the Univ. of Calif. at Berkeley (1947). In 1947 he settled in N.Y. He held fellowships at the MacDowell Colony (1948, 1950, 1951) and at Yaddo (1969). In 1974 he served as composer-in-residence of the Wolf Trap Farm Park in Vienna, Va. He publ. *Knowing the Score: Notes on Film Music* (1975). In his works, Bazelon made use of quaquaversal techniques, ranging from rudimentary triadic progressions to complex dodecaphonic structures infused with syncopated jazz rhythms.

WORKS: ORCH.: *Adagio and Fugue* for Strings (1947); *Concerto Overture* (1951; N.Y., March 21, 1965); Suite for Small Orch. (1953); syms.: *Short Symphony: Testament to a Big City* (1961; Washington, D.C., Dec. 4, 1962); No. 1 (1962; Kansas City, Mo., Oct. 26, 1963); No. 3 (1962); No. 4 (1965; 1st movement perf. as *Dramatic Movement for Orchestra*, Seattle, Feb. 21, 1966); No. 5 (1967; Indianapolis, May 8, 1970); No. 6 (1969; Kansas City, Mo., Nov. 17, 1970); No. 7, *Ballet for Orchestra* (1980); No. 8 for Strings (1986); No. 8 1/2 (1988); No. 9, *Sunday Silence* (1992); No. 10 for Narrator, Soprano, Chorus, and Orch. (1995; unfinished); Symphonie concertante for Clarinet, Trumpet, Marimba, and Orch. (1963; Williamston, Mass., April 26, 1985); *Overture to Shakespeare's Taming of the Shrew* (Washington, D.C., May 1964); *Excursion* (1965; Kansas City, Mo., March 5, 1966); *Dramatic Fanfare* (1970); *A Quiet Piece for a Violent Time* (New Orleans, Oct. 28, 1975); *Spirits of the Night* (1976); *De-Tonations* for Brass Quintet and Orch. (1978; N.Y., April 3, 1979); *Memories of a Winter Childhood* (1981; Harrisburg, Pa., Dec. 5, 1989); *Spires* for Trumpet and Small Orch. (1981; Lille, Feb. 6, 1989); *Tides* for Clarinet and Small Orch. (1982); *For Tuba with Strings Attached* for Tuba and Strings (1982; also for Tuba and String Quartet); Piano Concerto, *Trajectories* (1985); *Motivations* for Trombone and Orch. (1986); *Fourscore + 2* for 4 Solo Percussionists and Orch. (1987; Houston, April 26, 1989); *Midnight Music* for Symphonic Wind Band (1990; Machester, England, Oct. 14, 1992); *Prelude to Hart Crane's The Bridge* for Strings (1991); *Entre Nous* for Cello and Orch. (1992; N.Y., Feb. 6, 1994); *Fire and Smoke* for Timpani and Wind Band (1993; Aspen, Colo., July 4, 1994). **CHAMBER:** 3 string quartets (n.d., 1947, 1995); *5 Pieces* for Cello and Piano (1952); Chamber Concerto No. 1 for Flute, Clarinet, Trumpet, Tuba, Violin, Piano, and Percussion (1956; N.Y., Jan. 20, 1957); Brass Quintet (1963; N.Y., March 22, 1964); *Early American Suite* for Flute, Oboe, Clarinet, Bassoon, Horn, and Harpsichord or Piano (1965); Duo for Viola and Piano (1970); *Churchill Downs Chamber Concerto* (N.Y., Oct. 1970); *Propulsions*, percussion concerto for 7 Players (1974; Boston, April 26, 1976); Wind Quintet (N.Y., May 22, 1975); *Concatenations* for Viola and Percussion Quartet (1976; Boston, May 1, 1977); *Double Crossings* for Trumpet and Percussion (1976); *Sound Dreams* for Flute, Clarinet, Viola, Cello, Piano, and Percussion (Boston, Nov. 13, 1977); *Triple Play* for 2 Trombones and Percussion (1977; Sheffield, England, March 11, 1982); *Cross Currents* for Brass Quintet and Percussion (1978; Cambridge, Mass., Jan. 16, 1981); *3 Men on a Dis-Course* for Clarinet, Cello, and Percussion (1979; N.Y., April 9, 1989); *Partnership* for 5 Timpani and Marimba (N.Y., May 19, 1980); *For Tuba with Strings Attached* for Tuba and String Quartet (1982; N.Y., Jan. 10, 1985; also for Tuba and String Orch.); *Quintessentials* for Flute, Clarinet, Marimba, Percussion, and Brass (Baltimore, Nov. 3, 1983); Suite for Marimba (1983; N.Y., May 21, 1984); *Fusions* for Chamber Group (1983; Pittsburgh, Oct. 22, 1984); *Fairy Tale* for Viola and Chamber Ensemble (N.Y., Oct. 2, 1989); *Alliances* for Cello and Piano (1989); *Bazz Ma Tazz* for 8 Tenor Trombones, 4 Bass Trombones, and 6 Percussion (Boston, April 26, 1993). **PIANO:** 3 sonatas (1947; 1949–52; 1953); *Piano Suite for Young People* (2 vols., 1951); Sonatina (1952); *5 Pieces* (1952); *Imprints* (1978; N.Y., Feb. 10, 1981); *Re-Percussions* for 2 Pianos (1982; Akron, Ohio, Feb. 9, 1983); *Sunday Silence* (N.Y., Oct. 1, 1990). **VOCAL:** *Phenomena* for Soprano and Chamber Ensemble (1972); *Junctures* for Soprano and Orch. (1979); *Legends and Love Letters* for Soprano and Chamber Ensemble (Washington, D.C., Nov. 5, 1988); *Four . . . Parts of a World*, song cycle for Soprano and Piano (1991). **OTHER:** Many documentary film scores.

Bázlik, Miroslav, Slovak composer; b. Partizánská Lupča, April 12, 1931. He studied piano at the Bratislava Cons.; then took a course in composition with Cikker at the Bratislava Academy of Musical Arts, graduating in 1961. His musical idiom evolved along modern Romantic lines; in his later compositions, he resorted to serial techniques.

WORKS: OPERA: *Petr a Lucie* (1962–66; Bratislava, 1967). **ORCH.:** *Baroque Suite* for Small Orch. (1958); *Music* for Violin and Orch. (1961); *3 Pieces* for 14 Instruments (1964); *Bagatelles* for String Orch. or String Quartet (1972); *Pastorale* for Woodwinds and Harpsichord (1972). **CHAMBER:** *Music for Poetry* for Nonet, Harp, and Vibraphone (1966); *Pastorale* for Woodwinds and Harpsichord (1972); String Quartet (1974). **PIANO:** Sonata (1954); *Palette*, 5 bagatelles (1956). **VOCAL:** *5 Songs on Chinese Poetry* for Contralto, Flute, Piano, and Cello (1960); *Dvanást'* (The 12), oratorio (1967; Bratislava, Nov. 4, 1976); *Cantata Without Words* for Mezzo-soprano, Madrigal Ensemble, and Chamber Orch. (1972).

Beach, Mrs. H.H.A. (née **Amy Marcy Cheney**), important American composer; b. Henniker, N.H., Sept. 5, 1867; d. N.Y., Dec. 27, 1944. She was descended of early New England colonists, and was a scion of a cultural family. She entered a private school in Boston; studied piano with Ernest Perabo and Carl Baermann; received instruction in harmony and counterpoint from Junius W. Hill. She made her debut as a pianist in Boston on Oct. 24, 1883, playing Chopin's *Rondo* in E-flat major and Moscheles's G minor concerto under Neuendorff. On March 28, 1885, she made her first appearance with the Boston Sym. Orch. in Chopin's F minor concerto under Gericke. On Dec. 3, 1885, at the age of 18, she married Dr. H.H.A. Beach, a Boston surgeon, a quarter of a century older than she. The marriage was a happy one, and as a token of her loyalty to her husband, she used as her professional name Mrs. H.H.A. Beach. She began to compose modestly, mostly for piano, but soon embarked on an ambitious Mass, which was performed by the Handel and Haydn Soc. in Boston on Feb. 18, 1892, becoming the first woman to have a composition performed by that organization. On Oct. 30, 1896, her *Gaelic Symphony*, based on Irish folk tunes, was performed by the Boston Sym. Orch. with exceptional success. On April 6, 1900, she appeared as soloist with the Boston Sym. Orch. in the first performance of her Piano Concerto. She also wrote a great many songs in an endearing Romantic manner. When her husband died in 1910, she went to Europe; she played her works in Berlin, Leipzig, and Hamburg, attracting considerable attention as the first of her gender and national origin to be able to compose music of a European quality of excellence. She returned to the U.S. in 1914 and lived in N.Y. Her music, unpretentious in its idiom and epigonic in its historical aspect, retained its importance as the work of a pioneer woman composer in America.

WORKS: OPERA: *Cabildo* (1932; Athens, Ga., Feb. 27, 1947). **ORCH.:** *Eilende Wolken, Segler die Lüfte* for Alto and Orch. (N.Y., Dec. 2, 1892); *Bal masque* (N.Y., Dec. 12, 1893); *Gaelic Symphony* (1894; Boston, Oct. 30, 1896); Piano Concerto (1899; Boston, April 6, 1900); *Jephthah's Daughter* for Soprano and Orch. (1903). **CHAMBER:** Violin Sonata (1896; Boston, March 14, 1899); Piano Quintet (1907; Boston, Feb. 27, 1908); *Theme and Variations* for Flute and String Quartet (1916); String Quartet (1929); Piano Trio (1938). **PIANO:** Many pieces, including the popular *Valse-Caprice* (1889), *Fireflies* (1892), *Ballad* (1894), *The Hermit Thrush at Eve* (1922), and *The Hermit Thrust at Morn* (1922). **VOCAL: CHORAL:** Mass (1890; Boston, Feb. 7, 1892); *Festival Jubilate* for Chorus and Orch. (1891; Chicago, May 1, 1893); *The Chambered Nautilus* (1907); *The Canticle of the Sun* (1928); numerous other choral works, both sacred and secular; many songs, including the favorites *Ecstasy* (1893), *3 Browning Songs* (1900), *June* (1903), and *Shena Van* (1904).

BIBL.: P. Goetschius, *Mrs. H.H.A. B.* (Boston, 1906); B. Tuthill, "Mrs. H.H.A. B.," *Musical Quarterly* (July 1940); E. Merrill, *Mrs. H.H.A. B.: Her Life and Music* (diss., Univ. of Rochester, 1963); M. Eden, *Energy and Individuality in the Art of Anna Huntington, Sculptor, and A. B., Composer* (Metuchen, N.J., 1987); A. Block, "A. B.'s Music on Native American Themes," *American Music* (Summer 1990); J. Brown, *A. B. and her Chamber Music: Biography, Documents, Style* (Metuchen, N.J., 1994); W. Jenkins, *The Remarkable Mrs. B., American Composer: A Biographical Account Based on Her Diaries, Letters, Newspaper Clippings, and Personal Reminiscences* (Warren, Mich., 1994).

Beach, John Parsons, American composer; b. Gloversville, N.Y., Oct. 11, 1877; d. Pasadena, Calif., Nov. 6, 1953. He studied piano at the New England Cons. of Music in Boston; then took lessons with Gédalge in Paris and Malipiero in Venice. Returning to Boston, he took additional lessons with Loeffler. He held various teaching jobs; finally settled in Pasadena. His opera *Pippa's Holiday* was premiered in Paris in 1915, and his ballet *Phantom Satyr* was given in Asolo, Italy, July 6, 1925; another ballet, *Mardi Gras*, was premiered in New Orleans (Feb. 15, 1926). His orch. works include *Asolani* (Minneapolis, Nov. 12, 1926); *New Orleans Street Cries* (Philadelphia, April 22, 1927); *Angelo's Letter* for Tenor and Chamber Orch. (N.Y., Feb. 27, 1929). He also composed *Naïve Landscapes* for Piano, Flute, Oboe, and Clarinet (1917); *Poem* for String Quartet (1920); *Concert* for Violin, Viola, Cello, Flute, Oboe, and Clarinet (1929); many songs.

Beardslee, Bethany, American soprano; b. Lansing, Mich., Dec. 25, 1927. She studied at Michigan State Univ.; then received a scholarship to the Juilliard School of Music in N.Y., making her N.Y. debut in 1949. She soon became known as a specialist in modern music, evolving an extraordinary technique with a flutelike ability to sound impeccably precise intonation; she also mastered the art of *Sprechstimme*, which enabled her to give fine renditions of such works as Schoenberg's *Pierrot Lunaire*; she also was a brilliant performer of vocal parts in scores by Berg, Webern, and Stravinsky. In 1976 she joined the faculty of Westminster Choir College in Princeton, N.J.; in 1981–82 she was a prof. of music at the Univ. of Texas in Austin; after serving as performer-in-residence at the Univ. of Calif. at Davis (1982–83), she taught at Brooklyn College of the City Univ. of N.Y. (1983–84). She was married to **Jacques-Louis Monod** and, later, to **Godfrey Winham**.

Beattie, Herbert (Wilson), American bass and teacher; b. Chicago, Aug. 23, 1926. He studied voice with John Wilcox at the American Cons. of Music in Chicago and with Dick Marzzolo in N.Y.; he also studied at Colorado College (B.A., 1948), Westminster Choir College (M.M., 1950), and the Salzburg Mozarteum (1955). On Oct. 11, 1957, he made his debut at the N.Y. City Opera as Baron Douphol in *La Traviata*, where he sang regularly until 1972 and again from 1980 to 1984; he also sang opera in other cities in the U.S. and Europe, and toured as a concert artist. He taught at Syracuse Univ. (1950–52), Pennsylvania State Univ. (1952–53), the Univ. of Buffalo (1953–58), and at Hofstra Univ. (1959–82). Among his best roles were Mozart's Osmin, Sarastro, Leporello, and Don Alfonso, and Rossini's Dr. Bartolo and Mustafà. He also sang in many contemporary operas.

Becerra (-Schmidt), Gustavo, Chilean composer; b. Temuco, Aug. 26, 1925. He studied at the Santiago Cons. with Pedro Allende, and then with Domingo Santa Cruz. In 1949 he graduated from the Univ. of Chile, where he became a prof. in 1952; was its director of the Instituto de Extensión Musical (1959–63) and secretary-general of its music faculty (1969–71). From 1968 to 1970 he served as cultural attaché to the Chilean embassy in Bonn. In 1971 he received the Premio Nacional de Arte in music. His early works are set in the traditional neo-Classical manner, but soon he adopted an extremely radical modern idiom, incorporating dodecaphonic and aleatory procedures and outlining a graphic system of notation, following the pictorial representation of musical sounds of the European avant-garde, but introducing some new elements, such as indication of relative loudness by increasing the size of the notes on a music staff with lines far apart. His works include the opera *La muerte de Don Rodrigo* (1958); 3 syms. (1955, 1958, 1960); Violin Concerto (1950); Flute Concerto (1957); Piano Concerto (1958); 4 guitar concertos (1964–70); Concerto for Oboe, Clarinet, and Bassoon, with String Orch. (1970); 7 string quartets; Saxophone Quartet; 3 violin sonatas; Viola Sonata; 3 cello sonatas; Sonata for Double Bass and Piano; pieces for solo oboe and solo trombone; the oratorios *La Araucana* (1965) and *Lord Cochrane de Chile* (1967); numerous choral works.

Bechi, Gino, notable Italian baritone; b. Florence, Oct. 16, 1913; d. there, Feb. 2, 1993. He studied in Florence with Frazzi and Di Giorgi and in Alessandria. In 1936 he made his operatic debut as Germont in Empoli, and then sang in Rome (1938–52) and at Milan's La Scala (1939–44; 1946–53), where he acquired an admirable reputation. In 1950 he sang with the La Scala company during its visit to London's Covent Garden, and he returned to London in 1958 to sing at Drury Lane. In 1952 he appeared in Chicago and San Francisco. He also made appearances in musical films. In later years, he was active as a teacher and opera producer. Bechi was best known for his Verdi roles, among them Falstaff, Amonasro, Hamlet, Iago, and Nabucco.

Beck, Conrad, distinguished Swiss composer; b. Lohn, June 16, 1901; d. Basel, Oct. 31, 1989. He was a student of Andreae, Laquai, and Baldegger at the Zürich Cons.; after further training in Paris and Berlin, he settled in Basel in 1932 and served as director of the music division of the Radio (1939–66). In 1964 he was awarded the arts prize of the city. After composing in a late Romantic style, he developed a highly effective neo-Baroque means of expression.

WORKS: DRAMATIC: *La grande ourse*, ballet (1935–36); *St. Jakob an der Birs*, festival play (1943–44). **ORCH.:** 5 syms.: No. 1 (1925), No. 2, Sinfonietta (1926), No. 3 for Strings (1927), No. 4, *Concerto for Orchestra*, for Strings (1929), and No. 5 (1930); *Aeneas-Silvius-Sinfonie* (1957; Zürich, Feb. 25, 1958); Cello Concerto (1927); Concerto for String Quartet and Orch. (1929); *Innominata* (1931); *Konzertmusik* for Oboe and Strings (1933); Piano Concerto (1933); *Serenade* for Flute, Clarinet, and Strings (1935); *Ostinato* (1935–36); *Rhapsodie* for Piano, 4 Woodwinds, and Strings (1936); Violin Concerto (1940); Flute Concerto (1941); Concerto for Harpsichord and Strings (1942); Viola Concerto (1949); *Mouvement* (1953); *Suite concertante* for Wind, Double Bass, and Percussion (1961); *Concertato* (1964); Clarinet Concerto (1967–68); Chamber Concerto (1971); Concerto for Wind Quintet and Orch. (1976); *Drei Aspekte* for Chamber Orch. (1976); *Cercles* (1978–79); *Nachklänge* (1984). **CHAMBER:** 5 string quartets (1922, 1924, 1926, 1934, 1962); Duo for Violin and Flute (1927); 2 string trios (1928, 1946); Duo for Violin and Viola (1934); *3 Bilder aus dem Struwwelpeter* for Flute, Clarinet, Bassoon, and Piano (1934); Violin Sonata (1946); Cello Sonata (1954); Duo for 2 Violins (1960); Sonata for Flute, Oboe, Bassoon, and Violin (1970); piano pieces; organ music. **VOCAL:** *Requiem* (1930); *Oratorium* for Voice, Chorus, and Orch. (1934); *Der Tod zu Basel* for Speaker, Solo Voices, Chorus, and Orch. (1952; Basel, May 22, 1953); *Herbstfeuer* for Alto and Chamber Orch. (1956); *Die Sonnenfinsternis*, cantata for Alto and Chamber Orch. (Lucerne, Aug. 25, 1967); other cantatas, choral pieces, and songs.

BIBL.: W. Schuh and D. Larese, *C. B.: Eine Lebensskizze: Der Komponist und sein Werk* (Amriswil, 1972).

Beck, Jean-Baptiste, Alsatian-American musicologist; b. Gebweiler, Aug. 14, 1881; d. Philadelphia, June 23, 1943. He studied organ; received his Ph.D. at the Univ. of Strasbourg with the diss. *Die Melodien der Troubadours und Trouvères* (1908); later publ. a somewhat popularized ed. of it in French, *La Musique des troubadours* (Paris, 1910). Beck taught at the Univ. of Ill. from 1911 to 1914; then at Bryn Mawr College from 1914 to 1920. He settled in Philadelphia, where he taught at the Univ. of Pa., and from 1920 he taught at the Curtis Inst. of Music. In 1927 he initiated a project to publ. a Corpus Cantilenarum Medii Aevi, in 52 vols., but was able to bring out only 4 vols., under the subtitle *Les Chansonniers des troubadours et des trouvères* (all in French), containing phototype reproductions of medieval MSS, transcriptions in modern notation, and commentary: *Le Chansonnier cangé* (2 vols., Philadelphia, 1927) and *Le Manuscrit du roi* (2 vols., Philadelphia, 1938). Among his other important writings is an essay, "Der Takt in den Musikaufzeichnungen des XII. und XIII. Jahrhunderts," *Riemann Festschrift* (1909). Beck was an outstanding scholar of medieval vocal music; his application of the modal rhythms of the polyphony of that time to troubadour melodies was an important contribution to the problem of proper transcription into modern notation.

Beck, Sydney, American music librarian; b. N.Y., Sept. 2, 1906. He studied at the College of the City of N.Y., at N.Y. Univ., at the Inst. of Musical Art, and at the Mannes College of Music; during this period he took courses in violin and chamber music with Louis Svečenski, in composition with Wagenaar and Weisse, and in musicology with Sachs and Reese. In 1931 he became head of the Rare Book and Manuscript Collections of the N.Y. Public Library, holding this post until 1968. He also taught at the Mannes College of Music (1950–68). In 1968 he was appointed director of libraries at the New England Cons. of Music in Boston, retiring in 1976. He prepared eds. of works by F. Geminiani and J.M. Leclair.

Beck, Thomas Ludvigsen, Norwegian composer; b. Horten, Dec. 5, 1899; d. Olso, Sept. 9, 1963. He studied piano, organ, and composition at the Oslo Cons.; also took a course in theory in Leipzig. From 1930 until his death he was active as an organist, choral conductor, and music teacher in Oslo; was a member of the board of the Soc. of Norwegian Composers (1938–46). He wrote many cantatas, among them *Arnljot Gjelline* (1937), *Höifjell* (In the Mountains; 1945), and *Heilag framtid* (Holy Future; 1954); *Ballad on a Norwegian Folk Tune* for Orch. (1940); *3 Dances from Gudbrandsdal* for Orch. (Oslo, April 28, 1946); *Andante* for String Orch.; *Intrada* for Orch. or Piano; choruses; songs; film music.

Becker, Frank, American composer; b. Paterson, N.J., March 29, 1944. He studied with Joseph Wood at the Oberlin (Ohio) College Cons. of Music, and composition with Robert Palmer and jazz improvisation with Elston Husk. A Ford Foundation grant took him for 2 years to Wichita, Kans., where his works were frequently performed; he subsequently went to Japan, becoming famous in avant-garde circles as a composer, performer (on synthesizer), and producer. Since his return to the U.S. in 1981, he has written many film and television scores. Among his concert works are *Stonehenge* for Flute and Tape (a mixture of new age, minimalist, and pseudo-Japanese styles) and *Philiapaideia* for Orch. (1973), which won the Prix Francis Salabert in 1975.

Becker, Günther (Hugo), German composer; b. Forbach, Baden, April 1, 1924. He studied conducting with G. Nestler at the Badische Hochschule für Musik in Karlsruhe (1946–49), composition with W. Fortner in Heidelberg, and at the North-West German Academy of Music (1948–56), where he also studied choral conducting with K. Thomas (1953–55). He taught music at the Greek National School Anavryta in Athens (1956–58); also taught at the Goethe Inst. and the Dorpfeld Gymnasium there (1957–68). He then returned to Germany, where he founded the live electronic group Mega-Hertz (1969), and taught at the summer courses for new music in Darmstadt. He became a lecturer at the Musikhochschule Rheinland of the Robert Schumann Inst. in Düsseldorf (1973) and prof. of composition and live electronics at the Düsseldorf Hochschule für Musik (1974). In 1989 he retired. Becker's works, at first influenced by his sojourn in Greece, eventually gave way to a unique and uncompromising style utilizing all the resources of contemporary compositional processes.

WORKS: 3 string quartets (1963, 1967, 1988); *Nacht- und Traumgesänge* for Chorus and Orch. (1964; North German Radio, Hamburg, Feb. 16, 1965); *stabil-instabil* for Orch. (1965; West German Radio, Cologne, Oct. 28, 1966); *Correspondances I* for Clarinet and Chamber Orch. (Donaueschingen, Oct. 22, 1966) and *II* for Guitar, Harp, Harpsichord, and String Quartet (1968–69); *Griechische Tanzsuite* for Plucked String Orch. (Saarbrücken, Aug. 29, 1967); *Caprices concertants* for Mandolin, Mandola, Guitar, Percussion, and Plucked String Orch. (1968; Hannover, May 18, 1969); *Transformationen* for Orch., Live Electronic Ensemble, and Tape (Warsaw, Sept. 24, 1970); *Attitude* for Orch. (1972–73; Bonn, June 4, 1973); *Konzert* for Electronic Modulated Oboe and Orch. (1973–74; Munich, April 5, 1974); *Ihre Bosheit wird die ganze Erde zu einer Wuste machen*, sacred concerto for Speaker, Alto, Chorus, Organ, Instrumental Ensemble, and Tape (1978; Düsseldorf, Feb. 14, 1979); *Magnum Mysterium—Zeugenaussagen zur Auferstehung*, scenic oratorio (1979–80; Düsseldorf, May 4, 1980); *Ariosi* for Oboe, English Horn, Clarinet, Bass Clarinet, Vibraphone, and Marimbaphone (1982); *Parenthesen* for String Sextet (1982); *Un poco giocoso* for Bass Tuba and Chamber Ensemble (1983; Witten, April 27, 1984); *Doppelte Ebenen* for Violin and Viola (1984–85); *Reverenz 1985* for 4 Instruments (1985); *Zeitspuren* for 2 Pianos (1988); *trivalent* for Viola, Cello, and Double Bass (1988); *Hard Times* for Bassoon and Chamber Ensemble (1989); *Oh, Mr. Dolly, What a Terrible Noise* for Bass Clarinet and Tape (1990); *Psychogramme* for Trombone, Accordion, and Percussion (1993).

Becker, Gustave Louis, American pianist and teacher; b. Richmond, Texas, May 22, 1861; d. Epsom, Surrey, England, Feb. 25, 1959. He made his public debut at the age of 11; studied in N.Y. with Sternberg and at the Hochschule für Musik in Berlin (1888–91). Returning to N.Y., he became Rafael Joseffy's assistant at the National Cons. of Music of America. He continued his teaching activities privately. On May 23, 1952, the 80th anniversary of his public appearance as a child prodigy, he gave a piano recital in Steinway Hall in N.Y.; on his 94th birthday, May 22, 1955, he played at a concert in N.Y. arranged by his friends. He wrote 2 suites for String Quartet; *Herald of Freedom* for Chorus (1925); many vocal and piano pieces, about 200 numbers in all. He publ. pedagogic works: *Exercise for Accuracy; Superior Graded Course for the Piano; Musical Syllable System for Vocal Sight Reading*; and many magazine articles.

Becker, Heinz, prominent German musicologist; b. Berlin, June 26, 1922. He studied at the Berlin Hochschule für Musik, taking courses in clarinet, piano, conducting, and composition; he then enrolled at Humboldt Univ. in Berlin; received his Ph.D. in 1951 with the diss. *Zur Problematik und Technik der musikalischen Schlussgestaltung*; in 1956 he joined the musicological inst. of the Univ. of Hamburg as an assistant lecturer; he completed his Habilitation there with his *Studien zur Entwicklungsgeschichte der antiken und mittelalterlichen Rohrblattinstrumente* (1961; publ. in Hamburg, 1966). In 1966 he became a prof. of musicology at the Ruhr Univ. in Bochum, where he remained until his retirement in 1987. Apart from his professorial duties, he wrote music for the clarinet.

WRITINGS: *Der Fall Heine-Meyerbeer* (Berlin, 1958); ed. *Giacomo Meyerbeer: Briefwechsel und Tagebucher* (4 vols., Berlin, 1960–85); *Geschichte der Instrumentation*, in the Das Musikwerk series, XXIV (1964); *Beiträge zur Geschichte der Musikkritik* (Regensburg, 1965); *Beiträge zur Geschichte der Oper* (Regensburg, 1969); *Das Lokalkolorit in der Oper des 19. Jahrhunderts* (Regensburg, 1976); *Giacomo Meyerbeer in Selbstzeugnissen und Bilddokumenten* (Reinbek, 1980); with G. Becker, *Giacomo Meyerbeer: Ein Leben in Briefen* (Wilhelmshaven, 1983).

BIBL.: J. Schläder and R. Quandt, eds., *H. B.: Festschrift zum 60. Geburtstag* (Laaber, 1982).

Becker, (Jean Otto Eric) Hugo, famous German cellist; b. Strasbourg, Feb. 13, 1863; d. Geiselgasteig, July 30, 1941. He studied first with his father, Jean Becker (b. Mannheim, May 11, 1833; d. there, Oct. 10, 1884), a well-known cellist, and later with Grützmacher, Kündinger, Swert, and Piatti. He was a cellist in the Frankfurt am Main Opera orch. (1884–86) and a member of the Heermann quartet (1890–1906); taught at the Königliche Hochschule in Berlin (1909–29). He was not only a fine soloist but a remarkable ensemble player; was for many years a member of the Marteau-Dohnányi-Becker trio; also played with Ysaÿe and Busoni. Among his compositions are a Cello Concerto and smaller cello pieces. He publ. *Mechanik und Ästhetik des Violoncellspiels* (Vienna, 1929).

Becker, John J(oseph), remarkable American composer; b. Henderson, Ky., Jan. 22, 1886; d. Wilmette, Ill., Jan. 21, 1961. He studied at the Cincinnati Cons. (graduated, 1905); then at the Wisconsin Cons. in Milwaukee, where he was a pupil of Alexander von Fielitz, Carl Busch, and Wilhelm Middleschulte (Ph.D., 1923). From 1917 to 1927 he served as director of music at Notre Dame Univ.; was chairman of the fine arts dept. at the College of St. Thomas in St. Paul, Minn. (1929–35). He was subsequently Minnesota State Director for the Federal Music Project (1935–41) and prof. of music at Barat College of the Sacred Heart at Lake Forest, Ill. (1943–57); also taught sporadically at the Chicago Musical College. His early works are characterized by romantic moods in a somewhat Germanic manner. About 1930 he was drawn into the circle of modern American music; was on the editorial board of the *New Music Quarterly*, founded by Cowell, and became associated with Charles Ives. He conducted modern American works with various groups in St. Paul. Striving to form a style that would be both modern and recognizably American, he wrote a number of pieces for various instrumental groups under the title *Soundpiece*. He also developed a type of dramatic work connecting theatrical action with music. Becker's music is marked by sparse sonorities of an incisive rhythmic character contrasted with dissonant conglomerates of massive harmonies.

WORKS: DRAMATIC: *The Season of Pan*, ballet suite for Small Ensemble (c.1910); *The City of Shagpat*, opera (c.1926–27; unfinished); *Salome*, film opera (c.1931; unfinished); *Dance Figure: Stagework No. 1*, ballet for Soprano and Orch. (1932; includes music from *Salome*); *The Life of Man: Stagework No. 4*, ballet for Speaking Chorus and Orch. (1932–43; unfinished); *Abongo, a Primitive Dance: Stagework No. 2*, ballet for Wordless Voices and 29 Percussion Instruments (1933; N.Y., May 16, 1963); *A Marriage with Space: Stagework No. 3*, ballet for Speaking Chorus and Orch. (1935; arr. as Sym. No. 4, *Dramatic Episodes*, 1940); *Nostalgic Songs of Earth*, ballet for Piano (Northfield, Minn., Dec. 12, 1938); *Vigilante 1938*, ballet for Piano and Percussion (Northfield, Minn., Dec. 12, 1938); *Privilege and Privation: Stagework No. 5c*, opera (1939; Amsterdam, June 22, 1982); *Rain Down Death: Stagework No. 5a*, incidental music to the play by A. Kreymborg for Chamber Orch. (1939; also as *A Prelude to Shakespeare* for Orch., 1937, rev. as Suite No. 1 for Orch., 1939); *Dance for Shakespeare's Tempest*, incidental music for Piano and Chamber Orch. (1940; unfinished; arr. by M. Benaroyo as *The Tempest* for 2 Pianos, 1954); *When the Willow Nods: Stagework No. 5b*, incidental music to the play by A. Kreymborg for Speaker and Chamber Orch. (1940; includes music from *4 Dances* for Piano and from *Nostalgic Songs of Earth*; rev. as Suite No. 2 for Orch., 1940); *Antigone*, incidental music to the play by Sophocles for Orch. (1940–44); *Trap Doors*, incidental music to the play by A. Kreymborg for Speaking Chorus and Piano (n.d.; unfinished); *Deirdre: Stagework No. 6*, opera (1945; unfished); *Julius Caesar*, film score for Brass and Percussion (1949); *Faust: A Television Opera*, monodrama after Goethe for Tenor and Piano (1951; Los Angeles, April 8, 1985); *The Queen of Cornwall*, opera (1956; unfinished); *Madeleine et Judas*, incidental music to the play by R. Bruckberger for Orch. (1958; radio perf., Paris, March 25, 1959); *The Song of the Scaffold*, film score (1959; unfinished). **ORCH.:** Sym. No. 1, *Étude Primitive* (1912; Minneapolis, June 17, 1936); (2) *Cossack Sketches* (1912); *A Tartar Song* (c.1912); Sym. No. 2, *Fantasia tragica* (1920; not extant; rev. c.1937); Sym. No. 3, *Symphonia brevis* (1929; 1st complete perf., Minneapolis, May 20, 1937); *Concerto arabesque* for Piano and 12 Instruments or Small Orch. (1930; St. Paul, Minn., Dec. 7, 1931); Horn Concerto (1933; N.Y., Feb. 8, 1953); *Concertino Pastorale: A Forest Rhapsodie* for 2 Flutes and Orch. (1933; Cincinnati, Jan. 13, 1976); *Mockery: A Scherzo* for Piano and Dance Orch. (1933; 1st concert perf., N.Y., March 17, 1974); Viola Concerto (1937); Piano Concerto No. 2, *Satirico* (1938; St. Paul, Minn., March 28, 1939); 2 suites: No. 1 (1939; San Francisco, Jan. 15, 1983; from the incidental music to *Rain Down Death*) and No. 2 (1940; from the incidental music to *When the Willow Nods*); Sym. No. 5, *Homage to Mozart* (1942); *Victory March* (1942; from the Sym. No. 6); *The Snow Goose: A Legend of the Second World War* (1944); Violin Concerto (1948; Chattanooga, Jan. 18, 1983). **CHAMBER:** *Sonate American* for Violin and Piano (c.1925; South Bend, Ind., July 28, 1926); 8 *Soundpieces*: No. 1 for Piano Quartet (1932; N.Y., Nov. 13, 1933; also for Piano and String Quintet, 1933, and for Piano and String Orch., 1935), No. 2a, *Homage to Haydn*: String Quartet No. 1 (1936; also for String Orch., 1936), No. 3: Violin Sonata (1936; St. Paul, Minn., April 1, 1940), No. 4: String Quartet No. 2 (1937; Lake Forest, Ill., Oct. 19, 1947), No. 5: Piano Sonata (1937; St. Paul, Minn., April 13, 1943), No. 6: Sonata for Flute and Clarinet (1942; Chapel Hill, N.C., April 26, 1970), No. 7 for 2 Pianos (1949), and No. 8: String Quartet No. 3 (1959; unfinished). **PIANO:** Sonata, *The Modern Man I Sing* (c.1910); *The Mountains* (c.1912); *My Little Son, 18 Months Old: Studies in Child Psychology* (1924); *2 Architectural Impressions* (1924); *2 Chinese Miniatures* (1925; arr. for Orch. by R. Kraner, 1928); *4 Dances* (1938). **VOCAL:** *Rouge Bouquet* for Tenor, Men's Voices, Trumpet, and Piano (1917); *Out of the Cradle Endlessly Rocking*, cantata for Speaker, Soprano, Tenor, Chorus, and Orch. (1929; St. Cloud, Minn., July 19, 1931); *Missa symphonica* for Men's Voices (1933); Sym. No. 6, *Out of Bondage*, for Speaker, Chorus, and Orch. (1942); *Mass in Honor of the Sacred Heart* for 3 Equal Voices (1943); *Moments from the Passion* for Solo Voices, Chorus, and Organ (1945); *The 7 Last Words* for Women's or Men's Voices (1947); *Moments from the Liturgical Year* for Speaker, Speaking Chorus, Soloist, and Chorus of 3 Equal Voices (1948); Sym. No. 7 for Speaking Chorus, Women's Voices, and Orch. (1954; unfinished); also many solo songs. He orchestrated Ives's *General William Booth Enters Into Heaven* for Baritone, Men's Chorus, and Small Orch. (1934–35).

BIBL.: H. Cowell, "J. B.," *American Composers on American Music* (Stanford, Calif., 1933); idem, "J. B.: A Crusader from Kentucky," *Southern Literary Messenger*, I (1939); E. Becker, *J.J.*

B.: American Composer (MS, 1958); D. Gillespie, "J. B., Musical Crusader from St. Paul," *Musical Quarterly* (April 1976); idem, "J. B.'s Correspondence with Ezra Pound: The Origins of a Musical Crusader," *Bulletin of Research in the Humanities* (Spring 1980).

Becking, Gustav (Wilhelm), German musicologist; b. Bremen, March 4, 1894; d. during street fighting in Prague, May 8, 1945. He studied at the Univ. of Leipzig (Ph.D., 1920, with the diss. *Studien zu Beethovens Personalstil: Das Scherzothema*); then completed his Habilitation in 1922 at the Univ. of Erlangen with his *Der Musikalische Rhythmus als Erkenntnisquelle* (publ. in Augsburg, 1928). He taught at the Univ. of Erlangen (1922–29); then was a prof. at the Univ. of Utrecht (1929–30) and the German Univ. in Prague (from 1930). He wrote articles for music journals and ed. the collected works of E.T.A. Hoffmann (2 vols., Leipzig, 1922–23).

BIBL.: W. Kramolisch, *G. B. zum Gedächtnis: Eine Auswahl seiner Schriften und Beiträge seiner Schüler* (Tutzing, 1975).

Beckwith, John, prominent Canadian composer, teacher, writer on music, and pianist; b. Victoria, British Columbia, March 9, 1927. He began piano lessons as a child with Ogreta McNeill and Gwendoline Harper; after attending Victoria College (1944–45), he settled in Toronto, studying piano privately with Alberto Guerrero (1945–50) and at the Univ. of Toronto (Mus.B., 1947). He also received private composition lessons from Boulanger in Paris (1950–52). He completed his education at the Univ. of Toronto (Mus.M., 1961). In 1950 he made his debut as a pianist in a lecture-recital in Toronto. He was assoc. ed. of the *Canadian Music Journal* (1957–62), music reviewer for the *Toronto Star* (1959–62; 1963–65), and program annotator for the Toronto Sym. (1966–70). From 1952 to 1966 he taught theory at the Royal Cons. of Music of Toronto, and in 1952 joined the faculty at the Univ. of Toronto; in 1984 he was named Jean A. Chalmers Prof. of Canadian Music there, the first position of its kind created by a Canadian univ., and also founded and directed its Inst. for Canadian Music. In 1990 he retired as prof. emeritus. He was area ed. for Canada for *The New Grove Dictionary of Music and Musicians* (1972–80) and general ed. of the Canadian Composers/Compositeurs Canadiens study series (from 1975); he was also co-ed. of *The Modern Composer and His World* (with U. Kasemets; Toronto, 1961), *Contemporary Canadian Composers* (with K. MacMillan; Toronto, 1975), *Hello Out There!: Canada's New Music in the World, 1950–85* (with D. Cooper; Toronto, 1988), *Musical Canada: Words and Music Honouring Helmut Kallmann* (with F. Hall; Toronto, 1988), and *The Fifth Stream* (with P. Hatch; Toronto, 1991). In 1987 he was made a Member of the Order of Canada. His music is marked by pragmatic modernism, with ingenious applications of urban folklore and structural collage.

WORKS: DRAMATIC: *Night Blooming Cereus*, chamber opera (1953–58; radio premiere, Toronto, March 4, 1959; stage premiere, Toronto, April 5, 1960); *The Killdeer*, incidental music (1960); *The Shivaree*, opera (1965–66; 1978; Toronto, April 3, 1982); *Crazy to Kill*, opera (1987–88); *Taptoo!*, opera (1993–94). **ORCH.:** *Music for Dancing* (1949; rev. 1959); *Montage* (1953); *Fall Scene and Fair Dance* for Violin, Clarinet, and Strings (1956); *Concerto Fantasy* for Piano and Orch. (1958–60); *Flower Variations and Wheels* (1962); Concertino for Horn and Orch. (1963); *All the Bees and All the Keys* for Narrator and Orch. (1973); *A Concert of Myths* for Flute and Orch. (1982–83); *Peregrine* for Viola, Percussion, and Orch. (1989); *Round and Round* (1991–92). **BAND:** *Elastic Band Studies* (1969; rev. 1975); *For Starters* for 11 Brass Instruments (1984). **CHAMBER:** *3 Studies* for String Trio (1955–56); *Circle, with Tangents* for Harpsichord and 13 Solo Strings (1967); *Taking a Stand* for 5 Players, 8 Brass Instruments, 14 Music Stands, and 1 Platform (1972); *Musical Chairs* for String Quintet (1973); Quartet for 2 Violins, Viola, and Cello (1977); *Case Study* for Any 5 Instruments (1980); *Sonatina in 2 Movements* for Trumpet and Piano (1981); *Arctic Dances* for Oboe and Piano (1984); *College Airs* for String Quartet (1990); *Scene* for Clarinet, Trumpet, 2 Percussion, Piano, and Contrabassoon (1991); *After-images, after Webern* for Guitar and Cello (1994). **KEYBOARD: PIANO:** *Music for Dancing* for Piano, 4-hands (1948); *Novelette* (1951); *Études* (1983). **ORGAN:** *Upper Canadian Hymn Preludes* for Organ and Tape (1976–77). **OTHER KEYBOARD:** *Keyboard Practice* for 4 Players (1979). **VOCAL:** *5 Lyrics of the T'ang Dynasty* for High Voice and Piano (1947); *The Great Lakes Suite* for Soprano, Baritone, Clarinet, Cello, and Piano (1949); *4 Songs to Poems by e.e. cummings* for Soprano and Piano (1950); *Jonah* for 4 Soloists, Chorus, and Small Orch. (1963); *The Trumpets of Summer* for Speaker, 4 Soloists, Chorus, and 6 Instrumentalists (1964); *Sharon Fragments* for Chorus (1966); *Place of Meeting* for 3 Soloists, Chorus, and Orch. (1966–67); *The Sun Dance* for Speaker, 6 Soloists, 2 Choruses, Percussion, and Organ (1968); *Gas!* for 20 Speaking Voices (1969); *3 Motets on Swan's China* for Chorus (1980–81); *6 Songs to Poems by e.e. cummings* for Baritone and Piano (1980–82); *Mating Time* for 20 Solo Voices, Electric Piano, and Percussion (1981–82); *A Little Organ Concert* for Organ, Brass Quintet, and Chorus (1982); *Harp of David* for Chorus (1984–85); *Avowals* for Tenor and Keyboardist (1985); *Les Premiers hivernements* for Soprano, Tenor, and Early Instrumental Ensemble (1986); *Synthetic Trios* for Soprano, Clarinet, and Piano (1987); *Beep* for Soprano, Baritone, Chorus, and Percussion (1990); *The Hector* for Soprano and Early Instruments (1990). **COLLAGE:** *A Message to Winnipeg* for 4 Narrators, Clarinet, Violin, Piano, and Percussion (1960); *12 Letters to a Small Town* for 4 Narrators, Flute, Oboe, Guitar, and Piano or Harmonium (1961); *Wednesday's Child* for 3 Narrators, Soprano, Tenor, Flute, Viola, Piano, and Percussion (1962); *Canada Dash, Canada Dot* for Folksinger, 5 Narrators, Soprano, Contralto, Baritone, Bass, and Instruments (1965–67); *The Journals of Susanna Moodie* for 2 Keyboard Players and Percussion (1973); *"In the middle of ordinary noise . . ."*, auditory masque for Speaker, 2 Singers, 3 Instrumentalists, and Tape (1992).

Bedford, David (Vickerman), English composer, brother of **Steuart (John Rudolf) Bedford**; b. London, Aug. 4, 1937. He was the grandson of **Liza Lehmann**. After training in London at Trinity College of Music and with Berkeley at the Royal Academy of Music (1958–61), he completed his studies with Luigi Nono in Venice and worked in the RAI electronic music studio in Milan. Returning to England, he was active as a keyboardist and arranger with Kevin Ayers's rock band The Whole World. He was a teacher (1968–80) and composer-in-residence (1969–81) at Queen's College in London. From 1983 he was assoc. visiting composer at the Gordonstoun School in Scotland. In 1986 he became youth music director of the English Sinfonia in London, serving as its composer-in-assoc. from 1994. Bedford is a remarkably facile composer whose interests range from rock to art music, and from film scores to music for the young.

WORKS: DRAMATIC: SCHOOL OPERAS: *The Rime of the Ancient Mariner* (1978); *The Death of Baldur* (1979); *Fridiof's Saga* (1980); *The Ragnarok* (1982); *The Camlann Game* (1987); *The Return of Odysseus* (1988); *Anna* (1992–93); film scores; television music. **ORCH.:** *This One for You* (1965); *Gastrula* (1968); *Star's End* for Electric Guitar, Electric Bass Guitar, Percussion, and Orch. (1974); *Alleluia Timpanis* (1976); *Prelude for a Maritime Nation* (1981); Sym. for 12 Musicians (1981); *The Valley Sleeper, the Children, the Snakes and the Giant* for Chamber Orch. (1983); 2 syms.: No. 1 (1984) and No. 2 for Wind Band (1987); *Sun Paints Rainbows on the Vast Waves* for Wind Band (1984); *Sea and Sky and Golden Hill* for Wind Band (1985); *Ronde for Isolde* for Orch. or Wind Band (1986); *The Transfiguration* for Chamber Orch., Piano, and Percussion (1988); *Toccata for Tristan* for Brass Band (1989); *In Plymouth Town* for Chamber Orch. (1992); *Allison's Overture* (1992); *Susato Variations* (1992); *Allison's Concerto* for Trumpet and Orch. (1993); *The Goddess of Mahi River* for Sitar, Tabla, Flute, Cello, and Chamber Orch. (1994). **CHAMBER:** *5* for String Quintet (1963); *Trona* for 12 Players (1967); *Pentomino* for

Wind Quintet (1968); *Jack of Shadows* for 13 Players (1973); *Pancakes, with Butter, Maple Syrup, and Bacon, and the TV Weatherman* for Brass Quintet (1973); *Circe Variations* for Clarinet, Piano, Violin, and Cello (1976); *Fridiof Kennings* for Saxophone Quartet (1980); String Quartet (1981); Piano Sonata (1981); *Pentaquin* for Flute or Piccolo, Clarinet, Viola, Harp, and Percussion (1985); *For Tess* for Brass Quintet (1985); *Erkenne Mich* for Flute or Alto Flute, Oboe or English Horn, Bass Clarinet, and Vibraphone (1988); *Backings* for Soprano Saxophone and Tape (1990); *Cadenzas and Interludes* for 2 Clarinets, Viola, Cello, and Double Bass (1992). **OTHER INSTRUMENTAL:** *The Garden of Love* for Flute, Clarinet, Horn, Trumpet, Double Bass, and Rock Band (1969); *The Sword of Orion* for Flute, Clarinet, Violin, Cello, 4 Metronomes, and 32 Percussion Instruments (1970); *With 100 Kazoos* for Flute, Oboe, Clarinet, Bass Clarinet, Horn, Trumpet, Trombone, String Quartet, and 100 Kazoos Played by the Audience (1971); *Nurse's Song with Elephants* for 10 Acoustic Guitars and Singer (1971); *Variations on a Rhythm by Mike Oldfield* for 84 Percussion Instruments and Conductor (1973); *The Ones Who Walk Away From Omelas* for 9 Instruments, Electric Guitar, and Electric Bass Guitar (1976); *Verses and Choruses* for 2 Acoustic Guitars (1986). **VOCAL:** *A Dream of the 7 Lost Stars* for Chorus and Chamber Orch. (1964–65); *Music for Albion Moonlight* for Soprano and 6 Instruments (1965); *That White and Radiant Legend* for Soprano, Speaker, and 7 Instruments (1966); *The Tentacles of the Dark Nebula* for Tenor and 8 Instruments (1969); *Star Clusters, Nebulae, and Places in Devon* for Chorus and Brass or Brass Band (1971); *Holy Thursday with Squeakers* for Soprano, Electric Piano, Viola or Organ, Soprano Saxophone or Bassoon, and Percussion (1972); *When I Heard the Learned Astronomer* for Tenor and 14 Instruments (1972); *12 Hours of Sunset* for Chorus and Orch. (1974); *The Golden Wine is Drunk* for 16 Solo Voices (1974); *The Odyssey* for Chorus and Orch. (1976); *On the Beach at Night* for 2 Tenors, Piano, and Small Organ (1977); *The Way of Truth* for Chorus and Electronics (1977–78); *Of Beares, Foxes, and Many, Many Wonders* for Chorus and Orch. (1978); *The Song of the White Horse* for Chorus and Orch. (1978); *Requiem* for Soprano, Chorus, and Orch. (1980); *Vocoder Sextet* for Vocalist, Vocoder, Flute, Clarinet, Violin, and Viola (1981); *Of Stars, Dreams, and Cymbals* for Chorus (1982); *The Juniper Tree* for Soprano, Recorder, and Harpsichord (1982); *Into Thy Wondrous House* for Soprano, Children's Chorus, Chorus, and Orch. (1987); *The OCD Band and the Minotaur* for Soprano and 6 Instruments (1990); *Touristen Dachau* for Soprano, Men's Voices, and 6 Instruments (1992); *Charm of Grace* for 24 Voices (1994). **EDUCATIONAL:** *Seascapes* for Strings and 4 School Groups (1986); *Frameworks* for 2 Oboes, 2 Horns, Strings, and 4 School Orch. Groups (1989–90).

Bedford, Steuart (John Rudolf), English conductor, brother of **David (Vickerman) Bedford**; b. London, July 31, 1939. He was the grandson of **Liza Lehmann**. He received his training at the Royal Academy of Music in London and at Lancing College, Oxford. In 1967 he became conductor of the English Opera Group. After it was renamed the English Music Theatre Co. in 1975, he continued to conduct it until 1980. On June 16, 1973, he conducted the premiere of Britten's *Death in Venice* at the Aldeburgh Festival, where he subsequently conducted regularly. On Oct. 18, 1974, he made his Metropolitan Opera debut in N.Y. conducting the same opera, and remained on its roster until 1977. He was music director of the English Sinfonia from 1981 to 1992. With Oliver Knussen, he served as co-artistic director of the Aldeburgh Festival from 1989. From 1969 to 1980 he was married to **Norma Burrowes**.

Beecham, Sir Thomas, celebrated English conductor; b. St. Helens, near Liverpool, April 29, 1879; d. London, March 8, 1961. His father, Sir Joseph Beecham, was a man of great wealth, derived from the manufacture of the once-famous Beecham pills; thanks to them, young Beecham could engage in life's pleasures without troublesome regard for economic limitations. He had his first music lessons from a rural organist; from 1892 to 1897 he attended the Rossall School at Lancashire, and later went to Wadham College, Oxford. In 1899 he organized, mainly for his own delectation, an amateur ensemble, the St. Helen's Orchestral Soc.; also in 1899 he conducted a performance with the prestigious Halle Orch. in Manchester. In 1902 he became conductor of K. Trueman's traveling opera company, which gave him valuable practical experience with theater music. In 1905 he gave his first professional sym. concert in London, with members of the Queen's Hall Orch.; in 1906 he became conductor of the New Sym. Orch., which he led until 1908; then formed a group in his own name, the Beecham Sym. Orch., which presented its first concert in London on Feb. 22, 1909. In 1910 he presented his first season of opera at London's Covent Garden, and in subsequent seasons conducted there and at other London theaters. In 1915 he organized the Beecham Opera Co., by which time his reputation as a forceful and charismatic conductor was securely established in England. His audiences grew; the critics, impressed by his imperious ways and his unquestioned ability to bring out spectacular operatic productions, sang his praise; however, some commentators found much to criticize in his somewhat cavalier treatment of the classics. In appreciation of his services to British music, Beecham was knighted in 1916; with the death of his father, he succeeded to the title of baronet. But all of his inherited money was not enough to pay for Beecham's exorbitant financial disbursements in his ambitious enterprises, and in 1920 his operatic enterprise went bankrupt. He rebounded a few years later and continued his extraordinary career. On Jan. 12, 1928, he made his U.S. debut as a guest conductor of the N.Y. Phil., at which concert Vladimir Horowitz also made his U.S. debut as soloist. In 1929 he organized and conducted the Delius Festival in London, to which Delius himself, racked by tertiary syphilitic affliction, paralyzed and blind, was brought from his residence in France to attend Beecham's musical homage to him. From 1932 to 1939 he conducted at Covent Garden. In 1932 Beecham organized the London Phil.; contemptuous of general distaste for the Nazi regime in Germany, he took the London Phil. to Berlin in 1936 for a concert which was attended by the Führer in person. As the war situation deteriorated on the Continent, Beecham went to the U.S. in May 1940, and also toured Australia. In 1941 he was engaged as conductor of the Seattle Sym. Orch., retaining this post until 1943; he also filled guest engagements at the Metropolitan Opera in N.Y. from 1942 to 1944. In America he was not exempt from sharp criticism, which he haughtily dismissed as philistine complaints. On his part, he was outspoken in his snobbish disdain for the cultural inferiority of England's wartime allies, often spicing his comments with mild obscenities, usually of a scatological nature. Returning to England, he founded, in 1946, still another orch., the Royal Phil. In 1950 he made an extraordinarily successful North American tour with the Royal Phil. Beecham continued to conduct the orch. until ill health led him to nominate Rudolf Kempe as his successor in 1960. In 1957 Queen Elizabeth II made him a Companion of Honour. Beecham was married 3 times: to Utica Celestia Wells, in 1903 (divorced in 1942); to Betty Hamby (in 1943), who died in 1957; and to his young secretary, Shirley Hudson, in 1959. He publ. an autobiography, *A Mingled Chime* (London, 1943), and also an extensive biography of Delius (London, 1959; 2nd ed., rev., 1975). To mark his centennial, a commemorative postage stamp with Beecham's portrait was issued by the Post Office of Great Britain on Sept. 1, 1980. In 1964 the Sir Thomas Beecham Soc., dedicated to preserving his memory, was organized, with chapters in America and England. The Soc. publishes an official journal, *Le Grand Baton*, devoted to Beecham and the art of conducting. In spite of the occasional criticism directed at him, Beecham revealed a remarkable genius as an orchestra builder. In addition to his outstanding interpretations of Haydn, Mozart, Schubert, Richard Strauss, Delius, and Sibelius, he had a particular affinity for the works of French and Russian composers of the 19th century.

BIBL.: E. Smyth, *B. and Pharaoh* (London, 1935); N. Cardus, *Sir T. B.: A Memoir* (London, 1961); C. Reid, *T. B.: An Independent Biography* (London, 1961); H. Procter-Gregg, ed., *Sir T. B., Conductor and Impresario: As Remembered by His Friends and Colleagues* (Kendal, 1972; 2nd ed., 1976); H. Atkins and A. Newman, *B. Stories* (London, 1978); J. Gilmour, *Sir T. B.: The Seattle Years 1941–1943* (Ocean Shores, Wash., 1978); idem, *Sir T. B.: The North American Tour 1950* (Ocean Shores, Wash., 1979); A. Jefferson, *Sir T. B.: A Centenary Tribute* (London, 1979); special issue of *Le Grand Baton* (March-June 1979); J. Gilmour, *Sir T. B.—50 years in the "New York Times"* (London, 1988); 25th anniversary issue of *Le Grand Baton* (1989).

Beecroft, Norma (Marian), Canadian composer; b. Oshawa, Ontario, April 11, 1934. She studied piano with Gordon Hallett and Weldon Kilburn at the Royal Cons. of Music of Toronto (1952–58), during which period she also studied composition with John Weinzweig; following composition training from Copland and Foss at the Berkshire Music Center in Tanglewood (summer, 1958), she went to Rome to continue studies with Petrassi at the Accademia di Santa Cecilia (1959–62); she also attended Maderna's classes in Darmstadt (summers, 1960–61), and then Schaeffer's electronic music classes at the Univ. of Toronto (1962–63) before working with Davidovsky at the Columbia-Princeton Electronic Music Center (1964). She was active as a producer, host, and commentator for the CBC. With Robert Aitken, she founded the New Music Concerts in Toronto in 1971, which she oversaw until 1989. In her music, Beecroft has followed along modernistic paths. In a number of her works, she has effectively utilized 12-tone techniques and electronics.

WORKS: DRAMATIC: *Undersea Fantasy*, puppet show (1967); *Hedda*, ballet (1982); *The Dissipation of Purely Sound*, radiophonic opera (1988). **ORCH.:** *Fantasy* for Strings (1958); *2 Movements* (1958); *Improvvisazioni Concertanti No. 1* for Flute and Orch. (1961), *No. 2* (1971), and *No. 3* for Flute and Orch. (1973); *Pièce Concertante No. 1* (1966); *Jeu de Bach* for Oboe, Piccolo, Trumpet, Strings, and Tape (1985). **CHAMBER:** *Tre Pezzi Brevi* for Flute and Harp, or Guitar, or Piano (1960–61); *Contrasts* for Oboe, Viola, Xylorimba, Vibraphone, Percussion, and Harp (1962); *Rasas I* for Flute, Harp, String Trio, Percussion, and Piano (1968); *II and 7 for 5+* for Brass Quintet and Tape (1975); *Piece for Bob* for Flute and Tape (1975); *Collage '76* for Chamber Ensemble and Tape (1976); *Consequences for 5* for Piano, Synthesizer, and Live Electronics (1977); *Collage '78* for Bassoon, Piano, 2 Percussion, and Tape (1978); *Quaprice* for Horn, Percussion, and Tape (1980); *Cantorum Vitae* for Flute, Cello, 2 Pianos, Percussion, and Tape (1981); *Troissonts* for Viola and 2 Percussion (1981); *Jeu II* for Flute, Viola, and Tape (1985), *III* for Viola and Tape (1987), and *IV (Mozart)* for Fortepiano, Flute, Clarinet, Trumpet, Trombone, Horn, String Quintet, and Tape (1991); *Images* for Wind Quintet (1986); *Accordion Play* for Accordion and 2 Percussion (1989); *Hemispherics* for 9 Instruments (1990). **VOCAL:** *The Hollow Men* for Chorus (1956); *From Dreams of Brass* for Soprano, Narrator, Chorus, Orch., and Tape (1963–64); *Elegy* and *2 Went to Sleep* for Soprano, Percussion or Piano, and Tape (1967); *The Living Flame of Love* for Chorus (1968); *3 Impressions* for Chorus (1973); *Rasas II* (1973; rev. 1975) and *III* (1974) for Voice, Chamber Ensemble, and Tape; *Requiem Mass* for Soloists, Chorus, and Orch. (1989–90). **ELECTROACOUSTIC:** *Evocations: Images of Canada* (1991).

Beeson, Jack (Hamilton), American composer and teacher; b. Muncie, Ind., July 15, 1921. He studied with Burrill Phillips, Bernard Rogers, and Howard Hanson at the Eastman School of Music in Rochester, N.Y. (B.M., 1942; M.M., 1943), and with Bartók in N.Y. (1944–45). He pursued graduate work at Columbia Univ. (1945–48), where he was active as a teacher from 1945. From 1967 to 1988 he was the MacDowell Prof. of Music there, and he also served as chairman of its music dept. (1968–72). He held the American Prix de Rome (1948–50), a Fulbright fellowship (1949–50), and a Guggenheim fellowship (1958–59). In 1976 he was elected a member of the American Academy and Inst. of Arts and Letters. Beeson was particularly adept at writing operas.

WORKS: OPERAS: *Jonah* (1950); *Hello, Out There* (N.Y., May 27, 1954); *The Sweet Bye and Bye* (1956; N.Y., Nov. 21, 1957); *Lizzie Borden* (N.Y., March 25, 1965); *My Heart's in the Highlands*, chamber opera (1969; NET, March 17, 1970); *Captain Jinks of the Horse Marines*, romantic comedy (Kansas City, Mo., Sept. 20, 1975); *Dr. Heidegger's Fountain of Youth*, after Hawthorne (N.Y., Nov. 17, 1978); *Cyrano* (1990). **ORCH.:** *The Hippopotamus* for Very Small Orch. (1952; also for Voice and Piano, 1951); *Hymns and Dances* (1958; arr. from *The Sweet Bye and Bye*; also for Band, 1966); Sym. (1959); *Transformations* (1959); *Commemoration* for Band and Chorus ad libitum (1960); Fanfare for Brass, Wind, and Percussion (1963). **CHAMBER:** *Song* for Flute and Piano (1945); *Interlude* for Violin and Piano (1945; rev. 1951); Viola Sonata (1953); *Sonata canonica* for 2 Alto Recorders (1966); *The Hoosier Balks, The Hawkesley Blues* for 10 Instruments (1967). **PIANO:** 5 sonatas; *2 Diversions* (1944; rev. 1953); *Sketches in Black and White* (1958); *Round and Round* for Piano, 4-hands (1959). **ORGAN:** *Old Hundredth: Prelude and Doxology* (1972). **VOCAL:** *The Elephant* for Voice and Orch. (1953; also for Voice and Piano); *A Creole Mystery* for Voice and String Quartet (1970); *The Day's No Rounder Than its Angles Are* for Voice and String Quartet (1971); *Magicke Pieces* for Baritone, Chorus, 3 Winds, and Bells (1991); many other songs and choral pieces.

Beeth, Lola, German soprano; b. Kraków, Nov. 23, 1860; d. Berlin, March 18, 1940. She studied in Lemberg and then was a pupil of Louise Dustmann in Vienna, Pauline Viardot-García in Paris, Francesco Lamperti in Milan, and Rosa Deruda in Berlin. In 1882 she made her operatic debut as Elsa in *Lohengrin* at the Berlin Royal Opera, where she sang until 1888; then was a member of the Vienna Court Opera (1888–95). On Dec. 2, 1895, she made her Metropolitan Opera debut in N.Y. as Elsa, remaining on its roster for a season. After singing in London, St. Petersburg, Moscow, Monte Carlo, and Warsaw, she was again a member of the Vienna Court Opera (1898–1901). She then sang mainly in concerts and taught voice in Berlin.

Beglarian, Grant, Georgian-born American arts administrator and composer of Armenian descent; b. Tiflis, Dec. 1, 1927. He went to Teheran in 1934, and then to the U.S. in 1947, becoming a naturalized American citizen in 1954. After attending Boston Univ. (1947), he studied composition with Finney at the Univ. of Mich. (B.M., 1950; M.M., 1952; D.M.A., 1958) and with Copland at the Berkshire Music Center in Tanglewood (summer, 1959). He founded and was president of Music-Book Associates (1954–65) and director of the Contemporary Music Project of the Ford Foundation (1961–69). After serving as dean of the School of Performing Arts at the Univ. of Southern Calif. in Los Angeles (1969–82), he was president of the National Foundation for Advancement in the Arts in Miami (1982–91). In 1958 he won the George Gershwin Award, in 1959 and 1968 he received Ford Foundation Composer awards, and in 1961, 1963, and 1990 he was a resident at the MacDowell Colony.

WORKS: DRAMATIC: *Women of Troy*, incidental music (1949). **ORCH.:** *Symphony in 2 Movements* (1950); *Divertimento* (1957); *Sinfonia* (1961); *A Short Suite* (1968); *Diversions* for Viola, Cello, and Orch. (1972); *Sinfonia* for Strings (1974); *Partita* (1986). **BAND:** *Prelude and Allegro* (1955); Overture (1956); *1st Portrait* (1959); *A Hymn for Our Time* for Multiple Bands (1968). **CHAMBER:** Piano Quintet (1947); String Quartet (1948); Violin Sonata (1949); Cello Sonata (1951); (7) Duos for Flute and Viola (1954); (9) Duets for Violins (1955); *Music* for Bassoon and String Trio (1959); *2 Canzonas* for Trumpets and Trombones (1960); Woodwind Quintet (1966); *Fable, Foibles, and Fancies* for Cello (1971); *Variations on a Paganini Theme* for 3 Cellos (1975); *Ballad* for Cello (1978); *Elegy* for Cello (1979). **ORGAN:** Suite (1956). **VOCAL:** *Tell me Another One* for Baritone and Piano (1949); *12 Hungarian Songs* for Chorus and Orch. (1957); *A Christmas Carol* for Chorus (1959); *Motet* for

Chorus (1960); *Nurse's Song* for Chorus and Orch. (1960); . . . *And All the Hills Echoed* for Bass, Organ, Timpani, and Chorus (1968); *To Manitou* for Soprano and Orch. (1976).

Béhague, Gerard (Henri), French-born American musicologist; b. Montpellier, Nov. 2, 1937. He studied piano and composition at the National School of Music at the Univ. of Brazil, and at the Brazilian Cons. of Music in Rio de Janeiro; subsequently took courses in musicology at the Inst. de Musicologie at the Univ. of Paris with Chailley; moving to the U.S., he continued musicological studies with Gilbert Chase at Tulane Univ. (Ph.D., 1966). In 1974 he became a prof. of music at the Univ. of Texas in Austin. He made a specialty of American and Latin American music; ed. the journals *Ethnomusicology* (1974–78) and the *Latin American Music Review* (from 1980). He publ. *The Beginnings of Musical Nationalism in Brazil* (Detroit, 1971), *Music in Latin America: An Introduction* (Englewood Cliffs, N.J., 1977), and *Heitor Villa-Lobos: The Search of Brazil's Musical Soul* (Austin, Texas, 1994); also ed. *Performance Practice: Ethnomusicological Perspectives* (Westport, Conn., 1984). He contributed a number of articles to *The New Grove Dictionary of Music and Musicians* (1980).

Behm, Eduard, German composer and teacher; b. Stettin, April 8, 1862; d. Bad Harzburg, Feb. 6, 1946. He studied at the Leipzig Cons. He taught at the Erfurt Academy of Music; was director of the Scharwenka Cons. in Berlin (until 1901), and later a prof. there from 1917. He was awarded the Mendelssohn prize for a Sym. and the Bösendorfer prize for a Piano Concerto. He wrote the operas *Der Schelm von Bergen* (Dresden, 1899), *Marienkind* (1902), and *Das Gelobnis* (1914); a String Sextet, using the Stelzner Violotta; a Piano Trio; a Clarinet Quintet; 3 violin sonatas; a Violin Concerto; *Frühlingsidylle* for Violin and Orch.; men's choruses, songs, etc. Behm wrote a short autobiography, *Musik in Pommern* (1932).

Behrend, (Gustav) Fritz, German composer and teacher; b. Berlin, March 3, 1889; d. there, Dec. 29, 1972. He studied composition with H. van Eycken, P. Rufer, and Humperdinck, and piano with Breithaupt (1907–11). After serving as a coach at the Braunschweig Hoftheater (1911–12), he taught at the Ochs-Eichelberg Cons. (1918–42) and the Klindworth-Scharwenka Cons. in Berlin (1942–49). His compositions did not meet with favor during the Third Reich, but later they achieved a modicum of recognition.

WORKS: DRAMATIC: *König Renés Tochter* (1919); *Der schwangere Bauer* (1927); *Die lächerlichen Preziösen* (1928; Berlin, May 22, 1949); *Almansor* (1931); *Dornröschen* (1934); *Der Wunderdoktor* (1947); *Der fahrende Schüler im Paradies* (1949); *Der Spiegel* (1950); *Romantische Komödie* (1953). **ORCH.:** 7 syms.; *Rotkäppchensuite* (1912); *Lustspiel Overture* (1913); *Am Rhein* (1913); *Fantasie* for Piano and Orch. (1919); *Im Hochgebirge* (1920); *Penthesilea* (1926); *Lustspiel Overture* (1937); *Lustige Overture* (1947). **CHAMBER:** 7 string quartets; 2 piano trios (1923, 1929); Violin Sonata (1925); Cello Sonata (1925); Wind Quintet (1951); String Trio; Septet; Octet; piano pieces. **VOCAL:** Over 100 songs.

Behrend, Jeanne, American pianist, teacher, and composer; b. Philadelphia, May 11, 1911; d. there, March 20, 1988. She was a student of Hofmann (piano) and Scalero (composition) at the Curtis Inst. of Music in Philadelphia (graduated, 1934), where she later taught piano; also taught at the Juilliard School in N.Y. and at the Philadelphia College of Performing Arts (from 1969). She ed. piano music of Gottschalk (1956) and songs of Stephen Foster (1964). Among her works was the *Festival Fanfare: Prelude to the National Anthem*, a cantata, a String Quartet, piano pieces, and songs. She was married to **Alexander Kelberine**.

Behrend, Siegfried, German guitarist; b. Berlin, Nov. 19, 1933; d. Hausham, Sept. 20, 1990. His father, a guitar virtuoso, guided his early interest; at the age of 16, he entered the Klindworth-Scharwenka Cons. in Berlin, where he studied piano, composition, and conducting. He made his debut as a guitarist in Berlin in 1952; then toured Europe. He was particularly known for his performances of contemporary music, and commissioned many works for the guitar.

Behrens, Hildegard, noted German soprano; b. Varel, Oldenburg, Feb. 9, 1937. After obtaining a law degree from the Univ. of Freiburg im Breisgau, she studied voice with Ines Leuwen at the Freiburg im Breisgau Staatliche Hochschule für Musik. In 1971 she made her operatic debut as Mozart's Countess at the Freiburg im Breisgau City Theater; that same year she became a member of the opera studio of the Deutsche Oper am Rhein in Düsseldorf, becoming a full-fledged member of the company in 1972; also sang in Frankfurt am Main. In 1976 she made her debut at London's Covent Garden as Giorgetta in *Il Tabarro*. On Oct. 1, 1976, she made her first appearance at the Metropolitan Opera in N.Y. singing *Dich teure Halle* from *Tannhäuser* in a marathon concert, returning to make her formal debut there as Giorgetta on Oct. 15, 1976; in subsequent seasons, she returned to sing such roles as Fidelio, Elettra, Sieglinde, Isolde, Donna Anna, Brünnhilde, Berg's Marie, and Tosca. In 1983 she sang Brünnhilde at the Bayreuth Festival. She made her N.Y. recital debut in 1985.

Behrens, Jack, American composer and teacher; b. Lancaster, Pa., March 25, 1935. He was a student of Bergsma, Persichetti, and Mennin at the Juilliard School of Music in N.Y. (B.S., 1958; M.S., 1959), and then of Leon Kirchner and Sessions at Harvard Univ. (Ph.D., 1973); he also studied with Milhaud at the Aspen (Colo.) Music School (summer, 1962) and with Wolpe and Cage in Saskatchewan (summers, 1964–65). From 1962 to 1966 he taught at the Univ. of Saskatchewan, where he was head of the theory dept. at its cons. He taught at Simon Fraser Univ. (1966–70) and at Calif. State College in Bakersfield (1970–76). In 1976 he became a member of the faculty of music at the Univ. of Western Ontario, where he was chairman of the theory and composition dept. until 1980; he then served as dean of the faculty (1980–86). Behrens's music is in a sophisticated modern idiom, with judicious use of both serial and aleatoric procedures.

WORKS: OPERA: *The Lay of Thrym* (Regina, Saskatchewan, April 13, 1968). **ORCH.:** Trumpet Concerto (1955); *Introspection* for Strings (1956); *Declaration* (1964); *The Sound of Milo* (1970); Triple Concerto for Clarinet, Violin, Piano, and Orch. (1971); *Fantasy on Francis Hopkinson's My Days Have Been So Wondrous Free* for Small Orch. (1976); *New Beginnings* (1976); *A Greeting* (1977); *Fantasia on a Fragment* for Fortepiano and Chamber Orch. (1984); *Landmarks* (1991). **CHAMBER:** *Quarter Tone Quartet* for Strings (1960); *Green Centre* for Winds (1964; rev. 1990); *Serenades* for Flute, Clarinet, Piano, Violin, and Cello (1969); *Happy Birthday John Cage I and II* for Solo Instruments (1972); Clarinet Quintet (1974); *Bass Variants* for Double Bass (1977); *Dialogue* for Cello and Piano (1980); String Quartet, *In Nomine* (1980); *Fiona's Flute* for Flute and Piano (1982); *Well-tempered Duo* for Cello and Fortepiano (1984); *Reflections* for Viola and Clarinet (1990); *Reverberations* for Trumpet (1990). **PIANO:** *Passacaglia* (1964; rev. 1976); *Taos Portraits* (1976); *Music* for 2 Pianos (1979); *Aspects* for 3 Pianos (1983). **VOCAL:** *Early Song* for Tenor or Baritone, Flute, Oboe, Horn, Violin, and Viola (1965); *Looking Back* for Soprano, Flute, and Piano (1979); *A Fable—For the Whaling Fleets* for Narrator, Flute, Clarinet, Violin, Cello, and Piano (1985; rev. 1990); *I Have Mislaid Something* and *The Death of the Loch Ness Monster* for Baritone, Flute, and Piano (1985); many choral pieces.

Beilschmidt, Curt, German composer; b. Magdeburg, March 20, 1886; d. Leipzig, March 7, 1962. He studied in Magdeburg with Fritz Kauffmann; then in Leipzig (1905–09) with Stephan Krehl (theory), Adolf Ruthardt (piano), and Hans Sitt (violin). He served in the German army in World War I; returned to Leipzig in 1923 and founded a choral-symphonic group, which he continued to lead until 1954; also taught at the Leipzig Hochschule für Musik (1946–56). Among his works were the dance opera *Das Abenteuer im Walde* (Leipzig, March 13, 1918); the opera buffa *Meister Innocenz, Der schlaue Amor*

(Leipzig, July 6, 1921); the pastoral play *Der schlaue Amor* (Leipzig, 1921); the musical divertimento *Der Tugendwächter* (Halle, Oct. 14, 1927); and numerous works for orch. and chamber groups.

Beinum, Eduard (Alexander) van. See **Van Beinum, Eduard (Alexander).**

Bekker, (Max) Paul (Eugen), eminent German writer on music; b. Berlin, Sept. 11, 1882; d. N.Y., March 7, 1937. He studied violin with Rehfeld, piano with Sormann, and theory with Horwitz; began his career as a violinist with the Berlin Phil. He was music critic of the *Berliner Neueste Nachrichten* (1906–09) and of the *Berliner Allgemeine Zeitung* (1909–11); also served as chief music critic of the *Frankfurter Zeitung* from 1911. Later he became Intendant of the Kassel Stadttheater (1925); then in Wiesbaden (1927). In 1933 he left Germany, being unable to cope with the inequities of the Nazi regime. He publ. biographies of Oskar Fried (1907) and Jacques Offenbach (1909); also *Das Musikdrama der Gegenwart* (1909); Beethoven (1911; Eng. tr., 1926); *Das deutsche Musikleben, Versuch einer soziologischen Musikbetrachtung* (1916); *Die Sinfonie von Beethoven bis Mahler* (1918); *Franz Schreker* (1919); *Kunst und Revolution* (1919); *Die Weltgeltung der deutschen Musik* (1920); *Die Sinfonien G. Mahlers* (1921); *Richard Wagner* (1924; Eng. tr., 1931); *Von den Naturreichen des Klanges* (1924); *Musikgeschichte als Geschichte der musikalischen Formwandlungen* (1926); *Das Operntheater* (1930); *Briefe an zeitgenössische Musiker* (1932); *Wandlungen der Oper* (1934; Eng. tr., 1935, as *The Changing Opera*); *The Story of the Orchestra* (1936).

Bekku, Sadao, Japanese composer; b. Tokyo, May 24, 1922. He studied theoretical physics at the Univ. of Tokyo (1943–50); then studied composition with Milhaud, Rivier, and Messiaen at the Paris Cons. (1951–54). Returning to Japan, he became engaged in pedagogy; was also a member of the Japanese section of the ISCM from 1955 (president, 1968–73). His works are set in neo-Classical forms, with occasional use of authentic Japanese modalities. He publ. a book on the occult in music (Tokyo, 1971).

WORKS: OPERAS: *Le Dit les trois femmes*, opera buffa (Rome, 1964); *Prince Arima* (1963–67; Tokyo, March 13, 1967); *Aoi-no-ue* (1979). **ORCH.:** *Deux prières* (Tokyo, May 10, 1956); *Symphonietta* for Strings (Tokyo, Nov. 27, 1959); 4 syms. (1962, 1977, 1984, 1991); Violin Concerto (Tokyo Radio, Nov. 13, 1969); Viola Concerto (Tokyo, March 3, 1972); Piano Concerto (1981). **CHAMBER:** Trio for Oboe, Clarinet, and Bassoon (1953); Flute Sonata (1954); 2 *Japanese Suites*: No. 1 for Wind Quintet (1955) and No. 2 for 12 Instruments and Percussion (1958); String Quartet No. 1 (1955); Violin Sonata (1963–67); Viola Sonata (1969; arr. from the Violin Sonata). **PIANO:** Sonatina (1965); *Kaleidoscope*, suite (1966); *3 Paraphrases* (1968); *Sonatina in Classical Style* (1969). **VOCAL:** Choruses.

Belaiev, Victor (Mikhailovich), Russian musicologist and music critic; b. Uralsk, Feb. 6, 1888; d. Moscow, Feb. 16, 1968. He was a student of Liadov, Wihtol, and Glazunov at the St. Petersburg Cons. (graduated, 1914), where he was made a teacher (1913), senior lecturer (1916), and prof. of theory (1919). Shortly thereafter he settled in Moscow and became active with the Assn. for Contemporary Music. In addition to editing its journal, he wrote music criticism. He taught at the Moscow Cons. (1938–40; 1943–59), from which he received an honorary Ph.D. (1944). From 1959 he was a senior research fellow at the Inst. for the History of the Arts. He brought out brochures on various modern Russian composers; he also wrote a biography of Glazunov (Petrograd, 1922) and a collection of articles on Mussorgsky, Scriabin, and Stravinsky (Moscow, 1972). His most significant work is found in his articles on the music of central Asia.

Belkin, Boris, Russian-born Israeli, later Belgian violinist; b. Sverdlovsk, Jan. 26, 1948. He began violin lessons at age 6 and made his debut at 7; after training at Moscow's Central Music School, he completed his studies with Yankelevich and Andrievsky at the Moscow Cons.; he concurrently played throughout the Soviet Union. In 1972 he won 1st prize in the Soviet National Competition for violinists. In 1974 he emigrated to Israel and became a naturalized citizen. In 1975 he made his North American debut as soloist with the Montreal Sym. Orch. On April 22, 1975, he made his U.S. debut as soloist in the Tchaikovsky Concerto with the N.Y. Phil. He subsequently appeared with principal North American and European orchs. In later years, he made his home in Belgium, becoming a naturalized citizen of that country. He was particularly successful as an interpreter of 19th- and 20th-century violin masterworks.

Bell, Donald (Munro), Canadian bass-baritone; b. South Burnaby, British Columbia, June 19, 1934. He began his studies with Nancy Paisley Benn in Vancouver; after attending the Royal College of Music in London on scholarship (1953–55), he pursued training with Hermann Weissenborn in Berlin (1955–57); later he studied with Judith Boroschek in Düsseldorf (1967–76) and Richard Miller in Oberlin, Ohio (from 1985). He was only 14 when he was engaged to sing with the Vancouver Sym. Orch. In 1955 he appeared at the Glyndebourne Opera and the Berlin State Opera. In 1958 he made his recital debut at London's Wigmore Hall, and then appeared at the Bayreuth Festivals (1958–61). He made his Carnegie Hall debut in N.Y. in 1959. From 1964 to 1967 he was a member of the Deutsche Oper am Rhein in Düsseldorf, where he sang such roles as Don Giovanni, Count Almaviva, Wolfram, Amfortas, Kurwenal, and Gounod's Méphistophélès. He also sang at other European opera houses, but eventually became best known as a concert artist. In addition to the standard repertoire, he devoted much time to furthering the cause of contemporary music. After teaching at Carleton Univ. and the Univ. of Ottawa in 1977, he taught at the Univ. of Calgary from 1982.

Bell, Joshua, talented American violinist; b. Bloomington, Ind., Dec. 9, 1967. He first studied violin with Mimi Zweig, making his debut as a soloist with the Bloomington Sym. Orch. in 1975 at the age of 7; subsequently studied with Josef Gingold at the Indiana Univ. School of Music; also took summer courses with Ivan Galamian and a master class with Henryk Szeryng. He won the grand prize in the first annual Seventeen Magazine/General Motors National Concerto Competition in Rochester, N.Y., which led to his appearance as a soloist with the Philadelphia Orch. under Riccardo Muti on Sept. 24, 1982; he was the youngest soloist ever to appear with it at a subscription concert. In 1985 he made his Carnegie Hall debut in N.Y. as soloist with the St. Louis Sym. Orch. under Leonard Slatkin, and then toured Europe with them. In 1987 he was awarded the Avery Fisher Career Grant. In subsequent years, Bell appeared as a soloist with principal world orchs., and also gave solo recitals and played in chamber music settings. On Sept. 29, 1993, he was soloist in the premiere of Nicholas Maw's Violin Concerto with Roger Norrington and the Orch. of St. Luke's in N.Y.

Bell, W(illiam) H(enry), English composer; b. St. Albans, Aug. 20, 1873; d. Gordon's Bay, Cape Province, South Africa, April 13, 1946. He studied in his hometown; won the Goss Scholarship for the Royal College of Music in London (1889); studied organ with Stegall, violin with Burnett, piano with Izard, and composition with Corder and Stanford. He taught harmony at his alma mater (1903–12); in 1912, was appointed director of the South African College of Music in Cape Town and then dean of the music faculty at the Univ. of South Africa (1919), retiring in 1936. He was extremely critical of himself as a composer, and destroyed many of his MSS. Among his surviving works are the operas *Hippolytus* (1914) and *Isabeau* (1924); he also composed *Walt Whitman Symphony* (1899); Sym. No. 2 (1917–18); Sym. No. 3 (1918–19); *South African Symphony* (1927); Sym. in F minor (1932); *A Vision of Delight* (1906); *Arcadian Suite* (1908); symphonic poems: *Love among the Ruins* (1908), *The Shepherd* (1908), *La Fée des sources* (1912), and *Veldt Loneliness* (1921); Viola Concerto; Violin Sonata.

BIBL.: M. van Someren Godfrey, "The Symphonic Works of W.H. B.," *Musical Times* (May/June 1920); H. du Plessis, ed., *Letters from W.H. B.* (Cape Town and Johannesburg, 1973).

Bellezza, Vincenzo, Italian conductor; b. Bitonto, Bari, Feb. 17, 1888; d. Rome, Feb. 8, 1964. He studied piano with Alessandro Longo, composition with Nicola d'Arienzo, and conducting with Giuseppe Martucci at the Naples Cons. He made his conducting debut at the Teatro San Carlo in Naples in 1908; then conducted throughout Italy; also had guest engagements at Covent Garden, London (1926–30; 1935–36); served as guest conductor at the Metropolitan Opera in N.Y. (1926–35). After his return to Italy, he was on the staff of the Rome Opera.

Bellincioni, Gemma (Cesira Matilda), noted Italian soprano; b. Monza, Aug. 18, 1864; d. Naples, April 23, 1950. She studied with her father, the comic bass Cesare Bellincioni, and her mother, the contralto Carlotta Soroldoni. At age 15, she made her operatic debut in dell'Orefice's *Il segreto della Duchesa* at the Teatro della Società Filarmonica in Naples. After further studies with Luigia Ponti and Giovanni Corsi, she sang in Spain and Portugal (1882), and then in Rome (1885). In 1886 she made her first appearance at Milan's La Scala as Violetta, and that same year toured South America, where she became intimate with the tenor **Roberto Stagno**. In subsequent years, they toured together in opera and concert, although she never appeared in the U.S. On May 17, 1890, she created the role of Santuzza opposite Stagno's Turiddu at the Teatro Costanzi in Rome. On Nov. 17, 1898, she created the role of Fedora at Milan's Teatro Lirico. With Strauss conducting, she was the first to sing Salome in Italy in Turin in 1900, a role she subsequently sang more than 100 times. In 1911 she made her farewell operatic appearance as Salome in Paris, although she came out of retirement to sing opera in the Netherlands in 1924. She taught in Berlin (1911–15), Vienna (1931–32), and at the Naples Cons. (from 1932). Her autobiography was publ. as *Io ed il palcoscenico* (Milan, 1920).

BIBL.: B. Stagno-Bellincioni, *Roberto Stagno e G. B., intimi* (Florence, 1943).

Bělohlávek, Jiří, Czech conductor; b. Prague, Feb. 24, 1946. He studied piano with his father; also took cello lessons at the Prague Cons., and attended Sergiu Celibidache's master classes in conducting. In 1970 he won 1st prize in the Czech national competition for young conductors. From 1970 to 1972 he was assistant conductor of the Czech Phil. in Prague. He then was conductor of the Brno State Phil. (1972–77), with which he toured the U.S. In 1977 he was appointed chief conductor of the Prague Sym. Orch., a position he held until 1985. He appeared widely in Europe and abroad as a guest conductor; frequently was conductor with the Czech Phil., serving as its chief conductor from 1990 to 1992. From 1995 he was conductor of the newly-founded Prague Chamber Phil.

Bely, Victor, Russian composer; b. Berdichev, Jan. 14, 1904; d. Moscow, March 6, 1983. He studied composition at the Moscow Cons., then wrote some insignificant piano music and publ. a worthwhile collection of folk songs of the Ural region. He acquired particular notoriety as the organizer of the Procoll (Production Collective), with the purpose of initiating a system of composition *en masse*; from 1929 to 1932 he was also an active member of this so-called association of proletarian musicians. This kind of Communist extremism, however, proved unacceptable even from the official Soviet line, and Bely's organization was ingloriously dissolved. He eventually compromised by writing mass songs of social significance set to explosive revolutionary texts.

Ben-Dor, Gisèle (née **Buka**), Uruguayan conductor of Polish descent; b. Montevideo, April 26, 1955. Her parents emigrated to Uruguay after World War II. She commenced piano lessons at age 4 with Gloria Rodriguez and Santiago Baranda Reyes at the J.S. Bach Cons.; later received instruction in harmony and counterpoint from Yolanda Rizzardini. She was only 12 when she began conducting, and at 14 she was made music director of her school's choral and instrumental ensembles. In 1973 she accompanied her family to Israel, where she studied piano with Enrique Barenboim and composition with Arthur Gelbrun. She then studied orchestral conducting with S. Ronley Riklis and choral conducting with Avner Itai; also trained with Mendi Rodan in Jerusalem. Following further studies with Franco Ferrara at the Accademia Musicale Chigiana in Siena (1980), she completed her education at the Yale School of Music (M.A., 1982). In 1982 she made a notably successful debut with the Israel Phil.; subsequently appeared with other Israeli orchs. She was a Fellow Conductor of the Los Angeles Phil. Inst. and at the Berkshire Music Center in Tanglewood in 1985, and was awarded the Leonard Bernstein fellowship. In 1986 she won the Bartók Prize of the Hungarian TV conductor's competition. In 1987–88 she was assistant conductor of the Louisville Orch. From 1988 to 1991 she was resident conductor of the Houston Sym. Orch., where, during her tenure, she also served as music director of the Houston Youth Sym. and as acting music director of the Orch. at the Shepherd School of Music at Rice Univ. In 1991 she became music director of the Boston ProArte Chamber Orch. and of the Annapolis Sym. Orch. In Dec. 1993 she made an auspicious debut with the N.Y. Phil. when she was called in at the last minute to substitute for an ailing Kurt Masur. She conducted the concert without benefit of rehearsals and without scores, winning audience acclaim. In 1994 she became music director of the Santa Barbara Sym. Orch. while retaining her posts in Boston and Annapolis. As a guest conductor, she appeared widely in North America, Europe, and Israel.

Ben-Haim (real name, **Frankenburger**), **Paul,** eminent German-born Israeli composer and teacher; b. Munich, July 5, 1897; d. Tel Aviv, Jan. 14, 1984. He studied piano, composition (with Klose), and conducting at the Munich Academy of Arts (1915–20). He was assistant conductor to Walter and Knappertsbusch (1920–24) before serving as conductor in Augsburg (1924–31). With the advent of the Nazi regime in 1933, he emigrated to Tel Aviv and changed his surname to the Hebrew Ben-Haim. He was director of the Jerusalem Academy of Music (1949–54). In 1957 he was awarded the Israel State Prize. An automobile accident in 1972 brought a premature end to his creative work. Although his output followed generally along late Romantic lines, he also was influenced by the indigenous music of the Middle East, particularly of his adopted homeland. He was especially successful as a composer of vocal works.

WORKS: ORCH.: *Concerto Grosso* (1931); *Pan*, symphonic poem (1931); 2 syms.: No. 1 (1940; Tel Aviv, June 5, 1941) and No. 2 (1945; Tel Aviv, Feb. 2, 1948); *Evocation* for Violin and Orch. (1942); Concerto for Strings (1947); Piano Concerto (1949; Tel Aviv, Feb. 1, 1950); *Fanfare to Israel* (1950; also for Band); *From Israel* (1951); *The Sweet Psalmist of Israel* (1953; Tel Aviv, Oct. 18, 1956); *To the Chief Musician* (1958); Violin Concerto (1960; Tel Aviv, March 20, 1962); *Dance and Invocation* (1960; Tel Aviv, Feb. 2, 1961); *Capriccio* for Piano and Orch. (Tel Aviv., Sept. 25, 1960); Cello Concerto (1962; Limburg, Dec. 14, 1967); *The Eternal Theme* (1965; Tel Aviv, Feb. 12, 1966); *Divertimento* for Flute and Chamber Orch. (1971–72). **CHAMBER:** String Trio (1927); String Quartet (1937); Clarinet Quintet (1941); *Serenade* for Flute and String Trio (1952); Sonata for Solo Violin (1953); *3 Pieces* for Cello (1973); piano pieces, including a Sonata (1953). **VOCAL:** *Yoram*, oratorio (1931); Liturgical Cantata for Baritone, Chorus, and Orch. or Organ (1950); *A Book of Verses* for Chorus (1958); *Vision of a Prophet*, cantata for Tenor, Chorus, and Orch. (1959); *Lift up Your Heads*, motet for Soprano and 8 Instruments (1961); *3 Psalms* for Solo Voices, Chorus, and Orch. (1962); *A Hymn to the Desert* for Soprano, Baritone, Chorus, and Orch. (1963); *Myrtle Blossoms from Eden* for Soprano or Tenor, Alto or Baritone, and Piano or Chamber Orch. (1966); *Kabbalai Shabbat* (Friday Evening Service) for Soprano, Tenor, Chorus, and Organ or 9 Instruments (1967); *6 Sephardic Songs* for Chorus (1971).

BIBL.: J. Hirschberg, *P. B.-H.* (Tel Aviv, 1983; Eng. tr., 1990); H. Guttmann, *The Music of B.-H.: A Performance Guide* (Metuchen, N.J., 1992).

Ben-Yohanan, Asher, Israeli composer and pedagogue; b. Kávala, Greece, May 22, 1929. He went to Palestine in 1935 and studied composition with Ben-Haim in Tel Aviv; after studies with Reese and La Rue at N.Y. Univ. (1958–61), he continued his training in 1966 with Copland at the Berkshire Music Center in Tanglewood, Nono in Venice, and in Darmstadt; then studied at the Univ. of Mich. (M.M., 1970); was the Morse fellow in composition and a teacher at the Univ. of Cincinnati College-Cons. of Music (1970–71). He taught theory and literature at the Israel Cons. of Music (1962–69) and at the Telma Yellin Music and Arts School (1964–87), where he also was head of the music dept. until 1975; was prof. of theory and composition at Bar-Ilan Univ. (from 1973); also was chairman of the Israel Composers' League (1989–92).

WORKS: ORCH.: *Independence Day Parade* for Wind Band (1956); *Festive Overture* (1957); *2 Movements* (1959); *Music* (1967); Concertino for Strings (1973); *Variations* (1980; rev. 1989); *Meditations* for Chamber Orch. (1992). **CHAMBER:** String Quartet (1962–64); *Chamber Music for 6* (1968); *Quartetto Concertato* for Piano, Clarinet, Trombone, and Cello (1969–70); *Meditations on a Folk Song* for Piano, Flute, and Clarinet (1972); *3 Pieces for 3 Woodwinds* for Oboe, Clarinet, and Bassoon (1978); Woodwind Quintet (1985); *Divertimento* for Brass Trio (1988–89); *Hidden Feelings* for Harp (1990). **VOCAL:** *Ode to Jerusalem* for Chorus (1954); *Mosaic* for Soprano and 10 Players (1970–71); *Yefeh Nof* (O Fair Sight) for Chorus (1984).

Beňačková, Gabriela, prominent Czech soprano; b. Bratislava, March 25, 1947. After studies with Ondrej Francisci, she was a pupil of Tatiana Kresáková and Magda Móryová at the Cons. and of Janko Blaho at the Academy of Arts and Music in Bratislava. In 1969 she won the Dvořák vocal competition in Karlovy Vary, which led to her operatic debut as Prokofiev's Natasha at the Prague National Theater in 1970, where she sang regularly until 1981. She made her first appearance at London's Covent Garden in 1979 and at the Vienna State Opera in 1980; also sang in Cologne, Munich, Salzburg, N.Y., and other major music centers, in both opera and concert. In 1976 she was awarded the National Prize, and then received the titles of Artist of Merit (1979) and National Artist (1985) from her homeland. In 1988 she was made a Kammersängerin of the Vienna State Opera. She is highly regarded for her roles in operas by Smetana, Dvořák, and Janáček, and has also won admiration for her Manon, Tatiana, Marguerite, and Mimi.

Benatzky, Ralph (actually, **Rudolf Josef František**), Czech composer; b. Mährisch-Budwitz, June 5, 1884; d. Zürich, Oct. 16, 1957. He studied in Vienna, in Prague with Veit and Klinger, and in Munich with Mottl; he also took a Ph.D. in philology. After conducting at the Kleines Theater in Munich (1910–11), he went to Vienna as music director at the Kabarett Rideamus. He first gained notice as a composer for the theater with his operetta *Der lachende Dreibund* (Berlin, Oct. 31, 1913). His first notable success came with the operetta *Liebe im Schnee* (Vienna, Dec. 2, 1916), which was followed by the successful premieres of *Yuschi tanzt* (Vienna, April 3, 1920), *Apachen* (Vienna, Dec. 20, 1920), *Pipsi* (Vienna, Dec. 30, 1921), *Ein Märchen aus Florenz* (Vienna, Sept. 14, 1923), and *Adieu Mimi* (Vienna, June 9, 1926). From 1924 he also was active at the Grosses Schauspielhaus in Berlin, where he provided music for various productions, including the Johann Strauss pasticcio *Casanova* (Sept. 1, 1928) and *Die drei Musketiere* (Sept. 28, 1929). It was at that theater that he brought out his celebrated operetta *Im weissen Rössl* (Nov. 8, 1930), which was also made into a film in 1935. Among his other theater scores were *Cocktail* (Berlin, Dec. 15, 1930), *Zirkus Aimée* (Basel, March 5, 1932), *Bezauberndes Fräulein* (Vienna, May 24, 1933), *Deux sous de fleurs* (Paris, Oct. 6, 1933), *Das kleine Café* (Vienna, April 20, 1934), *Axel an der Himmelstur* (Vienna, Sept. 1, 1936), *Pairserinnin* (Vienna, May 7, 1937; rev. ver., Lucerne, Dec. 11, 1964), *Majestät-privat* (Vienna, Dec. 18, 1937), and *Der Silberhof* (Mainz, Nov. 4, 1941). During World War II, Benatzky lived in the U.S. After the War, he returned to Europe and finally settled in Switzerland.

Benda, Hans von, German conductor; b. Strasbourg, Nov. 22, 1888; d. Berlin, Aug. 13, 1972. He was a descendant of the Benda family of Bohemia. He studied at the Stern Cons. in Berlin; also at the Univs. of Berlin and Munich. He was director of music of the Berlin Radio (1926–33); then Intendant of the Berlin Phil. (1934–39); in 1939 he organized the Berlin Chamber Orch., with which he toured throughout Europe, South America, and the Far East. From 1954 to 1958 he served as director of music of Radio Free Berlin.

Bender, Paul, esteemed German bass-baritone and bass; b. Driedorf, July 28, 1875; d. Munich, Nov. 25, 1947. He was a student of Luise Reuss-Belce and Baptist Hoffmann in Berlin. In 1900 he made his operatic debut as the Hermit in *Der Freischütz* in Breslau; then was a principal member of the Munich Court Opera (1903–18), and its successor, the Bavarian State Opera (1918–33). In 1914 and 1924 he sang at London's Covent Garden. On Nov. 17, 1922, he made his Metropolitan Opera debut in N.Y. as Baron Ochs, remaining on its roster until 1927. In later years, he was a prof. of voice at the Munich Academy of Music. A greatly admired artist, Bender was made a Bavarian Kammersänger. He was equally successful in serious and buffo roles, being particularly noted for his Mozart and Wagner. In 1917 he created the role of Pope Pius V in Pfitzner's *Palestrina*. He was also a fine lieder artist and did much to promote the songs of Carl Loewe.

Benestad, Finn, distinguished Norwegian musicologist; b. Kristiansand, Oct. 30, 1929. He was educated at the Univ. of Oslo (M.A., 1953; Ph.D., 1961, with the diss. *Johannes Haarklou: Mannen og verket*; publ. in Oslo, 1961). After working as a teacher (1950–59) and a music critic (1953–61) in Oslo, he served as prof. of musicology at the Univ. of Trondheim (1961–64) and at the Univ. of Oslo (from 1965); also was a Fulbright scholar at the Univ. of Calif. at Los Angeles (1968–69). He was chairman of the collected works of Grieg, to which he contributed several vols. In 1979 he was made a member of the Norwegian Academy of Science and Letters.

WRITINGS (all publ. in Oslo unless otherwise given): *Waldemar Thrane: En pionér i norsk musikkliv* (1961); *Musikklaere* (1963; 5th ed., 1977); *Musikkhistorisk oversikt* (1965; 3rd ed., 1976); ed. with P. Krømer, *Festschrift til Olav Gurvin* (Oslo and Drammen, 1968); ed. *Norsk musikk: Studier i Norge*, vol. VI (1968); ed. *Skolens visebok* (1972); with others, *Aschehougs musikkverk* (1973–77); *Musikk og tanke: Hovedretninger i musikkestetikkens historie fra antikken til vår egen tid* (1976; 2nd ed., 1977); with D. Schjeldrup-Ebbe, *Edvard Grieg: Mennesket og kunstneren* (1980; Eng. tr., 1987, as *Edvard Grieg: The Man and the Artist*); with D. Schjeldrup-Ebbe, *Edvard Grieg Chamber Music: Nationalism, Universality, Individuality* (Oxford, 1993).

Bengtsson, Gustaf Adolf Tiburt(ius), Swedish conductor and composer; b. Vadstena, March 29, 1886; d. there, Oct. 5, 1965. He studied at the Stockholm Cons.; then in Berlin with Juon and in Leipzig with Riemann; subsequently was active in Karlstad as a composer and teacher; later was conductor in Linköping (1943–49).

WORKS: 3 syms. (1908, 1910, 1921); Violin Concerto; Cello Concerto; *Sinfonia concertante* for Violin, Viola, and Orch.; *Canone concertante* for Violin, Viola, and Chamber Orch. (1950); *Vettern*, symphonic poem (1950); String Quartet (1907); Piano Trio (1916); Violin Sonata; songs.

Bengtsson, (Lars) Ingmar (Olof), eminent Swedish musicologist; b. Stockholm, March 2, 1920; d. there, Dec. 3, 1989. He studied piano at the Stockholm Musikhögskolan and musicology at the univs. of Stockholm, Uppsala (Ph.D., 1955, with diss. *J.H. Roman och hans instrumentalmusik: Käll och stilkritiska studier*, publ. in Uppsala, 1955), and Basel. He appeared as a pianist and harpsichordist (1942–55); wrote music criticism for Stockholm's *Svenska Dagbladet* (1943–59); was a lecturer (1947–61) and a prof. (1961–85) at the Univ. of Uppsala. He served as president of the Swedish Soc. of Musicology (1961–85) and as ed.-in-chief of its journal, *Svensk tidskrift för musikforskning* (1962–71). In 1963 he became chairman of the complete ed. of Berwald's works. In 1965 he founded the Swedish Archives of the History of Music. He was honored with a Festschrift on his 50th (1970) and 65th (1985) birthdays.

WRITINGS: *Bach och hans tid* (Stockholm, 1946); *Från visa till symfoni* (Stockholm, 1947; 5th ed., 1973); with R. Danielson, *Handstilar och notpikturer i Kungl.: Musikaliska akademiens Roman-samling* (Uppsala, 1955); *Modern nordisk musik: Fjorton tonsättare om egna verk* (Stockholm, 1957); *Musikvetenskap: En oversikt* (Stockholm, 1973; 2nd ed., 1977); *Mr. Roman's Spuriosity Shop: A Thematic Catalogue of 503 Works (1213 Incipits and Other Excerpts) from ca. 1680–1750 by More Than Sixty Composers* (Stockholm, 1976); *Beräkning av intervall, stämningar, tempereringar m. m. med hjälp av räknedosa: Ett kompendium* (Uppsala, 1978); *Musikvidenskab—nu og i fremtiden* (Copenhagen, 1978); with E. Lomnäs and N. Castegren, *Franz Berwald: Die Dokumente seines Lebens* (Kassel, 1979); *Något om det heroiska i 1800-taets dikt och ton* (Lund, 1984).

Benguerel, Xavier, Spanish composer; b. Barcelona, Feb. 9, 1931. He was a pupil of Cristóbal Taltabull. His early works were influenced by French Impressionism; in 1958 he adopted the dodecaphonic techniques; then tilted toward extreme modernism.

WORKS: ORCH.: Concerto for Piano and Strings (1955); *Contrasts* for Chamber Orch. (1959); Concerto for 2 Flutes and Strings (1961); *Sinfonia continua* (Bilbao, Oct. 21, 1962); Violin Concerto (Barcelona, Oct. 9, 1965); *Sinfonia per a un Festival* (Barcelona, Oct. 30, 1966); *Sinfonia per a Petita Orquestra* (Hagen, Germany, April 24, 1967); *Sinfonia per a Gran Orquestra* (Barcelona, Oct. 2, 1968); *Dialogue orchestrale* (1969); *Musica riservata* for Strings (1969); *Consort Music* for Strings (1970); Organ Concerto (Baden-Baden, Sept. 17, 1971); Guitar Concerto (Kassel, Feb. 17, 1972); *Quasi una fantasia* for Cello and Chamber Orch. (Barcelona, Oct. 22, 1972); *Destructio* (Madrid, March 23, 1973); Percussion Concerto (1975). **CHAMBER:** 2 violin sonatas (1953, 1959); String Quartet No. 1 (1954); *4 estructuras: I* for Violin (1957), *II* for Flute (1959), *III* for Cello (1964), and *IV* for Piano (1966); *Successions* for Wind Quintet (1960); Duo for Clarinet and Piano (1963); *Musica* for 3 Percussionists (1967); *Test Sonata* for 17 Instruments and Percussion (1968); *Musica per a Oboe* for Oboe and Chamber Group (1968); *Crescendo* for Organ (1970); *Intento a dos* for Guitar and Percussion (1970); *Verses* for Guitar (1973); *Vermelia* for 4 Guitars (1976). **VOCAL:** *Nocturno de los avisos* for Soprano, Chorus, and Orch. (1963); *Paraule de Cada Dia* for Voice and Chamber Orch. (1967); *Arbor*, cantata for Soloists, 4 Speakers, Chorus, and Orch. (Barcelona, Oct. 22, 1972).

Benjamin, Arthur, admired Australian pianist, teacher, and composer; b. Sydney, Sept. 18, 1893; d. London, April 9, 1960. After studies in Brisbane, he completed his training at the Royal College of Music in London with Frederick Cliffe (piano) and Sir Charles Stanford (composition). He taught at the Sydney Cons. (1919–21) and the Royal College of Music (from 1926). After pursuing his career in Vancouver, British Columbia (1939–46), he returned to England. Benjamin was an adept composer who produced works in a readily accessible style.

WORKS: DRAMATIC: OPERAS: *The Devil Take Her* (London, Dec. 1, 1931); *Prima Donna* (1933; London, Feb. 23, 1949); *A Tale of 2 Cities* (1949–50; BBC, London, April 17, 1953); *Mañana*, television opera (1956); *Tartuffe* (1960; completed by A. Boustead; London, Nov. 30, 1964). **BALLET:** *Orlando's Silver Wedding* (London, May 1951). **ORCH.:** Piano Concertino (1927); *Light Music*, suite (1928–33); Violin Concerto (1932); *Heritage*, ceremonial march (1935); *Romantic Fantasy* for Violin, Viola, and Orch. (1937; London, March 24, 1938); *Overture to an Italian Comedy* (London, March 2, 1937); *Cotillon*, suite (1938); *2 Jamaican Pieces* (1938; includes the highly popular *Jamaican Rumba*; also for 1 or 2 Pianos); *Prelude to Holiday* (1940; Indianapolis, Jan. 17, 1941); Sonatina for Chamber Orch. (1940); Concerto for Oboe and Strings (transcribed from Cimarosa, 1942); Sym. No. 1 (1944–45; Cheltenham, June 30, 1948); Suite for Flute and Strings (transcribed from Scarlatti, 1945); *Elegy, Waltz and Toccata*, viola concerto (1945; also for Viola and Piano); *From San Domingo* (1945); *Caribbean Dance* (1946); *Ballade* for Strings (1947); *Concerto quasi una fantasia* for Piano and Orch. (Sydney, Sept. 5, 1950); Harmonica Concerto (London, Aug. 15, 1953); *North American Square Dances* for 2 Pianos and Orch. (Pittsburgh, April 1, 1955). **CHAMBER:** *3 Pieces* for Violin and Piano (1919); 2 string quartets (*Pastorale Fantasia*, 1924; 1959); Violin Sonatina (1924); Cello Sonatina (1938); *Le Tombeau de Ravel: Valse Caprice* for Clarinet or Viola and Piano (1949); *Divertimento* for Wind Quintet (1960). **PIANO:** Suite (1927); *2 Jamaican Songs* for 2 Pianos (1949). **VOCAL:** *3 Impressions* for Voice and String Quartet (1920); choral music; songs.

Benjamin, George (William John), gifted English composer, pianist, and conductor; b. London, Jan. 31, 1960. He was 7 when he began to study piano and 9 when he commenced composition lessons. After studies with Gellhorn in London (1974–76), he pursued training at the Paris Cons. (1976–78) with Messiaen (composition) and Loriod (piano); then continued composition studies with A. Goehr at King's College, Cambridge (1978–82), and also had lessons with Robin Holloway. From 1984 to 1987 he conducted research in electronic music at IRCAM in Paris. In 1979 he made his debut in London as a pianist. In 1980 he became the youngest composer ever to have a work performed at the London Proms when his *Ringed by the Flat Horizon* was given there. In subsequent years, he was active as a pianist and conductor in Europe, the U.S., and the Far East. He also was a visting prof. of composition at the Royal College of Music in London (from 1988) and principal guest artist of the Hallé Orch. in Manchester (from 1993). In his music, Benjamin has exploited the full range of compositional expression, from the traditional to electronics. His *Antara*, a complex synthesis of panpipe sonorities re-created in concerto form with IRCAM's famous 4X computer, was the subject of a 1987 documentary produced by the BBC.

WORKS: ORCH.: *Altitude* for Brass Band (1977); *Ringed by the Flat Horizon* (1979–80); *At First Light* for Chamber Orch. (1982); *Jubilation* (1985); *Antara* for 16 Players and Electronics (1987; rev. 1988–89); *Sudden Time* (1989–93); *Cascade* (1990); *Tribute in Memory of Olivier Messiaen* (1993); *3 Inventions* for Chamber Orch. (1995). **CHAMBER:** Violin Sonata (1976–77); Octet (1978); *Flight* for Flute (1979); Duo for Cello and Piano (1980); *Fanfare for Aquarius* for Chamber Ensemble (1983). **PIANO:** Sonata (1977–78); *Sortilèges* (1981); *3 Studies: Meditation on Haydn's Name* (1982), *Relativity Rag* (1984), and *Fantasy on Iambic Pentameter* (1985). **VOCAL:** *A Mind of Winter* for Soprano and Small Orch. (1981); *Upon Silence* for Mezzo-soprano and 5 Viols (1990). **TAPE:** *Panorama* (1985).

Benjamin, William E(mmanuel), Canadian music theorist, musicologist, and composer; b. Montreal, Dec. 7, 1944. He studied composition with Anhalt at McGill Univ. in Montreal (Mus.B., 1965) and with Babbitt, Cone, Westergaard, and Randall at Princeton Univ. (M.F.A., 1968; Ph.D., 1976, with the diss. *On Modular Equivalence as a Musical Concept*). After teaching at Wellesley College (1970–72) and the Univ. of Mich. (1972–78), he was assoc. (1978–83) and then full (from 1983) prof. at the Univ. of British Columbia, where he was head of the music school (1984–91). His writings on theory and analysis have been publ. in various journals. In his music, he strives to fashion a rational multidimensional musical space, in which dynamics, rhythm, and tonality are functional components in free serial arrangements.

WORKS: *A Midsummer Night's Dream*, incidental music to Shakespeare's play (1964); *The King of Siam*, incidental music to L. Angel's play (1965); *Mah Tovu*, hymn for Chorus (1965); *Variations* for 4 Players (1967); *At Sixes and Sevens*, sextet for Strings and Clarinets (1968); *2 Movements* for String Trio (1972); Piano Concerto (1970–75); *Square Waves* for Concert Band (1976–77); *2 Poems* for Contralto and Chamber Ensemble (1981); *The Unveiling*, incidental music to L. Angel's play (1982); *Sequences* for Guitar (1982).

Bennard, George, American hymn composer; b. Youngstown, Ohio, Feb. 4, 1873; d. Reed City, Mich., Oct. 10, 1958. He served as a Salvation Army officer from 1892 to 1907; subsequently traveled as an evangelist in the U.S. and Canada. He wrote a number of sacred songs, among them *God Bless Our Boys, The Old Rugged Cross*, and *Sweet Songs of Salvation*.

Bennett, Richard Rodney, prominent English composer; b. Broadstairs, Kent, March 29, 1936. He studied with Lennox Berkeley and Howard Ferguson at the Royal Academy of Music in London (1953–57) and with Boulez in Paris (1957–59). After serving as a prof. of composition at the Royal Academy of Music (1963–65), he devoted himself mainly to composition; also served as vice-president of the Royal College of Music in London (from 1983). In 1977 he was made a Commander of the Order of the British Empire. A prolific and facile composer, Bennett's output includes stage and concert works as well as film scores; in some of his compositions, he utilizes serial techniques.

WORKS: DRAMATIC: OPERAS: *The Ledge* (London, Sept. 11, 1961); *The Mines of Sulphur* (London, Feb. 24, 1965); *Penny for a Song* (London, Oct. 31, 1967); *All the King's Men*, children's opera (Coventry, March 28, 1969); *Victory* (London, April 13, 1970). **BALLETS:** *Jazz Calendar* (1963–64); *Isadora* (1980; London, April 30, 1981); *Noctuary* (1981; Armidale, New South Wales, June 3, 1985). Film scores, including *Murder on the Orient Express* (1974) and *Equus* (1977); also radio and television music. **ORCH.:** Horn Concerto (1956); *Journal* (1960); *Calendar* for Chamber Ensemble (London, Nov. 24, 1960); *Suite française* for Chamber Orch. (1961); *London Pastoral* for Chamber Ensemble (1961); *Nocturnes* for Chamber Orch. (1962); *A Jazz Calendar* for 12 Instruments (1963–64; produced as a ballet, London, 1968); *Aubade* (London, Sept. 1, 1964); 3 syms.: No. 1 (London, Feb. 10, 1966), No. 2 (N.Y., Jan. 18, 1968), and No. 3 (Worcester, Aug. 24, 1987); Piano Concerto (Birmingham, Sept. 19, 1968); Concerto for Guitar and Chamber Ensemble (London, Nov. 18, 1920); Concerto for Oboe and Strings (Aldeburgh Festival, June 6, 1971); Viola Concerto (N.Y., July 3, 1973); *Concerto for Orchestra* (Denver, Feb. 25, 1974); Violin Concerto (Birmingham, March 25, 1976); *Zodiac* (Washington, D.C., March 30, 1976); *Serenade* (London, April 24, 1977); *Acteon* for Horn and Orch. (London, Aug. 12, 1977); *Music* for Strings (Cheltenham, July 7, 1978); Double Bass Concerto (London, Oct. 15, 1978); *Sonnets to Orpheus* for Cello and Orch. (Edinburgh, Sept. 3, 1979); Harpsichord Concerto (St. Louis, Dec. 4, 1980); *Anniversaries* (London, Sept. 9, 1982); *Memento* for Flute and Strings (Windsor, Sept. 28, 1983); *Sinfonietta* (1984); *Moving into Aquarius* (1984; London, Jan. 23, 1985); *Reflections on a Theme of William Walton* for 11 Solo Strings (London, May 20, 1985); *Dream Dancing* (London, May 28, 1986); *Morning Music* for Symphonic Wind Ensemble (1986); Clarinet Concerto (1987); Marimba Concerto (Allentown, Pa., March 11, 1988); Saxophone Concerto (London, Oct. 14, 1988); *Diversions* (1989); *Flowers of the Forest* for Brass Band (1989); Percussion Concerto (1990); *Concerto for Stan Getz* for Saxophone and Orch. (1990); *Celebration* (1991); *The 4 Seasons* for Symphonic Wind Band (1991); *Variations on a Nursery Tune* (1992); Concerto for Trumpet and Wind Band (1993); Bassoon Concerto (London, April 4, 1995). **CHAMBER:** 4 string quartets (1952, 1953, 1960, 1964); Sonatina for Solo Flute (1954); *4 Improvisations* for Violin (1955); *Winter Music* for Flute and Piano (1960); Oboe Sonata (1961); Sonata for Solo Violin (1964); *Conversations* for 2 Flutes (1964); Trio for Flute, Oboe, and Clarinet (1965); Wind Quintet (1967–68); *5 Impromptus* for Guitar (1968); *Commedia I* for 6 Players (1972), *II* for Flute, Cello, and Piano (1972–73), *III* for 10 Instruments (1972–73), and *IV* for Brass Quintet (1972–73); *Scena II* for Cello (1973) and *III* for Basset Horn (1977); Oboe Quartet (1975); *Travel Notes* I for String Quartet (1975) and II for Wind Quartet (1976); Horn Sonata (1978); Violin Sonata (1978); *Metamorphoses* for String Octet (1980); *6 Tunes for the Instruction of Singing Birds* for Flute (1981); *Music* for String Quartet (1981); Sonatina for Solo Clarinet (1981); *After Syrinx I* for Oboe and Piano (1982) and *II* for Marimba (1984); Concerto for Wind Quintet (1983); Guitar Sonata (1983); *Serenade No. 2* for Ondes Martenot and Piano (1984); *Romances* for Horn and Piano (1985); Duo Concertante for Clarinet and Piano (1985); *Sonata After Syrinx* for Flute, Viola, and Harp (1985); *Sounds and Sweet Aires* for Flute, Oboe, and Piano (1985); Sonata for Wind Quintet and Piano (1986); *Lamento d'Arianna* for String Quartet (1986); Soprano Saxophone Sonata (1986); *After Ariadne* for Viola and Piano (1986); *Tender is the Night*, suite for Ondes Martenot and String Quartet (1987); *Arethusa* for Oboe and String Trio (1989); *Capriccio* for Cello and Piano (1990); Cello Sonata (1991); Bassoon Sonata (1991); *Arabesque* for Oboe (1992); Clarinet Quintet (1992). **PIANO:** Sonata (1954); *5 Studies* (1962–64); *Capriccio* for Piano, 4-hands (1968); *Scena I* (1973); *4-piece Suite* for 2 Pianos (1974); *Kandinsky Variations* for 2 Pianos (1977); *Impromptu on the Name of Haydn* (1981); *Noctuary: Variations on a Theme of Joplin* (1981); *Tango after Syrinx* (1985); *3 Romantic Pieces* (1988); *Partridge Pie* (1990); *Over the Hills and Far Away* for Piano Duet (1991). **VOCAL:** *The Approaches of Sleep* for 4 Voices and 10 Instruments (1959); *Soliloquy* for Voice and Jazz Ensemble (1966); *Epithalamion* for Chorus and Orch. (1966); *The Music That Her Echo Is*, cycle for Tenor and Piano (1967); *Jazz Pastoral* for Voice and Jazz Ensemble (1969); *Crazy Jane* for Soprano, Piano, Clarinet, and Cello (1968–69); *Sonnet Sequence* for Tenor and Instrumental Ensemble (1971); *The House of Sleep* for 6 Men's Voices (1971); *Tenebrae* for Baritone and Piano (1971); *Devotions* for Chorus (1971); *Nightpiece* for Soprano and Tape (1972); *Times Whiter Series* for Countertenor and Lute (1974); *Spells* for Soprano, Chorus, and Orch. (Worcester, Aug. 28, 1975); *Letters to Lindbergh* for Women's Voices and Piano Duet (1982); *Love Songs* for Tenor and Orch. (1984); *And Death Shall Have No Dominion* for Men's Chorus and Horn (1986); *Missa brevis* for Chorus (1990); *Sermons and Devotions* for 6 Men's Voices (1992).

BIBL.: S. Craggs, *R.R. B.: A Bio-Bibliography* (Westport, Conn., 1990).

Bennett, Robert Russell, American orchestrator, arranger, and composer; b. Kansas City, Mo., June 15, 1894; d. N.Y., Aug. 18, 1981. He was a member of a musical family: his father played in the Kansas City Phil. and his mother was a piano teacher. He studied in Kansas City with Carl Busch (1912–15), in Paris with Boulanger (1926–31), and in Berlin and London. In 1919 he orchestrated his first theatrical songs, and during the next 40 years reigned as the leading orchestrator of Broadway musicals. In all, he orchestrated about 300 such works, including ones by Kern, Gershwin, Porter, Rodgers, Berlin, and Loewe. His own music reveals not only a mastery of orchestration but a facile flow of melodies and rhythms in luscious harmonies. He publ. a book on orchestration, *Instrumentally Speaking* (N.Y., 1975).

WORKS: DRAMATIC: *Columbine*, pantomime ballet (1916); *Endimion*, operetta-ballet (1926; Rochester, N.Y., April 5, 1935); *An Hour of Delusion*, opera (1928); *Hold Your Horses*, musical play (N.Y., Sept. 25, 1933); *Maria Malibran*, opera (1934; N.Y., April 8, 1935); *The Enchanted Kiss*, opera (1944; WOR Radio, N.Y., Dec. 30, 1945); *Crystal*, opera (1972); incidental music and radio scores. **ORCH.:** Sym. No. 1 (1926); *Charleston Rhapsody* for Small Orch. (1926; N.Y., Feb. 18, 1931; rev. 1933); *Paysage* (1927; Rochester, N.Y., Dec. 15, 1933); *Abraham Lincoln Symphony: A Likeness in Symphony Form* (1929; Philadelphia, Oct. 24, 1931); *Sights and Sounds* (1929; Chicago, Dec. 13, 1938); March for 2 Pianos and Orch.

(Los Angeles, July 18, 1930; rev. 1950); *An Early American Ballade on Melodies of Stephen Foster* for Small Orch. (CBS, N.Y., April 15, 1932); *Concerto Grosso* for Dance Band and Orch. (Rochester, N.Y., Dec. 9, 1932); *6 Variations in Fox-trot Time on a Theme by Jerome Kern* for Chamber Orch. (N.Y., Dec. 3, 1933); *Adagio Eroico: To the Memory of a Soldier* (1932; Philadelphia, April 25, 1935); *Hollywood: Introduction and Scherzo* (NBC, N.Y., Nov. 15, 1936); *8 études* (CBS, N.Y., July 17, 1938); Concerto for Viola, Harp, and Orch. (1940; WOR Radio, N.Y., Feb. 27, 1941; rev. as Concerto for Harp, Cello, and Orch., 1959; N.Y., July 31, 1960); *Classic Serenade* for Strings (WOR Radio, N.Y., March 30, 1941); *Antique Suite* for Clarinet and Orch. (WOR Radio, N.Y., April 6, 1941); *Noctune and Appassionata* for Piano and Orch. (WOR Radio, N.Y., Aug. 18, 1941); *Symphony in D for the Dodgers*: Sym. No. 3 (WOR Radio, N.Y., May 16, 1941); Violin Concerto (WOR Radio, N.Y., Dec. 26, 1941); *The 4 Freedoms: A Symphony After 4 Paintings by Norman Rockwell* (NBC, N.Y., Sept. 26, 1943); Sym. No. 6 (1946); *A Dry Weather Legend* for Flute and Orch. (1946; Knoxville, Tenn., Feb. 19, 1947); *Overture to an Imaginary Drama* (Toronto, May 14, 1946); Piano Concerto (1947); *Concert Variations on a Crooner's Theme* for Violin and Orch. (Louisville, Nov. 30, 1949); *Overture to the Mississippi* (Boston, Jan. 14, 1950); *Kansas City Album: 7 Songs for Orchestra* (1949; Kansas City, Mo., Feb. 6, 1950); Concerto for Violin, Piano, and Orch. (1958; Portland, Ore., March 18, 1963); *A Commemoration Symphony: Stephen Collins Foster* for Soprano, Tenor, Chorus, and Orch. (Pittsburgh, Dec. 30, 1959); *Armed Forces Suite* (1959); Sym. No. 7 (1962; Chicago, April 11, 1963); *Harmonica Concerto* (1971). **WIND BAND OR ORCH.:** *Tone Poems* (1939); *Suite of Old American Dances* (1949); *Rose Variations* (1955); *Concerto grosso* (1957); *Symphonic Songs* (1957); *Ohio River Suite* (1959); *West Virginia Epic* (1960); *Kentucky* (1961); *Overture to Ty, Tris and Willie* (1961); *3 Humoresques* (c.1961); *Twain and the River* (1968); *Zimmer's American Greeting* (1974); *Autobiography* (1976). **CHAMBER:** Violin Sonata (1927); *Water Music* for String Quartet (1937); *Dance Scherzo* for Flute, Oboe, Clarinet, Horn, and Bassoon (1937); *Hexapoda* for Violin and Piano (1940); Clarinet Quartet (1941); *A Song Sonata* for Violin and Piano (1947); Trio for Flute, Cello, and Piano (1950); String Quartet (1956); Trio for Harp, Cello, and Flute (c.1960); Quintette for Accordion and String Quartet (1962); *Arabesque* for 2 Trumpets, Horn, Trombone, and Bass Trombone (1978); piano pieces; organ music. **VOCAL:** Choral works; songs.

BIBL.: G. Ferencz, *R.R. B.: A Bio-Bibliography* (Westport, Conn., 1990).

Benoist, André, French pianist; b. Paris, April 4, 1879; d. Monmouth Beach, N.J., June 19, 1953. He studied at the Paris Cons. with Pugno and Saint-Saëns; toured in Europe and America as accompanist to Casals, Heifetz, Albert Spalding, Tetrazzini, and other celebrated artists.

Benson, Joan, American keyboard player and teacher; b. St. Paul, Minn., Oct. 9, 1929. She studied at the Univ. of Ill. (B.Mus., M.Mus., 1951) and at Indiana Univ. (1953); then went to Europe, where she received additional instruction from Edwin Fischer, Guido Agosti et al., returning to the U.S. in 1960. She pursued a successful career as a versatile keyboard artist, becoming especially well known as a clavichordist and fortepianist through numerous tours of the U.S., Europe, and the Far East. Her repertoire extends from Renaissance pieces to modern music. As a teacher, she served on the faculties of Stanford Univ. (1970–76) and the Univ. of Oregon (1976–87).

Benson, Warren (Frank), esteemed American composer and teacher; b. Detroit, Jan. 26, 1924. He studied percussion and horn at Detroit's Cass Technical High School before pursuing training in theory at the Univ. of Mich. (B.M., 1949; M.M., 1951). After teaching percussion at the Univ. of Mich. (1943) and playing timpani in the Detroit Sym. Orch. (1946), he was a Fulbright music teacher at Anatolia College in Salonica, Greece (1950–52); returning to the U.S., he was director of the band and orch. at Mars Hill (N.C.) College (1952–53). He served as prof. of music and composer-in-residence at Ithaca (N.Y.) College (1953–67), where he was founder-director of its percussion ensemble. From 1967 until his retirement in 1993 he was prof. of composition at the Eastman School of Music in Rochester, N.Y.; from 1986 to 1988 he was also the Algur H. Meadows Distinguished Visiting Prof. of Composition at Southern Methodist Univ. in Dallas. In 1981–82 he held a Guggenheim fellowship. Benson has described his output as inclusive in nature, ranging from the tonal to the atonal in a style that remains uniquely his own. In addition to his idiomatic scores for percussion and wind ensemble, he has composed song cycles of high quality.

WORKS: DRAMATIC: *Odysseus*, dance-drama (Salonica, Greece, May 1951); *Bailando*, ballet (1965). **ORCH.:** *A Delphic Serenade* (1953); *5 Brief Encounters* for Strings (1961); Sym. for Drums and Wind Orch. (1962); *Theme and Excursions* for Strings (1963); *Chants and Graces* for Strings, Piccolo, Harp, and Percussion (1964); Horn Concerto (1971); *The Man With the Blue Guitar* (1980); *Beyond Winter: Sweet Aftershowers* for Strings (1981); Concertino for Flute, Strings, and Percussion (1983). **BAND:** *Transylvania Fanfare*, concert march (1953); *Night Song* (1958); *Juniperus* (1959); *Polyphonies* for Percussion (1960); *Remembrance* (1963); *The Leaves Are Falling* (1964); *Ginger Marmalade* (1978); Sym. No. 2, *Lost Songs* (1983); *Dawn's Early Light* (1987); *Meditation on I am for Peace* (1990). **WIND ENSEMBLE:** *Star-Edge* for Alto Saxophone and Wind Ensemble (1965); *Recuerdo* for Oboe or English Horn and Wind Ensemble (1965); *Helix* for Tuba and Wind Ensemble (1966); *The Solitary Dancer* (1966); *The Mask of Night* (1968); *The Passing Bell* (1974); *Wings* (1984); *Other Rivers* (1984); *Danzón-memory* (1991); *Adagietto* (1991); *Dux Variations* (1992); *Divertissement* (1993). **CHAMBER:** *Marche* for Woodwind Quartet (1955); Quintet for Oboe or Soprano Saxophone and Strings (1957); Percussion Trio (1957); Trio for Clarinet, Cello, and Piano (1959); *3 Pieces* for Percussion Quartet (1960); *Streams* for 7 Percussion (1961); *Wind Rose* for Saxophone Quartet (1967); 2 string quartets (1969, 1985); *Capriccio* for Piano Quartet (1972); *The Dream Net* for Alto Saxophone and String Quartet (1976); *Largo Tah* for Bass Trombone and Marimba (1977); *Winter Bittersweet* for 6 Percussion (1981); *Elegy* for Horn and Organ (1982); *Thorgard's Song* for Horn, Crotales, Chimes, Glockenspiel, and Vibraphone (1982); *Fair Game* for Clarinet, Trumpet, Violin, Cello, Piano, and Percussion (1986); *The Red Lion* for Vibraphone and Piano (1988); *Steps* for Brass Quintet (1988); many pieces for Solo Instrument. **VOCAL:** *Psalm XXIV* for Women's Voices and String Orch. (1957); *Love Is* for Antiphonal Choruses (1966); *Shadow Wood* for Soprano and Wind Ensemble or Chamber Orch. (1969; rev. 1992); *Nara* for Soprano, Flute, Piano and 2 Percussion (1970); *Songs of O* for Chorus, Brass Quintet, and Marimba (1974); *The Beaded Leaf* for Bass and Wind Orch. (1974); *Of Rounds* for Antiphonal Choruses and Chamber Ensemble (1975); *Earth, Sky, Sea* for Chorus, Flute, Bass Trombone, and Marimba (1975); *5 Lyrics of Louise Bogan* for Mezzo-soprano and Flute (1978); *Meditation, Prayer, and Sweet Hallelujah* for Antiphonal Choruses and Piano (1979); *Songs for the End of the World* for Mezzo-soprano, English Horn, Horn, Cello, and Marimba (1980); *Moon, Rain, and Memory Jane* for Soprano and 2 Cellos (1984); *Dos Antifonas Lindas* for Soprano, Mezzo-soprano, and Viola (1985); *Still* for Reader and Clarinet (1988); many other vocal works.

Bent, Ian D(avid), English musicologist; b. Birmingham, Jan. 1, 1938. He studied at St. John's College, Cambridge (B.A., 1961; B.Mus., 1962); subsequently taught at King's College, London. He received his Ph.D. in 1969 from the Univ. of Cambridge with the diss. *The Early History of the English Chapel Royal, c.1066–1327.* In 1975 he became a prof. of music at the Univ. of Nottingham. In 1982–83 he was visiting prof. at Harvard Univ., then was a visting prof. (1986–87) and a prof. (from

1987) at Columbia Univ. With his first wife, **Margaret Bent**, and B. Trowell, he edited the revised ed. of Dunstable's works in the Musica Britannica series. He was a senior consulting ed. of *The New Grove Dictionary of Music and Musicians* (1980). He ed. *Source Materials and the Interpretation of Music: A Memorial Volume to Thurston Dart* (London, 1981); also publ. *Music Analysis* (London and N.Y., 1987) and ed. *Music Analysis in the Nineteenth Century* (Cambridge and N.Y., vol. 1, 1994).

Bent, Margaret (Hilda), English musicologist; b. St. Albans, Dec. 23, 1940. She was an organ scholar at Girton College, Cambridge (B.A., 1962; B.Mus., 1963); also studied with Dart, receiving her Ph.D. in 1969 from the Univ. of Cambridge with the diss. *The Old Hall Manuscript: A Palaeographical Study.* She taught at King's College (1965–75); also, concurrently, at Goldsmiths' College from 1972. In 1975 she joined the faculty of Brandeis Univ. at Waltham, Mass. She joined the faculty of Princeton Univ. in 1981; she also served as president of the American Musicological Soc. (1985–86). In 1992 she became senior research fellow of All Souls College, Oxford. With A. Hughes, she ed. *The Old Hall Manuscript* in the Corpus Mensurabilis Musicae series, XLVI (1969–73); with her former husband, **Ian Bent**, and B. Trowell, she ed. the revised edition of Dunstable's works in the Musica Britannica series; also publ. a valuable study, *Dunstaple* (London, 1981).

Bentoiu, Pascal, Romanian composer and writer on music; b. Bucharest, April 22, 1927. He was a pupil of M. Jora in Bucharest (1943–48). After working at the Inst. for Folklore there (1953–56), he pursued research in ethnomusicology and aesthetics. He publ. 3 books on aesthetics: *Imagine şi sens* (Bucharest, 1971), *Deschideri spre lumea muzicii* (Bucharest, 1973), and *Gîndirea muzicală* (Bucharest, 1975), and a study of Enesco's works, *Capodopere enesciene* (Bucharest, 1984). As a composer, he won the State Prize in 1964, the Prix Italia of the RAI in 1968, and the Enesco Prize of the Romanian Academy in 1974. He was president of the Romanian Composers Union from 1990.

WORKS: OPERAS: *Amorul doctor* (The Love Doctor; 1964; Bucharest, Dec. 23, 1966); *Jertifirea Iphigeniei* (The Immolation of Iphigenia; Bucharest, Sept. 1968); *Hamlet* (1969; Bucharest, Nov. 19, 1971). **ORCH.:** Concert Overture (1948; rev. 1961); 2 piano concertos (1954, 1960); *Suite Transylvania* (1955); *Luceafărul* (The Morning Star), symphonic poem (1957); Violin Concerto (1958); *Bucharest Images* (1959); 8 syms. (1965, 1974, 1976, 1978, 1979, 1985, 1986, 1987); *Eminesciana III* (1976); Cello Concerto (1989). **CHAMBER:** Piano Sonata (1947; rev. 1957); 6 string quartets (1953–82); Violin Sonata (1962). **OTHER:** Vocal works.

Benton, Joseph. See **Bentonelli, Joseph (Horace).**

Benton, Rita, American musicologist and music librarian; b. N.Y., June 28, 1918; d. Paris, March 23, 1980. She studied with Friskin (piano diploma, 1938) and Wagenaar (theory) at the Juilliard School of Music in N.Y., at Hunter College in N.Y. (B.A., 1939), and musicology at the Univ. of Iowa (M.A., 1951; Ph.D., 1961), where she was a music librarian (from 1953) and a member of the music dept. faculty (from 1967). In 1962–63 she was president of the Music Library Assn. She ed. *Fontes artis musicae* (from 1976), publ. a catalogue of Pleyel's works (N.Y., 1977), and was general ed. of the *Directory of Music Research Libraries.* J. Halley collaborated with her on the study *Pleyel as Music Publisher: A Documentary Sourcebook of Early 19th-century Music* (Stuyvesant, N.Y., 1990).

Bentonelli (real name, **Benton**), **Joseph (Horace),** American tenor; b. Sayre, Okla., Sept. 10, 1898; d. Oklahoma City, April 4, 1975. Following the frequent practice among American singers, he adopted an Italian-sounding name when he embarked on a singing career. He was a student of Jean de Reszke in Paris. In 1925 he made his public debut with the de Reszke Ensemble in Nice. In 1934 he appeared at the Chicago Opera. On Jan. 10, 1936, he made his Metropolitan Opera debut in N.Y. as Massenet's Des Grieux, singing there until 1937. His repertoire included many leading Italian roles.

Bentzon, Jørgen, Danish composer, cousin of **Niels Viggo Bentzon**; b. Copenhagen, Feb. 14, 1897; d. Hørsholm, July 9, 1951. He studied composition with Carl Nielsen (1915–18). At the same time, he took courses in jurisprudence; subsequently he was attached to the Ministry of Justice in Denmark, and served as clerk of records of the Danish Supreme Court. He also taught piano and theory at a People's School of Music in Copenhagen. As a composer, he followed the Romantic trends current in Scandinavia; an influence of Nielsen pervades his music.

WORKS: OPERA: *Saturnalia* (Copenhagen, Dec. 15, 1944). **ORCH.:** *Dramatic Overture* (1923); *Variations on a Danish Folktune* for Piano, Strings, and Percussion (1928); 3 chamber concertos: No. 1, *Symphonic Trio,* for 3 instrumental groups of Violins, Horns, and Cellos (1928–29), No. 2, *Intermezzo Espressivo,* for Oboe, Clarinet, Horn, Bassoon, Strings, and Percussion (1935), and No. 3, for Clarinet and Chamber Orch. (1941); *Fotomontage,* overture (1934); *Variations* for Chamber Orch. (1935); *Cyklevise-Rhapsody* (1936); *Sinfonia seria* for School Orch. (1937); *Sinfonia buffa* for School Orch. (1939); 2 syms.: No. 1, *Dickens-Symphonie* (1939–40) and No. 2 (1946–47); *Sinfonietta* for Strings (1943). **CHAMBER:** 5 string quartets (1921–28); String Trio (1921); Sonatina for Flute, Clarinet, and Bassoon (1924); *Variazioni interrotti* for Clarinet, Bassoon, and String Trio (1925); Duo for Violin and Cello (1927); *Racconti 1–6* for 3 to 5 Instruments (1935–50). **PIANO:** *Variations* (1921); Sonata (1946). **VOCAL:** *En romersk Fortaelling* (A Roman Tale), cantata for Soloists, Chorus, and Piano (1937); *Mikrofoni No. 1* for Baritone, Flute, and Piano Trio (1937–39); songs; choruses.

Bentzon, Niels Viggo, prominent Danish pianist, pedagogue, and composer, cousin of **Jørgen Bentzon**; b. Copenhagen, Aug. 24, 1919. He began his piano training with his mother, and then took lessons with the jazz pianist Leo Mathisen; he subsequently studied piano with Christiansen, organ with Bangert, and theory with Jeppesen at the Copenhagen Cons. (1938–42). In 1943 he made his debut as a pianist, and later toured Europe and the U.S. He taught at the Århus Cons. (1945–49) and the Royal Danish Cons. of Music in Copenhagen (from 1949). Although a prolific composer, Bentzon also found time to write music criticism, publ. poetry, and paint. He publ. *Tolvtoneteknik* (Copenhagen, 1953) and *Beethoven: En skitse af et geni* (Copenhagen, 1970). His compositions follow along avant-garde lines for the most part, encompassing happenings, audio-visual scores, and graphic notation.

WORKS: DRAMATIC: OPERAS: *Faust III* (1961–62; Kiel, June 21, 1964); *Automaten* (1973; Kiel, May 3, 1974). **BALLETS:** *Metafor* (Copenhagen, March 31, 1950); *Kurtisanen* (The Courtesan; Copenhagen, Dec. 19, 1953); *Døren* (The Door; Copenhagen, Nov. 14, 1962); *Jenny von Westphalen* (Århus, Sept. 9, 1965); *Jubilacumsballet 800* (1968); *Duell* (Stockholm, Nov. 12, 1977). **ORCH.:** 22 numbered syms. (1942–91); 8 piano concertos (1947–82); 4 violin concertos (1951–76); 3 cello concertos (1956–82); 2 flute concertos (1963, 1976); concertos for Oboe (1952), Accordion (1962), Clarinet (1970–71), Viola (1973), Tuba (1975), etc. **CHAMBER:** 11 string quartets (1940–76); 7 violin sonatas (1940–73); 5 wind quintets (1941–57); 4 cello sonatas (1946–72); 8 sonatas for different solo wind instruments (1947–73); 4 quartets for 4 Flutes (1974–77); Harp Sonata (1986); *Trio Quartetto* for Violin, Cello, and Piano (1991); Quartet for Clarinet, Violin, Viola, and Cello (1993). **KEYBOARD:** 15 numbered piano sonatas (1940–81) and numerous other piano pieces; organ music. **OTHER:** Various vocal works and many occasional pieces.

Benzell, Mimi, American soprano; b. Bridgeport, Conn., April 6, 1922; d. Manhasset, Long Island, N.Y., Dec. 23, 1970. Her grandfather was a singer of Jewish folk songs in Russia before his emigration to America. She studied at Hunter College of the

City Univ. of N.Y. and with Olga Eisner at the Mannes College of Music in N.Y. In 1944 she made her operatic debut in Mexico City. On Dec. 3, 1944, she made her first appearance at the Metropolitan Opera in N.Y. in a concert, and then returned there to make her formal operatic debut as the Queen of the Night on Jan. 5, 1945; she remained on its roster until 1949. In subsequent years she pursued a career as a singer of popular music, winning her greatest success in the Broadway musical *Milk and Honey* (1961–63).

Benzi, Roberto, French conductor; b. Marseilles, Dec. 12, 1937. He began music training as a small child and in 1948 appeared as a youthful conductor in Bayonne and of the Colonne Orch. in Paris. He pursued academic studies at the Sorbonne in Paris and was a conducting pupil of Cluytens (1947–50). In 1954 he made his debut as an opera conductor, and in 1959 he made his first appearance at the Paris Opéra conducting *Carmen*. He subsequently made guest appearances in Europe, Japan, and North and South America. On Dec. 11, 1972, he made his Metropolitan Opera debut in N.Y. conducting *Faust*. From 1973 to 1987 he was music director in Bordeaux, and then was principal conductor and artistic advisor of Arnhem's Het Gelders Orch. from 1989. In 1966 he married **Jane Rhodes**.

Berberian, Cathy (Catherine), versatile American mezzo-soprano; b. Attleboro, Mass., July 4, 1925; d. Rome, March 6, 1983. She studied singing, dancing, and the art of pantomime; took courses at Columbia Univ. and N.Y. Univ.; then studied voice in Milan with Giorgina del Vigo. In 1957 she made her debut in a concert in Naples; attracted wide attention in 1958, when she performed John Cage's *Fontana Mix*, which demanded a fantastic variety of sound effects. Her vocal range extended to 3 octaves, causing one bewildered music critic to remark that she could sing both *Tristan* and *Isolde*. Thanks to her uncanny ability to produce ultrahuman (and subhuman) tones, and her willingness to incorporate into her professional vocalization a variety of animal noises, guttural sounds, grunts and growls, squeals, squeaks and squawks, clicks and clucks, shrieks and screeches, hisses, hoots, and hollers, she instantly became the darling of inventive composers of the avant-garde, who eagerly dedicated to her their otherwise unperformable works. She married one of them, **Luciano Berio**, in 1950, but their marriage was dissolved in 1964. She could also intone classical music. Shortly before her death, she sang her own version of the *Internationale* for an Italian television program commemorating the centennial of the death of Karl Marx (1983). She was an avant-garde composer in her own right; she wrote multimedia works, such as *Stripsody*, an arresting soliloquy of labial and laryngeal sounds, and an eponymously titled piano piece, *Morsicat(h)y*. Her integrity as a performer is reflected in her life-long insistance that her objective was always to meet the challenge of the new art of her time.

Berbié, Jane (real name, **Jeanne Marie-Louise Bergougne**), French mezzo-soprano; b. Villefranche-de-Lauragais, May 6, 1931. She received training at the Toulouse Cons. After making her operatic debut in 1958, she appeared at Milan's La Scala for the first time in Ravel's *L'Enfant et les sortilèges* in 1960. She appeared at the Glyndebourne Festivals (1969–71; 1983–84), the Aix-en-Provence Festivals (1969–70), London's Covent Garden (1971), and the Salzburg Festival (1974). From 1975 she sang at the Paris Opéra, and later at the Théâtre des Champs Elysées in Paris. She also appeared in other operatic centers in Europe and was a prof. at the Paris Cons. (from 1982). She was especially admired for her coloratura roles in operas by Mozart and Rossini.

Berezowsky, Nicolai (Nikolai Tikhonovich), talented Russian-born American violinist, conductor, and composer; b. St. Petersburg, May 17, 1900; d. (suicide) N.Y., Aug. 27, 1953. He studied at the court chapel in St. Petersburg (1908–16). After playing violin in the orchs. of the Saratov opera (1917–19) and Moscow's Bolshoi Theater (1919–20), he pursued violin training with Robert Pollack in Vienna. In 1922 he settled in the U.S. and in 1928 became a naturalized American citizen. He was a violinist in the orch. of the Capitol Theatre in N.Y. (1922–23) and the N.Y. Phil. (1923–29). In 1927 he studied with Paul Kochański (violin) and Rubin Goldmark (composition) at N.Y.'s Juilliard School of Music. He was assistant conductor with CBS (1932–36; 1941–46) and a member of the Coolidge String Quartet (1935–40). In 1948 he received a Guggenheim fellowship. His works followed along Romantic lines, with a later infusion of impressionistic harmonies.

WORKS: CHILDREN'S OPERA: *Babar the Elephant* (N.Y., Feb. 21, 1953). **ORCH.:** 4 syms.: No. 1 (Boston, March 16, 1931), No. 2 (Boston, Feb. 16, 1934), No. 3 (Rochester, N.Y., Jan. 21, 1937), and No. 4 (Boston, Oct. 22, 1943); *Hebrew Suite* (1929); Violin Concerto (Dresden, April 29, 1930); *Fantaisie* for 2 Pianos and Orch. (N.Y., Feb. 12, 1932); *Sinfonietta* (NBC, N.Y., May 8, 1932); *Concerto lirico* for Cello and Orch. (Boston, Feb. 22, 1935); *Toccata, Variations, and Finale* for String Quartet and Orch. (1937); *Introduction and Waltz* (N.Y., Oct. 15, 1939); Viola Concerto (1942); Clarinet Concerto (1942); *Soldiers on the Town* (N.Y., Nov. 25, 1943); *Christmas Festival Overture* (N.Y., Dec. 23, 1943); Harp Concerto (Philadelphia, Jan. 26, 1945); *Passacaglia* for Theremin and Orch. (N.Y., Feb. 29, 1948). **CHAMBER:** *Thème et variations* for Clarinet, Strings, and Piano (1926); 2 woodwind quintets (1928, 1937); 2 string quartets (1931, 1934); Suite for Wind Quintet (1941); *Sextet Concerto* for Strings (1951). **VOCAL:** *Gilgamesh*, cantata for Narrator, Soloists, Chorus, and Orch. (N.Y., May 16, 1947).

BIBL.: A. Berezowsky, *Duet with Nicky* (N.Y., 1943).

Berg, Alban (Maria Johannes), greatly significant Austrian composer whose music combined classical clarity of design and highly original melodic and harmonic techniques that became historically associated with the New Viennese School; b. Vienna, Feb. 9, 1885; d. there, Dec. 24, 1935. He played piano as a boy and composed songs without formal training. He worked as a clerk in a government office in Lower Austria; in 1904 he met Arnold Schoenberg, who became his teacher, mentor, and close friend; he remained Schoenberg's pupil for 6 years. A fellow classmate was Anton von Webern; together they initiated the radical movement known to history as the New or Second Viennese School of composition. In Nov. 1918 Schoenberg organized in Vienna the Soc. for Private Musical Performances (Verein für musikalische Privataufführungen) with the purpose of performing works unacceptable to established musical society. So as to emphasize the independence of the new organization, music critics were excluded from attendance. The society was disbanded in 1922, having accomplished its purpose. In 1925 Berg joined the membership of the newly created ISCM, which continued in an open arena the promotion of fresh musical ideas.

Berg's early works reflected the Romantic style of Wagner, Wolf, and Mahler; typical of this period were his *3 Pieces for Orchestra* (1913–15). As early as 1917 Berg began work on his opera *Wozzeck* (after the romantic play by Büchner), which was to become his masterpiece. The score represents an ingenious synthesis of Classical forms and modern techniques; it is organized as a series of purely symphonic sections in traditional Baroque forms, among them a passacaglia with 21 variations, a dance suite, and a rhapsody, all cast in a setting marked by dissonant counterpoint. Its first production at the Berlin State Opera on Dec. 14, 1925, precipitated a storm of protests and press reviews of extreme violence; a similarly critical reception was accorded to *Wozzeck* in Prague on Nov. 11, 1926. Undismayed, Berg and his friends responded by publishing a brochure incorporating the most vehement of these reviews so as to shame and denounce the critics. Leopold Stokowski, ever eager to defy convention, gave the first American performance of *Wozzeck* in Philadelphia on March 19, 1931; it aroused a great deal of interest and was received with cultured equanimity. Thereafter, performances of *Wozzeck* multiplied in Europe, and in due time the opera became recognized as a modern masterpiece. Shortly after the completion of *Wozzeck*, Berg wrote a *Lyric Suite* for String Quartet in 6 movements; it was first played in Vienna by the Kolisch Quartet on Jan. 8, 1927; in 1928 Berg arranged the 2nd, 3rd, and 4th movements for String Orch., which were performed in Berlin on Jan. 31, 1929. Rumors of a suppressed vocal part for the 6th movement of the suite, bespeaking Berg's secret affection for a married woman, Hanna Fuchs-Robettin, impelled Douglas M. Greene to institute a search for the original score; he discovered it in 1976 and, with the help of George Perle, decoded the vocal line in an annotated copy of the score that Berg's widow, understandably reluctant to perpetuate her husband's emotional aberrations, turned over to a Vienna library. The text proved to be Stefan Georg's rendition of Baudelaire's *De Profundis clamavi* from *Les Fleurs du mal*. Indeed, Berg inserted in the score all kinds of semiotical and numerological clues to his affection in a sort of symbolical synthesis. The *Lyric Suite* with its vocal finale was performed for the first time at Abraham Goodman House, N.Y., by the Columbia String Quartet and Katherine Ciesinski, mezzo-soprano, on Nov. 1, 1979.

Berg's 2nd opera, *Lulu* (1928–35), to a libretto derived from 2 plays by Wedekind, was left unfinished at the time of his death; 2 acts and music from the *Symphonische Stücke aus der Oper Lulu* of 1934 were performed posthumously in Zürich on June 2, 1937. Again, Berg's widow intervened to forestall any attempt to have the work reconstituted by another musician. However, Berg's publishers, asserting their legal rights, commissioned Friedrich Cerha to re-create the 3rd act from materials available in other authentic sources, or used by Berg elsewhere; the task required 12 years (1962–74) for its completion. After Berg's widow died in 1976, several opera houses openly competed for the Cerha version of the work; the premiere of the complete opera, incorporating this version, was first presented at the Paris Opéra on Feb. 24, 1979; the first American performance followed in Santa Fe, N.Mex., on July 28, 1979. As in *Wozzeck*, so in *Lulu*, Berg organized the score in a series of classical forms; but while *Wozzeck* was written before Schoenberg's formulation of the method of composition in 12 tones related solely to one another, *Lulu* was set in full-fledged dodecaphonic techniques; even so, Berg allowed himself frequent divagations, contrary to the dodecaphonic code, into triadic tonal harmonies.

Berg's last completed work was a Violin Concerto commissioned by Louis Krasner, who gave its first performance at the Festival of the ISCM in Barcelona on April 19, 1936. The score bears the inscription "Dem Andenken eines Engels," the angel being the daughter of Alma Mahler and Walter Gropius who died at an early age. The work is couched in the 12-tone technique, with free and frequent interludes of passing tonality.

WORKS: OPERAS: *Wozzeck*, after a play of Büchner, op. 7 (1917–22; Berlin, Dec. 14, 1925, E. Kleiber conducting; 1st U.S. perf., Philadelphia, March 19, 1931, Stokowski conducting; 1st British perf., London, Jan. 22, 1952, Kleiber conducting); *Lulu*, after Wedekind's plays *Erdgeist* and *Die Büchse der Pandora* (1928–35; Acts 1 and 2 complete, with Act 3 in short score; Acts 1 and 2, with music from the *Symphonische Stücke aus der Oper Lulu* [1934] to accompany the Act 3 death of Lulu, Zürich, June 2, 1937; 1st British perf., London, Oct. 1, 1962, L. Ludwig conducting; 1st U.S. perf., Santa Fe, N.Mex., Aug. 7, 1963, R. Craft conducting; 2nd version, with Act 3 realized by Friedrich Cerha, Paris, Feb. 24, 1979, Boulez conducting; 1st U.S. perf., Santa Fe, N.Mex., July 28, 1979, M. Tilson Thomas conducting; 1st British perf., London, Feb. 16, 1981, Sir Colin Davis conducting). **OTHER WORKS:** 70 lieder, including settings of Ibsen, Goethe, Rückert, Heine, Burns, and Rilke (1900–1905); *7 frühe Lieder* for Voice and Piano (1905–08; rev. and orchestrated 1928; Vienna, Nov. 6, 1928); *Variations on an Original Theme* for Piano (Vienna, Nov. 6, 1928); Piano Sonata, op. 1 (1907–08; Vienna, April 24, 1911; rev. 1920); *4 Lieder* for Medium Voice and Piano, op. 2 (1908–09; rev. 1920); String Quartet, op. 3 (1910; Vienna, April 24, 1911; rev. 1924); *5 Orchesterlieder nach Ansichtskartentexten von Peter Altenberg*, op. 4 (1912; 2 numbers perf. in Vienna, March 31, 1913, Schoenberg conducting; 1st complete perf., Rome, Jan. 24, 1953, Horenstein conducting); *4 Stücke* for Clarinet and Piano, op. 5 (1913; Vienna, Oct. 17, 1919); *3 Stücke* for Orch., op. 6. (1913–15; rev. 1929; 1st complete perf., Oldenburg, April 14, 1930); *3 Bruchstücke from Wozzeck* for Soprano and Orch., op. 7 (1923; Frankfurt am Main, June 11, 1924, Scherchen conducting); *Kammerkonzert* for Piano, Violin, and 13 Wind Instruments (the thematic material based on letter-notes in the names of Schoenberg, Webern, and Berg; 1923–25; Berlin, March 27, 1927, Scherchen conducting; its *Adagio*, scored for Violin, Clarinet, and Piano, was arranged in 1934); *Lyrische Suite* for String Quartet (1925–26; Vienna, Jan. 8, 1927, Kolisch Quartet; movements 2–4 arranged for String Orch., 1928; Berlin, Jan. 31, 1929, Horenstein conducting; with newly discovered vocal finale, N.Y., Nov. 1, 1979, Columbia String Quartet, K. Ciesinski mezzo-soprano); *Der Wein*, concert aria for Soprano and Orch., after Baudelaire (1929; Königsberg, June 4, 1930); *Symphonische Stücke aus der Oper Lulu* or *Lulu-Symphonie (Suite)*, in 5 movements, with soprano soloist in no. 3, *Lied der Lulu* (Berlin, Nov. 30, 1934, Kleiber conducting); Violin Concerto, *Dem Andenken eines Engels* (1935; Barcelona, April 19, 1936, L. Krasner soloist, Scherchen conducting); also piano arrangements of Schreker's *Der ferne Klang* (1911) and Schoenberg's *Gurrelieder* (1912), and the last 2 movements of the String Quartet, op. 10, for Voice and Piano. He also made an arrangement for chamber ensemble of J. Strauss's waltz *Wine, Women, and Song*.

WRITINGS: Berg contributed articles to many contemporary music journals; also wrote analyses for Schoenberg's *Gurrelieder, Kammersymphonie*, and *Pelleas und Melisande*.

BIBL.: The International A. B. Soc. of the Graduate Center of the City Univ. of N.Y. issues a newsletter. See also: special issue of *Eine Wiener Musikzeitschrift* (Vienna, 1936); W. Reich, *A. B.: Mit B.s eigenen Schriftem und Beiträgen von Theodor Wiesengrund-Adorno und Ernst Křenek* (Vienna, 1937); R. Leibowitz, *Schoenberg et son école* (Paris, 1947; Eng. tr., 1949, as *Schoenberg and His School*); H. Redlich, *A. B.: Versuch einer Würdigung* (Vienna, 1957; abr. Eng. tr., 1957, as *A. B.: The Man and His Music*); W. Reich, ed., *A. B.: Bildnis im Wort. Selbstzeugnisse und Aussagen der Freunde* (Zürich, 1959); K. Vogelsang, *A. B.: Leben und Werk* (Berlin, 1959); W. Reich, *A. B.: Leben und Werk* (Zürich, 1963; Eng. tr., 1965, as *The Life and Work of A. B.*); G. Perle, "Lulu: The Formal Design," *Journal of the American Musicological Society* (Summer 1964); H. Berg, ed., *A. B.: Briefe an seine Frau* (Vienna, 1965; Eng. tr., 1971, as *A. B.: Letters to His Wife*); T. Adorno, *A. B., der Meister des Kleinsten Übergangs* (Vienna, 1968; rev. ed., 1978); G. Ploebsch, *A. B.s "Wozzeck"; Dramaturgie und Musikalischer Aufbau* (Strasbourg, 1968); K. Schweizer, *Die Sonatensatzform im Schaffen A. B.s* (Stuttgart, 1970); M. Carner, *A. B.: The Man and the Work* (London, 1975; 2nd ed., rev., 1983); E. Hilmar, *Wozzeck von A. B.* (Vienna, 1975); V. Scherleiss, *A. B.* (Hamburg, 1975); D. Jarman, *The Music of A. B.* (Berkeley, 1979); K. Monson, *A. B.* (Boston, 1979); F. Grasberger and R. Stephan, eds., *Die Werke von A. B.: Handschriftenkatalog* (Vienna, 1981); R. Klein, ed., *A. B. Symposion, Wien 1980: Tagungsbericht* (Vienna, 1981); G. Perle, *The Operas of A. B.* (2 vols., Berkeley, 1981, 1985); J. Schmalfeldt, *B.'s Wozzeck: Harmonic Language and Dramatic Design* (London, 1983); E. Berg, *Der unverbesserliche Romantiker: A. B., 1885–1935* (Vienna, 1985); R. Hilmar, ed., *Katalog der Schriftstücke von der Hand A. B.s, der fremdschriftlichen und gedruckten Dokumente zur Lebensgeschichte und zu seinem Werk* (Vienna, 1985); P. Petersen, *A. B., Wozzeck: Eine semantische Analyse unter Einbeziehung der Skizzen und Dokumente aus dem Nachlass B.s* (Munich, 1985); J. Brand, C. Hailey, and D. Harris, eds., *The B.-Schönberg Correspondence* (N.Y., 1986); S. Rode, *A. B. und Karl Kraus: Zur geistigen Biographie des Komponisten der "Lulu"* (Frankfurt am Main, 1988); P. Hall, *A View of B.'s Lulu Through the Autograph Sources* (diss., Yale Univ., 1989); D. Jarman, *A. B.: "Wozzeck"* (Cambridge, 1989); idem ed., *The B. Companion* (Boston, 1990); H.-U. Fuss, *Musikalisch-*

dramatische Prozesse in den Opern A. B.s (Hamburg, 1991); D. Gable and R. Morgan, eds., *A. B.: Historical and Analytical Perspectives* (Oxford, 1991); D. Jarman, ed., *A. B.: Lulu* (Cambridge, 1991); R. Lorković, *Das Violinkonzert von A. B.: Analysen, Textkorrekturen, Interpretationen* (Winterthur, 1991); A. Pople, *B.: Violin Concerto* (Cambridge, 1991); C. Flores, *A B.: Musik als Autobiographie* (Wiesbaden, 1992); A. von Massow, *Halbwelt, Kultur und Natur in A. B.s "Lulu"* (Stuttgart, 1992); W. Gratzer, *Zur "wunderlichen Mystik" A. B.s: Eine studie* (Vienna, 1993); P. Hall, *A View of B.'s Lulu Through the Autograph Sources* (Berkeley, 1995); G. Perle, *"Style and Idea" in the Lyric Suite of A. B.* (Stuyvesant, N.Y., 1995).

Berg, Gunnar (Johnsen), Danish composer; b. St. Gallen (of Danish parents), Jan. 11, 1909; d. Bern, Aug. 25, 1989. He was taken to Denmark when he was 12 and began piano lessons. In 1936 he became a student in counterpoint of Jeppesen at the Copenhagen Cons. He later received training in piano from Hermann D. Koppel and Elisabeth Jürgens, and in theory from Herbert Rosenberg. In 1948 he went to Paris to study composition with Honegger at the École Normale de Musique, and he also received training in analysis from Messiaen. Upon his return to Denmark in 1958, he became active in avant-garde circles. Although he was awarded an annual grant by the Danish government in 1965 to pursue creative work, he became frustrated by the lack of acceptance of his music in Denmark and in 1980 he returned to Switzerland. Berg was the first Danish composer to write a serial composition in 1950 with his Suite for Cello. After 1958, he employed a *sui generis* serial technique in which each theme was a "cell" consisting of 5 to 10 notes, a model suggested by the experiments in cellular biology of the German bacteriologist Georg Gaffky (1850–1918).

WORKS: BALLET: *Mouture* (1953; rev. 1987). **ORCH.:** *Hymnos* for Strings (1946); *Passacaille* (1948; Århus, Sept. 7, 1980); *Essai acoustique III* for Piano and Orch. (1954); *5 Études* for Double String Orch. (1955–56; Stockholm, Sept. 26, 1960); *El triptico gallego* (1957; 1st complete perf., Copenhagen, May 31, 1960); *Mutationen* (1958; Danish Radio, Nov. 1, 1978); *37 Aspects* for Chamber Orch. (1959); *Pour piano et orchestre* (1959; Danish Radio, Sept. 29, 1966); *Frise* for Piano and Chamber Orch. (Copenhagen, May 17, 1961); *Uculang* for Piano and Orch. (1967; Danish Radio, April 15, 1969); *Aria* for Flute and Orch. (1980–81; Danish Radio, Feb. 2, 1984); *Etincelles* for Harpsichord and Brass Ensemble (1984–85). **CHAMBER:** *Duetto* for Flute and Oboe (1937); *Caprice* for Violin and Piano (1941; rev. 1951); Sonata for Flute and Clarinet (1942; rev. 1951); Sonata for Solo Violin (1945; rev. 1982); *Pièce* for Trumpet, Violin, and Piano (1949); Suite for Cello (1950); *Filandre* for Flute, Clarinet, and Violin (1953); *Prosthesis* for Saxophone and Piano (1954); *Trio d'Anches* for Oboe, Clarinet, and Bassoon (1955); *Belem* for Percussion and Piano, 4-hands (1956); *9 Duos* for Recorder and Cello (1957; rev. for Recorder and Guitar, 1984); *Petite Musique* for Flute, String Quartet, and Piano (1958; rev. 1960); *Pour 2 violoncelles et piano* (1958; rev. 1987); *Pour clarinette et violon* (1959); *Pour violon et piano* (1960); *Pour quintette à vent* (1962); *Pour quatuor à cordes* (1964–66); *Random* for Cello and Percussion (1968); *Tronqué* for Xylophone, Cello, and Piano (1969); *Agregats I* for Ondes Martenot (1970); *Monologue* for Trumpet (1975); *Fresques I–IV* for Guitar (1976–78); *Mouvements* for String Quartet (1979); *Melos I* for Guitar (1979); *Aerophones I–II* for Winds (1982–83); *Ar-Goat* for 2 Guitars (1984). **KEYBOARD: PIANO:** *Fantaisie* (1936; rev. 1968); *La Boite à musique* (1938); *Toccata-Interludium-Fuga* (1938); *Feldspath* (1942–44); *Variations sur une daina lithuanienne* (1946); Sonata (1945–47); *Cahier pour Léonie* (1951); *Cosmogonie* for 2 Pianos (1952); *Éclatements I–XV* (1954–61; 1987–88); *Gaffky's I–X* (1958–59). **ORGAN:** *Pour orgue* (1960); *Tantum ergo* (1978); *Melos II* (1979). **VOCAL:** *Le chemin de fer* for Voice, Flute, Clarinet, Violin, and Piano, 4-hands (1945; rev. 1950); *Tøbrud* for Voice, Violin, Clarinet, and Piano (1961); *Hyperion* for Voice and 10 Instruments (1977); *Graphos* for Voice, 2 Cellos, Percussion, and Piano (1987); solo songs.

BIBL.: J. Rossel, "G. B.—the Stranger in Danish Musical Circles," *Musical Denmark* (1979); idem, "Der ewige B.," *Dansk Musik Tidsskrift*, no. 3 (1989).

Berg, Josef, Czech composer; b. Brno, March 8, 1927; d. there, Feb. 26, 1971. He studied with Petrželka at the Brno Cons. (1946–50); was music ed. of Brno Radio (1950–53); wrote simple music for the Folk Art ensemble. Later he began using 12-tone techniques. His most original works are the operas *Odysseů návrat* (Odysseus's Return; 1962), *Evropská turistika* (European Tourism; 1963–64), *Eufrides před branami Thymen* (Euphrides in Front of the Gates of Tymenas; 1964), and *Johannes Doktor Faust* (1966). He also wrote 3 syms. (1950, 1952, 1955); Viola Sonata (1958); *Fantasia* for 2 Pianos (1958); Sextet for Piano, Harp, and String Quartet (1959); *Songs of the New Werther* for Bass-baritone and Piano (1962); Nonet for 2 Harps, Piano, Harpsichord, and Percussion (1962); *Sonata in Modo Classico* for Harpsichord and Piano (1963); *Organ Music on a Theme of Gilles Binchois* (1964); String Quartet (1966); *2 Canti* for Baritone, Instrumental Ensemble, Organ, and Metronome (1966); *Ó Corino* for 4 Solo Voices and Classical Orch. (1967); *Oresteia* for Vocal Quartet, Narrator, and Instrumental Ensemble (1967).

BIBL.: M. Štědroň, *J. B.* (Brno, 1992)

Berg, (Carl) Natanael, Swedish composer; b. Stockholm, Feb. 9, 1879; d. there, Oct. 14, 1957. He was a pupil of Julius Günther (voice) and J. Lindegren (counterpoint) at the Stockholm Cons. (1897–1900), but was essentially autodidact in composition; held state composer's fellowships for further studies in Berlin and Paris (1908–09), and in Vienna (1911–12); also took a degree in veterinary medicine (1902) and served as a veterinary surgeon in the Swedish Army until 1939. In 1918 he helped to found the Soc. of Swedish Composers, serving as its chairman until 1924. In 1932 he was elected a member of the Royal Swedish Academy of Music in Stockholm. His music is indulgent, reminiscent in its tumescent harmonies of Richard Strauss.

WORKS: OPERAS (all 1st perf. in Stockholm): *Leila* (1910; Feb. 29, 1912); *Engelbrekt* (1928; Sept. 21, 1929); *Judith* (1935; Feb. 22, 1936); *Brigitta* (1941; Jan. 10, 1942); *Genoveva* (1944–46; Oct. 25, 1947). **PANTOMIME-BALLETS:** *Älvorna* (1914); *Sensitiva* (1919); *Hertiginnans friare* (The Duchess's Suitors; 1920). **ORCH.:** Symphonic poems: *Traumgewalten* (1910); *Varde ljus!* (1914); *Reverenza* (1949); 5 syms.: No. 1, *Alles endet was entstehet* (1913), No. 2, *Årstiderna* (The Tides; 1916), No. 3, *Makter* (Power; 1917), No. 4, *Pezzo sinfonico* (1918; rev. 1939), and No. 5, *Trilogia delle passioni* (1922); Violin Concerto (1918); *Serenade* for Violin and Orch. (1923); Suite (1930); Piano Concerto (1931). **CHAMBER:** Piano Quintet (1917); 2 string quartets (1917, 1919). **VOCAL:** *Saul och David* for Baritone and Orch. (1907); *Eros' vrede* (Love's Wrath) for Baritone and Orch. (1911); *Mannen och kvinnan* (Man and Woman) for Soloists, Chorus, and Orch. (1911); *Predikaren* (The Preacher) for Baritone and Orch. (1911); *Israels lovsång* (Israel's Hymns), for Soloists, Chorus, and Orch. (1915); *Höga Visan* (The Song of Solomon) for Soloists, Chorus, and Orch. (1925); songs.

Berganza (Vargas), Teresa, admired Spanish mezzo-soprano; b. Madrid, March 16, 1935. She was a pupil of Lola Rodriguez Aragón in Madrid; after winning the singing prize at the Madrid Cons. in 1954, she made her debut in a Madrid concert in 1955; in 1957 she made her opertic debut as Dorabella at the Aix-en-Provence Festival. In 1958 she made her British debut as Cherubino at the Glyndebourne Festival, and that same year she sang at the Dallas Civic Opera. In 1960 she made her first appearance at London's Covent Garden as Rosina, and in 1962 her debut at the Chicago Lyric Opera as Cherubino, a role she repeated for her Metropolitan Opera debut in N.Y. on Oct. 11, 1967; she remained on its roster until 1969. She toured widely as a concert artist, winning particular distinction for her Spanish song recitals. In 1992 she participated in the gala ceremonies at the Olympic Games in Barcelona. In addition to her roles in operas by Mozart and Rossini, she was esteemed for her portrayals of Monteverdi's Ottavia, Purcell's Dido, and Bizet's Carmen. Her career is the subject of her book *Meditaciones de na Cantante* (Madrid, 1985).

Berge, Sigurd, Norwegian composer; b. Vinstra, July 1, 1929. He studied composition with Thorleif Eken at the Oslo Cons. and with Finn Mortensen (1956–59); later took courses in electronic music in Stockholm, Copenhagen, and Utrecht. From 1959 he taught at the Sagene College of Education. He served as chairman of the Norwegian Composers Union (1985–88). His output ranges from traditional works to electronic pieces.

WORKS: *Dances from Gudbrandsdal* for Orch. (1955–56); *Divertimento* for Violin, Viola, and Cello (1956); *Episode for* Violin and Piano (1958); *Pezzo orchestrale* (1958); *Rāga*, concerto-study in Indian music, for Oboe and Orch. (1959); *Sinus* for Strings and Percussion (1961); *Tamburo piccolo* for Strings and Percussion (1961); *Chroma* for Orch. (1963); *A* for Orch. (1964–65); *B* for Orch. (1965–66); Flute Solo (1966); Oboe Solo (1966); *Yang Guan* for Wind Quintet (1967); *Ballet* for 2 Dancers and Percussion (1967–68); *Gamma* for 7 Instruments (1970); *Epsilon* for Chamber Orch. (1970); *Delta* for Jazz Trio and Tape (1970); *Horn Call* for Horn (1972); *Between Mirrors* for Violin and Chamber Orch. (1977); *Music* for Orch. (1978); *Gudbrandskalsspelet*, music drama (1980); *Wind*, ballet (1981); *Music* for 4 Horns (1984); numerous electronic pieces.

Bergel, Erich, Romanian conductor; b. Rosenau, June 1, 1930. He studied in Bucharest. In 1959 he was appointed conductor of the Cluj Phil., but was shortly afterward (May 9, 1959) arrested and incarcerated on charges of subversive activities. After his release from prison on Oct. 4, 1962, he was engaged as a trumpet player by the Cluj Phil.; in 1966 he became its conductor. In 1971 he left Romania and settled in West Germany. In 1975 he made his American debut as guest conductor with the Houston Sym. Orch., serving as its principal guest conductor from 1979 to 1981. He publ. a disquisition on Bach's *Art of the Fugue* (Bonn, 1979; 1st vol. only).

Berger, Arthur (Victor), respected American composer and writer on music; b. N.Y., May 15, 1912. He studied piano (1923–28) and began composing while still in high school. After attending the City College of N.Y. (1928–30), he studied composition with Vincent Jones at N.Y. Univ. (B.S., 1934). He then continued his training at the Longy School of Music in Cambridge, Mass. (1935–37), and concurrently was a pupil of Piston, Archibald T. Davison, and Hugo Leichtentritt at Harvard Univ. (M.A., 1937). After further studies with Boulanger at the École Normale de Musique in Paris (1937–39), he taught at Mills College in Oakland, California (1939–42), where he also had composition lessons with Milhaud; then taught at Brooklyn College (1942–43), the Juilliard School of Music in N.Y., Brandeis Univ. (1953–80), and at the New England Cons. of Music in Boston (from 1979). He served as ed. of the *Musical Mercury* (1934–37) and as co-founder and ed. of *Perspectives of New Music* (1962–63); also was a music critic for the *Boston Transcript* (1943–47), *N.Y. Sun* (1943–46), and *N.Y. Herald Tribune* (1946–53). In addition to many articles in journals, he publ. a monograph on Copland (N.Y., 1953). In 1960 he held a Fulbright fellowship and in 1975–76 a Guggenheim fellowship. His musical idiom reveals the influence of divergent schools, including a *sui generis* serialism and the neo-Classical pragmatism of Stravinsky. His works, in whatever idiom, are characterized by strong formal structures; the title of one of his most cogent scores, *Ideas of Order* (1952), is a declaration of principles.

WORKS: ORCH.: *Serenade Concertante* for Violin and Chamber Orch. (1944; Rochester, N.Y., Oct. 24, 1945); *3 Pieces* for Strings (1945; N.Y., Jan. 26, 1946); *Ideas of Order* (1952; N.Y., April 11, 1953); *Polyphony* (Louisville, Nov. 17, 1956); Chamber Concerto (1960; N.Y., May 13, 1962; 3rd movement rev. as *Movement* for Orch., 1964; 1st, 2nd, and 3rd movements rev. as *Perspectives I, II,* and *III*, 1978). **CHAMBER:** Woodwind Quartet (1941); *3 Pieces* for String Quartet (1945); Duo No. 1 for Violin and Piano (1948), No. 2 for Violin and Piano (1950), No. 3 for Cello and Piano (1951), and No. 4 for Oboe and Clarinet (1952; arr. for Clarinet and Piano, 1957); *Chamber Music* for 12 Instruments (1956); String Quartet (1958); Septet for Flute, Clarinet, Bassoon, Violin, Viola, Cello, and Piano (1965–66; Washington, D.C., Nov. 25, 1966); Trio for Guitar, Violin, and Piano (1972); Piano Trio (1980); Woodwind Quintet (1984); *Diptych* for Flute, Clarinet, Violin, Cello, and Piano (1990); *Collage III* for Flute, Clarinet, Violin, Cello, Percussion, and Piano (1992). **PIANO:** *2 Episodes* (1933); *Entertainment Pieces*, ballet music (1940); *Fantasy* (1942); *Rondo* (1945); *Capriccio* (1945); *3 Bagatelles* (1946); *Partita* (1947); *Intermezzo* (1948); 4 2-part inventions (1948–49); 1-part invention (1954); *3 Pieces* for 2 Prepared Pianos (1961); *5 Pieces* (1969); *Composition* for Piano, 4-hands (1976); *An Improvisation for A*[aron] *C*[opland] (1981). **VOCAL:** *Words for Music, Perhaps* for Soprano or Mezzo-soprano, Flute, Clarinet, and Cello (1939–40); *Garlands* for Mezzo-soprano and Piano (1945); *Psalm XCII* for 4 Voices (1946); *Boo Hoo at the Zoo: Tails of Woe* for 2 Voices (1978); *5 Songs* for Tenor and Piano (1978–79); *Love, Sweet Animal* for 4 Voices and Piano, 4-hands (1982); *Ode of Ronsard* for Soprano and Piano (1987).

BIBL.: Festschrift in *Perspectives of New Music*, XVII/1 (1978); R. Lister, "A. B.: The Progress of a Method," *American Music* (Spring 1995).

Berger, Erna, distinguished German soprano; b. Cossebaude, near Dresden, Oct. 19, 1900; d. Essen, June 14, 1990. She was a student of Böckel and Melita Hirzel in Dresden. In 1925 she made her operatic debut as the first boy in *Die Zauberflöte* at the Dresden State Opera, where she sang until 1930. In Berlin she sang at the City Opera (1929) and the State Opera (from 1934); also appeared at the Bayreuth (1930–33) and Salzburg (1932–54) festivals. In 1934 she made her debut at London's Covent Garden as Marzelline, and sang there until 1938 and again in 1947. On Nov. 21, 1949, she made her Metropolitan Opera debut in N.Y. as Sophie, remaining on its roster until 1951. In 1955 she retired from the operatic stage but pursued a career as a lieder artist until 1968. From 1959 she was a prof. of voice at the Hamburg Hochschule für Musik. In 1985 the Berlin State Opera made her an honorary member. Her autobiography was publ. as *Auf Flügeln des Gesanges* (Zürich, 1988). Berger was an outstanding coloratura soprano. Among her other roles were the Queen of the Night, Rosina, Martha, Gilda, and Zerbinetta.

BIBL.: K. Höcker, *E. B.: Die singende Botschafterin* (Berlin, 1961).

Berger, Jean, German-born French, later American conductor, teacher, and composer; b. Hamm, Sept. 27, 1909. He studied musicicology with Egon Wellesz at the Univ. of Vienna and with Heinrich Besseler at the Univ. of Heidelberg (Ph.D., 1931), and then composition with Louis Aubert and Capdevielle in Paris, where he conducted the choir Les Compagnons de la Marjolaine and in 1935 became a naturalized American citizen. After teaching at the Conservatorio Brasileiro de Música in Rio de Janeiro (1939–41), he settled in the U.S., becoming a naturalized citizen in 1943. He taught at Middlebury (Vt.) College (1948–59), the Univ. of Ill. in Urbana (1959–61), and the Univ. of Colo. (1961–68). In 1964 he founded the John Sheppard Music Press in Boulder. He wrote mainly choral music in an accessible style. His best known work is the *Brazilian Psalm* for Chorus (1941).

WORKS: DRAMATIC: *Pied Piper*, musical play for Dancers, Solo Voices, Choruses, and Small Orch. (1968); *Birds of a Feather: An Entertainment* (1971); *Yiphth and his Daughter*, opera (1972); *The Cherry Tree Carol*, liturgical drama (1975). **ORCH.:** *Caribbean Concerto* for Harmonica and Orch. (St. Louis, March 10, 1942, Larry Adler soloist); *Creole Overture* (1949); *Petit Suite* for Strings (1952); *Short Overture* for Strings (1958); *Divertissement* for Strings (1970); *Short Symphony*

(1974); *Diversion* for Strings (1977). **CHAMBER:** Suite for Flute and Piano (1955); *Divertimento* for 3 Treble Instruments (1957); *6 Short Pieces* for Woodwind Quintet (1962); *Partita* for Woodwind Quintet (1970); piano pieces. **VOCAL: CHORAL:** *Le Sang des autres* (1937); *Brazilian Psalm* (1941); *Vision of Peace* (1949); *Magnificat* for Soprano, Chorus, Flute, and Percussion (1960); *Fiery Furnace*, dramatic cantata (1962); *Song of Seasons* for Soloists, Choruses, and Orch. (1967); *The Exiles* for 2 Voices, 2 Pianos, and Percussion (1976); also songs.

Berger, Roman, Slovak composer; b. Těšín, Aug. 9, 1930. He studied at the Katowice State College of Music (1949–52) and at the Bratislava Cons. (1952–56; 1960–65), where he taught piano (1955–66) and theory (1968–73; 1983–85); also worked at the musicological inst. of the Slovak Academy of Sciences (from 1976). He served as secretary of the Union of Slovak Composers (1967–69). In 1988 he was awarded the Herder Prize of Vienna. His works follow the tenets of the modern Viennese school of composition, formally well disciplined, melodically atonal, and harmonically complex.

WORKS: Trio for Flute, Clarinet, and Bassoon (1962); *Ukolébavka* (Lullaby) for Mezzo-soprano and Chamber Orch. (1962); Suite for Strings, Piano, and Percussion (1963); *Transformations* for Orch. (1965); *Memento* for Orch. (1974); *De Profundis* for Bass, Piano, Cello, and Electronics (1980); *Exodus* for Organ (1982); piano pieces; electronic works.

Berger, Theodor, Austrian composer; b. Traismauer an der Donau, May 18, 1905; d. Vienna, Aug. 21, 1992. He was a pupil of Korngold and Schmidt at the Vienna Academy of Music (1926–32). Under the influence of his teachers, he evolved a new Romantic style of composition.

WORKS: BALLETS: *Homerische Sinfonie* (1948); *Heiratsannoncen* (1958). **ORCH.:** *Malinconia* for Strings (1938); *Ballade* (1941); *Legende vom Prinzen Eugen* (1942); *Rondino giocoso* for Strings (1947); *Concerto manuale* for 2 Pianos, Marimbaphone, Metallophone, Strings, and Percussion (1951); *La parola* (1954); Violin Concerto (1954); *Sinfonia Parabolica* (1956); *Sinfonia Macchinale* (1956); *Symphonischer Triglyph* (1957); *Jahreszeiten*, sym. (1958). **CHAMBER:** 2 string quartets (1930, 1931). **VOCAL:** *Frauenstimmen im Orchester* for Women's Chorus, Harps, and Strings (1959); *Divertimento* for Men's Chorus, 7 Wind Instruments, and Percussion (1968).

Berger, Wilhelm Georg, Romanian composer; b. Rupea, Dec. 4, 1929; d. Bucharest, March 8, 1993. He studied at the Bucharest Cons. (1948–52); was a violist in the Bucharest Phil. (1948–57).

WORKS: ORCH.: *Symphonic Variations* (1958); Concerto for Strings (1958); 17 syms.: No. 1, *Lyric* (1960), No. 2, *Epic* (1963), No. 3, *Dramatic* (1964), No. 4, *Tragic* (1965), No. 5, *Solemn Music* (1968), No. 6, *Harmony* (1969), No. 7, *Energetic* (1970), No. 8, *The Morning Star*, with Chorus (1971), No. 9, *Melodie* (1973–74), No. 10, with Solo Organ (1975–76), No. 11, *Sarmizegetusa* (1976), No. 12, *To the Star*, for Strings (1978), No. 13, *Sinfonia solemnis* (1980), No. 14 (1980–84), No. 15 (1984–86), No. 16 (1986), and No. 17 (1986); 2 viola concertos (1960, 1962); *Rhapsodic Images* (1964); Violin Concerto (1965; Brussels, Jan. 11, 1966); Cello Concerto (1967); *Meditations*, cycle of variations for Chamber Orch. (1968); *Variations* for Wind Orch. (1968); Concerto for 2 Violas and Orch. (1968); *Concert Music* for Flute, Strings, and Percussion (1972); Concerto for Violin, Viola, and Orch. (1977); *Faust*, dramatic sym. (1981); *Horia*, symphonic poem (1985). **CHAMBER:** Viola Sonata (1953); 15 string quartets (1954, 1955, 1957, 1959, 1961, 1965, 1966, 1966, 1967, 1967, 1967, 1967, 1979, 1980, 1983); Nonet (1957); 2 violin sonatas (1959, 1977); Quintet for 2 Violins, Viola, Cello, and Piano (1968); Trio for Piano, Violin, and Cello (1977); Concerto for Solo Organ (1981); *7 Serious Pieces* for String Quartet (1986); *7 Dramatic Pieces* for String Quartet (1986). **VOCAL:** *Stefan Furtună*, oratorio (1958); songs.

Bergh, Arthur, American violinist, conductor, and composer; b. St. Paul, Minn., March 24, 1882; d. aboard the S.S. *President Cleveland* en route to Honolulu, Feb. 11, 1962. He studied violin; played in the Metropolitan Opera orch. (1903–08) and conducted concerts in N.Y. (1911–14); later worked for recording companies. Among his works are the opera *Niorada*; the melodramas, *The Raven* and *The Pied Piper of Hamelin*; the operettas *In Arcady* and *The Goblin Fair*; about 100 songs; violin pieces.

Berghaus, Ruth, German opera director; b. Dresden, July 2, 1927. She received training in dance at the Palucca School in Dresden (1947–50). In 1964 she became a choreographer with the Berliner Ensemble, serving as its Intendant (1971–77). She garnered notoriety as an opera director at the Berlin State Opera with her staging of *Il barbiere di Siviglia*. From 1980 to 1987 she was an opera director at the Frankfurt am Main Opera, where she oversaw outstanding productions of *Parsifal* (1982) and the *Ring* cycle (1985–87); also was active as a guest director in other European opera centers, including Brussels, Hamburg, Munich, and Vienna. In her productions, Berghaus has pursued a radical course laden with symbolism and satire. She was married to **Paul Dessau**.

BIBL.: S. Neef, *Das Theater der R. B.* (Berlin, 1989); K. Bertisch, *R. B.* (Frankfurt am Main, 1990).

Berglund, Joel (Ingemar), Swedish bass-baritone; b. Torsåker, June 4, 1903; d. Stockholm, Jan. 21, 1985. He was a pupil of John Forsell at the Stockholm Cons. (1922–28). In 1928 he made his operatic debut as Lothario in *Mignon* at the Royal Opera in Stockholm, where he was a member until 1949; he then made guest appearances there until 1964. He also sang in Venice, Chicago, Bayreuth (as the Dutchman, 1949), and other operatic centers. On Jan. 9, 1946, he made his Metropolitan Opera debut in N.Y. as Hans Sachs, remaining on its roster until 1949. He served as director of the Royal Opera in Stockholm (1949–52), and continued to make appearances in opera until his retirement in 1970.

Berglund, Paavo (Allan Engelbert), prominent Finnish conductor; b. Helsinki, April 14, 1929. After violin lessons from his grandfather, he pursued training at the Sibelius Academy in Helsinki, Vienna, and Salzburg. In 1949 he began his career as a violinist in the Finnish Radio Sym. Orch. in Helsinki. In 1952 he became conductor of the Helsinki Chamber Orch. In 1956 he was made assoc. conductor and in 1962 principal conductor of the Finnish Radio Sym. Orch. He was principal conductor of the Bournemouth Sym. Orch. (1972–79) and music director of the Helsinki Phil. (1975–79); then was principal guest conductor of the Scottish National Orch. in Glasgow (1981–85). He served as the conductor of the Stockholm Phil. from 1987 to 1991. From 1993 he was conductor of the Royal Danish Orch. in Copenhagen. Berglund has won distinction for his interpretations of the 20th-century masters of the sym., ranging from Sibelius to Shostakovich. He conducts left-handed.

Bergman, Erik (Valdemar), eminent Finnish composer, conductor, music critic, and pedagogue; b. Nykarleby, Nov. 24, 1911. He received training in musicology at the Univ. of Helsinki (1931–33) and in composition from Furuhjelm at the Helsinki Cons. (diploma, 1938). Following further studies with Tiessen at the Berlin Hochschule für Musik (1937–39), he studied with Vogel in Switzerland. Returning to Helsinki, he was conductor of the Catholic Church Choir (1943–50), the Akademiska Sangföreningen at the Univ. (1950–69), and the Sällskapet Muntra Musikanter (1951–78). As a music critic, he wrote for the *Nya Pressen* (1945–47) and *Hufvudstadsbladet* (1947–76). From 1963 to 1976 he was prof. of composition at the Sibelius Academy. In 1961 he received the International Sibelius Prize of the Wihuri Foundation. In 1982 he was made a Finnish Academician. In 1994 he was awarded the Nordic Council Music Prize for his opera *Det sjungande trädet* (The Singing Tree), which received its premiere in Helsinki on Sept. 3, 1995. Bergman ranks among the foremost Finnish composers of his era. He cultivates varied techniques, ranging from medieval modality to serialism. His major works have evolved along expressionistic lines.

WORKS: OPERA: *Det sjungande tradet* (The Singing Tree; 1986–88; Helsinki, Sept. 3, 1995). **ORCH.:** Suite for Strings (1938); *Burla* (1948); *Tre aspetti d'una serie dodecafonica* (Helsinki, Nov. 8, 1957); *Aubade* (1958; Helsinki, Nov. 20, 1959); *Simbolo* (1960; Helsinki, March 14, 1961); *Circulus* (Helsinki, May 21, 1965); *Colori ed improvvisazioni* (1973; Zeeland, Jan. 23, 1974); *Dualis* for Cello and Orch. (Helsinki, Sept. 19, 1978); *Birds in the Morning* for Flute and Orch. (Warsaw, Sept. 18, 1979); *Arctica* (Utrecht, Nov. 2, 1979; based on *Lapponia* for Mezzo-soprano, Baritone, and Chorus, 1975); Piano Concerto (1980–81; Helsinki, Sept. 16, 1981); *Ananke* (1981–82; Helsinki, Oct. 6, 1982); Violin Concerto (1982; Mainz, May 11, 1984); *Tutti e soli* for Chamber Orch. (Helsinki, April 3, 1990); *Sub Luna*, 4 noctures (Helsinki, Aug. 21, 1991); *Poseidon* (1992; Washington, D.C., March 3, 1994); *Fanfare* for Chamber Orch. (Porvoo, June 18, 1993); *Musica Marina* for Strings (Jakobstad, May 20, 1994). **CHAMBER:** Piano Trio (1937); Violin Sonata (1943); Suite for Guitar (1949); *3 Fantasies* for Clarinet and Piano (Helsinki, May 14, 1954); *Concertino da camera* for 8 Instruments (Helsinki, Nov. 24, 1961); *Soltafara* for Alto Saxophone and Percussion (1977; Helsinki, Jan. 16, 1978); *Dialogue* for Flute and Guitar (Savonlinna, July 22, 1977); *Midnight* for Guitar (London, Dec. 9, 1977); *Silence and Eruptions* for 10 Instruments (1979; Stockholm, May 16, 1980); *Janus* for Violin and Guitar (Jyväskylä, July 2, 1980); *Mipejupa* for Flute, Alto Saxophone, Guitar, and Percussion (Helsinki, June 20, 1981); String Quartet (Kuhmo, July 27, 1982); *Borealis* for 2 Pianos and Percussion (Washington, D.C., Nov. 19, 1983); *Quo Vadis* for Cello and Piano (1983; Helsinki, Aug. 31, 1984); *etwas rascher* for Saxophone Quartet (1985; Savonlinna, Aug. 10, 1986); *Karanssi* for Clarinet and Cello (Warsaw, Sept. 15, 1990); *Mana* for Violin, Cello, Clarinet, and Piano (Washington, D.C., Sept. 27, 1991); *Quint-essence* for Saxophone Quartet and Percussion (1993); *Attention!* for 5 Percussion (1993; Helsinki, Aug. 22, 1995); *Now* for Viola and Piano (1994; Lapland Festival, July 6, 1995); *Una Fantasia* for String Quartet and Piano (1994; Kuhmo, July 21, 1995). **KEYBOARD: PIANO:** *Intervalles* (1949; Zürich, Oct. 19, 1951); Sonatina (1950); *Espressivo* (Helsinki, Dec. 5, 1952); *Aspekter* (1963); *A propos de B-A-C-H* (Helsinki, March 21, 1977); *Omaggio a Cristoforo Colombo* (Helsinki, Nov. 29, 1991). **ORGAN:** *Exsultate* (1954). **HARPSICHORD:** *Energien* (1970; Helsinki, Nov. 26, 1971). **VOCAL:** *Majnätter* (May Nights) for Soprano and Orch. (Stockholm, May 20, 1946); *Ensamhetens sånger* (Songs of Solitude) for Mezzo-soprano, Baritone, and Orch. (1947); *Rubaiyat* for Baritone, Men's Chorus, and Orch. (1953); *Adagio* for Baritone, Men's Chorus, Flute, and Vibraphone (1957; Helsinki, May 10, 1958); *Svanbild* (Swan Picture) for Baritone, Vocal Quartet, and Men's Chorus (1958; Helsinki, April 15, 1959); *Aton* for Baritone, Reciter, Chorus, and Orch. (1959; Helsinki, April 29, 1960); *3 Galgenlieder* for Baritone, 2 Reciters, and Men's Chorus (1959); *4 Galgenlieder* for 3 Reciters and Speaking Chorus (1960; Zürich, Dec. 3, 1961); *Bauta* for Men's Chorus, Baritone, and Percussion (Helsinki, Nov. 25, 1961); *Sela* for Baritone, Chorus, and Chamber Orch. (Helsinki, Nov. 18, 1962); *Fåglarna* (Birds) for Baritone, Men's Chorus, Percussion, and Celesta (1962; Helsinki, April 6, 1963); *Barnets drom* (Child's Dream) for Child Reciter, 2 Men Speakers, Men's Chorus, and Recorder (Helsinki, Nov. 30, 1963); *Ha Li Bomp* for Reciter, Tenor, and Men's Chorus (1964; Helsinki, April 10, 1965); *En sådan Kväll* (Such an Evening) for Soprano and Chorus (1965; Turku, June 11, 1966); *Snö* (Snow) for Tenor, Men's Chorus, and Flute (1966); *Springtime* for Baritone and Chorus (1966; London, Feb. 22, 1967); *Jesurun* for Baritone, Men's Chorus, 2 Trumpets, 2 Trombones, and 3 Percussion (1967; Helsinki, May 10, 1968); *Annonssidan* (Small Ads) for Baritone, 3 Tenors, 25 Reciters, and Men's Chorus (1969); *Nox* for Baritone, Chorus, Flute, English Horn, and Percussion (Göteborg, April 20, 1970); *Requiem över en död diktare* (Requiem for a Dead Poet) for Baritone, Chorus, 2 Trumpets, 2 Trombones, 2 Percussion, and Organ (1970; Stockholm, May 19, 1975); *Missa in honorem Sancti Henrici* for Soloists, Chorus, and Organ (Helsinki, Sept. 5, 1971); *Hathor Suite* for Soprano, Baritone, Chorus, Flute, English Horn, Harp, and 2 Percussion (Helsinki, Nov. 27, 1971); *Bardo Thödol* for Reciter, Mezzo-soprano, Baritone, Chorus, and Orch. (1974; Helsinki, May 19, 1975); *Lapponia* for Mezzo-soprano, Baritone, and Chorus (Cambridge, Nov. 30, 1975; reworked as *Arctica* for Orch., 1979); *Bon Appétit!* for Reciter, Baritone, and Men's Chorus (1975); *Noa* for Baritone, Chorus, and Orch. (1976; Helsinki, Oct. 25, 1977); *Bim Bam Bum* for Reciter, Tenor, Men's Chorus, Flute, and Percussion (1976; Uppsala, April 23, 1977); *Voices in the Night* for Baritone and Men's Chorus (1977; Reykjavík, May 9, 1979); *Triumf att finnas till* (Triumph of Being Here) for Soprano, Flute, and Percussion (1978; Cologne, Jan. 25, 1979); *Gudarnas spar* (Tracks of the Gods) for Alto, Baritone, and Chorus (1978; Helsinki, March 2, 1980); *Tipitaka Suite* for Baritone and Men's Chorus (1980; Turku, April 3, 1982); *4 Vocalises* for Mezzo-soprano and Men's Chorus (1983; Helsinki, Nov. 24, 1986); *Lemminkainen* for Reciter, Mezzo-soprano, Baritone, and Chorus (1984; Helsinki, May 8, 1985); *Svep* (Sweep) for Reciter, Mezzo-soprano, Baritone, Chorus, and Instrumental Ensemble (1984; Helsinki, Feb. 5, 1985); *Bygden* (The Village) for Reciter, Soprano, Baritone, Chorus, Child Soprano, Children's Chorus, Instruments, Cowbells, Bottles, Gongs, etc. (1985); *Forsta maj* (May Day) for Tenor and Men's Chorus (1985; Helsinki, March 7, 1988); *Tule armaani* (Come, My Love) for Baritone and Men's Chorus (1988; Helsinki, Nov. 23, 1989); *Careliana* for 6 Men's Voices (1988; Joensuu, June 11, 1989); *Petrarca Suite* for Baritone and Chorus (Helsinki, Dec. 12, 1991); *Nein zur Lebensangst* for Reciter and Chamber Chorus (1991); *Tapiolassa* for Alto and Children's Chorus (1991; Helsinki, Nov. 23, 1993); *Den heliga oron* for Mezzo-soprano and String Qurtet (1994; Korsholm, June 19, 1995); *Aggadot* for Vocal Quartet and Instrumental Ensemble (1994; Joensuu, June 21, 1995); various other mixed and men's choruses; solo songs.

BIBL.: J. Parsons, *E. B.: A Seventieth Birthday Tribute* (London, 1981); A. Beyer, "In Search of Silence: A Meeting with E.B.," *Nordic Sounds*, 1 (1994).

Bergmans, Paul (Jean Étienne Charles Marie), Belgian librarian and musicologist; b. Ghent, Jan. 23, 1868; d. there, Nov. 14, 1935. He was educated at the Univ. of Ghent; also took courses in piano and violin at the Ghent Cons., and received private instruction in theory from Waelput. From 1885 until his death he wrote music criticism for *Flandre libérale*; in 1892 he became assistant librarian and in 1919 chief librarian at the Univ. of Ghent; in 1919 he also became the first holder of its chair in musicology, the first in a Belgian univ. In 1920 he was elected a member of the Académie Royale de Belgique.

WRITINGS: *Pierre Josephe Le Blau: Carillonneur de la ville de Gand au XVIIIe siècle* (Ghent, 1884); *Hendrick Waelput* (Ghent, 1886); *Variétés musicologiques* (Ghent, 1891–1901; Antwerp, 1920); *Analecte belgiques* (Ghent, 1896); *Les Imprimeurs belges à l'étranger* (Ghent, 1897; 2nd ed., 1922); *La Vie musicale gantoise au XVIIIe siècle* (Ghent, 1897); *L'Organiste des archiducs Albert et Isabelle: Peter Philips* (Ghent, 1903); *Nicolas Maiscocque: Musicien montois due XVIIe siècle* (Ghent, 1909); *Mélanges iconographiques, bibliographiques et historiques* (Ghent, 1912); *Les Musiciens de Courtrai et du Courtraisis* (Ghent, 1912); *La Biographie du compositeur Corneille Verdonck* (Brussels, 1919); *Henri Vieuxtemps* (Turnhout, 1920); *Le Baron Limnander de Nieuwenhove* (Brussels, 1920); *Quatorze lettres inédites du compositeur Philippe de Monte* (Brussels, 1921); *Tielman Susato* (Antwerp, 1923); *Les Origines belges de Beethoven* (Brussels, 1927); *Une Famille de musiciens belges du XVIIIe siècle: Les Loeillet* (Brussels, 1928); *La Typographie musicale en Belgique au XVIe siècle* (Brussels, 1930).

Bergonzi, Carlo, eminent Italian tenor; b. Polisene, near Parma, July 13, 1924. He studied with Grandini in Parma, where he also took courses at the Boito Cons. During World War II, he was imprisoned for his fervent anti-Fascist stance. After his liberation, he made his operatic debut in the baritone role of Rossini's Figaro in Lecce in 1948. In 1951 he made his debut as a tenor singing Andrea Chénier in Bari. He made his first appearance at Milan's La Scala in 1953 creating the title role in Napoli's *Masaniello*, and that same year he made his London debut as Alvaro at the Stoll Theatre. In 1962 he returned to London to make his Covent Garden debut in the same role. In 1955 he made his U.S. debut as Luigi in *Il Tabarro* at the Chicago Lyric Opera. On Nov. 13, 1956, he made his Metropolitan Opera debut in N.Y. as Radames, remaining on its roster until 1972, and again for the 1974–75, 1976–77, and 1978–83 seasons. He gave his farewell N.Y. concert at Carnegie Hall on April 17, 1994; he then bade farewell to Europe that same year in a series of concerts. He was blessed with a voice of remarkable beauty and expressivity. Among his many outstanding roles were Pollione, Rodolfo, Alfredo, Canio, Manrico, Nemorino, and Cavaradossi.

Bergsma, William (Laurence), notable American composer and pedagogue; b. Oakland, Calif., April 1, 1921; d. Seattle, March 18, 1994. His mother, a former opera singer, gave him piano lessons; he also practiced the violin. After the family moved to Redwood City, Bergsma entered Burlingame High School, where he had theory lessons. In 1937 he began to take lessons in composition with Hanson at the Univ. of Southern Calif. in Los Angeles. He composed a ballet, *Paul Bunyan*, and Hanson conducted a suite from it with the Rochester Civic Orch. in Rochester, N.Y., on April 29, 1939. Bergsma also took courses at Stanford Univ. (1938–40); from 1940 to 1944 he attended the Eastman School of Music in Rochester, studying general composition with Hanson and orchestration with Bernard Rogers. He graduated in 1942, receiving his M.M. degree in 1943. In 1944 Bergsma became an instructor in music at Drake Univ. in Des Moines. In 1946 and in 1951 he held Guggenheim fellowships. In 1946 he was appointed to the faculty of the Juilliard School of Music in N.Y., where he taught until 1963. From 1963 to 1971 Bergsma served as director of the School of Music of the Univ. of Wash. in Seattle, remaining as a prof. there until 1986. In 1967 he was elected to membership in the National Inst. of Arts and Letters. During his teaching activities he continued to compose, receiving constant encouragement from an increasing number of performances. His style of composition is that of classical Romanticism, having a strong formal structure without lapsing into modernistic formalism. The Romantic side of his music is reflected in his melodious lyricism. He never subscribed to fashionable theories of doctrinaire modernity.

WORKS: DRAMATIC: OPERAS: *The Wife of Martin Guerre* (N.Y., Feb. 15, 1956); *The Murder of Comrade Sharik* (1973; rev. 1978). **BALLETS:** *Paul Bunyan* (San Francisco, June 22, 1939); *Gold and the Senor Commandante* (Rochester, N.Y., May 1, 1942). **ORCH.:** Sym. for Chamber Orch. (Rochester, N.Y., April 14, 1943); 2 numbered syms.: No. 1 (1946–49; Radio Hilversum, April 18, 1950) and No. 2, *Voyages* (Great Falls, Mont., May 11, 1976); *Music on a Quiet Theme* (Rochester, N.Y., April 22, 1943); *A Carol on Twelfth Night*, symphonic poem (1953); *Chameleon Variations* (1960); *In Celebration: Toccata for the 6th Day*, commissioned for the inaugural-week concert of the Juilliard Orch. during the week of dedication of Phil. Hall at Lincoln Center for the Performing Arts (N.Y., Sept. 28, 1962); *Documentary 1* (1963; suite from a film score) and *2* (1967); *Serenade, To Await the Moon* for Chamber Orch. (La Jolla, Calif., Aug. 22, 1965); Violin Concerto (Tacoma, Wash., May 18, 1966); *Dances from a New England Album, 1852* for Small Orch. (1969); *Sweet Was the Song the Virgin Sung: Tristan Revisited*, variations and fantasy for Viola and Orch. (1977); *In Campo Aperto* for Oboe Concertante, 2 Bassoon, and Strings (1981). **CHAMBER:** *Showpiece* for Violin and Piano (1934); Suite for Brass Quartet (1940); 6 string quartets (1942, 1944, 1953, 1970, 1982, 1991); *Pieces for Renard* for Recorder and 2 Violas (1943); Concerto for Wind Quintet (1958); *Fantastic Variations on a Theme from Tristan und Isolde* for Viola and Piano (Boston, March 2, 1961); *Illegible Canons* for Clarinet and Piano (1969); *Changes for 7* for Wind Quintet, Percussion, and Piano (1971); *Clandestine Dialogues* for Cello and Percussion (1972); *Blatant Hypotheses* for Trombone and Piano (1977); Quintet for Flute and Strings (1979); *The Voice of the Coelacanth* for Horn, Violin, and Piano (1980); *Masquerade* for Wind Quintet (1986); *A Lick and a Promise* for Saxophone and Chimes (1988). **PIANO:** *3 Fantasies* (1943; rev. 1983); *Tangents* (1951); *Variations* (1984). **VOCAL:** *In a Glass of Water* (1945); *On the Beach at Night* (1946); *Confrontation*, after the Book of Job, for Chorus and 22 Instruments (Des Moines, Iowa, Nov. 29, 1963); *Wishes, Wonders, Portents, Charms* for Chorus and Instruments (N.Y., Feb. 12, 1975); *In Space* for Soprano and Instruments (Seattle, May 21, 1975); *I Told You So*, 4 songs for Voice and Percussion (1986).

Berinbaum, Martin, American trumpeter; b. Philadelphia, June 14, 1942. He studied with James Stamp at the Univ. of Southern Calif. in Los Angeles; then toured Europe and the Near East with the Roger Wagner Chorale; played 1st trumpet in the West Point Military Academy Band (1966–69); subsequently enrolled as a student of William Vachiano at the Juilliard School of Music in N.Y., graduating in 1970, and developed a career as a trumpet virtuoso.

Berio, Luciano, eminent Italian composer, conductor, and pedagogue; b. Oneglia, Oct. 24, 1925. Following initial training from his father, Ernesto Berio, he entered the Milan Cons. in 1945 to study composition with Paribeni and Ghedini, obtaining his diploma in 1950. He married **Cathy Berberian** in 1950 (marriage dissolved in 1964), who became a champion of his most daunting vocal works. In 1952 he attended Luigi Dallapiccola's course at the Berkshire Music Center in Tanglewood. After attending the summer course in new music in Darmstadt in 1954, he returned to Milan and helped to organize the Studio di Fonologia Musicale of the RAI with Maderna, remaining active with it until 1961. In 1956 he founded the journal *Incontri Musicali*, and also served as director of the concerts it sponsored until 1960. He taught composition at the Berkshire Music Center (1960, 1982), the Dartington Summer School (1961–62), Mills College in Oakland, California (1962–64), and Harvard Univ. (1966–67). From 1965 to 1972 he taught composition at the Juilliard School of Music in N.Y., where he also conducted the Juilliard Ensemble. From 1974 to 1979 he worked at IRCAM in Paris. He also gave increasing attention to conducting, eventually appearing as a guest conductor with leading European and North American orchs. In 1987 he became founder-director of Tempo Reale in Florence, a research, educational, and composition center. During the 1993–94 academic year, he was the Charles Eliot Norton Prof. of Poetry at Harvard Univ., and then served as its Distinguished Composer-in-Residence from 1994. In 1980 he was awarded an honorary doctorate from the City Univ. of London. He received the Premio Italia in 1982 for his *Duo*. In 1989 he was awarded the Ernst von Siemens-Musikpreis of Munich.

From the very beginning of his career as a composer, Berio embraced the ideals of the avant-garde. His early use of 12-tone writing was followed by imaginative explorations of aleatory, electronics, objets trouvés, and other contemporary means of expression. As one of the principal composers of his era, Berio has demonstrated a remarkable capacity for infusing new life into established forms. The theatrical nature of much of his music has rendered his vocal scores among the most challenging and significant works of their time. These works, like most of his output, have set daunting hurdles of virtuosity for the performer while demanding a level of tolerance from both critics and audiences alike.

WORKS: DRAMATIC: *Allez Hop*, racconto mimico for Mezzo-soprano, 8 Mimes, Ballet, and Orch. (1952–59; Venice, Sept. 23, 1959; rev. 1968); *Passaggio*, messa in scena for Soprano, 2 Choruses, and Orch. (1961–62; Milan, May 6, 1963); *Laborintus II* for Voices, Instruments, and Tape (1965); *Il combattimento di Tancredi e Clorinda*, after Monteverdi (1966); *Opera* for 10 Actors, 2 Sopranos, Tenor, Baritone, Vocal Ensemble, Orch., and Tape (1969–70; Santa Fe, N.M., Aug. 12, 1970; rev. version, Florence, May 28, 1977); *Per la dolce memoria de quel giorno*, ballet (1974); *La vera storia*, opera (1977–78; Milan, March 9, 1982); *Un re in ascolto*, azione musicale (1979–83; Salzburg, Aug. 7, 1984); *Duo*, imaginary theater for radio for Baritone, 2 Violins, Chorus, and Orch. (1982); *Naturale*, theater piece (1985–86); *Wir Bauen eine Stadt*, children's opera, after Hindemith (1987). **ORCH.:** *Preludio a una festa marina* for Strings (1944); Concertino for Clarinet, Violin, Harp, Celesta, and Strings (1951; rev. 1970); *Variazioni* for Chamber Orch. (1953–54; Hamburg, Feb. 23, 1955); *Nones* (1954; Rome, Oct. 15, 1955); *Mimusique No. 2* (1955); *Allelujah I* (1955–56) and *II* (1957–58; Rome, May 17, 1958); *Variazioni* for 2 Basset Horns and Strings, after Mozart (1956); *Divertimento* (Rome, Dec. 2, 1957; in collaboration with B. Maderna); *Tempi concertati* for Flute, Violin, 2 Pianos, and Other Instruments (1958–59); *Quaderni I* (1959), *II* (1961), and *III* (1962); *Chemins I* for Harp and Orch. (1965; based on *Sequenza II*), *III* for Viola and Orch. (1968; rev. 1973; based on *Chemins II*), *IIB* (1970), *IIC* for Bass Clarinet and Orch. (1972), *IV* for Oboe and Strings (1975; based on *Sequenza VII*), and *V* for Guitar and Chamber Orch. (1992); *Bewegung* (1971); *Still* (1971–73); Concerto for 2 Pianos and Orch. (1972–73); *Points on the Curve to Find . . .* for Piano and 23 Instruments (1974); *Eindrücke* (1973–74); *Il ritorno degli snovidenia* for Cello and 30 Instruments (1976–77); *Encore* (1978); 2 piano concertos: No. 1 (1979) and No. 2, *Echoing Curves* (1988); *Entrata* (San Francisco, Oct. 1, 1980); *Accordo* for 4 Wind Bands (1981); *Corale* for Violin, 2 Horns, and Strings (1981; based on *Sequenza VIII*); *Fanfara* (1982); *Requies* (1983–84; Lausanne, March 26, 1984; rev. 1985); *Voci* for Viola and 2 Instrumental Groups (1984); *Formazioni* (1986; Amsterdam, Jan. 15, 1987; rev. 1988); *Continuo* (1989); *Festum* (Dallas, Sept. 14, 1989). **CHAMBER:** *Divertimento* for Violin, Viola, and Cello (1947; rev. 1985); *Tre pezzi* for 3 Clarinets (1947); Wind Quintet (1948); Wind Quartet (1950–51; rev. 1951 as *Opus Number Zoo* for Wind Quintet); Sonatina for Flute, 2 Clarinets, and Bassoon (1951); *Due Pezzi* for Violin and Piano (1951; rev. 1966); *Study* for String Quartet (1952; rev. 1985); 2 string quartets (1956; 1986–93); *Serenata* for Chamber Ensemble (1957); *Sequenza I* for Flute (1958), *II* for Harp (1963), *V* for Trombone (1966), *VI* for Viola (1967), *VII* for Oboe (1969), *VIII* for Violin (1976), *IXa* for Clarinet (1980), *IXb* for Alto Saxophone (1981), *X* for Trumpet and Piano Resonance (1985), and *XI* for Guitar (1987–88); *Differences* for Flute, Clarinet, Harp, Viola, Cello, and Tape (1958); *Sincronie* for String Quartet (1963–64); *Gesti* for Recorder (1966); *Chemins II* for Viola and 9 Instruments (1967; based on *Sequenza VI*); *Memory* for Electric Piano and Electric Harpsichord (1970); *Autre Fois* for Flute, Clarinet, and Harp (1971); *Musica leggera* for Flute, Viola, and Cello (1974); *Les Mots sont allés* for Cello (1978); *Duetti* for 2 Violins (1979–82); *Lied* for Clarinet (1983); *Call-St. Louis Fanfare* for 5 Winds (1985; rev. 1987); *Ricorrenze* for Wind Quintet (1985–87); *Comma* for Clarinet (1987); *Psy* for Double Bass (1989); *Brin* for Guitar (1994; also for Piano, 1990). **KEYBOARD: PIANO:** *Pastorale* (1937); *Toccata* for Piano Duet (1939); *Petite Suite* (1947); *Cinque variazioni* (1952–53; rev. 1966); *Wasserklavier* (1965); *Sequenza IV* (1965–66); *Erdenklavier* (1969); *Luftklavier* (1985); *Feuerklavier* (1989); *Leaf* (1990); *Brin* (1990; also for Guitar, 1994). **ORGAN:** *Fa-Si* for Organ and Registration Assistants (1975). **HARPSICHORD:** *Rounds* (1966). **VOCAL:** *O bone Jesu* for Chorus (1946); *4 canzoni popolari* for Woman's Voice and Piano (1946–47); *Trio liriche greche* for Voice and Piano (1946–48); *Due canti siciliani* for Tenor and Men's Chorus (1948); *Ad Hermes* for Voice and Piano (1948); *Due pezzi sacri* for 2 Sopranos, Piano, 2 Harps, Timpani, and 12 Bells (1949); *Magnificat* for 2 Sopranos, Chorus, and Orch. (1949); *Opus Number Zoo* for Reciters and Wind Quintet (1951; rev. 1970; based on the Wind Quintet); *Deus meus* for Voice and 3 Instruments (1951); *El Mar la Mar* for Soprano, Mezzo-soprano, and 7 Instruments (1952); *Chamber Music* for Woman's Voice, Clarinet, Cello, and Harp (1953); *Epifanie* for Soprano or Mezzo-soprano and Orch. (1959–61; rev. 1965); *Circles* for Woman's Voice, Harp, and 2 Percussionists (1960); *Folk Songs* for Mezzo-soprano and 7 Instruments (1964; also for Mezzo-soprano and Orch., 1973); *Sequenza III* for Voice (1965); *O King* for Voice and 5 Instruments (1968); *Questo vuol dire che* for 3 Women's Voices, Small Chorus, and Tape (1968); *Sinfonia* for 8 Voices and Orch. (1968–69); *Air* for Soprano and Orch. (1969); *Melodrama* for Tenor and Instrumental Ensemble, after *Opera* (1970); *Agnus* for 2 Sopranos and 3 Clarinets (1971); *Bewegung II* for Baritone and Orch. (1971); *Recital for Cathy* for Mezzo-soprano and 17 Instruments (1971); *E Vó* for Soprano and Instrumental Ensemble (1972); *Cries of London* for 6 Voices (1973–74; also for 8 Voices, 1974–76); *Calmo (in memoriam Bruno Maderna)* for Mezzo-soprano and Chamber Orch. (1974; rev. 1988–89); *Coro* for 40 Voices and Instrumental Ensemble (1974–77); *Scena de La vera storia* for Mezzo-soprano, Bass, Chorus, and Orch. (1981); *Ecce: musica per musicologi* for Women's Voices, Men's Voices, and Bells (1987); *Ofanim* for Woman's Voice, 2 Children's Choruses, 2 Instrumental Groups, and Computer (1988–92); *Canticum novissimi testamenti II* for Soprano, Alto, Tenor, Bass, 4 Clarinets, and Saxophone Quartet (1989); *Epiphanies* for Soprano or Mezzo-soprano and Orch. (1991–92). **ELECTRONIC:** *Mutazioni* (1954); *Perspectives* (1957); *Momenti* (1957); *Thema (Omaggio a Joyce)* (1958); *Visage* (1961); *Chants paralleles* (1975); *Diario imaginario* (1975). **OTHER:** *Brahms-Berio, Op. 120, No. 1* for Clarinet or Viola and Orch. (1984–85); *Schubert-Berio: Rendering* for Orch. (1989; a restoration of fragments from a Schubert sym.); arrangements of various other works, including those by Verdi, Mahler, Weill, and Falla.

BIBL.: R. Dalmonte and B. Varga, *L. B.: Two Interviews* (London, 1985); D. Osmond-Smith, *B.* (Oxford, 1991); F. Menezes Filho, *L. B. et la phonologie: Une approche jakobsonienne de son oeuvre* (Frankfurt am Main, 1993).

Berkeley, Sir Lennox (Randall Francis), eminent English composer and teacher, father of **Michael (Fitzhardinge) Berkeley**; b. Boars Hill, May 12, 1903; d. London, Dec. 26, 1989. He was educated at Merton College, Oxford (1922–26), and then studied composition with Boulanger in Paris (1927–32). Returning to London, he worked for the BBC (1942–45) before serving as a prof. of composition at the Royal Academy of Music (1946–68). In 1957 he was made a Commander of the Order of the British Empire, in 1970 he received an honorary D.Mus. from the Univ. of Oxford, and in 1974 he was knighted. In his early works, Berkeley was influenced by the Parisian neo-Classicists and the music of Britten. He later developed a complex individual style that was broadly melodious, richly harmonious, and translucidly polyphonic.

WORKS: DRAMATIC: OPERAS: *Nelson* (1949–54; London, Sept. 22, 1954; orch. suite, 1955); *A Dinner Engagement* (Aldeburgh Festival, June 17, 1954); *Ruth* (London, Oct. 2, 1956); *Castaway* (Aldeburgh Festival, June 3, 1967). **BALLET:** *The Judgement of Paris* (1938). Also incidental music for plays and film scores. **ORCH.:** *Introduction and Dance* for Small Orch. (1926); 2 suites (1927, 1953); Concertino for Chamber Orch. (London, April 6, 1927); 2 sinfoniettas (1929, 1950); Sym. for Strings (1930–31; London, Dec. 14, 1931); 2 overtures (1934, Barcelona, April 23, 1936; 1947); *Mont Juic*, suite (1937; in collaboration with Britten); *Introduction and Allegro* for 2 Pianos and Orch. (1938); *Serenade* for Strings (1939); 4 syms.: No. 1 (1940; London, July 8, 1943), No. 2 (1956–58; Birmingham, Feb. 24, 1959), No. 3 (Cheltenham, July 9, 1969), and No. 4 (1976–78; London, May 30, 1978); Cello Concerto (1939; Cheltenham, July 17, 1983); *Divertimento* (1943); *Nocturne* (1946); Piano Concerto (1947); Concerto for 2 Pianos and Orch. (1948); Flute Concerto (1952; London, July 29, 1953); Concerto for Piano and Double String Orch. (1958; London, Feb. 11, 1959); *Overture for Light Orchestra* (1959); *Suite: A Winter's Tale* (1960); *5 Pieces* for Violin and Orch. (1961; London, July 3, 1962); Concerto for Violin and Chamber Orch. (1961); *Partita* for Chamber Orch. (1964–65); *Windsor Variations* for Chamber Orch. (1969); *Dialogue* for Cello and Chamber Orch. (1970);

Palm Court Waltz (1971); Sinfonia concertante for Oboe and Chamber Orch. (1973); *Antiphon* for Strings (1973); *Voices of the Night* (Birmingham, Aug. 22, 1973); Suite for Strings (1973–74); Guitar Concerto (London, July 4, 1974). **CHAMBER:** *Serenade* for Flute, Oboe, Violin, Viola, and Cello (1929); Suite for Flute, Oboe, Violin, Viola, and Cello (c.1930); 2 violin sonatas (1931, c.1933); 3 string quartets (1935, 1942, 1970); Trio for Flute, Oboe, and Piano (1935); Sonatina for Recorder or Flute and Piano (1939); String Trio (1943); Viola Sonata (1945); *Elegy* for Violin and Piano (1950); Trio for Violin, Horn, and Piano (1954); Sextet for Clarinet, Horn, and String Quartet (1955); Concertino for Recorder or Flute, Violin, Cello, and Harpsichord or Piano (1955); *Allegro* for 2 Treble Recorders (c.1955); *Diversions* for 8 Instruments (1964); Quartet for Oboe and String Trio (1967); *Introduction and Allegro* for Double Bass and Piano (1971); Duo for Cello and Piano (1971); Quintet for Winds and Piano (1974–75); Flute Sonata (1978); also many piano pieces, including a Sonata (1941–45); harpsichord music; organ pieces. **VOCAL:** *Jonah*, oratorio (1933–35); *Domini est Terra* for Chorus and Orch. (London, June 17, 1938); *4 Poems of St. Teresa of Avila* for Contralto and Strings (1947); *Stabat Mater* for 6 Solo Voices and 12 Instruments (1947; arranged for Voices and Small Orch. by M. Berkeley, 1978); *Colonus' Praise* for Chorus and Orch. (1948); *Variations on a Theme by Orlando Gibbons* for Tenor, Chorus, Strings, and Organ (1951); *4 Ronsard Sonnets*: Set 1 for 2 Tenors and Piano (1952) and Set 2 for Tenor and Orch. (London, Aug. 9, 1963); *Batter My Heart* for Soprano, Chorus, Organ, and Chamber Orch. (1962); *Signs in the Dark* for Chorus and Strings (1967); *Magnificat* for Chorus and Orch. (London, July 8, 1968); *Una and the Lion* for Soprano, Recorder, Viola da Gamba, and Harpsichord (1978–79); many other choral works and songs.

BIBL.: P. Dickinson, *The Music of L. B.* (London, 1988); M. Williamson, "Sir L. B. (1903–1989)," *Musical Times* (April 1990).

Berkeley, Michael (Fitzhardinge), English composer, son of **Sir Lennox (Randall Francis) Berkeley;** b. London, May 29, 1948. He was a chorister at Westminster Cathedral under the tutelage of George Malcolm; he also studied with his father at the Royal Academy of Music and then privately with Richard Rodney Bennett. He received the Guinness Prize for his *Meditations* for Chamber Orch. (1977); was assoc. composer to the Scottish Chamber Orch. (1979) and composer-in-residence at the London College of Music (1987–88). In 1995 he became artistic director of the Cheltenham Festival. His anti-nuclear oratorio *Or Shall We Die?* (1982) brought him to international attention. His music is austere while still projecting a firm relationship to the English New Romantic movement.

WORKS: DRAMATIC: *The Mayfly*, children's ballet (London, Sept. 30, 1984); *Baa-Baa Black Sheep*, opera (Cheltenham, July 7, 1993). **ORCH.:** *Meditations* for Chamber Orch. (1977); *Fantasia Concertante* for Chamber Orch. (1977); Concerto for Oboe and Chamber Orch. (Burnham Market, Aug. 20, 1977); *Primavera* (London, May 18, 1979); *Uprising*, sym. for Chamber Orch. (Edinburgh, Dec. 18, 1980); *Flames* (1980; Liverpool, Jan. 10, 1981); *The Vision of Piers the Ploughman* for Chamber Orch. (1981); *Gregorian Variations* (London, April 22, 1982); *The Romance of the Rose* for Chamber Orch. (1982); Concerto for Cello and Chamber Orch. (London, Feb. 20, 1983); Concerto for Horn and Chamber Orch. (Cheltenham, July 17, 1984); Organ Concerto (Cambridge, July 23, 1987); *Coronach* for Strings (1988); *Entertaining Master Punch* for Chamber Orch. (1991); Clarinet Concerto (1991); *Elegy* for Flute and Strings (1993); Viola Concerto (1994). **CHAMBER:** String Trio (1978); Violin Sonata (1979); *American Suite* for Flute or Recorder and Cello or Bassoon (1980); Chamber Sym. (London, Aug. 1, 1980); 4 string quartets (1981, 1984, 1987, 1995); Piano Trio (1982); *Music from Chaucer* for Brass Quintet (1983); Clarinet Quintet (1983); *Fierce Tears* for Oboe and Piano (1984); *A Mosaic for Father Popieluszko* for Violin and Guitar (1985); *For the Savage Messiah* for Piano Quartet and Bass (1985). **SOLO INSTRUMENTS:** *Strange Meeting* for Piano (1978); Organ Sonata (1979); *Iberian Notebook* for Cello (1980); *Worry Beads* for Guitar (1981); Guitar Sonata (1982); *The Snake* for English Horn (1990). **VOCAL:** *The Wild Winds* for Soprano and Small Orch. (London, Dec. 19, 1978); *Rain* for Tenor, Violin, and Cello (1979); *At the Round Earth's Imagin'd Corners* for Chorus (1980); *The Crocodile and Father William* for Chorus (1982); *Or Shall We Die?*, oratorio for Soprano, Baritone, Chorus, and Orch. (London, Feb. 6, 1983); *Songs of Awakening Love* for Soprano and Small Orch. (Cheltenham, July 15, 1986); *Verbum caro factum est* for Baritone, Chorus, and Organ (1987; Birmingham, Jan. 7, 1988); *The Red Macula* for Chorus and Orch. (Leeds, May 5, 1989); *Stupendous Stranger* for Chorus and Brass (1990).

Berlin, Irving (real name, **Israel Balin**), fabulously popular Russian-born American composer of hundreds of songs that became the musical conscience of the U.S.; b. Mogilev, May 11, 1888; d. N.Y., Sept. 22, 1989. Fearing anti-Semitic pogroms, his Jewish parents took ship when he was 5 years old and landed in N.Y. His father made a scant living as a synagogue cantor, and Izzy, as he was called, earned pennies as a newsboy. He later got jobs as a busboy, in time graduating to the role of a singing waiter in Chinatown. He learned to improvise on the bar piano and, at the age of 19, wrote the lyrics of a song, *Marie from Sunny Italy*. Because of a printing error, his name on the song appeared as Berlin instead of Balin. He soon acquired the American vernacular and, throughout his career, never tried to experiment with sophisticated language, thus distancing himself from his younger contemporaries, such as Gershwin and Porter. He was married in 1912, but his young bride died of typhoid fever, contracted during their honeymoon in Havana. He wrote a lyric ballad in her memory, *When I Lost You*, which sold a million copies. He never learned to read or write music, and composed most of his songs in F-sharp major for the convenience of fingering the black keys of the scale. To modulate into other keys, he had a special hand clutch built at the piano keyboard, so that his later songs acquired an air of technical variety. This piano is now installed at the Smithsonian Institution in Washington, D.C. His first biographer, Alexander Woollcott, fondly referred to him as a "creative ignoramus." Victor Herbert specifically discouraged Berlin from learning harmony for fear that he would lose his natural genius for melody, and also encouraged him to join ASCAP as a charter member, a position that became the source of his fantastically prosperous commercial success.

Berlin was drafted into the U.S. Army in 1917 but did not serve in military action. While in the army he wrote a musical revue, *Yip, Yip, Yaphank*, which contained one of his most famous tunes, *God Bless America*; it was for some reason omitted in the original show, but returned to glory when songster Kate Smith performed it in 1938. The song, patriotic to the core, became an unofficial American anthem. In 1925, when Berlin was 37 years old, he met Ellin Mackay, the daughter of the millionaire head of the Postal Telegraph Cable Co., and proposed to her. She accepted, but her father threatened to disinherit her if she married a Jewish immigrant. Money was not the object, for by that time Berlin was himself a contented millionaire. The yellow press of N.Y. devoted columns upon columns to the romance; they eventually married in a civil ceremony at the Municipal Building. Ironically, it was the despised groom who helped his rich father-in-law during the financial debacle of the 1920s, for while stocks fell disastrously, Berlin's melodies rose in triumph all over America. The marriage proved to be happy, lasting 62 years, until Ellin's death in July of 1988. Berlin was reclusive in his last years of life; he avoided making a personal appearance when members of ASCAP gathered before his house to serenade him on his 100th birthday.

Berlin was extremely generous with his enormous earnings. *God Bless America* brought in 3/4 of a million dollars in royalties, all of which was donated to the Boy and Girl Scouts of America. Another great song, *White Christmas*, which Berlin wrote for the film *Holiday Inn*, became a sentimental hit among American troops stationed in tropical bases in the Pacific during World War II; 115,000,000 records of this song and 6,000,000 copies of sheet music for it were sold in America. The homesick marines altered the first line from "I'm dreaming of a white Christmas" to "I'm dreaming of a white mistress," that particular commodity being scarce in the tropics. In 1954 Berlin received the Congressional Medal of Honor. His financial interests were taken care of by his publishing enterprise, Irving Berlin Music, Inc., founded in 1919, and also by ASCAP. According to some records, his income tax amounted to 91% of his total earnings.

WORKS: DRAMATIC (all first perf. in N.Y.): *Watch Your Step*, revue (Dec. 8, 1914); *Stop! Look! Listen!*, revue (1915); *The Century Girl*, revue (1916; with Victor Herbert); *Yip, Yip, Yaphank*, revue (Aug. 19, 1918); *Music Box Revue* (1921, 1922, 1923, 1924); *The Cocoanuts*, musical comedy (Dec. 8, 1925); *Ziegfeld Follies*, revue (1927); *Face the Music*, musical comedy (Feb. 17, 1932); *As Thousands Cheer*, revue (Sept. 30, 1933); *Louisiana Purchase*, musical comedy (May 28, 1940); *Me and My Melinda*, musical comedy (1942); *This Is the Army*, revue (July 4, 1942); *Annie Get Your Gun*, musical comedy (May 16, 1946); *Miss Liberty*, musical comedy (July 15, 1949); *Call Me Madam*, musical comedy (Oct. 12, 1950); *Mr. President*, musical play (Oct. 20, 1962). **FILM SCORES:** *The Cocoanuts* (1929); *Puttin' On the Ritz* (1929); *Top Hat* (1935); *Follow the Fleet* (1936); *On the Avenue* (1937); *Carefree* (1938); *Alexander's Ragtime Band* (1938); *Second Fiddle* (1939); *Holiday Inn* (1942); *This Is the Army* (1943); *Blue Skies* (1946); *Easter Parade* (1948); *Annie Get Your Gun* (1950); *Call Me Madam* (1953); *White Christmas* (1954); *There's No Business Like Show Business* (1954). **SONGS:** *Marie from Sunny Italy* (1907; lyrics only); *Alexander's Ragtime Band* (1911); *Everybody's Doing It Now* (1911); *When I Lost You* (1911); *God Bless America* (1918; rev. 1938); *Always* (1925); *Remember* (1925); *The Song Is Ended but the Melody Lingers On* (1927); *Russian Lullaby* (1927); *Blue Skies* (1927); *White Christmas* (1942).

BIBL.: A. Woollcott, *The Story of I. B.* (N.Y., 1925); D. Jay, *The I. B. Songography* (New Rochelle, N.Y., 1969); M. Freedland, *I. B.* (N.Y., 1974); I. Whitcomb, *I. B. and Ragtime America* (N.Y., 1987); L. Bergreen, *As Thousands Cheer: The Life of I. B.* (N.Y., 1990).

Berlinski, Herman, German-born American organist and composer; b. Leipzig, Aug. 18, 1910. He studied piano, theory, and conducting at the Leipzig Cons. (1927–32) and composition with Boulanger and piano with Cortot at the Paris École Normale de Musique (1934–38). In 1941 he settled in the U.S., and in 1947 became a naturalized American citizen. He pursued training in organ with Joseph Yasser at the Jewish Theological Seminary of America in N.Y. (Doctor of Sacred Music degree, 1960). From 1954 to 1960 he was assistant organist, and from 1960 to 1963 organist at N.Y.'s Temple Emanu-El; subsequently served as minister of music of the Washington, D.C., Hebrew Congregation (1963–77). On Nov. 14, 1981, he appeared in his native city of Leipzig for the first time in 48 years as a recitalist at the new Gewandhaus. His extensive output reflects dedication to liturgical musical expression.

WORKS: ORCH.: *Symphonic Visions* (1949); *Concerto da camera* (1952); Organ Concerto (1965); *Prayers for the Night* (1968). **CHAMBER:** *Chazoth*, suite for String Quartet and Ondes Martenot (1938); Flute Sonata (1941; rev. 1984); *Hassidic Suite* for Cello and Piano (1948); *Quadrille*, woodwind quartet (1952); String Quartet (1953); *Le Violon de Chagall*, violin sonata (1985); many organ pieces, including *The Burning Bush* (1956) and 11 sinfonias (1956–78). **VOCAL:** ORATORIOS: *Kiddush Ha-Shem* (1954–60); *Job* (1968–72; rev. 1984); *The Trumpets of Freedom* (Washington, D.C., Dec. 5, 1988). **CANTATAS:** *The Earth Is the Lord's* (1966); *Sing to the Lord a New Song* (1978); *The Beadle of Prague* (1983); *The Days of Awe* (1965–85; Washington, D.C., Sept. 22, 1985). Also songs.

BIBL.: M. Kratzanstein, "The Organ Music of H. B.," *American Organist* (April 1989).

Berlinski, Jacques, Polish-born American composer; b. Radom, Dec. 13, 1913; d. Reseda, Calif., March 17, 1988. He emigrated to France in 1931 and studied theory with Boulanger. During World War II, he served in an artillery unit in the French army. In 1948 he received a prize in an American composition contest for his *Symphony of Glory*, dedicated to Winston Churchill. He settled in the U.S. and became a naturalized American citizen in 1973. He wrote a choral sym., *America, 1976*, for the U.S. bicentennial (San Diego, May 6, 1976).

Berlioz, Gabriel Pierre, French composer; b. Paris, June 25, 1916. He studied in Paris with Roussel and d'Indy. He wrote a Viola Concerto (1935); *Francezaic*, comic opera (1939); 2 syms. (*Parisiènne*, 1942; 1953); *Jardin hante*, ballet (1943); Piano Trio (1944); *Divertissement* for Violin, Cello, Piano, and String Orch. (1945); Concerto for Kettledrums and Orch. (1951; Paris, Jan. 25, 1953); Bassoon Concerto (1952); pieces for tuba and piano, saxophone and piano, flute and piano, etc.

Berman, Boris, Russian pianist and teacher; b. Moscow, April 3, 1948. He was a student of Oborin at the Moscow Cons. (M.A., 1971). After making his debut in Moscow in 1965 and touring Russia, he emigrated to Israel (1973), where he taught at the Rubin Academy of Music in Tel Aviv (until 1979) and at its campus in Jerusalem (1976–79). In 1979 he went to the U.S. and served as artist-in-residence at Brandeis Univ. until 1981; subsequently taught at Indiana Univ. in Bloomington (1981–82) and at Boston Univ. (1982–84). In 1984 he joined the faculty of the Yale Univ. School of Music, where he was prof. and head of its piano dept. from 1986. He also pursued a global concert career, appearing as soloist with principal orchs., as a recitalist, and as a chamber music artist. His repertoire not only embraces the great masters, but also includes an extensive survey of modern composers. In addition to his performances of Stravinsky, Bartók, Ravel, Shostakovich, Stockhausen, Berio, and Schnittke, he has won particular distinction for his interpretations of the complete solo piano music of Prokofiev, including his exceedingly demanding transcriptions.

Berman, Lazar (Naumovich), brilliant Russian pianist; b. Leningrad, Feb. 26, 1930. He began music training in infancy with his mother, and at the age of 3 began piano lessons with Savshinsky. At age 7, he made his debut at the All-Union Festival for young performers in Moscow, where, at age 9, he became a pupil of Alexander Goldenweiser at the Central Music School, and later at the Cons. (graduated, 1953; master classes, 1953–57); he also studied at the Cons. with Theodore Gutmann. In 1951 he won the World Youth and Student Festival prize in East Berlin, and in 1956 took 5th prize at the Queen Elisabeth of Belgium competition in Brussels and 3rd prize at the Liszt competition in Budapest. From 1957 he pursued his career in earnest. In 1958 he made his London debut, but it was not until a highly successful tour of Italy in 1970 that he made his mark in the West. In 1971 he made his U.S. debut as soloist with the New Jersey Sym. Orch., and returned in 1976 to tour the U.S. to great critical acclaim. In subsequent years, he toured throughout the world. His titanic technique, astounding in bravura passages, does not preclude the beauty of his poetic evocation of lyric moods. His performances of Schumann, Liszt, Tchaikovsky, Scriabin, and Prokofiev are particularly compelling.

Bernac (real name, **Bertin**), **Pierre,** eminent French baritone and teacher; b. Paris, Jan. 12, 1899; d. Villeneuve-les-Avignon, Oct. 17, 1979. He received private voice lessons in Paris. He began his career as a singer rather late in life, being first engaged in finance as a member of his father's brokerage house in Paris. His musical tastes were decidedly in the domain of modern French songs; on May 2, 1926, he made his debut recital in Paris with a program of songs by Francis Poulenc and Georges Auric; at other concerts he sang works by Debussy, Ravel, Honegger, and Milhaud. Eager to learn the art of German lieder, he went to Salzburg to study with Reinhold von Warlich. Returning to Paris, he devoted himself to concerts and to teaching. He became a lifelong friend to Poulenc, who wrote many songs for him and acted as his piano accompanist in many tours through Europe and America. He also conducted master classes in the U.S. and was on the faculty of the American Cons. at Fontainebleau. He publ. a valuable manual, *The Interpretation of French Song* (N.Y., 1970; 2nd ed., 1976), and a monograph, *Francis Poulenc: The Man and His Songs* (N.Y., 1977).

Bernard, André, French trumpeter and conductor; b. Gap, April 6, 1946. He studied at the Grenoble Cons. (premier prix, 1964) and the Paris Cons. (premier prix, 1968); also had lessons in conducting with Giulini and Bartoletti. In 1968 he was a laureate in the Geneva competition; then pursued an international career as a trumpet virtuoso. He also appeared as a guest conductor with principal European orchs. In 1986 he conducted the Philharmonia Hungarica on a tour of the U.S.

Bernard, Robert, Swiss-born French composer, editor, and writer on music; b. Geneva, Oct. 10, 1900; d. Paris, May 2, 1971. He studied in Geneva with G.T. Strong, Barblan, and Lauber. In 1926 he settled in Paris; in 1937 he became a lecturer at the Schola Cantorum and a music critic; from 1939 to 1951 he was ed. of *La Revue Musicale.* He publ. monographs on Franck, Aubert, Roussel, and other French composers, and a *Histoire de la musique* (Paris, 1961–64).

WORKS: 3 operas: *Flen* (1918), *Le Chevalier au Barizel* (1919), and *Polyphème* (1929); Piano Concerto; Harp Concerto; Saxophone Quartet; Piano Trio; Trio for Oboe, Clarinet, and Trombone; piano pieces; songs.

Bernardi, Mario (Egidio), Canadian conductor; b. Kirkland Lake, Ontario, Aug. 20, 1930. He was sent to Italy when he was 6, where he studied piano, organ, and composition with Bruno Pasut at the Manzato Cons. in Treviso (1938–45), taking his examination in the latter year at the Venice Cons. He then took courses with Lubka Kolessa (piano) and Ettore Mazzoleni (conducting) at the Royal Cons. of Music of Toronto (1948–51), later studying conducting with Erich Leinsdorf at the Salzburg Mozarteum (1959). He began his career as a church organist and concert pianist; he also worked as a coach and conductor with the Royal Cons. Opera School in Toronto (from 1953). In 1957 he made his first appearance as a conductor with the Canadian Opera Co., and in 1963 he became assistant conductor at Sadler's Wells in London. In 1967 he made his U.S. debut conducting *La Bohème* at the San Francisco Opera. From 1969 to 1982 he served as the first music director of the new National Arts Centre Orch. in Ottawa; then was principal conductor of the CBC Vancouver Orch. (from 1983) and music director of the Calgary Phil. (1984–93). On Jan. 19, 1984, he made his Metropolitan Opera debut in N.Y. conducting Handel's *Rinaldo.* In 1972 he was made a Companion of the Order of Canada.

Berners, Lord (Sir Gerald Hugh Tyrwhitt-Wilson, Baronet), eccentric English composer, writer, and painter; b. Arley Park, Bridgnorth, Sept. 18, 1883; d. Farringdon House, Berkshire, April 19, 1950. He was mainly self-taught, although he received some music training in Dresden and England, and advice and encouragement from Stravinsky. He served as honorary attaché to the British diplomatic service in Constantinople (1909–11) and Rome (1911–19). Returning to England, he joined the literary smart set; he was on close terms with George Bernard Shaw, H.G. Wells, and Osbert Sitwell. He publ. half a dozen novels, including *The Girls of Radcliff Hall* (1937), *The Romance of a Nose* (1942), and *Far from the Madding War,* in which he portrays himself as Lord Fitzcricket. Berners affected bizarre social behavior; his humor and originality are reflected in his compositions, many of which reveal a subtle gift for parody. He wrote 2 autobiographical vols., *First Childhood* (London, 1934) and *A Distant Prospect* (London, 1945); he also had successful exhibitions of his oil paintings in London (1931, 1936).

WORKS: OPERA: *Le Carrosse du Saint-Sacrement* (Paris, April 24, 1924). **BALLETS:** *The Triumph of Neptune* (London, Dec. 3, 1926); *Luna Park* (London, March 1930); *A Wedding Bouquet* (London, April 27, 1937); *Cupid and Psyche* (London, April 27, 1939); *Les Sirènes* (London, Nov. 12, 1946). **ORCH.:** 3 pieces: *Chinoiserie, Valse sentimentale,* and *Kasatchok* (1919); *Fantaisie espagnole* (1920); Fugue (1928). **PIANO:** *3 Little Funeral Marches* (1914); *Le Poisson d'or* (1914); *Fragments psychologiques* (1915); *Valses bourgeoises* for Piano Duet (1915). **OTHER:** Film scores, including *Nicholas Nickleby* (1947); songs, including *Lieder Album,* after Heine (1913; *Du bist wie eine Blume* is set in accordance with the suggestion that the poem was not addressed to a lady but to a small white pig).

BIBL.: J. Holbrooke, *B.* (London, 1925); H. Bridgeman and E. Drury, *The British Eccentric* (N.Y., 1975); P. Dickinson, "Lord B., 1883–1950: A British avant-gardist at the time of World War I," *Musical Times* (Nov. 1983).

Bernet Kempers, Karel Philippus, Dutch musicologist; b. Nijkerk, Sept. 20, 1897; d. Amsterdam, Sept. 30, 1974. He studied with Sandberger at the Univ. of Munich (Ph.D., 1926, with the diss. *Jacobus Clemens non Papa und seine Motetten;* publ. in Augsburg, 1928) and completed his Habilitation at the Univ. of Amsterdam in 1929 with his *Herinneringsmotieven, leidmotieven, grondthema's.* He taught music history at the Royal Cons. in The Hague (1929–49) and at the Amsterdam Cons. (1934–53); was also privatdozent (1929–38), lecturer (1938–46), reader (1946–53), and prof. (1953–63) in musicology at the Univ. of Amsterdam. He was the ed. of the complete works of Clemens non Papa.

WRITINGS: *De italiaanse opera van Peri tot Puccini* (Amsterdam, 1929; Eng. tr., 1947); *Muziekgeschiedenis* (Rotterdam, 1932; 6th ed., 1965); *Meesters der Muziek* (Rotterdam, 1939; 6th ed., 1958); *Panorama der Muziek* (Rotterdam, 1948).

Bernheimer, Martin, German-born American music critic; b. Munich, Sept. 28, 1936. He was taken to the U.S. as a child in 1940 and became a naturalized American citizen in 1946. He studied at Brown Univ. (Mus.B., 1958); after attending the Munich Hochschule für Musik (1958–59), he studied musicology with Reese at N.Y. Univ. (M.A., 1961), where he also taught (1959–62). He was contributing critic of the *N.Y. Herald Tribune* (1959–62), contributing ed. of the *Musical Courier* (1961–64), temporary music critic of the *N.Y. Post* (1961–65), Kolodin's assistant at the *Saturday Review* (1962–65), and music ed. and chief music critic of the *Los Angeles Times* (1965–96). As a critic, Bernheimer possesses a natural facility and not infrequently a beguiling felicity of literary style; he espouses noble musical causes with crusading fervor, but he can also be aggressively opinionated and ruthlessly devastating to composers, performers, or administrators whom he dislikes; as a polemicist, he is a rara avis among contemporary critics, who seldom rise to the pitch of moral or musical indignation; he also possesses a surprising knowledge of music in all its ramifications, which usually protects him from perilous pratfalls. In 1974 and 1978 he won the ASCAP-Deems Taylor Award, and in 1982 the Pulitzer Prize for distinguished criticism.

Bernier, René, Belgian composer; b. Saint-Gilles, March 10, 1905; d. Brussels, Sept. 8, 1984. He studied at the Brussels Cons. and with Paul Gilson. With 7 other pupils of Gilson, he formed the Groupe des Synthetistes in 1925 with the aim of combining Classical forms with modern techniques. He was prof. of music history at the Mons Cons. (1945–70). In 1963 he was made a member of the Belgian Royal Academy.

WORKS: BALLETS: *Le Bal des ombres* (1954); *Symphonie en blanc* (1961; based on the *Sinfonietta* for Strings, 1957); *Tanagras* (1969). **ORCH.:** *Mélopées et Rythmes* (1932); *Ode à une Madone* (1938; rev. 1955); *Le Tombeau devant l'Escaut,* symphonic poem (1952); *Notturno* (1955); *Bassonnière* for Bassoon and Orch. (1956); *Sinfonietta* for Strings (1957); *Homage à sax* for Saxophone and Orch. (1958); *Reverdies* for Clarinet and Orch. (1960); *Interludes* (1966); *Ménestraudie* for Violin and Orch. (1970). **CHAMBER:** *Sonata à deux* for Flute and Harp (1939); Trio for Flute, Cello, and Harp (1942); piano pieces. **VOCAL:** *Présages* for Voice and Orch. (1942–46); *Liturgies* for

Chorus (1968); *Agnus Dei* for Voice and Keyboard Instrument (1983; also for Chorus and String Orch.); solo songs.

Bernstein, Elmer, talented American composer and conductor of film music; b. N.Y., April 4, 1922. He received piano lessons and then studied with Citkowitz, Sessions, Ivan Langstroth, and Wolpe; also attended N.Y. Univ. In 1942 he joined the U.S. Army Air Corps, and gained experience as an arranger and composer for the Armed Forces Radio Service. After his discharge, he was active as a concert pianist (1946–50) before finding his niche as a highly successful composer and conductor of film scores. His score for the film *Thoroughly Modern Millie* won an Academy Award in 1968; among his other film scores were *The Man with the Golden Arm* (1955), *The Ten Commandments* (1956), *Desire Under the Elms* (1958), *To Kill a Mockingbird* (1963), *Hawaii* (1966), *The Bridge at Remagen* (1969), *The Trial of Billy Jack* (1974), *Airplane!* (1980), *Ghostbusters* (1984), and *Da* (1988). He also wrote the musical *How Now, Dow Jones* (N.Y., Dec. 7, 1967), 3 orch. suites, chamber music, and songs.

Bernstein, Lawrence F., American musicologist; b. N.Y., March 25, 1939. He studied at Hofstra Univ. (B.S., 1960) and with LaRue and Reese at N.Y. Univ. (Ph.D., 1969, with the diss. *Cantus Firmus in the French Chanson for Two and Three Voices, 1500–1550*). He taught at the Univ. of Chicago (1965–70); was assoc. prof. (1970–81) and prof. (from 1981) of music at the Univ. of Pa., where he also was chairman of the music dept. (1972–73; 1974–77). He served as supervising ed. of the Masters and Monuments of the Renaissance series (from 1970), to which he contributed, and as ed.-in-chief of the *Journal of the American Musicological Society* (1975–77). In 1987–88 he held a Guggenheim fellowship. In addition to contributions to journals and other publications, he wrote articles for *The New Grove Dictionary of Music and Musicians* (1980).

Bernstein, Leonard (actually, **Louis**), prodigiously gifted American conductor, composer, pianist, and teacher; b. Lawrence, Mass., Aug. 25, 1918; d. N.Y., Oct. 14, 1990. He was born into a family of Russian-Jewish immigrants. When he was 16, he legally changed his given name to Leonard to avoid confusion with another Louis in the family. He was 10 when he began piano lessons with Frieda Karp. At age 13, he began piano training with Susan Williams at the New England Cons. of Music in Boston. When he was 14, he commenced piano studies with Heinrich Gebhard and his assistant, Helen Coates. In 1935 he entered Harvard Univ., where he took courses with Edward Burlingame Hill (orchestration), A. Tillman Merritt (harmony and counterpoint), and Piston (counterpoint and fugue). He graduated cum laude in 1939. On April 21, 1939, he made his first appearance as a conductor when he led the premiere of his incidental music to Aristophanes' *The Birds* at Harvard Univ. He then enrolled at the Curtis Inst. of Music in Philadelphia, where he studied with Reiner (conducting), Vengerova (piano), Thompson (orchestration), and Renée Longy (score reading), receiving his diploma in 1941. During the summers of 1940 and 1941, he was a pupil in conducting of Serge Koussevitzky at the Berkshire Music Center at Tanglewood, returning in the summer of 1942 as Koussevitzky's assistant. In 1942–43 he worked for the N.Y. publishing firm of Harms, Inc., using the pseudonym Lenny Amber (Amber being the Eng. tr. of the German Bernstein).

In Aug. 1943 Artur Rodzinski, then music director of the N.Y. Phil., appointed Bernstein as his assistant conductor. On Nov. 14, 1943, Bernstein substituted at short notice for ailing guest conductor Bruno Walter in a N.Y. Phil. concert which was broadcast to the nation by radio. He acquitted himself magnificently and was duly hailed by the press as a musician of enormous potential. Thus the most brilliant conducting career in the history of American music was launched, and Bernstein was engaged to appear as a guest conductor with several major U.S. orchs. On Jan. 28, 1944, he conducted the premiere of his first Sym., *Jeremiah*, with the Pittsburgh Sym. Orch. The score was well received and won the N.Y. Music Critics' Circle Award for 1944. That same year he brought out his ballet *Fancy Free*, followed by the musical *On the Town*, which scored popular and critical accolades. In 1945 he became music director of the N.Y. City Sym. Orch., a post he held until 1948. On May 15, 1946, he made his European debut as a guest conductor of the Czech Phil. in Prague. In 1947 he appeared as a guest conductor of the Palestine Sym. Orch. in Tel Aviv. During Israel's War of Independence in 1948, he conducted a series of concerts with it as the renamed Israel Phil. He then completed his 2nd Sym. for Piano and Orch., *The Age of Anxiety*, a score which reflected the troubled times. It was given its first performance by Koussevitzky and the Boston Sym. Orch. on April 8, 1949, with the composer at the piano. In 1951 Bernstein composed his first opera, *Trouble in Tahiti*. During the Israel Phil.'s first tour of the U.S. in 1951, he shared the conducting duties with Koussevitzky. Upon the latter's death that year, he was named his mentor's successor as head of the orch. and conducting depts. at the Berkshire Music Center, where he was active until 1953 and again in 1955. He also taught intermittently at Brandeis Univ. from 1951 to 1954. In 1953 he produced his successful Broadway musical *Wonderful Town*.

Bernstein was the first American conductor ever to appear as a guest conductor at Milan's La Scala when he led Cherubini's *Medea* in Dec. 1953. In 1954 he wrote the score for the Academy Award winning film *On the Waterfront*. That same year he made an indelible impact as an expositor/performer on the *Omnibus* television program. Returning to the theater, he composed his comic operetta *Candide*, after Voltaire, in 1956. Bernstein was appointed co-conductor (with Mitropoulos) of the N.Y. Phil. in 1956, and in 1958 he became its music director, the first American-born and trained conductor to attain that prestigious position. In 1957 he brought out his musical *West Side Story*, a significant social drama abounding in memorable tunes, which proved enduringly popular; in its film incarnation (1961), it won no less than 11 Academy Awards, including best film of the year. In the meantime, Bernstein consolidated his protean activities as music director of the N.Y. Phil. through his concerts at home and abroad, as well as his numerous recordings, radio broadcasts, and television programs. Indeed, he acquired a celebrity status rarely achieved by a classical musician. His televised N.Y. Phil. Young People's Concerts (1958–72) were extremely successful with viewers of all ages. In 1959 he took the N.Y. Phil. on a triumphant tour of 17 European and Near East nations, including the Soviet Union. On Jan. 19, 1961, he conducted the premiere of his *Fanfare* at the Inaugural Gala for President John F. Kennedy in Washington, D.C. Bernstein led the gala opening concert of the N.Y. Phil. in its new home at Phil. Hall at N.Y.'s Lincoln Center for the Performing Arts on Sept. 23, 1962. He then took the orch. on a transcontinental tour of the U.S. in 1963. On Dec. 10, 1963, he conducted the 1st performance of his 3rd Sym., *Kaddish*, with the Israel Phil. in Tel Aviv. The score reflects Bernstein's Jewish heritage, but is also noteworthy for its admixture of both 12-tone and tonal writing. On March 6, 1964, he made his Metropolitan Opera debut in N.Y. conducting *Falstaff*, which work he also chose for his Vienna State Opera debut on March 14, 1966. In 1967 he appeared for the first time as a guest conductor of the Vienna Phil. In subsequent years he became closely associated with it, appearing not only in Vienna but also on extensive tours, recordings, and films.

In 1969 Bernstein retired as music director of the N.Y. Phil. and was accorded the title of laureate conductor. Thereafter he made regular appearances with it in this honored capacity. From 1970 to 1974 he served as advisor at Tanglewood. For the opening of the John F. Kennedy Center for the Performing Arts in Washington, D.C., he composed his theater piece, *Mass* (Sept. 8, 1971), a challenging and controversial liturgical score. During the 1973–74 academic year, he was the Charles Eliot Norton Prof. of Poetry at Harvard Univ., where he gave a series of lectures later publ. as *The Unanswered Question* (1976). He returned to the genre of the musical in 1976 with his *1600*

Pennsylvania Avenue, but the work was not successful. On Jan. 19, 1977, he conducted at the Inaugural Concert for President Jimmy Carter in Washington, D.C. In 1983 Bernstein completed work on his opera *A Quiet Place*, which he considered his most important creative achievement. However, its premiere in Houston on June 17, 1983, was not a success. He then revised the work and incorporated it into his earlier opera *Trouble in Tahiti*. The revised version was premiered at Milan's La Scala on June 19, 1984, the first opera by an American composer ever accorded such a distinction. All the same, the opera remained problematic. In July-Aug. 1985 he toured as conductor with the European Community Youth Orch. in a "Journey for Peace" program to Athens, Hiroshima, Budapest, and Vienna. Bernstein also conducted celebratory performances of Beethoven's 9th Sym. to mark the opening of the Berlin Wall, first at the Kaiser Wilhelm Memorial Church in West Berlin (Dec. 23, 1989), and then at the Schauspielhaus Theater in East Berlin (telecast to the world, Dec. 25, 1989).

Increasingly plagued by ill health, Bernstein was compelled to announce his retirement from the podium on Oct. 9, 1990. His death just 5 days later (of progressive emphysema, complicated by a chronic pleurisy, eventuating in a fatal heart attack) shocked the music world and effectively brought to a close a unique era in the history of American music. Bernstein was afforded innumerable honors at home and abroad. Among his foreign decorations were the Order of the Lion, Commander, of Finland (1965); Chevalier (1968), Officier (1978), and Commandeur (1985), of the Légion d'honneur, of France; Cavaliere, Order of Merit, of Italy (1969); Grand Honor Cross for Science and Art of Austria (1976); and the Grand Order of Merit of the Italian Republic (1988). In 1977 he was made a member of the Swedish Royal Academy of Music in Stockholm, in 1981 of the American Academy and Inst. of Arts and Letters in N.Y., in 1983 of the Vienna Phil., and in 1984 of the N.Y. Phil. In 1987 he was awarded the Gold Medal of the Royal Phil. Soc. of London. He was made president of the London Sym. Orch. in 1987 and laureate conductor of the Israel Phil. in 1988. His 70th birthday was the occasion for an outpouting of tributes from around the world, highlighted by a major celebration at Tanglewood from Aug. 25 to 28, 1988. Bernstein's extraordinary musical gifts were ably matched by an abundance of spiritual and sheer animal energy, a remarkable intellect, and an unswerving commitment to liberal, and even radical, political and humanitarian ideals. As a composer, he revealed a protean capacity in producing complex serious scores on the one hand, and strikingly original and effective works for the Broadway musical theater on the other. All the same, it was as a nonpareil conductor and musical expositor that Bernstein so profoundly enlightened more than one generation of auditors. Ebullient and prone to podium histrionics of a choreographic expressivity, he was a compelling interpreter of the Romantic repertory. Bernstein had a special affinity for the music of Mahler, whose works drew from him unsurpassed readings of great beauty and searing intensity. He was also a convincing exponent of Haydn, Mozart, and Beethoven. Fortunately, many of Bernstein's greatest performances have been captured on recordings and video discs as a testament to the life and work of one of the foremost musicians of the 20th century.

WORKS: DRAMATIC: *The Birds*, incidental music to Aristophanes' play (1938; Cambridge, Mass., April 21, 1939, composer conducting); *The Peace*, incidental music to Aristophanes' play (1940; Cambridge, Mass., May 23, 1941); *Fancy Free*, ballet (N.Y., April 18, 1944, composer conducting); *On the Town*, musical comedy (Boston, Dec. 13, 1944, Goberman conducting); *Facsimile*, ballet (N.Y., Oct. 24, 1946, composer conducting; 2nd version as *Parallel Lives*, Milwaukee, Oct. 19, 1986; 3rd version as *Dancing On*, Zagreb, March 31, 1988); *Peter Pan*, incidental music to Barrie's play (N.Y., April 24, 1950); *Trouble in Tahiti*, opera (1951; Waltham, Mass., June 12, 1952, composer conducting); *Wonderful Town*, musical comedy (New Haven, Conn., Jan. 19, 1953); *The Lark*, incidental music to Anouilh's play, adapted by Lillian Hellman (Boston, Oct. 28, 1955); *Salomé*, incidental music to Wilde's play (CBS-TV, N.Y., Dec. 11, 1955; withdrawn); *Candide*, comic operetta (Boston, Oct. 29, 1956; rev. version, N.Y., Dec. 20, 1973, Mauceri conducting; operatic version, N.Y., Oct. 13, 1982, Mauceri conducting; rev., Glasgow, May 17, 1988, Mauceri conducting); *West Side Story*, musical (Washington, D.C., Aug. 19, 1957); *The Firstborn*, incidental music to Christopher Fry's play (N.Y., April 29, 1958; withdrawn); *Mass*, theater piece for Singers, Players, and Dancers (Washington, D.C., Sept. 8, 1971, Peress conducting; chamber version, Los Angeles, Dec. 26, 1972); *Dybbuk*, ballet (N.Y., May 16, 1974, composer conducting; retitled *Dybbuk Variations* for Orch.); *By Bernstein*, musical cabaret (N.Y., Nov. 23, 1975; withdrawn); *1600 Pennsylvania Avenue*, musical (Philadelphia, Feb. 24, 1976); *A Quiet Place*, opera (Houston, June 17, 1983, DeMain conducting; withdrawn; rev. version, incorporating *Trouble in Tahiti*, Milan, June 19, 1984, Mauceri conducting). **FILM SCORE:** *On the Waterfront* (1954).

ORCH.: 3 syms.: No. 1, *Jeremiah*, for Mezzo-soprano and Orch. (1942; Pittsburgh, Jan. 28, 1944, Tourel soloist, composer conducting), No. 2, *The Age of Anxiety*, for Piano and Orch. (Boston, April 8, 1949, composer soloist, Koussevitzky conducting; rev. version, N.Y., July 15, 1965, Entremont soloist, composer conducting), and No. 3, *Kaddish*, for Speaker, Soprano, Chorus, Boys' Choir, and Orch. (Tel Aviv, Dec. 12, 1963, Tourel soloist, composer conducting; rev. version, Mainz, Aug. 25, 1977, Caballé soloist, composer conducting); *Suite from Fancy Free* (1944; Pittsburgh, Jan. 14, 1945, composer conducting; withdrawn); *3 Dance Variations from Fancy Free* (N.Y., Jan. 21, 1946, composer conducting); *3 Dance Episodes from On the Town* (1945; San Francisco, Feb. 13, 1946, composer conducting); *Facsimile*, choreographic essay (1946; Poughkeepsie, N.Y., March 5, 1947, composer conducting); *Prelude, Fugue, and Riffs* for Clarinet and Jazz Ensemble (1949; CBS-TV, N.Y., Oct. 16, 1955, Benny Goodman soloist, composer conducting); *Serenade* for Violin, Harp, Percussion, and Strings (Venice, Sept. 12, 1954, Isaac Stern soloist, composer conducting); *Symphonic Suite from On the Waterfront* (Tanglewood, Aug. 11, 1955, composer conducting); *Overture to Candide* (1956; N.Y., Jan. 26, 1957, composer conducting); *Symphonic Dances from West Side Story* (1960; N.Y., Feb. 13, 1961, Foss conducting); *Fanfare* for the inauguration of President John F. Kennedy (Washington, D.C., Jan. 19, 1961, composer conducting); *Fanfare* for the 25th anniversary of N.Y.'s High School of Music and Art (N.Y., March 24, 1961); *2 Meditations from Mass* (Austin, Texas, Oct. 31, 1971, Peress conducting); *Meditation III from Mass* (Jerusalem, May 21, 1972, composer conducting; withdrawn); *Dybbuk Variations* (Auckland, New Zealand, Aug. 16, 1974, composer conducting); *3 Meditations from Mass* for Cello and Orch. (Washington, D.C., Oct. 11, 1977, Rostropovich soloist, composer conducting); *Slava!*, "a political overture" for Rostropovich (Washington, D.C., Oct. 11, 1977, Rostropovich conducting); *CBS Music* for the 50th anniversary of CBS (1977; CBS-TV, N.Y., April 1, 1978; withdrawn); *Divertimento* (Boston, Sept. 25, 1980, Ozawa conducting); *A Musical Toast*, in memory of Kostelanetz (N.Y., Oct. 11, 1980, Mehta conducting); *Halil*, nocturne for Flute and Orch. (Jerusalem, May 27, 1981, Rampal soloist, composer conducting).

CHAMBER: Trio for Violin, Cello, and Piano (1937); Violin Sonata (1940); *4 Studies* for 2 Clarinets, 2 Bassoons, and Piano (c.1940); Clarinet Sonata (1941–42; Boston, April 21, 1942, David Glazer clarinetist, composer pianist); *Brass Music* (1948); *Shivaree* for Double Brass Ensemble and Percussion (1969); *Red, White, and Blues* for Trumpet and Piano (1984; transcribed by P. Wastall from the song in *1600 Pennsylvania Avenue*).

PIANO: Sonata (1938); *Scenes from the City of Sin* for Piano, 4-hands (1939); *7 Anniversaries* (1943; Boston, May 14, 1944, composer pianist); *4 Anniversaries* (Cleveland, Oct. 1, 1948, Educie Podis pianist); *5 Anniversaries* (1949–51); *Touches* (1981); *Moby Diptych* (1981); *13 Anniversaries* (1988); *For Nicky, in Ancient Friendship* for Nicolas Slonimsky's 95th birthday (Los Angeles, April 27, 1989).

VOCAL: *Hashkiveinu* for Cantorial Solo (Tenor), Chorus, and Organ (N.Y., May 11, 1945); *Yigdal* for Chorus and Piano (1950);

Harvard Choruses for Men's Voices and Band (N.Y., March 7, 1957, Woodworth conducting; withdrawn); *Chichester Psalms* for Boy Soloist, Chorus, and Orch. (N.Y., July 15, 1965, composer conducting); *Suite from Candide* for Soloists, Chorus, and Orch. (Bloomington, Ind., April 9, 1977, Mauceri conducting); *Songfest* for 6 Singers and Orch. (1st complete perf., Washington, D.C., Oct. 11, 1977, composer conducting); *Olympic Hymn* for Chorus and Orch. (Baden-Baden, Sept. 23, 1981, Shallon conducting; withdrawn); *Jubilee Games* for Baritone and Orch. (N.Y., Sept. 13, 1986, composer conducting; rev. version, incorporating *Opening Prayer*, retitled as *Benediction*, Tel Aviv, May 31, 1988, composer conducting); *Opening Prayer* for Baritone and Orch. (N.Y., Dec. 15, 1986, composer conducting; retitled as *Benediction* and incorporated in the rev. version of *Jubilee Games*, Tel Aviv, May 31, 1988, composer conducting; in spite of this revision, *Opening Prayer* remains an independent work as well); *Missa brevis* for Countertenor or Septet of Solo Voices, Chorus, and Percussion (Atlanta, April 21, 1988, Shaw conducting).

SONGS (all for Voice and Piano unless otherwise given): *I Hate Music*, cycle of 5 children's songs (Lenox, Mass., Aug. 24, 1943, Tourel soloist, composer pianist); *Afterthought* (1945; N.Y., Oct. 24, 1948; withdrawn); *La Bonne Cuisine*, "4 recipes" (1947; N.Y., Oct. 10, 1948); *2 Love Songs*, after Rilke (1949; No. 1, N.Y., March 13, 1949; No. 2, N.Y., March 13, 1963); *Silhouette* (1951; Washington, D.C., Feb. 13, 1955); *On the Waterfront* (1954; withdrawn); *Get Hep!* (1955; withdrawn); *So Pretty* (N.Y., Jan. 21, 1968, Streisand soloist, composer pianist); *An Album of Songs* (1974; withdrawn); *My New Friends* (1979); *Piccola Serenata*, vocalise for Karl Böhm's 85th birthday (Salzburg, Aug. 27, 1979, Ludwig soloist, composer pianist); *Sean Song* for Voice and Violin, Viola, Cello, Harp, or Piano (1986); *My 12-tone Melody* for Irving Berlin's 100th birthday (N.Y., May 11, 1988, composer singer and pianist); *Arias and Barcarolles* for 4 Soloists and Piano, 4-hands (N.Y., May 9, 1988, Tilson Thomas and composer pianists).

WRITINGS: *The Joy of Music* (N.Y., 1959); *Leonard Bernstein's Young People's Concerts for Reading and Listening* (N.Y., 1961; rev. ed., 1970, as *Leonard Bernstein's Young People's Concerts*); *The Infinite Variety of Music* (N.Y., 1966); *The Unanswered Question: Six Talks at Harvard* (Cambridge, Mass., and London, 1976); *Findings* (N.Y., 1982).

BIBL.: J. Briggs, *L. B., The Man, His Work and His World* (Cleveland and N.Y., 1961); A. Holde, *L. B.* (Berlin, 1961); J. Gruen and K. Hyman, *The Private World of L. B.* (N.Y., 1968); P. Robinson, *B.* (N.Y., 1982); P. Gradenwitz, *L. B.: Eine Biographie* (Zürich, 1984; 2nd ed., 1990; Eng. tr., 1986); M. Freedland, *L. B.* (London, 1987); J. Peyser, *L. B.: A Biography* (N.Y., 1987); J. Gottlieb, ed., *L. B.: A Complete Catalog of His Works: Celebrating His 70th Birthday, August 25, 1988* (N.Y., 1988); J. Flugel, ed., *B. Remembered: A Life in Pictures* (N.Y., 1991); S. Chapin, *L. B.: Notes From a Friend* (N.Y., 1992); M. Secrest, *L. B.: A Life* (N.Y., 1994); W. Burton, ed., *Conversations About B* (Oxford, 1995).

Bernstein, Martin, American musicologist; b. N.Y., Dec. 14, 1904. He was educated at N.Y. Univ. (B.S., 1925; B.Mus., 1927); played the double bass in the N.Y. Sym. Orch. (1925–26), the N.Y. Phil. (1926–28), and the Chautauqua Sym. Orch. (1929–36). He was a member of the faculty of N.Y. Univ. (1926–72); then a prof. of music at Lehman College, City Univ. of N.Y. (1972–73). He publ. *Score Reading* (1932; 2nd ed., rev., 1947) and the successful textbook *An Introduction to Music* (N.Y., 1937; 3rd ed., rev., 1966, and 4th ed., rev., 1972 with M. Picker). A brother, Artie (actually, Arthur) Bernstein (b. N.Y., Feb. 3, 1909; d. Los Angeles, Jan. 4, 1964), a classically trained cellist, became a leading jazz bassist in the 1930s and '40s, playing with many big bands, including Jimmy Dorsey's; from 1939 to 1941 he was part of the Benny Goodman Sextet; after World War II, he became a studio musician.

BIBL.: E. Clinkscale and C. Brook, eds., *A Musical Offering: Essays in Honor of M. B.* (N.Y., 1977).

Béroff, Michel, French pianist; b. Épinal, May 9, 1950. After training at the Nancy Cons. (premier prix, 1962; prix d'excellence, 1963), he completed his studies with Loriod at the Paris Cons. (premier prix, 1966). In 1967 he made his Paris debut and won 1st prize in the Messiaen competition in Rouen; thereafter he toured internationally, appearing as a soloist with major orchs. and as a recitalist. While his large repertory embraces works from Mozart to the contemporary period, he has won particular notice for his performances of scores by Debussy, Stravinsky, Prokofiev, Bartók, and Messiaen.

Berry, Wallace (Taft), American composer and music theorist; b. La Crosse, Wis., Jan. 10, 1928; d. Vancouver, British Columbia, Nov. 16, 1991. He studied with Stevens at the Univ. of Southern Calif. in Los Angeles (B.Mus., 1949; Ph.D., 1956) and with Boulanger at the Paris Cons. (1953–54); then taught at the Univ. of Southern Calif. (1956–57), the Univ. of Mich. (1957–77), and (from 1978) the Univ. of British Columbia, where he was also head of the music dept. (1978–84). He served as president of the Soc. for Music Theory (1982–85). He publ. *Form in Music* (Englewood Cliffs, N.J., 1966; 2nd ed., rev., 1985), *Eighteenth-Century Imitative Counterpoint: Music for Analysis* (with E. Chudacoff; N.Y., 1969), *Structural Functions in Music* (Englewood Cliffs, N.J., 1975; 2nd ed., 1987), and *Musical Structure and Performance* (New Haven, Conn., 1989).

WORKS: DRAMATIC: *The Admirable Bashville*, chamber opera (1954). **ORCH.:** *4 Movements* for Chamber Orch. (1954); *Fantasy* (1958); *5 Pieces* for Small Orch. (1961); Piano Concerto (1964); *Canto Elegiaco* (1968); *Intonation: Victimis hominum inhumanitatis, in memoriam* (1972); *Acadian Images: 2 Movements* (1977–78). **CHAMBER:** Clarinet Sonata (1950); Suite for String Trio (1950); *3 Pieces on Arabic Songs* for Flute, Oboe, and Tom-tom (1950); Piano Quintet (1951); *Divertimento* for Harpsichord, Oboe, English Horn, and Cello (1952); 4 string quartets (1960, 1964, 1966, 1984); *Threnody* for Violin (1963–64); *Divertimento* for Wind Quintet, Piano, and Percussion (1964); Composition for Piano and Electronic Sounds (1967); Trio for Piano, Violin, and Cello (1970); *3 Essays in Parody* for Treble Instrument and Piano (1973); *Anachronisms* for Violin and Piano (1973); Piano Sonata (1975). **VOCAL:** *Spoon River*, 6 songs for Soprano, Bass-baritone, and Orch. (1952); *Canticle on a Judaic Text* for Soprano or Tenor and Orch. (1953); *No Man is an Island* for Chorus (1959); *3 Songs of April* for Soprano or Tenor and String Quartet (1959); *Heaven-haven* for Chorus (1960); *Spring Pastoral* for Chorus (1960); *Des visages de France* for Soprano, Mezzo-soprano, and Ensemble (1967); *Credo in unam vitam* for Tenor, Horn, Cello, and Chamber Ensemble (1969); *Lover of the Moon Trembling Now at Twilight* for Soprano or Tenor and Ensemble (1971); *Of the Changeless Night and the Stark Ranges of Nothing* for Mezzo-soprano, Cello, and Piano (1978–79); *The Moment: Summer's Night* for Mezzo-soprano and Piano (1985).

Berry, Walter, admired Austrian bass-baritone; b. Vienna, April 8, 1929. He studied engineering at the Vienna School of Engineering before pursuing vocal training with Hermann Gallos at the Vienna Academy of Music. In 1950 he made his debut at the Vienna State Opera in Honegger's *Jeanne d'Arc*, and subseuently sang there regularly; he also appeared at the Salzburg Festivals (from 1952). In 1957 he made his U.S. debut as Mozart's Figaro in Chicago. He made his Metropolitan Opera debut in N.Y. as Barak on Oct. 2, 1966, remaining on its roster until 1974 and returning for its 1975–76 and 1977–78 seasons. In 1976 he made his first appearance at London's Covent Garden as Barak. He also sang in Berlin, Munich, Paris, Tokyo, Buenos Aires, and elsewhere. In 1957 he married **Christa Ludwig**, with whom he appeared in opera and concert; they were divorced in 1970. In 1963 he was made an Austrian Kammersänger. Among his other roles were Leporello, Papageno, Telramund, Wotan, Escamillo, Baron Ochs, Wozzeck, and Dr. Schön.

BIBL.: P. Lorenz, *Christa Ludwig-W. B.: Eine Künstler Biographie* (Vienna, 1968).

Bersa, Blagoje, Croatian composer and teacher; b. Ragusa, Dec. 21, 1873; d. Zagreb, Jan. 1, 1934. He studied music in

Vienna, where he remained until 1919. He wrote 2 operas, *Fire* and *The Cobbler of Delft*; the symphonic poems *Sunny Fields*, *Ghosts*, and *Hamlet*; a String Quartet; a Piano Trio; and songs. Bersa was for many years a prof. of composition at the Zagreb Cons., influencing the development of a new generation of Croatian composers.

Bertini, Gary, Russian-born Israeli conductor and composer; b. Brichevo, May 1, 1927. He was taken to Palestine as a child and began violin lessons at age 16. After studies at the Milan Cons. (diploma, 1948), he continued his training with Seter and Singer at the Tel Aviv College of Music (diploma, 1951). He then went to Paris, where he studied at the Cons. and the École Normale de Musique, his principal mentors in composition being Honegger, Messiaen, and Boulanger; he also studied musicology at the Sorbonne with Chailley. Returning to Israel in 1954, he was music director of the Rinat (later Israel Chamber) Choir (1955–72), the Israel Chamber Ensemble Orch. (1965–75), and the Jerusalem Sym. Orch. (1977–86). He also served as principal guest conductor of the Scottish National Orch. in Glasgow (1971–81) and as artistic advisor of the Israel Festival (1976–83) and of the Detroit Sym. Orch. (1981–83). From 1983 to 1991 he was chief conductor of the Cologne Radio Sym. Orch. He also was Intendant and Generalmusikdirektor of the Frankfurt am Main Opera from 1987 to 1991, concurrently serving as chief conductor of its Museumgesellschaft concerts. In 1994 he became artistic director of the Israel Opera in Tel Aviv. Bertini has become well known for conducting 20th-century scores, including many first performances. As a composer, he has written stage music, incidental scores, orch. works, chamber music, and songs. In 1978 he was awarded the Israel State Prize for composition.

Bertouille, Gérard, Belgian composer; b. Tournai, May 26, 1898; d. Brussels, Dec. 12, 1981. He studied with Absil, Bourguignon, Marsick, and Souris. His music followed a median path in a restrained modern idiom.

WORKS: ORCH.: *Ouverture* (1937); *Prélude et Fugue* (1939); *Sinfonietta* (1942); 2 violin concertos (1942, 1970); 2 piano concertos (1946, 1953); 2 trumpet concertos (1946, 1973); 3 syms. (1947, 1955, 1977); *Sinfonia da Requiem* (1957); *Fantaisie-Passacaille* (1963); *Fantaisie Lyrique* (1969); Concerto for Strings (1974); Concerto for Flute, Oboe, and Strings (1977); *Ouverture romantique* for Band (1978). **CHAMBER:** 5 violin sonatas (1936, 1942, 1946, 1953, 1971); 6 string quartets (1939, 1941, 1942, 1953, 1953, 1957); 2 string trios (1943, 1945); Quartet for Flute and String Trio (1948); Trio for 2 Violins and Piano (1955); Wind Quintet (1969); *Fantaisie* for Piano Quartet (1978); piano music, including 2 sonatas (1945, 1978). **VOCAL:** *Requiem des hommes d'aujourd'hui* (1950); *Les Tentations de St. Antoine*, choreographic poem for Mezzo-soprano, Baritone, and Orch. (1958–59); songs.

Berutti (originally, **Beruti**), **Arturo,** Argentine composer of Italian descent; b. San Juan, March 27, 1862; d. Buenos Aires, Jan. 3, 1938. He received his early training in music with his father; then went to Leipzig, where he became a student of Jadassohn. He subsequently lived in Italy, where he composed 3 operas: *La Vendetta* (Vercelli, May 21, 1892), *Evangelina* (Milan, Sept. 19, 1893), and *Taras Bulba* (Turin, March 9, 1895). Returning to Argentina in 1896, he premiered the following operas in Buenos Aires: *Pampa* (July 27, 1897), *Yupanki* (July 25, 1899), *Khrise* (June 21, 1902), *Horrida Nox* (the 1st opera by a native Argentine composer, written to a Spanish libretto, to be produced in Argentina; July 7, 1908), and *Los Heroes* (Aug. 23, 1919).

Besanzoni, Gabriella, Italian mezzo-soprano; b. Rome, Sept. 20, 1888; d. there, June 6, 1962. She studied with Hilde Brizzi and Alessandro Maggi. In 1911 she made her operatic debut as a soprano in the role of Adalgisa in Viterbo; in 1913 she sang in Rome as Ulrica; appeared at the Teatro Colón in Buenos Aires from 1918. On Nov. 19, 1919, she made her Metropolitan Opera debut in N.Y. as Amneris, singing there for only 1 season. From 1923 to 1932 she appeared at Milan's La Scala, making her farewell appearance in Rome in 1939 in her finest role, Carmen. Among her other roles were Isabella, Cenerentola, Dalila, and Mignon.

Bessaraboff, Nicholas (Nikolai), Russian-born American writer on music; b. Voronezh, Feb. 12, 1894; d. N.Y., Nov. 10, 1973. He was trained as a mechanical engineer and a draftsman, but he also played the horn and became interested in the mechanics and acoustics of musical instruments. After the completion of his studies at the polytechnical inst. in St. Petersburg, he was sent in 1915 with a group of other Russian engineers to the U.S. in order to expedite the shipping of American military equipment for the Russian armed forces during World War I. He remained in the U.S. after the Russian Revolution of 1917, becoming a naturalized American citizen in 1927. He worked as a draftsman in Rochester, N.Y., at the same time doing extensive reading on the subject of musical instruments. In 1931 he moved to Boston, where he began cataloguing the collection of instruments in the Boston Museum of Fine Arts. In 1941 he publ. his magnum opus, *Ancient European Musical Instruments, An Organological Study of the Musical Instruments in the Leslie Lindsey Mason Collection at the Museum of Fine Arts, Boston.* In 1945 he officially changed his name to Nicholas Bessaraboff Bodley, adopting the maiden name of his American wife, Virginia Bodley.

BIBL.: D. Boyden, "N. B.'s *Ancient European Musical Instruments*," *Notes* (Sept. 1971).

Besseler, Heinrich, eminent German musicologist; b. Dortmund-Hörde, April 2, 1900; d. Leipzig, July 25, 1969. He was a pupil of Gurlitt at the Univ. of Freiburg im Breisgau (Ph.D., 1923, with the diss. *Beiträge zur Stilgeschichte der deutschen Suite im 17. Jahrhundert*; Habilitationsschrift, 1925, *Die Motettenkomposition von Petrus de Cruce bis Philipp von Vitry [ca. 1250–1350]*), Adler at the Univ. of Vienna, and Ludwig at the Univ. of Göttingen. He was a reader at the Univ. of Heidelberg (1928–48) and then prof. of musicology at the univs. of Jena (1948–56) and Leipzig (1956–65). Besseler was a distinguished authority on the music of the Middle Ages and the Renaissance. He wrote the important and influential study *Die Musik des Mittelalters und der Renaissance* (Potsdam, 1931), contributed valuable articles to various music journals and to *Die Musik in Geschichte und Gegenwart*, and ed. the collected works of Dufay, Ockeghem, and others of their era. His other writings include *Johann Sebastian Bach* (Stuttgart, 1935; 2nd ed., 1955); *Zum Problem der Tenorgeige* (Heidelberg, 1949); *Bourdon und Fauxbourdon: Studien zum Ursprung der niederländischen Musik* (Leipzig, 1950); *Fünf echte Bildnisse Johann Sebastian Bachs* (Kassel, 1956); with M. Schneider, *Musikgeschichte in Bildern* (Leipzig, 1961–68; W. Bachmann, co.-ed., 1968–69).

BIBL.: *Festschrift H. B. zum 60. geburtstag* (Leipzig, 1961).

Betti, Adolfo, Italian violinist; b. Bagni di Lucca, March 21, 1873; d. Lucca, Dec. 2, 1950. Of a musical family, he studied violin in Lucca; then with César Thomson in Liège (1892–96). In 1903 he became the 1st violinist of the Flonzaley Quartet, remaining with it until it was disbanded in 1929; this group presented some 2,500 concerts in America and about 500 in Europe. In 1933 Betti was awarded the Coolidge Medal for eminent services to chamber music in America. He taught in N.Y. before returning to Italy. He publ. *La vita e l'arte di Francesco Geminiani* (Lucca, 1933); also ed. Schubert's string quartets.

Bettinelli, Bruno, respected Italian composer and teacher; b. Milan, June 4, 1913. He studied harmony and counterpoint with Paribeni and orchestration with Bossi at the Milan Cons., taking diplomas in piano in 1931 and in composition and conducting in 1937; then pursued advanced training in composition with Frazzi at the Accademia Musicale Chigiana in Siena (1940). In 1941 he joined the faculty of the Milan Cons., where he was a prof. of composition from 1957 until his retirement in 1979. In 1961 he was made a member of the Accademia di Santa Cecilia in Rome and of the Accademia di Luigi Cherubini in Florence.

In his extensive output, he reveals particular skill in instrumental writing which reflects the best in the central European tradition with infusions of contemporary techniques, including the 12-tone method.

WORKS: OPERAS: *Il pozzo e il pendolo* (1957; Bergamo, Oct. 24, 1967); *La Smorfia* (Como, Sept. 30, 1959); *Count Down* (1969; Milan, March 26, 1970). **ORCH.:** *Movimento sinfonico* Nos. 1 (1938) and 2 (1945); *Sinfonia da camera* (1938); *Corale ostinato* (1938); *Due invenzioni* for Strings (1939); 7 syms. (1939; 1943; 1946; *Sinfonia breve*, 1954; 1975; 1976; 1978); 4 concertos (1940, 1951, 1964, 1988); *Fantasia concertante* for String Quartet and Orch. (1949); 2 piano concertos (1953, 1968); *Musica* for Strings (1958); *Preludio elegiaco* (1959); *Episodi* (1961); Concerto for 2 Pianos and Orch. (1962); *Varianti* (1970); *Musica per 12* (1973); *Studio* (1974); *Contrasti* (1979); *Divertimento* for Harpsichord and Orch. (1979); Concerto for Guitar, Strings, and Vibraphone (1981); Violin Concerto (1982–83); *Alternanze* (1983); *Omaggio a Stravinskij* for Chamber Orch. (1984); *Strutture* for Strings (1985); *Tre studi d'interpretazione* for Strings (1986). **CHAMBER:** 2 string quartets (1935, 1960); Cello Sonata (1951); *Improvvisazione* for Violin and Piano (1968); *Studio da concerto* for Clarinet (1971); Octet for 2 Flutes, Oboe, 2 Clarinets, 2 Bassoon, and Horn (1975); Violin Sonata (1980); Quintet for Flute, Oboe, Clarinet, Bassoon, and Horn (1984); *Ricercare a tre* for Piano, Clarinet, and Cello (1988); Trio for Violin, Cello, and Piano (1991); piano pieces; organ music; guitar pieces. **VOCAL:** *Messa di Requiem* (1942–43); *Cinque liriche di Montale* for Soprano and Chamber Ensemble (1948); *Sono una creatura*, cantata for Chorus and Orch. (1971); *In Nativitate Domini*, cantata for Soprano and Orch. (1982); *Terza Cantata* for Chorus and Orch. (1982–83); *Salmo IV*, cantata for Chorus and Orch. (1992); many other choral pieces and songs.

BIBL.: N. Castiglioni, *B. B.* (Milan, 1955); E. Gabellich, *Linguaggio Musicale di B. B.* (Milan, 1989).

Betts, Lorne, Canadian composer, music critic, and teacher; b. Winnipeg, Aug. 2, 1918; d. Hamilton, Ontario, Aug. 5, 1985. He studied piano, organ, and theory in Winnipeg, and was a pupil of Weinzweig in Toronto (1947–53) before settling in Hamilton, Ontario.

WORKS: OPERAS: *Riders to the Sea* (1955); *The Woodcarver's Wife* (1960). **ORCH.:** *Sinfonietta* (1952); 2 syms. (1954, 1961); 2 piano concertos (1955, 1957); *2 Abstracts* (1961); *Kanadario: Music for a Festival Occasion* (1966); *Variants* (1969); Suite (1975); Concerto for Cello, Piano, and Orch. (1976). **CHAMBER:** Violin Sonata (1948); Clarinet Sonata (1949); 3 string quartets (1950, 1951, 1970); String Trio (1959); Quartet for Flute, Clarinet, Bass Clarinet, and Celesta (1960); piano pieces, including a Sonata (1950). **VOCAL:** Choral works and songs.

Beversdorf, (Samuel) Thomas, American composer and teacher; b. Yoakum, Texas, Aug. 8, 1924; d. Bloomington, Ind., Feb. 15, 1981. He studied trombone and baritone horn with his father, a band director; later studied composition with Kent Kennan, Eric DeLamarter, and Anthony Donato at the Univ. of Texas (B.M., 1945), Rogers and Hanson at the Eastman School of Music in Rochester, N.Y. (M.M., 1946; D.M.A., 1957), Honegger and Copland at the Berkshire Music Center in Tanglewood (summer, 1947), and privately with Anis Fuleihan. He was a trombonist in the Rochester (N.Y.) Phil. (1945–46), the Houston Sym. Orch. (1946–48), and the Pittsburgh Sym. Orch. (1948–49). After teaching at the Univ. of Houston (1946–48), he was a prof. of music at the Indiana Univ. School of Music in Bloomington (1951–77).

WORKS: DRAMATIC: *Threnody: The Funeral of Youth*, ballet (Bloomington, Ind., March 6, 1963; also as *Variations* for Orch.); *The Hooligan*, opera (1964–69); *Metamorphosis*, opera (1968); *Vision of Christ*, mystery play (Lewisburg, Pa., May 1, 1971). **ORCH.:** 4 syms.: No. 1 (1946), No. 2 (1950), No. 3 for Winds and Percussion (Bloomington, Ind., May 9, 1954; also for Full Orch., Bloomington, Ind., Oct. 10, 1958), and No. 4 (1958); *Essay on Mass Production* (1946); *Mexican Portrait* (1948; rev. 1952); *Concerto Grosso* for Oboe and Chamber Orch. (1948; Pittsburgh, April 28, 1950); Concerto for 2 Pianos and Orch. (1951; Bloomington, Ind., March 17, 1967); *New Frontiers* (Houston, March 31, 1953); Violin Concerto, *Danforth* (1959); *Murals, Tapestries, and Icons* for Symphonic Band, Electric Bass, and Electric Piano (1975); Concerto for Tuba and Wind Orch. (Bloomington, Ind., Feb. 11, 1976). **CHAMBER:** Horn Sonata, *Christmas* (1945); 2 string quartets (1951, 1955); Tuba Sonata (1956); Trumpet Sonata (1962); Violin Sonata (1964–65); Flute Sonata (1965–66); Cello Sonata (1967–69); *La Petite Exposition* for Violin or Clarinet and 11 Strings (Dallas, Feb. 28, 1976); Sonata for Violin and Harp (1976–77); *Corelliana Variations* for 2 Flutes and Cello (1980).

Beyer, Frank Michael, German composer and pedagogue; b. Berlin, March 8, 1928. He received early music training from his father, a writer and amateur pianist; following studies in sacred music, he was a pupil of Pepping at the Berlin Staatliche Hochschule für Musik (1952–55). He was an assistant prof. (1960–68) and prof. (from 1968) at the Berlin Hochschule der Künste; was founder of the "musica nova sacra" concert series. He was a member of the Berlin Akademie der Künste, serving as director of its contemporary music section.

WORKS: BALLETS: *Geburt des Tanzes* (1987; Berlin, March 27, 1988); *Das Fenster* (1991). **ORCH.:** *Concerto for Orchestra* (1957); *Ode* (1963); Flute Concerto (1964); Organ Concerto (1967); *Versi* for Strings (Berlin, Oct. 7, 1968); *Rondeau imaginaire* (1972; Berlin, Sept. 20, 1973); *Concertino a tre* for Chamber Orch. (Schwetzingen, May 22, 1974); *Diaphonie* (1975; Nuremberg, Feb. 26, 1976); *Streicherfantasien* (1977; Berlin, March 12, 1980; also for String Quintet, Berlin, Sept. 18, 1978); *Griechenland* for 3 String Groups (1981; Berlin, June 22, 1982); *Deutsche-Tänze* for Cello, Double Bass, and Chamber Orch. (1982; Berlin, June 14, 1984; arranged from *Deutsche Tänze* for Cello and Double Bass, Vienna, Nov. 10, 1980); *Notre-Dame-Musik* (1983–84; Saarbrücken, Nov. 2, 1984); *Mysteriensonate* for Viola and Orch. (1986; Berlin, May 16, 1987); Concerto for Oboe and Strings (1986; Berlin, Oct. 7, 1987); *Musik der Frühe*, violin concerto (1993). **CHAMBER:** 3 string quartets (1957, 1969, 1985); Concerto for Organ and 7 Instruments (1966–69; arranged as Concerto for 5 Instruments, 1968); Wind Quintet (1972); Violin Sonata (1977); *De lumine* for 7 Players (1978); Trio for Oboe, Viola, and Harp (1980); *Passacaglia fantastica* for Violin, Cello, and Piano (1984); Sym. for 8 Players (Berlin, Feb. 6, 1989); *Sanctus* for Saxophone Quartet (1989); *Canciones* for Clarinet and Ensemble (1991); Clarinet Quintet (1992); *Nachstück* for Oboe and Piano (1993); *Nänie* for 2 Guitars (1994); piano pieces; organ works. **VOCAL:** Choral music, including *Maior Angelis*, cantata (1970).

Beyer, Johanna Magdalena, German-American composer and musicologist; b. Leipzig, July 11, 1888; d. N.Y., Jan. 9, 1944. She studied piano and theory in Germany. In 1924 she went to America and studied at the David Mannes School in N.Y., receiving a teacher's certificate in 1928. She also took private lessons with Dane Rudhyar, Ruth Crawford, Charles Seeger, and Henry Cowell. She wrote music and several plays for various projects in N.Y. During Cowell's term in San Quentin prison (1937–41), Beyer acted as his secretary and cared for his scores. Her compositional style was dissonant counterpoint.

WORKS: ORCH.: *March* for 14 Instruments (1935); *Cyrnab* for Chamber Orch. (1937); *Fragment* for Chamber Orch. (1937); *Symphonic Suite* (1937); *Dance for Full Orchestra (Status Quo)* (1938); *Elation* for Concert Band (1938); *Reverence* for Winds (1938); *Symphonic Movement I* (1939) and *II* (1941); *Symphonic Opus 3* (1939) and *5* (1940). **CHAMBER:** *Suite* for Clarinet *I* (1932) and *Ib* (1933); *Percussion Suite* (1933); Quintet for Woodwinds (1933); *Suite* for Clarinet and Bassoon (1933); *IV* for Percussion Ensemble (1935); Clarinet Sonata (1936); *Suite* for Bass Clarinet and Piano (1936?); *Movement* for Double Bass and Piano (1936); *Suite* for Violin and Piano (1937); *Suite* for Oboe and Bassoon (1937); *Movement* for Woodwinds (1938); *March* for 30 Percussion Instruments (1939); *Percussion*, op. 14 (1939); *Six Pieces* for Oboe and Piano (1939); *Three Movements* for Percussion Ensemble (1939); *Waltz* for Percussion Ensemble (1939); Trio for Woodwinds (1940?); 4 string quartets (1933–34; 1936; *Dance*, 1938; 1943?); *Music of the Spheres (Status Quo)* (1938). **PIANO:** *Clusters* or *New York Waltzes* (1931, 1936); *Gebrauchs-Musik* (1934); *Winter Ade and five other folk song settings* (1936); *Movement* for 2 Pianos (1936); *Dissonant Counterpoint* (1936?); *Suite for Piano* (1939); Sonatina (1943); *Prelude and Fugue* (n.d.); *Piano-Book, Classic-Romantic-Modern* (n.d.). **VOCAL: CHORAL:** *The Robin in the Rain* (1935); *The Federal Music Project* (1936); *The Main-Deep* (1937); *The People, Yes* (1937); *The Composers' Forum Laboratory* (1937). **SONGS:** *Sky-Pieces* (1933); 3 Songs (*Timber Moon; Stars, Songs, Faces; Summer Grass*) for Soprano, Piano, and Percussion (1933); *Ballad of the Star-Eater* for Soprano and Clarinet (1934); 3 Songs (*Total Eclipse; Universal-Local; To Be*) for Soprano and Clarinet (1934); *Have Faith!* for Soprano and Flute (3 versions; 1936–37).

Bialas, Günter, German composer and pedagogue; b. Bielschowitz, Silesia, July 19, 1907; d. Glonn, July 8, 1995. His father was the business manager of a local theater, and Bialas absorbed much music through personal connections with professional organizations. He studied in Breslau (1925–27) and with Trapp in Berlin (1927–33). After teaching composition at the Weimar Hochschule für Musik (1947), he was a teacher (1947–50) and a prof. (1950–59) of composition at the North-West German Academy of Music in Detmold; then was prof. of composition at the Munich Hochschule für Musik (1959–72). In 1967 he received the music prize of the Bavarian Academy of Fine Arts, and in 1971 the Culture Prize of Upper Silesia. He developed a style using serial procedures, with diversions into medieval and African modes.

WORKS: DRAMATIC: OPERAS: *Hero und Leander* (Mannheim, Sept. 8, 1966); *Die Geschichte von Aucassin und Nicolette* (1967–69; Munich, Dec. 12, 1969); *Der gestiefelte Kater* (1973–74; Schwetzingen, May 15, 1975; rev. version, Munich, July 18, 1987). **BALLET:** *Meyerbeer-Paraphrasen* (1971; Hamburg, May 12, 1974). **ORCH.:** *Kleine Konzertmusik* (1935); Viola Concerto (1940); Violin Concerto (1949); *Sinfonia piccola* (1960); Clarinet Concerto (1961); 2 cello concertos (1962, 1993); *Music in 2 Movements* for Harp and Strings (1966); *Concerto Lirico* for Piano and Orch. (1967); *Musik* for 11 Strings (1969); Chamber Concerto for Harpsichord or Piano and 13 Strings (1973); *Introitus—Exodus* for Organ and Orch. (1976); *Der Weg nach Eisenstadt*, "Haydn-Fantasy" for Small Orch. (1980); *Marschfantasie* (1988). **CHAMBER:** 3 string quartets (1936, 1949, 1969); Viola Sonata (1946); Violin Sonata (1946); Flute Sonata (1946); *Partita* for 9 Winds (1963); *Pastorale and Rondo*, nonet (1969); *Romanza e Danza*, octet (1971); *Assonanzen* for 12 Cellos (1978); Quintet for Harp and String Quartet (1983); *Andante (Herbstzeit)*, piano quartet (1984); 9 Bagatelles for Wind Trio, String Trio, and Piano (1984); 6 Bagatelles for Saxophone Quartet (1985–86); *Kunst des Kanons*, 10 pieces for 2 to 4 Saxophones (1992). **VOCAL:** *Indianische Kantate* for Baritone, Chamber Choir, and 8 Instruments (1951); *Oraculum*, cantata for Soprano, Tenor, Chorus, and Orch. (1953); *Symbolum* for Men's Chorus and Wind Quintet (1967); *Lamento di Orlando* for Baritone, Chorus, and Orch. (1986); *Matratzengruft*, Liedenspiel (1992).

BIBL.: G. Speer and H.-J. Winterhoff, *G. B. Meilensteine eines Komponistenlebens: Festschrift zum 70. Geburtstag* (Kassel, 1977); *G. B. zum 80. Geburtstag* (Dülmen, 1987); M. Holl and H. Schaefer, *Wort und Musik: Ausstellung zum 85. Geburtstag von G. B.: Bayerische Staatsbibliothek München, Musikabteilung, 15. July bis 4. September 1992* (Munich, 1992).

Bibalo, Antonio (Gino), Italian-born Norwegian composer of Slovak descent; b. Trieste, Jan. 18, 1922. After training with Luciano Gante (piano) and Giulio Viozzi (composition) at the Trieste Cons. (graduated, 1946), he went to London in 1953 to complete his composition studies with Elisabeth Luytens. In 1956 he settled in Norway and in 1967 became a naturalized Norwegian citizen. In 1991 he was awarded Norway's Prize for Culture for his opera *Macbeth* and was decorated with the St. Olaf Knight Cross of the King of Norway. In his music, Bibalo demonstrates a capacity for inventive tonal, melodic, and rhythmic writing with occasional excursions into serialism.

WORKS: DRAMATIC: OPERAS: *The Smile at the Foot of the Ladder* (1958–62; 1st complete perf. as *Das Lächeln am Fusse der Leiter*, Hamburg, April 6, 1965); *Frøken Julie* (Miss Julie; Århus, Sept. 8, 1975); *Askeladden* (Numskull Jack; 1976; Norwegian Radio, Dec. 26, 1977); *Gespenster* (Ghosts; Kiel, June 21, 1981); *Macbeth* (1989; Oslo, Sept. 29, 1990). **BALLETS:** *Pinocchio* (1967; Hamburg, Jan. 17, 1969); *Nocturne for Apollo* (1969); *Flammen* (1974). **ORCH.:** *Pitture Astratte* (1950–58); 2 piano concertos: No. 1 (1955; Oslo, Aug. 1, 1972) and No. 2 (1971; Bergen, April 27, 1972); 2 concerti da camera: No. 1 for Piano, Timpani, and Strings (1954) and No. 2 for Violin, Harpsichord, and Strings (1974); *Fantasia* for Violin and Orch. (1954); *Pour "Marguerite Infante"* (1955–70); *Concerto Allegorico* for Violin and Orch. (1957); *Serenata* for Chamber Orch. (1966); *Ouverture pour "Le Serviteure de deux maîtres"* (1968); 2 syms.: No. 1, *Sinfonia Notturna* (1968) and No. 2 (1978–79); *Per Clavicembalo, violino concertante e orchestra d'archi* (1974); *Freithoff Suite* (1974); *Musica* for Oboe, Strings, Percussion, and Harp (1986); Concertante for Wind Quintet and Orch. (1990). **CHAMBER:** *Autunnale* for Flute, Vibraphone, Double Bass, and Piano (1968); *Sonatina 1 A: Semplie* (1971) and *2 A: Astrale* (1972) for Flute, Oboe, Clarinet, Horn, and Bassoon; String Quartet (1972); *Sonata: Quasi una fantasia* for Accordion (1977); Sonata for Solo Violin (1978); *Study in Blue* for Guitar (1983); *The Savage*, "4 impressions" for 6 Players (1982–83); *Hvitt Landskap* for Violin, Cello, Flute, Clarinet, Piano, and Tape (1984); *Racconto d'una Stagione Alta* for Cello and Piano (1986); *4 Morceau* for 7 Players (1990); *Invenzione Evolutiva* for Double Bass (1990). **KEYBOARD: PIANO:** *3 Hommages* (1953); *4 Balkan Dances* (1956; also for Orch.); *Toccata* (1957); 2 sonatas (1974; *La Notte*, 1975); *Piano "Solo" in the Evening* (1977). **ORGAN:** *Prelude ed Elegia* (1989). **VOCAL:** *Elegie einer Raum-Zeit* for Soprano, Baritone, Chorus, and Orch. (1963); *Nocturne for Apollo: A Ballet of Requiem* for Chorus, Tape, and Orch. (1969); *Serenata* for Baritone and Men's Chorus (1971); *Cantico* for Mezzo-soprano and Tape (1983); *2 Intermezzi* for Baritone and Flute (1984–85); *Nocturne* for Voice and Piano (1988).

Bible, Frances, American mezzo-soprano; b. Sackets Harbor, N.Y., Jan. 26, 1927. She studied with Belle Julie Soudant and Queena Mario at the Juilliard School of Music in N.Y. (1939–47). She made her operatic debut as the Shepherd in *Tosca* at the N.Y. City Opera on Oct. 7, 1948, subsequently attaining a prominent place on its roster, singing principal roles there regularly until 1977. She was later a teacher (1979–82) and artist-in-residence (1982–83) at Rice Univ. in Houston. She was best known for her trouser and contemporary roles.

Bie, Oskar, German music critic; b. Breslau, Feb. 9, 1864; d. Berlin, April 21, 1938. He studied music with Philipp Scharwenka in Berlin; devoted himself principally to musical journalism, and publ. a number of informative monographs. In the spring of 1914, he accompanied Koussevitzky on his concert tour of the Volga and reported his impressions in a privately publ. illustrated ed. in 1920. Among his publications are *Das Klavier und seine Meister* (Munich, 1898; Eng. tr., 1899, as *A History of the Pianoforte and Pianoforte Players*); *Intime Musik* (Berlin, 1904); *Tanzmusik* (Berlin, 1905); *Der Tanz* (Berlin, 1906, 1919, 1925); *Die moderne Musik und Richard Strauss* (Berlin, 1906; Leipzig, 1916, 1925); *Die Oper* (Berlin, 1913); *Das Rätsel der Musik* (Leipzig, 1922); *Franz Schubert* (Berlin, 1925; Eng. tr., 1929, as *Schubert the Man*); *Das Deutsche Lied* (Berlin, 1926); *Richard Wagner und Bayreuth* (Zürich, 1931).

Biehle, (August) Johannes, German organist and pedagogue; b. Bautzen, June 18, 1870; d. there, Jan. 4, 1941. He studied at the Dresden Cons. After serving as organist and music director in Bautzen (1898–1914), he went to Berlin as a lecturer (from 1916) and a prof. (from 1922) of acoustics at the Technische Hochschule, and as a teacher of church music at the Univ. (from 1918); in 1927 he founded the Institut Beihle under the auspices of both institutions. He wrote the valuable studies "Theorie der pneumatischen Orgeltraktur und die Stellung des Spieltisches," *Sammelbände der Internationalen Musik-Gesellschaft*, XIII (1911) and *Theorie des Kirchenbaues* (Wittenberg, 1913). He was also a leading figure in the organ carillon movement.

BIBL.: E. Muller, ed., *Festschrift J. B.* (Leipzig, 1930); H. Biehle, "J. B. als Begrunder der Glockenwissenschaft," *Musik und Kirche*, XXXI (1961).

Bielawa, Herbert, American composer, pianist, and teacher; b. Chicago, Feb. 3, 1930. He studied music at home; from 1954 to 1956 he served in the U.S. Army in Germany, stationed in Frankfurt am Main, where he also studied conducting with Bruno Vondenhoff. He took courses in piano with Soulima Stravinsky at the Univ. of Ill. (B.M., 1954); then enrolled at the Univ. of Southern Calif. in Los Angeles, and took courses in composition with Ingolf Dahl (1960–61), Halsey Stevens (1961–64), and Ellis Kohs (1961–63); also studied music for cinema with Miklós Rosza and David Raksin. In 1966 he was appointed to the faculty of San Francisco State Univ.; in 1967 he established there the Electronic Music Studio; he retired in 1991. In his music, he makes unprejudiced use of the entire field of practical resources.

WORKS: *Concert Piece* for Orch. (1953); *Essay* for String Orch. (1958); *A Bird in the Bush*, chamber opera (1962); *Abstractions* for String Orch. (1965); *4 Legends* for Violins and Cellos (1967); *Divergents* for Orch. (1969); *Fluxbands* for 10 Instruments (1981); Duo for Violin and Harpsichord (1984); String Quartet (1989); *50/50* for Flute, Oboe, Clarinet, Bassoon, and Piano (1991); keyboard pieces; choral works; songs; electronic music.

Bierdiajew, Walerian, Polish conductor; b. Grodno, March 7, 1885; d. Warsaw, Nov. 28, 1956. He studied composition with Max Reger and conducting with Arthur Nikisch at the Leipzig Cons. He began his conducting career in Dresden in 1906; in 1908 he became regular conductor at the Maryinsky Opera Theater in St. Petersburg; then conducted in various Russian opera houses; from 1921 to 1925 he lived in Poland; from 1925 to 1930 he was again engaged as a conductor in Russia. In 1930 he was appointed prof. of conducting at the Warsaw Cons.; from 1947 to 1949 he was conductor of the Kraków Phil.; then taught at the Poznán Cons. (1949–54) and at the Warsaw Cons. (1954–56); also was director of the Warsaw Opera (1954–56).

Biggs, E(dward George) Power, eminent English-born American organist; b. Westcliff on Sea, Essex, March 29, 1906; d. Boston, March 10, 1977. He studied at the Royal Academy of Music in London, graduating in 1929. In 1930 he emigrated to the U.S. and became a naturalized American citizen in 1937. After making his N.Y. recital debut in 1932, he launched a career as one of the most distinguished concert organists of his time. He became particularly popular via his weekly CBS radio broadcasts (1942–58), his extensive recital tours, and his numerous recordings. His repertoire was vast, ranging from the great masters of the past to contemporary composers, among them Piston, Harris, Hanson, and Quincy Porter; Britten also wrote a work for him. Biggs refused to perform on electronic organs, which in his opinion vulgarized and distorted the classical organ sound. His style of performance had an unmistakable austerity, inspired by the Baroque school.

BIBL.: B. Owen, *E.P. B.: Concert Organist* (Bloomington, Ind., 1987).

Bigot, Eugène, French conductor; b. Rennes, Feb. 28, 1888; d. Paris, July 17, 1965. He studied violin and piano at the Rennes Cons. and later at the Paris Cons. In 1913 he was named chorus master at the Théâtre des Champs Élysées in Paris; subsequently toured Europe with the Ballets Suédois; also conducted the Paris Cons. Orch. (1923–25); then served as music director at the Théâtres des Champs-Élysées (1925–27). In 1935 he became president and director of the Concerts Lamoureux in Paris, a post he held until 1950; he also was principal conductor of the Paris Opéra-Comique (1936–47). From 1947 until his death he was chief conductor of the Paris Radio Orch.

Bijvanck, Henk, Dutch composer; b. Kudus, Java, Nov. 6, 1909; d. Heemstede, near Haarlem, Sept. 5, 1969. He studied composition with Franz Schmidt and piano with Andrassy in Vienna; was active as a pianist there; then taught piano at the Amsterdam Music Lyceum (1945–47). His works include: Piano Concerto (1943); *Liberation Symphony* (1944); *Lourdes Symphony* (1952); Sym. No. 2 (1965); chamber music; vocal works.

Bikel, Theodore, Austrian-born American singer and actor; b. Vienna, May 2, 1924. After the Anschluss in 1938, he fled with his family to Palestine; then made his way to London, where he studied at the Royal Academy of Dramatic Arts. He subsequently had a fine career as an actor on stage, screen, and television, concurrently establishing himself as a folksinger. In 1959 he scored a major Broadway success in the role of Georg von Trapp in the Rogers and Hammerstein musical *The Sound of Music.* He became a naturalized American citizen in 1961. He publ. an autobiography (N.Y., 1994).

Bilson, Malcolm, noted American pianist, fortepianist, and teacher; b. Los Angeles, Oct. 24, 1935. He studied at Bard College (B.A., 1957), the Vienna Academy of Music (1959), the Paris École Normale de Musique (1960), and the Univ. of Ill. (D.M.A., 1968). He championed the cause of performing works of the Classical era on original instruments or modern replicas. He toured widely in the U.S. and Europe, and was a founder of the Amade Trio (1974). He joined the faculty at Cornell Univ. in 1968. He is particularly esteemed for his insightful readings of the works of Haydn, Mozart, and Beethoven.

Bilt, Peter van der, Dutch bass-baritone; b. Jakarta, Dutch East Indies, Aug. 30, 1936; d. Amsterdam, Sept. 25, 1983. He studied in Amsterdam, where he made his operatic debut as Dulcamara in 1960. After appearing as Rossini's Don Basilio at the San Francisco Opera in 1963, he joined the Deutsche Oper am Rhein in Düsseldorf in 1964; made guest appearances in Vienna, Munich, Edinburgh, Los Angeles, and other music centers. Among his prominent roles were Don Giovanni, Figaro, Don Pasquale, Beckmesser, and Gianni Schicchi. He also sang widely in concerts.

Bimboni, Alberto, Italian-American pianist and composer; b. Florence, Aug. 24, 1882; d. N.Y., June 18, 1960. He studied in Florence; went to the U.S. in 1912 as an opera conductor. In 1930 he was appointed to the faculty of the Curtis Inst. of Music in Philadelphia; taught opera classes at the Juilliard School of Music in N.Y. from 1933; appeared as a pianist in concerts with Ysaÿe, John McCormack, and other celebrated artists. Among his compositions are the operas *Winona* (Portland, Oreg., Nov. 11, 1926), *Karin* (Minneapolis, 1928), *Il cancelleto d'oro* (N.Y., March 11, 1936), and *In the Name of Culture* (Rochester, N.Y., May 9, 1949), as well as numerous songs.

Binder, Abraham Wolfe, American composer and teacher; b. N.Y., Jan. 13, 1895; d. there, Oct. 10, 1966. He studied at Columbia Univ.; subsequently taught liturgical music at the Jewish Inst. of Religion in N.Y. He composed an opera, *A Goat in Chelm* (N.Y., March 20, 1960); a choral ballet, *Hora Vehodayah* (Praise and Dance); *The Legend of Ari* for Small Orch. (1963); and other symphonic works on Jewish themes.

Bindernagel, Gertrud, German soprano; b. Magdeburg, Jan. 11, 1894; d. Berlin, Nov. 3, 1932. She studied at the Magdeburg Cons., and then at the Berlin Hochschule für Musik (1913–17). At age 17, she began her career in Magdeburg, and then sang in Breslau (1917–19) and Regensburg (1919–20); subsequently appeared in Berlin at the State Opera (1920–27) and the Städtische Oper (from 1927); also made guest appearances in Barcelona, Munich, Hamburg, and Mannheim, becoming particularly admired as a Wagnerian. Following her performance of Brünnhilde in *Siegfried* at the Berlin Städtische Oper, she was fatally wounded by a gunshot delivered by her jealous husband, the banker Wilhelm Hintze.

Binenbaum, Janco, Bulgarian-French composer; b. Adrianopol, Dec. 28, 1880; d. Chevreuse, Seine-et-Oise, Feb. 4, 1956. He studied in Munich with Rheinberger and others; was active as a piano teacher in Germany and France, eventually settling in Chevreuse. He wrote a considerable amount of symphonic and chamber music in an impressionistic vein, colored with Balkan rhythms, none of which was publ., and little ever performed. Nonetheless, Binenbaum found sincere admirers of his works, among whom M.D. Calvocoressi was the most vocal.

Binet, Jean, Swiss composer; b. Geneva, Oct. 17, 1893; d. Trélex, Feb. 24, 1960. He studied in Geneva at the Univ. and at the Institut Jaques-Dalcroze; after training with Otto Barblan, William Montillet, and George Templeton Strong, he completed his studies with Ernest Bloch in N.Y., whom he helped to found the Dalcroze Rhythmic School and then the Cleveland Cons. He taught the Dalcroze method in Brussels (1923–29) before settling in Trélex; later was president of the Société Suisse des Auteurs et Editeurs (1951–60). His output was marked by a refined Gallic quality.

WORKS: DRAMATIC: BALLETS: *L'Ile enchantée* (1947); *Le printemps* (1950); incidental music. **ORCH.:** Concertino for Small Orch. (1927); *Suite d'airs et danses populaires suisses* for Small Orch. (1931); *Divertissement* for Violin and Small Orch. (1934; also for Violin and Piano); *4 danses* (1936); *3 pièces* for Strings (1939); *Cartes postales* for Small Orch. (1940); *Musique de mai* (1943); *6 pièces enfantines* for Small Orch. (1947); *Prélude symphonique* (1949); *Petit concert* for Clarinet and Strings (1950; also for Clarinet and Piano); *Suite grisonne* for Small Orch. (1951). **CHAMBER:** String Quartet (1927); Flute Sonatine (1942); *Kaval* for Flute and Piano (1945); *Sonate brève* for Violin and Piano (1946); *3 dialogues* for 2 Flutes (1957); *Variations sur un chant de Noël* for Bassoon and Piano (1957). **VOCAL:** Choral music and songs.

BIBL.: *Hommage à J. B.* (Nyon, 1961).

Bing, Sir Rudolf (Franz Joseph), prominent Austrian-born English opera manager; b. Vienna, Jan. 9, 1902. He studied at the Univ. of Vienna and took singing lessons. After working at the Darmstadt Landestheater (1928–30) and the Berlin Städtische Oper (1930–33), he went to England and joined the Glyndebourne Festival in 1934, where he then was its general manager (1936–49). In 1947 he also helped to found the Edinburgh Festival, which he led as artistic director until 1949. In 1946 he became a naturalized British subject. From 1950 to 1972 he was general manager of the Metropolitan Opera in N.Y. His tenure there was a distinguished, if at times controversial, one. His self assurance and acerbic wit added color to his clashes with the board of directors, celebrated artists, and the press. In 1971 he was knighted. He publ. the books *5,000 Nights at the Opera* (N.Y., 1972) and *A Knight at the Opera* (N.Y., 1981). His last years were blighted by Alzheimer's disease.

Bingham, Seth (Daniels), American organist, pedagogue, and composer; b. Bloomfield, N.J., April 16, 1882; d. N.Y., June 21, 1972. He studied with Horatio Parker at Yale Univ. (B.A., 1904; B.Mus., 1908) and with d'Indy, Widor, Guilmant, and Harry Jepson in Paris (1906–07). He taught at Yale Univ. (1908–19), Columbia Univ. (1919–54), and the Union Theological Seminary School of Sacred Music (1953–65); also was organist at N.Y.'s Madison Ave. Presbyterian Church (1913–53). His music was contrapuntal, occasionally chromatic, and, later, highly modal.

WORKS: OPERA: *La Charelzenn* (1917). **ORCH.:** *Pièce Gothique* for Organ and Orch. (1909); *Wall Street Fantasy* (1912; perf. as *Symphonic Fantasy,* N.Y., Feb. 6, 1916); *Tame Animal Tunes* for 18 Instruments (1918); *Memories of France,* suite (1920); Organ Concerto (Rochester, N.Y., Oct. 24, 1946); *Connecticut Suite* for Organ and Strings (Hartford, Conn., March 26, 1954); Concerto for Brass, Snare Drum, Organ, and Orch. (Minneapolis, July 12, 1954). **ORGAN:** Suite (1926); *Pioneer America* (1928); *Harmonies of Florence* (1929); *Carillon de Château-Thierry* (1936); *Pastoral Psalms* (1938); *12 Hymn-Preludes* (1942); *Variation Studies* (1950); *36 Hymn and Carol Canons* (1952); *Sonata for Prayer and Praise* (1960); *Ut Queant Laxis: Hymn to St. John the Baptist* (1962); *He Is Risen: Fantasy-Toccata on Easter Themes* (1962). **VOCAL:** *Wilderness Stone* for Narrator, Soli, Chorus, and Orch. (1933); *Canticle of the Sun* for Chorus and Organ or Orch. (1949); *Perfect Through Suffering* for Chorus and Organ (1971).

BIBL.: P. Basch, "S.D. B.: A Tribute," *Music: The A.G.O.—R.C.C.O. Magazine* (April 1972); M. Searle Wright, "S.D. B. 100th Anniversary: An Appreciation," *The American Organist* (June 1982).

Binički, Stanislav, Serbian composer and conductor; b. Jasika, near Kruševca, July 27, 1872; d. Belgrade, Feb. 15, 1942. He studied at the Univ. of Belgrade; later took courses in composition with Rheinberger in Munich. Returning to Belgrade, he helped organize the Serbian School of Music; was also active as an opera conductor. He composed a number of incidental pieces for the theater, the opera *Na uranku* (Dawn; Belgrade, Jan. 2, 1904), and choruses and songs.

Binkerd, Gordon (Ware), American composer and teacher; b. Lynch, Nebr., May 22, 1916. He studied piano in South Dakota, and composition with Bernard Rogers at the Eastman School of Music in Rochester, N.Y., and with Piston at Harvard Univ.; from 1949 to 1971, was a member of the faculty of the Univ. of Ill. He received a Guggenheim fellowship in 1959.

WORKS: ORCH.: 4 syms.: No. 1 (Urbana, March 20, 1955), No. 2 (Urbana, April 13, 1957), No. 3 (N.Y., Jan. 6, 1961), and No. 4 (St. Louis, Oct. 12, 1963; dismembered and reduced to a *Movement for Orchestra*); *A Part of Heaven,* 2 romances for Violin and Orch. (1972). **CHAMBER:** Cello Sonata (1952); Trio for Clarinet, Viola, and Cello (1955); 2 string quartets (1956, 1961); Violin Sonata (1977); String Trio (1979); 4 piano sonatas (1955, 1981, 1982, 1983). **VOCAL:** Choral works; songs.

Binkley, Thomas (Eden), American lutenist, wind player, and music scholar; b. Cleveland, Dec. 26, 1931; d. Bloomington, Ind., April 28, 1995. He studied at the Univ. of Ill. (B.M., 1956), then pursued postgraduate studies at the Univ. of Munich (1957–58) and the Univ. of Ill. (1958–59). His principal mentors were Dragan Plamenac, Claude Palisca, John Ward, Thrasybulos Georgiades, and George Hunter. From 1960 to 1980 he was director of the Studio der frühen Musik in Munich; also taught and performed in the medieval program at the Schola Cantorum Basiliensis in Basel (1973–77). In 1979 he became prof. of music and director of the Early Music Inst. at the Indiana Univ. School of Music in Bloomington. He served as general ed. of its book series Music: Scholarship and Performance, and of its monograph series Early Music Inst. Publications. He ed. the vol. *Willi Apel, Medieval Music: Collected Articles and Reviews* (Wiesbaden, 1986), and contributed articles to other publications. As a performing musician, he made appearances in major music centers in America and Europe.

Binns, Malcolm, English pianist and fortepianist; b. Gedling, Nottingham, Jan. 29, 1936. He studied at the Royal College of Music in London. He made his debut in London in 1957; subsequently appeared with the leading English orchs. and gave recitals. His vast repertory ranges from early music on the fortepiano to contemporary scores on the concert grand.

Birchard, Clarence C., American music publisher; b. Cambridge Springs, Pa., July 13, 1866; d. Carlisle, Mass., Feb. 27, 1946. He established his firm in Boston in 1901 and specialized in educational books for public schools; of these, a 10-book series, *A Singing School,* introduced lavish profusion of color in design and illustration; the firm also issued community songbooks, of which the most popular was *Twice 55 Community*

Songs (several million copies sold). The catalogue included scores by many American composers.

Biriukov, Yuri, Russian composer; b. Moscow, April 1, 1908; d. there, Nov. 1, 1976. He studied piano with Feinberg and composition with Miaskovsky at the Moscow Cons., graduating in 1936. Among his works are 2 operas, *Peasant Gentlewoman* (1947) and *Knight of the Golden Star* (1956); a ballet, *The Cosmonauts* (1962); a musical, *The Blue Express* (1971); a Sym. on Ingush themes (1968); 3 piano concertos (1941, 1945, 1970); 24 preludes and 4 toccatas for Piano; much music for the theater and films.

Birnie, Tessa (Daphne), New Zealand pianist and conductor; b. Ashburton, July 19, 1934. She studied piano with Paul Schramm in Wellington; then took lessons with Lefébure in Paris and K.U. Schnabel in Como; subsequently toured as a pianist in Australia and Asia; also played in the U.S. She organized the Sydney Camerata Orch. in 1963, appearing with it as both pianist and conductor; was founder-president of the Australian Soc. of Keyboard Music and founder of the journal *Key Vive Music.* In 1985 she was awarded the Medal of the Order of Australia.

Birtner, Herbert, German musicologist; b. Hamburg, June 16, 1900; d. in battle at Voronezh, Russia, Sept. 27, 1942. He first studied medicine; then took courses in musicology with Gurlitt and Kroyer; was an assistant lecturer at the Univ. of Leipzig (1924–28), and then was a prof. at the Univ. of Marburg (1938–40). In 1940 he was drafted into the German army. He contributed important studies on the music of the Reformation; his publ. works include *Joachim à Burck als Motettenkomponist* (Leipzig, 1924) and *Studien zur niederländisch-humanistischen Musikanschauung* (Marburg, 1929).

Birtwistle, Sir Harrison (Paul), eminent English composer; b. Accrington, Lancashire, July 15, 1934. He was a student of Frederick Thurston (clarinet) and Richard Hall (composition) at the Royal Manchester College of Music (1952–60), and then of Reginald Kell (clarinet) at the Royal Academy of Music in London (1960–61). After serving as director of music at the Cranbourne Chase School in Dorset (1962–65), he was a visiting prof. at Princeton Univ. (1966). Returning to England, he co-founded with Peter Maxwell Davies the Pierrot Players in 1967, a contemporary music ensemble, with which he remained active until 1970. He was a visiting prof. of music at Swarthmore College (1973–74) and the State Univ. of N.Y. at Buffalo (1975). Returning once more to England, he was active as music director at the National Theater in London from 1975. In 1987 he received the Grawemeyer Award of the Univ. of Louisville for his opera *The Mask of Orpheus.* He was knighted in 1988. In his compositions, Birtwistle departed completely from the folkloric trends popular in modern English music and adopted an abstract idiom, one marked by an expert handling of various elements in a thoroughly contemporary idiom. His operas constitute a significant contribution to the British stage.

WORKS: DRAMATIC: *Punch and Judy,* tragical comedy or comical tragedy (1966–67; Aldeburgh, June 8, 1968; rev. version, London, March 3, 1970); *Down by the Greenwood Side,* dramatic pastorale (1968–69; Brighton, May 8, 1969); *The Mask of Orpheus,* opera (1973–75; 1981–84; London, May 21, 1986); *Pulse Field: Frames, Pulses, and Interruptions,* ballet (Snape, June 25, 1977); *Bow Down,* music theater (London, July 4, 1977); *Yan, Tan, Tethera,* opera (1983–84; London, Aug. 7, 1986); *Gawain,* opera (1990–91; London, May 30, 1991); *The Second Mrs. Kong,* opera (1993–94; Glyndebourne, Oct. 21, 1994); incidental music. **ORCH.:** *Chorales* (1960–63; London, Feb. 14, 1967); *3 Movements with Fanfares* (London, July 8, 1964); *Nomos* for Amplified Flute, Amplified Clarinet, Amplified Horn, Amplified Bassoon, and Orch. (1967–68; London, Aug. 23, 1968); *An Imaginary Landscape* (London, June 2, 1971); *The Triumph of Time* (1971–72; London, June 1, 1972); *Grimethorpe Aria* for Brass Band (Harrogate, Aug. 15, 1973); *Melencolia I* for Clarinet, Harp, and 2 String Orchs. (Glasgow, Sept. 18, 1976); *Earth Dances* (1985–86; London, March 14, 1986); *Endless Parade* for Trumpet, Vibraphone, and Strings (1986–87; Zürich, May 1, 1987); *Machaut à ma Manière* (1988); *Salford Toccata* for Brass Band (Salford, April 12, 1989); *Gawain's Journey* (Vienna, Oct. 21, 1991); *Antiphonies* for Piano and Orch. (1992; Paris, May 5, 1993). **CHAMBER:** *Refrains and Choruses* for Wind Quintet (1957; Cheltenham, June 11, 1959); *3 Sonatas* for 9 Instruments (Aldeburgh, June 17, 1960); *The World Is Discovered* for 12 Instruments (London, March 5, 1961); *Entr'actes* for Flute, Viola, and Harp (1962; used in *Entr'actes and Sappho Fragments,* 1964); *Tragoedia* for 10 Instruments (Devon, Aug. 20, 1965); *Verses* for Clarinet and Piano (London, Oct. 1965); *Chorale from a Toy Shop* for Flute, Oboe or Clarinet, Clarinet or English Horn, Horn or Trombone, and Bassoon or Tuba (1967; Lewes, March 28, 1979; also for 2 Trumpets, Horn, Trombone, and Tuba, London, May 19, 1978); *3 Lessons in a Frame* for Piano, Flute, Clarinet, Violin, Cello, and Percussion (Cheltenham, July 17, 1967); *Linoi* for Clarinet and Piano (London, Oct. 11, 1968; 2nd version for Clarinet, Piano, Dancer, and Tape, London, April 22, 1969; 3rd version for Clarinet, Piano, and Cello, Sheffield, Nov. 12, 1973); *4 Interludes for a Tragedy* for Clarinet and Tape (without tape, London, Oct. 18, 1968; with tape, London, Feb. 10, 1969); *Verses* for Ensembles (1968–69; London, Feb. 12, 1969); *Some Petals from my Twickenham Herbarium* for Piccolo, Clarinet, Viola, Cello, Piano, and Bells (London, April 22, 1969); *Medusa* for Chamber Ensemble and Tape (Sheffield, Oct. 22, 1969; rev. version, London, March 3, 1970); *8 Lessons* for Keyboards (London, Jan. 13, 1970); *Signals* for Clarinet and Electronics (Edinburgh, Aug. 25, 1970); *Dinah and Nick's Love Song* for 3 Melody Instruments and Harp (1970; Sheffield, Oct. 26, 1972); *Tombeau in memoriam Igor Stravinsky* for Flute, Clarinet, Harp, and String Quartet (1971; London, June 17, 1972); *Chanson de Geste* for Amplified Sustaining Instrument and Tape (Perugia, July 1973); *For O, for O the Hobby Horse Is Forgot* for 6 Percussionists (1976; Tokyo, Feb. 10, 1978); *Silbury Air* for 15 Instruments (London, March 9, 1977); *Carmen Arcadiae Mechanicae Perpetuum* for 14 Instruments (1977; London, Jan. 24, 1978); Clarinet Quintet (1980; Huddersfield, Nov. 21, 1981); *Pulse Sampler* for Oboe and Claves (Huddersfield, Nov. 20, 1981); *Duets for Storab* for 2 Flutes (1983; London, March 25, 1984); *Secret Theatre* for 14 Instruments (London, Oct. 18, 1984); *Fanfare for Will* for 3 Trumpets, 4 Horns, 3 Trombones, and Tuba (London, July 10, 1987); *Ritual Fragment* for 14 Instruments (London, May 6, 1990); *An Interrupted Endless Melody* for Oboe and Piano (1991); *3 Movements* for String Quartet (1991–93; movement 1, Vienna, Nov. 18, 1991; movements 2–3, Antwerp, Nov. 8, 1993); *5 Distances* for Flute, Oboe, Clarinet, Bassoon, and Horn (1992; London, May 7, 1993). **VOCAL:** *Monody for Corpus Christi* for Soprano, Flute, Horn, and Violin (1959; London, April 5, 1960); *Narration: A Description of the Passing of a Year* for Chorus (1963; London, Feb. 14, 1964); *Entr'actes and Sappho Fragments* for Soprano and 6 Instruments (Cheltenham, July 11, 1964); *Ring a Dumb Carillon* for Soprano Playing Suspended Cymbals, Clarinet, and Percussion (1964–65; London, March 19, 1965); *Carmen Paschale,* motet for Chorus and Organ ad libitum (Aldeburgh, June 17, 1965); *The Visions of Francesco Petrarca* for Baritone, Mime Ensemble, Chamber Ensemble, and School Orch. (1965–66; York, June 15, 1966); *Monodrama* for Soprano, Speaker, and Chamber Ensemble (London, May 30, 1967); *Cantata* for Soprano and Chamber Ensemble (London, June 12, 1969); *Nenia: The Death of Orpheus* for Soprano, 3 Bass Clarinets, Piano, and Crotales (London, Nov. 20, 1970); *Meridian* for Mezzo-soprano, 2 3-part Soprano Choruses, and Instruments (1970–71; London, Feb. 26, 1971); *Prologue* for Tenor and 7 Instruments (London, April 18, 1971); *The Fields of Sorrow* for 2 Sopranos, Chorus, and 16 Instruments (Dartington, Aug. 7, 1971; rev. 1972); *Epilogue* for Baritone, Horn, 4 Trombones, and 6 Tam-tams (London, April 23, 1972); *La Plage: 8 Arias of Remembrance* for Soprano, 3 Clarinets, Piano, and Marimba (Sheffield, Oct. 26, 1972); *. . . agm . . .* for 16 Voices and 3 Instrumental Groups (1978–79; Paris, April 9, 1979); *Chorale Fragments from . . . agm . . .* for 16 Voices (London, April 5, 1979); *On the Sheer Threshold of the Night,* madrigal for 4 Solo Voices and Chorus (Hessian Radio, Frankfurt am Main, May 10, 1980); *Songs by Myself* for Soprano and 7 Instruments (London, Oct. 18, 1984); *Words Overheard* for Soprano and Chamber Orch. (Glasgow, Nov. 17, 1985); *4 Songs of Autumn* for Soprano and String Quartet (1987; London, Jan. 24, 1988); *An die Musik* for Soprano and 10 Instruments (London, May 4, 1988); *White and Light* for Soprano and 5 Instruments (Brighton, May 13, 1989); *4 Poems by Jaan Kaplinski* for Soprano and 13 Instruments (Aldeburgh, June 19, 1991); *Tenebrae* for Soprano and 5 Instruments (London, Sept. 18, 1992); *Night* for Soprano, 2 Choruses, Cello, and Double Bass (London, Sept. 18, 1992). **TAPE:** *Chronometer* (1971–72; London, April 24, 1972). **OTHER:** Pieces for young people; electronic music; arrangements.

BIBL.: M. Hall, *H. B.* (London, 1984).

Bischof, Rainer, Austrian composer; b. Vienna, June 20, 1947. He studied law, philosophy, art history, and pedagogy at the Univ. of Vienna (Ph.D., 1973); also composition at the Vienna Academy of Music (1965) and privately with Apostel (1967–72). After serving as president of the Austrian Composers Union (1984–86), he was a lecturer on aesthetics at the Vienna Hochschule für Musik (from 1987) and general secretary of the Vienna Sym. Orch. (from 1988). His music follows the tenets of the Second Viennese School.

WORKS: DRAMATIC: *Das Donauergeschenk,* chamber opera (1990; Vienna, June 22, 1991). **ORCH.:** *Deduktion* for Strings (1973–74); *Orchesterstücke* (1976–82); Concerto for Flute and Strings (1978–79; Innsbruck, Jan. 22, 1981); Double Concerto for Violin, Cello, and Orch. (1979–80; Zürich, June 9, 1983); Organ Concerto (1983–86; Vienna, March 5, 1987); *Largo Desolato* for Strings (1985); *Come uno sviluppo . . . stracci,* chamber sym. (1988–89); *Studie in PP* (1991). **CHAMBER:** Duo for Flute and Clarinet (1970); *Thema und 7 Variationen* for Oboe and Cello (1970); Wind Quartet for Flute, Clarinet, Horn, and Bassoon (1971); *Charakteristische Differenzen* for Violin and Piano (1974); *Studien zum Flöten-Konzert* for Flute (1978); *Musik* for 6 Recorders (1982–83); *Viola Tricolor,* 32 variations for Viola (1982); String Quartet (1983–86); *Trio Fragile 1985* for Violin, Cello, and Piano (1985); *Mallet Ricarcare* for Xylophone, Vibraphone, and Marimbaphone (1988); *Nightwoods* for Saxophone Quartet (1988); *Trio 89* for Violin, Cello, and Piano (1989); String Trio (1989–90); String Sextet (1989–90); *Hawa Naschira* for Violin (1990–91). **VOCAL:** Various works, including song cycles.

Bishop, Stephen. See **Kovacevich, Stephen.**

Bishop-Kovacevich, Stephen. See **Kovacevich, Stephen.**

Bismillah Khan, Indian shehnai player; b. Dumraon, March 21, 1916. He studied instrumental and vocal music; earned great renown in India; appeared as soloist at the Commonwealth Arts Festival in London in 1965, and later in other Western music centers.

Bissell, Keith (Warren), Canadian composer, music educator, and conductor; b. Meaford, near Owen Sound, Ontario, Feb. 12, 1912; d. Newmarket, near Toronto, May 9, 1992. He was a composition student of Leo Smith at the Univ. of Toronto (B.Mus., 1942), and later studied with Gunild Keetman and Carl Orff in Munich (1960). After teaching in Toronto schools (1934–48), he was assistant supervisor (1948) and then supervisor (1949–55) of school music in Edmonton. From 1955 to 1976 he served as supervisor of school music in Scarborough (part of metropolitan Toronto), where he introduced the Orff Schulwerk method. He also was conductor of the Scarborough Orff Ensemble (1960–73). In addition to his works for professional performance, he wrote much music for the young.

WORKS: DRAMATIC: *His Majesty's Pie,* operetta (1964); *The Centennial Play,* incidental music (1967); *A Musical Play,* operetta (1977); *The Miraculous Turnip,* children's opera (1980). **ORCH.:** *3 Pieces* for Strings (1960); *Under the Apple Boughs* for Horn and Strings (1962); Concertino for Piano and Strings (1962); *Adagio* for Small Orch. (1963); *Little Suite* for Trumpet and Strings (1963); *Divertimento* for Strings (1964); *Canada 1967* (1967); *Andante e Scherzo* for Chamber Orch. (1971); *Variations on a Canadian Folk Song* for Strings (1972); *3 Commentaries on Canadian Folk Songs* for Strings (1973); *Andante and Allegro* for Oboe and Strings (1976). **CHAMBER:** *Ballad* for Violin and Piano (1947); Violin Sonata (1948); *A Folk Song Suite* for Winds (1960); *Little Suite* for Trumpet and Piano (1962); *Serenade* for Wind Quintet (1972); Trio Suite for Trumpet, Horn, and Trombone (1973); Suite for Bassoon, String Quartet, and Percussion (1977); Suite for Brass Quintet (1977); Suite for Winds (1978); Horn Sonata (1978); *In the Modes* for Recorder and Percussion (1982); *3 Pieces* for 4 Recorders (1986). **VOCAL:** *People Look East,* cantata for Soloists, Chorus, and 4 Instruments (1965); *Let There Be Joy,* cantata for Soloists, Chorus, and 5 Instruments (1965); *Canada, Dear Home/Canada douce patrie* for Chorus and Orch. (1966); *A Bluebird in March* for Chorus and Orch. (1967); *The Passion According to St. Luke* for Soloists, Chorus, and Orch. (1970); *How the Loon Gots Its Necklace* for Narrator, String Quintet, and Percussion (1971); *Cantate Domino* for Women's Chorus and Chamber Orch. (1977); *Anniversary Cantata* for Chorus and Orch. (1978); *A Celebration of the Nativity* for Soloists, Chorus, and Chamber Orch. (1978); *Great Little One: Music for the Nativity* for Chorus and Orch. (1983); choruses; arrangements.

BIBL.: M. Irving, *K. B.: His Life, Career and Contribution to Music Education from 1912–76* (thesis, Univ. of Western Ontario, 1982).

Bitetti (Ravina), Ernesto (Guillermo), Argentine guitarist and teacher; b. Rosario, July 20, 1943. He studied guitar in Santa Fe; completed his education at the Univ. Nacional del Litoral (M. Mus., 1964). He made his debut in Rosario in 1958; then toured in the U.S., Europe, the Middle East, and the Orient. He taught at the Indiana Univ. School of Music in Bloomington from 1989. Several composers wrote guitar pieces especially for him.

Bitsch, Marcel, French composer; b. Paris, Dec. 29, 1921. He entered the Paris Cons. in 1939, studied composition with Busser, and won the 1st Prix de Rome in 1943 and the 2nd Prix de Rome in 1945. He wrote *Divertissement* for Flute, Clarinet, Oboe, and Bassoon (1947); *6 esquisses symphoniques* (1949); *Sinfonietta* (1950); 3 flute sonatas (1952); Piano Concertino (Paris, Nov. 28, 1954); vocal music.

Bittner, Julius, Austrian composer and music critic; b. Vienna, April 9, 1874; d. there, Jan. 9, 1939. He studied law and received music lessons from Josef Labor. After serving as a lawyer and judge in Wolkersdorf (1905–08) and Vienna (from 1908), he was employed in the Ministry of Justice (1920–22); later he was active as a music critic. As a composer, Bittner was most successful in writing operas on fairy tale or folklore subjects, often to his own libretti. He wrote many of his operatic roles and songs for his wife, the contralto Emilie Werner (1885–1963).

WORKS: DRAMATIC: OPERAS: *Die rote Gret* (Frankfurt am Main, Oct. 26, 1907); *Der Musikant* (1909; Vienna, April 12, 1910); *Der Bergsee* (1910; Vienna, Nov. 9, 1911; rev. 1938); *Die Kohlhaymerin* (1920; Vienna, April 9, 1921); *Mondnacht* (Berlin, Nov. 13, 1928); *Das Veilchen* (Vienna, Dec. 8, 1934). **OPERETTAS:** *Die silberne Tänzerin* (1926); *Général d'amour* (1926). Also Singspiels, a mimodrama, incidental music, and a ballet. **ORCH.:** 2 symphonic poems: *Vaterland* (1915); *Das Lied von den Bergan* (1930); *Österreichische Tänze* (1918); 2 syms. (1918, 1934). **CHAMBER:** 2 string quartets (1913, 1917); Cello Sonata (1915). **VOCAL:** Choral works and songs.

BIBL.: R. Specht, *J. B.: Eine Studie* (Munich, 1921); H. Ullrich, *J. B.* (Vienna, 1968).

Bjelinski, Bruno, Croatian composer and teacher; b. Trieste, Nov. 1, 1909. He studied in Zagreb at the Univ. (law) and at the Academy of Music, serving on the faculty of the latter (from 1945). His music was Romantically inclined.

WORKS: OPERA: *Pčelica Maja* (Maya the Bee; 1952). **ORCH.:** 5 syms.: No. 1, *Simfonija Ljeta* (Summer Sym.; Zagreb, Oct. 15, 1956), No. 2, *In Memoriam Poetae*, with Children's Chorus (1961), No. 3 (1964), No. 4 (1965), and No. 5 (1969); *Serenade* for Trumpet, Piano, Strings, and Percussion (1957); *Mediterranean Sinfonietta* (1959); *Sinfonietta brasileira* (1961); *Sinfonietta concertante* (1967); Horn Concertino (1967). **OTHER:** Chamber music, piano pieces, and songs.

Bjerre, Jens, Danish organist and composer; b. Århus, Oct. 13, 1903; d. Copenhagen, Jan. 3, 1986. He studied piano, organ, and theory at the Copenhagen Cons. (1919–23), and piano with Lévy in Paris. He was organist at Copenhagen's St. Stefanskirke (1933–55) and Garnisonskirke (1955–72).

WORKS: DRAMATIC: 2 ballets: *Kameliadaman* (1958; Copenhagen, March 27, 1960) and *Den hvide souper* (The White Supper; Danish Radio and TV, Dec. 27, 1964); incidental music. **ORCH.:** *Madrigal con Variazioni* (1948; Danish Radio, June 10, 1958); *Ouverture Parisienne* (1949). **CHAMBER:** *Mosaique musicale I* for Flute, Violin, and Cello (1936), *II* for English Horn, Violin, and Cello, (1955), and *III* for Flute, Violin, and Cello (1974); 2 violin sonatinas (1941, 1945); *Duo Concertante* for Cello and Piano (1942); *Serenade* for Flute, Oboe, and Viola (1943); Piano Trio (1946); Sonata for Solo Cello (1947); *Diapsalmata* for Cello and Piano (1953); *Dionysian Suite* for Oboe (1962); Trio for Flute, Cello, and Piano (1969); *Interludium* for Flute and Organ (1980). **ORGAN:** *Toccata con fughetta e ciacone* (1956). **VOCAL:** Choruses and songs.

Bjoner, Ingrid, Norwegian soprano; b. Kraakstad, Nov. 8, 1927. She studied pharmacy at the Univ. of Oslo (graduated, 1951) and pursued vocal training at the Oslo Cons. with Gudrun Boellemose, at the Frankfurt am Main Hochschule für Musik with Paul Lohmann, and in N.Y. with Ellen Repp. After making her operatic debut as the 3rd Norn and Gutrune with the Norwegian Radio in Oslo in 1956, she made her stage debut as Mozart's Donna Anna with the Norwegian National Opera in Oslo in 1957. She sang at the Stockholm Drottningholm Court Theater (1957), the Wuppertal Theater (1957–59), the Deutsche Oper am Rhein in Düsseldorf (1959–61), the Bayreuth Festival (1960), and the Bavarian State Opera in Munich (from 1961). On Oct. 28, 1961, she made her Metropolitan Opera debut in N.Y. as Elsa in *Lohengrin*, remaining on its roster until 1968 and returning again in 1971–72 and 1974–75. In 1967 she sang at London's Covent Garden and in 1974 she returned to N.Y. to sing the Duchess of Parma in the U.S. premiere of Busoni's *Doktor Faust* at Carnegie Hall. In subsequent years, she concentrated her career on European engagements. She also toured throughout the world as a concert singer. Later she served as a prof. at the Royal Danish Cons. of Music in Copenhagen (from 1991) and at the Norwegian Academy of Music in Oslo (from 1992). Bjoner was especially admired for her roles in operas by Wagner, Verdi, and Richard Strauss. She also won praise as Beethoven's Leonore, Iphigenia, and Turandot.

Björlin, (Mats) Ulf (Stefan), Swedish conductor and composer; b. Stockholm, May 21, 1933; d. West Palm Beach, Fla., Oct. 23, 1993. He studied with Igor Markevitch (conducting) in Salzburg and with Boulanger (composition) in Paris. Returning to Stockholm, he pursued an active career as a conductor and composer. After serving as director of music at the Royal Dramatic Theater there (1963–68), he conducted widely in Europe and North America. As a composer, he wrote some effective pieces for the theater.

WORKS: DRAMATIC: *Pinocchio*, children's musical (1966); *Om fem år*, opera (Stockholm, Oct. 27, 1967); *Den stora teatern* (Göteborg, Feb. 25, 1972); *Balladen om Kasper Rosenröd*, opera (Valberg-Karlstad, Nov. 15, 1972); *Kärlekin till Belisa*, radio opera (1981); *Tillfälle gör Tiufven*, opera buffa (1983); *Den främmande kvinnan*, opera (1983–84); incidental music. **ORCH.:** *Ekon* (1967); *Epitaph for Lars Görling* (1967); *Portrait of Raoul Wallenberg*, sym. for 3 Narrators, Choruses, and Orch. (1989; Palm Beach, Fla., April 25, 1990). **OTHER:** *Aft vaemod*, choreographic oratorio (1970); *Piae cantiones et alterae cantiones Septentrionales*, cantata for Soprano, Baritone, Chorus, and Orch. (1979); Wind Quintet (1983).

Björling, Jussi (actually, **Johan Jonatan**), eminent Swedish tenor; b. Stora Tuna, Feb. 5, 1911; d. Siarö, near Stockholm, Sept. 9, 1960. He studied voice with his father, a professional singer, making his first public appearance in 1916 as a member of the Björling Male Quartet, which included his father, David Björling (1873–1926), and 2 other brothers, Johan Olof "Olle" (1909–65) and Karl Gustaf "Gösta" (1912–57), both of whom pursued careers as singers; another brother, Karl David "Kalle" (1917–75), was also a singer. The Björling Male Quartet gave concerts throughout Sweden (1916–19); made an extensive tour of the U.S. (1919–21); then continued to sing in Sweden until 1926. Jussi Björling had an excellent professional training with John Forsell at the Royal Academy of Music in Stockholm. He made his operatic debut as the Lamplighter in *Manon Lescaut* at the Royal Theater in Stockholm on July 21, 1930, and remained there until 1939; also sang as a guest artist with the Vienna State Opera and the Dresden State Opera, and at the Salzburg Festival. He made his professional U.S. debut in a concert broadcast from Carnegie Hall in N.Y. on Nov. 28, 1937, and his first appearance with the Metropolitan Opera as Rodolfo in *La Bohème* on Nov. 24, 1938; he continued to sing there until 1941, when his career was interrupted by World War II. He resumed his appearances at the Metropolitan Opera in 1945 and sang there until 1954, and then again in 1956–57 and 1959. On March 15, 1960, he suffered a heart attack as he was preparing to sing the role of Rodolfo at the Royal Opera House, Covent Garden, London, but in spite of his great discomfort, went through with the performance. He appeared for the last time at a concert in Stockholm on Aug. 20, 1960. Björling was highly regarded for his fine vocal technique and his sense of style. He excelled in Italian and French roles, and also essayed some Russian operas. He wrote an autobiography, *Med bagaget i strupen* (Stockholm, 1945). The Jussi Björling Memorial Archive was founded in 1968.

BIBL.: J. Porter and H. Henrysson, *A J. B. Discography* (comprehensive, with biographical profile; Indianapolis, 1982; 2nd ed., rev., 1993).

Björling, Sigurd, Swedish baritone; b. Stockholm, Nov. 2, 1907; d. Helsingborg, April 8, 1983. He was a student of Louis Condé (1928–30); then of Torsten Lennartson at the Cons. (1933–34) and the Royal Opera School (1934–36) in Stockholm. In 1934 he made his operatic debut as Billy Jackrabbit in *La fanciulla del West* in Stockholm, where he continued to sing regularly until 1973. He also made guest appearances in various European opera centers. In 1950 he made his U.S. debut as Kurwenal with the San Francisco Opera. In 1951 he appeared at London's Covent Garden as Amfortas. On Nov. 15, 1952, he made his Metropolitan Opera debut in N.Y. as Telramund, singing there until 1953.

Bjôrnsson, Árni, Icelandic composer; b. Loni i Kelduhverfi, Dec. 23, 1905; d. Reykjavík, July 3, 1995. He studied theory, composition, piano, and organ at the Reykjavík College of Music; later went to England, where he enrolled at the Royal Manchester College of Music; subsequently returned to Reykjavík, where he joined the faculty of the College of Music. He composed orch. pieces and much choral music in a general Romantic vein.

Blacher, Boris, remarkable German composer; b. Newchwang, China (of half-German, quarter-Russian, and quarter-Jewish ancestry), Jan. 19, 1903; d. Berlin, Jan. 30, 1975. His family moved to Irkutsk, Siberia, in 1914, remaining there until 1920. In 1922 Blacher went to Berlin, where he studied architecture and then took a course in composition with F.E. Koch. From 1948 until 1970 he was prof. at the Hochschule für Musik in West Berlin, and from 1953 to 1970 served as its director. A prolific composer, Blacher was equally adept in classical and experimental forms and procedures. He initiated a system of "variable meters," with time signatures following the arithmetical progression, alternatively increasing and decreasing, with permutations contributing to metrical variety. For the theater he developed a sui generis "abstract opera," incorporating an element of organized improvisation. In 1960 he was appointed director of the Seminar of Electronic Composition at the Technological Univ. in Berlin, and subsequently made ample use of electronic resources in his own compositions.

WORKS: DRAMATIC: OPERAS: *Habemeajaja* (1929; not extant); *Fürstin Tarakanowa* (1940; Wuppertal, Feb. 5, 1941); *Romeo und Julia* (1943; Berlin Radio, 1947); *Die Flut* (1946; Berlin Radio, Dec. 20, 1946; stage premiere, Dresden, March 4, 1947); *Die Nachtschwalbe*, "dramatic nocturne" (Leipzig, Feb. 22, 1948; aroused considerable commotion because of its subject, dealing with prostitutes and pimps); *Preussisches Märchen*, ballet-opera (1949; Berlin, Sept. 23, 1952); *Abstrakte Oper No. 1* (Frankfurt Radio, June 28, 1953; stage premiere, Mannheim, Oct. 17, 1953; rev. version, Berlin, Sept. 30, 1957); *Rosamunde Floris* (Berlin, Sept. 21, 1960); *Zwischenfälle bei einer Notlandung*, "reportage in 2 phases and 14 situations" for Singers, Instruments, and Electronic Devices (1965; Hamburg, Feb. 4, 1966); *200,000 Taler* (Berlin, Sept. 25, 1969); *Yvonne, Prinzessin von Burgund* (1972; Wuppertal, Sept. 15, 1973); *Das Geheimnis des entwendeten Briefes* (1974; Berlin, Feb. 14, 1975). **BALLETS:** *Fest im Süden* (Kassel, Feb. 4, 1935); *Harlekinade* (1939; Krefeld, Feb. 14, 1940); *Das Zauberbuch von Erzerum* (1941; Stuttgart, Oct. 17, 1942; rev. version as *Der erste Ball*, Berlin, June 11, 1950); *Chiarina* (1946; Berlin, Jan. 22, 1950); *Hamlet* (1949; Munich, Nov. 19, 1950); *Lysistrata* (1950; Berlin, Sept. 30, 1951); *Der Mohr von Venedig* (Vienna, Nov. 29, 1955); *Demeter* (1963; Schwetzingen, June 4, 1964); *Tristan* (Berlin, Oct. 10, 1965). **INCIDENTAL MUSIC:** *Romeo and Juliet* (1951); *Lulu* (1952); *Georges Dandin* (1955); *War and Peace* (1955); *Robespierre* (1963); *Henry IV* (1970).

ORCH.: Concerto for 2 Trumpets and 2 String Orchs. (1931); *Kleine Marchmusik* (Berlin, Nov. 22, 1932); *Capriccio* (1933; Hamburg, May 14, 1935); Piano Concerto (Stuttgart, Nov. 13, 1935); *Divertimento* for Wind Instruments (1936; Berlin, Feb. 24, 1937); *Geigenmusik* for Violin and Orch. (1936); *Concertante Musik* (Berlin, Dec. 6, 1937); Sym. (1938; Berlin, Feb. 5, 1939); *Concerto da camera* for 2 Violins, Cello, and Strings (1939); *Hamlet*, symphonic poem (Berlin, Oct. 28, 1940); Concerto for Strings (1940; Hamburg, Oct. 18, 1942); *Partita* for Strings and Percussion (1945); *16 Variations on a Theme of Paganini* (Leipzig, Nov. 27, 1947); Concerto for Jazz Orch. (1947); 2 piano concertos: No. 1 (1947; Göttingen, March 20, 1948) and No. 2 (Berlin, Sept. 15, 1952); Violin Concerto (1948; Munich, Nov. 17, 1950); Concerto for Clarinet, Bassoon, Horn, Trumpet, Harp, and Strings (Berlin, June 14, 1950); *Dialog* for Flute, Violin, Piano, and Strings (1950); *Orchester-Ornament*, based on "variable meters" (Venice Festival, Sept. 15, 1953); *Studie im Pianissimo* (1953; Louisville, Sept. 4, 1954); *Zwei Inventionen* (Edinburgh Festival, Aug. 28, 1954); Viola Concerto (1954; Cologne, March 14, 1955); *Orchester-Fantasie* (1955; London, Oct. 12, 1956); *Hommage à Mozart* (Berlin, Dec. 10, 1956); *Music for Cleveland* (Cleveland, Nov. 21, 1957); *Musica giocosa* (Saarbrücken, April 30, 1959); *Variations on a Theme of Muzio Clementi* for Piano and Orch. (Berlin, Oct. 4, 1961); *Konzertstück* for Wind Quintet and Strings (Donaueschingen, Oct. 19, 1963); Cello Concerto (1964; Cologne, March 19, 1965); *Virtuose Musik* for Violin, 10 Wind Instruments, Percussion, and Harp (1966; Hanover, N.H., Aug. 19, 1967); arrangement of Bach's *Das musikalische Opfer* (1966); *Collage* (1968; Vienna, Oct. 5, 1969); Concerto for Trumpet and Strings (1970; Nuremberg, Feb. 11, 1971); Concerto for Clarinet and Chamber Orch. (1971; Schwetzingen, May 12, 1972); *Stars and Strings* for Jazz Ensemble and Strings (1972; Nuremberg, Jan. 12, 1973); *Poème* (1974; Vienna, Jan. 31, 1976); *Pentagram* for Strings (1974; Berlin, April 4, 1975).

CHAMBER: 5 string quartets: No. 1 (1930; Frankfurt am Main, Dec. 6, 1939), No. 2 (1940; Venice, 1941), No. 3 (1944), No. 4 (1951; Berlin, Jan. 25, 1953), and No. 5, *Variationen über einen divergierenden c-moll-Dreiklang* (1967; Berlin, March 8, 1968); Cello Sonata (1940); *Divertimento* for Trumpet, Trombone, and Piano (Berlin, Jan. 23, 1948); *Divertimento* for 4 Woodwinds (Munich, Sept. 28, 1951); Violin Sonata (1951; Berlin, Jan. 27, 1952); *2 Poems* for Vibraphone, Double Bass, Percussion, and Piano (1957; N.Y., Nov. 14, 1958); *Perpetuum mobile* for Violin (1963); Octet for Clarinet, Bassoon, Horn, and String Quintet (1965; Saarbrücken, Oct. 19, 1966); *4 Ornamente* for Violin and Piano (N.Y., Nov. 5, 1969); Piano Trio (1970); Sonata for 2 Cellos and 11 Instruments (Berlin, Dec. 26, 1972); *Blues espagnola and Rumba philharmonica* for 12 Cellos (1972; Tokyo, Oct. 28, 1973); Duo for Flute and Piano (1972); Quintet for Flute, Oboe, and String Trio (1973); *Tchaikovsky Variations* for Cello and Piano (1974).

PIANO: 2 sonatinas (1940, 1941); *3 pièces* (1943); *Ornamente, 7 Studies* (1950); Sonata (1951); 24 preludes (1974).

VOCAL: *Jazz-Koloraturen* for Soprano, Saxophone, and Bassoon (1929); *5 Sinnsprüche Omars des Zeltmachers* for Voice and Piano (1931); *Der Grossinquisitor*, oratorio (1942; Berlin, Oct. 14, 1947); 4 choruses to texts by Villon (1944); *Es taget vor dem Walde*, cantata (Berlin, June 29, 1946); *Francesca da Rimini* for Soprano and Violin (1954); *Träume vom Tod und vom Leben*, cantata (Wuppertal, June 5, 1955); *13 Ways of Looking at a Blackbird* for Voice and Strings (1957; Vienna, Jan. 11, 1959); *Après-lude*, 4 lieder for Voice and Piano (1958); *Die Gesänge des Seeräubers O'Rourke und seiner Geliebten Sally Brown* for Soprano, Cabaret Singer, Baritone, Speaker, Chorus, and Orch. (1958; Vienna, Oct. 5, 1959); *Requiem* for Soprano, Baritone, Chorus, and Orch. (1958; Vienna, June 11, 1959); *Jüdische Chronik* for Soloists, Chorus, and Orch. (1961; Cologne, Jan. 14, 1966; in collaboration with Dessau, K.A. Hartmann, Henze, and Wagner-Régeny); 5 Negro spirituals for Voice and Instruments (1962; Vienna, March 9, 1963); *Parergon to Eugene Onegin* for Mezzo-soprano and Chamber Ensemble (1966); *Nursery Rhymes* (1967); *For 7* for Soprano, Percussion, and Double Bass (1973).

ELECTRONIC: *Multiple Raumperspektiven* (1962); *Elektronische Studie über ein Posaunenglissando* (1962); *Persische elektronische Impulse* (1965); *Elektronisches Scherzo* (1965); *Musik für Osaka* (1969); *Ariadne*, duodrama for 2 Speakers and Electronics (1971).

BIBL.: F. Burt, "The Teaching and Ideas of B. B.," *Score*, No. 9 (1954); H. Stuckenschmidt, *B. B.* (Berlin, 1973); H. Henrich, *B. B., 1903–1975: Dokumente zu Leben und Werk* (Berlin, 1993); J. Hunkemöller, *B. B., der Jazz-Komponist* (Frankfurt am Main, 1994).

Blachut, Beno, Czech tenor; b. Wittkowitz, June 14, 1913; d. Prague, Jan. 10, 1985. He was a pupil of Luis Kadeřábek at the Prague Cons. (1935–39); in 1938 he made his operatic debut as Jeník in *The Bartered Bride* in Olomouc, where he sang until 1941; then was a leading member of the Prague National Theater; also sang in concerts. He was particularly esteemed for his portrayals of roles in operas by Smetana, Dvořák, and Janáček.

Black, Frank, American conductor; b. Philadelphia, Nov. 28, 1894; d. Atlanta, Jan. 29, 1968. He studied piano with Raphael Joseffy in N.Y.; then devoted himself chiefly to conducting radio orchs.; in 1928 he organized the music dept. of NBC, a post he held until 1948.

Black, Stanley, English pianist and conductor; b. London, June 14, 1913. He studied at the Matthay School of Music in London, and began his career as a jazz pianist and arranger; then was a conductor of the BBC Dance Orch. (1944–52); subsequently worked as a music director for films. In 1968–69 he was principal conductor of the BBC Northern Ireland Orch.; also appeared as a guest conductor with various orchs. in England. In 1971 he served as assoc. conductor of the Osaka Phil. In 1986 he was made an Officer of the Order of the British Empire.

Blackburn, Bonnie, American musicologist; b. Albany, N.Y., July 15, 1939. She studied at Wellesley College (B.A., 1961) and the Univ. of Chicago (M.A., 1963; Ph.D., 1970). She was a research assistant in the music dept. (1963–76) and visiting assoc. prof. at the Univ. of Chicago (1986); she also served as lecturer in the school of music at Northwestern Univ. (1987) and later was a visiting assoc. prof. at the State Univ. of N.Y. at Buffalo (1989–90). In 1988–89 she held a Guggenheim fellowship. In 1971 she married **Edward Lowinsky**, with whom she ed. the vol. *Josquin des Prez: Proceedings of the International Josquin Festival-Conference* (London, 1976). She contributed articles to *The New Grove Dictionary of Music and Musicians* (1980) and ed. *Johannis Lupi Opera Omnia* (3 vols., 1980–89) and *Music in the Culture of the Renaissance and Other Essays* by Edward E. Lowinsky (Chicago, 1989). She also publ. *Music for Treviso Cathedral in the Late Sixteenth Century: A Reconstruction of the Lost Manuscripts 29 and 30* (London, 1987). With Lowinsky and C. Miller, she ed. and tr. *A Correspondence of Renaissance Musicians* (Oxford, 1991).

Blackwood, Easley, American pianist, teacher, and composer; b. Indianapolis, April 21, 1933. He studied piano in his hometown and appeared as a soloist with the Indianapolis Sym. Orch. at age 14; studied composition during summers at the Berkshire Music Center (1948–50), notably with Messiaen in 1949; also with Bernhard Heiden at Indiana Univ. and Paul Hindemith at Yale Univ. (1949–51); received his M.A. from Yale in 1954; then went to Paris to study with Boulanger (1954–56). In 1958 he was appointed to the faculty of the Univ. of Chicago. Blackwood's music is marked by impassioned Romantic éclat and is set in a highly evolved chromatic idiom. He is also an accomplished pianist, particularly notable for his performances of modern works of transcendental difficulty. He publ. *The Structure of Recognizable Diatonic Tunings* (Princeton, N.J., 1986).

WORKS: ORCH.: 5 syms.: No. 1 (1954–55; Boston, April 18, 1958), No. 2 (1960; Cleveland, Jan. 5, 1961), No. 3 for Small Orch. (1964; Chicago, March 7, 1965), No. 4 (1973), and No. 5 (1978); Chamber Sym. for 14 Wind Instruments (1955); Clarinet Concerto (Cincinnati, Nov. 20, 1964); *Symphonic Fantasy* (Louisville, Sept. 4, 1965); Concerto for Oboe and Strings (1966); Violin Concerto (Bath, England, June 18, 1967); Concerto for Flute and Strings (Hanover, N.H., July 28, 1968); Piano Concerto (1969–70; Highland Park, Ill., July 26, 1970). **CHAMBER:** Viola Sonata (1953); 2 string quartets (1957, 1959); Concertino for 5 Instruments (1959); 2 violin sonatas (1960, 1973); *Fantasy* for Cello and Piano (1960); *Pastorale and Variations* for Wind Quintet (1961); Sonata for Flute and Harpsichord (1962); *Fantasy* for Flute, Clarinet, and Piano (1965). **OTHER:** *3 Short Fantasies* for Piano (1965); *Symphonic Episode* for Organ (1966); *Un Voyage à Cythère* for Soprano and 10 Players (1966); Piano Trio (1968); *12 Microtonal Études* for Synthesizer (1982).

Bláha, Ivo, Czech composer and teacher; b. Litomyšl, March 14, 1936. He was a student of Řídký and Sommer at the Prague Academy of Musical and Dramatic Arts (M.A., 1958), where he pursued postgraduate studies with Hlobil (1965–70); he also worked under Herzog and Kabeláč at the experimental studio of the Czech Radio in Plzeň (1969–70). He taught composition (1964–72) and was a reader on the film and television faculty (from 1967) of the Prague Academy of Musical and Dramatic Arts. In 1988 he completed his Habilitation there as a Dozent, and later was head of its dept. of sound creation of its film and television faculty (from 1993).

WORKS: DRAMATIC: Film and television scores. **ORCH.:** *Concerto for Orchestra* (1957); Percussion Concerto (1964); Violin Concerto (1968); *Per archi*, sinfonia (1977). **CHAMBER:** Wind Quintet (1956); 3 string quartets (1957, 1966, 1983); *3 Pieces* for Violin and Piano (1961); *Spring Plays*, suite for Wind Quintet (1962); *Sonatina semplice* for Trombone and Piano (1963); *Solitude*, sonata for Solo Violin (1965); *Music* for 5 Wind Instruments (1965); *Music to Pictures of a Friend* for Flute, Oboe, and Clarinet (1971); Cello Sonata (1972); *2 Inventions* for Flute (1974); *Variations on a Czech Folk Song* for 3 Flutes (1975); Duo for Bass Clarinet and Piano (1975); *With Respect for Old Maestros* for Violin and Piano (1978); *Violin* for Violin (1979); *Sonnets* for Brass Ensemble (1980); *Sonata transparenta* for Flute and Piano (1982); 2 sets of *Zoolessons* for Guitar (1984, 1987); *Imagination* for Violin and Piano (1988); *Sonata introspettiva* for Solo Viola (1989). **KEYBOARD: PIANO:** *3 Toccata Studies* (1967); *Rays* (1976); *Prelude for Cat* (1979). **ORGAN:** *Hymnus* (1980); *Vaults* (1986). **VOCAL:** *What's Beauty in the World*, cantata cycle for Children's Chorus and Chamber Orch. or Wind Quintet or Piano (1958); *Sentences About Life, Death, and Eternal Time* for Men's Chorus (1968); *Cet amour* for Speaker, Flute, Oboe, Clarinet, and Tape (1973–75); *Moravian Lullabies* for Soprano, Flute, and Piano (1982); various children's choral pieces.

Blake, David (Leonard), English composer and teacher; b. London, Sept. 2, 1936. He studied music at Gonville and Caius College, Cambridge (1957–60). After receiving a Mendelssohn scholarship, he studied with Hanns Eisler in East Berlin at the Deutsche Akademie der Künste (1960–61). In 1963–64 he was a Granada Arts Fellow at the Univ. of York, where he then was a lecturer (1964–71), senior lecturer (1971–76), and prof. (from 1976); from 1980 to 1983 he was also head of its music dept. He ed. *Hanns Eisler: A Miscellany* (1995). After composing in a tonal idiom and then in the 12-tone system, he experimented with a variety of styles, becoming drawn toward the use of oriental scales and aleatory methods.

WORKS: OPERAS: *Toussaint* (1976; London, Sept. 28, 1977; rev. 1982; London, Sept. 6, 1983); *The Plumber's Gift* (London, May 25, 1989). **ORCH.:** Sym. for Chamber Orch. (1966); *Metamorphoses* (1971); 2 violin concertos (London, Aug. 19, 1976; London, June 25, 1983); *Sonata alla Marcia* (London, May 17, 1978); *Scherzi ed Intermezzi* (Bedford, Nov. 17, 1984); *Pastoral Paraphrase* for Bassoon and Small Orch. (1986); *Mill Music* for Brass Band (1986); Cello Concerto (1989–93). **CHAMBER:** 3 string quartets (1962, 1973, 1982); *Sequence* for 2 Flutes (1967); Nonet (London, June 21, 1971; rev. 1978); *Scenes* for Cello (1972); *Arias* for Clarinet (1978); *Cassation* for Wind Octet (1979); *Scherzo and 2 Dances* for 7 Players (1981; York, Jan. 16, 1982); Clarinet Quintet (1980; Bradford, Jan. 29, 1981); *Capriccio* for 7 Players (1980; York, Jan. 14, 1981); *Fantasia* for Violin (1984); *Seasonal Variants* for 7 Players (Norwich, Oct. 18, 1985); *Night Music* for Saxophone Quartet (1990). **VOCAL:** 3 choruses, after Robert Frost (1964); *Beata l'Alma* for Soprano and Piano (1966); *What is the Cause?* for Chorus (1967); *Lumina* for Soprano, Baritone, and Orch. (1969); *The Bones of Chuang Tzu* for Baritone and Piano (1972); *In Praise of Krishna* for Soprano and 9 Players (Leeds, March 7, 1973); *From the Mattress Grave* for High Voice and 11 Players, after Heinrich Heine (1978; Durham, Feb. 3, 1979); *Change is Going to Come* for 2 Soloists, Chorus, and 4 Players (1982); *Rise, Dove* for Bass- baritone and Orch. (Manchester, Dec. 21, 1983).

Blake, Ran, American composer and teacher; b. Springfield, Mass., April 20, 1935. He studied at Bard College (B.A., 1960) and at Columbia Univ. (1960–62), where he attended classes in improvisation with William Russo; also took lessons with Gunther Schuller, who inculcated him in "3rd stream" music (1960–67); also took straight jazz instruction at the Lenox School of Jazz. From 1967 he taught at the New England Cons. of Music in Boston. He composed mostly for piano, employing combined jazz-Baroque techniques and sonorities; he also wrote many arrangements and improvisations on contemporary American songs.

Blake, Rockwell (Robert), gifted American tenor; b. Plattsburgh, N.Y., Jan. 10, 1951. He studied voice with Renata Booth as part of his high school education. Following attendance at the State Univ. of N.Y. at Fredonia, he received a scholarship to pursue vocal training at the Catholic Univ. of America in Washington, D.C.; completed his vocal studies in N.Y. He began his career singing with various small opera companies, first attracting notice when he appeared as Lindoro with the Washington, D.C., Opera in 1976; then sang with the Hamburg State Opera (1977–79) and the Vienna State Opera (1978). In 1978 he became the first recipient of the Richard Tucker Award. On Sept. 23, 1979, he made his N.Y. City Opera debut as Count Ory, and on Feb. 2, 1981, his Metropolitan Opera debut in N.Y. as Lindoro. He sang at the Chicago Lyric Opera and at the Rossini Opera Festival in Pesaro in 1983, at the San Francisco Opera in 1984, at the Paris Opéra in 1985, at the Paris Opéra-Comique and the Bavarian State Opera in Munich in 1987, and in Montreal and at the Salzburg Festival in 1989. In 1990 he appeared in the leading tenor role in Pergolesi's *Annibal* in Turin. In 1992 he sang James V in *La Donna del Lago* at Milan's La Scala. He also sang widely in concerts. Blessed with a remarkable coloratura, Blake won notable distinction as a true *tenore di grazia,* excelling in Mozart and Rossini.

Blancafort (de Rosselló), Manuel, Spanish composer; b. Barcelona, Aug. 12, 1897; d. there, Jan. 8, 1987. He studied in Barcelona with Lamote de Grignon. In his music, he cultivated national Catalan subjects while adhering to the impressionistic idiom set in neo-Classical forms. He wrote *Sardana sinfónica* for Orch. (1951); *Rapsódia catalana* for Cello and Orch. (1953); *Evocaciones,* symphonic suite (1969); and a number of piano pieces of a descriptive character.

Blanco, Juan, Cuban composer; b. Havana, June 29, 1920. He studied composition with José Ardévol; after a period of writing in traditional forms, he devoted himself to experimentation, making use of electronic devices with purposive spatial arrangement. In this manner he constructed *Texturas* for Orch. and Tape (1964), 4 sets of *Contrapunto espacial* for different groups spatially distributed (1965–70), and *Vietnam,* soundlike composition (1968).

Blank, Allan, American composer; b. N.Y., Dec. 27, 1925. He studied at the High School of Music and Art in N.Y.; subsequently at the Juilliard School of Music (1945–47), Washington Square College (B.A., 1948), the Univ. of Minnesota (M.A., 1950), and the Univ. of Iowa. He was a violinist in the Pittsburgh Sym. Orch. (1950–52); after teaching instrumental music in N.Y. high schools (1956–65), he taught at Western Illinois Univ. in Macomb (1966–68), Paterson (N.J.) State College (1968–70), Lehman College of the City Univ. of N.Y. (1970–77), and Virginia Commonwealth Univ. in Richmond (from 1978). He was also conductor (1984) and music director (1986–89) of the Richmond Community Orch. In his works, Blank strives for lyrical and dramatic expressivity complemented by clarity of line and richness of content.

WORKS: DRAMATIC: *Aria da capo,* chamber opera (1958–60); *The Magic Bonbons,* opera (1980–83); *The Noise,* opera (1985–86); incidental music to *Othello* (1983) and *Measure for Measure* (1984). **ORCH.:** *Concert Piece* for Band (1960–63); *Music for Orchestra* (1964–67); *Some Thank-You Notes* for Jazz Band (1970); *6 Miniatures and a Fantasia* (1972); *6 Significant Landscapes* for Chamber Orch. (1972–74); *Divertimento* for Tuba and Band (1979); *Kreutzer March* for Band (1981); Concertino for Bassoon and Strings (1984); Concertino for Strings (1987); *Overture for a Happy Occasion* (1987); Concerto for Clarinet and Strings (1990). **CHAMBER:** 3 string quartets (1958, 1981, 1989); Wind Quintet (1968–70); *Bicinium I* for Oboe and Bassoon, and *II* for Clarinet and Bassoon (1974); Trio for Trumpet, Horn, and Trombone (1975); *An American Medley* for Brass Quintet, Flute, and Percussion (1976); *Paganini Caprices* for 4 Horns, 3 Trumpets, 3 Trombones, and Tuba (1976); *Music* for Tubas (1977); *4 Inventions* for Bassoon and Piano (1979); *Fantasy on Cantillation Motives* for Violin, Viola, and Cello (1983); Trio for Flute, Cello, and Piano (1983); 2 Studies for Brass Quintet (1984); Concertino for 5 Players (1984–86); *Bicinium III* for Clarinet and Bass Clarinet (1986), *VI* for Violin and Cello (1993), and *VII* for 2 Violins (1993); *Forked Paths,* suite of 11 miniatures for Trumpet (1988); *Polymorphics* for Double Wind Quintet (1988); Sonata for Solo Violin (1990); *Divertimento* for Woodwind Quintet (1991); *3 Windgrams* for Flute, Clarinet, and Bassoon (1991); *Introduction and 3 Episodes* for Flute, Clarinet, and Bassoon (1991); *Around the Turkish Lady* for Alto Saxophone (1991); *4 Studies* for Contrabass (1992); *3 Bouquets* for Bassoon and Contrabass (1992); *A Twosome Frolic* for Violin and Cello (1993); *Elegy* for Violin and Organ (1993); *Dualisms* for Violin and Organ (1994). **PIANO:** *Rotation* (1959–60); *Restatement of Romance* (1973); Sonata (1992). **VOCAL:** *Esther's Monologue,* cantata for Soprano, Oboe, Viola, and Cello (1970); *Lines from Proverbs* for Chorus (1973); *Coalitions* for Soprano and 6 Instrumentalists (1975); *2 Holy Sonnets by John Donne* for Alto, Oboe, English Horn, Viola, and Harp (1977); *Some Funnies and Poems* for Narrator and Piano (1982); *Lines by Horace* for Chorus (1989); *Peace Cantata* for Chorus and Orch. or Piano (1989); *Friday Evening Service* for Soloist, Chorus, Organ, Flute, and Cello (1990); *A Shout of Praise* for Chorus (1993); *The Tide Rises, the Tide Falls* for Chorus and Piano (1994).

Blankenburg, Walter, German theologian and musicologist; b. Emleben, near Gotha, July 31, 1903; d. Schlüchtern, March 10, 1986. He was born into a family of Lutheran ministers. He received a classical education in Gotha and Altenburg (1914–22), and then pursued training in theology (1922–29) with Büchsel and Althaus in Rostock, Heim in Tübingen, and Barth and Hirsch in Göttingen. He also studied musicology and history with Ludwig and Brandl in Göttingen, with Gurlitt, Besseler, and Ritter in Freiburg im Breisgau, and with Schering and Blume in Berlin before completing his education with Zenck at the Univ. of Göttingen (Ph.D., 1940, with the diss. *Die innere Einheit Bachs Werke*). From 1930 to 1933 he was a music teacher in Rotenburg am Fulda and Kassel, and then was a pastor in Vaake from 1930 to 1937. He also was director of the Kasseler Singgemeinde Musik in Schlüchtern, and then was music director of the Evangelische Landeskirche of Kurhessen-Waldeck. He was ed. of the *Zeitschrift für Hausmusik* (1933–41), co-ed. of *Kirchenchordienst* (1935–42), and an ed. (1941–52) and ed.-in-chief (from 1952) of *Musik und Kirche.* In 1962 he was awarded an honorary doctorate in theology by the Univ. of Marburg. He was the author of the study *Einführung in Bachs h-moll Messe* (Kassel, 1950; 3rd ed., rev., 1974). With A. Dürr, he ed. Bach's *Weihnachtsoratorium* for the Neue Bach-Ausgabe (2nd series, VI, Kassel, 1960). He contributed many articles to journals and other publications, including the vols. *Geschichte der evangelischen Kirchenmusik* (Kassel, 2nd ed., rev., 1965; Eng. tr., 1974, as *Protestant Church Music: A History*) and *Kirchenmusik im Spannungsfeld der Gegenwart* (Kassel, 1968). Blankenburg's study *Johann Walter: Leben und Werk* was ed. by F. Brusniak and publ. posthumously (Tutzing, 1991).

Blanter, Matvei (Isaakovich), Russian composer; b. Pochep, Chernigov district, Feb. 10, 1903. He studied in Moscow with G. Conus; then devoted himself exclusively to the composition of light music. He wrote an operetta, *On the Banks of the Amur* (1939), and some incidental music. Of his songs, the most popular was *Katyusha* (famous during World War II), which combined the melodic inflection of the typical urban ballad with the basic traits of a Russian folk song. Blanter was regarded in Russia as a creator of the new Soviet song style.

BIBL.: V. Zak, *M. B.* (Moscow, 1971).

Blatný, Josef, Czech organist, pedagogue, and composer, father of **Pavel Blatný**; b. Brünn, March 19, 1891; d. there (Brno), July 18, 1980. He studied composition with Janáček at the Brünn Organ School (1909–12), and then was his assistant; subsequently was prof. of organ at the Brno Cons. (1928–56) and teacher of organ improvisation at the Janáček Academy of Music and Dramatic Arts in Brno (1947–55).

WORKS: *Sinfonia brevis* for String Orch. (1957); *2 Symphonic Dances* (1959); Chamber Sym. (1961); 3 violin sonatas (1925, 1957, 1968); 3 string quartets (1928, 1954, 1962); Suite for 2 Flutes, Clarinet, and Bassoon (1947); Piano Trio (1950); Piano Quartet (1968); Piano Sonata (1960); organ pieces; vocal music.

Blatný, Pavel, Czech pianist, conductor, teacher, and composer, son of **Josef Blatný**; b. Brno, Sept. 14, 1931. He began music studies with his father; then had instruction in piano and theory at the Brno Cons. (1950–55) and in musicology at the Univ. of Brno (1954–58); also took composition lessons with Bořkovec at the Prague Academy of Music (1955–59) and attended summer courses of new music at Darmstadt (1965–69); in 1968 he traveled to the U.S. and took lessons in jazz piano and composition at the Berklee College of Music in Boston. He became an exceedingly active musician in Czechoslovakia; wrote a vast number of works, some of them paralleling the development of "3rd-stream music" initiated in the U.S. by Schuller. He also gave countless piano recitals in programs of modern music, conducted a great many concerts, and participated in programs of the Czech Radio. In 1971 he was appointed chief of the music division of the television station in Brno; he also taught at the Janáček Academy of Music and Dramatic Arts in Brno (from 1979). He retired from these posts in 1991. In his later compositions, he turned to "serious" music, albeit with tonal manifestations.

WORKS: DRAMATIC: *Probádky lesa (Studánka a Domeček)* (Forest Tales [The Well and Little House]), 2 television operas for children (1975); 3 musicals. **3RD-STREAM MUSIC:** *Dialogue* for Soprano Saxophone and Jazz Orch. (1959–64); *Per orchestra sintetica* for Jazz and Classic Wind Orch. (1960); Concerto for Jazz Orch. (1962–64); *Étude* for Quarter Tone Trumpet (1964); *Tre per S+H* for Jazz Septet (1964); *10'30"* for Sym. Orch. (1965); *D-E-F-G-A-H-C* for Jazz Orch. (1968); *Quattro per Amsterdam* for Soprano, Chamber Orch., and Jazz Orch. (1969); *3 Pieces for E. Verschuaeren* for Big Band (1971); *Suite for Gustav Brom* (1972); *3 Sketches* for Chorus and Jazz Orch. (1973); *4 Movements* for Big Band (1973); *In Modo Classico* for String Quartet and Jazz Orch. (1973); *In Modo Archaico* for Piano and Jazz Orch. (1974); Concertino for Clarinet and Jazz Orch. (1974); *Picture* for Jazz Orch. (1976); *Trumpeters* for Jazz Orch. (1977); *Chime* for Jazz Orch. (1978); *Intermezzo* for Vocalist and Jazz Trio (1978); *Uno pezzo per due Boemi* for Bass Clarinet and Piano (1981); *Collage* for Jazz Orch. (1981); *Signals* for Big Band (1983); *Nenia* for Jazz Orch. (1985); *Jazz Roll Call* for Jazz Orch. (1986); *Dialogue* for Cello and Jazz Trio (1987); *Litany* for Jazz Orch. (1990). **ORCH.:** *Music* for Piano and Orch. (1955); *Concerto for Orchestra* (1956); Concerto for Chamber Orch. (1958); *Movement* for Strings (1976); *Circle* for Strings (1977); *2 Movements* for Brass Ensemble (1979); *Zvony* (The Bells), symphonic movement (1981); *Hommage à Gustav Mahler* (1982); Sym. (1984); *Collage—hommage à J.S. Bach* (1984); *Nenia for my Mother* (1985); *Jubilee Collage* (1986); *Anti-Variations on a Theme of Antonín Dvořák* (1990). **CHAMBER:** Suite for Winds and Piano (1958); *Suite 12* for Bass Clarinet and Piano (1961); *Debate* for Violin, Accordion, and Guitar (1971); *Scene for Brasses* for Brass Quintet (1972); *2:3* for Wind Quintet (1975); *Due pezzi per quintetto d'ottoni* (1978); *Musica cameralis per Ars cameralis* for Clarinet, Viola, and Piano (1981); *Groping* for Flute and Guitar (1982); *Circle* for Saxophone Quartet (1983); *. . . And a Little Song . . .* for Bass Clarinet and Piano (1986); *Dialogue* for Flute and Piano (1990). **VOCAL:** Cantatas: *The Willow Tree* (1980); *Christmas Eve* (1982); *The Noonday Witch* (1982); *The Water Sprite* (1988); *The Peculiar Loves* (1989); Mass (1993); songs.

Blaukopf, Kurt, Austrian musicologist; b. Czernowitz, Feb. 15, 1914. He studied theory with Wolpe and conducting with Scherchen in Vienna (1932–37); then went to Jerusalem, where he took courses in music history with Gerson-Kiwi (1940–42). He served as ed. of the periodical *Phono* (1954–65); in 1962 he became a lecturer in music sociology at the Vienna Academy of Music; from 1965 he was ed. of the periodical *HiFi Stereophonie* in Vienna. His writings include *Muziksoziologie* (Cologne, 1952; 2nd ed., 1972); *Grosse Dirigenten* (Teufen, 1953; Eng. tr., 1955); *Grosse Virtuosen* (Teufen, 1954; French tr., 1955); *Gustav Mahler, oder Zeitgenosse der Zukunft* (Vienna, 1969; Eng. tr., 1973); with H. Blaukopf, *Die Wiener Philharmoniker: Wesen, Werden, Wirken eines Grossen Orchesters* (Vienna, 1986; 2nd ed., 1992). He ed. *Gustav Mahler: Sein Leben, sein Werk und seine Welt in zeitgenossischen Bildern und Texten* (Vienna, 1976; 2nd ed., 1994; Eng. tr., 1976, as *Gustav Mahler: A Documentary Study*, rev. and enl., 1991); *Musik im Wandel der Gesellschaft: Grundzüge der Musiksoziologie* (Munich, 1982; Eng. tr., 1992, as *Musical Life in a Changing Society: Aspects of Music Sociology*).

BIBL.: I. Bontinck and O. Brusatti, eds., *Festschrift K. B.* (Vienna, 1975).

Blauvelt, Lillian Evans, American soprano; b. Brooklyn, March 16, 1874; d. Chicago, Aug. 29, 1947. She received violin lessons and made her debut at a recital in N.Y.'s Steinway Hall when she was 8; then entered the National Cons. of Music of America there at age 15 to pursue vocal training with Bouhy and Fürsch-Madi; continued studies in Paris with Bouhy before making her operatic debut in Gounod's *Mireille* in Brussels on Sept. 6, 1891. In 1899 she sang before Queen Victoria and in 1902 sang the coronation ode for Edward VII, who presented her with the Coronation Medal. In 1903 she made her first appearance at London's Covent Garden as Gounod's Marguerite. In later years, she appeared mainly in concerts. Following further training with **Alexander Savine**, whom she married in 1914, she created the title role in his opera *Xenia* (Zürich, May 29, 1919). She spent her last years as a voice teacher in N.Y. and Chicago.

Blažek, Zdeněk, Czech composer and teacher; b. Žarošice, May 24, 1905; d. Prague, June 19, 1988. He was a pupil of Petrželka at the Brno Cons. (1924–29) and of Suk at the Prague Cons. (1933–35). Returning to Brno, he was a teacher (1941–61) and director (1947–57) at the Cons., and then a teacher at the Purkyně Univ. (1961–70). His music evolved from Moravian folksongs.

WORKS: OPERAS: *Verchovina* (The Highlands; 1950–51; Brno, 1956); *R.U.R.* (1975). **ORCH.:** Suite for Strings (1934); *Funereal Music* for Strings, 2 Harps, Gong, and Timpani (1968); *Divertimento* for Strings (1971); *Lyric Suite* (1980); Horn Concerto (1981); *Malá*, suite for Chamber Orch. (1983); Bassoon Concerto (1985); Chamber Sym. with Solo Baritone (1986). **CHAMBER:** 8 string quartets (1943, 1947, 1956, 1967, 1969, 1977, 1981, 1986); String Quintet (1949); *4 Romantic Compositions* for Horn and Piano (1952); *4 Compositions* for Violin and Piano (1954); Horn Sonata (1964); Wind Quintet (1971); Violin Sonata (1982). **VOCAL:** 3 cantatas: *Song of My Native Land* (1938), *Ode to Poverty* (1958), and *Home* (1962); Requiem (1978); *Czech Christmas Mass* for Soloists, Chorus, and Orch. (1984); choruses; songs.

Blech, Harry, English violinist and conductor; b. London, March 2, 1910. He received music training at the Trinity College of Music in London and at the Royal Manchester College of Music. He was a violinist in the Halle Orch. in Manchester (1929–30) and the BBC Sym. Orch. in London (1930–36); organized the Blech String Quartet in 1933 (disbanded in 1950). In 1942 he founded the London Wind Players, in 1946 the London Symphonic Players, and in 1949 the London Mozart Players; conducted numerous concerts with these ensembles, mostly in programs of Haydn and Mozart. In 1964 he was made an Officer of the Order of the British Empire and in 1984 a Commander of the Order of the British Empire.

Blech, Leo, eminent German conductor and composer; b. Aachen, April 21, 1871; d. Berlin, Aug. 25, 1958. As a young man, he was engaged in a mercantile career; then studied briefly at the Hochschule für Musik in Berlin; returned to Aachen to conduct at the Municipal Theater (1893–99); also took summer courses in composition with Humperdinck (1893–96). He was subsequently engaged as opera conductor in Prague (1899–1906); then became conductor at the Berlin Royal Opera in 1906; was named Generalmusikdirektor in 1913. In 1923 he became a conductor of the Deutsches Opernhaus in Berlin; in 1924 was with the Berlin Volksoper, and in 1925 with the Vienna Volksoper. In 1926 he returned to Berlin as a conductor with the Staatsoper, remaining there until 1937;

was conductor of the Riga Opera (1937–41). From 1941 to 1949 he conducted in Stockholm. In 1949 he returned to Berlin and served as Generalmusikdirektor of the Städtische Oper, retiring with the title of Generalmusikdirektor in 1953. Blech was considered a fine interpreter of the standard German and Italian repertoire, particularly in the works of Wagner and Verdi. His own music was composed in the Wagnerian tradition; his knowledge and understanding of instrumental and vocal resources enabled him to produce competent operas; however, after initial successes, they suffered almost total oblivion.

WORKS: DRAMATIC: OPERAS: *Aglaja* (1893); *Cherubina* (1894); *Das war ich*, an "opera-idyl" (Dresden, Oct. 6, 1902); *Alpenkönig und Menschenfeind* (Dresden, Oct. 1, 1903; rev. as *Rappelkopf*, Berlin, Oct. 2, 1917); *Aschenbrödel* (Prague, 1905); *Versiegelt* (Hamburg, Nov. 4, 1908). **OPERETTA:** *Die Strohwitwe* (Hamburg, 1920). **ORCH.:** 3 symphonic poems: *Die Nonne, Waldwanderung*, and *Trost in der Natur.* **OTHER:** Choruses; piano pieces; songs.

BIBL.: E. Rychnowsky, *L. B.* (Prague, 1905); idem, *L. B.* (Leipzig, 1909); W. Jacob, *L. B.* (Hamburg, 1931).

Bledsoe, Jules, black American baritone and composer; b. Waco, Texas, Dec. 29, 1898; d. Los Angeles, July 14, 1943. He studied at the Chicago Musical College (B.A., 1919); then in Paris and Rome. Returning to America, he distinguished himself as a fine performer in musical comedies and opera. He sang the central role in the premiere of Jerome Kern's *Show Boat* (1927), appeared in grand opera as Rigoletto and Boris Godunov, and sang the title role in Gruenberg's *Emperor Jones.* As a composer, he wrote an *African Suite* for Orch. and several songs in the manner of Negro spirituals.

Blegen, Judith, American soprano; b. Lexington, Ky., April 27, 1940. She studied violin and voice at the Curtis Inst. of Music in Philadelphia (1959–64). In 1963 she went to Italy, where she studied with Luigi Ricci; then sang at the Nuremberg Opera (1963–66). She made a successful appearance at the Santa Fe Opera on Aug. 1, 1969, in the role of Emily in Menotti's satirical opera *Help! Help! the Globolinks!*, which was written especially for her. She made her Metropolitan Opera debut on Jan. 19, 1970, in N.Y. as Papagena, returning there regularly in subsequent seasons to sing such roles as Zerlina, Marzelline, Gilda, Sophie, Blondchen, Adele, Oscar, and Juliette. In 1975 she made her first appearance at London's Covent Garden, and in 1977 at the Paris Opéra.

Bleyle, Karl, German composer; b. Feldkirch, Vorarlberg, May 7, 1880; d. Stuttgart, June 5, 1969. He studied with Wehrle (violin) and S. de Lange (composition) in Stuttgart and with Thuille (composition) in Munich. He was active as a teacher and a theater conductor in Graz, Weimar, and Munich; in 1923 he returned to Stuttgart. Among his works are: 2 operas, *Hannele und Sannele* (Stuttgart, 1923) and *Der Teufelssteg* (Rostock, 1924); works for Soli, Chorus, and Orch., including *An den Mistral, Lernt Lachen, Mignons Beisetzung, Heilige Sendung, Die Höllenfahrt Christi, Ein Harfenklang, Prometheus, Trilogie der Leidenschaft*, and *Requiem*; numerous orch. pieces, including *Flagellantenzug, Gnomentanz, Siegesouverture, Reinecke Fuchs, Legende*, a Sym., and a Violin Concerto; chamber pieces, including a String Quartet and a Violin Sonata; also songs and piano pieces.

Bliss, Sir Arthur (Drummond), eminent English composer; b. London, Aug. 2, 1891; d. there, March 27, 1975. He studied counterpoint with Charles Wood at the Univ. of Cambridge (Mus.B., 1913), and then pursued training with Stanford, Vaughan Williams, and Holst at the Royal College of Music in London (1913–14). While serving in the British Army during World War I, he was wounded in 1916 and gassed in 1918. After the Armistice, he gained recognition as something of an *enfant terrible* with his *Madame Noy* for Soprano and 7 Instruments (1918) and *Rout* for Soprano and 10 Instruments (1920). With such fine scores as *A Colour Symphony* (1921–22), the *Introduction and Allegro* for Orch. (1926), the Oboe Quintet (1927), and the Clarinet Quintet (1932), he rose to prominence as a composer of great distinction. His music for H.G. Well's film *Things to Come* (1934–35) and the *Music* for Strings (1935) added luster to his reputation, which was further enhanced by his outstanding ballets *Checkmate* (1937), *Miracle in the Gorbals* (1944), and *Adam Zero* (1946). After a sojourn as a teacher in Berkeley, California (1939–41), Bliss served as director of music for the BBC in London (1942–44). In 1950 he was knighted and in 1953 he was made the Master of the Queen's Music. In 1969 he was made a Knight Commander of the Royal Victorian Order and in 1971 a Companion of Honour. G. Roscow ed. *Bliss on Music: Selected Writings of Arthur Bliss (1920–1975)* (Oxford, 1991).

WORKS: DRAMATIC: OPERAS: *The Olympians* (1944–49; London, Sept. 29, 1949); *Tobias and the Angel* (1958–59; BBC-TV, London, May 19, 1960). **BALLETS:** *Checkmate* (Paris, June 15, 1937); *Miracle in the Gorbals* (London, Oct. 26, 1944); *Adam Zero* (London, April 10, 1946); *The Lady of Shalott* (1957–58; Berkeley, Calif., May 2, 1958). **INCIDENTAL MUSIC:** *As You Like It* (1919); *The Tempest* (1921); *King Solomon* (1924). **FILM MUSIC:** *Things to Come* (1934–35); *Conquest of the Air* (1936–37); *Caesar and Cleopatra* (1944); *Men of Two World* (1945); *Presence au combat* (1945); *Christopher Columbus* (1949); *The Beggar's Opera* (1952–53); *Seven Waves Away* (1956). **ORCH.:** *2 Studies* (1920; London, Feb. 17, 1921); *Mêlée fantasque* (London, Oct. 13, 1921); *A Colour Symphony* (1921–22; Gloucester, Sept. 7, 1922; rev. version, London, April 27, 1932); *Twone, the House of Felicity* (London, March 15, 1923); *Elizabethan Suite* for Strings (1923); *Introduction and Allegro* (London, Sept. 8, 1926); *Hymn to Apollo* (Amsterdam, Nov. 28, 1926); *Music* for Strings (Salzburg, Aug. 11, 1935); Piano Concerto (1938–39; N.Y., June 10, 1939); *The Phoenix March: Homage to France, Aug. 1944* (Paris, March 11, 1945); Processional for the coronation of Queen Elisabeth II (London, June 2, 1953); Violin Concerto (1953–54; London, May 11, 1955); *Meditations on a Theme by John Blow* (Birmingham, Dec. 13, 1955); *Edinburgh*, overture (Edinburgh, Aug. 20, 1956); *Discourse* (Louisville, Oct. 23, 1957; rev. version, London, Sept. 28, 1965); *March of Homage in Honour of a Great Man* for Sir Winston Churchill (1961–62; BBC, London, March 30, 1962); Cello Concerto (1969–70; Aldeburgh, June 24, 1970); *Metamorphic Variations* (1972; London, April 21, 1973). **BRASS AND MILITARY BAND:** *Kenilworth Suite* (1936); *The First Guards*, march (1956); *The Belmont Variations* (1962); *The Linburn Air*, march (1964); various fanfares for royal and other occasions. **CHAMBER:** Violin Sonata (c.1914); 4 string quartets: No. 1 (Cambridge, May 30, 1914), No. 2 (1923–24), No. 3 (1940–41; N.Y., Jan. 13, 1944), and No. 4 (Edinburgh, Sept. 1, 1950); Piano Quartet (London, April 22, 1915); Piano Quintet (Paris, Nov. 26, 1919); *Conversations* for Flute, Oboe, Violin, Viola, and Cello (1920; London, April 20, 1921); *Allegro* for 2 Violins, Viola, and Piano (1923–24); *Andante tranquillo e legato* for Clarinet (1926–27); Oboe Quintet (Venice, Sept. 11, 1927); Clarinet Quintet (London, Dec. 19, 1932); Viola Sonata (London, May 9, 1933). **PIANO:** *Bliss* (1923); *Masks* (1924); *Toccata* (c.1925); *2 Interludes* (1925); Suite (1925); *The Rout Trot* (1927); *Study* (1927); Sonata (1952; London, April 24, 1953); *Miniature Scherzo* (1969); *Triptych* (1970); *A Wedding Suite* (1973). **VOCAL:** *Madame Noy* for Soprano and 7 Instruments (1918; London, June 23, 1920); *Rhapsody* for Mezzo-soprano, Tenor, and 7 Instruments (1919; London, Oct. 6, 1920); *Rout* for Soprano and 10 Instruments (London, Dec. 15, 1920); *2 Nursery Rhymes* for Soprano, Clarinet, and Piano (1920); Concerto for Piano, Tenor, Strings, and Percussion (London, June 11, 1921); *The Women of Yueh*, song cycle for Voice and Ensemble (N.Y., Nov. 11, 1923); *Pastoral: Lie Strewn the White Flocks* for Mezzo-soprano, Chorus, Flute, Timpani, and String Orch. (1928–29; London, May 8, 1929); *Serenade* for Baritone and Orch. (1929; London, March 18, 1930); *Morning Heroes*, sym. for Orator, Chorus, and Orch., dedicated to the composer's brother and all others who perished in battle (1929–30; Norwich, Oct. 22, 1930); *The Enchantress*, scene for Contralto and Orch. (Manchester, Oct. 2, 1951); *A Song of Welcome* for Soprano, Baritone, Chorus, and Orch. (London, May 15, 1954); *The Beatitudes,* cantata for Soprano, Tenor, Chorus, Organ, and Orch. (1960–61; Coventry, May 25, 1962); *Mary of Magdala,* cantata for Contralto, Bass, Chorus, and Orch. (1962; Worcester, Sept. 2, 1963); *The Golden Cantata* for Tenor, Chorus, and Orch. (1963; Cambridge, Feb. 18, 1964); *A Knot of Riddles,* song cycle for Baritone and 11 Instruments (Cheltenham, July 11, 1963); *The World Is Charged with the Grandeur of God,* cantata for Chorus, 2 Flutes, 3 Trumpets, and 4 Trombones (Blythburgh, June 27, 1969); *2 Ballads* for Children's or Women's Chorus and Piano or Small Orch. (1970); *Shield of Faith,* cantata for Soprano, Baritone, Chorus, and Organ (1974; Windsor, April 26, 1975); also unaccompanied vocal pieces.

BIBL.: S. Craggs, *A. B.: A Bio-Bibliography* (N.Y., 1988); A. Burn, "From Rebel to Romantic: The music of A. B.," *Musical Times* (Aug. 1991).

Bliss, P. Paul, American organist and composer; b. Chicago, Nov. 25, 1872; d. Oswego, N.Y., Feb. 2, 1933. He studied in Philadelphia; then went to Paris, where he was a pupil of Guilmant (organ) and Massenet (composition). Returning to America, he was active as an organist in Oswego; served as music director with the John Church Co. (1904–10) and the Willis Music Co. (from 1911). He composed 3 operettas: *Feast of Little Lanterns, Feast of Red Corn,* and *In India*; cantatas: *Pan on a Summer Day, 3 Springs,* and *The Mound-Builders*; piano suite, *In October*; many songs and choruses; also compiled *Graded Course for Piano* (4 vols.).

Blitzstein, Marc, significant American composer; b. Philadelphia, March 2, 1905; d. Fort de France, Martinique, Jan. 22, 1964. He studied piano and organ with Sternberg in Philadelphia. In 1921 he entered the Univ. of Pa. on a scholarship, but left the following year when he failed to meet the physical education requirements. He then studied piano with Siloti in N.Y. From 1924 1926 he was a composition student of Scalero at the Curtis Inst. of Music in Philadelphia. After further training with Boulanger in Paris and Schoenberg in Berlin (1926–28), he returned to the U.S. and wrote a few generic instrumental works in either a late Romantic or a more modern, Copland-influenced jazz style. However, he soon turned to creating works for the theater à la Brecht and Weill, in which "art for society's sake" and "social consciousness" of a fervent left-wing persuasion became the norm. Particularly notable was his play in music, *The Cradle Will Rock* (N.Y., June 16, 1937). In 1940–41 and 1941–42 he held Guggenheim fellowships. From 1942 to 1945 he served in the U.S. Army Air Force in England, where he was music director of the American Broadcasting Station for Europe. Upon his return to the U.S., he resumed composing for the theater. However, in the 1950s he was unable to sustain his musical standing as his unique blending of musical theater and opera went out of fashion, as did his penchant for social protest. During the last decade of his life, his works became more conventional. In 1959 he was elected to membership in the National Inst. of Arts and Letters. In 1960 he received a Ford Foundation grant to compose an opera on the subject of Sacco and Vanzetti for the Metropolitan Opera in N.Y., but the work was never finished. Two other operas were also left incomplete. Blitzstein died from injuries sustained after a savage beating by 3 sailors in an alley. Three arias, 1 each from his 3 unfinished operas, were premiered at a memorial concert conducted by Bernstein in N.Y., April 19, 1964. Blitzstein remains best known for his adaptation of Weill's *Die Dreigroschenoper* as *The Threepenny Opera* (Waltham, Mass., June 14, 1952). It opened off Broadway on March 10, 1954, and had a remarkable 6-year N.Y. run, becoming a classic of the American theater.

WORKS: DRAMATIC AND RADIO: *Svarga,* ballet (1924–25); *Jig-Saw,* ballet (1927–28); *Triple Sec,* opera-farce (1928; Philadelphia, May 6, 1929); *Parabola and Circula,* opera-ballet (1929); *Cain,* ballet (1930); *The Harpies,* satirical chamber opera (1931; N.Y., May 25, 1953); *The Condemned,* choral opera (1932); *The Cradle Will Rock,* "play in music" in 10 scenes with "social significance" (1936–37; N.Y., June 16, 1937, composer at the piano); *I've Got the Tune,* "radio song-play" (CBS, N.Y., Oct. 24, 1937); *No for an Answer,* short opera (1938–40; N.Y., Jan. 5, 1941); *The Guests,* ballet (1946–48; N.Y., Jan. 20, 1949; incorporates the unperformed ballet *Show,* 1946); *Regina,* musical theater to Hellman's play *The Little Foxes* (1946–49; tryout, New Haven, Oct. 6, 1949; N.Y. premiere, Oct. 31, 1949; rev. 1953 and 1958 for N.Y. opera house perfs.); *Reuben Reuben,* musical play (1949–55; Boston, Oct. 10, 1955); *Juno,* musical play (1957–59; N.Y., March 9, 1959); *Sacco and Vanzetti,* opera (1959–64; unfinished); *The Magic Barrel,* opera (1962–64; unfinished); *Idiots First,* opera (1962–64; unfinished but completed by L. Lehrman, 1973; piano score, Ithaca, N.Y., Aug. 1974). **INCIDENTAL MUSIC TO**: Shakespeare's *Julius Caesar* (1937), Büchner's *Danton's Death* (1938), Shaw's *Androcles and the Lion* (1946), Hellman's *Another Part of the Forest* (1946), Shakespeare's *King Lear* (2 versions, 1950, 1955), Jonson's *Volpone* (1956), Shakespeare's *A Midsummer Night's Dream* (1958) and *A Winter's Tale* (1958), and Hellman's *Toys in the Attic* (1960). **FILM SCORES:** *Hände* (1927); *Surf and Seaweed* (1931); *The Spanish Earth* (1936–37; in collaboration with V. Thomson); *Valley Town* (1940); *Native Land* (1940–41); *Night Shift* (1942); *The True Glory* (1944–45; not used). **OTHER:** Tr. and adaptation of Weill's *Die Dreigroschenoper* as *The Threepenny Opera* (1950–52; Waltham, Mass., June 14, 1952). **ORCH.:** *Sarabande* (1926); *Romantic Piece* (1930); Piano Concerto (1931; 1st perf. with orch., Brooklyn, Jan. 24, 1986); *Surf and Seaweed,* suite from the film (1931); *Orchestra Variations* (1934; N.Y., Oct. 9, 1988); *Freedom Morning* (London, Sept. 28, 1943); *Native Land,* suite from the film (1946; rev. 1958); *Lear: A Study* (1957–58; N.Y., Feb. 27, 1958; includes music from the 2 incidental scores to *King Lear*). **CHAMBER:** String Quartet, *The Italian* (1930); *Serenade* for String Quartet (1932; in 3 uncontrasted movements all marked Largo); *Discourse* for Clarinet, Cello, and Piano (1933; unfinished). **PIANO:** Sonata (1927); *Percussion Music for the Piano* (1928–29); *Scherzo* (1930); *Piano Solo* (1933); *Le monde libre* (1944); *The Guests,* suite from the ballet (1946–48). **VOCAL:** *Gods* for Mezzo-soprano and Strings, after Whitman (originally for Voice and Piano, 1926; rescored 1927; Philadelphia, Feb. 15, 1928); *A Word Out of the Sea,* cantata for Women's Chorus and Instrumental Ensemble, after Whitman (1928; 3 extant movements); *Is Five,* 5 songs for Soprano and Piano, after e.e. cummings (1929); *Invitation to Bitterness* for Men's Chorus and Supplementary Altos (1939); *The Airborne Symphony,* cantata for Tenor, Bass, Narrator, Men's Chorus, and Orch. (1943–46; N.Y., April 1, 1946, Orson Welles narrator, Bernstein conducting); *This is the Garden,* cantata (1956–57; N.Y., May 5, 1957); *Six Elizabethan Songs* for Voice and Piano (1958); *From Marion's Book,* 7 songs for Voice and Piano, after e.e. cummings (1960).

BIBL.: H. Brant, "M. B.," *Modern Music* (July 1946); R. Dietz, *The Operatic M. B.* (diss., Univ. of Iowa, 1970); S. Elliott, "A Committment to Causes," *N.Y. Times* (Oct. 9, 1988); E. Gordon, *Mark the Music: The Life and Work of M. B.* (N.Y., 1989).

Bloch, André, French composer; b. Wissembourg, Alsace, Jan. 18, 1873; d. Viry-Chatillon, Essome, Aug. 7, 1960. He studied at the Paris Cons. with Guiraud and Massenet; received the Premier Grand Prix de Rome in 1893. He was conductor of the orch. of the American Cons. at Fontainebleau. His works include the operas *Maida* (Aix-les-Baines, April 12, 1909), *Une Nuit de Noël* (1922), *Broceliande* (Paris, Nov. 23, 1925), and *Guignol* (Lyons, March 1, 1936); a ballet, *Feminaland* (1904); the symphonic poems *Kaa* (1933) and *L'Isba nostalgique* (1945); *Les Maisons de l'éternité* for Cello and Orch. (1930); *Concerto-Ballet* for Piano and Orch. (1943); and *Suite palestinienne* for Cello and Orch. (Paris, Nov. 14, 1948).

Bloch, Augustyn (Hipolit), Polish composer; b. Grudziądz, Aug. 13, 1929. After attending the Gdańsk School of Music (1946–50), he studied with Rączkowski (organ; 1950–55) and Szeligowski (composition; 1952–59) at the Warsaw Cons. He was a church organist in Gdańsk and Warsaw (1946–56), and a composer for the theater of the Polish Radio in Warsaw (1954–77). He served as vice-president of the Polish Composers Union (1977–79; 1983–87) and as chairman of the program committee of the Warsaw Autumn festivals (1979–87). His compositions, written in an accessible style, have won several competitions. In 1971 and 1985 he received awards from the Polish Ministry of Culture. In 1981 he was honored with the Polish Composers Union Award.

WORKS: DRAMATIC: *Voci*, ballet (1962; Polish TV, Sept. 20, 1967); *Awaiting*, ballet (1963; Warsaw, Sept. 9, 1964); *The Bullet*, ballet (1965); *Ayelet, Jephta's Daughter*, mystery-opera (1967; Warsaw, Sept. 22, 1968); *Gilgamesh*, ballet (1969); *Pan Żagtoba*, musical (1971); *Very Sleeping Beauty*, opera-ballet-pantomime (1973; Warsaw, Sept. 29, 1974); *The Mirror*, ballet-pantomime (1975). **ORCH.:** Concertino for Violin, Piano, Percussion, and Strings (1958); *Dialoghi* for Violin and Orch. (1964; Warsaw, Sept. 22, 1966); *Enfiando* (Bonn, Oct. 12, 1970); *Layers of Time* for 15 Strings (1978); *Oratorio* for Organ, Strings, and Percussion (1981–82); *Abide with Us, Lord* (1986; Warsaw, Sept. 26, 1987); *Upwards* (1993). **CHAMBER:** *Elegy* for Violin and Piano (1954); *Clarinetto divertente* for Clarinet (1976); *Notes* for Alto Saxophone (1981); *A Journey Through Europe on a Single Ticket* for 2 Pianos and 9 Percussion (1982); *Supplications* for Cello and Piano (1983); *A due* for Saxophone or Bass Clarinet and Vibraphone or Marimbaphone (1984); *Musica* for Clarinet and 4 Strings (1985); Duet for Violin and Cello (1986); *Musica* for 13 Instruments (1988); *Fanfare* for Winds (1991); Trio for Violin, Cello, and Piano (1992). **KEYBOARD: PIANO:** *Karol Szymanowski in memoriam*, variations (1953); *Filigrees* (1978). **ORGAN:** *Fantasia* (1953); Sonata (1954); *Jubilate* (1974); *Forte, piano e forte* (1985). **VOCAL:** *Espressioni* for Soprano and Orch. (1959); *Impressioni poetiche* for Men's Chorus and Orch. (1959); *Meditations* for Soprano, Organ, and Percussion (1961); *Salmo gioioso* for Soprano and 5 Instruments (1970); *Poem About Warsaw* for Reciter, Chorus, and Orch. (1974); *Wordsworth Songs* for Baritone and Chamber Orch. (1975–76; Warsaw, Sept. 20, 1978); *Just Some Music*, song cycle for Soprano and Orch. (1976–77); *Carmen biblicum* for Soprano and 9 Instruments (Witten, April 19, 1980); *Canti* for Chorus and Organ (1984); *For Thy Light Is Come* for Reciter, Chorus, Organ, and Orch. (1987; Hamburg, June 28, 1988); *Exaltabo Te, Domini* for Chorus (Warsaw, June 1, 1988); *Lauda* for Soprano, Alto, Percussion, and 4 Strings (1988); *Litany of Ostra Brama* for Chorus and Orch. (1989); *Thou Shall Not Kill*, meditations for Baritone, Cello, Chorus, and Orch. (1991).

Bloch, Ernest, remarkable Swiss-born American composer of Jewish descent, father of **Suzanne Bloch**; b. Geneva, July 24, 1880; d. Portland, Oreg., July 15, 1959. He studied solfeggio with Jaques-Dalcroze and violin with Louis Rey in Geneva (1894–97); then went to Brussels, where he took violin lessons with Ysaÿe and studied composition with Rasse (1897–99); while a student, he wrote a string quartet and a "symphonie orientale," indicative of his natural attraction to non-European cultures and coloristic melos. In 1900 he went to Germany, where he studied theory with Knorr at the Hoch Cons. in Frankfurt am Main and took private lessons with Ludwig Thuille in Munich; there he began the composition of his first full-fledged sym., in C-sharp minor, with its 4 movements orig. bearing titles expressive of changing moods. He then spent a year in Paris, where he met Debussy; Bloch's first publ. work, *Historiettes au crépuscule* (1903), shows Debussy's influence. In 1904 he returned to Geneva, where he began the composition of his only opera, *Macbeth*, after Shakespeare; another opera, *Jézabel*, on a biblical subject, never materialized beyond a few initial sketches. As a tribute to his homeland, he outlined the orch. work *Helvetia*, based on Swiss motifs, as early as 1900, but the full score was not completed until 1928. During the season 1909–10, Bloch conducted symphonic concerts in Lausanne and Neuchâtel. In 1916 he was offered an engagement as conductor on an American tour accompanying the dancer Maud Allan; he gladly accepted the opportunity to leave war-torn Europe, and expressed an almost childlike delight at the sight of the Statue of Liberty upon docking in the port of N.Y. Allan's tour was not successful, however, and Bloch returned to Geneva; in 1917 he received an offer to teach at the David Mannes School of Music in N.Y., and once more he went to America; he became a naturalized American citizen in 1924. This was also the period when Bloch began to express himself in music as an inheritor of Jewish culture, explicitly articulating his racial consciousness in several verbal statements. His *Israel Symphony*, *Trois poèmes juifs*, and *Schelomo*, a "Hebrew rhapsody" for Cello and Orch., mark the height of Bloch's greatness as a Jewish composer. In America, he found sincere admirers and formed a group of greatly talented students, among them Sessions, Ernst Bacon, George Antheil, Douglas Moore, Bernard Rogers, Randall Thompson, Quincy Porter, Halsey Stevens, Herbert Elwell, Isadore Freed, Frederick Jacobi, and Leon Kirchner. From 1920 to 1925 he was director of the Inst. of Music in Cleveland, and from 1925 to 1930, director of the San Francisco Cons. When the magazine *Musical America* announced in 1927 a contest for a symphonic work, Bloch won 1st prize for his "epic rhapsody" entitled simply *America*; Bloch fondly hoped that the choral ending extolling America as the ideal of humanity would become a national hymn; the work was performed with a great outpouring of publicity in 5 cities, but as happens often with prizewinning works, it failed to strike the critics and the audiences as truly great, and in the end remained a mere by-product of Bloch's genius. From 1930 to 1939 Bloch lived mostly in Switzerland; he then returned to the U.S. and taught classes at the Univ. of Calif. at Berkeley (1940–52); finally retired and lived at his newly-purchased house at Agate Beach, Oreg. In 1937 he was elected a member of the National Inst. of Arts and Letters, and in 1943 of the American Academy of Arts and Letters. In 1947 he was awarded the 1st Gold Medal of the American Academy of Arts and Sciences. In 1952 he received 2 N.Y. Music Critic's Circle awards for his String Quartet No. 3 and *Concerto Grosso No. 2*.

In his harmonic idiom, Bloch favored sonorities formed by the bitonal relationship of 2 major triads with the tonics standing at the distance of a tritone, but even the dissonances he employed were euphonious. In his last works of chamber music, he experimented for the first time with thematic statements of 12 different notes, but he never adopted the strict Schoenbergian technique of deriving the entire contents of a composition from the basic tone row. In his early Piano Quintet, Bloch made expressive use of quarter tones in the string parts. In his Jewish works, he emphasized the interval of the augmented second, without a literal imitation of Hebrew chants. Bloch contributed a number of informative annotations for the program books of the Boston Sym., N.Y. Phil., and other orchs.; he also contributed articles to music journals, among them "Man and Music" in *Musical Quarterly* (Oct. 1933). An Ernest Bloch Soc. was formed in London in 1937 to promote performances of his music, with Albert Einstein as honorary president and with vice-presidents including Sir Thomas Beecham, Havelock Ellis, and Romain Rolland.

WORKS: OPERA: *Macbeth* (1904–09; Paris, Nov. 30, 1910). **ORCH.:** *Vivre-Aimer*, symphonic poem (1900; Geneva, June 23, 1901); *Helvetia, the Land of Mountains and its People*, symphonic fresco (1900–1929; Chicago, Feb. 18, 1932); Sym. in C-sharp minor (1901–02; 1st complete perf., Geneva, 1910); *Hiver-printemps*, symphonic poems (1904–05; Geneva, Jan. 27, 1906); *Trois Poèmes juifs* (1913; Boston, March 23, 1917); *Schelomo*, Hebrew rhapsody for Cello and Orch. (1915–16; N.Y., May 3, 1917); Suite for Viola and Orch. (1919); *In the Night* (1922; orchestration of piano piece); *Poems of the Sea* (1922; orchestration of piano piece); *Concerto Grosso* No. 1 for Strings and Piano Obbligato (1924–25; Cleveland, June 1, 1925) and No. 2 for String Quartet and String Orch. (1952; BBC, London, April 11, 1953); *4 Episodes* for Chamber Orch. (1926); *Voice in the Wilderness*, symphonic poem with Cello Obbligato (1936; Los Angeles, Jan. 21, 1937); *Evocations*, suite (1937; San Francisco,

Feb. 11, 1938); Violin Concerto (1937–38; Cleveland, Dec. 15, 1938); *Bal Shem Suite* for Violin and Orch. (1939; N.Y., Oct. 19, 1941; orchestration of 1923 chamber piece); *Suite symphonique* (1944; Philadelphia, Oct. 26, 1945); *Concerto symphonique* for Piano and Orch. (1947–48; Edinburgh, Sept. 3, 1949); Concertino for Flute, Viola, and Strings (1948); *Scherzo fantasque* for Piano and Orch. (1948; Chicago, Dec. 2, 1950); *Suite hébraïque* for Viola or Violin and Orch. (1951; Chicago, Jan. 1, 1953); *In Memoriam* (1952); *Sinfonia breve* (1952; BBC, London, April 11, 1953); Sym. for Trombone and Orch. (1953–54; Houston, April 4, 1956); Sym. in E-flat major (1954–55; London, Feb. 15, 1956); *Proclamation* for Trumpet and Orch. (1955); *Suite Modale* for Flute and Strings (1956; Kentfield, Calif., April 11, 1965); *2 Last Poems ("Maybe")* for Flute and Chamber Orch.: *Funeral Music* and *Life Again?* (1958; anticipatory of death from terminal cancer). **CHAMBER:** 5 string quartets (1916, 1945, 1952, 1953, 1956); Suite for Viola and Piano (1919; also orchestrated); 2 violin sonatas (1920; *Poème mystique*, 1924); 2 piano quintets: No. 1 with the use of quarter tones (N.Y., Nov. 11, 1923) and No. 2 (N.Y., Dec. 6, 1957); *Baal Shem*, "3 Pictures of Chassidic Life" for Violin and Piano (1923; orchestrated 1939); *From Jewish Life* for Cello and Piano (1924); *Méditation hébraïque* for Cello and Piano (1924); *3 Nocturnes* for Piano Trio (1924); *Nuit exotique* for Violin and Piano (1924); *In the Mountains* for String Quartet (1925); *Night* for String Quartet (1925); *Paysages* for String Quartet (1925); *Prelude* for String Quartet (1925); *Abodah* for Violin and Piano (1929); *Melody* for Violin and Piano (1929); *2 Pieces* for String Quartet (1938, 1950); *Meditation and Processional* for Viola and Piano (1951); 3 suites for Cello (1956, 1956, 1957); 2 suites for Violin (1958); Suite for Viola (1958; last movement incomplete). **KEYBOARD: PIANO:** *Ex-Voto* (1914); *4 Circus Pieces* (1922); *In the Night* (1922; orchestrated); *Poems of the Sea* (1922; orchestrated); *Danse sacrée* (1923); *Enfantines* (1923); *Nirvana* (1923); *5 Sketches in Sepia* (1923); Sonata (1935); *Visions et Prophéties* (1936; piano reduction of parts of *Voice in the Wilderness*). **ORGAN:** *6 Preludes* (1949); *4 Wedding Marches* (1950). **VOCAL:** *Historiettes au crépuscule*, 4 songs for Mezzo-soprano and Piano (1903); *Poèmes d'automne*, songs for Mezzo-soprano and Orch. (1906); *Prelude and 2 Psalms* (Nos. 114 and 137) for Soprano and Orch. (1912–14); *Psalm 22* for Alto or Baritone and Orch. (1914); *Israel*, sym. for 5 Soloists and Orch. (1912–16; N.Y., May 3, 1917, composer conducting); *America: An Epic Rhapsody* for Chorus and Orch. (1926; N.Y., Dec. 20, 1928); *Avodath Hakodesh* for Baritone, Chorus, and Orch. (1930–33; Turin, Jan. 12, 1934).

BIBL.: G. Gatti, "E. B.," *Musical Quarterly* (Jan. 1921); R. Sessions, "E. B.," *Modern Music*, V/1 (1927); R. Stackpole, "E. B.," ibid.; M. Chiesa, *Bibliografia delle opere musicali di E. B.* (Turin, 1931); idem, *E. B.* (Turin, 1933); D. Newlin, "The Later Works of E. B.," *Musical Quarterly* (Oct. 1947); D. Kushner, "A Commentary on E. B.'s Symphonic Works," *Radford Review* (Summer 1967); M. Griffel, "Bibliography of Writings on E. B.," *Current Musicology*, 6 (1968); D. Kushner, "Catalogue of the Works of E. B.," *American Music Teacher* (Feb./March 1969); A. Knapp, "The Jewishness of B.: Subconscious or Conscious," *Proceedings of the Royal Music Association* (1970/71); D. Kushner, *E. B. and His Music* (Glasgow, 1973); S. Bloch and I. Heskes, *E. B., Creative Spirit: A Program Source Book* (N.Y., 1976); R. Strassburg, *E. B., Voice in the Wilderness: A Biographical Study* (Los Angeles, 1977); C. Wheeler, "E. B.'s Solo Piano Music," *American Music Teacher* (Nov./Dec. 1980); D. Sills, "B. Manuscripts at the University of California," *Notes* (Sept. 1985); idem, "B. Manuscripts at the Library of Congress," ibid. (June 1986); D. Kushner, *E. B.: A Guide to Research* (N.Y., 1988); W. Matz, *Musica humana: Versuch über E. B.s Philosophie der Musik* (Frankfurt am Main and N.Y., 1988).

Bloch, Suzanne, Swiss-American lutenist and harpsichordist, daughter of **Ernest Bloch;** b. Geneva, Aug. 7, 1907. She went to the U.S. with her father; studied there with him and with Sessions; then in Paris with Boulanger. She became interested in early music, which she championed on original instruments. With I. Heskes, she publ. *Ernest Bloch, Creative Spirit: A Program Source Book* (N.Y., 1976).

Blochwitz, Hans Peter, German tenor; b. Garmisch-Partenkirchen, Sept. 28, 1949. He received an engineering degree in computer science; after singing in amateur choruses and occasional concerts, he pursued a vocal career. In 1984 he made his operatic debut as Lensky at the Frankfurt am Main Opera; then sang in Brussels, Geneva, Hamburg, Milan, and Vienna. In 1987 he made his U.S. debut as the Evangelist in Bach's *St. Matthew Passion* with Solti and the Chicago Sym. Orch. In 1989 he made his first appearance at London's Covent Garden as Mozart's Ferrando, and that same year made his U.S. operatic debut in San Francisco as Mozart's Idamante. On Sept. 27, 1990, he appeared as Don Ottavio at his debut at the Metropolitan Opera in N.Y., and the following month made his U.S. recital debut in La Jolla, California; subsequently sang in opera and concert on both sides of the Atlantic. His impressive oratorio and concert repertoire ranges from Bach and Handel to Zemlinsky and Britten, with a noteworthy regard for the lieder of Schubert and Schumann. Among his operatic roles are Mozart's Tito, Tamino, and Belmonte, as well as Rossini's Count Almaviva and Donizetti's Nemorino.

Block, Michel, Belgian-born American pianist and teacher; b. Antwerp, June 12, 1937. He grew up in Mexico; made his debut as a soloist with the National Orch. in Mexico when he was 16; then went to N.Y., where he studied at the Juilliard School of Music. He made his N.Y. debut in 1959; then made a successful career as soloist with orchs. in the U.S. and Europe. In 1978 he became a teacher at the Indiana Univ. School of Music in Bloomington. In 1987 he became a naturalized American citizen.

Blom, Eric (Walter), eminent English writer on music; b. Bern, Switzerland, Aug. 20, 1888; d. London, April 11, 1959. He was of Danish and British descent on his father's side; his mother was Swiss. He was educated in England. He was the London music correspondent for the *Manchester Guardian* (1923–31); then was the music critic of the *Birmingham Post* (1931–46) and of *The Observer* in 1949; ed. *Music & Letters* from 1937 to 1950 and from 1954 to the time of his death; he was also ed. of the Master Musicians series. In 1955 he was made a Commander of the Order of the British Empire in recognition of his services to music and received the honorary degree of D.Litt. from Univ. of Birmingham. In his writings, Blom combined an enlightened penetration of musical aesthetics with a literary capacity for presenting his subjects and stating his point of view in a brilliant journalistic manner. In his critical opinions, he never concealed his disdain for some composers of great fame and renown, such as Rachmaninoff. In 1946 he was entrusted with the preparation of a newly organized and greatly expanded ed. of *Grove's Dictionary of Music and Musicians*, which was brought out under his editorship in 1954, in 9 vols., and for which Blom himself wrote hundreds of articles and tr. entries by foreign contributors. In 1946 Blom publ. his first lexicographical work, *Everyman's Dictionary of Music*, which went through several eds. before being thoroughly rev. by D. Cummings in 1988 as *The New Everyman Dictionary of Music*. His other books include *Stepchildren of Music* (1923); *The Romance of the Piano* (1927); *A General Index to Modern Musical Literature in the English Language* (1927; indexes periodicals for the years 1915–26); *The Limitations of Music* (1928); *Mozart* (1935; 6th ed., rev., 1974 by J. Westrup); *Beethoven's Pianoforte Sonatas Discussed* (1938); *A Musical Postbag* (1941; collected essays); *Music in England* (1942; rev. 1947); *Some Great Composers* (1944); *Classics, Major and Minor, with Some Other Musical Ruminations* (London, 1958).

Blomberg, Erik, Swedish composer and teacher; b. Järnskog, May 6, 1922. He was a student of Erland von Koch and Gunnar Bucht at the Stockholm Musikhögskolan (graduated, 1954); then devoted himself to composing and teaching. His compositions are in a progressive, post-Webern style.

WORKS: ORCH.: 8 syms.: No. 1, *4 dramatiska skisser*

(1966), No. 2, *3 studier i melodik* (1968), No. 3, *Associationskedjor* (1971), No. 4 (1973), No. 5 (1974), No. 6 (1982), No. 7 (1984), and No. 8, *Liten* (1992); *Dialog* for Piano and Orch. (1969); *Uppsaliensisk festmusik 1977* for Strings (1976); *Flykt* (1979); *Intoning* (1981); *Uttoning* (1981); *Sjuttonårsmelodik* (1992); *Artonårsmelodik* for Violin and Orch. (1992); *Chaconne* (1993); *Dansscen* (1993); *Lek* (1993); *Kväde 3* (1993); *Polonäs* (1994). **OTHER:** *Kompriment 1–20* for Various Instrumental Formations, ranging from small groups to orch. (1971–78); chamber music; piano pieces; much vocal music, including choral works and songs.

Blomdahl, Karl-Birger, significant Swedish composer; b. Växjö, Oct. 19, 1916; d. Kungsängen, near Stockholm, June 14, 1968. He studied composition with Hilding Rosenberg and conducting with Tor Mann in Stockholm; in 1946 he traveled in France and Italy on a state stipend; in 1954–55 he attended a seminar at Tanglewood on a grant of the American-Scandinavian Foundation. Returning to Sweden, he taught composition at the Stockholm Musikhögskolan (1960–64); in 1964 he was appointed music director at the Swedish Radio. He was an organizer (with Bäck, Carlid, Johanson, and Lidholm) of a "Monday Group" in Stockholm, dedicated to the propagation of an objective and abstract idiom as distinct from the prevalent type of Scandinavian romanticism. Blomdahl's early works are cast in a neo-Classical idiom, but he then turned to more advanced techniques, including the application of electronic resources. His 3rd Sym., *Facetter* (Facets), utilizes dodecaphonic techniques. In 1959 he brought out his opera *Aniara,* which made him internationally famous; it pictures a pessimistic future when the remnants of the inhabitants of the planet Earth, devastated by atomic wars and polluted by radiation, are forced to emigrate to saner worlds in the galaxy; the score employs electronic sounds, and its thematic foundation is derived from a series of 12 different notes and 11 different intervals. At the time of his death, Blomdahl was working on an opera entitled *The Saga of the Great Computer,* incorporating electronic and concrete sounds, and synthetic speech.

WORKS: DRAMATIC: *Vaknatten* (The Wakeful Night), theater music (1945); *Aniara,* opera (1957–59; Stockholm, May 31, 1959); *Minotaurus,* ballet (Stockholm, April 5, 1958); *Spel för åtta* (Game for 8), ballet (Stockholm, June 8, 1962; also as a choreographic suite for Orch., 1964); *Herr von Hancken,* comic opera (Stockholm, Sept. 2, 1965). **ORCH.:** *Symphonic Dances* (Göteborg, Feb. 29, 1940); Concert Overture (Stockholm, Feb. 14, 1942); Viola Concerto (Stockholm, Sept. 7, 1944); 3 syms.: No. 1 (1944; Stockholm, Jan. 26, 1945), No. 2 (1947; Stockholm, Dec. 12, 1952), and No. 3, *Facetter* (Facets; 1950; Frankfurt am Main, June 24, 1951); *Concerto Grosso* (Stockholm, Oct. 2, 1945); Concerto for Violin and Strings (Stockholm, Oct. 1, 1947); *Pastoral Suite* for Strings (1948); *Prelude and Allegro* for Strings (1949); Chamber Concerto for Piano, Winds, and Percussion (Stockholm, Oct. 30, 1953); *Sisyfos,* choreographic suite (Stockholm, Oct. 20, 1954; also as a ballet, Stockholm, April 18, 1957); *Fioriture* (Cologne, June 17, 1960); *Forma ferritonans* (Oxelösund, June 17, 1961). **CHAMBER:** Trio for Oboe, Clarinet, and Bassoon (1938); 2 string quartets (1939, 1948); 2 suites for Cello and Piano (1944, 1945); String Trio (1945); *Little Suite* for Bassoon and Piano (1945); *Dance Suite No. 1* for Flute, Violin, Viola, Cello, and Percussion (1948) and *No. 2* for Clarinet, Cello, and Percussion (1951); Trio for Clarinet, Cello, and Piano (1955). **PIANO:** *3 Polyphonic Pieces* (1945). **VOCAL:** *I speglarnas sal* (In the Hall of Mirrors), oratorio for Soloists, Chorus, and Orch. (1951–52; Stockholm, May 29, 1953); *Anabase* for Baritone, Narrator, Chorus, and Orch. (Stockholm, Dec. 14, 1956); *. . . resan i denna natt* (. . . the voyage in this night), cantata for Soprano and Orch. (Stockholm, Oct. 19, 1966). **ELECTRONIC:** *Altisonans* (1966).

BIBL.: G. Bucht, ed., *"Facetter" av och om K.-B. B.* (Stockholm, 1970; contains a complete catalogue of works with dates of 1st perfs.); R. Inglefield, "K.-B. B.: A Portrait," *Musical Quarterly* (Jan. 1972).

Blomstedt, Herbert (Thorson), prominent American-born Swedish conductor; b. Springfield, Mass. (of Swedish parents), July 11, 1927. He took courses at the Stockholm Musikhögskolan and at the Univ. of Uppsala; after conducting lessons with Igor Markevitch in Paris, he continued his training with Jean Morel at the Juilliard School of Music in N.Y. and with Leonard Bernstein at the Berkshire Music Center in Tanglewood, where he won the Koussevitzky Prize in 1953. In 1954 he made his professional conducting debut with the Stockholm Phil., then was music director of the Norrköping Sym. Orch. (1954–61); he subsequently held the post of first conductor of the Oslo Phil. (1962–68) while being concurrently active as a conductor with the Danish Radio Sym. Orch. in Copenhagen, where he served as chief conductor from 1967 to 1977. From 1975 to 1985 he was chief conductor of the Dresden Staatskapelle, with which he toured Europe and the U.S. (1979, 1983). From 1977 to 1983 he was chief conductor of the Swedish Radio Sym. Orch. in Stockholm. From 1985 to 1995 he was music director of the San Francisco Sym., leading it at its 75th-anniversary gala concert in 1986 and on a tour of Europe in 1987. In 1996 he became chief conductor of the North German Radio Sym. Orch. in Hamburg, and in 1998 music director of the Gewandhaus Orch. in Leipzig. He also appeared as a guest conductor with principal orchs. of the world.

Bloomfield, Theodore (Robert), American conductor; b. Cleveland, June 14, 1923. He studied conducting with Maurice Kessler and piano at the Oberlin (Ohio) College-Cons. of Music (Mus.B., 1944); then took courses in conducting at the Juilliard Graduate School in N.Y. with Edgar Schenkman; also studied piano with Claudio Arrau and conducting with Pierre Monteux. In 1946–47 he was apprentice conductor to George Szell at the Cleveland Orch.; then conducted the Cleveland Little Sym. and the Civic Opera Workshop (1947–52). He was subsequently music director of the Portland (Oreg.) Sym. (1955–59) and of the Rochester (N.Y.) Phil. (1959–63). He then was first conductor of the Hamburg State Opera (1964–66) and Generalmusikdirektor of Frankfurt am Main Opera (1966–68). From 1975 to 1982 he was chief conductor of the (West) Berlin Sym. Orch.

Blount, Herman. See **Sun Ra.**

Blum, Robert (Karl Moritz), Swiss composer and teacher; b. Zürich, Nov. 27, 1900; d. there, Dec. 10, 1994. He was a student of Andreae, Baldegger, Jarnach, Laquai, and Vogler at the Zürich Cons. (1912–22). After attending Busoni's master class in composition at the Prussian Academy of Arts in Berlin (1923), he returned to Switzerland and conducted various amateur orchs. and choirs. From 1943 to 1976 he taught counterpoint and composition at the Zürich Cons.

WORKS: DRAMATIC: *Amarapura,* opera (1924); film music. **ORCH.:** 10 syms. (1924–80); *4 Partite* (1929, 1935, 1953, 1967); *Passionskonzert* for Organ and Strings (1943); *Lamentatio angelorum* for Chamber Orch. (1943); *Overture on Swiss Folk Songs* (1944); Viola Concerto (1951); *Concerto for Orchestra* (1955); Oboe Concerto (1960); *Christ ist erstanden* (1962); Triple Concerto for Violin, Oboe, Trumpet, and Chamber Orch. (1963); *Concertante Symphonie* for Wind Quintet and Chamber Orch. (1964). **CHAMBER:** 3 string quartets; Flute Quartet (1963); Sonata for Flute and Violin (1963); *Divertimento* for 10 Instruments (1966); *Le Tombe di Ravenna* for 11 Winds (1968); Quartet for Clarinet and String Trio (1970); piano pieces; organ music. **VOCAL:** Oratorios; cantatas; Psalms; hymns; songs.

BIBL.: G. Fierz, *R. B.: Leben und Werk* (Zürich, 1967); G. Lehmann, *Zur Musik von R. B.* (Baden, 1973).

Blume, Friedrich, eminent German musicologist and editor; b. Schlüchtern, Jan. 5, 1893; d. there, Nov. 22, 1975. He was the son of a Prussian government functionary. He first studied medicine in Eisenach; in 1911 he went to the Univ. of Munich, where he began musicological studies; then went to the univs. of Leipzig and Berlin. During World War I, he served in the German army; he was taken prisoner by the British and spent

3 years in a prison camp in England. In 1919 he resumed his studies at the Univ. of Leipzig, where he took his Ph.D. in 1921 with the diss. *Studien zur Vorgeschichte der Orchestersuite im 15. und 16. Jahrhundert* (publ. in Leipzig, 1925); in 1923 he became a lecturer in music at the Univ. of Berlin; in 1925 he completed his Habilitation there with *Das monodische Prinzip in der protestantischen Kirchenmusik* (publ. in Leipzig, 1925); was made Privatdozent there that same year; also lectured in music history at the Berlin-Spandau School of Church Music from 1928 to 1934. In 1934 he joined the faculty of the Univ. of Kiel, where he was prof. from 1938 until his retirement in 1958; was then made prof. emeritus. In 1952 he was made a corresponding member of the American Musicological Soc. Blume was an authority on Lutheran church music; his *Die evangelische Kirchenmusik* was publ. in Bücken's *Handbuch der Musikwissenschaft*, X (1931; 2nd ed., rev., as *Geschichte der evangelischen Kirchenmusik*, 1965; Eng. tr., 1974, as *Protestant Church Music: A History*). He prepared a collected edition of the works of M. Praetorius (21 vols., Berlin, 1928–41); was general ed. of Das Chorwerk, a valuable collection of early polyphonic music (1929–38); also ed. of Das Erbe deutscher Musik (1935–43). In 1943 he was entrusted with the preparation of the monumental encyclopedia *Die Musik in Geschichte und Gegenwart* (14 vols., Kassel, 1949–68); following its publication, he undertook the further task of preparing an extensive supplement, which contained numerous additional articles and corrections; its publication was continued after his death by his daughter, Ruth Blume. He also wrote *Wesen und Werden deutscher Musik* (Kassel, 1944); *Johann Sebastian Bach im Wandel der Geschichte* (Kassel, 1947; Eng. tr., 1950, as *Two Centuries of Bach*); *Goethe und die Musik* (Kassel, 1948); *Was ist Musik?* (Kassel, 1959); *Umrisse eines neuen Bach-Bildes* (Kassel, 1962). His life's work was a study in the practical application of his vast erudition and catholic interests in musicological scholarship.

BIBL.: A. Abert and W. Pfannkuch, eds., *Festschrift F. B. zum 70. Geburtstag* (Kassel, 1963); G. Feder, "F. B. zum 80. Geburtstag," and G. Henle, "Zum 80. Geburtstag von F. B.," in *Haydn Studien* (Jan. 1973).

Blumenfeld, Harold, American composer; b. Seattle, Oct. 15, 1923. He studied composition with Bernard Rogers at the Eastman School of Music in Rochester, N.Y. (1941–43) and with Hindemith at Yale Univ. (B.M., 1949; M.M., 1950). He also studied conducting with Robert Shaw and Leonard Bernstein, and operatic stage direction with Boris Goldovsky at the Berkshire Music Center at Tanglewood, and in 1948–49 he attended the Salzburg Mozarteum and the Univ. and Cons. in Zürich. In 1951 he joined the faculty of Washington Univ. in St. Louis, where he was director of its opera studio until 1971. In 1971–72 he was a visiting prof. at Queens College of the City Univ. of N.Y., and then was again on the faculty of Washington Univ. from 1972 to 1989. Blumenfeld has concentrated on composing various vocal scores. His style is thoroughly contemporary in nature.

WORKS: OPERAS: *Amphitryon 4* (1962); *Fritzi* (1979); *Fourscore: An Opera of Opposites* (1980–86); *Breakfast Waltzes* (1991; St. Louis, March 25, 1994); *Seasons in Hell: A Life of Rimbaud* (1992–94; Cincinnati, Feb. 8, 1996). **ORCH.:** *Miniature Overture* (1958); *Contrasts* (1961–62); *Illuminations*, symphonic fragments after Rimbaud (1992; Cincinnati, April 15, 1993). **CHAMBER:** *Transformations* for Piano (1963); *Expansions* for Woodwind Quintet (1964); *Movements* for Brass Septet (1965). **VOCAL:** *See Here the Fallen* for Chorus and Orch. (1943); *3 Scottish Poems* for Men's Voices (1948–50); *War Lament* for Chorus and Guitar (1970); *Song of Innocence* for Tenor, Mezzo-soprano, Large Chorus, Chamber Chorus, and Orch. (1973); *Rilke* for Voice and Guitar (1975); *Circle of the Eye* for Medium Voice and Piano (1975); *Starfires* for Mezzo-soprano, Tenor, and Orch. (1975); *La vie antérieure* for Baritone, Mezzo-soprano, Tenor, and 13 Instruments (1976); *Voyages* for Baritone, Viola, Guitar, and 2 Percussion (1977); *Silentium* for Mezzo-soprano and Piano (1979); *La voix reconnue* for Tenor, Soprano, and Chamber Ensemble (1979); *La face cendrée* for Mezzo-soprano, Cello, and Piano (1981); *Charioteer of Delphi* for Mezzo-soprano or Baritone, Guitar, and Viola (1985); *Un carnet du damné* for Mezzo-soprano and Chamber Ensemble (1987); *Ange de flamme et de glace* for Baritone, 6 Instruments, and Tape (1990); *Mythologies* for Baritone, Speaker, and 7 Instruments (1991).

Blumental, Felicja, Polish-born Brazilian pianist; b. Warsaw, Dec. 28, 1911; d. Tel Aviv, Dec. 31, 1991. She studied composition with Szymanowski and piano with Drzewiecki and Joseph Goldberg at the Warsaw Cons. In 1942 she emigrated to Brazil and became a naturalized Brazilian citizen; in 1962 she returned to Europe. She became particularly known for her performances of works by rarely-heard composers of the past, especially Clementi, Czerny, and Hummel. She also commissioned scores from Villa-Lobos, Lutoslawski, and Penderecki.

Blumer, Theodor, German conductor and composer; b. Dresden, March 24, 1881; d. Berlin, Sept. 21, 1964. He studied at the Dresden Cons. He was active as a pianist, and from 1925 to 1931 as a conductor on Dresden Radio. From 1931 to 1942 he conducted radio broadcasts in Leipzig. He wrote several light operas, among them *Der Fünf-Uhr-Tee* (Dresden, 1911) and *Trau schau wem!*; also composed 3 syms.; several overtures; a considerable amount of chamber music, including duo sonatas, trios, quartets, quintets, and sextets, and a goodly amount of songs.

Boatwright, Helen (née **Strassburger**), American soprano and teacher; b. Sheboygan, Wis., Nov. 17, 1916. She began her training with Anna Shram Irving, and later studied with Marion Sims at Oberlin (Ohio) College. After making her operatic debut as Anna in an English language production of Nicolai's *Die lustigen Weiber von Windsor* at the Berkshire Music Center in 1942, she appeared in opera in Austin and San Antonio (1943–45). In 1943 she married **Howard Boatwright**, with whom she often appeared in concert. She taught in New Haven (1945–64), and in 1965 became adjunct prof. of voice at Syracuse Univ. In 1967 she made her N.Y. recital debut at Town Hall. She was prof. of voice at the Eastman School of Music in Rochester, N.Y. (1972–79) and at the Peabody Cons. of Music in Baltimore (1987–89); also gave master classes.

Boatwright, Howard (Leake, Jr.), American violinist, conductor, and composer; b. Newport News, Va., March 16, 1918. He studied violin with Israel Feldman in Norfolk. At age 17, he made his debut as soloist with the Richmond (Va.) Sym. Orch. From 1943 to 1945 he taught violin at the Univ. of Texas in Austin; then studied composition with Hindemith at Yale Univ. (1945–48), where he subsequently taught (1948–64); concurrently served as music director at St. Thomas' Church in New Haven, Conn. (1949–64). From 1964 to 1972 he was dean of the music school at Syracuse Univ.; then taught theory there. He continued to give violin recitals, usually with his wife, **Helen Boatwright**, whom he married in 1943. From 1950 to 1962 he was concertmaster of the New Haven Orch., and from 1957 to 1960 conducted the Yale Univ. Sym. He became greatly interested in the musical folklore of Eastern nations. In 1959 he went to India on grants from the Fulbright and Rockefeller foundations, and wrote 2 valuable monographs, *A Handbook of Staff Notation for Indian Music* and *Indian Classical Music and the Western Listener*, both publ. in Bombay in 1960. In his compositions, he revived the modalities of early church music, using modern harmonies and linear counterpoint. His best works are of this type, mostly written for chorus.

WORKS: ORCH.: *Variations* for Chamber Orch. (1949); Sym. (1976). **CHAMBER:** 2 string quartets (1947, 1975); *Serenade* for 2 String Instruments and 2 Wind Instruments (1952); Clarinet Quartet (1958); 12 pieces for Violin (1977); Clarinet Sonata (1980). **VOCAL:** Mass in C (1958); *The Passion According to St. Matthew* for Chorus (1962); *Canticle of the Sun* for Chorus (1963); *6 Prayers of Kierkegaard* for Soprano and Piano (1978); other choral works and songs.

Boatwright, McHenry, black American bass-baritone; b. Tennile, Ga., Feb. 29, 1928; d. N.Y., Nov. 5, 1994. He studied piano (B.Mus., 1950) and voice (B.Mus., 1954) at the New England Cons. of Music in Boston. In 1953 and 1954 he received Marian Anderson awards. In 1956 he made his formal concert debut in Boston, and in 1958 his first N.Y. concert appearance. After making his operatic debut as Arkel in *Pelléas et Mélisande* at the New England Opera Theater in 1958, he appeared with various opera companies and as a soloist with orchs. He created the central role in Schuller's opera *The Visitation* (Hamburg, Oct. 12, 1966).

Bockelmann, Rudolf (August Louis Wilhelm), German bass-baritone; b. Bodenteich, April 2, 1892; d. Dresden, Oct. 9, 1958. He studied in Celle and with Oscar Lassner, Soomer, and Karl Scheidemantel in Leipzig. In 1920 he made his operatic debut in Celle. In 1921 he sang the Herald in *Lohengrin* at the Leipzig Opera, where he appeared until 1926. From 1926 to 1932 he sang at the Hamburg City Theater. He also appeared at the Bayreuth Festivals (1928–42), London's Covent Garden (1929–30; 1934–38), and the Chicago Opera (1930–32). From 1932 to 1945 he was a member of the Berlin State Opera. Guest engagements also took him to Milan, Paris, Rome, Vienna, and Munich. His Nazi inclinations precluded engagements outside Germany after World War II. After teaching voice in Hamburg, he went to Dresden in 1955 as a prof. at the Hochschule für Musik. He was particularly esteemed as a Wagnerian, winning praise for his portrayals of Hans Sachs, Wotan, Kurwenal, Gunther, and the Dutchman.

Bodanzky, Artur, famous Austrian conductor; b. Vienna, Dec. 16, 1877; d. N.Y., Nov. 23, 1939. He studied at the Vienna Cons., and later with Zemlinsky. He began his career as a violinist in the Vienna Court Opera Orch. In 1900 he received his first appointment as a conductor, leading an operetta season in Budweis; in 1902 he became assistant to Mahler at the Vienna Court Opera; conducted in Berlin (1905) and in Prague (1906–09). In 1909 he was engaged as music director at Mannheim. In 1912 he arranged a memorial Mahler Festival, conducting a huge ensemble of 1,500 vocalists and instrumentalists. He conducted *Parsifal* at Covent Garden in London in 1914; his success there led to an invitation to conduct the German repertoire at the Metropolitan Opera in N.Y.; he opened his series with *Götterdämerung* (Nov. 18, 1915). From 1916 to 1931 he was director of the Soc. of Friends of Music in N.Y.; from 1919 to 1922 he also conducted the New Sym. Orch. He made several practical arrangements of celebrated operas (*Oberon, Don Giovanni, Fidelio,* etc.), which he used for his productions with the Metropolitan Opera. His style of conducting was in the Mahler tradition, with emphasis on climactic effects and contrasts of light and shade.

Bode, Rudolf, German acoustician and theorist of rhythmic gymnastics; b. Kiel, Feb. 3, 1881; d. Munich, Oct. 7, 1970. He studied physiology and philosophy at the Univ. of Leipzig, and theory at the Leipzig Cons. After attending the Dalcroze Inst. of Eurhythmics in Hellerau, he formulated a system of "rhythmic gymnastics." In 1911 he founded a school in Munich with courses embodying his body theories, intended to achieve perfect physical and mental health. He publ. *Der Rhythmus und seine Bedeutung für die Erziehung* (Jena, 1920); *Ausdruckgymnastik* (Munich, 1922; Eng. tr., 1931, as *Expressions-Gymnastic*); *Musik und Bewegung* (Kassel, 1930); *Energie und Rhythmus* (Berlin, 1939). He also wrote a manual of piano study as a rhythmic muscular action, *Rhythmus und Anschlag* (Munich, 1933).

Bodin, Lars-Gunnar, Swedish composer; b. Stockholm, July 15, 1935. He studied composition with Lennart Wenström (1956–60); attended the Darmstadt summer courses (1961); in 1972 he was composer-in-residence at Mills College in Oakland, California; in 1978 he became director of the Stockholm Electronic Music Studio. In collaboration with the Swedish concrete poet and composer Bengt Emil Johnson, he produced a series of "text-sound compositions."

WORKS: DANCE: *Place of Plays* (1967); *. . . from one point to any other point* (1968); *Händelser och handlingar* (1971). **CHAMBER:** *Music* for 4 Brass Instruments (1960); *Arioso* for Clarinet, Trombone, Cello, Piano, and Percussion (1962); *Semikolon: Dag Knutson in memoriam* for Horn, Trombone, Electric Guitar, Piano, and Organ (1963); *Calendar Music* for Piano (1964). **LIVE AND ELECTRONIC:** *My World—Is Your World* for Organ and Tape (1966); *Primary Structures* for Bassoon and Tape (1976); *Enbart för Kerstin* for Mezzo-soprano and Tape (1979); *Anima* for Soprano, Flute, and Tape (1984); *On Speaking Terms* for Trombone and Tape (1984); *Diskus* for Wind Quintet and Tape (1987). **ELECTRONIC:** *Place of Plays* (1967); *Winter Events* (1967); *Toccata* (1969); *Traces I* (1970) and *II* (1971); *Från borjan till slut* (1973); *Syner (Jorden, himlen, vindarna)* (1973); *Epilogue: Rapsodie de la seconde récolte* (1979); *Mémoires d'un temps avant la destruction* (1982); *For Jon II: Retrospective Episodes* (1986). **INTERMEDIA:** *Clouds* (1973–76). **TEXT-SOUND:** *Semikolon* (1965); *Fikonsnackarna* (1966); *En aptitretar—inga hundar i Kina* (1966); *Cybo I* and *II* (both 1967); *Dedicated to You I* (1970), *II* (1972), and *III* (1973); *For Jon (Fragments of a Time to Come)* (1977); *Nästan* (1977); *Plus* (1977); *For Jon III (They Extracted Their Extremities Plus for John)* (1982).

Bodky, Erwin, German-American music scholar; b. Ragnit, March 7, 1896; d. Lucerne, Dec. 6, 1958. He studied piano and theory in Berlin with Dohnányi and Juon; later attended classes of Richard Strauss and Busoni at the Meisterschule für Komposition (1920–22). He subsequently taught at the Scharwenka Cons. in Berlin. With the advent of the Nazi regime in 1933, Bodky went to Amsterdam, where he remained until 1938; then emigrated to the U.S., and taught at the Longy School of Music in Cambridge, Mass. (1938–48); in 1949 he was appointed a prof. at Brandeis Univ.

WRITINGS: *Der Vortag alter Klaviermusik* (Berlin, 1932); *Das Charakterstück* (Berlin, 1933); *The Interpretation of J.S. Bach's Keyboard Works* (Cambridge, Mass., 1960; also in Ger., Tutzing, 1970).

BIBL.: H. Slosbert et al., eds., *E. B.: A Memorial Tribute* (Waltham, Mass., 1965).

Bodley, Nicholas Bessaraboff. See **Bessaraboff, Nicholas.**

Bodley, Seóirse, Irish composer, teacher, conductor, and pianist; b. Dublin, April 4, 1933. He studied in Dublin at the Royal Irish Academy of Music and at Univ. College (B.M., 1955). Following training in Stuttgart (1957–59) with J.N. David (composition), Alfred Kreutz (piano), and Hans Müller-Kray (conducting), he returned to Dublin and took his D.Mus. at Univ. College (1960). In 1959 he joined its faculty, where he also conducted its chorus and orch., and founded its electro-acoustic studio. He appeared as a conductor with other Dublin ensembles, introducing many works to the city. His 2nd Sym., *Ceol,* inaugurated the National Concert Hall in Dublin on Sept. 9, 1981. Bodley was founding chairman of the Folk Music Soc. of Ireland and of the Assn. of Irish Composers. In 1982 he was made a member of Aosdána, Ireland's official body of distinguished artists. While Bodley has composed a number of works in which traditional Irish music is discernable, he has also written scores in an avant-garde mode, including serial techniques and novel instrumental combinations.

WORKS: ORCH.: *Music* for Strings (Dublin, Dec. 10, 1952); 5 syms.: No. 1 (1958–59; Dublin, Oct. 23, 1960), No. 2, *I Have Loved the Lands of Ireland* (1980; Dublin, Jan. 9, 1981), No. 3, *Ceol,* for Soprano, Mezzo-soprano, Tenor, Baritone, Semi-chorus, Children's Chorus, Orch., Speaker, and Audience (1980; Dublin, Sept. 9, 1981), No. 4 (1990–91; Parma, June 21, 1991), and No. 5, *The Limerick* (Limerick, Oct. 4, 1991); *Divertimento* for Strings (1961; Dublin, June 15, 1992); 2 chamber syms.: No. 1 (Paris, 1964, composer conducting) and No. 2 (Dublin, June 17, 1982, composer conducting); *Configurations* (1967; Dublin, Jan. 29, 1969); *A Small White Cloud Drifts over Ireland* (1975; Dublin, Jan. 5, 1976). **CHAMBER:** 2 string quartets: No. 1 (1968; Dublin,

Jan. 6, 1969) and No. 2 (1992; Dublin, May 21, 1993); *September Preludes* for Flute and Piano (1973; Dublin, Jan. 7, 1974); *Celebration Music* for 3 Trumpets and String Quartet (Dublin, Nov. 11, 1983; also for 3 Trumpets and String Orch.); Trio for Flute, Violin, and Piano (Dublin, July 6, 1986); *Phantasms* for Flute, Clarinet, Harp, and Cello (Dublin, Oct. 27, 1989). **PIANO:** *The Narrow Road to the Deep North* for 2 Pianos (Belfast, Feb. 17, 1972); *Aislingi* (Kilkenny, Aug. 29, 1977). **VOCAL:** *An Bás is an Bheatha* (Life and Death), song cycle for Chorus (1960; Dublin, Jan. 21, 1961); *Never to have lived is best,* song cycle for Soprano and Orch. (Dublin, June 11, 1965); *Ariel's Songs* for Soprano and Piano (1969; Dublin, Jan. 7, 1970); *Meditations on Lines from Patrick Kavanagh* for Alto and Orch. (1971; Dublin, June 30, 1972); *A Chill Wind* for Chorus (1977; Dublin, Jan. 12, 1978); *A Girl,* song cycle for Mezzo-soprano and Piano (Dublin, Oct. 17, 1978); *The Radiant Moment* for Chorus (Cork, April 26, 1979); *A Concert Mass* for Soprano, Mezzo-soprano, Tenor, Bass, Chorus, and String Orch. (1984; Dublin, May 4, 1990, composer conducting); *The Naked Flame* for Mezzo-soprano or Baritone and Piano (1987; Dublin, April 7, 1988); *Carta Irlandesa* (New from Ireland) for Mezzo-soprano or Baritone and Piano (Sligo, Sept. 4, 1988, composer pianist). **ELECTRO-ACOUSTIC:** *The Banshee* for Soprano, Mezzo-soprano, Tenor, Bass, and Electronics (Belfast, April 25, 1983).

Body, Jack (John Stanley), New Zealand composer, ethnomusicologist, teacher, and experimental photographer; b. Te Aroha, Oct. 7, 1944. He studied with Robin Maconie at the Univ. of Auckland (B.Mus., 1966; M.Mus., 1967), at Lilburn's electronic music studio in Wellington, in Cologne (1968), and with Koenig at the Inst. of Sonology at the Univ. of Utrecht (1969). After serving as a guest lecturer at the Akademi Musik Indonesia in Yogyakarta (1976–77), he was a lecturer at the Victoria Univ. School of Music in Wellington from 1980. As a composer, Body has ranged widely over the genres, from the use of traditional instruments to electro-acoustic music. He has been notably influenced by the music of South East Asia and East Asia, most especially of Indonesia. He has demonstrated a remarkable capacity for synthesizing non-Western musical materials with contemporary compositional techniques. In his experimental photography, he has explored relationships between sound and image.

WORKS: ORCH.: *4 Haiku* for Prepared Piano and 21 Solo Strings (1967); *Canzona* for Brass Band (1971); *23 Pages* (1972); *Hello François* (1976); *Melodies* (1983); *Little Elegies* (1985). **CHAMBER:** *Turtle Time* for Piano, Harp, Harpsichord, Organ, and Speaker(s) (1968); *Resonance Music* for 6 Percussionists and Electric Guitar (1974); *Bamboo Music* for 8 Players (1979); *3 Transcriptions* for String Quartet (1987); *Interior* for Chamber Ensemble and Tape (1987); *Epicycle* for String Quartet (1989); *Out of Africa* for 2 Guitars (1990); *Arum Manis* for String Quartet and Tape (1991); *3 Elegies* for Chamber Ensemble (1992). **VOCAL:** *Pater Noster* for 4 Soloists, Chorus, and Percussion (1973); *Carol to St. Stephen* for 3 Soloists and Chorus (1975); *Marvel not Joseph* for 2 Soloists and Chorus (1976); *Vox Populi* for Chorus and Tape (1981); *Love Sonnets of Michelangelo* for Soprano and Mezzo-soprano (1982); *Poems of Solitary Delights* for Voice and Orch. (1985); *5 Lullabies* for Chorus (1988); *Psalm 150* for Chorus (1992). **ELECTRO-ACOUSTIC:** *Kryptophones* (1973); *Musik dari Jalan* (Music from the Street; 1975); *Duets and Choruses* (1978); *Musik Anak-anak* (Children's Music; 1978); *Fanfares* (1981); *Jangkrik Genggong* (1985); *Musik mulut* (Mouth music; 1989); *Vox Humana* (1991). **OTHER:** *Lecture* for Actors and Various Media (1970); *Encounters* for Tape and Actors/Participants (1980); *Poi* for Tape (1982).

Boehe, Ernst, German conductor and composer; b. Munich, Dec. 27, 1880; d. Ludwigshafen, Nov. 16, 1938. He studied with Rudolf Louis and Ludwig Thuille in Munich. In 1907 he was assoc. conductor, with Courvoisier, of the Munich Volkssymphoniekonzerte; from 1913 to 1920 he was court conductor at Oldenburg; then conducted concerts in Ludwigshafen. His works are of a programmatic type, the orchestration emphasizing special sonorities of divided strings, massive wind instruments, and various percussive effects; his tone poems show a decisive Wagnerian influence, having a system of identification motifs. His most ambitious work was an orch. tetralogy on Homer's *Odyssey,* under the general title *Odysseus' Fahrten,* comprising *Odysseus' Ausfahrt und Schiffbruch* (Munich, Feb. 20, 1903), *Die Insel der Kirke, Die Klage der Nausikaa,* and *Odysseus' Heimkehr.* He also wrote the symphonic poem *Taormina* (Essen, 1906).

BIBL.: E. Istel, "E. B.," *Monographien moderner Musiker* (Leipzig, 1909).

Boehm, Karl. See **Böhm, Karl.**

Boelza, Igor (Feodorovich), Russian musicologist and composer; b. Kielce, Poland, Feb. 8, 1904; d. Moscow, Jan. 5, 1994. He received training in composition from Liatoshinsky at the Kiev Cons. (1922–25), and studied philology at the Univ. of Kiev. He was a teacher (1925–36) and a prof. (1936–41) at the Kiev Cons., and then settled in Moscow, where he was a prof. at the Cons. (1942–49). After taking his Ph.D. in 1951 with a diss. on Czech classical music at the Univ. of Moscow, he was on the staff of the Inst. for the History of the Arts (1954–61). Thereafter he was active with the Inst. of Slavonic Studies at the Academy of Sciences of the U.S.S.R. He wrote biographies of Mozart (Kiev, 1941), Borodin (Moscow, 1944; 2nd ed., 1946), Dvořák (Moscow, 1949), Karlowicz (Moscow, 1951), Glière (Moscow, 1955; 2nd ed., 1962), Vitězslav Novák (Moscow, 1957), Chopin (Moscow, 1960; 2nd ed., 1968), and Oginsky (Moscow, 1965). His most important work, however, was done on the history of Czech and Polish music, and included books on Czech classical opera (Moscow, 1951), the history of Polish music culture (Moscow, 1954–73), the history of Czech music culture (Moscow, 1959–73), and a study of Slav music (Moscow, 1965). Among his compositions were 5 syms., an overture, film scores, chamber music, and vocal works.

Boepple, Paul, Swiss-American choral conductor and pedagogue; b. Basel, July 19, 1896; d. Brattleboro, Vt., Dec. 21, 1970. He took courses at the Dalcroze Inst. in Geneva, and adopted the Dalcroze system in his own method of teaching music; from 1918 to 1926 he was a member of the faculty of the Inst. In 1926 he emigrated to the U.S.; directed the Dalcroze School of Music in N.Y. (1926–32); then taught at the Chicago Musical College (1932–34) and at the Westminster Choir School in Princeton, N.J. (1935–38); subsequently he taught at Bennington College in Vermont. As a choral conductor, he gave numerous performances of modern works.

Boero, Felipe, Argentine composer and teacher; b. Buenos Aires, May 1, 1884; d. there, Aug. 9, 1958. He studied with Pablo Berutti; received a government prize for further study in Europe, and attended the classes of Vidal and Fauré at the Paris Cons. (1912–14). Returning to Buenos Aires, he became active as a teacher. Among his operas, the following were first perf. at the Teatro Colón: *Tucumán* (June 29, 1918), *Ariana y Dionisios* (Aug. 5, 1920), *Raquela* (June 25, 1923), *Las Bacantes* (Sept. 19, 1925), *El Matrero* (July 12, 1929), and *Siripo* (June 8, 1937).

Boesch, Christian, Austrian baritone; b. Vienna, July 27, 1941. He pursued his training at the Vienna Hochschule für Musik, and in 1966 made his operatic debut at the Bern Stadttheater. He became a member of the Vienna Volksoper in 1975, later scoring notable success at the Salzburg Festival in 1978 for his portrayal of Papageno, a role he also chose for his Metropolitan Opera debut in N.Y. on Feb. 17, 1979. He later sang Wozzeck and Masetto at the Metropolitan.

Boesch, Rainer, Swiss composer, pianist, and teacher; b. Männedorf, Aug. 11, 1938. He received training in piano at the Geneva Cons. (diploma, 1960) and the Neuchâtel Cons. (diploma, 1965), and then in composition with Messiaen at the Paris Cons. (1966–68), where he received the premier prix in 1968 with the first electro-acoustic piece ever presented there.

After serving as director of the Lausanne Cons. (1968–72), he headed the new music dept. of the Institut de Hautes Études Musicales (1973–75). He settled in Geneva, where he founded the Studio ESPACES in 1976, a teaching and research organization. He also taught at the Institut Jaques-Dalcroze from 1976, overseeing its research center from 1989. In 1985 he co-founded the Swiss Centre for Computer Music, which he subsequently served as co-director. Boesch's large output embraces avant-garde usages, with a special regard for multimedia and electronic works.

WORKS: Cello Sonata (1955); Piano Pieces (1955–92); String Quartet (1960–61); *Désagrégation* for 12 Clarinets, 2 Tubas, Percussion, and Tape (1968); *Florès* for Instrumental Ensemble (1968); *Cendres*, piano concerto (1968–69); *Fêtes* for Chorus, Mimes, and Tape (1972); *Mécaniques* for Tape (1973); *Espaces*, opera (1975); *Transparences* for Orch. (1977); *Schriftzeichen für Kathrin* for Women's Voices, Piano, Orch., and Tape (1977); *Tissages* for Orch. (1978); *"***" (Suite II)*, multimedia piece (1978–89); Wind Quintet (1980); *Kreise* for Wind Orch. (1986); *Clavirissima* for Piano and Computer (1987); *Solisti* for Flute, Bassoon, 2 Saxophones, Double Bass, and Piano (1991).

Boesmans, Philippe, Belgian composer; b. Tongeren, May 17, 1936. He studied composition with Froidebise and Pousseur, and piano at the Liège Cons. (1954–62). His music adheres to the abstract trends of cosmopolitan modernism, with structural formulas determining the contents.

WORKS: *Étude I* for Piano (1963); *Sonance I* for 2 Pianos (1964) and *II* for 3 Pianos (1967); *Impromptu* for 23 Instruments (1965); *Corrélations* for Clarinet and 2 Instrumental Ensembles (Brussels, Sept. 16, 1967); *Explosives* for Harp and 10 Instrumentalists (1968); *Verticles* for Orch. (1969); *Blocage* for Voice, Chorus, and Chamber Ensemble (1970); *Upon La, Mi* for Voice, Amplified Horn, and Instrumental Ensemble (1970); *Fanfare* for 2 Pianos (1971); *Intervalles I* for Orch. (1972), *II* for Orch. (1973), and *III* for Voice and Orch. (1974); *Sur Mi* for 2 Pianos, Electric Organ, Crotale, and Tam-Tam (1974); *Multiples* for 2 Pianos and Orch. (1974); *Element—Extensions* for Piano and Chamber Orch. (1976); *Doublures* for Harp, Piano, Percussion, and 4 Instrumental Groups (1977); *Attitudes*, musical spectacle for Voice, 2 Pianos, Synthesizer, and Percussion (1977); Piano Concerto (1978); Violin Concerto (1979; Liège, Feb. 22, 1980); *Conversions* for Orch. (1980); *La Passion de Gilles*, opera (Brussels, Oct. 18, 1983); *Ricercar sconvolto* for Organ (1983); *Extase* for Orch. (1985); String Quartet (1989); *Reigen*, opera (1992).

Boettcher, Wilfried, German cellist and conductor; b. Bremen, Aug. 11, 1929; d. Uzes-Saint Siffret, France, Aug. 22, 1994. He studied cello with Arthur Troester at the Hamburg Hochschule für Musik (diploma, 1955) and with Pierre Fournier in Paris (1955–56). He was 1st cellist in the Bremen Radio Orch. (1948–50) and in the Hannover Opera orch. (1956–58). From 1958 to 1965 he was a prof. of cello at the Vienna Academy of Music. In 1959 he founded Die Wiener Solisten, which he conducted until 1966. From 1965 to 1974 he was a prof. at the Hamburg Hochschule für Musik. He also was chief conductor of the Hamburg Sym. Orch. (1967–71), and a conductor at the Hamburg State Opera (1970–73). From 1974 to 1978 he was principal guest conductor of the RAI Orch. in Turin. He also was a conductor at the Berlin Deutsche Oper (1975–82) and the Vienna State Opera (1977–82). In later years, he became closely associated as a conductor with several British orchs.

Boetticher, Wolfgang, noted German musicologist; b. Bad Ems, Aug. 19, 1914. He studied musicology at the Univ. of Berlin with Schering, Schünemann, Blume, and others; received his Ph.D. there in 1939 with the diss. *Robert Schumann: Einführung in Persönlichkeit und Werk* (publ. in Berlin, 1941); completed his Habilitation in musicology there in 1943 with his *Studien zur solistischen Lautenpraxis des 16. und 17. Jahrhunderts* (publ. in Berlin, 1943). In 1948 he joined the faculty of the Univ. of Göttingen; was prof. of musicology there from 1956 to 1959; from 1958 he also taught at the Technical Univ. in Clausthal. He is an acknowledged authority on the music of both the Renaissance and the 19th century; his writings on lute music, Orlando di Lasso, and Robert Schumann are particularly valuable.

WRITINGS: *Robert Schumann in seinen Schriften und Briefen* (Berlin, 1942); *Orlando di Lasso und seine Zeit* (2 vols., Kassel and Basel, 1958); *Von Palestrina zu Bach* (Stuttgart, 1959; 2nd ed., enl., 1981); *Dokumente und Briefe um Orlando di Lasso* (Kassel, 1960); *Aus Orlando di Lassos Wirkungskreis, Neue archivalische Studien zur Munchener Musikgeschichte* (Kassel and Basel, 1963); *Neue Forschungsergebnisse im Gebiet der musikalischen Renaissance* (Göttingen, 1964); *Die Familienkassette Schumanns in Dresden: Unbekannte Briefe an Robert und Clara Schumann* (Leipzig, 1974); *Robert Schumanns Klavierwerke: Entstehung, Urtext, Gestalt: Untersuchungen anhand unveröffentlichter Skizzen und biographischer Dokumente* (Wilhelmshaven, 1976–); *Geschichte der Motette* (Darmstadt, 1989).

BIBL.: H. Hüschen and D.-R. Moser, eds., *Convivium musicorum: Festschrift W. B. zum sechzigsten Geburtstag* (Berlin, 1974).

Bogatyrev, Anatoly (Vasilievich), Russian composer and teacher; b. Vitebsk, Aug. 13, 1913. He studied composition with Zolotarev at the Belorussian Cons. in Minsk, graduating in 1937; was an instructor there from 1948. He wrote 2 patriotic operas: *In the Forests of Polesye* (Minsk, Aug. 28, 1939) and *Nadezhda Durova* (Minsk, Dec. 22, 1956); 2 syms. (1946, 1947); Cello Concerto (1962); Double Bass Concerto (1964); cantatas.

Bogatyrev, Semyon (Semyonovich), Russian musicologist and composer; b. Kharkov, Feb. 15, 1890; d. Moscow, Dec. 31, 1960. He studied law at the Univ. of Kharkov, graduating in 1912; then went to St. Petersburg, where he enrolled at the Cons. in the composition classes of Kalafati and Wihtol and the orchestration class of Maximilian Steinberg. Upon graduating, he taught at the Kharkov Cons. (1917–19); subsequently was a lecturer at the Kharkov Inst. of Music and Drama (1922–41). In 1943 he was appointed to the faculty of the Moscow Cons., and remained there until his death. He publ. valuable manuals on double canon (Moscow, 1947) and retrograde counterpoint (Moscow, 1960). In 1957 Bogatyrev undertook the reconstruction and completion of Tchaikovsky's unfinished Sym. in E-flat major, which was publ. as the 7th Sym. His own compositions include works for orch., as well as 2 string quartets and 2 piano sonatas. A memorial vol. containing his writings was publ. in Moscow in 1972.

Bogdanov-Berezovsky, Valerian (Mikhailovich), Russian musicologist and composer; b. Starozhilovka, near St. Petersburg, July 17, 1903; d. Moscow, May 13, 1971. He studied with Maximilian Steinberg and Liapunov at the Leningrad Cons., graduating in 1927; taught there from 1945 to 1948, and was in charge of the artistic direction of the Leningrad Theater of Opera and Ballet from 1951 to 1962. He wrote operas: *The Frontier* (1941), *The Leningraders* (1943), and *Nastasia Filippovna*, after Dostoevsky's novel *The Idiot* (1964); several ballets, including *The Seagull*, after Chekhov (1959); 2 syms. (1933, 1953); Piano Concerto; Violin Concerto; some chamber music; choruses. He was known chiefly, however, as a critic and historian of Russian music; he wrote several monographs on Soviet composers and contributed numerous articles to Soviet journals.

BIBL.: I. Gusin, *V. B.-B.* (Leningrad, 1966).

Bogianckino, Massimo, Italian pianist, musicologist, and administrator; b. Rome, Nov. 10, 1922. He studied piano with Casella at the Accademia di Santa Cecilia in Rome and with Cortot at the École Normale de Musique in Paris; also took courses in musicology with Ronga at the Univ. of Rome and with P.M. Masson at the Sorbonne in Paris. He taught at the Carnegie Inst. in Pittsburgh (1948–51), the Pesaro Cons. (1951–57), and the Rome Cons. (1957–67). In 1967 he joined the faculty of the Univ. of Perugia. He served as artistic director of the Rome Opera (1963–68), the Spoleto Festival of Two Worlds (1968–71), La Scala in Milan (1972–74), and the Teatro Comunale in Florence (from 1975). From 1983 to 1985 he was director of the Paris Opéra; then was mayor of Florence. He wrote the vols. *L'arte clavicembalistica di Domenico Scarlatti* (Rome, 1956; Eng. tr., 1968, as *The Harpsichord Sonatas of Domenico Scarlatti*) and *Aspetti del teatro musicale in Italia e in Francia nell'età barocca* (Rome, 1968).

Boguslawski, Edward, Polish composer; b. Chorzów, Sept. 22, 1940. He studied composition with Szabelski in Katowice and with Haubenstock-Ramati in Vienna. In 1963 he joined the faculty of the State College of Music in Katowice. His music makes use of impressionistic techniques.

WORKS: *Intonazioni I* for 9 Instruments (1962) and *II* for Orch. (1967); *Apocalypse* for Narrator, Chorus, and Instruments (1965); *Signals* for Orch. (1965–66); *Metamorphoses* for Oboe, Clarinet, 2 Violins, Viola, and Cello (1967); *Canti* for Soprano and Orch. (1967); Concerto for Oboe, Oboe d'Amore, English Horn, Musette, and Orch. (1967–68); *Versions* for 6 Instruments (1968); *Musica per Ensemble MW-2* for Flute, Cello, and 2 Pianos (1970); Trio for Flute, Oboe, and Guitar (1970); *Per Pianoforte* (1971); *Capriccioso-Notturno* for Orch. (1972); *Impromptu* for Flute, Viola, and Harp (1972); *L'Être* for Soprano, Flute, Cello, and 2 Pianos (1973); *Pro Varsovia* for Orch. (1973–74); *Musica notturna* for Musette and Piano (1974); *Evocations* for Baritone and Orch. (1974); *Divertimento* for Chamber Ensemble (1975); Concerto for Oboe, Soprano, and Orch. (1975–76); *Beelzebub's Sonata*, chamber opera (Wroclaw, Nov. 19, 1977); *Musica concertante* for Saxophone and Orch. (1980; Warsaw, Sept. 24, 1986); Piano Concerto (1981; Katowice, Dec. 3, 1982); Symphonie Concertante for Violin and Chamber Orch. (1982); *Polonia*, symphonic poem for Violin and Orch. (Katowice, Oct. 5, 1984); *The Game of Dreams*, musical drama (1985); *Les Extrêmes se touchent* for Orch. (1986).

Boháč, Josef, Czech composer; b. Vienna, March 25, 1929. After training in Vienna, he was a student of Petrželka at the Janáček Academy of Music and Dramatic Art in Brno (1955–59). He later was active with Czech TV and the music publishing concern Panton. As a composer, he followed the median line of Central European modernism, with occasional resort to serial methods.

WORKS: DRAMATIC: *Námluvy* (The Courtship), comic opera (1967; Prague, March 18, 1971); *Goya*, opera (1972–77; Ostrava, Sept. 30, 1978); *Oči* (Eyes), television opera (1973; Czech TV, Prague, Oct. 5, 1974); *Zvířatka a Petrovští* (The Little Animals and Petrovští), opera (1980); *Zlatá svatba* (The Golden Wedding), comic opera (1981); *Rumcajs*, opera (1985). **ORCH.:** *Rhapsody* (1955); *Symphonic Overture* (1964); *Sinfonietta concertante* (1964–65); *Fragment* (1969); *Elegy* for Cello and Chamber Orch. (1969); *Suita drammatica* for Strings and Timpani (1969–70); *Southern Rainbow*, suite (1971); *February Overture* (1973); Piano Concerto (1974); Concerto for Violin and Chamber Orch. (1978); *Concertino Pastorale* for 2 Horns and Orch. (1978); *Concerto for Orchestra* (1983); *Dramatic Variants* for Viola and Orch. (1983). **CHAMBER:** Suite for String Quartet (1953); Cello Sonata (1954); String Trio (1965); *Sonetti per Sonatori* for Flute, Bass Clarinet, Percussion, and Piano (1974); *Sonata Giovane* for Piano (1983). **VOCAL:** *My Lute Sounds*, monodrama for Tenor, Soprano, and Nonet or Piano (1971); *Sonata Lirica* for Soprano, Strings, and Vibraphone (1982).

Böhm, Karl, renowned Austrian conductor; b. Graz, Aug. 28, 1894; d. Salzburg, Aug. 14, 1981. He studied law before enrolling at the Graz Cons., where he took lessons in piano and theory; subsequently he studied musicology with Mandyczewski at the the Univ. of Vienna. After service in the Austrian Army during World War I, he made his debut as a conductor at the Graz Opera in 1917. He then completed his training in law at the Univ. of Graz (Dr.Jur., 1919). In 1920 he was appointed 1st conductor at the Graz Opera. Although he never took formal lessons in conducting, he soon acquired sufficient technique to be engaged at the Bavarian State Opera in Munich (1921). In 1927 he was appointed Generalmusikdirektor in Darmstadt; having already mastered a number of works by Mozart, Wagner, and Richard Strauss, he included in his repertoire modern operas by Krenek and Hindemith. In 1931 he conducted *Wozzeck* by Berg, a performance which Berg himself warmly praised. From 1931 to 1933 Böhm held the post of Generalmusikdirektor of the Hamburg Opera; from 1934 to 1943 he was music director of the Dresden State Opera, where he gave the first performances of *Die schweigsame Frau* (June 24, 1935) and *Daphne* (Oct. 15, 1938), which Strauss dedicated to him. In 1943 he became director of the Vienna State Opera, but his tenure was a brief one due to its closure by the Nazis in 1944 and by its destruction by Allied bombing during the closing weeks of World War II in 1945. The rumors were rife of his at least passive adherence to the Nazis, although he categorically denied that he was ever a member of the party. After the War, he was not allowed by the Allied authorities to give performances pending an investigation of his political past; he was cleared and resumed his career in 1947. From 1950 to 1953 he conducted the German repertoire at the Teatro Colón in Buenos Aires. He then served again as director of the Vienna State Opera from 1954 to 1956. On Nov. 5, 1955, he conducted Beethoven's *Fidelio* at the opening of the reconstructed Vienna State Opera House. He made his first appearance in the U.S. with the Chicago Sym. Orch. on Feb. 9, 1956; on Oct. 31, 1957, he made his first appearance at the Metropolitan Opera in N.Y. with Mozart's *Don Giovanni*. He continued to conduct occasional performances at the Metropolitan until 1978. In 1961 he took the Berlin Phil. to the U.S., and in 1963–64 he made a tour in Japan with it. In 1975 he conducted an American tour with the Deutsche Oper of Berlin. In 1979 he took the Vienna State Opera on its first U.S. tour. He also conducted radio and television performances. Böhm received numerous honors and tokens of distinction, among them the Golden Mozart Memorial Medal from the International Mozarteum Foundation in Salzburg, the Brahms Medal from Hamburg, and the Brückner Ring from the Vienna Sym. Orch. On his 70th birthday, a Böhm Day was celebrated in Vienna, and he was granted the rare honorary title of Generalmusikdirektor of Austria; both his 80th and 85th birthdays were observed in Salzburg and Vienna. In 1977 he was elected president of the London Sym. Orch. Böhm was admired for his impeccable rendition of classical opera scores, particularly those of Mozart, in which he scrupulously avoided any suggestion of improper romanticization; he was equally extolled for his productions of the operas of Wagner and Richard Strauss, and he earned additional respect for his authoritative performances of the Austro-German orch. repertoire. He publ. *Begegnung mit Richard Strauss* (Munich, 1964) and a personal memoir, *Ich erinnere mich ganz genau* (Zürich, 1968; Eng. tr., 1992, as *A Life Remembered: Memoirs*).

BIBL.: F. Endler, *K. B.: Ein Dirigentenleben* (Hamburg, 1981); H. Hoyer, *K. B. an der Wiener Staatsoper: Eine Dokumentation* (Vienna, 1981).

Böhme, Kurt (Gerhard), distinguished German bass; b. Dresden, May 5, 1908; d. Munich, Dec. 20, 1989. He was a student of Adolf Kluge at the Dresden Cons. In 1930 he made his operatic debut as Caspar in *Der Freischütz* at the Dresden State Opera, where he remained as one of its principal artists until 1950; then was a member of the Bavarian State Opera in Munich. In 1936 he made his first appearance at London's Covent Garden with the visiting Dresden State Opera; later made regular appearances there from 1956 to 1970; he also was a guest artist in Vienna, Bayreuth, and Milan. On Nov. 11, 1954, he made his Metropolitan Opera debut in N.Y. as Pogner, and was again on its roster in 1956–57. Böhme was especially admired for his Wagnerian roles, but he also won great acclaim as Baron Ochs.

Bohnen, (Franz) Michael, noted German bass-baritone; b. Cologne, May 2, 1887; d. Berlin, April 26, 1965. He received training from Fritz Steinbach and Schulz-Dornburg at the Cologne Cons. In 1910 he made his operatic debut as Caspar in *Der Freischütz* in Düsseldorf. After singing in Wiesbaden (1912–13), he was a highly respected member of the Berlin Royal (later State) Opera from 1913 to 1921. He also made debuts in 1914 at London's Covent Garden and the Bayreuth Festival. On March 1, 1923, he made his Metropolitan Opera debut in N.Y. as the Tourist/Francesco in Schillings' *Mona Lisa,* remaining on its roster until 1932. On Jan. 19, 1929, he sang the leading role there in the U.S. premiere of Krenek's *Jonny spielt auf.* From 1933 to 1945 he sang at the Berlin Deutsches Opernhaus, and subsequently served as Intendant at the renamed Städtische Oper from 1945 to 1947. He was equally well versed in baritone and bass roles, numbering among his finest Sarastro, Wotan, King Marke, Hagen, Gurnemanz, Méphistophélès, Baron Ochs, and Scarpia.

Bohnke, Emil, Polish-born German violist and composer; b. Zduńska Wola, Oct. 11, 1888; d. in an automobile accident in Pasewalk, Pomerania, May 11, 1928. He studied at the Leipzig Cons.; then was a violist in various chamber music groups. He wrote a Violin Concerto, a Piano Trio, a String Quartet, and several violin sonatas.

Bois, Rob du, Dutch composer; b. Amsterdam, May 28, 1934. He had piano lessons as a child; then studied law; was mainly audodidact as a composer. His works are strongly contrapuntal in texture, following the classical Flemish tradition but applying ultramodern techniques, including serialism.

WORKS: ORCH.: Piano Concerto (1960; rev. 1968); *Cercle* for Piano, 9 Winds, and Percussion (1963); *Simultaneous* (1965); *Breuker Concerto* for 2 Clarinets, 4 Saxophones, and 21 String Players (1968); *A Flower Given to My Daughter* (1970); *Le Concerto pour Hrisanide* for Piano and Orch. (1971); *Allegro* for Strings (1973); *3 pezzi* (1973); Suite No. 1 (1973); Violin Concerto (1975); *Skarabee* (1977); *Zodiak* for Various Instruments (1977); Concerto for 2 Violins and Orch. (1979); *Sinfonia da camera* for Wind Orch. (1980); *My Daughter's Flower* for Brass Band (1982); *Luna* for Alto Flute and Orch. (1987–88). **CHAMBER:** 4 string quartets (1960–90); 7 pastorales: No. 1 for Oboe, Clarinet, and Harp (1960; rev. 1969), No. 2 for Recorder, Flute, and Guitar (1963; rev. 1969), No. 3 for Clarinet, Bongos, and Double Bass (1963; rev. 1969), No. 4 for Guitar (1963), No. 5 for String Quartet (1964; rev. 1966), No. 6 for Piano (1964), and No. 7 for Recorder (1964); Trio for Flute, Oboe, and Clarinet (1961); *Rondeaux per deux* for Piano and Percussion (1962; 2nd series for Piano, 4-hands, and Percussion, 1964); *3 Pieces* for Flute, Oboe, and Cello (1962); *Chants et contrepoints* for Wind Quintet (1962); *Espaces à remplir* for 11 Musicians (1963); Oboe Quartet (1964); 7 Bagatelles for Flute and Piano (1964); String Trio (1967); *Musica per quattro* for Horn, 2 Trumpets, and Trombone (1967); *Rounds* for Clarinet and Piano (1967); *Ranta Music* for Percussionist (1968); *Musique d'atelier* for Clarinet, Trombone, Cello, and Piano (1968); *Enigma* for Flute, Bass Clarinet, Piano, and Percussion (1969); *Trio agitato* for Horn, Trombone, and Tuba (1969); *Reflexions sur le jour ou Pérotin le Grand ressuscitera* for Wind Quintet (1969); *Polonaise* for a Pianist and a Percussionist (1971); *Fusion pour deux* for Bass Clarinet and Piano (1971); *The Dog Named Boo Has a Master Called Lobo* for Clarinet, Violin, and Piano (1972); *Because It Is* for 4 Clarinets (1973); *The 18th of June, Springtime, and Yet Already Summer* for 4 Saxophones (1974); *Melody* for Bass Clarinet and String Quartet (1974); *Springtime* for Piano and Wind Instruments (1978); *His Flow of Spirits is Something Wonderful* for Piano and Wind Instruments (1978); Violin Sonata (1980); Sonata for Solo Viola (1981); *Hyperion* for Clarinet, Horn, Viola, and Piano (1984); *Das Liebesverbot* for 4 Wagner Tubas (1986); *Symphorine* for Flute (1987).

Bok, Mary Louise Curtis, munificent American music patroness; b. Boston, Aug. 6, 1876; d. Philadelphia, Jan. 4, 1970. She inherited her fortune from Cyrus H.K. Curtis, founder of the Curtis Publishing Co. In 1917 she founded the Settlement School of Music in Philadelphia. In 1924 she established in Philadelphia the Curtis Inst. of Music and endowed it initially with a gift of $12.5 million in memory of her mother. The school had a faculty of the most distinguished American and European musicians, and it provided tuition exclusively on a scholarship basis; many talented composers and performers were among its students, including Leonard Bernstein, Samuel Barber, and Lukas Foss. She was first married to Edward W. Bok, in 1896, who died in 1930; in 1943 she married **Efrem Zimbalist**, who was director of the Curtis Inst. from 1941 until 1968. In 1932 she received an honorary doctorate from the Univ. of Pa., and, in 1934, an honorary doctorate from Williams College.

BIBL.: E. Viles, *M.L.C.B. Zimbalist: Founder of the Curtis Institute of Music and Patron of American Arts* (diss., Bryn Mawr College, 1983).

Bolcom, William (Elden), American pianist and composer; b. Seattle, May 26, 1938. He studied at the Univ. of Wash. in Seattle with John Verrall (B.A., 1958); took a course in composition with Milhaud at Mills College in Oakland, California (M.A., 1961); attended classes in advanced composition with Leland Smith at Stanford Univ. (D.M.A., 1964); also studied at the Paris Cons. (2nd prize in composition, 1965). He received Guggenheim fellowships in 1964–65 and 1968–69. He taught at the Univ. of Wash. in Seattle (1965–66), Queens College of the City Univ. of N.Y. (1966–68), and the N.Y. Univ. School of the Arts (1969–70). He joined the faculty of the school of music at the Univ. of Mich. in 1973; was made a full prof. in 1983. He was composer-in-residence of the Detroit Sym. Orch. (from 1987). In 1988 he won the Pulitzer Prize in Music for his *12 New Études* for Piano. In 1993 he was elected a member of the American Academy and Inst. of Arts and Letters. After absorbing a variety of techniques *sine ira et studio,* he began to experiment widely and wildly in serial thematics, musical collage, sophisticated intentional plagiarism, and microtonal electronics. He was also active as a pianist, recording and giving recitals of ragtime piano; in 1975 he married **Joan Morris**, with whom he appeared in concerts. He publ., with Robert Kimball, a book on the black American songwriting and musical comedy team of Noble Sissle and Eubie Blake, *Reminiscing with Sissle and Blake* (N.Y., 1973); also ed. the collected essays of George Rochberg, under the title *The Aesthetics of Survival: A Composer's View of Twentieth-Century Music* (Ann Arbor, Mich., 1984).

WORKS: DRAMATIC: *Dynamite Tonite,* actors' opera (N.Y., Dec. 21, 1963); *Greatshot,* actors' opera (1969); *Theatre of the Absurd* for Actor and Chamber Group (1970); *The Beggar's Opera,* an adaptation of John Gay's work, for Actors and Chamber Orch. (1978); *Casino Paradise,* musical theater opera (Philadelphia, April 1990); *McTeague,* opera (Chicago, Oct. 31, 1992). **ORCH.:** 5 syms.: No. 1 (1957), No. 2, *Oracles* (1964), No. 3 for Chamber Orch. (1979), No. 4 (1986; St. Louis, March 13, 1987), and No. 5 (1989; Philadelphia, Jan. 11, 1990); Concertante for Violin, Flute, Oboe, and Orch. (1961); *Concerto-Serenade* for Violin and Strings (1964); *Commedia* for "Almost" 18th-century Orch. (1971); *Summer Divertimento* for Chamber Orch. (1973); Piano Concerto (1976); *Humoresk* for Organ and Orch. (1979); *Ragomania* (1982); Violin Concerto (1983); *Fantasia concertante* for Viola, Cello, and Orch. (1985; Salzburg, Jan. 26, 1986); *Seattle Slew,* dance suite (1985–86; Seattle, March 5, 1986); *Spring Concertino* for Oboe and Chamber Orch. (1986–87; Midland, Mich., Nov. 7, 1987); *MCMXC Tanglewood* (Tanglewood, Aug. 4, 1990); *Fanfare: Converging on the Mountain* (Aspen, Colo., July 16, 1991); Clarinet Concerto (1991; N.Y., Jan. 3, 1992); *Lyric Concerto* for Flute and Orch. (St. Louis, Oct. 27, 1993); Concerto for 2 Left-handed Pianists and 2 Orchs. (1995). **CHAMBER:** 10 string quartets (1950–88); *Décalage* for Cello and Piano (1961); Octet for Flute, Clarinet, Bassoon, Violin, Viola, Cello, Contrabass, and Piano (1962); several works, each entitled *Session,* for various instrumental ensembles and mandatory drum play (1965, 1966, 1967); *Dream Music No. 2* for Harpsichord and Percussion (1966); Duets for Quintet of Flute, Clarinet, Violin, Cello, and Piano

(1971); *Whisper Moon* for Alto Flute, Clarinet, Violin, Cello, and Piano (1971); Duo Fantasy for Violin and Piano (1973); Piano Quartet (1976); violin sonatas no. 2 (1978), 3 (1992), and 4 (1995); *Afternoon,* rag suite for Clarinet, Violin, and Piano (1979); Brass Quintet (1980); *Aubade* for Oboe and Piano (1982); *Capriccio* for Cello and Piano (1985); *5 Fold 5* for Woodwind Quintet and Piano (1987); Cello Sonata (1990); Trio for Clarinet, Violin, and Piano (1993); many works for keyboard, including *Frescoes* for 2 Pianists, each doubling on a Harmonium and Harpsichord (Toronto, July 21, 1971); *12 New Études* for Piano (1977–86); *3 Gospel Preludes* for Organ (3 books; 1979–81); Sonata for 2 Pianos (Lafayette, Ind., April 6, 1994). **VOCAL:** *Songs of Innocence and of Experience* (1956–81; also for Soloists, Chorus, and Orch., 1982); *The Mask* for Piano and Chorus (Philadelphia, Oct. 12, 1990).

Boldemann, Laci, Finnish-born Swedish composer; b. Helsinki, April 24, 1921; d. Munich, Aug. 18, 1969. He studied piano and conducting at the Royal Academy of Music in London. At the outbreak of World War II in 1939, he went to Sweden and pursued piano training with Gunnar de Frumerie. After being compelled to return to Germany for army service, he saw action in the campaigns in the Soviet Union, Poland, and Italy before being captured by the Allies. He was a prisoner-of-war in the U.S. for 2 years; upon his release at the end of the War, he returned to Sweden to pursue his career as a composer. He was also active as a teacher and from 1963 to 1969 was secretary and treasurer of the Swedish Composers' Soc. Boldemann's output was the work of a solid craftsman who placed great store in lyrical invention.

WORKS: DRAMATIC: *Svart är vitt, sa kejsaren* (Black Is White, Said the Emperor), fairy tale opera (1964; Stockholm, Jan. 1, 1965); *Dårskapens timme* (Hour of Madness), opera-musical (Malmö, March 22, 1968); *Och så drommer han om Per Jonathan* (And He Dreams of Per Jonathan), operatic scene (Stockholm, Nov. 29, 1969). **ORCH.:** *La Danza,* overture (1949–50); *Sinfonietta* for Strings (1954); *Fantasia Concertante* for Cello and Orch. (1954); Piano Concerto (1956); Violin Concerto (1959); Sym. (1963; Munich, Jan. 13, 1964); Trumpet Concerto (1968; Malmö, Feb. 11, 1969); *Med bleck och med trä,* little wind overture (1969). **CHAMBER:** Violin Sonata (1950); *6 Small Pieces without Pedal* for Piano (1950); String Quartet (1950–57); *Canto elegiaco* for Cello and Piano (1962). **VOCAL:** *Lieder der Vergänglichkeit,* cantata for Baritone and Strings (1951); *4 Epitaphs* for Soprano and Strings (1952); *Notturno* for Soprano and Orch. (1958); *John Bauer,* oratorio (1967); songs.

Bolet, Jorge, brilliant Cuban-born American pianist; b. Havana, Nov. 15, 1914; d. Mountain View, Calif., Oct. 16, 1990. After training in Havana, he enrolled at the age of 12 as a scholarship student at the Curtis Inst. of Music in Philadelphia, where he studied with David Saperton (piano) and Fritz Reiner (conducting); he also studied piano with Leopold Godowsky (1932–33) and Moriz Rosenthal (1935). In 1935 he made his European debut in Amsterdam, and in 1937 his U.S. debut in Philadelphia. He then continued his training with Serkin. In 1937 he received the Naumburg Prize, which led to his successful N.Y. debut that same year. In 1938 he won the Josef Hofmann Award. After serving as Serkin's assistant at the Curtis Inst. (1939–42), he served in the military during World War II. Following the War, he pursued additional training with Abram Chasins and then began to tour. However, it was not until the early 1960s that he gained wide recognition as a virtuoso in the grand Romantic manner. In subsequent years, he toured all over the globe. He also served as prof. of music at the Indiana Univ. School of Music in Bloomington (1968–77), and then as head of the piano dept. at the Curtis Inst. (from 1977).

Bolling, Claude, outstanding French jazz pianist, bandleader, composer, and arranger; b. Cannes, April 10, 1930. He began formal piano training at age 12, receiving thorough grounding in the classical repertoire while mastering the jazz idiom; later he studied harmony and composition with Duruflé in Paris, where he immersed himself in the jazz scene. At age 16, he formed his first big band, and at 18, began his recording career with a Dixieland band. He soon made waves as a jazz musician, and later proved a successful composer for films, television, and the musical stage. He also worked with Duke Ellington, his mentor and friend, and many other noted jazz artists. In 1956 he organized another big band. He also made appearances as a jazz soloist, and later toured Europe and the U.S. with his own quintet. Bolling became a prominent figure in the crossover movement when he composed his Sonata for 2 Pianists (1970) for Jean-Bernard Pommier. His Suite for Flute and Jazz Piano Trio, written in 1975 for Jean-Pierre Rampal, became an internationally successful recording, attaining gold-record status in 1981. He also wrote *California Suite* (film score, 1976), Suite for Violin and Jazz Piano Trio (for Pinchas Zukerman; 1978), Suite for Chamber Orch. and Jazz Piano Trio (1983), and Suite for Cello and Jazz Piano Trio (for Yo-Yo Ma; 1984).

Bolshakov, Nikolai, Russian tenor; b. Kharkov, Nov. 23, 1874; d. Leningrad, Jan. 20, 1958. He studied in St. Petersburg; made his debut there with the Kharkov Opera Co. in 1899; in 1902 he went to Milan, where he studied voice with A. Brogi; then sang with the Maryinsky Theater in St. Petersburg (1906–29); participated in the spectacles of Diaghilev's "Russian Seasons" in Paris and London (1911–13); also gave recitals. From 1923 to 1953 he taught voice at the Leningrad Cons. He was noted for his interpretations of Faust and Don José.

Bombardelli, Silvije, Croatian conductor and composer; b. Split, March 3, 1916. He studied violin in Belgrade; returning to Split in 1945, he organized an orch. and also conducted opera. In his music, he applies modernistic procedures, including modified serial techniques.

WORKS: *Stranac* (The Stranger), ballet (Split, Jan. 25, 1956); *Plameni Vjetar* (The Flaming Wind) for Orch. and Speaking Chorus (Split, June 18, 1940); Sym. (Zagreb, Nov. 3, 1951); cantatas and choruses.

Bon, Maarten, Dutch pianist and composer; b. Amsterdam, Aug. 20, 1933. He graduated from the Muzieklyceum in Amsterdam in 1954; studied piano with T. Bruins and Spaanderman, and composition with Baaren; then gave recitals with his wife, the violinist Jeannelotte Hertzberger. His compositions, often whimsical, include *Capricboso y Obstinato* for Flute (1965); *Disturbing the Peace,* improvisation for 9 Players, more or less (1968–69); *Let's Go Out for a Drive (and Pollute the Air),* improvisation for Trombone, 3 Pianists, and Conductor (1970–74); *Free or Not* for 21 Wind Players (1972); *Sieben, jedenfalls sieben* for Chamber Ensemble (1976); *Display IV* for 6 Pianos and Piano Tuner (1980; rev. 1982) and *V* for 12 Cellos (1983); *Boréal* for Violin and Percussion Ensemble (1981); Solo for Clarinet (1983–86); *Canon a tre voci* for 3 Cellos (1988–93).

Bon, Willem Frederik, Dutch composer and conductor; b. Amersfoort, June 15, 1940; d. Nijeholtpade, April 14, 1983. He studied clarinet, conducting, and composition at the Amsterdam Cons. and the Royal Cons. of Music at The Hague, receiving a conducting diploma in 1971. In 1972 he became conductor of the Eindhoven Baroque Ensemble, and in 1973 was named an assistant conductor of the Concertgebouw Orch. in Amsterdam. At the time of his death, he taught composition at the Groningen Cons.

WORKS: DRAMATIC: *Eriks wonderbaarlijke reis* (Erik's Miraculous Journey), instrumental opera for Children, Narrator, and Orch. (1979). **ORCH.:** *Dialogues and Monologues* for Piano and Orch. (1968); *Nocturnes* for Strings (1968); *Variations on a Theme of Sweelinck* for Chamber Orch. (1969); 2 syms.: No. 1, *Usher Symphony,* after Poe (1968–70; originally intended as an opera) and No. 2, *Les Predictions* (1970); Concerto for Strings (1970); *Games* for 6 Wind Instruments, Piano, and Strings (1970); *To Catch a Heffalump* for Orch. and Tape (1971); *Circe,* prelude (1972); *Passacaglia in Blue* for 12 Wind Instruments and Double Bass (1972); *Aforismen* for 15 Strings (1972); Concerto for Oboes (Oboe, Oboe d'Amore, and Heckelphone) and Strings (1974); Sym. for Strings (1982). **CHAMBER:** 2 wind quintets (1963–66; 1969); Cello Sonata (1966); *Sunphoneion I* for Flute, Vibraphone, and Piano (1968); *Sans paroles* for Clarinet, Bass Clarinet, and String Trio (1970); *Petite trilogie* for Trumpet (1970); Sonata for Solo Bassoon (1970); *Riflessioni* for Flute and Harp (1971); *5 tours de passe-passe* for Flute and Piano (1971); *Allegorie* for Harp (1972); *3 Saturnien* for Piano Trio (1981). **PIANO:** *Miniatures* (1966). **VOCAL:** *3 poèmes de Verlaine* for Mezzo-soprano, Flute, Cello, and Piano (1967); *Missa brevis* for Chorus and 9 Wind Instruments (1969); *Jadis et naguère* for Mezzo-soprano, Clarinet, Violin, and Piano (1970); *1999, 4 Prophesies of Nostradamus* for Soprano and Orch. (1973); *Le Grand Age Millième*, 4 quatrains after Nostradamus, for Men's Chorus (1974); *Les Quatre Saisons de Verlaine*, each for a different Vocal Soloist and Orch.: *Le Printemps* for Soprano, *L'Été* for Alto, *L'Automne* for Baritone, and *L'Hiver* for Tenor (1976–79); *Silence*, after Poe, for Mezzo-soprano, Wind Quintet, and Piano (1978); *Dag* (Hello), 4 songs for Mezzo-soprano and Percussion (1979).

BIBL.: E. Vermeulen, "B.: Usher Symphony," *Sonorum Speculum*, No. 48 (Autumn 1971).

Bonaventura, Anthony di, American pianist and teacher, brother of **Mario di Bonaventura**; b. Follansbee, W.Va., Nov. 12, 1930. A precocious talent, he made his debut at age 13 as soloist in the Beethoven 3rd Piano Concerto with the N.Y. Phil. At age 18, he became a pupil of Vengerova at the Curtis Inst. of Music in Philadelphia, graduating at 24. He then launched an ambitious career as a soloist with American and European orchs.; also played numerous recitals. He commissioned several composers of the avant-garde to write special works for him, among them Luciano Berio, Milko Kelemen, and György Ligeti. In 1973 he was appointed to the piano faculty of Boston Univ.

Bonaventura, Arnaldo, Italian musicologist; b. Livorno, July 28, 1862; d. Florence, Oct. 7, 1952. He studied law, violin, and theory, but made musicology his career. He was a prof. of music history and librarian at the Florence Istituto Musicale until 1932; then became director and prof. of music history and aesthetics at the Florence Cons.

WRITINGS: *Manuale di storia della musica* (Livorno, 1898; 10th ed., 1920); *Elementi di estetica musicale* (Livorno, 1905; 3rd ed., 1926, as *Manuale di estetica musicale*); *Dante e la musica* (Livorno, 1904); *Storia degli stromenti musicali* (Livorno, 1908; many other eds.); *Niccolo Paganini* (Modena, 1911; 3rd ed., 1925); *Saggio storico sul teatro musicale italiano* (Livorno, 1913); *Storia e letteratura del pianoforte* (Livorno, 1918); *Verdi* (Paris, 1923); *Bernardo Pasquini* (Ascoli Piceno, 1923); *Manuale di cultura musicale* (Livorno, 1924); *"Mefistofele" di Boito* (Milan, 1924); *Giacomo Puccini: L'uomo-l'artista* (Livorno, 1925); *Storia del violino, dei violinisti e della musica per violino* (Milan, 1925); *L'opera italiana* (Florence, 1928); *Domenico del Mela* (Burgo San Lorenzo, 1928); *Musicisti livornesi* (Livorno, 1930); *Boccherini* (Milan and Rome, 1931); *Rossini* (Florence, 1934).

Bonaventura, Mario di, American conductor, music educator, and music publisher, brother of **Anthony di Bonaventura**; b. Follansbee, W.Va., Feb. 20, 1924. He studied violin; was a pupil in composition in Paris of Boulanger (1947–53) and in conducting at the Salzburg Mozarteum and in Paris of Igor Markevitch; received instruction in piano accompaniment at the Paris Cons., and won the Lili Boulanger Memorial Prize in composition (1953). He was music director of the Ft. Lauderdale Sym. Orch. (1959–62); then taught at Dartmouth College (1962–74), where he served as director of its Congregation of the Arts, a summer contemporary music festival (1963–70); after serving as vice-president and director of publications at G. Schirmer/Associated Music Publishers, N.Y. (1974–79), he was director of the Boston Univ. School of Music (1980–82).

Bonavia, Ferruccio, Italian-English writer on music and composer; b. Trieste, Feb. 20, 1877; d. London, Feb. 5, 1950. He studied violin in Trieste and Milan; in 1898 he went to England; earned his living as a violinist; mastered the English language and became music critic of the *Manchester Guardian* and of the *London Daily Telegraph*. He publ. a monograph on Verdi (London, 1930; 2nd ed., 1947); miniature biographies of Mozart (1938) and Rossini (1941); and a fanciful book of imaginary conversations, *Musicians in Elysium* (1949). He composed a Violin Concerto, a String Octet, a String Quartet, and some songs.

Bonci, Alessandro, Italian tenor; b. Cesena, Feb. 10, 1870; d. Viserba, Aug. 8, 1940. He studied with Carlo Pedrotti and Felice Coen in Pesaro, and with Delle Sedie in Paris. On Jan. 20, 1896, he made his operatic debut as Fenton in Parma; after appearances at Milan's La Scala (1897) and London's Covent Garden (debut as Rodolfo, 1900), he toured throughout Europe. On Dec. 3, 1906, he sang Lord Arthur Talbot in *I Puritani* at the opening of the new Manhattan Opera House in N.Y. On Nov. 22, 1907, he made his Metropolitan Opera debut in N.Y. as the Duke of Mantua, and remained on its roster until 1910. He later sang in Chicago (1919–21) and at the Teatro Costanzi in Rome (1922–23) before settling in Milan as a voice teacher. Among his best roles were Count Almaviva, Ottavio, Wilhelm Meister, and Rodolfo. He also appeared in German lieder recitals.

Bond, Carrie (Minetta) Jacobs, American composer; b. Janesville, Wis., Aug. 11, 1862; d. Los Angeles, Dec. 28, 1946. She was naturally gifted in music and painting, and improvised songs to her own words at the piano. She organized a music-selling agency and publ. her own songs under the imprint Carrie Jacobs Bond and Son. Although deficient in musical training, she succeeded in producing sweet melodies in lilting rhythms with simple accompaniments that became extremely popular in America. Her most successful song was *A Perfect Day* (1910), which sold more than 8 million copies of sheet music. Among her other successful songs were *I Love You Truly* (1901), *Just a-wearyin' for You* (1901), and *God Remembers When the World Forgets* (1913). Her autobiography appeared as *The Roads of Melody* (1927).

Bond, Victoria, American conductor and composer; b. Los Angeles, May 6, 1945. Her father was a physician and an opera singer and her mother was a pianist. Following initial music instruction from her mother, she attended the Mannes School of Music in N.Y. and pursued piano training with Reisenberg. Returning to Los Angeles, she studied composition with Ingolf Dahl at the Univ. of Southern Calif. (B.M.A., 1968), and also worked with Paul Glass. Upon returning to N.Y., she pursued studies in composition with Sessions and in conducting with Morel, Ehrling, Karajan, Leonard Slatkin, and Blomstedt at the Juilliard School (M.M.A., 1975; D.M.A., 1977), where she also was an assistant to Pierre Boulez and the first woman to take a doctorate in orchestral conducting. She was an Exxon-Arts Endowment conductor with the Pittsburgh Sym. Orch. (1978–80), and concurrently was music director of the Pittsburgh Youth Orch. From 1982 to 1986 she was music director of the Empire State Youth Orch. in Albany, and from 1982 to 1988 music director of the Bel Canto Opera in N.Y. She was music director of the Roanoke Sym. Orch. (1986–95) and artistic director of Opera Roanoke (1989–95). As a guest conductor, she appeared widely in the U.S., Europe, and Asia. She has made special effort to champion out-of-the-ordinary repertoire, including scores by women composers.

WORKS: DRAMATIC: OPERA: *Gulliver* (1988; rev. 1995 as *Travels*). **MUSIC THEATER:** *Everyone is Good for Something.* **BALLETS:** *Equinox* (1978); *Other Selves* (1979); *Sandburg Suite* (1980); *Great Gallopin Gottschalk* (1981). **ORCH.:** *Ringing* (Houston, July 4, 1986); *Urban Bird*, alto saxophone concerto (San Francisco, April 3, 1993); *Thinking Like a Mountain* (1994). **CHAMBER:** *Dreams of Flying*, string quartet (1994); **VOCAL:** *Tarot* for Chorus and Percussion Orch. (1978); *Molly ManyBloom* for Soprano and String Quartet (1990); song cycles.

Bondeville, Emmanuel (Pierre Georges) de, French composer; b. Rouen, Oct. 29, 1898; d. Paris, Nov. 26, 1987. He studied organ in Rouen and composition at the Paris Cons. He served as music director of the Eiffel Tower radio station (1935–49), artistic director of the Monte Carlo Opera (1945–49), and director of the Paris Opéra (1952–70). In 1959 he was elected a member of the Académie des Beaux-Arts of the Institut de France.

WORKS: 3 operas: *L'École des maris* (Paris, June 19, 1935), *Madame Bovary* (Paris, June 1, 1951), and *Antoine et Cléopâtre* (Rouen, March 10, 1974); symphonic triptych after Rimbaud's *Illuminations*: *Le Bal des pendus* (Paris, Dec. 6, 1930), *Ophélie* (Paris, March, 29, 1933) and *Marine* (Paris, March 11, 1934); *Symphonie lyrique* (1957); *Symphonie choréogaphie* (1965); choral pieces; songs; Piano Sonata.

Bondon, Jacques (Lauret Jules Désiré), French composer; b. Boulbon, Bouches-du-Rhône, Dec. 6, 1927. He studied violin and painting. In 1945 he settled in Paris, where he was a student of Dandelot, Koechlin, Milhaud, and Rivier. In 1963 he became a member of the music committee of the ORTF. In 1981 he became director of the Georges Bizet Cons. In 1979 he won the composition prize of the Institut de France. After early experimentation with ultramodern techniques, he tergiversated to prudential modernism.

WORKS: DRAMATIC: *Mélusine au rocher*, radio opera (1968; Luxembourg, Oct. 30, 1969); *Ana et l'albatros*, opera (Metz, Nov. 21, 1970); *i. 330*, opera-ballet (Nantes, May 20, 1975). **ORCH.:** *La Coupole* (1954); *Le Taillis ensorcelé* (1954); Ondes Martenot Concerto (1955); *Concert de printemps* for Piano, Strings, and Percussion (1957); *Suite indienne* (1958); *Giocoso* for Violin and Strings (1960); *Musique pour un autre monde* (1962); *Fleurs de feu* (1965); *Concerto de Mars* for Guitar and Orch. (1966); *Concerto de Molines* for Violin and Orch. (1968); *Lumières et formes animées* for Strings (1970); *Symphonie latine* (1973); *Concerto solaire* for 7 Brass Instruments and Orch. (1977); *Concerto d'octobre* for Clarinet and Strings (1978); *Symphonie concertante* for Piano and Winds (1979); *Concerto con fuoco* for Guitar and Strings (1981); *Concerto pour un ballet* for Flute and Orch. (1982). **CHAMBER:** *Sonatine d'été* for Violin and Piano (1953); *Kaléidoscope* for Ondes Martenot, Piano, and Percussion (1957); String Quartet (1959); *Le Soleil multicolore* for Flute, Harp, and Viola (1970); *Mouvements chorégraphiques* for Flute and Piano (1971); *Musique pour un jazz différent* for Percussion Quartet (1971); *Les Folklores imaginaires* for Wind Quintet (1986; also for Guitar, Flute, and Violin). **VOCAL:** *Le Résurrection*, oratorio (1975); *Les Monts de l'étoile* for Soprano, String Quartet, and Piano (1978; also for Soprano and Orch.); *Le Chemin de croix*, oratorio (1989).

BIBL.: M.-J. Chauvin, "Entretien avec J. B.," *Courrier Musical de France* (Jan./April 1970).

Bonelli (real name, **Bunn), Richard,** American baritone; b. Port Byron, N.Y., Feb. 6, 1887; d. Los Angeles, June 7, 1980. He studied at Syracuse Univ. and with Arthur Alexander and Jean de Reszke in Paris. On April 21, 1915, he made his operatic debut as Valentine at the Brooklyn Academy of Music. After appearances at the Monte Carlo Opera, Milan's La Scala, and in Paris, he sang with the Chicago Opera (1925–31). On Dec. 1, 1932, he made his Metropolitan Opera debut in N.Y. as Germont, remaining on its roster until 1945. Thereafter he taught at the Curtis Inst. of Music in Philadelphia and in N.Y. He was best known for his Verdi roles, but also was praised for his portrayals of Wolfram, Tonio, and Sharpless.

Bongartz, Heinz, German conductor; b. Krefeld, July 31, 1894; d. Dresden, May 2, 1978. He studied in Krefeld, and then at the Cologne Cons. with Fritz Steinbach (conducting), Otto Neitzel (composition), and Elly Ney (piano). In 1923 he became director of the Mönchen-Gladbach Opera. With Oskar Fried, he was conductor of the Blüthner-Orch. in Berlin (1924–26). After conducting in Meiningen (1926–31), he was music director in Gotha (1931–33), 1st conductor in Kassel (1933–37), Generalmusikdirektor in Saarbrücken (1937–44), and chief conductor of the Pfalz Orch. in Ludwigshafen (1944–46). In 1946–47 he was a prof. at the Leipzig Hochschule für Musik. From 1947 to 1964 he was chief conductor of the Dresden Phil.

Boninsegna, Celestina, Italian soprano; b. Reggio Emilia, Feb. 26, 1877; d. Milan, Feb. 14, 1947. Without the benefit of vocal training, she made her debut at the age of 15 at Reggio Emilia as Norina; then enrolled at the Pesaro Cons.; her official debut took place in Fano in 1896, when she appeared as Gilda; then sang in Milan, Rome, Genoa, and South America; also at London's Covent Garden (1904, 1905). On Dec. 21, 1906, she made her Metropolitan Opera debut in N.Y. as Aida, but remained on the roster for only that 1 season. In 1909–10 she sang with the Boston Opera. Following her retirement, she taught voice; spent her last years in the Casa di Riposo in Milan.

Bónis, Ferenc, Hungarian musicologist; b. Miskolc, May 17, 1932. He was educated at the Budapest Academy of Music, studying composition with Szervánszky, Bartha, Kodály, and Szabolcsi (Ph.D., 1958, with the diss. *Mosónyi Mihály*). He was an ed. with Hungarian Radio (1950–52; 1957–70); became director of its programs in music for young audiences in 1970. From 1961 to 1973 he was engaged in musicological research at the Hungarian Academy of Sciences; was made a lecturer at the Budapest Academy of Music in 1972. He became ed. of *Magyar Zenetudomány* in 1959, and also of *Magyar Zenetörteneti Tanulmányok* in 1968.

WRITINGS: *Erkel Ferenc* (Budapest, 1953; 2nd ed., 1954); *Bartók élete képekben* (Budapest, 1956; 4th ed., 1980; Ger. tr., 1964; French tr., 1964; Eng. tr., 1964, as *Béla Bartók: His Life in Pictures*); *Kadósa Pál* (Budapest, 1965); ed. *Tóth Aladár válogatott zenekritikai* (Budapest, 1968); *Bartók Béla élete képekben és documentumokban* (Budapest, 1972; Ger. tr., 1972; Eng. tr., 1972, as *Béla Bartók: His Life in Pictures and Documents*).

Bonner, Eugene (MacDonald), American composer and music critic; b. Jacksonville, N.C., 1889; d. Taormina, Sicily, Dec. 8, 1983. He studied at the Peabody Cons. of Music in Baltimore and received training in piano with Bachner and Hutcheson, in organ with Philips, and in composition with Bois and Brockway; during a European sojourn (1911–17), pursued studies in composition and instrumentation with Scott, Lehmann, and Bedford; during a 2nd European sojourn, took courses in instrumentation and conducting with Wolff in Paris (1921–27). Returning to the U.S., he became music ed. of *Outlook Magazine* (1927–29); subsequently was a music critic for the *Brooklyn Eagle*, the *Daily Mirror*, *Cue Magazine*, and the *N.Y. Herald Tribune*, and managing ed. of the *Musical Record*. In 1955 he settled in Taormina.

WORKS: DRAMATIC: OPERAS: *Barbara Frietchie* (1921); *Celui qui Épousa une Femme Muette* (1923); *The Venetian Glass Nephew* (1927); *The Gods of the Mountain* (1936); *Frankie and Johnnie* (1945). **INCIDENTAL MUSIC TO:** *The Young Alexander* (1929). **ORCH.:** *White Nights* (1925); *Taormina*, little suite (1939); Concertino for Piano and String Orch. (1945). **CHAMBER:** Piano Quintet (1925); *Suite Sicilienne* for Violin and Piano (1926). **VOCAL:** *Whispers of Heavenly Death*, 3 songs for Voice and Orch. (1922); *Flûtes* for Voice and 4 Instruments (1923).

Bonnet, Joseph (Élie Georges Marie), eminent French organist, pedagogue, and composer; b. Bordeaux, March 17, 1884; d. Ste. Luce-sur-Mer, Quebec, Aug. 2, 1944. He studied with his father, organist at Ste. Eulalie; at the age of 14, he was appointed regular organist at St. Nicholas, and soon after at St. Michel; entered the class of Guilmant at the Paris Cons. and graduated with 1st prize. In 1906 he won the post of organist at St. Eustache over many competitors. After extensive tours on the Continent and in England, he became organist of the Concerts du Conservatoire as successor to Guilmant in 1911, which position he retained until 1939. He made his American debut in N.Y. (Jan. 30, 1917), followed by successful tours of the U.S. In 1940 he fled France and went to the U.S., finally settling in Quebec as a teacher at the Cons. He wrote many pieces for his instrument, and ed. for publication all the works played in his series of N.Y. concerts as *Historical Organ Recitals* (6 vols.); also publ. an anthology of early French organ music (N.Y., 1942).

BIBL.: H. Gaul, "B., Bossi, Karg-Elert. Three Apercus," *Musical Quarterly* (July 1918).

Bonney, Barbara, American soprano; b. Montclair, N.J., April 14, 1956. She received training in Canada and with Walter Raninger at the Salzburg Mozarteum. In 1979 she became a member of the Darmstadt Opera, where she made her first appearance as Anna in *Die lustigen Weiber von Windsor*; among her subsequent roles were Blondchen, Adina, Cherubino, Gilda, Massenet's Manon, and Natalie in Henze's *Der Prinz von Homburg*. In 1983–84 she appeared with the Frankfurt am Main Opera, the Hamburg State Opera, and the Bavarian State Opera in Munich. In 1984 she made her first appearance at London's Covent Garden as Sophie. In 1985 she made her debut at Milan's La Scala as Pamina. She made her Metropolitan Opera debut in N.Y. on March 3, 1988, as Najade in *Ariadne auf Naxos*, where she returned to sing Adele and Sophie. In 1989 she made her first appearance at the Chicago Lyric Opera as Adele. She also pursued a successful concert career. Her husband is **Håkan Hagegård.**

Bonsel, Adriaan, Dutch flutist and composer; b. Hilversum, Aug. 4, 1918. He studied at the Amsterdam Cons.; appeared as a flute soloist in recitals and with various orchs.

WORKS: ORCH.: Suite for Flute and Strings (1946); *Folkloristic Suite* (1948); Clarinet Concerto (1950); 2 syms. (1956, 1957); *Divertimento* for Small Orch. (1957); *S.O.S.*, overture (1962); *Vrede-Oorlog-Vrede? (Peace-War-Peace?) Moto-perpetuo?* (1975); *Suite voor bamboe* (1988); *Sinfonietta* for Amateur Orch. (1990). **CHAMBER:** 2 wind quintets (1949, 1953); *Elegy* for Viola (1961); *Concert Études* for Flute (1963); *Musica* for Flute, Cello, and Piano (1971); *Anthriscus Sylvestris*, divertimento for 12 Flutes (1974); Octet for Winds (1975); *Intrada* for Horn, 2 Trumpets, 2 Trombones, and Tuba (1982); 3 pieces for Flute (1984).

Bonynge, Richard (Alan), noted Australian conductor; b. Sydney, Sept. 29, 1930. He studied piano at the New South Wales Conservatorium of Music in Sydney and at the Royal College of Music in London, beginning his career as a pianist. After marrying **Joan Sutherland** in 1954, he devoted himself to helping her master the bel canto operatic repertoire. In 1962 he made his conducting debut in a concert with his wife in Rome; he then made his debut as an opera conductor with a performance of *Faust* in Vancouver (1963). He made his first appearance at London's Covent Garden in 1964, leading a performance of *I Puritani*. On Dec. 12, 1966, he made his Metropolitan Opera debut in N.Y., conducting *Lucia di Lammermoor*, with his wife in the title role. In subsequent years he conducted concerts and operas throughout the world. He was music director of the Australian Opera in Sydney from 1976 to 1986. In 1977 he was made a Commander of the Order of the British Empire.

BIBL.: Q. Eaton, *Sutherland & B.: An Intimate Biography* (N.Y., 1987).

Bookspan, Martin, American music critic, administrator, and broadcaster; b. Boston, July 30, 1926. He was educated at the Boston Music School (violin and theory) and Harvard College (B.S. in German literature, 1947). He was executive director of the New England Opera Theater (1952–54); from 1956 to 1968, held various administrative positions with WQXR Radio in N.Y. In 1968 he was named coordinator for the sym. and concert activities of ASCAP. He was host and commentator for the Boston Sym. and Pops radio broadcasts (1957–68); from 1975 to 1988 he was host, commentator, and executive producer for the N.Y. Phil. radio broadcasts; from 1976 also commentator for the "Live from Lincoln Center" PBS telecasts. He was a permanent member of the panel of critics for the "First Hearing" radio program; was a contributing ed. to *Stereo Review Magazine* (1958–76); also wrote for the *N.Y. Times* (1963–65). He publ. *101 Masterpieces of Music and Their Composers* (N.Y., 1968); *Zubin: The Zubin Mehta Story* (N.Y., 1978); *André Previn: A Biography* (Garden City, N.Y., 1981).

Boone, Charles, American composer and writer on music; b. Cleveland, June 21, 1939. He studied with Schiske at the Vienna Academy of Music (1960–61); took private lessons with Krenek and Weiss in Los Angeles (1961–62); attended the Univ. of Southern Calif. in Los Angeles (B.M., 1963) and San Francisco State College (M.A., 1968); served as chairman of the San Francisco Composers' Forum and coordinator of the Mills College Performing Group and Tape Music Center. From 1975 to 1977 he was composer-in-residence in Berlin under the sponsorship of the Deutscher Akademischer Austauschdienst. In addition to composing, Boone has been active as a writer on contemporary music. His music creates a sonic environment on purely structural principles, employing serial matrices, coloristic contrasts, and spatial parameters of performing instruments, with resulting styles ranging from lyrical pointillism to static sonorism.

WORKS: *3 Motets* for Chorus (1962–65); *Oblique Formation* for Flute and Piano (1965); *Starfish* for Flute, Clarinet, 2 Percussion, 2 Violins, and Piano (1966); *A Cool Glow of Radiation* for Flute and Tape (1966); *The Edge of the Land* for Orch. (1968); *Not Now* for Clarinet (1969); *Zephyrus* for Oboe and Piano (1970); *Vermilion* for Oboe (1970); Quartet for Clarinet, Violin, Cello, and Piano (1970); *Chinese Texts* for Soprano and Orch. (1971); *First Landscape* for Orch. (1971); *Vocalise* for Soprano (1972); *Second Landscape* for Chamber Orch. (1973; also for Orch., 1979); *Raspberries* for 3 Percussion (1974); *Linea Meridiana* for 10 Instruments (1975); *San Zeno/Verona* for Chamber Ensemble (1976); *Fields/Singing* for Soprano and Chamber Ensemble (1976); *Shunt* for 3 Percussion (1978); *String Piece* for String Orch. (1978); *Streaming* for Flute (1979); *Little Flute Pieces* (1979); *Springtime* for Oboe (1980); *Winter's End* for Soprano, Countertenor, Viola da Gamba, and Harpsichord (1980); *Slant* for Percussion (1980); *The Watts Tower* for Percussion (1981); *Trace* for Flute and 10 Instruments (1981–83); *Weft* for 6 Percussion (1982); *Drum Bug* for Mechanical Woodblocks (1983); *The Khaju Bridge* for Soprano, Trumpet, Double Bass, Electric Organ, Percussion, and Tape (1984); *Drift* for Flute, Oboe, Clarinet, Piano, Violin, Viola, Cello, and Double Bass (1984); *Solar One* for Flute and Trumpet (1985); *The Timberline, and Other Pieces* for Carillon (1987–89); *Silence and Light* for String Quartet (1989–90); *Morphosis* for Percussion Quartet (1989–90).

Booren, Jo van den, Dutch composer; b. Maastricht, March 14, 1935. He studied trumpet with Marinus Komst and composition with Kees van Baaren and Klaus Huber; was active as an orch. trumpet player. In his music, he pursues the goal of sonorous structuralism.

WORKS: Trio for Oboe, Clarinet, and Bassoon (1960); Sonata for 3 Clarinets (1962); *Suite dionysienne* for English Horn and String Orch. (1963–64); *Estremi* for Oboe, Violin, Viola, and Cello (1967); *Spectra* for Wind Quintet (1967); *Capriccio* for Brass Orch. (1968); *Spiel I* for Oboe and Electronic Sound (1969); *Strofa I* for Cello (1969), *II* for Trumpet (1970), and *III* for Horn (1972); *Equilibrio* for Flute (1970); *Ballade* for Oboe (1971); *Intrada Festiva* for 4 Horns, 4 Trumpets, and 4 Trombones (1971); *Akirob* for Flute, Violin, and Viola (1972); *Potpourri 1973* for Brass Quintet (1973); 3 syms.: No. 1, *Sinfonia jubilata* (1975), No. 2 (1983), and No. 3, *Short Symphony* (1987); 3 flute quartets (1978, 1980, 1980); *Display* for Saxophone Quartet and Symphonic Band (1986); *Passage* for Orch. (1987); Sextet for 2 Clarinets, 2 Bassoon, and 2 Horns (1987); Sonata for Solo Violin (1988); Concerto for Saxophone Quartet and Orch. (1989); *Meditazione* for Large Ensemble (1990); *Rofena* for Wind Orch. (1990); Flute Concerto (1991); Organ Concerto (1991); Violin Concerto (1992); *Cirkels I* for Accordion Orch. (1993) and *II* for Wind Band and String Orch. (1993).

Borchard, Adolphe, French pianist and composer; b. Le Havre, June 30, 1882; d. Paris, Dec. 13, 1967. He studied at the

Paris Cons. with Diémer and Lenepveu, where he won prizes for piano (1903) and composition (1905, 1907); toured extensively as a pianist, making his American debut in 1910; later settled in Paris as director of various musical activities sponsored by the French government. He composed *Es Kual Herria* (The Basque Country) for Piano and Orch. (1922); *En marge de Shakespeare* for Orch. (1923); *L'Élan* for Orch. (1923); *Sept estampes amoureuses* for Orch. (1927); numerous songs.

Borck, Edmund von, talented German composer; b. Breslau, Feb. 22, 1906; in battle near Nettuno, Italy, Feb. 16, 1944. He studied composition in Breslau (1920–26), and music history at the Univ. of Berlin; held several positions as opera conductor in Berlin and Frankfurt am Main; then taught theory and composition in Berlin until drafted into the army in 1940. His progress as a composer was rapid; his early works indicated an innate and original creative ability, and his death in combat was a great loss to German music. His style of composition is neo-Classical, with strong contrapuntal structure; the rather austere and reticent mode of expression assumes in Borck's music a colorful aspect through a variety of melodic and rhythmic devices, often in a rhapsodically romantic vein.

WORKS: Alto Saxophone Concerto (1932); Violin Sonata (1932); *Orchesterstücke* (1933); *Ländliche Kantate* (1934); *Concerto for Orchestra* (1936); Sextet for Flute and Strings (1936); *Kleine Suite* for Flute (1938); *2 Fantasiestücke* for Orch. (1940); Piano Concerto (1941); *Orphika*, "an Apollonian transformation" for Orch. (1941); *Napoleon*, opera (1942).

Boretz, Benjamin (Aaron), American composer, editor, and music critic; b. N.Y., Oct. 3, 1934. He studied piano and cello, and received lessons in conducting from Julius Rudel and in harpsichord from Erwin Bodky; he also took courses at Brooklyn College (B.A., 1954), Brandeis Univ. (M.F.A., 1957), and Princeton Univ. (M.F.A., 1960; Ph.D., 1970). Among his composition mentors were Berger, Fine, Foss, Milhaud, and Sessions. He held many academic appointments, including N.Y. Univ. (1964–69), Columbia Univ. (1969–72), and Bard College (from 1973). He was music critic for the *Nation* (1962–69), and, with Berger, founded *Perspectives of New Music* (1961), serving as its co-ed. until 1964, and then as its ed. until 1983, again from 1994. With Edward T. Cone, he co-ed. *Perspectives on Schoenberg and Stravinsky* (1968; 2nd ed., rev., 1972), *Perspectives on American Composers* (1971), *Perspectives on Contemporary Music Theory* (1972), and *Perspectives on Performance and Notation* (1976). With J.K. Randall, he publ. the collection *Being About Music* (1995). His compositions include a *Concerto Grosso* for String Orch. (1956); Violin Concerto (1956); *Divertimento* for 5 Instruments (1957); String Quartet (1958); *Group Variations I* for Orch. (1967) and *II* for Computer (1970–74; re-realized 1993); *Liebeslied* for Piano (1974); *". . . my chart shines high where the blue milk's upset . . ."* for Piano (1978); *Language, as a Music: 6 Marginal Pretexts for Composition* for Speaker, Piano, and Prerecorded Tape (1980); *Soliloquy I* for Piano (1981); *music/consciousness/gender* for Voice, Recorded Voices, Computer-generated Sound, Acoustic Sound, and Video Images (1994). He also composed a series of works in sound score, the "notation" being in the form of sound on tape.

Borg, Kim, Finnish bass, teacher, and composer; b. Helsinki, Aug. 7, 1919. He studied voice with Heikki Teittinen in Helsinki (1936–41; 1945–47), where he also received training in theory and composition with Leo Funtek and Aarre Merikanto, and then pursued vocal studies with Andrejewa de Skilondz in Stockholm (1950–59). He also studied biochemistry at the Helsinki Inst. of Technology (diploma, 1946). In 1947 he made his formal concert debut in Helsinki, and in 1951 his formal operatic debut in Århus as Colline in *La Bohème*. In addition to his concert appearances, he sang regularly in opera in Helsinki and Copenhagen (1952–70), Stockholm (1963–75), and Hamburg (1964–70). On Oct. 30, 1959, he made his Metropolitan Opera debut in N.Y. as Count Almaviva, remaining on its roster until 1962. In 1961 he appeared as Boris Godunov in Moscow. He retired from the stage in 1980. From 1972 to 1989 he was a prof. at the Royal Danish Cons. of Music in Copenhagen. He publ. the books *Suomalainen laulajanaapinen* (ABC for a Finnish Singer; Helsinki, 1972) and *Muistelmia* (Memoirs; Helsinki, 1992). Among his compositions were 2 syms., *Sinfonietta* for Strings, a Trombone Concerto, a Concerto for Double Bass and Strings, chamber music, a *Stabat Mater*, and songs. He also prepared orchestrations of Mussorgsky's *Songs and Dances of Death* and *Without Sun*, and of Wolf's *Michelangelo Lieder*. In addition to Boris Godnunov, he also had success in such roles as Osmin, Don Giovanni, King Marke, Hans Sachs, Don Carlos, Pimen, Gremin, Rossini's Don Basilio, and Debussy's Arkel.

Borgatti, Giuseppe, Italian tenor; b. Cento, March 17, 1871; d. Reno, Lago Maggiore, Oct. 18, 1950. He studied with Alessandro Busi in Bologna; made his operatic debut as Faust in Castelfranco Veneto in 1892; in 1896 he sang the title role in *Andrea Chenier* at Milan's La Scala; also sang in Wagner's operas. He retired from the stage in 1914 owing to glaucoma, becoming totally blind in 1923. He publ. an autobiography, *La mia vita d'artista* (Bologna, 1927). His daughter, Renata Borgatti (b. Bologna, March 2, 1894; d. Rome, March 10, 1964), was a pianist.

Borge, Victor (real name, **Borge Rosenbaum**), variously talented Danish-born American pianist and inborn musical humorist; b. Copenhagen, Jan. 3, 1909. He began his training with his father, Bernhard Rosenbaum (1847–1932), and appeared in recital in Copenhagen at the age of 8. After further studies with Schiøler there, he pursued training with Petri and Lamond in Vienna and Berlin. From 1922 to 1934 he appeared as a concert pianist. Although he commanded a fine facility and prestidigital velocity at the keyboard, he failed to develop the necessary *Sitzfleisch* for a virtuoso concert career. However, in 1931 he began presenting a type of humorous piano concert sui generis, garnering success not only in Denmark but also throughout Europe. Hitler and his goosestepping cohorts provided Borge with fertile comedic material. After the Nazis occupied Denmark in 1939 and placed Borge at the top of their blacklist, he deemed it prudent to leave Europe for N.Y. in 1940. In 1948 he became a naturalized American citizen. An appearance on Bing Crosby's "Kraft Music Hall" radio program in 1941 proved so successful, that he returned for 56 consecutive weeks. In 1945 he played at N.Y.'s Carnegie Hall. He had his own "Victor Borge Show" on radio in 1946. In 1953 he opened his own one-man show on Broadway, billed as "comedy in music," which ran for 849 rib-tickling performances. In succeeding years, he toured extensively and with great success. He later took up conducting, and appeared with various U.S. orchs. in both light and serious programs. His mastery of idiomatic English and his remarkable gift for improvising jokes were aided and abetted by his sepulchral voice, capable of imitating everything from bassos to ornithological coloratura sopranos. Thus superbly equipped, he continued to delight audiences well into his 80s. Indeed, his video *Victor Borge: Then and Now* (1993) proved a best-seller. He publ. the books *My Favorite Intermissions* (1971) and *My Favorite Comedies in Music* (1980).

BIBL.: H. Temianka, "V. B. Zooms toward 80," *Musical America* (Jan. 1989).

Borgioli, Armando, Italian baritone; b. Florence, March 19, 1898; d. in an air raid on the Milan-Modena train near Codogno, Jan. 20, 1945. He made his debut as Amonasro at the Teatro Carcano in Milan in 1925; then sang at Milan's La Scala and London's Covent Garden. On Jan. 22, 1932, he made his Metropolitan Opera debut in N.Y., as Carlo in *La forza del destino*, remaining on the company's roster until 1935. He was best known for his dramatic roles in Verdi's operas.

Borgioli, Dino, Italian tenor; b. Florence, Feb. 15, 1891; d. there, Sept. 12, 1960. He studied in Florence with Eugenio Giachetti. In 1914 he made his operatic debut as Arturo in *I Puri-*

tani at Milan's Teatro Corso; appeared in various Italian opera houses, including Milan's La Scala (debut as Ernesto in *Don Pasquale*, 1918). After singing with Melba on her farewell tour of Australia (1924), he made his first appearance at London's Covent Garden as Edgardo in 1925, continuing to sing there until 1939. In 1932 he sang Cavaradossi in San Francisco, a role he again sang in Chicago in 1933. On Dec. 31, 1934, he made his Metropolitan Opera debut in N.Y. as Rodolfo, but sang with the company for only that 1 season. In 1937 he sang Ottavio at the Glyndebourne Festival. From 1939 he taught voice in London, eventually retiring to Florence. His roles in operas by Mozart and Rossini were particularly esteemed.

Bori, Lucrezia (real name, **Lucrecia Borja y Gonzalez de Riancho**), distinguished Spanish soprano; b. Valencia, Dec. 24, 1887; d. N.Y., May 14, 1960. She studied at the Valencia Cons. and with Melchior Vidal in Milan. She made her operatic debut in Rome at the Teatro Adriano on Oct. 31, 1908, as Micaëla; then sang in Milan, in Naples, and, in 1910, in Paris as Manon Lescaut with the Metropolitan Opera Co.; then made a European tour. In 1911 she sang at La Scala in Milan; made her debut at the Metropolitan Opera in N.Y. as Manon Lescaut on Nov. 11, 1912, and sang there until the end of the 1914–15 season. After a period of retirement occasioned by a vocal affliction, she reappeared in 1919 at Monte Carlo as Mimi, returning to the Metropolitan in 1921 in the same role. Thereafter she appeared in N.Y. with increasing success and popularity until the end of the 1935–36 season, when she retired from opera. Among her finest roles were Juliette, Despina, Massenet's Manon, Mélisande, Violetta, Norina, and Mimi.

Borkh, Inge (real name, **Ingeborg Simon**), famous German soprano; b. Mannheim, May 26, 1917. She first appeared as a stage actress, then decided upon a singing career. She studied at the Milan Cons. and at the Mozarteum in Salzburg. She made her debut as Czipra in Johann Strauss's *Zigeunerbaron* at the Lucerne Opera in 1940, remaining a member there until 1944; then sang at the Bern Opera until 1951. She made her American debut at the San Francisco Opera in 1953; on Jan. 24, 1958, she appeared at the Metropolitan Opera in N.Y. as Salome, returning to its roster for the 1960–61 and 1970–71 seasons. In 1959 she made her first appearance at London's Covent Garden, also as Salome. She made her farewell operatic appearance at the Munich Festival in 1988. Her other notable roles included Leonore, Eglantine, Lady Macbeth, and Elektra.

Bořkovec, Pavel, Czech composer; b. Prague, June 10, 1894; d. there, July 22, 1972. He originally studied philosophy, and turned to composition rather late in life; took lessons with Křička and Foerster in 1919; from 1925 to 1927 he attended master classes of Suk at the Prague Cons. From 1946 to 1964 he was on the faculty of the Academy of Musical Arts in Prague. His early works were in the manner of Dvořák and Suk; later he experienced the influence of neo-Classicism and adopted dissonant counterpoint.

WORKS: DRAMATIC: OPERAS: *The Satyr* (1937–38; Prague, Oct. 8, 1942); *Paleček* (Tom Thumb; 1945–47; Prague, Dec. 17, 1958). **BALLET:** *Krysař* (The Pied Piper; 1939; concert perf., Prague, Jan. 15, 1941; 1st stage perf., Oct. 8, 1942). **ORCH.:** *Stmívaní* (Twilight), symphonic poem (1920); 3 syms. (1926–27; 1955; 1959); *The Start*, symphonic allegro (1929; Prague, March 26, 1930); 2 piano concertos (1931; 1949–50); Violin Concerto (1933); *Partita* (1936); Concerto Grosso for 2 Violins, Cello, Orch., and Piano (1941–42); *2 Symphoniettas* for Chamber Orch. (1944; 1963–68); Cello Concerto (1950–51). **CHAMBER:** Piano Quartet (1922); 5 string quartets (1924; 1928; 1940; 1947; 1961–62); Sonata for Solo Viola (1931); Wind Quintet (1932); 2 violin sonatas (1934, 1956); Nonet (1941–42); Violin Sonatina (1942); *Intermezzo* for Horn and Piano (1965). **PIANO:** Suite (1930); *Partita* (1935); *2 Pieces* (1941–42). **VOCAL:** *Jen jedenkrat* (Only Once), melodrama (1921); *Stadion* (The Stadium) for Voice, Wind Quintet, and Piano (1929); *Love Songs* for Voice and Piano or Small Orch., after Goethe and Villon (1932); *5 Songs*, after Pasternak (1935); *6 Madrigals about Time* for Chorus (1957); *Silentium Turbatum*, symphonic movement for Alto, Orch., and Electric Guitar (Prague, Feb. 28, 1965); *Te Deum* for Soli, Chorus, and Orch. (1968).

Bornefeld, Helmut, German organist and composer; b. Stuttgart-Untertürkheim, Dec. 14, 1906; d. Heidenheim, Feb. 11, 1990. He studied organ, piano, and composition at the Hochschule für Musik in Stuttgart; then was organist and choirmaster in Heidenheim. With Siegfried Reda, he organized the Heidenheim Arbeitstage für Neue Kirchenmusik in 1946, and remained actively engaged in its activities until 1960. His compositions include numerous sacred and secular choral pieces, chamber music, and organ pieces.

WRITINGS: *Das Positiv* (Kassel, 1941); *Orgelbau und neue Orgelmusik* (Kassel, 1952); *Orgelspiegel* (Kassel, 1966).

Bornschein, Franz (Carl), American composer, conductor, and teacher; b. Baltimore, Feb. 10, 1879; d. there, June 8, 1948. He spent his entire career in his native city, where he first studied violin with Lawrence Rosenberger and Julius Zech; subsequently he studied violin with Joan Van Hulsteyn and harmony with Phillip Kahmer and Otis Boise at the Peabody Cons. of Music (diploma, 1902). In 1905 he joined its preparatory dept. and also was made the local correspondent of *Musical America*. From 1910 to 1913 he was music critic of the Baltimore *Sun*. In 1919 he became a teacher of violin, conducting, and composition at Peabody, remaining on its faculty until his death. He also conducted various local orch. and choral groups. Bornschein had modest success as a composer of choral works, some of which appeared under the pseudonym Frank Fairfield. His tone poems on American subjects were favorably received.

WORKS: DRAMATIC: *Mother Goose's Goslings*, children's operetta (1918); *Willow Plate*, operetta (1932); *Song of Songs*, opera (1934). **ORCH.:** *The Phantom Canoe* (Baltimore, Nov. 24, 1916); *The Sea God's Daughter* (Chicago, Feb. 10, 1924); *Old Louisiana* (1930); *Southern Nights* (Washington, D.C., March 1, 1936); *Leif Ericson* (Baltimore, Feb. 23, 1936); *Moon over Taos* (1939); *The Earth Sings* (1939); *The Mission Road* (1939); *Ode to the Brave* (1939); 2 violin concertos; numerous suites for Youth Orch. **CHAMBER:** String Quartet (1900); Piano Quintet (1904); *Pan Dances* for Flute and Strings (1933); *Appalachian Legend* for Cello and Piano (1940); *The Sprite* for Harp (1945); 22 duos for Violin and Piano; keyboard pieces. **VOCAL:** *Deodate*, oratorio; 7 cantatas; 27 anthems; more than 80 choruses; 30 songs.

Borovsky, Alexander, Russian-American pianist; b. Mitau, March 18, 1889; d. Waban, Mass., April 27, 1968. He first studied with his mother (a pupil of Safonov), then with A. Essipova at the St. Petersburg Cons., winning the Rubinstein Prize in 1912. He taught master classes at the Moscow Cons. from 1915 to 1920; then gave recitals in Turkey, Germany, France, and England. He was a soloist with virtually all major European orchs.; he also made several successful tours in South America. In 1941 he settled in the U.S., and became a prof. at Boston Univ. (1956).

Borowski, Felix, English-American composer, music critic, and teacher; b. Burton, March 10, 1872; d. Chicago, Sept. 6, 1956. He studied violin with his father, a Polish émigré; took lessons with various teachers in London, and at the Cologne Cons.; then taught in Aberdeen, Scotland. His early *Russian Sonata* was praised by Grieg, which provided impetus to his progress as a composer. In 1897 he accepted a teaching engagement at the Chicago Musical College; was its president from 1916 to 1925. Subsequently he became active in musical journalism; in 1942 he was appointed music ed. of the *Chicago Sun*; also served as program annotator for the Chicago Sym. Orch. (from 1908). He also taught musicology at Northwestern Univ. (1937–42). Among his many musical works, the violin piece *Adoration* became widely popular. Borowski revised G.P.

Upton's *The Standard Operas* in 1928, and *The Standard Concert Guide* in 1930.

WORKS: DRAMATIC: *Boudour,* ballet-pantomime (Chicago, Nov. 25, 1919); *Fernando del Nonsensico,* satiric opera (1935). **ORCH.:** Piano Concerto (Chicago, 1914); *Allegro de concert* for Organ and Orch. (Chicago, 1915); *Peintures* (Chicago, Jan. 25, 1918); *Le Printemps passionné,* symphonic poem (Evanston, Ill., 1920); *Youth,* fantasy-overture (Evanston, Ill., May 30, 1923); *Ecce Homo,* symphonic poem (N.Y., Jan. 2, 1924); *Semiramis,* symphonic poem (Chicago, Nov. 13, 1925); 3 syms.: No. 1 (Chicago, March 16, 1933), No. 2 (Los Angeles, July 22, 1936), and No. 3 (Chicago, March 29, 1939); *The Little Match Girl* for Narrator and Orch., after Andersen (1943); *Requiem for a Child* (1944); *The Mirror,* symphonic poem (Louisville, Nov. 27, 1954). **CHAMBER:** 3 string quartets; many pieces for violin, organ, and piano. **VOCAL:** Songs.

Børresen, (Aksel Ejnar) Hakon, Danish composer; b. Copenhagen, June 2, 1876; d. there, Oct. 6, 1954. He studied with Svendsen; was awarded the Ancker scholarship for composition in 1901. He was president of the Danish Composers Soc. from 1924 to 1949. His compositions include the operas *Den Kongelige Gaest* (Copenhagen, Nov. 15, 1919) and *Kaddara* (Copenhagen, March 16, 1921); *Tycho Brahes Dröm,* ballet (Tycho Brahe's Dream; Copenhagen, March 1, 1924); 3 syms.; Violin Concerto; chamber music; piano works; songs.

Borris, Siegfried, respected German music scholar, pedagogue, and composer; b. Berlin, Nov. 4, 1906; d. there, Aug. 23, 1987. He studied economics at the Univ. of Berlin (1925–27), where he then pursued training in musicology with Arnold Schering (Ph.D., 1933, with the diss. *Kirnbergers Leben und Werk*); he also studied composition with Paul Hindemith at the Berlin Hochschule für Musik (1927–29), where he subsequently taught (1929–33). After teaching privately, he rejoined its faculty as a lecturer in music history in 1945; he also was director of Berlin's Julius Stern Inst. from 1967. He composed in an accessible style, highlighted by an effective use of folk music.

WORKS: DRAMATIC: 2 radio operas: *Hans im Glück* (1947) and *Hirotas und Gerline* (1948); *Die Rübe,* Märchenoper (1953); *Frühlingsgesellen,* Liederspiel (1951); *Ruf des Lebens,* scenic cantata (1954); *Das letzte Spiel,* ballet (1955). **ORCH.:** Suite (1938); 5 syms. (1940, 1940, 1942, 1943, 1943); *Aeolische Suite* for Strings (1943); Concertino for English Horn and Strings (1949); *Divertimento* for 5 Winds and Strings (1951); Concerto for Harpsichord, Flute, Bassoon, and Strings (1952); Concertino for Flute and Strings (1953); Concertino for Accordion and Orch. (1955); Concerto for Violas da Gamba, 3 Woodwind Instruments, and Strings (1957); Piano Concerto (1962); *Hymnus* for Oboe and Orch. (1964); *Concerto for Orchestra* (1964); Organ Concerto (1965); Saxophone Concerto (1966); Horn Concerto (1967); Concerto for Strings (1968); *Evolution* for 19 Winds, 3 Double Basses, Harp, and Percussion (1972). **CHAMBER:** Oboe Quartet (1938); Wind Quintet (1938); 3 string quartets (1938, 1941, 1953); Wind Octet (1941); Octet for Clarinet, Bassoon, Horn, and Strings (1960); Piano Quintet (1960); Wind Sextet (1966); also 15 sonatas, 16 duos, 16 trios, and many keyboard pieces. **VOCAL:** Sacred works, including *Missa "Dona nobis pacem"* (1953), *Weihnachtsmotette* (1955), and *Psalm CXXXV* for Solo Voices, Chorus, and Orch. (1963); secular works, including 14 sets of lieder.

WRITINGS: *Praktische Harmonielehre* (Berlin, 1938; 2nd ed., rev., 1972); *Der grosse Acker* (Berlin, 1946); *Beiträge zu einer neuen Musikkunde* (Berlin, 1947–48); *Einführung in die moderne Musik* (Halle, 1951); *Klingende Elementarlehre* (Berlin, 1951; 2nd ed., 1973); *Modern Jazz* (Berlin, 1962); *Die Oper im 20. Jahrhundert* (Wolfenbüttel, 1962–73); *Der Schlüssel zur Musik von heute* (Düsseldorf, 1967); *Musikleben in Japan* (Kassel, 1967); *Die grossen Orchester* (Düsseldorf, 1969).

Borroff, Edith, American musicologist and composer; b. N.Y., Aug. 2, 1925. She was educated at the Oberlin Cons., the American Cons. of Music in Chicago (B.Mus, 1946; M.M., 1948), and the Univ. of Mich. (Ph.D., 1958). She taught at Milwaukee-Downer College (1950–54), Hillsdale College in Michigan (1958–62), the Univ. of Wisc. (1962–66), Eastern Michigan Univ. (1966–72), and the State Univ. of N.Y. at Binghamton (1973–92).

WRITINGS: *Elisabeth Jacquet de La Guerre* (1966); *The Music of the Baroque* (1970); *Music in Europe and the United States: A History* (1971; 2nd ed., 1989); ed. *Notations and Editions (A Book in Honor of Louise Cuyler)* (1974); with M. Irvin, *Music in Perspective* (1976); *Three American Composers* (1986); *American Opera: A Checklist* (1992); *Music Melting Round: A History of Music in the United States* (1995).

WORKS: 4 string quartets; String Trio (1943); *Variations* for Cello and Piano (1944); Quintet for Clarinet and Strings (1948); 2 cello sonatas (1949, 1993); *Sonatina giocoso* for Viola and Piano (1953; also for Violin and Piano, 1980); *Spring over Brooklyn,* musical (1954); Horn Sonata (1955); *Variations and Theme* for Oboe and Piano (1956); *Voices in Exile,* 3 canons for Flute and Viola (1962); *IONS: 14 Pieces in the Form of a Sonnet* for Flute and Piano (1968); *The Sun and the Wind,* musical fable (1974–76); *Game Pieces,* suite for Woodwind Quintet (1980); Concerto for Marimba and Small Orch. (1981); Trio for Tenor Saxophone, Piano, and Percussion (1982); Trio for Violin, Cello, and Piano (1983); *The Elements,* sonata for Violin and Cello (1987); *Comic Miniatures,* suite for Violin and Piano (1988); *Mottoes,* suite for 8 Saxophones (1989); *32 Variations in the Form of a Sonata* for Clarinet and Piano (1991); piano pieces; organ music; choral pieces; songs.

BIBL.: J. Regier, *The Organ Compositions of E. B.: An Introduction* (diss., Univ. of Okla., 1993).

Bortkiewicz, Sergei (Eduardovich), Russian pianist and composer; b. Kharkov, Feb. 28, 1877; d. Vienna, Oct. 25, 1952. He was a pupil of Liadov at the St. Petersburg Cons. (1896–99); later studied with Jadassohn in Leipzig (1900–1902). He made his debut as a pianist in Munich in 1902, and subsequently made concert tours of Germany, Australia, Hungary, France, and Russia. From 1904 to 1914 he lived in Berlin, and taught at the Klindworth-Scharwenka Cons.; then returned to Russia; was in Vienna from 1920 to 1929, in Berlin from 1929 to 1934, and again in Vienna from 1934. His compositions include an opera, *Acrobats*; 2 syms.; *Austrian Suite* and *Yugoslav Suite* for Orch.; 4 piano concertos; Violin Concerto; Cello Concerto; piano pieces; songs. He was the author of the book *Die seltsame Liebe Peter Tschaikowskys und der Nadezhda von Meck* (1938).

Börtz, Daniel, Swedish composer; b. Osby, Hässleholm, Aug. 8, 1943. He studied composition privately with Fernström and Rosenberg, and then at the Stockholm Musikhögskolan with Blomdahl (1962–65) and Lidholm (1965–68); he also received training in violin from Barkel and Grünfarb, and later in electronic music from Koenig at the Univ. of Utrecht. From 1972 to 1979 he was secretary of the Swedish Composer's Soc. He taught at the Stockholm Musikhögskolan from 1987. Börtz's works, which reflect the state of contemporary usages, nevertheless display an individualistic approach to melodic and harmonic writing.

WORKS: DRAMATIC: *Muren—Vägen—Ordet,* liturgical opera (1971–72); *Landskab med flod,* chamber opera (1972); *Den heliga Birgittas död och Mottagande i himmelen,* liturgical opera (Lund, Oct. 7, 1973); *Bacchanterna,* opera (1988–90; Stockholm, Nov. 2, 1991). **ORCH.:** *Intrada* (1964); *In memoriam di . . .* (1969); 11 syms. (1973; 1974–75; 1975–76; 1976–77; 1980–81; 1981–83; 1984–86; 1987–88; 1990–91; 1992; 1993–94); Concerto for Violin, Bassoon, and Chamber Orch. (1974); *Concerto grosso* No. 1 (1977–78) and No. 2 for Wind Orch. (1981); *October Music* for Strings (1978); Concerto for Bassoon, Winds, and Percussion (1978–79); Concerto for Cello and Chamber Orch. (1980); Concerto for Piano, Percussion, and Chamber Orch. (1981–82); Violin Concerto (1985); Oboe Concerto (1986); *Parodos* (1987). **CHAMBER:** *5 Preludes* for Flute (1964); *Monologhi I* for Cello (1965–66), *II* for Bassoon (1966), *III* for Violin (1967), and *IV* for

Piano and Tape (1970); 3 string quartets (1966; 1971; 1985–87). **VOCAL:** *Il canto dei canti di Salomone* for Soprano and Instruments (1965); *Voces* for 3 Voices, Orch., and Tape (1968); *Josef K* for Narrator, 8 Soli, Chorus, and Orch., after Kafka (1969); *Night Winds* for Vocal Quartet (1972); *Nightflies* for Mezzo-soprano and Chamber Ensemble (1973); *Fläcker av liv* for 2 Narrators, Soli, Chorus, and Orch. (1979–80).

Borup-Jørgensen, (Jens) Axel, Danish composer; b. Hjörring, Nov. 22, 1924. He studied with Rachlew (piano), and with Schierbeck and Jersild (orchestration) at the Royal Danish Cons. of Music in Copenhagen (1946–51); later attended the summer sessions in new music at Darmstadt (1959, 1962). His works came to reflect the ideals of Fortner, Ligeti, and Stockhausen.

WORKS: ORCH.: Concertino for Piano, Flute, Bassoon, and Strings (1948–49); *Fantasy* for Flute and Strings (1949); Clarinet Concerto (1949–50); *Chamber Concerto* for Violin and Small Orch. (1951); *Sommasvit* for Strings (1957); *Cretaufoni* (1960–61); *Insulae* for Strings (1961–62); *Stykker* (1963–65); *Marin* (1963–70); *Nordic Summer Pastorale* for Small Orch. (1964); *Déjà vu* for Guitar and Strings (1983). **CHAMBER:** 5 string quartets (1950; 1951; 1954–55; 1960; 1965); Viola Sonata (1952–53); *Partita* for Viola (1953–54); *Improvisations* for String Quartet (1955); *Music* for Percussion and Viola (1955–56); *Microorganisms* for String Quartet (1956); Sonatina for 2 Violins (1958); *Sonata breve* for Viola and Piano (1959–60); *Mobile* for Viola, Marimba, and Piano (1961); *Vinterstykke* for String Quartet (1967); *Tagebuch im Winter* for Flute, String Quartet, and Piano (1970–72); *Distichon* for Violin and Piano (1972–73); *Malinconia* for String Quartet (1972–74); *Recostruzioni* for Wind Quintet (1973–74); *Carambolage* for Piano, Electric Guitar, and Percussion (1976–77); *Musica Autumnalis* for Winds, Percussion, and Electric Organ (1977); Piano Quintet (1978); *Periphrasis* for Flute and Percussion (1979); *Favola* for Flute and Harp (1980); *La Primavera* for 2 Percussionists (1982); *Coast of Sirens* for 7 Instruments and Tape (1985); Trio for Clarinet, Cello, and Piano (1988–90); *2 Movements* for Harp (1993). **PIANO:** *7 Preludes* (1958–59); *Winter Pieces* (1959); *Vinter-epigrammer* (1975); *Epigrammer* (1976); *Thalatta, Thalatta* (1988). **VOCAL:** *Pocket Oratorium* for 16 Voices and Instruments (1963–64); *Marin* for 24 Men's Voices (1969); songs.

Bory, Robert, Swiss writer on music; b. Geneva, April 1, 1891; d. Nyon, Oct. 9, 1960. He studied jurisprudence while at the same time taking courses in composition with Jaques-Dalcroze and conducting with Gustave Doré. Pursuing a legal career, he became a judge in Nyon in 1934. He publ. pictorial eds. on Mozart, Beethoven, Wagner, Liszt, and Chopin.

WRITINGS: *Une Retraite romantique en Suisse: Liszt et la Comtesse d'Agoult* (Geneva, 1923; 2nd ed., 1930); *La Vie de Franz Liszt par l'image* (Geneva, 1936); *Liszt et ses enfants, Blandine, Cosima et Daniel* (Paris, 1936); *Richard Wagner: Sein Leben und sein Werk in Bildern* (Frauenfeld, 1938); *La Vie et l'oeuvre de Wolfgang-Amadeus Mozart par l'image* (Geneva, 1948; Eng. tr., 1948); *La Vie de Frédéric Chopin par l'image* (Geneva, 1951); *Le Séjour en Suisse de Wolfgang-Amadeus Mozart en 1766* (Lausanne, 1956); *La Vie et l'oeuvre de Beethoven par l'image* (Zürich, 1960; Eng. tr., 1966).

Bos, Coenraad Valentyn, Dutch pianist and pedagogue; b. Leiden, Dec. 7, 1875; d. Chappaqua, N.Y., Aug. 5, 1955. He was a pupil of Julius Rontgen at the Amsterdam Cons. (1892–95); later studied in Berlin. With Jan van Veen (violin) and Jan van Lier (cello), he formed a trio in Berlin which enjoyed an enviable reputation during its active period (1896–1910). His masterly accompaniments on a tour with Ludwig Wüllner attracted more than ordinary attention, and made him one of the most celebrated accompanists both in Europe and in the U.S., where he eventually settled. He was the accompanist of Culp, Hempel, Traubel, Kreisler, Schumann-Heink, Casals, Gerhard, Thibaud, Farrar, and many others. He taught at the Juilliard School of Music in N.Y. from 1934 to 1952. In collaboration with Ashley Pettis, he publ. *The Well-Tempered Accompanist* (1949).

Boschot, Adolphe, French music critic; b. Fontenay-sous-Bois, near Paris, May 4, 1871; d. Paris, June 1, 1955. He was music critic of *Echo de Paris* from 1910, and of *Revue Bleue* from 1919; founded, with Théodore de Wyzewa, the Paris Mozart Soc.; was elected to the Institut de France in 1926, succeeding Widor as permanent secretary of the Académie des Beaux-Arts. His greatest work is an exhaustive biography of Berlioz in 3 vols.: *La Jeunesse d'un romantique, Hector Berlioz, 1803–31* (Paris, 1906; rev. ed., 1946), *Un Romantique sous Louis-Philippe, Hector Berlioz, 1831–42* (Paris, 1908; rev. ed., 1948), and *Le Crépuscule d'un romantique, Hector Berlioz, 1842–69* (Paris, 1913; rev. ed., 1950). Other books are *Le Faust de Berlioz* (1910; new ed., 1945); *Carnet d'art* (1911); *Une Vie romantique, Hector Berlioz* (an abridgement of his 3-vol. work, 1919; 27th ed., 1951; also in Eng.; definitive ed., 1965); *Chez les musiciens* (3 vols., 1922–26); *Entretiens sur la beauté* (1927); *La Lumière de Mozart* (1928); *Le Mystère musical* (1929); *La Musique et la vie* (2 vols., 1931–33); *Théophile Gautier* (1933); *Mozart* (1935); *La Vie et les oeuvres d'Alfred Bruneau* (1937); *Musiciens-Poètes* (1937); *Maîtres d'hier et de jadis* (1944); *Portraits de musiciens* (3 vols., 1946–50); *Souvenirs d'un autre siècle* (1947). Boschot tr. into French the librettos of several of Mozart's operas. He was also prominent as a poet; publ. the collections *Poèmes dialogués* (1901) and *Chez nos poètes* (1925).

Boscovich, Alexander Uriah, significant Israeli composer; b. Klausenburg, Transylvania, Aug. 16, 1907; d. Tel Aviv, Nov. 13, 1964. He studied in Budapest; later enrolled at the Vienna Academy of Music, where he studied piano with Victor Ebenstein and composition with Richard Stöhr; then went to Paris, where he took courses with Paul Dukas and Boulanger; also had a few lessons in piano with Alfred Cortot. From 1930 to 1938 he was engaged as conductor at the State Opera in Cluj; in 1938 he emigrated to Palestine; taught at the Tel Aviv Cons. (1945–64); wrote music criticism for the Israeli newspaper *Haaretz*. In his music, Boscovich incorporated quasi-oriental motifs in the framework of Western music; in several works, he made use of authentic Jewish folk songs, adorning them with modernistic harmonies. In this manner he wrote his most popular piece, *Chansons populaires juives* for Orch. (Haifa, March 15, 1938; orig. entitled *The Golden Chain*). Other works: Violin Concerto (1942); Oboe Concerto (1943); *Adonai Ro'i* (The Lord Is My Shepherd) for Alto Voice and Orch. (1946); *Semitic Suite* for Piano (1947; also for 2 Pianos, and for Orch.); *Piccola suite* for Flute, Snare Drum, and String Orch. (1956–57); *Psalm* for Violin and Piano (1957; contains thematic material from the Violin Concerto); *Cantico di ma'alot* (Song of Ascent) for Orch. (1960); *Bal Yisrael* (Daughter of Israel), cantata for Tenor, Chorus, and Orch. (1960–61); *With Joy and Gladness* for 2 Violins, with optional Drum and Triangle (1961); *Piece* for Oboe and Harpsichord (1961–62); *Lament* for Violin or Cello, and Piano (1962); *Concerto da camera* for Violin and Chamber Ensemble (1962); *Ornaments* for Flute and 4 Orch. Groups (1964).

Bose, Fritz, German musicologist; b. Messenthin, July 26, 1906; d. Berlin, Aug. 16, 1975. He studied at the Humboldt Univ. in Berlin, where his teachers included Abert and Schering (musicology), Hornbostel (ethnomusicology), and Sachs (organology); received his Ph.D. there in 1934 with the diss. *Die Musik der Uitoto* (publ. in Berlin, 1934). He was a lecturer of the Univ. of Berlin from 1934 to 1945; in 1953 he was named director of the history dept. of the Institut für Musikforschung in Berlin, retiring in 1971; he also taught at the Technical Univ. of Berlin (1963–67). In 1966 he founded the Deutsche Gesellschaft für Musik des Orients, which he headed until 1972. He also served as ed. of the *Jahrbuch für musikalische Volks- und Völkerkunde* from 1963 until his death. He wrote the study *Musikalische Völkerkunde* (Freiburg im Breisgau and Zürich, 1953).

Bose, Hans-Jürgen von, German composer; b. Munich, Dec. 24, 1953. He went to Frankfurt am Main and studied at the Hoch Cons. (1969–72) and with Hans Engelmann (composition) and Klaus Billing (piano) at the Hochschule für Musik

(1972–75). In 1980 and 1985 he held scholarships at the Villa Massimo in Rome. In 1986 he was elected a member of the Akademie der Künste in Berlin.

WORKS: DRAMATIC: *Blütbund*, chamber opera (1974; Hamburg, June 8, 1977); *Das Diplom*, comic opera (1975; Ulm, Nov. 26, 1976); *Die Nacht aus Blei*, ballet (1980–81; Berlin, Nov. 1, 1981; rev. 1988; Wiesbaden, March 23, 1991); *Die Leiden des jungen Werthers*, lyrical scenes (1983–84; Schwetzingen, April 30, 1986); *Chimäre*, opera (Aachen, June 11, 1986); *Werther-Szenen*, ballet (1988; Schweinfurt, April 26, 1989); *63: Dream Palace*, opera (1989; Munich, May 6, 1990); *Medea*, ballet (Zürich, Feb. 20, 1994). **ORCH.:** *Morphogenesis* (1975; Baden-Baden, Sept. 12, 1976); Sym. No. 1 (1976; Munich, March 10, 1978); *Musik für ein Haus voll Zeit* for Large Chamber Orch. (1978; Kiel, April 9, 1979); *Travesties in a Sad Landscape* for Chamber Orch. (London, Nov. 19, 1978); *Symphonic Fragment* for Tenor, Baritone, Bass, Chorus, and Orch. (Darmstadt, June 1, 1980); *Variationen* for 15 Strings (1980; Frankfurt am Main, March 29, 1981; rev. 1990; Berlin, Jan. 25, 1991); *Idyllen* (1982–83; Berlin, April 23, 1983); *Symbolum* for Organ and Orch. (1985; Munich, May 27, 1988); *Labyrinth I* (1987; Stuttgart, March 4, 1991); *. . . Other Echoes Inhabit the Garden* for Oboe and Orch. (Donaueschingen, Oct. 16, 1987); *Prozess* for Chamber Orch. (1987–88; Radio France, Paris, March 5, 1988); *Zwei Studien* (Saarlandischer Rundfunk, Saarbrucken, May 28, 1989);*Concertino per il H.W.H.* for Chamber Orch. (Munich, Sept. 29, 1991); *Scene* for Chamber Orch. (London, Oct. 8, 1991). **CHAMBER:** 3 string quartets: No. 1 (1973), No. 2 (1976–77), and No. 3 (1986–89; Saarbrücken, May 25, 1989); *Threnos—Hommage à Bernd Alois Zimmermann* for Viola and Cello (1975); Sonata for Solo Violin (1975); String Trio (1978); *Solo* for Cello (1978–79); *. . . vom Wege abkommen* for Cello (1981–82); *Drei Studien* for Violin and Piano (1986; Paris, April 24, 1988); *Drei Epitaphe* for Wind Sextet (Berlin, Sept. 12, 1987); Nonett (Salzburg, Aug. 21, 1988); *Befragung* for Clarinet, 2 Violins, Viola, Cello, and Double Bass (1988; Mönchengladbach, June 5, 1989); *Edge* for Violin (Berlin, Nov. 17, 1989). **PIANO:** *Labyrinth II* (1987; Frankfurt am Main, Jan. 8, 1988); *Origami*, 2 episodes for Piano, 4-hands (1991; Deutschlandsberg, Oct. 18, 1992). **VOCAL:** *Todesfuge* for Baritone, Chorus, and Organ (1972; Frankfurt am Main, Nov. 10, 1991); 3 Songs for Tenor and Chamber Orch. (1977); *Guarda el canto* for Soprano and String Quartet (1981–82); *Sappho-Gesänge* for Mezzo-soprano and Piano or Chamber Orch. (1982); *. . . im Wind gesprochen* for Soprano, 2 Narrators, Chorus, Organ, and Chamber Orch. (1984–85; Stuttgart, Sept. 20, 1985); *Sonnet XLII* for Baritone and String Quartet, after Shakespeare (1985; Hamburg, Feb. 7, 1986); *5 Gesänge* for Baritone and 10 Instruments, after García Lorca (1986; Cologne, Feb. 6, 1987); *Karfreitags-Sonett* for Chorus (1986); *Sechs deutsche Volkslieder* for Baritone and 8 Instruments (Berlin, Oct. 18, 1988); *Vier Lieder* for Soprano and 10 Instruments (Berlin, Oct. 18, 1988); *Achalm* for Soprano and 7 Instruments (Frankfurt am Main, Sept. 8, 1989); *Love after Love* for Soprano and Orch. (1990–91; Hamburg, Oct. 13, 1991); *Ein Brudermord* for Baritone, Accordion, Cello, and Tape (Stuttgart, Nov. 8, 1991); *In hora mortis* for Speaker and String Orch. (1991; Cologne, March 10, 1992); *Siete Textos de Miguel Angel Bustos* for Soprano, Accordion, and Cello (Digne-les-Bains, Oct. 11, 1991).

Boskovsky, Willi, noted Austrian violinist and conductor; b. Vienna, June 16, 1909; d. Visp, Switzerland, April 21, 1991. He entered the Vienna Academy of Music at age 9 to study violin with Mayrecker and Moravec, graduating at 17 with the Fritz Kreisler Prize. He made appearances as a soloist until 1939, although he joined the Vienna Phil. in 1933; from 1939 to 1971 he was one of its concertmasters. In 1937 he founded the Boskovsky Quartet, and in 1948 the Vienna Octet, with which he remained active until 1958. From 1954 to 1979 he served as conductor of the New Year's Day Concerts of the Vienna Phil., which brought him international recognition through its radio and television broadcasts. From 1969 he also was chief conductor of the Vienna Strauss Orch., and likewise conducted the Vienna Mozart Ensemble.

Bosmans, Henriëtte (Hilda), Dutch pianist and composer; b. Amsterdam, Dec. 5, 1895; d. there, July 2, 1952. She studied piano with her mother at the Amsterdam Cons., and embarked on a career as a pianist. In 1927 she took lessons in composition with Willem Pijper. In her music, she cultivated an agreeable neo-Classical idiom, with coloristic éclat, suggesting the techniques and devices of French Impressionism; wrote many songs to texts by French poets.

WORKS: Violin Sonata (1918); Cello Sonata (1919); Piano Trio (1921); 2 cello concertos (1922, 1924); *Poem* for Cello and Orch. (1926); String Quartet (1928); Piano Concertino (1928; Geneva, April 6, 1929); *Konzertstück* for Flute and Orch. (1929); *Konzertstück* for Violin and Orch. (1934); *Doodenmarsch* (March of the Dead) for Narrator and Chamber Orch. (1946); piano pieces.

Bosse, Gustave, German publisher; b. Vienenburg, Feb. 6, 1884; d. Regensburg, Aug. 27, 1943. He founded his firm in 1912 at Regensburg; publ. *Zeitschrift für Musik* (from 1929) and *Deutsche Musikbücherei* (a collection of music books).

BIBL.: S. Lieberwirth, *G. B.: Ein Leben am ersten Pult* (Leipzig, 1987).

Bosseur, Jean-Yves, French composer and writer on music; b. Paris, Feb. 5, 1947. He studied privately with Stockhausen and Pousseur; later was active as a producer for Radio-France. His compositions, marked by experimentation without specific serial procedures, include a symphonic suite, *Un Arraché de partout*, for Brass, Hammond Organ, 2 Electric Guitars, Vibraphone, Xylorimba, Marimbaphone, and Percussion (1967; Paris, March 22, 1968); *Interstices* for 24 Strings (1971); *In extremis* for Orch. (1975); *Frau Linke Quartett* for String Quartet (1975); *Instants de mémoire* for Piano, Clarinet, Flute, Violin, and Cello (1977–78); *Satie's Dream* for Voice and Chamber Ensemble, after Kenneth White (1980–81); *Empreintes Nocturnes* for Piano, after Satie (1981); *Ton Bale* for Wind Orch. (1985); *Stream* for Accordion (1989); *Hong-Kong Variations* for Instrumental Group (1990); *Mémoires d'oubli* for Orch., Voice, and Tape, after Bernard Noël (1990–91); *Portrait de Geneviève Asse* for Harpsichord, Harp, and Cello (1991); Mass (1995); also ballets and film music. Bosseur is also a prolific writer of articles and books on current music and musical life; among his most valuable publications are *Musique, passion d'artistes* (1988; Eng. tr., 1991), *Le Sonore et le visuel* (1992; Eng. tr., 1993), and *John Cage* (1995).

Bossi, (Marco) Enrico, Italian organist, pianist, pedagogue, and composer, father of **(Rinaldo) Renzo Bossi**; b. Salò, Brescia, April 25, 1861; d. at sea (en route from America to Europe), Feb. 20, 1925. Son and pupil of the organist Pietro Bossi of Morbegno (1834–96), he studied at the Liceo Rossini in Bologna (1871–73), and at Milan (1873–81) under Sangali (piano), Fumagalli (organ), Campanari (violin), Boniforti (counterpoint), and Ponchielli (composition). He was maestro di cappella and organist at Como Cathedral (1881–89), prof. of organ and harmony in the Royal Cons. San Pietro at Naples (until 1896), prof. of advanced composition and organ at the Liceo Benedetto Marcello in Venice (1896–1902), director of the Liceo Musicale at Bologna (1902–12), and director of the Music School of the Accademia di Santa Cecilia in Rome (1916–23); toured Europe, England, and the U.S. as a pianist and organist. He wrote *Metodo di studio per l'organo moderno* (Milan, 1893).

WORKS: 3 operas: *Paquita* (Milan, 1881), *Il Veggente* (Milan, 1890; rev. version as *Il Viandante*, Mannheim, 1896), and *L'Angelo della notte*; *Giovanna d'Arco*, mystery place (1913); *Intermezzi Goldoniani* for String Orch.; *Concertstück* for Organ and Orch.; *Inno di Gloria* for Chorus and Organ; *Tota pulchra* for Chorus and Organ; *Missa pro Sponso et Sponsa* (Rome, 1896); *Il Cieco* for Solo, Chorus, and Orch. (1897); *Canticum Canticorum*, biblical cantata; *Il Paradiso Perduto* for Chorus and Orch.

(Augsburg, 1903); *Surrexit pastor*, motet; *Primavera classica* for Chorus; String Trio; Piano Trio; etc.

BIBL.: H. Gaul, "Bonnet, B., Karg-Elert, Three Apercus," *Musical Quarterly* (July 1918); E. Dagnino, *M.E. B., Cenni biografici* (Rome, 1925); L. Orsini, *Fascicolo commemorativo* (Milan, 1926); G. Paribeni, L. Orsini, and E. Bontempelli, *M.E. B.: Il Compositore, l'organista, l'uomo* (Milan, 1934); F. Mompellio, *M.E. B.* (Milan, 1952).

Bossi, (Rinaldo) Renzo, Italian conductor, teacher, and composer, son of **(Marco) Enrico Bossi**; b. Como, April 9, 1883; d. Milan, April 2, 1965. He studied in Venice and in Leipzig; took a course in conducting with Nikisch; conducted at various cities in Italy; in 1916 he was appointed instructor at the Verdi Cons. in Milan.

WORKS: DRAMATIC: OPERAS: *Passa la ronda* (Milan, March 3, 1919); *Volpino il calderaio* (Milan, Nov. 13, 1925); *La rosa rossa* (Parma, Jan. 9, 1940). **BALLET:** *Il trillo del diavolo* (1948). **ORCH.:** Sym.; Violin Concerto. **OTHER:** Many, many minor pieces for various instruments.

BIBL.: F. Mompellio, *M.E. B.* (Milan, 1952); S. Pintacuda, *R. B.* (Milan, 1955).

Bostelmann, Otto, German-American composer; b. Hamburg, Aug. 22, 1907; d. Santa Barbara, Calif., March 16, 1981. He settled in the U.S. in 1926; studied with Wesley La Violette in Los Angeles; organized the Bohemian Composers Group there in 1957. His works comprise 3 syms., 3 "crescendi" for Orch., and much chamber music.

Botstein, Leon, Swiss-born American educator, historian, and conductor; b. Zürich, Dec. 14, 1946. After graduating from the High School of Music and Art in N.Y. (1963), he studied history at the Univ. of Chicago (B.A., 1967) and Harvard Univ. (A.M., 1968; Ph.D., 1985). He lectured on history at Boston Univ. (1969) and was president of Franconia (N.H.) College (1970–75); also was founder-principal conductor of the White Mountain Festival of the Arts (1973–75). In 1975 he became both president and prof. of history and music history at Bard College in Annandale-on-Hudson, N.Y., where he also was artistic director of the Bard Music Festival (from 1990). While retaining these positions, he also pursued a conducting career; was co-conductor (1982–89) and conductor (1989–92) of the Hudson Valley Phil. Chamber Orch. in Poughkeepsie, N.Y., and also principal guest conductor of the Hudson Valley Phil. (1991–92). From 1992 he was conductor of the American Sym. Orch. in N.Y. In 1992 he became the revitalizing ed. of the *Musical Quarterly*. His provocative articles, essays, and reviews, ranging from the current state of education in America to music history, have appeared in various newspapers, magazines, and professional journals. He publ. *Judentum und Modernität: Essays zur Rolle der Juden in der Deutschen und Österreichischen Kultur 1848–1938* (Vienna, 1991).

Botstiber, Hugo, Austrian music scholar; b. Vienna, April 21, 1875; d. Shrewsbury, England, Jan. 15, 1941. He was a pupil of R. Fuchs, Zemlinsky, H. Rietsch, and Guido Adler in Vienna, where he subsequently held administrtive posts until emigrating to England in 1939. He ed. the *Musikbuch aus Österreich* (1904–11); publ. *Joseph Haydn und das Verlagshaus Artaria* (with Franz Artaria; Vienna, 1911); *Geschichte der Ouvertüre* (Leipzig, 1913); and *Beethoven im Alltag* (Vienna, 1927); completed C. Pohl's biography of J. Haydn (Vol. III, Leipzig, 1927). Of particular interest to American musicians is his article "Musicalia in der New York Public Library" in the bulletin of the Société Internationale de Musique (Oct. 1903), calling international attention for the first time to the important music collection of the N.Y. Public Library.

Bottenberg, Wolfgang (Heinz Otto), German-born Canadian composer and teacher; b. Frankfurt am Main, May 9, 1930. He entered the Jesuit order in 1952 and taught himself theory and organ. After graduating from the Theologische Hochschule Vallender (1957), he emigrated to Canada in 1958 and became a naturalized Canadian citizen in 1964. He studied theory with R.A. Stangeland at the Univ. of Alberta (B.Mus., 1961), and then completed his training with Huston, Takács, and Cooper at the Univ. of Cincinnati (M.Mus., 1962; D.M.A., 1970). He taught at the Acadia Univ. in Wolfville, Nova Scotia (1965–73) and at Concordia Univ. in Montreal (from 1973). His interest in early music prompted him to organize the Acadia Medieval Ensemble in Montreal in 1974. In addition to early music, Bottenberg's works have been notably influenced by Hindemith. He makes eclectic use of tonal, atonal, and serial resources.

WORKS: OPERA: *Inook* (1986). **ORCH.:** *Passacaglia* for Chamber Orch. (1961; rev. 1971); *Fantasia* for Trumpet and Small Orch. (1966); *A Suite of Carols* (1967; orchestration of *3 English Carols* for Piano Duet, 1963); *Sinfonietta* (1970; orchestration of Sonata for Piano Duet, 1961); *Fantasia Serena* (1973; Halifax, Dec. 1, 1980); Concerto for Organ and Small Orch. (1975; Guelph, July 18, 1979); Concertino for Tenor Saxophone and Strings (1989); *Festival Overture* (1990); *Prelude, Aria, and Fugue* for Strings (1992; Montreal, April 22, 1993). **CHAMBER:** *Sonata with Variations on a South German Folk Song* for 2 Alto Recorders and Piano (1959; rev. 1972); Quartet for Flute, 2 Clarinets, and Bassoon (1960); Trio for Flute, Clarinet, and Piano (1960–63); Trio for Flute, Clarinet, and Bassoon (1963); *Variables* for Recorder Player, Woodwind Quartet, and String Quintet (1964); Trio for 3 Recorders (1964); *Ciacona* for Alto Recorder and Harpsichord or Piano (1964; rev. 1977); String Quartet (1968); *Divertimento* for Flute Quartet (1968); *Dialogue* for Alto Recorder and Harpsichord or Piano (1971; rev. 1972); Octet (1972; Montreal, Feb. 21, 1985); *Fa So La Ti Do Re* for Soprano Saxophone or Clarinet and String Quartet (1972; Radio Hilversum, Jan. 17, 1984); Sonata for Flute and Clarinet (1972); *Partita* for Guitar, Recorder Quartet, and Viola da Gamba (1978); *Sonata Modalis* for Clarinet or Viola and Piano (Montreal, Nov. 22, 1979); *Overture for Broken Consort* for Flute, Clarinet, Violin, Cello, and Guitar (1981; San Francisco, March 29, 1982); *Fanfare* for Brass Quintet (1982); *5 for 5* for Woodwind Quintet (1983; Montreal, Feb. 21, 1985); *Reflections of Summer* for Flute, Viola, and Guitar (1983); *Canzona Festiva "O Canada"* for 16 Horns (Montreal, Dec. 15, 1989); Suite for Recorder Quartet and Optional Percussion (Montreal, May 17, 1989); Trio for Viola, Cello, and Piano (1991); *Toccata* for Clarinet and 4 Sounds Tracks (1991; also for 5 Clarinets). **KEYBOARD: PIANO:** Sonata for Piano Duet (1961; orchestrated as *Sinfonietta*, 1970); *3 English Carols* for Piano Duet (1963; orchestrated as *A Suite of Carols*, 1967); *Moods of the Modes* (1973); *3 Sketches* (1981); Pieces for Piano Duet (1988); *Elements of Nature* for 2 Pianos (1990). **ORGAN:** *Triptych* (1967); *Sonata "Ave Maris Stella"* (1990). **VOCAL:** *Duineser Kantate/Duino Cantata* for Baritone, Chorus, and Small Orch. (1962); *The World is a Rainbow*, secular cantata for Soprano or Tenor or Boy Soprano, Chorus, and Woodwind Quintet (1966); *Those Passions . . . Which Yet Survive*, cantata for Bass and 7 Instruments (1968); *Ritual* for Chorus and Orch. (1970); *Eine Weihnachtliche Hausmusik* for Medium Voice, 2 Alto Recorders, and Piano or Piano Duet (1973); *Canadian Madrigals* for Chorus (1983); *Cunctipotens Genitor Deus* for Chorus and Orch. (1990); songs.

WRITINGS: *Building a Treble Viola da Gamba* (Montreal, 1980); ed. *Florilegium Cantionum Mensuralium* (2 vols., Montreal, 1982); *Reading Early Music from Original Notation* (Montreal, 1983).

Bottje, Will Gay, American flutist, teacher, and composer; b. Grand Rapids, June 30, 1925. He studied flute (B.S., 1947) and received instruction in composition (M.S., 1948) from Vittorio Giannini at the Juilliard School of Music in N.Y.; then pursued training with Hank Badings in Holland and Boulanger in Paris (1952–53); subsequently was a pupil of Bernard Rogers and Hanson (composition), Joseph Mariano (flute), and Paul White (conducting) at the Eastman School of Music in Rochester, N.Y. (D.M.A., 1955); later worked at the Univ. of Utrecht electronic music studios (1962–63) and at the Stockholm Stiftlesen (1973).

He taught at the Univ. of Mississippi (1955–57) before serving as prof. of theory and composition at Southern Illinois Univ. in Carbondale (1957–81), where he founded an electronic music studio (1965). His music is of a highly experimental nature, awash with corrosive dissonances in a manner influenced primarily by developments cultivated in the Northern avant-garde music laboratories.

WORKS: OPERAS: *Altgeld* (Carbondale, Ill., March 6, 1968); *Root!* (1971). **ORCH.:** 7 syms. (1946–70); *The Ballad Singer* (1951); Concerto for Flute, Trumpet, Harp, Strings, and Percussion (1955); Piccolo Concertino (1956); *Theme and Variations* (1958); Concerto for Trumpet, Trombone, and Winds (1959); Piano Concerto (1960); *Sinfonietta* (1960); *Sinfonia Concertante* for Brass Quintet and Winds (1961); *Rhapsodic Variations* for Viola, Piano, and Strings (1962); *Chiaroscuros* (1975); *Mutations* for Small Orch. (1977); Tuba Concerto (1977); *Songs From the Land Between the Rivers* (1980); Concerto for Oboe, Bassoon, and Orch. (1981); *Scenes From the West Shore* (1983); *Commentaries* for Guitar and Orch. (1983); Concerto for 2 Flutes and Orch. (1984); Concerto for Oboe, Violin, and Orch. (1984). **CHAMBER:** 4 string quartets (1950, 1959, 1962, 1982); Quintet for Flute and Strings (1954); 2 wind quintets (1957, 1984); Trumpet Sonata (1959); Cello Sonata (1959); Saxophone Quartet (1963); *Modalities I* for Saxophone Quartet and Tape (1970) and *II* for Clarinet and Tape (1971); *Modules I* for Clarinet and Piano (1973) and *II* for Double Bass and Piano (1976); Sym. for Cello and Piano, 4-hands (1978–79); Guitar Sonata (1980); Oboe Sonata (1981); Harpsichord Sonata (1981). **VOCAL:** Song cycles.

Boucourechliev, André, Bulgarian-born French writer on music and composer; b. Sofia, July 28, 1925. After training at the Sofia State Academy of Music (1946–49), he pursued studies in Paris at the École Normale de Musique (1949–51) and received piano instruction from Gieseking at the Saarbrücken Cons. (1955). Returning to Paris, he became a naturalized French citizen in 1956 and was active mainly as a music critic and composer. He wrote a number of orch. and chamber pieces in an advanced idiom. Among his books are *Schumann* (Paris, 1957; Eng. tr., 1959), *Chopin: A Pictorial Biography* (London, 1963), *Beethoven* (Paris, 1963), *Stravinsky* (Paris, 1982; Eng. tr., 1987), and *Essai sur Beethoven* (Arles, 1991).

Boudreau, Robert (Austin), American trumpeter and conductor; b. Bellingham, Mass., April 25, 1927. He studied trumpet with Georges Mager of the Boston Sym. Orch. and with William Vacchiano at the Juilliard School of Music in N.Y. He then taught music at Ithaca College (1951–52), Lehigh Univ. (1952–53), and Duquesne Univ. (1955–57). In 1957 he founded in Pittsburgh the American Wind Sym. Orch., specializing in contemporary music; it commissioned works from numerous composers with its performances taking place aboard the *Point Counterpoint II*, a floating arts center.

Boué, Geori (actually, **Georgette**), French soprano; b. Toulouse, Oct. 16, 1918. After studying at the Toulouse Cons., she settled in Paris, where she sang with success in opera and operetta; in 1942 she made her first appearance at the Opéra as Marguerite, and subsequently appeared there regularly; also toured in Europe. She was married to **Roger Bourdin**. Although she was particularly esteemed for her French roles, she also sang Violetta, Leonore, Salome, Tosca, Desdemona and Cio-Cio-San.

Boughton, Rutland, English composer; b. Aylesbury, Jan. 23, 1878; d. London, Jan. 24, 1960. He studied at the Royal College of Music in London with Stanford and Davies; without obtaining his diploma, he engaged in professional activity; was for a time a member of the orch. at the Haymarket Theatre in London; taught at the Midland Inst. in Birmingham (1905–11); also conducted a choral society there. He became a firm believer in the universality of arts along Wagnerian lines; formed a partnership with the poet Reginald Buckley; their book of essays, *The Music Drama of the Future*, expounding the neo-Wagnerian idea, was publ. in 1911. To carry out these plans, Boughton organized stage festivals at Glastonbury, helped by his common-law wife, Christina Walshe. Boughton's opera, *The Immortal Hour*, was performed there on Aug. 26, 1914; his choral music drama, *The Birth of Arthur*, had a performance there in 1920; these productions were staged with piano instead of an orch. After an interruption during World War I, Boughton continued the Glastonbury festivals until 1926. In 1927 he settled in the country, in Gloucestershire. He continued to compose, however, and produced a number of stage works, as well as instrumental pieces. His ideas of universal art had in the meantime been transformed into concepts of socialist realism, with an emphasis on the paramount importance of folk music as against formal constructions. He publ. *The Death and Resurrection of the Music Festival* (1913); *The Glastonbury Festival Movement* (1922); *Bach, the Master* (1930); *Parsifal: A Study* (1920); *The Nature of Music* (1930); *The Reality of Music* (1934).

WORKS: DRAMATIC: *The Birth of Arthur* (1909; Glastonbury, Aug. 16, 1920); *The Immortal Hour* (1913; Glastonbury, Aug. 26, 1914); *The Round Table* (Glastonbury, Aug. 14, 1916); *The Moon Maiden*, choral ballet for girls (Glastonbury, April 23, 1919); *Alkestis*, music drama (Glastonbury, Aug. 26, 1922); *The Queen of Cornwall*, music drama (Glastonbury, Aug. 21, 1924); *May Day*, ballet (1926); *The Ever Young*, music drama (1928; Bath, Sept. 9, 1935); *The Lily Maid*, opera (Gloucester, Sept. 10, 1934); *Galahad*, music drama (1944); *Avalon*, music drama (1946). **ORCH.:** *The Skeleton in Armour*, symphonic poem with Chorus (1898); *The Invincible Armada*, symphonic poem (1901); *A Summer Night* (1902); 3 syms. (*Oliver Cromwell*, 1904; *Deirdre*, 1927; 1937); *Love and Spring* (1906); *Midnight* (1907); Trumpet Concerto (1943). **CHAMBER:** Violin Sonata (1921); Quartet for Oboe and Strings (1930); String Trio (1944); Piano Trio (1948); Cello Sonata (1948). **VOCAL:** *Song of Liberty* for Chorus and Orch. (1911); *Bethlehem*, choral drama (1915); *Pioneers* for Tenor, Chorus, and Orch. (1925); many choral pieces.

BIBL.: *The Self-Advertisement of R. B.* (c.1909); H. Antcliffe, "A British School of Music Drama: The Work of R. B.," *Musical Quarterly* (Jan. 1918); M. Hurd, *Immortal Hour: The Life and Period of R. B.* (London, 1962; 2nd ed., rev. and enl., 1993, as *R. B. and the Glastonbury Festivals*); idem, "The Glastonbury Festivals," *Musical Times* (Aug. 1984).

Boughton, William (Paul), English conductor; b. Birmingham, Dec. 18, 1948. He studied cello at the Guildhall School of Music in London, with Maurice Eisenberg in the U.S., and with Milos Sadlo at the Prague Academy of Music; after a brief career as a cellist with the Royal Phil., the London Sinfonietta, and several BBC orchs., he turned to conducting. In 1980 he founded the English String Orch. in Worcester, which made a major tour of Europe in 1986; he also was artistic director of the Malvern Festival (1983–88) and principal conductor of the Jyväskylä Sym. Orch. in Finland (1986–93). He appeared as guest conductor with many British orchs. His repertoire ranges from Haydn to Tippett.

Boukoff, Yuri, Bulgarian-born French pianist; b. Sofia, March 1, 1923. After training with Brzoniowski and Stoyanov in Sofia, he went to Paris and pursued studies with Nat at the Cons. (premier prix, 1946); also received guidance from Enesco, Edwin Fischer, and Marguerite Long. After winning prizes in the Geneva (1947), Long-Thibaud (1949), and Queen Elisabeth of Belgium (1952) competitions, he pursued an international career as a virtuoso. In 1964 he became a naturalized French citizen. Although he excelled in performances of works from the Romantic era, Boukoff also championed modern composers ranging from Prokofiev to Menotti.

Boulanger, Lili (Juliette Marie Olga), talented French composer, sister of **Nadia (Juliette) Boulanger**; b. Paris, Aug. 21, 1893; d. Mézy, Seine-et-Oise, March 15, 1918. She studied composition with Vidal at the Paris Cons. (1909–13), attracting considerable attention when she won the Grand Prix de Rome at graduation with her cantata *Faust et Hélène*, becoming the first woman to receive this distinction. Her early death at the age of 24 was lamented by French musicians. Her talent, delicate and poetic, continued the tradition of French Romanticism on the borderline of Impressionism. Besides her prize-winning cantata, she wrote 2 symphonic poems, *D'un soir triste* and *D'un matin de printemps*; her opera to Maeterlinck's play *La Princesse Maleine* remained incomplete. She also wrote several choral works with orch.: *Soir sur la plaine; Hymne au soleil; La Tempête; Les Sirènes; Sous bois; La Source; Pour les funérailles d'un soldat; 3 psaumes; Vieille prière bouddhique*; *Pie Jesu*, sacred chorus for Voice, Strings, Harp, and Organ; cycle of 13 songs to texts of Francis Jammes, *Clairières dans le ciel*; some flute pieces.

BIBL.: C. Mauclair, "La Vie et l'oeuvre de L. B.," *Revue Musicale* (Aug. 1921); P. Landormy, "L. B.," *Musical Quarterly* (Oct. 1930); R. Dumesnil, *Portraits de musiciens français* (Paris, 1938); E. Lebeau, *L. B.* (Paris, 1968); L. Rosenstiel, *The Life and Works of L. B.* (Rutherford, 1978).

Boulanger, Nadia (Juliette), illustrious French teacher, sister of **Lili (Juliette Marie Olga) Boulanger**; b. Paris, Sept. 16, 1887; d. there, Oct. 22, 1979. Both her father and grandfather were teachers at the Paris Cons.; her mother, the Russian Countess Myshetskaya, was a professional singer, and it was from her that Boulanger received her first music lessons. She entered the Paris Cons., where she studied organ with Guilmant and Vierne, and composition with Gabriel Fauré; she graduated with prizes in organ and theory; in 1908 she received the 2nd Prix de Rome for her cantata *La Sirène*; she completed the composition of the opera by Raoul Pugno, *La Ville Morte*, left unfinished at his death; also composed cello music, piano pieces, and songs. Realizing that she could not compare with her sister Lili in talent as a composer, she devoted herself to teaching, and it was in that capacity that she found her vocation. She was assistant in a harmony class at the Paris Cons. (1909–24); was engaged as a teacher at the École Normale de Musique in Paris (1920–39); when the American Cons. was founded in 1921 at Fontainebleau, she joined its faculty as a teacher of composition and orchestration, becoming its director in 1950. She also had a large class of private pupils from all parts of the world, many of whom achieved fame; among Americans who went to Paris to study with her were Copland, Harris, Piston, Virgil Thomson, Elliott Carter, David Diamond, Elie Siegmeister, Irving Fine, Easley Blackwood, Arthur Berger, John Vincent, and Harold Shapero; others were Igor Markevitch, Jean Françaix, Lennox Berkeley, and Dinu Lipatti. Not all of her students were enthusiastic about her methods; some of them complained about the strict, and even restrictive, discipline she imposed on them; but all admired her insistence on perfection of form and accuracy of technique. Her tastes were far from the catholicity expected of teachers; she was a great admirer of Stravinsky, Debussy, and Ravel, but had little appreciation of Schoenberg and the modern Vienna School. She visited the U.S. several times; played the organ part in Copland's Organ Sym. (which she advised him to compose) with the N.Y. Sym. Orch., under the direction of Walter Damrosch (Jan. 11, 1925), and was the first woman to conduct regular subscription concerts of the Boston Sym. Orch. (1938) and of the N.Y. Phil. (Feb. 11, 1939). During World War II, she stayed in America; taught classes at Radcliffe College, Wellesley College, and the Juilliard School of Music in N.Y.; returning to Paris in 1946, she took over a class in piano accompaniment at the Cons.; continued her private teaching as long as her frail health permitted; her 90th birthday was celebrated in Sept. 1977, with sincere tributes from her many students in Europe and America.

BIBL.: A. Kendall, *The Tender Tyrant. N. B.: A Life Devoted to Music* (London, 1977); B. Mosaingeon, *Mademoiselle: Entretiens avec N. B.* (Luynes, 1980; Eng. tr., 1985); L. Rosenstiel, *N. B.: A Life in Music* (N.Y., 1982); J. Spycket, *N. B.* (Lausanne, 1987; Eng. tr., 1992).

Boulez, Pierre, celebrated French composer and conductor; b. Montbrison, March 26, 1925. He studied composition with Messiaen at the Paris Cons., graduating in 1945; later took lessons with René Leibowitz, who initiated him into the procedures of serial music. In 1948 he became a theater conductor in Paris; made a tour of the U.S. with a French ballet troupe in 1952. In 1954 he organized in Paris a series of concerts called "Domaine Musical," devoted mainly to avant-garde music. From 1962 he pursued a career as a guest conductor. In 1966 he conducted *Parsifal* at the Bayreuth Festival, returning there until 1969. In 1969 he became principal guest conductor of the Cleveland Orch. In 1971 he was engaged as music director of the N.Y. Phil., a choice that surprised many and delighted many more. From the outset he asserted complete independence from public and managerial tastes, and proceeded to feature on his programs works by Schoenberg, Berg, Webern, Varèse, and other modernists, giving a relatively small place to Romantic composers. This policy provoked the expected opposition on the part of many subscribers, but the management decided not to oppose Boulez in his position as music director of the orch. The musicians themselves voiced their full appreciation of his remarkable qualities as a professional of high caliber, but they also described him derisively as a "French correction," with reference to his extraordinary sense of rhythm, perfect pitch, and memory, but a signal lack of emotional participation in the music. In America, Boulez showed little interest in social amenities and made no effort to ingratiate himself with men and women of power. His departure in 1977 and the accession of the worldly Zubin Mehta as his successor were greeted with a sigh of relief, as an antidote to the stern regimen imposed by Boulez. While attending to his duties at the helm of the N.Y. Phil., Boulez accepted outside obligations; from 1971 to 1975 he served as chief conductor of the London BBC Sym. Orch.; then conducted the *Ring* cycle for the centenary celebrations at the Bayreuth Festivals (1976–80). He established residence in Paris, where he had founded, in 1974, the Inst. de Recherche & Coordination Acoustique/Musique, a futuristic establishment generously subsidized by the French government; in this post he could freely carry out his experimental programs of electronic techniques with the aid of digital synthesizers and a complex set of computers capable of acoustical feedback. He served as its director until 1992. In 1989 he was awarded the Praemium Imperiale prize of Japan for his various contributions to contemporary music. On Dec. 7, 1992, he conducted Debussy's *La Mer* as part of the 150th anniversary concert of the N.Y. Phil., which was televised live to the nation by PBS. In 1995 he was named principal guest conductor of the Chicago Sym. Orch.

Boulez's music is an embodiment of futuristic techniques; it is fiendishly difficult to perform and even more difficult to describe in the familiar terms of dissonant counterpoint, free serialism, or indeterminism. He specifically disassociated himself from any particular modern school of music. He even publ. a pamphlet with the shocking title *Schoenberg est mort*, shortly after Schoenberg's actual physical death; he similarly distanced himself from other current trends. He is the author of *Stocktakings from an Apprenticeship* (Oxford, 1991).

WORKS: DRAMATIC: *Le Soleil des Eaux*, music for a radio play for Voice and Orch. (1948; rev. as a cantata for Soprano, Tenor, Bass, and Chamber Orch., 1948; withdrawn; rev. for Soprano, Tenor, Bass, Chorus, and Orch., 1958; rev. for Soprano, Chorus, and Orch., 1965); *L'Orestie*, incidental music (1948); *Symphonie Mécanique*, film music for Tape (1955); *Le Crépuscule de Yang Koui-Feï*, incidental music for radio (1967); *Ainsi parla Zarathoustra*, incidental music (1974). **ORCH.:** *Polyphonie X* for 18 Solo Instruments (Donaueschingen, Oct. 6, 1951); *Doubles* (1957–58; Paris, March 16, 1958; expanded as *Figures-Doubles-Prismes*, 1963 and 1968); *Poésie pour pouvoir* for 2 Orchs. and Tape (Donaueschingen, Oct. 19, 1958, composer and H. Rosbaud conducting); *Tombeau* (1959–62); *Domaines* for Clarinet and 21 Instruments (1961–68; Brussels, Dec. 20, 1968, composer conducting; also for Solo Clarinet, 1961); *Éclat* for 15 Instruments (Los Angeles, March 26, 1965;

expanded as *Éclats/Multiples* for 27 Instruments, 1966–in progress); *Livre pour Cordes* (1968; based on *Livre pour quatuor* for String Quartet, 1948–49); *. . . explosante-fixe . . .* (1971; also for 2 Instruments and Electronics, 1972, and for Flute and Electronics, 1989); *Mémoriales* (1973–75); *Rituel in memoriam Bruno Maderna* (1974–75; London, April 2, 1975, composer conducting); *Notations* (Paris, June 18, 1980; based on *12 Notations* for Piano, 1945); *Répons* for 24 Players, 6 Instrumental Soloists, Chamber Ensemble, Computers, and Live Electronics (Donaueschingen, Oct. 18, 1981); *Initiale*, fanfare for 7 Brass Instruments (1987); *Dérive II* for 11 Instruments (1988) and *III*, fanfare for Brass Instruments, for Solti's 80th birthday (Chicago, Nov. 21, 1992, composer conducting). **CHAMBER:** Flute Sonatine (1946); *Livre pour quatuor* for String Quartet (1948–49; rev. 1989; also as *Livre pour Cordes* for Orch., 1968); *Strophes* for Flute (1957); *Domaines* for Clarinet (1961; also for Clarinet and 21 Instruments, 1961–68); *Messagesquisse* for Solo Cello and 6 Cellos (1976); *Pour le docteur Kalmus* for Clarinet, Flute, Violin, Cello, and Piano (1977); *Dérive I* for Flute, Clarinet, Violin, Cello, Vibraphone, and Piano (1984); *Dialogue de l'ombre double* for Clarinet and Electronics (1984); *Mémoriale ("... explosante fixe . . ." originel)* for Flute and 8 Instruments (1985); *Anthems* for Violin (1991). **PIANO:** *12 Notations* (1945; utilized in *Notations* for Orch., 1980); 3 sonatas: No. 1 (1946), No. 2 (1946–48; Paris, April 29, 1950), and No. 3 (1955–57); Sonata for 2 Pianos (Paris, April 29, 1950); *Structures I* (1951–53) and *II* (1956–61) for 2 Pianos. **VOCAL:** *Le Visage nuptial* for Soprano, Alto, 2 Ondes Martenot, Piano, and Percussion (1946–47; rev. for Soprano, Alto, Women's Chorus, and Orch., 1951–52, and for Soprano, Mezzo-soprano, Chorus, and Orch. 1985–89); *Le Soleil des Eaux*, cantata for Soprano, Tenor, Bass, and Chamber Orch. (1948; withdrawn; based on music for a radio play for Voice and Orch., 1948; rev. for Soprano, Tenor, Bass, Chorus, and Orch., 1958; rev. for Soprano, Chorus, and Orch., 1965); *Le Marteau sans Maître* for Alto, Alto Flute, Guitar, Vibraphone, Xylorimba, Percussion, and Viola (1953–55; rev. 1957); *Improvisation sur Mallarmé* for Soprano, Harp, Bells, Vibraphone, and Percussion (1957; also for Soprano and Orch., 1962), *II* for Soprano, Celesta, Harp, Piano, Bells, Vibraphone, and Percussion (1957), and *III* for Soprano and Orch. (1959; rev. 1983–84); *Pli selon pli (Don, Improvisation sur Mallarmé I-III, Tombeau)* for Soprano and Orch. (1957–90); *Don* for Soprano and Piano (1960; also for Soprano and Orch., 1962, rev. 1989–90); *Tombeau* for Soprano and Orch. (1959–60); *cummings ist der dichter* for 16 Solo Voices and 24 Instruments (1970; rev. 1986). **TAPE:** *Études I, sur un son, II, sur sept songs* (1951–52).

BIBL.: A. Goléa, *Rencontres avec P. B.* (Paris, 1958); J. Peyser, *B., Composer, Conductor, Enigma* (N.Y., 1976); R. Miller, *Pli selon pli: P. B. and the "New Lyricism"* (diss., Case Western Reserve Univ., 1978); P. Griffiths, *B.* (N.Y., 1979); D. Jameux, *P. B.* (Paris, 1984; Eng. tr., 1990); J. Hausler, ed., *Festschrift P. B.* (Vienna, 1985); T. Hirsbrunner, *P. B. und sein Werk* (Laaber, 1985); W. Glock, ed., *P. B.: A Symposium* (London, 1986); P. Stacey, *B. and the Modern Concept* (Lincoln, Nebr., 1987); P. McCallum, "An Interview with P. B.," *Musical Times* (Jan. 1989); D. Gable, "B.'s Two Cultures: The Post-War European Synthesis and Tradition," *Journal of the American Musicological Society* (Fall 1990); L. Koblyakov, *P. B.: A World of Harmony* (Chur and N.Y., 1990); J.-J. Nattiez and F. Davoine, eds., *P. B./John Cage: Correspondance et documents* (Winterthur, 1990; Eng. tr., 1993); G. Born, *Rational Music: IRCAM, B., and the Institutionalisation of the Avant-Garde* (Berkeley, 1995).

Bouliane, Denys, Canadian composer; b. Grand-Mère, near Trois-Rivières, Quebec, May 8, 1955. He was a student of Jacques Hétu, Alain Gagnon, and José Evangelista (composition), Roger Bédard (analysis), and Jeanne Landry (counterpoint) at Laval Univ. (B.Mus., 1977; M.Mus., 1979); following further training under Kagel at the Cologne Hochschule für Musik (1980), he completed his studies with Ligeti at the Hamburg Hochschule für Musik (to 1985). From 1980 he was active at the West German Radio in Cologne. In 1987 he was awarded the Jules Léger Prize and in 1991 the 1st Prix Serge-Garant. Bouliane's works are post-modern in nature, marked by a remarkable facility with a broad range of techniques, ranging from Gregorian chant to jazz.

WORKS: ORCH.: *Douze Tiroirs de demi-vérités pour alléger votre descente* for Piano and Orch. (1982; rev. 1984); *Une Foire imaginée* for Percussion and Orch. (1982); *Le Cactus rieur et la demoiselle qui souffrait d'une soif insatiable* (1986); *Concerto for Orchestra* (1989). **CHAMBER:** Wind Quintet (1976); *Climats* for Percussion, 6 Winds, 3 Strings, and Piano (1978); *Jeux de société* for Wind Quintet and Piano (1983); *Comme un silène entr'ouvert* for 4 Winds, Harp, Piano, Double Bass, and Tape (1983–85); *Rituel lapidaire en souvenance . . .* for English Horn and Vibraphone (1984; rev. 1985); *À propos . . . et le baron perche?* for 9 Winds and Double Bass (1985); *. . . a certain chinese cyclopoedia . . .* for Wind Quintet (1986); *Nouvelle Oeuvre pour ensemble* for 7 Winds, 2 Synthesizers, 2 Percussion, and 5 Strings (1989). **VOCAL:** *Quatre Chants* for Soprano, Piano, and Cello (1975); *Jappements à la lune* for Chorus and Orch. (1982); *Das Affendlied* for Soprano (1988).

OTHER: *Paraphrase en pente douce sur Le Hareng Saur de Charles Cros* for Tape (1984); *Organum* for Slides and Tape (1985); *Pilu, wo bist du?* for Children's Game and Tape (1985).

BIBL.: P. Wilson, "La Musique du réalisme magique: Portrait du compositeur D. B.," *Sonances* (Winter 1987–88).

Boult, Sir Adrian (Cedric), eminent English conductor; b. Chester, April 8, 1889; d. London, Feb. 22, 1983. His mother, a professional writer on music, gave him piano lessons; at age 12 he received some instruction in music from a science teacher, H.E. Piggott, at the Westminster School in London. At 19 he entered Christ Church, Oxford, and sang in the Oxford Bach Choir; then he studied with Hans Sitt at the Leipzig Cons. (1912–13), and also attended rehearsals and concerts of that city's Gewandhaus Orch. under Nikisch and sang in the Gewandhaus Choir. Upon his return to England, he took his D.Mus. at Oxford and joined the staff of London's Covent Garden in 1914. In 1916 he appeared as guest conductor with the Liverpool Phil. and in 1918 with the London Sym. Orch. During the autumn season of 1919, he was principal conductor of Diaghilev's Ballets Russes in London, and from 1919 to 1924 he was conductor of the British Sym. Orch., an ensemble made up of former soldiers in the British army. In 1919 he also became a teacher of conducting at the Royal College of Music in London, a post he retained until 1930. From 1924 to 1930 he was music director of the City of Birmingham Orch.; he also was music director of the Bach Choir from 1928 to 1931.

In 1930 he was appointed director of music for the BBC in London, and retained that important position until 1942. He was also charged with organizing the BBC Sym. Orch., which he conducted in its first concert on Oct. 22, 1930. He subsequently served as its chief conductor until 1950. Under his discerning guidance, it became one of the principal radio orchs. in the world. He led it on several tours abroad, including a notably successful one to Paris, Vienna, Zürich, and Budapest in 1936. During these years, he also appeared as guest conductor with the Vienna Phil. (1933), the Boston Sym. Orch. (1935), the NBC Sym. Orch. in N.Y. (1938), the N.Y. Phil. (leading it in the premieres of Bax's 7th Sym. and Bliss's Piano Concerto at the 1939 World's Fair, June 9 and 10, respectively), the Chicago Sym. Orch. (1939), and the Concertgebouw Orch. of Amsterdam (1945). From 1942 to 1950 he was assoc. conductor of the Henry Wood Promenade Concerts in London. He was music director of the London Phil. from 1950 to 1957 and led it on a major tour of the Soviet Union in 1956. In 1959–60 he was again music director of the City of Birmingham Sym. Orch., and from 1962 to 1966 he once more taught conducting at the Royal College of Music. In 1937 he was knighted, and in 1969 was made a Companion of Honour. In 1944 he was awarded the Gold Medal of the Royal Phil. Soc. He was conductor at the coronations of King George VI in 1937 and Queen Elizabeth II in 1953.

Boult's style of conducting was devoid of glamorous self-assertion; his ideal was, rather, to serve music with a minimum of display, and for this he was greatly respected by the musicians he led. Throughout his long and distinguished career he championed the cause of British music. He was particularly esteemed for his performances of the works of Vaughan Williams, whose *Pastoral Symphony* (Jan. 26, 1922), 4th Sym. (April 10, 1935), and 6th Sym. (April 21, 1948) received their premiere performances under his direction in London.

WRITINGS: *The Point of the Stick: A Handbook on the Technique of Conducting* (Oxford, 1920); *Thoughts on Conducting* (London, 1963); *My Own Trumpet*, an autobiography (London, 1973).

BIBL.: J. Moore, ed., *Music and Friends: Letters to A. B.* (London, 1979); H. Simeone and S. Mundy, eds., *Sir A. B., Companion of Honour: A Tribute* (Tunbridge Wells, 1980); M. Kennedy, *A. B.* (London, 1987).

Bour, Ernest, French conductor; b. Thionville, April 20, 1913. After music studies at home, he entered the Univ. of Strasbourg, where he took courses in classical languages; later studied conducting with Fritz Munch and Hermann Scherchen. From 1935 to 1939 he was music director of Radio Strasbourg, and then of the Mulhouse Orch. (1941–47). From 1950 to 1964 he was music director of the Strasbourg Orch. From 1964 to 1979 he served as chief conductor of the Southwest Radio Sym. Orch. of Baden-Baden. In 1976 he was appointed principal conductor of the Radio Kamerorkest in Hilversum. Bour was particularly noted for his championship of contemporary music.

Bourdin, Roger, French baritone; b. Lavallois, June 14, 1900; d. Paris, Sept. 14, 1973. He studied at the Paris Cons.; made his operatic debut as Lescaut in *Manon* in 1922 at the Paris Opéra-Comique; also sang at the Paris Opéra. He made his Covent Garden debut in London in 1930 as Debussy's Pélleas. He was married to **Geori Boué**.

Bourguignon, Francis de, Belgian composer; b. Brussels, May 29, 1890; d. there, April 11, 1961. He was a student of Dubois and Edgar Tinel (composition) and Arthur de Greef (piano) at the Brussels Cons.; after touring extensively as a pianist, he pursued composition studies with Paul Gilson in Brussels (1925). With 7 other students of Gilson, he formed the Groupe des Synthétistes to promote contemporary music. From 1939 to 1955 he taught at the Brussels Cons.

WORKS: DRAMATIC: *La Mort d'Orphé*, ballet (1928); *Congo*, radio play (1936); *Le Mauvais Pari*, chamber opera (1937). **ORCH.:** Piano Concertino (1927); *2 esquisses sud-américaines* (1928); *Fête populaire* (1929); *Le Jazz vainqueur*, symphonic poem (1929); *Prélude and Dance* (1929); *Éloge de la folie* (1934); Sym. (1934); *Oiseaux de nuit* (1937); *Puzzle*, suite (1938); *Fantasy on 2 Themes of Eugène Ysaÿe* for Piano and Orch. (1938); *Sinfonietta* (1939); *Berceuse* (1940); Suite for Viola and Orch. (1940); *Juventus*, suite (1941); *Recuerdos: 2 impressions sud-américaines* (1943); *Concerto Grosso* (1944); Violin Concerto (1947); Piano Concerto (1949); *Récitatif et Ronde* for Trumpet and Orch. (1951); Concertino for Piano and Chamber Orch. (1952); Concerto for 2 Pianos and Orch. (1953); *Ouverture martiale* (1960). **CHAMBER:** String Trio; Piano Trio; 2 string quartets; Oboe Quintet; piano suites. **VOCAL:** *La Nuit*, oratorio (1945); choral pieces; songs.

BIBL.: A. Vandernoot, *F. d.B.* (Brussels, 1949).

Boutry, Roger, French pianist, conductor, and composer; b. Paris, Feb. 27, 1932. He studied at the Paris Cons.; received 1st prize as a pianist at age 16, 1st prize as a conductor at age 21, and the Premier Prix de Rome at age 22. In 1963 he was awarded the Grand Prix Musical of the City of Paris. He embarked on a successful career as a pianist, touring in Europe, Russia, and Australia; as a conductor, he appeared with several orchs. in France, and served as conductor of l'Orchestre de la Garde Républicaine from 1972.

WORKS: Piano Concerto (1954); *Rapsodie* for Piano and Orch. (1956); *Ouverture-Tableau* for Orch. (1959); *Divertimento* for Saxophone and Orch. (1964); *Concerto-Fantaisie* for 2 Pianos and Orch. (Paris, Feb. 16, 1967); *Intermezzi* for Chamber Orch. (1970); Flute Concerto; Quartet for Trombones; 2 sextets; *Pastels et contours* for 5 Harps; also didactic pieces for various instruments.

Bovet, Joseph, Swiss priest, teacher, conductor, and composer; b. Sâles, Gruyère, Oct. 7, 1879; d. Clarens, Feb. 10, 1951. He studied in Romont, Fribourg, and Einsiedeln, and at the Seckau Benedictine monastery; then became a priest and taught music at the Fribourg diocesan seminary. He was made conductor at the Fribourg Cathedral and conducted various choral groups; from 1909 to 1923 he was also conductor of the Fribourg sym. concerts. He wrote much church music for choral forces, music for plays, and part songs.

BIBL.: *Hommage à l'abbé B.* (Fribourg, 1947); R. Loup, *L'abbé B.: Barde du pays* (Lausanne, 1952).

Bovy, Vina (real name, **Malvina Johanna Pauline Félicité Bovi van Overberghe**), Belgian soprano; b. Ghent, May 22, 1900; d. there, May 16, 1983. She studied piano and voice at the Ghent Cons. (1915–17). In 1917 she made her debut in *Hänsel und Gretel* in Ghent; sang at the Théâtre Royal de la Monnaie in Brussels (1920–23) and at the Teatro Colón in Buenos Aires (1927); had guest engagements in Barcelona, Madrid, Monte Carlo, Venice, Milan, Rome, and Paris. On Dec. 24, 1936, she made her Metropolitan Opera debut in N.Y. as Violetta, remaining on its roster until 1938. From 1947 to 1955 she was director of the Ghent Opera. Among her best roles were Gilda, Manon, Lakmé, Juliette, Pamina, Desdemona, and Elsa.

BIBL.: J. Deleersnyder, *V. B.* (Ghent, 1965).

Bowen, (Edwin) York, English composer and teacher; b. London, Feb. 22, 1884; d. Hampstead, Nov. 23, 1961. He studied at the Royal Academy of Music in London, where he won the Erard and Sterndale Bennett scholarships; his teachers were T. Matthay (piano) and F. Corder (composition). Upon graduation, he was appointed instructor in piano there. A prolific composer, Bowen wrote 3 syms.; 3 piano concertos; Violin Concerto; Viola Concerto; Rhapsody for Cello and Orch.; symphonic poems (*The Lament of Tasso*, *Eventide*, etc.); orch. suites; many practical piano pieces in miniature forms. Bowen was the author of a manual, *Pedalling the Modern Pianoforte* (London, 1936).

BIBL.: M. Watson, *Y. B.: A Centenary Tribute* (London, 1984).

Bowles, Paul (Frederic), American man of letters and composer; b. N.Y., Dec. 30, 1910. He became fascinated with pictorial arts, belles lettres, and the vocal projection of poetry as a child, and when he was 8 he also began to study music. At 17, he had his first poem publ. in the literary review *transition.* In 1929 he made his way to Paris, where he was dazzled by its intellectual resplendence and the insouciant milieu of the Left Bank. Returning to N.Y., his hypnopomping musical talent manifested itself and in 1930 he became a student of Copland. In 1931 he returned to Paris, where he continued his studies with Copland and had a few lessons with Boulanger. He became a habitué of the circle surrounding Gertrude Stein and Alice B. Toklas, but his wanderlust led him to visit Berlin and North Africa. The latter sojourn proved the turning point in his artistic career, both as a composer and as a man of letters. After composing several orch., chamber, and vocal scores, Bowles attracted attention with his ballet *Yankee Clipper* (1936). During the following 2 decades, he proved adept at composing film scores and incidental music for plays. In 1941 he received a Guggenheim fellowship, which resulted in his opera *The Wind Remains* (1941–43), after García Lorca. His psychological attraction to exotic lands prompted him to return to North Africa in 1947, which remained the center of his activities for the rest of his life with occasional sojourns to various lands abroad. Among his later compositions was the opera *Yerma* (1948–55), also after García Lorca. As a composer, he found his métier in works reflecting American, Mexican, and North African elements. Bowles soon became best known, however, as a writer, when in 1949 he publ. the first of his many bone-chilling novels, *The Sheltering Sky.* He also wrote short stories and made trs. of native works about North Africa. His autobiography was publ. as *Without Stopping* (1972). The vol. *Paul Bowles: Music* (1995) is a collection of essays, interviews, and reviews. Bowles was married to the novelist and playwright Jane Auer, who died in 1973.

WORKS: DRAMATIC: OPERAS: *Denmark Vesey* (1938); *The Wind Remains* (1941–43); *Yerma* (1948–55). **BALLETS:** *Yankee Clipper* (1936); *The Ballroom Guide* (1937); *Pastorela* (1941); *Colloque sentimental* (1944). Also incidental music to plays and various film scores. **ORCH.:** *Iquitos* (1933); *Pastorale, Havanaise et Divertissement* (1933); Suite (1933); *Romantic Suite* (1939); Concerto for 2 Pianos, Winds, and Percussion (1947); *Danza mexicana* (1947). **CHAMBER:** Sonata for Oboe and Clarinet (1930); Flute Sonata (1932); Violin Sonata (1934); Piano Trio (1936); *Melodia* for 11 Instruments (1937); *Music for a Farce* for Clarinet, Trumpet, Percussion, and Piano (1938); *Prelude and Dance* for Wind, Brass, Percussion, and Piano (1947); many piano pieces, including Sonata for 2 Pianos (1949). **VOCAL:** *Scènes d'Anabase* for Tenor, Oboe, and Piano (1932); *Par le détroit,* cantata for Soprano, 4 Men's Voices, and Harmonium (1933); *3 Pastoral Songs* for Tenor, Piano, and Strings (1944); *A Picnic Cantata* for 4 Soloists, 2 Pianos, and Percussion (1952); many songs for Voice and Piano; see P. Garland, ed., *Paul Bowles: Selected Songs* (Santa Fe, N.M., 1984).

BIBL.: G. Dagel, "A Nomad in New York: P. B., 1933–48," *American Music* (Fall 1989); C. Sawyer-Lauçanno, *An Invisible Spectator: A Biography of P. B.* (N.Y., 1989).

Bowman, James (Thomas), notable English countertenor; b. Oxford, Nov. 6, 1941. He was educated at New College, Oxford (Dip.Ed., 1964; M.A. in history, 1967) and received vocal instruction in London from De Rentz and Manen. In 1967 he made his operatic debut as Britten's Oberon at Aldeburgh with the English Opera Group. From 1967 he sang with the group regularly in London, and also was a member of the Early Music Consort (1967–76). In 1970 he appeared in *Semele* at the Sadler's Wells Opera there, and continued to sing there after it became the English National Opera in 1974. He sang Endymion in *La Calisto* at the Glyndebourne Festival in 1970, and sang there regularly until 1974. On July 12, 1972, he created the role of the Priest in Maxwell Davies's *Taverner* at London's Covent Garden. Britten then wrote the role of Apollo for him in *Death in Venice* (Aldeburgh, June 16, 1973). On July 7, 1977, he created the role of Astron in Tippett's *The Ice Break* at Covent Garden. In subsequent years, Bowman continued to appear regularly in England but he also was engaged in opera and concert appearances in Europe and abroad.

Boyd, Anne (Elizabeth), Australian composer; b. Sydney, April 10, 1946. She studied flute at the New South Wales Cons. (1960–63) and composition at the Univ. of Sydney (1963–66); concluded her studies at York Univ. in England (Ph.D., 1972). She was a lecturer at the Univ. of Sussex (1975–77); served as head of the music dept. at the Univ. of Hong Kong (1980–88).

WORKS: *Air and Variations* for Flute and Piano (1960); Trio for Flute, Violin, and Piano (1962); *Infinity* for Piano (1964); *L'Altro* for Orch. (1964); *Exegesis No. 1* for 4 Flutes and 2 Piccolos (1964); *Synchrony No. 1,* trio for Oboe, Clarinet, and Bassoon (1964); *Chelidiones* for Flute, Piccolo, and Tape (1965); *3 Piano Pieces* (1965); *The Fall of Icarus* for Flute, Clarinet, Cello, and Piano (1966); Trio for Oboe, Violin, and Cello (1966); *The Stairway,* ballet for 4 Instruments and Percussion (1968); 2 string quartets (*The 4th Generation,* 1968; 1973); *Games* for Any Number of Players (1969); *As Far as Crawls the Toad* for 5 Young Percussionists (1970); *Hidden in a White Cloud* for Wind Quintet, or for Flutes and Cellos (1970); *The Voice of the Phoenix* for Piano, Guitar, and Harp (all amplified), 10 Percussionists, Orch. with Augmented Woodwinds, and VCS-3 Synthesizer ad libitum (1971); *Greetings to Victor McMahon* for 12 Flutes (1971); *The Metamorphoses of the Solitary Female Phoenix* for Wind Quintet, Piano, and Percussion (1971); *The Rose Garden,* theater piece (1972); *Anklung I* for Piano (1974) and *II* for Violin (1980); *Bencharong* for Strings (1976); *The Death of Captain Cook,* oratorio (1978); *The Little Mermaid,* children's opera (1978); *The Beginning of the Day,* children's opera (1980).

Boydell, Brian (Patrick), prominent Irish composer; b. Dublin, March 17, 1917. He took courses in music at the Evangelical Church Music Inst. of the Univ. of Heidelberg, with Hadley and Howells at the Royal College of Music in London (1938–39), at the Royal Irish Academy of Music in Dublin, and at the Univ. of Dublin (D.Mus., 1959); subsequently was a prof. of music there (1962–82). He was made a Commendatore della Repubblica Italiana for his services to Italian Renaissance music (1983) and a member of Aosdana for general contributions to the creative arts in Ireland. He publ. the study *Rotunda Music in Eighteenth-Century Dublin* (Dublin, 1992). His music reveals an assured command of traditional compositional techniques.

WORKS: ORCH.: Sym. for Strings (1945); *5 Joyce Songs* (1946); *In Memoriam Mahatma Gandhi* (1948); Violin Concerto (1953); *The Wooing of Etain,* 2 suites (1954); *Elegy and Capriccio* for Clarinet and Strings (1955); *Megalithic Ritual Dances* (1956); *Meditation and Fugue* (1956); *Ceól Cas Corach* (Cas Corach's Music; 1958); *Shielmartin Suite* (1958); *Richard's Riot* (1961); *Symphonic Inscapes* (1968); *Jubilee Music* (1976); *Partita Concertante* for Violin, Harp, and Orch. (1978); *A Wild Dance for Ceól Chumann na nóg* (1982); *Masai Mara* (1988). **CHAMBER:** Oboe Quintet (1940); String Trio (1944); Cello Sonata (1945); 3 string quartets (1950, 1957, 1969); Quintet for Flute, Harp, and String Trio (1960); *4 Sketches* for 2 Irish Harps (1962); *A Pack of Fancies for a Travelling Harper* (1970); *5 Mosaics* for Violin and Piano or Harp (1972); *5 Blows* for Brass Quintet (1984); *An Album of Pieces for the Irish Harp* (1989); *Adagio and Scherzo* for String Quartet (1991); also many piano pieces. **VOCAL:** *An Easter Carol* for Chorus (1940); *Shatter Me, Music* for Chorus (1952); *The Deer's Cry* for Baritone and Orch. (1957); *Noël* for Chorus and Orch. (1960); *Mors et vita* for Soloists, Chorus, and Orch. (1960–61); *A Terrible Beauty is Born* for Narrator, Soloists, Chorus, and Orch. (1965); *4 Yeats Poems* for Soprano and Orch. (1965); *Mouth Music* for Chorus (1974); *The Small Bell,* cantata (1980); *The Carlow Cantata or The Female Friend* (1985); *Under No Circumstances: An Historical Entertainment* for 2 Soloists, Narrator, Chorus, and Orch. (1987; Dublin, March 10, 1988); songs.

Boyden, David D(odge), American musicologist; b. Westport, Conn., Dec. 10, 1910; d. Berkeley, Sept. 18, 1986. He studied at Harvard Univ. (A.B., 1932; M.A., 1938), then joined the faculty of the Univ. of Calif. at Berkeley, remaining there until 1975. He publ. *A Manual of Counterpoint Based on Sixteenth-century Practice* (N.Y., 1944; 2nd ed., 1953), *The History and Literature of Music, 1750 to the Present* (N.Y., 1948), *An Introduction to Music* (N.Y., 1956; 2nd ed., 1970), and *The History of Violin Playing from Its Origins to 1761* (London, 1965).

Boykan, Martin, American composer, teacher, and pianist; b. N.Y., April 12, 1931. He studied composition with Piston at Harvard Univ. (B.A., 1951), Copland at the Berkshire Music Center at Tanglewood (summers, 1949–50), and Paul Hindemith at the Univ. of Zürich (1951–52) and Yale Univ. (M.M., 1953). He also had lessons in piano from Steuermann. From 1957 to 1970 he was active as a pianist. In 1957 he joined the faculty of Brandeis Univ., where he later was a prof. of composition. He also was a visiting prof. of composition at Columbia Univ. (1988–89) and N.Y. Univ. (1993). In 1994 he was a senior Fulbright lecturer at Bar-Ilan Univ. in Israel. He held Fulbright (1953–55) and Guggenheim (1984) fellowships, and also won the American Academy in Rome prize (1972). His music is marked by a predominate lyrical line and emotional breadth.

WORKS: ORCH.: Concerto for 13 Players (1971); Sym. for Baritone and Orch. (1989; Salt Lake City, April 9, 1993). **CHAM-**

BER: Trio for Violin, Viola, and Cello (1948); String Quartet (1949); 3 numbered string quartets (1967, 1974, 1984); Flute Sonata (1950); Duo for Violin and Piano (1951); Flute Quintet (1953); Trio for Violin, Cello, and Piano (1975); *Nocturne* for Cello, Piano, and Percussion (1991); *Eclogue* for Flute, Horn, Viola, Cello, and Piano (1991); *Echoes of Petrarch* for Flute, Clarinet, and Piano (1992); Cello Sonata (1992); *Impromptu* for Violin (1993); Violin Sonata (1994). **KEYBOARD: PIANO:** 2 sonatas (1986, 1990); *Pastorale* (1993). **ORGAN:** *Prelude* (1964). **VOCAL:** *Psalm 128* for Chorus (1965); *Elegy* for Soprano and 6 Instruments (1982); *Shalom Rav* for Baritone, Chorus, and Organ (1985); *Epithalamion* for Baritone, Violin, and Harp (1987); *Voyages* for Soprano and Piano (1992); *Sea Gardens*, 4 songs for Soprano and Piano (1993); *3 Psalms* for Soprano and Piano (1993).

Boyle, George Frederick, American pianist, teacher, and composer; b. Sydney, Australia, June 29, 1886; d. Philadelphia, June 20, 1948. He received his early musical training from his parents; in 1905 he went to Berlin, where he took piano lessons with Busoni. He began his career as an accompanist. In 1910 he settled in the U.S.; taught piano at the Peabody Cons. of Music in Baltimore (1910–22), the Curtis Inst. of Music in Philadelphia (1924–26), and the Inst. of Musical Art in N.Y. (1927–39). He wrote *Aubade* for Orch. (St. Louis, March 5, 1916); Piano Concerto (Worcester Festival, Sept. 28, 1911); Cello Concerto (Washington, D.C., Feb. 7, 1918); 3 piano trios; Violin Sonata; Viola Sonata; Cello Sonata; about 100 piano pieces and 50 songs.

BIBL.: I. Peery, *G.F. B.: Pianist, Teacher, Composer* (diss., Peabody Cons. of Music, 1987).

Bozay, Attila, Hungarian composer and teacher; b. Balatonfűzfő, Aug. 11, 1939. He studied in Budapest at the Bartók Cons. (1954–57) and then with Farkas at the Academy of Music, graduating in 1962. After serving as a music producer for the Hungarian Radio (1963–66), he went to Paris on a UNESCO scholarship in 1967. Returning to Budapest, he devoted himself fully to composition and later taught at the Academy of Music. In 1968 and 1979 he received the Erkel Prize. In 1984 he was made a Merited Artist by the Hungarian government. In 1988 he received the Bartók-Pásztory Award.

WORKS: OPERAS: *Küngisz királynö* (Queen Kungisz; 1968–69); *Csongor és Tünde* (1979–84; Budapest, Jan. 20, 1985). **ORCH.:** *Pezzo concertato No. 1* for Viola and Orch. (1965) and *No. 2* for Zither and Orch. (1974–75); *Pezzo sinfonico No. 1* (1967) and *No. 2* (1975–76); *Pezzo d'archi* (1968; rev. 1974); *Gyermekdalok* (Children's Songs) for 18 Strings (1976); *Variazioni* (1977); *Improvisations No. 3* for Prepared Piano and Strings (1987). **CHAMBER ENSEMBLE:** *Sorozat* (Series; 1970); *A malom* (The Mill; 1972–73). **CHAMBER:** Duo for 2 Violins (1958); *Episodi* for Bassoon and Piano (1959); Trio for Violin, Viola, and Cello (1960; rev. 1966); Wind Quintet (1962); 2 string quartets (1964, 1971); *Két tétel* (2 Movements) for Oboe and Piano (1970); *Improvisations No. 2* for Recorders and String Trio (1976); *Tükör* (Mirror) for Zither and Cimbalom (1977); Violin Sonata (1987–88); various pieces for Solo Instrument, including many for Piano. **VOCAL:** *Papírszeletek* (Paper Slips) for Soprano, Clarinet, and Cello (1962); *Kiáltások* (Outcries) for Tenor, Violin, Cello, Clarinet, Horn, and Piano (1963); *Trapéz és korlát* (Trapeze and Parallel Bars), cantata for Tenor, Chorus, and Orch. (1966); *Lux perpetua*, motet for Chorus (1969); *Két tájkép* (2 Landscapes) for Baritone, Flute, and Zither (1970–71); 24 Children's or Women's Choruses (1985).

Božič, Darijan, Slovenian composer; b. Slavonski Brod, April 29, 1933. He studied composition with Škerjanc and conducting with Švara at the Ljubljana Academy of Music (1958–61); upon graduation, served as an opera conductor and artistic director of the Slovenian Phil. (1970–74); later was a prof. at the Univ. of Maribor (1988–95), and then director of SNG Opera in Ljubljana (from 1995). His music was at first influenced by jazz; later he adopted radical serial techniques.

WORKS: DRAMATIC: *Baletska jednočinka*, ballet (1957); *Humoreske*, opera (1958); *Spoštovanja vredna vlačuga*, opera (1960); *Polineikes*, collage (1966); *Gluha okna*, ballet (1967); *Ares Eros*, opera (1970); *Lizistrata*, opera (1975); *King Lear*, opera (1985). **ORCH.:** Piano Concerto (1956); Saxophone Concerto (1958); Trombone Concerto (1960); Trumpet Concerto (1961); Sym. (1964–65); *Audiostructures* for Piano and Orch.; *Audiospectrum* (1972). **CHAMBER:** *Sonata in Cool I* for Flute and Piano (1961), *II* for Clarinet and Piano (1961), and *III* for Flute, Bass Clarinet, and Harp (1965); *Pop-art-music* for String Quartet, Piccolo, and 2 Metronomes (1969); *Audiogemi I–IV* for String Quartet (1974). **VOCAL:** *Trije dnevni Ane Frank* (3 Days of Anne Frank) for 2 Narrators and Synthetic Sound (1963); *Gregora strniše* for Narrator and 7 Instruments (1965); *Kriki* (Cries) for Narrator, Brass Quintet, and Tape (1966); *Requiem (to the Memory of a Murdered Soldier—My Father)*, sound collage for Narrator, Chorus, Instruments, and Concrete Sounds (1969).

Bozza, Eugène, French composer and conductor; b. Nice, April 4, 1905; d. Valenciennes, Sept. 28, 1991. He studied at the Paris Cons.; received the Grand Prix de Rome in 1934. From 1939 to 1948 he was conductor of the Opéra-Comique in Paris; then moved to Valenciennes, where he was appointed director of the local cons.

WORKS: DRAMATIC: *Fête romaine*, ballet (1942); *Jeux de plage*, ballet (1946) *Léonidas*, opera (1947); *Beppo ou le Mort dont personne ne voulait*, comic opera (1963); *La Duchesse de Langeais*, lyric drama (Lille, 1967). **ORCH.:** Violin Concerto (1938); Saxophone Concerto (1939); *Rhapsodie niçoise* for Violin and Orch. (1942); Concertino for Bassoon and Chamber Orch. (1944); *Ballade* for Trombone and Orch. (1944); Cello Concerto (1947); Sym. (1948); *5 Mouvements* for Strings (1970). **CHAMBER:** *Luciolles* for 6 Clarinets; *Suite française* for 5 Woodwind Instruments; *3 Pieces* for 5 Trombones; other compositions for unusual instrumental combinations.

Bradford, Alex, black American gospel singer and composer; b. Bessemer, Ala., Jan. 23, 1927; d. Newark, N.J., Feb. 15, 1978. He became a singer with the Protective Harmoneers, a children's gospel group, when he was 13; he also appeared on his own program on a local radio station. He later took courses at the Snow Hill (Ala.) Inst., where he worked as a student teacher and picked up the unearned title of "professor," which he used the rest of his life. After working with his own group, the Bradford Singers, he joined forces with Willie Webb and made the successful recording *Every Day and Every Hour* (1950); then organized the all-male Bradford Specials. Following the success of his own song *Too Close to Heaven*, which he recorded in 1953, he toured extensively. He also appeared in Langston Hughes's *Black Nativity* in 1961, and went on to Broadway, where he starred in *Don't Bother Me, I Can't Cope* (1972) and *Your Arms Too Short to Box with God* (1976).

Bradley, Gwendolyn, black American soprano; b. N.Y., Dec. 12, 1952. She received training at the North Carolina School of the Arts in Winston-Salem, N.C., the Curtis Inst. of Music in Philadelphia, and the Philadelphia Academy of Vocal Arts. In 1976 she made her operatic debut as Verdi's Nannetta at the Lake George (N.Y.) Opera, and on Feb. 20, 1981, she made her first appearance at the Metropolitan Opera in N.Y. as the Nightingale in *L'Enfant et les Sortilèges*, returning there to sing such roles as Blondchen, Gilda, and Offenbach's Olympia in subsequent years. She made her European debut at the Corfu (Greece) Festival in 1981, and later was guest artist with opera companies in Cleveland, Philadelphia, Amsterdam, Glyndebourne, Hamburg, Berlin, Monte Carlo, and Nice. She also appeared as a soloist with many distinguished orchs.

Bradshaw, Merrill (Kay), American composer and pedagogue; b. Lyman, Wyo., June 18, 1929. He was educated at Brigham Young Univ. (A.B., 1954; M.A., 1955) and the Univ. of Ill. (M.M., 1956; D.M.A., 1962). From 1957 he taught at Brigham Young Univ. As a member of the Mormon Church, he contributed a great deal to the formulation of classical Mormon music.

WORKS: MUSICAL: *The Title of Liberty* (1975). **ORCH.:** Piano Concerto (1955); 5 syms.: No. 1 (1957), No. 2 (1962), No. 3 (1967), No. 4 (1968), and No. 5 (1978; Auckland, New Zealand, July 4, 1979); *Facets* (1965); *Feathers* (1968); *4 Mountain Sketches* (1974); *Nocturnes and Revels* (1974); *Lovers and Liars* (1976); *Homages,* viola concerto (Provo, July 14, 1979); Violin Concerto (Provo, March 5, 1981); Double Concerto (1994). **CHAMBER:** *Dialogue* for Flute and Horn (1956); 2 string quartets (1957, 1969); Violin Sonata (1957); Suite for Viola (1967); Suite for Oboe and Piano (1966); Brass Quintet (1969); Nocturne for 2 Horns and Strings (1977). **PIANO:** *6 Bagatelles* (1958); *Moments* (1968); *20 Mosaics* (1972); *6 plus 4* for 10 Pianos (1976). **VOCAL:** *The Restoration,* oratorio (Provo, March 23, 1974); *Love and Death, 4 Elizabethan Lyrics* for Soprano, Viola, and Strings (Provo, Sept. 10, 1982); choruses; hymns; Psalms; ballads.

Braein, Edvard Fliflet, Norwegian composer and conductor; b. Kristiansund, Aug. 23, 1924; d. Oslo, April 30, 1976. He was of a musical family; his grandfather was an organist and choirmaster, and his father, Edvard Braein (1887–1957), was a composer, organist, and conductor. He studied at the Oslo Cons., graduating in 1943; then studied conducting with Grüner-Hegge and composition with Brustad; later took private lessons with Rivier in Paris (1950–51). Upon returning to Oslo, he was active mainly as a choral conductor.

WORKS: DRAMATIC: *Anne Pedersdotter,* opera (Oslo, 1971); *Den stundeslose* (The Wastrel), opera buffa (Oslo, 1975); *The Little Matchstick Girl,* ballet (1976; unfinished). **ORCH.:** *Towards the Sea* for Chamber Orch. (1947); Concert Overture (1948); 3 syms. (1949–50; 1951–54; 1967); *Serenade* (1951–52); *Adagio* for Strings (1953); *Capriccio* for Piano and Orch. (1956–57); *Divertimento* for Flute and Orch. (1958); *Symphonic Prelude* (1959); *Largo* for Strings (1960–61); *Intrata* (1961); *Overture in Miniature* (1962); *Little Serenade* (1963); *Ritmico e melodico* (1971); *Til Arendal,* festival overture (1972); *Havljom* (Echo from the Sea; 1973). **CHAMBER:** Violin Sonata (1940); *The Merry Musicians* for Clarinet, Violin, Viola, and Cello (1947); *Divertimento* for Clarinet, Violin, Viola, and Cello (1962); String Trio (1964); *Humoresque* for Chamber Ensemble (1966).

Braga, (Antônio) Francisco, Brazilian conductor, pedagogue, and composer; b. Rio de Janeiro, April 15, 1868; d. there, March 14, 1945. He played clarinet in military bands in Rio de Janeiro; at the age of 18, he composed an overture, which was played at the inauguration of the Soc. of Popular Concerts there on Jan. 5, 1887. He then went to Paris, where he studied with Massenet; also traveled in Germany and Italy. Influenced mainly by Massenet and Mascagni, Braga wrote the opera *Jupira* (Rio de Janeiro, March 20, 1899). From 1908 until 1933 he conducted sym. concerts in Rio de Janeiro. His symphonic works include the programmatic pieces *Insomnia, Cauchemar,* and *Paysage.* Braga was the teacher of many Brazilian composers and contributed much to the musical culture of his country.

BIBL.: T. Gomes, *F. B.* (Rio de Janeiro, 1937); *Exposição comemorativa do centenario do nascimento de F. B.* (Rio de Janeiro, 1968).

Bragard, Roger, Belgian musicologist; b. Huy, Nov. 21, 1903; d. Brussels, Dec. 15, 1985. He studied philology at the Univ. of Liège; then went to Paris, where he studied musicology with Pirro and composition with d'Indy. Returning to Belgium, he taught music history at the Brussels Cons. He publ. the valuable *Histoire de la musique belge* (3 vols., 1946, 1949, 1956).

Brăiloiu, Constantin, distinguished Romanian-born French ethnomusicologist; b. Bucharest, Aug. 25, 1893; d. Geneva, Dec. 20, 1958. He studied music in Lausanne, with Gédalge at the Paris Cons. (1912–14), and in Romania. After a period as a composer and music critic, he turned to ethnomusicological research. In 1921 he became a prof. of music history and aesthetics at the Académie Royale de Musique in Bucharest, and later taught at the Académie de Musique Religieuse de la Sainte Patriarchie (1929–35). In 1926 he became secretary-general of the Soc. of Romanian Composers, where he founded its folklore archives in 1928; it later became the Institutul de Folclor şi Ethnografie. From 1943 to 1946 he served as attaché at the Romanian Embassy in Bern. With Eugène Pittard, he founded the international folk music archives in Geneva in 1944. In 1948 he went to Paris and in 1956 he became a naturalized French citizen. He was a member of the Centre National de la Recherche Scientifique, and pursued research at the Musée de l'Homme and at the Sorbonne's Inst. of Musicology. His article "Esquisse d'une méthode de folklore musical (organisation d'archives)," *Revue de Musicologie,* XI (1931; Eng. tr. in *Ethnomusicology,* XIV, 1970) is a valuable guide to his approach to the synoptic transcription of music. Among his other important articles were "Le rythme aksak," *Revue de Musicologie,* XXX (1951), "Sur une mélodie russe," *Musique russe* (vol. II, Paris, 1953), and "Le rythme enfantin: Notions liminaires," *Cercle international d'études ethno-musicologigues: Wegimont 1954.* He also engaged in valuable fieldwork, which he preserved on recordings.

BIBL.: J. Chailley, "Hommage à C. B.," *Revue des études roumaines,* VII–VIII (1961); special B. issue of *Cercetări de muzicologie,* II (1970).

Brailowsky, Alexander, noted Russian-born French pianist; b. Kiev, Feb. 16, 1896; d. N.Y., April 25, 1976. After study with his father, a professional pianist, he continued his training at the Kiev Cons., graduating with a gold medal in 1911. Following advanced studies with Leschetizky in Vienna (1911–14) and Busoni in Zürich, he completed his training with Planté in Paris, where he made his debut in 1919. In 1926 he became a naturalized French citizen. He presented a complete cycle of Chopin's works in Paris (1924), which he repeated several times. He made a highly successful world tour; made his American debut at Aeolian Hall in N.Y. on Nov. 19, 1924; made a coast-to-coast tour of the U.S. in 1936; first gave the Chopin cycle in America during the 1937–38 season, in 6 recitals in N.Y. In 1960 he played the Chopin cycle again in N.Y. and Brussels in honor of the 150th anniversary of Chopin's birth.

Brain, Alfred (Edwin), English-born American horn player and teacher, brother of **Aubrey (Harold)** and uncle of **Dennis Brain**; b. London, Oct. 24, 1885; d. Los Angeles, March 29, 1966. After studying horn with his father, he pursued training with Borsdorf at the Royal Academy of Music in London (1901–04). He played in the Scottish Orch. in Glasgow (1904–08); then was principal horn in the Queen's Hall Orch. (1908–16; from 1919) and also was a member of the London Sym. Orch. (from 1919). After serving as co-principal horn in the N.Y. Sym. Orch. (1922–23), he was 1st horn in the Los Angeles Phil. (1923–34; 1936–37) and the Cleveland Orch. (1934–36); was again a member of the Los Angeles Phil. (1943–44); also played in Hollywood film studios. In 1930 he became a naturalized American citizen.

Brain, Aubrey (Harold), English horn player and teacher, brother of **Alfred (Edwin)** and father of **Dennis Brain**; b. London, July 12, 1893; d. there, Sept. 20, 1955. He studied horn with his father, and then at the Royal College of Music in London with Borsdorf (1911–13). In 1911 he was made principal horn in the New Sym. Orch. in London; in 1913 he played in the orch. of the Beecham Opera Co. From 1922 to 1930 he was a member of the orch. of the Royal Phil. Soc. and the Queen's Hall Orch. in London; also pursued a solo career from 1923, and held the posts of co-principal (1923–24), principal (1924–28), and again co-principal (1928–29) horn in the London Sym. Orch. From 1930 to 1945 he was principal horn in the BBC Sym. Orch. in London. He later played in the Philharmonia Orch. in London (1948–50). From 1923 to 1955 he was prof. of horn at the Royal Academy of Music in London.

Brain, Dennis, phenomenal English horn player, son of **Aubrey (Harold)** and nephew of **Alfred (Edwin) Brain**; b. London, May 17, 1921; d. in an automobile accident in Hatfield, Sept. 1, 1957. He received piano lessons as a child and took up the bugle in his school cadet band. In 1936 he began studying the horn at home with his father, who continued as his teacher when he entered the Royal Academy of Music in London that same year; he also had instruction there in piano, organ, and conducting. While still a student, he launched his professional career in 1938 playing 2nd horn to his father in a concert under Adolf Busch in London. With the outbreak of World War II in 1939, he enlisted in the Royal Air Force and played principal horn in its sym. orch. for the duration of the conflict. In the meantime, he completed his training at the Royal Academy of Music in 1940. From 1942 to 1947 he was principal horn in the National Sym. Orch. in London; he also was a valuable member of the New London Orch., the London Wind Players, and the London Baroque Ensemble. In 1945 he became principal horn of the Philharmonia Orch. in London, a post he held with great distinction for the rest of his life. He also served as principal horn of the Royal Phil. in London from 1946 to 1948, and again from 1950 to 1954. From 1949 he was principal horn of the London Mozart Players. In addition to his various orch. duties, he toured as a virtuoso soloist and was active with his own wind quintet and trio. Brain was duly recognized as the foremost horn player of his time, and following his tragic death he became a legend. His lips were insured for £10,000. Among his legendary performances captured on recordings are the 4 Mozart and the 2 Strauss horn concertos, all of which were classical best-sellers in his lifetime and remain unsurpassed for their perfection of execution. From 1942 several noted composers wrote works especially for him, among them Britten (*Serenade* for Tenor, Horn, and Strings), Seiber (*Notturno* for Horn and Strings), Hindemith (Horn Concerto), Jacob (Horn Concerto), Arnold (2nd Horn Concerto), and Searle (*Aubade* for Horn and Orch.). It can only be imagined how profoundly the modern horn repertoire would have been enhanced in succeeding decades had Brain lived an average lifetime.

BIBL.: S. Pettitt, *D. B.: A Biography* (London, 1976).

Braithwaite, Nicholas (Paul Dallon), English conductor, son of **(Henry) Warwick Braithwaite**; b. London, Aug. 26, 1939. He studied at the Royal Academy of Music in London, at the Bayreuth Festival master classes, and with Swarowsky in Vienna. He was assoc. conductor of the Bournemouth Sym. Orch. (1967–70), assoc. principal conductor of the Sadler's Wells Opera in London (1970–74), and music director of the Glyndebourne Touring Opera (1976–80). After serving as principal guest conductor of the Manchester Camerata (1977–84), he was its principal conductor (1984–91). He also was music director of the Stora Theater Opera and Ballet in Göteborg (1981–84), chief conductor of the Adelaide Sym. Orch. (1987–91), and dean of the Victorian College of the Arts in Melbourne (1988–91). He then was chief conductor of the Tasmanian Sym. orch. (from 1991).

Braithwaite, (Henry) Warwick, New Zealand conductor, father of **Nicholas (Paul Dallon) Braithwaite**; b. Dunedin, Jan. 9, 1896; d. London, Jan. 18, 1971. He studied at the Royal Academy of Music in London; won the Challen Gold Medal and the Battison Hayes Prize. He began his career as a conductor with the O'Mara Opera Co.; then conducted with the British National Opera Co. He was assistant music director of the BBC; then went to its Cardiff studio in Wales as music director; also conducted the Cardiff Musical Soc. (1924–31). He was a founder of the Welsh National Orch. From 1932 to 1940 he was a conductor at the Sadler's Wells Opera in London; then he led the Scottish Orch. in Glasgow (1940–46). Later he was a ballet conductor at the Royal Opera, Covent Garden, in London (1950–53); then conducted the National Orch. of New Zealand and served as artistic director of the National Opera of Australia (1954–55). From 1956 to 1960 he was music director of the Welsh National Opera; then was again a conductor at Sadler's Wells until 1968. He publ. *The Conductor's Art* (London, 1952).

Brancour, René, French music critic; b. Paris, May 17, 1862; d. there, Nov. 16, 1948. Educated at the Paris Cons., he became curator of its collection of musical instruments; in 1906, began a course of lectures on aesthetics at the Sorbonne; also wrote newspaper criticism. A brilliant writer, he poured invective on the works of composers of the advanced school; his tastes were conservative, but he accepted French music of the Impressionist period. He wrote biographies of Félicien David (1911) and Méhul (1912) in the series Musiciens Célèbres; of Massenet (1923) and Offenbach (1929) in Les Maîtres de la Musique. Other books were *La Vie et l'oeuvre de Georges Bizet* (1913), *Histoire des instruments de musique* (1921), and *La Marseillaise et le chant du départ.*

Brand, Max(imilian), Austrian-born American composer; b. Lemberg, April 26, 1896; d. Langenzersdorf, near Vienna, April 5, 1980. He became a student of Franz Schreker in Vienna in 1919, and continued as his student in Berlin in 1920. He also received instruction from Alois Hàba and Erwin Stein. Brand's early use of 12-tone methods is revealed in his *Fünf Balladen nach Gedichten von Else Lasker-Schüler* (1927). He scored a sensation when he brought out his first opera, *Maschinist Hopkins* (Duisburg, April 13, 1929), which subsequently was performed throughout Europe. This expressionistic score of the "machine era" served as a remarkable precursor to Berg's *Lulu.* Brand pursued his interest in avant-garde expression by founding Vienna's Mimoplastisches Theater für Ballett and by serving as co-director of the Raimund Theater, where he oversaw the Wiener Opernproduktion company. He also was associated with Eisler in producing experimental films. As a Jew, Brand's works were banned by the Nazis in Germany in 1933. After the Anschluss in Austria in 1938, he was compelled to flee to Brazil. In 1940 he went to the U.S. and in 1944 became a naturalized American citizen. He was active in N.Y. as director of the Music and Theatre Wing, Caravan of East and West. Around 1958 he began to experiment with electronics. In 1975 he returned to Austria and was active in his own electronic music studio.

WORKS: DRAMATIC: *Maschinist Hopkins,* opera (1928; Duisburg, April 13, 1929); *Kleopatra,* opera (1932–38); *Requiem,* opera (1933); *Die Chronik,* scenic cantata (1938); *The Gate,* scenic oratorio (N.Y., May 23, 1944); *Stormy Interlude,* opera (1955); ballets; incidental music. **ORCH.:** *Eine Nachtmusik* for Chamber Orch. (1923); *The Wonderful 1-Hoss Shay,* symphonic poem (Philadelphia, Jan. 20, 1950); *Night on the Bayous of Louisiana,* tone poem (1953). **CHAMBER:** String Trio (1923); *Piece* for Flute and Piano (1940). **VOCAL:** *Nachtlied* for Soprano and Orch. (1922); *Kyrie Eleison* for Chorus (1940); songs. **ELECTRONIC:** *The Astronauts, An Epic in Electronics* (1962); *Ilian 1 & 2* (1966).

BIBL.: C. Bennett, "Maschinist Hopkins: A Father for Lulu?," *Musical Times* (Sept. 1986); T. Brezinka, "M. B.: Sein Leben und sein Werk," *Arbeit der Hochschule für Musik und darstellende Kunst in Wien im Rahmen des Ergänzungsstudiums* (Vienna, 1989).

Brandts-Buys, Jan (Willem Frans), Dutch composer; b. Zutphen, Sept. 12, 1868; d. Salzburg, Dec. 7, 1933. He was a pupil of M. Schwarz and A. Urspruch at the Raff Cons. in Frankfurt am Main; lived for a time in Vienna; later settled in Salzburg. His first opera, *Das Veilchenfest* (Berlin, Dec. 3, 1909), met with opposition; a second opera, *Das Glockenspiel* (Dresden, Dec. 4, 1913), was received more kindly; while a third, *Die drei Schneider von Schönau* (Dresden, April 1, 1916), was quite successful. Subsequent operas were *Der Eroberer* (Dresden, Jan. 14, 1918), *Micarême* (Vienna, Nov. 14, 1919), *Der Mann im Mond* (Dresden, June 18, 1922), *Traumland* (Dresden, Nov. 24, 1927), and *Ulysses* (German radio, March 12, 1937). He also wrote a ballet, *Machinalität* (Amsterdam, 1928); 2 piano concertos; a *Konzertstück* for Cello and Orch.; chamber music; piano pieces; songs.

Brannigan, Owen, English bass; b. Annitsford, March 10, 1908; d. Newcastle upon Tyne, May 9, 1973. He studied at the Guildhall School of Music in London (1934–42), where he won its gold medal in 1942. In 1943 he made his operatic debut as Sarastro with the Sadler's Wells Opera in London, where he sang until 1948 and again from 1952 to 1958; also appeared at the Glyndebourne Festivals (1947–49), at London's Covent Garden, and with the English Opera Group. He became closely associated with the music of Britten, in whose operas he created Swallow in *Peter Grimes* (1945), Collatinus in *The Rape of Lucretia* (1946), Superintendent Budd in *Billy Budd* (1947), Noye in *Noye's Fludde* (1958), and Bottom in *A Midsummer Night's Dream* (1960). He also sang in oratorio, concerts, and lighter fare. In 1964 he was made a Member of the Order of the British Empire.

Branscombe, Gena, Canadian-born American choral conductor and composer; b. Picton, Ontario, Nov. 4, 1881; d. N.Y., July 26, 1977. She attended the Chicago Musical College, where she studied piano with Rudolph Ganz and composition with Felix Borowski, receiving her B.A. in 1900; in 1909 she went to Berlin, where she took a course with Humperdinck. Returning to America, she took conducting lessons with Frank Damrosch and Albert Stoessel. She became a naturalized American citizen in 1910. In 1934 she organized the Branscombe Chorale, a women's ensemble that she conducted until 1954. She composed mostly choral works, often to her own texts; of these the most notable are *A Wind from the Sea*, after Longfellow (c.1924), *Pilgrims of Destiny* (1926), *The Phantom Caravan*, after Banning (c.1927), *Youth of the World* (c.1932), and *Coventry's Choir*, after Alvarez (c.1944). She also composed a symphonic suite, *Quebec* (1928), and some 150 songs.

Brant, Henry, innovative American composer and pioneer of spatial music; b. Montreal (of American parents), Sept. 15, 1913. He learned the rudiments of music from his father; in 1929 the family moved to N.Y., where Brant studied elementary theory with Leopold Mannes at the Inst. of Musical Art and also took private lessons in advanced composition with Wallingford Riegger and George Antheil. He further learned the elements of conducting from Fritz Mahler. Having absorbed the totality of quaquaversal techniques of composition, he proceeded to teach others at various institutions of progressive musical learning. In 1982 he settled in Santa Barbara, California. In 1979 he was elected a member of the American Academy and Inst. of Arts and Letters. An audacious explorer of sonic potentialities, he drew without prejudice upon resources ranging from kitchen utensils to tin cans in search of superior cacophony. He became a pioneer in the field of spatial music, in which participating instruments were to be placed at specified points in space.

WORKS: *Angels and Devils* for a Merry Murmuration of Innumerable Flutes (N.Y., Feb. 6, 1933); *Whoopee in D Major* (1938); *The Great American Goof*, ballet (N.Y., Jan. 11, 1940); Saxophone Concerto (1941; N.Y., May 12, 1945); *All Souls' Carnival* for Flute, Violin, Cello, Piano, and Accordion (1947); *Millennium No. 1* for Trumpets, Chimes, and Bells (1950), *No. 2* for Multiple Brass and Percussion (1954), *No. 3* for Brass and Percussion (1957), and *No. 4* for Brass (1964); *From Bach's Menagerie* for Saxophone Quartet (1974); *Behold the Earth*, Requiem cantata (1951); *Feuerwerk* for Speaker, Fireworks, and Instruments (1961); *Horizontals Extending* for 2 Chamber Orchs., Jazz Drummer, and 3 Karate Artists (1981); *Desert Forest* for Orch. (Atlanta, May 23, 1985); *A Concord Symphony*, orchestration of Charles Ives's *Concord Sonata* (Ottawa, June 16, 1995, composer conducting). **NONDESCRIPT ENSEMBLES:** *5 & 10 Cent Store Music* for Violin, Piano, and Kitchen Hardware (1932); *Hommage aux frères Marx* for Solo Tin Whistle and Other Plebeian Contraptions (1938); *Kitchen Music* for Water Glasses, Bottles, and Assorted Junk (1946); *Machinations* for Flageolet, Double Ocarina, Ceramic Flute, Steel Harp, and What Have You (1970); *Solar Moth*, a pheromone to attract tonal insects (1979). **SPATIAL WORKS:** *Encephalograms* for Soprano and 7 Instruments (1955); *In Praise of Learning* for 16 Sopranos and 16 Percussionists (1958); *Mythical Beasts* for Soprano and 16 Instruments (1958); *Barricades* for Tenor and 9 Instruments (1961); *Verticals Ascending* for 2 Separate Instrumental Groups (1968); *6 Grand Pianos Bash Plus Friends* (1974); *American Weather* for Winds and Percussion (1976); *Cerberus* for Double Bass, Piccolo, Soprano, and Mouth Organ (1978); Piano Concerto for Piano, 16 Women's Voices, and Orch. (1978); *Revenge before Breakfast* for 2 Woodwinds, 2 Strings, 2 Percussion, and Piano (1982); *Meteor Farm* for Orch., Jazz Band, Gamelans, West African Drums, South Indian Singers, and 2 Western Sopranos (1982); Piano Concerto for 16 Women, Piano, and Orch. (1978); *Brant aan de Amstel*, water spectacle for Holland for 100 Flutes, 4 Jazz Drummers, 3 Choruses, 4 Street Organs, 4 Church Carillons, and 3 Bands (1984); *Knot-holes, Bent Nails & a Rusty Saw* for Anyone and Anybody Accompanied by Some Sonorous Garbage (1985); *Northern Lights over the Twin Cities* for 2 Choruses, Bagpipe Band, and 5 Pianos (1985); *An Era Any Time of Year* for a Walking Baritone Accompanied by Piano Strings Pizzicato and Other Things (1987); *Instant Sygyzy* for 2 String Quartets and Whatnot (1987); *Ghost Nets*, concerto for Double Bass with 2 Chamber Seines Equipped with Imaginary Sinkers and Floats (1988); *Prisons of the Mind*, a "spatial sym." (Dallas, April 12, 1990).

Branzell, Karin Maria, noted Swedish contralto; b. Stockholm, Sept. 24, 1891; d. Altadena, Calif., Dec. 14, 1974. She was a pupil of Thekla Hofer in Stockholm, Louis Bachner in Berlin, and Enrico Rosati in N.Y. In 1912 she made her operatic debut as Prince Sarvilaka in d'Albert's *Izeÿl* in Stockholm, where she sang at the Royal Opera until 1918; then was a member of the Berlin State Opera until 1923. On Feb. 6, 1924, she made her Metropolitan Opera debut in N.Y. as Fricka in *Die Walküre*, and remained on the roster until 1944; sang there again in 1951. She also appeared at the Bayreuth Festivals (1930–31), London's Covent Garden (1935; 1937–38), and the San Francisco Opera (1941). In later years she taught at the Juilliard School of Music in N.Y. The exceptional range of her voice allowed her to sing both contralto and soprano roles. Although especially known for such Wagnerian roles as Ortrud, Venus, Erda, Brangäne, and the *Walküre* Brünnhilde, she also was admired as Amneris, Dalila, Herodias, and Clytemnestra.

Braslau, Sophie, American contralto; b. N.Y., Aug. 16, 1892; d. there, Dec. 22, 1935. She studied with Arturo Buzzi-Peccia. On Nov. 27, 1913, she made her Metropolitan Opera debut in N.Y. as the voice in *Parsifal*, followed by her formal debut there the next day as Fyodor in *Boris Godunov*; remained on its roster until 1920, creating Cadman's Shanewis on March 23, 1918. She gave concerts throughout the U.S., and in 1931 made a tour of Europe. In 1934 she sang for the last time in N.Y.

Brassens, Georges, French chansonnier; b. Sète, Herault, Oct. 22, 1921; d. there, Oct. 29, 1981. He began his career as a chansonnier, accompanying himself on the guitar in a repertoire of his own songs, which he called "lyrisme plébéien"; indeed, his texts voiced proletarian discontent, as revealed by such titles as *La Mauvaise Réputation*, *Le Pornographe*, and *Je suis un voyou*, calculated to shock the self-contented bourgeoisie. But the Establishment apparently did not recoil from these verbal blows, and in 1967 the Académie Française honored him with a poetry prize. He also wrote a novel, *La Tour des miracles* (Paris, 1953).

BIBL.: J. Charpentreau, *G. B. et la poésie quotidienne de la chanson* (Paris, 1960); A. Larue, *B., ou La Mauvaise Herbe* (Paris, 1970); J. Sermonte, *G. B.* (Paris, 1988); L. Calvet, *G. B.* (Paris, 1991); J. Vassal, *G. B., ou, La chanson d'abord* (Paris, 1991).

Brauer, Evald, Estonian flutist and composer; b. Väinjärve, July 26, 1904; d. Tallinn, Oct. 20, 1961. He studied flute at the Tallinn Cons., and then taught flute there (1935–40). He also publ. a textbook on flute playing in the Estonian language (1939). His compositions are set in an acceptable academic manner, with Estonian motifs lending an air of authenticity. In this ethnically colored idiom he wrote *Estonian Capriccio* for Orch. (1936); a symphonic poem, *Mahtra* (1958); overtures and choruses.

Braun, Carl, German bass; b. Meisenheim, Prussia, June 2, 1885; d. Hamburg, April 19, 1960. He studied with Hermann Gausche in Kreuznach and later with Eugen Robert Weiss. He sang at the Wiesbaden Opera (1906–11) and at the Vienna Court Opera (1911–12); then was engaged at the Berlin City Opera (1912–14). He also appeared at the Bayreuth Festivals (1906–31). On Feb. 8, 1913, he made his American debut at the Metropolitan Opera in N.Y. as King Marke, but was dismissed as an enemy alien in the spring of 1917 when the U.S. entered the war against Germany. In 1922–23 he made a South American tour; also sang in the U.S. in 1928 and 1931. In 1933 he was engaged as a stage director at the German Opera in Berlin, and in 1935–36 held similar posts at the Berlin Volksoper and at the Danzig Municipal Theater. In 1937 he retired from the stage and was thereafter active mainly as a concert agent in Hamburg. He was particularly esteemed for his Wagnerian roles.

Braun, Peter Michael, German composer, teacher, pianist, and conductor; b. Wuppertal, Dec. 2, 1936. He was a pupil of Frank Martin, Zimmermann, and Herbert Eimert at the Cologne Hochschule für Musik and of Klebe at the Detmold Hochschule für Musik. In 1978 he became a prof. of composition and theory at the Heidelberg-Mannheim Hochschule für Musik. His style is governed by structural considerations.

WORKS: ORCH.: *Seliger Kontrapunt* for Strings (1952; 1988–91); *Scherzo* (1956–91); *Exkursion* (1958–71); *Interstellar* for 4 Orch. Groups (1959); *Transfer* (1965–68); *Variete* (1965–69); *Landschaft* (1966–71); *Problems and Solutions* for Strings (1973–74); *Junctim* (1974–75; rev. 1988); *Ambiente* (1974–76); *Serenata Palatina* (1975–82); *Ballett* for Orch. and Speaker ad libitum (1980–87); *Recherche* (1983–85). **CHAMBER:** *Zwei Fantasien* for 4 Recorders (1952–83); *Fantasie-Quartett* for Horns (1952–84); String Quartet (1957); Piano Trio (1958); *Terms* for Chamber Ensemble (1962–71); *Miró* for Flute and Piano, after 3 paintings of Joan Miró (1976; rev. 1989); *Drei Choräle* for 4 Trombones or 3 Cellos and Double Bass or 4 Bassoons and Contrabassoon (1979); *Man liebt Brahms*, 2 retrospectives for Violin and Cello (1986; also for Violin and Harp, 1987); Duo for Violin and Piano (1988; also for Flute and Piano, 1989); *Kontemplation* "on minimal art" for Flute or Violin and Piano or Harp (1988); *Hommage à Brandenbourg* for 7 Instruments (1988–91); *Arc-en-ciel* for Bass or Alto Flute (1992); piano pieces; organ music. **VOCAL:** *Kle-Sito* for Soprano, Guitar, and 2 Percussionists (1960–61); *Entelechie* for 6 Solo Voices or Chorus and Orch. (1972); *Kashima Kiko* for Alto or Baritone and Small Orch. (1977); *Arie* for Soprano and Orch. (1977–80); *Alborada* for Soprano and Orch. (1987); choral pieces; songs. **ELECTRONICS:** *Ereignisse: Hommage à Edgard Varèse* (1966–68); *Essay*, 3 pieces (1971); *Klangsonden* (1976).

Braunfels, Walter, German composer and pedagogue; b. Frankfurt am Main, Dec. 19, 1882; d. Cologne, March 19, 1954. He studied piano in Vienna with Leschetizky and composition in Munich with Thuille. In 1925 he became a co-director of the Hochschule für Musik in Cologne. With the advent of the Nazi regime in 1933, he was compelled to abandon teaching; after the collapse of the Third Reich in 1945, he reorganized the Hochschule für Musik in Cologne and served as its director until 1950. He excelled mainly as an opera composer; the following operas are notable: *Falada* (Essen, May 24, 1906); *Prinzessin Brambilla* (Stuttgart, March 25, 1909; rev. 1931); *Ulenspiegel* (Stuttgart, Nov. 9, 1913); *Die Vögel*, after Aristophanes (Munich, Dec. 4, 1920; his most successful opera); *Don Gil von den grünen Hosen* (Munich, Nov. 15, 1924); *Der glaserne Berg* (Krefeld, Dec. 4, 1928); *Galatea* (Cologne, Jan. 26, 1930); *Der Traum, Ein Leben* (1937); *Die heilige Johanna* (1942); also a mystery play, *Verkündigung*, after Paul Claudel (1936). He further wrote 2 piano concertos; Organ Concerto; *Revelation of St. John* for Tenor, Double Chorus, and Orch.; piano music and songs. He believed in the artistic and practical value of Wagnerian leading motifs; in his harmonies he was close to Richard Strauss, but he also applied impressionistic devices related to Debussy.

Bravničar, Matija, Slovenian composer and teacher; b. Tolmin, Feb. 24, 1897; d. Ljubljana, Nov. 25, 1977. After service in the Austrian army (1915–18) he was a violinist at the opera theater in Ljubljana; meanwhile he studied composition at the Cons. there, graduating in 1932. He was director of the Ljubljana Academy of Music (1945–49) where he later taught composition (1952–68); was president of the Soc. of Slovenian Composers (1949–52) and of the Union of Yugoslavian Composers (1953–57). In his works, he cultivated a neo-Classical style, with thematic material strongly influenced by the melorhythmic inflections of Slovenian folk music.

WORKS: DRAMATIC: *Pohujšanje v dolini Sentflorijanski* (Scandal in St. Florian's Valley), opera buffa (Ljubljana, May 11, 1930); *Stoji, stoji Ljubljanca*, satirical revue (Ljubljana, Dec. 2, 1933); *Hlapec Jernij in njegova pravica* (Knight Jernej and His Justice), opera (Ljubljana, Jan. 25, 1941). **ORCH.:** *Hymnus Slavicus* (1931; Ljubljana, May 14, 1932); *Kralj Matjaž* (King Mattias), overture (Ljubljana, Nov. 14, 1932); *Slavik Dance Burlesques* (1932); *Divertissements* for Piano and Strings (1933); *Belokranjska rapsodija* (1938); *Simfonična antiteza* (Symphonic Antithesis; 1940; Ljubljana, Feb. 9, 1948); 3 syms.: No. 1 (1947; Ljubljana, Feb. 20, 1951), No. 2 (1951; Ljubljana, Oct. 27, 1952), and No. 3 (1956); *Kurent*, symphonic poem (1950); *Plesne metamorfoze* (1955); *Marcia-Rondo* (1960); Violin Concerto (1961; Llubljana, Feb. 7, 1963); Horn Concerto (1963); *Fantasia rapsodica* for Violin and Orch. (1967); *Simfonični plesi* (Symphonic Dances; 1969). **CHAMBER:** *Elegie* for Horn and Piano (1929); 2 wind quintets (1930, 1968); Trio for Flute, Clarinet, and Bassoon (1930); *Dialog* for Cello and Piano (1965); Sonata for Solo Violin (1966).

Braxton, Anthony (Delano), black American jazz alto saxophonist, contrabass clarinetist, composer, and teacher; b. Chicago, June 4, 1945. He studied with Jack Gell at the Chicago School of Music (1959–64) and also attended the Chicago Musical College (1963–66) before studying philosophy at Roosevelt Univ. (1966–68). In 1966 he became a member of the Assn. for the Advancement of Creative Musicians. In 1967 he founded the Creative Construction Co. with Leroy Jenkins and Leo Smith. That same year he recorded the album *For Alto*, the first album ever devoted to the solo saxophone. In 1970 he performed with Musica Elettronica Viva, the improvisation group, and in 1970–71 with Circle, Chick Corea's free-jazz quartet. Thereafter he was active as a solo artist and leader of his own small groups. As such, he made many recordings. After teaching at Mills College in Oakland, California (1985–90), he was a prof. of music at Wesleyan Univ. in Middletown, Conn. (from 1990). He publ. *Tri-Axium Writings* (3 vols., 1985) and *Composition Notes* (5 vols., 1988). In addition to his superb handling of the alto saxophone and the contrabass clarinet, he mastered all of the saxophone and clarinet family as well as various percussion instruments. In his vast output of compositions, he has produced both jazz and notated scores which reveal a remarkable blending of African-American and European experiences.

BIBL.: G. Lock, *Forces in Motion: A. B. and the Meta-Reality of Creative Music* (London, 1988); R. Radano, *New Musical Figurations: A. B.'s Cultural Critique* (Chicago, 1993); P. Wilson, *A. B.: Sein Leben, seine Musik, seine Schallplatten* (Schaftlach, 1993).

Bream, Julian (Alexander), noted English guitarist and lutenist; b. London, July 15, 1933. He was educated at the Royal College of Music in London. He made his debut at the age of 17. In 1960 he founded the Julian Bream Consort; also directed the Semley Festival of Music and Poetry from 1971. Through his numerous concerts and recordings, he has helped to revive interest in Elizabethan lute music. He was named an Officer of the Order of the British Empire in 1964, and a Commander of the Order of the British Empire in 1985.

BIBL.: T. Palmer, *J. B.: A Life on the Road* (London, 1982).

Brecher, Gustav, German conductor and editor; b. Eichwald, near Teplitz, Bohemia, Feb. 5, 1879; d. (suicide) Ostend, May 1940. His family moved to Leipzig in 1889, where he studied with Jadassohn. His first major work, the symphonic poem *Rosmersholm,* was introduced by R. Strauss at a Liszt-Verein concert in Leipzig (1896), where Brecher subsequently made his debut as a conductor (1897). He was a vocal coach and occasional conductor of operas in Leipzig (1898); also conducted in Vienna (1901), and served as 1st conductor in Olmütz (1902), Hamburg (1903), and Cologne (1911–16); then was in Frankfurt am Main (1916–24) and Leipzig (1924–33). He committed suicide with his wife aboard a boat off the Belgian coast while attempting to flee from the advancing Nazi troops. His compositions include a symphonic fantasia, *Aus unserer Zeit.* He was the author of *Über die veristische Oper; Analysen zu Werken von Berlioz und Strauss;* and *Über Operntexte und Opernübersetzungen* (1911).

Brecknock, John, English tenor; b. Long Eaton, Nov. 29, 1937. He studied with Frederic Sharp and Dennis Dowling at the Birmingham School of Music. In 1967 he made his debut as Alfred in *Die Fledermaus* at the Sadler's Wells Opera in London, and continued to sing there with fine success; also appeared at the Glyndebourne Festival (1971) and at London's Covent Garden (debut as Fenton, 1974). On March 23, 1977, he made his Metropolitan Opera debut in N.Y. as Tamino. He also appeared in various European operatic centers. Although best known for such roles as Mozart's Belmonte and Ottavio, Rossini's Count Almaviva and Comte Ory, and Verdi's Duke of Mantua, he also sang in contemporary roles.

Bredemeyer, Reiner, German composer; b. Velez, Colombia, Feb. 2, 1929; d. Berlin, Dec. 5, 1995. He studied composition with Karl Höller at the Akademie der Tonkunst in Munich (1949–53); then took courses with Wagner-Regény at the Akademie der Künste in East Berlin (1955–57). In 1961 he was appointed conductor of the German Theater in East Berlin; in 1978 he joined the faculty of the Akademie der Künste there. In his music he was an astute experimenter, but he adhered to the tenets of classical forms and avoided the extremes of modernism.

WORKS: DRAMATIC: *Leben der Andrea,* opera after Brecht's *Galileo* (1971); *Die Galoschenoper,* after *The Beggar's Opera* (1978); *Candide,* after Voltaire (1981–82; Halle, Jan. 12, 1986). **ORCH.:** *Integration* (1961); *Variante* (1962); Violin Concerto (1963); *Komposition* for 56 Strings (1964); *Spiel* (1964); *Schlagstück* 3 for Orch. and 3 Percussion Groups (1966); *Bagatellen für B.* for Piano and Orch. (1970); *Spiel zu 45* (1970); *Piano und . . . ,* piano concerto (1972); *Oktoberstück* (1973); Sym. (1974); *Anfangen—aufhören* (1974); Double Concerto for Harpsichord, Oboe, and Orch. (1974); *2 tempi* for Flute, Recorder, and Strings (1976); *Auftakte* for 3 Orch. Groups (1976); Concerto for Oboe and Strings (1977); *4 Pieces* (1979); *9 Bagatelles* for Strings (1984); *3 Pieces* for 2 Orch. Groups (1986); Horn Concerto (1986); *Sonatas I–III* (1988); *Vermasseltes Doppel, NOK,* oboe concerto (1994). **CHAMBER:** Quintet for Flute, Clarinet, Violin, Cello, and Double Bass (1956); Concertino for 12 (1957); Octet (1959); 2 woodwind quintets (1959, 1969); *Schlagstück 1* for Percussionist (1960), *2* for Piano and Percussion (1965), and *5* for Piano and Percussion (1970); 3 string quartets (1961, 1968, 1983); String Quintet (1962); *5 Pieces* for Oboe and 3 Bassoons (1964); *6 Serenades* for various instrumental combinations (1966–80); *Pointing* for 18 String Instruments (1966); Sonata for Violin, Viola, and Piano (1967); *Schlagquartett* for Piano, Double Bass, and 2 Percussionists (1967); *Ab 14* for Piano and 13 String Instruments (1971); *(Cello)^2* for Cello and Tape (1971); *8 Pieces* for String Trio (1971); *6 Solos* for Various Instruments (1973–80); *(Oboe)^2* for Oboe and Tape (1975); *Grosses Duet* for 2 Instrumental Groups (1975); *Piano und . . .^{5}* for Piano, Flute, Horn, Trombone, Cello, and Double Bass (1976); *Interludium* for Soprano Saxophone, Flute, Cello, Double Bass, and Percussion (1977); *Piano und . . .^{6}* for Piano, 2 Cellos, Wind Instrument, and 3 Percussionists (1977); *Still Leben? mit Gitarre* for Guitar and 4 Trombones (1978); *5 Blechstücke* for 2 Trumpets and 2 Trombones (1979); *D für Paul Dessau* for 15 String Instruments (1980); *Septet 80* for 2 Oboes, Cello, Double Bass, Percussion, Trombone, and Harpsichord (1980); *Septet 87* for 2 Guitars, Percussion, and String Quartet (1987); *Vorwahl 522 (Kein Anschluss unter dieser Nummer?)* for Chamber Ensemble (1989). **VOCAL:** *Cantata* for Alto and Women's Chorus (1961); *Wostock* for Chorus and Orch. (1961); *Karthago* for Chorus and Chamber Ensemble (1961); *Sätze und Sentenzen* for Chorus and Orch. (1963); *Canto* for Alto, Men's Chorus, and 10 Instruments (1965); *Synchronisiert-Asynchron* for Soprano, Oboe, Bassoon, Cello, Piano, Percussion, and Tape (1975); *Zum 13. 7. (Für Schönberg)* for Woman's Voice, Clarinet, Saxophone, and Percussion (1976); *Cantata 2* for 16 Voices and 16 Instruments (1977); *Madrigal, Rezitativ und Arie* for Tenor and 8 Instruments (1979); *Das Alltägliche* for Soprano, Tenor, and Orch. (1980); *Musica Vivarese* for Soprano, Bass Chorus, and Instruments (1982); *Die Winterreise* for Baritone, Horn, and Piano, after Wilhelm Müller (1984); *Lieder auf der Flucht* for Mezzo-soprano and Piano (1986); *Die schöne Müllerin* for Baritone, String Quartet, and Horn Quartet, after Müller (1986; Berlin, Feb. 21, 1987); *Post-modern* for Chorus and 4 Horns (1988).

Brediceanu, Tiberiu, Romanian composer, administrator, and music editor; b. Lugoj, Transylvania, April 2, 1877; d. Bucharest, Dec. 19, 1968. He studied music mainly in Romania; was director of the Astra Cons. in Brasov (1934–40) and director-general of the Romanian Opera in Bucharest (1941–44). He publ. valuable collections of Romanian songs and dances, including 170 Romanian folk melodies, 810 tunes of the Banat regions, and 1,000 songs of Transylvania.

WORKS: Operas: *Poemul muzical etnografic* (1905; rev. and retitled *Romania in port, joc si cintec,* 1929) and *La şezătoare* (1908); *Seara mare,* lyric scene (1924); *Învierea,* pantomime (1932); *La seceriş* (1936); *4 Symphonic Dances* (1951); 2 suites for Violin and Piano (1951); piano pieces; songs.

Brehm, Alvin, American double-bass player, conductor, and composer; b. N.Y., Feb. 8, 1925. He studied with Fred Zimmerman (double bass) and Giannini (orchestration) at the Juilliard School of Music in N.Y. (1942–43); then with Riegger (composition) at Columbia Univ. (M.A., 1951). After making his debut as a double-bass player (1942), he performed with the Pittsburgh Sym. Orch. (1950–51), the Contemporary Chamber Ensemble (1969–73), the Group for Contemporary Music (1971–73), the Philomusica Chamber Music Soc. (1973–83), and the Chamber Music Soc. of Lincoln Center (1984–89). After making his debut as a conductor (1947), he was active in promoting contemporary music. He was founder-conductor of the Composer's Theatre Orch. (1967), and also taught at the State Univ. of N.Y. at Stony Brook (1968–75), the Manhattan School of Music (1969–75), and the State Univ. of N.Y. at Purchase (from 1981), where he also was head of its music division (1981–90).

WORKS: DRAMATIC: *The Final Theory,* chamber opera (1994). **ORCH.:** *Hephaestus Overture* (1966); Concertino for Violin and Strings (1975); Piano Concerto (1977); Double Bass Concerto (1982); Tuba Concerto (1982). **CHAMBER:** *Divertimento* for Trumpet, Horn, and Trombone (1962); *Dialogues* for Bassoon and Percussion (1964); *Divertimento* for Woodwind Quintet (1965); Brass Quintet (1967); *Colloquy and Chorale* for Bassoon Quartet (1974); Cello Sonata (1974); *Quarks* for Flute, Bassoon, String Quartet, and Piano (1976); Sextet for Piano and Strings (1976); *A Pointe at His Pleasure* for Renaissance Instruments (1979); *AYU Variations* for Flute and Guitar (1980); *Tre canzone* for Viola and Piano (1980); *La bocca della verità* for Flute, Clarinet, Violin, Cello, and Piano (1983); Sextet for Woodwind Quintet and Piano (1984); *Children's Games* for Flute, Clarinet, Violin, Viola, Cello, and Piano (1984–85); *Circles* for Piano (1991); *Lion's Den* for Violin and Percussion (1992).

Brehme, Hans (Ludwig Wilhelm), German composer; b. Potsdam, March 10, 1904; d. Stuttgart, Nov. 10, 1957. He studied piano in Berlin with Wilhelm Kempff; taught at Stuttgart and elsewhere. A highly diligent composer, he wrote music in many genres; the idiom of his compositions is fundamentally Classical, with a generous admixture of moderately modern harmonies. He wrote an opera, *Der Uhrmacher von Strassburg* (1941); operetta, *Versiegelten Bürgermeister* (1944); 2 syms.; 2 piano concertos; Flute Concerto; *Triptycon* for Orch., on a theme by Handel (highly successful); Sextet for Flute, Clarinet, Horn, Violin, Viola, and Cello; Clarinet Quintet; Saxophone Sonata; several works for Accordion.

Breithaupt, Rudolf (Maria), German pianist, pedagogue, and music scholar; b. Braunschweig, Aug. 11, 1873; d. Ballenstedt, April 2, 1945. He studied jurisprudence, philosophy, and musicology before taking piano lessons with Teichmüller at the Leipzig Cons.; then went to Berlin and was appointed piano teacher at the Stern Cons. He publ. studies on piano playing: *Die natürliche Klaviertechnik* (Leipzig, 1905; French tr., 1923); *Die Grundlagen der Klaviertechnik* (Leipzig, 1906; French tr., 1908; Eng. tr., 1909; Russian tr., 1929); and *Praktische Studien* (1916–21). He also publ. *Musikalische Zeit und Streitfragen* (Berlin, 1906).

Brel, Jacques, Belgian-born French singer and songwriter; b. Brussels, April 8, 1929; d. Paris, Oct. 9, 1978. He rose to fame in France in the 1950s as a singer and writer of popular songs which emphasized such themes as unrequited love, loneliness, death, and war. In 1967 he quit the concert stage and turned to the theater, as a producer, director, and actor. In 1968 the composer Mort Shuman brought Brel's songs to Broadway in his musical *Jacques Brel Is Alive and Well and Living in Paris.* The title proved ironic; stricken with cancer, Brel abandoned his career in 1974 and made his home in the Marquesas Islands; in 1977 he returned to Paris to record his final album, *Brel.*

BIBL.: P. Berruer, *J. B. va bien: Il dort aux Marquises* (Paris, 1983); J. Lorcey and J. Monserrat, *J. B.* (Paris, 1984); O. Todd, *J. B., Une Vie* (Paris, 1984); P. Baton, *J. B.* (Brussels, 1990); J. Beaucarne, *B.* (Paris, 1990); T. Weick, *Die Rezeption des Werkes von J. B.* (Frankfurt am Main, 1991).

Brelet, Gisèle (Jeanne Marie Noémie), French musicologist and pianist; b. Fontenay-le-Comte, Vendée, March 6, 1915; d. Sèvres, June 21, 1973. She studied piano at the Nantes Cons. and at the Paris Cons.; also took courses in biology and philosophy at the Sorbonne in Paris (Ph.D., 1949). In 1950 she became director of the Bibliothèque Internationale de Musicologie. She wrote the studies *Esthétique et création musicale* (Paris, 1947), *Le Temps musical* (Paris, 1949), and *L'Interprétation créatrice* (Paris, 1951).

Brendel, Alfred, eminent Austrian pianist; b. Wiesenberg, Jan. 5, 1931. He studied in Zagreb with Dezelić (piano) and Dugan (harmony), and in Graz with Kaan (piano) and Michl (composition); he pursued piano training in Basel with Paul Baumgartner, and also attended the master classes of Edwin Fischer in Lucerne and Eduard Steuermann in Salzburg. After making his debut in Graz in 1948, he captured 4th prize in the Busoni competition in Bolzano in 1949. In 1960 he made a notable impression as soloist with the Vienna Phil. at the Salzburg Festival, and then garnered critical acclaim by presenting cycles of all the Beethoven piano sonatas in London in 1962 and in N.Y. in 1963. He subsequently pursued a distinguished international career, appearing as a soloist with the major orchs. and as a recitalist. In 1974 he settled in London. In 1991 he appeared as soloist in Beethoven's *Choral Fantasy* at the gala concert marking the 100th anniversary of N.Y.'s Carnegie Hall. He received many honors, including an honorary knighthood from Queen Elizabeth II of England in 1989. In addition to his discerning performances of Mozart, Beethoven, Schubert, and Liszt, Brendel has also played works outside the Viennese classical tradition, including those by Stravinsky, Bartók, and Schoenberg. He is also an engaging writer, as revealed in his *Musical Thoughts and Afterthoughts* (London, 1976; 2nd ed., 1982) and *Music Sounded Out: Essays, Lectures, Interviews, Afterthoughts* (London, 1990).

Brendel, Wolfgang, German baritone; b. Munich, Oct. 20, 1947. After vocal studies, he began his career in Kaiserslautern. He joined the Bavarian State Opera in Munich in 1971, and became Kammersanger there in 1977. On Nov. 20, 1975, he made his Metropolitan Opera debut in N.Y. as Count Almaviva in *Le nozze di Figaro*; then appeared at the San Francisco Opera as Rodrigo in *Don Carlo* (1979), at Milan's La Scala as Count Almaviva (1981), at the Chicago Lyric Opera as Miller in *Luisa Miller* (1982), and at the Bayreuth Festival as Wolfram in *Tannhäuser* (1985). He made his debut at London's Covent Garden as Conte Di Luna in *Il Trovatore* on Oct. 12, 1985. He appeared in opera centers throughout Europe and the U.S.; his most noted roles include Rossini's Figaro, Papageno, Eugene Onegin, Amfortas, Silvio, and Pelléas.

Brenta, Gaston, Belgian composer; b. Brussels, June 10, 1902; d. there, May 30, 1969. He studied theory with Paul Gilson; in 1925 he and 7 other pupils of Gilson formed the Belgian Groupe des Synthétistes, advocating a more modern approach to composition. From 1931 he was associated with the Belgian Radio; from 1953 to 1967 he was music director of the French Services there. His music follows the traditions of cosmopolitan Romanticism, with exotic undertones.

WORKS: DRAMATIC: *Le Khâdi dupé*, opera (Brussels, Dec. 16, 1929); 2 radio dramas: *Aucassin et Nicolette* (1934) and *Heracles* (1955); 3 ballets: *Zo'har* (1928); *Florilège de Valses* (1940); *Candide* (1955); *Le Bal chez la Lorette* (1954), which forms a part of *Les Bals de Paris,* a large ballet consisting of passages contributed by several Belgian composers. **ORCH.:** *Variations sur un thème congolais* (1926); *Nocturne* (1934); *Arioso et Moto Perpetuo* (1940); *War Music* (1946); Sym. (1946); *In Memoriam Paul Gilson* (1950); *Farandole burlesque* (1951); 2 piano concertos (1952, 1968); Concertino for Trumpet, Strings, and Timpani (1958); *Saxiana,* concertino for Saxophone, Strings, Timpani, and Piano (1962); *Airs variés pour de belles écouteuses* for Bassoon and Strings (1963); *Pointes sèches de la Belle Époque* for Piano and Strings (1964); *Matinée d'été* (1967). **CHAMBER:** String Quartet (1939); *Melopée* for Violin and Piano (1945); *Le Soldat fanfaron,* suite for Quintet (1952); Concertino for 5 Winds, Double Bass, Piano, and Percussion (1963); piano pieces.

Bresgen, Cesar, Austrian composer and teacher of German descent; b. Florence, Oct. 16, 1913; d. Salzburg, April 7, 1988. He studied organ, piano, conducting, and composition at the Munich Academy of Music (1930–36), his mentors being Emmanuel Gatscher, Gottfried Rüdinger, and Joseph Haas. In 1936 he won the Felix Mottl Prize for composition. After working in the music division of the Bavarian Radio in Munich, he settled in Salzburg in 1939 and organized his own music school; he also taught composition at the Mozarteum. He served in the army during World War II, and then was a church organist and choir director in Mittersill. In 1947 he returned to the Salzburg Mozarteum as prof. of composition. In 1974 he was awarded the Austrian State Prize for music. He publ. the books *Musikalische Dokumentation* (Vienna, 1982) and *Die Improvisation in der Musik* (Wilhelmshaven, 1983), as well as folk song collections. As a composer, Bresgen acquired a notable facility for writing effective *Gebrauchsmusik.*

WORKS: DRAMATIC: *Der Goggolore,* Singspiel (1937–39; unfinished); *Dornröschen,* Singspiel (Strasbourg, April 15, 1942); *Paracelsus,* opera (1942–43); *Das Urteil des Paris,* komisches Singspiel (Göttingen, Jan. 31, 1943); *Der Igel als Brautigam,* children's opera (Esslingen, Nov. 3, 1948; rev. version, Nuremburg, Nov. 13, 1951); *Visiones amantis* or *Der Wolkensteiner,* Ludus tragicus (1951; Bremen Radio, Feb. 17, 1964; 1st stage perf., Innsbruck, Dec. 20, 1971); *Niño fliegt mit Niña,* "insect comedy" for Children (Munich, May 14, 1953); *Brüderlein Hund,* children's opera (Nuremberg, Nov. 12, 1953); *Der ewige Arzt,* Mystereinspiel (Schwyz, Feb. 10, 1956); *Ercole,* opera (Hamburg Radio, 1956); *Der Mann im Mond,* musical fairy tale (Nuremberg, May 22, 1960); *Die alte Lokomotive,* scenic cantata (Munich, Oct. 7, 1960); *Die Schattendiebe* or *Ali und der Bilderdiebel,* children's Singspiel (Vienna, April 13,

1962); *Bastian der Faulpelz,* musical pantomime (Hamburg, 1966); *Trubloff,* Singspiel (1970); *Der Engel von Pra,* opera (Salzburg, Dec. 25, 1978; rev. 1985); *Pilatus,* opera (Villach, Aug. 2, 1980); *Krabat,* Singspiel (1982); *Albolina, oder der Kampf der Geister um die Morgenrote,* musical fairy tale (Villach, July 12, 1987). **ORCH.:** Chamber Concerto for Guitar and Small Orch. (1962); *Elegie* for 12 Cellos (1979); *Ballade* for Violin, Harpsichord, and 13 Strings (1983); *Impressioni nella notte* for Small Orch. (1984); Clarinet Concerto (1986); *Magnalia Dei,* symphonic metamorphosis for Orch. and Speaker (1987). **OTHER:** Chamber music and choral pieces.

BIBL.: D. Larese, *C. B.* (Amriswil, 1968); R. Lück, *C. B.* (Vienna, 1974).

Bresnick, Martin, American composer and teacher; b. N.Y., Nov. 13, 1946. He studied at N.Y.'s High School of Music and Art; then was a pupil of Arnold Franchetti at the Hartt School of Music in Hartford, Conn. (B.A., 1967), of Leland Smith and John Chowning at Stanford Univ. (M.A., 1968; D.M.A., 1972), and of Einem and Cerha at the Vienna Academy of Music on a Fulbright fellowship (1969–70); also studied with Ligeti. After teaching at the San Francisco Cons. of Music (1971–72) and Stanford Univ. (1972–75), he was a prof. of composition at the Yale Univ. School of Music (from 1975). He received grants from the NEA (1974, 1979), held the Rome Prize fellowship (1975–76), took 1st prize in the Premio Ancona (1980) and in the International Sinfonia Musicale Competition (1982), and received various commissions. Bresnick, his wife, and 5 other patrons were the victims of random violence on the evening of Aug. 7, 1994, when they were stabbed by a man gone beserk in a New Haven restaurant. Fortunately, all victims survived.

WORKS: ORCH.: *Ocean of Storms* (1970); *Wir Weben, Wir Weben* for Strings (1978; also for Chamber Ensemble or String Sextet); *One* (1986); *Little Suite* for Amateur String Orch. (1987); *Pontoosuc* (1989); *Angelus Novus* (1991); *Sinfonia* (1992). **CHAMBER:** Trio for 2 Trumpets and Percussion (1966); 3 string quartets (1968, 1984, 1992); *Introit* for 8 Woodwinds and 8 Brass Instruments (1969); *Musica* for 9 Instruments (1972); *B's Garland* for 8 Cellos (1973); *Conspiracies* for Solo Flute and 4 Other Flutes (1979); *High Art* for Piccolo and Toy Piano (1983); *Bread & Salt* for 14 Instruments (1984); *Tent of Miracles* for Solo Baritone Saxophone and 3 Other Baritone Saxophones (1984); *Just Time* for Woodwind Quintet (1985); Trio for Violin, Cello, and Piano (1988); *Tucket* for Brass Quintet (1990). **VOCAL:** *Where is the Way* for Chorus (1970); *Ants* for Soprano, Mezzo-soprano, Tenor, Baritone, 5 Actor/Mimes, Woodwind Quintet, String Quartet, Double Bass, Percussion, and Harp (1976); *Der Signâl* for Soprano, Alto, Mezzo-soprano, Narrator or Tape, and 8 Instruments (1982); *3 Choral Songs* (1986); *New Haven, Woodstock* for Chorus (1993); *Falling* for Mezzo-soprano and Piano or Orch. (1994).

Bressler, Charles, American tenor; b. Kingston, Pa., April 1, 1926. After studies with Lucia Dunham, Sergius Kagen, and Marjorie Schloss at the Juilliard School of Music in N.Y. (graduated, 1950; postgraduate diploma, 1951), he became a founding member of the N.Y. Pro Musica, with which he toured widely (1953–63). He also was a founding member of the N.Y. Chamber Soloists (from 1957); likewise appeared with the Santa Fe Opera and the Washington (D.C.) Opera Soc., and toured Europe as a concert artist. He taught at various schools, including N.Y.'s Mannes College of Music (from 1966) and Manhattan School of Music (from 1978). He was best known for his performances of early music, but also had success in contemporary roles.

Bretan, Nicolae, remarkable Romanian composer; b. Năsăud, April 6, 1887; d. Cluj, Dec. 1, 1968. He studied at the Klausenburg Cons., composition and voice with Farkas, and violin with Gyémánt (1906–08); then at the Vienna Academy of Music (1908–09) and at the Magyar Királyi Zeneakademia in Budapest (1909–12) with Siklos (theory) and Szerémi (violin). His primary career was that of an opera singer, performing baritone parts at the opera houses in Bratislava, Oradea, and Cluj between 1913 and 1944, also acting as a stage director. At the same time, he surprisingly asserted himself as a composer of operas and lieder in an effective veristic manner, marked by a high degree of professional expertise and considerable originality.

WORKS: Operas: *Luceafărul* (The Evening Star; in Romanian; tr. by the composer into Hungarian and German; Cluj, Feb. 2, 1921); *Golem* (in Hungarian; tr. by the composer into Romanian and German; Cluj, Dec. 23, 1924); *Eroii de la Rovine* (in Romanian; Cluj, Jan. 24, 1935); *Horia* (in Romanian; also tr. into German by the composer; Cluj, Jan. 24, 1937); *Arald* (in Romanian; 1939); *Requiem*; mystery play, *An Extraordinary Seder Evening* (in Hungarian; also tr. into Eng.); *Mein Liederland,* about 230 songs to Romanian, Hungarian, and German texts.

Brett, Philip, English-born American musicologist; b. Edwinstowe, Oct. 17, 1937. He studied at King's College, Cambridge (B.A., 1958; Mus.B., 1961), and after a brief period at the Univ. of Calif. at Berkeley, completed his training at Cambridge (Ph.D., 1965). He joined the faculty at the Univ. of Calif. at Berkeley in 1966, where he was a prof. (1978–90) and chairman of the music dept. (1988–90). In 1979 he became a naturalized American citizen. He was prof. of music at the Univ. of Calif. at Riverside from 1991. With Thurston Dart, he prepared The English Madrigalists (1956; a rev. ed. of Fellowes's The English Madrigal School); he also was general ed. of the new critical edition of the works of Byrd. He publ. the useful study *Peter Grimes* (Cambridge, 1983) and ed. with E. Wood and G. Thomas *Queering the Pitch: The New Gay and Lesbian Musicology* (1994).

Bréval, Lucienne (real name, **Berthe Agnes Lisette Schilling**), Swiss-born French soprano; b. Männedorf, Nov. 4, 1869; d. Paris, Aug. 15, 1935. She studied piano at the Lausanne Cons. and the Geneva Cons. and voice with Wartot at the Paris Cons., making her operatic debut at the Paris Opéra as Selika in *L'Africaine* on Jan. 20, 1892; subsequently was a principal singer there for 25 years. In 1899 she sang at London's Covent Garden, and on Jan. 16, 1901, made her Metropolitan Opera debut in N.Y. as Chimène in *Le Cid,* remaining on the company's roster until 1902. She excelled in the French repertoire.

Brevik, Tor, Norwegian composer, conductor, and music critic; b. Oslo, Jan. 22, 1932. He studied violin, viola, and theory at the Oslo Cons. before completing his training in Sweden. In 1958 he founded the Oslo Youth Chamber Orch. He was also active as a music critic.

WORKS: DRAMATIC: *Contrasts,* ballet (1964); *Da kongen kom til Spilliputt,* opera (1973). **ORCH.:** *Adagio and Fugue* for Strings (1958); Overture (1958); *Serenade* for Strings (1959); *Chaconne* (1960); Concertino for Clarinets and Strings (1961); *Canto elegiaco* (1964); Chamber Concerto for Strings (1967); *Intrada* (1969); *Romance* for Violin and Orch. (1972; also for Violin and Piano); *Andante cantabile* for Violin and Strings (1975); Viola Concerto (1982); *Sinfonietta* (1989); *Sinfonia Brevik* (1991); *Music* (1993). **CHAMBER:** *Music* for Violin (1963); *Divertimento* for Wind Quintet (1964); *Adagio religioso* for Horn (1967); String Quartet (1967); *Music* for 4 Strings (1968); Septet (1977); *Fantasy* for Flute (1979); *Serenade* for 10 Winds (1994). **VOCAL:** *Elegy* for Soprano, Viola, Double Bass, and Percussion (1964); *Light of Peace* for Soli, Chorus, and String Quartet or Orch. (1980); choruses; songs.

Bréville, Pierre (-Onfroy de), French composer, teacher, and music critic; b. Bar-le-Duc, Feb. 21, 1861; d. Paris, Sept. 24, 1949. He studied at the Paris Cons. with Théodor Dubois (1880–82) and later with César Franck. He was a prof. of counterpoint at the Paris Schola Cantorum from 1898 to 1902; was active also as a music critic. He completed (with d'Indy and others) Franck's unfinished opera *Ghiselle*; in his own music, he followed the traditions of French Romanticism. His opera, *Eros Vainqueur,* was premiered in Brussels on March 7, 1910; he also wrote an overture to Maeterlinck's play *La Princesse Maleine,* and to his *Les Sept Princesses*; also composed the orch. suites *Nuit de décembre* and *Stamboul,* as well as numerous choral pieces.

Brewster, W(illiam) Herbert, Sr., black American gospel songwriter; b. Somerville, Tenn., July 2, 1899; d. Memphis, Oct. 14, 1987. He had a fine baritone voice and served as an evangelist in a Baptist church in Memphis. He also acquired a reputation as a writer of religious songs. His chant *Surely God Is Able* was probably the first composition in gospel-singing usage to employ triple meter within the time signature of 12/8. Some of his moralistic songs, such as *How I Got Over*, sold over a million copies.

Brey, Carter, American cellist; b. Glen Ridge, N.J., Sept. 19, 1954. He was a student of Laurence Lesser (1972–74) and Stephen Kates (1974–76) at the Peabody Inst. in Baltimore, and of Aldo Parisot (1977–78) at Yale Univ. After winning 1st prize in the duo category with pianist Barbara Weintraub at the Munich International Competition in 1978, he took 3rd prize in the first Rostropovich International Cello Competition in Paris in 1981. In 1982 he won the Young Concert Artists Auditions and made his formal debut at the Kennedy Center in Washington, D.C. In 1984 he received an Avery Fisher Career Grant. From 1983 he pursued a successful career as a soloist with the major orchs., as a recitalist, and as a chamber music player. In addition to the standard cello repertory, Brey has made a special effort to perform contemporary scores.

Brian, Havergal, English composer of extreme fecundity and longevity; b. Dresden, Staffordshire, Jan. 29, 1876; d. Shoreham-by-the-Sea, Sussex, Nov. 28, 1972. He studied violin, cello, and organ with local teachers; left school at age 12 to earn his living and help his father, who was a potter's turner. At the same time he taught himself elementary theory and also learned French and German without an instructor. From 1904 to 1949 he engaged in musical journalism. He attained a reputation in England as a harmless eccentric possessed by inordinate ambitions to become a composer; he attracted supporters among English musicians, who in turn were derided as gullible admirers of a patent amateur. But Brian continued to write music in large symphonic forms; some of his works were performed, mostly by non-professional organizations; amazingly enough, he increased his productivity with age; he wrote 22 syms. after reaching the age of 80, and 7 more after the age of 90. The total number of syms. at the time of his death was 32. Finally, English musicians, critics, conductors, and concert organizations became aware of the Brian phenomenon, and performances, mostly posthumous, followed. A Havergal Brian Soc. was formed in London, and there were a few timorous attempts to further the Brian cause outside of England. The slow acceptance of Brian's music was not due to his overindulgence in dissonance. Quite the contrary is true; Brian was not an innovator; he followed the Germanic traditions of Richard Strauss and Mahler in the spirit of unbridled grandiosity, architectural formidability, and rhapsodically quaquaversal thematicism. Brian's modernism tended to be programmatic, as in the ominous whole-tone progressions in his opera *The Tigers*, illustrating the aerial attacks on London by zeppelins during World War I. Brian's readiness to lend his MSS to anyone showing interest in his music resulted in the loss of several of his works; a few of them were retrieved after years of search.

WORKS: OPERAS: *The Tigers*, to his own libretto (1916–19; lost until 1977; BBC, May 3, 1983); *Turandot*, to a German libretto after Schiller (1950–51); *The Cenci*, after Shelley (1952); *Faust*, after Goethe (1955–56); *Agamemnon*, to an English libretto after Aeschylus (1957; London, Jan. 28, 1972). **ORCH.:** *Tragic Prelude* (1899–1900; not extant); *Burlesque Variations on an Original Theme* (1903; lost until 1974; Hull, March 13, 1980); *For Valour*, concert overture (1904; rev. 1906; London, Oct. 8, 1907); *Hero and Leander*, symphonic poem (1904–05; Hanley, Dec. 3, 1908; not extant); 5 English Suites: No. 1 (1904–06; Leeds, Jan. 12, 1907), No. 2, *Night Portraits* (1915; not extant), No. 3 (1919–21; Bournemouth, March 16, 1922), No. 4, *Kindergarten* (1924; London, July 5, 1977), and No. 5, *Rustic Scenes* (1953); *Fantastic Variations on an Old Rhyme* (1907; 1st movement of *A Fantastic Symphony*; rev. 1912; Brighton, April 28, 1921); *Festal Dance* (1908; 3rd movement of *A Fantastic Symphony*; Birmingham, Dec. 14, 1914); *In Memoriam* (1910; Edinburgh, Dec. 26, 1921); *Comedy Overture* No. 1: *Doctor Merryheart* (1911–12; Birmingham, Jan. 3, 1913), No. 2: *The Tinker's Wedding* (1948; BBC, Glasgow, June 25, 1950, and No. 3: *The Jolly Miller* (1962; Philadelphia, Nov. 15, 1974); 32 syms.: No. 1, *The Gothic*, in 2 parts of 3 movements each (Part II is a setting of the *Te Deum*) for 4 Vocal Soloists, 4 Mixed Choruses, Children's Chorus, 4 Brass Bands, and Very Large Orch. (1919–27; amateur perf., London, June 24, 1961; professional perf., London, Oct. 30, 1966), No. 2 (1930–31; Brighton, May 19, 1973), No. 3 (1931–32; BBC, Oct. 18, 1974), No. 4, *Das Siegeslied*, a German setting of *Psalm 68* in the Lutheran version, for Soprano, Double Mixed Chorus, and Orch. (1932–33; BBC, July 3, 1967), No. 5, *Wine of Summer*, for Baritone and Orch. (1937; London, Dec. 11, 1969), No. 6, *Tragica* (1948; BBC, Sept. 21, 1966), No. 7 (1948; BBC, March 13, 1968), No. 8 (1949; BBC, Feb. 1, 1954), No. 9 (1951; BBC, March 22, 1958), No. 10 (1953–54; BBC, Nov. 3, 1958), No. 11 (1954; BBC, Nov. 5, 1959), No. 12 (1957; BBC, Nov. 5, 1959), No. 13 (1959; BBC, May 14, 1978), No. 14 (1959–60; BBC, May 10, 1970), No. 15 (1960; BBC, May 14, 1978), No. 16 (1960; BBC, June 18, 1975), No. 17 (1960–61; BBC, May 14, 1978), No. 18 (1961; London, Feb. 26, 1962), No. 19 (1961; BBC, Dec. 31, 1976), No. 20 (1962; London, Oct. 5, 1976), No. 21 (1963; BBC, May 10, 1970), No. 22, *Brevis* (1964–65; BBC, Aug. 15, 1971), No. 23 (1965; Galesburg, Ill., Oct. 4, 1973), No. 24 (1965; BBC, June 18, 1975), No. 25 (1965–66; BBC, Dec. 31, 1976), No. 26 (1966; Stoke on Trent, May 13, 1976), No. 27 (1966; BBC, March 18, 1979), No. 28 (1967; BBC, Oct. 5, 1973), No. 29 (1967; Stoke on Trent, Nov. 17, 1976), No. 30 (1967; London, Sept. 24, 1976), No. 31 (1968; London, March 18, 1979), and No. 32 (1968; London, Jan. 28, 1971); 2 violin concertos: No. 1 (1934; stolen and presumed destroyed) and No. 2 (1934–35; London, June 20, 1969); *Elegy* (1954; London, Feb. 17, 1977); Cello Concerto (1964; London, Feb. 5, 1971); *Concerto for Orchestra* (1964; Leeds, April 12, 1975); *Ave Atque Vale*, legend (1968).

CHAMBER: *Legend* for Violin and Piano (1919); *Festival Fanfare* for Brass (1967; originally *Fanfare for the Brass*; Urbana, Ill., May 7, 1972).

PIANO: *3 Illuminations* (1916); *Double Fugue* in E major (1924); *Prelude and Fugue* in C minor (1924); *Prelude and Fugue* in D major and D minor (1924); *John Dowland's Fancy*, prelude (1934).

VOCAL: *Requiem* for Baritone, Chorus, and Orch. (1897; not extant); *Psalm 23* for Tenor, Chorus, and Orch. (1904; full score not extant; reconstructed 1945; Hove, March 10, 1973); *By the Waters of Babylon* for Baritone, Chorus, and Orch. (1905; rev. 1909; Hanley, April 18, 1907; full score not extant); *Carmilhan*, dramatic ballad for Soloists, Chorus, and Orch. (1906; not extant); *The Vision of Cleopatra*, cantata for Soloists, Chorus, and Orch. (1907; Southport, Oct. 14, 1909; full score destroyed by fire); *Pilgrimage to Kevlaar*, ballad for Chorus and Orch. (1913–14; not extant); *Prometheus Unbound*, lyric drama for Soloists, Double Chorus, and Orch., after Shelley (1937–44; full score not extant); choruses; over 100 songs.

BIBL.: R. Nettel, *Ordeal by Music: The Strange Experience of H. B.* (London, 1945); L. Foreman, ed., *H. B.: A Collection of Essays* (London, 1969); M. MacDonald, *H. B.: Perspective on the Music* (London, 1972); idem, *The Symphonies of H. B.* (3 vols., London, 1974–83); K. Eastaugh, *H. B.: The Making of a Composer* (London, 1976); L. Foreman, *H. B. and the Performance of His Orchestral Music: A History and a Sourcebook* (London, 1976); R. Nettel, *H. B. and His Music* (London, 1976); P. Rapoport, *Opus Est* (London, 1979).

Briccetti, Thomas (Bernard), American conductor and composer; b. Mt. Kisco, N.Y., Jan, 14, 1936. He studied piano with Jean Dansereau and composition with Barber, Mennin, and Hovhaness; attended the Eastman School of Music in Rochester, N.Y. (1955). In 1959–60 he held the Prix de Rome, and then

Ford Foundation Composer's fellowships (1961–63). He was music director of the St. Petersburg (Fla.) Sym. Orch. (1963–68) and the Florida Sun Coast Opera (1964–68). He was assoc. conductor of the Indianapolis Sym. Orch. (1968–72). From 1971 to 1978 he was music director of the Ft. Wayne (Ind.) Phil.; also of the Cleveland Inst. of Music Univ. Circle Orch. (1972–75). He was music director of the Omaha Sym. Orch. and Nebraska Sinfonia (1975–83). After serving as principal guest conductor of the Stavanger Sym. Orch. and Radio Ensemble (1986–87), he was artistic director of the Orch. Stabile in Bergamo (from 1988) and principal conductor of the Orch. Sinfonica in Umbria (from 1988). His compositions include *Eurydice*, opera; Sym.; Violin Concerto; *The Fountain of Youth*, overture; *Illusions*, symphonic poem; String Quartet; Flute Sonata; Piano Sonata; choral music; songs.

Brice, Carol (Lovette Hawkins), black American contralto; b. Sedalia, N.C., April 16, 1918; d. Norman, Okla., Feb. 15, 1985. She received training at Palmer Memorial Inst. in Sedalia, at Talladega (Ala.) College (B.Mus., 1939), and from Francis Rogers at the Juilliard School of Music in N.Y. (1939–43). She first attracted attention when she sang in *The Hot Mikado* at the N.Y. World's Fair (1939); she was also chosen to sing at a concert for President Roosevelt's 3rd inauguration in 1941 and was the first black American to win the Naumburg Award (1943). Among her many stage roles were Addie in *Regina*, Maude in *Finian's Rainbow*, Maria in *Porgy and Bess*, Queenie in *Showboat*, and Harriet Tubman in *Gentlemen, Be Seated*. She was a member of the Vienna Volksoper (1967–71), then taught at the Univ. of Okla. (from 1974). With her husband, the baritone Thomas Carey, she founded the Cimarron Circuit Opera Co.

Brice, Fanny (real name, **Fannie Borach**), American comedienne and singer; b. N.Y., Oct. 29, 1891; d. Los Angeles, May 29, 1951. After singing in her parents' tavern, she toured the burlesque circuit, where she was discovered by Florenz Ziegfeld, who featured her in his *Follies of 1910*. Subsequently she appeared in other eds. of the Follies, and in Broadway musicals. Her most notable film role was her self-portrayal in *The Great Ziegfeld* (1936); in the *Ziegfeld Follies of 1934*, she also created the role of little Baby Snooks, a character she continued to portray on radio from 1938 until her death. Her 3rd husband was Billy Rose, the producer and songwriter (married, 1929; divorced, 1938). Her career was the subject of the 1964 Broadway musical *Funny Girl*, which was later made into a film starring Barbra Streisand (1968).

BIBL.: N. Katkov, *The Fabulous F.* (N.Y., 1951).

Bricken, Carl Ernest, American composer, conductor, and pianist; b. Shelbyville, Ky., Dec. 28, 1898; d. Sweet Briar, Va., Jan. 25, 1971. He studied with Scalero at the Mannes School of Music in N.Y.; pursued training at Yale Univ., in Vienna, and with Alfred Cortot at the École Normale de Musique in Paris. He taught at the Mannes School of Music (1925–28) and at the Inst. of Musical Art in N.Y.; in 1931 he organized the music dept. at the Univ. of Chicago, and was its chairman until becoming prof. of music at the Univ. of Wisc. in 1938. After serving as conductor of the Seattle Sym. Orch. (1944–48), he taught at Sweet Briar College (1954–63) before devoting himself to painting. He wrote 3 syms., and other orch. works, chamber music, and piano pieces.

Brico, Antonia, Dutch-American pianist, conductor, and teacher; b. Rotterdam, June 26, 1902; d. Denver, Aug. 3, 1989. She studied at the Univ. of Calif. at Berkeley (graduated, 1923); after piano studies with Stojowski in N.Y., she studied conducting at the Berlin Hochschule für Musik and privately with Muck. Overcoming general skepticism concerning women conductors, she raised funds to conduct a special concert of the Berlin Phil. on Jan. 10, 1930, which aroused some curiosity. On Aug. 1, 1930, she conducted the Los Angeles Phil. at the Hollywood Bowl. She then pursued her career in N.Y., where she was founder-conductor of the Women's Sym. Orch. (1934–38). In 1938 she became the first woman to conduct the N.Y. Phil. In 1941 she settled in Denver, where she founded and conducted her own semiprofessional Antonia Brico Sym. Orch., making her last appearance on the podium in 1985. In the film documentary *Antonia* (1974), she eloquently pleaded for the feminist cause in music and especially in conducting.

Bridge, Frank, distinguished English composer; b. Brighton, Feb. 26, 1879; d. Eastbourne, Jan. 10, 1941. He studied composition with Stanford at the Royal College of Music in London (1899–1903). He was active as a violinist and violist in several string quartets, among them the Joachim, Grimson, and English string quartets. In 1910–11 he was conductor of the New Sym. Orch. in London, and in 1913 he conducted at Covent Garden there. In 1923 he toured the U.S. conducting his own works. As a composer, Bridge received recognition only in the last years of his life. After his death, greater appreciation arose, particularly in his homeland. In his early works, he followed the paths of Delius, Ireland, and Bax. After World War I, he pursued a more adventuresome route, influenced by the Second Viennese School, although never embracing serialism. Among his most remarkable advanced works are the 3rd and 4th string quartets. Benjamin Britten, his ardent student and admirer, composed his *Variations on a Theme of Frank Bridge* after the latter's *Idyll* No. 2 for String Quartet.

WORKS: DRAMATIC: *The 2 Hunchbacks*, incidental music (London, Nov. 15, 1910, composer conducting); *The Pageant of London* (1911); *Threads*, incidental music (London, Aug. 23, 1921); *In the Shop*, children's ballet (1921); *The Christmas Rose*, opera (1919–29; London, Dec. 8, 1931, composer conducting). **ORCH.:** *Berceuse* for Violin and Strings (1901; London, June 20, 1902); *Coronation March* (1901); *Valse intermezzo à cordes* for Strings (1902); *Trois Morceau d'orchestre* (1902); *Serenade* (1903); *Symphonic Poem* (1903; London, May 20, 1904, composer conducting); *Norse Legend* (1905); *Rosemary* (1906); *Dramatic Overture* (c.1906); *Isabella* (London, Oct. 3, 1907); *Dance Rhapsody* (London, July 21, 1908, composer conducting); *An Irish Melody* for Strings (1908; also for String Quartet); Suite for Strings (1909–10); *The Sea* (1911; London, Sept. 24, 1912); *Dance Poem* (1913; London, March 16, 1914, composer conducting); *Lament* for Strings (London, Sept. 15, 1915); *Summer* (1914–15; London, March 13, 1916, composer conducting); *2 Poems* (1915; London, Jan. 1, 1917, composer conducting); *2 Old English Songs* for Strings (London, Sept. 26, 1916, composer conducting); *Sir Roger de Coverley* (London, Oct. 21, 1922, composer conducting; also for String Orch., 1938); *Vignettes de danse* for Small Orch. (1925; BBC, Glasgow, May 12, 1941); *Canzonetta* for Small Orch. (1926); *There is a willow grows aslant a brook* for Small Orch. (London, Aug. 20, 1927, composer conducting); *Enter Spring* (Norwich, Oct. 27, 1927, composer conducting); *Oration, concerto elegiaco* for Cello and Orch. (1930; BBC, Jan. 16, 1936, Florence Hooten soloist, composer conducting); *Phantasm* for Piano and Orch. (1931; London, Jan. 10, 1934, Kathleen Long soloist, composer conducting); *Todessehnsucht (Come Sweet Death)* for Strings (1936); *Rebus* (1940; London, Feb. 23, 1941); Sym. for Strings (1940; unfinished; 1st movement, Aldeburgh Festival, June 20, 1979). **CHAMBER:** 2 piano trios: No. 1 (London, Nov. 14, 1900) and No. 2 (1928–29; London, Nov. 4, 1929); String Quintet (London, Dec. 4, 1901); *Scherzo phantastick* for 2 Violins, Viola, and Cello (1901; London, June 27, 1907); 1 unnumbered string quartet (1900; London, March 14, 1901); 4 numbered string quartets: No. 1 (1906; London, June 16, 1909), No. 2 (1914–15; London, Nov. 4, 1915), No. 3 (1925–27; Vienna, Sept. 17, 1927), and No. 4 (1937; Pittsfield, Mass., Sept. 23, 1938); Piano Quartet (1902; London, Feb. 23, 1903); 2 violin sonatas: No. 1 (1904) and No. 2 (1932; London, Jan. 18, 1934); *Elégie* for Cello and Piano (1904; Kensington, March 6, 1908); 2 piano quintets: No. 1 (1905; London, May 28, 1907) and No. 2 (London, May 29, 1912); *Phantasie* for String Quartet (1905; London, June 22, 1906); *3 Idylls* for String Quartet (1906; London, March 8, 1907); String Sextet (1906–12; London, June 18, 1913); *Phantasy* for Piano Trio

(1907; London, April 27, 1909); *Allegro appassionato* for Viola and Piano (c.1907; London, Nov. 24, 1909); 3 sets of *Miniatures* for Violin, Cello, and Piano (c.1908; Exeter, Nov. 7, 1913); *Phantasy* for Piano Quartet (1910; London, Jan. 21, 1911); *2 Pieces* for 2 Violas (1911–12; London, March 18, 1912); Cello Sonata (1913–17; London, July 13, 1917); *Rhapsody* for 2 Violins and Viola (1928; Aldeburgh Festival, June 24, 1965); *Divertimenti* for Flute, Oboe, Clarinet, and Bassoon (1934; rev. 1937–38; Washington, D.C., April 14, 1940); Viola Sonata (c.1935; unfinished). **KEYBOARD: PIANO:** *2 capriccios* (1905); *Dramatic fantasia* (1906); *3 sketches* (1906); *3 Poems* (1913–14); *4 Characteristic Pieces* (1917); *A Fairy Tale* (1917); 3 sets of *Miniature pastorals* (1917, 1921, 1921); *3 Improvisations* for Piano, Left-hand (1918); *The Hour Glass* (1919–20); Sonata (1924; London, Oct. 15, 1925, Myra Hess pianist); *In Autumn* (1924); *Winter pastoral* (1925). **ORGAN:** *3 Pieces* (c.1905); 2 books of *Organ Pieces* (1905, 1912); *Lento: Im memoriam C(harles) H(ubert) H(astings) P(arry)* (1918); *3 Pieces* (1939). **VOCAL:** *Music when soft voices die* for Chorus (1904); *A Prayer* for Chorus and Orch. (1916; London, Jan. 1919, composer conducting; also for Chorus and Organ); *A Litany* for Women's Chorus (1918); *Evening Primrose* for Women's Chorus and Piano (1923); *Golden Slumbers* for Women's Voices (1923); solo songs.

BIBL.: P. Pirie, *F. B.* (London, 1971); A. Payne and L. Foreman, *F. B.* (London, 1976); P. Hindmarsh, *F. B.: A Thematic Catalogue* (London, 1983); A. Payne, *F. B.: Radical and Conservative* (London, 1984); K. Little, *F. B.: A Bio-Bibliography* (N.Y., 1991).

Brilioth, Helge, Swedish tenor; b. Vaxjo, May 7, 1931. He studied at the Stockholm Musikhögskolan, the Accademia di Santa Cecilia in Rome, and the Salzburg Mozarteum. In 1958 he made his operatic debut in the baritone role of Bartolo in Paisiello's *Il Barbiere di Siviglia* in Stockholm; then sang in Bielefeld (1962–64). After further training in Stockholm, he made his debut as a tenor there in 1965 in the role of Don José. In 1969 he made his first appearance at the Bayreuth Festival as Siegmund. He sang Siegfried in *Götterdämmerung* at the Salzburg Easter Festival in 1970. On Nov. 14, 1970, he made his Metropolitan Opera debut in N.Y. as Parsifal, where he remained on the roster until 1974. He subsequently concentrated his career in Europe.

Brînduş, Nicolae, Romanian composer, writer on music, and teacher; b. Bucharest, April 16, 1935. He studied piano (1952–57) and composition (1960–64) at the Bucharest Cons., and then attended intermittent summer courses in new music in Darmstadt (1969–80); later he worked at IRCAM in Paris (1985). After serving as pianist of the Ploieşti Phil. (1960–69), he taught chamber music at the Bucharest Cons. (1969–81). In 1981 he became an ed. of the journal *Musica.* He also was a prof. of chamber music at the Bucharest Cons. from 1992. In 1993 he lectured on contemporary music in N.Y., Washington, D.C., Los Angeles, and other U.S. cities. After serving on the executive committee of the ISCM (1991–93), he was president of its Romanian section (from 1994). He publ. the theoretical vol. *Interferenţe* (Interrelations; Bucharest, 1984). Among his honors are the prizes of the Romanian Composers and Musicologists Union (1974), the Romanian Radio and TV (1975, 1977), and the Romanian Academy (1977). In his compositions, Brînduş has explored the utilization of modal and serial elements, improvisation, and electronics. He is also a leading advocate of the syncretic form known as instrumental theater.

WORKS: DRAMATIC: *Logodna* (The Betrothal), opera-pantomime (1964–66; Bucharest, Feb. 9, 1975); *La Ţigănci* (With the Gypsy Girls), opera (1978–85; Bucharest, June 19, 1987). **INSTRUMENTAL THEATER:** *Kitsch-N* for Clarinet and Tape (1974; Warsaw, Sept. 1979); *Infrarealism* for Voice, Clarinet, and Piano (1975); *Languir me fais* for Percussionist (1979); *Prolegomene I* (1981) and *II* (1988) for Tenor and Piano or Bass and Double Bass; *Ouvédennerode* for Saxophone, Double Bass, and Tape (1993). **ORCH.:** *6 Miniatures* (1962–70; Braşov, June 4, 1970); *3 Pieces* (1964; Cluj-Napoca, May 14, 1966); *Music* for Chamber Orch. (1964; Tîrgu Mureş, May 5, 1966); *Phtora I-Durations* (1968; Bucharest, May 10, 1973); *Inscription* (1969; Arad, June 4, 1971); *Antiphonia* for String Chamber Orch. (Zagreb, May 4, 1971); *Match II-Monody I and Polyphony II* for Chamber Orch. and Tape (Warsaw, Sept. 1973); 2 piano concertos: No. 1, *Dialogos* (1978; Iaşi, May 1979) and No. 2 (1993); Concerto for 2 Pianos and Orch. (1983; Timişoara, May 28, 1984); *Sineuphonia I* for 2 Organs, Orch., and Tape (1986–87; Chişinau, April 1994). **CHAMBER:** *Cantus Firmus-Phtora III* for Keyboard Instrument(s) and Other Instruments or Voices (1970); *Waves* for Piano, Violin, Viola, Cello, Clarinet, and Percussion (Darmstadt, July 1972); *Melopedia and Fugue* for Bassoon (1981); *Rhythmòdia,* concerto for Solo Percussion (1982). **PIANO:** *Pieces* (1962); *Ostinato* (1962); Sonata for 2 Pianos (1963). **VOCAL:** *Pintea Viteazul* for Tenor, Chorus, and Orch. (1964; rev. 1970); *The Ballad Symphony* (1964–78); *7 Psalms* for Baritone, Piano, and Percussion (1965); *Strigoii* for Soloists, Narrator, Chorus, Orch., and Tape (1966; Bucharest, Jan. 9, 1975); *Mărturie,* cantata for Chorus and Orch. (1967; Bucharest, Feb. 16, 1971); *Domnişoara Hus,* cantata for Voices and Orch. (1968; Bucharest, Feb. 12, 1970); *Vă stau vasale simetrii,* cantata for Chorus and orch. (1971); *Eroii de la Plevna,* cantata for Bass-baritone, Chorus, and Orch. (1976; Iaşi, April 8, 1977); *Voinicul şi calul* for Tenor, Baritone, Chorus, and Orch. (1978).

Britain, Radie, American composer and teacher; b. Silverton, Texas, March 17, 1899; d. Palm Desert, Calif., May 23, 1994. After studying piano at the American Cons. in Chicago (B.M., 1924), she studied theory and composition with Noelte in Munich and organ with Dupré in Paris (1924–26); then continued her studies with Noelte in Chicago, and also had instruction in piano from Godowsky and organ from Yon. She taught harmony and composition at Chicago's Girvin Inst. of Music (1930–34); after teaching at the Chicago Cons. (1934–39), she taught piano and composition in Hollywood (1940–60). She publ. the book *Composer's Corner* (1978). Her autobiography appeared posthumously as *From Ridin' Herd to Writing Symphonies* (1995). Most of her compositions followed along traditional lines, inspired by various American subjects.

WORKS: DRAMATIC: *Ubiquity,* musical drama (1937); *Happyland,* children's operetta (1946); *Carillon,* opera (1952); *The Spider and the Butterfly,* children's operetta (1953); *Kuthara,* chamber opera (1960; Santa Barbara, June 24, 1961); *The Dark Lady Within,* drama with music (1962); *Western Temperament,* drama with music (telecast, Omaha, June 2, 1963); 4 ballets. **ORCH.:** *Prelude to a Drama* (1928; Chicago, Jan. 31, 1937); *Symphonic Intermezzo* (Chicago, Jan. 8, 1928); *Heroic Poem* (1929; Rochester, N.Y., March 3, 1932); *Rhapsodic Phantasie* for Piano and Orch. (1933; Chicago, April 24, 1938); *Nocturn* for Small Orch. (1934; Chicago, Nov. 10, 1940); *Light* (1935; Chicago, Nov. 29, 1938); *Southern Symphony* (1935; Chicago, March 4, 1940); *Ontonangon Sketches* (1939); *Saturnale* (1939); Suite for Strings (1940; Rochester, N.Y., Oct. 23, 1945); *Phantasy* for Oboe and Orch. (1942; Amarillo, Tex., April 22, 1958); *We Believe* (1942; Madrid, March 19, 1961); *Serenata Sorrentina* for Small Orch. (1946; Amarillo, Tex., April 8, 1947); *Cactus Rhapsody* (1953; Washington, D.C., April 4, 1960); *Cowboy Rhapsody* (Amarillo, Tex., April 11, 1956); *Cosmic Mist Symphony* (1962; Houston, April 18, 1967); *Pyramids of Giza* (1973; N.Y., Feb. 20, 1976); *Anwar Sadat (In Memory)* (1982); *Earth of God* for Strings (1984); *Sam Houston* (1987); *Texas* (1987). **CHAMBER:** *Epic Poem* for String Quartet (1927); String Quartet (1934; Chicago, Nov. 3, 1940); *Chipmunks* for Woodwind, Harp, and Percussion (1940); *Phantasy* for Oboe and Piano (1942; also for Oboe, Harp, and Piano); *Serenade* for Violin and Piano (1944); *Barcarola* for Violin and Piano (1948; also for Voice and 8 Cellos, 1958); *In the Beginning* for 4 Horns (1962); *Hebraic Poem* for String Quartet (1976); *Ode to NASA* for Brass Quintet (1981); *Soul of the Sea* for Cello and Piano (1984); many piano pieces, including a Sonata (1958). **VOCAL:** Choral works, song cycle, and solo songs.

BIBL.: W. and N. Bailey, *R. B.: A Bio-Bibliography* (N.Y., 1990).

Britten, (Edward) Benjamin, Lord Britten of Aldeburgh, renowned English composer; b. Lowestoft, Suffolk, Nov. 22, 1913; d. Aldeburgh, Dec. 4, 1976. He grew up in moderately prosperous circumstances; his father was an orthodontist, his mother an amateur singer. He played the piano and improvised facile tunes; many years later he used these youthful inspirations in a symphonic work which he named *Simple Symphony.* In addition to piano, he began taking viola lessons with Audrey Alston. At the age of 13, he was accepted as a pupil in composition by Frank Bridge, whose influence was decisive on Britten's development as a composer. In 1930 he entered the Royal College of Music in London, where he studied piano with Arthur Benjamin and Harold Samuel, and composition with John Ireland until 1933. He progressed rapidly; even his earliest works showed a mature mastery of technique and a fine talent for lyrical expression. His *Fantasy Quartet* for Oboe and Strings was performed at the Festival of the ISCM in Florence on April 5, 1934. He became associated with the theater and the cinema and began composing background music for films. In 1936 he met Peter Pears. From 1937 they appeared in joint recitals, remaining intimate as well as professional companions until Britten's death. With the outbreak of World War II in 1939, Britten went to the U.S.; he returned to England in the spring of 1942; was exempted from military service as a conscientious objector. After the War, he organized the English Opera Group (1947), and in 1948 the Aldeburgh Festival, in collaboration with Eric Crozier and Pears; this Festival became an important cultural institution in England, serving as the venue for the first performances of many of Britten's own works, often under his direction; he also had productions at the Glyndebourne Festival. In his operas, he observed the economic necessity of reducing the orch. contingent to 12 performers, with the piano part serving as a modern version of the Baroque ripieno. This economy of means made it possible for small opera groups and univ. workshops to perform Britten's works; yet he succeeded in creating a rich spectrum of instrumental colors, in an idiom ranging from simple triadic progressions, often in parallel motion, to ultrachromatic dissonant harmonies; on occasion he applied dodecaphonic procedures, with thematic materials based on 12 different notes; however, he never employed the formal design of the 12-tone method of composition. A sui generis dodecaphonic device is illustrated by the modulatory scheme in Britten's opera *The Turn of the Screw,* in which each successive scene begins in a different key, with the totality of tonics aggregating to a series of 12 different notes. A characteristic feature in his operas is the inclusion of orch. interludes, which become independent symphonic poems in an impressionistic vein related to the dramatic action of the work. The cries of seagulls in Britten's most popular and musically most striking opera, *Peter Grimes,* create a fantastic quasi-surrealistic imagery. Britten was equally successful in treating tragic subjects, as in *Peter Grimes* and *Billy Budd,* comic subjects, exemplified by his *Albert Herring,* and mystical evocation, as in his *The Turn of the Screw.* He was also successful in depicting patriotic subjects, as in *Gloriana,* composed for the coronation of Queen Elizabeth II. He possessed a flair for writing music for children, in which he managed to present a degree of sophistication and artistic simplicity without condescension. In short, Britten was an adaptable composer who could perform a given task according to the specific requirements of the occasion. He composed a "realization" of Gay's *Beggar's Opera.* He also wrote modern "parables" for church performance, and produced a contemporary counterpart of the medieval English miracle play *Noye's Fludde.* Among his other works is the remarkable *War Requiem,* a profound tribute to the dead of many wars. In 1952 Britten was made a Companion of Honour, in 1965 he received the Order of Merit, and in 1976 he became the first English composer to be created a life peer, becoming Lord Britten of Aldeburgh. In collaboration with Imogen Holst, Britten wrote *The Story of Music* (London, 1958) and *The Wonderful World of Music* (Garden City, N.Y., 1968; rev. ed., 1970).

WORKS: OPERAS: *Paul Bunyan* (N.Y., May 5, 1941; rev. 1974; BBC, Feb. 1, 1976; Aldeburgh, June 14, 1976); *Peter Grimes* (London, June 7, 1945; Tanglewood, Aug. 6, 1946, Bernstein conducting); *The Rape of Lucretia* (Glyndebourne, July 12, 1946); *Albert Herring* (Glyndebourne, June 20, 1947, composer conducting); *The Beggar's Opera,* a new realization of the ballad opera by John Gay (Cambridge, May 24, 1948, composer conducting); *The Little Sweep,* or *Let's Make an Opera,* "an entertainment for young people" with optional audience participation (Aldeburgh, June 14, 1949); *Billy Budd* (1st version in 4 acts; London, Dec. 1, 1951, composer conducting; rev. version in 2 acts, 1960; BBC, Nov. 13, 1960); *Gloriana* (London, June 8, 1953, Pritchard conducting); *The Turn of the Screw,* chamber opera (Venice, Sept. 14, 1954, composer conducting); *Noye's Fludde,* 1-act children's opera (Aldeburgh, June 18, 1958); *A Midsummer Night's Dream* (Aldeburgh, June 11, 1960, composer conducting); *Curlew River,* church parable (Aldeburgh, June 12, 1964, composer conducting); *The Burning Fiery Furnace,* church parable (Aldeburgh, June 9, 1966, composer conducting); *The Prodigal Son,* church parable (Aldeburgh, June 10, 1968, composer conducting); *Owen Wingrave* (BBC-TV, May 16, 1971, composer conducting; stage premiere, London, May 10, 1973); *Death in Venice* (Aldeburgh, June 16, 1973); 2 realizations of operas by Purcell: *Dido and Aeneas* (London, May 1, 1951, composer conducting) and *The Fairy Queen,* a shortened version for concert perf. (Aldeburgh, June 25, 1967); a ballet, *The Prince of the Pagodas* (London, Jan. 1, 1957, composer conducting).

ORCH.: *Sinfonietta* (1932; London, Jan. 31, 1933); *Simple Symphony* (Norwich, March 6, 1934, composer conducting); *Soirées musicales,* suite from Rossini (1936); *Variations on a Theme of Frank Bridge* for Strings (Salzburg, Aug. 27, 1937); *Mont Juic,* suite of Catalan dances (1937; BBC, Jan. 8, 1938; in collaboration with L. Berkeley); Piano Concerto (London, Aug. 18, 1938; rev. 1945; with an added 3rd movement, Cheltenham, July 2, 1946); Violin Concerto (1939; N.Y., March 28, 1940); *Young Apollo* for Piano, String Quartet, and Strings (Toronto, Aug. 27, 1939); *Canadian Carnival* (1939; BBC, June 6, 1940); *Sinfonia da Requiem* (1940; N.Y., March 29, 1941); *An American Overture* (1942); *Diversions* for Piano, Left-hand, and Orch. (1940; Philadelphia, Jan. 16, 1942, Paul Wittgenstein soloist; rev. 1954); *Matinées musicales,* suite from Rossini (1941); *Scottish Ballad* for 2 Pianos and Orch. (Cincinnati, Nov. 28, 1941); *Prelude and Fugue* for 18 Strings (London, June 23, 1943); *4 Sea Interludes,* from *Peter Grimes* (Cheltenham, June 13, 1945); *The Young Person's Guide to the Orchestra,* variations and fugue on a theme of Purcell (Liverpool, Oct. 15, 1946); Symphonic Suite from *Gloriana* (Birmingham, Sept. 23, 1954); *Pas de six* from *The Prince of the Pagodas* (Birmingham, Sept. 26, 1957); *Cello Symphony* (1963; Moscow, March 12, 1964; Rostropovich soloist, composer conducting); *The Building of the House,* overture for the opening of the Maltings concert hall (Aldeburgh, June 2, 1967, composer conducting); *Suite on English Folk Tunes* (1974; Aldeburgh, June 13, 1975); *Lachrymae, Reflections on a Song of John Dowland* for Viola and Strings (1976; Recklinghausen, May 3, 1977).

CHAMBER: *Quartettino* for String Quartet (1930; London, May 23, 1983); 1 unnumbered string quartet (1931; rev. 1974; Aldeburgh, June 7, 1975); 3 numbered string quartets: No. 1 (Los Angeles, Sept. 21, 1941), No. 2 (London, Nov. 21, 1945), and No. 3 (1975; Aldeburgh, Dec. 19, 1975); *Phantasy* in F minor for String Quintet (July 22, 1932); *Phantasy* for Oboe and String Trio (1932; Florence, April 5, 1934); Suite for Violin and Piano (1935; London, Jan. 27, 1936); *2 Insect Pieces* for Oboe and Piano (1935; Manchester, March 7, 1979); *3 Divertimenti* for String Quartet (London, Feb. 25, 1936); *Temporal Variations* for Oboe and Piano (London, Dec. 15, 1936); *Lachrymae, Reflections on a Song of John Dowland* for Viola and Piano (Aldeburgh, June 20, 1950); *6 Metamorphoses* for Oboe (Thorpress, June 14, 1951); *Alpine Suite* for 3 Recorders (1955); Cello

Sonata (Aldeburgh, July 7, 1961); *Nocturnal* for Guitar (1963; Aldeburgh, June 12, 1964); *3 Suites* for Cello: No. 1 (1964; Aldeburgh, June 27, 1965), No. 2 (1967; Aldeburgh, June 17, 1968), and No. 3 (1971; Aldeburgh, Dec. 21, 1974); *Gemini Variations* for Flute, Violin, and Piano, 4-hands (Aldeburgh, June 19, 1965); Suite for Harp (Aldeburgh, June 24, 1969).

PIANO: 5 waltzes (1923–25; rev. 1969); *Holiday Diary*, suite (1934); *Sonatina romantica* (1940; Aldeburgh, June 16, 1983).

VOCAL: *A Hymn to the Virgin*, anthem for Mixed Voices (1930; Lowestoft, Jan. 5, 1931); *A Boy Was Born*, choral variations (1933; BBC, Feb. 23, 1934; rev. 1955); *Friday Afternoons* for Children's Voices (1935); *Te Deum in C* (1935; London, Jan. 27, 1936); *Our Hunting Fathers*, symphonic cycle for High Voice and Orch. (Norwich, Sept. 25, 1936, composer conducting); *On This Island*, 5 songs, to texts by W.H. Auden (BBC, London, Nov. 19, 1937); *4 Cabaret Songs*, to texts by W.H. Auden (1937–39); *Ballad of Heroes* for High Voice, Chorus, and Orch. (London, April 5, 1939); *Les Illuminations* for High Voice and Strings, to poems by Rimbaud (1939; London, Jan. 30, 1940); *7 Sonnets of Michelangelo* for Tenor and Piano (1940; London, Sept. 23, 1942); *Hymn to St. Cecilia* for 5-part Chorus (London, Nov. 22, 1942); *A Ceremony of Carols* for Treble Voices and Harp (Norwich, Dec. 5, 1942); *Rejoice in the Lamb* for Chorus, Soloists, and Organ (Northampton, Sept. 21, 1943); *Serenade* for Tenor, Horn, and Strings (London, Oct. 15, 1943); *Festival Te Deum* (1944; Swindon, April 24, 1945); *The Holy Sonnets of John Donne* for High Voice and Piano (London, Nov. 22, 1945); *Canticle I, "My Beloved Is Mine"* for High Voice and Piano (Aldeburgh, Nov. 1, 1947); *A Charm of Lullabies* for Mezzo-soprano and Piano (1947; The Hague, Jan. 3, 1948; orchestrated by Colin Matthews; Indianapolis, Jan. 17, 1991, Forrester soloist, Leppard conducting); *Saint Nicolas*, cantata (Aldeburgh, June 5, 1948); *Spring Symphony* for Soloists, Chorus, and Orch. (Amsterdam, July 9, 1949); *5 Flower Songs* for Chorus (Dartington, South Devon, April 3, 1950); *Canticle II, Abraham and Isaac* (Nottingham, Jan. 21, 1952); *Choral Dances* from *Gloriana* (1953); *Winter Words* for High Voice and Piano, to poems by Thomas Hardy (Harewood House, Leeds, Oct. 8, 1953); *Canticle III, Still Falls the Rain*, for Tenor, Horn, and Piano, after Edith Sitwell (London, Jan. 28, 1955); *Songs from the Chinese* for High Voice and Guitar (1957; Aldeburgh, June 17, 1958); *Nocturne* for Tenor, Obbligato Instruments, and Strings, to English poems (Leeds, Oct. 16, 1958); *6 Hölderlin Fragments* for Voice and Piano (Schloss Wolfsgarten, Nov. 20, 1958); *Cantata accademica* for Soloists, Chorus, and Orch. (1959; Basel, July 1, 1960); *Missa Brevis in D* for Boys' Voices and Organ (London, July 22, 1959); *War Requiem*, after the Latin Requiem Mass and 9 poems of Wilfred Owen, for Soloists, Chorus, and Orch. (Coventry, May 30, 1962, composer conducting); *Cantata Misericordium* for Soloists, Small Chorus, and Orch., for the centenary of the International Red Cross (Geneva, Sept. 1, 1963); *Songs and Proverbs of William Blake* for Baritone and Piano (Aldeburgh, June 24, 1965); *Voices for Today*, anthem for Chorus, for the 20th anniversary of the United Nations (triple premiere, N.Y., Paris, and London, Oct. 24, 1965); *The Poet's Echo* for High Voice and Piano, after Pushkin (Moscow, Dec. 2, 1965); *The Golden Vanity*, vaudeville for Boys' Voices and Piano (1966; Aldeburgh, June 3, 1967, with the Vienna Boys' Choir); *Children's Crusade*, ballad for Children's Voices and Orch., after Brecht (1968; London, May 19, 1969); *Who Are These Children?*, song cycle for Tenor and Piano (1969; Edinburgh, May 4, 1971); *Canticle IV, Journey of the Magi*, after T.S. Eliot, for Tenor, Counter-tenor, Baritone, and Piano (Aldeburgh, June 26, 1971); *Canticle V, The Death of St. Narcissus* for Tenor and Harp, after T.S. Eliot (1974; Schloss Elmau, Bavaria, Jan. 15, 1975); *Sacred and Profane*, 8 medieval lyrics for Chorus (Aldeburgh, Sept. 14, 1975); *A Birthday Hansel* for Voice and Harp, after Robert Burns (1975; Cardiff, March 19, 1976); *Phaedra*, cantata for Mezzo-soprano and Chamber Orch. (1975; Aldeburgh, June 16, 1976); *Welcome Ode* for Children's Chorus and Orch. (1976; Ipswich, July 11, 1977); *8 British Folksongs* arranged for Voice and Orch.; *6 French Folksongs* arranged for Voice and Orch.; 6 vols. of British folksong arrangements, with Piano Accompaniment (1943–61); realizations of Purcell's *Orpheus Brittanicus*, with Peter Pears; *4 chansons françaises* for High Voice and Orch. (1928; 1st perf. in concert form at Aldeburgh, June 10, 1980).

BIBL.: E. White, *B. B.* (London, 1948; 3rd ed., rev., 1983); D. Mitchell and H. Keller, eds., *B. B.: A Commentary of His Works from a Group of Specialists* (London, 1952); *Tribute to B. B. on His 50th Birthday* (London, 1963); I. Holst, *B.* (London, 1966; rev. ed., 1970); M. Hurd, *B. B.* (London, 1966); P. Young, *B.* (London, 1966); P. Howard, *The Operas of B. B.* (N.Y., 1969); A. Kendall, *B. B.* (London, 1973); D. Mitchell, *B. B., 1913–1976: A Pictorial Biography* (N.Y., 1978); P. Evans, *The Music of B. B.* (London, 1979); D. Herbert, ed., *The Operas of B. B.* (London, 1979); A. Blyth, *Remembering B.* (London, 1981); R. Duncan, *Working with B.: A Personal Memoir* (Welcombe, Devon, 1981); C. Headington, *B.* (London, 1981); M. Kennedy, *B.* (London, 1981; rev. ed., 1993); A. Whittall, *The Music of B. and Tippett: Studies in Themes and Techniques* (Cambridge, 1982; 2nd ed., 1990); P. Brett, *Peter Grimes* (Cambridge, 1983); C. Palmer, ed., *The B. Companion* (London, 1984); P. Alexander, "The Process of Composition of the Libretto of B.'s 'Gloriana','" *Music & Letters* (April 1986); B. Britten, *My Brother B.* (Bourne End, 1987); S. Corse, *Opera and the Uses of Language: Mozart, Verdi, and B.* (London and Toronto, 1987); J. Evans, P. Reed, and P. Wilson, eds., *A B. Source Book* (Aldeburgh, 1987); D. Mitchell, *B. B.: Death in Venice* (Cambridge, 1987); P. Alexander, "A Study of the Origins of B.'s 'Curlew River'," *Music & Letters* (April 1988); M. Cooke, "B. and the shō," *Musical Times* (May 1988); P. Reed, *The Incidental Music of B. B.: A Study and Catalogue of His Music for Film, Theatre and Radio* (diss., Univ. of East Anglia, 1988); C. Hindley, "Love and Salvation in B.'s 'Billy Budd'," *Music & Letters* (Aug. 1989); P. Reed, "A Cantata for Broadcasting: B.'s 'The Company of Heaven'," *Musical Times* (June 1989); C. Hindley, "Contemplation and Reality: A Study of B.'s 'Death in Venice'," *Music & Letters* (Nov. 1990); D. Mitchell and P. Reed, eds., *Letters from a Life: Selected Letters and Diaries of B. B.* (2 vols., Berkeley, 1991); H. Carpenter, *B. B.: A Biography* (London, 1992); P. Banks, ed., *B.'s 'Gloriana': Essays and Sources* (Woodbridge, Suffolk, 1993); M. Cook and P. Reed, eds., *B. B.: Billy Budd* (Cambridge, 1993); P. Banks, ed., *The Making of Peter Grimes: The Facsimile of B.'s Composition Draft: Studies* (2 vols., Woodbridge, Suffolk, 1995); C. Mark, *Early B. B.: A Study of Stylistic and Technical Evolution* (Hamden, Conn., 1995); P. Reed, ed., *On Mahler and B.: Essays in Honour of Donald Mitchell on his Seventieth Birthday* (Woodbridge, Suffolk, 1995).

Brkanović, Ivan, Croation composer; b. Skaljari, Dec. 27, 1906; d. Zagreb, Feb. 20, 1987. He studied with Bersa at the Zagreb Academy of Music (graduated, 1935) and Léfebvre at the Paris Schola Cantorum; then taught in Zagreb secondary schools (1935–51) and was a visiting prof. at the Sarajevo Academy of Music (1957–62). His works utilized thematic materials derived from national folk music, but his harmonic idiom followed along modern lines.

WORKS: DRAMATIC: OPERAS: *Ekvinocij* (Equinox; 1945; Zagreb, Oct. 4, 1950); *Zlato Zadra* (The Gold of Zadar; Zagreb, April 15, 1954). **BALLET:** *Heloti* (1959; Zagreb, March 17, 1963). **ORCH.:** 5 syms. (1935, 1946, 1947, 1948, 1949); Concertino for Strings (1955); *Sarajevska svita* (1957; Zagreb, Jan. 20, 1958). **CHAMBER:** 2 string quartets (1933, 1938); piano pieces. **VOCAL:** *Triptych* for Soloists, Chorus, and Orch. (1936); *Dalmatinski diptihon* for Soloists, Chorus, and Orch. (1953); 3 cantatas: *Bosnanska sjećanja* (1961), *Zelena zmija lujbavi* (1964), and *Snatrenje* (1967); *Ho po mukah Ambroza Matije Gupca zvanog Beg* (The Torturous Journey of Ambrose Matija Gubec, Named Beg), scenic oratorio (Zagreb, Dec. 13, 1974).

Broadstock, Brenton (Thomas), Australian composer and teacher; b. Melbourne, Dec. 12, 1952. He studied at Monash Univ. (B.A., 1976), Memphis (Tenn.) State Univ. (M.M., 1980), the Univ. of Sydney (with Sculthorpe; postgraduate composition diploma, 1981), Trinity College in London (A.Mus., 1981), and the Univ. of Melbourne (D.Mus., 1989). In 1988 he served as the 1st composer-in-residence of the Melbourne Sym. Orch. and in 1989 joined the faculty of the Univ. of Melbourne. He publ. the vol. *Sound Ideas: Australian Composers born since 1950* (Sydney, 1995). In his music, Broadstock follows a stylistically diverse course frequently marked by adventuresome harmonies, dense and complex textures, and aleatoric structures. In his opera *Fahrenheit 451* (1992), he explores the potentials of electronic sound. He also reveals a deep social consciousness in such scores as his 3 syms.: No 1, *Toward the Shining Light* (1988), was prompted by the severe mental and physical handicaps of his first-born son; No. 2, *Stars in a Dark Night* (1989), was inspired by the letters of Ivor Gurney; and No. 3, *Voices from the Fire* (1991), was his coming to terms with genocide.

WORKS: DRAMATIC: *Fahrenheit 451*, opera (1992); *That Eye the Sky*, film score (1993). **ORCH.:** *Festive Overture* (1981); *The Mountain* (1984); *Expedition* for Strings (1985); *Aurora Australis* (1985); Tuba Concerto (1985); *Battlements* (1986); Piano Concerto (1987); 3 syms.: No. 1, *Toward the Shining Light* (Melbourne, May 21, 1988), No. 2, *Stars in a Dark Night* (Melbourne, Nov. 11, 1989), and No. 3, *Voices from the Fire* (1991; Melbourne, July 2, 1992); *Nearer and Farther* for Horn and Strings (1991); *In a Brilliant Blaze* for Chamber Orch. (1993). **BRASS BAND:** *St. Aelred*, rhapsody (1981); *Click*, festival march (1982); *Rutherford Variations* (1990). **CHAMBER:** 4 string quartets (n.d., 1981, n.d., 1990); *Aureole 1* for Flute and Piano (1982), *2* for Bass Clarinet (1983), *3* for Oboe and Piano (1984), and *4* for Piano (1984); *Beast from Air* for Trombone and Percussion (1985); Wind Quartet, *Down the Emperor's Road* (1986); *And No Birds Sing* for Flute, Clarinet, Violin, Piano, and Percussion (1987); *In Chains* for Alto Flute and Guitar (1990); *Deserts Bloom . . . Lakes Die* for Wind Octet and Double Bass (1990); *Pennscapes* for Clarinet, Viola, Cello, and Piano (1994); *Celebration* for Flute, Clarinet, Piano, 2 Violins, Viola, and Cello (1994–95). **PIANO:** *In the Silence of Night* (1989); *Giants in the Land* (1991; also for Organ). **VOCAL:** *Etheu Fugaces* for Soprano, Flute, Clarinet, Violin, Cello, Piano, and Percussion (1981); *The Songs I Had* for Soprano and Trombone (1989).

Brockway, Howard A., American pianist, teacher, and composer; b. Brooklyn, Nov. 22, 1870; d. N.Y., Feb. 20, 1951. He studied with K. Barth (piano) and O. Boise (composition) in Berlin (1890–95). He taught privately in N.Y. (1895–1903; 1910–25), and at the Peabody Cons. of Music in Baltimore (1903–10) and the David Mannes School of Music in N.Y. (from 1925). With L. Wyman, he ed. 2 vols. of Appalachian folk songs: *Lonesome Tunes* (N.Y., 1916) and *20 Kentucky Mountain Songs* (Boston, 1920).

WORKS: Sym. (Berlin, Feb. 23, 1895); *Sylvan Suite* for Orch. (Boston, April 6, 1901); *Cavatina* and *Romanza* for Violin and Orch.; Suite for Cello and Orch.; Violin Sonata; *Moment musical* for Violin and Piano; many piano pieces.

Brod, Max, significant Czech-born writer and composer; b. Prague, May 27, 1884; d. Tel Aviv, Dec. 20, 1968. In Prague he associated himself with Kafka and other writers of the New School, and himself publ. several psychological novels. He studied music at the German Univ. in Prague and became a music critic for various Czech and German publs. In 1939 he emigrated to Tel Aviv, where he continued his literary and musical activities. Among his compositions are *Requiem Hebraicum* (1943); *2 Israeli Peasant Dances* for Piano and Small Orch. (Tel Aviv, April 24, 1947); several piano suites and 14 song cycles. He wrote an autobiography, *Streitbares* Leben (Munich, 1960); also a biography of Janáček (Prague, 1924), and a book on music in Israel (Tel Aviv, 1951).

Broder, Nathan, American musicologist and editor; b. N.Y., Dec. 1, 1905; d. there, Dec. 16, 1967. He studied at the College of the City of N.Y. In 1945 he became assoc. ed. of the *Musical Quarterly*, a position he held until his death; from 1946 to 1952 he was lecturer in music at Columbia Univ.; from 1959 to 1962, adjunct prof. of music there. In 1956 he received a Guggenheim fellowship, and in 1961 a Ford Foundation grant. From 1963 until his death he was music ed. of W.W. Norton & Co.; also in 1963–64, president of the American Musicological Soc. He publ. a monograph on Samuel Barber (N.Y., 1954); ed. Mozart's piano sonatas and fantasies (Bryn Mawr, 1956); compiled *The Collector's Bach* (Philadelphia, 1958); was co-editor (with Paul Henry Lang) of *Contemporary Music in Europe* (N.Y., 1965).

Brodie, Paul (Zion), noted Canadian saxophonist and teacher; b. Montreal, April 10, 1934. He studied saxophone with Larry Teal at the Univ. of Mich. in Ann Arbor (M.Mus., 1958) and with Marcel Mule in Paris (1959), making his N.Y. recital debut in 1960 at Town Hall. He taught briefly at the Royal Cons. of Music of Toronto (1959–60), then became founder-director of the Brodie School of Music and Modern Dance in Toronto (1961–79); he was also on the faculty of the Univ. of Toronto (1968–73). In 1969 he helped to found the World Saxophone Congress. From 1972 to 1979 he toured with his own Paul Brodie Saxophone Quartet, and then devoted himself to touring as a soloist around the globe. From 1982 he taught at York Univ.

Broekman, David, Dutch-born American conductor and composer; b. Leiden, May 13, 1899; d. N.Y., April 1, 1958. He studied with Anrooy in The Hague and conducted at the Royal Opera there. After playing violin in the N.Y. Phil (1924–26), he went to Hollywood and contributed soundtracks for several films, including *All Quiet on the Western Front* and *The Phantom of the Opera*; also conducted pageants and was music director of Universal Pictures (1929–31), Columbia Pictures (1931–34), and CBS radio station KHJ (1934–41). After World War II, he conducted sym. orchs. and was music director of various television shows; conducted the contemporary concert series "Music in the Making" at N.Y.'s Cooper Union (1952–57), introducing John Becker's Horn Concerto, among other works. He wrote a satirical autobiographical novel, *The Shoestring Symphony* (N.Y., 1948), exhibiting a mandatory jaundiced view of Hollywood.

WORKS: 3 short operas: *Barbara Allen* (1953), *The Stranger* (1953), and *The Toledo War* (1954); 2 syms.: No. 1 (1934) and No. 2 (1941–44; Cincinnati, March 7, 1947); Violin Concerto (1953); Concerto for Piano, Percussion, and Orch. (1955); String Quartet (1954); Piano Sonata; 5 études for Piano.

Brogue, Roslyn, American composer; b. Chicago, Feb. 16, 1919; d. Beverly, Mass., Aug. 1, 1981. She studied languages at the Univ. of Chicago and music at Radcliffe College (Ph.D., 1947). In 1944 she married her private student **Ervin Henning**. Her music followed dodecaphonic precepts.

WORKS: Trio for Oboe, Clarinet, and Bassoon (1946); Suite for Small Orch. (1947); Suite for Recorders (1949); Piano Quartet (1949); String Quartet (1951); Trio for Violin, Clarinet, and Piano (1953); many songs with varied instrumental accompaniments.

Broman, Natanael, Swedish pianist and composer; b. Kolsva, Dec. 11, 1887; d. Stockholm, Aug. 27, 1966. He studied at the Stockholm Cons. (1902–11) and later in Berlin. From 1925 to 1951 he was in charge of the music division of Stockholm Radio. He was highly regarded as a pianist. In his compositions, he followed the neo-Romantic trend with a strong undertow of Scandinavian melos. He composed a symphonic poem, *Fritiof och Ingeborg* (1912); some violin pieces; and a number of songs.

Broman, Sten, eminent Swedish violinist, conductor, music critic, and composer; b. Uppsala, March 25, 1902; d. Lund, Oct. 29, 1983. He studied violin with Henri Marteau, conducting with Zemlinsky, and composition with Finke at the German Academy of Music in Prague; pursued training in musicology with Wagner at the Univ. of Fribourgh and with Kurt Sachs at the Univ. of Berlin; in 1926 he received his licentiate degree from the Univ. of Lund. He was the influential music critic of *Sydsvenksa Dagbladet* (1930–67); in 1937 he founded the Skåne Quartet, and later was a member of the Piano Quartet (1948–51); also conducted the Malmö Phil. Soc. (1946–66). From 1930 to 1962 he was president of the Swedish section of the ISCM. As a composer, he followed a median line of Scandinavian Romanticism; beginning around 1960 he adopted serial techniques and later experimented with electronic sound.

WORKS: DRAMATIC: *Malmö Dances*, ballet (1952); film music. **ORCH.:** *Choral Fantasia* (1931); *Gothic Suite* for Strings (1932); 9 syms.: No. 1, *Sinfonia ritmica* (Malmö, March 20, 1962), No. 2 (Stockholm, Nov. 16, 1963), No. 3 (Malmö, April 27, 1965), No. 4 (1965; Detroit, Nov. 17, 1966), No. 5 for Soprano and Orch. (Stockholm, April 19, 1968), No. 6, with Taped Organ Sounds (Lund, Sweden, Oct. 13, 1970), No. 7, with Electronic Sound (Stockholm, May 5, 1972), No. 8 (Stockholm, April 5, 1975), and No. 9 (Swedish Radio, June 15, 1977); *Sententia crevit* for Orch. and Concrete Sound Tape (Lund, June 13, 1968); Overture (1979). **CHAMBER:** *Canon* for Piano (1929); 4 string quartets (1929, 1933, 1970, 1973); Duo for Violin and Viola (1932); 3 suites for Viola and Piano (1935, 1937, 1942); Sextet for Strings, Percussion, and Piano (1963); Septet for Percussion, Celesta, and Piano (1968); Brass Concerto (Malmö, Nov. 11, 1971). **VOCAL:** *Musica Cathedralis* for Soprano, Bass, 3 Choruses, Orch., 2 Organs, and Tape (Lund, April 4, 1973).

Bronarski, Ludwik (Ryszard Marian), Polish-Swiss musicologist; b. Lemberg, April 13, 1890; d. Fribourg, Nov. 9, 1975. He traveled to Vienna, where he studied musicology with Adler and Dietz at the Univ. (1909–13), later completing his training with Peter Wagner at the Univ. of Fribourg (Ph.D., 1919, with the diss. *Die Lieder der heiligen Hildegard*; publ. in Zürich, 1922); he subsequently received a law diploma (1926). He taught at the Fribourg Cons. (1946–67). With J. Turczyński, he ed. the Paderewski edition of Chopin's works (21 vols., Warsaw, 1949–63).

WRITINGS: *Harmonika Chopina* (Warsaw, 1935); *Études sur Chopin* (2 vols., Lausanne, 1944–46; 2nd ed., 1947–48); *Chopin et l'Italie* (Lausanne, 1946); *Szkice Chopinowskie* (Chopin Sketches; Kraków, 1961).

Bronfman, Yefim, admired Russian-born Israeli, later American pianist; b. Tashkent, April 10, 1958. He began his training with his mother, a piano teacher; after the family emigrated to Israel in 1973, he took up formal study at the Rubin Academy of Music in Tel Aviv. In 1976 he appeared at the Marlboro (Vt.) Music Festival; then pursued additional training with Serkin at the Curtis Inst. of Music in Philadelphia and at the Juilliard School in N.Y. As a soloist with the Israel Phil., he toured the U.S. (1976), Australia (1978), and South America (1979); also appeared as a soloist with major U.S. and European orchs. In 1982 he made his N.Y. recital debut. He became a naturalized American citizen in 1989. In 1991 he was awarded the Avery Fisher Prize, giving his first recital at N.Y.'s Avery Fisher Hall in 1993. His expansive repertoire extends from Scarlatti to works from the contemporary era.

Brons, Carel, Dutch composer; b. Groningen, Jan. 1, 1931; d. Hilversum, May 16, 1983. He studied piano with Luctor Ponse, organ with Cor Batenburg, and theory with Johan Vetter (1949–55). He worked for Radio Holland (1954–72); from 1958 he also was music director of the Hilversum Radio. He adopted versatile idioms in his compositions, making occasional use of serial methods.

WORKS: ORCH.: *Varianten* (1966; orchestration of organ work); *Epitaphium* (1967); *Music* for Strings (1969); *They Are Telling Us* for 2 Harps and Chamber Orch. (1976–78); *Symphonic Fantasy* for Organ and Orch. (1980). **CHAMBER:** *Balletto* for Wind Quintet (1961); *Dialogs I* for Oboe and Piano (1962) and *II* for Flute and Harp (1967); 3 string quartets (1962, 1969, 1977); *Serenata I* for Flute (1963), *II* for Oboe, Clarinet, and Bassoon (1964), and *III* for 4 Clarinets (1974); *Mutazione* for Wind Quintet (1964); *Monologue I* for Oboe (1967), *II* for Flute (1967), *III* for Clarinet (1968), *IV* for Bassoon (1968; rev. 1974), and *V* for Trumpet (1970); Concertino for Clarinet, Violin, and Piano (1977); *Gentle Vision* for Flute and Piano (1978); *Threnody* for Flute (1978); *Ballade '81* for Saxophone Quartet (1981); *Springtime Music* for 11 Instruments (1982–83). **KEYBOARD: PIANO:** *Imaginations I–III* (1966, 1966, 1974); *Telling a Story 1* (1970) and *2* for Young Pianists (1978). **ORGAN:** *Invenzione* (1963); *Reflecties* (1965); *Varianten* (1965; orchestrated 1966); *Prismen* (1967); *Astrabikon* (1968); *Cyclus* (1969); *Litany* (1971); *Reflections* for 2 Organs (1975); Suite (1979); *Structures in Music* (1980). **VOCAL:** *Vox mea*, cantata for Soprano, Chorus, Instrumental Soloists, and Orch. (1974–76).

Bronsgeest, Cornelis, Dutch baritone; b. Leiden, July 24, 1878; d. Berlin, Sept. 22, 1957. He studied with Schulz-Dornburg in Berlin and Stockhausen in Frankfurt am Main. In 1900 he made his operatic debut in Magdeburg, singing there until 1903; then sang with the Hamburg Opera (1903–06). In 1906 he made his first appearance in Berlin at the Royal Opera as Amonasro; continued to sing in Berlin until 1935. In 1914 he made his London debut as Papageno at the Drury Lane Theatre; in 1919–20, made a tour of North America. From 1924 to 1933 he served as director of opera broadcasts of the Berlin Radio. After World War II, he returned to Berlin to assist in restoring the operatic life of the city.

Bronskaya, Evgenya (Adolfovna), outstanding Russian soprano; b. St. Petersburg, Feb. 1, 1882; d. there (Leningrad), Oct. 12, 1953. She first studied with her mother, E. de Hacke; then in Milan with Teresa Arkel; made her operatic debut in Tiflis in 1901; subsequently sang in Kiev (1902–03) and in Moscow (1904–05). From 1907 to 1910 she sang with a traveling Italian opera troupe, performing in Italy, France, and the U.S. (Boston, Chicago, and Philadelphia). Returning to Russia, she was a member of the Maryinsky Theater in St. Petersburg (1910–23); from 1923 to 1950 she taught voice at the Leningrad Cons. She was a brilliant coloratura soprano, particularly impressive in the roles of Lucia, Gilda, and Violetta.

Brook, Barry S(helley), eminent American musicologist; b. N.Y., Nov. 1, 1918. He studied piano privately with Mabel Asnis, then entered the Manhattan School of Music, where he was a student of Louise Culver Strunsky in piano, of Hugh Ross in conducting, and of Sessions in composition. He subsequently studied at the City College of the City Univ. of N.Y. (B.S., social sciences, 1939), then took courses in musicology with Lang at Columbia Univ. (M.A., 1942, with the diss. *Clément Janequin*). From 1942 to 1945 he was a member of the U.S. Air Corps. Selecting as his major subject French music history, he went to Paris, where he studied at the Sorbonne (Ph.D., 1959, with the diss. *La Symphonie française dans la seconde moitié du XVIII*[e] *siècle*). In 1945 he became a prof. at Queens College of the City Univ. of N.Y. He also was a lecturer at Brooklyn College (1945–46) and a prof. at Hunter College (1954) of the City Univ. of N.Y. In 1967 he became a prof. of music and executive officer of the Ph.D. program at the Graduate School and Univ. Center of the City Univ. of N.Y., leaving these posts in 1989 to become director of the univ.'s Center for Music Research and Documentation. He also taught at the Inst. de Musicologie at the Univ. of Paris (1967–68), the Eastman School of Music in Rochester, N.Y. (1973), the Univ. of Adelaide (1974), the Juilliard School in N.Y. (from 1977), the Centre National de la Recherche Scientifique in Paris (1983), and the Univ. of Alabama (1987). He served as ed. in chief of *RILM* [Répertoire International de Littérature Musicale] *Abstracts of Music Literature* (from 1966), *The Symphony 1720–1840* (61 vols., N.Y., 1979–86), and *French Opera in the 17th and 18th Centuries* (75 vols., N.Y., 1984–); with F. Degrada and H. Hucke, he was general ed. of *Giovanni Battista Pergolesi Complete Works/Opere Complete* (18 vols., N.Y., 1986–). In 1954–55 he held a Ford Foundation fellowship, in 1958–59 a Fulbright Research scholarship, and in 1961–62 and 1966–67 Guggenheim fellowships. In 1965 he became the first American to receive the Dent Medal of the Royal Musical Assn. of England, in 1972 he was made a Chevalier of the Order of Arts and Letters of France, in 1978 he was awarded the Smetana Medal of Czechoslovakia, and in 1989 he became the first non-Scandinavian musicologist to be elected to membership in the Royal Swedish Academy of Music. He especially distinguished himself as an authority on 17th- and 18th-century music and on musical bibliography.

WRITINGS: *La Symphonie française dans la seconde moitié du XVIIIe siècle* (3 vols., Paris, 1962); *The Breitkopf Thematic Catalogue, 1762–1787* (N.Y., 1966); ed. *Musicology and the Computer; Musicology 1960–2000: A Practical Program* (N.Y., 1970); ed. with E. Downes and S. Van Solkema, *Perspectives in Musicology: The Inaugural Lectures of the Ph.D. Program in Music at the City University of New York* (N.Y., 1972; 2nd ed., rev., 1975); *Thematic Catalogues in Music: An Annotated Bibliography* (N.Y., 1972).

Brook, Peter (Stephen Paul), noted English opera producer; b. London, March 21, 1925. He was educated at the Univ. of Oxford. He then worked briefly at London's Covent Garden in producing opera; from 1962 he was a co-director of the Royal Shakespeare Co.; from 1970 he spent much time in Paris with his Centre International de Créations Théâtrales, where he attempted to synthesize theatrical elements in a total media art. In 1981 he produced in Paris a modernistically compressed version of *Carmen,* which he also staged in N.Y. in 1983.

BIBL.: J. Trewin, *P. B.* (London, 1971).

Brooks, Patricia, American soprano; b. N.Y., Nov. 7, 1937; d. Mount Kisco, N.Y., Jan. 22, 1993. She studied at the Manhattan School of Music in N.Y.; also took dance lessons with Martha Graham. She made her operatic debut as Marianne in *Der Rosenkavalier* at the N.Y. City Opera on Oct. 12, 1960; also sang with opera companies in San Francisco, Chicago, New Orleans, Philadelphia, Houston, and Santa Fe. She made her Covent Garden debut in London in 1969 as Shemakhan in *The Golden Cockerel.* In 1978 she retired from the operatic stage and taught at the State Univ. of N.Y. in Purchase until 1981. Among her best roles were Gilda, Lucia, Violetta, Massenet's Manon, Sophie, and Mélisande.

Broome, (William) Edward, English-born Canadian choral conductor, organist, teacher, and composer; b. Manchester, Jan. 3, 1868; d. Toronto, April 28, 1932. He studied in Wales with Roland Rogers (organ and piano, 1876–90) and Jules Riviere (conducting); was awarded a piano diploma from the Royal Academy of Music in London (1884) and was made a Fellow of the Guild of Organists (1889). After settling in Canada, he was awarded the B.Mus. from Trinity College, Toronto (1901) and the D.Mus. from the Univ. of Toronto (1908). He served as organist-choirmaster at churches in Brockville, Ontario (1893–95), Montreal (1895–1906), Toronto (1906–25), and Calgary (1926–27). From 1907 he taught at the Toronto Cons. of Music. In 1910 he founded the Toronto Oratorio Soc., which he conducted until 1925. He won 8 1st prizes in composition in the Welsh Eisteddfods, including one for his dramatic cantata *The Siege of Cardiff Castle* (1908). Among his other works were the cantata *The Hymn of Trust* (1910), various other sacred pieces, and songs.

Broqua, Alfonso, Uruguayan composer; b. Montevideo, Sept. 11, 1876; d. Paris, Nov. 24, 1946. He studied with Vincent d'Indy at the Schola Cantorum in Paris, where he settled. His works are characterized by a fine feeling for exotic material, which he presented in the brilliant manner of French modern music.

WORKS: DRAMATIC: *Cruz del Sur,* opera (1918); *Thelen at Nagouëy,* Inca ballet (1934); *Isabelle,* romantic ballet (1936). **OTHER:** *Tabaré,* poetic cycle for Soli, Women's Chorus, and Piano or Orch. (1908); *Poema de las Lomas,* triptych for Piano (1912); Piano Quintet; *3 cantos del Uruguay* for Voice, Flute, and 2 Guitars (1925); *Cantos de Parana* for Voice and Guitar (1929); *Evocaciones Criollas,* 7 pieces for Guitar (1929); *3 préludes Pampéens* for Piano (1938; also for orch.).

Brosa, Antonio, Spanish violinist; b. Canonja, Tarragona, June 27, 1894; d. Barcelona, March 26, 1979. He studied in Barcelona and Brussels; then went to London, where he founded the Brosa String Quartet in 1925; made tours of Europe and the U.S. with it until 1938; then concentrated on a career as a soloist. He lived in the U.S. during World War II, returning to Europe in 1946. He was the soloist in the premiere of Britten's Violin Concerto in N.Y. on March 28, 1940.

Brott, Alexander, prominent Canadian conductor, violinist, teacher, and composer, father of **Boris** and **Denis Brott**; b. Montreal, March 14, 1915. Following violin lessons with Alfred De Seve, he studied with Maurice Onderet (violin) and Douglas Clarke (composition) at the McGill Cons. (Licentiate in Music, 1932) in Montreal; subsequently pursued training with Jacobsen (violin), Willeke (chamber music), Bernard Wagenaar (composition), and Stoessel (conducting) at the Juilliard School of Music in N.Y. (1934–39). He was a violinist in the Montreal Orch. (1930–34; 1939–41); then was concertmaster (1945–48) and assistant conductor (intermittently 1948–61) of the Montreal Sym. Orch. From 1939 to 1985 he was on the faculty of McGill Univ. In 1939 he founded the McGill String Quartet and in 1945 the McGill Chamber Orch. He appeared as a guest conductor throughout North America and Europe. From 1965 to 1981 he was artistic director of the Kingston (Ontario) Sym. In 1985 he founded the Montreal Young Virtuosi. In 1979 he was made a member of the Order of Canada, and in 1987 Chevalier de l'Ordre national du Québec. In his music he follows the Romantic tradition, with impressionistic harmonies imparting an aura of modernity.

WORKS: BALLET: *Le Corriveau* (1966). **ORCH.:** *Oracle* (1938); *War and Peace* (1944); *Concordia* (1946); *From Sea to Sea,* suite (1947); Concerto for Violin and Chamber Orch. (Montreal, March 7, 1950); *Delightful Delusions* (1950); *Prelude to Oblivion* for Chamber Orch. (1951); *Fancy and Folly* (1953); *Scherzo* (1954); *Analogy in Anagram* (1955); *Arabesque* for Cello and Chamber Orch. (1957); *3 Astral Visions* for Strings (1959); *Spheres in Orbit* (1960); *Martlet's Muse* (1962); *Circle, Triangle, 4 Squares* for Strings (1963); *Profundium Praedictum* for Double Bass or Viola or Cello, and String Orch. (1964); *Paraphrase in Polyphony,* variants based on a recently unearthed 10-bar canon written by Beethoven in 1825 (Montreal, Nov. 3, 1967); *The Young Prometheus,* 12 preludes and fugues based on Beethoven sketches (1969); *The Emperor's New Clothes* for Narrator and Orch. (Kingston, Ontario, Feb. 21, 1971); *Cupid's Quandary,* violin concerto (1975); *Evocative Provocations,* cello concerto (1975); *Hymn II Her* for Flute, Bassoon, and Strings (1977); *My Mother—My Memorial* (1978); *Curioso Furioso* for Strings (1982); *Trivial Trifles* for Strings (1984). **CHAMBER:** Quintet for Recorder and String Quartet (1940); String Quartet (1941); *Critic's Corner* for String Quartet and Percussion (1950); *5 Miniatures* for 8 Players (1950); *Vignettes en caricature* for Piano (1952); *Sept for 7* for Narrator, String Trio, Clarinet, Saxophone, and Piano (1955); *3 Acts for 4 Sinners* for Saxophone Quartet (1961); *Mutual Salvation Orgy* for Brass Quintet (1962); *Berceuse* for Saxophone Quartet (1962); *3 on a Spree* for Flute, Oboe, and Harp (1963); *Mini-Minus* for Clarinet, Bassoon, Trumpet, Trombone, Violin, Double Bass, and Percussion (1968); *Spasms for 6* for 6 Percussionists (1971); *Saties-Faction* for String Quartet (1972); *Shofar* for Cello (1976); *Double Entente* for String Quartet (1976); *Prisms* for Flute and Guitar (1984). **VOCAL:** *Israel* for Chorus and Orch. (1956); *The Vision of Dry Bones* for Baritone, Piano, and Strings (1958); *World Sophisticate* for Soprano, Brass Quintet, and Percussion (1962); *Centennial Celebration* for Narrator, Women's Chorus, and Strings (1967).

Brott, Boris, Canadian conductor, son of **Alexander** and brother of **Denis Brott**; b. Montreal, March 14, 1944. He received training in violin from his father, and took courses at the Montreal Cons. (1957–61). After conducting studies with Pierre Monteux in Hancock, Maine (summer, 1956), he pursued training with Igor Markevitch at the Instituto Nacional de Bellas Artes in Mexico City, where he took 1st prize in the Pan-American conducting competition in 1958. He was founder-conductor of the Phil. Youth Orch. in Montreal (1959–61). After winning 3rd prize in the Liverpool conducting competition in 1962, he was assistant conductor of the Toronto Sym. Orch. (1963–65). From 1964 to 1969 he was music director of the Northern Sinfonia Orch. in Newcastle upon Tyne, and also was a conductor of the Royal Ballet at London's Covent Garden (1966–68). From 1967 to 1972 he was music director of Lakehead Univ. in Thunder Bay, Ontario. In 1968 he was one of the four 1st prize winners in the Mitropoulos conducting competition in N.Y., and in 1968–69 he was an assistant conductor of the N.Y. Phil., where he profited from the tutelage of Bernstein. In 1969 he became music director of the Hamilton (Ontario) Phil., a post he retained until 1990. In 1970–71 he was interim music director of the Kitchener Waterloo Sym. Orch. in Ontario. From 1970 to 1973 he was music director of the Regina (Saskatchewan) Sym. Orch. He served as chief conductor of the BBC Welsh Sym. Orch. in Cardiff from 1972 to 1977, and also was principal conductor of the CBC Winnipeg Orch. from 1976 to 1983. He was founder-conductor and music advisor of Symphony Nova Scotia in Halifax from 1983 to 1986. In 1988 he founded the Boris Brott Summer Music Festival in Hamilton, subsequently serving as its artistic director. With his father, he served as co-conductor of the McGill Chamber Orch. in Montreal from 1989. He likewise was music director of the Ventura County (Calif.) Sym. Orch. from 1992. As a guest conductor, he appeared with leading orchs. around the world. In 1987 he received the Order of Canada and in 1990 he was made a Knight of Malta.

Brott, Denis, Canadian cellist and teacher, son of **Alexander** and brother of **Boris Brott**; b. Montreal, Dec. 9, 1950. He studied with Walter Joachim at the Montreal Cons. (1959–67), Zara Nelsova in Aspen (1963–68), Janos Starker at Indiana Univ. (1968–71), and Gregor Piatigorsky at the Univ. of Southern Calif. in Los Angeles (1971–75); he then completed his training with Leonard Rose in N.Y., Maurice Gendron in Paris, and André Navarra in Siena. In 1967 he won 1st prize at the Merriweather Post Competition in Washington, D.C.; then placed 1st in the Montreal Sym. Orch. Concours that same year, which led to his debut with that orch. in the Dvořák Concerto (1967). During his seasons at the Marlboro (Vt.) Festival (1972–75), he attended Casal's master classes. He toured widely as a soloist in North America and Europe; from 1980 to 1989 he was a member of the Orford String Quartet. He taught at the Univ. of North Carolina (1975–77), the Royal Cons. of Music of Toronto (from 1978), the Univ. of Toronto (1980–89), and the Montreal Cons. (from 1989).

Brouwenstijn, Gré (actually, **Gerarda Demphina Van Swol**), Dutch soprano; b. Den Helder, Aug. 26, 1915. She studied at the Amsterdam Music Lyceum, then made her operatic debut as 1 of the 3 ladies in *Die Zauberflöte* in Amsterdam (1940); joined the Netherlands Opera there in 1946. She made her debut at London's Covent Garden as Aida in 1951, and continued to make regular appearances there until 1964; also sang at the Bayreuth Festivals (1954–56), Buenos Aires's Teatro Colón (1958), and the Chicago Lyric Opera (1959); made her farewell appearance in *Fidelio* in Amsterdam in 1971. She was best known for her Verdi and Wagner roles.

Brouwer, Leo, noted Cuban guitarist, conductor, and composer; b. Havana, March 1, 1939. He began music training in Havana, where he made his debut as a guitarist in 1955. In 1959 he went to the U.S. to study composition at the Juilliard School of Music in N.Y. and guitar at the Hartt School of Music in Hartford, Conn. Returning to Havana, he became a leading figure in avant-garde music circles. He also pursued a distinguished career as a guitar virtuoso, traveling all over the world. He likewise appeared as a conductor in his homeland and abroad. In 1972 he was in Berlin under the auspices of the Deutscher Akademischer Austauschdienst. In 1984 a guitar competition was founded in his honor in Japan. He served as music director of the Orquesta de Córdoba in Spain from 1992. Brouwer was the first Cuban composer to embrace aleatory and open forms. His extensive output includes theater music, ballets, film scores, orch. works, chamber music, vocal scores, many guitar pieces, etc.

Brown, A(lfred) Peter, learned American musicologist; b. Chicago, April 30, 1943. He was educated at Northwestern Univ. in Evanston, Ill. (B.M.E., 1965; M.M., 1966; Ph.D., 1970, with the diss. *The Solo and Ensemble Keyboard Sonatas of Joseph Haydn: A Study of Structure and Style*); he later pursued postdoctoral work at N.Y. Univ. (1970), and held a Guggenheim fellowship (1978–79). He joined the faculty of Indiana Univ. in Bloomington in 1974, devoting much of his research to 18th-century music.

WRITINGS: With J. Berkenstock and C. Brown, *Joseph Haydn in Literature: A Bibliography* (Munich, 1974); *Carlo d'Ordonez (1734–1786): A Thematic Catalog* (Detroit, 1978); *Performing Haydn's The Creation: Reconstructing the Earliest Renditions* (Bloomington, Ind., 1985); *Haydn's Keyboard Music: Sources and Style* (Bloomington, Ind., 1986); with R. Griscom, *The French Music Publisher Guera of Lyon: A Dated List* (Detroit, 1987).

Brown, David (Clifford), English musicologist; b. Gravesend, July 8, 1929. He studied at the Univ. of Sheffield (B.A., 1951; B.Mus., 1952); then was music librarian at the Univ. of London Library, Senate House (1959–62). In 1962 he was appointed a lecturer at the Univ. of Southampton; was prof. of musicology there from 1983 to 1989. He was awarded a Ph.D. in 1971 by the Univ. of Southampton for his book *Thomas Weelkes: A Biographical and Critical Study* (London, 1969). He also wrote *John Wilbye* (London, 1974) and then specialized in Russian music; publ. *Mikhail Glinka* (London, 1974) and an extended 4-vol. biography of Tchaikovsky (1978–91), the merits of which are marred by an easy acceptance of the questionable theory that Tchaikovsky committed suicide. Later he publ. *Tchaikovsky Remembered* (London and Boston, 1993). He contributed articles on Russian music to *The New Grove Dictionary of Music and Musicians* (1980).

Brown, Earle (Appleton, Jr.), significant American composer; b. Lunenburg, Mass., Dec. 26, 1926. He took courses in engineering and mathematics at Northeastern Univ. in Boston, and then studied theory with Kenneth McKillop (from 1946) and composition with Roslyn Brogue (from 1947), graduating from the Schillinger School in 1950. From 1952 to 1955 he was associated with the Project for Music for Magnetic Tape in N.Y. He soon adopted the most advanced compositional techniques, experimenting with serial methods as well as aleatory forms. He was fascinated by the parallelism in abstract expressionism in painting, mobile sculptures, and flexible musical forms, which prompted him to develop the idea of graphic notation in 1952 and of open form in 1953. Brown professes no *parti pris* in his approach to techniques and idioms of composition, whether dissonantly contrapuntal or serenely triadic. Rather, his music represents a mobile assemble of plastic elements, in open-ended or closed forms. As a result, his usages range from astute asceticism and constrained constructivism to soaring sonorism and lush lyricism, *sine ira et studio*. Brown has had many lectureships and received many honors. He served as composer-in-residence at the Peabody Cons. of Music in Baltimore (1968–73), the Aspen (Colo.) Music Festival (1971, 1975, 1981), the Rotterdam Phil. and Cons. (1974), the Calif. Inst. of the Arts (1974–83), the American Academy in Rome (1987) et al. He also was a visiting prof. at the Basel Academy of Music (1975), the State Univ. of N.Y. at Buffalo (1975), the Univ. of Calif. at Berkeley (1976), the Univ. of Southern Calif. in Los Angeles (1978), Yale Univ. (1980–81; 1986–87) et al. In 1965–66 he held a Guggenheim fellowship. He was given an honorary doctorate in music by the Peabody Cons. of Music in 1970. From 1986 to 1989 Brown was president of the American Music Center in N.Y.

WORKS: *Fugue* for Piano (1949); *Home Burial* for Piano (1949); Trio for Clarinet, Bassoon, and Piano (1949; unfinished); *Passacaglia* for Piano (1950); *Strata* for 2 Pianos (1950); String Quartet (1950); *3 Pieces* for Piano (1951); *Perspectives* for Piano (1952); *Music* for Violin, Cello, and Piano (1952); *Folio* for Unspecified Instruments (1952–53: *October 1952, November 1952 [Synergy], December 1952, MM 87 and MM 135,* and *Music for Trio for 5 Dancers*; arranged for Chamber Ensemble, 1981); *Music for "Tender Buttons"* for Speaker, Flute, Horn, and Harp (1953); Octet I (1952–53) and II (1957) for 8 Tapes; *25 Pages* for 1 to 25 Pianos (1953; N.Y., April 14, 1954); *4 Systems* for Unspecified Instruments (1954; arranged for Chamber Ensemble, 1981); *Indices* for Chamber Orch. (1954); *Music* for Cello and Piano (1954–55); *4 More* for Piano (1956); *Pentathis* for Flute, Bass Clarinet, Trumpet, Trombone, Harp, and Piano Quartet (1957–58); *Holograph I* for Flute, Piano, and Percussion (1959); *Available Forms I* for 18 Musicians (1961) and *II* for Large Orch. and 2 Conductors (1962); *Light Music* for Large Orch., Lights, and Electronics (1961); *Novara* for Flute, Bass Clarinet, Trumpet, Trombone, Harp, and Piano Quartet (1962); *From Here* for 4 Sopranos, 4 Altos, 4 Tenors, 4 Basses, and 20 Instruments (1963); *Times 5* for Flute, Trombone, Harp, Violin, Cello, and 4-track Tape (1963); *Corroboree* for 3 or 2 Pianos (1964); *9 Rarebits* for 1 or 2 Harpsichords (1965); *String Quartet 1965* (1965); *Calder Piece* for 4 Percussion and Mobile (1963–66); *Modules I–II* (1966) and *III* (1969) for Orch.; *Event: Synergy II* for 11 Woodwind and 8 Strings (1967–68); *Small Piece for Large Chorus* (1969–70); *Syntagm III* for Flute, Bass Clarinet, Vibraphone, Marimba, Harp, Piano, Violin, and Cello (1970); *New Piece Loops* for 17 Instruments (1971–72); *Time Spans* for Large Orch. (1972); *Centering* for Violin and Chamber Orch. (1973); *Sign Sounds* for 18 Instruments (1972); *Cross Sections and Color Fields* for Orch. (1975); *Windsor Jambs (Transients)* for Mezzo-soprano, Flute, Clarinet, Piano, Percussion, Violin, Viola, and Cello (1980); *Folio II* for Unspecified Instruments (1981); *Sounder Rounds* for Orch. (1982; Saarbrücken, May 12, 1983, composer conducting); *Tracer* for Flute, Oboe, Bassoon, Violin, Cello, Double Bass, and 4-track Tape (1984; Berlin, Feb. 8, 1985).

BIBL.: P. Quist, *Indeterminate Form in the Works of E. B.* (diss., Peabody Cons. of Music, 1984); K. Potter, "E. B. in Context," *Musical Times* (Dec. 1986).

Brown, Eddy, American violinist; b. Chicago, July 15, 1895; d. Abano Terme, Italy, June 14, 1974. He was given his first violin lessons by his father; then was taken to Europe, and studied in Budapest with Hubay. He won a violin competition at the age of 11 playing the Mendelssohn Concerto in Budapest. He then proceeded to London, and eventually to Russia, where he became a pupil of Auer. Returning to the U.S. in 1915, he made several transcontinental tours; was a soloist with the N.Y. Phil., the Chicago Sym. Orch., the Philadelphia Orch., and the Boston Sym. Orch. In 1922 he founded the Eddy Brown String Quartet; in 1932 he became president of the Chamber Music Soc. of America, which he organized. He became active in educational programs over the radio; was music director of the Mutual Broadcasting System (1930–37) and of station WQXR in N.Y. (1936–55). From 1956 to 1971 he was artistic coordinator of the Univ. of Cincinnati College-Cons. of Music.

Brown, Howard Mayer, American musicologist; b. Los Angeles, April 13, 1930; d. Venice, Feb. 21, 1993. He studied composition with Piston and musicology with Otto Gombosi at Harvard Univ. (B.A., 1951; M.A., 1954; Ph.D., 1959, with the diss. *Music in the French Secular Theater, 1400–1550;* publ. in Cambridge, Mass., 1963); also studied in Vienna (1951–53) and later held a Guggenheim fellowship in Florence (1963–64). He was a member of the faculty at Wellesley College (1958–60); in 1960 he was appointed to the staff of the Univ. of Chicago, where he subsequently was made a prof. (1967) and chairman of the music dept. (1970). From 1972 to 1974 he taught at King's College, Univ. of London; then returned to the Univ. of Chicago. In 1989 he was made an honorary member of the American Musicological Soc. He publ. *Instrumental Music Printed before 1600: A Bibliography* (Cambridge, Mass., 1965), *Embellishing Sixteenth-Century Music* (London, 1976), and *Music in the Renaissance* (Englewood Cliffs, N.J., 1976). In 1970 he was named ed. of the compendium *Italian Opera, 1640–1770: Major Unpublished Works in a Central Baroque and Early Classical Tradition* (N.Y., 1977 et seq.). With S. Sadie, he ed. *Music Before 1600* (Basingstoke, 1989) and *Music After 1600* (Basingstoke, 1989).

Brown, Iona, English violinist and conductor; b. Salisbury, Wiltshire, Jan. 7, 1941. She studied violin as a child; in 1955 she joined the National Youth Orch. of Great Britain, remaining a member for 5 years; she also studied with Hugh Maguire in London, Remy Principe in Rome, and Henryk Szeryng in Paris and Nice. From 1963 to 1966 she played in the Philharmonia Orch. of London; in 1964 she joined the Academy of St. Martin-in-the-Fields, and served as its director from 1974. In 1980 she was named music director of the Norwegian Chamber Orch. in Oslo. She also was music advisor (1986–87) and music director (1987–92) of the Los Angeles Chamber Orch. She was made an Officer of the Order of the British Empire in 1986.

Brown, Maurice J(ohn) E(dwin), English writer on music; b. London, Aug. 3, 1906; d. Marlborough, Sept. 27, 1975. He was educated at the Univ. of London (B.Sc., 1929; B.Mus., 1939); then pursued a career as a high-school and grammar-school teacher; concurrently devoted himself to research, studying various aspects of the life and works of Schubert; his *Schubert: A Critical Biography* (London, 1958; Ger. tr., 1969) is a standard source; he was also an authority on Chopin. In addition to many articles for music periodicals, he wrote *Schubert's Variations* (London, 1954); *Chopin: An Index of His Work in Chronological Order* (London, 1960); *Essays on Schubert* (London, 1966); with O.E. Deutsch, *Schubert: Die Erinnerungen seiner Freunde* (Leipzig, 1966); *Schubert Songs* (London, 1967); *Schubert Symphonies* (London, 1970).

Brown, Merton (Luther), American composer; b. Berlin, Vt., May 5, 1913. He studied both piano and violin; moved to N.Y. in 1935 and took piano lessons with Anne Hull, and studied composition privately with Wallingford Riegger (1939–42) and Carl Ruggles (1943–45). From 1949 to 1967 he lived in Rome; then settled in Boston. His music is set in dense, dissonant counterpoint without negating the lyrical flow of melody.

WORKS: *Consort for 4 Voices,* scored for 2 Pianos (N.Y., April 21, 1947); Piano Sonata (1948); *Chorale* for Strings (1948); *Duo in 3 Movements* for Violin and Piano (1956); *Concerto breve per archi* (Naples, Jan. 23, 1960); *Metamorfosi per piano* (1965); *Dialogo* for Cello and Piano (1970); *Concertino* for String Orch. (1974); *Divertimento* for Piano, 4-hands (1975); *5 Pieces* for Clarinet and Piano (1976); *Psalm 13* (1976).

Brown, Newel Kay, American composer and pedagogue; b. Salt Lake City, Feb. 29, 1932. He studied composition with Leroy Robertson at the Univ. of Utah (B.F.A., 1953; M.F.A., 1954) and with Howard Hanson, Wayne Barlow, and Bernard Rogers at the Eastman School of Music in Rochester, N.Y. (Ph.D., 1967). From 1961 to 1967 he taught at Centenary College for Women at Hackettstown, N.J.; from 1967 to 1970 he was on the faculty of Henderson State College, Arkadelphia, Ark.; in 1970 he became prof. of composition at North Texas State Univ. in Denton. As a member of the Mormon Church, he wrote a number of choral works which entered the permanent repertoire; his Mormon children's choral work, *I Hope They Call Me on a Mission* (1968), was tr. into 17 languages.

WORKS: Saxophone Sonata (1968); *4 Pieces* for Flute and Clarinet (1968); Suite for 2 Trumpets (1968); Trombone Sonata (1969); Woodwind Quintet (1969); *Hopkins Set* for Baritone and Trombone (1971); *Postures* for Bass Trombone and Piano (1972); *Glaser Set* for Mezzo-soprano, Trumpet, Clarinet, and

Piano (1974); *Anagrams* for Trumpet, Marimba, and Percussion (1977); *Windart I* for Tuba, Soprano, and Piano (1978) and *II* for Euphonium, 6 Clarinets, Vibraphone, and Percussion (1980); *4 Meditations* for Bass Voice, Alto Saxophone, and Percussion (1981); numerous sacred songs and choruses.

Brown, Rayner, American organist, teacher, and composer; b. Des Moines, Iowa, Feb. 23, 1912. He studied at the Univ. of Southern Calif. in Los Angeles (B.Mus., 1938; M.Mus., 1947); his mentors included Ingolf Dahl, Hanns Eisler, and Lucien Cailliet. He was organist at Wilshire Presbyterian Church (1941–77) and a prof. of music at Biola Univ. in La Mirada, California (1950–77).

WORKS: ORCH.: 6 syms. (1952, 1957, 1958, 1980, 1982, 1982); 7 organ concertos (1959, 1966, 1980, 1980, 1982, 1983, 1986); Concerto for Clarinet and Wind Orch. (1979); Concerto for Bass Trombone and Wind Orch. (1981); Clarinet Concerto (1984); Concerto for Violin, Harp, and Orch. (1987); Concert for Organ Duet and Orch. (1989); also various pieces for Wind Orch. and band music. **CHAMBER:** 3 sonatas for Flute and Piano (1944, 1959, 1985); Quartet for Violin, Viola, Cello, and Piano (1947); String Quartet (1953); 4 brass quintets (1957, 1960, 1981, 1985); Violin Sonata (1977); Sonata for 6 Trombones (1980); Tuba Quartet (1980); Trio for Cello, Trumpet, and Piano (1982); Sonata for Violin and Harp (1986); Sonata for English Horn and Organ (1989); Sonata for Harp and Organ (1990); various piano pieces; numerous organ works, including 35 sonatinas (1945–80) and 20 sonatas (1958–87). **VOCAL:** Cantatas and other pieces.

Browning, John, brilliant American pianist; b. Denver, May 22, 1933. His father was a professional violinist, his mother an accomplished pianist. Browning studied with her from childhood; played a Mozart piano concerto at the age of 10, and was accepted as a student by Rosina Lhévinne, who was giving a master course in Denver at the time. The family later moved to Los Angeles, where Browning became a private student of Lee Pattison. He soon moved to N.Y., where he entered the class of Lhévinne at the Juilliard School of Music; in 1954 he received the $2,000 Steinway Centennial Award. In 1955 he won the Leventritt Award. He made his N.Y. Phil. debut in 1956; then went to Brussels to compete for the International Piano Competition sponsored by Queen Elisabeth; he won 2nd prize, after Vladimir Ashkenazy, who received 1st prize. Returning to the U.S., he developed a nonstop career of uninterrupted successes. On Sept. 24, 1962, he gave the premiere of Samuel Barber's Piano Concerto with the Boston Sym. Orch., conducted by Erich Leinsdorf at Lincoln Center for the Performing Arts in N.Y. The work became his honorific cachet; it was modern, it was difficult to play, but he performed it hundreds of times in subsequent years. He also performed virtually the entire standard repertoire of piano concertos from Beethoven to Prokofiev. His engagements as a recitalist took him all over the globe, and he frequently appeared with the foremost orchs. as a soloist.

Brownlee, John (Donald Mackensie), Australian baritone; b. Geelong, Jan. 7, 1900; d. N.Y., Jan. 10, 1969. He was a pupil of Gilly in Paris, where he made his operatic debut as Nilakantha in *Lakmé* at the Théâtre Lyrique in 1926. On June 8, 1926, he first appeared at London's Covent Garden as Marcello during Melba's farewell concert. From 1927 to 1936 he was a member of the Paris Opéra; also sang at the Teatro Colón in Buenos Aires (1931) and the Glyndebourne Festivals (1935–39). On Feb. 17, 1937, he made his Metropolitan Opera debut in N.Y. as Rigoletto, and continued to sing there until 1957. He also sang in Chicago (1937–38; 1945), San Francisco (1940–50), and again at Covent Garden (1949–50). From 1953 to 1967 he was president of the American Guild of Musical Artists. He founded the Empire State Music Festival near Ellenville, N.Y., in 1955. In 1956 he became president of the Manhattan School of Music, and then was its president from 1966 until his death. Among his most prominent roles were Don Giovanni, Count Almaviva, Papageno, Alfonso, Iago, and Scarpia.

Brubeck, Howard R(engstorff), American composer and teacher; b. Concord, Calif., July 11, 1916; d. La Jolla, Calif., Feb. 16, 1993. He received piano lessons from his mother, who was a pianist; he then studied at San Francisco State College (B.A., 1938) and with Milhaud at Mills College in Oakland, Calif. (M.A., 1941). After serving as Milhaud's assistant (1944–50), he taught at San Diego State College (1950–53); he then was chairman of the music dept. (from 1953) and dean of humanities (from 1966) at Palomar College before retiring in 1978. He was the brother of Dave (David Warren) Brubeck (b. Concord, Calif., Dec. 6, 1920), the prominent jazz pianist, bandleader, and composer.

WORKS: ORCH.: *Gigue* for Strings (1939); *California Suite* (1945); *The Devil's Disciple,* overture (1954); *4 Dialogues* for Jazz Ensemble and Orch. (1956); *Symphonic Movement on a Theme of Robert Kurka* (1958); *The Gardens of Versailles* (1960). **VOCAL:** *Alleluia* for Soprano, Chorus, and Chamber Orch. (1944); *Elizabethan Suite* for Women's Chorus and Chamber Orch. (1944); choruses; songs. **OTHER:** Stage pieces, chamber music, piano pieces, and arrangements.

Bruce, (Frank) Neely, American pianist, conductor, music scholar, and composer; b. Memphis, Tenn., Jan. 21, 1944. He studied piano with Roy McAllister at the Univ. of Alabama (B.M., 1965); then was a pupil in piano (M.M., 1966) of Soulima Stravinsky and in composition (D.M.A., 1971) of Ben Johnston at the Univ. of Ill., where he also taught (1968–74). In 1974 he joined the faculty at Wesleyan Univ., where he also conducted the Wesleyan Singers. In 1977 he founded the American Music/Theatre Group, an ensemble devoted to the performance of American music from all eras.

WORKS: DRAMATIC: *Pyramus and Thisbe,* chamber opera (1964–65); *The Trials of Psyche,* opera (1970–71); *Americana, or, A New Tale of the Genii,* opera (1978–83); incidental music to plays and films; dance scores. **ORCH.:** *Quodlibet on Christmas Tunes* for Chamber Orch. (1963); Percussion Concerto (1967); Concerto for Violin and Chamber Orch. (1974); *Atmo-Rag* for Chamber Orch. (1987); *Santa Ynez Waltz* for Chamber Orch. (1989); *Trio* for 3 Rock Bands (1988–94); *Orion Rising* (1988–97); *1, 2, Ready, Go!* for Chamber Orch. (1991); *Barnum's Band* for Large Wind Ensemble (1991–92); *Songs of Zion Recycled* for Tuba and Orch. (1992–93; Hartford, Ct., June 5, 1993). **CHAMBER:** Trio for Violin, Viola, and Cello (1963); Quintet for Flute, Clarinet, English Horn, Bass Clarinet, and Bassoon (1967); *Rondo* for Flute, Tuba, and Piano (1976); *Jesus Christ is Risen Today,* Easter partita for 2 Horns, 2 Trumpets, 2 Trombones or Baritone Horns, and Organ (1980); *The Hartford and Middletown Waltzes* for Violin and Piano (1986); *Music for Emeline* for 8 Instruments (1989); *Narrative Objects* for Oboe, Clarinet, Bassoon, and 2 Alto Saxophones (1991); *Brass Bouquet* for Brass Instruments (1992); *Analogues* for Violin and Alto Saxophone (1993); *Wild Oysters II* for Electric Cello (1993); *4 + 1* for String Quartet and Piano (1994). **KEYBOARD: PIANO:** *Variations on a Polonaise* (1969); 6 sonatas; *Introduction and Variations* (1978); *Furniture Music in the Form of 50 Rag Licks* (1980); 9 nocturnes; *Siagi Tamu Tango, or, Tango Rue Jardin* (1984); *Homage to Charlie* (1985); *Piano Rock Album* (1989–91); *2 Moods* (1990). **ORGAN:** *Variations and Interludes* (1968); *Homage to Maurice* (1986); *Pink Music* (1989–92). **HARPSICHORD:** *A Book of Pieces for the Harpsichord* (1968–85). **VOCAL:** *Psalms of the Nativity,* oratorio for Mezzo-soprano, Tenor, Baritone, Chorus, and Chamber Orch. (1972–89); *There was a child went forth . . .* for Men's Chorus, Piano, Percussion, and Flute (1972); *A Feast of Fat Things,* cantata for Soprano and 7 Instruments (1977); *Perfumes and Meanings* for 16 Solo Voices (1980); *The Plague: A Commentary on the Work of the Fourth Horseman* for 4 Solo Voices and Tape (1983–84); *6 Whitman Settings* for 12 Solo Singers and 12 Instruments (1986–87); *The Dream of the Other Dreamers* for 4 Singers and 2 SPX 90s (1987); *Hamm Harmony,* 38 Psalm and fuguing tunes (1988–92); *8 Ghosts* for 4 Singers and 4 SPX 90s (1989); *2+2+2* for 6 Singers (1989); *Hugomotion,* oratorio for

Soloists, Chorus, and Orch. (1989–95); *Emily's Flowers*, 24 vocal pieces (1991–92); *Tanglewood*, oratorio for Soloists, 2 Choruses, and Orch. (1993); also various solo songs in sets or cycles.

Bruchollerie, Monique de la, French pianist and teacher; b. Paris, April 20, 1915; d. there, Dec. 15, 1972. She studied with Isidor Philipp; graduated from the Paris Cons. at the age of 13; toured widely as a concert pianist; also was active as a teacher. In 1964 she made a bold proposal to modernize the piano as a performing instrument by constructing a crescent-shaped keyboard to facilitate simultaneous playing in high treble and low bass. She also prophetically proposed to install electronic controls enabling the pianist to activate a whole chord by striking a single key.

Bruči, Rudolf, Serbian conductor, teacher, and composer; b. Zagreb, March 30, 1917. He studied in Vienna with Uhl; returning to Serbia, he became a teacher and conductor in Novi Sad. In his works, he employs polytonal and atonal devices which culminate in free dodecaphony.

WORKS: *Maskal*, symphonic suite (1955); *Concerto for Orchestra* (Belgrade, Nov. 25, 1959); *Čovek je vidik bez kraja*, cantata (Belgrade, Dec. 21, 1961); *Srbija*, cantata (Belgrade, May 24, 1962); *Sinfonia lesta* (1965); *Sinfonietta* for Strings (1965); *Salut au monde*, oratorio (1967); Sym. No. 3 (1969); Concerto for Clarinet and Strings (1970); Concertino for Orch. (1970).

Bruck, Charles, Romanian-born French conductor and pedagogue; b. Timişoara, May 2, 1911; d. Hancock, Maine, July 16, 1995. He studied at the Vienna Cons., then took courses with Perlemuter (piano) and Boulanger (composition) at the Paris École Normale de Musique; he also received instruction in conducting from Pierre Monteux (1934). In 1939 he became a naturalized French citizen. After winning the conducting competition of the Orch. Symphonique de Paris (1936), he served as its assistant conductor; he later conducted at the Cannes and Deauville Casinos (1949–50), the Netherlands Opera in Amsterdam (1950–54), the Strasbourg Radio Sym. Orch. (1955–65), and the Orch. Philharmonique de l'ORTF in Paris (1965–70); subsequently he was director of Monteux's conducting school in Hancock, Maine until his death.

Brückner-Rüggeberg, Wilhelm, German conductor and pedagogue; b. Stuttgart, April 15, 1906; d. Hamburg, April 1, 1985. He studied with August Schmid-Lindner and Siegmund von Hausegger in Munich, where he began his career as chorus master at the Bavarian State Opera in 1928. After conducting in various German music centers, he was a guest conductor with the Hamburg State Opera in 1936–37; subsequently was on its roster from 1938 to 1971. He taught at the Hamburg Hochschule für Musik, becoming a prof. in 1955.

Brüggen, Frans, distinguished Dutch recorder player, flutist, and conductor; b. Amsterdam, Oct. 30, 1934. He studied the recorder with Kees Otten and flute at the Amsterdam Muzieklyceum; in addition, took courses in musicology at the Univ. of Amsterdam. He then launched a major career as a virtuoso performer of music for the recorder; as a flute soloist, he was equally at home in performances of the Baroque masters and contemporary avant-garde composers; also gave informative lectures and illustrative performances of recorder music in Europe, and taught at the Royal Cons. in The Hague. In 1981 he founded the Orch. of the 18th Century, which he conducted with fine success on both sides of the Atlantic. He also was artistic director of the Netherlands Radio Chamber Orch. in Hilversum (1991–94) and joint principal guest conductor of the Orch. of the Age of Enlightenment in London (from 1992).

Brugnoli, Attilio, Italian composer and teacher; b. Rome, Sept. 7, 1880; d. Bolzano, July 10, 1937. He studied piano and composition at the Naples Cons. with Paolo Serrao (graduated, 1900); won the Rubinstein Prize in Paris (1905); taught at the conservatories of Parma (1907–21) and Florence (1921–37). His compositions include a Piano Concerto (1905); Violin Concerto (1908); piano suite, *Scene napolitane* (1909), and other works for Piano; songs; also a pedagogic work, *Dinamica pianistica* (Milan, 1926).

Brumby, Colin (James), Australian composer, conductor, and teacher; b. Melbourne, June 18, 1933. He was educated at the Melbourne Univ. Conservatorium of Music (B.Mus., 1957; D.Mus., 1971); he also received training in composition in Santiago de Compostela (1962), London (1962–64), and Rome (1972–73), and studied computer music at Stanford Univ. (1974). He was music director of the Victorian Chamber Players (1956), the South Melbourne Sym. Orch. (1957), and the Queensland Opera (1969–71). In 1964 he joined the faculty of the Univ. of Queensland, where he was an assoc. prof. from 1977; he also was music director of its Musical Soc. (1966–68; 1977–86). After composing in an approved atonal style, Brumby forsook that path in 1974 to embrace an adventuresome tonal style. In both atonal and tonal scores, melodic writing is a salient feature.

WORKS: DRAMATIC: OPERAS: *The 7 Deadly Sins* (Brisbane, Sept. 12, 1970); *The Marriage Machine* (1971; Sydney, Jan. 28, 1972); *La Donna* (1986); *Lorenzaccio* (1986–87); *Fire on the Wind* (1990); *Summer Carol* (1990). **BALLETS:** *Bunyip*, television ballet (1966); *Cinderella*, after Rossini (Brisbane, Dec. 10, 1975); *Masques* (Brisbane, Aug. 18, 1980); *Alice, Memories of Childhood* (1987). Also operettas for children, incidental music, and film scores. **ORCH.:** Concerto for Viola and Strings (1960); *Antipodea* (1962); *Partite* for Clarinet and Strings (Brisbane, June 20, 1962); *Fibonacci Variations* (1964); *Mediterranean Suite* (1964); 2 violin concertos: No. 1 (1969; Brisbane, Feb. 28, 1970) and No. 2 (Brisbane, Aug. 1983); *Litanies of the Sun* (1970; Brisbane, May 28, 1971); *The Phoenix and the Turtle* (Canberra, Oct. 6, 1974); Horn Concerto (1974; Brisbane, April 2, 1975); Flute Concerto (1976; Brisbane, Feb. 23, 1977); *Entradas* (1978); *Musagettes* (Brisbane, Oct. 2, 1978); *Festival Overture on Australian Themes* (1981; Adelaide, Feb. 17, 1982); 2 syms.: No. 1 (Brisbane, April 7, 1982) and No. 2, *Mosaics of Ravenna* (1993); *Paean* (Sydney, July 3, 1982); Bassoon Concerto (Adelaide, Nov. 16, 1983); *South Bank Overture* (1984; Brisbane, April 23, 1985); Guitar Concerto (Brisbane, May 22, 1985); Piano Concerto (Perth, Sept. 17, 1985); Oboe Concertino (Brisbane, June 29, 1987); Clarinet Concerto (1988; Brisbane, July 21, 1989); *Scena* for English Horn and Strings (1988); Viola Concerto, *Tre aspetti di Roma* (1990); Trumpet Concerto (1991); *West End Overture* (1993); Concerto for Organ and Strings (1994). **CHAMBER:** *4 Exotic Pieces* for Flute and Harp (1961); Wind Quintet (1964); String Quartet (1969); *Player Chooses* for 3 Instruments and Keyboard (1973); *Chiaroscuro* for Clarinet, Cello, and Piano (1977); Suite for Double Basses (1978); *Haydn Down Under* for Bassoon and String Quartet (1980); *The 7 Ages of Man* for Wind Quintet and Optional Narrator (1981); Clarinet Sonatina (1982); Bassoon Sonata (1984); Piano Quartet (1985); Flute Sonatina (1985); *4 Aphorisms* for Clarinet and Piano (1986); *Mundoolun* for English Horn and Piano (1988); *Borromeo Suite* for Flute and Guitar (1990); *Gardens of the Villa Taranto* for Flute and Guitar (1991). **VOCAL:** *3 Italian Songs* for High Voice and String Quartet (1968); *Gilgamesh* for Narrator, Chorus, Brass, and Percussion (1968); *Charlie Bubble's Book of Hours* for Soloists, Chorus, and Orch. (1969); *Bring Out Your Christmas Masks* for Soloists, Chorus, Dancers, Actors, Orch., and Organ (Brisbane, Dec. 10, 1969); *Ballade for St. Cecilia* for Soloists, Chorus, and Orch. (1970); *Celebrations and Lamentations* for 4 Choruses, Wind, Brass, and Percussion (Brisbane, May 25, 1972); *This Is the Vine* for Soloists, Chorus, and Orch. (1972; Melbourne, Feb. 24, 1973); *Orpheus Beach* for Soprano, Baritone, and Orch. (Brisbane, Oct. 10, 1978); *3 Baroque Angels* for Chorus and Orch. (1979); *Festival Mass* for Chorus, Wind, Brass, and Percussion (Brisbane, Aug. 11, 1984); *Psalm 148* for Chorus and Band (Brisbane, Aug. 11, 1984); *Great Is Truth and Mighty Above All Things* for Baritone, Chorus, and Orch. (Brisbane, May 10,1985); *Stabat mater dolorosa* for Soprano, Baritone, and String Trio (1986); *The Ballad of Sydney Hospital*, cantata for Mezzo-soprano, Baritone, Chorus, and Orch. (Sydney, Nov. 15, 1988); *The Ballad of Charlie Blow*, cantata for Women's Chorus, Mixed Chorus, and Orch. (1988); *Canti Pisani* for Medium Voice and Orch. (1989); *A Special Inheritance*, cantata for Women's Voices and Orch. (1990); *The Trenchant Troubadour*, song cycle for Medium Voice and Piano (1991).

Brun, Fritz, Swiss conductor, teacher, and composer; b. Lucerne, Aug. 18, 1878; d. Grosshöchstetten, Nov. 29, 1959. He studied in Lucerne (1892–95) and at Cologne (1896–1901); settled in Bern (1909), where he taught at the Cons. and conducted the Bern Sym. Orch. until 1943.

WORKS: ORCH.: 10 syms. (1908–53); *Variations* for Piano and String Orch. (1944); Piano Concerto (1944); Cello Concerto; *Rhapsodie* for Orch. (1958). **CHAMBER:** 4 string quartets (1898, 1921, 1943, 1949); Violin Sonata (1906); Cello Sonata (1953).

BIBL.: *Kleine Festgabe für F. B.* (Bern, 1941).

Brün, Herbert, German composer and teacher; b. Berlin, July 9, 1918. In 1936 he went to Jerusalem, where he studied with Wolpe and Pelleg at the Cons. until 1938; after attending Columbia Univ. in N.Y. (1948–49), he pursued research on the applications of electroacoustic and electronic methods of sound production in Paris, Cologne, and Munich (1955–62). He taught at the Univ. of Ill. (1963–88). Among his writings are *Über Musik und Zum Computer* (1971) and *My Words and Where I Want Them* (1986). In his music, he explores the potentialities of computers as a catalytic factor for advanced techniques; the titles of his works often suggest paradoxical logic.

WORKS: Concertino for Orch. (1947); 3 string quartets (1952, 1957, 1961); *Mobile* for Orch. (1958); *Gestures for 11* for 11 Instruments (1964); *Soniferous Loops* for Instruments and Tape (1964); *Non sequitur*, group of works for Varying Ensembles (1966); Trio for Trumpet, Trombone, and Percussion (1968); Nonet (1969); *6 for 5 by 3 in Pieces* for Oboe, English Horn, Clarinet, and Bass Clarinet (1971); *Twice Upon 3 Times* for Bass Clarinet and Tuba (1980). **ELECTRONIC:** *Anepigraphe* (1958); *Klänge unterwegs* (1962); *Futility 1964* (1964); *Infraudibles* (1968); *Piece of Prose* (1972); *Dust* (1976); *More Dust* (1977); *Dustiny* (1978); *A Mere Ripple* (1979); *U-turn-to* (1980); *I Told You So* (1981). **COMPUTER:** *Mutatis mutandis* (1968); *Polyplots* (1971); *Links* (1973).

Brunelle, Philip, American conductor, organist, and choral scholar; b. Albert Lea, Minn., July 1, 1943. He was educated at the Univ. of Minnesota. From 1968 to 1985 he was music director of the Minnesota Opera, where he conducted operas by various American composers. In 1969 he was named organist and choirmaster at the Plymouth Congregational Church in Minneapolis, where he quickly organized and became artistic director of the Plymouth Music Series of Minnesota, a distinguished and innovative series widely known for its diversified programming. As a guest conductor, Brunelle appeared with various American orchs. and opera companies. After making his European conducting debut at the Aldeburgh Festival in 1983, he made guest conducting appearances in several European music centers. In 1991 he founded and served as artistic director of the Ensemble Singers, which also made occasional appearances with his Plymouth Music Series. In 1994 he conducted the Ensemble Singers in successful engagements in Nuremberg, Leipzig, and Prague. In addition to his performing career, Brunelle served as a visiting prof. at the Univ. of Minnesota School of Music and contributed a regular column to *The American Organist*. He has prepared eds. of several major choral works. In 1982 he was awarded the Kodály Medal by the Hungarian government. In 1988 he received Sweden's Stig Andersson Award and in 1989 the King of Sweden presented him with the Royal Order of the Polar Star. He was awarded honorary doctorates from St. Olaf College in Northfield, Minn. (1988) and from Gustavus Adolphus College in St. Peter, Minn. (1993). Brunelle's repertoire is expansive, ranging from early music to contemporary scores. Among modern composers he champions are Copland, Argento, Hemberg, Shchedrin, Susa, and Larsen.

Brunold, Paul, French pianist, organist, and writer on music; b. Paris, Oct. 14, 1875; d. there, Sept. 14, 1948. He was a pupil of Marmontel (piano) and Lavignac (theory) at the Paris Cons.; later studied with Paderewski. In 1915 he became organist at St. Gervais, in Paris. With H. Expert, he ed. the *Anthologie des maîtres français du clavecin des XVIIe et XVIIIe siècles*; with A. Tessier, he brought out a complete edition of Chambonnières's works; he also ed. 2 vols. of works by Dieupart (*6 Suites pour clavecin* and *Airs et Chansons*). He publ. the book *Histoire du grand orgue de l'Église St. Gervais à Paris* (1934).

Brunswick, Mark, American composer and teacher; b. N.Y., Jan. 6, 1902; d. London, May 25, 1971. He studied with Goldmark and Ernest Bloch; then lived in Europe (1925–38), during which time he studied with Boulanger in Paris and was active in Vienna. Returning to the U.S., he served as chairman of the National Committee for Refugee Musicians (1938–43); was president of the American section of the ISCM (1941–50) and of the College Music Assn. (1953). After teaching at Black Mountain College (1944) and Kenyon College (1945), he was chairman of the music dept. at the City College of N.Y. (1946–67).

WORKS: OPERA: *The Master Builder*, after Ibsen. (1959–67; unfinished). **ORCH.:** Sym. (1945; Minneapolis, March 7, 1947); *Air with Toccata* for Strings (1967). **CHAMBER:** *2 Movements* for String Quartet (1926); *Fantasia* for Viola (1932); *7 Trios* for String Quartet (1956); Septet for Wind Quintet, Viola, and Cello (1957); Quartet for Violin, Viola, Cello, and Double Bass (1958). **VOCAL:** *Lysistrata* for Soprano, Women's Voices, and Orch. (1930); *Eros and Death*, choral sym. for Mezzo-soprano, Chorus, and Orch. (1932–54); *4 Madrigals and a Motet* (1960); *5 Madrigals* for Chorus (1965); songs.

BIBL.: M. Gideon, "The Music of M. B.," *American Composers Alliance Bulletin*, XIII/1 (1965).

Bruscantini, Sesto, Italian baritone; b. Porto Civitanova, Dec. 10, 1919. He studied law; then went to Rome to study music with Luigi Ricci. He made his debut at La Scala in Milan in 1949, singing the bass role of Don Geronimo in Cimarosa's *Il matrimonio segreto*. He then sang at several festivals in Glyndebourne (1951–54); in 1952 he appeared at the Salzburg Festival. In 1961 he made his U.S. debut with the Chicago Lyric Opera. On Feb. 2, 1981, he made his Metropolitan Opera debut in N.Y. as Taddeo in *L'Italiana in Algeri*, and sang there until 1983. He was particularly renowned for his buffo roles. In 1953 he married **Sena Jurinac**.

Brusilovsky, Evgeni (Grigorievich), Russian composer and pedagogue; b. Rostov-na-Donu, Nov. 12, 1905; d. Moscow, May 9, 1981. He studied composition with Maximilian Steinberg at the Leningrad Cons., graduating in 1931. In 1933 he was commissioned by the Leningrad Union of Composers to go to Kazakhstan to promote music education there and to help native composers write music based on their own ethnic sources. Brusilovsky taught at the Alma-Ata Cons. of Music. He wrote a number of works making use of native motifs; particularly notable are his operas on folk subjects.

WORKS: OPERAS (all 1st perf. in Alma-Ata): *Kyz-Zhybek* (1934); *Zhalbyr* (1935; 2nd version, 1938; 3rd version, 1946); *Er-Targyn* (1937; 2nd version, 1954); *Ayman-Sholpan* (1938); *Altyn Styk* (1940); *Guard, Alga!* (1942); *Amangeldy* (1945); *Dudaray* (1953); *The Inheritors* (1963). **BALLET:** *Bayan-Slu* (1971). **ORCH.:** 8 syms. (1931, 1932, 1944, 1957, 1961, 1965, 1969, 1972); Piano Concerto (1948); Trumpet Concerto (1967); Viola Concerto (1969). **CHAMBER:** 2 string quartets (1944, 1952); piano pieces; educational studies for various instruments. **VOCAL:** Numerous choruses and songs.

Brusilow (real name, **Brusilovsky**), **Anshel,** American violinist, conductor, and teacher; b. Philadelphia, Aug. 14, 1928. He studied violin with Zimbalist at the Curtis Inst. of Music in

Philadelphia (1943) and with Jani Szanto at the Philadelphia Musical Academy (diploma, 1947), and conducting with Monteux (1944–54). In 1944 he made his debut as a violinist with Ormandy and the Philadelphia Orch. He served as concertmaster of the New Orleans Sym. Orch. (1954–55), assoc. concertmaster of the Cleveland Orch. (1955–59), and concertmaster of the Philadelphia Orch. (1959–66); was founder-conductor of the Philadelphia Chamber Orch. (1961–65) and the Chamber Sym. of Philadelphia (1966–68). After serving as resident conductor (1970–71) and executive director and conductor (1971–73) of the Dallas Sym. Orch., he taught at North Texas State Univ. in Denton (1973–82), Southern Methodist Univ. in Dallas (1982–89), and the Univ. of North Texas at Denton (from 1989).

Bruson, Renato, distinguished Italian baritone; b. Este, near Padua, Jan. 13, 1936. He received training at the Padua Cons. In 1961 he made his operatic debut as Count Di Luna in Spoleto, and then sang in various Italian music centers. On Feb. 1, 1969, he made his Metropolitan Opera debut in N.Y. as Enrico in *Lucia di Lammermoor.* In 1972 he made his first appearance at Milan's La Scala as Antonio in *Linda di Chamounix.* He made his debut at London's Covent Garden as Renato in *Un ballo in maschera* in 1976. In 1982 he sang Falstaff in Los Angeles. He appeared as Don Giovanni at the Berlin Deutsche Oper in 1988. In 1990 he sang Montfort in *Les Vespres siciliennes* at N.Y.'s Carnegie Hall. He appeared as Germont at Covent Garden in 1995. His guest engagements also took him to Vienna, Munich, Chicago, Hamburg, Paris, San Francisco, and other cities.

Brusselmans, Michel, Belgian composer; b. Paris (of Belgian parents), Feb. 12, 1886; d. Brussels, Sept. 20, 1960. He studied with Huberti, Tinel, and Gilson at the Brussels Cons.; won the Agniez Prix in 1914 for his symphonic poem *Hélène de Sparte.* In 1922 he became ed. for the Paris music publisher Jamin, and spent most of his life in France. His music is Romantic in inspiration and programmatic in content.

WORKS: BALLETS: *Les Néréides* (1911); *Kermesse flamande* (1912); *Les Sylphides* (on themes of Chopin). **ORCH.:** *Ouverture fériale* (1908); *Scènes Breugheliennes* (1911); *Hélène de Sparte,* symphonic poem (1914); *Télémaque a Gaulus* for Chamber Orch. (1923); 3 syms. (1924; 1934; *Levantine,* 1956–57); *Esquisses flamandes* (1927); *Légende du gapeau* for Horn and Orch. or Piano (1930); *Rhapsodie flamande* (1931); *Scènes provençales* (1931); *Suite phrygienne* (1932); *Suite d'après les Caprices de Paganini* (1936); *Suite divertissement* (1937); *Rhapsodie* for Horn and Orch. (1938); Organ Concerto (1938); *Ouverture héroïque* (1942); *Sinfonietta* (1954). **CHAMBER:** Violin Sonata (1915); Cello Sonata (1916); *Prelude and Fugue* for 8 Winds (1923); *Visages de Paris* for Piano (1946). **VOCAL:** *Jésus,* oratorio (1936); *Psaume LVI* for Soprano, Chorus, and Orch. (1954); songs.

Brustad, Bjarne, Norwegian violinist, violist, conductor, and composer; b. Christiania, March 4, 1895; d. there (Oslo), May 22, 1978. He studied at the Christiania Cons.; then took violin lessons with Flesch in Berlin (1915–16). From 1919 to 1922 he was a violinist in the Oslo Phil., and from 1929 to 1943 he played first viola there. He also conducted orchs. in Oslo; in 1951 he received a government life pension. His music is Romantic in its essence, and traditional in form.

WORKS: OPERA: *Atlantis* (1945). **ORCH.:** 4 violin concertos (1922–61); Concertino for Viola and Chamber Orch. (1932); 9 syms. (1948, 1951, 1953, 1957, 1967, 1970, 1971, 1972, 1973); Clarinet Concerto (1970). **CHAMBER:** 3 string quartets (1919, 1929, 1959); 3 sonatas for Solo Violin (1935, 1956, 1957); Trio for Clarinet, Violin, and Viola (1938); Trio for Clarinet, Violin, and Bassoon (1947); Violin Sonata (1950); *Divertimento* for Flute (1958).

Bruynèl, Ton, Dutch composer; b. Utrecht, Jan. 26, 1934. He studied piano at the Utrecht Cons.; then worked in the studio for electronic music at the Univ. of Utrecht; in 1957 he organized a private electronic music studio. Most of his compositions involve instruments in combination with electronics, and some require theatrical visualizations.

WORKS: *Resonance I* (1960–62) and *II* (1963), theater pieces; *Reflexes* for Birma Drum (1961); *Relief* for Organ and 4 Sound Tracks (1964); *Mobile* for 2 Sound Tracks (1965); *Milieu* for 2 Sound Tracks and Organ (1965–66); *Arc* for Organ and 4 Sound Tracks (1966–67); *Mekaniek* for Wind Quintet and 2 Sound Tracks (1967); *Decor,* ballet score (1967); *Signs* for Wind Quintet, 2 Sound Tracks, and Video Projection (1969); *Ingredients* for Piano and Sound Tracks (1970); *Intra I* for Bass Clarinet and Sound Track (1971); *Elegy* for Woman's Voice and 2 Sound Tracks (1972); *Looking Ears* for Bass Clarinet, Grand Piano, and Sound Tracks (1972); *Phases* for 4 Sound Tracks and Orch. (Utrecht, Jan. 10, 1975); *Soft Song* for Oboe and 2 Sound Tracks (1975); *Dialogue* for Bass Clarinet and Sound Tracks (1976); *Translucent I* for String Quartet and Sound Tracks (1977) and *II* for String Orch. and Sound Tracks (1978); *Toccare* for Piano and Sound Tracks (1979); *From the Tripod* for Loudspeakers, Women, and Listeners (1981); *John's Lullaby* for Chorus, Tape, and Orch. (1985); *Continuation* for Chorus and Tape (1985); *Nocturno en Pedraza* for Flute and Sound Tracks (1988); *Ascolta* for Soloist and Chorus (1989); *Tarde* for Cello (1992); *Le Jardin* for Alto Flute, Harpsichord, and Woman's Voice (1992).

Bruzdowicz, Joanna, Polish-French composer; b. Warsaw, May 17, 1943. She studied piano with Irena Protasewicz and Wanda Losakiewicz, and composition with Sikorski at the Warsaw Cons. (M.A., 1966). She then pursued training in composition in Paris with Boulanger, Messiaen, and Schaeffer (1968–70), where she was active with the Groupe de Recherches Musicales of the ORTF. She later made her home in Belgium while pursuing activities as a composer, music critic, and teacher. Her output ranges the spectrum from traditional scores to electronic pieces.

WORKS: DRAMATIC: OPERAS: *In der Strafkolonie* or *La Colonie Pénitentiaire* (Tours, 1972; rev. version, Liège, Oct. 9, 1986); *Les Troyennes* (Paris, 1973; Polish version, Warsaw, July 20, 1979); *Bramy Raju* (The Gates of Paradise; Warsaw, Nov. 1987); *Tides and Waves* (1991–92; Barcelona, June 1992). **BALLET:** *Le Petit Prince* (Brussels, Dec. 10, 1976). **CHILDREN'S MUSICAL:** *En attendant Anaïs* (Brussels, Dec. 6, 1987). Many film and theater scores. **ORCH.:** *Impressions* (1966); *Suite in memoriam Sergei Prokofiev* (1966–67); *Eclairs* (1969); Piano Concerto (1974; Paris, Feb. 23, 1975); Sym. (Paris, April 30, 1975); Violin Concerto (1975; Radio France, Feb. 11, 1978); *Aquae sextiae,* suite for Winds (Aix-en-Provence, July 12, 1978); Double Bass Concerto (1982; Łódź, March 1984); *4 Season's Greetings* for Soloists and String Chamber Orch. (1988–89; Poznań, April 2, 1989); *The Cry of the Phoenix,* cello concerto (Lublin, Sept. 16, 1994). **CHAMBER:** Wind Quintet (1966); *Per Due* for Violin and Piano (1966); *Epigrams* for Violin (1966); *Esquisses* for Flute, Viola, Cello, and Piano (1969); *Stigma* for Cello (1969; Paris, Dec. 1970); *Episode* for Piano and 13 Strings (1973); *Ette* for Clarinet (1974); *Einklang* for Harpsichord and Organ (1975); Trio for Variable Instrumentation (1975); *Fantasia Hermantica on the Theme S'A'B'B'E* for Viola and Piano (1979); *Tre contre tre* for Flute, Oboe, Viola, and 3 Percussion (1979); *Marlos Grosso Brasileiras* for Flute, Violin, Harpsichord, and Tape (1980); *Trio dei Due Mondi* for Violin, Cello, and Piano (1980; Radio Fance, Jan. 1981); *Dum Spiro Spero* for Flute and Tape (Brussels, May 1981); *Para y contra* for Double Bass and Tape (Brussels, Sept. 1981); *Trio per Trio* for Flute, Violin, and Harpsichord (Brussels, Sept. 15, 1981); *Dreams and Drums* for Percussionist (Santa Barbara, Calif., March 1982); 2 string quartets: No. 1, *La Vita* (Brussels, April 1983) and No. 2, *Cantus Aeternus* (Warsaw, May 10, 1988); *Oracle* for Bassoon and Tape (1982; Paris, March 1983); *Aurora Borealis* for Harp and Organ (Bergen, May 22, 1988); Sonata for Solo Violin, *Il Ritorno* (Zagreb, April 25, 1990); *Je me souviens* for Marimba (Montreal, Dec. 17, 1990); Violin Sonata, *Spring in America* (N.Y., April 20, 1994). **PIANO:** *Erotiques* (1966); *Esitana* for 2 Pianos or Piano,

4-hands (1973); *An der Schönen Blauen Donau* for 2 Pianos and Tape (1973–74); *October Sonata* (1978). **VOCAL:** *Niobe* for Speaker, Soprano, and 5 Instruments (1966); *Sketches from the Harbor* for Mezzo-soprano, Flute, Piano, and 3 Percussion (1967); *Jour d'ici et d'ailleurs* for Vocal Quartet, Chorus, Speaker, and Chamber Ensemble (1971); *A Claire Voix* for Chorus, 4 Instruments, and Tape (1973); *Urbi et Orbi*, cantata for Tenor, Children's Chorus, 2 Trumpets, 2 Trombones, and Organ (Stuttgart, June 23, 1985); *La Espero*, cantata for Soprano, Baritone, and 7 Instruments (Kraków, March 25, 1990); *On Prayer* for Soprano and Piano (WFMT, Chicago, Nov. 21, 1990); *Stabat Mater* for Chorus (Los Angeles, April 3, 1993). **OTHER:** *Ek-Stasis*, electro-acoustic piece with mimes (1969); *Phobos*, electronic piece (1969); *Homo Faber*, electronic trilogy (1971–75); *Inner Space-Outer Space*, electronic piece (1978); *Bartókalia*, electronic piece (1979); *Neue Kinderszenen*, electronic suite for children (1980).

Bryars, (Richard) Gavin, significant English composer and teacher; b. Goole, Yorkshire, Jan. 16, 1943. He studied composition privately with Cyril Ramsey (1959–61) and George Linstead (1963–65) in England, and with Ben Johnston (1968) in the U.S.; also at the Univ. of Sheffield (B.A. in philosophy, 1964) and at the Northern School of Music (1964–66). After teaching at the Northampton College of Technology (1966–67), the Portsmouth College of Art (1969–70), and the Leicester Polytechnic (1970–85), he was prof. of music at De Montford Univ. (from 1985). In 1981 he founded his own Gavin Bryars Ensemble, with which he toured widely. Bryar's output is generally experimental in nature. His works are indeterminate, replete with repetition, and often utilize electronics. His warmth and humor is evidenced in his *The Sinking of the Titanic* (1969), a multimedia, meditative collage work composed of excerpts from pieces the drowning orch. might have been playing. His poignant *Jesus' Blood Never Failed Me Yet*, originally composed for Ensemble and Tape (1971), became an international success in its later version for Orch. and Tape (1994), incorporating the raspy voice of Tom Waits. Bryars has also collaborated with a number of well-known musicians, including Brian Eno, Steve Reich, and Cornelius Cardew, as well as with the preeminent American theater director, Robert Wilson.

WORKS: DRAMATIC: *Irma*, opera (1977; realization of a work by Tom Phillips); *Medea*, opera (1982; rev. version, Lyons, Oct. 23, 1984); *Dr. Ox's Experiment*, opera (1988–95); other theater music, dance scores, and incidental music. **ORCH.:** *2nd Suite from Irma* for Piano and Strings (1978); *3 Studies on Medea* (1983); *Eglisak* for Chamber Orch. (1984–85; Strasbourg, Oct. 10, 1985); *By the Vaar* for Double Bass, Bass Clarinet, Percussion, and Strings (London, April 6, 1987); *The Green Ray* for Soprano Saxophone and Chamber Orch. (Swanage, July 6, 1991); *The North Shore* for Viola, Strings, Harp or Piano, and Percussion (London, July 30, 1994; also for Viola and Piano, 1993); *Jesus' Blood Never Failed Me Yet* for Orch. and Tape (Winnipeg, Feb. 5, 1994; also for Ensemble and Tape, 1971). **INSTRUMENTAL:** *The Sinking of the Titantic* for Ensemble (1969; London, Dec. 11, 1972); *The Squirrel and the Ricketty-Racketty Bridge* for 2 Guitars (1 Players) or Multiples of Same (1971; London, Dec. 11, 1972); *Jesus' Blood Never Failed Me Yet* for Ensemble and Tape (1971; London, Dec. 11, 1972; also for Orch. and Tape, 1994); *The Cross-Channel Ferry* for Up to 12 Players (Paris, Nov. 16, 1979); *Les Fiançailles* for Piano, String Quintet, and 2 Percussionists (Vienna, May 22, 1983); *Allegrasco* for Soprano Saxophone or Clarinet and Piano (Leicester, Dec. 7, 1983; also for Clarinet or Soprano Saxophone and Ensemble, Ghent, Nov. 10, 1986); 4 string quartets, including No. 1, *Between the National and the Bristol* (Vienna, Oct. 8, 1985), No. 2 (Huddersfield, Dec. 1, 1990), and No. 4, *A Man in a Room, Gambling*, for Pre-recorded Voice and String Quartet (1992; London, June 3, 1993); *Viennese Dance No. 1* for Horn, Percussion, and Optional String Trio (1985; Paris, Nov. 20, 1986); *Sub Rosa* for Clarinet, Recorder, Vibraphone, Piano, Violin, and Double Bass (Ghent, Nov. 10, 1986); *The Old Tower of Löbenicht* for Violin or Viola, Bass Clarinet, Tenor Horn, Cello, Double Bass, 2 Percussionists, Piano, and Electric Guitar (London, June 13, 1987); *Alaric I or II* for Saxophone Quartet (Leicester, Oct. 3, 1989); *After the Requiem* for Electric Guitar, 2 Violas, and Cello (1990); *4 Elements* for Ensemble (1990; Oxford, Nov. 16, 1994); *Die Letzten Tage* for 2 Violins (Seville, April 19, 1992); *Aus den Letzten Tagen* for 2 Violins, Cello, Clarinet, 2 Percussionists, and Electric Keyboard (1992); *The Archangel Trip* for Ensemble (Bristol, April 18, 1993); *The North Shore* for Viola and Piano (Edinburgh, Oct. 19 1993; also for Viola, String Orch., Harp or Piano, and Percussion, 1994); *3 Elegies* for 9 Clarinets (1993); *Suite from Wonderlawn* for Electric Guitar, Viola, Cello, and Amplified Double Bass (London, Dec. 6, 1994). **PIANO:** *Out of Zaleski's Gazebo* for 2 Pianos, 6- or 8-hands (Louvain, Dec. 12, 1977); *My First Homage* for 2 Pianos (N.Y., Nov. 11, 1978). **VOCAL:** *On Photography* for Chorus, Harmonium, and Piano (1983); *Effarene* for Soprano, Mezzo-soprano, 2 Pianos, and 2 Percussionists (London, March 23, 1984); *Pico's Flight* for Soprano and Orch. (Egham, Feb. 25, 1986; also for Soprano and Chamber Orch., Leicester, Feb. 11, 1990); *Glorious Hill* for Male Alto, 2 Tenors, and Baritone (Lewes, Aug. 10, 1988); *Incipit Vita Nova* for Male Alto, Violin, Viola, and Cello (Leicester, April 1, 1989); *Cadman Requiem* for Male Alto, 2 Tenors, Baritone, 2 Violas, Cello, and Optional Double Bass (Lyons, May 17, 1989); *The Black River* for Soprano and Organ (Leicester, Jan. 22, 1991); *The White Lodge* for Low Mezzo-soprano, Electronics, and Tape (London, Sept. 21, 1991; also for Low Contralto, 2 Violins, Viola, Cello, 2 Double Basses, 2 Percussionists, and Electric Keyboard, Paris, Dec. 9, 1992); *The Adnan Songbook (No. 5)* for Soprano, Clarinet, Bass Clarinet, Viola, Cello, and Double Bass (London, Nov. 8, 1992); *The War in Heaven* for Soprano, Male Alto, Semi Chorus, Chorus, and Orch. (London, April 29, 1993).

Brymer, Jack, distinguished English clarinetist; b. South Shields, Jan. 27, 1915. He studied at the Univ. of London; then served in the Royal Air Force in World War II. In 1947 he joined the Royal Phil. in London as principal clarinet; then held this position with the BBC Sym. Orch. there (1963–71) and the London Sym. Orch. (1971–86). He was director of the London Wind Soloists; was prof. at the Royal Academy of Music, London (1950–59); then taught at Kneller Hall (1967–71) and the Guildhall School of Music in London (from 1982). In 1960 he was made an Officer of the Order of the British Empire. He wrote an autobiography, *From Where I Sit* (1979); also publ. *In the Orchestra* (1987).

Bryn-Julson, Phyllis (Mae), esteemed American soprano; b. Bowdon, N.Dak., Feb. 5, 1945. She studied piano, organ, violin, and voice at Concordia College, Moorehead, Minn.; then spent several summers at the Berkshire Music Center at Tanglewood and completed her studies at Syracuse Univ. On Oct. 28, 1966, she made her formal debut as soloist in Berg's *Lulu Suite* with the Boston Sym. Orch., and in 1976 made her operatic debut as Malinche in the U.S. premiere of Sessions's *Montezuma* in Boston. She often appears in recital with her husband, the organist Donald Sutherland. In addition to teaching at Kirkland-Hamilton College in Clinton, N.Y., and at the Univ. of Maryland, she conducted master classes on both sides of the Atlantic. She is particularly renowned as a concert singer, at ease with all periods and styles of music.

Bucchi, Valentino, Italian composer and pedagogue; b. Florence, Nov. 29, 1916; d. Rome, May 9, 1976. He studied composition with Frazzi and Dallapiccola, and music history with Torrefranca at the Univ. of Florence, graduating in 1944; subsequently held teaching posts at the Florence Cons. (1945–52; 1954–57), the Venice Cons. (1952–54), and the Perugia Cons. (1957–58); was music director of the Accademia Filarmonica Romana (1958–60) and artistic director of the Teatro Comunale in Bologna (1963–65); was director of the Florence Cons. (1974–76). In his works, he continued the national Italian tradition of the musical theater, while attempting to modernize the polyphony of the Renaissance along the lines established by Malipiero.

WORKS: DRAMATIC: OPERAS: *Il giuoco del barone* (Florence, Dec. 20, 1944); *Il Contrabasso* (Florence, May 20, 1954); *Una notte in Paradiso* (Florence, May 11, 1960); *Il coccodrillo* (Florence, May 9, 1970). **BALLETS:** *Racconto siciliano* (Rome, Jan. 17, 1956); *Mirandolina* (Rome, March 12, 1957). **ORCH.:** *Ballata del silenzio* (1951); *Concerto lirico* for Violin and Strings (1958); *Concerto grottesco* for Double Bass and Strings (1967). **CHAMBER:** String Quartet (1956); Solo Clarinet Concerto (1969); *Ison* for Cello (1971). **VOCAL:** *Colloquio corale* for Narrator, Soloist, Chorus, and Orch. (1971).

Bucci, Mark, American composer; b. N.Y., Feb. 26, 1924. He attended St. John's Univ. in N.Y. (1941–42); after private training in composition from Tibor Serly (1942–45), he continued his studies with Frederick Jacobi and Vittorio Giannini at the Juilliard School of Music in N.Y. (B.S., 1951) and with Copland at the Berkshire Music Center in Tanglewood. In 1953–54 and 1957–58 he held Guggenheim fellowships. His modern, lyrical style is particularly effective in his stage works.

WORKS: DRAMATIC: OPERAS: *The Boor* (N.Y., Dec. 29, 1949); *The Dress* (N.Y., Dec. 8, 1953); *Sweet Betsy from Pike* (N.Y., Dec. 8, 1953); *Tale for a Deaf Ear* (Tanglewood, Aug. 5, 1957); *The Hero* (N.Y., Sept. 24, 1965); Midas (1981). **MUSICALS:** *Caucasian Chalk Circle* (1948); *The Thirteen Clocks* (1953); *The Adamses* (1956); *Time and Again* (1958); *The Girl from Outside* (1959); *Chain of Jade* (1960); *Pink Party Dress* (1960); *The Old Lady Shows Her Medals* (1960); *Cheaper by the Dozen* (1961); *Johnny Mishuga* (1961); *Our Miss Brooks* (1961); *The Best of Broadway* (1961); *Ask Any Girl* (1967); *Second Coming* (1976). **INCIDENTAL MUSIC TO:** *Cadenza* (1947); *Elmer and Lily* (1952); *Summer Afternoon* (1952); *The Western* (1954); *The Sorcerer's Apprentice* (1969). **OTHER:** Film scores; Concerto for Kazoo and Orch. (1959; N.Y., March 26, 1960; renamed *Concerto for a Singing Instrument*); Flute Concerto; choral music; songs.

Buchanan, Isobel, Scottish soprano; b. Glasgow, March 15, 1954. She studied at the Royal Scottish Academy of Music and Drama in Glasgow, graduating in 1974. In 1976 she made her operatic debut as Pamina with the Australian Opera in Sydney, where she sang until 1978 when she made her Glyndebourne Festival debut in the same role and as Micaëla at the Vienna State Opera. In 1979 she appeared at London's Covent Garden and at the Santa Fe (N.Mex.) Opera. In 1981 she sang at the Aix-en-Provence Festival. In subsequent years, she appeared with various opera companies and toured widely as a concert artist. Among her most admired roles are Adina, Zerlina, Donna Elvira, Susanna, and Fiordiligi.

Bucharoff (actually, **Buchhalter**), **Simon,** Russian-American pianist and composer; b. Berdichev, April 20, 1881; d. Chicago, Nov. 24, 1955. He settled in America as a youth; studied piano with Paolo Gallico in N.Y., and later with Julius Epstein and Emil von Sauer in Vienna. He occupied various teaching posts; lived principally in Chicago and Hollywood. He publ. *The Modern Pianist's Textbook* (N.Y., 1931). Among his works were the operas *A Lover's Knot* (Chicago, Jan. 15, 1916) and *Sakahra* (Frankfurt am Main, Nov. 8, 1924; rev. 1953); also symphonic poems (*Reflections in the Water, Drunk, Doubt; Joy Sardonic*).

Buchbinder, Rudolf, Austrian pianist; b. Leitmeritz, Dec. 1, 1946. He studied with Bruno Seidlhofer at the Vienna Academy of Music; in 1965 he made a tour of North and South America; in 1966 he won a special prize awarded at the Van Cliburn Competition; then made a tour with the Vienna Phil., and also appeared as a soloist in Paris, Milan, Madrid, and London. In 1975 he made a tour of Japan and the U.S. with the Vienna Sym. Orch.; in addition, he taught piano at the Basel Academy of Music. He subsequently toured extensively, appearing as a soloist with leading orchs and as a recitalist.

Buchla, Donald (Frederick), American electronic-instrument designer and builder, composer, and performer; b. Southgate, Calif., April 17, 1937. After studying physics at the Univ. of Calif. at Berkeley (B.A., 1961), he became active with the San Francisco Tape Music Center, where in 1966 he installed the first Buchla synthesizer. That same year he founded Buchla Associates in Berkeley for the manufacture of synthesizers. In addition to designing and manufacturing electronic instruments, he also installed electronic-music studios at the Musikhögskolan in Stockholm and at IRCAM in Paris, among other institutions. In 1975 he became co-founder of the Electric Weasel Ensemble, a live electronic-music group, and in 1978 he became co-director of the Artists' Research Collective in Berkeley. He held a Guggenheim fellowship in 1978.

WORKS: With electronic instruments: *Cicada Music* for some 2,500 Cicadas (1963); *5 Video Mirrors* for Audience of 1 or More (1966); *Anagnorisis* for 1 Performer and Voice (1970); *Harmonic Pendulum* for Buchla Series 200 Synthesizer (1972); *Garden* for 3 Performers and Dancer (1975); *Keyboard Encounter* for 2 Pianos (1976); *Q* for 14 Instruments (1979); *Silicon Cello* for Amplified Cello (1979); *Consensus Conduction* for Buchla Series 300 Synthesizer and Audience (1981); also an orchestration of D. Rosenboom's *How Much Better If Plymouth Rock Had Landed on the Pilgrims* for 2 Buchla Series 300 Synthesizers (1969).

Bucht, Gunnar, Swedish composer, musicologist, and pedagogue; b. Stocksund, Aug. 5, 1927. He studied composition with Blomdahl (1947–51) and also took courses in musicology at the Univ. of Uppsala (Ph.D., 1953); later pursued training in composition with Orff in Germany (1954), Petrassi in Italy (1954–55), and Deutsch in Paris (1961–62). He taught at the Univ. of Stockholm (1965–69), and then was in the diplomatic service as cultural attaché at the Swedish Embassy in Bonn (1970–73). From 1975 to 1985 he was a prof. of composition at the Stockholm Musikhögskolan, serving as its director from 1987 to 1993. From 1963 to 1969 he was chairman of the Soc. of Swedish Composers. In 1964 he was elected to membership in the Royal Swedish Academy of Music in Stockholm. His music retains traditional forms while adopting diverse modern techniques.

WORKS: DRAMATIC: *Tronkrävarna* (The Pretenders), opera (1961–64; Stockholm, Sept. 10, 1966); *Jerikos murar* (The Walls of Jericho), opera-oratorio (1966–67; reworked as an electronic piece). **ORCH.:** *Introduction and Allegro* for Strings (1950); *Meditation* for Piano and Orch. (1950); 11 syms.: No. 1 (1952; Swedish Radio, Dec. 6, 1953), No. 2 (1953), No. 3 (1954; Swedish Radio, April 17, 1955), No. 4 (1957–58; Stockholm, April 3, 1959), No. 5 (1960; Stockholm, Jan. 14, 1962), No. 6 (1961–62; Stockholm, Nov. 20, 1963), No. 7 (1970–71; Norrköping, March 26, 1972), No. 8 (1982–83; Stockholm, Sept. 13, 1984), No. 9 (1988–90; Stockholm, Oct. 31, 1990), No. 10, *Sinfonie gracieuse ou l'Apothéose de Berwald* (1993), and No. 11 (1993–94); 2 cello concertos (1954; 1989–90); *Symphonic Fantasy* (1955); *Divertimento* (1955–56); *Couplets et Refrains* (1960); *Strangaspel* for Strings (1965); *Winter Organ* (1974); *Journées Oubliées* (1975; Stockholm, April 25, 1976); *Au delà* (1977; Stockholm, March 14, 1979); Violin Concerto (1978; Stockholm, Nov. 5, 1980); *The Big Band—and After* (1979; Swedish Radio, April 3, 1981); *Georgica* (1980; Swedish Radio, Feb. 11, 1983); *Ein Clairobscur* for Chamber Orch. (1980–81); Sinfonia Concertante for Flute, Viola, Harp, and Orch. (1981–82; Norrköping, Jan. 13, 1983); *Fresques mobiles* (1985–86; Swedish Radio, Jan. 28, 1989); *Tonend bewegte Formen* (1987); *Konsert för Arholma* for Strings (1989); Piano Concerto (1994). **CHAMBER:** String Quintet (1949–50); 2 string quartets (1951, 1959); *5 Bagatelles* for String Quartet (1953); Sonata for Piano and Percussion (1955); *Quintetto amichevole* for Winds (1976); *A huit mains* for Flute, Violin, Cello, and Harpsichord (1976); *Bald från mitt gulsippeänge* for Clarinet and Piano (1985; also for Harpsichord, 1988); *Unter vollem Einsatz* for Organ and 5 Percussion (1986–87). **PIANO:** *Theme and Variations* (1949); 2 sonatas

(1951, 1959). **VOCAL:** *La fine della diaspora* for Chorus and Orch. (1958; Stockholm, Oct. 4, 1963); *Eine lutherische Messe* for Soloists, Mixed and Children's Choruses, and Orch. (1972–73); *Music for Lau* for Children's Chorus, Winds, Percussion, Double Basses, and Tape (1974–75); cantatas; choruses; songs.

Büchtger, Fritz, German composer; b. Munich, Feb. 14, 1903; d. in an automobile accident in Starnberg, Dec. 26, 1978. He was a student of Beer-Walbrunn and Waltershausen at the Munich Akadamie der Tonkunst (1923–26). He was active as a choral conductor and teacher, and also in the promotion of contemporary music until the advent of the Nazi regime, when he was compelled to change course. After the collapse of the Third Reich, he again embraced the cause of contemporary music, helping to found the Studio for New Music in Munich in 1948. In 1953 he became president of the Musikalischen Jugend Deutschlands, and was a prominent figure in music education. In 1953 he received the music prize of the City of Munich and in 1977 the Schwabinger Kunstpreis. In his music, Büchtger developed a dodecaphonic technique which he adroitly utilized even in his sacred music.

WORKS: DRAMATIC: *O Mensch, gib acht!,* Kalenderspiel (1939); *Der Spielhansl,* musical play (1946). **ORCH.:** *Muzik zu einer Feier* for Strings (1932); *Musik* for Little Orch. (1935); *Kleines festliches Vorspiel* (1939); Concerto for Strings (1952); *Studien* (1956); *Concerto for Orchestra* (1957); Concertino I for Oboe, Violin, Cello, and Strings (1960) and II for Piano, Winds, Strings, Vibraphone, and Percussion (1962); Concerto for Violin and Strings (1963); *Stufen* (1966); *Musik* for Strings (1967); *Schichten-Bögen* (1969); *Ascensio* (1973). **CHAMBER:** 6 string quartets (1948, 1958, 1967, 1969, 1972, 1973); *Strukturen* for Nonet (1968); *Stück* for Oboe and String Quartet (1971); Quartet for Violin, Viola, Cello, and Piano (1972); *Nyktodia* for Wind Octet (1972); Piano Trio (1974); piano pieces; organ music. **VOCAL: CANTATAS:** *Der Name des Menschen* for Chorus and Orch. (1931); *Flamme* for Baritone, Chorus, and Orch. (1932); *Bergfahrt* for Baritone, Men's Chorus, Piano, and Small Orch. (1939); *Es werden Zeichen geschehen* for Chorus and Small Orch. (1969). **ORATORIOS:** *Der weisse Reiter* for Baritone, Chorus, and Orch. (1948); *Das gläserne Meer* for Baritone, Chorus, and Orch. (1953); *Die Auferstehung* for Chorus and Orch. or Strings and Organ (1954); *Die Verklärung* for Baritone, Women's Voices, and Strings (1956); *Die Himmelfahrt Christi* for Baritone, Chorus, and Orch. or Strings and Organ (1957); *Pfingsten* for Baritone, Chorus, and Orch. (1957); *Das Weihnachtsoratorium* for Voices, Flute, Oboe, and Strings (1959); *Johannes der Taufer* for Baritone, Chorus, and Orch. (1961). **OTHER WORKS WITH VOICES:** *Serenata im Walde* for Men's Chorus and Orch. (1935); *Hymnen an das Licht* for Baritone or Medium Woman's Voice and Orch. (1938); *Drusus* for Soloists, Chorus, and Orch. (1943); *Das Gesicht des Hesekiel* for Baritone, Women's Voices, and 15 Instruments (1972); numerous choruses and solo songs.

BIBL.: L. Wismeyer, *F. B.* (Regensburg, 1963); A. Ott, ed., *F. B. 1973* (Munich, 1974; new ed., 1988, as *F. B. 1903–1978*); K. Hübler, *F. B. und die neue Musik in München* (Munich, 1983); K.-R. Danler et al., *F. B.* (Tutzing, 1989).

Buck, Ole, Danish composer; b. Copenhagen, Feb. 1, 1945. Though largely self-taught, he began to compose energetically at an early age. As such, he forged his own remarkably independent style marked by carefully constructed forms, refined expression, and melodic invention.

WORKS: BALLET: *Felix Luna* (1970–71). **ORCH.:** Overture (1966); *Preludes I–IV* (1967); *Punctuations* (1968); *Granulations I* (1971); *Pastorals* (1975); *White Flower Music II* (1991); *Rivers and Mountains* (1993–94). **CHAMBER:** *White Flower Music* for 2 Flutes, 2 Clarinets, and Trumpet (1965); *Fioriture* for Flute and Piano (1965); *Signes* for Wind Quintet (1967); *Summer Trio* for Flute, Cello, and Guitar (1968); *Masques* for 6 Percussion Groups (1969); *Sonnabend* for Flute, Oboe, Horn, and Violin (1971); *14 Preludes* for Flute and Guitar (1972); *Kindergarten* for Flute, Oboe, Horn, and Violin (1972); *Friendless* for Wind Quintet (1972); *Days and Days* for Violin, Viola, and Cello (1976); *Chamber Music I* (1979) and *II* (1982) for Chamber Ensemble; *Maya* for Flute and Percussion (1980); *Carols* for Oboe, Clarinet, Saxophone, and Bassoon (1980; rev. 1994); *Canaries* for Recorder, Harpsichord, and Cello (1981); *Gurre Trio* for Flute, Viola, and Double Bass (1982); *Aquarelles* for Chamber Ensemble (1983); *Pan* for Flute and Piano (1983); *Gymel* for Recorder and Spinet (1983); *Primavera* for Flute, Viola, and Guitar (1984); *Ommagio a Antonio Vivaldi* for Guitar (1984); *Consonante* for Recorder (1985); *Rejang* for Percussionist (1986); *Landscapes I* (1992) and *II* (1994) for Chamber Ensemble; *Reyong* for Organ and Percussion (1992); *Mikrokosmos* for String Quartet (1992); *Veryovochkoy* for 2 Accordions and Percussion (1993); *Petite Suite* for Descant Recorder and Guitar (1993); *Sonata in 2 Parts* for Violin and Cello (1993). **KEYBOARD: PIANO:** *Flos forum* for 2 Pianos (1985); Sonatina (1985). **ORGAN:** *Sumer is icumen in* (1970). **VOCAL:** *Calligraphy* for Soprano and Chamber Orch. (1964); *Merle* for Mezzo-soprano (1967); *Fairies* for Soprano and Orch. (1972); *Songbook* for Soprano and 10 Instruments (1972–73); *Mana* for Chorus and 6 Percussionists (1987).

Buck, Sir Percy Carter, English organist and teacher; b. London, March 25, 1871; d. there, Oct. 3, 1947. He studied at the Guildhall School of Music and the Royal College of Music in London; subsequently served as a church organist. From 1901 to 1927 he was music director at the Harrow School; was prof. of music at Trinity College in Dublin (1910–20) and at the Univ. of London (1925–37); also taught at the Royal College of Music in London. He was knighted in 1937. His works include an overture for Orch., *Coeur de Lion*; String Quartet; Piano Quintet; sonatas; piano pieces, etc. He was the author of *Ten Years of University Music in Oxford* (1894; with Mee and Woods); *Unfigured Harmony* (1911); *Organ Playing* (1912); *First Year at the Organ* (1912); *The Organ: A Complete Method for the Study of Technique and Style; Acoustics for Musicians* (1918); *The Scope of Music* (1924); *Psychology for Musicians* (1944); also was ed. of the introductory vol. and vols. I and II of the 2nd edition of the *Oxford History of Music.*

Bücken, Ernst, eminent German musicologist; b. Aachen, May 2, 1884; d. Overath, near Cologne, July 28, 1949. He studied musicology at the Univ. of Munich with Sandberger and Kroyer; also took courses in composition with Courvoisier; received his Ph.D. there in 1912 with the diss. *Anton Reicha; Sein Leben und seine Kompositionen* (publ. in Munich, 1912); completed his Habilitation at the Univ. of Cologne in 1920 with his *Der heroische Stil in der Oper* (publ. in Leipzig, 1924); was a prof. there from 1925 to 1945; then retired to Overath. His elucidation of musical styles remains an important achievement in his work as a musicologist; as such, he ed. the monumental Handbuch der Musikwissenschaft in 10 vols., which began publication in 1927; for this series he contributed *Musik des Rokokos und der Klassik* (1927), *Die Musik des 19. Jahrhunderts bis zur Moderne* (1929–31), and *Geist und Form im musikalischen Kunstwerk* (1929–32); he was also editor of the series Die grossen Meister der Musik from 1932. His further writings include *Tagebuch der Gattin Mozarts* (Munich, 1915); *München als Musikstadt* (Leipzig, 1923); *Führer und Probleme der neuen Musik* (Cologne, 1924); *Musikalische Charakterköpfe* (Leipzig, 1924); ed. *Handbuch der Musikerziehung* (Potsdam, 1931); *Ludwig van Beethoven* (Potsdam, 1934); *Richard Wagner* (Potsdam, 1934; 2nd ed., 1943); *Deutsche Musikkunde* (Potsdam, 1935); *Musik aus deutscher Art* (Cologne, 1936); *Musik der Nationen* (Leipzig, 1937; 2nd ed., rev. as *Geschichte der Musik,* ed. by J. Völckers, 1951); ed. *Richard Wagner: Die Hauptschriften* (Leipzig, 1937); *Das deutsche Lied: Probleme und Gestalten* (Hamburg, 1939); *Robert Schumann* (Cologne, 1940); *Wörterbuch der Musik* (Leipzig, 1940); *Musik der Deutschen: Eine Kulturgeschichte der deutschen Musik* (Cologne, 1941); *Wolfgang Amadeus Mozart: Schöpferische Wandlungen* (Hamburg, 1942); *Richard Strauss* (Kevelaar, 1949).

BIBL.: W. Kahl, "E. B.," *Die Musikforschung,* III (1950).

Buckley, Emerson, American conductor; b. N.Y., April 14, 1916; d. Miami, Nov. 17, 1989. He studied at Columbia Univ. (B.A., 1936), where he began his career as conductor of its Grand Opera (1936–38). He subsequently was conductor of the Palm Beach (Fla.) Sym. Orch. (1938–41), the N.Y. City Sym. Orch. (1941–42), the San Carlo Opera in N.Y. (1943–45), and WOR Radio in N.Y. (1945–54). In 1950 he became music director of the Miami Opera, and from 1973 to 1985 he was its artistic director and resident conductor; also served as music director of the Fort Lauderdale Sym. Orch. (later the Phil. Orch. of Florida) from 1963 to 1986. In 1963 he received the Alice M. Ditson Award for conducting. He was principally known as a favorite conductor on tour with Pavarotti. With his silver hair and goatee he cut a striking figure when he appeared in Pavarotti's film *Yes, Giorgio!* (1982); the film was unsuccessful, but Buckley's appearance produced an impression. He was also the conductor in a film documentary about Pavarotti, entitled *A Distant Harmony.*

Buckner, Thomas, leading American baritone, composer, and producer; b. N.Y., Aug. 13, 1941. After brief studies at Yale Univ., he took both B.A. (1964) and M.A. (1965) degrees in English literature at the Univ. of Santa Clara in California; also took courses in linguistics at Stanford Univ. He then devoted himself to vocal training, numbering among his mentors W.A. Mathieu, Martial Singher, Alden Gilchrist, Marion Cooper, and Raymond Beegle; also studied Indian music with Ali Akbar Kahn at the American Soc. for Eastern Arts in Berkeley, California (1967–67). Buckner was active in Berkeley from 1967 to 1983, where he founded and directed the 1750 Arch Concerts (1972–80) and 1750 Arch Records (1973–83); he also was co-founder/director (with Robert Hughes) of the 23-piece Arch Ensemble, which specialized in 20th-century music. From 1989 he curated the World Music Institute's "Interpretations" series in N.Y. While Buckner's repertoire spans the ages, he has become a stalwart proponent of the avant-garde, appearing in first performances of works by David First, Annea Lockwood, Henry Threadgill, Somei Satoh, Jin Hi Kim, and David Behrman, among many others; he is known particularly for his lengthy association with Robert Ashley, in whose *Perfect Lives* trilogy (*Atalanta [Acts of God]* [1982], and *eL/Aficionado* [1987] and *Improvement [Don Leaves Linda]* [1984–85] from *Now Eleanor's Idea*) he created critically-acclaimed leading roles. Through these and other performances, including a number of noteworthy recitals in N.Y. and frequent appearances with the improvisational group "Act of Finding," the experimental group "Roscoe Mitchell New Chamber Ensemble," and the pianist Joseph Kubera, Buckner has earned the critical sobriquet *"the* voice of the Downtown (N.Y.) new music scene." Among his many recordings are 2 solo compilations, *Full Voice Spectrum* (1992) and *Sign of Our Times* (1995), both featuring works written especially for him, as well as *Pilgrimage* (1995; with the "Roscoe Mitchell New Chamber Ensemble") and *Act of Finding* (1995; with Ratzo B. Harris, Bruce Arnold, and Tom Hamilton). As a composer, Buckner creates primarily structured improvisations, in both solo (*Resonances*, 1995) and ensemble (*In Moments of Great Passion* for Improvising Baritone and String Orch., after John Ralston Saul's *Voltaire's Bastards*; N.Y., Dec. 19, 1995) settings.

Buczek, Barbara, Polish composer; b. Kraków, Jan. 9, 1940; d. there, Jan. 21, 1993. She spent her entire career in Kraków, where she studied piano with Kazimierz Mirski and was a student of Maria Bilińska-Riegerowa at the music school. She then pursued training with Ludwik Stefanski (piano diploma, 1965) and Boguslaw Schaeffer (composition diploma, 1974) at the Academy of Music, where she later served on the faculty.

WORKS: ORCH.: *3 Pieces* for Chamber Orch. (1968); *Metaphonie* (1970); *2 Impressions* (1970); *Anekumena*, concerto for 89 Instruments (1974; Warsaw, Sept. 25, 1975); *Labirynt* (1974); *Assemblage* for Alto Flute and Strings (1975); *Simplex* (1976); Violin Concerto (1979; Turin, June 13, 1986); *Dikolon* (Salzburg, May 11, 1985); Concerto for Cello, Chorus, and Orch. (1985); *Les sons ésotériques* for Flute, Orch., and Tape (1985; Salzburg, Aug. 5, 1989); *Fantasmagorie* for Chamber Orch. (1992). **CHAMBER:** 2 string quartets (1968; *Transgressio*, 1985); Wind Quintet (1969; Kraków, April 3, 1980); Quintet for Saxophone, Flute, Horn, Cello, and Vibraphone (1971); Sextet for Violin, Flute, Soprano, Cello, and 2 Pianos (1974); Duodecet for Strings (1976; Gdańsk, Jan. 20, 1984); *Eidos I* for Violin (1977), *II* for Tuba (1977; also for Tuba and Piano, 1984), *III* for Bassoon (1979), and *IV* for Piano (1992); *Hypostase I*, quintet for Soprano, Flute, Vibraphone, Cello, and Saxophone (1978; Kraków, Feb. 4, 1980), *II* for Violin Sextet (1985; Salzburg, June 27, 1990), and *III* for Mezzo-soprano and Chamber Group (1985); *Primus inter pares* for Flute, Saxophone, Clarinet, Trombone, Violin, and Double Bass (1985). **VOCAL:** Vocal Concerto for 12 Voices (1969); *Desunion* for Soprano and Double Bass (1982); *Motet* for Reciters, Baritone, Instruments, and Tape (1984).

Buczynski, Walter (Joseph), Canadian composer, pianist, and teacher; b. Toronto, Dec. 17, 1933. After studies with Earle Moss (piano) and Ridout (theory) at the Royal Cons. of Music of Toronto, he had lessons in composition with Milhaud and Charles Jones at the Aspen (Colo.) Music School (summer 1956); he then studied piano with Lhévinne in N.Y. (1958–59) and Drzewiecki in Warsaw (1959, 1961), and composition with Boulanger in Paris (1960, 1962). He taught piano and theory at the Royal Cons. of Music of Toronto (from 1962), and piano, theory, and composition at the Univ. of Toronto (from 1969); until 1977 he also pursued an active career as a pianist. His early penchant for satirical and humorous expression eventually mellowed as he pursued a more lyrical but still adventuresome path.

WORKS: DRAMATIC: *Mr. Rhinoceros and His Musicians*, children's opera (1965); *Do Re Mi*, children's opera (1967); *From the Buczynski Book of the Living*, chamber opera (1972); *Naked at the Opera*, chamber opera (1978). **ORCH.:** *Beztitula* for Piano and Orch. (1964); *4 Arabesques and Dance* for Flute and Strings (1964); *3 Thoughts* (1964); *Triptych* (1964); *4 Movements* for Piano and Strings (1969); *7 Miniatures* (1970); *A Work for Dance* (1970); *Zeroing In No. 2 (Distractions and Then)* (1971), *No. 4 (Innards and Outards)* for Soprano, Piano, and Orch. (1972), and *No. 3* for String Quartet and Orch. (1973); *3 against Many* for Flute, Clarinet, Bassoon, and Orch. (1973); *Ars Romantica* for Chamber Orch. (1976); *Lyric I* for Piano and Orch. (1976), *II* for Piano and Orch. (1983), *III* for Cello and Orch. (1984), *V* for Oboe and Strings (1988), and *VII* for Viola and Orch. (1991); *Rhapsody* for 2 Horns and Strings (1976); *3 Serenades* (1976); *Legends* for Strings (1976); Piano Concerto (1979); Violin Concerto (1980); *Fantasy on Themes from the Past* for Accordion and Strings (1980; rev. 1984); *Prayer and Dance* for Clarinet, String Quartet, and String Orch. (1982); Sym. (1986). **CHAMBER:** Trio for Violin, Cello, and Piano (1954); *Divertimento* for Violin, Cello, Clarinet, and Bassoon (1957); *Elegy: In Memoriam Kathleen Parlow* for Violin and Piano (1963); *Trio/67* for Mandolin, Clarinet, and Cello (1967); Duo for Double Bass and Piano (1974); *Quartet/74* for Flute, Clarinet, Cello, and Harpsichord (1974); Sextet for Flute, Clarinet, Violin, Cello, and 2 Percussion (1974); *Trio/74* for Harp, Bass Clarinet, and Double Bass (1974); *Olympics '76* for Brass Quintet (1976); *Sonata Belsize* for Accordion (1977); Violin Sonata (1979); *. . . Winds . . .* for Flute, Cello, Celesta, Harpsichord, and Percussion (1982); Cello Sonata (1982); Sonata for Violin and Cello (1983); Piano Quintet (1984); *Gemini Quartet* for Oboe, Violin, Viola, and Cello (1986); *Divertissement No. 2* for Harp, Accordion, and Vibraphone (1987) and *No. 3: Impressions and Memories* for Percussion Quintet (1988); String Quartet No. 3 with Soprano (1987). **PIANO:** *Aria and Toccata* (1963); *Amorphus* (1964); Suite (1964); 3 sonatas (1967, 1972, 1991); *Zeroing In* for Pianist-Speaker and Tape (1971) and *No. 5 (Dictionary of Mannerisms)* (1972); *27 Pieces for a 27 Minute Show* (1973); *Zeroing In—Zeroing Out* for Piano and Tape (1977); *Monogram* (1978); *Lyric Ii* (1984); *August Collection*, 24 preludes (1987); *Mosaics* (1988). **VOCAL:** *Mass with Outside*

Prayers for Chorus and Wind Quintet (1976); *The Tales of Nanabozho* for Speaker and Wind Quintet (1976); *Psalm 51* for Soloists, Chorus, and Orch. (1977); *Missa brevis* for Chorus, String Quartet, and Brass Quartet (1977); *Resurrection II* for Baritone, Clarinet, Violin, Viola, Cello, Accordion, and Percussion (1980); *Songs of War* for Tenor, Baritone, and Piano (1983); *Remembrances of Latin Texts* for Chorus (1988).

Budashkin, Nikolai, Russian composer; b. Lubakhovka, Aug. 6, 1910; d. Moscow, Jan. 31, 1988. After working as a blacksmith, he went to Moscow and took a course with Miaskovsky at the Cons. He specialized in music for popular Russian instruments in symphonic combinations; he wrote 2 concertos for Domra and Orch. (1944, 1947); Concert Variations for Balalaika and Orch., on a Russian folk song (1946); and works for ensembles consisting entirely of such instruments. His early *Festive Overture* (1937) achieved considerable success in Russia.

Budd, Harold (Montgomery), iconoclastic American composer, pianist, and poet; b. Los Angeles, May 24, 1936. He grew up in the Mojave desert town of Victorville. He studied composition and acoustics with Gerald Strang and Aurelio de la Vega at San Fernando Valley State College (later Calif. State Univ. at Northridge; B.A., 1963) and with Ingolf Dahl at the Univ. of Southern Calif. in Los Angeles (M.Mus., 1966). From 1970 to 1976 he taught at the Calif. Inst. of the Arts. He received NEA grants in 1974 and 1979. In 1992 he made a tour of Europe with Bill Nelson; another followed, in 1994, with Hector Zazou. Budd's compositions since the early 1970s, including his *Madrigals of the Rose Angel* for Topless Female Chorus, Harp, Percussion, Celesta, and Lights (1972), challenged the avant-garde with their prettiness and surface decoration. By the early 1980s, he began to use the recording studio as an instrument, producing 7 albums in rapid succession, including two on his own Cantil label, *The Serpent (In Quicksilver)* (1981), and *Abandoned Cities* (1984), as well as collaborations with Brian Eno, *The Plateaux of Mirror* (1980) and *The Pearl* (1984), and The Cocteau Twins, *The Moon And The Melodies* (1986). His later *Lovely Thunder* (1986), co-produced with Michael Hoenig, was his last album before departing for London, where he resided from 1987 to 1990; *The White Arcades* (1988) is his sole recorded work as an expatriate. He also created two gallery installations, including "Blue Room with Flowers and Gong" for Los Angeles's Institute of Contemporary Art, for which his *Gypsy Violin* (1985) was composed. Upon his return to the U.S., Budd composed the pieces comprising his *By the Dawn's Early Light* (1991), which signals both his departure from studio-produced albums and a return to more formal modes of composition: through-composed text settings and predetermined structures. The genesis of this work, scored for Guitar, Pedal Steel Guitar, Viola, Harp, and Voice, is a journal of poems Budd began writing in response to his exposure to the work and words of the Italian painter Sandro Chia, six of which are recorded in the composer's voice. Other recordings include *The Pavilion of Dreams* (1978), *Music For 3 Pianos* (1992; with Ruben Garcia and Daniel Lentz), *She Is A Phantom* (1994), *Through The Hill* (1994; with Andy Partridge), *Glyph* (1995; with Hector Zazou), and *Walk Into My Voice: American Beat Poetry* (1995; with Lentz). Although Budd is best known for his recordings, his career as a composer predates his recorded works by nearly two decades. To this earlier period belong such minimalist scores as *Analogies from Rothko* for Orch. (1964); *September Music* (1967); *November* (1967); *Black Flowers*, "quiet chamber ritual for 4 performers," to be staged in semidarkness on the threshold of visibility and audibility (1968); *Intermission Piece* (1968); *1 Sound* for String Quartet glissando (1968); *Mangus Colorado* for Amplified Gongs (1969; Buffalo, Feb. 4, 1970); *Lovely Thing* for Piano, with instructions to the player: "Select a chord—if in doubt call me (in lieu of performance) at 213–662-7819 for spiritual advice" (Memphis, Tenn., Oct. 23, 1969); *Lovely Thing* for Strings (1969); *California 99* (1969); *The Candy-Apple Revision* (1970; an unspecified D-flat major chord); and *Lirio*, a 24-hour marathon for Solo Gong (1971).

Budden, Julian (Midforth), English musicologist; b. Holylake, Cheshire, April 9, 1924. He was educated at Queen's College, Oxford (B.A., 1948; M.A., 1951) and the Royal College of Music, London (B.Mus., 1955); from 1951 he worked for the BBC, serving as a producer for music programs (1955–70), chief producer for opera (1970–76), and music organizer for external services (1976–83). His studies of 19th-century Italian opera are important; especially valuable is *The Operas of Verdi* (3 vols., London, 1973–81; rev. ed., 1992). He also publ. the biography *Verdi* (London, 1985; rev. ed., 1993). In 1991 he received the Order of the British Empire.

Buelow, George J(ohn), American musicologist; b. Chicago, March 31, 1929. He studied piano with Ganz at the Chicago Musical College, where he received M.B. (1950) and M.M. (1951) degrees; then studied musicology with Martin Bernstein, Sachs, and Reese at N.Y. Univ. (Ph.D., 1961, with the diss. *Johann David Heinichen, "Der General-bass in der Composition": A Critical Study with Annotated Translation of Selected Chapters*). In 1961 he joined the faculty of the Univ. of Calif. at Riverside; then was prof. of music at the Univ. of Kentucky in Louisville (1968–69) and Rutgers Univ. (1969–77). In 1977 he became prof. of musicology at Indiana Univ. in Bloomington. He is particularly noted for his studies of 17th- and 18th-century German music. He publ. *Thorough-bass Accompaniment according to Johann David Heinichen* (Berkeley, 1966; 3rd ed., rev., 1992), *New Mattheson Studies* (with H. Marx; Cambridge, 1984), and *The Late Baroque Era: From the 1680s to 1740* (Basingstoke, 1993).

BIBL.: T. Mathiesen and B. Rivera, eds., *Festa Musicologica: Essays in Honor of G.J. B.* (Stuyvesant, N.Y., 1995).

Bughici, Dumitru, Romanian composer; b. Iaşi, Nov. 14, 1921. He received initial training at the Iaşi Cons. (1935–38), and later studied at the Leningrad Cons. (1950–55), where his teachers included Schnittke and Arapov. In 1955 he joined the faculty of the Bucharest Cons. In 1988 he went to Jerusalem, where he was active as a teacher and composer.

WORKS: BALLETS: *The Fight of Light against Darkness* (1965); *Energy* (1965); *The Liberation of the Village* (1980). **ORCH.:** *The Poem of New Life* (1953); 2 violin concertos (1955, 1977); *Evocation*, symphonic poem (1956); 4 sinfoniettas (1958, 1962, 1969, 1979); *The Heroic Poem* (1959); 11 syms. (1961; 1964, rev. 1967; 1966; 1972; 1977; 1978–79; 1983; 1984; 1985; 1985; 1987–90); *Bolero* (1963); *The Monument*, symphonic poem (1964); *Partita* (1965); *Dramatic Dialogues* for Flute and Strings (1967); *Sonata* for Strings (1970); *Melody, Rhythm, Color*, jazz concerto (1970); *A Poem to Love* (1971); *Symphonic Fantasia in Jazz Rhythm* (1974); Cello Concerto (1974); Trumpet Concerto (1975); Piano Concertino (1975); *5 Musical Images* (1977); *Choreographic Tableaux*, symphonic suite (1978); Simfonie Concertante No. 1 for String Quartet and Orch. (1979–80) and No. 2 for Flute, Oboe, Clarinet, Bassoon, Strings, and Percussion (1980–81); Flute Concerto (1985). **CHAMBER:** Suite for Violin and Piano (1953); Scherzo for Cello and Piano (1953); 5 string quartets (1954; 1968; 1971; 1976–77; 1978); 3 trios for Violin, Cello, and Piano (1961 1976, 1983); 2 violin sonatas (1963, 1981); Sonata for Solo Violin (1968); *Quartet-Fantasia* (1968–69); *Triptych* for Violin and Piano (1970); 2 brass quintets (1975, 1981); *Fantasia* for Xylophone and Double Bass (1980); Septet (1980–81); piano pieces.

Buhlig, Richard, American pianist and teacher; b. Chicago, Dec. 21, 1880; d. Los Angeles, Jan. 30, 1952. He studied in Chicago, and in Vienna with Leschetizky (1897–1900); made his recital debut in Berlin (1901); then toured Europe and the U.S. (American debut with the Philadelphia Orch. in N.Y., Nov. 5, 1907). In 1918 he was appointed teacher of piano at the Inst. of Musical Arts in N.Y. He eventually settled in Los Angeles as a performer and teacher.

Bujarski, Zbigniew, Polish composer; b. Muszyna, Aug. 21, 1933. He studied composition with Wiechowicz and conducting with Wodiczko at the State College of Music in Kraków.

WORKS: *Burning Bushes*, cycle for Soprano, and Chamber Ensemble or Piano (1958); *Triptych* for String Orch. and Percussion (1959); *Synchrony I* for Soprano and Chamber Ensemble (1959) and *II* for Soprano, Chorus, and Orch. (1960); *Zones* for Chamber Ensemble (1961); *Kinoth* for Orch. (1963); *Chamber Composition* for Voice, Flute, Harp, Piano, and Percussion (1963); *Contraria* for Orch. (1965); *El Hombre* for Soprano, Mezzo-soprano, Baritone, Chorus, and Orch. (1969–73; Warsaw, Sept. 21, 1974); *Musica domestica* for 18 String Instruments (1977); Concerto for Strings (1979; Warsaw, Sept. 10, 1980); *Similis Greco*, symphonic cycle (1979–83); *Quartet on the Advent* (1984); *Quartet for the Resurrection* (1990).

Buketoff, Igor, American conductor; b. Hartford, Conn., May 29, 1915. He studied at the Univ. of Kansas (1931–32), the Juilliard School of Music in N.Y. (B.S., 1935; M.S., 1941), and the Los Angeles Cons. In 1942 he won the first Alice M. Ditson Award for Young Conductors. He was music director of the Chautauqua Opera (1941–47), the N.Y. Phil. Young People's Concerts (1948–53), the Fort Wayne (Ind.) Phil. (1948–66), the Iceland Sym. Orch. in Reykjavík (1964–65), the St. Paul (Minn.) Opera (1968–74), and the Texas Chamber Orch. (1980–81). He also taught at the Juilliard School of Music (1935–45), the Chautauqua School of Music (1941–47), Columbia Univ. (1943–47), Butler Univ. (1953–63), and the Univ. of Houston (1977–79). Buketoff was notably active in the promotion of contemporary music.

Bukofzer, Manfred F(ritz), eminent German-born American musicologist; b. Oldenburg, March 27, 1910; d. Oakland, Calif., Dec. 7, 1955. He studied at the Hoch Cons. in Frankfurt am Main, and at the Univs. of Heidelberg, Berlin, and Basel (Ph.D., 1936, with the diss. *Geschichte des englischen Diskants und des Fauxbourdons nach den theoretischen Quellen*; publ. in Strasbourg, 1936); also took courses with Hindemith in Berlin. He lectured in Basel (1933–39); also at Oxford and Cambridge Univs. In 1939 he settled in the U.S., becoming a naturalized American citizen in 1945. He taught at Case Western Reserve Univ. in Cleveland (1940–41). In 1941 he became a member of the faculty of the Univ. of Calif. at Berkeley where, a year before his untimely death, he was appointed chairman of its music dept. His numerous publications are distinguished by originality of historical and musical ideas coupled with precision of factual exposition; having mastered the English language, he was able to write brilliantly in British and American publications; he was also greatly esteemed as a teacher. Bukofzer ed. the works of Dunstable (Vol. VIII of Musica Britannica, 1953; 2nd ed., rev., 1970 by M. Bent, I. Bent, and B. Trowell).

WRITINGS: *Sumer Is Icumen In: A Revision* (Berkeley, 1944); *Music in the Baroque Era* (N.Y., 1947); *Studies in Medieval and Renaissance Music* (N.Y., 1950); *The Place of Musicology in American Institutions of Higher Learning* (N.Y., 1957); *Music of the Classic Period, 1750–1827* (Berkeley, 1958).

BIBL.: D. Boyden, "In Memoriam: M.F. B.," *Musical Quarterly* (July 1956).

Buller, John, English composer; b. London, Feb. 7, 1927. He studied music as a child, beginning formal composition lessons in 1959 with Anthony Milner in London. He served as composer-in-residence at the Univ. of Edinburgh (1975–76) and at Queens Univ. in Belfast (1985–86).

WORKS: *The Cave* for Flute, Clarinet, Trombone, Cello, and Tape (1970); *2 Night Pieces from Finnegans Wake* for Soprano, Flute, Clarinet, Piano, and Cello (1971); *Finnegans Floras* for 14 Voices, Hand Percussion, and Piano (1972); *Poor Jenny* for Flutes and Percussion (1973); *Le terrazze* for 14 Instruments and Tape (1974); *The Mime of Mick, Nick, and the Maggies* for Soprano, Tenor, Baritone, Chorus, Orch., and Speaker or Tape (1976; London, Feb. 6, 1978); *Proenca* for Mezzo-soprano, Electric Guitar, and Orch. (London, Aug. 6, 1977); *Sette spazi* for 2 Clarinets, Violin, Cello, and Piano (1978); *The Theatre of Memory* for Orch. (London, Sept. 7, 1981); *Kommos* for Voices and Electronics (St. Bartholomew's Festival, June 21, 1982); *Towards Aquarius* for 15 Players and Tape (London, Nov. 1, 1983); *A la fontana del vergier* for Countertenor, 2 Tenors, and Baritone (1984); *Of 3 Shakespeare Sonnets* for Mezzo-soprano, Flute, Clarinet, Harp, 2 Violins, Viola, and Cello (London, June 12, 1985); *Bakxai*, opera (1991–92); *Bacchae Metrics* for Orch. (1993).

Bullock, Sir Ernest, English organist and educator; b. Wigan, Sept. 15, 1890; d. Aylesbury, May 24, 1979. He studied organ with Bairstow in Leeds; also took courses at the Univ. of Durham (B.Mus., 1908; D.Mus., 1914). After serving as suborganist at Manchester Cathedral (1912–15), he was organist and choirmaster at Exeter Cathedral (1919–27). In 1928 he was named organist and Master of the Choristers at Westminster Abbey, and as such participated in several coronations. He became Gardiner Prof. of Music at the Univ. of Glasgow in 1941. He was then director of the Royal College of Music in London from 1952 until his retirement in 1960. He was knighted by King George VI in 1951.

Bumbry, Grace (Melzia Ann), greatly talented black American mezzo-soprano and soprano; b. St. Louis, Jan. 4, 1937. She attended Boston Univ. and Northwestern Univ., and pursued vocal training with Lehmann at the Music Academy of the West in Santa Barbara (1955–58) and with Bernac in Paris. With Martina Arroyo, she was co-winner of the Metropolitan Opera auditions in 1958. In 1960 she made a notably successful operatic debut as Amneris at the Paris Opéra. In 1961 she became the first black American singer to appear at the Bayreuth Festival when she sang Venus in *Tannhäuser*. In 1963 she made her Covent Garden debut in London as Eboli, and her Chicago Lyric Opera debut as Ulrica. In 1964 she sang Lady Macbeth at her first appearance at the Salzburg Festival. She made her Metropolitan Opera debut in N.Y. as Eboli on Oct. 7, 1965, and subsequently sang there regularly. From 1970 she concentrated on the soprano repertoire. Among her distinguished roles at the Metropolitan were Carmen (1967), Santuzza (1970), Tosca (1971), Salome (1973), Venus (1977), Leonora in *Il Trovatore* (1982), and Gershwin's Bess (1985). In 1990 she sang Berlioz's Cassandre at the opening of the Opéra de la Bastille in Paris. In 1995 she sang Cherubini's Medea in Athens. She also appeared as a soloist with major orchs.

Bunger, Richard Joseph, American pianist and composer; b. Allentown, Pa., June 1, 1942. He studied at Oberlin (Ohio) College Cons. of Music (B.Mus., 1964) and the Univ. of Ill. (M.Mus., 1965). In 1973 he was appointed to the faculty of Calif. State College, Dominguez Hills. He became absorbed in the modern techniques of composition, particularly in the new resources provided by the prepared piano; publ. an illustrated vol., *The Well-Prepared Piano* (1973), with a foreword by John Cage. He also evolved a comprehensive notational system called "Musiglyph," which incorporates standard musical notation and musical graphics indicating special instrumental techniques. He is the inventor of the "Bungerack," a music holder for the piano, particularly convenient for scores of large size.

Bunin, Revol, Russian composer; b. Moscow, April 6, 1924; d. there, July 4, 1976. He was a student at the Moscow Cons., graduating in 1945 in the class of Shostakovich; in 1947 he became an assistant to Shostakovich at the Leningrad Cons. A prolific composer, he wrote an opera, *Masquerade*; 8 syms.; 2 string quartets; other chamber music; and film scores.

Bunin, Vladimir, Russian composer; b. Skopin, Riazan district, July 24, 1908; d. Moscow, March 23, 1970. He studied at the Moscow Cons. with A. Alexandrov, graduating in 1938. His compositions, which followed the traditions of Russian classicism, include 2 syms. (1943, 1949); Violin Concerto (1953);

Piano Concerto (1965); *Poem about Lenin* for Orch. (1969); many piano pieces and songs.

Burg (real name, **Bartl**), **Robert,** German baritone; b. Prague, March 29, 1890; d. Dresden, Feb. 9, 1946. He studied with Hans Pokorny in Prague, where he made his operatic debut at the German Theatre (1915). After appearing in Augsburg (1915–16), he was a member of the Dresden Court (later State) Opera from 1916 to 1944; in addition to his Verdi roles there, he created the roles of Busoni's Doktor Faust (1925) and Hindemith's Cardillac (1926). He also sang at the Bayreuth Festivals (1933–42), where he was heard as Alberich, Klingsor, and Kothner, and made guest appearances in Munich, Berlin, Vienna, and other European cities.

Burganger, Judith, first-rank American pianist; b. Buffalo, March 17, 1939. She studied at the Staatliche Hochschule für Musik in Stuttgart (diploma, 1961; M.M., 1965); subsequently won 1st prize in Munich's International Piano Competition. She performed with major U.S. orchs., including the Cleveland Orch. and the Chicago Sym. She has also been praised for her ensemble performances and for her recitals. She held teaching positions at the Cleveland Inst. of Music, Carnegie-Mellon Univ., and Florida Atlantic Univ. (from 1980).

Burge, David (Russell), American pianist, teacher, and composer; b. Evanston, Ill., March 25, 1930. He studied at Northwestern Univ. (B.M., 1951; M.M., 1952) and at the Eastman School of Music in Rochester, N.Y. (D.M.A., 1956); then studied piano with Pietro Scarpini in Florence, Italy, on a Fulbright scholarship (1956–57). He made annual concert tours of the U.S. from 1959; from 1962 to 1972 he taught at the Univ. of Colo., in 1965 becoming the conductor of the Boulder Phil., a position he held until 1972, when he joined the faculty of the Eastman School of Music. He gave premiere performances of many works by American composers. His own compositions include *Sources II* for Violin, Cello, and Piano (1966) and *III* for Clarinet and Percussion (1967); *Aeolian Music* for Flute, Clarinet, Piano, Violin, Cello, and Tape (1968); *That no one knew* for Violin and Orch. (1969); and a number of piano pieces. He publ. *Twentieth-Century Piano Music* (N.Y., 1990).

Burgess, Anthony (real name, **John Anthony Burgess Wilson**), celebrated English novelist, critic, and composer; b. Manchester, Feb. 25, 1917; d. London, Nov. 22, 1993. He studied language and literature at the Univ. of Manchester (B.A., 1940); he also played piano in jazz combos and taught himself to compose by a close study of the Classical masters. He was active as a teacher in England and the Far East; later was writer-in-residence at the Univ. of North Carolina at Chapel Hill (1969–70), visiting prof. at Princeton Univ. and Columbia Univ. (1970), and distinguished prof. at City College of the City Univ. of N.Y. (1972–73). As a novelist, Burgess made a notable impression with his disturbing *A Clockwork Orange* (1962), which was followed by such novels as the *Napoleon Symphony* (1974) and his major literary achievement, *Earthly Powers* (1980). Among his other writings were *This Man and Music* (1982) and the autobiography, *Little Wilson and Big God* (1987). As a composer, he produced a respectable body of works notable for being refreshingly rhythmical and tonal, but not without quirky quartal harmonies and atonal diversions.

WORKS: OPERA: *Blooms of Dublin* (1981). **ORCH.:** Sym. (1937); *Sinfonietta* for Jazz Combo (1941); *Gibraltar*, symphonic poem (1944); Cello Concerto (1944); *Song of a Northern City* for Piano and Orch. (1947); *Ascent of F6* for Dance Band (1947); *The Adding Machine* for Dance Band (1949); *Partita* for Strings (1951); *Ludus Multitonalis* for Recorder Consort (1951); Concertino for Piano and Percussion (1951); *Sinfoni Melayu* (1956); Concerto for Flute and Strings (1960); *Passacaglia* (1961); Sym. in C (1975); Piano Concerto (1976); *A Glasgow Overture* (1985); *Mr. Burgess's Almanac* (1988); *Petite Symphonie pour Strasbourg* (1988); *Concerto Grosso* for 4 Guitars and Orch. (1988); *Marche pour une Révolution* (1989). **CHAMBER:** Cello Sonata (1944); *Cyrano de Bergerac* for Flute, Trumpet, Cello, Percussion, and Keyboard (1970); 2 guitar quartets (1984, 1987). **PIANO:** 2 sonatas (1946, 1951). **VOCAL:** *The Brides of Enderby* for Voice, Flute, Oboe, Cello, and Piano (1976); *Man Who Has Come Through* for Voice, Flute, Oboe, Cello, and Piano (1984); *La Piaggia del Pineto* for Voice and Piano (1988).

Burgess, Sally, South African-born English mezzo-soprano; b. Durban, Oct. 9, 1953. She was a student of Alan at the Royal College of Music in London; later pursued private training with Studholme, Salaman, and Veasey. In 1976 she began her career as a soprano with her formal debut as a soloist in the Brahms *Requiem* in London. In 1977 she made her first appearance at the English National Opera there as Bertha in *Euryanthe*, returning there in subsequent years to sing such roles as Zerlina, Cherubino, Micaëla, Massenet's Charlotte, Mimi, and Strauss's Composer. In 1978 she made her Wigmore Hall Recital debut in London, and thereafter became well known via her many concert engagements. In 1983 she made her debut as a mezzo-soprano at London's Covent Garden as Siebel; also appeared that year at Glyndebourne as Smeraldina in Prokofiev's *The Love for 3 Oranges.* In 1986 she sang Carmen at the English National Opera, and also appeared with Opera North. She sang Fricka in *Die Walküre* at Glasgow's Scottish Opera in 1991, returning there in 1992 as Annius in *La Clemenza di Tito.*

Burghauser, Jarmil, distinguished Czech composer, conductor, and musicologist; b. Písek, Oct. 21, 1921. After training in composition with Křička (1933–37) and Jeremiáš (1937–40), he pursued studies in conducting at the Prague Cons. with Doležil and Dědeček (graduated, 1944), and then at its master school with Talich (graduated, 1946); subsequently he took courses in musicology and psychology at the Charles Univ. in Prague, but quit his studies in protest against the Communist coup in 1948; it was not until 1991 that he presented his diss. and was awarded his Ph.D. He served as chorus master and conductor at the National Theater in Prague from 1946 to 1950, and thereafter devoted himself principally to composition and scholarship. Following the Soviet-bloc invasion of his homeland in 1968 and the restoration of hard-line Communist rule, he became suspect. Although he had done valuable work on the critical edition of Dvořák's works, his name was not acknowledged in the new vols. In order to get his music before the public, he took the pseudonym Michal Hájků. From 1978 to 1989 to was choirmaster at St. Margaret's church in Prague. Following the overthrow of the Communist regime by the "Velvet Revolution" in 1989, Burghauser became a leading figure in the restoration of the musical life of his country by serving as chairman of the Guild of Composers and as a member of the rehabilitation committee of the Ministry of Culture. In addition to his valuable work on the critical edition of Dvořák's compositions, he also ed. works for the critical editions of the music of Janáček, Smetana, and Fibich. In his own compositions, he developed a style which he described as harmonic serialism. Under his pseudonym, he composed an interesting series of works in the style of earlier periods which he called "Storica apocrifa della musica Boema."

WORKS: DRAMATIC: *Lakomec* (The Miser), opera (1949; Liberec, May 20, 1950); *Karolinka a lhář* (Caroline and the Liar), opera (1950–53; Olomouc, March 13, 1955); *Honza a čert* (Honza and the Devil), ballet (Ostrava, Nov. 23, 1954; rev. 1960); *Sluha dvou pánů* (Servant of 2 Masters), ballet (1957; Prague, May 9, 1958); *Most* (The Bridge), anti-opera (1963–64; Prague, March 31, 1967); *Tristam a Izalda*, ballet (1969). **ORCH.:** Syms.: No. 1 (1933; rev. 1974); No. 2 (1935; rev. 1979); No. 3 (1936; rev. 1959); *Indiánská symfonie* (1974); Sinfonia in F (1980); *Jarní rondo* (Spring rondo) for Small Orch. (1937; rev. 1970); Suite for Chamber Orch. (1939; rev. 1977); Concerto for Wind Quintet and Strings (1942; Prague, Feb. 12, 1948); *Toccata* for Small Orch. (1947); *Symphonic Variations on We Greet the Spring* (1952); Symphonic Suite (1955); *Sedm reliéfů* (7 Reliefs; 1962; Prague, Feb. 19, 1963); *Cesty* (Ways) for Strings,

Percussion, and Bowed Instruments (1964; Prague, Feb. 21, 1965); *Barvy v čase* (Colors in Time) for Small Orch. (Wexford, Ireland, Oct. 25, 1967); *Strom života* (The Tree of Life; 1968; Graz, Oct. 22, 1969); *Rožmberská suita* (Rožmberk Suite) for Small Orch. (1972); Concerto for Guitar and Strings (1978); *Ciaconna per il fine d'un tempo* for Piano and Orch. (1982). **CHAMBER:** *Romance* for Violin and Piano (1933; rev. 1984); 5 trios for 2 Oboes and Bassoon (1933–83); 5 string quartets (1934, rev. 1953; 1937, rev. 1953; 1941; 1944; 1944–51); 2 suites for 6 Clarinets (1938, 1970); 2 trios for Flute, Viola, and Guitar (1938, rev. 1967; 1962); 2 piano trios (1938, rev. 1982; 1940); Nonet (1942); *Možnosti* (Possibilities) for Clarinet, Cimbalom, and Percussion (1965); *10 Sketches* for Flute (1965); *Patero zamyšlení* (5 Reflections) for Violin and Guitar (1966); *Pět barevných střepin* (5 Colored Splinters) for Harp (1966); Violin Sonata, *Neveselé vyprávění* (Cheerless Tale; 1970); *Stanze dell'ansietà e speranza* for Flute, Oboe, Violin, Viola, Cello, and Harpsichord (1971); *Soumraky a svítání* (Dusks and Dawns) for Bass Clarinet and Piano (1971); *Plochy a čáry* (Areas and Lines) for Violin, Guitar, and Cello (1972); *Jitřní hudba* (Morning Music) for Flute and Guitar (1974); *Partita* for 2 Flutes, Guitar, and Cello (1976); *Lobkovitz Trio* for Flute, Guitar, and Cello (1977); *Vchynice Trio* for Flute, Violin, and Cello (1978); *Parthia czeská* for Recorder, Lute, and Viola da Gamba (1978); *Coree regales* for Early Instruments (1978); *Sonata da chiesa* for Flute, Oboe, Violin, Viola, Cello, and Harpsichord (1979); String Trio (1982); *Alejí času* (By the Alley of Time) for Trumpet, Horn, and Trombone (1982); *Pianot, rabbia e conforto* for Cello and Piano (1982); *Tre ricercari* for 9 Instruments (1983); Viola Sonata (1985); *Recitativo e terzetto* for Flute, Violin, and Cello (1989); *Tesknice* (Nostalgia) *II* for Violin and Cimbalom (1989); numerous works for 1 or 2 Guitars. **VOCAL:** *Utrpení a vzkříšení* (Suffering and Resurrection), vocal sym. (1937–46; Prague, May 26, 1946); *Věčná oblaka* (Eternal Clouds), cantata (1942); *Tajemný trubač* (The Mystic Trumpeter), cantata after Walt Whitman (1944); *Česká* (Czech), cantata (1952); *Země zamyšlená* (Thoughtful Earth), cantata (1966; Prague, March 24, 1968); *Pašije podle Lukáše* (St. Luke Passion) for Soloists and Chorus (1977); *Proprium de Nativiatate* for Soloists, Chorus, and Orch. (1978); *Missa brevis pastoralis* for Soloists, Chorus, and Orch. (1980); *V zemi české* (In the Czech Country) for Reciters, Chorus, and Orch. (1982); choruses; song cycles.

WRITINGS (all publ. in Prague): *Orchestrace Dvořákových Slonvanských tanců* (Orchestration of Dvořák's Slavonic Dances; 1959); *Antonín Dvořák: Tematický katalog, bibliografie, přehled života a díla* (Antonín Dvořák: Thematic Catalog, Bibliography, Survey of Life and Work; 1960); *Nejen pomníky* (Not Monuments Only; 1966); *Antonín Dvořák* (1966); with A. Špelda, *Akustické základy orchestrace* (Acoustic Basis of Orchestration; 1967; Ger. tr., 1971); completion of J. Rychlik's *Moderni instrumentace* (Modern Instrumentation; 1968); *Česká interpretační tradice* (Czech Tradition of Interpretation; 1982).

Burgin, Richard, Polish-born American violinist, conductor, and teacher; b. Warsaw, Oct. 11, 1892; d. Gulfport, Fla., April 29, 1981. He made his debut as soloist with the Warsaw Phil. when he was 11; after touring the U.S. as a soloist in 1907, he studied with Auer at the St. Petersburg Cons. (1908–12). He was concertmaster of the Helsinki Sym. Orch. (1912–15) and the Christiania Phil. (1916–19). From 1920 to 1962 he was concertmaster of the Boston Sym. Orch.; was made its assistant conductor in 1927 and assoc. conductor in 1943. He also was head of the string dept. of the New England Cons. of Music in Boston, a teacher of violin at Boston Univ., and teacher of conducting at the Berkshire Music Center in Tanglewood. From 1963 to 1972 he was prof. of violin at Florida State Univ. in Tallahassee; also played in the Florestan Quartet. Burgin was particularly esteemed as a teacher. In 1940 he married **Ruth Posselt**.

Burgon, Geoffrey (Alan), English composer; b. Hambledon, July 15, 1941. He was a student of Peter Wishart (composition) and Bernard Brown (trumpet) at the Guildhall School of Music in London. After playing trumpet in various orchs., jazz ensembles, and theater orchs. (1964–71), he devoted himself to composing and to conducting for films and television. His scores for the television series *Tinker, Tailor, Soldier, Spy* (1979) and *Brideshead Revisited* (1981) established his reputation. He has demonstrated special talent in composing works for vocal forces.

WORKS: DRAMATIC: OPERA: *Hard Times* (1991). **MUSIC THEATER:** *Epitaph to Sir Walter Raleigh* (1968; London, Feb. 8, 1969); *Joan of Arc* (1970); *The Fall of Lucifer* (1977); *Mirandola* (1980–81); *Orpheus* (Wells, July 17, 1982). **BALLETS:** *The Golden Fish* (1964); *Ophelia* (1964); *The Calm* (1974); *Running Figures/Goldberg's Dream* (Leeds, March 25, 1975); *Step at a Time* (London, Nov. 4, 1976); *Persephone* (1979); *Lamentations and Praises* (Jerusalem, Aug. 7, 1979); *Mass* (1984; London, Sept. 16, 1985); *The Trial of Prometheus* (1988); film and television scores. **ORCH.:** Concerto for Strings (1963; Bath, June 6, 1977); *5 Pieces* for Strings (1967); *Gendling* (London, July 11, 1968); *Alleluia Nativitas* (London, Feb. 17, 1970); *Cantus Alleluia* (1973; London, April 10, 1974); *May Day Prelude* (London, May 1, 1977); *Brideshead Variations* (London, March 21, 1982; also for Brass or Concert Band); Trumpet Concerto (1993); *The Turning World* for Trumpet, Percussion, and Strings (1993). **CHAMBER:** *Fanfares and Variants* for 2 Trumpets and 2 Trombones (1969); *Gloria* for 6 Instruments (1973); *3 Nocturnes* for Harp (1974); *4 Guitars* (1977); *4 Horns* (1977); Oboe Quartet (1980); *Sanctus Variations* for 2 Trumpets and Organ (1980); *Chamber Dances* (1981–82); *Little Missenden Variations* for Clarinet, English Horn, Horn, and Bassoon (1984); *Fanfare* for Horns, Trumpets, Trombones, and Tuba (1985). **VOCAL:** *Cantata on Medieval Latin Texts* for Countertenor, Flute, Oboe, and Bassoon (1964); *Acquainted with Night* for Countertenor, Strings, Harp, and Percussion (1965); *Think on Dredful Domesday* for Voices and Orch. (1969); *Magnificat* for Voices and Orch. (1970); *The Golden Eternity* for Voices and Orch. (1970); *This Endris Night* for Tenor, Women's Voices, and Brass (1972); *Canciones del Alma* for 2 Countertenors and 13 Solo Strings (1975); *Requiem* for Soprano, Countertenor, Tenor, Chorus, and Orch. (Hereford, Aug. 26, 1976); *Veni Spiritus* for Soprano, Baritone, Chorus, and Orch. (1978–79); *Magnificat and Nunc Dimittis* for 2 Sopranos, Trumpet, Organ, and Strings (1979); *Hymn to St. Thomas of Hereford* for Chorus and Orch. (1981; Hereford, Aug. 22, 1982); *The World Again* for Soprano and Orch. (1982–83; London, Oct. 9, 1984); *Revelations* for Soprano, Tenor, Baritone, Chorus, and Orch. (1984; London, April 13, 1985); *Title Divine* for Soprano and Orch. (1986; London, April 22, 1987); *A Vision* for Tenor and String Orch. (1991); many other choral pieces and songs.

Burgstaller, Alois, German tenor; b. Holzkirchen, Sept. 21, 1871; d. Gmund, April 19, 1945. He was trained as a watchmaker, and also sang; encouraged by Cosima Wagner, he made a serious study of singing, and performed the roles of Siegfried, Siegmund, Erik, and Parsifal at the Bayreuth Festivals (1896–1902). He made his American debut at the Metropolitan Opera in N.Y. as Siegmund in *Die Walküre* on Feb. 12, 1903; remained on its roster until his final appearance, again as Siegmund, on Jan. 14, 1909. He also sang the title role in the first staged American performance of *Parsifal*, in N.Y., on Dec. 24, 1903, in violation of the German copyright; as a result, he was permanently banned from Bayreuth. In 1910 he returned to Germany.

Burian, Emil František, Czech composer and stage director, nephew of **Karl Burian**; b. Pilsen, June 11, 1904; d. Prague, Aug. 9, 1959. His father was a baritone and his mother a singing teacher. He received his training at the Prague Cons., where he attended Foerster's master class in composition (graduated, 1927). Even before graduating, he was active in avant-garde quarters in Prague as a stage director, dramatist, actor, and musician. With his mother, he presented concerts of new music from 1920. In 1924 he organized Přítomnost, a society for contemporary music. In 1927 he organized the Voice Band, which sang according to prescribed rhythm but without definite pitch; it attracted considerable attention at the Sienna ISCM Festival on Sept. 12, 1928. Betwen 1929 and 1932 he was active in Brno and Oloumoc. In 1933 he founded his own D 34 theater in Prague. During the Nazi occupation, Burian's theater was shut down and he was placed in a concentration camp. After his liberation, he was a director in Brno (1945–46). In 1946 he returned to Prague and served that year as director of the Karlín musical theater. His long-standing commitment to the political Left led to his being made a deputy in the post-World War II National Assembly. As a composer, he followed an eclectic path, finding inspiration in Czech folk art, jazz, the music of Les Six, and Dada. Between the 2 World Wars, he was one of the leading figures in the Czech avant-garde. After World War II and the installation of the Communist regime, he embraced the tenets of socialist realism. His writings, all publ. in Prague, include *O moderní ruské hudbě* (1926); *Polydynamika* (1926); *Jazz* (1928); *Památník bratří Burianů* (Almanac of the Burian Brothers; 1929); *Pražská dramaturgie* (1938); *Emil Burian* (1947); *Karel Burian* (1948); *Divadlo za našich dnů* (The Theater of Our Days; 1962).

WORKS: DRAMATIC: OPERAS: *Alladine a Palomid* (1923; rev. version, Prague, Oct. 14, 1959); *Před slunce východem* (Before Sunrise; Prague, Nov. 24, 1925); *Bubu z Montparnassu* (Bubu from Montparnasse; (1927); *Mastičkář* (The Quack; Prague, May 23, 1928; rev. by R. Krátký, 1955); *Milenci z kiosku* (The Lovers from the Market Stall; Prague, Nov. 13, 1935); *Maryša* (Brno, April 16, 1940); *Opera z pouti* (Country Fair Scenes; Prague, Jan. 28, 1956); *Račte odpusdit* (Please Forgive Me; Prague, Oct. 13, 1956). Also ballets and film scores. **ORCH.:** *Suita poetica* (5 separate movements: 1925, 1947, 1950, 1951, 1953); Suite for Oboe and Strings (1928); *Reminiscence*, symphonic suite (1929–36); 2 syms. (*Siréna*, 1947; 1948); Accordion Concerto (1949); *Overture to Socialism* (1950). **CHAMBER:** Trio for Flute, Viola, and Cello (1924); *From Youth*, string sextet (1924); Duo for Violin and Cello (1925); 8 string quartets (1927, 1929, 1940, 1947, 1947, 1948, 1949, 1951); *Variations* for Wind Quintet (1928); *Of Warm Nights*, suite for Violin and Piano (1928); *Passacaglia* for Violin and Viola (1929); *4 Pieces* for Wind Quintet (1929); Wind Quintet (1930); Suite for Cello and Piano (1935); *Sonata romantica* for Violin and Piano (1938); *Lost Serenade* for Flute and Piano (1940); Duo for Violin and Piano (1946); *Fantasie* for Violin and Piano (1954). **PIANO:** *American Suite* for 2 Pianos (1926); Sonata (1927); *Echoes of Czech Dances* (1953); Sonatina (1954). **VOCAL:** *Cocktails*, song cycle for Voice and Jazz Band (1926); *Requiem* for Voice Band and Jazz Band (1927); *May*, cantata for Voice Band, Harp, 2 Pianos, and Timpani (1936); *Children's Songs*, song cycle for Voice and Chamber Orch. (1937).

BIBL.: B. Srba, *Poetické divadlo E.F. B.* (The Poetic Theater of E.F. B.; Prague, 1971); I. Kladiva, *E.F. B.* (Prague, 1982).

Burian, Karl (Karel), noted Czech tenor, uncle of **Emil František Burian**; b. Rusínov, near Rakovník, Jan. 12, 1870; d. Senomaty, Sept. 25, 1924. He studied with Franz Piwoda in Prague and Felix von Kraus in Munich. On March 28, 1891, he made his operatic debut as Jeník in *The Bartered Bride* in Brünn; then sang in Reval (1892–94), Aachen (1894–95), Cologne (1895–96), Hannover (1897–98), and Hamburg (1898–1902). From 1902 to 1911 he was a principal member of the Dresden Court Opera, where he created the role of Herod in Strauss's *Salome* (Dec. 9, 1905). On Nov. 30, 1906, he made his Metropolitan Opera debut in N.Y. as Tannhäuser, remaining on its roster until 1913; during this period, he used the name Carl Burrian. He also sang at the Bayreuth Festivals, where he was greatly admired. In later years, he appeared at the Vienna Court Opera, in Budapest, and in Prague. He was famous for his portrayal of Tristan; among his other distinguished roles were Parsifal, Siegmund, and both Siegfrieds.

Burk, John N(aglee), American writer on music; b. San Jose, Calif., Aug. 28, 1891; d. Boston, Sept. 6, 1967. He graduated from Harvard Univ. (A.B., 1916). In 1934 he succeeded Philip Hale as program annotator of the Boston Sym. Orch. He ed. Hale's Boston Sym. program notes (1935) and annotated *Letters of Richard Wagner*, from the Burrell Collection (N.Y., 1950). He was the author of the books *Clara Schumann, A Romantic Biography* (N.Y., 1940), *The Life and Works of Beethoven* (N.Y., 1943), and *Mozart and His Music* (N.Y., 1959).

Burkhard, Paul, Swiss conductor and composer; b. Zürich, Dec. 21, 1911; d. Zell, Sept. 6, 1977. He was trained at the Zürich Cons. After working at the Bern City Theater (1932–34), he was resident composer at the Zürich Theater (1939–44). From 1944 to 1957 he conducted the Zürich Radio Orch. As a composer, he was successful mainly with light theater pieces. His *Der schwarze Hecht* (Zürich, April 1, 1939) was partially reworked by Erik Charell as *Feuerwerk* (Munich, May 16, 1950), and became internationally known via its song, *O, mein Papa.* Among his other theater pieces were *Hopsa* (Zürich, Nov. 30, 1935; rev. version, Wiesbaden, Oct. 12, 1957), *Dreimal Georges* (Zürich, Oct. 3, 1936), *Die Frauen von Coraya* or *Der Paradies der Frauen* (Stettin, Feb. 19, 1938), *Casanova in der Schweiz* (Zürich, 1942), *Tic-Tac* (1942), *Die Pariserin* (1946; Zürich, Dec. 31, 1957), *Die kleine Niederdorfoper* (Zürich, Dec. 31, 1951), *Bunbury* (1963; Basel, Oct. 7, 1965), *Die Schneekönigin* (Zürich, 1964) and *Regenbogen* (Basel, Nov. 30, 1977). He also wrote various works for young people, including the Christmas opera *Ein Stern geht auf aus Jakob* (Hamburg, Dec. 6, 1970) and religious plays.

BIBL.: P. Flury and P. Kaufmann, *O mein Papa . . . P. B.: Leben und Werk* (Zürich, 1979).

Burkhard, Willy, significant Swiss composer and pedagogue; b. Leubringen bei Biel, April 17, 1900; d. Zürich, June 18, 1955. After graduating from the Muristalden teachers's training college, he took up music studies with E. Graf in Bern; he then pursued training with Karg-Elert and Teichmüller in Leipzig (1921), Courvoisier in Munich (1922–23), and d'Ollone in Paris (1923–24). He taught theory at the Bern Cons. (1928–33), and later theory and composition at the Zürich Cons. (1942–55). His music was neo-Classical in form and strongly polyphonic; his astringent linear idiom was tempered by a strong sense of modal counterpoint. He made an especially important contribution to church music.

WORKS: OPERA: *Die Schwarze Spinne* (1947–48; Zürich, May 28, 1949; rev. 1954). **ORCH.:** 2 violin concertos: No. 1 (1925) and No. 2 (1943; Zürich, Jan. 26, 1946); 2 syms. (1926–28; Sym. in 1 Movement, 1944); *Ulenspiegel Variations* (1932); *Fantasy* for Strings (1934); *Small Serenade* for Strings (1935); Concerto for Strings (1937); *Toccata* for Strings (1939); *Laupen-Suite* (1940); Concertino for Cello and Strings (1940); Organ Concerto (1945); *Hymne* for Organ and Orch. (1945); *Concertante Suite* (1946); *Piccola sinfonia giocosa* for Small Orch. (1949); *Fantasia mattutina* (1949); *Toccata* for 4 Winds, Percussion, and Strings (Zürich, Dec. 7, 1951); *Sonata da camera* for Strings and Percussion (1952); Viola Concerto (1953); Concertino for 2 Flutes, Harpsichord, and Strings (1954). **CHAMBER:** String Trio (1926); Piano Trio (1936); Violin Sonatina (1936); Suite for 2 Violins (1937); Sonata for Solo Viola (1939); String Quartet in 1 Movement (1943); *Serenade* for 8 Instruments (1945); *Romance* for Horn and Piano (1945); Violin Sonata (1946); Cello Sonata (1952); *Serenade* for Flute and Clarinet (1953); Suite for Flute (1954–55). **KEYBOARD: PIANO:** Sonata (1942); *6 Preludes* (1954–55). **ORGAN:** *Fantasie* (1931); *Choral-Triptychon* (1953). **VOCAL: ORATORIOS:** *Das Gesicht Jesajas* (1933–35; Basel, Feb. 18, 1936); *Das Jahr* (1940–41; Basel, Feb. 19, 1942). **CANTATAS:** *Biblische Kantate* (1923); *Till Ulenspiegel* (1929); *Vorfrühling* (1930); *Spruchkantate* (1933); *Genug ist nicht genug* (1938–39; Basel, June 11, 1940); *Lob der Musik* (1939); *Cantate Domino* (1940); *Heimatliche Kantate* (1940); *Psalmen-Kantate* (1952); various other cantatas. **OTHER:** *Te Deum* for Chorus, Trumpet, Trombone, Kettledrum, and Organ (1931); *Das ewige Brausen* for Bass and Chamber Orch. (1936); *Psalm 93* for Chorus and Organ (1937); *Kreuzvolk der Schweiz* for Chorus and Organ (1941); *Magnificat* for Soprano and Strings (1942); *Cantique de notre terre* for Soloists, Chorus, and Orch. (1943); *Mass* for Soprano, Bass,

Chorus, and Orch. (Zürich, June 28, 1951); *Psalm 148* for Chorus and Instruments (1954).

BIBL.: H. Zurlinden, *W. B.* (Erlenbach, 1956); E. Mohr, *W. B.: Leben und Werk* (Zürich, 1957); S. Burkhard and F. Indermühle, *W. B. (17. April 1900–18. Juni 1955) Werkverzeichnis* (Liebefeld, 1968).

Burlas, Ladislav, Slovak composer; b. Trnava, April 3, 1927. He studied general music subjects at the Univ. of Bratislava (1946–51) and composition with A. Moyzes at the Bratislava Cons. and the Academy of Music, graduating in 1955; then taught theory at Comenius Univ. in Bratislava. He publ. monographs on J.L. Bella (Bratislava, 1953) and A. Moyzes (Bratislava, 1956).

WORKS: ORCH.: *Symphonic Triptych* (1957); *Epitaph* (1958); *Bagatelles* for Strings (1960); *Planctus* for Strings (1968); Concertino for Percussion and Winds (1971). **CHAMBER:** *The Singing Heart,* string sextet (1960); Sonata for Solo Violin (1968); *Music* for String Quartet (1968–69); String Quartet No. 2 (1973). **VOCAL:** Cantatas; choruses; songs.

Burleigh, Cecil, American composer, violinist, and teacher; b. Wyoming, N.Y., April 17, 1885; d. Madison, Wis., July 28, 1980. He studied violin and theory as a child; after training with Anton Witek (violin) and Hugo Leichtentritt (composition) at the Klindworth-Scharwenka Cons. in Berlin (1903–05), he studied with Émile Sauret (violin) and Felix Borowski (composition) at the Chicago Musical College (1905–07). From 1907 to 1909 he toured as a soloist with orchs. and as a recitalist in North America. He taught violin at the Western Inst. of Music and Drama in Denver (1909–11), violin and theory at Morningside College in Sioux City, Iowa (1911–14), and at Montana State Univ. in Missoula. In 1919 he went to N.Y. to study violin with Auer, composition with Ernest Bloch, and orchestrtion with Rothwell, concurrently pursuing his career as a violinist. He taught violin, theory, and composition at the Univ. of Wis. in Madison from 1921 to 1955.

WORKS: ORCH.: 3 violin concertos: No. 1 (1912), No. 2, *Indian* (1918; Cleveland, March 13, 1921), and No. 3 (1927); *Mountain Pictures* (1917–19); *Evangeline* (1918); *The Village Dance* (1921; based on a piano piece); *2 Sketches from the Orient* for Band (1927; based on a piano piece); *Leaders of Men* (1943); 3 syms.: *Creation, Prophecy,* and *Revelation* (c.1944; Madison, Wis., May 1, 1955); *From the Muses* for Small Orch. (1945). **CHAMBER:** *4 Rocky Mountain Sketches* for Violin and Piano (1914); *Scherzando fantastique* for Violin and Piano (1921); 2 violin sonatas (*The Ascension,* 1914; *From the Life of St. Paul,* 1926); *6 Nature Studies* for Violin and Piano (1915); *4 Prairie Sketches* for Violin and Piano (1916); *Hymn to the Ancients* for Piano Quintet (1940); *2 Essays* for String Quartet, *Illusion* and *Transition* (1945); piano pieces. **VOCAL:** About 65 songs.

BIBL.: J. Howard, *C. B.* (N.Y., 1929).

Burleigh, Harry Thacker, black American baritone, composer, and arranger; b. Erie, Pa., Dec. 2, 1866; d. Stamford, Conn., Sept. 12, 1949. He studied at the National Cons. in N.Y. In 1894 he became baritone soloist at St. George's Church in N.Y.; retired in 1946. He gained wide popularity for his arrangements of *Heav'n, Heav'n, Deep River,* and *Go Down Moses.* On May 16, 1917, the National Assn. for the Advancement of Colored People awarded him the Spingarn Medal for highest achievement by an American citizen of African descent during the year 1916.

WORKS: *6 Plantation Melodies* for Violin and Piano (1901); *Southland Sketches* for Violin and Piano; *From the Southland* for Piano; *Jubilee Songs* of the United States of America (1916); *Old Songs Hymnal* (1929).

BIBL.: "In Retrospect . . . H.T. B. (1866–1949)," *Black Perspective in Music* (Sept. 1974); A. Simpson, *Hard Trials: The Life and Music of H.T. B.* (Metuchen, N.J., 1990).

Burmeister, Richard, German composer, pianist, and teacher; b. Hamburg, Dec. 7, 1860; d. Berlin, Feb. 19, 1944. He studied with Liszt in Weimar, Rome, and Budapest, accompanying him on his travels; later taught at the Hamburg Cons., the Peabody Inst. in Baltimore, the Dresden Cons. (1903–06), and the Klindworth-Scharwenka Cons. in Berlin (1907–25). Burmeister also made extensive concert tours of Europe and the U.S. His works include the symphonic fantasy *Die Jagd nach dem Glück;* Piano Concerto; *Romanza* for Violin and Orch.; *The Sisters* for Alto and Orch. and other vocal pieces; piano music. He also rescored Chopin's F-minor Concerto, Liszt's *Mephisto Waltz* and 5th Rhapsody (with new orch. accompaniment), and Weber's *Konzertstück* for Piano and Orch.

Burrian, Carl. See **Burian, Karl.**

Burritt, Lloyd (Edmund), Canadian composer; b. Vancouver, June 7, 1940. He was a student of Coulthard (composition) and Hultberg (electronic music) at the Univ. of British Columbia (B.M., 1963; M.M., 1968); he also took courses in composition with Jacob and Howells at the Royal College of Music in London (1963–65) and in conducting with Schuller, Leinsdorf, Bernstein, and Dee Hiatt at the Berkshire Music Center in Tanglewood (summers, 1965–66). His works follow an expressionist path.

WORKS: MUSIC THEATER AND MULTIMEDIA: *Acid Mass* for Film, Tape, and Dancers (1969); *Electric Soul,* tape piece for Dancers (1970); *Electric Chair* for Actress, Alto Saxophone, and Tape (1971); *Altar of the Sun* for Actors, Singers, Dancers, Chorus, Flute, Horn, Percussion, and Piano (North Vancouver, April 3, 1983; concert version as *Francis of Assisi Suite*); *The Hobbit* for Actors, Singers, Dancers, Chorus, Flute, Horn, Percussion, and Piano (North Vancouver, Dec. 19, 1984; concert version as *The Hobbit Suite*). **ORCH.:** Sym. (1964); *Assassinations* for Orch. and Tape (Vancouver, Dec. 1, 1968); *Electric Tongue* for Orch. and Tape (Vancouver, May 30, 1969); *Cicada* for Orch. and Tape (Calgary, April 5, 1970; also for Concert Band); *New York* for Orch. and Tape (1970); *Overdose* for Orch. and Tape (Ottawa, Feb. 15, 1971); *Spectrum* for Strings, Piano, and Tape (Vancouver, Aug. 13, 1972); *Symphonic Overture* (1980). **CHAMBER:** Piano Sonatina (1961); Violin Sonata (1963); *Icon* for Organ and Tape (1970); *Memo to RCCO* [Royal College of Canadian Organists] for Organ and Tape (1972); *Memo to NFBC* [National Film Board of Canada] for Keyboard and Tape (1972). **VOCAL:** *3 Autumn Songs* for Mezzo-soprano and Orch. (1965; Vancouver, Feb. 27, 1968; also for Mezzo-soprano and Piano); *Landscapes* for Soprano, Alto, and Tape (1967; also as *Landscapes 3* for Soprano, Violin, and Tape); *The Hollow Men* for Girl and Boy Speakers, Soprano, Alto, Tenor, Bass, Semi-Chorus, Chorus, 13 Instrumentalists, and Tape (Vancouver, April 5, 1968); *Once Again . . . Pop!* for Non-singing Chorus and Tape (1969); *4 Winter Haiku* for Baritone and Tape (1969); *Rocky Mountain Grasshopper* for Chorus, Concert Band, and Tape (North Vancouver, May 27, 1971); *David* for Boy Soprano, Tenor, Baritone, Children's Voices, Chorus, Orch., and Tape (Vancouver, Nov. 5, 1977); *Rise of the Phoenix* for Voice or Voices and Instruments (1979); *Song for Marshall McLuhan* for Bass-baritone, Chorus, and Orch. (Vancouver, April 30, 1986); *Crystal Earth* for Soprano, Chorus, and Concert Band (1987; North Vancouver, Oct. 24, 1988).

Burrowes, Norma (Elizabeth), Welsh soprano; b. Bangor, April 24, 1944. She studied at the Queen's Univ. in Belfast and with Flora Nielsen and Rupert Bruce-Lockhart at the Royal Academy of Music in London. In 1970 she made her professional operatic debut as Zerlina with the Glyndebourne Touring Opera Co., and that same year she made her first appearance at London's Covent Garden as Fiakermilli in *Arabella.* From 1971 she sang at the Sadler's Wells (later the English National) Opera in London, and also appeared at the Salzburg, Glyndebourne, Aix-en-Provence, and other festivals. On Oct. 12, 1979, she made her Metropolitan Opera debut in N.Y. as Blondchen. She also toured widely as a concert singer. In 1982 she retired from the operatic stage. From 1969 to 1980 she was married to **Steuart Bedford**.

Burrows, (James) Stuart, Welsh tenor; b. Pontypridd, Feb. 7, 1933. He was educated at Trinity College, Carmarthen. After winning a prize at the National Eisteddfod of Wales in 1959, he appeared as a concert singer. In 1963 he made his operatic debut as Ismaele in *Nabucco* at the Welsh National Opera in Cardiff. In 1967 he made his first appearance at London's Covent Garden as Beppe, and subsequently sang there regularly. He made his U.S. debut as Tamino at the San Francisco Opera that same year. In 1970 he sang for the first time at the Vienna State Opera and the Salzburg Festival. On April 13, 1971, he made his Metropolitan Opera debut in N.Y. as Ottavio, and continued to make occasional appearances there until 1982. He also toured extensively as a concert artist. Among his other esteemed roles were Faust, Alfredo, Belmonte, Lensky, Ernesto, and Rodolfo.

Burt, Francis, English composer and teacher; b. London, April 28, 1926. He studied with Ferguson and Berkeley at the Royal Academy of Music in London (1948–51), and then with Blacher in Berlin (1951–54). After winning the Mendelssohn Scholarship in 1954, he completed his studies in Rome (1954–55). In 1956 he settled in Vienna, where he was a prof. of composition at the Hochschule für Musik and Darstellende Kunst from 1973 to 1993. In 1973 he received the Körner Prize. He was awarded the Würdigungspreis for music in 1978 and in 1981 he received the music prize of the City of Vienna. He was awarded the Great Silver Medal of Honor in 1992 for services to the Republic of Austria.

WORKS: DRAMATIC: OPERAS: *Volpone oder Der Fuchs* (1952–58; Stuttgart, June 2, 1960; rev. 1960–61); *Barnstable oder Jemand auf dem Dachboden* (1967–69; Kassel, Nov. 30, 1969). **BALLET:** *Der Golem* (1959–63; Hannover, Jan. 31, 1965). **ORCH.:** *Jamben* (1953; Baden-Baden, March 2, 1955); *Espressione Orchestrale* (1958–59; Vienna, Dec. 18, 1959); *Fantasmagoria* (London, Aug. 23, 1963); *Morgana* (1983–86; Vienna, April 16, 1986). **CHAMBER:** 2 string quartets (1951–52; 1992–93); *Serenata Notturna* for Oboe, Clarinet, and Bassoon (1952); Duo for Clarinet and Piano (1954); *For William* for 9 Players (1988); *Echoes* for 9 Players (1988–89; Vienna, March 1, 1989); *Hommage à Jean-Henri Fabre* for 5 Players (1993–94). **PIANO:** *Musik* for 2 Pianos (1953). **VOCAL:** *2 Songs of David* for Chorus (1951); *Hute* and *7 Lieder nach Gedichten von Carl Sandburg* for Medium Voice and Piano (1952); *The Skull,* cantata for Tenor and Piano (1953–54; also for Tenor and Orch., 1955); *Bavarian Gentians* for Vocal Quartet and Piano (1956); *Unter der Blanken Hacke des Monds* for Baritone and Orch. (1974–76; Munich, Nov. 18, 1976); *Und GOtt der HErr sprach* for Mezzo-soprano, Baritone, Bass, 2 Choruses, and Orch. (1976–83; Vienna, Jan. 25, 1984).

BIBL.: H. Krones, *Musikalisches Dokumentation F. B.* (Vienna, 1980).

Burton, Stephen Douglas, American composer and teacher; b. Whittier, Calif., Feb. 24, 1943. He studied at the Oberlin (Ohio) College Cons. of Music (1960–62), with Henze at the Salzburg Mozarteum, and at the Peabody Cons. of Music in Baltimore (M.M., 1974). In 1969 he was awarded a Guggenheim fellowship. After teaching at the Catholic Univ. of America in Washington, D.C. (1970–74), he joined the faculty of George Mason Univ. in Fairfax, Va., in 1974, serving as a prof. there from 1983. He publ. *Orchestration* (1982). While his music draws upon the totality of modern resources, it remains faithful to the directness, energy, and spirit of the American experience.

WORKS: DRAMATIC: *The Nightingale and the Rose,* chamber ballet (1968; also as *Eurydice* for Violin, Clarinet, Trombone, Piano or Celesta, and Percussion, 1977); *No Trifling with Love,* opera (1970); *An American Triptych,* 3 1-act operas: *Maggie,* after Crane, *Dr. Heidegger's Experiment,* after Hawthorne, and *Benito Cereno,* after Melville (1974–75; Alexandria, Va., July 29, 1988); *The Starchild,* children's opera (1975); *The Duchess of Malfi,* opera (1975–78; Vienna, Va., Aug. 18, 1978); *Finisterre,* dance piece (Newport, R.I., Aug. 21, 1977); *The Merchant of Venice,* incidental music to Shakespeare's play (1988); *Brotherhood,* music theater (1991–92). **ORCH.:** *Sinfonia per Roma* (1963); Concerto for Violin and Chamber Orch. (1965; also as Concerto for Violin and Piano); 7 syms.: No. 1 (1967; Berlin, Jan. 31, 1968), No. 2, *Ariel,* for Baritone or Mezzo-soprano and Baritone and Orch., after Sylvia Plath (Washington, D.C., Oct. 19, 1976), No. 3, *Songs of the Tulpehocken,* for Tenor and Orch. (Reading, Pa., Feb. 22, 1976), No. 4, *Homage to Bach,* for Organ and Orch. (1980), No. 5, *Prelude* (1981), No. 6, *I Have a Dream,* for Soprano, Narrator, Chorus, and Orch. (Washington, D.C., May 17, 1987), and No. 7, *The Tempest: Homage to Shakespeare* (Long Island, N.Y., March 1988); *Dithyramb* (Washington, D.C., Oct. 10, 1972); *Stravinskiana,* flute concerto (Chicago, Feb. 14, 1972; also for Flute and Piano); *Variations on a Theme by Mahler* for Chamber Orch. (Washington, D.C., Oct. 10, 1982); *Fanfare for Peace* (Washington, D.C., Sept. 1983); *Pied Piper Overture* (Washington, D.C., Feb. 1, 1983); *Ode* (1986). **CHAMBER:** *Notturno/Elegy* for Cello (1972); *Partita* for Violin (1972); *Burlesque* for Clarinet, Piano, and String Quartet (1972); String Quartet, *Quartet Fantasy* (Washington, D.C., Feb. 9, 1974); Trio for Violin, Cello, and Piano (1975); *Rhapsody* for Alto Saxophone and Piano (London, July 28, 1975); *3 Poems* for Flute (1976); *Fantocciata,* trio sonata/collage for Flute, Oboe, and Harpsichord or Piano (1976); *Divertimento* for Wind Quintet (1976); *Dances* for Flute and Guitar (1984). **VOCAL:** *Ode to a Nightingale* for Soprano and Orch. (1962; Berlin, Oct. 9, 1963); *Requiem Mass* for 6 Soloists, Chorus, and Orch., in memory of President John F. Kennedy (1963); *6 Hebrew Melodies after George Gordon, Lord Byron* for Medium Voice and String Quintet (1967; also for Medium Voice and Piano, 1973); *Sérénade* for Soprano, Flute, Harp, and String Quartet (1967); *Los Desastres de la Guerra* for Men's Chorus, Organ, Piano, and Percussion (1971); *Sechs Lieder nach Gedichten von Hermann Hesse* for High Voice and Piano (Washington, D.C., May 26, 1974; also for High Voice and 13 Instruments, 1977); *Requiescat* for Chorus (1975); *From Noon to Starry Night* for Chorus and Chamber Orch. (1989).

Bury, Edward, Polish composer and teacher; b. Gniezno, Sept. 18, 1919. He studied composition with Sikorski and conducting at the Warsaw Cons. (1937–44); from 1945 to 1954 he taught at the Kraków Cons. He publ. books on conducting (1961) and score reading (1971).

WORKS: ORCH.: *Czech Fantasy* for Piano and Orch. (1948); *Little Suite* (1950); *Triptych* (1952); Violin Concerto (1954); *Concert Overture* (1954); *Suita giocosa* (1956); *Maski* (Masks), fantastic suite (1957); 8 syms.: No. 1, *Symfonia wolności* (Freedom Sym.; 1960), No. 2 for 6 Concertante Instruments and Orch. (1962), No. 3, *Mówi Prezydent John F. Kennedy* (President John F. Kennedy Speaks) for Male Speaker, Women's Speaking Chorus, Mixed Chorus, and Orch. (1964), No. 4, *De timpani a tutti,* for Bass, Chorus, Tape, and Orch. (1966–67), No. 5, *Bohaterska* (Heroic; 1969), No. 6, *Pacem in terris,* to a text from the encyclical of Pope John XXIII, for Narrator, Church Bells, and Orch. (1972), No. 7 (1977), and No. 8 (1980). **OTHER:** Chamber music; piano pieces; *The Millennium Hymn* for Chorus and Orch. (1965); choruses.

Busch, Adolf (Georg Wilhelm), noted German violinist, brother of **Hermann** and **Fritz Busch**; b. Siegen, Westphalia, Aug. 8, 1891; d. Guilford, Vt., June 9, 1952. He studied in Cologne and Bonn; then served as concertmaster of the Vienna Konzertverein (1912–18); subsequently taught at the Hochschule für Musik in Berlin. In 1919 he organized the Busch Quartet and the Busch Trio (with his younger brother, Hermann, and his son-in-law, Rudolf Serkin). The Busch Quartet gained renown with the appointment of Gosta Andreasson and Karl Doktor as members; Busch's brother Hermann became cellist in the Busch Trio in 1926 and in the Busch Quartet in 1930. Adolf Busch went to Basel in 1927; in 1939 he emigrated to America. In 1950 he organized the Marlboro School of Music in Vermont. His *Adolf Busch: Briefe, Bilder, Erinnerungen* (Walpole, N.H., 1991) was publ. posthumously in German and in English.

Busch, Fritz, eminent German conductor, brother of **Adolf (Georg Wilhelm)** and **Hermann Busch**; b. Siegen, Westphalia, March 13, 1890; d. London, Sept. 14, 1951. He studied at the Cologne Cons. with Steinbach, Boettcher, Uzielli, and Klauwell; was then conductor of the Deutsches Theater in Riga (1909–10); in 1912 he became music director of the city of Aachen, and then of the Stuttgart Opera in 1918. In 1922 he was named Generalmusikdirektor of the Dresden State Opera; during his tenure, he conducted many notable productions, including the premieres of Strauss's *Intermezzo* and *Die ägyptische Helena*. On Nov. 27, 1927, he made his U.S. debut as a guest conductor with the N.Y. Sym. Orch. In 1933 he was dismissed from his Dresden post by the Nazi government; leaving Germany, he made many appearances as a conductor with the Danish Radio Sym. Orch. and the Stockholm Phil.; from 1934 to 1939 he served as music director of the Glyndebourne Festivals; from 1940 to 1945 he was active mainly in South America. On Nov. 26, 1945, he made his first appearance with the Metropolitan Opera in N.Y., conducting *Lohengrin*; he continued on its roster until 1949. He was equally distinguished as an operatic and symphonic conductor, becoming particularly renowned for his performances of Mozart. He wrote an autobiography, *Aus dem Leben eines Musikers* (Zürich, 1949; Eng. tr., 1953, as *Pages from a Musician's Life*).

BIBL.: G. Busch, *F. B., Dirigent* (Frankfurt am Main, 1970); B. Dopheide, *F. B.* (Tutzing, 1970).

Busch, Hermann, noted German cellist, brother of **Adolf (Georg Wilhelm)** and **Fritz Busch**; b. Siegen, Westphalia, June 24, 1897; d. Bryn Mawr, Pa., June 3, 1975. He studied at the Cologne Cons. and the Vienna Academy of Music; played cello in the Vienna Sym. Orch. (1923–27); in 1926 he became a member of the Busch Trio; was also a member of the renowned Busch Quartet from 1930 until the death of his brother Adolf in 1952. During his last years of life, he taught at the Marlboro School of Music in Vermont.

Busch, William, English pianist and composer; b. London, June 25, 1901; d. Woolacombe, Devon, Jan. 30, 1945. He was educated in the U.S. and England; then studied in Germany with Leonid Kruetzer (piano) and Hugo Leichtentritt (theory). He made his debut in London (Oct. 20, 1927). His music shows competent craftsmanship; among his works are: Piano Concerto (1939); Cello Concerto (1941); Piano Quartet (1939); piano pieces.

Bush, Alan (Dudley), English composer and teacher; b. London, Dec. 22, 1900; d. Watford, Oct. 31, 1995. He was a student of Corder (composition) and Matthay (piano) at the Royal Academy of Music in London (1918–22); also received private training in piano from Moiseiwitsch (1924–29) and Schnabel (1928), and in composition from Ireland (1927–32); also studied musicology with Wolf and Blume at the Univ. of Berlin (1929–31). From 1925 to 1978 he was prof. of composition at the Royal Academy of Music. He also was active as a pianist and conductor. In 1935 he joined the Communist Party, to which he remained deeply committed. In 1936 he founded the Workers' Music Assn., which he served as president from 1941 to 1976. In 1947–48 he was chairman of the Composers Guild of Great Britain. He publ. *Strict Counterpoint in the Palestrina Style* (London, 1948), *In My Seventh Decade* (London, 1970), and *In My Eighth Decade* (London, 1980). His early works were highly modern, utilizing a thematic style in which every note retains thematic importance. After World War II, tonal elements were added.

WORKS: DRAMATIC: OPERAS: *Wat Tyler* (1948–51; [East] Berlin Radio, April 3, 1952); *Men of Blackmoor* (1954–55; Weimar, Nov. 18, 1956); *The Sugar Reapers* (1961–63; Leipzig, Dec. 11, 1966); *Joe Hill: The Man Who Never Died* (1966–68; East Berlin, Sept. 29, 1970); also operas for young people. **BALLETS:** *His Wars or Yours* (1935); *Mining* (1935). **ORCH.:** *Symphonic Impressions* (1927; London, Nov. 11, 1930); *Dance Overture* for Military Band (1930; orchestrated 1935); Piano Concerto, with Baritone Solo and Men's Chorus in the finale (1937); 4 syms.: No. 1 (1941; London, July 24, 1942), No. 2, *Nottingham* (Nottingham, June 27, 1949), No. 3, *Byron Symphony*, for Baritone, Chorus, and Orch. (1959–60), and No. 4, *Lescaux Symphony* (1983); *Meditation on a German Song of 1848* for Violin and Strings (1941; also for Violin and Piano); *Overture: Festal Day* (1942); *Fantasia on Soviet Themes* (1942; London, July 27, 1945); *English Suite* for Strings (1945–46); *Overture "Resolution"* (1946); *Homage to William Sterndale Bennett* for Strings (1946); *Piers Plowman's Day* (1946–47; Prague Radio, Oct. 16, 1947); Violin Concerto (London, July 16, 1948); Concert Suite for Cello and Orch. (1952); *Defender of Peace* (Vienna Radio, May 24, 1952); *Dorian Passacaglia and Fugue* (1959); *Variations, Nocturne and Finale on an English Sea-Song* for Piano and Orch. (1962); *Partita Concertante* (1965); *Time Remembered* for Chamber Orch. (1969); *Africa* for Piano and Orch. (1972); *Concert Overture for an Occasion* (1972); *Liverpool Overture* (1973); *Festival March for British Youth* (1973); *Song Poem and Dance Poem* for Strings (1986). **CHAMBER:** String Quartet (1923; London, Dec. 4, 1924); Piano Quartet (1924); *Dialectic* for String Quartet (1929; London, March 22, 1935); *3 Concert Studies* for Piano, Violin, and Cello (1947); *Autumn Poem* for Horn and Piano (1954); *3 African Sketches* for Flute and Piano (1960); *Prelude, Air, and Dance* for Violin, String Quartet, and Percussion (1963–64); *Serenade* for String Quartet (1969); *Suite of 6* for String Quartet (1975); Concertino for 2 Violins and Piano (1981); Piano Quintet (1984); Octet (1985); many piano pieces, including 3 sonatas (1921, 1970, 1986). **VOCAL:** *The Winter Journey* for Soprano, Baritone, Chorus, String Quintet, and Harp (1946); *Lidice* for Chorus (1947); *Voices of the Prophets* for Tenor and Piano (1953); *The Ballad of Freedom's Soldier* for Tenor, Bass-baritone, Chorus, and Orch. (1953); *The Alps and Andes of the Living World* for Speaker, Tenor, Chorus, and Orch. (1968); *Africa Is My Name* for Mezzo-soprano, Chorus, and Piano or Orch. (1976); *The Earth in Shadow* for Chorus and Orch. (1982); *Mandela Speaking* for Chorus and Orch. (1985); many other choral works and songs.

BIBL.: R. Stevenson, ed., *Time Remembered—A. B.: An 80th Birthday Symposium* (Kidderminster, 1981).

Bush, Geoffrey, English composer and teacher; b. London, March 23, 1920. He received training in composition from Ireland and then pursued his education at Balliol College, Oxford (B.Mus., 1940; D.Mus., 1946). After lecturing in the extra-mural dept. at the Univ. of Oxford (1947–52), he tutored in the extra-mural dept. at the Univ. of London (1952–80), where he subsequently served as music consultant (1984–87). He also was a visiting prof. at King's College, Univ. of London (1969–89). In 1957 he was chairman of the Composers Guild of Great Britain. He ed. works for Musica Britannica and for the collected edition of Elgar's works. He publ. *Musical Creation and the Listener* (London, 1954; rev. 1967), *Left, Right and Centre: Reflections on Composers and Composing* (London, 1983), and *An Unsentimental Education* (London, 1990). His works are written in an engaging neo-Classical style.

WORKS: DRAMATIC: *The Blind Beggar's Daughter*, opera (1952; rev. 1964); *If the Cap Fits*, opera (Cheltenham, July 12, 1956); *The Equation*, opera (1967; BBC Radio, Feb. 7, 1976); *Lord Arthur Savile's Crime*, theater piece (1972; BBC Radio, July 27, 1986); *The Cat who went to Heaven*, music theater (1974); *Love's Labours Lost*, opera (1988). **ORCH.:** *Natus est Immanuel* for Strings (1939); *Rhapsody* for Clarinet and Strings (1940; also for Clarinet and String Quartet or Piano); *The Spanish Rivals*, overture (1941); *Divertimento* for Strings (1943); Sinfonietta Concertante for Cello and Small Orch. (1943; BBC, Sept. 28, 1945); *In Praise of Salisbury* (1944); *The Rehearsal*, overture (1945); Concerto for Oboe and Strings (1948); *2 Miniatures* for Strings (1948); *Yorick*, overture (1949); Concertino No. 1 for Piano and Orch. (1953; London, Feb. 11, 1961); 2 syms.: No. 1 (Cheltenham, July 8, 1954) and No. 2, *The Guilford* (1957); Concerto for Light Orch. (1958); *Hornpipe for St. Cecilia's Day* (Birmingham, Nov. 22, 1960); *Old London*, suite for Concert

Band (1961); Concerto for Trumpet, Piano, and Strings (1962; London, Dec. 16, 1963); *Finale for a Concert* (1964); *Music* (1967); *Consort Music: 6 Victorian Sketches* for Strings (1987). **CHAMBER:** Violin Sonata (1945; BBC, Oct. 31, 1949); Trio for Oboe, Bassoon, and Piano (Canterbury, Nov. 18, 1952); *Dialogue* for Oboe and Piano (London, March 25, 1960); *Homage to Matthew Locke* for 3 Trumpets and 3 Trombones (1962); Wind Quintet (1963); Concertino No. 2 for Piano and 12 Players (1976); *Tributes: 5 Respectful Pieces* for Clarinet and Piano (1986); *Pavans and Galliards* for Wind Quintet (1992); piano pieces; organ music. **VOCAL:** *A Christmas Cantata* for Soprano, Chorus, Oboe, and Strings (1947); *A Summer Serenade* for Tenor, Chorus, Piano, Timpani, and Strings (1948); *Twelfth Night, an Entertainment* for Tenor, Chorus, and Chamber Orch. (1950); *Farewell, Earth's Bliss* for Baritone and String Quartet or String Orch. (1950); *In Praise of Mary* for Soprano, Chorus, and Orch. (Hereford, Sept. 7, 1955); *Songs of Wonder* for High Voice and Piano or String Orch. (1959); *A Lover's Progress* for Tenor, Oboe, Clarinet, and Bassoon (London, April 26, 1961); *Cantata Piccola* for Baritone, Chorus, Strings, and Harpsichord or Piano (1965); *Daffydd in Love* for Baritone, Chorus, and Piano (1974); *Phantoms* for Soprano, Girls' or Boys' Chorus, and Instrumental Ensemble or Brass Band (1978); *Love's Labours Lost* for Soprano, Baritone, and Orch. (1986); *4 Chaucer Settings* for Baritone, Oboe, and Piano (1987); many other choral pieces; various other songs, including *Archy at the Zoo* for High Voice and Piano (1994).

Busoni, Ferruccio (Dante Michelangiolo Benvenuto), greatly admired Italian-German pianist, pedagogue, and composer; b. Empoli, near Florence, April 1, 1866; d. Berlin, July 27, 1924. Busoni grew up in an artistic atmosphere: his father played the clarinet and his mother, Anna Weiss, was an amateur pianist. He learned to play the piano as a child; at the age of 8, he played in public in Trieste. He gave a piano recital in Vienna when he was 10, and included in his program some of his own compositions. In 1877 the family moved to Graz, where Busoni took piano lessons with W. Mayer. He conducted his *Stabat Mater* in Graz at the age of 12. At 15 he was accepted as a member of the Accademia Filarmonica in Bologna; he performed there his oratorio *Il sabato del villaggio* in 1883. In 1886 he went to Leipzig and undertook a profound study of Bach's music. In 1889 he was appointed a prof. of piano at the Helsinki Cons., where among his students was Sibelius (who was a few months older than his teacher). At that time, Busoni married Gerda Sjostrand, whose father was a celebrated Swedish sculptor; their 2 sons became well-known artists. In 1890 Busoni participated in the Rubinstein Competition in St. Petersburg, winning 1st prize with his *Konzertstück* for Piano and Orch. On the strength of this achievement, he was engaged to teach piano at the Moscow Cons. (1890–91). He then accepted the post of prof. at the New England Cons. of Music in Boston (1891–94); however, he had enough leisure to make several tours, maintaining his principal residence in Berlin. During the season of 1912–13, he made a triumphant tour of Russia. In 1913 he was appointed director of the Liceo Musicale in Bologna. The outbreak of the World War I in 1914 forced him to flee to the U.S.; after a tour of the country, he moved to neutral Switzerland. In 1923 he went to Paris, and then returned to Berlin, remaining there until his death. In various cities, at various times, he taught piano in music schools; among his students were Brailowsky, Ganz, Petri, Mitropoulos, and Grainger. Busoni also taught composition, numbering Weill, Jarnach, and Vogel among his pupils. He exercised great influence on Varèse, who was living in Berlin when Busoni was there; Varèse greatly prized Busoni's advanced theories of composition.

Busoni was a philosopher of music who tried to formulate a universe of related arts; he issued grandiloquent manifestos urging a return to classical ideals in modern forms; he sought to establish a unifying link between architecture and composition; in his eds. of Bach's works, he included drawings illustrating the architectonic plan of Bach's fugues. He incorporated his innovations in his grandiose piano work *Fantasia contrappuntistica*, which opens with a prelude based on a Bach chorale and closes with a set of variations on Bach's name, B-A-C-H (i.e., B-flat, A, C, B-natural). In his theoretical writings, he proposed a system of 113 different heptatonic modes, and also suggested the possibility of writing music in exotic scales and subchromatic intervals; he expounded those ideas in his influential essay *Entwurf einer neuen Aesthetik der Tonkunst* (Trieste, 1907; Eng. tr. by T. Baker, N.Y., 1911). Busoni's other publications of significance were *Von der Einheit der Musik* (1923; in Italian, Florence, 1941; in Eng., London, 1957) and *Über die Möglichkeiten der Oper* (Leipzig, 1926). Despite Busoni's great innovations in his own compositions and his theoretical writing, however, the Busoni legend is kept alive not through his music but mainly through his sovereign virtuosity as a pianist. In his performances, he introduced a concept of piano sonority as an orch. medium; indeed, some listeners reported having heard simulations of trumpets and French horns sounded at Busoni's hands. The few extant recordings of his playing transmit a measure of the grandeur of his style, but they also betray a tendency, common to Busoni's era, toward a free treatment of the musical text, surprisingly so, since Busoni preached an absolute fidelity to the written notes. On concert programs Busoni's name appears most often as the author of magisterial and eloquent transcriptions of Bach's works. His gothic transfiguration for piano of Bach's *Chaconne* for Unaccompanied Violin became a perennial favorite of pianists all over the world.

Busoni was honored by many nations. In 1913 he received the order of Chevalier de la Légion d'honneur from the French government, a title bestowed on only 2 Italians before him: Rossini and Verdi. In 1949 a Concorso Busoni was established. Another international award honoring the name of Busoni was announced by the Accademia di Santa Cecilia of Rome, with prizes given for the best contemporary compositions; at its opening session in 1950, the recipient was Stravinsky.

WORKS: OPERAS: *Sigune* (1885–88); *Die Brautwahl* (1906–11; Hamburg, April 12, 1912); *Arlecchino* (1914–16; Zürich, May 11, 1917, composer conducting); *Turandot* (1916–17; Zürich, May 11, 1917, composer conducting); *Doktor Faust* (1916–23; unfinished; completed by Jarnach, 1924–25; Dresden, May 21, 1925). **ORCH.:** *Symphonic Suite* (Trieste, June 9, 1883); *Introduction and Scherzo* for Piano and Orch. (1882–84); *Concert Fantasy* for Piano and Orch. (1888–89; Leipzig, June 10, 1890, composer soloist, Reinecke conducting; rev. as *Symphonic Tone Poem*, Boston, April 14, 1893); *Konzertstück* for Piano and Orch. (1889–90; St. Petersburg, Aug. 27, 1890, composer soloist, Moritz Köhler conducting); Suite No. 2, *Geharnischte* (1894–95; Berlin, Oct. 8, 1897, composer conducting; rev. 1903; Berlin, Dec. 1, 1904, composer conducting); Violin Concerto (1896–97; Berlin, Oct. 8, 1897, Henri Petri soloist, composer conducting); *Lustspielouvertüre* (Berlin, Oct. 8, 1897, composer conducting; rev. 1904; Berlin, Jan. 11, 1907, composer conducting); Concerto for Piano, Men's Chorus, and Orch. (1901–04; Berlin, Nov. 10, 1904, composer soloist, Muck conducting); *Turandot*, incidental music (1905; Berlin, Oct. 26, 1911; not extant); *Turandot*, suite from the opera (Berlin, Oct. 21, 1905, composer conducting); *Berceuse élégiaque: Des Mannes Wiegenlied am Sarge seiner Mutter* (1909; N.Y., Feb. 21, 1911, Mahler conducting); *Die Brautwahl*, suite from the opera (1912; Berlin, Jan. 3, 1913, Fried conducting); *Nocturne symphonique* (1912–13; Berlin, March 12, 1914, composer conducting); *Indianische Fantasie* for Piano and Orch. (1913–14; Berlin, March 12, 1914, composer soloist, Alexis Birnbaum conducting); *Rondò arlecchinesco* (1915; Rome, March 5, 1916, composer conducting); *Gesang vom Reigen der Geister*, study for Small Orch. from the *Indianisches Tagebuch* No. 2 (1915); Concertino for Clarinet and Small Orch. (Zürich, Dec. 9, 1918); *Sarabande und Cortège*, 2 studies for *Doktor Faust* (1918–19; Zürich, March 31, 1919); *Divertimento* for Flute and Orch. (1920; Berlin, Jan. 13, 1921, Henrik de Vries soloist, composer conducting); *Tanzwalzer* (1920; Berlin, Jan. 13, 1921, composer conducting); *Romanza e scherzoso* for Piano and Orch. (Basel, Dec. 10, 1921).

CHAMBER: 1 unnumbered Violin Sonata (1876); 2 numbered violin sonatas: No. 1 (c.1889) and No. 2 (Helsinki, Sept. 30, 1898); 4 string quartets (1876; 1881; c.1884; Leipzig, Jan. 28, 1888); Concerto for Piano and String Quartet (1878); Suite for Clarinet and Piano (1878); Suite for Clarinet and String Quartet (1878–81); *Solo dramatique* for Clarinet and Piano (1879); *Serenade* for Cello and Piano (1883); Short Suite for Cello and Piano (1885); *4 Bagatelles* for Violin and Piano (1888); *Kulsatelle*, 10 short variations on a Finnish folk song for Cello and Piano (1889); *Albumleaf* for Flute or Muted Violin and Piano (1916); *Elegy* for Clarinet and Piano (1919–20). **PIANO:** 8 sonatas (1875, 1877, 1877, 1877, 1880, 1880 [not extant], 1883, n.d.); *5 Pieces* (1877); *Suite campestre* (1878); (4) *Danze antiche* (1878–79); *3 Pieces in the Old Style* (1880); *24 Préludes* (1881); *Una festa di villaggio*, 6 pieces (1881); *Danza notturna* (1882); *Macchiette medioevali* (1882–83); *5 Études* (c.1882–88); *6 Elegies* (1907); *Fantasia nach Johann Sebastian Bach* (London, Oct. 16, 1909, composer pianist); *An die Jugend*, 4 pieces (1909); *Fantasia contrappuntistica*, after J.S. Bach (Basel, Sept. 30, 1910, composer pianist); 6 sonatinas (1910, 1912, 1915, 1917, 1918, 1920); *Indianisches Tagebuch*, book I (1915); *Improvisation* on the Bach chorale *Wie wohl ist mir, o Freund der Seele* for 2 Pianos (1916); *3 Albumleaves* (1917, 1921, 1921); *Klavierübung in fünf Teilen* (1, 1917; 2, 1917–18; 3, 1919–21; 4, 1897; 5, 1922); *Nocturne* (1918); *Toccata* (1920); *Perpetuum mobile* (1922); *5 kurze Stücke zur Pflege des polyphonischen Spiels* (1923); *Prélude et étude en arpèges* (1923); *Klavierübung in zehn Büchern* (1923–24).

VOCAL: Mass for 4 Voices (1879); *Requiem* for Soloists, Chorus, and Orch. (1881); *4 Pieces* for Soloists, Men's Chorus, and Orch. (1882); *Il sabato del villaggio*, cantata for Soloists, Chorus, and Orch. (1882; Bologna, March 22, 1883); *2 Songs* for Voice and Piano, after Byron (1883); *So lang man jung* for Tenor, Men's Chorus, and Orch. (1884); *Unter den Linden* for Voice and Small Orch. (1893); *Altoums Gebet* for Baritone and Small Orch. (1917); *Lied des Méphistophélès* for Baritone and Small Orch., after Goethe (1918); *Lied des Unmuts* for Baritone and Piano or Orch. (1918); *Zigeunerlied* for Baritone and Orch. (1923); *Schlecter Trost* for Baritone and Orch. (1924).

OTHER: Cadenzas to concertos by Mozart, Beethoven, Weber, and Brahms; transcriptions of numerous works by J.S. Bach, Mozart, Liszt et al.

BIBL.: H. Leichtentritt, *F. B.* (Leipzig, 1916); idem, "F. B. as a Composer," *Musical Quarterly* (Jan. 1917); H. Pfitzner, *Futuristengefahr* (Munich, 1917); G. Selden-Goth, *F. B.* (Vienna, 1922); A. Cottlow, "My Years with B.," *Musical Observer* (June 1925); S. Nadel, *F. B.* (Leipzig, 1931); E. Dent, *F. B., A Biography* (London, 1933); G. Gatti, "The Stage Works of F. B.," *Musical Quarterly* (July 1934); A. Santelli, *B.* (Rome, 1939); G. Guerrini, *F. B., La vita, la figura, l'opera* (Florence, 1944); H. Stuckenschmidt, *F. B., Zeittafel eines Europaers* (Zürich, 1967; Eng. tr., 1970, *F. B.: Chronicle of a European*); H. Meyer, *Die Klaviermusik F. B.s* (Zürich, 1969); H. Kosnick, *B., Gestaltung durch Gestalt* (Regensburg, 1971); J. Kindermann, *Thematisch-chronologisches Verzeichnis der musikalischen Werke von F. B.* (Regensburg, 1980); S. Sablich, *B.* (Turin, 1982); A. Beaumont, *B. the Composer* (London, 1985); L. Sitsky, *B. and the Piano: The Works, the Writings, and the Recordings* (N.Y., 1986); A. Beaumont, ed. and tr., *F. B.: Selected Letters* (London, 1987); A. Riethmüller, *F. B.s Poetik* (Mainz and London, 1988); M.-A. Roberge, *F. B.: A Bio-Bibliography* (Westport, Conn., 1991).

Büsser, (Paul-) Henri, esteemed French conductor, pedagogue, and composer; b. Toulouse, Jan. 16, 1872; d. Paris, Dec. 30, 1973. He received initial music instruction as a choirboy at the Toulouse Cathedral under Aloys Kunc; at age 13, he was taken to Paris, where he studied with A. Georges at the School of Religious Music; he then pursued training at the Cons. (1889–92) as a pupil of Franck and Widor (organ) and Guiraud (composition); he also received advice from Gounod. In 1892 he became organist at St. Cloud, near Paris. In 1893 he won the Prix de Rome with his cantata *Antigone*. Returning to Paris, he became conductor at the Théâtre du Chateau d'Eau in 1900, and at the Opéra-Comique in 1902; he was conductor at the Opéra (1905–39; 1946–51). In 1904 he became head of the vocal ensemble class at the Cons., and subsequently was prof. of composition there from 1931 to 1948. In 1938 he was elected to membership in the Académie. He married **Yvonne Gall** in 1958. Büsser was an accomplished composer for the theater. He also orchestrated Debussy's *Petite Suite* (1907), *Printemps* (1912), *La cathédrale engloutie* (1917), and other pieces. His writings comprise *Traité d'instrumentation* (with Guiraud; Paris, 1933), *De "Pelléas" aux "Indes galantes"* (Paris, 1955), and *Gounod* (Lyons, 1961).

WORKS: DRAMATIC: *Les accordailles*, opéra comique (1890); *Les Marivaudages*, pantomime (1891); *Daphnis et Chloë*, scenic pastorale (c.1896; Paris, Dec. 14, 1897); *Le miracle des perles*, drame lyrique (1898); *Blanc et noir*, pantomime (Paris, 1900); *Colomba*, drame lyrique (c.1910; Nice, Feb. 4, 1921); *Les noces corinthiennes*, tragédie lyrique (1916–18; Paris, May 10, 1922); *La pie borgne*, comédie lyrique (Aix-les-Bains, Aug. 5, 1927); *La carosse du Saint-Sacrement*, comédie lyrique (Paris, June 2, 1948); *Roxelane*, comédie lyrique (Mulhouse, Jan. 31, 1948); *Diafoirus 60*, farce musicale (Lille, April 4, 1963); *La Vénus d'Ille*, drame lyrique (Lille, April 15, 1964). **ORCH.:** *A la villa Médicis* (c.1895); *Suite funambulesque* (1900); *Hercule au jardin des Hespérides* (1900). **OTHER:** Magnificat; masses; motets; choruses; songs; piano pieces; organ music.

Bussotti, Sylvano, important Italian composer, opera director, and stage designer; b. Florence, Oct. 1, 1931. He began violin lessons at a very early age and also took up painting while still a youth. At the age of 9, he entered the Florence Cons., where he was a student in harmony and counterpoint of Roberto Lupi and in piano of Dallapiccola. His training there was soon interrupted by World War II. After the War, he pursued composition study on his own (1949–56) before continuing his training in Paris with Max Deutsch (1956–58). He also attended courses in new music at Darmstadt (summers, 1958–61). In 1964–65 he was active in the U.S. on a Rockefeller Foundation grant. In 1972 he studied in Berlin under the auspices of the Deutscher Akademischer Austauschdienst. He taught at the Academy of Fine Arts in L'Aquila (1971–74), and then served as artistic director of the Teatro La Fenice in Venice (1975). He was artistic consultant to the Puccini Festival in Torre del Lago (1979–81), and later its artistic director. From 1980 he taught at the Fiesole School of Music. He publ. *I miei teatri: Diario segreto, diario pubblico, alcuni saggi* (Palermo, 1981). Bussotti's early interest in painting continued later in life; his visual works have been exhibited around the globe. As a composer, he found his exploration of serialism, indeterminacy, and other modern means of expression too restrictive. He thus charted a revolutionary course which led him to embrace an anarchistic aestheticism. In 1976 he established his own production company, "Bussottioperaballet," which, from 1984 to 1992, operated as a festival in Genazzano. From his *Lorenzaccio* (1972), much of Bussotti's energies have gone into operas, both his own (which often draw heavily upon earlier compositions) and the standard repertory, which he has explored as a director and stage designer in most luxurious terms. He has also continued to create films and to write poetry, and has elevated himself to Italian celebrity status through his flamboyant direction of the musical section of the Venice Biennale, of which his last, highly controversial term was 1991.

WORKS: DRAMATIC: *Juvenilia*, ballet (1951–53; Segromigno, Aug. 5, 1983); *La Passion selon Sade*, chamber mystery (Palermo, Sept. 5, 1965); *Lorenzaccio*, romantic melodrama (1968–72; Venice, Sept. 7, 1972); *Raramente*, choreographic mystery (Florence, Feb. 4, 1971); *Bergkristall*, ballet (1972–74; concert premiere, North German Radio, Hamburg, May 15, 1973; stage premiere, Rome, June 8, 1974); *Syro-Sadun-Settimino*, monodance (Royan, March 1974); *Oggetto amato*, dance piece (1975; Milan, April 7, 1976); *Phaidra/Heliogabalus*, ballet (1975–80; Turin, Feb. 15, 1981); *Nottetempo*, lyric drama (Milan, April 7, 1976); *Le* *rarita', potente*, lyric representation (1976–78; Treviso, Oct. 12, 1979); *Autotono*, divertimento (1977; Treviso, Oct. 12, 1979); *Le Racine*, theater piece (Milan, Dec. 9, 1980); *Miró, L'uccello luce*, ballet-pantomime (Venice, Sept. 25, 1981); *Cristallo di Rocca*, ballet (Milan, June 10, 1983); *Phèdre*, lyric tragedy (Rome, April 19, 1988); *L'Ispirazione*, melodrama (Florence, May 25, 1988). **ORCH.:** *. . . et due voci* (1958–85); *Mit einem gewissen sprechenden Ausdruck* for Chamber Orch. (1961–63); *I semi di Gramsci*, symphonic poem for String Quartet and Orch. (1962–71; Rome, April 22, 1972); *Lorenzaccio Symphony I* for Soprano and Orch. (Royan, March 28, 1974) and *II* (Rome, Dec. 17, 1978); *Il catalogo è questo I–IV* (1976–88); *Le bal Miró* (1981; Rome, Dec. 20, 1986); *Timpani* (1985; Rome, Jan. 12, 1986); *Nuit du faune, Concerti con figuro* (1991). **CHAMBER:** *Breve* for Ondes Martenot (1958–72); *Phrase à trois* for String Trio (1960); *Fragmentations* for Harp (1962); *Rara (eco sierologico)* for Violin, Viola, Cello, Double Bass, and Guitar (1964–67); *Rara (dolce)* for Flute and Mime (1966); *Solo* for Various Instrumental Combinations (1967; Danish Radio, Feb. 3, 1968); *Marbre pour cordes* for 11 Strings (London, Nov. 10, 1967); *Ultima rara (pop song)* for Solo Guitar or Guitar and 3 Speakers (1969); *Quartetto Gramsci* for String Quartet (1971; Siena, Aug. 26, 1974); *Rondò di scena* for 4 Flutes (1975); *Ripetente* for 8 Instrumentalists (Milan, Feb. 12, 1976); *Gran Duo* for Cello and Piano (1977–78); *Passo d'uomo* for Piccolo, Timpani, and Percussion (Rome, Dec. 17, 1978); *Tramonto* for Flute, Horn, and Clarinet (1978; L'Aquila, March 5, 1979); *"Dai, dimmi, su!"* for 11 Instruments (1978); *3 Lovers' Ballet* for Violin, Cello, and Piano (1978); *Brutto, ignudo* for Bass Clarinet (1979); *Accademia* for Flute and Piano (1980; Fiesole, June 22, 1981); *Nudo disteso* for Viola (1980); *Naked Angel Face* for Double Bass (Pisa, Nov. 13, 1982); *La Vergine ispirata* for Harpsichord and Another Harmony Instrument (1982; Paris, March 21, 1983); *Due concertanti I* for Piccolo and Double Bass (1983); *Qu'un corps défiguré* for Viola, Oboe, Bassoon, Trombone, and Percussion (Rome, June 14, 1986); *Concerto a L'Aquila* for Piano and 9 Instruments (London, July 5, 1986); *Andante favorito* for String Quartet (1988). **PIANO:** *La Recherche de bal perdu* (1953–57); *Musica per amici* (1957; rev. 1971); *Piano Pieces for David Tudor* (1959); *Pour clavier* (1961); *Tableaux vivants* for 2 Pianos (1964); *Foglio d'album* (1970); *Novelletta* (1972–73); *Brillante* (1975); *Olof Palme* (1987). **VOCAL:** *Nympheo* for Voices and Instruments (1937–84); *Autunno* for 4 Voices (1950–53); *Poesia di depisis* for Soprano and 15 Instruments (1954; Siena, Aug 27, 1975); *Nottetempo con lo scherzo e una rosa* for Voice and Chamber Orch. (1954–57); *El carbonero* for 5 Voices (1957); *Due voci* for Soprano, Ondes Martenot, and Orch. (1958); *Pièces de chair II* for Baritone, Woman's Voice, Piano, and Instruments (1958–60; Paris, Oct. 22, 1970); *Torso (Letture di Braibanti)* for Voice and Orch. (1960–63); *Memoria* for Voices and Orch. (1962); *Siciliano* for 12 Men's Voices (1962); *Il nudo* for Voice and 5 Instruments (1963); *"Extraits de concert"* for Voice and Ensemble (1965; Milan, Feb. 28, 1966); *Cinque frammenti all'Italia* for Mixed Voices and Chorus (1967–68; Venice, Sept. 14, 1968); *Julio Organum Julii* for Reciter and Organ (1968); *The Rara Requiem* for Vocal Group, Chorus, Guitar, Cello, Wind Orch., Piano, Harp, and Percussion (Venice, Sept. 13, 1969; rev. 1970); *Aria di Mara* for Soprano and Orch. (Milan, July 9, 1973); *Lachrimae* for Voices (1978); *Citazione con quartina per Maurice* for Baritone and Piano (1981); *In memoriam (Cathy Berberian)* for Voice, Flute, Viola, and Piano (Genazzano, Sept. 8, 1984); *Pianino* for Boy's Voice and Piano (1987); *Lingue ignote* for Bass and 7 Instruments (1993–94); *Furioso* for Mezzo-soprano and Orch. (Vienna, May 28, 1994); *Unerbittliches Denkgesetz* for Bass, Flute, Trumpet, and Piano (Rome, Jan. 20, 1994).

BIBL.: F. Degrada, *S. B. e il suo teatrale* (Milan, 1976); M. Bucci, *L'opera di S. B.* (Florence, 1988).

Bustabo, Guila, American violinist; b. Manitowoc, Wis., Feb. 25, 1917. She was a child prodigy; played at a benefit concert in Chicago at the age of 4; at age 10, she was a soloist with the N.Y. Phil., performing a Wieniawski concerto (Nov. 2, 1929). She studied with Persinger in N.Y. and with Enesco and Hubay in Europe. From 1964 to 1970 she was on the faculty of the Innsbruck Cons. in Austria.

Bustini, Alessandro, Italian composer and teacher; b. Rome, Dec. 24, 1876; d. there, June 23, 1970. He studied at the Accademia di Santa Cecilia in Rome with Sgambati (piano), Renzi (organ), and Falchi (composition), graduating in 1897. He was subsequently appointed to its faculty, and was its president from 1952 to 1964. His works, all written in the traditional Italian manner, include the opera *Maria Dulcis* (Rome, April 15, 1902); 2 syms. (1899, 1909); *Le Tentazioni*, symphonic poem (1914); *Le Stagioni* for Violin and Chamber Orch. (1934); 2 string quartets; songs; piano works.

Buswell, James Oliver (, IV), American violinist, conductor, and teacher; b. Fort Wayne, Ind., Dec. 4, 1946. He studied violin with Galamian at the Juilliard School of Music in N.Y., then pursued academic training at Harvard Univ. (B.A., 1970). In 1963 he made his debut as a violinist in St. Louis, and in 1967 made his N.Y. recital debut; subsequently toured as a soloist, recitalist, and chamber music player; later was a member of the Buswell-Parnas-Luvisi Trio, and also made appearances as a conductor. He taught at the Univ. of Arizona in Tucson (1972–73), the Indiana Univ. School of Music in Bloomington (1974–86), and the New England Cons. of Music in Boston (from 1986).

Butt, Dame Clara (Ellen), notable English contralto; b. Southwick, Sussex, Feb. 1, 1872; d. North Stoke, Oxfordshire, July 13, 1936. She studied with J.H. Blower at the Royal College of Music in London; later took lessons with Bouhy in Paris and Gerster in Berlin. She made her operatic debut as Ursula in Sullivan's *Golden Legend* (London, Dec. 7, 1892); then sang at the music festivals at Hanley and Bristol. She visited the U.S. in 1899 and 1913; in 1913–14 she made a world tour with her husband, R. Kennerley Rumford, a baritone. Several composers wrote works for her, among them Elgar (*Sea-Pictures*) and H. Bedford (*Romeo and Juliet*). In 1920 she was made a Dame Commander of the Order of the British Empire.

BIBL.: W. Ponder, *C. B.* (London, 1928).

Butterley, Nigel (Henry), Australian composer, pianist, and teacher; b. Sydney, May 13, 1935. He attended the New South Wales State Conservatorium of Music in Sydney (1952–55), his principal mentors being Frank Warbrick (piano) and Raymond Hanson (composition); later he pursued training in composition with Priaulx Rainier in London (1962). In 1966 he won the Prix Italia for his choral work *In the Head the Fire*. He was active as a pianist, especially as a proponent of contemporary music. He also was on the music staff of the Australian Broadcasting Commission. From 1973 to 1991 he was a lecturer at the Newcastle Conservatorium. In 1991 he received the Australian Creative Artists' Fellowship and was made a Member of the Order of Australia. As a composer, Butterley pursues a thoroughly individualistic style, notable for its assured technical command and penchant for lyricism.

WORKS: DRAMATIC: *In the Head the Fire*, radio piece (1966); *Watershore*, radio piece (1978); *Lawrence Hargrave Flying Alone*, opera (Sydney, Sept. 24, 1988). **ORCH.:** *Meditations of Thomas Traherne* (1968); *Pentad* (1968); *Refractions* (1969); *Explorations* for Piano and Orch. (1970); Violin Concerto (1970; rev. 1975); *Fire in the Heavens* (1973); Sym. (1980); *Goldengrove* for Strings (1982; rev. 1993); *In Passing* (1982); *From Sorrowing Earth* (Sydney, Aug. 21, 1991); *Poverty* (1992); *The Woven Light* (1994). **CHAMBER:** *Laudes* for 8 Instruments (1963); 3 string quartets (1965, 1974, 1980); *The White-Throated Warbler* for Sopranino Recorder or Flute or Piccolo and Harpsichord or Piano (1965); *Variations* for Wind Quintet and Piano (1967); *Voices* for Wind Quintet (1971); *Fanfare and Processional* for 4 Trumpets, 2 Trombones, and 2 Timpani (1977); *Evanston Song* for Flute and Piano (1978); Trio for Clarinet, Cello, and Piano (1979); *Forest I* for Viola and Piano (1990) and *II* for Trumpet and Piano (1993); *The Wind Stirs Gently* for Flute and Cello (1992). **KEYBOARD: PIANO:** *Arioso, Toccata, Comment on a Popular Song* (1960); *Grevillea* (1962; rev. 1985); *Letter From Hardy's Bay* (1971); *Uttering Joyous Leaves* (1981); *Lawrence Hargrave Flying Alone* (1981); *Il Gubbo* (1987). **ORGAN:** *3 Pieces* (1961, 1979, 1989). **VOCAL:** *The True Samaritan* for Chorus (1958; rev. 1976); *Carmina: 4 Latin Poems of Spring* for Medium Voice and Wind Quintet (1968; rev. 1990); *Sometimes with One I Love* for Soprano, Baritone, Male Speaker, Flute, Clarinet, Horn, 2 Cellos, and Piano (1976); *The Owl* for Soprano, Flute, Clarinet, Violin or Viola, Cello, Piano, and Percussion (1983); *There Came a Wind like a Bugle* for Chorus (1987); *The Woven Light* for Soprano and Orch. (1993); various other choral pieces and songs.

Butterworth, George (Sainton Kaye), talented English composer; b. London, July 12, 1885; d. in the battle of the Somme, near Pozières, Aug. 5, 1916. He learned to play the organ at school in Yorkshire, then studied with Dunhill at Eton (1899–1904) and at Trinity College, Oxford (1904–08). He then taught at Radley and wrote music criticism for *The Times* of London; with C. Sharpe and Vaughan Williams, he became an ardent collector of folk songs, which were incorporated into several of his compositions; also helped to prepare Vaughan Williams's *London Symphony*, which was dedicated to his memory. To strengthen his technique, he studied with Parratt (organ), Sharpe (piano), and Wood (harmony) at the Royal College of Music in London (1910–11). At the outbreak of World War I, he enlisted in the British army and was posthumously awarded the Military Cross for bravery. His death was greatly lamented. Before he left for France, he destroyed many of his MSS, including those of a Violin Sonata and a *Barcarolle* for Orch. that had been much praised.

WORKS: ORCH.: *2 English Idylls* (Oxford, Feb. 8, 1912); *A Shropshire Lad*, rhapsody (originally titled *The Cherry Tree*, prelude; Leeds, Oct. 2, 1913); *The Banks of Green Willow*, idyll (West Kirby, Feb. 27, 1914). **CHAMBER:** Suite for String Quartet (n.d.). **VOCAL:** *I fear thy kisses*, after Shelley (1909); 6 songs from *A Shropshire Lad*, after Housman (London, June 20, 1911); *Requiescat*, after Wilde (1911); *Bredon Hill*, after Housman (1912); *I will make you brooches*, after Stevenson (n.d.); *Love blows as the wind blows*, after Henley, for Baritone and String Quartet or Piano or Orch. (1914). **CHORAL:** *On Christmas Night* (1902); *We get up in the morn* (1912); *In the highlands*, after Stevenson (1912); *11 Folk Songs from Sussex* (1912); *Morris Dances* (with Sharpe; 1913).

BIBL.: *G. B. 1885–1916* (1916); I. Copley, *G. B. and His Music: A Centennial Tribute* (London, 1985).

Butting, Max, German composer; b. Berlin, Oct. 6, 1888; d. there, July 13, 1976. He studied organ in Berlin and composition in Munich. Returning to Berlin, he was a successful teacher, but in 1933 was deprived of his various positions for political reasons, being the former ed. of a socialist publication. He was able to return to his professional activities after the end of World War II. In 1948 he was appointed a lecturer in the music division of the East Berlin Radio; in 1968 he received an honorary doctor's degree from Humboldt Univ. in East Berlin. His music is animated by polyphonic purposefulness and is marked by rhythmic vitality and lyric meditation. Since many of his works were destined for amateur performances, Butting shunned modernistic involvements; however, in his 9th and 10th syms. he applied dodecaphonic structures.

WORKS: OPERA: *Plautus im Nonnenkloster* (Leipzig, Oct. 3, 1959). **ORCH.:** 10 syms. (1922–63); *Sinfonietta, with Banjo* (1929); Flute Concerto (1950); *Symphonic Variations* (1953); *Sinfonietta* (1960); Piano Concerto (1965); *Legende* (1966); *Triptychon* (1967); *Concert Overture* (1973). **CHAMBER:** 10 string quartets (1914–71); String Quintet (1916); Quintet for Violin, Viola, Cello, Oboe, and Clarinet (1921); Wind Quintet (1925); Piano Trio (1947); String Trio (1952); many piano pieces. **VOCAL:** Choruses; songs.

BIBL.: D. Brennecke, *Das Lebenswerk M. B.s* (Leipzig, 1973).

Buttykay (real name, **Gálszécsy és Butykai**), **Ákos,** Hungarian pianist, teacher, and composer; b. Halmi, July 22, 1871; d. Debrecen, Oct. 26, 1935. He studied in Budapest, where he took courses in law and also attended the Academy of Music; he pursued training in piano and composition in Weimar. After touring as a pianist, he taught piano at the Budapest Academy of Music (1907–22). He won success as a theater composer with his operetta *A bolygó görög* (The Wandering Greek; Budapest, Oct. 19, 1905). After composing the theater scores *A harang* (Budapest, Feb. 1, 1907), *Csibészkirály* (Budapest, Feb. 21, 1907), and *Hamupipőke* (Budapest, Oct. 26, 1912), he composed his most successful operetta, *Az ezüst sirály* (The Silver Seagull; Budapest, Feb. 6, 1920). His *Olivia hercegnő* was chosen to open the new Főváriosi Operettszinház in Budapest on Dec. 23, 1922. Among his other works were 2 syms. (1900, 1902); *Magyar Suite* for Orch. (1900); *Magyar Rhapsody* for Orch. (1931); chamber music; piano pieces; songs.

Bychkov, Semyon, Russian-born American conductor; b. Leningrad, Nov. 30, 1952. He was the brother of **Yakov Kreizberg**. He attended the Glinka Choir School in Leningrad as a youth; subsequently studied with Ilya Musin at the Leningrad Cons., graduating in 1974. In 1975 he emigrated to the U.S., where he received an Artist Diploma from the Mannes College of Music in N.Y. in 1976. From 1980 to 1985 he was music director of the Grand Rapids Sym. Orch. In 1983 he became a naturalized American citizen. After serving as assoc. conductor (1980–81) and principal guest conductor (1981–85) of the Buffalo Phil., he was its music director (1985–89). He subsequently was music director of the Orchestre de Paris (from 1989), and also was principal guest conductor of the orch. of the Maggio Musicale Fiorentino (from 1992) and of the St. Petersburg Phil. (from 1992).

Bylsma, Anner, Dutch cellist; b. The Hague, Feb. 17, 1934. He studied cello with Carel Boomkamp at the Royal Cons. of Music in The Hague, receiving the Prix d'excellence in 1957; subsequently won the Pablo Casals Competition in Mexico City (1959). After serving as principal cellist of Amsterdam's Concertgebouw Orch. (1962–68), he devoted himself to an international career as a soloist and recitalist. He taught at his alma mater and at Amsterdam's Sweelinck Cons., and was the Erasmus Scholar at Harvard Univ. in 1982. His repertoire is comprehensive, ranging from the Baroque and early Classical periods (utilizing original instruments) to contemporary scores.

Byrne, David, Scottish-born American musician; b. Dumbarton, May 14, 1952. He was taken to the U.S. when he was 6. In 1970–71 he attended the Rhode Island School of Design, where he developed his dominant conviction that dance, song, instrumental music, drama, and cinema were parts of a total art. As his own medium he selected modern dance music and vocal works, stretching in style from folk music to rock. He frequented the popular cabarets and dance halls of N.Y., where he absorbed the essence of urban folklore and the rhythmic ways of natural musicians. He joined the group Talking Heads in 1975 as lead singer, guitarist, and composer, which made a specialty of exotic rhythms, especially Caribbean dance tunes, merengue, salsa, bomba, and cha-cha; from Colombia they took cambia; from Brazil, the classical samba. Much of the music that Byrne concocts of these elements is multilingual; one of his albums is titled *Speaking in Tongues* (1983). Byrne also favors African sounds, such as that of the Nigerian juju. The titles of his own songs are fashionably nonsensical, e.g., *Stop Making Sense*, which seems to make plenty of sense to his public. He is an accomplished guitarist, and as a performer displays unbounded physical energy, allowing himself a free voice that ranges from a hiccup to a cry, while urging the accompanying chorus to intone such anarchistic declarations as "Don't Want to Be Part of Your World." The devotion that Byrne has for modern dance is exemplified by the remarkable score he wrote for *The Catherine Wheel*, choreographed by Twyla Tharp; it possesses the widely differing ingredients of new-wave rock and spiritual soul music, masculine and rough on the one hand and elegiac and devotional on the other. The resulting complex has also the additional element of African percussion. Taken as a whole, it represents a synthesis of urban beat and largely unrelated Eastern rhythms. The Talking Heads disbanded in 1989. His 1989 album, *REI MOMO* (promoted in concert at the Brooklyn Academy of Music as part of the New Music America Festival), consists of songs that, backed by a 16-piece band, combine Latin and pop styles. In 1992 he brought out the succesful album *Uh-Oh*. It was followed by his *David Byrne* album in 1994. There is a hypnopompic quality in his inspiration as a composer, asymptotically lying in both reality and irreality, like a half-waking state.

BIBL.: K. Emerson, "D. B.: Thinking Man's Rock Star," *N.Y. Times Magazine* (May 5, 1985).

Caamaño, Roberto, Argentine composer, pedagogue, and pianist; b. Buenos Aires, July 7, 1923. He studied piano and composition at the Conservatorio Nacional de Música in Buenos Aires; toured as a pianist in Latin America, North America, and Europe (1944–61). He concentrated his activities in Buenos Aires, where he was on the faculties of the Universidad del Litoral (1949–52), the Conservatorio Nacional de Música (1956–74), and the Universidad Católica Argentina (from 1964); he also was artistic director of the Teatro Colón (1961–64). In 1969 he became a member of the Accademia Nacional de Bellas Artes; in 1971 he received the Gran Premio of the Argentine Sociedad de Autores y Compositores. He publ. the valuable compendium *Historia del Teatro Colón* (3 vols., Buenos Aires, 1969) and *Apuntes para la formación del pianista profesional* (Buenos Aires, 1979).

WORKS: ORCH.: *Variaciones americanas* (1953–54; Buenos Aires, July 10, 1955); Bandoneón Concerto (Buenos Aires, Aug. 2, 1954); 2 piano concertos: No. 1 (1957; Washington, D.C., April 18, 1958) and No. 2 (Buenos Aires, Aug. 9, 1971); *Tripartita* for Wind Orch. (1966); Harp Concerto (1973–74; Washington, D.C., May 1, 1974); Guitar Concerto (Buenos Aires, Nov. 30, 1974). **CHAMBER:** 2 string quartets (1945, 1947); Piano Quintet (1962); various piano pieces. **VOCAL:** *Magnificat* for Chorus and Orch. (1954; Louisville, Ky., March 25, 1955); *Cantata de la paz* for Chorus and Orch. (Buenos Aires, July 3, 1966); *Canto a San Martin* for Reciter, Chorus, and Orch. (1979; Buenos Aires, June 13, 1980); *Te Deum* for Chorus and Orch. (1980; Buenos Aires, Nov. 28, 1981); songs.

BIBL.: N. Ceñal, "R. C. (1923)," *Revista del Instituto de Investigación Musicológica Carlos Vega*, No. 7 (Buenos Aires, 1986).

Caballé, Montserrat, celebrated Spanish soprano; b. Barcelona, April 12, 1933. She was a pupil of Eugenia Kemeny, Conchita Badia, and Napoleone Annovazzi at the Barcelona Conservatorio del Liceo; after her graduation in 1953, she made her operatic debut in Reus, near Barcelona, in *La Serva Padrona.* She then sang in Basel (1956–59) and Bremen (1959–62), and also made guest appearances in Vienna as Salome and Donna Elvira (1958), Milan's La Scala as a Flowermaiden in *Parsifal* (1960), where she sang major roles from 1969, and Mexico City as Massenet's Manon (1962). She made a brilliant U.S. debut on April 20, 1965, when she substituted for Marilyn Horne in a concert performance of *Lucrezia Borgia* at N.Y.'s Carnegie Hall. After appearing as the Marschallin and the Countess at the Glyndebourne Festival (summer 1965), she made her Metropolitan Opera debut in N.Y. on Dec. 22, 1965, as Gounod's Marguerite. In subsequent years, she returned to the Metropolitan Opera regularly, eliciting extraordinary praise for such roles as Desdemona, Norma, Violetta, Liù, Mimi, Aida, Adriana Lecouvreur, and Tosca, among others. She also sang with various other opera companies, including debut appearances as Violetta at the Chicago Lyric Opera (1970) and London's Covent Garden (1972). In addition, she toured extensively as a concert artist. Her performances of operas in concert allowed her to survey not only Wagner but roles seldom heard. On Sept. 24, 1989, she created the role of Queen Isabella in Balada's *Cristóbal Colón* in Barcelona, where, in 1992, she also appeared at the opening gala ceremonies at the Olympic Games. The great beauty of Caballé's voice was ably complemented by an extraordinary vocal technique, one equally suited for the opera house and concert hall. Few singers of her day could match her command of such a large repertory, which ranged from standard to contemporary opera, and from art songs to zarzuela. In 1964 she married the Spanish tenor Bernabé Martí (b. 1934).

Cacioppo, George (Emanuel), innovative American composer; b. Monroe, Mich., Sept. 24, 1927; d. Ann Arbor, Mich., April 4, 1984. He studied with Ross Lee Finney at the Univ. of Mich. in Ann Arbor (M.A., 1952) and later with Roberto Gerhard there (1960); also with Leon Kirchner at the Berkshire Music Center in Tanglewood. In 1960 he helped to organize the ONCE Festival in Ann Arbor, with which he was active until

1968; was an announcer and engineer at the Univ. of Mich. radio station (1960–84), and also taught periodically at the Univ. (1970–80). His interests in astronomy, mathematics, and poetry consumed him after 1970. His compositions written between 1960 and 1970 concern themselves with pitch relationships and with total-sound spectrums.

WORKS: *Fantasy* for Violin and Piano (1950); *Music* for 2 Trumpets and Strings (1951); Piano Sonata: *In Memoriam Béla Bartók* (1951); *Overture and Elegy* for Orch. (1952–53); String Trio (1960); *Bestiary I: Eingang* for Soprano, Piano, and 4 Percussionists (1961); 11 piano pieces for any number of pianos, with their realizations on tape sounding synchronously, or nonsynchronously, and lasting any practical, or impractical, length of time, 2 of which are subtitled: No. 3, *Cassiopeia* (1962) and No. 11, *Informed Sources* (1970); *2 Worlds* for Soprano and 7 Instruments (1962); *Mod 3* for Flute, Double Bass, and Percussion (1963); *Moved Upon Silence* for 6 Percussionists (1963); *The Advance of the Fungi* for Textless Men's Chorus, 3 Clarinets, 3 Trombones, 2 Horns, and Percussion (1964); *Time on Time in Miracles* for Soprano, 2 Horns, 2 Trombones, Cello, Piano, and Percussion (1964); *Holy Ghost Vacuum, or America Faints* for Electric Organ (Ann Arbor, March 29, 1966, composer organist); *K* for Live Electric Organs, Pianos, and Sound Modifiers (1967; rev. as *K-2*, 1968); *Dream Concert* for Organ, Voice, and Percussionist (1976).

Cadman, Charles Wakefield, important American composer; b. Johnstown, Pa., Dec. 24, 1881; d. Los Angeles, Dec. 30, 1946. His great-grandfather was the hymn composer Samuel Wakefield (1799–1895). After studies with William Steiner (organ), Edwin L. Walker (piano), and Leo Oehmler (theory), he received training in theory and conducting from Luigi von Kunits and Emil Paur. From 1908 to 1910 he was music ed. and critic of the *Pittsburgh Dispatch*. His interest in American Indian music resulted in various lecture-performance tours in the U.S. and Europe with the Cherokee-Creek Indian Princess Tsianina Redfeather. In 1916 he settled in Los Angeles as a composer and teacher. Cadman wrote an opera based on the life of Redfeather, *Shanewis or The Robin Woman*, which was premiered at the Metropolitan Opera in N.Y. on March 23, 1918.

WORKS: DRAMATIC: *The Land of the Misty Water*, opera (1909–12; rev. as *Ramala*); *Shanewis or The Robin Woman*, opera (N.Y., March 23, 1918); *The Sunset Trail*, operatic cantata (Denver, Dec. 5, 1922); *The Garden of Mystery*, opera (N.Y., March 20, 1925); *The Ghost of Lollypop Bay*, operetta (1926); *Lelawala*, operetta (1926); *A Witch of Salem*, opera (Chicago, Dec. 8, 1926); *The Belle of Havana*, operetta (1928); *South in Sonora*, operetta (1932); *The Willow Tree*, radio score (NBC, Oct. 3, 1932); film scores. **ORCH.:** *Thunderbird Suite* (1914); *Oriental Rhapsody* (1917); *Prairie Sketches* (1923; arranged from a piano piece, 1906); *To a Vanishing Race* for Strings (1925); *Hollywood Suite* (1932); *Dark Dancers of the Mardi Gras* for Piano and Orch. (1933); *Trail Pictures* (1934); *American Suite* for Strings (1936); *Suite on American Folktunes* (1937); Sym., *Pennsylvania* (1939–40; Los Angeles, March 7, 1940); *Aurora Borealis* for Piano and Orch. (1944); *A Mad Empress Remembers* for Violin and Orch. (1944); *Huckleberry Finn Goes Fishing*, overture (1945). **CHAMBER:** Piano Trio (1914); Violin Sonata (1932); Piano Quintet (1937). **PIANO:** *Melody* (1905); *Prairie Sketches* (1906; also for Orch., 1923); *Idealized Indian Themes* (1912); Sonata (1915); *Oriental Suite* (1921). **VOCAL:** *The Vision of Sir Launfal* for Men's Chorus (1909); *The Father of Waters* for Chorus (1928); *The Far Horizon* for Chorus (1934); sacred anthems; song cycles; numerous solo songs.

BIBL.: J. Porte, "C.W. C.: An American Nationalist," *The Chesterian*, no. 39 (1924); N. Fielder, *Complete Musical Works of C.W. C.* (Los Angeles, 1951; catalog); H. Perison, *C.W. C.: His Life and Works* (diss., Eastman School of Music, 1978); idem, "The 'Indian' Operas of C.W. C.," *College Music Symposium*, XXII/2 (1982).

Caduff, Sylvia, Swiss conductor; b. Chur, Jan. 7, 1937. She studied at the Lucerne Cons., receiving a piano diploma in 1961; then attended Karajan's conducting classes at the Berlin Cons.; continued conducting studies with Kubelik, Matačić, and Otterloo in Lucerne, Salzburg, and Hilversum. She made her debut with the Tonhalle Orch. of Zürich. After winning 1st prize in the 1966 Mitropoulos conducting competition in N.Y., she was an assistant conductor under Bernstein with the N.Y. Phil. (1966–67); then taught conducting at the Bern Cons. (1972–77). In 1977 she became the first woman in Europe to be appointed a Generalmusikdirektor, when she took that position with the orch. of the city of Solingen. She left that position in 1985.

Cage, John (Milton, Jr.), singularly inventive and much beloved American composer, writer, philosopher, and visual artist of ultramodern tendencies; b. Los Angeles, Sept. 5, 1912; d. N.Y., Aug. 12, 1992. His father, John Milton Cage, Sr., was an inventor, and his mother, Lucretia Harvey, was active as a clubwoman and columnist in Southern California. He studied piano with his Aunt Phoebe and Fannie Charles Dillon in Los Angeles, showing particular interest in the music of Edvard Grieg. He had early aspirations to be either a minister or a writer, and, representing Los Angeles High School in 1927, won the Southern California Oratorical Contest at the Hollywood Bowl with his essay "Other People Think," a plea for Pan-American conscience by the (North) American people. After brief studies at Pomona College in Claremont, California (1928–30), he traveled to Europe, where he studied architecture with Ernö Goldfinger and piano with Lazare Lévy in Paris; also traveled throughout Biskra, Majorca, Madrid, and Berlin (1930–31), painting, writing poetry, and producing his first musical compositions, which he abandoned prior to his return to California. He continued writing, painting, and composing on his own, supporting himself as a gardener in an auto court in Santa Monica and also lecturing on modern art and music to housewives. He then studied composition with Richard Buhlig, developing a method of composition employing two twenty-five tone ranges, which appear in his early *Solo with Obbligato Accompaniment of Two Voices in Canon, and Six Short Inventions on the Subjects of the Solo* (1933–44; rev. 1963). At the suggestion of Henry Cowell, he pursued studies in harmony with Adolph Weiss; he also studied modern harmony, contemporary music, and Oriental and folk music with Cowell at the New School for Social Research in N.Y. Cage's studies culminated with counterpoint lessons from Schoenberg (1934), both privately and at the Univ. of Southern Calif.; he also attended Schoenberg's classes in counterpoint and analysis at the Univ. of Calif., Los Angeles. On June 7, 1935, Cage married Xenia Andreyevna Kashevaroff. Through his brief association with the filmmaker Oskar Fischinger, Cage became interested in noise, subsequently developing methods of writing complex rhythmic structures for percussion music; he then joined a modern dance group at the Univ. of Calif., Los Angeles, as an accompanist and percussion composer. He and Xenia also studied bookbinding with Hazel Dreis, and formed a quartet of bookbinders for playing percussion music.

During the summer of 1937, Cage was on the faculty of Mills College in Oakland, California, where he worked as a composer for Marian Van Tuyl. He then moved to Seattle as composer-accompanist for Bonnie Bird's modern dance classes at the Cornish School, where he met Merce Cunningham, who was a dance student there. He organized a percussion orchestra, collected musical instruments, and made tours throughout the Northwest; it was in Seattle that Cage also met Morris Graves, and arranged for an exhibition of his work; he also arranged exhibitions of the work of Alexej Jawlensky, Kandinsky, Klee, and Mark Tobey. In 1939 he gave concerts of percussion music with Lou Harrison in San Francisco; he also worked as a recreational leader for the Works Progress Administration there, and composed his *First Construction (in Metal)* for 6 Percussionists (Seattle, Dec. 9, 1939). He began developing Cowell's piano technique of making use of tone clusters and playing directly on the body of the instrument or on the strings, which culminated in his invention of the "prepared piano"; by placing objects (screws, copper coins, rubber erasers, etc.) on and between the piano strings, he was able to significantly alter the tone color of individual keys and thus transform the piano into a percussion orchestra. His first prepared piano piece was music to accompany a dance by Syvilla Fort, *Bacchanale* (1938; rev. version, Seattle, April 28, 1940). The instrument rapidly gained acceptance among avant-garde composers, and in 1949, after the N.Y. premiere by Maro Ajemian of his *Sonatas and Interludes* for Prepared Piano (1946–48), he received a grant from the Guggenheim Foundation and a $1,000 award from the National Academy of Arts and Letters for having "extended the boundaries of music."

In 1941 Cage went to Chicago, where, at the invitation of László Moholy-Nagy, he taught a class in experimental music at the School of Design. He also accompanied dance classes of Katherine Manning there, and gave a concert of percussion music at the Arts Club. Commissioned by CBS ("Columbia Workshop") to create a radio program, he composed *The City Wears a Slouch Hat* for 4 Percussion and Sound Effects, to a text by Kenneth Patchen (Chicago, May 31, 1942). He then moved to N.Y. (1942), where he began a lengthy association with Cunningham, who had since relocated to N.Y. to perform with Martha Graham; Cage and Cunningham would collaborate for nearly 50 years on works that introduced radical innovations in musical and choreographic composition. When the Merce Cunningham Dance Co. was formed in 1953, Cage served as its first music director, a position he maintained for more than 30 years. It was also during this period that Cage met Marcel Duchamp through Max Ernst and Peggy Guggenheim. He became interested in chess, and later played demonstration games with Duchamp on a chessboard designed by Lowell Cross to operate on aleatory principles with the aid of a computer (*Reunion*; Toronto, March 5, 1968). During this period Cage also gave a concert at the Museum of Modern Art, the first in a series of New York recitals that established his reputation. After his divorce from Xenia in 1945, he moved to N.Y.'s Lower East Side; having a "crisis of faith" about composition, he began what became a life-long study of Eastern philosophies, first (Indian philosophy and music) with the visiting Indian musician and teacher Gira Sarabhai, and then (Zen Buddhism) with Daisetz Teitaro Suzuki, whose classes he attended at Columbia Univ. He also made numerous tours with Cunningham, and received an important commission from Lincoln Kirstein and the Ballet Soc., resulting in *The Seasons* (N.Y., May 18, 1947). In 1948 Cage taught at Black Mountain College in North Carolina, where he met R. Buckminster Fuller, Richard and Louise Lippold, Elaine and Willem de Kooning, and Joseph Albers, among others. In 1949 he spent 3 months in Europe, where he appeared in concerts and dance recitals with Cunningham; he also met Pierre Boulez; their subsequent correspondence was publ. as *Pierre Boulez/John Cage: Correspondance et documents* (J.-J. Nattiez and F. Davoine, eds., Winterthur, 1990). Returning to N.Y., Cage participated in the formation, with Robert Motherwell and others, of the Artists Club. Dating from this period are also his "Lecture on Nothing" and "Lecture on Something," and his *String Quartet in Four Parts* (1949–50).

In 1950 Cage began developing means for composition with chance operations. He came under the influence of the *I Ching*, or "Book of Changes," one of the most influential books in the Chinese canon, which became his sole director as a composer, poet, and visual artist for the remainder of his life. An extremely significant collaboration stemming from this period, and extending throughout the decade in the realization of the first of his *I Ching* chance-determined compositions, was with the pianist David Tudor, who was able to reify Cage's exotic inspirations, works in which the performer shares the composer's creative role. Tudor also became closely associated with the Merce Cunningham Dance Co., and thus he and Cage had a close working relationship of some 40 years' duration. In 1950 Cage completed a score for Herbert Matter's film, *Works of Calder* for Prepared Piano and Tape (1949–50), which received 1st prize from the Woodstock Art Film Festival. He also composed his *Concerto for Prepared Piano and Chamber Orchestra* (1950–51; N.Y., Jan. 1952) as well as his *Imaginary Landscape No. 4* for 24 Performers on 12 Radios, commissioned by the New Music Soc. and presented at Columbia Univ.'s McMillin Theater on May 10, 1951. It was during this period as well that he began a life-long friendship with Robert Rauschenberg. In 1952, at Black Mountain College, Cage presented a theatrical event historically marked as the earliest Happening; participants in this protypical adventure included Cunningham, Charles Olson, Rauschenberg, M.C. Richards, and Tudor. Cage's seminal *Music of Changes* was given its premiere performance by Tudor at the Cherry Lane Theater on Jan. 1, 1952. In this year, he also composed his first piece for tape as a score for a dance by Jean Erdman, *Imaginary Landscape No. 5* (N.Y., Jan. 18, 1952). Influenced at the Black Mountain Happening by Rauschenberg's all-black and all-white paintings, Cage composed his notoriously tacet *4'33"* (1952); the ultimate freedom in musical expression, Cage's work is heard in 3 movements (indicated by the pianist's closing and reopening of the piano key cover), during which no sounds are intentionally produced. It was first performed by Tudor in Woodstock, N.Y., on Aug. 29, 1952. A decade later Cage created a second "silent" piece, *0'00"*, "to be played in any way by anyone," presented for the first time in Tokyo on Oct. 24, 1962. Any sounds produced by the listeners are automatically regarded as integral to the piece, so that the wisecrack about the impossibility of arriving at a fair judgment of such a silent piece, since one cannot tell what music is not being played, is invalidated by the uniqueness of Cage's art.

In 1954 Cage moved with Tudor, Richards, and Karen Weinrib to a cooperative community established by Paul and Vera Williams in Rockland County, N.Y. He also made a concert tour of Europe (Donaueschingen, Cologne, Paris, Brussels, Stockholm, Zürich, Milan, and London) with Tudor, and, upon his return, met Jasper Johns, who would remain a life-long friend and associate. He also began work on his *Music for Piano* series (ranging from *Music for Piano 1*, 1952, to *Music for Piano 85* for Piano and Electronics, 1962), using the imperfections in manuscript paper to guide his composition. From 1956 to 1960 he taught occasional classes at the New School for Social Research, where his students included George Brecht, Al Hansen, Dick Higgins, Toshi Ichiyanagi, Allan Kaprow, and Jackson Mac Low. In 1958 an historically significant 25-year retrospective concert of his music was given at N.Y.'s Town Hall. He then spent a summer in Europe teaching a class in experimental music at Darmstadt and giving concerts and lectures elsewhere, including "Indeterminacy, New Aspects of Form in Instrumental and Electronic Music" at the Brussels World Fair. In Italy he composed *Fontana Mix* for any Sound Sources or Actions (1958; Rome, Jan. 5, 1959); he also appeared on an Italian quiz show, "Lascia o Raddoppia," as a mushroom expert, winning $6,000; in his 5 performances he presented his *Amores* for Prepared Piano and 3 Percussionists (1936; rev. version, N.Y., Feb. 7, 1943), *Sounds of Venice* for Various Stage Properties and Tape (Milan, Jan. 1959), and *Water Walk* for Piano and Various Stage Properties (Milan, Jan. 1959).

Returning to N.Y. in 1959, Cage again taught at the New School for Social Research, this time 3 specific courses: (1) mushroom identification, (2) the music of Virgil Thomson, and (3) experimental composition. In 1960–61 he was a fellow at the Center for Advanced Studies at Wesleyan Univ. in Middletown, Connecticut, where he completed his first book, *Silence* (1961), which has since become a classic study in 20th-century musical aesthetics. He also met Norman O. Brown. In 1961 he was commissioned by the Montreal Festivals Soc. to write the orch. piece *Atlas Eclipticalis* for 1 to 86 Specified Instruments (1961–62; Montreal, Aug. 3, 1961). In 1962 he founded, with Esther Dam, Ralph Ferrara, Lois Long, and Guy G. Nearing, the N.Y. Mycological Soc. He also made an extensive concert tour of Japan with Tudor. In 1963 he directed the first N.Y. performance of *Vexations* by Erik Satie, a composer to whom he expressed almost life-long devotion. He also made a world tour with the Merce Cunningham Dance Co. Other activities in the late 1960s included the formation, with Johns, of the philanthropic Foundation for Contemporary Performance Arts in N.Y.; he also was composer-in-residence at the Univ. of Cincinnati. In 1967 he publ. *A Year From Monday.* It was during this period also that he met the controversial Canadian media philosopher Marshall McLuhan, whose ideas resonated strongly in Cage, as well as Wendell Berry, who introduced him to the *Journals* of Henry David Thoreau, which subsequently appeared, in various guises, in many of Cage's works. He also was an assoc. at the Center for Advanced Study at the Univ. of Ill., where he created *HPSCHD* for 1 to 7 Amplified Harpsichords and 1 to 51 Tapes (1967–69; Champaign-Urbana, Ill., May 16, 1969; in collaboration with L. Hiller). In 1969 he was an artist-in-residence at the Univ. of Calif., Davis; he also publ. *Notations* (with A. Knowles), and executed his first visual work (with Calvin Sumsion), *Not Wanting to Say Anything About Marcel*, at Hollander's Workshop in N.Y. In 1970 he was again, this time as an advanced fellow, at the Center for Advanced Studies at Wesleyan Univ.

Throughout the 1970s Cage traveled extensively and produced works in a variety of media. With Lois Long he publ. *Mushroom Book*, and also made a European tour with Tudor. In 1973 he publ. *M: Writings '67-'72.* In 1974–75 he composed his *Etudes Australes* (Witten, April 23 and 25, 1982), using star charts as his guide; in 1978 he created color etchings entitled *Score Without Parts (40 Drawings by Thoreau): Twelve Haiku*, incorporating drawings by Thoreau. Also from the 1970s were his *Child of Tree* (Detroit, Mich., March 8, 1975) and *Branches* (1976), both scored for Percussion and Amplified Plant Materials, as well as his *Lecture on the Weather* for 12 Amplified Voices, optionally with Instruments, Tape, and Film (1975; Toronto, Feb. 26, 1976), a lavish audio-visual work commissioned by the Canadian Broadcasting Corp. on the occasion of American's Bicentennial, combining collages of spoken texts by Thoreau, a film by Luis Frangella, and weather recordings by Marianne Amacher. He also composed *Renga* for 78 Instruments or Voices or combinations thereof (1975–76; Boston, Sept. 29, 1976) and *Apartment House 1776* for 4 Voices, optionally on Tape, and any number of Instruments (Boston, Sept. 29, 1976). He then began reading the works of James Joyce, being particularly influenced by *Finnegans Wake.* On the advice of Yoko Ono, he also began following the macrobiotic diet, which significantly improved his health. In 1977 he began work on his mammoth *Freeman Etudes* for Violin, composed for Paul Zukofsky and dedicated to Betty Freeman and completed with the assistance of James Pritchett only shortly before their premiere in Zürich on June 29, 1991; also from this period was his *Inlets* for 3 Performers using Water-filled Conch Shells, Blown Conch Shell, and the sound of fire (Seattle, Sept. 10, 1977). At the encouragement of Kathan Brown in 1978, Cage began making prints at Crown Point Press in Oakland (later San Francisco), California; Cage returned there annually until his death in 1992, producing such works as *Seven Day Diary* (1978), *Dereau* (1982), *Where There is Where There—Urban Landscape* (1987), *Dramatic Fire* (1989), and *Smoke Weather Stone Weather* (1991); Cage also produced a series of unique pencil rock tracings on handmade Indian paper, entitled *Where R = Ryoanji* (1983–92). Also in 1978 was the publication of his *Writing Through Finnegans Wake* (with A. Knowles) and the composition of his lively *Alla Ricerca del Silenzio Perduto* (a.k.a. *Il Treno*) for Prepared Train (1977; Bologna and vicinity, June 26–28, 1978).

In 1979 Cage worked at Paris's IRCAM (with David Fullemann) to complete his *Roaratorio, an Irish Circus on Finnegans Wake*, a quintessential realization of his _______, _________*Circus On* _______ for Voice, Tape, and any number of Musicians, optionally on tape, a means of translating any book into music; the work was commissioned by Klaus Schöning at the Westdeutscher Rundfunk, Cologne, and premiered in Donaueschingen on Oct. 20 of that same year. In 1980 his *Third* and *Fourth Writings Through Finnegans Wake* appeared; in 1981–82 he composed his fanciful hörspiel, *James Joyce, Marcel Duchamp, Erik Satie: Ein Alphabet* (Westdeutscher Rundfunk, Cologne, July 6, 1982). In 1981 he wrote *Composition in Retrospect* (Cambridge, Mass., 1993), and also composed *Thirty Pieces for Five Orchestras* (Pont-à-Mousson, Nov. 22, 1981) and *Dance/4 Orchestras* (Mission San Juan Bautista, Calif., Aug. 22, 1982). He also gave a night-long reading of his *Empty Words: Writings '73-'78* (Middletown, Conn., 1979) over National Public Radio. In 1982 his scores and prints were exhibited for the first time at the Whitney Museum of American Art in N.Y. and at the Philadelphia Museum of Art. In 1984 he began extensive work with the computer, employing programs made for him by Andrew Culver and Jim Rosenberg, producing his first computer-assisted mesostic poem, after Allen Ginsburg's *Howl.*

In 1987 several large-scale works were completed and premiered, including Cage's only installation, *Voiceless Essay*, based on texts from Thoreau's *Essay on Civil Disobedience* and ambient sounds. He also completed *Europeras 1 & 2* for any number of Voices, Chamber Orch., Tape, and Organ ad libitum (1984–87; Frankfurt am Main, Dec. 12, 1987), a chance-determined, musico-dramatic staged collage self-referentially comprised of excerpts from extant operas across historical time. The scheduled opening of *Europeras 1 & 2* on Nov. 15, 1987 was delayed and its location changed due to a fire, reportedly set by a vagrant in search of food, which devastated the Frankfurt am Main Opera House. He also produced works for and attended numerous 75th birthday celebrations worldwide, including a week-long event at the Los Angeles Festival. Also from this year was his *Two* for Flute and Piano, the first in a series of "number pieces," each utilizing a flexible notation system of his devising called "time-bracket notation;" "time-bracket notation" would be his method of choice for virtually all compositions henceforth. In 1988 he extended his activities as a visual artist further with a series of watercolors with Ray Kass at the Mountain Lake Workship in Roanoke, Virginia. In 1988–89 he held the prestigious Charles Eliot Norton Chair at Harvard Univ., for which he wrote and delivered 6 large-scale, quasi-autobiographical mesostic poems incorporating the writings of Fuller, Thoreau, McLuhan et al.; these poems (or lectures), with texts from interspersed seminars with students, were later publ. as *I–VI* (Boston, 1990). In 1989 a joint exhibition, "Dancers on a Plane: John Cage, Merce Cunningham, Jasper Johns," was presented in London and Liverpool. In 1990 Cage's watercolors were exhibited as "New River Watercolors" at the Phillips Collection in Washington, D.C. Cage also saw the premiere of his *Fourteen* for Piano and Small Orch. (Zürich, May 12, 1990) and his *Europeras 3 & 4* for at least 6 Voices, 2 Pianos, at least 6 Performers with 12 Gramophones and 1 Phonograph, and Tape and Light Operators at London's Almeida Music Festival (June 17, 1990). His *Europera 5* followed in 1991, a somewhat diminutive version in the *Europeras* series for 2 Voices, Piano, Phonograph, and Sound and Light Operators (Buffalo, N.Y., April 18, 1991). The Scottish National Orch. produced a week of Cage music. Cage also began designing, in collaboration with curator Julie Lazar, his continually changing work for museum, *Rolywholyover A Circus*, which was seen successively, after his death, in Los Angeles, Houston, N.Y., Mito (Japan), and Philadelphia. In 1991 Cage attended the John Cage-James Joyce Zürich June Festival, where his *Europeras 1 & 2* was performed at the Zürich Opera; also premiered there was *Beach Birds*, his final collaboration with Cunningham. During this period, Cage also made suites of handmade paper and edible drawings with Bernie Toale at Rugg Toad Papers in Boston, Mass.

In 1992, the last year of his life, Cage attended innumerable 80th birthday celebrations around the world. He also composed a remarkable number of scores, including orch. works for the Hessischer Rundfunk (Frankfurt am Main), the Westdeutscher Rundfunk (Cologne), and the American Composers Orch. (N.Y.)., as well as some 20 compositions, most of them "number pieces," for various smaller ensembles. He also completed his first and only film, the strikingly minimalist *One[11]*, with Henning Lohner. Shortly before his 80th birthday and his scheduled departure for Frankfurt am Main to attend the extensive birthday celebrations planned in both Frankfurt and Cologne, on Aug. 11, 1992, Cage collapsed in the N.Y. loft he shared with Cunningham; he died peacefully the following afternoon, on Aug. 12, 1992, without gaining consciousness, of a massive stroke.

Cage's influence, while unquestionably profound, has likely yet to be fully felt. With the passing years, he departed from the pragmatism of precise musical notation and circumscribed ways of performance, electing instead to mark his creative intentions in graphic symbols, pictorial representations, generalized and often poetic instructions, and flexible time relationships. His principal contribution to the history of music was his establishment of the principle of indeterminacy in composition; by adapting Zen Buddhist meditative practices to composition, Cage succeeded in bringing both authentic spiritual ideas and a liberating attitude of play to the enterprise of Western art. His aesthetic of chance also, uniquely, produced a body of what might be called "once-only" works, any 2 performances of which can never be the same. In an effort to reduce the subjective element in composition, Cage developed methods of selecting the components of his pieces by chance, early on through the throwing of coins or dice and later through the use of various random number generators on the computer, and especially the program known as *IC*, designed by Cage's assistant, Andrew Culver, to simulate the coin oracle of the *I Ching*; the result is a system of total serialism, in which all elements pertaining to acoustical pulses, pitch, noise, duration, relative loudness, tempi, combinatory superpositions, etc., are determined by referring to previously drawn correlating charts. Thus, Cage's works did not originate in psychology, motive, drama, or literary purpose, but, rather, were just sounds, free of judgments about whether they are musical or not, free of fixed relations, and free of memory and taste.

Cage was also a brilliant writer, much influenced by the manner, grammar, syntax, and glorious illogic of Gertrude Stein. While his books did not appear until the early 1960s (with the exception of the co-authored *Virgil Thomson: His Life in Music*; with K. Hoover, N.Y., 1959), he was early on a frequent reviewer and contributor on music and dance to such periodicals as *Perspectives of New Music* and *Modern Music*, the latter under the guiding editorship of his close friend, Minna Daniel (née Lederman); he also was an assoc. ed. of the short-lived magazine *Possibilities*. Of singular importance to the field, however, was his development of a style of poetry he called "mesostic" (the name suggested by Norman O. Brown, to differentiate from the clearly related "acrostic"), which uses an anchoring, generating string of letters down the center of the page that spell a name, a word, or line of text relating (or not) to the subject matter of the poem. Cage's mesostic poems, analogously indeterminate with respect to their composition to his musical works of the period, were eventually also composed via computer, the "source material" pulverized and later enhanced by Cage into semi-coherent, highly evocative poetic texts; the most extensive example is found in the 6 lectures comprising the afore-mentioned *I–VI*, composed for Harvard Univ. He also collaborated on a number of other projects, including *The First Meeting of the Satie Society*, with illustrations by Johns, Cy Twombly, Rauschenberg, Sol LeWitt, Mell Daniel, Thoreau, and Cage himself, coordinated by Benjamin Schiff and publ. in 1993 by the Limited Editions Club.

Cage was elected to the American Academy and Inst. of Arts and Letters in 1968 and to the American Academy of Arts and Sciences in 1978; he was inducted into the more exclusive branch of the Academy, the American Academy of Arts and Letters, in 1989. In 1981 he received the Mayor's Award of Honor in N.Y. City. He was named Commander of the Order of Arts and Letters by the French Minister of Culture in 1982, and received an Honorary Doctorate of Performing Arts from the Calif. Inst. of the Arts in 1986. In the summer of 1989 he was guest artist at International Festivals in Leningrad and Moscow, at which he presented works entitled *Music for ____* (1984; rev. 1987), incorporating flexible time-bracket notation, which he conducted chironomically. In late 1989 he traveled to Japan to receive, in traditional and quite formal Japanese dress, the highly prestigious and lucrative Kyoto Prize.

WORKS: DRAMATIC: *Music for Marriage at the Eiffel Tower* for Piano and Toy Instruments (Seattle, March 24, 1939; in collaboration with H. Cowell and G. McKay); *The City Wears a Slouch Hat*, music for a radio play for 4 Percussion and Sound Effects, to a text by K. Patchen (Chicago, May 31, 1942); *Works of Calder*, music for a film for Prepared Piano and Tape (1949–50); *Black Mountain Piece* for 3 Voices, Piano, Dancer, Gramophone, Radios, Films, Slides, and Painter (Black Mountain, N.C., Summer, 1952); *Water Music* for Piano and Various Stage Properties (N.Y., May 2, 1952); *Sounds of Venice* for Various Stage Properties and Tape (Milan, Jan. 1959); *Water Walk* for Piano and Various Stage Properties (Milan, Jan. 1959); *Theatre Piece* for 1 to 8 Performers (N.Y., March 7, 1960); *Mewanemooseicday*, musical exhibition around the music of Erik Satie (Davis, Calif., Nov. 21, 1969); *Dialogue* for 2 Performers (c.1970); *Song Books* for Any Number of Performers (Paris, Oct. 26, 1970); *Demonstration of the Sounds of the Environment* for 300 people silently following a chance-determined path (Milwaukee, Fall 1971); *Alla Ricerca del Silenzio Perduto* for Prepared Train (1977; Bologna and vicinity, June 26–28, 1978); *Silent Environment* for an indeterminate closed space (1979; Berlin, Jan. 20, 1980); *Evéne/EnvironneMetzment* for an audience possibly producing sounds (Metz, Nov. 21, 1981); *Europeras 1 & 2* for any number of Voices, Chamber Orch., Tape, and Organ ad libitum (1985–87; Frankfurt am Main, Dec. 12, 1987); *Europeras 3 & 4* for at least 6 Voices, 2 Pianos, at least 6 Performers with 12 Gramophones and 1 Phonograph, and Tape and Light Operators (London, June 17, 1990); *Europera 5* for 2 Voices, Piano, Phonograph, and Sound and Light Operators (Buffalo, N.Y., April 18, 1991). **RADIO PLAYS:** *James Joyce, Marcel Duchamp, Erik Satie: Ein Alphabet* (1981–82; Westdeutscher Rundfunk, Cologne, July 6, 1982); *Klassik nach Wunsch* (Westdeutscher Rundfunk, Cologne, April 23, 1982); *Fifteen Domestic Minutes* (National Public Radio, Nov. 5, 1982); *HMCIEX* (1983–84; Westdeutscher Rundfunk, July 10, 1984); *Empty Mind* (Westdeutscher Rundfunk, Cologne, Feb. 15, 1987). **FILM:** *One[11]* (1992; may be performed with *103* for Orch.).

ORCH.: *The Seasons* (N.Y., May 18, 1947); *Concerto for Prepared Piano and Chamber Orchestra* (1950–51; N.Y., Jan. 1952); *Etcetera* for Chamber Orch. (Paris, Nov. 6, 1973); *Exercise* (Rome, 1973; rev. 1984); *Quartets I–VIII* for Small Orch. (1976; Aptos, Calif., Aug. 20, 1977); *Quartets I–VIII* for Chamber Orch. (1976; St. Paul, Minn., May 31, 1978); *Quartets I–VIII* for Full Orch. (1976; Bonn, Dec. 9, 1977); *Quartets I, V and VI* for Concert Band and 12 Amplified Voices (1976); *Thirty Pieces for Five Orchestras* (Pont-à-Mousson, Nov. 22, 1981); *Dance/4 Orchestras* (Mission San Juan Bautista, Calif., Aug. 22, 1982); *A Collection of Rocks* for Chorus and Orch. (1984; Zagreb, April 19, 1985); *Etcetera 2/4 Orchestras* (1985; Tokyo, Dec. 8, 1986); *Twenty-Three* for Strings (Putney, Vt., July 1988); *101* (1988; Boston, April 6, 1989); *108* (Stuttgart, Nov. 30, 1991); *103* (1991; Cologne, Sept. 19, 1992; may be performed with the film *One[11]*); *Twenty-Eight* for 28 Woodwind and Brass Instruments, *Twenty-Six* for 26 Violins, and *Twenty-Nine* for 2 Timpani, 2 Percussion, Piano, 10 Violas, 8 Cellos, and 6 Double Basses (1991; Frankfurt am Main, Sept. 5, 1992); *Eighty* (1992); *Sixty-Eight* (Frankfurt am Main, Nov. 6, 1992); *Fifty-Eight* for Concert Band (Graz, Oct. 11, 1992); *Seventy-Four* (N.Y., Nov. 8, 1992).

CHAMBER: *Sonata for Clarinet* (1933); *Allemande* for Clarinet (1934); *Duet for Flutes* (1934); *Six Short Inventions* for Alto Flute, Clarinet, Trumpet, Violin, 2 Violas, and Cello (1934–58; N.Y., May 15, 1958); *Quest* for Various Amplified Objects and Piano (Los Angeles, April 28, 1935); *Three Pieces for Flute Duet* (1935); *String Quartet* (1936); *Amores* for Prepared Piano and 3 Percussionists (1936; rev. version, N.Y., Feb. 7, 1943); *Music for Wind Instruments* for Flute, Oboe, Clarinet, Horn, and Bassoon

(1938); *Fads and Fancies in the Academy* for Piano and 4 Percussionists (Oakland, Calif., July 27, 1940); *Four Dances* for Voice, Prepared Piano, and Percussion (1942–43; N.Y., Jan. 16, 1943); *She Is Asleep* for 4 Percussionists, Voice, and Prepared Piano (1943; N.Y., May 15, 1958); *Four Walls* for Piano and Voice (Steamboat Springs, Colo., Aug. 22, 1944); *Prelude for Six Instruments in A minor* for Flute, Bassoon, Trumpet, Piano, Violin, and Cello (1946); *Nocturne for Violin and Piano* (N.Y., Oct. 23, 1947); *String Quartet in Four Parts* (1949–50; Black Mountain, N.C., Aug. 12, 1950); *Six Melodies for Violin and Keyboard* for Violin and Piano (1950; Cambridge, Mass., Nov. 1959); *Sixteen Dances* for Flute, Trumpet, 4 Percussion, Piano, Violin, and Cello (1950–51; N.Y., Jan. 21, 1951); *Inlets* for 3 Performers using Water-filled Conch Shells, Blown Conch Shell, and the sound of fire (Seattle, Sept. 10, 1977); *Cheap Imitation* for Violin (Nov. 5, 1977); *Chorals for Violin Solo* (1978); *Pools* for Performer using Water-filled Conch Shells and Tape (1977–78; Amsterdam, June 15, 1978); *Sounday* for Violin, Piano, Voice, 9 Performers with Amplified Plant Materials and Water-filled Conch Shells, Blown Conch Shell, and Tape (1977–78; Amsterdam, June 15, 1978); *Freeman Etudes* for Violin (1977–90; Zürich, June 29, 1991); *Thirty Pieces for String Quartet* (1983; Darmstadt, July 27, 1984); *Haikai* for Flute and Zoomoozophone (1984; N.Y., March 9, 1985); *Eight Whiskus* for Violin (1985; N.Y., April 23, 1986); *Improvisation A + B* for Voice, Clarinet, Trombone, Percussion, and Cello (1986); *Haikai* for Gamelan (1986); *Two* for Flute and Piano (1987); *Seven* for Flute, Clarinet, Percussion, Piano, Violin, Viola, and Cello (Boston, Nov. 18, 1988); *Four* for String Quartet (1989); *Three* for 3 Recorder Players (1989; Speyer, July 27, 1990); *Fourteen* for Piano, Flute, Bass Flute, Clarinet, Bass Clarinet, Horn, Trumpet, 2 Percussionists, 2 Violins, Viola, Cello, and Double Bass (Zürich, May 12, 1990); *One*^{6} for Violin (1990); *Seven*^{2} for Bass Flute, Bass Clarinet, Bass Trombone, 2 Percussionists, Cello, and Double Bass (Erlangen, Sept. 25, 1990); *One*^{8} for Cello (Stuttgart, Nov. 30, 1991); *Eight* for Flute, Oboe, Clarinet, Bassoon, Horn, Trumpet, Trombone, and Tuba (Washington, D.C., May 14, 1991); *Five*^{2} for English Horn, 2 Clarinets, Bass Clarinet, and Timpani (1991; Cologne, Jan. 19, 1992); *Four*^{3} for 1 or 2 Pianos, 12 Rainsticks, and Violin or Oscillator (Zürich, June 20, 1991); *One*^{9} for Shō (1991; Japan, Jan. 18, 1992); *Two*^{3} for Shō and Water-filled Conch Shells (1991); *Two*^{4} for Violin and Piano or Shō (Washington, D.C., Nov. 15, 1991); *Five*^{3} for Trombone and String Quartet (1991; Middelburg, The Netherlands, June 28, 1992); *Five*^{4} for 2 Saxophones and 3 Percussionists (1991; Witten, April 25, 1992); *Five*^{5} for Flute, 2 Clarinets, Bass Clarinet, and Percussion (1991); *Four*^{5} for Saxophone Quartet or multiples thereof (1991); *Ten* for Flute, Oboe, Clarinet, Trombone, Percussion, Piano, and String Quartet (1991; Amsterdam, Feb. 24, 1992); *Two*^{5} for Trombone and Piano (1991; Frankfurt am Main, Jan. 30, 1992); *One*^{10} for Violin (1992; Baltimore, Md., April 4, 1993); *Two*^{6} for Violin and Piano (Orléans, Dec. 5, 1992); *Thirteen* for Flute, Oboe, Clarinet, Bassoon, Trumpet, Trombone, Tuba, 2 Xylophones, and String Quartet (1992; Gütersloh, Feb. 17, 1993). **PERCUSSION:** *Quartet* (1935; Seattle, 1938); *Trio* (1936); *Imaginary Landscape No. 1* for 4 Percussionists (Seattle, Spring 1939); *First Construction (in Metal)* for 6 Percussionists (Seattle, Dec. 9, 1939); *Second Construction* for 4 Percussionists (Portland, Ore., Feb. 14, 1940); *Imaginary Landscape No. 2* for 4 Percussionists (Seattle, May 7, 1940; withdrawn); *Living Room Music* for 4 Percussionists (1940); *Third Construction* for 4 Percussionists (San Francisco, May 14, 1941); *Double Music* for 4 Percussionists (San Francisco, May 14, 1941; in collaboration with L. Harrison); *Imaginary Landscape No. 3* for 6 Percussionists (Chicago, March 1, 1942); *Imaginary Landscape No. 2* for 5 Percussionists (San Francisco, May 7, 1942); *Credo in Us* for 4 Percussionists (Bennington, Vt., Aug. 1, 1942); *27'10.554" for a Percussionist* (1956; Munich, Feb. 2, 1962); *Child of Tree* for Percussionist using Amplified Plant Materials (Detroit, Mich., March 8, 1975); *Branches* for any number of Percussionists using Amplified Plant Materials (1976); *R/13 (Where R = Ryoanji)* for Percussionist using found objects (Viitasaari, July 1983); *But what about the noise of crumpling paper which he used to do in order to paint the series of "Papiers froissés" or tearing up paper to make "Papiers déchirés?" Arp was stimulated by water (sea, lake, and flowing waters like rivers), forests* for 3 to 10 Percussionists (1985); *One*^{4} for Percussionist (1990); *Three*^{2} for 3 Percussionists (1991); *Six* for 6 Percussionists (1991; The Hague, June 19, 1992); *Four*^{4} for 4 Percussionists (1991; N.Y., Summer 1992). **KEYBOARD: PIANO AND PREPARED PIANO:** *Etudes* (c.1931); *Three Easy Pieces* (1933); *Music for Xenia* (1934); *Two Pieces for Piano* (c.1935; rev. 1974); *Metamorphosis* (Seattle, Oct. 10, 1938); *Bacchanale* (1938; rev. version, Seattle, April 28, 1940); *Four Songs of the Moment* (Seattle, May 7, 1940); *Spiritual* (Seattle, May 7, 1940); *Jazz Study* (c.1942); *Dance* (1942); *Opening Dance* (Minneapolis, Minn., Feb. 20, 1942); *Totem Ancestor* (N.Y., Oct. 20, 1942); *And the Earth Shall Bear Again* (N.Y., Dec. 6, 1942); *Primitive* (1942); *In the Name of the Holocaust* (1942; Chicago, Feb. 14, 1943); *Shimmera* (1942; Chicago, Feb. 14, 1943); *Lidice* (N.Y., Jan. 20, 1943); *Ad Lib* (Chicago, Feb. 14, 1943); *Our Spring Will Come* (1943); *A Room* (1943); *Chess Pieces* (1943); *Meditation* (1943); *Tossed As It Is Untroubled* (1943; N.Y., April 5, 1944); *Triple-Placed No. 1* (1943; N.Y., April 5, 1944); *The Perilous Night* (1943–44; N.Y., April 5, 1944); *Prelude for Meditation* (1944); *Root of an Unfocus* (N.Y., April 5, 1944); *Spontaneous Earth* (N.Y., April 5, 1944); *Tripled-Paced No. 2* (1944); *The Unavailable Memory of* (N.Y., April 5, 1944); *A Valentine Out of Season* (1944); *A Book of Music* for 2 Prepared Pianos (1944; N.Y., Jan. 21, 1945); *Crete* (c.1945); *Dad* (c.1945); *Thin Cry* (c.1945); *Soliloquy* (N.Y., Jan. 9, 1945); *Experiences No. 1* for 2 Pianos (N.Y., Jan. 9, 1945); *Mysterious Adventure* (N.Y., Jan. 9, 1945); *Three Dances* for 2 Prepared Pianos (1944; rev. version, N.Y., Jan. 21, 1945); *Daughters of the Lonesome Isle* (1945; Bronxville, N.Y., Feb. 27, 1946); *The Feast* (1946); *Foreboding* (1946); *Ophelia* (Bronxville, N.Y., Feb. 27, 1946); *Encounter* (N.Y., May 12, 1946); *Two Pieces for Piano* (1946); *Sonatas and Interludes* (1946–48; Black Mountain, N.C., April 6, 1948); *Music for Marcel Duchamp* (1947); *Dream* (Black Mountain, N.C., Aug. 20, 1948); *Orestes* (Black Mountain, N.C., Aug. 20, 1948); *Suite for Toy Piano* (Black Mountain, N.C., Aug. 20, 1948); *Haikus* (1950–51); *Music of Changes* (1951; N.Y., Jan. 1, 1952); *Waiting* (N.Y., Feb. 4, 1952); *Seven Haiku* (1951–52); *Two Pastorales* (1951–52; N.Y., Feb. 10, 1952); *For M.C. and D.T.* (Norwalk, Conn., Aug. 1952); *Music for Piano 1* (N.Y., Dec. 16, 1952); *Music for Piano 2* (1953; N.Y., Jan. 10, 1954); *Music for Piano 4–19* for any number of Pianos (Baton Rouge, La., June 23, 1953); *Music for Piano 3* (1953); *Music for Piano 20* (1953); *34'46.776" for a Pianist* and *31'57.9864" for a Pianist* (Donaueschingen, Oct. 17, 1954); *Music for Piano 21–36/37–52* for any number of Pianos (New City, N.Y., Oct. 15, 1955); *Music for Piano 53–68* for any number of Pianos (Notre Dame, Ind., May 18, 1956); *Music for Piano 69–84* for any number of Pianos (1956); *Winter Music* for 1 to 20 Pianos (1956–57; N.Y., Jan. 12, 1957); *For Paul Taylor and Anita Dencks* (N.Y., Oct. 20, 1957); *TV Köln* (Cologne, Oct. 6 or 7, 1958); *Music for Amplified Toy Pianos* (Middletown, Conn., Feb. 25, 1960); *Music for Piano 85* for Piano with Electronics (1962); *Electronic Music for Piano* for any number of Pianos with Electronics (Stockholm, Sept. 1964); *Cheap Imitation* (1969; N.Y., Jan. 8, 1970); *Etudes Australes* (1974–75; Witten, April 23 and 25, 1982); *Furniture Music Etcetera* for 2 Pianos (1980); *Perpetual Tango* (1984); *One* (1987; Essen, Feb. 27, 1988); *Swinging* (1989); *Two*^{2} for 2 Pianos (1989; N.Y., May 4, 1990); *One*^{2} for Pianist using 1 to 4 Pianos (Huddersfield, Nov. 21, 1989); *The Beatles 1962–1970* for Piano and Tapes (1990); *One*^{5} (1990). **ORGAN:** *Some of The Harmony of Maine* (1978; Essen, Nov. 8, 1980); *Souvenir* (1983; San Francisco, June 29, 1984); *Organ*^{2}*/Aslsp* (Metz, Nov. 21, 1987). **CARILLON:** *Music for Carillon No. 1* (1952; N.Y., May 15, 1958), *No. 2* (1954), *No. 3* (1954), *No. 4* (1961), and *No. 5* (1967).

VOCAL: *Greek Ode* for Voice and Piano (Santa Monica, Calif., Nov. 1932); *The Preacher* for Voice and Piano (Santa Monica, Calif., Nov. 1932); *Three Songs* for Voice and Piano

(1932–33); *Five Songs for Contralto* for Voice and Piano (1938); *Ho to AA* for Voice and Piano (1939); *A Chant with Claps* for Voice with Handclaps (c.1940); *America Was Promises* for Voice and Piano, 4-hands (Seattle, May 7, 1940); *The Wonderful Widow of Eighteen Springs* for Voice and Piano (N.Y., May 5, 1942); *Forever and Sunsmell* for Voice and 2 Percussionists (N.Y., Oct. 20, 1942); *Experiences No. 2* for Voice (1948); *A Flower* for Voice and Piano (1950); *Solo for Voice 1* (N.Y., May 25, 1958); *Aria* for Voice (1958; Rome, Jan. 5, 1959); *Solo for Voice 2* (Lenox, Mass., Aug. 12, 1960); *Sixty-Two Mesostics re Merce Cunningham* for Voice (1971); *Les Chants de Maldoror Pulvérisés par l'Assistance Même* for a Francophone Audience of no more than 200 persons (1971); *Lecture on the Weather* for 12 Amplified Voices, with optional Instruments, Tape, and Film (1975; Toronto, Feb. 26, 1976); *Hymns and Variations* for 12 Amplified Voices (Bonn, June 10, 1979); *Litany for the Whale* for 2 Voices (1980); *Ear for Ear* for 2 or More Voices (N.Y., April 8, 1983); *Nowth upon Nacht* for Voice and Piano (1984); *Eight Whiskus* for Voice (1984; N.Y., May 14, 1985); *Selkus²* for Voice (1984); *Mirakus²* for Voice (1984); *Sonnekus²* for Voice (Bonn, March 31, 1985); *Wishing Well* for 4 Voices (1986); *Four Solos for Voice* for any solo from or combination of Soprano, Mezzo-soprano, Tenor, and Bass (N.Y., June 29, 1988); *Four²* for Chorus (1990); *One¹²* for Voice (Perugia, June 22, 1992).

TAPE: *Imaginary Landscape No. 5* (N.Y., Jan. 18, 1952); *Williams Mix* (1952; Urbana, Ill., March 22, 1953); *Music for The Marrying Maiden* (N.Y., June 15, 1960); *Rozart Mix* (Waltham, Mass., May 1965); *Bird Cage* (1972); *Newport Mix* (Cincinnati, Spring 1967); *Cassette* (N.Y., Dec. 7, 1977); *Improvisation III* (N.Y., Feb. 26, 1980); *Improvisation IV* (London, June 30, 1980; rev. 1982); *Instances of Silence* (March 16, 1982); *Stratified Essay* (1987); *Voiceless Essay* (1987); *Mozart Mix* (1991). **ELECTRONIC MEDIA:** *Imaginary Landscape No. 4* for 24 Performers on 12 Radios (N.Y., May 10, 1951); *Speech 1955* for 5 Radios and Newsreader (1955); *WBAI* for Tapes and Phonodiscs or Amplifiers (N.Y., Feb. 1960); *Cartridge Music* for 1 to 40 Players using Amplified Small Sounds and Piano or Cymbal (Bremen, Sept. 15, 1960); *Variations V* for any number of Performers using Photo-electric Cells and Electronic Sound Sources (N.Y., July 23, 1965); *Variations VI* for any number of Performers using Photo-electric Cells and Electronic Sound Sources (Washington, D.C., April 27, 1966); *Reunion* for Electronic Chessboard and Electronic Equipment activited by a game of chess (Toronto, March 5, 1968); *0'00" No. 2* for Amplified Playing Area activated by a game involving 2 or more persons (1968); *Program (KNOBS) for the Listener* for Phonodisc and Amplifier (1969; in collaboration with L. Hiller); *33 1/3* a large number of Phonodiscs and at least 12 Turntables to be operated by the audience (Davis, Calif., Nov. 21, 1969); *Variations VII* for any number of Musicians using Photo-electric Cells and Electronic Equipment (N.Y., Oct. 15, 1966; rev. 1972); *Telephones and Birds* for 3 Performers using Telephones and Tapes (N.Y., Jan. 18, 1977); *Address* for Phonodiscs and 12 Turntables to be operated by the audience, 5 Performers using Cassette Machines, and Electric Bell (N.Y., Dec. 7, 1977); *Paragraphs of Fresh Air* for Voice and 4 Instrumentalists also operating Tapes, Cassettes, Phonodiscs or Microphones, and Telephone (1979); *Concerto Grosso* for 4 Television Sets and 12 Radios (1979; Berlin, Jan. 20, 1980); *Rocks* for any combination of at least 6 Radios, Television Sets, Phonodiscs, and Cassettes ad libitum with machines emitting relatively fixed sounds (1986); *Sculptures Musicales* for any number of groups of indeterminate Sound Sources, each group consisting of at least 3 different sounds (Berkeley, Sept. 23, 1989); *One³* for Performer amplifying the sound of an auditorium to feedback level (Kyoto, Nov. 1989).

OTHER: VARIABLE INSTRUMENTATION: *In a Landscape* for Piano or Harp (Black Mountain, N.C., Aug. 20, 1948); *59 1/2" for a String Player* for Violin, Viola, and Cello or Double Bass (1953; San Antonio, May 7, 1962); *26'1.1499" for a String Player* for Violin, Viola, and Cello or Double Bass (1953–55; New City, N.Y., Oct. 15, 1955); *Radio Music* for 1 to 8 Radios (N.Y., May 30, 1956); *Concert for Piano and Orchestra* for any solo from or combination of Piano, Flute, Clarinet, Bassoon, Trumpet, Trombone, Tuba, 3 Violins, 2 Violas, Cello, and Double Bass, with optional Conductor (1957–58; N.Y., May 15, 1958); *Atlas Eclipticalis* for 1 to 86 Specified Instruments (Montreal, Aug. 3, 1961); *HPSCHD* for 1 to 7 Amplified Harpsichords and 1 to 51 Tapes (1967–69; Champaign-Urbana, Ill., May 16, 1969; in collaboration with L. Hiller); *Cheap Imitation* for 24 to 95 Specified Instruments (1970–72; The Hague, May 13, 1972 [declared public rehearsal by the composer]); *Etudes Boreales* for Cello and/or Piano (1978); *A House Full of Music* for Music School Students performing their repertoire simultaneously (1981–82; Bremen, May 10, 1982); *Postcard from Heaven* for 1 to 20 Harps (Minneapolis, Sept. 1982); *Musicircus for Children* for Children performing their repertoire simultaneously (Turin, May 19, 1984); *Aslsp* for Piano or Organ (College Park, Md., July 14, 1985); *Ryoanji* for any solo from or combination of Voice, Flute, Oboe, Trombone, Double Bass ad libitum with Tape, and Obbligato Percussionist or any 20 Instruments (1983–85); *Hymnkus* for any solo from or combination of Voice, Alto Flute, Clarinet, 2 Saxophones, Bassoon, Trombone, 2 Percussionists, Accordion, 2 Pianos, Violin, and Double Bass (1986); *Music for ____* for any solo from or combination of Voice, Flute, Oboe, Clarinet, Horn, Trumpet, Trombone, 4 Percussionists, 2 Pianos, 2 Violins, Viola, and Cello (New Milford, Conn., Aug. 15, 1984; rev. 1987); *cComposed Improvisation* for any solo from or combination of Snare Drum, Steinberger Bass Guitar, and One-sided Drums, with or without Jangles (1987–90); *Scottish Circus* for any Scottish or Irish Folk Instruments (Glasgow, Sept. 20, 1990). **INDETERMINATE SOUND SOURCES:** Music-based mathematical formulae (1930–31); *Sonata for Two Voices* (1933); *Solo with Obbligato Accompaniment of Two Voices in Canon, and Six Short Inventions on the Subjects of the Solo* (1933–44; rev. 1963); *Composition for Three Voices* (1934); *Party Pieces* for any Instruments encompassing specified ranges (c.1945; in collaboration with H. Cowell, L. Harrison, and V. Thomson); *4'33"* (Woodstock, N.Y., Aug. 29, 1952); *Haiku* (1958); *Variations I* (Greensboro, N.C., March 15, 1958); *Music Walk* for 1 or More Performers at a single Piano using Radios and other Auxiliary Sound Sources (Düsseldorf, Oct. 14, 1958); *Fontana Mix* for any Sound Sources or Actions (1958; Rome, Jan. 5, 1959); *Variations II* (N.Y., March 24, 1961); *0'00"* for 1 Performer (Tokyo, Oct. 24, 1962); *Variations III* (1962–63; Berlin, Jan. 1963); *Variations IV* (Los Angeles, July 17, 1963); *Musicircus* for any number of Performers willing to perform in the same place and time (Champaign-Urbana, Ill., Nov. 17, 1967); *Variations VIII* for any number of Performers possibly producing sounds with machines (1968; rev. 1976 and 1978); *Sound Anonymously Received* for Unsolicited Instrument (Davis, Calif., Nov. 21, 1969; rev. 1978); *Score (40 Drawings by Thoreau) and 23 Parts* for any Instruments or Voices or combinations thereof and Tape (Saint Paul, Minn., Sept. 28, 1974); *Renga* for 78 Instruments or Voices or combinations thereof (1975–76; Boston, Sept. 29, 1976); *Apartment House 1776* for 4 Voices, optionally on Tape, and any number of Instruments (Boston, Sept. 29, 1976); *49 Waltzes for the Five Boroughs* (1977); *A Dip in the Lake* (1978); *______, __ ______ Circus on ______* for Voice, Tape, and any number of Musicians, optionally on tape (Donaueschingen, Oct. 20, 1979); *Vis-à-Vis* for 2 Musicians (1986; in collaboration with T. Takemitsu); *Five* for 5 Voices or Instruments or combination thereof encompassing specified ranges (Middelburg, The Netherlands, June 27, 1988); *Five Stone Wind* for 3 Performers (Avignon, July 30, 1988); *One⁷* (1990); *Five Hanau Silence* for environmental sounds of Hanau (1991); *Four⁶* (1990–92; N.Y., July 23, 1992).

WRITINGS: With K. Hoover, *Virgil Thomson: His Life and Music* (N.Y., 1959); *Silence: Lectures and Writings* (Middletown, Conn., 1961); *A Year from Monday: New Lectures and Writings* (Middletown, Conn., 1967); *To Describe the Process of Composition Used in Not Wanting to Say Anything about Marcel* (Cincinnati, 1969); with A. Knowles, *Notations* (N.Y., 1969); *M: Writings '67–'72* (Middletown, Conn., 1973); *Writings through Finnegans Wake* (N.Y., 1978; includes *Writing for the Second*

Time through Finnegans Wake); *Empty Words: Writings '73–'78* (Middletown, Conn. 1979); with D. Charles, *For the Birds* (Boston, 1981); with S. Barron, *Another Song* (N.Y., 1981); W. Diamond and C. Hicks, eds., *John Cage: Etchings 1978–1982* (Oakland, Calif., 1982); with L. Long, *Mud Book* (N.Y., 1982; 2nd ed., 1988); *Themes and Variations* (N.Y., 1982); *X: Writings '79–'82* (Middletown, Conn., 1983); *I–VI* (Cambridge, Mass., 1990); *Composition in Retrospect* (Cambridge, Mass., 1993); R. Kostelanetz, ed., *John Cage, Writer: Previously Uncollected Pieces* (N.Y., 1993).

BIBL.: C. Tomkins, "Profiles: J. C.— Figures in an Imaginary Landscape," *New Yorker* (Nov. 1964); S. Kubota, *Marcel Duchamp and J. C.* (N.Y., 1968); L. Hiller, "Programming the 'I Ching' Oracle," *Computer Studies in the Humanities and Verbal Behavior*, III/3 (1970); R. Kostelanetz, ed., *J. C.* (N.Y., 1970; new ed., 1991); E. Snyder, *J. C. and Music since World War II: A Study in Applied Aesthetics* (diss., Univ. of Wisc., 1970); W. Duckworth, *Expanding Notational Parameters in the Music of J. C.* (diss., Univ. of Ill., 1972); R. Bunger, *The Well-Prepared Piano* (Colorado Springs, Colo., 1973; 2nd ed., San Pedro, Calif., 1981); J. Davies, *Two aspects of the American avant-garde: Charles Ives and J. C.* (diss., Univ. of Wales, Cardiff, 1973); L. Ferrero, *Le Idée di J. C.* (diss., Univ. of Turin, 1974); M. Nyman, *Experimental Music: C. and Beyond* (N.Y., 1974); J. Francis, *Structure in the Solo Piano Music of J. C.* (diss., Florida State Univ., 1976); F. Hoogerwerf, "C. contra Stravinsky, or delineating the aleatory aesthetic," *International Review of the Aesthetics and Sociology of Music*, VII/2 (1976); D. Charles, *Gloses sur J. C.* (Paris, 1978); H.-K. Metzger and R. Riehn, *J. C.* (Munich, 1978); S. Smith, "The Early Percussion Music of J. C.," *The Percussionist*, XVI/1 (1978); M. Fürst-Heidtmann, *Das präparierte Klavier des J. C.* (Regensburg, 1979); R. Hobbs, "Possibilities," *Art Criticism*, I/2 (1979); T. DeLio, "C.'s *Variations II*: The Morphology of a Global Structure," *Perspectives of New Music*, XIX (1980); M. Perloff, *The Poetics of Indeterminacy: Rimbaud to Cage* (Princeton, N.J., 1980); F. Bayer, *De Schönberg à Cage: Essai sur la notion d'espace sonore dans la musique contemporaine* (Paris, 1981); P. Griffiths, *C.* (N.Y., 1981); N. Crohn Schmitt, "J. C. in a New Key," *Perspectives of New Music*, XX/1–2 (1981–82); K. Brown, "Changing Art: A Chronicle Centered on J. C.," in W. Diamond and C. Hicks, eds., *John Cage: Etchings 1978–1982* (Oakland, Calif., 1982); M. Froment-Meurice, *Les intermittences de la raison: Penser C., entendre Heidegger* (Paris, 1982); P. Gena and J. Brent, eds., *A J. C. Reader: In Celebration of His 70th Birthday* (N.Y., 1982); H. Kepler, *J. C. und der Zen-Buddhismus* (diss., Univ. of Marburg, 1982); K. Schöning, *Roaratorio: Eine irischer Circus über Finnegans Wake* (Königstein, 1982); K. Shimoda, "C. and Zen," *Contact*, 55 (1982); R. Stevenson, "J. C. on His 70th Birthday: West Coast Background," *Inter-American Review*, V/1 (Fall 1982); S. Husarik, "J. C. and Lejaren Hiller: HPSCHD, 1969," *American Music*, I/2 (1983); T. DeLio, *Circumscribing the Open Universe: Essays on C., Feldman, Wolff, Ashley and Lucier* (Washington, D.C., 1984); D. Campana, *Form and Structure in the Music of J. C.* (diss., Northwestern Univ., 1985); T. Holmes, *Annotated Discography of the Music of J. C.* (Cherry Hill, N.J., 1986); J. Petkus, *The Songs of J. C. (1932–1970)* (diss., Univ. of Conn., 1986); S. Hilger, *C. and Cunningham: Eine Entwicklungsgeschichte von Musik und Tanz auf dem Weg einer beziehungsreichen Beziehungslosigkeit* (diss., Univ. of Bonn, 1987); R. Kostelanetz, ed., *Conversing with C.* (N.Y., 1987); P. van Emmerik, *A C. Documentary* (thesis, Univ. of Amsterdam, 1988); E. Pedrini, *J. C. Happening and Fluxus* (Florence, 1988); J. Pritchett, *The Development of Chance Techniques in the Music of J. C., 1950–1956* (diss., N.Y. Univ., 1988); R. Fleming and W. Duckworth, eds., *J. C. at Seventy-Five* (London and Toronto, 1989); N. Crohn Schmitt, "J. C., Nature, and Theater," in *Actors and Onlookers: Theater and Twentieth-Century Scientific Views of Nature* (Evanston, Ill., 1990); H.-K. Metzger and R. Riehn, eds., special issue of *Musik-Konzept* (2 vols.; Frankfurt am Main, 1990; includes list of works, discography, and extensive bibliography); J.-J. Nattiez and F. Davoine, eds., *Pierre Boulez/J. C.: Correspondance et documents* (Winterthur, 1990; Eng. tr., 1993; Ger. tr., 1995; Japanese tr., 1996); L. Austin, "An Interview with J. C. and Lejaren Hiller," *Computer Music Journal* (Winter 1992); W. Fetterman, *J. C.'s Theatre Pieces: Notations and Performances* (diss., N.Y. Univ., 1992); L. Kuhn, *J. C.'s "Europeras 1 & 2": The Musical Means of Revolution* (diss., Univ. of Calif., Los Angeles, 1992); D. Revill, *The Roaring Silence: J. C.: A Life* (N.Y., 1992); *Rolywholyover A Circus*, "box" accompanying the Los Angeles Museum of Contemporary Art exhibition of the same name (N.Y., 1992; contains new and reprinted essays by C., A. d'Harnoncourt, J. Lazar, L. Kuhn, J. Retallack, M. Swed, M. McLuhan, A. Weil, E. Snyder, and D.T. Suzuki); J.-Y. Bosseur, *J. C.* (Paris, 1993); R. Kostelanetz, ed., *Writings About J. C.* (Ann Arbor, 1993); J. Pritchett, *The Music of J. C.* (Cambridge, 1993); L. Kuhn, "Synergetic Dynamics in J. C.'s *Europeras 1 & 2*," *Musical Quarterly* (Spring 1994); G. Leonard, *Into the Light of Things: The Art of the Commonplace from Wordsworth to J. C.* (Chicago, 1994); D. Patterson, "C. and Beyond: An Annotated Interview with Christian Wolff," *Perspectives of New Music* (Summer 1994); M. Perloff and C. Junkerman, *J. C: Composed in America* (Chicago, 1994); W. Duckworth, *Talking Music: Conversations with J. C., Philip Glass, Laurie Anderson, and Five Generations of American Experimental Composers* (N.Y., 1995); R. Kostelanetz, *C. Ex(Plain)ed* (N.Y., 1995); J. Retallack, *MUSICAGE: C. Muses on Art, Music, Poetry* (Middletown, Conn., 1995); C. Shultis, "Silencing the Sounded Self: J. C. and the Intentionality of Nonintention," *Musical Quarterly* (Summer 1995); D. Patterson, *J. C., 1942–1954: A Language of Changes* (diss., Columbia Univ., 1996).

Cahier, Sarah (Jane Layton-Walker), American contralto; b. Nashville, Jan. 8, 1870; d. Manhattan Beach, Calif., April 15, 1951. She studied in Indianapolis. After singing in concert and church settings under the name Mrs. Morris Black, she pursued training with Jean de Reszke in Paris, Gustav Walter in Vienna, and Amalie Joachim in Berlin. In 1904 she made her operatic debut in Nice, and then was a member of the Vienna Court Opera (1906–11). On Nov. 20, 1911, she was a soloist in the premiere of Mahler's *Das Lied von der Erde* in Munich. She then made her Metropolitan Opera debut in N.Y. under the name Sarah Charles-Cahier, having married Charles Cahier in 1905, singing Azucena on April 3, 1912; she remained on its roster until 1913. She subsequently devoted herself to concert engagements, and later taught in Sweden, Salzburg, and N.Y. Among her best known roles were Carmen, Amneris, and Fricka.

Cahill, Teresa (Mary), English soprano; b. Maidenhead, July 30, 1944. She trained at the Guildhall School of Music and the Royal Academy of Music in London. In 1967 she made her operatic debut as Rosina with the Phoenix Opera Co. in London; from 1970 she appeared at the Glyndebourne Festivals and at Covent Garden in London; also sang with the Welsh National Opera in Cardiff and Scottish National Opera in Glasgow. In 1972 she appeared for the first time at the Santa Fe Opera, in 1976 at Milan's La Scala, and in 1981 with the Philadelphia Opera. She also pursued an active career as a concert singer. Her operatic repertoire includes roles in operas by Mozart, Verdi, and R. Strauss.

Cailliet, Lucien, exceptional French-born American composer, arranger, and conductor; b. Châlons-sur-Marne, May 22, 1891; d. Woodland Hills, Calif., Jan. 3, 1985. He gained experience as an instrumentalist and bandmaster in the French Army, and received training at the Dijon Cons. and from Fauchet, Caussade, and Pares at the Paris Cons. (graduated, 1913). In 1915 he emigrated to the U.S. and in 1923 became a naturalized citizen. In 1919 he joined the Philadelphia Orch. as a clarinetist, and also was active with it as an arranger (several of his arrangements appeared under Stokowski's cognomen, with the approval of Cailliet). He also taught at the Curtis Inst. of Music in Philadelphia. In 1937 he was awarded a doctorate in music by the Philadelphia Musical Academy. From 1938 to 1945 he taught orchestration, counterpoint, and conducting at the Univ.

of Southern Calif. in Los Angeles. Between 1945 and 1957 he wrote some 25 film scores for Hollywood. He also made appearances as a guest conductor. From 1957 to 1976 he was educational and musical director of the G. Leblanc Corp. He prepared an orchestration of Mussorgsky's *Pictures at an Exhibition* (1937); among his original works were *Memories of Stephen Foster* for Orch. (1935), *Variations on "Pop Goes the Weasel"* for Orch. (1938), band music, and clarinet pieces.

BIBL.: L. Fisher, "L. C.: His Contribution to the Symphonic Band, Orchestra, and Ensemble Literature," *Journal of Band Research*, XVIII/2 (1983; with complete list of works).

Cairns, David (Adam), English music critic; b. Loughton, Essex, June 8, 1926. After study at Winchester and Trinity College, Oxford (1945–48), and Princeton Univ. (1950–51), he devoted himself mainly to music criticism, writing for the *Financial Times* of London (1962–67), the *New Statesman* (1967–70), and the *Sunday Times* of London (from 1973), where he served as chief music critic (from 1983). He was particularly noted for his work on Berlioz; he prepared a tr. of Berlioz's *Les Soirées de l'orchestre* (1963), tr. and ed. Berlioz's memoirs (1969; 2nd ed., 1977), and wrote the study *Berlioz, Vol. 1: The Making of an Artist* (1989). He also publ. a collection of his own journalistic writings, *Responses* (1973).

Calabro, Louis, American composer and conductor; b. N.Y., Nov. 1, 1926. He studied with Persichetti at the Juilliard School of Music in N.Y. (graduated, 1952; postgraduate diploma, 1953). In 1955 he was appointed to the faculty at Bennington (Vt.) College. In 1971 he founded the Sage City Sym. in North Bennington. He received Guggenheim fellowships in 1954 and 1959 and NEA fellowships in 1973 and 1976.

WORKS: ORCH.: Concerto for Strings (1950); *Statement* (1951); Piano Concerto (1953); 3 syms. (1956; also for Strings, 1957; 1959–60); *10 Short Pieces* for Strings (1961); *Triple Concerto* for 3 Cellos and Orch. (1971); *The Young Pianist's Concertino* for Piano and Strings (1972); *Threnody* for Strings (1973); *Invention* for Symphonic Band (1975); *Eos* for English Horn and Strings (1977). **CHAMBER:** Trio for Clarinet, Cello, and Piano (1949); Piano Trio (1952); Violin Sonata (1953); 2 string quartets (1954, 1968); *Bodas de Sangre* for Piano, Violin, Clarinet, Cello, Timpani, and Guitar (1955); Sonata for Solo Cello (1956); *Dynamogeny* for Viola and Piano (1958); *Co-Instances—Music without Order* for Piano, Cello, Violin, and Clarinet (1958); *Environments* for Clarinet and 12 Brasses (1969); *Memoirs: Part 1* for Bassoon and Percussion (1973); *3 Pieces* for Piccolo (1973); *Rare Birds* for Narrator and Flute (1976); *Kusehani* for 12 Players (1976). **PIANO:** Sonatina (1952); Sonata (1954); *Diversities* (1966); *Piano Variations* (1968). **VOCAL:** *Dadacantatadada* for Blues Singer and Orch. (1964); *Epitaphs* for Chorus and Orch. (1967); *Latitude 15.09ºN (Longitude 108.5ºE)*, oratorio (1970); *Voyage*, Bicentennial work for Chorus and Orch. (1974–75); *Lunarlied* for Chorus and Strings (1976); songs.

Calcaño, José Antonio, Venezuelan composer and musicologist; b. Caracas, March 23, 1900; d. there, Sept. 11, 1980. After studies at the Escuela Superior de Música in Caracas, he went to Bern for further training. Returning to Venezuela, he was appointed to the faculty of the Univ. of Caracas where he organized an indigenous Coro Creole; he later taught at the Escuela de Música Padre Sojo. His works include a ballet, *Mirando en Rusia*, a Sym., 2 string quartets, and choruses; he also arranged classical music for various ensembles, and publ. several informative books, among them a historical survey of music in Caracas, *400 años de música caraqueña* (Caracas, 1967).

Caldwell, Sarah, remarkable American conductor and operatic impresario; b. Maryville, Mo., March 6, 1924. She studied at the Univ. of Ark. and at Hendrix College, and then was a violin pupil of Richard Burgin at the New England Cons. of Music in Boston; she also studied viola with Georges Fourel at the Berkshire Music Center in Tanglewood (summer, 1946), where she returned in 1947 to stage Vaughan Williams's *Riders to the Sea.* After studying with and serving as assistant to Boris Goldovsky, she was head of the Boston Univ. opera workshop (1952–60). In 1958 she founded the Boston Opera Group, which became the Opera Co. of Boston in 1965, which played a prominent role in the musical life of the city for some 25 years. In addition to standard operatic fare, Caldwell conducted the U.S. stage premieres of such modern operas as Schoenberg's *Moses und Aron* (Nov. 30, 1966), Prokofiev's *War and Peace* (May 8, 1974), Sessions's *Montezuma* (March 31, 1976), and Tippett's *The Ice Break* (May 18, 1979). She also was the first woman to conduct at the Metropolitan Opera in N.Y. (*La Traviata*, Jan. 13, 1976). She returned to the Metropolitan Opera in 1978 to conduct *L'Elisir d'Amore.* She also appeared as a guest conductor with various U.S. orchs.

Cale, John, English vocalist, composer, instrumentalist, and producer; b. Garnant, South Wales, Dec. 3, 1940. He was educated at Goldsmiths' College, London, and in N.Y. with Copland and La Monte Young. He was a founding member, with Lou Reed, of the N.Y. band Velvet Underground, whose album *White Light, White Heat* (1967) shows classical and avant-garde influences. His first solo album was *Vintage Violence* (1969); he subsequently collaborated with Terry Riley on *The Church of Anthrax* (1971) and *The Alchemy in Peril* (1972), and with Brian Eno on *June 1, 1974.* As a producer, he was a major influence on British punk.

Callas, Maria (real name, **Maria Anna Sofia Cecilia Kalogeropoulos**), celebrated American soprano; b. N.Y., Dec. 3, 1923; d. Paris, Sept. 16, 1977. Her father was a Greek immigrant. The family returned to Greece when she was 13; she studied voice at the Royal Academy of Music in Athens with Elvira de Hidalgo, and made her debut as Santuzza in the school production of *Cavalleria rusticana* in Nov. 1938. Her first professional appearance was in a minor role in Suppé's *Boccaccio* at the Royal Opera in Athens when she was 16; her first major role, as Tosca, was there in July 1942. She returned to N.Y. in 1945; she auditioned for the Metropolitan Opera and was offered a contract, but decided instead to go to Italy, where she made her operatic debut in the title role of *La Gioconda* (Verona, Aug. 3, 1947). She was encouraged in her career by Tullio Serafin, who engaged her to sing Isolde and Aida in various Italian productions. In 1951 she became a member of La Scala in Milan. She was greatly handicapped by her absurdly excessive weight (210 lbs.); by a supreme effort of will, she slimmed down to 135 pounds; with her classical Greek profile and penetrating eyes, she made a striking impression on the stage; in the tragic role of Medea in Cherubini's opera she mesmerized the audience by her dramatic representation of pity and terror. Some critics opined that she lacked a true bel canto quality in her voice and that her technique was defective in coloratura, but her power of interpretation was such that she was soon acknowledged to be one of the greatest dramatic singers of the century. Her personal life was as tempestuous as that of any prima donna of the bygone era. In 1949 she married the Italian industrialist Giovanni Battista Meneghini, who became her manager, but they separated 10 years later. Her romance with the Greek shipping magnate Aristotle Onassis was a recurrent topic of sensational gossip. Given to outbursts of temper, she made newspaper headlines when she walked off the stage following some altercation, or failed to appear altogether at scheduled performances, but her eventual return to the stage was all the more eagerly welcomed by her legion of admirers. After leaving La Scala in 1958, she returned there from 1960 to 1962. She also sang at London's Covent Garden (1952–53; 1957–59; 1964), in Chicago (1954–56), and Dallas (1958–59). Perhaps the peak of her success was her brilliant debut at the Metropolitan Opera in N.Y. as Norma on Oct. 29, 1956. Following a well-publicized disagreement with its management, she quit the company only to reach an uneasy accommodation with it to return as Violetta on Feb. 6, 1958; that same year she left the company again, returning in 1965 to sing Tosca before abandoning the operatic stage altogether. In

1971–72 she gave a seminar on opera at the Juilliard School in N.Y., which was enthusiastically received. In 1974 she gave her last public performances in a series of concerts with Giuseppe di Stefano; she then returned to Europe. She died suddenly of a heart attack in her Paris apartment. Her body was cremated and her ashes scattered on the Aegean Sea. Callas was nothing short of a phenomenon, one whose popularity has only increased with time. One radio commentator's characterization of Callas was that "If an orgasm could sing, it would sound like Maria Callas." She excelled particularly in roles by Rossini, Bellini, Donizetti, and Verdi.

BIBL.: E. Gara and R. Hauert, *M. C.* (Geneva, 1957; Eng. tr., 1958); E. Callas, *My Daughter M. C.* (N.Y., 1960); G. Jellinek, *C.* (N.Y., 1960); M. Picchetti and M. Teglia, *El arte de M. C.* (Buenos Aires, 1969); S. Galatopoulos, *C.—La Divina: Art That Conceals Art* (London, 1963; 3rd ed., rev. and aug., 1976, as *C.: Prima donna assoluta*); J. Ardoin and G. Fitzgerald, *C* (N.Y., 1974); H. Wisneski, *M. C.: The Art Behind the Music* (N.Y., 1975); J. Ardoin, *The C. Legacy: The Complete Guide to Her Recordings* (N.Y., 1977; 2nd ed., rev., 1982; new ed., 1991); P.-J. Rémy, *C.: Une vie* (Paris, 1978); idem, *M. C.: A Tribute* (N.Y., 1978); S. Segalini, *C.: Les images d'une voix* (Paris, 1979; Eng. tr., 1981); S. Linakis, *Diva: The Life and Death of M. C.* (Englewood Cliffs, N.J., 1980); C. Verga, *M. C.: Mito e malinconia* (Rome, 1980); C. Chiarelli, *M. C.: Vita, immagini, parole, musica* (Venice, 1981); G. Menghini, *M. C. mia moglie* (Milan, 1981; Eng. tr., 1982); A. Stassinopoulos, *M. C.: The Woman Behind the Legend* (N.Y., 1981); D. Lowe, ed., *C., as They Saw Her* (N.Y., 1986); R. La Rochelle, *C.: La diva et le vinyle* (Montreal, 1987); N. Stancioff, *M. C. Remembered* (N.Y., 1987); J. Callas, *Sisters: A Revealing Portrait of the World's Most Famous Diva* (London and N.Y., 1989); J. Kesting, *M. D.* (Düsseldorf, 1990; Eng. tr., 1993); R. Allegri, *La vera storia di M. C.: Con documenti inediti* (Milan, 1991); A. Petrolli, *La divina C.: Vita ed arte* (Trento, 1991); M. Di Stefano, *C. nemica mia* (Milan, 1992); M. Scott, *M. C.* (Boston, 1992); E. Kanthou, *M. C.* (Wilhelmshaven, 1993); F. Rohmer, *C.: Gesichter eines Mediums* (Munich, 1993); B. Tosi, *Casta diva: L'incomparable C.* (Parma, 1993).

Callaway, Paul (Smith), American organist and conductor; b. Atlanta, Ill., Aug. 16, 1909. After attending Westminster College in Fulton, Mo. (1927–29), he studied organ with Tercius Noble in N.Y. (1930–35), with Leo Sowerby in Chicago (1936), and with Marcel Dupré in Paris. He was organist and choirmaster at St. Thomas's Chapel in N.Y. (1930–35) and at St. Mark's Chapel in Grand Rapids (1935–39); then was organist and music director of the Cathedral Church of St. Peter and St. Paul in Washington, D.C. (1939–42; 1946–77); also was music director of the Opera Soc. of Washington, D.C. (1956–57) and of the Lake George Opera Festival in Glens Falls, N.Y. (1967–77).

Calligaris, Sergio, Argentine-born Italian pianist, teacher, and composer; b. Rosario, Jan. 22, 1941. He commenced piano lessons with Domingo Scarafia; in 1964 he became a student of Arthur Loesser at the Cleveland Inst. of Music (artist's diploma, 1966), where he also taught, and then completed his training with Guido Agosti at the Accademia di Santa Cecilia in Rome. In 1969 he became a teacher of piano at Calif. State Univ. in Los Angeles; in 1973 he founded the American Academy of the Arts in Verona, serving as its first artistic director. In 1974 he became a naturalized Italian citizen and began teaching at the Cons. of San Pietro a Majello in Naples; from 1977 he taught at the Alfredo Casella Cons. in L'Aquila. His playing is distinguished by a Romantic élan and virtuoso technique. As a composer, he blends Romantic and post-Romantic styles into a thoroughly contemporary idiom.

WORKS: ORCH.: Concerto for Strings (1989); *Danze Sinfoniche: Omaggio a Bellini* (1990); Piano Concerto (1992). **CHAMBER:** *Tema e Sete Variazioni*, trio for Oboe or Violin, Bassoon or Cello, and Harpsichord or Piano (1958; rev. 1976); Cello Sonata (1978); Suite for Cello and Harpsichord or Piano (1981); *Suite Classica* for Flute or Violin and Piano (1983); *Suite da Requiem No. 1* for Violin, Horn, and Piano (1984) and *No. 2* for 2 Pianos, 4 Timpani ad libitum, and Chorus ad libitum (1985); Suite for Cello (1991). **PIANO:** *Il quaderno pianistico di Renzo* (1978); *24 studi* (1978–80); *Scene coreografiche* for Piano Duet or 2 Pianos (1979); *Passacaglia* for 3 Pianos, after Bach (1983); *BHS*, divertimento on music by Bach, Handel, and Scarlatti for 2 Pianos and Women's Voices ad libitum (1984–85); *Vivaldiana*, divertimento on themes by Vivaldi for 2 Pianos (1986); *Due danze concertanti* for 2 Pianos (1986). **OTHER:** Various vocal pieces.

Calvé (real name, **Calvet de Roquer**), **(Rosa-Noémie) Emma,** famous French soprano; b. Decazeville, Aveyron, Aug. 15, 1858; d. Millau, Jan. 6, 1942. She studied voice with Puget in Paris and with Marchesi and Laborde. She made her operatic debut as Marguerite in Gounod's *Faust* at the Théâtre Royal de la Monnaie in Brussels on Sept. 23, 1881; then sang at the Opéra-Comique in Paris 3 years later. She sang at La Scala in Milan and at other Italian opera houses from 1886; appeared at Covent Garden in London from 1892 to 1904. She made her American debut at the Metropolitan Opera in N.Y. as Santuzza on Nov. 29, 1893, and remained on its staff until 1904; her greatest role was that of Carmen. Subsequently she sang at the Manhattan Opera (1907–09), in Boston (1912), and in Nice (1914) before retiring from the operatic stage; she continued to give concerts until 1927. Her life was made the subject of a novel by Gustav Kobbé, *Signora, A Child of the Opera House* (N.Y., 1903). She publ. an autobiography, in Eng., *My Life* (N.Y., 1922); she later publ. an additional vol. of memoirs, *Sous tous les ciels j'ai chanté* (Paris, 1940).

BIBL.: A. Gallus, *E. C., Her Artistic Life* (N.Y., 1902); A. Lebois, "Hommagla à E.C. (1858–1942)," *Annales, Faculté des lettres de Toulouse* (Sept. 1967).

Calvocoressi, Michel Dimitri, eminent Greek writer on music; b. Marseilles, Oct. 2, 1877; d. London, Feb. 1, 1944. He studied music in Paris, but was mostly autodidact; also pursued study in the social sciences. In 1914 he settled in London. He wrote music criticism and correspondences for French and other journals. He mastered the Russian language and became an ardent propagandist of Russian music; made excellent trs. into English and French of Russian and German songs. Among his books are *La Musique russe* (Paris, 1907); *The Principles and Methods of Musical Criticism* (London, 1923; rev. 1933); *Musical Taste and How to Form It* (London, 1925); *Musicians' Gallery: Music and Ballet in Paris and London* (London, 1933); also monographs on Liszt (Paris, 1906), Mussorgsky (Paris, 1908), Glinka (Paris, 1911), Schumann (Paris, 1912), and Debussy (London, 1941); a new extensive biography of Mussorgsky was posth. publ. (London, 1946). With G. Abraham, he publ. the valuable *Masters of Russian Music* (London, 1936).

Cambreling, Sylvain, French conductor; b. Amiens, July 2, 1948. He received training in music at the Paris Cons. In 1975 he became assistant conductor of the Orchestre de Lyon; also conducted opera in Lyon; beginning with the 1979–80 season, he appeared regularly as a conductor at the Paris Opéra. In 1981 he became joint music director (with John Pritchard) of the Théâtre Royal de la Monnaie in Brussels. He also conducted at the Glyndebourne Festival, the Frankfurt am Main Opera, La Scala in Milan, in the U.S., and in Canada. On Jan. 9, 1986, he made his Metropolitan Opera debut in N.Y. conducting *Roméo et Juliette.* In 1993 he became chief conductor of the Frankfurt am Main Opera.

Camden, Archie (actually, **Archibald Leslie),** virtuoso English bassoonist; b. Newark-upon-Trent, March 9, 1888; d. Wheathampstead, Feb. 16, 1979. He studied at the Royal Manchester College of Music. In 1906 he joined the Halle Orch. of Manchester, where he played 1st bassoon from 1914 to 1933; during the same period, he taught bassoon at the Royal Manchester College of Music. In 1933 he joined the BBC Sym. Orch. in London; then played with the Royal Phil. (1946–47); finally was a member of the London Mozart Players (1954–71). Camden did much to establish the bassoon as a solo instrument; his performances of works by Vivaldi, Mozart, and Weber were outstanding. His autobiography was publ. as *Blow by Blow* (London, 1982).

Cameron, (George) Basil, English conductor; b. Reading, Aug. 18, 1884; d. Leominster, June 26, 1975. He studied with Tertius Noble in York (1900–1902) and with Joachim (violin) and Max Bruch (composition) at the Berlin Hochschule für Musik (1902–06). After playing violin in the Queen's Hall Orch. in London, he Germanized his name as Basil Hindenberg and was conductor of the Torquay orch. (1912–16). With the outbreak of World War I in 1914, he deemed it prudent to revert to his real name. After conducting the Hastings orch. (1923–30), he served as co-conductor (with Dobrowen) of the San Francisco Sym. Orch. (1931–34). From 1932 to 1938 he was conductor of the Seattle Sym. Orch. He then returned to England and conducted at the London Promenade Concerts. After World War II, he appeared as a guest conductor in England and on the Continent. In 1957 he was made a Commander of the Order of the British Empire.

Campanella, Michele, Italian pianist; b. Naples, June 5, 1947. He was educated at the Naples Cons., winning the Casella Competition while a student there in 1966; then taught at the Milan Cons. (1969–73), and subsequently made tours as soloist with leading orchs. of Europe and the U.S. From 1987 he taught master classes at the Accademia Musicale Chigiana in Siena. His performances of the Romantic and modern repertoire have won critical praise.

Campo (y Zabaleta), Conrado del, distinguished Spanish composer and teacher; b. Madrid, Oct. 28, 1878; d. there, March 17, 1953. He was a student of Hierro, Monasterio, Fontanilla, and Serrano at the Madrid Cons.; he also studied with Chapí. Having become proficient as a violinist and violist, he played in the sym. orch. at the Teatro Real in Madrid, and was a member of the Quarteto Francés and the Quinteto de Madrid. He helped to organize the orch. of the National Radio, which he conducted from 1947 to 1951. He served as prof. of harmony (1915–23) and of composition (1923–53) at the Madrid Cons., where his outstanding students included Cristóbal Halffter and Domingo Santa Cruz. While Spanish national traits are prominent in his works, he also adapted German Romantic sonorities.

WORKS: DRAMATIC: OPERAS: *El final de Don Alvaro* (Madrid, March 4, 1911); *La dama desconocida* (1911); *La tragedia del beso* (Madrid, May 18, 1915); *Los amantes de Verona* (1916); *Dies irae* (1917); *El Avapiés* (Madrid, March 8, 1919; in collaboration with A. Barrios); *Fantochines* (Madrid, 1924); *Leonor Telles* (1927); *El árbol de los ojos* (1931); *Lola la piconera* (Barcelona, Nov. 14, 1950); *El pájaro de dos colores* (1951); some 25 zarzuelas; film scores. **ORCH.: TONE POEMS:** *Antes las ruinas* (1899); *La divina comedia* (1905–08); *Granada* (1912); *Airiños, aires . . .* (1916); *Kasida* (1920); *Evocación medieval* (1924); *Ofrenda a los caidos* (1938); *Evocación y nostalgia de los molinos de viento* (1952). **OTHER WORKS FOR ORCH.:** *Madrileña*, overture (1920); *Bocetos castellanos*, suite (1929); *Evocación de Castilla* for Piano and Orch. (1931); *Suite madrileña* (1934); *Aragonesa*, overture (1935); Violin Concerto (1938); *Fantasia castellana* for Piano and Orch. (1939); Suite for Violin and Chamber Orch. (1940); *Asturiana*, overture (1942); *El viento en Castilla*, suite (1942); *El la Pradera*, suite (1943); Cello Concerto (1944). **CHAMBER:** 12 string quartets (1904–52); *El Cristo de la Vega* for Reciter and String Quartet (1907); *Caprichos románticos* for String Quartet (1908); Violin Sonata (1949); Piano Quintet (1952); piano pieces. **VOCAL:** Sacred music and songs.

BIBL.: T. Borrás, *C. d.C.* (Madrid, 1954).

Campoli, Alfredo, Italian-born English violinist; b. Rome, Oct. 20, 1906; d. London, March 27, 1991. He was a pupil of his father, a prof. at the Accademia di Santa Cecilia in Rome; then settled in England while still a child. After making his London debut at the age of 10, he toured throughout England, receiving the gold medal at the London Music Festival in 1919. In 1938 he made his first appearance at the London Promenade Concerts. He also was active with his own orch., which featured lighter works. From 1945 he pursued a career as a violin virtuoso, making his U.S. debut in N.Y. in 1953. In subsequent years, he toured the globe. He was admired for his finely-wrought interpretations of the standard repertory, but he also promoted 20th-century English works, including those by Elgar and Bliss.

Campora, Giuseppe, Italian tenor; b. Tortona, Sept. 30, 1923. He studied voice in Genoa and Milan. In 1949 he made his operatic debut in Bari as Rodolfo; in 1951 he joined Milan's La Scala and also sang with other Italian opera houses. He made his Metropolitan Opera debut in N.Y. as Rodolfo on Jan. 20, 1955, and remained on the roster until 1959; was again on its roster from 1963 to 1965. Among his best known roles were Enzo, Massenet's Des Grieux, Gounod's Faust, Cavaradossi, Edgardo, and Alfredo.

Campos-Parsi, Héctor, Puerto Rican composer; b. Ponce, Oct. 1, 1922. He studied in Ponce, then at the Univ. of Puerto Rico in Río Piedras (1938–44). After taking courses at the New England Cons. of Music in Boston (1947–50) and with Copland and Messiaen at the Berkshire Music Center in Tanglewood (summers 1949–50), he studied with Boulanger in Fontainebleau (1951–53). Returning to Puerto Rico in 1955, he was active as a composer, poet, journalist, music critic, television commentator, and concert manager. In some of his works, he utilized Puerto Rican folk music. In other pieces, he embraced aleatory procedures and electronics.

WORKS: BALLETS: *Incidente* (1949); *Melos* (1951); *Juan Bobo y las fiestas* (1957); *Urayoán* (1958); *Areyto boriken* (1974); *De Diego* (1974). **ORCH.:** *Divertimento de Sur* for Flute, Clarinet, and Strings (1953); *Oda a Cabo Rojo* (1959); *Rapsodia elegíaca* for Strings (1960); *Kollagia* for Orch., Percussion, and Tape (1963); *Dúo trágico* for Piano and Orch. (1964); *Tiempo sereno* for Strings (1983); *Trés Madrigales* for Soprano and Strings (1983); *Tissú* for Accordion and Small Orch. (1984); *Tureyareito* (1984); *Eglogas* for Baritone and Strings (1988). **CHAMBER:** *Serenata* for String Trio (1949); Violin Sonata (1949); *Música* for 3 Violins (1949); String Quartet (1950); *Dialogantes* for Violin and Piano (1952); Violin Sonatina (1953); *Música per la stagione estiva* for 2 Flutes and Piano (1956); *El secreto* for Flute, Oboe, 2 Clarinets, Cello, and Piano (1957); *Petroglifos* for Piano Trio (1966); *Arawak* for Cello and Tape (1970); *Sleeping Beauty* for Flute, Harp, and 2 Pianos (1978); *Fanfare for an American Festival* for 3 Trumpets, 2 Trombones, and Percussion (1982); *Sonetos Sagrados* for Soprano, Flute, Oboe, Clarinet, Bassoon, and Horn (1986); piano pieces.

BIBL.: F. Caso, *H. C.-P. in the History of Twentieth-Century Music in Puerto Rico* (diss., Indiana Univ., 1972).

Camps, Pompeyo, Argentine composer; b. Paraná, Oct. 27, 1924. After playing piano in bands in his native town, he settled in Buenos Aires in 1947, where he studied with Jaime Pahissa and adopted his "intertonal system" of convertible counterpoint. In 1964 Camps modified this technique by incorporating serial procedures. He was also active as a music critic.

WORKS: Piano Sonata (1954); 2 string quartets (1957, 1974); *La pendiente*, opera (1959); *Fantasia* for Strings (1961); *The Ballad of Reading Gaol* for Men's Chorus, Narrator, and Orch. (1964); *Sinfónia para un poeta* for Baritone and Orch. (1967); *Tríptico arcáico* for Flute, Viola, Cello, and Guitar (1961); *Danzas* for Percussion (1966); *Reflejos* for 13 Brasses and Percussion (1968); *Ciudad sin tregua* for String Quartet (1974); songs; piano pieces.

Camussi, Ezio, Italian composer; b. Florence, Jan. 16, 1877; d. Milan, Aug. 11, 1956. He studied in Rome with Falchi and Sgambati; later with Massenet in Paris and at the Liceo Musicale in Bologna.

WORKS: OPERAS: *La Dubarry* (Milan, Nov. 7, 1912); *I fuochi di San Giovanni* (Milan, March 27, 1920); *Il donzello, Scampolo* (Trieste, Feb. 22, 1925); *Il volto della Virgine* (Bari,

Jan. 23, 1937); also *La principessa lontana, I Romanzeschi,* and *Intermezzi giocosi* for Puppet Theater. **ORCH.:** *Balletto sinfonico; Pantomima romantica; Suita romanesca; Intermezzi Goldoniani; Fantasticherie* for Small Orch.; *Festival Miniature Overture; Scene medioevali* for Violin and Orch. **VOCAL:** Songs.

Canal, Marguerite, French composer; b. Toulouse, Jan. 29, 1890; d. there, Jan. 27, 1978. She studied at the Paris Cons. with Paul Vidal; in 1920 she won the Grand Prix de Rome for her symphonic scene *Don Juan.* In 1919 she was appointed to the faculty of the Paris Cons. Her works include a Violin Sonata (1922); *Spleen* for Cello and Chamber Ensemble (1926); several piano pieces; about 100 songs.

Caniglia, Maria, Italian soprano; b. Naples, May 5, 1905; d. Rome, April 16, 1979. She was a pupil of Roche at the Naples Cons. In 1930 she made her operatic debut in Turin as Chrysothemis, and later that year made her first appearance at Milan's La Scala as Maria in Pizzetti's *Lo Straniero.* She continued to sing at La Scala until 1943, and again from 1948 to 1951; also appeared with the company on its visits to London's Covent Garden (1937, 1939, 1950). On Nov. 21, 1938, she made her Metropolitan Opera debut in N.Y. as Desdemona, but returned to Europe in 1939. In 1939 she married **Pino Donati**. Among her best known roles were Tosca, Aida, Alice Ford, the 3 Leonoras, Maria Boccanegra, and Adriana Lecouvreur. She also created the title role in Respighi's *Lucrezia* (Milan, Feb. 24, 1937).

Canino, Bruno, Italian pianist, harpsichordist, teacher, and composer; b. Naples, Dec. 30, 1935. He studied with Calace and Bettinelli at the Milan Cons., then toured widely in Europe, the U.S., and Japan. He was a member of the Trio di Milano, and also made many duo piano appearances with Antonio Ballista. From 1961 he taught at the Milan Cons. He was especially known as a proponent of contemporary music; he also wrote some orch. pieces and chamber music in a fairly advanced style.

Cannon, (Jack) Philip, English composer and teacher; b. Paris (of English-French parents), Dec. 21, 1929. He was educated in England; studied composition with Imogen Holst; then at the Royal College of Music in London with Gordon Jacob and Vaughan Williams. He subsequently took lessons with Paul Hindemith. From 1957 to 1959 he lectured at the Univ. of Sydney; in 1960 he joined the staff of the Royal College of Music in London.

WORKS: 2 Rhapsodies for Piano (1943); 2 string quartets (1944, 1964); String Trio (1945); *In the Time of the Breaking of Nations* for Voice and Piano Quintet (1945); *Fantasia* for String Quartet (1946); Sextet for Flute, Oboe, and String Quartet (1946); Sinfonietta for Chamber Orch. (1947); *Symphonic Study: Spring* for Orch. (1949); *Songs to Delight* for Women's Chorus and Strings (1950); *Sinfonietta* for Strings (1952); *5 Chansons de Femme* for Soprano and Harp (1952); *L'Enfant s'amuse,* suite for Piano (1954); *Sonatine champêtre* for Piano (1959); Sonata for 2 Pianos (1960); *Son of Science,* cantata for Boys' Voices, Chorus, Tenor, Piano, Percussion, and Strings (Aylesbury, Dec. 2, 1961); *Fanfare to Youth* for 8 Trumpets (1963); *Morvoren,* opera (London, July 15, 1964); *Kai-kaus (A Persian Suite)* for Chamber Group (1965); *Lacrimae mundi* for Piano Trio (1974); *Son of Man* for Chorus and Orch. (Liverpool, June 26, 1975); *Lord of Light,* oratorio (1980).

Cantelli, Guido, brilliant Italian conductor; b. Novara, April 27, 1920; d. in an airplane crash in Orly, near Paris, Nov. 24, 1956. A gifted child, he was given a place in his father's military band when he was a small boy; appeared as organist at the local church from age 10, and made his debut as a pianist at age 14. He pursued formal studies with Pedrollo and Ghedini at the Milan Cons. He then was conductor of Novara's Teatro Coccia in 1941, but was compelled to give up his post and join the Italian army in 1943. When he refused to support the Fascist cause, he was sent to the Nazi-run Stettin labor camp (1943–44); after being transferred to Bolzano, he escaped to Milan, but was captured and sentenced to death. He was saved by the liberation of his homeland in 1944. After World War II, he conducted at Milan's La Scala; Toscanini heard his performances and was sufficiently impressed to invite him as guest conductor with the NBC Sym. Orch. in N.Y. He made his American debut on Jan. 15, 1949, and subsequently conducted there regularly. From 1951 he also made appearances as a conductor with the Philharmonia Orch. in London. Cantelli was one of the most gifted conductors of his generation. A perfectionist, he conducted both rehearsals and concert and operatic performances from memory. He was able to draw the most virtuosic playing from his musicians. A few days before his death, he was appointed artistic director of La Scala.

BIBL.: L. Lewis, *G. C.: Portrait of a Maestro* (London, 1981).

Cantelo, April (Rosemary), English soprano; b. Purbrook, April 2, 1928. She studied piano and voice at the Royal College of Music in London; was subsequently a member of the New English Singers and the Deller Consort; also appeared in opera with the Glyndebourne Opera and the English Opera Group; she also gave solo recitals. From 1949 to 1964 she was married to **Colin Davis**.

Canteloube (de Malaret), (Marie-) Joseph, French pianist, composer, and writer on music; b. Annonay, near Tournon, Oct. 21, 1879; d. Grigny, Seine-et-Oise, Nov. 4, 1957. His name was simply Canteloube, but he added "de Malaret" after the name of his ancestral estate. He studied piano in Paris with Amélie Doetzer and composition with Vincent d'Indy at the Schola Cantorum. He became an ardent collector of French folk songs and arranged and publ. many of them for voice with instrumental accompaniment. His *Chants d'Auvergne* (4 sets for Voice, with Piano or Orch., 1923–30) are frequently performed. Among his other albums, *Anthologie des chants populaires français* (4 sets, 1939–44) is a comprehensive collection of regional folk songs. He also publ. a biography of d'Indy (Paris, 1949).

WORKS: 2 operas: *Le Mas* (1910–13; Paris, April 3, 1929) and *Vercingetorix* (1930–32; Paris, June 26, 1933); symphonic poem: *Vers la princesse lointaine* (1910–11); 3 symphonic sketches: *Lauriers* (Paris, Feb. 22, 1931), *Pièces françaises* for Piano and Orch. (1935), and *Poème* for Violin and Orch. (1937); *Rustiques* for Oboe, Clarinet, and Bassoon (1946).

BIBL.: L. Boursiac, *C.* (Toulouse, 1941); F. Gougniaud-Taginel, *J. C.: Chantre dela terre* (Béziers, 1988).

Capdevielle, Pierre, French composer and pianist; b. Paris, Feb. 1, 1906; d. Bordeaux, July 9, 1969. He studied at the Paris Cons. with Gédalge and Paul Vidal, and privately with Vincent d'Indy. He composed an opera, *Les Amants captifs* (1947–50); a lyric tragedy, *Fille de l'homme* (Paris Radio, Nov. 9, 1967); the orch. works *Incantation pour la mort d'un jeune spartiate* (1931), *Ouverture pour le pédant joué* (1943), and *Cantate de la France retrouvée* (1946); 3 syms. (1936; 1942; Chamber Sym., 1953); *Épaves retrouvées,* 4 symphonic tableaux (1955); *Concerto del Dispetto* for Piano and Orch. (1959); Sonata Concertante for Trombone and Piano (1963); *Sonatine pastorale* for Flute and Piano; String Quartet; etc.

Cape, Safford, American-Belgian choral conductor; b. Denver, June 28, 1906; d. Brussels, March 26, 1973. He studied in Europe, principally in Brussels, with Charles Van den Borren, whose daughter he married. In 1933 he established in Brussels a music society, Pro Musica Antiqua, with which he gave numerous performances of choral and instrumental works by medieval and Renaissance composers until his retirement in 1967.

Capecchi, Renato, Italian baritone; b. Cairo (of Italian parents), Nov. 6, 1923. He was a student in Milan of Ubaldo Carrozzi. After making his debut on the Italian Radio (1948), he made his stage debut as Amonasro in 1949 in Reggio Emilia. From 1950 he sang at Milan's La Scala. On Nov. 24, 1951, he made his Metropolitan Opera debut in N.Y. as *Germont père,* remaining on its roster until 1954. In 1975 he returned there, and then made occasional visits. Between 1953 and 1983 he was a regular guest at the Verona Arena. In 1962 he made his debut at London's Covent Garden as Melitone, and sang there again in 1973. In 1977 and 1980 he appeared as Falstaff at Glyndebourne. His guest appearances took him not only all over Italy but to Berlin, Paris, Munich, Moscow, Stuttgart, Stockholm, and other European music centers. His vast repertoire included hundreds of roles, ranging from the traditional to the contemporary. He was particularly successful as a buffo artist, winning special praise for his portrayals of Rossini's Figaro, Dr. Bartolo, Dulcamara, Don Pasquale, and Gianni Schicchi.

Capell, Richard, English writer on music; b. Northampton, March 23, 1885; d. London, June 21, 1954. He studied cello in London and at the Lille Cons. He was music critic for the *London Daily Mail* (1911–33); then joined the *Daily Telegraph*; during World War II, was its war correspondent in the French, Greek, and Italian campaigns. From 1928 to 1933 he was an ed. of the *Monthly Musical Record*; from 1950 to 1954 he edited *Music & Letters*. In 1946 he was made an Officer of the Order of the British Empire. He publ. *Schubert's Songs* (London, 1928; 3rd ed., rev., 1973 by M. Cooper), a biography of Gustav Holst (London, 1928), and *Opera* (London, 1930; 2nd ed., aug., 1948).

Capet, Lucien, distinguished French violinist and teacher; b. Paris, Jan. 8, 1873; d. there, Dec. 18, 1928. He studied at the Paris Cons. with J.P. Maurin (1888–93), graduating with the premier prix. From 1896 to 1899 he was concertmaster of the Lamoureux Orch.; from 1899 to 1903 he taught violin at the Cons. of Ste. Cecile in Bordeaux. In 1904 he founded the celebrated Capet Quartet in Paris, playing 1st violin in it until 1921, specializing particularly in the Beethoven quartets. In 1907 he became a teacher at the Paris Cons. In 1924 he was appointed director of the Inst. de Violon in Paris. He composed *Le Rouet*, symphonic poem; *Prélude religieux* for Orch.; *Devant la mer* for Voice and Orch.; *Poème* for Violin and Orch.; 5 string quartets; 2 violin sonatas; 6 violin études. He publ. *La Technique supérieure de l'archet* (Paris, 1916); *Les 17 Quatuors de Beethoven*; also a philosophical work, *Espérances*.

Caplet, André, French composer and conductor; b. Le Havre, Nov. 23, 1878; d. Paris, April 22, 1925. He studied violin in Le Havre, and played in theater orchs. there and in Paris; entered the Paris Cons. (1896), where he studied with Leroux and Lenepveu; in 1901 he received the Grand Prix de Rome for his cantata *Myrrha*. His *Marche solennelle* for the centennial of the Villa Medicis was performed in Rome (April 18, 1903). He was active in France as a choral and operatic conductor; conducted the first performance of Debussy's *Le Martyre de St. Sébastien* (Paris, May 22, 1911); also conducted the Boston Opera Co. (1910–14) and in London at Covent Garden (1912). Caplet was wounded in action while serving in the French Army during World War I, which seriously impaired his life and greatly curtailed his subsequent musical activities. His music is unequivocally impressionistic, with a lavish use of whole-tone scales and parallel chord formations; he combined this impressionism with neo-archaic usages and mystic programmatic ideas. He was a close friend of Debussy, with whom he collaborated on several of his orch. works and even completed sections left unfinished by Debussy. Their correspondence was publ. in Monaco in 1957.

WORKS: *Rêverie* for Flute and Piano (1897); *Myrrha*, cantata (1901); Double Wind Quintet (Paris, March 9, 1901); *Marche solennelle* (Rome, April 18, 1903); *Elégie* for Cello and Piano (1903); *The Masque of the Red Death* for Harp and Orch. (Paris, March 7, 1909; arranged as *Conte fantastique* for Harp and String Quartet, 1919; Paris, Dec. 29, 1923); Septet for 3 Women's Voices and String Quartet (1909); *Inscriptions champêtres* for Chorus (1914); *Douamont* for Military Band (1917); Mass for 3 Voices (1920); *Hymne à la naissance du matin* for Chorus and Orch. (1920); *Epiphanie* for Cello and Orch. (Paris, Dec. 29, 1923); *Le miroir de Jésus* for Mezzo-soprano, Women's Chorus, Harp, and Strings (1923; Paris, May 1, 1924); *A la française* and *A l'espagnole*, divertissements for Harp (1924); various choral works, songs, and piano pieces.

BIBL.: M. Brillant, Roland-Manuel, and A. Hoeree, "A. C., musicien mystique," *La Revue Musicale* (July 1925); *A. C.* (Paris, 1976).

Capobianco, Tito, Argentine-born American opera director and administrator; b. La Plata, Aug. 28, 1931. He received training in law and philosophy in La Plata and in music at the Univ. of Buenos Aires. In 1953 he launched his career as an opera director with a production of *Pagliacci* in La Plata. Moving to Buenos Aires, he was technical director at the Teatro Colón (1958–62) and general director of the Teatro Argentino (1959–61); subsequently was artistic director of the Cincinnati Opera Festival (1961–65) and the Cincinnati Opera (1962–65). In 1966 he began staging operas at the N.Y. City Opera, where he was resident stage director from 1967. In 1975 he organized the Las Palmas Festival in the Canary Islands. He also became artistic director of the San Diego Opera in 1975, serving as its general director from 1977. In 1983 he became general director of the Pittsburgh Opera. He was prof. of acting and interpretation at the Academy of Vocal Arts in Philadelphia (1962–68); in 1967 he founded the American Opera Center at the Juilliard School of Music in N.Y., serving as its director until 1969. He was director of opera studies and festival stage director at the Music Academy of the West in Santa Barbara (from 1983), and prof. of acting, staging, and interpretation at the Graduate School of Music at Yale Univ. (from 1983). In many of his operatic stagings, he collaborated with his wife, the choreographer Elena Denda.

Capoianu, Dumitru, Romanian composer; b. Bucharest, Oct. 19, 1929. He studied at the Bucharest Cons. (1941–53) with Jora, Mendelsohn, Vancea, Andricu, and Rogalski. From 1969 to 1973 he was manager of the Georges Enesco Phil.

WORKS: DRAMATIC: Musicals, ballets, and film scores. **ORCH.:** 2 suites (1953, 1954); *Divertissement* for 2 Clarinets and Strings (1956); Violin Concerto (1957); *Cinematographic Variations* (1965); *Moto perpetuo* for Solo Violin or Group of Violins and Orch. (1972); *Chemari '77* (1977); *Muzica de ambianta* (1980); *Fațete*, symphonic jazz suite (1986). **CHAMBER:** Wind Quintet (1950); Viola Sonata (1952); 2 string quartets (1954, 1959); Trio for Violin, Viola, and Cello (1968); Sonata for Solo Harp (1978); *Arcuri*, trio for Viola, Cello, and Piano (1982); Sonata for Solo Cello (1982). **VOCAL:** *Valses ignobles et sentimentales du tout . . .* for Mezzo-soprano and String Orch. (1986); choral pieces; solo songs.

Cappuccilli, Piero, admired Italian baritone; b. Trieste, Nov. 9, 1929. He studied with Luciano Doaggio in Trieste. In 1957 he made his operatic debut at Milan's Teatro Nuovo as Tonio. On March 26, 1960, he made his Metropolitan Opera debut in N.Y. as Germont père, but then pursued his career in Europe. In 1964 he made his first appearance at Milan's La Scala as Donizetti's Ashton, and subsequently sang there regularly with notable success. He made his debut at London's Covent Garden as Germont père in 1967, and returned there in 1976 as a member of the La Scala company. In 1969 he made his first appearance at the Chicago Lyric Opera as Francesco in *I Due Foscari*. He made his debut at the Salzburg Festival as Posa in 1975. In 1978 he sang Simon Boccanegra in Paris. While continuing to sing in various Italian operatic centers, he also appeared as a guest artist throughout Europe. Among his other fine roles were Iago, Renato, Rigoletto, Nabucco, Escamillo, and Macbeth.

Caprioli, Alberto, Italian composer, conductor, teacher, and writer on music; b. Bologna, Nov. 16, 1956. He studied composition with Franco Margola (1973–79) and Camillo Togni (diploma, 1983) and conducting with Piero Guarino (1977–78) at the Padua Cons. He also studied conducting with Tito Gotti at the Bologna Cons. (diploma, 1979), with Kondrashin in Hilversum (1978), and with Suitner (1979–83) and Cerha (diploma, 1983) at the Vienna Academy of Music. His training in composition was completed with Schaeffer at the Salzburg Mozarteum

(1986–88). In 1984 he became a teacher of conducting at the Bologna Cons., where he held that chair from 1988. From 1990 he was one of the collaborators on the critical edition of Maderna's works. In 1992 he founded the Progetto Esperia in Bologna, a new music laboratory. His writings have appeared in various publications. In his music, Caprioli has followed a contemporary path which includes the use of tape and live electronics.

WORKS: *Elegia* for Piano (1974; Ravenna, Feb. 22, 1987); *Sette Frammenti dal diario* for Piano (1974; South German Radio, Stuttgart, June 24, 1987); *Les Adieux de vent* for Piano (1974; Bologna, Sept. 6, 1988); *Abendlied (omaggio a Gustav Mahler)* for Soprano and Orch. (1977; Parma, May 5, 1978); *Sonetti di Shakespeare* for Voice and Chamber Ensemble (Austrian Radio, Salzburg, Oct. 4, 1983); Trio for Piano, Violin, and Cello (Austrian Radio, Salzburg, Sept. 28, 1984); *del celeste confine* for String Quartet (1985; Kraków, April 7, 1987); *Serenata per Francesca* for 6 Players (Austrian Radio, Salzburg, Sept. 27, 1985); *A la dolce ombra* for Violin, Cello, and Piano (1985; Perugia, Jan. 28, 1987); *Dialogue* for Double Bass and 2 String Quartets (Undine, Oct. 2, 1986); *Per lo dolce silentio de la notte* for Piano and Tape (Salzburg, May 25, 1987); *Symphoniae I/II* (Salzburg, May 5, 1988) and *III* (Salzburg, Aug. 4, 1989) for Violin; *Due Notturni d'obliò* for Chamber Ensemble (Stuttgart, Sept. 10, 1988); *. . . il vostro pianto aurora o luna* for Flute, Clarinet, Horn, Guitar, and Vibraphone (Paris, Dec. 11, 1988); *Intermedio I* for Amplified Flute and Live Electronics (Klagenfurt, March 9, 1989); *Vor dem singenden Odem (alla memoria di Luigi Nono)* for Flute, Clarinet, Violin, Cello, and Piano (Perugia, May 31, 1990; rev. version, Bologna, April 8, 1992); *Sette frammenti dal Kyrie per Dino Campana* for Soli, Chorus, and Orch. (Stuttgart, Aug. 25, 1991); *"John-Cage"-Variations* for Bass Flute, Bass Clarinet, Violin, Cello, and Piano (Trieste, Sept. 25, 1991); *À quinze ans* for Cello (Bratislava, Oct. 22, 1991); *Anges*, paraphrase after Schumann, for Alto Flute, Viola, and Harp (Siena, Aug. 26, 1993); *Folâtre (Notturno di rosa)* for 2 Guitars (1993); *L'ascesa degli angeli ribelli* for Voice and Instruments (Bologna, Feb. 8, 1994); *Dittico baciato* for Chorus and Orch. (Bologna, Nov. 15, 1994).

Capuana, Franco, Italian conductor, brother of **Maria Capuana**; b. Fano, Sept. 29, 1894; d. while conducting Rossini's *Mose* at the Teatro San Carlo, Naples, Dec. 10, 1969. He studied composition at the Naples Cons. He began his career as an opera conductor in 1915; from 1930 to 1937 he was music director of the Teatro San Carlo in Naples; from 1937 to 1940, and again from 1946 to 1949, he was a conductor at La Scala in Milan, then its music director (1949–52). He specialized in Italian verismo operas, but also excelled in the operas of Wagner, Strauss, and several modern composers.

BIBL.: B. Cagnoli, *L'arte musicale di F. C.* (Milan, 1983).

Capuana, Maria, Italian contralto, sister of **Franco Capuana**; b. Fano, 1891; d. Cagliari, Feb. 22, 1955. She studied voice and piano at the Cons. San Pietro a Majella in Naples. In 1918 she made her operatic debut in Naples as Urbain in *Les Huguenots*; in 1920 she sang Brangäne in Turin, and in 1922 made her first appearance at Milan's La Scala as Ortrud, where she successfully sang various Wagnerian roles. She also appeared in other major Italian music centers, as well as in Barcelona, Lisbon, Cairo, and the Teatro Colón in Buenos Aires. Among her finest non-Wagnerian roles were Amneris and Herodias.

Caracciolo, Franco, Italian conductor; b. Bari, March 29, 1920. He studied composition and piano at the Cons. in San Pietro a Majella in Naples and conducting with Molinari at the Accademia di Santa Cecilia in Rome. In 1949 he went to Naples as conductor of the Alessandro Scarlatti Orch. In 1964 he settled in Milan as principal conductor of RAI, retiring in 1987. In his programs, Caracciolo revived many of the forgotten orch. works of Italian composers; he also conducted contemporary works.

Carapetyan, Armen, eminent Persian-born American musicologist of Armenian descent; b. Isfahan, Oct. 11, 1908; d. Francestown, N.H., Sept. 5, 1992. He studied at the American College in Tehran (diploma, 1927); after receiving training in violin and composition in Paris and N.Y., he continued composition studies with Malipiero; then took courses in musicology at Harvard Univ. (M.A., 1940; Ph.D., 1945, with the diss. *The "Musica nova" of Adriano Willaert, with Reference to the Humanistic Society of Sixteenth-Century Venice*). In 1945 he became founder-director of the American Inst. of Musicology with headquarters in Rome and Cambridge, Mass., where he diligently pursued his labors until 1980; he served as general ed. of Corpus Mensurabilis Musicae, Corpus Scriptorum de Musica, and Musicological Studies and Documents, and was ed. of the journal *Musica Disciplina* (from 1946). He contributed numerous important articles on the music of the Middle Ages and the Renaissance to U.S. and European journals. In 1979 he was made an honorary member of the American Musicological Soc.

Cardew, Cornelius, English composer of extreme avant-garde tendencies; b. Winchcombe, Gloucester, May 7, 1936; d. in a road accident in London, Dec. 13, 1981. He studied composition with Ferguson at the Royal Academy of Music in London (1953–57); in 1957 he went to Cologne and worked at the electronic studio there as an assistant to Stockhausen (1958–60). Returning to England, he organized concerts of experimental music. From 1963 to 1965 he had private lessons with Petrassi in Rome. In 1967 he was appointed to the faculty of the Royal Academy of Music in London. In 1969, together with Michael Parsons and Howard Skempton, he organized the Scratch Orch., a heterogeneous group for performances of new music, militantly latitudinarian and disestablishmentarian. Under the influence of the teachings of Mao Zedong, Cardew renounced his modernistic past as a bourgeois deviation detrimental to pure Marxism, and subsequently attacked his former associate, Stockhausen, in a book ominously entitled *Stockhausen Serves Imperialism* (London, 1974). He also repudiated his own magnum opus, *The Great Learning*, which was orig. performed at the 1968 Cheltenham Festival, scored for a non-singing chorus to the words of Ezra Pound's tr. of Confucius, a chorus which was admonished to bang on tapped stones, to whistle and shriek, but never to stoop to vocalizing. In the revised version of the work, he appended to the title the slogan "Apply Marxism-Leninism-Mao Zedong Thought in a living way to the problems of the present." This version was first performed by the Scratch Orch. at a Promenade Concert in London on Aug. 24, 1972. His other works include *Volo Solo* for Any Handy Musical Instrument (1965); *3 Winter Potatoes* for Piano and various assorted Concrete Sounds, as well as for Newspapers, Balloons, Noise, and People Working (London, March 11, 1968); *The East is Red* for Violin and Piano (1972); and *The Old and the New* for Soprano, Chorus, and Orch. (1973). He also publ. several pamphlets containing some confusing confutations of Confucius. In addition, he compiled a seminal manual, *Scratch Music* (London, 1970).

Cardus, Sir (John Frederick) Neville, English writer on music and cricket; b. Manchester, April 3, 1888; d. London, Feb. 28, 1975. He studied singing, then turned to journalism; wrote essays on numerous subjects, but primarily on cricket and music. In 1917 he joined the staff of the *Manchester Guardian*; then was its chief music critic (1927–39); from 1939 to 1947 he was in Australia, writing on cricket and music for the *Sydney Morning Herald.* Returning to London, he became music critic for the *Manchester Guardian* in 1951. He received the Wagner Medal of the City of Bayreuth in 1963; was knighted in 1967. His literary style is quasi-Shavian in its colloquial manner and stubborn persuasion.

WRITINGS: *Music for Pleasure* (1942); *Ten Composers* (1945; 2nd ed., aug., 1958 as *A Composers' Eleven*); *Autobiography* (1947); *Second Innings: More Autobiography* (1950); *Talking of Music* (1957); *Sir Thomas Beecham: A Memoir* (1961); *Gustav Mahler: His Mind and His Music* (1965); *The Delights of Music: A Critic's Choice* (1966); *Full Score* (1970).

BIBL.: R. Daniels, ed., *Conversations with C.* (London, 1976);

C. Brookes, *His Own Man: The Life of N. C.* (London, 1985); A. Lamb, "C. Reaches His Century," *Musical Times* (April 1988).

Carelli, Emma, esteemed Italian soprano; b. Naples, May 12, 1877; d. in an automobile accident in Montefiascone, near Rome, Aug. 17, 1928. She was a pupil of her father, the composer B. Carelli, at the Cons. San Pietro a Majella in Naples. In 1895 she made her operatic debut in Altamura in Mercadante's *La Vestale.* After singing in various Italian opera houses, she made her debut at Milan's La Scala in 1899 as Desdemona; in 1901 she was the first to sing the role of Tatiana in Italy. She then sang throughout Europe, and also appeared at the Teatro Colón in Buenos Aires and in Rio de Janeiro. In 1910 she married Walter Mocchi, the director of Rome's Teatro Costanzi, where she was the first to sing Elektra in Italy in 1912. She succeeded her husband as its director (1912–26). Among her most acclaimed roles were Iris and Zazá.

Carewe, John (Maurice Foxall), English conductor; b. Derby, Jan. 24, 1933. After studies with W. Goehr, Deutsch, and Boulez at the Guildhall School of Music in London, and with Messiaen at the Paris Cons., he organized the New Music Ensemble (1958). He was also on the staff of Morley College (1958–66) and was principal conductor of the BBC Welsh Sym. Orch. in Cardiff (1966–71); he subsequently was music director of the Brighton Phil. Soc. (1974–87) and principal conductor of the Fires of London (1980–84). From 1993 to 1996 he was music director of the City Theater and Robert Schumann Phil. in Chemnitz.

Caridis, Miltiades, Greek conductor; b. Gdańsk (of Greek parents), May 9, 1923. He studied at the Athens Cons. and with Swarowsky at the Vienna Academy of Music, where he received his conducting diploma in 1947; he also studied conducting with Karajan and Scherchen. He conducted opera in Graz (1945–59), Bregenz (1947–48), and Cologne (1959–62). Cardis was chief conductor of the Philharmonia Hungarica in Marl kreis Recklinghausen (1960–67), with which he toured the U.S. in 1964 and 1967. After serving as chief conductor of the Oslo Phil. (1969–75), he was Generalmusikdirektor of the Duisburg Sym. Orch. (1975–81); then was chief conductor of the Niederösterreichisches Tonkünstler Orch. in Vienna (1981–85).

Carlid, Göte, Swedish composer; b. Högbo, Dec. 26, 1920; d. Stockholm, June 30, 1953. He was a philosophy student at the Univ. of Uppsala; then served as a municipal librarian in Enköping (1946–48) and Sollentuna (1948–50). As a composer, he was largely autodidact, but from the outset he adopted a modern idiom, making use of impressionistic and expressionistic techniques. His last works before his early death show a learned approach to many of the problems of new music.

WORKS: *Monologues* for Piano (1944–50); *Notturno* for String Orch. (1945); *3 Songs* for Woman's Voice, Flute, Clarinet, and Cello (1946–49); *Small Pieces* for Piano (1947); Piano Sonata (1948); *Quartetto elegiaco* for String Quartet (1948); *A Little Tea Music* for Flute, 2 Clarinets, and Cello (1949); *Mass* for Strings (1949); *Triad* for Saxophone and Piano (1950); *Hymnes à la beauté* for Chorus and Orch. (1952); *The Music Bus* for Soli, Children's Chorus, and Instruments (1952).

Carlos, Wendy (née **Walter**), American organist, composer, and electronics virtuoso; b. Pawtucket, R.I., Nov. 14, 1939. He played piano as a child; later studied with Ron Nelson at Brown Univ. (A.B., 1962) and with Luening, Ussachevsky, and Beeson at Columbia Univ. (M.A., 1965). In 1964 he began working with Robert Moog in perfecting the Moog Synthesizer. The result of their experiments with versified tone-colors was a record album under the title *Switched-on Bach* (1968), which became unexpectedly successful, selling some million copies. This was followed in 1969 by *The Well-Tempered Synthesizer,* engineered entirely by Carlos. Then, at the age of 32, he suddenly became aware of his sexual duality, a woman's psyche imprisoned in a man's body. To remedy this sundering nature, he underwent a transsexual operation; on St. Valentine's Day, Feb. 14, 1979, he officially changed his first name from Walter to Wendy. She/he described his sexual tergiversation in a candid interview in *Playboy* (May 1979), illustrated with photographs "before and after." In 1992 Carlos brought out the album *Switched-on Bach 2000.*

WORKS: *Noah,* opera (1964–65); *Timesteps* for Synthesizer (1970); *Sonic Seasons* for Synthesizer and Tape (1971); *Pompous Circumstances* for Synthesizer or Orch. (1974–75); *Variations on Dies irae* for Orch. (1980); film scores, including *A Clockwork Orange* (1971), *The Shining* (1978–80), and *TRON* (1981–82); some chamber music and other pieces.

Carlson, Claudine, French-American mezzo-soprano; b. Mulhouse, Feb. 26, 1937. She studied in California and at the Manhattan School of Music in N.Y. with Jennie Tourel and Esther Andreas; then embarked on a successful career as a concert singer. On April 18, 1968, she made her first appearance at the N.Y. City opera as Cornelia in *Giulio Cesare.* She made her Metropolitan Opera debut in N.Y. as Geneviève in *Pelléas et Mélisande* on Oct. 11, 1977, and sang there again in 1981. Gifted with a voice of fine quality, she gained particular renown in the French repertoire.

Carlstedt, Jan, Swedish composer; b. Orsa, June 15, 1926. He studied composition with Lars-Erik Larsson at the Stockholm Musikhogskolan (1948–52), then pursued studies at the Royal College of Music in London (1952–53) and in Rome (1953–54). Returning to Stockholm, he became active in furthering the cause of modern music; was founder-chairman of the Contemporary Music Assn. in Stockholm (1960) and secretary of the Soc. of Swedish Composers (1961–63). In 1964 he was elected a member of the Royal Swedish Academy of Music in Stockholm.

WORKS: 5 string quartets (1951–52; 1966; 1967; 1972; 1977); 2 syms.: No. 1 (1952–54; rev. 1960; Stockholm, Oct. 4, 1961) and No. 2, in memory of Martin Luther King, Jr. (1968; N.Y., Dec. 20, 1970); String Trio (1955–56); Sonata for String Orch. (1956); Sonata for 2 Violins (1956); *12 Miniatures* for Violin, Clarinet, and Cello (1958); 8 Duets for 2 Violins (1958); *Sinfonietta* for Wind Quintet (1959); Sonata for Solo Violin (1959); *Ballata* for Cello (1960); *Divertimento* for Oboe and String Trio (1962); Wind Quintet (1962); *Pentastomos* for Wind Quintet (1972–73); *Metamorfoser* for Flute, Oboe, Violin, and Cello (1974); *Trittico* for Oboe and String Orch. (1980); *Nocturne* for 4 Cellos (1983); *Intrada* for Orch. (1985); *Metamorphosi* for Strings (1986); *Missa pro defunctis: Lacrimosa* for Chorus (1989); *Ballad to Stephen Foster* for Chorus (1990).

Carlyle, Joan (Hildred), English soprano; b. Wirral, April 6, 1931. She studied in London, making her operatic debut as Frasquita at London's Covent Garden in 1955. She continued to sing there regularly until 1969 in such roles as Mimi, Nedda, Sophie, Arabella, Pamina, Desdemona, Britten's Titania, and Tippett's Jenifer; she also appeared at the Edinburgh Festival, the Glyndebourne Festival, the Vienna State Opera, the Bavarian State Opera in Munich, and the Teatro Colón in Buenos Aires.

Carmirelli, Pina (actually, **Giuseppina**), Italian violinist; b. Varzi, Jan. 23, 1914; d. Carpena, Feb. 27, 1993. She studied at the Milan Cons., graduating in 1930, and at the Accademia di Santa Cecilia in Rome. She began her concert career in 1937; in 1949 she founded the Boccherini Quintet, and in 1954 the Carmirelli Quartet, with which she toured throughout Europe. From 1975 to 1986 she was concertmaster of I Musici. She was also active as a teacher in Italy and the U.S.

Carner, Mosco, Austrian-born English writer on music and conductor; b. Vienna, Nov. 15, 1904; d. Cornwall, Aug. 3, 1985. He studied at the New Vienna Cons., and then musicology with Adler at the Univ. of Vienna (Ph.D., 1928, with the diss. *Studien zur Sonatenform bei Robert Schumann*). After conducting opera in Opava (1929–30) and Gdańsk (1930–33), he emigrated to England and became a naturalized British subject. He devoted himself mainly to writing music criticism in London, and later was music critic of *Time and Tide* (1949–62) and the *Evening News* (1957–61).

WRITINGS (all publ. in London unless otherwise given): *Dvořák* (1941); Vol. 2 of *A Study of 20th-Century Harmony* (1942); *Of Men and Music* (1944); *The Waltz* (1948); *Puccini: A Critical Biography* (1958; 3rd ed., rev., 1992); *Alban Berg: The Man and the Work* (1975; 2nd ed., rev., 1983); *Madam Butterfly* (1979); *Major and Minor* (1980); *Hugo Wolf Songs* (1982); *Tosca* (Cambridge, 1985).

Carneyro, Claudio, Portuguese composer and teacher; b. Oporto, Jan. 27, 1895; d. there, Oct. 18, 1963. He studied composition with Lucien Lambert at the Oporto Cons. and later in Paris with Widor (1919–22) and Dukas (1934). He taught composition at the Oporto Cons. (1922–58); was its director from 1955 to 1958. In his music, he made use of authentic Portuguese motives, adorning them by sonorous impressionistic harmonies.

WORKS: ORCH.: *Pregões romarias e processões* (1928); *Memento* for Strings (1933); *Cantarejo e dancara* (1938); *Pavana e gelharda* for Strings (1939); *Catavento* for Piano and Chamber Orch. (1942); *Portugalesas* (1949); *Khroma* for Viola and Orch. (1954); *Roda dos degredados* for Violin and Orch. (1960); *Bailadeiras* (1962); *Gradualis* (1962). **CHAMBER:** Piano Quartet (1914); *Partita* for String Trio (1928–35); Violin Sonata (1929); String Quartet (1947); *Poemas em prosa* for Piano (1930–31). **VOCAL:** Choruses; songs.

Carol-Berard, French composer and music theorist; b. Marseilles, April 5, 1881; d. Paris, Dec. 13, 1942. He studied with Albeniz in Barcelona; then settled in Paris. His music, impressionistic with an oriental flavor, remains largely unpubl. He evolved a theory of "chromophonie" (color in movement) and wrote several papers on the subject in *La Revue Musicale* and other publications. He also wrote poetry under the pseudonym Olivier Realtor.

WORKS: *Symphonie dansée*; *Symphonie des forces mécaniques*; *L'Oiseau des îles*, lyric piece; 3 piano suites: *Égypte, D'une existence ânterieure*, and *Extrême-Asie*; humorous piano pieces: *Les Heures civiles et militaires* and *L'Élégie à jouer dans une cave*; a number of songs to poems of Verlaine and Mallarmé.

Carpenter, John Alden, important American composer; b. Park Ridge, Ill., Feb. 28, 1876; d. Chicago, April 26, 1951. He studied in Chicago with Amy Fay and W.C.E. Seeboeck, and then with J.K. Paine at Harvard Univ. (B.A., 1897). During a trip to Rome (1906), he had some lessons with Elgar, and then completed his training in Chicago with B. Ziehn (1908–12). He was employed in his father's shipping supply business, later serving as its vice-president (1909–36). In subsequent years, he devoted himself entirely to composition. In 1918 he was elected a member of the National Inst. of Arts and Letters, and received its Gold Medal in 1947. In 1942 he was elected a member of the American Academy of Arts and Letters. Carpenter gained success as a composer with his first orch. score, the humorous suite *Adventures in a Perambulator* (1914). Adopting mildly modernistic techniques, he was notably successful in his works on American subjects with a tinge of ragtime and jazz elements. His "jazz pantomime" *Krazy Kat* (1921), after the well-known comic strip by George Herriman, proved an immediate success. It was followed by his *Skyscrapers* (1923–24), "a ballet of American life," which retains its historical interest as a period piece. Among his orch. works, the most notable is his symphonic poem *Sea Drift* (1933), after Whitman. Carpenter also distinguished himself as a composer of songs.

WORKS: DRAMATIC: *The Birthday of the Infanta*, ballet (1917; rev. version, Chicago, Dec. 23, 1919; suite, 1930, rev. 1940; concert suite, 1949); *Krazy Kat*, "jazz pantomime" (Chicago, Dec. 23, 1921; rev. 1940); *Skyscrapers*, ballet (1923–24; N.Y., Feb. 19, 1926); incidental music. **ORCH.:** Suite (c.1906–09); *Berceuse* for Small Orch. (1908); *Adventures in a Perambulator*, suite (1914; Chicago, March 19, 1915); Piano Concertino (1915; Chicago, March 10, 1916; rev. 1948); 2 syms.: No. 1, *Sermons in Stones* (Norfolk, Conn., June 5, 1917; rev. version, Chicago, Oct. 24, 1940) and No. 2 (N.Y., Oct. 22, 1942); *A Pilgrim Vision*, symphonic poem (Philadelphia, Nov. 23, 1920); *Jazz Orchestra Pieces: Oil and Vinegar* (1925–26); *Patterns* for Piano and Orch. (Boston, Oct. 21, 1932); *Sea Drift*, symphonic poem after Whitman (Chicago, Nov. 30, 1933; rev. 1944); Violin Concerto (1936; Chicago, Nov. 18, 1937); *Danza* (1937; also for Piano, 1947); *The Anxious Bugler*, symphonic poem (N.Y., Nov. 17, 1943); *Blue Gal* for Cello and Orch. (1943); *The 7 Ages*, suite after Shakespeare (N.Y., Nov. 29, 1945); *Carmel Concerto* for Piano and Orch. (1948). **CHAMBER:** Violin Sonata (1911; N.Y., Dec. 11, 1912); String Quartet (1927); Piano Quintet (1934). **PIANO:** Sonata (1897); *Polonaise américaine* (1912); *Little Indian* (1916); *Little Dancer* (1917); *Tango américaine* (1920); *Diversions* (1922). **VOCAL:** *Songs of Faith* for Chorus and Orch. (1931; rev. 1936); *Song of Freedom* for Chorus and Orch. (1941); *Song of David* for Women's Voices, Cello, and Orch. (1951; unfinished); song cycles, including *Gitanjali* (1913) and *Water Colors* (1918); many solo songs.

BIBL.: F. Borowski, "J.A. C.," *Musical Quarterly* (Oct. 1930); O. Downes, "J.A. C., American Craftsman," ibid.; T. Pierson, *The Life and Music of J.A. C.* (diss., Univ. of Rochester, 1952); J. O'Connor, *J.A. C.: Bio-Bibliography* (Westport, Conn., 1994).

Carpitella, Diego, Italian ethnomusicologist; b. Reggio di Calabria, June 12, 1924. After receiving an arts degree from the Univ. of Rome in 1947, he made an extensive collection of documents and field recordings of the music of central and southern Italy; 2 of his recordings were released in collaboration with Alan Lomax in 1957. He publ. studies on the musics of Tunisia, Brazil, Uruguay, and Argentina, popular and jazz music, and general issues of ethnomusicology. He taught at the univs. of Trent, Chieti, and Rome (from 1975); organized Italy's 1st ethnomusicology congress in 1974. His writings include *Musica popolare e musica di consumo* (1955), *La musica nei rituali sardi dell'argia* (1967), and *Musica e tradizione orale* (1973).

Carré, Marguerite (née **Marthe Giraud**), French soprano; b. Cabourg, Aug. 16, 1880; d. Paris, Dec. 26, 1947. She studied at the Bordeaux Cons. and the Paris Cons. In 1899 she made her operatic debut as Mimi in Nantes; in 1901 she joined the Paris Opéra-Comique, where she appeared in such roles as Manon, Mélisande, Louise, Madama Butterfly, and Pamina, and where she created roles in operas by Charpentier, Leroux, and Rabaud. In 1914 she married Albert Carré, director of the Opéra-Comique; they divorced in 1924 but remarried upon her retirement in 1929.

Carreno, Inoceñte, Venezuelan composer; b. Porlamar, Dec. 28, 1919. He studied horn, clarinet, piano, and theory in Caracas; graduated in composition in 1946; subsequently became engaged in pedagogical work; also played the horn in the Caracas Sym. Orch. and conducted choruses. His works include a symphonic poem, *El Pozo* (1946); *Suite Breve* for String Orch. (1947); *Margariteña*, suite for Orch. (1954); Concerto for Horn and Strings (1958); *Sinfonieta satirica* for 11 Instruments (1965); *Dialogo* for Flute and Chamber Orch. (1965); chamber music and choruses.

Carreño, (Maria) Teresa, famous Venezuelan pianist; b. Caracas, Dec. 22, 1853; d. N.Y., June 12, 1917. As a child, she studied with her father, an excellent pianist; driven from home by a revolution, the family settled in N.Y. in 1862, where she studied with Gottschalk. At the age of 8, she gave a public recital in N.Y. (Nov. 25, 1862). She began her career in 1866, after studying with G. Mathias in Paris and A. Rubinstein. She lived mainly in Paris from 1866 to 1870; then in England. She developed a singing voice and made an unexpected appearance in opera in Edinburgh as the Queen in *Les Huguenots* (May 24, 1872) in a cast that included Tietjens, Brignoli, and Mario; was again in the U.S. in 1876, when she studied voice in Boston. For the Bolivar centenary celebration in Caracas (Oct. 29, 1885), she appeared as singer, pianist, and composer of the festival hymn, written at the request of the Venezuelan government; hence the frequent but erroneous attribution to Carreño of the national hymn of Venezuela, *Gloria al bravo pueblo* (the music of which was actually composed in 1811 by J. Landaeta, and officially adopted as the Venezuelan national anthem on May 25, 1881). In Caracas she once again demonstrated her versatility, when for the last 3 weeks of the season she conducted the opera company managed by her husband, **Giovanni Tagliapietra**. After these musical experiments, she resumed her career as a pianist; made her German debut in Berlin, Nov. 18, 1889; in 1907 toured Australia. Her last appearance with an orch. was with the N.Y. Phil. (Dec. 8, 1916); her last recital appearance was in Havana (March 21, 1917). She impressed her audiences by the impetuous élan of her playing, and was described as "the Valkyrie of the piano." She was married 4 times: to **Émile Sauret** (June 1873), to the baritone Giovanni Tagliapietra (1876), to **Eugène d'Albert** (1892–95), and to Arturo Tagliapietra, a younger brother of Giovanni (June 30, 1902). Early in her career, she wrote a number of compositions, including a String Quartet; *Petite danse tsigane* for Orch.; 39 concert pieces for piano; a waltz, *Mi Teresita*, which enjoyed considerable popularity; and other small pieces. She was one of the first pianists to play MacDowell's compositions in public; MacDowell took lessons from her in N.Y. She was greatly venerated in Venezuela; her mortal remains were solemnly transferred from N.Y., where she died, and reburied in Caracas, on Feb. 15, 1938.

BIBL.: M. Milinowski, *T. C.* (New Haven, 1940); A. Marquez Rodriguez, *Esbozo biográfico de T. C.* (Caracas, 1953); R. Marciano, *T. C.* (Kassel, 1990).

Carreras, José (Maria), celebrated Spanish tenor; b. Barcelona, Dec. 5, 1946. He studied with Jaime Puig at the Barcelona Cons. before completing his training with Juan Ruax. In 1970 he made his operatic debut as Flavio in *Norma* in Barcelona, and later that year appeared as Gennaro opposite Caballé's Lucrezia Borgia. In 1971 he won the Verdi Competition in Parma, where he made his Italian debut as Rodolfo. He also made his first appearance in London that year singing Leicester in a concert performance of *Maria Stuarda*. On March 15, 1972, he made his U.S. debut as Pinkerton at the N.Y. City Opera, where he remained on the roster until 1975. In 1973 he sang for the first time at the San Francisco Opera as Rodolfo. He made his Metropolitan Opera debut in N.Y. on Nov. 18, 1974, as Cavaradossi, and subsequently returned there regularly. In 1975 he sang for the first time at Milan's La Scala as Riccardo. In 1976 he made his first appearances at the Salzburg Festival (as Don Carlos) and at the Chicago Lyric Opera (as Riccardo). In addition to his engagements with principal opera houses of the world, Carreras pursued a notably successful career as a concert artist. However, in 1987 he was stricken with acute lymphocytic leukemia. Following exhaustive medical treatment, he was able to resume his career in 1988 when he appeared at a special Barcelona outdoor concert before an audience of 150,000 admirers. That same year he founded the José Carreras Leukemia Foundation in Barcelona. In 1989 he appeared in recitals in Seattle and N.Y., and also returned to the operatic stage as Jason in Cherubini's *Medea* in Mérida, Spain. On Sept. 24, 1989, he created the title role in Balada's *Cristóbal Colón* in Barcelona. On July 7, 1990, he appeared in a spectacular concert with fellow tenors Plácido Domingo and Luciano Pavarotti in Rome, with Zubin Mehta conducting. The event was telecast live to the world and subsequently became a best-selling video and compact disc. In 1992 Carreras served as musical director of the opening and closing ceremonies at the Barcelona Olympic Games. On July 16, 1994, he again appeared in concert with Domingo, Pavarotti, and Mehta in Los Angeles in another spectacular telecast event. His autobiography was publ. as *Singen mit der Seele* (Munich, 1989; Eng. tr., 1991, as *Singing from the Soul*). The title aptly describes his approach not only to singing but to living the life of one of the world's favorite tenors.

BIBL.: J. Pérez Senz, *J. C. El placer de cantar: Un retrato autobiográfico* (Barcelona, 1988).

Carrillo (-Trujillo), Julián (Antonio), Mexican composer; b. Ahualulco, San Luis Potosí, Jan. 28, 1875; d. Mexico City, Sept. 9, 1965. He was of Indian extraction; lived mostly in Mexico City, where he studied violin with Pedro Manzano and composition with Melesio Morales. He graduated from the National Cons. in 1899 and received a government stipend for study abroad as a winner of the President Diaz Prize. He took courses at the Leipzig Cons. with Hans Becker (violin), Jadassohn (theory), and Hans Sitt (orchestration); he also played violin in the Gewandhaus Orch. under Nikisch. From 1902 to 1904 he studied at the Ghent Cons., winning 1st prize as violinist. He returned to Mexico in 1905 and made numerous appearances as a violinist; also conducted concerts; was appointed general inspector of music and director of the National Cons. (1913–14; 1920–24). He visited the U.S. many times, and conducted his works in N.Y. and elsewhere. During his years in Leipzig, he wrote a Sym., which he conducted there in 1902; at the same time, he began experimenting with fractional tones and developed a theory which he named *Sonido 13*, symbolically indicating divisions beyond the 12 notes of the chromatic scale. He further devised a special number notation for quarter tones, eighth tones, and sixteenth tones, and constructed special instruments for their realization, such as a harpzither with 97 strings to the octave; he also publ. several books dealing with music of fractional tones, and ed. a monthly magazine, *El Sonido 13*, in 1924–25.

WORKS: OPERAS: *Ossian* (1903); *Matilda* (1909); *Zultil* (1922). **ORCH.:** 3 syms. (1901, 1905, 1948); 3 syms. for fractional tones (1926); Triple Concerto for Violin, Flute, Cello, and Orch. (1918); Concertino for Violin, Guitar, Cello, Piccolo, and Harp in fractional tones, with Orch. in normal tuning (1926; Philadelphia, March 4, 1927); *Horizontes* for Violin, Cello, and Harp in fractional tones, and Orch. (1947; Pittsburgh, Nov. 30, 1951); Concertino, *Metamorfoseador Carrillo*, for Piano in third tones and Orch. (1950; Brussels, Nov. 9, 1958); Concerto for Cello in quarter and eighth tones and Orch. (1954; Brussels, Nov. 9, 1958); *Balbuceos* for Piano in sixteenth tones and Chamber Orch. (Houston, March 18, 1960); 2 concertos for Violin in quarter tones and Orch. (1963, 1964). **CHAMBER:** String Sextet (1902); Piano Quintet (1918); 4 atonal quartets (1928–48); *Preludio a Cristóbal Colón* for Soprano, with 5 Instruments in fractional tones (Mexico City, Feb. 15, 1925); Sonata in Quarter Tones for Guitar (1925); also sonatas for string instruments in quarter tones, with piano. **OTHER:** *Mass for Pope John XXIII* for Chorus (1962).

WRITINGS: *Julián Carrillo, Su vida y su obra* (Mexico City, 1945); *Leyes de metamorfósis musicales* (Mexico City, 1949).

BIBL.: A. Pike, "The Discoveries and Theories of J. C., 1875–1965," *Inter-American Music Bulletin*, IV (1966).

Carroli, Silvano, Italian baritone; b. Venice, Feb. 22, 1939. He trained at the opera school of the Teatro La Fenice in Venice and with Marcello and Mario del Monaco. After making his operatic debut as Schanuard in Venice in 1963, he sang in various Italian music centers. In 1972 he made his U.S. debut as Tonio in Dallas. As a member of Milan's La Scala company, he toured the U.S. in 1976 and Japan in 1981. In 1977 he made his debut at London's Covent Garden as Jack Rance, and returned there in later seasons. In 1978 he made his first appearance at the Chicago Lyric Opera. On Oct. 28, 1983, he made his Metropolitan Opera debut in N.Y. as Don Carlo in *La Forza del Destino*. In 1984 he sang at the Paris Opéra. His guest engagements also took him to Vienna, Barcelona, Brussels, Munich, and Berlin. Carroli is especially associated with roles in Italian opera, but he also sings roles to fine effect in operas by Mozart and Wagner.

Carron (real name, **Cox), Arthur,** English tenor; b. Swindon, Dec. 12, 1900; d. there, May 10, 1967. He joined London's Old Vic Theatre in 1929; also sang in London at the Sadler's Wells Opera until 1935 and at Covent Garden (1931, 1939). In 1936 he went to the U.S., where he won the Metropolitan Opera Auditions of the Air, and made his debut with the Metropolitan on May 29, 1936, as Canio in *Pagliacci*; he was chosen to sing the role of Nolan in the world premiere of Walter Damrosch's *The Man without a Country* on May 12, 1937; remained on the roster of the Metropolitan until 1946; then returned to England, where he sang at Covent Garden until 1951. Among his other roles were Tristan, Tannhäuser, Siegmund, Otello, and Manrico.

Carse, Adam (von Ahn), English composer and writer on music; b. Newcastle upon Tyne, May 19, 1878; d. Great Missenden, Buckinghamshire, Nov. 2, 1958. He studied with F. Corder and Burnett at the Royal Academy of Music in London. From 1909 to 1922 he taught music at Winchester College, then taught harmony and composition at the Royal Academy of Music (1923–40). He assembled a collection of about 350 wind instruments, which he presented to the Horniman Museum in London in 1947. A catalog of this collection was publ. in 1951.

WORKS: 2 symphonic poems: *The Death of Tintagiles* (London, 1902) and *In a Balcony* (London, Aug. 26, 1905); 2 syms. (London, July 3, 1906; London, Nov. 19, 1908, rev. 1909); 2 orch. suites: *The Merry Milkmaids* (1922) and *The Nursery* (1928); *Judas Iscariot's Paradise*, ballade for Baritone, Chorus, and Orch. (1922); 2 sketches for Strings (1923); *Barbara Allen* for Strings; *Norwegian Fantasia* for Violin and Orch.; *The Lay of the Brown Rosary*, dramatic cantata; numerous choruses; chamber music; piano pieces; songs.

WRITINGS: *The History of Orchestration* (London, 1925); *Orchestral Conducting* (London, 1929); *Musical Wind Instruments* (London, 1939); *The Orchestra in the 18th Century* (Cambridge, 1940; 2nd ed., 1950); *The Orchestra from Beethoven to Berlioz* (Cambridge, 1948); *The Orchestra* (London, 1948); *18th Century Symphonies* (London, 1951); *The Life of Jullien* (Cambridge, 1951).

Cartan, Jean, talented French composer; b. Nancy, Dec. 1, 1906; d. Bligny, March 26, 1932. His father was the famous mathematician Elie Cartan. He studied with Marcel Rousseau; then with Paul Dukas at the Paris Cons. His works, composed within the brief period of 6 years, showed extraordinary promise, and his death at the age of 25 was mourned as a great loss to French music. He left a cantata, *Pater Noster*, 2 string quartets; a Sonatina for Flute and Clarinet (Oxford, July 25, 1931); piano pieces and several cycles of songs.

BIBL.: A. Roussel, "J. C.," *La Revue Musicale*, XIII (1932).

Carter, Elliott (Cook, Jr.), outstanding American composer and teacher; b. N.Y., Dec. 11, 1908. After graduating from the Horace Mann High School in N.Y. in 1926, Carter entered Harvard Univ., majoring in literature and languages; at the same time, he studied piano at the Longy School of Music in Cambridge, Mass. In 1930 he devoted himself exclusively to music at Harvard, taking up harmony and counterpoint with Piston, and orchestration with Hill; also attended in 1932 a course given there by Holst. He obtained his M.A. in 1932, and then went to Paris, where he studied with Boulanger and at the École Normale de Musique, receiving a *licence de contrepoint*; in the interim, he learned mathematics, Latin, and Greek. In 1935 he returned to America; was music director of the Ballet Caravan (1937–39); gave courses in music and also in mathematics, physics, and classical Greek at St. John's College in Annapolis, Md. (1940–44); then taught at the Peabody Cons. of Music in Baltimore (1946–48). He was on the faculty of Columbia Univ. (1948–50), Queens College of the City Univ. of N.Y. (1955–56), and Yale Univ. (1960–62). In 1963 he was composer-in-residence at the American Academy in Rome, and in 1964 held a similar post in West Berlin. In 1967–68 he was a prof.-at-large at Cornell Univ. He held Guggenheim fellowships in 1945–46 and 1950–51, and the American Prix de Rome in 1953. In 1965 he received the Creative Arts Award from Brandeis Univ. In 1953 he received 1st prize in the Concours International de Composition pour Quatuor à Cordes in Liège for his 1st String Quartet; in 1960 he received the Pulitzer Prize in Music for his 2nd String Quartet, which also received the N.Y. Music Critics Circle Award and was further elected as the most important work of the year by the International Rostrum of Composers. He again won the Pulitzer Prize in Music, for his 3rd String Quartet, in 1973. In 1985 he was awarded the National Medal of Arts by President Ronald Reagan. In 1987 he was made a Dommandeur dans l'Ordre des Arts des Lettres of France. In 1991 he was named a Commendatore of the Order of Merit in Italy. Carter's reputation as one of the most important American composers grew with each new work he produced; Stravinsky was quoted as saying that Carter's Double Concerto was the first true American masterpiece. The evolution of Carter's compositional style is marked by his constant preoccupation with taxonomic considerations. His early works are set in a neo-Classical style. He later absorbed the Schoenbergian method of composition with 12 equal tones. Finally he developed a system of serial organization in which all parameters, including intervals, metric divisions, rhythm, counterpoint, harmony, and instrumental timbres, become parts of the total conception of each individual work. In this connection, he introduced the term "metric modulation," in which secondary rhythms in a polyrhythmic section assume dominance expressed in constantly changing meters, often in such unusual time signatures as 10/16, 21/8, etc. Furthermore, he assigns to each participating instrument in a polyphonic work a special interval, a distinctive rhythmic figure, and a selective register, so that the individuality of each part is clearly outlined, a distribution which is often reinforced by placing the players at a specified distance from one another. E. and K. Stone ed. *The Writings of E. C.: An American Composer Looks at Modern Music* (N.Y., 1977).

WORKS: DRAMATIC: OPERA: *Tom and Lily* (1934; withdrawn). **BALLETS:** *Pocahontas* (Keene, N.H., Aug. 17, 1936; withdrawn; orch. version, 1938–39; N.Y., May 24, 1939); *The Minotaur* (N.Y., March 26, 1947). **INCIDENTAL MUSIC TO:** Sophocles's *Philoctetes* (1931; Cambridge, Mass., March 15, 1933); Plautus's *Mostellaria* (Cambridge, Mass., April 15, 1936); Shakespeare's *Much Ado About Nothing* (1937; withdrawn). **ORCH.:** Sym. (1937; withdrawn); *Prelude, Fanfare, and Polka* for Small Orch. (1938); Sym. No. 1 (1942; Rochester, N.Y., April 27, 1944; rev. 1954); *Holiday Overture* (1944; rev. 1961); *Elegy* for Strings (1952; N.Y., March 1, 1953; arranged from the *Elegy* for Cello and Piano, 1943); *Variations for Orchestra* (1954–55; Louisville, April 21, 1956); Double Concerto for Harpsichord, Piano, and 2 Chamber Orchs. (N.Y., Sept. 6, 1961); Piano Concerto (1964–65; Boston, Jan. 6, 1967); *Concerto for Orchestra* (1968–69; N.Y., Feb. 5, 1970); *A Symphony of 3 Orchestras* (1976; N.Y., Feb. 17, 1977); *Penthode* for 5 Instrumental Quartets (1984–85; London, July 26, 1985); *3 Occasions* (1986–89; 1, *A Celebration of Some 100 × 150 Notes*, 1986; Houston, April 10, 1987; 2, *Remembrance*, Tanglewood, Aug. 10, 1988; 3, *Anniversary*, London Oct. 5, 1989); Oboe Concerto (1986–87; Zürich, June 17, 1988); Violin Concerto (San Francisco, May 2, 1990); *Partita* (1993; Chicago, Feb. 17, 1994); *Adagio Tenebroso* (1994; London, Sept. 13, 1995). **CHAMBER:** *Canonic Suite* for 4 Alto Saxophones (1939; rev. for 4 Clarinets, 1955–56; rev. for 4 Saxophones, 1981); *Pastoral* for English Horn or Viola or Clarinet and Piano (1940); *Elegy* for Cello and Piano (1943; arranged for String Quartet, 1946, for String Orch., 1952, and for Viola and Piano, 1961); Piano Sonata (1945–46; N.Y. radio broadcast, Feb. 16, 1947); Woodwind Quintet (1948; N.Y., Feb. 21, 1949); Cello Sonata (1948; N.Y., Feb. 27, 1950); *8 Etudes and a Fantasy* for Flute, Oboe, Clarinet, and Bassoon (1949–50; N.Y., Oct. 28, 1952); *8 Pieces for 4 Timpani* for 1 Performer (1950–66); 4 string quartets: No. 1 (1950–51; N.Y., Feb. 26, 1953), No. 2 (1959; N.Y., March 25, 1960), No. 3 (1971; N.Y., Jan. 23, 1973), and No. 4 (Miami, Sept. 17, 1986); Sonata for Flute, Oboe, Cello, and Harpsichord (1952; N.Y., Nov. 19, 1953); *Canon for 3: In memoriam Igor Stravinsky* for 3 Equal Instruments (1971; N.Y., Jan. 23, 1972); Duo for Violin and Piano (1973–74; N.Y., March 21, 1975); Brass Quintet for 2 Trumpets, Horn, and 2 Trombones (BBC, London, Oct. 20, 1974); *A Fantasy About Purcell's "Fantasia Upon One Note"* for 2 Trumpets, Horn, and 2 Trombones (1974; N.Y., Jan. 13, 1975); *Birthday Fanfare for Sir William Glock's 70th* for 3 Trumpets, Vibraphone, and Glockenspiel (London, May 3, 1978); *Night Fantasies* for Piano

(Bath, June 2, 1980); Triple Duo for Violin, Cello, Flute, Clarinet, Piano, and Percussion (1982–83; N.Y., April 23, 1983); *Changes* for Guitar (N.Y., Dec. 11, 1983); *Canon for 4: Homage to William* [Glock] for Flute, Bass Clarinet, Violin, and Cello (Bath, June 8, 1984); *Esprit rude/esprit doux* for Flute and Clarinet (1984; Baden-Baden, March 31, 1985); *Riconoscenza per Goffredo Petrassi* for Violin (Pontino, June 15, 1984); *Birthday Flourish* for 5 Trumpets or Brass Quintet (San Francisco, Sept. 14, 1988); *Enchanted Preludes* for Flute and Cello (N.Y., May 16, 1988); *Con leggerezza pensosa* for Clarinet, Violin, and Cello (Latina, Italy, Sept. 29, 1990); Quintet for Piano and Winds (1991; Cologne, Sept. 13, 1992); *Scrivo in Vento* for Flute (Avignon, July 20, 1991); *Bariolage* for Harp (Geneva, March 23, 1992); *Immer Neu* for Oboe and Harp (Sermoneta, Italy, June 30, 1992); *Immer Song* for Oboe (Witten, April 25, 1992); 3 preceding works constitute *Trilogy* for Oboe and Harp (Sermoneta, June 30, 1992); *Gra* for Clarinet (Sermoneta, June 4, 1993); *Figment* for Cello (1994; N.Y., May 8, 1995). **VOCAL:** 11 madrigals for 3 to 8 Voices (1937); *Heart Not So Heavy as Mine* for Chorus (1938; N.Y., March 31, 1939); *The Defense of Corinth* for Speaker, Men's Voices, and Piano, 4-hands (1941; Cambridge, Mass., March 12, 1942); 3 poems of Robert Frost for Mezzo-soprano or Baritone and Piano (1943; also for Soprano or Tenor and Chamber Orch., 1975); *Warble for Lilac Time* for Soprano or Tenor and Piano or Small Orch. (1943; Saratoga Springs, N.Y., Sept. 14, 1946; rev. 1954); *Voyage* for Mezzo-soprano or Baritone and Piano (1943; N.Y., March 16, 1947; also for Small Orch., 1975; rev. 1979); *The Harmony of Morning* for Women's Voices and Small Orch. (1944; N.Y., Feb. 25, 1945); *Musicians Wrestle Everywhere* for Mixed Voices and Strings ad libitum (1945; N.Y., Feb. 12, 1946); *A Mirror on Which to Dwell* for Soprano and 9 Players (1975; N.Y., Feb. 24, 1976); *Syringa* for Mezzo-soprano, Bass, and 11 Players (N.Y., Dec. 10, 1978); *In Sleep, in Thunder* for Tenor and 14 Players (1981; London, Oct. 27, 1982); *Of Challenge and of Love* for Soprano and Piano (1995).

BIBL.: A. Edwards, *Flawed Words and Stubborn Sounds: A Conversation with E. C.* (N.Y., 1971); *E. C.: A 70th Birthday Tribute* (London, 1978); D. Schiff, *The Music of E. C.* (N.Y., 1983); C. Rosen, *The Musical Languages of E. C.* (Washington, D.C., 1984); D. Harvey, *The Later Music of E. C.: A Study in Music Theory and Analysis* (N.Y., 1989); E. Restagno, *E. C.: In Conversation with Enzo Restagno for Settemre Musica 1989* (N.Y., 1991); A. Edwards, C. Rosen, and H. Holliger, *Entretiens avec E. C.* (Geneva, 1992).

Carterette, Edward (Calvin), respected American psychologist and acoustician; b. Mount Tabor, N.C., July 10, 1921. He studied mathematics at the Univ. of Chicago and psychology at Harvard Univ. and Indiana Univ. in Bloomington (Ph.D., 1957). After conducting research at MIT, Indiana Univ., and the Univ. of Calif. at Berkeley, he joined the faculty of the Univ. of Calif. at Los Angeles as prof. of experimental psychology (1968). He is noted for his studies in psychoacoustics and music cognition; he was assoc. ed. of the journal *Music Perception* (from 1982), and his books and numerous publ. articles include studies on perception of non-Western instruments, as well as the psychoacoustics of rhythm and musical memory.

Caruso, Enrico (actually, **Errico**), great Italian tenor; b. Naples, Feb. 25, 1873; d. there, Aug. 2, 1921. While attending the Scuola sociale e serale in Naples, he received some training in oratorio and choral singing. By the age of 11, he was serving as principal soloist in its choir. He also received lessons from Amelia Tibaldi Nicola. In 1891 he began vocal training with Guglielmo Vergine, who remained a mentor until 1895. In 1894 he was engaged to sing in *Mignon* at the Teatro Mercadante in Naples, but at the piano rehearsal he proved a dismal failure at sight-reading and was dismissed. Caruso finally made his operatic debut at the Teatro Nuovo in Naples in Mario Morelli's *L'Amico Francesco* on March 15, 1895. He then sang Turiddu and Faust in Caserta, and subsequently Faust, the Duke of Mantua, and Alfredo at the Teatro Bellini in Naples. After successful appearances in Cairo as Edgardo, Enzo Grimaldo, and Puccini's Des Grieux, he returned to Naples to sing Bellini's Tebaldo at the Teatro Mercadente. While engaged in Salerno (1896–97), he received vocal coaching from the conductor Vincenzo Lombardi. On May 29, 1897, he scored a fine success as Enzo Grimaldo at the opening of the Teatro Massimo in Palermo. He then won accolades as Rodolfo at the Teatro Goldoni in Livorno on Aug. 14, 1897. During the 1897–98 season, he sang at the Teatro Lirico in Naples with increasing success. The decisive turning point in his career came at that theater on Nov. 17, 1898, when he created the role of Loris in Giordano's *Fedora.* On Jan. 27, 1899, he made his first appearance in St. Petersburg as Alfredo, where he sang until 1900. He sang Loris at his debut in Buenos Aires on May 14, 1899, and continued to appear there until 1901, returning again in 1915 and 1917. On March 6, 1900, he made his first appearance in Moscow at a concert at the Bolshoi Theater, and then made his stage debut there as Radames on March 11. Caruso first sang at La Scala in Milan on Dec. 26, 1900, as Rodolfo. After appearing in the premiere of Mascagni's *Le Maschere* there on Jan. 17, 1901, he scored an enormous success there as Nemorino on Feb. 17. On March 11, 1902, he sang in the premiere of Franchetti's *Germania* there. His La Scala success prompted the Gramophone & Typewriter Co. of England to make a series of recordings of him in Milan in 1902–03. Caruso's fame was greatly enhanced through these and other recordings, especially those made with the Victor Talking Machine Co. of the U.S. between 1904 and 1920. On May 14, 1902, he made a notable British debut as the Duke of Mantua at Covent Garden in London. He appeared there again from 1904 to 1907, and in 1913–14. On Nov. 6, 1902, he sang in the premiere of Cilea's *Adriana Lecouvreur* at the Teatro Lirico in Milan. Caruso made an auspicious U.S. debut as the Duke of Mantua at the Metropolitan Opera in N.Y. on Nov. 23, 1903. For the rest of his career, he remained a stellar artist on its roster, appearing not only with the company in N.Y. but widely on tour. In his 18 seasons with the company, he sang 39 roles in 862 performances.

In addition to the Italian repertoire, Caruso won great success in such French roles as Massenet's Des Grieux, Saint-Saëns's Samson, Bizet's Don José, and Meyerbeer's Raoul. He also created the role of Jack Rance in Puccini's *La Fanciulla del West* on Dec. 10, 1910. Caruso chose his famous portrayal of the Duke of Mantua for his debut appearances at the Dresden Court Opera (May 8, 1904), the Vienna Court Opera (Oct. 6, 1906), and the Berlin Royal Opera (Oct. 23, 1907). His success in Vienna led Emperor Franz Joseph I to make him an Austrian Kammersänger in 1906, and he returned there to sing in 1907 and again from 1911 to 1913. He also continued to appear at the Berlin Royal Opera until 1909. In 1910 Kaiser Wilhelm II made him a German Kammersänger. From 1911 to 1913 he again sang at the Berlin Royal Opera. With the outbreak of World War I in 1914, Caruso concentrated his career mainly on the Metropolitan Opera, where he had become an idolized figure. He also made various appearances as a concert artist. On Dec. 11, 1920, while singing Nemorino at the Brooklyn Academy of Music, he was stricken with a throat hemorrhage. He managed to sing through the 1st act, but the remainder of the performance had to be cancelled. Although in great physical distress, he insisted on meeting his contractual obligation to sing Eléazar at the Metropolitan on Christmas Eve, 1920. This was his last public appearance. A severe pleurisy necessitated several debilitating surgeries. On May 28, 1921, he set sail to his beloved Italy, where he died 8 weeks later.

Caruso was richly blessed with a voice of extraordinary beauty and refinement, with unsurpassed breath control and impeccable intonation. Following surgery to remove a node from his vocal cords in 1909, his voice took on the darker characteristics of the baritone range. Caruso's earnings were astounding in his day. During his highest paid season at the Metropolitan (1907–08), he received $140,000. His concert fees were most lucrative, and eventually reached $15,000 per appearance. His recordings likewise became a gold mine. For his last contract with the Victor Talking Machine Co. in 1919, he was guaranteed an annual payment of $100,000 per year, in addition to royalties. In spite of his great wealth, however, he never lost his common touch and gave generously to various causes. And as much as he loved to sing, he loved life even more. Unfortunately, his private life was wracked by numerous ill-fated love affairs, several of which led to unsavory court proceedings and widespread press coverage and gossip. In 1897 he became intimate with the soprano (Vittoria Matilde) Ada Giachetti (b. Florence, Dec. 1, 1874; d. Rio de Janeiro, Oct. 16, 1946), the wife of the wealthy manufacturer Gino Botti. Their liaison produced 2 sons, the younger of whom, Enrico (Roberto Giovanni) Caruso, Jr. (b. Castello, near Florence, Sept. 7, 1904; d. Jacksonville, Fla., April 9, 1987), had a brief career as a tenor and actor. Caruso was also attracted to Ada's younger sister, the soprano Rina Giachetti, with whom he became intimate in 1906. It was also in 1906 that he was accused of making improper advances to a woman at N.Y.'s Central Park Zoo, which became known as the "monkey-house incident." Although Caruso pleaded not guilty and had a corroborating eye-witness, he was found guilty as charged and fined $10. He lost on appeal and paid the fine in 1907. In 1908 Ada deserted him for the family chauffeur. The bitter conflict which ensued between them culminated in a rancorous court battle in Milan in 1912. Caruso found solace in Rina, then in Dorothy Park Benjamin, whom he married in N.Y. on Aug. 20, 1918. Caruso's colorful life was the subject of the fictionalized film biography, *The Great Caruso* (1951), starring Mario Lanza. On Feb. 27, 1987, the U.S. Postal Service issued a commemorative stamp in his honor, with appropriate ceremonies at the Metropolitan Opera in N.Y., attended by his son, Enrico Caruso, Jr.

BIBL.: S. Fucito and B. Beyer, *C. and the Art of Singing* (N.Y., 1922); P. Key, *E. C.: A Biography* (Boston, 1922); D. Caruso and T. Goddard, *Wings of Song: The Story of C.* (N.Y., 1928; British ed., 1928, as *Wings of Song: An Authentic Life Story of E. C.*); N. Daspuro, *E. C.* (Milan, 1938); P. Suardon, *E. C.* (Milan, 1938); D. Caruso, *E. C.: His Life and Death* (N.Y., 1945); H. Steen, *C.: Eine Stimme erobert die Welt* (Essen-Steele, 1946); E. Gara, *C.: Storia di un emigrante* (Milan, 1947); T. Ybarra, *C.: The Man of Naples and the Voice of Gold* (N.Y., 1953); F. Robinson, *C.: His Life in Pictures* (N.Y., 1957); J.-P. Mouchon, *E. C., 1873–1921, sa vie et sa voix: Étude psycho-physiologique, physique, phonétique et esthétique* (Langres, 1966; Eng. tr., 1974); S. Jackson, *C.* (N.Y., 1972); H. Greenfield, *C.* (N.Y., 1983); M. Scott, *The Great C.* (N.Y., 1988); E. Caruso, Jr. and A. Farkas, *E. C.: My Father and My Family* (Portland, Oreg., 1990); H. Greenfield, *C.: An Illustrated Life* (North Pomfret, Vt., 1991); S. Fucito, *C. and the Art of Singing* (Mineola, N.Y., 1995).

Carvalho, Eleazar de, Brazilian conductor and composer; b. Iguatú, July 28, 1912; d. São Paulo, Sept. 12, 1996. His father was of Dutch extraction and his mother was part Indian. He studied in Fortaleza at the Apprentice Seaman's School; later joined the National Naval Corps in Rio de Janeiro and played tuba in the band. In 1941 he became assistant conductor of the Brazilian Sym. Orch. in Rio de Janeiro. In 1946 he went to the U.S. to study conducting with Koussevitzky at the Berkshire Music Center in Tanglewood, and Koussevitzky invited him to conduct a pair of concerts with the Boston Sym. Orch. Carvalho demonstrated extraordinary ability and musicianship by leading all rehearsals and the concerts without score in a difficult program; his sense of perfect pitch was exceptional. He subsequently conducted a number of guest engagements with orchs. in America and in Europe. From 1963 to 1968 he was music director of the St. Louis Sym. Orch.; during his tenure, he introduced many modern works into his programs, much to the discomfiture of the financial backers of the orch. From 1969 to 1973 he was conductor of the Hofstra Univ. Orch. in Hempstead, N.Y., which offered him a more liberal aesthetic climate; then returned to Brazil, where he became artistic director of the São Paulo State Sym. Orch. He married **Jocy de Oliveira**.

WORKS: 2 operas: *Descuberta do Brasil* (Rio de Janeiro, June 19, 1939) and *Tiradentes* (Rio de Janeiro, Sept. 7, 1941); *Sinfonia branca* (1943); 3 symphonic poems: *A Traicao* (1941), *Batalha Naval de Riachuelo* (1943), and *Guararapes* (1945); 3 overtures; 2 trios; 2 string quartets; Violin Sonata; songs.

Casabona, Francisco, Brazilian composer and pedagogue; b. São Paulo, Oct. 16, 1894; d. there, May 24, 1979. He studied in Brazil; then attended classes of Alessandro Longo (piano), Camillo de Nardis (theory), and Giovanni Barbieri (composition) at the Naples Cons. Returning to Brazil, he became a prof. at the São Paulo Cons. In his music, Casabona followed an Italianate expressive style, excelling equally in vocal and instrumental works.

WORKS: 2 comic operas: *Godiamo la Vita* (Rome, 1917) and *Principessa dell'Atelier* (Naples, 1918); 3 symphonic poems: *Nero* (1915), *Crepúsculo Sertanejo* (1926), and *Noite de São João* (1934); 2 sinfonias (1937, 1940); *La Fable d'Einstein* for Orch. (1946); *Maracatú*, Afro-Brazilian dance (1964); Violin Sonata; piano pieces; choruses and songs.

Casadesus, François Louis, French conductor and composer, brother of **Henri** and **Marius Casadesus**; b. Paris, Dec. 2, 1870; d. there, June 27, 1954. He studied at the Paris Cons. He conducted the Opéra and the Opéra-Comique of Paris on tour in France (1890–92); in 1895 he conducted the Opéra on a European tour; he was the founder and director (1918–22) of the American Cons. at Fontainebleau; later was active as a radio conductor and wrote music criticism. A collection of valedictory articles was publ. in honor of his 80th birthday (Paris, 1950).

WORKS: 4 operas: *Cachaprès* (Brussels, 1914), *La Chanson de Paris* (1924), *Bertran de Born* (Monte Carlo, 1925), and *Messie d'Amour* (Monte Carlo, 1928); *Symphonie scandinave*; *Au beau jardin de France* for Orch.; Sym.; smaller compositions for Orch.; numerous songs.

Casadesus, Gaby (née **Gabrielle L'Hôte**), French pianist and teacher; b. Marseilles, Aug. 9, 1901. She studied with Louis Diémer and Marguerite Long at the Paris Cons., where she won the premier prix in 1917; she then toured widely as a soloist, and later in duo concerts with her husband, **Robert Casadesus**. She served on the faculties of the Salzburg Mozarteum, the Paris Schola Cantorum, and the American Cons. in Fontainebleau. In 1975 she helped organize the Robert Casadesus International Piano Competition in Cleveland, which became the Cleveland International Piano Competition in 1994. Her career is the subject of the vol. *Mes noces musicales: Conversation avec Jacqueline Muller* (Paris, 1989).

Casadesus, Henri, French violinist, brother of **François** and **Marius Casadesus**; b. Paris, Sept. 30, 1879; d. there, May 31, 1947. He studied with Lavignac and Laforge in Paris; from 1910 to 1917 he was a member of the Capet Quartet; he was a founder and director of the Société Nouvelle des Instruments Anciens, in which he played the viola d'amore; subsequently toured in the U.S. His collection of rare and ancient instruments were housed in the museum of the Boston Sym. Orch.

Casadesus, Jean (Claude Michel), French pianist, son of **Robert (Marcel)** and **Gaby Casadesus**; b. Paris, July 7, 1927; d. in an automobile accident near Renfrew, Ontario, Canada, Jan. 20, 1972. He studied piano with his parents; at the outbreak of World War II, he went to the U.S. and studied at Princeton Univ. He won the contest for young soloists held by the Philadelphia Orch. in 1946; then appeared as soloist with the N.Y. Phil. and with major European orchs.

Casadesus, Jean-Claude, French conductor, nephew of **Robert (Marcel)** and **Gaby Casadesus**; b. Paris, Dec. 7, 1935. He studied at the Paris Cons.; in 1959 he received the premier prix as a percussion player there; he was then engaged as timpanist of the Concerts Colonne (until 1968) and of the Domaine Musical in Paris; also studied conducting with Dervaux at the École Normale de Musique in Paris (premier prix, 1965) and with Boulez in Basel. In 1969 he became resident conductor of the Opéra and of the Opéra-Comique in Paris. In 1971 he became assistant conductor to Dervaux with the Orchestre Philharmonique des Pays de la Loire in Angers. In 1976 he founded the Lille Phil.; also appeared as a guest conductor with various orchs. and opera houses in Europe. He was made an officer of the National Order of Merit for his services to French culture.

Casadesus, Marius, French violinist and composer, brother of **François** and **Henri Casadesus**; b. Paris, Oct. 24, 1892; d. there, Oct. 13, 1981. He studied at the Paris Cons., graduating in 1914 with the premier prix in violin; subsequently toured in Europe and America; gave numerous sonata recitals with his nephew, **Robert Casadesus**. He was a founding member of the Société Nouvelle des Instruments Anciens (1920–40), organized with the purpose of reviving early string instruments, such as the Quinton and Diskantgambe. He wrote a number of pieces for the violin, some choral music, and songs, but his most notorious contribution to violin literature was the so-called *Adelaide Concerto,* supposedly composed by Mozart when he was 10 years old and dedicated to the oldest daughter of Louis XV, Adelaide (hence the nickname). It was performed in Paris on Dec. 24, 1931, with considerable publicity, but skepticism arose when Casadesus failed to produce either the MS or a contemporary copy of it. In 1977, in the course of a litigation for his copyright as the arranger of the "Adelaide Concerto," Casadesus admitted that the piece was entirely of his own hand.

Casadesus, Robert (Marcel), eminent French pianist and composer; b. Paris, April 7, 1899; d. there, Sept. 19, 1972. A scion of a remarkable musical family, he absorbed music at home from his earliest childhood. His uncles were **Henri**, **Marius**, and **François Casadesus**; another uncle, Marcel Louis Lucien (1882–1917), was a cellist, and his aunt Rose was a pianist. He received his formal musical education studying piano with Diemer and composition with Leroux at the Paris Cons. From 1922 he toured extensively; after the outbreak of World War II in 1939, he went to the U.S.; taught classes at various schools. After the war, he taught at the American Cons. at Fontainebleau. He was a prolific composer; wrote 7 syms., of which the last was performed posth. in N.Y. on Nov. 8, 1972. He appeared with his wife, **Gaby Casadesus**, in his Concerto for 2 Pianos and Orch. with the N.Y. Phil. on Nov. 25, 1950. He also wrote a Concerto for 3 Pianos and String Orch., which he performed for the first time with his wife and his son Jean in N.Y., July 24, 1965. As a pianist, Casadesus was distinguished for his Gallic sense of balance and fine gradation of tonal dynamics. In 1975 the 1st Robert Casadesus International Piano Competition was held in Cleveland to honor his memory. In 1994 it was reorganized as the Cleveland International Piano Competition.

BIBL.: S. Stookes, *The Art of R. C.* (London, 1960); E. Feder, "R. C.: Composer, Performer, Pedagogue," *Ovation* (Aug. 1983).

Casals, Pablo (actually, **Pau Carlos Salvador Defilló**), great Spanish cellist; b. Vendrell, Catalonia, Dec. 29, 1876; d. San Juan, Puerto Rico, Oct. 22, 1973. Legend has it, supported by Casals himself, that he was conceived when Brahms began his B-flat Major Quartet, of which Casals owned the original MS, and that he was born when Brahms completed its composition. This legend is rendered moot by the fact that the quartet in question was completed and performed before Casals was even born. But even the ascertainable facts of the life of Casals make it a glorious tale. His father, the parish organist and choirmaster in Vendrell, gave Casals instruction in piano, violin, and organ. When Casals was 11, he first heard the cello performed by a group of traveling musicians, and decided to study the instrument. In 1888 his mother took him to Barcelona, where he enrolled in the Escuela Municipal de Música. There he studied cello with José García, theory with José Rodoreda, and piano with Joaquín Malats and Francisco Costa Llobera. His progress as a cellist was nothing short of prodigious, and he was able to give a solo recital in Barcelona at the age of 14, on Feb. 23, 1891; he graduated with honors in 1893. Albéniz, who heard him play in a café trio, gave him a letter of introduction to Count Morphy, the private secretary to María Cristina, the Queen Regent, in Madrid. Casals was asked to play at informal concerts in the palace, and was granted a royal stipend for composition study with Tomás Bretón. In 1893 he entered the Cons. de Música y Declamación in Madrid, where he attended chamber music classes of Jésus de Monasterio. He also played in the newly organized Quartet Soc. there (1894–95). In 1895 he went to Paris and, deprived of his stipend from Spain, earned a living by playing 2nd cello in the theater orch. of the Folies Marigny. He decided to return to Spain, where he received, in 1896, an appointment to the faculty of the Escuela Municipal de Música in Barcelona; he was also principal cellist in the orch. of the Gran Teatro del Liceo. In 1897 he appeared as soloist with the Madrid Sym. Orch., and was awarded the Order of Carlos III from the Queen. His career as a cello virtuoso was then assured. In 1899 he played at the Crystal Palace in London, and later for Queen Victoria at her summer residence at Cowes, Isle of Wight. On Nov. 12, 1899, he appeared as a soloist at a prestigious Lamoureux Concert in Paris, and played with Lamoureux again on Dec. 17, 1899, obtaining exceptional success with both the public and the press. He toured Spain and the Netherlands with the pianist Harold Bauer (1900–1901); then made his first tour of the U.S. (1901–2). In 1903 he made a grand tour of South America. On Jan. 15, 1904, he was invited to play at the White House for President Theodore Roosevelt. In 1906 he became associated with the talented young Portuguese cellist Guilhermina Suggia, who studied with him and began to appear in concerts as Mme. P. Casals-Suggia, although they were not legally married. Their liaison was dissolved in 1912; in 1914 Casals married the American socialite and singer Susan Metcalfe; they were separated in 1928, but did not divorce until 1957. Continuing his brilliant career, Casals organized, in Paris, a concert trio with the pianist Cortot and the violinist Thibaud; they played concerts together until 1937. Casals also became interested in conducting, and in 1919 he organized, in Barcelona, the Orquesta Pau Casals and led its first concert on Oct. 13, 1920. With the outbreak of the Spanish Civil War in 1936, the Orquesta Pau Casals ceased its activities. Casals was an ardent supporter of the Spanish Republican government, and after its defeat vowed never to return to Spain until democracy was restored. He settled in the French village of Prades, on the Spanish frontier; between 1939 and 1942 he made sporadic appearances as a cellist in the unoccupied zone of southern France and in Switzerland. So fierce was his opposition to the Franco regime in Spain that he declined to appear in countries that recognized the totalitarian Spanish government, making an exception when he took part in a concert of chamber music in the White House on Nov. 13, 1961, at the invitation of President John F. Kennedy, whom he admired. In 1950 he resumed his career as conductor and cellist at the Prades Festival, organized in commemoration of the bicentennial of the death of Bach; he continued leading the Prades Festivals until 1966. He made his permanent residence in 1956, when he settled in San Juan, Puerto Rico (his mother was born there when the island was still under Spanish rule). In 1957 an annual Festival Casals was inaugurated there. During all these years, he developed energetic activities as a pedagogue, leading master classes in Switzerland, Italy, Berkeley, Calif., and Marlboro, Vt., some of which were televised. Casals was also a composer; perhaps his most effective work is *La sardana,* for an ensemble of cellos, which he composed in 1926. His oratorio *El pessebre* (The Manger) was performed for the first time in Acapulco, Mexico, on Dec. 17, 1960. One of his last compositions was the *Himno a las Naciones Unidas* (Hymn of the United Nations); he conducted its first performance in a special concert at the United Nations on Oct. 24, 1971, 2 months before his 95th birthday. On Aug. 3, 1957, at the age of 80, Casals married his young pupil Marta Montañez; following his death, she married the pianist Eugene Istomin, on Feb. 15, 1975. Casals did not live to see the liberation of Spain from the Franco dictatorship, but he was posthumously honored by the Spanish government under King Juan Carlos I, which issued in 1976 a commemorative postage stamp in honor of his 100th birthday.

BIBL.: L. Littlehales, *P. C.* (N.Y., 1929; rev. ed., 1948); A. Conte, *La Légende de P. C.* (Perpignan, 1950); J. Corredor, *Conversations with C.* (London, 1956); A. Seiler, *C.* (Olten, 1956); P. and A. Kahn, *Joys and Sorrows: Reflections by P. C. as Told to Albert E. Kahn* (N.Y., 1970); H. Kirk, *P. C. A Biography* (N.Y., 1974); D. Blum, *C. and the Art of Interpretation* (London, 1977); J. Lloyd Webber, ed., *Song of the Birds: Sayings, Stories, and Impressions of P. C.* (London, 1985); J. Corredor, *P. C.* (Barcelona, 1991); J. Hargrove, *P. C.: Cellist of Conscience* (Chicago, 1991); R. Baldock, *P. C.* (London, 1992); H. Garza, *P. C.* (N.Y., 1993).

Casanova, André, French composer; b. Paris, Oct. 12, 1919. He studied with Paul Baumgartner (piano) and Leibowitz (composition) in Paris. In 1960 he was the winner of the Queen Marie-José composition competition. In 1977 he received the Prix de la Fondation des Éditions Durand. His music generally followed along neo-Classical lines, with some atonal deviations.

WORKS: DRAMATIC: *Le Livre de la Foi jurée*, lyric piece (1964); *La Clé d'argent*, lyric drama (1965); *Le Bonheur dans le crime*, lyric drama (1969); *La Coupe d'or*, opera (1970). **ORCH.:** 3 syms.: No. 1 (1949), No. 2 for Chamber Orch. (1952; Nice, Feb. 20, 1971), and No. 3, *Dithyrambe*, for Tenor and Orch. (1964; Paris, Feb. 13, 1973); *Ballade* for Clarinet and Chamber Orch. (1954–55); Piano Concertino (1958); *Notturno* (1959); *Capriccio* for Oboe and Chamber Orch. (1960); *Anamorphoses* (1961; Strasbourg, June 21, 1969); Violin Concerto (1963); Concerto for Trumpet and Strings (1966); *Strophes* (1968); Organ Concerto (1972); *Épisodes* for Violins and Strings (1972); Guitar Concerto (1973); *Récitatifs* (1973; Nice, Feb. 2, 1974); *Idylles* (1976); *Partita* (1979); *Sinfonietta* (1981); *Sinfonia* (1981); Cello Concerto (1982–83); *Ein musikalisches Opfer* (1984–85); *Rhapsodie concertante* for Viola and Chamber Orch. (1987); Piano Concerto (1988–91); *Ephemeris* (1989); *Expressions* for Strings (1991); *Musique* for Brass and Strings (1991). **CHAMBER:** *4 Bagatelles* for Wind Quintet (1955); String Trio (1966); 6 string quartets (1967, 1985, 1985, 1990, 1991, 1992); Quintet for Piano and Winds (1970: Trio for Piano, Violin, and Cello (1972); *5 Pièces* for Cello (1972); Sextet for Clarinet, String Quartet, and Double Bass (1978–83); Violin Sonata (1988); String Quintet (1988); piano pieces. **VOCAL:** *Cavalier seul* for Baritone and Strings (1964); *Rituels* for Voice and Instrumental Ensemble (1972–82); *Esquisses pour une tragédie* for Soprano, Baritone, and Instrumental Ensemble (1979); *Deutsches Gesänge* for Baritone and Orch. (1980); songs.

Casavola, Franco, Italian composer; b. Modugno, July 13, 1891; d. Bari, July 7, 1955. He studied in Rome with Respighi; abandoning his academic pursuits, he joined the Futurist movement, and composed music glorifying the mechanical age; he also wrote futurist poetry. Among his works in this genre are a ballet, *Fantasia meccanica*, and *La danza dell'elica* for Flute, Clarinet, Violin, Percussion, Wind Machine, and Blasting Machine. At a later period, he veered toward musical realism with Romantic overtones. He wrote the operas *Il gobbo del califfo* (Rome, May 4, 1929), *Astuzie d'amore* (Bari, Jan. 28, 1936), and *Salammbô* (1948); also 2 ballets, *L'alba di Don Giovanni* (1932) and *Il castello nel bosco* (1931).

Casazza, Elvira, Italian mezzo-soprano; b. Ferrara, Nov. 15, 1887; d. Milan, Jan. 24, 1965. She studied in Ferrara and Milan; made her debut in Varese in 1909; then sang at La Scala in Milan (1915–42); also sang at Covent Garden, London (1926, 1931). After her retirement in 1948, she taught voice in Rome and then in Pesaro. Her most noted role was Mistress Quickly.

Casella, Alfredo, outstanding Italian composer and teacher; b. Turin, July 25, 1883; d. Rome, March 5, 1947. He began to play the piano at the age of 4 and received his early instruction from his mother; in 1896 he went to Paris, and studied with Diémer and Fauré at the Cons.; won the premier prix in piano in 1899. He made concert tours as a pianist in Europe; appeared as a guest conductor with European orchs.; taught piano classes at the Paris Cons. from 1912 to 1915; returned to Rome and was appointed a prof. of piano at the Accademia di Santa Cecilia. In 1917 he founded the Società Nazionale di Musica (later the Società Italiana di Musica Moderna; from 1923 the Corporazione delle Musiche Nuove, Italian section of the ISCM). On Oct. 28, 1921, Casella made his American debut with the Philadelphia Orch. in the triple capacity of composer, conductor, and piano soloist; he also appeared as a guest conductor in Chicago, Detroit, Cincinnati, Cleveland, and Los Angeles; was conductor of the Boston Pops from 1927 to 1929, introducing a number of modern works, but failing to please the public. In 1928 he was awarded the 1st prize of $3,000 from the Musical Fund Soc. in Philadelphia; in 1934 he won the Coolidge Prize. In 1938 he returned to Italy. Apart from his activities as pianist, conductor, teacher, and composer, Casella was a prolific writer on music, and contributed numerous articles to various publications in Italy, France, Russia, Germany, and America; he possessed an enlightened cosmopolitan mind, which enabled him to penetrate the musical cultures of various nations; at the same time, he steadfastly proclaimed his adherence to the ideals of Italian art. In his music, he applied modernistic techniques to earlier forms; his style may be termed neo-Classical, but in his early years he cultivated extreme modernism.

WORKS: DRAMATIC: OPERAS: *La donna serpente* (Rome, March 17, 1932); *La favola d'Orfeo* (Venice, Sept. 6, 1932); *Il deserto tentato* (Florence, May 6, 1937). **BALLETS:** *Il convento veneziano* (1912; Milan, Feb. 7, 1925); *La Giara*, "choreographic comedy" (Paris, Nov. 19, 1924); *La camera dei disegni*, for children (Rome, 1940); La rosa del sogno (Rome, 1943). **ORCH.:** 3 syms. (1905; 1908–09; Chicago, March 27, 1941); Suite in C (1909); *Italia*, rhapsody (Paris, April 23, 1910); *Le Couvent sur l'eau*, symphonic suite based on the ballet *Il convento veneziano* (Paris, April 23, 1914); *Elegia eroica* (Rome, Jan. 21, 1917); *Pagine di guerra* (1916); *Pupazzetti*, 5 pieces for Puppets (1918); *A notte alta* for Piano and Orch. (1921; also for Piano, 1917); *Partita* for Piano and Orch. (N.Y., Oct. 29, 1925); *Scarlattiana*, on themes by Scarlatti, for Piano and Orch. (N.Y., Jan. 22, 1927); *Concerto romano* for Organ and Orch. (N.Y., March 11, 1927); Violin Concerto (Moscow, Oct. 8, 1928); *Introduzione, Aria e Toccata* (Rome, April 5, 1933); Concerto for Trio and Orch. (Berlin, Nov. 17, 1933); Concerto (Amsterdam, 1937); *Paganiniana*, on themes by Paganini (Vienna, 1942). **CHAMBER:** *Barcarola e scherzo* for Flute and Piano (1904); 2 cello sonatas (1907, 1927); *Siciliana e burlesca* for Flute and Piano (1914; also for Piano Trio, 1917); *5 pezzi* for String Quartet (1920); Concerto for String Quartet (1923–24; also for String Orch.); *Serenata* for Clarinet, Bassoon, Trumpet, Violin, and Cello (1927); *Sinfonia* for Clarinet, Trumpet, Cello, and Piano (1932); Piano Trio (1933). **PIANO:** Many pieces, including 2 series of stylistic imitations, *À la manière de . . . :* Wagner, Fauré, Brahms, Debussy, Strauss, and Franck (1911), and (in collaboration with Ravel) Borodin, d'Indy, Chabrier, and Ravel (1913); Sonatina (1916); *A notte alta* (1917; also for Piano and Orch., 1921); *11 pezzi infantili* (1920); *2 ricercari sul nome Bach* (1932); 3 pieces for Pianola (1918). **VOCAL:** *Notte di Maggio* for Voice and Orch. (Paris, March 29, 1914); *L'Adieu à la vie*, cycle of 4 Hindu lyrics after Tagore's *Gitanjali* (1915; also for Voice and Orch., 1926); *4 favole romanesche* (1923); *Ninna nanna popolare genovese* (1934); *3 canti sacri* for Baritone and Orch. (1943); *Missa solemnis pro pace* (1944).

WRITINGS: *L'evoluzione della musica* (publ. in Italian, French, and Eng. in parallel columns; 1919); *Igor Stravinsky* (1926; new ed., 1951); *"21 & 26"* (1931); *Il pianoforte* (1938); *I segreti della Giara* (1941; Eng. tr., 1955, as *Music in My Time: The Memoirs of Alfredo Casella*); *La tecnica dell'orchestra contemporanea* (completed by V. Mortari; 1950).

BIBL.: L. Cortese, *A. C.* (Genoa, 1935); special issue of *Rassegna Musicale* in honor of C.'s 60th birthday (May–June 1943); G. Gatti, "In Memory of A. C.," *Musical Quarterly* (July 1947); F. d'Amico & G. Gatti, eds., *A. C.* (Milan, 1958).

Casimiri, Raffaele Casimiro, Italian musicologist and composer; b. Gualdo Tadino, Nov. 3, 1880; d. Rome, April 15, 1943.

He studied in Padua. He founded the ecclesiastical magazines *Psalterium* (1907) and *Sacri Concentus*; also *Note d'Archivio* (1924). His specialty was polyphonic music of the time of Palestrina, whose collected works he ed. (1939–42). He contributed numerous articles to Italian publications; some of his findings on Palestrina have been disputed; his ingenious hoax, which he unveiled in *Note d'Archivio* of March 1924, claiming a discovery of a notebook of Palestrina establishing the date of Palestrina's birth, was deliberately contrived to confute his learned colleagues; he exposed it in a series of scurrilous letters. He also composed 2 oratorios, several masses, motets, and offertories.

BIBL.: E. Dagnino, "R. C.," *Rassegna Musicale* (April 1943).

Casken, John (Arthur), English composer and teacher; b. Barnsley, Yorkshire, July 15, 1949. He was a student of Joubert and Dickinson at the Univ. of Birmingham (1967–71), and then pursued training in Warsaw with Dobrowolski and Lutoslawski (1971–73). He subsequently lectured at the Univ. of Birmingham (1973–79), the Huddersfield Polytechnic (1979–81), and Univ. of Durham (1981–92); then was prof. of music at the Univ. of Manchester (from 1992). His early works were influenced by Lutoslawski but he later tended toward eclecticism.

WORKS: CHAMBER OPERA: *Golem* (1986–88; London, June 28, 1989). **ORCH.:** *Arenaria* for Flute and 13 Players (1976); *Tableaux des trois ages* (1976–77); Piano Concerto (1980–81; Manchester, Jan. 24, 1982); *Masque* (Windsor, Oct. 9, 1982); *Erin* for Double Bass and Small Orch. (1982–83); *Orion over Farne* (Glasgow, Sept. 17, 1984); *Maharal Dreaming* (Darlington, May 12, 1989); Cello Concerto (1991); *Darting the Skiff* for Strings (1993); *Cor d'oeuvre*, overture (1993). **CHAMBER:** *Kagura* for 13 Wind Instruments (1972–73); *Music for the Crabbing Sun* for Flute, Oboe, Cello, and Harpsichord (1974); *Music for a Tawny-Gold Day* for Viola, Alto Saxophone, Bass Clarinet, and Piano (1975–76); *Thymehaze* for Alto Recorder and Piano (1976); *Amarantos* for 9 Instruments (1977–78; London, Dec. 12, 1978); *Melanos* for 8 Instruments (1979); *A Belle Pavine* for Violin and Tape (1980); 2 string quartets: No. 1 (1981–82; London, Feb. 2, 1982) and No. 2 (1993); *Eructavit* for 10 Instruments (Durham, Nov. 26, 1982); *Fonteyn Fanfares* for 12 Brass (1982); *Taerset* for Clarinet and Piano (1982–83); *Piper's Linn* for Small Pipes and Tape (1983–84); *Clarion Sea* for 2 Trumpets, Horn, Trombone, and Tuba (1984–85; Birmingham, May 5, 1985); *Vaganza* for Chamber Group (St. Albans, July 12, 1985); Piano Quartet (1989–90; Birmingham, Nov. 24, 1990); *Infanta Marina* for Chamber Ensemble (1993–94). **VOCAL:** *Firewhirl* for Soprano and 7 Instruments (1979–80; Bath, May 25, 1980); *To Fields We Do Not Know* for Chorus (1983–84); *The Land of Spices* for Chorus (1990); *A Gathering* for Chorus (1991); *Sharp Thorne* for 4 Solo Voices (1991–92); *Still Mine* for Baritone and Orch. (1991–92); *Sunrising* for Chorus (1993).

Cassado (Moreau), Gaspar, distinguished Spanish cellist; b. Barcelona, Sept. 30, 1897; d. Madrid, Dec. 24, 1966. He was the son of Joaquin Cassadó (Valls) (b. Mataró, near Barcelona, Sept. 30, 1867; d. Barcelona, March 25, 1926), a well-known organist and composer. Gaspar Cassado studied cello with Casals; toured Europe; made his U.S. debut in N.Y. on Dec. 10, 1936; made a U.S. tour in 1949. He composed a Cello Sonata, a Cello Concerto, and other pieces for his instrument. His *Catalonian Rhapsody* for Orch. was performed by the N.Y. Phil. on Nov. 8, 1928. He also made arrangements for cello and orch. of a Mozart horn concerto and Weber's Clarinet Concerto.

Cassel, (John) Walter, American baritone and teacher; b. Council Bluffs, Iowa, May 15, 1910. He studied voice with Harry Cooper in Council Bluffs, where he also received training in trumpet and piano; after attending Creighton Univ. in Omaha, he pursued vocal studies with Frank La Forge in N.Y. In 1938 he began singing on radio shows, and on Dec. 12, 1942, made his Metropolitan Opera debut in N.Y. as Brétigny in *Manon*, remaining on its roster until 1945, and then again from 1954 to 1970 and in 1973–74. On March 21, 1948, he made his first appearance at the N.Y. City Opera as Escamillo, singing there regularly until 1954, and then intermittently until 1969. He taught at Indiana Univ. in Bloomington (from 1974). While he proved equally at home in both serious and light roles, he was best known for his roles in operas by Wagner and R. Strauss. He sang the role of Horace Tabor in the first performance of Douglas Moore's *The Ballad of Baby Doe* (1956).

Cassilly, Richard, American tenor; b. Washington, D.C., Dec. 14, 1927. He studied at the Peabody Cons. in Baltimore. After singing Michele in Menotti's *The Saint of Bleecker Street* in N.Y. (1955), he made his N.Y. City Opera debut as Vakula in Tchaikovsky's *The Golden Slippers* (Oct. 13, 1955); was on its roster until 1959, and again from 1960 to 1963 and from 1964 to 1966. He made his European debut in Sutermeister's *Raskolnikoff* in Geneva (1965) and that same year sang at the Hamburg State Opera, where he appeared regularly (1966–77). He was concurrently a member of London's Covent Garden (1968–78) and also sang in major European opera centers. He made his Metropolitan Opera debut in N.Y. as Radames on Jan. 20, 1973. He resumed his association with the Metropolitan Opera in 1978, and subsequently appeared there in such roles as Tannhäuser, Don José, Tristan, Samson, Otello, Jimmy Mahoney in *Mahagonny*, and Captain Vere in *Billy Budd*.

Cassuto, Álvaro (Leon), Portuguese conductor and composer; b. Oporto, Nov. 17, 1938. He studied violin and piano as a small child; then took courses in composition with Artur Santos and Lopes Graça. In the summers of 1960 and 1961 he attended classes in new music in Darmstadt with Ligeti, Messiaen, and Stockhausen, and at the same time had instruction in conducting with Karajan. He further studied conducting with Pedro de Freitas Branco in Lisbon and Franco Ferrara in Hilversum. In 1964 he took his Ph.D. in law at the Univ. of Lisbon and in 1965 his M.A. in conducting at the Vienna Academy of Music. In 1969 he received the Koussevitzky Prize at Tanglewood. He served as an assistant conductor of the Gulbenkian Orch. in Lisbon (1965–68) and with the Little Orch. in N.Y. (1968–70). In 1970 he was appointed permanent conductor of the National Radio Orch. of Lisbon, and in 1975 was elected its music director. In 1974 he was appointed a lecturer in music and conductor of the Sym. Orch. of the Univ. of Calif. at Irvine, remaining there until 1979. From 1979 to 1985 he was music director of the Rhode Island Phil. in Providence, and from 1981 to 1987 the music director of the National Orchestral Assn. in N.Y. In 1987 he founded the Nova Filarmonia Portuguesa in Lisbon, which he conducted until 1993. In 1993 he founded the Portuguese Sym. Orch. in Lisbon at the behest of the Portuguese government, serving as its artistic director and principal conductor. He also was guest conductor of numerous orchs. in Europe, South America, and the U.S. A progressive-minded and scholarly musician, Cassuto amassed a large repertoire of both classical and modern works, displaying a confident expertise. He is also a composer of several orch. works in a modern idiom, as well as of chamber pieces.

WORKS: *Sinfonia breve No. 1* (Lisbon, Aug. 29, 1959) and *No. 2* (1960); *Variations* for Orch. (1961); *Permutations* for 2 Orchs. (1962); String Sextet (1962); Concertino for Piano and Orch. (1965); *Cro (mo-no)fonia* for 20 String Instruments (1967); *Canticum in Tenebris* for Soloists, Chorus, and Orch. (1968); *Evocations* for Orch. (1969); *Circle* for Orch. (1971); *In the Name of Peace*, opera (1971); *Song of Loneliness* for 12 Players (1972); *To Love and Peace*, symphonic poem (1973); *Homage to My People*, suite for Band, on Portuguese folk songs (1977); *Return to the Future* for Orch. (1985); *4 Seasons or Movements* for Piano and Orch. (1987).

Castagna, Bruna, Italian mezzo-soprano; b. Bari, Oct. 15, 1905; d. Pinamar, Argentina, July 10, 1983. She was a student of Scognamiglio in Milan. In 1925 she made her operatic debut as the Nurse in *Boris Godunov* in Mantua; that same year she made her first appearance at Milan's La Scala as Suzuki, and then sang there until 1928 and again from 1932 to 1934; also appeared at the Teatro Colón in Buenos Aires (1927–30). On March 2, 1936, she made her Metropolitan Opera debut in N.Y. as Amneris, remaining there until 1940, and then returning in 1943 and 1945. She eventually settled in Argentina. In addition to her roles in Verdi's operas, she became well known for her portrayals of Carmen, Adalgisa, Santuzza, and Dalila.

Castaldi, Alfonso, Romanian composer and teacher; b. Maddalone, April 23, 1874; d. Bucharest, Aug. 6, 1942. He studied at the Naples Cons. with Francisco Cilea and Umberto Giordano; taught at the Bucharest Cons. (1904–40), and was greatly esteemed as a pedagogue. He wrote several operas in an Italianate style; also the symphonic poems *Thalassa* (1906) and *Marsyas* (1907); a Sym. (1920); 3 string quartets; other chamber music; and numerous choruses.

Castaldo, Joseph, American composer; b. N.Y., Dec. 23, 1927. He studied in N.Y. and was active as a clarinetist; he then took composition classes at the Accademia di Santa Cecilia in Rome (1947). Returning to the U.S., he had special courses with Giannini at the Manhattan School of Music in N.Y. and with Persichetti at the Philadelphia Cons. (B.M., M.M.), where he subsequently was appointed chairman of composition and theory (1960); when it merged with the Philadelphia Musical Academy in 1966, he assumed the presidency; he continued in this capacity (until 1983) when it became the Philadelphia College of Performing Arts (1976). Among his works are *Lacrimosa I* (1976) and *II* (1977) for Strings; Cello Concerto (1984); *Theoria* for Wind Ensemble, Piano, and Percussion (1971; rev. 1972); *Flight*, cantata (1960); 2 string quartets; *Dichotomy* for Woodwind Quintet; and choruses.

Castelnuovo-Tedesco, Mario, greatly significant Italian-born American composer; b. Florence, April 3, 1895; d. Los Angeles, March 16, 1968. He studied piano with Edoardo del Valle, and then continued his training at the Florence Cons., where he took diplomas in piano (1910) and in composition in Pizzetti's class (1913). He attained considerable eminence in Italy between the 2 world wars, and his music was often heard at European festivals. Political events forced him to leave Italy; in 1939 he settled in the U.S. and in 1946 became a naturalized American citizen. He became active as a composer for films in Hollywood, but continued to write large amounts of orch. and chamber music. His style is remarkably fluent and adaptable, often reaching rhapsodic eloquence.

WORKS: DRAMATIC: *La mandragola*, opera (Venice, May 4, 1926); *The Princess and the Pea*, overture with Narrator (1943); *Bacco in Toscana*, dithyramb for Voices and Orch. (Milan, May 8, 1931); *Aucassin et Nicolette*, puppet show with Voices and Instruments (1938; Florence, June 2, 1952); *All's Well That Ends Well*, opera (1959); *Saul*, biblical opera (1960); *Il Mercante di Venezia*, opera (Florence, May 25, 1961); *The Importance of Being Earnest*, chamber opera (1962); *The Song of Songs*, scenic oratorio (Hollywood, Aug. 7, 1963); *Tobias and the Angel*, scenic oratorio (1965). **BIBLICAL ORATORIOS:** *Ruth* (1949); *Jonah* (1951). **ORCH.:** 3 violin concertos: No. 1, *Concerto italiano* (1925; Rome, Jan. 31, 1926), No. 2, *The Prophets* (N.Y., April 12, 1933), and No. 3 (1939); 2 piano concertos: No. 1 (Rome, Dec. 9, 1928) and No. 2 (N.Y., Nov. 2, 1939); *Variazioni sinfoniche* for Violin and Orch. (1930); Cello Concerto (1934; N.Y., Jan. 31, 1935); 2 guitar concertos (1939, 1953); *Cipressi* (Boston, Oct. 25, 1940; arranged from the piano piece, 1920); *Poem* for Violin and Orch. (1942); *The Birthday of the Infanta* (1942; New Orleans, Jan. 28, 1947); *Indian Songs and Dances*, suite (Los Angeles, Jan. 7, 1943); *An American Rhapsody* (1943); *Serenade* for Guitar and Orch. (1943); *Octoroon Ball*, ballet suite (1947); *Noah's Ark*, movement for Narrator and Orch., from *Genesis*, a suite, with other movements by Schoenberg, Stravinsky, Toch, Milhaud, Tansman, and N. Shilkret, who commissioned the work (Portland, Oreg., Dec. 15, 1947); Concerto for 2 Guitars and Orch. (1962); overtures. **CHAMBER:** *Signorine: 2 profili* for Violin and Piano (1918); *Ritmi* for Violin and Piano (1920); *Capitan Fracassa* for Violin and Piano (1920); *Notturno adriatico* for Violin and Piano (1922); *I nottambuli* for Cello and Piano (1927); Cello Sonata (1928); 2 piano trios (1928, 1932); 3 string quartets (1929, 1948, 1964); *Sonata quasi una fantasia* for Violin and Piano (1929); *The Lark* for Violin and Piano (1930); 2 piano quintets (1932, 1951); *Toccata* for Cello and Piano (1935); *Capriccio diabolico* for Guitar (1935; later arranged as a guitar concerto); Concertino for Harp and 7 Instruments (1937); *Ballade* for Violin and Piano (1940); *Divertimento* for 2 Flutes (1943); Sonata for Violin and Viola (1945); Clarinet Sonata (1945); Sonatina for Bassoon and Piano (1946); Quintet for Guitar and Strings (1950); Sonata for Viola and Cello (1950); *Fantasia* for Guitar and Piano (1950); *Concerto da camera* for Oboe and Strings (1950); Sonata for Violin and Cello (1950); Sonata for Cello and Harp (1966); numerous guitar pieces. **PIANO:** *English Suite* (1909); *Questo fu il carro della morte* (1913); *Il raggio verde* (1916); *Alghe* (1919); *I naviganti* (1919); *La sirenetta e il pesce turchino* (1920); *Cantico* (1920); *Vitalba e Biancospino* (1921); *Epigrafe* (1922); *Alt-Wien* (1923); *Piedigrotta* (1924); *Le stagioni* (1924); *Le danze del Re David* (1925); *3 poemi campestri* (1926); *3 corali su melodie ebraiche* (1926); Sonata (1928); *Crinoline* (1929); *Candide*, 6 pieces (1944); *6 canoni* (1950). **SONGS:** *Le Roy Loys* (1914); *Ninna-Nanna* (1914); *Fuori i barbari* (1915); *Stelle cadenti* (1915); *Coplas* (1915); *Briciole* (1916); *3 fioretti di Santo Francesco* (1919; also with Orch.); *Girotondo de golosi* (1920); *Etoile filante* (1920); *L'infinito* (1921); *Sera* (1921); 33 Shakespearean songs (1921–25); *2 preghiere per i bimbi d'Italia* (1923); *1830* (1924); *Scherzi*, 2 series (1924–25); *Indian Serenade* (1925); *Cadix* (1926); *3 Sonnets from the Portuguese* (1926); *Laura di Nostra Donna* (1935); *Un sonetto di Dante* (1939); *Recuerdo* (1940); *Le Rossignol* (1942); *The Daffodils* (1944). **CHORAL:** 2 madrigals (1915); *Lecho dodi*, synagogue chant for Tenor, Men's Voices, and Organ (1936); *Sacred Synagogue Service* (1943); *Liberty, Mother of Exiles* (1944).

BIBL.: G. Rossi-Daria, "M. C.-T.," *Chesterian* (Jan.-Feb. 1926); N. Rossi, *Complete Catalogue of Works by M. C.-T.* (N.Y., 1977); B. Scalin, *Operas by M. C.-T.* (diss., Northwestern Univ., 1980).

Castéra, René d'Avezac, French composer; b. Dax, Landes, April 3, 1873; d. Angoume, Landes, Oct. 8, 1955. He studied at the Paris Schola Cantorum with d'Indy and Guilmant. In 1902 he founded the Édition Mutuelle for the publication of works by French composers. He wrote an opera, some symphonic pieces, a Piano Trio, Violin Sonata, songs, and character pieces for piano.

Castiglioni, Niccolò, Italian composer and teacher; b. Milan, July 17, 1932; d. there, Sept. 7, 1996. He took courses in piano and composition at the Milan Cons., and also was a student at the Salzburg Mozarteum; from 1958 to 1965 he was active at the summer courses in new music in Darmstadt. In 1966–67 he was composer-in-residence at the Center for the Creative and Performing Arts at the State Univ. of N.Y. in Buffalo, and then taught composition at the univs. of Michigan (1967), Washington in Seattle (1968–69), and California at San Diego (1970). In 1970 he returned to Italy. After teaching in Trento (1976–78), he joined the faculty of the Milan Cons. (1978). His music was pragmatically modernistic, making use of a vast panorama of styles, ranging from neo-Classical to post-Webern and beyond.

WORKS: DRAMATIC: OPERAS: *Uomini e no* (1955); *Attraverso lo specchio* (RAI, Oct. 1, 1961) *Jabberwocky*, chamber opera (1962); *Sweet* (1968); *3 Mystery Plays*, opera triptych (Rome, Oct. 2, 1968); *Oberon, the Fairy Prince* (1980; Venice, Oct. 10, 1981); *The Lord's Masque* (1980; Venice, Oct. 10, 1981). **BALLETS:** *Inverno in-ver* (1973; rev. version, Palermo, Feb. 3, 1978); *Beth-Daleth* (Florence, May 21, 1980). **ORCH.:** *Concertino per la notte di Natale* (1952; San Remo, Dec. 24, 1979); 4 syms.: No. 1 for Soprano and Orch. (Venice, Sept. 15, 1956), No. 2 (1956–57; RAI, Nov. 23, 1957), No. 3, *Sinfonia con giardino* (1977–78; RAI, Turin, March 23, 1979), and No. 4, *Sinfonia con rosignolo* for Soprano and Orch. (1989; Parma, May 18,

1991); *Ouverture in tre tempi* (1957); *Sequenze* (1959); *Rondels* (1960–61); *Concerto for Orchestra* (1963); *La Chant du signe*, flute concerto (1969); *Arabeschi* for Flute, Piano, and Orch. (1971–72); *Quadlibet*, little concerto for Piano and Chamber Orch. (1976; Paris, May 2, 1978); *Couplets* for Harpsichord and Orch. (1978–79; Saarbrücken, July 6, 1979); *Sinfonietta* for Soprano and Small Orch. (1980; Milan, March 28, 1982); *Cavatina* for Piccolo and Orch. (1981–82; RAI, Rome, March 17, 1990); *Zweihundertfünfzig Jahre*, for the 250th anniversary of Haydn's birth (Trento, Feb. 3, 1982); *Morceaux lyriques* for Oboe and Orch. (1982; Warsaw, Sept. 21, 1984); *Fiori di ghiaccio*, piano concerto (1983; Milan, Jan. 29, 1984); *Small is Beautiful* (RAI, Naples, Nov. 9, 1984); *Intermezzo* for Chamber Orch. (Milan, Nov. 29, 1987); *Märchen, Traum und Legende* (1987–88; Rome, April 23, 1989); *Conductus* (1988; Paris, March 1, 1989); *Ricordo di Julius Bissier* (1989; Berlin, Feb. 12, 1991); *Fantasia concertata* for Piano and Orch. (1991); *Altisonanza* (1992). **CHAMBER:** *Movimento continuato* for Piano and 11 Instruments (1958–59); *Tropi* for 6 Players (1959); *Ode* for 2 Pianos, Winds, and Percussion (1966); *Masques* for 12 Instruments (1967); *The New Melusine* for String Quartet (1969); *Quilisma* for 2 Violins, Viola, Cello, and Piano (1977); *Doppio Coro* for 10 Winds (1977); *Motetto* for 10 Winds (1978); *Beth* for Clarinet and 5 Instruments (1979); *Daleth*, sonatina for Clarinet and Piano (1979); *Musica vneukokvhaja* for Piccolo (1981); *Rima* for Oboe and Piano (1984); *Musichetta* for 10 Instruments (1988); *Gorgheggio* for Piano and 8 Instruments (1988); *Risognanze* for 16 Instruments (1989; RAI, Turin, April 27, 1992); *Filastrocca* for Wind Quintet (1989); *Romanze* for String Quartet (1990; London, Oct. 28, 1991); *Romanzetta* for Flute (1990); *Gruezi* for Oboe (1990); *Momenti musicali* for 7 Instruments (1991); *Cronaca del Ducato di Urbino* for 6 Percussionists (1991; Geneva, March 29, 1992); *Capriccio* for 11 Instruments (Lanciano, Aug. 14, 1991); *Cassazione* for Wind Quintet (1991; Schwetzingen, May 28, 1992); *Sic* for Flute and Guitar (Basel, Sept. 5, 1992); *Intonazione* for Flute, Oboe, Violin, and Cello (1992; Geneva, March 1993). **PIANO:** *Omaggio a Edvard Grieg* for 2 Pianos (Brescia, June 13, 1981); *Come io passo l'estate*, suite (1983; La Spezia, March 10, 1984); *He* (1990). **VOCAL:** *Elegia* for Soprano and 19 Instruments (1957); *A Solemn Music* for Soprano and Chamber Orch. (1963; rev. 1964–65 as *A Solemn Music II*); *Gyro* for Chorus and 9 Instruments (1963); *Figure*, mobile for Voice and Orch. (1965); *Canzoni* for Soprano and Orch. (1966); *Dickinson-Lieder* for Soprano and Small Orch. (1977; Basel, Feb. 5, 1979); *Le favole di Esopo*, oratorio for Chorus and Orch. (1979; Milan, March 14, 1980); *Salmo XIX* for Soli, Chorus, and Orch. (1979–80; Perugia, Sept. 26, 1980); *Sacro concerto* for Soli, Chorus, and Orch. (Venice, Oct. 5, 1982); *Geistliches Lied* for Soprano and Orch. (RAI, Naples, March 13, 1983); *Mottetto* for Soprano and Orch. (1987; RAI, Milan, Feb. 25, 1988); *Hymne* for 12 Voices (1988–89); *Veni Sancte Spiritus* for Soli, Chorus, and Orch. (1990; RAI, Milan, May 2, 1991); *Cantus planus* for 2 Sopranos and 7 Instruments (part 1, Geneva, Aug. 26, 1990; part 2, 1990–91, Geneva, May 14, 1991); *Osterliedlein* for Voice and Instruments (1990); *Stabat Mater* for Men's Chorus and Instruments (Copenhagen, Nov. 16, 1992); other choral works and songs.

BIBL.: R. Cresti, *Linguaggio musicale di N. C.* (Milan, 1991).

Castilla, Alberto, Colombian composer; b. Bogota, April 9, 1883; d. Ibague, June 10, 1937. He studied engineering; was at one time connected with the government of Colombia. In 1898 he settled in Tolima, where he founded a music school. He wrote a number of songs, some of which achieved popularity. In 1954 the Colombian government issued a postage stamp in his honor.

Castleman, Charles (Martin), American violinist and teacher; b. Quincy, Mass., May 22, 1941. A wunderkind from the cradle, he began violin lessons at the age of 4 with Ondříček. At 6 he appeared as a soloist with Fiedler and the Boston Pops Orch., and at 9 made his solo recital debut in Boston. He then was a pupil of Ivan Galamian at the Curtis Inst. of Music in Philadelphia (1957–63), and also received counsel from Josef Gingold, Henryk Szeryng, and David Oistrakh. After attending Harvard College, he played in the New String Trio of N.Y. (1972–75) and then in the Raphael Trio; also taught at the Eastman School of Music in Rochester, N.Y. (from 1975). He appeared as a soloist with major orchs. in the U.S. and Europe, and also gave solo recitals and played much chamber music.

Caston, Saul (real name, **Solomon Cohen**), American trumpeter and conductor; b. N.Y., Aug. 22, 1901; d. Winston-Salem, N.C., July 28, 1970. He studied trumpet with Max Schlossberg in N.Y.; then was a student of Abram Chasins (piano), Scalero (composition), and Reiner (conducting diploma, 1935) at the Curtis Inst. of Music in Philadelphia, where he also taught trumpet (1924–42). He was 2nd (1918–23) and then 1st (1923–45) trumpet in the Philadelphia Orch., where he also was assoc. conductor (1936–45). After conducting the Reading Sym. Orch. (1941–44), he was conductor of the Denver Sym. Orch. (1944–64).

Castro, José María, Argentine cellist, conductor, and composer, brother of **Juan José** and **Washington Castro**; b. Avellaneda, near Buenos Aires, Dec. 15, 1892; d. Buenos Aires, Aug. 2, 1964. He studied cello and composition in Buenos Aires. From 1913 he played in orchs. and chamber music ensembles, and later was solo cellist in the Orquesta Filharmónica of the Asociación del Profesorado Orquestal (1922–27). He was titular conductor of the Orquesta Filarmónica in Buenos Aires (1930–42), and also conducted the municipal band there (1933–53).

WORKS: DRAMATIC: BALLETS: *Georgia* (1937; Buenos Aires, June 2, 1939); *El sueño de la botella* (1948); *Falarka* (La Plata, Oct. 27, 1951). **MONODRAMA:** *La otra voz* (1953; Buenos Aires, Sept. 24, 1954). **ORCH.:** *Concerto grosso* (1932; Buenos Aires, June 11, 1933); *Obertura para una ópera cómica* (1934; Buenos Aires, Nov. 9, 1936); Piano Concerto (Buenos Aires, Nov. 17, 1941; rev. 1955); *Concerto for Orchestra* (1944); Concerto for Cello and 17 Instruments (1945; Buenos Aires, April 8, 1949); *Tres pastorales* (Buenos Aires, Sept. 30, 1945); *El libro de los sonetos* (1947); *Suite de cinco piezas* (1948); *Arietta con variazioni* (1948); *Preludio y Toccata* (1949); *Tema coral con variaciones* (1952; Buenos Aires, June 27, 1954); Concerto for Violin and 18 Instruments (1953; Buenos Aires, July 6, 1954); Piano Concerto (1955); *Diez improvisaciones breves* (1957; Buenos Aires, May 9, 1959); *Preludio, Tema con variaciones y Final* (1959; Buenos Aires, Aug. 18, 1960); *Sinfonía de Buenos Aires* (1963; Buenos Aires, June 26, 1966). **CHAMBER:** Concerto for Violin and Piano (1917); Violin Sonata (1918); Sonata Cello and Violin (1933); Sonata for 2 Cellos (1938); 3 string quartets (1943, 1947, 1956); *Tres estudios* for Cello and Piano (1946); *Tres piezas* for Cello and Piano (1947); *Sonata poética* for Violin and Piano (1957); many solo piano pieces, including 6 sonatas (1919; 1924; 1927; 1931; *Sonata de Primavera*, 1939; *Sonata dramática*, 1944). **VOCAL:** *Cinco liricas* for Voice and Orch. (1958); *Con la patria adentro* for Tenor and Orch. (1964; Buenos Aires, Aug. 26, 1965); many songs with piano.

BIBL.: N. Ceñal, "J.M. C. (1892–1964)," *Revista del Instituto de Investigación Musicológica Carlos Vega*, no. 7 (Buenos Aires, 1986).

Castro, Juan José, eminent Argentine composer and conductor, brother of **José Maria** and **Washington Castro**; b. Avellaneda, near Buenos Aires, March 7, 1895; d. Buenos Aires, Sept. 3, 1968. After study in Buenos Aires, he went to Paris, where he took a course in composition with Vincent d'Indy. Returning to Argentina in 1929, he organized in Buenos Aires the Orquesta de Nacimiento, which he conducted; in 1930 he conducted the ballet season at the Teatro Colón; conducted opera there from 1933; also became music director of the Asociación del Profesorado Orquestal and Asociación Sinfónica, with which he gave first local performances of a number of modern works. In 1934 he received a Guggenheim Foundation grant. From 1947 to 1951 he conducted in Cuba and Uruguay; from 1952 to 1953 he was principal conductor of the Victorian Sym. Orch. in Melbourne, Australia; from 1956 to 1960 he was conductor of the Orquesta Sinfónica Nacional in Buenos Aires; from 1959 to 1964 he was director of the Puerto Rico Cons. in San Juan. Castro was proficient in all genres of composition, but his works were rarely performed outside South America, and he himself conducted most of his symphonic compositions. His most notable success outside his homeland came when he won the prize for the best opera in a La Scala competition in Milan with his *Prosperpino e lo straniero* (in Spanish as *Prosperpina y el extranjero*) in 1952.

WORKS: DRAMATIC: OPERAS: *La Zapatera prodigiosa* (Montevideo, Dec. 23, 1949); *Prosperpina e lo straniero* (Milan, March 17, 1952); *Bodas de sangre* (Buenos Aires, Aug. 9, 1956); *Cosecha negra* (1961). **BALLETS:** *Mekhano* (Buenos Aires, July 17, 1937); *Offenbachiana* (Buenos Aires, May 25, 1940). **ORCH.:** *Dans le jardin des morts* (Buenos Aires, Oct. 5, 1924); *A una madre* (Buenos Aires, Oct. 27, 1925); *La Chellah*, symphonic poem (Buenos Aires, Sept. 10, 1927); 5 syms.: No. 1 (1931), No. 2, *Sinfonía biblica*, for Chorus and Orch. (1932), No. 3, *Sinfonía Argentina* (Buenos Aires, Nov. 29, 1936), No. 4, *Sinfonía de los campos* (Buenos Aires, Oct. 29, 1939), and No. 5 (1956); *Allegro, Lento y Vivace* (1931); *Anunciación, Entrada a Jerusalem, Golgotha* (Buenos Aires, Nov. 15, 1932); Piano Concerto (1941); *Corales criollos No. 3*, symphonic poem (1953); *Suite introspectiva* (1961; Los Angeles, June 8, 1962); Violin Concerto (1962). **CHAMBER:** Violin Sonata (1914); Cello Sonata (1916); String Quartet (1942). **PIANO:** 2 sonatas (1917, 1939); *Corales criollos Nos. 1 and 2* (1947). **VOCAL:** *Epitafio en ritmos y sonidos* for Chorus and Orch. (1961); *Negro* for Soprano and Orch. (1961); songs.

BIBL.: R. Arizaga, *J.J. C.* (Buenos Aires, 1963).

Castro, Washington, Argentine conductor, teacher, and composer, brother of **José Maria** and **Juan José Castro**; b. Buenos Aires, July 13, 1909. He studied cello; from 1947 he devoted himself mainly to conducting and teaching.

WORKS: ORCH.: *Sinfonía primaveral* (1956); Piano Concerto (1960); *Sinfonía breve* for Strings (1960); *Concerto for Orchestra* (1963); *Rhapsody* for Cello and Orch. (1963); *3 Pieces* (1970). **CHAMBER:** 3 string quartets (1945, 1950, 1965); piano pieces. **VOCAL:** Songs.

Catunda, Eunice, Brazilian pianist and composer; b. Rio de Janeiro, March 14, 1915. She studied piano and harmony; took special courses in modern music and orchestration with Guarnieri and H.J. Koellreuter; in 1948 she went to Europe and studied conducting with Scherchen. In 1946 she joined the modernistic group Musica Viva; in 1973 she was appointed a lecturer at the Univ. of Brasilia. Her compositions include *Hommage à Schönberg* for Chamber Ensemble (1949); Piano Concerto (1955); *Seresta* for 4 Saxophones (1958); several piano pieces; and songs.

Caturla, Alejandro Garcia, Cuban composer; b. Remedios, March 7, 1906; d. there (assassinated), Nov. 12, 1940. He studied with Pedro Sanjuán in Havana; then with Boulanger in Paris (1928). He was founder (1932) and conductor of the Orquesta de Conciertos de Caibarién (chamber orch.) in Cuba; served as district judge in Remedios. In Caturla's music, primitive Afro-Cuban rhythms and themes are treated with modern techniques and a free utilization of dissonance.

WORKS: Suite of 3 Cuban dances: *Danza del tambor*, *Motivos de danzas*, and *Danza Lucumi* (Havana, 1928); *Bembe* for 14 Instruments (Paris, 1929); *Dos poemas Afro-Cubanos* for Voice and Piano (Paris, 1929; also arranged for Voice and Orch.); *Yambo-O*, Afro-Cuban oratorio (Havana, Oct. 25, 1931); *Rumba* for Orch. (1931); *Primera suite cubana* for Piano and 8 Wind Instruments (1930); *Manita en el Suelo*, "mitologia bufa Afro-Cubana" for Narrator, Marionettes, and Chamber Orch. (1934).

BIBL.: A. Salazar, "La obra musical de A. C.," *Revista Cubana* (Jan. 1938); N. Slonimsky, "C. of Cuba," *Modern Music* (Jan. 1940); R. Nodal Consuegra, "La figure de A. G. C. en la musica cubana," *Exilo* (Summer 1971).

Cauchie, Maurice, French musicologist; b. Paris, Oct. 8, 1882; d. there, March 21, 1963. He was first a physicist and chemist; after 1917 he devoted himself exclusively to music, specializing in the study of French music of the 16th and 17th centuries. He ed. the collected works of Clément Janequin; wrote *La Pratique de la musique* (1948); publ. numerous essays in French magazines on Ockeghem, Attaingnant, Janequin, Cléreau, Costeley, Boesset, Couperin, Gluck, Beethoven et al.; compiled a thematic index of the works of François Couperin (1949).

Caussade, Georges, esteemed French pedagogue; b. Port-Louis, Ile Maurice, Nov. 20, 1873; d. Chanteloupe-les-Vignes, Yvelines, Aug. 5, 1936. He studied at the Paris Cons., where he won the premier prix in harmony (1891) and in counterpoint and fugue (1896), and then the Prix de Rome with his scene lyrique, *Frédégonde* (1897). He taught counterpoint (from 1905) and fugue (from 1921) at the Paris Cons. Caussade had many distinguished pupils, including his wife, **Simone Plé-Caussade**, who succeeded him at the Cons. in 1928. He publ. the influential treatise *Technique de l'harmonie* (Paris, 1931).

Cavalieri, Lina (actually, **Natalina**), famous Italian soprano; b. Viterbo, Dec. 25, 1874; d. in an air raid on Florence, Feb. 8, 1944. As a young woman of striking beauty, she became the cynosure of the Paris boulevardiers via her appearances in cafés (1893) and at the Folies-Bergère (1894). During a trip to Russia in 1900, she married Prince Alexander Bariatinsky, who persuaded her to take up an operatic career. After studying in Paris, she made a premature debut as Nedda at the Teatro São Carlo in Lisbon (1900); at her 2nd appearance, the audience's disapproval brought the performance to a halt. She and the Prince then parted company, but she continued vocal studies with Maddalena Mariani-Masi in Milan, returning successfully to the stage as Mimi at the Teatro San Carlo in Naples (1900); she then sang in St. Petersburg and Warsaw (1901). In 1905 she was chosen to create the role of L'Ensoleillad in Massenet's *Chérubin* in Monte Carlo, and on Dec. 5, 1906, she made her Metropolitan Opera debut in N.Y. as Fedora, winning subsequent praise for her dramatic portrayals there of Tosca and Mimi. In 1907, after divorcing her husband, she contracted a lucrative marriage with the American millionaire Winthrop Chandler, but left him in a week, precipitating a sensational scandal that caused the Metropolitan to break her contract; she made her farewell appearance there in a concert on March 8, 1908. She sang at London's Covent Garden (1908), N.Y.'s Manhattan Opera House (1908), the London Opera House (1911), and the Chicago Grand Opera (1913–14; 1921–22). She married **Lucien Muratore** in 1913, but abandoned him in 1919; she then married Paolo D'Arvanni, making her home at her Villa Cappucina near Florence. Among her other fine roles were Adriana Lecouvreur, Manon Lescaut, and Salomé in *Hérodiade*. She publ. an autobiography, *La mie verità* (1936). She was the subject of an Italian film under the telling title *La Donna più bella dello mondo* (1957), starring Gina Lollobrigida.

Cavallo, Enrica, Italian pianist; b. Milan, May 19, 1921. She was educated at the Verdi Cons. in Milan. She married the Italian violinist Franco Gulli; in 1947 they formed the noted Gulli-Cavallo Duo; in subsequent years, they toured all over the world; in addition, she taught at the Verdi Cons. In 1973 she was appointed to the faculty of the Indiana Univ. School of Music in Bloomington.

Cazden, Norman, American pianist, musicologist, and composer; b. N.Y., Sept. 23, 1914; d. Bangor, Maine, Aug. 18, 1980. He studied piano with Ernest Hutcheson and composition with Bernard Wagenaar at the Juilliard Graduate School (teacher's diploma, 1932); then attended City College in N.Y. (B.S., 1943); he later studied composition with Piston and Copland and took courses in musicology at Harvard Univ. (Ph.D., 1948, with the diss. *Musical Consonance and Dissonance*). From 1926 he was active as a pianist. He taught at the Univ. of Maine in Orono (1969–80). He wrote *A Book of Nonsense Songs* (N.Y., 1961), and, with H. Haufrecht and N. Studer, *Folk Songs of the Catskills* (Albany, 1982). His compositions reflect some interesting technical ideas in a general format of acceptable modernity.

WORKS: DRAMATIC: *The Lonely Ones*, ballet (1944); *Dingle Hill*, dramatic cantata (1958); incidental music to *The Merry Wives of Windsor* (1962) and *The Tempest* (1963). **ORCH.:** *6 Definitions* (1930–39); *Preamble* (1938); *On the Death of a Spanish Child* (1939); *3 Dances* (1940); *Stony Hollow* (1944); Sym. (1948); *3 Ballads* (1949); *Songs from the Catskills* for Band (1950); *Woodland Valley Sketches* (1960); *Adventure* (1963); Chamber Concerto for Clarinet and Strings (1965); Viola Concerto (1972). **CHAMBER:** String Quartet (1936); Concerto for 10 Instruments (1937); 3 chamber sonatas for Clarinet and Viola (1938); Quartet for Clarinet and String Trio (1939); String Quintet (1941); Horn Sonata (1941); Flute Sonata (1941); Suite for Violin and Piano (1943); Suite for 2 Trumpets, Horn, Baritone Horn, Trombone, and Tuba (1954); Quintet for Oboe and String Quartet (1960); *2 Elizabethan Suites* for 2 Trumpets, Horn, Trombone, and Tuba (1964) and for String Quartet (1965); Wind Quintet (1966); Piano Trio (1969); Bassoon Sonata (1971); English Horn Sonata (1974); Tuba Sonata (1974). **OTHER:** Choral works and folk-music arrangements.

Cebotari (real name, **Cebutaru**), **Maria,** outstanding Moldavian soprano; b. Kishinev, Bessarabia, Feb. 23, 1910; d. Vienna, June 9, 1949. She sang in a church choir; from 1924 to 1929 she studied at the Kishinev Cons.; then went to Berlin, where she took voice lessons with Oskar Daniel at the Hochschule für Musik. In 1929 she sang with a Russian émigré opera troupe in Bucharest and in Paris. In 1931 she made an auspicious debut as Mimi at the Dresden State Opera, where she was a principal member until 1943; also appeared at the Salzburg Festival. In 1936 she joined the Berlin State Opera, singing with it until 1944; from 1946 she was a member of the Vienna State Opera. She also filled guest engagements in other European opera houses. She had a large repertoire which included the standard soprano roles, among them Violetta, Madama Butterfly, Pamina, and Manon; she also gave brilliant performances in modern operas; Richard Strauss greatly prized her abilities, entrusting to her the role of Aminta in the premiere of his *Die schweigsame Frau* (Dresden, June 24, 1935). Thanks to her cosmopolitan background, she sang the part of Tatiana in Russian in Tchaikovsky's opera *Eugene Onegin* and the part of Antonida in Glinka's *A Life for the Tsar*. She also appeared in films. She was married to the Russian nobleman Count Alexander Virubov; after their divorce in 1938, she married the film actor Gustav Diessl.

BIBL.: A. Mingotti, *M. C., Das Leben einer Sängerin* (Salzburg, 1950).

Ceccato, Aldo, Italian conductor; b. Milan, Feb. 18, 1934. He studied at the Verdi Cons. in Milan (1948–55), with Albert Wolff and Willem van Otterloo in the Netherlands (1958), and at the Berlin Hochschule für Musik (1959–62). In 1960 he served as assistant to Celibidache at the Accademia Musicale Chigiana in Siena. In 1964 he won 1st prize in the RAI conducting competition, and in 1969 he made his U.S. debut at the Chicago Lyric Opera and his first appearance at London's Covent Garden. He was music director of the Detroit Sym. Orch. (1973–77) and Generalmusikdirektor of the Hamburg State Phil. (1975–83); then was music director of the Bergen Sym. Orch. (1985–89) and chief conductor of the Hannover Radio Orch. (1985–89). He subsequently was chief conductor of the Slovak Phil. in Bratislava (1990–91), the RAI Orch. in Turin (from 1990), and the Orquesta Nacional de España in Madrid (1991). His father-in-law was **Victor de Sabata**.

Ceely, Robert (Paige), American composer; b. Torrington, Conn., Jan. 17, 1930. He studied at the New England Cons. of Music (B.Mus., 1954), with Milhaud and Leon Kirchner at Mills College (M.A., 1955), with Sessions at the Berkshire Music Center at Tanglewood (1955), and with Sessions, Babbitt, and Cone (analysis) and Strunk (musicology) at Princeton Univ. (1957–59); he later attended summer courses in contemporary music in Darmstadt (1962, 1964), and seminars in electronic music and digital sound synthesis in the U.S. He taught at the U.S. Naval School of Music (1955–57), Robert College in Istanbul (1961–63), the New England Cons. of Music (from 1967), Emmanuel College (1969–73), and Northeastern Univ. (1984–85). He publ. *Electronic Music Resource Book* (1983).

WORKS: String Trio (1953); Wind Quintet (1954); *Composition for 10 Instruments* (1963); *Stratti* for Tape (1963); *Elegia* for Tape (1964); *Vonce* for Tape (1967); *Logs* for 2 Double Basses (1968); *Kyros*, theatrical documentary for Viola, Optics, and Tape (1969); *Beyond the Ghost Spectrum*, ballet (1969); *Mitsyn 1971* for Tape (1971); *Slide Music* for Trombone Quartet (1974); *La Fleur, les fleurs* for Tape (1975); *Rituals* for 40 Flutes (1978); *Flee, Floret, Florens* for 15 Solo Voices (1979); *Piano Piece* (1980); *Bottom Dogs* for 4 Double Basses (1981); *Roundels* for Wind Ensemble and Tape (1981); *Totems* for Oboe and Tape (1982); *Dialogues* for Flute (1983); *Infractions* for Tape (1985); *Minute Rag* for Piano (in honor of Gunther Schuller's 60th birthday; 1985); *Pitch Dark* for Jazz Ensemble (1985); *Synoecy* for Clarinet and Tape (1986); *Timeshares* for Percussion Ensemble (1989); *Special K*, variations for Piano (1989); *Post hoc, ergo propter hoc* for Bass Clarinet (1989); *Harlequin* for Double Bass and Tape (1990); *Hypallage* for Trumpet and Tape (1990); *Asyndeton* for Piano and Tape (1993).

Cehanovsky, George, Russian baritone, b. St. Petersburg, April 14, 1892; d. Yorktown Heights, N.Y., March 25, 1986. He was a member of the Russian navy in World War I; after the war, he studied voice with his mother, a professional singer. He made his professional debut as Valentin in *Faust* in Petrograd in 1921. In 1923 he emigrated to the U.S., and in 1926 joined the roster of the Metropolitan Opera in N.Y., with which he remained until 1966. He filled 96 different roles during his long career; however, most were secondary roles, and thus he never reached the rank of celebrity. In 1956 he married **Elisabeth Rethberg**.

Čelanský, Ludvík Vítězslav, Czech conductor and composer; b. Vienna, July 17, 1870; d. Prague, Oct. 27, 1931. He studied at the Prague Cons.; then conducted theater orchs. in Pilsen and Zagreb. Returning to Prague, he made the Czech Phil. into an independent organization (1901), and conducted its first season and again in 1918–19; he also conducted opera and concerts abroad.

WORKS: *Camille*, opera (Prague, Oct. 23, 1897); *Adam, Noë, Moïse*, symphonic trilogy (1915–19); church music; songs.

Celibidache, Sergiu, transcendently endowed Romanian conductor; b. Roman, June 28, 1912; d. Paris, Aug. 14, 1996. He studied at the Berlin Hochschule für Musik, where his teachers included Kurt Thomas, Heinz Thiessen, Fritz Stein, and Heinz Gmeindl; he also took courses in musicology with Schering and Schünemann at the Univ. of Berlin. In 1945 he was appointed conductor of the Berlin Phil. as successor to Furtwängler; he continued in that capacity until Furtwängler formally resumed his position in 1952. After engagements as a guest conductor throughout Europe, he was chief conductor of the Swedish Radio Sym. Orch. in Stockholm (1964–71), the Stuttgart Radio Sym. Orch. (1971–77), and the Orch. National de France in Paris (1973–75). In 1979 he became Generalmusikdirektor of the Munich Phil. He also went to the U.S., where he was engaged as conductor of the student orch. at the Curtis Inst. of Music in Philadelphia (1983–84). So remarkable was his progress with this student group that he was engaged to make a formal U.S. debut as a conductor with it at Carnegie Hall in N.Y. on Feb. 27, 1984, at which he astonished the audience and the critics with his mastery of a diversified program of works by Rossini, Wagner, Debussy, and Prokofiev. In 1989 he took the Munich Phil. on an 11-city tour of the U.S., winning extraordinary acclaim. A cosmopolitan existentialist, Celibidache lectured on musical phenomenology at the Univ. of Mainz; he also composed in his leisure time, producing 4 syms., a Piano Concerto, and a variety of minor pieces. In spite of his cult-like following, however, Celibidache's career remained a singular one. After leaving his Berlin post, his appointments and guest engagements were confined to orchs. of the 2nd rank due to his exorbitant demand for unlimited rehearsal time. He also disdained commercial recordings so that his performances were preserved only thanks to the radio stations which taped his concerts throughout his career. In 1988 he relented and allowed video discs to be made of several of his performances.

BIBL.: K. Weiler, *C.: Musiker und Philosoph* (Munich, 1993).

Celis, Frits, Belgian conductor and composer; b. Antwerp, April 11, 1929. He studied composition at the Royal Flemish Cons. in Antwerp and harp at the Brussels Cons.; also attended the summer conducting course at the Mozarteum in Salzburg (1949–51) and similar courses at the Hochschule für Musik in Cologne (1953–54). He then conducted at the Théâtre Royal de la Monnaie in Brussels (1954–59). In 1960 he was appointed to the faculty of the Royal Flemish Cons. of Antwerp.

WORKS: *Music* for Strings (1951); Violin Sonata (1951); String Trio (1958); *De Geestelijke bruiloft* for Voice, and Piano or Chamber Orch. (1958); Cello Sonata (1963); *Élégie* for Orch. (Antwerp, Dec. 8, 1967); *3 Symphonic Movements* (1969); *Toccata* for Oboe and Piano (1972); *Episodes* for Viola and Harpsichord (1973); *Variazioni* for Chamber Orch. (1974); Trio for Flute, Viola, and Harp (1977); 3 syms.: No. 1 (1979), No. 2 (1986), and No. 3, *Incanti* (1987); *Cantilena* for Orch. (1980); *Preludio e Narrazione* for Soprano and Orch. (1983); *Musica per Undici* for 10 Percussionists and Synthesizer (1984); Sonatina for Oboe, Clarinet, and Bassoon (1986); *Incantations* for Clarinet Choir (1987); *A Hypocritical Funeral March* for Brass Quartet (1987); Quartet for Flute, Violin, Viola, and Cello (1987); choruses; songs.

Celletti, Rodolfo, Italian music critic; b. Rome, June 13, 1917. He obtained a law degree from the Univ. of Rome; then devoted himself to music criticism, writing for various newspapers in Milan. He also ed. the valuable reference work *Le grandi voci: Dizionario critico-biografico dei cantanti* (Rome, 1964).

Celona, John, American composer and teacher; b. San Francisco, Oct. 30, 1947. He studied at San Francisco State Univ. (B.Mus., 1970; M.A., 1972) and the Univ. of Calif. at San Diego (Ph.D., 1977); also attended the Univ. of Pittsburgh and Indiana Univ. His principal mentors were Henry Onderdonk, Xenakis, and Gaburo. He was active as a tenor saxophonist, and also was founder-director of several new music ensembles, among them the Networks Orch. In 1977 he joined the faculty of the Univ. of Victoria in British Columbia, where he taught composition and conducted its new music ensemble, Sonic Lab. His output embraces not only the more traditional contemporary modes of expression, but also avant-garde jazz, pop, and world musics. He has created several arresting electro-acoustic pieces.

WORKS: ORCH.: *Module* (1971). **CHAMBER:** *Proportions: Networks* for Any Large Ensemble (1970); *Multiphony III: Gradients* for Tenor Trombone (1973) and *I: Transforms* for Amplified String Quartet (1974); *Voicings* for Double Bass (1977); *Music on 1 Timbre* for Any Large Ensemble and Tape (1979); *Moving Points* for 11 Instruments (1979); *This Space* for 5 Instruments (1981); *Instrument Flying* for Marimba and Tape (1982); *Primitive Cool Suite* for Percussionist and Tape (1985); *Distant Drummer* for Bass Clarinet, Synthesizers, Electric Bass, and Acoustic/Digital Drums (1986); *Emerald Soft* for Percussion, Processed Voice, and Tape (1986); *Glassbowls* for Gamelan Percussion and Tape (1987); *Hermosa* for Latin Percussion and Live Digital Keyboard/Sampler System (1988–89); *sum over histories* for Amplified Spatial Sextet, Piano, RAAD Violin, and Yamaha DX/Proteus Keyboard (1990); *Also Ran* for Processed Acoustic Percussion, Interactive/Electronic Drumming, and Mathews/Boie Radio Drum (1990–91); *Voce Mod* for Flute and Computer-controlled Effects Processing (1990–91); *Twilight Magellan (to Miles Davis)* for 6 Instruments and Electronics (1992); *Electraglide With Dragon* for Gamelan Ensemble and Computer-generated Polyphony (1993). **KEYBOARD:** *Player Piano I* for 3 Pianos (1977); *Tracking* for Piano (1978); *Elan B* for Keyboard and Electronics (1988); *Srivox Filonga* for Keyboard and Electronics (1988). **VOCAL:** *Round: Hodie Illuxit Nobies . . .* for Chorus (1971; rev. 1977). **ELECTRO-ACOUSTIC:** *Timbral-Orchestral* (1976); *Music in Circular Motions* (1981); *Possible Orchestras (at the 21st Harmonic)* (1984); *Cordes de Nuit* (1987); *Pacific Rims* (1987).

Čeremuga, Josef, Czech composer; b. Ostrava, June 14, 1930. He studied composition with Řídký and Dobiáš and quarter-tone music with A. Hába at the Prague Academy of Music (1950–53); after completing his postgraduate studies there (1953–56), he joined its faculty in 1960, serving in a variety of capacities. His works reflect modern Czech and Russian styles, with broad neo-Romantic melos sharpened by euphonious dissonances.

WORKS: DRAMATIC: OPERA: *Juraj Čup* (1958–60; Prague, April 27, 1963). **BALLET:** *Princezna se zlatou hvězdou na čele* (The Princess with a Golden Star on Her Forehead; 1980–82). **ORCH.:** 3 syms. (1952; 1966–67; 1975); 2 violin concertos (1955; 1970–80); *3 Symphonic Frescoes* (1958–59); Piano Concerto (1962; Teplice, Jan. 21, 1963); *Hommage aux étudiants,* overture (1964); *Concerto da camera* for Wind Quintet and Strings (1970–71); *Festive Overture* (1977); *Prague Symfonietta* (1977); *3 Silesian Dances* (1977–80); Concerto for Piano, Trumpet, and Orch. (1982). **CHAMBER:** 3 string quartets (1956, 1961, 1973); Piano Trio (1959–60); Cello Sonata (1957); Viola Sonata (1961); *4 Pictures* for Clarinet and Accordion (1961); 2 wind quintets (1964, 1967); Quintet for Flute, Oboe, Violin, Viola, and Cello (1975); *Faun's Moods* for Flute, Guitar, and Marimba (1980); *Dialogue* for Cello and Piano (1982). **VOCAL:** Songs.

Cerha, Friedrich, notable Austrian composer and pedagogue; b. Vienna, Feb. 17, 1926. He was a student of Prihoda (violin) and Uhl (composition) at the Vienna Academy of Music (1946–51), and also took courses in philosophy and musicology at the Univ. of Vienna (Ph.D., 1950). With Kurt Schwertsik, he founded the new music ensemble Die Reihe. In 1960 he became a lecturer at the Vienna Academy of Music, where he also was director of its electronic music studio until 1969; he subsequently was assoc. prof. (1969–70) and prof. (from 1970) of music there. In 1986 he was awarded the Austrian State Prize. Cerha completed the 3rd act of Berg's unfinished opera *Lulu* (1962–78), which was first given in its finished version in Paris on Feb. 24, 1979. He has also produced a considerable output of avant-garde scores notable for their innovative blending of contemporary techniques and traditional idioms.

WORKS: OPERAS: *Baal,* after Brecht (1974–81; Salzburg, Aug. 7, 1981; suite of songs, North German Radio, Hamburg, Jan. 22, 1982); *Der Rattenfänger* (1984–86). **ORCH.:** Concerto for Strings (1947–49); Sym. (1947–50; 1st movement perf. as *Sinfonia in un movimento,* 1950); *Tryptichon* for Flute, Oboe, Clarinet, Horn, and Strings (1948–51); *Konzertante Sinfonie* for Piano and Orch. (1950–53); *Relazioni fragili* for Harpsichord and Chamber Orch. (1956–57; Vienna, May 16, 1960); *Espressioni fondamentali* (1957; Berlin, Nov. 17, 1960); *Intersecazioni I* (1959–61) and *II* (1959–73; Graz, Oct. 16, 1973) for Violin and Orch.; *Fasce* (1959; fair-copied, 1967–68, 1972–73, and 1975; Graz, Oct. 8, 1975); *Mouvements I–III* for Chamber Orch. (1960); *Spiegel I–VII* (1960–61; fair-copied, 1961–71; 1st complete perf., Graz, Oct. 9, 1972); *Symphonien* for Winds and Timpani (1964); *Langegger Nachtmusik I* (1969) and *II* (1970); Sym. (1975); Double Concerto for Violin, Cello, and Orch. (1975–76); Double Concerto for Flute, Bassoon, and Orch. (1982; Graz, Oct. 7, 1983); Flute Concerto (1986); *Monumentum: für Karl Prantl* (1987–88). **CHAMBER:** 2 string quartets (1948, 1951); *Aria und Fuge* for 8 Winds (1949); String Trio (1952); Horn Sonata (1952); *Ricercar, Toccata, Passacaglia* for Flute, Viola d'Amore, and Lute or Harpsichord (1953); *Deux* *éclats en réflexion* for Violin and Piano (1956); *Formation et solution* for Violin and Piano (1956–57); *Enjambements* for 7 Instruments (1959); *Fünf kleine Stücke* for Clarinet and Piano (1960–64); *Sieben Anekdoten* for Flute and Piano (1960–64); *Fantasien nach Cardew's Herbst 60* for 7 Instruments (1962–63); *Phantasma 63* for Chamber Group (1963); *Catalogue des objets trouvés* for Chamber Group (1968–69); *Curriculum* for 13 Instruments (1972–73); *Fier musikalische Grafiken* for Any Instrumentation (1973); *Quellen* for Ensemble (1992). **PIANO:** *Klavierbuch für Roswitha* (1952–53); *Klavierstücke 58* (1958); *Elégie* (1964); *Adaxl-Suite* (1970); *Netzwerke-Phantasie* (1988). **VOCAL:** *Sonnengesang des heiligen Franz von Assisi* for Soloists, Chorus, Harp, and String Orch. (1947–49); *Rubaijat des Omar Khajjam* for Chorus (1949–54); *An die Herrscher der Welt* for Soloists and Chorus (1950–51); *Fragment aus dem I-Ging* for Soloists, Chorus, and Orch. (1952); *Exercises* for Baritone, Speakers, and Chamber Orch. (1962–68); *Verzeichnis* for 4 Sopranos, 4 Altos, 4 Tenors, and 4 Basses (1969); *Keintate I* (1982) and *II* (1983–84) for Medium Voice and 11 Instruments; *Nachtgesang* for Tenor and Orch. (1984); *Requiem für Rikke* for Tenor and Orch. (1984–89; based on *Der Rattanfänger*); *Eine Art Chanson* for Amplified Medium Voice, Piano, Percussion, and Double Bass (1985).

Černý, Ladislav, Czech violist and teacher; b. Pilsen, April 13, 1891; d. Dobřiš, July 13, 1975. He studied violin at the Prague Cons.; then played viola in the opera orch. in Ljubljana (1916–21); returning to Prague, he organized the Zik Quartet, known as the Prague Quartet from 1929; was a member until his death. He taught at the Prague Cons. (1940–46); from 1946 to 1973 he was a prof. at the Prague Music Academy. Hindemith dedicated his Sonata for Solo Viola to him.

Cerovsek, Corey, remarkable Canadian violinist of Austrian descent; b. Vancouver, April 24, 1972. A child prodigy, he began violin lessons at the age of 4 with John Loban, making his debut as soloist with the Calgary Phil. when he was 9; subsequently was invited to appear with all the leading Canadian orchs. and many of the foremost U.S. orchs. In the meantime, he continued his training with Charmain Gadd and Richard Goldner at Western Washington Univ. in Bellingham. At 12, the Royal College of Music of Toronto awarded him its gold medal for excellence and Josef Gingold accepted him as his student at the Indiana Univ. School of Music in Bloomington, the youngest student ever accepted there. While at Indiana Univ., he took his B.Sc. in music and mathematics (1984), his M.Mus. (1988), and his D.Mus (1991). In 1987 he made his London debut, and thereafter made tours of Europe. His career as a soloist with orchs., as a recitalist, and as a chamber music player have taken him to the world's principal music centers. He has also made appearances with his sister, Katja (b. Vienna, Oct. 1, 1969), a pianist.

Cerquetti, Anita, Italian soprano; b. Montecosaro, near Macerata, April 13, 1931. After training in Perugia, she made her operatic debut in 1951 as Aida in Spoleto; then sang in various Italian opera houses. In 1955 she made her U.S. debut at the Chicago Lyric Theatre. In 1958 she scored a major success when she substituted for Callas in the role of Norma at the Rome Opera, and that same year she made her first appearance at Milan's La Scala as Abigaille. Her promising career was cut short by a debilitating illness which compelled her to retire in 1961.

Cervetti, Sergio, Uruguayan-born American composer and teacher; b. Dolores, Nov. 9, 1940. He received training in piano from José Maria Martino Rodas in Mercedes and from Hugo Balzo in Montevideo, and in composition from Carlos Estrada at the National Cons. in Montevideo and from Guido Santórsola. From 1962 to 1967 he pursued studies at the Peabody Cons. of Music in Baltimore, where he had further training in composition from Stefans Grové and Ernst Krenek. In 1969–70 he was composer-in-residence at the Deutscher Akademischer Austauschdienst in West Berlin. With the dancer Kenneth Rinker, he co-founded the Berlin Dance Ensemble, with whom he collaborated in various dance scores in subsequent years. In 1970 he settled in N.Y. and worked in electronic music with Davidovsky and Ussachevsky at Columbia Univ.; also taught at Brooklyn College. In 1972 he became a prof. at the Tisch School of the Arts at N.Y. Univ., where he taught advanced courses in electronic and 20th-century music. In 1979 he became a naturalized American citizen. In his early works, Cervetti employed serial and expressionist styles. Around 1970 he became more adventuresome and turned to aleatory and electronics with minimalist and nationalistic excursions.

WORKS: ORCH.: *Orbitas* (1967); *Plexus* for Small Orch. (1971); Trumpet Concerto (1977); *Las Indias Olvidades*, concerto for Harpsichord and 11 Instruments (1990; Alicante, Sept. 27, 1992); Piano Concerto (1994). **CHAMBER:** String Trio (1963); *Cinco Episodios*, piano trio (1966); *Zinctum* for String Quartet (1968); *. . . de la tierra . . .* for Ensemble (1972); *El Rio de los Pajaros Pintados* for Bandoneon and Tape (1978); *Music for Rachel* for Ensemble (1979); 3rd String Quartet (1990). **KEYBOARD: PIANO:** 2 sonatas (1964, 1989); *Estudios Australes* (1989). **HARPSICHORD:** *Candombe* (1984); *Llanto y Muerte* (1988); *Alberada y Hard Rock* (1993). **VOCAL:** *El Carro de Heno* for Chorus and Orch. (1967); *Cantata Duraciones* (1967); *Lux Lucet in Tenebris* for Chorus (1970); *4 Fragments of Pablo Neruda* for Soprano, Oboe, Guitar, Cello, and Percussion (1970); *Madrigal III* (1975) and *IV* (1985); *4 Fragments of Isadora*, song cycle for Soprano and Piano (1979); *7 Songs of Orfila Bardesio* for Voice and Piano (1989); *Leyenda* for Soprano and Orch. (1991); *El triunfo de la Muerte*, song cycle for Voice and Piano (1993); *No Longer Very Clear*, aria for Soprano, String Quartet, and Harpsichord (WNYC-FM, N.Y., June 13, 1994). **ELECTRO-ACOUSTIC:** *Wind Devil* (1983); *Manhattan* (1984); *Enclosed Time* (1985); *Night Trippers* (1986); *Transatlantic Light* (1987); *The Hay Wain* (1987); *Inez de Castro* (1988). **OTHER:** *Cocktail Party* for Amplified Instruments, Piano obbligato, and a "variable number of guests" (1970).

Cesana, Otto, Italian-American composer; b. Brescia, July 7, 1899; d. N.Y., Dec. 9, 1980. He went to the U.S. as a young man, and studied music with Julius Gold in California. He specialized in writing film music without, however, relinquishing his more ambitious pursuits. He wrote 6 syms. and 6 concertos: 1 for Clarinet, 1 for Trumpet, 1 for Trombone, 1 for Piano, 1 for 2 Pianos, and 1 for 3 Pianos; also composed a ballet, *Ali Baba and the 40 Thieves*, and a jazzy piece entitled *Swing Septet* (Indianapolis, Jan. 23, 1942). He was the author of several manuals, among them *Course in Modern Harmony* (1939), *Course in Counterpoint* (1940), and *Voicing the Modern Dance Orchestra* (1946).

Cezar, Corneliu, Romanian composer; b. Bucharest, Dec. 22, 1937. He studied composition at the Bucharest Cons. with Ciortea, Jora, Mendelsohn, and Vieru.

WORKS: DRAMATIC: *Galileo Galilei*, opera (1962; Bucharest, Dec. 16, 1964); *Pinocchio*, theater piece (1983). **ORCH.:** *Cronika* for Orch. and Tape (Bucharest, Feb. 1, 1968); *Alpha Lirae* (1984). **CHAMBER:** Piano Sonata (1959); Quartet for Flute, Violin, Viola, and Bassoon (1959); *Taaroa* for Narrator, 2 Prepared Pianos, Carillon on Tape, and Clarinet (1968). **TAPE:** *AUM* (1970); *Rota* (1978); *Ziua fără sfîrşit* (1978).

Chadabe, Joel, American composer; b. N.Y., Dec. 12, 1938. He studied with Will Mason at the Univ. of North Carolina at Chapel Hill (B.A., 1959) and Elliott Carter at Yale Univ. (M.M., 1962), then taught at the State Univ. of N.Y. at Albany (from 1965), served as consultant to Bennington (Vt.) College (from 1971), and was president of Intelligent Computer Music Systems, Inc. (from 1986). In 1964 he held a Ford Foundation fellowship, later receiving grants, commissions, or awards from the NEA (1976, 1985, 1988), Rockefeller Foundation (1977), N.Y. Foundation for the Arts (1985), and the Fulbright Commission (travel grant, 1988). From 1978 to 1987 he was president of Composer's Forum, Inc. In 1994, with Paul Lansky and Neil

Rolnick, he founded the Electronic Music Foundation in Albany, N.Y. His articles on electronic music have appeared in various journals, including *Computer Music Journal* and *Contemporary Music Review.* His compositions make use of a variety of electronic and computer technologies.

WORKS: *Prelude to Naples* for 4 Instruments (1965); *Street Scene* for English Horn, Tape, and Projections (1967); *Ideas of Movement at Bolton Landing* for Electronic Sounds on Tape (1971); *Shadows and Lines* for Electronic Sounds on Tape (1972); *Flowers* for Stringed Instrument and Electronic Sounds on Tape (1975); *Settings for Spirituals* for Singer and Computer-generated Accompaniment (1977); *Solo* for Computer/Synthesizer (1978; rev. 1981); *Scenes from Stevens* for Computer/Synthesizer System (1979); *Rhythms* for Computer/Synthesizer System and Percussion (1980); *Variation* for Piano (1983); *Follow Me Softly* for Computer/Synthesizer System and Percussion (1984); *The Long Ago and Far Away Tango* for Piano (1984); *Bar Music* for Computer/Synthesizer (1985); *Several Views of an Elusive Lady* for Soprano and Electronic Sounds on Tape (1985); *Many Mornings Many Moods* for Percussion, Electronics, and Orch. (1988); *After Some Songs* for Computer/Synthesizer and Solo Instruments (1994).

Chadwick, George Whitefield, eminent American composer and teacher; b. Lowell, Mass. Nov. 13, 1854; d. Boston, April 4, 1931. He began musical training with his brother. From the time he was 15, he was active as an organist, and in 1872 he became a Congregational church organist. He also pursued organ training with Dudley Buck and Eugene Thayer at the New England Cons. of Music in Boston. After serving as a prof. of music at Olivet College in Michigan (1876–77), he went to Leipzig to study privately with Jadassohn, and then entered the Cons. there in 1878. His *Rip Van Winkle* overture and his 2nd String Quartet were selected as the finest works at the annual Cons. concerts in 1879. He then pursued training with Rheinberger at the Munich Hochschule für Musik (1879–80). Upon his return to Boston in 1880, he devoted himself mainly to composing and teaching. He also was active as an organist, as a pianist (prinicipally in programs of his own works), and as a symphonic and choral conductor. He served as director and conductor of the Springfield (1890–99) and Worcester (1897–1901) festivals. In 1882 he became a teacher at the New England Cons. of Music. In 1897 he became its director, and proceeded to make it one of the most distinguished conservatories in the U.S. Many noted American composers were Chadwick's pupils. In 1898 he was elected a member of the National Inst. of Arts and Letters, and in 1909 of the American Academy of Arts and Letters, which awarded him its gold medal in 1928. Chadwick was one of the leading American composers of his day. While he is usually regarded as a pillar of the "Boston Classicists," his most important works actually reveal attempts to find a new American style, albeit one reflecting the tenets of late Romanticism. Among his most important works were the verismo opera *The Padrone* (1912–13), the 2nd Sym. (1883–85), the *Symphonic Sketches* (1895–1904), the symphonic ballad *Tom O'Shanter* (1914–15), the 4th String Quartet (1896), and various songs.

WORKS: DRAMATIC: *The Peer and the Pauper,* comic operetta (1884); *A Quiet Lodging,* operetta (Boston, April 1, 1892); *Tabasco,* burlesque opera (1893–94; Boston, Jan. 29, 1894); *Judith,* lyric drama (1899–1900; Worcester Festival, Sept. 23, 1901); *Everywoman: Her Pilgrimage in Quest of Love,* incidental music (1910; Hartford, Conn., Feb. 9, 1911); *The Padrone,* opera (1912–13; concert perf., Thomaston, Conn., Sept. 29, 1995); *Love's Sacrifice,* pastoral opera (1916–17; Chicago, Feb. 1, 1923). **ORCH.:** *Rip Van Winkle,* overture (Leipzig, March 18, 1879; rev. 1920s); *Schön München,* waltz (1880; Boston, Jan. 7, 1881); 3 syms.: No. 1 (1881; Boston, Feb. 23, 1882). No. 2 (1883–85; 1st complete perf., Boston, Dec. 10, 1886), and No. 3 (1893–94; Boston, Oct. 19, 1894); *Andante* for Strings (Boston, April 13, 1892); *Thalia: Overture to an Imaginary Comedy* (1882; Boston, Jan. 12, 1883); *Melpomene: Overture to an Imaginary Tragedy* (Boston, Dec. 23, 1887); *A Pastoral Prelude* (1890; Boston, Jan. 30, 1892); *Serenade* (1890); *Tabasco March* for Band or Orch. (Boston, Jan. 29, 1894); *Symphonic Sketches* (1895–1904; Boston, Feb. 7, 1908); *Adonais,* overture (1899; Boston, Feb. 2, 1900); *Euterpe,* overture (1903; Boston, April 22, 1904); *Cleopatra,* symphonic poem (1904; Worcester Festival, Sept. 29, 1905); *Sinfonietta* (Boston, Nov. 21, 1904); *Suite symphonique* (1905–09; Philadelphia, March 29, 1911); *Theme, Variations, and Fugue* for Organ and Orch. (Boston, Nov. 13, 1908); *Everywoman Waltz* (1909); *Aphrodite,* symphonic fantasy (1910–11; Norfolk Festival, June 4, 1912); *Tam O'Shanter,* symphonic ballad (1914–15; Norfolk Festival, June 3, 1915); *Angel of Death,* symphonic poem (1917–18; N.Y., Feb. 9, 1919); *Jericho March* (c.1919); *Elegy: In Memoriam Horatio Parker* (1920); *Anniversary Overture* (Norfolk Festival, June 7, 1922); *Tre pezzi* (1923). **CHAMBER:** 5 string quartets: No. 1 (Leipzig, May 29, 1878), No. 2 (1878; Leipzig, May 30, 1879), No. 3 (c.1885; Boston, March 9, 1887), No. 4 (Boston, Dec. 21, 1896), and No. 5 (1898; Boston, Feb. 12, 1901); Piano Quintet (1887; Boston, Jan. 23, 1888); *Romanze* for Cello and Piano (1911); *Easter Morn* for Violin or Cello and Piano (c.1914); *Fanfare* for 3 Trumpets, 3 Trombones, and Timpani (Boston, Nov. 3, 1925); piano pieces; organ music. **VOCAL: CHORUS AND ORCH.:** *The Viking's Last Voyage* (Boston, April 22, 1881); *Dedication Ode* (1883); *Lovely Rosabelle,* ballad (Boston, Dec. 10, 1899); *The Pilgrims* (1890; Boston, April 2, 1891); *Phoenix Expirans,* cantata (1891; Springfield Festival, May 5, 1892); *Ode* for the Opening of the World's Columbian Exposition (Chicago, Oct. 21, 1892); *The Lily Nymph,* dramatic cantata (1894–95; N.Y., Dec. 7, 1895); *Ecce jam noctis* (New Haven, Conn., June 30, 1897); *Noel* (1907–08; Norfolk Festival, June 2, 1909); *Land of Our Hearts* (1917; Norfolk Festival, June 4, 1918); *Fathers of the Free* (c.1927); *Commemoration Ode* (c.1928); many other accompanied and unaccompanied choral works, both sacred and secular. **SOLO VOICE AND ORCH.:** *The Miller's Daughter* for Baritone and Orch. (1886; San Francisco, May 18, 1887); *Lochinar* for Baritone and Orch. (Springfield Festival, May 7, 1896); *Aghadoe* for Alto and Orch. (1910). Also many solo songs with piano or organ accompaniment.

WRITINGS: *Harmony: A Course of Study* (Boston, 1897; many subsequent eds.); *Key to the Textbook on Harmony* (Boston, 1902).

BIBL.: C. Engel, "G.W. C.," *Musical Quarterly* (July 1924); A. Langley, "C. and the New England Conservatory," ibid. (Jan. 1935); V. Yellin, *The Life and Operatic Works of G.W. C.* (diss., Harvard Univ., 1957); idem, "C., American Realist," *Musical Quarterly* (Jan. 1975); idem, *C.: Yankee Composer* (Washington, D.C., and London, 1990); B. Faucett, *The Symphonic Works of G.W. C.* (diss., Florida State Univ., 1992).

Chailley, Jacques, eminent French musicologist; b. Paris, March 24, 1910. He studied composition with Boulanger, Delvincourt, and Busser, musicology with Pirro, Rokseth, and Smijers, and conducting with Mengelberg and Monteux; he also took courses in medieval French literature at the Sorbonne in Paris (1932–36; Ph.D., 1952, with 2 dissertations: *L'École musicale de Saint-Martial de Limoges jusqu'à la fin du XIe siècle* [publ. in Paris, 1960] and *Chansons de Gautier du Coinci* [publ. as *Les Chansons à la Vierge de Gautier de Coinci* in *Monuments de la musique ancienne,* XV, 1959]). He was general secretary (1937–47), vice-principal (1947–51), and prof. of the choral class (1951–53) at the Paris Cons.; from 1952 to 1979 he was director of the Inst. of Musicology at the Univ. of Paris; also taught at the Paris Lycée La Fontaine (1951–69); from 1962 to 1981 he was director of the Schola Cantorum. He wrote authoritatively on many subjects, including medieval music, the music of ancient Greece, music history, and the music of Bach, Mozart, Wagner, and others. He also composed 2 operas, a ballet, orch. works, including 2 syms. (1942–47; 1980–84), and chamber music.

WRITINGS (all publ. in Paris unless otherwise given): *Petite Histoire de la chanson populaire française* (1942); with H. Challan, *Théorie complète de la musique* (1949); *Histoire musicale* *du Moyen Âge* (1950; 3rd ed., 1984); *Les Notations musicales nouvelles* (1950); *La Musique médiévale* (1951); *Traité historique d'analyse musicale* (1951; 2nd ed., 1977, as *Traité historique harmonique*); *Formation et transformations du langage musical* (1954); *Chronologie musicale: I, années 300 à 1599* (1955); ed. *Précis de musicologie* (1958; 2nd ed., rev., 1984); *L'Imbroglio des modes* (1960); *40,000 ans de musique: L'Homme à la découverte de sa musique* (1961; Eng. tr., 1964, as *40,000 Years of Music: Man in Search of Music*); *Les Passions de J.S.* Bach (1963; 2nd ed., rev., 1984); *Tristan et Isolde de Wagner* (1963; 2nd ed., 1972); ed. *Alia musica* (1965); *Expliquer l'harmonie?* (Lausanne, 1967); *La Musique et le signe* (Lausanne, 1967); *"La Flûte enchantée," opéra maçonnique: Essai d'explication du livret et de la musique* (1968; 2nd ed., aug., 1983; Eng. tr., 1971, as *The Magic Flute, Masonic Opera*); *"L'Art de la fugue" de J.S. Bach. Étude critique des sources* (I, 1971, II, 1972); *Le "Carnaval" de Schumann* (1971); *Cours d'histoire de la musique* (4 vols., 1972–90); *Les Chorals d'orgue de Bach* (1974); *La Musique* (Tours, 1975); *Le Voyage d'hiver de Schubert* (1975); *Solfège-déchiffrage pour les jeunes pianistes* (1975); *Traité d'harmonie au clavier* (1977); *Parsifal de R. Wagner, opéra initiatique* (1979); *La Musique grecque antique* (1979); *De la musique à la musicologie . . . a l'occasion de son 70e anniversaire* (1980); *Eléments de philologie musicale* (2 vols., 1985); with J. Viret, *Le Symbolisme de la gamme* (1988); *Propos sans orthodoxie* (1989).

Chailly, Luciano, prominent Italian music administrator, teacher, and composer, father of **Riccardo Chailly**; b. Ferrara, Jan. 19, 1920. He studied violin in Ferrara (diploma, 1941) and pursued academic training at the Univ. of Bologna (B.A., 1943); after composition studies with R. Bossi at the Milan Cons. (diploma, 1945), he studied with Hindemith in Salzburg (1948). He was director of music programming for the RAI (1950–67), and artistic director of Milan's La Scala (1968–71), Turin's Teatro Regio (1972), Milan's Angelicum (1973–75), and Verona's Arena (1975–76). He was again associated with La Scala (from 1977) and was artistic director of the Genoa Opera (1983–85); he also taught at the Milan Cons. (1968–83). In 1989–90 he was artistic director of the RAI orch. and choir in Turin. His music is composed in a communicative neo-Classical idiom, with some dodecaphonic incrustations and electronic effects.

WORKS: DRAMATIC: OPERAS: *Ferrovia soprelevata* (Bergamo, Oct. 1, 1955); *Una domanda di matrimonio* (Milan, May 22, 1957); *Il canto del cigno* (Bologna, Nov. 16, 1957); *La riva delle Sirti* (Monte Carlo, March 1, 1959); *Procedura penale* (Como, Sept. 30, 1959); *Il mantello* (Florence, May 11, 1960); *Era proibito* (Milan, March 5, 1963); *L'Idiota* (1966–67; Rome, Feb. 14, 1970); *Vassiliev* (Genoa, March 16, 1967); *Markheim* (Spoleto, July 14, 1967); *Sogno (ma forse no)* (Trieste, Jan. 28, 1975); *Il libro dei reclami* (Vienna, May 29, 1975); *La Cantatrice calva* (Vienna, Nov. 5, 1985). **BALLETS:** *Fantasmi al Grand-Hotel* (Milan, 1960); *Il cappio* (Naples, 1962); *L'urlo* (Palermo, 1967); *Shee* (Melbourne, 1967); *Anna Frank* (Verona, 1981); *Es-Ballet* (1983). **INSTRUMENTAL:** *Toccata* for Orch. (1948); *12 Sonate tritematiche* (for various instrumentations; 1951–61); *Sequenze dell'artide* for Orch. (1961); *Piccole serenate* for Strings (1967); *Contrappunti a quattro dimensioni* for Orch. (1973); *Newton-Variazioni* for Chamber Orch. (1979); *Es-Konzert* for Orch. (1980); *Psicosi* for Instruments and Percussion (1980); *Es-Kammerkonzert* for Small Instrumental Group (1983); chamber works; piano pieces. **OTHER:** Choral works; songs; music for television.

BIBL.: R. Cresti, *Linguaggio musicale di L. C.* (Milan, 1993).

Chailly, Riccardo, noted Italian conductor, son of **Luciano Chailly**; b. Milan, Feb. 20, 1953. He studied composition with his father, and then with Bruno Bettinelli at the Milan Cons.; he also studied conducting with Piero Guarino in Perugia, Franco Caracciolo in Milan, and Franco Ferrara in Siena. He was assistant conductor of the sym. concerts at Milan's La Scala (1972–74); his international career began with his U.S. debut at the Chicago Lyric Opera conducting *Madama Butterfly* (1974); he subsequently was a guest conductor at the San Francisco Opera, Milan's La Scala, London's Covent Garden, and the Vienna State Opera. He made his Metropolitan Opera debut in N.Y. with *Les Contes d'Hoffmann* on March 8, 1982. From 1982 to 1989 he was chief conductor of the (West) Berlin Radio Sym. Orch., which he led on its first tour of North America in 1985; he also was principal guest conductor of the London Phil. (1982–85) and artistic director of the Teatro Comunale in Bologna (1986–89). In 1988 he became chief conductor of the Concertgebouw Orch. of Amsterdam, which was renamed the Royal Concertgebouw Orch. that same year by Queen Beatrix in honor of its 100th anniversary. Chailly is one of the leading conductors of his generation, and has won praise for his performances in both the opera pit and the concert hall.

Chaix, Charles, French organist, teacher, and composer; b. Paris, March 26, 1885; d. Thonex, near Geneva, Feb. 16, 1973. He studied music at the École Niedermeyer in Paris; in 1904 he went to Geneva, where he studied with Otto Barblan at the Cons., graduating in 1908. He subsequently was on its faculty (1910–14; again from 1918). He combined his pedagogical activities with service as a church organist; also conducted advanced classes in counterpoint at the Lyons Cons. He retired from teaching in 1961. His works include 2 syms. (1914, 1928); Piano Quintet (1941); String Quartet (1948); choral works. He publ. a treatise on harmony, *Éléments d'écriture musicale* (Geneva, 1935).

Chajes, Julius, Polish-American pianist and composer; b. Lemberg, Dec. 21, 1910; d. Royal Oak, Mich., Feb. 24, 1985. He studied piano and composition in Vienna. In 1937 he emigrated to the U.S. and became director of music at the Jewish Community Center in Detroit, for which most of his later compositions were written. He wrote several cantatas on biblical subjects, many of which were performed in Vienna.

Chalabala, Zdeněk, noted Czech conductor; b. Uherské Hradiště, April 18, 1899; d. Prague, March 4, 1962. He studied composition with Novák in Prague, then took courses in violin, conducting, and composition at the Brno Cons., where his principal teachers were Janáček and Neumann. He was conductor of the Slovak Phil. in Brno (1924–25), the National Theater in Brno (1925–29), where he served as music director (1929–36), and the Prague National Theater (1936–45), and chief conductor of the Ostrava Opera (1945–49), the Brno National Theater (1949–52), and the Slovak National Theater in Bratislava (1952–53). In 1953 he returned to the Prague National Theater as chief conductor, a post he held with distinction until his death.

Chaliapin, Feodor (Ivanovich), celebrated Russian bass; b. near Kazan, Feb. 13, 1873; d. Paris, April 12, 1938. He was born into a poverty-ridden peasant family, and thus was compelled to work in menial jobs from an early age and had little opportunity for formal schooling. While still a youth, he began to travel with various opera and operetta companies as a chorister and eventually appeared in stage roles. In 1890 he made his formal operatic debut as the Stolnik in *Halka* with the Semyonov-Smarsky company in Ufa. During his travels, he was accompanied by the writer Maxim Gorky, who also sang in a chorus; together they made their way through the Russian provinces, often walking the railroad tracks when they could not afford the fare. Chaliapin's wanderings took him to Tiflis, where his extraordinary vocal gifts deeply impressed the tenor and vocal pedagogue Dimitri Usatov (1847–1913), who taught him free of charge in 1892–93. After appearances in Tiflis in 1893–94, Chaliapin went to St. Petersburg and sang with Panayev's company in 1894. He then was a member of the St. Petersburg Imperial Opera from 1894 to 1896. He subsequently went to Moscow, where he sang with Mamontov's company (1896–99), producing a great impression with his portrayals of Boris Godunov, Ivan Susanin, Varlaam, Dosifey, Ivan the Terrible, Holofernes in Serov's *Judith*, the Viking Guest in *Sadko*, and the Miller in Dargomyzhsky's *Rusalka*. On Dec. 7, 1898, he created the role of Salieri in Rimsky-Korsakov's *Mozart and Salieri* with Mamontov's company. During this time, Chaliapin also acquired fame as a concert singer. In 1899 he joined Moscow's Bolshoi Theater, where he served as its principal bass until 1914. His first appearance outside his homeland was at Milan's La Scala in 1901 when he sang Boito's Mefistofele. He returned to La Scala in 1904, 1908, 1912, 1929–30, and 1933. From 1905 to 1937 he made frequent appearances in Monte Carlo, where he created the title role in Massenet's *Don Quichotte* on Feb. 19, 1910. On July 25, 1905, he made his London debut at a private concert, and returned there to sing in the Russian seasons at Drury Lane in 1913 and 1914. He made his Metropolitan Opera debut in N.Y. as Mefistofele on Nov. 20, 1907. However, his dramatic characterizations failed to evoke sympathetic response from N.Y. audiences and critics, so he went to Paris to sing in Diaghilev's Russian seasons in 1908, 1910, and 1913. After the Russian Revolution, he became soloist and artistic director of the Petrograd Opera in 1918. He also was made a People's Artist by the Soviet government, but he soon became estranged by the course of events in his homeland and in 1921 settled in Paris. On Dec. 9, 1921, he made a triumphant return to the Metropolitan Opera with his compelling portrayal of Boris Godunov, and thereafter sang there with notable acclaim until 1929. From 1922 to 1924 he also sang with the Chicago Opera. In 1926 and in 1928–29 he appeared at London's Covent Garden, and in 1931 he returned to London to sing at the Lyceum Theatre. On March 3, 1935, he gave his farewell concert performance in N.Y.; his operatic farewell followed in Monte Carlo in 1937 when he once again sang Boris Godunov. Chaliapin made many recordings and appeared in film versions of *Tsar Ivan the Terrible* (1915) and *Don Quixote* (1933). He wrote *Stranitsiiz moyey zhizni: Avtobiografiya* (Leningrad, 1926; Eng. tr., 1927, as *Pages from My Life*) and *Maska i dusha: Moi sorok let na teatrakh* (Paris, 1932; Eng. tr., 1932, as *Man and Mask*). Chaliapin was one of the foremost singing actors ever to grace the operatic stage. He dominated every scene in which he appeared as much by his remarkable dramatic gifts as by his superlative vocal prowess. Even in his last years, when this prowess declined, he never failed to move audiences by the sheer intensity of his performances.

BIBL.: M. Yankovsky, *C.* (Leningrad, 1972); V. Borovsky, *C.: A Critical Biography* (N.Y., 1988).

Challender, Stuart, Australian conductor; b. Hobart, Tasmania, Feb. 19, 1947; d. Sydney, Dec. 13, 1991. After training at the Univ. of Melbourne, he served as music director of the Victorian Opera Co. in Melbourne, and of the Melbourne Youth Orch. He then pursued studies in Hamburg, with Ferrera in Siena, and with Kelterborn and Celibidache in Zürich. He served as assistant conductor of the operas in Nuremberg and Zürich (1970–74), as a conductor at the Lucerne Opera (1974–76), and as resident conductor of the Basel Opera (1976–80). From 1980 to 1986 he was resident conductor of the Australian Opera in Sydney, and also artistic director of the contemporary music ensemble, the Seymour Group (1981–83). In 1985 he made his U.S. debut conducting *Eugene Onegin* at the San Diego Opera. In 1986 he became principal guest conductor of the Sydney Sym. Orch., and in 1987 its chief conductor. In 1987 he made his English debut with the Royal Phil. of London. In 1988 he made a successful tour of the U.S. with the Sydney Sym. Orch. After contracting AIDS, he continued to pursue his career and returned to London in 1991 to conduct *Rusalka* at the English National Opera. Shortly before his death, he was named an Officer of the Order of Australia.

Chaminade, Cécile (Louise Stéphanie), French composer and pianist; b. Paris, Aug. 8, 1857; d. Monte Carlo, April 13, 1944. She was a pupil of Lecouppey, Savard, and Marsick; later studied composition with Godard. She became successful as a concert pianist; wrote a great number of agreeable piano pieces, in the salon style, which acquired enormous popularity in France, England, and America. She made her American debut playing the piano part of her *Concertstück* with the Philadelphia Orch. (Nov. 7, 1908); also wrote a lyric sym., *Les Amazones* (Antwerp, April 18, 1888); 2 orch. suites; 2 piano trios; more than 200 piano pieces in a Romantic style.

BIBL.: M. Citron, *C. C.: A Bio-Bibliography* (Westport, Conn., 1988).

Chamlee, Mario (real name, **Archer Cholmondeley**), American tenor; b. Los Angeles, May 29, 1892; d. there, Nov. 13, 1966. He studied with Achille Alberti in Los Angeles, where he made his operatic debut as Edgardo in 1916. After singing with Scotti's company, he made his Metropolitan Opera debut in N.Y. as Cavaradossi on Nov. 22, 1920, remaining on its roster until 1928. Following engagements in Europe, he was again on the Metropolitan's roster (1932–34; 1935–39). Among his prominent roles were Pinkerton, Count Almaviva, Boito's Faust, Turiddu, Alfredo, and Hageman's Caponsacchi, which he created on Feb. 4, 1937. In later years he was primarily active as a voice teacher.

Champagne (actually, **Desparois dit Champagne**), **Claude (Adonaï)**, Canadian composer; b. Montreal, May 27, 1891; d. there, Dec. 21, 1965. He studied violin, piano, and composition in Montreal; then went to Paris, where he took courses in composition with Gédalge, Koechlin, and Laparra (1921–28). He then taught at McGill Univ. in Montreal (1932–41). From 1942 to 1962 he served as assistant director of the Conservatoire de Musique du Québec à Montreal. In his music, he followed the modern French tradition.

WORKS: *Hercule et Omphale*, symphonic poem (1918; Paris, March 31, 1926); *Prélude et Filigrane* for Piano (1918); *Suite canadienne* for Chorus and Orch. (Paris, Oct. 20, 1928); *Habanera* for Violin and Piano (1929); *Danse villageoise* for Violin and Piano (1929; also orchestrated); *Quadrilha brasileira* for Piano (1942); *Images du Canada français* for Chorus and Orch. (1943; Montreal, March 9, 1947); *Evocation* for Small Orch. (1943); *Gaspesia* for Orch. (1944; rev. as *Symphonie gaspesienne*, 1945); Piano Concerto (1948; Montreal, May 30, 1950); String Quartet (1951); *Paysanna* for Small Orch. (1953); *Suite miniature* for Flute, Cello, and Harpsichord (1958; rev. as *Concertino grosso* for String Orch., 1963); *Altitude* for Chorus, Orch., and Ondes Martenot (1959; Toronto, April 22, 1960); organ pieces; songs.

Chance, Michael, English countertenor; b. Penn, Buckinghamshire, March 7, 1955. He was educated as a choral scholar at King's College, Cambridge. He first made a name for himself as a concert artist via appearances with British ensembles, mainly as an exponent of early music. In 1983 he made his operatic debut at the Buxton Festival as Cavalli's Apollo. His European operatic debut followed in 1985 in Lyons as Handel's Andronicus; subsequently sang opera in various European music centers, appearing in both early and modern roles. His engagements as a concert artist took him all over Europe and North America, and were greeted with critical accolades for his naturally cultivated vocal gifts.

Chang, Sarah, gifted American violinist; b. Philadelphia, Dec. 10, 1980. She was born to Korean parents who saw to it that she received training in violin from the age of 4; at 5, she began to perform in public in Philadelphia. In 1987 she received the Starling Scholarship at the Juilliard School in N.Y., where she studied with Dorothy DeLay and Hyo Kang. She soon came to the attention of Zubin Mehta, who was so taken by her extraordinary musicianship that he invited her to make her N.Y. Phil debut under his direction in 1988 as soloist in Paganini's 1st Violin Concerto. In 1991 she was a soloist with Muti and the Philadelphia Orch. at its 90th anniversary gala concert. In 1992 she became the youngest recipient of the "Concert for Planet Earth" at the Rio de Janeiro Earth Summit. By the time she was 15, she had appeared as a soloist with many of the most prestigious orchs. of the world, among them the Chicago Sym. Orch., the Los Angeles Phil., the Pittsburgh Sym. Orch., the San Francisco Sym., the London Sym. Orch., the Gewandhaus Orch. of Leipzig, and the Berlin Phil. She also performed at many principal festivals. On May 24, 1995, she was soloist in the Mendelssohn Violin Concerto with Kurt Masur and the N.Y. Phil., which appearance was telecast live to the nation by PBS.

Chanler, Theodore Ward, American composer; b. Newport, R.I., April 29, 1902; d. Boston, July 27, 1961. He studied in Boston with Hans Ebell (piano) and with Arthur Shepherd (composition); then at the Cleveland Inst. of Music with Ernest Bloch; later took courses at the Univ. of Oxford (1923–25); also studied with Boulanger in Paris. He returned to America in 1933 and wrote music criticism; taught at the Peabody Cons. of Music in Baltimore (1945–47) and then at the Longy School in Cambridge, Mass. In 1944 he held a Guggenheim fellowship. His music, mostly in smaller forms, is distinguished by a lyrical quality; his songs are particularly expressive; he employed the modern idiom of polytonal texture without overloading the harmonic possibilities; the melody is free, but usually within tonal bounds.

WORKS: DRAMATIC: *The Pot of Fat*, chamber opera (Cambridge, Mass., May 8, 1955); *Pas de Trois*, ballet (1942). **CHAMBER:** Violin Sonata (1927); violin pieces; piano music, including *5 Short Colloquies* (1936), *Toccata* (1939), *The Second Joyful Mystery* for 2 Pianos (1942), and *A Child in the House* (1949); organ pieces. **VOCAL:** Mass for 2 Women's Voices and Organ (1930) and other choral works; about 50 songs.

BIBL.: E. Nordgren, *An Analytical Study of the Songs of T. C. (1902–1961)* (diss., N.Y. Univ., 1980).

Chantavoine, Jean (François Henri), French writer on music; b. Paris, May 17, 1877; d. Mussy-sur-Seine, July 16, 1952. He studied music history with Friedlaender in Berlin (1898, 1901–02). He was music critic of *Revue Hebdomadaire* (1903–20) and *Excelsior* (1911–21); in 1923 he was appointed General Secretary of the Paris Cons., a post he held until 1937. He ed. the biographical series Les Maîtres de la Musique, to which he contributed the monographs on Beethoven (1906) and Liszt (1910; 6th ed., 1950); publ. *Musiciens et poètes* (1912); *De Couperin à Debussy* (1921); *Les Symphonies de Beethoven* (1932); *Petit guide de l'auditeur de musique* (1947); *Mozart dans Mozart* (1948).

Chapin, Schuyler G(arrison), American music administrator; b. N.Y., Feb. 13, 1923. He received training from Boulanger at the Longy School of Music in Cambridge, Mass. (1940–41). After working for NBC (1941–51), Tex and Jinx McCary Enterprises (1951–53), and Columbia Artists Management (1953–59), he was head of the Masterworks Division of Columbia Records (1959–63); he later was associated with N.Y.'s Lincoln Center for the Performing Arts, and, from 1969 to 1971, was executive producer for Amberson Enterprises. He then was general manager of N.Y.'s Metropolitan Opera (1972–75). From 1976 to 1987 he served as dean of Columbia Univ.'s School of the Arts. He was vice-president of worldwide concert and artist activities for Steinway and Sons (1990–92). In 1994 he became chairman of cultural affairs for the city of N.Y. He publ. his memoirs as *Musical Chairs: A Life in the Arts* (1977). He also publ. *Leonard Bernstein: Notes From a Friend* (1992).

Chapuis, Michel, distinguished French organist and pedagogue; b. Dole, Jan. 15, 1930. After initial training in Dole, he studied in Paris with René Mahlherbe and Édouard Souberbielle at the École César Franck, and then with Dupré at the Cons. (premiers prix in organ and improvisation, 1951). He was active as a church organist in Paris and also toured as a concert artist; from 1956 to 1979 he was a prof. at the Strasbourg Cons., then at the Besançon Cons. (1979–86), and at the Paris Cons. (from 1986). As a performer, he is especially known as an interpreter of the music of the French and German Baroque masters. He has been in the forefront in France in his efforts to restore and build organs.

Charles, Christophe G(illes), multitalented French sound sculptor and installation artist; b. Marseilles, Jan. 20, 1964. He was born into an intellectual family: his grandfather was a magistrate and specialist of Islamic law (author of the book *Le Japon au rendez-vous de l'Occident*), and both parents are prominent French philosophers, covering, in their specializations, both Occident and Orient. Christophe Charles studied at the Institut National des Langues Orientales (1984–89; 1989–96); also with Henning Christiansen at the Hamburg Hochschule für Bildende Künste (1985–86), the Nagoya Univ. Language Center (1987–88), the Nihon Univ. Faculty of Arts in Tokyo, and with Yamaguchi Katsuhiro and others at the Tsukuba Univ. Faculty of Arts (1991–96; Ph.D., 1996, with a diss. on experimental cinema and video in Japan). His works fall into 3 overlapping categories determined by both relations of sounds to space and by possibilities for participation: 1: "audiographics," in which recycled sounds progress without visual counterpart; 2: "sound and light installations," interactive, multimedia works, in 2- or 3-dimensions; and 3: "undirected concerts," wherein sound is activated by movement in space. In all cases, there is strong reliance upon computer technology; original materials are mostly sampled, coupled with (real and unintended) environmental sounds. While Charles's works are nonhierarchical with respect to materials and open-ended with respect to form, both structure and development are often highly evident. Overall, his aesthetic explores the limits of intention (desire) and nonintention (chance), inviting participants to become aware of other layers of perception (silence).

WORKS: *Kalkutta Kreis*, soundscapes from Calcutta and Hamburg, with piano chords (Marseilles, 1984); *Sound Wall*, feedback (Hamburg, 1986); *Der Hirt auf dem Felsen*, soundscapes from Hamburg, Marseilles, and Paris (Marseilles, 1986); *Silo*, with bells, grain silo, and wind (Hamburg, 1986); *Unter den Linden*, with rain, bells, birds, metal wire, and flute (1987; Nagoya, 1988); *Fanbai*, soundscapes of Japan and Korea, with Buddhist chants, voices, bells, and gongs (Tokyo, 1988); *From Circle From Sound*, soundscapes from Japan, Korea, and India, with Buddhist chants, voices, bells, stones, and bamboo (Nagoya, 1988); *The Relation between Matter and Mind*, with Buddhist chants, insects, and (activating) footsteps on stones (Berlin, 1989); *Touch for Sound*, with (activating) brushes on canvas (1988; Eindhoven, 1990); *Next Point/Joyamai*, soundscapes from Calcutta and Puri, with trumpet, rain, ocean waves, stones, flutes, bamboo, electric guitar, and bells (Göttingen, 1991); *World Time*, installation involving soundscapes from Europe, Asia, Africa, America, and Oceania, with landscape images (Nagoya, 1992); *Next Point/Europe*, soundscape from Calcutta, with rain, Rør, piano, tuba, Buddhist chants, and Sibelius's 4th Sym.'s violin (Nice, 1992); *Next Point/let it hold itself up*, soundscapes from Calcutta and Puri, with trumpet, rain, ocean waves, stones, flutes, metal plates, bamboo, electric guitar, and bells (1991; Nagoya, 1993); *Time Out*, soundscapes from Calcutta and Puri, with trumpet, rain, ocean waves, stones, metal pieces, bamboos, electric guitar, and bells (Kanagawa, 1993); *Kiryû Symphon*, installation involving soundscapes of Kiryû City, with manual and mechanical looms, sounds of Japanese papermaking (Washi), metalworking, pottery, woodcutting, and animal sounds (Kiryû, 1993); *Dog*, soundscapes from Tokyo, Africa, and India, with bells, Kayagum, Yokobue, ocean waves, violins, synthesized sounds, percussion, and animal sounds (Seoul, 1994); *Deposition Yokohama*, soundscapes of Yokohama and Hamburg, with *Time Out*, *Dog*, and voices of Demetrio Stratos and Joseph Beuys (Stuttgart, 1994; also as an installation, Yokohama, 1995); *Undirections*, installation involving soundscapes from Africa and India, with percussion, animal sounds, hammers, stones, and Rør (Kyoto, 1995).

Charles, Ernest, American composer; b. Minneapolis, Nov. 21, 1895; d. Beverly Hills, April 16, 1984. He began his career as a singer in Broadway revues and in vaudeville; also wrote songs in an appetizing semi-classical genre, suitable for recitals. His first success came in 1932 when John Charles Thomas sang his song *Clouds* in a N.Y. recital. Encouraged, Charles subsequently composed about 50 solo songs, many of which made the top listing among recitalists: *Let My Song Fill Your Heart; My Lady Walks in Loneliness; When I Have Sung My Songs; If You Only Knew; Sweet Song of Long Ago; Oh, Lovely World.*

BIBL.: L. Wolz, "The Songs of E. C.," *NATS Bulletin* (March/April 1983).

Charpentier, Gustave, famous French composer; b. Dieuze, Lorraine, June 25, 1860; d. Paris, Feb. 18, 1956. He studied at the Paris Cons. (1881–87), where he was a pupil of Massart (violin), Pessard (harmony), and Massenet (composition). He received the Grand Prix de Rome in 1887 with his cantata *Didon.* He evinced great interest in the social problems of the working classes, and in 1900 formed the society L'OEuvre de Mimi Pinson, devoted to the welfare of the poor, which he reorganized during World War I as an auxiliary Red Cross society. His fame is owed to one amazingly successful opera, *Louise,* a "roman musical" to his own libretto (his mistress at the time was also named Louise, and like the heroine of his opera, was employed in a dressmaking shop), which was premiered at the Opéra-Comique in Paris on Feb. 2, 1900. The score is written in the spirit of naturalism and includes such realistic touches as the street cries of Paris vendors. Its success was immediate, and it entered the repertoire of opera houses all over the world. Encouraged, Charpentier wrote a sequel under the title *Julien* (Paris, June 4, 1913), but it failed to arouse comparable interest.

BIBL.: A. Homonet, *Louise* (Paris, 1922); M. Delmas, *G. C. et le lyrisme français* (Paris, 1931); K. Hoover, "G. C.," *Musical Quarterly* (July 1939).

Charpentier, Jacques, French composer and organist; b. Paris, Oct. 18, 1933. He studied piano with Maria Cerati-Boutillier; then lived in Calcutta (1953–54), where he made a study of Indian music; prepared a valuable thesis, *Introduction à l'étude de la musique de l'Inde.* Upon his return to Paris, he studied composition with Aubin and analysis with Messiaen at the Cons. In 1954 he was appointed organist at the church of St.-Benoit-d'Issy; in 1966 he was named chief inspector of music of the French Ministry of Cultural Affairs, and in 1975 Inspector General of the Secretariat of State for Culture. In 1974 he was named official organist of the Church of St. Nicolas du Chardonnet in Paris. From 1979 to 1981 he was director of music, lyric art, and dance in the French Ministry of Culture. Several of his works are based on Hindu melorhythms.

WORKS: DRAMATIC: *La Femme et son ombre,* ballet (1967); *Béatrice de Planisoles,* opera (Aix en Provence, July 23, 1971). **ORCH.:** Violin Concerto (1953); 7 syms.: No. 1, *Symphonie breve,* for Strings (1958), No. 2, *Sinfonia sacra,* for Strings (1965), No. 3, *Shiva Nataraja* (Shiva—the King of the Dance; 1968; Paris, March 2, 1969), No. 4, *Brasil,* in homage to Villa-Lobos (1973), No. 5, *Et l'imaginaire se mit à danser* (1977), No. 6 for Orch. and Organ (1979), and No. 7, *Acropolis* (1985); Ondes Martenot Concerto (1959); *Alla francese,* concertino for Ondes Martenot, Strings, and Percussion (1959–60); Octuple Concerto for 8 Winds and Strings (1963); *Prélude pour la Genèse* for Strings (1967); *Récitatif* for Violin and Orch. (1968); 10 concertos: No. 1 for Organ and Strings (1969), No. 2 for Guitar and Strings (1970), No. 3 for Harpsichord and Strings (1971), No. 4 for Piano and Strings (1971), No. 5 for Saxophone and Strings (1975), No. 6 for Oboe and Strings (1975), No. 7 for Trumpet and Strings (1975), No. 8 for Horn and Strings (1976), No. 9 for Cello and Strings (1976), and No. 10 for Clarinet and Strings (1983); Trumpet Concerto (1976). **CHAMBER:** 2 string quartets (1955, 1956); Piano Quintet (1955); Ondes Martenot Quartet (1958); *Suite karnatique* for Ondes Martenot (1958); *Prelude and Allegro* for Bass Saxophone and Piano (1959); *Lalita* for Ondes Martenot and Percussion (1961); *Pour Diane* for Horn and Piano (1962); *Pour Syrinx* for Flute and Piano (1962); *Mouvement* for Flute, Cello, and Harp (1965); *Gavambodi 2* for Saxophone and Piano (1966); *Pour le Kama Soutra* for Percussion Ensemble (1969); *Pour une Apsara* for 2 Harps (1970); *Esquisses* for Flute and Piano (1972); *Tu dors mais mon coeur veille* for Violin (1974); *Et le jour vint . . .* for 13 Instruments (1977); *Vitrail pour un temps de guerre* for Winds (1982). **KEYBOARD: PIANO:** *Toccata* (1954); *Études karnatiques* (4 cycles, 1957–61). **ORGAN:** *Messe* (1964); *Répons* (1968). **VOCAL:** *4 Psaumes de Toukaram* for Soprano and Orch. (1957); *Tantum ergo* for 4 Voices and Orch. (1962); *La Croisade des pastoureaux,* oratorio (1964); *Musique pour un Zodiaque,* oratorio (1971); *La Genèse,* oratorio (1973); *Une Voix pour une autre* for 2 Women's Voices, Flute, Clarinet, and Percussion (1974); *Te Deum* (1978); *Prélude pour une nuit étoilée* for Chorus and Orch. (1986); *Le Miroir de Marie-Madeleine* for Soprano, Women's Voices, and Orch. (1988).

Charpentier, Raymond (Louis Marie), French composer and music critic; b. Chartres, Aug. 14, 1880; d. Paris, Dec. 27, 1960. He studied composition with Gédalge. From 1921 to 1943 he was music director of the Comedie Française in Paris; then was active on the French radio (1944–50). He wrote some 20 scores of incidental music for plays produced at the Comedie Française as well as a comic opera, *Gerard et Isabelle* (Paris, 1912); several symphonic overtures; 2 string quartets; Wind Quartet; Viola Sonata; piano pieces; songs.

Charteris, Richard, Australian musicologist; b. Chatham Islands, New Zealand, June 24, 1948. He studied at Victoria Univ. in Wellington (B.A., 1970), the Univ. of Canterbury (M.A., 1972), and the Univ. of London (Ph.D., 1976, with the diss. *John Coprario (Cooper) c. 1575–1626: A Study and Complete Critical Edition of His Instrumental Music).* He was Rothmans Research Fellow in the music dept. at the Univ. of Sydney (1976–78) and served as chief investigator of the Australian Research Grants Scheme (1981–86) and its successor, the Australian Research Council (from 1986). His scholarly interests include English and Italian music of the 16th and 17th centuries.

WRITINGS: *John Coprario: A Thematic Catalogue of His Music with a Biographical Introduction* (N.Y., 1977); *A Catalogue of the Printed Books on Music, Printed Music and Music Manuscripts in Archbishop Marsh's Library, Dublin* (Kilkenny, 1982); *Alfonso Ferrabosco the Elder (1543–1588): A Thematic Catalogue of His Music with a Biographical Calendar* (N.Y., 1984); ed., *Altro Polo: Essays on Italian Music in the Cinquecento* (Sydney, 1990).

Chasalow, Eric (David), American composer; b. Buffalo, May 25, 1955. He studied at Bates College (B.A., 1977); also had training in composition from W.T. McKinley at the New England Cons. of Music in Boston (1975–76); subsequently studied composition with Davidovsky and Beeson and flute with Sollberger at Columbia Univ. (M.A., 1979; D.M.A., 1985). In 1985 he became a teacher of composition at Brandeis Univ., where he also directed its Electro-Acoustic Music Studio. He was executive director of the Guild of Composers (1980–85) and the Music Alliance (1988–90) in N.Y. He held an NEA composer's fellowship (1983), a Guggenhiem fellowship (1986–87), and a Fromm Foundation commission (1993).

WORKS: ORCH.: *Medusa Rising* (1977); *At the Still Point* (1979); *Leaping to Conclusions* for Chamber Orch. (1987). **CHAMBER:** *Advent of the Wyvern* for Bassoon (1975); *The Inscriptions in the Air* for Brass Octet (1976); *Clones I–V* for Flute, Cello, and Piano (1976–77); *Chambers* for 4 Flutes (1978); *Anti-Chambers* for Flute (1979); *Versus and Fragments* for Horn, Percussion, and Electronic Sounds (1979); *Falling Forward* for Flute (1980); *2 From 3* for Violin, Cello, and Piano (1980); *Returning to the Point* for Flute, Violin, Viola and Cello (1981); *A Circumstance of Dancing* for Flute and 11 Instruments (1982–84); *Hanging in the Balance* for Cello and Electronic Sounds (1983); *Over the Edge* for Flute and Electronic Sounds (1986); *Fast Forward* for Percussion and Electronic Sounds (1988); String Quartet (1989–90); *Winding Up* for Horn (1990); *In the Works* for Flute, Clarinet, Violin, Cello, Percussion, and Piano (1993). **PIANO:** *Groundwork* (1986); *Little Word* (1991). **VOCAL:** *Words* for Chorus (1980); *The Furies* for Soprano and Electronic Sounds (1984); songs. **TAPE:** *The Glass*

Bead Game (1975); *Anthrax* (1976); *Between 2* (1977); *This Way Out* (1991); *The Fury of Rainstorms* (1992).

Chase, Gilbert, eminent American musicologist; b. Havana (of American parents), Sept. 4, 1906; d. Chapel Hill, N.C., Feb. 22, 1992. He studied at Columbia Univ. and at the Univ. of North Carolina at Chapel Hill. From 1929 to 1935 he lived in Paris and was active as a music correspondent for British and American music periodicals. In 1935 he returned to the U.S.; during 1940–43, he was consultant on Spanish and Latin American music at the Library of Congress in Washington, D.C.; simultaneously was active in an advisory capacity to musical radio programs. From 1951 to 1953 he was cultural attaché at the American Embassy in Lima, and from 1953 to 1955 served in the same capacity in Buenos Aires. He then was director of the School of Music at the Univ. of Okla. (1955–57); from 1958 to 1960 he was cultural attaché in Belgium; from 1960 to 1966 he was a prof. of music and director of Latin American studies at Tulane Univ. in New Orleans. From 1961 to 1969 he was director of the Inter-American Inst. for Musical Research, serving as ed. of its yearbook (1964–76). In 1963 he organized the 1st Inter-American Conference on Musicology in Washington, D.C. In 1955 the Univ. of Miami bestowed upon him the title of Honorary Doctor of Letters. He also taught at the State Univ. of N.Y. in Buffalo (1973–74) and at the Univ. of Texas in Austin from 1975 to 1979.

WRITINGS: *The Music of Spain* (N.Y., 1941; 2nd ed., 1959; in Spanish, Buenos Aires, 1943); *America's Music: From the Pilgrims to the Present* (N.Y., 1955; 3rd ed., rev., 1983; also tr. into German, French, Portuguese, and Spanish); *Introducción a la musica americana contemporánea* (Buenos Aires, 1958); *A Guide to the Music of Latin America* (Washington, D.C., 1962); *The American Composer Speaks: A Historical Anthology, 1770 to 1965* (Baton Rouge, 1966); *Two Lectures in the Form of a Pair: 1, Music, Culture and History; 2, Structuralism and Music* (Brooklyn, 1973); *Roger Reynolds: Profile of a Composer* (N.Y., 1982).

Chasins, Abram, multitalented American pianist, teacher, writer on music, broadcaster, and composer; b. N.Y., Aug. 17, 1903; d. there, June 21, 1987. He was a student of Hutcheson (piano) and Goldmark (composition) at N.Y.'s Juilliard School of Music; he also was a protégé of Hofmann, and later studied analysis with Tovey in London (1931). From 1926 to 1936 he taught at the Curtis Inst. of Music in Philadelphia, and later privately. He also was active as a pianist and composer. His most popular work for piano was the *3 Chinese Pieces* (1928; orchestrated 1929), which became a favorite encore piece with piano virtuosos. Chasins was soloist in the first performances of his 2 piano concertos (Philadelphia, Jan. 18, 1929 and March 3, 1933). From 1941 to 1965 he presented classical music broadcasts on WQXR in N.Y. In 1949 he married his pupil **Constance Keene**, with whom he subsequently appeared in duo recitals. In 1972 he became musician-in-residence at the Univ. of Southern Calif. in Los Angeles, where he also was director of its radio station, KUSC (1972–77).

WRITINGS (all publ. in N.Y.): *Speaking of Pianists* (1957; 3rd ed., rev., 1981); *The Van Cliburn Legend* (1959); *The Appreciation of Music* (1966); *Music at the Crossroads* (1972); *Leopold Stokowski: A Profile* (1979).

Chatman, Stephen (George), American composer; b. Faribault, Minn., Feb. 28, 1950. He was a pupil of Walter Aschaffenburg and Joseph Wood at the Oberlin Cons. (B.M., 1972) and of Finney, Bassett, Bolcom, and Kurtz at the Univ. of Mich. in Ann Arbor (M.M., 1973). After working with Stockhausen at the Cologne Hochschule für Musik on a Fulbright scholarship (1974), he completed his education at the Univ. of Mich. in Ann Arbor (D.M.A., 1977). In 1976 he joined the faculty of the Univ. of British Columbia in Vancouver, where he subsequently was a prof. from 1986.

WORKS: ORCH.: *2 Followers of Lien* (1973); *Occasions* (1975–77); *Grouse Mountain Lullaby* (1978); *They All Replied* (1978); *Crimson Dream* (1982–83); *Mirage* (1987). **CHAMBER:** *Music* for Timpani, Alto Flute, Trombone, and Piano (1971); *O lo velo* for Alto Saxophone and Percussion (1973); *On the Contrary* for Clarinet and 9 Players (1973–74); *Quiet Exchange* for Alto Saxophone or Clarinet and Percussion (1976); *Northern Drones* for Viola and Percussion (1976); *Outer Voices* for 8 Players (1978); *Variations on "Home on the Range"* for String Quartet or Saxophone Quartet (1979); *Nocturne* for Flute, Violin, Viola, and Cello (1980); *Screams and Whimpers* for Saxophone Quartet (1981); *Gossamer Leaves* for Clarinet and Piano (1981); *Fanfare* for 3 Trumpets and 3 Trombones (1982). **VOCAL:** *Whisper, Baby* for Chorus, Piano, and Percussion (1975); *And There Will Be Signs* (1977); *Moonset* for Chorus, 5 Percussion, and Organ (1979); *You Have Ravished My Heart* (1981); *Elizabethan Spring* (1983); songs.

Chaun, František, Czech composer and painter; b. Kaplice, Jan. 26, 1921; d. Prague, Dec. 31, 1981. A pharmacist by profession and a painter by avocation, he studied music privately with Feld and Slavický in Prague (1954–61). Stylistically and ideologically, he modeled his works after those of Stravinsky, with both the parody and classical formality in a curiously synthetic design.

WORKS: ORCH.: *Fantasy* (1960); *Sinfonietta Concertante* for Bassoon, Strings, and Piano (1963); *Kafka Trilogy* (Prague, Nov. 26, 1968); *Ghiribizzo* for Piano and Orch. (1969); *Sinfonietta buffa* (1970); *Hommage à Dubuffet*, double concerto for Violin, Cello, Strings, 2 Oboes, and 2 Horns (1970; Prague, March 4, 1971); *Pět obrázků* (5 Pictures; 1971; Prague, March 24, 1974); *Obrázek* (Little Picture; 1980; Prague, March 27, 1981). **OTHER:** Choral, chamber, and piano pieces.

Chávez (y Ramírez), Carlos (Antonio de Padua), distinguished Mexican composer and conductor; b. Calzada de Tacube, near Mexico City, June 13, 1899; d. Mexico City, Aug. 2, 1978. He studied piano as a child with Pedro Luis Ogazón; then studied harmony with Juan B. Fuentes and Manuel Ponce. He began to compose very early in life; wrote a Sym. at the age of 16; made effective piano arrangements of popular Mexican songs and also wrote many piano pieces of his own. His first important work was a ballet on an Aztec subject, *El fuego nuevo* (1921), commissioned by the Secretariat of Public Education of Mexico. Historical and national Mexican subject matter remained the primary source of inspiration in many of his works, but he rarely resorted to literal quotations from authentic folk melodies; rather, he sublimated and distilled the melorhythmic Mexican elements, resulting in a sui generis style of composition. In 1922–23 he traveled in France, Austria, and Germany, and became acquainted with the modern developments in composition. The influence of this period on his evolution as a composer is reflected in the abstract titles of his piano works, such as *Aspectos*, *Energía*, and *Unidad*. Returning to Mexico, he organized and conducted a series of concerts of new music, giving 1st Mexican performances of works by Stravinsky, Schoenberg, Satie, Milhaud, and Varèse. From 1926 to 1928 he lived in N.Y. In 1928 he organized the Orquesta Sinfónica de Mexico, of which he remained the principal conductor until 1949. Works of modern music occupied an important part in the program of this orch., including 82 1st performances of works by Mexican composers, many of them commissioned by Chávez; Silvestre Revueltas was among those encouraged by Chávez to compose. During his tenure as conductor, Chávez engaged a number of famous foreign musicians as guest conductors, as well as numerous soloists. In 1948 the orch. was renamed the Orquesta Sinfónica Nacional; it remains a permanent institution. Chávez served as director of the Conservatorio Nacional de Música from 1928 to 1933 and again in 1934; he was general director of the Instituto Nacional de Bellas Artes from 1946 to 1952. Beginning in 1936 Chávez conducted a great number of concerts with major American orchs., and also conducted concerts in Europe and South America. Culturally, he maintained a close connection with progressive artists and authors of Mexico, particularly the painter Diego Rivera; his *Sinfonía proletaria* for Chorus and Orch. reflects his political commitment. In 1958–59 he was the Charles Eliot Norton Prof. of Poetry at Harvard Univ.; these lectures were publ. as *Musical Thought* (Cambridge, Mass., 1960); Chávez also publ. a book of essays, *Toward a New Music* (N.Y., 1937).

WORKS: DRAMATIC: OPERA: *Panfilo and Lauretta* (1953; in Eng., N.Y., May 9, 1957; rev. Spanish version as *El Amor propiciado*, Mexico City, Oct. 28, 1959; later retitled *The Visitors*). **BALLETS:** *El fuego nuevo* (1921; Mexico City, Nov. 4, 1928); *Los cuatro soles* (1925; Mexico City, July 22, 1930); *Caballos de Vapor* (1926; 1st perf. in Eng. as *HP*, i.e., *Horsepower*, Philadelphia, March 31, 1932); *Antígona* (Mexico City, Sept. 20, 1940; 1st perf. as incidental music for Sophocles' *Antigone*, 1932); *La hija de Cólquide* (1943; 1st perf. as accompaniment to the Martha Graham Dance Company as *Dark Meadow*, N.Y., Jan. 23, 1946); *Pirámide* (1968). **ORCH.:** *Sinfonía* (1915); *Cantos de Méjico* for Mexican Orch. (1933); 7 syms.: No. 1, *Sinfonía de Antígona*, derived from his incidental music for *Antigone* (Mexico City, Dec. 15, 1933), No. 2, *Sinfonía India* (1935; broadcast, N.Y., Jan. 23, 1936), No. 3 (1951; Caracas, Dec. 11, 1954), No. 4, *Sinfonía romántica* (1952; Louisville, Feb. 11, 1953), No. 5 for Strings (Los Angeles, Dec. 1, 1953), No. 6 (1961; N.Y., May 7, 1964), and No. 7 (1960; unfinished); *Obertura republicana* (Mexico City, Oct. 18, 1935); Concerto for 4 Horns (Washington, D.C., April 11, 1937; rev. 1964); Piano Concerto (1938–40; N.Y. Phil., Jan. 1, 1942); *Cuatro nocturnos* for Soprano, Contralto, and Orch. (1939); Toccata (1947); Violin Concerto (1948; Mexico City, Feb. 29, 1952); *Soli No. 3* for Bassoon, Trumpet, Viola, Timpani, and Orch. (Baden-Baden, Nov. 24, 1965); *Resonancias* (Mexico City, Sept. 18, 1964); *Elatio* (Mexico City, July 15, 1967); *Discovery* (Aptos, Calif., Aug. 24, 1969); *Clio*, symphonic ode (Houston, March 23, 1970); *Initium* (1972; Akron, Ohio, Oct. 9, 1973); *Mañanas Mexicanas* (1974; orig. for Piano, 1967); *Sonante* for Strings (1974); Trombone Concerto (1975–76; Washington, D.C., May 9, 1978). **CHAMBER:** Piano and String Sextet (1919); 3 string quartets (1921, 1932, 1944); *3 Pieces* for Guitar (1923); Violin Sonatina (1924); Cello Sonatina (1924); *Energía* for 9 Instruments (1925; Paris, June 11, 1931); Sonata for 4 Horns (1929); 3 of 4 pieces under the generic title *Soli* (No. 1 for Oboe, Clarinet, Trumpet, and Bassoon, 1933; No. 2 for Wind Quintet, 1961; No. 4 for Brass Trio, 1966); *3 Espirales* for Violin and Piano (1934); *Xochipilli Macuilxochitl* for 4 Wind Instruments and 6 Percussionists (N.Y., May 16, 1940); *Toccata* for 6 Percussionists (1942; Mexico City, Oct. 31, 1947); 2 of 3 instrumental pieces, under the generic title *Invention* (No. 2 for String Trio, 1965; No. 3 for Harp, 1967), introducing an inductive method of thematic illation in which each musical phrase is the logical consequent of the one immediately preceding it; *Upingos* for Oboe (1957); *Fuga HAG,C* for Violin, Viola, Cello, and Double Bass (1964); *Tambuco* for 6 Percussionists (1964); *Variations* for Violin and Piano (1969). **PIANO:** 6 sonatas (*Sonata fantasía*, 1917; 1919; 1928; 1941; 1960; 1961); *Berceuse* (1918); *7 Madrigals* (1921–22); *Polígonos* (1923); *Aspectos I* and *II* (1923); Sonatina (1924); *Blues* (1928); *Fox* (1928); *Paisaje* (1930); *Unidad* (1930); *10 Preludes* (1937); *Fugas* (1942); *4 Études* (1949); *Left Hand Inversions of 5 Chopin Études* (1950); *Invention* No. 1 (1958); *Estudio a Rubinstein*, in minor seconds (1974); *5 caprichos* (1975–76). **VOCAL: CHORAL:** *Tierra mojada* for Chorus, Oboe, and English Horn (Mexico City, Sept. 6, 1932); *El Sol* for Chorus and Orch. (Mexico City, July 17, 1934); *Sinfonía proletaria (Llamadas)* for Chorus and Orch. (Mexico City, Sept. 29, 1934); *La paloma azul* for Chorus and Chamber Orch. (1940); *Prometheus Bound*, cantata (1956; Aptos, Calif., Aug. 27, 1972). **VOICE AND ORCH.:** *Cuatro nocturnos* for Soprano, Contralto, and Orch. (1939). **VOICE AND PIANO:** *3 exágonos* (1923); *Inutil epigrama* (1923); *Otros 3 exágonos* (1924); *3 poemas* (1938); *La casada infiel* (1941).

BIBL.: H. Weinstock, "C. C.," *Musical Quarterly* (Oct. 1936); R. Morillo, *C. C., vida y obra* (Buenos Aires, 1960); R. Halffter, compiler, *C. C., Catalogo completo de sus obras* (Mexico City, 1971); R. Parker, *C. C., Mexico's Modern-Orpheus* (Boston, 1983); idem, "Copland and C.: Brothers-in-Arms," *American Music* (Winter 1987); G. Carmona, ed., *Epistolario selecto de C. C.* (Mexico City, 1989); R. Parker, "C. C.'s *Opus Ultimum*: The Unfinished Cello Concerto," *American Music* (Winter 1993).

Chaynes, Charles, French composer and broadcasting administrator; b. Toulouse, July 11, 1925. He first studied violin at the Toulouse Cons., and then entered the Paris Cons., where he took courses in violin with Gabriel Bouillon, in chamber music with Joseph Calvet, in composition with Milhaud and Rivier, and in harmony and fugue with N. and J. Gallon (Grand Prix de Rome, 1951, with the cantata *Et l'homme vit se rouvrir les portes*). After composing at the French Academy in Rome (1952–55), he returned to Paris and joined the ORTF as a radio producer in 1956; he then was director of its France-Musique (1965–75) before serving as its chief of the music service (1975–90). As a composer, Chaynes has pursued an independent course in which free atonality is enlivened by infusions of East Asian and African modes of expression.

WORKS: OPERAS: *Erzsebet* (Paris, March 28, 1983); *Noces de sang* (1986); *Jocaste* (1993). **ORCH.:** *Divertissement* for Strings (1949); *Danses symphoniques* (1951); Concerto for Strings (1953); *Ode pour une mort tragique* (1953–54; Vichy, June 25, 1954); Sym. (1955); Concerto for Trumpet and Chamber Orch. (1956); Violin Concerto (1958; ORTF, March 14, 1961); *Deuxième Concerto* (1960; Monte Carlo, Nov. 25, 1962); *Quatre illustrations pour "La Flute de jade"* for Flute and Orch. (Aix-en-Provence, July 23, 1960); Piano Concerto (1961; Paris, Feb. 17, 1966); *Expressions contrastées* (1965; Strasbourg, June 23, 1966); Organ Concerto (1966); *Irradiations* for Violin, Cello, Harpsichord, and Strings (1968; Bordeaux, June 9, 1969); *Transmutations* (1969; Besançon, Sept. 4, 1971); *Lieu de lumière* (1972); *Mazapan* (1973; Paris, June 7, 1974); *Peintures noires* (1974; Paris, April 27, 1975); *Visions concertantes* for Guitar and Strings (Besançon, Sept. 11, 1976); *Les Caractères illisibles* for Chamber Orch. (1978; Paris, Jan. 21, 1980); Clarinet Concerto (Orléans, Dec. 2, 1979); *Visages Myceniens* (1983); *Litanies* (1988); *Via ercolensi*, flute concerto (1991). **CHAMBER:** Violin Sonata (1952); *Serenade* for Wind Quintet (1954); *Lied, Scherzando et Final* for Double Bass and Piano (1957); *Variations sur Tanka* for Flute and Piano (1962); *Trois Études linéaires* for Chamber Group (1963); *Commentaires concertants* for Chamber Group (1964); *Concordances* for Percussion and Piano (1967); String Quartet (1970); *Séquences pour l'Apocalypse* for 6 Instruments (1971–72); *Tarquinia* for Ondes Martenot, Piano, and Percussion (1973); *Valeurs transposées* for Chamber Group (1979); *Lorsque Cecile chantait* for 5 Instruments (1983). **VOCAL:** *Et l'homme vit se rouvrir les portes*, cantata (1951); *Par ces Chemins du coeur*, 6 prayers for Soprano and Orch. or Piano (1953); *Joie aux âmes* for 4 Soloists and 5 Instruments (1962); *Quatres Poèmes de Sappho* for Soprano and String Trio (1968); *Pour un Monde Noir* for Soprano and Orch. (1976–78); *Oginoha* for Soprano, Flute, Celtic Harp, and Percussion (1986).

Cheek, John (Taylor), American bass-baritone; b. Greenville, S.C., Aug. 17, 1948. He received a B.Mus. degree from the North Carolina School of the Arts; then studied in Siena with Gino Bechi at the Accademia Musicale Chigiana, where he received the Diploma of Merit; he subsequently served in the U.S. Army. He made his professional debut in 1975. On June 6, 1977, he made his first appearance with the Metropolitan Opera as Ferrando during the company's visit to the Wolf Trap Farm Park; then made his formal debut with the company in N.Y. as the physician in *Pelléas et Mélisande* on Oct. 11, 1977; he later sang Pimen in *Boris Godunov*, Ferrando in *Il Trovatore*, Wurm in *Luisa Miller*, Klingsor in *Parsifal*, and also Panthée in *Les Troyens* at the opening-night celebration of the Metropolitan's centenary season in 1983–84. In 1987 he won the North Carolina Arts Prize.

Chemin-Petit, Hans (Helmuth), German composer and teacher; b. Potsdam, June 24, 1902; d. Berlin, April 12, 1981. His family was of remote French origin; both his father and grandfather were professional musicians. He studied cello in

Berlin with Hugo Becker and composition with Paul Juon; subsequently was mostly active as a cello teacher; was on the staff of the Berlin Hochschule für Musik and later at the Akademie der Künste; in 1968 he was appointed director of its music dept. As a composer, he followed the median line of neo-Classicism.

WORKS: CHAMBER OPERAS: *Der gefangene Vogel* (1927); *Lady Monika* (1930); *König Nicolo* (1962); *Die Komödiantin* (1968); *Die Rivalinnen* (1970). **ORCH.:** 2 syms. (1932, 1949); Cello Concerto (1932); *Concerto for Orchestra* (1944); Concerto for Organ, Strings, and Kettledrums (1963); *Musik* (1968). **OTHER:** 2 recorder sonatas (1958, 1960); Symphonic Cantata (1967); other cantatas; church music; piano pieces.

BIBL.: A Witte, *H. C.-P.* (Berlin, 1987).

Cherbuliez, Antoine-Élisée, Swiss musicologist; b. Mulhouse, Alsace, Aug. 22, 1888; d. Zürich, Oct. 15, 1964. He studied science at the Univ. of Strasbourg and took private organ lessons with Albert Schweitzer. He studied music with his grandfather Adolphe Koekkert in Geneva, and took courses at the Zürich Cons. From 1913 until 1916 he studied privately with Max Reger in Jena. He served for a time as an organist; in 1923 he was appointed instructor in musicology at the Univ. of Zürich. He wrote some chamber music and choruses, but devoted his energies mainly to writing. He publ. *Gedankliche Grundlagen der Musikbetrachtung* (Zürich, 1924); *Zum problem der religiösen Musik* (Basel, 1924); *Die Anwendung der Sievers'schen Theorien auf die musikalische Interpretation* (Zürich, 1925); *Peter Cornelius* (Zürich, 1925); *Die Schweiz in der deutschen Musikgeschichte* (Zürich, 1926); *Geschichte der Musikpedagogik in der Schweiz* (Bern, 1943); biographies of Bach, Handel, Haydn, Chopin, Grieg, Verdi, and Tchaikovsky; monographs on Mozart, Beethoven, and Brahms; many articles for musical journals.

Chéreau, Patrice, prominent French theater, film, and opera producer; b. Lézigne, Maine-et-Loire, Nov. 2, 1944. He was a leading theater producer from 1964, serving as co-director of the Théâtre National Populaire (1979–81) and director of the Théâtre des Amandiers in Nanterre (from 1982). As an opera producer, he caused a major stir with his deconstructionist version of the centennial mounting of Wagner's *Ring* cycle at the Bayreuth Festival (1976–80); he also produced the premiere staging of the 3-act version of Berg's *Lulu* in Paris (1979) and brought out *Wozzeck* there (1992). In 1994 he staged *Don Giovanni* at the Salzburg Festival. He publ. the book *Si tant que l'opéra soit du théâtre: Notes sur le mise en scène de la création mondiale de l'oeuvre integrale d'Alban Berg "Lulu"* (Toulouse, 1992).

Cherepnin. See **Tcherepnin.**

Cherkassky, Shura (Alexander Isaakovich), remarkable Russian-born American pianist; b. Odessa, Oct. 7, 1909; d. London, Dec. 17, 1995. He began piano training with his mother; while still a child, he was taken by his family to the U.S., where he continued his studies with Josef Hofmann at the Curtis Inst. of Music in Philadelphia. After making his debut in Baltimore at the age of 11, he appeared as a soloist with Walter Damrosch and the N.Y. Sym. Orch. and performed at the White House in Washington, D.C. (1923); he made his first tour abroad in 1928 with visits to Australia and South Africa. Following a major tour of Europe in 1946, he pursued extensive tours to most of the major music centers in the world. In 1976 he went to Russia for a series of acclaimed concerts, and returned there in 1977 and 1987. He gave many recitals at N.Y.'s 92nd Street Y, which honored him in 1986 with the establishment of the Shura Cherkassky Recital Award to be given annually to a gifted young pianist. On Dec. 2, 1991, he celebrated his 80th year with a recital at N.Y.'s Carnegie Hall in a program of works by Schumann, Chopin, Bach-Busoni, Tchaikovsky-Pabst, Josef Hofmann, and well-received encores. As one of the last representatives of the hallowed Romantic school of piano virtuosity, Cherkassky regaled audiences with a bravura technique and singing tone in the grand Russian manner.

Cherney, Brian, Canadian composer and teacher; b. Peterborough, Ontario, Sept. 4, 1942. He studied composition with Weinzweig and Dolin, and piano with Margaret Miller Brown and Jacques Abram at the Univ. of Toronto (B.M., 1964; M.M., 1967; Ph.D., 1974); he also attended the summer courses for new music in Darmstadt (1966, 1969). He taught theory and composition at the Univ. of Victoria (1971–72) and then at McGill Univ. (from 1972). He publ. a biography of Harry Somers (Toronto, 1975). While Cherney's output reflects the influence of the avant-garde, he has developed a thoroughly individualistic style in which structural factors are complemented by a fine poetic sense.

WORKS: ORCH.: 2 sets of *Variations* (1962, 1967); Violin Concerto (1964); *6 Miniatures* for Oboe and Strings (1968); *7 Images* for 22 Players (1971); *Adieux* (1980); *Into the Distant Stillness . . .* (1984); *Illuminations* for Strings (1987); *Final Furnishings* for Oboe and Orch. (1989); *Transfiguration* (1990). **CONCERT BAND:** *In the Stillness between . . .* (1982). **CHAMBER:** Violin Sonata (1961); Quintet for Alto Saxophone and String Quartet (1962); *Interlude and Variations* for Wind Quintet (1965); Suite for Viola and Piano (1965); Wind Quintet (1965); 3 string quartets (1966, 1970, 1985); *Kontakion: Quiet Music for 11 Players* (1969); *Notturno* for Wind Quintet (1974); Chamber Concerto for Viola and 10 Players (1975); *Tangents I* for Cello and Tape (1975) and *II* for Oboe and Tape (1975–76); String Trio (1976); *Group Portrait—with Piano* for Wind Quintet (1978); *Trois petites pièces desséchées . . . en forme de sandwich* for Viola and Piano (1979); *Triolet* for Flute, Harp, and Bassoon (1980); *Playing for Time* for Oboe, Percussion, and Piano (1981); *Beyond the 7th Palace* for Viola and Percussion (1982); *Gan Eden* for Violin and Piano (1983); *River of Fire* for Oboe d'Amore and Harp (1983); *Accord* for Recorder, Oboe, and Cello (1985); *In Stillness Ascending* for Viola and Piano (1986); *In the Stillness of the Summer Wind* for Oboe and String Quartet (1987); *Dunkle Stimmen . . . am Rande der Nacht* for Viola, Cello, and Double Bass (1988); *Le Fil d'Ariane* for Guitar and Percussion (1988); *6 Miniatures* for Oboe and Piano (1989); *Doppelgänger* for 2 Flutes (1991); *In the Stillness of September 1942* for English Horn and 9 Strings (1992); also pieces for various Solo Instruments. **PIANO:** *6 Miniatures* (1965); *Fantasy* (1966); Sonata (1966); *Jest* (1967); *Intervals, Shapes, Patterns* (1968); *Pieces for Young Pianists* (1968); *Elegy for a Misty Afternoon* (1971); *Mémoires, reflets et rêves d'ailleurs . . .* (1977–79; rev. 1980 as *Dans le crépuscule du souvenir*); *In the Stillness of the 7th Autumn* (1983). **ORGAN:** *Gothic Scenes and Interludes* (1983–87). **VOCAL:** *2 Songs* for Soprano and Chamber Orch. (1963); *Mobile IV* for Soprano and Chamber Ensemble (1969); *Eclipse* for Soprano, Flute, and Piano (1972); *The Garden of Earthly Delights* for Tenor, Wind Quintet, Optional Harpsichord or Spinet, Optional Chimes, and Offstage Piano (1979).

Chernov, Vladimir, Russian baritone; b. Moscow, Sept. 22, 1953. He received training at the Moscow Cons. (graduated, 1981) and at the opera school at Milan's La Scala. He won prizes in the Tchaikovsky (Moscow, 1982), Bussetto (1983), and Helsinki (Tito Gobbi prize, 1984) competitions. In 1983 he became a member of the Kirov Theater in Leningrad, where he excelled in the baritone repertoire. In 1985 he made his first tour of England and Ireland as a soloist with the Moscow Radio Sym. Orch. His U.S. debut followed in 1988 when he sang Marcello with the Opera Co. of Boston. In 1990 he appeared as Figaro at London's Covent Garden. He sang Posa at the Metropolitan Opera in N.Y. in 1992. In 1995 he made his debut at Milan's La Scala as Stankar in *Stiffelio.* His guest engagements also took him to many other leading opera houses in Europe and North America. In addition to the Russian repertoire, Chernov has won special praise for his roles in the Italian and French repertoire.

Cheslock, Louis, English-born American composer, violinist, and teacher; b. London, Sept. 9, 1898; d. Baltimore, July 19, 1981. He was taken to the U.S. as a child and became a citizen through the naturalization of his father. He studied at the Peabody Cons. of Music in Baltimore, taking diplomas in violin (1917), harmony (1919), and composition (1921). After teaching violin there (1916–22), he remained on its faculty as a teacher of theory and composition (1922–76). He also was a violinist in the Baltimore Sym. Orch. (1916–37). His music was basically neo-Romantic, although in later years he experimented with modern elements ranging from jazz to dodecaphony. He publ. an *Introductory Study on Violin Vibrato* (Baltimore, 1931) and ed. *H.L. Mencken on Music* (N.Y., 1961).

WORKS: DRAMATIC: *The Jewel Merchants*, opera (1930; Baltimore, Feb. 26, 1940); *Cinderella*, ballet (Baltimore, May 11, 1946; rev. 1958). **ORCH.:** Violin Concerto (1921; Baltimore, Feb. 25, 1926); 3 tone poems: *Cathedral at Sundown*, *'Neath Washington Monument*, and *At the Railway Station* (1922; Chicago, April 29, 1923); Symphonic Prelude (1927); *Serenade* for Strings (1930); Sym. (1932); *Themes and Variations* for Horn and Orch. (1934); Horn Concerto (1936); *The Legend of Sleepy Hollow* (1936; Baltimore, May 2, 1978); *Rhapsody in Red and White: An American Divertissement* (1941); *Set of 6* for Small Orch. (1946); Suite for Oboe and Strings (1953); *Homage à Mendelssohn* for Strings (1960). **CHAMBER:** Violin Sonata (1917); Piano Sonatina (1932); *Shite Ami I* for String Quartet and Harp (1932) and *II* for Violin, Cello, and Harp (1932); String Quartet (1941); Cello Sonatina (1943); Concertinetto for Brass, Piano, and Percussion (1954); *Descant* for Clarinet (1970). **VOCAL:** *Psalm CL* for Chorus (1931); *David*, oratorio for Chorus (1937); *3 Period Pieces* for Chorus (1940); *The Congo*, oratorio for Chorus (Akron, Ohio, Oct. 30, 1942); song cycles; solo songs; anthems; part songs.

BIBL.: E. Sprenkle, *The Life and Works of L. C.* (diss., Peabody Cons. of Music, 1979).

Chevreuille, Raymond, Belgian composer; b. Brussels, Nov. 17, 1901; d. Montignies-le-Tilleul, May 9, 1976. He took a course in harmony at the Brussels Cons., but was largely self-taught in composition. From 1936 to 1959 he was employed as a sound engineer at the Belgian Radio. His style of composition embodies distinct elements of French impressionism; his searing melodies and rich harmonies are often housed within a framework of emancipated tonality, often verging on polytonal syncretism.

WORKS: DRAMATIC: CHAMBER OPERA: *Atta Troll* (1952). **BALLETS:** *Jean et les Argayons* (1934); *Cendrillon* (1946); *La Bal chez la portière* (1954); *Spéléomagie*, miniature ballet for TV (1959). **SYMPHONIC RADIO PLAYS:** *D'un diable de briquet* (1950); *L'Élixir du révérend père Gaucher* (1951). **ORCH.:** 3 piano concertos (1937, 1952, 1968); *Mouvements symphoniques* (1938); 9 syms.: No. 1 (1939), No. 2, *Symphonie des souvenirs*, with Soloists and Optional Chorus (Brussels, Nov. 23, 1945), No. 3 (Brussels, June 25, 1952), No. 4, *Short Symphony* (1952), No. 5, *Symphonie printanière* (1954), No. 6 (1957), Sym. for Chamber Orch. (1958), No. 7 (1964), and No. 8 (1970); 2 cello concertos (1940, 1965); 3 violin concertos (1941, 1953, 1965); Concerto for Oboe, Clarinet, Bassoon, and Orch. (1943); Double Concerto for Piano, Saxophone or Viola, and Orch. (1946); *Concerto for Orchestra* (1947); *Divertissement* for Chamber Orch. (1948); *Barbe-Bleue* (1949); Horn Concerto (Brussels, July 12, 1950); Trumpet Concerto (1954); *Récréation de midi* for Strings (1955); *Mouvements*, suite for Brass (1956); *Carnaval à Ostende*, suite (1959); *Presto Giocoso* (1961); *Concerto Grosso* for 2 Trumpets and Orch. (1961); Concerto for Flute and Chamber Orch. (1961); *Bruegel, peintre des humbles*, suite (1963); Concerto for Clarinet, Strings, and Percussion (1968); *2 Airs* (1971). **CHAMBER:** 6 string quartets (1930, 1934, 1934, 1939, 1943, 1945); Piano Trio (1936); String Trio (1937); Piano Quartet (1938); Cello Sonata (1941); *Divertissement* for Wind Quintet (1942); *Musiques lilliputiennes* for 4 Flutes (1942); Quartet for 4 Cellos (1942); *Variations* for Violin and Piano (1946); *Récit et Air gai* for Clarinet and Piano (1950); 5 Bagatelles for String Quartet (1952); *Serenade* for Wind Quintet (1958); Wind Quartet (1964); Trio for Flute, Viola, and Double Bass or Piano (1961); Clarinet Quintet (1968). **VOCAL: CANTATAS:** *Le Fléau* (1930); *Le Cantique de soleil* (1941); *L'Éléphant et le papillon* (1941); *La Dispute des orgues* (Brussels, Jan. 10, 1942); *Évasions* (1942); *Saisons* (1943); also *Prière pour les condamnés à mort* for Narrator and Orch. (Brussels, Oct. 14, 1945); *Assonances* for Narrator and Chamber Orch. (1962); *Rhapsody* for Woman's Voice and Chamber Orch. (1969).

Chiara, Maria(-Rita), Italian soprano; b. Oderzo, near Venice, Nov. 24, 1939. She studied with Antonio Cassinelli, who later became her husband, and with Maria Carbone. In 1965 she made her operatic debut in Venice as Desdemona. She subsequently appeared with the Bavarian State Opera in Munich and with the Vienna State Opera (1970); her debut at London's Covent Garden came in 1973 as Liù. In 1977 she made her U.S. debut as Manon Lescaut at the Chicago Lyric Opera; her Metropolitan Opera debut in N.Y. followed on Dec. 16, 1977, as Violetta. In 1985 she appeared as Aida at Milan's La Scala. She sang Amelia in *Un Ballo in Maschera* in Naples in 1989. In 1991 she appeared as Leonora in *Il Trovatore* in Turin. Among her most noted roles are Anna Bolena, Maria Stuarda, Amelia Boccanegra, Aida, and Elisabeth de Valois.

Chiari, Giuseppe, Italian composer; b. Florence, Sept. 26, 1926. He studied piano; organized the group Musica e Segno in association with Sylvano Bussotti; participated in the Fluxus festival in Wiesbaden (1962), and in avant-garde manifestations in N.Y. (1964) and at the Centre de Musique in Paris (1965). In his productions, he follows the most latitudinarian and disestablishmentarian trends of metadadaistic fragmentationarianism, both in tonal and verbal structures. He publ. *Musica senza contrappunto*, a varitype anthology of disjected observations (Rome, 1969). In it he launched the slogan "Musica gestuale," which deals with audiovisual and tactile events, volitional as well as aleatory. Among his compositions are *Intervalli* for Piano (1956); *Per arco* for Cello (1962); *Teatrino* for Actor-Pianist, Rubber Dolls, Alarm Clocks, and Handsaw (1963); and *Don't Trade Here* for Action Theater (1965).

Chihara, Paul (Seiko), American composer; b. Seattle, July 9, 1938. As an American of Japanese descent, he was relocated with his family to Minadkoka, Idaho, after the Japanese attack on Pearl Harbor in 1941. He received piano lessons as a child, and then studied English literature at the Univ. of Wash. (B.A., 1960) and at Cornell Univ. (M.A., 1961; D.M.A., 1965), where he also received instruction in composition from Robert Palmer; he also studied composition with Boulanger in Paris (1962–63), Ernst Pepping in Berlin (1965–66), and Schuller at the Berkshire Music Center at Tanglewood (summer, 1966). From 1966 to 1975 he taught at the Univ. of Calif. at Los Angeles. After serving as the Andrew W. Mellon Prof. at the Calif. Inst. of Technology (1975), he taught at the Calif. Inst. of the Arts (1976). He was composer-in-residence of the San Francisco Ballet in 1980. Chihara has explored serial techniques, occasionally adopting aleatory procedures. An oriental influence may be seen in a number of his scores.

WORKS: DRAMATIC: BALLETS: *Shinju* (Lover's Suicide; 1975); *Mistletoe Bride* (1978); *The Infernal Machine* (1978–80; rev. as the musical *Oedipus Rag*); *The Tempest* (1980); film and television scores. **ORCH.:** Viola Concerto (1963); *Forest Music* (1968; Los Angeles, May 2, 1971); *Windsong* for Cello and Orch. (1971); *Grass* for Double Bass and Orch. (1971; Oberlin, Ohio, April 14, 1972); *Ceremony III* for Flute and Orch. (1973), *IV* (1973), and *V, Symphony in Celebration* (1973–75; Houston, Sept. 8, 1975); Concerto for String Quartet and Orch. (1980); Saxophone Concerto (1980; Boston, Jan. 30, 1981); Sym. No. 2, *Birds of Sorrow* (1981; Los Angeles, March 10, 1982). **CHAMBER:** *Logs* for Double Bass (1966); *Branches* for 2 Bassoons and Percussion (1966); *Driftwood* for String Quartet (1967); *Redwood* for Viola and Percussion (1967); *Willow, Willow* for Bass Flute, Tuba, and Percussion (1968); *Logos XVI* for Amplified String Bass and Tape (1970); *Ceremony I* for Oboe, 2 Cellos, Double Bass, and Percussion (1971) and *II* for Amplified Flute, 2 Amplified Cellos, and Percussion (1972); Piano Trio

(1974); *Elegy* for Piano Trio (1974); *The Beauty of the Rose is in its Passing* for Bassoon, 2 Horns, Harp, and Percussion (1976); String Quartet, *Primavera* (1977); Sinfonia Concertante for 9 Instruments (1980); *Sequoia* for String Quartet and Tape (1984). **VOCAL:** *Magnificat* for 6 Women's Voices (1965); *Psalm XC* for Chorus (1965); *Nocturne* for 24 Solo Voices (1966); *Ave Maria—Scarborough Fair* for 6 Men's Voices (1971); *Missa Carminum* for 8 Voices (1975).

Childs, Barney (Sanford), American composer; b. Spokane, Wash., Feb. 13, 1926. He studied intermittently with Leonard Ratner, Carlos Chávez, Copland, and Elliott Carter; obtained a B.A. degree in English from the Univ. of Nevada (1949), an M.A. from the Univ. of Oxford as a Rhodes Scholar (1955), and a Ph.D. in literature from Stanford Univ. (1959). He taught English at the Univ. of Arizona (1956–65); then served as dean of Deep Springs College in California (1965–69). From 1969 to 1971 he taught theory and composition at Wisconsin College-Cons. in Milwaukee; in 1971 he joined the faculty at Johnston College of the Univ. of Redlands in California; was a prof. there from 1973 to 1994. Not overly concerned with public tastes and current fashions of cosmopolitan styles, Childs cultivates indeterminate structures. He ed., with Elliott Schwarz, *Contemporary Composers on Contemporary Music* (N.Y., 1967).

WORKS: 6 *Interbalances* for Various Groups (1941–64); 2 violin sonatas (1950, 1956); 5 wind quintets (1951–69); 8 string quartets (1951–74); 2 syms. (1954, 1956); *Concerto da camera* for Trumpet and Woodwinds (1951); Trio for Flute, Oboe, and Clarinet (1952); Quartet for Clarinet and Strings (1953); Bassoon Sonata (1953); Concerto for English Horn, Strings, Harp, and Percussion (1955); Quartet for Bassoons (1958); Oboe Sonata (1958); Brass Trio (1959); Flute Sonata (1960); Trombone Sonata (1961); Quartet for Flute, Oboe, Double Bass, and Percussion (1964); *6 Events* for Band (1965); Music for Piano and Strings (1965); *The Golden Bubble* for Double Bass Sarrusophone and Percussion (1967); *Music* for 6 Tubas (1969); *Keet Seel* for Chorus (1970); Concerto for Clarinet and Orch. (1970); *Supposes: Imago Mundi* for Band (1970); *When Lilacs Last in the Dooryard Bloom'd . . .* for Soloists, Chorus, and Band (1971); Trio for Clarinet, Cello, and Piano (1972); *Of Place, as Altered* for 5 Clarinets (1972); *Of Place, as Particular* for Soprano and Tape (1973); *Concert Piece for Tuba and Band* (1973); Quintet for Winds, Harp, and Percussion (1974); *The Golden Shore* for Band (1974); *Lanterns and Candlelight* for Marimba and Soprano (1975); *A Question of Summer* for Tuba and Harp (1976); *4 Pieces for 6 Winds* for Wind Quintet and Saxophone (1977); *Quartet/Fantasy* for 4 Tubas (1977); *September with Band* for Band (1978); *Featuring: "Mighty" Joe Nowhere und die Greater Wairopi All'Stars* for 7 Equal Instruments (1978); *Overture to Measuring a Meridian* for Wind Sextet and Percussion (1978); *7 Quiet Studies* for Percussion (1978); *6 Gamut Studies* for Marimba (1978); *Mosaic on a Theme of Balakirev* for Alto Saxophone (1979); *A Continuance, in 7 Parts* for Band (1979); *Clay Music* for 4 Players on special handmade clay instruments (1980); *!BANANA FLANNEL-BOARD!—the Historic 1st Album* for 3 Readers and Tape Delay (1980); *Orrery* for Band (1980); *13 Classic Studies for the Contrabass* (1981); *The Edge of the World* for Bass Clarinet and Organ (1981); *Real Music* for 2 Clarinets (1981); *81 Licks for Trombone* (1983); *Pastorale* for Bass Clarinet and Tape (1983); *Sunshine Lunchh, & Like Matters* for Bass Clarinet, Baritone, Percussion, and Electronic Music Machine (1984; "Lunchh" is the emphatically designated rendering by the composer); Horn Octet (1984); *Instant Winners* for E-flat Clarinet (1986); *A Box of Views* for Wind Quintet and Piano (1988); Concerto for Timpani and Orch. (1989); *Fantasy Variations* for Violinist Who Also Reads (1991); *Quite a row of them sitting there* for Clarinet and Piano (1992); *Intrada: Be someone else* for Saxophone Quartet (1992).

Chilingirian, Levon, Cypriot violinist; b. Nicosia, May 28, 1948. After studies in Nicosia, he pursued formal training at the Royal College of Music in London and with M. Parikian. With the pianist Clifford Benson, he won 1st prize in the BBC Beethoven Competition in 1969 and in the Munich International Competition in 1971; they toured widely in recital from 1970. In 1971 he organized the Chilingirian String Quartet, which acquired a fine reputation.

Chiriac, Mircea, Romanian composer; b. Bucharest, May 19, 1919. He studied harmony with Otescu and Jora at the Bucharest Cons. (1936–45); in 1966 he was appointed to its faculty.

WORKS: BALLETS: *Iancu Jianu* (1959–63; Bucharest, Feb. 7, 1964); *Văpaia* (1973–74; Bucharest, Feb. 17, 1974). **ORCH.:** *Nocturne* (1945); 2 rhapsodies (1951, 1955); *Festival Overture* (1953); *Poem* for Violin and Orch. (1954); *Bucureştiul de altă dată* (1957); *Sinfonietta* (1965); Concerto for Strings (1966); *Simfonie de camera* (1969); *Prelude, Intermezzo, and Toccata*, symphonic triptych (1971); *Divertissement* for Strings (1971); *Variations* for Piano and Orch. (1978); *Thalassa*, symphonic poem (1982). **CHAMBER:** 4 string quartets (1945; 1972; 1980; 1984–85); Trio for Piano, Violin, and Cello (1975); Clarinet Sonata (1981); Quintet for Flute, Oboe, Clarinet, Horn, and Bassoon (1982). **VOCAL:** *Terra Daciae*, 3 poems for Tenor and Orch. (1977); *Ars poetica*, 5 poems for Tenor and Orch. (1980); other songs.

Chisholm, Erik, Scottish composer and conductor; b. Glasgow, Jan. 4, 1904; d. Rondebosch, South Africa, June 7, 1965. He first studied music in Glasgow; then in London and in Edinburgh with Donald Tovey (composition) and Puishnov (piano); received his Mus.Bac. in 1931, and his Mus.Doc. in 1934 from the Univ. of Edinburgh. He was conductor of the Glasgow Grand Opera Soc. from 1930 to 1939; in 1940 he joined the Carl Rosa Opera Co. as conductor; in 1945 he founded the Singapore Sym. Orch.; in 1946 he was appointed prof. of music and director of the South African College of Music at Cape Town Univ.; also conducted operas in South Africa. His book, *The Operas of Leos Janáček*, was publ. posth. (N.Y., 1971). Chisholm's style of composition was marked by considerable complexity; elements of oriental scale formations are notable.

WORKS: DRAMATIC: OPERAS: *The Feast of Samhain* (1941); *The Inland Woman* (Cape Town, Oct. 21, 1953); *Dark Sonnet*, after O'Neill (Cape Town, Oct. 20, 1952); *Simoon*, after Strindberg (1953); *Dark Sonnet* and *Simoon* were later combined with a 3rd short opera, *Black Roses*, with a libretto by the composer, to form a trilogy entitled *Murder in 3 Keys* (N.Y., July 6, 1954). **BALLETS:** *The Pied Piper of Hamelin* (1937); *The Forsaken Mermaid* (1940); *The Earth Shapers* (1941); *The Hoodie* (1947). **ORCH.:** *Straloch Suite* (1933); 2 syms. (1938, 1939); *Piobaireachd Concerto* for Piano and Orch. (1940); *Pictures from Dante* (1948); *Hindustani Concerto* for Piano and Orch. (Cape Town, Nov. 22, 1949); Violin Concerto (Cape Town, March 18, 1952); *Concerto for Orchestra* (Cape Town, March 29, 1952). **CHAMBER:** Double Trio for Clarinet, Bassoon, Trumpet, Violin, Cello, and Double Bass; piano pieces. **VOCAL:** *The Adventures of Babar* for Narrator and Orch. (1940); choral works; songs.

Chlubna, Osvald, Czech composer; b. Brünn, June 22, 1893; d. there (Brno), Oct. 30, 1971. Following attendance at the Czech Technical College (1911–13) and the Commercial Academy (1913–14), he studied composition with Janáček at the Brno Organ School (1914–15); he later attended Janáček's master class in Brno (1923–24). Although Chlubna made his living as a bank clerk until 1953, he devoted much time to composing. He also taught at the Cons. (1919–35; 1953–59) and at the Janáček Academy of Music (1956–58) in Brno. His works followed along Romantic lines, being notable for their lyrical and rhapsodic elements. Chlubna orchestrated Act 3 of Janáček's 1st opera, *Šárka*. With B. Bakala, he rev. and reorchestrated Janáček's last opera, *Z mrtvého domu* (From the House of the Dead), for its posthumous premiere. He also completed Janáček's unfinished symphonic poem, *Dunaj* (The Danube). His multi-vol. study of Janáček's compositional style remains in MS.

WORKS: OPERAS: *Pomsta Catullova* (Catullus's Revenge; 1917; Brno, Nov. 30, 1921; rev. 1959); *Alladina a Palomid čili Síla touhy* (Alladina and Palomid, or The Power of Desire; 1921–22; Brno, Jan. 31, 1925); *Nura* (1928–30; Brno, May 20, 1932); *V den počátku* (In the Day of the Beginning; Brno, Jan. 24, 1936); *Freje pana z Heslova* (The Affairs of the Lord of Heslov; 1939; Brno, Jan. 28, 1949); *Jiří z Kunštátu a Poděbrad* (Jiří of Kunštát and Poděbrady; 1941); *Kolébka* (The Cradle; 1952); *Eupyros* (n.d.). **ORCH.:** *Distance and Dreams* (1916); *Sinfonietta* (1924); 3 syms.: No. 1, *Symphony of Life and Love* (1927), No. 2, *Brno Symphony* (1946), and No. 3 (1960); *From the Hillsides, Mountains, and Forests* (1934); Piano Concerto (1937); Cello Concerto (1938); *Nature and Man: From the Spring, Summer Serenade,* and *Autumn Carnival* (1949–53); Violin Concerto (1950); *This Is My Country: The Fountains of Brno, Macocha Ravine, Oh, Upwards, Boys, Upwards!, Pernštejn Castle,* and *My Land is Beautiful* (1955–57). **CHAMBER:** 5 string quartets (1925, 1928, 1933, 1963, 1969); Sonata for Violin and Cello (1925); Violin Sonata (1948); Cello Sonata (1948); piano pieces. **VOCAL:** Cantatas; choral cycles; song cycles.

BIBL.: M. Černohorská, *O. C.* (Brno, 1963).

Chmura, Gabriel, Polish-born Israeli conductor; b. Wroclaw, May 7, 1946. His family emigrated in 1955 to Israel, where he studied piano, theory, and composition at the Tel Aviv Academy of Music; he then studied conducting with Dervaux in Paris (1968), Ferrara in Siena (1969), and Swarowsky in Vienna (1969–71). He won the Gold Medal at the Cantelli Competition in Milan and 1st prize at the Karajan Competition in Berlin in 1971; he subsequently served as Karajan's assistant until 1973. He was Generalmusikdirektor in Aachen (1974–82) and of the Bochum Sym. Orch. (from 1982), and appeared throughout Europe as a guest conductor, making his North American debut with the N.Y. Phil. in 1980. From 1987 to 1990 he was principal conductor and music director of the National Arts Centre Orch. in Ottawa.

Chojnacka, Elisabeth, Polish-born French harpsichordist; b. Warsaw, Sept. 10, 1939. She studied in her homeland and then with Van de Wiele in Paris. In 1968 she took 1st prize in the Vercelli competition, and subsequently pursued a career as a harpsichord virtuoso. She won particular distinction for her championship of contemporary music, commissioning many works for her instrument from such composers as Bussotti, Donatoni, Górecki, C. Halffter, Ligeti, and Xenakis.

Chomiński, Józef Michal, eminent Polish musicologist; b. Ostrów, near Przemyśl, Aug. 24, 1906; d. Feb. 20, 1994. He took courses in musicology with Chybiński and in ethnography with Adam Fischer at the Univ. of Lwów (1926–31; M.A., 1931; Ph.D., 1936); he completed his Habilitation in 1949 at the Univ. of Poznań. He taught at the Poznań music school (1945–48) and the Univ. of Warsaw (1947–76), and also served as chairman of the music division in the art inst. of the Polish Academy of Sciences (1951–68). He ed. *Muzyka* (1956–71) and the Monumenta Musicae in Polonia series (1964–71).

WRITINGS: *Preludia Chopina* (Kraków, 1950); ed. with Z. Lissa, *Muzyka polskiego Odrodzenia* (Music of the Polish Renaissance; Warsaw, 1953; 4th ed., 1958); ed. with K. Wilkowska-Chomińska, *Formy muzyczne* (Kraków; vol. I, *Male formy instrumentalne* [Small Instrumental Forms], 1954; 2nd ed., aug., 1983; vol. II, *Wielkie formy instrumentalne* [Large Instrumental Forms], 1956; vol. III, *Piesn* [Song], 1974; vol. IV, *Opera i drama* [Opera and Drama], 1976; vol. V, *Wielkie formy wokalne* [Large Vocal Forms], 1984); ed. with Z. Lissa, *Kultura muzyczna Polski ludowej 1944–1955* (Musical Culture of the People's Republic of Poland 1944–1955; Kraków, 1957); ed., *Historia muzyki powszechnij* (A General History of Music; Kraków, 1957–64); *Historia harmonii i kontrapunktu* (3 vols., Kraków, 1958, 1962, 1988); *Sonaty Chopina* (Kraków, 1960); ed., *Z zycia i twórczości Karola Szymanowskiego* (Life and Works of Karol Szymanowski; Kraków, 1960); ed., *Slownik muzyków polskich* (A Dictionary of Polish Music; Kraków, 1964–67); *Muzyka Polski ludowej* (Music in the People's Republic of Poland; Warsaw, 1968); *Studia nad twórczościa Karola Szymanowskiego* (Kraków, 1969); *Chopin* (Kraków, 1978); with T. Turo, *Katalog dziel Fryderyka Chopina: A Catalog of the Works of Frederick Chopin* (Kraków, 1990).

Chookasian, Lili, American contralto; b. Chicago, Aug. 1, 1921. She studied with Phillip Manuel, then made her concert debut as soloist in Mahler's 3rd Sym. with Bruno Walter and the Chicago Sym. Orch. (1957). Her operatic debut followed as Adalgisa at the Arkansas Opera Theater in Little Rock (1959), and, after additional training with Rosa Ponselle, she made her Metropolitan Opera debut in N.Y. as La Cieca in *La Gioconda* (March 9, 1962). She remained on the Metropolitan roster until 1978, where she again was a member from 1979. She made her first European appearance at the Bayreuth Festival in 1963 and in subsequent years sang widely in both opera and concert performances, appearing often in contemporary works.

Chorzempa, Daniel (Walter), American organist, harpsichordist, pianist, and composer; b. Minneapolis, Dec. 7, 1944. He was educated at the Univ. of Minnesota (Ph.D., 1971, with a diss. on Reubke); then enrolled at the Hochschule für Musik in Cologne; became a member of the Studio für Elektronische Musik in Cologne in 1970, and composed works for the medium. He also toured extensively as a keyboard virtuoso from 1968.

Chotzinoff, Samuel, Russian-American pianist and music critic; b. Vitebsk, July 4, 1889; d. N.Y., Feb. 9, 1964. He was taken to America as a child; studied piano with Oscar Shack and theory with Daniel Gregory Mason at Columbia Univ., graduating in 1912. He subsequently became an expert accompanist; toured with Zimbalist and Heifetz. He served as music critic of the *N.Y. World* (1925–30) and the *N.Y. Post* (1934–41). He then occupied various teaching and administrative positions; was for several years music director of NBC. He wrote a novel on Beethoven's life, entitled *Eroica*; a book of reminiscences, *A Lost Paradise* (1955); and a monograph, *Toscanini, an Intimate Portrait* (N.Y., 1956). His autobiographical *Days at the Morn and A Little Night Music* was publ. posth. (1964).

Chou Wen-chung, remarkable Chinese-born American composer; b. Chefoo, June 29, 1923 (corresponding to May 16, 1923, according to the lunar calendar in the Chinese Year of the Bear). He studied civil engineering at the National Univ. in Chungking (1941–45), then went to the U.S. on a scholarship to study architecture. Turning his attention to music, he studied composition with Slonimsky in Boston (1946–49), Luening at Columbia Univ. (M.A., 1954), and Varèse in N.Y. (1949–54); he also held 2 Guggenheim fellowships (1957, 1959). In 1958 he became a naturalized U.S. citizen. He was composer-in-residence at the Univ. of Ill. in Urbana (1958), and on the faculties of Brooklyn College (1961–62), Hunter College (1963–64), and Columbia Univ. (from 1964). In 1982 he became an elected member of the Inst. of the American Academy and Inst. of Arts and Letters. His music combines Chinese elements of structure and scale formation with free dissonant counterpoint related to Varèse's theory of "organized sound."

WORKS: ORCH.: *Landscapes* (1949; San Francisco, Nov. 19, 1953); *All in the Spring Wind* (1952–53); *And the Fallen Petals* (1954; Louisville, Feb. 9, 1955); *In the Mode of Chang* for Chamber Orch. (1956; N.Y., Feb. 2, 1957); *Metaphors* for Winds (1960–61); *Riding the Wind* for Winds (1964); *Pien*, chamber concerto for Piano, Percussion, and Winds (1966); *Beijing in the Mist* (1985); Cello Concerto (N.Y., Jan. 10, 1993). **CHAMBER:** Suite for Harp and Wind Quintet (1950); *2 Miniatures from the T'ang Dynasty* for 10 Instruments (1957); *To a Wayfarer* for Clarinet, Harp, Percussion, and Strings (1958); *Soliloquy of a Bhiksuni* for Trumpet, Brass, and Percussion (1958); *The Dark and the Light* for Piano, Percussion, Violin, Viola, Cello, and Double Bass (1964); *Yü Ko* for 9 Instruments (1965);

Ceremonial for 3 Trumpets and 3 Trombones (1968); *Yün* for 2 Pianos, 2 Percussion, and Wind Sextet (1969); *Echoes from the Gorge* for Chamber Group (N.Y., April 27, 1989); *Windswept Peaks* for Violin, Cello, Clarinet, and Piano (1990). **VOCAL:** 7 *Poems of the T'ang Dynasty* for Soprano or Tenor, 7 Winds, Piano, and Percussion (1951; N.Y., March 16, 1952); *Poems of White Stone* for Chorus and Instrumental Ensemble (1958–59). **OTHER:** Film scores.

Chowning, John, American composer; b. Salem, N.J., Aug. 22, 1934. He studied at Wittenberg Univ. in Springfield, Ohio (B.M., 1959), with Boulanger in Paris (1959–62), and at Stanford Univ. (Ph.D., 1966), where he was a member of the faculty and served as director of both its Computer Music and Acoustics Group (1966–74) and its Center for Computer Research in Music and Acoustics (from 1975). A leading figure in computer-music circles, he utilized frequency modulation in his development of "Chowning FM." His works for computer-generated quadraphonic sound include *Sabelithe* (1972), *Turenas* (1972), *Stria* (1977), and *Phōnē* (1981).

BIBL.: C. Roads, "J. C. on Composition," *Composers and the Computer* (Los Altos, Calif., 1985).

Christensen, Dieter, German ethnomusicologist; b. Berlin, April 17, 1932. He studied with Reinhard and Dräger at the Free Univ. of Berlin (Ph.D., 1957, with a diss. on the music of New Guinea), then was curator and director of the ethnomusicology department of the Folk Museum of Berlin (1958–71) and prof. of music and director of the Center for Studies in Ethnomusicology at Columbia Univ. His research has focused upon the musics of Oceania, Mexico, and West Africa, and the methodology and history of ethnomusicology. He publ. *Kurdish Folk Music from Western Iran* (1965), "On the Preservation of Arab Music," *II. Internationaler Kongress für arabische Musik* (1969), and "Musical Style and Social Context in Kurdish Songs," *Asian Music* (1975), as well as a series of pamphlets (with Gerd Kock) on Micronesian dance.

Christian, Palmer, American organist and teacher; b. Kankakee, Ill.,May 3, 1885; d. Ann Arbor, Mich., Feb. 19, 1947. After training with Clarence Dickinson in Chicago, he studied with Straube in Leipzig (1909–10) and Guilmant in Paris (1910–11). He began his career as a church organist, and then was municipal organist in Denver (1920–21). From 1924 until his death he was organist and prof. of organ at the Univ. of Mich. in Ann Arbor. He also made frequent recital tours and appeared as a soloist with leading U.S. orchs.

Christiansen, F(redrik) Melius, esteemed Norwegian-American choral conductor, teacher, and composer, father of **Olaf Christiansen**; b. Eidsvold, April 1, 1871; d. Northfield, Minn., June 1, 1955. He emigrated to the U.S. in 1888. After conducting the Scandinavian Band in Marinette, Wis. (1890–92), he studied at Augsburg College and then at the Northwestern Cons. of Music in Minneapolis (graduated, 1894); then pursued training at the Leipzig Cons. (1897–99). In 1903 he was made head of the music dept. at St. Olaf College in Northfield, Minn., where he founded the St. Olaf Choir in 1911, serving as its conductor until 1942. Under his guidance, it became one of the finest choral groups in the U.S. Christiansen excelled as a conductor of a cappella choral forces. He made numerous arrangements of Lutheran chorales and Norwegian folk melodies for 4-part chorus, and also ed. the St. Olaf Choir series (12 vols., Minneapolis, 1919–44). Among his original works were an oratorio, 3 cantatas, and instrumental pieces, including 2 sets of organ music.

BIBL.: L. Bergmann, *Music Master of the Middle West: The Story of F.M. C. and the St. Olaf Choir* (Minneapolis, 1944); R. Hanson, *An Analysis of Selected Choral Works of F.M. C.* (diss., Univ. of Ill., 1970).

Christiansen, Olaf, American choral conductor and teacher, son of **F(redrik) Melius Christiansen**; b. Minneapolis, Aug. 12, 1901; d. Northfield, Minn., April 12, 1984. He was trained by his father, whom he succeeded in 1942 as conductor of the St. Olaf Choir in Northfield, a position he held with distinction until 1968. Christiansen also trained many choral conductors.

Christie, William (Lincoln), esteemed American-born French harpsichordist, conductor, and teacher; b. Buffalo, Dec. 19, 1944. He learned to play the piano and organ before studying harpsichord with Igor Kipnis at the Berkshire Music Center in Tanglewood; took courses in music and art history at Harvard Univ. (B.A., 1966); then studied harpsichord with Ralph Kirkpatrick, organ with Charles Krigbaum, and musicology with Claudio Palisca and Nicholas Temperley at Yale Univ. (M.Mus., 1970). After a brief teaching assignment at Dartmouth College (1970–71), he went to France and became a member of the Five Centuries Ensemble (1971–75) and the Concerto Vocale (from 1972); he also made appearances as a recitalist. In 1978 he founded Les Arts Florissants, a vocal and instrumental ensemble that won distinction for performances of the French and Italian Baroque repertoire. He taught at the Sommer Akademie für alte Musik in Innsbruck (1977–83) and in 1982 became the first American prof. at the Paris Cons.

Christoff, Boris (Kirilov), celebrated Bulgarian bass; b. Plovdiv, May 18, 1914; d. Rome, June 28, 1993. He sang in the Gusla Choir in Sofia, where he was heard by King Boris, who made it possible for him to go to Rome to study with Stracciari; he later studied in Salzburg with Muratti. He made his debut in a concert in Rome in 1946; that same year he made his operatic debut there at the Teatro Argentina as Colline in *La Bohème*. He made his first appearance at La Scala in Milan in 1947, at Covent Garden in London in 1949, and his U.S. debut as Boris Godunov with the San Francisco Opera on Sept. 25, 1956. During his distinguished career, he appeared with many leading opera houses, singing most of the principal bass roles in the operas of Verdi, as well as such roles as Gurnemanz, Ivan Susanin, Hagen, Rocco, Konchak, and King Mark. He was most renowned for his dramatic portrayal of Boris Godunov, which recalled the interpretation of Chaliapin. His brother-in-law was **Tito Gobbi**.

BIBL.: F. Barker, *Voice of the Opera: B. C.* (London, 1951); G. Lauri-Volpi, *Voci parallele: B. C.* (Milan, 1955); O. Dejkova, *B. D.* (Sofia, 1965); A. Bozhkov, *B. Khristov* (Sofia, 1985); V. Pravchanska-Ivanova and N. Pravchanski, *Sreshti s B. Khristov* (Sofia, 1990).

Christoff, Dimiter, Bulgarian composer; b. Sofia, Oct. 2, 1933. He studied composition with M. Goleminov at the Bulgarian State Cons. in Sofia (1951–56), where he later taught (from 1970). He was also vice-president of the Bulgarian Composers Union (1972–85) and general secretary of the International Music Council of UNESCO (1975–79).

WORKS: OPERAS: *Game* (1978); *The Golden Fish Line*, chamber opera (1984). **ORCH.:** 3 piano concertos (1954, 1983, 1994); *Sinfonietta* for Strings (1956); *Poem* (1957); 3 syms. (1958, 1964, 1969); *Overture* (1961); *Symphonic Episodes* (1962); Violin Concerto (1966); *Chamber Suite* for Flute, Piccolo, and Chamber Orch. (1966); Cello Concerto (1969); *Concert Miniatures* (1970); *Overture with Fanfares* (1974); *Quasi una fantasia-gioco* (1981); *Game* for Cello and Orch. (1983); *Perpetui mobili in pianissimi* (1987). **CHAMBER:** *Suite* for Wind Quintet (1953); *2 Dances* for Trumpet and Piano (1960); Sonata for Solo Cello (1965); Concerto for 3 Small Drums and 5 Instruments (1967); String Quartet (1970); Quartet for Flute, Viola, Harp, and Harpsichord (1973). **PIANO:** 4 sonatas (1962, 1974, 1974, 1974). **VOCAL:** Choruses; songs.

Christopher, Cyril (Stanley), English organist and composer; b. Oldbury, Worcestershire, June 23, 1897; d. Sutton Coldfield, March 31, 1979. He studied organ with Alfred Hollins; held numerous posts as a church organist and a choral conductor; also taught theory at the Birmingham School of Music. He wrote mainly for chorus; among his instrumental works are Fantasy-Trio for Clarinet, Violin, and Piano (1939); Trio for Oboe, Bassoon, and Piano (1954); Oboe Sonata (1956); *Sere-*

nade for Wind Instruments, Cello, and Double Bass (1967); 2 short symphonic poems, *Midsummer Night* and *The Lone Shore.*

Christophers, Harry, English conductor; b. Goudhurst, Kent, Dec. 26, 1953. He received his initial training at the Canterbury Cathedral Choir School, and later pursued his education at Magdalen College, Oxford. In 1977 he organized the esteemed choral aggregation The Sixteen, which he led in a vast repertory from Palestrina to contemporary composers. In 1989 he toured Great Britain, Europe, Japan, and Brazil with his group, and in 1992 he toured the globe with it. He also made appearances as a guest conductor throughout Great Britain and Europe.

Christoskov, Peter, Bulgarian composer and violinist; b. Sofia, March 8, 1917. He studied violin at the Bulgarian State Cons. in Sofia, graduating in 1936; then went to Berlin, where he continued violin studies; returning to Sofia, he was appointed head of the instrumental dept. of the Bulgarian State Cons. In his works, he often applies the asymmetrical rhythms of Bulgarian folk songs, using dissonant harmonies for coloristic effects.

WORKS: *Moto Perpetuo* for String Orch. (1956); 2 violin concertos (1958, 1961); *Concerto for Orchestra* (1964); *Children's Album* for Violin and Chamber Orch. (1966); *Aria and Toccata* for Violin and Orch. (1967); *Concerto-Improvisation* for Cello and Orch. (1970); Piano Concerto (1972); *Symphonic Sketches* (1973); *Concerto-Poem* for Cello and Orch. (1973).

Christou, Jani, remarkable Greek composer; b. Heliopolis, Egypt (of Greek parents), Jan. 8, 1926; d. in an automobile accident near Athens, Jan. 8, 1970. He studied at Victoria College in Alexandria; then took courses in philosophy under Wittgenstein at King's College, Cambridge (M.A., 1948); concurrently studied composition with Hans Redlich in Letchworth (1945–48); then enrolled in the summer courses of the Accademia Musicale Chigiana in Siena (1949–50); during the same period, he attended Karl Jung's lectures on psychology in Zürich. Christou returned to Alexandria in 1951; then lived on his family estate on the island of Chios. He evolved a system of composition embracing the totality of human and metaphysical expression, forming a "philosophical structure" for which he designed a surrealistic graphic notation involving a "psychoid factor," symbolized by the Greek letter psi; aleatory practices are indicated by the drawing of a pair of dice; a sudden stop, by a dagger, etc. His score *Enantiodromia* (Opposed Pathways) for Orch. (1965; rev. 1968; Oakland, Calif., Feb. 18, 1969), in such a graphic notation, is reproduced in the avant-garde publication *Source,* 6 (1969). His notation also includes poetry, choreographic acting, special lighting, film, and projection meant to envelop the listener on all sides. At his death, he left sketches for a set of 130 multimedia compositions of a category he called *Anaparastasis* ("proto-performances, meant to revive primeval rituals as adapted to modern culture").

WORKS: *Phoenix Music* for Orch. (1948–49); 3 syms.: No. 1 (1950; London, April 29, 1951), No. 2 for Chorus and Orch. (1954–58), and No. 3 (1959–62); *Latin Mass* for Chorus, Brass, and Percussion (1953; Athens, Sept. 26, 1971); *David's Psalms* for Baritone, Chorus, and Orch. (1953); *6 Songs* for Voice and Piano, after T.S. Eliot (1955; orchestrated 1957); Gilgamesh, oratorio (1958); *Patterns and Permutations* for Orch. (1960; Athens, March 11, 1963); *Toccata* for Piano and Orch. (1962); *The 12 Keys* for Mezzo-soprano and Chamber Ensemble (1962); *The Breakdown,* opera (1964); *Tongues of Fire,* Pentecost oratorio (Oxford, June 27, 1964); *Enantiodromia* (Opposed Pathways) for Orch. (1965; rev. 1968; Oakland, Calif., Feb. 18, 1969); *Mysterion,* oratorio for Soli, 3 Choruses, Actors, Orch., and Tape, to ancient Egyptian myths (1965–66); *Praxis for 12* for 11 Strings and Pianist-Percussionist-Conductor (Athens, April 18, 1966; also as *Praxis* for 44 Strings and Pianist-Percussionist-Conductor); *Oresteia,* "super-opera," after Aeschylus (1967–70; unfinished). Performable works from the cycle *Anaparastasis* are: *The Strychnine Lady* for Female Violist, 2 groups of Massed Strings, Brass, Percussion, Tapes, Metal Sheet, Sound-producing Objects and Toys, Red Cloth, and 5 Actors (Athens, April 3, 1967); *Anaparastasis I (Astron)* for Baritone and Instrumental Ensemble (Munich, Nov. 12, 1968); *Anaparastasis III (The Pianist)* for Actor, Variable Instrumental Ensemble, and 3 Stereo Tapes (Munich, Nov. 13, 1969); *Epicycle* for Variable Instrumental Ensemble that may take a chiliad or a hebdomad, a nanosecond or a quindecillion of non-zero moments to perform (concise version, Athens, Dec. 15, 1968; extended version, Athens, Dec. 20, 1968); stage music for *The Persians* (1965), *The Frogs* (1966), and *Oedipus Rex* (1969).

BIBL.: J. Papaioannou, *J. C. and the Metaphysics of Music* (London, 1970).

Christov, Dobri. See **Khristov, Dobri.**

Chung, Kyung-Wha, brilliant Korean violinist, sister of **Myung-Wha** and **Myung-Whun Chung**; b. Seoul, March 26, 1948. She began violin study as a small child; made her orch. debut in Seoul at the age of 9, playing the Mendelssohn Concerto; in 1961 she went to the U.S., where she studied with Ivan Galamian at the Juilliard School of Music in N.Y. In 1967 she shared 1st prize with Pinchas Zukerman in the Leventritt Competition. In 1968 she appeared as soloist with the N.Y. Phil.; made her European debut in 1970 with the London Sym. Orch. She subsequently toured regularly throughout the world as a virtuoso of the first rank. She gave numerous trio concerts with her sister and brother, and also appeared as a soloist with her brother acting as conductor.

Chung, Myung-Wha, gifted Korean-born American cellist, sister of **Kyung-Wha** and **Myung-Whun Chung**; b. Seoul, March 19, 1944. She studied cello in Seoul; made her orch. debut there in 1957; in 1961 she went to the U.S., where she studied with Rose at the Juilliard School of Music in N.Y. (B.A., 1965); then attended a master class given by Gregor Piatigorsky at the Univ. of Southern Calif. in Los Angeles. She made her U.S. debut in San Francisco (1967) and her European debut in Spoleto (1969); she won 1st prize in the Geneva Competition (1971), the same year she became a naturalized American citizen. She appeared as soloist with orchs. in Europe and America; also played trio concerts with her sister and brother.

Chung, Myung-Whun, talented Korean-born American conductor and pianist, brother of **Myung-Wha** and **Kyung-Wha Chung**; b. Seoul, Jan. 22, 1953. He played piano as a child, making his debut as soloist with the Seoul Phil. when he was 7; he then went to the U.S., where he studied with Nadia Reisenberg (piano) and Carl Bamberger (conducting) at the Mannes College of Music in N.Y., and at the Juilliard School (diplomas in piano and conducting, 1974); he received additional tutelage in conducting there from Sixten Ehrling (1975–78). He made his conducting debut in Seoul (1971), subsequently winning 2nd prize in piano at the Tchaikovsky Competition in Moscow (1974). He became a naturalized American citizen in 1973. He pursued a dual career as a pianist and conductor; he gave trio concerts with his sisters; was assistant conductor of the Los Angeles Phil. (1978–81), and chief conductor of the Saarland Radio Sym. Orch. in Saarbrücken (1984–90). On Feb. 21, 1986, he made his Metropolitan Opera debut in N.Y. conducting *Simon Boccanegra.* In 1989 he became music director-designate and in 1990 was confirmed in the position of music director of the new Opéra de la Bastille in Paris. While his tenure was initially successful, the election of a new French government led to a change in the administration of the Opéra. Although Chung's tenure as music director was to extend to the year 2000, the new administration in 1994 sought to end his tenure by 1997, freeze his salary, and deny him artistic control of the Opéra. His refusal to accept these altered terms led to an abrupt dismissal, although he conducted the opening performances of the season in Oct. 1994 with *Simon Boccanegra* before taking leave of the embattled company.

Chusid, Martin, American musicologist; b. N.Y., Aug. 19, 1925. He studied at the Univ. of Calif. at Berkeley (B.A., 1950; M.A.,

1955; Ph.D., 1961, with the diss. *The Chamber Music of Schubert*). Chusid taught at the Univ. of Southern Calif. in Los Angeles (1959–63) and at N.Y. Univ. (from 1963), where he also served as chairman of the music dept. (1967–70), assoc. dean of the graduate school of arts and sciences (1970–72), and director of the American Inst. for Verdi Studies (from 1976). He edited the Norton Critical Score ed. of Schubert's *Unfinished Symphony* (N.Y., 1968; 2nd ed., 1971), and was a contributor to the new critical ed. of Verdi's complete works; he also edited *A Catalog of Verdi's Operas* (Hackensack, N.J., 1974) and, with W. Weaver, *The Verdi Companion* (N.Y., 1979).

Chybiński, Adolf (Eustachy), eminent Polish musicologist; b. Kraków, April 29, 1880; d. Poznań, Oct. 31, 1952. After attending the Univ. of Kraków, he pursued musicological studies with Sandberger and Kroyer at the Univ. of Munich (Ph.D., 1908, with the diss. *Beiträge zur Geschichte des Taktschlagens*; publ. in Kraków, 1912); he also studied composition privately with Thuille in Munich (1905–7) and completed his Habilitation at the Univ. of Lemberg in 1912 with his *Teoria mensuralna w polskiej literaturze muzycznej pierwszej polowy XVI wieku* (Mensural Theory in Polish Music Literature of the 1st Half of the 16th Century; publ. in Kraków, 1912). He joined the faculty of the Univ. of Lemberg (later Lwów) in 1912, and was prof. of theory at the Lemberg (later Lwów) Cons. from 1916. In 1945 he became director of the musicological inst. at the Univ. of Poznań, a position he retained until his death. Chybiński particularly distinguished himself as an authority on Polish music history. He ed. several Polish music journals and prepared a number of early Polish compositions for publication, including works by G.G. Gorczycki, Jan of Lublin, and M. Zielenski. His autobiography, *W czasach Straussa i Tetmajera* (In the Time of Strauss and Tetmajer), was publ. posth. (Kraków, 1959). On his 50th birthday, he was honored with a Festschrift (Kraków, 1930), and again on his 70th birthday (Kraków, 1950).

WRITINGS: "Tabulatura organowa Jana z Lublina" (The Organ Tablature of Jan of Lublin), Kwartalnik muzyczny, I (1911–13); "Przyczynki bio- i bibliograficzne do dawnej muzyki polskiej" (Bio- and Bibliographical Contributions to Early Polish Music), *Przegląd muzyczny*, II, nos. 1, 4, and 5 (1926) and V, nos. 2 and 11 (1929); "Z dziejow muzyki polskiej do 1800 roku" (The History of Polish Music to 1800), *Muzyka*, IV/7–9 (1927); *Grzegorz Gerwazy Gorczycki. Cz. I: Życie, dzialalność, dziela* (A Study of His Life and Music; Poznań, 1928); "Stosunki muzyczne Polski z Francją w XVI stuleciu" (Musical Relations between Poland and France in the 16th Century), *Przegląd muzyczny*, IV, nos. 3 and 4 (1928; also publ. separately, Poznań, 1928); *Mieczyslaw Karlowicz* (Warsaw, 1939; 2nd ed., aug., 1949); *Slownik muzykow dawnej Polski do roku 1800* (A Dictionary of Early Polish Musicians to 1800; Kraków, 1949).

Ciamaga, Gustav, Canadian composer; b. London, Ontario, April 10, 1930. He studied theory with Weinzweig and Beckwith at the Univ. of Toronto (1953–56) and studied composition and musicology with Berger, Shapero, and Irving Fine at Brandeis Univ. In 1963 he was appointed to the music faculty at the Univ. of Toronto, where he was director of its electronic music studio. His electronic scores include: *Ottawa 1967* (1966); *Curtain Raiser* (1969); *1-Part Invention* (1965); 8 *2-Part Inventions* (1965–70); *Ragamuffin Nos. 1* and *2* (1967); he wrote several scores of computer music, among them *Canon for Stravinsky* (1972); also *Solipsism while Dying* for Voice, Instruments, and Tape (1972).

Ciani, Dino, Italian pianist; b. Fiume, June 16, 1941; d. in an automobile accident in Rome, March 28, 1974. He first studied in Genoa with Marta del Vecchio; after further training at the Rome Cons., he received advanced instruction from Cortot at the Accademia Musicale Chigiana in Siena, in Lausanne, and in Paris (1958–62). In 1961 he took 2nd prize in the Liszt-Bartók competition in Budapest, and thereafter toured internationally. He was admired for his expansive repertoire, which ranged from the classics to the contemporary era.

Ciccolini, Aldo, distinguished Italian pianist and pedagogue; b. Naples, Aug. 15, 1925. He began piano lessons at a very early age; at 9, he was granted entrance to the Naples Cons., where he studied piano with Paolo Denza, taking 1st prize in 1940; he also took 1st prize in composition there in 1943. In 1941 he made his debut as soloist in Chopin's F minor Concerto in Naples. In 1947 he became a prof. of piano at the Naples Cons. He was co-winner of the Grand Prize in the Long-Thibaud Competition in 1949. On Nov. 2, 1950, he made his U.S. debut as soloist in Tchaikovsky's 1st Piano Concerto with the N.Y. Phil., and subsequently pursued a notable international career. He was a prof. at the Paris Cons. (1971–88). Ciccolini maintains a comprehensive repertoire, which extends from Bach to contemporary composers. His virtuoso technique is enhanced by a particularly refined lyricism.

Ciesinski, Katherine, American mezzo-soprano, sister of **Kristine Ciesinski**; b. Newark, Del., Oct. 13, 1950. She studied at Temple Univ. (B.M., 1972; M.M., 1973) and at the Curtis Inst. of Music in Philadelphia (opera diploma, 1976); she won 1st prize in the Geneva International Competition (1976) and Grand Prize in the Paris International Competition (1977). She made her concert debut with the Philadelphia Orch. (1974) and her operatic debut as Leonora in *La Favorita* with the Opera Co. of Philadelphia (1975). She sang Erika in Barber's *Vanessa* at the Spoleto Festival U.S.A. (1978), then gained wide recognition as Countess Geschwitz in the first U.S. production of the 3-act version of Berg's *Lulu* at the Santa Fe Opera (1979). In 1988 she sang in the premiere performance of Argento's *The Aspern Papers* in Dallas. She made her Metropolitan Opera debut in N.Y. as Nicklausse in *Les contes d'Hoffmann* in 1988. As a concert artist, she appeared with leading orchs. in both North America and Europe; she also gave duo recitals with her sister. Among her prominent roles are Ottavia in *L'Incoronazione di Poppea*, Laura in *La Gioconda*, Eboli in *Don Carlos*, Dalila in *Samson et Dalila*, Charlotte in *Werther*, Octavian in *Der Rosenkavalier*, and the Composer in *Ariadne auf Naxos*.

Ciesinski, Kristine, American soprano, sister of **Katherine Ciesinski**; b. Wilmington, Del., July 5, 1952. She studied at Temple Univ. (1970–71), the Univ. of Delaware (1971–72), and Boston Univ. (1973–74; B.A., 1974); in 1977 she won the Gold Medal in the Geneva International Competition and 1st prize in the Salzburg International Competition. She made her N.Y. concert debut as a soloist in Handel's Messiah (1977) and her European operatic debut as Baroness Freimann in Lortzing's *Der Wildschütz* at the Salzburg Landestheater (1979), remaining on its roster until 1981; was subsequently a member of the Bremen State Opera (1985–88). She made guest appearances with the Cleveland Opera (1985), Glasgow's Scottish National Opera (1985), Toronto's Canadian Opera Co. (1986), Leeds's Opera North (1986), the Augsburg Opera (1986), Cardiff's Welsh National Opera (1986), Munich's Bavarian State Opera (1989), London's English National Opera (1989–93), and Milan's La Scala (1992). She also sang extensively in concerts, often appearing with her sister. Her finest roles include Iphigénie, Medea, Beethoven's Leonora, Cassandra, La Wally, Eva, Elisabeth in *Tannhäuser*, Chrysothemis, Ariadne, Salome, and Tosca. She married **Norman Bailey** in 1985.

Cigna, Gina (real name, **Ginetta Sens**), French soprano of Italian descent; b. Paris, March 6, 1900. She was a pupil of Calvé, Darclée, and Storchio. After making her operatic debut as Freia at Milan's La Scala in 1927, she was on its roster (1929–43); also appeared at London's Covent Garden (1933; 1936–37; 1939). On Feb. 6, 1937, she made her Metropolitan Opera debut in N.Y. as Aida, and sang there until 1938 in such roles as Leonora in *Il Trovatore*, Gioconda, Norma, Donna Elvira, and Santuzza. After World War II, she taught voice in Milan; also was on the faculty of the Royal Cons. of Music of Toronto (1953–57).

Cikker, Jan, eminent Slovak composer and pedagogue; b. Banská Bystrica, July 29, 1911; d. Bratislava, Dec. 21, 1989. He was a student of Křička (composition), Dědeček (conducting), and Wiedermann (organ) at the Prague Cons. (1930–35), where he then attended Novák's master class in composition (1935–36); he concurrently studied musicology at the Univ. of Prague, and then pursued conducting studies with Weingartner in Vienna (1936–37). After settling in Bratislava, he was prof. of theory at the Cons. (1938–51) and prof. of composition at the Academy of Music and Dramatic Arts (1951–81). In 1955, 1963, and 1975 he was awarded state prizes. In 1966 he was named a National Artist by his homeland, and that same year was awarded the Herder Prize of the Univ. of Vienna. In 1979 he received the UNESCO Prize. In a number of his works, Cikker utilized Slovak melodies. In others, he moved toward expressionism and eventually embraced serial procedures. His works for the stage were particularly notable.

WORKS: OPERAS: *Juro Jánošík* (1953; Bratislava, Nov. 10, 1954; rev. version, Bratislava, May 7, 1956); *Beg Bajazid* (Bajazet Bey; 1956; Bratislava, Feb. 16, 1957); *Mr. Scrooge*, after Dickens (1957–59; 1st perf. as *Evening, Night, and Morning*, Kassel, Oct. 5, 1963); *Vzkriesenie* (Resurrection), after Tolstoy (1961; Prague, May 18, 1962); *Hra o láske a smrti* (A Play of Love and Death), after Romain Rolland (1968; Munich, Aug. 1, 1969); *Coriolanus* (1971; Prague, April 4, 1974); *Rozsudok: Zemetrasenie v Chile* (The Sentence: Earthquake in Chile; 1978; Bratislava, Oct. 8, 1979); *Obliehanie Bystrice* (The Siege of Bystrica; 1981; Bratislava, Oct. 8, 1983); *Zo života hmyzu* (From the Life of Insects; 1986; Bratislava, Feb. 21, 1987). **ORCH.:** 3 syms.: No. 1 (1930; arranged from the Piano Sonata, 1927), No. 2, *Jarná symfónia* (Spring Sym., 1937), and No. 3, *Symfónia 1945* (1974; Bratislava, May 22, 1975); *Epitaf*, symphonic poem (1931; rev. 1973); *Prologue symphonique* (1934); *Capriccio* (1936); *Symphonietta* (1939; arranged from the Piano Sonatine, 1933); *O živote* (About Life), cycle of 3 symphonic poems: *Leto* (Summer; 1941), *Vojak a matka: Boj* (Soldier and Mother: Battle; 1943), and *Ráno* (Morning; 1944–46); Piano Concertino (1942); *Slovenská suita* (1943); *Spomienky* (Recollections) for 5 Winds and Strings (1947); *Dramatická fantázia* (1957); *Meditácie na tému Heinricha Schütza* (Meditations on a Theme of Heinrich Schütz; 1964); *Orchestrálne štúdie k činohre* (Orchestral Studies on a Drama; 1965); *Hommage à Beethoven* (1970); *Variácie na slovenskú l'udovú pieseň* (Variations on a Slovak Folk Song; 1970); *Paleta* (Palette; 1980). **CHAMBER:** 1 unnumbered string quartet (1928); 2 numbered string quartets (1935, 1935); Suite for Violin and Viola (1935); *Domovina* (Homeland) for String Quartet (1986). **PIANO:** Sonata (1927); Sonatine (1933); *Variácie* (Variations; 1935); *V samote* (Dance of Solitude; 1939); *Tatranské potoky* (The Tatra Streams), 3 Études (1954); *Čo mi deti rozprávali* (What Children Told Me), 15 aquarelles (1957); *Variácie* (Variations), on a Slovak folk song (1973). **VOCAL:** *Vianočná kantata* (Christmas Cantata) for Chorus and Piano (1930); *Vel'konočná kantata* (Easter Cantata) for Chorus and Orch. (1931); *Cantus filiorum*, cantata for Bass, Chorus, and Orch. (1939); *O mamičke* (About Mother), song cycle for Voice and Piano (1940); *Óda na radosť* (Ode to Joy), oratorio for Soloists, Reciter, Chorus, and Orch. (1982).

BIBL.: J. Samko, *J. C.* (Bratislava, 1955).

Cilèa, Francesco, Italian composer and pedagogue; b. Palmi, Calabria, July 23, 1866; d. Varazze, Nov. 20, 1950. He studied at the Naples Cons. (1881–89) with Cesi (piano) and Serrao (composition); taught piano there (1894–96); then harmony at the Istituto Musicale in Florence (1896–1904); was head of the Palermo Cons. (1913–16) and of the Cons. di San Pietro a Majella in Naples (1916–35). He was a member of the Reale Accademia Musicale in Florence (1898) and a knight of the Order of the Crown of Italy (1893).

WORKS: OPERAS: *Gina* (Naples, Feb. 9, 1889); *La Tilda* (Florence, April 7, 1892); *L'Arlesiana* (Milan, Nov. 27, 1897; rev. version, Milan, Oct. 22, 1898); *Adriana Lecouvreur* (Milan, Nov. 6, 1902); *Gloria* (Milan, April 15, 1907); *Il matrimonio selvaggio* (1909). **OTHER:** *Poema sinfonico* for Soloist, Chorus, and Orch. (Genoa, July 12, 1913); Piano Trio (1886); Cello Sonata (1888); *Variations* for Violin and Piano (1931); piano pieces; songs.

BIBL.: E. Moschino, *Sulle opere di F. C.* (Milan, 1932); C. Gaianus, *F. C. e la sua nuova ora* (Bologna, 1939); T. d'Amico, *F. C.* (Milan, 1960).

Cillario, Carlo Felice, Italian conductor; b. San Rafael, Argentina, Feb. 7, 1915. He began music training in Buenos Aires, then studied violin and composition at the Bologna Cons. After making appearances as a violinist, he received instruction in conducting from Enesco; he then went to Russia, where he continued his studies at the Odessa Cons. He made his conducting debut at the Odessa Opera (1942), and after World War II embarked on a far-flung career as an operatic and sym. conductor, making guest appearances in the leading music centers of Europe and North and South America. He was music director of the Australian Opera in Sydney (1969–71), serving as its principal guest conductor and music consultant from 1987.

Cimara, Pietro, Italian conductor and composer; b. Rome, Nov. 10, 1887; d. Milan, Oct. 1, 1967. He was a student of Respighi at the Accademia di Santa Cecilia in Rome. In 1916 he made his conducting debut in Rome, where he conducted until 1927. On March 11, 1932, he made his Metropolitan Opera debut in N.Y. conducting *Lucia di Lammermoor*, remaining on its roster until 1937; was again on its roster (1938–50; 1952–57). He composed many songs.

Ciortea, Tudor, Romanian composer and teacher; b. Braşov, Dec. 11, 1903; d. Bucharest, Oct. 13, 1982. He studied with J. Jongen in Brussels, Boulanger and Paul Dukas in Paris, and with Otescu at the Bucharest Cons., where he subsequently taught (1941–71).

WORKS: ORCH.: *Suită maramureşeană* (1949); *Passacaglia and Toccata* (1957); Concerto for Strings (1958; Bucharest, Jan. 2, 1960); *Variations on a Popular Theme* for Piano and Orch. (1969); Clarinet Concerto (1972; Bucharest, June 6, 1974). **CHAMBER:** Violin Sonata (1946); Cello Sonata (1946; rev. 1958); Trio for Violin, Cello, and Piano (1949; rev. 1978); 6 string quartets (1952, 1954, 1975, 1977, 1981, 1981); Piano Quintet (1957); Flute Sonata (1961; rev. 1966); Clarinet Sonata (1962); Trumpet Sonata (1964); Quintet for Clarinet, Violin, Viola, Cello, and Piano (1970); Brass Quintet (1970); Sextet for Flute, Oboe, Clarinet, Horn, Cello, and Double Bass (1982); various piano pieces, including 3 sonatas (1949, 1953, 1959) and a Sonatina (1960). **VOCAL:** Numerous songs.

Cipra, Milo, Croatian composer and pedagogue; b. Vares, Oct. 13, 1906; d. Zagreb, July 9, 1985. He was a pupil of Bersa at the Zagreb Academy of Music (graduated, 1933), where he later taught (from 1941) and served as its dean (1961–71). His early works followed traditional song patterns of Croatia while sustaining the formal elements of universal classicism, but he later adopted more modern methods.

WORKS: ORCH.: *Sinfonietta* (1934; rev. 1946); 2 syms. (1948, 1952); *Dubrovački Divertimento* for Chamber Orch. (1955–56); Concerto for Strings (1956); *Sunčev put* (Sun's Way) for Wind Orch., Piano, Harp, and Percussion (1958–59); *3 susreta* (Encounters; 1961); *Epitaf* (1961); *Leda*, symphonic pantomime (1965); *Triptih dalmatinskih gradova* (Triptych of Dalmation Cities; Zagreb, Dec. 10, 1976). **CHAMBER:** 5 string quartets (1930, 1932, 1935, 1938, 1972); Piano Trio (1937); Violin Sonata (1944); Cello Sonata (1946); *Musica sine nomine* for 5 Winds, Piano, and Voice (1963); *Svitanje* (Aubade) for Wind Quintet (1965). **PIANO:** Sonata (1954). **VOCAL:** Songs.

Cirino, Giulio, Italian bass; b. Rome, Feb. 15, 1880; d. there, Feb. 26, 1970. He made his operatic debut in Rome in 1903; subsequently sang at La Scala in Milan; was on the roster of the Teatro Colón in Buenos Aires from 1909 to 1923; retired from the stage in 1935. He was particularly successful in buffo roles of the Italian repertoire, but he also sang in Wagner's operas.

Cisneros, Eleanora de (née **Broadfoot**), American mezzo-soprano; b. Brooklyn, Nov. 1, 1878; d. there (N.Y.), Feb. 3,

1934. She received training from Francesco Fanciulli and Adeline Murio-Celli in N.Y. Under the name Eleanor Francis, she made her operatic debut as Siebel at N.Y.'s American Theater in 1898. Her talent was recognized by Jean de Reszke, who arranged for her Metropolitan Opera debut as Rossweise in *Die Walküre* during the company's visit to Chicago on Nov. 24, 1899, under the name Eleanor Broadfoot. Her formal debut with the company followed in N.Y. in the same role on Jan. 5, 1900; she remained on its roster for the season. In 1901 she married Cuban Count Francesco de Cisneros and took his name professionally. After further training with Angelo Tabadello in Paris, she made her European debut in Turin in 1902. She then appeared at London's Covent Garden (1904–08) and at Milan's La Scala, where she created the role of Candia in Franchetti's *La figlia di Iorio* (1906); she also appeared in the first mountings there of Tchaikovsky's *The Queen of Spades* (1906) and Strauss's *Salome* (1906) and *Elektra* (1909). She was the principal artist with the Manhattan Opera House (1906–08), and also appeared at the Bayreuth Festival (1908). She sang in Chicago (1910–13; 1915–16), and also with Melba's opera company in London and Australia in 1911. In subsequent years, she concentrated her career in Europe. In 1932 she gave her farewell performance in Cleveland. In addition to her Wagnerian roles, she had success as Gioconda, Azucena, Santuzza, and Carmen.

Citkowitz, Israel, Polish-born American composer and teacher; b. Skierniewice, Feb. 6, 1909; d. London, May 4, 1974. He was taken to the U.S. as a child and became a naturalized citizen. After studies with Copland and Sessions in N.Y., he pursued training with Boulanger in Paris (1927–31); then wrote music criticism. From 1939 to 1969 he taught at N.Y.'s Dalcroze School of Music, and then settled in London. He wrote a String Quartet (1932), *Andante tranquillo* for String Quartet (1932), *Movements* for String Quartet, and a Piano Sonatine (1929), but was best known for his choral pieces *The Lamb* (1936) and *Songs of Protest* (1936), and for his song cycles and solo songs.

Ciuciura, Leoncjusz, Polish composer; b. Grodzisk Mazowiecki, July 22, 1930. He studied with Szeligowski at the State College of Music in Warsaw. All of his works are essays in combinatorial permutation with optional instrumental or vocal additions, subtractions, multiplications, or divisions.

WORKS: *Canti al fresco* for 9 Women's Voices and Instrumental Ensemble (1961); *Concertino de camera* for Chamber Orch. (1961); *Ornament* for Flute, Bassoon, Clarinet, and Strings (1962); *Penetrations* for 4 Orch. Groups, 4 Conductors, and Composer (1963); *Spirale I per uno* for Baritone and 36 Percussion Instruments (1964) and *II per uno e più* for Optional Instrumental Ensemble (1964); *Emergenza* for 3 Orch. Groups, 3 Conductors, and Composer (1964); *Incidenti* for Optional Voices and Instrumental Ensemble (1964); *Per 5* for any combination of Flute, Oboe, Horn, Bassoon, and Trumpet (1972); *Creatoria I* and *II* for Optional Voice or Instrument or Groups of Instruments or Voices (1975); *Music* for Flute and 8 Instruments (1976).

Civil, Alan, noted English horn player and teacher; b. Northampton, June 13, 1929; d. London, March 19, 1989. He studied with Aubrey Brain in London and with Willy von Stemm in Hamburg. Returning to London, he was principal horn of the Royal Phil. (1952–55), and later co-principal horn, with Dennis Brain, of the Philharmonia Orch. (1955–57); after Brain's tragic death, he was principal horn (1957–66); from 1966 to 1988 he was principal horn of the BBC Sym. Orch. In 1966 he became a prof. of horn at the Royal College of Music in London. In 1979 he became president of the British Horn Soc. He was made a member of the Order of the British Empire in 1985.

Claflin, (Alan) Avery, American composer; b. Keene, N.H., June 21, 1898; d. Greenwich, Conn., Jan. 9, 1979. He studied law and banking, and also received instruction in music at Harvard Univ. from Davison. In 1919 he joined the employ of the French-American Banking Corp. in N.Y., later serving as its president (1947–54). His best known work was an amusing choral piece on a text of the Internal Revenue Service, *Lament for April 15* (Tanglewood, Aug. 11, 1955).

WORKS: OPERAS: *The Fall of Usher* (1920–21); *Hester Prynne* (1929–33); *La grande bretèche*, after Balzac (1946–48; NBC Radio, Feb. 3, 1957); *Uncle Tom's Cabin* (1961–64). **ORCH.:** *Moby Dick Suite* (1929; also for 2 Pianos); *Chapter III: A Symphony* (1934–36); *Concerto Allegro* (1938); Sym. No. 2 (1941–43); *Fishbone Punch* (1945; also for 2 Pianos, 1953); *Teen Scenes* for Strings (1954–55); *4 Pieces for Orchestra*: Sym. No. 3 (1956); Piano Concerto: *Concerto giocoso* (1957; also for 2 Pianos, 6-hands). **CHAMBER:** Piano Trio (1922); String Quartet (1937). **VOCAL:** *Mary of Nazareth* for Chorus and Organ (1948–51); *Lament for April 15* for Chorus (Tanglewood, Aug. 11, 1955).

Clapham, John, English musicologist; b. Letchworth, July 31, 1908; d. Bristol, Nov. 9, 1992. He studied cello with Douglas Cameron, and took courses in harmony and counterpoint at the Royal Academy of Music in London; then studied at the Univ. of London (B.Mus., 1934; D.Mus., 1946). He was a lecturer at the Univ. College of Wales in Aberystwyth (1946–62); then was senior lecturer (1962–69) and lecturer (1969–73) at the Univ. of Edinburgh. He distinguished himself in studies of Czech music.

WRITINGS: *Antonín Dvořák: Musician and Craftsman* (London, 1966); *Smetana* (London, 1972); *Dvořák* (Newton Abbot, 1979).

Clapp, Philip Greeley, American composer and pedagogue; b. Boston, Aug. 4, 1888; d. Iowa City, April 9, 1954. He studied piano with his aunt Mary Greeley James (1895–99) and violin with Jacques Hoffman in Boston (1895–1905); also took lessons in theory with John Marshall (1905). He then entered Harvard Univ., studying theory and composition with Spalding, Converse, and Edward Burlingame Hill (B.A., 1908; M.A., 1909; Ph.D., 1911). He also studied composition and conducting in Stuttgart with Max von Schillings (1909–10). He was a teaching fellow at Harvard (1911–12); was music director at Dartmouth College (1915–18); in 1919 he was appointed director of the music dept. at the Univ. of Iowa, and remained at that post for the rest of his life. Clapp was a prolific composer and a competent teacher; he was also a brilliant pianist, but did not develop a concert career; he also appeared as a conductor of his own works and was in charge of the univ. orch. at Iowa City. His music was conceived in an expansive Romantic idiom much influenced by the modern German style of composition, and yet introducing some advanced melodic and harmonic patterns, such as harmonies built on fourths.

WORKS: OPERAS: *The Taming of the Shrew* (1945–48); *The Flaming Brand* (1949–53). **ORCH.:** *Norge*, symphonic poem (Cambridge, Mass., April 29, 1909); 12 syms.: No. 1, in E major (1910; Waterloo, Iowa, April 27, 1933, composer conducting), No. 2, in E minor (Boston, April 10, 1914, composer conducting), No. 3, in E-flat major (Boston, April 6, 1917, composer conducting), No. 4, in A major (1919; rev. 1941), No. 5, in D major (1926; rev. 1941; Iowa City, July 26, 1944, composer conducting), No. 6, in B major, *Golden Gate* (1926; San Jose, Calif., June 5, 1951), No. 7, in A major (Boston, March 22, 1931, composer conducting), No. 8, in C major (1930; rev. 1941; N.Y., Feb. 7, 1952), No. 9, in E-flat minor, *The Pioneers* (1931; Iowa City, July 16, 1939), No. 10, in F major, *Heroic* (1935; Iowa City, May 23, 1951, composer conducting), No. 11, in C major (1942; rev. 1950), and No. 12, in B-flat major (1944); *Song of Youth*, symphonic poem (1910); *Dramatic Poem* (Cambridge, Mass., April 24, 1912, composer conducting); *Summer*, prelude (St. Louis, Jan. 16, 1914); *Overture to a Comedy* (1933; Cleveland, Dec. 28, 1940); *A Highly Academic Diversion* on 7 Notes for Chamber Orch. (Iowa City, Feb. 17, 1933, composer conducting); *Fantasy on an Old Plain Chant* for Cello and Orch. (Iowa City, Jan. 17, 1940); Concerto for 2 Pianos and Orch. (Iowa City, Dec. 20, 1945). **CHAMBER:** Violin Sonata (1909); String Quartet (1909); Suite for Brass Sextet (1938); Concerto Suite for 4 Trombones (1939); *Prelude and Finale* for Woodwind Quintet

(1939). **VOCAL:** Numerous choral works, among them *A Chant of Darkness* for Chorus and Orch., to a text by Helen Keller (1919–24; rev. 1929, 1932–33; Iowa City, April 16, 1935, composer conducting).

BIBL.: D. Holcomb, *P.G. C.* (Iowa City, 1972); C. Calmer, *P.G. C.: The Later Years (1909–54)* (diss., Univ. of Iowa, 1992).

Clark, Edward, English conductor; b. Newcastle upon Tyne, May 10, 1888; d. London, April 29, 1962. He studied in Paris, in Vienna, and in Berlin with Schoenberg. He led the orch. for Diaghilev's London seasons (1924–26); was with the BBC (1927–36); in 1940 he founded the North Eastern Regional Orch. in Newcastle. In 1947 he was elected president of the International Soc. for Contemporary Music. He was married to **Elizabeth Lutyens**.

Clark, Melville Antone, American harpist and harp manufacturer; b. Syracuse, N.Y., Sept. 12, 1883; d. there, Dec. 11, 1953. His uncle was the well-known instrument maker, Melville Clark (1850–1918). He received his first instruction on the harp from his father; then was a pupil of Van Veachton Rogers (1896–99) and of John Aptommas in London (1908). While on a tour of Great Britain in 1908, he acquired a small Irish harp, formerly the property of the poet Thomas Moore; by the application of acoustic principles, he improved the model and succeeded in producing a small, portable harp (39 inches high) of considerable tone volume. He founded the Clark Harp Manufacturing Co. in Syracuse, which turned out the first small Irish harps in 1913; on a tour of the U.S. with John McCormack (1913–14), he demonstrated the possibilities of the new instrument; he took out 14 patents for improvements on the portable harp, and also developed a new method of pedaling the concert harp. He gave about 4,000 recitals in the U.S., Canada, and England; was co-founder of the Syracuse Sym. Orch. and president of the Clark Music Co. (1910). He authored several manuals, including *How to Play the Harp*, *Romance of the Harp*, and *Singing Strings*.

Clarke, Henry Leland, American composer and teacher; b. Dover, N.H., March 9, 1907. He received training in piano, organ, and violin before pursuing his education at Harvard Univ. (M.A., 1929), where he studied composition with Holst (1931–32; Ph.D., 1947, with a diss. on John Blow). He also studied with Boulanger at the École Normale de Musique in Paris (1929–31) and with Weisse and Luening in Bennington, Vt., and N.Y. (1932–38). Clarke taught at Bennington (Vt.) College (1936–38), Westminster Choir College in Princeton, N.J. (1938–42), the Univ. of Calif. at Los Angeles (1947–58), and the Univ. of Wash. in Seattle (1958–77). He publ. the book *Sound and Unsound: Ideas on Music* (Seattle, 1973). In his compositions, he developed such innovations as "Intervalescent Counterpoint" (with interval values constantly changing one voice to another), "Lipophony" (with certain notes systematically omitted), "Word Tones" (whenever a word recurs, it is assigned to the same pitch), and "Rotating Triskaidecaphony" (a 12-tone series returning to note 1 for the 13th note, with the next row starting and ending on note 2, etc.).

WORKS: OPERAS: *The Loafer and the Loaf* (1951; Los Angeles, May 1, 1956); *Lysistrata* (1968–72; Marlboro, Vt., Nov. 9, 1984). **ORCH.:** *Lyric Sonata* for Strings (1932; rev. 1960); *Monograph* (1952); *Saraband for the Golden Goose* (1957); *Points West* for Wind and Percussion (1960; also for Full Orch., 1970); *Encounter* for Viola and Orch. (1961); *Variegation* (1961). **CHAMBER:** 3 string quartets (1928, 1956, 1958); *Danza de la muerte* for Oboe and Piano (1937); *Nocturne* for Viola and Piano (1955); *A Game That 2 Can Play* for Flute and Clarinet (1959); *Concatenata (Quodlibet)* for Wind Quintet (1969); *Danza de la vida* for Oboe and Piano (1975); *3 From Foster, Fuguing Trio* for Flute, Violin, and Cello (1980–81); *Drastic Measures* for Trombone (1982); *Salute to Justin Morgan* for Flute, Violin, and Harpsichord (1982); much piano and organ music. **VOCAL: CHORAL:** *No Man is an Island*, after Donne (1951); *The Young Dead Soldiers*, after MacLeish (1970); *These are the Times that Try Men's Souls*, after Paine (1976); *Choose Life*, after *Deuteronomy* 30:19 (1983); *The Sun Shines Also Today*, after Emerson (1983); *We Believe*, after Von Odgen Vogt (1984); *The Earth Mourns*, after *Isaiah* 24 (1984); many songs.

BIBL.: O. Daniel, *H.L. C.* (N.Y., 1970).

Clarke, Rebecca (Thacher), English-born American composer and violist; b. Harrow, Aug. 27, 1886; d. N.Y., Oct. 13, 1979. She studied violin with Hans Wessely at the Royal Academy of Music (1902–04) and composition with Stanford at the Royal College of Music (1904–10) in London; she then switched to the viola, taking a few private lessons from Tertis and becoming the first female member of Henry Wood's Queen Hall Orch. (1912). In 1928 she formed the English Ensemble, with which she played until 1929. She married **James Friskin** in 1944; she then lived in N.Y. Her music, comprising entirely chamber works, was quite advanced, being on the fringe of atonality in outline, but remaining firmly rooted in English Impressionism. For some of her compositions, she used the name Anthony Trent.

WORKS: Violin Sonata (1909); *Morpheus* for Viola and Piano (1917); Viola Sonata (1919); Piano Trio (1921); String Quartet (1924); *Epilogue* for Cello and Piano (1921); *Chinese Puzzle* for Violin and Piano (1921); *Rhapsody* for Cello and Piano (1923); *Midsummer Moon* for Violin and Piano (1924); *3 Old English Songs* for Voice and Piano (1924); *3 Irish Country Songs* for Voice and Violin (1926); *Prelude, Allegro, and Pastorale* for Clarinet and Viola (1941; Berkeley, Calif., Aug. 6, 1942); *Combined Carols* for String Quartet and Strings (1941); *Passacaglia on an Old English Tune* for Viola and Piano (1941); over 60 songs.

BIBL.: M. Ponder, "R. C.," *Journal of the British Music Society* (1983); C. MacDonald, "R. C.'s Chamber Music," *Tempo* (March 1987).

Claussen, Julia (née **Ohlson**), Swedish mezzo-soprano; b. Stockholm, June 11, 1879; d. there, May 1, 1941. She studied at the Royal Academy of Music in Stockholm (1897–1902); then in Berlin with Friedrich (1903–05). She made her operatic debut as Leonora in *La Favorite* at the Stockholm Opera (Jan. 19, 1903); was engaged there from 1903 until 1932; made her debut at Covent Garden in London in 1914; was a member of the Chicago Opera Co. (1912–14; 1915–17). She made her first appearance at the Metropolitan Opera in N.Y. as Dalila on Nov. 23, 1917, and remained on its roster until 1929; in 1934 she returned to Stockholm as a teacher at the Cons.

Clemencic, René, Austrian recorder player, harpsichordist, conductor, and composer; b. Vienna, Feb. 27, 1928. He took courses in musicology at the Sorbonne in Paris, the Collège de France, and the Univ. of Vienna (Ph.D., 1956); studied recorder, harpsichord, and theory with H. Staeps, harpsichord with E. Harich-Schneider, early music with J. Mertin, analysis with E. Ratz, and theory with J. Polnauer in Vienna; he also received recorder training from J. Collette in Nijmegen and from L. Hoffer v. Wintersfeld and W. Nitschke in Berlin. In 1958 he founded the Musica Antiqua in Vienna, which became the Ensemble Musica Antiqua in 1959; with this group, he gave performances of music from the Middle Ages to the Baroque, utilizing authentic instruments. In 1969 he founded the Clemencic Consort, and led it in a vast repertoire, extending from the medieval period to the avant-garde. He also taught at the Vienna Academy of Music and authored 2 books, *Old Musical Instruments* (London, 1968; also in German) and *Carmina Burana, Kommentar zur Gesamtausgabe der Melodien* (Munich, 1979).

WORKS: *Fantasia Dodekafonica* for Recorder (1964); *Maraviglia I* for Recorder (1968), *II* for Recorder (1968), *III/Iter Exstaticum* for Speaker and Chamber Ensemble (1968), *IV/Lucerna Eius* for Chamber Ensemble (1969), and *V* for Voice and 4 Players (1972); *Bicinia Nova* for 2 Recorders or Piccolo Flutes (1969); *Experience One* for Recorder, Harpsichord, and Tape (1971); *Nova Bicinia Nova* for 2 Recorders (1971); *Sesostris I*, monodrama for Speaker and 5 Players (1970) and *II* for Speaker, 2 Loudspeakers, 4 Singers, and Chamber Ensemble

(1976); *Chronos I* for Recorder, Violin, and Tape (1971), *II* for 4 Recorders (1975), and *III* for 4 Instruments (1976); *Flauto Magico I* for Recorder (1978) and *II* for Recorder and Strings (1984); *Realitäten* for Voice and Chamber Ensemble (1979); *Musik zum "Urfaust"* for Voice and Chamber Ensemble (1980); *Sicut Navis* for Cello and Piano (1981); *Missa Mundi (Ossiacher Marienmesse)* for 5 Voices, Chorus, and Orch. (1981); *Musik zu "Tolldreiste Szenen"* for Voice and Chamber Ensemble (1981); *Stufen* for Countertenor and 5 Instruments (1981); *Musik zum "Prinz von Homburg"* for Orch. (1983); *Unus Mundus* for 10 Instruments and Tape (1986); *Requiem pro Vivis et Mortuis* for 5 Voices, Chorus, and Orch. (1986–87); *Drachenkampf* for Speaker and 7 Players (1987); *Estasi* for 6 Percussionists (1988); *Passatempo* for Brass and Wind Quintet (1989); *Musica Instrumentalis* for Chamber Ensemble (1989); *Musica Hermetica* for 2 Violins and Tape (1989).

Clemens, Hans, German tenor; b. Bicken-Gelsenkirchen, July 27, 1890; d. Montrose, Colo., Aug. 25, 1958. After successful appearances in Germany and at Covent Garden in London, he went to the U.S. He made his Metropolitan Opera debut in N.Y. as the Steersman in *Der Fliegende Holländer* (Nov. 1, 1930); appeared also in other Wagnerian roles, being particularly effective as David in *Die Meistersinger von Nürnberg*. In 1938 he settled in Los Angeles as a vocal teacher.

Clementi, Aldo, prominent Italian composer and pedagogue; b. Catania, May 25, 1925. He began training in piano at age 13 and in composition at age 16 in Catania. He pursued piano studies with Giovanna Ferro at the Conservatorio di Santa Cecilia in Rome (diploma, 1946), and then attended Scarpini's master class at the Accademia Musicale Chigiana in Siena (1947). From 1945 to 1952 he also studied composition with Alfred Sangiorgi in Catania and Bolzano, who introduced him to 12-tone writing. Following further composition studies with Petrassi at the Conservatorio di Santa Cecilia (1952–54; diploma, 1954), he attended the summer courses in new music at Darmstadt (1955–62) and was active at the Studio di Fonologia in Milan (1956–62). From 1971 to 1992 he taught theory at the Univ. of Bologna. Among his honors were 1st prize in the ISCM competition in 1963 for his *Sette scene* for Chamber Orch. and the Abbiati Prize in 1992 for his opera *Interludi: Musica per il Mitro di Eco e Narciso*. Clementi is one of the leading avant-garde composers of Europe. As such, he sees his main task as that of creating works which fulfill his vision of contemporary music as a vehicle for the dissolution of music as we know it.

WORKS: DRAMATIC: *College*, azione musicale (Rome, May 14, 1962); *Blitz*, azione musicale (Royan, April 18, 1973); *Collage 4*, azione mimo-visiva (1979; Florence, May 30, 1981); *Finale*, azione lirica (Rome, Oct. 13, 1984); *Interludi: Musica per il Mito di Eco e Narciso*, opera (Gibellina, July 23, 1992); *Carillon*, opera (1994). **ORCH.:** *Tre studi* for Chamber Orch. (1956–57; Darmstadt, July 27, 1957); *Episodi* (1958; Brussels Radio, Jan. 13, 1959); *Sette scene* for Chamber Orch. (1961; Florence, May 20, 1964); *Informel* (1961–63; Palermo, Oct. 1, 1963); *Variante B* (1963; Venice, Sept. 12, 1964); *Sinfonia da camera* for Chamber Orch. (Milan, April 21, 1974); Concerto for Piano, 24 Instruments, and 12 Carillons (1975; Milan, Feb. 12, 1976); Concerto for Double Bass, Orch., and 12 Carillons (Royan, March 21, 1976); *Clessidra* for Chamber Orch. (Bergamo, May 22, 1976); Concerto for Violin, 40 Instruments, and 12 Carillons (Brescia, June 8, 1977); *Capriccio* for Viola and 24 Instruments (1979–80; RAI, Naples, April 4, 1980); *Halleluja* (RAI, Naples, Oct. 8, 1982); *Das Alte Jahr* for Chamber Orch. (Milan, April 27, 1985); *O du selige* (RAI, Naples, Dec. 6, 1985); *Berceuse* (1989); *Romanza* for Piano and Orch. (RAI, Rome, March 16, 1991). **CHAMBER:** Flute Sonatina (1950; Bergamo, June 6, 1983); Sonata for Trumpet, Guitar, and Piano (1955; Zürich, June 2, 1957); *Concertino in form di variazioni* for 9 Instruments (1956; London, May 27, 1957); *Ideogrammi 1* for 16 Instruments (1959; Palermo, May 13, 1960) and *2* for Flute and 17 Instruments (1959; Venice, Sept. 21, 1960); *Triplum* for Flute, Oboe, and Clarinet (1960; Darmstadt, Sept. 2, 1961); *Informel 1* for 11 Instrumentalists (1961; Venice, Sept. 6, 1970) and *2* for 15 Instruments (1962; Venice, April 16, 1963); *Reticolo: 11* for 11 Instruments (Venice, Sept. 6, 1966), *4* for String Quartet (1968; Warsaw, Sept. 28, 1969), and *12* for 12 Strings (1970; Como, Sept. 20, 1971); *Intermezzo* for 14 Instruments and Prepared Piano (Naples, June 17, 1977); *Sphinxs* for Violin, Viola, and Cello (Naples, June 15, 1978); String Quartet (1978; Venice, Oct. 1, 1979); *L'Orologio di arceua* for 13 Instrumentalists (Venice, Sept. 30, 1979); *Pastorale en Rondeau* for 2 Violins, Viola, Harpsichord, and Carillons (Perugia, June 21, 1981); Concerto for 16 Instruments (1981–82; Champigny, April 18, 1983); *Aeb* for 17 Instruments (RAI, Naples, May 13, 1983); *Adagio* for Quintet and Prepared Piano (Naples, Nov. 22, 1983); *Ouverture* for 12 Instruments (Chiusa di Chianciano, July 22, 1984); *Scherzo* for Flute, Clarinet, Violin, and Viola (1985; Zürich, Nov. 22, 1987); Concerto for Piano and 14 Instruments (1986; Genoa, Feb. 2, 1987); *Prélude: Hommage à Ravel* for 12 Instruments (Montpellier, July 21, 1987); *Fantasia* for 4 Guitars (Sermoneta, June 24, 1988); *Cantabile* for 12 Instrumentalists (Siena, Aug. 23, 1988); *Sei canoni* for Flute and Harpsichord (1990); *1492* for 16 Instruments (Latina, June 30, 1992); *Settimino* for 7 Instruments (Milan, April 22, 1993); *C.A.G.* for Flute, Violin, Vibraphone, and Guitar (Bologna, May 4, 1993); *. . . Im Himmelreich* for 9 Instruments (Amsterdam, May 16, 1994); *G.F.F. . . .* for 5 Instruments (Rome, May 18, 1994); *Albumblatt* for Flute, Guitar, and Vibraphone (Rome, May 29, 1995); *"C.A.B.E."* for Flute and Violin (Sermoneta, June 9, 1995); piano pieces; organ music. **VOCAL:** *Due poesie* for Voice and Piano (1946); Cantata for Reciter, Soprano, Chorus, and Chamber Orch. (1954); *Variante A* for Chorus and Orch. (1964; Venice, Sept. 9, 1976); *Silben* for Woman's Voice, Clarinet, Violin, and 2 Pianos (1966; Rome, March 1, 1968); *Otto frammenti* for Soprano, Countertenor, Organ, Lute, and Viola da Gamba (Naples, June 17, 1978); *Im Frieden dein, O Herre mein* for 8 Voices (Bologna, Sept. 7, 1980); *Cent sopirs* for Chamber Chorus and Orch. (RAI, Rome, April 16, 1983); *Ach ich fühl's* for Voice and 15 Instruments (Milan, April 21, 1985); *Mottetto su re, mi . . .* for 18 Women's Voices (1989); *Cantilena* for Voice and Double Bass (1989–90); *The Plaint* for Woman's Voice and 13 Instruments (Melbourne, May 22, 1992); *Rapsodia* for Soprano, Contralto, and Orch. (Stuttgart, April 24, 1994); *Vocalizzo* for Voice and Instrumental Groups (Sermoneta, June 10, 1994). **ELECTRONIC:** *Collage 2* (1960; Venice, April 15, 1962) and *3: Dies irae* (1966–67; RAI, Aug. 27, 1967); *Studio per una passacaglia* (Milan, May 3, 1993).

BIBL.: R. Cresti, *A. C.: Studio monografico e intervista* (Milan, 1990).

Cleobury, Nicholas (Randall), English conductor, organist, pianist, and harpsichordist, brother of **Stephen (John) Cleobury**; b. Bromley, June 23, 1950. He was educated at Worcester College, Oxford. After serving as assistant organist at Chichester Cathedral (1971–72) and Christ Church, Oxford (1972–76), he was chorus master at the Glyndebourne Festival (1976–79); was also assistant director of the BBC Singers in London (1977–80). He was the principal opera conductor at the Royal Academy of Music in London from 1980 to 1987. In 1989 he became artistic director of the Cambridge Sym. Orch., a position he retained when it became the Britten Sinfonia in 1992. As a guest conductor, he appeared with all of the major British orchs. and also toured in Europe, North America, and Australia. He also was frequently engaged as an opera conductor in England.

Cleobury, Stephen (John), English conductor and organist, brother of **Nicholas (Randall) Cleobury**; b. Bromley, Dec. 31, 1948. He received training at St. John's College, Cambridge (M.A.,; Mus.B.). After serving as organist at St. Matthew's, Northampton (1971–74), he was sub-organist at Westminster Abbey in London (1974–78); then was master of music at Westminster Cathedral (1979–82). In 1982 he became director of music at King's College, Cambridge. He became well known via his many tours as conductor of the King's College Choir, as well as through its annual live worldwide broadcast each Christmas Eve of the Festival of 9 Lessons and Carols. From 1990 to 1992 he served as president of the Royal College of Organists. In 1995 he became chief conductor of the BBC Singers in London.

Clercx, Suzanne, Belgian musicologist; b. Houdeng-Aimeries, June 7, 1910; d. Liège, Sept. 27, 1985. She studied at the Univ. of Liège; took courses in musicology with Charles van den Borren; obtained her Ph.D. in 1939 with the diss. *Essai sur l'évolution de la musique instrumentale dans les Pays-Bas au XVIII siècle.* She was then a librarian at the Royal Cons. in Brussels (1941–49); in 1945 she was appointed lecturer at the Univ. of Liège; became a prof. in 1966, where she was active until 1975; in 1980 she was made prof. emeritus. In 1952 she was made a corresponding member of the American Musicological Soc.

WRITINGS: *Henri-Jacques de Croes* (Brussels, 1940); *Grétry, 1741–1813* (Brussels, 1944); *Le Baroque et la musique* (Brussels, 1948); *Pierre van Maldère* (Brussels, 1948); *Johannes Ciconia: Un Musicien liégeois et son temps* (Brussels, 1960).

Cleva, Fausto (Angelo), Italian-born American conductor; b. Trieste, May 17, 1902; d. while conducting at the odeum of Herodes Atticus in Athens, Aug. 6, 1971. He studied at the Trieste Cons. and the Milan Cons. After making his conducting debut with *La Traviata* at the Teatro Carcano in Milan in 1920, he emigrated to the U.S. and became a naturalized citizen in 1931. In 1921 he joined the staff of the Metropolitan Opera in N.Y., where he later was chorus master (1935–42). On Dec. 4, 1938, he made his first appearance there as a conductor in a Sunday evening concert. His formal debut with the company followed on Feb. 14, 1942, when he conducted *Il Barbiere di Siviglia.* He then conducted at the San Francisco Opera (1942–44; 1949–55) and was music director of the Cincinnati Summer Opera (1943–63). He also rejoined the roster of the Metropolitan Opera in 1950, where he conducted every season until his death

Cleve, Halfdan, Norwegian pianist, teacher, and composer; b. Kongsberg, Oct. 5, 1879; d. Oslo, April 6, 1951. He studied with his father, an organist, and with Winter-Hjelm in Christiania; then continued his studies in Berlin with O. Raif and with the Scharwenka brothers (1899–1903). He made his debut as a pianist in Berlin (1902); then settled in Christiania in 1910 as a pianist and teacher. His compositions include 5 piano concertos (1902, 1904, 1906, 1910, 1916); Piano Quintet; Violin Sonata; Ballade for Cello and Piano; many piano pieces and songs.

Cleveland, James, black American gospel singer and composer; b. Chicago, Dec. 5, 1931; d. Los Angeles, Feb. 9, 1991. He was reared in a gospel milieu in which he was encouraged to develop his natural talent for music by the pianist Roberta Martin. He was a pianist and singer with the group the Caravans and then formed his own Gospel Chimes in 1959; he also became a licensed minister of the Church of God in Christ. His song *Grace Is Sufficient* (1948) became a gospel standard; his album *Peace Be Still* (1963) added further to his renown. In 1970 he founded the Cornerstone Institutional Baptist Church, for which he also served as pastor.

Cliburn, Van (actually, **Harvey Lavan, Jr.**), brilliant American pianist; b. Shreveport, La., July 12, 1934. His mother, Rildia Bee Cliburn, was a pupil of Arthur Friedheim; she was his only teacher until 1951, when he entered the Juilliard School of Music in N.Y. as a student of Rosina Lhévinne, graduating in 1954. He was 4 when he made his first public appearance in Shreveport; after winning the Texas State Prize in 1947, he appeared as a soloist with the Houston Sym. Orch. In 1948 he won the National Music Festival Award, in 1952 the Dealy Award and the Kosciuszko Foundation Chopin prize, in 1953 the Juilliard School of Music concerto competition, and in 1954 the Roeder Award and the Leventritt competition in N.Y.; that same year he appeared as a soloist with the N.Y. Phil. In 1958 he captured 1st prize at the Tchaikovsky Competition in Moscow, the first American to achieve this feat; upon his return to N.Y., he received a hero's welcome in a ticker-tape parade. In subsequent years he toured extensively, appearing as a soloist with leading orchs. and as a recitalist. In 1978 he withdrew from public performances, but appeared again in 1987 as a recitalist in a concert for President Reagan and Soviet General Secretary Gorbachev at the White House in Washington, D.C. In 1989 he appeared as soloist in the Liszt and Tchaikovsky 1st piano concertos with the Philadelphia Orch.; that same year he accepted Gorbachev's invitation to perform in Moscow, and on Sept. 8 was the soloist with Eduardo Mata and the Dallas Sym. Orch. in the gala opening of the Morton H. Meyerson Sym. Center. In the summer of 1994 he toured the U.S. as soloist with the Moscow Phil. Van Cliburn's playing combines a superlative technique with a genuine Romantic sentiment, particularly effective in the music of Tchaikovsky and Rachmaninoff. The Van Cliburn International Piano Competition was organized in 1962 and is held quadrennially in Fort Worth, Texas, the home of the Van Cliburn Foundation.

BIBL.: A. Chasins, *The V. C. Legend* (N.Y., 1959); H. Reich, *V. C.* (Nashville, Tenn., 1993).

Closson, Ernest, Belgian writer on music; b. St. Josse ten Noode, near Brussels, Dec. 12, 1870; d. Brussels, Dec. 21, 1950. He was self-taught in music. He occupied various posts as an archivist; was assistant curator for the collection of musical instruments (1896–1924), chief curator (1924–35), and a teacher (1912–35) at the Brussels Cons.; also taught at the Mons Cons. (1917–35). From 1920 to 1940 he was music critic of *L'Indépendance Belge.* In some of his writings, he used the pen name Paul Antoine.

WRITINGS: *Siegfried de Wagner* (1891); *Edvard Grieg* (1892); *La Musique et les arts plastiques* (1897); *20 Noëls français anciens* (1911); *Le Manuscrit dit des basses-danses de la Bibliothèque de Bourgogne* (1912); *Notes sur la chanson populaire en Belgique* (1913); *Esthétique musicale* (1921); *L'Élément flamand dans Beethoven* (1928; 2nd ed., 1946; Eng. tr., 1936).

BIBL.: *Mélanges C.* (Brussels, 1948).

Cluytens, André, noted Belgian-born French conductor; b. Antwerp, March 26, 1905; d. Neuilly, near Paris, June 3, 1967. He studied piano at the Antwerp Cons. His father, conductor at the Théâtre Royal in Antwerp, engaged him as his assistant (1921); later he conducted opera there (1927–32). He then settled in France, and became a naturalized French citizen in 1932. He served as music director at the Toulouse Opera (1932–35); in 1935 he was appointed opera conductor in Lyons. In 1944 he conducted at the Paris Opéra; in 1947 he was appointed music director of the Opéra-Comique in Paris. In 1949 he was named conductor of the Société des Concerts du Conservatoire de Paris. In 1955 he became the first French conductor to appear at the Bayreuth Festival. On Nov. 4, 1956, he made his U.S. debut in Washington, D.C., as guest conductor of the Vienna Phil. during its first American tour. In 1960 he became chief conductor of the Orchestre National de Belgique in Brussels, a post he held until his death. Cluytens was highly regarded as an interpreter of French music.

BIBL.: B. Gavoty, *A. C.* (Geneva, 1955).

Cluzeau-Mortet, Luis, Uruguayan composer; b. Montevideo, Nov. 16, 1889; d. there, Sept. 28, 1957. He studied piano and theory with his maternal grandfather. Cluzeau-Mortet played piano and viola in radio bands in Montevideo and also composed industriously. His music was marked by Romantic influences, with occasional excursions into cautious modernism. All of his orch. works were first performed by the radio orch. SODRE in Montevideo, of which he was a member: *Llanuras* (Oct. 14, 1944); *Rancherío* (Aug. 2, 1947); *Artigas* (Aug. 13, 1955); *Sinfonía del Este* (unfinished; a movement, *La laguna negra,* was played on Aug. 16, 1958, as a posthumous act of homage); *Fantasía concerto* for Piano and Chamber Orch. He also wrote *4 ritmos criollos* for String Quartet; *Bagatelas criollas* for 4 Flutes; songs and piano pieces.

Coates, Albert, eminent English conductor; b. St. Petersburg, Russia (of an English father and a mother of Russian descent), April 23, 1882; d. Milnerton, near Cape Town, South Africa, Dec. 11, 1953. He went to England for his general education; enrolled in science classes at the Univ. of Liverpool, and studied organ with an elder brother who was living there at the time. In 1902 he entered the Leipzig Cons., studying cello with Julius Klengel, piano with Teichmüller, and conducting with Nikisch; served his apprenticeship there and made his debut as conductor in Offenbach's *Les Contes d'Hoffmann* at the Leipzig Opera in 1904. In 1905 he was appointed (on Nikisch's recommendation) chief conductor of the opera house at Elberfeld; from 1907 to 1909 he was a joint conductor at the Dresden Court Opera (with Schuch); then at Mannheim (1909–10, with Bodanzky). In 1911 he received the appointment at the Imperial Opera of St. Petersburg, and conducted many Russian operas. From 1919 he conducted in England, specializing in Wagner and the Russian repertoire; was a proponent of Scriabin's music. Having made his first appearance at London's Covent Garden in 1914 with *Tristan und Isolde*, he conducted there regularly from 1919. From 1919 to 1921 he was principal conductor of the London Sym. Orch. In 1920 he made his American debut as guest conductor of the N.Y. Sym. Orch.; during 1923–25, he led conducting classes at the Eastman School of Music in Rochester, N.Y., conducted the Rochester Phil., and appeared as guest conductor with other American orchs. Subsequent engagements included a season at the Berlin State Opera (1931) and concerts with the Vienna Phil. (1935). In 1938 he conducted for the last time at Covent Garden. In 1946 he settled in South Africa, where he conducted the Johannesburg Sym. Orch. and taught at the Univ. of South Africa at Cape Town. Coates was a prolific composer, but his works had few performances. He was, however, one of the most outstanding, if unheralded, conductors of his generation; he excelled in the Romantic operatic and symphonic repertoire, conducting particularly memorable performances of Russian music and Wagner's music dramas.

BIBL.: S. Stroff, "A. C.," *Le Grand Baton* (March 1980).

Coates, Edith (Mary), English mezzo-soprano; b. Lincoln, May 31, 1908; d. Worthing, Jan. 7, 1983. She studied at Trinity College of Music in London and with Carey and Borgioli. In 1924 she joined the Old Vic Theatre in London, where she sang major roles from 1931 to 1946. In 1937 she appeared at London's Covent Garden, where she was on the roster until 1939 and again from 1947 to 1963. She sang in the premieres of Britten's *Peter Grimes* (1945) and *Gloriana* (1953), and of Bliss's *The Olympians* (1949). Among her other roles were the Countess in *The Queen of Spades*, Carmen, Delila, Amneris, Ortrud, and Azucena. In 1977 she was made an Officer of the Order of the British Empire.

Coates, Eric, English composer and violist; b. Hucknall, Nottinghamshire, Aug. 27, 1886; d. Chichester, Dec. 21, 1957. He took instruction at the Royal Academy of Music in London with Tertis (viola) and Corder (composition). He was a member of the Hambourg String Quartet, with which he made a tour of South Africa (1908); was 1st violist in the Queen's Hall Orch. in London (1912–19). In 1946 he visited the U.S., conducting radio performances of his works; in 1948 he toured in South America. A detailed account of his career appears in his autobiography *Suite in Four Movements* (London, 1953). As a composer, Coates specialized in semi-classical works for orch. His valse serenade *Sleepy Lagoon* (1930) attained enormous popularity all over the world, and was publ. in numerous arrangements. His *London Suite* (1933) was equally successful, its *Knightsbridge* movement becoming one of the most frequently played marches in England and elsewhere. He further wrote an orch. suite, *4 Centuries* (1941), tracing typical historical forms and styles in 4 sections (*Fugue, Pavane, Valse,* and *Jazz*); *3 Elizabeths* for Orch.; a great number of songs and instrumental pieces.

BIBL.: G. Self, *In Town Tonight: A Centenary Study of the Life and Music of E. C.* (London, 1986).

Coates, Gloria, American composer and painter; b. Wausau, Wis., Oct. 10, 1938. She was a student of Helen Gunderson and Kenneth Klaus at Louisiana State Univ., of Alexander Tcherepnin at the Salzburg Mozarteum, and of Luening and Beeson at Columbia Univ. She also received training in voice, musicology, art, and theater. After working as an actress, singer, and teacher, she settled in Munich in 1969 and devoted herself to composition and painting. In 1971 she founded the German-American Contemporary Music Series in Munich and Cologne, serving as its director until 1983. Her music is compact and dense, replete with euphonious dissonances in the framework of involute counterpoint. In 1978 she gained wide recognition with the premiere of her *Music on Open Strings* at the Warsaw Autumn Festival. In 1979 she became the first non-socialist composer to have a commissioned work performed at the East Berlin Festival.

WORKS: ORCH.: 8 syms.: No. 1, *Music on Open Strings*, for Strings (1973–74; Warsaw, Sept. 20, 1978), No. 2, *Music in Abstract Lines* or *Illuminatio in Tenebris* (1987; N.Y., Nov. 16, 1989), No. 3, *Symphony Nocturne*, for Strings (1976–85; Heidelberg, June 24, 1988), No. 4, *Chiaroscuro* (1990), No. 5 (1985; based on *3 Mystical Songs* for Chorus and Chamber Orch.), No. 6, *Music in Microtones* (1986; Boston, Nov. 6, 1987), No. 7 (1990–91), and No. 8, *Indian Sounds* (1991; based on *Indian Sounds* for Voices and Chamber Orch., 1991–92); *Planets: 3 Movements for Orchestra* (1974; Hannover, Feb. 2, 1975; also as *Planets, Nonett*, or *Halley's Comet* for Chamber Orch., Rome, March 23, 1980); *Sinfonietta della Notte* (1980; Lund, July 4, 1982); *Transitions* for Chamber Orch. (1984–85; Munich, June 23, 1985); *Meteor March* for Wind Orch. (1986); *Resistances* (1987); *The Quinces's Quandary* for Chamber Orch. (1994). **CHAMBER:** *Glissando Quartet* or *Passacaglia Fugue* for String Quartet (1962); *St. Joan Overture* for Organ and Percussion (1963); Trio for 3 Flutes (1966); 5 string quartets (1966; *Mobile*, 1972; 1975–76; 1977; 1988–89); *May the Morning Star Rise* for Viola and Organ (1973–74); *6 Movements* for String Quartet (1978); *Valse Triste* or *Valse Macabre* for Chamber Ensemble (1980); *Lunar Loops I* for 2 Guitars (1986) and *II* for 2 Guitars and Percussion (1988); *In a Zen Monastery* for 3 Percussion (1988); *Lichtsplitter I* for Flute, Harp, and Viola (1988–89) and *II* for Flute, Harp, Viola, and Percussion (1990); *In the Glacier* for 10 Flutes (1992); *Königshymne* for 10 Flutes and Percussion (1993); *Night Music* for Saxophone, Piano, and Gongs (1993); *Transfer 482* for Harp, Flute, Viola, and 2 Percussion (1993); *Druid Drones on a Celtic Ruins* for Brass and Percussion (1994). **VOCAL:** *Voices of Women in Wartime*, cantata for Soprano and Chamber Orch. (1973); *The Force for Peace in War*, cantata for Soprano and Chamber Orch. (1974–89); *Fonte di Rimini*, sinfonia brevis for Soli, Chorus, and Orch. (1975–84); *The Elements* for Chorus and Orch. (1975–86); *Vita* or *Anima della terra* for Soli, Chorus, and Orch. (1976–84); *3 Mystical Songs* for Chorus and Chamber Orch. (1985; also as Sym. No. 5); *Emily Dickinson Songs* for Voice and Orch. (1989); *Wir Tönen Allein* for Soprano and Chamber Orch. (1989–91); *Rainbow Across the Night Sky* for Women's Voices, Violin, Viola, and Percussion (1991); *Indian Sounds* for Voices and Chamber Orch. (1991–92; also as Sym. No. 8); choral pieces; song cycles; solo songs.

Coates, John, English tenor; b. Girlington, Yorkshire, June 29, 1865; d. Northwood, Middlesex, Aug. 16, 1941. He studied with his uncle, J.G. Walton, at Bradford; sang as a small boy at a Bradford church; began serious study in 1893, and took lessons with William Shakespeare in London. He sang baritone parts in Gilbert & Sullivan operettas, making his debut at the Savoy Theatre in London in *Utopia Limited* (1894); toured in the U.S. with a Gilbert & Sullivan company. He made his debut in grand opera as Faust at London's Covent Garden (1901); also sang Lohengrin in Cologne and other German cities with considerable success; later sang nearly all the Wagner roles in English with the Moody-Manners Co., the Carl Rosa Co., and with

Beecham (1910); from 1911 to 1913 he toured with Quinlan's opera company in Australia and South Africa. He served in the British army during World War I; in 1919, he returned to London, devoting himself chiefly to teaching; he also gave recitals of songs by English composers. In 1926–27 he made a concert tour of the U.S.

Cobelli, Giuseppina, Italian soprano; b. Maderno, Lake Garda, Aug. 1, 1898; d. Barbarano di Salò, Aug. 10, 1948. She studied in Bologna, Cologne, and Hamburg. In 1924 she made her operatic debut as Gioconda in Piacenza; after singing with the Italian Opera in the Netherlands, she joined Milan's La Scala in 1925, where she was one of its principal artists until deafness compelled her to leave the company in 1942. She was notably successful in such Wagnerian roles as Isolde, Sieglinde, and Kundry, as well as in the standard and modern Italian repertory.

Cochereau, Pierre, eminent French organist, pedagogue, and composer; b. St. Mandé, near Paris, July, 9, 1924; d. Lyons, March 5, 1984. He studied piano with Marius-François Gaillard and Marguerite Long (1933–36), and then organ with Marie-Louise Girod (1938) and Paul Delafosse (1941); in 1944 he entered the Paris Cons., where he took lessons in organ with Marcel Dupré, in harmony with Henri Challon and Duruflé, in fugue with N. Gallon, in composition with Aubin, and in music history with Dufourcq, winning various prizes. From 1942 to 1954 he was organist at St. Roch in Paris. In 1955 he became organist at Notre Dame in Paris, which position he held with great distinction for the rest of his life. He also made numerous recital tours of Europe, North and South America, Japan, and Australia, winning critical acclaim for his mastery of improvisation. He also served as director of the conservatories in Le Mans (1950–56), Nice (1961–80), and Lyons (from 1980). Among his works were a Sym. (1957), 2 organ concertos, a Piano Quintet, and various solo organ pieces.

BIBL.: D. Briggs, "P. C.: legacy of an organist," *Musical Times* (May 1989).

Cochran, William, American tenor; b. Columbus, Ohio, June 23, 1943. He studied at Wesleyan Univ. and with Singher at the Curtis Inst. of Music in Philadelphia. He made his Metropolitan Opera debut in N.Y. as Vogelsang in *Die Meistersinger von Nürnberg* on Dec. 21, 1968. In 1970 he joined the Frankfurt am Main Opera, where he subsequently sang principal roles in both standard and contemporary operas.

Cockshott, Gerald Wilfred, English composer; b. Bristol, Nov. 14, 1915; d. London, Feb. 3, 1979. He specialized in English literature; was head of the English dept. at Whittingehame College, Brighton (1948–64), and at Ifield Grammar School, Crawley, Sussex (1965–78). He studied composition privately with Vaughan Williams; became active primarily as a writer on musical subjects. His music is transparently tonal and impressed with melorhythms of English folk songs.

WORKS: OPERAS: *Apollo and Persephone* (N.Y., Feb. 22, 1956); *A Faun in the Forest* (Westport, Conn., Aug. 9, 1959). **ORCH.:** Sym. (1949); *Serenade* for Flute and Strings (1952). **OTHER:** *3 Pieces on Appalachian Folk Tunes* for Cello and Piano (1962); songs; carols; choruses; numerous arrangements.

Coelho, Rui, Portuguese composer; b. Alcaçer do Sal, March 3, 1891; d. Lisbon, May 5, 1986. He was a student of Colaço (piano) and of Ferreira and Borba (composition) at the Lisbon Cons., and then of Humperdinck, Bruch, and Schoenberg in Berlin (1910–13) and of Vidal at the Paris Cons. Upon his return to Lisbon, he devoted himself mainly to composition and music criticism; he also made appearances as a pianist and conductor. His compositions were predicated upon nationalist principles.

WORKS: DRAMATIC: OPERAS: *O serão da infanta* (1913); *Crisfal* (1919); *Auto do berço* (1920); *Rosas de todo o ano* (1921; Lisbon, May 30, 1940); *Belkiss* (1923; Lisbon, June 9, 1928); *Inês de Castro* (1925; Lisbon, Jan. 15, 1927), *Cavaleiro das mãos irresistíveis* (1926); *Freira de beja* (1927); *Entre giestas* (Lisbon, 1929); *Tá-mar* (Lisbon, 1936); *Dom João IV* (Lisbon, Dec. 1, 1940); *A feira* (1942); *A rosa de papel* (Lisbon, Dec. 18, 1947); *Auto da barca do inferno* (1949; Lisbon, Jan. 15, 1950); *Inês Pereira* (Lisbon, April 5, 1952); *O vestido de noiva* (1958; Lisbon, Jan. 4, 1959); *Auto da alma* (1960); *Orfeu em Lisboa* (1964–66); *Auto da barca da glória* (1970). **BALLETS:** *Princesa dos sapatos de ferro* (1912); *O sonho da princesa na rosa* (1916); *A história de carochinha* (1916); *Bailado do encantemento* (1917); *O sonho da pobrezinha* (1921); *A feira* (1921); *Bailado africano* (1930); *Inêz de Castro* (1939); *Passatempo* (1940); *Dom Sebastião* (1943); *Festa na aldeia* (1966). **ORCH.:** 5 *Sinfonia camoneana* (1912, 1917, 1948, 1951, 1957); 4 symphonic poems: *Nun' Alvares* (1922), *Alcaçer* (1925), *Rainha santa* (1926), and *O castelo de Lisboa* (1962); 4 *Suite portuguesa* (1925, 1927, 1928, 1956); 2 *Pequena sinfonia* (1929, 1932); *Cenas bíblicas* (1933); 2 *Rapsódia portuguesa* (1934, 1942); *Fantasia portuguesa* for Violin and Orch. (1935); 2 piano concertos (1939, 1948); 3 syms. (1939, 1955, 1956); *Egypcienne* for Violin and Orch. (1950); *Rapsódia de Lisboa* (1961); *Viagens na minha terra,* 4 suites (1964–67); *Sinfonia henriquina, prólogo* (1966); *Sinfonia de além mar* (1969). **CHAMBER:** 2 violin sonatas (1910, 1923); *Largo* for 2 Violas, Cello, and Piano (1911); Piano Trio (1916); String Quartet (1942); piano pieces. **VOCAL:** *Fátima,* oratorio (1931); *Missa a Santa Terezinha* (1934); *Oratória de paz* (1967); songs.

BIBL.: *R. C.: Sua acção e sua obras de 1910 a 1967* (Lisbon, 1967).

Coertse, Mimi, South African soprano; b. Durban, June 12, 1932. She studied in Johannesburg and Vienna. She made her debut with the Vienna State Opera on tour in Naples in 1955; then sang in Basel and at the Teatro San Carlo in Naples. In 1957 she became a member of the Vienna State Opera; she also appeared in London, Cologne, Rome, Brussels, and other major European music centers.

Coeuroy, André (real name, **Jean Bélime**), distinguished French writer on music; b. Dijon, Feb. 24, 1891; d. Chaumont, Haute-Marne, Nov. 8, 1976. After training at the Dijon Cons., he went to Paris to study at the Lycée Louis le Grand and at the École Normale Supérieure (1911–14), where he took a degree in German; he also studied harmony and counterpoint with Reger in Leipzig (1910) and took a course in philology at the Univ. of Munich (1912–13). With Henry Prunières, he founded *La Revue Musicale* in 1920, with which he remained active until 1937. He also wrote music criticism for various newspapers and journals. His expertise in philology was reflected in his writings on music.

WRITINGS (all publ. in Paris): *La Musique française moderne* (1921); *Musiciens, 10 bois de Gimel* (1921); *La Walkyrie* (1922); *Musique et littérature* (1923); *Weber* (1924); *La Musique religieuse en France* (1925); with A. Schaeffner, *Le Jazz* (1926); with J. Mercier, *Panorama de la Radio* (1929); with R. Jardiller, *Histoire de la musique par le disque* (1931); *Petite histoire des Concerts Colonne* (1931); *Les grands Concerts spirituels* (1933); *La Littérature française et ses rapports avec la musique* (1930–41); *La Musique et le peuple en France* (1942); *Histoire générale du jazz* (1943); *Les Lieder de Schubert* (1948); *Robert Schumann* (1949); *La Musique et ses formes* (1950); *Chopin* (1951); *Dictionnaire critique de la musique ancienne et moderne* (1956); *Wagner et l'esprit romantique* (1965).

Cohen, Harriet, distinguished English pianist; b. London, Dec. 2, 1895; d. there, Nov. 13, 1967. She studied piano with her parents, then took an advanced course in piano with Matthay; she made her first public appearance as a solo pianist at the age of 13. She then engaged in a successful career in England, both as a soloist with major orchs. and in chamber music concerts. She made a specialty of early keyboard music, but also played many contemporary compositions; Vaughan Williams, Arnold Bax, and other English composers wrote works for her. After damaging her right hand in 1948, she played works for the left-hand alone. In 1938 she was made a Commander of the Order of the

British Empire. She publ. a book on piano playing, *Music's Handmaid* (London, 1936; 2nd ed., 1950). Her memoirs, *A Bundle of Time*, were publ. posthumously (London, 1969).

Cohen, Isidore (Leonard), American violinist and teacher; b. N.Y., Dec. 16, 1922. He studied violin with Galamian and chamber music with Salmond and Letz at the Juilliard School of Music in N.Y. (B.S., 1948). After playing in the Schneider (1952–55) and Juilliard (1958–66) quartets, he was a member of the Beaux Arts Trio (1968–93), with which he toured internationally; he also appeared as a soloist with orchs. and as a recitalist. He taught at the Marlboro (Vt.) Music School (from 1957), at the Juilliard School of Music (1957–65), and at the Mannes College of Music in N.Y. (1970–88).

BIBL.: N. Delbanco, *The Beaux Arts Trio: A Portrait* (London, 1985).

Cohen, Joel (Israel), American lutenist and conductor; b. Providence, R.I., May 23, 1942. He took courses in composition and musicology at Brown Univ. (B.A., 1963) and Harvard Univ. (M.A., 1965), then studied theory and composition with Boulanger in Paris (1965–67). In 1968 he became conductor of the Boston Camerata, which he led in works from the medieval, Renaissance, and Baroque eras.

Cohn, Arthur, versatile American composer, conductor, lexicographer, and publishing executive; b. Philadelphia, Nov. 6, 1910. He studied violin and later took a course in composition at the Juilliard School of Music in N.Y. with Rubin Goldmark. Returning to Philadelphia, he was director of the Edwin A. Fleisher Collection at the Free Library (1934–52). From 1942 to 1965 he conducted the Sym. Club of Philadelphia; also the Germantown Sym. Orch. (1949–55), the Philadelphia Little Sym. (1952–56), and the Haddonfield (N.J.) Sym. Orch. (1958–91). From 1956 to 1966 he was head of symphonic and foreign music at Mills Music Co., and from 1966 to 1972 held a similar position with MCA Music. In 1972 he was appointed Director of Serious Music at Carl Fischer. He publ. *The Collector's Twentieth-Century Music in the Western Hemisphere* (N.Y., 1961); *Twentieth-Century Music in Western Europe* (N.Y., 1965); *Musical Quizzical* (N.Y., 1970); *Recorded Classical Music: A Critical Guide to Compositions and Performances* (N.Y., 1981); *The Encyclopedia of Chamber Music* (N.Y., 1990).

WORKS: 6 string quartets (1928–45); *5 Nature Studies* (1932); *Retrospections* for String Orch. (Philadelphia, April 3, 1935); *Music* for Brass Instruments (1935); Suite for Viola and Orch. (1937); *Machine Music* for 2 Pianos (1937); *4 Preludes* for String Orch. (N.Y., May 26, 1937); *4 Symphonic Documents* (1939); *Music for Ancient Instruments* (1939); Quintuple Concerto for 5 Ancient Instruments and Modern Orch. (1940); Flute Concerto (1941); *Variations* for Clarinet, Saxophone, and String Orch. (1945); *Music* for Bassoon (1947); *Quotations in Percussion* for 103 Instruments for 6 Players (1958); *Kaddish* for Orch. (1964); Percussion Concerto (1970).

Cohn, James (Myron), American musicologist, inventor, and composer; b. Newark, N.J., Feb. 12, 1928. He studied with Barlow at the Eastman School of Music in Rochester, N.Y. (1940–41), Harris at Cornell Univ. (1941–43), and Wagenaar at the Juilliard School of Music in N.Y. (B.S., 1949; M.S., 1950); later pursued postgraduate studies with Ruth Anderson at Hunter College of the City Univ. of N.Y. (1973). He was a musicologist for ASCAP from 1954 to 1984. Cohn invented devices that can be applied to keyboards or fingerboards to control pitch, intonation, loudness, vibrato, and tremolo.

WORKS: OPERA: *The Fall of the City* (1952; Athens, Ohio, July 8, 1955). **ORCH.:** *Sinfonietta* (1946); Piano Concertino (1946); 8 syms.: No. 1 (1947), No. 2 (1949; Brussels, Dec. 11, 1953), No. 3 (1955; Detroit, Dec. 17, 1959), No. 4 (1956; Florence, Oct. 1, 1960), No. 5 (1959), No. 6 (1965), No. 7 (1967), and No. 8 (1978); *Homage*, overture (1959); *Variations on "The Wayfaring Stranger"* (1960; Detroit, Oct. 4, 1962); *Enchanted Journey* (1961); *Prometheus*, overture (1962); Concerto for Concertina and Strings (1966); *The Little Circus* (1974) (9) *Miniatures* (1975); *A Song of the Waters* (1976); *March-Caprice* for Bassoon and Strings (1982); Concerto for Clarinet and Strings (1986). **CHAMBER:** Septet for Winds and Strings (1947); Sextet for Winds and Piano (1948); 3 string quartets, including Nos. 2 (1950) and 3 (1961); *Sonata Romantica* for Double Bass or Cello and Piano (1952; also for Bassoon and Piano, 1978); Sonata for Solo Cello (1953); Sonata for Solo Violin (1959); Flute Sonata (1974); *Sonata Robusta* for Bassoon and Piano (1980); *Concerto da Camera* for 5 Instruments (1982); *The Goldfinch Variations* for 3 Treble Instruments (1984); Viola Sonata (1987); Oboe Sonata (1988); Trio for Piano, Violin, and Cello (1988); Horn Sonata (1988). **PIANO:** *12 Variations on an Original Theme* (1944); 5 sonatas (1947, 1956, 1964, 1981, 1986). **VOCAL:** Choral pieces.

Colding-Jørgensen, Henrik, Danish composer, organist, and choirmaster; b. Riisskov, March 21, 1944. He studied composition with Holmboe at the Royal Danish Cons. of Music in Copenhagen, graduating in 1966; then taught organ in Copenhagen (1967–70) and theory at the Odense Cons. (1969–75). In 1975 he became active as a church organist and choirmaster in Copenhagen. From 1977 to 1985 he was chairman of the board of the Holstebro Electronic Music Studio.

WORKS: ORCH.: Sym. No. 1 (1965); *At elske musikken* (To Love Music; 1975; Copenhagen, May 6, 1976); *Ballade* for Tuba and Chamber Orch. (1979); *Nuup Kangerlua* (1985) *Le Alpi nel Cuore* (1988). **CHAMBER:** *Divertimento* for 8 Instruments (1964); String Quartet No. 1 (1965); *Sinusrhapsodie* for 2 Cellos (1968); *Avnstrup Suite* for Recorder, Violin, and Guitar (1969); *Mourn* for Guitar (1969); *Suite à deux* for Flute and Clarinet (1971); *Cello* for Cello (1972); *Solo Grande* for Percussion (1972); *Balancer* for Violin and Percussion (1974); *Puer natus* for 5 Tubas (1976); *Boast* for Tuba (1980); *Recitative and Fugue* for Piano and Cello (1983); *Swimmings* for Viola and Piano (1985); *Toccata, Aria e Minuetto* for Oboe (1986). **ORGAN:** *Logbogsblade* (Logbook Sheets; 1969); Magnus (1972). **VOCAL:** *Lapidary Landscapes* for Mezzo-soprano, Bass-baritone, Oboe, English Horn, Viola, Cello, and Percussion (1965); *På din taerskel* (At Your Doorstep) for Contralto and Orch. (1966); *Enfance III* for Contralto, Horn, and Harp (1967) and *IV* for Contralto and Piano (1968); *Barbare* for 6 Soloists, Chorus, and Orch. (1967; Copenhagen Radio, Jan. 21, 1972); *Altid noget andet* (Always Something Else) for Tenor and Viola d'Amore (1973); *Ava Maria* for Contralto (1974); *Fra først af* (From the Beginning) for Chorus, Trumpet, Trombone, and Organ (1975); *Victoria through the Wood* for Alto and Orch. (1975); *Det er mig der vaelter* (It Is I Who Am Overturned) for Soprano, Mezzo-soprano, and Organ (1980); *Enfance II* for Mezzo-soprano and Bass Clarinet (1983); *Sic Enim* for Mezzo-soprano and Organ (1985); 2 songs by Keats for Soprano and Guitar (1988).

Cole, Rossetter Gleason, American composer, organist, and teacher; b. near Clyde, Mich., Feb. 5, 1866; d. Lake Bluff, Ill., May 18, 1952. After training in harmony from Francis York in Ann Arbor, he studied engineering and the liberal arts, including music with Calvin Cady, at the Univ. of Mich. (graduated, 1888). He won a scholarship to pursue training at the Berlin Königliche Meisterschule in 1890, where he studied organ with Middelschulte, violin with Bruch, conducting with Gustav Kogel, and composition and counterpoint with Heinrich van Eyken. Upon his return to the U.S. in 1892, he became a prof. and head of the music dept. at Riper College in Wisconsin; then was a prof. at Grinnel College in Iowa (1894–1901). After teaching privately in Chicago (1901–07), he was a prof. at the Univ. of Wisc. (1907–09). He then taught again privately in Chicago (from 1909). During these years, he also was active as a church organist. In 1915 he became head of the theory dept. at the Cosmopolitan School in Chicago, where he was dean from 1935. From 1939 to 1941 he was president of the Soc. of American Musicians. He prepared the vol. *Choral and Church Music* (1916) in the Art of Music series.

WORKS: DRAMATIC: *Hiawatha's Wooing*, melodrama

(1904); *King Robert of Sicily*, melodrama (1906); *Pierrot Wounded* (1917); *The Maypole Lovers*, opera (1919–31; 2 orch. suites, 1934, 1942). **ORCH.:** *Symphonic Prelude* (1914; Chicago, March 11, 1915); *Rhapsody* (1941–42); *Pioneer Overture* (1918; Chicago, March 14, 1919); *Heroic Piece* for Organ and Orch. (1923; Chicago, Feb. 11, 1924; also for Orch., 1938). **CHAMBER:** Violin Sonata (1891); *Ballade* for Cello and Piano (1905–06); *3 Songs* for Cello and Piano (1922); various piano and organ pieces. **VOCAL: CANTATAS:** *The Passing of Summer* (1887–88; rev. 1902); *The Broken Troth* (1917); *The Rock of Liberty* (1920); also part songs; about 40 solo songs.

Cole, Ulric, American pianist and composer; b. N.Y., Sept. 9, 1905; d. Bridgeport, Conn., May 21, 1992. She studied piano with her mother (1910–12) and with Homer Grunn (1912–23) in Los Angeles, and then went to N.Y., where she was a student of George Boyle (piano) and Goetschius (composition) at the Inst. of Musical Art (1923–24), and of Josef Lhévinne (piano) and Goldmark (composition) at the Juilliard Graduate School (1924–27); she completed her training in Paris with Boulanger in 1927. From 1924 she made tours of the U.S. as a pianist, often performing her own works, which included 2 piano concertos, a *Divertimento* for Piano and Strings (Cincinnati, March 31, 1939, composer soloist), chamber music, and many piano pieces.

Cole, Vinson, black American tenor; b. Kansas City, Mo., Nov. 20, 1950. He studied at the Curtis Inst. of Music in Philadelphia, where he sang Werther while still a student in 1975; then was an apprentice at the Santa Fe Opera, and was chosen to create the role of Innis Brown in Ulysses Kay's *Jubilee* in Jackson, Miss., in 1976; that same year he made his European debut as Belmonte with the Welsh National Opera in Cardiff. From 1976 to 1980 he appeared at the Opera Theatre of St. Louis. He sang Nicolai's Fenton at the N.Y. City Opera in 1981. Other operatic engagements took him to Paris, Salzburg, Stuttgart, Naples, and Marseilles. As a concert artist, he toured widely in the U.S. and abroad, appearing with major orchs. Among his admired operatic portrayals are Gluck's Orfeo, Percy in *Anna Bolena*, Des Grieux in *Manon*, Lensky, Gounod's Faust, and Bizet's Nadir.

Coleman, Ornette, innovative black American jazz saxophonist and composer; b. Fort Worth, Texas, March 9, 1930. He took up the alto saxophone at the age of 14 and the tenor saxophone at 16. While in high school, he played in its band and with local groups, and also formed his own rhythm and blues band. After graduation, he continued to work with local groups and began to travel throughout the South. He pursued training in harmony and theory on his own, and then at the Lenox (Mass.) School of Jazz in 1959. In 1958 he formed his own jazz group, and soon gained wide recognition via such recordings as *The Shape of Jazz to Come* (1959), *Change of the Century* (1959), and *Free Jazz* (1960). In subsequent years, he toured extensively in the U.S. and Europe. As a composer, Coleman wrote both jazz and concert works, including *Forms and Sounds* for Woodwind Quintet (1965), *Skies of America* for Orch. (1972), and *Sex Spy* (1977).

BIBL.: J. Litweiler, *O. C.: A Harmolodic Life* (N.Y., 1992).

Coleridge-Taylor, Samuel, important English composer, conductor, and teacher; b. London, Aug. 15, 1875; d. Croydon, Sept. 1, 1912. His father was a black Sierra Leone physician and his mother was English. After violin lessons with Joseph Beckwith in Croydon, he entered the Royal College of Music in London in 1890 to continue his violin training; in 1892 he became a composition student of Stanford there, and in 1893 he won a composition scholarship; before completing his studies in 1897, he had several of his works premiered there. His first public success came with his Ballade in A minor for Orch., which was premiered at the Three Choirs Festival in Gloucester on Sept. 14, 1898. It was soon followed by what proved to be his most successful score, the cantata *Hiawatha's Wedding Feast*, which was first performed under Stanford's direction at the Royal College of Music on Nov. 11, 1898. It was subsequently performed widely in Europe and the U.S. Although he continued to compose in earnest, he never duplicated this popular success. He also was active as a conductor, leading various orchestral and choral aggregations. He likewise was engaged in teaching, serving as prof. of composition at Trinity College of Music (from 1903) and at the Guildhall School of Music (from 1910) in London. In 1904, 1906, and 1910 he visited the U.S. While greatly influenced by Dvořák, Coleridge-Taylor's works also reveal a fascination with black subjects and melodies.

WORKS: DRAMATIC: *Dream Lovers*, operatic romance (1898); *The Gitanos*, cantata-operetta (1898); *Thelma*, opera (1907–09). Incidental music to Stephen Phillips's *Herod* (1900), *Ulysses* (1901–02), *Nero* (1906), and *Faust* (1908); also to Noyes's *The Forest of Wild Thyme* (1910) and Shakespeare's *Othello* (1910–11). **ORCH.:** *Ballade* for Violin and Orch. (1895); Sym. (London, March 6, 1896); *Legende* for Violin and Orch. (1897); *4 Characteristic Waltzes* (1899); *Ballade* (Gloucester, Sept. 13, 1898); *Romance* for Violin and Orch. (c.1899); *Solemn Prelude* (Worcester, Sept. 13, 1899); (4) *Scenes from an Everyday Romance*, suite (London, May 24, 1900); *Idyll* (Gloucester, Sept. 11, 1901); *Toussaint l'Ouverture* (London, Oct. 26, 1901); *Ethiopa Saluting the Colours*, march (1902); *4 Novelletten* for Strings, Tambourine, and Triangle (1903); *Symphonic Variations on an African Air* (London, June 14, 1906); *Fantasiestück* for Cello and Orch. (New Brighton, July 7, 1907); *A Lovely Little Dream* for Strings and Harmonium (c.1909); *The Bamboula*, rhapsodic dance (Norfolk, Conn., June 1, 1910); *Petite suite de concert* (1910); Violin Concerto (Norfolk, Conn., June 1912); *From the Prairie*, rhapsody (1914). **CHAMBER:** (3) *Hiawathan Sketches* for Violin and Piano (1893); Piano Quintet (c.1893); Clarinet Sonata (c.1893); Nonet for Piano, Strings, and Woodwinds (1894); *Suite de* [4] *pièces* for Violin, Piano, and Organ (1894); (5) *Fantasiestücke* for String Quartet (1895); *2 Romantic Pieces* for Violin and Piano (c.1895); Clarinet Quintet (1895); String Quartet (1896); *Gypsy Suite* for Violin and Piano (1897); *Valse Caprice* for Violin and Piano (1898); *Ballade* for Violin and Piano (1907); *Variations on an Original Theme* for Cello (1907); Violin Sonata (1912); *Variations* for Cello and Piano (publ. 1918); also many piano pieces, including *2 Moorish Tone-pictures* (1897); *African Suite* (1897); *3 Silhouettes* (1897); *24 Negro Melodies* (1905); (4) *Scènes de ballet* (1906); (5) *Forest Scenes* (1907); *Three-fours*, valse suite (1909). **VOCAL:** Scenes from *The Song of Hiawatha*, cantata (1: *Hiawatha's Wedding Feast* for Tenor, Chorus, and Orch., London, Nov. 11, 1898; 2: *The Death of Minnehaha* for Soprano, Baritone, Chorus, and Orch., Hanley, Oct. 26, 1899; 3: Overture, Norwich, Oct. 6, 1899; 4: *Hiawatha's Departure* for Soprano, Tenor, Baritone, Chorus, and Orch., London, March 22, 1900); *The Soul's Expression*, 4 sonnets for Chorus and Orch. (Hereford, Sept. 13, 1900); *The Blind Girl of Castél*, cantata for Soprano, Baritone, Chorus, and Orch. (Leeds, Oct. 9, 1901); *Meg Blane*, rhapsody for Mezzo-soprano, Chorus, and Orch. (Sheffield, Oct. 3, 1902); *The Atonement*, sacred cantata for Soloists, Chorus, and Orch. (Hereford, Sept. 10, 1903); *5 Choral Ballads* for Baritone, Chorus, and Orch. (Norwich, Oct. 25, 1905); *Kubla Khan*, rhapsody for Mezzo-soprano, Chorus, and Orch. (1905); *Endymion's Dream*, cantata for Soprano, Tenor, Chorus, and Orch. (1909; Brighton, Feb. 4, 1910); *Bon-bon Suite*, cantata for Baritone, Chorus, and Orch. (1909); *A Tale of Old Japan*, cantata for Soloists, Chorus, and Orch. (London, Dec. 6, 1911); also works for Solo Voice, including *Zara's Ear-rings* for Voice and Orch. (1895) and songs, part songs, and choruses with piano accompaniment.

BIBL.: W. Berwick Sayers, *S. C.-T., Musician: His Life and Letters* (London, 1915; 2nd ed., rev., 1927); J. Coleridge-Taylor, *S. C.-T.: A Memory Sketch* (London, 1942); idem, *C.-T.: Genius and Musician* (London, 1943); W. Tortolano, *S. C.-T.: Anglo-Black Composer, 1875–1912* (Metuchen, N.J., 1977); A. Coleridge-Taylor, *The Heritage of S. C.-T.* (London, 1979); J. Green, "A Note on C.-T.'s Origins," *Musical Times* (Aug. 1985); S. Butterworth, "C.-T.: New Facts for Old Fiction," ibid. (April 1989); J. Thompson, *S. C.-T.: The Development of His Composi-*

tional Style (Metuchen, N.J., 1994); G. Self, *The Hiawatha Man: S. C.-T.* (Brookfield, Vt., 1995).

Colgrass, Michael (Charles), American composer; b. Chicago, April 22, 1932. He received training in percussion and composition at the Univ. of Ill. (Mus.B., 1956), and also studied composition with Foss at the Berkshire Music Center in Tanglewood (summers, 1952, 1954) and Milhaud at the Aspen (Colo.) Music School (summer, 1953); he then took private composition lessons with Riegger (1958–59) and Ben Weber (1959–62) in N.Y. After working as a freelance solo percussionist in N.Y. (1956–67), he settled in Toronto, where he devoted himself fully to composition. In 1964 and 1968 he held Guggenheim fellowships, and in 1978 he was awarded the Pulitzer Prize in Music for his *Déjà vu*, a concerto for 4 Percussionists and Orch. In his output, he has utilized various styles and techniques, with percussion often playing a significant melorhythmic role.

WORKS: DRAMATIC: *Virgil's Dream*, music theater (1967); *Nightingale, Inc.*, comic opera (1971); *Something's Gonna Happen*, children's musical (1978). **ORCH.:** *Divertimento* for 8 Drums, Piano, and Strings (1960); *Rhapsodic Fantasy* for 15 Drums and Orch. (1965); *Sea Shadow* (1966); *As Quiet as . . .* (1966); *Auras* for Harp and Orch. (1973); *Concertmasters* for 3 Violins and Orch. (1975); *Letter from Mozart* (1976); *Déjà vu* for 4 Percussionists and Orch. (1977); *Delta* for Clarinet, Violin, and Percussion Orch. (1979); *Memento* for 2 Pianos and Orch. (1982); *Chaconne* for Viola and Orch. (Toronto, Sept. 27, 1984); *Demon* for Amplified Piano, Percussion, Tape, Radio, and Orch. (1984); *The Schubert Birds* (1989); *Snow Walker* for Organ and Orch. (1990); *Arctic Dreams* for Symphonic Band (1991). **CHAMBER:** *3 Brothers* for 9 Percussion (1951); *Percussion Music* for 4 Percussion (1953); *Chamber Music* for 4 Drums and String Quartet (1954); Percussion Quintet (1955); *Variations* for 4 Drums and Viola (1957); *Fantasy Variations* for Solo Percussion and 6 Percussion (1960); *Rhapsody* for Clarinet, Violin, and Piano (1962); *Light Spirit* for Flute, Viola, Guitar, and Percussion (1963); *Night of the Raccoon* for Harp, Flute, Keyboard, and Percussion (1978); *Flashbacks* for 5 Brass (1979); *Winds of Nagual—A Musical Fable* for Wind Ensemble (Boston, Feb. 14, 1985); *Strangers: Irreconcilable Variations* for Clarinet, Viola, and Piano (1986); String Quartet, *Folklines* (1987); piano pieces. **VOCAL:** *The Earth's a Baked Apple* for Chorus and Orch. (1969); *New People* for Mezzo-soprano, Viola, and Piano (1969); *Image of Man* for 4 Solo Voices, Chorus, and Orch. (1974); *Theatre of the Universe* for Solo Voices, Chorus, and Orch. (1975); *Best Wishes, U.S.A.* for 4 Solo Voices, Double Chorus, 2 Jazz Bands, Folk Instruments, and Orch. (1976).

Collaer, Paul, Belgian pianist and writer on music; b. Boom, June 8, 1891; d. Brussels, Dec. 10, 1989. He studied science at the Univ. of Brussels. From 1937 to 1953 he was director of the Brussels Radio, where he promoted performances of modern music.

WRITINGS: *Stravinsky* (1930); *J.S. Bach* (1936); *Signification de la musique* (1943); *Darius Milhaud* (1947); *La Musique moderne* (1955; amplified ed., 1963, as *A History of Modern Music*); with A. Van der Linden, *Atlas historique* (1960); *Ozeanien* (1965); *Amerika; Eskimo und indianische Bevolkerung* (1967); *La Musique populaire traditionelle en Belgique* (1974); *Musique traditionelle Sicilienne* (2 vols., 1981).

Collard, Jean-Philippe, French pianist; b. Mareuil-sur-Ay, Jan. 27, 1948. He began piano studies as a child; then studied at the Paris Cons. with Pierre Sancan, graduating at age 16 with a premier prix; subsequently won several honors, including 3rd prize in the Long-Thibaud Competition in 1969. Collard appeared as soloist with leading European orchs. and in recitals. He made his American debut in 1973 with the San Francisco Sym.; then made a number of coast-to-coast tours of the U.S.

Colles, H(enry) C(ope), eminent English music scholar; b. Bridgnorth, Shropshire, April 20, 1879; d. London, March 4, 1943. He studied at the Royal College of Music in London with Parry (music history), Walter Alcock (organ), and Davies (theory). Subsequently he received an organ scholarship to Worcester College, Oxford; then entered the Univ. of Oxford, obtaining his B.A. (1902), Mus.Bac. (1903), and M.A. (1907) degrees; later received an honorary Mus.Doc. (1932). In 1905 he became music critic of the Academy; from 1905 to 1911 he was assistant music critic and from 1911 to 1943 chief music critic of the *Times*; in 1919 he was appointed teacher of music history and criticism at the Royal College of Music; was also music director of Cheltenham Ladies' College. He was the editor of the 3rd and 4th eds. of *Grove's Dictionary of Music and Musicians* (1927–29 and 1939–40); also edited vol. VII of *The Oxford History of Music* (1934).

WRITINGS: *Brahms* (1908); *The Growth of Music: A Study in Music History for Schools* (3 vols., 1912–16; 3rd ed., 1956); *Voice and Verse, a Study in English Song* (1928); *The Chamber Music of Brahms* (1933); *English Church Music* (1933); *The Royal College of Music; A Jubilee Record, 1883–1933* (1933); *On Learning Music* (1940); *Walford Davies* (1942); *Essays and Lectures* (1945).

Collet, Henri, French music critic and composer; b. Paris, Nov. 5, 1885; d. there, Nov. 23, 1951. He was a pupil of J. Thibaut and Barès in Paris; then studied Spanish literature with Menéndez Pidal in Madrid, continuing his music studies under Olmeda. He coined the title Les Six Français for a group of young French composers comprising Auric, Durey, Honegger, Milhaud, Poulenc, and Tailleferre.

WORKS: *El Escorial*, symphonic poem; *Danses castillanes* for Orch.; *Gitanerías* for Orch.; *La cueva di Salamanca*, orch. intermezzo; *Rhapsodie castillane* for Viola and Orch.; *Impressions (Vers Burgos)* for String Quartet; *Romería castellana* for Woodwinds; Piano Quintet; String Quartet; *Trio castillan*; *Sonata castillane* for Violin and Piano; many songs.

WRITINGS: *Un tratado de Canto de órgano (siglo XVI°) MS. en la Biblioteca Nacional de Paris* (Madrid, 1913); *Le Mysticisme musical espagnol au XVI*e *siècle* (Paris, 1913); *Tomas Luis de Victoria* (Paris, 1914); *Albéniz et Granados* (Paris, 1925; 2nd ed., 1948); *L'Essor de la musique espagnole au XX*e *siècle* (Paris, 1929).

Collier, Marie, Australian soprano; b. Ballarat, April 16, 1926; d. in a fall from a window in London, Dec. 7, 1971. She studied with Wielaert and Gertrude Johnson in Melbourne, where she made her operatic debut as Santuzza; she then completed her training in Milan with Ugo Benvenuti Giusti (1955–56). In 1956 she made her first appearance at London's Covent Garden as Musetta, where she sang regularly until her death; she also appeared at the Sadler's Wells Opera in London. From 1965 to 1968 she sang at the San Francisco Opera. On March 17, 1967, she created the role of Christine Mannon in Levy's *Mourning Becomes Electra* at her Metropolitan Opera debut in N.Y.; she remained on its roster until 1968, and then returned for the 1969–70 season. Collier was highly regarded for her performances of contemporary operas, excelling in such roles as Kát'a Kabanová, Emilia Marty in *The Makropoulos Case*, Jenůfa, Marie in *Wozzeck*, Katerina Izmailova, Walton's Cressida, and Hecuba in Tippett's *King Priam*, which she created.

Collier, Ron(ald William), Canadian composer, arranger, conductor, trombonist, and teacher; b. Coleman, near Lethridge, Alberta, July 3, 1930. He studied in Vancouver (1943–50), where he played trombone in the Kitsilano Boys' Band; following composition training with Gordon Delamont in Toronto (1951–54), he became the first jazz composer to receive a Canada Council grant, which allowed him to pursue studies with George Russell and Hall Overton in N.Y. (1961–62). He played trombone in dance bands and orchs., and eventually led his own jazz groups and big band. In 1972 he became composer-in-residence at Humber College in Toronto, where he taught composition and arranging from 1974. Collier was a principal figure in the 3rd Stream movement in Canada.

WORKS: Sonata for Piano and Jazz Quintet (c.1955); *The*

City for Narrator-Singer and Orch. (1960); *Requiem for JFK* for Big Band (1964); *Hear Me Talkin' to Ya* for Narrator-Singer and Octet (1964; in collaboration with Don Francks); *Aurora Borealis*, ballet (1966); *Carneval* for Narrator, Flugelhorn, and Orch. (1969); *Celebration* for Piano and Orch. (1972; in collaboration with Duke Ellington); *Humber Suite* for Big Band (1973); *Jupiter* for Big Band (1974); *Reflections on 3* for Wind Sym. (1980); *Never in Nevis* for Big Band (1983); *4 Kisses* for Big Band (1983); *To Prussia with Love and a Little Jive* for Jazz Ensemble (1988); also film and television scores; arrangements.

Collingwood, Lawrance (Arthur), English conductor and composer; b. London, March 14, 1887; d. Killin, Perthshire, Dec. 19, 1982. He studied at the Guildhall School of Music in London and later at Exeter College, Oxford (1907–11). In 1912 he went to Russia and took courses at the St. Petersburg Cons. with Glazunov, Wihtol, Steinberg, and Tcherepnin; in 1918 he returned to England and became active as a conductor; was principal conductor (1931–41) and music director (1941–47) at Sadler's Wells in London. In 1948 he was made a Commander of the Order of the British Empire. His compositions include 2 operas, *Macbeth* (London, April 12, 1934) and *The Death of Tintagiles* (concert perf., London, April 16, 1950); Piano Concerto; Piano Quartet; 2 piano sonatas.

Collins, Anthony (Vincent Benedictus), English conductor and composer; b. Hastings, Sept. 3, 1893; d. Los Angeles, Dec. 11, 1963. He studied violin at the Royal College of Music in London, and composition there with Holst; was then a violist in the London Sym. Orch. and in the orch. of the Royal Opera House, Covent Garden; from 1936 he pursued a career as conductor, appearing with the Carl Rosa Opera Co., the Sadler's Wells Opera, and the London Sym. Orch. From 1939 to 1945 he conducted and composed for films in the U.S. After pursuing his career again in England (1945–53), he settled in the U.S. He wrote 4 operas, 2 syms., 2 violin concertos, chamber music, and various lighter pieces.

Collins, Michael, remarkable English clarinetist; b. London, Jan. 27, 1962. He commenced clarinet training when he was 10, and later pursued his studies with David Hamilton at the Royal College of Music in London; later was a student of Thea King. While still a student, he attracted notice as winner of the BBC-TV Young Musician of the Year prize. In 1984 he made his debut at the London Promenade concerts as soloist in Thea Musgrave's Clarinet Concerto, and that same year he appeared for the first time at N.Y.'s Carnegie Hall. In 1985 he became the youngest prof. ever appointed to the faculty of the Royal College of Music. In 1988 he became principal clarinetist of the Philharmonia Orch. in London. In addition to his appearances as a virtuoso soloist with orchs., he also played in many chamber music settings and appeared in duo recitals with Mikhail Pletnev. His extensive repertoire, ranging from the masters to contemporary composers, showcases a musician whose virtuosity is equalled by impeccable taste.

Collum, Herbert, German organist, harpsichordist, conductor, and composer; b. Leipzig, July 18, 1914. He studied organ with Straube and Ramin at the Hochschule für Musik in Leipzig; also piano with Adolf Martienssen and composition with J.N. David. In 1934 he became organist of the Kreuzkirche in Dresden; founded the Collum Concerts (1935) and the Collum Choir (1946) of Dresden. He was a distinguished interpreter of the music of Bach, both as organist and as harpsichordist; he also composed concertos for harpsichord and many vocal works.

Colombo, Pierre, Swiss conductor; b. La Tour-de-Peilz, May 22, 1914. He received training in piano, voice, and flute, and also pursued studies in science at the Univ. of Lausanne; he studied conducting at the Basel Cons. (diploma, 1942), his principal mentors being Scherchen and H. Münch; he also studied with Krauss. He conducted choral groups and in 1950 founded the Geneva Chamber Orch. After conducting the Johannesburg (South Africa) Sym. Orch. (from 1953), he was an administrator with the Geneva Radio (from 1955). He also appeared as a guest conductor throughout Europe.

Coltrane, John (William), remarkable black American jazz tenor and soprano saxophonist, bandleader, and composer; b. Hamlet, N.C., Sept. 23, 1926; d. Huntington, N.Y., July 17, 1967. While growing up in Highpoint, N.C., he learned to play the E-flat alto horn, clarinet, and alto saxophone, and then pursued training in Philadelphia at the Ornstein School of Music and the Granoff Studios. In 1945 he launched his professional career, working as an alto and tenor saxophonist with various musicians, including Dizzy Gillespie (1949–51). After turning decisively to the tenor saxophone, he played with Johnny Hodges's septet (1953–54) before gaining distinction as a master of his instrument as a member of Miles Davis's quintet (1955–57). He then expanded his mastery to include the soprano saxophone, and played with Thelonious Monk's quartet (1957) and again with Davis (1958–60). In 1960 he organized his own innovative quartet. Coltrane was a controversial figure, but his importance as a major contributor to the avant-garde jazz movement of his era is duly recognized by jazz cognoscente.

BIBL.: C. Simpkins, *C.: A Biography* (N.Y., 1975); J. Thomas, *Chasin' the Trane: The Music and Mystique of J.C.* (Garden City, N.Y., 1975); B. Cole, *J. C.* (N.Y., 1976; new ed., 1993); D. Baker, *The Jazz Style of J. C.* (Lebanon, Ind., 1980); B. Priestly, *J. C.* (London, 1987); E. Nisenson, *Ascension: J. C. and His Quest* (N.Y., 1993); G. Putschögl, *J. C. und die Afro-Amerikanische Oraltradition* (Graz, 1993).

Colvig, William, American instrument maker and performer; b. Medford, Oreg., March 13, 1917. He was born into a musical family; he studied piano from the age of 6 and played in bands and orchs. during his formal studies at the Univ. of Calif. at Berkeley and the College of the Pacific in Stockton. In 1967 he initiated an association with the composer Lou Harrison, for whom he has built many instruments, including psalteries, harps, flutes, monochords, and several complete gamelans; he performed on these instruments in many of Harrison's compositions, as well as on traditional instruments in concerts and lectures. His instruments have been used by the San Francisco Sym. and San Francisco Opera Co., among others; he built the gamelans housed at the Univ. of Calif. at Berkeley and at Mills College in Oakland.

Comden, Betty (real name, **Elizabeth Cohen**), prominent American librettist, lyricist, and musician; b. N.Y., May 3, 1915. She received her education at N.Y. Univ. (B.S., 1938). She began her career as a member of the Revuers, a N.Y. nightclub act, where she first became associated with Adolph Green. Their first major success as co-authors came with the Broadway musical *On the Town* (1945), after Leonard Bernstein's ballet *Fancy Free*. After working with Jule Styne on *Two on the Aisle* (1951), they produced their finest screenplays with *Singin' in the Rain* (1952) and *The Band Wagon* (1953). Returning to Broadway, they collaborated with Bernstein on *Wonderful Town* (1953). They then resumed their collaborative efforts with Styne, producing such notable scores as *Peter Pan* (1954), *Bells Are Ringing* (1956), *Do Re Mi* (1960), and *Hallelujah Baby!* (1967). Their success continued with their collaboration with Charles Strouse on *Applause* (1970) and with Cy Coleman on *On the Twentieth Century* (1978), both scores receiving Tony Awards; they garnered a 2nd Tony Award for their collaboration with Coleman on *The Will Rogers Follies* (1991). The remarkable team of Comden and Green proved to be the longest running in the history of the American theater. In 1991 they received Kennedy Center Honors. Comden was the author of the vol. *Off Stage* (Oxford, 1995).

BIBL.: A. Robinson, *B. C. and Adolph Green: A Bio-Bibliography* (Westport, Conn., 1993).

Comet, Catherine, French conductor; b. Fontainebleau, Dec. 6, 1944. She studied at the Paris Cons. (1958–63), where she took a premier prix in piano; concurrently received private training in analysis, harmony, counterpoint, and fugue from

Boulanger before pursuing conducting studies with Morel at the Juilliard School of Music N.Y. (1964–68), where she received B.A. and M.A. degrees. In 1966 she won 1st prize in the Besançon conducting competition, and in 1967 she made her professional conducting debut with the Lille Radio Sym. Orch. at the Besançon Festival. In 1970–71 she was an assistant to Boulez with the BBC Sym. Orch. in London. She was conductor of the Paris Opéra Ballet from 1972 to 1975; from 1979 to 1981 she was music director of the Univ. of Wisc. sym. and chamber orchs. in Madison. After serving as the Exxon-Arts Endowment Conductor of the St. Louis Sym. Orch. (1981–84), she was assoc. conductor of the Baltimore Sym. Orch. (1984–86). In 1986 she became music director of the Grand Rapids (Mich.) Sym. Orch. In 1988 she was named co-recipient of the Seaver/NEA Conductors Award. From 1990 to 1992 she was music director of the American Sym. Orch. in N.Y. Comet has appeared with fine success as a guest conductor with principal North American orchs., including those of Boston, Chicago, Cincinnati, Detroit, Minneapolis, Philadelphia, San Francisco, Toronto, and Washington, D.C.

Comissiona, Sergiu, prominent Romanian-born American conductor; b. Bucharest, June 16, 1928. He studied conducting with Silvestri and Lindenberg, making his conducting debut at the age of 17 in Sibiu in a performance of Gounod's *Faust.* He became a violinist in the Bucharest Radio Quartet (1946), and then in the Romanian State Ensemble (1947), where he was subsequently assistant conductor (1948–50) and music director (1950–55). From 1955 to 1959 he was principal conductor of the Romanian State Opera in Bucharest. Being Jewish, he was moved to emigrate to Israel, where he was music director of the Haifa Sym. Orch. (1960–66) and founder-director of the Ramat Gan Chamber Orch. (1960–67). In 1963 he appeared in North America as conductor of the Israel Chamber Orch., and, in 1965, as guest conductor of the Philadelphia Orch. He then was music director of the Göteborg Sym. Orch. (1966–77), music adviser of the Northern Ireland Orch. in Belfast (1967–68), and music director of the Baltimore Sym. Orch. (1969–84). On July 4, 1976, he became a naturalized U.S. citizen. He was music director of the Chautauqua (N.Y.) Festival Orch. (1976–80), music advisor of the Temple Univ. Festival in Ambler (1977–80), and music advisor of the American Sym. Orch. in N.Y. (1977–82). He served as artistic director (1980–83), music director-designate (1983–84), and music director (1984–88) of the Houston Sym. Orch. From 1982 he was chief conductor of the Radio Phil. Orch. in Hilversum. In 1987–88 he was also music director of the N.Y. City Opera, and then was chief conductor of the Helsinki Phil. from 1990. He likewise served as music director-designate (1990–91) and music director (1991–94) of the Vancouver (B.C.) Sym. Orch.

Cone, Edward T(oner), American composer, pianist, teacher, and writer on music; b. Greensboro, N.C., May 4, 1917. He studied composition with Sessions at Princeton Univ. (B.A., 1939; M.F.A., 1942); also took piano lessons with Jeffrey Stoll, Karl Ulrich Schnabel, and Eduard Steuermann. He joined the faculty of Princeton Univ. in 1946; was made an assoc. prof. in 1952 and a full prof. in 1960, retiring in 1985. He received a Guggenheim fellowship in 1947. In addition to composing and teaching, he gave piano recitals. He was also active as a writer; was ed. of the periodical *Perspectives of New Music* (1966–72).

WRITINGS: *Musical Form and Musical Performance* (N.Y., 1968); *The Composer's Voice* (Berkeley, 1974); co-ed. (with B. Boretz), *Perspectives on Schoenberg and Stravinsky* (Princeton, 1968), *Perspectives on American Composers* (N.Y., 1971), and *Perspectives on Notation and Performance* (N.Y., 1975); ed. *Roger Sessions on Music* (Princeton, 1979); P. Morgan, ed., *Music: A View from Delft: Selected Essays* (Chicago, 1989).

WORKS: ORCH.: Sym. (1953); Elegy (1953); *Nocturne and Rondo* for Piano and Orch. (1955–57); Violin Concerto (1959); *Music* for Strings (1964); *Variations* (1967–68); *Cadenzas* for Violin, Oboe, and Strings (1979). **CHAMBER:** 2 string quartets (1939–49); 2 violin sonatas (1940, 1948); *Rhapsody* for Viola and Piano (1947); Piano Trio (1951); Piano Quintet (1960); *Funereal Stanzas* for Wind Quintet (1965); String Sextet (1966); *Capriccio* for String Quartet (1981); Piano Quartet (1983). **PIANO:** *Fantasy* (1950); *Prelude, Passacaglia and Fugue* (1957); *Fantasy* for 2 Pianos (1965). **VOCAL:** *Scarabs* for Soprano and String Quartet (1948); Philomela for Soprano and Chamber Ensemble (1954–70); *Around the Year* for Madrigal Group and String Quartet (1956); songs.

Confalonieri, Giulio, Italian music critic, pedagogue, and composer; b. Milan, May 23, 1896; d. there, June 29, 1972. He studied at the Univ. of Milan (graduated, 1920) and received training in composition from Alfano at the Bologna Cons. (diploma, 1921). After further studies with Dukas in Paris (1922), he lived in London (1923–26) before returning to Milan to pursue his career. He wrote the opera *Rosaspina* (Bergamo, Sept. 9, 1939); other stage music; orch. pieces; chamber music. He publ. *Prigionia di un artista: Il romanzo di Luigi Cherubini* (2 vols., Milan, 1948), *Guida alla musica* (Milan, 1950; 2nd ed., 1958, as *Storia della musica*), and *Come la musica* (Turin, 1966).

Confrey, Zez (Edward Elezear), American pianist and composer of light music, especially of a style known as "novelty piano"; b. Peru, Ill., April 3, 1895; d. Lakewood, N.J., Nov. 22, 1971. He studied at the Chicago Musical College and privately with Jessie Dunn and Frank Denhart. He appeared as piano soloist, along with George Gershwin, at Paul Whiteman's concert "Experiment in Modern Music" (1924), at which Gershwin's *Rhapsody in Blue* was premiered.

WORKS: *Kitten on the Keys* (1921); *Stumbling* (1922); *Dizzy Fingers, Valse Mirage,* and *3 Little Oddities* (1923); *Concert Etude* (1922); *Buffoon* (1930); *Grandfather's Clock* (1933); *Oriental Fantasy* (1935); *Ultra Ultra* (1935); *Rhythm Venture* (1936); *Della Robbia* (1938); etc.

Conley, Eugene, American tenor; b. Lynn, Mass., March 12, 1908; d. Denton, Texas, Dec. 18, 1981. He studied with Harriet Barrows and Ettore Verna. After making his operatic debut as the Duke of Mantua at the Brooklyn Academy of Music (1940), he sang with the San Carlo Opera Co.; later appeared in Chicago (1942) and at Milan's La Scala (1949). On Jan. 25, 1950, he made his Metropolitan Opera debut in N.Y. as Faust, remaining on its roster until 1956. He made guest appearances in San Francisco, Stockholm, at Paris's Opéra-Comique, and at London's Covent Garden. From 1960 to 1978 he was artist-in-residence at North Texas State Univ. in Denton. Among his best known roles were Edgardo, Rodolfo, Pinkerton, and Tom Rakewell.

Conlon, James (Joseph), American conductor; b. N.Y., March 18, 1950. He studied at the High School of Music and Art in N.Y., and then was a pupil in conducting of Morel at the Juilliard School of Music in N.Y. (B.M., 1972). After making his formal conducting debut with *Boris Godunov* at the Spoleto Festival in 1971, he conducted at the Juilliard School (1972–75). On April 12, 1974, he became the youngest conductor ever to lead a subscription concert of the N.Y. Phil. On Dec. 11, 1976, he made his Metropolitan Opera debut in N.Y. conducting *Die Zauberflöte,* and remained on its roster until 1980; was again on its roster from 1981 to 1983. He served as music director of the Cincinnati May Festival (from 1979) and chief conductor of the Rotterdam Phil. (1983–91). In 1989 he became chief conductor of the Cologne Opera; in 1991 he also was made Generalmusikdirektor of the city of Cologne and chief conductor of the Gürzenich Orch. there. He likewise was music advisor (1995–96) and principal conductor (from 1996) of the Opéra de la Bastille in Paris.

Connell, Elizabeth, Irish mezzo-soprano, later soprano; b. Port Elizabeth, South Africa, Oct. 22, 1946. She was a student of Otakar Kraus at the London Opera Centre. In 1972 she won the Maggie Teyte Prize and made her operatic debut at the Wexford Festival as Varvara in *Kát'a Kabanová.* In 1975 she sang with the Australian Opera in Sydney, and from 1975 to 1980 she was a member of the English National Opera in London, where she won notice as Eboli and Herodias. In 1976 she made her debut at London's Covent Garden as Verdi's Viclinda, and in 1980 at the Bayreuth Festival as Ortrud. In 1983 she turned to soprano roles, and in 1984 appeared as Electra at the Salzburg Festival and as Norma in Geneva. On Jan. 7, 1985, she made her Metropolitan Opera debut in N.Y. as Vitellia, and then returned to Covent Garden to sing Leonora in *Il Trovatore* and Leonore in *Fidelio*.

Connolly, Justin (Riveagh), English composer and teacher; b. London, Aug. 11, 1933. He was a student of Fricker and Boult at the Royal College of Music in London. He then held a Harkness fellowship at Yale Univ., where he studied with Powell (1963–65) and also taught. Returning to London, he was prof. of theory and composition at the Royal College of Music (1966–89). As a composer, Connolly has followed the structural techniques of the avant-garde, with notable influence from Babbitt and Carter.

WORKS: DRAMATIC: *Chimaera* for Dancer, Alto, Baritone, Chorus, Piano, Percussion, and Cello (1979; rev. 1981). **ORCH.:** *Antiphonies* (n.d.); *Rebus* (1970); *Anima* for Viola and Orch. (1974); *Diaphony* for Organ and Orch. (1977); Sym. (1991). **CHAMBER:** *Cinquepaces* for Brass Quintet (n.d.); a series of pieces under the titles *Obbligati, Triads*, and *Tesserae* (1966–69); *Sestina A* and *B* for Chamber Ensemble (1972; rev. 1978); *Celidh* for 4 Violins (1976); *Nocturnal* for Flutes, Piano, Percussion, and Double Bass (1990); piano pieces. **VOCAL:** *The Marriage of Heaven and Hell* for Soloists, Chorus, and Orch. (n.d.); *Poems of Wallace Stevens I* for Soprano and 7 Players (1967) and *II* for Soprano, Clarinet, and Piano (1970); *Regeneration* for Chorus and Brass (1977); *Sentences* for Chorus, Brass, and Organ (1979); *Waka* for Mezzo-soprano and Piano (1981); *Spelt from Sibyl's Leaves* for 6 Solo Voices and Ensemble (1989); *Cantata* for Soprano and Piano (1991).

Consoli, Marc-Antonio, Italian-born American composer; b. Catania, May 19, 1941. He studied with Rieti at the N.Y. College of Music (B.M., 1966), with Krenek at the Peabody Cons. of Music in Baltimore (M.M., 1967), and with Goehr at the Yale Univ. School of Music (M.M., 1971; D.M.A., 1977); he also took courses with Schuller and Crumb at the Berkshire Music Center in Tanglewood, with Donatoni at the Accademia Musicale Chigiana in Siena, and at the Warsaw Cons. He became a naturalized U.S. citizen in 1967. He was founder-director of the Musica Oggi Ensemble (1978–80) and served as a church music director and organist (from 1988). He was also ed. of the Hargail Music Press (1978–84) and ed. and publisher of Rinaldo Music Press (from 1983). From 1990 he was adjunct assistant prof. at N.Y. Univ. His honors include Guggenheim fellowships (1971, 1979), NEA grants (1979, 1981, 1985), and an award from the American Academy and Inst. of Arts and Letters (1975).

WORKS: BALLETS: *Naked Masks: 3 Frescoes from a Dream* (N.Y., Dec. 13, 1980); *The Last Unicorn* (1981; N.Y., Feb. 24, 1989). **ORCH.:** *Profiles* (1973); *Music for Chambers* (1974; Hilversum, Sept. 13, 1975); *Odefonia* (1976; N.Y., May 23, 1978); *Afterimages* (1982; N.Y., June 2, 1983); Cello Concerto (N.Y., May 9, 1988); *Arie Mutate* (1990). **CHAMBER:** *Brazilian Fantasy* for Clarinet and Piano (1965); Sonatina for Tenor Saxophone and Piano (1965); *Interactions I* for 6 Instruments (Tanglewood, Aug. 12, 1970), *II* for Flute and Harp (New Haven, Conn., April 30, 1971), *III* for Violin, Cello, and Piano (College Park, Md., March 22, 1971), *IV: The Aftermath* for 5 Instruments (New Haven, Conn., Dec. 12, 1971), and *V: The Consequences* for Flute and String Quartet (1972); *Sciuri novi I* for Flute (Siena, Aug. 28, 1974) and *II* for Contrabass and Tape (1975; Royan, March 23, 1976); *Music for Chambers* for 3 Groups of Instruments (1974; Helsinki, May 10, 1978); *Ellipsonics* for 1 to 4 Players and Optional Slides, Lights, Mimes, and/or Dancers (1974; Pamparato, Italy, July 10, 1975); *Tre fiori musicali* for Flute and Guitar (1978; N.Y., April 30, 1980); *Orpheus's Meditation* for Guitar (1981; N.Y., May 4, 1982); *Saxlodie* for Alto Saxophone and Piano (Warsaw, Oct. 20, 1981); 2 string quartets: No. 1 (1983; N.Y., April 25, 1984) and No. 2 (1990); *Sans parole I* for Cello (1983) and *II* for Violin (N.Y., Nov. 10, 1988); *Lauda* for Violin, Cello, and Piano (San Diego, Dec. 7, 1985); *Reflections* for Clarinet, Alto Saxophone, Trombone, Contrabass, and Percussion (N.Y., March 10, 1986). **VOCAL:** *Equinox I* (Baltimore, May 23, 1967) and *II* (Tanglewood, Aug. 14, 1968) for Soprano Ensemble; *Isonic* for Soprano, Flute, 2 Pianos, and Percussion (Graz, Oct. 26, 1970); *Canti trinacriani* for Baritone, Orch., and Tape (1975; Royan, March 2, 1976); *Tre canzoni* for Soprano or Mezzo-soprano, Flute, and Cello (N.Y., May 18, 1976); *Vuci siculani* for Mezzo-soprano, Flute, Clarinet, Guitar, and String Quartet (N.Y., Dec. 12, 1979); *Fantasia celeste* for Soprano, Flute, Clarinet, Violin, Cello, Piano, and Percussion (Boston, April 4, 1983); *6 Ancient Greek Lyrics* for Soprano or Mezzo-soprano, Flute, Cello, and Piano (N.Y., Dec. 10, 1984); *Musiculi II* for Women's Voices and Orch. (1985–86; N.Y., Feb. 19, 1991) and *IV* for Chorus and Orch. (1990–92); *The Light Cantata* for Soprano or Mezzo-soprano, Narrator, Mixed Chorus, Treble Chorus, and Orch. (N.Y., Dec. 4, 1986); *Greek Lyrics* for Soprano, Chorus, Piano, and Strings (N.Y., June 5, 1988); choruses; solo songs.

Constant, Franz, Belgian composer and pianist; b. Montignies-le-Tilleul, Nov. 17, 1910. He studied at the Charleroi Academy of Music and at the Brussels Cons. with M. Maas, L. Jongen, Bourguignon, and Absil; he also studied with Tomasi in Paris. He became a concert pianist and formed a successful duo with his wife, Jeanne Pellaerts. In 1947 he was appointed to the faculty of the Brussels Cons. As a composer, Constant blends the modalities of the classical Belgian School with coloristic harmonies.

WORKS: ORCH.: *Rhapsodie* for Violin and Orch. (1962); Saxophone Concerto (1963); Trumpet Concerto (1965); *Sinfonietta* for Flute, Oboe, and Strings (1968); *Fantasia* for Saxophone and Orch. (1969); Concertino for Flute and Strings (1970); Violin Concerto (1971); *Rhapsodie* (1973); *Expressions* for Violin, Piano, and Strings (1973); Clarinet Concertino (1975); *Ballade du sud* for 2 Pianos and Orch. (1979); *Mouvement rhapsodie* for Double Bass and Orch. (1980); *Musique* for Saxphone Quartet and Strings (1981); *Quattro movimenti sinfonici* (1983); Concerto for Accordion and Wind Orch. (1985); Concerto for Brass and Wind Orch. (1987). **CHAMBER:** *Allegro* for Trumpet and Piano (1959); *4 séquences* for 4 Saxophones (1962); *Impressions* for 4 Clarinets (1964); Flute Sonata (1967); *Évocation* for Flute and Piano (1969); *Suo tempore* for Violin and Piano (1969); *Dialogue* for Clarinet and Piano (1970); *Sonatine picturale* for Clarinet and Piano (1970); *Couleur provençale* for Horn and Piano (1970); *Pour la guitare I* and *II* (1971); *5 Miniatures* for Violin, Flute, and Piano (1971); Piano Quartet (1971); *Divertissement* for Bassoon and Piano (1972); *Rythme et expression* for Violin, Saxophone, Piano, and Percussion (1972); *Musique à deux* for Flute and Guitar (1973); *Musica lyrica* for Flute, Violin, and Piano or Harpsichord (1976); *Suite en trio* for Flute, Violin, and Piano (1977); *Rhapsodie d'été* for Clarinet Octet and Percussion (1977); *Odyssée* for Cello and Piano (1982); *Sonate à trois* for 2 Violins and Piano (1983); *Triptyque* for 2 Pianos and Percussion (1984); String Quartet (1985); *Impromptu* for Alto Saxophone and Piano (1987); many piano pieces. **VOCAL:** *Jeanne de Naples*, cantata for Soprano, Narrator, Children's Voices, Speaking and Singing Choruses, and Orch. (1972); *Histoires du dimanche* for Children's Chorus, and Piano or Ensemble of 11 Instruments (1973); songs.

Constant, Marius, Romanian-born French conductor, composer, and teacher; b. Bucharest, Feb. 7, 1925. He first studied at the Bucharest Cons., where he took prizes in piano, harmony, counterpoint, and composition. In 1946 he settled in Paris and eventually became a naturalized French citizen. He was a student of Honegger, and also at the Cons. of Messiaen, Aubin, and Boulanger (premiers prix in composition and analysis, 1949), and at the École Normale de Musique of Fournet (conducting degree, 1949). He was active with the Groupe de

Recherches Musicales du Club d'Essai de la Radio (1952–54), and was co-founder and director of the program France-Musique (1954–66); he also was chief conductor of the Ballets de Roland Petit (1957–63). In 1963 he founded Ars Nova, a contemporary music ensemble, which he served as music director until 1971. From 1973 to 1978 he was director of dance at the Paris Opéra. He was prof. of orchestration at the Paris Cons. (1979–88), and also taught composition and analysis at Stanford Univ. in California. Constant has won a number of honors for his compositions, including the Italia Prize (1952, 1987), the Koussevitzky Prize (1962), the Grand Prix National de la Musique (1969), and the "Victoires" de la Musique (1991). In 1993 he was elected a member of the Académie des Beaux-Arts, succeeding to the chair of Messiaen. In his compositions, Constant at first wrote along impressionistic lines; he later adopted a more advanced style in which he often made use of both serial and aleatory procedures.

WORKS: DRAMATIC: OPERAS: *Le Souper* (Besançon, Sept. 9, 1969); *Le jeu de Sainte Agnès* (Besançon, Sept. 6, 1974); *La Tragédie de Carmen* (Paris, Nov. 5, 1981); *Impressions de Pélléas* (Paris, Nov. 13, 1992). **BALLETS:** *Cyrano de Bergerac* (Paris, April 17, 1959); *Eloge de la folie* (Paris, March 11, 1966); *Paradis perdu* (London, Feb. 27, 1967); *Candide* (1970; Hamburg, Jan. 20, 1971); *Septentrion* (Marseilles, May 15, 1975); *Nana* (Paris, May 6, 1976); *L'Ange bleu* (Berlin, June 8, 1985). **FILM:** *Napoléon* (1992). **TELEVISION:** *Twilight Zone*, signature theme (1959). **ORCH.:** *Musique de concert* for Alto Saxophone and Chamber Orch. (1955); *24 Préludes* (Paris, March 24, 1959); *Turner*, 3 essays (Aix-en-Provence, July 17, 1961); *Chaconne et Marche militaire* (Philadelphia, March 28, 1968); *Winds* for 14 Instruments (Aix-en-Provence, July 11, 1968); *Strings* for Electric Guitar and 12 Strings (1969; also for Harpsichord and 12 Strings, 1972); *Candide* for Harpsichord and Orch. (1970; Geneva, May 5, 1971); *Faciebat Anno 1973* for 24 Violins and Orch. (Aix-en-Provence, July 17, 1973); 3 syms.: No. 1, *Nana-Symphonie* (1976–80; Besançon, Sept. 12, 1980), No. 2, Sym. for Winds (Montreal, March 17, 1978), and No. 3, *Brevissima* (Madrid, Feb. 27, 1992); *Concerto Gli Elementi* for Trombone and Orch. (1977); *Stress* for Jazz Trio and Orch. (Châteauvallon, Aug. 21, 1977; in collaboration with M. Solal); Concertante for Alto Saxophone and Orch. (1978); *Harpalycée* for Harp and Strings (1980; also for Harp and String Quartet); *103 Regards dans l'eau* for Violin and Orch. (1981; also for Violin and 12 Instruments, 1983); *Perpetuo* (1986); *Texas Twilight* (1986); *Choruses and Interludes* for Horn, Orch., and Jazz Quartet (1987; Rheims, June 3, 1988); Barrel Organ Concerto (Cannes, April 10, 1988); *Konzertstück* for Oboe and Orch. (Toulon, May 30, 1990); *Hämeenlinna: An Imaginary Landscape* (Helsinki, May 23, 1991). **BAND:** *L'inaguration de la maison* (1985). **CHAMBER:** Trio for Oboe, Clarinet, and Bassoon (1950); *Trois complexes* for Double Bass and Piano (1951); *Moulins à prières* for 2 Harpsichords (1969); *Equal* for 5 Percussionists (1970); *Quatorze stations* for Percussionist (1970); *9 Mars 1971: Hommage à Jean-Pierre Guezec* for Piccolo and Glockenspiel (1971); *Pour flûte et un instrument* (1972); *Silètes* for Harpsichord (1973); *Psyché* for 2 Pianos and 2 Percussion (1975); *For Clarinet* (1975); *9 Pièces* for Flute and Piano (1978); *Alleluias* for Trumpet and Organ (1980); *D'une élégie slave* for Guitar (1981); *Recitativo* for Viola (1983); *Pierres-Jewels* for 3 Cellos (1984); *Die Trennung* for String Quartet (1990); *Phantasma* for Violin and Piano (1990); *Blues-Variations* for Guitar and Electric Guitar (1990); *Matines* for Organ (1992). **VOCAL:** *Chants de Maldoror* for Narrator and Orch. (Vicenza, Sept. 17, 1962).

Constantinescu, Dan, Romanian composer; b. Bucharest, June 10, 1931. He studied with Negrea, Rogalski, and Jora at the Bucharest Cons., where he later was an instructor in theory.

WORKS: ORCH.: *Divertissement in a Classical Style* for Strings (1954); *Toma Alimos*, ballad (1955); *Partita* (1957); Concerto for Piano and Strings (1963); Chamber Sym. (1968); *Sinfonia Concertante* (1970); Concerto for 2 Pianos and Orch. (1972); Sym. for Strings (1973). **CHAMBER:** Trio for Violin, Clarinet, and Piano (1964); Cello Sonata (1964); Clarinet Sonata (1965); *Variations* for Piano and String Trio (1966); String Quartet (1967); *Mişcări* for Clarinet, Violin, Viola, and Cello (1974); String Sextet (1976). **VOCAL:** Songs.

Constantinescu, Paul, eminent Romanian composer and pedagogue; b. Ploieşti, July 13, 1909; d. Bucharest, Dec. 20, 1963. He studied with Castaldi, Jora, Cuclin, and Brăiloiu at the Bucharest Cons. (1928–33) and with Schmidt and Marx in Vienna (1934–35). Returning to Bucharest, he taught at the academy for religious music (1937–41) and then was a prof. of composition at the Cons. from 1941 until his death. In 1932 he received the Enesco prize and in 1956 the Romanian Academy prize. Constantiescu made use of folk and liturgical elements in his works, developing a style marked by an assured command of form and modal harmony. He did much to chart the course for the post-Enesco generation of Romanian nationalist composers.

WORKS: DRAMATIC: *O noapte furtunoasă*, comic opera (1934; rev. 1950; Bucharest, May 19, 1951); *Nunta în Carpaţi*, choreographic poem (Bucharest, May 5, 1938); *Pană Lesnea Rusalim*, opera (1954–55; Cluj-Napoca, June 26, 1956). **ORCH.:** *Suită românească* (1930–36; rev. 1942); *Jocuri româneşti* (1936); *Burlescă* for Piano and Orch. (1937; Bucharest Radio, March 7, 1938); *Simfonietă* (1937; Bucharest Radio, March 16, 1938); 2 syms.: No. 1 (1944; Bucharest, May 18, 1947; rev. 1955) and No. 2, *Simfonie ploieşteană* (Ploieşti, Sept. 29, 1961); *Variatuni libere asupra unei melodii bizantine din sec. XIII* for Cello and Orch. (1946; rev. 1951); Concerto for Strings (1947; rev. 1955; Bucharest, Feb. 16, 1956); *Rapsodia II* (1949; Bucharest, Oct. 15, 1950); *Baladă haiducească* for Cello and Orch. (1950; Bucharest, Dec. 23, 1951); *Suită bucovineană* (1951); Piano Concerto (1952; Bucharest, May 16, 1953); *Juventus*, overture (1952); *Rapsodie oltenească* (1957); Violin Concerto (1957; Brasov, May 21, 1958); *Înfrăţire*, choreographic rhapsody (Bucharest, Aug. 20, 1959); Harp Concerto (1960; Bucharest, May 4, 1961); Triple Concerto for Violin, Cello, Piano, and Orch. (Bucharest, Dec. 28, 1963). **CHAMBER:** *2 Studii în stil bizantin* for Violin, Viola, and Cello (1929); Quintet (1932); Violin Sonatina (1933); *Sonatină bizantină* for Solo Cello or Viola (1940); *Cîntec vechi pe 2 melodii din Anton Pann* for Cello and Piano (1952); piano pieces. **VOCAL:** *Isarlîk* for Soprano and Orch. (1936); *Ryga Crypto şi Lapona Enigel* for Soli, Reciter, and Orch. (1936; rev. 1951; Bucharest, June 1, 1966); *Byzantinisches Passions und Osteroratorium* for Soli, Chorus, and Orch. (1943; Bucharest, March 3, 1946; rev. 1948); *Byzantinisches Weihnachtoratorium* for Soli, Chorus, and Orch. (Bucharest, Dec. 21, 1947); *Uliţa noastră*, 7 songs for Baritone and orch. (1960); other songs.

BIBL.: V. Tomescu, *P. C.* (Bucharest, 1967).

Contiguglia, Richard and **John**, brilliant American duo-pianists; b. identical twins, N.Y., April 13, 1937. They began taking piano lessons in early childhood, and grew in parallel congruence; they played in a duo recital in public when they were 6, and continued to develop in close consanguinity; they composed music for 2 pianos and transcribed solo works for their concerts. When they were 12, Percy Grainger invited them to play at one of his recitals; he subsequently befriended them and gave them valuable advice; later they took piano lessons with Jean Wilder and with Bruce Simonds at Yale Univ.; upon graduation, they received a Ditson Fellowship, which enabled them to study with Dame Myra Hess in London. They made their professional debut in London in 1962, playing piano 4-hands; in 1964 they made a major European tour. In addition to the standard literature for duo-pianos, they performed piano transcriptions for 2 pianos and for piano 4-hands of obscure works. In 1971 they gave an all-Liszt concert in London, which included his piano transcription of his symphonic poems *Mazeppa* and *Orpheus*, and of his arrangements of excerpts from Bellini's *Norma* and *La Sonnambula* and Mozart's *Don Giovanni*. In 1972 they played Liszt's transcriptions of Beethoven's 9th Sym.

in London, arousing considerable curiosity, and repeated this exhibition in N.Y. in 1974. They gave the first performance of Liszt's *Grosses Konzertstück über Mendelssohn's "Lieder ohne Worte"* for 2 Pianos, composed in 1834, in Utrecht on Oct. 19, 1986. They further played duo-piano works by Bartók and Grainger. For a brief period, they split their original fetal name into 2 fungible parts, Conti-Guglia.

Contilli, Gino, Italian composer and teacher; b. Rome, April 19, 1907; d. Genoa, April 4, 1978. He studied at the Accademia di Santa Cecilia in Rome with Respighi. He taught at the Messina Liceo Musicale (1942–66) and was director of the Genoa Cons. (from 1966).

WORKS: OPERA: *Saul* (1941). **ORCH.:** 2 concertos (1936, 1942); *Sinfonia italiana* (1938); *Espressioni sinfoniche* (Venice, Sept. 21, 1960); *Preludi* (1966). **CHAMBER:** Violin Sonata (1947). **VOCAL:** *La notte* for Voice and Small Ensemble (1950); *In Lunam*, cantata (1957; RAI, Nov. 20, 1964); *Offerta musicale* for Soprano and 5 Instruments (1959); *Immagini sonore* for Soprano and 11 Instruments (1964).

BIBL.: G. Zaccaro, *G. C.* (Milan, 1980).

Conus, Sergei, Russian-American pianist and composer; b. Moscow, Oct. 18, 1902. He studied music with his father, Julius Conus (b. Moscow, Feb. 1, 1869; d. Malenki, Ivanov District, Jan. 3, 1942), with his uncle, Leo Conus, and with Oskar Riesemann. In 1920 he went to Paris, where he studied piano with Cortot and Philipp; then lived in Serbia, Bulgaria, and Poland. He was again in France from 1937 to 1949, and in Morocco from 1949 to 1959; then settled in America, where he taught piano at the Boston Cons. His compositions are mostly for piano (24 preludes, many miniatures, a concerto); he also wrote a Sym. His style is characteristically Russian, closely resembling that of Rachmaninoff.

Converse, Frederick Shepherd, distinguished American composer and teacher; b. Newton, Mass., Jan. 5, 1871; d. Westwood, Mass., June 8, 1940. After graduating from Harvard Univ. (1893), he studied music in Boston with Carl Baermann and Chadwick (1894–96), then in Munich at the Royal Academy of Music with Rheinberger (graduated, 1898). Returning to Boston, he taught harmony at the New England Cons. of Music (1900–1902; 1920–36; dean, 1931–37) and was a composition instructor at Harvard Univ. (1901–07). He received a Mus.Doc. from Boston Univ. (1933); became a member of the American Academy of Arts and Letters (1937). His early works reflect the influence of academic German training; later he began to apply more advanced harmonies; in his *Flivver 10 Million*, written to glorify the 10 millionth Ford car, he adopted a frankly modern idiom, modeled after Honegger's *Pacific 231*. He sketched some material for a 5th Sym. in 1937, but did not complete it. He renumbered his syms. in 1936, calling his previously unnumbered Sym. No. 1 and upping Nos. 1, 2, and 3 by one, giving the title of Sym. No. 5 to the undeveloped sketches for that work. But his Syms. Nos. 2, 3, and 4 were premiered, respectively, as Nos. 1, 2, and 3.

WORKS: OPERAS: *The Pipe of Desire* (1905; Boston, Jan. 31, 1906); *The Sacrifice* (1910; Boston, March 3, 1911); *Sinbad the Sailor* (1913); *The Immigrants* (1914). **ORCH.:** Syms.: D minor (Munich, July 14, 1898), No. 1 (c.1919; Boston, Jan. 30, 1920), No. 2 (1921; Boston, April 21, 1922), No. 3 (1936), and No. 6 (Indianapolis, Nov. 29, 1940); *Youth*, overture (1895; rev. 1897); *Festival March* (1899); *Festival of Pan* (1899; Boston, Dec. 21, 1900); *Endymion's Narrative* (1901; Boston, April 9, 1903); *Night and Day* (1901; Boston, Jan. 21, 1905); Violin Concerto (1902); *Euphrosyne*, overture (1903); *The Mystic Trumpeter* (1904; Philadelphia, March 3, 1905); *Ormazd*, tone poem (1911; St. Louis, Jan. 26, 1912); *Ave atque vale*, tone poem (1916; St. Louis, Jan. 26, 1917); *Fantasia* for Piano and Orch. (1922); *Song of the Sea*, tone poem (1923; Boston, April 18, 1924); *Elegiac Poem* (1925; Cleveland, Dec. 2, 1926); *Flivver 10 Million*, epic tone poem (1926; Boston, April 15, 1927); *California*, descriptive tone poem (1927; Boston, April 6, 1928); *American Sketches*, symphonic suite (1928; Boston, Feb. 8, 1935); Piano Concertino (1932); *Salutation*, concert march (1935); *3 Old-fashioned Dances* for Chamber Orch. (1938); *Rhapsody* for Clarinet and Orch. (1938); *Haul Away, Jo!*, variations on an American sea shanty (1939). **CHAMBER:** 3 string quartets (1896, rev. 1901; 1904; 1935); Septet for Clarinet, Bassoon, Horn, Piano, and String Trio (1897); Piano Trio (1932); *Prelude and Intermezzo* for Brass Sextet (1938); *2 Lyric Pieces* for Brass Quintet (1939); piano pieces. **VOCAL: ORATORIOS:** *Job*, dramatic poem for Soli, Chorus, and Orch. (Worcester Festival, Oct. 2, 1907); *Hagar in the Desert*, dramatic narrative for Low Voice and Orch. (Hamburg, 1908). **CANTATAS:** *The Peace Pipe* (1914); *The Answer of the Stars* (1919); *The Flight of the Eagle* (1930). *OTHER VOCAL: La Belle Dame sans merci*, ballade for Baritone with Orch. (1902); *Psalm, I Will Praise Thee, O Lord* (1924); choruses; songs.

BIBL.: R. Severence, *The Life and Works of F.S. C.* (diss., Boston Univ., 1932); R. Garofalo, *The Life and Works of F.S. C. (1871–1940)* (diss., Catholic Univ. of America, Washington, D.C., 1969).

Conyngham, Barry (Ernest), Australian composer and teacher; b. Sydney, Aug. 27, 1944. He studied jurisprudence before taking private composition lessons with Meale; in 1966 he entered the New South Wales State Conservatorium in Sydney, and then took his M.A. under Sculthorpe at the Univ. of Sydney, and subsequently his D.Mus. at the Univ. of Melbourne. In 1970 he pursued private lessons with Takemitsu in Japan and in 1972–73 postdoctoral studies at the Univ. of Calif. in San Diego. After teaching at the Univ. of New South Wales and the National Inst. of Dramatic Art (1968–70), and at the Univ. of Western Australia (1971), he was a visiting fellow at Princeton Univ. (1973–74) and composer and researcher in residence at the Univ. of Aix-Marseilles (1974–75). From 1975 to 1990 he taught at the Univ. of Melbourne. He served as prof. and head of the School of Creative Arts at the Univ. of Wollongong in New South Wales from 1990. Both jazz and Japanese influences are evident in his work; he has also written much electronic music.

WORKS: DRAMATIC: *Ned*, opera (1975–78); *The Apology of Bony Anderson*, opera (1978); *Fly*, opera (1981–84); *The Oath of Bad Brown Bill*, children's opera (1985); *Vast*, ballet (1987; Melbourne, March 4, 1988); *Diamentina Ghosts*, music theater (1988); *Bennelong*, music theater (1988). **ORCH.:** *Crisis: Thoughts in a City* for 2 String Orchs. and 3 Percussion (1968); *5 Windows* (1969); *Ice Carving* for Violin and 4 String Orchs. (1970); *Water . . . Footsteps . . . Time* for Amplified Tam-tam, Electric Guitar, Harp, Piano, and 2 Orchs. (1970–71); *6* for 6 Percussion and Orch. (1971); *Without Gesture* for Percussion, Harp, Piano, and Orch. (1973); *Sky* for Strings (1977); Percussion Concerto (1977); *Shadows of Noh*, double bass concerto (1978); *Mirages* (1978); *Horizons: Concerto for Orchestra* (1981); *Southern Cross*, double concerto for Violin, Piano, and Orch. (1981); *Dwellings* for Small Orch. (1982); Concerto for Cello and Strings (1984); *Recurrences* for Organ, Celesta, 2 Pianos, Electric Piano, and Orch. (1986); *Vast I: The Sea* (1987), *II: The Coast* (1987), *III: The Centre* (1987), and *IV: The Cities* (1987); *Glimpses of Bennelong* for Chamber Orch. (1987); *Monuments*, piano concerto (Albany, N.Y., May 19, 1989); *Waterways*, viola concerto (1989); *Cloudlines*, harp concerto (1990); *Decades* (Sydney, Sept. 9, 1992). **CHAMBER:** *Jazz Ballet* for 5 Instruments (1964); Cello Sonata (1965); *Dialogue* for String Trio (1967); *Lyric Dialogue* for 5 Flutes, Oboe, and Cello (1967); *Prisms* for 6 Violins (1968); *3* for 2 Percussion and String Quartet (1970); *5* for Wind Quintet (1970–71); *Snowflake* for Keyboard Player (1973); *Playback* for Double Bass or Cello and Tape (1973); String Quartet (1979); *Viola* for Viola (1981); *Journeys* for Reed Player and Tape (1981); *Voicings* for Flute, Trombone, Percussion, Piano, and Tape (1983); *Preview* for Cello (1984); *Streams* for Harp, Flute, and Viola (1988). **VOCAL:** *Farben* for Chorus (1968); *From Voss* for Amplified Woman's Voice, Harp, and Percussion (1973); *Edward John*

Eyre for Narrator and Chorus (1973); *Bony Anderson* for Baritone and Chamber Group (1978); *Basho* for Soprano and Chamber Group (London, Oct. 13, 1981); *Imaginary Letters* for Voices (1981); *Antipodes* for Soprano, Tenor, Baritone, Didgeridoo, Chorus, and Orch. (1984–85); *Matilda* for Soloists, Chorus, and Orch. (1988).

Cook, Will Marion, black American conductor and composer; b. Washington, D.C., Jan. 27, 1869; d. N.Y., July 19, 1944. He entered the Oberlin (Ohio) Cons. to study violin when he was 13, continuing his studies with Joachim in Germany and at the National Cons. in N.Y. He had a brief career as a concert violinist before devoting himself to composition for the black musical theater in N.Y.; he was director and composer for the Bert Williams-George Walker productions (1900–1908) and founded his own "syncopated" sym. orch. (1918), with which he toured extensively. In his later years, he was active mainly as a conductor and teacher in N.Y.

WORKS: MUSICALS (all 1st perf. in N.Y.): *Clorindy, or the Origin of the Cakewalk* (July 5, 1898); *Jes' Lak White Fo'ks* (1899); *The Cannibal King* (1901); *In Dahomey* (Feb. 18, 1903; in collaboration with others); *The Southerners* (May 23, 1904); *Abyssinia* (Feb. 10, 1906; in collaboration with others); *Bandana Land* (Feb. 3, 1908; in collaboration with others); *The Traitor* (March 1913; in collaboration with others); *Darkeydom* (Oct. 23, 1915; in collaboration with others); *Swing Along* (1929; in collaboration with W. Vodery). **OTHER:** Choral works; songs.

Cooke, Arnold (Atkinson), English composer and pedagogue; b. Gomersal, Yorkshire, Nov. 4, 1906. He studied with Dent at Caius College, Cambridge (B.A., 1928; B.Mus., 1929), returning there to take his D.Mus. in 1948; he also studied with Hindemith at the Berlin Hochschule für Musik (1929–32). He served as prof. of harmony, counterpoint, and composition at the Royal Manchester College of Music (1933–38), and later at Trinity College of Music in London (1947–77); in 1953 he also was chairman of the Composers Guild of Great Britain. His works are composed in an agreeable tonal idiom.

WORKS: DRAMATIC: OPERAS: *Mary Barton* (1949–52); *The Invisible Duke* (1975). **BALLET:** *Jabez and the Devil* (1962). **ORCH.:** *Concert Overture* No. 1 (1934) and No. 2, *The Processional* (1946); Piano Concerto (1939–40); 6 syms. (1946–47; 1963; 1967; 1974; 1978–79, London, July 17, 1981; 1983–84); Concerto for Strings (1948); Concerto for Oboe and Strings (1954); *Sinfonietta* for Chamber Orch. (1954); Concerto for Clarinet and Strings (1955); Concerto for Recorder or Flute and Strings (1956); Violin Concerto (1958); Concerto for Small Orch. (1966); *Variations on a Theme of Dufay* (1966); *York Suite* (1972); Cello Concerto (1972–73); *Repton Fantasia* (1984); *Concerto for Orchestra* (1986). **CHAMBER:** Cello Sonata (1925–26); 2 numbered cello sonatas (1941; 1979–80); String Quartet (1927–28); 5 numbered string quartets (1933, 1947, 1967, 1976, 1978); Quintet for Harp, Flute, Clarinet, Violin, and Cello (1932); Quartet for Flute and String Trio (1936); Viola Sonata (1936–37); 2 violin sonatas (1939, 1951); Piano Trio (1944); Quartet for Oboe and String Trio (1948); Piano Quartet (1949); String Trio (1950); Quintet for Horn, Violin, 2 Violas, and Piano (1955); 3 oboe sonatas (1957, 1959, 1962); Clarinet Sonata (1959); Wind Quintet (1961); Quintet for Clarinet and String Quartet (1962); Quartet for Flute, Clarinet, Cello, and Piano (1964); Quartet-Sonata for Recorder, Violin, Cello, and Harpsichord (1964); Trio for Clarinet, Cello, and Piano (1965); Quintet for Piano and String Quartet (1969); Harmonica Sonata (1970); Septet for 7 Clarinets (1971); Quartet for 4 Clarinets (1977); Trio for Oboe, Clarinet, and Bassoon (1984); Alto Flute Sonata (1985); Bassoon Sonata (1987); Sonata for Flute and Harp (1988); also piano and organ music. **VOCAL:** Cantatas: *Holderneth* (1933–34) and *Ode on St. Cecilia's Day* (1964); anthems; choruses; songs.

Cooke, Deryck (Victor), English writer on music; b. Leicester, Sept. 14, 1919; d. Thornton Heath, Oct. 26, 1976. He studied composition with Hadley and Orr at the Univ. of Cambridge (B.A., 1940; M.A., 1943; Mus.B., 1947) and then worked in the BBC music dept. (1947–59; 1965–76). He prepared a performing version of the odd-numbered movements of Mahler's 10th Sym. for a BBC broadcast on Dec. 19, 1960. The composer's widow, Alma, forbade any further broadcasts or performances, but was eventually convinced of the merits of the score and supplied Cooke with 24 unpubl. pages of fragments with which he completed the sym. (new version, London, Aug. 13, 1964). Further revisions were made with the assistance of Colin and David Matthews before the work was publ. in 1976. Since then the Mahler-Cooke version has been performed throughout the world.

WRITINGS (all publ. in London): *The Language of Music* (1959); *Mahler 1860–1911* (1960; rev. and enl. ed., 1980, as *Gustav Mahler: An Introduction to His Music*); *I Saw the World End: A Study of Wagner's Ring* (1979); *Variations: Essays on Romantic Music* (1982).

Cooke, Francis Judd, American composer and teacher; b. Honolulu, Dec. 28, 1910. He learned to play piano, organ, and cello; after graduating from Yale Univ. (1933), he studied with Loeffler in Medfield, Mass. (1934–35) before completing his training with Tovey at the Univ. of Edinburgh (graduated, 1937). He taught at the New England Cons. of Music in Boston (1939–70), Yale Univ. (1959–60), and Wellesley College (1973–79); was also organist and choir director at the First Parish Church in Lexington, Mass. (1955–81). He composed in an accessible, neo-Classical style.

WORKS: Horn Sonata (1968); *Roque Island March* for Orch. (c.1971); *Sposalizio* for Viola and Piano (1983); *Fagotti a Quattro* for Bassoon Quartet (1986–89); Piano Quartet (1987); *Variations* for Orch. (1988); *Fantasia Veneziana* for Brass Quintet (1988); *The House of Christmas*, cantata for 2 Soloists, Chorus, and Instruments (1989); *Chaikovskik* for Woodwind Quintet (1989); Concertino for Oboe and Woodwind Quartet (1989–90); *Symphony 1990* (1990); *Concerto non Grosso* for Chamber Ensemble (WGBH, Boston, Feb. 28, 1990); String Quartet (1990); numerous pieces for Chorus and Organ; songs.

Cooke, James Francis, American writer on music and composer; b. Bay City, Mich., Nov. 14, 1875; d. Philadelphia, March 3, 1960. He studied with R.H. Woodman and W.H. Hall; then went to Germany in 1900, where he continued his studies with Meyer-Olbersleben and H. Ritter. As ed. of the *Etude* (1908–49), he brought it to a high degree of popularity by promoting special features. He composed a number of successful piano pieces, including *White Orchids, Moon Mist, Ballet Mignon, Sea Gardens*, and *Italian Lake Suite*, as well as songs.

WRITINGS: *A Standard History of Music* (1910); *Great Pianists on Piano Playing* (4th ed., 1914); *Mastering the Scales and Arpeggios* (1913); *Musical Playlets for Children* (1917); *Great Singers on the Art of Singing* (1921); *Great Men and Famous Musicians* (1925); *Young Folks' Picture-History of Music* (1925); *Light, More Light* (1925); *Johannes Brahms* (1928); *Claude Debussy* (1928); *Musical Travelogues* (1934); *How to Memorize Music* (1947); also plays and poems.

Coolidge, Elizabeth (Penn) Sprague, generous American music patronesss; b. Chicago, Oct. 30, 1864; d. Cambridge, Mass., Nov. 4, 1953. In 1918 she established the Berkshire Festivals of Chamber Music in Pittsfield, Mass., which were held annually under her auspices; she later sponsored the Elizabeth Sprague Coolidge Foundation in the Library of Congress in Washington, D.C., created in 1925 for the purpose of producing concerts and music festivals, awarding prizes, etc., under the administration of the Music Division of the Library. Numerous composers were commissioned to write music for it. The auditorium of the Library of Congress was likewise her gift. In 1932 she founded the Elizabeth Sprague Coolidge Medal "for eminent services to chamber music," awarded annually (until 1949). She also initiated performances of modern and classical chamber music throughout the U.S. and Europe. Her sponsorship of the appearances of artists in the U.S. and abroad (the Pro Arte,

Coolidge, Roth quartets, etc.) was an important factor in the development of musical life in the U.S. In recognition of her many cultural contributions, she was made honorary M.A. (Yale Univ., Smith College, Mills College), L.D. (Mt. Holyoke College), Mus.Doc. (Pomona College), and LL.D. (Univ. of Calif.). She also received the Cobbett Medal and various foreign decorations.

BIBL.: W. Bedford, *E.S. C.: The Education of a Patron of Chamber Music: The Early Years* (diss., Univ. of Missouri, 1964); J. Rosenfeld, *E.S. C.: A Tribute on the One Hundredth Anniversary of Her Birth* (n.p., 1964).

Cooper, Emil (Albertovich), respected Russian conductor of English descent; b. Kherson, Dec. 20, 1877; d. N.Y., Nov. 16, 1960. He studied at the Odessa Cons., with Hellmesberger, Jr., and Nikisch in Vienna, and with Taneyev in Moscow. In 1896 he made his conducting debut in Odessa. He then conducted in Kiev (1899–1906), and at Moscow's Bolshoi and Zimin theaters (1904). On Oct. 7, 1909, he conducted the premiere of Rimsky-Korsakov's *The Golden Cockerel* in Moscow. From 1909 to 1911 he conducted Diaghilev's Russian seasons in Paris, and also appeared at London's Covent Garden. He continued to conduct in Russia until 1923, and then in Riga (1925–28). From 1929 to 1932 he conducted at the Chicago Opera, and then in Europe. In 1939 he returned to the Chicago Opera, remaining with it until his Metropolitan Opera debut in N.Y. on Jan. 26, 1944, conducting *Pelléas et Mélisande.* He remained on the roster there until 1950, and then conducted the Montréal Opera Guild. In addition to the Russian repertory, he was esteemed for his interpretations of Wagner.

Cooper, Imogen, English pianist, daughter of **Martin (Du Pré) Cooper**; b. London, Aug. 28, 1949. Following studies with Kathleen Long, she pursued training at the Paris Cons. with Jacques Février and Yvonne Lefébure, where she won the premier prix in 1967. In 1969 and 1970 she had master classes with Brendel in Vienna. In 1969 she won the Mozart Memorial Prize. After making her first appearance at the London Promenade Concerts in 1973, she appeared as a soloist with various British orchs. and as a recitalist. In 1984 she made her U.S. debut in Los Angeles. Subsequently she appeared with major orchs. at home and abroad, and pursued an active recital career. Cooper has won particular notice for her sensitive interpretations of Mozart, Schubert, and the French masters.

Cooper, Kenneth, versatile American harpsichordist, pianist, conductor, musicologist, and pedagogue; b. N.Y., May 31, 1941. After training at N.Y.'s High School of Music and Art, he studied harpsichord with Sylvia Marlowe at the Mannes College of Music (1960–63) and pursued his education with Lang, Moore, and Luening at Columbia Univ. (B.A., 1962; M.A., 1964; Ph.D., 1971). In 1965 he made his debut as a harpsichordist at London's Wigmore Hall; his U.S. debut followed in 1973 at N.Y.'s Alice Tully Hall. In subsequent years, he toured widely in the U.S. and abroad. He taught at Barnard College (1967–71) and Brooklyn College of the City Univ. of N.Y. (1971–73); then served as prof. of harpsichord at the Mannes College of Music (1975–85), visiting specialist in performance practice at Montclair (N.J.) State College (1977–92), artist-in-residence at Columbia Univ. (from 1983), and director of Graduate Seminars in Baroque practice and conductor of the Baroque Orch. at the Manhattan School of Music (from 1984). His comprehensive repertory embraces works from the early keyboard era to the avant-garde.

Cooper, Martin (Du Pré), English writer on music, father of **Imogen Cooper**; b. Winchester, Jan. 17, 1910; d. Richmond, Surrey, March 15, 1986. He studied at Hertford College, Oxford (B.A., 1931) and with Wellesz in Vienna (1932–34). He then was music critic for the London *Mercury* (1935–38), *Daily Herald* (1946–50), and the *Daily Telegraph* (1950–54; chief music critic, 1954–76); also was ed. of the *Musical Times* (1953–56).

WRITINGS (all publ. in London unless otherwise given): *Gluck* (1935); *Bizet* (1938); *Opéra comique* (1949); *Profils de musiciens anglais* (Paris, 1950); *French Music from the Death of Berlioz to the Death of Fauré* (1951); *Russian Opera* (1951); ed. *The Concise Encyclopedia of Music and Musicians* (1958; 3rd ed., rev., 1975); ed. vol. X, *The Modern Age 1890–1960,* in *The New Oxford History of Music* (1974); D. Cooper, ed., *Judgements of Value: Selected Writings on Music* (Oxford, 1988; includes many of Cooper's writings).

Cooper, Paul, American composer and teacher; b. Victoria, Ill., May 19, 1926. He received instruction from Kanitz, Stevens, and Sessions at the Univ. of Southern Calif. in Los Angeles (B.S., 1950; M.A., 1953; D.M.A., 1956), and from Boulanger in Paris at the Cons. and the Sorbonne (1953–54). He was a teacher (1955–65) and a prof. (1965–68) of music at the Univ. of Mich., where he also was chairman of the music dept. (1966–68); then was prof. of composition at the Univ. of Cincinnati College-Cons. of Music (1969–74) and subsequently at the Shepherd School of Music at Rice Univ. in Houston (from 1974). He held Guggenheim fellowships (1965, 1972). He publ. *Perspectives in Music Theory* (1973; 2nd ed., 1981). In his works, Cooper follows an eclectic course in which he utilizes various styles in an original manner.

WORKS: DRAMATIC: *Mysterion* for Soprano, Narrator, Chamber Orch., and Optional Dancers (1988). **ORCH.:** 6 syms.: No. 1, *Concertant,* for Solo Woodwind, Brass, String Quartet, Percussion, and Strings (1966), No. 2, *Antiphons,* for Oboe and Symphonic Winds (1971), No. 3, *Lamentations,* for Strings (1971), No. 4, *Landscape,* for Flute, Trumpet, Viola, and Orch. (1973–75), No. 5, *Symphony in 2 Movements* (1982–83; Houston, Sept. 10, 1983), and No. 6, *In Memoriam* (1987); 2 violin concertos (1967; 1980–82); *Liturgies* for Symphonic Woodwinds, Brass, and Percussion (1968); *A Shenandoah: For Ives' Birthday* for Flute, Trumpet, Viola, and Orch. (1974); *Descants* for Viola and Orch. (1975); *Homage* for Flute, Trumpet, Viola, and Orch. (1976); Cello Concerto (1976–78); *Variants* (1978); Flute Concerto (1980–81); Organ Concerto (1982); Saxophone Concerto (1982); Duo Concertante for Violin, Viola, and Orch. (1985); *Jubilate* for Symphonic Woodwinds, Brass, and Percussion (1985–86); Double Concerto for Violin, Viola, and Orch. (1985–87). **CHAMBER:** 6 string quartets (1952, rev. 1978; 1954, rev. 1979; 1959; 1963–64; 1973; 1977); Viola Sonata (1961); Violin Sonata (1962); Sonata for [3] Flutes [1 Player] and Piano (1962–63); 2 cello sonatas (1962–63; 1965); Double Bass Sonata (1964); *Concert for 4* for Flute, Oboe, Harpsichord, and Double Bass (1965); *Concert for 5* for Wind Quintet (1965); *Epitaphs* for Alto Flute, Harp, and Double Bass (1969); *Soliloquies* for Violin and Piano (1970); *Variants II* for Viola and Piano (1972); *Chimera* for Violin, Viola, Cello, and Piano (1973); *Concert for 3* for Clarinet, Cello, and Piano (1977); *Canons d'Amour* for Violin and Viola (1981); *Canti* for Viola and Piano (1981); *Chamber Music I* for 6 Instruments (1982; rev. as *Chamber Music II,* 1983); *4 Impromptus* for Alto Saxophone and Piano (1983); *Variants IV* for Alto Saxophone and Piano (1986); *Tre voci,* trio for Violin, Cello, and Piano (1986); also piano pieces and organ music. **VOCAL:** *Credo* for Double Chorus and Orch. (1970); *Cantigas* for Soprano, Double Chorus, and Orch. (1972); *Refrains* for Soprano, Baritone, Double Chorus, and Orch. (1976); *Celebration* for Chamber Chorus, Organ, Speaker, and Congregational Singing (1983); *Voyagers* for Chorus and Orch. (1983); *Omnia tempus habent* for Chorus and Organ (1987); song cycles.

Coover, James B(urrell), American music librarian and pedagogue; b. Jacksonville, Ill., June 3, 1925. He was educated at the Univ. of Northern Colorado (B.A., 1949; M.A., 1950) and the Univ. of Denver (M.A., 1953). He was associated with the Bibliographical Center for Research in Denver (1951–53), serving as its assistant director (1952–53); he then was director of the George Sherman Dickinson Music Library at Vassar College (1953–67). Subsequently he was prof. of music and director of the music library at the State Univ. of N.Y. at Buffalo from 1967. He also served as president (1959–60) and executive board member (1987–90) of the Music Library Assn.

WRITINGS: *Music Lexicography* (Denver, 1952; 3rd ed., rev. and enl., 1971); with R. Colvig, *Medieval and Renaissance Music on Long-Playing Records* (Detroit, 1964; 2nd ed., 1973); *Provisional Checklist of Priced Antiquarian Catalogues Containing Musical Materials* (Buffalo, 1981); *Musical Instrument Collections* (Detroit, 1981; rev. ed., 1987, as *Antiquarians' Catalogues of Musical Interest*); *Music Publishing, Copyright and Piracy in Victorian England, 1881–1906* (London, 1985); ed., with C. Bradley, *Richard S. Hill: Tributes from Friends* (1987); *Music at Auction: Puttick & Simpson (of London), 1794–1971* (1988).

Cope, David (Howell), eclectic American writer, composer, and teacher; b. San Francisco, May 17, 1941. He was educated at Arizona State Univ. and the Univ. of Southern Calif. in Los Angeles; then served on the faculties of Miami Univ. of Ohio and at the Univ. of Calif. at Santa Cruz. He is well known for his didactic books on contemporary composition, which include *New Directions in Music* (Dubuque, 1971; 6th ed., rev., 1993), *New Music Composition* (N.Y., 1977), and *Computer Analysis of Musical Style* (N.Y., 1990). Among his compositions are *Threshold and Visions* for Orch. (1977), *Experiments in Musical Intelligence* (1988), and *Cradle Falling*, opera for Soprano and Orch. (1989).

Copland, Aaron, greatly distinguished and exceptionally gifted American composer; b. N.Y., Nov. 14, 1900; d. North Tarrytown, N.Y., Dec. 2, 1990. He was educated at the Boys' High School in Brooklyn, and began piano study with Leopold Wolfsohn, Victor Wittgenstein, and Clarence Adler as a young child. In 1917 he commenced lessons in harmony and counterpoint with Rubin Goldmark in N.Y., and soon began to compose. His first publ. piece, *The Cat and the Mouse* for Piano (1920), subtitled *Scherzo humoristique*, shows the influence of Debussy. In 1920 he entered the American Cons. in Fontainebleau, where he studied composition and orchestration with Boulanger. Returning to America in 1924, he lived mostly in N.Y.; became active in many musical activities, not only as a composer but also as a lecturer, pianist, and organizer in various musical societies. He attracted the attention of Serge Koussevitzky, who gave the first performance of his early score *Music for the Theater* with the Boston Sym. Orch. in 1925; Koussevitzky then engaged Copland as soloist in his Piano Concerto in 1927; the work produced a considerable sensation because of its jazz elements, and there was some subterranean grumbling among the staid subscribers to the Boston Sym. concerts. Koussevitzky remained Copland's steadfast supporter throughout his tenure as conductor of the Boston Sym., and later as the founder of the Koussevitzky Music Foundation. In the meantime, Walter Damrosch conducted in N.Y. Copland's Sym. for Organ and Orch., with Boulanger as soloist. Other orchs. and their conductors also performed his music, which gained increasing recognition. Particularly popular were Copland's works based on folk motifs; of these the most remarkable are *El Salón México* (1933–36) and the American ballets *Billy the Kid* (1938), *Rodeo* (1942), and *Appalachian Spring* (1944). A place apart is occupied by Copland's *Lincoln Portrait* for Narrator and Orch. (1942), with texts arranged by the composer from speeches and letters of Abraham Lincoln; this work has had a great many performances, with the role of the narrator performed by such notables as Adlai Stevenson and Eleanor Roosevelt. His patriotic *Fanfare for the Common Man* (1942) achieved tremendous popularity and continued to be played on various occasions for decades; Copland incorporated it in toto into the score of his 3rd Sym. He was for many years a member of the board of directors of the League of Composers in N.Y.; with Sessions, he organized the Copland-Sessions Concerts (1928–31), and was also a founder of the Yaddo Festivals (1932) and of the American Composers' Alliance (1937); was also a participant in such organizations as the Koussevitzky Music Foundation, the Composers Forum, the Cos Cob Press, etc. He was head of the composition dept. at the Berkshire Music Center at Tanglewood from 1940 to 1965, and from 1957 to 1965 was chairman of the faculty. He lectured extensively and gave courses at The New School for Social Research in N.Y. and at Harvard Univ. (1935 and 1944); was the Charles Eliot Norton Lecturer at Harvard in 1951–52. He was the recipient of many awards: Guggenheim fellowship (1925–27); RCA Victor award of $5,000 for his *Dance Symphony*; Pulitzer Prize in Music and N.Y. Music Critics' Circle Award for *Appalachian Spring* (1945); N.Y. Music Critics' Circle Award for the 3rd Sym. (1947); Oscar award for the film score *The Heiress* from the Academy of Motion Picture Arts and Sciences (1950); Gold Medal for Music from the American Academy of Arts and Letters (1956); Presidential Medal of Freedom (1964); Howland Memorial Prize of Yale Univ. (1970); he was also decorated with a Commander's Cross of the Order of Merit in West Germany; was elected to honorary membership of the Accademia di Santa Cecilia in Rome. He held numerous honorary doctor's degrees: Princeton Univ. (1956); Brandeis Univ. (1957); Wesleyan Univ. (1958); Temple Univ. (1959); Harvard Univ. (1961); Rutgers Univ. (1967); Ohio State Univ. (1970); N.Y. Univ. (1970); Columbia Univ. (1971). About 1955 Copland developed a successful career as a conductor, and led major sym. orchs. in Europe, the U.S., South America, and Mexico; he also traveled to Russia under the auspices of the State Dept. In 1982 the Aaron Copland School of Music was created at Queens College of the City Univ. of N.Y. In 1983 he made his last appearance as a conductor in N.Y. His 85th birthday was widely celebrated; Copland attended a special concert given in his honor by Zubin Mehta and the N.Y. Phil., which was televised live by PBS. He was awarded the National Medal of Arts (1986). As a composer, Copland made use of a broad variety of idioms and techniques, tempering dissonant textures by a strong sense of tonality. He enlivened his musical textures by ingenious applications of syncopation and polyrhythmic combinations; but in such works as Piano Variations, he adopted an austere method of musical constructivism. He used a modified 12-tone technique in his Piano Quartet (1950) and an integral dodecaphonic idiom in the score of *Connotations* (1962).

WORKS: DRAMATIC: *Grohg*, ballet (1922–25; not perf.; material incorporated into *Dance Symphony*); *Hear Ye! Hear Ye!*, ballet (Chicago, Nov. 30, 1934); *The 2nd Hurricane*, play-opera for high school (1936; N.Y., April 21, 1937); *Billy the Kid*, ballet (Chicago, Oct. 16, 1938); *From Sorcery to Science*, music for a puppet show (N.Y., May 12, 1939); *Rodeo*, ballet (N.Y., Oct. 16, 1942); *Appalachian Spring*, ballet (Washington, D.C., Oct. 30, 1944); *The Tender Land*, opera (N.Y., April 1, 1954); *Dance Panels*, ballet (1959; rev. 1962; Munich, Dec. 3, 1963; arranged for Piano, 1965). **FILM MUSIC:** *The City* (1939); *Of Mice and Men* (1939); *Our Town* (1940); *North Star* (1943); *The Cummington Story* (1945); *The Red Pony* (1948); *The Heiress* (1948); *Something Wild* (1961). **INCIDENTAL MUSIC TO PLAYS:** *Miracle at Verdun* (1931); *The 5 Kings* (1939); *Quiet City* (1939).

ORCH.: *Music for the Theater* (Boston, Nov. 20, 1925); Sym. for Organ and Orch. (N.Y., Jan. 11, 1925; rev. version without organ, designated as Sym. No. 1, 1928; Berlin, Dec. 9, 1931; also as *Prelude* for Chamber Orch., 1934); Piano Concerto (1926; Boston, Jan. 28, 1927); *Symphonic Ode* (1927–29; composed for the 50th anniversary of the Boston Sym. Orch.; Boston, Feb. 19, 1932; rev. 1955 for the 75th anniversary of the Boston Sym. Orch. and rededicated to the memory of Koussevitzky; Boston, Feb. 3, 1956); *A Dance Symphony* (1930; based on the ballet *Grohg*; Philadelphia, April 15, 1931); *Short Symphony* (Sym. No. 2) (1932–33; Mexico City, Nov. 23, 1934); *Statements* (1932–35; 1st complete perf., N.Y., Jan. 7, 1942); *El Salón México* (1933–36; Mexico City, Aug. 27, 1937); *Music for Radio (Prairie Journal)*, subtitled *Saga of the Prairie* (CBS, N.Y., July 25, 1937); *An Outdoor Overture* (N.Y., Dec. 16, 1938; arr. for Band, 1941); *Quiet City*, suite from the film for English Horn, Trumpet, and Strings (1939; N.Y., Jan. 28, 1941); *John Henry* for Chamber Orch. (CBS, N.Y., March 5, 1940; rev. 1952); *Our Town*, suite from the film (CBS, N.Y., June 9, 1940); *Billy the Kid*, suite from the ballet (NBC, N.Y., Nov. 9, 1940); *Lincoln Portrait* for Speaker and Orch. (Cincinnati, May 14, 1942); *Rodeo*, 4 dance episodes from the ballet (1942; Boston, May 28,

1943); *Music for Movies* for Chamber Orch. (from the films *The City, Of Mice and Men,* and *Our Town*; 1942; N.Y., Feb. 17, 1943); *Fanfare for the Common Man* for Brass and Percussion (1942; Cincinnati, March 12, 1943); *Letter from Home* (N.Y. broadcast, Oct. 17, 1944; rev. 1962); *Variations on a Theme by Eugene Goossens* (with 9 other composers; 1944; Cincinnati, March 23, 1945); *Appalachian Spring,* suite from the ballet (N.Y., Oct. 4, 1945); *Danzón Cubano* (orig. for 2 Pianos, 1942; orch. version, 1944; Baltimore, Feb. 17, 1946); Sym. No. 3 (1944–46; Boston, Oct. 18, 1946); Concerto for Clarinet, Strings, Harp, and Piano (1947–48; N.Y., Nov. 6, 1950); *The Red Pony,* suite from the film (Houston, Nov. 1, 1948); *Preamble for a Solemn Occasion* for Speaker and Orch. (N.Y., Dec. 10, 1949; arr. for Organ, 1953; arr. for Band, 1973); *Orchestral Variations* (orch. version of the *Piano Variations*; 1930; 1957; Louisville, March 5, 1958); *Connotations* (commissioned for the opening of Phil. Hall, Lincoln Center, N.Y., Sept. 23, 1962); *Music for a Great City* (symphonic suite descriptive of life in N.Y. City; London, May 26, 1964); *Emblems* for Band (1964); *Down a Country Lane* for School Orch. (London, Nov. 20, 1964); *Inscape* (commissioned by the N.Y. Phil. and 1st perf. by that orch. at the Univ. of Mich., Ann Arbor, Sept. 13, 1967); *Inaugural Fanfare* (Grand Rapids, Mich., June 1969; rev. 1975); *3 Latin American Sketches: Estribillo, Paisaje mexicano, Danza de Jalisco* (N.Y., June 7, 1972); *Proclamation* (1982; orchestrated by P. Ramey, 1985; N.Y., Nov. 14, 1985).

CHAMBER: *Capriccio* for Violin and Piano; *Poem* for Cello and Piano; *Lament* for Cello and Piano; *Preludes* for Violin and Piano; String Quartet (unfinished); Piano Trio (unfinished); *Rondino* for String Quartet (1923; N.Y., Oct. 18, 1984); *Nocturne* for Violin and Piano (1926); *Ukelele Serenade* for Violin and Piano (1926); *Lento molto* for String Quartet (1928); *Vitebsk, Study on a Jewish Theme* for Piano Trio (1928; N.Y., Feb. 16, 1929); *Elegies* for Violin and Viola (1932); Sextet for Clarinet, Piano, and String Quartet (arranged from *Short Symphony*; 1932–33; 1937; N.Y., Feb. 26, 1939); Violin Sonata (1942–43); Quartet for Piano and Strings (Washington, D.C., Oct. 29, 1950); *Nonet* for 3 Violins, 3 Violas, and 3 Cellos (1960; Washington, D.C., March 2, 1961); *Duo* for Flute and Piano (1971); *Threnody I: Igor Stravinsky, In Memoriam* for Flute and String Trio (1971) and *II: Beatrice Cunningham, In Memoriam* for G-Flute and String Trio (1973); *Vocalise* for Flute and Piano (arrangement of *Vocalise*; 1928; 1972).

PIANO: *Moment musical* (1917); *Danse caracteristique* for Piano Duet or Orch. (1918); *Waltz Caprice* (1918); *Sonnets, 1–3* (1918–20); *Moods (3 esquisses): Amertume, pensif, jazzy* and *Petit portrait,* a supplement (1920–21); Piano Sonata in G major (1920–21); *Scherzo humoristique: Le Chat et la souris* (1920); Passacaglia (1921–22); *Sentimental Melody* (1926); *4 Piano Blues* (1926–48); *Piano Variations* (1930; orch. version, 1957); *Sunday Afternoon Music (The Young Pioneers)* (1935); Piano Sonata (1939–41; Buenos Aires, Oct. 21, 1941, composer pianist); Piano Fantasy (1952–57); *Down a Country Lane* (1962); Rodeo (arrangement from the ballet; 1962); *Danza de Jalisco* for 2 Pianos (1963; orch. version, 1972); *Dance Panels* (arrangement from the ballet; 1965); *In Evening Air* (excerpt arranged from the film score *The Cummington Story*; 1969); *Night Thoughts (Homage to Ives)* (1972); *Midsummer Nocturne* (1977); *Midday Thoughts* (1982); *Proclamation* (1982).

VOCAL: CHORAL: 4 Motets (1921); *The House on the Hill* for Women's Voices (1925); *An Immorality* for Soprano, Women's Voices, and Piano (1925); *What Do We Plant?* for Women's Voices and Piano (1935); *Lark* for Bass and Chorus (1938); *Las agachadas* for Chorus (1942); *Song of the Guerrillas* for Baritone, Men's Voices, and Piano (1943); *The Younger Generation* for Chorus and Piano (1943); *In the Beginning* for Mezzo-soprano and Chorus (commissioned for the Harvard Symposium; Cambridge, Mass., May 2, 1947); *Canticle of Freedom* (1955; rev. 1965). **SONGS:** *Melancholy* (1917); *Spurned Love* (1917); *After Antwerp* (1917); *Night* (1918); *A Summer Vacation* (1918); *My Heart Is in the East* (1918); *Simone* (1919); *Music I Heard* (1920); *Old Poem* (1920); *Pastorale* (1921); *As It Fell upon a Day* (1923); *Poet's Song* (1927); *Vocalise* (1928); *12 Poems of Emily Dickinson* (1949–50); *Old American Songs* for Voice and Orch. (arrangements in 2 sets, 1950 and 1952); *Dirge in Woods* (1954).

WRITINGS: *What to Listen for in Music* (N.Y., 1939; 2nd ed., 1957; tr. into German, Italian, Spanish, Dutch, Arabic, and Chinese); *Our New Music* (N.Y., 1941; 2nd ed., rev. and enl. as *The New Music, 1900–1960,* N.Y., 1968); *Music and Imagination,* a collection of lectures delivered at Harvard Univ., 1951–52 (Cambridge, Mass., 1952); *Copland on Music* (N.Y., 1960); an autobiography, *Copland* (with V. Perlis; 2 vols., N.Y., 1984, 1989).

BIBL.: P. Rosenfeld, *An Hour with American Music* (Philadelphia, 1929); T. Chanler, "A. C.," in H. Cowell, ed., *American Composers on American Music* (Stanford, 1933); A. Berger, *A. C.* (N.Y., 1953); J. Smith, *A. C.: His Work and Contribution to American Music* (N.Y., 1955); R. Goldman, "A. C.," *Musical Quarterly* (Jan. 1961); E. Cone, "Conversation with A. C.," *Perspectives of New Music* (Spring/Summer 1968); C. Peare, *A. C. His Life* (N.Y., 1969); D. Hamilton, "A. C.: A Discography of the Composer's Performances," *Perspectives of New Music* (Fall/Winter 1970); special issue of *Tempo,* devoted to C. on the occasion of his 70th birthday (Winter 1970/71); B. Northcott, "Notes on C.," *Musical Times* (Nov. 1980); Q. Hilliard, *A Theoretical Analysis of the Symphonies of A. C.* (diss., Univ. of Florida, 1984); N. Butterworth, *The Music of A. C.* (N.Y., 1985); P. Ramey, "A. C.: Genial Patriarch of American Music," *Ovation* (Nov. 1985); J. Skowronski, *A. C.: A Bio-Bibliography* (Westport, Conn., 1985); R. Parker, "C. and Chavez: Brothers-in-Arms," *American Music* (Winter 1987).

Copley, John (Michael), English opera director; b. Birmingham, June 12, 1933. He studied with Joan Cross at the National School of Opera in London. He was active in London as a stage manager at the Sadler's Wells Opera, where he first turned to directing with his staging of *Il Tabarro* in 1957; he then worked at Covent Garden, where he garnered success with his production of *Così fan Tutte* in 1968; from 1971 to 1988 he was resident opera director there, and also was active at the English National Opera. As a guest opera director, he staged works at the San Francisco Opera, the Australian Opera in Sydney, the Santa Fe Opera, and the Metropolitan Opera in N.Y. His respect for the score at hand and the singers engaged, combined with imaginative direction, have made Copley's productions notably successful.

Coppens, Claude A(lbert), Belgian pianist, teacher, and composer; b. Schaerbeek, Dec. 23, 1936. He studied at the Brussels Cons. (1944–52), and with Jacques Fevrier and Marguerite Long in Paris, completing his education at the Univ. of Brussels (doctorate in law, 1960). He was active as a teacher at the conservatories in Brussels, Antwerp, and Ghent.

WORKS: *Symetries A* for 9 Instruments (1960–61); Piano Sonata (1964); *Due sinfonie per tre gruppi* (1965–66); *Concerting Variations* for Violin and 9 Instruments (1970); *Gedichtje van St. Niklaas,* cantata for Boy's Chorus and Small Orch. (1970–71); *The Horn of Plenty,* musical play (1978); Saxophone Quartet (1979–80); Sonata for Flute and Cello (1981–82); *Skiai* for Trombone and Percussion (1982); *XIII Pages for XIII Clarinets: Portrait of the Artist as a Young-Old Man* for Clarinet Orch. (1982–83); *. . . un coup de des jamais n'abolira le hasard . . .* for Marimba and Clarinet Orch. (1984; also for Harpsichord and String Orch.); *Logoganic Patterns* for Double Percussion (1984).

Coppola, Piero, admired Italian conductor; b. Milan, Oct. 11, 1888; d. Lausanne, March 13, 1971. He studied at the Milan Cons. (graduated, 1909). After conducting in various Italian operatic centers, he conducted in London in 1914. During World War I, he pursued his career in Scandinavia. In 1921 he went to Paris, where he won distinction as music director of the recording firm La Voix de son Maître (1923–34), with whom he made a number of pioneering recordings. In 1930 he was awarded the Chevalier of the French Légion d'honneur for his services to French music. He conducted throughout Europe until World War II; after the war, he conducted in Switzerland and Italy. He also composed, producing 2 operas, *Sirmione* and *Nikita* (1914), a Sym. (Paris, Nov. 13, 1924, composer conducting), and the symphonic sketch *La Ronde sous la cloche* (1924).

BIBL.: W. Holmes, "Episodes in the Life and Times of an Artist: The Story of P. C.," *Le Grand Baton* (Sept.–Dec. 1973).

Corboz, Michel (-Jules), Swiss conductor; b. Marsens, Feb. 14, 1934. He was educated at the École Normale in Fribourg; then became a director of church music in Lausanne (1953), where he organized the Ensemble Vocal et Instrumental de Lausanne (1968), with which he has given numerous performances of Baroque vocal and orch. music.

Corder, Frederick, English composer, teacher, and writer on music; b. London, Jan. 26, 1852; d. there, Aug. 21, 1932. He studied at the Royal Academy of Music in London (1873–75); after winning the Mendelssohn Scholarship in 1875, he pursued training with Hiller in Cologne (1878–79). He conducted the Brighton Aquarium concerts (1880–82); then was prof. of composition (from 1888) and curator (from 1889) of the Royal Academy of Music. Among his outstanding students were Bantock, Bax, and Holbrooke. With his wife, Henrietta Luisa (née Walford) Corder, he made the 1st Eng. trs. of Wagner's *Parsifal* (1879), *Die Meistersinger von Nürnberg* (1882), *Der Ring des Nibelungen* (1882), *Tristan und Isolde* (1882), and *Lohengrin* (1894). His own compositions followed along late Romantic lines. His son, Paul Corder (b. London, Dec. 14, 1879; d. there, Aug. 6, 1942), was a composer and teacher. He studied with his father at the Royal Academy of Music, and taught there from 1907. Among his works were stage pieces, orch. music, piano pieces, and songs.

WORKS: DRAMATIC: *La morte d'Arthur*, opera (1877–78); *A Storm in a Teacup*, operetta (1880; Brighton, Feb. 18, 1882); *Nordisa*, opera (1886; Liverpool, Jan. 26, 1887); *Ossian*, opera (1905); incidental music. **ORCH.:** *Evening on the Sea Shore* (1876); *Im Schwarzwald*, suite (1876); *Ossian*, overture (1882); *Nocturne* (1882); *Prospero*, overture (1885); *Roumanian Suite* (1887); *Pippa Passes* (1897); *Elegy* for 24 Violins and Organ (1908); *A Fairy Tale* (1913). **CHAMBER:** *Rümanische Weisen* for Violin and Piano (1883). **VOCAL:** *Des Sängers Fluch*, declamation for Voice and Piano (1883); (4) *River Songs* for 3 Women's Voices (1884); *The Bridal of Triermain* for Soli, Chorus, and Orch. (1886); *Margaret: The Blind Girl of Castel-Cuillé* for Soprano, Alto, Women's Voices, and Piano (1888); *The Grand Panjandrum* for Chorus (1898); other choral pieces and songs; folk song arrangements.

WRITINGS (all publ. in London): *Exercises in Harmony and Counterpoint* (1891); *A Plain and Easy Guide to Music: or The New "Morely"* (1893; 3rd ed., 1920); *The Orchestra and How to Write for it* (1896); *Recitation with Music* (1897); *Modern Musical Composition* (1909); *Beethoven and his Music* (1912); *Wagner and his Music* (1912); *A History of the Royal Academy of Music from 1822 to 1922* (1922); *Beethoven* (1922); *Wagner* (1922; 2nd ed., 1948); *Ferencz Liszt* (1925).

Cordero, Roque, Panamanian composer, teacher, and conductor; b. Panama, Aug. 16, 1917. After training in Panama, he won a scholarship in 1943 to the Univ. of Minnesota, where he had lessons in conducting from Mitropoulos; he also studied counterpoint and composition with Krenek at Hamline Univ. in St. Paul, and pursued training in conducting with Chappel at the Berkshire Music Center in Tanglewood and with Barzin in N.Y. Returning to Panama, he was prof. of composition at the National Inst. of Music (1950–66), where he served as its director (1953–64); he also was conductor of the National orch. (1964–66). He taught at Indiana Univ. in Bloomington (1966–69) and at Illinois State Univ. in Normal (1972–87). As a conductor, he toured internationally. Cordero received various awards and commission as a composer, and in 1949 he received a Guggenheim fellowship. After composing in a basically tonal idiom, he developed a modified 12-tone technique in 1946.

WORKS: DRAMATIC: 2 ballets. **ORCH.:** *8 Miniatures* (1944; rev. 1948); *Obertura panamena No. 2* (1944); Piano Concerto (1944); 4 syms. (1945, 1946, 1965, 1986); *Movimento sinfonico* for Strings (1946); *Rapsodia campesina* (1949); *5 mensajes breves* (1959); Violin Concerto (1962); *Circunvoluciones y moviles* for 57 Instruments (1967); Concertino for Viola and Strings (1968); *Elegy* for Strings (1973); *Momentum jubilo* (1973); *6 Mobiles* (1974–75); *Overture of Salutation* (1980); *Poetic Nocturne of the Min River* (1981). **CHAMBER:** Violin Sonatine (1946); Quintet for Flute, Clarinet, Violin, Viola, and Piano (1949); 4 string quartets (1960, 1968, 1973, 1983); Cello Sonata (1962); *3 Short Messages* for Viola and Piano (1966); *Permutaciones 7* for Clarinet, Trumpet, Timpani, Piano, Violin, Viola, and Double Bass (1967); *Paz, Paix, Peace* for 4 Trios and Harp (1969); *Variations and Theme for 5* for Wind Quartet and Horn (1975); *Soliloquios No. 1* for Flute (1975), *No. 2* for Saxophone (1976), *No. 3* for Clarinet (1976), *No. 4* for Percussion (1981), and *No. 5* for Double Bass (1981); *Double Concerto without Orchestra* for Violin and Piano (1978); *Music for 5 Brass* (1980); *Petite Mobiles* for Bassoon and Trios (1983); *Serenatas* for Flute, Clarinet, Viola, and Harp (1987). **PIANO:** *Sonatina ritmica* (1943); *Rhapsody* for 2 Pianos (1945); *Sonata breve I* (1946) and *II* (1966); *3 Piececillas para Alina* (1978); Sonata (1985). **VOCAL:** *Cantata for Peace* (1975–79); choral pieces.

BIBL.: R. Sider, "R. C.: The Composer and his Style," *Inter-American Music Bulletin*, no. 61 (1971).

Cordon, Norman, American baritone; b. Washington, N.C., Jan. 20, 1904; d. Chapel Hill, N.C., March 1, 1964. He attended the Fishburne Military School; later studied at the Univ. of North Carolina and at the Nashville Cons. of Music; was a voice student of Gaetano de Lucas and Hadley Outland. He sang with the San Carlo Opera Co.; in 1933 he made his debut as Scarpia at the Civic Opera in Chicago, of which he was a member until 1936; on May 13, 1936, he made his Metropolitan Opera debut in N.Y. as Monterone, remaining on its roster until 1946; he also appeared with the San Francisco Opera, the Cincinnati Summer Opera, and on Broadway.

Corelli, Franco, outstanding Italian tenor; b. Ancona, April 8, 1921. He studied naval engineering at the Univ. of Bologna; in 1947 he entered the Pesaro Cons. to study voice; dissatisfied with the academic training, he left the Cons. and proceeded to learn the repertoire by listening to recordings of great singers. He made his operatic debut at the Spoleto Festival in 1952 as Don José; then sang at the Rome Opera in 1953 and at Milan's La Scala in 1954; he appeared at London's Covent Garden in 1957. On Jan. 27, 1961, he made his Metropolitan Opera debut in N.Y. as Manrico in *Il Trovatore*; while continuing on its roster until 1975, he also appeared with major opera houses worldwide. Among his finest roles were Radames, Ernani, Don Alvaro, Raoul, and Calaf.

BIBL.: M. Boagno, *F. C.: Un uomo, una voce* (Parma, 1990).

Corena, Fernando, Swiss bass; b. Geneva, Dec. 22, 1916; d. Lugano, Nov. 26, 1984. He studied in Geneva and with Enrico Romani in Milan; after making his operatic debut in 1937, he sang with the radio and municipal theater in Zürich. He first gained wide notice as Varlaam in Trieste in 1947, and subsequently was invited to sing with major opera houses in Europe and the U.S.; he made his Metropolitan Opera debut in N.Y. as Leporello (Feb. 6, 1954), and remained on its roster until 1979. He first appeared at London's Covent Garden on May 16, 1960, as Dr. Bartolo in *Il Barbiere di Siviglia*. He was particularly known for his buffo roles. Among his other roles were Don Pasquale, Dulcamare, Alfonso, Osmin, and Gianni Schicchi.

Corigliano, John, American violinist, father of **John (Paul) Corigliano**; b. N.Y., Aug. 28, 1901; d. Norfolk, Conn., Sept. 1, 1975. He was a student of Giacomo Quintano, Alois Trnka, and Auer. After making his N.Y. debut in 1919, he toured as a soloist. He was concertmaster of the CBS Sym. Orch. (1934–35), and then assistant concertmaster (1935–43) and concertmaster (1943–66) of the N.Y. Phil.; thereafter he was concertmaster of the San Antonio Sym. Orch.

Corigliano, John (Paul), notable American composer and teacher, son of **John Corigliano**; b. N.Y., Feb. 16, 1938. While still a child, he began to play the piano and to try his hand at composing. During his high school years, he studied orchestration on his own by listening to recordings with scores in hand. He then was a student of Luening at Columbia Univ. (B.A., 1959) and of Giannini at the Manhattan School of Music. He worked as a music programmer in N.Y. for WQXR-FM and WBAI-FM (1959–64), as an assoc. producer of music programs for CBS-TV (1961–72), and as music director of the Morris Theater in N.J. (1962–64). After teaching at the College of Church Musicians in Washington, D.C. (1968–71), he was on the faculties of the Manhattan School of Music (from 1971) and of Lehman College of the City Univ. of N.Y. (from 1973), where he later held the title of Distinguished Prof. (from 1986). He also taught at the Juilliard School in N.Y. (from 1991). Corigliano established his considerable reputation as a composer with his Clarinet Concerto (N.Y., Dec. 6, 1977). From 1987 to 1990 he served as the first composer-in-residence of the Chicago Sym. Orch. His deeply-felt Sym. No. 1, dedicated to the victims of AIDS, was premiered by that orch. under Barenboim's direction on March 15, 1990. The highly successful premiere and subsequent recording of the score brought Corigliano international acclaim. His opera, *The Ghosts of Versailles*, added further lustre to his reputation at its critically-acclaimed premiere by the Metropolitan Opera in N.Y. under Levine's direction on Dec. 19, 1991. Corigliano has won many honors and awards and received major commissions. In 1968–69 he held a Guggenheim fellowship. In 1989 the American Academy and Inst. of Arts and Letters gave him its award for music, and in 1991 he was elected to its membership. He also won the Grawemeyer Award in 1991 from the Univ. of Louisville for his Sym. No. 1. In his diverse output, Corigliano has produced a body of music notable for its remarkable originality and craftsmanship. Despite the apparent dissonant freedom of his polyphonic writing, his music retains a firm tonal anchorage.

WORKS: DRAMATIC: *The Naked Carmen*, electric rock opera (1970; transcription of Bizet's *Carmen*); *The Ghosts of Versailles*, grand opera buffa (N.Y., Dec. 19, 1991); incidental music for plays; film scores. **ORCH.:** *Elegy* (1965; San Francisco, June 1, 1966); *Tournaments* (1965; Louisville, Jan. 11, 1980); Piano Concerto (San Antonio, April 7, 1968); *Gazebo Dances* for Concert Band (Evansville, Ind., May 6, 1973; also for Orch., 1974; Woodbury, N.J., Feb. 20, 1981; also for Piano, 4-hands, 1972); *Aria* for Oboe and Strings (1975; 4th movement of the Oboe Concerto, 1975; also for Oboe and String Quintet, 1985); Oboe Concerto (N.Y., Nov. 9, 1975); *Voyage* for Strings (1976; Rockland County, N.Y., April 22, 1977; also for Flute and Strings, London, Nov. 26, 1983; also for Flute and String Quintet, 1988); Clarinet Concerto (N.Y., Dec. 6, 1977); *Pied Piper Fantasy*, flute concerto (1981; Los Angeles, Feb. 4, 1982); *Promenade Overture* (Boston, July 10, 1981); *3 Hallucinations* (1981; Syracuse, N.Y., Jan. 22, 1982; based on the film score for *Altered States*); *Summer Fanfare: Echoes of Forgotten Rites* (Miami, June 21, 1982); *Fantasia on an Ostinato* (N.Y., Sept. 18, 1986; also for Piano, 1985); *Campagne di Ravello: A Celebration Piece for Sir Georg Solti* (Chicago, Oct. 9, 1987); Sym. No. 1 (1988–89; Chicago, March 15, 1990); *Troubadours: Variations* for Guitar and Chamber Orch. (St. Paul, Minn., Oct. 8, 1993); *Fanfares to Music* (1994; also for 11 Instruments, 1993). **CHAMBER:** Violin Sonata (1963; Spoleto, July 10, 1964); *Scherzo* for Oboe and Percussion (1975); *Aria* for Oboe and String Quintet (1985; also for Oboe and String Orch., 1975); *Phantasmagoria* for Cello and Piano (Washington, D.C., May 1993); *Fanfare to Music* for 11 Instruments (N.Y., Oct. 20, 1993; also for Orch., 1994); *Amen* for Double Brass Ensemble (1994; also for Chorus). **PIANO:** *Kaleidoscope* for 2 Pianos (1959; Spoleto, June 28, 1961); *Gazebo Dances* for Piano, 4-hands (1972; N.Y., Feb. 24, 1985; also for Concert Band, 1973, and for Orch., 1974); *Étude Fantasy* (Washington, D.C., Oct. 9, 1976); *Fantasia on an Ostinato* (Fort Worth, May 24, 1985; also for Orch., 1986). **VOCAL:** *Petit Fours* for Voice and Piano (1959); *Fern Hill* for Mezzo-soprano, Chorus, and Orch. (1960–61; Washington, D.C., Dec. 11, 1965; also for String Orch., N.Y., Dec. 19, 1961); *Poem in October* for Tenor and 8 Instruments (N.Y., Oct. 25, 1970; also for Tenor and Orch., Washington, D.C., April 24, 1976); *Poem on His Birthday* for Baritone, Chorus, and Orch. (Washington, D.C., April 14, 1976; also for Baritone, Chorus, and Piano); the preceding 3 works constitute *A Dylan Thomas Trilogy*, choral sym. for Soloists, Chorus, and Orch. (1st complete perf., Washington, D.C., April 24, 1976); *What I Expected Was . . .* for Chorus, Brass, and Percussion (Tanglewood, Aug. 16, 1962); *The Cloisters* for Voice and Piano (N.Y., Nov. 15, 1965; also for Voice and Orch., Washington, D.C., May 2, 1976); *Christmas at the Cloisters* for Chorus and Organ or Piano (1966; NBC-TV, Dec. 25, 1967); *L'Invitation au Voyage* for Chorus (1971; San Antonio, May 13, 1972); *Wedding Song* for Medium Voice, Melody Instrument, and Organ (1971); *Creations* for Narrator and Orch. (1972; rev. version, Milwaukee, Oct. 3, 1984); *A Black November Turkey* for Chorus (1972; San Antonio, Jan. 20, 1973); *Psalm No. 8* for Chorus and Organ (San Antonio, Oct. 18, 1976); *3 Irish Folksong Settings* for Voice and Flute (N.Y., June 18, 1988); *Of Rage and Remembrance* for Mezzo-soprano, Men's Chorus with 12 Chimes, Timpani, 8 Cellos, and 4 Double Basses (Seattle, March 29, 1991); *Amen* for Chorus (Montreat, N.C., June 19, 1994; also for Double Brass Ensemble).

BIBL.: M. Humphrey, *J. C.* (N.Y., 1989; rev. ed., 1994).

Corner, Philip (Lionel), American composer, performer, and teacher; b. N.Y., April 10, 1933. He studied with Mark Brunswick at the City College of N.Y. (B.A., 1955), then pursued training in philosophy with Messiaen at the Paris Cons. (2nd prix, 1957), composition with Otto Luening and Henry Cowell at Columbia Univ. (M.A., 1959), and piano with Dorothy Taubman (1961–75). While serving in the U.S. Army in South Korea (1959–60), he became immersed in Asian music; upon his discharge, he was active with various avant-garde groups in N.Y., and also taught at Rutgers Univ. (from 1972). One of the earliest minimalists, Corner has extended his compositional horizon to include both Western and non-Western forms of expression, carefully recorded in his own graphic notation. He publ. *I Can Walk through the World as Music* (1980).

WORKS: ORCH.: *This Is It . . . This Time* (1959). **INSTRUMENTAL:** *Sang-teh* (1959); *Air Effect* (1961); *Certain Distilling Processes* (1962); *Pond* (1968); *OM Emerging* (1970); *OM series* (1970–74); *Elementals* (1976). **GAMELAN** (works in open score): *Gamelan* (1975); *Gamelan II* (1975); *Gamelan IX* (1975); *The Barcelona Cathedral* (1978); *Gamelan P. C.* (1979); *Gamelan LY* for Gamelan Ensemble, Erhu, and Clarinet (1979); *Gamelan IRIS* for Gamelan Ensemble and Flute (1980); *Gamelan CONCERT!O* for Gamelan Ensemble, Harpsichord, and Electric Guitar (1980); *Gamelan CORN* for Violin (1982); *Gamelan ANTIPODE* for Violin (1984). **OTHER:** Theater pieces; electronic works; piano music.

Correa de Azevedo, Luis Heitor, Brazilian musicologist; b. Rio de Janeiro, Dec. 13, 1905; d. Paris, Nov. 10, 1992. He studied at the Instituto Nacional de Música in Rio de Janeiro; in 1932 he was appointed librarian there; in 1939 he became prof. of national folklore; in 1943 he organized the Centro de Pesquisas Folklóricas at the Escuela Nacional de Música; from 1947 to 1965 he was head of the music division of UNESCO in Paris. In 1942 he was made a corresponding member of the American Musicological Soc. He publ. valuable studies on Brazilian music: *Escala, ritmo e melodia na música dos Indios brasileiros* (Rio de Janeiro, 1938); *Relação das operas de autores brasileiros* (Rio de Janeiro, 1938); *A música brasileira e seus fundamentos* (Washington, D.C., 1948); *Música e músicos do Brasil* (Rio de Janeiro,

1950); *150 años de música no Brasil* (Rio de Janeiro, 1956); *La Musique en Amérique latine* (Paris, 1957); also several informative articles in Brazilian, French, and American magazines.

Corsaro, Frank (Andrew), American theater, musical, and opera director and administrator; b. N.Y., Dec. 22, 1924. He received training in drama at Yale Univ., graduating in 1947. From 1955 he oversaw various stage productions on Broadway. He also directed opera at the N.Y. City Opera from 1958. In 1977 he was named artistic director of the Actor's Studio in N.Y. His dramatically compelling opera productions have been staged throughout the U.S., Europe, and Australia.

Cortés, Ramiro, Jr., American composer and teacher; b. Dallas, Nov. 25, 1933; d. Salt Lake City, July 2, 1984. He was a student of Henry Cowell in N.Y. (1952), of Donovan at Yale Univ. (1953–54), and of Halsey Stevens and Ingolf Dahl at the Univ. of Southern Calif. in Los Angeles (B.M., 1955); after training with Petrassi in Rome on a Fulbright fellowship (1956–58), he completed his studies with Sessions at Princeton Univ. (1958) and with Giannini at the Juilliard School of Music in N.Y. (M.M., 1962). He taught in Los Angeles at the Univ. of Calif. (1966–67), and at the Univ. of Southern Calif. (1967–72); in 1972–73 he was composer-in-residence at the Univ. of Utah, where he subsequently served as a teacher and chairman of its theory and composition dept. (1973–84). In his works to the late 1960s, he followed strict serial procedures; later he became less dogmatic in approach.

WORKS: DRAMATIC: OPERAS: *The Christmas Garden*, children's opera (1955); *Prometheus* (1960); *The Eternal Return* (1981). **MUSICAL:** *The Patriots* (1975–76; rev. 1978). Also incidental music and dance scores. **ORCH.:** *Night Music* for Chamber Orch. (1954); *Sinfonia sacra* (1954; N.Y., April 9, 1955; rev. 1959); *Yerma*, symphonic portrait (1955); *Xochitl* (1955; Los Angeles, April 22, 1956); Chamber Concerto for Cello and 12 Winds (1957–58; rev. 1978); Sym. (1953–58); *Sinfonia breve* (1955–58); *Meditation* for Strings (1961); *The Eternal Return* (1963; rev. 1965); Concerto for Violin and Strings (1964–65; rev. 1983); *Charenton*, suite for Chamber Orch. (1968–71); Concerto for Harpsichord and Strings (1970–71); *Movements in Variation* (1972); Piano Concerto (1975); *Symphonic Celebration* (1979); *Contrasts* for Symphonic Band (1979–80); *Music* for Strings (1983). **CHAMBER:** *Elegy* for Flute and Piano (1952); *Divertimento* for Flute, Clarinet, and Bassoon (1953); Piano Quintet (1953); Piano Trio (1959; rev. 1965); 2 string quartets (1962, 1983); *The Brass Ring* for 2 Trumpets and 3 Trombones (1967); Duo for Flute and Oboe (1967); Wind Quintet (1967–68); *3 Movements* for 5 Wind Instruments (1968); Capriccio for Woodwind Quintet (1971); Violin Sonata (1971–72); Cello Sonata (1976–77); *Charenton Variations* for 11 Instruments (1978); *Little Suite* for 8 Instruments (1978); Trumpet Sonata (1978); Suite for Violin and Piano (1980); Trio for Clarinet, Cello, and Piano (1981); *Bridges* for Wind Ensemble (1982); piano pieces, including 3 sonatas (1954–79). **VOCAL:** Choral works; song cycles.

Cortese, Luigi, Italian composer; b. Genoa, Nov. 19, 1899; d. there, June 10, 1976. He studied with Mario Ferrari in Genoa, Casella in Rome, and Gédalge in Paris. From 1951 to 1964 he served as director of the Istituto Musicale in Genoa. He was active as a music critic. He publ. the monographs *Alfredo Casella* (1935), *Il Bolero di Ravel* (1944), and *Chopin* (1949).

WORKS: OPERAS: *Prometeo* (1941–47; Bergamo, Sept. 22, 1951); *La notte veneziana* (1953–55; Turin Radio, 1955); *Le notte bianche* (1970). **ORCH.:** *Prelude and Fugue* (1940); *Canto notturno* (1940); Sym. (1953–56); Violin Concerto (1961); *Fantasia* (1964); *Sinfonia Sacra: Inclina, Domine, aurem tuam* for Chorus and Orch. (1967; Turin, April 24, 1969). **CHAMBER:** Violin Sonatina (1935); Horn Sonata (1955); Cello Sonata (1960); *Improvviso* for Viola and Piano (1966); *Invenzione* for 2 Flutes (1973); numerous piano pieces. **VOCAL:** *David*, oratorio (1938; Genoa, Feb. 20, 1941); *4 odes de Ronsard* for Voice and Orch. (1948–57; Naples, Aug. 4, 1961); *3 Salmi* for Soprano and Orch. (1975); solo songs.

Cortis, Antonio, Spanish tenor; b. on a ship between Oran and Altea, Aug. 12, 1891; d. Valencia, April 2, 1952. He went to Madrid, where he sang in the children's (1901–05) and adult (from 1911) choruses at the Teatro Real; he was soon singing operatic roles in Barcelona and Valencia. He made appearances in South America (from 1917) and in Italy (1919), and was a member of the Chicago Opera (1924–32) and the San Francisco Opera (1925–26). In 1931 he sang at London's Covent Garden, and from 1935 pursued his career in Spain; he made his farewell appearance as Cavaradossi in Saragossa (1951). Held in high esteem in his homeland, Cortis became known as the Spanish Caruso. Among his most prominent roles were Radames, Canio, Don José, Edgardo, and Andrea Chénier.

Cortot, Alfred (Denis), famous French pianist, conductor, and teacher; b. Nyon, Switzerland (of a French father and a Swiss mother), Sept. 26, 1877; d. Lausanne, June 15, 1962. He was a pupil at the Paris Cons., and studied with Decambes, Rouquou, and Diémer; he won the 1st prize for piano in 1896; the same year he made his debut in Paris, playing Beethoven's C-minor Concerto at one of the Colonne concerts, and won signal success; he went to Bayreuth (1898) and studied Wagner's works with J. Kniese, and acted as répétiteur at the festivals from 1898 to 1901. Returning to Paris, he began a most active propaganda for the works of Wagner; on May 17, 1902, he conducted the French premiere of *Götterdämmerung* at the Théâtre du Château d'Eau, and in the same year established the Association des Concerts A. Cortot, which he directed for 2 years, educating the public to an appreciation of Wagner; in 1904 he became conductor of the orch. concerts of the Société Nationale and of the Concerts Populaires at Lille (until 1908). In 1905, together with Jacques Thibaud (violin) and Pablo Casals (cello), he formed a trio, which soon gained a great European reputation, and which continued to perform until 1937. From 1907 to 1918 he was a prof. of piano at the Paris Cons. With A. Mangeot, he founded the École Normale de Musique in Paris in 1919, and subsequently served as its director. Cortot toured widely as a soloist and recitalist in Europe and the U.S. until the outbreak of World War II. During the German occupation of France, he was a highly visible artist and was associated with the cultural policies of the Vichy regime. After the liberation, he was compelled to make an accounting of his activities, but was soon allowed to resume his concert career. He subsequently gave numerous concerts until his farewell appearance at the Prades Festival in 1958. He was awarded the Gold Medal of the Royal Phil. Soc. of London in 1923 and was made a Commandeur de la Légion d'honneur of France in 1934. Among his outstanding pupils were Haskil, Solomon, Bachauer, and Lipatti. Although Cortot was technically a highly wayward pianist, he succeeded in infusing his readings of the Romantic repertory with a rare insight and poetic patina.

WRITINGS: *Principes rationnels de la technique pianistique* (French and Eng., Paris, 1928; American ed., Boston, 1930); *La Musique française de piano* (vol. I, 1930; Eng. tr., 1932; vol. II, 1932); *Cours d'interpretátion* (vol. I, Paris, 1934; Eng. tr., 1937); *Aspects de Chopin* (Paris, 1949; Eng. tr., 1951).

BIBL.: B. Gavoty, *A. C.* (Paris, 1977).

Cosma, Viorel, Romanian musicologist; b. Timişoara, March 30, 1923. He studied composition with Jora, I. Dumitrescu, P. Constantinescu, and Rogalski, and musicology with Vancea in Bucharest; then taught at the Cons. there (from 1951). In addition to monographs on Romanian composers, he publ. *Muzicieni Români* (1965; 2nd ed., rev. and enl., 1970); *Interpreti români lexicon* (1977); *Două milenii de muzică pe pămîntul României* (2 Millennia of Music in the Land of Romania; 1977); *De la cîntecul zavarei la imnurile unitătii nationale* (From Songs of Revolt to the Hymns of Unity; 1978); *A Concise History of Romanian Music* (1982); *Exegeze muzicologice* (Musicological Studies; 1984); *40 de ani în fotoliul de orchestră* (40 Years in the Concert Halls; 1986); *Muzucieni din România: Lexicon bio-bibliografic* (1988–90).

BIBL.: M. Marinescu, "V. C.: Portrait," *Muzica* (Bucharest, 1988).

Cossa, Dominic, American baritone and teacher; b. Jessup, Pa., May 13, 1935. He studied at the Univ. of Scranton (B.S. in psychology, 1959), the Univ. of Detroit (M.A., 1961), the Detroit Inst. of Musical Arts, and the Philadelphia Academy of Vocal Arts, his principal vocal mentors being Anthony Marlowe, Robert Weede, and Armen Boyajin. On Oct. 13, 1961, he made his first appearance at the N.Y. City Opera as Morales in *Carmen*, and subsequently sang leading baritone roles there. On Jan. 30, 1970, he made his Metropolitan Opera debut in N.Y. as Silvio, and remained on its roster until 1975; he returned for the 1978–79 season. He also appeared as a guest artist with other U.S. opera companies and in Europe. He taught at the Manhattan School of Music in N.Y. and at the Univ. of Maryland. Among his best roles were Rossini's Figaro, Lescaut, Germont, Marcello, Rigoletto, and Dr. Malatesta.

Cossotto, Fiorenza, distinguished Italian mezzo-soprano; b. Crescentino, April 22, 1935. After training at the Turin Cons., she studied in Milan at the La Scala opera school with Ettore Campogalliani. While still a student, she sang at La Scala before making her formal operatic debut there as Sister Mathilde in *Les Dialogues des Carmélites* on Jan. 26, 1957; continued to sing there regularly until 1973, winning special praise for her Verdi roles and as Donizetti's Leonora. In 1958 she commenced an international career with her appearance in Wexford as Donizetti's Giovanna Seymour; she then made debuts at the Vienna State Opera (as Maddalena, 1958), London's Covent Garden (as Néris in *Médée*, 1959), and the Chicago Lyric Opera (as Donizetti's Leonora, 1964). On Feb. 6, 1968, she made her Metropolitan Opera debut in N.Y. as Amneris, and continued to sing there with distinction in succeeding years in such roles as Adalgisa, Eboli, Mistress Quickly, Laura, and Carmen. In 1958 she married **Ivo Vinco**.

Cossutta, Carlo, Italian tenor; b. Trieste, May 8, 1932. He was a student of Manfredo Miselli, Mario Melani, and Arturo Wolken in Buenos Aires, where he made his operatic debut as Alfredo in 1956. In 1958 he made his first appearance at the Teatro Colón in Buenos Aires as Cassio, and created the title role in Ginastera's *Don Rodrigo* there in 1968. In 1963 he appered as Cassio at his Chicago Lyric Opera debut, and, in 1964, as the Duke of Mantua at his debut at London's Covent Garden. On Feb. 17, 1973, he made his first appearance at the Metropolitan Opera in N.Y. as Pollione, where he sang for one season and then returned for the 1978–79 season. He also sang in Milan, Paris, Berlin, Munich, Hamburg, Philadelphia, Boston, and San Francisco. Among his other roles were Otello, Don Carlos, Turiddu, Cavaradossi, and Manrico.

Costa, Mary, American soprano; b. Knoxville, Tenn., April 5, 1932. She was trained at the Los Angeles Cons. of Music. She pursued work in films (was the voice of Walt Disney's Sleeping Beauty) and television commercials before taking up a serious vocal career. In 1958 she made her operatic debut with the Los Angeles Opera, and in 1959 she made her first appearance with the San Francisco Opera. On Jan. 6, 1964, she made her Metropolitan Opera debut in N.Y. as Violetta, and returned there for occasional appearances until 1978. She also sang at the Glyndebourne Festival, London's Covent Garden, the Leningrad Opera, the Bolshoi Theater in Moscow, the Cincinnati Opera, the Philadelphia Opera et al. She also appeared as a soloist with orchs. and as a recitalist around the world. In 1972 she starred in the film *The Great Waltz.* She founded the Knoxville (Tenn.) Opera Co. in 1978. In 1979 the Mary Costa Scholarship was established at the Univ. of Tenn. Among her best known roles were Manon, Rosalinde, Musetta, and Alice Ford.

Cotapos (Baeza), Acario, Chilean composer; b. Valdivia, April 30, 1889; d. Santiago, Nov. 22, 1969. He studied music in Santiago; in 1916 he went to N.Y., where he took lessons with various teachers, including Bloch. He lived in France until 1934; then went to Spain to work in defense of the Loyalists during the Spanish Civil War; in 1939 he returned to Chile. An experimenter by nature, Cotapos adopted an advanced quasi-serial technique of monothematic mottoes of 8 or more notes. He wrote a music drama, *Voces de gesta* (1933); several symphonic preludes; String Quartet; *Sonata fantasia* for Piano (1924); songs; piano pieces.

Čotek, Pavel, Czech composer; b. Fryšava, March 12, 1922. He studied at the Prague Cons. and the Janáček Academy in Brno; then was active as a choirmaster and music critic.

WORKS: ORCH.: *Concertino grosso* for Oboe, Clarinet, Horn, and Strings (1964); *Symphonic Etudes* (1965); Concerto for 2 Solo Percussionists and Orch. (1968); *Responsoria* for Organ and Orch. (1969). **CHAMBER:** *3 Romantic Compositions* for Horn and Piano (1954); *Dance Suite* for Wind Quintet (1955); Suite for Violin and Piano (1958); *3 Compositions* for Flute and Piano (1962); Violin Sonata (1962); *Chamber Music* for String Quartet and Percussion (1963); *5 Short Movements* for Clarinet and Piano (1964–69); *Wind Music* for Piccolo, Trumpet, Bass Trumpet, Bass Trombone, and Piano (1970); *Agoge* for Viola and Piano (1973); *Causerie* for Bass Clarinet and Piano (1980). **VOCAL:** *Portrait of a Bird*, melodrama for 2 Narrators, Flute, Viola, Bass Clarinet, Celesta, and Harp (1963); choruses; songs.

Cotrubaş, Ileana, outstanding Romanian soprano; b. Galaţi, June 9, 1939. After studies at the Scolă Specială de Muzică (1952–57) and with Eugenia Elinescu and Constantin Stroescu at the Bucharest Cons. (1957–63), she made her operatic debut as Yniod in *Pelléas et Mélisande* in Bucharest (1964). She took 1st prize in both the 's-Hertogenbosch (1965) and Munich Radio (1966) competitions, and then completed her studies at the Vienna Academy of Music (1967). She appeared at the Salzburg Festival in 1967, then was a member of the Frankfurt am Main Opera (1968–71). In 1969 she appeared as Mélisande at the Glyndebourne Festival and as Pamina at the Vienna State Opera, where she subsequently appeared regularly; she was made an Austrian Kammersängerin in 1981. In 1973 she made her U.S. debut as Mimi at the Chicago Lyric Opera; she then sang in Paris (1974) and at Milan's La Scala (1975). On March 23, 1977, she made her Metropolitan Opera debut in N.Y. in the role of Mimi. In addition to her appearances at the world's leading opera houses and festivals, she also toured extensively as a concert artist until her retirement in 1989. Among her other notable roles were Amina, Susanna, Norina, Adina, Violetta, Gilda, Marguerite, Elisabetta, Antonia, and Micaëla.

Coulthard, Jean, Canadian composer and teacher; b. Vancouver, Feb. 10, 1908. She began her studies with her mother, Jean (Blake; née Robinson) Coulthard (b. Moncton, New Brunswick, Aug. 13, 1882; d. Vancouver, July 16, 1933), a pianist and teacher. Following lessons with Jan Cherniavsky (piano) and Frederick Chubb (theory) in Vancouver (1924–28), she continued her training on scholarship at the Royal College of Music in London (1928–30), where she was a composition student of R.O. Morris and Vaughan Williams; still later she worked with Arthur Benjamin (1939), Bernard Wagenaar (1945, 1949), and Gordon Jacob (1965–66). After serving as head of the music dept at St. Anthony's College (1934–36) and Queen's Hall School (1936–37) in Vancouver, she was a lecturer (1947–57) and senior instructor (1957–73) in composition at the Univ. of British Columbia. In 1978 she was named an Officer of the Order of Canada. Coulthard's well-crafted works follow along traditional lines.

WORKS: DRAMATIC: *Excursion*, ballet (1940); *The Return of the Native*, opera (1956–79); *The Devil's Fanfare*, ballet (1958). **ORCH.:** *A Winter's Tale* for Strings (1940); *Convoy*, later retitled *Song to the Sea*, overture (1941); 4 syms.: No. 1 (1951), No. 2, *This Land*, choral sym. for Soli, Chorus, and Orch. (1966–67), No. 3, *Lyric Symphony*, for Bassoon and Chamber Orch. (1975), and No. 4, *Autumn Symphony*, for Strings (originally titled *Symphonic Images*, 1984–85); *A Prayer for Elizabeth* for Strings (1953); *Rider on the Sands* (1953); *The Bird of Dawn-*

ing Singeth All Night Long (1960); *Fantasy* for Violin, Piano, and Orch. (1961); *Serenade or a Meditation and 3 Dances* for Strings (1961); Piano Concerto (1963); *Endymion* (1964); *Kalamalka: Lake of Many Colors* (1974); *Canada Mosaic* (1974); *Burlesca* for Piano and Strings (1977); Symphonic Ode for Violin and Chamber Orch. (1977); *Symphonic Image: Vision of the North* for Strings (1989). **CHAMBER:** 2 violin sonatinas (1945); *Music on a Quiet Song* for Flute and Strings (1946); Cello Sonata (1947); Oboe Sonata (1947); 3 string quartets: No. 1 (1948; rev. 1952), No. 2, *Threnody* (1954; rev. 1969), and No. 3 (1981); 3 violin sonatas: No. 1, *Duo Sonata* (1952), No. 2, *Correspondence* (1964), and No. 3, *Á la jeunesse* (1981); Piano Quartet, *Sketches from a Mediaeval* (1957); *Sonata Rhapsody* for Viola and Piano (1962); *Ballad of the North* for Violin and Piano (1965–66); *Divertimento* for Flute, Oboe, Clarinet, Horn, Bassoon, and Piano (1968); *Lyric Trio* for Piano Trio (1968); *Lyric Sonatina* for Bassoon and Piano (1969); *Lyric Sonatina* for Flute and Piano (1971); *The Birds of Lansdowne* for Piano Trio and Tape (1972); *12 Essays on a Cantabile Theme* for 2 String Quartets (1972); *Music on a Scottish Folk Song* for Violin and Guitar (1974); *Lyric Sonatina* for Clarinet and Piano (1976); *Fanfare Sonata* for Trumpet and Piano (1978); *Shizen: 3 Nature Sketches from Japan* for Oboe and Piano (1979); *Pas de Deux*, sonatina for Flute and Bassoon (1980); *Fantasy Sonata* for Horn and Piano (1983); *Lyric Sonatina* for Guitar (1984); *Dopo Botticelli* for Cello and Piano (1985); *Duo Sonata* for Violin and Cello (1989); numerous piano pieces, including 2 sonatas (1947, 1986). **VOCAL:** *Night Wind* for Alto and Piano (1951; rev. for Soprano and Orch.); *2 Visionary Songs* for Soprano, Flute, and Strings (1968); *Songs from the Distaff Muse I* for Soprano, Alto, and Cello (1972) and *II* for Soprano, Alto, and Piano (1974); *Serenade* for Alto and Violin (1977); *Vancouver Lights: A Soliloquy* for Soprano, Baritone, Chorus, and Orch. (1980); *Fanfare Overture* for Chorus and Orch. (1985); *Shelley Portrait* for Alto, Flute, Clarinet, Cello, and Piano (1987); *When Tempests Rise*, cantata for Soli, Chorus, and Orch. (based on the opera *The Return of the Native*, 1988); choruses; other songs.

Cour, Niels la, Danish composer and teacher; b. Copenhagen, Nov. 14, 1944. He studied at the Royal Danish Cons. of Music in Copenhagen (1964–69), with Kayser (composition and orchestration, 1973–74), and at the Conservatorio di Santa Cecilia in Rome (1975). After teaching at the Odense Cons. of Music (1968–77), he was on the faculty of the Royal Danish Cons. of Music (from 1978). He has written much effective choral music.

WORKS: ORCH.: *Mythos* for Strings (1969); *Imago* (1971); *Symphonic Fragments* (1973–74); *Divertimento* (1976); Sym. (1980–82); *Preludio boreale* (1983–84). **CHAMBER:** *Imago* for 6 Instruments (1967); 6 string quartets: No. 1, *Das innere Licht* (1968), No. 2, *Mild und leise* (1969), No. 3, *Communio* (1970–71), No. 4, *Quatuor classique* (1971–72), No. 5 (1977), and No. 6 (1977–78); *5 Stilleben* for Viola and Piano (1968); 2 wind quintets (1972–73; 1975); Trio for Violin, Cello, and Piano (1979); *Enetanker* for Guitar (1983). **KEYBOARD: PIANO:** *Praeludium* (1979). **ORGAN:** *Archetypon* (1970); *3 Intermezzi* (1973–74); *De profundis* (1974); *Suite solenne* (1980). **VOCAL:** *Vinger* for Women's Chorus (1973); 5 Motets for Chorus (1977); Requiem-cantata for Chorus and Organ (1981–82); 3 Latin Motets for Chorus (1982); *Francis of Assisi's Prayer* for Women's or Mixed Chorus (1984); *4 Salmi* for Chorus (1985); 3 Latin Motets for Chorus (1988); *Tantum ergum sacrementum* for Chorus (1989); *Missa brevis* for Soli and Chorus (1989); *Sursum corda* for Chorus (1991).

Couraud, Marcel, French conductor; b. Limoges, Oct. 20, 1912; d. Loches, Sept. 14, 1986. He studied organ with Marchal in Paris, then enrolled in theory courses at the École Normale de Musique there; also took lessons in composition with Boulanger and in conducting with Munch. In 1945 he formed the Marcel Couraud Vocal Ensemble, which he conducted until 1954; then conducted in Stuttgart. In 1967 he was appointed artistic director of the ORTF choirs in Paris; subsequently was founder-conductor of the Groupe Vocal de France (1976–78).

Courboin, Charles (Marie), prominent Belgian-American organist, pedagogue, and organ designer; b. Antwerp, April 2, 1884; d. N.Y., April 13, 1973. He was a student of Blockx and Mailly at the Brussels Cons. In 1904 he emigrated to the U.S. and served as an organist in Oswego and Syracuse, N.Y., and in Springfield, Mass. He became well known as an organist and concert organizer at the Wanamaker dept. stores in N.Y. and Philadelphia; he also made tours of North America. In 1942 he became head of the organ dept. at the Peabody Cons. of Music in Baltimore. From 1943 to 1970 he was organist and music director at St. Patrick's Cathedral in N.Y. He designed and dedicated many organs in the U.S.

Coward, Sir Noel, English playwright and author of musical comedies; b. Teddington, Middlesex, Dec. 16, 1899; d. Port Maria, Jamaica, March 25, 1973. At the age of 11, he appeared on the stage, and was associated with the theater ever after, in the triple capacity of actor, playwright, and producer. Having had no formal education in music, he dictated his songs to a musical amanuensis. Among the musical comedies for which he wrote both words and music are *This Year of Grace* (N.Y., Nov. 7, 1928); *Bitter-Sweet* (London, July 12, 1929); *Conversation Piece* (London, Feb. 16, 1934); *Operette* (London, Feb. 17, 1938); *Pacific 1860* (London, Dec. 19, 1946); *Ace of Clubs* (London, July 7, 1950); *After the Ball* (London, June 10, 1954); *Sail Away* (N.Y., Oct. 3, 1961); 51 songs from his musical plays are publ. in the *Noel Coward Song Book* (N.Y., 1953) with the author's introduction. He also publ. an autobiography, *Present Indicative* (London, 1937); 2nd vol., *Future Indefinite* (London, 1954). He was knighted in 1970.

BIBL.: C. Lesley (N. C.'s valet-companion), *Remembered Laughter* (N.Y., 1976); G. Payn and S. Morley, eds., *The N. C. Diaries* (London, 1982); S. Citron, *N. and Cole: The Sophisticates* (Oxford, 1993).

Cowell, Henry (Dixon), remarkable and innovative American composer; b. Menlo Park, Calif., March 11, 1897; d. Shady, N.Y., Dec. 10, 1965. His father, of Irish birth, was a member of a clergyman's family in Kildare; his mother was an American of progressive persuasion. Cowell studied violin with Henry Holmes in San Francisco; after the earthquake of 1906, his mother took him to N.Y., where they were compelled to seek support from the Soc. for the Improvement of the Condition of the Poor; they returned to Menlo Park, California, where Cowell was able to save enough money, earned from menial jobs, to buy a piano. He began to experiment with the keyboard by striking the keys with his fists and forearms; he named such chords "tone clusters" and at the age of 13 composed a piece called *Adventures in Harmony*, in which they appear. Later he began experimenting in altering the sound of the piano by placing various objects on the strings, and also by playing directly under the lid of the piano *pizzicato* and *glissando*, thus anticipating the later development of the "prepared piano." He first exhibited these startling innovations on March 5, 1914, at the San Francisco Musical Soc. at the St. Francis Hotel, much to the consternation of its members. The tone clusters per se were not new; they were used for special sound effects by composers in the 18th century to imitate thunder or cannon fire. Vladimir Rebikov applied them, for example, in his piano piece *Hymn to Inca*, and Charles Ives used them in his *Concord Sonata* to be sounded by covering a set of white or black keys with a wooden board. However, Cowell had a priority by systematizing tone clusters as harmonic amplifications of tonal chords, and he devised a logical notation for them. These tone clusters eventually acquired legitimacy in the works of many European and American composers. Cowell also extended the sonorities of tone clusters to instrumental combinations and applied them in several of his symphonic works. In the meantime, Cowell began taking lessons in composition with E.G. Strickland and Wallace Sabin at the Univ. of Calif. at Berkeley, and later with Frank Damrosch at the Inst. of Musical Art in N.Y., and, privately, with Charles Seeger (1914–16). After brief service in the U.S. Army in 1918, where he was employed first as a cook and later as arranger for its Band, he became engaged professionally to give a series of lectures on new music, illustrated by his playing his own works on the piano. In 1928 he became the first American composer to visit Russia, where he attracted considerable attention; some of his pieces were publ. in a Russian ed., the first such publications by an American. Upon his return to the U.S., he was appointed lecturer on music at the New School for Social Research in N.Y.

In 1931 Cowell received a Guggenheim fellowship, and went to Berlin to study ethnomusicology with Hornbostel. This was the beginning of his serious study of ethnic musical materials. He had already experimented with Indian and Chinese devices in some of his works; in his *Ensemble for Strings* (1924), he included Indian thundersticks. In 1931 he formed a collaboration with Leon Theremin, then visiting the U.S.; with his aid he constructed an ingenious instrument, the Rhythmicon, which made possible the simultaneous production of 16 different rhythms on 16 different pitch levels of the harmonic series. He demonstrated the Rhythmicon at a lecture-concert in San Francisco on May 15, 1932. He also composed an extensive work entitled *Rhythmicana* for it, but it did not receive a performance until Dec. 3, 1971, at Stanford Univ., using advanced electronic techniques. In 1927 Cowell founded the *New Music Quarterly* for publication of ultramodern music, mainly by American composers.

Cowell's career was brutally interrupted in 1936, when he was arrested in California on charges of homosexuality (then a heinous offense) involving the impairment of the morals of a minor. Lulled by the deceptive promises of a wily district attorney of a brief confinement in a sanatorium, Cowell pleaded guilty to a limited offense; he was vengefully given a maximum sentence of imprisonment, up to 15 years. Incarcerated at San Quentin, he was assigned to work in a jute mill, but indomitably continued to write music. Thanks to interventions on his behalf by a number of eminent musicians, he was paroled in 1940 to Percy Grainger as a guarantor of his good conduct; he obtained a full pardon on Dec. 9, 1942, from the governor of California, Earl Warren, after it was discovered that the evidence against him was largely contrived. On Sept. 27, 1941, he married Sidney Robertson, a noted ethnomusicologist. He then resumed his full activities as an ed. and instructor; he held teaching positions at the New School for Social Research in N.Y. (1940–62), the Univ. of Southern Calif. in Los Angeles, Mills College in Oakland, California, and the Peabody Cons. of Music in Baltimore (1951–56); he was also appointed adjunct prof. of summer classes at Columbia Univ. (1951–65). In 1951 Cowell was elected a member of the National Academy of Arts and Letters; he received an honorary Mus.D. from Wilmington College (1953) and from Monmouth (Ill.) College (1963). In 1956–57 he undertook a world tour with his wife through the Near East, India, and Japan, collecting rich primary materials for his compositions, which by now had acquired a decisive turn toward the use of ethnomusicological melodic and rhythmic materials, without abandoning, however, the experimental devices which were the signposts of most of his works. In addition to his symphonic and chamber music, Cowell publ. in 1930 an important book, *New Musical Resources.* He also ed. a symposium, *American Composers on American Music* (Stanford, Calif., 1933). In collaboration with his wife, he wrote a biography of Charles Ives (1955).

WORKS: DRAMATIC: *The Building of Bamba,* pageant (Halcyon, near Pismo Beach, Calif., Aug. 18, 1917). *O'Higgins of Chile,* opera (1949; unfinished); *The Commission,* "operatic episode" (1954; Woodstock, N.Y., Sept. 26, 1992).

16 HYMN AND FUGUING TUNES (based on fuguing tunes of William Billings): No. 1 for Band (1943); No. 2 for String Orch. (1944); No. 3 for Orch. (1944); No. 4 for 3 Instruments (1944); No. 5 for String Orch. (1945; version for Orch. incorporated into Sym. No. 10); No. 6 for Piano (1946); No. 7 for Viola and Piano (1946); No. 8 for String Quartet or String Orch. (1947–48); No. 9 for Cello and Piano (1950); No. 10 for Oboe and Strings (1955); No. 11, became *7 Rites of Music* for Men's Chorus and Orch. (1956); No. 12 for 3 Horns (1957); No. 13 for Trombone and Piano (1960); No. 14 for Organ (1961); No. 15A, a duet for the anniversary of his marriage (Sept. 27, 1961); No. 15B for 2 Violins or Any Combination (2 versions, 1 with a more extended ground bass); No. 16 for Violin and Piano (1965; N.Y., Oct. 6, 1966; also for Violin and Orch.).

20 SYMS.: No. 1 (1916–17); No. 2, *Anthropos* (Mankind; 1938); No. 3, *Gaelic Symphony* (1942); No. 4, *Short Symphony* (1946; Boston, Oct. 24, 1947); No. 5 (1948; Washington, D.C., Jan. 5, 1949); No. 6 (1950–55; Houston, Nov. 14, 1955); No. 7 (Baltimore, Nov. 25, 1952); No. 8, *Choral,* for Chorus and Orch. (1952; Wilmington, Ohio, March 1, 1953); No. 9 (1953; Green Bay, Wis., March 14, 1954); No. 10 for Chamber Orch. (1953; U.S. premiere, N.Y., Feb. 24, 1957); No. 11, *The 7 Rituals of Music* (1953; Louisville, May 29, 1954); No. 12 (1955–56; Houston, March 28, 1960); No. 13, *Madras Symphony,* for Small Orch. and 3 Indian Instruments (1957–58; Madras, India, March 3, 1959); No. 14 (1960–61; Washington, D.C., April 27, 1961); No. 15, *Thesis* (Bowling Green, Ky., Oct. 7, 1961); No. 16, *Icelandic Symphony* (1962; Reykjavík, March 21, 1963); No. 17 (1962–63; 1st movement perf. as *Lancaster Overture,* Lancaster, Pa., 1963); No. 18 (1964); No. 19 (Nashville, Tenn., Oct. 18, 1965); No. 20 (1965).

OTHER WORKS FOR ORCH.: *Vestiges* (1914–20); *Some Music* (1915); *Some More Music* (1915–16); *Communication* (1920); *Sinfonietta* for Small Orch. (1924–28; Boston, Nov. 23, 1931, Slonimsky conducting); *Irish Suite* for Solo String, Percussion, and Piano (1928; Boston, March 11, 1929, Slonimsky conducting; a scoring of the piano pieces *The Banshee, Leprechaun,* and *Fairy Bells* with Chamber Orch. accompaniment); Piano Concerto (1929; Havana, Dec. 28, 1930; 1st complete U.S. perf., Omaha, Oct. 12, 1978); *Polyphonica* for 12 Instruments (1930); Synchrony (1930; Paris, June 6, 1931, Slonimsky conducting); *Reel No. 1* and *No. 2* (1930, 1932); *2 Appositions* for Strings (1931); *Rhythmicana,* Concerto for Rhythmicon and Orch. (1931; Palo Alto, Calif., Dec. 3, 1971); 3 pieces for Chamber Orch.: *Competitive Sport, Steel and Stone,* and *Heroic Dance* (1931); *4 Continuations* for Strings (1933); *Old American Country Set* (1937; Indianapolis, Feb. 28, 1940); *Celtic Set* (Selinsgrove, Pa., May 6, 1938); *American Melting Pot* (1939); *Symphonic Set* (1939; orchestration of *Toccanta*); *Shoonthree* (Sleep Music; 1939; also for Band); *Pastoral & Fiddler's Delight* (1940; N.Y., July 26, 1949, Stokowski conducting); *Ancient Desert Drone* (1940); *Tales of Our Countryside* for Piano and Orch. (1940; Atlantic City, May 11, 1941; composer soloist, Stokowski conducting; based on piano pieces written 1922–30); *Vox Humana* (1940); *Little Concerto* for Piano and Orch. or Band (1942; also known as *Concerto piccolo*); Suite for Piano and Strings (1943); *American Pipers* (1943); *United Music* (1944); *Big Sing* (1945); *Festival Overture* for 2 Orchs. (1946); *Saturday Night at the Firehouse* (1948); *Aria* for Violin and Strings (1952); *Rondo* (1953); *Ballad* for Strings (1955); *Variations* (1956); *Persian Set* for 12 Instruments (1956–57); *Music 1957* (1957); *Ongaku* (1957; Louisville, March 26, 1958); *Antiphony* for 2 Orchs. (1958; Kansas City, Mo., Nov. 14, 1959); Percussion Concerto (1958; Kansas City, Jan. 7, 1961); *Mela and Fair* (New Delhi, India, Dec. 11, 1959); *Characters* (1959); *Chiaroscuro* (1960; Guatemala City, Oct. 13, 1961); *Variations on Thirds* for 2 Solo Violas and Strings (1960); *Concerto brevis* for Accordion and Orch. (1960); Harmonica Concerto (1960); *Air and Scherzo* for Saxophone and Small Orch. (1961); *Duo concertante* for Flute, Harp, and Orch. (Springfield, Ohio, Oct. 21, 1961); 2 koto concertos: No. 1 (1963; Philadelphia, Dec. 18, 1964) and No. 2 (Hanover, N.H., May 8, 1965); *Concerto grosso* for 5 Instruments and Orch. (1963; Miami Beach, Jan. 12, 1964); Harp Concerto (1965); Carol (1965; new orchestration of slow movement of Koto Concerto No. 1).

OTHER WORKS FOR BAND: *A Curse and a Blessing* (1938); *Shoonthree* (1940; also for Orch.); *Celtic Set* (1943; orig. for

Orch., 1938); *Animal Magic* (1944); *Grandma's Rumba* (1945); *Fantasie* (West Point, N.Y., May 30, 1952); *Singing Band* (1953).

OTHER WORKS FOR VOICE: *The Thistle Flower* for Women's Voices (1928); *Vocalise* for Voice, Flute, and Piano (1937); *Chrysanthemums* for Soprano, 2 Saxophones, and 4 Strings (1937); *Toccanta* for Soprano, Flute, Cello, and Piano (1938); *The Coming of Light* for Chorus (1939); *Fire and Ice*, after Frost, for 4 Male Soloists and Orch. or Band (1942); Sonatina for Baritone, Violin, and Piano (1942); *American Muse* for Soprano, Alto, and Piano (1943); *To America* for Chorus (1947); *The Commission*, cantata for 4 Soloists and Orch. (1954); *. . . if He Please* for Mixed and either Boys' or Women's Choruses and Orch. (1954); Septet for 5 Voices without words, Clarinet, and Piano (1955–56); *A Thanksgiving Psalm from the Dead Sea Scrolls* for Men's Chorus and Orch. (1956; orig. *Hymn and Fuguing Tune* No. 11); *Edson Hymns and Fuguing Tunes* for Chorus and Orch. (1960); *The Creator* for Chorus and Orch. (1963); *Ultima Actio* for Chorus (1965).

OTHER CHAMBER WORKS: *Quartet Romantic* for 2 Flutes, Violin, and Viola (1915–17); 5 string quartets: No. 1, *Pedantic* (1915–16), No. 2, *Movement* (1928), No. 3, *Mosaic* (1935), No. 4, *United* (1936), and No. 5 (1956; rev. 1962); also the unnumbered *Quartet Euphometric* (1916–19); other pieces; also unnumbered *Ensemble* for 2 Violins, Viola, 2 Cellos, and 3 Thundersticks (1924; version for String Orch. without Thundersticks, 1959); *7 Paragraphs* for String Trio (1925); Suite for Violin and Piano (1927); *Exultation* for 10 Strings (1928); Suite for Wind Quintet (1930); 3 works for Percussion: *Pulse, Return,* and *Ostinato Pianissimo* (1930–34); *6 Casual Developments* for Clarinet and Piano (1935); *Sound-form* for Dance for Flute, Clarinet, Bassoon, and Percussion (1936); *Sarabande* for Oboe, Clarinet, and Percussion (1937); *Trickster Coyote* for Flute and Percussion (1941); *Action in Brass* for 5 Brasses (1943); Violin Sonata (1945; rev. 1947); Saxophone Quartet (1946); *Tall Tale* for Brass Sextet (1947); *Set for 2* for Violin and Piano (1948); *4 Declamations and Return* for Cello and Piano (1949); *Set of 5* for Violin, Piano, and Percussion (1951); *Set* for Harpsichord, Flute, Oboe, and Cello (1953); *Set of 2* for Harp and Violin (1955); *Homage to Iran* for Violin and Piano (1957); *Iridescent Rondo* for Accordion (1959); *Air and Scherzo* for Saxophone and Piano (1961); Quartet for Flute, Oboe, Cello, and Harp (1962); *Gravely and Vigorously,* in memory of John F. Kennedy, for Cello (1963; orig. the *Hymn and Fuguing Tune* No. 17); *26 Simultaneous Mosaics* for Violin, Cello, Clarinet, Piano, and Percussion (N.Y., Dec. 1, 1964); Piano Trio (1965); *Cleistogamy* (self-pollinating flowerlets), a collection of pieces written between 1941 and 1963.

PIANO: *The Tides of Manaunaun* (1912); *Advertisements* (1914; rev. 1959); *Dynamic Motion* (1914); *6 Ings: Floating-Fleeting-Wafting-Seething-Frisking-Scooting* (1916); *It Isn't It* (1922); *The Snows of Fujiyama* (1922); *Aeolian Harp* (1923); *Piece* for Piano with Strings (Paris, 1924); *The Banshee* (1925); *Lilt of the Reel* (1925); *Sinister Resonance* (1925); *Tiger* (1927); *2 Woofs* (1930); *Hilarious Curtain Opener and Ritournelle* (1937); hundreds of other pieces with similar fanciful titles; also some organ pieces.

WRITINGS: *New Musical Resources* (N.Y., 1930); ed., *American Composers on American Music: A Symposium* (Stanford, Calif., 1933); with S. Cowell, *Charles Ives and His Music* (N.Y., 1955).

BIBL.: N. Slonimsky, "H. C.," in *American Composers on American Music: A Symposium* (Stanford, Calif., 1933; reprinted, N.Y., 1962); M. Goss, *Modern Music-Makers* (N.Y., 1952); H. Weisgall, "The Music of H. C.," *Musical Quarterly* (Oct. 1959); O. Daniel, "H. C.," *Stereo Review* (Dec. 1974); R. Mead, *H. C.'s New Music, 1925–1936* (N.Y., 1981); M. Manion, *Writings about H. C.: An Annotated Bibliography* (N.Y., 1982); W. Lichtenwanger, *The Music of H. C.: A Descriptive Catalog* (Brooklyn, 1986); M. Hicks, "The Imprisonment of H. C.," *Journal of the American Musicological Society* (Summer 1991); S. Johnson, "H. C., John Varian, and Halcyon," *American Music* (Spring 1993).

Cowie, Edward, English-born Australian composer, conductor, teacher, and painter; b. Birmingham, Aug. 17, 1943. He studied with Fricker and took his B.Ed. at the Univ. of London (1964); after training from A. Goehr (1964–68), he worked with Lutoslawski in Poland (1971); he also studied at the Trinity College of Music in London (L.T.C.L., 1968), and at the univs. of Southampton (B.Mus., 1970; D.Mus., 1979) and Lancaster (Ph.D., 1983). From 1974 to 1983 he was senior lecturer at the Univ. of Lancaster; in 1979 he also was a visiting prof. at the Univ. of Kassel. From 1983 to 1986 he was composer-in-residence at the Royal Liverpool Phil., and from 1983 to 1989 prof. of creative arts at the Univ. of Wollongong in New South Wales. In 1988 he became a naturalized Australian citizen. In 1989–90 he was prof. of creative arts at James Cook Univ. in Queensland. He then served as artistic director and prof. of arts fusion of the Australian Arts Fusion Centre in Brisbane (from 1991). He also was active as a conductor. His talent as a painter has been highlighted in various exhibitions. As a composer, his technique ranges from static triadic tonality to serialistic atonality; reflections of nature, including birdsong, and a preoccupation with form, are pervasive aspects of his works.

WORKS: DRAMATIC: *Commedia*, opera (1976–78); *Kate Kelly's Roadshow,* music theater (1982). **ORCH.:** 2 clarinet concertos (1969, 1975); *Moon, Sea, and Stars* (1974); *Leviathan,* symphonic poem (1975); *Columbine* (1976); Piano Concerto (1976–77); *L'Or de la trompette d'été* for 18 Strings (1977); *Concerto for Orchestra* (1980–81); *Leonardo* for Strings (1980–81); 2 numbered syms.: No. 1, *The American* (1980–81; Liverpool, Feb. 1, 1984) and No. 2, *The Australian* (1982); *Choral Symphony: Symphonies of Rain, Sea, and Speed* for Baritone, Chorus, and Orch. (1981–82); Concerto for Harp and Strings (1983); *Atlas* (1984; Liverpool, May 13, 1986); *15-Minute Australia* for Youth Orch. (1985); Cello Concerto (1992). **CHAMBER:** 4 string quartets (1973, 1976, 1980, 1981); *Cathedral Music* for Brass (1976); *Harlequin* for Harp (1977); *Commedia Lazzis* for Guitar (1977); *Kelly-Nolan-Kelly* for Clarinet (1980); *Cartoon Music* for Percussion, Keyboard, Violin, and Cello (1984); Flute Quartet (1991). **PIANO:** *Piano Variations* (1976; rev. 1981); *The Falls of Clyde* for 2 Pianos (1976); *Kelly Variations* (1980); Sonata (1985). **VOCAL:** *Shinko-Kinshu* for High Voice and Instruments (1968; rev. 1972); *Gesangbuch* for 24 Voices Unaccompanied or With Instruments (1971); *Endymion Nocturnes* for Tenor and String Quartet (1973; also for Tenor, Horn, and Strings, 1981); *A Charm of Finches* for Soprano and 3 Flutes (1973); *Leighton Moss* for Chorus and Chamber Orch. (1974–75); *Columbine* for Soprano and Chamber Orch. (1979); *Missa Brevis* for Chorus and Organ (1982); *Avium Cencentus* for Chorus (1988); *The Roof of Heaven* for Tenor, 2 Oboes, 2 Horns, and Strings (1988); *'48* for High Voice and Chamber Ensemble (1992).

Cox, Jean, American tenor; b. Gadsen, Ala., Jan. 16, 1922. After attending the Univ. of Alabama and the New England Cons. of Music in Boston, he studied with Kitsamer in Frankfurt am Main, Ricci and Bertelli in Rome, and Lorenz in Munich. In 1951 he made his operatic debut as Lensky with the New England Opera Theater in Boston. In 1954 he made his European operatic debut as Rodolfo in Spoleto, and then sang in Kiel (1954–55) and Braunschweig (1955–59). He appeared at the Bayreuth Festivals (1956–75), at the Hamburg State Opera (1958–73), and at the Mannheim National Theater (from 1959). As a guest artist, he sang with various European opera houses, including the Paris Opéra (as Siegmund, 1971) and at London's Covent Garden (as Siegfried, 1975). In the U.S. he appeared at the Chicago Lyric Opera (1964, 1970, 1973) and made his Metropolitan Opera debut in N.Y. as Walther von Stolzing on April 2, 1976, where he sang for the season before concentrating his career in Europe. He sang various Wagnerian roles, as well as Fra Diavolo, Don Carlos, Othello, Strauss's Herod and Bacchus, and the Cardinal in *Mathis der Maler.*

Cox, John, English opera director and administrator; b. Bristol, March 12, 1935. He was educated at Oxford, where he produced the first British staging of *L'enfant et les sortilèges* in

1958. In 1959 he was an assistant at the Glyndebourne Festival. In 1965 he launched his professional career with his staging of *L'enfant et les sortilèges* at the Sadler's Wells Opera in London, and worked there regularly from 1969. From 1971 to 1981 he was director of production at the Glyndebourne Festival, where he excelled in the staging of operas by Richard Strauss. Following his tenure as general administrator and artistic director of Glasgow's Scottish Opera (1981–86), he was director of production at Covent Garden from 1988. His inventive productions have been seen on the Continent, in the U.S., and Australia.

Crabbé, Armand (Charles), Belgian baritone; b. Brussels, April 23, 1883; d. there, July 24, 1947. He studied with Demest and Gilles at the Brussels Cons. (1902–04), and then with Cottone in Milan. In 1904 he made his operatic debut as the Nightwatchman in *Die Meistersinger von Nürnberg* at the Théâtre Royal de la Monnaie in Brussels. From 1906 to 1914 he sang at London's Covent Garden, and returned there in 1937. On Nov. 5, 1907, he made his U.S. debut as Escamillo at N.Y.'s Manhattan Opera; after appearances with the Chicago Grand Opera (1910–14), he sang at Milan's La Scala (1915–16; 1928–31), in Buenos Aires (1916–26), and in Belgium. In his last years, he taught voice in Brussels. With Auguste Maurage, he composed the opera *Les Noces d'or.* He publ. the books *Conseils sur l'art du chant* (Brussels, 1931) and *L'art d'Orphée* (Brussels, 1933). Among his many roles were Rossini's Figaro, Silvio, Beckmesser, Rabaud's Mârouf, Ford, and Valentin.

Craft, Robert (Lawson), American conductor and writer on music; b. Kingston, N.Y., Oct. 20, 1923. He studied at the Juilliard School of Music in N.Y. (B.A., 1946) and the Berkshire Music Center in Tanglewood; took courses in conducting with Monteux. In 1947 he conducted the N.Y. Brass and Woodwind Ensemble. He was conductor of the Evenings-on-the-Roof and the Monday Evening Concerts in Los Angeles (1950–68). A decisive turn in his career was his encounter with Stravinsky in 1948, whom he greatly impressed by his precise knowledge of Stravinsky's music; gradually he became Stravinsky's closest associate. He was also instrumental in persuading Stravinsky to adopt the 12-tone method of composition, a momentous turn in Stravinsky's creative path. He collaborated with Stravinsky on 6 vols. of a catechumenical and discursive nature: *Conversations with Igor Stravinsky* (N.Y., 1959); *Memories and Commentaries* (N.Y., 1960); *Expositions and Developments* (N.Y., 1962); *Dialogues and a Diary* (N.Y., 1963); *Themes and Episodes* (N.Y., 1967); *Retrospections and Conclusions* (N.Y., 1969). Resentful of frequent referral to him as a musical Boswell, Craft insists that his collaboration with Stravinsky was more akin to that between the Goncourt brothers, both acting and reacting to an emerging topic of discussion, with Stravinsky evoking his ancient memories in his careful English, or fluent French, spiced with unrestrained discourtesies toward professional colleagues on the American scene, and Craft reifying the material with an analeptic bulimia of quaquaversal literary, psychological, physiological, and culinary references in a flow of finely ordered dialogue. His other publications include *Prejudices in Disguise* (N.Y., 1974); *Stravinsky in Photographs and Documents* (with Vera Stravinsky; London, 1976; N.Y., 1978); *Current Convictions: Views and Reviews* (N. Y., 1977); *Present Perspectives* (N.Y., 1984); *Stravinsky: Glimpses of a Life* (N.Y., 1992). He also tr. and ed. *Stravinsky, Selected Correspondence* (2 vols., N.Y., 1982, 1984).

BIBL.: J. Peyser, "Stravinsky-C., Inc.," *American Scholar,* LII (1983).

Craighead, David, highly regarded American organist and pedagogue; b. Strasburg, Pa., Jan. 24, 1924. He was a student of Alexander McCurdy at the Curtis Inst. of Music in Philadelphia (B.M., 1946). He began his career as a church organist, then taught at Westminster Choir College in Princeton, N.J. (1945–46) and at Occidental College in Los Angeles (1948–55). From 1955 to 1992 he was prof. of organ and chairman of the organ dept. at the Eastman School of Music in Rochester, N.Y., where he taught again in 1993. He made extensive tours of the U.S. as a concert artist, giving numerous world premieres.

Cras, Jean Émile Paul, French composer; b. Brest, May 22, 1879; d. there, Sept. 14, 1932. He grew up in a musical atmosphere and when still a child began to compose; he took lessons with Henri Duparc, under whose influence he composed a number of miniatures in an impressionistic vein; he was at his best in lyrical songs and instrumental pieces. He pursued a career in the French navy, attaining the rank of vice admiral.

WORKS: *Polyphème,* opera (Paris, Dec. 28, 1922); *Journal de Bord,* symphonic suite (1927); *Légende* for Cello and Orch. (1929); Piano Concerto (1931); chamber music; songs.

Crass, Franz, German bass-baritone; b. Wipperfurth, Feb. 9, 1928. He was a student of Glettenberg at the Cologne Hochschule für Musik. In 1954 he made his operatic debut as Amonasro in Krefeld, and then sang in Hannover (1956–62), Bayreuth (1959–73), and Cologne (1962–64). He was a member of the Hamburg State Opera (from 1964), and also appeared at the Vienna State Opera, the Bavarian State Opera in Munich, at La Scala in Milan, and at Covent Garden in London. He was particularly known for his roles in operas by Mozart and Wagner, as well as for his appearances as a concert artist.

Crawford, Robert (McArthur), Canadian-American baritone, conductor, and composer; b. Dawson, Yukon Territory, July 27, 1899; d. N.Y., March 12, 1961. He studied at Princeton Univ., and also took courses at the Juilliard Graduate School in N.Y. and at the American Cons. at Fontainebleau. Returning to the U.S., he held various posts as a choral teacher and conductor. He composed several orch. suites and songs, of which the most popular is *The U.S. Air Force* ("Off we go . . .").

Crawford, Ruth (Porter), gifted American composer, folk music researcher, and teacher; b. East Liverpool, Ohio, July 3, 1901; d. Chevy Chase, Md., Nov. 18, 1953. She studied at the School of Musical Art in Jacksonville, Fla., where she then served on its faculty as a piano teacher (1918–21). In 1921 she enrolled at the American Cons. in Chicago, where she received training in piano from Heniot Lévy and Louise Robyn, and in theory and composition from John Palmer and Adolf Weidig. After additional piano studies with Djane Lavoie-Herz, as well as teaching posts at the American Cons. (1925–29) and the Elmhurst (Ill.) College of Music (1926–29), she went to N.Y. to pursue training in composition with **Charles Seeger**, whom she married in 1931. A Guggenheim fellowship in 1930 allowed her to complete her studies in Berlin and Paris. Upon her return to the U.S., she devoted much time to folk music research and to teaching young children. She transcribed, arranged, and ed. hundreds of folk songs from the collection at the Library of Congress in Washington, D.C., and publ. the collections *American Folksongs for Children* (Garden City, N.Y., 1948), *Animal Folksongs for Children* (Garden City, N.Y., 1950), and *American Folk Songs for Christmas* (Garden City, N.Y., 1953). As a composer, Crawford wrote several bold and insightful works in an experimental tonal style. While she anticipated many techniques of the future avant-garde, her last works took on a less dissonant voice and were notably influenced by her folk music research.

WORKS: ORCH.: Suite for Small Orch. (1926); *Rissolty Rossolty* (1939). **CHAMBER:** Violin Sonata (Chicago, May 22, 1926); Suite for 5 Winds and Piano (1927; rev. 1929; Cambridge, Mass., Dec. 14, 1975); Suite No. 2 for Strings and Piano (1929); *4 Diaphonic Suites* for Various Instruments (1930); String Quartet (1931; N.Y., Nov. 13, 1933); Suite for Wind Quintet (Washington, D.C., Dec. 2, 1952). **PIANO:** 5 preludes (1924–25); 4 preludes (1927–28); *Piano Study in Mixed Accents* (1930). **VOCAL:** *Adventures of Tom Thumb* for Narrator and Piano (1925); 5 songs for Voice and Piano, after Sandburg (1929); 3 chants: No. 1, *To an Unkind God,* for Women's Chorus, No. 2, *To an Angel,* for Soprano and Chorus, and No. 3, for Soprano, Alto, and

Women's Chorus (all 1930); 3 songs for Alto, Oboe, Percussion, Piano, and Optional Orch., after Sandburg: No. 1, *Rat Riddles* (N.Y., April 21, 1930), No. 2, *In Tall Grass* (Berlin, March 10, 1932), and No. 3, *Prayers of Steel* (Amsterdam, June 14, 1933); 2 Ricercari for Voice and Piano: No. 1, *Sacco, Vanzetti* and No. 2, *Chinaman, Laundryman* (both 1932).

BIBL.: C. Seeger, "R. C.," in H. Cowell, ed., *American Composers on American Music* (Stanford, Calif., 1933); S. Cowell, "R.C. Seeger," *Journal of the International Folk Music Council,* VII (1955); M. Gaume, *R.C. S.: Memoirs, Memories, Music* (Metuchen, N.J., 1986); R. Wilding-White, "Remembering R.C. Seeger: An Interview with Charles and Peggy Seeger," *American Music* (Winter 1988); J. Tick, "R. C.'s 'Spiritual Concept': The Sound-Ideals of an Early American Modernist," *Journal of the American Musicological Society* (Summer 1991); J. Straus, *The Music of R.C. Seeger* (Cambridge, 1995).

Creatore, Giuseppe, Italian-American conductor; b. Naples, June 21, 1871; d. N.Y., Aug. 15, 1952. He was a pupil of d'Arienzo and De Nardis at the Naples Cons. After conducting the Naples municipal band (1888–96), he went to the U.S. in 1900. In 1902 he founded his own band in N.Y., with which he toured North America; he also was head of his own opera company (1918–23). He was conductor of the N.Y. City Symphonic Orch. (1936–40) and the N.Y. State Symphonic Band (1937–40), remaining active as a conductor until 1946.

Crespin, Régine, outstanding French soprano, later mezzo-soprano; b. Marseilles, Feb. 23, 1927. She studied pharmacology; then began taking voice lessons with Suzanne Cesbron-Viseur and Georges Jouatte in Paris. She made her debut in Mulhouse as Elsa in 1950 and then sang at the Paris Opéra from 1951, where she quickly rose to prominence. She acquired a reputation as one of the best Wagnerian singers; she sang Kundry at the Bayreuth Festivals (1958–60); appeared also at La Scala in Milan, at Covent Garden in London, and on Nov. 19, 1962, made her debut with the Metropolitan Opera in N.Y. in the role of the Marschallin; she remained with the Metropolitan until her farewell appearance as Mme. De Croissy in *Dialogues of the Carmelites* on April 16, 1987. From 1977 until her retirement in 1991 she sang mezzo-soprano roles. Her memoires were publ. as *La vie et l'amour d'une femme* (Paris, 1980). She sang the parts of Elsa in *Lohengrin*, Sieglinde in *Die Walküre*, and Amelia in *Un ballo in maschera*; also appeared as a concert singer. Her sonorous, somewhat somber voice suited dramatic parts excellently.

Cresswell, Lyell (Richard), New Zealand composer; b. Wellington, Oct. 13, 1944. He was educated at Victoria Univ. of Wellington (B.Mus., 1968), the Univ. of Toronto (Mus.M., 1970), the Univ. of Aberdeen (Ph.D., 1974), and the Inst. of Sonology at the Univ. of Utrecht (1974–75). After teaching at the Univ. of Glasgow, he was music organizer for the Chapter Arts Centre in Cardiff (1978–80). He was the Forman Fellow in Composition at the Univ. of Edinburgh (1980–82) and the Cramb Fellow in Composition at the Univ. of Glasgow (1982–85); in 1978 he won the Ian Whyte Award and in 1979 the Australasian Performing Rights Assn. Silver Scroll for his contributions to New Zealand music. His works were selected as outstanding compositions by the UNESCO International Rostrum of Composers in 1979, 1981, and 1988. He was the featured composer at Musica Nova in Glasgow (1984), the Sonorities Festival of 20th-Century Music in Belfast (1985), the Asian Music Festival in Tokyo (1990), and the New Zealand International Festival of the Arts (1990, 1994). While Cresswell utilized aleatoric methods and electronic means in his early works, he later developed a style in which textural and structural components became the focus of attention. He also found inspiration in New Zealand and Scottish sources, and extended his reach to include various folk and ethnic materials. In some of his works, he displayed an engaging wit and humor.

WORKS: ORCH.: *Salm* (1977; Aberdeen, Jan. 30, 1979); *The Magical Wooden Head* (Denedin, Sept. 20, 1980); *O!* (1983, Wellington, March 12, 1983); Cello Concerto (Glasgow, Sept. 22, 1984); *Speak for us, great sea* (Belfast, April 28, 1985); *Akarana Karaka* (1989; Auckland, June 7, 1990); *Ixion* (Edinburgh, Aug. 12, 1989); *Ylur* (1990–91; Kirkwall, June 23, 1991); *Major Ricketts* for Brass Band (1991; Manchester, Feb. 16, 1992). **CHAMBER:** String Quartet (Edinburgh, Dec. 3, 1981); *Le Sucre du Printemps* for 6 Bass Clarinets and 3 Contrabass Clarinets (1982; Amsterdam, Jan. 19, 1983); *The Pumpkin Massacre* for 12 Solo Strings (1987; Napier, April 15, 1989); *Passacaglia* for Large Chamber Ensemble (1988; Edinburgh, April 16, 1989); Brass Sextet (1988; Edinburgh, March 9, 1989); *Atta* for Cello (Ferrara, Oct. 3, 1993). **KEYBOARD: PIANO:** *The Grammar of Solitude* (1985–88; Paris, May 25, 1989); *Who's Afraid of Red, Yellow, and Blue* (Middelburg, July 7, 1993). **HARPSICHORD:** *Bisbigliando* (1993; Viitasaari, July 10, 1994). **VOCAL:** *Prayer for the cure of a sprained back* for Mezzo-soprano (1979; Christchurch, March 12, 1982); *7 Shaker Songs* for Baritone and Piano (Stroud, Oct. 16, 1980); *O Let the Fire Burn* for Chorus (Wellington, April 25, 1981); *8 Shaker Songs* for Soprano and Piano (1985; London, June 17, 1986); *To Aspro Pano Sto Aspro* for Chorus (1985; Glasgow, May 12, 1986); *A Modern Ecstasy* for Mezzo-soprano, Baritone, and Orch. (1986; Glasgow, May 6, 1989); *Words for Music* for Mezzo-soprano (1989; London, Feb. 6, 1990); *Voices of Ocean Winds* for Chorus and Orch. (1989; Wellington, March 23, 1990); *Il Suono di Enormi Distanze* for Mezzo-soprano and Large Ensemble (1992–93; Glasgow, May 7, 1993).

Creston, Paul (real name, **Giuseppe Guttoveggio**), American composer, organist, and teacher; b. N.Y., Oct. 10, 1906; d. San Diego, Aug. 24, 1985. He received training in piano from Randegger and Déthier and in organ from Yon, but lacked formal instruction in theory or composition. Although he composed tentatively in his youth, he did not embark upon a serious career as a composer until he was 26 when he wrote his *5 Dances* for Piano. From 1934 to 1967 he was organist at St. Malachy's Church in N.Y. In 1938 he held a Guggenheim fellowship. In 1941 his first sym. won the N.Y. Music Critics' Circle Award, and thereafter he received various awards and commissions. He taught at the N.Y. College of Music (1963–67), and then was a prof. of music and composer-in-residence at Central Washington State College in Ellensburg (1968–75). Among his writings were *Principles of Rhythm* (1964), *Creative Harmony* (1970), and *Rational Metric Notation* (1979). Creston's large output was marked by a harmonic and rhythmic idiom of considerable complexity, principally in his instrumental writing. He avoided illogical binary meters and proposed such time signatures as 6/12 or 3/9 in several of his works.

WORKS: ORCH.: *Partita* for Flute, Violin, and Strings (1937); *Threnody* (1938); *2 Choric Dances* (1938); 6 syms.: No. 1 (1940; N.Y., Feb. 22, 1941), No. 2 (1944; N.Y., Feb. 15, 1945), No. 3 (Worcester Festival, Oct. 27, 1950), No. 4 (1951; Washington, D.C., Jan. 30, 1952), No. 5 (1955; Washington, D.C., April 4, 1956), and No. 6 for Organ and Orch. (1981; Washington, D.C., June 28, 1982); Marimba Concertino (1940); Saxophone Concerto (1941; N.Y., Jan. 27, 1944); *A Rumor*, symphonic sketch (N.Y., Dec. 13, 1941); *Fantasy* for Piano and Orch. (1942); *Frontiers* (Toronto, Oct. 14, 1943); *Poem* for Harp and Orch. (1945); *Fantasy* for Trombone and Orch. (1947; Los Angeles, Feb. 12, 1948); Piano Concerto (1949); Concerto for 2 Pianos and Orch. (1951; Montevallo, Ala., Nov. 18, 1968); *Walt Whitman*, symphonic poem (1952); *Invocation and Dance* (1953; Louisville, May 15, 1954); *Dance Overture* (1954); 2 violin concertos: No. 1 (1956; Detroit, Jan. 14, 1960) and No. 2 (Los Angeles, Nov. 17, 1960); *Lydian Ode* (1956); *Toccata* (1957); Accordion Concerto (1958); *Janus* (Denver, July 17, 1959); *Corinthians: XIII*, symphonic poem (1963; Phoenix, March 30, 1964); *Choreografic Suite* (1965); *Pavane Variations* (La Jolla, Calif., Aug. 21, 1966); *Chthonic Ode* (1966; Detroit, April 6, 1967); *Thanatopsis* (1971); *Square Dance 76* for Wind Sym. Orch. (1975); Suite for Strings (1978); *Sadhana* for Cello and Orch. (Los Angeles, Oct. 3, 1981). **CHAMBER:** *3 Poems from Walt Whitman* for Cello and Piano (1934); Suite for Saxophone and Piano (1935); String Quartet (1936); Suite for Viola and Piano (1937); Suite for Violin and Piano (1939); Saxophone Sonata (1939); Suite for Flute, Viola, and Piano (1952); Suite for Cello and Piano (1956); Concertino for Piano and Wind Quintet (1969); *Ceremonial* for Percussion Ensemble (1972); *Rapsodie* for Saxophone and Piano or Organ (1976); Suite for Saxophone Quartet (1979); Piano Trio (1979); piano works. **VOCAL:** 3 chorales, after Tagore (1936); Requiem for Tenor, Bass, and Organ (1938); *Dance Variations* for Soprano and Orch. (1942); *Psalm XXIII* for Soprano, Chorus, and Piano (1945); Missa solemnis for Chorus and Organ or Orch. (1949); *Adoro te*, mass for Women's or Mixed Chorus and Piano (1952); *The Celestial Vision* for Men's Chorus (1954); *Isaiah's Prophecy*, Christmas oratorio (1962); *Nocturne* for Soprano, Wind Quintet, String Quintet, and Piano (1964); *The Psalmist* for Alto and Orch. (1967); *Cum jubilo*, mass for Chorus (1968); *Hyas Illahee* for Chorus and Orch. (1969); *Leaves of Grass* for Chorus and Piano (1970); *Thanksgiving Anthem* for Chorus and Orch. (1982).

BIBL.: H. Cowell, "P. C.," *Musical Quarterly* (Oct. 1948); W. Simmons, "P. C.: Maintaining a Middle Course," *Music Journal*, XXXIV/10 (1976).

Crews, Lucile, American composer; b. Pueblo, Colo., Aug. 23, 1888; d. San Diego, Calif., Nov. 3, 1972. She studied at the New England Cons. of Music in Boston, then with Boulanger in Paris and Hugo Kaun in Berlin. She wrote a symphonic poem, *To an Unknown Soldier* (1926); a miniature opera, *Ariadne and Dionysus* (1935); a "grand opera," *800 Rubles* (1926); Suite for Strings and Woodwinds; Viola Sonata; piano pieces; songs.

Crimi, Giulio, Italian tenor; b. Paterno, May 10, 1885; d. Rome, Oct. 29, 1939. He made his debut in Palermo in 1910 as Manrico; then sang at Covent Garden in London (1914). On Nov. 13, 1918, he made his Metropolitan Opera debut in N.Y. as Radames; on Dec. 14, 1918, he sang there in the premieres of Puccini's *Gianni Schicchi* (as Rinuccio) and *Il Tabarro* (as Luigi); continued to sing there until 1921; also made appearances in Chicago (1916–18; 1922–24); then sang in Milan and Rome. After his retirement in 1928, he taught voice; one of his most famous pupils was Tito Gobbi.

Crist, Bainbridge, American composer and teacher; b. Lawrenceburg, Ind., Feb. 13, 1883; d. Barnstable, Mass., Feb. 7, 1969. He studied piano and flute; later law at George Washington Univ. (LL.B.). He went to Europe to complete his musical training (theory with P. Juon in Berlin and C. Landi in London, and singing with William Shakespeare. He taught singing in Boston (1915–21) and Washington, D.C. (1922–23); returned to Europe (1923) and spent 4 years in Florence, Paris, Lucerne, and Berlin; then settled in Washington, D.C. Crist devoted much time to teaching. He was the author of *The Art of Setting Words to Music* (N.Y., 1944).

WORKS: DRAMATIC: *Le Pied de la momie*, choreographic drama (1915); *Pregiwa's Marriage*, Javanese ballet (1920); *The Sorceress*, choreographic drama (1926). **ORCH.:** *Egyptian Impressions*, suite (Boston Pops, June 22, 1915); *Abhisarika* for Violin and Orch. (1921); *Intermezzo* (1921); *Chinese Dance* (1922); *Arabian Dance* (1922); *Nautch Dance* (1922); *Dreams* (1924); *Yearning* (1924); *Nocturne* (1924); *An Old Portrait* (1924); *La Nuit revécue* (1933; N.Y., March 8, 1936); *Vienna 1913* (1933); *Frivolité* (1934); *Hymn to Nefertiti* (1936); *Fête espagnole* (1937); *American Epic 1620*, tone poem (Washington, D.C., Feb. 28, 1943). **VOCAL: VOICE AND ORCH.:** *A Bag of Whistles* (1915); *The Parting*, poem (1916); *Rhymes* (1917); *O Come Hither!* (1918); *Drolleries* (1920); *Colored Stars*, suite of 4 songs (1921); *Remember* (1930); *The Way That Lovers Use* (1931); *Noontime* (1931); *Evening* (1931); *By a Silent Shore* (1932); also choral works. **OTHER:** Piano pieces; songs.

BIBL.: J. Howard, *B. C.* (N.Y., 1929).

Cristoforeanu, Florica, Romanian soprano; b. Rimnicu-Sarat, Aug. 16, 1887; d. Rio de Janeiro, March 1, 1960. She studied at the Milan Cons. with Filippi and Bodrilla; made her debut in Capodistria in 1908 as Lucia; then sang operetta in Bucharest and Milan (1909–19). From 1927 to 1932 she appeared at Milan's La Scala; also sang in Rome (1928–34) and in South America. She retired in 1940. In addition to her classical roles, she was known for her performances of works by contemporary Italian composers.

Crocker, Richard L(incoln), American musicologist; b. Roxbury, Mass., Feb. 17, 1927. He studied with Schrade at Yale Univ. (B.A., 1950; Ph.D., 1957, with the diss. *The Repertoire of Proses at St. Martial de Limoges*); later conducted research in England and France on a Guggenheim fellowship (1969–70). He taught at his alma mater (1955–63), then joined the faculty of the Univ. of Calif. at Berkeley (from 1963). He publ. *A History of Musical Style* (N.Y., 1966), with A. Basart, *Listening to Music* (N.Y., 1971), and *The Early Medieval Sequence* (Berkeley and Los Angeles, 1977); he also ed., with D. Hiley, vol. II: *The Early Middle Ages to 1300* in *The New Oxford History of Music* (Oxford, 1990).

Crockett, Donald, American composer, conductor, and teacher; b. Pasadena, Calif., Feb. 18, 1951. He studied composition at the Univ. of Southern Calif. in Los Angeles (B.M., 1974; M.M., 1976) and at the Univ. of Calif. at Santa Barbara (Ph.D., 1981). From 1981 to 1984 he was composer-in-residence of the Pasadena Chamber Orch. In 1984 he joined the faculty of the Univ. of Southern Calif. to teach theory and composition and as music director of its Contemporary Music Ensemble. In 1994 he became prof. of theory and composition there; also was composer-in-residence of the Los Angeles Chamber Orch. (from 1991). In 1991 he received a Kennedy Center Friedheim Award, and in 1994 the Goddard Lieberson Fellowship of the American Academy of Arts and Letters.

WORKS: ORCH.: *Melting Voices* (1986; N.Y., March 1990); Concerto for Piano and Wind Ensemble (1988); *Wedge* (1990); *Antiphonies* for Chamber Orch. (1992; Los Angeles, March 1993); Cello Concerto (1993); *Roethke Preludes* (1994; Los Angeles, 1995). **CHAMBER:** Trio for Flute, Cello and Harp (1980); *4 Songs of a Nomad Flute* for Harpsichord (1984); *The Melting Voice* for Chamber Ensemble (1986); 2 string quartets: No. 1, *Array* (1987) and No. 2 (1993); *to be sung on the water* for Violin and Viola (1988); *Pilgrimage* for Piano (1988); *Still Life with Bell* for Chamber Ensemble (1989); *Celestial Mechanics* for Oboe and String Quartet (1990). **VOCAL:** *Occhi dell'alma mia* for High Voice and Guitar (1977); *Lyrikos* for Tenor and Orch. (1979); *The Pensive Traveller* for High Voice and Piano (1981); *Vox in Rama* for Double Chorus and Orch. (1983); *White Night* for Chorus (1984); *The Tenth Muse* for Soprano and Orch. (1986); *Ecstatic Songs*, part 1, for High Voice and Piano (1989); *The Cinnamon Peeler* for Mezzo-soprano and Chamber Ensemble (1993).

Croiza, Claire, French mezzo-soprano and teacher; b. Paris, Sept. 14, 1882; d. there, May 27, 1946. After training at the Paris Cons., she made her operatic debut in Nancy in 1905 in de Lara's *Messalina*. In 1906 she joined the Théâtre Royal de la Monnaie in Brussels. From 1908 she was a member of the Paris Opéra, where she was especially admired for her roles in operas by Gluck, Berlioz, Bizet, and Strauss. In 1922 she joined the faculty of the École Normale de Musique in Paris, and from 1934 she taught at the Paris Cons. Her performances of the French song repertory were highly regarded, particularly her interpretations of Fauré, Duparc, and Debussy. B. Bannerman ed. and tr. *The Singer as Interpreter: Claire Croiza's Master Classes* (London, 1989).

BIBL.: B. Bannerman, "Recollections of C. C.," *Bulletin of the British Institute of Recorded Sound*, no. 1 (1956); J.-M. Nectoux, ed., *C. C. 1882–1946* (Paris, 1984).

Crooks, Richard (Alexander), American tenor; b. Trenton, N.J., June 26, 1900; d. Portola Valley, Calif., Sept. 29, 1972. He studied voice with Sydney H. Bourne and also took lessons with Frank La Forge; was a boy soprano (later tenor) soloist in N.Y. churches. He made his debut with the N.Y. Sym. Orch. under Damrosch in 1922; then gave concerts in London,

Vienna, Munich, Berlin, and the U.S. (1925–27). On Sept. 20, 1927, he made his stage debut as Cavaradossi at the Hamburg Opera; made his American debut in the same role with the Philadelphia Grand Opera Co. (Nov. 27, 1930); made his debut at the Metropolitan Opera in N.Y. as Des Grieux (Feb. 25, 1933), where he continued to sing until 1942. He toured Australia (1936–39); gave concerts from coast to coast in the U.S. and Canada; appeared in recitals, as an orch. soloist, and in festivals.

Crosby, John (O'Hea), American conductor, opera impresario, and music educator; b. N.Y., July 12, 1926. He received instruction in violin and piano from his mother, and later studied composition with Hindemith at Yale Univ. (B.A., 1950) and conducting with Rudolph Thomas at Columbia Univ. and Monteux in Hancock, Maine. From 1951 to 1956 he was on the staff of the N.Y. City Opera. In 1956 he founded the Opera Assn. of New Mexico, later renamed the Santa Fe Opera. During his long tenure as its general director and resident conductor, he gave premiere performances of numerous operas by American and foreign composers. Crosby was also president of the Manhattan School of Music in N.Y. (1976–85) and of Opera America (from 1976).

Cross, Joan, English soprano, opera producer, and teacher; b. London, Sept. 7, 1900; d. Aldeburgh, Dec. 12, 1993. She received training from Holst at St. Paul's Girls School and from Dawson Freer at Trinity College of Music in London. In 1924 she became a member of the chorus at the Old Vic Theatre in London; in 1931 she joined the Sadler's Wells Opera in London, where she was principal soprano until 1946. In 1946 she helped to found the English Opera Group, with which she was active as both a soprano and producer. In 1948 she co-founded the Opera School, which became the National School of Opera in 1955. In 1951 she was made a Commander of the Order of the British Empire. Cross became particularly known for her roles in Britten's operas, in which she created Ellen Orford in *Peter Grimes* (1945), the Female Chorus in *The Rape of Lucretia* (1946), Lady Billows in *Albert Herring* (1947), Elizabeth I in *Gloriana* (1953), and Mrs. Grose in *The Turn of the Screw* (1954).

Cross, Lowell (Merlin), American composer and electro-musicologist; b. Kingsville, Texas, June 24, 1938. He studied mathematics and music at Texas Technological Univ., graduating in 1963; then entered the Univ. of Toronto, obtaining his M.A. in musicology in 1968; attended classes of Marshall McLuhan in environmental technology there; took a course in electronic music with Myron Schaeffer and Gustav Ciamaga. After teaching electronic music and working as a research assoc. at the electronic music studio there (1967–68), he was director and a teacher at the Mills Tape Music Center (1968–69) and a consulting artist and engineer with Experiments in Art and Technology, Inc. (1968–70). In 1971 he joined the faculty of the Univ. of Iowa, where he served as a prof. from 1981. Eschewing any preliminary serial experimentation, Cross espoused a cybernetic totality of audiovisual, electronic, and theatrical arts. He compiled a manual, *A Bibliography of Electronic Music* (Toronto, 1967; 3rd ed., rev., 1970). As a pioneer in astromusicology, he created the selenogeodesic score *Lunar Laser Beam* (broadcast as a salutatory message on Nicolas Slonimsky's 77th birthday, April 27, 1971, purportedly via Leningrad, the subject's birthplace; the Sea of Tranquillity on the moon; and the Ciudad de Nuestra Señora Reina de Los Angeles in California).

WORKS: *4 Random Studies* for Tape (1961); *0.8 Century* for Tape (1962); *Eclectic Music* for Flute and Piano (1964); *Antiphonies* for Tape (1964); *After Long Silence* for Soprano and Tape (1964); *3 Etudes* for Tape (1965); *Video I* and *II* for Variable Media, including Tape, Audio System, Oscilloscope, and Television (1965–68); *Musica Instrumentalis* for Acoustical Stereophonic Instruments, Monochrome and Polychrome Television (1965–68); *Video III* for Television and Phase-derived Audio System (1968); *Reunion* for Electronic Chessboard (constructed by Cross and first demonstrated in Toronto, March 5, 1968, the main opponents in the chess game being John Cage and Marcel Duchamp, who won readily); *Video/Laser I–IV* for Laser Deflection System (1969–80); *Electro-Acustica* for Instruments, Laser Deflection System, Television, and Phase-derived Audio System (1970–71).

Cross, Ronald, American instrumentalist, conductor, musicologist, and composer; b. Fort Worth, Texas, Feb. 18, 1929. He studied at the Guilmant Organ School in N.Y.; then received further training in organ from Harold Friedell in N.Y. and attended the master classes of E. Power Biggs and Virgil Fox; he also learned to play various wind and string instruments. He pursued his education at Centenary College of Louisiana (B.A., 1950) and took courses in musicology with Reese and Sachs, and in composition with Philip James at N.Y. Univ. (M.A., 1953; Ph.D., 1962); he also studied at the Venice Cons., the Univ. of Florence, the Accademia Musicale Chigiana in Siena, the Univ. of Siena, and the Univ. of Vienna (on a Fulbright fellowship, 1955–57). In addition to serving as an organist and choirmaster in N.Y. churches, he appeared in concerts as a keyboard, wind, and string player and as a conductor. After teaching at Notre Dame College of Staten Island (1958–68), he was an assoc. prof. (1968–75) and a prof. (from 1975) at Wagner College in N.Y., where he led its Collegium Musicum and later served as chairman of its music dept. (1981–84). His compositions include vocal and chamber pieces. He contributed articles to various publications and ed. the works of Mattaeus Pipelare (3 vols., Rome, 1966–67).

Crosse, Gordon, English composer; b. Bury, Lancashire, Dec. 1, 1937. He studied music history with Wellesz at the Univ. of Oxford (graduated, 1961), where he continued his research under Frank Harrison in 1961–62; he then studied with Petrassi at the Accademia di Santa Cecilia in Rome (1962). After working as senior music tutor in the extra-mural dept. at the Univ. of Birmingham (1964–66), he served as its Haywood fellow in music (1966–69). From 1969 to 1976 he was a fellow in music at the Univ. of Essex, and in 1973 composer-in-residence at King's College, Cambridge. In 1976 he was awarded the Cobbett Medal. In subsequent years, Crosse devoted himself to composition. His research into early music, combined with his love of literature, resulted in dramatic, vocal, and instrumental works notable for their rich expressivity in a strongly defined personal style.

WORKS: DRAMATIC: OPERAS: *Purgatory* (Cheltenham, July 7, 1966); *The Grace of Todd* (1967–68; Aldeburgh, June 7, 1969); *The Story of Vasco* (1968–73; London, March 13, 1974); *Potter Thompson* (1972–73; London, Jan. 9, 1975). **BALLETS:** *Wildboy* (Washington, D.C., Dec. 12, 1980); *Young Apollo* (London, Nov. 17, 1984). **ORCH.:** *Elegy* for Small Orch. (1959–61; Manchester, April 1962); 2 violin concertos: No. 1, *Concerto da camera* (1962; BBC, 1966; 1st concert perf., London, Feb. 18, 1968) and No. 2 (1969; Oxford, Jan. 29, 1970); Concerto for Chamber Orch. (1962; Budapest, July 3, 1968); *Symphonies* for Chamber Orch. (1964; Birmingham, Feb. 13, 1965); Sinfonia concertante (Cheltenham, Feb. 13, 1965; rev. as Sym. No. 1, 1975–76); *Ceremony* for Cello and Orch. (London, Aug. 4, 1966); *Ouvert: Clos* for Chamber Orch. (London, Sept. 15, 1969); *Some Marches on a Ground* (Norwich, Oct. 14, 1970); *Ariadne* for Oboe and Small Orch. (1971–72; Cheltenham, July 11, 1972); *Thel* for Flute, 2 Horns, and Strings (1974–76; Aldeburgh, June 27, 1978); *Epiphany Variations* or *Mag and Nunc* (1975); *Play Ground,* ballet suite (Manchester, March 2, 1978); *Dreamsongs* (Edinburgh, Aug. 20, 1979; based on the chamber piece, 1973); Cello Concerto, *In Memoriam Luigi Dallapiccola* (Cheltenham, July 7, 1979); *Elegy and Scherzo alla Marcia* for Strings (1980; Snape, June 24, 1981; adapted from the String Quartet, 1979); *Array* for Trumpet and Strings (London, Aug. 9, 1986); *Quiet!* for Wind Band (1987). **CHAMBER:** *Villanelles* for Wind Quintet, Violin, and Cello (1959; rev. version, London, Nov. 23, 1974); *3 Inventions* for Flute and Clarinet (1959); *Canto* for 6 Instruments (1961; rev. 1963); 2 sets of *Studies* for String Quartet (1972–73; 1977); *Dreamsongs* for Clarinet, Oboe,

Bassoon, and Piano (1973; also for Orch., 1979); String Quartet (1979; London, Nov. 24, 1980); *Rhymes and Reasons*, trio for Clarinet, Cello, and Piano (1980; Huntingdon, Nov. 17, 1982); *Peace for Brass* for 10 Instruments (1980; King's Lynn, July 29, 1981); *Fear No More* for Oboe, Oboe d'amore, and English Horn (1980; London, Oct. 5, 1981); *A Wake* for Flute, Clarinet, Cello, and Piano (Aldeburgh, June 16, 1982); *Watermusic* for Treble, Descant, and Sopranino Recorders and Piano (Glasgow, Dec. 3, 1982); *Wavesongs* for Cello and Piano (Oxford, Oct. 30, 1983); *Chime* for 2 Trumpets, Trombone, Horn, and Tuba (1983); Trio for Violin, Cello, and Piano (1985; London, April 4, 1986); Oboe Quintet (Birmingham, Dec. 3, 1988). **VOCAL:** *Corpus Christi Carol* for Soprano or Tenor, Clarinet, and String Quartet (1961; London, Dec. 18, 1964); *For the Unfallen* for Tenor, Horn, and Strings (1963; Liverpool, Sept. 17, 1968); *Changes: A Nocturnal Cycle* for Solo Voices and Orch. (1965–66); *The Covenant of the Rainbow* for Chorus, Organ, and Piano, 4-hands (Northampton, Sept. 20, 1968); *Memories of Morning: Night* for Mezzo-soprano and Orch. (London, Dec. 8, 1971); *Celebration* for Unison Voices, Mixed Chorus, and Orch. (1972; London, Sept. 16, 1974); *World Within* for Narrator, Mezzo-soprano, and 10 Instruments (1976; London, April 17, 1977); *Verses in Memoriam David Munrow* for Countertenor, Recorder, Cello, and Harpsichord (1979); *Voices from the Tomb* for Medium Voice and Piano (1979; London, Oct. 21, 1980); *Harvest Songs* for Double Chorus, Junior Chorus, and Orch. (Manchester, July 18, 1980); *Dreamcanon* for Alto, Chorus, Piano, Electric Piano, and Percussion (London, Nov. 11, 1981); *Wintersong* for 6 Soloists and Optional Percussion (London, Nov. 26, 1982); *A Wake Again* for 2 Countertenors, 2 Recorders, Cello, and Harpsichord (1985; N.Y., April 13, 1986); *Armada Echoes* for 2 Countertenors, Tenor, 2 Baritones, and Bass (Plymouth, July 10, 1988). **OTHER:** *Meet My Folks!* for Speaker, Children's Voices, and 8 Instruments (1964); *Rats Away!* for Children's Voices and 6 Instruments (1964); *Ahmet the Woodseller* for Unison Voices, Percussion, and 8 Instruments (1964–65); *The Demon of Adachigahara* for Narrator, Children's Voices, and Orch. (1967); *Wheel of the World*, entertainment (1969–72; Aldeburgh, June 5, 1972); *The History of the Flood* for Children's Voices and Harp (1970); *Matthew Mark Luke and John* for Children's Chorus and Harp (London, Dec. 6, 1970); *Holly from the Bongs*, nativity (1973; Manchester, Dec. 9, 1974).

Crossley, Paul (Christopher Richard), English pianist; b. Dewsbury, Yorkshire, May 17, 1944. He was an organ scholar at Mansfield College, Oxford; also studied piano with Fanny Waterman in Leeds. In 1967 he received a scholarship from the French government to continue his studies with Messiaen and Yvonne Loriod. In 1968 he made his first major tour, garnering praise in England and on the Continent. In subsequent years, he performed regularly in England, and also made tours of Europe, North America, and Japan, often in programs of contemporary works. From 1988 to 1994 he was joint artistic director of the London Sinfonietta. Among composers whose works he has championed are Fauré, Ravel, Berg, Janáček, Poulenc, Messiaen, and Tippett.

Crossley-Holland, Peter, English ethnomusicologist and composer; b. London, Jan. 28, 1916. He studied physiology at St. John's College, Oxford (B.A., 1936; M.A., 1941); then took courses in composition with Ireland, Seiber, and Julius Harrison at the Royal College of Music in London (B.Mus., 1943); subsequently pursued postgraduate work in Indian music at the London School of Oriental and African Studies. From 1943 to 1945 he was regional director of the British Arts Council; from 1948 to 1963 he was engaged in the music division of the BBC; then became assistant director of the Inst. of Comparative Music Studies and Documentation in Berlin. In 1969 he joined the faculty at the Univ. of Calif. at Los Angeles; he became a prof. there in 1972, retiring in 1984. In 1965 he became ed. of the *Journal of the International Folk Music Council.* As an ethnomusicologist, Crossley-Holland concentrated mostly on Celtic, Tibetan, and native American music. He ed. *Music in Wales* (London, 1948) and *Artistic Values in Traditional Music* (Berlin, 1966); also publ. *Music: A Report on Musical Life in England* (London, 1949). He also composed songs and pieces for chorus and for recorders.

Crozier, Catharine, esteemed American organist and pedagogue; b. Hobart, Okla., Jan. 18, 1914. She was educated at the Eastman School of Music in Rochester, N.Y. (B.M., 1936; artist's diploma, 1938; M.M., 1941); among her mentors were Joseph Bonnet, Yella Pessl, and **Harold Gleason**, to whom she was later married. In 1941 she made her formal debut at the Washington (D.C.) National Cathedral. After World War II, she pursued an international career as a concert organist. She taught organ (1938–55) and was head of the organ dept. (1953–55) at the Eastman School of Music; then served as prof. of organ at Rollins College in Winter Park, Fla. (1955–69). She maintained an exhaustive repertory, which she fully committed to memory. She particularly championed the cause of contemporary organ music.

Cruft, Adrian (Francis), English double-bass player, teacher, and composer; b. Mitcham, Surrey, Feb. 10, 1921; d. Hill Head, Hampshire, Feb. 20, 1987. He first studied double bass with his father, Eugene (John) Cruft (b. London, 1887; d. there, June 4, 1976). In 1938 he was awarded the Boult conducting scholarship at the Royal College of Music in London, where he studied conducting with W.H. Reed and Reginald Goodall, clarinet with Frederick Thurston, piano with Arthur Benjamin, and composition with Jacob and Rubbra. From 1947 to 1969 he played double bass in various London orchs. In 1966 he was chairman of the Composer's Guild of Great Britain. In 1972 he became a prof. of theory and composition at the Royal College of Music, and also taught at the Guildhall School of Music in London (1972–75). His output followed along traditional lines.

WORKS: *Partita* for Small Orch. (1951); *Actaeon*, overture (1952); Concertino for Clarinet and Strings (1955); *Divertissement* for Orch. (1959); *Tamburlaine*, overture (1962); *Prospero's Island*, fantasy overture (1962); *Divertimento* for String Orch. (1963); *Meditation on the Passion Chorale* for String Orch. (1973); orch. suites; much brass music, including pieces for band and other ensembles; chamber music; sacred and secular choral works; many pieces for young performers, including the melodrama *The Horse Trough* (1974), the vaudeville opera *The Eatanswill Election* (1981), and the "operina" *Dr. Syn* (1983).

Crumb, George (Henry, Jr.), distinguished and innovative American composer; b. Charleston, W.Va., Oct. 24, 1929. He studied music at home; began composing while in school, and had some of his pieces performed by the Charleston Sym. Orch. He then took courses in composition at Mason College in Charleston (B.M., 1950); later enrolled at the Univ. of Ill. (M.M., 1952) and continued his studies in composition with Finney at the Univ. of Mich. (D.M.A., 1959); in 1955 he received a Fulbright fellowship for travel to Germany, where he studied with Blacher at the Berlin Hochschule für Musik. He further received grants from the Rockefeller (1964), Koussevitzky (1965), and Coolidge (1970) foundations; in 1967 he held a Guggenheim fellowship, and also was given the National Inst. of Arts and Letters Award. In 1968 he was awarded the Pulitzer Prize in Music for his *Echoes of Time and the River.* From 1959 to 1964 he taught piano and occasional classes in composition at the Univ. of Colo. in Boulder; in 1965 he joined the music dept. of the Univ. of Pa. where he was subsequently the Annenberg Prof. of the Humanities (1983–96). In his music, Crumb is a universalist. Nothing in the realm of sound is alien to him; no method of composition is unsuited to his artistic purposes; accordingly, his music can sing as sweetly as the proverbial nightingale, and it can be as rough, rude, and crude as a primitive man of the mountains. His vocal parts especially demand extraordinary skills of lungs, lips, tongue, and larynx to produce such sound effects as percussive tongue clicks, explosive shrieks, hissing, whistling, whispering, and sudden shouting of verbal irrelevancies, interspersed with portentous syllabification, disparate phonemes, and rhetorical logorrhea. In startling contrast, Crumb injects into his sonorous kaleidoscope citations from popular works, such as the middle section of Chopin's *Fantaisie-Impromptu*, Ravel's *Bolero*, or some other "objet trouvé." In his instrumentations, Crumb is no less unconventional. Among the many unusual effects to be found in his scores is an instruction to the percussion player to immerse the loudly sounding gong into a tub of water, having an electric guitar played with glass rods over the frets, or telling wind instrumentalists to blow soundlessly through their tubes. Spatial distribution also plays a role: instrumentalists and singers are assigned their reciprocal locations on the podium or in the hall. Like many composers who began their work around the middle of the 20th century, Crumb first adopted the Schoenbergian idiom, seasoned with pointillistic devices. After these preliminaries, he wrote his unmistakably individual *Madrigals*, to words by Federico García Lorca, scored for voice and instrumental groups. There followed his extraordinary *Ancient Voices of Children*, performed for the first time at a chamber music festival in Washington, D.C., on Oct. 31, 1970; the text is again by Lorca; a female singer intones into the space under the lid of an amplified grand piano; a boy's voice responds in anguish; the accompaniment is supplied by an orch. group and an assortment of exotic percussion instruments, such as Tibetan prayer stones, Japanese temple bells, a musical saw, and a toy piano. His equally remarkable *Makrokosmos* calls for equally unusual effects; in several movements, the pianist is instructed to vocalize at specified points of time. Crumb's most grandiose creation is *Star-Child*, which calls for gargantuan forces, including a large orch., 2 children's choruses, and 8 additional percussion players performing on all kinds of utensils, such as pot lids, and also iron chains and metal sheets, as well as ordinary drums; it had its first performance under the direction of Pierre Boulez with the N.Y. Phil. on May 5, 1977.

WORKS: Sonata for Solo Cello (1955); *Variazioni* for Orch. (1959; Cincinnati, May 8, 1965); *5 Pieces for Piano* (1962); *Night Music I* for Soprano, Piano or Celesta, and Percussion, after Federico García Lorca (1963; Paris, Jan. 30, 1964); *4 Nocturnes (Night Music II)* for Violin and Piano (1963; Buffalo, N.Y., Feb. 3, 1965); *Madrigals, Book I* for Soprano, Contrabass, and Vibraphone, after García Lorca (1965; Philadelphia, Feb. 18, 1966); *Madrigals, Book II* for Soprano, Flute, and Percussion, after García Lorca (1965; Washington, D.C., March 11, 1966); *11 Echoes of Autumn, 1965 (Echoes I)* for Violin, Alto Flute, Clarinet, and Piano (Brunswick, Maine, Aug. 10, 1966); *Echoes of Time and the River (Echoes II: 4 Processionals for Orchestra)* (Chicago, May 26, 1967); *Songs, Drones, and Refrains of Death* for Baritone, Electric Guitar, Electric Contrabass, Amplified Piano (and Amplified Harpsichord), and 2 Percussionists, after García Lorca (1968; Iowa City, Iowa, March 29, 1969); *Madrigals, Book III* for Soprano, Harp, and 1 Percussion Player, after García Lorca (1969; Seattle, March 6, 1970); *Madrigals, Book IV* for Soprano, Flute, Harp, Contrabass, and Percussion, after García Lorca (1969; Seattle, March 6, 1970); *Night of the 4 Moons* for Alto, Alto Flute, Banjo, Electric Cello, and Percussion, after García Lorca (Washington, Pa., Nov. 6, 1969); *Black Angels (13 Images from the Dark Land: Images I)* for Electric String Quartet (Ann Arbor, Mich., Oct. 23, 1970); *Ancient Voices of Children* for Soprano, Boy Soprano, Oboe, Mandolin, Harp, Electric Piano (and Toy Piano), and 3 Percussionists, after García Lorca (Washington, D.C., Oct. 31, 1970); *Lux aeterna* for 5 Masked Players for Soprano, Bass Flute (and Soprano Recorder), Sitar, and 2 Percussionists (1971; Richmond, Va., Jan. 16, 1972); *Vox balaenae (Voice of the Whale)* for 3 Masked Players for Electric Flute, Electric Cello, and Amplified Piano (1971; Washington, D.C., March 17, 1972); *Makrokosmos, Volume I (12 Fantasy-Pieces after the Zodiac for Amplified Piano)* (1972; Colorado Springs, Feb. 8, 1973); *Makrokosmos, Volume II (12 Fantasy-Pieces after the Zodiac for Amplified Piano)* (1973; N.Y., Nov. 12, 1974); *Music for a Summer Evening (Makrokosmos III)* for 2 Amplified Pianos and 2 Percussionists (Swarthmore, Pa., March 30, 1974); *Dream Sequence (Images II)* for Violin, Cello, Piano, Percussion, and 2 Offstage Musicians playing Glass Harmonica (1976); *Star-Child*, parable for Soprano, Antiphonal Children's Voices, Men's Speaking Chorus, Bell Ringers, and Large Orch., demanding the coordinating abilities of 4 conductors (N.Y., May 5, 1977, under the general direction of Pierre Boulez); *Celestial Mechanics (Makrokosmos IV)*, cosmic dances for Amplified Piano, 4-hands (N.Y., Nov. 18, 1979); *Apparition*, elegiac songs and vocalises for Soprano and Amplified Piano, after Walt Whitman (1979; N.Y., Jan. 13, 1981); *A Little Suite for Christmas, A.D. 1979* for Piano (Washington, D.C., Dec. 14, 1980); *Gnomic Variations* for Piano (1981); *Pastoral Drone* for Organ (1982); *Processional* for Piano (1983); *A Haunted Landscape* for Orch. (N.Y., June 7, 1984); *The Sleeper* for Mezzo-soprano and Piano, after Poe (N.Y., Dec. 4, 1984); *An Idyll for the Misbegotten* for Amplified Flute and 3 Percussionists (1985; Toronto, Nov. 16, 1986); *Federico's Little Songs for Children* for Soprano, Flute, and Percussion, after Lorca (1986; Philadelphia, June 12, 1988); *Zeitgeist* for 2 Amplified Pianos (1987; Duisburg, Jan. 17, 1988); *Quest* for Guitar, Soprano Saxophone, 2 Percussion, Harp, and Contrabass (1990; rev. version, Vienna, Oct. 31, 1994); *Easter Dawning* for Carillon (1991; Dayton, Ohio, June 12, 1992).

BIBL.: D. Cope, *G. C.: A Biography* (N.Y., 1984; with annotated list of works compiled by D. Gillespie); D. Gillespie, ed., *G. C.: Profile of a Composer* (N.Y., 1986).

Cruz, Ivo, Portuguese conductor, music educator, and composer; b. Corumbá, Brazil, May 19, 1901; d. Lisbon, Sept. 8, 1985. He was trained in law at the Univ. of Lisbon (1919–24); then pursued studies in conducting and composition with Richard Mors and August Reuss in Munich (1925–30), where he also studied musicology at the Univ. He was founder-conductor of the Lisbon Phil. (1937–71) and director of the Lisbon Cons. (1938–71).

WORKS: BALLET: *Pastoral: Poemas de amore e saudade* (1942). **ORCH.:** *Nocturnos da Lusitania* (1928); 2 piano concertos: No. 1, *Coimbra* (1945) and No. 2, *Lisboa* (1946); 2 syms.: *Sinfonia de Amadis* (1952) and *Sinfonia de Quelez* (1964); *Idilio de Miraflores* (1952). **CHAMBER:** Violin Sonata (1922); piano pieces. **VOCAL:** Song cycles and solo songs.

Cruz-Romo, Gilda, Mexican soprano; b. Guadalajara, Feb. 12, 1940. She studied at the Cons. of Mexico, making her debut there in 1962. On May 8, 1970, she appeared at the Metropolitan Opera in N.Y. as Maddalena in *Andrea Chénier*, continued to sing there in subsequent seasons; also sang in Chicago, Houston, and Dallas. In Europe, she appeared in London, Milan, Moscow, Paris, and Vienna. Her large repertory included both Verdi Leonoras, Violetta, Amelia, Aida, Elisabeth de Valois, Cherubini's Medea, Donna Anna, Cio-Cio San, Manon, Suor Angelica, and Tosca.

Crzellitzer, Franz, German-born Israeli composer; b. Berlin-Charlottenburg, Nov. 1, 1905; d. Tel Aviv, Jan. 27, 1979. In 1934 he settled in Tel Aviv.

WORKS: BALLET-PANTOMIME: *The Pied Piper of Hamelin* (1944–46). **ORCH.:** *Charaktermarsch* (1939); 2 unnumbered syms. (1940–41; 1968–70); *Improvisation* (1951); *3 Suites* for Strings (1952; 1968–74; 1974); *2 Symphonic Fantasies* (1958, 1959); *Fantasy* for Violin and Orch. (1960); *Fantasy* for Cello and Orch. (1962); Concerto for 2 Pianos and Orch. (1966); Trumpet Concerto (1967); Viola Concerto (1967); *Capriccio* for Piano and Chamber Orch. (1970); Concertino for Clarinet and Strings (1971); *Concert Piece* for Trombone and Orch. (1971); *Sinfonietta* (1972); *Concert Piece* for Horn, Clarinet, and Strings (1972); *Die Wüste* (1974); Concertino for Bassoon and Strings (1975); Concertino for Flute and Strings (1975); Concertino for Violin and Strings (1976); *Concert Piece* for Organ and Orch. (1976); *Concert Piece* (1977). **CHAMBER:** 2 violin sonatas (1948); Piano Quintet (1949); 2 string quartets (1954, 1963); Oboe Quartet (1955); Wind Quintet (1966); 2 piano trios (1968, 1971); Cello Sonata (1971); Flute Sonata (1972); Trio for Horn, Violin, and Piano (1973); Viola Sonata (1974); Brass Quintet

(1975). **KEYBOARD: PIANO:** *5 Preludes* (1947); *7 Preludes* (1968–69); *Theme and Variations* (1973); *Toccata and 2 Études* (1976). **ORGAN:** *Passacaglia* (1972).

Cuclin, Dimitrie, Romanian composer and pedagogue; b. Galați, April 5, 1885; d. Bucharest, Feb. 7, 1978. He studied with Kiriac, Castaldi, and Dinicu at the Bucharest Cons. (1904–07), and then in Paris at the Cons. and at the Schola Cantorum with Widor and d'Indy (1908–14). After teaching at the Brooklyn College of Music (1922–30), he returned to his homeland to serve as a prof. at the Bucharest Cons. (1930–48). His prolific output reflected the influence of the French and German Romantic tradition.

WORKS: DRAMATIC: OPERAS: *Soria* (1910–11); *Traian și Dochia* (1921); *Agamemnon* (1922); *Bellérophon* (1925); *Meleagridele* (1958). **BALLET:** *Tragedie în pădure* (1962). **ORCH.:** 20 syms. (1910–32; 1938; 1942; 1944; 1947; 1948; 1948; 1948; 1949; 1949; 1950; 1951; 1951; 1952; 1954; 1959; 1965; 1967; 1971; 1972); *Triptic* (1928); *Suite Miscellanea* (1932); Piano Concerto (1939); *Rapsodie prahoveană* (1944); *Dansuri românești* (1961); Clarinet Concerto (1968). **CHAMBER:** 3 string quartets (1913, 1948, 1949); Violin Sonata (1923); Trio for Piano, Violin, and Cello (1924); Sonata for Flute and Cello (1953); Trio for Clarinet, Trumpet, and Bassoon (1954); Quintet for Flute, English Horn, Piano, Trombone, and Tuba (1955); Quartet for 2 Violins, Viola, and Clarinet (1955); Trio for Harp, Cello, and Double Bass (1955); various suites; 5 piano sonatas (1909–57). **VOCAL:** *David și Goliath*, oratorio (1928); *Cetatea-i pe stîncă*, cantata (1959); many songs.

Cudworth, Charles (Cyril Leonard), English librarian and musicologist; b. Cambridge, Oct. 30, 1908; d. there, Dec. 26, 1977. He served at the Music Division of the Library of the Univ. of Cambridge from 1943; from 1946 to 1973 he was curator of the Pendlebury Library of Music there; in 1965 he was elected a Fellow of the Univ. College at Cambridge; in 1968 he was a visiting prof. at the Univ. of Southern Calif. in Los Angeles. His specialty was the music of the 18th century. He publ. *Thematic Index of English Eighteenth Century Overtures and Symphonies* (London, 1953) and *Handel* (London, 1972); he also contributed numerous valuable articles to British and American music journals.

BIBL.: C. Hogwood and R. Luckett, eds., *Music in Eighteenth-century England: Essays in Memory of C. C.* (Cambridge, 1983).

Cuénod, Hugues (-Adhémar), notable Swiss tenor; b. Corseaux-sur-Vevey, June 26, 1902. He received training at the Ribaupierre Institut in Lausanne, at the conservatories in Geneva and Basel, and in Vienna. He commenced his career as a concert singer. In 1928 he made his stage debut in *Jonny spielt auf* in Paris, and in 1929 he sang for the first time in the U.S. in *Bitter Sweet.* From 1930 to 1933 he was active in Geneva, and then in Paris from 1934 to 1937. During the 1937–39 seasons, he made an extensive concert tour of North America. From 1940 to 1946 he taught at the Geneva Cons. In 1943 he resumed his operatic career singing in *Die Fledermaus* in Geneva. He subsequently sang at Milan's La Scala (1951), the Glyndebourne Festival (from 1954), and London's Covent Garden (1954, 1956, 1958). Cuénod pursued his career into old age, making his belated debut at the Metropolitan Opera in N.Y. as the Emperor in *Turandot* just 3 months before his 85th birthday. In his 87th year, he appeared as Monsieur Taupe in *Capriccio* at the Geneva Opera in 1989. Among his finest roles were Mozart's Basilio, the Astrologer in *The Golden Cockerel*, and Sellem in *The Rake's Progress.* He was particularly known for his championship of early music and of the French song repertory.

Cugley, Ian (Robert), Australian composer; b. Melbourne, June 22, 1945. He studied with Sculthorpe and Maxwell Davies at the Univ. of Sydney (1963–66). In 1967 he was appointed to the faculty of the Univ. of Tasmania; he also was percussionist in the Tasmanian Sym. Orch., and organized Spectrum, a contemporary music ensemble. His music represents a curious polarization of techniques, in which starkly primitive melorhythms enter a tangential relationship with total serialism.

WORKS: *Variations* for Flute, Oboe, and Horn (1963); *Adagio* for 4 Horns or String Quartet (1964); *Pan, the Lake* for Flute, Horn, Cello, Strings, and Percussion, including 8 Indonesian Kulintang Gongs (1965); Prelude for Orch. (1965); Sonata for Flute, Viola, and Guitar or Harp (1966); *Canticle of All Created Things* for Chorus, Harp, and Percussion (1966); *Canticle II (In Cenerem Reverteris)* for Soli, Chorus, and Orch. (1967); *5 Variants* for Strings (1968); *3 Pieces* for Chamber Orch. (1968); *The 6 Days of Creation*, cantata (1969); Chamber Symphony for 11 Wind Instruments (1971); *Aquarelles* for Piano (1972); Sonata Movement for Violin and Piano (1972); Violin Concerto (1973); numerous works for school orchs.; 3 electronic studies (1967–72); sacred music.

Culp, Julia, Dutch contralto; b. Groningen, Oct. 6, 1880; d. Amsterdam, Oct. 13, 1970. She first studied violin as a child; then became a voice pupil of Cornelia van Zanten at the Amsterdam Cons. (1897), and later of Etelka Gerster in Berlin. She made her formal debut in Magdeburg in 1901; her tours of Germany, Austria, the Netherlands, France, Spain, and Russia were highly successful, establishing her as one of the finest singers of German lieder. Her American debut took place in N.Y. on Jan. 10, 1913; for many years, she visited the U.S. every season.

Culshaw, John (Royds), English recording producer; b. London, May 28, 1924; d. there, April 27, 1980. He studied music while serving in the British army. From 1954 to 1967 he was manager and chief producer with the Decca Record Co.; from 1967 to 1975 he held the same post with the BBC. He was awarded the rank of Officer of the Order of the British Empire in 1966. He made a mark in the recording industry by introducing the stereo-reproduction process, which created a 3-dimensional effect. His principal achievement was the stereophonic recording of *Der Ring des Nibelungen*, issued by Decca under the direction of Solti. Culshaw related the background of this undertaking in his books *Ring Resounding* (London, 1967) and *Reflections on Wagner's Ring* (London, 1976). His other publications are *Sergei Rachmaninov* (London, 1949) and *A Century of Music* (London, 1952). He also publ. an autobiography, *Odyssey of a Recording Pioneer: Putting the Record Straight* (N.Y., 1981).

Culver, (David) Andrew, inventive American-Canadian composer, instrument maker, and performer; b. Morristown, N.J., Aug. 30, 1953. He studied composition with John Rea and Bengt Hambraeus, electronic music with Alcides Lanza, and sound recording with Wieslaw Woczcyk at McGill Univ. in Montreal (B.M., 1977; M.M., 1980); subsequently he was a founding member of SONDE, a Canadian music design and performance ensemble. He pioneered the musical application of R. Buckminster Fuller's tensegrity structural principle, devising richly resonant music sculptures that vibrate synergistically. His output takes 4 forms: stage performances by music sculpture ensemble, interactive music sculpture installations, computer-displayed text and electroacoustic music projections, and scores for traditional instruments. His solo stage works include *Viti* (1981) and *Music with Tensegrity Sound Source #5* (1983), which he has performed in Europe, Canada, and the U.S.; his *Hard Lake Frozen Moon* (1989), for 2 performers active in an elaborate stage environment built up of 19 sound sources, was commissioned by Toronto's New Music Concerts and the Laidlaw Foundation. His *Quasicrystals . . .* (1989), developed with pianist Thomas Moore at the Yellow Springs Inst. for Contemporary Studies and the Arts, is a work for 2 performers on separate and complex itineraries within a field of 21 amplified, hanging music sculptures. Chance-composed lighting is an essential, determining element of these and other works. Culver has also created public installations of interactive music sculptures, including those at the Staten Island Children's Museum (1983) and the Children's Museum of Manhattan (1989–91). From 1984 to 1992, Culver worked with John Cage, developing computer programs toward the realization of Cage's musical and poetic processes. His programs ic and tic, computer simulations of the coin oracle of the *I Ching*, were used in all aspects of the composition and direction of Cage's *Europeras 1 & 2* (1987).

Cummings, David (Michael), English music lexicographer; b. London, Oct. 10, 1942. After taking his B.Ed. degree at Sidney Webb College in London (1975), he entered the mundane profession of British schoolteacher. His passion for music and its elucidation led him to wade perilously in the backwaters of musicography with the ineluctable mission to correct the errors of his predecessors and contemporaries. From 1980 he served as an advisor and contributor to various standard music reference works, and also wrote articles and reviews for music journals. He was ed. of *The New Everyman Dictionary of Music* (6th ed., 1988; new ed., rev., 1995 as *The Hutchinson Encyclopedia of Music*). With D. McIntire, he was co-consultant ed. of the *International Who's Who in Music* (12th ed., 1990), and subsequently served as its ed. (14th and 15th eds., 1992–96).

Cundell, Edric, English composer and conductor; b. London, Jan. 29, 1893; d. Ashwell, Hertfordshire, March 19, 1961. He studied at Trinity College of Music in London, where he later taught; was active as a horn player and pianist, and also conducted amateur groups. In 1935 he founded the Edric Cundell Chamber Orch.; in 1938 he was made director of the Guildhall School of Music in London; retired in 1959. In 1949 he was made a Commander of the Order of the British Empire.

WORKS: Sym.; symphonic poems: *Serbia* (1919) and *The Tragedy of Deirdre* (1922); *Our Dead* for Tenor and Orch. (1922); Piano Concerto; Piano Quartet, String Sextet, String Quartet, Rhapsody for Viola and Piano; piano pieces; songs.

Cunningham, Arthur, black American composer; b. Piermont, N.Y., Nov. 11, 1928. He commenced piano studies at the age of 6 and was composing for his own jazz group when he was 12; he later received formal training at Fisk Univ. (B.A., 1951), Columbia Univ. Teachers College (M.A., 1957), and the Juilliard School of Music. In addition to composing, he was active as a teacher and conductor. His output runs the gamut of styles and techniques, ranging from serious to rock.

WORKS: *Adagio* for Oboe and Strings (1954); *Night Lights* for Orch. (1955); *Lights across the Hudson*, tone poem (1956); *The Beauty Part*, musical (1963); *Violetta*, musical (1963); *Dialogues* for Piano and Chamber Orch. (1966); *Ballet* for String Quartet and Jazz Quartet (1968); *His Natural Grace*, rock opera (1969); *Harlem Suite*, ballet (1971); Double-bass Concerto (1971); *The Prince* for Baritone and Orch. (1973); *Rooster Rhapsody* for Narrator and Orch. (1975); *Crispus Attucks* for Band (1976); *Night Bird* for Voice, Jazz Quintet, and Orch. (1978); also chamber pieces, piano pieces, choral part songs and suites, and songs.

Curran, Alvin, American composer; b. Providence, R.I., Dec. 13, 1938. He studied piano and trombone in his youth, later receiving training in composition from Ron Nelson at Brown Univ. (B.A., 1960) and from Carter and Powell at Yale Univ. (M.Mus., 1963). He went to Rome (1965), where he founded the Musica Elettronica Viva ensemble for the performance of live electronic music with Richard Teitelbaum and Frederic Rzewski; the ensemble later evolved to include all manner of avant-garde performance practices. His compositions range from tape works to experimental pieces using the natural environment.

WORKS: *Music for Every Occasion*, 50 monodic pieces for Any Use (1967–77); *Songs and Views from the Magnetic Garden* for Voice, Flugelhorn, Synthesizer, and Tape (1973–75); *Light Flowers, Dark Flowers* for Piano, Ocarina, Synthesizer, and Tape (1974–77); *The Works* for Voice, Piano, Synthesizer, and Tape (1977–80); *The Crossing* for 4 Sopranos, Chorus, 7 Instruments, and Tape (1978); *Maritime Rites*, environmental concerts for Choruses in Rowboats, Ship, and Foghorns (1981); *Natural History* for Tape (1984); *Maritime Rites Satellite Music*, 10 radio concerts for the Sounds of the Eastern U.S. Seaboard and Soloists (1984–85); *Electric Rags I* for Piano and Computer-controlled Synthesizers (1985) and *II* for Saxophone Quartet and Computer Electronics (1989); *For Four or More* for Amplified String Quartet and Computer-controlled Synthesizers (1986); *Waterworks* for 22 Computer-controlled Ship Horns, Brass Bands, and Fireworks (1987); *Edible Weeds* for String Quartet, Flute, Oboe, Clarinet, Bassoon, Trombone, Electric Bass, and Keyboards (1988); *Crystal Psalms* for 6 Choruses, Percussion, Instrumental Ensembles, Accordions, Shofars, and Tape (1988); *Vsto for Giacinto* for String Quartet (1989); *7 Articles* for 10 Instruments (1989).

Curry, Arthur Mansfield, American composer and pedagogue; b. Chelsea, Mass., Jan. 27, 1866; d. Atlanta, Dec. 30, 1953. He studied with Franz Kneisel (violin) and Edward MacDowell (composition); taught at the New England Cons. of Music in Boston (1915–39).

WORKS: *Blomidon*, overture (Worcester, Mass., 1902); *Atala*, symphonic poem (Boston, April 21, 1911); *The Winning of Amarac*, Celtic legend for Narrator, Women's Chorus, and Orch. (Boston, 1934); choruses; piano pieces; many songs.

Curtin, Phyllis (née **Smith**), esteemed American soprano and teacher; b. Clarksburg, W.Va., Dec. 3, 1921. She studied at Wellesley College (B.A., 1943) and received vocal instruction from Olga Avierino, Joseph Regnaeas, and Goldovsky. In 1946 she made her operatic debut as Lisa in *The Queen of Spades* with the New England Opera Theatre in Boston. Her recital debut followed in 1950 at N.Y.'s Town Hall. On Oct. 22, 1953, she made her first appearance with the N.Y. City Opera as Fräulein Burstner in Gottfried von Einem's *The Trial*, where she remained on the roster until 1960; then returned in 1962, 1964, and 1975–76. She also made appearances at the Teatro Colón in Buenos Aires (1959), the Glyndebourne Festival (1959), the Vienna State Opera (1960–61), and at La Scala in Milan (1962). On Nov. 4, 1961, she made her Metropolitan Opera debut in N.Y. as Fiordiligi, remaining on its roster for the season; she returned for the 1966–70 and 1972–73 seasons. Her tours as a soloist with orchs. and as a recitalist took her all over the globe until her retirement in 1984. She taught at the Aspen (Colo) School of Music and the Berkshire Music Center in Tanglewood. After serving as prof. of voice at the Yale Univ. School of Music (1974–83), she was prof. of voice and dean of the school of the arts at Boston Univ. (from 1983); in 1992 she retired as its dean but continued to teach there. Curtin became well known for such roles as Mozart's Countess, Donna Anna, Rosalinde, Eva, Violetta, Alice Ford, Salome, and Ellen Orford. She also created Floyd's Susannah (1955) and Cathy in *Wuthering Heights* (1958).

Curtis, Alan (Stanley), American musicologist, harpsichordist, fortepianist, and conductor; b. Mason, Mich., Nov. 17, 1934. He studied at Michigan State Univ. (B.Mus., 1955) and the Univ. of Ill. (M.Mus., 1956; Ph.D., 1963); also studied harpsichord with Gustav Leonhardt in Amsterdam (1957–59). He joined the faculty of the Univ. of Calif. at Berkeley in 1960, becoming a full prof. in 1970. As a conductor, Curtis became well known as a specialist in 17th and 18th century opera, leading performances throughout Europe and the U.S. He wrote *Sweelinck's Keyboard Music: A Study of English Elements in Seventeenth-century Dutch Composition* (London and Leiden, 1969); he also ed. *Pièces de clavecin* by L. Couperin (1970) and by Balbastre (1980), and Monteverdi's *L'incoronazione di Poppea* (1989).

Curtiss, Mina (née **Kirstein**), American writer on music; b. Boston, Oct. 13, 1896; d. Bridgeport, Conn., Nov. 1, 1985. She was educated at Smith College (M.A., 1918), where she later was an assoc. prof. of English literature (1920–34). Apart from her literary publications, she contributed articles to the *Musical Quarterly*; she also wrote *Bizet and His World* (N.Y., 1958). In 1977 she publ. a memoir, *Other People's Letters*.

Curtis-Smith, Curtis O(tto) B(ismarck), American composer, pianist, and teacher; b. Walla Walla, Wash., Sept. 9, 1941. He studied piano with David Burge at Whitman (Wash.) College (1960–62) and Gui Mombaerts at Northwestern Univ. (B.M.,

1964; M.M., 1965), and composition with Kenneth Gaburo (1966) and Bruno Maderna (1972) at the Berkshire Music Center in Tanglewood. He taught at Western Michigan Univ. in Kalamazoo (from 1968), making concurrent appearances as a recitalist and soloist with various orchs. Among his honors are the Koussevitzky Prize (1972), the Gold Medal of the Concorso Internazionale di Musica e Danza G.B. Viotti (1975), NEA grants (1975, 1980), the Prix du Francis Salabert (1976), annual ASCAP awards (from 1977), a Guggenheim fellowship (1978–79), an American Academy and Inst. of Arts and Letters award (1978), and Michigan Council for the Arts grants (1981, 1984). In 1972 he developed the technique of "piano bowing," heard in his *Rhapsodies* and *Unisonics*, in which a fishing line is drawn across the strings of the instrument to produce continuous single and clustered pitches. He later utilized Sub-Saharan African polyrhythms and melodies.

WORKS: ORCH.: *Winter Pieces* for Chamber Orch. (1974); *(Bells) Belle de Jour* for Piano and Orch. (1974–75); *The Great American Symphony (GAS!)* (1981); *Songs and Cantillations* for Guitar and Orch. (1983); *Chaconne à son goût* (1984); *Celebration* (1986); *Passacaglia* (1986); *". . . Float Wild Birds, Sleeping"* (1988); Concerto for Piano, Left-hand, and Orch. (1990); Violin Concerto (1994). **CHAMBER:** 3 string quartets (1964, 1965, 1980); *A Song of the Degrees* for 2 Pianos and Percussion (1972); *5 Sonorous Inventions* for Violin and Piano (1973); *Unisonics* for Alto Saxophone and Piano (1977); *Partita* for Chamber Ensemble (1977); *Ensembles/Solos* for Piano and Chamber Ensemble (1977); *Tonalities* for Clarinet and Percussion (1978); *Plays and Rimes* for Piano and Brass Quintet (1979); *Sundry Dances* for Winds and Brass (1979–80); *Black and Blue* for Brass Quintet (1979); 2 piano trios (1982, 1992); *Ragmala: A Garland of Ragas* for Guitar and String Quartet (1983); *Sardonic Sketches* for Wind Quintet (1986); *Fantasy Pieces* for Violin and Piano (1987); *5 Pieces* for Piano and Percussion (1988); Sextet for Piano and Winds (1991); *African Laughter*, sextet for Flute, Oboe, Clarinet, Violin, Viola, Cello, and Piano (1994); pieces for solo instrument. **PIANO:** *Pianacaglia* (1967); *Trajectories* (1967–68); *Piece du jour* (1971); *Rhapsodies* (1973); *Tristana Variations* (1975–76); *For Gatsby (Steinway #81281)* (1982). **VOCAL:** *Till Thousands Thee. Lps. A Secular Alleluia without . . .* for 6 Sopranos, 2 Trumpets, and Percussion (1969); *Passant. Un. Nous passons. Deux. De notres somme passons. Trois.* for 19 Voices, Chamber Ensemble, and Electronics (1970); *Canticum Novum/Desideria* for 6 Sopranos, 4 Tenors, and Chamber Ensemble (1971); *Comedie* for 2 Sopranos and Chamber Orch. (1972); *Beastly Rhymes* for Chorus (1983–84); *Chansons innocentes* for Soprano and Piano (1987); *A Civil War Song Cycle* for Mezzo-soprano or Soprano and Piano (1987); *The Shimmer of Evil* for Baritone and Chamber Ensemble or Piano (1989); *The Mystic Trumpeter* for Baritone, Men's Chorus, Trumpet, and Organ (1991); *Gold Are My Flowers*, cantata/melodrama for Soprano, Baritone, and Chamber Group (1992). **OTHER:** Tape pieces.

Curzon, Sir Clifford (Michael), eminent English pianist; b. London, May 18, 1907; d. there, Sept. 1, 1982. His father was an antique dealer; both he and his wife were music-lovers and they encouraged their son's studies, first as a violinist, and then as a pianist. In 1919 he enrolled at the Royal Academy of Music in London, where he studied piano with Charles Reddie and Katharine Goodson; he won 2 scholarships and the Macfarren Gold Medal. At the age of 16, he garnered praise as a soloist in Bach's Triple Concerto at a Henry Wood Promenade Concert in London. He was only 19 when he was given a post as a teacher at the Royal Academy of Music, but he decided to continue his studies and went to Berlin (1928), where he was tutored by Schnabel, and then to Paris (1930), where he took courses with Landowska in harpsichord and with Boulanger in general music culture. On Feb. 26, 1939, he made an auspicious American debut in N.Y., and in subsequent years made regular concert tours in the U.S. Curzon was a scholarly virtuoso with a formidable technique. His interpretations of Mozart and Beethoven were particularly notable, but he also was praised for his congenial interpretations of works by Romantic composers, especially Schubert, Schumann, and Brahms. In 1958 he was made a Commander of the Order of the British Empire. He received the degree of D.Mus. *honoris causa* from the Univ. of Leeds in 1970. He was knighted in 1977. In 1980 he received the Gold Medal of the Royal Phil. Soc. in London. In 1931 he married **Luccile Wallace**.

Curzon, (Emmanuel-) Henri (-Parent) de, French music critic and writer; b. Le Havre, July 6, 1861; d. Paris, Feb. 25, 1942. He was keeper of the government archives at Paris from 1892 until 1926; then became librarian of the Opéra-Comique; also was music critic of the *Gazette de France* (1889–1918).

WRITING: *Les Dernières Années de Piccini à Paris* (1890); *La Légende de Sigurd dans l'Edda; L'Opéra d'Ernest Reyer* (1890); *Musiciens du temps passé* (1893); *Croquis d'artistes* (1898); *Les Lieder de Schubert* (1899); *État sommaire des pièces et documents concernant la musique* (1899); *Guide de l'amateur d'ouvrages sur la musique* (1901); *Felipe Pedrell et "Les Pyrénées"* (1902); *Les Lieder de Beethoven* (1905); *Essai de bibliographie mozartienne* (1906); *Grétry, biographie critique* (1907); *L'Évolution lyrique au théâtre* (1908); *Meyerbeer, Biographie critique* (1910); with A. Soubies, *Documents inédits sur le "Faust" de Gounod* (1912); *Mozart, Biographie critique* (1914); *Rossini* (1920); *L'Oeuvre de Richard Wagner à Paris et ses interprètes* (1920); *Ambroise Thomas* (1921); *Jean-Baptiste Fauré* (1923); *Ernest Reyer* (1924); *Jean Elleviou* (1930); *Cosima Wagner et Bayreuth* (1930); *Berlioz, L'Homme et le musicien* (1932).

Custer, Arthur, American composer; b. Manchester, Conn., April 21, 1923. He studied engineering at the Univ. of Hartford (1940–42); after graduating in music from the Univ. of Conn. at Storrs (1949), he pursued training with Pisk at the Univ. of Redlands in Calif. (1949–51), Bezanson at the Univ. of Iowa (1952–55), and Boulanger (1960–62). He taught at Kansas Wesleyan Univ. (1952–55) and the Univ. of Omaha (1955–58); then was assistant dean of fine arts at the Univ. of Rhode Island (1962–65) and dean of the Philadephia Musical Academy (1965–67). After serving as director of the St. Louis Metropolitan Educational Center for the Arts (1967–70), he was director (1970–73) and composer-in-residence (1973–75) of the Arts in Education Project of the Rhode Island State Council on the Arts.

WORKS: Sextet for Woodwinds and Piano (1959); *Colloquy* for String Quartet (1961); *Sinfonia de Madrid* (Madrid, April 28, 1962); *Cycle* for a Heterogeneous Ensemble (1963); Concertino for 2nd Violin and Strings, in reality his String Quartet No. 2 (1964); *2 Movements* for Wind Quintet (1964); *Permutations* for Violin, Clarinet, and Cello (1967); Concerto for Brass Quintet (1968); *Rhapsodality Brass!* for Orch. (1969); *Interface I* for String Quartet and 2 Recording Engineers, being his String Quartet No. 3 (1969) and *II* for Ensemble, Slide Projectors, and Audience (1976); *Rhapsodality Brown!* for Piano (1969); *Parabolas* for Trombone and Percussion (1969); *Parabolas* for Viola and Piano (1969); *Doubles* for Violin and Chamber Orch. (1972; rev. 1975); *Eyepiece* for Oboe and Tape (1974); *Sweet 16* for Clarinet and Piano (1976).

Cuvillier, Charles (Louis Paul), French composer; b. Paris, April 24, 1877; d. there, Feb. 14, 1955. He studied privately with Fauré and Messager, and with Massenet at the Paris Cons. He then devoted himself to the musical theater, bringing out his first light stage work, *Avant-hier matin* (Paris, Oct. 20, 1905; rev. version as *Les Adam*, Paris, Feb. 20, 1913). Its success led to the Parisian premieres of his *Son p'tit frère* (April 10, 1907; rev. version as *Laïs, ou la courtisane amoureuse*, 1930), *Afgar, ou Les Loisirs andalous* (April 10, 1909), and *Les Muscadines* (April 28, 1910; rev. version as *La Fausse Ingénue*, Paris, March 17, 1918). Following premieres of *L'Astronome et l'étoile* (Buenos Aires, July 1911) and *Les Trois Sultanes* (Monca, Jan. 1912), he brought out one of his most ambitious works, *Der lila Domino* (Leipzig, Feb. 3, 1912). His *Sappho* (Paris, Feb. 27, 1912; rev. version as *La République des vierges*, Paris, Sept. 6,

1917) was followed by his *La Reine s'amuse* (Marseilles, Dec. 31, 1912; rev. version as *La Reine joyeuse*, Paris, Nov. 1, 1918), a notably successful score which featured the famous waltz *Ah! la troublante volupté*. *La Reine s'amuse* was a great success in London in its adapted version as *The Naughty Princess*. Among Cuvillier's other stage works were *Flora Bella* (Munich, Sept. 5, 1913), *The Sunshine of the World* (London, Feb. 18, 1920), *Bob et moi* (Paris, April 6, 1924), *Qui êtes vous?* (Monte Carlo, Nov. 13, 1926), and *Boulard et ses filles* (Paris, Nov. 8, 1929).

Cuyler, Louise (Elvira), American musicologist; b. Omaha, March 14, 1908. She studied at the Eastman School of Music in Rochester, N.Y. (B.M., 1929; Ph.D., 1948) and at the Univ. of Mich. (M.M., 1933), where she was a member of the staff from 1929 to 1975, with wartime leave (1942–45) for service with the American Red Cross in the Pacific. In 1975 she went to Smith College as Neilson Distinguished Prof. She contributed a number of informative papers to various scholarly publications, among them "Mozart's Quartets Dedicated to Haydn" in the memorial vol. for Curt Sachs (N.Y., 1965) and "Music in Biographies of Emperor Maximilian" in the Festschrift for Gustave Reese (N.Y., 1966); she also ed. Isaac's *Choralis Constantinus*, Part III (Ann Arbor, Mich., 1950), and *Five Polyphonic Masses of Heinrich Isaac* (Ann Arbor, 1956). She publ. *The Emperor Maximilian I and Music* (London, 1973) and *The Symphony* (N.Y., 1973; 2nd ed., 1995).

BIBL.: E. Borroff, ed., *Notations and Editions: A Book in Honor of L. C.* (Dubuque, Iowa, 1974).

Czekanowska, Anna, Polish ethnomusicologist; b. Lwów, June 25, 1929. She studied with Chybiński at the Univ. of Poznán (1947–52) and with Chomiński at the Univ. of Warsaw (Ph.D., 1958; Habilitation, 1968). In 1969 she joined the ethnomusicology faculty at the Univ. of Warsaw and in 1975 became director of the Inst. of Musicology. Her research has focused on Slavonic music; among her publications are *Ethnografia muzyczna: Metodologia i metodyka* (Musical Ethnography: Methodology and Methods; 1971) and "Principles of Construction of Ancient Slavic Songs," *Narodno stvaraštvo* (1972).

Czerwenka, Oskar, Austrian bass; b. Vöcklabruck bei Linz, July 5, 1924. He was a student of O. Iro in Vienna. In 1947 he made his operatic debut as the Hermit in *Der Freischütz* in Graz. He joined the Vienna State Opera in 1951, where he became successful in such roles as Baron Ochs, Osmin, and Kecal in *The Bartered Bride*, and in operas by Lortzing; in 1961 he was made an Austrian Kammersänger. From 1953 he also appeared at the Salzburg Festival. In 1959 he sang Baron Ochs at the Glyndebourne Festival and, on Dec. 26 of that year, made his Metropolitan Opera debut in N.Y. in the same role. He also appeared in Hamburg, Berlin, Munich, Frankfurt am Main, Cologne, and Stuttgart. He also appeared widely as a concert artist. He publ. the book *Lebenszeiten-Ungebetene Briefe* (Vienna, 1987).

Cziffra, György, noted Hungarian-born French pianist; b. Budapest, Sept. 5, 1921; d. Morsang-sur-Orge, Jan. 15, 1994. He studied with Dohnányi at the Budapest Academy of Music; his education was interrupted by World War II, when he served in the Hungarian army; after the war, he continued his studies at the Budapest Academy of Music with Ferenczi, but was once more distracted from music when he was arrested in 1950 for his rebellious political views. He was released from jail in 1953, but was again endangered by the abortive Hungarian revolt in 1956. Convinced that he could have no peace under Communist rule, he went to Paris, where he made successful appearances as a pianist; in 1968 he became a naturalized French citizen. In 1973 he founded the St.-Frambourg Royal Chapel Foundation in Senlis to assist young musicians and artists. He was best known for his interpretations of works of the Romantic repertoire; especially brilliant were his renditions of the music of Liszt. He publ. *Des canons et des fleurs* (Paris, 1977).

Czukay, Holger, German new-wave composer; b. Danzig, March 24, 1938. A musical iconoclast, Czukay fell through the cracks of both jazz and classical instruction until he studied with Stockhausen (1962); he subsequently went to Switzerland, where he encountered rock music through the guitarist Michael Karoli, with whom he formed the pioneer new-wave group Can (1968–78). Can followed the early Stockhausen aesthetic, utilizing "found" music from shortwave radio as well as the techniques of tape splicing and the collage of ethnic music. Czukay anticipated trends in alternative pop music not apparent to most people until well into the 1980s; the ethnic-based constructions in his Forgery series of the 1970s were acknowledged by David Byrne and Brian Eno as an influence in their collaboration, *My Life in the Bush of Ghosts*.

Czyż, Henryk, Polish conductor and composer; b. Grudziadz, June 16, 1923. He studied law at Torun Univ.; then went to the Poznán Academy of Music, where he studied conducting with Bierdiajew and composition with Szeligowski. In 1952 he was appointed conductor at the Poznán Opera; from 1953 to 1956 he conducted the Polish Radio and Television Sym. Orch. in Katowice. He was subsequently chief conductor of the Łódż Phil. (1957–60); from 1964 to 1968 he conducted the Kraków Phil.; from 1971 to 1974 served as Generalmusikdirektor of the Düsseldorf Sym. Orch.; from 1972 to 1980 he was again chief conductor of the Łódż Phil. He made his American debut with the Minnesota Orch. in 1973. From 1980 to 1995 he was a prof. at the Warsaw Academy of Music. Among his works were the stage pieces *Białowłosa* (The Girl with the Flaxen Hair; Warsaw, Nov. 24, 1962; rev. version, Łódż, Oct. 2, 1971); *Knyolog w rozterce* (Cynologist at a Loss; Polish TV, 1965; stage premiere, Kraków, Nov. 19, 1967), and *Inge Bartsch* (Warsaw, Dec. 11, 1982); several orch. works, including *Étude* (1949) and Symphonic Variations (1952), etc.

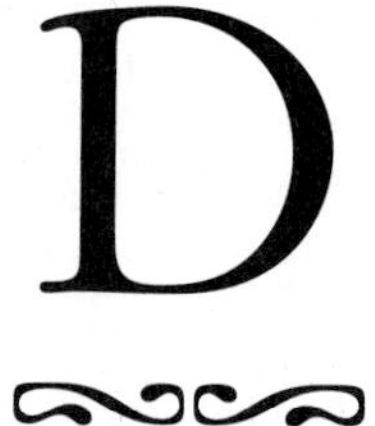

Da-Oz, Ram (real name, **Avraham Daus**), German-born Israeli composer; b. Berlin, Oct. 17, 1929. He went to Palestine as a child in 1934; studied oboe and piano at the Cons. in Tel Aviv, and composition with André Hajdu at the Music Academy there. He lost his eyesight during the Israeli war for independence in 1948.

WORKS: ORCH.: *Von Trauer und Trost* (1960); Concerto for Violin and Strings (1961); *Dmuyoth umassechot* (Changing Phantoms), movements for Chamber Ensemble (1967); *Quartet* for Narrator and Small Orch. (1970); *Rhapsody on a Jewish Yemenite Song* for Piano and Strings (1971); *3 Romances* for Violin and Small Orch. (1975); *Introduction and Passacaglia* (1981). **CHAMBER:** 4 string quartets (1955–70); Violin Sonata (1960); String Trio (1961); Suite for Harpsichord, Flute, Oboe, and Cello (1963); Piano Trio (1963); Dialogue for 2 Clarinets (1965); *Illumination* for Violin (1966); *Improvisation on a Song* for 10 Instruments (1968); *4 Miniatures* for Recorders and Piano (1975); *Divertimento* for Brass Quartet (1977). **PIANO:** 2 sonatas (1955; *Movimenti quasi una sonata,* 1963); *5 Contrasts* (1958); *Capriccio* (1960); *8 Little Pictures* (1962); *Aspects* (1969); *Bells* (1973); *Mood Ring* (1976); *Pictures in Procession* (1979); *RuTaNoWa* (1980). **OTHER:** Songs.

D'Accone, Frank A(nthony), American musicologist; b. Somerville, Mass., June 13, 1931. He studied with Geiringer and Read at Boston Univ. (B.Mus., 1952; M.Mus., 1953), then with Pirrotta, Merritt, and Piston at Harvard Univ. (M.A., 1955; Ph.D., 1960). He taught first at the State Univ. of N.Y. at Buffalo (1960–68); also was a visiting prof. at the Univ. of Calif. at Los Angeles (1965–66), to which he returned as a prof. of music in 1968. He is ed. of the *Music of the Florentine Renaissance* in the Corpus Mensurabilis Musicae series, XXXII (1966 et seq.); he also publ. *Alessandro Scarlatti's "Gli equivoci nel sambiante": The History of a Baroque Opera* (N.Y., 1985).

Dadelsen, Georg von, distinguished German musicologist; b. Dresden, Nov. 7, 1918. He studied musicology at the Univ. of Kiel at Humboldt Univ. in Berlin, and at the Free Univ. of Berlin (Ph.D., 1951, with the diss. *Alter Stil und alte Techniken in der Musik des 19. Jahrhunderts*); completed his Habilitation at the Univ. of Tübingen in 1958 with his *Beiträge zur Chronologie der Werke J.S. Bachs* (publ. in Trossingen, 1958). He was an assistant lecturer at the Univ. of Tübingen (1952–58); was then prof. of musicology at the Univ. of Hamburg (1960–71); from 1971 he held the same title at the Univ. of Tübingen. He is particularly noted for his valuable contributions to the study of Bach's music.

WRITINGS: *Bemerkungen zur Handschrift J.S. Bachs, seiner Familie und seines Kreises* (Trossingen, 1957); *Editionsrichtlinien musikalischer Denkmäler und Gesamtausgaben* (Kassel, 1967); A. Feil and T. Kohlhase, eds., *Über Bach und anderes: Aufsätze und Vortrage, 1957–1982* (Laaber, 1983).

BIBL.: *Acht klein Präludien und Studien über Bach: G.v. D. zum 70. Geburtstag am 17. November 1988* (Wiesbaden, 1992).

Daffner, Hugo, German composer and musicologist; b. Munich, June 2, 1882; d. in the concentration camp in Dachau, Oct. 9, 1936. He studied composition with Thuille and musicology with Sandberger and Kroyer at the Royal Academy in Munich (Ph.D., 1904, with the diss. *Die Entwicklung des Klavierkonzerts bis Mozarts*; publ. in Leipzig, 1908); subsequently took private lessons with Reger. He conducted opera in Munich from 1904 to 1906; was active as a music critic in Königsberg and Dresden; decided to study medicine, and obtained the degree of M.D. in 1920; in 1924 he went to live in Berlin as a practicing physician. He became a victim of the Nazi program of extermination of Jews. Among his works were 3 operas: *Macbeth, Truffaldino,* and *Der eingebildete Kranke;* 2 syms.; 2 string quartets; 2 piano trios; 2 piano quintets; various other pieces.

Dahl, Ingolf, distinguished German-born American pianist, conductor, pedagogue, and composer of German-Swedish descent; b. Hamburg, June 9, 1912; d. Frutigen, near Bern, Aug.

6, 1970. After composition training with Jarnach at the Cologne Hochschule für Musik (1930–32), he went to Zürich and studied musicology at the Univ. and conducting with Andreae at the Cons. (1932–36). In 1938 he emigrated to the U.S., becoming a naturalized American citizen in 1943. In 1944 he received additional training from Boulanger. In 1945 he joined the faculty of the Univ. of Southern Calif. in Los Angeles, where he also conducted its sym. orch. until 1958, and again in 1968–69. During the summers from 1952 to 1957, he oversaw his own Tanglewood Study Group at the Berkshire Music Center. During the summers from 1964 to 1966, he served as director and conductor of the Ojai Festival. In 1954 and 1968 he held Guggenheim fellowships, and in 1964 he received the Alice M. Ditson Award. As a performer, Dahl was an active champion of contemporary music. He became associated with Stravinsky, who influenced him in his direction as a composer. With his Piano Quartet (1957), Dahl adopted serial techniques which he utilized inventively in such works as his Sinfonietta for Concert Band (1961) and his *Aria Sinfonica* (1965).

WORKS: ORCH.: Concerto for Alto Saxophone and Wind Orch. (1949; rev. 1953); Symphony concertante for 2 Clarinets and Orch. (1952); *The Tower of Saint Barbara*, symphonic legend (1954; Louisville, Jan. 29, 1955); Sinfonietta for Concert Band (1961); *Aria sinfonica* (Los Angeles, April 15, 1965); *Quodlibet on American Folktunes* (1965; arranged from the piece for 2 Pianos, 8-hands, 1953); *4 Intervals* for Strings (1967; arranged for Piano, 4-hands, 1967); *Elegy Concerto* for Violin and Chamber Orch. (1970; completed by D. Michalsky, 1971). **CHAMBER:** *Allegro and Arioso* for Woodwind Quartet (1942); *Music for Brass Instruments*, brass quintet (1944); *Variations on a Swedish Folktune* for Flute (1945; rev. 1962; arranged for Flute and Alto Flute, 1970); *Concerto a tre* for Violin, Cello, and Clarinet (1946); Duo for Cello and Piano (1946; rev. 1948); *Notturno* for Cello and Piano (1946); *Divertimento* for Viola and Piano (1949); *Couperin Variations* for Recorder or Flute and Harpsichord or Piano (1957); Piano Quartet (1957); *Serenade* for 4 Flutes (1960); Piano Trio (1962); Duettino concertante for Flute and Percussion (1966); *IMC Fanfare* for 3 Trumpets and 3 Trombones (1968); *Fanfare on A and C* [for Aaron Copland] for 3 Trumpets, Horn, Baritone, and Trombone (1969); *Sonata da camera* for Clarinet and Piano (1970); 5 duets for 2 Clarinets (1970); *Little Canonic Suite* for Violin and Viola (1970); *Variations on a French Folksong* for Flute and Piano (1970). **PIANO:** *Rondo* for Piano, 4-hands (1938); *Prelude and Fugue* (1939); *Pastorale montano* (1943); *Hymn and Toccata* (1947); *Quodlibet on American Folktunes* for 2 Pianos, 8-hands (1953; arranged for Orch., 1965); *Sonata seria* (1953); *Sonatina alla marcia* (1956); *Fanfares* (1958); *Sonata pastorale* (1959); *Reflections* (1967). **VOCAL:** Choruses and songs.

BIBL.: J. Berdahl, *I. D.: His Life and Works* (diss., Univ. of Miami, 1975).

Dahl, Viking, Danish organist and composer; b. Osby, Oct. 8, 1895; d. Stockholm, Jan. 5, 1945. He studied organ at the Stockholm Cons. (1915–19); concurrently he took courses in art history. In 1920 he went to Paris, where he had lessons in modern dance with Isadora Duncan and in composition with Koechlin; he later completed his studies in Copenhagen and Berlin. In 1921 he went to Lund as a music teacher, and from 1926 he served as organist of Varberg Church. After composing in both impressionist and expressionist styles, he turned to Swedish folk music for inspiration. His first work, the *Oriental Suite* for Orch. (1919), was followed by his choreographic poem *Maison de fous* (Paris, 1920), which attracted considerable attention. His early promise as a composer, however, was not fulfilled.

Dahlhaus, Carl, eminent German musicologist and editor; b. Hannover, June 10, 1928; d. Berlin, March 13, 1989. He studied musicology at the Univ. of Göttingen with Gerber; also at the Univ. of Freiburg with Gurlitt; received his Ph.D. from the Univ. of Göttingen in 1953 with the diss. *Studien zu den Messen Josquins des Prés.* He was a dramatic adviser for the Deutsches Theater in Göttingen from 1950 to 1958; from 1960 to 1962, was an ed. of the *Stuttgarter Zeitung*; then joined the Inst. für Musikalische Landesforschung of the Univ. of Kiel; completed his Habilitation there in 1966 with his *Untersuchungen uber die Entstehung der harmonischen Tonalität* (publ. in Kassel, 1968; Eng. tr., 1991, as *Studies on the Origin of Harmonic Tonality*). In 1966–67 he was a research fellow at the Univ. of Saarbrücken; in 1967 he became prof. of music history at the Technical Univ. of Berlin. In 1984 he was made a corresponding member of the American Musicological Soc. He was the ed.-in-chief of the complete edition of Wagner's works, which began publication in 1970; he was also an ed. of the Supplement to the 12th edition of the *Riemann Musik-Lexikon* (2 vols., Mainz, 1972, 1975); with Hans Eggebrecht, of the *Brockhaus-Riemann Musik-Lexikon* (2 vols., Wiesbaden and Mainz, 1978–79); and of *Pipers Enzyklopadie des Musiktheaters* (from 1986); in addition, he was co-ed. of the *Neue Zeitschrift für Musik* (1972–74), *Melos/NZ für Musik* (1975–78), *Musik und Bildung* (1978–80), and *Musica* (from 1981). He was one of the foremost musicologists of the 2nd half of the 20th century. A scholar of great erudition, he wrote authoritatively and prolifically on a vast range of subjects, extending from the era of Josquin to the present day.

WRITINGS: *Musikästhetik* (Cologne, 1967; 4th ed., 1986; Eng. tr., 1982, as *Aesthetics of Music*); *Studien zur Trivialmusik des 19. Jahrhunderts* (Regensburg, 1967); *Analyse und Werturteil* (Mainz, 1970; Eng. tr., 1983, as *Analysis and Value Judgment*); *Das Drama Richard Wagners als musikalisches Kunstwerk* (Regensburg, 1970); *Richard Wagner: Werk und Wirkung* (Regensburg, 1971); *Wagners Konzeption des musikalischen Dramas* (Regensburg, 1971); *Richard Wagners Musikdramen* (Velber, 1971; 2nd ed., 1985; Eng. tr., 1979, as *Richard Wagner's Music Dramas*); *Wagner's Ästhetik* (Bayreuth, 1971); *Zwischen Romantik und Moderne: Vier Studien zur Musikgeschichte des späteren 19. Jahrhunderts* (Munich, 1974; Eng. tr., 1980, as *Between Romanticism and Modernism: Four Studies in the Music of the Later Nineteenth Century*); *Grundlagen der Musikgeschichte* (Cologne, 1977; Eng. tr., 1983, as *Foundations of Music History*); *Die Idee der absoluten Musik* (Kassel, 1978; Eng. tr., 1989, as *The Idea of Absolute Music*); *Schönberg und andere: Gesammelte Aufsätze zur Neuen Musik* (Mainz, 1978; Eng. tr., 1988, as *Schoenberg and the New Music*); *Die Musik des 19. Jahrhunderts* (Wiesbaden, 1980; 2nd ed., 1988; Eng. tr., 1989, as *Nineteenth-Century Music*); *Musikalischer Realismus: Zur Musikgeschichte des 19. Jahrhunderts* (Munich and Zürich, 1982; Eng. tr., 1985, as *Realism in Nineteenth Century Music*); with H. de la Motte-Haber, *Systematische Musikwissenschaft* (Laaber, 1982); *Vom Musikdrama zur Literaturoper: Aufsätze zur neueren Operngeschichte* (Munich and Salzburg, 1983); with J. Deathridge, *Wagner* (London, 1984); *Die Musiktheorie im 18. und 19. Jahrhundert: Erster Teil: Grundzüge einer Systematik* (Darmstadt, 1984); *Die Musik des 18. Jahrhunderts* (Laaber, 1985); with R. Katz, *Contemplating Music: Source Readings in the Aesthetics of Music* (N.Y., 1987); *Ludwig van Beethoven und seine Zeit* (Laaber, 1987; 2nd ed., 1988; Eng. tr., 1991, as *Ludwig van Beethoven: Approaches to His Music*); *Klassische und romantische Musikästhetik* (Laaber, 1988).

BIBL.: H. Danuser et al., eds., *Das musikalische Kunstwerk: Geschichte, Ästhetik, Theorie: Festschrift C. D. zum 60. Geburtstag* (Laaber, 1988); M. Zimmermann, ed., *Oper nach Wagner: In memoriam C. D.* (Laaber, 1993).

Dahms, Walter, German music critic; b. Berlin, June 9, 1887; d. Lisbon, Oct. 5, 1973. He studied with Adolf Schultze in Berlin (1907–10), then engaged in music criticism; also composed some minor piano pieces and songs. About 1935 he went to Lisbon, where he changed his name to Gualtério Armando, and continued to publ. books on music in the German language, but for some unfathomable reason he persistently denied his identity. The reasons for his leaving Germany are obscure; he was not a Jew (in fact, he wrote some anti-Semitic articles, directed against Schoenberg and others, as early as 1910), and presumably had nothing to fear from the Nazi government, unless he regarded it as unduly liberal. A clue to his true identity was the synonymity of his first names in German (Walter) and in Portuguese (Gualtério).

WRITINGS: *Schubert* (Berlin, 1912); *Schumann* (1916); *Mendelssohn* (1919); *Die Offenbarung der Musik: Eine Apotheose Friedrich Nietzsches* (Munich, 1921); *Musik des Südens* (1923); *Paganini* (Berlin, 1960); *Liszt* (Berlin, 1961); *Wagner* (Berlin, 1962).

D'Albert, Eugène. See **Albert, Eugen d'.**

Dalberto, Michel (Jean Jacques), French pianist; b. Paris, June 2, 1955. He was a student at the Paris Cons., his principal mentors being Vlado Perlemuter, Raymond Trouard, and Jean Hubeau. In 1975 he won the Clara Haskil prize and the Salzburg Mozart competition, and in 1978 captured 1st prize in the Leeds competition. After making his formal debut as soloist with Leinsdorf and the Orchestre de Paris in 1980, he pursued a global career as a soloist with orchs., recitalist, and chamber music player.

Dalby, (John) Martin, Scottish composer and broadcasting administrator; b. Aberdeen, April 25, 1942. He was a violist in the National Youth Orch. of Great Britain before attending the Royal College of Music in London on scholarship, where he studied viola with Riddle and composition with Howells (1960–63); additional scholarships allowed him to pursue studies in Italy (1963–65). From 1965 to 1971 he was a music producer with the BBC in London; after serving as the Cramb Research Fellow in composition at the Univ. of Glasgow (1971–72), he held the position of head of music with the BBC in Scotland (from 1972).

WORKS: ORCH.: *Waltz Overture* (1965); 2 syms. (1970, 1983); *Concerto Martin Pescatore* for Strings (1971); *The Tower of Victory* (Glasgow, Sept. 22, 1973); Viola Concerto (London, Sept. 6, 1974); *El Ruiseñor* (1979); Chamber Sym.: *O Bella e Vaga Aurora* (Edinburgh, Sept. 10, 1982); *Nozze di Primavera* (1984); *A Plain Man's Hammer* for Symphonic Wind Ensemble (1984). **CHAMBER:** Piano Trio (1967); *Commedia* for Clarinet, Violin, Cello and Piano (1969); *Whisper Music* for Chamber Ensemble (1971); *Cancionero para una Mariposa* for Chamber Ensemble (1971); String Quintet (1972); *Yet Still She is the Moone* for Brass Septet (1973); *Paginas* for Treble Recorder and Harpsichord (1973); *Unicorn* for Violin and Piano (1975); *Aleph* for Chamber Ensemble (1975); *Almost a Madrigal* for Winds and Percussion (1977); *The Dancer Eduardova* for 6 Players (1978); *Man Walking,* serenade for Octet (1981); *De Patre ex Filio,* octet for Winds and Strings. (1988). **PIANO:** 2 sonatas (1985, 1989). **VOCAL:** *Requiem for Philip Sparrow* for Mezzo-soprano, Chorus, 3 Oboes, and Strings (1967); *Cantica* for Soprano or Tenor, Clarinet, Viola, and Piano (1969); *The Keeper of the Pass* for Soprano, 3 Clarinets, Percussion, and Piano (1971); *Orpheus* for Chorus, Optional Narrator, and 11 Instruments (1972); *Cantigas del Cancionero* for 5 Solo Voices (1972); *El Remanso del Pitido* for 12 Solo Voices (1974); *Ad Flumina Babyloniae,* motet for Chorus (1975); *Beauty a Cause* for 12 or 16 Voices and Instrumental Ensemble (1977; Glasgow, Feb. 13, 1978); *Coll for the Hazel Tree* for Chorus and Electronics (1979); *Antoinette Alone* for Mezzo-soprano and Piano (1980; BBC Radio, Sept. 19, 1981).

Dalcroze, Emile Jaques. See **Jaques-Dalcroze, Emile.**

Dale, Benjamin (James), English composer and teacher; b. Crouch Hill, July 17, 1885; d. London, July 30, 1943. He studied at the Royal Academy of Music in London with F. Corder; was organist at St. Stephen's, Ealing; then taught composition at the Royal Academy of Music.

WORKS: *The Tempest,* overture (1902); Piano Sonata (1905); suites for Piano and Viola (1907); *Before the Paling of the Stars* for Chorus and Orch. (1912); *Songs of Praise* for Chorus and Orch. (1923); *The Flowing Tide* for Orch. (1924; 1943); *Rosa mystica* and *Cradle Song* for Chorus; 2 songs (after Shakespeare) for Voice and Viola obbligato; Sextet for Violas; Violin Sonata; piano pieces; songs; etc.

Dale, Clamma, black American soprano; b. Chester, Pa., July 4, 1948. She studied at the Philadelphia Settlement Music School, and later with Hans Heinz, Alice Howland, and Cornelius Reed at the Juilliard School of Music in N.Y. (B.Mus., 1970; M.S., 1975). On Feb. 20, 1973, she appeared as St. Teresa I in *4 Saints in 3 Acts* in the Mini-Met staging at N.Y.'s Manhattan Forum. On Sept. 30, 1975, she made her N.Y. City Opera debut as Antonia in *Les Contes d'Hoffmann,* and subsequently appeared with opera companies throughout North America and abroad; she also toured extensively as a concert artist. Among her principal roles were Pamina, Countess Almaviva, Nedda, Musetta, Liù, and Gershwin's Bess.

Dal Farra, Ricardo, Argentine composer and electroacoustic music performer; b. Buenos Aires, Nov. 19, 1957. He was educated in Buenos Aires. He served as prof. of electroacoustic composition at the Conservatorio Municipal de Música, co-director of the Electronic Music Laboratory of the Sociedad Argentina de Educación Musical (ISME), and director of the radio program "Musica Electroacustica y por Computadora" on LSI Radio Municipal de Buenos Aires. His compositions, processed live in performance, involve sophisticated computer programming and the most modern techniques for producing and manipulating synthesized sound. Among these are 2 tape pieces, *Estudio sobre ritmo y espacio* (1982) and *Karma* (1986), *Ancestros* for Aerophones and Electroacoustic Processors (1986), several works for Guitar and Electroacoustic Processors, including *Integrados* (1986), *Double* (1986), and *Clones* (1986), and *G* (*I. Gravitacional* and *II. Inercial*) for MIDI Guitar and a DX7 Digital Synthesizer (1987).

Dalis, Irene, American mezzo-soprano, teacher, and operatic administrator; b. San Jose, Calif., Oct. 8, 1925. She studied at San Jose State Univ. (A.B., 1946; M.S., 1957) and at Columbia Univ. Teachers College (M.A., 1947); received vocal training from Edyth Walker (1947–50) and Paul Althouse (1950–51) in N.Y., and from Otto Müller (1952) in Milan. In 1953 she made her operatic debut as Eboli in *Don Carlo* at the Oldenburg Landestheater; sang with the Städtische Oper in Berlin (1955–60). On March 16, 1957, she made her Metropolitan Opera debut in N.Y. as Eboli, and continued to sing there regularly until 1977. She also made guest appearances at Covent Garden in London, the Chicago Lyric Opera, and the Bayreuth Festivals. In 1976 she became a prof. of music at San Jose State Univ.; she also directed its opera workshop, which served as the nucleus for the fully professional Opera San Jose, with Dalis as executive director (1984–88) and artistic director (from 1988).

Dallapiccola, Luigi, eminent Italian composer and pedagogue; b. Pisino, Istria, Feb. 3, 1904; d. Florence, Feb. 19, 1975. He took piano lessons at an early age in Pisino. After training in piano and harmony in Trieste (1919–21), he studied with Ernesto Consolo (piano diploma, 1924) and Vito Frazzi (composition diploma, 1931) at the Florence Cons., where he subsequently was a distinguished member of the faculty (1934–67). A collection of his essays appeared as *Appunti incontri meditazioni* (Milan, 1970). As a composer, Dallapiccola adopted dodecaphonic procedures but added considerable innovations, such as the use of mutually exclusive triads and thematic structure and harmonic progressions. He particularly excelled in his handling of vocal lines in a complex modern idiom.

WORKS: DRAMATIC: OPERAS: *Volo di notte* (1937–39; Florence, May 18, 1940); *Il Prigioniero* (1944–48; rev. version, Turin Radio, Dec. 4, 1949; stage premiere, Florence, May 20, 1950); *Ulisse* (1959–68; in Ger. as *Odysseus,* Berlin, Sept. 29, 1968. **BALLET:** *Marsia* (1942–43; Venice, Sept. 9, 1948). **ORCH.:** *Partita* (1930–32; Florence, Jan. 22, 1933); *Piccolo Concerto per Muriel Couvreaux* for Piano and Chamber Orch. (1939–41; Rome, May 1, 1941); *Due pezzi* (1947; based on the *Due studi* for Violin and Piano); *Tartiniana* for Violin and Chamber Orch. (1951; Bern, March 4, 1952); *Variazioni per* *orchestra* (1953–54; Louisville, Oct. 2, 1954; orchestration of *Quaderno musicale di Annalibera* for Piano); *Piccola musica notturna* (Hannover, June 7, 1954; also for 8 Instruments, 1961); *Tartiniana seconda* for Violin and Chamber Orch. (1956; Turin Radio, March 15, 1957; orchestration of the piece for Violin and Piano); *Dialoghi* for Cello and Orch. (1959–60; Venice, Sept. 17, 1960); *3 Questions with 2 Answers* (1962; New Haven, Conn., Feb. 5, 1963; based on *Ulisse*). **CHAMBER:** *Ciaccona, Intermezzo e Adagio* for Cello (1945); *Due studi* for Violin and Piano (1946–47; also used in the *Due pezzi* for Orch.); *Tartiniana seconda* for Violin and Piano (1955–56; also for Violin and Chamber Orch.); *Piccola musica notturna* for 8 Instruments (1961; also for Orch.). **PIANO:** *Musica* for 3 Pianos (1935); *Sonatina canonica* (1942–43); *Quaderno musicale di Annalibera* (1952, rev. 1953; also for Orch.; transcribed for organ by R. Shackelford, 1970). **VOCAL:** *Due canzoni di Grado* for Mezzo-soprano, Small Women's Chorus, and Small Orch. (1927); *Dalla mia terra*, song cycle for Mezzo-soprano, Chorus, and Orch. (1928); *Due laudi di Fra Jacopone da Todi* for Soprano, Baritone, Chorus, and Orch. (1929); *La Canzone del Quarnaro* for Tenor, Men's Chorus, and Orch. (1930); *Due liriche del Kalewala* for Tenor, Baritone, Chamber Chorus, and 4 Percussion (1930); *3 studi* for Soprano and Chamber Orch. (1932); *Estate* for Men's Chorus (1932); *Rhapsody* for Voice and Chamber Orch. (1934); *Divertimento in quattro esercizi* for Soprano, Flute, Oboe, Clarinet, Viola, and Cello (1934); *Cori di Michelangelo I* for Chorus (1933), *II* for Women's Chorus and 17 Instruments (1935), and *III* for Chorus and Orch. (1936); *3 laudi* for Soprano and Chamber Orch. (1936–37); *Canti di prigionia* for Chorus, 2 Pianos, 2 Harps, and Percussion (1938–41; 1st complete perf., Rome, Dec. 11, 1941); *Liriche greche I: Cinque frammenti di Saffo* for Voice and 15 Instruments (1942), *II: Due liriche di Anacreonte* for Soprano, 2 Clarinets, Viola, and Piano (1945), and *III: Sex carmina Alcaei* for Soprano and 11 Instruments (1943); *Roncesvals* for Voice and Piano (1946); *Quattro liriche di Antonio Machado* for Soprano and Piano (1948; also for Soprano and Chamber Orch., 1964); *3 poemi* for Soprano and Chamber Ensemble (1949); *Job*, biblical drama for 5 Singers, Narrator, Chorus, Speaking Chorus, and Orch. (1949–50; Rome, Oct. 30, 1950); *Canti di liberazione* for Chorus and Orch. (1951–55; Cologne, Oct. 28, 1955); *Goethe-Lieder* for Woman's Voice and 3 Clarinets (1953); *An Mathilde*, cantata for Woman's Voice and Orch. (1955); *5 canti* for Baritone and 8 Instruments (1956); *Concerto per la notte di Natale dell'anno 1956* for Soprano and Chamber Orch. (1956; Tokyo, Oct. 11, 1957); *Requiescant* for Chorus, Children's Chorus, and Orch. (1957–58; North German Radio, Hamburg, Nov. 17, 1959); *Preghiere* for Baritone and Chamber Orch. (Berkeley, Calif., Nov. 10, 1962); *Parole di San Paolo* for Medium Voice and Chamber Ensemble (Washington, D.C., Oct. 10, 1969); *Sicut umbra . . .* for Mezzo-soprano and 4 Instrumental Groups (1969–70; Washington, Oct. 30, 1970); *Tempus destruendi/Tempus aedificandi* for Chorus (1970–71); *Commiato* for Soprano and Chamber Ensemble (Murau, Austria, Oct. 15, 1972).

BIBL.: B. Zanolini, *L. D.: La conquista di un linguaggio* (Padua, 1974); D. Kamper, *Gefangenschaft und Freiheit: Leben und Werk des Komponisten L. D.* (Cologne, 1984); A. Quattrocchi, ed., *Studi zu L. D.: Un Seminario* (Lucca, 1993).

Dallapozza, Adolf, Italian-born Austrian tenor; b. Bolzano, March 14, 1940. His parents settled in Austria when he was 5 months old. He received his musical education at the Vienna Cons.; then joined the Chorus of the Volksoper; in 1962 he made his debut as soloist in the role of Ernesto in Donizetti's *Don Pasquale*. In 1967 he became a member of the Vienna State Opera; also sang with the Bavarian State Opera in Munich and made appearances in Milan, Basel, Hamburg, Zürich, and Buenos Aires. In 1976 the President of Austria made him a Kammersänger. He is highly regarded for his versatility, being equally competent in opera, oratorio, and operetta.

Dalla Rizza, Gilda, Italian soprano; b. Verona, Oct. 2, 1892; d. Milan, July 4, 1975. She received her musical training in Bologna, where she made her operatic debut as Charlotte in *Werther* in 1912; in 1915 she sang at La Scala in Milan; Puccini so admired her singing that he created the role of Magda in *La Rondine* for her (Monte Carlo, March 27, 1917). She sang in Rome (1919), at London's Covent Garden (1920), and again at La Scala (1923–39); then taught voice at the Venice Cons. (1939–55). Her students included Anna Moffo and Gianna d'Angelo. She was married to the tenor Agostino Capuzzo (1889–1963). Her most famous role was Violetta.

BIBL.: P. Badoer, *G.d. R.: La cantante prediletta di Giacomo Puccini* (Abano Terme, 1991).

Dal Monte, Toti (real name, **Antonietta Meneghelli**), outstanding Italian soprano; b. Mogliano, near Treviso, June 27, 1893; d. Pieve di Soligo, Treviso, Jan. 26, 1975. She studied piano at the Venice Cons., then voice with Barbara Marchisio. She made her operatic debut at La Scala in Milan as Biancafiore in Zandonai's *Francesca da Rimini* in 1916, and then sang throughout Italy. After a brilliant appearance as Gilda at La Scala in 1922, she pursued a notably acclaimed career in Europe, singing in Paris, Vienna, London, and Berlin with extraordinary success. On Dec. 5, 1924, she made her Metropolitan Opera debut in N.Y. as Lucia, remaining on its roster for 1 season; she also sang at the Chicago Civic Opera (1924–28) and at London's Covent Garden (1926). She continued to sing in opera until World War II, after which she made her farewell performance at the Verona Arena in 1949; thereafter she taught voice. She publ. an autobiography, *Una voce nel mondo* (Milan, 1962). Her other remarkable roles included Cio-Cio-San, Mimi, and Stravinsky's Nightingale.

Dalmorès, Charles (real name, **Henry Alphonse Boin**), French tenor; b. Nancy, Jan. 1, 1871; d. Los Angeles, Dec. 6, 1939. After taking 1st prizes at the local Cons. for solfeggio and horn at 17, he received from the city of Nancy a stipend for study at the Paris Cons., where he took 1st prize for horn at 19; played in the Colonne Orch. and the Lamoureux Orch.; at 23, became a prof. of horn at the Lyons Cons. His vocal teacher was Dauphin. His stage debut as a tenor took place on Oct. 6, 1899, at Rouen as Siegfried; later he sang at the Théâtre Royal de la Monnaie in Brussels (1900–1906) and at London's Covent Garden (1904–05; 1909–11). On Dec. 7, 1906, he made his debut as Faust at the Manhattan Opera House in N.Y., then was with the Chicago Opera Co. (1910–18). His repertoire was large, and included Wagnerian as well as French operas; in Chicago he sang Tristan and the title role in the 1st performance of *Parsifal* to be presented there.

Damase, Jean-Michel, French composer and pianist; b. Bordeaux, Jan. 27, 1928. He was a student of Delvincourt at the Paris Cons. and winner of the Grand Prix de Rome in 1947. He made appearances as a pianist while devoting time to composition. In 1954 he made his first appearance in the U.S. as a pianist-composer in N.Y.

WORKS: DRAMATIC: BALLETS: *Le Saut du Tremplin* (1944); *La Croqueuse de diamants* (1950); *Piège de lumière* (1952); *Lady in the Ice* (1953); *Le prince du désert* (1955); *Balance à trois* (1955); *La boucle* (1957); *Othello* (1957); *La noce forcaine* (1961); *Suite monégasgue* (1964). **OTHER:** *Colombe*, lyric comedy (Bordeaux, May 5, 1961); *Le Tendre Eleonore*, opera-bouffe (1962); *Eurydice*, lyric comedy (Bordeaux, May 26, 1972); *L'héritière*, opera (1974). **ORCH.:** *Interludes* (1948); *Rhapsody* for Oboe and Strings (1948); 2 piano concertos (1950; Paris, Feb. 6, 1963); *Concert Piece* for Saxophone, Clarinet, and Chamber Orch. (1950); Concertino for Harp and Strings (1951); Sym. (1954); Violin Concerto (1955; Paris, Dec. 22, 1956); Flute Concerto (1993). **CHAMBER:** Quintet for Violin, Viola, Cello, Flute, and Harp (1947); Trio for Flute, Harp, and Cello (1949); Piano Quartet (1967); piano pieces. **OTHER:** Songs.

Dambois, Maurice, Belgian cellist and teacher; b. Liège, March 30, 1889; d. there, Nov. 12, 1969. He studied at the Liège Cons. (1899–1905), winning prizes in piano, harmony, chamber music, fugue, and cello. He made his debut at the age of 12 in

Saint-Saëns's A-minor Concerto; toured Germany (1905), England (1906–08), France, Portugal, and the Netherlands. He was appointed director of the Académie de Musique in Liège (1910) and prof. of cello at the Brussels Cons. (1912). After the outbreak of World War I in 1914, he went to England (until 1916); went to the U.S. in 1917 with Ysaÿe; made his American debut in N.Y., April 21, 1917, followed by successful tours. In 1926 he settled in Brussels, and resumed his post as prof. of cello at the Cons., retaining it for 30 years.

Damerini, Adelmo, Italian musicologist; b. Carmignano, near Florence, Dec. 11, 1880; d. there, Oct. 12, 1976. He studied with Edgardo Binelli and Giannotto Bastianelli. He held teaching positions at the American Methodist Inst. in Rome, the Palermo Cons. (1922), and the Boito Cons. in Parma; from 1933 to 1962 he was a prof. at the Cherubini Cons. in Florence.

WRITINGS: *Origine e svolgimento della sinfonia* (Pistoia, 1919); *Le sinfonie di Beethoven* (Rome, 1921); *Lorenzo Perosi* (Rome, 1924; 2nd ed., rev., 1953); *Classicismo e romanticismo nella musica* (Florence, 1942); *Il R. Conservatorio di musica "Luigi Cherubini" di Firenze* (Florence, 1942); *L'Istituto Giovanni Pacini di Lucca* (Florence, 1942); *Boezio: Pensieri sulla musica* (Florence, 1955); *Profilo delle grandi epoche musicale* (Milan, 1955); *Guglielmo de Machaut e l' "Ars nova" italiana* (Florence, 1960); with G. Roncaglia, *Volti musicali di Falstaff* (Siena, 1961); *Luigi Cherubini nel II centenario della nascita* (Florence, 1962).

Damrosch, Frank (Heino), German-American conductor and teacher, brother of **Walter (Johannes) Damrosch**; b. Breslau, June 22, 1859; d. N.Y., Oct. 22, 1937. He was the son of the eminent German-American conductor and violinist, Leopold Damrosch (b. Posen, Oct. 22, 1832; d. N.Y., Feb. 15, 1885). He studied piano and composition in his youth; in 1871 he went with his family to N.Y., then went to Denver, where he conducted the Chorus Club (1882–85) and was supervisor of music in the public schools (1884–85). Returning to N.Y., he was chorus master and assistant conductor at the Metropolitan Opera (1885–91). After studying composition with Moszkowski in Berlin (1891), he returned to N.Y. and organized the People's Singing Classes in 1892, which he conducted as the People's Choral Union (1894–1909). In 1893 he founded the Musical Art Soc., a professional chorus devoted to the performance of a cappella choral works, which he led until 1920; he also conducted the Oratorio Soc. (1898–1912). From 1898 to 1912 he conducted a series of sym. concerts for young people that were continued by his brother Walter; he also served as supervisor of music in N.Y. public schools (1897–1905). In 1905 he established the splendidly equipped Inst. of Musical Art, which, in 1926, became affiliated with the Juilliard School of Music; he retained his position as dean until his retirement in 1933. He received the degree of D.Mus. (honoris causa) from Yale Univ. in 1904. He publ. *Popular Method of Sight-Singing* (N.Y., 1894), *Some Essentials in the Teaching of Music* (N.Y., 1916), and *Institute of Musical Art, 1905–1926* (N.Y., 1936).

BIBL.: L. and R. Stebbins, *F. D.* (1945); G. Martin, *The D. Dynasty: America's First Family of Music* (N.Y., 1983).

Damrosch, Walter (Johannes), distinguished German-American conductor, music educator, and composer, brother of **Frank (Heino) Damrosch**; b. Breslau, Jan. 30, 1862; d. N.Y., Dec. 22, 1950. He was the son of the eminent German-American conductor and violinist, Leopold Damrosch (b. Posen, Oct. 22, 1832; d. N.Y., Feb. 15, 1885). He received lessons in piano and composition before going to N.Y. with his family in 1871, where he continued his music studies. During the 1884–85 season of the Metropolitan Opera, he served as his father's assistant. When his father fell ill, he received some deathbed coaching from him and made his Metropolitan Opera debut conducting *Tannhäuser* on Feb. 11, 1885, just 4 days before his father succumbed. He remained on the roster of the Metropolitan Opera until 1891, and also served as his father's successor as conductor of the Oratorio Soc. of N.Y. (1885–98) and the Sym. Soc. of N.Y. (from 1885). In 1887 he pursued training in conducting with Bülow in Frankfurt am Main. In 1894 he founded the Damrosch Opera Co. in N.Y., which he conducted in performances of German operas until 1899, both there and in other major U.S. cities. From 1900 to 1902 he was again on the roster of the Metropolitan Opera. He was conductor of the N.Y. Phil. in 1902–03. After the reorganization of the Sym. Soc. of N.Y. in 1903, he was its conductor until it merged with the N.Y. Phil. in 1928. In 1920 he conducted the Sym. Soc. of N.Y. on a major tour of Europe. In 1912 he took over the sym. concerts for young people originally organized by his brother, and he also conducted young people's concerts with the Sym. Soc. of N.Y. His interest in music education prompted him to utilize the medium of radio to further the cause of music appreciation; on Oct. 19, 1923, he conducted the Sym. Soc. of N.Y. in its first radio broadcast from Carnegie Hall. In 1926 he inaugurated a regular series of radio broadcasts, which were later aired as the "NBC Music Appreciation Hour" throughout the U.S. and Canada from 1928 to 1942. He also served as musical counsel to NBC from 1927 to 1947. Damrosch conducted the U.S. premieres of Tchaikovsky's 4th and 6th syms. as well as scores by Wagner, Mahler, and Elgar. He also conducted premieres of works by American composers, including Gershwin's *An American in Paris.* He received honorary doctorates from Columbia Univ. (1914), Princeton Univ. (1929), N.Y. Univ. (1935) et al. In 1929 he was awarded the David Bispham medal. In 1932 he was elected to membership in the American Academy of Arts and Letters, and in 1938 he received the gold medal. His autobiography was publ. as *My Musical Life* (N.Y., 1923; 2nd ed., 1930).

WORKS: DRAMATIC: OPERAS: *The Scarlet Letter* (Boston, Feb. 10, 1896); *The Dove of Peace,* comic opera (Philadelphia, Oct. 15, 1912); *Cyrano de Bergerac* (N.Y., Feb. 27, 1913; rev. 1939); *The Man without a Country* (May 12, 1937); *The Opera Cloak* (N.Y., Nov. 3, 1942). **INCIDENTAL MUSIC TO:** Euripides' *Iphigenia in Aulis* (Berkeley, 1915) and *Medea* (Berkeley, 1915); Sophocles' *Electra* (N.Y., 1917). **OTHER:** *Manila Te Deum* (N.Y., 1898); *An Abraham Lincoln Song* for Baritone, Chorus, and Orch. (1935); *Dunkirk* for Baritone, Men's Chorus, and Chamber Orch. (NBC, May 2, 1943); chamber music; songs.

BIBL.: W. Henderson, "W. D.," *Musical Quarterly* (Jan. 1932); G. Damrosch Finletter, *From the Top of the Stairs* (Boston, 1946); F. Himmelein, *W. D.: A Cultural Biography* diss., Univ. of Virginia, 1972); M. Goodell, *W. D. and his Contributions to Music Education* (diss., Catholic Univ. of America, 1973); G. Martin, *The D. Dynasty: America's First Family of Music* (N.Y., 1983).

Dan, Ikuma, Japanese composer; b. Tokyo, April 7, 1924. He studied at the Tokyo Music Academy with K. Shimofusa and S. Moroi. After teaching at the Tokyo Music School (1947–50), he was active as a film music director and composer.

WORKS: DRAMATIC: OPERAS: *Yûzuru* (The Twilight Crane; 1950–51; Tokyo, Jan. 30, 1952; rev. 1956); *Kikimimizukin* (The Listening Cap; 1954–55; Tokyo, March 18, 1955); *Yang Kwei-fei* (1957–58; Tokyo, Dec. 11, 1958); *Chanchiki* (Cling-Clang; 1961–63); *Hikarigoke* (1972; Osaka, April 27, 1972). **DANCE DRAMA:** *Futari Shizuka* (1961). **ORCH.:** Symphonic Poem (1948); 6 syms. (1949–50; 1955–56; 1959–60; 1964–65; 1965; 1970); *Sinfonia burlesca* (1953; Tokyo, Jan. 26, 1959); *The Silken Road,* dance suite (1953–54; Tokyo, June 23, 1955); *Journey through Arabia,* symphonic suite (1958); *Olympic Games Overture* (1964); *Festival Overture* (1965); Concerto Grosso for Harpsichord and Strings (1965); *Japanese Poem No. 1* (Tokyo, Sept. 25, 1967); *A Letter from Japan No. 2* (1969); *Rainbow Tower* (1970). **CHAMBER:** String Trio (1947); Piano Sonata (1947); String Quartet (1948); *Divertimento* for 2 Pianos (1949). **VOCAL:** *Hymn to the Sai-kai* for Chorus and Orch. (1969); choruses.

Danckert, Werner, German musicologist; b. Erfurt, June 22, 1900; d. Krefeld, March 5, 1970. He studied natural science and mathematics at the Univ. of Jena, then musicology at the Univ.

of Leipzig with Riemann and Abert, at the Univ. of Erlangen with Becking, and at the Leipzig Cons. with Schering. He received his Ph.D. in 1924 at the Univ. of Erlangen with the diss. *Geschichte der Gigue* (publ. in Leipzig, 1924); he completed his Habilitation at the Univ. of Jena in 1926 with his *Personale Typen des Melodiestils* (publ. in an enl. ed. as *Ursymbole melodischer Gestaltung* in Kassel, 1932). He was Becking's assistant at the Univ. of Erlangen (1924–25); then taught piano at the Weimar Academy of Music (1929–32) and was a music critic in Erfurt (1932–37). He became a lecturer at the Univ. of Berlin in 1937, prof. in 1939, and head of the musicology dept. in 1943; then was in Graz (1943–45). He was a prof. at the Univ. of Rostock in 1950, but returned to West Germany that same year.

WRITINGS: *Beiträge zur Bachkritik* (Kassel, 1934); *Das europäische Volkslied* (Berlin, 1939; 2nd ed., 1970); *Grundriss der Volksliedkunde* (Berlin, 1939); *Claude Debussy* (Berlin, 1950); *Goethe: Der mythische Urgrund seiner Weltenschau* (Berlin, 1951); *Offenes und geschlossenes Leben: Zwei Daseinsaspekte in Goethes Weltenschau* (Bonn, 1963); *Unehrliche Leute: Die verfemten Berufe* (Bern and Munich, 1964); *Das Volkslied im Abendland* (Bern and Munich, 1966); *Tonreich and Symbolzahl in Hochkulturen und in der Primitivenwelt* (Bonn, 1966); *Symbol, Metaphor, Allegorie im Lied der Völker* (Bonn, 1977).

Danco, Suzanne, admired Belgian soprano; b. Brussels, Jan. 22, 1911. She began her training at the Brussels Cons.; after winning the Vienna vocal competition (1936), she studied with Fernando Carpi in Prague. She then went to Italy, where she made her debut as a concert artist in 1940. In 1941 she made her operatic debut as Fiordiligi in Genoa, and later sang in various Italian operatic centers. She had much success at Milan's La Scala, where she sang in the local premieres of *Peter Grimes* (as Ellen Orford, 1947) and *Oedipus Rex* (as Jocasta, 1948). From 1948 to 1951 she appeared at the Glyndebourne Festivals. She sang in the U.S. for the first time in 1950. In 1951 she appeared as Mimi at London's Covent Garden. In later years, she concentrated on concert engagements and also was active as a teacher at the Accademia Musicale Chigiana in Siena. Among her other notables roles were Donna Anna, Mélisande, and Berg's Marie. She was especially praised as a concert artist, excelling in the French repertory, particularly in works by Berlioz, Debussy, and Ravel.

Dandara, Liviu, Romanian composer; b. Miorcani, near Botoşani, Dec. 3, 1933. He studied with Paul Constantinescu, Ion Dumitrescu, and Tudor Ciortea at the Bucharest Cons. (1953–59).

WORKS: ORCH.: *Sinfonietta lirica* (1958); *Ouverture solennelle* (1959); Suite (1962); *Divertissement* (1964); *Expresii umane* (1968); *Spatii*, stereophonic music for 32 Instruments and Amplifiers (1971); Piano Concerto (1972). **CHAMBER:** *3 Slow Movements* for Clarinet and Piano (1963); *Ipostaze* for Wind Quartet (1966); Sonata for Solo Clarinet (1966); *Dialoguri cu axa timpului* for Flute, Violin, Piano, and Percussion (1968); *Pentaedre per la "Musica Nova,"* quintet for Clarinet, Violin, Viola, Cello, and Piano (1969); *Bamba!* for Wind Instruments or Voices and Percussion (1971); *Trei stari despre liniste* for Violin and Piano (1980). **PIANO:** *Miniatures* (1959); Sonatina (1961); Toccata (1965); *Sonata brevis* (1966); *Quadriforium* for Piano and Tape (1970). **OTHER:** Choral pieces; songs; film music.

Dandelot, Georges (Edouard), French composer and teacher; b. Paris, Dec. 2, 1895; d. St.-Georges de Didonne, Charente-Maritime, Aug. 17, 1975. He studied with Widor at the Paris Cons.; later took lessons with Dukas and Roussel. He was in the French army during World War I, and received the Croix de Guerre for valor. In 1919 he became an instructor at the École Normale de Musique in Paris; in 1942, was appointed a prof. at the Paris Cons. Dandelot composed an oratorio, *Pax* (1st prize at the International Exposition in Paris, 1937); 2 operas: *Midas* (1947) and *L'Ennemi* (1948); 3 ballets: *Le Souper de famine* (1943), *Le Jardin merveilleux* (1944), and *Pierrot et la rose* (1948); Sym. (1941); Piano Concerto (Paris, Jan. 7, 1934); *Concerto romantique* for Violin and Orch. (1944); chamber music; songs.

Daneau, Nicolas, Belgian composer and teacher; b. Binche, June 17, 1866; d. Brussels, July 12, 1944. He studied at the Ghent Cons. with Adolphe Samuel, graduating in 1892; won the 2nd Prix de Rome in 1895. He was director of the Tournai Cons. (1896–1919), and of the Mons Cons. (1919–31). His daughter, Suzanne Daneau (b. Tournai, Aug. 17, 1901; d. there, Nov. 29, 1971), was his pupil. She wrote orch. works, chamber music, and piano pieces, mostly based on native folk songs.

WORKS: DRAMATIC: *Linario*, lyric drama (Tournai, 1906); *Myrtis*, opera-idyll (Tournai, 1910); *Le Sphynx*, opera; *La Brute*, lyric drama. **ORCH.:** *Villes d'Italie*; *Adima et Hevah*; *Arles*; *Mardi-Gras*; *Petite suite*. **CHAMBER:** Suite for Violin and Piano; String Quartet; Piano Quintet.

BIBL.: L. Beatrice, *D.; Histoire d'une famille d'artistes* (Brussels, 1944).

Dang Thai Son (actually, **Son Thai Dang**), Vietnamese pianist; b. Hanoi, July 2, 1958. He began piano lessons at age 5 with his mother, a piano teacher at the Hanoi Cons., where he became a student in 1965; his studies were interrupted by the American bombing campaign during the Vietnam War, and he and his mother fled to the village of Xuan Phu, where he continued his training. After the War, he took his degree at the Hanoi Cons. (1976). He then went to Moscow to pursue his studies at the Cons. with Natanson, graduating in 1983; subsequently completed his training with Bashkirov (1983–86). In 1980 he won 1st prize in the Chopin Competition in Warsaw in the wake of the controversial decision by the jury to eliminate his fellow competitor Ivo Pogorelich in the final round. Dang's victory was significant, since with it he became the first Asian pianist to win 1st prize in such a prestigious competition. In 1981 he made his debut in Paris, followed by debuts in London in 1984 and in Berlin in 1985. In 1989 he made his U.S. debut in a recital at N.Y.'s 92nd Street Y. In 1991 he settled in Canada while continuing to pursue an international career. His repertoire ranges from Haydn to Prokofiev.

Daniel-Lesur, Jean Yves (real name, **Daniel Jean Yves Lesur**), prominent French composer and pedagogue; b. Paris, Nov. 19, 1908. He spent his entire life in Paris, where he studied at the Cons. (1919–29) with J. Gallon and Caussade (harmony and fugue), Armand Ferté (piano), and Tournemiere (organ and composition). He was assistant organist at St. Clotilde (1927–37) and organist at the Benedictine Abbey (1935–39; 1942–44). With Messiaen, Baudrier, and Jolivet, he founded the Groupe Jeune France in 1936. He taught counterpoint (1935–64) and was director (1957–62) of the Schola Cantorum. He was responsible for music information for the French Radio (from 1939) and was music councilor for the French TV (from 1968). From 1969 to 1971 he was inspector general of music for the Ministry of Culture. He was administrator of the Réunion des Théâtres Lyriques Nationaux from 1971 to 1973. With B. Gavoty, he publ. *Pour ou contre la musique moderne* (Paris, 1957). He was made a Commandeur de la Légion d'honneur and a Commandeur de l'Ordre National du Merité et Commandeur des Arts et Lettres. In 1982 he was made a member of the Académie des Beaux-Arts. In his compositions, Daniel-Lesur perfected an ascetic modal style.

WORKS: DRAMATIC: OPERAS: *Andrea del Sarto* (1968; Marseilles, Jan. 24, 1969); *Ondine* (Paris, April 26, 1982); *La Reine morte* (1987). **BALLETS:** *L'Infante et le monstre* (1938; in collaboration with A. Jolivet); *Le Bal du destin* (1956). Also film scores. **ORCH.:** *Hommage à J.S. Bach* for Strings (1933); *Suite française* (1935); *Passacaille* for Piano and Orch. (1937); *Pastorale* for Chamber Orch. (1938); *Ricercare* (1939); *L'Étoile de Seville*, suite for Chamber Orch. (1941); *Variations* for Piano and Strings (1943); *Andrea del Sarto*, symphonic poem (1947; Paris, June 21, 1949); *Ouverture pour un festival* (1951); *Concerto da camera* for Piano and Chamber Orch. (1953); *Sérénade* for Strings (1954); *Symphonie de danses* for Piano, Timpani, and Strings (1958); *Symphonie d'ombre et de lumière* (1964); *Fantaisie concertante* for Cello and Orch. (1992; Paris, Sept. 1994). **CHAMBER:** Suite for 3 Woodwinds (1939); Suite for String Quartet (1940); Suite for Piano Quartet (1943); *Suite médiévale* for Flute, Harp, and String Trio (1944); *Élégie* for 2 Guitars (1956); *Nocturne* for Oboe and Piano (1974); *Encore un instant de bonheur* for Instrumental Ensemble (1993). **KEYBOARD: PIANO:** *Les carillons*, suite (1930); *Le village imaginaire* for 2 Pianos (1947); *Ballade* (1948); *Fantaisie* for 2 Pianos (1962). **ORGAN:** Various pieces. **VOCAL:** *Quatre lieder* for Voice and Orch. (1933–39); *Chansons cambodgiennes* for Voice and Chamber Orch. (1947); *L'Annociation*, cantata for Tenor, Speaker, Chorus, and Chamber Orch. (1952); *Cantique des cantiques* for Chorus (1953); *Cantique des colonnes* for Women's Chorus and Orch. (1954–57); *Messe du jubilé* for Chorus, Organ, 3 Trumpets, and Timpani (1960; also for Chorus and Orch., 1962); *Chanson de mariage* for Women's Chorus (1964); *Dans la nuit* for Soprano, Baritone, and Orch. (1988); *Le voyage d'automne* for Chorus and Orch. (1990); many other choral pieces and songs.

BIBL.: S. Gut, *Le Group Jeune France* (Paris, 1977).

Daniel, Minna (née **Lederman**), legendary American editor and writer on music; b. N.Y., March 3, 1896; d. there, Oct. 29, 1995. She studied music and dance professionally before taking a degree at Barnard College (1917) and beginning her career as a journalist. In 1923 she joined the newly-formed League of Composers, and in 1924 helped launch its *Review*, which in 1925 became *Modern Music*, the first American journal to serve as a literary forum for contemporary composers. During her tenure as its sole ed. (1924–46), she encouraged a generation of American composer-critics, publishing essays and reviews by such musical activists as Thomson, John Cage, Elliott Carter, Blitzstein, and Bowles; she also publ. articles by Berg, Schoenberg, and Bartók. The journal attained an international reputation. In 1975 she established the Archives of Modern Music at the Library of Congress in Washington, D.C. In 1983 she publ. the informative chronicle *The Life and Death of a Small Magazine*. She also ed. *Stravinsky in the Theatre* (N.Y., 1949; 3rd ed., 1975).

Daniel, Oliver, American music administrator and writer on music; b. De Pere, Wis., Nov. 24, 1911; d. Scarsdale, N.Y., Dec. 30, 1990. He attended St. Norbert College in West De Pere (1925–29), then studied piano in Europe and at the New England Cons. of Music in Boston. He was active as a pianist and as a piano teacher until becoming music director of the educational division of CBS radio in 1942; he was head of the concert-music division of BMI (1954–77) and was associated with the International Music Council of UNESCO (from 1958). With Stokowski, he founded the Contemporary Music Soc. in 1952; later was active with various other organizations, including the American Music Center, the Charles Ives Soc., and the American Composers Orch. He wrote a column for the *Saturday Review* (1957–68); also contributed to other journals. He ed. various collections of works by early American composers and publ. the study *Leopold Stokowski: A Counterpoint of View* (1982).

Daniélou, Alain, French musicologist; b. Paris, Oct. 4, 1907; d. Lausanne, Jan. 27, 1994. He devoted himself mainly to the study of Asian music. He lectured at the Univ. of Benares (1949–54); was director of research in Madras (1954–56) and at the Inst. of Indology in Pondicherry (1956–59). In 1959 he was appointed instructor at the École Française d'Extrême Orient in Paris. In 1963 he assumed the post of director of the International Inst. for Comparative Studies.

WRITINGS: *Introduction to the Study of Musical Scales* (London, 1943); *Northern Indian Music* (2 vols., Calcutta, 1949, 1953; 2nd ed., rev., 1968, as *The Ragas of Northern Indian Music*); *La Musique du Cambodge et du Laos* (Pondicherry, 1957); *Traité de musicologie comparée* (Paris, 1959); *Purānas: Textes des Purānas sur la théorie musicale* (Pondicherry, 1959); *Bharata, Muni, Le Gitālamkāra* (Pondicherry, 1960); *Inde* (Paris, 1966); *Sémantique musicale* (Paris, 1967); *La Situation de la musique et des musiciens dans les pays d'orient* (Florence, 1971; Eng. tr., 1971).

Danielpour, Richard, American composer; b. N.Y., Jan. 28, 1956. He studied at Oberlin (Ohio) College, then at the New England Cons. of Music in Boston (B.M., 1980) before pursuing graduate studies in composition with Mennin and Persichetti at the Juilliard School in N.Y. (M.M., 1982; D.M.A., 1986) and piano studies with Hollander and Lettvin. He taught at the College of New Rochelle and Marymount Manhattan College (1984–88). In 1989 he was a guest composer at the Accademia di Santa Cecilia in Rome. In 1991–92 he was composer-in-residence of the Seattle Sym. Orch., and in 1994 of the Santa Fe (N.Mex.) Chamber Music Festival. Danielpour's music exhibits a modern Romantic tenor and is often programmatically derived.

WORKS: BALLET: *Anima Mundi* (1995; also a concert suite). **ORCH.:** 3 syms.: No. 1, *Dona Nobis Pacem* (1984; rev. 1985), No. 2, *Visions*, for Soprano, Tenor, and Orch., after Dylan Thomas (1986; San Francisco, Dec. 19, 1986), and No. 3, *Journey Without Distance*, for Soprano, Chamber Chorus, and Orch., after Schumann (1989–90; Akron, Feb. 24, 1990); *First Light* for Chamber Orch. (1988; also for Orch., 1989); *The Awakened Heart* (1990); 2 piano concertos: No. 1, *Metamorphosis* (N.Y., April 21, 1990) and No. 2 (1993; N.Y., March 30, 1994); *Song of Remembrance* (1991); *Toward the Splendid City* (1992); Cello Concerto (San Francisco, Sept. 14, 1994). **CHAMBER:** 3 string quartets (n.d., withdrawn; *Shadow Dances*, 1993; *Psalms of Sorrow*, 1994); *Urban Dances I* (1989) and *II* (1993) for Brass Quintet; Piano Quintet (1988). **PIANO:** *Piano Fantasy* (1980); *The Enchanted Garden* (1992). **VOCAL:** *Prologue and Prayer* for Chorus and String Orch. (1982; rev. 1988); *Sonnets to Orpheus I* for Soprano and Ensemble (1992) and *II* for Baritone and Ensemble (1994).

Daniels, Barbara, American soprano; b. Newark, Ohio, May 7, 1946. She studied at Ohio State Univ. (B.Mus., 1969) and the Univ. of Cincinnati College-Cons. of Music (M.A., 1971). In 1973 she made her operatic debut as Susanna in *Le nozze di Figaro* at the West Palm Beach (Fla.) Opera; then was a member of the Innsbruck Landestheater (1974–76), Kassel Staatstheater (1976–78), and Cologne Opera (1978–82). In 1978 she appeared as Rosalinde at London's Covent Garden, and on Sept. 30, 1983, she made her Metropolitan Opera debut in N.Y. as Musetta, also making guest appearances at the Vienna State Opera, the Chicago Lyric Opera, the Paris Opéra, and the Bavarian State Opera in Munich. Among her other roles are Violetta, Alice Ford, Massenet's Manon, and Micaëla.

Daniels, Mabel Wheeler, American composer; b. Swampscott, Mass., Nov. 27, 1878; d. Boston, March 10, 1971. She studied at Radcliffe College (B.A., 1900), with Chadwick in Boston, and with Thuille in Munich (1904–05). She was director of the Radcliffe Glee Club (1911–13) and head of music at Simmons College in Boston (1913–18). In 1931 she held a MacDowell fellowship, and was awarded honorary doctorates from Boston Univ. (1939), Wheaton College (1957), and the New England Cons. of Music (1958). Daniels became best known as a composer of choral music. Her experiences abroad were captured in her *An American Girl in Munich: Impressions of a Music Student* (Boston, 1905).

WORKS: DRAMATIC: OPERETTAS: *A Copper Complication* (1900); *The Court of Hearts* (1900; Cambridge, Mass., Jan. 2, 1901); *The Show Girl* (1902; in collaboration with D. Stevens). **OPERA SKETCH:** *Alice in Wonderland Continued* (Brookline, Mass., May 20, 1904). **ORCH.:** Suite for Strings (1910); *Deep Forest* for Small Orch. (N.Y., June 3, 1931; arranged for Full Orch., 1934; Boston, April 16, 1937); *Pirates' Island* (1934; Harrisburg, Pa., Feb. 19, 1935); *In memoriam* (1945); *Digressions*, ballet for Strings (1947); Overture (1951). **CHAMBER:** *Pastoral Ode* for Flute and Strings (1940); *3 Observations* for 3 Woodwinds (1943); *4 Observations* for 4 Strings (1945); Violin Sonata (n.d.). **VOCAL: CHORAL WITH ORCH.:** *The Desolate City*, with baritone solo (1913); *Peace with a Sword* (1917); *Songs of Elfland* (St. Louis, Feb. 2, 1924); *The Holy Star* (1928); *A Holiday Fantasy* (1928); *Exultate Deo* (Boston, May 31, 1929); *The Song of Jael*, with soprano solo (1937; Worcester, Oct. 5, 1940); *A Psalm of Praise* (Cambridge, Mass., Dec. 3, 1954). **OTHER CHORAL:** *In Springtime*, cycle for Women's Voices (1910); *Eastern Song* and *The Voice of My Beloved* for Women's Voices, Piano, and 2 Violins (both 1911); *Flowerwagon* for Women's Chorus and Piano (1914); *The Girl Scouts Marching Song* (1918); *Oh God of all our Glorious Past* (1930); *Through the Dark the Dreamers Came* for Women's or Mixed Chorus (c.1930; rev. 1961); *The Christ Child* for Chorus and Piano (1931); *A Night in Bethlehem* (1954). Also numerous songs.

Dankevich, Konstantin, eminent Ukrainian composer and teacher; b. Odessa, Dec. 24, 1905; d. Kiev, Feb. 26, 1984. He studied with Zolotarev at the Odessa Cons., graduating in 1929. In 1942 he was made artistic director of the Red Army Ensemble of Songs and Dance in Tbilisi. From 1944 to 1953 he was a prof. of composition at the Odessa Cons.; in 1953 he was appointed to the faculty of the Kiev Cons. In his works, Dankevich utilized motifs of Ukrainian and Russian folk songs. He first attracted attention with his opera *Bogdan Khmelnitsky* (Kiev, Jan. 29, 1951), on a subject from Ukrainian history, which was attacked for its libretto and its unsuitable music; Dankevich revised the score, after which it gained favorable notices in Russia. He also wrote the opera *Nazar Stodolya* (Kharkov, May 28, 1960). His most popular score was *Lileya*, a ballet (1939). Other works included 2 syms. (1937, 1945), several overtures, and patriotic choruses, including *Poem of the Ukraine* (1960) and the ideological cantata to his own words, *The Dawn of Communism Has Risen over Us* (1961). A monograph on him was publ. in Ukrainian in Kiev (1959).

Dankworth, John (Philip William), English alto saxophonist, clarinetist, bandleader, and composer-arranger; b. London, Sept. 20, 1927. He studied at the Royal Academy of Music in London (1944–46); then played alto saxophone and clarinet in jazz groups; formed his own septet in 1950, then his own jazz orch. in 1953. After his marriage to **Cleo Laine** in 1958, he toured with her, appearing as a guest conductor in England and the U.S. His compositions include *Improvisations* (1959; with M. Seiber); *Escapade* (1967); *Tom Sawyer's Saturday* for Narrator and Orch. (1967); String Quintet (1971); Piano Concerto (1972). In 1974 he was made a Commander of the Order of the British Empire.

BIBL.: G. Collier, *Cleo and J.* (London, 1976).

Danon, Oskar, Serbian conductor; b. Sarajevo, Feb. 7, 1913. He was educated at the Prague Cons. and the Univ. of Prague (Ph.D., 1938). In 1940 he became a conductor at the Belgrade Opera; was its director (1945–60). He also conducted throughout Europe, both opera and sym. concerts.

Danuser, Hermann, eminent German musicologist; b. Frauenfeld, Switzerland, Oct. 3, 1946. After training at the Hochschule für Musik and the Univ. in Zürich (graduated, 1973), he went to Berlin and completed his education at the Hochschule der Künste (1974–82) and the Technical Univ. (Habilitation, 1982). He taught musicology at the Hochschule für Musik und Theater in Hannover (1982–88) and at the Albert-Ludwigs-Univ. in Freiburg-im-Breisgau (1988–93). In 1992 he became coordinator of research for the Paul Sacher Stiftung in Basel and in 1993 prof. of musicology at the Humboldt Univ. in Berlin. Danuser is an authority on the music of the 20th century. Among his books are *Musikalische Prosa* (1975), *Die Musik des 20. Jahrhunderts* (1986), *Gustav Mahler: Das Lied von der Erde* (1986), and *Gustav Mahler und seine Zeit* (1991).

D'Arányi, Jelly. See **Arányi, Jelly d'.**

Darclée, Hariclea (real name, **Haricly Hartulary**), Romanian soprano; b. Braila, June 10, 1860; d. Bucharest, Jan. 10, 1939. She studied in Bucharest and Paris; made her debut as Marguerite at the Paris Opéra in 1888; then sang at La Scala in Milan, creating La Wally on Jan. 20, 1892; also sang in Rome, N.Y., St. Petersburg, Moscow, and in South America before retiring in 1918. She was particularly distinguished for her Italian repertoire; she created the role of Tosca (Rome, Jan. 14, 1900); also was known for her performances of roles in Wagner's operas.

Darcy, Robert, French-born Belgian cellist and composer; b. Paris, Nov. 10, 1910; d. Schaerbeek, near Brussels, June 6, 1967. He obtained the Premier Prix in cello at the Lyons Cons. (1928); studied composition with Francis Bousquet and Paul Vidal. He played the cello in orchs. in Paris and Brussels. Mobilized in 1939, he was taken prisoner of war in June 1940; while in captivity, he organized a prisoners' orch.; after his release he returned to Belgium, becoming a naturalized citizen in 1949. His style is rooted in neo-Classicism, with an admixture of atonal elements.

WORKS: ORCH.: *Scherzo* (1923); *Rêverie* (1931); *7 Sketches* for Small Orch. (1933); Suite for Wind Orch. (1935); Suite for Strings (1936); Concerto for 4 Cellos and Wind Orch. (1936); *Piece* for 2 Cellos and Orch. (1937); *Fantasie* for Cello and Orch. (1937); *3 Marines* (1939); Concerto for 4 Saxophones and Orch. (1939); *Danses mosanes* (1943); Trumpet Concerto (1948); Piano Concerto (1951); Sym. (1953); *Concerto for Orchestra* (1965). **CHAMBER:** 3 quartets for 4 Cellos (1935–37); 3 string quartets (1936–50); *Caprice* for Wind Quintet (1936); Sextet for Winds (1937); *6 Pieces* for 4 Cellos (1937); Trio for Oboe, Clarinet, and Bassoon (1938); Quartet for 4 Saxophones (1938); Bassoon Sonata (1948); Piece for Wind Quintet (1962). **VOCAL:** Songs.

Darke, Harold (Edwin), English organist, teacher, and composer; b. London, Oct. 29, 1888; d. Cambridge, Nov. 28, 1976. He studied with Parratt (organ) and Stanford (composition) at the Royal College of Music in London, where he served as a prof. of organ (1919–69); he also was organist at St. Michael's Church, Cornhill (1916–41; 1945–66) and at King's College, Cambridge (1941–45). In 1966 he was made a Commander of the Order of the British Empire. He wrote sacred music, organ and piano pieces, and songs.

BIBL.: G. Beechley, "H. D.'s Church Music," *Musical Times* (Aug. 1988).

Darnton, (Philip) Christian, English composer; b. near Leeds, Oct. 30, 1905; d. Hove, April 14, 1981. He began piano lessons at the age of 4 and began composing at 9; after studies with F. Corder, Sr., at the Brighton School of Music, he went to London for studies with Craxton (piano) at the Matthay School and Dale (composition) at the Royal Academy of Music; later was a student of Wood (composition) and Rootham (theory) at Caius College, Cambridge (1923–26), Jacob at the Royal College of Music, London (1927), and Butting in Berlin (1928–29). He publ. *You and Music* (Harmondsworth, 1939; 2nd ed., 1946).

WORKS: *Fantasy Fair*, opera; 3 syms.; 2 piano concertos; *Suite concertante* for Violin and Chamber Orch. (1938); *5 Orchestral Pieces* (Warsaw, April 14, 1939); *Jet Pilot*, cantata (1950); *Concerto for Orchestra* (1970–73).

Darré, Jeanne-Marie, French pianist and teacher; b. Givet, July 30, 1905. She studied with Marguerite Long and Isidor Philipp in Paris. After numerous concerts in France and elsewhere in Europe, she made her U.S. debut in N.Y. (1962); then made a successful series of tours in the U.S., appearing with major American orchs. In 1958 she became a teacher at the Paris Cons. A virtuoso in the grand manner, Darré produced a sensation by playing several piano concertos on a single night.

Dart, (Robert) Thurston, eminent English musicologist and keyboard player; b. London, Sept. 3, 1921; d. there, March 6, 1971. He studied keyboard instruments at the Royal College of Music in London (1938–39); also took courses in mathematics at Univ. College, Exeter (B.Sc., 1942). In 1947 he became an assistant lecturer in music at the Univ. of Cambridge, then a full lecturer in 1952, and finally a prof. of music in 1962. In 1964 he was named King Edward Prof. of Music at King's College of the Univ. of London. As a performing musician, he made numerous appearances on the harpsichord; also appeared as organist and performer on Baroque keyboard instruments. He served as ed. of the *Galpin Society Journal* (1947–54) and secretary of the documentary ed. *Musica Britannica* (1950–65). His magnum opus was *The Interpretation of Music* (London, 1954; 5th ed., 1984; Ger. tr., 1959, as *Practica musica*; Swedish tr., 1964). He also ed. works by Morley, Purcell, John Bull, and others.

BIBL.: I. Bent, ed., *Source Materials and the Interpretation of Music: A Memorial Volume to T. D.* (London, 1981).

Darvos, Gábor, Hungarian composer; b. Szatmárnémeti, Jan. 18, 1911; d. Budapest, Feb. 18, 1985. He studied bassoon and composition (with Kodály) at the Budapest Academy of Music (1926–32). After a South American sojourn (1939–48), he returned to Budapest and worked at the Hungarian Radio (1949–60); he also was ed.-in-chief of *Editio Musica Budapest* (1955–57) and artistic director of Hungaroton Records (1957–59); subsequently he was music advisor to Artisjus, the Hungarian Copyright Office (1960–72). In 1955 he was awarded the Erkel Prize.

WORKS: ORCH.: *Improvisations symphoniques* for Piano and Orch. (1963; rev. as *Fantázia* for Piano and Chamber Ensemble, 1983); *Szimfonikus etűdök* (Symphonic Etudes; 1984). **CHAMBER:** *Rotation for 5* for Vibraphone, Marimbaphone, Guitar, Cimbalom, and Piano (1967); *Magánzárka* (Solitary Confinement) for Pecussion and Tape (1970). **VOCAL:** *Medália* (Medal) for Soprano, Percussion, Keyboard Instruments, and Tape (1965); *A Torony* (The Tower) for Voices and Instruments (1967; also for Chorus and Tape, 1984); *Passiózene* (Passion Music) for Voices and Tape (1974–78); *Bánat* (Grief) for Baritone, Orch., and Tape (1978). **TAPE:** *Preludium* (1970); *Reminiszcenciák* (Reminiscences; 1979); *Poèmes électroniques* (1982–83).

D'Ascoli, Bernard, blind French pianist; b. Aubagne, Nov. 18, 1958. He was stricken with blindness at the age of 3, but by the time he was 11 he was able to read music via Braille, which allowed him to pursue studies at the Marseilles Cons. (1973–77). In 1978 he won 1st prize in the Maria Canals competition in Barcelona, and in 1981 he took 3rd prize in the Leeds competition. In 1981 he made his Paris debut at the Salle Cortot, followed by his first appearance in London in 1982. In 1983 he made his Australian debut in Sydney, and in 1985 his U.S. debut as soloist with the Houston Sym. Orch. He played for the first time in Vienna in 1986 and in Tokyo in 1988. In addition to his engagements with leading orchs. of the day, he also appeared widely as a recitalist.

Dashow, James (Hilyer), American composer; b. Chicago, Nov. 7, 1944. After studies with Babbitt, Cone, Kim, and Randall at Princeton Univ. (B.A., 1966), with Berger, Boykan, and Shifrin at Brandeis Univ. (M.F.A., 1969), and with Petrassi at the Accademia di Santa Cecilia in Rome (diploma, 1971), he founded the Forum Players (1971–75), a contemporary chamber music group. He served as director of the Studio di Musica Elettronica Sciadoni in Rome (from 1975). From 1982 to 1989 he taught computer music at the Centro di Sonologia Computazionale at the Univ. of Padua; also was guest lecturer in various European and U.S. cities. He was a producer of contemporary music programs for the RAI from 1985 to 1992. In 1969 he held a Fulbright fellowship; later accolades included grants from the NEA (1976, 1981) and the Rockefeller Foundation (1982), an award from the American Academy and Inst. of Arts and Letters (1984), and a Guggenheim fellowship (1989).

WORKS: *Songs of Despair* for Soprano and 11 Instruments (1968–69); *Transformations* for Dance and Electronics (1969); *Astrazioni Pomeridiane* for Orch. (1970–71); *BURST!* for Soprano and Electronics (1971); *Maximus* for Soprano, 3 Wind Players, Piano, and Percussion (1972–73); *At Delphi* for Soprano and Electronics (1975); *Whispers out of Time* for Electronics (1975–76); *Effetti collaterali* for Clarinet and Computer-generated Electronics (1976); *Il piccolo principe*, opera (1981–82); *Songs from a Spiral Tree* for Mezzo-soprano, Flute, and Harp (1984–86); *Oro, argento, and legno* for Flute and Computer (1987); *Archimede*, theater piece (1988); *Disclosures* for Cello and Computer (1988–89); *4/3*, trio for Violin, Cello, and Piano (1989–91); *Ritrono a Delfi* for Alto Flute and Electronics (1990); *Reconstructions* for Harp and Computer (1992); *A Sheaf of Times*, septet for Flute, Clarinet, Harp, Percussion, Piano, Violin, and Cello (1992–94); *Morfologie* for Trumpet and Computer (1993).

Daugherty, Michael, American composer; b. Cedar Rapids, Iowa, April 28, 1954. He studied with Wuorinen at the Manhattan School of Music (M.A., 1976) and with Druckman, Brown, Reynolds, Rands, and Evans at Yale Univ. (M.M.A., 1982; D.M.A., 1986); then traveled to Hamburg, where he studied with Ligeti at the Hochschule für Musik (1982–84). He also studied at IRCAM on a Fulbright fellowship (1978–80). He received an NEA Composition Fellowship in 1980; subsequently joined the faculty at the Oberlin (Ohio) College Cons. of Music (1986), becoming director of its Summer Electronic Music Workshop.

WORKS: ORCH.: *5 Seasons* (1980); *Mxyzptlk* for 2 Flute Soloists and Chamber Orch. (1988; Cleveland, Feb. 6, 1989); *Oh Lois!* (St. Paul, Minn., April 4, 1989); *Lex* (1990). **CHAMBER ENSEMBLE:** *Future Music, Part I* (1984); *Future Funk* (1985); *Piano Plus* (1985); *Re: Percussion* (1986); *Blue Like an Orange* (1987); *SNAP!* (1987); *Bounce I* (1988); *Lex* (1989). **OTHER:** Synthesizer and computer pieces.

d'Avalos, Francesco, Italian composer, conductor, and teacher; b. Naples, April 11, 1930. He received lessons in piano from age 12 from Vincenzo Vitale, and then studied orchestration with Renato Parodi. He pursued training in philosophy at the Univ. of Naples, and also studied composition at the Cons. of San Pietro a Majella in Naples (diploma with high honors, 1955) and conducting with Kempen, Celibidache, and Ferrara at the Accademia Musicale Chigiana in Siena. After making his conducting debut with the RAI Orch. in Rome in 1964, he appeared as a guest conductor in Italy and Europe. He taught at the Bari Cons. before joining the faculty of the Cons. of San Pietro a Majella in 1979. As a composer, d'Avalos followed an avant-, later post-avant-, garde path. As a conductor, he strives to preserve the composer's intentions even in the face of received tradition. He has won particular distinction for his performances of the Italian symphonic repertoire of the 19th and early 20th centuries.

WORKS: MUSIC DRAMA: *Maria di Venosa* (1992). **ORCH.:** *Psyché and Eros*, suite (1947); *Music* for Orch. and Piano Concertante (1948); *Music for Imaginary Drama* (1951); 2 syms.: No. 1 for Soprano and Orch. (1955) and No. 2 for Soprano and Orch. (1991); *Studio sinfonico* (1956; rev. 1982); *Hymne an die Nacht* (1958); *Qumrān* (1966). **CHAMBER:** String Quintet (1960); Quintet for Piano and Strings (1967). **VOCAL:** *3 Songs on Japanese Poems* for Soprano and Orch. (1953); *Vexilla Regis* for Chorus and Orch. (1960); *The River Wang* for Soprano, Double String Orch., and 2 Flutes (1961); *Lines* for Soprano and Orch. (1963); *Die stille Stadt* for Soprano, String Orch., and Timpani (1995).

Davico, Vincenzo, Italian composer; b. Monaco, Jan. 14, 1889; d. Rome, Dec. 8, 1969. He was a student of Cravero in Turin and of Reger in Leipzig. After living in Paris (1918–40), he settled in Rome.

WORKS: DRAMATIC: OPERAS: *La dogaressa* (1919; Monte Carlo, Feb. 26, 1920); *Berlingaccio* (1931); *La principessa prigioniera* (Bergamo, Sept. 29, 1940). **BALLETS:** *L'agonia della rosa* (Paris, May 2, 1927); *Narciso* (San Remo, Feb. 19, 1935). **ORCH.:** *Polifemo* (1910); *La principessa lontana*, suite (1911); *Impressioni pagane* (1916); *Poema erotico* (1913); *Impressioni romane* (1913); *Impressioni antiche* (1916); *Poemetti pastorali* (1926). **CHAMBER:** Cello Sonata (1909); Piano Trio (1911);

Sonatina rustica for Violin and Piano (1926); *10 variazioni senza tema* for Cello and Piano (n.d.); *Soliloqui* for Cello and Piano (1945); piano pieces. **VOCAL:** *La tentazione di San Antonio* for Soli, Chorus, and Orch. (1921); *Cantata breve* for Baritone, Chorus, and Orch. (1945); *Requiem per la morte d'un povero* for Soli, Chorus, and Orch. (1949–50); songs.

BIBL.: C. Valabrega, *La lirica da camera di V. D.* (Rome, 1953).

Dávid, Gyula, Hungarian composer and teacher; b. Budapest, May 6, 1913; d. there, March 14, 1977. He studied with Kodály at the Budapest Academy of Music (graduated, 1938). He was a violist in several orchs. (1938–45), and also a conductor at the National Theater in Budapest (until 1949); then taught chamber music at the Academy of Music (1950–60; 1967–77) and the Béla Bartók Music School (1964–67). In 1952 and 1955 he received the Erkel Prize, and in 1957 the Kossuth Prize. His compositional practices ranged from free use of folk melodies to strict 12-tone procedures.

WORKS: DRAMATIC: *Nádasban* (In the Reeds), ballet (1961); much incidental music. **ORCH.:** 4 syms. (1948, 1958, 1960, 1970); *Balettzene* (Ballet Music; 1948); *Tánczene* (Dance Music; 1950); Viola Concerto (1950); *Színházi zene* (Theater Music; 1955); Sinfonietta (1960); Concerto Grosso for Viola and Strings (1963); Violin Concerto (1966); Horn Concerto (1971); *Ünnepi nyitány* (Festive Overture; 1972). **CHAMBER:** 5 wind quintets (1949, 1955, 1964, 1967, 1968); Flute Sonata (1954); 2 string quartets (1962, 1973); *Preludio* for Flute and Piano (1964); *Miniatűrök* (Miniatures) for Brass Sextet (1968); Viola Sonatina (1969); Trio for Violin, Cello, and Piano (1972); *Pezzo* for Viola and Piano (1974). **PIANO:** Sonata (1955). **VOCAL:** *Felhőtlen ég* (Cloudless Skies), cantata for Chorus and Orch. (1964); *A rózsa lágolás* (The Rose is Aflame) for Woman's Voice, Flute, and Viola (1966); *Égő szavakkal* (With Flaming Words), cantata for Chorus and Orch. (1969); choruses.

BIBL.: J. Breuer, *D. G.* (Budapest, 1966).

David, Hans T(heodor), German-American musicologist; b. Speyer, Palatinate, July 8, 1902; d. Ann Arbor, Mich., Oct. 30, 1967. He was educated at the univs. of Tübingen, Göttingen, and Berlin (Ph.D., 1928, with the diss. *Johann Schobert als Sonatenkomponist*; publ. in Borna, 1928). In 1933 he went to the Netherlands, and in 1936 he emigrated to the U.S. In 1937 he joined the staff at the N.Y. Public Libary, and in 1939 became a lecturer at N.Y. Univ.; after serving as a prof. and head of the musicology dept. at Southern Methodist Univ. in Dallas (1945–50), he was prof. of music history at the Univ. of Mich. at Ann Arbor (from 1950). He was highly regarded as a Bach scholar.

WRITINGS: With A. Rau, *A Catalog of Music of American Moravians, 1742–1842, from the Archives of the Moravian Church at Bethlehem* (Bethlehem, Pa., 1938); *Bach's 'Musical Offering': History, Interpretation and Analysis* (N.Y., 1945); ed. with A. Mendel, *The Bach Reader* (N.Y., 1945; 2nd ed., rev., 1966).

David, Johann Nepomuk, outstanding Austrian composer and teacher, father of **Thomas Christian David**; b. Eferding, Nov. 30, 1895; d. Stuttgart, Dec. 22, 1977. He studied with Joseph Marx at the Vienna Academy of Music (1921–22). After serving as a schoolteacher, organist, and choirmaster in Wels (1924–34), he joined the faculty of the Leipzig Landeskonservatorium (later the Hochschule für Musik) in 1934, becoming its director in 1942. He was subsequently director at the Salzburg Mozarteum (1945–48). In 1948 he was appointed prof. of composition at the Musikhochschule in Stuttgart, serving until 1963. In 1978 the International Johann Nepomuk David Soc. was organized in Stuttgart. His mastery of counterpoint is revealed in all of his works, which are polyphonic in structure.

WRITINGS (all publ. in Göttingen unless otherwise given): *Die Jupitersymphonie* (1953); *Die zweistimmigen Inventionen von Johann Sebastian Bach* (1957); *Die dreistimmigen Inventionen von Johann Sebastian Bach* (1959); *Das wohltemperierte Klavier: Versuch einer Synopsis* (1962); *Der musikalische Satz im Spiegel der Zeit* (Graz, 1963).

WORKS: ORCH.: Concerto Grosso for Chamber Orch. (1923); Flute Concerto (1934); 2 partitas (1935, 1939); 8 numbered syms.: No. 1 in A minor (1936), No. 2 (1938), No. 3 (1940), No. 4 (1945), No. 5 (1951; Stuttgart, May 3, 1952), No. 6 (1954; Vienna, June 22, 1955), No. 7 (1956; Stuttgart, Oct. 10, 1957), and No. 8 (1964–65; Stuttgart, Nov. 20, 1965); *Kume, kum, geselle min*, divertimento on old folk songs (1938); *Variationen über ein Thema von Johann Sebastian Bach* (1942); *Symphonische Variationen über ein Thema von Heinrich Schütz* (1942); 3 concertos for Strings: No. 1 (1950), No. 2 (1951) and No. 3 (1974; Berlin, Feb. 20, 1975); 2 violin concertos: No. 1 (1952; Stuttgart, April 25, 1954) and No. 2 (1957; Munich, April 22, 1958); *Deutsche Tänze* for Strings (1953; Wiesbaden, July 7, 1954); *Sinfonia preclassica super nomen H-A-S-E* (1953; St. Veit, Carinthia, Oct. 16, 1954); *Sinfonia breve* (1955; Baden-Baden, March 4, 1956); *Melancholia* for Viola and Chamber Orch. (1958; Lucerne, Aug. 31, 1961); *Magische Quadrate* (1959; Recklinghausen, March 23, 1960); *Sinfonia per archi* (1959; Linz, Nov. 30, 1960); *Spiegelkabinett*, waltz (Dresden, Nov. 20, 1960); Organ Concerto (1965; Cologne, Nov. 28, 1966); *Variationen über ein Thema von Josquin des Prés* for Flute, Horn, and Strings (1966; Munich, April 17, 1969); Concerto for Violin, Cello, and Small Orch. (1969); *Chaconne* (1972). **CHAMBER:** String Trio (1935); *Duo concertante* for Violin and Cello (1937); Sonata for Flute, Viola, and Guitar (1940); Trio for Flute, Violin, and Viola (1942); solo sonatas for Flute (1942), Violin (1943), Viola (1943), Cello (1944), and Lute (1944); Sonata for Flute and Viola (1943); Sonata for 2 Violins (1945); 4 string trios (1945, 1945, 1948, 1948); Clarinet Sonata (1948); Sonata for 3 Cellos (1962); Sonata No. 2 for Solo Violin (1963); Trio for Flute, Violin, and Cello (1974). **ORGAN:** *Ricercare* (1925); *Chaconne* (1927); *2 Hymnen* (1928); *Passamezzo and Fugue* (1928); *Toccata and Fugue* (1928); *Fantasia super "L'homme armé"* (1929); *Preambel und Fuge* (1930); *Das Choralwerk* (21 vols., 1932–73); *2 Fantasias and Fugue* (1935); *Ricercare* (1937); *Introitus, Chorale and Fugue on a Theme of Bruckner* for Organ and 9 Wind Instruments (1939); *Chaconne and Fugue* (1962); *Toccata and Fugue* (1962); *Partita über B-A-C-H* (1964); *12 Orgelfugen durch alle Tonarten* (1968); *Partita* (1970); *Partita* for Violin and Organ (1975). **SACRED VOCAL:** *Stabat Mater* for 6-part Chorus (1927); *Deutsche Messe* for Chorus (1952; Leipzig, Feb. 19, 1953); *Missa choralis (de Angelis) ad quattuor voces inaequales* (1953; Linz, Jan. 17, 1954); *Requiem chorale* for Soloists, Chorus, and Orch. (1956; Vienna, June 11, 1957); *Ezzolied*, oratorio for Soloists, Chorus, and Orch. (1957; Berlin, May 17, 1960); *O, wir armen Sunder*, cantata for Alto, Chorus, and Organ (1966); *Mass* (1968); *Komm, Heiliger Geist*, cantata for 2 Choruses and Orch. (1972; Linz, March 26, 1974); also motets.

BIBL.: R. Klein, *J.N. D.* (Vienna, 1964); H. Bertram, *Material—Struktur—Form: Studien zur musikalischen Ordnung bei J.N. D.* (Wiesbaden, 1965); H. Stuckenschmidt, *J.N. D.* (Wiesbaden, 1965); G. Sievers, ed., *Ex Deo nascimur: Festschrift zum 75. Geburtstag von J.N. D.* (Wiesbaden, 1970); W. Dallmann, *J.N. D.: Das Choralwerk für Orgel* (Bern, 1994).

David, José, French composer, son of **Léon David**; b. Sables-d'Olonne, Jan. 6, 1913. He entered the Paris Cons. in 1933; studied with Fauchet, Jacques de la Presle, and Büsser; also had lessons with Dupré (organ) and Emmanuel (music history). He collaborated with N. Obouhov in *Traité d'harmonie tonale et atonale* (Paris, 1947).

WORKS: *Impressions de Vendée* for Piano (1944; also for Orch.); *La Ballade de Florentin Prunier* for Voice, Violin, Cello, and Piano (1947); *Symphonie* for Ondes Martenot and Orch. (1948); *Jacquet le Prioux*, ballet (1950); Violin Sonata (1955); *Laudate dominum* for 3 Men's Voices and Organ (1960); *2 Poems* for Voice and Piano (1973).

David, Karl Heinrich, Swiss composer; b. St. Gallen, Dec. 30, 1884; d. Nervi, Italy, May 17, 1951. He studied in Cologne and

Munich; taught at the Basel Cons. (1910–14); then at Cologne and Berlin (1914–17); in 1918, returned to Switzerland. He was the ed. of the *Schweizer Musikzeitung* in Zürich (1928–41).

WORKS: OPERAS: *Aschenputtel* (Basel, Oct. 21, 1921); *Der Sizilianer* (Zürich, Oct. 22, 1924); *Jugendfestspiel* (Zürich, June 8, 1924); *Traumwandel* (Zürich, Jan. 29, 1928); *Weekend*, comic opera (1933). **ORCH.:** Piano Concerto (1929); *Ballet* (1931); *Pezzo sinfonico* (1945); Concerto for Saxophone and Strings (1947); *Symphonie de la côte d'argent* (1948); *Mascarade*, overture (1950); *Andante and Rondo* for Violin and Chamber Orch. **CHAMBER:** *2 Pieces* for Piano and 9 Woodwinds; Viola Suite; Piano Trio; Quartet for Saxophone, Violin, Cello, and Piano (1946); Duet for Horn and Piano (1951). **VOCAL:** *Das hohe Lied Salomonis* for Soprano, Tenor, Women's Chorus, and Orch.; songs.

David, Léon, French tenor, father of **José David**; b. Sables-d'Olonne, Dec. 18, 1867; d. there, Oct. 27, 1962. He studied at the Nantes Cons. and later at the Paris Cons. He made his debut at the Opéra-Comique in Paris in 1892; appeared subsequently in Brussels, Monte Carlo, Marseilles, Bordeaux, Cairo, Lisbon, Bucharest, and other cities. From 1924 to 1938 he was a prof. of singing at the Paris Cons.

David, Thomas Christian, noted Austrian composer and teacher, son of **Johann Nepomuk David**; b. Wels, Dec. 22, 1925. He was a choirboy at Leipzig's Thomaskirche and studied with his father at the Leipzig Hochschule für Musik before studying musicology at the Univ. of Tübingen (1948). He taught flute at the Salzburg Mozarteum (1945–48) and was founder-director of the South German Madrigal Choir (1952–57); he then went to Vienna, where he taught harmony and composition at the Academy of Music (from 1957), later serving as prof. of harmony at the Hochschule für Musik (from 1973) and director of the Austrian Composers Soc. (from 1986). He also taught at the Univ. of Teheran and was director of the Iranian Television Orch. (1967–73). He made various appearances as a flutist, harpsichordist, pianist, choral director, and conductor. David received several awards for his compositions, which are noted for their innovative, modernistic uses of contrapuntal devices.

WORKS: OPERAS: *Atossa* (1968); *Der Weg nach Emmaus* (Alpbach, Aug. 28, 1982); *Als Oedipus kam* (1986). **ORCH.:** *Divertimento* for Strings (1951); *Serenade* for Strings (1957); Concerto No. 1 for Strings (1961; Munich, Sept. 20, 1962); Concerto for 12 Strings (1964); Sym. No. 1 (1965); Concerto (1967); Concerto No. 2 for Strings (1971; Teheran, Jan. 10, 1973); Concerto No. 3 for Strings (1974; Linz, Nov. 30, 1975); *Entrada* (1975); *Sinfonia giacosa* (1975); Concerto grosso (1978; Prague, Feb. 21, 1982); *Duplum* for Wind Orch. (East Lansing, Mich., June 3, 1983); *Festival Prologue* (1982). **CONCERTOS WITH ORCH.:** Piano (1960); Clarinet (1961); 5 Brass Instruments and Strings (1962); Violin (1962; Munich, May 26, 1965); Violin (No. 1, 1962; Munich, May 26, 1965; No. 2, 1986); Guitar and Chamber Orch. (1963); Violin and Strings (Teheran, Sept. 3, 1970); Oboe (1975; Hagen, March 18, 1976); Organ (1976; Vienna, Dec. 11, 1981); 2 Violins and Strings (1977; Hagen, March 8, 1979); Bass (1979; Hagen, Oct. 16, 1980); 3 Violins and Strings (1981); Flute (1982; Vienna, March 3, 1983); Cello (1983; Vienna, March 20, 1987); Violin, Clarinet, and Piano (1983; N.Y., May 1, 1984); Sinfonia Concertante for Violin, Clarinet, Piano, and Wind Orch. (1986). **CHAMBER:** 5 string quartets (1952, 1953, 1954, 1965, 1967); Quartet for Flute and String Trio (1958); Concerto for 9 Instruments (1961; Vienna, Feb. 28, 1962); Quintet for Clarinet and String Quartet (1963); 3 Intermezzi for Violin and Piano (1964); 2 wind quintets (1966, 1979); Cello Sonata (1970); Trio for Violin, Clarinet, and Piano (1977); *Tricinium* for Flute, English Horn or Viola, and Cello (1977); Quartet for Oboe and String Trio (1979); Sonata for Violin and Viola (1980); Sonata for Clarinet and Violin (1980); Sonata for Flute and Clarinet (1980); Sonata for Cello and Guitar (1982); Trio for Violin, Viola, and Cello (1984); Toccata for 9 Flutes (1985); Trio for Violin, Cello, and Piano (1985); Trio for Flute, Viola, and Guitar (1985); Quintet for 2 Flutes, Violin, Cello, and Piano (1987); many works for solo instruments. **VOCAL:** 10 madrigals (1950–82); *Wer ist es*, motet (1960); *Missa in honorem Mariae* (1965); *Das Lied des Menschen*, oratorio (1975; Gumersbach, May 1978); *Die Vogel*, cantata for Soprano, Flute, Clarinet, and Piano (1981); *Und wir haben erkannt*, motet (1982); also 15 songs (1963–86).

Davidenko, Alexander, Russian composer; b. Odessa, April 13, 1899; d. Moscow, May 1, 1934. He organized, with Bely, the Procoll (Production Collective of Composers) in Russia in 1925. His most important work is the opera *1905* (1929–33; with B. Shekhter); another opera, *Down the Cliff*, was left incomplete. He also composed workers's songs.

BIBL.: N. Martynov, ed., *A. D.* (Leningrad, 1968).

Davidovich, Bella, esteemed Russian-born American pianist and pedagogue, mother of **Dmitry Sitkovetsky**; b. Baku, July 16, 1928. Her maternal grandfather was concertmaster of the Baku opera orch. and her mother was a pianist. She began formal piano training when she was 6; at age 9 she appeared as soloist in the Beethoven 1st Piano Concerto in Baku. In 1939 she was sent to Moscow to pursue studies with Igumnov, with whom she subsequently studied at the Cons. (1946–48), where she completed her training with Yakov Flier (1948–54). In 1949 she captured joint 1st prize at the Chopin Competition in Warsaw, which launched her upon a highly successful career in Russia and Eastern Europe; she was a soloist each season with the Leningrad Phil. (1950–78) and taught at the Cons. (1962–78). In 1967 she made her first appearance outside Russia, playing in Amsterdam; in 1971 she made a tour of Italy. Following the defection of her son to the West in 1977, she was refused permission to perform there by the Soviet government. In 1978 she emigrated to the U.S., becoming a naturalized American citizen in 1984. In 1979 she made an acclaimed debut in a recital at N.Y.'s Carnegie Hall. In 1982 she joined the faculty of the Juilliard School in N.Y. but continued to pursue an international career. In 1988 she and her son visited Russia, being the first émigrés to be invited to perform there by Goskontsert since the Gorbachev era of reform was launched.

Davidovsky, Mario, Argentine composer and teacher; b. Buenos Aires, March 4, 1934. He studied composition and theory with Guillermo Graetzer in Buenos Aires and also took courses with Teodor Fuchs, Erwin Leuchter, and Ernesto Epstein; then continued his training with Babbitt at the Berkshire Music Center in Tanglewood (summer, 1958). He worked at the Columbia-Princeton Electronic Music Center (from 1960) and taught at the Univ. of Mich. (1964), the Di Tella Inst. of Buenos Aires (1965), the Manhattan School of Music in N.Y. (1968–69), Yale Univ. (1969–70), City College of the City Univ. of N.Y. (1968–80), Columbia Univ. (1981–94), where he served as director of the Columbia-Princeton Electronic Music Center, and Harvard Univ. (from 1994). He held 2 Guggenheim fellowships (1960, 1971) and in 1971 received the Pulitzer Prize in Music for his *Synchronisms No. 6* for Piano and Electronics. In 1982 he was elected a member of the Inst. of the American Academy and Inst. of Arts and Letters. Davidovsky's method of composition tends toward mathematical parameters; his series of 8 compositions entitled *Synchronisms* derives from the numerical coordinates of acoustical elements; electronic sound is integral to most of his work.

WORKS: ORCH.: Concertino for Percussion and Strings (1954); *Suite sinfonica para "El payaso"* (1955); *Serie sinfonica* (1959); *Contrastes No. 1* for Strings and Electronics (1960); *Pianos* (1961); *Transientes* (1972); *Synchronisms No. 7* for Orch. and Electronics (1973); *Consorts* for Symphonic Band (1980); *Divertimento* for Cello and Orch. (1984); Concertante for String Quartet and Orch. (Philadelphia, March 8, 1990). **CHAMBER:** 4 string quartets (1954, 1958, 1976, 1980); Quintet for Clarinet and Strings (1955); *3 Pieces* for Woodwind Quintet (1956); *Noneto* for 9 Instruments (1956); Trio for Clarinet, Trumpet, and Viola (1962); *Synchronisms No. 1* for Flute and Electronics (1963), *No. 2* for Flute, Clarinet, Violin, Cello, and Electronics (1964), *No. 5* for Percussion Ensemble and Electronics (1969), *No. 6* for Piano and Electronics (1970), and *No. 8* for Woodwind Quintet and Electronics (1974); *Inflexions* for Chamber Ensemble (1965); *Junctures* for Flute, Clarinet, and Violin (1966); *Music* for Violin (1968); *Chacona* for Violin, Cello, and Piano (1971); *Pennplay* for 16 Players (1978); String Trio (1982); *Capriccio* for 2 Pianos (1985). **VOCAL:** *Synchronisms No. 4* for Men's Voices or Mixed Chorus and Electronics (1967); *Scenes from Shir-ha-shirim* for Soprano, 2 Tenors, Baritone, and Chamber Orch. (1975); *Romancero* for Soprano, Flute, Clarinet, Violin, and Cello (1983). **TAPE:** 3 studies (1961, 1962, 1965).

Davidson, Lyle, American composer; b. Randolph, Vt., Feb. 25, 1938. He studied at the Univ. of Vermont (1956–58), the New England Cons. of Music in Boston (B.M., 1962; M.M., 1964), Brandeis Univ., and Boston Univ. He was active in avant-garde circles, composing pieces for the theater, dance, and films. His output utilized various contemporary techniques, including the use of electronics.

Davidson, Tina, American composer; b. Stockholm (of American parents), Dec. 30, 1952. She studied piano at the State Univ. of N.Y. at Oneonta (1962–70) and at the School of Music in Tel Aviv (1971), and composition with Brant, Fine, and Nowak at Bennington (Vt.) College (1972–76). From 1978 to 1989 she was assoc. director of RELÂCHE, a Philadelphia-based ensemble for the performance of contemporary music, with which she was active until the late 1980s. From 1981 to 1985 she taught piano at Drexel Univ. She was composer-in-residence of the Orch. Soc. of Philadelphia (1992–94) and of Opera Delaware in Wilmington (1994–97). Her music is replete with colorful sonoric effects and extra-musical influences.

WORKS: *Recollections of Darkness*, string trio (1975); *2 Beasts from the Forest of Imaginary Beings* for Narrator and Orch. (1975; Bennington, Vt., April 20, 1976); *Complex* for Wind Orch. (1977); *Man-Faced-Scarab* for Soprano, Flute, Clarinet, and Oboe (1978); *Witches' Hammer* for Voice and Percussion (1979); *Dancers* for Orch. (Philadelphia, May 25, 1980); Quintet for Alto Flute, Bass Clarinet, Viola, Cello, and Double Bass (1981); Piano Concerto (1981; Philadelphia, Feb. 28, 1983); *Unicorn/Tapestry* for Voice, Cello, and Tape (1982); *Wait for the End of Dreaming* for 2 Baritone Saxophones and Double Bass (1983–85); *Day of Rage* for Piano (1984); *Blood Memory: A Long Quiet after the Call* for Cello and Orch. (1985; Bennington, Vt., June 1, 1986); *Never Love a Wild Thing* for Variable Ensemble (1986); *Star Myths* for Piano or Variable Ensemble (1987); *Cassandra Sings* for String Quartet (1988); *In the Darkness I Find a Face (It is Mine)* for Orch. (1989); *Blue Dawn (The Promised Fruit)* for 3 Winds and Piano (1989); *The Selkie Boy* for Orch. (1991); *They Come Dancing* for Orch. (1994; Roanoke, Va., Jan. 23, 1995).

Davies, Ben(jamin) Grey, Welsh tenor; b. Pontardawe, near Swansea, South Wales, Jan. 6, 1858; d. Bath, England, March 28, 1943. After winning 1st prize for solo singing at the Swansea Eisteddfod in 1877, he studied at the Royal Academy of Music in London (1878–80) under Randegger, Sr., and Fiori, winning the bronze, silver, and gold medals for best declamatory English singing. His debut was in Birmingham, Oct. 11, 1881, in *The Bohemian Girl.* He created the title role in Sullivan's *Ivanhoe* (London, Jan. 31, 1891). In 1892 he made his debut at London's Covent Garden as Faust. He made his first appearance in the U.S. at the Chicago World's Fair in 1893, then was mainly active as a concert and oratorio singer. He sang regularly at the Handel Festivals until 1926.

Davies, Dennis Russell, significant American conductor; b. Toledo, Ohio, April 16, 1944. He studied piano with Lonny Epstein and Sascha Gorodnitzki and conducting with Morel and Mester at the Juilliard School of Music in N.Y. (B.Mus., 1966; M.S., 1968; D.M.A., 1972), where he also taught (1968–71) and was co-founder (with Berio) of the Juilliard Ensemble (1968–74). He was music director of the Norwalk (Conn.) Sym. Orch. (1968–73), the St. Paul (Minn.) Chamber Orch. (1972–80), the Cabrillo (Calif.) Music Festival (1974–91), and the American Composers Orch. in N.Y. (from 1977). In 1978 he made his first appearance at the Bayreuth Festival, conducting *Der fliegende Holländer.* He was Generalmusikdirektor of the Württemberg State Theater in Stuttgart (1980–87), principal conductor and director of Classical music programming at the Saratoga (N.Y.) Performing Arts Center (1985–88), and Generalmusikdirektor of Bonn (1987–95), where he was chief conductor of the Orchester der Beethovenhalle and of the Opera. In 1994 he led the orch. on a tour of North America. From 1991 to 1996 he was music director of the Brooklyn Academy of Music and principal conductor of the Brooklyn Phil. He likewise was chief conductor of the Stuttgart Chamber Orch. (from 1995) and the Austrian Radio Sym. Orch. in Vienna (from 1996). In 1987 he received the Alice M. Ditson conductor's award. Davies has acquired a notable reputation as a champion of contemporary music.

Davies, Fanny, English pianist; b. Guernsey, June 27, 1861; d. London, Sept. 1, 1934. She studied at the Leipzig Cons. with Reinecke and Paul (piano) and Jadassohn (theory) in 1882–83, and at the Hoch Cons. in Frankfurt am Main with Clara Schumann (1883–85); she also was a pupil of Scholz (fugue and composition). Her London debut took place at the Crystal Palace on Oct. 17, 1885; she then made successful tours in England, Germany, France, and Italy. Her performances of the works of Robert Schumann and Brahms were particularly admired.

Davies, Hugh (Seymour), English composer and instrument inventor; b. Exmouth, April 23, 1943. He was a pupil of Rubbra at the Univ. of Oxford (1961–64) and subsequently an assistant to Stockhausen as well as a member of his electronic music group (1964–66); then was director of the electronic music studio at Goldsmiths' College, Univ. of London (1967–86), and subsequently was active as a consultant researcher. In addition to works for traditional instruments, he wrote music utilizing instruments of his own invention, tape, and electronics.

WORKS: *Contact* for Piano (1963); *Vom ertrunkenen Mädchen* for Soprano, Flute, Clarinet, and Piano (1964); Quintet for Electronics (1967–68); *Interfaces* for Tape and Electronics (1967–68); *Kangaroo* for Organ (1968); *Beautiful Seaweeds* for Players, Dancers, and Slides (1972–73); Wind Trio (1973–75); *The Musical Educator* for Speaker, Players, Dancers, and Slides (1974); *Natural Images* for Tape (1976); *Melodic Gestures* for Flute, Violin, Cello, and Piano (1978); *Ex una voce* for Tenor and Synthesizer (1979). **SPECIALLY-CONSTRUCTED INSTRUMENTS:** *Shozyg I, II, I + II* (1968); *Spring Song* (1970); *Gentle Springs* (1973); *Music for Bowed Diaphragms* (1973); *My Spring Collection* (1975); *Salad* (1977); *The Search for the Music of the Spheres* (1978); *At Home* (1978).

Davies, (Albert) Meredith, English organist, conductor, and music educator; b. Birkenhead, July 30, 1922. He studied at the Royal College of Music in London and was an organ scholar at Keble College, Oxford, later becoming organist at St. Albans Cathedral (1947) and at Hereford Cathedral (1949). He then pursued conducting studies with Previtali at the Accademia di Santa Cecilia in Rome (1954, 1956). He was organist at New College, Oxford (1956–60), assoc. conductor (1957–59) and deputy music director (1959–60) of the City of Birmingham Sym. Orch., and director of the City of Birmingham Choir (1957–64). Davies was music director of the English Opera Group in London (1963–5) and of the Vancouver (B.C.) Sym. Orch. (1964–71), and also chief conductor of the BBC Training Orch. in London (1969–72). He was conductor of the Royal Choral Soc. of London (1972–85) and of the Leeds Phil. (1975–84). From 1979 to 1988 he was principal of Trinity College of Music in London. In 1982 he was made a Commander of the Order of the British Empire.

Davies, Sir Peter Maxwell, distinguished English composer and conductor; b. Manchester, Sept. 8, 1934. He studied at the Royal Manchester College of Music (graduated, 1952) and at the Univ. of Manchester (Mus.B., 1956). In 1957 he won an Italian government scholarship to study in Rome with Petrassi. After serving as director of music at Cirencester Grammar School (1959–62), he received a Harkness fellowship to pursue studies with Sessions and Babbitt at Princeton Univ. (1962–64). In 1966 he was composer-in-residence at the Univ. of Adelaide. In 1967 he became co-founder (with Harrison Birtwistle) of the Pierrot Players in London, a contemporary music ensemble. In 1970 it was renamed the Fires of London, and Davies remained its artistic director until 1987. In 1970 he made his residence on the island of Hoy, Orkney, where, in 1977, he founded the St. Magnus Festival of Orkney, serving as its artistic director, and, from 1986, its president. From 1979 to 1983 he also was director of Music of the Dartington Hall Summer School. In 1985 he became composer-in-residence and assoc. conductor of the Scottish Chamber Orch. in Glasgow, with which he toured widely. In 1992 he assumed similar positions with the BBC Phil. in Manchester and the Royal Phil. in London. Davies received honorary doctorates from various institutions of higher learning, among them the univs. of Edinburgh (1979), Aberdeen (1981), Manchester (1983), and Bristol (1984). In 1981 he was made a Commander of the Order of the British Empire and in 1987 he was knighted.

In his works, Davies combines seemingly incongruous elements, which include reverential evocations of medieval hymnody, surrealistic depictions of historical personages, and hedonistic musical theatrics. Among his most arresting works in this synthetic manner is his *8 Songs for a Mad King* (1969), a fantastic suite of heterogeneously arranged pieces representing the etiology of the madness of King George III; at the other end of the spectrum is his *Vesalii Icones* (1969), inspired by the anatomical drawings of Christ's Passion and Resurrection by the Renaissance artist Vesalius. In his later scores, he often found inspiration in the Orkney landscape and literary heritage.

WORKS: DRAMATIC: OPERAS: *Taverner* (1962–70; London, July 12, 1972); *The Martyrdom of St. Magnus* (1976; Orkney, June 18, 1977); *The Lighthouse* (1979; Edinburgh, Sept. 2, 1980); *Resurrection* (1987; Darmstadt, Sept. 18, 1988); *Redemption* (1988); *The Doctors of Myddfai* (1993–96). **MUSIC THEATER:** *8 Songs for a Mad King* for Baritone, Flute, Clarinet, Keyboards, Percussion, Violin, and Cello (London, April 22, 1969); *Vesalii Icones* for Dancer, Cello, Flute, Clarinet, Piano, Percussion, and Viola (London, Dec. 9, 1969); *Blind Man's Bluff* for Mime, Soprano, Mezzo-soprano, and Small Orch. (London, May 29, 1972); *Miss Donnithorne's Maggot* for Female Singer, Flute, Clarinet, Violin, Cello, Piano, Percussion, and 4 Mechanical Metronomes (Adelaide, March 9, 1974); *Salome*, ballet (Copenhagen, Nov. 10, 1978; concert suite, London, March 16, 1979); *Le Jongleur de Notre Dame* for Mime, Baritone, Flute, Clarinet, Violin, Cello, Piano, Percussion, and Children's Band (Orkney, June 18, 1978); *The Yellow-Cake Revue*, anti-nuclear cabaret for Singer and Piano (Orkney, June 21, 1980); *The Medium*, monodrama for Mezzo-soprano (Orkney, July 21, 1981); *The No. 11 Bus* for Mime, 2 Dancers, Mezzo-soprano, Tenor, Baritone, Flute, Clarinet, Violin, Cello, Piano, and Percussion (London, March 20, 1984); *Caroline Mathilde*, ballet (1990).

ORCH.: *Prolation* (1958; Rome, June 10, 1959); 2 fantasias on an In Nomine of John Taverner (London, Sept. 13, 1962; London, April 30, 1965); *Sinfonia* for Chamber Orch. (London, May 1962); *St. Thomas Wake Foxtrot for Orchestra on a Pavan by John Bull* (Dortmund, June 2, 1969); *Wordles Blis* (London, Aug. 28, 1969); *The Boy Friend*, film suite (London, Dec. 11, 1971); 5 syms.: No. 1 (1976; London, Feb. 2, 1978), No. 2 (1980; Boston, Feb. 26, 1981), No. 3 (1984; Manchester, Feb. 19, 1985), No. 4 (London, Sept. 10, 1989), and No. 5 (1993–94; London, Aug. 10, 1994); Sinfonia Concertante for Wind Quintet and Chamber Orch. (1982; London, Aug. 12, 1983); *Sinfonietta accademica* (Edinburgh, Oct. 6, 1983); *An Orkney Wedding, with Sunrise* for Bagpipes and Orch. (Boston, May 10, 1985); Violin Concerto (1985; Kirkwall, Orkney, June 21, 1986); *Jimmack the Postie* (Kirkwall, June 22, 1986); 10 *Strathclyde* concertos: No. 1 for Oboe and Orch. (Glasgow, April 29, 1987), No. 2 for Cello and Orch. (1988; Glasgow, Feb. 1, 1989), No. 3 for Horn, Trumpet, and Orch. (1989; Glasgow, Jan. 19, 1990), No. 4 for Clarinet and Orch. (1990), No. 5 for Violin, Viola, and Orch. (Glasgow, March 13, 1991), No. 6 for Flute and Orch. (1991), No. 7 for Double Bass and Orch. (Glasgow, Nov. 25, 1992), No. 8 for Bassoon and Orch. (1993), No. 9 for Chamber Orch. (1994), and No. 10 for Chamber Orch. (1995); Trumpet Concerto (Hiroshima, Sept. 21, 1988); *Ojai Festival Overture* (Ojai, Calif., June 1, 1991); *Sir Charles: His Pavan* (1992); *A Spell for Green Corn: The MacDonald Dances* (1993); *Chat Moss* (1993).

CHAMBER: Movement for String Quartet (1952; London, May 23, 1983); Trumpet Sonata (1955); *Stedman Doubles* for Clarinet and Percussion for 1 Player (1956; rev. 1968); Clarinet Sonata (1956; Darmstadt, July 20, 1957); *Alma redemptoris mater* for Flute, Oboe, 2 Clarinets, Bassoon, and Horn (Dartington, Aug. 7, 1957); *St. Michael* for 17 Wind Instruments (1957; London, July 13, 1959); Sextet for Flute, Clarinet, Harpsichord, Percussion, Viola, and Cello (1958; rev. as a Septet with the addition of a guitar, 1972); *Ricercar and Doubles on "To Many a Well"* for Flute, Oboe, Clarinet, Bassoon, Horn, Harpsichord, Viola, and Cello (1959); String Quartet (London, Nov. 1961); *Shakespeare Music* for 11 Instruments (London, Dec. 8, 1964); *7 in Nomine* for 10 Instruments (London, Dec. 3, 1965); *Antechrist* for Piccolo, Bass Clarinet, 3 Percussionists, Violin, and Cello (London, May 30, 1967); *Hymnos* for Clarinet and Piano (1967); *Stedman Caters* for Flute, Clarinet, Harpsichord, Viola, Cello, and Percussion (London, May 30, 1968); *Eram quasi agnus* for 7 Wind Instruments, Handbells, and Harp (London, June 10, 1969); *Canon in memoriam Igor Stravinsky* for Flute, Clarinet, Harp, and String Quartet (broadcast, April 6, 1972); *Hymn to St. Magnus* for Flute, Clarinet, Piano, Viola, Cello, and Percussion (London, Oct. 13, 1972); *Renaissance Scottish Dances* for Flute, Clarinet, Guitar, Violin, Cello, and Percussion (Dartington, July 29, 1973); *Si quis diligit Me* for Alto Flute, Clarinet, Celesta, Crotales, Viola, and Cello (Dartington, July 29, 1973); *All Sons of Adam* for Alto Flute, Clarinet, Celesta, Guitar, Marimba, Viola, and Cello (London, Feb. 20, 1974); *Psalm 124* for Flute, Bass Clarinet, Glockenspiel, Marimba, Guitar, Violin, and Cello (Dartington, July 28, 1974); *Ave Maris Stella* for Flute, Clarinet, Piano, Marimba, Viola, and Cello (Bath, May 27, 1975); *3 Studies for Percussion* for 11 Players (1975); *My Lady Lothian's Lilt* for Alto Flute, Bass Clarinet, Viola, Cello, Percussion, and Mezzo-sorpano Obbligato (Dartington, Aug. 20, 1975); *Kinloche His Fantassie* for Flute, Clarinet, Harpsichord, Glockenspiel, Violin, and Cello (Dartington, Aug. 19, 1976); *Runes from a Holy Island* for Alto Flute, Clarinet, Celesta, Percussion, Viola, and Cello (broadcast, Nov. 6, 1977); *A Mirror of Whitening Light* for 14 Instruments (London, March 23, 1977); *Our Father Whiche in Heaven Art* for Flute, Clarinet, Celesta, Marimba, Violin, and Cello (Dartington, Aug. 18, 1977); *Little Quartet No. 2* for String Quartet (1977; rev. version, Canton, N.Y., Nov. 12, 1987); *A Welcome to Orkney* for Flute, Oboe, Clarinet, Bassoon, Horn, 2 String Quartets, and Double Bass (Orkney, June 20, 1980); *Little Quartet No. 1* for String Quartet (1980; Dartington, July 26, 1982); *The Bairns of Brugh* for Piccolo, Bass Clarinet, Piano, Marimba, Viola, and Cello (Bergen, May 30, 1981); Quintet for 2 Trumpets, Horn, Trombone, and Tuba (1981; Boston, March 19, 1982); *Image, Reflection, Shadow* for Flute, Clarinet, Cimbalom, Piano, Violin, and Cello (Lucerne, Aug. 22, 1981); *The Pole Star*, march for 2 Trumpets, Horn, Trombone, and Tuba (1982; Dartington, Aug. 18, 1983); *Birthday Music for John* for Flute, Viola, and Cello (Swansea, Oct. 13, 1983); Sonatine for Violin and Cimbalom (London, June 8, 1984); *Unbroken Circle* for Alto Flute, Bass Clarinet, Piano, Viola, and Cello (Bath, June 1, 1984); *Dowland: Farewell—A Fancye* for Alto Flute, Bass Clarinet, Viola, Cello, Piano, and Marimba (1986; London, Jan. 20, 1987); *Mishkenot* for 9 Players (London, May 3, 1988). **SOLO INSTRUMENTS:** *Solita* for Flute (1969); *Turris campanarum sonatium* for Percussion (1971); *The Door of the Sun* for Viola (1975); *The Kestrel Paced Round the Sun* for Flute (1975); *The 7 Brightnesses* for

Clarinet (1975); *3 Organ Voluntaries* (1976); *Nocturne* for Alto Flute (1979); Piano Sonata (1981); *Hill Runes* for Guitar (1981); *Sea Eagle* for Horn (1982); Organ Sonata (1982); Guitar Sonata (1984); *First Grace of Light* for Oboe (1991).

VOCAL: *5 Motets* for Soprano, Alto, Tenor, Bass, Chorus, and 16 Instruments (1959; London, March 1, 1965); *O magnum mysterium* for Chorus, Organ, and Ensemble (Cirencester, Dec. 8, 1960); *Ave Maria, Hail Blessed Flower* for Chorus (1961); *Te lucis ante terminum* for Chorus and 12 Instruments (Cirencester, Nov. 30, 1961); *Leopardi Fragments* for Soprano, Mezzo-soprano, and 8 Instruments (London, July 1962); *Veni sancte spiritus* for Soprano, Alto, Tenor, Bass, Chorus, and Orch. (1963; Cheltenham, July 10, 1964); *Ecce manus tradentis* for Soprano, Alto, Tenor, Bass, Chorus, and Ensemble (Wiltshire, Aug. 20, 1965); *Revelation and Fall* for Soprano and 16 Instruments (1965; London, Feb. 26, 1968; rev. 1980); *Notre Dame des Fleurs* for Soprano, Mezzo-soprano, Countertenor, and 6 Instruments (1966; London, March 17, 1973); *Missa super L'Homme Armé* for Voice and 6 Players (1968; London, April 22, 1969); *From Stone to Thorn* for Mezzo-soprano and 4 Instruments (Oxford, June 30, 1971); *Stone Litany: Runes from a House of the Dead* for Mezzo-soprano and Orch. (Glasgow, Sept. 22, 1973); *Fiddlers at the Wedding* for Mezzo-soprano and 4 Instruments (1973; Paris, May 3, 1974); *Dark Angels* for Mezzo-soprano and Guitar (1974); *Anakreontika* for Mezzo-soprano and 4 Instruments (London, Sept. 17, 1976); *The Blind Fiddler* for Mezzo-soprano and 6 Instruments (Edinburgh, Feb. 20, 1976); *Norn pater noster* for Chorus and Organ (1977); *Westerlings* for Chorus (1977); *Black Pentecost* for Baritone, Mezzo-soprano, and Orch. (1979; London, May 11, 1982); *Solstice of Light* for Tenor, Chorus, and Organ (Orkney, June 18, 1979); *Into the Labyrinth* for Tenor and Chamber Orch. (Kirkwall, June 22, 1983); *1 Star, at Last* for Chorus (Cambridge, Dec. 24, 1984); *Excuse Me* for Mezzo-soprano and 5 Instruments (1985; London, Feb. 26, 1986); *House of Winter* for Chorus (Orkney, June 23, 1986); *Sea Runes* for Chorus (N.Y., Nov. 16, 1986); *Winterfold* for Mezzo-soprano and 7 Instruments (1986; London, Jan. 20, 1987); *Hallelujah! The Lord Almightie* for Chorus and Organ (Edinburgh, June 11, 1989); *Hymn to the Word of God* for Soloists and Chorus (1990); *Corpus Christi, with Cat and Mouse* for Chorus (1993); *A Holy Calendar* for Chorus (1993).

OTHER: Various works for young people.

BIBL.: P. Griffiths, *P.M. D.* (London, 1982); M. Seabrook, *Max: The Life and Music of P.M. D.* (London, 1994).

Davies, Ryland, Welsh tenor; b. Cwm, Ebbw Vale, Feb. 9, 1943. He studied at the Royal Manchester College of Music. He made his operatic debut as Almaviva in 1964 with the Welsh National Opera; then sang in Glasgow, Glyndebourne, and London (1969). He sang in San Francisco in 1970; made his Metropolitan Opera debut in N.Y. on Oct. 15, 1975, as Ferrando in *Così fan tutte.* He appeared in major European operatic centers, and also toured widely as a concert singer. Among his best known roles were Tamino, Don Ottavio, Belmonte, Lensky, Nemorino, and Pelléas. From 1966 to 1981 he was married to **Anne Howells**.

Davies, Tudor, Welsh tenor; b. Cymmer, Nov. 12, 1892; d. London, April 2, 1958. He studied in Cardiff and at the Royal Academy of Music in London. He appeared at the Old Vic; joined the British National Opera Co. in 1922; created the title role in *Hugh the Drover* by Vaughan Williams (London, July 14, 1924); in 1928 he sang in the U.S. with the Civic Opera in Philadelphia. He then was a principal singer with the Old Vic and the Sadler's Wells Opera (1931–41); was a member of the Carl Rosa Opera Co. (1941–46); also appeared in concerts.

Davies, Sir (Henry) Walford, eminent Welsh organist, music educator, and composer; b. Oswestry, Sept. 6, 1869; d. Wrington, Somerset, March 11, 1941. He was a pupil of Parratt at St. George's Chapel in Windsor, where he served as his assistant (1885–90); then studied with Parry and Stanford at the Royal College of Music in London, where he subsequently taught (1895–1903). He was conductor of the Bach Choir (1903–7); held positions as organist at Christ Church, Hampstead (1891–98), the Temple Church (1898–1918), and St. George's Chapel (1927–32); was a prof. of music at the Univ. of Wales (1919–26). Between 1924 and 1934 he led the novel broadcasting series "Music Lessons in Schools." He was knighted in 1922, and in 1934 was appointed Master of the King's Musick. He publ. *The Musical Outlook in Wales* (London, 1926), *The Pursuit of Music* (London, 1935), and *Music and Worship* (with H. Grace; London, 1935). As a composer, Davies is remembered for his *Solemn Melody* for Organ and Strings (1908) and his march for the Royal Air Force (1917); he also wrote a Sym. (1911), *Conversations* for Piano and Orch. (London, Oct. 14, 1914), overtures, choral music, chamber music, songs, and many pieces for school performance.

BIBL.: H. Colles, *W. D., A Biography* (London, 1942); D. Allsobrook, *Music for Wales: W. D. and the National Council of Music, 1918–1941* (Cardiff, 1992).

Davis, Andrew (Frank), esteemed English conductor; b. Ashridge, Hertfordshire, Feb. 2, 1944. He studied piano at the Royal Academy of Music in London, and after taking organ lessons with Peter Hurford and Piet Kee, was an organ scholar at King's College, Cambridge (1963–67). He then received instruction in conducting from Franco Ferrara at the Accademia di Santa Cecilia in Rome. Following a successful guest conducting engagement with the BBC Sym. Orch. in London in 1970, he served as assistant conductor of the BBC Scottish Sym. Orch. in Glasgow until 1973, making his debut as an opera conductor that same year at the Glyndebourne Festival. He was assoc. conductor of the New Philharmonia Orch. in London (1973–75) and principal guest conductor of the Royal Liverpool Phil. (1974–76). In 1974 he made his North American debut as a guest conductor with the Detroit Sym. Orch. He then was music director of the Toronto Sym. (1975–88), which, under his guidance, acquired a fine international reputation via major tours of North America, Europe, the People's Republic of China, and Japan. In 1982 he inaugurated the orch.'s new home, the Roy Thomson Hall in Toronto, in a gala concert. After completing his tenure, he served as the orch.'s conductor laureate from 1988 to 1990. In 1988 he was named chief conductor of the BBC Sym. Orch. in London and music director of the Glyndebourne Festival. In 1994 he conducted the 100th anniversary season of the Henry Wood Promenade Concerts in London with the BBC Sym. Orch. His 3rd marriage was to **Gianna Rolandi**. In 1992 he was made a Commander of the Order of the British Empire. His vast repertoire encompasses works from virtually every era, all of which display his wide sympathies, command of technique, and musical integrity.

Davis, Anthony, black American composer and pianist; b. Paterson, N.J., Feb. 20, 1951. He studied at Yale Univ. (B.A., 1975), proving himself to be an extremely facile jazz pianist; was co-founder of Advent (1973), a free jazz ensemble that included trombonist George Lewis, and then played in trumpeter Leo Smith's New Delta Ahkri band (1974–77). He also played in N.Y. with violinist Leroy Jenkins (1977–79) and with flutist James Newton, both active proponents of the Assn. for the Advancement of Creative Musicians. His compositions, while strictly notated, are improvisational in tone. His opera *X,* based on the life of Malcolm X, was premiered in Philadelphia in 1985; a performance followed in 1989 at N.Y.'s Lincoln Center. On June 14, 1992, his opera *Tania,* inspired by the Patty Hearst-Symbionese Liberation Army exploits, was performed for the first time in Philadelphia. Among his many recordings are *Of Blues and Dreams* (1978), *Hidden Voices* (with J. Newton; 1979), and *Under the Double Moon* (with J. Hoggard; 1982).

Davis, Carl, American conductor and composer; b. N.Y., Oct. 28, 1936. He was educated at the New England Cons. of Music in Boston and at Bard College (B.A.), his mentors in composition in the U.S. being Paul Nordoff and Hugo Kauder; also studied with Per Nørgård in Copenhagen. He became active in

England as a conductor and composer. From 1984 to 1987 he was principal conductor of the Bournemouth Pops. In 1987–88 he was assoc. conductor of the London Phil. He composed much stage, film, and television music. He also collaborated with Paul McCartney on the *Liverpool Oratorio* (1991).

WORKS: DRAMATIC: OPERA: *Peace* (1978). **TELEVISION OPERAS:** *The Arrangement* (1967); *Orpheus in the Underground* (1976). **MUSICALS:** *The Projector* (1971); *Pilgrim* (1975); *Cranford* (1976); *Alice in Wonderland* (1977); *The Wind in the Willows* (1986); *Kip's War* (1987). **BALLETS:** *Dances of Love and Death* (1981); *Fire and Ice* (1986); *The Portrait of Dorian Gray* (1987); *A Simple Man* (1987); *Liaisons Amoureuses* (1989); *Lipizzaner* (1989); *A Christmas Carol* (1992); *Savoy Suite* (1993). **FILM SCORES:** *The French Lieutenant's Woman* (1981); *Champions* (1984); *King David* (1985); *Girl in a Swing* (1988); *Scandal* (1988); *The Rainbow* (1988); *Frankenstein Unbound* (1989); *Fragments of Isabella* (1990); *Crucifer of Blood* (1991); *Raft of the Medusa* (1992); *The Voyage* (1993); *The Trial* (1993); also scores for various silent films, including *Napoleon* (1980), *Thief of Baghdad* (1984), *Ben Hur* (1987), and *City Lights* (1988). **ORCH.:** *Lines on London*, sym. (1980); *Overture on Australian Themes* (1981); Clarinet Concerto (1984); *Fantasy* for Flute, Strings, and Harpsichord (1985); *Glenlivet Fireworks Music* (1987); *The Pigeon's Progress* for Narrator and Orch. (1988); *A Duck's Diary* for Narrator and Orch. (1990); *The Town Fox* for Narrator and Orch. (1990). **VOCAL:** *The Most Wonderful Birthday of All* for Soprano and Orch. (1985); *Liverpool Oratorio* for Voices and Orch. (1991; in collaboration with P. McCartney).

Davis, Sir Colin (Rex), eminent English conductor; b. Weybridge, Sept. 25, 1927. He studied clarinet at the Royal College of Music in London, and played in the band of the Household Cavalry while serving in the army. He began his conducting career with the Kalmar Chamber Orch. and the Chelsea Opera Group; in 1958 he conducted a performance of *Die Entführung aus dem Serail* in London; from 1961 to 1965 he served as music director of Sadler's Wells. He made his U.S. debut as a guest conductor with the Minneapolis Sym. Orch. on Dec. 30, 1960; subsequently had engagements with the N.Y. Phil., the Philadelphia Orch., and the Los Angeles Phil. From 1972 to 1983 he served as principal guest conductor of the Boston Sym. Orch. On Jan. 20, 1967, he made his Metropolitan Opera debut in N.Y. conducting *Peter Grimes.* From 1967 to 1971 he was chief conductor of the BBC Sym. Orch. in London. In 1965 he conducted at the Royal Opera at Covent Garden; he succeeded Solti as its music director in 1971. Among his notable achievements was a production at Covent Garden of the *Ring* cycle between 1974 and 1976; in 1977 he became the first British conductor to appear at the Bayreuth Festival, conducting *Tannhäuser.* He conducted the Royal Opera during its tours in South Korea and Japan in 1979, and in the U.S. in 1984. In 1983 he was appointed chief conductor of the Bavarian Radio Sym. Orch. in Munich, which he led on a tour of North America in 1986. In 1986 he stepped down as music director at Covent Garden to devote himself fully to his duties in Munich and to pursue far-flung engagements as a guest conductor with major orchs. and opera houses of the world. In 1988 he was named to an international chair at the Royal Academy of Music. In 1993 he stepped down from his Munich position. In 1995 he became principal conductor of the London Sym. Orch. From 1998 he was also principal guest conductor of the N.Y. Phil. Davis is an authoritative interpreter of such masters as Mozart, Berlioz, Sibelius, and Stravinsky. He has also championed the cause of his British contemporaries, most notably Sir Michael Tippett. He was made a Commander of the Order of the British Empire in 1965, and was knighted in 1980. From 1949 to 1964 he was married to **April Cantelo**.

BIBL.: A. Blyth, *C. D.* (London, 1972).

Davis, Ivan, American pianist and teacher; b. Electra, Texas, Feb. 4, 1932. He studied piano with Silvio Scionti at North Texas State Univ. in Denton and later at the Accademia di Santa Cecilia in Rome with Carlo Zecchi. He also took private lessons with Horowitz, beginning in 1961. He obtained 1st prizes at the Busoni Competition in Bolzano (1958), the Casella Competition at Naples (1958), and the Franz Liszt Competition in N.Y. (1960). On Oct. 21, 1959, he made his N.Y. recital debut at Town Hall, and subsequently toured throughout the U.S. After making his London debut in 1966, he played on the Continent. In addition to serving on the faculty of the Univ. of Miami in Coral Gables (from 1966), he was a visiting prof. at the Indiana Univ. School of Music in Bloomington (1971–72); he also gave master classes in various locales throughout the U.S. His repertoire ranges from Scarlatti to Gershwin, showing special affinity for the works of Schumann, Chopin, Liszt, and Tchaikovsky.

Davis, John David, English composer and teacher; b. Birmingham, Oct. 22, 1867; d. Estoril, Portugal, Nov. 20, 1942. He studied in Frankfurt am Main and in Brussels. After returning to England in 1889, he taught in various schools in Birmingham; in 1905, was appointed prof. of composition at the Guildhall School of Music in London. He wrote an opera on a Russian subject, *The Zaporoges* (Birmingham, May 7, 1895); also a concert overture, *Germania*, 2 string quartets, 2 violin sonatas, piano pieces, and songs.

Davis, Miles (Dewey, III), famous black American jazz trumpeter, bandleader, and composer; b. Alton, Ill., May 25, 1926; d. Santa Monica, Calif., Sept. 28, 1991. He grew up in East St. Louis, Ill., where he began playing the trumpet at 13 and had lessons with Elwood Buchanan. Even before graduating from high school, he had professional stints in St. Louis. In 1944 he entered the Juilliard School of Music in N.Y. to pursue formal training, but he also frequented the jazz haunts of the city. In 1945 he quit Juilliard, and soon began playing and recording with Charlie Parker's quintet. He also toured with the bands of Benny Carter and Billy Eckstein. In 1948 he set out on his own with a bop group. With the arranger Gil Evans, he made a series of nonet recordings (1949–50), later collected and reissued as the album *Birth of the Cool* (1957). In 1954 his recording of *Walkin'* demonstrated his mastery of blues improvisation in a hard bop style; in 1955 he caused a sensation at the Newport Jazz Festival. In subsequent years, he performed and recorded with various small jazz groups. With his albums *Milestones* (1958) and *Kind of Blue* (1959; with the singles *So What* and *Flamenco Sketches*), Davis left bop behind and adopted a style marked by slow-moving modal harmonies. From 1964 to 1970 the Davis quintet included the saxophonist and composer Wayne Shorter, who proved an influential collaborator. Davis's penchant for intensive improvisation and rhythmic flexibility were showcased in such albums as *E.S.P.* (1965), *Sorcerer* (1967), and *Nefertiti* (1967). He then shifted focus once again and pursued the fusion style of jazz, notable for its use of acoustic sounds à la electronic instruments, improvisation, and rock. During this period, he brought out the bestselling album *Bitches Brew* (1969). After incorporating black American, African, Indian, and Brazilian elements into an original funk style, he dropped out of the jazz scene for health reasons from 1975 to 1980. In 1981 he was featured in the album *The Man with the Horn.* In 1982 he suffered a major stroke but, amazingly, fought his way back to health and made an extensive tour of Europe later that year; in 1983 he brought out yet another fine album, *Star People.* Always searching for new avenues of expression, Davis adapted songs by such rock stars as Michael Jackson and Cyndi Lauper. In July 1991, just 2 months before his death, he performed at the North Sea Jazz Festival in the Netherlands. With Q. Troupe, he publ. *Miles: The Autobiography* (N.Y., 1989). Davis was married and divorced 3 times. His 3rd wife (1981–88) was the actress Cicely Tyson.

BIBL.: M. James, *M. D.* (London, 1961); L. Feather, *From Satchmo to M.* (N.Y., 1972); B. Cole, *M. D.: A Musical Biography* (N.Y., 1974); I. Carr, *M. D.: A Critical Biography* (London, 1982; U.S. ed., 1982, as *M. D.: A Biography*); J. Chambers, *Milestones I: The Music and Times of M. D. to 1960* (Toronto, 1984); idem, *Milestones II: The Music and Times of M. D. Since 1960* (Toronto, 1985); R. Williams, *M. D.: The Man in the Green Shirt* (N.Y., 1993).

Davison, A(rchibald) T(hompson), eminent American music educator; b. Boston, Oct. 11, 1883; d. Brant Rock, Mass., Feb. 6, 1961. He studied at Harvard Univ. (B.A., 1906; M.A., 1907; Ph.D., 1908, with the diss. *The Harmonic Contributions of Claude Debussy*); then took lessons in organ with Widor in Paris (1908–9). Returning to America, he was organist and choirmaster at Harvard Univ. (1910–40); conducted the Harvard Glee Club (1912–33) and the Radcliffe Choral Soc. (1913–28); he began teaching at Harvard in 1917 as assistant prof.; subsequently he was assoc. prof. (1920–29), prof. of choral music (1929–40), and the James Edward Ditson Prof. of Music (1940–54). He held numerous honorary degrees, including those of D.Mus. at Williams College and the Univ. of Oxford; Fellow of the Royal College of Music, London; Litt.D. from Washington Univ. (1953); and L.H.D. from Temple Univ. (1955). He wrote 2 comic operas, the musical comedy *The Girl and the Chauffeur* (Boston, April 16, 1906), the *Tragic Overture*, and the symphonic poem *Hero and Leander*. His greatest achievement, however, was as an educator and popularizer of musical subjects: his lectures on music appreciation were broadcast and enjoyed considerable success among radio listeners. He was assoc. ed., with T. Surette, of a multivol. collection of vocal and instrumental pieces, the Concord Series of Educational Music, for which he made numerous arrangements.

WRITINGS (all publ. in Cambridge, Mass., unless otherwise given): *Protestant Church Music in America* (Boston, 1920; 2nd ed., enl., 1933); *Music Education in America* (N.Y., 1926); *Choral Conducting* (1940); *The Technique of Choral Composition* (1946); ed. with W. Apel, *Historical Anthology of Music* (vol. I, 1946; 2nd ed., rev., 1950; vol. II, 1950); *Bach and Handel: The Consummation of the Baroque in Music* (1951); *Church Music: Illusion and Reality* (1952); *Words and Music: A Lecture Delivered to the Whittal Pavilion of the Library of Congress* (Washington, D.C., 1954).

BIBL.: *Essays on Music in Honor of A.T. D. by his Associates* (Cambridge, Mass., 1957); D. Tovey, *A.T. D.: Harvard Musician and Scholar* (diss., Univ. of Mich., 1979).

Davy, Gloria, black American soprano; b. N.Y., March 29, 1931. She was a student of Belle Julie Soudent at the Juilliard School of Music in N.Y. (1948–53) and of Victor de Sabata in Milan. In 1953 she sang in the touring production of *Porgy and Bess*. On April 2, 1954, she appeared as the Countess in the U.S. premiere of *Capriccio* in N.Y. She made her European operatic debut in Nice as Aida in 1957, a role she repeated for her Metropolitan Opera debut in N.Y. on Feb. 12, 1958. She remained on the Metropolitan roster until 1961, appearing as Pamina, Nedda, and Leonora in *Il Trovatore*. Aida was her debut role at the Vienna State Opera in 1959 and at London's Covent Garden in 1960. From 1961 she appeared at the Berlin Deutsche Oper, singing such roles as Aida, Fiordiligi, Donna Anna, Cio-Cio-San, Donna Elvira, and Salome. She also pursued guest engagements in other European operatic centers (1963–69). From 1975 to 1985 she made regular concert tours in Europe. In 1983 she made her London recital debut at Wigmore Hall. She served as a prof. at the Indiana Univ. School of Music in Bloomington from 1985 to 1993.

Dawson, Frederick, English pianist and teacher; b. Leeds, July 16, 1868; d. Lymm, Cheshire, Oct. 23, 1940. He studied with his father, and later with Hallé and Dannreuther; by age 10 he could play the complete Bach "48" from memory. After additional guidance from A. Rubinstein, he pursued a successful career in his homeland and in Europe. He also taught at the Royal Manchester College of Music (from 1893) and at London's Royal College of Music. Dawson's repertory was extensive, embracing the early English virginalists through the French Impressionists of his own era. He publ. the study *The Pianoforte* (Glasgow, 1922).

Dawson, Ted, Canadian composer and teacher; b. Victoria, British Columbia, April 28, 1951. After training in violin, piano, and composition at the Victoria School of Music, he studied composition with Brian Cherney and Rudolf Komorous at the Univ. of Victoria (B.Mus., 1972); concurrently played viola in the Victoria Sym. Orch. He then pursued graduate studies in electronic music and composition with Gustav Ciamaga at the Univ. of Toronto (1972); he was also a student of Hambraeus and Lanza at McGill Univ. in Montreal (M.M.A., 1974) and took courses in music and visual arts at the Univ. of Toronto (1984), where he obtained his honors specialist certificate in music (1987). His advanced education was completed at the State Univ. of N.Y. at Buffalo (Ph.D., 1994). He taught at Concordia Univ. (1974–78) and Vanier College (1978–80) in Montreal, and then was assistant prof. at Queen's Univ. in Kingston, Ontario (1987–88) and at Brock Univ. in St. Catharines, Ontario (1988–90).

WORKS: *Pentad* for String Quartet (1971); *Concerto grosso I* for Quadraphonic Tape or Amplified Viola, Amplified Bassoon, Trombone, Percussion, and Stereo Tape (1973–74) and *II* for 5 Instrumental Soloists and Orch. (1973); *Chameleon* for Amplified Flute (1974–75); *The Land of Nurr* for Electronics (1975); *The Clouds of Magellan* for 3 Slide Projectors, Computerized Dissolver, Synchronization Tape, and Quadraphonic Audiotape (1976–77); *Binaries in Lyrae* for 4 Dancers, 2 Amplified Percussion Ensembles, Amplified Piano, and Lights (1977–78); *Megatherium* for 2 Amplified Pianos, Synthesizer, and Audiotape (1977–78); *Binaries* for 4 Optional Dancers, 2 Amplified Percussion, and Amplified Piano (1980); *Joint Actions* for Female Dancers and Double Bass (1980–81); *Traces in Glass* for Flute, Piano, and Percussion (1986); *5 Songs from the Late T'ang* for Baritone and Orch. (1987–88; also for Voice, Piano, and Percussion); *Portraits in a Landscape* for Tape (1988); *China Beach* for Amplified Piano and Tape (1992); Sym. No. 1 (1992–94).

Dawson, William Levi, black American composer; b. Anniston, Ala., Sept. 26, 1898; d. Tuskegee, Ala., May 2, 1990. He ran away from home at 13 to enter the Tuskegee Inst.; later played trombone on the Redpath Chautauqua Circuit; graduated from the Tuskegee Inst. in 1921; studied with Carl Busch in Kansas City and at the American Cons. in Chicago (M.A., 1927). He played 1st trombone in the Chicago Civic Orch. (1926–30); then conducted the Tuskegee Choir. Among his works was a *Negro Folk Symphony* (Philadelphia, Nov. 16, 1934; rev. 1952); *Out in the Fields* for Soprano and Orch. (1928); *Scherzo* for Orch. (1930); *A Negro Work Song* for Orch. (1940); Piano Trio (1925); Violin Sonata (1927); many choral part songs; numerous arrangements of spirituals and black folk songs.

BIBL.: J. Spady, *W.L. D.: A Umum Tribute* (Philadelphia, 1981).

Deák, Csaba, Hungarian-born Swedish composer; b. Budapest, April 16, 1932. He studied clarinet and composition at the Béla Bartók Cons. in Budapest (1949–55) and composition with Ferenc Farkas at the Budapest Academy of Music (1955–56); he subsequently went to Sweden, where he took composition lessons with Hilding Rosenberg. He also studied composition, clarinet, and conducting at the Ingesund School of Music in Arvika; he received his music teacher's certification from the Stockholm Musikhögskolan (1969). He taught at the Swedish State School of the Dance in Stockholm (from 1969) and at the Univ. of Göteborg (1971–74).

WORKS: DRAMATIC: *Fäderna* (The Fathers), chamber opera (Stockholm, Oct. 16, 1968); *Etude on Spring*, electronic ballet (1970); *Lucie's Ascent into Heaven*, an "astrophonic minimelodrama" (1973); *Bye-bye, Earth, A Play about Death* (1976–77); theater music. **ORCH.:** *Eden* for Symphonic Band (1978); *The Piper's Wedding* for Wind Quintet and Symphonic Band (1979); *Vivax* (1982); *5 Short Pieces* for Symphonic Band (1983); *Farina Pagus* for Symphonic Band (1983); *Concerto Maeutro* (1989); *Gustadolphory* for Symphonic Band (1989); *Ad Nordiam Hungarica* for Chamber Orch. (1991); Concerto for Clarinet and Wind Orch. (1992). **CHAMBER:** 2 string quartets (1959, 1967); *Duo Suite* for Flute and Clarinet (1960); *Air* for

Violin and Piano (1961); *121* for Winds, Percussion, and Double Bass (1969); Trio for Flute, Cello, and Piano (1971); *Andante och Rondo* for Wind Quintet (1973); *Verbunk* for Brass Sextet (1976); *Hungarian Dances* for Wind Quintet (1977); Octet for Wind Quintet and String Trio (1977); *Herykon* for Brass Quintet (1981); *Massallians* for Trumpet, Trombone, Brass Ensemble, and Percussion (1985); Saxophone Quartet (1986); Saxophone Quintet (1988); Quartet for Tubas (1990); *Magie noire* for Clarinet and String Quartet (1993); *Novem* for Saxophone Quartet and Brass Quintet (1994); piano pieces. **VOCAL:** Choral works; songs.

Dean, Stafford (Roderick), English bass; b. Kingswood, Surrey, June 20, 1937. He studied at Epsom College and at the Royal College of Music in London; also received private lessons from Howell Glynne and Otakar Kraus. He first sang with Opera for All (1962–64); in 1964 he made his debut at the Glyndebourne Festival as Lictor in *L'Incoronazione de Poppea*, and at Sadler's Wells in London as Zuniga, where he appeared regularly until 1970; in 1969 he made his debut at London's Covent Garden as Masetto, and remained on its roster. On Feb. 6, 1976, he made his Metropolitan Opera debut in N.Y. as Figaro. He also sang opera in Chicago, San Francisco, Toronto, Hamburg, Berlin, Vienna, Paris, and other cities, and likewise toured widely as a concert artist. His extensive repertoire includes such roles as Sarastro, Leporello, Osmind, Sparafucile, and King Philip. He married **Anne Howells**.

Dean, Winton (Basil), English writer on music; b. Birkenhead, March 18, 1916. He pursued studies in the liberal arts at King's College, Cambridge (B.A., 1938; M.A., 1941); took private music lessons with Philip Radcliffe; then devoted himself to musicological research. He publ. several valuable biographical essays on Handel, Bizet, and others. In 1989 he was made a corresponding member of the American Musicological Soc.

WRITINGS: *Bizet* (London, 1948; 2nd ed., rev., 1965, as *Georges Bizet: His Life and Work*; 3rd ed., 1976); *Carmen* (London, 1949); *Franck* (London, 1950); *Introduction to the Music of Bizet* (London, 1950); *Handel's Dramatic Oratorios and Masques* (London, 1959; rev. ed., 1990); *Handel and the Opera Seria* (Berkeley, 1969); with J. Knapp, *Handel's Operas 1704–1726* (Oxford, 1987; 2nd ed., rev., 1995); *Essays on Opera* (Oxford, 1990).

BIBL.: N. Fortune, ed., *Music and Theatre: Essays in Honour of W. D.* (Cambridge, 1987).

De Angelis, Nazzareno, noted Italian bass; b. Aquila, Nov. 17, 1881; d. Rome, Dec. 14, 1962. As a boy, he sang in the Sistine and Justine chapel choirs in Rome. He made his operatic debut in Aquila in 1903; then appeared with major Italian opera houses. In 1909–10 he was on the roster of the Manhattan Opera House in N.Y.; then of the Chicago Opera (1910–11; 1915–20); later made appearances with the Rome Opera (until 1938); also gave song recitals. He was regarded as one of the most cultured bass singers of the Italian school of opera, and he was equally appreciated in Wagnerian roles.

De Boeck, August, Belgian organist, pedagogue, and composer; b. Merchtem, May 9, 1865; d. there, Oct. 9, 1937. He went to Brussels to study organ at the Cons., and also had lessons in orchestration from Gilson. He was active as a church organist in Brussels, where he also was a teacher of organ (1893–1902) and of harmony (1920–30) at the Cons. He also taught organ at the Royal Flemish Cons. in Antwerp (1909–21) and was director of the Mechelen Cons. (1920–30). De Boeck's compositions generally followed along the lines of the French Impressionists.

WORKS: DRAMATIC: OPERAS: *Théroigne de Mérincourt* (Antwerp, Jan. 1901); *Winternachtsdroom* (Antwerp, Dec. 1902); *De Rijndwergen* (Antwerp, Oct. 1906); *Reinaert de Vos* (Antwerp, Jan. 1, 1909); *La Route d'Emeraude* (Ghent, Feb. 1921). **OPERETTAS:** *Papa Poliet* (1914–18); *Totole* (1929). **BALLETS:** *Cendrillon* (1895); *La Phalène* (1896). **INCIDENTAL MUSIC TO:** G. Eekhoud's *La Chevalière d'Eon* (1894); R. Verhulst's *Jesus de Nazarener* (1909). **ORCH.:** *Rhapsodie dahoméenne* (1893); Sym. (1896); *Fantaisie op twee vlaamse volksliederen* (1923); Violin Concerto (1925); *In the schuur* (1937). **CHAMBER:** Pieces for Solo Instrument and Piano; piano music; organ pieces. **VOCAL:** 3 masses; 13 cantatas; 38 motets; spiritual choral songs; secular songs.

BIBL.: F. Rasse, *A. D.B.* (Brussels, 1943).

Debussy, (Achille-)Claude, great French composer whose music created new poetry of mutating tonalities and became a perfect counterpart of new painting in France; b. St.-Germain-en-Laye, Aug. 22, 1862; d. Paris, March 25, 1918. Mme. Mauté de Fleurville, the mother-in-law of the poet Verlaine, prepared him for the Paris Cons.; he was admitted at the age of 10 and studied piano with Marmontel (2nd prize, 1877) and solfège with Lavignac (3rd medal, 1874; 2nd, 1875; 1st, 1876). He further took courses in harmony with Emile Durand (1877–80) and practiced score reading under Bazille. In 1880 Marmontel recommended him to Mme. Nadezhda von Meck, Tchaikovsky's patroness. She summoned him to Interlaken, and they subsequently visited Rome, Naples, and Fiesole. During the summers of 1881 and 1882, Debussy stayed with Mme. von Meck's family in Moscow, where he became acquainted with the syms. of Tchaikovsky; however, he failed to appreciate Tchaikovsky's music and became more interested in the idiosyncratic compositions of Mussorgsky. Back in France, he became friendly with Mme. Vasnier, wife of a Paris architect and an amateur singer.

Debussy made his earliest professional appearance as a composer in Paris on May 12, 1882, at a concert given by the violinist Maurice Thieberg. In Dec. 1880 he enrolled in the composition class of Guiraud at the Paris Cons. with the ambition of winning the Grand Prix de Rome; after completing his courses, he won the 2nd Prix de Rome in 1883. Finally, on June 27, 1884, he succeeded in obtaining the Grand Prix de Rome with his cantata *L'Enfant prodigue*, written in a poetic but conservative manner reflecting the trends of French Romanticism. During his stay in Rome, he wrote a choral work, *Zuleima* (1885–86), after Heine's *Almanzor*, and began work on another cantata, *Diane au bois*. Neither of these 2 incunabulae was preserved. His choral suite with orch., *Printemps* (1887), failed to win formal recognition. He then set to work on another cantata, *La Damoiselle élue* (1887–89), which gained immediate favor among French musicians.

In 1888 Debussy visited Bayreuth, where he heard *Parsifal* and *Die Meistersinger von Nürnberg* for the first time, but Wagner's grandiloquence never gained his full devotion. What thoroughly engaged his interest was the oriental music that he heard at the Paris World Exposition in 1889. He was fascinated by the asymmetric rhythms of the thematic content and the new instrumental colors achieved by native players; he also found an inner valence between these oriental modalities and the verses of certain French impressionist poets, including Mallarmé, Verlaine, Baudelaire, and Pierre Louÿs. The combined impressions of exotic music and symbolist French verses were rendered in Debussy's vocal works, such as *Cinq poèmes de Baudelaire* (1887–89), *Ariettes oubliées* (1888), *Trois mélodies* (1891), and *Fêtes galantes* (1892). He also wrote *Proses lyriques* (1892–93) to his own texts. For the piano, he composed *Suite bergamasque* (1890–1905), which includes the famous *Clair de lune*. In 1892 he began work on his instrumental *Prélude à l'après-midi d'un faune*, after Mallarmé, which comprises the quintessence of tonal painting with its free modal sequences under a subtle umbrage of oscillating instrumentation. The work was first heard in Paris on Dec. 22, 1894; a program book cautioned the audience that the text contained sensuous elements that might be distracting to young females. It was about that time that Debussy attended a performance of Maeterlinck's drama *Pelléas et Mélisande*, which inspired him to begin work on an opera on that subject. In 1893 there followed *Trois chansons de Bilitis*, after prose poems by Louÿs, marked by exceptional sensuality of the text in a musical context of free modality; a later work, *Les Chansons de Bilitis* for 2 harps, 2 flutes, and celesta, was heard in Paris in 1901 as incidental music to accompany recited and mimed neo-Grecian poetry of Louÿs. Between 1892 and 1899 Debussy worked on *3 Nocturnes* for orch.: *Nuages, Fêtes,* and *Sirènes.*

As the 20th century dawned, Debussy found himself in a tangle of domestic relationships. A tempestuous liaison with Gabrielle Dupont (known as Gaby Lhéry) led to a break, which so distressed Gaby that she took poison. She survived, but Debussy sought more stable attachments; on Oct. 19, 1899, he married Rosalie Texier, with whom he made his first attempt to form a legitimate union. But he soon discovered that like Gaby before her, Rosalie failed to satisfy his expectations, and he began to look elsewhere for a true union of souls. This he found in the person of Emma Bardac, the wife of a banker. He bluntly informed Rosalie of his dissatisfaction with their marriage. Like Gaby 7 years before, Rosalie, plunged into despair by Debussy's selfish decision, attempted suicide; she shot herself in the chest but missed her suffering heart. Debussy, now 42 years old, divorced Rosalie on Aug. 2, 1905. Bardac and her husband were divorced on May 4, 1905; Debussy married her on Jan. 20, 1908. They had a daughter, Claude-Emma (known as "Chouchou"), born Oct. 15, 1905; she was the inspiration for Debussy's charming piano suite, *Children's Corner* (the title was in English, for Chouchou had an English governess). She survived her father by barely a year, dying of diphtheria on July 14, 1919.

With his opera *Pelléas et Mélisande,* Debussy assumed a leading place among French composers. It was premiered at the Opéra-Comique in Paris on April 30, 1902, after many difficulties, including the open opposition of Maeterlinck, who objected to having the role of Mélisande sung by the American soprano Mary Garden, whose accent jarred Maeterlinck's sensibilities; he wanted his mistress, Georgette Leblanc, to be the first Mélisande. The production of the opera aroused a violent controversy among French musicians and littérateurs. The press was vicious in the extreme: "Rhythm, melody, tonality, these are 3 things unknown to Monsieur Debussy," wrote the doyen of the Paris music critics, Arthur Pougin. "What a pretty series of false relations! What adorable progressions of triads in parallel motion and fifths and octaves which result from it! What a collection of dissonances, sevenths and ninths, ascending with energy! . . . No, decidedly I will never agree with these anarchists of music!" Camille Bellaigue, who was Debussy's classmate at the Paris Cons., conceded that *Pelléas et Mélisande* "makes little noise," but, he remarked, "it is a nasty little noise." The English and American reports were no less vituperative, pejorative, and deprecatory. "Debussy disowns melody and despises harmony with all its resources," opined the critic of the *Monthly Musical Record* of London. Echoing such judgments, the *Musical Courier* of N.Y. compared Debussy's "disharmony" with the sensation of "an involuntary start when the dentist touches the nerve of a sensitive tooth." And the American writer James Gibbons Huneker exceeded all limits of permissible literary mores by attacking Debussy's physical appearance. "I met Debussy at the Café Riche the other night," he wrote in the N.Y. *Sun,* "and was struck by the unique ugliness of the man. . . . [H]e looks more like a Bohemian, a Croat, a Hun, than a Gaul." These utterances were followed by a suggestion that Debussy's music was fit for a procession of headhunters of Borneo, carrying home "their ghastly spoils of war."

Debussy's next important work was *La Mer,* which he completed during a sojourn in England in 1905. It was first performed in Paris on Oct. 15, 1905. Like his String Quartet, it was conceived monothematically; a single musical idea permeated the entire work despite a great variety of instrumentation. It consists of 3 symphonic sketches: *De l'aube à midi sur la mer, Jeux de vagues,* and *Dialogue du vent et de la mer. La Mer* was attacked by critics with even greater displeasure than *Pelléas et Mélisande.* The American critic Louis Elson went so far as to suggest that the original title was actually "Le Mal de mer," and that the last movement represented a violent seizure of vomiting. To summarize the judgment on Debussy, a vol. entitled *Le Cas Debussy* was publ. in Paris in 1910. It contained a final assessment of Debussy as a "déformateur musical," suffering from a modern nervous disease that affects one's power of discernment.

Meanwhile, Debussy continued to work. To be mentioned is the remarkable orch. triptych, *Images* (1906–12), comprising *Gigues, Ibéria,* and *Rondes de printemps.* In 1908 he conducted a concert of his works in London; he also accepted engagements as conductor in Vienna (1910), Turin (1911), Moscow and St. Petersburg (1913), and Rome, Amsterdam, and The Hague (1914). Among other works of the period are the piano pieces, *Douze préludes* (2 books, 1909–10; 1910–13) and *Douze études* (2 books, 1915). *En blanc et noir,* for 2 pianos, dates from 1915. On May 15, 1913, Diaghilev produced Debussy's ballet *Jeux* in Paris. On May 5, 1917, Debussy played the piano part of his Violin Sonata at its premiere in Paris with violinist Gaston Poulet. But his projected tour of the U.S. with the violinist Arthur Hartmann had to be abandoned when it was discovered that Debussy had irreversible colon cancer. Surgery was performed in Dec. 1915, but there was little hope of recovery. The protracted 1st World War depressed him; his hatred of the Germans became intense as the military threat to Paris increased. He wrote the lyrics and the accompaniment to a song, *Noël des enfants,* in which he begged Santa Claus not to bring presents to German children whose parents were destroying the French children's Christmas. To underline his national sentiments, he emphatically signed his last works "musicien français." Debussy died on the evening of March 25, 1918, as the great German gun, "Big Bertha," made the last attempt to subdue the city of Paris by long-distance (76 miles) bombardment.

Debussy emphatically rejected the term "impressionism" as applied to his music. But it cannot alter the essential truth that like Mallarmé in poetry, he created a style peculiarly sensitive to musical mezzotint, a palette of half-lit delicate colors. He systematically applied the oriental pentatonic scale for exotic evocations, as well as the whole-tone scale (which he did not invent, however; earlier samples of its use are found in works by Glinka and Liszt). His piece for piano solo, *Voiles,* is written in a whole-tone scale, while its middle section is set entirely in the pentatonic scale. In his music, Debussy emancipated discords; he also revived the archaic practice of consecutive perfect intervals (particularly fifths and fourths). In his formal constructions, the themes are shortened and rhythmically sharpened, while in the instrumental treatment the role of individual solo passages is enhanced and the dynamic range made more subtle.

WORKS: CHORAL, DRAMATIC, AND LITERARY: *Hymnis,* cantata (1880; unfinished); *Daniel,* cantata for 3 Voices (1880–84); *Printemps* for Women's Chorus and Orch. (1882; publ. as *Salut printemps,* 1928); *Le Gladiateur,* cantata (June 22, 1883); *Invocation* for 4 Men's Voices and Orch. (1883; publ. 1957); *L'Enfant prodigue,* cantata for Soprano, Tenor, Baritone, Chorus, and Orch. (Paris, June 27, 1884; reorchestrated 1905 and 1908); *Printemps* for Chorus (1884); *Diane au bois,* cantata (1884–86; unfinished); *La Damoiselle élue,* cantata for Soprano, Mezzo-soprano, Women's Chorus, and Orch. (1887–89; Paris, April 7, 1893); *Axel,* music for a scene to Villiers de l'Isle Adam's drama (1889); *Rodrigue et Chimène,* opera (1890–92; piano score only, partially lost; reconstructed by Richard Smith and orchestrated by Edison Denisov; Lyons, May 14, 1993); *Pelléas et Mélisande,* opera (1893–95; 1901–02; Paris, April 30, 1902, Messager conducting); *F.E.A. (Frères en art),* play written with René Peter (1896–1900; unfinished); *Esther et la maison des fous,* text for a dramatic work (1900); *Le Diable dans le beffroi,* opera after Poe's *The Devil in the Belfry* (1902–03; unfinished; only notes for the libretto and sketch for Scene I extant); *Trois chansons de Charles d'Orléans* for Chorus (2 pieces composed in 1898 incorporated into score of 1908; Paris, April 9, 1909, composer conducting); *Masques et Bergamasques,* scenario for a ballet (1910); *La Chute de la maison Usher,* opera after Poe's *The Fall of the House of Usher* (1908–18; unfinished; only sketches and final version of the libretto and incomplete vocal score extant); *Le Martyre de Saint-Sébastien*, incidental music to the mystery play by d'Annunzio for Soprano, 2 Contraltos, Chorus, and Orch. (Paris, May 22, 1911); *Jeux*, ballet (1912; Paris, May 15, 1913, Monteux conducting); *Khamma*, ballet (1912; Paris, Nov. 15, 1924, Pierné conducting); *Ode à la France*, cantata for Solo, Chorus, and Orch. (1916; completed from the sketches by M.-F. Gaillard; piano score, 1928; orch. score, 1954).

ORCH.: *Intermezzo*, after Heine's *Intermezzo* (1882); *Suite d'orchestre* (1883–84); *Printemps*, symphonic suite for Orch. and Chorus (1887; full score destroyed in a fire; later reduction for voices and piano, 5-hands, by Durand, 1904; definitive version reorchestrated by Büsser, 1913; Paris, April 18, 1913, Rhené-Baton conducting); *Fantaisie* for Piano and Orch. (1889; London, Nov. 20, 1919, Coates conducting); *Prélude à l'après-midi d'un faune* (1892–94; Paris, Dec. 22, 1894, Doret conducting); *Nocturnes: Nuages; Fêtes; Sirènes* (the latter with wordless women's chorus) (1892–99; *Nuages* and *Fêtes*, Paris, Dec. 9, 1900, Chevillard conducting; 1st complete perf., Paris, Oct. 27, 1901, Chevillard conducting); *Danse sacrée* and *Danse profane* for Harp and Strings (1903; Paris, Nov. 6, 1904); *La Mer*, 3 symphonic sketches: 1, *De l'aube à midi sur la mer*, 2, *Jeux de vagues*, 3, *Dialogue du vent et de la mer* (1903–05; Paris, Oct. 15, 1905, Chevillard conducting); *King Lear*, incidental music to Shakespeare's play: *Fanfare* and *Sommeil de Lear* (1904; Paris, Oct. 30, 1926, Wolff conducting; also notes in MS for 6 other pieces); *Images: Gigues* (1909–12); *Ibéria* (1906–08); *Rondes de printemps* (1908–09) (orchestration of *Gigues* completed by Caplet; *Gigues*, Paris, Jan. 26, 1913, Pierné conducting; *Ibéria*, Paris, Feb. 20, 1910, Pierné conducting; *Rondes de printemps*, Paris, March 2, 1910, composer conducting).

CHAMBER: Trio in G major for Piano, Violin, and Cello (1880); *Intermezzo* for Cello and Piano (1882); *Scherzo* for Cello and Piano (1882); String Quartet (Paris, Dec. 29, 1893); *Chansons de Bilitis*, incidental music for the poems of Louÿs for 2 Flutes, 2 Harps, and Celesta (1900; Paris, Feb. 7, 1901); *Rapsodie* for Saxophone and Piano (1903–05; unfinished; piano accompaniment orchestrated by Roger-Ducasse; Paris, May 14, 1919, Caplet conducting); *Prèmiere rapsodie* for Clarinet and Piano (1909–10; Paris, Jan. 16, 1911; orchestrated by the composer, 1910); *Petite pièce* for Clarinet and Piano (1910); *Syrinx* for Flute (Paris, Dec. 1, 1913); Cello Sonata (1915; 1st confirmed perf., London, March 4, 1916); Sonata for Flute, Viola, and Harp (1915; Paris, Dec. 10, 1916 [private perf.]); Sonata for Piano and Violin (1916–17; Paris, May 5, 1917, composer pianist, Poulet violinist).

PIANO: SOLO PIANO: *Danse bohémienne* (1880); *Deux arabesques* (1880); *Rêverie; Ballade; Danse* (orchestrated by Ravel); *Valse romantique*; *Nocturnes* (1890); *Suite bergamasque: Prélude; Menuet; Clair de lune; Passepied* (1890–1905); *Mazurka* (1891); *Pour le piano: Prélude; Sarabande* (orchestrated by Ravel); *Toccata* (1896–1901; Paris, Jan. 11, 1902, Viñes pianist); *Estampes: Pagodes; Soirée dans Grenade; Jardins sous la pluie* (1903; 1st complete perf., Paris, Jan. 9, 1904, Viñes pianist); *D'un cahier d'esquisses* (1903; Paris, April 20, 1910, Ravel pianist); *Masques* (1904) and *L'Isle joyeuse* (1904; orchestrated by B. Molinari; Paris, Feb. 18, 1905, Viñes pianist); *Images*, 1st series: *Reflets dans l'eau; Hommage à Rameau; Mouvement* (1905; Paris, March 3, 1906, Viñes pianist); *Children's Corner: Doctor Gradus ad Parnassum; Jimbo's Lullaby; Serenade for the Doll; Snow Is Dancing; The Little Shepherd; Golliwog's Cake-walk* (1906–08; Paris, Dec. 18, 1908, Harold Bauer, pianist; orchestrated by Caplet); *Images*, 2nd series: *Cloches à travers les feuilles; Et la lune descend sur le temple qui fut; Poissons d'or* (1907–08; Paris, Feb. 21, 1908, Viñes pianist); *Le Petit Nègre* (1909); *Hommage à Haydn* (1909; Paris, March 11, 1911); *Douze préludes*, Book I: *Danseuses de Delphes* (Paris, May 25, 1910, composer pianist); *Voiles* (Paris, May 25, 1910, composer pianist); *Le Vent dans la plaine; Les Sons et les parfums tournent dans l'air du soir; Les Collines d'Anacapri* (Paris, Dec. 26, 1909, Viñes pianist); *Des Pas sur la neige; Ce qu'a vu le Vent d'Ouest; La Fille aux cheveux de lin; La Sérénade interrompue* (Paris, Jan. 14, 1911, Viñes pianist); *La Cathédrale engloutie* (Paris, May 25, 1910, composer pianist); *La Danse de Puck; Minstrels* (1909–10); *La Plus que lente* (1910; orchestrated by the composer, 1912); *Douze préludes*, Book II: *Brouillards; Feuilles mortes; La Puerta del Vino; Les Fées sont d'exquises danseuses; Bruyères; General Lavine—eccentric; La Terrasse des audiences du clair de lune; Ondine; Hommage à S. Pickwick, Esq., P.P.M.P.C.; Canope; Les Tierces alternées; Feux d'artifice* (1910–13); *La Boîte a joujoux*, children's ballet (1913; Paris, Dec. 10, 1919, Inghelbrecht conducting); *Berceuse héroïque pour rendre hommage à S.M. le Roi Albert I de Belgique et à ses soldats* (1914; orchestrated by the composer, 1914; Paris, Oct. 26, 1915, Chevillard conducting); *Douze études*, Book I: *Pour les cinq doigts; Pour les tierces; Pour les quartes; Pour les sixtes; Pour les octaves; Pour les huit doigts* (1915); *Douze études*, Book II: *Pour les degrés chromatiques; Pour les agréments; Pour les notes répétées; Pour les sonorités opposées; Pour les arpèges; Pour les accords* (1915; both books perf. Dec. 14, 1916, Walter Morse Rummel pianist). **PIANO DUET:** *Symphonie en si* (1 movement, 1880; intended for orch.; Paris, Jan. 27, 1937); *Triomphe de Bacchus* (1882; intended as an orch. interlude; orchestrated by Gaillard, 1927); *Petite suite: En bateau; Cortège; Menuet; Ballet* (1889); *Marche écossaise sur un thème populaire* (The Earl of Ross March; 1891; orchestrated by the composer, Paris, Oct. 22, 1913, Inghelbrecht conducting); *Six epigraphes antiques: Pour invoquer Pan, dieu du vent d'été; Pour un tombeau sans nom; Pour que la nuit soit propice; Pour la danseuse aux crotales; Pour l'Egyptienne; Pour remercier la pluie au matin* (1900–1914; also for piano solo; orchestrated by Ansermet). **2 PIANOS:** *Lindaraja* (1901; Paris, Oct. 28, 1926); *En blanc et noir* (3 pieces; 1915; Paris, Dec. 21, 1916, composer and Roger-Ducasse pianists).

SONGS (author of text precedes date of composition): *Ballade à la lune* (Alfred de Musset; 1876?); *Beau soir* (Paul Bourget; 1876?); *Fleur des eaux* (Maurice Bouchor; 1876?); *Nuit d'étoiles* (Théodore de Banville; 1876?); *Fleur des blés* (André Girod; 1877); *Mandoline* (Paul Verlaine); *La Belle au bois dormant* (Vincent Hypsa); *Voici que le printemps* (Bourget); *Paysage sentimental* (Bourget; all composed 1880–83); *L'Archet* (Charles Cros); *Séguedille* (J.L. Vauthier); *Les Roses; Chanson espagnole* (for 2 voices); *Rondel chinois*, 3 songs on poems by Gourget: *Regret; Romance d'Ariel; Musique*, 6 songs on poems by Banville: *Caprice; Aimons-nous; O floraison divine des lilas; Souhait; Sérénade; Fête galante*, 3 songs on poems by Leconte de Lisle: *La Fille aux cheveux de lin; Jane; Eclogue* (for soprano and tenor); *Il dort encore* (from Banville's *Hymnis*); *Coquetterie posthume* (Théophile Gautier); *Flots, palmes, sables* (Armand Renaud; all composed 1880–84); *Zéphyr* (Banville; 1881); *En sourdine* (Verlaine; 1st version, 1882); *Rondeau* (Musset; 1882); *Pantomime* (Verlaine); *Clair de lune* (Verlaine); *Pierrot* (Banville); *Apparition* (Stéphane Mallarmé; all composed 1882–84); *Cinq poèmes de Baudelaire: Le Balcon; Harmonie du soir; Le Jet d'eau* (piano accompaniment orchestrated by the composer); *Recueillement; La Mort des amants* (all composed 1887–89); *Ariettes oubliées* (Verlaine); *C'est l'extase . . . ; Il pleure dans mon coeur . . . ; L'ombre des arbres . . . ; Chevaux de bois; Green; Spleen* (all composed 1888); *Deux romances* (Bourget): *Romances; Les Cloches* (1891); *Les Angélus* (G. le Roy; 1891); *Dans le jardin* (Paul Gravolet; 1891); *Trois mélodies* (Verlaine): *La mer est plus belle . . . ; Le Son du cor s'afflige . . . ; L'Echelonnement des haies* (1891); *Fêtes galantes* (Verlaine), 1st series: *En sourdine; Fantoches; Clair de lune (1892); Proses lyriques (composer); De rêve; De grêve; De fleurs; De soir* (1892–93); *Trois chansons de Bilitis* (Pierre Louÿs): *La Flûte de Pan; La Chevelure; Le Tombeau des Naïades* (1897); *Fêtes galantes* (Verlaine), 2nd series: *Les Ingénus; Le Faune; Colloque sentimental* (1904); *Trois chansons de France: Rondel: Le temps a laissé son manteau . . .* (Charles d'Orléans); *La Grotte* (Tristan Lhermite; identical to *Auprès de cette grotte sombre*, below); *Rondel: Pour ce que plaisance est morte . . .* (Charles d'Orléans; all composed

1904); *Le Promenoir des deux amants* (Lhermite): *Auprès de cette grotte sombre . . . ; Crois mon conseil . . . ; Je tremble en voyant ton visage* (1910); *Trois ballades de François Villon* (orchestrated by the composer); *Ballade de Villon à s'amye; Ballade que feit Villon à la requeste de sa mère pour prier Nostre-Dame; Ballade des femmes de Paris* (1910); *Trois poèmes de Stéphane Mallarmé: Soupir; Placet futile; Eventail* (1913); *Noël des enfants qui n'ont plus de maison* (composer; 1915).

WRITINGS: Debussy contributed numerous critical articles to *La Revue Blanche, Gil Blas, Musica, La Revue S.I.M.* et al. A selection of these, some abridged, appeared as *Monsieur Croche, antidilettante* (Paris, 1921; 2nd ed., 1926; Eng. tr., 1927, as *Monsieur Croche the Dilettante-Hater*, 2nd ed., 1962; new ed. by F. Lesure as *Monsieur Croche et autres écrits*, Paris, 1971; Eng. tr., 1977, as *D. on Music: The Critical Writings of the Great French Composer C. D.*).

BIBL.: SOURCE MATERIAL: A periodical, *Cahiers D.*, began publication in 1974 (issued by the Centre de Documentation C. D. in St.-Germain-en-Laye, France). F. Lesure has prepared a *Catalogue de l'oeuvre de C. D.* (Geneva, 1977). The *Oeuvres complètes* began publication in 1986. Other sources include the following: A. Martin, *C. D.: Chronologie de sa vie et de ses oeuvres* (Paris, 1942); A. Gauthier, *D.: Documents iconographiques* (Geneva, 1952); *Catalogue de la collection Walter Straram: Manuscrits de C. D.* (Rambouillet, 1961); F. Lesure, *C. D., Catalogue de l'Exposition* (Paris, 1962); C. Abravanel, *C. D.: A Bibliography* (Detroit, 1974); F. Lesure, *Iconographie musicale: D.* (Geneva, 1974); M. Rolf, "Orchestral Manuscripts of C. D.: 1892–1905," *Musical Quarterly* (Fall 1984); J. Briscoe, *C. D.: A Guide to Research* (N.Y., 1990).

CORRESPONDENCE: J. Duran, ed., *Lettres de C. D. à son éditeur* (Paris, 1927); *Correspondance de C. D. et P.-J. Toulet* (Paris, 1929); J. André-Messager, ed., *La Jeunesse de Pelléas: Lettres de C. D. à André Messager* (Paris, 1938); *C. D.: Lettres à deux amis: 78 lettres inédites à Robert Godet et G. Jean-Aubry* (Paris, 1942); H. Borgeaud, ed., *Correspondance de C. D. et Pierre Louÿs* (Paris, 1945); E. Lockspeiser, ed., *Lettres inédites de C. D. à André Caplet* (Monaco, 1957); P. Vallery-Radot, ed., *Lettres de C. D. à sa femme Emma* (Paris, 1957); F. Lesure, ed., "C. D.: Textes et documents inédits," *Revue de Musicologie*, XLVIII (1962); idem, "Lettres inédites de C. D. à Pierre Louÿs," ibid., LVII (1971); idem, ed., *C. D.: Correspondance 1884–1918* (Paris, 1980; rev. ed., 1993)

BIOGRAPHICAL: L. Liebich, *C.-A. D.* (London, 1908); L. Laloy, *C. D.* (Paris, 1909; 2nd ed., aug., 1944); G. Jean-Aubry, "C. D.," *Musical Quarterly* (Oct. 1918); idem, "Some Recollections of D.," *Musical Times* (May 1918); J.-G. Prod'homme, "C.-A. D.," *Musical Quarterly* (Oct. 1918); E. Vuillermoz, *C. D.* (Paris, 1920); R. Jardillier, *C. D.* (Dijon, 1922); A. Suarés, *D.* (Paris, 1922; 2nd ed., aug., 1936); R. Paoli, *D.* (Florence, 1924; 2nd ed., 1947); F. Shera, *D. and Ravel* (London, 1925); F. Gysi, *C. D.* (Zürich, 1926); R. van Santen, *D.* (The Hague, 1926; 2nd ed., 1947); C. Koechlin, *D.* (Paris, 1930); R. Peter, *C. D.* (Paris, 1931; 2nd ed., aug., 1944); L. Vallas, *C. D. et son temps* (Paris, 1932; 2nd ed., 1958; Eng. tr., 1973); E. Decsey, *C. D.* (Graz, 1936); E. Lockspeiser, *D.* (London, 1936; 5th ed., rev., 1980); idem, "Mussorgsky and D.," *Musical Quarterly* (Oct. 1937); O. Thompson, *D., Man and Artist* (N.Y., 1937); H. Strobel, *C. D.* (Zürich, 1940; 3rd ed., rev., 1948); L. Vallas, *A.-C. D.* (Paris, 1944); R. Paoli, *D.* (Florence, 1947; 2nd ed., 1951); G. Ferchault, *C. D., musicien français* (Paris, 1948); H. Harvey, *C. of France: The Story of D.* (N.Y., 1948); R. Malipiero, *D.* (Brescia, 1948); J. van Ackere, *C. D.* (Antwerp, 1949); R. Myers, *D.* (London, 1949); W. Danckert, *C. D.* (Berlin, 1950); G. and D.-E. Inghelbrecht, *C. D.* (Paris, 1953); V. Seroff, *D., Musician of France* (N.Y., 1956); E. Vuillermoz, *C. D.* (Geneva, 1957); M. Dietschy, "The Family and Childhood of D.," *Musical Quarterly* (July 1960); J. Barraqué, *D.* (Paris, 1962; Eng. tr., 1972); E. Lockspeiser, *D.: His Life and Mind* (2 vols., London, 1962 and 1965; rev. ed., Cambridge, 1978); Y. Tiénot and O. d'Estrade-Guerra, *D.: L'Homme, son oeuvre, son milieu* (Paris, 1962); A. Goléa, *D.* (Paris, 1965); P. Young, *D.* (London, 1966); G. Gourdet, *D.* (Paris, 1970); R. Nichols, *D.* (London, 1973); C. Goubault, *C. D.* (Paris, 1986); L. Knödler, *D.* (Haarlem, 1989); R. Nichols, *D. Remembered* (London and Boston, 1992); C. Timbrell, "C. D. and Walter Rummel: Chronicle of a Friendship, with New Correspondence," *Music & Letters* (Aug. 1992).

CRITICAL, ANALYTICAL: L. Gilman, *D.'s "Pelléas et Mélisande"* (N.Y., 1907); F. Santoliquido, *Il Dopo-Wagner, C. D. e Richard Strauss* (Rome, 1909); C. Caillard and J. de Bérys, *Le Cas D.* (Paris, 1910); G. Setaccioli, *D. é un innovatore?* (Rome, 1910); D. Chennevière, *C. D. et son oeuvre* (Paris, 1913); C. Paglia, *Strauss, D., e compagnia bella* (Bologna, 1913); A. Lualdi, "C. D. La sua Arte e la sua Parabola," *Rivista Musicale Italiana*, XXV/2 (1918); E. Newman, "The Development of D.," *Musical Times* (May and Aug. 1918); A. Cortot, "La Musique de piano de D.," *La Revue Musicale*, I (1920; Eng. tr., 1922, as *The Piano Music of D.*); G. Gatti, "The Piano Works of C. D.," *Musical Quarterly* (July 1924); J. Palache, "D. as Critic," ibid.; M. Emmanuel, *Pelléas et Mélisande* (Paris, 1926); L. Vallas, *Les Idées de C. D., musicien français* (Paris, 1927; Eng. tr., 1929, as *The Theories of C. D.*); M. Dumesnil, *How to Play and Teach D.* (N.Y., 1932); A. Liess, *C. D. Das Werk in Zeitbild* (2 vols., Strasbourg, 1936); H. Kolsch, *Der Impressionismus bei D.* (Düsseldorf, 1937); E. Lockspeiser, "D.'s Unpublished Songs," *Radio Times* (Sept. 23, 1938); A. Liess, *C. D. und das deutsche Musikschaffen* (Würzburg, 1939); A. Jakobik, *Die assoziative Harmonik in den Klavier-Werken C. D.s* (Würzburg, 1940); G. Schaeffner, *C. D. und das Poetische* (Bern, 1943); A. Gauthier, *Sous l'influence de Neptune: Dialogues avec D.* (Paris, 1945); J. d'Almendra, *Les Modes grégoriens dans l'oeuvre de C. D.* (Paris, 1948); E. Decsey, *D.s Werke* (Graz, 1949); V. Jankélévitch, *D. et le mystère* (Neuchâtel, 1949; 2nd ed., 1962); E. Robert Schmitz, *The Piano Works of C. D.* (N.Y., 1950; 2nd ed., 1966); J. van Ackere, *Pelléas et Mélisande* (Brussels, 1952); A. Goléa, *Pelléas et Mélisande, analyse poetique et musicale* (Paris, 1952); A. Schaeffner, "D. et ses rapports avec la musique russe," in P. Souvtchinsky, ed., *Musique russe* (Vol. I, Paris, 1953); H. Büsser, *De Pelléas aux Index galantes* (Paris, 1955); O. d'Estrade-Guerra, "Les Manuscrits de Pelléas et Mélisande," *La Revue Musicale*, no. 235 (1957); M. Long, *Au piano avec C. D.* (Paris, 1960; Eng. tr., 1972); M. Dietschy, *La Passion de C. D.* (Neuchâtel, 1962; Eng. tr., 1990, as *A Portrait of C. D.*); E. Lockspeiser, *D. et Edgar Poe* (Monaco, 1962); "Souvenir et présence de D.," *La Revue Belge de Musicologie*, XVI (1962); E. Lockspeiser, "D.'s Concept of the Dream," *Proceedings of the Royal Musical Association*, LXXXIX (1962–63); F. Lesure, "C. D. after His Century," *Musical Quarterly* (July 1963); "C. D. 1862–1962: Livre d'or," *La Revue Musicale*, no. 258 (1964); S. Jarocinski, *D., a impresionizm i symbolizm* (Kraków, 1966; French tr., 1971; Eng. tr., 1976, as *D.: Impressionism and Symbolism*); P. Ruschenburg, *Stilkritische Untersuchungen zu den Liedern C. D.s* (diss., Univ. of Hamburg, 1966); E. Hardeck, *Untersuchungen zu den Klavierliedern C. D.s* (Regensburg, 1967); R. Park, *The Later Style of C. D.* (diss., Univ. of Mich., 1967); V. Jankélévitch, *La Vie et la mort dans la musique de D.* (Neuchâtel, 1968); F. Dawes, *D. Piano Music* (London, 1969); W. Austin, ed., *D.: Prelude to "The Afternoon of a Faun"* (Norton Critical Score ed., containing background, criticism, and analysis; N.Y., 1970); D. Cox, *D.'s Orchestral Music* (London, 1974); C. Zenck, *Versuch über die wahre Art D. zu analysieren* (Munich, 1974); A. Whittall, "Tonality and the Whole-tone Scale in the Music of D.," *Music Review*, XXXVI (1975); V. Jankélévitch, *D. et le mystère de l'instant* (Paris, 1976); A. Wenk, *D. and the Poets* (Berkeley and Los Angeles, 1976); R. Holloway, *D. and Wagner* (London, 1979); R. Orledge, "D.'s Piano Music: Some Second Thoughts and Sources of Inspiration," *Musical Times* (Jan. 1981); M. Cobb, ed., *The Poetic D.: A Collection of His Song Texts and Selected Letters* (annotated; Boston, 1982); E. Lang-Becker, *D. Nocturnes* (Munich, 1982); R. Orledge, *D. and the Theatre* (Cambridge, 1982); R. Howat, *D. in Proportion: A Musical Analysis* (Cambridge, 1983); J. Trilling, *Untersuchungen zur Rezeption C. D.s in der zeitgenössischen Musikkritik* (Tutzing, 1983); A. Wenk, *C. D. and Twentieth-Century Music* (Boston, 1983); D. Grayson, "The Libretto of D.'s

'Pelléas et Mélisande'," *Music & Letters* (March 1985); R. Orledge, "D. et 'La "Girl" anglaise': The Legend of 'Khamma'," *Musical Times* (March 1986); idem, "The Genesis of D.'s 'Jeux'," ibid. (Feb. 1987); H. Ferguson, "D.'s Emendations to 'Pelléas'," ibid. (Aug. 1988); G.-P. Biasih, *Montale, D., and Modernism* (Princeton, N.J., 1989); R. Nichols and R. Smith, *C. D.: Pelléas et Mélisande* (Cambridge, 1989); R. Parks, *The Music of C. D.* (New Haven and London, 1989); R. Beyer, *Organale Satztechniken in den Werken von C. D. und Maurice Ravel* (Wiesbaden, 1992); F. Lesure, *C. D. avant "Pelléas" ou Les Années symbolistes* (Paris, 1992); J. Arndt, *Der Einfluss der javanischen Gamelan-Musik auf Kompositionen von C. D.* (Frankfurt am Main and N.Y., 1993); idem, *Einheitlichkeit versus Widerstreit: Zwei gründsätzlich verschiedene Gestaltungsarten in der Musik C. Ds* (Frankfurt am Main and N.Y., 1993).

Decadt, Jan, Belgian composer; b. Ypres, June 21, 1914; d. Harelbeke, June 5, 1995. He studied with Joseph Ryelandt at the Ghent Cons., and later with Jean Absil in Brussels. He was director of the music school in Harelbeke from 1945, and in 1957 was appointed prof. of fugue at the Antwerp Cons.; from 1971 he taught composition at the Ghent Cons. His musical style was marked by strong polyphonic structures with impressionistic coloration.

WORKS: *Variations on "Sir Halewijn"* for Orch. (1943); *Ballada op een boom* (Ballade on a Tree) for Soprano, Flute, Oboe, and String Trio (1945); *Habanera* for Orch. (1947); Piano Concerto (1953); Sym. No. 1 (1958); *Constant Permeke,* cantata (1963); *Monographie musicale d'un grand peintre* for Orch. (Johannesburg, Nov. 17, 1964); *Concerto Overture* for Flute, Oboe, and String Orch. (1964); Suite for Trumpet and Chamber Orch. (1967); *Petite planète* for Narrator, Soprano, Flute, Viola, and Cello (1967); *Concertante Fantasia* for Oboe and Piano (1970); *Introduction and Capriccio* for Clarinet and Piano (1972); Saxophone Concerto (1973); Quartet for Saxophones (1974); *Wens-album* for Flute and Clarinet (1976); *Kleine fanfare* for Brass Band (1981); *Naar Wiegeland* for Voice and Piano (1986).

Decaux, Abel, French organist, teacher, and composer; b. Auffay, 1869; d. Paris, March 19, 1943. He studied organ with Widor and Guilmant and composition with Massenet at the Paris Cons. He served as organist at the church of Sacré-Coeur in Montmartre; then was prof. of organ at the Paris Schola Cantorum; from 1923 to 1937 he taught organ at the Eastman School of Music in Rochester, N.Y. Decaux composed very little, but he attracted posthumous attention by the discovery, and performance, of his group of piano pieces under the title *Clairs de lune* (the plural being of the essence): *Minuit passe, La Ruelle, Le Cimétière,* and *La Mer,* written between 1900 and 1907 and publ. in 1913, which seem to represent early examples of piano writing usually associated with Debussy and Ravel; the similarity of styles is indeed striking, which indicates that Impressionism was "in the air," and in the ears, of impressionable French musicians early in the new century.

Decker, Franz-Paul, German conductor; b. Cologne, June 23, 1923. He was a student of Jarnach and Papst at the Cologne Hochschule für Musik (1941–44) and of Bücken and Fellerer at the Univ. of Cologne. After conducting in Gniessen (1944–46), he was music director in Krefeld (1946–50), 1st conductor (1950–53) and city music director (1953–56) in Wiesbaden, and Generalmusikdirektor in Bochum (1956–64). From 1962 to 1968 he was chief conductor of the Rotterdam Phil. From 1967 to 1975 he was music director of the Montreal Sym. Orch. He served as principal guest conductor and music adviser of the Calgary (Alberta) Phil. (1975–77), as artistic adviser of the Winnipeg Sym. Orch. (1981–82), and as principal guest conductor of the New Zealand Sym. Orch. in Wellington (1984–85; 1986–88). From 1986 to 1992 he was principal conductor of the Orquestra Ciutat de Barcelona, which position he held again from 1994 to 1996. He also was principal guest conductor of the National Arts Centre Orch. in Ottawa from 1991 to 1997.

Decoust, Michel, French composer and administrator; b. Paris, Nov. 19, 1936. He was a student at the Paris Cons. (1956–65) of Dandelot (harmony), Desportes (counterpoint), Milhaud and Rivier (composition), Fourestier (conducting), and Messiaen (analysis), winning the Grand Prix de Rome in 1963. He also studied with Stockhausen in Cologne and Boulez in Basel. In 1967 he organized the Orchestre Philharmonique des Pays de la Loire in Angers, which he supervised until 1970. After serving as head of music of the Maison de la Culture in Rennes (1970–72), he was founder-director of the Pantin Cons. (1972–76). From 1976 to 1979 he was head of the education dept. of IRCAM in Paris, and then was chief inspector for musical research of the French Ministry of Culture from 1979 to 1991. In 1992 he became director general of music, dance, and dramatic art in Montpellier.

WORKS: ORCH.: *Mouvement* for Strings and Percussion (1964); *Polymorphie* (1967); *Si et si seulement* (1972); *Interférence* (1974); *T.H.T.* (1982); *Lierre* for Strings (1986); *De la gravitation suspendue des mémoires* (1986); *Hommage à Maurice Ravel* (1987); *Synopsis* (1989); Violin Concerto (1990); *Onyx* (1990). **CHAMBER:** *Mobile* for Percussion (1965); *Intéraction* for String Trio (1967); *Sun* for Viola or Violin and 12 Strings (1971); *Iambe* for 14 Instrumentalists (1976); *Sinfonietta* for 10 Instrumentalists (1983); *Folio 4* for Percussion Quartet (1984); *Sonnet* for 12 Instrumentalists (1985); *Ouverture* for Flute, English Horn, Bassoon, Violin, and Harpsichord (1986); *Fruits de la passion* for 10 Instrumentalists (1987); *Travelling Ariane* for Flute and Harp (1990); *Lignes* for Clarinet and String Quartet (1992). **VOCAL:** *Les Hommes sur la terre* for Tenor, Baritone, and Orch. (1963); *Horizon remarquable* for Soprano and Orch. (1964); *Les Rois mages* for Voice and Orch. (1964); *Relevé d'esquisses* for Soprano, Piano, Clarinet, Trombone, and Cello (1964–82); *Et, ée* for Chorus and Orch. (1973); *L'Application des lectrices aux champs* for Soprano and Orch. (1977); *Traits* for Soprano, Clarinet, Horn, Piano, and Cello (1982); *Aubes incendiées* for Soprano and 12 Instrumentalists (1985); *Je, qui d'autre* for Soprano, Tenor, Bass, and 14 Instrumentalists (1987); *Dodici voci* for 12 Voices (1989).

Decreus, Camille, French pianist, teacher, and composer; b. Paris, Sept. 23, 1876; d. Fontainebleau, Sept. 26, 1939. He studied piano with Pugno at the Paris Cons. (premier prix, 1895). After making his debut in Paris in 1906, he toured in Europe and the U.S. as a solo artist and accompanist; was director of the American Cons. in Fontainebleau (from 1924). He wrote piano pieces and songs.

Decsényi, János, Hungarian composer; b. Budapest, March 24, 1927. He studied in Budapest with Sugár at the Cons. (1948–52) and with Szervánszky at the Academy of Music (1952–56). From 1951 he was active with the Hungarian Radio, becoming head of its dept. of serious music and director of its electronic music studio. In 1986 he was made a Merited Artist by the Hungarian government.

WORKS: DRAMATIC: *Képtelen történet* (An Absurd Story), ballet (1962); *Az orr* (The Nose), pantomime (1979). **ORCH.:** *Divertimento* for Harpsichord and Chamber Orch. (1959); *Csontváry-képek* (Csontváry Pictures; 1967); *Melodiae hominis* for Chamber Orch. (1969); *Gondolatok—nappal, éjszaka* (Thoughts—by Day, by Night; 1971); *Kommentárok Marcus Aureliushoz* (Commentaries on Marcus Aurelius) for 16 Solo Strings (1973); *Double* for Chamber Orch. (1974); *Variations* for Piano and Orch. (1976); *Concerto boemo* (1976); *Concerto grosso* for Chamber Orch. (1978); *A tücsökszót ki érti meg?* (Who Understands the Speech of Crickets?) for Chamber Orch. and Tape (1983); Cello Concerto (1984); *A harmadik* (The 3rd One) for 15 Solo Strings (1985); 2 syms. (1986, 1993). **CHAMBER:** String Trio (1955); *Sonatina pastorale* for Flute and Piano (1956); String Quartet (1978). **VOCAL:** *Szerelem* (Love) for Soprano and Orch. (1957); *A gondolat játékai* (The Plays of Thought), cantata for Soprano and Chamber Orch. (1972); *Sírfelirat Aquincumból* (Epitaph from Aquincum) for Soprano,

Electric Organ, and 16 Solo Strings (1979); *Weöres Sándor tizenkettedik szimfóniája* (The 12th Symphony of Sandor Weöres) for Soprano and Percussion (1980). **ELECTRONIC:** *Kövek* (Stones; 1987); *Prospero szigete* (Prospero's Island; 1989).

Decsey, Ernst (Heinrich Franz), German-born Austrian writer on music; b. Hamburg, April 13, 1870; d. Vienna, March 12, 1941. He studied law in Vienna (doctorate, 1894), then composition with Bruckner and Robert Fuchs at the Vienna Cons. He was active as a music critic in Graz and in Vienna. He was the author of a major biography of Hugo Wolf (4 vols., Berlin, 1903–06; abridged 1-vol. ed., 1921). He also wrote *Anton Bruckner* (Berlin, 1920); *Johann Strauss* (Berlin, 1922; 2nd ed., 1947); *Franz Lehár* (Vienna, 1924); *Franz Schubert* (Vienna, 1924); *Maria Jeritza* (Vienna, 1931); *Claude Debussy* (2 vols., Graz, 1936); and *Debussys Werke* (Graz and Vienna, 1948).

DeFabritiis, Oliviero (Carlo), Italian conductor; b. Rome, June 13, 1902; d. there, Aug. 12, 1982. He studied with Setaccioli and Refice. He made his conducting debut at the Teatro Adriano in Rome in 1920; subsequently was a conductor at the Rome Opera (1934–61). He made numerous guest appearances with major European opera houses; also conducted in the U.S.

Defauw, Désiré, Belgian conductor; b. Ghent, Sept. 5, 1885; d. Gary, Ind., July 25, 1960. He was a violin pupil of Johan Smit. From 1914 to 1918 he led his own quartet, the Allied Quartet of London. He was prof. of conducting at the Brussels Cons. and conductor of its concerts (from 1926); he also conducted his own concert series in Brussels and was founder-conductor of the Orchestre National de Belgique there in 1937. In 1940 he went to Canada, where he was music director of the Montreal Sym. Orch. (1941–53); he was also music director of the Chicago Sym. Orch. (1943–47) and then of the Gary (Ind.) Sym. Orch. (1950–58).

BIBL.: M. Herzberg, *D. D.* (Brussels, 1937).

Defossez, René, Belgian conductor, pedagogue, and composer; b. Spa, Oct. 4, 1905; d. Brussels, May 20, 1988. He studied with Rasse at the Liège Cons., winning the Belgian Prix de Rome in 1935 with his opera-cantata *Le Vieux Soudard.* He was conductor at the Théâtre Royal de la Monnaie in Brussels (1936–59) and prof. of conducting at the Brussels Cons. (1946–71). In 1969 he was elected a member of the Royal Belgian Academy.

WORKS: DRAMATIC: OPERA: *Le Subterfuge improvisé* (1938). **OPERA-CANTATAS:** *La Conversion de St. Hubert* (1933); *Le Vieux Soudard* (1935). **BALLETS:** *Floriante* (1942); *Le Sens du divin* (1947); *Le Rêve de l'astronome* (1950); *Les Jeux de France* (1959); *Le Regard* (1970). **BALLET-CANTATA:** *Le Pêcheur et son âme* (1965). **HISTORIC FRESCO:** *Lièges libertes* (1981). **ORATORIOS:** *Bê Pretimps d'amour* (1939); *La Frise empourprée* (1939). **ORCH.:** *Aquarium* (1927); *Images sous-marines* (1930); *Symphonie wallonne* (1935); *Poème romantique* for Strings (1935); *Amaterasu* (1935); *Variations* for Piano and Orch. (1939); *Adagio et Scherzo* for Flute and Orch. (1941); *Recitativo et Allegro* for Trumpet and Orch. (1945); *Marche funebre* (1946); Trombone Concerto (1948); Violin Concerto (1951); Piano Concerto (1956; rev. for 2 Pianos, 1963); *La Chasseur d'images* (1966); *Sinfonietta de printemps* (1975). **CHAMBER:** 2 String Quartets (1934, 1950); Wind Trio (1946); *Petit quartet* for Violin, Piano, Saxophone, and Percussion (1973); piano pieces. **VOCAL:** Choruses and songs.

DeGaetani, Jan(ice), remarkable American mezzo-soprano; b. Massillon, Ohio, July 10, 1933; d. Rochester, N.Y., Sept. 15, 1989. She studied at the Juilliard School of Music in N.Y. with Sergius Kagan. Upon graduation, she joined the Contemporary Chamber Ensemble, with which she developed a peculiar technique essential for performance of ultramodern vocal works. She devoted herself to a detailed study of Schoenberg's *Pierrot lunaire,* which became one of her finest interpretations. She mastered the most challenging techniques of new vocal music, including fractional intervals. She also mastered foreign languages so as to be able to perform a wide European repertoire. She became a faithful interpreter of the most demanding works by modern composers, among them Boulez, Crumb, Druckman, Maxwell Davies, Ligeti, Carter, and Davidovsky. She also developed a fine repertoire of Renaissance songs, and soon became a unique phenomenon as a lieder artist, excelling in an analytical capacity to express the most minute vocal modulations of the melodic line while parsing the words with exquisite intellectual penetration of their meaning, so that even experienced critics found themselves at a loss of superlatives to describe her artistry. From 1973 she taught at the Eastman School of Music. With N. and R. Lloyd, she publ. the useful vol. *The Complete Sightsinger* (1980).

Degen, Helmut, German composer and teacher; b. Aglasterhausen, near Heidelberg, Jan. 14, 1911; d. Trossingen, Oct. 2, 1995. He studied piano, composition, and conducting at the Hochschule für Musik in Cologne; then took courses at the Univ. of Bonn with Schiedermair and Schrade. He taught at the Duisburg Cons., and at the Trossingen Hochschulinstitut für Musik. His music was couched in a well-defined, neo-Classical idiom, with strong points of reference to Baroque forms. He publ. a *Handbuch der Formenlehre* (Regensburg, 1957).

WORKS: ORCH.: Piano Concerto (1940); Organ Concerto (1943); Concertino for 2 Clarinets and Orch. (1944); Cello Concerto (1945); 3 syms. (1945, 1947, 1948); *Symphonisches Spiel I* (1956), *II* for Violin, Cello, Piano, and Orch. (1957), and *III* (1960); *Triptychon* (1952). **CHAMBER:** 2 string quartets (1941, 1950); Piano Trio (1943); Concerto for Harpsichord and 6 Instruments (1945); Trio for Flute, Viola, and Clarinet (1950); Saxophone Sonata (1950); Nonet for Wind Instruments and Strings (1951); 4 piano sonatas; numerous concert studies. **VOCAL:** Choruses.

Degrada, Francesco, esteemed Italian musicologist; b. Milan, May 23, 1940. He studied piano, composition, and conducting at the Milan Cons., obtaining a simultaneous arts degree from the Univ. of Milan (1964), where he was a prof. (from 1976). He joined the music history faculty of the Univ. of Milan in 1964, where he was prof. (from 1976) and director of the arts dept. (from 1983); also taught at the Milan Cons. (1966–73) and gave lectures at various European and U.S. univs., including N.Y. Univ. (1986). His interest in Baroque music led him to organize the chamber group Complesso Barocco di Milan in 1967, with which he was associated as director and harpsichordist until 1976. His research ranges from the Renaissance period to the contemporary era. In addition to numerous scholarly articles in various publications, he has also ed. works by Pergolesi, Vivaldi, Durante, D. Scarlatti, and Sarti.

WRITINGS: *Al gran sole carico d'amore: Per un nuovo teatro musicale* (Milan, 1974; 2nd ed., 1977); *Sylvano Bussotti e il suo teatro* (Milan, 1976); *Antonio Vivaldi da Venezia all'Europa* (Milan, 1977); *Il palazzo incantato: Studi sulla tradizione del melodramma dal Barocco al Romanticismo* (2 vols., Florence, 1979); *Vivaldi veneziano europeo* (Florence, 1980); ed. *Studi Pergolesiani/Pergolesi Studies* (2 vols., N.Y., 1986, 1988); *Andrea Gabrieli e il suo tempo* (Florence, 1988).

De Grassi, Alex, American composer and guitarist; b. Yokosuka, Japan, Feb. 13, 1953. He is a cousin of **William Ackerman**. De Grassi began playing guitar at the age of 13, inspired by folk-blues guitarists John Renbourn and Burt Jansch. His first recording (1978) was one of the first releases on Ackerman's Windham Hill label, and as such is one of the earliest New Age recordings. De Grassi's guitar music shares stylistic traits with that of his cousin, although it is somewhat brighter and more syncopated. He is a "crossover" artist who has received awards in both folk and jazz categories. His highly successful *Altiplano* (1987) was his first release on a label other than Windham Hill; it shows a considerably freer style and wider range of jazz and ethnic influences. De Grassi has toured North America and Europe, performing at venues including N.Y.'s Carnegie Hall, Davies Sym.

Hall in San Francisco, and the Kennedy Center in Washington, D.C. Among his works are *Turning: Turning Back* for Guitar (1978), *Slow Circle* for Guitar (1979), *Clockwork* for Guitar and Other Instruments (1981), *Southern Exposure* for Guitar (1983), and *Altiplano* for Guitar and Other Instruments (1987).

De Guide, Richard, Belgian composer and pedagogue; b. Basècles, March 1, 1909; d. Brussels, Jan. 12, 1962. He was a student of Paul Gilson and Jean Absil. After working at the Institut National de Radiodiffusion (1938–45), he was director of the music academy of Woluwé-St. Pierre in Brussels (1946–61); he also taught at the Liège Cons. (1950–53) and the Mons Cons. (1961). He publ. *Jean Absil: Vie et oeuvre* (Tournai, 1965).

WORKS: BALLET: *Les Danaïdes* (1956). **ORCH.:** *Mouvements symphoniques* (1938); 3 syms.: No. 1 (1943), No. 2 for Organ and Orch. (1951), and No. 3 for Strings, Harp, and Timpani (1957); *Vincti non devicti*, symphonic poem (1948); Piano Concerto, *Le Téméraire* (1952); *Le Tombeau de Montaigne*, suite (1955); *Hommage à Hindemith* for Chamber Orch. (1958). **CHAMBER:** *Concerto for 11* for Winds and Percussion (1940); Duo for 2 Trumpets (1944); Duo for 2 Violins (1945); *Speciosa miracula*, sextet for Winds and Piano (1948); *2 nomes* for Flute (1951); *Les caractères du trombone*, suite for Trombone and Piano (1958). **KEYBOARD: PIANO:** *Humoresque* (1927); *Préludes and Toccata* (1949); *4 symptômes* for Piano, left-hand (1960). **ORGAN:** *Préludes* (1942). **VOCAL:** *Illustration pour un Jeu de l'Oie* for Voice and Piano or Orch. (1939–41).

Deis, Carl, American organist, music editor, and composer; b. N.Y., March 7, 1883; d. there, July 24, 1960. He studied piano at home from early childhood under the guidance of his father, who was a trombone player; then was a pupil at the National Cons. of Music of America and the N.Y. College of Music. In 1906 he became a choral conductor and voice teacher at various private schools in N.Y.; was engaged as organist at the Soc. for Ethical Culture (1919–33). In 1917 he was appointed music ed. of G. Schirmer, Inc., a position he held until his retirement in 1953. He wrote several attractive songs, among them *New Year's Day, The Flight of the Moon, Come Down to Kew, The Drums*, and *Were I a Star.*

Dejoncker, Theodore, Belgian composer; b. Brussels, April 11, 1894; d. Asse, July 10, 1964. He studied with Gilson. In 1925 he founded, with 7 other composers, the progressive Groupe des Synthétistes.

WORKS: *Sinfonia la classica* (1939); *Symphonie burlesque*; *Symphonie romantique*; *Brutus*, overture; *Prologue symphonique*; *Portrait de Bernard Shaw* for Orch.; String Quartet; Saxophone Quartet; String Trio (1960).

De Jong, Conrad J(ohn), American composer; b. Hull, Iowa, Jan. 13, 1934. He studied trumpet at North Texas State Univ. in Denton, majoring in music education (B.M.Ed., 1954); later studied composition with Heiden at Indiana Univ. in Bloomington (M.M., 1959); subsequently took lessons with Ton de Leeuw in Amsterdam (1969). He was appointed to the music faculty of the Univ. of Wisc. in River Falls in 1959.

WORKS: *Unicycle* for Harpsichord or Piano (1960); *3 Studies* for Brass Septet (1960); *Music* for 2 Tubas (1961); *Essay* for Brass Quintet (1963); String Trio (1964); *Fun and Games* for Any Instrument with Piano (1966; rev. 1970); *Aanraking* (Contact) for Trombone (1969); *Hist Whist* for Soprano, Flute, Viola, and Percussion (1969); *Grab Bag* for Tuba Ensemble (1970); *Resound*, trio for Flute, Guitar, and Percussionist or Half-Track Stereo Tape with Tape Delay System and 35mm Slide Projection (1974); 3 Short Variation Fanfares for Brass Quintet (1980); *La Dolorosa* for English Horn (1982).

Dela, Maurice (real name, **Albert Phaneuf**), Canadian composer and organist; b. Montreal, Sept. 9, 1919; d. there, April 28, 1978. He studied organ and theory with Raoul Paquet before taking courses in theory and composition with Séverin Moisse and Claude Champagne at the Cons. de Musique du Quebec à Montreal (1943–47). He also studied orchestration with Sowerby in Chicago and J.-J. Gagnier in Montreal. He subsequently was a church organist in the province of Quebec, a composer and arranger for the CBC (1951–65), and a teacher in Montreal. His music is pragmatic in style and idiom, tending toward Baroque consistency but energized by an injection of euphonious dissonance.

WORKS: ORCH.: *Ballade* for Piano and Orch. (1945); Piano Concerto (1946); *Le Chat, la belette et le petit lapin* for Narrator and Orch. (1950; rev. 1965); *Les Fleurs de Glais* for Narrator and Orch. (1951); *Scherzo* (1952); *Adagio* for Strings (1956); Piano Concertino (1962); *2 esquisses* (1962); *Projection* (1966); 2 syms. (1968, 1972); *3 Dances* (1971); *Triptyque* (1973); *Suite 437* for Band (1977). **CHAMBER:** *Petite suite maritime* for Wind Instruments (1946); Suite for Flute, Cello, and Piano (1953–54); 2 string quartets (1960, 1963); *Divertissement* for Brass Quintet (1962); *Miniatures* for 3 Recorders (1968). **PIANO:** *Hommage* (1950); *2 Impromptus* (1964). **VOCAL:** *Ronde* for Soprano and Small Orch. or Piano (1949); songs; arrangements of folk songs of Quebec province.

Delacôte, Jacques, French conductor; b. Remiremont, Vosges, Aug. 16, 1942. He studied flute at the Nancy Cons. (1956–60) and the Paris Cons. (1960–63), and then conducting with Swarowsky at the Vienna Academy of Music (1965–70). In 1971 he won the Mitropoulos Competition in N.Y., which led to his formal debut with the N.Y. Phil. in 1972. He subsequently appeared as a conductor with major orchs. and opera houses on both sides of the Atlantic.

Delage, Maurice (Charles), French composer; b. Paris, Nov. 13, 1879; d. there, Sept. 19, 1961. He took lessons with Ravel. Subsequently he made voyages to the Orient, and was greatly impressed with Japanese art. His music reveals oriental traits in subject matter as well as in melodic progressions. An ardent follower of Debussy's principles, Delage wrote music in a highly subtilized manner with distinctive instrumental colors. Among his compositions were *Conte par la mer*, symphonic poem (1908); songs, with Small Orch.: *4 poèmes hindous* (1921); *Roses d'Octobre* (1922); *7 Hai-Kaï* (1923); *3 chants de la jungle* (1935); *2 fables de La Fontaine* (1949); *In Morte* (1951); and String Quartet (1948).

De Lamarter, Eric, American organist, conductor, music critic, teacher, and composer; b. Lansing, Mich., Feb. 18, 1880; d. Orlando, Fla., May 17, 1953. He studied organ with Fairclough in St. Paul, Middelschulte in Chicago, and Guilmant and Widor in Paris (1901–02), and was a graduate of Albion College in Michigan (1900); then held several organ positions in Chicago, notably with the 4th Presbyterian Church (1914–36). He was music critic for the *Chicago Inter-Ocean* (1901–14), the *Chicago Record-Herald* (1905–08), and the *Chicago Tribune* (1909–10); he also taught at Olivet College (1904–05), Chicago Musical College (1909–10), Univ. of Missouri, Ohio State Univ., and the Univ. of Texas. He was assistant conductor of the Chicago Sym. Orch. and conductor of the Chicago Civic Orch. (1918–36).

WORKS: DRAMATIC: *The Betrothal*, incidental music (N.Y., Nov. 19, 1918); ballet music. **ORCH.:** 4 syms.: No. 1 (1913; Chicago, Jan. 23, 1914), No. 2 (Philadelphia, June 5, 1925), No. 3 (1931; Chicago, Feb. 16, 1933), and No. 4 (1932); *The Faun*, overture (Chicago, Nov. 18, 1913); *Serenade* (1915); *Masquerade*, overture (1916); *Fable of the Hapless Folktune* (Chicago, April 6, 1917); 2 organ concertos: No. 1 (Chicago, April 2, 1920) and No. 2 (Chicago, Feb. 24, 1922); *Weaver of Tales* for Organ and Chamber Orch. (1926); *The Black Orchid*, suite from *The Dance of Life*, ballet (Chicago, Feb. 27, 1931); *Serenade near Taos* (N.Y., Jan. 11, 1938); *The Giddy Puritan*, overture (original title, *They, Too, Went t'Town*, 1921; NBC, June 6, 1938); *Huckleberry Finn*, overture (1948); *Ol' Kaintuck*, overture (1948); *Cluny*, dialogue for Viola and Orch. (1949). **OTHER:** Chamber music; organ works; songs.

Delamont, Gordon (Arthur), Canadian composer; b. Moose Jaw, Saskatchewan, Oct. 27, 1918; d. Toronto, Jan. 16, 1981. He studied trumpet and played in his father's band in Vancouver;

played in dance orchs. and led his own dance band (1945–49). His works are all in the jazz idiom. For jazz orch., he wrote *Allegro and Blues* (1962), *Ontario Suite* (1965), *Centum* (1966), *Song and Dance* (1967), and *Collage No. 3* (1967). He also wrote *Portrait of Charles Mingus* for Octet (1963), *3 Entertainments* for Saxophone Quartet (1969), *Moderato and Blues* for Brass Quintet (1972), and *Conversation* for Flugelhorn and Alto Saxophone (1977). He publ. *Modern Arranging Techniques* (N.Y., 1965), *Modern Harmonic Techniques* (2 vols., N.Y., 1965), *Modern Contrapuntal Techniques* (N.Y., 1969), *Modern Twelve-Tone Techniques* (N.Y., 1973), and *Modern Melodic Techniques* (N.Y., 1976).

De Lancie, John (Sherwood), prominent American oboist and teacher; b. Berkeley, Calif., July 26, 1921. His father was an electrical engineer and an amateur clarinet player; his brother played the violin. In 1935 he won an audition for the Philadelphia Orch., and was also accepted to study oboe in the class of Tabuteau at the Curtis Inst. of Music in Philadelphia (1936–40). He was engaged as oboist with the Pittsburgh Sym. Orch. (1940–42). In 1942 he was drafted into the U.S. Army as a member of the U.S. Army Band. De Lancie was sent to Algiers, to Eisenhower's headquarters; he was subsequently employed by the Office of Strategic Services. After World War II, De Lancie joined the Philadelphia Orch. (1946), serving as its principal oboist (1954–74). In 1977 he was appointed director of the Curtis Inst. of Music, retiring in 1985. He rapidly advanced to the position of one of the greatest virtuosos on his instrument. An interesting episode in his career concerns his meeting with Richard Strauss in Munich in 1945, during which he asked Strauss why he had not composed an oboe concerto, in view of the fact that there were so many beautiful oboe solos in many of his works. This suggestion bore fruit, but De Lancie was not the first to play it; the first performance was given by Marcel Saillet on Feb. 26, 1946, in Zürich. De Lancie did, however, commission and give first performances of a number of works, including Jean Françaix's *L'Horloge de Flore* and Benjamin Lee's Oboe Concerto.

Delaney, Robert (Mills), American composer and teacher; b. Baltimore, July 24, 1903; d. Santa Barbara, Calif., Sept. 21, 1956. He studied music in the U.S., in Italy, and in Paris (1922–27) with Capet (violin) and Boulanger and Honegger (composition). He held a Guggenheim fellowship in 1929; in 1933 he received a Pulitzer Traveling Fellowship for his music to Stephen Vincent Benet's *John Brown's Body.* He then occupied various teaching posts.

WORKS: *Don Quixote Symphony* (1927); *John Brown's Song,* choral sym. (1931); *Night* for Chorus, String Orch., and Piano (1934); *Adagio* for Violin and Strings (1935); *Work 22,* overture (1939); Sym. No. 1 (1942); *Western Star* for Chorus and Orch. (1944); orch. suites; 3 string quartets.

Delannoy, Marcel, French composer; b. La Ferté-Alais, July 9, 1898; d. Nantes, Sept. 14, 1962. He took lessons with Gédalge and Honegger. He wrote an effective stage work, *Poirier de Misère* (Paris, Feb. 21, 1927), which obtained excellent success. Other works are the ballet-cantata *Le Fou de la dame* (concert perf., Paris, Nov. 9, 1928; stage perf., Geneva, April 6, 1929); *Cinderella,* ballet (Chicago, Aug. 30, 1931; rev. as *La Pantoufle de vair,* Paris, May 14, 1935); Sym. (Paris, March 15, 1934); *Ginevra,* comic opera (Paris, July 25, 1942); *Arlequin radiophile,* chamber opera (Paris, April 1, 1946); *Puck,* fairy opera after Shakespeare (Strasbourg, Jan. 29, 1949); *Concerto de mai* for Piano and Orch. (Paris, May 4, 1950); *Travesti,* ballet (Enghien-les-Bains, June 4, 1952); Sym. for Strings and Celesta (1952–54); *Les Noces fantastiques,* ballet (Paris, Feb. 9, 1955); *Le Moulin de la galette,* symphonic poem (1958).

DeLay, Dorothy, greatly respected American violin pedagogue; b. Medicine Lodge, Kans., March 31, 1917. Her father was a cellist and her mother a pianist; she attended Oberlin College (1933–34) before pursuing violin studies with Michael Press at Michigan State Univ. (B.A., 1937) and Louis Persinger and Raphael Bronstein at the Juilliard Graduate School of Music in N.Y. (diploma, 1941). She established herself as one of the foremost violin teachers in the world; after working as an assistant to Ivan Galamian, she taught at the Juilliard School of Music (from 1947), Sarah Lawrence College (1948–87), the Meadowmount School of Music in Westport, N.Y. (1948–70), the Aspen (Colo.) Music School (from 1971), the Univ. of Cincinnati College-Cons. of Music (from 1974), the Philadelphia College of the Performing Arts (1977–83), and the New England Cons. of Music in Boston (1978–87); she also conducted master classes all over the world. Among her most celebrated pupils were Itzhak Perlman, Shlomo Mintz, and Cho-Liang Lin.

BIBL.: B. Sand, "D. D.: Teaching Genius," *Musical America* (May 1988).

Delcroix, Léon Charles, Belgian composer; b. Brussels, Sept. 15, 1880; d. there, Nov. 14, 1938. He studied piano with J. Wieniawski, organ with A. Mailly, and composition with Ysaÿe in Brussels and Vincent d'Indy in Paris. He conducted theater orchs. in Belgium (1909–27); then devoted himself to composition. He wrote a biography of J. Wieniawski (Brussels, 1908).

WORKS: DRAMATIC: *Ce n'était qu'un rêve*; *La Bacchante,* ballet (Ghent, 1912); *Le Petit Poucet,* opera (Brussels, Oct. 9, 1913). **ORCH.:** Sym. (won the award of the Belgian Academy); *Le Roi Harald*; *Çunacépa*; *Soir d'été à Lerici*; *Le Val harmonieux*; *Rapsodie languedocienne*; *Marche cortège*; *Sérénade* for Clarinet, Piano, and Orch.; *Elégie et Poème* for Violin and Orch. **OTHER:** Many chamber music works (quartets, quintets, sonatas, etc.); piano pieces; church music; songs.

Delden, Lex van, Dutch composer and writer on music; b. Amsterdam, Sept. 10, 1919; d. there, July 1, 1988. He studied medicine at the Univ. of Amsterdam and was autodidact in composition. He contributed articles to various Dutch and foreign publications, and also served as music ed. of the newspaper *Het Parool* (from 1947); he likewise was president of the Soc. of Dutch Composers. He was a prolific composer who wrote in a basically tonal style.

WORKS: ORCH.: 8 syms.: No. 1, *De stroom, Mei 1940* (The Torrent; May 1940) for Soprano, Chorus, 8 Instruments, and Percussion (1952; for Orch., 1954), No. 2, *Sinfonia giocosa* (1953), No. 3, *Facetten* (Facets; 1955), No. 4 (1957), No. 5 (1959), No. 6 (1963), No. 7, *Sinfonia concertante,* for 11 Winds (1964), and No. 8 for Strings (1964); Harp Concerto (1951–52); Trumpet Concerto (1956); Concerto for 2 Oboes and Orch. (1959); Piano Concerto (1960); Concerto for 2 String Orchs. (1961); Flute Concerto (1965); Concerto for Violin, Viola, Double Bass, and Orch. (1965); Concerto for 2 Soprano Saxophones and Orch. (1967); *Musica sinfonica* (1967); Concerto for Percussion, Celesta, and Strings (1968); Concerto for Electronic Organ and Orch. (1973); Concerto for Violin, 15 Winds, and Percussion (1978); *Musica di catasto* for Strings (1981; also for String Quintet). **CHAMBER:** Trio for Piano, Violin, and Viola (1944); Piano Sonata (1949); *Kleine Suite* for 12 Harps (1951; in collaboration with M. Flothius); 3 string quartets (1954, 1965, 1979); Quartet for Flute, Violin, Viola, and Cello (1957); Sonata for Solo Cello (1958); Violin Sonata (1964); *Fantasia* for Harp and 8 Winds (1965); 2 trios for Violin, Cello, and Piano (1969, 1988); *Sestetto* for String Sextet (1971); *Nonetto per Amsterdam* for Clarinet, Bassoon, Horn, 2 Violins, Viola, Cello, Double Bass, and Piano (1975); *Quintetto* for Brass Quintet (1981); *Tomba* for 4 Saxophones (1985). **VOCAL:** 3 oratorios: *De Vogel Vrijheid* (The Bird of Freedom; 1955), *Anthropolis* (1962), and *Icarus* (1963); choral pieces; songs.

de Leone, Francesco (Bartolomeo), American conductor, pedagogue, and composer; b. Ravenna, Ohio (of Italian parents), July 28, 1887; d. Akron, Ohio, Dec. 10, 1948. He studied at Dana's Musical Inst., Warren, Ohio (1901–03), and at the Royal Cons. of Naples (1903–10); returning to the U.S., he settled in Akron, Ohio, where he founded the de Leone School of Music and organized and directed the music dept. of the Univ. of Akron; also conducted the Akron Sym. Orch. He wrote the operas *Alglala* (Akron, May 23, 1924); *A Millionaire Caprice* (in Italian; Naples, July 26, 1910); *Cave Man Stuff*, operetta; *Princess Ting-Ah-Ling*, operetta; the sacred musical dramas *Ruth*, *The Prodigal Son*, *The Golden Calf*, and *David*; *The Triumph of Joseph*, oratorio; the orch. pieces *6 Italian Dances*, *Italian Rhapsody*, and *Gibraltar Suite*; over 400 songs; piano pieces.

Delgadillo, Luis (Abraham), Nicaraguan composer; b. Managua, Aug. 26, 1887; d. there, Dec. 20, 1961. He studied at the Milan Cons.; returning to Nicaragua, he became a band conductor and opened a music school, which later became a cons. His music is permeated with native rhythm and melos; virtually all of his output is descriptive of some aspect of Latin American culture and history.

WORKS: ORCH.: *Sinfonia indigena* (1921); *Sinfonia mexicana* (1924); *Teotihuácan* (1925); *Sinfonia incaica* (1926; Caracas, May 20, 1927); *Sinfonia serrana* (1928); 12 short syms. (all 1953); *Obertura Debussyana* (1955); *Obertura Schoenbergiana* (1955). **OTHER:** 7 string quartets; piano pieces; church music.

DeLio, Thomas, American composer and music theorist; b. N.Y., Jan. 7, 1951. He studied composition at the New England Cons. of Music in Boston (B.M., 1972) and at Brown Univ., in an interdisciplinary program involving music, mathematics, and visual art (Ph.D., 1979, with the diss. *Structural Pluralism*). He taught at Clark Univ. (1977), the New England Cons. of Music (1977–80), and the Univ. of Maryland (from 1980). He was co-founder and co-ed. of the journal *Sonus* (1980–85); his articles have appeared in various other art and music journals. His research focuses on open structures and mathematical concepts in composition. As a composer, he has created live electronic sound installations and computer-aided compositions; among his works are *Text* for Piano (1985), *Against the silence . . .* for Percussion and Tape (1985), and *contrecoup . . .* for Chamber Ensemble (1989). He publ. *Circumscribing the Open Universe* (Lanham, Md., 1983); ed. *Contiguous Lines: Issues and Ideas in the Music of the '60s and '70s* (Lanham, Md., 1985).

Delius, Frederick (actually, **Fritz Theodor Albert**), significant English composer of German parentage; b. Bradford, Jan. 29, 1862; d. Grez-sur-Loing, France, June 10, 1934. His father was a successful merchant, owner of a wool company; he naturally hoped to have his son follow a career in industry, but did not object to his study of art and music. Delius learned to play the piano and violin. At the age of 22 he went to Solano, Fla., to work on an orange plantation owned by his father; a musical souvenir of his sojourn there was his symphonic suite *Florida*. There he met an American organist, Thomas F. Ward, who gave him a thorough instruction in theory; this study, which lasted 6 months, gave Delius a foundation for his further progress in music. In 1885 he went to Danville, Va., as a teacher. In 1886 he enrolled at the Leipzig Cons., where he took courses in harmony and counterpoint with Reinecke, Sitt, and Jadassohn. It was there that he met Grieg, becoming his friend and admirer. Indeed, Grieg's music found a deep resonance in his own compositions. An even more powerful influence was Wagner, whose principles of continuous melodic line and thematic development Delius adopted in his own works. Euphonious serenity reigns on the symphonic surface of his music, diversified by occasional resolvable dissonances. In some works, he made congenial use of English folk motifs, often in elaborate variation forms. Particularly successful are his evocative symphonic sketches *On Hearing the First Cuckoo in Spring*, *North Country Sketches*, *Brigg Fair*, and *A Song of the High Hills*. His orch. nocturne *Paris: The Song of a Great City* is a tribute to a city in which he spent many years of his life. Much more ambitious in scope is his choral work *A Mass of Life*, in which he draws on passages from Nietzsche's *Also sprach Zarathustra*.

Delius settled in Paris in 1888; in 1897 he moved to Grez-sur-Loing, near Paris, where he remained for the rest of his life, except for a few short trips abroad. In 1903 he married the painter Jelka Rosen. His music began to win recognition in England and Germany; he became a favorite composer of Sir Thomas Beecham, who gave numerous performances of his music in London. But these successes came too late for Delius; a syphilitic infection which he had contracted early in life eventually grew into an incurable illness accompanied by paralysis and blindness; as Beecham phrased it, "Delius had suffered a heavy blow in the defection of his favorite goddess, Aphrodite Pandemos, who had returned his devotions with an affliction which was to break out many years later." Still eager to compose, he engaged as his amanuensis the English musician Eric Fenby, who wrote down music at the dictation of Delius, including complete orch. scores. In 1929 Beecham organized a Delius Festival in London (6 concerts; Oct. 12 to Nov. 1, 1929) and the composer was brought from France to hear it. In the same year Delius was made a Companion of Honour by King George V and an Hon.Mus.D. by Oxford. A film was made by the British filmmaker Ken Russell on the life and works of Delius. However, he remains a solitary figure in modern music. Affectionately appreciated in England, in America, and to some extent in Germany, his works are rarely performed elsewhere.

WORKS: DRAMATIC: *Zanoni*, incidental music after Bulwer Lytton (1888; unfinished); *Irmelin*, opera (1890–92; Oxford, May 4, 1953); *The Magic Foundation*, lyric drama (1893–95; BBC, London, Nov. 20, 1977); *Koanga*, lyric drama (1895–97; Elberfeld, March 30, 1904); *Folkeraadet*, incidental music to G. Heiberg's drama (Christiania, Oct. 18, 1897); *A Village Romeo and Juliet*, lyric drama (1899–1901; Berlin, Feb. 21, 1907); *Margot la Rouge*, lyric drama (1902; concert perf. BBC, London, Feb. 21, 1982; stage perf., St. Louis, June 8, 1983); *Fennimore and Gerda*, opera (1908–10; Frankfurt am Main, Oct. 21, 1919); *Hassan, or The Golden Journey to Samarkand*, incidental music to J. Flecker's drama (1920–23; Darmstadt, June 1, 1923; full version, London, Sept. 20, 1923).

ORCH.: *Florida*, suite (1887; private perf., Leipzig, 1888; rev. 1889; public perf., London, April 1, 1937); *Hiawatha*, tone poem (1888; unfinished; excerpt, Norwegian TV, Oslo, Jan. 13, 1984); *Suite* for Violin and Orch. (1888; BBC, Feb. 28, 1984); *Rhapsodic Variations* (1888; unfinished); *Idylle de Printemps* (1889); *Suite d'orchestre* (1889); 3 Small Tone Poems: *Summer Evening*, *Winter Night [Sleigh Ride]*, and *Spring Morning* (1889–90; Westminster, Nov. 18, 1946); *Légendes* for Piano and Orch. (1890; unfinished); *Petite suite d'orchestre* for Small Orch. (1890; Stratford-upon-Avon, May 13, 1978); *Paa vidderne* (On the Heights), symphonic poem after Ibsen (1890–91; Christiania, Oct. 10, 1891); *Légende* for Violin and Orch. (1895?; London, May 30, 1899); *Over the Hills and Far Away*, fantasy overture (1895–97; Elberfeld, Nov. 13,1897); *Appalachia: American Rhapsody* (1896; London, Dec. 10, 1986; rev. as *Appalachia: Variations on an Old Slave Song* for Baritone, Chorus, and Orch.; 1902–03; Elberfeld, Oct. 15, 1904); Piano Concerto in C minor (1st version in 3 movements, 1897; Elberfeld, Oct. 24, 1904; 2nd version in 1 movement, 1906; London, Oct. 22, 1907); *La Ronde se déroule*, symphonic poem after H. Rode (London, May 30, 1899; rev. 1901, as *Lebenstanz* [Life's Dance]; Düsseldorf, Jan. 21, 1904; 2nd rev., 1912; Berlin, Nov. 15, 1912); *Paris: A Nocturne (The Song of a Great City)* (1899; Elberfeld, Dec. 14, 1901); *Brigg Fair: An English Rhapsody* (Basel, 1907); *In a Summer Garden*, rhapsody (London, Dec. 11, 1908; rev., Boston, April 19, 1912); *A Dance Rhapsody*, No. 1 (1908; Hereford, Sept. 8, 1909) and No. 2 (1916; London, Oct. 20, 1923); *2 Pieces* for Small Orch: *On Hearing the 1st Cuckoo in Spring* (1912) and *Summer Night on the River* (1911; Leipzig, Oct. 23, 1913); *North Country Sketches* (1913–14; London, May 10, 1915); *Air and Dance* for Strings (private perf., London, 1915; public perf., London, Oct. 16, 1929); Double Concerto for Violin, Cello, and Orch. (1915–16; London, Feb. 21, 1920); Violin Concerto (1916; London, Jan. 30, 1919); *Eventyr (Once upon a Time)*, ballad after Asbjørnsen (1917; London, Jan. 11, 1919); *A Song before Sunrise* for Small Orch. (1918; London, Sept. 19, 1923); *Poem of Life and Love* (1918); Cello Concerto (1920–21; Frankfurt am Main, Jan. 30, 1921); *A Song of Summer* (1929–30; London, Sept. 7, 1931); *Caprice and Elegy* for Cello and Chamber Orch. (1930); *Irmelin Prelude* (1931; London, Sept. 23, 1935); *Fantastic Dance* (1931; London, Jan. 12, 1934).

CHAMBER: 2 string quartets: No. 1 (1888; unfinished) and No. 2 (original version in 3 movements, London, Nov. 17, 1916; rev. version in 4 movements, London, Feb. 1, 1919); *Romance* for Violin and Piano (1889); Violin Sonata in B major (1892; private perf., Paris, 1893); 3 numbered violin sonatas: No. 1 (1905, 1914; Manchester, Feb. 24, 1915), No. 2 (1923; London, Oct. 7, 1924), and No. 3 (London, Nov. 6, 1930); *Romance* for Cello and Piano (1896; Helsinki, June 22, 1976); Cello Sonata (1916; London, Oct. 31, 1918); *Dance* for Harpsichord (1919). **PIANO:** *Zum Carnival Polka* (1885); *Pensées mélodieuses* (1885); *Valse* and *Rêverie* (1889–90; unfinished); *Badinage* (1895?); *5 Pieces* (1922–23); *3 Preludes* (1923; London, Sept. 4, 1924).

VOCAL: *6 German Partsongs* for Chorus (1885–87); *Paa vidderne* (On the Heights) for Reciter and Orch., after Ibsen (1888; Norwegian TV, Oslo, May 17, 1983); *Sakuntala* for Tenor and Orch. (1889); *Twilight Fancies* for Voice and Piano (1889; orchestrated 1908; Liverpool, March 21, 1908); *The Bird's Story* for Voice and Piano (1889; orchestrated 1908; Liverpool, March 21, 1908); *Maud*, 5 songs for Tenor and Orch., after Tennyson (1891); *2 songs* for Voice and Piano, after Verlaine (1895; later orchestrated); *7 Danish Songs* for Voice and Orch. or Piano (1897; 5 songs, London, March 30, 1899); *Mitternachtslied Zarathustras* for Baritone, Men's Chorus, and Orch., after Nietzsche (1898; London, May 30, 1899); *The Violet* for Voice and Piano (1900; orchestrated 1908; Liverpool, March 21, 1908); *Summer Landscape* for Voice and Piano (1902; orchestrated 1903); *Appalachia: Variations on an Old Slave Song* for Baritone, Chorus, and Orch. (1902–03; Elberfeld, Oct. 15, 1904; rev. of *Appalachia: American Rhapsody* for Orch., 1896; London, Dec. 10, 1986); *Sea Drift* for Baritone, Chorus, and Orch., after Whitman (1903–04; Essen, May 24, 1906); *A Mass of Life* for Soprano, Alto, Tenor, Baritone, Chorus, and Orch., after Nietzsche's *Also sprach Zarathustra* (1904–05; partial perf., Munich, June 4, 1908; complete perf., London, June 7, 1909); *Songs of Sunset* for Mezzo-soprano, Baritone, Chorus, and Orch., after E. Dowson (1906–07; London, June 16, 1911); *Cynara* for Baritone and Orch. (1907, 1929; London, Oct. 18, 1929); *On Craig Ddu* for Chorus (1907; Blackpool, 1910); *Wanderer's Song* for Men's Chorus (1908); *Midsummer Song* for Chorus (1908); *La Lune blanche* for Voice and Orch. or Piano, after Verlaine (1910); *An Arabesque* for Baritone, Chorus, and Orch. (1911; Newport, Monmouthshire, May 28, 1920); *The Song of the High Hills* for Wordless Chorus and Orch. (1911–12; London, Feb. 26, 1920); *2 Songs for Children* (1913); *I-Brasîl* for Voice and Orch. or Piano (1913; Westminster, Nov. 21, 1946); *Requiem* for Soprano, Baritone, Chorus, and Orch. (1913–14; London, March 23, 1922); *To Be Sung of a Summer Night on the Water*, 2 songs for Wordless Chorus (1917; London, June 28, 1921); *The splendour falls on castle walls* for Chorus, after Tennyson (1923; London, June 17, 1924); *A Late Lark* for Tenor and Orch. (1924, 1929; London, Oct. 12, 1929); *Songs of Farewell* for Chorus and Orch., after Whitman (1930; London, March 21, 1932); *Idyll: Once I passed through a populous city* for Soprano, Baritone, and Orch., after Whitman (1932; London, Oct. 3, 1933; based on *Margot la Rouge*). **SOLO SONGS:** *Over the Mountains High* (1885); *Zwei braune Augen* (1885); *Der Fichtenbaum* (1886); *5 Songs from the Norwegian: Slumber Song, The Nightingale, Summer Eve, Longing,* and *Sunset* (1888); *Hochgebirgsleben* (1888); *O schneller, mein Ross* (1888); *Chanson de Fortunio* (1889); *7 Songs from the Norwegian: Cradle Song, The Homeward Journey, Evening Voices, Sweet Venevil, Minstrel, Love Concealed,* and *The Bird's Story* (1889–90; Nos. 3 and 7 orchestrated); *Skogen gir susende, langsom besked* (1890–91); *4 Songs*, after Heine: *Mit deinen blauen Augen, Ein schöner Stern, Hör' ich das Liedchen klingen,* and *Aus deinen Augen* (1890–91); *3 Songs*, after Shelley: *Indian Love Song, Love's Philosophy,* and *To the Queen of My Heart* (1891); *Lyse Naetter* (1891); *Jeg havde en nyskaare Seljeflo/jte* (1892–93); *Nuages* (1893); *2 Songs*, after Verlaine: *Il pleure dans mon coeur* and *Le ciel est, pardessus le toit* (1895; also orchestrated); *The page sat in the lofty tower* (1895?); *7 Danish Songs: Summer Nights, Through Long, Long Years, Wine Roses, Let Springtime Come, Irmelin Rose, In the Seraglio Garden,* and *Silken Shoes* (1896–97; also orchestrated); *Traum Rosen* (1898?); *Im Glück wir lachend gingen* (1898?); *4 Songs*, after Nietzsche: *Nach neuen Meeren, Der Wanderer, Der Einsame,* and *Der Wanderer und sein Schatten* (1898); *The Violet* (1900; also orchestrated); *Autumn* (1900); *Black Roses* (1901); *Jeg ho/rer i Natten* (1901); *Summer Landscape* (1902; also orchestrated); *The nightingale has a lyre of gold* (1910); *La Lune blanche*, after Verlaine (1910; also orchestrated); *Chanson d'automne*, after Verlaine (1911); *I-Brasîl* (1913; also orchestrated); *4 Old English Lyrics: It was a lover and his lass, So white, so soft is she, Spring, the sweet spring,* and *To Daffodile* (1915–16); *Avant que tu ne t'en ailles*, after Verlaine (1919, 1932).

BIBL.: P. Heseltine, *F. D.* (London, 1923; 2nd ed., rev., 1952); R. Hull, *F. D.* (London, 1928); E. Blom, "D. and America," *Musical Quarterly* (July 1929); C. Delius, *F. D., Memories of My Brother* (London, 1935); E. Fenby, *D. as I Knew Him* (London, 1936; 3rd ed., 1966); A. Hutchings, *D., A Critical Biography* (London, 1948); T. Beecham, *F. D.* (London, 1959; 2nd ed., rev., 1975); G. Jahoda, *The Road to Samarkand: F. D. and His Music* (N.Y., 1969); E. Fenby, *D.* (London, 1971); W. Randel, "F. D. in America," *Virginia Magazine of History & Biography* (July 1971); L. Carley and R. Threlfall, *D. and America* (London, 1972); A. Jefferson, *D.* (London, 1972); R. Lowe, *F. D., 1862–1934; A Catalogue of the Music Archives of the D. Trust, London* (London, 1974); L. Carley, *D.: The Paris Years* (London, 1975); C. Palmer, *D.: Portrait of a Cosmopolitan* (London, 1976); C. Redwood, ed., *A D. Companion* (London, 1976; 2nd ed., 1980); L. Carley and R. Threlfall, *D.: A Life in Pictures* (London, 1977; 2nd ed., 1984); R. Threlfall, *F. D. (1862–1934): A Catalogue of the Compositions* (London, 1977); C. Redwood, *Flecker and D.: The Making of "Hassan"* (London, 1978); L. Carley, *D.: A Life in Letters:* vol. I, *1862–1908* (London, 1983; Cambridge, Mass., 1984) and vol. II, *1909–1934* (Aldershot, 1988); *D. 1862–1934* (50th anniversary brochure by the D. Trust, London, 1984); R. Threlfall, *F. D.: A Supplementary Catalogue* (London, 1986); P. Jones, *The American Source of D.' Style* (N.Y., 1989); L. Carley, ed., *Grieg and D.: A Chronicle of their Friendship in Letters* (N.Y., 1993).

Della Casa, Lisa, noted Swiss soprano; b. Burgdorf, Feb. 2, 1919. She commenced vocal studies with Margarete Haeser in Zürich when she was 15. She made her operatic debut as Cio-Cio-San in Solothurn-Biel (1941), then was a member of the Zürich Stadttheater (1943–50). She made her first appearance at the Salzburg Festival as Zdenka in 1947, then appeared as the Countess in *Le nozze di Figaro* at the Glyndebourne Festival in 1951. That same year she sang Sophie and Arabella, her most celebrated portrayal, in Munich. She subsequently was a leading member of the Vienna State Opera (1952–74). She made her Metropolitan Opera debut in N.Y. as Mozart's Countess on Nov. 20, 1953, and continued to sing there with distinction until 1968. Della Casa was chosen to sing the role of the Marschallin at the opening of the new Salzburg Festspielhaus (1960). She was held in great esteem for her remarkable portrayals of roles in operas by Mozart and Richard Strauss.

BIBL.: D. Debeljević, *Ein Leben mit L. d. C.* (Zürich, 1975).

Della Corte, Andrea, eminent Italian musicologist; b. Naples, April 5, 1883; d. Turin, March 12, 1968. He was self-taught in music; devoted himself mainly to musical biography and analysis. He taught music history at the Turin Cons. (1926–53) and at the Univ. of Turin (1939–53). From 1919 to 1967 he was music critic of *La Stampa*.

WRITINGS: *Paisiello* (Turin, 1922); *Saggi di critica musicale* (Turin, 1922); *L'opera comica italiana del 1700* (2 vols., Bari, 1923); *Piccola antologia settecentesca, XXIV pezzi inediti o rari* (Milan, 1925); with G. Gatti, *Dizionario di musica* (Turin, 1925; 6th ed., 1959); *Disegno storico dell'arte musicale* (Turin, 1927; 5th ed., 1950); *Antologia della storia della musica* (2 vols., Turin, 1927–29; 4th ed., 1945); *Niccolò Piccinni* (Bari, 1928);

Scelta di musiche per lo studio della storia (Milan, 1928; 3rd ed., 1949); *La vita musicale di Goethe* (Turin, 1932); with G. Pannain, *Storia della musica* (Turin, 1936; 4th ed., 1964); with G. Pannain, *Vincenzo Bellini* (Turin, 1936); *Ritratto di Franco Alfano* (Turin, 1936); *Pergolesi* (Turin, 1936); *Un Italiano all'estero: Antonio Salieri* (Turin, 1937); *Tre secoli di opera italiana* (Turin, 1938); *Verdi* (Turin, 1939); *Toscanini* (Vicenza, 1946); *Satire e grotteschi di musiche e di musicisti d'ogni tempo* (Turin, 1947); *Le sei pi belle opere di Verdi: Rigoletto, Il Trovatore, La Traviata, Aida, Otello, Falstaff* (Milan, 1947); *Gluck* (Florence, 1948); *Baldassare Galuppi* (Siena, 1949); *Arrigo Serato* (Siena, 1949); *L'interpretazione musicale e gli interpreti* (Turin, 1951).

Deller, Alfred (George), English countertenor; b. Margate, May 31, 1912; d. Bologna, July 16, 1979. He studied voice with his father; began singing as a boy soprano, later developing the alto range. He sang in the choirs of the Canterbury Cathedral (1940–47) and at St. Paul's in London. In 1950 he formed his own vocal and instrumental ensemble, the Deller Consort, acting as conductor and soloist in a repertoire of early English music. This unique enterprise led to a modest revival of English madrigals of the Renaissance. In 1963 he founded the Stour Music Festival in Kent. Britten wrote the part of Oberon in his *A Midsummer Night's Dream* for him. In 1970 Deller was named a Commander of the Order of the British Empire.

BIBL.: M. and M. Hardwick, *A. D.: A Singularity of Voice* (London, 1968; 2nd ed., rev., 1982).

Dello Joio, Norman, able American composer and teacher; b. N.Y., Jan. 24, 1913. His family's original name was Ioio. His father, grandfather, and great-grandfather were church organists. Dello Joio acquired skill as an organist and pianist at home; at the age of 12, he occasionally substituted for his father on his job at the Church of Our Lady of Mount Carmel in N.Y. He took additional organ lessons from his well-known godfather, **Pietro Yon**, and studied piano with Gaston Déthier at the Inst. of Musical Art in N.Y. (1933–38); in the meantime, he played jazz piano in various groups in N.Y. From 1939 to 1941 he studied composition with Wagenaar at the Juilliard School of Music in N.Y.; in 1941 he enrolled in the summer class of composition led by Hindemith at the Berkshire Music Center in Tanglewood; he continued to attend Hindemith's courses at Yale Univ. from 1941 to 1943. During this period, he wrote several works of considerable validity, among them a piano trio, a ballet entitled *The Duke of Sacramento*, a Magnificat, a Piano Sonata, and other pieces. He taught composition at Sarah Lawrence College (1945–50); held 2 consecutive Guggenheim fellowships (1944, 1945); and composed music with utmost facility and ingratiating felicity. His *Concert Music* was premiered by the Pittsburgh Sym. Orch., conducted by Fritz Reiner, on Jan. 4, 1946, and his *Ricercari* for Piano and Orch. was introduced by the N.Y. Phil. on Dec. 19, 1946, with George Szell conducting, with the piano part played by Dello Joio himself. There followed a number of major works in a distinctive Joioan manner, some of them deeply rooted in medieval ecclesiasticism, profoundly liturgical, and yet overtly modern in their neo-modal moderately dissonant counterpoint. He also exhibited a flair for writing on topical American themes, ranging from impressions of the Cloisters in N.Y. to rhythmic modalities of Manhattan's Little Italy. On May 9, 1950, at Sarah Lawrence College, he produced his first opera, *The Triumph of Joan*; he later used its thematic material in a sym. in 3 movements, *The Triumph of St. Joan*, originally titled *Seraphic Dialogue*. He then wrote another opera on the subject of St. Joan, to his own libretto, *The Trial of Rouen*, first performed on television, by the NBC Opera Theater, April 8, 1956; still another version of the St. Joan theme was an opera in which Dello Joio used the original title, *The Triumph of St. Joan*, but composed the music anew; it had its premiere at the N.Y. City Opera on April 16, 1959. In 1957 Dello Joio received the Pulitzer Prize in Music for his *Meditations on Ecclesiastes*, scored for string orch.; it was first performed in Washington, D.C., on Dec. 17, 1957, but the material was used previously for a ballet, *There Is a Time*. In 1961 he produced an opera, *Blood Moon*, brought out by the San Francisco Opera, to a scenario dealing with the life and times of an adventurous actress, Adah Menken, who exercised her charms in New Orleans at the time of the Civil War. Returning to liturgical themes, Dello Joio composed three masses (1968, 1975, 1976). He continued his activities as a teacher; from 1956 to 1972 he was on the faculty of the Mannes College of Music in N.Y.; from 1972 to 1979 he taught at Boston Univ. He held honorary doctorates in music from Lawrence College in Wisconsin (1959), Colby College in Maine (1963), and the Univ. of Cincinnati (1969). He received the N.Y. Music Critics' Circle Award in 1947 and 1959.

WORKS: DRAMATIC: *Prairie*, ballet (1942; arranged from the Sinfonietta, 1941); *The Duke of Sacramento*, ballet (1942); *On Stage*, ballet (1945); *Diversion of Angels*, ballet (New London, Conn., Aug. 13, 1948; for Martha Graham); *The Triumph of Joan*, opera (1949; Bronxville, N.Y., May 9, 1950; withdrawn); *The Triumph of St. Joan Symphony*, ballet (Louisville, Dec. 5, 1951; based on the opera *The Triumph of St. Joan*; rechoreographed as *Seraphic Dialogue* [by Martha Graham], 1955); *The Ruby*, opera (1953; Bloomington, Ind., May 13, 1955); *The Tall Kentuckian*, incidental music to B. Anderson's play (Louisville, June 15, 1953); *The Trial at Rouen*, opera (1955; NBC-TV, April 8, 1956; rev. as *The Triumph of St. Joan*, N.Y., April 16, 1959); *There is a Time*, ballet (1956; arranged from *Meditations on Ecclesiastes* for Strings, 1956); *Air Power*, television music (1956–57; arranged as a symphonic suite, 1957); *Profile of a Composer*, television music (CBS-TV, Feb. 16, 1958; includes *Ballad of the 7 Lively Arts*); *Here is New York*, television music (1959; includes excerpts from *New York Profiles*; arranged as an orch. suite); *The Saintmaker's Christmas Eve*, television music (1959); *Vanity Fair*, television music (1959); *Women's Song*, ballet (1960; arranged from the Harp Concerto, 1945); *Anthony and Cleopatra*, incidental music to Shakespeare's play (1960); *Time of Decision*, television music (1962); *The Louvre*, television music (1965; arranged for Band, 1965); *A Time of Snow*, ballet (1968; arranged for Band as *Songs of Abelard*, 1969); *The Glass Heart*, ballet (1968; arranged from *Meditations on Ecclesiastes* for Strings, 1956); *Satiric Dances for a Comedy by Aristophanes* for Band (1974; Concord, Mass., July 17, 1975); *As of a Dream*, masque (1978).

ORCH.: Piano Concertino (1938; withdrawn); Flute Concertino (1938; withdrawn); *Ballad* for Strings (1940; withdrawn); Concerto for 2 Pianos and Orch. (1941; withdrawn); Sinfonietta (1941; arranged as the ballet *Prairie*, 1942); Harmonica Concerto (1942; withdrawn); *Magnificat* (1942); *To a Lone Sentry* for Chamber Orch. (1943); *Concert Music* (1944; Pittsburgh, Jan. 4, 1946); *On Stage* (Cleveland, Nov. 23, 1945; arranged from the ballet); Harp Concerto (1945; N.Y., Oct. 20, 1947; arranged as the ballet *Women's Song*, 1960); *3 Ricercari* for Piano and Orch. (N.Y., Dec. 19, 1946); *Serenade* (1947–48; Cleveland, Oct. 20, 1949; arranged as the ballet *Diversion of Angels*, 1948); *Variations, Chaconne and Finale (3 Symphonic Dances)* (1947; Pittsburgh, Jan. 30, 1948); *Concertato* for Clarinet and Orch. (Chautauqua, May 22, 1949; arranged for Clarinet and Piano, 1949); *New York Profiles* (La Jolla, Calif., Aug. 21, 1949); *Epigraph* (1951; Danver, Jan. 29, 1952); *Meditations on Ecclesiastes* for Strings (1956; Washington, D.C., Dec. 17, 1957; arranged as the ballets *There is a Time*, 1956, and *The Glass Heart*, 1968); *A Ballad of the 7 Lively Arts* for Piano and Orch. (1957); *Fantasy and Variations* for Piano and Orch. (1961; Cincinnati, March 9, 1962); *Variants on a Medieval Tune* for Band (Durham, N.C., May 8, 1963); *From Every Horizon* for Band (1964); *Antiphonal Fantasy on a Theme of Vincenzo Albrici* for Organ, Brass, and Strings (1965); *Air* for Strings (1967); *Fantasies on a Theme by Haydn* (1968; Little Rock, Ark., June 3, 1969); *Homage to Haydn* (1968–69); *Songs of Abelard* for Band (1969; arranged from the ballet *A Time of Snow*, 1968); *Choreography* for Strings (1972); *Concertante* for Band (1973); *Lyric Fantasies* for Viola and Strings (1973); *Colonial Ballads* for Band (1976); *Colonial Variants: 13 Profiles of the Original Colonies* (Philadelphia, May 27, 1976); *Arietta* for Strings (1978);

Caccia for Band (1978); *Ballabili* (1981); *Air and Roulade* for Band (1984); *East Hampton Sketches* for Strings (1984); *Variants on a Bach Chorale* (1985).

CHAMBER: Piano Trio (1937; withdrawn); Quartet for 4 Bassoons (1937; withdrawn); Cello Sonata (1937; withdrawn); Violin Sonata (1937; withdrawn); *Colloquy* for Violin and Piano (1938; withdrawn); Violin Sonata (1938; withdrawn); Woodwind Quintet (1939; withdrawn); Woodwind Trio (1940; withdrawn); *Fantasia on a Gregorian Theme* for Violin and Piano (1942); Sextet for 3 Recorders and String Trio (1943); Trio for Flute, Cello, and Piano (1944); *Duo concertante* for Cello and Piano or 2 Pianos (1945); *Variations and Capriccio* for Violin and Piano (1948); *Concertante* for Clarinet and Piano (1949; arranged from the *Concertato* for Clarinet and Orch., 1949); *Colloquies* for Violin and Piano (1963); *Bagatelles* for Harp (1968); *The Developing Flutist* for Flute and Piano (1972); *3 Essays* for Clarinet and Piano (1974); String Quartet (1974); Trumpet Sonata (1979); *Reflections on a Christmas Tune* for Woodwind Quintet (1981). **PIANO:** 3 sonatas (1933, 1944, 1948); *Prelude to a Young Dancer* (1943); *Prelude to a Young Musician* (1943); 2 *Nocturnes* (1946); *Aria and Toccata* for 2 Pianos (1952); *Family Album* for Piano, 4-hands (1962); *Night Song* (1963); *5 Images* for Piano, 4-hands (1967); *Capriccio on the Interval of a Second* (1968); *Stage Parodies* for Piano, 4-hands (1974); *Diversions* (1975); *Salute to Scarlatti* (1979; also for Harpsichord); *Concert Variations* (1980); *Song at Springtide* for Piano, 4-hands (1984).

VOCAL: *Chicago* for Chorus, after Sandburg (1939; withdrawn); *Vigil Strange* for Chorus and Piano, 4-hands (1941); *The Mystic Trumpeter* for Chorus and Horn, after Whitman (1943); *A Jubilant Song* for Women's Voices and Piano, after Whitman (1945); *Symphony for Voices* for Chorus, after Benet (1945; rev. as *Song of Affirmation* for Soprano, Narrator, Chorus, and Orch., 1953); *A Fable* for Tenor, Chorus, and Piano, after Lindsay (1946); *Madrigal* for Chorus and Piano, after Rossetti (1947); *The Bluebird* for Chorus and Piano (1950); *A Psalm of David* for Chorus, Strings, Brass, and Percussion (1950); *Song of the Open Road* for Chorus, Trumpet, and Piano, after Whitman (1952); *The Lamentation of Saul* for Baritone and Orch. or Sextet, after D.H. Lawrence (1954); *O Sing Unto the Lord (Psalm 98)* for Men's Voices and Organ (1958); *To St. Cecilia* for Chorus and Piano or Brass, after Dryden (1958); *Prayers for Cardinal Newman* for Chorus and Organ (1960); *The Holy Infant's Lullaby* for Unison Voices and Organ (1961); (4) *Songs of Walt Whitman* for Chorus and Orch. (1966); *Proud Music of the Storm* for Chorus, Brass, and Organ, after Whitman (1967); *Years of the Modern* for Chorus, Brass, and Percussion, after Whitman (1968); *Mass* for Chorus, Brass, and Organ or Piano (1969); *Evocations: Visitation at Night* for Chorus, Optional Children's Voices, and Orch. or Piano (1970); *Evocations: Promise of Spring* for Chorus, Optional Children's Voices, and Orch. or Piano (1970); *O Come to Me, My Love* for Chorus and Piano, after Rossetti (1972); *Psalm of Peace* for Chorus, Trumpet, Horn, and Organ or Piano (1972); *The Poet's Song* for Chorus and Piano, after Tennyson (1973); *Mass in Honor of the Eucharist* for Chorus, Cantor, Congregation, Brass, and Organ (1975); *Songs of Remembrance* for Baritone and Orch. (1977); *The Psalmist's Meditation* for Chorus and Organ or Piano (1979); *Hymns Without Words* for Chorus and Piano or Orch. (1980); *Love Songs at Parting* for Chorus and Piano (1981); *I Dreamed of an Invincible City* for Chorus and Piano or Organ (1984); *Nativity* for Soloists, Chorus, and Orch. (1987).

BIBL.: T. Bumgardner, *N. D. J.* (Boston, 1986).

Delmar, Dezso, Hungarian-American composer; b. Timişoara, July 14, 1891; d. Contra Costa Co., Calif., Oct. 20, 1985. He studied piano with Bartók and theory with Kodály at the Royal Academy of Music in Budapest, graduating in 1913; concurrently took courses in jurisprudence, obtaining a law degree. He served in the Austro-Hungarian army in World War I; after demobilization, he devoted himself entirely to music. He went to the U.S. in 1922; lived in N.Y. until 1929, then moved to Los Angeles; in 1946 he settled in Sacramento as a teacher of piano and theory. His works include *Hungarian Sketches* for Orch. (1947); Sym. (1949); 3 string quartets, String Trio, Violin Sonata; choral music; many piano pieces and songs. His works reflect the melorhythmic modalities of Hungarian folk music.

Del Mar, Norman (René), respected English conductor, teacher, and writer on music; b. London, July 31, 1919; d. Bushey, Feb. 6, 1994. He studied composition with Morris and Vaughan Williams at the Royal College of Music in London, and also had lessons in conducting with Lambert. In 1944 he founded the Chelsea Sym. Orch., with which he championed rarely performed works in England. He also played horn in and was assistant conductor of the Royal Phil. In London (1947–48). From 1949 to 1955 he was principal conductor of the English Opera Group, and from 1953 to 1960 conductor and prof. at the Guildhall School of Music in London. In 1954–55 he was conductor with the Yorkshire Sym. Orch. After serving as principal conductor of the BBC Scottish Sym. in Glasgow (1960–65), he was principal guest conductor of the Göteborg Sym. Orch. (1969–73). In 1972 he joined the faculty of the Royal College of Music, where he taught conducting and conducted its First Orch. He also conducted the chamber orch. of the Royal Academy of Music in London (1973–77) and was principal conductor of the Academy of the BBC (1974–77), a training ensemble. After serving as principal guest conductor of the Bournemouth Sinfonietta (1982–85), he was artistic director of the Århus Sym. Orch. (1985–88). In 1990 he retired from the faculty of the Royal College of Music. In 1975 he was made a Commander of the Order of the British Empire. Among his writings were *Paul Hindemith* (London, 1957), *Modern Music and the Conductor* (London, 1960), *Richard Strauss: A Critical Commentary of His Life and Works* (3 vols., London, 1962, 1968, 1972), *Anatomy of the Orchestra* (London, 1981), *A Companion to the Orchestra* (London, 1987), *Conducting Beethoven: Volume I: The Symphonies* (Oxford, 1992) and *Volume 2: Overtures, Concertos, Missa Solemnis* (Oxford, 1993), and *Conducting Brahms* (Oxford, 1993). His son, Jonathan Del Mar (b. London, Jan. 7, 1951), is also a conductor. He studied at Christ Church, Oxford (M.A., 1972), the Royal College of Music (diploma, 1976), and the Accademia di Santa Cecilia in Rome (1977). He appeared as a guest conductor with various British orchs.

Delmas, Jean-François, famous French bass-baritone; b. Lyons, April 14, 1861; d. St. Alban de Monthel, Sept. 29, 1933. He was a pupil of Bussine and Obin at the Paris Cons., where he won the premier prix for singing in 1886. He made his operatic debut at the Paris Opéra in 1886 as St.-Bris in *Les Huguenots*; then was a regular member there until his retirement in 1927, idolozed by the public, and unexcelled as an interpreter of Wagner, in whose works he created the principal bass parts in several French premieres; he created also the chief roles in Massenet's *Le Mage* (1891) and *Thaïs* (1894), Leroux's *Astarté* (1901), Saint-Saëns's *Les Barbares* (1901), and Erlanger's *Le Fils de l'étoile* (1904). In addition to his enormous French repertoire, Delmas also sang in the operas of Gluck, Mozart, and Weber.

Delmas, Marc-Jean-Baptiste, talented French composer; b. St. Quentin, March 28, 1885; d. Paris, Nov. 30, 1931. He was a pupil of Vidal and Leroux; won the Prix de Rossini (1911), the Grand Prix de Rome (1919), the Chartier Prix for chamber music, the Prix Cressent, and other awards for various compositions. He wrote the books *Georges Bizet* (Paris, 1930), *Gustave Charpentier et le lyrisme française* (Coulommiers, 1931), and *Massenet, sa vie, ses oeuvres* (Paris, 1932).

WORKS: OPERAS: *Jean de Calais* (1907); *Laïs* (1909); *Stéfano* (1910); *Cyrca* (1920); *Iriam* (1921); *Anne-Marie* (1922); *Le Giaour* (1925). **ORCH.:** *Les Deux Routes* (1913); *Au pays wallon* (1914); *Le Poète et la fée* (1920); *Le Bateau ivre* (1923); *Penthésilée* (1922); *Rapsodie ariegéoise* for Cello and Orch. **OTHER:** Chamber music; piano pieces.

Del Monaco, Mario, renowned Italian tenor; b. Florence, July 27, 1915; d. Mestre, near Venice, Oct. 16, 1982. His father was a government functionary, but his mother loved music and sang. Del Monaco haunted provincial opera theaters, determined to be a singer; indeed, he sang a minor part in a theater in Mondolfo, near Pesaro, when he was only 13. Rather than take formal voice lessons, he listened to operatic recordings; at 19 he entered the Rossini Cons. in Pesaro, but left it after an unhappy semester of academic vocal training with unimaginative teachers. In 1935 he won a prize in a singing contest in Rome. In 1939 he made his operatic debut as Turriddu in Pesaro. On Jan. 1, 1941, he made his Milan debut as Pinkerton, but had to serve time out in the Italian army during World War II. After the war's end, he developed a busy career singing opera in a number of Italian theaters, including La Scala of Milan. In 1946 he sang at the Teatro Colón in Buenos Aires, and also in Rio de Janeiro, Mexico City, and at London's Covent Garden. On Sept. 26, 1950, he sang the role of Radames at the San Francisco Opera in his first appearance in the U.S.; on Nov. 27, 1950, he made his Metropolitan Opera debut in N.Y. as Des Grieux in *Manon Lescaut*; he continued to sing at the Metropolitan until 1958 in virtually every famous tenor part, including Don José, Manrico, Cavaradossi, Canio, Andrea Chénier, Otello, etc. In 1973 he deemed it prudent to retire, and he spent the rest of his life in a villa near Venice, devoting his leisure to his favorite avocations, sculpture and painting. Del Monaco was buried in his Otello costume, while the funeral hymns were intoned in his own voice on a phonograph record.

Delmotte, Roger, French trumpeter; b. Roubaix, Sept. 20, 1925. He studied with M. Leclercq at the Roubaix Cons., and then with E. Foveau at the Paris Cons., where he won the premier prix for trumpet. After winning 1st prize in the Geneva competition in 1950, he became 1st trumpeter in the Opéra orch. and the Concerts Lamoureux in Paris in 1951. He soon established himself as a soloist with orchs. and as a recitalist; also was active as a teacher. While he won particular distinction for his performances of the Baroque repertory, Delmotte did much to further the cause of the contemporary trumpet literature through commissions and first performances.

Delna (real name, **Ledan**), **Marie,** French contralto; b. Meudon, near Paris, April 3, 1875; d. Paris, July 23, 1932. She was a pupil of Laborde and Savary in Paris, where she made her debut at the Opéra-Comique on June 9, 1892, as Dido in Berlioz's *Les Troyens*; sang there for 6 years with great success; she also appeared at London's Covent Garden in 1894. She sang at the Paris Opéra (1898–1901) and at Milan's Teatro Lirico (1898–1901); then again at the Opéra-Comique. In 1903 she married a Belgian, A.H. de Saone, and retired temporarily from the stage; her reappearance at the Opéra-Comique in 1908 was greatly acclaimed and after that she was a prime favorite. On March 5, 1910, she sang Gluck's Orfeo at her Metropolitan Opera debut in N.Y. and later Marcelline in Bruneau's *L'Attaque du moulin* at the New Theater, making a deep impression; then returned to Paris, where she continued to sing at the Opéra-Comique until her retirement in 1922.

Delogu, Gaetano, Italian conductor; b. Messina, April 14, 1934. He studied violin as a child, then music and law (degree 1958) at the Univ. of Catania; also studied conducting with Ferrara in Rome and Venice. After winning 1st prize in the Florence (1964) and Mitropoulos (1968) competitions, he appeared as a guest conductor in Europe and the U.S. He was music director of the Teatro Massimo in Palermo (1975–78) and the Denver Sym. Orch. (1979–86). In 1995 he became music director of the Prague Sym. Orch.

De Los Angeles, Victoria. See **Los Angeles** (real name **Gómez Cima**), **Victoria de.**

Del Tredici, David (Walter), outstanding American composer and teacher; b. Cloverdale, Calif., March 16, 1937. He studied piano with Bernhard Abramowitsch (1954–60); also composition with Shifrin and Elston at the Univ. of Calif. at Berkeley (B.A., 1959). In the summer of 1958, he pursued training in piano at the Aspen (Colo.) Music School, where he also attended Milhaud's composition seminar. He continued his studies in composition with Kim and Sessions at Princeton Univ. (M.F.A., 1963) and had private lessons with Helps in N.Y. In 1964 he completed his graduate studies at Princeton Univ., and also attended the Berkshire Music Center in Tanglewood that summer, returning there in 1965. In 1966–67 he held a Guggenheim fellowship, and during those summers he was composer-in-residence at the Marlboro (Vt.) Festival. From 1968 to 1972 he taught at Harvard Univ. In 1973 he taught at the State Univ. of N.Y. at Buffalo, and later that year became a teacher at Boston Univ. In the summer of 1975 he also was composer-in-residence at Aspen. In 1984 he became a teacher at City College of the City Univ. of N.Y. He also was composer-in-residence at the American Academy in Rome in 1985, and from 1988 to 1990 he held that title with the N.Y. Phil. In 1991 he was made a prof. at the Manhattan School of Music in N.Y. In 1992 he was the featured composer at the Pacific Music Festival in Sapporo, Japan. Del Tredici has received various awards, commissions, and honors. In 1968 he received an award from the American Inst. of Arts and Letters. In 1973 and 1974 he held NEA grants. In 1980 he was awarded the Pulitzer Prize in Music for his *In Memory of a Summer Day* for Amplified Soprano and Orch. His *Happy Voices* for Orch. won a Friedheim Award in 1982. In 1984 he was elected a member of the American Academy and Inst. of Arts and Letters. Among Del Tredici's first scores to attract notice were those inspired by James Joyce, including *I Hear an Army* for Soprano and String Quartet (Tanglewood, Aug. 12, 1964), which immediately caught the fancy of the cloistered but influential cognoscenti, literati, and illuminati, and *Night Conjure-Verse* for Soprano, Mezzo-soprano, and Chamber Ensemble, which Del Tredici conducted in its San Francisco premiere on March 2, 1966. In these and other Joyce-inspired works, he plied a modified dodecaphonic course in a polyrhythmic context, gravid with meaningful pauses without fear of triadic encounters. However, Del Tredici achieved his greatest fame with a series of brilliant tone pictures after Lewis Carroll's *Alice in Wonderland*, in which he projected, in utter defiance of all modernistic conventions, overt tonal proclamations, fanfares, and pretty tunes that were almost embarrassingly attractive, becoming melodiouser and harmoniouser with each consequent tone portrait. His *Final Alice* for Amplified Soprano, Folk Group, and Orch. (Chicago, Oct. 7, 1976) secured his international reputation as a composer of truly imaginative gifts, whose embrace of tonality is evinced in scores replete with brilliant harmonies and resplendent colors.

WORKS: *Soliloquy* for Piano (Aspen, Colo., Aug. 1958); *4 Songs on Poems of James Joyce* for Voice and Piano (1958–60; Berkeley, March 1, 1961); *2 Songs on Poems of James Joyce* for Voice and Piano (1959; rev. 1978; Washington, D.C., Feb. 11, 1983); String Trio for Violin, Viola, and Cello (Berkeley, May 21, 1959); *Fantasy Pieces* for Piano (1959–60); *Scherzo* for Piano, 4-hands (1960); String Quartet (1961–63; unfinished); *I Hear an Army* for Soprano and String Quartet (Tanglewood, Aug. 12, 1964); *Night Conjure-Verse* for Soprano, Mezzo-soprano or Countertenor, and Chamber Ensemble, after Joyce (1965; San Francisco, March 2, 1966); *Syzygy* for Soprano, Horn, and Orch., after Joyce (1966; N.Y., July 6, 1968); *The Last Gospel* for Woman's Voice, Rock Group, Chorus, and Orch. (1967; San Francisco, June 15, 1968; rev. version, Milwaukee, Oct. 3, 1984); *Pop-Pourri* for Amplified Soprano, Rock Group, Chorus, and Orch., after Carroll (La Jolla, Calif., July 28, 1968; rev. 1973); *An Alice Symphony* for Amplified Soprano, Folk Group, and Orch., after Carroll (1969; rev. 1976; movements 1 and 4, *Illustrated Alice*, for Amplified Soprano and Orch., San Francisco, Aug. 8, 1976; movements 2 and 3, *In Wonderland*, for Amplified Soprano, Folk Group, and Orch., Aspen, July 29, 1975; 1st complete perf., Tanglewood, Aug. 7, 1991); *Adventures Underground* for Amplified Soprano, Folk Group, and

Orch., after Carroll and Isaac Watts (1971; Buffalo, N.Y., April 13, 1975; rev. 1977); *Vintage Alice: Fantascene on A Mad Tea Party* for Amplified Soprano, Folk Group, and Orch., after Carroll, Jane Taylor, and *God Save the Queen* (Saratoga, Calif., Aug. 5, 1972); *Final Alice* for Amplified Soprano, Folk Group, and Orch., after Carroll, William Mee, and an unknown author (1974–75; Chicago, Oct. 7, 1976); *Child Alice* for Amplified Soprano(s) and Orch., after Carroll (1977–81; part 1, *In Memory of a Summer Day*, St. Louis, Feb. 23, 1980; part 2, *Quaint Events*, Buffalo, Nov. 19, 1981, *Happy Voices*, San Francisco, Sept. 16, 1980, and *All in the Golden Afternoon*, Philadelphia, May 8, 1981; 1st complete perf., N.Y., April 27, 1986); *Acrostic Song* from *Final Alice* for High Voice and Piano (Lenox, Mass., Aug. 21, 1982; also for Medium Voice and Piano, 1982; Chorus and Piano, N.Y., Nov. 19, 1983; Flute and Piano, N.Y., Feb. 12, 1985; Chorus and Piano or Harp, N.Y., May 16, 1986; Soprano and 10 Instruments, N.Y., Dec. 15, 1987; etc.); *Acrostic Paraphrase* for Harp, after the *Acrostic Song* from *Final Alice* (Tempe, Ariz., June 22, 1983); *Virtuoso Alice*, grand fantasy on a theme from *Final Alice* for Piano (1984; N.Y., Nov. 10, 1987); *March to Tonality* for Orch. (Chicago, June 13, 1985); *Haddock's Eyes* for Amplified Soprano and 10 Instruments, after Carroll and Thomas Moore (1985; N.Y., May 2, 1986); *Tattoo* for Orch. (1986; Amsterdam, Jan. 30, 1987); *Steps* for Orch. (N.Y., March 8, 1990); *Brass Symphony* for Brass Quintet (1992); *Dum Dee Tweedle* for Voices and Orch., after Carroll (1993).

De Luca, Giuseppe, notable Italian baritone; b. Rome, Dec. 25, 1876; d. N.Y., Aug. 26, 1950. He studied with Vinceslao Persichini at the Accademia di Santa Cecilia in Rome. He made his first professional appearance in Piacenza (Nov. 6, 1897) as Valentine in *Faust*; then sang in various cities of Italy; from 1902, was chiefly in Milan at the Teatro Lirico, and from 1903 at La Scala; he created the principal baritone role in the premieres of *Adriana Lecouvreur* at the Teatro Lirico (Nov. 6, 1902) and *Madama Butterfly* at La Scala (Feb. 17, 1904). He made his Metropolitan Opera debut in N.Y. as Figaro in *Il barbiere di Siviglia* on Nov. 25, 1915, with excellent success, immediately establishing himself as a favorite; on Jan. 28, 1916, he sang the part of Paquiro in the premiere of *Goyescas* by Granados, at the Metropolitan, of which he was a member until 1935. After a sojourn in Italy, he returned to the U.S. in 1940, and made a few more appearances at the Metropolitan, his vocal powers undiminished by age; he made his farewell appearance in a concert in N.Y. in 1947. He sang almost exclusively the Italian repertoire; his interpretations were distinguished by fidelity to the dramatic import of his roles and he was praised by critics for his finely graduated dynamic range and his mastery of *bel canto*.

Delune, Louis, Belgian composer; b. Charleroi, March 15, 1876; d. Paris, Jan. 5, 1940. He studied with Tinel at the Brussels Cons.; won the Belgian Prix de Rome with his cantata *La Mort du roi Reynaud* (1905); then traveled as accompanist for César Thomson. He lived for many years in Paris, and wrote most of his works there, including *Symphonie chevaleresque*, the opera *Tania*, a ballet, *Le Fruit défendu*, Piano Concerto, and violin pieces.

Delvaux, Albert, Belgian composer; b. Louvain, May 31, 1913. He studied at the Louvain Cons. and then completed his training with Joseph Leroy at the Liège Cons. He won a 3rd prize (1957, for *Esquisses*) and a 1st prize (1961, for *Sinfonia burlesca*) in the Queen Elisabeth International Composition Competition in Brussels.

WORKS: ORCH.: *5 Pieces* for Strings (1942); *Scherzo* (1942); Symphonic Poem (1943); Symphonic Suite (1948); Symphonic Variations (1948); *Sinfonietta* (1952); Concerto for Cello and Chamber Orch. (1957); *Concerto da camera* for Chamber Orch. (1957); *Sinfonia burlesca* (1960); *5 Bagatelles* for Chamber Orch. (1960); *Miniatures* (1960); 2 violin concertos (1961, 1974); *Sinfonia concertante* for Violin, Viola, and Strings (1963); *Mouvement symphonique* (1966); Concerto for Flute, Oboe, Clarinet, Bassoon, and Chamber Orch. (1967); *Sinfonia* (1969); Concerto for Violin, Cello, and Strings (1970); *Introduction et Allegro* for Strings (1971); *Divertimento* for Strings (1981); Concerto for Viola and Chamber Orch. (1984); *Sinfonia in Sol* (1986); *Capriccio* (1988). **CHAMBER:** 2 string trios (1939, 1961); Sonata for Flute, Oboe, Clarinet, and Bassoon (1940); 4 string quartets (1943, 1945, 1955, 1961); Trio for Oboe, Clarinet, and Bassoon (1948); *5 Impromptus* for Flute, Oboe, Clarinet, and Piano (1959); Violin Sonata (1962); *Sonata a 4* for 4 Clarinets or Flute, Oboe, Clarinet, and Bassoon (1964); *Walliser Suite* for Wind Quintet (1966); *Cassazione* for Violin, Oboe, Clarinet, and Cello (1966); *Andante e Scherzando* for Violin and Piano (1972); Cello Sonatine (1978); Sonatine for Guitar and Flute (1981); Saxophone Quartet (1982); *Adagio-Scherzo* for Violin, Flute, Viola, Cello, and Harp (1982); Duo for Flute and Harp (1985); Duo for Clarinets (1987). **VOCAL:** *Hero et Léandre* for Soloists, Chorus, and Orch. (1941); choruses; songs.

Delvincourt, Claude, outstanding French composer and music educator; b. Paris, Jan. 12, 1888; d. in an automobile accident in Orbetello, Italy, April 5, 1954. He studied with Boëllmann, Büsser, Caussade, and Widor at the Paris Cons.; in 1913 he received the Prix de Rome for his cantata *Faust et Hélène* (sharing the prize with Lili Boulanger). He was in the French army during World War I, and on Dec. 31, 1915, suffered a crippling wound. He recovered in a few years, and devoted himself energetically to musical education and composition. In 1931 he became director of the Versailles Cons.; in 1941 he was appointed director of the Paris Cons. His music was distinguished by strong dramatic and lyric qualities; he was most successful in his stage works.

WORKS: *Offrande à Siva*, choreographic poem (Frankfurt am Main, July 3, 1927); *La Femme à barbe*, musical farce (Versailles, June 2, 1938); *Lucifer*, mystery play (Paris, Dec. 8, 1948); 2 orch. suites from the film score *La Croisière jaune*: *Pamir* (Paris, Dec. 8, 1935) and *Films d'Asie* (Paris, Jan. 16, 1937); *Ce monde de rosée* for Voice and Orch. (Paris, March 25, 1935); chamber music; piano pieces.

BIBL.: W. Landowski, *L'Oeuvre de C. D.* (Paris, 1947).

Delz, Christoph, Swiss-born German composer and pianist; b. Basel, Jan. 3, 1950; d. there, Sept. 13, 1993. He began studies in performance and counterpoint early, completing a concert pianist diploma before finishing school. He then studied with Stockhausen (composition), Aloys Kontarsky (piano), and Wangenheim (conducting) at the Cologne Hochschule für Musik (1974–81). His compositions involved musical collage, theatrical gestures, eclectically combined styles, and revolutionary agendas, and were performed at ISCM World Music Days in Cologne, Paris, Donaueschingen, Venice, and London. In 1983 he received the Music Prize of the City of Cologne.

WORKS: Piano Quartet (1975–76; Bonn, Nov. 25, 1977); *Kölner Messe* for Tape and Chorus (1977–81; Cologne, Nov. 4, 1983); *Im Dschungel, Ehrung für Rousseau den Zöllner* for Large Orch. (1981–82; Donaueschingen, Oct. 16, 1983); String Quartet (1982; Witten, April 28, 1985); *Arbeitslieder* for Soli, Chorus, Piano, and Wind Quintet (1983–84; Venice, Nov. 23, 1985); Piano Concerto (1984–85; London, Feb. 22, 1986); *Solde, Lecture d'après Lautréamont* for Soli, Chorus, and Percussion (1985–86); *2 Nocturnes* for Piano and Orch. (1986); *Jahreszeiten* for Piano, Small Orch., and Tape (1988–89); *Joyce-Fantasy* for Soprano, Chorus, 2 Pianos, and Harmonium (1990).

De Main, John (Lee), American conductor; b. Youngstown, Ohio, Jan. 11, 1944. He studied with Adele Marcus (piano; B.A., 1966) and Jorge Mester (conducting; M.S., 1968) at the Juilliard School of Music in N.Y. He was an assistant conductor at the WNET opera project in N.Y. and in 1972 at the N.Y. City Opera. After serving as assoc. conductor of the St. Paul (Minn.) Chamber Orch. (1972–74), he became music director of the Texas Opera Theater in 1975, the touring company of the Houston Grand Opera. In 1978 he was appointed principal conductor of the Houston Grand Opera, serving as its music director from 1980 to

1994; he also was principal conductor of the Chatauqua (N.Y.) Opera (1982–87) and music director of Opera Omaha (1983–91). He was music director of the Madison (Wis.) Sym. Orch. from 1994. In addition to conducting rarely-heard works, De Main gave many premiere performances of contemporary operas.

DeMarinis, Paul, American composer; b. Cleveland, Oct. 6, 1948. He was educated at Antioch (Ohio) College (B.A., 1971) and Mills College in Oakland, California, where he studied with Robert Ashley (M.F.A., 1973) and subsequently taught composition and computer art (1973–78). He also taught at Wesleyan Univ. (1979–81) and San Francisco State Univ. (1987–89), and was a sound designer for Atari video games (1982–84). As a performer, he has appeared solo and in collaboration with such artists as Ashley and David Tudor. He is best known for his performance works, computer/sound installations, and interactive electronic inventions. His computer audio-graphics systems have been installed at the Museum of Contemporary Art in Chicago and at the Wadsworth Atheneum; he has also created permanent audio installations at the Exploratorium in San Francisco and at the Boston Children's Museum. Much of his later work, such as *Kokole* (1985) and *I Want You* (1986), involves computer-processed speech. Among his installations are *Pygmy Gamelan* (Paris, N.Y., Los Angeles, 1976–80), *Music Room/Faultless Jamming* (San Francisco, Boston, 1982), and *Laser Disk* (Eindhoven, Netherlands, 1989).

Demarquez, Suzanne, French composer and writer on music; b. Paris, July 5, 1899; d. there, Oct. 23, 1965. She studied at the Paris Cons. She composed chamber music, including a sprightly Flute Sonatine (1953). She publ. *André Jolivet* (Paris, 1958), *Manuel de Falla* (Paris, 1963; Eng. tr., 1968), and *Hector Berlioz* (Paris, 1969).

Demény, Desiderius, Hungarian composer; b. Budapest, Jan. 29, 1871; d. there, Nov. 9, 1937. He was a pupil of V. Herzfeld and S. von Bacho; was ordained as a priest at Gran in 1893; became court chaplain (1897); on 3 different occasions he won the Géza Zichy Prize (with *Ungarische Tanzsuite, Festouvertüre,* and *Rhapsodie*); in 1902 he founded *Zeneközlöny,* an important Hungarian music journal. Among his compositions were 8 masses; *Hungarian Suite* for Chorus; *Scherzo* for Men's Chorus; *2 Bilder aus Algier*; *Serenata sinfonica*; *Der sieghafte Tod,* operetta; several melodramas; many other choral and vocal works, including about 100 songs (most to German texts).

Demessieux, Jeanne, distinguished French organist and pedagogue; b. Montpellier, Feb. 14, 1921; d. Paris, Nov. 11, 1968. At the age of 12, she played organ at the church of St.-Esprit; she studied at the Paris Cons. with Tagliaferro, J. and N. Gallon, and Dupré, winning premiers prix in harmony (1937), piano (1938), and fugue and counterpoint (1940). She gave her first public recital in Paris in 1946; then toured widely in Europe; made her first highly successful visit to the U.S. in 1953. In 1952 she became a prof. at the Liège Cons.; also served as organist at the Madeleine in Paris from 1962. She possessed a phenomenal technique and was regarded as one of the most brilliant improvisers on the organ.

Demian, Wilhelm, Romanian composer and conductor; b. Braşov, June 22, 1910. He studied in his hometown (1925–28) and in Vienna (1929–33); from 1935 to 1940 he conducted the Phil. in Cluj; after 1949 he was conductor of the Hungarian State Opera there. His music is marked by a distinct neo-classical idiom in the manner of the modern German school. Among his works are Sym. (1947); Piano Concertino (1953); Violin Concerto (1956); *Liberté,* cantata (1957); Oboe Concerto (1963); *Capcana,* opera (1964); *Attention! On tourne!,* musical (1972).

Demidenko, Nikolai, Russian pianist; b. Aniskino, July 1, 1955. He was a pupil of Bashkirov at the Moscow Cons. After winning 2nd prize at the Montreal competition in 1976 and 3rd prize at the Tchaikovsky competition in Moscow in 1978, he toured throughout his homeland as a soloist with orchs. and as a recitalist. In 1985 he made his British debut as soloist on tour with the Moscow Radio Sym. Orch.; subsequently returned to appear as soloist with the principal British orchs. In 1990 he settled in England and became a teacher at the Yehudi Menuhin School. In 1992 he made his first appearance at the London Promenade Concerts as soloist in Rachmaninoff's 4th Piano Concerto. In 1993 he won critical acclaim for a series of 6 recitals at London's Wigmore Hall in which he surveyed the piano repertoire from the standard literature to contemporary works with virtuosic aplomb and interpretative insight.

Demougeot, (Jeanne Marguerite) Marcelle (Decorne), remarkable French soprano; b. Dijon, June 18, 1871; d. Paris, Nov. 24, 1931. She studied in Dijon and Paris. She made her debut at the Paris Opéra in 1902 as Donna Elvira; and sang there until 1925. She was one of the foremost French Wagnerian sopranos of her time, noted for her Brünnhilde, Elisabeth, Kundry, and Venus.

Dempster, Stuart (Ross), American trombonist and composer; b. Berkeley, Calif., July 7, 1936. He studied at San Francisco State College (B.A. in perf., 1958; M.A. in composition, 1967) and also had private trombone instruction from A.B. Moore, Orlando Giosi, and John Klock. He taught at the San Francisco Cons. of Music (1961–66) and at Calif. State College at Hayward (1963–66); in 1968 he joined the faculty of the Univ. of Wash. in Seattle. From 1962 he made tours as a trombone virtuoso. He received a Fulbright-Hays Award as a senior scholar in Australia (1973) and a Guggenheim fellowship (1981). He has made a special study of trombone music, both past and present, and has commissioned and premiered many works for his instrument. His interests also include non-Western instruments, especially the Australian didjeridu. He publ. the study *The Modern Trombone: A Definition of Its Idioms* (Berkeley, Calif., 1979).

WORKS: 5 pieces for Brass Quintet (1957–59); Bass Trombone Sonata (1961); *Adagio and Canonic Variations* for Brass Quintet (1962); *Chamber Music 12* for Voice and Trombones (1964); *The Road Not Taken* for Voice, Chorus, and Orch. (1967); *10 Grand Hosery,* mixed media ballet (1971–72); *Life Begins at 40,* concert series and musical gallery show (1976); *Didjeridervish* for Didjeridu (1976); *Hornfinder* for Trombone and Audience (1982); *Aix en Providence* for Multiple Trombones (1983); *JDBBBDJ* for Didjeridu and Audience (1983); *Sound Massage Parlor* for Didjeridu, Garden Hoses, Shell, and Audience (1986); *SWAMI* (State of Washington as a Musical Instrument), performance piece for the state of Washington centennial (1987–89); *Milanda Embracing* for Mixed Ensemble (1993–94); *Underground Overlays* for Conch Shells, Chanters, and Tape (1994–95); *Caprice* for Unicycle-Riding Trombonist (1995).

Demus, Jörg (Wolfgang), Austrian pianist; b. St. Polten, Dec. 2, 1928. At the age of 11, he entered the Vienna Academy of Music; also took lessons in conducting with Swarowsky and Josef Krips and in composition with Joseph Marx; continued his piano studies with Gieseking at the Saarbrücken Cons.; then worked with Kempff, Michelangeli, Edwin Fischer, and Nat. He made his debut at the age of 14 in Vienna; made his London debut in 1950; then toured South America (1951). In 1956 he won 1st prize in the Busoni Competition in Bolzano. Apart from his solo recitals, he distinguished himself as a lieder accompanist to Dietrich Fischer-Dieskau and other prominent singers. Demus assembled a large collection of historic keyboard instruments; publ. a book of essays, *Abenteuer der Interpretation* (1967), and, with Paul Badura-Skoda, an analysis of Beethoven's piano sonatas (1970). In 1977 he was awarded the Beethoven Ring and in 1979 the Mozart Medal of Vienna.

Demuth, Norman, English composer, writer on music, and teacher; b. South Croydon, July 15, 1898; d. Chichester, April 21, 1968. He was a student of Parratt and Dunhill at the Royal College of Music in London, and then continued private studies with Dunhill. After military service during World War I (1915–17), he was active as a church organist and later conducted in provincial music centers. He became prof. of composition at the Royal Academy of Music in London in 1930; with the exception of his military service in World War II, he retained this post throughout his life. Demuth's high regard for French music led to his being made a corresponding member of the Institut. In 1951 he became an officer of the French Académie and in 1954 a chevalier of the Légion d'honneur. In his compositions, he followed a course set by d'Indy and Roussel.

WORKS: DRAMATIC: OPERAS: *Conte venitien* (1947); *Le Flambeau* (1948); *Volpone* (1949); *The Oresteia* (1950); *Rogue Scapin* (1954). **BALLETS:** *The Temptation of St. Anthony* (1937); *Planetomania* (1940); *Complainte* (1946); *Bal des fantômes* (1949); *La débutante* (1949). Also incidental music and film scores. **ORCH.:** *Cortège* (1931); *Introduction and Allegro* (1936); Violin Concerto (1937); 2 partitas (1939, 1958); *2 War Poems* for Piano and Orch. (1940); *Valse graves et gaies* (1940); Concertino for Flute and Strings (1941); *Fantasy and Fugue* (1941); *Divertimento No. 1* for Strings (1941) and *No. 2* (1943); *Elegiac Rhapsody* for Cello and Small Orch. (1942); *Threnody* for Strings (1942); *Overture for a Victory* (1943); Piano Concerto (1943); *Suite champêtre* (1945); *Overture for a Joyful Occasion* (1946); Concertino for Piano and Small Orch. (1947); Concerto for Piano, Left-hand, and Orch. (1947); *Legend* for Piano, Left-hand, and Orch. (1949); 4 syms.: No. 1 (1949), No. 2 (1950), No. 3 for Strings (1952), and No. 4 (1956–57); 2 symphonic studies (1949, 1950); *Mouvement symphonique* for Ondes Martenot and Orch. (1952); *Ouverture à la française* (1952); *Ballade* for Viola and Orch. (1953); *Variations symphonique* (1954); *François Villon* (1956); Cello Concerto (1956); Concert Overture (1958); *Sinfonietta* (1958). **MILITARY BAND:** Saxophone Concerto (1938); *The Sea* (1939); *Regimental March of the Royal Pioneer Corps* (1943). **CHAMBER:** 3 violin sonatas (1937, 1938, 1948); *Serenade* for Violin and Piano (1938); Flute Sonata (1938); Cello Sonata (1939); Sonatina for 2 Violins (1939); Sonatine for Flute, Oboe, and Piano (1946); *Capriccio* for Violin and Piano (1948); Trio for Flute, Oboe, and Bassoon (1949); String Trio (1950); String Quartet (1950); *Lyric Trio* for Flute, Oboe, and Piano (1953); Suite for Flute, Oboe, and Harpsichord (1954); Quartet for Flute and Piano Trio (1955); *Suite de printemps* for Violin and Piano (1955); *Le souper du roi* for Wind, Drums, and Harpsichord (1956); *Divertissement* for Flute and Piano Trio (1957); *Pastoral Fantasy* for Piano Quartet (1957); *Primavera* for Flute and Piano Trio (1958); piano pieces; organ works. **VOCAL:** *3 Poems* for Soprano and Strings (1941); *3 Poems* for Voice and Strings (1944); *Pan's Anniversary* for Chorus and Orch. (1952); *Sonnet* for Baritone, Chorus, and Orch. (1953); *Requiem* for Chorus (1954); numerous part songs; many solo songs.

WRITINGS (all publ. in London unless otherwise given): *The Gramophone and How to Use it* (1945); *Albert Roussel* (1947); *Ravel* (1947); *An Anthology of Musical Criticism* (1948); *César Franck* (1949); *Paul Dukas* (1949); *The Symphony: Its History and Development* (1950); *A Course in Musical Composition* (1950–58); *Gounod* (1951); *Musical Trends in the 20th Century* (1952); *Musical Forms and Textures* (1953); *French Piano Music* (1958); *French Opera: Its Development to the Revolution* (Horsham, 1963).

Denéréaz, Alexandre, Swiss composer and musicologist; b. Lausanne, July 31, 1875; d. there, July 25, 1947. He studied at the Lausanne Cons. with Blanchet and at the Dresden Cons. with Draeseke and Doring; in 1896 he was appointed a prof. at the Lausanne Cons.; also taught musicology at the Univ. of Lausanne. He publ. an original theory of harmony. He was also the author, with C. Bourgues, of *La Musique et la vie intérieure: Histoire psychologique de l'art musical* (appendix entitled *L'Arbre généalogique de l'art musical*; 1919). Among his compositions were 3 syms.; many symphonic poems; cantatas; Concerto Grosso for Orch. and Organ; string quartets; organ works; music to René Morax's *La Dime.*

Denis, Didier, French composer; b. Paris, Nov. 5, 1947. He studied at the Paris Cons. with Challan (harmony), Bitsch (counterpoint and fugue), Messiaen (analysis), and Rivier (composition), where he won several premiers prix (1958–71). He then was active at the Villa Medici in Rome under the auspices of the French Academy (1971–73). From 1982 to 1991 he was an inspector of music for the French Ministry of Culture. In 1992 he became a prof. of composition at the Toulouse Cons.

WORKS: OPERA: *Urbicande* (in preparation). **ORCH.:** *Chants de Tse Yeh* for Piano and Chamber Ensemble (1969); *Urbicande symphonie* (1985–88). **CHAMBER:** Trio for Flute, Clarinet, and Bassoon (1966); *Fugue indoue* for 2 Groups of Percussion (1968); *Triangle au soleil à 7 branches* for Jazz Quartet and 11 Instrumentalists (1969); *Amore stelle* for Flute and Viola (1983); *Ivre de t'aimer beaucoup, ivre de t'aimer d'amour, ivre de t'aimer trente et une fois d'amour* for Cello and 23 Winds (1987). **VOCAL:** *Sagesse, force, beauté, l'amour* for Soprano, 12 Instruments, and Percussion (1967); *Cinq fois je t'aime* for Reciter, Soprano, and Orch. (1968); *C'est pas une raison* for Soprano, Tenor, Instrumental Ensemble, and Tape (1970); *Obscur et fronçé comme un oeillet violet* for 2 Sopranos, 42 Voices, and 6 Instrumentalists (1972); *Les Herbes folles de la campagne* for Soprano, Lute, and 71 Guitars (1975); *Khamaïleôn* for Soprano and 3 Clarinets (1986); *Les Temps sont révolus* for Voice and Instrument (1991); *A la grâce de Dieu* for Soprano, Children's Chorus, and 10 Instruments (1992).

Denisov, Edison, remarkable, innovative Russian composer; b. Tomsk, April 6, 1929. He was named after Thomas Alva Edison by his father, an electrical engineer. He studied mathematics at the Univ. of Moscow, graduating in 1951, and composition at the Moscow Cons. with Shebalin (1951–56). In 1959 he was appointed to the faculty of the Cons. An astute explorer of tonal possibilities, Denisov writes instrumental works of an empirical genre. The titles of his pieces reveal a lyric character of subtle nuances, often marked by impressionistic colors.

WORKS: DRAMATIC: *Soldier Ivan,* opera (1959); *L'Ecume des jours,* lyric drama (1981); *Confession,* ballet (1984). **ORCH.:** 2 syms. (1955, 1988); *Sinfonietta on Tadzhik Themes* (1957); *Peinture* (Graz, Oct. 30, 1970); Cello Concerto (Leipzig, Sept. 25, 1973); Flute Concerto (Dresden, May 22, 1976); Violin Concerto (Milan, July 18, 1978); Piano Concerto (Leipzig, Sept. 5, 1978); *Partita* for Violin and Orch. (Moscow, March 23, 1981); Concerto for Bassoon, Cello, and Orch. (1982; Venice, Sept. 24, 1984); *Tod ist ein langer Schlaf,* variations on a theme by Haydn, for Cello and Orch. (Moscow, May 30, 1982); Chamber Sym. (Paris, March 7, 1983); *Epitaphe* for Chamber Orch. (Reggio Emilia, Sept. 11, 1983); *Colin et Chloé,* suite from the opera *L'Ecume des jours* (Moscow, Oct. 17, 1983); Concerto for 2 Violas, Harpsichord, and Strings (1984); *5 Paganini Caprices* for Violin and Strings (1985); *Happy End* for Strings (1985); Viola Concerto (1986; utilized in the Saxophone Concerto, 1993); Oboe Concerto (1986); *Glocken im Nebel* (1988); Clarinet Concerto (1989); Saxophone Concerto (1993; based on the Viola Concerto); Concerto for Flute, Harp, and Orch. (1995). **CHAMBER:** Sonata for 2 Violins (1958); *Musique* for 11 Wind Instruments and Timpani (Leningrad, Nov. 15, 1965); String Quartet No. 2 (1961); Violin Sonata (1963); *Crescendo e diminuendo* for Harpsichord and 12 Strings (Zagreb, May 14, 1967); *Ode in Memory of Ché Guevara* for Clarinet, Piano, and Percussion (Moscow, Jan. 22, 1968); *Musique romantique* for Oboe, Harp, and String Trio (Zagreb, May 16, 1969); *3 Pieces* for Cello and Piano (1969); String Trio (1969); *D-S-C-H,* a monogram for Shostakovich (1969); Wind Quintet (1969); *Silhouettes* for Flute, 2 Pianos, and Percussion (1969); *Chant des oiseaux* for Prepared Piano and Tape (1969); Alto Saxophone Sonata (1970); Piano Trio (1971); Cello Sonata (1971); *Solo per flauto* (1971); *Solo per oboe* (1971); *Canon in Memory of Igor Stravinsky* for Flute, Clarinet, and Harp (1971); Sonata for Solo Clarinet (1972); *3 Pieces* for Harpsichord and Percussion (1972); *2 Pieces* for Alto Saxophone and Piano (1974); *Choral varié* for Trombone and Piano (1975); *Aquarelle* for 24 Strings (1975); *4 Pieces* for Flute and Piano (1977); *Concerto piccolo* for 4 Saxophones and 6 Percussionists (Bordeaux, April 28, 1979); Sonata for Flute and Guitar

(1977); Sonata for Solo Violin (1978); Concerto for Solo Guitar (1981); Trio for Oboe, Cello, and Harpsichord (1981); Sonata for Solo Bassoon (1982); Sonata for Violin and Organ (1982); *Musique de chambre* for Viola, Harpsichord, and Strings (1982); *5 études* for Bassoon (1983); Sonata for Flute and Harp (1983); *Es ist genug*, variations for Viola and Piano on a theme of Bach (1984); *Diane dans le vent d'automne* for Viola, Vibraphone, Piano, and Double Bass (1984); Quintet for Clarinet and Strings (1987); Quintet for Piano and Strings (1987); *3 Pieces* for Percussion (1989); *Variations on a Theme of Mozart* for 8 Flutes (1990); Octet (1992); *Dedicare* for Flute, Clarinet, and String Quartet (1992); Quintet for 4 Saxophones and Piano (1992). **KEYBOARD: PIANO:** *Variations* (1961); *3 Pieces* for Piano, 4-hands (1967); *Signes en blanc* (1974). **HARPSICHORD:** *Feuilles mortes*. **VOCAL:** *Canti di Catulli* for Bass and 3 Trombones (1962); *Soleil des Incas* for Soprano and Instrumental Ensemble (Leningrad, Nov. 30, 1964); *Chansons italiennes* for Soprano, Flute, Horn, Violin, and Harpsichord (1966); *Pleurs* for Soprano, Piano, and Percussion (1966); *5 Geschichten vom Herrn Keuner* for Tenor and 7 Instruments (1968); *Automne*, 13 poems (1969); 2 songs for Soprano and Piano (1970); *Chant d'automne* for Soprano and Orch. (Zagreb, May 16, 1971); *La Vie en rouge* for Voice, Flute, Clarinet, Violin, Cello, and Piano (1973); *Requiem* for Soprano, Tenor, Chorus, and Orch. (Hamburg, Oct. 30, 1980); *Colin et Chloé*, suite from the opera *L'Ecume des jours*, for Soloists, Chorus, and Orch. (1981); *Lumière et ombres* for Bass and Piano (1982); *Ton image charmante* for Voice and Orch. (1982); *Venue du printemps* for Chorus (1984); *Aus plus haut des cieux* for Voice and Chamber Orch. (1986); *Eternal Light* for Chorus (1988). **ORCHESTRATIONS:** Mussorgsky: *Nursery Songs*, *Sunless*, and *Songs and Dances of Death*; Mossolov: *Advertisements* arranged for Voice and Orch.; Debussy's opera *Rodrique et Chimène* (Lyons, May 15, 1993); several Schubert dances.

BIBL.: J.-P. Armengaud, *Entretiens avec E. D.: Un compositeur sous le regime communist* (Paris, 1993).

Dennée, Charles (Frederick), American pianist and pedagogue; b. Oswego, N.Y., Sept. 1, 1863; d. Boston, April 29, 1946. He studied piano with A.D. Turner and composition with S.A. Emery at the New England Cons. of Music in Boston; also studied piano with Hans von Bülow during von Bülow's last visit to the U.S. (1889–90). In 1883 he was appointed a teacher of piano at the New England Cons. of Music; an accident to his right wrist caused his retirement in 1897. He was among the first to give illustrated lecture-recitals in the U.S. A selection of his essays was publ. as *Musical Journeys* (Brookline, Mass., 1938); he also publ. a manual, *Progressive Technique*. Some of his teaching pieces achieved steady popularity with piano students.

Denny, William D(ouglas), American composer, teacher, violist, and conductor; b. Seattle, July 2, 1910; d. Berkeley, Calif., Sept. 2, 1980. He studied at the Univ. of Calif. at Berkeley (B.A., 1931; M.A., 1933) before pursuing training in composition with Dukas in Paris (1933–35) and as a Horatio Parker Fellow at the American Academy in Rome (1939–41). He taught at his alma mater (1938–39), at Harvard Univ. (1941–42), and at Vassar College (1942–44); returning to his alma mater, he served as a prof. (1945–78) and as chairman of the music dept. (1972–75). In his well-crafted output, he favored complex contrapuntal textures and dissonant harmonies.

WORKS: ORCH.: *Bacchanale* (1935); Concertino (1937; San Francisco, April 25, 1939); 3 syms.: No. 1 (CBS, May 1939), No. 2 (1949; San Francisco, March 22, 1951), and No. 3 (1955–57; San Francisco, Jan. 16, 1963); *Sinfonietta* (1940); Suite for Chamber Orch. (1940); Overture for Strings (1945; San Francisco, May 2, 1946); *Praeludium* (1946; San Francisco, Feb. 5, 1947); *Introduction and Allegro* (1956). **CHAMBER:** 3 string quartets (1937–38; 1952; 1955); Viola Sonata (1943–44); String Trio (1965). **ORGAN:** *Partita* (1958); *Toccata, Aria, and Fugue* (1966). **CHORAL:** *Most Glorious Lord of Life*, cantata (1943); 3 motets (1946–47).

Densmore, Frances, American ethnomusicologist; b. Red Wing, Minn., May 21, 1867; d. there, June 5, 1957. She studied at the Oberlin (Ohio) Cons. (hon. M.A., 1924); then took courses with Leopold Godowsky (piano) and J.K. Paine (counterpoint). She began the study of Indian music in 1893 at the World's Fair in Chicago, continuing privately until 1907, when she began systematic research for the Bureau of American Ethnology (Smithsonian Institution), including an exhaustive study of the Cheyenne, Arapaho, Maidu, Santo Domingo Pueblo, and New Mexican Indian tribes. She lectured extensively on Indian music, and publ. a number of books and articles on the subject. A Frances Densmore ethnological library was established at Macalester College in St. Paul, Minn.

WRITINGS: *Chippewa Music*, a collection of Indian songs (2 vols., 1910–13); *Poems from Sioux and Chippewa Songs* (words only; 1917); *Tetom Sioux Music* (1918); *Indian Action Songs* (1921); *Northern Ute Music* (1922); *Mandan and Hidatfa Music* (1923); *The American Indians and Their Music* (1926; 2nd ed., 1937); *The Music of the Tule Indians of Panama* (1926); *Some Results of the Study of American Indian Music* (reprinted from the *Journal of the Washington Academy of Sciences*, XVIII/14; 1928); *Pawnee Music* (1929); *Papago Music* (1929); *What Intervals Do Indians Sing?* (reprinted from the *American Anthropologist*, April/June, 1929); *Yaman and Yaqui Music* (*U.S. Bureau of American Ethnology*, Bulletin 110; 1932); *Menominee Music* (ibid., Bulletin 102; 1932); *Cheyenne and Arapaho Music* (1936); *Alabama Music* (1937); *Music of Santo Domingo Pueblo, New Mexico* (1938); *Nootka and Quileute Music* (1939); *Music of the Indians of British Columbia* (1943); *Choctaw Music* (1943); *Seminole Music* (1956).

Dent, Edward J(oseph), eminent English musicologist, teacher, and music critic; b. Ribston, Yorkshire, July 16, 1876; d. London, Aug. 22, 1957. He studied with C.H. Lloyd at Eton College; then went to Cambridge to continue his studies with Charles Wood and Stanford (Mus.B., 1899; M.A., 1905); he was elected a Fellow of King's College there in 1902, and subsequently taught music history, harmony, counterpoint, and composition until 1918. He was also active in promoting operatic productions in England by preparing translations of libretti for performances at Cambridge, particularly of the operas of Mozart. From 1918 he wrote music criticism in London. In 1919 he became one of the founders of the British Music Soc., which remained active until 1933. The ISCM came into being in 1922 largely through his efforts, and he served as its president until 1938 and again in 1945; he also was president of the Société Internationale de Musicologie from 1931 until 1949. In 1926 he was appointed prof. of music at Cambridge, a position he held until 1941. He was made an honorary Mus.D. at the Univ. of Oxford (1932), Harvard (1936), and Cambridge (1947). In 1937 he was made a corresponding member of the American Musicological Soc. After his death, the Royal Musical Assn. created, in 1961, the Dent Medal, which is given annually to those selected for their important contributions to musicology. A scholar of the widest interests, Dent contributed numerous articles to music journals, encyclopedias, dictionaries, and symposia.

WRITINGS: *Alessandro Scarlatti* (London, 1905; 2nd ed., rev. by F. Walker, 1960); *Mozart's Operas: A Critical Study* (London, 1913; 3rd ed., rev., 1955); *Terpander, or Music and the Future* (London, 1926); *Foundations of English Opera: A Study of Musical Drama in England during the Seventeenth Century* (Cambridge, 1928); *Ferruccio Busoni* (London, 1933; 2nd ed., 1966); *Handel* (London, 1934); *Opera* (Harmondsworth, 1940; 5th ed., rev., 1949); *Notes on Fugue for Beginners* (Cambridge, 1941); *A Theatre for Everybody: The Story of the Old Vic and Sadler's Wells* (London, 1945; 2nd ed., rev., 1946); *The Rise of Romantic Opera* (ed. by W. Dean; Cambridge, 1976); *Selected Essays* (ed. by H. Taylor; Cambridge, 1979).

BIBL.: L. Haward, "E.J. D.: Bibliography," *Music Review*, VII (1946; publ. separately, Cambridge, 1956); W. Dean, "E. J. D.: A Centenary Tribute," *Music & Letters* (Oct. 1976); P. Radcliffe, *E.J. D.: A Centenary Memoir* (Rickmansworth, 1976).

Denzler, Robert, Swiss conductor and composer; b. Zürich, March 19, 1892; d. there, Aug. 25, 1972. He studied with

Andreae at the Zürich Cons.; after further training in Cologne, he was an assistant at Bayreuth. He was music director of the Lucerne (1912–15) and then of the Zürich Opera (1915–27); after serving as 1st conductor of the Berlin Städtische Oper (1927–32), he was again music director of the Zürich Opera (1934–47). He composed a Piano Concerto, suites, and songs.

De Peyer, Gervase (Alan), English clarinetist, conductor, and teacher; b. London, April 11, 1926. He studied with Frederick Thurston at the Royal College of Music in London and with Louis Cahuzac in Paris (1949). He then pursued an international career as a clarinet virtuoso; served as 1st clarinetist of the London Sym. Orch. (1955–72), was founder-conductor of the Melos Sinfonia, and assoc. conductor of the Haydn Orch. in London. He taught at the Royal Academy of Music in London (from 1959) and performed with the Chamber Music Soc. of Lincoln Center in N.Y. (1969–89). He gave master classes all over the globe and also commissioned a number of works for clarinet.

DePreist, James (Anderson), greatly talented black American conductor, nephew of **Marian Anderson**; b. Philadelphia, Nov. 21, 1936. He studied at the Univ. of Pa. (B.S., 1958; M.A., 1961) and with Persichetti at the Philadelphia Cons. of Music (1959–61). He conducted the Contemporary Music Guild in Philadelphia (1959–62); then was a music specialist for the U.S. State Dept. During a tour of the Far East in 1962, he was stricken with poliomyelitis, but persevered in his career; conducted in Bangkok (1963–64). In 1964 he won 1st prize in the Mitropoulos conducting competition in N.Y., then was assistant conductor of the N.Y. Phil. (1965–66). He was principal guest conductor of the Sym. of the New World in N.Y. (1968–70). In 1969 he made his European debut with the Rotterdam Phil. After serving as assoc. conductor (1971–75) and principal guest conductor (1975–76) of the National Sym. Orch. in Washington, D.C., he was music director of L'Orchestre Symphonique de Québec (1976–83). He was music director of the Oregon Sym. Orch. in Portland (from 1980), principal conductor designate (1990–91) and principal conductor (from 1991) of the Malmö Sym. Orch., and chief conductor of the Orchestre Philharmonique de Monte Carlo (from 1994). DePreist has won critical accolades for his impeccable performances of an extensive orch. repertoire. He has also publ. 2 vols. of poetry, *This Precipice Garden* (1987) and *The Distant Siren* (1989).

Déré, Jean, French composer; b. Niort, June 23, 1886; d. Sainte Suzanne, Mayenne, Dec. 6, 1970. He studied at the Paris Cons. with Caussade, Diémer, and Widor; won the 2nd Prix de Rome (1919). Among his works were the symphonic poem *Krischna*; incidental music for Marlowe's *Faustus*; *3 esquisses* for Piano and Orch.; chamber music; piano pieces; songs.

De Rensis, Raffaello, Italian music critic; b. Casacalenda, Campobasso, Feb. 17, 1879; d. Rome, Nov. 3, 1970. He founded the weekly magazine *Musica* in 1908; wrote music criticism in daily newspapers. He publ. *Il cantore del popolo, Beniamino Gigli* (Rome, 1934); *Franco Faccio e Verdi* (Milan, 1934); *Ottorino Respighi* (Turin, 1935); *Ermanno Wolf-Ferrari* (Milan, 1937); *Arrigo Boito* (Florence, 1942); *Umberto Giordano e Ruggiero Leoncavallo* (Siena, 1949); *Francesco Cilea* (Palmi, 1950); *Musica vista* (Milan, 1960).

Dermota, Anton, Austrian tenor of Slovenian descent; b. Kropa, June 4, 1910; d. Vienna, June 22, 1989. After training at the Ljubljana Cons., he was a student in Vienna of Elisabeth Rado. In 1934 he made his operatic debut in Cluj; in 1936 he joined the Vienna State Opera, where he sang regularly during the next 40 years; in 1946 he was made a Kammersänger and in 1955 he sang Florestan at the reopening celebration of the restored Vienna State Opera house. He also sang at the Salzburg Festival, Milan's La Scala, the Paris Opéra, and London's Covent Garden, and appeared as a concert artist. In 1966 he became a prof. at the Vienna Academy of Music. He was best known for his roles in Mozart's operas, but he also was admired as Des Grieux, Lensky, Rodolfo, and Palestrina.

Dernesch, Helga, Austrian soprano; b. Vienna, Feb. 3, 1939. She was educated at the Vienna Cons. She made her operatic debut at the Bern Stadttheater in 1961; then sang in Wiesbaden and Cologne; subsequently appeared at the Bayreuth Festivals. In 1969 Herbert von Karajan chose her for his Salzburg Easter Festival; in 1970 she made her debut at Covent Garden, London; also sang with the Hamburg State Opera, the Berlin Städtische Oper, and the Vienna State Opera. She sang many Wagnerian dramatic roles and those of Richard Strauss; from 1979 she turned her attention to mezzo-soprano parts. From 1982 she sang at the San Francisco Opera. On Oct. 14, 1985, she made her Metropolitan Opera debut in N.Y. as Mussorgsky's Marfa. In 1990 she appeared as Verdi's Mistress Quickly in Los Angeles. She sang Strauss's Clytemnestra at the Opéra de la Bastille in Paris in 1992. She married **Werner Krenn**.

De Rogatis, Pascual, Argentine composer and teacher; b. Teora, Italy, May 17, 1880; d. Buenos Aires, April 2, 1980. He studied piano and composition with Alberto Williams and violin with Pietro Melani and Rafael Albertini in Buenos Aires, where he then devoted himself to teaching and composing.

WORKS: DRAMATIC: *Huemac*, lyric drama (1913–14; Buenos Aires, July 22, 1916); *La novia del hereje* or *La Inquisición en Lima*, opera (c.1924; Buenos Aires, June 13, 1935); incidental music; dance scores. **ORCH.:** *Suite árabe* (1902; Buenos Aires, Oct. 10, 1904); *Danza de las dríades* (1902); *Preludio sinfónico* (1903; Buenos Aires, Oct. 10, 1904); *Oriental* (1903; Buenos Aires, Nov. 20, 1905); *Marcha heroica* (1904); symphonic poems: *Marko y el hada* (1905), *Paisaje otoñal* (1905), *Belkiss en la selva* (1906), *Zupay* (1910), *Atipac: Escenas de la selva americana* (c.1920), and *La fiesta del Chiqui* (1935); *Segunda oda de Safo* (1906); *América* c.1920); *Fantasía indígena* (1920); *Suite americana* (1924; Buenos Aires, Aug. 24, 1926); *Estampas argentinas* (1942). **OTHER:** Chamber music, mostly for Solo Piano; *Oratorio laico* for Soprano, Tenor, Chorus, and Orch. (1910; Buenos Aires, May 5, 1928); many songs with piano.

BIBL.: C. Munoz, "P. d.R. (1880–1980)," *Revista del Instituto de Investigación Musicológica Carlos Vega*, No. 7 (Buenos Aires, 1986).

Dervaux, Pierre, noted French conductor and teacher; b. Juvisy-sur-Orge, Jan. 3, 1917; d. Marseilles, Feb. 20, 1992. He studied at the Paris Cons. with Philipp, Armand Ferté, Nat, J. and N. Gallon, and Samuel-Roussel. After conducting at the Paris Opéra-Comique (1945–53), he was permanent conductor at the Paris Opéra (1956–70); from 1958 he was also president and chief conductor of the Concerts Colonne in Paris. He was music director of the Orchestre Symphonique de Québec (1968–71), the Orchestre Philharmonique des Pays de la Loire (1971–78), and in Nice (1979–82). He taught at the École Normale de Musique in Paris (1964–86), the Montreal Cons. (1965–72), and the Nice Academy (1971–82). Dervaux was especially admired for his brilliant and colorful interpretations of the French repertoire. He also composed, producing 2 syms., concertos, chamber music, and piano pieces.

Derzhinskaya, Xenia (Georgievna), notable Russian soprano; b. Kiev, Feb. 6, 1889; d. Moscow, June 9, 1951. She was a pupil of F. Pash and M. Marchesi in Kiev. After appearing in concerts there, she settled in Moscow and sang at the Narodniy Dom Opera (1913–15), and subsequently was a leading member of the Bolshoi Theater (1915–48); also pursued a concert career, and taught voice at the Moscow Cons. (1947–51). In 1937 she was named a People's Artist of the USSR. She won high praise in her homeland for her compelling portrayals of roles in Russian operas.

BIBL.: E. Grosheva, *X.G. D.* (Moscow, 1952).

De Sabata, Victor (actually, **Vittorio**), outstanding Italian conductor and composer; b. Trieste, April 10, 1892; d. Santa Margherita Ligure, Dec. 11, 1967. He studied with Michele Saladino and Giacomo Orefice at the Milan Cons. (1901–11). An extremely versatile musician, he could play piano with considerable élan, and also took lessons on cello, clarinet, oboe, and bassoon. He was encouraged in his career as a conductor by Toscanini; at the same time, he began to compose operas; his first production was *Il Macigno*, which was first performed at La Scala in Milan on March 30, 1917. His symphonic poem *Juventus* (1919) was conducted at La Scala by Toscanini. De Sabata's style of composition involved Romantic Italian formulas, with lyric and dramatic episodes receiving an equal share of attention. In the meantime, he filled engagements as an opera and sym. conductor in Italy. In 1927 he conducted concerts in N.Y. and Cincinnati, in 1936 he conducted at the Vienna State Opera, in 1939 he was a guest conductor with the Berlin Phil., and in 1946 he conducted in Switzerland. On April 21, 1946, he was invited to conduct a sym. concert in London, the 1st conductor from an "enemy country" to conduct in England after World War II. He then was a guest conductor with the Chicago Sym. Orch. in 1949, and with the N.Y. Phil. and the Boston Sym. Orch. in 1950. He became popular with American audiences, and in 1952 was engaged to conduct in N.Y., Philadelphia, Washington, D.C., Baltimore, St. Louis, and Detroit. In 1953 he conducted in Philadelphia, Los Angeles, San Francisco, and Santa Barbara, California. On Feb. 18, 1957, he conducted at the funeral of Toscanini; this was his last appearance on the podium. He was the father-in-law of **Aldo Ceccato**. As a conductor, De Sabata acquired a brilliant reputation in both operatic and symphonic repertoire. He was an impassioned and dynamic conductor who excelled particularly in the works of Verdi and Wagner.

WORKS: DRAMATIC: *Il Macigno*, opera (Milan, March 30, 1917; 2nd version, Driada, Turin, Nov. 12, 1935); *Lisistrata*, opera (1920); *Le mille e una notte*, ballet (Milan, Jan. 20, 1931); theater music for Max Reinhardt's production of *The Merchant of Venice* (Venice, July 18, 1934). **ORCH:** 3 symphonic poems: *Juventus* (1919), *La notte di Platon* (1924), and *Gethsemani* (1925).

BIBL.: R. Mucci, *V. d.S.* (Lanciano, 1937); T. Celli, *L'arte di V. d.S.* (Turin, 1978).

Desarzens, Victor, Swiss conductor; b. Château d'Oex, Oct. 27, 1908; d. Lausanne, Feb. 13, 1986. After studies with Porta (violin) and Hoesslin (conducting) at the Lausanne Cons., he completed his training with Enesco. He began his career as 1st violinist in the Orchestre de la Suisse Romande in Geneva and as a chamber music player. In 1942 he founded a chamber ensemble in Lausanne, which later became the Lausanne Chamber Orch., which he led until 1973 in radio broadcasts and tours of Europe. He also was music director of the Winterthur Musikkollegium (1945–76).

Desderi, Ettore, Italian composer and pedagogue; b. Asti, Dec. 10, 1892; d. Florence, Nov. 23, 1974. He studied with Luigi Perrachio at the Turin Cons. and then with Franco Alfano in Bologna. From 1933 to 1941 he was director of the Liceo Musicale in Alessandria and, from 1941 to 1951, a teacher of composition at the Milan Cons. From 1951 to 1963 he was director of the Bologna Cons. He publ. *La musica contemporanea* (Turin, 1930) and numerous articles in Italian and German journals.

WORKS: *Intermezzi all' Antigone* for Orch. (1924); *Job*, biblical cantata (1927); *Sinfonia davidica* for Soli, Chorus, and Orch. (1929); Violin Sonata; Cello Sonata; many choral works.

BIBL.: A. Bonacorsi, "E. D.," *Il Pianoforte* (July 1926); M. Rinaldi, *E. D.* (Tivoli, 1943); *A E. D. nel suo 70 compleanno* (Bologna, 1963).

De Segurola, Andrés (Perello), Spanish bass; b. Valencia, March 27, 1874; d. Barcelona, Jan. 22, 1953. He studied with Pietro Farvaro in Barcelona, where he made his operatic debut in 1898 at the Teatro Liceo. On Oct. 10, 1901, he made his first appearance with the Metropolitan Opera in a concert during the company's visit to Toronto, and 2 days later sang Laurent in *Roméo et Juliet* there; his debut with the company in N.Y. came on March 3, 1902, as the King in *Aida*, and he remained on its roster until the end of the season; then was again on its roster from 1909 to 1920. He later appeared in films and taught in Hollywood (1931–51) before settling in Barcelona. Among his most prominent roles were Basilio, Alvise, Varlaam, Colline, Sparafucile, and Geronte in *Manon Lescaut*. G. Creegan ed. *Through My Monocle: Memoirs of the Great Basso Andreas de Segurola* (Steubenville, Ohio, 1991).

Deshevov, Vladimir, Russian composer; b. St. Petersburg, Feb. 11, 1889; d. there (Leningrad), Oct. 27, 1955. He studied with Steinberg and Liadov at the St. Petersburg Cons. Many of his themes were drawn from folk sources. Among his works were the revolutionary operas *The Red Hurricane* (Leningrad, Oct. 29, 1924), *Ice and Steel*, based on the Kronstadt rebellion of 1921 (Leningrad, May 17, 1930), and *The Hungry Steppe*, about socialist distribution of land in Uzbekistan.

Des Marais, Paul (Emile), American composer; b. Menominee, Mich., June 23, 1920. He studied with Sowerby in Chicago (1937–41), Boulanger in Cambridge, Mass. (1941–42) and Paris (1949), and Piston at Harvard Univ. (B.A., 1949; M.A., 1953). He received the Lili Boulanger prize (1947–48), the Boott prize in composition from Harvard (1949), and a John Knowles Paine Traveling Fellowship (1949–51). After teaching at Harvard (1953–56), he was on the faculty of the Univ. of Calif. at Los Angeles (from 1956), where he received the Inst. of Creative Arts Award (1964–65); he later received the Phoebe Ketchum Thorne award (1970–73). He publ. the study *Harmony* (1962) and contributed articles to *Perspectives of New Music*. His early music was oriented toward neo-classicism, with pandiatonic excrescences in harmonic structures. He later moved to a free combination of serial and non-serial elements, functioning on broad tonal planes.

WORKS: DRAMATIC: *Epiphanies*, chamber opera (1968); *Orpheus*, theater piece for Narrator and Instruments (1987); incidental music to Dryden's *A Secular Masque* (1976), Shakespeare's *A Midsummer Night's Dream* (1976), Sophocles' *Oedipus* (1978), G.B. Shaw's *St. Joan* (1980), Dryden's *Marriage à la Mode* (1981), Shakespeare's *As You Like It* (1983), and G. Etherege's *The Man of Mode* (1984). **DANCE:** *Triplum* for Organ and Percussion (1981); *Touch* for 2 Pianos (1984). **CHAMBER:** 2 piano sonatas (1947, 1952); *Theme and Changes* for Harpsichord (1953); *Capriccio* for 2 Pianos and Percussion (1962); *2 Movements* for 2 Pianos and Percussion (1972; rev. and enl. as *3 Movements*, 1975); *Baroque Isles: The Voyage Out* for 2 Keyboard Percussionists (1986); *The French Park* for 2 Guitars (1988). **CHORAL:** *Polychoric Mass* for Voices (1949); *Motet* for Voices, Cellos, and Double Basses (1959); *Psalm 121* for Chorus (1959); *Organum 1–6* for Chorus, Organ, and Percussion (1972; rev. and enl. 1980); *Brief Mass* for Chorus, Organ, and Percussion (1973); *Seasons of the Mind* for Chorus, Piano 4-hands, and Celesta (1980–81). **VOCAL:** *Le Cimetière marin* for Voice, Keyboards, and Percussion (1971); solo songs.

Desmond, Astra, English mezzo-soprano and teacher; b. Torquay, April 10, 1893; d. Faversham, Aug. 16, 1973. She studied in London at Westfield College and with Blanche Marchesi at the Royal Academy of Music. Following additional training in Berlin, she returned to London and made her recital debut in 1915. While she made some appearances with the Carl Rosa Opera Co., she devoted herself principally to the concert and oratorio repertory; was a prof. of voice at the Royal Academy of Music (from 1947). In 1949 she was made a Commander of the Order of the British Empire. Her interpretations of English music, particularly works by Elgar and Vaughan Williams, were outstanding. Having mastered 12 languages, she also excelled as an interpreter of the Scandinavian song literature.

Désormière, Roger, brilliant French conductor; b. Vichy, Sept. 13, 1898; d. Paris, Oct. 25, 1963. He studied with Koechlin in Paris. After serving as music director of the Paris Ballets Suédois (1924–25) and the Ballets Russes (1925–29), he was conductor (from 1936) and director (1944–46) of the Opéra-Comique; in 1945–46 he also was assoc. director of the Paris Opéra. In

1946–47 he was a guest conductor with the BBC Sym. Orch. in London, and in 1949 he returned to that city with the Opéra-Comique to conduct *Pelléas et Mélisande* at Covent Garden. He also appeared as a guest conductor of opera and sym. throughout Europe. Désormière was an outstanding interpreter of the French repertory. He also championed 20th-century French music, conducting premieres of works by Satie, Koechlin, Roussel, Milhaud, Poulenc, Messiaen, Boulez et al. After being stricken with aphasia and other disorders, he abandoned his career in 1952.

BIBL.: D. Mayer and P. Souvchinsky, *R. D. et son temps* (Monaco, 1966).

Dessau, Paul, prominent German composer; b. Hamburg, Dec. 19, 1894; d. Königs Wusterhausen, near Berlin, June 27, 1979. He studied violin with Florian Zajic at the Klindworth-Scharwenka Cons. in Berlin (1910–12), and then returned to Hamburg to study piano and score reading with Eduard Behm and composition with Max Loewengard. In 1912 he became co-répétiteur at the Hamburg City Theater, and then went to Bremem in 1913 as an operetta conductor at the Tivoli Theater. After military service during World War I, he returned to Hamburg in 1918 as conductor and composer at the Kammerspiele. He was co-répétiteur and conductor at the Cologne Opera (1919–23) and at the Mainz City Theater (1923–25), and then was 1st conductor at the Berlin Städtische Oper from 1925. When the Nazis came to power in 1933, Dessau lost his post and made his way to Paris, where he came into contact with René Leibowitz and 12-tone music. In 1939 he went to the U.S. While in N.Y., he commenced a long collaboration with Bertolt Brecht. In 1944 he went to Hollywood, where he composed for films. He also composed the music for his most successful collaboration with Brecht, *Mutter Courage und ihre Kinder* (1946). In 1948 he settled in East Germany, where he continued to work with Brecht until the latter's death in 1956. In 1952 Dessau was made a member of the German Academy of Arts, becoming vice-president and prof. there in 1959. He taught at the Zeuthen school, near Berlin, from 1960. In 1953, 1956, 1965, and 1974 he was awarded state prizes by the German Democratic Republic, and in 1964 he received its National Order of Merit. His wife was **Ruth Berghaus**. In his earliest scores, Dessau pursued expressionist and neo-Classical precepts. He then developed an interest in Jewish folk music while exploring 12-tone music. His association with Brecht led him into more popular modes of expression. His works after settling in East Germany are imbued with the progressive ideals of socialist realism, but with increasing serial applications.

WORKS: DRAMATIC: OPERAS: *Giuditta* (1910–12; unfinished); *Orpheus 1930/31*, radio operetta (Berlin, 1931; rev. as *Orpheus und der Bürgmeister*); *Die Reisen des Glücksgotts* (1945; unfinished); *Das Verhöor des Lukullus* (1949; Berlin, March 17, 1951; rev. version as *Die Verurteilung des Lukullus*, Berlin, Oct. 12, 1951); *Puntila* (1956–59; Berlin, Nov. 15, 1966); *Lanzelot* (1967–69; Berlin, Dec. 19, 1969); *Einstein* (1971–73; Berlin, Feb. 16, 1974); *Leonce und Lena* (1977–78; Berlin, Nov. 24, 1979). **INCIDENTAL MUSIC TO:** Brecht's *99%*, later retitled *Furcht und Elend des Dritten Reiches* (1938), *Mutter Courage und ihre Kinder* (1946), *Der gute Mensch von Sezuan* (1947), *Herr Puntila und sein Knecht* (1949), *Mann ist Mann* (1951), and *Der kaukasische Kreidekreis* (1953–54); also Goethe's *Faust*, part I (1949) and *Urfaust* (1952), F. Wolf's *Der arme Konrad* (1951), J. Becher's *Der Weg nach Fussen* (1956), Shakespeare's *Coriolanus* (1964), Weiss's *Vietnam-Diskurs* (1968), and Müller's *Zement* (1973). Also film scores, tanzscenen, lehrstücke, and schulstücke. **ORCH.:** 2 syms.: No. 1 (1926) and No. 2 (1934; rev. 1962); *Trauermarsch* for Winds (1953); *Sinfonischer Marsch*, retitled *Sozialistische Festouvertüre* (1953; rev. 1963); 4 sets of *Orchestermusik*: No. 1, *1955* (1955), No. 2, *Meer dur Stürme* (1967), No. 3, *Lenin* (1970), and No. 4 (1973); *In memoriam Bertolt Brecht* (1957); *Bach-Variationen* (1963); *Divertimento* for Chamber Orch. (1964). **CHAMBER:** Concertino for Violin, Flute, Clarinet, and Horn (1924); *Lustige Variationen über Hab mein' Wagen vollgeladen* for Clarinet, Bassoon, and Harpsichord (1928; rev. for Clarinet, Bassoon, and Piano, 1953); 5 string quartets (1932; 1942–43; 1943–46; 1948; 1955); *Hebräische Melodie* for Violin and Piano (1935); *Burleske* for Cello and Piano (1932); Suite for Saxophone and Piano (1935); *Jewish Dance* for Violin and Piano (1940); *2 Kanons* for Flute, Clarinet, and Bassoon (1942); *Arie* for Cello and Piano (1950); *5 Tanzstücke* for Mandolin, Guitar, and Accordion (1951); *Quattrodramma 1965* for 4 Cellos, 2 Pianos, and 2 Percussion (1965); *3 Stücke* for 2 Trumpets or Clarinets and Trombone or Bassoon (1975). **PIANO:** Sonata (1914; rev. 1948); *12 Studien* (1932); *10 Kinderstücke* (1934; rev. 1953); *Zwölfton Versuche* (1937); *Guernica* (1938); *11 Jüdische Volktänze* (1946); *Klavierstück über BACH* (1948); *5 Studien für Anfänger* (1948); Sonatine (1955); *3 Intermezzi* (1955); *Klavierstücke für Maxim* (1955–63). **VOCAL: ORATORIOS AND CANTATAS:** *Haggada* for Soli, Chorus, Children's Chorus, and Orch. (1936; rev. 1962); *2 Gebete* for Voice, Chorus, and Organ (1939); *Jeworechecho* for Baritone, Chorus, and Organ (1941); *Internationale Kriegsfibel* (1944–45); *Deutsches Miserere* for Soli, Chorus, Children's Chorus, Orch., Organ, and Trautonium (1944–47); *An die Mütter und an die Lehrer* for Mezzo-soprano, Speaker, Chorus, 3 Trumpets, 2 Pianos, and Timpani (1950); *Appell* for Soli, Speaker, Chorus, Children's Chorus, and Orch. (1951–52); *Die Erziehung der Hirse* for Baritone, Speaker, Chorus, Youth Chorus, and Orch. (1952; rev. 1954); *Lilo Herrmann* for Sprechstimme, Small Chorus, Flute, Clarinet, Trumpet, Violin, Viola, and Cello (1953); *Hymne auf den Beginn einer neuen Geschichte der Menschheit* for Soprano, Speaker, Chorus, 3 Pianos, 2 Harps, Double Bass, Timpani, and Percussion (1959; rev. 1964); *Jüdische Chronik* for Baritone, Speaker, Chamber Chorus, and Small Orch. (1960; in collaboration with Blacher, Hartmann, Henze, and Wagner-Régeny); *Margurer Bericht* for Baritone, Chorus, Children's Chorus, and Orch. (1961); *Appell der Arbeiterklasse* for Alto, Tenor, Chorus, and Orch. (1961); *Requiem für Lumumba* for Soprano, Baritone, Speaker, Chorus, and Instruments (1963); *Geschäftsbericht* for 4 Soli, Speaker, Chorus, and Instruments (1967). **OTHER VOCAL:** *Psalm XV* (1927); *Psalm XIII* (1930–31); *Chormusik mit Schlagzeug* (1930–31); *Ausmarsch* (1933); *Hawel Hawalim* for Chorus and Piano or Organ (1939); *Grabschrift für Gorki* for Unison Men's Voices and Winds (1947); *Grabschrift für Rosa Luxemburg* for Chorus and Orch. (1948); *Grabschrift für Karl Liebknecht* for Chorus and Orch. (1948); *Proletarier aller Länder, vereinigt euch!* (1948); *3 Chorlieder* for Chorus and Orch. (1949); *Grabschrift für Lenin* for Chorus and Orch. (1951); *Dreistimmiger Kanon für Otto Nagel* (1959); *Sang der Gesänge* for Chorus and Percussion (1963); much solo vocal music.

WRITINGS: *Musikarbeit in der Schule* (Berlin, 1968); *Aus Gesprächen* (Leipzig, 1975); *Notizen und Noten* (Leipzig, 1974); F. Hennenberg, ed., *Opern* (Berlin, 1976).

BIBL.: F. Hennenberg, *D.-Brecht: Musikalische Arbeiten* (Berlin, 1963); idem, *P. D.: Eine Biographie* (Leipzig, 1965); idem, *Für Sie porträtiert: P. D.* (Leipzig, 1974; 2nd ed., 1981).

Dessoff, Margarethe, Austrian choral conductor; b. Vienna, June 11, 1874; d. Locarno, Switzerland, Nov. 19, 1944. She was trained at the Frankfurt am Main Cons. After championing the cause of early vocal music in Europe, she went to N.Y. and in 1924 founded the Adesdi Chorus, a women's chorus, and in 1928 a mixed chorus; they were amalgamated under her direction in 1930 as the Dessoff Choirs. In 1936 she settled in Switzerland.

Destinn, Emmy (real name, **Emilie Pavlína Kittlová**), famous Czech soprano; b. Prague, Feb. 26, 1878; d. České Budějovice, Jan. 28, 1930. She first studied the violin; her vocal abilities were revealed later by Marie Loewe-Destinn, whose 2nd name she adopted as a token of appreciation. She made her debut as Santuzza at the Kroll Opera in Berlin (July 19, 1898) and was engaged at the Berlin Royal Opera as a regular member until 1908. She specialized in Wagnerian operas, and became a protégée of Cosima Wagner in Bayreuth, where she sang for the first time in 1901 as Senta; because of her ability to cope with difficult singing parts, Richard Strauss selected her for the title role in the Berlin and Paris premieres of his *Salome.* She made her London debut at Covent Garden on May 2, 1904, as Donna Anna; her success in England was spontaneous and unmistakable, and she continued to sing opera in England until the outbreak of World War I. She made her American debut in *Aida* with the Metropolitan Opera in N.Y. on Nov. 16, 1908, and remained with the company until 1916, and then was on its roster again from 1919 to 1921. She retired from the opera stage in 1926 but continued to make concert appearances until shortly before her death. For a few years following World War I, she used her Czech name, Ema Destinnová, but later dropped it. She was a versatile singer with a pure soprano voice of great power; her repertoire included some 80 parts. A film biography of her life, *The Divine Emma,* was produced in Czechoslovakia in 1982.

BIBL.: L. Brieger-Wasservogel, *E. D. und Maria Laiba* (1908); A. Rektorys, *Ema D.ová* (Prague, 1936); M. Martínková, *Život Emy D.ová* (Pilzen, 1946); V. Holzknecht and B. Trita, *E. D.ová ve slovech a obrazech* (E. D. in Words and Pictures; Prague, 1972); M. Pospíšil, *Veliké srdce: Život a umění Emy Destinové* (A Great Heart: The Life and Art of E. D.; Prague, 1974; with discography).

Déthier, Edouard, Belgian-American violinist and teacher, brother of **Gaston-Marie Déthier**; b. Liège, April 25, 1886; d. N.Y., Feb. 19, 1962. He studied at the Liège Cons. (1895–1901); then at the Brussels Cons. (1901–02), where he subsequently taught (1902–04). He settled in the U.S. in 1906, appearing with principal orchs.; taught at the Inst. of Musical Art and at the Juilliard Graduate School in N.Y.

Déthier, Gaston-Marie, Belgian-American organist, pedagogue, and composer, brother of **Edouard Déthier**; b. Liège, April 18, 1875; d. N.Y., May 26, 1958. He studied at the Liège Cons. At age 11, he became organist at the Church of St. Jacques in Liège. In 1894 he went to N.Y. as organist of St. Francis Xavier, where he remained until 1907. From 1904 to 1945 he taught organ and piano at the Inst. of Musical Art; then taught privately. He composed numerous organ pieces.

Detoni, Dubravko, Croatian pianist and composer; b. Križevci, Feb. 22, 1937. He graduated in piano from the Zagreb Academy of Music in 1960; studied with Cortot in Siena (1960–61); then took lessons in composition with Šulek at the Zagreb Academy of Music, graduating in 1965; had advanced studies with Bacewicz and Lutoslawski at the experimental studio of the Polish Radio in Warsaw (1966–67) and with Stockhausen and Ligeti in Darmstadt. He was the founder and artistic leader of ACEZANTEZ, the Ensemble of the Center for New Tendencies in Zagreb. His music rejects all established formulas and seeks new conceptions in sound through serial, aleatory, and musical-theater resources.

WORKS: *Passacaglia* for 2 Pianos and Strings (1962); *Musica a cinque* for Orch. (1962); *Preobrazbe* (Transfigurations) for Orch. (1963; Zagreb, June 7, 1965); *Dramatski prolog* for Orch. (1965); *Stravaganze* for Wind Quintet (1966); *Likovi i plohe* (Forms and Surfaces) for Chamber Orch. (1967; Graz, Sept. 26, 1968); *Phonomorphia 1* for Electronic and Concrete Sounds (1967), *2* for Piano and Tape (1968), and *3* for Voices, Instrumental Ensemble, and Tape (1969); *Grafika I* for Organ (1968), *II* for Chamber Ensemble (1968), *III* for Vocal Ensemble, 6 Flutes, Ondes Martenot, Organ, and Piano (1969), *IV* for ad libitum Chamber Ensemble (1971), and *V*, instrumental "theater" for Chamber Ensemble (1972; Graz, Oct. 14, 1973); *Assonanze No. 1* for Cello and Piano (1968) and *No. 2* for Cello and Orch. (1971); *Elucubrations* for Piano and Orch. (1969; Zagreb, Jan. 7, 1970); *Forte-Piano, Arpa, Crescendo* for 2 Pianos and Percussion (1969); *Notturni* for 4 Vocal Groups, 4 Instrumental Ensembles, Organ, and Tape (1970); *Monos 1–3*, cycle for variable orchestration (1970–72); *Einflüsse* for 2 Cellos and Orch. (1971); *Music, or Tract about the Superfluous* for Narrating Actor, Organ, Piano, Percussion, Clarinet, and Orch. (1973); *10 Beginnings* for String Quartet (1973); *Dokument 75* for Chamber Ensemble (1975); *Fragment 75* for Chamber Ensemble (Graz, Oct. 11, 1975).

Dett, R(obert) Nathaniel, distinguished black American composer, conductor, and anthologist; b. Drummondville, Quebec, Oct. 11, 1882; d. Battle Creek, Mich., Oct. 2, 1943. He came from a musical family; both his parents were amateur pianists and singers. In 1893 the family moved to Niagara Falls, N.Y., where Dett studied piano with local teachers. He earned his living by playing at various clubs and hotels, then enrolled at the Oberlin (Ohio) Cons., where he studied piano with Howard Handel Carter and theory with Arthur E. Heacox and George Carl Hastings (B.Mus., 1908). He also conducted a school choir; eventually, choral conducting became his principal profession. He taught at Lane College in Jackson, Tenn. (1908–11), the Lincoln Inst. in Jefferson, Mo. (1911–13), the Hampton Inst. in Virginia (1913–32), and Bennett College in Greensboro, N.C. (1937–42). Concerned about his lack of technical knowledge in music, he took lessons with Karl Gehrkens at Oberlin in 1913; also attended classes at Columbia Univ., the American Cons. of Music in Chicago, Northwestern Univ., the Univ. of Pa., and, during the academic year 1919–20, at Harvard Univ., where he studied composition with Foote. In 1929 he pursued training with Boulanger at the American Cons. in Fontainebleau; during 1931–32, he attended the Eastman School of Music in Rochester, N.Y. (M.Mus., 1932). In the meantime, he developed the Hampton Choir, which toured in Europe in 1930 with excellent success, receiving encomiums in England, France, Belgium, the Netherlands, Germany, and Switzerland. He also periodically led his choir on the radio; in 1943 he became a musical adviser for the USO, and worked with the WAC (Women's Army Corps) on service duty at Battle Creek. His dominating interest was in cultivating Negro music, arranging Negro spirituals, and publishing collections of Negro folk songs. All of his works were inspired by black melos and rhythms; some of his piano pieces in the Negro idiom became quite popular, among them the suite *Magnolia* (1912), *In the Bottoms* (1913), which contained the rousing *Juba Dance*, and *Enchantment* (1922). He also wrote a number of choral pieces, mostly on biblical themes, such as the oratorios *The Chariot Jubilee* (1921) and *The Ordering of Moses* (Cincinnati, May 7, 1937). His choruses *Listen to the lambs, I'll never turn back no more,* and *Don't be weary, traveler,* became standards in the choral repertoire. He publ. the anthologies *Religious Folk Songs of the Negro* (1926) and *The Dett Collection of Negro Spirituals* (4 vols., 1936). His piano compositions were ed. by D.-R. de Lerma and V. McBrier (Evanston, Ill., 1973).

BIBL.: M. Stanley, "R.N. D. of Hampton Institute," *Musical America* (July 1918); V. McBrier, *R.N. D.: His Life and Works: 1882–1943* (Washington, D.C., 1977); J. Spencer, "R.N. D.'s Views on the Preservation of Black Music," *Black Perspective in Music,* X (1982); A. Simpson, *Follow Me: The Life and Music of R.N. D.* (Metuchen, N.J., 1993).

Deutekom, Cristina (real name, **Stientje Engel**), notable Dutch soprano; b. Amsterdam, Aug. 28, 1931. She was a student of Johan Thomas and Coby Riemersma at the Amsterdam Cons. In 1962 she made her operatic debut as the Queen of the Night in Amsterdam, a role she subsequently sang with great distinction at her Metropolitan Opera debut in N.Y. on Sept. 28, 1967; was again on its roster (1973–75). She subsequently sang in principal opera houses of the world, becoming equally adept in both coloratura and dramatic roles. Deutekom excelled particularly in the operas of Mozart, Rossini, Bellini, Donizetti, and Verdi.

Deutsch, Diana, significant English-born American music psychologist; b. London, Feb. 15, 1938. She studied theory and composition in London; received a 1st-class honors B.A. in psychology from Oxford (1959) and a Ph.D. in psychology from the Univ. of Calif. at San Diego (1970), where she became a research psychologist at its Center for Human Information Processing. In 1989 she obtained professorial status there. She conducted highly creative research in psychoacoustics and the psychology of music. Her work has included extensive study of auditory illusions and paradoxes; she also created a model of the process of analyzing musical shape that received widespread attention. She ed. *The Psychology of Music* (N.Y., 1982), and in 1983 founded the journal *Music Perception*, of which she served as ed. Among her important articles are "An Auditory Illusion," *Nature*, 1251 (1974), "Internal Representation of Pitch Sequences in Tonal Music," *Psychological Review*, lxxxviii (1981), and "Pitch Class and Perceived Height: Some Paradoxes and Their Implications," *Explorations in Music, the Arts and Ideas*, ed. by Narmour and Solie (N.Y., 1988).

Deutsch, Max, Austrian-born French composer, conductor, and pedagogue; b. Vienna, Nov. 17, 1892; d. Paris, Nov. 22, 1982. He studied composition privately with Schoenberg; also took courses at the Univ. of Vienna. He began his career conducting operetta in Vienna; in 1923 he went to Berlin, where he organized his own orch. group concentrating mainly on modern music, emulating Schoenberg's Soc. for Private Performances of Vienna. In 1925 he settled in Paris, where he founded a Jewish theatrical ensemble, Der Jiddische Spiegel; also conducted concerts of modern music. From 1933 to 1935 he was in Madrid, where he was in charge of a film enterprise; in 1939 he went to France; after service in the Foreign Legion (until 1945), he returned to Paris, where he devoted himself to teaching, using Schoenberg's method. In 1960 he founded the Grands Concerts de la Sorbonne. In his compositions, Deutsch pursued novel ideas; he was the first to write a complete film sym., in 5 movements, for the production of the German film *Der Schutz* (1923); he furthermore composed 2 syms. and a choral sym., *Prière pour nous autres mortels.*

Deutsch, Otto Erich, eminent Austrian musicologist; b. Vienna, Sept. 5, 1883; d. there, Nov. 23, 1967. He studied literature and art history at the univs. of Vienna and Graz; was art critic of Vienna's *Die Zeit* (1908–09); then served as an assistant at the Kunsthistorisches Institut of the Univ. of Vienna (1909–12); later was a bookseller, and then music librarian of the important collection of Anthony van Hoboken in Vienna (1926–35). In 1939 he emigrated to England and settled in Cambridge; in 1947 he became a naturalized British subject, but returned to Vienna in 1951. A scholar of impeccable credentials, Deutsch was an acknowledged authority on Handel, Mozart, and Schubert; his documentary biographies of these composers constitute primary sources; he was also responsible for initiating the critical edition of Mozart's letters, which he ed. with W. Bauer and J. Eibl as *Mozart: Briefe und Aufzeichnungen* (7 vols., Kassel, 1962–75).

WRITINGS: *Schubert-Brevier* (Berlin, 1905); *Beethovens Beziehungen zu Graz* (Graz, 1907); *Franz Schubert: Die Dokumente seines Lebens und Schaffens* (in collaboration, 1st with L. Scheibler, then with W. Kahl and G. Kinsky), which was planned as a comprehensive work in 3 vols. containing all known documents, pictures, and other materials pertaining to Schubert, arranged in chronological order, with a thematic catalog, but of which only 2 vols. were publ.: vol. III, *Sein Leben in Bildern* (Munich, 1913), and vol. II, part 1, *Die Dokumente seines Lebens* (Munich, 1914; Eng. tr. 1946, by E. Blom, as *Schubert: A Documentary Biography*; American ed., 1947, as *The Schubert Reader: A Life of Franz Schubert in Letters and Documents*; 2nd German ed., 1964, enl., in the *Neue Ausgabe sämtlicher Werke of Schubert*); *Franz Schuberts Briefe und Schriften* (Munich, 1919; Eng. tr., 1928; 4th German ed., Vienna, 1954); *Die historischen Bildnisse Franz Schuberts in getreuen Nachbildungen* (Vienna, 1922); *Die Originalausgaben von Schuberts Goethe-Liedern* (Vienna, 1926); *Franz Schubert: Tagebuch: Faksimile der Originalhandschrift* (Vienna, 1928); *Mozart und die Wiener Logen* (Vienna, 1932); with B. Paumgartner, *Leopold Mozarts Briefe an seine Tochter* (Salzburg, 1936); *Das Freihaustheater auf der Wieden 1787–1801* (Vienna, 1937); *Wolfgang Amadé Mozart: Verzeichnis aller meiner Werke. Faksimile der Handschrift mit dem Beiheft "Mozarts Werkverzeichnis 1784–1791"* (Vienna, 1938; Eng. tr., 1956); *Schubert: Thematic Catalogue of All His Works in Chronological Order* (with D. Wakeling; London, 1951; Ger tr. as *Franz Schubert: Thematisches Verzeichnis seiner Werke*, in the *Neue Ausgabe sämtlicher Werke of Schubert* in a rev. ed., 1978); *Handel: A Documentary Biography* (N.Y., 1954; London, 1955); *Franz Schubert: Die Erinnerungen seiner Freunde* (Leipzig, 1957; Eng. tr., 1958); *Mozart: Die Dokumente seines Lebens* (Kassel, 1961; Eng. tr., 1965, as *Mozart: A Documentary Biography*; 2nd ed., 1966; supplement, 1978); *Mozart und seine Welt in zeitgenössischen Bildern* (completed by M. Zenger, Kassel, 1961).

BIBL.: *O.E. D. zum 75. Geburtstag* (Vienna, 1958); W. Gerstenberg, J. LaRue, and W. Rehm, eds., *Festschrift O.E. D.* (Kassel, 1963); J. Stone, "More on the Mozart Puzzles," *Musical Times* (July 1988).

Devčić, Natko, Croatian composer; b. Glina, June 30, 1914. He studied piano and composition at the Zagreb Academy of Music, graduating in 1939; later studied with Marx in Vienna (1949–50), Rivier in Paris (1953), and attended courses led by Boulez at Darmstadt (summer, 1965); also researched the potentials of electronic sound with Davidovsky at the Columbia-Princeton Electronic Music Studio in N.Y. (1966–67). His early works are based on folk resources; later he experimented with advanced techniques.

WORKS: DRAMATIC: *Labinska vještica* (The Witch of Labin), opera (Zagreb, Dec. 25, 1957); *Dia . . .* , ballet (Zagreb, May 20, 1971). **ORCH.:** *Scherzo* (1936); *Nocturne* (1941; rev. 1956); *Istarska suite* (Zagreb, Dec. 8, 1948); Sym. (1953); *Balada* for Piano and Orch. (1953); *Concertino* for Violin and Chamber Orch. (1958); *Prolog* for Winds and Percussion (1965); *Fibula* for 2 Orchs. (Zagreb, May 12, 1967); Concerto for Voice, Ondes Martenot, and Chamber Ensemble (Graz, Oct. 23, 1969); *Panta rei* (All Things Change, a motto of Heraclitus) for Piano and Orch. (1973); *Entre nous* (Zagreb, March 26, 1975). **CHAMBER:** *8 Minutes* for Piano and Chamber Ensemble (1965); *Odrazi* (Reflections) for Chamber Ensemble (1965); *Micro-tune* for Viola and Piano (1971); *Structures transparentes* and *Structures volantes* for Harp (1966, 1971). **PIANO:** *Sonata-Fantasy* (1940); *Koraci* (Steps; 1962); *Micro-suite* (1965). **VOCAL:** *Kantata o bezimenima* (Cantata about a Nameless One) for Chamber Chorus and 12 Instruments (1959); *Ševa* (The Lark), cantata (Zagreb, March 30, 1960); *Igra rijeci* (Play of Words) for 2 Narrators, Chorus, Instrumental Ensemble, and Tape (Zagreb, May 9, 1969). **TAPE:** *Columbia 68* (1968).

De Vito, Gioconda, Italian violinist and teacher; b. Martina Franca, July 26, 1907; d. Rome, Oct. 24, 1994. After training with Principe in Pesaro (1918–21), she made her debut in Rome in 1923; in 1932 she won 1st prize in the Vienna competition; following World War II, she pursued a major European career until retiring in 1961. She taught at the Bari Cons. (1925–34), in Rome at the Cons. (1934–45) and the Accademia di Santa Cecilia (1945–58), and in Siena at the Accademia Musicale Chigiana (1949). She was admired for her interpretations of the standard repertory; she was also the dedicatee of Pizzetti's Violin Concerto.

Devlin, Michael (Coles), American bass-baritone; b. Chicago, Nov. 27, 1942. He studied at Louisiana State Univ. (Mus.B., 1965) and received vocal training from Norman Treigle and Daniel Ferro in N.Y. In 1963 he made his operatic debut as Spalanzani in *Les Contes d'Hoffmann* in New Orleans, and in 1966 he made his first appearance at the N.Y. City Opera as the Hermit in the U.S. premiere of Ginastera's *Don Rodrigo*, continuing on its roster until 1978. In 1974 he made his British debut at the Glyndebourne Festival as Mozart's Almaviva; he first sang at London's Covent Garden in 1975, then appeared at the Holland Festival, the Frankfurt am Main Opera, and the Bavarian State Opera in Munich in 1977. On Nov. 23, 1978, he made his

Metropolitan Opera debut in N.Y. as Escamillo, and subsequently returned there regularly. In later years, he sang with opera companies in San Francisco, Hamburg, Paris, Monte Carlo, Dallas, Chicago, Los Angeles, and other cities. He also appeared as a soloist with the world's major orchs.

De Vocht, Lodewijk, Belgian conductor, teacher, and composer; b. Antwerp, Sept. 21, 1887; d. 's Gravenzel, near Antwerp, March 27, 1977. He spent his entire career in Antwerp, where he was a student of Gilson and Mortelmans at the Royal Flemish Cons. He became a violinist in the orch. of the Société des Concerts Nouveaux in 1903, serving as its conductor from 1921; he also was choirmaster at the Cathedral (1912–50) and founder-conductor of the Chorale Caecilia (1915–68). From 1921 to 1953 he taught at the Royal Flemish Cons., and also was conductor of its concerts (1935–53). De Vocht's works were composed in a Romantic vein.

WORKS: ORCH.: 3 syms.; Violin Concerto (1944); Cello Concerto (1955); Recorder Concerto (1957); symphonic poems. **CHAMBER:** Wind Trio (1955); *Suite champêtre* for Guitar (1971–73); 2 piano sonatas; organ preludes and fugues. **VOCAL:** *Primavera* for Soprano, Tenor, Chorus, and Orch. (1963–65); *Scaldis aeterna*, cantata (1966); choruses; songs.

DeVoto, Mark (Bernard), American composer, teacher, writer on music, pianist, and conductor; b. Cambridge, Mass., Jan. 11, 1940. His father was the American novelist, journalist, historian, and critic Bernard (Augustine) DeVoto. He studied at the Longy School of Music (1946–56), then with Thompson, Piston, Pirrotta, and Ward at Harvard Univ. (B.A., 1961), with Foss at the Berkshire Music Center in Tanglewood (summer, 1959), and with Sessions, Kim, Babbitt, and Cone at Princeton Univ. (M.F.A., 1963; Ph.D., 1967, with the diss. *Alban Berg's Picture-Postcard Songs*). He taught at Reed College (1964–68), Portland State Univ. (1968), the Univ. of New Hampshire (1968–81), and Tufts Univ. (from 1981), where he was director of its sym. orch. He was founding ed. of the International Alban Berg Soc. newsletter (1968–75); also rev. and augmented Piston's *Harmony* (4th ed., 1978; 5th ed., 1987).

WORKS: ORCH.: 4 piano concertos: No. 1 (1956), No. 2 (1965–66), No. 3, *The Distinguished Thing* (1968), and No. 4 with Symphonic Wind Ensemble, Women's Voices, and Viola obbligato (1983); *Night Songs and Distant Dances* (1962); *3 Little Pieces* (1964); *Interior Dialogue* (1991). **CHAMBER:** *2 Etudes* for Piano, Left-hand (1970); Quartet for Flute, Clarinet, Guitar, and Harp (1987); *Lux benigna* for Euphonium, Violin, Organ, and Piano (1988); *Zvon* for Flute, Violin, and Piano (1992); String Quartet No. 2 (1993). **VOCAL:** *Planh* for 6 Solo Voices and 5 Instruments (1960); *3 Edgar Allan Poe Songs* for Soprano, Concertina, Guitar, Harpsichord, and 8 Flutes (1967; rev. 1970); *Fever-Dream Vocalise* for Soprano, Flute, Cello, Piano, and Percussion (1968); *Ornieres* for Soprano, Piano, Organ, and Percussion Ensemble (1974); *The Caucasian Chalk Circle* for Voices and 9 Instruments (1979–80); *H* for Reciter and Flute Choir (1981); *Psalm 98* for Chorus, 2 Trumpets, and 2 Trombones (1983); *Herbstlieder*, 6 songs for Mezzo-soprano and Piano (1986); *Hodayot* for Chorus and Orch. (1989–90). **OTHER:** Orch. and band arrangements.

Devreese, Frédéric, Belgian conductor and composer, son of **Godefroid Devreese**; b. Amsterdam, June 2, 1929. He studied first at the Mechelen Cons.; then took courses in composition from Poot and conducting from Defossez at the Brussels Cons.; subsequently studied with Pizzetti at the Accademia di Santa Cecilia in Rome (1952–55). Returning to Belgium, he became associated with the Flemish TV as program director.

WORKS: DRAMATIC: OPERAS: *Willem van Saeftinghe* (Brussels TV, Sept. 28, 1964; 1st stage perf., Antwerp, Nov. 21, 1964); *De vreemde ruiter* (1966). **BALLETS:** *Mascarade* (1955; Aix-les-Bains, France, 1956); *L'Amour de Don Juan* (1973). **ORCH.:** 4 piano concertos (1949; 1952; 1955–56; 1983); Violin Concerto (1951); Sym. (1953); *Mouvement lent* for Strings (1953); *Recitativo et Allegro* for Trumpet and Orch. (1959); *Mouvement vif* for Strings (1963); *Evocation*, suite (1967); *Divertimento* for Strings (1970); *Prelude* (1981); Suite for Brass Band (1985); *Gemini, bewegingen* (1986); *L'Oeuvre au noir*, suite (1988); *Variations and Theme* for Strings (1991). **CHAMBER:** *Complainte* for Cello or Oboe, and Piano (1951); Quintet for Flute, Clarinet, Bassoon, Piano, and Percussion (1957); *Ensorbeelden*, suite for Brass Quintet (1972); Suite No. 2 for Brass Quintet (1981); *5 Divertimenti* for 4 Saxophones (1985); piano pieces. **VOCAL:** Choruses.

Devreese, Godefroid, Belgian conductor, teacher, and composer, father of **Frédéric Devreese**; b. Kortrijk, Jan. 22, 1893; d. Brussels, June 4, 1972. He studied at the Brussels Cons. with Ysaÿe and César Thomson (violin) and Rasse and Gilson (composition). He was a conductor of the Antwerp Opera (1919–20); was a violinist with the Concertgebouw Orch. in Amsterdam (1925–30) and director of the Mechelin Cons. (1930–58), concurrently giving courses at the Brussels Cons. (1944–59).

WORKS: BALLET: *Tombelène* (1927). **ORCH.:** *Poème héroïque* (1923); *Symphonic Variations on a Popular Scottish Theme* (1923); Concertino for Cello and Chamber Orch. (1926); *In memoriam* (1928); 2 violin concertos (1936, 1970); Piano Concerto (1938); 4 syms.: No. 1, *Gothique* (1944), No. 2, *Goethe*, for Chorus and Orch. (1952), No. 3, *Sinfonietta* (1962), and No. 4 (1965–66); *Rhapsodie* for Clarinet and Orch. (1948); *Allegro* for Trumpet and Orch. (1950); Suite (1953); *Sinfonietta* for Strings (1962); *6 Variations on a Popular Theme* for Strings (1963); *Capriccio* for Violin and Strings (1963). **CHAMBER:** Violin Sonata (1924); Cello Sonata (1926); String Quartet (1937); Piano Trio (1950). **PIANO:** *Scherzo de concert* (1921); *Danse lente* (1924); 7 sonatinas (1944–45); Sonata (1945). **VOCAL:** *Stabat mater* for Soprano, Chorus, and Orch. (1965); *Te Deum* for Chorus and Orch. (1967; Brussels, March 30, 1973); songs.

De Waart, Edo (actually, **Eduard**). See **Waart, Edo** (actually, **Eduard**) **de.**

Dexter, John, English opera director; b. Derby, Aug. 2, 1925; d. London, March 23, 1990. He worked in London in the theater and in films; from 1957 to 1972 he was associated with the English Stage Company, and also was assoc. director of the National Theatre from 1963. In 1966 he staged his first opera, *Benvenuto Cellini*, at London's Covent Garden. After staging operas in Hamburg (1969–72) and Paris (1973), he was director of production at the Metropolitan Opera in N.Y. (1974–81), where his memorable achievements included *Dialogues des Carmélites* and *Lulu* (1977), *Billy Budd* (1978), *Aufstieg und Fall der Stadt Mahagonny* (1979), and the triple bill of Satie's *Parade*, Poulenc's *Les mamelles de Tirésias*, and Ravel's *L'enfant et les sortilèges* (1981). From 1981 to 1984 he served as production advisor at the Metropolitan. **Deyo, Felix,** American composer and pianist, 2nd cousin of **Ruth Lynda Deyo**; b. Poughkeepsie, N.Y., April 21, 1888; d. Baldwin, N.Y., June 21, 1959. He studied piano with his mother, Mary Forster Deyo (1857–1947), then at the Brooklyn Cons. of Music; after graduation, he taught there (1911–39). In 1939 he became director of the Baldwin (Long Island) Cons. of Music. He wrote 3 syms.: *A Lyric Symphony* (Babylon, Long Island, Dec. 8, 1949), *An Ancient Symphony*, and *A Primeval Symphony*; also 2 piano sonatas, a Violin Sonata, and numerous piano pieces of a programmatic nature (*Flight of the Dodo Bird*, etc.). His wife, Asta Nygren Deyo (1898–1953), was a piano teacher.

Deyo, Ruth Lynda, American pianist and composer, 2nd cousin of **Felix Deyo**; b. Poughkeepsie, N.Y., April 20, 1884; d. Cairo, March 4, 1960. She studied piano with William Mason and Teresa Carreño and composition with MacDowell. She made her debut at the age of 9 at the World's Columbian Exposition in Chicago (1893); made her concert debut in Berlin (March 23, 1904); subsequently played with major orchs. in the U.S. and in Europe; appeared in recitals with Kreisler and Casals. In 1925 she settled in Egypt and devoted herself mainly to composition. In 1930 she completed the full score of an opera on Egyptian themes, *The Diadem of Stars*, to a libretto by her husband, Charles Dalton; its *Prelude* was perf. by Stokowski and the Philadelphia Orch. (April 4, 1931).

D'Haene, Rafaël, Belgian composer and teacher; b. Gullegem, Sept. 29, 1943. He studied piano with E. del Pueyo in Brussels and composition with Dutilleux in Paris (Licence de Composition, 1968) and Legley at the Chapelle Musicale Reine Elisabeth in Brussels. In 1970 he became prof. of counterpoint and fugue at the Brussels Cons. and prof. of musical analysis at the Chapelle Musicale Reine Elisabeth.

WORKS: *9 Stukken* for Piano (1967–68); *Werk uit Roemenie,* lieder cycle for Baritone (1969); *Miroir des vanités* for Chorus (1970); Trumpet Sonata (1970); String Quartet (1971); *Klage der Ariadne,* cantata for Soli, Chorus, and Orch. (1971–72); *Capriccio* for Orch. (1972); *5 Orchestral Lieder* (1972); *Praeludia* for Orch. (1974); *Impressions,* lieder cycle for Mezzo-soprano (1980); *Canzone* for Piano (1983); *Lettres persanes* for Orch. (1986); *Cassazione,* piano trio (1986); *Sonette an Orpheus,* 3 lieder for Soprano and Orch. (1987).

D'Hoedt, Henri-Georges, Belgian composer; b. Ghent, June 28, 1885; d. Brussels, May 14, 1936. He was a student of Emile Mathieu and Leo Moeremans. He became director of the Louvain Cons. in 1924, serving until his death. He was one of the first Belgian composers to depart from late-19th-century Romanticism and come under the influence of French Impressionism.

WORKS: *Klaas au Pays de Cocagne,* opera (Antwerp, 1926); *Les Brèves Chroniques de la vie bourgeoise,* satirical symphonic study (1934); *Narcisse* for Orch.; *L'Ile de Cythère* for Chorus and Orch.; *La Vocation de Siddartha,* symphonic trilogy; *Dionysos,* symphonic poem; *Poème pantagruélique* for Orch.; chamber music.

D'Hooghe, Clement (Vital Ferdinand), noted Belgian organist, pedagogue, and composer; b. Temse, April 21, 1899; d. Wilrijk, near Antwerp, April 1, 1951. He studied classics at the Episcopal College of St. Niklaas (1913–17); after training in organ with Paepen, harmony and composition with Wambach, De Boeck, and Mortelmans, and orchestration with Gilson at the Antwerp Cons. (1918–27), he studied organ improvisation with Dupré in Paris. From 1926 until his death, D'Hooghe was organist at St. Paul's in Antwerp. As a recitalist, he acquired an outstanding reputation as a virtuoso. From 1942 he also was a prof. at the Antwerp Cons.

WORKS: *Preludium* for Orch. (1928); *Variations on a Swedish Song* for Orch. (1936); Piano Concerto (1949); Piano Quartet (1939); String Quartet (1944); Cello Sonata (1945); choral works; songs; children's pieces.

Diaghilev, Sergei (Pavlovich), famous Russian impresario; b. Gruzino, Novgorod district, March 31, 1872; d. Venice, Aug. 19, 1929. He was associated with progressive artistic organizations in St. Petersburg, but his main field of activity was in western Europe. He established the Ballets Russes in Paris in 1909; he commissioned Stravinsky to write the ballets *The Firebird, Petrouchka,* and *Le Sacre du printemps*; also commissioned Prokofiev, Milhaud, Poulenc, Auric, and other composers of the younger generation. Ravel and Falla also wrote works for him. The great importance of Diaghilev's choreographic ideas lies in the complete abandonment of the classical tradition; in this respect he was the true originator of the modern dance.

BIBL.: A. Haskell, *D., His Artistic and Private Life* (London, 1935); V. Kamenev, *Russian Ballet through Russian Eyes* (London, 1936); S. Lifar, *S. D.: His Life, His Work, His Legend* (London, 1940); C. Beaumont, *The D. Ballet in London, A Personal Record* (London, 1940); S. Grigoriev, *The D. Ballet* (London, 1953); R. Buehle, *In Search of D.* (N.Y., 1956); B. Kochno, *D. and the Ballets Russes* (N.Y., 1970); R. Buckle, *D.* (N.Y., 1979).

Diamond, David (Leo), eminent American composer; b. Rochester, N.Y., July 9, 1915. After attending the Cleveland Inst. of Music (1927–29), he was a student of Rogers at the Eastman School of Music in Rochester, N.Y. (1930–34); he then studied at the New Music School and the Dalcroze Inst. in N.Y. (1934–36) with Boepple and Sessions. In 1936 he went to Paris to pursue studies with Boulanger, and during the summers of 1937 and 1938 he attended the American Cons. in Fontainebleau; he also studied with Ribaupierre and Scherchen. While in Paris, he became associated with the most important musicians and writers of his time, including Stravinsky, Ravel, Roussel, and Milhaud. His *Psalm* for Orch. (1936) won the Juilliard Publication Award in 1937 and brought him wide recognition. In 1941 he received the Prix du Rome and in 1942 the American Academy in Rome Award. With his *Rounds* for Strings (1944), he established himself as one of America's most important composers. This highly successful score won the N.Y. Music Critics' Circle Award in 1944. In subsequent years, Diamond received various commissions and had his works performed by major conductors. After serving as the Fulbright Prof. at the Univ. of Rome (1951–52), he settled in Florence. In 1961 and 1963 he was the Slee Prof. at the State Univ. of N.Y. at Buffalo. In 1965 he moved to the U.S. and taught at the Manhattan School of Music in N.Y. until 1968, serving as chairman of its music dept. in 1967–68. In 1970 he was a visiting prof. at the Univ. of Colo. in Boulder. In 1971–72 he was composer-in-residence at the American Academy in Rome. He then was prof. of composition and lecturer in graduate studies at the Juilliard School in N.Y. from 1973. In 1983 he also was a visting prof. at the Univ. of Denver. From 1991 to 1994 he was composer-in-residence at the Tisch Center for the Arts in N.Y. In 1938, 1941, and 1958 he held Guggenheim fellowships. In 1966 he was elected to membership in the National Inst. of Arts and Letters. In 1985 he received the William Schuman Lifetime Achievement Award and in 1991 the Edward MacDowell Gold Medal. In 1995 he received the Medal of Arts from President William Clinton. As a composer, Diamond developed an original and recognizable style of harmonic and contrapuntal writing with the clearest sense of tonality. The element of pitch, often inspired by natural folklike patterns, is strong in all of his music. He later adopted a modified dodecaphonic method, while keeping free of doctrinaire serialism. His orch., chamber, and vocal output constitutes a significant contribution to 20th-century American music.

WORKS; DRAMATIC: OPERA: *The Noblest Game* (1971–75). **MUSICAL COMEDY:** *Mirandolina* (1958). **MUSICAL FOLK PLAY:** *The Golden Slippers* (N.Y., Dec. 5, 1965). **DANCE DRAMA:** *Icaro* (1937). **BALLETS:** *A Myriologue* (1935); *Formal Dance* (N.Y., Nov. 10, 1935); *Dance of Liberation* (1936; N.Y., Jan. 23, 1938); *Tom* (1936); *Duet* (1937); *Prelude* (1937); *The Dream of Audubon* (1941); *Labyrinth* (N.Y., April 5, 1946). **INCIDENTAL MUSIC TO:** Shakespeare's *The Tempest* (1944; N.Y., Jan. 25, 1945; rev. 1946 and 1968) and *Romeo and Juliet* (1947; rev. 1950; N.Y., March 10, 1951); Williams's *The Rose Tattoo* (1950–51; N.Y., Feb. 3, 1951. **FILM SCORES:** *A Place to Live* (1941); *Dreams that Money can Buy* (1943); *Strange Victory* (1948); *Anna Lucasta* (1949); *Lippold's the Sun* (1965); *Life in the Balance* (1966). **RADIO SCORES:** *Hear it Now* (1942); *The Man Behind the Gun* (1942).

ORCH.: *Divertimento* for Piano and Small Orch. (1935); *Threnody* (1935); *Variations on a Theme by Erik Satie* (1935–36); *Psalm* (Rochester, N.Y., Dec. 10, 1936); Suite No. 1 from the ballet *Tom* (1936); 3 violin concertos: No. 1 (1936; N.Y., March 24, 1937), No. 2 (1947; Vancouver, Feb. 29, 1948), and No. 3 (1967–68; N.Y., April 1, 1976); *Aria and Hymn* (1937); *Variations on an Original Theme* for Chamber Orch. (1937; Rochester, N.Y., April 23, 1940); Overture (1937); Cello Concerto (1938; Rochester, N.Y., April 30, 1942); *Heroic Piece* for Chamber Orch. (Zürich, July 29, 1938); *Elegy in Memory of Maurice Ravel* for Brass, Harp, and Percussion (Rochester, N.Y., April 28, 1938; rev. for Strings and Percussion, 1938–39); *Music* for Double Strings, Brass, and Timpani (1938–39; rev. 1968); *Concert Piece* (1939; N.Y., May 16, 1940); Concerto for Chamber Orch. (Yaddo, N.Y., Sept. 7, 1940); 11 syms.: No. 1 (1940–41; N.Y., Dec. 21, 1941), No. 2 (1942; Boston, Oct. 13, 1944), No. 3 (1945; Boston, Nov. 3, 1951), No. 4 (1945; Boston,

Jan. 23, 1948), No. 5 (1951; rev. 1964; N.Y., April 26, 1966), No. 6 (1951–54; Boston, March 8, 1957), No. 7 (1959; N.Y., Jan. 26, 1962), No. 8 (1960; N.Y., Oct. 26, 1961), No. 9 for Baritone and Orch. (N.Y., Nov. 17, 1985), No. 10 (in progress), and No. 11 (N.Y., Dec. 3, 1992); *Ballade* for Chamber Orch. (1935); *Rounds* for Strings (Minneapolis, Nov. 24, 1944); *The Enormous Room* (1948; Cincinnati, Nov. 19, 1949); *Timon of Athens*, symphonic portrait (Louisville, 1949); Piano Concerto (1949–50; N.Y., April 28, 1966); *Ceremonial Fanfare* for Brass and Percussion (1950); *Sinfonia Concertante* (1954–56; Rochester, N.Y., March 7, 1957); *Diaphony* for Organ, Brass, 2 Pianos, and Timpani (1955; N.Y., Feb. 22, 1956; rev. for Organ and Orch., 1968); *The World of Paul Klee* (1957; Portland, Oreg., Feb. 15, 1958); *Elegies* for Flute, English Horn, and Strings (1962–63); Piano Concertino (1964–65); *Music* for Chamber Orch. (1969–70); *A Buoyant Music*, overture No. 2 (1970); *Sinfonietta* (1989; Koger, July 20, 1990); *Kaddish* for Cello and Orch. (1989; Seattle, April 9, 1990).

CHAMBER: *6 Pieces* for String Quartet (1935); *Partita* for Oboe, Bassoon, and Piano (1935); Chamber Sym. for Clarinet, Bassoon, Trumpet, Viola, and Piano (1935–36); *Chamber Music for Young People* for Violin and Piano (1936); Cello Sonata (1936; rev. 1938); Concerto for String Quartet (1936); Quintet for Flute and Piano Quartet (1937); String Trio (1937); Violin Sonatina (1937); 2 piano quartets (1938, 1972); 9 string quartets (1940; 1943–44; 1946; 1951; 1960; 1962; 1963–64; 1964; 1966); 2 violin sonatas (1943–46; 1981); *Canticle* for Violin and Piano (1946); *Perpetual Motion* for Violin and Piano (1946); *Chaconne* for Violin and Piano (1948); Quintet for Clarinet, 2 Violas, and 2 Cellos (1950); Piano Trio (1951); Sonata for Solo Violin (1954–59); Sonata for Solo Cello (1956–59); Wind Quintet (1958); *Night Music* for Accordion and String Quartet (1961); Nonet for 3 Violins, 3 Violas, and 3 Cellos (1961–62); Accordion Sonata (1963); *Introduction and Dance* for Accordion (1966). **PIANO:** *4 Gymnopedies* (1937); Concerto for 2 Pianos (1942); *The Tomb of Melville* (1944–49); Sonata (1947); *A Private World* (1954–59); *Then and Now* (1962); *Alone at the Piano* (1967); *Prelude, Fantasy, and Fugue* (1983).

VOCAL: *2 Elegies* for Voice and String Quartet (1935); *This Is the Garden* for Chorus (1935); *4 Ladies*, song cycle (1935; rev. 1962); *Vocalise* for Voice and Viola (1935); *Paris this April Sunset* for Women's Chorus, Cello, and Double Bass (1937); *3 Madrigals*, after James Joyce, for Chorus (1937); *The Mad Maid's Song* for Voice, Flute, and Harpsichord (1937; rev. 1953); *Somewhere I Have Never Travelled* for Voice and Orch. (1938); *3 Epitaphs*, song cycle (1938); *5 Songs from The Tempest* (1944); *Young Joseph*, after Thomas Mann, for Women's Chorus and String Orch. (1944); *L'Ame de Claude*, song cycle setting extracts from Debussy's letters to Jacques Durand (1949); *The Martyr* for Men's Chorus and Optional Orch. (1950; rev. 1964); *Mizmor L'David*, sacred service for Tenor, Chorus, and Organ (1951); *The Midnight Meditation*, song cycle (1951); *Ahavah*, symphonic eulogy for Male Narrator and Orch. (1954); *2 Anthems* for Chorus (1955); *Prayer for Peace* for Chorus (1960); *This Sacred Ground* for Baritone, Chorus, Children's Chorus, and Orch. (1962); *We Two*, song cycle (1964); *To Music*, choral sym. for Tenor, Bass-baritone, Chorus, and Orch. (1967); *A Secular Cantata* for Tenor, Baritone, Chorus, and Small Orch. (1976; N.Y., Feb. 5, 1977); *A Song for Hope* for 8 Solo Voices and Orch. (1978).

BIBL.: V. Kimberling, *D. D.: A Bio-bibliography* (Metuchen, N.J., 1987); C. Shore, ed., *D. D.: A Musical Celebration* (Stuyvesant, N.Y., 1995).

Dianda, Hilda, Argentine composer; b. Córdoba, April 13, 1925. She studied in Europe with Scherchen and Malipiero; from 1958 to 1962 she worked at Radiodiffusion Française in Paris. Upon returning to Argentina, she devoted herself to composition and organization of concerts of ultramodern music.

WORKS: 3 string quartets (1947, 1960, 1962); Concertante for Cello and Chamber Orch. (1952); Trio for Flute, Oboe, and Bassoon (1953); Wind Quintet (1957); *Díptico* for 16 Instruments (1962); *Núcleos* for String Orch., 2 Pianos, and Percussion (1964); works for various ensembles under the generic titles *Resonancias* and *Ludus* (1964–69).

Dianin, Sergei, Russian writer on music; b. St. Petersburg, Dec. 26, 1888; d. Davidovo, Oct. 26, 1968. A son of Borodin's assistant in chemistry, he became a mathematician by profession; having access to Borodin's archives, he publ. 4 vols. of Borodin's letters (Moscow, 1928, 1936, 1949, 1950) and a vol. devoted to Borodin's life, materials, and documents (Moscow, 1955; 2nd ed., 1960; Eng. tr., 1963).

Dianov, Anton, Russian composer; b. Moscow, Feb. 19, 1882; d. there, March 25, 1939. He was a pupil of the Moscow Cons., graduating in 1912. In 1920 he became director of the Music School in Moscow. He wrote effective piano pieces, music for violin and piano (*Lyrische Fragmente*), and many songs.

Díaz, Justino, noted Puerto Rican bass; b. San Juan, Jan. 29, 1940. He studied at the Univ. of Puerto Rico (1958–59) and at the New England Cons. of Music in Boston (1959–62); he also received training from Frederick Jagel. In 1957 he made his debut as Ben in Menotti's *The Telephone* in San German, Puerto Rico, and in 1961 appeared with the New England Opera Theater in Boston. After winning the Metropolitan Opera Auditions of the Air, he made his debut with the company in N.Y. as Monterone on Oct. 23, 1963; was chosen to create the role of Antony in Barber's *Antony and Cleopatra* at the opening of the new Metropolitan Opera house at Lincoln Center on Sept. 16, 1966. He made guest appearances in Salzburg, Hamburg, Vienna, Munich, Milan, and other European music centers. On Sept. 10, 1971, he appeared in the premiere of Ginastera's *Beatrix Cenci*, which inaugurated the opera house at the Kennedy Center in Washington, D.C. On March 4, 1973, he made his N.Y. City Opera debut as Francesco in the same opera. In 1976 he made his first appearance at London's Covent Garden as Escamillo; appeared there as Jack Rance in 1994 and as Scarpia in 1995. In 1987 he sang Iago in Zeffirelli's film version of *Otello*.

di Bonaventura, Anthony. See **Bonaventura, Anthony di.**

di Bonaventura, Mario. See **Bonaventura, Mario di.**

Dichter, Misha, talented American pianist; b. Shanghai (of Polish-Jewish refugees), Sept. 27, 1945. He was reared in Los Angeles; at the age of 15, he won a contest of the Music Educators National Conference, Western Division. While attending the Univ. of Calif. at Los Angeles, he enrolled in a master class conducted by Rosina Lhévinne; later joined her class at the Juilliard School of Music in N.Y. In 1966 he entered the Tchaikovsky Competition in Moscow and won 2nd prize, scoring popular acclaim among Russian audiences. Returning to the U.S., he made his Boston Sym. Orch. debut as soloist at the Tanglewood Festival in 1966; numerous appearances with major American and European orchs. followed; he also gave recitals. His wife, Cipa (b. Rio de Janeiro, May 20, 1944), is also a fine pianist with whom he often appeared in duo recitals. Dichter's natural predilections lie in the Romantic repertoire; his playing possesses a high emotional appeal; but he also can render full justice to Classical masterpieces.

Dick, Marcel, Hungarian-American violist, conductor, pedagogue, and composer, b. Miskolcz, Aug. 28, 1898; d. Cleveland Heights, Ohio, Dec. 13, 1991. His great-uncle was the prominent Hungarian violinist Eduard Reményi (b. Miskolc, Jan. 17, 1828; d. San Francisco, May 15, 1898). He was a pupil of Joseph Bloch (violin) and Kodály (composition) at the Royal Academy of Music in Budapest. After playing violin in the Budapest Phil., he was 1st violist in the Vienna Sym. Orch. (1924–27); he also played in the Kolisch and Rosé Quartets. In 1934 he settled in the U.S.; after serving as 1st violist in the Detroit Sym. Orch., he held that position with the Cleveland Orch. (1943–49). In 1946 he joined the faculty of the Cleveland Inst. of Music, where he was head of the theory dept. from

1948 until his retirement in 1973. As a composer, he was influenced by the 12-tone system of his friend Schoenberg. Among his works were a Sym. (Cleveland, Dec. 14, 1950), a Sym. for 2 String Orchs. (1964), chamber music, and vocal pieces.

Dickie, Murray, Scottish tenor; b. Bishopton, April 3, 1924; d. Cape Town, June 19, 1995. After studies in Glasgow, he pursued training with Dino Borgioli in London, Stefan Pollmann in Vienna, and Guido Farinelli in Milan. In 1947 he made his operatic debut as Count Almaviva in London, where he appeared at the Cambridge Theatre (1947–49) and at Covent Garden (1949–52). He sang at the Glyndebourne Festivals (1950–54), the Vienna State Opera (from 1951), and the Salzburg Festivals (from 1955). On Oct. 18, 1962, he made his Metropolitan Opera debut in N.Y. as David in *Die Meistersinger von Nürnberg*, remaining on the roster until 1965; he was again on its roster (1966–67; 1970–72). He became well known for his buffo roles.

Dickinson, Clarence, distinguished American organist, pedagogue, and composer; b. Lafayette, Ind., May 7, 1873; d. N.Y., Aug. 2, 1969. After training at Miami Univ in Oxford, Ohio, and at Northwestern Univ. in Chicago, he studied in Berlin and Paris, his principal mentors being Moszkowski (piano), Guilmant (organ) and Pierné (composition). He was organist at St. James's Episcopal Church in Chicago before settling in N.Y. in 1909 as organist at the Brick (Presbyterian) Church; in 1912 he became prof. of church music at the Union Theological Seminary, where he founded its School of Sacred Music in 1928 and served as its director until 1945. With his wife, the writer Helen Adell Dickinson, he publ. the book *Excursions in Musical History* (1917) and ed. a collection of Moravian anthems (1954). He ed. the influential series Historical Recitals for Organ (50 numbers) and a hymnal for the Presbyterian Church (1933), and publ. *Technique and Art of Organ Playing* (1922). Among his compositions were the operas *The Medicine Man* and *Priscilla*; the *Storm King Symphony* for Organ and Orch. (1921); much sacred music, including various anthems; many organ pieces.

Dickinson, George Sherman, American music educator; b. St. Paul, Minn., Feb. 9, 1888; d. Chapel Hill, N.C., Nov. 6, 1964. He studied at Oberlin College (B.A., 1909), the Oberlin Cons. of Music (Mus.Bac., 1910), and Harvard Univ. (M.A., 1912); also studied with Kaun and Juon in Berlin (1913–14). He taught at the Oberlin Cons. of Music from 1914 to 1916 and was a member of the faculty of Vassar College from 1922 to 1953. He wrote *The Growth and Use of Harmony* (vol. 4 of *Fundamentals of Musical Art*; N.Y., 1927); *Classification of Musical Compositions* (Poughkeepsie, 1938); *The Pattern of Music* (Poughkeepsie, 1939); *Music as a Literature: An Outline* (Poughkeepsie, 1953); *The Study of Music as a Liberal Art* (Poughkeepsie, 1953); *The Study of the History of Music in the Liberal Arts College* (N.Y., 1953); *A Handbook of Style in Music* (N.Y., 1965).

Dickinson, Meriel, English mezzo-soprano, sister of **Peter Dickinson**; b. Lytham St. Annes, Lancashire, April 8, 1940. She studied piano and voice in England, and also attended the Vienna Academy of Music. After making her London debut in 1964, she devoted herself mainly to the performance of modern music; her brother toured with her as accompanist, and also composed a number of works for her. In 1986 she made her N.Y. debut in Berio's *Laborintus*.

Dickinson, Peter, English composer, pianist, and teacher, brother of **Meriel Dickinson**; b. Lytham St. Annes, Lancashire, Nov. 15, 1934. After taking his M.S. at Queen's College, Cambridge (1957), he studied with Wagenaar at the Juilliard School of Music in N.Y. (1958–60). He lectured at the College of St. Mark and St. John in London (1962–66). After serving as a music tutor in the extramural dept. of the Univ. of Birmingham (1966–67), he was a lecturer in music on its faculty (1970–74). In 1974 he became the 1st prof. of music at the Univ. of Keele, which position he retained until 1984. He then was a prof. at Goldsmiths' College, Univ. of London, from 1991. He toured widely as accompanist to his sister, for whom he composed various works. As a composer, he was particularly influenced by Satie, ragtime, blues, and jazz. He developed what he described as "style modulation," a layering of serious and popular styles. His interest in literature facilitated his preparation of deft settings of vocal texts.

WRITINGS: Ed. *Twenty British Composers* (London, 1975); *The Music of Lennox Berkeley* (London, 1988).

WORKS: ORCH.: *Monologue* for Strings (1959); *5 Diversions* (1969); *Transformations* (Cheltenham, July 3, 1970); Organ Concerto (Gloucester, Aug. 22, 1971); Concerto for Strings, Percussion, and Electronic Organ (1971); Piano Concerto (1978–84; Cheltenham, July 22, 1984); Violin Concerto (1986; Leeds, Jan. 31, 1987); *Jigsaws* (1988); *Merseyside Echoes* (1988). **CHAMBER:** 2 string quartets: No. 1 (1958; rev. 1974) and No. 2 with Tape or Piano (1975); *Juilliard Dances* for 8 Instruments (1959); Violin Sonata (1961); *Baroque Trio* for Flute, Oboe, and Harpsichord (1962); *Music* for Oboe and Chamber Organ (1962); *4 Duos* for Flute or Oboe and Cello (1962; rev. 1978); *Fanfares and Elegies* for 3 Trumpets, 3 Trombones, and Organ (1967); *Translations* for Recorder, Viola da Gamba, and Harpsichord (1971); *Recorder Music* for Recorder and Tape or 2 Recorders (1973); *Solo for Baryton* with Tape and Viola da Gamba or 2nd Baryton (1976); *Aria* for Horn, Oboe, Clarinet, and Bassoon (1977); *Hymns, Rags, and Blues* for Violin, Clarinet, and Piano (1985); *London Rags* for 2 Trumpets, Horn, Trombone, and Tuba (1986). **PIANO:** *Piano Variations* (1957; renamed *Vitalitas Variations*); *Paraphase II* (1967); *Rags, Blues, and Parodies* (1970–86); *Sonatas* for Piano and Tape (1987). **VOCAL: CHORAL:** *4 Hopkins Poems*, with Soprano, Baritone, and Organ (1960–64); *Martin of Tours*, with Tenor, Baritone, Chamber Organ, and Piano Duet (1966); *The Dry Heart* (1967); *Outcry*, with Contralto and Orch. (1969); *Late Afternoon in November* for 16 Solo Voices (1975). **SACRED:** *Jesus Christ Is Risen Today* for Chorus (1955); 2 motets (1963); *Magnificat and Nunc Dimittis* for Voices and Organ (1963); *Mass* (1965); *A Mass of the Apocalypse* for Chorus, Speaker, Percussion, and Piano (London, July 15, 1984). **OTHER VOCAL:** *Elegy* for Countertenor, Cello, and Harpsichord (1966); *Winter Afternoons*, cantata for 6 Solo Voices and Double Bass (1970); *Surrealist Landscape* for High Voice, Piano, and Tape (1973); *Lust* for Voices and Optional Tape (1974); *A Memory of David Munrow* for 2 Countertenors, 2 Recorders, Viola da Gamba, and Harpsichord (1977); *Reminiscences* for Mezzo-soprano, Saxophone, and Piano (1978); *The Unicorns* for Soprano and Brass Band (1982); *Larkin's Jazz* for Speaker-Singer and Chamber Group (1989); numerous songs with keyboard accompaniment.

Di Domenica, Robert (Anthony), American composer, flutist, and teacher; b. N.Y., March 4, 1927. He studied music education at N.Y. Univ. (B.S., 1951), composition with Riegger and Josef Schmid, and flute with Harold Bennett (1949–55). He was a flutist with various orchs. and ensembles, and also taught flute. In 1969 he joined the faculty of the New England Cons. of Music in Boston, where he was an assoc. dean (1973–76) and dean (1976–78), and then a teacher of theory and composition (from 1978). In 1972 he held a Guggenheim fellowship. In 1994 the Robert Di Domenica Collection was completed at the Library of Congress in Washington, D.C. In his works, he follows a serial course while utilizing such diverse elements as jazz and American popular music.

WORKS: OPERAS: *The Balcony* (1972; Boston, June 16, 1990); *The Scarlet Letter* (1986); *Beatrice Cenci* (1993). **ORCH.:** Sym. (1961; Boston, Nov. 15, 1972); Concerto for Violin and Chamber Orch. (1962; N.Y., April 15, 1965); 2 piano concertos (1963, 1982); Concerto for Wind Quintet, Strings, and Timpani (1964; Boston, May 7, 1981); *Music* for Flute and Strings (1967; Boston, Nov. 16, 1980); *Variations on a Theme by Gunther Schuller* for Chamber Orch. (1983; Boston, Dec. 11, 1984); *Dream Journeys* (1984; Plymouth, Mass., Oct. 5, 1985); *Variations and Soliloquies* (1988); *Gone Are the Rivers and Eagles*

(1992). **CHAMBER:** Sextet for Wind Quintet and Piano (1957); Flute Sonata (1957); Quartet for Flute, Violin, Horn, and Piano (1959); Quartet for Flute, Violin, Viola, and Cello (1960); String Quartet (1960); *Variations on a Tonal Theme* for Flute (1961); Wind Quintet with Soprano Voice (1963); Quintet for Clarinet and String Quartet (1965); Trio for Flute, Bassoon, and Piano (1966); Violin Sonata (1966); *Saeculum aureum* for Flute, Piano, and Tape (1967); Alto Saxophone Sonata (1968); *Music for Stanzs* for Flute, Clarinet, Bassoon, Horn, and Tape (1981). **PIANO:** Sonatina (1958); *4 Movements* (1959); *11 Short Pieces* (1973); *Improvisations* (1974); *The Art of the Row* (1989; Boston, Dec. 12, 1990). **VOCAL:** *The First Kiss of Love* for Soprano and Piano (1960); *4 Short Songs* for Soprano and 6 Instruments (1975); *Black Poems* for Baritone, Piano, and Tape (1976); *Songs from Twelfth Night* for Tenor, Flute, Viola da Gamba, and Harpsichord (1976); *Sonata after Essays for Piano* for Soprano, Baritone, Piano, Flute, and Tape (1977; also as *Concord Revisited* for Soprano, Baritone, Piano, Chamber Orch., and Tape, 1978); *Arrangements* for Soprano, 6 Instruments, and Tape (1979); *The Holy Colophon* for Soprano, Tenor, Chorus, and Orch. (1980; Boston, Oct. 11, 1983); *Hebrew Melodies* for Soprano, Violin, and Piano (1983).

Didur, Adamo, famous Polish bass; b. Wola Sekowa, near Sanok, Galicia, Dec. 24, 1874; d. Katowice, Jan. 7, 1946. He studied with Wysocki in Lemberg and Emmerich in Milan, where he made his concert debut in 1894; later that year he made his operatic debut as Méphistophélès in Rio de Janeiro. He sang at the Warsaw Opera (1899–1903), Milan's La Scala (1903–06), London's Covent Garden (1905), and Buenos Aires's Teatro Colón (1905–08). On Nov. 4, 1907, he made an auspicious N.Y. debut as Alvise at the Manhattan Opera; his Metropolitan Opera debut followed as Ramfis on Nov. 16, 1908, and he remained on its roster as one of its leading artists until 1932. He then returned to Poland; his appointment as director of the Warsaw Opera in 1939 was aborted by the outbreak of World War II. He later settled in Katowice as a voice teacher, founding an opera company (1945) and becoming director of the Cons. His portrayals of Leporello and Boris Godunov were particularly memorable.

Diemer, Emma Lou, American composer, keyboard player, and teacher; b. Kansas City, Mo., Nov. 24, 1927. She was a pupil of Donovan and Hindemith at Yale Univ. (B.M., 1949; M.M., 1950), of Toch and Sessions at the Berkshire Music Center in Tanglewood (summers, 1954, 1955), and of Rogers, Hanson, and Craighead at the Eastman School of Music in Rochester, N.Y. (Ph.D., 1960). She was composer-in-residence for the Ford Foundation Young Composers Project in Arlington, Va. (1959–61) and also on the faculties of the Univ. of Maryland (1965–70) and the Univ. of Calif. at Santa Barbara (1971–91). From 1990 she was composer-in-residence of the Santa Barbara Sym. Orch. In 1992 she won a Kennedy Center Friedheim Award.

WORKS: ORCH.: 4 syms. (1953; 1955; *On American Indian Themes*, 1959; *Symphonie antique*, 1961); 2 piano concertos (1953, 1991); Concerto for Harpsichord and Chamber Orch. (1958); *Pavane* for Strings (1959); *Youth Overture* (1959); *Rondo Concertante* (1960); *Festival Overture* (1961); Flute Concerto (1963); *Fairfax Festival Overture* (1967); *Concert Piece* for Organ and Orch. (1977); *Winter Day* (1982); Trumpet Concerto (1983; rev. as a violin concerto, 1983); *Suite of Homages* (1985); *Serenade* for Strings (1988); Marimba Concerto (1990); *Santa Barbara Overture* (1995). **BAND:** *Brass Menagerie*, suite (1960); *La Rag* (1981). **CHAMBER:** Violin Sonata (1949); Piano Quartet (1954); Flute Sonata (1958); Woodwind Quintet No. 1 (1960); Sextet for Piano and Woodwind Quintet (1962); Toccata for Flute Chorus (1968); *Music* for Woodwind Quartet (1972); Trio for Flute, Oboe, Harpsichord, and Tape (1973); *Pianoharpsichordorgan* for 1 or 3 Performers (1974); *Movement* for Flute, Oboe, Clarinet, and Piano (1976); *Quadralogue* for Flute Quartet (1978); *Summer of 82* for Cello and Piano (1982); String Quartet No. 1 (1987); *Catch-A-Turian* for Violin and Piano (1988; also for Flute and Piano, 1994); *Laudate* for Trumpet and Organ (1990); *A Quiet, Lovely Piece* for Clarinet and Piano (1991); Sextet for Flute, Oboe, Clarinet, Violin, Cello, and Piano (1992); piano pieces; organ music. **OTHER:** Choral works; songs; electronic scores.

Diepenbrock, Alphons (Johannes Maria), eminent Dutch composer; b. Amsterdam, Sept. 2, 1862; d. there, April 5, 1921. He received training in piano, violin, and voice. As a composer, he was autodidact, having made a thorough study of 16th-century Netherlands polyphony, Beethoven's late string quartets, and Wagner's music. He pursued his education at the Univ. of Amsterdam, where he studied classical literature (graduated, 1888, with a thesis on Seneca). After teaching classics at the 's-Hertogenbosch grammar school, he returned to Amsterdam in 1894 as a private teacher of Latin and Greek. He also pursued his career as a composer, eventually developing a personal style in which Wagnerian elements were entertwined with impressionistic modalities à la Debussy (from 1910). Diepenbrock was a notable composer of sacred music, creating such outstanding works as the *Missa in die festo* (1891) and the *Te Deum* (1897). Among his other distinguished vocal works were the 2 *Hymnen an die Nacht* (1899) and *Die Nacht* (1911). His incidental scores were also noteworthy. He left a number of incomplete MSS at his death. E. Reeser ed. his letters and documents as *Alphons Dieprenbrock: Brieven en documenten* (4 vols., Amsterdam, 1962–74).

WORKS: INCIDENTAL MUSIC TO: Verhagen's *Marsyas* (1910); J. van der Vondel's *Gijsbrecht van Aemstel* (1912); Aristophanes's *The Birds* (1917); Goethe's *Faust* (1918); Sophocles's *Electra* (1920). **ORCH.:** *Akademische feestmarsch* (1882; orchestrated by C. Dopper); *Hymne* for Violin and Orch. (1917); ballet suite (1918). **VOCAL:** *5 Gesänge nach Goethe* for Chorus (1884); *Avenue Maria* for Voice and Piano or Organ (1889); *Jesu dulcis memoria* for Voice and Piano or Organ (1890); *Missa in die festo* for Chorus and Organ (1891; Kyrie and Gloria orchestrated, 1913); *Les elfes* for Chorus and Orch. (1896); *Caelestis urbs Jerusalem, Stabat mater dolorosa,* and *Stabat mater speciosa* for Chorus (1897); *Te Deum* for Soli, Chorus, and Orch. (1897); *Wenige wissen das Geheimnis der Liebe* for Voice and Organ (1898; also for Soprano, Wind Quintet, and Double Bass, 1915); *Wenn ich nur hae* for Voice and Organ (1898); *2 Hymnen an die Nacht* for Voice and Orch. (1899); *Carmen saeculare* for Chorus (1901); *Tantum ergo* for Chorus and Organ (1901); *Vondel's vaart naar Agrippina* for Voice and Orch. (1903); *Den uil* for Chorus (1903); *Christus is opgestanden* for Chorus (1903); *De grote hone en de kleine kat* for Chorus (1903); *Im grossen Schweigen* for Baritone and Orch. (1906); *Veni creator Spiritus* for Chorus (1906); *Hymnus de Sanctu Spiritu* for Chorus and Organ (1906); *Hymne aan Rembrandt* for Chorus and Orch. (1906); *Die Nacht* for Alto and Orch. (1911); *Berceuse* for Mezzo-soprano, Cello, and Piano (1912); *Bruiloftslied* for Soprano, Alto, Oboe, Triangle, Violin, Viola, and Cello (1912); *Lydische Nacht* for Voice and Orch. (1913); *Ecce guomodo moritur* for Chorus (1913); *Come raggio di sol* for Soprano and Wind Quintet (1917); many solo songs.

BIBL.: E. Reeser, "A. D.," *Sonorum speculum*, XII (1962).

Dieren, Bernard van, Dutch-English composer and writer; b. Rotterdam, Dec. 27, 1887; d. London, April 24, 1936. He began playing the violin at an early age but later pursued his enthusiasm for literature and science. As a composer, he was self-taught. In 1909 he settled in 1909 in England, where he devoted much time to writing criticism for continental newspapers and magazines. Among his writings were a study of the sculptor Jacob Epstein (London, 1920) and an interesting collection of essays, *Down Among the Dead Men* (London, 1935). As a composer, he developed a highly personal style of harmonic and contrapuntal complexity.

WORKS: OPERA: *The Tailor* (1917). **ORCH.:** *Elegy* for Cello and Orch. (1908); *Beatrice Cenci* (1909); Overture (1916); *Serenade* for Small Orch. (c.1923); *Anjou*, overture (1935); Sym. (unfinished). **CHAMBER:** *Canzonetta* for Violin and Piano (c.1907); *Impromptu Fantasiestück* for Violin (1909); 6 string quartets (1912, 1917, 1918, 1923, 1927, 1928); *Sonata tyroica* for Violin and Piano (1913); Sonata for Solo Cello (1929); *Duettino* for 2 Violins (1933); Sonata for Solo Violin (1935). **PIANO:** *6 Sketches* (1911); *Toccata* (1912); *12 Netherlands Melodies* (1918); *Tema con variazione* (1928). **VOCAL:** *Balsazar* for Chorus and Orch. (1908); *Chinese Symphony* for 5 Soli, Chorus, and Orch. (1914); *Diaphonia* for Baritone and Chamber Orch. (1916); *2 Poems* for Speaker and String Quartet (1917); *2 Songs* for Baritone and String Quartet (1917); *Les propous des beuveurs* for Chorus and Orch. (1921); *Sonetto VII of Edmund Spenser's Amoretti* for Tenor and Chamber Orch. (1921); various other songs.

BIBL.: E. Davis, "B. v.D.," *Musical Quarterly* (April 1938); A. Chisolm, *B. v.D.: An Introduction* (London, 1984); H. Davies, "B. v.D. (1887–1936)," *Musical Times* (Dec. 1987); idem, "B. v.D., Philip Heseltine and Cecil Gray: A Significant Affiliation," *Music & Letters* (Jan. 1988).

Diether, Jack, Canadian-American musicologist; b. Vancouver, British Columbia, Feb. 26, 1919; d. N.Y., Jan. 22, 1987. He was educated at the Univ. of British Columbia. He served in the Canadian army and air force during World War II. In 1955 he settled in the U.S.; was employed at the Pickwick Bookshop in Hollywood and at G. Schirmer's music store in N.Y. In the meantime, he wrote for music journals, concentrating on the clarification of obscure periods in the lives and works of Bruckner and Mahler; contributed valuable articles to the journal of the Bruckner Soc. of America, *Chord and Discord*, of which he became ed. in 1969; also wrote annotations for orch. programs and phonograph records. From 1975 to 1987 he was music critic of N.Y.'s *The Westsider*.

Di Giuseppe, Enrico, American tenor; b. Philadelphia, Oct. 14, 1932. He was a pupil of Richard Bonelli at the Curtis Inst. of Music in Philadelphia and of Hans Heinz at the Juilliard School of Music in N.Y. In 1959 he made his operatic debut as Massenet's Des Grieux in New Orleans; then toured with the Metropolitan Opera National Co. On March 18, 1965, he made his first appearance at the N.Y. City Opera as Michele in Menotti's *The Saint of Bleecker Street*; he then sang there regularly from 1967 to 1981. He made his Metropolitan Opera debut in N.Y. as Turiddu on June 20, 1970, where he later sang many Italian and French roles. He also sang opera in other major U.S. operatic centers and toured as a concert artist. Among his finest portrayals were Mozart's Ferrando and Almaviva, Bellini's Pollione, Verdi's Alfredo, Massenet's Werther, and Puccini's Pinkerton.

Dijk, Jan van, Dutch pianist, teacher, and composer; b. Oostzaan, June 4, 1918. He studied composition with Pijper in Rotterdam (1936–46); gave piano recitals; taught at the Brabant Cons. in Tilburg from its founding in 1955, and at the Royal Cons. of Music in The Hague from 1961. A prolific composer, he wrote hundreds of works. He also produced music in the 31-tone system devised by the Dutch physicist Adriaan Fokker.

WORKS: OPERAS: *Flying Dutchman* (1953); *Protesilaus and Laodamia* (1968). **ORCH.:** Concertino for Flute, Piano, Percussion, and Strings (1938); 3 sinfoniettas (1940, 1952, 1956); *Cassatio* for Strings and Piano obbligato (1943); 8 syms. (1944–92); *Capriccio* for Viola and Orch. (1946); 4 piano concertinos (1948–49; 1953; 1966; 1966); Concertino for 2 Pianos and String or Wind Orch. (1949); *Suite pastorale* for Oboe, English Horn, and Small Orch. (1953); *3 Suites da Sonar* (1954, 1955, 1958); *Cortège en Rondeau* (1955); Saxophone Concertino (1956); *Toccata* for Strings (1957); Concertino for Recorder and Chamber Orch. (1958); *Serenade* for Winds, Percussion, and Piano (1959); *4 Bagatelles* (1960); Concertino for Accordion and Strings (1960); Dance Suite for Orch. and Jazz Combo (1961); *17 Projections* (1962); Double Bass Concerto (1962); *Salon symphonique* (1963); Concerto for Piano, 4-hands, and Small Orch. (1963); *Contrasts* for Orch. and Jazz Combo (1964); *Décorations et décompositions* (1964); *Duetto accompagnato* for Saxophone, Trombone, and Strings (1964); 2 serenades for Small Orch. (1966, 1970); *Jardin public* for Flute and Orch. (1967); Triple Concerto for Flute, Recorder, Harpsichord, and Orch. (1968); *Makedonski* for Chamber Orch. (1969); *2 Résumés* for Piano and Small Orch. (1970); *Touch after Finish* for Trumpet, Organ, Piano, and Strings (1971); *Fantaisie* for Double Bass and Orch. (1972); *About* (1973); *Kleine Concertante* for 2 Flutes and Chamber Orch. (1974); *Affiche pour la réouverture du magasin* (1974); *Accomplishement* for Small Orch. (1975); *Sinfonia e Fughetta* (1976); *Parties sur l'amitié* (1977); Pianola Concerto (1978); *5 Miniatures* (1986–91). **CHAMBER:** 5 string quartets (1940, 1941, 1942, 1965, 1974); *Divertimento* for Clarinet, Viola, and Cello (1941); Septet (1949–50); Piano Trio (1950); *Divertimento* for 2 Violins and Cello (1951); Duo for Cello and Piano (1953); Cello Sonatina (1953); Violin Sonatina (1953); Saxophone Sonata (1953); Sonatina for Violin and Piano (1954); *Serenade* for Trumpet and Horn (1955); Suite for 2 Flutes and Piano (1957); 2 sonatas for Solo Flute (1961, 1966); *Musica sacra I* for 2 Violins, Viola, and Organ (1966), *II* for Flute, Cello, and Piano (1968), and *III* for Clarinet, Violin, and Piano (1975); *Musique à trois* for Flute, Recorder, and Harpsichord (1967); Sonata for Solo Violin (1968); *Quintetto* for Mandolin, Bass Clarinet, Percussion, Organ, and Piano (1969); *4 Caprices* for Accordion (1969); *Pet* for Flute, Saxophone, Trumpet, Violin, and Double Bass (1973); *Concertino à 3* for Flute, Violin and Viola (1975). **PIANO:** Sonata (1942); 18 sonatinas (1944–74); Rondino (1955); Sonatina for Piano, 4-hands (1956); *2 Kantieks* (1964, 1976); *Couple* (1969); *Something* for 2 Piano Players (1969); *Partita piccola* (1970); *Alba Communis* (1973); *3 Inventions* (1976). **31-TONE PIECES:** *7 Pieces* for Organ (1948); *Musica per organo trentunisono I* for 31-tone Organ (1950–51) and *II*, 7 pieces for 31-tone Organ (1957); Concertino for Trombone, Violin, and Cello (1961). **VOCAL:** *Jaergetijde* for Chorus and Orch. (1944); *Het masker van den Rooden Dood* for Narrator and Chamber Orch. (1952); *Zwartbaard* for Men's Chorus and Orch. (1953); *De Kommandeur* for Soloists, Narrator, Boys' Chorus, and String Quartet or String Orch. (1958); *Heer en Knecht*, cantata (1963); *Coornhert*, cantata (1964); *Quodlibet* for Chorus and Orch. (1967); *Pros romaious*, cantata (1968); *Ars vivendi* for Chorus and Orch. (1977); *Onbeduidende polka en twee wiegeliedjes* for Chorus and Orch. (1985); *Nijmegen, Nijmegen* for Chorus and Orch. (1985).

Diller, Angela, American pianist and pedagogue; b. Brooklyn, Aug. 1, 1877; d. Stamford, Conn., April 30, 1968. She studied music at Columbia Univ. with MacDowell and Goetschius; also with Johannes Schreyer in Dresden. From 1899 to 1916 she was head of the theory dept. of the Music School Settlement in N.Y.; from 1916 to 1921, was an administrator at the David Mannes School in N.Y.; then director of the Diller-Quaile School of Music in N.Y. (1921–41); also was on the faculty of the Univ. of Southern Calif. in Los Angeles (1932), Mills College in Oakland, California (1935), and the New England Cons. of Music in Boston (1936–37). She was co-founder, with Margarethe Dessoff, of the Adesdi Chorus and A Cappella Singers of N.Y. With E. Quaile, K. Stearns Page, and Harold Bauer, she ed. many educational music works. In 1953 she received a Guggenheim fellowship. She publ. *First Theory Book* (1921), *Keyboard Harmony Course* (4 vols., 1936, 1937, 1943, 1949), and *The Splendor of Music* (1957).

Dilling, Mildred, noted American harpist and teacher; b. Marion, Ind., Feb. 23, 1894; d. N.Y., Dec. 30, 1982. She studied with Louise Schellschmidt-Koehne and later, in Paris, with Henriette Renie. After her concert debut in Paris (1911), she played in N.Y. (1913) with the Madrigal Singers of the MacDowell Chorus; appeared in joint recitals in Europe with de Reszkes and Yvette Guilbert, and in the U.S. with Alma Gluck and Frances Alda; toured the U.S. and Great Britain many times; also made concert tours in South America, the Middle East, and the Orient. She had numerous private pupils who became well-known harp players; her most famous student was the comedian Harpo Marx. She cultivated calluses on her fingers to achieve sonority. Dilling was the owner of a large collection of harps which she acquired in different parts of the world. She publ. *Old Tunes for New Harpists* (1934) and *30 Little Classics for the Harp* (1938).

BIBL.: E. Kahn, Jr., "The Harp Lady," *New Yorker* (Feb. 3, 1940).

Dillon, Fannie Charles, American pianist and composer; b. Denver, March 16, 1881; d. Altadena, Calif., Feb. 21, 1947. She studied at Claremont College in Pomona, California, and in Berlin (1900–06) with Godowsky, Kaun, and Urban; later in N.Y. with Rubin Goldmark. She made her debut as a pianist in 1908; taught at Pomona College (1910–13), and from 1918 to 1941 in Los Angeles high schools. Her orch. works included *Celebration of Victory* (1918), *The Cloud* (1918), *The Alps* (1920), and *Chinese Symphonic Suite* (1936); she also wrote piano pieces, including the popular *Birds at Dawn* (1917).

Dillon, Henri, French composer; b. Angers, Oct. 9, 1912; d. in combat in Indochina on July 9, 1954. He studied at the Military School in St.-Cyr; was in the army during World War II. He was largely self-taught in music, and adopted a classical style of composition, derived mainly from the melodic patterns of French folk songs.

WORKS: ORCH.: Cello Concerto (1949); Violin Concerto (1949); *Arlequin*, divertimento for Strings (1949); Viola Concerto (1952); Concerto for 2 Trumpets and Orch. (1953). **CHAMBER:** Saxophone Sonata (1949); Violin Sonata (1952); Concerto for 2 Pianos (Paris, Dec. 15, 1952); *Cassation* for 12 Wind Instruments (1953); various works for piano, including a Sonata (1953).

Dillon, James, Scottish composer; b. Glasgow, Oct. 29, 1950. He attended the Glasgow School of Art (1967–68) and the Polytechnic of Central London (1972–73); then studied acoustics, music, and linguistics at the Polytechnic of North London (1973–76). He was active at the summer courses in new music in Darmstadt (1982, 1984, 1986, 1988). In 1986 he pursued research in computer music at IRCAM in Paris and was a visiting lecturer at the State Univ. of N.Y. in Stony Brook. In 1986–87 he was a lecturer at Goldsmith's College, Univ. of London. As a composer, Dillon was largely autodidact. In his music, he pursued a course marked by diversity and complexity.

WORKS: ORCH.: *Windows and Canopies* (1985); *Überschreiten* (1986); *helle Nacht* (1986–87); *La femme invisible* for Chamber Orch. (1989); *Introitus* for 12 Strings, Tape, and Live Electronics (1989–90); *L'oeuvre au noir* for Chamber Orch. and Live Electronics (1990); *Ignis noster* (1991–92); *Vernal Showers* for Violin and Chamber Orch. (1992); *Blitzschlag* for Flute and Orch. (1994). **CHAMBER:** *Crossing Over* for Clarinet (1978); *Ti˘re-Ti˘ke-Dha* for Drummer (1979); *. . . Once Upon a Time* for 8 Instruments (1980); *Who do you love* for Flute, Clarinet, Woman's Voice, Percussion, Violin, and Cello (1980–81); *Parjanya-Vata* for Cello (1981); *Come live with me* for Flute, Oboe, Mezzo-soprano, Piano, and Percussion (1981); *East 11th St. N.Y. 10003* for 6 Percussionists (1982); 2 string quartets (1983, 1991); *Zone (. . . de azul)* for 8 Instruments (1983); *Le Rivage* for Flute, Oboe, Clarinet, Horn, and Bassoon (1984); *Sgothan* for Flute (1984); *Diffraction* for Piccolo (1984); *Shrouded Mirrors* for Guitar (1988); *Del Cuatro Elemento* for Violin (1988): *L'ECRAN parfum* for 6 Violins and 3 Percussionists (1988); *éileadh sguaibe* for 9 Instrumentalists and Live Electronics (1990); Trio for Violin, Viola, and Cello (1990–91); *Siorram* for Viola (1992); *Lumen naturae* for Violin, Viola, and Cello (1992). **PIANO:** *Dillug-Kefitsab* (1976); *Spleen* (1980). **VOCAL:** *Evening Rain* for Voice (1981); *A Roaring Flame* for Woman's Voice and Double Bass (1981–82); *(Time Lag Zerø)* for Woman's Voice and Viola (1982); *L'évolution du vol* for Woman's Voice, Clarinet, 2 Percussionists, Piano, and Double Bass (1993); *Viriditas* for 16 Solo Voices (1993); *Oceanos* for 16 Voices, Orch., and Electronics (1994).

Dimas de Melo Pimenta, Emanuel, Brazilian composer, architect, and urban planner; b. São Paulo, June 3, 1957. He studied at the Braz Cubas Univ. in São Paulo (degree in architecture and urbanism, 1985); in 1986 he settled in Lisbon, where he began and quickly aborted postgraduate studies in art history at the Universidade Nova; also studied Zen techniques of composition, gagaku, rāgas, and occidental music with Koellreutter, and learned to play alto and soprano flutes; in 1993 he completed an M.B.A. degree at the European Univ. His compositions, in particular the tape works, represent an eclectic incorporation of unusual source materials and utilization of novel compositional methods; from the 1970s he applied computer technologies and from the mid-1980s both Virtual Reality and Cyperspace technologies to both music and architecture. His career has spanned the arts to include graphic and urban design, photography, and creative writing; he publ. 2 highly creative theoretical treatises, *Tapas: Architecture and the Unconscious* (São Paulo, 1985) and *Virtual Architecture* (England, 1991); among his important articles is "How Many Senses Do We Need?," *Art and Technology* (Calouste Gulbenkian Foundation, Lisbon, 1993). Exhibits of his graphic scores have been shown at the São Paulo Cultural Centre (1984), the Calouste Gulbenkian Foundation in Lisbon (1987), the Bibliothèque Nationale de Paris (1993), the Computer Art Museum in Seattle (1993), and the National Gallery of Budapest (1994). Several of his musical scores were commissioned by the Merce Cunningham Dance Company, including *Microcosmos* (1993–95).

WORKS: ACOUSTIC: *Spheres* for Large Ensemble (1981); *Cantos* for Ensemble (1982); *Quartet 1* for Bass Clarinet, Tenor Saxophone, Clarinet, and Flute (1984) and *2* for Piano, Flute, Clarinet, and Cello (1984); *Concert* for 2 Musicians and 1 Piano (1985). **ELECTROACOUSTIC:** *Spheres III* for Ensemble and Tape (1981–82); *O vazio deita as unhas de fora e morde no veu estendido a beira da imagem* for Chorus, Percussion, Keyboards, and Tape (1982); *Frankenstern*, minimal opera for 20 TV Sets, Videos, Soprano, 2 Mezzo-sopranos, Baritone, Piano, and Tape (São Paulo, Dec. 12, 1984); *20 TV Sets and a Priest* for 20 TV Sets and Tape (1984); *A Bao a Qu* for Ensemble, Synthesizers, Video Score, and Tape (1985); *Concert for Only 1 Cricket*, with Brazilian forest sounds (1986); *Factory* for 2 Tenors and Tape, based on a fragment from Mozart's *Don Giovanni* (1986–87). **MAGNETIC TAPE:** *Emiedrico* (1981); *La Mer* (1984; also an acoustic version, 1985); *Airports*, environmental piece using white noise (1984); *Spaces* (1984); *Short Waves 1985*, utilizing radio emissions (1985), and *SBb(r)* (1986), both for the Merce Cunningham Dance Co.; *On Bartók*, based on the 1st movement of Bartók's *Music for Strings, Percussion, and Celesta* (1986); *Stones*, using indigenous Brazilian instruments (1988). **DIGITAL TAPE:** *Music from 144 Voices* (1987); *Webern Variation* (1987); *Sun*, using the structure of the sound waves from the sun (1987); *Plan*, using sound particles of medieval instruments from 8th- to 11th-century Islamic music from Andalusia, structured on patterns first used by Palestrina (1987); *Twilight*, based on gagaku music (1987); *wHALLtz*, using 32 loudspeakers from 3 structural fragments of J. Strauss, Jr.'s *Kaiserwalzer* (1987); *Crossing Over* (1988); *Beethoven Quartet*, based on a fragment from Beethoven's Quartet, op. 130 (1988); *Strange Loopings*, following Kurt Gödel's theorem (1988); *Musak*, "kitsch music" for supermarkets, elevators, shopping centers, postal centers, etc. (1988); *Constellations* for 4 or 20 Computer-controlled Marimbas (2 versions; 1989); *Dipak*, based on an ancient North Indian evening rāga (1989); *Finnegans* for Voice and Computer (1989); *Music for Nothing*, "constructed from a graphical complex drawn from the frontiers of chaos" (1989); *Gravity Sound Waves and Gravitational Sounds*, based on Michel Henon's attractor (both 1990); *Microcosmos*, created from micro-particles of a ferrous mineral (1993–95).

Dimitrova, Ghena, Bulgarian soprano; b. Beglj, May 6, 1941. She studied with Christo Brumbarov at the Bulgarian State Cons. in Sofia; then sang with the Sofia Opera. After winning 1st prize in the Sofia Competition in 1970, she scored a major success as Amelia in *Un ballo in maschera* in Parma (1972); subsequently held engagements in France, Spain, South America, Moscow, Vienna, and Rome. In 1983 she made her London debut in a concert performance of *La Gioconda*; later that year she appeared as Turandot at Milan's La Scala. In 1984 she sang at N.Y.'s Carnegie Hall and at the Salzburg Festival; later operatic roles included Turandot at London's Covent Garden (1985) and Leonora in *Il Trovatore* at the San Francisco Opera (1986). On Dec. 14, 1987, she made her Metropolitan Opera debut in N.Y. as Turandot. In 1992 she appeared as Leonora in *La Forza del Destino* in Naples. Among her other roles were Aida, Norma, Santuzza, and Tosca.

Dimov, Bojidar, Bulgarian composer; b. Lom, Jan. 31, 1935. He studied composition with Veselin Stoyanov in Sofia and with Karl Schiske in Vienna. In 1968 he settled in Cologne, where he founded a group for promotion of new music called Trial and Error. His compositions followed the experimental method symbolized by the name of this group, striving to obtain a pragmatic modern style and technique.

WORKS: *Incantations I–III* for Soprano and Chamber Orch. (1963–69); *Komposition I* for Piano (1963), *II* for String Quartet (1964), and *III* for Orch. (1967–68); *Continuum: Trauerminuten für Dana Kosanova* for Chamber Orch., commemorating a 15-year-old Czech girl student killed in the course of the Soviet invasion of Czechoslovakia in 1968 (Graz, Oct. 25, 1969); *Raumspiel* for Piano and Chamber Orch. (1969); *Symphonies* for Voice and Chamber Orch. (1970); *Dual* for 7 Instruments (1971).

Dimov, Ivan, Bulgarian composer; b. Kazanlak, Dec. 13, 1927. He studied composition with Goleminov at the Bulgarian State Cons. in Sofia, graduating in 1953; then took courses in advanced composition at the Moscow Cons.

WORKS: DRAMATIC: OPERAS: *They Have Stolen the Council* (1966); *The Emigrant* (1973). **BALLET:** *Laughter of Africa* (1966). **OTHER:** *Pieces* for Oboe and Piano (1955); *Kardjalii*, dance drama for Orch. (1959); Violin Concertino (1961); *Dramatic Poem* for Orch. (1964); String Quartet (1971); *Miniatures* for Piano (1973); choruses; songs.

D'Indy, Vincent. See **Indy, Vincent d'.**

Dinerstein, Norman (Myron), American music educator and composer; b. Springfield, Mass., Sept. 18, 1937; d. Cincinnati, Dec. 23, 1982. He studied at Boston Univ. (B.M., 1960), the Hartt College of Music in Hartford, Conn. (M.M., 1963), and Princeton Univ. (Ph.D., 1974); also took courses at the Berlin Hochschule für Musik (1962–63), the Berkshire Music Center in Tanglewood (summers, 1962, 1963), and in Darmstadt (1964). He was then on the faculties of Princeton Univ. (1965–66), the New England Cons. of Music in Boston (1968–69; 1970–71), Hartt College (1971–76), and the Univ. of Cincinnati College-Cons. of Music (1976–81), where he was dean (1981–82).

WORKS: *4 Movements* for 3 Woodwind Instruments (1961); *Terzetto* for Brass Trio (1961); *Cassation* for Orch. (1963); *Serenade* for Oboe, Clarinet, Harp, Violin, and Cello (1963); *Schir ha Schirim* for Chorus and Orch. (1963); *Intermezzo* for Orch. (1964); *Pezzi piccoli* for Flute and Viola (1966); *Contrasto* for Orch. (1968); *Sequoia* for Jazz Ensemble (1969); *Refrains* for Orch. (1971); *The Answered Question* for Wind Ensemble (1972); *Songs of Remembrance* for Soprano and Strings (1976–79); *Tubajubalee* for Tuba Ensemble (1978);*Golden Bells* for Chorus and Orch. (1980–82; completed by M. Schelle); also choral music; song cycles; piano pieces.

Dineşcu, Violeta, Romanian-born German composer, teacher, and writer on music; b. Bucharest, July 13, 1953. She studied at the Bucharest Cons. (B.A. in composition, piano, and pedagogy, 1977; M.A. in composition, 1978). After teaching at the George Enescu Music School in Bucharest (1978–82), she settled in West Germany and in 1989 became a naturalized German citizen. From 1987 to 1990 she taught at the Heidelberg Cons. for Church Music, and from 1989 to 1991 at the Frankfurt am Main Cons. In 1990 she joined the faculty of the Bayreuth Academy of Music. She contributed articles on music to publs. in Europe and the U.S. In her compositions, melodic and rhythmic elements are complemented by a concern for mathematical exactitude, the exploration of sound potentials, and the utilization of electronic instruments.

WORKS: DRAMATIC: OPERAS: *Hunger and Thirst*, chamber opera (1985; Freiburg-im-Breisgau, Feb. 1, 1986); *Der 35. Mai*, children's opera (Mannheim, Nov. 30, 1986); *Eréndira*, chamber opera (1992); *Schachnovelle*, opera (1994). **BALLET:** *Der Kreisel* (Ulm, May 26, 1985). **FILM:** *Tabu*, music for the F. Murnau film of 1931 (Frankfurt am Main, April 5, 1988). **ORCH.:** *Transformation* (1978); *Anna Perenna* (1979); *Memories* for Strings (1980); *Akrostichon* (1983); *Map 67* for Chamber Orch. (1987); *Fresco* for Youth Orch. (1989). **CHAMBER:** Sonata for Woodwind and Piano (1973); *Satya I* for Violin (1981), *II* for Bassoon (1981), *III* for Double Bass (1981), *IV* for Clarinet (1981), and *V* for Bassoon, Clarinet, Violin, and Double Bass (1981); *Echos II* for Piano and Percussion (1982); *Alternances* for Wind Quintet (1982); *Nakris* for Saxophone Quartet (1985); *Melismen* for Recorder Quintet (1985); *Quasaar Paal 2* for Mutabor (Computer Organ) and Cello (1985); *New Rochelle* for DX7 Synthesizer (1987); Trio for Oboe, Clarinet, and Bassoon (1987); *Loc Maria* for Organ and Percussion (1987); *Ostrov I* for Viola Quartet (1987) and *II* for Clarinet Quartet (1988); *Din Terra Lonhdana* for String Quartet (1987); *Terra Lohndana* for Chamber Ensemble (1988); *Kata* for Flute and Piano (1989); *. . . wenn der freude thränen flessen . . .* for Cello and Piano (1990); *Lichtwellen* for Clarinet (1991); *Trautropfen* for Clarinet and Piano (1992). **VOCAL:** *Bewitch Me Into a Silver Bird!* for Chorus and Orch. (1975); *Mondnacht* for Voice and Organ (1985); *Zebaoth* for Baritone and 2 Organs (1986); Concertino for Voice and Orch. (1986; Ulm, March 5, 1987); *Mondnächte* for Voice, Saxophone, and Percussion (1986); *Donis Nobis Pacem* for Voice, Percussion, and Cello (1987); Concertino for Voice and Orch. (Baden-Baden, Aug. 26, 1988); also various choruses and solo songs.

Dinicu, Grigoraş, Romanian violinist and composer; b. Bucharest, April 3, 1889; d. there, March 28, 1949. He was of a family of musicians; in 1902 he studied violin with Flesch, who taught at the Bucharest Cons. At his graduation in 1906, Dinicu played a violin piece of his own based on popular Romanian rhythms, *Hora staccato*; Jascha Heifetz made a virtuoso arrangement of it in 1932. Subsequently Dinicu played in hotels, restaurants, nightclubs, and cafés in Bucharest and in western Europe. He also composed numerous other pieces of light music in the gypsy and Romanian manner.

Di Stefano, Giuseppe, noted Italian tenor; b. Motta Santa Anastasia, near Catania, July 24, 1921. He was a pupil of Adriano Torchi and Luigi Montesanto in Milan. During World War II, he was conscripted into the Italian army but in 1943 he went AWOL to Switzerland, where he was interned as a refugee. After making appearances on the Swiss radio and in concert in 1944, he returned to Italy and made his operatic debut in 1946 as Massenet's Des Grieux in Reggio Emilia, a role he also chose for his first appearance at Milan's La Scala the following year. He made his Metropolitan Opera debut in N.Y. on Feb. 25, 1948, as the Duke of Mantua; he remained on its roster until 1952, appearing as Rossini's Almaviva, Faust, Nemorino, Rinuccio in *Gianni Schicchi*, Alfredo, Rodolfo, and Pinkerton; he returned for the 1955–56 and 1964–65 seasons. From 1948 to 1952 he appeared in Mexico City. In 1950 he made his San Francisco Opera debut as Rodolfo. From 1952 to 1961 he was a principal member at La Scala, where he appeared as Radames, Canio, and Turiddu, and where he created the role of Giuliano in Pizzetti's *Calzare d'Argento* in 1961. In 1954 he made his first appearance at the Lyric Theatre of Chicago as Edgardo. His British debut followed in 1957 as Nemorino at the Edinburgh Festival. In 1961 he made his debut at London's Covent Garden as Cavaradossi. He also sang at the Vienna State Opera, the Berlin State Opera, the Paris Opéra, and the Teatro Colón in Buenos Aires. In 1973–74 he made a concert tour of the world with Maria Callas.

Distler, Hugo, distinguished German composer, organist, choral conductor, and pedagogue; b. Nuremberg, June 24, 1908; d. (suicide) Berlin, Nov. 1, 1942. He was a student of Martienssen (piano), Ramin (organ), and Grabner (harmony) at the Leipzig Cons. (1927–31). In 1931 he became organist at St. Jakobi in Lübeck. In 1937 he became a lecturer at the Württemberg Hochschule für Musik in Stuttgart, where he also conducted its 2 choirs. In 1940 he was called to Berlin as prof. at the Hochschule für Musik, where he also conducted its choir from 1941. In 1942 he was also named conductor of the State and Cathedral Choir. Despite the prominence Distler achieved as a performing musician and teacher, the Nazi's disdain for his work led him to take his own life. He is now recognized as one of the most significant German composers of his generation. While his works remain tonally anchored, they reveal an innovative harmonic sense.

WORKS: ORCH.: Concerto for Harpsichord and Strings (1935; Hamburg, April 29, 1936); *Konzertstück* for Piano and Orch. (1937; Oldenburg, Feb. 11, 1955). **CHAMBER:** *Kammermusik* for 6 Instruments (1927); *Sonata über alte deutsche Volkslieder* for 2 Violins and Piano (1938); String Quartet (1939). **PIANO:** *Kleine Sonate* (1927); *Konzertante Sonate* for 2 Pianos (1931); *Elf kleine Klavierstücke für die Jugend* (1936); *Konzertstück* for 2 Pianos (1940). **ORGAN:** 2 partitas (1932, 1935); *Sieben kleine Orgelchoralbearbeitungen* (1938); Sonata (1938–39). **VOCAL: SACRED:** *Deutsches Choralmesse* (1932); *Der Jahrkreis* for Chorus (1932–33); *Choralpassion* for Soloists and Chorus (Berlin, March 29, 1933); *Die Weihnachtsgeschichte* for Soloists and Chorus (1933); *Liturgische Sätze* for Chorus (1933–35); *Wo Gott zum Haus nit gibt sein Gunst,* cantata for Chorus, 2 Oboes, Strings, and Harpsichord (1934); *Geistliche Chormusik,* 9 motets for Chorus (1934–41); *Drei geistliche Konzerte* for Soprano and Organ or Harpsichord (1938); *Nun danket all und bringet Ehr,* cantata for Soloists, Chorus, Strings, and Organ (1941); many other works. **SECULAR:** *An die Natur,* cantata for Soprano, Chorus, Piano or Harpsichord, and Strings (Pyrmont, Aug. 16, 1933); *Das Lied von der Glocke* for Baritone, Chorus, and Orch. (1933); *Neues Chorliederbuch* for Chorus (1936–38); *Mörike-Chorliederbuch* for Chorus (1938–39; Graz, June 26, 1939); *Lied am Herde,* cantata for Bass or Baritone and Chamber Orch. (1941; Berlin, Feb. 3, 1942; also for Baritone or Alto and Piano); *Kleine Sommerkantate* for 2 Sopranos and String Quartet (1942); various other works.

BIBL.: U. von Rauchhaupt, *Die vokale Kirchenmusik H. D.s* (Gütersloh, 1963); L. Palmer, *H. D. and His Church Music* (St. Louis, 1967); U. Herrmann, *H. D.—Rufer und Mahner* (Berlin, 1972); A Sievers, *Der Kompositionsstil H. D.s dargestellt an Beispielen aus dem Mörike-Chorliederbuch* (Wiesbaden, 1989); H. Grabner et al., *H. D.* (Tutzing, 1990).

Dittrich, Paul-Heinz, German composer and teacher; b. Gornsdorf, Dec. 4, 1930. He studied composition at the Leipzig Hochschule für Musik (1951–56; diploma, 1958), and then attended Wagner-Régeny's master classes at the Academy of Arts in East Berlin (1958–60). From 1960 to 1976 he taught at the Hanns Eisler Hochschule für Musik in East Berlin, returning there as a prof. of composition in 1990. In 1991 he founded the Bandenburgische Colloquium für Neue Musik in Zeuthen. He received the Artist's Prize in 1981 and the National Prize in 1988 of the German Democratic Republic. In 1983 he became a member of the Academy of Arts in East Berlin, serving as secretary of its music section from 1990. His works astutely utilize modern forms and technical idioms, while observing and preserving the pragmatic elements of instrumental and vocal writing.

WORKS: Violin Sonata (1954); *Passacaglia* for Orch. (1955); 4 string quartets (1958–59; 1982; 1987; 1991–92); *Divertimento* for Chamber Orch. (1959); 9 Pieces for Orch. (1960); *Kammermusik I* for Flute, Oboe, Clarinet, Bassoon, Piano, and Tape (1970), *II* for Oboe, Cello, Piano, and Tape (1973), *III* for Baritone and Wind Quintet (1974), *IV* for Soprano, 7 Instruments, and Live Electronics (1977), *V* for Wind Quintet and Live Electronics (1976–77), *VI* for Oboe, Engish Horn, Trombone, Viola, Cello, Double Bass, Piano, and Percussion (1980), *VII* for 5 Speakers, Wind Quintet, and Harpsichord (1985), *VIII* for Oboe, Cello, and Piano (1988), *IX* for Flute, Clarinet, Cello, Harpsichord, Speaker, and Tape (1988), *X* for Flute, Bass Clarinet, and Piano (1989), and *XI* for Soprano, Cello, Piano, and Wind Quintet (1990); *Memento vitae* for Baritone, 12 Vocalists, 4 Choral Groups, and Percussion (1971–73); *Vokalblätter* for Soprano and 12 Vocalists (1972–73); *Areae Sonantes* for 3 Vocal Groups and Orch. (1972–73); Cello Concerto (1974–75; Berlin, Feb. 24, 1976); *Cantus I* for Orch. (1975; Hamburg, Dec. 20, 1977) and *II* for Soprano, Cello, Orch., Tape, and Live Electronics (1977); *Laudatio Pacis* for Reciter, 4 Soloists, Chorus, and Vocal Ensemble (1975; Berlin, Oct. 3, 1993; in collaboration with S. Gubaidulina and M. Kopelent); *Illuminations* for Orch. (1976; Royan, April 3, 1977); *Concert avec plusieurs instruments* No. 1 for Harpsichord and 7 Instruments (1976), No. 2 for Viola, Cello, and 2 Orch. Groups (1977–78; Metz, Nov. 18, 1978), No. 3 for Flute, Oboe, Orch., and Live Electronics (1978–79; Dresden, May 31, 1979), No. 4 for Piano and Orch. (1983; Warsaw, Sept. 25, 1984), No. 5 for Flute and 7 Cellos (1984), No. 6 for Oboe and Chamber Orch. (1985; Berlin, Nov. 15, 1991), No. 7 for Oboe, Trombone, Cello, 2 Pianos, 4 Speakers, 4 Percussion, and Chamber Orch. (1989), and No. 8 for Cello and Chamber Orch. (1992); *Engfürung* for 6 Vocalists, 6 Instrumentalists, Orch., Live Electronics, and Tape (Donaueschingen, Oct. 16, 1981); *Etym* for Orch. (1981–82; Leipzig, Oct. 2, 1984); *Memento mori* for Baritone, Double Chorus, and Percussion (1985; Stuttgart, March 15, 1988); *Spiel* for 3 Speakers, 3 Singers, 11 Instrumentalists, and Live Electronics (1986–87; Berlin, Nov. 17, 1987); *Hymnischer Entwurf* for Speaker and Orch. (1987; Dresden, June 10, 1989); *Poesien,* opera (1987–91).

Dixon, (Charles) Dean, black American conductor; b. N.Y., Jan. 10, 1915; d. Zug, near Zürich, Nov. 3, 1976. He showed a musical talent as a child and began to take violin lessons. At the age of 17, he organized at his high school in the Bronx a group called the Dean Dixon Sym. Soc. He studied violin at the Juilliard School of Music in N.Y. (1932–36); on a conducting fellowship, he took lessons with Albert Stoessel at the Juilliard Graduate School (1936–39); also enrolled in academic classes at Columbia Univ. Teachers College, receiving an M.A. in 1939. On May 7, 1938, he made his professional conducting debut at N.Y.'s Town Hall; that same year, he also founded the N.Y. Chamber Orch. Eleanor Roosevelt became interested in his career, and helped him to obtain some conducting engagements, including an appearance with the N.Y. Phil. at the Lewisohn Stadium on Aug. 10, 1941, making him the first of his race to conduct this orch. In 1944 Dixon organized the American Youth Orch., which had a limited success. In 1949 he went to Europe in the hopes of securing wider opportunities. These hopes were fully realized; he was engaged as music director of the Göteborg Sym. Orch. (1953–60), the Hessian Radio Sym. Orch. in Frankfurt am Main (1961–70), and the Sydney (Australia) Sym. Orch. (1964–67). Returning briefly to the U.S. in 1970, he was guest conductor for a series of N.Y. Phil. summer concerts in Central Park, then returned to Europe and settled in Switzerland in 1974. His career was cut short when he underwent open-heart surgery in 1975.

Dixon, James, American conductor; b. Estherville, Iowa, April 26, 1928. He studied at the Univ. of Iowa (B.M., 1952; M.M., 1956). He was conductor of the U.S. 7th Army Sym. Orch. in Germany (1951–54), the Univ. of Iowa Sym. Orch. in Iowa City (1954–59), and the New England Cons. of Music in Boston (1959–61). In 1962 he returned to the Univ. of Iowa Sym. Orch. as conductor; from 1965 he also served as conductor of the Tri-City Sym. Orch. in Davenport, Iowa, and Rock Island, Ill. In addition, he was assoc. conductor of the Minneapolis Sym. Orch. (1961–62). He was the recipient of the Gustav Mahler Medal in 1963.

Dlugoszewski, Lucia, innovative American composer, performer, teacher, and inventor; b. Detroit, June 16, 1931. She studied piano with Agelageth Morrison at the Detroit Cons. (1940–46); after courses in physics at Wayne State Univ. in Detroit (1946–49), she went to N.Y. and studied analysis with Salzer at the Mannes College of Music (1950–53); she also had lessons in piano with Grete Sultan and in composition with Varèse. The latter greatly influenced her, as did the N.Y. School of painters and poets. In an effort to expand her compositional parameters, she invented several instruments. Her most noteworthy creation was the so-called timbre piano (c.1951), a revamped conventional piano activated by striking the strings with mallets, or having the strings bowed and picked. She became especially successful as a composer for the dance, and was closely associated with the Erick Hawkins Dance Co. From 1960 she was also with the Foundation for Modern Dance. In 1966 she received the National Inst. of Arts and Letters Award and in 1977 she became the first woman to receive the Koussevitzky International Recording Award for her *Fire Fragile Flight.*

WORKS: DRAMATIC: OPERAS: *Tiny Opera* (1953); *The Heidi Songs* (1970). **DANCE:** *Openings of the Eye* (1952); *Here and Now with Watchers* (1954–57); *8 Clear Places* (1958–60); *Cantilever* (1964); *To Everyone Out There* (1964); *Geography of Noon* (1964); *Lords of Persia* No. 1 (1965), No. 2 (1968), and No. 3 (1971); *Dazzle on a Knife's Edge* (1966); *Tight Rope* (1968); *Agathlon Algebra* (1968); *Black Lake* (1969); *Of Love . . . Or He is a Cry, She Is His Ear* (1971); *Angels of the Inmost Heaven* (1972); *Avanti* (1983); *The Woman Deunde Amor* (1984–85). Also incidental music and film scores. **ORCH.:** *Orchestra Structure for the Poetry of Everyday Sounds* (1952); *Orchestral Radiant Ground* (1955); *Arithmetic Points* (1955); *Flower Music for Left Ear in a Small Room* (1956); *Instants in Form and Movements* for Timbre Piano and Chamber Orch. (1957); *Suchness Concerto* for Orch. of Invented Percussion (1958–60); *4 Attention Spans* (1964); *Beauty Music 3* for Timbre Piano and Chamber Orch. (1965); *Quick Dichotomies* for 2 Trumpets, Clarinet, and Orch. of Invented Percussion (1965); *Naked Flight Nageire* for Chamber Orch. (1966); *Hanging Bridges* (1968; also for String Quartet); *Kitetail Beauty Music* for Violin, Timbre Piano, and Orch. of Invented Percussion (1968); *Naked Swift Music* for Violin, Timbre Piano, and Orch. of Invented Percussion (1968); *Skylark Concert: An Evening of Music* for Chamber Orch. (1969–70); *Kireji: Spring and Tender Speed* (1972); *Tender Theatre Flight Nageire* for Brass Quintet and Percussion Orch. (1972–79); *Abyss and Caress* for Trumpet and Small Orch. (1975); *Amor New Tilting Night* for Chamber Orch. (1978); *Startle Transparent Terrible Freedom* (1981); *Quidditas Sorrow Terrible Freedom* (1983–84); *Duenda Amor* (1983–84). **CHAMBER:** Flute Sonata (1950); *Transparencies No. 1* for Harp (1952), *No. 2* for Flute (1952), *No. 3* for Harp and Violin (1952), and *No. 4* for String Quartet (1952); *Naked Wabin* for 6 Instruments (1956); *Flower Music* for String Quartet (1959); *Rates of Speed in Space* for Ladder Harp and Quintet (1959); *Delicate Accidents in Space* for Unsheltered Rattle Quintet (1959); *Concert of Man Rooms and Moving Space* for Flute, Clarinet, Timbre Piano, and 4 Unsheltered Rattles (1960); *Archaic Aggregates* for Timbre Piano, Ladder Harps, Tangent and Unsheltered Rattles, and Gongs (1961); *Beauty Music* for Clarinet, Percussion, and Timbre Piano (1965); *Suchness with Radiant Ground* for Clarinet and Percussion (1965); *Balance Naked Flung* for 5 Instrumentaliss (1966); *Naked Quintet* for Brass (1967); *Leap and Fall, Quick Structures* for 2 Trumpets, Clarinet, 2 Violins, and Percussion (1968); *Space Is a Diamond* for Trumpet (1970); *Swift Diamond* for Timbre Piano, Trumpet, and Invented Percussion (1970); *Velocity Shells* for Timbre Piano, Trumpet, and Invented Percussion (1970); *pure Flight Air* for String Quartet (1970); *Amor Elusive Empty August* for Woodwind Quintet (1979); *Cicada Terrible Freedom* for Flute, String Quintet, and Bass Trombone (1980–81); *Wilderness Elegant Tilt* for 11 Instruments (1981–84); *Quidditas* for String Quartet (1984–85). **VOCAL:** *Fire Fragile Flight* for Voice and Orch. (1973).

Dobbs, Mattiwilda, black American soprano and teacher; b. Atlanta, July 11, 1925. She was educated at Spelman College in Atlanta (B.A., 1946) and at Columbia Univ. (M.A., 1948); pursued vocal training with Lotte Leonard in N.Y. (1946–50) and Bernac in Paris (1950–52). In 1948 she won the Marian Anderson scholarship contest and made her debut as a concert artist; in 1951 she won 1st prize in singing in the Geneva Competition. After appearing in opera and recitals in Holland (1952), she sang at Milan's La Scala, the Glyndebourne Festival, and London's Covent Garden (1953). In 1955 she appeared at the San Francisco Opera; on Nov. 9, 1956, she made her Metropolitan Opera debut in N.Y. as Gilda. In 1957 she made her first appearance at the Royal Swedish Opera in Stockholm; also sang at the Hamburg State Opera (1961–63; 1967). In addition to her operatic and concert engagements in the U.S. and Europe, she also toured in Australia, New Zealand, and Israel. She was a visiting prof. at the Univ. of Texas in Austin (1973–74); then was a prof. at the Univ. of Ill. (1975–76), the Univ. of Georgia (1976–77), and Howard Univ. in Washington, D.C. (1977–91).

Dobiáš, Václav, Czech composer; b. Radčice, near Semily, Sept. 22, 1909; d. Prague, May 18, 1978. He studied violin and composition at the Prague Cons., where he also took courses in microtonal music with A. Hába, and wrote a *Lento* for 3 Harps (1940) and a Violin Concerto (1941) making use of quarter tones. After 1945 he became involved in the political problems of musical education; in conformity with the ideology of the Communist Party, he began to write music for the masses in the manner of socialist realism; in 1958 he was elected to the Central Committee of the Communist Party and was a member of the National Assembly from 1960 to 1969.

WORKS: ORCH.: Chamber Sym. (1939); 2 numbered syms. (1943, 1956–57); Sinfonietta (1946–47; rev. 1962); Sonata for Piano, Wind Quintet, Strings, and Timpani (1947); *The Grand Procession,* symphonic poem (1948). **CHAMBER:** 4 string quartets (1931, 1936, 1938, 1942); Violin Sonata (1936); Cello Sonata (1939); *Říkadla* (Rhymes) for 9 Instruments (1938); *Pastoral Wind Quintet* (1943); *4 Nocturnes* for Cello and Piano (1944); *Quartettino* for String Quartet (1944); *Dance Fantasy* for 9 Instruments (1948). **PIANO:** 2 sonatas (1931, 1940). **VOCAL:** Cantatas; mass choruses; songs.

BIBL.: J. Štilec, *V. D.* (Prague, 1985).

Dobos, Kálmán, Hungarian composer and pianist; b. Szolnok, July 22, 1931. Although he became blind in 1945, he began his training in music that same year; he studied composition with Viski at the Budapest Academy of Music (graduated, 1957). From 1958 he made tours as a pianist; also worked in the music dept. of the Hungarian Radio.

WORKS: DRAMATIC: Incidental music to radio plays and films. **ORCH.:** Sym. (1957); *3 Hungarian Dances* (1964); *Hangjelenségek* (Sound Phenomena; 1968). **CHAMBER:** Cello Sonata (1956); *Adagio and Fugue* for String Quartet (1959); *2 Movements* for Violin, Cello, and Piano (1960); *Musica da camera* for Violin and Piano (1962); String Trio (1963); *Megnyilatkozások* (Manifestations) for String Quartet, Piano, and Percussion (1969); *Belső mozdulatok* (Inner Movements) for Clarinet, Piano, and Percussion (1970); *Vetületek* (Projections) for 4 Percussionists (1975); Sonatina for 2 Horns (1976); *Összefüggések* (Connections) for Cello, Piano, and Percussion (1985). **KEYBOARD: PIANO:** Sonata (1957); *Meditation* (1964); *Variations on a Hungarian Folk Song* (1972); *Ringató* (Rocking) (1972). **ORGAN:** *Variations and Fugue* (1974); *Variációk Szent István emlékére* (Variations in Memory of St. Stephen; 1988). **VOCAL:** *Emlékezés* (Remembrance) for Voice and Orch. (1959); *Villanások* (Flashes) for Soprano, Violin, Cello, and Piano (1963); *Hungarian Folk Songs from Moldavia* for Mezzo-soprano and Chamber Ensemble (1974); sacred and secular choral works; songs.

Dobronić, Antun, Croatian composer and teacher; b. Jelsa, island of Hvar, April 2, 1878; d. Zagreb, Dec. 12, 1955. He studied music with Novák in Prague; then returned to Yugoslavia, and in 1921 was appointed a prof. at the Zagreb Cons. He wrote many stage works, among them the operas *Ragusean Diptych*; *The Man of God*; *Mara*; *Dubrovnički triptihon* (1925); *Udovica Rozlinka* (1934); *Rkac* (1938); *Goran* (1944); also a ballet, *The Giant Horse*; 8 syms.; 2 symphonic poems: *Au long de l'Adriatique* (1948) and *Les Noces* (1949); chamber music in the national style, including a Piano Quintet, subtitled *Bosnian Rhapsody*; 5 string quartets; choruses and songs.

Dobrowen, Issay (Alexandrovich) (real name, **Ishok Israelevich Barabeichik**), distinguished Russian conductor; b. Nizhny-Novgorod, Feb. 27, 1891; d. Oslo, Dec. 9, 1953. His orphaned mother was adopted by Israil Dobrovel; Issay Dobrowen changed his legal name, Dobrovel, to Dobrowein, and later to Dobrowen. He studied at the Nizhny-Novgorod Cons. as a small child (1896–1900); then entered the Moscow Cons. and studied with Igumnov (piano) and Taneyev (composition); went to Vienna for additional training with Godowsky (piano). Returning to Moscow, he made his conducting debut at the Kommisarzhevsky Theater in 1919; then conducted at the Bolshoi Theater (1921–22); in 1922 he led the Dresden State Opera in the German premiere of Mussorgsky's opera *Boris Godunov*; subsequently conducted at the Berlin Volksoper (1924–25) and the Sofia Opera (1927–28). In 1931 he made his American debut conducting the San Francisco Sym. Orch.; was guest conductor with the Minneapolis Sym. Orch., the Philadelphia Orch., and the N.Y. Phil. He was a regular conductor of the Budapest Opera from 1936 to 1939; at the outbreak of World War II he went to Sweden, where he won his greatest successes as conductor and producer at the Stockholm Royal Theater (1941–45). From 1948 he conducted at La Scala in Milan. In 1952 he conducted at London's Covent Garden. He was a prolific composer; wrote several piano concertos and pieces for piano solo, in a Romantic vein; also an orch. fairy tale, *1,001 Nights* (Moscow, May 27, 1922).

Dobrowolski, Andrzej, Polish composer and teacher; b. Lwów, Sept. 9, 1921; d. Graz, Aug. 8, 1990. He studied organ, clarinet, and voice at the Warsaw Cons., then composition with Malawski and theory with Lobaczewska at the Kraków State College of Music (1947–51). He taught at the Warsaw State College of Music (1954–75), then was a prof. of composition at the Graz Hochschule für Musik (from 1976), serving as head of its faculty of composition, theory, and conducting (from 1980). His music is a paradigm of modern structuralism and textural abstraction.

WORKS: ORCH.: *Symphonic Variations* (1949); *Overture* (1950); Bassoon Concerto (1953); Sym. No. 1 (1955); *Music* for Strings and 4 Groups of Wind Instruments (1964); *Music* for Strings, 2 Groups of Wind Instruments, and 2 Loudspeakers (1967); *Music 1* (1968), *2: Amar* (1970), *3* (1972–73), *4: A-La* (1974), *5: Passacaglia* (1978–79), and *6* (1981–82); *Music* for Chamber Orch. (1982–83); *Music* for Orch. and Oboe (1984–85); *Flütchen* for Chamber Ensemble and Reciter (1986). **OTHER:** Trio for Oboe, Clarinet, and Bassoon (1956); Studies for Oboe, Trumpet, Bassoon, and Double Bass (1959); *Passacaglia from 40 to 5*, electronic music (1959); *Music* for Tape No. 1 (1962); *Music* for Tape and Oboe (1965); *Krabogapa* for 4 Instruments (1969); *Music* for Tape and Piano (1971); *Music* for Chorus, 2 Groups of Winds, Double Basses, and Percussion (1975); *Music* for Tape and Double Bass (1977); *Music* for 3 Accordions, Mouth Harmonicas, and Percussion (1977); *Music* for Tape and Clarinet (1980); *Musik für Grazer Bläserkreis* for 8 Trumpets, 8 Horns, 8 Trombones, and Percussion (1984).

Dodge, Charles (Malcolm), American composer and teacher; b. Ames, Iowa, June 5, 1942. He studied composition with Hervig and Bezanson at the Univ. of Iowa (B.A., 1964), Milhaud at the Aspen (Colo.) Music School (summer, 1961), and Schuller at the Berkshire Music Center in Tanglewood (summer, 1964), where he also attended seminars given by Berger and Foss. He then studied composition with Chou Wen-chung and Luening, electronic music with Ussachevsky, and theory with William J. Mitchell at Columbia Univ. (M.A., 1966; D.M.A., 1970). He was a teacher at Columbia Univ. (1967–69; 1970–77) and Princeton Univ. (1969–70); was assoc. prof. (1977–80) and prof. (1980–95) of music at Brooklyn College and the graduate center of the City Univ. of N.Y. In 1993–94 and again from 1995 he served as a visiting prof. of music at Dartmouth College. He was president of the American Composers Alliance (1971–75) and the American Music Center (1979–82). In 1972 and 1975 he held Guggenheim fellowships. In 1974, 1976, 1987, and 1991 he held NEA composer fellowships. With T. Jerse, he publ. *Computer Music: Synthesis, Composition, and Performance* (N.Y., 1985).

WORKS: *Composition in 5 Parts* for Cello and Piano (1964); *Solos and Combinations* for Flute, Clarinet, and Oboe (1964); *Folia* for Chamber Orch. (1965); *Rota* for Orch. (1966); *Changes* for Computer Synthesis (1970); *Earth's Magnetic Field* for Computer Synthesis (1970); *Speech Songs* for Computer-Synthesized Voice (1972); *Extensions* for Trumpet and Computer Synthesis (1973); *The Story of Our Lives* for Computer-Synthesized Voice (1974; also for Videotape, 1975); *In Celebration* for Computer-Synthesized Voice (1975); *Palinode* for Orch. and Computer Synthesis (1976); *Cascando*, radio play by Samuel Beckett (1978); *Any Resemblance Is Purely Coincidental* for Piano and Computer-Synthesized "Caruso Voice" (1980); *Han motte henne i parken*, radio play by Richard Kostelanetz (1981); *He Met Her in the Park*, radio play by Richard Kostelanetz (1982); *Distribution, Redistribution* for Violin, Cello, and Piano (1983); *Mingo's Song* for Computer-Synthesized Voice (1983); *The Waves* for Soprano and Computer Synthesis (1984); *Profile* for Computer Synthesis (1984); *Roundelay* for Chorus and Computer Synthesis (1985); *A Postcard from the Volcano* for Soprano and Computer Synthesis (1986); *Song without Words* for Computer Synthesis (1986); *A Fractal for Wiley* for Computer Synthesis (1987); *Viola Elegy* for Viola and Computer Synthesis (1987); *Clarinet Elegy* for Bass Clarinet and Computer Synthesis (1988); *Wedding Music* for Violin and Computer Synthesis (1988); *Allemande* for Computer Synthesis (1988); *The Voice of Binky* for Computer Synthesis (1989); *Imaginary Narrative* for Computer Synthesis (1989); *Hoy (In His Memory)* for Voice and Computer Synthesis (1990); *The Village Child*, puppet theater (1992); *The One and the Other* for Chamber Orch. (1993; Los Angeles, April 11, 1994); *Concert Études* for Violin and Computer Synthesis (N.Y., April 12, 1994).

BIBL.: E. Thieberger, "An Interview with C. D.," *Computer Music Journal* (Spring 1995).

Dodgson, Stephen (Cuthbert Vivian), English composer; b. London, March 17, 1924. He studied with R.O. Morris at the Royal College of Music in London, where he subsequently taught (1965–82). He was also active as a broadcaster.

WORKS: OPERA: *Margaret Catchpole* (1979). **ORCH.:** 2 concertos for Guitar and Chamber Orch. (1959, 1972); Bassoon Concerto (1969); Wind Sym. (1974); Clarinet Concerto (1983); *Capriccio Concertante: All Hallows' Eve* for Clarinet and Large Symphonic Wind Ensemble (1984); Trombone Concerto (1986). **CHAMBER:** 2 string trios (1951, 1964); Suite for Wind Quintet (1965); Quintet for Piano and String Quartet (1966); 2 piano trios (1967, 1973); Cello Sonata (1968); Quintet for Guitar and String Quartet (1973); Trio for Oboe, Bassoon, and Piano (1973); String Quartet (1986); 3 piano sonatas (1959, 1975, 1983); numerous solo works for guitar, harpsichord, lute, etc. **VOCAL:** *Cadilly* for 4 Singers and Wind Quintet (1968); *Te Deum* for Chorus (1972); *Magnificat* for Soloists and Orch. (1975); *In Wilde America*, cantata for Soloists, Chorus, and 8 Instrumentalists (1977); *Epigrams from a Garden* for Contralto and Clarinet Choir (1977); *Sir John*, cantata for Chorus and Horn Trio (1980); songs.

Doebler, Curt, German organist, teacher, and composer; b. Kottbus, Jan. 15, 1896; d. Berlin, June 19, 1970. He studied organ with A. Dreyer. From 1919 to 1932 he was organist and choirmaster at the Catholic church in Charlottenburg; after occupying various positions as an organist and a teacher elsewhere, he returned to Charlottenburg (1950). In his music,

Doebler attempted to establish a modern style based on Palestrina's polyphony. His numerous choruses enjoyed success in Germany in their day.

Doenhoff, Albert von, American pianist and composer; b. Louisville, Ky., March 16, 1880; d. N.Y., Oct. 3, 1940. He studied at the Cincinnati College of Music and then in N.Y. with Rafael Joseffy. He made his professional debut in N.Y. on March 8, 1905; subsequently developed a successful career as a concert pianist. He publ. many pieces for piano and pedagogical material.

Doflein, Erich, German musicologist; b. Munich, Aug. 7, 1900; d. Kirchzarten, Oct. 29, 1977. He received training in music from Auerbach, Kaminski, and Praetorius, in musicology from Schneider, in art history from Pinder, and in philosophy from Hönigswald in Breslau and Munich; in 1924 he received his Ph.D. at the Univ. of Breslau with the diss. *Über Gestalt und Stil in der Musik*; he then completed his studies with Gurlitt and Erpf in Freiburg im Breisgau. In 1928 he helped to found an institute for private music teachers there, where he taught; he then taught at the Breslau music school (1941–44); in 1947 he became a prof. and acting director of the newly-founded Freiburg im Breisgau Hochschule für Musik, remaining on its faculty until 1965; in 1948 he also helped to found the Institut für Neue Musik und Musikerzeihung in Bayreuth, which later removed to Darmstadt, where he served as its president (1956–60). Doflein was especially active in the field of music pedagogy. With his wife Elma, he publ. the valuable *Geigenschulwerk* (Mainz, 1931; 2nd ed., 1951; Eng. tr., 1957).

BIBL.: L. Abraham, ed., *E. D. Festschrift* (Mainz, 1972).

Döhl, Friedhelm, German composer and teacher; b. Göttingen, July 7, 1936. He was a pupil of Fortner at the Freiburg im Breisgau Hochschule für Musik (1956–64) and pursued his academic studies at the Univ. of Göttingen (Ph.D., 1966, with the diss. *Weberns Beitrag zur Stilwende der neuen Musik*; publ. in Munich, 1976). After lecturing at the Düsseldorf Hochschule für Musik (1965–68), he was principal lecturer (1969–72) and prof. (1972–74) at the Musicological Inst. of the Free Univ. in Berlin; then was founder-director of the studio for electronic music, for music and theater, and for non-European music at the Basel Academy of Music (1974–82). He served as a prof. of composition at the Lübeck Hochschule für Musik from 1983, and as its director from 1991. Döhl's earliest creative efforts were heavily influenced by Webern and Schoenberg; he later developed an innovative style notable for both exploration of color and experimental instrumentation.

WORKS: DRAMATIC: OPERA: *Medea* (1987–90). **BALLETS:** *Ikaros* (1977–78); *Fiesta* (1982). **ORCH.:** *Zorch*, concerto for 3 Open Pianos and Big Band (1972); Sym. for Cello and Orch. (1980–81); *Tombeau: Metamorphose* (1982–83); *Passion* (1984); *Winterreise* for Strings (1986; also for String Quintet, 1985). **CHAMBER:** Duo for Violin and Piano (1961); *Varianti*, octet for Flute, Oboe, Clarinet, Bassoon, and String Quartet (1961); *Klangfiguren* for Wind Quintet (1962); *Canto W* for Flute (1962); *Oculapis: Reflexe* for Flute and Piano (1962); *Albumblätter* for 1 to 10 Flutes (1963); *Julianische Minuten* for Flute and Piano (1963); Toccata for Flute, Trumpet, Harpsichord, and Piano (1964); *Tappeto: Impressionen* for Cello and Harp (1967); *Pas de deux* for Violin and Guitar (1968); *Klang-Szene I* for 2 Electric Organs, Live Electronics, 4 Groups of Loudspeakers, Props, and Lights (1970) and *II* for 5 Ensembles, Live Electronics, Props, and Lights (1971); *Textur I* for Flute (1971); String Quartet (1971–72); *Sotto voce* for Flute, Cello, and Piano (1973); *Der Abend/Die Nacht* for Flute and Cello (1979); *Conductus* for 4 Percussion (1980); *5 Pieces* for Flute (1980); *2 Songs of Palamidi* for Flute and Guitar (1980); *Nachklänge* for Guitar (1981); *Ballet mécanique (Hommage à la laveuse inconnue)* for 2 Flutes, 2 Clarinets, Cello, Piano, and Percussion (1984); *Nachtfahrt* for Open Piano (Tape ad libitum) and Percussion (1984); *Winterreise*, string quintet (1985; also for String Orch., 1986); *Kadenz* for Cello (1986–87); *Missa (Medea-Interpolation)* for 2 Trombones and 3 Percussion (1989); *Posaunen im Raum (Medea-Material I)* for Trombone Ensemble (1990); *Flöten im Raum (Medea-Material II)* for Flute Ensemble (1990); *Medeas Lied* for Chamber Ensemble (1991); *Moin moin* for 7 Percussion and 4 Trombones (1993). **KEYBOARD: PIANO:** 4 sonatas (1959, 1960, 1961, 1962); *Klangmodell I* and *II* (1971); *Textur II* (1971); *Cadenza* for 1 to 3 Open Pianos (1972); *Odradek* for 2 Open Pianos (1976); *8 Porträts* (1977–78); *3 Traumstücke* (1978); *7 Haiku* (1979); *Bruchstücke zur Winterreise* (1985); *"Und wenn die Stimme . . ."* (1986); *4 Bagatellen* (1989). **ORGAN:** *Improvisation I* (1962): *Fragment (Kyrie eleison)* (1980); *Gloria: Fragment II* (1986). **VOCAL:** *Hälfte des Lebens* for Chorus and Instruments (1959); *7 Haiku* for Soprano, Flute, and Piano (1963); *Fragment: Sybille* for Baritone, Flute, Viola, Cello, and Piano (1963); *Epitaph: Tich Yuang Tuc* for Soprano, Clarinet, and Chamber Ensemble (1963); *Melancolia: Magische Quadrate* for Soprano, Chorus, and Orch. (1967–68); *". . . wenn aber . . .": 9 Fragmente* for Baritone and Piano (1969); *Süll: Mikrodrama I* for Speaker, Flute, and Props (1972); *A & O (Textur III): Mikrodrama II* for Speaker, Microphone, Loudspeaker, Props, and Tape ad libitum (1973); *Anna K. Informationen über einen Leichenfund: Mikrodrama III* for Speaker, Tape, Bass Drum, and Cello (1974); *Szene über einen kleinen Tod* for Woman's Voice, Flute, and Cello, and Cymbal and Tape ad libitum (1975); *Unterwegs: 7 Stationen* for Soprano and Piano (1978); *Auf schmalem Grat*, Requiem for 6 Voices and Tam-tam (1978); *Itke-Songs* for Voice and Accordion, or Guitar, or Piano (1978); *Medea: Monolog* for Soprano and Chamber Orch. (1979–80).

Dohnányi, Christoph von, eminent German conductor of Hungarian descent, grandson of **Ernst (Ernő) von Dohnányi**; b. Berlin, Sept. 8, 1929. He began to study the piano as a child; his musical training was interrupted by World War II. His father, Hans von Dohnányi, a jurist, and his uncle, Dietrich Bonhoeffer, the Protestant theologian and author, were executed by the Nazis for their involvement in the July 20, 1944, attempt on Hitler's life. After the war, he studied jurisprudence at the Univ. of Munich; in 1948 he enrolled at the Hochschule für Musik in Munich, and won the Richard Strauss Prize for composition and conducting. Making his way to the U.S., he continued his studies with his grandfather at Florida State Univ. at Tallahassee; also attended sessions at the Berkshire Music Center at Tanglewood. Returning to Germany, he received a job as a coach and conductor at the Frankfurt am Main Opera (1952–57). Progressing rapidly, he served as Generalmusikdirektor in Lübeck (1957–63) and Kassel (1963–66), chief conductor of the Cologne Radio Sym. Orch. (1964–70), and director of the Frankfurt Opera (1968–77). From 1977 to 1984 he was Staatsopernintendant of the Hamburg State Opera. In 1984 he assumed the position of music director of the Cleveland Orch., having been appointed music director designate in 1982, succeeding Lorin Maazel. In the meantime, he had engagements as a guest conductor of the Vienna State Opera, Covent Garden in London, La Scala in Milan, the Metropolitan Opera in N.Y., the Berlin Phil., the Vienna Phil., and the Concertgebouw Orch. in Amsterdam. In 1992 the Cleveland Orch., under Dohnányi's direction, became the resident orch. of the Salzburg Festival, the first time this honor was bestowed upon an American orch. On Dec. 12, 1993, he conducted Beethoven's 9th Sym. in a gala concert at Cleveland's Public Auditorium marking the 75th anniversary of the founding of the Cleveland Orch. He also was principal guest conductor of the Philharmonia Orch. in London from 1994. As both a sym. and opera conductor, Dohnányi has proved himself a master technician and a versatile musician capable of notably distinguished interpretations of all types of music, from Baroque to the avant-garde. He is married to **Anja Silja**.

Dohnányi, Ernst (Ernő) von, eminent Hungarian pianist, composer, conductor, and pedagogue, grandfather of **Christoph von Dohnányi**; b. Pressburg, July 27, 1877; d. N.Y., Feb. 9, 1960. He began his musical studies with his father, an amateur cellist; then studied piano and theory with Károly

Forstner. In 1894 he entered the Royal Academy of Music in Budapest, where he took courses in piano with Thomán and in composition with Koessler. In 1896 he received the Hungarian Millennium Prize, established to commemorate the thousand years of existence of Hungary, for his sym. He graduated from the Academy of Music in 1897, and then went to Berlin for additional piano studies with d'Albert. He made his debut in a recital in Berlin on Oct. 1, 1897; on Oct. 24, 1898, he played Beethoven's 4th Piano Concerto in London; then followed a series of successful concerts in the U.S. Returning to Europe, he served as prof. of piano at the Hochschule für Musik in Berlin (1908–15). He then returned to Budapest, where he taught piano at the Royal Academy of Music; served briefly as its director in 1919, when he was appointed chief conductor of the Budapest Phil. In 1928 he became head of the piano classes at the Academy of Music; in 1934 he became its director. In 1931 he assumed the post of music director of the Hungarian Radio. As Hungary became embroiled in the events of World War II and partisan politics which invaded even the arts, Dohnányi resigned his directorship in 1941, and in 1944 he also resigned his post as chief conductor of the Budapest Phil. Personal tragedy also made it impossible for him to continue his work as a musician and teacher: both of his sons lost their lives; one of them, the German jurist Hans von Dohnányi, was executed for his role in the abortive attempt on Hitler's life; the other son was killed in combat. Late in 1944 he moved to Austria. At the war's end, rumors were rife that Dohnányi used his influence with the Nazi overlords in Budapest to undermine the position of Bartók and other liberals, and that he acquiesced in anti-Semitic measures. But in 1945 the Allied occupation authorities exonerated him of all blame; even some prominent Jewish-Hungarian musicians testified in his favor. In 1947–48 he made a tour of England as a pianist; determined to emigrate to America, he accepted the position of piano teacher at Tucumán, Argentina; in 1949 he became composer-in-residence at Florida State Univ. in Tallahassee.

Dohnányi was a true virtuoso of the keyboard, and was greatly esteemed as a teacher; among his pupils were Solti, Anda, and Vázsonyi. His music represented the terminal flowering of European Romanticism, marked by passionate eloquence of expression while keeping within the framework of Classical forms. Brahms praised his early efforts. In retrospect, Dohnányi appears as a noble epigone of the past era, but pianists, particularly Hungarian pianists, often put his brilliant compositions on their programs. His most popular work with orch. is *Variations on a Nursery Song*; also frequently played is his Orch. Suite in F-sharp minor. Dohnányi himself presented his philosophy of life in a poignant pamphlet under the title *Message to Posterity* (Jacksonville, Fla., 1960).

WORKS: DRAMATIC: *Der Schleier der Pierrette*, pantomime (1908–09; Dresden, Jan. 22, 1910); *Tante Simona*, comic opera (1911–12; Dresden, Jan. 10, 1913); *A vajda tornya* (The Tower of the Voivod), opera (1915–22; Budapest, March 19, 1922); *Der Tenor*, comic opera (1920–27; Budapest, Feb. 9, 1929). **ORCH.:** 1 unnumbered sym. (1896; Budapest, June 3, 1897); 2 numbered syms.: No. 1 (1900–1901; Manchester, Jan. 30, 1902) and No. 2 (1943–44; London, Nov. 23, 1948; rev. 1953–56; Minneapolis, March 15, 1957); *Zrinyi*, overture (1896; Budapest, June 3, 1897); 2 piano concertos: No. 1 (1897–98; Budapest, Jan. 11, 1899) and No. 2 (1946–47; Sheffield, England, Dec. 3, 1947); *Konzertstück* for Cello and Orch. (1903–04; Budapest, March 7, 1906); Suite (1908–09; Budapest, Feb. 21, 1910); *Variationen über ein Kinderlied* for Piano and Orch. (1913; Berlin, Feb. 17, 1914, composer soloist); 2 violin concertos: No. 1 (1914–15, Copenhagen, March 5, 1919) and No. 2 (1949–50; San Antonio, Jan. 26, 1952); *Unnepi nyitány* (Festival Overture; 1923); *Ruralia hungarica* (Budapest, Nov. 17, 1924, composer conducting); *Szimfonikus percek* (Symphonic Minutes; 1933); *Suite en valse* (1942–43); Concertino for Harp and Chamber Orch. (1952); *American Rhapsody* (1953; Athens, Ohio, Feb. 21, 1954, composer conducting). **CHAMBER:** 2 piano quintets (1895, 1914); 3 string quartets (1899, 1906, 1926); Cello Sonata (1899); *Serenade* for String Trio (1902); Violin Sonata (1912); Sextet for Piano, Clarinet, Horn, and String Trio (1935); *Aria* for Flute and Piano (1958); *Passacaglia* for Flute (1959). **PIANO:** 4 Pieces (1896–97); Waltz for Piano, 4-hands (1897); *Variations and Fugue on a Theme of E(mma) G(ruber)* (1897); *Gavotte and Musette* (1898); *Passacaglia* (1899); 4 rhapsodies (1902–03); *Winterreigen*, 10 bagatelles (1905); *Humoresken in Form einer Suite* (1907); 3 Pieces (1912); Fugue for Piano, Left-hand or 2 Hands (1913); *Suite im alten Stil* (1913); 6 Concert Etudes (1916); *Variations on a Hungarian Folk Song* (1917); *Pastorale*, Hungarian Christmas song (1920); *Suite en valse* for 2 Pianos (1945); 6 Pieces (1945); *3 Singular Pieces* (1951); didactic pieces. **VOCAL:** *Magyar hiszekegy* (Hungarian Credo) for Tenor, Chorus, and Orch. (1920); *Missa in Dedicatione Ecclesiae* (Mass of Szeged) for Soloist, Chorus, Organ, and Orch., for the consecration of Szeged Cathedral (Szeged, Oct. 25, 1930); *Cantus vitae*, symphonic cantata (1939–41); *Stabat Mater* for 3 Soloists, Children's Chorus, and Orch. (1952–53; Wichita Falls, Texas, Jan. 16, 1956); songs.

BIBL.: V. Papp, *D. E.* (Budapest, 1927); M. Reuth, *The Tallahassee Years of E. v.D.* (diss., Florida State Univ., 1962); L. Podhradszky, "The Works of E. D.," *Studia musicologica Academiae scientiarum hungaricae*, VI (1964); B. Vázsonyi, *D. E.* (Budapest, 1971).

Doire, René, French composer; b. Evreux, June 13, 1879; d. Paris, July 9, 1959. He studied in Rouen and later in Paris with Widor and Vincent d'Indy; he then was engaged as a bandleader in the casinos of various French spas. He composed an opera, *Morituri* (1903); *Vision d'Espagne* for Violin and Orch. (1916); *Dramatico* for Piano and Orch. (1923); Violin Sonata (1918); *Reflets de jeunesse*, song cycle for Voice and Piano or Orch. (1902); and solo songs.

Dokshitcher, Timofei, Russian trumpeter and pedagogue; b. Nezhin, Dec. 13, 1921. He was a student in Moscow of Vassilenki and at the Gnessin Inst. of Vasilevski and Tabakov; he later studied conducting with Ginzburg at the Moscow Cons. (1952–57). From 1945 to 1983 he was principal trumpet in the orch. of the Bolshoi Theater in Moscow; he also pursued a solo career, and from 1971 served as a prof. at the Moscow Cons. In addition to championing the works of contemporary Russian composers, he also prepared transcriptions for his instrument.

Doktor, Paul (Karl), distinguished Austrian-born American violist and pedagogue; b. Vienna, March 28, 1919; d. N.Y., June 21, 1989. He studied with his father, Karl Doktor, violist of the renowned Busch Quartet; graduated as a violinist at the Academy of Music in Vienna in 1938, but subsequently changed to viola, and in 1942 received the 1st prize at the Geneva Competition. From 1939 to 1947 he was solo violist of the Lucerne Orch.; emigrated to the U.S. in 1947; in 1948 he made his U.S. debut at the Library of Congress in Washington, D.C.; in 1952 he became a naturalized American citizen. In 1953 he was appointed to the faculty of the Mannes College of Music in N.Y.; taught at the Philadelphia Musical Academy from 1970 and the Juilliard School from 1971. He commissioned several composers to write works for his instrument, including Piston and Quincy Porter; he also prepared various transcriptions for viola and ed. a number of viola pieces by other composers.

Dolega-Kamiénski. See **Kamiénski, Lucian.**

Dolin, Samuel (Joseph), Canadian composer and teacher; b. Montreal, Aug. 22, 1917. He received training in piano and theory in Montreal, and then pursued his education at the Univ. of Toronto (B.Mus., 1942). In 1945 he joined the staff of the Toronto Cons. of Music, where he studied composition with Weinzweig. He also studied piano and had lessons in composition with Krenek before completing his education at the Univ. of Toronto (D.Mus., 1958). Dolin continued to serve on the staff at the Cons. as a teacher for 50 years, founding its electronic music studio in 1966. He served as vice-president

(1967–68) and president (1969–73) of the Canadian League of Composers, and also as chairman (1970–74) of the Canadian section of the ISCM. In 1984 he was founding artistic director of the Canadian Contemporary Music Workshop. Dolin's music ranges widely in scope, from the traditional in manner to multimedia scores.

WORKS: DRAMATIC: *Casino (Greed)*, opera (1966–67); *Drakkar*, entertainment for Narrator, Mezzo-soprano, 2 Baritones, 2 Dancers, Chamber Ensemble, 2 Synthesizers, and Amplifiers (1972; Toronto, Feb. 17, 1973); *Golden Section: The Biography of a Woman* for Soprano, Dancer, Slides, Narrator, Lighting, and Orch. (1981); *Hero of Our Time* for Baritone, Men's Chorus, Dancers, and Orch. (1985). **ORCH.:** Sinfonietta (1950); *Serenade* for Strings (1951); 3 syms. (1956, 1957, 1976); *Isometric Variables (Bassooneries in Free Variations)* for Bassoon and Strings (1957); Sonata for Strings (1962); *Fantasy* for Piano and Chamber Orch. (1967); Piano Concerto (1974); Accordion Concerto (1984); Concerto for Oboe, Cello, and Orch. (1989). **CHAMBER:** Violin Sonata (1960); *Portrait* for String Quartet (1961); *Georgian Bay*, concerto grosso for Percussion, Accordion, and Tape (1970); Sonata for Solo Accordion (1970); Sonata for Violin and Tape (1973); Sonata for Flute and Tape (1973); Sonata for Cello and Tape (1973); *Adikia* for 1 to 5 Accordions and Tape (1975); *Prelude, Interlude, and Fantasy* for Cello (1976); Duo Concertante for Free Bass Accordion and Guitar (1977); Cello Sonata (1978); Trio for Violin, Cello, and Piano (1980); *Blago's Trio* for Flute, Clarinet, and Bassoon (1980); *Sonata Fantasia* for Baroque Flute and Fortepiano (1980); Brass Quintet (1981); *Psalmody* for Oboe (1982); *2 Vocalises* for 2 Cellos (1990). **PIANO:** *4 Miniatures* (1943); *3 Preludes* (1949); Sonata (1950); *Little Suite* (1954); *Little Toccata* (1959); Sonatina (1959); *Slightly Square Round Dance* (1966); *If* (1972); *Prelude for John Weinzweig* (1973); *Queekhoven and A. J.* (1975). **VOCAL:** 3 song sets (1951); *Chloris* for Voice and Piano (1951); *The Hills of Hebron* for Chorus and Piano (1954); *Marchbankantata* for Baritone, Chorus, Piano, and Synthesizer (1971); *Mass* for 6 Voices, Congregation, and Organ (1972); *Deuteronomy XXXII* for Voice and Flute (1977).

Dolmetsch, (Eugène) Arnold, eminent French-born English music scholar and instrumentalist, father of **Carl Frederick Dolmetsch**; b. Le Mans, Sarthe, Feb. 24, 1858; d. Haslemere, Surrey, Feb. 28, 1940. His father and maternal grandfather maintained an organ and piano workshop in Le Mans in which he was apprenticed in the construction and repair of instruments. He received piano lessons at age 4, then took violin lessons from an itinerant violinist, and later from his uncle. After his father's death in 1874, he carried on the family business. In 1878, however, he eloped to Nancy with Marie Morel, a widow 10 years his senior; following the birth of their daughter, they proceeded to London, where they were married (May 28, 1878). In 1879 he went to Brussels to study violin with Vieuxtemps; he then came under the influence of Gevaert at the Brussels Cons., where he also studied harmony and counterpoint with Kufferath and piano with de Greef (1881–83); also learned to play the viola d'amore. Upon his return to London, he took courses in violin with Henry Holmes, in harmony and counterpoint with Frederick Bridge, and in composition with Parry at the Royal College of Music (1883–85). From 1885 to 1889 he was an assistant violin teacher at Dulwich College; he also spent much time researching and copying early MSS in the Royal College of Music library, and later in the British Library. He began collecting old books on early music, and proceeded to collect and restore viols; he also taught his wife, daughter, and selected pupils to play the instruments, and presented concerts of Elizabethan music. Expanding his activities still more widely, he set about restoring a variety of keyboard instruments, and later learned to build the instruments himself. At the invitation of Bridge, he performed the music of Byrd, Bull, Purcell, Locke, Lawes, Jenkins, and Simpson at Bridge's lecture at Gresham College on Nov. 21, 1890; this was the first time the music of these early composers had been played on original instruments in modern times. On April 27, 1891, he gave a notable "Concert of Ancient Music of the XVI and XVII Centuries" in London, playing works on the viols, lute, and harpsichord, assisted by 2 vocal soloists. He worked industriously to establish himself as an authority on early music and instruments, a distinguished performer, and a skilled craftsman; his cause was championed by George Bernard Shaw. Dolmetsch and his wife separated in 1893 and were divorced in 1899. From 1895 he lived with his divorced sister-in-law, Elodie, a fine keyboard player; in 1899 they were married. Dolmetsch, his wife, and Mabel Johnston, a player on the viola da gamba and the violone, made their U.S. debut in N.Y. on Jan. 6, 1903. Dolmetsch and his 2nd wife were divorced later that year, at which time he married Johnston; with Kathleen Salmon, his pupil and a harpsichordist, they made an extensive U.S. tour in 1904–05. He was hired by Chickering & Sons of Boston in 1905 to oversee the manufacture of early keyboard instruments, viols, and lutes. From 1906 to 1911 he lived in Cambridge, Mass.; he also continued to give concerts. In 1911 he began working at the Gaveau factory in Fontenay-sous-Bois, near Paris. In 1914 he returned to England and settled in Haslemere in 1917, where he maintained a workshop and built the first modern recorder (1918). In 1925 he organized the Haslemere Festivals, where he and his family presented annual concerts. In 1927 the Dolmetsch Foundation was organized by his pupils and friends with the goal of furthering his work. Its journal, *The Consort*, began publication in 1929. Dolmetsch was awarded the cross of the Légion d'honneur of France (1938) and an honorary doctorate in music from the Univ. of Durham (1939). He prepared eds. of early music, including *Select English Songs and Dialogues of the 16th and 17th Centuries* (2 vols., London, 1898, 1912), *English Tunes of the 16th and 17th Centuries for Treble Recorder in F and Pieces for 2, 3 and 4 Recorders* (Haslemere, 1930), *Select French Songs from the 12th to the 18th Century* (London, 1938), and *The Dolmetsch Collection of English Consorts* (ed. by P. Grainger; N.Y., 1944). He also contributed articles to journals and publ. the book *The Interpretation of the Music of the XVII and XVIII Centuries* (London, 1915; 2nd ed., 1946). U. Supper ed. *A Catalogue of the Dolmetsch Library* (Haslemere, 1967).

BIBL.: R. Donington, *The Work and Ideas of A. D.* (Haslemere, 1932); P. Grainger, "A. D., Musical Confucius," *Musical Quarterly* (April 1933); W. McNaught, "A. D. and His Work," *Musical Times* (April 1940); N. Ferguson, "The Development of the D. Movement," *Hinrichsen's Musical Year Book* (1947); M. Dolmetsch, *Personal Recollections of A. D.* (London, 1958); E. Herrin, "A. D.," *The Consort* (July 1958); M. Campbell, *D.: The Man and His Work* (London and Seattle, 1975).

Dolmetsch, Carl Frederick, French recorder player, instrument maker, and scholar, son of **(Eugène) Arnold Dolmetsch**; b. Fontenay-sous-Bois, near Paris, Aug. 23, 1911. He received a thorough musical education from his father. He was only 7 when he made his first public appearance, and only 8 when he made his first tour. In 1937 he became director of the Society of Recorder Players. In 1940 he succeed his father as director of the Haslemere Festivals. From 1940 to 1976 he served as chairman of the firm Arnold Dolmetsch, Ltd. In 1971 he became director of the Dolmetsch International Summer School. He was chairman of Dolmetsch Musical Instruments from 1982. As a recorder player, he made regular tours of Europe and North and South America. He also commissioned scores for his instrument and prepared many recorder editions. He was the author of *Recorder and German Flute during the 17th and 18th Centuries* (London, 1960). In 1954 he was made a Commander of the Order of the British Empire.

Dolphy, Eric (Allan), black American jazz alto saxophonist, bass clarinetist, and flutist; b. Los Angeles, June 20, 1928; d. Berlin, June 29, 1964. He took up the clarinet in early childhood, later studying music at Los Angeles City College. After working with local groups, including Chico Hamilton's quintet (1958–59), he went to N.Y., where he performed with Charles

Mingus's Quartet (1959–60). He co-led a quintet with Booker Little (1961), then worked with John Coltrane, John Lewis, and again with Mingus. He was a master at improvisation, excelling in both jazz and "3rd-stream" genres. His repertoire included several avant-garde works, including Varèse's *Density 21.5*.

BIBL.: V. Simosko and B. Tepperman, *E. D.: A Musical Biography and Discography* (Washington, D.C., 1974); R. Horricks, *The Importance of Being E. D.* (Tunbridge Wells, 1989).

Dolukhanova, Zara, Russian mezzo-soprano of Armenian descent; b. Moscow, March 5, 1918. She studied with private teachers. She joined the Moscow Radio staff in 1944. A lyric singer, she excelled in the Romantic Russian repertoire. In 1959 she made her first American tour, enjoying great acclaim; she toured America again in 1970. In 1966 she was awarded the Lenin Prize.

Domanínská (real name, **Klobásková**), **Libuše,** Czech soprano; b. Brno, July 4, 1924. She was a student at the Brno Cons. of Hana Pírková and Bohuslav Sobeský. In 1945 she made her operatic debut as Blaženka in Smetana's *Tajemství*, and continued to sing there until 1955. In 1955 she became a member of the Prague National Theater, where she was a principal artist until 1985. She also was a member of the Vienna State Opera (1958–68) and a guest artist with other European opera companies. She likewise pursued an active concert career. In 1966 she was made an Artist of Merit and in 1974 a National Artist by the Czech government. In addition to her roles in operas by Mozart, Verdi, and Puccini, she won particular praise for her portrayals in operas by Czech and Russian masters.

Domanský, Hanuš, Slovak composer; b. Nový Hrozenkov, March 1, 1944. He studied composition with Jan Duchaň at the Brno Cons. and with Kardoš at the Bratislava Academy of Musical Arts, where he graduated in 1970. He later was active with the Czech Radio in Bratislava. His music combines the Czech tradition of Janáček with techniques of Stravinsky and Berg. His Sym. (1980) received the Slovak Composers Award in 1983.

WORKS: ORCH.: Concerto piccolo (1970); Sym. (1980); Piano Concerto (1984). **CHAMBER:** *Music* for Trumpet, Flute, and Bass Clarinet (1966); Piano Sonata (1967); String Quartet (1968); *Musica giocosa* for Violin and Piano (1971); *Dianoia* for Violin (1976); *A Fragment of a Sonata* for Piano (1977); *Bagatelles* for Piano (1978); *Dithyrambs* for Piano (1980). **VOCAL:** *About Winter*, cantata for Narrator, Children's Chorus, and Orch. (1968); *Fiat lux*, oratorio for Narrator, Soprano, Chorus, and Orch. (1970); *Disobedient Chants* for Children's Chorus (1971); *Klapancie* (Versifying) for Chorus and Percussion (1972); *Recruit Songs* for Men's Chorus (1978); also songs.

Domarkas, Ionas, Lithuanian composer; b. Lengiru, May 23, 1934. He studied at the Lithuanian Cons. in Vilna, and was subsequently active in radio broadcasting and teaching. Among his works are *Symphonic Dances* for Orch. (1969); a Violin Sonata (1972); and several pieces for clarinet, oboe, and bassoon, as well as for piano.

Domgraf-Fassbänder, Willi, German baritone, father of **Brigitte Fassbänder**; b. Aachen, Feb. 9, 1897; d. Nuremberg, Feb. 13, 1978. He first studied in Aachen, where he made his operatic debut (1922), then with Jacques Stückgold and Paul Bruns in Berlin and with Giuseppe Borgatti in Milan. He sang in Berlin, Düsseldorf, and Stuttgart, and was a leading member of the Berlin State Opera from 1928 until the end of World War II; he also appeared at the Glyndebourne Festivals (1934–35; 1937). After the war, he sang in Hannover, Vienna, Munich, and Nuremberg, serving as chief producer at the latter opera house (1953–62). He also taught at the Nuremberg Cons. (from 1954). Among his finest roles were Figaro, Papageno, and Guglielmo.

Domingo, Plácido, famous Spanish tenor and able conductor; b. Madrid, Jan. 21, 1941. His parents were zarzuela singers; after a tour of Mexico, they settled there and gave performances with their own company. Plácido joined his parents in Mexico at the age of 7 and began appearing with them in various productions while still a child; he also studied piano with Manuel Barajas in Mexico City and voice with Carlo Morelli at the National Cons. there (1955–57). He made his operatic debut in the tenor role of Borsa in *Rigoletto* with the National Opera in Mexico City in 1959. His first major role was as Alfredo in *La Traviata* in Monterrey in 1961; that same year he made his U.S. debut as Arturo in *Lucia di Lammermoor* with the Dallas Civic Opera; then was a member of the Hebrew National Opera in Tel Aviv (1962–64). He made his first appearance with the N.Y. City Opera as Pinkerton in *Madama Butterfly* on Oct. 17, 1965. On Aug. 9, 1966, he made his Metropolitan Opera debut as Turiddu in a concert performance of *Cavalleria rusticana* at N.Y.'s Lewisohn Stadium; his formal debut on the stage of the Metropolitan followed on Sept. 28, 1968, when he essayed the role of Maurice de Saxe in *Adriana Lecouvreur*, establishing himself as one of its principal members. He also sang regularly at the Vienna State Opera (from 1967), Milan's La Scala (from 1969), and London's Covent Garden (from 1971). His travels took him to all the major operatic centers of the world, and he also sang for recordings, films, and television. He also pursued conducting. He made his formal debut as an opera conductor with *La Traviata* at the N.Y. City Opera on Oct. 7, 1973, and on Oct. 25, 1984, he appeared at the Metropolitan Opera, conducting *La Bohème*. He commissioned Menotti's opera *Goya* and sang the title role at its premiere in Washington, D.C., on Nov. 15, 1986. In 1987 he sang Otello at the 100th anniversary performances at La Scala. On New Year's Eve 1988 he appeared as a soloist with Zubin Mehta and the N.Y. Phil. in a gala concert televised live to millions, during which he also conducted the orch. in the overture to *Die Fledermaus*. On July 7, 1990, he participated in a celebrated concert with fellow tenors José Carreras and Luciano Pavarotti in Rome, with Mehta conducting. The concert was telecast live to the world and subsequently became a best-selling video and compact disc. In 1992 he appeared at the opening gala ceremonies of the Olympic Games in Barcelona. In 1993 he sang Parsifal at the Bayreuth Festival with extraordinary success. Domingo celebrated his 25th anniversary with the Metropolitan Opera singing Siegmund in Act 1 of *Die Walküre* in a performance broadcast live on radio throughout the world on Sept. 27, 1993. On July 16, 1994, he again appeared in concert with Carreras, Pavarotti, and Mehta in Los Angeles, which spectacle was telecast live to the world. In 1994 Domingo was named principal guest conductor of the Los Angeles Opera. In 1996 he assumed the position of artistic director of the Washington (D.C.) Opera. One of the best-known lyric tenors of his era, Domingo has gained international renown for his portrayals of such roles as Cavaradossi, Des Grieux, Radames, Don Carlo, Otello, Don José, Hoffmann, Canio, and Samson. He publ. an autobiography, *Plácido Domingo: My First Forty Years* (N.Y., 1983).

BIBL.: D. Snowman, *The World of P. D.* (London, 1985); L. Fayer, *Von Don Carlos bis Parsifal: P. D., 25 Jahre an der Wiener Staatsoper* (Vienna, 1992); R. Stefoff, *P. D.* (N.Y., 1992).

Dominguez, Oralia, Mexican contralto; b. San Luis Potosí, Oct. 15, 1927. She studied at the National Cons. in Mexico City, during which time she made her first appearance as a singer in Debussy's *La Damoiselle élue*. After making her stage debut at the Mexico City Opera in 1950, she made her European debut at a concert at London's Wigmore Hall in 1953, and then toured in France, Spain, Germany, and the Netherlands; that same year she appeared as Princess de Bouillon in *Adrienne Lecouvreur* at Milan's La Scala. She then sang opera in Naples, Brussels, Vienna, and Paris. In 1955 she created the role of Sosostris in Tippett's *A Midsummer Marriage* at London's Covent Garden, and then appeared regularly at the Glyndebourne Festivals from 1955 to 1964. She was a member of the Deutsche Oper am Rhein in Düsseldorf from 1960. She also appeared as soloist with major orchs. and as a recitalist.

Dömling, Wolfgang, German musicologist; b. Munich, Dec. 20, 1938. He was educated at the Univ. of Munich, where he took his Ph.D. with the diss. *Der mehrstimmigen Balladen, Rondeaux und Virelais von Guillaume de Machaut* (publ. in the *Münchner Veröffentlichung zur Musikgeschichte*, XVI, Tutzing, 1970). From 1977 he was a prof. at the Univ. of Hamburg. Dömling has pursued studies in music of the Middle Ages, of the 19th century, and of the early 20th century. In addition to his articles in journals, he wrote *Hector Berlioz: Die symphonisch-dramatischen Werke* (Stuttgart, 1979), *Igor Strawinsky: Studien zu Ästhetik und Kompositionstechnik* (with T. Hirsbrunner; Laaber, 1985), and "Kunstwerk der Zukunft—Gegenwart der Moderne: Über einige Aspekte der französisch Wagner-Rezeption" in the Floros Festschrift (Wiesbaden, 1990).

Donalda (real name, **Lightstone**), **Pauline,** Canadian soprano; b. Montreal, March 5, 1882; d. there, Oct. 22, 1970. The original family name was Lichtenstein, which her father changed to Lightstone when he became a British subject. She received her first musical training at Royal Victoria College in Montreal, and then was a private pupil of Duvernoy in Paris. She made her operatic debut as Massenet's Manon in Nice, Dec. 30, 1904; the next year she appeared at the Théâtre Royal de la Monnaie in Brussels and at Covent Garden in London; in 1906–07 she appeared at the Manhattan Opera House in N.Y., and in London and Paris, mainly in oratorios and concerts. From the time of her retirement in 1922 until 1937 she had a singing school in Paris; in 1937 she returned to Montreal. In 1938 she presented her valuable music library (MSS, autographs, and music) to McGill Univ. In 1942 she founded the Opera Guild in Montreal, serving as its president until it ceased operations in 1969. In 1967 she was made an Officer of the Order of Canada. Her stage name was taken in honor of Sir Donald Smith (later Lord Strathcona), who endowed the Royal Victoria College and was her patron.

BIBL.: C. Brotman, *P. D.* (Montreal, 1975).

Donath, Helen (née **Erwin**), American soprano; b. Corpus Christi, Texas, July 10, 1940. After attending Del Mar College in Corpus Christi, she studied voice with Paola Novikova and Maria Berini. She then joined the Cologne Opera studio, where she made her formal operatic debut as Inez in *Il Trovatore* in 1960. From 1963 to 1967 she sang at the Hannover Opera, and then joined the Bavarian State Opera in Munich in 1967, where she quickly rose to prominence. In 1971 she made her U.S. operatic debut as Sophie at the San Francisco Opera. In 1979 she made her first appearance at London's Covent Garden as Anne Trulove. She also appeared as a guest artist in Salzburg, Vienna, Hamburg, Berlin, Bayreuth, Milan, and Zürich. In 1990 she was made a Bavarian Kammersängerin. Among her many roles were Susanna, Zerlina, Ilia in *Idomeneo*, Marcelline in *Fidelio*, Ännchen in *Der Freischütz*, Micaëla, Mélisande, and Mimi.

Donati, Pino, Italian opera director, administrator, and composer; b. Verona, May 9, 1907; d. Rome, Feb. 24, 1975. After studying violin, he received instruction in composition from Paribeni. He was an opera director at the Verona Arena (1936–43), in Lisbon (1946–50), and in Bologna (1950–56). In 1958 he became artistic director of the Chicago Lyric Opera; from 1964 until his death he served as its co-artistic director with Bruno Bartoletti; from 1968 he also was director of the Florence Opera. In 1939 he married **Maria Caniglia**. Among his works were the operas *Corradino lo Svevo* (Verona, April 4, 1931) and *Lancillotto del lago* (Bergamo, Oct. 2, 1938), and chamber music.

Donato, Anthony, American violinist, conductor, teacher, and composer; b. Prague, Nebr., March 8, 1909. He studied violin with Gustave Tinlot, conducting with Goossens, and composition with Hanson, Royce, and Rogers at the Eastman School of Music in Rochester, N.Y. (B.M., 1931; M.M., 1937; Ph.D., 1947). After playing violin in the Rochester Phil. (1927–31) and the Hochstein Quartet (1929–31), he served as head of the violin depts. at Drake Univ. (1931–37), Iowa State Teachers College (1937–39), and the Univ. of Texas (1939–46); he then was prof. of theory and composition at Northwestern Univ. (1947–76), where he also conducted its chamber orch. (1947–58). He publ. a valuable textbook on notational techniques, *Preparing Music Manuscripts* (Englewood Cliffs, N.J., 1963). As a composer, Donato was particularly successful writing choral works and piano pieces.

WORKS: OPERA: *The Walker Through Walls* (1964; Evanston, Ill., Feb. 26, 1965). **ORCH.:** 2 sinfoniettas (1936, 1959); *Elegy* for Strings (1938); 2 syms. (1944, 1945); *Mission San José de Aguaya* (1945); *Prairie Schooner*, overture (1947); Suite for Strings (1948); *The Plains* (1953); *Episode* (1954); *Solitude in the City* for Narrator and Orch. (1954); *Serenade* for Small Orch. (1962); *Centennial Ode* (Omaha, Dec. 11, 1967; for Nebraska's centennial); *Improvisation* (1968); *Discourse* for Flute and Strings (1969; also for Flute and Piano). **CHAMBER:** 2 violin sonatas (1938, 1949); 4 string quartets (1941, 1947, 1951, 1975); *Drag and Run* for Clarinet, 2 Violins, and Cello (1946); *Pastorale and Dance* for 4 Clarinets (1947); Sonatine for 3 Trumpets (1949); Horn Sonata (1950); Wind Quintet (1955); *Prelude and Allegro* for Trumpet and Piano (1957); Piano Trio (1959); Clarinet Sonata (1966); *Discourse I* for Flute and Piano (1969; also for Flute and Strings) and *II* for Saxophone and Piano (1974); many piano pieces. **VOCAL:** *March of the Hungry Mountains* for Tenor, Chorus, and Small Orch. (1949); *Last Supper* for Baritone and Chorus (1952); *The Congo* for Soprano, Chorus, and Orch. (1957); *Prelude and Choral Fantasy* for Men's Voices, 2 Trumpets, 2 Trombones, Percussion, and Organ (1961); *Blessed is the Man* for Chorus, Brass Quartet, and Organ (1970); many songs.

Donatoni, Franco, noted Italian composer and pedagogue; b. Verona, June 9, 1927. He commenced his musical training with Piero Bottagisio at the Verona Liceo Musicale. After further studies in composition with Desderi at the Milan Cons. (1946–48), he was a student of Liviabella at the Bologna Cons., where he took diplomas in composition and band orchestration (1949), choral music (1950), and composition (1951). He pursued advanced composition studies with Pizzetti at the Accademia di Santa Cecilia in Rome (graduated, 1953), and then attended the summer courses in new music in Darmstadt (1954, 1956, 1958, 1961). He taught at the Bologna Cons. (1953–55), the Turin Cons. (1956–69), and the Milan Cons. (1969–78) before holding the chair in advanced composition at the Accademia di Santa Cecilia. He also taught advanced composition at the Accademia Musicale Chigiana in Siena (from 1970), and was concurrently on the faculty of the Univ. of Bologna (1971–85). In addition, he taught at the Civica Scuola in Milan, the Perosi Academy in Biella, and the Forlanini Academy in Brescia; also gave master classes. He publ. the vols. *Questo* (1970), *Antecedente X* (1980), *Il sigaro di Armando* (1982), and *In-oltre* (1988). In addition to his memberships in the Accademia Nazionale di Santa Cecilia and the Accademia Filarmonica of Rome, the French government honored him as a Commandeur of l'Ordre des Arts et des Lettres in 1985. As a composer, Donatoni was deeply influenced by Schoenberg, Boulez, and Stockhausen, particularly in his mature aleatoric style. His gifts as a master of his craft are most fully revealed in his orch. works and chamber music, which are notable for their imaginative manipulation of sonorities and colors.

WORKS: DRAMATIC: OPERA: *Atem* (1983–84; Milan, Feb. 16, 1985). **BALLET:** *La lampara* (1957).

ORCH.: Concertino for Brass, Timpani, and Strings (1952); Concerto for Bassoon and Strings (1952); Overture for Chamber Orch. (1953); Sinfonia for Strings (1953); *Divertimento I* for Violin and Chamber Orch. (1954) and *II* for Strings (Venice, Sept. 10, 1965); *Musica* for Chamber Orch. (1955); *Strophes* (1959; RAI, Jan. 30, 1960); *Sezioni* (1960; North German Radio, Hamburg, May 14, 1962); *Puppenspiel I* (1961; Palermo, Oct. 8, 1962) and *II* for Flute and Orch. (Valdagno, Sept. 17, 1966); *Per orchestra* (1962; Warsaw, Sept. 24, 1963); *Black and White* for Strings (1964; Palermo, Sept. 6, 1965); *Doubles II* (1970; Venice, Jan. 15, 1971); *To Earle I* for Chamber Orch. (1970; Bolzano,

Feb. 2, 1971) and *II* (1971–72; Kiel, Sept. 2, 1972); *Voci* (1972–73; Rome, Feb. 3, 1974); *Espressivo* for Oboe and Orch. (1974; Royan, March 24, 1975); *Duo per Bruno* (1974–75; West German Radio, Cologne, Sept. 19, 1975); *Portrait* for Harpsichord and Orch. (1976–77; Radio France, Paris, Oct. 6, 1977); *Le ruisseau sur l'escalier* for Cello and Chamber Orch. (1980; Paris, April 30, 1981); *Sinfonia Op. 63 "Anton Webern"* (Naples, May 13, 1983); *Diario '83* for 4 Trumpets, 4 Trombones, and Orch. (1983–84; Milan, Feb. 16, 1985); *Eco* for Chamber Orch. (1985–86); Concerto grosso for Orch. and Electronics (Bologna, June 5, 1992).

CHAMBER: *Quartetto I* (1950), *II* (1958; Florence, March 23, 1962), and *IV* (Palermo, Oct. 5, 1963) for String Quartet; Viola Sonata (1952); Harp Sonata (1953); *Movimento* for Harpsichord, Piano, and 9 Instruments (Milan, Nov. 30, 1959); *For Grilly* for 7 Instrumentalists (Rome, May 24, 1960); *Asar* for 10 Strings (1964); *Etwas ruhiger im Ausdruck* for Flute, Clarinet, Violin, Cello, and Piano (1967; Rome, Feb. 1, 1968); *Souvenir I*: Chamber Sym. for 15 Instruments (Venice, Sept. 12, 1967) and *II: Orts* for 14 Instruments and Speaker ad libitum (Paris, March 21, 1969); *Solo* for 10 Strings (1969); *Estratto I* for Piano (1969; Trieste, Feb. 19, 1970), *II* for Piano, Harpsichord, and Harp (Brescia, June 9, 1970), *IV* for 8 Instruments (Rome, Feb. 3, 1974), and *III* for Piano and Wind Octet (1975; Milan, Feb. 12, 1976); *Lied* for 13 Instruments (1972; Siena, Sept. 3, 1973); *Jeux pour deux* for Harpsichord and Organ (1973; Royan, March 28, 1975); *Duetto* for Harpsichord (Brescia, June 5, 1975); *Lumen* for 6 Instruments (Siena, Aug. 27, 1975); *Ash* for 8 Instruments (Siena, Aug. 27, 1976); *Musette per Lothar* for Musette (Siena, Aug. 27, 1976); *Toy* for 2 Violins, Viola, and Harpsichord (Turin, June 23, 1977); *Algo* for Guitar (Milan, Nov. 2, 1977); *Ali* for Viola (Paris, June 26, 1978); *Spiri* for 10 Instruments (Rome, June 18, 1978); *About . . .* for Violin, Viola, and Guitar (Siena, Aug. 25, 1979); *Argot* for Violin (Siena, Aug. 25, 1979); *Nidi I* for Piccolo (Venice, Sept. 26, 1979) and *II* for Baroque Tenor Flute (1992); *Marches I* for Harp (Berkeley, Nov. 25, 1979) and *II* for Harp, 3 Women's Voices ad libitum, and Chamber Ensemble (Alessandria, Sept. 18, 1990); *Clair* for Clarinet (Siena, Aug. 26, 1980); *Tema* for Chamber Ensemble (1981; Paris, Feb. 8, 1982); *Small* for Piccolo, Clarinet, and Harp (Siena, Aug. 25, 1981); *The Heart's Eye* for String Quartet (Venice, Oct. 7, 1981); *Fili* for Flute and Piano (Venice, Oct. 7, 1981); *Lame* for Cello (Siena, Aug. 26, 1982); *Feria I* for 5 Flutes, 5 Trumpets, and Organ (Bologna, Sept. 24, 1982) and *II* for Organ (Milan, June 17, 1992); (28) *François Variationen* for Piano (1983–89); *Rima* for Piano (Cortona, July 9, 1983); *Alamari* for Cello, Double Bass, and Piano (Siena, Aug. 29, 1983); *Ala* for Cello and Double Bass (1983; Siena, Aug. 23, 1985); *Ronda* for Violin, Viola, Cello, and Piano (La Rochelle, June 24, 1984); *Lem* for Double Bass (Sesto San Giovanni, March 31, 1984); *Ombra* for Bass Clarinet (Certaldo, July 26, 1984); *Darkness* for 6 Percussionists (Strasbourg, Sept, 18, 1984); *Cadeau* for 11 Instruments (Turin, July 7, 1985); Septet for 2 Violins, 2 Violas, and 2 Cellos (Cremona, Sept. 22, 1985); *Omar* for Vibraphone (Siena, Aug. 23, 1985); *Refrain I* for 8 Instruments (Amsterdam, July 7, 1986) and *II* for Chamber Ensemble (Melbourne, Sept. 29, 1991); *Arpège* for 6 Instruments (1986; Paris, March 30, 1987); *Flag* for 13 Instruments (Milan, May 9, 1987); *Ave* for Piccolo, Glockenspiel, and Celesta (Strasbourg, Oct. 3, 1987); *Short* for Trumpet (Cosenza, May 9, 1988); *La souris sans sourire* for String Quartet (1988; Paris, Dec. 18, 1989); *Cloche I* for 2 Pianos, 8 Winds, and 2 Percussion (1988–89; Strasbourg, Sept. 19, 1989), *II* for 2 Pianos (Rome, Oct. 1, 1990), and *III* for Chamber Ensemble (Ravenna, July 21, 1991); *Frain* for 8 Instruments (1989); *Soft* for Bass Clarinet (Fermo, July 31, 1989); *Midi* for Flute (Turin, Sept. 27, 1989); *Hot* for Soprano or Tenor Saxophone and Chamber Ensemble (Metz, Nov. 17, 1989); *Blow* for Wind Quintet (1989; Milan, Feb. 11, 1990); *Caglio* for Violin (Milan, Nov. 28, 1989); *Chantal* for Harp, Flute, Clarinet, and String Quartet (Geneva, July 12, 1990); *Het* for Flute, Bass Clarinet, and Piano (Siena, Aug. 22, 1990); *Rasch* for Saxophone Quartet (Graz, Oct. 6, 1990); *Spice* for Violin, Clarinet, Cello, and Piano (1990; London, Feb. 19, 1991); *Holly* for Chamber Ensemble (1990; Toronto, March 22, 1991); *Bok* for Bass Clarinet and Marimba (1990; Rome, April 8, 1991); *Sweet* for Flute (1992); *Sincronie* for Piano and Cello (Huddersfield, Nov. 28, 1992).

VOCAL: *Il libro dei sette sigilli* for Soloists, Chorus, and Orch. (1951); *Serenata* for Woman's Voice and 16 Instruments (Milan, April 11, 1959); *Madrigale* for Chorus and Percussion Quartet (1968); *Arie* for Voice and Orch. (1978; RAI, Rome, March 15, 1980); *. . . ed insieme bussarono* for Woman's Voice and Piano (Strasbourg, Nov. 7, 1978); *De Pres* for Woman's Voice, 2 Piccolos, and 3 Violins (Radio France, Paris, Feb. 9, 1980); *L'ultima sera* for Woman's Voice and 5 Instruments (1980; Radio France, Paris, June 18, 1981); *Abyss* for Woman's Voice, Flute, and Instruments (Metz, Nov. 18, 1983); *In cauda* for Chorus and Orch. (1983; Cologne, Dec. 6, 1991); *She* for 3 Sopranos and 6 Instruments (Rome, Sept. 24, 1983); *Still* for High Soprano and 6 Instruments (Milan, April 21, 1985); *O si ride* for 12 Vocalists (1987; Paris, May 19, 1988); *Cinis* for Woman's Voice and Piano (Strasbourg, Sept. 21, 1988); *Åse: Algo II* for Woman's Voice and Guitar (1990); *Aahiel* for Soprano or Mezzo-soprano, Clarinet, Vibraphone or Marimba, and Piano (1992).

TAPE: *Quartetto III* (1961; Venice, April 15, 1962).

BIBL.: G. Mazzola Nangeroni, *F. D.* (Milan, 1989).

Dönch, Karl, German bass-baritone; b. Hagen, Jan. 8, 1915; d. Vienna, Sept. 16, 1994. He studied at the Dresden Cons., then made his operatic debut in Görlitz (1936). He sang in Reichenberg, Bonn, and Salzburg, later becoming a member of the Vienna State Opera (1947) and making regular appearances at the Salzburg Festivals (from 1951). He was a guest artist at the Berlin Städtische Oper, the Deutsche Oper am Rhein in Düsseldorf, Milan's La Scala, and the Teatro Colón in Buenos Aires. On Jan. 22, 1959, he made his Metropolitan Opera debut in N.Y. as Beckmesser; was on its roster from 1962 to 1965 and again from 1966 to 1969. From 1973 to 1986 he was director of the Vienna Volksoper. In addition to the standard Austro-German repertoire, Dönch sang in several contemporary works, including Liebermann's *Penelope* (1954) and Frank Martin's *Tempest* (1956).

Dong, Kui, innovative Chinese composer; b. Beijing, Feb. 14, 1967. She began piano lessons at the age of 4 with her mother, a coloratura soprano with the Chamber Orch. of the Central Philharmonic Soc. in Beijing. She studied composition and theory with Mingxin Du and Zuqing Wu at the Central Cons. of Music in Beijing (B.A., 1987; M.A., 1989); in 1991 she entered the doctoral program in composition and computer music composition at Stanford Univ., where her principal mentors were John Chowning, Chris Chafe, Leland Smith, and Wayne Peterson. Her compositions have won numerous awards, including the 1st prize National Music Award for Music and Dance in Beijing (1990) and 1st prize in Boston's Alea III International Competition (1994); in 1995 she held the Gerald Oshita Stipend for Composers in the Artists in Residence Program at the Djerassi Foundation in Woodside, California. In 1995 she received a Young Composers Award. Her music video, *The Horizon* (1993), was funded by a research grant from the Asia-Pacific National Fund.

WORKS: *Piano Suite* (Beijing, Sept. 4, 1984); *Sigui* for Sanxian, Bamboo Flute, and Chinese Percussion (Beijing, Sept. 4, 1984); *Chen* for Piano Duet (1986); *Imperial Concubine Yang* for Orch. (1988–89; Beijing, Feb. 9, 1989); *Zhang Jing Tang* for Orch. (Beijing, Dec. 14, 1989); *Four Image Songs* (1990); *Eclipse I*, computer-generated tape music installation (1992; San Jose, Calif., Nov. 13, 1993); *Prelude, Fugue, and Postlude* for Piano (Stanford, Calif., Dec. 14, 1992); *The Horizon*, music video (1993); *The Blue Melody* for Violin, Cello, Flute, Clarinet, and Piano (Stanford, Calif., May 12, 1993); *Invisible Scenes I* for String Orch. (Windsor, Canada, Nov. 4, 1994); *Flying Apples*, computer algorhythmic composition for quadraphonic tape (Stanford, Calif., July 12, 1994); *Cycle of Light* for 12 Musicians (1995); Clarinet Concert (1995–96).

Donington, Robert, distinguished English musicologist; b. Leeds, May 4, 1907; d. Firle, Sussex, Jan. 20, 1990. He studied at Queen's College, Oxford (B.A., 1930; B. Litt., 1946); also took a course in composition with Wellesz at Oxford; became associated with Arnold Dolmetsch in his workshop in Haslemere and studied the technique of early instruments; contributed to the revival of Elizabethan instruments and music. He was a member of the English Consort of Viols (1935–39); then played with the London Consort (1950–60); in 1956 he founded the Donington Consort, and led it until 1961. He lectured extensively in the U.S. He was made a Commander of the Order of the British Empire in 1979.

WRITINGS: *The Work and Ideas of Arnold Dolmetsch* (Haslemere, 1932); with E. Hunt, *A Practical Method for the Recorder* (2 vols., London, 1935); *The Instruments of Music* (London, 1949; 4th ed., rev., 1982, as *Music and Its Instruments*); *Music for Fun* (London, 1960); *Tempo and Rhythm in Bach's Organ Music* (London, 1960); *The Interpretation of Early Music* (N.Y., 1963; 3rd ed., rev., 1974; corrected ed., 1989); *Wagner's "Ring" and Its Symbols* (London, 1963; 3rd ed., rev. and enl., 1974); *A Performer's Guide to Baroque Music* (London, 1973); *String-playing in Baroque Music* (London, 1977); *The Opera* (London, 1978); *The Rise of Opera* (London, 1981); *Baroque Music: Style and Performance: A Handbook* (London, 1982); *Opera and Its Symbols: The Unity of Words, Music, and Singing* (London, 1991).

Donner, Henrik Otto, Finnish composer; b. Tampere, Nov. 16, 1939. He studied composition at the Sibelius Academy in Helsinki with Fougstedt and Kokkonen; then attended seminars in electronic music in Bilthoven, the Netherlands; also took private lessons with Ligeti. He played trumpet in jazz bands and later in his own band. After serving as head of entertainment and music for the Finnish Broadcasting Co. (1970–74), he was managing director of Love Records (1976–79).

WORKS: *3 Pieces* for Flute and Piano (1962); *Cantata profana* (1962); *Ideogramme I* for Flute, Clarinet, Trombone, Percussion, and 12 Radios (1962) and *II* for 20 Musicians, Tape Recording, and Promenade Room (1963); *For Emmy 2* for 3 Women's Voices and Amplified Chamber Ensemble (1963); *Kinetique* for Jazz Band and Chamber Ensemble (1964); *Moonspring, or Aufforderung zum . . . or Symphony 1*, "Hommage à Ives," for Strings, Guitar, Harp, and Hammond Organ (1964); *6 Bagatelles* for String Quartet (1965); *Gilbert*, musical (1965); *To Whom It May Concern* for Orch. and Jazz Drums (1966); *XC* for Soprano, Chorus, and Chamber Orch. (1969); String Quartet No. 1, with Baritone (1970); *In the Afternoon* for Viola (1971); *Notte* for Guitar (1971); *Etyd för sommarvind* (Etude for Summer Wind) for Men's Chorus (1971); film music.

Donohoe, Peter (Howard), English pianist and conductor; b. Manchester, June 18, 1953. He began piano study at the age of 4 and later attended Chetham's School of Music in Manchester (1964–71); at age 12, he made his debut as soloist in Beethoven's 3rd Piano Concerto in Manchester; after attending the Univ. of Leeds (1971–72), he studied at the Royal Manchester College of Music (1972–73) and the Royal Northern College of Music (1973–76) before completing his training with Loriod at the Paris Cons. (1976–77). In 1979 he made his first appearance at the London Promenade Concerts. After winning joint 2nd-prize in the Tchaikovsky Competition in Moscow in 1982, he pursued a global career as a soloist with orchs., a recitalist, and a chamber music player. As a conductor, he served as artistic director of the Northern Chamber Orch. (1984–87) and as founder-conductor of the Manchester Sinfonietta (from 1986). As a piano virtuoso, Donohoe has won accolades for both his fine performances of the standard repertoire and for his championship of an extensive modern repertoire, ranging from Stravinsky and Prokofiev to Messiaen and Muldowney.

Donostia, José Antonio de (real name, **José Gonzalo Zulaica y Arregui**), Spanish organist, musicologist, and composer; b. San Sebastián, Jan. 10, 1886; d. Lecároz, Navarre, Aug. 30, 1956. He studied with Echazarra at the Lecároz Franciscan College, Esquerrá in Barcelona, Gaviola in San Sebastián, and Cools and Roussel in Paris. He worked in Toulouse (1936), Paris (1939–40), and Bayonne (1941–43) as an organist and choirmaster, then became head of the folklore dept. of Barcelona's Spanish Inst. of Musicology (1943), where he brought out monographs and eds. of Basque folk song.

WORKS: CHAMBER: 12 romanzas for Violin and Piano (1905–10); String Quartet (1906); *3 piezas* for Cello and Piano (1906); *La Quête héroïque de Graal* for 4 Ondes Martenot and Piano (1938); *Página romántica* for Violin and Piano (1941); piano pieces; organ music. **VOCAL:** *Les Trois Miracles de Ste. Cécile* for Chorus and Orch. (1920); *La Vie profonde de St. François d'Assise* for Chorus and Orch. (1926); *Le Noël de Greecio* for Chorus and Orch. (1936); *Poema de la Pasión* for 2 Sopranos, Chorus, and English Horn (1937); *Missa pro defunctis* for Chorus and Organ (1945).

WRITINGS: *La música popular vasca* (Bilbao, 1918); *Euskel eres-sorta* (Bilbao, 1922); *Essai d'une bibliographie musicale populaire basque* (Bayonne, 1932); *Música y músicos en el pais vasco* (San Sebastián, 1951); *El "Moto proprio" y la canción popular religiosa* (San Sebastián, 1954); *Euskal-erriko otoitzak* (San Sebastián, 1956).

BIBL.: J. de Riezu, *J.A. d.D.* (Pamplona, 1956).

Donovan, Richard Frank, American organist, conductor, teacher, and composer; b. New Haven, Conn., Nov. 29, 1891; d. Middletown, Conn., Aug. 22, 1970. He studied music at Yale Univ. and at the Inst. of Musical Art in N.Y. (M.B., 1922); also took lessons in organ with Widor in Paris. Returning to America, he served as organist in several N.Y. churches; from 1923 to 1928 he was on the faculty of Smith College; in 1928 he was appointed to the School of Music at Yale Univ., where he later was a prof. of theory (1947–60). From 1936 to 1951 he conducted the New Haven Sym. Orch.; was also organist and choirmaster of Christ Church in New Haven. As a composer, Donovan adopted a modern polyphonic style in his choral works, while his instrumental scores often reveal impressionistic traits.

WORKS: ORCH.: *Smoke and Steel*, symphonic poem (1932); Sym. for Chamber Orch. (1936); *New England Chronicle*, overture (1947); *Passacaglia on Vermont Folk Tunes* (1949); Sym. (1956); *Epos* (1963). **CHAMBER:** *Wood-Notes* for Flute, Harp, and Strings (1925); Sextet for Wind Instruments and Piano (1932); 2 piano trios (1937, 1963); Serenade for Oboe, Violin, Viola, and Cello (1939); *Terzetto* for 2 Violins and Viola (1950); Woodwind Quartet (1953); *Soundings* for Trumpet, Bassoon, and Percussion (1953); *Music for 6* (1961). **KEYBOARD:** 2 suites for piano (1932, 1953); much organ music. **CHORAL:** *Fantasy on American Folk Ballads* for Men's Voices and Piano (1940); *Mass* for Unison Voices, Organ, 3 Trumpets, and Timpani (1955); *Forever, O Lord* for Chorus (1965).

Dooley, William (Edward), American baritone; b. Modesto, Calif., Sept. 9, 1932. He was a pupil of Lucy Lee Call at the Eastman School of Music in Rochester, N.Y., and of Viktoria Prestel and Hedwig Fichtmüller in Munich. In 1957 he made his operatic debut as Rodrigo in *Don Carlos* in Heidelberg; after singing at the Bielefeld Stadttheater (1959–62), he was a member of the Berlin Deutsche Oper (from 1962), where he sang in the premieres of Sessions's *Montezuma* (1964), Reimann's *Gespenstersonate* (1984), and Rihm's *Oedipus* (1987). In 1964 he appeared at the Salzburg Festival, returning there in 1966 to sing in the premiere of Henze's *The Bassarids*. On Feb. 15, 1964, he made his Metropolitan Opera debut in N.Y. as Eugene Onegin, remaining on its roster until 1977. His engagements as a concert artist took him to many of the principal North American and European music centers. Among his prominent roles were Pizarro, Kothner, Escamillo, Macbeth, Amonasro, Telramund, Mandryka, Nick Shadow, and Wozzeck.

Doorslaer, Georges van, Belgian music scholar; b. Mechelen, Sept. 27, 1864; d. there, Jan. 16, 1940. He studied medicine;

music was his avocation. In association with Charles van den Borren, he began a detailed study of early Belgian music; became particularly interested in the history of the carillon. He wrote numerous articles on Philippe de Monte, and ed. his works with van den Borren (31 vols., Bruges, 1927–39; reprint 1965).

WRITINGS: *La vie et les oeuvres de Philippe de Monte* (Brussels, 1921); *Le Carillon de la Tour de Saint-Rombaut à Malines* (Mechelen, 1926); *De Beiaard van Aalst* (Mechelen, 1926); *La corporation et les ouvrages des orfèvres malinois* (Antwerp, 1935).

BIBL.: P. Verheyden, "In Memoriam Dr. G. v.D., 1864–1940," *Bulletin du Cercle Archéologique de Malines*, XLV (1940; with list of writings).

Dopper, Cornelis, Dutch conductor and composer; b. Stadskanaal, near Groningen, Feb. 7, 1870; d. Amsterdam, Sept. 18, 1939. He was a student of Jadassohn and Reinecke at the Leipzig Cons. (1887–90). After serving as a coach and conductor with the Netherlands Opera in Amsterdam (1896–1903), he was conductor of the Savage Opera Co., with which he toured North America. From 1908 to 1931 he held the post of 2nd conductor under Mengelberg with the Concertgebouw Orch. in Amsterdam. He introduced youth concerts to the Netherlands. His well-crafted scores were composed in a late Romantic vein.

WORKS: DRAMATIC: OPERAS: *Het blinde meisje von Castel Cuillé* (1892; The Hague, Dec. 17, 1894); *Frithof* (1895); *William Ratcliff* (1896–1901; Weimar, Oct. 19, 1909); *Het eerekruis* (1902; Amsterdam, Jan. 9, 1903); *Don Quichotte* (unfinished). **BALLET:** *Meidevorn*. **ORCH.:** 7 syms.: No. 1, *Diana* (1896), No. 2 (1903), No. 3, *Rembrandt* (1892), No. 4, *Symphonietta* (1906), No. 5, *Symphonia epica* (1914), No. 6, *Amsterdam* (1912), and No. 7, *Zuiderzee* (1919); *Ciaconna gotica* (Amsterdam, Oct. 24, 1920); overtures; concertos; suites. **OTHER:** Chamber music; piano pieces; choral works; songs.

Doran, Matt (Higgins), American composer and teacher; b. Covington, Ky., Sept. 1, 1921. He was a student at Los Angeles City College and of Toch, Kubik, and Eisler at the Univ. of Southern Calif. in Los Angeles (B.M., 1947; D.M.A., 1953); he also received training in flute and played in several orchs. He taught at Del Mar College in Corpus Christi (1953–55) and at Ball State Univ. in Muncie (1956–57); he then was an instructor (1957–66) and a prof. (from 1966) at Mount St. Mary College in Los Angeles.

WORKS: OPERAS: 10 operas, including *The Committee* (1953; Corpus Christi, May 25, 1955) and *The Marriage Counselor* (Los Angeles, March 12, 1977). **ORCH.:** 4 syms. (1946, 1959, 1977, 1979); Flute Concerto (1953); Horn Concerto (1954); Piano Concerto (1975); Cello Concerto (1976); Double Concerto for Flute, Guitar, and Strings (Los Angeles, May 21, 1976). **CHAMBER:** *Poem* for Flute and Piano (1965); Clarinet Sonata (1967); Sonatina for Flute and Cello (1968); Quartet for Oboe, Clarinet, Bassoon, and Viola (1970); Trio for Flute, Clarinet, and Piano (1979–80); flute pieces; piano music. **VOCAL:** *Eskaton*, oratorio for Soloists, Chorus, Orch. (1976); songs.

Doráti, Antal, distinguished Hungarian-born American conductor and composer; b. Budapest, April 9, 1906; d. Gerzensee, near Bern, Nov. 13, 1988. He studied with Leo Weiner, both privately and at the Franz Liszt Academy of Music in Budapest, where he also received instruction in composition from Kodály (1920–24). He was on the staff of the Budapest Opera (1924–28); after conducting at the Dresden State Opera (1928–29), he was Generalmusikdirektor in Münster (1929–32). In 1933 he went to France, where he conducted the Ballets Russes de Monte Carlo, which he took on a tour of Australia (1938). He made his U.S. debut as guest conductor with the National Sym. Orch. in Washington, D.C., in 1937. In 1940 he settled in the U.S., becoming a naturalized citizen in 1947. He began his American career as music director of the American Ballet Theatre in N.Y. (1941–44); after serving as conductor of the Dallas Sym. Orch. (1945–49), he was music director of the Minneapolis Sym. Orch. (1949–60). From 1963 to 1966 he was chief conductor of the BBC Sym. Orch. in London; then of the Stockholm Phil. (1966–70). He was music director of the National Sym. Orch. in Washington, D.C. (1970–77), and of the Detroit Sym. Orch. (1977–81); was also principal conductor of the Royal Phil. in London (1975–79). He made numerous guest conducting appearances in Europe and North America, earning a well-deserved reputation as an orch. builder. His prolific recording output made him one of the best-known conductors of his time. His recordings of the Haydn syms. and operas were particularly commendable. In 1984 he was made an honorary Knight Commander of the Order of the British Empire. In 1969 he married **Ilse von Alpenheim**, who often appeared as a soloist under his direction. His autobiography was publ. as *Notes of Seven Decades* (London, 1979).

WORKS: *Divertimento* for Orch.; *Graduation Ball*, ballet, arranged from the waltzes of Johann Strauss; *The Way of the Cross*, dramatic cantata (Minneapolis, April 19, 1957); 2 syms.: No. 1 (Minneapolis, March 18, 1960) and No. 2, *Querela pacis* (Detroit, April 24, 1986); *7 Pieces* for Orch. (1961; perf. as a ballet, *Maddalena*); Piano Concerto (1974; Washington, D.C., Oct. 28, 1975); Cello Concerto (Louisville, Oct. 1, 1976); chamber music.

BIBL.: J. Ayres, "A. D., 1906–1988," *Le Grand Baton* (Dec. 1991).

Doret, Gustave, Swiss composer and conductor; b. Aigle, Sept. 20, 1866; d. Lausanne, April 19, 1943. He received his first instruction at Lausanne; studied violin with Joachim in Berlin (1885–87); then entered the Paris Cons. as a pupil of Marsick (violin) and Dubois and Massenet (composition). He was conductor of the Concerts d'Harcourt and of the Société Nationale de Musique in Paris (1893–95); at the Opéra-Comique (1907–09); also appeared as a visiting conductor in Rome, London, and Amsterdam. In his music, Doret cultivated the spirit of Swiss folk songs; his vocal writing is distinguished by its natural flow of melody. He publ. *Musique et musiciens* (1915), *Lettres à ma nièce sur la musique en Suisse* (1919), *Pour notre indépendance musicale* (1920), and *Temps et contretemps* (1942).

WORKS: DRAMATIC: OPERAS: *Maedeli* (1901); *Les Armaillis* (Paris, Oct. 23, 1906; rev. version, Paris, May 5, 1930); *Le Nain du Hasli* (Geneva, Feb. 6, 1908); *Loÿs*, dramatic legend (Vevey, 1912); *La Tisseuse d'Orties* (Paris, 1926); incidental music. **OTHER:** *Voix de la Patrie*, cantata (1891); *Les Sept Paroles du Christ*, oratorio (1895); *La Fête des vignerons* (1905); String Quartet; Piano Quintet; about 150 songs.

BIBL.: J. Dupérier, *G. D.* (Paris, 1932).

Dorfmann, Ania, Russian-American pianist and teacher; b. Odessa, July 9, 1899; d. N.Y., April 21, 1984. As a very young child in Russia, she teamed up with Jascha Heifetz in duo recitals; then was accepted at the age of 12 at the Paris Cons., where her teacher was Isidor Philipp. She returned to Russia just before the Revolution, but was able to leave again in 1920; she toured in Europe as a concert pianist; in 1936 she emigrated to America, giving her first American recital in N.Y. on Nov. 27, 1936. On Dec. 2, 1939, she appeared as a soloist with Toscanini and the NBC Sym. Orch. in N.Y. She then devoted herself mainly to teaching; was on the faculty of the Juilliard School of Music in N.Y. from 1966.

Dorian, Frederick (real name, **Friedrich Deutsch**), eminent Austrian-born American music scholar; b. Vienna, July 1, 1902; d. Pittsburgh, Jan. 24, 1991. He studied musicology with Adler at the Univ. of Vienna (Ph.D., 1925, with the diss. *Die Fugenarbeit in den Werken Beethovens*; publ. in *Studien zur Musikwissenschaft*, XIV, 1927); also took piano lessons with Steuermann and studied composition privately with Webern. He was also closely associated with Schoenberg; Dorian's family apartment housed the headquarters of the famous Soc. for Private Musical Performances, organized by Schoenberg, Berg, and Webern. He also took courses in conducting, achieving a high degree of professionalism. He served as music critic of the *Berliner Mor-*

genpost (1930–33), the *Frankfurter Zeitung* (1934), and the *Neues Wiener Journal* (1935–36). In 1936 he emigrated to the U.S., becoming a naturalized citizen in 1941. From 1936 to 1954 he was a member of the Carnegie-Mellon Univ. (formerly Carnegie Inst. of Technology) in Pittsburgh; there he organized an opera dept., and conducted its inaugural performance; from 1971 to 1975 he served as Andrew Mellon Lecturer there. From 1975 to 1977 he was visiting lecturer on music history at the Curtis Inst. of Music in Philadelphia. In 1978 he gave lectures on musicology at the Hebrew Univ. in Jerusalem. He also served, from 1945, as program annotator for the Pittsburgh Sym. Orch. program magazine.

WRITINGS: *Hausmusik alter Meister* (3 vols., Berlin, 1933); *The History of Music in Performance* (N.Y., 1942; 2nd ed., 1966); *The Musical Workshop* (N.Y., 1947); *Commitment to Culture* (Pittsburgh, 1964).

Doring, Ernest N(icholas), American violin specialist; b. N.Y., May 29, 1877; d. Fort Worth, Texas, July 9, 1955. He studied violin and viola as a child. After working for John Friedrich & Brother in N.Y. (1893–1926), he was employed by the Rudolph Wurlitzer Co. in N.Y. and Chicago (1926–37). In 1937 he founded his own business in Evanston, Ill.; in 1941 it was purchased by William Lewis & Son in Chicago, which employed Doring until his death. In 1938 he founded the journal *Violins*, which later that year was renamed *Violins and Violinists*; it continued to appear until 1960. He publ. *How Many Strads?* (Chicago, 1945) and *The Guadagnini Family of Violin Makers* (Chicago, 1949).

Dostal, Nico(laus Josef Michäel), Austrian composer; b. Korneuburg, Nov. 25, 1895; d. Vienna, Oct. 27, 1981. He was the nephew of Hermann Dostal (1874–1930), a composer of operettas and military marches. After studies in Linz and Vienna, he was active at the Innsbruck City Theater; then conducted in St. Pölten, Romania, and Salzburg. In 1924 he went to Berlin and was active as an arranger and orchestrator of operettas, and as a composer of songs for the theater and films. In 1927 he became a conductor at the Theater am Nollendorfplatz, where he scored a fine success with his first operetta *Clivia* (Dec. 23, 1933). It was followed by the successful operettas *Die Vielgeliebt* (March 5, 1935), *Monika* (Stuttgart, Oct. 3, 1937), *Die ungarische Hochzeit* (Stuttgart, Feb. 4, 1939), and *Manina* (Berlin, Nov. 28, 1942). Among his well-received postwar scores was *Doktor Eisenbart* (Nuremberg, March 29, 1952). His autobiography was publ. as *Ans Ende deiner Träume kommst du nie: Berichte, Bekenntniss, Betrachtungen* (Innsbruck, 1982).

WORKS: MUSIC THEATER: *Clivia* (Berlin, Dec. 23, 1933); *Die Vielgeliebte* (Berlin, March 5, 1935); *Prinzessin Nofretete* (Cologne, Sept. 12, 1936); *Extrablätter* (Bremen, Feb. 17, 1937); *Monika* (Stuttgart, Oct. 3, 1937); *Die ungarische Hochzeit* (Stuttgart, Feb. 4, 1939); *Die Flucht ins Glück* (Stuttgart, Dec. 23, 1940); *Die grosse Tänzerin* (Chemnitz, Feb. 15, 1942); *Eva im Abendkleid* (Chemnitz, Nov. 21, 1942); *Manina* (Berlin, Nov. 28, 1942); *Süsse kleine Freundin* (Wuppertal, Dec. 31, 1949); *Zirkusblut* (Leipzig, March 3, 1950); *Der Kurier der Königin* (Hamburg, March 2, 1950); *Doktor Eisenbart* (Nuremberg, March 29, 1952); *Der dritte Wunsch* (Nuremberg, Feb. 20, 1954); *Liebesbriefe* (Vienna, Nov. 25, 1955); *So macht man Karriere* (Nuremberg, April 29, 1961); *Rhapsodie der Liebe* (Nuremberg, Nov. 9, 1963).

Doubrava, Jaroslav, Czech composer; b. Chrudim, April 25, 1909; d. Prague, Oct. 2, 1960. He was a student of Otakar Jeremiáš (1931–37). During the German occupation of his homeland, he was active in the partisan movement. After the liberation in 1945, he joined the staff of the Czech Radio in Prague, where he served as head of music (1950–55). Among his compositions are particularly well-crafted works for the theater.

WORKS: DRAMATIC: OPERAS: *Sen noci svatojanské* (A Midsummer Night's Dream; 1942–49; Opava, Dec. 21, 1969); *Křest svatého Vladimíra* (The Conversion of St. Vladimir; 1949–50; unfinsihed); *Líný Honza* (Lazy Honza; 1952; unfinished); *Balada o lásce* (Ballad of Love) or *Láska čarovana* (Love Bewitched), opera-ballad (1960; orchestrated by J. Hanuš; Prague, June 21, 1962). **BALLETS:** *Král Lávra* (King Lavra; 1951); *Don Quijote* (1955). **ORCH.:** 3 syms.: No. 1, *Chorální* (1938–40), No. 2, *Stalingradská* (1943–44), and No. 3, *Tragická* (1956–58); *Partisan March* (1945); *Festive March* (1945); *Autumn Pastorale* (1960; arranged from his unfinished 4th Sym. by O. Macha). **CHAMBER:** 2 violin sonatas (1942, 1958); Sonata for Solo Violin (1942). **PIANO:** Suite (1937); Sonatina (1938); Sonata (1948–49); children's pieces. **VOCAL:** *Poselství* (The Message), oratorio (1939–40); *Bala o krásné smrti* (Ballad of a Beautiful Death), cantata (1941); song cycles.

Dougherty, Celius (Hudson), American pianist and composer; b. Glenwood, Minn., May 27, 1902; d. Effort, Pa., Dec. 22, 1986. After training in piano and composition with Ferguson at the Univ. of Minnesota, he was a piano scholarship student of J. Lhévinne and Goldmark at the Juilliard School of Music in N.Y. He toured as an accompanist to noted singers of the day, several of whom championed his songs; he also toured in duo-piano recitals with Vincent Ruzicka, giving first performances of works by Stravinsky, Schoenberg, Berg, Hindemith et al. Among his compositions were *Many Moons*, opera (Poughkeepsie, N.Y., Dec. 6, 1962); Piano Concerto (1922); String Quartet (1938); Violin Sonata (1928); 2 pianos sonatas (1925, 1934); *Music from Seas and Ships*, sonata for 2 Pianos (1942–43); and more than 100 songs.

BIBL.: J. Bender, *The Songs of C. D.* (thesis, Univ. of Minnesota, 1981).

Douglas, Barry, Irish pianist; b. Belfast, April 23, 1960. He studied clarinet, cello, and organ, and also received piano lessons from Felicitas Lewinter; he then attended the Belfast School of Music, winning a scholarship to continue training with John Barstow at the Royal College of Music in London, and with Maria Curcio. In 1981 he made his London debut, subsequently winning the Silver Medal at the Arthur Rubinstein Competition in Israel (1983), the Bronze Medal at the Van Cliburn Competition in Fort Worth (1985), and the Gold Medal at the Tchaikovsky Competition in Moscow (1986). In 1988 he made his N.Y. recital debut at Carnegie Hall. During the 1988–89 season, he toured in the U.S., concluding his engagements with an appearance as soloist with the St. Louis Sym. Orch. at N.Y.'s Lincoln Center. He subsequently toured throughout the world.

Douglas, Clive (Martin), Australian conductor and composer; b. Rushworth, Victoria, July 27, 1903; d. Melbourne, April 29, 1977. He received lessons in violin, piano, orchestration, and conducting before pursuing training with Nickson and Heinze at the Univ. of Melbourne Conservatorium of Music (Mus.B., 1934). In 1936 he joined the conducting staff of the Australian Broadcasting Commission, appearing as a conductor with its orchs. in Hobart (1936–41) and Brisbane (1941–47), and then as assoc. conductor in Sydney (1947–53) and assoc. and resident conductor in Melbourne (1953–66). In 1953 he received the Coronation Medal, in 1958 he was awarded a Doctor of Music degree from the Univ. of Melbourne, and in 1963 he was made a Life Fellow of the International Inst. of Arts and Letters. In many of his scores, Douglas made use of aboriginal melorhythmic patterns.

WORKS: DRAMATIC: *The Scarlet Letter*, opera (1925–29; unfinished); *Ashmadai*, operetta (1929; 1934–35; 1st public perf. in a radio broadcast, Melbourne, Aug. 17, 1936); *Kaditcha* or *A Bush Legend*, operetta (1937–38; ABC, Tasmania, June 22, 1938; rev. 1956); *Corroboree*, ballet from the operetta *Kaditcha* (1939); *Eleanor*, *Maid Rosamond*, and *Henry of Anjou*, opera trilogy (1941–43); documentary film scores; music for radio and television. **ORCH.:** *Symphonic Fantasy* (1938); *Carwoola* (1939); *Meet the Orchestra*, educational suite (1944); 3 syms. (*Jubilee*, 1950; *Namatjira*, 1956; 1963); *Sturt 1829* (1952); *Essay* for Strings (1952); *Wangadilla Suite* (1954); *Festival in Natal*

(1954); *Greet the Orchestra*, educational suite (1955); *Olympic Overture* (1956); *Coolawidgee*, miniature suite for Small Orch. (1957); *Sinfonietta: Festival of Perth* (1961); *Variations Symphoniques* (1961); *Fanfare Overture* (1961); *Divertimento II* for 2 Pianos and Small Orch. (1962; rev. 1967); *4 Light Orchestra Pieces* (1964); *3 Frescoes* (1969); *Movement in C Major on a Theme of Alfred Hill* (1969); *Pastoral* (1970); *Carnival* (1970); *Discourse* for Strings (1971). **CHAMBER:** *Divertimento I* for Woodwind Quintet (1962–65). **VOCAL:** *The Hound of Heaven* for Baritone, Chorus, and Orch. (1933; rev. 1938); *5 Pastels* for Soprano, Celesta, and Strings (1952); *The Lakes of Tasmania* for Voice and Orch. (1954); *Song Landscape* for Soprano or Tenor and String Orch. (1955); *Terra Australia* for Narrator, Soprano, Chorus, and Orch. (1959).

Dounias, Minos, Greek violinist, musicologist, and music critic; b. Cetate, Romania, Sept. 26, 1900; d. Athens, Oct. 20, 1962. He studied at Robert College in Constantinople, where he received instruction in violin, and with Moser and Kulenkampff at the Berlin Hochschule für Musik (1921–26); then studied musicology with Abert and Schering at the Univ. of Berlin (Ph.D., 1932, with the diss. *Die Violinkonzerte Giuseppe Tartinis*; publ. in Wolfenbüttel, 1935; 2nd ed., 1966). He settled in Athens in 1936, where he taught at Pierce College, wrote music criticism, and made appearances as a violinist. He was particularly active in the promotion of early music.

Dounis, Demetrius Constantine, Greek-American violinist and teacher; b. Athens, Dec. 7, 1886; d. Los Angeles, Aug. 13, 1954. He studied violin with Ondricek in Vienna and simultaneously enrolled as a medical student at the Univ. of Vienna; made several tours as a violinist in Europe; after World War I, he was appointed prof. at the Salonika Cons. He then lived in England and eventually settled in America; established his N.Y. studio in 1939; went to Los Angeles in 1954. He originated the technique of the "brush stroke," in which the bow is handled naturally and effortlessly. He wrote numerous manuals.

BIBL.: V. Leland, *D. Principles of Violin Playing* (London, 1949); C. Costantakos, *D.C. D.: His Method in Teaching the Violin* (N.Y., 1988).

Downes, Sir Edward (Thomas), respected English conductor; b. Birmingham, June 17, 1924. After studies at the Univ. of Birmingham (M.A., 1944), he took courses in horn and composition at the Royal College of Music in London (1944–46); in 1948 he received the Carnegie Scholarship and pursued training in conducting with Scherchen. He was an assistant conductor with the Carl Rosa Opera (1950–52); he then was on the conducting staff at London's Covent Garden (1952–69), where he led an extensive repertoire of standard and modern scores, including his own translation of Shostakovich's *Katerina Ismailova* (1963); he also conducted Wagner's *Ring* cycle there (1967). In 1972 he became musical director of the Australian Opera in Sydney, inaugurating the new Sydney Opera House in 1973 with his own translation of Prokofiev's *War and Peace.* In 1976 he left this post, and in 1980 became principal conductor of the BBC Northern Sym. Orch. in Manchester, a post he retained in 1983 when it was renamed the BBC Phil. In 1992 he left this post, having been appointed assoc. music director and principal conductor at Covent Garden in 1991. In 1986 he was made a Commander of the Order of the British Empire, and in 1991 he was knighted.

Downes, Edward O(lin) D(avenport), American music critic and lecturer, son of **(Edwin) Olin Downes**; b. Boston, Aug. 12, 1911. He studied at Columbia Univ. (1929–30), the Univ. of Paris (1932–33), the Univ. of Munich (1934–36, 1938), and Harvard Univ. (Ph.D., 1958, with the diss. *The Operas of Johann Christian Bach as a Reflection of the Dominant Trends in "opera seria," 1750–1780*). Under the tutelage of his father, he embarked upon a career as a music critic; wrote for the *N.Y. Post* (1935–38), the *Boston Transcript* (1939–41), and the *N.Y. Times* (1955–58); was program annotator for the N.Y. Phil. (from 1960); from 1958 to 1996 he acted as quizmaster for the Metropolitan Opera broadcasts. He was a lecturer at Wellesley College (1948–49), Harvard Univ. (1949–50), and the Univ. of Minnesota (1950–55). After serving as musicologist-in-residence at the Bayreuth master classes (1959–65), he was prof. of music history at Queens College of the City Univ. of N.Y. (1966–81) and at N.Y. Univ. (1981–86). From 1986 he was a prof. of music at the Juilliard School.

WRITINGS: *Verdi, The Man in His Letters* (tr. of Werfel and Stefan's *Giuseppe Verdis Briefe*, Berlin, 1926; N.Y., 1942); *Adventures in Symphonic Music* (N.Y., 1943); ed. with B. Brook and S. van Solkema, *Perspectives in Musicology* (N.Y., 1972); *The New York Philharmonic Guide to the Symphony* (N.Y.,1976; 2nd ed., 1981, as *Guide to Symphonic Music*).

Downes, (Edwin) Olin, eminent American music critic, father of **Edward O(lin) D(avenport) Downes**; b. Evanston, Ill., Jan. 27, 1886; d. N.Y., Aug. 22, 1955. He studied piano at the National Cons. of Music of N.Y. and was a pupil in Boston of Louis Kelterborn (history and analysis), Carl Baermann (piano), Homer Norris and Clifford Heilman (theory), and John Marshall (music criticism). After establishing himself as a music critic of the *Boston Post* (1906–24), he was the influential music critic of the *N.Y. Times* from 1924 until his death. He was also active as a lecturer and served as quizmaster of the Metropolitan Opera broadcasts. His valuable collection of letters (about 50,000) to and from the most celebrated names in 20th-century music history is housed at the Univ. of Georgia. Downes did much to advance the cause of Strauss, Stravinsky, Sibelius, Prokofiev, and Shostakovich in the U.S. In 1937 he received the order Commander of the White Rose of Finland and in 1939 an honorary Mus.Doc. from the Cincinnati Cons. of Music.

WRITINGS (all publ. in N.Y.): *The Lure of Music* (1918); ed. *Select Songs of Russian Composers* (1922); *Symphonic Broadcasts* (1931); *Symphonic Masterpieces* (1935); ed. *Ten Operatic Masterpieces, From Mozart to Prokofiev* (1952); *Sibelius the Symphonist* (1956); I. Downes, ed., *Olin Downes on Music* (1957).

BIBL.: G. Goss, *Jean Sibelius and O. D.: Music, Friendship, Criticism* (Boston, 1995).

Downes, Ralph (William), English organist, organ designer, and teacher; b. Derby, Aug. 16, 1904; d. London, Dec. 24, 1993. He studied at the Royal College of Music in London (1922–25); then was an organ scholar at Keble College, Oxford. Making his way to the U.S., he was music director and organist at Princeton Univ. (1928–36); he then returned to London, where he became organist of Brompton Oratory; in 1948 he became resident organist of the London Phil. He was appointed a prof. at the Royal College of Music in 1954. He designed many notable organs, including the instrument for London's Royal Festival Hall. He publ. the vol. *Baroque Tricks: Adventures with the Organ Builders* (Oxford, 1983). In 1969 he was made a Commander of the Order of the British Empire.

Downey, John (Wilham), American composer and teacher; b. Chicago, Oct. 5, 1927. He was a pupil of Tarnovsky (piano) and Stein (composition) at De Paul Univ. in Chicago (B.M., 1949) and of Ganz, Rieti, Krenek, and Tcherepnin at the Chicago Musical College (M.M., 1951); he then went to Paris, where he studied with Milhaud, Boulanger, and Messiaen at the Cons. (1952) and with Chailley and Jankélévitch at the Sorbonne (docteur dès lettres, 1957). After teaching at De Paul Univ., Chicago City College, and Roosevelt Univ., he was prof. of composition and composer-in-residence at the Univ. of Wisc. in Milwaukee (from 1964). He publ. the study *La musique populaire dans l'oeuvre de Béla Bartók* (1966). In 1980 he was made a Chevalier de l'Ordre des Arts et Lettres of France. In his music, Downey adopted modified serial techniques and also utilized electronic and computer-generated sounds.

WORKS: DRAMATIC: *Ageistics*, ballet (1967); incidental music to Shakespeare's *Twelfth Night* (1971). **ORCH.:** *La Joie de la paix* (1956); *Chant to Michelangelo* (1958); Concerto for Harp and Chamber Orch. (1964); *Jingalodeon* (1968); *Prospectations III–II–I* for 3 Orchs. (1970); *Symphonic Modules 5*

(1972); *Tooter's Suite* for Youth Orch. (1973); *The Edge of Space* for Bassoon and Orch. (1978; also for Bassoon and Piano); *Discourse* for Oboe, Harpsichord, and Strings (1984; N.Y., Jan. 15, 1987); Double Bass Concerto (1985; Sydney, Sept. 1987); *Declamations* (Albany, N.Y., Dec. 6, 1985); *Call for Freedom* for Symphonic Winds (1989); *Ode to Freedom* (Milwaukee, Oct. 1992); Sym. No. 1 (Chicago, March 1993); *Yad Vashem: An Impression* for Chamber Orch. (Milwaukee, June 8, 1994). **CHAMBER:** String Trio (1953); Violin Sonata (1954); Wind Octet (1954); 2 string quartets (1964, 1975); Cello Sonata (1966); *Eartheatrics* for 8 Percussionists (1967); *Agort* for Woodwind Quintet (1967); *Almost 12* for Wind Quintet, String Quintet, and Percussion (1970); *Ambivalences I* for Any Chamber Combination (1972); *Crescendo* for Percussion Ensemble (1977); *High Clouds and Soft Rain* for 24 Flutes (1977); Duo for Oboe and Harpsichord (1981); *Portrait* No. 2 for Clarinet and Bassoon (1983) and No. 3 for Flute and Piano (1984); Piano Trio (1984); *Prayer* for Violin, Viola, and Cello (1984); *Recombinance* for Double Bass and Piano (1985); *Rough Road* for Flute and Guitar (1994; WFMT-FM, Chicago, Jan. 15, 1995); *Angel Talk* for 8 Cellos (1995). **PIANO:** 2 sonatas (1949, 1951); *Adagio lyrico* for 2 Pianos (1953); *Eastlake Terrace* (1959); *Edges* (1960); *Pyramids* (1961); *Ambivalences II* (1973); *Portrait* No. 1 (1982); *Memories* (1991). **VOCAL:** *Lake Isle of Innisfree* for High Voice and Piano (1963); *What If?* for Chorus, Timpani, and 8 Brass (1973); *A Dolphin* for High Voice, Alto Flute, Viola, Piano, and Percussion (1974); *Tangents*, jazz oratorio for Soprano, Chorus, String Quintet, Electric Guitar, and Percussion (1981); *Psalm 100* for Chorus (1989); *Meni Odnakovo* for Bass and Orch. (1990).

Doyen, Albert, French composer and choral conductor; b. Vendresse, Ardennes, April 3, 1882; d. Paris, Oct. 22, 1935. He studied composition with Widor at the Paris Cons. In 1917 he established the choral society Fêtes du Peuple. Among his works are a Sym., an ode in memory of Zola, String Quartet, Piano Trio, Violin Sonata, and numerous choral compositions.

Draga, Gheorghe, Romanian composer; b. Bîrsa-Aldeşti, April 26, 1935. He studied with Vancea, Vieru, and Ion Dumitrescu at the Bucharest Cons. (1957–63).

WORKS: Piano Sonata (1962); Clarinet Sonata (1963); *Se construieşte lumea noastra*, cantata (1963); Sym. (1965); *Cantata festiva* (1967); *Concert Music* for Orch. (1968); String Quartet (1968); *Eterofonii* for Strings, Brass, and Percussion (1969); Concert Overture (1969); Prelude for Orch. (1971); *Stejarul românesc*, cantata (1976); *Sarmizegetusa*, symphonic poem (1983).

Dräger, Hans-Heinz, German-born American musicologist; b. Stralsund, Dec. 6, 1909; d. Austin, Texas, Nov. 9, 1968. He studied musicology with Blume, Schering, Hornbostel, Schünemann, and Sachs at the Univ. of Berlin (Ph.D., 1937, with the diss. *Die Entwicklung des Streichbogens und seine Anwendung in Europa*; publ. in Kassel, 1937), completing his Habilitation at the Univ. of Kiel in 1946 with his *Prinzip einer Systematik der Musikinstrumente* (publ. in Kassel, 1948). While in Berlin, he was active with the State Inst. for German Music Research (1937–38) and at the State Museum of Musical Instruments (1938–39); also was lecturer in organology at the Hochschule für Musik (1939). He was prof. of musicology at the univs. of Greifswald (1947–49) and Rostock (1948–49), at Humboldt Univ. in East Berlin (1949–53), and at the Free Univ. in West Berlin (1953–61). In 1955 he was a visiting prof. at Stanford Univ. He settled in the U.S. in 1961, becoming a naturalized citizen in 1966; he was on the musicology faculty at the Univ. of Austin (1961–66).

BIBL.: H.-B. Dietz, "In Memoriam H.-H. D. (1909–68)," *Die Musikforschung*, XXII (1969).

Drăgoi, Sabin V(asile), eminent Romanian composer, folklorist, and pedagogue; b. Selişte, June 18, 1894; d. Bucharest, Dec. 31, 1968. He studied harmony with Zirra in Iaşi (1918–19), theory with Bena and counterpoint with Klee in Cluj (1919–20), and composition with Novák, conducting with Ostrčil, and music history with Krupka in Prague (1920–22). After teaching music in Deva (1922–24), he was director of the Timişoara Cons. (1925–43) and then a teacher at the Cluj Cons. (1943–45). He served as prof. of folklore at the Cons. (1950–52) and as director of the Folklore Inst. (1950–64) in Bucharest. He received the Enesco prize 3 times (1922, 1923, 1928) and the Romanian Academy prize (1933). His extensive folklore research in the Banat and in Transylvania is often reflected in his compositions.

WORKS: DRAMATIC: *Năpasta* (Disaster), opera (1927; Bucharest, May 30, 1928; rev. 1958; Bucharest, Dec. 23, 1961); *Constantin Brîncoveanu*, scenic oratorio (1929; Bucharest, Oct. 25, 1935); *Kir Ianulea*, comic-fantastic opera (1930–38; Cluj-Napoca, Dec. 22, 1939); *Horia*, historical opera (1945; rev. 1959); *Păcală*, comic opera (1954–56; Brasov, May 6, 1962); film music. **ORCH.:** *3 Tablouri simfonice* (1921); *Memento mori—La groapa lui Scărlătescu* (1923); *Divertisment rustic* (1928); *Divertisment sacru* for Chamber Orch. (1933); Piano Concerto (1940–41; Bucharest, Feb. 14, 1943); *Rapsodia din Belint* (1942; Bucharest, Dec. 12, 1943); *2 Dansuri pe tempe populare mureşene* (1942); *Petrecere populară*, suite (1950); *La Mislea—La moartea unei tovarăşe căzute în ilegalitate*, symphonic poem (1951); *Mitrea Cocor*, suite (1953); *Suită făgărăşană* (1954); *Suită de 7 dansuri populare* (1960); *Suită tătară* (1961); *Suită lipoveana* (1962). **CHAMBER:** 2 string quartets (1920, 1922); Violin Sonata (1949); *Dixtour* for Winds, Strings, and Piano (1955). **PIANO:** *Suită de dansuri populare* (1923); *8 Miniaturi* (1923); *Mica suită: In memoriam Béla Bartók* (1955); *30 Colinde* (1958); *10 Miniaturi* (1960); *12 Miniaturi* (1966). **VOCAL:** *Povestea neamului* for Chorus and Orch. (1936; Bucharest, Nov. 10, 1938); *Balada celor patru mineri* for Soli, Chorus, and Orch. (1950); *Mai multă lumina*, cantata for Chorus and Orch. (1951); *Povestea bradului*, oratorio for Soli, Chorus, and Orch. (1952); *Cunună—Serbarea secerişului*, cantata for Soli, Chorus, and Orch. (1959).

BIBL.: N. Rădulescu, *S.V. D.* (Bucharest, 1971).

Dragon, Carmen, American conductor, composer, and arranger; b. Antioch, Calif., July 28, 1914; d. Santa Monica, Calif., March 28, 1984. He learned to play piano and other instruments; after studies at San Jose State College, he found his niche as a successful conductor, composer, and arranger for films, radio, and recordings; he also conducted pop concerts and served as conductor of the Glendale (Calif.) Sym. Orch. (from 1963). His son, Daryl Dragon (b. Los Angeles, Aug. 27, 1942), was one-half of the popular music team of Captain and Tennille.

Drake, Alfred (real name, **Alfredo Capurro**), esteemed American baritone, actor, and director; b. N.Y., Oct. 7, 1914; d. there, July 25, 1992. He sang in a Brooklyn church choir and then in the glee club at Brooklyn College, from which he graduated in 1935. He began his career as a chorus singer. His rich baritone voice caught the attention of Rodgers and Hart, who cast him in a supporting role in their Broadway musical *Babes in Arms* (1937). After further stage appearances, he was chosen by Rodgers and Hammerstein to create the role of Curly in the award-winning musical *Oklahoma!* in 1943, which made Drake a star on Broadway and also winner of the Drama Critics' Circle Award. Following appearances on stage in *Sing Out, Sweet Land* (1944), *The Beggar's Holiday* (1946), and *The Cradle Will Rock*, and in the film *Tars and Spars* (1946), he again won critical accolades when he created the role of Fred Graham in Cole Porter's Broadway musical *Kiss Me, Kate* in 1948. In 1953 he scored another Broadway triumph when he created the role of Haji in the musical *Kismet*, for which he won a 2nd Drama Critics' Circle Award as well as a Tony Award. In later years, he pursued a career mainly as a fine dramatic actor and director. In 1973 he again won accolades as Honore Lachalles in the revival of *Gigi*. In 1981 he was inducted into the Theatre Hall of Fame. In 1990 he was awarded the Tony Honor of Excellence for his contributions to the American theater.

Drangosch, Ernesto, Argentine pianist, teacher, and composer; b. Buenos Aires, Jan. 22, 1882; d. there, June 26, 1925.

He studied in Buenos Aires with Alberto Williams and Aguirre, and in Berlin with Bruch, Humperdinck, and Ansorge; later toured Europe and America as a pianist. Returning to Buenos Aires in 1905, he founded his own cons.

Dranishnikov, Vladimir, Russian conductor and composer; b. St. Petersburg, June 10, 1893; d. Kiev, Feb. 6, 1939. He studied at the St. Petersburg Cons. with Essipova (piano), Steinberg, Liadov, and Wihtol (composition), and Nikolai Tcherepnin (conducting). He was employed as a rehearsal pianist at the St. Petersburg Imperial Opera (1914–18); in 1918, became conductor there, earning great esteem for his skill in both the classical and the modern repertoire; he conducted the first Soviet performance of Berg's *Wozzeck*, and of numerous Soviet operas. In 1930 he was appointed conductor of the Kiev Opera. He wrote symphonic works and choruses.

Draper, Charles, English clarinetist and pedagogue; b. Odcombe, Somerset, Oct. 23, 1869; d. Surbiton, Oct. 21, 1952. He studied with his brother and with Henry Lazarus, and then was a scholarship student at the Royal College of Music in London. He was active in London, where he joined the Crystal Palace Orch. in 1895; he also played in the orch. of the Phil. Soc. and in 1905 became a founding member of the New Sym. Orch.; from 1895 to 1940 he taught at the Guildhall School of Music. Through his appearances as a soloist and chamber music player, he played a decisive role in establishing the clarinet as a worthy solo instrument. His nephew, Haydn (Paul) Draper (b. Penarth, Glamorganshire, Wales, Jan. 21, 1889; d. London, Nov. 1, 1934), was also a clarinetist and pedagogue. After training with his father, he entered the Royal College of Music in London on a scholarship in 1908 and studied with his uncle and with Julian Egerton. He played principal clarinet in the Queen's Hall Orch. in London, and later was a member of the London Wind Quintet; from 1923 he was a teacher at the Royal Academy of Music in London, where he was mentor to Reginald Kell.

BIBL.: P. Weston, "C. D.: The Grandfather of English Clarinetists," *Music Teacher*, XLVIII (1969); idem, *Clarinet Virtuosi of the Past* (London, 1971).

Drdla, Franz (actually, **František Alois**), Bohemian violinist and composer; b. Saar, Moravia, Nov. 28, 1868; d. Badgastein, Sept. 3, 1944. After training with Bennewitz (violin) and Foerster (composition) at the Prague Cons. (1880–82), he studied at the Vienna Cons. (1882–88) with J. Hellmesberger, Jr. (violin) and Krenn and Bruckner (composition), winning 1st prize for violin and the medal of the Gesellschaft der Musikfreunde. He was a violinist in the orch. of the Vienna Court Opera (1890–93); after serving as concertmaster of the orch. of the Theater an der Wien (1894–99), he made successful tours as a violinist in Europe (1899–1905) and the U.S. (1923–25). His lighter pieces for violin and piano won enormous popularity in their day, especially his *Serenade No. 1* (1901), *Souvenir* (1904), and *Vision*. He also wrote the operettas *Zlatá sít* (1st perf. as *Das goldene Netz*, Leipzig, 1916; rev. as *Bohyně lásky* [The Goddess of Love], Brno, 1941) and *Komtesa z prodejny* (1st perf. as *Die Ladenkomtesse*, Brünn, 1917), and a Violin Concerto (1931).

BIBL.: J. Květ, *F. D.* (Ždár nad Sázavou, 1968).

Dreier, Per, Norwegian conductor; b. Trondheim, Dec. 25, 1929. He studied conducting with Paul van Kempen and Willem van Otterloo at the Royal Cons. of Music in The Hague. He made his debut with the Trondheim Sym. Orch. in 1953. He then was a conductor at the Württemberg State Theater at Stuttgart (1953–57) and chief conductor and artistic director of the Århus Sym. Orch. (1957–73); also served as chief conductor of the Jutland Opera (1957–71). Dreier has done much to promote contemporary Norwegian music.

Drejsl, Radim, Czech composer; b. Dobruska, April 29, 1923; d. (suicide) Prague, April 20, 1953. He studied piano at the Prague Cons. and composition with Bořkovec at the Prague Academy of Musical Arts (1946–50). From 1949 until his death he was music director of the Vít Nejedlý Army Artistic Ensemble.

WORKS: 2 piano suites (1945, 1946); 2 piano sonatas (1946, 1947); Flute Sonatina (1947); Bassoon Sonatina (1948); *Spring* for Wind Quintet (1948); Sym. for Strings (1948); Piano Concerto (1948–49); *Dožínková Suite* (Harvest Home Suite) for Oboe or English Horn and Piano (1949–50); military marches; choruses; songs.

Dresden, Sem, notable Dutch composer and pedagogue; b. Amsterdam, April 20, 1881; d. The Hague, July 30, 1957. He studied composition with Zweers at the Amsterdam Cons., and then composition and conducting with Pfitzner at the Stern Cons. in Berlin (1903–05). Returning to Amsterdam, he was conductor of the Motet and Madrigal Soc. (1914–26); he also taught composition at (1919–24) and was director (1924–37) of the Cons. In 1937 he became director of the Royal Cons. of Music in The Hague, but was removed from his position by the Nazi occupation authorities in 1940; upon the liberation in 1945, he was restored to his position, which he held until 1949. He publ. *Het Muziekleven in Nederlands sinds 1880* (Amsterdam, 1923) and *Stromingen en Tegenstromingen in de Muziek* (Haarlem, 1953); he also rev. Worp's *Algemeene Muziekleer* (Groningen, 1931; 9th ed., 1956). His compositions reveal both German and French influences with a distinctive Dutch strain.

WORKS: DRAMATIC: OPERA: *François Villon* (1956–57; orchestrated by J. Mul; Amsterdam, June 15, 1958). **OPERETTA:** *Toto* (1945). **ORCH.:** *Theme and Variations* (Amsterdam, March 29, 1914); 2 violin concertos (1936, 1942); Symphonietta for Clarinet and Orch. (1938); Oboe Concerto (1939); Piano Concerto (1942–46); Flute Concerto (1949); *Dansflitsen* (Dance Flashes; The Hague, Oct. 20, 1951); Organ Concerto (1952–53). **CHAMBER:** 2 piano trios (1902, 1942); Violin Sonata (1905); Trio for 2 Oboes and English Horn (1912); 2 cello sonatas (1916, 1942); Sonata for Flute and Harp (1918); String Quartet (1924); Sonata for Solo Violin (1943); Suite for Cello (1943–47); piano pieces; organ music. **VOCAL:** *Chorus tragicus* for Chorus, 5 Trumpets, 2 Bugles, and Percussion (1927); *4 Vocalises* for Mezzo-soprano and 7 Instruments (1935); *O Kerstnacht* for Chorus and Strings (1939); *Chorus symphonicus* for Soprano, Tenor, Chorus, and Orch. (1943–44; rev. 1955); *Psalm 99* for Chorus, Organ, and 4 Trombones (1950); *St. Antoine*, oratorio (1953); *Psalm 84* for Soprano, Tenor, Chorus, and Orch. (1954); *Carnival Cantata* for Soprano, Men's Chorus, and Orch. (1954); *De wijnen van Bourgondië* (The Wines of Burgundy) for Chorus and Orch. (1954); *St. Joris*, oratorio (1955); *Catena musicale* for Soprano, Woodwind Quartet, String Trio, and Orch. (1956); *Rembrandt's "Saul and David"* for Soprano and Orch. (1956); choruses; songs.

BIBL.: J. Wouters, "S. D.," *Sonorum Speculum* (Winter 1965).

Dresher, Paul (Joseph), American composer and performer; b. Los Angeles, Jan. 8, 1951. He studied at the Univ. of Calif. at Berkeley (B.A., 1977) and composition with Erickson, Reynolds, and Oliveros at the Univ. of Calif. at San Diego (M.A., 1979); also received training in Ghanaian drumming, Javanese and Balinese gamelan, and North Indian classical music. In 1984 he founded the Paul Dresher Ensemble. His awards include an NEA grant (1979), the Goddard Lieberson fellowship of the American Academy and Inst. of Arts and Letters (1982), and a Fulbright fellowship (1984). In addition to orch. and chamber works, he has written experimental operatic and theater pieces (many in collaboration with theater director George Coates), as well as various electroacoustic taped scores for use in theater, dance, video, radio, and film. As a composer, his intent has been to integrate the more traditional formal aspects of music with what he terms a "pre-maximalist" vocabulary.

WORKS: Guitar Quartet (1975); *Z* for Soprano, 6 Percussion, and Tape (1978); *Liquid and Stellar Music*, live perf. solo piece (1981); *The Way of How*, music theater (1981); *Dark Blue Circumstance*, live perf. solo piece for Electric Guitar and Electronics (1982); *Casa Vecchia* for String Quartet (1982); *Are Are*, music theater (1983); *Seehear,* music theater (1984); *re:act:ion* for Orch. (1984); *Was Are/Will Be,* staged concert piece (1985); *Freesound* (1985–88); *Slow Fire,* music theater/opera (1985–88); *Figaro Gets a Divorce,* theater score (1986); *The Tempest,* theater score (1987); *Shelflife,* live perf. dance piece (1987); *Rhythmia,* tape piece for Dance (1987); *Loose the Thread,* dance piece for Violin, Piano, and Percussion (1988); *Power Failure,* music theater/opera (1988–89); *Pioneers,* music theater/opera (1989–90; Spoleto Festival, May 26, 1990); *Awed Behavior,* music theater (1992–93; Los Angeles, May 1, 1993); *Din of Iniquity* for 6 Instruments (1994); *Stretch* for 6 Instruments (1995).

Dressel, Erwin, German pianist, conductor, and composer; b. Berlin, June 10, 1909; d. there, Dec. 17, 1972. He studied in Berlin with Klatte at the Stern Cons. and with Juon at the Hochschule für Musik. He was active in Berlin as a pianist, theater conductor, arranger, and composer.

WORKS: OPERAS: *Der arme Columbus* (Kassel, Feb. 19, 1928); *Der Kuchentanz* (Kassel, May 18, 1929); *Der Rosenbusch der Maria* (Leipzig, June 23, 1930); *Die Zwillingsesel* (Dresden, April 29, 1932); *Jery und Bätely* (Berlin, 1932); *Die Laune der Verliebten* (Hamburg and Leipzig, 1949); *Der Bar* (Bern, 1963). **ORCH.:** 4 syms. (1927, 1929, 1932, 1948); Concerto for Oboe, Clarinet, Bassoon, and Orch. (1951); Clarinet Concerto (1961); *Cassation* (1961); *Variationen-Serenade* for Piano and Orch. (1962); *Caprice fantastique* (1963); Saxophone Concerto (1965); Viola Concerto (1969). **CHAMBER:** 2 string quartets; String Trio; piano pieces. **VOCAL:** Choral music; songs.

Drew, James, multifaceted American composer, playwright, pianist, and teacher; b. St. Paul, Minn., Feb. 9, 1929. He studied at the N.Y. School of Music (1954–56), with Varèse (1956), and with Riegger (1956–59). Following further training at Tulane Univ. (M.A., 1964), he pursued postgraduate studies at Washington Univ. in St. Louis (1964–65). In 1972–73 he held a Guggenheim fellowship. He taught at Northwestern Univ. (1965–67), Yale Univ. (1967–73), the Berkshire Music Center at Tanglewood (summer, 1973), Louisiana State Univ. (1973–76), Calif. State Univ. at Fullerton (1976–77), and the Univ. of Calif. at Los Angeles (1977–78). As a composer and playwright, Drew has pursued an active career outside of academia. Except for master classes and lectures, he has worked since 1980 on independent projects for the theater, concert stage, and film. His Grey Wolf Atelier International, which is devoted to the arts education of children, parents, and teachers, was founded in 1993. With his colleague, the educator Mary Gae George, the Atelier operates in Florida, Utah, Indiana, and the Netherlands.

WORKS: DRAMATIC: *Toward Yellow,* ballet (1970); *Mysterium,* television opera (1974–75); *Crucifixus Domini Christi* (1975); *Suspense Opera* (1975); *Dr. Cincinnati* (1977); *5 O'Clock Ladies* (1981); *Himself, the Devil* (1982); *Whisper,* video piece (1982); *Becket: The Final Moments,* automated drama (1984); *One Last Dance,* theater and/or video piece (1985); *Blue in Atlantis,* audio-theater piece (1986); *"Live" from the Black Eagle* (1987–88); *Rat's Teeth* (1989); *Surprise Operas* (1989); *Theater of Phantom Sounds* (1993); *The Voice* (1995); *Club Berlin is Closed: Hello?,* theater piece (1995). **ORCH.:** *Passacaglia* (1957); *Contrappunto* (1965); 3 syms.: No. 1 for Chamber Orch. (1968), No. 2 for Chorus and Orch. (Norfolk, Va., Aug. 20, 1971), and No. 3 (1977; Providence, R.I., April 6, 1991); *Symphonies* for Orch., Chorus, and 3 Conductors (1969); 2 violino grande concertos (1969, 1993); *October Lights* (New Haven, Conn., Oct. 18, 1969); *Metal Concerto* for Percussion (N.Y., Feb. 2, 1971); Percussion Concerto (1972–73; N.Y., March 21, 1973); *West Indian Lights* (Tanglewood, Aug. 9, 1973); Viola Concerto (1973); *Metal Assemblage* for Wind Orch. (1976); Violin Concerto (1977); Sinfonia for Strings (1980); Concerto for 2 Violins and Orch. (1981); *St. Mark Triple Concerto* for Violin, Cello, Piano, and Brass or Winds (1981); *Open/Closed Forms* for Chamber Orch. (1983); *Courtyard Music* for Chamber Orch. and Kinisones (1983); *Faustus: An Epilogue* for 2 Pianos, Viola, and Chamber Orch. (1984); *Donaldsonville: Steeples, Whistles, Fog* (1988); Piano Concerto, *The Celestial Cabaret* (1991); *Inaudible Answers* (1992); Concerto for Cello and Chamber Orch. (1994); *Walden Songs* for Chamber Orch. (1994). **CHAMBER:** *Indigo Suite* for Piano, Double Bass, and Percussion (1959); *Divisiones* for 6 Percussion (1962); Piano Trio (1962); *Polifonica I* for Flute, Clarinet, Oboe, String Quartet, and Piano (1963) and *II* for Flute and Percussion (1966); *Almost Stationary* for Piano Trio (1971); *Gothic Lights* for Brass (1972); 3 string quartets (1972–75; 1977; 1989); *Epitaphium pour Stravinsky* for 3 Trombones, Horn, Tuba, and Piano (1973); *Trio for the Fiery Messengers* for Piano Trio (1979); Violin Sonata (1979); Cello Sonata (1980); Sonata for Solo Viola (1983); *American Elegy* for Brass Quintet (1983); *Chartres Street Processional* for Brass (1986); *The Bejesus Redemption Psalter* for Percussion (1987); *Lincoln Center Blues* for Any Instrument or Piano (1987); *Some Sad Songs and Marches* for Brass (1988); *Antitangoes* for Flute and Contrabass (1992); *Book of Lights* for Clarinet, Cello, Viola, and Piano (1993); *Elephants Coming* for String Quartet (1994); *Sacred Dances of the Tunnel Saints* for 2 Pianos and 2 Percussionists (1995). **VOCAL:** *The Lute in the Attic* for Voice, Flute, Clarinet, Cello, and 3 Gongs (1963); *The Fading of the Visible World,* oratorio for Soprano, Tenor, Bass, Chorus, and Orch. (1975); *The Orangethorpe Aria* for Soprano, Piano Trio, and Clarinet (1978); *Trinity* for Soprano and Chamber Ensemble (1983); *Dublin Dream Songs* for Soprano and Percussionist (1992); *Many Moons, Many Winters* for Soprano and String Orch. (1994).

Dreyfus, George (actually, **Georg**), German-born Australian bassoonist, conductor, and composer; b. Wuppertal, July 22, 1928. He emigrated to Australia in 1939. He studied clarinet and bassoon at the Melbourne Conservatorium, then completed his training at the Vienna Academy of Music (1955–56). He played in various Australian orchs., including the Melbourne Sym. Orch. (1953–64); in 1958 he founded the New Music Ensemble in Melbourne, which became the George Dreyfus Chamber Orch. in 1970. In 1976 he held the Prix de Rome of the German Academy in Rome, and in 1983 was artist-in-residence at the Tianjin Cons. of Music in China. He publ. an autobiography, *The Last Frivolous Book* (Sydney, 1984).

WORKS: DRAMATIC: OPERAS: *Garni Sands* (1965–66; Sydney, July 12, 1972); *The Takeover,* school opera (1969); *The Gilt-Edged Kid* (1970; Melbourne, April 11, 1976); *The Lamentable Reign of Charles the Last,* "pantopera" (1975; Adelaide, March 23, 1976). **MUSICALS:** *Smash Hit!* (1980); *The Sentimental Bloke* (Melbourne, Dec. 17, 1985). **MIME-DRAMA:** *The Illusionist* (1972). **ORCH.:** *Music for Music Camp* (1967); 2 syms. (1967, 1976); *Jingles,* 5 pieces (1968); *. . . and more Jingles,* 5 further pieces (1972); *Hallelujah for Handel* for Brass Band or Orch. (1976); *Symphonie concertante* for Bassoon, Violin, Viola, Cello, and Strings (1978); *Grand Ridge Road,* suite for Small Orch. (1980); *Folk Music* with Large Orch. (1982); *German Teddy,* sym. for Mandolin Orch. (1984; Wuppertal, April 27, 1986); *Euroa Hooray!,* overture for Concert Band (1985). **CHAMBER:** Trio for Flute, Clarinet, and Bassoon (1956); *The Seasons* for Flute, Viola, and Percussion (1963); 2 wind quintets (1965, 1968); Sextet for Didjeridu and Wind Quintet (1971); *Old Melbourne* for Bassoon and Guitar (1973). **VOCAL:** *Galgenlieder* for Baritone, Flute, Clarinet, Bassoon, and Violin (1957); *Songs Comic and Curious* for Baritone, Flute, Oboe, Clarinet, Horn, and Bassoon (1959); *Wilhelm Busch Lieder* for High Voice and Wind Trio (1959); *Music in the Air* for Baritone, Flute, Viola, and Percussion 91961); *From Within Looking Out* for Soprano, Flute, Viola, Vibraphone, and Celesta (1962); *Ned Kelly Ballads* for Folksinger, 4 Horns, and Rhythm Section (1964); *Song of the Maypole,* cantata for Children's Choruses and Orch. (1968); *Homage to Igor Stravinsky* for Chorus (1968); *Reflections in a Glass House* for Narrator, Children's Chorus, and Orch. (1969); *Mo* for Baritone, String Orch., and Continuo (1972); *Ein Kaffeekonzert* for Soprano and Piano Trio (1977); *Terrigal* for Chorus and Orch. (1977); *Ballad of the Drover* for Children's Voices (1979); *An Australian Folk Mass* (1979); *Cele-*

bration, cantata for Women's Voices, Piano, and Orch. (1981); *Charles Rasp*, cantata for Men's Chorus, Children's Chorus, Pop Singer, and Concert Band (1984); *The Box Hill Gloria*, cantata for Chorus, Children's Chorus, Pop Singer, Concert Band, Brass Band, Pipe Band, and String Orch. (1986).

Dreyfus, Huguett (Pauline), French harpsichordist; b. Mulhouse Nov. 30, 1928. She studied in Paris at the École Normale de Musique and with Dufourcq at the Cons. (graduated, 1950) before pursuing advanced training with Gerlin at the Accademia Musicale Chigiana in Siena (1953). After winning the 1st medal in harpsichord at the Geneva competition in 1958, she toured internationally; also was a prof. at the Paris Schola Cantorum (from 1967). While she has concentrated on the music of Bach, Couperin, Scarlatti, and Rameau, her repertory also includes adventuresome scores by contemporary composers.

Driessler, Johannes, German composer and pedagogue; b. Friedrichsthal, Jan. 26, 1921. He received training in organ, choral conducting, and theory from Karl Rahner at the Saarbrücken Cons. and in composition from William Maler at the Cologne Cons. In 1946 he became a teacher of church music at the North West German Music Academy in Detmold, where he was a prof. of composition (from 1958) and deputy director (1960–83). He was especially adept at composing choral works in an acceptable tonal idiom.

WORKS: OPERAS: *Claudia amata* (1952); *Prinzessin Hochmut* (1952); *Der Umfried*, youth opera (1957); *Doktor Luzifer Trux* (1958). **ORCH.:** Piano Concerto (1953); Cello Concerto (1954); *Ikarus*, sym. for 2 Soloists, Chorus, and Orch. (1960); 3 numbered syms.: No. 1, *Dum spiro spero* (1964), No. 2, *Dum ludo laudo* (1966), and No. 3, *Amo dum vivo*, for Strings and Percussion (1969); Concerto for String Trio and Orch. (1963). **ORGAN:** *20 Choralsonaten* (1954–55). **VOCAL: ORATORIOS:** *Dein Reich komme* (1949); *Gaudia mundana* (1951); *De profundis* for Soloists, 2 Choruses, Winds, Timpani, and Piano (1950–52); *Darum seid getrost* (1954); *Der Lebendige* (1956); *Der grosse Lobgesang* for Mezzo-soprano, Chorus, Winds, and Brass (1959). **OTHER VOCAL:** *Denn dein Reich komme*, cantata for Soloists, 2 Choruses, and Instruments (1947); *Sinfonia sacra* for Chorus (1948); *Christe eleison*, Passion motet (1948); *Triptychon*, cantata for Chorus and Small Orch. (1950); *12 Spruchmotetten und 10 Spruchkanons* for Chorus (1950); *Balduin Brummsel*, cantata for Soloists and Orch. (1952); *Altenberger Messe* for Chorus and Winds (1955); *Markus-Passion* for Chorus (1955); *2 Concerti sacri* for Soloist and Organ (1961).

Dring, Madeleine, English violinist, pianist, singer, and composer; b. Hornsey, Sept. 7, 1923; d. London, March 26, 1977. She studied violin at the Junior Dept. of the Royal College of Music in London, and also acquired professional skill as a pianist, singer, and actress. She took courses in composition at the Royal College of Music with Howells and Vaughan Williams. She developed a knack for writing attractively brief pieces. She also wrote a short opera, *Cupboard Love*, several trios, a suite for Harmonica and Piano, and incidental music for radio and television.

Drinker, Henry S(andwith, Jr.), American music scholar and translator; b. Philadelphia, Sept. 15, 1880; d. Merion, Pa., March 9, 1965. He was a lawyer by profession, but devoted much time to musical pursuits. He founded the Accademia dei Dilettanti di Musica in his home in 1930, which gave performances of choral music ranging from the 17th to the 20th centuries until it was disbanded in 1960. He also founded the Drinker Library of Choral Music, which he later donated to the Free Library of Philadelphia. He tr. the texts of 212 cantatas by Bach, as well as the *St. Matthew Passion*, the *St. John Passion*, the *Christmas Oratorio*, the *Easter Oratorio*, and the *Magnificat*; also all of Mozart's choral music, all of Schumann's songs, all of the solo songs of Schubert and Wolf, and the complete vocal works of Brahms. His wife, Sophie (Lewis) (née Hutchinson) Drinker (b. Philadelphia, Aug. 24, 1888; d. Chestnut Hill, Pa., Sept. 6, 1967) was a champion of women in music; she publ. *Music and Women* (1948) and *Brahms and His Women's Choruses* (1952).

WRITINGS: *The Chamber Music of Johannes Brahms* (Philadelphia, 1932); *Bach's Use of Slurs in Recitativo Secco* (Merion, Pa., 1946); *Drinker Library of Choral Music: Catalogue* (Philadelphia, 1957); *Accademia dei Dilettanti di Musica, 1930–1960* (Merion, Pa., 1960).

Drozdov, Anatoly, Russian pianist, pedagogue, writer on music, and composer; b. Saratov, Nov. 4, 1883; d. Moscow, Sept. 10, 1950. He studied piano with Nikolai Dubasov at the St. Petersburg Cons., graduating in 1909. He was a prof. of piano at the Ekaterinoder Cons. (1911–16), the Saratov Cons. (1918–20), and the Moscow Cons. (1920–24). Drozdov publ. many articles on music and composed 2 piano sonatas and other piano works, as well as chamber pieces. His brother, Vladimir Drozdov (b. Saratov, June 6, 1882; d. N.Y., March 10, 1960), was a pianist and composer. He studied with Essipova at the St. Petersburg Cons. (graduated, 1904) and with Leschetizky in Vienna. After serving as a piano teacher (1907–14) and prof. (1914–17) at the St. Petersburg Cons., he taught in the Ukraine (1918–23) before leaving the country for the West. He composed pieces for piano, including 3 sonatas.

Druckman, Jacob (Raphael), outstanding American composer and teacher; b. Philadelphia, June 26, 1928; d. New Haven, Conn., May 24, 1996. He received lessons in theory, composition, and violin from Gessensway (1938–40) and in solfège and score reading from Longy (1945). During the summers of 1949 and 1950, he attended the composition course of Copland at the Berkshire Music Center at Tanglewood. He pursued his studies with Persichetti, Mennin, and Wagenaar at the Juilliard School of Music in N.Y. (B.S., 1954; M.S., 1956), and with Aubin at the École Normale de Musique in Paris on a Fulbright fellowship (1954–55). Later he did research in electronic music at the Columbia-Princeton Electronic Music Center (1965–66) and at the ORTF in Paris (1968). From 1957 to 1972 he taught at the Juilliard School of Music. He also taught at Bard College (1961–67) and was an assoc. director of the Columbia-Princeton Electronic Music Center (1967). In 1971–72 he was director of the electronic music studio at the Yale Univ. School of Music. After serving as assoc. prof. of composition at Brooklyn College of the City Univ. of N.Y. (1972–76), he was chairman of the music dept. of the Yale Univ. School of Music (from 1976), where he again was director of the electronic music studio (from 1976). He was president of the Koussevitzky Music Foundation from 1981. In 1982 he was in residence at the American Academy in Rome. From 1982 to 1986 he was composer-in-residence of the N.Y. Phil. He was president of the Aaron Copland Music Fund for Music from 1991. In 1957–58 and 1968–69 he held Guggenheim fellowships. In 1972 he won the Pulitzer Prize in Music for his *Windows* for Orch. He received the Brandeis Univ. Creative Arts Award in 1975. In 1978 he was elected to membership in the Inst. of the American Academy and Inst. of Arts and Letters. In his distinguished body of works, Druckman demonstrated an assured handling of various contemporary means of expression, ranging from 12-tone procedures and electronics to traditional and new Romantic elements. His mastery of orchestration was particularly notable.

WORKS: DRAMATIC: *Spell*, ballet (1951); *Interlude*, ballet (1953); *Suite*, ballet (1953); *Performance*, ballet (1960); *Measure for Measure*, incidental music to Shakespeare's play (1964); *Look Park*, film score (1970); *Traite du rossignol*, film score (1970). **ORCH.:** *Music for the Dance* (1949); Concerto for Strings (1951); *Volpone Overture* (1953); Concerto for Violin and Small Orch. (1956); *Odds and Evens: A Game* for Children's Orch. (1966); *Windows* (Chicago, March 16, 1972); *Incenters* for Trumpet, Horn, Trombone, and Orch. (Minneapolis, Nov. 23, 1973; also for Chamber Ensemble, 1968); *Mirage* (St. Louis, March 4, 1976); *Chiaroscuro* (1976; Cleveland, March 14, 1977); Viola Concerto (N.Y., Nov. 2, 1978); *Aureole* (N.Y., June 6, 1979); *Prism* (Baltimore, May 21, 1980); *A Birthday Bouquet* (N.Y., April 26, 1986); *Athanor* (N.Y., May

8, 1986); *Paean* (1986; Houston, Jan. 3, 1987); *In Memoriam Vincent Persichetti* (N.Y., Dec. 6, 1987); *Variation on Bernstein's "New York, New York"* (Tanglewood, Aug. 28, 1988); *Brangle* (Chicago, March 28, 1989); *Nor Spell Nor Charm* for Chamber Orch. (Los Angeles, March 2, 1990); *Shog* (Paris, Feb. 21, 1991); *Summer Lightning* (Tanglewood, July 19, 1991); *Seraphic Games* (Costa Mesa, Calif., April 25, 1992); *Demos* (Brussels, Dec. 31, 1992); *With Bells On*, fanfare for Symphonic Winds and Percussion (Los Angeles, March 31, 1994). **CHAMBER:** 3 string quartets: No. 1 (1948), No. 2 (N.Y., Dec. 13, 1966), and No. 3 (Milwaukee, Nov. 17, 1981); Duo for Violin and Piano (1949; Tanglewood, Aug. 1950); *Divertimento* for Clarinet, Horn, Harp, Violin, Viola, and Cello (1950; N.Y., March 1953); *Animus I* for Trombone and Tape (Annandale-on-Hudson, N.Y., May 23, 1966) and *III* for Clarinet and Tape (Paris, Oct. 23, 1969); *Incenters* for Chamber Ensemble (New Brunswick, N.J., May 7, 1968; also for Trumpet, Horn, Trombone, and Orch., 1973); *Valentine* for Double Bass (N.Y., Nov. 19, 1969); *Orison* for Organ and Tape (1969; N.Y., Jan. 19, 1970); *Delizie contente che l'alme beate* for Wind Quintet and Tape (N.Y., Dec. 13, 1973); *Other Voices* for Brass Quintet (Aspen, Colo., July 20, 1976); *Tromba Marina* for 4 Double Basses (N.Y., Dec. 29, 1981); *Reflections on the Nature of War* for Marimba (Washington, D.C., Nov. 7, 1986); *Dance With Shadows* for Brass Quintet (1989); *Come Round* for Chamber Ensemble (Santa Fe, N.M., Aug. 16, 1992); Duo for Violin and Cello (Charonne, France, June 17, 1994). **VOCAL:** *Laude* for Baritone, Flute, Viola, and Cello (1952); *The Simple Gifts* for Chorus and Piano (1954); *4 Madrigals* for Chorus (1958; N.Y., March 6, 1959); *Dark Upon the Harp* for Mezzo-soprano, Brass Quintet, and Percussion (1962); *Antiphonies I, II,* and *III* for 2 Choruses (1963; *I* and *II*, N.Y., Feb. 28, 1964; *III*, Tanglewood, July 30, 1976); *The Sound of Time* for Soprano and Piano (N.Y., Dec. 3, 1964; also for Soprano and Orch., Provincetown, Mass., July 25, 1965); *Dance of the Maidens* for Chorus, Organ, and Percussion (1965); *Hymnus referamus* for Chorus, Organ, and Percussion (1965); *Psalm 89* for Chorus, Organ, and Percussion (1965); *Shir Shel Yakov: Sabbath Eve Service* for Tenor, Chorus, and Organ (N.Y., April 21, 1967); *Animus II* for Soprano, 2 Percussionists, and Tape (1968; Paris, Feb. 2, 1970) and *IV* for Tenor, Instrumental Ensemble, and Tape (Paris, Sept. 29, 1977); *Lamia* for Soprano and Orch. (Albany, N.Y., April 20, 1974; rev. version, N.Y., Oct. 17, 1975; also for Soprano and Small Orch., St. Paul, Minn., Nov. 7, 1986); *Bō* for 3 Women's Voices, Marimba, Harp, and Bass Clarinet (N.Y., March 3, 1979); *Vox Humana* for Soprano, Mezzo-soprano, Tenor, Bass, Chorus, and Orch. (1982–83; Washington, D.C., Oct. 25, 1983); *Nor Spell* for Mezzo-soprano and English Horn (Aspen, Colo., July 19, 1990); *Counterpoise* for Soprano and Orch. (Philadelphia, April 28, 1994).

Drury, Stephen, American pianist; b. Spokane, Wash., April 13, 1955. His mother taught him piano; he then went to Harvard Univ., where he worked at the Electronic Music Studio. In 1977 he continued his piano studies in N.Y. with William Masselos; then returned to Harvard and organized an Experimental Music Festival, during which he gave a complete performance of Satie's *Vexations.* He also played the piano sonatas of Ives and piano pieces by Cage. While preoccupied with avant-garde music, Drury also took occasional lessons in classical piano with Arrau in N.Y. On the musical far-out frontier, he became a member of a conceptual team called Beaux Eaux Duo.

Drzewiecki, Zbigniew, distinguished Polish pianist and pedagogue; b. Warsaw, April 8, 1890; d. there, April 11, 1971. After preliminary training in Warsaw, he studied with C. Prohaska at the Vienna Academy of Music (1909–11) and privately with Maria Prentner (1911–15). He had a few private lessons with Paderewski (1928). In 1916 he made his debut as a soloist with the Warsaw Phil.; he taught at the Warsaw Academy of Music (1916–44; 1945–68) and at the Lvov Cons. (1930–40); in 1945 he founded the Kraków Cons., where he was rector (1945–50) and teacher (until 1968). His fame as a pedagogue reached beyond his homeland; his students included Roger Woodward from Australia and Fou Ts'ong from China. He was active in ISCM activities in Poland and served as a jurist for the Chopin Piano Competition, in which 1st prizes were captured by his students Halina Czerny-Stefanska (1949) and Adam Harasiweicz (1955).

BIBL.: S. Kisielewski, *Z. D.* (Kraków, 1973).

Dubensky, Arcady, Russian-American violinist and composer; b. Viatka, Oct. 15, 1890; d. Tenafly, N.J., Oct. 14, 1966. He learned to play the violin in his youth, and then was a student of Hřímalý (violin), Ilyinsky (composition), and Arends (conducting) at the Moscow Cons. (1904–09; diploma, 1909). After playing 1st violin in the Moscow Imperial Opera orch. (1910–19), he settled in N.Y. in 1921 and was a violinist in the N.Y. Sym. Orch. (1922–28) and the N.Y. Phil. (1928–53). While he composed in a conservative idiom, he made adroit use of unusual instrumental combinations.

WORKS: DRAMATIC: OPERAS: *Romance with Double Bass* (1916; N.Y., Oct. 31, 1936); *Downtown* (1930); *On the Highway* (1936); *2 Yankees in Italy* (1944). **INCIDENTAL MUSIC TO:** Tarkington's *Mowgli* (1940). **ORCH.:** Sym. (1916); *Russian Bells*, symphonic poem (N.Y., Dec. 29, 1927); *Intermezzo and Complement* (1927); *From Old Russia* (1927); *Gossips* for Strings (Philadelphia, Nov. 24, 1928); *Caprice* for Piccolo and Orch. (1930); *The Raven* for Narrator and Orch. (1931); *Prelude and Fugue* (1932; Boston, April 12, 1943); *Fugue* for 18 Violins (Philadelphia, April 1, 1932); *Tom Sawyer*, overture (Philadelphia, Nov. 29, 1935); *Political Suite: Russian Monarchy, Nazi and Fascist, Communist* (radio broadcast, N.Y., Sept. 17, 1936); *Serenade* (1936); *Rondo and Gigue* for Strings (1937); *Fantasy on a Negro Theme* for Tuba and Orch. (1938); *Stephen Foster: Theme, Variations, Finale* (1940; Indianapolis, Jan. 31, 1941); *Orientale* (1945); *Fugue* for 34 Violins (1948); *Concerto grosso* for 3 Trombones, Tuba, and Orch. (1949); *Trumpet Overture* for 18 Toy Trumpets and 2 Bass Drums (N.Y., Dec. 10, 1949); Trombone Concerto (1953). **CHAMBER:** 2 string quartets (1932, 1954); *Variations* for 8 Clarinets (1932); *Theme and Variations* for 4 Horns (1932); String Sextet (1933); *Prelude and Fugue* for 4 Double Basses (1934); Suite for 4 Trumpets (1935); Suite for 9 Flutes (1935); *Song of November* for Oboe and Piano (1950).

Dubois, Pierre-Max, French composer; b. Graulhet, Tarn, March 1, 1930; d. Rocquencourt, Aug. 29, 1995. He studied at the Tours Cons., obtaining a prize in piano at the age of 15; later studied composition with Milhaud at the Paris Cons. In 1955 he won the Grand Prix de Rome and the music prize of the City of Paris.

WORKS: DRAMATIC: *Impressions foraines*, ballet (1951); *Le Docteur OX*, ballet-bouffe, after Jules Verne (Lyons, Feb. 23, 1964); *Cover Girls*, choreographic spectacle (1965); *Comment causer*, "opéra pouf (1970); *Les Suisses*, opera (1972); *Hommage à Hoffnung*, ballet (1980). **ORCH.:** *Impressions foraines* (1949); *Divertissement* for Saxophone and Orch. (1952); *Sérénades* for Bassoon and Orch. (1953); *Capriccio* for Violin and Orch. (1954); 2 violin concertos: No. 1 (1955; Strasbourg, June 20, 1957) and No. 2 (1964); Cello Concerto (1958); Concerto for Saxophone and Strings (1959); 2 syms.: No. 1, *Drame pour Epidaure* (1960) and No. 2, *Symphonie-Sérénade* for Strings (1964); *Concerto italien* for 2 Pianos and Orch. (1962); Concerto for Violin, Piano, and Orch. (Besançon, Sept. 15, 1963); *Musique pour un Western* (1964); *Concerto ironico* for Bassoon and Orch. (1968); Concertino for 4 Saxophones and Orch. (1969); *Beaujency concerto* for Clarinet and Orch. (1969); *Sinfonia militaire* (1969); *Beaugency-Concerto* for Clarinet and Orch. (1969); Bass Clarinet Concerto (1978); *Suite concertante* for Wind Quintet and Orch. (1980); *Hommage à Rabelais*, overture (1981). **CHAMBER:** *Concertstück* for Saxophone and Piano (1955); Quartet for 4 Horns (1961); Quartet for 4 Flutes (1961); Quartet for 4 Trombones (1961); Quartet for 4 Clarinets (1962); *Pop Variations* for Flute and Piano (1971); *Le cinéma muet* for Horn, Trumpet, Trombone, and Tuba (1972); *Coïncidence* for Clarinet and Piano (1977); *Les Nouvelles Saisons* for Double Wind Quintet and Piano (1982).

Dubrovay, László, Hungarian composer; b. Budapest, March 23, 1943. He studied at the Bartók Cons. and the Academy of Music in Budapest (graduated, 1966), his principal mentors being István Szelényi, Ferenc Szabó, and Imre Vincze; then continued his training in West Germany on a scholarship from the Deutscher Akademischer Austauschdienst, receiving instruction in composition from Stockhausen and in electronic music from Hans-Ulrich Rumpert (1972–74). Returning to Budapest, he taught theory at the Academy of Music (from 1976); was awarded the Erkel Prize (1985). In some of his works, he utilizes electronic and computer resources.

WORKS: DRAMATIC: *Il ricatto*, opera (1991); *The Sculptor*, dance-play (1993). **ORCH.:** *Verificazione* (1970); *Succession* (1974); Concerto for 11 Strings (1979); Concerto for Flute and 45 Strings (1981); Concerto for Trumpet and 15 Strings (1981); Concerto for Piano, Orch., and Synthesizer (1982); Piano Concerto (1984); *Variations on an Oscillating Line* (1987); *Deserts* for Brass Orch. (1987); Triple Concerto for Tuba, Trombone, Trumpet, and Orch. (1989); March for Winds (1990). **CHAMBER:** *Cinque pezzi* for Bassoon and Piano (1967); *Sei duo* for Violin and Percussion (1969); 2 brass quintets (1971, 1980); 2 wind quintets (1972, 1983); *Magic Squares* for Violin and Cimbalom (1975); *Matuziáda* Nos. 1 to 5 for 4 Flutes (1975–76); *Geometrum II*: String Quartet No. 2 (1976); *Numberplay No. 1* for 20 Players (1976); *Interferences No. 1* for 2 Cimbaloms (1976); *Music* for 2 Cimbaloms (1977); Brass Septet for 3 Trumpets, Horn, 2 Trombones, and Tuba (1980); String Quartet No. 3 (1983); Octet for Clarinet, Bassoon, Horn, and String Quartet (1985–87). **OTHER:** Pieces for solo instrument, chorus, live electronics, computer, and tape.

Duchâble, François-René, French pianist; b. Paris, April 22, 1952. He was a pupil of Joseph Benvenutti and Madeleine Giraudeau-Basset at the Paris Cons. At age 16, he received 11th prize at the Queen Elisabeth of Belgium competition in Brussels, and in 1973 won the Prix de la Fondation Sacha Schneider, which led to his first major engagement in Paris at the Salle Gaveau. In 1980 he won critical accolades as soloist in Bartók's 3rd Piano Concerto with Karajan and the Berlin Phil., and thereafter pursued an international career as a virtuoso.

Duckles, Vincent H(arris), American musicologist; b. Boston, Sept. 21, 1913; d. Berkeley, Calif., July 1, 1985. He began his training at the Univ. of Calif., Berkeley (A.B., 1936); after studies at Columbia Univ. (M.A. in music education, 1937; Ed.D., 1941), he pursued training once more at the Univ. of Calif., Berkeley (B.L.S., 1949; Ph.D., 1953, with the diss. *John Gamble's Commonplace Book*); also held Fulbright senior research scholarships at the Univ. of Cambridge (1950–51) and at the Univ. of Göttingen (1957–58), and a grant-in-aid from the American Council of Learned Societies for research in Europe (1964–65). He was a music librarian (1949–57), assoc. prof. (1957–60), and prof. (1960–81) at the Univ. of Calif., Berkeley. In 1982 he was made an honorary member of the American Musicological Soc. He specialized in 17th-century English song literature, music bibliography, and the history of musical scholarship. He publ. the valuable and enduring source *Music Reference and Research Materials: An Annotated Bibliography* (N.Y., 1964; 4th ed., rev., 1988 by M. Keller; rev. 1994).

BIBL.: P. Elliott and M. Roosa, "V. D. (1913–1985): A Bibliography of His Publications," *Notes* (Dec. 1987).

Duckworth, William (Ervin), American composer, pianist, teacher, and writer on music; b. Morganton, N.C., Jan. 13, 1943. He studied with Mailman (composition) at East Carolina Univ. (B.M., 1965) and with Johnston (composition), Robert Gray (trombone), and Charles Leonhard (education) at the Univ. of Ill. (M.S., 1966; D.M.Ed., 1972, with the diss. *Expanding Notational Parameters in the Music of John Cage*). He was founder-director of the Assn. of Independent Composers and Performers (1969–72) and president of the Media Press (1969–72). From 1973 he taught at Bucknell Univ. He was also active as a pianist. In his highly diversified output as a composer, Duckworth has imaginatively utilized pop, jazz, minimalist, and other elements to forge a remarkable personal style of expression. His *The Time Curve Preludes* for Piano (1977–78) mark the beginning of postminimalism; in his *Gathering Together/Revolution* for Mallet Percussion, Drums, and Keyboards (1992–93), he created the first chance-determined postminimalist "moment form."

WRITINGS: With E. Brown, *Theoretical Foundations of Music* (1978); *A Creative Approach to Music Fundamentals* (1981; 5th ed., 1994); ed. with R. Fleming, *John Cage at Seventy-Five* (1989); *Talking Music: Conversations with 5 Generations of American Experimental Composers* (1995); *Sound and Light: La Monte Young and Marian Zazeela* (1996).

WORKS: *An Unseen Action* for Flute, Prepared Piano, and 4 Percussion (1966; Cleveland, May 17, 1968); *Gambit* for Percussion and Tape (1967); *Non-ticking Tenuous Tintinnabule Time* for 4 Electric Metronomes and Percussion Quartet (Hamilton, N.Y., Oct. 15, 1968); *Introjection* for Guitar (1968); *A Peace for 20 Voices* (1968); *A Ballad in Time and Space* for Tenor Saxophone and Piano (1968); *Knight to King's Bishop 4* for Dancer and Gong (1968); *The Sleepy Hollow Elementary School Band* for 20 to 60 Instrumentalists (1968); *Pitch City* for Any 4 Wind Players (1969); *Western Exit* for Movie, Slides, Announcer, and Chamber Ensemble (1969); *Memories of You . . .* for Any Instrumentation (1969); *When in Eternal Lines to Time Thou Grow'st* for Orch. (1970; Philadelphia, June 22, 1974); *Walden* for Any Number of Instruments, Dancers, Readers, Slides, and Movies and/or Lights (1971; Hartford, Dec. 10, 1972); *Walden Variations* for Any Number of Instruments, Dancers, Readers, Slides, Movies and/or Lights (1971; Urbana, March 14, 1972); *Sound World I* for 3 or More Instrumentalists (1972; Chapel Hill, N.C., Sept. 27, 1973); *A Mass for These Forgotten Times* for Chorus (1973); *Gymel* for 4 Mallet Percussionists or Keyboards (1973); *7 Shades of Blue* for Flute, Clarinet, Violin, Cello, and Piano (Brunswick, Maine, April 29, 1974); *A Summer Madrigal* for Flute, Violin, Piano, 2 Percussion, and Rock Singer (1976); *Silent Signals* for Percussion Quartet (1976); *A Book of Hours* for Flute, Violin, Clarinet, Cello, and Piano (Brunswick, Maine, Oct. 17, 1976); *The Last Nocturn* for Piano (1976); *The Time Curve Preludes* (1977–78; Middletown, Ct., Feb. 6, 1979); *Year* for Amplified Prepared Piano and Slides (1979); *Music in 7 Regions* for Amplified Piano or Synthesizer (1979; Philadelphia, June 17, 1983); *Southern Harmony* for Chorus (1980–81; 1st complete perf., Lewisburg, Pa., Feb. 28, 1992); *Simple Songs About Sex and War* for Voice and Piano (1983–84; Huddersfield, England, Nov. 29, 1987); *Songs of the Pale Horseman* for Chorus and Live Electronics (1984; rev. 1985 and 1990); *Tango Voices* for Piano (Oslo, Aug. 19, 1984); *Imaginary Dances* for Piano (1985; rev. 1988); *31 Days* for Any Solo Woodwind (1986); *Music in the Combat Zone* for Soprano and Chamber Ensemble (Philadelphia, Nov. 1, 1986); *Polking Around* for Accordion (1986; arranged for Ensemble by G. Klucevsek, 1988); *12 Words* for Solo Instrument or Voice and 4 Similar Instruments (1989–90; N.Y., March 24, 1990); *Slow Dancing in Yugoslavia* for Accordion (WNYC-FM, N.Y., March 21, 1990); *Blue Rhythm* for Violin/Flute, Cello, and Piano (1990; Philadelphia, Feb. 3, 1991); *Their Song* for Baritone and Piano (1991; N.Y., May 13, 1993); *Gathering Together* for 2 Keyboards and 2 Mallet Percussion (Rome, Sept. 21, 1992); *Revolution* for 2 Pianos and 4 Percussion, amplified (1992–93; N.Y., March 25, 1993).

Ducloux, Walter (Ernest), Swiss-born American conductor and teacher; b. Kriens, April 17, 1913. He was educated at the Univ. of Munich (Ph.D., 1935) and studied conducting at the Vienna Academy of Music (diploma, 1937). After conducting in Lucerne (1937–39), he emigrated to the U.S. and became a naturalized citizen in 1943. He appeared as a conductor in the U.S. and Europe; also served on the faculties of the Univ. of Southern Calif. in Los Angeles (1953–68) and the Univ. of Texas in Austin (from 1968). He was music director of the Austin (Texas) Sym. Orch. (1973–75) and the Austin (Texas) Lyric Opera (from 1986).

Dudarova, Veronika, Russian conductor; b. Baku, Dec. 5, 1916. After training in Baku, she attended the Leningrad Cons. and studied conducting with Anosov and Ginzburg at the Moscow Cons. (graduated, 1947). She then was a conductor with the State Sym. Orch. of the U.S.S.R. in Moscow. In 1960 she became its chief conductor, the first woman in Russia to attain such a position. She conducted it throughout the country, and also abroad. After conducting in Istanbul (from 1989), she returned to Moscow and was founder-conductor (from 1991) of the Sym. Orch. of Russia. In 1960 she was made a People's Artist of the U.S.S.R. in recognition of her pioneering career as a woman conductor in Russia.

Duesing, Dale, American baritone; b. Milwaukee, Sept. 26, 1947. He studied voice at Lawrence Univ. in Appleton, Wis. Following appearances in Bremen (1972) and Düsseldorf (1974–75), he sang in the premiere of Imbrie's *Angle of Repose* in San Francisco in 1976; that same year, made his first appearance at the Glyndebourne Festival as Strauss's Olivier. On Feb. 22, 1979, he made his Metropolitan Opera debut in N.Y. as Strauss's Harlekin, returning there in later seasons as Rossini's Figaro, as Pelléas, and as Billy Budd; also sang opera in Seattle, Santa Fe, Chicago, Houston, Brussels, Barcelona, Salzburg, and Milan. Duesing won critical acclaim when he created the tasking role of I in the premiere of Schnittke's *Zhizn s Idiotom* (Life with an Idiot) in Amsterdam in 1992. Among his other operatic roles are Guglielmo, Eugene Onegin, Belcore, Wolfram, and Janáček's Goryanshikov.

Dufallo, Richard (John), American conductor; b. East Chicago, Ind., Jan. 30, 1933. He played clarinet as a youngster; then enrolled at the American Cons. of Music in Chicago. He subsequently studied composition with Foss at the Univ. of Calif., Los Angeles; in 1957 he joined the Improvisation Chamber Ensemble organized by Foss, and showed an exceptional talent for controlled improvisation in the ultramodern manner. He then joined Foss as his assoc. conductor with the Buffalo Phil. (1962–67); also served on the faculty of the State Univ. of N.Y. at Buffalo (1963–67), where he directed its Center of Creative and Performing Arts. He attended a conducting seminar with William Steinberg in N.Y. (1965); Boulez gave him additional instruction in Basel (1969). In 1967 he went to Japan and other Asian countries as assistant tour conductor with the N.Y. Phil. In 1971 he made his European conducting debut in Paris. He served as conductor of the "Mini-Met," an adjunct to the Metropolitan Opera in N.Y. (1972–74), and was director of the series of new music sponsored by the Juilliard School in N.Y. (1972–79). From 1970 to 1985 he was artistic director of the Aspen Music Festival's Conference on Contemporary Music. From 1980 to 1982 he also served as artistic adviser of Het Gelders Orkest in Arnhem, the Netherlands. In 1984–85 he was acting director of the Aspen Inst. Italia in Rome. He appeared as a guest conductor with many orchs. in the U.S. and Europe, securing a reputation as an advocate of contemporary music. He publ. the book *Trackings: Composers Speak with Richard Dufallo* (N.Y. and Oxford, 1989).

Dufourcq, Norbert, distinguished French music historian and organist; b. St. Jean-de-Braye, Loiret, Sept. 21, 1904; d. Paris, Dec. 19, 1990. He was educated at the Sorbonne, where he studied history and geography, then at the École Nationale des Chartes (1924–28), graduating as an archivist-paleographer; also studied piano and music history with Gastoué (1913–20), organ with Marchal (1920–40), and harmony, counterpoint, and fugue with Marie-Rose Hublé. He took his Ph.D. at the Univ. of Paris in 1935 with the diss. *Esquisse d'une histoire de l'orgue en France: XIIIe–XVIIIe siècles* (publ. in Paris, 1935). He was a teacher of history at the Collège Stanislas in Paris (1935–46); also prof. of music history and musicology at the Paris Cons. (1941–76). In addition to other teaching positions, he appeared as an organist. He ed. performing and scholarly eds. of works for the organ and harpsichord of 17th- and 18th-century French composers.

WRITINGS (all publ. in Paris): *Documents inédits pour servir à l'histoire de l'orgue* (1935); *Les Clicquot, facteurs d'orgues du Roy* (1942; 2nd ed., 1990); ed. *La Musique des origines à nos jours* (1946); *Jean-Sébastien Bach: Génie allemand, génie latin?* (1947; 2nd ed., 1949); *Jean-Sébastien Bach, le maître de l'orgue* (1948; 2nd ed., 1973); *L'Orgue* (1948; 5th ed., 1976); *César Franck* (1949); *La Musique française* (1949; 2nd ed., aug., 1970); *Le Clavecin* (1949; 2nd ed., 1967); *Autour de Coquard, César Franck et Vincent d'Indy* (1952); *Nicolas Lebègue, organiste de la Chapelle Royale* (1954); ed. with F. Raugel and A. Machabey, *Larousse de la musique* (1957); *Jean-Baptiste Boesset, surintendant de la Musique du Roi* (1963); ed *La Musique: Les hommes, les instruments, les hommes* (1965); *Le livre de l'orgue français, 1589–1789* (6 vols., 1969–82); with M. Benoit and B. Gagnepain, *Les Grandes Dates de l'histoire de la musique* (1969; 2nd ed., 1975).

BIBL.: M. Benoît, ed., "N. D. (1904–1990)," *L'Orgue,* nos. 49–50 (1993).

Dufranne, Hector (Robert), Belgian bass-baritone; b. Mons, Oct. 25, 1870; d. Paris, May 3, 1951. He studied in Brussels, making his operatic debut there at the Théâtre Royal de la Monnaie as Valentine in *Faust* (Sept. 9, 1896); then went to Paris as a member of the Opéra-Comique (1899–1909) and the Opéra (from 1909). He also sang at the Manhattan Opera in N.Y. (1908–10), the Chicago Grand Opera (1910–22), and London's Covent Garden (1914); he retired from the stage in 1939. He created roles in several French operas, including Golaud in Debussy's *Pelléas et Mélisande* (1902).

Dugan, Franjo, Croatian organist, teacher, and composer; b. Krapinica, Sept. 11, 1874; d. Zagreb, Dec. 12, 1948. After studies with Bruch in Berlin, he was cathedral organist (1912–48) and a teacher at the Cons. in Zagreb. He publ. manuals on orchestration and musical form. His compositions included choral works and chamber music.

Duhamel, Antoine, French composer; b. Valmondois, near Paris, July 30, 1925. He was the son of the writer Georges Duhamel and of the actress Blanche Albane. He studied at the Paris Cons. with Messiaen, Dufourcq, and de la Presle, but pursued his major training privately with Leibowitz who provided him with a thorough grounding in modern techniques. Although he composed some concert works, he devoted much time to the theater. In addition to film and television scores, he wrote much stage music. Among the latter were *L'ivrogne* (1952; Tours, 1984); *Gala de cirque* (Strasbourg, 1965); *Lundi, Monsieur, vous serez riche* (Paris, Jan. 23, 1969); *L'opéra des oiseaux* (Lyons, May 19, 1971); *Ubu à l'opéra* (Avignon, July 16, 1974); *Gambara* (Lyons, June 2, 1978); *Le cirque impérial* (Avignon, July 30, 1979); *Les travaux d'Hercule* (Vaise, June 15, 1981); *Le transsibérien* (1983); *Le scieur de long* (Tours, March 9, 1984); *Quatrevingt-treize* (Fourvières, July 10, 1989); *Les Adventures de Sinbad le marin* (Colmar, Feb. 12, 1991).

Dukas, Paul, famous French composer and teacher; b. Paris, Oct. 1, 1865; d. there, May 17, 1935. From 1882 to 1888 he was a student at the Paris Cons., studying under Mathias (piano), Dubois (harmony), and Guiraud (composition); won 1st prize for counterpoint and fugue in 1886, and the 2nd Prix de Rome with a cantata, *Velléda* (1888). He began writing music reviews in 1892; was music critic of the *Revue Hebdomadaire* and *Gazette des Beaux-Arts.* In 1906 he was made a Chevalier of the Légion d'honneur. From 1910 to 1913, and again from 1928 to 1935, he was prof. of the orch. class at the Cons.; in 1918, was elected Debussy's successor as a member of the *Conseil de l'enseignement supérieur* there; also taught at the École Normale de Musique. Although he was not a prolific composer, Dukas wrote a masterpiece in his orch. scherzo *L'Apprenti Sorcier,* his opera *Ariane et Barbe-Bleue* is one of the finest French operas in the impressionist style. Among his other notable works are the Sym. in C major and the ballet *La Péri.* Shortly before his death, he destroyed several MSS of his unfinished compositions.

WORKS: DRAMATIC: OPERA: *Ariane et Barbe-Bleue* (1899–1906; Paris, May 10, 1907). **BALLET:** *La Péri* (1911–12; Paris, April 22, 1912). **ORCH.:** 3 overtures: *King Lear* (1883), *Götz von Berlichingen* (1884), and *Polyeucte* (1891); Sym. in C major (1896; Paris, Jan. 3, 1897); *L'Apprenti Sorcier*, scherzo (Paris, May 18, 1897). **OTHER:** *Villanelle* for Horn and Piano (1906); piano music, including a Sonata (1899–1901), *Variations, Interlude et Finale (sur un thème de Rameau)* (1903), *Prélude élégiaque* (1908), and *La Plainte au loin du faune* (1920); *Sonnet de Ronsard* for Voice (1924). With Saint-Saëns, he completed Guiraud's opera *Frédégonde*.

BIBL.: G. Samazeuilh, *P. D.* (Paris, 1913; 2nd ed., 1936); V. d'Indy, *Emmanuel Chabrier et P. D.* (Paris, 1920); G. Samazeuilh, *P. D., musicien français* (Paris, 1936); D. issue of the *Revue Musicale* (May–June 1936); G. Favre, *P. D.: Sa vie, son oeuvre* (Paris, 1948); N. Demuth, *P. D.* (London, 1949); G. Favre, *L'Oeuvre de P. D.* (Paris, 1969); idem, ed., *Correspondance de P. D.* (Paris, 1971); W. Moore, *The Significance of Late Nineteenth-Century French Wagnérisme in the Relationship of P. D. and Edouard Dujardin: A Study of Their Correspondence, Essays on Wagner, and D.'s Opera Ariane et Barbe-Bleue* (diss., Univ. of Texas, 1986).

Duke, John (Woods), American pianist, pedagogue, and composer; b. Cumberland, Md., July 30, 1899; d. Northampton, Mass., Oct. 26, 1984. He studied piano with Harold Randolph and composition with Gustav Strube at the Peabody Cons. of Music in Baltimore (1915–18), then studied piano with Franklin Cannon and composition with Howard Brockway and Bernard Wagenaar in N.Y.,; later received instruction in piano from Schnabel in Berlin and in composition from Boulanger in Paris (1929). He was assistant prof. (1923–38) and prof. (1938–67) of music at Smith College in Northampton, Mass., becoming prof. emeritus at his retirement. He composed over 200 songs, some of which are outstanding contributions to the genre.

WORKS: DRAMATIC: *Captain Lovelock*, opera (Hudson Falls, N.Y., Aug. 18, 1953); *The Sire de Maledroit*, opera (Schroon Lake, N.Y., Aug. 15, 1958); *The Yankee Pedlar*, operetta (Schroon Lake, N.Y., Aug. 17, 1962). **ORCH.:** Concerto for Piano and Strings (1938); *Carnival Overture* (1940). **CHAMBER:** Suite for Solo Viola (1933); *Fantasy* for Violin and Piano (1936); String Trio (1937); 2 string quartets (1941, 1967); Piano Trio (1943). **VOCAL:** Choral works; more than 200 songs, including major cycles to poems of Emily Brontë and Emily Dickinson.

Duke, Vernon. See **Dukelsky, Vladimir (Alexandrovich).**

Dukelsky, Vladimir (Alexandrovich), versatile Russian-born American composer who used the name **Vernon Duke**; b. Parfianovka, Oct. 10, 1903; d. Santa Monica, Calif., Jan. 16, 1969. He was a student of Glière (1916–19) and Dombrovsky (1917–19) at the Kiev Cons. After living in Constantinople (1920–21), he went to N.Y. in 1922 and to Paris in 1924, where Diaghilev commissioned him to write the ballet *Zéphyr et Flore* (Monte Carlo, April 28, 1925); he also found a champion in Koussevitzky, who conducted his works in Paris and later in Boston. After composing for the London stage (1926–29), he returned to N.Y. and studied orchestration with Schillinger (1934–35). In 1936 he became a naturalized American citizen. Upon settling in the U.S., Dukelsky pursued a dual career as a composer of both serious and popular music. At George Gershwin's suggestion, he adopted the name Vernon Duke for his popular scores, and in 1955 he dropped his real name entirely. He scored his greatest success with the Broadway musical *Cabin in the Sky* (Oct. 25, 1940), which was also made into a film (1943). His amusing autobiography was publ. as *Passport to Paris* (Boston, 1955); he also wrote the polemical book *Listen Here! A Critical Essay on Music Depreciation* (N.Y., 1963).

WORKS: DRAMATIC (all perf. in N.Y. unless otherwise given): **REVUES:** *Walk a Little Faster* (Dec. 7, 1932); *Ziegfeld Follies of 1934* (Jan. 4, 1934); *Ziegfeld Follies of 1936* (Jan. 30, 1936); *The Show is On* (Dec. 25, 1936); *Dancing in the Streets* (Boston, 1943); *Sweet Bye and Bye* (New Haven, Conn., Oct. 10, 1946); *Two's Company* (Dec. 15, 1952). **OPERETTA:** *Yvonne* (London, May 22, 1926; in collaboration with J. Gilbert). **MUSICAL COMEDY:** *The Yellow Mask* (London, Feb. 8, 1928). **MUSICALS:** *Cabin in the Sky* (Oct. 25, 1940; film version in collaboration with H. Arlen, 1943); *Banjo Eyes* (Dec. 25, 1941); *The Lady Comes Across* (Jan. 9, 1942); *Jackpot* (Jan. 13, 1944); *Sadie Thompson* (Nov. 16, 1944). **OPERAS:** *Mistress into Maid* (Santa Barbara, Calif., 1958); *Zenda* (San Francisco, Aug. 1963). **INCIDENTAL MUSIC:** *Time Remembered* (1957). **BALLETS:** *Zéphyr et Flore* (Monte Carlo, April28, 1925); *Public Gardens* (Chicago, March 8, 1935); *Le bal des blanchisseuses* (Paris, Dec. 19, 1946); *Emperor Norton* (San Francisco, 1957); *Lady Blue* (1961). **FILM SCORES:** *April in Paris* (1952); *She's Working Her Way Through College* (1952); also completed G. Gershwin's *The Goldwyn Follies* (1938). **ORCH.:** Piano Concerto (1924); 3 syms.: No. 1 (1927–28; Paris, June 14, 1928), No. 2 (1928–30; Boston, April 25, 1930), and No. 3 (Brussels Radio, Oct. 10, 1947); *Ballade* for Piano and Chamber Orch. (1931); Violin Concerto (Boston, March 19, 1943); *Ode to the Milky Way* (1945; N.Y., Nov. 18, 1946); Cello Concerto (1945; Boston, Jan. 4, 1946); *Variations on an Old Russian Chant* for Oboe and Strings (1958). **CHAMBER:** Trio (Variations) for Flute, Bassoon, and Piano (1930); *Capriccio mexicano* for Violin and Piano (1939); *Etude* for Violin and Bassoon (1939); *3 Pieces* for Flute, Oboe, Clarinet, Bassoon, and Piano (1946); *Nocturne* for 6 Wind Instruments and Piano (1947); 2 violin sonatas (1948, 1960); String Quartet (1956). **PIANO:** Sonata (1928); *2 pièces* (1930); *Printemps* (1931); *N.Y. Nocturne* (1939); *Surrealist Suite* (1940); *Vieux carré* (1940); *Homage to Boston* (1943); *3 Caprices* (1944); *Music for Moderns* for 6 Players (1944); *Parisian Suite* (1955); *Souvenir de Venise* (1955); *Serenade to San Francisco* (1956). **VOCAL:** *Dushenka* for Women's Voices and Orch. (1927); *Epitaph* for Soprano, Chorus, and Orch. (Boston, April 15, 1932); *Dédicaces* for Soprano, Piano, and Orch. (1934; Boston, Dec. 16, 1938); *The End of St. Petersburg*, oratorio (1937; N.Y., Jan. 12, 1938); *Moulin-Rouge* for Soprano, 6 Voices, and Piano (1944); *Paris aller et retour*, cantata for Chorus and Piano (1948). **SONGS:** *Triolets for the North*, song cycle (1922); (8) *Poèsies de Hyppolite Bogdanovitch* (1927–30); *5 poèsies* (1930); *I'm Only Human After All* (1930); *Autumn in N.Y.* (1935); *3 Chinese Songs* (1937); *5 Victorian Songs* (1942); *5 Victorian Street Ballads* (1944); *Ogden Nash's Musical Zoo*, 20 songs (1947); *La bohème et mon coeur*, 7 songs (1949); *A Shropshire Lad*, 6 songs (1949); 4 songs (1955).

BIBL.: N. Slonimsky, "V. D.," *Modern Music* (March 1927); I. Stravinsky, "A Cure for V.D.," *Listen* (Sept. 1964).

Dumesnil, Maurice, French-American pianist and teacher; b. Angoulême, Charente, April 20, 1886; d. Highland Park, Mich., Aug. 26, 1974. He studied at the Paris Cons. with Philipp, graduating in 1905. He received personal coaching from Debussy in playing Debussy's piano works, and was subsequently considered an authority on the subject. He publ. *How to Play and Teach Debussy* (1933) and *Claude Debussy, Master of Dreams* (1940). Apart from his principal occupation as a piano teacher, he was also active as a conductor in Mexico (1916–20); eventually settled in N.Y.

Dumesnil, René (Alphonse Adolphe), French writer; b. Rouen, June 19, 1879; d. Paris, Dec. 24, 1967. He studied literature at the Sorbonne in Paris; was active as a literary critic. Besides his publications dealing with literature, he wrote a number of books on music.

WRITINGS: *Le Rythme musical* (1921; 2nd ed., 1949); *Le Monde des musiciens* (1924); *Le Don Juan de Mozart* (1927; 2nd ed., 1955); *Musiciens romantiques* (1928); *Richard Wagner* (1929); *La Musique contemporaine en France* (1930; 2nd ed., 1949); with P. Hemardinquer, *Le Livre du disque* (1931); *Histoire illustrée de la musique* (1934); *Portraits de musiciens français* (1938); *La Musique romantique française* (1944); *La Musique en France entre les deux guerres* (1946); *L'Envers de la musique* (1949); *Histoire illustrée du théâtre lyrique* (1954); *Richard*

Wagner (1954; a much larger work than his 1929 edition); *L'Opéra* (1964); *Mozart présent dans ses oeuvres lyriques* (1965).

BIBL.: G. van der Kemp, *Notice sur la vie et les travaux de R. D.* (Paris, 1970).

Dumitrescu, Gheorghe, Romanian composer and teacher, brother of **Ion Dumitrescu**; b. Oteşani, Dec. 28, 1914; d. 1995. He studied with Cuclin, Perlea, and Jora at the Bucharest Cons. (1935–41). He was active as a violinist, conductor, and composer at the National Theater in Bucharest (1935–46), and was composer-counselor for the Armatei artistic ensemble (1947–57). In 1951 he was appointed a prof. at the Bucharest Cons. He won the Enesco prize 3 times (1942, 1943, 1946) and was awarded the Great Prize of the Romanian Composers Union (1985). He was especially adept at writing music for the stage.

WORKS: DRAMATIC: *Tarsiţa şi Rosiorul*, operetta (1949; Bucharest, Dec. 12, 1950); *Ion Vodă cel Cumplit*, opera (1955; Bucharest, April 12, 1956); *Decebal*, musical tragedy (1957); *Răscoala*, popular music drama (Bucharest, Nov. 20, 1959); *Fata cu garoafe*, opera (Bucharest, May 6, 1961); *Meşterul Manole*, opera-legend (1970; Bucharest, Oct. 4, 1971); *Geniu pustiu*, opera (1973); *Vlad Tepeş*, musical drama (1974); *Orfeu*, lyric tragedy (1976–77); *Luceafărul*, ballet-opera (concert perf., Bucharest, Dec. 29, 1981); *Marea iubire*, opera (concert perf., Dec. 13, 1982); *Ivan Turbincă*, opera (1983); *Prometheu*, lyric tragedy (1985); *Mihai Viteazul*, music drama (1986). **ORCH.:** 4 syms.: No. 1 (1945), No. 2 for Chorus and Orch. (1962), No. 3 (1965), and No. 4 (1970); *Poemul psaltic* (1939); *Poemul rustic* (1939); *Poemul amurgului* (1941); *Poemul vesel* (1941); *Poemul trist* (1941); 4 suites: No. 1, *Pitorească* (1942), No. 2 (1943), No. 3, *A primăverii* (1944), and No. 4, *Cîmpeneasca* (1963); *Uvertură eroică* (1943); Cello Concerto (1947). **CHAMBER:** 2 piano sonatas (1938, 1939); Viola Sonata (1939); Violin Sonata (1939); Piano Quintet (1940); piano pieces. **VOCAL: ORATORIOS:** *Tudor Vladimirescu* (1950); *Griviţa* (1963); *Zori le de aur* (1964); *Din lumea cor dor, în cea fără dor* (1966); *Pămînt dezrobit* (1968); *Soarele neatîrnării* (1976); *Marea trecere* (1979); *Memento mori* (1984); many cantatas; songs.

Dumitrescu, Ion, Romanian composer and teacher, brother of **Gheorghe Dumitrescu**; b. Oteşani, June 2, 1913. He was a student of Castaldi (harmony), Cuclin (composition), Jora (counterpoint, fugue, and composition), and Perlea (conducting) at the Bucharest Cons. (1934–41). He was active as a composer and conductor at the National Theater in Bucharest from 1940 to 1947. He taught at the Bucharest Cons. from 1944. From 1963 to 1977 he also was chairman of the Romanian Composers Union. He received prizes of the Romanian Academy in 1957 and the Romanian Composers Union in 1979. His works are in a traditional style.

WORKS: DRAMATIC: Film music. **ORCH.:** 3 suites (1938, 1940, 1944); *2 Pieces* (1940); *Poeme* for Cello and Orch. (1940); Sym. (1948; Bucharest, May 8, 1949); *Symphonic Prelude* (Bucharest, Feb. 3, 1952); Concerto for Strings (1956); *Muntele Retezat*, suite (1956); Sinfonietta (Bucharest, Oct. 19, 1957). **CHAMBER:** *Suită în stil vechi* for Viola and Piano (1939); String Quartet (1949). **PIANO:** Sonata (1938); Sonatina (1940); *2 Pieces* (1942). **VOCAL:** Songs.

Dunayevsky, Isaak, Russian composer; b. Lokhvitza, near Poltava, Jan. 30, 1900; d. Moscow, July 25, 1955. He studied piano as a child; then entered the Kharkov Cons. and studied violin with Joseph Achron. He devoted himself mainly to popular music; some songs from his operettas and film scores have become famous. At one time he experimented with jazz rhythms. He received many honors from the Soviet government, including, in 1941, the Stalin Prize for his music to the film *The Circus*.

BIBL.: L. Danilevich, *I. D.* (Moscow, 1947); A. Chernov, *I. D.* (Moscow, 1961).

Dunbar, W. Rudolph, black flutist, conductor, teacher, and writer; b. Nabaclis, British Guiana, April 5, 1907; d. London, June 10, 1988. He was clarinetist in the British Guiana Militia Band (1916–19); then went to the U.S., where he studied clarinet, piano, and composition at the Inst. of Musical Art in N.Y. (graduated, 1924). He pursued further training in Paris with Louis Cahuzac, Gaubert, and Vidal, and in Vienna with Weingartner. In 1931 he settled in London, becoming the first black musician to conduct a band on the BBC (1934) and the London Phil. (April 26, 1942). While working as a newspaper correspondent with the Allies in France, he appeared as conductor with the Pasdeloup Orch. in Paris (Nov. 18, 1944); in 1945 he conducted the Berlin Phil. He subsequently devoted himself mainly to the cause of racial justice and wrote extensively on international affairs. In 1964 he became the first black musician to conduct in the Soviet Union.

BIBL.: "In Retrospect: W.R. D.," *Black Perspective in Music*, IX (1981).

Duncan, (Robert) Todd, black American baritone; b. Danville, Ky., Feb. 12, 1903. He was educated at Butler Univ. in Indianapolis (B.A., 1925) and at Columbia Univ. Teachers College (M.A., 1930); then taught voice at Howard Univ. in Washington, D.C. (until 1945). In 1934 he made his operatic debut with the Aeolian Opera in N.Y. as Alfio in *Cavalleria rusticana*. On Oct. 10, 1935, he created the role of Porgy in Gershwin's *Porgy and Bess* in N.Y., and subsequently sang in revivals of the score. He was the first black American to become a member of a major opera company when he made his appearance at the N.Y. Opera City on Sept. 28, 1945, as Tonio. He appeared as Stephen Kumalo in Weill's *Lost in the Stars* (1949–50), winning both the Donaldson and N.Y. Drama Critics' Circle awards in 1950.

Dunhill, Thomas (Frederick), English composer, teacher, and writer on music; b. London, Feb. 1, 1877; d. Scunthorpe, Lincolnshire, March 13, 1946. He entered the Royal College of Music in London in 1893, and studied with Franklin Taylor (piano) and Stanford (theory); in 1905 he was appointed a prof. there. In 1907 he founded the Concerts of British Chamber-Music, which he oversaw until 1916. He publ. *Chamber Music* (1912), *Mozart's String Quartets* (2 vols., 1927), *Sullivan's Comic Operas* (1928), and *Sir Edward Elgar* (1938).

WORKS: DRAMATIC: OPERAS: *The Enchanted Garden* (London, March 1928); *Tantivy Towers* (London, Jan. 16, 1931); *Happy Families* (Guildford, Nov. 1, 1933). **BALLETS:** *Gallimaufry* (Hamburg, Dec. 11, 1937); *Dick Whittington* (n.d.). **CHAMBER:** *Phantasy* for String Quartet; Piano Quintet; Quintet for Violin, Cello, Clarinet, Horn, and Piano; Quintet for Horn and String Quartet; Piano Quartet; Viola Sonata; 2 violin sonatas; violin pieces; cello pieces. **VOCAL:** *The Wind among the Reeds*, song cycle for Tenor and Orch.

Dunkley, Ferdinand (Luis), English-American organist and composer; b. London, July 16, 1869; d. Waldwick, N.J., Jan. 5, 1956. He studied at the Royal Academy of Music in London with Parry, Bridge, Martin, Gladstone, Sharpe, and Barnett; then was organist of St. Jude's, London (1885–87) and of St. Aubyn's, London (1888–93). In 1893 he was engaged as music director at St. Agnes' School in Albany, N.Y.; was organist at Temple Sinai, New Orleans (1924–34); in 1934 he was appointed a prof. at Loyola Univ., New Orleans. He made his last public appearance on his 82nd birthday, when he gave an organ recital.

WORKS: *The Wreck of the Hesperus*, ballade for Soli, Chorus, and Orch.; choral works: *Praise the Lord* (1919); *Green Branches* (1919); *God is my strong salvation* (1921); *Street Cries* (1924); *Blessed is the man* (1937); etc.

Dunlap, Arlene, American pianist and teacher; b. Seattle, Nov. 22, 1937. She studied at the Univ. of Wash. (B.A., 1960). After moving to Santa Barbara, California in 1969, she became active as a teacher. She also performed widely, specializing in new music; composers who have written works for her include Daniel Lentz, Gary Eister, Michael John Fink, and Harold Budd; from the 1970s she was particularly active in performance ensembles organized by Lentz. She has recorded extensively as a keyboardist, vocalist, and conductor, both in ensembles and as a soloist; also has given numerous lecture-recitals. She composed music for film, video, and dance, as well as collected pedagogical pieces for beginning piano students. She is married to **Richard Dunlap**.

Dunlap, Richard, American pianist, composer, and performer; b. Seattle, Dec. 7, 1939. He studied with Spencer Moseley and Alden Mason at the Univ. of Wash. (B.F.A., 1966; M.F.A., 1968). After moving to Santa Barbara, California in 1969, he became active as a performer; he also was lecturer (1969–72) and assistant prof. (1972–77) at the Univ. of Calif. at Santa Barbara, and a visiting artist at the Univ. of Nevada, Las Vegas (1973), the Univ. of Hawaii, Hilo (1974), Ohio State Univ. (1979), Arizona State Univ. West in Phoenix (1994) et al. Dunlap has performed widely in solo and group performances ("Soundworks" [1978] and "Soundworks 2" [1992], "Intersphere" [1981], and "History of Animals" [1992]), as well as in exhibitions of his own design ("Three for Icarus" [1975], "Of This Time, Of This Place" [1983), "Constructures: New Perimetrics in Abstract Painting" [1985], "V. Forest '94" [1992], and "In the Spirit of FLUXUS" [1994]). He is married to **Arlene Dunlap**.

Dunn, James Philip, American organist, teacher, and composer; b. N.Y., Jan. 10, 1884; d. Jersey City, N.J., July 24, 1936. He studied at the College of the City of N.Y. (B.A., 1903) and with MacDowell, Leonard McWhood, and Rybner at Columbia Univ. (M.A., 1905). He was active as an organist in Catholic churches in N.Y. and Jersey City, and also devoted time to teaching and writing on music.

WORKS: DRAMATIC: *The Galleon* (1918); *Lyric Scenes* (n.d.). **ORCH.:** *Lovesight*, symphonic poem (1919); *The Confessions of St. Augustine* (1925); *Overture on Negro Themes* (1925); *We*, tone poem commemorating Lindbergh's transatlantic flight (N.Y., Aug. 27, 1927); Sym. (1929); *The Barber's Six Brothers: Passacaglia and Theme Fugatum* (1930); *Choral* (1930). **CHAMBER:** Piano Quintet (1910); Violin Sonata (1912); Piano Trio (1913); 2 string quartets (1913); *Variations* for Violin and Piano (1915); much piano and organ music. **VOCAL:** *Annabel Lee* for Voice and Orch. (1913); *The Phantom Drum*, cantata for Soli, Women's Voices, and Orch. (1918); *It was a lover and his lass* for Women's Chorus and Orch. (1918); *The Music of Spring* for Women's Voices and Piano or Orch. (1918); *Marquesan Isle* for Women's Voices and Piano (1923; also for Voices and Orch. or Jazz Band, 1924); *Song of the Night* for Chorus (1923); *Salve Regina* for Women's Chorus (1924); part songs; solo songs.

BIBL.: J. Howard, *Studies of Contemporary American Composers: J.P. D.* (N.Y., 1925).

Dunn, John, English violinist and composer; b. Hull, Feb. 16, 1866; d. Harrogate, Dec. 18, 1940. He received his instruction from his brother, who was conductor of the Hull Theatre Orch.; then was a pupil at the Leipzig Cons. of Schradieck (violin) and Jadassohn (theory); toured England and Germany. He wrote a Violin Concerto and a spate of short violin pieces. He publ. *Manual of Violin Playing* (London, 1898).

Dunn, John Petri, Scottish pianist, teacher, and writer on music; b. Edinburgh, Oct. 26, 1878; d. there, Feb. 4, 1931. He studied in London with Matthay; toured Europe as accompanist of Jan Kubelik in 1904; later was a prof. at the Stuttgart and Kiel conservatories. In 1914 he returned to Great Britain; was a prof. of music at the Univ. of Edinburgh from 1920 until his death.

WRITINGS: *Ornamentation in the Works of Chopin* (London, 1921); *A Student's Guide for Orchestration* (London, 1928); *The Basis of Pianoforte Playing* (London, 1933).

Dunn, Mignon, American mezzo-soprano; b. Memphis, Tenn., June 17, 1931. She attended Southwestern Univ. in Memphis and the Univ. of Lausanne; at 17 she was awarded a Metropolitan Opera scholarship and pursued vocal training in N.Y. with Karin Branzell and Beverley Johnson. In 1955 she made her operatic debut as Carmen in New Orleans, and then appeared as Maddalena in Chicago later that year; on March 28, 1956, she made her N.Y. City Opera debut as the 4th Lady in Walton's *Troilus and Cressida*, remaining on its roster until 1957; sang there again in 1972 and 1975. On Oct. 29, 1958, she made her Metropolitan Opera debut in N.Y. as the Nurse in *Boris Godunov*; in subsequent seasons she appeared in more than 50 roles there, including Amneris, Azucena, Fricka, Herodias, Marina, and Ortrud. She also made guest appearances in San Francisco, London, Paris, Berlin, Hamburg, Milan, and Vienna. In 1972 she married the conductor Kurt Klippstatter.

Dunn, Susan, American soprano; b. Malvern, Ark., July 23, 1954. She was educated at Hendrix College in Arkansas and at Indiana Univ. in Bloomington. In 1982 she made her operatic debut as Aida in Peoria. After winning the Richard Tucker Award in 1983, she attracted favorable notice as Sieglinde in a concert performance of Act I of *Die Walküre* at N.Y.'s Carnegie Hall in 1985. She subsequently appeared with the Chicago Lyric Opera, the Washington (D.C.) Opera, the Houston Grand Opera, and the San Francisco Opera. In 1986 she made her European operatic debut in Bologna as Hélène in *Les vêpres siciliennes*; also sang Aida at Milan's La Scala and appeared at the Vienna State Opera. On Feb. 5, 1990, she made her debut at the Metropolitan Opera in N.Y. as Leonora in *Il Trovatore*.

Dunn, Thomas (Burt), American conductor; b. Aberdeen, S.Dak., Dec. 21, 1925. He studied at the Peabody Cons. of Music, Johns Hopkins and Harvard Univs., and the Amsterdam Cons.; his teachers included Fox and Biggs (organ) and Shaw (choral conducting) in the U.S., and Leonhardt (harpsichord) and Anton van der Horst (conducting) in the Netherlands. He began his career as a church music director in Baltimore and Philadelphia; in 1959 he was appointed director of the Cantata Singers in N.Y.; also organized the Festival Orch. there, which he led from 1959 to 1969. From 1967 to 1986 he was music director of the Handel and Haydn Soc. of Boston. He taught at the Indiana Univ. School of Music in Bloomington from 1990.

Dupin, Paul, French composer; b. Roubaix, Aug. 14, 1865; d. Paris, March 6, 1949. He worked in a factory; then was a menial clerk, but turned to music against all odds; took some lessons with Emile Durand, and then proceeded to compose with fanatic compulsion, seeing some 200 of his works published. Among his compositions were about 500 canons for 3–12 voices, as well as 40 string quartets entitled *Poèmes*; he wrote much other chamber music, some pretty piano pieces with fanciful titles (*Esquisse fuguées*, *Dentelles*), and an opera, *Marcelle*, which he later renamed *Lyszelle*. He was much admired in Paris for his determination, but his works were rarely performed.

BIBL.: R. Rolland, "P. D.," *Bulletin Français de la S.I.M.* (Dec. 15, 1908); C. Koechlin, "D.," *Revue Musicale*, IV (1923); P. Ladmirault, *Les Choeurs en canon de P. D.: Notice biographique et analytique* (Paris, 1925).

DuPré, Jacqueline, renowned English cellist; b. Oxford, Jan. 26, 1945; d. London, Oct. 19, 1987. She entered the London Cello School at the age of 5; while still a child, she began studies with her principal mentor, William Pleeth, making her first public appearance on British television when she was 12. She was awarded a gold medal upon graduation from the Guildhall School of Music in London (1960); also studied with Casals in Zermatt, Switzerland, with Tortelier at Dartington Hall and in Paris, and with Rostropovich in Moscow. After winning the Queen's Prize (1960), she made her formal debut in a recital at London's Wigmore Hall on March 1, 1961. She made her North American debut at N.Y.'s Carnegie Hall as soloist in Elgar's Cello Concerto with Doráti and the BBC Sym. Orch. on May 14, 1965, an appearance that electrified the audience and elicited rapturous critical reviews. On June 15, 1967, she married in Jerusalem **Daniel Barenboim**, with whom she subsequently performed. In 1973 she was diagnosed as having multiple sclerosis, at which time she abandoned her career. She later gave master classes as her health permitted. In 1976 she was made an Officer of the Order of the British Empire, and in 1979 was awarded an honorary doctorate in music by the Univ. of London. The Jacqueline DuPré Research Fund was founded to assist in the fight against multiple sclerosis. Her life was the subject of a Broadway play, *Duet for One* (1981).

BIBL.: W. Wordsworth, ed., *J. d.P.: Impressions* (N.Y., 1983; 2nd ed., 1989); C. Easton, *J. d.P.: A Biography* (London, 1989).

Dupré, Marcel, celebrated French organist, pedagogue, and composer; b. Rouen, May 3, 1886; d. Meudon, near Paris, May 30, 1971. At age 7, he began his musical studies with his father, Albert Dupré, a church organist; at 12, he became organist at St. Vivien in Rouen, and also began private organ lessons with Guilmant in Paris. In 1902 he entered the Paris Cons., where he studied piano with Diémer (premier prix, 1905), organ with Guilmant and Vierne (premier prix, 1907), and fugue with Widor (premier prix, 1909); he also received training in composition from Widor, winning the Grand Prix de Rome in 1914 with his cantata *Psyché*. He was interim organist at Notre-Dame in 1916; in 1920 he gave a cycle of 10 recitals of Bach's complete organ works at the Paris Cons., playing from memory; that same year, he became assistant organist under Widor at St. Sulpice. On Nov. 18, 1921, he made his U.S. debut in N.Y., followed by a transcontinental tour, performing 94 recitals in 85 American cities; a 2nd U.S. tour in 1923 included 110 concerts; he made his 10th tour of the U.S. in 1948. In 1939 he gave 40 concerts in Australia on his world tour. He had, meanwhile, been appointed prof. of organ at the Paris Cons. in 1926; in 1934 he succeeded Widor as organist at St. Sulpice, continuing there until his death at the age of 85. He became general director of the American Cons. in Fontainebleau in 1947 and was appointed director of the Paris Cons., in succession to Delvincourt, in 1954 (until 1956). Dupré wrote his work, the oratorio *La Vision de Jacob*, at the age of 14; it was performed on his 15th birthday at his father's house in Rouen, in a domestic production assisted by a local choral society. Most of his organ works are products of original improvisations. Thus *Symphonie-Passion*, improvised at the Wanamaker organ in Philadelphia (Dec. 8, 1921), was written down much later and performed in its final version at Westminster Cathedral in London (Oct. 9, 1924). Similarly, *Le Chemin de la Croix* was improvised in Brussels (Feb. 13, 1931) and performed in a definitive version in Paris the following year (March 18, 1932). Among precomposed works were 2 syms. for Organ: No. 1 (Glasgow, Jan. 3, 1929) and No. 2 (1946); Concerto for Organ and Orch. (Groningen, April 27, 1938, composer soloist); *Psalm XVIII* (1949); 76 chorales and several a cappella choruses; also numerous "verset-préludes." He was the author of *Traité d'improvisation à l'orgue* (Paris, 1925), *Méthode d'orgue* (Paris, 1927), and *Manuel d'accompagnement du plain-chant gregorien* (Paris, 1937). R. Kneeream ed. and tr. his autobiography as *Recollections* (Melville, N.Y., 1975).

BIBL.: R. Delestre, *L'Oeuvre de M. D.* (Paris, 1952); B. Gavoty and R. Hauert, *M. D.* (Geneva, 1955); M. Murray, *M. D.: The Work of a Master* (Boston, 1985); C. Colleney, *M. D., 1886–1971, ou, Le cause de l'orgue* (Bordeaux, 1987).

Dupuis, Albert, eminent Belgian composer; b. Verviers, March 1, 1877; d. Brussels, Sept. 19, 1967. He studied piano, violin, and flute at the Verviers Cons. before pursuing training with Vincent d'Indy and others at the Paris Schola Cantorum (1897–99). Returning to his homeland, he won the Belgian Prix de Rome in 1903 with his cantata *La chanson d'Halewyn*, which was premiered in Brussels on Nov. 25 of that year; it later was rev. as the opera of the same title and premiered in Antwerp on Feb. 14, 1914. In 1907 he became director of the Verviers Cons., which post he held until 1947. He distinguished himself as a composer for the theater, in a style reflecting his French training.

WORKS: OPERAS: *Idylle* (Verviers, March 5, 1895); *Bilitis* (Verviers, Dec. 21, 1899); *Jean-Michel* (1901–02; Brussels, March 5, 1903); *Martille* (1904; Brussels, March 3, 1905); *Fidélaine* (Liège, March 30, 1910); *Le château de la Bretêche* (Nice, March 28, 1913); *La chanson d'Halewyn* (Antwerp, Feb. 14, 1914; based on the cantata of the same title, 1903); *La passion* (Monte Carlo, April 2, 1916); *La délivrance* (Verviers, Dec. 19, 1918); *La barrière* (Verviers, Feb. 26, 1920); *La victoire* (Brussels, March 28, 1923); *Un drame sous Philippe II* (Liège, Dec. 29, 1926); *Hassan* (Antwerp, Nov. 5, 1931); *Ce n'était qu'un rêve* (Antwerp, Jan. 26, 1932). **ORCH.:** 2 syms. (1904; 1922–23); *Fantaisie rhapsodique* for Violin and Orch. (1906); *Poème oriental* for Cello and Orch. (1924); Cello Concerto (1926); *Epitaphe* (1929); *Aria* for Viola and Orch. (1933); Piano Concerto (1940); *Caprice rhapsodique* (1941); Violin Concerto (1944). **CHAMBER:** Violin Sonata; String Quartet; 2 piano trios; Piano Quartet; many piano pieces. **VOCAL:** Oratorios; cantatas; choruses; songs.

BIBL.: J. Dor, *A. D.* (Liège, 1935); R. Michel, *Un grand musicien belge méconnu: A. D.* (Verviers, 1967).

Durey, Louis (Edmond), French composer; b. Paris, May 27, 1888; d. St. Tropez, July 3, 1979. He received training in solfège, harmony, counterpoint, and fugue from Léon Saint-Requier at the Paris Schola Cantorum (1910–14); he was self-taught in orchestration. In 1936 he joined the French Communist Party. During the German occupation (1940–44), he was a member of the Résistance. He was secretary-general of the Fédération Musicale Populaire (1937–56) and of the Assn. Française des Musiciens Progressistes (from 1948); he also wrote music criticism for the Paris Communist newspaper *L'Humanité* (from 1950). In 1961 he received the Grand Prix de la Musique Française. Although Durey was one of Les Six, he early on adopted a distinct path as a composer. His works owe much to the examples of Satie and Stravinsky. He was at his best writing chamber and vocal works.

WORKS: DRAMATIC: *Judith*, monodrama for Voice and Piano (1918); *L'occasion*, comic opera (1923–25; Strasbourg Radio, May 22–25, 1974); *L'intruse*, puppet play (1936); *Feu la mère de madame*, radio score (1945); *Chant des partisans coréens*, incidental music (1952); film scores. **ORCH.:** *Carillons* (1919; orchestration of a piano duet, 1916); *Neige* (1919; orchestration of a piano duet, 1918); *Pastorale* (1920); *Fantasie concertante* for Cello and Orch. (1947); *Ile-de-France*, overture (1955); Concertino for Piano, 16 Winds, Double Bass, and Timpani (1956); *Mouvement symphonique* for Piano and Strings (1963); Sinfonietta for Strings (1966); *Dilection* for Strings (1967); *Obsession* (1970; orchestration of a piano piece, 1968). **CHAMBER:** 3 string quartets (1917, 1922, 1928); String Trio (1919); Sonatine for Flute and Piano (1929); *Trio-sérénade* for Violin, Viola, and Cello (1955); *Les soirées de Valfère* for Wind Quintet (1963); *Octophonies* for 8 Strings (1965); *Divertissement* for 3 Winds (1966); *Nicolios et la flûte* for Flute and Harp (1968). **PIANO:** *Carillons* for Piano Duet (1916; orchestrated 1919); *Neige* for Piano Duet (1918; orchestrated 1919); *Romance sans paroles* (1919); *3 Préludes* (1920); 3 sonatines (1926); *Nocturne* (1928); *10 Inventions* (1928); *De l'automne 53* (1953); *Auto-portraits* (1967); *Obsession* (1968; orchestrated 1970). **VOCAL:** *Eloges* for Soprano, Alto, Tenor, Bass, and Chamber Orch. (1917–62; also for Soli, Chorus, and Orch.); *Le printemps au fond de la mer* for Voice and 10 Winds (1920);*Cantate de la prison* for Voice and Piano or Orch. (1923); *3 chansons musicales* for Chorus (1948); *La guerre et la paix* for Tenor, Bass, Chorus, and 8 Instruments (1949); *La longue marche* for Tenor, Chorus, and Orch. (1949); *Paix aux hommes par millions* for Soprano, Chorus, and Orch. (1949); *Cantate à Ben-Ali* for Tenor, Chorus, and Piano or Chamber Orch. (1952); *3 poèmes* for Baritone and Piano or Orch. (1953); *10 choeurs de métiers* for Chorus and 6 Instruments ad libitum (1957); *Cantate de la rose et de l'amour* for Soprano and Piano or String Orch. (1965); many other vocal pieces.

BIBL.: F. Robert, *L. D.: L'aîné des Six* (Paris, 1968); J. Roy, *Le groupe des six: Poulenc: Poulenc, Milhaud, Honegger, Auric, Tailleferre, D.* (Paris, 1994).

Durkó, Zsolt, prominent Hungarian composer; b. Szeged, April 10, 1934. He was a student of Farkas at the Budapest Academy of Music (1955–60) and of Petrassi at the Accademia di Santa Cecilia in Rome (1961–63). After teaching at the Budapest Academy of Music (1971–77), he was active with the

Hungarian Radio (from 1982). In 1978 he won the Kossuth Prize, and in 1983 the Bartók-Pasztory Award. He was made a Merited Artist in 1983 and an Outstanding Artist in 1987 by the Hungarian government. His varied output reveals an assured craftsmanship and imaginative use of traditional forms in a contemporary style.

WORKS: OPERA: *Mózes* (1972–77; Budapest, May 15, 1977). **ORCH.:** *Episodi sul tema B-A-C-H* (1962–63); *Organismi* for Violin and Orch. (1964); *Una rapsodia ungherese* for 2 Clarinets and Orch. (1964–65); *Cantilene* for Piano and Orch. (1968); *Concerto for Orchestra* (1970); *Ballad* for Youth Orch. (1970); *Fantázia és utójáték* (Fantasy and Postlude) for Youth Orch. (1979); *Quattro dialoghi* for 2 Percussion Soloists and Orch. (1979); *Refrains* for Violin and Chamber Orch. (1979); Piano Concerto (1980); *Ornamenti 1* (1984) and *2* (1985); Violin Concerto (1992–93). **CHAMBER ENSEMBLE:** *Colloides* for Flute and Chamber Ensemble (1969); *Iconography No. 2* for Horn and Chamber Ensemble (1971); *Chamber Music* for 2 Pianos and 11 Strings (1972–73); *Turner Illustrations* for Violin and 14 Instruments (1976); *Impromptus* for Flute and Chamber Ensemble (1983); *Téli zene* (Winter Music) for Horn and Chamber Ensemble (1984). **CHAMBER:** *11 pezzi per quartetto d'archi* (1962); *Improvvisazioni* for Wind Quintet (1965); 2 string quartets (1966, 1969); *Symbols* for Horn and Piano (1968–69); *Quartetto d'ottoni* (1970); *Iconography No. 1* for 2 Bass Viols or Cellos and Harpsichord (1971); *Fire Music* for Flute, Clarinet, Piano, and String Trio (1971); *Serenata* for 4 Harps (1973); *Varianti* for Viola and Piano (1974); 8 Duos for 2 Horns (1977); 5 Pieces for Tuba and Piano (1978); *Movements* for Tuba and Piano (1980); *3 Essays* for Clarinet and Piano (1983); Sinfonietta for 10 Brass Instruments (1983); *Clair-obscure* for Organ and Trumpet (1984); Sextet for 5 Clarinets and Piano (1987); Woodwind Octet (1988); also piano pieces and organ music. **VOCAL:** *Fioriture* for Chamber Chorus and Orch. (1966); *Altamira* for Chamber Chorus and Orch. (1967–68); *Halotti beszed* (Burial Prayer), oratorio for Tenor, Baritone, Chorus, and Orch. (1967–72); *Hat tanulmány* (6 Studies) for Chorus and Piano (1970–72); *Cantata No. 1* for Baritone, Chorus, and Orch. (1971) and *No. 2* for Chorus and Orch. (1972); *Hét dallamrajz* for Chorus and Piano (1972); *Széchenyi Oratorio* for Baritone, Chorus, and Orch. (1981–82); *Pillanatképek a Kalevalából* for Chorus (1986); *Ilmarinen* for Chorus (1986); *3 English Verses* for Mezzo-soprano and 12 Instruments (1991).

BIBL.: E. Olsvay, "A Conversation with Z. D.," *Hungarian Music Quarterly*, III/3–4 (1992).

Durlet, Emmanuel, Belgian pianist, teacher, and composer; b. Antwerp, Oct. 11, 1893; d. there, Feb. 7, 1977. He studied piano with Frans Lenaerts; took a course in Vienna with Godowsky (1912–14). Returning to Belgium, he developed a brilliant career as a pianist; gave a cycle of all 32 sonatas by Beethoven. He held the post of prof. of advanced piano playing at the Antwerp Cons. (1920–59). Among his works are a Piano Concerto, a Violin Concerto, a Violin Sonata, and numerous teaching pieces for piano in a Romantic vein, as well as songs.

Dürr, Alfred, distinguished German musicologist and editor; b. Berlin, March 3, 1918. He was educated at the Univ. of Göttingen (Ph.D., 1950, with the diss. *Studien über die frühen Kantaten Johann Sebastian Bachs*; publ. in Leipzig, 1951). In 1951 he became a research assistant at the Johann-Sebastian-Bach-Inst. in Göttingen; from 1962 to 1981 he served as its director, and continued to be associated with it until 1983. He was a member of the Akademie der Wissenschaften in Göttingen from 1976. He was an ed. of the *Bach-Jahrbuch* and also ed. works for the Bach *Neue Ausgabe sämtlicher Werke*. In 1988 he was elected a corresponding member of the American Musicological Soc.

WRITINGS: *Johann Sebastian Bach, Weihnachts oratorium* (Munich, 1967); *Die Kantaten von Johann Sebastian Bach* (Kassel and Munich, 1971; 5th ed., rev., 1985); *Johann Sebastian Bach: Seine Handschrift-Abbild seines Schaffens* (Wiesbaden, 1984); *Im Mittelpunkt Bach: Ausgewählte Aufsätze und Vorträge* (Kassel, 1988); *Die Johannes-Passion von Johann Sebastian Bach: Entstehung, Überlieferung, Werkeinführung* (Kassel and Munich, 1988); *Bachs Werk vom Einfall bis zur Drucklegung* (Wiesbaden, 1989).

BIBL.: W. Rehm, ed., *Bachiana et alia musicologica: Festschrift A. D. zum 65. Geburtstag am 3. Marz 1983* (Kassel and N.Y., 1983).

Dürr, Walther, German musicologist; b. Berlin, April 27, 1932. He was educated at the Univ. of Tübingen, where he took his Ph.D. in 1956 with the diss. *Studien zu Rhythmus und Metrum im italienisch Madrigal, insbesondere bei Luca Marenzio*. From 1964 he was one of the editors of the new and exhaustive critical ed. of the works of Schubert. He also was a prof. at the Univ. of Tübingen from 1977. W. Aderhold and W. Litschauer ed. the vol. *Zeichen-Setzung: Aufsätze zur musikalisch Poetik* (Kassel, 1992) in honor of his 60th birthday.

WRITINGS: *Franz Schuberts Werke in Abschriften: Liederalben und Sammlungen* (Kassel, 1975); *Das deutsch Sololied im 19. Jahrhundert* (Wilhelmshaven, 1984); with A. Feil and W. Litschauer, *Reclams Musikführer "Franz Schuberts"* (Stuttgart, 1991); *Sprache und Musik: Geschichte, Gattungen, Analysemodelle* (Kassel, 1994).

Duruflé, Maurice, noted French organist, teacher, and composer; b. Louviers, Eure, Jan. 11, 1902; d. Paris, June 16, 1986. He studied piano and organ with local teachers; in 1919 he went to Paris, where he studied organ with Tournemire, Guilmant, and Vierne. In 1920 he enrolled at the Paris Cons., where he took courses in organ with Gigout (premier prix, 1922), harmony with Jean Gallon (premier prix, 1924), fugue with Caussade (premier prix, 1924), and composition with Dukas (1928). In 1930 he was appointed organist of the church of St. Etienne-du-Mont in Paris. In 1943 he became a prof. at the Paris Cons., remaining on its staff until 1969. Duruflé composed a number of sacred works and organ pieces. His best known compositions are a Requiem (1947) and a Mass (1967).

Dushkin, Samuel, Polish-American violinist; b. Suwalki, Dec. 13, 1891; d. N.Y., June 24, 1976. He was taken to America as a child and was adopted by the composer Blair Fairchild, who gave him his primary musical education; then received training in violin from Remy and in composition from Ganaye at the Paris Cons. He studied violin with Auer in N.Y. and later took several lessons with Kreisler. He made his European debut as a violinist in 1918, and subsequently toured widely in Europe and America. In 1928 he became associated with Stravinsky and helped him to solve the technical problems in the violin part of his Violin Concerto; was the soloist in the performance of this work in Berlin on Oct. 23, 1931, with Stravinsky conducting. He also gave the performance of Stravinsky's *Duo concertant* for Violin and Piano, with Stravinsky playing the piano part (Berlin, Oct. 28, 1932). He recounted the details of these collaborations in his article "Working with Stravinsky," publ. in the Merle Armitage collection *Stravinsky* (N.Y., 1936). He publ. teaching manuals for violin, and also ed. works for violin ranging from the Baroque to the Classical periods (several "ed." works were later discovered to be by Dushkin).

Dutilleux, Henri, distinguished French composer and teacher; b. Angers, Jan. 22, 1916. He was a student at the Paris Cons. (1933–38) of J. and N. Gallon (harmony and counterpoint), Büsser (composition), and Emmanuel (music history), winning the Grand Prix de Rome in 1938. He pursued his career in Paris, where he worked for the French Radio (1944–63) and was a prof. of composition at the École Normale de Musique (1961–70). In 1970–71 he was a guest prof. at the Paris Cons. In 1967 he was awarded the Grand Prix National de la Musique. In 1987 he received the Prix Maurice Ravel for his complete works. He was awarded the Praemium Imperial of Japan in 1994. In 1995 he was composer-in-residence at the Tanglewood Festival of Contemporary Music. Dutilleux developed a thoroughly individualistic contemporary style of composition, marked by a meticulous craftsmanship.

WORKS: DRAMATIC: *L'anneau du roi*, lyric scene (1938); *Petite Lumière et L'Ourse*, music for a radio play (1944); *Les Hauts de Hurle-vent*, incidental music (1945; orch. suite, 1945); *La Princesse d'Élide*, incidental music (1946); *Monsieur de Pourceaugnac*, incidental music (1948); *Hernani*, incidental music (1952); *Le Loup*, ballet (Paris, March 18, 1953); film scores. **ORCH.:** *Sarabande* (1941); *Danse fantastique* (1943); 2 syms.: No. 1 (Paris, June 7, 1951) and No. 2, *Le Double* (1957–59; Boston, Dec. 11, 1959); *Sérénade* (1956); *Métaboles* (1962–64; Cleveland, Jan. 14, 1965); *Tout un monde lointain . . .*, cello concerto (1967–70; Aix-en-Provence, July 25, 1970); *Timbres, espace, mouvement ou "La nuit étoilée"* (1977–78; Washington, D.C., Jan. 10, 1978); *L'Arbre des songes*, violin concerto (1980–85; Paris, Nov. 5, 1985); *Mystère de l'insant* for 24 Strings, Cimbalom, and Percussion (1986–89); *Instantanées* for Strings (1988). **CHAMBER:** *Suite de concert* for String Quartet, Wind Quartet, and Piano (1937); *Sarabande et cortège* for Bassoon and Piano (1942); Flute Sonatine (1943); Oboe Sonata (1947); *Choral, cadence et fugato* for Trombone and Piano (1950: *Ainsi la nuit*, string quartet (1974–76); *Trois strophes sur le nom de SACHER* for Cello (1982); *Les Citations*, diptyque for Oboe, Harpsichord, Double Bass, and Percussion (1991). **PIANO:** *Au gré des ondes* (1946); *Bergerie* (1946); Sonata (1946–48); *Blackbird* (1950); *Tous les chemins* (1961); *Résonances* (1965); *Figures de Résonances* for 2 Pianos (1970); *Deux Preludes* (1973–88); *Petit air à dormir debout* (1983); *Le jeu des contraires* (1988). **VOCAL:** *Gisèle*, cantata for Soprano, Tenor, Bass, and Orch. (1936); *Quatre mélodies* for Medium Voice and Piano (1942; also for Medium Voice and Orch., 1954); *La Geôle* for Medium Voice and Piano or Orch. (1944); *Deux Sonnets* for Medium Voice and Piano (1944–50); *Chanson de la déportée* for Voice and Piano (1945); (2) *Chansons de bord* for Children's Chorus (1950); *San Francisco Night* for Soprano and Piano (1963); *Hommage à Nadja Boulanger* for Soprano, Mezzo-soprano, Clarinet, and Zither (1964).

BIBL.: P. Mari, *H. D.* (Paris, 1973; 2nd ed., 1988); R. Jacobs, *H. D.* (Paris, 1974); D. Humbert, *H. D.: L'oeuvre et le style musical* (Paris, 1985); C. Glayman, *H. D.: Mystère et memoire des sons* (Paris, 1993).

Dutoit, Charles (Edouard), outstanding Swiss conductor; b. Lausanne, Oct. 7, 1936. He took courses in violin, piano, and conducting at the Lausanne Cons., graduating at age 17; he then pursued training in conducting with Baud-Bovy at the Geneva Cons. (prize, 1958), with Galliera at the Accademia Musicale Chigiana in Siena (diploma, 1958), and with Munch at the Berkshire Music Center in Tanglewood (summer, 1959). He was a choral conductor at the Univ. of Lausanne (1959–63), and then conducted the Lausanne Bach Choir. After appearing as a guest conductor with the Bern Sym. Orch. in 1963, he served as its 2nd conductor (1964–66) and music director (1966–78); he also was chief conductor of the Zürich Radio Orch. (1964–66), assoc. conductor of the Zürich Tonhalle Orch. (1966–71), and conductor of the National Sym. Orch. in Mexico City (1973–75) and the Göteborg Sym. Orch. (1976–79). On Aug. 31, 1972, he made his U.S. debut conducting at the Hollywood Bowl. In subsequent years, he made extensive guest conducting tours of Europe, North and South America, Australia, Japan, and Israel. In 1977 he became music director of the Orchestre Symphonique de Montréal, which gained international recognition under his guidance. He also was principal guest conductor of the Minnesota Orch. in Minneapolis (from 1983). On Dec. 21, 1987, he made his Metropolitan Opera debut in N.Y. conducting *Les Contes d'Hoffmann*. While retaining his position in Montreal, he also served as chief conductor of the Orchestre National de France in Paris (from 1990). He likewise was chief conductor of the NHK (Japan Broadcasting Corp.) Sym. Orch. in Tokyo (from 1996). Dutoit's extensive repertoire embraces works from the Baroque era to modern scores, but he has won a particularly notable reputation as a consummate interpreter of French music. He was married 3 times, his 2nd wife being **Martha Argerich**.

BIBL.: G. Nicholson, *C.D.: Le Maître de l'orchestre* (Lausanne, 1986).

Duval, Denise, French soprano; b. Paris, Oct. 23, 1921. She studied at the Bordeaux Cons. In 1941 she made her operatic debut as Lola at the Bordeaux Grand Théâtre. In 1944 she joined the Folies Bergères in Paris, where she won notice; in 1947 she was chosen to create Thérese in Poulenc's *Les Mamelles de Tirésias* at the Paris Opéra-Comique, where she also created Elle in his *La Voix Humaine* in 1959; she also appeared regularly at the Paris Opéra. In 1953 she sang in N.Y., in 1960 at the Edinburgh Festival (as Elle), and in 1962 at the Glyndebourne Festival (as Mélisande); she also made guest appearances in Milan, Cologne, Brussels, Amsterdam, Geneva, and Buenos Aires. After retiring in 1965, she taught voice in Paris. Among her other roles were Massenet's Salomé, Ravel's Concepción, and Poulenc's Blanche.

Duvosel, Lieven, Belgian composer; b. Ghent, Dec. 14, 1877; d. Sint-Martens-Latem, April 20, 1956. He studied in Antwerp and Paris; lived in Berlin (where Nikisch and R. Strauss performed his works), later in The Hague and Haarlem. His most representative work is the symphonic cycle in 5 parts *Leie*: 1. *De Morgen*; 2. *De Leie*; 3. *De Liefde aan der Leie*; 4. *Kerstnacht (Christmas)*; and 5. *Het Leieland*. Other compositions include 3 syms., *Den Avond* (Evening), symphonic poem, *Wereldwee* (World's Grief), many cantatas, choruses, and songs.

BIBL.: F. van Durme, *L. D.* (Antwerp, 1943); E. Collumbien, *Lijst der werken van D.* (Ghent, 1950).

Dux, Claire, German-American soprano; b. Witkowicz, Aug. 2, 1885; d. Chicago, Oct. 8, 1967. She was a student of Maria Schwadtke, Adolf Deppe, and Teresa Arkel in Berlin before completing her training in Milan. In 1906 she made her operatic debut as Pamina in Cologne, singing there until 1911. From 1911 to 1918 she was a member of the Berlin Royal Opera; she also sang in London, where she was the British Sophie at Covent Garden (1913) and appeared as Pamina at Drury Lane (1914). After singing at Stockholm's Royal Theater (1918–21), she was a member of the Chicago Grand (later Civic) Opera (1921–22; 1923–24); she also toured the U.S. with the German Opera Co. In 1926 she married her 3rd husband, the wealthy Chicagoan Charles H. Swift, and retired from the operatic stage. She then sang in concerts until making her farewell in Berlin in 1932.

Dvarionas, Balis, Lithuanian composer, conductor, and teacher; b. Leipaia, June 19, 1904; d. Vilnius, Aug. 23, 1972. He studied at the Leipzig Cons. with Teichmüller (piano) and Karg-Elert (composition); also received training in piano from Petri at the Berlin Hochschule für Musik and in conducting from Abendroth. In 1926 he went to Kaunas and taught piano there until 1940; in 1947 he became a prof. at the Lithuanian Cons. in Vilnius; also conducted the Lithuanian Phil. there (1940–41; 1958–61). Among his works are: Sym. (1947); Violin Concerto (1948; received a State Prize); 2 piano concertos (1958, 1962); opera, *Dalia* (1959); many choral works. He wrote the music for the national anthem of the Lithuanian Soviet Socialist Republic (1950).

BIBL.: Y. Gaudrimas, *B. D.* (Moscow, 1960).

Dvořáček, Jiří, prominent Czech composer and pedagogue; b. Vamberk, June 8, 1928. He studied organ at the Prague Cons. (1943–47) and composition with Řídký and Dobiáš at the Prague Academy of Music (1949–53), where he subsequently taught (from 1953), later serving as a prof. of composition and chairman of the composition dept. (1979–90). In 1983 he was made an Artist of Merit by the Czech government. From 1987 to 1989 he was president of the Union of Czech Composers and Concert Artists. His works represent a median course of Central European modernism.

WORKS: OPERA: *Ostrov Afrodity* (Aphrodite's Island; 1967; Dresden, Feb. 13, 1971). **ORCH.:** 2 syms. (1953, 1985); *Symphonic Suite* (1958); *Overture* (1958); *Concertante Suite* (1962);

Ex post, symphonic movement for Piano and Orch. (1963); *Quattro episodi*, symfonietta (1971); *Žija a zpívám* (I Am Living and Singing), cantata for Soloists, Chorus, Reciter, Children's Chorus, and Orch. (1978); *Giubilo* (1983); Violin Concerto (1989). **CHAMBER:** *Sonata Capricciosa* for Violin and Piano (1956); *Invention* for Trombone and Piano or Small Orch. (1961); *Meditations* for Clarinet and Percussion (1964); *Music* for Harp (1970); *Due per duo*, 2 rondos for Horn and Piano (1970); Brass Quintet (1973); Trumpet Sonata (1977); Organ Sonata (1979); Accordion Sonata (1979); *Tema con Variazioni per trombone e pianoforte* (1980); *Prague Transformations* for Wind Quintet (1981); *Partita* for Oboe and Bassoon (1986); *Partita piccola* for Violin, Guitar, and Harmonica (1987); *3 Movements* for String Quartet (1990).

Dvořáková, Ludmila, Czech soprano; b. Kolin, July 11, 1923. She was a pupil of Jarmila Vavrdova at the Prague Cons. (1942–49). In 1949 she made her operatic debut as Kát'a Kabanová in Ostrava, and then appeared in Bratislava and at the Smetana Theater in Prague from 1952; was a member of the Prague National Theater (1954–57). In 1956 she made her appearance at the Vienna State Opera, and from 1960 she sang at the Berlin State Opera; she also sang at the Bayreuth Festivals (1965–71) and at London's Covent Garden (1966–71). On Jan. 12, 1966, she made her Metropolitan Opera debut in N.Y. as Beethoven's Leonore, remaining on its roster until 1968. In addition to her roles in Czech operas, she was admired for her Wagner, Verdi, and Strauss.

Dvorský, Peter (actually, **Petr**), Czech tenor; b. Partizánske, Sept. 25, 1951. He graduated from the Bratislava Cons. in 1973, making his operatic debut in *Eugene Onegin* at the Slovak National Theater in Bratislava that same year. After winning 5th prize at the Tchaikovsky Competition in Moscow (1974) and prize at the Geneva Competition (1975), he sang in Bratislava, Prague, Budapest, Moscow, Vienna, Milan, and London. On Nov. 15, 1977, he made his Metropolitan Opera debut in N.Y. as Alfredo. He appeared at London's Covent Garden from 1978. In 1986 he was made an Austrian Kämmersanger. He won particular praise for his performances in operas by Smetana, Dvořák, and Janáček; also sang in operas by Verdi and Puccini with distinction.

BIBL.: D. Štilichová, *P. D.* (Bratislava, 1991).

Dyer-Bennet, Richard, English-born American singer; b. Leicester, Oct. 6, 1913; d. Monterey, Mass., Dec. 14, 1991. He emigrated to the U.S. in 1925 and became a naturalized citizen in 1935. He studied voice with Cornelius Reid and guitar with José Rey De La Torre. He made his concert debut in N.Y. in 1944; also sang in nightclubs. In 1970 he joined the State Univ. of N.Y. at Stony Brook as an instructor in the theater arts dept. He acquired popularity mainly as a singer of English and American ballads, but he was also praised for his performance of Schubert song cycles, especially *Die schöne Müllerin* in his own tr., under the title "The Lovely Milleress."

Dyer, Louise. See **Hanson-Dyer, Louise** (née **Dyer**).

Dykema, Peter (William), American music pedagogue; b. Grand Rapids, Mich., Nov. 25, 1873; d. Hastings-on-Hudson, N.Y., May 13, 1951. He studied law at the Univ. of Mich. (B.S., 1895; M.L., 1896); then took lessons in voice and in theory at the Inst. of Musical Art in N.Y. (1903–05) and studied with Edgar Stillman Kelley in Berlin (1911–12). He was music supervisor at the N.Y. Ethnical Culture School (1903–13); from 1913 to 1924 he was prof. of music and chairman of the public school music dept. at the Univ. of Wisc.; from 1924 to 1939 he was a prof. of music education at Teachers College, Columbia Univ. He publ. a number of music handbooks for schools, among them *Twice 55 Community Songs* (6 vols., 1919–27); *School Music Handbook* (1931; rev. ed., 1955, by H. Cundiff); *Singing Youth* (1935); *Golden Key Orchestral Series* (1937); with N. Church, *Modern Band Training Series* (1938); with K. Gehrkens, *The Teaching and Administration of High School Music* (1941).

BIBL.: H. Eisenkramer, *P.W. D.: His Life and Contribution to Music Education* (diss., Univ. of Mich., 1963); H. Dengler, *Music for All: A Biography of P.W. D.* (Baltimore, 1994).

Dyson, Sir George, English composer and pedagogue; b. Halifax, Yorkshire, May 28, 1883; d. Winchester, Sept. 28, 1964. He was a scholarship student in organ and composition at the Royal College of Music in London (1900–1904), and then continued his training in Italy and Germany (1904–1908). After serving as music master at Osborne, Marlborough, Rugby, and Wellington, he was director of music at Winchester College (1924–37); he subsequently was director of the Royal College of Music (1938–52). In 1941 he was knighted and in 1953 he was made a Knight Commander of the Royal Victorian Order. He publ. *The New Music* (1924), *The Progress of Music* (1932), and the candid autobiography *Fiddling While Rome Burns: A Musician's Apology* (1954). C. Palmer ed. *Dyson's Delight: An Anthology of Sir George Dyson's Writings and Talks on Music* (London, 1989).

WORKS: Sym. (1937); Violin Concerto (1943); 2 concerti for Strings (1949); chamber music; piano pieces; cantatas: *In Honour of the City* (1928), *The Canterbury Pilgrims* (1931; overture perf. as *At the Tabard Inn*, 1946), *St. Paul's Voyage to Melita* (1933), and *Quo Vadis?* (1939); songs; pedagogical pieces.

BIBL.: C. Palmer, *G. D.: A Centenary Appreciation* (Borough Green, 1984).

Dzegelenok, Alexander (Mikhailovich), Russian composer; b. Moscow, Aug. 24, 1891; d. there, Jan. 31, 1969. He studied piano (diploma, 1914) and composition (with Koreshchenko, 1918) at the Music and Drama School of the Moscow Phil. Soc. In 1919 he organized the Moscow People's Cons., serving as its director (1920–21); then taught piano at the Moscow Technical School of Music (1926–34).

WORKS: DRAMATIC: *Niyazgyul*, opera (1941); film scores. **ORCH.:** *Egipet* (Egypt; 1921); 2 cello concertos (1929, 1936); *Chapayev*, march-ballad (1933; also for Band, 1938); *Na golubom ozere* (On the Blue Sea; 1936); Sinfonia (1944); *Vostochnaya syuita* (Eastern Suite, 1951). **BAND:** *Geroicheskaya syuita* (1948); *Prazdnichnaya uvertyura* (Festival Overture; 1948); *Stalingradskaya bitva* (The Battle of Stalingrad; 1950); *Muzhestvo* (Courage), sym. (1972); many other pieces; arrangements. **CHAMBER:** Piano Trio (1926); *2 Pieces* for Violin and Piano (1933); *Poeme-paysage* for Violin and Piano (1953). **PIANO:** *March-Humoresque* (1924); *Humoresque* (1925); *Poem* (1925); *Mazurka* (1925). **VOCAL:** Songs.

Dzerzhinsky, Ivan (Ivanovich), Russian composer; b. Tambov, April 9, 1909; d. Leningrad, Jan. 18, 1978. He went to Moscow and studied piano with Yavorsky at the First Music School (1925–29) and composition with Gnessin at the Gnessin Music School (1929–30); he then went to Leningrad to pursue training in composition with Popov and Riazanov at the Central Music School (1930–32) and with Asafiev at the Cons. (1932–34). While still a student, he composed his first opera, *Tikhiy Don* (Quiet Flows the Don). After its failure in an opera competition, he sought the assistance of Shostakovich who helped him to revamp the score. It received its premiere in Leningrad on Oct. 22, 1935. After Stalin attended a performance of the work in Moscow on Jan. 17, 1936, the Soviet propaganda machine was set in motion to proclaim it a model for the development of the so-called "song opera" in the socialist realist manner. Dzerzhinsky's limited compositional gifts frustrated him in repeating this signal success, although he continued to compose a large catalog of music. He held various administrative positions with the Union of Soviet Composers from 1936, serving on its central committee from 1948.

WORKS: DRAMATIC: OPERAS: *Tikhiy Don* (Quiet Flows the Don; 1932–34; Leningrad, Oct. 22, 1935; rev. version, Leningrad, Nov. 7, 1947); *Podnyataya tselina* (Virgin Soil Upturned; Moscow, Oct. 23, 1937; rev. version, Perm, May 30, 1964); *Volochayevskiye dni* (Volochayev Days; 1939); *Groza* (The Storm; 1940–55; concert perf., Moscow, April 17, 1956);

Krov naroda (The Blood of the People; 1941; Orenburg, Jan. 21, 1942); *Nadezhda Svetlova* (1942; Orenburg, Sept. 8, 1943); *Metel (v zimnyuyu noch)* (The Blizzard [on a Winter's Night]), comic opera (Leningrad, Nov. 24, 1946); *Knyaz-ozero* (The Prince Lake), folk opera (Leningrad, Oct. 26, 1947); *Daleko ot Moskvï* (Far from Moscow; Leningrad, July 19, 1954; rev. version, Leningrad, Nov. 8, 1954); *Sudba cheloveka* (The Fate of a Man; 1959; Moscow and Leningrad, Oct. 17, 1961); *Grigori Melekhov* (Leningrad, Nov. 4, 1967); incidental music; film scores. **ORCH.:** 3 piano concertos (1932, 1934, 1945); *Povest o partizane* (Tale About a Partisan), symphonic poem (1934); *Ermak*, symphonic poem (1949). **OTHER:** Many vocal works; piano pieces.

BIBL.: O. Tompakova, *Ocherk o zhizni i tvorchestve I.I. D.* (Study of the Life and Work of I. I. D.; Leningrad, 1964); S. Aksyuk, ed., *I. D.: Stati, vospominaniya* (I. D.: Articles, Reminiscences; Moscow, 1988).

Eames, Emma (Hayden), famous American soprano; b. Shanghai, China, Aug. 13, 1865; d. N.Y., June 13, 1952. Her mother, who was her first teacher, took her to America as a child; she then studied with Clara Munger in Boston and with Marchesi in Paris. She made her operatic debut at the Paris Opéra on March 13, 1889, as Juliette in Gounod's *Roméo et Juliette*, singing there until 1891. On April 7, 1891, she made her first appearance at London's Covent Garden as Marguerite, and continued to sing there until 1901. On Nov. 9, 1891, she made her first appearance with the Metropolitan Opera as Elsa in *Lohengrin* during its visit to Chicago. On Dec. 14, 1891, she made her formal debut with the company as Juliette in N.Y. She remained with the Metropolitan until 1909, appearing as Marguerite in *Faust*, Desdemona in *Otello*, Elisabeth in *Tannhäuser*, Aida, Tosca, and Donna Anna in *Don Giovanni*. In 1911–12 she was a member of the Boston Opera, and then retired from the operatic stage. She received the Jubilee Medal from Queen Victoria, and was decorated by the French Academy with the order of Les Palmes Académiques. Her emotional life was turbulent; she married the painter Julian Story in 1891, but they were separated in the midst of a widely publicized scandal; in 1911 she married **Emilio de Gogorza**, but left him too. She publ. an autobiography, *Some Memories and Reflections* (N.Y., 1927).

Earhart, Will, American music educator; b. Franklin, Ohio, April 1, 1871; d. Los Angeles, April 23, 1960. From 1900 to 1912 he was a school supervisor in various localities in Ohio and Indiana; in 1912 he went to Pittsburgh, where he was director of music in the public schools (1912–40); was also founder and head of public school music at the Univ. of Pittsburgh (1913) and a lecturer on music education at the Carnegie Inst. of Technology. He publ. a number of books on musical education, among them *Music in the Public Schools* (1914); with O. McConathy, *Music in Secondary Schools* (1917); *Music to the Listening Ear* (1932); *The Meaning and Teaching of Music* (1935); and with C. Boyd, *Elements of Music Theory* (2 vols., 1938); ed. *Art Songs for High Schools* (1910); and *The School Credit Piano Course* (1918).

BIBL.: F. McKernan, *W. E.: His Life and Contributions to Music Education* (diss., Univ. of Southern Calif., Los Angeles, 1956).

Easdale, Brian, English composer; b. Manchester, Aug. 10, 1909; d. Oct. 30, 1995. He studied at the Royal College of Music in London (1925–33). He became interested in theatrical music; wrote 3 operas, *Rapunzel* (1927), *The Corn King* (1935), and *The Sleeping Children* (1951); incidental music to Shakespeare's plays; also several film scores, of which the most successful was *The Red Shoes* (1948). Other works include a Piano Concerto (1938) and several orch. pieces of a descriptive nature (*Dead March*; *The Phoenix*; *Bengal River*, etc.); *Cavatina* for Brass Ensemble (1961); *Missa coventrensis* (1962) for the consecration of Coventry Cathedral; songs.

Eastman, George, prominent American industrialist and philanthropist; b. Waterville, N.Y., July 12, 1854; d. (suicide) Rochester, N.Y., March 14, 1932. He perfected a process for making dry plates for photocopy (1880) and in 1884 founded the Eastman Dry Plate and Film Co., which in 1892 became the Eastman Kodak Co., subsequently one of the leading companies of its kind in the world. A munificent philanthropist, he gave away more than $75 million to various scientific, educational, and cultural organizations. He founded the Eastman School of Music of the Univ. of Rochester (1921), and also endowed the Eastman Theatre. He took his own life after learning that he had cancer.

Easton, Florence (Gertrude), English soprano; b. South Bank, Yorkshire, Oct. 25, 1882; d. N.Y., Aug. 13, 1955. She studied with Agnes Larkcom at the Royal Academy of Music in London and with Elliott Haslam in Paris; in 1903 she made her operatic debut as the Shepherd in *Tannhäuser* with the Moody-Manners Co. in Newcastle upon Tyne; toured the U.S. with Savage's opera company in 1904–05 and 1906–07. She was a member of the Berlin Royal Opera (1907–13) and the Hamburg Opera (1912–16); after singing with the Chicago Grand Opera (1915–17), she made her Metropolitan Opera debut in N.Y. as Santuzza on Dec. 7, 1917, remaining on its roster until 1929; she created the role of Lauretta in *Gianni Schicchi* there in 1918. In 1927 and 1932 she sang at London's Covent Garden and in 1934 appeared at Sadler's Wells Opera in London. She then returned to the Metropolitan Opera in 1936 as Brunnhilde in *Die Walküre* before retiring from the stage.

Eaton, John (Charles), American composer and teacher; b. Bryn Mawr, Pa., March 30, 1935. He studied composition with Babbitt, Cone, and Sessions at Princeton Univ. (1953–59; B.A., M.F.A.). He also received training in piano from Steuermann, Erich Kahn, and Frank Sheridan. In 1959, 1960, and 1962 he held American Prix de Rome prizes. In 1962 and 1965 he held Guggenheim fellowships. In 1970 he became composer-in-residence at the Indiana Univ. School of Music in Bloomington, where he was assoc. prof. (1971–73) and prof. (1973–91). In 1976–77 he was composer-in-residence at the American Academy in Rome. In 1990 he received the MacArthur Award. He was a prof. at the Univ. of Chicago from 1991. He publ. the book *Involvement with Music: New Music since 1950* (1976). Eaton has made use of various modern resources in his compositions, including electronics. In some pieces, he has employed the Syn-Ket, a synthesizer invented by Paolo Ketoff.

WORKS: DRAMATIC: *Ma Barker*, opera (1957); *Heracles*, opera (1964; Turin, Oct. 10, 1968); *Myshkin*, television opera (1971; Bloomington, Ind., April 23, 1973); *The 3 Graces*, theater piece (1972); *The Lion and Androcles*, children's opera (1973; Indianapolis, May 1, 1974); *Danton and Robespierre*, opera (Bloomington, Ind., April 21, 1978); *The Cry of Clytaemnestra*, opera (1979; Bloomington, Ind., March 1, 1980); *The Tempest*, opera (1983–85; Santa Fe, July 27, 1985); *The Reverend Jim Jones*, opera (1988); *Peer Gynt*, theater piece (1990; Chicago, May 29, 1992); *Let's Get This Show on the Road: An Alternative View of Genesis*, opera (Chicago, Dec. 8, 1993); *Don Quixote*, theater piece (1994). **ORCH.:** *Tertullian Overture* (1958); *Concert Piece* for Syn-Ket and Orch. (1966); Sym. No. 2 (1980–81); *Remembering Rome*, sinfonietta for Strings (Bloomington, Ind., March 1, 1987). **CHAMBER:** String Quartet (1958); *Encore Piece* for Flute and Piano (1959); Trumpet Sonata (1959); *Adagio and Allegro* for Flute, Oboe, and Strings (1960); *Concert Piece 1* for Clarinet and Piano (1960) and *2* for Syn-Ket (1966); *Epigrams* for Clarinet and Piano (1960); *Concert Music* for Clarinet (1961); *Variations* for Flute (1964); *Vibrations* for Flute, 2 Oboes, and 2 Clarinets (1967); *Thoughts for Sonny* for Trumpet (1968); *Sonority Movement* for Flute and 9 Harps (1971); Piano Trio, *In Memoriam Mario Cristini* (1971); *Burlesca* for Tuba and Piano (1981); *Fantasy Romance* for Cello and Piano (1989); *2 Plaudits for Ralph Shapey* for Flute, Oboe, and Cello (1991); *Salome's Flea Circus* for Clarinet and Piano (1994). **PIANO:** *Variations* (1957); *Microtonal Fantasy* for 2 Pianos (1965). **VOCAL:** *Song Cycle* for Voice and Piano, after Donne (1956); *Songs for R.P.B.* for Voice, Piano, and Synthesizer (1964); *Thoughts on Rilke* for Soprano, 2 Syn-Kets, Syn-Mill, and Reverberation Plate (1966); *Blind Man's Cry* for Soprano, Syn-Ket, Moog Synthesizer, Syn-Mill, and 2 Tapes (1968); Mass for Soprano, Clarinet, and Synthesizers (1969); *Ajax* for Baritone and Orch. (1972); *Guillen Songs* for Voice and Piano (1974); *Oro* for Voice and Synthesizers (1974); *Land of Lampedusa* for Mezzo-soprano, Soprano, Piano, and Synthesizers (1974); *Lullaby for Estela* for Voice and Piano (1975); Duo for Chorus (1977); *A Greek Vision* for Soprano, Flute, and Electronics (1982); *El Divino Narciso*, cantata for Soprano, Mezzo-soprano, Tenor, Flute, 2 Percussionists, Cello, and Optional Electronics (1989); *A Packet for Emily and Bill* for Mezzo-soprano or Soprano, Clarinet, and Electronics or Piano (1991); *Notes on Moonlight* for Soprano, Mezzo-soprano, and Chamber Ensemble (1991); *Trumpet Voluntary* for Soprano and Brass Quintet (1991); *Songs of Desperation and Comfort* for Mezzo-soprano and Chamber Orch. (1993; Cleveland, May 9, 1994); *Lettere* for Mezzo-soprano, Flute, Harp, and String Quartet (1994; Chicago, April 21, 1995). **OTHER:** *Soliloquy* for Synthesizer (1967); Duet for Syn-Ket and Synthesizer (1968); *Genesis* for Eaton-Moog Multiple-Touch-Sensitive Keyboard (1992).

Ebel, Arnold, German composer, organist, and choral conductor; b. Heide, Holstein, Aug. 15, 1883; d. Berlin, March 4, 1963. He studied at the Univ. of Berlin; also took private lessons with Max Bruch; from 1909 he was active in Berlin as an organist, choral conductor, and teacher; served as president of the German Composers' Assn. (1920–33, and again from 1949). He wrote numerous piano pieces and songs; also a *Sinfonietta giocosa* for Orch.

Eben, Petr, Czech composer, pianist, and teacher; b. Žamberk, Jan. 22, 1929. He studied with František Rauch (piano) and Pavel Bořkovec (composition) at the Prague Academy of Music (1948–52). From 1955 to 1990 he taught music history at the Charles Univ. in Prague, and also served as prof. of composition at the Royal Northern College of Music in Manchester (1978–79); he then taught at the Prague Academy of Music (from 1990). Eben was imprisoned during the Nazi occupation of his homeland, and then endured the suffocating Communist regime until its undoing by the "velvet revolution" in 1989. As a composer, he found solace in plainchant and folk music, thus his liturgical works and organ music represent significant aspects of his oeuvre.

WORKS: DRAMATIC: *Faust*, incidental music to Goethe's play (1976); *Hamlet*, incidental music to Shakespeare's play (1977); *Curses and Blessings*, ballet (1983). **ORCH.:** 2 organ concertos: No. 1, *Symphonia gregoriana* (1954) and No. 2 (1982); Piano Concerto (1962); *Vox clamantis* for 3 Trumpets and Orch. (1969); *Night Hours*, concertante sym. (1975); *Prague Nocturne: Hommage à W.A. Mozart* (1983). **CHAMBER:** Oboe Sonata (1950); *Suita balladica* for Cello and Piano (1955); *Sonatina semplice* for Violin or Flute and Piano (1955); *Duetti per due trombe* (1956); *Duettinos* for Soprano Instrument and Piano (1963); *Ordo modalis* for Oboe and Harp (1964); *Quintettto per stromenti a fiato*, wind quintet (1965); *Fantasia vespertina* for Trumpet and Piano (1967); *Variations on Chorale*, brass quintet (1968–69); *Music* for Oboe, Bassoon, and Piano (1970); *Windows* for Trumpet and Organ (1976); *"Wood and Wind,"* sonata for Flute and Marimba (1978); *Tabulatura nova* for Guitar (1979); *Mutationes* for Organ and Piccolo (1980); String Quartet (1981); *Fantasia* for Viola and Organ (1982); *Landscapes of Patmos* for Organ and Percussion (1984); *Opponents* for Clarinet, Piano, and Percussion (1985); Piano Trio (1986); *Risonanza* for Harp (1986); *Tres iubilationes* for 4 Brass Instruments and Organ (1987); Harpsichord Sonata (1988); Nonet (1988); *2 Movements* for Trombone and Organ (1988); Piano Quintet (1991–92). **ORGAN:** *Sunday Music* (1957–59); *Laudes* (1964); 10 chorale overtures (1971); 2 chorale fantasias (1972); *Faust*, 9-part cycle (1979–80); *Versetti* (1982); *Hommage à Dietrich Buxtehude* (1987); *Job*, 8-part cycle (1987); *Biblical Dances* (1990–91); *2 Festive Preludes* (1992). **PIANO:** Sonata (1951); *Differences and Contrasts*, 11 "motion" études (1969); *Letters to Milena* (1990). **VOCAL:** *6 Love Songs* for Medium Voice and Piano (1951); *Missa adventus et quadragesimae* for Men's Chorus and Organ (1952); *The Lover's Magic Spell* for Woman's Voice and Chorus (1957); *Love and Death* for Chorus (1957–58); *6 Songs on Rainer Maria Rilke* for Low Voice and Piano (1961); *Unkind Songs* for Alto and Viola (1963); *Apologia Socratus* for Alto, Baritone, Chorus, Children's Chorus, and Orch. (1967); *Trouvere Mass* for Chorus, Guitar, and Recorders (1968–69); *Cantica Comeniana* for Mixed or Women's Chorus (1970); *Pragensia* for Chamber Chorus and Renaissance Instruments (1972); *Salve Regina* for Chorus (1973); *Greek Dictionary* for Women's Chorus and Harp (1974); *Honor to Charles IV* for Men's Chorus and Orch. (1978); *Missa cum populo* for Chorus, Congregation, 4 Brass Instruments, and Organ (1981–82); *Cantico delle creature* for Chorus (1987); *Prague Te Deum* for Chorus and Brass Instruments or Organ (1990); *Verba sapientiae* for

Chorus (1991); *Holy Signs* for Chorus, Wind Ensemble, and Organ (1992–93).

BIBL.: K. Vondrovicová, *P. E.* (Prague, 1993).

Eberhardt, Siegfried, German violin pedagogue; b. Frankfurt am Main, March 19, 1883; d. Zwickau, June 29, 1960. He studied violin with Dessau at the Stern Cons. in Berlin, and then with Serato; was a teacher of violin at the Stern Cons. (1908–33), and then its director (1933–35); then lived in Halle and Lübeck; in 1945, founded the Hochschule für Theater und Musik in Halle and the Zwickau Academy.

WRITINGS: With C. Flesch, *Der beseelte Violinton* (1910); *Absolute Treffsicherheit auf der Violine* (1911); *Virtuose Violin-Technik* (1921); *Paganinis Geigenhaltung* (1921); *Die Lehre der organischen Geigenhaltung* (1922); with G. Eberhardt, *Der natürliche Weg zur höchsten Virtuosität* (1923–24); *Der Körper in Form und Hemmung* (1926); *Hemmung und Herrschaft auf dem Griffbrett* (1931); *Wiederaufstieg oder Untergang der Kunst der Geigen* (1956).

BIBL.: K. Schröter, *Flesch-E., Naturwidrige oder natürliche Violintechnik?* (Leipzig, 1924).

Ebert, (Anton) Carl, noted German opera producer and administrator; b. Berlin, Feb. 20, 1887; d. Santa Monica, Calif., May 14, 1980. He studied acting with Max Reinhardt; then appeared in theaters in Berlin and Frankfurt am Main. In 1927 he became general administrator of the State Theater in Darmstadt and began to produce operas there. He then held a similar post at the Berlin City Opera (1931–33); he left Germany when the Nazis came to power. Ebert was one of the founders of the Glyndebourne Festival (1934), serving as its artistic director until 1939; in 1936 he organized the Turkish National School for Opera and Drama in Ankara, serving as its director until 1947; then was again artistic director at Glyndebourne (1947–59). He was also a prof. and head of the opera dept. at the Univ. of Southern Calif., Los Angeles (1948–54). He subsequently was administrator of the Berlin Städtische Oper (1956–61). As a producer, he gave much importance to the fusion of the music with the dramatic action on stage.

Eckardt, Hans, distinguished German musicologist; b. Magdeburg, Oct. 9, 1905; d. Berlin, Feb. 26, 1969. He studied philology in Leipzig, took courses in musicology with Sachs, Hornbostel, and Schünemann at the Univ. of Berlin, and received his Ph.D. in 1932 at the Univ. of Heidelberg with the diss. *Die Musikanschauung der französischen Romantik* (publ. in Kassel, 1935). He then went to Japan, where he taught at the Imperial Univ. in Fukuoka (1932–35); after studies at the Univ. of Tokyo (1936–37), he served as director of the Japanese-German Research Inst. of Cultural History in Kyoto (1938–45) and was a teacher at St. Thomas's Philosophical College there (1946–47). Upon his return to Germany, he completed his Habilitation in 1954 at the Free Univ. of Berlin with his *Das Kokonchomonshû des Tachibana Narisve als musikgeschichtliche Quelle* (publ. in Wiesbaden, 1956), joining its faculty as a lecturer in 1958 and as a prof. in 1964. He was an authority on Japanese music, and contributed many articles to both Japanese and German publications.

Eckerberg, (Axel) Sixten (Lennart), Swedish conductor, pianist, and composer; b. Hjältevad, Sept. 5, 1909; d. Göteborg, April 9, 1991. After training at the Stockholm Cons. (1927–32), he studied conducting with Weingartner in Basel (1932–34) and piano with Sauer in Vienna and Philipp in Paris. From 1937 to 1969 he was chief conductor of the Göteborg Radio Orch. His autobiography was publ. as *Musiken och mitt lif* (Stockholm, 1970). In his compositions, his contrapuntal writing tended toward the austere with occasional impressionist elements.

WORKS: DRAMATIC: *Ånger*, musical (1972; Swedish Radio, July 22, 1975); *Det stora bankränet*, opera (1975); *Uppståndelse*, opera (1975–76). **ORCH.:** *Melodi* for Piano and Strings (1935); 3 syms. (1941; 1943–45; 1966); *Sommarmusik* (1941); *Sub luna* (1942); 3 piano concertos (1943, 1949, 1971); *Visione* (1961); Piano Concertino (1962); *La danza della vita* (1970); *Promenade Suite* for Winds and Percussion (1971); *Sagan om asarna* (1971); *Serenade* (1972); *Skogssuset* (1973); Cello Concerto (1974). **OTHER:** *Nocturne* for Alto and Orch. (1970–71); chamber music; piano pieces.

Eckert, Rinde, American avant-garde vocalist, librettist, and composer; b. Mankato, Minn., Sept. 20, 1951. He studied at the Univ. of Iowa (B.M., 1973) and Yale Univ. (M.M., 1975), then was on the faculty of the Cornish Inst. (1980–82) and resident stage director of the Cornish Opera Theater. Since 1980 he has worked primarily with the composer Paul Dresher, and is principal performer and collaborator on their American opera trilogy (*Slow Fire* [1985–88], *Power Failure* [1989], and *Pioneers*). He was also principal performer and collaborator on the *How Trilogy* with George Coates Performance Works (*The Way of How* [1981], *are are* [1983], and *Seehear* [1984]; music by Dresher). Other works with Dresher include *Was Are/Will Be* (1983–85), *Shelf Life* (1987, with choreographer Margaret Jenkins), and *Secret House* (1990, with the Oberlin Dance Collective). His intense vocal style indicates both classical and rock training; his libretti are complex explorations, drenched with verbal paradox, of the pressure and instability of contemporary life. Among his own musical compositions are a radio opera, *Shoot the Moving Things* (1987), *Shorebirds Atlantic* for Voice, Harmonica, and Tape (1987), and *Dry Land Divine* for Voice, Accordion, Harmonica, and Electronics (1988).

Eckhardt-Gramatté, S(ophie)-C(armen) "Sonia," Russian-born Canadian violinist, pianist, teacher, and composer; b. Moscow, Jan. 6, 1899; d. in a traffic accident in Stuttgart, Dec. 2, 1974. Her mother, a former pupil of Anton and Nikolai Rubinstein, gave her piano lessons in Paris (1906–08). She then studied violin with Alfred Brun and Guillaume Rémy, piano with S. Chenée, and chamber music with Vincent d'Indy and Chevillard at the Paris Cons. (1909–13); while still a student, she gave concerts in Paris, Geneva, and Berlin, appearing as both a violinist and a pianist; she later received additional violin training from Huberman. In 1920 she married the painter Walter Gramatté; they lived in Barcelona (1924–26), but spent most of their time in Germany, where she toured as a duo pianist with Edwin Fischer in 1925. Her husband died in 1929. During the 1929–30 season, she toured the U.S., settling again in Germany in 1934, where she married the art critic Ferdinand Eckhardt; she assumed the name Eckhardt-Gramatté in 1939. She took additional courses in composition from Max Trapp at Berlin's Preussische Akademie (from 1936). The couple went to Vienna in 1939 and to Winnipeg in 1953. In 1958 she became a naturalized Canadian citizen. Her works are marked by an impressive craftsmanship.

WORKS: ORCH.: 3 piano concertos (1925, 1946, 1967); 2 syms. (1939; Manitoba, 1969–70); *Capriccio concertante* (1940); *Markantes Stück* for 2 Pianos and Orch. (1946–50); Concertino for Strings (1947); Triple Concerto for Trumpet, Clarinet, Bassoon, Strings, and Timpani (1949); Bassoon Concerto (1950); 2 violin concertos (1951, 1952); *Concerto for Orchestra* (1953–54); *Symphony-Concerto* for Piano and Orch. (1966–67). **CHAMBER:** 4 suites for Violin (1922–68); 6 piano suites (1923–52); *10 Caprices* for Violin (1924–34); Concerto for Violin (1925); *6 Caprices* for Piano (1934–36); 3 string quartets (1938; 1943; 1962–64); 2 duos for 2 Violins (1944); Duo for Viola and Cello (1944); Duo for 2 Cellos (1944); Wind Quartet (1946); 2 string trios (1947); *Ruck-Ruck Sonata* for Clarinet and Piano (1947; rev. 1962); Wind Trio (1947); 2 violin sonatas (1950, 1951); *Duo concertante* for Flute and Violin (1956); *Duo concertante* for Cello and Piano (1959); Wind Quintet (1962–63); Nonet (1966); Piano Trio (1967); Woodwind Trio (1967); Concertino for Viola da Gamba and Harpsichord (1971); *Fanfare* for 8 Brasses (1971).

BIBL.: L. Watson, "S.C. E.-G.," *The Canadian Music Educator* (Fall 1975); F. Eckhardt, *Music from Within: A Biography of the Composer S.C. E.-G.* (Manitoba, 1985).

Eckstein, Pavel, Czech musicologist; b. Opava, April 27, 1911. He studied jurisprudence at Charles Univ. in Prague, graduating in 1935; received his musical education there. During the German occupation (1941–45), he was in a concentration camp in Łódź, but survived and returned to Prague, where he became active as an organizer of music festivals, an ed., and a writer on music. From 1969 to 1992 he was artistic advisor of the Prague National Theater, and subsequently was chief dramaturg there from 1992. Among his books are *Czechoslovak Opera* (Prague, 1964) and *The Czechoslovak Contemporary Opera—Die tschechoslowakische zeitgenössische Oper* (Prague, 1967).

Eda-Pierre, Christiane, esteemed French soprano; b. Fort-de-France, Martinique, March 24, 1932. She studied at the Paris Cons., graduating with 3 premiers prix in 1957. In 1958 she made her operatic debut in Nice as Leila in *Les pêcheurs de Perles*; after singing Pamina at the Aix-en-Provence Festival (1959), she went to Paris and made debuts at the Opéra-Comique (as Lakmé, 1961) and the Opéra (as Lucia di Lammermoor, 1962). In 1966 she made her first appearance at London's Covent Garden as Teresa in *Benvenuto Cellini*. She appeared as Mozart's Countess with the Paris Opéra during its visit to N.Y. in 1976. On April 3, 1980, she made her Metropolitan Opera debut in N.Y. as Mozart's Constanze, and returned there for the 1981–82 season. In 1983 she created the role of the Angel in Messiaen's St. François d'Assise in Paris. She also served as a prof. of voice at the Paris Cons. (from 1977). Among her other admired roles were Rameau's Dardanus, the Queen of the Night, Berlioz's Hero, Zerbinetta, Gilda, and Milhaud's Médée.

Eddy, (Hiram) Clarence, distinguished American organist, pedagogue, and composer; b. Greenfield, Mass., June 23, 1851; d. Winnetka, Ill., Jan. 10, 1937. After training with Dudley Buck in Hartford, Conn. (1867), he studied organ with Haupt and piano with Löschhorn in Berlin (1871–74). He subsequently acquired a notable reputation as a virtuoso through his frequent concert tours of North America and Europe; he also was active as a church organist and as a teacher. In addition to the standard organ repertoire, he programmed works by American composers, including his son. He prepared a tr. of Haupt's treatise on the theory of counterpoint and fugue (1876), and also publ. *The Church and Concert Organist* (2 vols., 1882, 1885), *The Organ in Church* (1887), and *A Method for Pipe Organ* (1917). His reminiscences appeared in *The Diapason* (April 1932–May 1933).

Eddy, Nelson, popular American baritone; b. Providence, R.I., June 29, 1901; d. Miami Beach, March 6, 1967. He received training from Bispham and in N.Y. from Vilonat, and later studied in Dresden and Paris. In 1922 he made his stage debut, and subsequently appeared in operatic and light operatic roles. He soon found his métier as a popular singer on the radio, and also pursued a successful career as a singing actor with Jeanette MacDonald in the films *Naughty Marietta* (1935), *Rose Marie* (1936), *Maytime* (1937), *The Girl of the Golden West* (1938), *Sweethearts* (1939), *New Moon* (1940), *Bittersweet* (1940), and *I Married an Angel* (1942). In subsequent years, he made occasional concert appearances.

BIBL.: E. Knowles, *Films of Jeanette MacDonald and N. E.* (South Brunswick, N.J., 1975); G. Lulay, *N. E., America's Favorite Baritone: An Authorized Biographical Tribute* (Wheeling, Ill., 1990); L. Kiner, *N. E.: A Bio-Discography* (Methuchen, N.J., 1992).

Edel, Yitzhak, Polish-born Israeli composer, choral conductor, and teacher; b. Warsaw, Jan. 1, 1896; d. Tel Aviv, Dec. 14, 1973. He learned to play the violin as a youth, and later pursued training in theory and composition with Rytel and Statkowsky at the Warsaw Cons. (graduated, 1928). Emigrating to Palestine in 1929, he taught and was choir director at the Lewinsky Teacher's Seminary until 1965. His output was profoundly influenced by Jewish folk and liturgical music. Among his works were the orch. pieces *Capriccio* (1948), *Israeli Dance* (1950), and *Sinfonietta rusticana* (1969); chamber music; piano pieces; various choral works, including the folk cantata *Lamitnadvim ba'am* (To the People's Volunteers) for Tenor, Chorus, and Orch. (1957); songs; folk song arrangements.

Edelmann, Otto (Karl), noted Austrian bass-baritone; b. Brünn am Gebirge, near Vienna, Feb. 5, 1917. He studied with Lierhammer and Graarud at the Vienna Academy of Music, making his operatic debut as Mozart's Figaro in Gera in 1937; he then sang in Nuremberg (1938–40). After military service during World War II, he resumed his career as a leading member of the Vienna State Opera from 1947. He also sang at the Bayreuth Festival, the Salzburg Festival, La Scala in Milan, the Hamburg State Opera, the Edinburgh Festival, and other major operatic centers. On Nov. 11, 1954, he made his Metropolitan Opera debut in N.Y. as Hans Sachs, a role in which he particularly excelled; he continued to sing there regularly until 1976. His most famous role was that of Baron Ochs in *Der Rosenkavalier*.

BIBL.: S.-M. Schlinke, *O. E.: Ein Meistersinger aus Wien* (Vienna, 1987).

Edelmann, Sergei, remarkable Russian-born pianist; b. Lwów, July 22, 1960. He trained with his father, the head of the piano dept. at the Lwów Cons., then made his public debut at the age of 10 as soloist in Beethoven's 1st Piano Concerto with the Lwów Phil. After emigrating to the U.S. in 1979, he continued his studies with Firkušny at the Juilliard School in N.Y., and with Claude Frank at the Aspen School of Music. In subsequent years, he performed as soloist with the principal orchs. of North America and Europe, and also gave recitals. Blessed with an extraordinary virtuoso technique, he is esteemed for his performances of the Romantic repertoire.

Eder, Helmut, Austrian composer and pedagogue; b. Linz, Dec. 26, 1916. He studied at the Linz teacher training inst. (diploma, 1937). In 1938 he entered the Austrian Army. During his service in World War II, he was taken prisoner of war. After his release, he studied with Hindemith in Salzburg (1947, 1950), Orff in Munich (1953–54), and J.N. David in Stuttgart (1954). From 1950 to 1967 he was prof. of theory at the Linz Cons. He subsequently was prof. of composition at the Salzburg Mozarteum from 1967. In 1962 he was awarded the Austrian State Prize. In 1963 he received the Theodor Körner Prize for music. He was awarded the Würdigungspreis in 1972. In 1986 he was made an honorary member of the Austrian Composers Guild.

WORKS: DRAMATIC: OPERAS: *Ödipus* (1958); *Der Kardinal* (1962); *Die weisse Frau* (1968); *Konjugationen 3*, television opera (1969); *Der Aufstand* (1975); *Georges Dandin oder Der betrogene Ehemann* (1978–79); *Mozart in New York* (1989–90; Salzburg, Aug. 15, 1991).

BALLETS: *Moderner Traum* (Linz, Sept. 29, 1957); *Anamorphose* (1963; Linz, June 22, 1966); *Die Irrfahrten des Odysseus* (1964–65). **ORCH.:** *Präludium und Ricercar* for Strings (1949; Linz, May 16, 1950); 5 syms.: No. 1 (1950), No. 2 (Vienna, Jan. 31, 1962), No. 3 for Strings (1959), No. 4, *Choral* (1973–75; Vienna, Oct. 15, 1977), and No. 5, *Organ* (1979–80; Salzburg, Aug. 13, 1980); *Musica semplice* for Flute, Harpsichord, and Strings (1953); *Tanzreihen*, ballet suite (1954; Linz, Jan. 24, 1956); *Musik* for 2 Trumpets and Strings (1955); Concerto for Piano, 15 Winds, Double Basses, and Percussion (1956); *Pezzo sereno* (1958); *Concerto semiserio* for 2 Pianos and Orch. (1960); Oboe Concerto (1962); 3 violin concertos: No. 1 (1963; Vienna, Feb. 10, 1964), No. 2 for Violin and Strings (1964; Linz, Jan. 31, 1967), and No. 3 (1981–82; Munich, Jan. 21, 1983); *Danza a solatio* (1963; Linz, Jan. 27, 1964); *Concerto a dodici per* [12] *archi* (Vienna, Oct. 22, 1963); *Nil admirari* (1966; Linz, Oct. 2, 1967); *Syntagma* (Vienna, Oct. 6, 1967); Concerto for Bassoon and Chamber Orch. (Vienna, June 4, 1968); *L'Homme armé*, organ concerto (1968–69; Nuremberg, July 5, 1969); *Metamorphosen* for Flute, Oboe, String Quartet, and Orch. (1970; Salzburg, Jan. 31, 1971); *Memento* for Positive Organ, String Quartet, and String Orch. (1970; Bayreuth, May 22, 1971);

Melodia-ritmica for Strings (Linz, Dec. 13, 1973); *Pastorale* for Strings (Linz, Nov. 30, 1974); *Jubilatio* (Linz, Dec. 26, 1976); *Serenade* for 6 Horns and 46 Strings (1977); Double Concerto for Cello, Double Bass, and Orch. (1977–78; Saarbrücken, May 21, 1979); Cello Concerto (Linz, Sept. 5, 1981); *Concerto A. B.* for Chamber Orch. (1982; Linz, March 17, 1983; also for Orch., 1983; Vienna, March 14, 1984); *Notturni . . . von Tänzern, Träumen und allerlei Vogelsang* for Flute, Oboe, and Strings (Munich, Sept. 29, 1983); *Haffner Concerto* for Flute and Orch. (1983–84; Salzburg, Jan. 31, 1985); Concertino for Classical Orch. (1984; Graz, April 14, 1986); *Pièce de concert* for Strings (1984); *Schwanengesang* for Cello and Chamber Orch. (Linz, Nov. 22, 1987); *Stracci II*, chamber sym. (Vienna, May 14, 1993). **CHAMBER:** Trio for Violin, Viola, and Cello (Vienna, Jan. 8, 1957); 3 wind quintets: No. 1 (1958; Linz, May 6, 1959), No. 2, *Septuagesima instrumentalis* (1968–69; Mannheim, June 11, 1969), and No. 3, *Begegnung* (1987–88; Berlin, Sept. 29, 1989); *Ottetto breve* for Flute, Oboe, Clarinet, Bassoon, 2 Violins, Viola, and Cello (1960; Vienna, Feb. 12, 1961); *Impressioni* for String Quartet (Linz, Oct. 4, 1966); Wind Septet, *Hommage à Johannes Kepler* (1970; ORF, Linz, April 16, 1971); Piano Trio (Salzburg, May 24, 1971); *So-no-ro I* for Clarinet, Viola, Piano or Celesta, and Organ (1974; Salzburg, April 23, 1975) and *II* for Clarinet, Bass Clarinet, Cello, Double Bass, Guitar, and Piano (Hamburg, Dec. 1, 1977); *Litzlberg Serenade* for 2 Clarinets, Trumpet, Horn, and Bassoon (1976; Litzlberg, July 29, 1986); *Suite mit intermezzi* for 11 Winds (1979; London, May 29, 1981); 4 Pieces for 2 Violins (1980; Linz, June 14, 1981); 6 Bagatelles for 3 Violins (1980); Clarinet Quintet (1982; Berlin, Feb. 18, 1984); Quartet for Flute and String Trio (1983; Vienna, Jan. 9, 1984); String Quartet (1985); *Aulodie* for Flute, Bassoon or Cello, Double Bass, and Percussion (Cardiff, Nov. 21, 1986); *Gedanken* for Horn, Violin, and Piano (Vienna, April 26, 1993); piano pieces; organ music. **VOCAL:** *Drei Tierlieder* for High Voice and Orch. (1966); *Cadunt umbrae* for Alto, 8 Women's Voices, Orch., and Tape (1973–74; Salzburg, May 22, 1974); *Non sum qualis eram*, oratorio for Soprano, Baritone, Bass, Chorus and Orch. (1975; Salzburg, Dec. 10, 1976); *Divertimento* for Soprano and 2 Orch. Groups (Salzburg, Aug. 14, 1976); . . . *Missa est* for 3 Soloists, 2 Choruses, and 3 Orch. Groups (Salzburg, Aug. 23, 1986); *Dir, Seele des Weltalls*, cantata for 2 Tenors, Bass, Men's Chorus, and Orch. (Vienna, June 7, 1991); *Gebet und Verzweiflung* for Chorus and Orch. (1992–93); *Herbstgesänge* for Chamber Chorus and 7 Instruments (Vienna, Nov. 25, 1993).

BIBL.: G. Gruber and G. Kraus, *H. E.* (Vienna, 1988).

Edlund, Lars, Swedish organist, conductor, teacher, and composer; b. Karlstad, Nov. 6, 1922. He studied in Arvika and at the Stockholm Musikhögskolan (1942–47). After serving as an organist in Tranås and Södertälje (1948–60), he taught aural training at the Stockholm Musikhögskolan until 1971; then devoted himself to performing and composing. He publ. 2 influential books, *Modus novus: Lärobok i fritonal melodiläsning* (New method: Textbook in atonal melody reading: 1963) and *Modus vetus: Gehörstudier i dur/moll-tonalitet* (Old method: Ear training in major/minor tonalities; 1967), which have guided his path as a composer. He won particular distinction for his choral music. Among his works are a chamber opera, *Flickan i ögat* (1979); chamber music, including 2 string quartets (1980–81; 1993); piano pieces; organ music; *Elegi* for Chorus (1971); *Missa Sancti Nicolai* for Soloists, Chorus, and Percussion (Stockholm, July 10, 1979); *Adonai* for Baritone, Chorus, Organ, and Percussion (1983). His son, Mikael Edlund (b. Tranås, Jan. 19, 1950), is also a composer.

Edmunds, John (actually, **Charles Sterling**), American composer and music scholar; b. San Francisco, June 10, 1913; d. Berkeley, Dec. 9, 1986. He studied with Scalero at the Curtis Inst. of Music in Philadelphia, Piston at Harvard Univ. (M.A., 1941), Harris at Cornell Univ., Luening at Columbia Univ., and Goldsbrough and Dart in England. He taught at Syracuse Univ. (1946–47), and was co-founder of the Campion Soc. in San Francisco (1946–53), notable for its annual Festival of Unfamiliar Music. After serving as head of the Americana collection at the N.Y. Public Library (1957–61), he taught at the Univ. of Calif. at Berkeley (1965–66). In 1951 he held a Fulbright scholarship and in 1969 a Guggenheim fellowship. As a music scholar, Edmunds devoted much time to preparing *The Major Epoch of English Song: The 17th-Century from Dowland to Purcell* (12 vols., 1940–76), an unpublished collection of more than 300 songs arranged for voice and piano as realized from lute tablatures and figured basses. He also publ. *The Garden of the Muses* (N.Y., 1985). As a composer, he was especially successful as a songwriter. Among his other works were masques, ballets, and choral music.

Edvaldsdóttir, Sigrún, Icelandic violinist; b. Reykjavík, Jan. 13, 1967. She commenced violin training when she was 5; undertook formal studies with Gudný Gudmundsdóttir at the Reykjavík College of Music, graduating at 17 as the youngest person ever with a soloist diploma. She then went to the U.S. to study with Roland and Almita Amos, and then with Jascha Brodsky and Jaime Laredo at the Curtis Inst. of Music in Philadelphia (B.M., 1988). In 1987 she took 2nd prize in the Leopold Mozart competition in Augsburg; in 1988 she won 5th prize in the Carl Nielsen competition in Denmark; in 1990 she captured the Bronze Medal at the Sibelius Competition in Helsinki. In 1988 she became 1st violinist of the newly founded Miami (Fla.) String Quartet. She also pursued a career as a soloist and as a recitalist.

Edwards, Ross, Australian composer; b. Sydney, Dec. 23, 1943. He studied at the New South Wales State Conservatorium of Music in Sydney (1959–62), the Univ. of Sydney (1963), and the Univ. of Adelaide (B.Mus., 1968; M.Mus., 1971), his principal mentors being Meale and Sculthorpe. A Commonwealth postgraduate scholarship enabled him to pursue studies in London with Maxwell Davies. He also studied with Veress. After serving as senior tutor (1973–76) and lecturer (1976–80) in composition at the New South Wales State Conservatorium of Music, he was composer-in-residence at the Univ. of Wollongong (1983). In 1989 he was made the Australia Council's Don Banks fellow. In 1990 he received the D.Mus. degree from the Univ. of Sydney. He held 2 Australian Creative Artists fellowships. Edwards has developed a highly imaginative style of composition. In his works, designated as his "sacred series," an austere meditative aura prevails. In other scores he has been much influenced by the sounds of the natural world, including those of insects and birds.

WORKS: DRAMATIC: *Christina's World*, chamber opera (1983; rev. 1989); *Sensing*, television dance score (1993). **ORCH.:** *Mountain Village in a Clearing Mist* (1973); Piano Concerto (1982); Violin Concerto, *Maninyas* (Sydney, Aug. 9, 1988); *Yarrageh: Nocturne* for Solo Percussion and Orch. (Sydney, July 19, 1989); *Aria and Transcendental Dance* for Horn and Strings (1990); *Symphony Da Pacem Domine* (1991; Perth, Aug. 7, 1992); Concerto for Guitar and Strings (Darwin, July 8, 1995). **CHAMBER:** *Monos I* for Cello (1970) and *II* for Piano (1970); *Shadow D-Zone* for Flute, Clarinet, Piano, Percussion, Violin, and Cello (1977); *The Tower of Remoteness* for Clarinet and Piano (Sydney, Dec. 15, 1978); *Laikan* for Flute, Clarinet, Piano, Percussion, Violin, and Cello (1979); *10 Little Duets* for Recorder Duet (1982); *Marimba Dances* for Marimba (1982); *Maninya II* for String Quartet (1982), *III* for Wind Quintet (1985), and *IV* for Clarinet, Trombone, and Marimba (1985); *Reflections* for Piano and 3 Percussion (1985); *Ecstatic Dances* for 2 Flutes (1990); *Booroora* for Clarinet, Percussion, and Double Bass (1990); *Prelude and Dragonfly Dance* for Percussion Quartet (1991); *Black Mountain Duos* for 2 Cellos (1992); *Veni Creator Spiritus* for String Octet (Perth, Nov. 2, 1993); *Ulpirra* for Recorder (1993); *Laughing Rock* for Cello (1993–94); *Enyato I* for String Quartet (1994) and *II* for Viola (1994). **VOCAL:** *5 Carols from Quem Quaeritis* for Women's Chorus (1967); *Antifon* for Chorus, Brass Sextet, Organ, and 2 Tam-tams (1973); *The Hermit of Green Light*, song cycle for Countertenor and Piano (1979); *Ab Estasias Foribus* for Chorus (1980–87); *Maninya I* for Countertenor and

Cello (1981–86) and *V* for Countertenor and Piano (1986); *Flower Songs* for Chorus and 2 Percussion (1987); *Dance Mantra* for 6 voices and Drum (1992).

Edwards, Sian, talented English conductor; b. Sussex, May 27, 1959. She studied horn before entering the Royal Northern College of Music in Manchester, where she turned to conducting; following studies with Sir Charles Groves and Norman Del Mar, and in the Netherlands with Neeme Järvi, she pursued diligent training with Ilya Musin at the Leningrad Cons. (1983–85). In 1984 she won the Leeds Competition and subsequently appeared as a guest conductor with principal British orchs. In 1986 she made her first appearance as an operatic conductor at Glasgow's Scottish Opera with Weill's *Mahogonny.* In 1987 she conducted *La Traviata* at the Glyndebourne Festival. She became the first woman ever to conduct at London's Covent Garden when she led a performance of Tippett's *The Knot Garden* in 1988; that same year she conducted the premiere of Turnage's *Greek* at the Munich Biennale. In 1989 she made her U.S. debut as a guest conductor with the St. Paul (Minn.) Chamber Orch.; she continued to conduct at Covent Garden, leading performances of *Rigoletto* (1989), *Il Trovatore* (1990), and *Carmen* (1991). From 1993 to 1995 she was music director of the English National Opera in London.

Effinger, Cecil, American composer; b. Colorado Springs, July 22, 1914; d. Boulder, Colo., Dec. 22, 1990. He took courses in mathematics at Colorado College (B.A., 1935); then studied harmony and counterpoint with Frederick Boothroyd in Colorado Springs (1934–36). He then studied composition with Wagenaar in N.Y. (1938) and Boulanger in Fontainebleau (1939), where he was awarded the Stoval composition prize. He was oboist in the Colorado Springs Sym. Orch. (1932–41) and the Denver Sym. Orch. (1937–41); taught at Colorado College (1936–41) and the Colorado School for the Blind (1939–41). During World War II, he conducted the 506th Army Band (1942–45), then taught at the American Univ. in Biarritz, France (1945–46). After teaching at Colorado College (1946–48), he was music ed. of the *Denver Post* (1947–48); then was head of the composition dept. (1948–81) and composer-in-residence (1981–84) at the Univ. of Colo. in Boulder. In 1954 he patented a practical music typewriter as the "Musicwriter." In his music he maintained a median modern style, making use of polytonal and atonal procedures, without abandoning the basic sense of tonality.

WORKS: DRAMATIC: *Pandora's Box,* children's opera (1961); *Cyrano de Bergerac,* opera (Boulder, July 21, 1965); *The Gentleman Desperado,* music theater (1976); incidental music. **ORCH.:** *Concerto Grosso* (1940); *Western Overture* (1942); Concertino for Organ and Small Orch. (1945); 2 Little Syms. (1945, 1958); Suite for Cello and Chamber Orch. (1945); 5 syms. (1946–58); Piano Concerto (1946); *Lyric Overture* (1949); *Pastorale* for Oboe and Strings (1949); Sym. Concertante for Harp, Piano, and Orch. (1954); *Tone Poem on the Square Dance* (1955); Trio Concertante for Trumpet, Trombone, Horn, and Chamber Orch. (1964; also for 2 Pianos, 1968); *Landscape I* for Brass and Strings (1966) and *II* (1984); Violin Concerto (1972); *Toccata* for Chamber Orch. (1980); band pieces. **CHAMBER:** 6 string quartets (1943, 1944, 1948, 1963, 1985; No. 2, n.d., unfinished); Viola Sonata (1944); 3 piano sonatas (1946, 1949, 1968); Piano Trio (1973); *Intrada* for Brass Quintet (1982); Flute Sonata (1985); also band music. **VOCAL: ORATORIOS:** *The Invisible Fire* for Soloists, Chorus, and Orch. (1957); *Paul of Tarsus* for Chorus, Strings, and Organ (1968). **CANTATAS:** *Cantata for Easter* for Chorus and Organ (1971); *Cantata Opus 111: From Ancient Prophets* for Chorus, Wind, Cello, and Double Bass (1983); other vocal works.

Egge, Klaus, prominent Norwegian composer; b. Gransherad, Telemark, July 19, 1906; d. Oslo, March 7, 1979. He was a student of Larsen (piano), Sandvold (organ), and Valen (composition) in Oslo, and later of Gmeindl (composition) at the Berlin Hochschule für Music (1937–38). From 1945 to 1972 he was president of the Soc. of Norwegian Composers. In 1949 he was awarded a government life pension. His works were conditioned by Scandinavian modalities, within a framework of euphonious and resonantly modernistic harmonies. He liked to sign his scores with the notes E-g-g-e, a motto which also occasionally served as a basic theme.

WORKS: BALLET: *Fanitullen* (Devil's Dance; 1950). **ORCH.:** 3 piano concertos: No. 1 (Oslo, Nov. 14, 1938), No. 2 (Oslo, Dec. 9, 1946), and No. 3 (Bergen, April 25, 1974); 5 syms.: No. 1, *Lagnadstonar* (Sounds of Destiny; Oslo, Oct. 4, 1945), No. 2, *Sinfonia giocosa* (Oslo, Dec. 9, 1949), No. 3, *Louisville Symphony* (Louisville, Ky., March 4, 1959), No. 4, *Sinfonia seriale sopra B.A.C.H.-E.G.G.E.* (Detroit, March 28, 1968), and No. 5, *Sinfonia dolce quasi passacaglia* (Oslo, Sept. 27, 1969); *Tårn over Oslo,* overture (1950); Violin Concerto (Oslo, Nov. 5, 1953); Cello Concerto (Oslo, Sept. 9, 1966). **CHAMBER:** Violin Sonata (1932); String Quartet (1933; rev. 1963); 2 piano sonatas: No. 1, *Draumkvede* (Dream Vision; 1933) and No. 2, *Patética* (1955); 3 *Fantasies* for Piano (1939); 2 wind quintets (1939, 1976); Piano Trio (1941); Duo concertante for Violin and Viola (1950); Harp Sonatina (1974). **VOCAL:** *Sveinung Vreim* for Soli, Chorus, and Orch. (Oslo, Dec. 1, 1941); *Elskhugskvaede* (Love Song) for Voice and Strings (1942); *Draumar i stjernesno* (Starsnow Dreams), 3 songs for Soprano and Orch. (1943); *Fjell-Norig* (Mountainous Norway) for Voice and Orch. (Oslo, Oct. 1, 1945); *Noreg-songer* (The Norway Song) for Chorus and Orch. (Oslo, May 2, 1952); choruses; other songs.

Eggebrecht, Hans Heinrich, eminent German musicologist and editor; b. Dresden, Jan. 5, 1919. He attended the Gymnasium in Schleusingen, of which his father was superintendent; was drafted into the army during World War II, and was severely wounded; then studied music education in Berlin and Weimar; he received his teacher's certificate in 1948. He subsequently studied musicology with H.J. Moser, R. Münnich, and M. Schneider; received his Ph.D. in 1949 from the Univ. of Jena with the diss. *Melchior Vulpius.* He was assistant lecturer under Vetter in music history at the Univ. of Berlin from 1949 to 1951; then did lexicographical work in Freiburg and taught musicology at the Univ. there (1953–55); he completed his Habilitation there in 1955 with his *Studien zur musikalischen Terminologie* (publ. in Mainz, 1955; 2nd ed., 1968). He was Privatdozent at the Univ. of Erlangen (1955–56) and taught musicology at the Univ. of Heidelberg (1956–57). From 1961 to 1988 he was prof. of musicology at the Univ. of Freiburg im Breisgau. In 1964 he became ed. of the *Archiv für Musikwissenschaft.* One of his major musicological contributions was his publication of the vol. on musical terms and historical subjects (*Sachteil*) for the 12th ed. of the *Riemann Musik-Lexikon* (Mainz, 1967), in which he settles many debatable points of musical terminology. Equally important has been his editorship of the *Handwörterbuch der musikalischen Terminologie* from 1972. He also was an ed. of the *Brockhaus-Riemann Musik-Lexikon* with Carl Dahlhaus (2 vols., Wiesbaden and Mainz, 1978–79; supplement, 1989) and of Meyers *Taschenlexikon Musik* (3 vols., Mannheim, 1984).

WRITINGS: *Heinrich Schütz: Musicus poeticus* (Göttingen, 1959); *Ordnung und Ausdruck im Werk von Heinrich Schütz* (Kassel, 1961); *Die Orgelbewegung* (Stuttgart, 1967); *Schütz und Gottesdienst* (Stuttgart, 1969); *Versuch über die Wiener Klassik: Die Tanzszene in Mozarts Don Giovanni* (Wiesbaden, 1972); *Zur Geschichte der Beethoven-Rezeption: Beethoven 1970* (Wiesbaden, 1972); *Musikalische Denken: Aufsätze zur Theorie und Ästhetik der Musik* (Wilhelmshaven, 1977); *Die Musik Gustav Mahlers* (Munich, 1982); *Bachs Kunst der Fuge: Erscheinung und Deutung* (Munich, 1984; Eng. tr., 1993); *Die mittelalterliche Lehre von der Mehrstimmigkeit* (Darmstadt, 1984); *Musik im Abendland: Prozesse und Stationen vom Mittelalter bis zur Gegenwart* (Munich, 1991); *Orgelbau und Orgelmusik in Russland* (Kleinblittersdorf, 1991); *Zur Geschichte der Beethoven-Rezeption* (Laaber, 1994).

BIBL.: W. Breig, R. Brinkmann, and E. Budde, eds., *Analysen: Beiträge zu einer Problemgeschichte des Komponierens. Festschrift für H.H. E. zum 65. Geburtstag* (Stuttgart, 1984).

Eggen, Arne, Norwegian organist and composer, brother of **Erik Eggen**; b. Trondheim, Aug. 28, 1881; d. Baerum, near Oslo, Oct. 26, 1955. He studied at the Christiania Cons. (1903–05) and then with Straube (organ) and Krehl (composition) at the Leipzig Cons. (1906–07). He toured Norway and Sweden giving organ recitals; from 1927 to 1945 he was president of the Soc. of Norwegian Composers. In 1934 he received a government life pension.

WORKS: 2 operas: *Olav Liljekrans* (1931–40; Oslo, 1940) and *Cymbeline* (1943–48; Oslo, Dec. 7, 1951); Sym. (Christiania, March 4, 1920); *King Olav*, oratorio (Oslo, March 30, 1933); *Chaconne* for Organ or Orch. (1917); 2 violin sonatas; Piano Trio; Cello Sonata; Suite for Violin and Piano; organ music; piano pieces; many songs.

Eggen, Erik, Norwegian music scholar and composer, brother of **Arne Eggen;** b. Trondheim, Nov. 17, 1877; d. Ringsaker, June 7, 1957. He studied theory with Hilde (1895), and later pursued his education at the Univ. of Oslo (Ph.D., 1925). He was a school teacher (1898–1939); was also ed. of *Norsk toneblad* (1910–17) and devoted much time to the study of folk music. His writings include *Edvard Grieg* (Christiania, 1911) and *Norsk musikksoge* (Christiania, 1923). Among his compositions are *Norsk Rapsodi* for Orch., a cantata, and choral pieces.

Eggerth, Martha (real name, **Márta Eggert**), Hungarian soprano; b. Budapest, April 17, 1912. She was only 12 when she began appearing in juvenile roles in light theater performances in Budapest. In 1930 she attracted favorable notice in the title role of *Das Veilchen vom Montmartre* in Vienna, and in subsequent years had a notably successful career both on stage and in films. Her theater engagements took her all over Europe and to N.Y., where she was notably successful in *The Merry Widow* with her husband, **Jan Kiepura**. She pursued her career to an advanced age, appearing in her 80th year in Stolz's *Servus Du* in Vienna.

Egk (real name, **Mayer**), **Werner,** significant German composer; b. Auchsesheim, near Donauwörth, May 17, 1901; d. Inning, near Munich, July 10, 1983. Rumor had it that he took the name Egk as a self-complimentary acronym for "ein grosser (or even ein genialer) Komponist." Egk himself rejected this frivolous suspicion, offering instead an even more fantastic explanation that Egk was a partial acronym of the name of his wife Elisabeth Karl, with the middle guttural added "for euphony." He studied piano with Anna Hirzel-Langenhan and composition with Carl Orff in Munich, where he made his permanent home. Primarily interested in theater music, he wrote several scores for a Munich puppet theater; was also active on the radio; then wrote ballet music to his own scenarios and a number of successful operas. He was also active as an opera conductor and music pedagogue. He conducted at the Berlin State Opera from 1938 to 1941, and was head of the German Union of Composers from 1941 to 1945. He was commissioned to write music for the Berlin Olympiad in 1936, for which he received a Gold Medal. He also received a special commission of 10,000 marks from the Nazi Ministry of Propaganda. The apparent favor that Egk enjoyed during the Nazi reign made it necessary for him to stand trial before the Allied Committee for the de-Nazification proceedings in 1947; it absolved him of political taint. From 1950 to 1953 he was director of the Berlin Hochschule für Musik. As a composer, Egk continued the tradition of Wagner and Richard Strauss, without excluding, however, the use of acidulous harmonies, based on the atonal extension of tonality. The rhythmic investiture of his works is often inventive and bold. He publ. a vol. of essays under the title *Musik, Wort, Bild* (Munich, 1960).

WORKS: DRAMATIC: *Columbus*, radio opera (1932; Bavarian Radio, Munich, July 13, 1933; 1st stage perf., Frankfurt am Main, Jan. 13, 1942); *Die Zaubergeige*, opera (Frankfurt am Main, May 19, 1935; rev. version, Stuttgart, May 2, 1954); *Peer Gynt*, opera (Berlin, Nov. 24, 1938); *Joan von Zarissa*, ballet (1939; Berlin, Jan. 20, 1940); *Circe*, opera (1945; Berlin, Dec. 18, 1948; rev. version as *17 Tage und 4 Minuten*, Stuttgart, June 2, 1966); *Abraxas*, ballet (South West Radio, Baden-Baden, Dec. 7, 1947; 1st stage perf., Munich, June 6, 1948); *Ein Sommertag*, ballet (Berlin, June 11, 1950); *Die chinesische Nachtigall*, ballet (Munich, May 6, 1953); *Irische Legende*, opera (Salzburg, Aug. 17, 1955; rev. 1970); *Der Revisor*, opera (Schwetzingen, May 9, 1957); *Die Verlobung in San Domingo*, opera (Munich, Nov. 27, 1963); *Casanova in London*, ballet (Munich, Nov. 23, 1969). **ORCH.:** Kleine Symphonie (1926); *Geigen Musik* for Violin and Orch. (1936); *Olympische Festmusik* (Berlin, Aug. 1, 1936); 2 sonatas (1948, 1969); *Französische Suite*, after Rameau (1949; Munich, Jan. 28, 1950; as a ballet, 1952); *Allegria*, suite (South West Radio, Baden-Baden, April 25, 1952; as a ballet, 1953); *Variationen über ein Karibisches Thema* (1959; Baden-Baden, Jan. 18, 1960; as the ballet *Danza*, 1960); *Moria* (1972; Nuremberg, Jan. 12, 1973); *Spiegelzeit* (1979); *Ouvertüre: Musik über eine verschollene Romanze* (1980); *Nachtanz über ein Thema aus den 16. Jahrhundert* (1982). **CHAMBER:** Piano Trio (1922); String Quartet (1924); String Quintet (1924); String Quintet (1924); Piano Sonata (1947); *Polonaise und Adagia* for 9 Instruments (1975); *5 Stücke* for Wind Quintet (1975). **VOCAL:** *Furchtlosigkeit und Wohlwollen*, oratorio for Tenor, Chorus, and Orch. (1931; Baden-Baden, April 3, 1936; rev. 1959); *Quattro canzoni* for Tenor and Orch. (1932; rev. 1955); *Natur-Liebe-Tod* and *Mein Vaterland*, cantatas (both perf. in Göttingen, June 26, 1937); *La Tentation de Saint Antoine* for Alto, String Quartet, and String Orch. (Baden-Baden, May 18, 1947; as a ballet, 1969); *Chanson et Romance* for Soprano and Chamber Orch. (Aix-en-Provence, July 19, 1953); *Nachtgefühl*, cantata for Soprano and Orch. (1975).

BIBL.: B. Kohl and E. Nölle, eds., *W. E.: Das Bühnenwerk* (Munich, 1971); E. Krause, *W. E.: Oper und Ballet* (Wilhelmshaven, 1971).

Egmond, Max (Rudolf) van, admired Dutch bass-baritone; b. Semarang, Java, Feb. 1, 1936. He studied with Tine van Willingen-de Lorme and took prizes in the 's Hertogenbosch (1959), Brussels (1962), and Munich (1964) competitions. He then pursued a distinguished career as a concert and oratorio artist, touring extensively in Europe and North America. From 1973 he also taught singing at the Amsterdam Musieklyceum. He was particularly associated with Baroque music, excelling in the works of Bach.

BIBL.: J. Müller, *M. v. E., toonaangevend kunstenaar* (Zutphen, 1984).

Egorov, Youri, Russian pianist; b. Kazan, May 28, 1954; d. Amsterdam, April 15, 1988. He learned to play the piano as a child in Kazan, and later was a pupil of Zak at the Moscow Cons. In 1971 he won 4th prize in the Long-Thibaud competition in Paris, and in 1974 3rd prize in the Tchaikovsky competition in Moscow. In 1976 he left his homeland and settled in the Netherlands. He made his N.Y. debut in 1978 and appeared for the first time in England in 1980. In subsequent years, he appeared with many of the principal orchs. of the world and as a recitalist. His career was cut tragically short by AIDS. He was particularly admired for his performances of the Romantic repertory.

Ehlers, Alice (Pauly), Austrian-born American harpsichordist and teacher; b. Vienna, April 16, 1887; d. Los Angeles, March 1, 1981. She studied piano with Leschetizky in Vienna; during World War I, she took lessons in harpsichord with Landowska in Berlin. In 1936 she emigrated to the U.S. and became a naturalized citizen in 1943. From 1941 to 1967 she taught harpsichord at the Univ. of Southern Calif. in Los Angeles; she also gave courses at the Juilliard School of Music in N.Y. and the Univ. of Calif. in Berkeley. She continued to appear in concert as a harpsichordist and gave occasional performances even as a nonagenarian.

BIBL.: K. and A. Bergel, trs. and eds., *Albert Schweitzer and A. E.: A Friendship in Letters* (Lanham, Md., 1991).

Ehmann, Wilhelm, German musicologist; b. Freistatt, Dec. 5, 1904; d. Freiburg im Breisgau, April 16, 1989. He studied musicology at the univs. of Freiburg and Leipzig; received his Ph.D. in 1934 with the diss. *Adam von Fulda als Vertreter der ersten deutschen Komponisten-Generation* (publ. in Berlin, 1936) from the Univ. of Freiburg; completed his Habilitation there with his *Der Thibaut-Behaghel-Kreis* in 1937. From 1934 to 1940 he was on the faculty of the Univ. of Freiburg; from 1940 to 1945 he taught at the Univ. of Innsbruck. In 1948 he founded and became director of the church-music school in Westphalia (later named the Hochschule für Kirchenmusik); he retired in 1972. He also taught at the Univ. of Munster (1948–54).

WRITINGS: *Die Chorführung* (2 vols., Kassel, 1949; 3rd ed., 1956; vol. II, in Eng., Minneapolis, 1936); *Tibilustrium: Das geistliche Blasen, Formen und Reformen* (Kassel, 1950); *Erziehung zur Kirchenmusik* (Gütersloh, 1951); *Erbe und Auftrag musikalischer Erneuerung: Entromantisierung der Singbewegung* (Kassel, 1951); *J.S. Bach in unserem Leben* (Wolfenbüttel, 1952); *Das Chorwesen in der Kulturkrise* (Regensburg, 1953); *Kirchenmusik, Vermächtnis und Aufgabe* (Darmstadt, 1958); *Alte Musik in der neuen Welt* (Darmstadt, 1961); *Der Bläserchor: Besinnung und Aufgabe* (Kassel, 1969).

Ehrenberg, Carl (Emil Theodor), German conductor, teacher, and composer; b. Dresden, April 6, 1878; d. Munich, Feb. 26, 1962. He studied with Draeseke at the Dresden Cons. (1894–98); from 1898 on was engaged as a conductor in Germany; from 1909 to 1914 he conducted concerts in Lausanne; from 1915 to 1918 he was 1st conductor at the Augsburg Opera; then conducted at the Berlin State Opera (1922–24). Subsequently he was a prof. at the Cologne Hochschule für Musik (1924–35) and at the Akademie der Tonkunst in Munich (1935–45).

WORKS: 2 operas: *Und selig sind* (1904) and *Anneliese* (1922); several overtures; 2 syms.; Sinfonietta; Cello Concerto; 4 string quartets; Piano Trio; Wind Quartet; String Trio; Violin Sonata; many choruses; songs; piano pieces.

BIBL.: A. Würz, "Komponist, Dirigent, Musikerzieher: Zu C. E.s 75. Geburtstag," *Zeitschrift für Musik*, CXIII (1953).

Ehrlich, Abel, German-born Israeli composer and teacher; b. Cranz, Sept. 3, 1915. He began violin lessons at the age of 6, and later was a student at the Zagreb Academy of Music (1934–38). After emigrating to Palestine, he studied composition with Rosowsky at the Jerusalem Academy of Music (1939–44); later he attended the Darmstadt summer courses in new music under Stockhausen, Nono et al. (1959, 1961, 1963, 1967). He taught composition in various Israeli academies, conservatories, and teacher training colleges; from 1966 to 1982 he was on the faculty of the Univ. of Tel Aviv. He received many awards and prizes for his works. In 1989 he was awarded the Israeli government prize. In his early works, he adhered to a Romantic line with infusions of Middle Eastern themes. Later he adopted an advanced idiom marked by a personal amalgam of traditional Jewish cantillation and serialism.

WORKS: DRAMATIC: *Immanuel Haromi*, musical spectacle (1971); *Dead Souls*, opera bouffa (1978). **ORCH.:** *A Game of Chess* for Jazz Orch. (1957); *And Though Thou Set Thy Nest Among the Stars* (1969); *Evolution* (1970); *Deliver Them That Are Drawn Unto Death* for Strings (1970); *7 Minutes* for Strings and Percussion (1971); *Divertimento* for Oboe, Clarinet, 2 Horns, and Strings (1971); *Carolus-Music* (1975); *Azamer Bishvahin*, 5 pieces for Small Orch. (1977). **CHAMBER:** 6 string quartets (1947, 1947, 1952, 1962, 1967, 1969); *Testimony* for 2 Flutes (1961); *Riv* for Violin (1962); *Secrets* for Flute (1963); 4 wind quintets (1966–70); *Music* for Cello (1970); *Improvisations with a Game in Hell* for String Trio (1970); Trio for Horn, Cello, and Percussion (1970); Trio for Violin, Flute, and Bassoon (1971); Trio for Horn, Violin, and Piano (1972); *Djerba Dance Song* for Oboe (1973); *Music* for Violin, Cello, Piano, and 2 Tape Recorders (1974); *The Beauty from Marseilles* for Harp (1977). **PIANO:** *Reincarnations* (1965); Sonata (1973); *Music* (1980); *Signature* (1982). **VOCAL:** *The Towers and the Shadows* for Narrator, Singers, and Instruments (1960); *The Writing of Hezekiah* for Soprano, Violin, Oboe, and Bassoon (1962; also for Soprano and Chamber Orch.); *Echa* for Chorus and Chamber Orch. (1970); *The Unicorn* for 12 Singers, 3 Percussionists, and 3 Oboes (1971); *Job 7, 11–16* for Baritone, Chorus, and Orch. (1971); *Ne subito . . .* for Chorus and Orch. (1971); *arp-music* for Baritone, Mime, 8 Instruments, and Electro-acoustics (1971); *For the Memory of Them is Forgotten* for Chorus and 5 Instruments (1973); *A Vision of God* for 8 Groups, each consisting of Soprano, Alto, Violin, and Viola (1975); *Let Us Proclaim*, oratorio for Soloists, Chorus, and Orch. (1982); *Giordano Bruno*, semi-oratorio (1986); *Because You Are My Kinsman* for Soprano, Cello, and Piano (1989); *Job*, oratorio (1990).

Ehrling, (Evert) Sixten, noted Swedish conductor; b. Malmö, April 3, 1918. He studied piano, organ, composition, and conducting at the Royal Academy of Music's Cons. in Stockholm. After a brief career as a concert pianist, he joined the staff of the Royal Opera in Stockholm as a rehearsal pianist, and made his conducting debut there in 1940. He then took conducting lessons with Karl Böhm in Dresden (1941) and, after the end of World War II, with Albert Wolff in Paris. In 1942 he was appointed conductor in Göteborg; in 1944 he became a conductor at the Royal Opera in Stockholm, where he served as chief conductor from 1953 to 1960. From 1963 to 1973 he was music director of the Detroit Sym. Orch.; then headed the orch. conducting class at the Juilliard School in N.Y. In 1978 he became music adviser and principal guest conductor of the Denver Sym. Orch., and from 1979 to 1985, he was its principal guest conductor; he was also artistic adviser to the San Antonio Sym. Orch. (1985–88). He was chief conductor and musical advisor of the orchs. at the Manhattan School of Music in N.Y. from 1993.

Eichheim, Henry, American composer and violinist; b. Chicago, Jan. 3, 1870; d. Montecito, near Santa Barbara, Calif., Aug. 22, 1942. He received elementary musical training from his father, Meinhard Eichheim, a cellist in the Theodore Thomas Orch.; then studied with Becker, L. Lichtenberg, and S. Jacobson at the Chicago Musical College. After a season as a violinist in the Thomas Orch. in Chicago, he was a member of the Boston Sym. Orch. (1890–1912); then devoted himself to concert work and composition. He made 5 trips to the Orient (1915, 1919, 1922, 1928, mid-1930s) and collected indigenous instruments, which he subsequently used in his orch. music. All of his works are based on oriental subjects, with their harmonic idiom derived from Debussy and Scriabin.

WORKS: DRAMATIC: *The Rivals*, ballet (1924; Chicago, Jan. 1, 1925; rev. as *Chinese Legend* for Orch., Boston, April 3, 1925); *A Burmese pwé*, incidental music (N.Y., March 16, 1926). **ORCH.:** *Oriental Impressions* or *The Story of the Bell* (1919–22; Boston, March 24, 1922; rev. of a piano piece, 1918–22); *Malay Mosaic* (1924; N.Y., March 1, 1925); *Impressions of Peking* and *Korean Sketch* for Chamber Orch. (Venice, Sept. 3, 1925); *Java* (Philadelphia, Nov. 8, 1929); *Bali* (Philadelphia, April 20, 1933). **CHAMBER:** 2 violin sonatas (1892–95; 1934); String Quartet (1895); violin music; piano pieces. **VOCAL:** *The Moon, My Shadow, and I* for Soprano and Orch. (1926); songs.

Eichhorn, Kurt (Peter), German conductor; b. Munich, Aug. 4, 1908; d. Murnau am Staffelsee, June 29, 1994. He studied with Hermann Zilcher; made his professional debut at the Bielefeld Opera in 1932. In 1941 he conducted at the Dresden State Opera. After World War II, he returned to Munich as a conductor at the Gärtnerplatz Theater; also conducted at the Bavarian State Opera. From 1967 to 1975 he served as chief conductor of the Munich Radio Orch.

Eimert, (Eugen Otto) Herbert, German musicologist and composer; b. Bad Kreuznach, April 8, 1897; d. Cologne, Dec. 15, 1972. He took courses with Abendroth, Bölsche, and Othegraven at the Cologne Cons. (1919–24) and studied musicology with Bücken, Kahl, and Kinsky at the Univ. of Cologne (Ph.D., 1931, with the diss. *Musikalische Formstrukturen im 17. und 18. Jahrhundert*; publ. in Augsburg, 1932). He worked for the Cologne Radio from 1927 until the advent of the Nazis in 1933;

after the fall of the Third Reich in 1945, he resumed his activities (until 1965); was founder-director of its electronic music studio (1951–62). He served as a prof. at the Cologne Hochschule für Musik (1965–71). He composed a number of electronic works. His important writings include *Atonale Musiklehre* (Leipzig, 1924), *Lehrbuch der Zwölftontechnik* (Wiesbaden, 1950; 6th ed., 1966), and *Grundlagen der musikalischen Reihentechnik* (Vienna, 1963). With H. Humpert, he ed. *Das Lexikon der elektronischen Musik* (Regensburg, 1973).

Einem, Gottfried von, outstanding Austrian composer; b. Bern, Switzerland, Jan. 24, 1918; d. Obern Duvenbach, Austria, July 12, 1996. He was taken to Germany as a child and pursued academic studies in Plön and Ratzeburg. In 1938 he was arrested and briefly imprisoned by the Gestapo, but that same year he became a coach at the Bayreuth Festival and at the Berlin State Opera. After studying composition with Blacher in Berlin (1941–42), he went to the Dresden State Opera in 1944 as resident composer and musical advisor. Later that year he settled in Austria, where he studied counterpoint with J.N. David. From 1963 to 1972 he taught at the Vienna Hochschule für Musik. He also served as president of the Austrian Soc. of Authors, Composers, and Music Publishers (1965–70). Einem publ. the books *Das musikalische Selbstporträt von Komponisten, Dirigenten, Sängerinnen und Sänger unserer Zeit* (Hamburg, 1963) and *Komponist und Gesellschaft* (Karlsruhe, 1967). He achieved an original mode of expression within tonal parameters which allowed him to explore a remarkable range of dynamic, rhythmic, and harmonic effects. He excelled as a composer of dramatic scores, but he also revealed himself as a distinguished composer of instrumental music.

WORKS: DRAMATIC: OPERAS: *Dantons Tod* (1944–46; Salzburg, Aug. 6, 1948); *Der Prozess* (1950–52; Salzburg, Aug. 17, 1953); *Der Zerrissene* (1961–64; Hamburg, Sept. 17, 1964); *Der Besuch der alten Dame* (1970; Vienna, May 23, 1971); *Kabale und Liebe* (1975; Vienna, Dec. 17, 1976); *Jesu Hochzeit* (Vienna, May 18, 1980); *Tulifant* (1989–90; Vienna, Oct. 30, 1990). **BALLETS:** *Prinzessin Turandot* (1942–43; Dresden, Feb. 5, 1944); *Rondo von goldenen Kalb* (1950; Hamburg, Feb. 1, 1952); *Pas de coeur* (Munich, July 22, 1952); *Glück, Tod und Traum* (1953; Alpbach, Aug. 23, 1954); *Medusa* (Vienna, Jan. 16, 1957; rev. 1971). **ORCH.:** *Capriccio* (1942–43; Berlin, March 3, 1943); *Concerto for Orchestra* (1943; Berlin, April 3, 1944); *Orchestermusik* (Vienna, June 21, 1948); *Serenade* for Double String Orch. (1949; Berlin, Jan. 30, 1950); *Meditations* (Louisville, Nov. 6, 1954); Piano Concerto (1955; Berlin, Oct. 6, 1956); *Wandlungen* (1956); *Symphonic Scenes* (1956; Boston, Oct. 11, 1957); *Ballade* (1957; Cleveland, March 20, 1958); *Tanz-Rondo* (Munich, Nov. 13, 1959); 4 syms.: No. 1, *Philadelphia Symphony* (1960; Vienna, Nov. 11, 1961), No. 2, *Wiener Symphonie* (1976; Minneapolis, Nov. 16, 1977), No. 3, *Münchner Sinfonie* (1985), and No. 4 (1988); *Nachstück* (1960; Kassel, Nov. 16, 1962); Violin Concerto (1966–67; Vienna, May 31, 1970); *Hexameron* (1969; Los Angeles, Feb. 19, 1970); *Bruckner Dialog* (1971; Linz, March 23, 1974); *Arietten* for Piano and Orch. (1977; Berlin, Feb. 20, 1978); *Ludi Leopoldini*, variations on a theme of Emperor Leopold I (Berlin, Oct. 12, 1980); Organ Concerto (1981; Linz, Feb. 1, 1983); *Fraktale*, "Concerto Philharmonico" for the 150th anniversary of the Vienna Phil. (Vienna, Oct. 18, 1992). **CHAMBER:** Violin Sonata (1947); 5 string quartets (1975; 1977; 1980; 1981; 1989–91); Sonata for Solo Violin (1975); Wind Quintet (1976); Sonata for Solo Viola (1980); *Steinbeis Serenade*, octet (1981); Sonata for Solo Double Bass (1982); String Trio (1985); Cello Sonata (1987); *Sonata enigmatica* for Double Bass (1988); Flute Quartet (1988); Trio for Violin, Clarinet, and Piano (1992); *Jeux d'amour* for Horn and Piano (1993); *Karl-Hartwig Kaltners Malerei* for 4 Brass Instruments (1993). **VOCAL:** *Hymnus* for Alto, Chorus, and Orch. (1949; Vienna, March 31, 1951); *Das Stundenlied* for Chorus and Orch. (1958; Hamburg, March 1, 1959); *Von der Lieb* for Soprano or Tenor and Orch. (Vienna, June 18, 1961); *Kammergesänge* for Mezzo-soprano, Baritone, and Small Orch. (1965); *Geistliche Sonata* for Soprano, Trumpet, and Organ (1971–73); *Rosa mystica* for Baritone and Orch. (1972; Vienna, June 4, 1973); *An die Machgebornen* for Alto, Baritone, Chorus, and Orch. (1973–75; N.Y., Oct. 24, 1975); *Gute Ratschläge*, cantata for Soloists, Chorus, and Guitar (1982); *Missa Claravallensis* for Chorus, Winds, and Percussion (1987–88); *Alchemistenspiegel* for Baritone and Orch. (Bregenz, July 30, 1990); song cycles; solo songs.

BIBL.: D. Hartmann, *G. v. E.* (Vienna, 1967); H. Hopf and B. Sonntag, eds., *G. v. E.: Ein Komponist unseres Jahrhunderts* (Münster, 1989); K. Lezak, *Das Opernschaffen G.v. E.s.* (Vienna, 1990).

Einstein, Alfred, eminent German-born American musicologist; b. Munich, Dec. 30, 1880; d. El Cerrito, Calif., Feb. 13, 1952. He studied law before pursuing training in composition with Beer-Walbrunn at the Munich Akademie der Tonkunst and in musicology with Sandberger at the Univ. of Munich (Ph.D., 1903, with the diss. *Zur deutschen Literatur für Viola da Gamba in 16. und 17. Jahrhundert*; publ. in Leipzig, 1905). He greatly distinguished himself as the 1st ed. of the *Zeitschrift für Musikwissenschaft* (1918–33); he also was the music critic of the *Münchner Post* (until 1927) and of the *Berliner Tageblatt* (1927–33). After Hitler came to power in 1933, he went to England. Following an Italian sojourn, he emigrated to the U.S. in 1939 and became a naturalized American citizen in 1945. From 1939 to 1950 he was prof. of music history at Smith College in Northampton, Mass. Einstein was an outstanding music scholar, ed., and critic. Although some of his writings have been superseded by later scholarship, they remain brilliant in style, vivid and richly metaphorical, and capable of conveying to the reader an intimate understanding of music of different eras. His study *The Italian Madrigal* (1949) was a particularly notable achievement. Einstein was the ed. of the rev. editions of Riemann's *Musik Lexikon* (Berlin, 9th ed., 1919; 10th ed., 1922; 11th ed., aug., 1929); he also ed. Riemann's *Handbuch der Musikgeschichte* (Leipzig, 2nd ed., rev., 1929) and prepared an augmented German tr. of Eaglefield-Hull's *Dictionary of Modern Music* (1924) as *Das neue Musiklexikon* (Berlin, 1926). His rev. of Köchel's *Chronologisch-thematisches Verzeichnis sämtlicher Tonwerke Wolfgang Amade Mozarts* (Leipzig, 3rd ed., 1937; reprint, with supplement, Ann Arbor, 1947) was valuable in its day. He contributed many scholarly articles to learned journals, Jahrbücher, Festschrifte et al. He likewise ed. works by Marenzio, Gluck, Antico, and Mozart, as well as *The Golden Age of the Madrigal* (N.Y., 1942).

WRITINGS: *Geschichte der Musik* (Leipzig, 1917; 6th ed., rev., 1953; Eng. tr., 1936; 5th ed., 1948, as *A Short History of Music*); *Heinrich Schütz* (Kassel, 1928); *Gluck* (London, 1936; Ger. ed., 1954); *Greatness in Music* (N.Y., 1941; Ger. ed., 1951, as *Grösse in der Musik*); *Mozart: His Character, His Work* (N.Y., 1945; 4th ed., 1959; Ger. ed., 1947; 2nd ed., rev., 1953); *Music in the Romantic Era* (N.Y., 1947; 2nd ed., 1949; Ger. ed., 1950, as *Die Romantik in der Musik*); *The Italian Madrigal* (Princeton, N.J., 1949); *Schubert: A Musical Portrait* (N.Y., 1951; Ger. ed., 1952); P. Lang, ed., *Essays on Music* (N.Y., 1956; 2nd ed., rev., 1958); *Von Schütz bis Hindemith* (Zürich and Stuttgart, 1957); *Nationale und Universale Musik* (Zürich and Stuttgart, 1958); C. Dower, ed., *Alfred Einstein on Music: Selected Music Criticisms* (N.Y. 1991).

BIBL.: O. Kinkeldey, "To A. E.," *Notes* (Dec. 1950).

Eiríksdóttir, Karólína, Icelandic composer; b. Reykjavík, Jan. 10, 1951. She studied composition with Thorkell Sigurbjornsson at the Reykjavík College of Music and with George Wilson and William Albright at the Univ. of Mich. (M.M., 1978); taught at the Kopavogur School of Music and the Reykjavík College of Music. In 1985 she received an Icelandic Artists' Grant. Her music is stark and austere, laden with northern Romanticism.

WORKS: DRAMATIC: *Someone I Have Seen*, chamber opera (1988). **ORCH.:** *Notes* (1978; Ann Arbor, Mich., March 1, 1979);

Sónans (Reykjavík, Oct. 15, 1981); *5 Pieces* for Chamber Orch. (Reykjavík, April 30, 1983); Sinfonietta (Reykjavík, Nov. 3, 1985); *Rhapsody* for Chamber Orch. (1990); *Klifur* (1991). **CHAMBER:** *IVP* for Flute, Violin, and Cello (1977); *Nabulations* for 2 Flutes, 2 Trumpets, 2 Trombones, 2 Percussion, Violin, and Double Bass (1978); *Fragments* for Flute, Oboe, Clarinet, Horn, Harp, Percussion, Violin, Viola, and Cello (1979); *In vultus solis* for Violin (1980); *Ylir* for Bassoon, Horn, Trumpet, Trombone, 2 Violins, Viola, Cello, and Harpsichord (1981); *The Blue Maid* for Clarinet, Violin, and Piano (1983); *6 Movements* for String Quartet (1983); Trio for Violin, Cello, and Piano (1987); *Hringhenda* for Clarinet (1989); *Whence This Calm?* for Guitar (1990); *Mutanza* for Wind Quintet and Harpsichord (1991); *Spring Verse* for Harpsichord (1991). **PIANO:** *A Kind of Rondo* (1984); *Finger Travels* (1986); *Rhapsody* (1986). **VOCAL:** *6 Poems from the Japanese* for Mezzo-soprano, Flute, and Cello (1977); *Some Days* for Soprano, Flute, Clarinet, Cello, and Piano (1982; also for Soprano, Flute, Clarinet, Cello, Guitar, and Harpsichord, 1991); *2 Miniatures* for Chorus (1983); *Land Possessed by Poems* for Baritone and Piano (1987); *Ungadei* for Chorus (1991); *Winter* for Chorus (1991).

Eisenberg, Maurice, outstanding German-born American cellist and pedagogue; b. Königsberg, Feb. 24, 1900; d. while teaching a cello class at the Juilliard School of Music in N.Y., Dec. 13, 1972. He was taken to the U.S. as a child; studied violin; then, at the age of 12, took up the cello. He played as a youth in café orchs., and studied at the Peabody Cons. of Music in Baltimore. He was a cellist of the Philadelphia Orch. (1917–19); then joined the N.Y. Sym. Orch. He went to Europe in 1927 and studied in Berlin with Hugo Becker; in Leipzig with Julius Klengel; in Paris with Alexanian, where he also took lessons in harmony and counterpoint with Boulanger; and in Spain with Casals. He then taught at the École Normale de Musique in Paris (1929–39); then appeared with major sym. orchs. and taught at various colleges. With M. Stanfield, he publ. *Cello Playing of Today* (1957).

Eisler, Hanns (Johannes), remarkable German composer; b. Leipzig, July 6, 1898; d. Berlin, Sept. 6, 1962. He began to study music on his own while still a youth, then studied with Weigl at the New Vienna Cons. and later privately with Schoenberg (1919–23); he also worked with Webern. In 1924 he won the Vienna Arts Prize. He went to Berlin in 1925 and taught at the Klindworth-Scharwenka Cons. In 1926 he joined the German Communist Party; after the Nazis came to power in 1933, he left Germany; made visits to the U.S. and was active in Austria, France, England, and other European countries. He taught at the New School for Social Research in N.Y. (1935–36; 1937–42) and at the Univ. of Calif. in Los Angeles (1942–48); then left the U.S. under the terms of "voluntary deportation" on account of his Communist sympathies. In 1949 he settled in East Berlin and became a prof. at the Hochschule für Musik and a member of the German Academy of the Arts. Under Schoenberg's influence, Eisler adopted the 12-tone method of composition for most of his symphonic works. However, he demonstrated a notable capacity for writing music in an accessible style. His long association with Bertolt Brecht resulted in several fine scores for the theater; he also worked with Charlie Chaplin in Hollywood (1942–47). His songs and choral works became popular in East Germany. He composed the music for the East German national anthem, *Auferstanden aus Ruinen*, which was adopted in 1949. His writings include *Composing for the Films* (with T. Adorno; N.Y., 1947), *Reden und Aufsätze* (Berlin, 1959), and *Materialen zu einer Dialektik der Musik* (Berlin, 1973). G. Mayer ed. his *Musik und Politik* (2 vols., Berlin, 1973 and Leipzig, 1982).

WORKS: DRAMATIC: *Johannes Faustus*, opera (Berlin, March 11, 1953); some 38 scores of incidental music, to works by Brecht (*Rote Revue*, 1932; *Die Rundköpfe und die Spitzköpfe*, 1934–36; *Furcht und Elend des dritten Reiches*, 1945; *Galileo Galilei*, 1947; *Tage der Kommune*, 1950; *Die Gesichte der Simone Machard*, 1957; *Schweyk im zweiten Weltkrieg*, 1943–59), by Feuchtwanger (*Kalkutta, 4.Mai*, 1928), by Ernst Toller (*Feuer aus den Kesseln*, 1934; *Peace on Earth*, 1934), by Ben Jonson (*Volpone*, 1953), by Aristophanes (*Lysistrata*, 1954), by Shakespeare (*Hamlet*, 1954), by Schiller (*Wilhelm Tell*, 1961), etc.; some 42 film scores (*None but the Lonely Heart*, 1944; *Woman on the Beach*, 1947; *Der Rat der Götter*, 1950; *Fidelio*, 1956; *The Witches of Salem*, 1957; *Trübe Wasser*, 1959; etc.). **CHAMBER:** 3 piano sonatas (1923, 1924, 1943); *Divertimento* for Wind Quintet (1923); Duo for Violin and Cello (1924); Piano Sonatine (1934); *Präludium und Fuge über BACH* for String Trio (1934); Sonata for Flute, Oboe, and Harp (1935); Violin Sonata (1937); String Quartet (1938); 2 nonets (1939, 1941); 2 septets (1940, 1947); *14 Arten, den Regen zu beschreiben* for Flute, Clarinet, Violin, Cello, and Piano (1940); piano albums for children, etc. **VOCAL: CHORUS AND ORCH.:** *Tempe der Zeit*, cantata (1929); *Die Massnahme* (1930); *Die Mutter* (1931); *Kalifornische Ballade*, cantata (1934; based on a radio score); *Deutsche Sinfonie* for Soloists, 2 Speakers, Chorus, and Orch. (Paris, June 25, 1937); *Lenin*, Requiem (1936–37); *Mitte des Jahrhunderts*, cantata (1950); *Bilder aus der "Kriegsfibel"* (1957). **VOICE AND ORCH.:** *Glückliche Fahrt* for Soprano and Orch. (1946); *Rhapsodie* for Soprano and Orch. (1949); *Die Teppichweber von Kujan-Bulak*, cantata for Soprano and Orch. (1957); *Es lächelt der See* for Soprano, Tenor, and Orch. (1961); *Ernste Gesänge*, 7 songs for Baritone and Strings (1936–62); also works for Voice and Smaller Ensembles, including 9 works entitled *Kammerkantate* (1937); many songs with piano. **OTHER:** 6 orch. suites drawn from films (1930–33); other orch. works drawn from films and stage pieces, including 5 *Orchesterstücke* (1938) and *Kammersinfonie* (1940).

A collected ed. of his compositions and writings was undertaken by the German Academy of the Arts in East Berlin in association with the Hanns Eisler Archive.

BIBL.: H. Brockhaus, *H. E.* (Leipzig, 1961); N. Notowicz, *H. E.: Quellennachweise* (Leipzig, 1966); H. Bunge, *Fragen Sie mehr über Brecht: H. E. im Gespräch* (Munich, 1970); E. Klemm, *H. E.: Für Sie porträtiert* (Leipzig, 1973); A. Betz, *H. E.: Musik einer Zeit* (Munich, 1976; Eng. tr., 1982, as *H. E.: Political Musician*); M. Grabs, *H. E.: Kompositionen, Schriften, Literatur: Ein Handbuch* (Leipzig, 1984); D. Blake, *H. E.: A Miscellany* (London, 1995).

Eisler, Paul, Austrian pianist, conductor, and composer; b. Vienna, Sept. 9, 1875; d. N.Y., Oct. 16, 1951. He was a pupil of Bruckner at the Vienna Cons. He conducted in Riga, Vienna, and at the Metropolitan Opera in N.Y. (1916–17; 1920–29); also made numerous tours as an accompanist to Caruso, Ysaÿe, and others. He composed several operettas, including *Spring Brides*, *The Sentinel*, *The Little Missus*, and *In the Year 1814*.

Eisma, Will (Leendert), Dutch violinist and composer; b. Sungailiat, Dutch East Indies, May 13, 1929. He received violin lessons from his father, and then studied violin and counterpoint at the Rotterdam Cons. (1948–53); he also had private composition lessons with Kees van Baaren, and later studied violin with André Gertler and composition with Goffredo Petrassi at the Accademia di Santa Cecilia in Rome (1959–61); he also took a course in electronic music in Utrecht. Eisma was a violinist in the Rotterdam Phil. (1953–59), the Società Corelli Chamber Orch. (1960–61), and the Hilversum Radio Chamber Orch. (1961–89); he also organized his own electronic music studio in 1973. His output is in an uncompromisingly modern idiom.

WORKS: ORCH.: 3 concertos (1958, 1959, 1960); Concerto for 2 Violins and Orch. (1961); *Taurus* (1963); *Volumina* (1964); *Diaphora* (1964); *Vanbridge Concerto* for Horn and Orch. (1970); *Little Lane*, oboe concerto (1973); *Le Choix du costume est libre* for String Trio and Chamber Orch. (1974); *Metselwerk* for Percussion and Orch. (1979); *Indian Summer*, English horn concerto (1981); *Suara-suara pada waktu fajar* (Voices at Daybreak) for Gamelan-Slendro and Orch. (1985); *Silver Plated*

Bronze for Double Bass and Orch. (1986); *Passo del diavolo* (1988; rev. 1990). **CHAMBER:** Septet (1959); String Quintet (1961); *Archipel* for String Quartet (1964); *Fontemara* for Wind Quintet (1965); *La Sonorité suspendue* for String Trio (1970); *Concert à vapeur* for Violin, Tape, and Synthesizer (1974); *Mandi* for Brass Ensemble (1981); *Adventures of a Shawl* for 9 Instruments (1984); *Kalos* for String Quartet and Piano (1987). **VOCAL:** *Orchestral Music with Voice* for Soloists, Chorus, and Orch. (1969); *Le Gibet* for Baritone, 7 Instruments, and Live Electronics (1971); *Le Cheval mort* for Mezzo-soprano, Bass Clarinet, Piano, Percussion, 2 Synthesizers, and Tape (1976); *Du Dehors—Du Dedans* for Mezzo-soprano and Orch. (1983).

Ek, (Fritz) Gunnar (Rudolf), Swedish cellist, organist, and composer; b. Åsarum, June 21, 1900; d. Lund, June 21, 1981. After training in Lund, he studied with Gustaf Hägg and Otto Olsson (cello and organ) and Ernst Ellberg (composition) at the Stockholm Cons. (1920–26). He was a cellist in the orch. of the Swedish film industry (1928–37); after serving as organist in Ostra Eneby, near Norrköping (1938–42), he was organist and director of music at All Saint's Church in Lund; he also was cellist in the Skåne Quartet. His output reveals a sure hand at contrapuntal writing.

WORKS: ORCH.: 3 syms.: No. 1 (1922–24; rev. 1940), No. 2 (1928–30), and No. 3 (1931–32); *Svensk fantasi* (1935); *Fantasi* for Violin and Orch. (1936); *Koralsvit* (1936); *Fantasy and Fugue* for Strings (1939–40; rev., 1963, as *Fantasy, Fugue, and Coda*); Concert Overture (1940); Piano Concerto (1944); *Dorisk Suite* for Strings and 5 Winds (1966; rev. 1968–69); *Variations on a Chorale Theme* for Strings (1969); Concertino for Strings (1971). **CHAMBER:** Wind Octet (1970); Organ Suite (1966); organ pieces. **VOCAL:** *Doomsday Cantata* (1946); *Dig vare lov och pris, O Krist,* choral fantasy with organ and strings (1950; Malmö, Dec. 13, 1964); songs.

Ekier, Jan (Stanislaw), Polish pianist, teacher, editor, and composer; b. Kraków, Aug. 29, 1913. After studies at the Univ. of Kraków, he received instruction in piano from Drzewiecki and in composition from Sikorski at the Warsaw Cons. (1934–39). He toured as a pianist, and also was a prof. of piano at the Warsaw Cons. (from 1955). He served as ed. of the "National Edition" of Chopin's works. Among his works were orch. pieces, chamber music, and vocal works.

Eklund, Hans, prominent Swedish composer and teacher; b. Sandviken, July 1, 1927. He studied at the Stockholm Musikhogskolan with Åke Uddén and Lars-Erik Larsson (1947–52) and with Ernst Pepping in Berlin (1954) before completing his training in Rome (1957). He was prof. of harmony and counterpoint at the Stockholm Musikhögskolan (from 1964). In 1975 he was elected a member of the Royal Swedish Academy of Music; in 1985 he was awarded the degree of Litteris et Artibus from the King of Sweden. Edlund's large output is notable for its imaginative handling of traditional forms.

WORKS: RADIO OPERA: *Moder Svea* (Mother Svea; Swedish Radio, Oct. 7, 1972). **ORCH.:** *Variations* for Strings (1952); *Symphonic Dances* (1954); *Musica da camera*: No. 1 for Cello and Chamber Orch. (1955), No. 2, *Art Tatum in Memoriam,* for Trumpet, Piano, Percussion, and Strings (1956), No. 3 for Violin and Chamber Orch. (1957), No. 4 for Piano and Orch. (1959), No. 5, *Fantasia,* for Cello and Strings (1970), and No. 6 for Oboe and Chamber Orch. (1970); 10 syms.: No. 1, *Sinfonia seria* (1958), No. 2, *Sinfonia breve* (1964), No. 3, *Sinfonia rustica* (1967–68), No. 4, *Hjalmar Branting in Memoriam,* for Narrator and Orch. (1973–74), No. 5, *Quadri* (1978), No. 6, *Sinfonia senza speranza* (1983), No. 7, *La Serenata* (1984), No. 8, *Sinfonia grave* (1985), No. 9, *Sinfonia introvertita* (1992–93), and No. 10, *sine nomine* (1994); *Introduzione-Versioni e Finale* for Strings (1962–63); *Facce* (1964); *Toccata* (1966); *Interludio* (1967); *Primavera* for Strings (1967); *Pezzo elegiaco* for Cello, Percussion, and Strings (1969); *Introduction and Allegro* for Harpsichord and Strings (1972); Concerto for Trombone, Winds, and Percussion (1972); *Variazioni pastorali* for Strings (1974); Chamber Concerto for Violin and Strings (1977); Horn Concerto (1979); Concerto for Clarinet and Strings (1980); Concerto for Tuba and Brass Orch. (1980); Concerto for Clarinet, Cello, and Orch. (1983); *Fantasie breve* (1986); *Divertimento* (1986); *L'estate* for Strings (1986); *Concerto Grosso* for String Quartet and String Orch. (1987); *Due pezzi* (1988); *Mesto per archi* (1989); *Apertura* (1991). **CHAMBER:** 4 string quartets (withdrawn, 1954, 1960, 1964); 2 sonatas for Solo Violin (1956, 1982); *Improvisata* for Wind Quintet (1958); Piano Trio (1963); *4 Temperamenti* for 4 Clarinets (1963); *Sommarparafras* for Wind Quintet (1968); *Serenade* for Mixed Quintet (1978); *Omaggio à San Michele* for 4 Saxophones (1981); *5 Pieces* for Clarinet (1983), Oboe (1983), Bassoon (1983), and Double Bass (1984); *Serenade* for 10 Brass Instruments (1986); *Serenata* for Flute and Piano (1990); piano pieces; organ music. **VOCAL:** *Den fula ankungen* for Soloists, Children's Chorus, and Orch. (1976); *Requiem* for 2 Soloists, Chorus, and Orch. (1978; Stockholm, Nov. 24, 1979); *Homofoni* for Chorus (1987); *3 Sea Poems* for Chorus (1988).

Ekman, Karl, Finnish pianist and conductor; b. Kaarina, near Åbo, Dec. 18, 1869; d. Helsinki, Feb. 4, 1947. He studied in Helsinki (1889–92); from 1892 to 1895 he was a pupil of H. Barth in Berlin and A. Grünfeld in Vienna. In 1895 he became a piano teacher at the Helsinki Cons., and from 1907 to 1911 he was director there; from 1912 to 1920 he was conductor of the orch. at Åbo. He arranged Swedish and Finnish folk songs, and ed. a piano method; publ. a biography of Sibelius (Stockholm, 1935; Eng. tr., 1936). His wife, Ida (b. Helsinki, April 22, 1875; d. there, April 14, 1942), was a concert singer; she studied in Helsinki, Paris, and Veinna; distinguished herself by her performances of Sibelius's songs.

El-Dabh, Halim (Abdul Messieh), Egyptian-born American composer; b. Cairo, March 4, 1921. He studied piano and Western music at the Sulcz Cons. in Cairo (1941–44), then went to the U.S. in 1950 on a Fulbright fellowship, studying with Copland and Irving Fine at the Berkshire Music Center at Tanglewood and taking graduate degrees from the New England Cons. of Music and Brandeis Univ. In 1961 he became a naturalized American citizen. He taught at Haile Selassie Univ. in Ethiopia (1962–64), Howard Univ. (1966–69), and Kent State Univ. (from 1969), where he later also was co-director of its Center for the Study of World Musics (from 1979). His compositions reveal Afro-Arab influences, especially in their rhythmic structures and their incorporation of unusual percussive devices. He publ. *The Derabucca: Hand Techniques in the Art of Drumming* (1965).

WORKS: DRAMATIC: *Clytemnestra,* epic dance drama (for Martha Graham; 1958); *The Egyptian Series: Lament of the Pharaohs, Pyramid Rock to the Sky, Gloria Aton,* and *Prayer to the Sphinx* for Solo Voices, Chorus, and Orch. (1960); *The Islamic Series: Allahu Akbar, Al-khaheera, Ya Leiyly, Saladin and the Citadel,* and *The Nile* for Voices ad libitum and Orch. (1960); *Theodora in Byzantium* (1965); *Black Epic,* opera-pageant (1968); *Opera Flies* (1971); *Ptahmose and the Magic Spell,* opera trilogy: *The Osiris Ritual, Aton, the Ankh, and the World,* and *The 12 Hours Trip* (1972–73); *Drink of Eternity,* opera-pageant (1981). **ORCH.:** 3 syms. (1950, 1952, 1956); Concerto for Darabukka or Timpani and Strings (1954); *Fantasia-Tahmeel* for Darabukka or Timpani and Strings (1954); *Bacchanalia* (1958); *Tahmeela* for Flute and Chamber Orch. (1958–59); *Nomadic Waves* for Double Wind Orch. and Percussion; *Unity at the Cross Road*; Concerto for Darabukka, Clarinet, and Strings (1981); *Rhapsodia egyptia-brasileira* (1985). **OTHER:** Chamber music; piano pieces; choruses.

Elder, Mark (Philip), prominent English conductor; b. Hexham, June 2, 1947. He studied in Bryanston and played bassoon in the National Youth Orch. before pursuing his education at the Univ. of Cambridge (B.A., M.A.). In 1969–70 he was on the music staff of the Wexford Festival. In 1970 he became an assistant conductor at the Glyndebourne Festival, serving as chorus master until 1972. From 1972 to 1974 he was a staff conductor at the Australian Opera in Sydney. In 1974 he became a conductor at the English National Opera in London. He made his debut at London's Covent Garden in 1976 conducting *Rigoletto*. In 1977 he became assoc. conductor at the English National Opera, and subsequently served as its music director from 1979 to 1993. During his tenure there, Elder conducted the British premieres of several operas by masters of the past as well as the world premieres of operas by contemporary composers. From 1980 to 1983 he was principal guest conductor of the London Mozart Players, and, from 1982 to 1985, of the BBC Sym. Orch. in London. In 1981 he made his first appearance at the Bayreuth Festival conducting *Die Meistersinger von Nürnberg*. He made his U.S. debut as a guest conductor of the Chicago Sym. Orch. in 1983. In 1988 he conducted *Le Nozze di Figaro* at the Metropolitan Opera in N.Y. From 1989 to 1994 he was music director of the Rochester (N.Y.) Phil. In 1992 he became principal guest conductor of the City of Birmingham Sym. Orch. In 1989 he was made a Commander of the Order of the British Empire.

Elgar, Sir Edward (William), great English composer; b. Broadheath, near Worcester, June 2, 1857; d. Worcester, Feb. 23, 1934. He received his earliest music education from his father, who owned a music shop and was organist for the St. George's Roman Catholic Church in Worcester; he also took violin lessons from a local musician. He rapidly acquired the fundamentals of theory and served as arranger with the Worcester Glee Club, becoming its conductor at the age of 22; simultaneously he accepted a rather unusual position for a young aspiring musician with the County of Worcester Lunatic Asylum at Powick, where he was for several years in charge of the institution's concert band; he was also engaged in various other musical affairs. In 1885 he succeeded his father as organist at St. George's. He married in 1889 and moved to Malvern, where he stayed from 1891 to 1904. During these years, he conducted the Worcestershire Phil. (1898–1904); in 1905 he accepted the position of Peyton Prof. of Music at the Univ. of Birmingham, and in 1911–12 served as conductor of the London Sym. Orch. He then settled in Hampstead. His wife died in 1920, at which time he returned to Worcester.

Elgar's first signal success was with the concert overture *Froissart* (Worcester, Sept. 9, 1890). His cantata *The Black Knight* was produced at the Worcester Festival (April 18, 1893) and was also heard in London at the Crystal Palace (Oct. 23, 1897); the production of his cantata *Scenes from the Saga of King Olaf* at the North Staffordshire Music Festival (Oct. 30, 1896) attracted considerable attention; he gained further recognition with his *Imperial March* (1897), composed for the Diamond Jubilee of Queen Victoria; from then on, Elgar's name became familiar to the musical public. There followed the cantata *Caractacus* (Leeds Festival, Oct. 5, 1898) and Elgar's great masterpiece, the oratorio *The Dream of Gerontius* (Birmingham Festival, Oct. 14, 1900). He began to give more and more attention to orch. music. On June 19, 1899, Hans Richter presented the first performance of Elgar's *Variations on an Original Theme* (generally known as the *Enigma Variations*) in London. This work consists of 14 sections, each marked by initials of fancied names of Elgar's friends; in later years, Elgar issued cryptic hints as to the identities of these persons, which were finally revealed. He also stated that the theme itself was a counterpoint to a familiar tune, but the concealed subject was never discovered; various guesses were advanced in the musical press from time to time; a contest for the most plausible answer to the riddle was launched in America by the *Saturday Review* (1953), with dubious results. The success of the *Enigma Variations* was followed (1901–30) by the production of Elgar's *Pomp and Circumstance* marches, the first of which became his most famous piece through a setting to words by Arthur Christopher Benson, used by Elgar in the *Coronation Ode* (1902) as *Land of Hope and Glory*; another successful orch. work was the *Cockaigne Overture* (London, June 20, 1901). Elgar's 2 syms., written between 1903 and 1910, became staples in the English orch. repertoire. His Violin Concerto, first performed by Fritz Kreisler (London, Nov. 10, 1910), won notable success; there was also a remarkable Cello Concerto (London, Oct. 26, 1919, Felix Salmond soloist, composer conducting).

The emergence of Elgar as a major composer about 1900 was all the more remarkable since he had no formal academic training. Yet he developed a masterly technique of instrumental and vocal writing. His style of composition may be described as functional Romanticism; his harmonic procedures remain firmly within the 19th-century tradition; the formal element is always strong, and the thematic development logical and precise. Elgar had a melodic gift, which asserted itself in his earliest works, such as the popular *Salut d'amour*; his oratorios, particularly *The Apostles*, were the product of his fervent religious faith (he was a Roman Catholic). He avoided archaic usages of Gregorian chant; rather, he presented the sacred subjects in a communicative style of secular drama. Elgar was the recipient of many honors. He was knighted in 1904. He received honorary degrees of Mus.Doc. from Cambridge (1900), Oxford (1905), and Aberdeen (1906); also an LL.D. from Leeds (1904). During his first visit to the U.S., in 1905, he received a D.Mus. degree from Yale Univ.; in 1907 he was granted the same degree from the Univ. of Western Pa. (now the Univ. of Pittsburgh). He received the Order of Merit in 1911; was made a Knight Commander of the Royal Victorian Order in 1928 and a baronet in 1931; was appointed Master of the King's Musick in 1924. He was not a proficient conductor, but appeared on various occasions with orchs. in his own works; during the 3rd of his 4 visits to the U.S. (1905, 1906, 1907, 1911), he conducted his oratorio *The Apostles* (N.Y., 1907); also led the mass chorus at the opening of the British Empire Exhibition in 1924. His link with America was secured when the hymnlike section from his first *Pomp and Circumstance* march became a popular recession march for American high school graduation exercises.

WORKS: DRAMATIC: OPERA: *The Spanish Lady*, op. 89 (unfinished; sketches date from 1878; 15 excerpts orchestrated by Percy M. Young; BBC, London, Dec. 4, 1969). **INCIDENTAL MUSIC TO:** *Grania and Diarmid*, op. 42 (Yeats and Moore; Dublin, Oct. 1901); *The Starlight Express*, op. 78 (Blackwood and Pearn; London, Dec. 29, 1915); *King Arthur* (Binyon; London, March 12, 1923); *Beau Brummel* (Matthews; Birmingham, Nov. 5, 1928, composer conducting). **MASQUE:** *The Crown of India*, op. 66 (1902–12; London, March 11, 1912; as a suite for Orch., Hereford Festival, Sept. 11, 1912, composer conducting). **BALLET:** *The Sanguine Fan*, op. 81 (London, March 20, 1917). **ORCH.:** *Introductory Overture for Christy Minstrels* (Worcester, June 12, 1878, composer conducting); *Minuet-grazioso* (Worcester, Jan. 23, 1879); Suite in D major for Small Orch. (1882; 1st complete perf., Birmingham, March 1, 1888; rev. as *3 Characteristic Pieces*, op. 10 [1899]: No. 1, *Mazurka*, No. 2, *Serenade mauresque*, and No. 3, *Contrasts: The Gavotte A.D. 1700 and 1900*); *Sevillana*, op. 7 (Worcester, May 1, 1884; rev. 1889); *Salut d'amour (Liebesgruss)*, op. 12 (1888; London, Nov. 11, 1889); *Froissart*, concert overture, op. 19 (Worcester, Sept. 9, 1890, composer conducting); *Serenade* in E minor for Strings, op. 20 (1892; 1st complete perf., Antwerp, July 23, 1896); *Sursum corda* for Strings, Brass, and Organ, op. 11 (Worcester, April 9, 1894); *Minuet* for Small Orch., op. 21 (orig. for Piano, 1897; orchestrated 1899; New Brighton, July 16, 1899); *Chanson de matin*, op. 15, No. 1, and *Chanson de nuit*, op. 15, No. 2 (orig. for Violin and Piano, c.1889–90; orchestrated 1901; London, Sept. 14, 1901); *Imperial March*, op. 32 (London, April 19, 1897, A. Manns conducting; for Queen Victoria's Diamond Jubilee); *Variations on an Original Theme (Enigma Variations)*, op. 36 (1898–99; London, June 19, 1899, Richter conducting); *Serenade lyrique* for Small Orch. (London, Nov. 27, 1900); *Pomp and Circumstance*, 5 marches for Sym. Orch., op. 39: No. 1, in D major (1901), No. 2, in A minor (1901; Liverpool, Oct. 19, 1901, A. Rodewald conducting), No. 3, in C minor (1904; London, March 8, 1905, composer conducting), No. 4, in G major (London, Aug. 24, 1907, H. Wood conducting), and No.

5, in C major (London, Sept. 20, 1930, H. Wood conducting); *Cockaigne (In London Town)*, concert overture, op. 40 (London, June 20, 1901, composer conducting); *Dream Children*, 2 pieces for Small Orch., op. 43 (London, Sept. 4, 1902; also for Piano); *In the South (Alassio)*, concert overture, op. 50 (1903–04; London, March 16, 1904, composer conducting); *Introduction and Allegro* for String Quartet and String Orch., op. 47 (1904–05; London, March 8, 1905, composer conducting); *The Wand of Youth*, 2 suites for Orch., comprising the last revision of his music for a children's play composed c.1867: Suite No. 1, op. 1A (London, Dec. 14, 1907, H. Wood conducting) and Suite No. 2, op. 1B (Worcester, Sept. 9, 1908, composer conducting); Sym. No. 1, in A-flat major, op. 55 (1907–08; Manchester, Dec. 3, 1908, Richter conducting); *Elegy* for Strings, op. 58 (London, July 13, 1909); Concerto in B minor for Violin and Orch., op. 61 (1909–10; London, Nov. 10, 1910, Fritz Kreisler soloist, composer conducting); *Romance* for Bassoon and Orch., op. 62 (1910; Herefordshire Orch. Soc., Feb. 16, 1911); Sym. No. 2, in E-flat major, op. 63 (1903–10; London, May 24, 1911, composer conducting); *Coronation March*, op. 65 (Westminster Abbey, London, June 22, 1911; for the coronation of King George V); Carissima for Small Orch. (1913; 1st public perf., London, Feb. 15, 1914); *Falstaff*, symphonic study in C minor with 2 interludes, op. 68 (1902–13; Leeds Festival, Oct. 1, 1913, composer conducting); *Sospiri* for Strings, Harp, and Organ, op. 70 (London, Aug. 15, 1914, H. Wood conducting); *Carillon*, recitation with Orch., op. 75 (London, Dec. 7, 1914, composer conducting); *Polonia*, symphonic prelude, op. 76 (London, July 6, 1915, composer conducting); *Une Voix dans le desert*, recitation with Orch., op. 77 (1915; London, Jan. 29, 1916, composer conducting); *Le Drapeau belge*, recitation with Orch., op. 79 (London, April 14, 1917, H. Harty conducting); Concerto in E minor for Cello and Orch., op. 85 (London, Oct. 26, 1919, Felix Salmond soloist, composer conducting; later arranged as a viola concerto by Lionel Tertis; Hereford Festival, Sept. 6, 1933, Tertis soloist, composer conducting); *Empire March* (Wembley, April 23, 1924, composer conducting); *Severn Suite* for Brass Band, op. 87 (London, Sept. 27, 1930; also for Orch., 1932; 1st public perf., Worcester, Sept. 7, 1932, composer conducting); *Nursery Suite* (London, Aug. 20, 1931, composer conducting; also arranged as a ballet, *Ninette de Valois*, by C. Lambert; London, March 21, 1932, Lambert conducting); *Mina* for Small Orch. (1933). @EN1: **CHAMBER:** *Promenades* for Wind Quintet (1878); *Romance* for Violin and Piano, op. 1 (1878; Worcester, Oct. 20, 1885); *Harmony Music* for Wind Quintet (1879); String Quartet, op. 8 (1887; MS destroyed); Violin Sonata, op. 9 (1887; MS destroyed); *Allegretto on GEDGE* for Violin and Piano (1888); *Liebesahnung* for Violin and Piano (1889); *La Capricieuse* for Violin and Piano, op. 17 (1891); *Very Melodious Exercises in the 1st Position* for Violin, op. 22 (1892); *Études caractéristiques pour violon seul*, op. 24 (1882–92); Sonata in E minor for Violin and Piano, op. 82 (1918; 1st public perf., London, March 21, 1919); String Quartet in E minor, op. 83 (1918; 1st public perf., London, May 21, 1919); Quintet in A minor for Strings and Piano, op. 84 (1918–19; 1st public perf., London, May 21, 1919).

KEYBOARD: PIANO: *Rosemary* (1882); *May Song* (1901); *Concert Allegro*, op. 46 (London, Dec. 2, 1901); *Skizze* (1903); *In Smyrna* (1905); Sonatina (1932); *Adieu* (1932); *Serenade* (1932). **ORGAN:** *11 Vesper Voluntaries*, op. 14 (1889); Sonata in G major, op. 28 (Worcester Cathedral, July 8, 1895).

VOCAL: ORATORIOS: *The Light of Life (Lux Christi)*, op. 29 (Worcester Festival, Sept. 10, 1896, composer conducting); *The Dream of Gerontius*, op. 38 (1899–1900; Birmingham Festival, Oct. 3, 1900, Richter conducting; although commonly listed as an oratorio, Elgar did not designate it as such); *The Apostles*, op. 49 (Birmingham Festival, Oct. 14, 1903, composer conducting); *The Kingdom*, op. 51 (1901–06; Birmingham Festival, Oct. 3, 1906, composer conducting). **CANTATAS:** *The Black Knight*, op. 25 (Worcester Festival, April 18, 1893, composer conducting); *Scenes from the Saga of King Olaf*, op. 30 (1894–96; North Staffordshire Music Festival, Hanley, Oct. 30, 1896, composer conducting); *Caractacus*, op. 35 (Leeds Festival, Oct. 5, 1898, composer conducting). **OTHER VOCAL:** *Salve Regina* (1878); *Domine salvan fac* (1878); *Tantum ergo* (1878); *O salutaris hostia* for 4-part Chorus (1880); *Credo*, in E minor (1880); *4 Litanies for the Blessed Virgin Mary* for Chorus (1882); *Ave, Verum Corpus (Jesu, Word of God Incarnate)*, op. 2, No. 1 (1887); *Ave Maria (Jesu, Lord of Life and Glory)*, op. 2, No. 2 (1887); *Ave Maris Stella (Jesu, Meek and Lowly)*, op. 2, No. 3 (1887); *Ecce sacerdos magnus* for Chorus and Organ (Worcester, Oct. 9, 1888); *My Love Dwelt in a Northern Land*, part-song for Mixed Voices (Tenbury Musical Soc., Nov. 13, 1890); *Spanish Serenade (Stars of the Summer Night)* for Mixed Voices, op. 23 (1891; with orch. accompaniment, 1892; Herefordshire Phil. Soc., April 7, 1893); *Scenes from the Bavarian Highlands*, 6 choral songs with Piano or Orch., op. 27 (piano version, 1895; orch. version, 1896; Worcester Festival, April 21, 1896, composer conducting); *The Banner of St. George*, ballad for Chorus and Orch., op. 33 (London, March 14, 1895; 2nd version, London, May 18, 1897); *Te Deum and Benedictus* for Chorus and Organ, op. 34 (Hereford Festival, Sept. 12, 1897); *Sea-Pictures*, song cycle for Contralto or Mezzo-soprano and Orch., op. 37 (1897–99; Norwich Festival, Oct. 5, 1899, Clara Butt soloist, composer conducting); *To Her Beneath Whose Steadfast Star*, part-song for Mixed Voices (Windsor Castle, May 24, 1899; dedicated to Queen Victoria); *Weary Wind of the West*, part-song for Mixed Voices (1902; Morecambe Festival, May 2, 1903); *Coronation Ode* for Soloists, Chorus, and Orch., op. 44 (Sheffield Festival, Oct. 2, 1902, composer conducting); *5 Part-Songs from the Greek Anthology* for Men's Voices, op. 45 (1902; London, April 25, 1904); *Evening Scene*, part-song for Mixed Voices (1905; Morecambe Festival, May 12, 1906); *4 Part-Songs* for Mixed Voices, op. 53 (1907); *The Reveille* for Men's Voices, op. 54 (1907; Blackpool Music Festival, Oct. 17, 1908); *Angelus (Tuscany)*, part-song for Mixed Voices, op. 56 (1909; London, Dec. 8, 1910); *Go, Song of Mine* for Chorus, op. 57 (Hereford Festival, Sept. 9, 1909); song cycle with Orch., op. 59, Nos. 3, 5, and 6 (Nos. 1, 2, and 4 not composed; 1909–10; London, Jan. 24, 1910, Muriel Foster soloist, composer conducting); *O hearken thou, offertory* for Chorus and Orch., op. 64 (Westminster Abbey, London, June 22, 1911; for the coronation of King George V); *Great Is the Lord (Psalm 48)*, anthem for Mixed Voices, op. 67 (1910–12; Westminster Abbey, London, July 16, 1912); *The Music Makers*, ode for Soloists, Chorus, and Orch., op. 69 (1902–12; Birmingham Festival, Oct. 1, 1912, composer conducting); *Give unto the Lord (Psalm 29)*, anthem for Mixed Voices, Organ, and Orch., op. 74 (St. Paul's Cathedral, London, April 30, 1914); 2 choral songs for Mixed Voices, op. 71 (1914); *Death on the Hills*, choral song for Mixed Voices, op. 72 (1914); 2 choral songs for Mixed Voices, op. 73 (1914); *The Spirit of England* for Soloists, Chorus, and Orch., op. 80 (1915–17; 1st complete perf., London, Nov. 24, 1917, composer conducting); *The Wanderer* for Men's Voices (1923); *Zut, zut, zut* for Men's Voices (1923); also many solo songs.

A collected ed. of his works, *The Elgar Complete Edition*, ed. by Jerrold Northrop Moore and Christopher Kent, commenced publication in 1981.

BIBL.: The Elgar Soc. of England began issuing the *Elgar Society Newsletter* in 1973; it became the *Elgar Society Journal* in 1979. Other writings include: R. Buckley, *Sir E. E.* (London, 1904; new ed., 1925); E. Newman, *E.* (London, 1906); J. Porte, *Sir E. E.* (London, 1921); J. Shera, *E.'s Instrumental Works* (London, 1931); B. Maine, *E., His Life and Works* (2 vols., London, 1933); J. Porte, *E. and His Music* (London, 1933); A. Sheldon, *E. E.* (London, 1933); A.H. Fox-Strangways, "E.," *Music & Letters* (Jan. 1934); R. Powell, "E.'s Enigma," ibid. (July 1934); special Elgar issue of *Music & Letters* (Jan. 1935); C. Barber, "Enigma Variations," ibid. (April 1935); W. Reed, *E. as I Knew Him* (London, 1936; new ed., 1973); Mrs. R. Powell, *E. E.: Memories of a Variation* (London, 1937; 2nd ed., 1947; rev. ed., 1994, by C. Powell); W. Reed, *E.* (London, 1939); W. Anderson, *Introduction to the Music of E.* (London, 1949); D. McVeagh, *E. E., His Life and Music* (London, 1955); P. Young, *E., O.M.* (London,

1955; new ed., 1973); idem, ed., *Letters of E. E. and Other Writings* (London, 1956); idem, ed., *Letters to Nimrod from E. E.* (London, 1965); M. Kennedy, *Portrait of E.* (London, 1968; 2nd ed., rev., 1982); R. Fiske, "The Enigma: A Solution," *Musical Times* (Nov. 1969); M. Hurd, *E.* (London, 1969); E. Sams, "E.'s Cipher Letter to Dorabella," *Musical Times* (Feb. 1970); idem, "Variations on an Original Theme (Enigma)," ibid. (March 1970); I. Parrott, *E.* (London, 1971); C. Kent, *E. E.: A Composer at Work: A Study of His Creative Processes as Seen through His Sketches and Proof Corrections* (diss., King's College, Univ. of London, 1978); S. Mundy, *E.: His Life and Times* (Tunbridge Wells, 1980); G. Hodgkins, *Providence and Art: A Study of E.'s Religious Beliefs* (London, 1982); C. Kent, "E.'s Third Symphony: The Sketches Reconsidered," *Musical Times* (Aug. 1982); M. De-la-Noy, *E. the Man* (London, 1983); C. Redwood, ed., *An E. Companion* (Ashbourne, 1983); R. Anderson, "E. and Some Apostolic Problems," *Musical Times* (Jan. 1984); D. Bury, *E. and the Two Mezzos* (London, 1984); J. Dibble, "Parry and E.: A New Perspective," *Musical Times* (Nov. 1984); D. Hudson, "E.'s Enigma: The Trail of Evidence," ibid.; J. Northrop Moore, *E. E.: A Creative Life* (Oxford, 1984); idem, *Spirit of England: E. E. and His World* (London, 1984); N. Reed, "E.'s Enigmatic Inamorata," *Musical Times* (Aug. 1984); M. Portnoy, "The Answer to E.'s Enigma," *Musical Quarterly*, No. 2 (1985); P. Young, "E. and the Spanish Lady," *Musical Times* (May 1986); C. Grogan, "E.'s Rejected Apostle," ibid. (Feb. 1988); J. Moore, ed., *E. E.: The Windflower Letters: Correspondence with Alice Caroline Stuart Wortley and Her Family* (Oxford, 1989); C. Weaver, *The Thirteenth Enigma? The Story of E. E.'s Early Love* (London, 1989); R. Anderson, *E. in Manuscript* (London, 1990); R. Monk, ed., *E. Studies* (Aldershot, 1990); J. Northrop Moore, *E. E.: Letters of a Lifetime* (Oxford, 1990); C. Kent, *E. E.: A Guide to Research* (N.Y., 1993); R. Monk, ed., *E. E.: Music and Literature* (Aldershot, 1993); S. Craggs, *E. E.: A Source Book* (Aldershot, 1995); P. Young, *E., Newman and the Dream of Gerontius: In the Tradition of English Catholicism* (Brookfield, Vt., 1995).

Elías, Alfonso de, Mexican pianist, conductor, pedagogue, and composer, father of **Manuel Jorge de Elías;** b. Cuernavaca, Aug. 30, 1902; d. Mexico City, Aug. 19, 1984. He was a student of José Velasquez (piano), Gustavo Campa (orchestration), and Rafael Tello (composition) at the National Cons. in Mexico City (1915–27). He was active as a pianist and conductor, and also taught in Mexico City at the Universidad Autónoma (from 1958) and at the National Cons. (from 1963). His works were in a thoroughly Romantic style.

WORKS: BALLET: *Las Biniguendas de plata* (1933). **ORCH.:** *El jardín encantado,* symphonic triptych (1924); 3 syms. (1926, 1934, 1968); *Variaciones sobre un tema mexicano* (1927); 2 symphonic poems: *Leyenda mística del Callejón del Ave María* (1930) and *Cacahuamilpa* (1940). **CHAMBER:** 2 string quartets (1930, 1961); Violin Sonata (1932); Organ Sonata (1963). **VOCAL:** Various works, including masses and motets.

Elías, Manuel Jorge de, Mexican composer, son of **Alfonso de Elías**; b. Mexico City, June 5, 1939. He received his early musical training from his father; he then entered the Autonomous National Univ. of Mexico and the National Cons. in Mexico City, where he studied piano, organ, flute, violin, and cello (1959–62); attended a class in electronic music at Columbia Univ. in N.Y. (1974); returning to Mexico, he founded in 1976 the Inst. of Music of the Univ. of Veracruz. In 1991 he became director of the Música de Bellas Arts. His music is hedonistically pragmatic and structurally precise, but allows interpolation of aleatory passages.

WORKS: *Suite romantica,* 10 pieces for Piano (1954–56); *Pequeños corales* for Chorus (1954–57); *Suite de miniaturas* for Wind Quartet (1957); *Sonata breve* for Piano (1958); *Estampas infantiles,* suite for Strings (1959); Sinfonietta (1958–61); *Vitral No. 1* for Chamber Orch. (1962), *No. 2* for Chamber Orch. and Tape (1967), and *No. 3* for Orch. (Mexico City, Nov. 7, 1969); *Divertimento* for Percussion (1963); *Jabel,* ballet for 2 Pianos (1964); *Aforismo No. 1, Pájaros perdidos* for Chorus (1963) and *No. 2* for Flute and Tape (1968); *Guanajuato,* overture-divertimento for Orch. (1964); *Impresiones sobre una estampa colonial,* divertimento for Orch. (1965); *Ciclos elementarios* for Wind Quartet (1965); *Speculamen* for 2 Violins, 2 Violas, 3 Cellos, and Double Bass (1967); *Elegía heroica,* symphonic poem (1967); *Memento* for Recorder, Chorus, Strings, and Narrator (1967); String Quartet No. 1 (1967); *Música nupcial* for Contralto and Brass or Strings (1967); 2 sonatas for solo violin (1968, 1969); *Pro pax* for Tape (1968); *3 Quimeras* for 2 Pianos (1969, 1973, 1974); *3 Kaleidoscopios* for Organ (1969, 1973, 1974); *Sonante No. 1* for Piano (1971), *No. 2* for Clarinet (1970), *No. 3* for Trumpet, Trombone, and Horn (1970; also for Orch., 1974), *No. 4* for Orch. (Mexico City, March 26, 1971), *No. 5* for Orch. (Mexico City, Nov. 24, 1972), *No. 6, Homenaje a Neruda,* for Strings (1973), and *No. 7* for Orch. (Brussels, Dec. 1974); *Parametros I* for Synthesizer (1971); *Ludus* for 3 Choruses (1972–73); *Concertante No. 1* for Violin and Orch. (1973); *Música domestica* for Recorder and Percussion (1973); *Sine nomine* for String Quartet and Piano (1975); *Jeux* for Horn, Trumpet, and Bassoon (1975); *Obertura-Poema* for Soloists, Chorus, Organ, and Wind Orch. (1975); *Fax Music* for Winds (1990); *Tri-Neos* for Clarinet, Bassoon, and Piano (1991); further choruses; songs.

Elias, Rosalind, American mezzo-soprano; b. Lowell, Mass., March 13, 1930. She began her training at the New England Cons. of Music in Boston; during her student days there, she sang Poppaea in *L'incoronazione di Poppea,* and also appeared with the Boston Sym. Orch.; she then studied at the Berkshire Music Center in Tanglewood. After singing with the New England Opera Co. (1948–52), she completed her training in Italy with Luigi Ricci and Nazareno de Angelis. Following engagements at Milan's La Scala and Naples' Teatro San Carlos, she made her Metropolitan Opera debut in N.Y. as Grimgerde in *Die Walküre* on Feb. 23, 1954; she created roles there in Barber's *Vanessa* (Erika, 1958) and *Antony and Cleopatra* (Charmian, 1966), remaining on its roster for over 30 years. She also made guest appearances in Europe and toured as a concert artist. Among her other roles were Dorabella, Rosina, Cherubino, Giordano's Bersi, Carmen, and Octavian.

Eliasson, Anders, Swedish composer; b. Borlänge, April 3, 1947. He was a pupil of Ingvar Lidholm (composition) and Valdemar Söderholm (harmony and counterpoint) at the Stockholm Musikhögskolan (1966–72); he also studied with Ligeti. In 1983 he was awarded the Royal Swedish Academy of Music prize in Stockholm. His music reveals a searching exploration of new forms while retaining conventional compositional techniques.

WORKS: DRAMATIC: *En av oss,* church opera (1974); *Backanterna,* incidental music to Euripides (Swedish Radio, April 4, 1982). **ORCH.:** *Glasdans* (1973; Swedish TV, Jan. 9, 1974); *Canti in lontananza* for Chamber Orch. (Swedish Radio, Oct. 1, 1977); *Impronta* (1978; Norrköping, Sept. 22, 1979); *Turnings* (1978; Swedish Radio, June 13, 1979); *Desert Point* for Strings (1981; Växjö, Feb. 13, 1982); Concerto for Bassoon and Strings (1981; Stockholm, Feb. 19, 1983); *Sinfonia da camera* (Swedish Radio, Aug. 14, 1984); Sym. No. 1 (1986; Swedish Radio, Feb. 6, 1987); *Ostacoli* for Strings (1987); *Fantasia* (1988); *Intermezzi* for Chamber Orch. (1988; Stockholm, Feb. 14, 1989); *Sinfonia concertante*: Sym. No. 3 (Trondheim, Nov. 16, 1989); *Farfalle e ferro,* concerto for Horn and Strings (1991; Göteborg, May 3, 1992). **CHAMBER:** *Melos* for String Quartet (1970); *Picknick* for Wind Quintet (1972); a series of works titled *Disegno*: for Piano, 4-hands, Cello, and Xylophone (1974), String Quartet (1975), 2 Trumpets, Horn, 2 Trombones, and Tuba (1975), Cello (1975), Clarinet (1982), Harpsichord (1982), Trombone (1984), Flute (1984), Piano (1984), String Quartet and Harpsichord (1984), and Piano (1987); *La Fièvre* for Wind Quintet (1978); *Malaria* for Clarinet, Trumpet, Trombone, Percussion, and Double Bass (1978); *Ombra* for Clarinet and String Quartet (1980); *Notturno* for Bass Clarinet, Cello, and Piano (1981); *Senza risposte* for Flute, Violin, Cello, and Piano (1983);

Dai cammini misteriosi for 2 Oboes, Bassoon, Harpsichord, and Double Bass (1983); *Sotto il segno del sole* for Chamber Group (1987); *Fogliame*, quartet for Piano and String Trio (1990); *Stämmor* for String Quartet (1991).

VOCAL: *Hymn* for 6 Men's Voices, Winds, and Percussion (1970); *Då sade man . . . och nu* for Soprano, Bass Clarinet, Cello, Vibraphone, and Tam-tam (1972); *Inför logos* for Soprano, Alto, Tenor, Bass, and Tape (1973); *Den gröna rosen*, cantata for Soprano, Saxophone Quartet, and Percussion (1976); *Canto del vagabondo in memoria di Carolus Linnaeus* for Soprano, Women's Chorus, and Orch. (1979; Swedish Radio, Nov. 28, 1980); *Breathing Room: July* for Chorus (1984).

Elizalde, Federico, Spanish conductor and composer; b. Manila, Philippines (of Spanish parents), Dec. 12, 1908; d. there, Jan. 16, 1979. He studied piano at the Madrid Cons. (1st prize, 1923), law at Stanford Univ., and composition with Ernest Bloch. In 1930 he became conductor of the Manila Sym. Orch. and in 1948 president of the Manila Radio. His works include *Paul Gauguin*, opera (1948); *Sinfonia Concertante* (Barcelona, April 23, 1936); Violin Concerto (1943); Piano Concerto (1947); chamber music.

Elkan, Henri, Belgian-American conductor and music publisher; b. Antwerp, Nov. 23, 1897; d. Philadelphia, June 12, 1980. After study at the Antwerp and Amsterdam conservatories, he emigrated to the U.S. in 1920; subsequently conducted performances of the Philadelphia Grand Opera Co. (1928–36). In 1926 he founded the Henri Elkan Music Publishing Co. in Philadelphia; in 1928 he was joined by Adolphe Vogel, a cellist in the Philadelphia Orch., and the company became the Elkan-Vogel Music Publishing Co.; the partnership was dissolved in 1952, and in 1956 Elkan formed a publishing firm once again under his own name.

Elkus, Albert (Israel), American composer and teacher, father of **Jonathan (Britton) Elkus**; b. Sacramento, April 30, 1884; d. Oakland, Feb. 19, 1962. He studied at the Univ. of Calif. (M.Lit., 1907); also studied piano with Hugo Mansfeldt and Oscar Weil in San Francisco, and later with Harold Bauer and Josef Lhévinne; went to Vienna, where he took lessons in conducting with Franz Schalk and counterpoint with Karl Prohaska; then took courses with Robert Fuchs and Georg Schumann in Berlin. Returning to the U.S., he taught at Dominican College in San Rafael, California (1924–31); was on the faculty of the San Francisco Cons. (1923–25; 1933–37), serving as its director (1951–57); he also taught at Mills College in Oakland (1929–44) and at the Univ. of Calif. at Berkeley (1935–51). Among his compositions are *Concertino on Lezione III of Ariosto* for Cello and Strings (1917); *Impressions from a Greek Tragedy* for Orch. (San Francisco, Feb. 27, 1921); *I Am the Reaper*, chorus for Men's Voices (1921).

Elkus, Jonathan (Britton), American conductor, pedagogue, and composer, son of **Albert (Israel) Elkus**; b. San Francisco, Aug. 8, 1931. He studied composition with Cushing and Denny at the Univ. of Calif. in Berkeley (B.A., 1953), Ernst Bacon and L. Ratner at Stanford Univ. (M.A., 1957), and Milhaud at Mills College in Oakland, California (1957). He taught at Lehigh Univ. in Bethlehem, Pa. (1957–73), and also conducted its bands. After serving as director of music (1979–85) and chairman of the humanities dept. (1985–89) at Cape Cod Academy in Osterville, he was chairman of the history dept. at Stuart Hall School in Stauton (1989–92). In 1992 he became director of bands at the Univ. of Calif. at Davis. He publ. *Charles Ives and the American Band Tradition: A Centennial Tribute* (Exeter, England, 1974).

WORKS: DRAMATIC: OPERAS: *The Outcasts of Poker Flat* (1959; Bethlehem, Pa., April 16, 1960); *Medea* (1963; Milwaukee, Nov. 13, 1970); *The Mandarin* (N.Y., Oct. 26, 1967); *Helen in Egypt* (Milwaukee, Nov. 13, 1970). **MUSICALS:** *Tom Sawyer* (San Francisco, May 22, 1953); *Treasure Island* (1961); *A Little Princess* (1980). Also incidental music. **BAND:** *Camino Real* (1955); *Serenade* for Horn, Baritone Horn, and Band (1957); *CC Rag* (1974); *The Apocalypse*, rag (1974); *Pipers on Parade* (1976); *Chiaroscuro*, suite (1977); *Cal Band March* (1978); many transcriptions and arrangements. **CHAMBER:** *3 Sketches* for 2 Clarinets and Bassoon (1954); *The Charmer*, rag for Clarinet, Trombone, and Piano (1972); piano pieces; organ music.

Ellberg, Ernst (Henrik), Swedish composer and pedagogue; b. Söderhamm, Dec. 11, 1868; d. Stockholm, June 14, 1948. He studied with J. Lindberg (violin) and J. Dente (composition) at the Stockholm Cons. (1886–92), and then held a state composer's fellowship (1894–96). From 1887 to 1905 he was a violist in the Royal Orch. in Stockholm; he taught composition, counterpoint, and orchestration at the Stockholm Cons. (1904–33), and then taught military musicians there until 1943. In 1912 he was made a member of the Swedish Royal Academy of Music, and in 1916 he was granted the title of prof. Ellberg was an influential teacher. His music is steeped in the Romantic tradition. Among his compositions are the operas *Den röda liljan* (The Red Lily) and *Rassa*; ballets; *Introduction and Fugue* for Strings (1891); a Sym. (1896); also overtures; chamber music; songs for Men's Chorus.

Eller, Heino, noted Estonian composer and pedagogue; b. Yuryev, March 7, 1887; d. Tallinn, June 16, 1970. He studied law at the Univ. of St. Petersburg (1908–12). Following service in the army during World War I, he studied violin and composition (with Kalafati) at the Petrograd Cons. (graduated, 1920). After teaching theory and composition at the Tartu Higher Music School (1920–40), he was prof. of composition at the Tallinn Cons. (1940–70). In 1957 he was honored with the title of People's Artist of the Estonian S.S.R. In 1965 he was awarded the prize of the Estonian Republic. Eller was one of the principal founders of the modern Estonian national school of music. Many of his students became prominent figures in the musical life of Estonia. Eller's works adhered to Classical precepts but explored modern harmonic and timbral usages.

WORKS: ORCH.: *Fantasy* for Violin and Orch. (1916; rev. 1963); 6 symphonic poems: *Twilight* (1918); *Dawn* (1918); *Nocturnal Sounds* (1920); *Apparitions* (1924); *The Eagle's Flight* (1949); *The Singing Fields* (1951); *Symphonic Scherzo* (1921); Violin Concerto (1933; rev. 1965); 3 syms. (1936, 1947, 1961); *White Night*, symphonic suite (1939); *Dance Suite* (1942); *5 Pieces* for Strings (1953); Sinfonietta for Strings (1965); *Episode from Revolutionary Times* (n.d.). **CHAMBER:** 2 violin sonatas (1922, 1946); 5 string quartets (1925, 1930, 1945, 1954, 1959); many violin pieces; pieces for Cello and Harp. **PIANO:** 4 sonatas (1920, 1938, 1944, 1958); about 200 other pieces.

BIBL.: H. Sepp, *H. E. i klaverilooming* (Tallinn, 1958); idem, ed., *H. E. sonas ja pildis* (H. E. in Words and Pictures; Tallinn, 1967).

Elling, Catharinus, Norwegian organist, composer, and writer on music; b. Christiania, Sept. 13, 1858; d. there (Oslo), Jan. 8, 1942. He studied in Christiania, Leipzig (1877–78), and with Herzogenberg at the Berlin Hochschule für Musik (1886–87). Returning to Christiania in 1896, he taught counterpoint and composition at the Cons. until 1908; he was also active as a choral conductor (1897–1901) and as a church organist (1909–26). In 1898 he received a government subvention to study Norwegian folk songs, which resulted in essays and books; he also wrote biographies of Bull, Grieg, Svendsen, and Kjerulf.

WORKS: *Kosakkerne* (The Cossacks), opera (1890–94); 2 syms. (1890, 1897); *Norwegian Suite* for Orch. (1904); Violin Concerto (1919); *Den forlorne søn* (The Prodigal Son), oratorio (1895–96); incidental music to plays; chamber music; songs.

BIBL.: Ø. Gaukstad, *Melodi- og tekstregister til C. E.s optegnelser av folkemusikk* (Oslo, 1963).

Ellington, "Duke" (actually, **Edward Kennedy**), famous black American jazz pianist, bandleader, and composer; b. Washington, D.C., April 29, 1899; d. N.Y., May 24, 1974. He played ragtime as a boy; worked with various jazz bands in Washington, D.C., during the 1910s and early 1920s, and in 1923 went to

N.Y., where he organized a "big band" (orig. 10 pieces) that he was to lead for the next half-century, a band that revolutionized the concept of jazz: no longer was jazz restricted to small combos of 4–6 "unlettered" improvisers; with the Ellington band, complex arrangements were introduced, requiring both improvising skill and the ability to read scores; eventually these scores were to take on the dimensions and scope of classical compositions while retaining an underlying jazz feeling. In the early days, his chief collaborator in composition and arrangements was trumpeter James "Bubber" Miley; baritone saxophonist Harry Carney, another arranger, was with the band from its inception until Ellington's death; from 1939 the main collaborator was pianist-composer Billy Strayhorn. Ellington possessed a social elegance and the gift of articulate verbal expression that inspired respect, and he became known as "Duke" Ellington. He was the first jazz musician to receive an honorary degree from Columbia Univ. (1973). He was also the recipient of the Presidential Medal of Freedom (1969). He made several European trips under the auspices of the State Dept.; toured Russia in 1970 and also went to Latin America, Japan, and Australia. So highly was he esteemed in Africa that the Republic of Togo issued in 1967 a postage stamp bearing his portrait. His remarkable career is highlighted in his book *Music Is My Mistress* (Garden City, N.Y., 1973). After his death, his band was led by his son Mercer Ellington (b. Washington, D.C., March 11, 1919; d. Copenhagen, Feb. 8, 1996). He composed more than 1,000 works, including *East St. Louis Toodle-Oo* (1926); *Black and Tan Fantasy* and *Creole Love Song* (1927); *Mood Indigo* (1930); *Sophisticated Lady* (1932); *Diminuendo and Crescendo in Blue* (1937); *Black, Brown and Beige* (1943); *Liberian Suite* (1948); *My People*, commissioned for the 100th anniversary of the Emancipation Proclamation (1963); *1st Sacred Concert* (San Francisco, 1965); *2nd Sacred Concert* (N.Y., 1968); *The River*, ballet (1970); *Queenie Pie*, musical (unfinished; completed by others; Philadelphia, Sept. 20, 1986).

BIBL.: B. Ulanov, *D. E.* (N.Y., 1946); P. Gammond, *D. E., His Life and Music* (London, 1958); S. Dance, *The World of D. E.* (N.Y., 1970); D. Jewell, *D., A Portrait of D. E.* (N.Y., 1977); D. George, *The Real D. E.* (London, 1982); R. Frankl, *D. E.* (N.Y., 1988); G. Brown, *D. E.* (Englewood Cliffs, N.J., 1990); K. Rattenbury, *E. E.: Jazz Composer* (London and New Haven, 1990); M. Tucker, *E.: The Early Years* (Urbana, 1991); K. Smith, *D. E.* (Los Angeles, 1992); K. Stratemann, *D. E., Day by Day and Film by Film* (Copenhagen, 1992); J. Hasse, *Beyond Category: The Life and Genius of D. E.* (N.Y., 1993); M. Tucker, ed., *The D. E. Reader* (Oxford, 1993); E. Stwertka, *D. E.: A Life of Music* (N.Y., 1994).

Ellinwood, Leonard (Webster), American musicologist; b. Thomaston, Conn., Feb. 13, 1905; d. Washington, D.C., July 8, 1994. He studied at Aurora (Ill.) College (B.A., 1926) and with Charles Warren Fox at the Eastman School of Music in Rochester, N.Y. (M.Mus., 1934; Ph.D., 1936, with the diss. *The Works of Francesco Landini*). He taught at Michigan State College (1936–39); then was a cataloguer at the Library of Congress in Washington, D.C., where he later was head of its humanities division (1970–75). He publ. *Musica Hermanni Contracti* (Rochester, N.Y., 1936), *Bio-bibliographical Index of Musicians in the U.S.A. Since Colonial Times* (Washington, D.C., 1941; 2nd ed., 1956), and *The History of American Church Music* (N.Y., 1953); he also ed. Landini's works (Cambridge, Mass., 1939) and Tallis's English sacred music in the Early English Church Music series, XII–XIII (1971–72).

Elliott, Paul, English tenor; b. Macclesfield, Cheshire, March 19, 1950. He was a choral scholar at Magdalen College, Oxford (1969–72), later pursuing his education at the Univ. of Oxford (B.A., 1973; M.A., 1977). His principal vocal teachers were David Johnston and Peter Pears. He served as vicar choral at St. Paul's Cathedral (1972–75) and sang with various choral and early music groups, including the John Alldis Choir (1972–76), the Deller Consort (1973–82), the Monteverdi Choir (1973–78), and the Academy of Ancient Music (from 1973); also was a founding member of the Hilliard Ensemble (1974–84) and the London Early Music Group (1976–79). From 1984 to 1989 he sang with the Newberry Consort in Chicago. He toured widely as a solo concert artist, and also sang in opera, scoring success as Handel's Acis in St. Gallen (1984) and as Mozart's Belmonte in Chicago (1988). In 1987 he joined the faculty of the Indiana Univ. School of Music in Bloomington.

Ellis, Brent, American baritone; b. Kansas City, Mo., June 20, 1946. He studied with Edna Forsythe (1962–65), Marian Freschl (1965–71), and Daniel Ferro in N.Y. (from 1971), where he also attended classes at the Juilliard School of Music (1965–67; 1970–72). In 1965 he made his first appearance at the Santa Fe Opera, where he later sang regularly (1972–82); also appeared at the Houston Grand Opera (1972–81). In 1973 he won both the WGN Radio Auditions of the Air and the Montreal International Competition, and on April 28, 1974, made his N.Y. City Opera debut as Ottone in L'incoronazione di Poppea; then sang with the Chicago Lyric Opera (1974), the San Francisco Opera (1974–78), the Boston Opera (1975–83), the Glyndebourne Festival (1977–78), the Hamburg State Opera (1977–79), and the Vienna State Opera (1977–79). On Oct. 25, 1979, he made his Metropolitan Opera debut in N.Y. as Silvio in *Pagliacci*. From 1984 he sang at the Cologne Opera. In 1988 he made his first appearance at London's Covent Garden as Rigoletto.

Ellis, Don(ald Johnson), American trumpeter, bandleader, arranger, and composer; b. Los Angeles, July 25, 1934; d. there, Dec. 17, 1978. He studied composition with Gardner Read at Boston Univ. and with John Vincent at the Univ. of Calif. at Los Angeles, and trumpet in Boston, N.Y., and Los Angeles. He played trumpet in various bands, including those of Charlie Barnet (1958) and Maynard Ferguson (1959), and was also 1st trumpeter in the National Sym. Orch. in Washington, D.C. In 1961 he organized his own trio, and in 1962 his own quartet; he later led his own orch. in Los Angeles. He was equally at home in serious and popular music. His major work was *Contrasts* for Trumpet and 2 Orchs. (1965). He won a Grammy Award for his arrangement of music from the film *The French Connection* (1973).

BIBL.: A. Agostinelli, *D. E.: A Man for Our Time (1934–1978)* (Providence, R.I., 1984).

Ellis, Osian (Gwynn), Welsh harpist and teacher; b. Fynnongroew, Feb. 8, 1928. He received training at the Royal Academy of Music in London. He played in the Melos Ensemble and was solo harpist with the London Sym. Orch.; acquired a fine reputation as a concert artist via engagements as a soloist with the foremost orchs. and as a recitalist around the globe. From 1959 to 1989 he was also prof. of harp at the Royal Academy of Music. In 1971 he was made a Commander of the Order of the British Empire. In addition to the standard harp literature, Ellis commissioned works for his instrument from Britten, Hoddinott, Mathias, Menotti, Schuman, and others. He publ. *The Story of the Harp in Wales* (1991).

Elman, Mischa (actually, **Mikhail Saulovich**), remarkable Russian-born American violinist; b. Talnoy, Jan. 20, 1891; d. N.Y., April 5, 1967. At the age of 6, he was taken by his father to Odessa, where he became a violin student of Fidelmann and a pupil of Brodsky. His progress was extraordinary, and when Leopold Auer heard him play in 1902, he immediately accepted him in his class at the St. Petersburg Cons. In 1904 he made his debut in St. Petersburg with sensational acclaim; on Oct. 14, 1904, he made a brilliant Berlin debut; on March 21, 1905, he made his first appearance in London to great acclaim. On Dec. 10, 1908, he made his U.S. debut as soloist in an extraordinary performance of the Tchaikovsky concerto with Altschuler and the Russian Sym. Orch. in N.Y., and was hailed as one of the greatest virtuosos of the time; he played with every important sym. orch. in the U.S. In the following years, he played all over the world, and, with Jascha Heifetz, became a synonym for violinistic prowess. His playing was the quintessence of Romantic interpretation; his tone was mellifluous but resonant; he excelled particularly in the concertos of Mendelssohn, Tchaikovsky, and Wieniawski; but he could also give impressive performances of Beethoven and Mozart. He publ. several violin arrangements of Classical and Romantic pieces, and he also composed some playable short compositions for his instrument. His father publ. a sentimental book, *Memoirs of Mischa Elman's Father* (N.Y., 1933). In 1923 Elman became a naturalized American citizen.

BIBL.: A. Kozinn, *M. E. and the Romantic Style* (Chur and N.Y., 1990).

Elmendorff, Karl (Eduard Maria), eminent German conductor; b. Düsseldorf, Oct. 25, 1891; d. Hofheim am Taunus, Oct. 21, 1962. He was a student of Steinbach and Abendroth at the Cologne Hochschule für Musik. After conducting opera in Düsseldorf, Mainz, Hagen, and Aachen, he held the post of 1st conductor at the Berlin State Opera and the Bavarian State Opera in Munich (from 1925). He won distinction as a conductor at the Bayreuth Festivals (1927–42); he also was Generalmusikdirektor in Kassel and Wiesbaden (1932–35), and then conducted in Mannheim (1935–42), at the Berlin State Opera (1937–45), and at the Dresden State Opera (1942–45); he subsequently was Generalmusikdirektor in Kassel (1948–51) and Wiesbaden (1951–56). Elmendorff was greatly esteemed as a Wagnerian.

Elmo, Cloe, Italian mezzo-soprano; b. Lecce, April 9, 1910; d. Ankara, May 24, 1962. She was a pupil of Chibaudo at the Accademia di Santa Cecilia in Rome; after winning the Vienna singing competition (1932), she pursued training with Rinolfi and Pedrini. In 1934 she made her operatic debut as Santuzza in Cagliara, and then was a valued member of Milan's La Scala (1936–43). On Nov. 14, 1947, she made her Metropolitan Opera debut in N.Y. as Azucena, remaining on its roster until 1949. From 1951 to 1954 she again sang at La Scala, and then taught voice at the Ankara Cons. Her repertoire included both standard and contemporary roles in Italian operas.

Elmore, Robert Hall, American organist, teacher, and composer; b. Ramapatnam, India (of American parents), Jan. 2, 1913; d. Ardmore, Pa., Sept. 22, 1985. He studied with Pietro Yon (organ) and Harl McDonald (composition), at the Royal Academy of Music in London (licentiate, 1933), and at the Univ. of Pa. (B.Mus., 1937). He taught organ at Philadelphia's Clarke Cons. of Music (1936–53) and Musical Academy (from 1939), and composition at the Univ. of Pa. (from 1940); he also was organist at various churches. His *It Began at Breakfast* was the first televised opera by an American composer.

WORKS: *It Began at Breakfast*, opera (Philadelphia, Feb. 8, 1941); 2 tone poems: *Valley Forge* (Philadelphia, April 9, 1937) and *Prelude to Unrest*; 2 orch. suites: *3 Colors* and *Legend of Sleepy Hollow*; Organ Concerto, String Quartet; organ pieces; sacred music; songs.

Eloy, Jean-Claude, French composer; b. Mont-Saint-Aignan, Seine-Maritime, June 15, 1938. He studied in Paris at the Schola Cantorum, and then at the Cons. with Lucette Descaves and Nat (premier prix in piano, 1957), Février (premier prix in chamber music, 1958), N. Gallon (premier prix in counterpoint, 1959), Martenot (premier prix in Ondes Martenot, 1960), and Milhaud (2nd prix in composition, 1961). He also attended the summer courses in new music in Darmstadt (1957, 1960, 1961), where he workd with Stockhausen, Messiaen, Pousseur, and Scherchen. From 1961 to 1963 he studied with Boulez in Basel. In 1972–73 he worked at the Cologne electronic music studio under Stockhausen. From 1971 to 1987 he was a producer for Radio-France in Paris. In 1963 he won the Prix de la Biennale of Paris and in 1981 the Prix national de la musique. From his earliest works, he adopted the advanced techniques of serialism, being particularly influenced by Boulez, Varèse, and Webern.

WORKS: ORCH.: *Étude III* (1962); *Équivalences* for 18 Instruments (1963); *Polychronies I* and *II* (1964); *Macles* for 6 Instrumental Groups (1967); *Faisceaux-Diffractions* for 28 Instruments (1978); *Fluctuante-Immuable* (1977; Paris, May 5, 1978). **VOCAL:** *Cantate* for Soprano and Instruments (1961); *Chants pour une ombre* for Soprano and 9 Instruments (1961); *Kâmakalâ* for 5 Choruses and 3 Orch. Ensembles, and 3 Conductors (1971); *Kshara-Akshara* for Soprano Chorus, 3 Orch. Ensembles, and 3 Conductors (1974); *A l'approche du feu méditant . . .* for 2 Buddhist Monk Choruses and Gagaku Ensemble (Tokyo, Sept. 30, 1983); *Anâhata* for 2 Soloists, 3 Gagaku Instruments, Percussion, Electronics, and Concrete Sounds (1984–86; Paris, Nov. 19, 1986); *Sappho Hikètis* for 2 Women's Voices and Electronics (Paris, Oct. 24, 1989); *Butsumyôe* for 2 Women's Voices (Paris, Oct. 24, 1989); *Erkos* for Woman's Voice, Percussion, and Electro-acoustic Environment (1990–91); *Rosa, Sonia . . .* for 2 Women's Voices (1991); *Gaia* for Soprano and Electro-acoustic Environment (1991–92). **OTHER:** *Shanti* for Electronics (Royan, March 23, 1974); *Gaku-no-Michi* for Electronics and Concrete Sounds (1977–78); *Poème-Picasso* for Electronics (1978); *Étude IV: Points-lignes-paysages* for Electronics (1978–80); *Yo-In* for Electronics (1980); *. . . d'une étoile oubliée* for Electronics and Percussion (1986).

Elschek, Oskár, Slovak ethnomusicologist; b. Bratislava, June 16, 1931. He studied musicology and aesthetics at the Univ. of Bratislava (degree, 1954), then became a member of the Musicology Inst. of the Slovak Academy of Sciences. In 1963 he was appointed ed.-in-chief of *Slovenská Hudba*, and in 1967 he co-ed. the *Annual Bibliography of European Ethnomusicology*. His publications include studies of Slovak and European folk music, organology, and the sociology of music. With his wife Alica Elscheková (b. Bratislava, Nov. 21, 1930), he wrote books on Slovak folk music (1956, 1962) and ed. the 1st vol. of Bartók's folk songs (1959). He publ., with A. Elschekova, *Úvod do štúdia slovenskej l'udovej hudby* (Introduction to the Study of Slovak Folk Music; Bratislava, 1962). He also publ. *Slovenské l'udové píst'aly a d'alšie aerofóny* (Bratislava, 1991).

Elson, Arthur, American writer on music, son of **Louis (Charles) Elson**; b. Boston, Nov. 18, 1873; d. N.Y., Feb. 24, 1940. After training from his father, he studied at the New England Cons. of Music in Boston, Harvard Univ. (graduated, 1895), and the Mass. Inst. of Technology (graduated, 1897). He served as music critic of the *Boston Advertiser* (from 1920).

WRITINGS: *A Critical History of the Opera* (1901; new ed., 1926, as *A History of Opera*); *Orchestral Instruments and Their Use* (1902; new ed., 1930); *Woman's Work in Music* (1903; new ed., 1931); *Modern Composers of Europe* (1905; new ed., 1922); *Music Club Programs from All Nations* (1906; new ed., 1928); *The Musician's Guide* (1913); *The Book of Musical Knowledge* (1915; new ed., 1934); *Pioneer School Music Course* (1917).

Elson, Louis (Charles), American music historian, father of **Arthur Elson**; b. Boston, April 17, 1848; d. there, Feb. 14, 1920. He studied voice with Kreissmann at Boston and theory with Karl Gloggner Castelli in Leipzig. Returning to Boston, he was music ed. of the *Boston Advertiser* (1886–1920); was a teacher (from 1880) and head of the theory dept. (from 1881) at the New England Cons. of Music. He was ed.-in-chief of the *University Encyclopedia of Music* (10 vols., 1912). In his music criticism, he attacked the modernists with vicious eloquence, reserving the choicest invective for Debussy; he called *La Mer* "Le Mal de Mer," and said that the faun of *L'Après-midi d'un faune* needed a veterinary surgeon. His widow endowed a memorial fund for the presentation of lectures on music at the Library of Congress in Washington, D.C., in 1945.

WRITINGS: *Curiosities of Music* (1880); *The History of German Song* (1888); *The Theory of Music* (1890; rev. by F. Converse, 1935); *European Reminiscences, Musical and Otherwise* (1891; new ed., 1914); *The Realm of Music* (1892); *Great Composers and Their Work* (1898); *The National Music of America and Its Sources* (1899; new ed., rev. by A. Elson, 1924); with P. Hale, *Famous Composers and Their Works* (1900); *Shakespeare in Music* (1901); *The History of American Music* (1904; 2nd ed., 1915; rev. by A. Elson, 1925); *Elson's Music Dictionary* (1905); *Elson's Pocket Music Dictionary* (1909); *Mistakes and Disputed*

Points in Music (1910); *Women in Music* (1918); *Children in Music* (1918).

BIBL.: *Lectures on the History and Art of Music: The L.C. E. Memorial Lectures at the Library of Congress, 1946–1963* (Washington, D.C., 1969).

Elston, Arnold, American composer; b. N.Y., Sept. 30, 1907; d. Vienna, June 6, 1971. He studied harmony and counterpoint with Goldmark in N.Y. and took courses at City College (B.A., 1930) and Columbia Univ. (M.A., 1932); after composition studies with Webern in Vienna (1932–35), he continued his training at Harvard Univ. (Ph.D., 1939), while concurrently studying conducting with Fiedler in Boston (1939). He taught at the Longy School of Music in Cambridge, Mass. (1939–40), the Univ. of Oregon (1941–58), and the Univ. of Calif. at Berkeley (1958–71). He wrote the books *Music and Medicine* (1948) and *A Modern Guide to Symphonic Music* (1966).

WORKS: *Suite* for Orch. (1931); 2 string quartets (1932, 1961); *Variations* for String Quartet (1934); *Sweeney Agonistes,* chamber opera (1948–50); *Chorus for Survival,* chamber cantata for Soprano, Baritone, Chorus, and 7 Instruments (1954–55); *The Love of Don Perlimplin,* opera (1957–58); *Great Age, Behold Us,* cantata for Chorus and Orch. (1965–66); Piano trio (1967); *Prelude, Paean and Furioso* for Orch. (1967–71); piano music.

Elvira, Pablo, Puerto Rican baritone; b. Santurce, Sept. 24, 1937. He studied voice at the Puerto Rico Cons., becoming a finalist in the Metropolitan Opera auditions in 1966. He taught at the Indiana Univ. School of Music in Bloomington (1966–74), where he made his formal debut as Rigoletto (1968). On Feb. 23, 1974, he made his first appearance at the N.Y. City Opera as Germont, where he sang regularly in subsequent seasons. He made his Metropolitan Opera debut in N.Y. as Rigoletto on March 22, 1978. In addition to his operatic engagements, he also sang frequently in concert. Among his finest roles were Rossini's Figaro, Don Carlo, Renato, Leoncavallo's Tonio, and Puccini's Lescaut.

Elwell, Herbert, American composer, teacher, and music critic; b. Minneapolis, May 10, 1898; d. Cleveland, April 17, 1974. He studied at the Univ. of Minnesota; then took courses with Bloch in N.Y. (1919–21) and Boulanger in Paris (1921–24); received a Prix de Rome in 1923; from 1924 to 1927 he held a fellowship at the American Academy in Rome. Returning to the U.S., he held a post as teacher of composition at the Cleveland Inst. of Music (1928–45); from 1932 to 1964 he served as music critic for the *Cleveland Plain Dealer.*

WORKS: BALLET: *The Happy Hypocrite* (1925; orch. suite, Rome, May 21, 1927). **ORCH.:** *The Centaur* (1924); *Orchestral Sketches* (1937); *Introduction and Allegro* (N.Y., July 12, 1942); *Ode* (1950); *Concert Suite* for Violin and Orch. (1957). **CHAMBER:** Piano Quintet (1923); Violin Sonata (1927); 2 string quartets (1929, 1937); *Variations* for Violin and Piano (1951); piano pieces, including a Sonata (1926). **VOCAL:** *I Was with Him,* cantata for Tenor, Men's Chorus, and 2 Pianos (1937; Cleveland, Nov. 30, 1942); *Blue Symphony* for Voice and String Quartet (1944; Cleveland, Feb. 2, 1945); *Lincoln: Requiem Aeternam* for Baritone, Chorus, and Orch. (1946; Oberlin, Feb. 16, 1947); *Pastorale* for Voice and Orch. (1947; Cleveland, March 25, 1948); *Watch America* for Chorus (1951); *The Forever Young* for Voice and Orch. (Cleveland, Oct. 29, 1953); songs.

BIBL.: F. Koch, "H. E. and his Music," *Bulletin of the National Association of Teachers* (Dec. 1971).

Emery, Walter (Henry James), English organist and writer; b. Tilshead, Wiltshire, June 14, 1909; d. Salisbury, June 24, 1974. He studied organ at the Royal Academy of Music in London; then was engaged as a church organist; from 1937 to 1969 he was an associate at Novello & Co. in the editorial dept. He publ. *The St. Matthew Passion: Its Preparation and Performance* (with Sir Adrian Boult; London, 1949); *Bach's Ornaments* (London, 1953); *Editing Early Music: Notes on the Preparation of Printer's Copy* (with T. Dart and C. Morris; London, 1963); commentaries on Bach's organ works; etc.

Emmanuel, (Marie François) Maurice, eminent French music scholar, pedagogue, and composer; b. Bar-sur-Aube, May 2, 1862; d. Paris, Dec. 14, 1938. He received his primary education in Dijon; then studied at the Paris Cons. (1880–87) with Savard, Dubois, Delibes, and Bourgault-Ducoudray; then specialized in the musical history of antiquity under Gevaert in Brussels; also studied ancient languages at the Sorbonne in Paris, becoming a licencié ès lettres (1887) and a docteur ès lettres (1895) with the theses *De saltationis disciplina apud Graecos* (publ. in Latin, Paris, 1895) and *La Danse grecque antique d'après les monuments figurés* (Paris, 1896; Eng. tr., 1916, as *The Antique Greek Dance after Sculptured and Painted Figures*), completing his study of composition with Guiraud. He was a prof. of art history at the Lycée Racine and Lycée Lamartine (1898–1905) and maitre de chapelle at Ste.-Clotilde (1904–07); in 1909 he succeeded Bourgault-Ducoudray as prof. of music history at the Paris Cons., and held this post until 1936.

WRITINGS: *Histoire de la langue musicale* (2 vols., Paris, 1911; new ed., 1928); *Traité de l'accompagnement modal des psaumes* (Lyons, 1912); with R. Moissenet, *La Polyphonie sacrée* (Dijon, 1923); *Pelléas et Mélisande de Claude Debussy* (Paris, 1926; 2nd ed., 1950); *César Franck* (Paris, 1930); *Anton Reicha* (Paris, 1936).

WORKS: DRAMATIC: *Pierrot Peintre,* pantomime (1886); *Prométhée enchaîné,* opera (1916–18); *Salamine,* opera (1921–23; 1927–28; Paris, June 28, 1929); *Amphitryon,* opéra-bouffe (1936; Paris, Feb. 20, 1937). **ORCH.:** *Ouverture pour un conte gai* (1890); *Zinagesca* for 2 Piccolos, 2 Pianos, Timpani, and Strings (1902); 2 syms.: No. 1 (1919) and No. 2, *Bretonne* (1930–31); *Le poème du Rhône,* symphonic poem (1938). **CHAMBER:** Cello Sonata (1887); Violin Sonata (1902); String Quartet (1903); Sonata for Flute, Clarinet, and Piano (1907); Sonata for Cornet, Bugle, and Piano (1936). **PIANO:** 6 sonatinas (1893, 1897, 1920, 1920, 1925, 1925).

BIBL.: M. Béclard d'Harcourt, "L'oeuvre musical de M. E.," *La revue musicale,* no. 152 (1935); special issue of ibid., no. 206 (1947).

Emsheimer, Ernst, German-born Swedish ethnomusicologist; b. Frankfurt am Main, Jan. 15, 1905. He studied musicology with Adler and Fischer at the Univ. of Vienna (1924) and the Univ. of Freiburg im Breisgau (Ph.D., 1927), then became musicological consultant in Leningrad at the National Academy for the History of Art, the Hermitage Collection, and the Museum of Ethnography (1932–36), where he led a field recording expedition into the northern Caucasus (1936). He settled in Stockholm in 1937, becoming musicological adviser to the Museum of Ethnography. From 1949 to 1973 he was director of the Museum of Music History in Stockholm; under his direction, it became an important center of Swedish musical and musicological activity. He is co-founder of the *Handbücher der Europäischen Volksmusikinstrumente.* He publ. *Studia ethnomusicologica eurasiatica* (Stockholm, 1964 et seq.; collected writings).

Enacovici, George, Romanian composer, teacher, and violinist; b. Focşani, May 4, 1891; d. Bucharest, Jan. 26, 1965. He studied at the Bucharest Cons. with Kiriac and Castaldi (1905–12); studied composition with Vincent d'Indy, and violin at the Schola Cantorum in Paris (1914–18). He taught violin at the Bucharest Cons. (1919–54) and was concertmaster of the Bucharest Phil. (1920–21) and the Bucharest Radio Orch. (1928–33).

WORKS: *Intermezzo* for String Orch. and Harp (1912); *Poem* for Violin and Orch. (1920); *Suite in a Romanian Style* for Orch. (1928); *Symphonic Episode* (1933); *Rapsodie romana* for Orch. (1934); *Amfitrita,* symphonic poem (1940); *Arlequinada,* capriccio for 2 Violins and Chamber Orch. (1941); Sym. (1954); Violin Concerto (1956); 3 string quartets; Violin Sonata; Piano Sonata; minor pieces in various genres.

Enesco, Georges (real name, **George Enescu**), famous Romanian violinist, conductor, teacher, and composer; b. Liveni-Virnav,

Aug. 19, 1881; d. Paris, May 4, 1955. He began to play the piano when he was 4, taking lessons with a Gypsy violinist, Nicolas Chioru, and began composing when he was 5; then studied with Caudella in Iaşi. On Aug. 5, 1889, he made his formal debut as a violinist in Slănic, Moldavia. In the meantime, he had enrolled in the Cons. of the Gesellschaft der Musikfreunde in Vienna (1888), where he studied violin with S. Bachrich, J. Grün, and J. Hellmesberger, Jr.; piano with L. Ernst; harmony, counterpoint, and composition with R. Fuchs; chamber music with J. Hellmesberger, Sr.; and music history with A. Prosnitz, winning 1st prizes in violin and harmony (1892). After his graduation (1894), he entered the Paris Cons., where he studied violin with Marsick and J. White, harmony with Dubois and Thomas, counterpoint with Gédalge, composition with Fauré and Massenet, and early music with Diémer, winning 2nd accessit for counterpoint and fugue (1897) and graduating with the premier prix for violin (1899). At the same time, he also studied cello, organ, and piano, attaining more than ordinary proficiency on each. On June 11, 1897, he presented in Paris a concert of his works, which attracted the attention of Colonne, who brought out the youthful composer's op. 1, *Poème roumain*, the next year. Enesco also launched his conducting career in Bucharest in 1898. In 1902 he first appeared as a violinist in Berlin and also organized a piano trio; in 1904 he formed a quartet. On March 8, 1903, he conducted the premiere of his 2 *Romanian Rhapsodies* in Bucharest, the first of which was to become his most celebrated work. He soon was appointed court violinist to the Queen of Romania. In 1912 he established an annual prize for Romanian composers, which was subsequently won by Jora, Enacovici, Golestan, Otescu, and others. In 1917 he founded the George Enescu sym. concerts in Iaşi. After the end of World War I, he made major tours as a violinist and conductor; he also taught violin in Paris, where his pupils included Menuhin, Grumiaux, Gitlis, and Ferras. He made his U.S. debut in the triple role of conductor, violinist, and composer with the Philadelphia Orch. in N.Y. on Jan. 2, 1923; he returned to conduct the N.Y. Phil. on Jan. 28, 1937. He led several subsequent concerts with it with remarkable success; led it in 14 concerts in 1938, and also appeared twice as a violinist; he conducted 2 concerts at the N.Y. World's Fair in 1939. The outbreak of World War II found him in Romania, where he lived on his farm in Sinaia, near Bucharest. He visited N.Y. again in 1946 as a teacher. On Jan. 21, 1950, during the 60th anniversary season of his debut as a violinist, he gave a farewell concert with the N.Y. Phil. in the multiple capacity of violinist, pianist, conductor, and composer, in a program comprising Bach's Double Concerto (with Menuhin), a violin sonata (playing the piano part with Menuhin), and his 1st *Romanian Rhapsody* (conducting the orch.). He then returned to Paris, where his last years were marked by near poverty and poor health. In July 1954 he suffered a stroke and remained an invalid for his remaining days.

Although Enesco severed relations with his Communist homeland, the Romanian government paid homage to him for his varied accomplishments. His native village, a street in Bucharest, and the State Phil. of Bucharest were named in his honor. Periodical Enesco festivals and international performing competitions were established in Bucharest in 1958. Enesco had an extraordinary range of musical interests. His compositions include artistic stylizations of Romanian folk strains; while his style was neo-Romantic, he made occasional use of experimental devices, such as quarter tones in his opera, *Oedipe*. He possessed a fabulous memory and was able to perform innumerable works without scores. He not only distinguished himself as a violinist and conductor, but he was also a fine pianist and a gifted teacher.

WORKS: OPERA: *OEdipe*, op. 23 (1921–31; Paris, March 10, 1936). **ORCH.:** 3 unnumbered syms. (1895, 1896, 1898); 5 numbered syms.: No. 1, op. 13 (1905; Paris, Jan. 21, 1906), No. 2, op. 17 (1912–14; Bucharest, March 28, 1915), No. 3, op. 21, for Chorus and Orch. (1916–18; Bucharest, May 25, 1919; rev. 1921), No. 4 (1934; unfinished), and No. 5 for Tenor, Women's Chorus, and Orch. (1941; unfinished); *Uvertura tragica* (1895); *Ballade* for Violin and Orch. (1896); *Uvertura triumfală* (1896); Violin Concerto (Paris, March 26, 1896); *Fantaisie* for Piano and Orch. (1896; Bucharest, March 26, 1900); Piano Concerto (1897; unfinished); 2 *Suites roumaines*: No. 1 (1896; unfinished) and No. 2 (1897); *Poème roumain*, op. 1, for Wordless Chorus and Orch. (1897; Paris, Feb. 9, 1898); *Pastorale* for Small Orch. (Paris, Feb. 19, 1899); *Symphonie concertante* for Cello and Orch., op. 8 (1901; Paris, March 14, 1909); 2 *Rhapsodies roumaines*, op. 11 (1901; Bucharest, March 8, 1903); 2 *Intermezzi* for Strings, op. 12 (1902–03); Suite No. 1, op. 9 (1903; Paris, Dec. 11, 1904); *Suite châtelaine*, op. 17 (1911; unfinished); Suite No. 2, op. 20 (1915; Bucharest, March 27, 1916); Suite No. 3, op. 27, *Villageoise* (1938; N.Y., Feb. 2, 1939); *Concert Overture*, op. 32, "sur des thèmes dans le caractère populaire roumain" (1948; Washington, D.C., Jan. 23, 1949); *Symphonie de chambre* for 12 Instruments, op. 33 (1954; Paris, Jan. 23, 1955); *Vox maris*, symphonic poem, op. 31 (c.1929–55; Bucharest, Sept. 10, 1964). **CHAMBER:** 2 piano quintets: No. 1 (1895) and No. 2, op. 29 (1940); 3 numbered sonatas for Violin and Piano: No. 1, op. 2 (1897), No. 2, op. 6 (1899), and No. 3, "dans le caractère populaire roumain" (1926); 2 cello sonatas: No. 1, op. 26 (1898) and No. 2, op. 26 (1935); 2 piano trios (1897, 1916); *Aubade* for String Trio (1899); Octet for 4 Violins, 2 Violas, and 2 Cellos, op. 7 (1900); *Dixtuor* for Wind Instruments, op. 14 (1906); *Au soir*, nocturne for 4 Trumpets (1906); *Konzertstück* for Viola and Piano (1906); 2 piano quartets: No. 1, op. 16 (1909) and No. 2, op. 30 (1943–44); 2 string quartets: No. 1, op. 22 (1916–20) and No. 2, op. 22 (1950–53); other chamber works. **PIANO:** *Introduzione* (1894); *Ballade* (1894); *Praeludium* (1896); *Scherzo* (1896); 3 suites: No. 1, op. 3, "dans le style ancien" (1897), No. 2, op. 10 (1901–3), and No. 3, op. 18, *Pièces impromptues* (1913–16); *Variations on an Original Theme* for 2 Pianos, op. 5 (1898); *Impromptu* (1900); *Pièce sur le nom de Fauré* (1922); 2 sonatas: No. 1, op. 24 (1924) and No. 2, op. 24 (1933–35; incorrectly publ. as "No. 3"). **VOCAL:** *La Vision de Saul*, cantata (1895); *Ahasverus*, cantata (1895); *L'Aurore*, cantata (1897–98); *Waldgesang* for Chorus (1898); Cantata for Soprano and Orch. (1899); about 25 songs, many to words by the Queen of Romania, who wrote poetry in German under the pen name Carmen Sylva.

BIBL. (all publ. in Bucharest unless otherwise given): M. Costin, *G. E.* (1938); V. Cheorghiu, *Un muzician genial: G. E.* (1944); F. Brulez, *G. E.* (1947); B. Gavoty, *Yehudi Menuhin—G. E.* (Geneva, 1955); A. Tudor, *E.* (1956); L. Voiculescu, *G. E. i opera şa Oedip* (1956); A. Tudor, *G. E.: Viaţâ in imagini* (1959; French tr., 1961); *G. E. on the 80th Anniversary of His Birth* (1961); G. Bălan, *G. E.: Mesajul—estetica* (1962); idem, *E.* (1963; German tr., 1964); F. Foni, *N. Missir, M. Voicana, and E. Zottoviceanu, G. E.* (1964); B. Kotlyarov, *G. E.* (Moscow, 1965); E. Ciomac, *E.* (1968); M. Voicana et al., eds., *G. E.: Monografie* (2 vols., 1971); R. Draghici, *G. E.* (Bacau, 1973); M. Voicana, ed., *Enesciana*, I (1976; in French, German, and Eng.); A Cosmovici, *G. E. în lumea muzicii şi în familie* (1990); N. Malcolm, *G. E.: His Life and Music* (London, 1990); V. Cosma, *G.E.: Cronica unei vieţi zbuciumstei* (1991).

Engel, Carl, distinguished American musicologist of German descent; b. Paris, July 21, 1883; d. N.Y., May 6, 1944. He was educated at the univs. of Strasbourg and Munich, and also was a composition pupil of Thuille in Munich. In 1905 he emigrated to the U.S. and in 1917 became a naturalized American citizen. He was music ed. for the Boston Music Co. (1909–22), head of the music division of the Library of Congress in Washington, D.C. (1922–34), and president of G. Schirmer, Inc., in N.Y. (1929–32; 1934–44). From 1922 he contributed to the *Musical Quarterly*, serving as its eminent ed. from 1929 to 1942. In 1937–38 he was president of the American Musicological Soc. A writer of brilliance and wide learning, he publ. the essay collections *Alla Breve, from Bach to Debussy* (N.Y., 1921) and *Discords Mingled* (N.Y., 1931). He also was a composer, producing chamber music, piano pieces, and songs.

BIBL.: G. Reese, ed., *A Birthday Offering to C. E.* (N.Y., 1943).

Engel, Hans, eminent German musicologist; b. Cairo, Egypt, Dec. 20, 1894; d. Marburg, May 15, 1970. He studied at the Akademie der Tonkunst in Munich with Klose and at the Univ. of Munich with Sandberger (Ph.D., 1925, with the diss. *Die Entwicklung des deutschen Klavierkonzertes von Mozart bis Liszt*; publ. in Leipzig, 1927); completed his Habilitation at the Univ. of Greifswald in 1926; then taught there (1926–35). He was on the faculty of the Univ. of Königsberg (1935–46) and the Univ. of Marburg (1946–63).

WRITINGS: *Carl Loewe* (Greifswald, 1934); *Franz Liszt* (Potsdam, 1936); *Deutschland und Italien in ihren musikgeschichtlichen Beziehungen* (Regensburg, 1944); *Johann Sebastian Bach* (Berlin, 1950); *Musik der Völker und Zeiten* (Hannover, 1952; rev. ed., 1968); *Luca Marenzio* (Florence, 1956); *Musik in Thüringen* (Cologne and Graz, 1966).

Engel, Karl (Rudolf), esteemed Swiss pianist and pedagogue; b. Basel, June 1, 1923. He was a student of Baumgartner at the Basel Cons. (1942–45) and of Cortot at the École Normale de Musique in Paris (1947–48). After winning 2nd prize in the Queen Elisabeth of Belgium Competition in Brussels in 1952, he toured internationally as a soloist with orchs., a recitalist, and a chamber music performer. He became especially known for his complete cycles of the Mozart piano sonatas and concertos, and the Beethoven piano sonatas. He also distinguished himself as an accompanist, often appearing in lieder recitals with Dietrich Fischer-Dieskau, Hermann Prey, and Peter Schreier. From 1959 to 1986 he was prof. of piano at the Hannover Hochschule für Musik.

Engel, Lehman, American conductor, composer, and writer on music; b. Jackson, Miss., Sept. 14, 1910; d. N.Y., Aug. 29, 1982. He attended the Univ. of Cincinnati and studied composition at the Cincinnati Cons. of Music (1927–29) before completing his training in N.Y. with Goldmark at the Juilliard Graduate School (1930–34) and with Sessions (1931–37). After conducting his own Lehman Engel Singers and the Madrigal Singers (1935–39), he concentrated on conducting and composing for the serious and popular N.Y. theater.

WORKS: DRAMATIC: OPERAS: *The Pierrot of the Minuet* (1927; Cincinnati, April 3, 1928); *Malady of Love* (N.Y., May 27, 1954); *The Soldier* (1955; concert perf., N.Y., Nov. 25, 1956).

MUSICAL COMEDIES: *Golden Ladder* (Cleveland, May 28, 1953); *Serena* (1956). **BALLETS:** *Ceremonials* (1932; N.Y., May 13, 1933); *Phobias* (N.Y., Nov. 18, 1932); *Ekstasis* (1933); *Transitions* (N.Y., Feb. 19, 1934); *Imperial Gesture* (1935); *Marching Song* (1935); *Traditions* (1938); *The Shoe Bird* (1967; Jackson, Miss., April 20, 1968). Also incidental music to over 50 plays and some film scores. **ORCH.:** 2 syms. (1939, 1945); *Overture for the End of the World* (1945); Viola Concerto (1945); *Jackson*, overture (Jackson, Miss., Feb. 13, 1961). **CHAMBER:** String Quartet (1933); Cello Sonata (1945); Violin Sonata (1953). **VOCAL:** *The Chinese Nightingale*, cantata (1928); *The Creation* for Narrator and Orch. (1945); choruses.

WRITINGS (all publ. in N.Y.): *This Bright Day* (autobiography; 1956; 2nd ed., rev., 1974); *Planning and Producing the Musical Show* (1957; 2nd ed., rev., 1966); *The American Musical Theatre: A Consideration* (1967; 2nd ed., rev., 1975); *The Musical Book* (1971); *Words with Music* (1972); *Getting Started in the Theater* (1973); *Their Words are Music: The Great Lyricists and Their Lyrics* (1975); *The Critics* (1976); *The Making of a Musical* (1977); *Getting the Show On: The Complete Guidebook for Producing a Musical in Your Theatre* (1983).

Engelmann, Hans Ulrich, German composer and pedagogue; b. Darmstadt, Sept. 8, 1921. He had piano lessons while in high school; he then took courses in composition with Fortner in Heidelberg (1945–49); from 1948 to 1950 he attended the classes of Leibowitz and Krenek in Darmstadt; also enrolled at the Univ. of Frankfurt am Main (1946–52), taking classes in musicology (with Gennrich and Osthoff) and philosophy (with Adorno). In 1952 he received his Ph.D. there with a diss. on Bartók's *Mikrokosmos* (publ. in Würzburg, 1953). In 1949 he held a Harvard Univ. stipend at the Salzburg Seminar in American Studies; was active in radio programming and in composition for films and for the theater in Iceland (1953–54), and then was theater composer in Darmstadt (1954–61). In 1969 he was appointed an instructor at the Frankfurt am Main Hochschule für Musik. His early works are impregnated by chromaticism with an impressionistic tinge. He adopted the 12-tone method of composition, expanding it into a sui generis "field technique" of total serialism, in which rhythms and instrumental timbres are organized systematically. In his theater music, he utilizes aleatory devices, *musique concrète*, and electronic sonorities.

WORKS: DRAMATIC: *Ballet colore* (1948); *Doktor Fausts Hollenfahrt*, chamber opera (1949–50; North German Radio, Hamburg, Jan. 11, 1951); *Noche de luna*, ballet (1958); *Operette*, music theater (1959); *Verlorener Schatten*, opera (1960); *Serpentina*, ballet (1962–63); *Der Fall Van Damm*, opera (1966–67; West German Radio, Cologne, June 7, 1968); *Ophelia*, multimedia theater piece (Hannover, Feb. 1, 1969); *Revue*, music theater piece (1972–73); much incidental music; film scores. **ORCH.:** *Kaleidoskop*, suite (1941); Concerto for Cello and Strings (1948); *Musik* for Strings, Brass, and Percussion (1948); *Impromptu* (1949); *Leopoldskron*, divertimento for Chamber Orch. (1949); *Orchester-Fantasie* (1951; rev. as Sym. No. 1, 1963); *Partita* (1953); *Strukturen* for Chamber Orch. (1954); *Fünf Orchesterstücke* (1956); *Polifonica* for Chamber Orch. (1957); *Ezra Pound Music* (1959); *Trias* for Piano, Orch., and Tape (1962); *Shadows* (1964); *Sonata* for Jazz Orch. (1967); *Capricciosi* (1968); *Sinfonies* (Sym. No. 2; 1968); *Sinfonia da camera* for Chamber Orch. (1981); *Stele für Büchner*, canto sinfonico for Soloists, Chorus, and Orch. (1986). **CHAMBER:** Cello Sonata (1948); String Quartet (1952); *Integrale* for Saxophone and Piano (1954); *Timbres* for Harp, Celesta, Piano, Percussion, and Tape (1963); *Mobile II* for Clarinet and Piano (1968); *Modelle I oder "I Love You Babi"* for Amplified Instruments (1970) and *II* for Trombone and Percussion Ensemble (1970); *Les chansons* for Chamber Group (1982); *Duettini* for Piano and Percussion (1985); *Inter-Lineas* for Alto Saxophone and Marimba, Vibraphone, or Percussion (1985); piano pieces. **VOCAL:** *Die Mauer*, dramatic cantata for Soloists, Chorus, and Orch. (1954; North German Radio, Hamburg, Oct. 4, 1955; stage premiere, Darmstadt, March 21, 1960); *Die Freiheit*, cantata for Soloists, Speaker, Chorus, and Orch. (1957); *Metall*, cantata for Soloists, Speaker, Chorus, and Orch. (1958); *Nocturnes* for Soprano and Chamber Orch. (1958); *Incanto* for Soprano, Soprano Saxophone, and Percussion (1959); *Manifest von Menschen*, oratorio for Soloists, Speaker, Chorus, and Orch. (1966); *Missa popularis* for Soloists, Chorus, Brass, Winds, Kettledrums, and Percussion (1980).

BIBL.: K. Carius et al., *Commedia humana: H.U. E. und sein Werk* (Wiesbaden, 1985).

Engerer, Brigitte, French pianist; b. Tunis, Oct. 27, 1952. She was taken to Paris at an early age, where at 6 she became a pupil of Lucette Descaves and made her public debut; after further training at the Paris Cons., she completed her studies with Stanislav Neuhaus at the Moscow Cons. (graduated, 1975). She won prizes at the Long-Thibaud Competition in Paris (6th, 1969), the Tchaikovsky Competition in Moscow (6th, 1974), and the Queen Elisabeth of Belgium Competition in Brussels (3rd, 1978). Engerer appeared as a soloist with the world's leading orchs. and gave recitals in the major music centers.

English, Granville, American composer; b. Louisville, Jan. 27, 1895; d. N.Y., Sept. 1, 1968. He studied with Borowski, Reuter, and Gunn at the Chicago Musical College (B.M., 1915), and with Boulanger, Haubiel, Riegger, and Serly. He taught in Chicago and N.Y., and in 1961 was composer-in-residence at Baylor Univ.

WORKS: DRAMATIC: FOLK OPERA: *Wide, Wide River*. **BALLET:** *Sea Drift*. **ORCH.:** *The Ugly Duckling* (1924); *Ballet Fantasy* (1937); *Among the Hills* (Oklahoma City, March 9, 1952); *Mood Tropicale* (Baltimore, Feb. 5, 1955); *Evenings by* *the Sea* (Port Washington, N.Y., Jan. 20, 1956). **OTHER:** Chamber music, choral works, and songs.

Englund, Einar (Sven), prominent Finnish composer, pedagogue, pianist, and music critic; b. Ljugarn, Gotland (Sweden), June 17, 1916. He studied composition with Carlson and Palmgren, instrumentation with Funtek, and piano with Paavola and Linko at the Sibelius Academy in Helsinki (1933–41); after military service (1941–45), he was awarded a stipend to continue his training with Copland at the Berkshire Music Center in Tanglewood (summer, 1949). From 1957 to 1976 he was music critic of the Helsinki Swedish newspaper *Hufvudstadsbladet.* He was also active as a pianist, often performing his own works in Finland and abroad. From 1958 to 1982 he was on the faculty of the Sibelius Academy, and in 1978 was elected to membership in the Royal Swedish Academy of Music. He has produced a distinguished body of instrumental music in a well-crafted neo-Classical style.

WORKS: BALLETS: *Sinuhe* (1953); *Odysseus* (1959). **ORCH.:** Syms.: No. 1, *The War Symphony* (1946; Helsinki, Jan. 17, 1947), No. 2, *The Blackbird Symphony* (1947; Helsinki, Oct. 8, 1948), No. 3 (1969–71; Helsinki, May 12, 1972), No. 4, *The Nostalgic* (Helsinki, Oct. 26, 1976), No. 5, *Fennica* (Helsinki, Dec. 6, 1977). No. 6, *Aphorisms*, for Chorus and Orch. (1984; Helsinki, March 12, 1986), and No. 7 (1988); *Epinikia*, symphonic poem (1947); *The Wall of China*, concert suite from the music to Max Frisch's play (1949); Cello Concerto (1954; Helsinki, May 17, 1955); *4 Dance Impressions* (1954); 2 piano concertos: No. 1 (1955; Helsinki, March 2, 1956, composer soloist) and No. 2 (1974; Helsinki, Feb. 4, 1975, composer soloist); Violin Concerto (1981; Tampere, March 26, 1982); *Serenade* for Strings (1983; Kaustinen, Feb. 15, 1984); Flute Concerto (1985; Helsinki, Sept. 16, 1986); *Lahti-fanfaari* (Lahti, Aug. 28, 1986); *Juhlasoitto "1917"* (1986; Turku, Nov. 12, 1987); *Odeion*, overture (1987; Mikkeli, Nov. 18, 1988); Clarinet Concerto (1991). **CHAMBER:** Quintet for Piano and Strings (1941); *Introduzione e Capriccio* for Violin and Piano (1970); *Divertimento upsaliensis* for Wind Quintet, String Quintet, and Piano (1978); Violin Sonata (1979); *De profundis* for 14 Brass Instruments (1980); Concerto for 12 Cellos (1980–81); Cello Sonata (1982); Trio for Piano, Violin, and Cello (1982); String Quartet (1985); also works for solo instruments, including Piano Sonata No. 1 (1978); *Arioso interrotto* for Violin (1979); *Pavane e Toccata* for Piano (1983); *Viimeinen saari* (The Last Island) for Cello (1986); Intermezzo for Oboe (1987). **OTHER:** Choral pieces; music for films, plays, and radio.

Enna, August (Emil), eminent Danish composer; b. Nakskov, May 13, 1859; d. Copenhagen, Aug. 3, 1939. He was taken to Copenhagen as a child, and learned to play piano and violin; had sporadic instruction in theory; later became a member of a traveling orch. and played with it in Finland (1880). Upon his return to Copenhagen, he taught piano and played for dancers; in 1883 he became music director of Werner's Theatrical Soc. and wrote his first stage work, *A Village Tale*, which he produced the same year. After these practical experiences, he began to study seriously; took lessons with Schjorring (violin), Matthesson (organ), and Rasmussen (composition) and soon publ. a number of piano pieces, which attracted the attention of Gade, who used his influence to obtain a traveling fellowship for Enna; this made it possible for Enna to study in Germany (1888–89) and acquire a complete mastery of instrumental and vocal writing. He followed the German Romantic school, being influenced mainly by Weber's type of opera, and by Grieg and Gade in the use of local color; the first product of this period was his most successful work, the opera *Heksen* (The Witch), premiered in Copenhagen (Jan. 24, 1892), then in Germany.

WORKS (all 1st perf. in Copenhagen unless otherwise given): **OPERAS:** *Agleia* (1884); *Heksen* (The Witch; Jan. 24, 1892); *Kleopatra* (Feb. 7, 1894); *Aucassin og Nicolette* (Feb. 2, 1896); *Den lille pige med svovlstikkerne* (The Match Girl; Nov. 13, 1897); *Lamia* (Antwerp, Oct. 3, 1899); *Ung Elskov* (as *Heisse Liebe*, Weimar, Dec. 6, 1904); *Prinsessen paa aerten* (Princess and the Pea; Århus, Sept. 15, 1900); *Nattergallen* (The Nightingale; Nov. 10, 1912); *Gloria Arsena* (April 15, 1917); *Børnene fra Santa Fé* (The Children from Santa Fé; March 16, 1918); *Komedianter* (Comedians; April 8, 1920); *Don Juan Mañara* (April 17, 1925); *Afrodites praestinde* (Aphrodite's Priestess; 1925); *Ghettoens dronning* (The Queen of the Ghetto; 1932). **BALLETS:** *The Shepherdess and the Chimney Sweep* (Oct. 6, 1901); *St. Cecilia's Golden Shoe* (Dec. 26, 1904); *The Kiss* (Oct. 19, 1927). **ORCH.:** 2 syms. (1886, 1908); Violin Concerto (1897); *Hans Christian Andersen*, overture (1905). **OTHER:** Choral pieces.

Eno, Brian (Peter George St. John le Baptiste de la Salle), English composer, musician, and producer; b. Woodbridge, Suffolk, May 15, 1948. Although interested in tape recorders and recorded music at an early age, he received no formal music training, studying art at Ipswich and Winchester art schools (1964–69); he then became involved in avant-garde experiments, performing works by LaMonte Young and Cornelius Cardew. He helped found the art-rock band Roxy Music in 1971, leaving it 2 years later for a solo career that resulted in 4 modestly successful progressive-rock albums during the mid-1970s. In 1975, while confined to bed after being struck by a London taxi, he was also struck by the pleasures of minimalism, shifting his style to what he has termed "ambient," a sort of high-art Muzak. He has collaborated with David Bowie, Talking Heads, U2, and Harold Budd. In 1979 he became interested in video, subsequently producing "video paintings" and "video sculptures" used as ambient music in galleries, museums, airport terminals, and private homes. His music has influenced both New Wave and New Age genres. With R. Mills, he publ. *More Dark than Shark* (London, 1986). Among his works are *Another Green World* (1975); *Discreet Music* (1975); *Before and after Science* (1977); *Music for Airports* (1978); *The Plateaux of Mirror* (with H. Budd; 1980); and *On Land* (1984).

BIBL.: E. Tamm, *B. E.: His Music and the Vertical Color of Sound* (Boston, 1989).

Enríque, Manuel, significant Mexican composer, violinist, and teacher; b. Ocotlan, June 17, 1926; d. Mexico City, April 26, 1994. He was 6 when he began violin lessons with his father, and 5 years later he started composing. He studied violin with Ignacio Camarena at the Guadalajara Cons. (1935–45) and composition with Bernal Jiménez in Morelia (1952–55). From 1949 to 1955 he was concertmaster of the Guadalajara Sym. Orch. He then continued his training with Mennin (composition) and Galamian (violin) at the Juilliard School of Music in N.Y. (1955–57), and also had private theory lessons with Wolpe (1957). Later he pursued research at the Columbia-Princeton Electronic Music Center (1971). Enríquez was assistant concertmaster of the National Sym. Orch. of Mexico (1958–65) and concertmaster of the National Sym. Chamber Orch. (from 1965). He also taught violin and composition at the National Cons. in Mexico City (1964–75), where he served as director (1972–74). From 1977 to 1988 he was director of CENIDIM (the National Searching and Information Music Center). After serving as music director of the National Inst. of Fine Arts (1988–92), he taught at the Univ. of Calif. at Los Angeles (1992–94). Enríquez was a leading composer of the post-Chávez generation in Mexico. His early works show the influences of Hindemith, Bartók, and jazz. After his U.S. studies, his music progressed into the vanguard of severe constructivism, employing dodecaphony, serialism, sonorism, indeterminacy, and graphic notation.

WORKS: DRAMATIC: *Mixteria* for Actress, 4 Musicians, and Tape (1970); *Trauma* for Actress/Dancer, Musicians, Dancers, and Tape (1974); *La Casa del Sol* for Musicians, Dancers, Actors, and Tape (1976). **ORCH.:** *Música Incidental* (1952); 2 violin concertos (1955, 1966); Suite for Strings (1957); 2 syms. (1957, 1962); *Preámbulo* (1961); *Obertura Lírica* (1963); *Transición* (1965); *Poema* for Cello and Strings (1966); *Trayectorias* (1967); *Si Lebet* (1968); *Ixamatl* (Donaueschingen, Oct. 19, 1969); Piano Concerto (1970; Mexico City, March 19, 1971); *El y . . . ellos* for

Violin and Orch. Ensemble (1971); *Encuentros* for Strings and 4 Percussionists (1972); *Ritual* (1973); *Corriente Alterna* (1977); *Raíces* (1977); *Fases* (1978); *Concierto Barroco* for 2 Violins, Strings, and Harpsichord (1978); *Interminado sueño* (1981); *Manantial de soles* (1984); Cello Concerto (1990); Concerto for 2 Guitars and Orch. (1992). **CHAMBER:** Suite for Violin and Piano (1949); 5 string quartets (1959; 1967; 1974; 1984; *Xopan cuicatl*, 1988); *Divertimento* for Flute, Clarinet, and Bassoon (1962); 4 Pieces for Viola and Piano (1962); *Pentamúsica* for Wind Quintet (1963); *3 Formas Concertantes* for Violin, Cello, Clarinet, Bassoon, Horn, Piano, and Percussion (1964); Violin Sonata (1964); *Ambivalencia* for Violin and Cello (1967); *Concierto para 8* for 7 Musicians and Conductor (1968); *Diptico I* for Flute and Piano (1969) and *II* for Violin and Piano (1971); *Móvil II* for Violin With or Without Tape (1969); *3 × Bach* for Violin and Tape (1970); *Monólogo* for Trombone (1971); *á . . . 2* for Violin and Piano (1972); Piano Trio (1974); *Tlachtli* for Violin, Cello, Flute, Clarinet, Horn, Trombone, and Piano (1976); *Conuro* for Double Bass and Tape (1976); *Tzicuri* for Cello, Clarinet, Trombone, and Piano (1976); *Políptico* for 6 Percussionists (1983). **KEYBOARD: PIANO:** *A Lapiz* (1965); *Módulos* for 2 Pianos (1965); *Móvil I* (1968–69); *Para Alicia* (1970); *1 × 4* for Piano, 4-hands (1975); *Hoy de ayer* (1981). **ORGAN:** *Imaginario* (1973). **VOCAL:** *Ego*, cantata for Woman's Voice, Flute, Cello, Piano, and Percussion (1966); *Contravox* for Chorus, 2 Percussionists, and Tape (1977). **ELECTRONIC:** *La Reunión de los Saurios* (1971); *Láser I* (1972); *Música para Federico Silva* (1974); *Cantos de los Volcanos* (1977); *Interecos* (1984).

Enthoven, (Henri) Emile, Dutch composer; b. Amsterdam, Oct. 18, 1903; d. N.Y., Dec. 26, 1950. He studied composition with Wagenaar at the Royal Cons. of Music in The Hague and with Schreker in Berlin. At the age of 14, he wrote an adolescent but well-crafted sym., which Mengelberg performed with the Concertgebouw Orch. in Amsterdam (1918). But this precocious success was not a manifestation of enduring talent; his later works lacked originality. Soon he abandoned composition altogether and took up jurisprudence; in 1939 he emigrated to N.Y. Among his works are 3 syms. (1917, 1924, 1931) and a Violin Concerto (1920).

Entremont, Philippe, eminent French pianist and conductor; b. Rheims, June 6, 1934. He began his training with his parents, both of whom were musicians; after piano lessons with Rose Aye and Marguerite Long (1944–46), he entered the Paris Cons. as a pupil of Jean Doyen, winning the premier prix for solfège at 12, for chamber music at 14, and for piano at 15. At 17, he made his formal debut as a pianist in Barcelona. In 1951 he won 5th prize and in 1953 the joint 2nd prize in the Long-Thibaud Competition in Paris, and in 1952 he also was a finalist in the Queen Elisabeth of Belgium Competition in Brussels. In 1953 he won accolades for his first concerts in the U.S. and thereafter toured with notable success as a virtuoso around the world. From 1967 he also pursued a career as a conductor. In 1976 he became music director of the Vienna Chamber Orch., which he led on many tours. He also served as music adviser and principal conductor (1980–81) and as music director (1981–86) of the New Orleans Phil.; he then was principal conductor (1986–87), music director-designate (1987–88), and music director (1988–89) of the Denver Sym. Orch. From 1988 to 1990 he was music director of the Colonne Orch. in Paris while retaining his duties with the Vienna Chamber Orch.; in 1993 he also became principal guest conductor of the Netherlands Chamber Orch. in Hilversum. His performances, both as a pianist and conductor, reveal a discriminating Gallic sensibility.

Eötvös, Peter, Hungarian conductor and composer; b. Székelyudvarhely, Jan. 2, 1944. He studied composition with Pál Kardos at the Budapest Academy of Music (1958–65) and conducting at the Cologne Hochschule für Musik (1966–68). From 1966 he worked closely with Stockhausen, and was also associated with the electronic music studio of Cologne's West German Radio (1971–79). From 1974 he appeared as a guest conductor in contemporary programs with major European orchs. He became music director of the Ensemble InterContemporain in Paris in 1979, a position he held until 1992. He also was principal guest conductor of the BBC Sym. Orch. in London (1985–88). In 1992 he was named a prof. and director of the new music ensembles at the Karlsruhe Hochschule für Musik. In 1994 he became co-principal conductor (with Ton Koopman) of the Netherlands Radio Chamber Orch. in Hilversum.

WORKS: *Moro Lasso*, comedy madrigal for 5 Soloists (1963; rev. version, 1972; Witten, April 28, 1974); *Hochzeitsmadrigal*, comedy madrigal for 6 Soloists (1963; rev. version, 1976; Metz, Nov. 20, 1976); *Windsequenzen* for Wind Instruments and Amplification (Budapest, Dec. 23, 1975); *Intervalles-Intérieurs* for Various Instruments (1981; La Rochelle, March 11, 1982); *Endless 8* for Voices, Percussion, 2 Organs, and Electric Guitar (Paris, Dec. 5, 1981); *Pierre-Idyll I* for Chamber Ensemble (1984; Baden-Baden, March 31, 1985; for Pierre Boulez's 60th birthday) and *II* for Violin, Cello, Double Bass, and Orch. (1990); *Chinese Opera* for Chamber Orch. (Paris, Nov. 17, 1986); *Szenen* for String Quartet (1992); *Triangel* for Percussionist and 27 Players (1994); *Psalm 151* for Percussion and Orch. (1994); *Psychokosmos* for Orch. (1994); also works for television and film.

Eppert, Carl, American composer and conductor; b. Carbon, Ind., Nov. 5, 1882; d. Milwaukee, Oct. 1, 1961. He studied with Harris and Wells at the American Cons. in Chicago, and then with Kaun, Nikisch, and Kunwald in Berlin (1907–14). After conducting the Seattle Grand Opera, he led the Milwaukee Civic Orch. (1921–26) and was head of the theory and composition dept. at the Wisconsin Cons. in Milwaukee (1921–23).

WORKS: OPERA: *Kaintuckee* (1915). **ORCH.:** *Arabian Suite* (1915); *Serenade* for Strings (1917); 4 symphonic poems: *The Pioneer* (1925), *Traffic* (NBC, May 8, 1932; later used as the 1st movement of the Sym. No. 1), *City Shadows*, and *Speed* (both Rochester, N.Y., Oct. 30, 1935); *Concert Waltz* (1930); 7 syms. (1934–45);*Escapade* (1937; Indianapolis, Jan. 3, 1941); *Ballet of the Vitamins* (1937–38); Concerto grosso for Flute, Oboe, Clarinet, Bassoon, and Strings (1940); *2 Symphonic Impressions* (Chicago, Feb. 13, 1941); also band pieces. **CHAMBER:** Violin Sonata (1912); 2 string quartets (1927, 1935); 3 woodwind quintets (1935, 1935, 1936); Woodwind Quartet (1937). **VOCAL:** Choral music.

Epstein, David M(ayer), American composer, conductor, and writer on music; b. N.Y., Oct. 3, 1930. He learned to play the piano and clarinet and took part in jazz bands. He studied at Antioch College (A.B., 1952); then took courses with Carl McKinley and Francis Judd Cooke at the New England Cons. of Music (M.M., 1953), with Irving Fine, Shapero, and Berger at Brandeis Univ. (M.F.A., 1954), and with Babbitt and Sessions at Princeton Univ. (M.F.A., 1956; Ph.D., 1968, with the diss. *Schoenberg's Grundgestalt and Total Serialism: Their Relevance to Homophonic Analysis*). In 1955–56 he took lessons in composition with Milhaud in Aspen. In conducting, his mentors were Max Rudolf, Izler Solomon, and Szell. He taught at Antioch College (1957–62); became an assoc. prof. of music at the Mass. Inst. of Technology in 1965; was named a prof. there in 1971. He has also served as music director of the M.I.T. Sym. Orch. from 1965. In addition, he was music director of the Harrisburg (Pa.) Sym. Orch. (1974–78). In 1983 he was appointed conductor of the New Orch. of Boston. From 1983 to 1988 he was a member of the Herbert von Karajan Musikgespräche in Vienna and at the Salzburg Easter Festival. He publ. *Beyond Orpheus: Studies in Musical Structure* (Cambridge, Mass., 1979) and *Shaping Time: Music, the Brain, and Performance* (New York, 1995), which won the ASCAP-Deems Taylor Award. In his music, he follows a serial method, cleansed of impurities and reduced to a euphonious, albeit contrapuntally dissonant, idiom.

WORKS: ORCH.: *Movement* (1953); Sym. (1958); *Sonority-Variations* (1968); *Ventures*, 3 Pieces for Symphonic Wind Ensemble (Rochester, N.Y., Dec. 11, 1970); Cello Concerto (1979). **CHAMBER:** Piano Trio (1953); String Trio (1964); String

Quartet (1971). **VOCAL:** *Excerpts from a Diary*, song cycle (1953); *The Seasons*, song cycle to poems by Emily Dickinson (1956); *Night Voices* for Narrator, Children's Chorus, and Orch. (1974); *The Concord Psalter* for Chorus (1979); *The Lament of Job* for Chorus (1982). **OTHER:** *Piano Variations* (1961); film music.

Equiluz, Kurt, esteemed Austrian tenor and teacher; b. Vienna, June 13, 1929. He received instruction in piano and violin as a child, and was a member of the Vienna Boys Choir (from 1939). In 1944 he entered the Vienna Academy of Music, where he studied with Hubert Jelinek (harp), Adolf Vogel (voice), and Ferdinand Grossmann (choral conducting). He then was a member of the Vienna Academy Chamber Choir (1946–51), and in 1949 won the Vienna Mozart Competition. In 1950 he joined the Vienna State Opera chorus, making his debut as a solo artist in 1957 and subsequently singing roles in operas by Mozart, Beethoven, and Strauss. However, it was as an oratorio and lieder artist that he acquired an international reputation, excelling particularly in the works of Bach. In 1980 he was made an Austrian Kammersänger. In 1964 he joined the faculty of the Graz Hochschule für Musik, and in 1981 the faculty of the Vienna Hochschule für Musik.

Erb, Donald (James), significant American composer and teacher; b. Youngstown, Ohio, Jan. 17, 1927. His family moved to Cleveland when he was a child; he studied cornet with a local musician. After a period of service in the U.S. Navy, he enrolled at Kent State Univ. in Ohio, where he continued to study trumpet and also took courses in composition with Harold Miles and Kenneth Gaburo (B.S., 1950), earning his living by playing trumpet in dance bands. In 1950 he entered the Cleveland Inst. of Music, in the class of Marcel Dick (M.M., 1953). On June 10, 1950, he married Lucille Hyman, and went with her to Paris to study with Boulanger (1952). Returning to Cleveland, he was engaged as a member of the faculty of the Cleveland Inst. of Music (1953). In 1961 he moved to Bloomington, Ind., where he studied composition with Bernhard Heiden at Indiana Univ., receiving his doctorate in music in 1964. In 1964–65 he was an assistant prof. of composition at Bowling Green (Ohio) State Univ. In 1965 he received a Guggenheim fellowship. From 1965 to 1967 he was a visiting assistant prof. for research in electronic music at Case Inst. of Technology in Cleveland; from 1966 to 1981, composer-in-residence at the Cleveland Inst. of Music; in 1975–76, visiting prof. of composition at Indiana Univ. in Bloomington. From 1969 to 1974 he served as staff composer at the Bennington Composers Conference in Vermont. After holding the chair of Meadows Prof. of Composition at Southern Methodist Univ. in Dallas (1981–84), he was prof. of music at the Indiana Univ. School of Music (1984–87); then was prof. of composition at the Cleveland Inst. of Music (from 1987). From 1982 to 1986 he was president of the American Music Center. From 1988 to 1991 he was composer-in-residence of the St. Louis Sym. Orch. In 1991 he was resident composer at the American Academy in Rome. He was composer-in-residence at the Aspen (Colo.) Music Festival (summer, 1993) and of the Atlantic Center for the Arts (1995). As a composer, Erb is exceptionally liberal in experimenting in all useful types of composition, from simple folklike monody to the strict dodecaphonic structures; as a former trumpeter in jazz bands, he also makes use of the jazz idiom as freely as of neo-Classical pandiatonic techniques. His most popular composition, *The 7th Trumpet* for Orch., is an epitome of his varied styles. He furthermore applies electronic sound in several of his works. In his band compositions, he achieves an extraordinary degree of pure sonorism, in which melody, harmony, and counterpoint are subordinated to the purely aural effect. He also cleverly introduces strange-looking and unusual-sounding musical and unmusical and antimusical instruments, such as euphonious goblets, to be rubbed on the rim, and telephone bells. Thanks to the engaging manner of Erb's music, even when ultradissonant, his works safely traverse their premieres and endure through repeated performances.

WORKS: ORCH.: Chamber Concerto for Piano and Strings (1958; Chicago, Feb. 12, 1961); *Symphony of Overtures* (1964; Bloomington, Ind., Feb. 11, 1965); Concerto for Solo Percussion and Orch. (Detroit, Dec. 29, 1966); *Christmasmusic* (Cleveland, Dec. 21, 1967); *The 7th Trumpet* (Dallas, April 5, 1969); *Klangfarbenfunk I* for Orch., Rock Band, and Electronic Sounds (Detroit, Oct. 1, 1970); *Autumnmusic* for Orch. and Electronic Sounds (New Haven, Conn., Oct. 20, 1973); *Treasures of the Snow* (1973; Bergen, N.J., June 8, 1974); *Music for a Festive Occasion* for Orch. and Electronic Sounds (1975; Cleveland, Jan. 11, 1976); Cello Concerto (1975; Rochester, N.Y., Nov. 4, 1976); Trombone Concerto (St. Louis, March 11, 1976); Concerto for Keyboards and Orch. (1978; Akron, Ohio, March 23, 1981); Trumpet Concerto (1980; Baltimore, April 29, 1981); *Sonneries* (1981; Rochester, N.Y., March 18, 1982); *Prismatic Variations* (1983; St. Louis, Jan. 28, 1984); Contrabassoon Concerto (1984; Houston, March 15, 1985); Clarinet Concerto (1984); *Concerto for Orchestra* (Atlanta, Sept. 12, 1985); Concerto for Brass and Orch. (1986; Chicago, April 16, 1987); *Solstice* for Chamber Orch. (Cleveland, June 3, 1988); Sym. for Winds (1989; Elmhurst, Ill., May 11, 1990); *Ritual Observances* (St. Louis, April 30, 1991); Violin Concerto (1992; Grand Rapids, Mich., April 16, 1993); *Evensong* (1993; Cleveland, May 5, 1994).

CHAMBER: 2 string quartets (1960, 1989); Quartet for Flute, Oboe, Alto Saxophone, and Double Bass (1961); Sonata for Harpsichord and String Quartet (1961); *Dance Pieces* for Violin, Piano, Trumpet, and Percussion (1963); *Hexagon* for Flute, Alto Saxophone, Trumpet, Trombone, Cello, and Piano (1963); *Antipodes* for String Quartet and Percussion Quartet (1963); *Phantasma* for Flute, Oboe, Double Bass, and Harpsichord (1965); *Diversion for 2 (other than sex)* for Trumpet and Percussion (1966); *Andante* for Piccolo, Flute, and Alto Flute (1966); Trio for Violin, Electric Guitar, and Cello (1966); *Reconnaissance* for Violin, Double Bass, Piano, Percussion, and 2 Electronic Setups (1967); *Trio for 2* for Alto Flute or Percussion, and Double Bass (1968); *Harold's Trip* to the Sky for Viola, Piano, and Percussion (1972); Quintet for Violin, Cello, Flute, Clarinet, and Piano (1976); Trio for Violin, Percussion, and Piano (1977); Sonata for Clarinet and Percussion (1980); *3 Pieces* for Harp and Percussion (1981); *Déjà vu*, 6 études for Double Bass (1981); *The St. Valentine's Day Brass Quintet* (1981); *Aura* for String Quintet (1981); *The Last Quintet* for Woodwinds (1982); *The Devil's Quickstep* for Flute, Clarinet, Violin, Cello, Percussion, Keyboards, and Harp (1982); *Fantasy for Cellist and Friends* (1982); *Adieu* for Bass Clarinet and 2 Percussionists (1984); *The Rainbow Snake* for Trombone, 2 Percussion, Keyboards, and Tape (1985); *Views of Space and Time* for Violin, Keyboards, Harp, 2 Percussion, and Amplification (1987); *A Book of Fanfares* for Brass Quintet (1987); *The Watchman Fantasy* for Amplified Piano with Digital Delay, Violin, and Synthesizer (1988); *Woody* for Clarinet (1988); *4 Timbre Pieces* for Cello and Double Bass (1989); *5 Red Hot Duets* for 2 Contrabassoons (1989); *Celebration Fanfare* for 13 Instruments (1990); *Drawing Dawn the Moon* for Piccolo and Percussion (1991); *Illwarra Music* for Bassoon and Piano (1992); Sonata for Solo Violin (1994); *Remembrances* for 2 Trumpets (1994); *Changes* for Clarinet and Piano (1994); Harp Sonata (1995).

VOCAL: *Cummings Cycle* for Chorus and Orch. (1963); *Fallout?* for Narrator, Chorus, String Quartet, and Piano (1964); *God Love You Now* for Chorus, Hand Percussion, and Harmonicas (1971); *New England's Prospect* for Choruses, Narrator, and Orch. (Cincinnati, May 17, 1974).

ELECTRONIC SOUND: *Reticulation* for Symphonic Band and Electronic Tape (1965); *Stargazing* for Band and Electronic Tape (1966); *Fission* for Electronic Tape, Soprano Saxophone, Piano, Dancers, and Lights (1968); *In No Strange Land* for Tape, Trombone, and Double Bass (1968); *Basspiece* for Double Bass and 4 tracks of prerecorded Double Bass (1969); *Souvenir* for Tape, Instruments, Lights, etc. (1970); *Z milosci do Warszawy* for Piano, Clarinet, Cello, Trombone, and Electronic Sound (1971); *The Purple-roofed Ethical Suicide Parlor* for Wind Ensemble and Electronic Sound (1972); *The Towers of Silence* for Electronic Quintet (1974).

Erb, John Lawrence, American music educator and composer; b. Reading, Pa., Feb. 5, 1877; d. Eugene, Oreg., March 17, 1950. He studied at the Metropolitan College of Music in N.Y. (1894–99). He was director of the Wooster, Ohio, Cons. (1905–13) and of the School of Music, Univ. of Ill. (1914–21); was lecturer at the American Inst. of Applied Music in N.Y. (1921–24); from 1923 he was at the Conn. College for Women. He publ. *Brahms* (1895; 1905; rev. ed., London, 1934); *Hymns and Church Music* (1911); *Elements of Harmony* (1911); *Elementary Theory* (1911); *Music Appreciation for the Student* (1926); *Select Songs for the Assembly* (1931). He also composed songs, piano pieces, organ music, anthems, and music for pageants.

Erb, Karl, noted German tenor; b. Ravensburg, July 13, 1877; d. there, July 13, 1958. He was self-taught. He made his debut in Stuttgart in 1907; then sang in Lübeck (1908–10), Stuttgart (1910–13), and Munich (1913–25); later embarked on a series of appearances as a concert and oratorio singer. He was best known for his portrayal of roles in the works of Mozart; he created the title role in Pfitzner's *Palestrina* (1917). From 1921 to 1932 he was married to **Maria Ivogün**.

Erbse, Heimo, German composer; b. Rudolstadt, Thuringia, Feb. 27, 1924. He studied in Weimar, and in Berlin with Boris Blacher; in 1957 he moved to Salzburg.

WORKS: Sonata for 2 Pianos (1951); *Capriccio* for Piano, Strings, and Percussion (1952); Piano Trio (1953); *12 Aphorismen* for Flute, Violin, and Piano (1954); *Sinfonietta giocosa* (1955); *Dialog* for Piano and Orch. (1955); *Tango-Variationen* for Orch. (1958); *Julietta*, opera semi-seria (Salzburg, Aug. 17, 1959); Wind Quartet (1961); 2 piano concertos (1962, 1991); 5 syms. (1963–64; 1969–70; n.d.; 1992; 1993); *Der Herr in Grau*, comic opera (1966); *5 Songs* for Baritone and Orch. (1969); *Musik für Nonett* (1970–71); *4 Gesänge aus den Anakreontischen Liedern* for Soprano or Tenor, Flute, and Harpsichord (1977); String Quartet No. 2 (1987); Sextet for Winds and Piano (1991); Clarinet Sonata (1993).

Erdélyi, Miklós, Hungarian conductor; b. Budapest, Feb. 9, 1928; d. there, Sept. 2, 1993. He studied at the Franz Liszt Academy of Music in Budapest (1946–50) with Ferencsik (conducting), Zalánfy (organ), and Kókai (composition). After making his conducting debut in Budapest in 1947, he was music director of the Hungarian Radio Choir there (1950–52). In 1951 he became a répétiteur at the Hungarian State Opera in Budapest, where he was a conductor from 1959. He also appeared as a guest conductor in various European music centers, and in 1972 made his U.S. debut as a guest conductor with the San Antonio Sym. Orch. He was the author of *Schubert* (Budapest, 1963; 2nd ed., 1979).

Erede, Alberto, Italian conductor; b. Genoa, Nov. 8, 1908. After training in Genoa and at the Milan Cons., he studied conducting with Weingartner in Basel (1929–31) and Busch in Dresden (1930). In 1930 he made his debut at the Accademia di Santa Cecilia in Rome; then was on the staff of the Glyndebourne Festival (1934–39); he also conducted the Salzburg Opera Guild (1935–38). In 1937 he made his U.S. debut with the NBC Sym. Orch. in N.Y. After serving as chief conductor of the RAI Orch. in Turin (1945–46), he was music director of the New London Opera Co. (1946–48). On Nov. 11, 1950, he made his Metropolitan Opera debut in N.Y. conducting *La Traviata*, remaining on its roster until 1955; he conducted there again in 1974. He was Generalmusikdirektor of the Deutsche Oper am Rhein in Düsseldorf (1958–62). In 1968 he conducted *Lohengrin* at the Bayreuth Festival. He subsequently was active as a guest conductor in Europe, and in 1975 became artistic director of the Paganini Competition in Genoa.

Erickson, Robert, American composer and teacher; b. Marquette, Mich., March 7, 1917. He studied with Wesley La Violette at the Chicago Cons. and with Krenek at Hamline Univ. in St. Paul (B.A., 1943; M.A., 1947); in 1950 he attended a seminar in composition under Sessions at the Univ. of Calif. at Berkeley. In 1966 he held a Guggenheim fellowship. He taught at the College of St. Catherine in St. Paul, Minn. (1947–53), at San Francisco State College (1953–54), at the Univ. of Calif. at Berkeley (1956–58), and at the San Francisco Cons. of Music (1957–66). From 1967 to 1987 he was a prof. of composition at the Univ. of Calif. at San Diego. In his early works, he utilized serial techniques; after exploring electronic music, he resumed non-electronic means of expression. He publ. *The Structure of Music: A Listener's Guide to Melody and Counterpoint* (1955) and *Sound Structure in Music* (1975).

WORKS: *Introduction and Allegro* for Orch. (Minneapolis, March 11, 1949); Piano Sonata (1948); 2 string quartets (1953, 1956); Piano Trio (1953); *Divertimento* for Flute, Clarinet, and Strings (1953); *Fantasy* for Cello and Orch. (1953); *Variations* for Orch. (1957); Duo for Violin and Piano (1959); Chamber Concerto (1960); Concerto for Piano and 7 Instruments (1963); *Sirens and Other Flyers* for Orch. (1965); *Ricercar a 5* for Trombone and Tape (1966); *Scapes*, a "contest for 2 groups" (1966); *Birdland* for Electronic Tape (1967); *Ricercar a 3* for Double Bass and Electronic Tape (1967); *Cardenitas*, dramatic aria for Singer, Mime, Conductor, 7 Musicians, and Stereophonic Prerecorded Tape (1968); *Pacific Sirens* for Instruments and Tape (1969); *Rainbow Rising* for Orch. (1974); *The Idea of Order at Key West* for Voice and Instruments (1979); *East of the Beach* for Small Orch. (1980); *Auroras* for Orch. (1982); *Taffytime* for Large Ensemble (1983); *Mountain* for Mezzo-soprano and Chamber Orch. (1983); *Sierra* for Tenor or Baritone and Chamber Orch. (1984); *Solstice* for String Quartet (1984–85).

Ericson, Eric, distinguished Swedish choral conductor, organist, and pedagogue; b. Borås, Oct. 26, 1918. He studied at the Stockholm Musikhögskolan (1941–43) and at the Basel Schola Cantorum (1943–49). He served as an organist and choirmaster in Stockholm churches, including the Jakobskirche from 1949. In 1945 he became conductor of the Swedish Radio Chamber Choir in Stockholm, which he subsequently conducted as the expanded Swedish Radio Choir from 1951 to 1984. He also was conductor of the noted men's choir Orphei Dränger in Uppsala from 1951 to 1985. In 1952 he became a teacher and in 1968 a prof. at the Stockholm Musikhögskolan. In 1995 he received the Nordic Council Music Prize. Ericson was an inspirational choral conductor and influential pedagogue.

BIBL.: L. Reimers and B. Wallner, eds., *Choral Music Perspectives: Dedicated to E. E.* (Stockholm, 1993).

Erkin, Ulvi Cemal, Turkish composer and teacher; b. Constantinople, March 14, 1906; d. Ankara, Sept. 15, 1972. He studied piano with Philipp in Paris and composition with Boulanger in Fontainebleau. Returning to Turkey, he became a piano instructor at the Ankara Cons. His works include *Bayram*, tone poem (Ankara, May 11, 1934); 2 syms. (Ankara, April 20, 1946; 1948–51); Violin Concerto (Ankara, April 2, 1948); chamber music; piano pieces.

d'Erlanger, Baron François Rodolphe, French ethnomusicologist and composer; b. Boulonge-sur-Seine, June 7, 1872; d. Sidi bou Said, Tunisia, Oct. 29, 1932. He settled in Tunis in 1910; from 1924, assisted by Arab scholars and musicians, he made intensive study of Arabic music, translating many major theoretical treatises. His most important work, the source collection *La Musique arabe* (6 vols., Paris, 1930–59), was intended to spark a Renaissance of Arab music and its study; the 1st 4 vols. contain translations of writings from the 10th to 16th centuries, and the last 2 vols. codify contemporary theory. Most of his books were publ. posthumously; they became primary sources on Arab music, as they include translations, transcriptions, and extended analytic studies. His own compositions were written according to Arab theoretical principles.

WRITINGS (all publ. in Paris): *La Musique arabe* (6 vols., 1930–59); *Chants populaires de l'Afrique du nord* (1931); *Mélodies tunisiennes, hispano-arabes, arabo-berbères, juives, nègres* (1937).

d'Erlanger, Baron Frédéric, French-born English composer; b. Paris, May 29, 1868; d. London, April 23, 1943. He was born into the family of French bankers. He studied music with Ehmant in Paris; then settled in London, where he was active as a banker and a composer. In 1897 he assumed the pseudonym Regnal, formed by reading backward the last 6 letters of his name.

WORKS: DRAMATIC: OPERAS: *Jehan de Saintre* (Aix-les-Bains, Aug. 1, 1893); *Inez Mendo* (London, July 10, 1897); *Tess* (Naples, April 10, 1906); *Noël* (Paris, Dec. 28, 1910). **BALLET:** *Les cent baisers* (London, 1935). **ORCH.:** *Suite symphonique* (1895); Violin Concerto (London, March 12, 1903); *Concerto symphonique* for Piano and Orch. (1921). **CHAMBER:** Piano Quintet; String Quartet; Violin Sonata.

Ermler, Mark, Russian conductor; b. Leningrad, May 5, 1932. He studied with Khaiken and Rabinovich at the Leningrad Cons., graduating in 1956. In 1952 he made his debut with the Leningrad Phil., and in 1953 his debut as an opera conductor with *Die Entführung aus dem Serail* in Leningrad. From 1956 he was on the conducting staff of the Bolshoi Theater in Moscow, where he led a vast operatic and ballet repertoire; also appeared with the company on its tours to Montreal (1967), Paris and Tokyo (1970), Milan (1974), N.Y. and Washington, D.C. (1975), Berlin (1980), and other major music centers. As a guest conductor, he appeared throughout Europe, North America, and Japan.

Ernesaks, Gustav (Gustavovich), Estonian composer and conductor; b. Chariu, Dec. 12, 1908; d. Tallinn, Jan. 24, 1993. He was a pupil of A. Kapp at the Tallinn Cons. He subsequently was active as a composer and conductor. Among his works were several operas, music for films and plays, choruses, and songs.

Ernster, Desző, Hungarian bass; b. Pécs, Nov. 23, 1898; d. Zürich, Feb. 15, 1981. He studied in Budapest and Vienna; then sang in Plauen, Gera, and Düsseldorf; in 1929 he appeared at the Berlin State Opera, in 1931 at the Bayreuth Festival, and in 1933 at the Vienna State Opera; then was a member of the Graz City Theater (1935–36). He made his first visit to the U.S. during the 1938–39 season, when he sang in N.Y. with the Salzburg Opera Guild. During World War II, he was interned in a concentration camp. On Nov. 20, 1946, he made his Metropolitan Opera debut in N.Y. as Marke in *Tristan und Isolde*; remained on its roster until 1964; was also a member of the Deutsche Oper am Rhein in Düsseldorf (1950–67).

BIBL.: J. Fábián, *E.* (Budapest, 1969).

Erpf, Hermann (Robert), German musicologist and composer; b. Pforzheim, April 23, 1891; d. Stuttgart, Oct. 17, 1969. He studied with Wolfrem in Heidelberg (1909–11) and with Riemann at the Univ. of Leipzig (Ph.D., 1913, with the diss. *Der Begriff der musikalischen Form*; publ. in Stuttgart, 1914). He taught at Pforzheim (1919–23) and at the Univ. of Freiburg am Breisgau (1923–25); was assistant director at the Academy of Speech and Music in Münster (1925–27); was in charge of the Folkwangschule in Essen (1927–43). From 1943 to 1945, and again from 1952 to 1956, he was director of the Hochschule für Musik in Stuttgart. He composed choral pieces, chamber music, and songs.

WRITINGS: *Entwicklungszuge in der zeitgenössischen Musik* (Karlsruhe, 1922); *Studien zur Harmonie- und Klangtechnik der neueren Musik* (Leipzig, 1927; 2nd ed., 1969); *Harmonielehre in der Schule* (Leipzig, 1930); *Vom Wesen der neuen Musik* (Stuttgart, 1949); *Neue Wege der Musikerziehung* (Stuttgart, 1953); *Gegenwartskunde der Musik* (Stuttgart, 1954); *Form und Struktur in der Musik* (Mainz, 1967).

Ershov, Ivan (Vasilievich), celebrated Russian tenor; b. Maly Nesvetai, near Novocherkassk, Nov. 20, 1867; d. Tashkent, Nov. 21, 1943. He studied voice in Moscow with Alexandrova-Kochetova and in St. Petersburg with Gabel and Paleček. In 1893 he made his operatic debut at the Maryinsky Theater in St. Petersburg as Faust, which became one of his most popular roles; then went to Italy and took voice lessons with Rossi in Milan; appeared in Turin as Don José in *Carmen.* He returned to Russia in 1894 and joined the Kharkov Opera; in 1895 he became a member of the Maryinsky Opera Theater in St. Petersburg, and served with it until 1929. He achieved fabulous success as the greatest performer of the tenor roles in the Russian repertoire, and he also was regarded by music critics and audiences as the finest interpreter of the Wagnerian operas; he sang Siegfried, Tannhäuser, Lohengrin, and Tristan with extraordinary lyric and dramatic penetration; as an opera tenor in his time, he had no rivals on the Russian stage. In 1929, at the age of 62, he sang Verdi's Otello; he also appeared in oratorio and solo recitals. From 1916 to 1941 he taught voice at the Petrograd (Leningrad) Cons. At the beginning of the siege of Leningrad in 1941, Ershov was evacuated with the entire personnel of the Cons. to Tashkent in Central Asia, where he died shortly afterward.

BIBL.: V. Bogdanov-Berezovsky, *I. E.* (Leningrad, 1951).

Erskine, John, American pianist, educator, and writer on music; b. N.Y., Oct. 5, 1879; d. there, June 1, 1951. He studied piano with Carl Walter and composition with MacDowell; then took up an academic and literary career, becoming highly successful as a novelist and essayist. He was educated at Columbia Univ. (B.A., 1900; M.A., 1901; Ph.D., 1903; LL.D., 1929); was a prof. of English there (1909–37), then prof. emeritus. In 1923 he resumed piano study under Ernest Hutcheson; played as soloist with the N.Y. Sym. Orch. and the Baltimore Civic Orch.; was president of the Juilliard School of Music in N.Y. (1928–37); and president of the Juilliard Music Foundation from 1948 until his death. He was ed. of *A Musical Companion* (1935). He publ. *Is There a Career in Music?* (N.Y., 1929); *Song without Words: The Story of Felix Mendelssohn* (1941); *The Philharmonic-Symphony Society of N.Y., Its First Hundred Years* (N.Y., 1943); *What Is Music?* (Philadelphia, 1944); *The Memory of Certain Persons* (Philadelphia, 1947); *My Life as a Teacher* (N.Y., 1948); *My Life in Music* (N.Y., 1950).

Eschenbach (real name, **Ringmann**), **Christoph,** remarkably talented German pianist and conductor; b. Breslau, Feb. 20, 1940. His mother died in childbirth; his father, the musicologist Heribert Ringmann, lost his life in battle soon thereafter; his grandmother died while attempting to remove him from the advancing Allied armies; placed in a refugee camp, he was rescued by his mother's cousin, who adopted him in 1946. He began studying piano at age 8 with his foster mother; his formal piano training commenced at the same age with Eliza Hansen in Hamburg, and continued with her at the Hochschule für Musik there; he also studied piano with Hans-Otto Schmidt in Cologne, and received instruction in conducting from Brückner-Ruggeberg at the Hamburg Hochschule für Musik. In 1952 he won 1st prize in the Steinway Piano Competition; after winning 2nd prize in the Munich International Competition in 1962, he gained wide recognition by capturing 1st prize in the 1st Clara Haskil Competition in Montreux (1965). In 1966 he made his London debut; following studies with Szell (1967–69), the latter invited him to make his debut as soloist in Mozart's Piano Concerto in F major, K. 459, with the Cleveland Orch. on Jan. 16, 1969. In subsequent years, he made numerous tours as a pianist, appearing in all of the major music centers of the world. He also gave duo concerts with the pianist Justus Frantz. In 1972 he began to make appearances as a conductor; made his debut as an opera conductor in Darmstadt with *La Traviata* in 1978. He pursued a successful career as both a pianist and a conductor, sometimes conducting from the keyboard. After serving as Generalmusikdirektor of the Rheinland-Pfalz State Phil. (1979–81), he was 1st permanent guest conductor of the Zürich Tonhalle Orch. (1981–82); then was its chief conductor (1982–85). In 1988 he became music director of the Houston Sym. Orch. He also served as music director of the Ravinia Festival in Chicago from 1995. Eschenbach maintains a varied repertoire, as both a pianist and a conductor; his sympathies range from the standard literature to the cosmopolitan avant-garde.

BIBL.: W. Erk, ed., *Für C. E. zum 20. Februar 1990: Eine Festgabe* (Stuttgart, 1990).

Escher, Rudolf (George), noted Dutch composer; b. Amsterdam, Jan. 8, 1912; d. De Koog, March 17, 1980. He studied harmony, violin, and piano at the Toonkunst Cons. in Rotterdam (1931–37); was a student in composition of Pijper (1934); worked in the electronic music studios in Delft (1959–60) and in Utrecht (1961). He taught at the Amsterdam Cons. (1960–61) and at the Inst. for Musical Science at the Univ. of Utrecht (1964–75). In 1977 he was awarded the Johan Wagenaar Prize for his compositions. Escher's music was very much influenced by the modern French school.

WORKS: ORCH.: *Sinfonia in memoriam Maurice Ravel* (1940); *Musique pour l'esprit en deuil* (1941–43; Amsterdam, Jan. 19, 1947); *Passacaglia* (1945; withdrawn); Concerto for Strings (1947–48; withdrawn); *Hymne de Grand Meaulnes* (1950–51); 2 syms. (1953–54; 1958; rev. 1964 and 1971); *Summer Rites at Noon* for 2 facing Orchs. (1962–68); orchestration of Debussy's *6 épigraphes antiques* for Piano Duet (1976–77; Hilversum Radio, July 6, 1978). **CHAMBER:** *Sonata concertante* for Cello and Piano (1943); Sonata for 2 Flutes (1944); Sonata for Solo Cello (1945); Trio for Oboe, Clarinet, and Bassoon (1946); Sonata for Solo Flute (1949); Violin Sonata (1950); *Le Tombeau de Ravel* for Flute, Oboe, Violin, Viola, Cello, and Harpsichord (1952); *Air pour charmer un lezard* for Flute (1953); Trio for Violin, Viola, and Cello (1959); Wind Quintet (1966–67); *Monologue* for Flute (1969); Sonata for Solo Clarinet (1973); *Sinfonia* for 10 Instruments (1976); Flute Sonata (1975–77); Trio for Clarinet, Viola, and Piano (1978). **PIANO:** Sonata No. 1 (1935); *Arcana musae dona*, suite (1944); *Habanera* (1945); *Due voci* (1949); *Non troppo*, 10 easy pieces (1949); Sonatina (1951). **VOCAL:** *Nostalgies* for Tenor and Orch. (1951; rev. 1961); *Le Vrai Visage de la paix* for Chorus (1953; rev. 1957); *Song of Love and Eternity* for Chorus (1955); *Ciel, air et vents* for Chorus (1957); *Univers de Rimbaud* for Tenor and Orch. (1970).

Escobar, Roberto, Chilean composer and musicologist; b. Santiago, May 11, 1926. He studied at the Escuela Moderna de Música in Santiago and at the Manhattan School of Music in N.Y. In 1972 he was a senior Fulbright scholar at Columbia Univ., and in 1976–77 at the Univ. of Missouri. From 1974 he held chairmanships at the Univ. of Chile in Santiago, where he became a Distinguished Prof. in 1981; he also was made a prof. extraordinary at the Catholic Univ. in Valparaiso that same year. He served as president of the Asociación Nacional de Compositores (1974–77) and the Sociedad Chilena de Filosofía (1985–88). Among his books are *Músicos sin pasado* (Barcelona, 1971), *Filosofía en Chile* (Santiago, 1976), and *Teoria de Chileno* (Santiago, 1981).

WORKS: ORCH.: *Diferencias Sinfonicas* (1962); *Laberinto* for 4 Voices, 16 Instruments, and Percussion (1971); *Symphonia de Fluminis*, choral sym. (1992); *Sinfonia Andres Bello*, choral sym. for the 150th anniversary of the Univ. of Chile (Santiago, Oct. 9, 1993). **CHAMBER:** *Cuarteto Estructural* for String Quartet (1966); *Ceremonia de Percusion*, Mass for Percussion and Guitar (1974); *Cuarteto Funcional* for String Quartet (1979); *The Tower of the Winds* for String Quartet (1992); pieces for Solo Instruments.

Escot, Pozzi (Olga), Peruvian-born American composer of French-Moroccan descent; b. Lima, Oct. 1, 1931. She studied with Andrés Sás at the Sás-Rosay Academy of Music in Lima (1949–53); she also took courses in mathematics at San Marcos Univ. there (1950–52). She emigrated to the U.S. in 1953, becoming a naturalized citizen in 1963; she studied with Bergsma at the Juilliard School of Music in N.Y. (B.S., 1956; M.S., 1957) and with Jarnach at the Hamburg Hochschule für Musik (1957–61). She taught at the New England Cons. of Music in Boston (1964–67; 1980–81) and at Wheaton College in Norton, Mass. (from 1972), where she was director of its electronic music studio; she also lectured at the univs. of Peking and Shanghai (1984). She ed. the journal *Sonus* (from 1980). With her husband, Robert Cogan, she wrote *Sonic Design: The Nature of Sound and Music* (Englewood Cliffs, N.J., 1976) and *Sonic Design: Practice and Problems* (Englewood Cliffs, N.J., 1981). Her musical idiom follows the tenets of modern structural formalism with modified serial procedures.

WORKS: ORCH.: 3 syms. (*Little Symphony*, 1952–53; Sym. for Strings, 1955; 1957); *Sands . . .* for 5 Saxophones, Electric Guitar, 17 Violins, 9 Double Basses, and Percussion (1965); Concerto for Piano and Chamber Orch. (1982). **CHAMBER:** *Cristhos: Trilogy No. 2* for Alto Flute, Contrabassoon, 3 Violins, and Percussion (1963); *Neyrac lux* for 2 Guitars and Electric Guitar (1978); *Trio in memoriam Solrac* for Violin, Cello, and Piano (1984); *Mirabilis I* for Viola and Tape (1990) and *II* for Piano, Percussion, and Clarinet (1992); *Jubilation* for String Quartet (1991); *Bels Dous Amics*, trio for Violin, Cello, and Piano (1993). **PIANO:** *Differences* (2 groups; 1960–61; 1963); *Interra I* for Piano, Tape, Lights, and Film (1968) and *II* for Piano, Left-hand and Tape (1980). **VOCAL:** *3 Poems of Rilke* for Narrator and String Quartet (1959); *Lamentus: Trilogy No. 1* for Soprano, 2 Violins, 2 Cellos, Piano, and 3 Percussion (1962); *Visione: Trilogy No. 3* for Soprano, Speaker, Flute or Piccolo, Alto Flute, Alto Saxophone, Double Bass, and Percussion (1964); *Ainu* for 4 Ensembles of 5 Voices (1970; also for 1 Voice, 1978); *Missa triste* for 3 Women's Choruses and 3 Optional Treble Instruments (1981); *Your Kindled Valors Bend* for Alto, Clarinet, and Piano (1989).

Eshpai, Andrei (Yakovlevich), Russian composer and pianist, son of **Yakov (Andreievich) Eshpai;** b. Kozmodemiansk, May 15, 1925. He studied piano with Safranitsky and composition with Miaskovsky and Golubev (1948–53) at the Moscow Cons., where he completed his training in composition with Khatchaturian (1953–56). From 1965 to 1970 he was on its faculty. He made tours as a pianist throughout Russia and abroad. In 1986 he received the Lenin Prize. His output, which includes both serious and light scores, is written in an accessible style. He has made use of folk motifs of the Mari nation.

WORKS: DRAMATIC: Operettas; musicals; ballets, including *The Circle* (1980; Kuibishev, Feb. 23, 1981); incidental music to plays; many film scores. **ORCH.:** *Symphonic Dances* (1951); *Hungarian Melodies* for Violin and Orch. (1952); 2 piano concertos (1954, 1972); 7 syms. (1959; 1962; 1964; 1982; 1985–86; 1988–89; 1991); *Concerto for Orchestra* (1967); *Festival Overture* for Chorus and Orch. (1970); Oboe Concerto (1982); Concerto for Saxophone, Soprano, and Orch. (1986); Viola Concerto (1988); Cello Concerto (1989); Violin Concerto No. 3 (1990); Violin Concerto No. 4 (1991); Flute Concerto (1994). **CHAMBER:** 2 violin sonatas (1966, 1970); String Quartet (1992).

Eshpai, Yakov (Andreievich), Russian composer of Mari descent, father of **Andrei (Yakovlevich) Eshpai**; b. near Zvenigorodsk, Oct. 30, 1890; d. Moscow, Feb. 20, 1963. He studied violin and singing in Kazan, and later at the Moscow Cons. He publ. important collections of national songs of the Ural region, particularly of the Mari ethnic group; also wrote vocal and instrumental music on native themes.

Esplá (y Triay), Oscar, Spanish music educator and composer; b. Alicante, Aug. 5, 1886; d. Madrid, Jan. 6, 1976. He began his musical studies in Alicante, and then pursued training in engineering and philosophy at the Univ. of Barcelona (1903–11); subsequently he studied with Reger in Meiningen and Munich (1912) and Saint-Saëns in Paris (1913). In 1930 he became a prof. at the Madrid Cons., serving as its director (1936–39); was also president of the Junta Nacional de Música y Teatros Líricos (1931–34). He became director of the Laboratoire Musical Scientifique in Brussels in 1946; returning to Spain, he became director of his own cons. in Alicante (1958). He publ. *El arte y la musicalidad* (Alicante, 1912), *Fundamento estético de las actividades del espíritu* (Munich, 1915), and *Función musical y* *música contemporánea* (Madrid, 1955). A. Iglesias ed. *Escritos de Oscar Esplà* (3 vols., 1977–86). His compositions show the influence of Spanish folk music; he utilized his own Levantine scale in his works.

WORKS: DRAMATIC: OPERAS: *La bella durmiente* (Vienna, 1909); *La balteira* (N.Y., 1935); *Plumes au vent* (1941); *El pirata cautivo* (Madrid, 1974); *Calixto y Melibea* (1974–76). **SCENIC CANTATA:** *Nochebuena del diablo* for Soprano, Chorus, and Orch. (1923). **BALLETS:** *Ciclopes de Ifach* (1920?); *El contrabandista* (Paris, 1928); *Fiesta* (1931; unfinished). **ORCH.:** *El sueño de Eros*, symphonic poem (1904); *Suite levantina* (1911; rev. as *Poema de miños*, 1914); *Don Quijote velando las armas*, symphonic episode (1924); *Schubertiana* (1928); *El ámbito de la danza* (1929–34); 2 *suites folklóricas* for Chamber Orch. (1932, 1934); *Concierto de cámara* (1937); *Sonata del sur* for Piano and Orch. (1943–45); *Sinfonía aitana* (Madrid, Oct. 31, 1964); *Sinfonia de retaguardia* (1969–76). **CHAMBER:** Violin Sonata (1915); Piano Trio (1917); 2 string quartets (1920, 1943); *Sonata concertante* (1939); *Lírica española* for Piano and Instruments (1952–54); organ music. **VOCAL:** Choral pieces; cantatas.

BIBL.: E. García Alcázar, *O. E.y.T.: (Alicante, 5-8-1886–Madrid, 6-1-1976): Estudio monográfico documental* (Alicante, 1993).

Esposito, Michele, Italian composer, pianist, and conductor; b. Castellammare di Stabia, near Naples, Sept. 29, 1855; d. Florence, Nov. 23, 1929. He studied at the Cons. San Pietro e Majella at Naples with Cesi (piano) and Serrao (theory); then gave piano concerts in Italy; in 1882 he was engaged as a piano teacher at the Royal Irish Academy of Music in Dublin; he organized the Dublin Orch. Soc. in 1899 and conducted it until 1914, and again in 1927. He composed several works on Irish subjects: Irish operetta, *The Post Bag* (London, Jan. 27, 1902); incidental music for *The Tinker and the Fairy* (Dublin, 1910); *Suite of Irish Dances* for Orch.; 2 Irish rhapsodies; several arrangements of Irish melodies. He received 1st prizes for his cantata *Deirdre* (Irish Festival, Dublin, 1897); and *Irish Symphony* (Irish Festival, Dublin, 1902); also wrote 2 string quartets, 2 violin sonatas, cello sonatas, etc.

BIBL.: K. van Hoek, "M. E., Maestro of Dublin," *Irish Monthly* (June 1943).

Esswood, Paul (Lawrence Vincent), English countertenor; b. West Bridgford, June 2, 1942. He studied with Gordon Clinton at the Royal College of Music in London (1961–64), and then was a lay vicar at Westminster Abbey until 1971. In 1965 he made his formal debut as a countertenor in a BBC performance of Handel's *Messiah*; his operatic debut followed in Cavalli's *Erismena* in Berkeley, California, in 1968. In 1967 he co-founded the Pro Cantione Antiqua, an a cappella male vocal group, but he also continued to pursue his solo career, appearing at many major European festivals. He also was a prof. at the Royal College of Music (1977–80) and at the Royal Academy of Music (from 1985). While he was best known for his performances of such early masters as Monteverdi, Cavalli, Purcell, Bach, and Handel, he also appeared in modern works, including the premieres of Penderecki's *Paradise Lost* (Chicago, Nov. 29, 1978) and Glass's *Akhnaten* (Stuttgart, March 24, 1984).

Estes, Simon (Lamont), noted black American bass-baritone; b. Centerville, Iowa, Feb. 2, 1938. He sang in a local Baptist church choir as a child, then studied voice with Charles Kellis at the Univ. of Iowa and on scholarship at N.Y.'s Juilliard School of Music. He made his operatic debut as Ramfis at the Berlin Deutsche Oper (1965); after winning a silver medal at the Tchaikovsky Competition in Moscow (1966), he appeared with the San Francisco Opera and the Chicago Lyric Opera, but was mainly active as a concert artist. On June 10, 1976, he made his first appearance with the Metropolitan Opera as Oroveso in *Norma* during the company's visit to the Wolf Trap Farm Park in Vienna, Va. However, it was not until he sang the Dutchman at the Bayreuth Festival in 1978 that his remarkable vocal gifts began to be widely appreciated. He subsequently appeared as the Dutchman throughout Europe to notable acclaim. In 1980 he made his U.S. recital debut at N.Y.'s Carnegie Hall, and in 1981 returned to the Metropolitan Opera roster, singing Wotan opposite Birgit Nilsson's Brünnhilde in a concert performance of Act III of *Die Walküre* in N.Y. He finally made his formal stage debut with the company there as the Landgrave on Jan. 4, 1982. In 1985 he returned to sing Porgy in *Porgy and Bess*. He sang Wotan in the *Ring* cycle at the Metropolitan Opera from 1986 to 1988. In 1990 he appeared in the title role of the musical *King* in London. His comprehensive operatic and concert repertoire ranges from Handel to spirituals.

Estévez, Antonio, Venezuelan composer; b. Calabozo, Jan. 3, 1916; d. Caracas, Nov. 26, 1988. He studied composition with Sojo and oboe at the Caracas Escuela de Música y Declamación (1934–44), composition with Copland at the Berkshire Music Center in Tanglewood, and electronic music in Paris. Among his works were *Suite Llanera* for Orch. (1942); *Concerto for Orchestra* (1949–50); choruses; piano pieces; *Cosmovibrafonía*, electronic pieces (1968).

Estrada, Carlos, Uruguayan conductor, music educator, and composer; b. Montevideo, Sept. 15, 1909; d. there, May 7, 1970. He was a student in Montevideo of Adelina Pérez Montero (piano), Carlos Correa Luna (violin), and Manuel Fernández Espiro (harmony, counterpoint, and composition), and at the Paris Cons. of Roger-Ducasse and Büsser (composition), N. Gallon (counterpoint and fugue), and Paray, Wolff, and Gaubert (conducting). He was active in Montevideo as a conductor, and also was director of the National Cons. (1954–68). Among his works were *L'Annonce faite à Marie*, opera (1943); 2 syms. (1951, 1967); *Daniel*, oratorio (1942); chamber music; piano pieces.

Estrada, Julio, Mexican composer, theoretician, historian, and pedagogue; b. Mexico City (of exiled Spanish parents), April 10, 1943. He studied in Mexico with del Castillo, de Elías, de Tercero, and Julian Orbón (1955–63), in Germany with Gerhard Muench (1963–65), and in Paris (1965–69) with Boulanger, Barraine, Raffi Ourgandjian, Messiaen, Jean E. Marie, Pousseur, and Xenakis; then returned briefly to Germany, where he studied with Stockhausen at the Kölner Kurse für Neue Musik and with Ligeti at the Darmstadter Musikferienkurse. Upon his return to Mexico in 1970, he worked at Radio Universidad. He created several new-music ensembles, including Pro-Música Nueva and Compañía Musical de Repertorio Nuevo, introducing to Mexico the works of Cage, Ligeti, Oliveros, Riley, Stockhausen, and others. From 1973 he taught in the Escuela Nacional de Musica at the Universidad Nacional Autónoma de México. He was the first full-time music researcher at the Instituto de Investigaciones Estéticas (from 1976) and the first music scholar to be appointed by the Mexican Education Ministry as Investigador Nacional (1984–87; 1987–90). He was general ed. of *La música de Mexico* (10 vols., 1984); he also publ. a collection of essays on new Latin American and Mexican music, *Reunión entre tiemps* (1990). His work with Jorge Gil in the Finite Group's Theory and Boolean Algebra Applications in Music (resulting in *Música y teoriá de Grupos Finitos, 3 variables booleanas* [1984]) was the first instance in Mexico in which musicians used computers as both a theoretical and a precompositional tool. Estrada also posited his general theory of intervallic cycles as a hierarchical system applied to musical systems based on scales in his *El espectro interválico, una teoría general de la interválica y sus aplicaciones al estudio precompositional y al análisis musical del gregoriano a la música actual* (1990). He conceives of musical composition as a field where new solutions can be obtained from an objective order and organization according to its inner characteristics of discontinuity or continuity; his own compositions demand the invention of new technical and theoretical models coming out of "the primordial needs of fantasy." Profoundly political, Estrada identifies the act of composition with the act of liberation, with "the permissiveness of musical ideas becoming at the same time the powerful exigency of a true, almost phonographic representation of each detail belonging to sounds already internally experienced."

WORKS: *Persona* (1969); *Solo* (1970); *Memorias, para teclado* (1971); *Melódica* (1973); *Canto mnémico, fuga en 4 dimensiones* (1973; rev. 1983); *Canto tejido* for Piano (1974); *Canto naciente* for 3 Trumpets, 2 Cornets, 2 Trombones, and Tuba (1975–78); *Canto oculto* for Violin (1977); *Canto alterno* for Cello (1978); *Diario* for 15 Stringed Instruments (1980); *eua'on I* for Tape (1981) and *II* for Orch. (1983); *eolo'oolin* for 6 Percussionists (1981–82); *yuunohui'yei* for Cello (1983); *ishini'ioni* for String Quartet (1984–90); *yuunohui'nahui* for Double Bass (1985); *yuunohui'ce* for Violin (1990); *yuunohui'ome* for Viola (1990).

Etcheverry, Henri-Bertrand, French bass-baritone; b. Bordeaux, March 29, 1900; d. Paris, Nov. 14, 1960. He studied in Paris, where he made his operatic debut as Ceprano in *Rigoletto* at the Opéra in 1932; from 1937 he was a member of the Paris Opéra-Comique, and he also sang at London's Covent Garden (1937, 1949). He was greatly admired for his portrayal of Golaud; among his other notable roles were Don Giovanni, Wotan, Boris Godunov, and Gounod's Méphistophélès and Friar Lawrence.

Etler, Alvin (Derald), American oboist, teacher, and composer; b. Battle Creek, Iowa, Feb. 19, 1913; d. Northampton, Mass., June 13, 1973. He studied at the Univ. of Ill., with Shepherd at Case Western Reserve Univ., and with Hindemith at Yale Univ. (M.B., 1944), where he also taught (1942–46). He later taught at Cornell Univ. (1946–47), the Univ. of Ill. (1947–49), and Smith College (1949–73). He held 2 Guggenheim fellowships (1940, 1941). He was the author of *Making Music: An Introduction to Theory* (N.Y., 1974). His music is marked by stately formality of design.

WORKS: ORCH.: *Music* for Chamber Orch. (1938); 2 sinfoniettas (1940, 1941); *Passacaglia and Fugue* (1947); Concerto for String Quartet and Strings (1948); Sym. (1951); *Dramatic Overture* (1956); *Concerto for Orchestra* (1957); *Elegy* for Small Orch. (1959); Concerto for Wind Quintet and Orch. (1960; Tokyo, Oct. 18, 1962); *Triptych* (1961); Concerto for Clarinet and Chamber Ensemble (1962; N.Y., Dec. 20, 1965); Concerto for Brass Quintet, Strings, and Percussion (1967); Concerto for String Quartet and Orch. (Milwaukee, June 13, 1968); *Convivialities* (1968); Concerto for Cello and Chamber Group (N.Y., March 2, 1971). **CHAMBER:** Suite for Oboe, Violin, Viola, and Cello (1936); Sonata for Oboe, Clarinet, and Viola (1944); Bassoon Sonata (1951); 2 clarinet sonatas (1952, 1969); Oboe Sonata (1952); 2 wind quintets (1955, 1957); Cello Sonata (1956); Concerto for Violin and Wind Quintet (1958); Sonata for Viola and Harpsichord (1959); 2 string quartets (1963, 1965); Brass Quintet (1963); *Sonic Sequence* for Brass Quintet (1967). **VOCAL:** *Onomatopoesis* for Men's Chorus, Winds, Brass, and Percussion (1965).

BIBL.: P. Shelden, *A. E. (1913–1973); His Career and His Two Sonatas for Clarinet* (diss., Univ. of Maryland, 1978).

Eto, Toshiya, Japanese violinist and teacher; b. Tokyo, Nov. 9, 1927. He was a student of Suzuki in Japan and of Zimbalist at the Curtis Inst. of Music in Philadelphia, where he taught (1953–61) before joining the Toho School of Music in Tokyo. In 1951 he made his U.S. debut at N.Y.'s Carnegie Hall and in 1968 his British debut in London.

Ettinger, Max (Markus Wolf), German conductor and composer; b. Lemberg, Dec. 27, 1874; d. Basel, July 19, 1951. He studied with Herzogenberg in Berlin and with Thuille and Rheinberger at the Munich Akademie der Tonkunst. After conducting in Munich (1900–1920), Leipzig (1920–29), and Berlin (1929–33), he settled in Switzerland in 1938.

WORKS: OPERAS: *Judith* (Nuremberg, Nov. 24, 1921); *Der eifersüchtige Trinker* (Nuremberg, Feb. 7, 1925); *Juana* (Nuremberg, Feb. 7, 1925); *Clavigo* (Leipzig, Oct. 19, 1926); *Frühlings Erwachen* (Leipzig, April 14, 1928); *Dolores* (1930–31). **VOCAL:** *Weisheit des Orients*, oratorio for 4 Soloists, Chorus, and Orch. (1924); *Das Lied von Moses* for 4 Soloists, Chorus, and Orch. (1934–35); *Königen Esther* for Chorus (1940–41); *Jiddisch Leben* for Chorus (1942); *Jewish Requiem* (1947). **OTHER:** Chamber music and songs.

BIBL.: E. Jucker, "Das Work M. E.s," *Schweizerische Musikzeitung/Review musicale suisse*, XCIII (1953).

Eulenburg, Ernst (Emil Alexander), German music publisher, father of **Kurt Eulenburg**; b. Berlin, Nov. 30, 1847; d. Leipzig, Sept. 11, 1926. He studied at the Leipzig Cons. In 1874 he established in Leipzig the publishing house bearing his name; after his acquisition of Payne's *Kleine Partitur-Ausgabe* (1891), he enormously increased the scope of that publication so that large orch. scores could be included. Upon his death, the firm was taken over by his son.

Eulenburg, Kurt, German music publisher, son of **Ernst (Emil Alexander) Eulenburg;** b. Berlin, Feb. 22, 1879; d. London, April 10, 1982. He was apprenticed by his father and joined the Eulenburg firm in 1911. Upon his father's death in 1926, he became sole owner. He expanded the dept. of miniature scores and also publ. Urtext eds. of many of Mozart's scores. In 1939 he went to Switzerland. That same year, he organized a new company in London, where he settled in 1945. He opened branches in Zürich in 1947 and in Stuttgart in 1950. The ed. was acquired by Schott in 1957, but Eulenburg remained active until his retirement in 1968. Schott then assumed control of the London division.

Europe, James Reese, black American conductor and composer; b. Mobile, Ala., Feb. 22, 1881; d. (murdered) Boston, May 10, 1919. He studied violin and piano in childhood in Washington, D.C.; then went to N.Y., where he was active as a director of musical comedies, founding the Clef Club (1910), a union and contracting agency for black musicians. He also founded the Clef Club sym. orch., which gave performances of works by black composers at Carnegie Hall (1912–14). He was music director and composer for the dancers Irene and Vernon Castle (1914–17), and is credited with composing the first foxtrot for them. He also wrote songs for musicals and composed dances and marches for his orchs. and bands. He was stabbed to death by a disgruntled drummer in his band.

BIBL.: R. Badger, *A Life in Ragtime: A Biography of J.R. E.* (Oxford, 1995).

Evangelisti, Franco, Italian composer; b. Rome, Jan 21, 1926; d. there, Jan. 28, 1980. He studied with Daniele Paris in Rome (1948–53) and Harald Genzmer at the Freiburg-im-Breisgau Hoschschule für Musik (1953–56); he also attended the Darmstadt summer courses in new music with Eimert and Stockhausen, and worked at the electronic music studios in Cologne and Warsaw. He was active in new music circles in Rome, where he became president of Nuova Consonanza in 1961; he taught there at the Accademia di Santa Cecilia (1968–72), the Conservatorio dell'Aquila (1969–75), and the Conservatorio Santa Cecilia (1974–80). Evangelisti was the author of the book *Dal silenzio ad una nuova musica* (Palermo, 1967).

WORKS: DRAMATIC: *Die Schachtel* (1963). **ORCH.:** *Variazioni* (1955); *Ordini* (1955); *Random or not Random* (1962); *Condensazioni* (1962); *3 strutture* (1963). **CHAMBER:** *4!* for Violin and Piano (1955); *Proiezioni sonore* for Piano (1956); *Proporzioni* for Flute (1958); *Aleatorio* for String Quartet (1960); *Spazio a 5* for Percussion, Voices, and Electronics (1961). **ELECTRONIC:** *Incontri di fasce sonore* (1957); *Campi integrati* (1959).

Evans, Anne, esteemed English soprano; b. London, Aug. 20, 1941. She was a student of Ruth Packer at the Royal College of Music in London and of Maria Carpi, Herbert Graf, and Lofti Mansouri at the Geneva Cons. After singing secondary roles at the Geneva Grand Théâtre, she returned to London in 1968 to join the Sadler's Wells Opera (later the English National Opera), where she was notably successful in such roles as Mimi, Tosca, Elsa, the Marschallin, and Sieglinde; she also appeared with the Welsh National Opera in Cardiff as Senta, Chrysothemis, the Empress, Donna Anna, and Brünnhilde (1985). Her Brünnhilde elicited critical acclaim when the company visited London's Covent Garden in 1986, which role she also sang at the Bayreuth Festival for the first time in 1989. On Feb. 6, 1992, she made her Metropolitan Opera debut in N.Y. as Elisabeth in *Tannhäuser.* In 1993 she appeared as Isolde with the Welsh National Opera in Cardiff, and then with the company at London's Covent Garden. She appeared as the Marschallin at the English National Opera in 1994. In 1996 she sang Brünnhilde at Covent Garden.

Evans, Edwin, Jr., English writer on music, son of **Edwin Evans, Sr.**; b. London, Sept. 1, 1874; d. there, March 3, 1945. His father was the organist and writer on music Edwin Evans, Sr. (1844–1923). Edwin Evans Jr. studied for a business career; was engaged in telegraphy, railroads, and finance from 1889 to 1913; then devoted himself exclusively to musical pursuits. He was music critic of the *Pall Mall Gazette* (1912–23) and the *Daily Mail* (1933–45); was one of the founders of the ISCM (1922); in 1938 he was elected its president, retaining this post until his death. He wrote *Tchaikovsky* (London, 1906; 3rd ed., rev., 1966); *The Margin of Music* (London, 1924); *Music and the Dance* (London, 1948).

Evans, Sir Geraint (Llewellyn), distinguished Welsh baritone; b. Pontypridd, South Wales, Feb. 16, 1922; d. Aberystwyth, Sept. 19, 1992. He began to study voice in Cardiff when he was 17, and, after serving in the RAF during World War II, resumed his vocal studies in Hamburg with Theo Hermann; then studied with Fernando Carpi in Geneva and Walter Hyde at the Guildhall School of Music in London. He made his operatic debut as the Nightwatchman in *Die Meistersinger von Nürnberg* at London's Covent Garden (1948); thereafter was a leading member of the company. He also sang at the Glyndebourne Festivals (1949–61). In 1959 he made his U.S. debut with the San Francisco Opera; first appearances followed at Milan's La Scala (1960), the Vienna State Opera (1961), the Salzburg Festival (1962), N.Y.'s Metropolitan Opera (debut as Falstaff; March 25, 1964), and the Paris Opéra (1975). In 1984 he made his farewell operatic appearance as Dulcamara at Covent Garden. He was also active as an opera producer. In 1959 he was made a Commander of the Order of the British Empire and was knighted in 1969. With N. Goodwin, he publ. an entertaining autobiography, *Sir Geraint Evans: A Knight at the Opera* (London, 1984). His finest roles included Figaro, Leporello, Papageno, Beckmesser, Falstaff, Don Pasquale, and Wozzeck.

Everding, August, German opera director and administrator; b. Bottrop, Oct. 31, 1928. He received training in piano and also took courses in Germanic studies, philosophy, theology, and dramaturgy at the univs. of Bonn and Munich. From 1959 he worked regularly at the Munich Kammerspiele, later serving as its Intendant (1963–73). From 1973 to 1977 he was Intendant at the Hamburg State Opera, and from 1977 to 1982 at the Bavarian State Opera in Munich, where he subsequently was Generalintendant of the Bavarian State Theater (1982–93). In 1993 he became founder-president of the Bavarian Theater Academy. In addition to staging operas during his tenures in Hamburg and Munich, he worked as a guest opera director at the Bayreuth Festival, the Savonlinna Festival, London's Covent Garden, N.Y.'s Metropolitan Opera, and other music centers. He publ. *Mir ist die Ehre widerfahren: An-Reden, Mit-Reden, Aus-Reden, Zu-Reden* (Munich, 1985) and *Wenn für Romeo der letzte Vorhang fällt: Theater, Musik, Musiktheater: Zur aktuellen Kulturszene* (Munich, 1993).

BIBL.: K. Seidel, *Die ganze Welt ist Bühne: A. E.* (Munich, 1988).

Evett, Robert, American composer and writer on music; b. Loveland, Colo., Nov. 30, 1922; d. Takoma Park, Md., Feb. 3, 1975. He studied with Roy Harris in Colorado Springs (1941–47) and with Persichetti at the Juilliard School of Music in N. Y. (1951–52). He was chairman of the music dept. of the Washington (D.C.) Inst. of Contemporary Arts (1947–50), and then was book ed. and music critic for the *New Republic* (1952–68); he also was a contributing critic on books and music for the *Washington Star* (1961–75), and then its book ed. (1970–75). His compositions were basically neo-Classical in nature, with an infusion of dissonant harmonic writing.

WORKS: ORCH.: Concertino (1952); Concerto for Small Orch. (1952); Cello Concerto (1954); *Variations* for Clarinet and Orch. (1955); Piano Concerto (1957); 3 syms.: No. 1 (1960), No. 2, *Billy Ascends,* for Voices and Orch. (Washington, D.C., May 7, 1965), and No. 3 (Washington, D.C., June 6, 1965); Harpsichord Concerto (Washington, D.C., April 25, 1961); *Anniversary Concerto 75* (Washington, D.C., Oct. 19, 1963); *The Windhover* for Bassoon and Orch. (Washington, D.C., May 20, 1971); *Monadnock,* dance music (1975). **CHAMBER:** Clarinet Sonata (1948); Piano Quintet (1954); Duo for Violin and Piano (1955); Cello Sonata (1955); Viola Sonata (1958); 2 violin sonatas (1960; 1975, unfinished); Piano Quartet (1961); Oboe Sonata (1964); *Fantasia on a Theme by Handel* for Piano, Violin, and Cello (1966). **KEYBOARD: PIANO:** *5 Capriccios* (1943–49); 4 sonatas (1945, 1952, 1953, 1956); *Chaconne* (1950); *Toccata* for 2 Pianos (1959); *Ricercare* for 2 Pianos (1961); *6 Études* (1961). **ORGAN:** Trio Sonata (1953). **HARPSICHORD:** Sonata (1961). **VOCAL:** *The Mask of Cain* for 2 Baritones, Soprano, and Harpsichord (1949); *Mass* for Voices and Organ (1950); *Billy in the Darbies* for Baritone, Clarinet, String Quartet, and Piano (1958); *The 5 Books of Life* for 2 Baritones, Soprano, and Harpsichord (1960); *Requiem* for Chorus (1973); choruses; songs.

Evseyev, Sergei, Russian composer and pedagogue; b. Moscow, Jan. 24, 1893; d. there, March 16, 1956. He studied piano with Medtner as a youth; then entered the Moscow Cons., where he continued to study piano with Goldenweiser and also attended classes in composition with Taneyev; upon graduation, he devoted himself to teaching theory at the Moscow Cons. His compositions included 3 syms. (1925, 1933, 1943); 2 piano concertos (1932); Clarinet Concerto (1943); 2 string quartets (1935, 1945); Dramatic Sonata for Cello and Piano (1941); many piano pieces.

Evstatieva, Stefka, Bulgarian soprano; b. Rousse, May 7, 1947. She was a pupil of Elena Kiselova at the Bulgarian State Cons. in Sofia. In 1971 she made her operatic debut as Amelia at the Rousse Opera, where she was a member until 1979; was also a member of the Bulgarian State Opera in Sofia from 1978. In 1980 she made her first appearance with the Royal Opera, Covent Garden, London as Desdemona during its visit to Manchester; in 1981 she sang with the company in London as Donna Elvira. After engagements in Berlin and Vienna in 1982, and in Milan and Paris in 1983, she made her Metropolitan Opera debut in N.Y. as Elisabeth in *Don Carlos* on April 9, 1984. In 1984 she appeared with the San Francisco Opera. In subsequent years, she sang with many of the principal opera houses of Europe and North America, and also toured as a concert artist. Among her other roles were Donna Elvira, Leonora, Aida, Mimi, Suor Angelica, Tosca, Madeleine de Coigny, and Lisa in *The Queen of Spades.*

Ewen, David, Polish-born American writer on music; b. Lemberg, Nov. 26, 1907; d. Miami Beach, Dec. 28, 1985. He was taken to the U.S. in 1912 and pursued his training in N.Y. at City College and Columbia Univ.; also studied theory with Max Persin. He was music ed. of *Reflex Magazine* (1928–29), *The American Hebrew* (1935), and *Cue* (1937–38), and then was active with the publ. firm of Allen, Towne, and Heath (1946–49); in 1965 he joined the faculty of the Univ. of Miami, which awarded him an honorary D.Mus. in 1974; in 1985 he received the ASCAP Award for Lifetime Achievement in Music. Ewen publ. more than 80 books during a career of some 50 years, including *The Book of Modern Composers* (1942; 3rd ed.,

1961, as *The New Book of Modern Composers*); *Encyclopedia of the Opera* (1955; 2nd ed., rev., 1971 as *New Encyclopedia of the Opera*); *Panorama of American Popular Music* (1957); *Complete Book of the American Musical Theater* (1958; 3rd ed., rev., 1976 as *New Complete Book of the American Musical Theater*); *Encyclopedia of Concert Music* (1959); *The Story of America's Musical Theater* (1961; 2nd ed., rev., 1968); *Popular American Composers: From Revolutionary Times to the Present* (1962; supplement, 1972); *The Complete Book of Classical Music* (1963); *The Life and Death of Tin Pan Alley* (1964); *American Popular Songs: From the Revolutionary War to the Present* (1966); *Great Composers: 1300–1900* (1966); *Composers Since 1900* (1969; supplement, 1981); *Great Men of American Popular Song* (1970; 2nd ed., rev., 1972); *Mainstreams of Music* (4 vols., 1972–75); *All the Years of American Popular Music* (1977); *Musicians Since 1900* (1978); *American Composers: A Biographical Dictionary* (1982).

Ewing, Maria (Louise), noted American mezzo-soprano and soprano; b. Detroit, March 27, 1950. She commenced vocal training with Marjorie Gordon, continuing her studies with Steber at the Cleveland Inst. of Music (1968–70), and later with Tourel and O. Marzolla. In 1973 she made her professional debut at the Ravinia Festival with the Chicago Sym. Orch., and subsequently was engaged to appear with various U.S. opera houses and orchs.; she also appeared as a recitalist. On Oct. 14, 1976, she made her Metropolitan Opera debut in N.Y. as Cherubino, and returned there to sing such roles as Rosina, Dorabella, Mélisande, Blanche in *Dialogues des carmelites*, and Carmen. In 1976 she made her first appearance at Milan's La Scala as Mélisande; in 1978 she made her Glyndebourne Festival debut as Dorabella, and returned there as a periodic guest. In 1986 she sang Salome in Los Angeles and appeared in *The Merry Widow* in Chicago in 1987. In 1988 she sang Salome at London's Covent Garden, a role she sang to enormous critical acclaim in Chicago that same year; she returned there as Tosca in 1989 and Susanna in 1991. After a dispute over artistic matters at the Metropolitan Opera in 1987, she refused to sing there until 1993 when she returned as Dido. She was married for a time to **Sir Peter Hall**.

Expert, (Isidore-Norbert-) Henry, eminent French music librarian and editor; b. Bordeaux, May 12, 1863; d. Tourettes-sur-Loup, Alpes-Maritimes, Aug. 18, 1952. He settled in Paris in 1881 and studied with Franck and Gigout. He taught at the École Nationale de Musique Classique (1902–05) and at the École des Hautes Sociales. In 1909 he became deputy librarian and in 1921 chief librarian at the Paris Cons., retiring in 1933. He ed. the valuable collections *Les maîtres musiciens de la renaissance française* (23 vols., Paris, 1894–1908) and *Monuments de la musique française au temps de la renaissance* (10 vols., Paris, 1924–29; new ed. by B. Loth and J. Chailley, 1958 et seq.). The Assn. des Amis d'Henry Expert et de la Musique Française Ancienne was founded after his death and sponsored the publ. of his MS transcriptions as *Maîtres anciens de la musique française* (Paris, 1966 et seq.).

Eyser, Eberhard, German violist and composer; b. Kwidzyn, Poland, Aug. 1, 1932. He studied composition at the Hannover Hochschule für Musik (1952–57); his principal mentor was Fritz von Bloh, but he also attended the Salzburg Mozarteum, the Accademia Musicale Chigiana in Siena, and seminars with Xenakis, Maderna, and Scherchen. He was a violist in the Hannover Opera orch. (1956–57), the Stuttgart Radio Sym. Orch. (1957–61), and the Royal Theater orch. in Stockholm (from 1961).

WORKS: DRAMATIC: OPERAS: *Molonne*, chamber opera (Stockholm, Oct. 27, 1970); *Abu Said, Kalifens son* (1970–76; Stockholm, March 10, 1976); *Sista resan*, chamber opera (1972–73; Vadstena, July 24, 1974); *Carmen 36*, chamber opera (1972–77); *Det djupa vattnet*, lyric scene (1979); *Sensommardag*, chamber opera (1979); *Sista dagen på jorden*, chamber opera (1979); *Altaret* (1980); *Bermuda-Triangeln* (1981); *Der letzte Tag auf Erden* (1979–82); *Rid i natt* (1982–91); *Destination Mars*, chamber opera (1983); *Das gläserne Wand*, chamber opera (1985); *Herr Karls likvaka*, madrigal-opera (1985–88); *The Picture of Dorian Gray* (1986); *Intimate Letters*, chamber opera (1989). **BALLET:** *Golgata* (1983). **ORCH.:** *Metastrophy* (1965); *Symphonie orientale* for Chamber Orch. (1974); Piano Concerto (1974–77); *Sima*, symphonic variations (1977); 3 sinfoniettas (1977, 1979, 1993); *Burloni* for Wind Orch. (1985); *Aneio noma* (1988); *Itabol* (1989); *Giuochi dodecafonici* for Wind Orch. (1990); *Stoccasta* (1992). **CHAMBER:** *Podema* for String Quartet (1969); Sonata for Bass Clarinet, Cymbal, and Piano (1972); Sonata for Solo Bassoon (1973); *Ottoletto* for 8 Clarinets (1975); 5 saxophone quartets (1976–89); *Submarine Music* for Bass Clarinet and Tape (1979); *Umoett* for Guitar, 2 Violins, Viola, and Cello (1983); *Tonadas* for Horn, Violin, 2 Violas, and Cello (1986); *Quintette à la mode dodecaphonique* for Saxophones (1988); *Trio à la mode dodecaphonique* for Oboe, Alto Saxophone, and Cello (1989); Violin Sonata (1989); *Panteod* for String Quartet (1990); *Igomantra*, viola sonata (1992); *Litalö: Hommage à Arvo Pärt* for String Quartet (1992). **VOCAL:** *The Vineyard*, scenic cantata for Soloists and Orch. (1993).

Eysler (actually, **Eisler**), **Edmund,** noted Austrian composer; b. Vienna, March 12, 1874; d. there, Oct. 4, 1949. He was a student of Door (piano), R. Fuchs (harmony and counterpoint), and J.N. Fuchs (composition) at the Vienna Cons. He made Vienna the center of his activities, beginning with the premiere of his operetta *Bruder Straubinger* (Feb. 20, 1903). Its waltz song *Kussen ist keine Sund* became celebrated. Success continued with *Pufferl* (Feb. 10, 1905), *Die Schützenliesel* (Oct. 7, 1905), *Künstlerblut* (Oct. 20, 1906), and *Vera Violetta* (Nov. 30, 1907). Further success attended his *Der unsterbliche Lump* (Oct. 14, 1910), *Der Natursänger* (Dec. 22, 1911), *Der Frauenfresser* (Dec. 23, 1911), *Der lachende Ehemann* (March 19, 1913), and *Ein Tag im Paradies* (Dec. 23, 1913). Even during World War I, his works were produced unabated: *Die—oder keine* (Oct. 9, 1915), *Wenn zwei sich lieben* (Oct. 29, 1915), *Warum geht's denn jetzt?* (July 5, 1916), *Hanni geht's tanzen* (Nov. 7, 1916), and *Graf Toni* (March 2, 1917). After the War, Eysler brought out a steady stream of additional scores. His greatest postwar success came with *Die goldene Meisterin* (Sept. 13, 1927), which was acclaimed as one of his finest scores. His last major success came with *Ihr erster Ball* (Nov. 21, 1929). As a Jew, Eysler was compelled to go into hiding during World War II. After the War, his status was restored as one of Vienna's master melodists of the operetta genre.

WORKS: MUSICAL THEATER (all 1st perf. in Vienna unless otherwise given): *Das Gastmahl des Lucullus* (Nov. 23, 1901); *Bruder Straubinger* (Feb. 20, 1903); *Pufferl* (Feb. 10, 1905); *Die Schützenliesel* (Oct. 7, 1905); *Phryne* (Oct. 6, 1906); *Künstlerblut* (Oct. 20, 1906); *Vera Violetta* (Nov. 30, 1907); *Ein Tag auf dem Mars* (Jan. 17, 1908); *Das Glücksschweinchen* (June 26, 1908); *Johann der Zweite* (Oct. 3, 1908); *Der junge Papa* (Feb. 3, 1909); *Lumpus und Pumpus* (Jan. 21, 1910); *Der unsterbliche Lump* (Oct. 14, 1910); *Der Zirkuskind* (Feb. 18, 1911); *Der Natursänger* (Dec. 22, 1911); *Der Frauenfresser* (Dec. 23, 1911); *Der lachende Ehemann* (March 19, 1913); *Ein Tag im Paradies* (Dec. 23, 1913); *Komm, deutscher Brüder* (Oct. 4, 1914); *Der Kriegsberichterstatter* (Oct. 9, 1914; in collaboration with others); *Frühling am Rhein* (Oct. 10, 1914); *Der Durchgang der Venus* (Nov. 28, 1914); *Die—oder keine* (Oct. 9, 1915); *Wenn zwei sich lieben* (Oct. 29, 1915); *Das Zimmer der Pompadour* (Dec. 1, 1915); *Warum geht's denn jetzt?* (July 5, 1916); *Hanni geht's tanzen* (Nov. 7, 1916); *Der berühmte Gabriel* (Nov. 8, 1916); *Graf Toni* (March 2, 1917); *Der Aushilfsgatte* (Nov. 7, 1917); *Leute von heute* (June 22, 1918; in collaboration with R. Stolz and A. Werau); *Der dunkel Schatz* (Nov. 14, 1918); *Der fidele Geiger* (Jan. 17, 1919); *Rund um die Bühne* (March 1, 1920); *Der König heiratet* (April 1920); *Wer hat's gemacht* (Oct. 1, 1920); *La bella Mammina* (Rome, April 9, 1921; German version as *Die schöne Mama*, Vienna, Sept. 17, 1921); *Die fromme Helene* (Dec. 22, 1921); *Die Parliamentskathi* (April 15, 1922);

Fräulein Sopherl, die schöne vom Markt (May 19, 1922); *Schummel macht alles* (July 1, 1922); *Drei auf einmal* (March 29, 1923); *Der ledige Schwiegersohn* (April 20, 1923); *Vierzehn Tage (im) Arrest* (June 16, 1923); *Lumpenlieschen* (May 21, 1923); *Das Land der Liebe* (Aug. 27, 1926); *Die goldene Meisterin* (Sept. 13, 1927); *Ihr erster Ball* (Nov. 21, 1929); *Das Strumpfband der Pompadour* (Augsburg, March 16, 1930); *Durchlaucht Mizzi* (Dec. 23, 1930); *Die schlimme Paulette* (Augsburg, March 1, 1931); *Zwei alte Wiener* (Feb. 12, 1932); *Die Rakete* (Innsbruck, Dec. 23, 1932); *Donauliebchen* (Dec. 25, 1932); *Das ist der erste Liebe(lei)* (Dec. 23, 1934); *Wiener Musik* (Dec. 22, 1947). **OTHER:** 2 operas: *Der Hexenspiegel* (1900) and *Hochzeitspräludium* (1946); ballet: *Schlaraffenland* (1899); dances; piano pieces; songs.

BIBL.: K. Ewald, *E. E.: Ein Musiker aus Wien* (Vienna, 1934); R. Prosl, *E. E.* (Vienna, 1947).

Fabini, (Felix) Eduardo, Uruguayan violinist and composer; b. Solís del Mataojo, May 18, 1882; d. Montevideo, May 17, 1950. He studied violin at the Conservatorio la Lira in Montevideo, and later as a student of César Thomson (violin) and Auguste de Boeck (composition) at the Brussels Cons. (1900–1903), winning 1st prize for violin; then gave concerts as a violinist in South America and in the U.S. (1926). He eventually returned to Montevideo, and was active there as a composer and educator. His music is inspired entirely by South American folklore; the idiom is mildly modernistic, with lavish use of whole-tone scales and other external devices of Impressionism.

WORKS (all 1st perf. in Montevideo): **BALLETS:** *Mburucuyá* (April 15, 1933); *Mañana de Reyes* (July 31, 1937). **ORCH.:** *Campo,* symphonic poem (April 29, 1922); *La isla de los Ceibos,* overture (Sept. 14, 1926); *Melga sinfónica* (Oct. 11, 1931); *Fantasia* for Violin and Orch. (Aug. 22, 1929). **OTHER:** Piano pieces; choral works; songs.

BIBL.: R. Lagarmilla, *E. F.* (Montevideo, 1954); G. Paraskevaídis, *E. F.: La obra sinfónica* (Montevideo, 1992).

Fachiri, Adila (née **d'Arányi),** Hungarian-born English violinist, sister of **Jelly d'Arányi;** b. Budapest, Feb. 26, 1886; d. Florence, Dec. 15, 1962. She was the grandniece of the renowned Hungarian-born violinist, conductor, pedagogue, and composer Joseph Joachim (b. Kittsee, near Pressburg, June 28, 1831; d. Berlin, Aug. 15, 1907). She studied with Hubay at the Royal Academy of Music in Budapest before completing her training with Joachim in Berlin (1905–07), who gave her a 1715 Stradivarius violin. In 1906 she made her debut in Vienna. In 1909 she made her British debut in Haslemere, settling in London in 1913 and marrying the lawyer Alexander Fachiri. In addition to her appearances as a soloist with orchs. and as a chamber music artist, she gave concerts with her sister until 1960.

BIBL.: J. Macleod, *The Sisters d'Arányi* (London, 1969).

Faerber, Jörg, German conductor; b. Stuttgart, June 18, 1929. He studied at the Stuttgart Hochschule für Musik. He then began his career in Stuttgart as a theater conductor. In 1960 he founded the Württemberg Chamber Orch. in Heilbronn, and subsequently established it as one of the finest ensembles of its kind in Europe. He was especially distinguished as an interpreter of the Baroque repertoire.

Fagan, Gideon, South African conductor and composer; b. Somerset West, Cape Province, Nov. 3, 1904; d. Cape Town, March 21, 1980. He studied at the South African College of Music in Cape Town with W.H. Bell (1916–22) and later in London at the Royal College of Music (1922–26), where his teachers were Boult and Sargent (conducting) and Vaughan Williams (composition). Fagan established residence in London, where he led theatrical companies, arranged light music for broadcasts and films, and acted as guest conductor with the BBC and other orchs. In 1949 he returned to South Africa, where he became active as arranger and conductor at the Johannesburg Radio (SABC); later was its head of music (1963–66). He also taught composition and conducting at the Univ. of Cape Town (1967–73). In 1979 he received the Medal of Honor of the South African Academy for Science and Art.

WORKS: ORCH.: *Ilala,* symphonic poem (1941); *South African Folk-tune Suite* (1942); *5 Orchestral Pieces* (1948–49); *Concert Overture* (1954); *Heuwelkruin* (Hill Crest), suite for Piano and Orch. (1954); *Albany,* overture (1970); *Ex unitate vires,* symphonic sketch (1970); Suite for Strings (1974); *Karoosimfonie* (1976–77). **CHAMBER:** *Nocturne* for Woodwinds and Strings (1926); Nonet (1958); *Quintics* for 5 Brasses (1975); piano pieces. **VOCAL:** *Tears,* symphonic poem for Soloist, Chorus, and Orch. (1954); *My Lewe,* 6 poems for Baritone, Flute, Clarinet, Piano, and String Quartet (1969); *Een vaderland,* oratorio (1977–78); songs.

Failoni, Sergio, Italian conductor; b. Verona, Dec. 18, 1890; d. Sopron, July 25, 1948. He received his musical education in Verona and Milan. He conducted opera throughout Italy; from 1932 he made appearances at La Scala in Milan. From 1928 to

1947 he was chief conductor of the State Opera in Budapest. In 1947 he was invited to make his debut at the Metropolitan Opera in N.Y.; however, he suffered a stroke and died the following year. He was regarded as one of the leading interpreters of the Italian repertoire.

Fairchild, Blair, American composer; b. Belmont, Mass., June 23, 1877; d. Paris, April 23, 1933. He studied composition with J.K. Paine and Walter Spalding at Harvard Univ. (B.A., 1899); then took courses with Giuseppe Buonamici in Florence. From 1901 to 1903 he was an attaché in the American embassies in Turkey and Persia. From 1905 he lived mostly in Paris, where he continued his musical studies with Widor. Influenced by his travels in the Orient, and fascinated by the resources of exotic melos and rhythm, he wrote a number of pieces for orch. and for piano, and many songs in a pseudo-oriental manner; despite the imitative qualities of his music, Fairchild must be regarded as one of the few Americans who tried to transplant exotic folkways, both in subject matter and in melodic turns.

WORKS: DRAMATIC: *Dame Libellule*, ballet-pantomime (1919). **ORCH.:** *East and West*, tone poem (1908); *Légende* for Violin and Orch. (1911); 3 symphonic poems: *Tamineh* (1913), *Zál* (1915), and *Shah Féridoûn* (1915); *Étude symphonique* for Violin and Orch. (1922); *Rhapsodie on Old Hebrew Melodies* for Violin and Orch. (1924); *6 chants nègres* (Boston, Dec. 6, 1929; orchestrated from piano pieces). **CHAMBER:** 2 violin sonatas (1908, 1919); String Quintet (1909); Piano Trio (1910); String Quartet (1911); *Concerto de Chambre* for Violin, Piano, and String Quartet (1911). **VOCAL:** *Stornelli Toscani* for Voice and Piano (n.d.); *12 Persian Folk Songs* for Voice and Piano (1904); *5 Greek Sea Prayers* for Voice and Piano (1913).

BIBL.: W. Upton, "Our Musical Expatriates," *Musical Quarterly* (Jan. 1928).

Faith, Percy, Canadian-born American conductor, arranger, and composer; b. Toronto, April 7, 1908; d. Los Angeles, Feb. 9, 1976. He took up violin at age 7 and piano at 10. After training at Toronto's Canadian Academy, he entered the Toronto Cons. of Music at 14 to study with Frank Welsman. At 18, he abandoned his hopes for a career as a concert pianist after his hands were severely burned in an accident, and pursued training in composition with Louis Waizman. From 1927 he was active as a conductor and arranger of popular music for Canadian radio programs. In 1940 he settled in the U.S. and in 1945 became a naturalized American citizen. He was music director of "The Carnation Contented Hour" on NBC Radio (1940–47), Coca-Cola's "The Pause That Refreshes" on CBS Radio (1946–49), and "The Woolworth Hour" on CBS Radio (1955–57). He also was an arranger-conductor for Columbia Records in N.Y. (1950–59) and Los Angeles (1960–76). Although he wrote an operetta, *The Gandy Dancer* (1943), orch. works, choral music, and piano pieces, he was especially adept as a composer, arranger, and orchestrator of popular music. He wrote the film scores for *Love Me or Leave Me* (1955), *Tammy Tell Me True* (1961), *I'd Rather Be Rich* (1964), *The Love Goddesses* (1964), *The Third Day* (1965), and *The Oscar* (1966). Among his 45 albums, he attained gold status with *Viva* (1957), *Bouquet* (1959), and *Themes for Young Lovers* (1963). He also captured Grammy Awards in 1960 and 1969.

Falabella (Correa), Roberto, Chilean composer; b. Santiago, Feb. 13, 1926; d. there, Dec. 15, 1958. He was paralyzed by polio as a child. He pursued his studies with Lucila Césped (1945–46), Alfonso Letelier (1949–50), Gustavo Becerra (1952), and Miguel Aguilar and Esteban Eitler (1956–57). His music was Classical in form, Romantic in content, and modernistic in technique.

WORKS: DRAMATIC: *Epitafios fúnebres*, chamber opera (1952); *Del diario morir*, miniature opera (1954); *El peine de oro*, ballet (1954); *Andacollo*, ballet (1957). **ORCH.:** Sym. (1955); *2 divertimenti* for Strings (1955); *Emotional Studies* (1957; also for Piano). **CHAMBER:** *Dueto* for Flute and Violin (1952); Violin Sonata (1954); Cello Sonata (1954); String Quartet (1957). **PIANO:** 2 sonatas (1951, 1954); *Preludios episódicos* (1953); *Impresiones* (1955); *Retratos* (1957). **VOCAL:** *Palimpsestos* for Contralto, Bassoon, Horn, and Percussion (1954); *La Lámpara en la tierra*, cantata for Baritone and Orch. (1958).

Falcinelli, Rolande, French organist, teacher, and composer; b. Paris, Feb. 18, 1920. She was a student at the Paris Cons. of Samuel-Rousseau, Plé-Caussade, Büsser, and Dupré, taking premiers prix in harmony (1938), fugue (1939), and organ (1942), and the 2nd Prix de Rome (1942). In 1945 she became organist of the basilica at Sacré-Coeur de Montmarte in Paris. She also appeared as a recitalist. In 1948 she became prof. of organ at the American Cons. in Fontainebleau, then at the École Normale de Musique in Paris in 1951, and subsequently at the Paris Cons. in 1955, where she retired in 1986. Her output included organ music and vocal pieces.

Falik, Yuri, greatly talented Russian cellist and composer; b. Odessa, July 30, 1936. He studied cello with A. Strimer at the Leningrad Cons.; in 1962 he won 1st cello prize at the International Competition in Helsinki. He composed music from adolescence; in 1955 he enrolled in the composition class of Boris Arapov at the Leningrad Cons., graduating in 1964. He subsequently joined the staff of the Leningrad Cons., teaching both cello and composition. In his music, Falik reveals a quasi-Romantic quality, making use of tantalizingly ambiguous melodic passages approaching the last ramparts of euphonious dissonance. His angular rhythms, with their frequently startling pauses, suggest a theatrical concept.

WORKS: DRAMATIC: *Till Eulenspiegel*, "mystery ballet" (1967); *Oresteia*, choreographic tragedy (1968); *Les Fourberies de Scapin*, opéra bouffe (Tartu, Dec. 22, 1984). **ORCH.:** Concertino for Oboe and Chamber Orch. (1961); Sym. for Strings and Percussion (1963); 2 concertos for Orch. (1967; *Symphonic Études*, 1977); *Music* for Strings (1968); *Easy Symphony* (1971); Violin Concerto (1971); *Elegiac Music in Memoriam Igor Stravinsky* for Chamber Orch. (1975). **CHAMBER:** 7 string quartets (1955–93); Trio for Oboe, Cello, and Piano (1959); Wind Quintet (1964); *The Tumblers* for 4 Woodwinds, 2 Brasses, and 19 Percussion Instruments (1966); *Inventions* for Vibraphone, Marimba, and 5 Tam-tams (1972); *English Divertimento* for Flute, Clarinet, and Bassoon (1978). **VOCAL:** *Solemn Song*, cantata (1968); *Winter Songs* for Chorus (1975); 3 concertos for Chorus (1979, 1987, 1988); *Russian Orthodox Liturgical Songs* for Soloists and Chorus (1990–92); songs.

Falkner, Sir (Donald) Keith, English bass-baritone and pedagogue; b. Sawston, Cambridgeshire, March 1, 1900; d. Bungay, Suffolk, May 17, 1994. He studied at New College, Oxford, and with Plunkett Greene in London, Lierhammer in Vienna, Grenzebach in Berlin, and Dossert in Paris. From 1923 to 1946 he was active mainly as a concert singer, appearing principally in oratorios. After serving as visiting prof. (1950–51), assoc. prof. (1951–56), and prof. (1956–60) at Cornell Univ., he was director of the Royal College of Music in London (1960–74). He was joint artistic director of the Kings Lynn Festival (1981–83). In 1974 he was knighted.

Fall, Leo(pold), notable Austrian composer; b. Olmütz, Feb. 2, 1873; d. Vienna, Sept. 16, 1925. He began his musical training with his father, Moritz Fall (1840–1922), a military bandmaster and composer. At 14, he enrolled at the Vienna Cons. to study violin and piano, and also had courses in harmony and counterpoint with J.N. Fuchs and R. Fuchs. He was active as a theater conductor in Berlin (1894–96), and then was conductor of the Centralhallen-Theater in Hamburg (1896–98). Returning to Berlin, he conducted in theaters before becoming music director of the Intimes-Theater, a cabaret. There he brought out his comic opera *Paroli* (Oct. 4, 1902). After the failure of his grand opera *Irrlicht* (Mannheim, 1905), Fall concentrated his efforts on lighter stage works. Although his first operetta *Der Rebell* (Vienna, Nov. 28, 1905) was a failure at its premiere, its revised version as *Der liebe Augustin* (Berlin, Feb. 3, 1912) was a resounding success. In the meantime, Fall scored his first unqualified success with *Der fidele Bauer* (Mannheim, July 25, 1907). With *Die Dollarprinzessin* (Vienna, Nov. 2, 1907), Fall also was acclaimed in Great Britain and America, establishing him as one of the principal operetta composers of his time. His *Die geschiedene Frau* (Vienna, Dec. 23, 1908) was so successful that it was heard around the world. His success continued with *Das Puppenmädel* (Vienna, Nov. 4, 1910), *Die schöne Risette* (Vienna, Nov. 19, 1910), *Die Sirene* (Vienna, Jan. 5, 1911), and *The Eternal Waltz* (London, Dec. 22, 1911). During World War I, Fall continued to compose, producing the outstanding *Die Kaiserin* or *Fürstenliebe* (Berlin, Oct. 16, 1916) and the popular *Die Rose von Stambul* (Vienna, Dec. 2, 1916). With the war over, Fall turned out the notable scores *Der goldene Vogel* (Dresden, May 21, 1920), *Die spanische Nachtigall* (Berlin, Nov. 18, 1920), and *Die Strassensängerin* (Berlin, Sept. 24, 1921). His greatest postwar success came with his *Madame Pompadour* (Berlin, Sept. 9, 1922), which became an international favorite. His brother, Richard Fall (b. Gewitsch, April 3, 1882; d. in the concentration camp in Auschwitz about Nov. 20, 1943), was also a composer. He wrote operettas, revues, and film scores. Among his best known stage works were *Der Wiener Fratz* (Vienna, Jan. 1, 1912), *Der Weltenbummler* (Berlin, Nov. 18, 1915), *Die Puppenbaronessen* (Vienna, Sept. 1, 1917), and *Grossstadtmärchen* (Vienna, Jan. 10, 1920).

WORKS: MUSIC THEATER: *Lustige Blätter* (Hamburg, July 25, 1896); *1842* or *Der grosse Brand* (Hamburg, Aug. 1, 1897); *Der Brandstifter* (Berlin, Jan. 1, 1899); *Die Jagd nach dem Glück* (Berlin, Feb. 1, 1900); *'ne feine Nummer* (Berlin, Feb. 16, 1901; in collaboration with V. Hollander); *Paroli* or *Frau Denise* (Vienna, Oct. 4, 1902); *Der Rebell* (Vienna, Nov. 28, 1905; rev. version as *Der liebe Augustin*, Berlin, Feb. 3, 1912); *Der Fuss* (Chemnitz, Sept. 18, 1906); *Der fidele Bauer* (Mannheim, July 25, 1907); *Die Dollarprinzessin* (Vienna, Nov. 2, 1907); *Die geschiedene Frau* (Vienna, Dec. 23, 1908); *Brüderlein fein* (Berlin, Dec. 31, 1908); *Die Schrei nach der Ohrfeige* (1909); *Brüderlein fein* (Vienna, Dec. 1, 1909); *Das Puppenmädel* (Vienna, Nov. 4, 1910); *Die schöne Risette* (Vienna, Nov. 19, 1910); *Die Sirene* (Vienna, Jan. 5, 1911); *The Eternal Waltz* (London, Dec. 11, 1911); *Die Studentengräfin* (Berlin, Jan. 18, 1913); *Der Nachtschnellzug* (Vienna, Dec. 18, 1913); *Jung England* (Berlin, Feb. 14, 1914; rev. version as *Frau Ministerpräsident*, Dresden, Feb. 3, 1920); *Der künstliche Mensch* (Berlin, Oct. 2, 1915); *Die Kaiserin* or *Fürstenliebe* (Berlin, Oct. 16, 1915); *Tantalus im Dachstüberl* (Würzburg, March 26, 1916); *Seemansliebchen* (Berlin, Sept. 4, 1916; in collaboration with F. Warnke); *Die Rose von Stambul* (Vienna, Dec. 2, 1916); *Der goldene Vogel* (Dresden, May 21, 1920); *Die spanische Nachtigall* (Berlin, Nov. 18, 1920); *Die Strassensängerin* (Berlin, Sept. 24, 1921); *Der heilige Ambrosius* (Berlin, Nov. 3, 1921); *Madame Pompadour* (Berlin, Sept. 9, 1922); *Der süsse Kavalier* (Vienna, Dec. 11, 1923); *Jugend im Mai* (Dresden, Oct. 22, 1926); *Rosen aus Florida* (Vienna, Feb. 22, 1929; arranged by E. Korngold). **OTHER:** Waltzes; songs.

BIBL.: W. Zimmerli, *L.F.* (Zürich, 1957).

Falla (y Matheu), Manuel (Maria) de, great Spanish composer; b. Cadíz, Nov. 23, 1876; d. Alta Gracia, Córdoba province, Argentina, Nov. 14, 1946. He studied piano with his mother; after further instruction from Eloisa Galluzo, he studied harmony, counterpoint, and composition with Alejandro Odero and Enrique Broca; then went to Madrid, where he studied piano with José Tragó and composition with Felipe Pedrell at the Cons. He wrote several zarzuelas, but only *Los amores de la Inés* was performed (Madrid, April 12, 1902). His opera *La vida breve* won the prize of the Real Academia de Bellas Artes in Madrid in 1905, but it was not premiered until 8 years later. In 1905 he also won the Ortiz y Cussó Prize for pianists. In 1907 he went to Paris, where he became friendly with Debussy, Dukas, and Ravel, who aided and encouraged him as a composer. Under their influence, he adopted the principles of Impressionism without, however, giving up his personal and national style. He returned to Spain in 1914 and produced his tremendously effective ballet *El amor brujo* (Madrid, April 2, 1915). It was followed by the evocative *Noches en los jardines de España* for Piano and Orch. (Madrid, April 9, 1916). In 1919 he made his home in Granada, where he completed work on his celebrated ballet *El sombrero de tres picos* (London, July 22, 1919). Falla's art was rooted in both the folk songs of Spain and the purest historical traditions of Spanish music. Until 1919 his works were cast chiefly in the Andalusian idiom, and his instrumental technique was often conditioned by effects peculiar to Spain's national instrument, the guitar. In his puppet opera *El retablo de maese Pedro* (1919–22), he turned to the classical tradition of Spanish (especially Castilian) music. The keyboard style of his Harpsichord Concerto (1923–26), written at the suggestion of Wanda Landowska, reveals in the classical lucidity of its writing a certain kinship with Domenico Scarlatti, who lived in Spain for many years. Falla became president of the Instituto de Espana in 1938. When the Spanish Civil War broke out, and General Franco overcame the Loyalist government with the aid of Hitler and Mussolini, Falla left Spain and went to South America, never to return to his homeland. He went to Buenos Aires, where he conducted concerts of his music. He then withdrew to the small locality of Alta Gracia, where he lived the last years of his life in seclusion, working on his large scenic cantata *Atlántida.* It remained unfinished at his death and was later completed by his former pupil Ernesto Halffter.

WRITINGS: *Escritos sobre música y músicos* (ed. by F. Sopeña; Madrid, 1950; 3rd ed., 1972; Eng. tr., 1979, as *On Music and Musicians*); *Cartas a Segismondo Romero* (ed. by P. Recuero; Granada, 1976); *Correspondencia de Manuel de Falla* (ed. by E. Franco; Madrid, 1978).

WORKS: DRAMATIC: *La vida breve*, opera (1904–05; Nice, April 1, 1913); *El amor brujo*, ballet (1914–15; Madrid, April 2, 1915; concert version, 1916); *El corregidor y la molinera*, farsa mimica (1916–17; Madrid, April 7, 1917; rev. and expanded as *El sombrero de tres picos*); *El sombrero de tres picos*, ballet (rev. and expanded from *El corregidor y la molinera*; 1918–19; 2 orch. suites, 1919; London, July 22, 1919); *El retablo de maese Pedro*, puppet opera (1919–22; concert perf., Seville, March 23, 1923; private stage perf. in the salon of Princess de Poligna, Paris, June 25, 1923; public stage perf., Paris, Nov. 13, 1923); *Atlántida*, cantata escenica (1925–46; unfinished; completed by E. Halffter; Milan, June 18, 1962; rev. and perf. in concert form, Lucerne, Sept. 9, 1976); also several zarzuelas, including *Los amores de la Inés* (Madrid, April 12, 1902); incidental music, and a comic opera, *Fuego fatuo* (1918–19). **ORCH.:** *Noches en los jardines de España* for Piano and Orch. (1909–15; Madrid, April 9, 1916); Concerto for Harpsichord or Piano, Flute, Oboe, Clarinet, Violin, and Cello (1923–26; Barcelona, Nov. 4, 1926); *Homenajes*, 4 pieces: 1, *à Cl. Debussy* (orig. for Guitar as *Le Tombeau de Claude Debussy*, 1920); 2, *Fanfare sobre el nombre de E.F. Arbós* (1933); 3, *à Paul Dukas* (orig. for Piano as *Pour le tombeau de Paul Dukas*, 1935); 4, *Pedrelliana* (1924–39); 1st performance of entire suite, Buenos Aires, Nov. 18, 1939. **CHAMBER:** *Melodía* for Cello and Piano (1897–99); *Mireya* for Flute and Piano Quartet (1899); Piano Quartet (1899); *Romanza* for Cello and Piano (1899); *Serenata andaluza* for Violin and Piano (1899; not extant); *Fanfare pour une fête* (1921). **PIANO:** *Nocturno* (1899); *Serenata andaluza* (1899); *Canción* (1900); *Vals-capricho* (1900); *Cortejo de gnomos* (1901); *Suite fantástica* (1901; not extant); *Hoja de album* (1902); *Pièces espagnoles: Aragonesa, Cubana, Montanesa*, and *Andaluza* (1902–8); *Allegro de concierto* (1903); *Fantasía bética* (1919); *Canto de los remeros del Volga* (1922); *Pour le tombeau de Paul Dukas* (1935; orch. version as *Homenajes*). **GUITAR:** *Homenaje "Le Tombeau de Claude Debussy"* (1920; orch. version as *Homenajes*). **VOCAL:** *Dos rimas* (1899–1900); *Preludios* (1900); *Tus ojillo negros* (1902); *Trois mélodies* (1909); *Siete canciones populares españolas* (1914–15); *Oracion de las madres que tienen a sus hijos en brazos* (1914); *El pan de ronda* (1915); *Psyché* for Voice, Flute, Harp, and String Trio (1924); *Soneto a Córdoba* for Voice and Harp or Piano (1927).

BIBL.: E. Istel, "M. d.F.," *Musical Quarterly* (Oct. 1926);

J. Trend, *M. d.F. and Spanish Music* (N.Y., 1929; new ed., 1934); Roland-Manuel, *M. d.F.* (Paris, 1930); G. Chase, "F.'s Music for Piano Solo," *Chesterian* (1940); A. Sagardia, *M. d.F.* (Madrid, 1946); J. Thomas, *M. d.F. en la Isla* (Palma, 1947); J. Jaenisch, *M. d.F. und die spanische Musik* (Zürich and Freiburg im Breisgau, 1952); L. Campodonico, *F.* (Paris, 1959); R. Arizaga, *M. d.F.* (Buenos Aires, 1961); E. Molina Fajardo, *M. d.F. y el "cante jondo"* (Granada, 1962); J. Viniegra, *M. d.F.: Su vida intima* (Cádiz, 1966); A. Saeardia, *Vida y Obra de M. d.F.* (Madrid, 1967); J. Grunfeld, *M. d.F.: Spanien und die neue Musik* (Zürich, 1968); M. Orozco, *M. d.F.: Biografia illustrada* (Barcelona, 1968); A. Campoamor Gonzalez, *M. d.F., 1876–1946* (Madrid, 1976); R. Crichton, *M. d.F.: Descriptive Catalogue of His Works* (London, 1976); B. James, *M. d.F. and the Spanish Musical Renaissance* (London, 1979); R. Crichton, *F.* (London, 1982); G. Chase and A. Budwig, *M. d.F.: A Bibliography and Research Guide* (N.Y., 1986); J. de Persia, *Los últimos años de M. d.F.* (Madrid, 1989); T. Garms, *Der Flamenco und der spanische Folklore in M. d.F.s Werken* (Wiesbaden, 1990); K. Pahlen, *M. d.F. und der Musik in Spaniern* (Mainz, 1993).

Falletta, JoAnn, American conductor; b. N.Y., Feb. 27, 1954. She began classical guitar and piano lessons at age 7; in 1972 she entered the Mannes College of Music in N.Y. to continue her guitar studies but the next year became a conducting student of Sung Kwak (B.M., 1976; M.A., 1978). In 1982 she entered the Juilliard School in N.Y. on a conducting scholarship, completing her advanced training with Mester and Ehrling (M.M. 1983; D.M.A., 1989). From 1978 to 1990 she was music director of the Queens (N.Y.) Phil.; was also music director of the Denver Chamber Orch. (1983–92) and assoc. conductor of the Milwaukee Sym. Orch. (1985–88). In 1985 she won both the Stokowski and Toscanini conducting awards. From 1986 to 1995 she was music director of the Bay Area Women's Phil. in San Francisco, with which she presented works by women composers of all eras. She concurrently served as music director of the Long Beach (Calif.) Sym. Orch. (from 1989) and the Virginia Sym. Orch. in Norfolk (from 1991). As a guest conductor, she appeared with orchs. in the U.S. and abroad.

Fano, (Aronne) Guido Alberto, Italian composer, teacher, and writer on music; b. Padua, May 18, 1875; d. Tauriano di Spilimbergo, Friuli, Aug. 14, 1961. He was a pupil of Orefice and Pollini in Padua, then of Martucci at the Bologna Liceo Musicale (composition diploma, 1897); received a law degree from the Univ. of Bologna (1901). He taught piano at the Bologna Liceo Musicale (1900–1905); then was director of the conservatories in Parma (1905–12), Naples (1912–16), and Palermo (1916–22); subsequently taught piano at the Milan Cons. (1922–38; 1945–47).

WORKS: DRAMATIC: *Astraea,* poema drammatico; *Juturna,* dramma musicale. **ORCH.:** *La tentazione di Gesù,* symphonic poem; overture (1912); *Andante e allegro con fuoco* for Piano and Orch. (1936); *Impressioni sinfoniche da Napoleone* (1949). **OTHER:** Chamber music, piano pieces, and songs.

WRITINGS: *Pensieri sulla musica* (Bologna, 1903); *Nella vita del ritmo* (Naples, 1916); *Lo studio del pianoforte* (3 vols., Milan, 1923–24).

Farberman, Harold, American conductor and composer; b. N.Y., Nov. 2, 1929. He was educated at the Juilliard School of Music in N.Y. (diploma, 1951) and the New England Cons. of Music in Boston (B.S., 1956; M.S., 1957). He was a percussionist in the Boston Sym. Orch. (1951–63) and conductor of the New Arts Orch. in Boston (1955–63); then was conductor of the Colorado Springs (Colo.) Phil. (1967–68) and the Oakland (Calif.) Sym. Orch. (1971–79); subsequently was principal guest conductor of the Bournemouth Sinfonietta (from 1986). In 1975 he became founder-president of the Conductors' Guild. In 1980 he organized the Conductors' Inst. at the Univ. of West Virginia, which removed to the Univ. of South Carolina in 1987.

WORKS: DRAMATIC: *Medea,* chamber opera (1960–61; Boston, March 26, 1961); *If Music Be,* mixed media piece (1965); *The Losers,* opera (N.Y., March 26, 1971); ballets; film scores. **ORCH.:** Concerto for Bassoon and Strings (1956); Sym. (1956–57); Timpani Concerto (1958); *Impressions* for Oboe, Strings, and Percussion (1959–60); Concerto for Alto Saxophone and Strings (1965); *Elegy, Fanfare, and March* (1965); Violin Concerto (1976); *The You Name it March* (1981); *Shapings* for English Horn, Strings, and Percussion (1984); *A Summer's Day in Central Park* (1987; N.Y., Jan. 21, 1988). **CHAMBER:** *Variations* for Percussion and Piano (1954); *Variations on a Familiar Theme* for Percussion (1955); *Music Inn Suite* for 6 Percussion (1958); String Quartet (1960); *Progressions* for Flute and Percussion (1961); *Quintessence* for Woodwind Quintet (1962); Trio for Violin, Piano, and Percussion (1963); *For Eric and Nick* for Chamber Group (1964); *Images for Brass* for 2 Trumpets, Horn, Trombone, and Tuba (1964); *The Preacher* for Electric Trumpet and 4 Percussion (1969); *Alea* for 6 Percussion (1976); Duo for English Horn and Percussion (1981). **VOCAL:** *Evolution* for Soprano, Horn, and 7 Percussion (1954); *Greek Scene* for Mezzo-soprano, Piano, and Percussion (1957; also for Mezzo-soprano and Orch.); *August 30, 1964-N.Y. Times* for Mezzo-soprano, Piano, and Percussion (1964); *War Cry on a Prayer Feather* for Soprano, Baritone, and Orch. (1976).

Fariñas, Carlos, Cuban composer and teacher; b. Cienfuegos, Nov. 28, 1934. He was a student of Ardévol and Gramatges at the Havana Cons., of Copland at the Berkshire Music Center at Tanglewood (summer, 1956), and of Pirumov and Rogal-Levitski at the Moscow Cons. (1961–63); later he worked in Berlin on a grant from the Deutscher Akademischer Austauschdienst (1975–77). After serving as director of the Conservatorio Alejandro García Caturla in Havana (1963–67), he was head of the music dept. of the Biblioteca Nacional de Cuba there (1967–77). In 1978 he joined the faculty of music at the Instituto Superior de Arte de Cuba in Havana, where he was founder-director of the Estudio de Música Electroacustica y por Computadoras (from 1989). His works are generally cast along avant-garde lines. While he used Afro-Cuban folk sources for inspiration in some of his works, he eventually embraced the most technologically advanced means of expression, including electronic and computer-processed scores.

WORKS: DRAMATIC: OPERA: *Escenas* (1990). **BALLETS:** *Despertar* (1959–60); *Yagruma* (1975). **ORCH.:** *Música* for Strings (1957); *Relieves* for 5 Orch. Groups (1969); *Muros rejas y vitrales* (1969–71); *El bosque ha echado a andar* (1976); *Punto y tonadas* for Strings (1981); *Nocturno de enero* (1989); *En tres partes* for Cuban Lute and Strings (1990). **CHAMBER:** Sonata for Violin and Cello (1961); String Quartet (1962–63); *Tiento I* for Clarinet, Guitar, Piano, and Percussion (1966) and *II* for 2 Pianos and Percussion (1969); *In rerum natura* for Clarinet, Violin, Cello, and Harp (1972); *Tatomaitee* for String Quartet and Percussion (1972); Concerto for Violin and 2 Percussion (1976); *Impronta* for Piano, 4 Percussion, and Tape (1985); guitar pieces. **PIANO:** (6) *Preludios* (1953–64); *6 Sones sencillos* (1956–64); *Atanos* (1972); *Alta gracia* (1984); *Sonero* (1992); *Conjuro: John Cage in memoriam* (1993). **OTHER:** Choral pieces; multimedia music; tape pieces.

Farjeon, Harry, English composer; b. Hohokus, N.J. (of English parents), May 6, 1878; d. London, Dec. 29, 1948. He was a son of the English novelist B.L. Farjeon, and grandson of the famous actor Joseph Jefferson. He was educated in England, taking music lessons with Landon Ronald and John Storer; then studied composition with Corder at the Royal Academy of Music in London; won the Lucas Medal and other prizes. In 1903 he became an instructor at the Royal Academy of Music.

WORKS: *Floretta,* opera (1899); *The Registry Office,* operetta (1900); *A Gentleman of the Road,* operetta (1902); Piano Concerto (1903); *Hans Andersen Suite* for Small Orch. (1905); *Summer Vision,* symphonic poem (not extant); 2 song cycles: *Vagrant Songs* and *The Lute of Jade.*

Farkas, Ferenc, prominent Hungarian composer and teacher; b. Nagykanizsa, Dec. 15, 1905. He began to study piano as a child; took courses with Leo Weiner and Albert Siklós at the Academy of Music in Budapest (1922–27); a state scholarship enabled him to study with Respighi at the Accademia di Santa Cecilia in Rome (1929–31). Returning to Hungary, he was a music teacher at the municipal school in Budapest (1935–41); from 1941 to 1944 he taught at the Cluj Cons.; was director of the music school in Székesfehérvár (1946–48); from 1949 to 1975 he was a prof. of composition at the Academy of Music in Budapest. In 1950 and 1991 he was awarded the Kossuth Prize and in 1960 the Erkel Prize; was made Merited Artist (1965) and Honored Artist (1970) of the Hungarian People's Republic. He also received the Herder Prize of Hamburg (1979) and was made a Cavaliere dell'Ordine della Repubblica Italiana (1985).

WORKS: DRAMATIC: *The Magic Cupboard*, comic opera (1938–42; Budapest, April 22, 1942; also a separate overture, 1952); *The Sly Students*, ballet (1949); *Csinom Palkó*, musical play (1950; rev. 1960); *Vidróczki*, radio ballad (1959; rev. as an opera, 1964); *Piroschka*, musical comedy (1967); *Story of Noszty Junior with Mari Tóth*, musical comedy (1971); *Panegyricus*, ballet (1972); *A Gentleman from Venice*, opera (1980). Also incidental music and film scores. **ORCH.:** *Fantasy* for Piano and Orch. (1929); *Divertimento* (1930); Harp Concertino (1937; rev. 1956); *Dinner Music* for Chamber Orch. (1938); *Rhapsodia carpathiana* (1940); *Marionette's Dance Suite* (1940–41); *Musica pentatonica* for Strings (1945); *Musica dodecatonica*, later renamed *Prelude and Fugue* (1947); Piano Concertino (1947–49); *Lavotta*, suite (1951); Sym. (1951–52); *Scherzo sinfonico* (1952); *Symphonic Overture* (1952); *Sketches from the Bukk* (1955); *Piccola musica di concerto* for Strings (1961); *Trittico concertato* for Cello and Strings (1964); *Gyász és vígasz* (Planctus et Consolationes; 1965); *Concerto all'Antica* for Baryton or Viola da Gamba, and Strings (1965); *Serenata concertante* for Flute and Strings (1967); *Festive Overture* (1972); *Variazioni classiche* (1975–76); *Ouverture philharmonique* (1977–78); *Musica serena* for Strings (1982); *Musica giocosa*, suite (1982); Concertino for Trumpet and Strings (1984). **CHAMBER:** 3 violin sonatinas (1930, 1931, 1959); *Alla danza ungherese* for Cello or Violin and Piano (1934); *Scherzino and Intermezzo* for Recorder and Piano (1940); *Serenade* for Wind Quintet (1951); *Antiche danze ungheresi* for Wind Quintet (1953); *Sonata a due* for Viola and Cello (1961); Serenade for Flute and 2 Violins (1965); String Quartet (1970–72); *Tower Music of Nyirbátor* for 3 Trumpets, 4 Horns, 3 Trombones, and Tuba (1974); Trio for Violin, Cello, and Piano (1979); 10 Studies for 2 Violins (1982); *Trigon* for Flute, Bassoon, and Piano (1988). **VOCAL:** *Cantata lirica* for Chorus and Orch. (1945); *Cantus Pannonicus* for Soprano, Chorus, and Orch. (Budapest, April 3, 1959); *Flying Flags* for Soprano, Baritone, Men's Chorus, and Orch. (1972–73); *Aspirationes principis* for Tenor, Baritone, and Orch. (1974–75); *Vita poetae* for Men's Trio, Chorus, and Instruments (1976); *Ad Musicam* for Chorus (1981); songs.

BIBL.: J. Ujfalussy, *F. F.* (Budapest, 1969).

Farkas, Philip (Francis), American horn player and teacher; b. Chicago, March 5, 1914; d. Bloomington, Ind., Dec. 21, 1992. After study with Louis Defrasne in Chicago, he was 1st horn player in the Kansas City Phil. (1933–36), the Chicago Sym. Orch. (1936–41; 1947–60), the Cleveland Orch. (1941–45; 1946–47), and the Boston Sym. Orch. (1945–46). He taught at the Indiana Univ. School of Music in Bloomington (1960–82) and founded his own publishing company, Wind Music, Inc.; also authored *The Art of French Horn Playing* (1956), *The Art of Brass Playing* (1962), and *A Photographic Study of 40 Virtuoso Horn Players' Embouchures* (1970).

BIBL.: M. Stewart, ed., *P.: The Legacy of a Master* (Northfield, Ill., 1990).

Farley, Carole Ann, talented American soprano; b. Le Mars, Iowa, Nov. 29, 1946. She studied at the Indiana Univ. School of Music (Mus.B., 1968), with Reid in N.Y., and on a Fulbright scholarship with Schech at the Munich Hochschule für Musik (1968–69). In 1969 she made her debut at the Linz Landestheater and also her U.S. debut at N.Y.'s Town Hall; subsequently appeared as a soloist with major orchs. of the U.S. and Europe, and sang with the Welsh National Opera (1971–72), the Cologne Opera (1972–75), the Strasbourg Opera (1975), the N.Y. City Opera (1976), and the Lyons Opera (1976–77). She made her formal Metropolitan Opera debut in N.Y. as Lulu on March 18, 1977, and continued to sing there in later seasons; she also sang at the Zürich Opera (1979), the Deutsche Oper am Rhein in Düsseldorf (1980–81; 1984), the Chicago Lyric Opera (1981), the Florence Maggio Musicale (1985), and at the Teatro Colón in Buenos Aires (1989). In addition to her esteemed portrayal of Lulu, which she essayed over 80 times in various operatic centers, she also sang Poppea, Donna Anna, Violetta, Massenet's Manon, Mimi, and various roles in Richard Strauss's operas. She married **José Serebrier** in 1969.

Farmer, Henry George, Irish conductor, music scholar, and composer; b. Birr, Jan. 17, 1882; d. Law, Scotland, Dec. 30, 1965. After instruction in piano, violin, and harmony with Vincent Sykes in Birr, he went to London and studied with Henry Tonking, Mark Andrews, and F.A. Borsdorf. In 1895 he became a violinist and clarinetist in the Royal Artillery Orch., later serving as its 1st horn (1902–10); he also conducted in theaters and in 1911 founded the Irish Orch. of London. In 1914 he went to Glasgow and completed his education at the Univ. From 1914 to 1947 he was conductor of the Empire Theatre Orch. in Glasgow; he also was founder–conductor of the Glasgow Sym. Orch. (1919–43). In 1949 he was awarded an honorary doctorate in music by the Univ. of Glasgow. He wrote valuable books on the music of the Middle East. Among his compositions were a ballet and other theater pieces, overtures, and chamber music.

WRITINGS: *Memoirs of the Royal Artillery Band* (1904); *The Rise and Development of Military Music* (1912); *Heresy in Art* (1918); *The Arabian Influence on Musical Theory* (1925); *The Arabic Musical Manuscripts in the Bodleian Library* (1925); *Byzantine Musical Instruments in the Ninth Century* (1925); *A History of Arabian Music to the XIIIth Century* (1929); *Historical Facts for the Arabian Musical Influence* (1930); *Music in Medieval Scotland* (1930); *Music in Scotland* (1931); *The Organ of the Ancients from Eastern Sources, Hebrew, Syriac and Arabic* (1931); *Studies in Oriental Musical Instruments (1931); An Old Moorish Lute Tutor* (1933); *Al-Farabi's Arabic-Latin Writings on Music* (1934); with H. Smith, *New Mozartiana: The Mozart Relics in the Zavertal Collection at the University of Glasgow* (1935); *Turkish Instruments of Music in the Seventeenth Century* (1937); *The Sources of Arabian Music* (1940; 2nd ed., rev., 1965); *Instruments of Music: History and Development* (1941); *Maimonides on Listening to Music* (1941); *Music: The Priceless Jewell* (1942); *Sa'adyah Gaon on the Influence of Music* (1943); *The Glen Collection of Musical Instruments* (1945); *The Minstrelsy of the Arabian Nights* (1945); *Music in 18th Century Scotland* (1946); *A History of Music in Scotland* (1947); *Handel's Kettledrums and Other Papers on Military Music* (1950; 2nd ed., rev., 1960); *Military Music* (1950); *Music Making in the Olden Days: The Story of the Aberdeen Concerts, 1748–1801* (1950); *Cavaliere Zavertal and the Royal Artillery Band* (1951); *Oriental Studies, Mainly Musical* (1953); *The History of the Royal Artillery Band* (1954); *British Bands in Battle* (1965).

Farnadi, Edith, Hungarian pianist and teacher; b. Budapest, Sept. 25, 1921; d. Graz, Dec. 14, 1973. She entered the Budapest Academy of Music at the age of 9; studied with Bartók and Weiner. She made her debut at age 12; was granted her diploma at 16. She made appearances with the violinists Hubay and Huberman; taught at the Budapest Academy of Music; then became a teacher in Graz.

Farnam, (Walter) Lynnwood, outstanding Canadian organist and pedagogue; b. Sutton, Quebec, Jan. 13, 1885; d. N.Y., Nov. 23, 1930. He studied piano in Dunham, and then held the Lord Strathcona Scholarship to the Royal College of Music in London (1900–1904), where he was a student of Franklin Taylor (piano) and Parratt and W.S. Hoyte (organ). He was organist in Montreal at St. James' Methodist Church (1904–05) and at the Church of St. James the Apostle (1905–08), and then organist-choirmaster at Christ Church Cathedral (1908–13); he also was active as a recitalist and in 1912–13 taught at the McGill Cons. After serving as organist at Boston's Emmanuel Church (1913–18), he went to N.Y. as organist at the Fifth Ave. Presbyterian Church (1919–20) and then at the Church of the Holy Communion (1920–30). His recital tours took him all over North America, England, and France. In addition to teaching in N.Y., he was on the faculty of the Curtis Inst. of Music in Philadelphia (1927–30). Farnam's recital repertoire was extraordinary, ranging from the pre-Bach masters to his own era. He played the complete works of Bach, and also of many Romantic composers, among them Franck and Brahms. Louis Vierne's 6th Organ Sym. (1931) is dedicated to Farnam's memory.

BIBL.: J. Rizzo, "L.F.—Master Organist of the Century," *Diapason* (Dec. 1974 and Jan. 1975); J. Conner, "L.F.: A Centennial Remembrance," *American Organist* (Nov. 1985).

Farncombe, Charles (Frederick), English conductor; b. London, July 29, 1919. He first studied engineering at the Univ. of London (B.Sc., 1940); after military service in World War II, he enrolled at the Royal School of Church Music, Canterbury, and the Royal Academy of Music, London. In 1955 he organized the Handel Opera Soc., serving as its music director and conductor. From 1970 to 1979 he was chief conductor of the Drottningholm Court Theater in Stockholm; then was music director of the London Chamber Opera (1983–95) and the Malcolm Sargent Festival Choir (from 1986). In 1977 he was made a Commander of the Order of the British Empire.

Farquhar, David (Andross), New Zealand composer and teacher; b. Cambridge, New Zealand, April 5, 1928. He studied with Douglas Lilburn, at Canterbury College, and at Victoria College (B.A., B.Mus., 1948); went to England and took his M.A. at Emmanuel College, Cambridge (1951), completing his training with Benjamin Frankel at the Guildhall School of Music in London (1951–52). Returning to New Zealand, he was a lecturer (1953–76) and prof. of music (1976–93) at Victoria Univ. of Wellington; in 1974 he was founding president of the Composers Assn. of New Zealand. His music is contrapuntal in structure and neo-Romantic in mood.

WORKS: DRAMATIC: OPERAS: *A Unicorn for Christmas* (1962); *Shadow* (1970; Wellington, Sept. 19, 1988); incidental music. **ORCH.:** *Epithalamion Overture* (1954); *Ring round the Moon*, dance suite (1957); *Evocation* (1957); 3 syms.: No. 1 (1959; Wellington, Aug. 13, 1960; 1st sym. by a New Zealand composer given a public premiere), *Bells in Their Seasons*, choral sym. (1974), and No. 2 (Wellington, Nov. 5, 1983); *Harlequin Overture* (1959); *Anniversary Suite No. 1* (1961) and *No. 2* (1965); *Elegy* for Strings (1961); *Echoes and Reflections* for Strings (1974); *March* for Clarinet and Strings (1984). **CHAMBER:** 2 string quartets (1949, 1989); *Serenade* for Wind Quartet (1951); *Elegy* for Wind Trio (1965); *Notturno* for Brass Quintet (1966); Concerto for Wind Quintet (1967); *Scenes and Memories* for Violin, Piano, and Percussion (1972); *3 Pieces* for Double Bass (1976); *Concerto for 6* for Flute, Clarinet, Vibraphone, Piano, Violin, and Cello (1987); String Quartet (1989).

Farrar, Ernest (Bristow), English organist and composer; b. London, July 7, 1885; d. in the battle of the Somme, France, Sept. 18, 1918. He studied at the Royal College of Music in London with Stanford and Parratt; served as organist of the English Church in Dresden (1909); then at various churches in England (1910–14). His orch. suite English *Pastoral Impression* won the Carnegie Award; he further wrote the orch. pieces *The Open Road, Lavengro, The Forsaken Merman*, and *Heroic Elegy;* also *3 Spiritual Studies* for Strings; variations on an old English sea song for Piano and Orch.; the cantatas *The Blessed Damozel* and *Out of Doors*; chamber music; organ preludes; songs; etc.

Farrar, Geraldine, celebrated American soprano; b. Melrose, Mass., Feb. 28, 1882; d. Ridgefield, Conn., March 11, 1967. She studied music with Mrs. J.H. Long of Boston; took lessons with Emma Thursby in N.Y., Trabadello in Paris, and Graziani in Berlin; made a successful debut at the Berlin Royal Opera on Oct. 15, 1901, as Marguerite, under the direction of Karl Muck; then studied with Lilli Lehmann. She sang at the Monte Carlo Opera (1903–06). Her career in Europe was well established before her American debut as Juliette at the Metropolitan Opera in N.Y. (Nov. 26, 1906); she remained on the roster for 16 years; made her farewell appearance in *Zaza* on April 22, 1922, but continued to sing in concert; gave her last public performance at Carnegie Hall in N.Y. in 1931. Her greatest success was Cio-Cio-San, which she sang opposite Caruso's Pinkerton in *Madama Butterfly* at its American premiere at the Metropolitan on Feb. 11, 1907; she subsequently sang this part in America more than 100 times. Her interpretation of Carmen was no less remarkable. She also appeared in silent films between 1915 and 1919; her film version of *Carmen* aroused considerable interest. On Feb. 8, 1916, she married the actor Lou Tellegen, from whom she was subsequently divorced. She made adaptations of pieces by Kreisler, Rachmaninoff, and others, for which she publ. the lyrics. She wrote an autobiography, *Such Sweet Compulsion* (N.Y., 1938), which had been preceded in 1916 by *Geraldine Farrar: The Story of an American Singer.*

BIBL.: E. Wagenknecht, *G. F.: An Authorized Record of Her Career* (Seattle, 1929); E. Nash, *Always First Class: The Career of G. F.* (Washington, D.C., 1982); A. Truxall, ed., *All Good Greetings, G. F.: Letters of G. F. to Ilka Marie Stolker, 1946–1958* (Pittsburgh, 1991).

Farrell, Eileen, brilliant American soprano; b. Willimantic, Conn., Feb. 13, 1920. Her parents were vaudeville singers; she received her early vocal training with Merle Alcock in N.Y., and later studied with Eleanor McLellan. In 1940 she sang on the radio; in 1947–48 she made a U.S. tour as a concert singer; toured South America in 1949. Her song recital in N.Y. on Oct. 24, 1950, was enthusiastically acclaimed and secured for her immediate recognition. She was soloist in Beethoven's 9th Sym. with Toscanini and the NBC Sym. Orch.; also appeared many times with the N.Y. Phil. She made her operatic debut as Santuzza with the San Carlo Opera in Tampa, Fla., in 1956. In 1958 she joined the San Francisco Opera and in 1957 became a member of the Lyric Opera of Chicago. On Dec. 6, 1960, she made a successful debut with the Metropolitan Opera in N.Y. as Gluck's Alcestis; she remained on its roster until 1964; then returned in 1965–66. She was a Distinguished Prof. of Music at the Indiana Univ. School of Music in Bloomington from 1971 to 1980; then held that title at the Univ. of Maine in Orono from 1983 to 1985.

Farwell, Arthur (George), American composer and music educator; b. St. Paul, Minn., April 23, 1872; d. N.Y., Jan. 20, 1952. He studied at the Mass. Inst. of Technology, graduating in 1893; then studied music with Homer Norris and George Chadwick in Boston, Humperdinck and Pfitzner in Berlin (1897–99), and Guilmant in Paris. He was a lecturer on music at Cornell Univ. (1899–1901); from 1909 to 1914 he was on the editorial staff of *Musical America*, and also directed municipal concerts in N.Y. City (1910–13); then was director of the Settlement Music School in N.Y. (1915–18). He was acting head of the music dept. at the Univ. of Calif., Berkeley (1918–19); in 1919 he founded the Santa Barbara Community Chorus, which he conducted until 1921; later taught theory at Michigan State College in East Lansing (1927–39). Farwell was a pioneer in new American music, and tirelessly promoted national ideas in art. He contributed to various ethnological publications. From 1901 to 1911 he operated the Wa-Wan Press (Newton, Mass.), a periodical (quarterly, 1901–07; monthly, 1907–11) that printed piano and vocal music of "progressive" American composers of the period, the emphasis being on works that utilized indigenous (black, Indian, and cowboy) musical materials. Disillusioned about commercial opportunities for American music, including his own, he established at East Lansing, in 1936, his own lithographic handpress, with which he printed his music, handling the entire process of reproduction, including the cover designs, by himself.

WRITINGS: *A Letter to American Composers* (N.Y., 1903); with W. Dermot Darby, *Music in America in The Art of Music, IV* (N.Y., 1915).

WORKS: ORCH.: *The Death of Virginia,* symphonic poem (1894); *Academic Overture: Cornell* (1900); *Dawn,* fantasy on Indian themes (1904; orig. for Piano); *The Domain of Hurakan* (1910; orig. for Piano); *Symbolistic Study No. 3,* after Whitman's *Once I Passed Through a Populous City* (1905; rev. 1921; Philadelphia, March 30, 1928); *Symphonic Poem on March! March!* for Orch. and Chorus ad libitum (1921); *The Gods of the Mountain,* suite from the incidental music to Dunsany's play (1928; Minneapolis, Dec. 13, 1929); Concerto for 2 Pianos and Strings (1931; CBS, May 28, 1939; orig. *Symbolistic Study No. 6: Mountain Vision* for Piano); *Rudolph Gott Symphony* (1932–34); *Navao Dance No. 1* (1944; orig. for Piano); *The Heroic Breed, in memoriam General Patton* (1946). **CHAMBER:** *Fugue Fantasy* for String Quartet (1914); String Quartet, *The Hako* (1922); Violin Sonata (1927; rev. 1935); Piano Quintet (1937); Suite for Flute and Piano (1949); Cello Sonata; many piano pieces. **VOCAL:** Many pieces for Chorus and Orch., school choruses, and songs; music for pageants and masques, including *Caliban* for MacKaye's Shakespeare tercentenary masque (1915) and incidental music to C.W. Stevenson's *The Pilgrimage Way* (1920–21). **OTHER:** Collections of American Indian melodies and folk songs of the South and West; arrangements of American Indian melodies.

BIBL.: E. Waters, "The Wa-Wan Press: An Adventure in Musical Idealism," *A Birthday Offering to Carl Engel* (N.Y., 1943); E. Kirk, *Toward American Music: A Study of the Life and Music of A.G. F.* (diss., Univ. of Rochester, 1958); B. Farwell et al., *Guide to the Music of A. F. and to the Microfilm Collection of His Work* (Briarcliff Manor, N.Y., 1971); E. Culbertson, "A. F.'s Early Efforts on Behalf of American Music, 1889–1921," *American Music* (Summer 1987); T. Stoner, "'The New Gospel of Music': A. F.'s Vision of Democratic Music in America," ibid. (Summer 1991); E. Culbertson, *He Heard America Singing: A. F., Composer and Crusading Music Educator* (Metuchen, N.J., 1992).

Fasano, Renato, Italian conductor; b. Naples, Aug. 21, 1902; d. Rome, Aug. 3, 1979. He studied piano and composition at Naples, specializing in Renaissance music. In 1941 he founded the Collegium Musicum Italicum of Rome and in 1947 he organized the distinguished chamber group I Virtuosi di Roma, leading its performances on European tours. In 1957 he also founded the Piccolo Teatro Musicale Italiano; in 1960 he was named director of the Accademia di Santa Cecilia in Rome. Fasano was greatly esteemed for his effort to revive a proper appreciation of Italian music of the Renaissance period.

Fassbänder, Brigitte, noted German mezzo-soprano, daughter of **Willi Domgraf-Fassbänder;** b. Berlin, July 3, 1939. She studied with her father and attended the Nuremberg Cons. (1952–61). In 1961 she made her operatic debut as Nicklausse in *Les Contes d'Hoffman* at the Bavarian State Opera in Munich, where she became one of its most esteemed members. In 1970 she was honored as a Bavarian Kammersängerin. She appeared as Carmen at the San Francisco Opera in 1970, as Octavian at London's Covent Garden in 1971, and as Brangäne at the Paris Opéra in 1972. From 1972 to 1978 she appeared regularly at the Salzburg Festivals. On Feb. 16, 1974, she made her Metropolitan Opera debut in N.Y. as Octavian, returning there as Fricka in *Die Walküre* in 1986. In 1989 she sang Clytemnestra at the Salzburg Festival, returning in 1990 as Clairon in *Capriccio.* On Jan. 9, 1994, she made her N.Y. recital debut at Alice Tully Hall. In 1995 she retired. While her operatic repertoire ranged from Gluck to contemporary scores, she won special distinction for her roles in operas by Mozart and Strauss. She also pursued a distinguished concert career.

Fassbender, Zdenka, Bohemian soprano; b. Děčín, Dec. 12, 1879; d. Munich, March 14, 1954. She studied voice in Prague with Sophie Löwe-Destinn; made her operatic debut in Karlsruhe in 1899; from 1906 to 1919 she was one of the principal singers at the Munich Opera; she also sang at Covent Garden in London (1910, 1913). Felix Mottl married her on his deathbed to sanction their long-standing alliance.

Faull, Ellen, American soprano and teacher; b. Pittsburgh, Oct. 14, 1918. She studied at the Curtis Inst. of Music in Philadelphia and at Columbia Univ. She made her debut as Donna Anna in *Don Giovanni* with the N.Y. City Opera on Oct. 23, 1947, establishing herself as one of its principals, singing there regularly until 1979. She also appeared in San Francisco, Boston, and Chicago, and as a soloist with many U.S. orchs. Faull taught at N.Y.'s Manhattan School of Music (from 1971) and the Juilliard School (from 1981). She was particularly noted for her roles in Italian operas.

Fauré, Gabriel (-Urbain), great French composer and pedagogue; b. Pamiers, Ariège, May 12, 1845; d. Paris, Nov. 4, 1924. His father was a provincial inspector of primary schools; noticing the musical instinct of his son, he took him to Paris to study with Louis Niedermeyer; after Niedermeyer's death in 1861, Fauré studied with Saint-Saëns, from whom he received thorough training in composition. In 1866 he went to Rennes as organist at the church of St.-Sauveur; returned to Paris on the eve of the Franco-Prussian War in 1870, and volunteered in the light infantry. He was organist at Notre Dame de Clignancourt (1870), St.-Honoré d'Elyau (1871), and St.-Sulpice (1871–74). He then was named deputy organist (to Saint-Saëns, 1874), choirmaster (1877), and chief organist (1896) at the Madeleine. In 1896 he was appointed prof. of composition at the Paris Cons. He was an illustrious teacher; among his students were Ravel, Enesco, Koechlin, Roger-Ducasse, Florent Schmitt, and Nadia Boulanger. In 1905 he succeeded Théodore Dubois as director and served until 1920. Then, quite unexpectedly, he developed ear trouble, resulting in gradual loss of hearing. Distressed, he made an effort to conceal it but was eventually forced to abandon his teaching position. From 1903 to 1921 he wrote occasional music reviews in *Le Figaro* (a selection was publ. as *Opinions musicales,* Paris, 1930). He was elected a member of the Académie des Beaux Arts in 1909, and in 1910 was made a Commander of the Legion d'honneur. Fauré's stature as a composer is undiminished by the passage of time. He developed a musical idiom all his own; by subtle application of old modes, he evoked the aura of eternally fresh art; by using unresolved mild discords and special coloristic effects, he anticipated procedures of Impressionism; in his piano works, he shunned virtuosity in favor of the Classical lucidity of the French masters of the clavecin; the precisely articulated melodic line of his songs is in the finest tradition of French vocal music. His great *Requiem* and his *Élégie* for Cello and Piano have entered the general repertoire.

WORKS: DRAMATIC: *Barnabé,* opéra-comique (1879; unfinished; not perf.); *Caligula,* op. 52, incidental music to a play by A. Dumas père (Paris, Nov. 8, 1888); *Shylock,* incidental music to a play by E. de Haraucourt, after Shakespeare, op. 57 (Paris, Dec. 17, 1889); *La Passion,* incidental music to a play by Haraucourt (Paris, April 21, 1890); *Le Bourgeois Gentilhomme,* incidental music to a play by Molière (1893); *Pelléas et Mélisande,* incidental music to a play by Maeterlinck, op. 80 (London, June 21, 1898); *Prométhée,* tragédie lyrique, op. 82 (Béziers, Aug. 27, 1900); *Le Voile du bonheur,* incidental music to a play by Clémenceau, op. 88 (Paris, Nov. 4, 1901); *Pénélope,* drame lyrique (Monte Carlo, March 4, 1913); *Masques et bergamasques,* comédie musicale, op. 112 (Monte Carlo, April 10, 1919). **ORCH.:** *Suite d'orchestre,* op. 20 (1865–74; 1st movement publ. in 1895 as *Allegro symphonique,* op. 68, in an arrangement for Piano, 4-hands, by L. Boëllmann); Violin Concerto, op. 14 (1878–79; 2nd movement destroyed); *Berceuse* for Violin and Orch., op. 16 (1880; original version for Violin and Piano, 1879); *Ballade* for Piano and Orch., op. 19 (Paris, April 23, 1881; original version for Solo Piano, 1877–79); *Romance* for Violin and Orch., op. 28 (1882; original version for Violin and Piano, 1877); Sym. in D minor, op. 40 (1884; Paris, March 15, 1885); *Pavane* for Orch. and Chorus ad libitum, op. 50 (1887; Paris, March 28, 1888); *Shylock*, suite from the incidental music, op. 57 (1890); *Menuet* in F major (1893); *Élégie* for Cello and Orch., op. 24 (1896?; original version for Cello and Piano, 1880); *Pelléas et Mélisande*, suite from the incidental music, op. 80 (1898); *Jules César*, suite after *Caligula*, op. 52 (1905); *Dolly*, suite, op. 56 (an orchestration by H. Rabaud [1906] of the pieces for Piano, 4-hands, 1894–97); *Fantaisie* for Piano and Orch., op. 111 (1918–19; Paris, March 14, 1919); *Masques et bergamasques*, suite from the comédie musicale, op. 112 (1919); *Chant funéraire* (1921). **CHORAL: SACRED:** *Super flumina* for Chorus and Orch. (1863); *Cantique de Jean Racine* for Chorus and Organ, op. 11 (1865; rev. version for Chorus, Harmonium, and String Quintet, 1866); *Cantique à St. Vincent de Paul* (1868; not extant); *Tu es Petrus* for Baritone, Chorus, and Organ (1872?); *Messe basse* for Soloists, Women's Chorus, Harmonium, and Violin (1881); *Messe de Requiem* (1886–87; orig. in 5 movements for Soprano, Chorus, Organ, String Ensemble, and Timpani; Madeleine, Paris, Jan. 16, 1888; expanded to 7 movements, adding a Baritone Solo, Horns, and Trumpets, c.1889; full orch. version, c.1900); *Tantum ergo* in E major for Chorus, 3 Children's Voices, Solo Voices, and Organ, op. 65, no. 2 (1894); *Sancta mater* for Tenor, Chorus, and Organ (1894); *Tantum ergo* in F major for Soprano, Chorus, and Organ (1904). **SECULAR:** *Les Djinns* for Chorus and Orch., op. 12 (1875?); *La Naissance de Vénus* for Soloists, Chorus, and Orch., op. 29 (1882; Paris, April 3, 1886); etc. **CHAMBER** (all 1st perf. in Paris unless otherwise given): 2 violin sonatas: No. 1, op. 13 (1875–76; Jan. 27, 1877) and No. 2, op. 108 (1916–17; Nov. 10, 1917); 2 piano quartets: No. 1, op. 15 (1876–79; Feb. 14, 1880; rev. 1883) and No. 2, op. 45 (1885–86; Jan. 22, 1887); *Romance* for Violin and Piano, op. 28 (1877; Feb. 3, 1883; 2nd version for Violin and Orch., 1882); *Berceuse* for Violin and Piano, op. 16 (1879; Feb. 14, 1880; 2nd version for Violin and Orch., 1880); *Élégie* for Cello and Piano, op. 24 (1880; Dec. 15, 1883; 2nd version for Cello and Orch., 1896?); *Papillon* for Cello and Piano, op. 77 (1884?); *Petite pièce* for Cello, op. 49 (1887?); 2 piano quintets: No. 1, op. 89 (1887–95; 1903–5; Brussels, March 23, 1906) and No. 2, op. 115 (1919–21; May 21, 1921); *Romance* for Cello and Piano, op. 69 (1894); *Andante* for Violin and Piano, op. 75 (1897; Jan. 22, 1898); *Sicilienne* for Cello or Violin and Piano, op. 78 (1898); *Fantaisie* for Flute and Piano, op. 79 (July 28, 1898; orchestrated by L. Aubert, 1957); *Sérénade* for Cello and Piano, op. 98 (1908); 2 cello sonatas: No. 1, op. 109 (1917; Jan. 19, 1918) and No. 2, op. 117 (1921; May 13, 1922); Piano Trio, op. 120 (1922–23; May 12, 1923); String Quartet, op. 121 (1923–24; June 12, 1925). **SONGS:** *Le Papillon et la fleur*, op. 1, no. 1 (V. Hugo; 1861); *Mai*, op. 1, no. 2 (Hugo; 1862); *Rêve d'amour*, op. 5, no. 2 (Hugo; 1862); *L'Aube nait* (Hugo; 1862); *Puisque j'ai mis lèvre* (Hugo; 1862); *Tristesse d'Olympio* (Hugo; 1865); *Dans les ruines d'une abbaye*, op. 2, no. 1 (Hugo; 1866); *Les Matelots*, op. 2, no. 2 (T. Gautier; 1870); *Lydia*, op. 4, no. 2 (Leconte de Lisle; 1870); *Hymne*, op. 7, no. 2 (C. Baudelaire; 1870); *Seule!*, op. 3, no. 1 (Gautier; 1871); *L'Absent*, op. 5, no. 3 (Hugo; 1871); *L'Aurore* (Hugo; 1871); *La Rançon*, op. 8, no. 2 (Baudelaire; 1871); *Chant d'automne*, op. 5, no. 1 (Baudelaire; 1871); *La Chanson de pêcheur*, op. 4, no. 1 (Gautier; 1872); *Aubade*, op. 6, no. 1 (L. Pomey; 1873); *Tristesse*, op. 6, no. 2 (Gautier; 1873); *Barcarolle*, op. 7, no. 3 (M. Monnier; 1873); *Ici-bas!*, op. 8, no. 3 (S. Prudhomme; 1874); *Au bord de l'eau*, op. 8, no. 1 (Prudhomme; 1875); *Sérénade toscane*, op. 3, no. 2 (1878); *Après un rêve*, op. 7, no. 1 (1878); *Sylvie*, op. 6, no. 3 (P. de Choudens; 1878); *Nell*, op. 18, no. 1 (Leconte de Lisle; 1878); *Le Voyageur*, op. 18, no. 2 (A. Silvestre; 1878); *Automne*, op. 18, no. 3 (Silvestre; 1878); *Poème d'un jour*, op. 21 (C. Grandmougin; 1878); *Les Berceaux*, op. 23, no. 1 (Prudhomme; 1879); *Notre amour*, op. 23, no. 2 (Silvestre; 1879); *Le Secret*, op. 23, no. 3 (Silvestre; 1880–81); *Chanson d'amour*, op. 27, no. 1 (Silvestre; 1882); *La Fée aux chansons*, op. 27, no. 2 (Silvestre; 1882); *Aurore*, op. 39, no. 1 (Silvestre; 1884); *Fleur jetée*, op. 39, no. 2 (Silvestre; 1884); *Le Pays des rêves*, op. 39, no. 3 (Silvestre; 1884); *Les Roses d'Ispahan*, op. 39, no. 4 (Leconte de Lisle; 1884); *Noël*, op. 43, no. 1 (V. Wilder; 1886); *Nocturne*, op. 43, no. 2 (Villiers de l'Isle Adam; 1886); *Les Présents*, op. 46, no. 1 (Villiers de l'Isle Adam; 1887); *Clair de lune*, op. 46, no. 2 (P. Verlaine, 1887); *Larmes*, op. 51, no. 1 (J. Richepin; 1888); *Au cimetière*, op. 51, no. 2 (Richepin; 1888); *Spleen*, op. 51, no. 3 (Verlaine; 1888); *La Rose*, op. 51, no. 4 (Leconte de Lisle; 1890); *Chanson and Madrigal*, op. 57 (Haraucourt; 1889); *En prière* (S. Bordèse; 1889); *Cinq mélodies "de Venise,"* op. 58 (Verlaine): *Mandoline; En sourdine; Green; À Clymène; C'est l'extase* (1891); *Sérénade du Bourgeois gentilhomme*, op. posth. (Molière; 1893); *La Bonne Chanson*, op. 61 (Verlaine): *Une Sainte en son auréole; Puisque l'aube grandit; La Lune blanche luit dans les bois; J'allais par des chemins perfides; J'ai presque peur, en vérité; Avant que tu ne t'en ailles; Donc, ce sera par un clair jour d'été; N'est-ce pas?; L'Hiver a cessé* (1892–94); *Prison*, op. 83, no. 1 (Verlaine; 1894); *Soir*, op. 83, no. 2 (A. Samain; 1894); *Le Parfum impérissable*, op. 76, no. 1 (Leconte de Lisle; 1897); *Arpège*, op. 76, no. 2 (Samain; 1897); *Mélisande's Song*, op. posth. (Maeterlinck; tr. by Mackail; 1898); *Dans la forêt de septembre*, op. 85, no. 1 (C. Mendès; 1902); *La Fleur qui va sur l'eau*, op. 85, no. 2 (Mendès; 1902); *Accompagnement*, op. 85, no. 3 (Samain; 1902); *Le Plus Doux Chemin*, op. 87, no. 1 (Silvestre; 1904); *Le Ramier*, op. 87, no. 2 (Silvestre; 1904); *Le Don silencieux*, op. 92 (J. Dominique; 1906); *Chanson*, op. 94 (H. de Regnier; 1906); *Vocalise-étude* (1907); *La Chanson d'Ève*, op. 95 (C. Van Lerberghe; 1906–10); *Le Jardin clos*, op. 106 (Van Lerberghe; 1914); *Mirage*, op. 113 (Baronne A. de Brimont; 1919); *C'est la paix*, op. 114 (G. Debladis; 1919); *L'Horizon chimérique*, op. 118 (J. de la Ville de Mirmont; 1921). **PIANO** (all for Solo Piano unless otherwise given): *3 romances sans paroles*, op. 17 (1863); *Intermède symphonique* for Piano, 4-hands (1869; included as the Ouverture in *Masques et bergamasques*, op. 112); *Gavotte* (1869; also in the Sym., op. 20, and *Masques et bergamasques*, op. 112); *Prélude et fugue* (1869; fugue the same as op. 84, no. 6); *8 pièces brèves*, op. 84 (1869–1902); *Nocturne* No. 1, op. 33, no. 1 (1875), No. 2, op. 33, no. 2 (1880), No. 3, op. 33, no. 3 (1882), No. 4, op. 36 (1884), No. 5, op. 37 (1884), No. 6, op. 63 (1894), No. 7, op. 74 (1898), No. 9, op. 97 (1908), No. 10, op. 99 (1908), No. 11, op. 104, no. 1 (1913), No. 12, op. 107 (1915), and No. 13, op. 119 (1921); *Ballade*, op. 19 (1877–79; 2nd version for Piano and Orch., 1881); *Mazurka*, op. 32 (1878); *Barcarolle* No. 1, op. 26 (1880), No. 2, op. 41 (1885), No. 3, op. 42 (1885), No. 4, op. 44 (1886), No. 5, op. 66 (1894), No. 6, op. 70 (1896), No. 7, op. 90 (1905), No. 8, op. 96 (1906), No. 9, op. 101 (1909), No. 10, op. 104, no. 2 (1913), No. 11, op. 105 (1913), No. 12, op. 106bis (1915), and No. 13, op. 116 (1921); *Impromptu* No. 1, op. 25 (1881), No. 2, op. 31 (1883), No. 3, op. 34 (1883), No. 4, op. 91 (1905–06), and No. 5, op. 102 (1909); *Valse-caprice* No. 1, op. 30 (1882), No. 2, op. 38 (1884), No. 3, op. 59 (1887–93), and No. 4, op. 62 (1893–94); *Souvenirs de Bayreuth: Fantaisie en forme de quadrille sur les thèmes favoris de l'Anneau de Nibelung* for Piano, 4-hands, op. posth. (with Messager; 1888); *Dolly*, pieces for Piano, 4-hands, op. 56 (1894–97; orchestrated by H. Rabaud, 1906); *Allegro symphonique* for Piano, 4-hands, op. 68 (an arrangement by L. Boëllmann [1895] of the 1st movement of the *Suite d'orchestre*, op. 20 [c.1865]); *Thème et variations*, op. 73 (1895; orchestrated by Inghelbrecht, 1955); *9 préludes*, op. 103 (1909–10).

BIBL.: Special issue of *Musica*, no. 77 (1909); L. Vuillemin, *G. F. et son oeuvre* (Paris, 1914); special issue of *La Revue Musicale*, III/11 (1922); L. Aguettant, *La Génie de G. F.* (Lyons, 1924); A. Copland, "G. F.: A Neglected Master," *Musical Quarterly* (Oct. 1924); A. Bruneau, *La Vie et les oeuvres de G. F.* (Paris, 1925); C. Koechlin, *G. F.* (Paris, 1927; Eng. tr., 1945; 2nd ed., 1949); P. Fauré-Fremiet, *G. F.* (Paris, 1929; 2nd ed., aug., 1957); G. Servières, *G. F.* (Paris, 1930); V. Jankélévitch, *G. F. et ses mélodies* (Paris, 1938; 3rd ed., aug., 1974, as *G. F. et l'inexprimable*); G. Faure, *G. F.* (Paris, 1945); C. Rostand, *L'Oeuvre de G. F.* (Paris, 1945); special issue of *La Revue Musicale* (May

1945); N. Suckling, *F.* (London, 1946); M. Favre, *G. F.s Kammermusik* (Zürich, 1949); V. Jankélévitch, *Le Nocturne: F., Chopin et la nuit, Satie et le matin* (Paris, 1957); E. Vuillermoz, *G. F.* (Paris, 1960; Eng. tr., 1969); M. Long, *Au piano avec G. F.* (Paris, 1963); J.-M. Nectoux, *F.* (Paris, 1972; 2nd ed., aug., 1986); idem, *Phonographie de G. F.* (Paris, 1979; documents, articles, and iconography); R. Orledge, *G. F.* (London, 1979); J.-M. Nectoux, ed., *G. F.: Correspondance* (Paris, 1980); idem, *G. F.: His Life through His Letters* (London, 1984); J. Rutter, "In Search of the Real F. Requiem," *American Organist* (Nov. 1984; provides an in-depth chronology of the *Requiem* as it is known today); J. Barrie Jones, tr. and ed., *G. F.: A Life in Letters* (London, 1989); R. Tait, *The Musical Language of G. F.* (N.Y. and London, 1989); J. Nectoux, *G. F.: Le voix du clair-obscur* (Paris, 1990; Eng. tr., 1991, as *G. F.: A Musical Life*); C. Breitfeld, *Form und Struktur in der Kammermusik von G. F.* (Kassel, 1992).

Favero, Mafalda, Italian soprano; b. Portamaggiore, near Ferrara, Jan. 6, 1903; d. Milan, Sept. 3, 1981. She studied at the Bologna Cons. with Alessandro Vezzani. Under the stage name of Maria Bianchi, she made her operatic debut in 1926 in Cremona as Lola; in 1927 she made her formal operatic debut as Liù in Parma. In 1928 she made her first appearance at Milan's La Scala as Eva in *Die Meistersinger von Nürnberg,* and subsequently sang there regularly until 1943, then again from 1945 to 1950. In 1937 and 1939 she appeared at London's Covent Garden. On Nov. 24, 1938, she made her Metropolitan Opera debut in N.Y. as Mimi, remaining on its roster for a season. Among her finest roles were Mimi, Adriana Lecouvreur, Manon, and Thaïs.

BIBL.: I. Buscaglia, *M.F. nella vita e nell'arte* (1946).

Fayer, Yuri, Russian conductor; b. Kiev, Jan. 17, 1890; d. Moscow, Aug. 3, 1971. After attending the Kiev Cons., he studied violin and composition at the Moscow Cons. He played in various orchs. before conducting opera in Riga (1909–10); in 1916 he joined the orch. of the Bolshoi Theater in Moscow, where he was assistant conductor (1919–23) and chief conductor (1923–63) of its ballet; he toured with it in Europe, the U.S., and China. His memoirs were publ. in 1970.

Feder, (Franz) Georg, German musicologist; b. Bochum, Nov. 30, 1927. He studied composition in Bochum; subsequently studied musicology at the Univs. of Tübingen, Göttingen, and Kiel; received his Ph.D. from the Univ. of Kiel in 1955 with the diss. *Bachs Werke in ihren Bearbeitungen 1750–1950, I: Die Vokalwerke.* In 1957 he became assistant to Jens Peter Larsen at the Joseph-Haydn-Inst. in Cologne; he succeeded Larsen as its director in 1960; as such, he became chief ed. of the complete edition of Haydn's works; he also served as ed. of the publication *Haydn-Studien* from 1965. He publ. *Musikphilologie: Eine Einführung in die musikalische Textkritik, Hermeneutik und Editionstechnik* (Darmstadt, 1987).

Federhofer, Hellmut, eminent Austrian musicologist; b. Graz, Aug. 6, 1911. He studied piano and theory in Graz; then continued his studies at the Vienna Academy of Music with Stöhr and Kabasta, graduating in 1936 with a diploma in conducting. He also took private lessons in composition with Berg, Sauer, and Jonas. He took courses in musicology with Orel and Lach at the Univ. of Vienna; received his Ph.D. there in 1936 with the diss. *Akkordik und Harmonik in frühen Motetten der Trienter Codices.* From 1937 to 1944 he was State Librarian. He completed his Habilitation in 1944 at the Univ. of Graz with his *Musikalische Form als Ganzheit* (publ. as *Beiträge zur musikalischen Gestaltanalyse,* Graz, 1950). He became Privatdozent at the Univ. of Graz in 1945; in 1951 prof. of musicology. In 1962 he became director of the Musicological Inst. at the Johannes Gutenberg Univ. in Mainz. That same year he became ed. of *Acta Musicologica.* In 1986 he became editorial director of the new critical edition of the works of Fux. His books include *Musikpflege und Musiker am Grazer Habsburgerhof der Erzherzöge Karl und Ferdinand von Innerösterreich (1564–1619)* (Mainz, 1967), *Neue Musik: Ein Literaturbericht* (Tutzing, 1977), *Akkord und Stimmfuhrung in den Musiktheoretischen Systemen von Hugo Riemann, Ernst Kurth und Heinrich Schenker* (Vienna, 1981), *Musikwissenschaft und Musikpraxis* (Vienna, 1985), and *Motivtechnik von Johannes Brahms und Arnold Schönbergs Dodekaphonie* (Vienna, 1989). He also ed. *Heinrich Schenker als Essayist und Kritiker: Gesammelte Aufsätze, Rezensionen und kleine Berichte aus den Jahren 1891–1901* (Hildesheim, 1990).

BIBL.: C.-H. Mahling, ed., *Florilegium Musicologicum: H. F. zum 75. Geburtstag* (Tutzing, 1988).

Fedorov, Vladimir (Mikhailovich), Russian-born French music librarian, scholar, and composer; b. near Chernigov, Aug. 18, 1901; d. Paris, April 9, 1979. After training at the Univ. of Rostov, he settled in Paris and studied with Gédalge (counterpoint and fugue) and Vidal (composition) at the Cons. (1921–30), and with Pirro (musicology) at the Sorbonne (1921–32). He was librarian at the Sorbonne (1933–39), and then was head of the music division of the Bibliothèque Nationale (1946–66); he also was librarian at the Cons. (1958–64). In 1951 he founded the International Assn. of Music Libraries (IAML), serving as its vice-president (1955–62) and president (1962–65), and as ed. of its journal, *Fontes Artis Musicae* (1954–75). He publ. a biography of Mussorgsky (Paris, 1935) and was one of the eds. of the *Encyclopédie de la Musique* (3 vols., Paris, 1958–61). Among his compositions were chamber music and piano pieces.

BIBL.: H. Heckmann and W. Rehm, eds., "Mélanges offerts à V.F.," *Fontes Artis Musicae,* XIII (1966).

Fedoseyev, Vladimir (Ivanovich), prominent Russian conductor; b. Leningrad, Aug. 5, 1932. He studied with N. Reznikov at the Gnesin Inst. in Moscow (graduated, 1957) and with L. Ginzburg at the Moscow Cons. (graduated, 1971). He conducted an orch. of native instruments (1959–74) and was principal conductor of the Grand Orch. of the All-Union Radio and Television in Moscow (from 1974). He is distinguished for his interpretations of 19th-century Russian music as well as for his work with indigenous music. In 1970 he was awarded the Glinka Prize, and in 1973 was made a National Artist of the Russian S.F.S.R.

Feghali, José, Brazilian pianist; b. Rio de Janeiro, March 28, 1961. He began piano lessons as a child, appearing for the first time in public when he was only 5; at age 8, was a soloist with the Brazilian Sym. orch. in Rio de Janeiro. In 1976 he went to London to study with Maria Curcio, and then pursued training with Christopher Elton on scholarship at the Royal Academy of Music. After capturing 1st prize in the Van Cliburn Competition in Ft. Worth in 1985, he was engaged as a soloist with the world's principal orchs. and as a recitalist. He also served as artist-in-residence at Texas Christian Univ. in Ft. Worth.

Fehr, Max, Swiss musicologist; b. Bulach, near Zürich, June 17, 1887; d. Winterthur, April 27, 1963. He studied at the Univ. of Zürich with Eduard Bernoulli (Ph.D., 1912). In 1917 he became librarian, and in 1923 president, of the Allgemeine Musikgesellschaft of Zürich; he retired as librarian in 1957. In addition to his scholarly works on music, he wrote a satirical novelette, *Die Meistersinger von Zürich* (Zürich, 1916).

WRITINGS: *Spielleute im alten Zürich* (Zürich, 1916); *Unter Wagners Taktstock* (Winterthur, 1922); *Geschichte des Musikkollegiums Winterthur, I. Teil: 1629–1830* (Winterthur, 1929); *Richard Wagners Schweizer Zeit* (2 vols., Aarau, 1934, 1953); *Die Familie Mozart in Zürich* (Zürich, 1942); *Die wandernden Theatertruppen in der Schweiz: Verzeichnis der Truppen, Aufführungen und Spieldaten für das 17. und 18. Jahrhundert* (Einsiedeln, 1949); with L. Caflisch, *Der junge Mozart in Zürich* (Zürich, 1952); *Musikalische Jagd* (Zürich, 1954).

BIBL.: E. Nievergelt, *M. F.* (Zürich, 1968).

Feicht, Hieronim, Polish musicologist; b. Mogilno, near Poznań, Sept. 22, 1894; d. Warsaw, March 31, 1967. He studied theology; then composition in Kraków, and musicology with

Chybiński at the Univ. of Lwów (Ph.D., 1925); later completed his Habilitation at the Univ. of Poznań (1946). He taught at the Kraków Cons. from 1927 to 1930 and again from 1935 to 1939; in the interim he was a prof. at the State College of Music in Warsaw (1930–32). From 1946 to 1952 he was chairman of the musicology dept. at the Univ. of Wroclaw; was rector of the State College of Music in Wroclaw (1948–52), and a prof. of music history at the Univ. of Warsaw (1952–64). He publ. important essays on Polish music: *Musik-historische Bemerkungen über die Lemberger Handschriften des Bogarodzica-Liedes* (Poznań, 1925); *Wojciech Debolecki, Ein polnischer Kirchenkomponist aus der 1. Hälfte des 17. Jahrhunderts* (Lwów, 1926); *Polifonia renesansu* (Kraków, 1957); also ed. works by Polish composers. A festschrift was publ. in honor of his 70th birthday in 1964.

Feinberg, Samuel, eminent Russian pianist, pedagogue, and composer; b. Odessa, May 26, 1890; d. Moscow, Oct. 22, 1962. He moved to Moscow in 1894; studied piano with Goldenweisser at the Cons.; also took theory lessons with Zhilayev; graduated in 1911. In 1922 he was appointed prof. of piano at the Cons., holding this post until his death; also gave piano recitals in Russia in programs emphasizing new Russian music; he performed all of Beethoven's sonatas and the complete set of Bach's *Wohl-temperiertes Clavier,* as well as Chopin and Schumann. As a composer, he limited himself almost exclusively to piano music, which was influenced mainly by Chopin and Scriabin in its fluidity and enhanced tonality.

WORKS: ORCH.: 3 piano concertos (1931; 1944; 1947, rev. 1951). **PIANO:** 12 sonatas (1915, 1916, 1917, 1918, 1921, 1923, 1924, 1933, 1939, 1940, 1954, 1960); 2 fantasias (1916–17; 1924); 4 preludes (1922); 3 preludes (1923); 2 suites (1926, 1936). **VOCAL:** Various songs.

BIBL.: V. Belayev, *S. F.* (Moscow, 1927; in Russian and German).

Feinhals, Fritz, distinguished German baritone; b. Cologne, Dec. 4, 1869; d. Munich, Aug. 30, 1940. He studied in Milan and Padua. He made his operatic debut in Essen in 1895 as Silvio; in 1898 he joined the Munich Court (later State) Opera, where he remained until his retirement in 1927. On Nov. 18, 1908, he made his debut at the Metropolitan Opera in N.Y. as Wotan in *Die Walküre,* but was on its roster for only the 1908–09 season. He also made appearances in London, Paris, and Vienna. He was a Wagnerian singer par excellence; his portrayal of Wotan was imperious in its power; he was also successful in the role of Hans Sachs. He also excelled in operas by Mozart and Verdi.

Feinstein, Michael (Jay), American singer and remarkably facile pianist; b. Columbus, Ohio, Sept. 7, 1956. He began playing piano by ear when he was 5, later being largely self-taught via the huge record collection he acquired while growing up. After graduating from high school, he worked in various Columbus locales before moving to Los Angeles (1976), where he was assistant to Ira Gershwin (1977–83), who proved an inspiring mentor. In 1984 he accompanied Liza Minnelli on Johnny Carson's "The Tonight Show," later pursuing a highly lucrative solo career on the supper club circuit, making appearances at posh social events, on television, and with U.S. orchs. He was a significant contributor to the revitalized interest in the 1980s in the songs of Gershwin, Berlin, and other composers of the era between the two World Wars.

Felciano, Richard, American composer; b. Santa Rosa, Calif., Dec. 7, 1930. He studied with Milhaud at Mills College in Oakland, California (1952) and subsequently at the Paris Cons. (1953–55). As a student living in San Francisco, he supported himself by singing in a liturgical choir of men and boys, during which time he twice sang the complete liturgical year in Dominican chant and from neumatic notation. This experience had a profound effect on his style, even in orchestral and electronic music, and it was reinforced by several residencies at the Abbey of Solesmes while he was a student in Paris. After a period of service in the U.S. Army, he studied privately with Dallapiccola in Florence. While there, he met and married Rita Baumgartner, a native of Zürich, who later, as Rita Felciano, became a recognized American dance critic. In 1959 he took his Ph.D. at the Univ. of Iowa. In 1964 he received a Ford Foundation fellowship to serve as composer-in-residence to Cass Technical High School in Detroit, during which time he composed a number of works for student ensembles, some of which employed aleatory techniques and graphic notation. Returning to San Francisco in 1965, he received a series of commissions for the Roman Catholic liturgy in the wake of the liberalizing directives of the 2nd Vatican Council (1964). One of these commissions, *Pentecost Sunday,* introduced electronic sound into liturgical music and assumed a permanent place in its repertory. In 1967 he was appointed resident composer to the National Center for Experiments in Television in San Francisco, a pioneering effort by the Rockefeller Foundation to explore television as a non-documentary, non-narrative medium. As a participant in this project, he created *Linearity,* a television piece for harp and live electronics, the first musical work using the technical properties of a television system as an instrumental component. In the same year, he joined the music faculty of the Univ. of Calif. at Berkeley. In 1968 he received a Guggenheim fellowship and in 1971 a 2-year fellowship from the Ford Foundation as composer-in-residence to the City of Boston. During that residency, he created a 14-channel electronic environment with light sculptures of his own design for Boston City Hall and *Galactic Rounds* (1972), an orchestral work whose climax deploys rotating trumpets and trombones to create Doppler shifts, an early indication of his interest in acoustics which was to become pronounced in later decades. In 1974 he received an award from the American Academy of Arts and Letters and in 1975 was a resident fellow at the Rockefeller Foundation's International Study and Conference Center in Bellagio. From 1974 to 1978 he served as a panelist for the NEA and from 1976 to 1980 was an Art Commissioner for the City of San Francisco. In 1976 he was commissioned to compose a work joining an Eastern with a Western instrument for the 12th World Congress of the International Musicological Society at Berkeley, a pioneering forum in the growth of East-West studies in music. The result was *In Celebration of Golden Rain* (1977) for Indonesian gamelan and pipe organ, a work which addressed the conflicting scales, design, and intent of the instruments of these 2 cultures as a problem of symbiosis rather than one of fusion, making a philosophical as well as a musical statement. Many subsequent works show the influence of non-Western cultures. In 1982–83 he was active at IRCAM in Paris, where his encounter with the new field of cognitive psychology in its musical applications gave a scientific articulation to a lifelong interest in acoustics. He returned to Berkeley and in 1987 founded the Center for New Music and Audio Technologies (CNMAT), an interdisciplinary facility linking music, cognitive psychology, linguistics, computer science, and architecture. His music reflects an acute interest in acoustics and sonority, and an attempt to cast them in ritual, architectural, or dramatic forms.

WORKS: CHAMBER OPERA: *Sir Gawain and the Green Knight* (San Francisco, April 4, 1964).

ORCH.: *Mutations* (1966); *Galactic Rounds* (1972); *Orchestra* (San Francisco, Sept. 24, 1980); Organ Concerto (1986); *Camp Songs* for Chamber Orch. (1992); Sym. for Strings (1993); *Overture Concertante* for Clarinet and Orch. (1995).

CHAMBER: *Evolutions* for Clarinet and Piano (1962); *Contractions,* mobile for Woodwind Quintet (1965); *Aubade* for String Trio, Harp, and Piano (1966); *Spectra* for Double Bass and Flutes (1967); *In Celebration of Golden Rain* for Indonesian Gamelan and Western Pipe Organ (1977); *from and to, with* for Violin and Piano (1980); *Crystal* for String Quartet (1981); *Of Things Remembered* for Harp, Flute, and Viola (1981); *Salvador Allende* for String Quartet, Clarinet, and Percussion (1983); *Volkan* for 5 Flutes (1 Player) (1983); *Pieces of Eight* for Double Bass and Organ (1984); *Dark Landscape* for English Horn (1985); *Lontano* for Harp and Piano (1986); *Constellations* for

Multiple Brass Quintets and Horn Choir (1987); *Shadows* for 6 Players (1987); *Masks* for Flute and Trumpet (1989); *Palladio* for Violin, Piano, and Percussion (1989); *Primal Balance* for Contrabass and Flute (1991); *Cante jondo* for Bassoon, Clarinet, and Piano (1993); String Quartet (1995).

KEYBOARD: PIANO: *Gravities* for Piano, 4-hands (1965); *5 Short Piano Pieces* (1986). **ORGAN:** *On the Heart of the Earth* (1976).

VOCAL: *The Eyes of All* for Voices (1955); *Communion Service* for 2 Equal Voices and Organ (1961); *A Christmas Madrigal* for Chorus and Brass Ensemble (1964); *4 Poems from the Japanese* for Women's Voices, 5 Harps, and Percussion (1964); *The Captives* for Chorus and Orch. (1965); *Give Thanks to the Lord*, anthem for Small Chorus (1966); *Short Unison Mass* for Voices and Organ (1966); *Pentecost Sunday: Double Alleluia* for Unison Chorus, Organ, and Electronic Sounds (1967); *Glossolalia* for Baritone, Organ, Percussion, and Electronic Sounds (1967); *Songs of Darkness and Light* for Chorus and Organ (1970); *Te Deum* for Soloists, 3 Boy Sopranos, Chorus, Marimba, and Organ (1974); *Alleluia to the Heart of (the) Matter* for 2 Equal Voices and Organ (1976); *The Seasons* for Chorus (1978); *The Tuning of the Sky* for Voices (1978); *Lumen* for Soprano and Organ (1980); *Mass for Catherine of Siena* for Chorus and Organ (1981); *Furies* for 3 Sopranos and 3 Flutes (1988); *Mad With Love* for Unison and Mixed Chorus and Handbells (1993); *Streaming/Dreaming* for Soprano (1994); *Vac* for Woman's Voice, Clarinet, Violin, Cello, and Piano (1995).

ELECTRONIC SOUND: *Words of St. Peter* for Chorus, Organ, and Electronic Sounds (1965); *Crasis* for Flute, Clarinet, Violin, Cello, Piano, Harp, Percussion, and Electronic Sounds (1967); *Noösphere I* for Alto Flute and Electronic Tape (1967); *Background Music*, theater piece for Harp and Live Electronics (1969); *6 Electronic Dances* (1969); *The Architect and the Emperor of Assyria*, electronic score for Arrabal's play (1969); *Quintet, "Frames and Gestures"* for String Quartet, Piano, and Electronic Sounds (1970); *Lamentations for Jani Christou* for 12 Instruments and Electronic Sounds (1970); *Sic Transit* for Equal or Mixed Voices, Organ, Electronic Sounds, and Light Sources (1970); *Litany* for Organ and Electronic Tape (1971); *Signs* for Chorus, Electronic Sounds, and 3 Slide Projectors (1971); *Out of Sight* for Chorus, Organ, and Electronic Sounds (1971); *God of the Expanding Universe* for Organ and Electronic Sounds (1971); *Ekagrata* for Organ, 2 Drummers, and Electronic Sounds (1972); *I Make My Own Soul From All the Elements of the Earth* for Organ and Electronic Sounds (1972); *Stops* for Organ and Electronic Sounds (1972); *The Angels of Turtle Island* for Soprano, Flute, Violin, Percussion, and Live Electronics (1972); *2 Public Pieces* for Unison Voices and Electronic Sounds (1972); *The Passing of Enkidu* for Chorus, Piano, Percussion, and Electronic Sounds (1973); *Hymn of the Universe* for Chorus and Electronic Sounds (1973); *Susani* for Chorus, Organ, Belltree, and Electronic Sounds (1974); *Chöd* for Violin, Cello, Contrabass, 2 Percussion, Piano, and Live Electronics (1975); *And From the Abyss* for Tuba and Electronic Sounds (1975); *Windows in the Sky* for Unison Chorus, Organ, and Electronic Sounds (1976); *Alleluia to the Heart of Stone* for Reverberated Recorder (1984); *The Hollow Woods* for 2 Recorders and Live Electronics (1989); *Responsory* for Man's Voice and Interactive Live Electronics (1991); *A Japanese Songbook* for Soprano and Electronic Sounds (1992).

OTHER: VIDEO: *Instruments of Violence* (1967); *Linearity* for Harp and Live Electronics (1968); *Mother Goose: A Parable of Man* (1970); *Point of Inflection* (1971); *The Place for No Story* (1972); also *Trio for Speaker, Screen, and Viewer*, interactive piece for broadcast television (1968); *Islands of Sound*, environmental music for 14 Carillons (1975); *Berlin Feuerwerkmusik* for 3 Mobile Carillons at Berlin's Tempelhof Airfield (1987).

Feld, Jindřich, Czech composer; b. Prague, Feb. 19, 1925. He studied violin and viola with his father, a prof. of violin at the Prague Cons.; he then took courses in composition there with Hlobil (1945–48) and with Řídký at the Prague Academy of Music (1948–52); he also studied musicology, aesthetics, and philosophy at the Charles Univ. in Prague (Ph.D., 1952). His 4th string quartet was awarded the State Prize in 1968. In 1968–69 he was a visiting prof. at the Univ. of Adelaide. During this time, he composed his *Dramatic Fantasy: The Days of August*, an orch. score in protest to the Soviet invasion of his homeland. From 1972 to 1986 he was a prof. of composition at the Prague Cons. He subsequently was head of the music dept. of the Czech Radio from 1990 to 1992. After composing works reflective of the Czech tradition, he developed a distinctive voice utilizing a variety of modern compositional methods.

WORKS: DRAMATIC: *Poštácká pohádka* (The Postman's Tale), children's opera (1956). **ORCH.:** *Divertimento* for Strings (1950); *Furiant* (1950); *Concerto for Orchestra* (1951; rewritten 1957); *Comedy Overture* (1953); Flute Concerto (1954); *Rhapsody* for Violin and Wind Orch. (1956); Concerto for Chamber Orch. (1957); Sonata for Flute and Strings (1957–65); Cello Concerto (1958); Bassoon Concerto (1959); *May 1945*, dramatic overture (1960); Suite for Chamber Strings (1961); *Thuringian Overture* (1961); *3 Frescoes* (1963); *Concert Music* for Oboe, Bassoon, and Orch. (1964); *Concert Piece* for Horn and Orch. (1966); *Serenata giocosa* for Chamber Orch. (1966); 2 syms. (1967, 1983); *Dramatic Fantasy: The Days of August* (1968–69); Oboe Concerto (1970); Chamber Sinfonietta for Strings (1971); *Concert Suite* for Bass Clarinet, Piano, Strings, and Percussion (1972); Piano Concerto (1973); Trombone Concerto (1975); Accordion Concerto (1975); *Partita piccola* for Accordion Orch. (1976); Violin Concerto (1977); *Evocations* for Accordion Orch. and Percussion (1978); *Serenade* for Chamber Strings (1979); *Concert Fantasy* for Flute, Strings, and Percussion (1980); Saxophone Concerto (1980); Harp Concerto (1982); *H.C. Andersen's Fairy Tales* for Accordion Orch. (1984); *Fresco* for Symphonic Wind Band (1985); Concertino for Flute, Piano, and Orch. (1991). **CHAMBER:** 16 string quartets (1949, 1952, 1962, 1965, 1979; 1993); 2 wind quintets (1949, 1968); Suite for Clarinet and Piano (1949); Sonatina for 2 Violins (1953); *4 Pieces* for Flute (1954); *Elegy and Burlesque* for Cello and Piano (1954–55); Viola Sonata (1955); *Rhapsody* for Violin and Piano (1956); Flute Sonata (1957); Chamber Suite for Nonet (1960); Trio for Violin, Viola, and Cello (1961); Duo for Flute and Bassoon or Bass Clarinet (1962); Trio for Flute, Violin, and Cello (1963); *Caprices* for Wind Quartet and Guitar (1964); Suite for Accordion (1965); Bassoon Sonatina (1969); Brass Quintet (1970); Clarinet Sonatina (1970); Trio for Violin or Flute, Cello, and Piano (1972); Cello Sonata (1972); *5 Stylistic Studies* for String Quartet, Flute, and Harp (1974); Guitar Sonata (1974); *Suite Rhapsodica* for Clarinet (1976); *Toccata and Passacaglia* for Harp (1976); *Partita canonica* for 3 Trumpets and 3 Trombones (1977); *Epigrams* for Piccolo Flute, Tuba, and Harp (1977); *Serenade* for 4 Horns (1978); *Music* for 2 Accordions (1979); *Cassation* for 9 Flutes (1980); Concert Duo for 2 Flutes (1981); Saxophone Quartet (1981); *Elegy* for Soprano Saxophone or Oboe and Piano (1981); Oboe or Soprano Saxophone Sonata (1982); *Introduction and Allegro* for Accordion and Percussion (1983); *Concert Music* for Viola and Flute (1983; also for Quinton and Piano, 1988); Quartettino for Recorder Quartet (1985); Sonatina for Flute and Harp (1986); *Concerto da camera* for 2 String Quartets (1987); Trio for Oboe, Clarinet, and Bassoon (1987); Duo for Violin and Cello or Viola (1989). **KEYBOARD: PIANO:** *Prelude and Toccata* (1958–59); Sonata (1972). **ORGAN:** *Rhapsody* (1963). **VOCAL:** *Laus Cantus* for Soprano and String Quartet (1985); *COSMAE CHRONICA BOEMORUM*, oratorio-cantata for Soloists, Chorus, and Orch. (1988); choruses; songs.

Feldbrill, Victor, Canadian conductor; b. Toronto, April 4, 1924. He received training in violin from Sigmund Steinberg (1936–43) and in theory from Weinzweig (1939) before studying conducting at the Toronto Cons. of Music with Mazzoleni (1942–43), during which time he was conductor of the Univ. of Toronto Sym. Orch. Following training in harmony and composition with Howells at the Royal College of Music and in conducting with Ernest Read at the Royal Academy of Music in

London, he was concertmaster and assistant conductor of the Royal Cons. of Music of Toronto Sym. Orch. and Opera Co. (1946–49). He studied violin with Kathleen Parlow (1945–49), took his artist diploma from the Univ. of Toronto (1949), was a conducting student at the Berkshire Music Center in Tanglewood (summer, 1947), of Monteux in Hancock, Maine (summers, 1949–50), and of Otterloo and Zallinger in Salzburg (summer, 1956). He played 1st violin in the Toronto Sym. Orch. (1949–56) and the CBC Sym. Orch. (1952–56). In 1952 he became founder-conductor of the Canadian Chamber Players. In 1956–57 he was assistant conductor of the Toronto Sym. Orch. From 1958 to 1968 he was music director of the Winnipeg Sym. Orch. He served on the staff of the Univ. of Toronto from 1968 to 1982. He also was director of the youth programming of the Toronto Sym. (1968–78); from 1973 to 1977 he was likewise the resident conductor of the Toronto Sym. He was founder-conductor of the Toronto Sym. Youth Orch. (1973–78). From 1979 to 1981 he was acting music director of the London (Ontario) Sym. Orch. He was a prof. at the Tokyo National Univ. of Art and Music from 1981 to 1987. He served as interim music advisor (1990–91), as music director (1991–93), and as principal guest conductor (from 1993) of the Hamilton (Ontario) Phil. In appreciation for his yeoman service in the cause of promoting contemporary Canadian music, he was made an Officer of the Order of Canada in 1985.

Feldbusch, Eric, Belgian cellist, music educator, and composer; b. Grivegnée, March 2, 1922. He studied cello at the Liège Cons. (1934–39); later took courses in composition with Quinet and Legley (1947–48). He was director of the Mons Cons. (1963–72) and of the Brussels Cons. (1974–87).

WORKS: DRAMATIC: *Orestes*, opera (1969); *El Diablo Cojuelo*, ballet (1972). **ORCH.:** *Variations sur un air connu* (1955); *Contrastes* (1956); *Les Moineaux de Baltimore*, suite (1958); *Adagio* for Strings (1958); *Adagio* for 3 Cellos and String Orch. (1960); *Mosaïque* for Strings (1961); *Overture* for Strings (1961); *Shema Israël* for Strings (1962); *Ode à des enfants morts* (1965–66); Violin Concerto (1967); *Fantaisie-Divertissement* (1967); *Piccola musica* for Strings (1971); *Pointes Sèches* (1977); *Triade* for Chamber Orch. (1977); *Itinéraire* (1982); *Dichroisme II* (1983); *Concertante* for 2 Pianos and Orch. (1986); Cello Concerto (1988). **CHAMBER:** *Aquarelles* for Wind Quintet (1947); 4 string quartets (1955, 1958, 1963, 1971); Sonata for Violin and Cello (1955); *Cadence and Allegro* for Cello and Piano (1956); Violin Sonata (1957); Piano Trio (1958); *Variations extra-formelles* for Cello and Piano (1959); Trio for Flute, Violin, and Cello (1961); Duo for Flute and Viola (1963); Septet for Soprano, 2 Violins, Double Bass, Flute, Trumpet, and Percussion (1969); piano pieces. **OTHER:** Vocal works.

Felderhof, Jan (Reindert Adriaan), Dutch composer and pedagogue; b. Bussum, near Amsterdam, Sept. 25, 1907. He studied violin with Felice Togni and Hendrik Rynbergen (diploma, 1931) and theory and composition with Sem Dresden (diploma, 1933) at the Amsterdam Cons.; he later studied with Chris Bos at the Utrecht Cons. (diploma, 1958). He taught at the Amsterdam Cons. (1934–54; 1958–68), where he was adjunct director (1968–73); he also taught at the Bussum music school (1944–54), served as director of the Rotterdam Cons. (1954–55), and taught at the Utrecht Cons. (1956–67). In 1970 he was made a Knight of the Order of Oranje Nassau by the Dutch government. His works have an agreeable veneer of simple musicality, and all are excellently written.

WORKS: OPERA: *Vliegvuur* (Wildfire; 1959–64; Dutch Radio, Nov. 10, 1965). **ORCH.:** *Music* for 15 Winds and Percussion (1930); *5 Dance Sketches* (1930); 2 sinfoniettas (1932, 1962); Suite for Flute and Small Orch. (1933); *Rhapsodie* for Oboe and Small Orch. (1937); Sym. (1949); *Ouverture* (1955); Concerto for Flute, Strings, and Percussion (1955); *Omaggio* (1974); *Complimento* for Strings (1975); *Introduction and Rondo* (1980); *Chanterelle* (1985); *Nostalgic Suite* (1989). **CHAMBER:** 3 violin sonatas (1932, 1939, 1965); 4 string quartets (1932, 1936, 1938, 1957); Suite for Flute and Piano (1933); String Trio (1934); Cello Sonata (1935); Piano Trio (1936); *Divertimento* for Brass Quartet (1950); Violin Sonatina (1953); *Rondo* for Oboe, Clarinet, and Bassoon (1960); Trio for 3 Different Clarinets (1968); Suite for Flute, Oboe, and Piano (1974); Sonata for 2 Violins and Piano (1977); *Andante* for Flute, Oboe, and Harp (1983); Sonatine for Flute, Oboe, and Harp (1988); piano pieces, including 5 sonatinas (1933–62); organ music. **VOCAL:** *Tot wien zullen wij henengaan* (To Whom Shall We Make Our Way), cantata (1935; rev. 1941); *Groen is de gong* for Chorus and Orch. (1977); *Composite* for Women's Chorus, Flute, and Harp (1984); songs.

Feldhoff, Gerd, German baritone; b. Radervormwald, near Cologne, Oct. 29, 1931. He studied at the Northwest Music Academy in Detmold. He made his operatic debut in Essen in 1959 as Figaro in *Le nozze di Figaro*; then sang at the Städtische Oper in Berlin, the Hamburg State Opera, and the Frankfurt am Main Opera. From 1968 to 1978 he appeared at the Bayreuth Festivals. He made his Metropolitan Opera debut in N.Y. as Kaspar in *Der Freischütz* on Sept. 28, 1971. He was especially noted as a dramatic baritone; he also made tours as a concert artist.

Feldman, Ludovic, Romanian composer and violinist; b. Galați, June 6, 1893; d. Bucharest, Sept. 11, 1987. He studied violin in Galați, with Klenck at the Bucharest Cons. (1910–11), and with Ondříček at the New Vienna Cons. (1911–13). He was a violinist in the Phil. and in the orch. of the State Opera in Bucharest (1926–40). Following training in composition with Jora in Bucharest (1941–42), he devoted himself fully to composing.

WORKS: ORCH.: 5 suites (1948; 1949; 1951–52; 1960; 1960); *Fantezie concertantă* for Cello and Orch. (1949); *Poem concertant* for Violin and Orch. (1950–51); Concerto for Flute and Chamber Orch. (1953); Concerto for 2 String Orchs., Celesta, Piano, and Percussion (Brasov, Oct. 15, 1958); 5 Symphonic Pieces (1960–61); *Sonată concertantă* for Violin and Chamber Orch. (1964); *Variațiuni simfonice* (1966; Bucharest, June 14, 1967); *Simfonie concertantă* for Chamber Orch. (1971; Paris, Jan. 11, 1973); *Simfonie omagială* (1978; Bucharest, June 6, 1983); *Poem simfonie* (1981). **CHAMBER:** 2 suites for Violin and Piano (1947, 1948); Flute Sonata (1952); 2 viola sonatas (1953, 1965); String Trio (1955); String Quartet (1957); 2 quintets (1956–57; 1977); Violin Sonata (1962–63); Cello Sonata (1963–64); *Improvizație*, trio for Violin, Cello, and Piano (1979); piano pieces.

BIBL.: D. Dediu, *Episoade și viziuni: L.F.* (Bucharest, 1991).

Feldman, Morton, significant American composer and pedagogue; b. N.Y., Jan. 12, 1926; d. Buffalo, Sept. 3, 1987. At 12, he began piano lessons with Vera Maurina-Press. In 1942 he commenced composition lessons with Riegger, and in 1944 with Wolpe. In 1950 he was befriended by Cage, and soon moved in the circles of such musicians as Brown, Wolff, and Tudor, and such abstract expressionist painters as Rothko, Guston, Kline, Pollock, and Rauschenberg. The influence of these musicians and painters was pronounced, but Feldman pursued his own path as a composer. In his *Projections* series (1950–51), he first utilized graph notation. In 1953 he abandoned it, only to resort to it again from time to time between 1958 and 1967. In his *Durations* series (1960–61), he utilized what he described as "race-course" notation in which exact notation for each instrumental part still allows for relative freedom in durations and vertical coordination. About 1979 he began to compose works of extended duration, producing in his 2nd String Quartet (1983) a score which can run for almost 6 hours. In 1966 Feldman held a Guggenheim followship. He received awards from the National Inst. of Arts and Letters in 1970 and from the Koussevitzky Foundation in 1975. From 1973 until his death he was the Edgard Varèse Prof. at the State Univ. of N.Y. at Buffalo, where he was a major influence as both a composer and a teacher. W. Zimmermann ed. a collection of his writings as *Morton Feldman Essays* (Kerpen, 1985).

WORKS: *Journey to the End of Night* for Soprano or Tenor, Flute, Clarinet, Bass Clarinet, and Bassoon (1947); *Only* for

Voice (1947); *Illusions* for Piano (1949); *Piece* for Violin and Piano (1950); *2 Intermissions* for Piano (1950); *Projection I* for Cello (1950), *II* for Flute, Trumpet, Piano, Violin, and Cello (1951), *III* for 2 Pianos (1951), *IV* for Violin and Piano (1951), and *V* for 3 Flutes, Trumpet, 2 Pianos, and 3 Cellos (1951); *4 Songs to e.e. cummings* for Soprano, Piano, and Cello (1951); *Jackson Pollock*, film score (1951); *Marginal Intersection* for Orch. (1951); *Structures* for String Quartet (1951); *Extensions I* for Violin and Piano (1951), *II* (withdrawn), *III* for Piano (1952), and *IV* for 3 Pianos (1952–53); *Intersection I* for Orch. (1951), *II* for Piano (1951), *III* for Piano (1953), and *IV* for Cello (1953); *Intermission V* for Piano (1952) and *VI* for Piano or 2 Pianos (1953); *Piano Piece* (1952, 1955, 1956a, 1956b, 1963, 1964); *11 Instruments* for Flute, Alto Flute, Horn, Trumpet, Bass Trumpet, Trombone, Tuba, Vibraphone, Piano, Violin, and Cello (1953); *Intersection* for Tape (1953); *3 Pieces* for Piano (1954); *2 Pieces* for 2 Pianos (1954); *3 Pieces* for String Quartet (1954, 1954, 1956); *2 Pieces for 6 Instruments* for Flute, Alto Flute, Horn, Trumpet, Violin, and Cello (1956); *Piano (3 Hands)* (1957); *Piece for 4 Pianos* (1957); *2 Pianos* (1957); *Ixion* for 10 Instruments (1958; N.Y., April 14, 1966); *Out of "Last Pieces"* for Orch. (1958); *Piano 4 Hands* (1958); *2 Instruments* for Horn and Cello (1958); *Atlantis* for 17 Instruments (1959; also for 10 Instruments); *Last Pieces* for Piano (1959); *The Swallows of Salangan* for Chorus and 23 Instruments (1960); *Durations I* for Alto Flute, Piano, Violin, and Cello (1960), *II* for Cello and Piano (1960), *III* for Tuba, Piano, and Violin (1961), *IV* for Violin, Cello, and Vibraphone (1961), and *V* for Horn, Celesta, Piano, Harp, Vibraphone, Violin, and Cello (1961); *Structures* for Orch. (1960–62); *Intervals* for Bass-baritone, Trombone, Cello, Vibraphone, and Percussion (1961); *The Straits of Magellan* for Flute, Horn, Trumpet, Piano, Amplified Guitar, Harp, and Double Bass (1961); *2 Pieces* for Clarinet and String Quartet (1961); *For Franz Kline* for Soprano, Horn, Piano, Tubular Bells, Violin, and Cello (1962); *The O'Hara Songs* for Bass-baritone, Tubular Bells, Piano, Violin, Viola, and Cello (1962); *Christian Wolff in Cambridge* for Chorus (1963); *De Kooning* for Horn, Percussion, Piano, Violin, and Cello (1963); *Rabbi Akiba* for Soprano and 10 Instruments (1963); *Vertical Thoughts I* for 2 Pianos (1963), *II* for Violin and Piano (1963), *III* for Soprano, Flute, Horn, Trumpet, Trombone, Tuba, 2 Percussion, Piano, Celesta, Violin, Cello, and Double Bass (1963), *IV* for Piano (1963), and *V* for Soprano, Tuba, Percussion, Celesta, and Violin (1963); *Chorus and Instruments I* for Chorus, Horn, Tuba, Percussion, Piano, Celesta, Violin, Cello, and Double Bass (1963) and *II* for Chorus, Tuba, and Tubular Bells (1967); *The King of Denmark* for Percussion (1964); *Numbers* for Flute, Horn, Trombone, Tuba, Percussion, Piano, Celesta, Violin, Cello, and Double Bass (1964); *4 Instruments* for Tubular Bells, Piano, Violin, and Cello (1965); *2 Pieces* for 3 Pianos (1966); *First Principles I* (1966) and *II* (1966–67) for 19 Instruments; *In Search of an Orchestration* for Orch. (1967); *False Relationships and the Extended Ending* for Trombone, Tubular Bells, 3 Pianos, Violin, and Cello (1968); *Between Categories* for 2 Tubular Bells, 2 Pianos, 2 Violins, and 2 Cellos (1969); *On Time and the Instrumental Factor* for Orch. (1969; Dallas, April 24, 1971); *Madame Press Died Last Week at Ninety* for 12 Instruments (1970); *The Viola in My Life I* for Viola, Flute, Percussion, Piano, Violin, and Cello (London, Sept. 19, 1970), *II* for Viola, Flute, Clarinet, Percussion, Celesta, Violin, and Cello (1970), *III* for Viola and Piano (1970), and *IV* for Viola and Orch. (Venice, Sept. 16, 1971); *I Met Heine in the Rue Fürstenberg* for Mezzo-soprano, Flute, Clarinet, Percussion, Piano, Violin, and Cello (1971); *Rothko Chapel* for Soprano, Alto, Chorus, Percussion, Celesta, and Viola (1971; Houston, April 1972); *3 Clarinets, Cello, and Piano* (1971; BBC, London, March 1972); *Chorus and Orchestra I* (1971; Cologne, March 1973); and *II* for Soprano, Chorus, and Orch. (1972; London, Jan. 5, 1973); *Cello and Orchestra* (1972); *Pianos and Voices II*, renamed *Pianos and Voices* for 5 Pianos and 5 Women's Voices (1972); *Voices and Instruments I* for Chorus, 2 Flutes, English Horn, Clarinet, Bassoon, Horn, Timpani, Piano, and Double Bass (Dartington, Aug. 11, 1972) and *II* for 3 Women's Voices, Flute, 2 Cellos, and Double Bass (1972); *Voice and Instruments I* for Soprano and Orch. (1972; Berlin, March 14, 1973) and *II* for Woman's Voice, Clarinet, Cello, and Double Bass (1974); *For Frank O'Hara* for Flute, Clarinet, 2 Percussion, Piano, Violin, and Cello (1973); *String Quartet and Orchestra* (1973); *Voices and Cello* for 2 High Voices and Cello (1973); *Instruments I* for Alto Flute, Piccolo, Oboe, English Horn, Trombone, Percussion, and Cello (1974), *II* for Flute, Piccolo, Alto Flute, Oboe, English Horn, Clarinet, Bass Clarinet, Trumpet, Trombone, Tuba, Percussion, Harp, Piano, and Double Bass (1974), *III* for Flute, Oboe, and Percussion (1977), and *IV: Why Patterns?* for Violin, Piano, and Percussion (1978; also for Flute, Alto Flute, Percussion, and Piano (1979); *4 Instruments* for Violin, Viola, Cello, and Piano (1975); *Piano and Orchestra* (1975); *Elemental Procedures* for Soprano, Chorus, and Orch. (1976; West German Radio, Cologne, Jan. 22, 1977); *Oboe and Orchestra* (1976); *Orchestra* (Glasgow, Sept. 18, 1976); *Routine Investigations* for Oboe, Trumpet, Piano, Viola, Cello, and Double Bass (1976); *Voice, Violin, and Piano* (Holland Festival, June 2, 1976); *Neither*, monodrama for Soprano and Orch. (Rome, May 13, 1977); *Piano* (1977); *Flute and Orchestra* (1977–78); *Spring of Chosroes* for Violin and Piano (1978); 2 string quartets: No. 1 (1979; N.Y., May 4, 1980) and No. 2 (Toronto, Dec. 4, 1983); *Violin and Orchestra* (1979; Hessian Radio, Frankfurt am Main, April 12, 1984); *Principal Sound* for Organ (1980); *The Turfan Fragments* for Chamber Orch. (1980; Swiss-Italian Radio, Lugano, March 26, 1981); Trio for Violin, Viola, and Piano (1980); *Bass, Clarinet, and Percussion* for Clarinet, Percussion, and Double Bass (1981; Middelburg, July 1, 1982); *Triadic Memories* for Piano (London, Oct. 5, 1981); *Untitled Composition*, later named *Patterns in a Chromatic Field* for Cello and Piano (1981; Middelburg, July 1982); *For John Cage* for Violin and Piano (N.Y., March 1982); *3 Voices* for 3 Sopranos or 3 Solo Voices and Tape (1982; Valencia, Calif., March 1983); *Clarinet and String Quartet* (Newcastle upon Tyne, Oct. 9, 1983); *Crippled Symmetry* for Flute, Bass Flute, Vibraphone, Glockenspiel, Piano, and Celesta (1983; Berlin, March 1984); *For Philip Guston* for Flute, Alto Flute, Percussion, Piano, and Celesta (1984; Buffalo, April 21, 1985); *For Bunita Marcus* for Piano (Middelburg, June 1985); *Violin and String Quartet* (1985); *Piano and String Quartet* (Los Angeles, Nov. 2, 1985); *Coptic Light* for Orch. (N.Y., May 30, 1986); *For Christian Wolff* for Flute, Piano, and Celesta (Darmstadt, July 1986); *For Stefan Wolpe* for Chorus and 2 Vibraphones (1986; River Falls, Wis., April 30, 1987); *Palais de Mari* for Piano (N.Y., Nov. 20, 1986); *Samuel Beckett, Words and Music* for a radio play for 2 Flutes, Vibraphone, Piano, Violin, Viola, and Cello (N.Y., March 1987); *Piano, Violin, Viola, Cello* (Middelburg, July 4, 1987).

BIBL.: K. Potter, *An Introduction to the Music of M.F.* (diss., Univ. of Wales, Cardiff, 1973); T. DeLio, *Circumscribing the Open Universe: Essays on Cage, F., Wolff, Ashley and Lucier* (Washington, D.C., 1984).

Felix, Václav, prominent Czech composer and pedagogue; b. Prague, March 29, 1928. He studied composition with Bořkovec and Dobiáš at the Prague Academy of Music (graduated, 1953), then did postgraduate study in theory with Janeček (1953–56); he completed his education at the Charles Univ. in Prague (Ph.D. in philosophy, 1957; Candidatus scientiarum, 1961). He was ed. of *Hudební Rozhledy* in Prague (1959–61). In 1960 he joined the faculty of the Prague Academy of Music, where he was head of the theory and music history dept. (1979–85), dean of the music faculty (1985–90), and a prof. (1985–92). From 1978 to 1989 he was vice president of the central committee of the Union of Czech Composers and Concert Artists. He received the prize of the Czech Minister of Culture (1976), was made an Artist of Merit (1978), and received the prize of the Union of Czech Composers and Concert Artists (1980) and the National Prize (1986). His music follows the golden mean of agreeable Central European modernism.

WORKS (all 1st perf. in Prague unless otherwise given):

OPERAS: *Nesmělý Kasanova aneb Čím zrají muži* (Shy Casanova or What Makes Men Ripe; 1966; Dec. 13, 1967); *Inzerát* (The Advertisement; Brno, April 25, 1975); *Mariana* (1982; April 11, 1985). **ORCH.:** *Concerto romantico* for Violin, Clarinet or Viola, Harp, and Strings (Oct. 19, 1953); *Fantasy* for Clarinet and Orch. (1959; March 30, 1960); *Concertant Variations* (1962; Feb. 17, 1963); Suite for Strings (1969); *Joyful Overture* (1971; March 8, 1972); *Concert Waltz* (1973); 6 syms.: No. 1 for Woman's Voice and Orch. (1974; May 25, 1975), No. 2 for Small Orch. (1981; Karlovy Vary, March 19, 1982), No. 3 for Chorus and Orch. (1986; March 10, 1988), No. 4 (Nov. 12, 1987), No. 5 for Chamber Orch. (1987), and No. 6 for Large Wind Orch. (1990); Concertino for Flute and Strings (1976; Jan. 18, 1977); *Labor Victorious*, gala overture for Large Wind Orch. (1977; March 8, 1978); Double Concerto for Cello or Bass Clarinet, Piano, and Strings (1978; March 17, 1979); *Symphonic Variations on a Czech Recruit Song* for Large Wind Orch. (1979; March 23, 1980); *Summer Day Romance* for Clarinet and Orch. (1979; Teplice, July 3, 1980); Trumpet Concerto (1984; Poděbrady, May 20, 1986); Cello Concerto (1990). **CHAMBER:** 3 piano trios (1955, 1956, 1962); Cello Sonata (1960); String Trio (1961); *The Story of Snow White*, quintet for Harp and String Quartet (1963); *Sonata a tre* for Violin, Viola, and Harp (1967); *Sonata da Requiem* for Horn or Bass Clarinet and Piano (1969); Wind Quintet (1972); Brass Quintet (1972); Trio for Violin, Horn, and Piano (1973); Trio for Clarinet, Cello, and Piano (1977); *Sonata Lirica* for Oboe and Piano (1978); *Quartetto amoroso* for 2 Violins, Viola, and Cello (1979); *Sonata Capricciosa* for Flute and Piano (1981); *We Have a Baby at Home*, suite for Flute, Violin, and Piano (1984); *A Small Afternoon* for Flute, Viola, and Cello (1985); *Sonata concertante* for Viola and Piano (1989); *Sonata Melodiosa* for English Horn and Piano (1993) piano pieces, including 3 sonatinas (1969) and *Sonata poetica* (1988). **VOCAL:** 3 cantatas: *The Celebration* (1963), *Where Do the Months Come From?* (1965), and *Always Generous* (1980; Olomouc, Sept. 3, 1981); other works.

Fellegara, Vittorio, Italian composer and teacher; b. Milan, Nov. 4, 1927. He received training in physics and mathematics at the Univ. (1945–50) and in theory from Chailly at the Verdi Cons. (graduated, 1951) in Milan. Thereafter he was active as a composer and teacher.

WORKS: BALLET: *Mutazioni* (1962; Milan, Jan. 27, 1965; as 4 symphonic fragments, Copenhagen, May 28, 1964). **ORCH.:** *Concerto for Orchestra* (1952; RAI, Feb. 28, 1957); *Concerto breve* for Chamber Orch. (Milan, Dec. 15, 1956); *Sinfonia 1957* (1957; Rome, June 28, 1958); *Serenata* for Chamber Orch. (Rome, May 24, 1960; also for 9 Instruments); *Frammenti I* for Chamber Orch. (1960; Palermo, May 21, 1961) and *II: Variazioni* for Chamber Orch. (Milan, April 17, 1961); *Studi in forma di variazioni* for Chamber Orch. (Piacenza, May 23, 1978); *Trauermusik* for Strings (1978; Bergamo, April 6, 1982); *You Wind of March* for Flute and Orch. (1979; Verona, May 21, 1988); *Berceuse* for Flute and Chamber Orch. (1982; also for Flute and Piano, 1980); *Primo vere* for Piano and Chamber Orch. (1988; Ancona, Jan. 26, 1991; also for Piano and Small Orch., Frankfurt am Main, Feb. 25, 1992). **CHAMBER:** *Ottetto* for Winds (1953; Donaueschingen, Oct. 15, 1955); *Serenata* for 9 Instruments (1960; also for Chamber Orch.); *Berceuse* for Flute and Piano (1980; also for Flute and Chamber Orch., 1982); *Wiegenlied* for Clarinet and Piano (Siena, Aug. 25, 1981; also for Clarinet Concertante and 8 Winds, 1982; Bergamo, March 30, 1985); *Contrasti* for Chamber Ensemble (1982; Bergamo, March 26, 1983); *Wintermusic* for Violin, Cello, and Piano (1983; Bergamo, March 17, 1984); *Eisblumen* for Guitar (1985); *Der Musensohn* for Oboe (1985); *Herbstmusik: Omaggio a Mahler* for String Quartet (1986; Bergamo, April 11, 1987); *Stille Nacht* for Organ and 9 Winds (Bergamo, Oct. 6, 1990); *Arabeschi* for Harp (1991); *Pampas Flash* for Chamber Ensemble (1992); *Winterzeit* for Guitar Quartet (1992). **PIANO:** *Invenzioni* (1949); *Ricercare fantasia* (1951; Milan, May 30, 1952); *Preludio, fuga e postludio* (1952–53; Bayreuth, Aug. 4, 1953); *Omaggio a Bach* (Brescia, June 7, 1975). **VOCAL:** *Requiem di Madrid* for Chorus and Orch. (1958; RAI, Turin, Oct. 17, 1959); *Dies irae* for Chorus and Instruments (1959; RAI, Milan, April 11, 1973); *Epitaphe* for 2 Sopranos and 5 Instrumentalists (Venice, Sept. 12, 1964); Cantata for 2 Women's Voices and Orch. (Donaueschingen, Oct. 23, 1966); *Madrigale* for Vocal Quintet and Instruments (Milan, Nov. 25, 1969; also for Small Chorus and Chamber Orch.); *Notturno* for Soprano, Contralto, Men's Chorus, and Orch. (1971; RAI-TV, Nov. 29, 1975); *Chanson* for Soprano and Chamber Orch. (1974; RAI, Milan, Oct. 1, 1975); *Zwei Lieder* for Women's Chorus (1974); *Shakespearian Sonnet* for Chorus and Timpani ad libitum (1985).

Fellerer, Karl Gustav, eminent German musicologist and editor; b. Freising, July 7, 1902; d. Munich, Jan. 7, 1984. He studied at the Regensburg School of Church Music and took courses in composition with Heinrich Schmid and Joseph Haas in Munich; then studied musicology at the Univ. of Munich with Sandberger and at the Univ. of Berlin with Hornbostel, Abert, Wolf, and Sachs; received his Ph.D. in 1925 from the Univ. of Munich with the diss. *Beiträge zur Musikgeschichte Freisings von den ältesten christlichen Zeiten bis zur Auflösung des Hofes 1803* (Freising, 1926); completed his Habilitation in 1927 at the Univ. of Munster with his *Der Palestrina stil und seine Bedeutung in der vokalen Kirchenmusik des 18. Jahrhunderts* (Augsburg, 1929). In 1927 he became a lecturer at the Univ. of Munster; in 1931 he was made a prof. at the Univ. of Fribourg in Switzerland; in 1934 he became head of the dept. of musicology at the Univ. of Munster; in 1939 he was named prof. of music history at the Univ. of Cologne; he retired in 1970. Fellerer distinguished himself as an outstanding authority on the history of music of the Roman Catholic church; he contributed valuable studies on the music of the Middle Ages, the Renaissance, and the 19th century; he also served as ed. of several important music journals and other publications. His 60th birthday was honored by the publication of 3 Festschrifts, and another Festschrift was publ. in honor of his 70th birthday.

WRITINGS: *Die Deklamationsrhythmik in der vokalen Polyphonie des 16. Jahrhunderts* (Düsseldorf, 1928); *Orgel und Orgelmusik: Ihre Geschichte* (Augsburg, 1929); *Palestrina* (Regensburg, 1930; 2nd ed., rev., 1960); *Studien zur Orgelmusik des ausgehenden 18. und frühen 19. Jahrhunderts* (Kassel, 1932); *Beiträge zur Choralbegleitung und Choralverarbeitung in der Orgelmusik des ausgehenden 18. und beginnenden 19. Jahrhunderts* (Leipzig, 1932); *Die Aufführung der katholischen Kirchenmusik in Vergangenheit und Gegenwart* (Einsiedeln, 1933); *Mittelalterliches Musikleben der Stadt Freiburg im Uechtland* (Regensburg, 1935); *Der gregorianische Choral im Wandel der Jahrhunderte* (Regensburg, 1936); *Giacomo Puccini* (Potsdam, 1937); *Geschichte der katholischen Kirchenmusik* (Düsseldorf, 1939); *Deutsche Gregorianik im Frankenreich* (Regensburg, 1941); *Edvard Grieg* (Potsdam, 1942); *Einführung in die Musikwissenschaft* (Berlin, 1942; 2nd ed., rev., 1953); *Georg Friedrich Händel: Leben und Werk* (Hamburg, 1953); *Mozarts Kirchenmusik* (Salzburg, 1955); *Soziologie der Kirchenmusik* (Cologne, 1963); *Bearbeitung und Elektronik als musikalisches Problem in Urheberrecht* (Berlin and Frankfurt am Main, 1965); *Klang und Struktur in der abendländischen Musik* (Cologne, 1967); *Das Problem Neue Musik* (Krefeld, 1967); *Monodie und Polyphonie in der Musik des 16. Jahrhunderts* (Brussels, 1972); *Der Stilwandel in der abendländischen Musik um 1600* (Cologne, 1972); *Geschichte der katholischen Kirchenmusik* (Kassel, 1972–76); *Max Bruch* (Cologne, 1974); *Der Akademismus in der deutschen Musik des 19. Jahrhunderts* (Opladen, 1976); *Die Kirchenmusik W.A. Mozarts* (Laaber, 1985).

Fellowes, E(dmund) H(orace), eminent English musicologist and editor; b. London, Nov. 11, 1870; d. Windsor, Dec. 20, 1951. He was educated at Winchester College and Oriel College, Oxford (B.Mus. and M.A., 1896); his teachers in music were P. Buck, Fletcher, and L. Straus. He was ordained in 1894, and then served as assistant curate in Wandsworth, London (until 1897); after serving as minor canon and precentor of Bristol

Cathedral (1897–1900), he became minor canon at St. George's Chapel, Windsor Castle, a position he held until his death; he was also choirmaster there (1924–27). He was honorary librarian of St. Michael's College, Tenbury Wells (1918–48); was also a lecturer at various English univs. His importance rests upon his valuable writings on and eds. of early English music. He received honorary Mus.D. degrees from the Univs. of Dublin (1917), Oxford (1939), and Cambridge (1950); was made a Companion of Honour by King George VI in 1944.

EDITIONS: The English Madrigal School (36 vols., 1913–24; 2nd ed., rev., 1956, by T. Dart as The English Madrigalists); The English School of Lutenist Song Writers (32 vols., 1920–32; 2nd ed., partly rev., 1959–66, by T. Dart as The English Lutesongs; 3rd ed., rev., 1959–); with P. Buck, A. Ramsbotham, and S. Warner, Tudor Church Music (10 vols., 1922–29; appendix, 1948, by Fellowes); The Collected Works of William Byrd (20 vols., London, 1937–50; 2nd ed., rev., 1962– , by T. Dart, P. Brett, and K. Elliott).

WRITINGS: *English Madrigal Verse, 1588–1632* (Oxford, 1920; 3rd ed., rev. and enl., 1967); *The English Madrigal Composers* (Oxford, 1921; 2nd ed., 1948); *William Byrd: A Short Account of His Life and Work* (Oxford, 1923; 2nd ed., 1928); *The English Madrigal School: A Guide to Its Practical Use* (London, 1924); *Orlando Gibbons: A Short Account of His Life and Work* (Oxford, 1925; 2nd ed., 1951, as *Orlando Gibbons and His Family*); *The English Madrigal* (Oxford, 1925); *The Catalogue of Manuscripts in the Library of St Michael's College, Tenbury* (Paris, 1934); *William Byrd* (a larger study than the 1923 monograph; Oxford, 1936; 2nd ed., 1948); *Organists and Masters of the Choristers of St George's Chapel in Windsor Castle* (London and Windsor, 1939); *English Cathedral Music from Edward VI to Edward VII* (London, 1941; 5th ed., rev., 1969); with E. Pine, *The Tenbury Letters* (London, 1942); *Memoirs of an Amateur Musician* (London, 1946).

Felsenstein, Walter, influential Austrian opera producer; b. Vienna, May 30, 1901; d. East Berlin, Oct. 8, 1975. He studied at a Graz technical college; then went to Vienna, where he enrolled in drama courses at the Burgtheater. In 1923 he appeared as an actor in Lübeck. In 1925 he became dramatic adviser and producer in Beuthen, Silesia; in 1927 he was called to Basel to become chief opera and drama producer at the Stadttheater; in 1929 he went to Freiburg im Breisgau as both actor and dramatic adviser and producer. He served as chief producer at the Cologne Opera in 1932 and at the Frankfurt am Main Opera in 1934. Despite his differences with the policies of the Nazi authorities, he was able to continue producing operas and dramas. From 1938 to 1940 he produced plays in Zürich; he then served as producer in Berlin (1940–44); he was drafted by the military despite his age, and served for a year. From 1947 until his death he was director of the Komische Oper in East Berlin. During his tenure, the Komische Oper established itself as one of the best opera houses of Europe; his productions of *Die Fledermaus, Carmen, Le nozze di Figaro, Otello, Les Contes d'Hoffmann*, and *Die Zauberflöte* were artistically of the first rank. He also made operatic films and gave courses on theater arts. Among his students were the opera producers Götz Friedrich and Joachim Herz. With S. Melchinger, he compiled *Musiktheater* (Bremen, 1961); with G. Friedrich and J. Herz, he publ. *Musiktheater: Beiträge zur Methodik und zu Inszenierungs-Konzeptionen* (Leipzig, 1970).

BIBL.: R. Münz, *Untersuchungen zum realistischen Musiktheater W. F.s* (diss., Humboldt Univ., Berlin, 1964); G. Friedrich, *W. F.: Weg und Werk* (Berlin, 1967); P. Fuchs, ed. and tr., *The Music Theater of W. F.: Collected Articles, Speeches and Interviews by F. and Others* (N.Y., 1975); I. Kobán, ed., *W. F.: Theater: Gespräche, Briefe, Dokumente* (Berlin, 1991).

Feltsman, Vladimir, prominent Russian-born American pianist; b. Moscow, Jan. 8, 1952. He was born into a musical family; his father, Oskar Feltsman, was a composer of popular music. He began taking piano lessons at the age of 6 from his mother, and then enrolled at Moscow's Central Music School, completing his training with Yakov Flier at the Moscow Cons. At age 11, he made his debut as a soloist with the Moscow Phil., and at 15 he won 1st prize in the Prague Concertino Competition. After capturing joint 1st prize in the Long-Thibaud Competition in Paris in 1971, he pursued a successful career as a soloist with major Soviet and Eastern European orchs.; he made particularly successful appearances in works in the Romantic repertoire, his specialty, in Japan (1977) and France (1978). His auspicious career was interrupted by the Soviet authorities when, in 1979, he applied for a visa to emigrate to Israel with his wife. His application was denied and he subsequently was allowed to give concerts only in remote outposts of the Soviet Union. With the support of the U.S. ambassador, he gave several private concerts at the ambassador's official residence in Moscow; in 1984 one of these was surreptitiously recorded and later released by CBS Masterworks. When his plight became a cause célèbre in the West, Feltsman was allowed to give his first Moscow recital in almost a decade (April 21, 1987). In June 1987 he was granted permission to emigrate, and in Aug. 1987 went to the U.S., where he accepted an appointment at the State Univ. of N.Y. at New Paltz. On Sept. 27, 1987, he gave a special concert at the White House for President Reagan, and on Nov. 11, 1987, gave his first N.Y. recital in Carnegie Hall. He subsequently appeared as a soloist with various orchs. and as a recitalist. In 1995 he became a naturalized American citizen.

Felumb, Svend Christian, Danish oboist and conductor; b. Copenhagen, Dec. 25, 1898; d. there, Dec. 16, 1972. He studied in Copenhagen with L. Nielsen and Bruce, and in Paris with Blenzel and Vidal. From 1924 till 1947 he was an oboist in the Danish Royal Orch. in Copenhagen. From 1947 to 1962 he conducted the Tivoli Orch. in Copenhagen. He was the founder of the Ny Musik society in Copenhagen and a leader of the movement for modern national Danish music.

Fenby, Eric (William), English composer; b. Scarborough, April 22, 1906. He studied piano and organ; after a few years as an organist in London, he went (1928) to Grez-sur-Loing, France, as amanuensis for Frederick Delius, taking down his dictation note by note, until Delius's death in 1934. He publ. his experiences in a book entitled *Delius as I Knew Him* (London, 1936; 4th ed., N.Y., 1981). He was director of music of the North Riding Training School (1948–62); from 1964, was a prof. of composition at the Royal Academy of Music in London. In 1964 he was made an Officer of the Order of the British Empire. Because of the beneficent work he undertook, he neglected his own compositions; however, he wrote some pleasant music for strings. He also publ. the books *Menuhin's House of Music* (London, 1969) and *Delius* (London, 1971).

BIBL.: C. Redwood, ed., *A Delius Companion: A 70th Birthday Tribute to E. F.* (London, 1976).

Fennell, Frederick, noted American conductor and teacher; b. Cleveland, July 2, 1914. He first began conducting at the National Music Camp in Interlochen, Mich. (summers, 1931–33), and then studied at the Eastman School of Music in Rochester, N.Y., (B.M., 1937; M.M., 1939), where he subsequently conducted various ensembles (1939–65). He also was founder-conductor of the Eastman Wind Ensemble (from 1952), which he developed into one of the premier groups of its kind. After serving as conductor-in-residence at the Univ. of Miami School of Music in Coral Gables (1965–80), he was conductor of the Kosei Wind Orch. in Tokyo (from 1984). He publ. *Time and the Winds* (Kenosha, Wis., 1954) and *The Drummer's Heritage* (Rochester, N.Y., 1956).

BIBL.: R. Rickson, *Fortissimo: A Bio-Discography of F.F.: The First Forty Years, 1953 to 1993* (Cleveland, 1993).

Fennelly, Brian, American composer and teacher; b. Kingston, N.Y., Aug. 14, 1937. After attending Union College in Schenectady, N.Y. (M.E. in mechanical engineering, 1958; B.A., 1963), he was a student of Mel Powell, Gunther Schuller, and Allen Forte at Yale Univ. (M.M., 1965; Ph.D., 1968, with the diss. *A*

Descriptive Notation for Electronic Music). From 1968 he was a prof. of music at N.Y. Univ. In 1975, 1977, and 1980 he received grants from the Martha Baird Rockefeller Fund. He held NEA Composer fellowships in 1977, 1979, and 1985. In 1980 he received a Guggenheim fellowship. In his music, Fennelly follows the American traditions set by Sessions and Carter, while often reflecting the influence of jazz and the inspiration of nature. He strives for maximum expressivity and structural rigor, extending from the virtuosic possibilities of a solo instrument to the coloristic potential of the full orch.

WORKS: ORCH.: *In Wildness is the Preservation of the World*, Thoreau fantasy (1975); *Thoreau Fantasy No. 2* (1984–85); Concert Piece for Trumpet and Orch. (1976); *Quintuplo* for Brass Quintet and Orch. (1977–78); *Scintilla prisca* for Cello and Orch. (1980); *Tropes and Echoes* for Clarinet and Orch. (1981); Concerto for Saxophone and Strings (1983–84); *Fantasy Variations* (1984–85); *Lunar Halos: Paraselenae* (1990); *A Thoreau Symphony* (1992–96). **CHAMBER:** Suite for Double Bass (1963; rev. 1981); Duo for Violin and Piano (1964); *For Solo Flute* (1964; rev. 1976); *2 Movements* for Oboe, Clarinet, Trumpet, and Trombone (1965); *Diversions* for Violin (1968; rev. 1981); Wind Quintet (1967); *Evanescences* for Alto Flute, Clarinet, Violin, Cello, and Tape (1969); String Quartet (1971); *Tesserae I* for Harpsichord (1971), *II* for Cello (1972), *III* for Viola (1976), *IV* for Double-bass Trombone (1976), *V* for Tuba (1980), *VI* for Trumpet (1976), *VII* for Clarinet (1979), *VIII* for Alto Saxophone (1980), and *IX* for Percussion (1981); *Prelude and Elegy* for Brass Quintet (1973); *Consort I* for Trombone Quintet (1976); *Empirical Rag* for Brass Quintet (1977; also for other instruments); *Canzona and Dance* for Clarinet, Violin, Viola, Cello, and Piano (1982–83); *3 Intermezzi* for Bass Clarinet and Marimba (1983); *Triple Play* for Violin, Cello, and Piano (1984); *Corollary I: Coralita* for Horn and Piano (1986), *II* for Alto Saxophone and Piano (1987–88), and *III* for Trumpet and Piano (1989); Trio No. 2 for Violin, Cello, and Piano or Harpsichord (1986–87); 2 brass quintets: No. 1 (1987) and No. 2, *Locking Horns* (1993); piano pieces. **VOCAL:** *Songs with Improvisation* for Mezzo-soprano, Clarinet, and Piano (1964; rev. 1969); *Psalm XIII* for Chorus and Brass (1965); *Festive Psalm* for Chorus, Narrator, Organ, and Tape (1972); *Praise Yah* for Chorus and Organ (1974); *Winterkill* for Chorus and Piano (1981); *2 Poems of Shelley* for Chorus (1982); *Keats on Love* for Chorus and Piano (1989); *Proud Music* for Chorus, Organ, 2 Trumpets, and 2 Trombones (1994); *Soon Shall the Winter's Foil* for Chorus (1994). **ELECTRONIC:** *Sunyata* (1970).

Ferand, Ernst (Thomas), Hungarian musicologist; b. Budapest, March 5, 1887; d. Basel, May 29, 1972. He studied composition at the Royal Academy of Music in Budapest (diploma, 1911), and then was a student of Jaques-Dalcroze in Hellerau, near Dresden (1913–14); he also took courses in music history, psychology, and philosophy at the Univ. of Budapest, and later in musicology and psychology at the Univ. of Vienna (Ph.D., 1937, with the diss. *Die Improvisationspraxis in der Musik*; publ. as *Die Improvisation in der Musik*, Zürich, 1938). After teaching at the Fodor Cons. of Music in Budapest (1912–19), he was director of the Dalcroze School in Hellerau (1920–25) and of the Hellerau-Laxenburg College, near Vienna (1925–38); he then taught at the New School for Social Research in N.Y. (1939–65). In addition to valuable articles in journals, he publ. a harmony textbook (Budapest, 1914) and *Die Improvisation in Beispielen aus neun Jahrhunderten abendländischer Musik* (Cologne, 1956; 2nd ed., rev., 1961; Eng. tr., 1961, in Das Musikwerk, XII).

Ferchault, Guy, French musicologist; b. Mer, Loire-et-Cher, Aug. 16, 1904; d. Paris, Nov. 14, 1980. He studied with C. Lalo, Pirro, and Masson at the Cons. and philosophy at the Sorbonne (graduated, 1942) in Paris. He held teaching positions in music education in Paris, Orléans (1941), Poitiers (1942–49), Tours (1948–51), and Roubaix (from 1952); from 1943 to 1967 he was also a prof. of music history at the Cons. Régional de Musique in Versailles, and then at St. Maur.

WRITINGS: *Henri Duparc, Une Amitié mystique, d'après ses lettres à Francis Jammes* (Paris, 1944); *Les Créatures du drame musical: De Monteverdi à Wagner* (Paris, 1944); *Introduction à l'esthétique de la mélodie* (Gap, 1946); *Claude Debussy, musicien français* (Paris, 1948); *Faust, J.-S. Bach et l'esthétique de son temps* (Zürich, 1950).

Fere, Vladimir, Russian composer and ethnomusicologist; b. Kamyshin, May 20, 1902; d. Moscow, Sept. 2, 1971. He studied piano with Goldenweiser and composition with Glière and Miaskovsky at the Moscow Cons. (1921–29). In 1936 he went to Frunze, Kirghizia, where he composed, in collaboration with Vlasov, a number of operas based on native folk motifs, all first premiered there: *Golden Girl* (May 1, 1937); *Not Death but Life* (March 26, 1938); *Moon Beauty* (April 15, 1939); *For People's Happiness* (May 1, 1941); *Patriots* (Nov. 6, 1941); *Son of the People* (Nov. 8, 1947); *On the Shores of Issyk-Kul* (Feb. 1, 1951); *Toktogul* (July 6, 1958); *The Witch* (1965); *One Hour before Dawn* (1969). He also wrote several symphonic pieces on Kirghiz themes; numerous choruses; chamber music.

Ferencsik, János, noted Hungarian conductor; b. Budapest, Jan. 18, 1907; d. there, June 12, 1984. He studied organ and theory at the Budapest Cons.; became répétiteur at the Hungarian State Opera (1927), and subsequently conductor there (from 1930); he was also an assistant at the Bayreuth Festivals (1930, 1931). He was chief conductor of the Hungarian Radio and Television Sym. Orch. (1945–52), the Hungarian State Sym. Orch. (1952–84), and the Budapest Phil. (1953–76); also appeared as a guest conductor in Europe and North America. He was awarded the Kossuth Prize (1951, 1961); the Order of the Banner was bestowed upon him by the Hungarian government on his 70th birthday. He was a persuasive interpreter of the Hungarian repertoire.

Ferenczy, Oto, Slovak composer; b. Brezovica nad Torysou, March 30, 1921. He studied philosophy, aesthetics, and musicology at the Comenius Univ. in Bratislava (Ph.D., 1945); was mainly self-taught in composition. In 1951 he joined the staff of the Bratislava Academy of Music and Dramatic Arts; from 1962 to 1966 was its rector; subsequently was prof. of theory there until 1990. From 1982 to 1987 he served as president of the Union of Slovak Composers. His music, expertly crafted, is entrenched well within the inoffensive idiom of Central European neo-Classicism.

WORKS: COMIC OPERA: *Nevšedna humoreska* (An Uncommon Humoresque; 1966–67). **ORCH.:** *Merry-Making*, dance suite (1951); *Hurbanovská*, overture (1952); *Serenade* for Harp, Flute, Clarinet, Bassoon, and Strings (1955); *Capriccio* for Piano and Orch. (1957); *Elegy* (1957); *Finale* (1958); *Partita* for Chamber Orch. (1963–65); *Symphonic Prologue* (1973); Overture (1977); Piano Concerto (1978). **CHAMBER:** *Music* for 4 String Instruments (1947; rev. 1973); Concerto for 9 Instruments (1949); String Quartet (1962); Violin Sonata (1964); Concertino for 12 Instruments (1965); piano pieces. **VOCAL:** *The Star of the North*, cantata (1960); choruses; solo songs.

Ferguson, Donald (Nivison), American music educator; b. Waupun, Wis., June 30, 1882; d. Minneapolis, May 11, 1985. He studied at the Univ. of Wisc. (B.A., 1904); then went to London, where he studied composition with Josef Holbrooke and piano with Michael Hambourg (1905–08); later studied at the Univ. of Minnesota (M.A., 1922) and at the Univ. of Vienna (1929–30). In 1913 he joined the faculty of the Univ. of Minnesota; was named full prof. in 1927; he retired in 1950, but returned to teach as prof. emeritus there from 1953 to 1956. Concurrently he was head of the music dept. at Macalester College in St. Paul (1950–59). From 1930 to 1960 he served as program annotator for the Minneapolis Sym. Orch.

WRITINGS: *A History of Musical Thought* (N.Y., 1935; 3rd ed., rev., 1959); *A Short History of Music* (N.Y., 1943); *Piano Music of 6 Great Composers* (N.Y., 1947); *Masterworks of the Orchestral Repertoire* (Minneapolis, 1954); *Music as Metaphor; The Elements of Expression* (Minneapolis, 1960); *Image and*

Structure in Chamber Music (Minneapolis, 1964); *The Why of Music* (Minneapolis, 1969).

BIBL.: J. Slettom, "D. F. at 100: A Life in Music," *Minnesota Monthly* (Sept. 1982).

Ferguson, Howard, Irish pianist, musicologist, and composer; b. Belfast, Oct. 21, 1908. He studied piano with Harold Samuel; he also took courses in composition with R.O. Morris and in conducting with Sargent at the Royal College of Music in London (1924–28). From 1948 to 1963 he was a prof. of composition at the Royal Academy of Music in London. His music is neo-Classical in its idiom; in some of his compositions he makes use of English, Scottish, and Irish folk songs.

EDITIONS: *W. Tisdall: Complete Keyboard Works* (London, 1958); *Style and Interpretation: An Anthology: Early Keyboard Music: England and France; Early Keyboard Music: Germany and Italy; Classical Piano Music; Romantic Piano Music; Keyboard Duets* (2 vols., London, 1963–71); *Style and Interpretation: Sequels: Early French Keyboard Music, I, II; Early Italian Keyboard Music, I, II; Early German Keyboard Music, I, II; Early English Keyboard Music, I, II* (8 vols., London, 1966–71); with C. Hogwood, *W. Croft: Complete Harpsichord Works* (2 vols., London, 1974); *Anne Cromwell's Virginal Book, 1638* (London, 1974); *F. Schubert, Piano Sonatas* (London, 1979); *Keyboard Works of C.P.E. Bach* (4 vols., London, 1983).

WORKS: *5 Irish Folktunes* for Cello or Viola and Piano (1927); *2 Ballads* for Baritone, Chorus, and Orch. (1928–32); 2 violin sonatas (1931, 1946); *3 Medieval Carols* for Voice and Piano (1932–33); *4 Short Pieces* for Clarinet or Viola and Piano (1932–36); *3 Sketches* for Flute and Piano (1932–52); Octet for Clarinet, Bassoon, Horn, String Quartet, and Double Bass (1933); *5 Pipe Pieces* for 3 Bamboo Pipes (1934–35); *Partita* for Orch. (1935–36; also for 2 Pianos); Flute Sonata (1938–40); *4 Diversions on Ulster Airs* for Orch. (1939–42); *5 Bagatelles* for Piano (1944); *Chauntecleer*, ballet (1948); Concerto for Piano and Strings (1950–51; London, May 29, 1952, Myra Hess soloist); *Discovery* for Voice and Piano (1951); *2 Fanfares* for 4 Trumpets and 3 Trombones (1952); *Overture for an Occasion* for Orch. (1952–53); *5 Irish Folksongs* for Voice and Piano (1954); *Amore langueo* for Tenor, Chorus, and Orch. (1955–56); *The Dream of the Rood* for Soprano or Tenor, Chorus, and Orch. (1958–59); piano pieces.

BIBL.: A. Burn, "The Music of H. F.," *Musical Times* (Aug. 1983); H. Cobbe, "H. F. at 80," ibid. (Oct. 1988); A. Ridout, ed., *The Music of H. F., a Symposium* (London, 1989).

Fernândes, Armando José, Portuguese composer and teacher; b. Lisbon, July 26, 1906; d. there, May 3, 1983. He studied piano with Rey Colaço and Varela Cid, composition with A. da Costa Ferreira, and musicology with Freitas Branco at the Lisbon Cons.; after training in piano with Cortot and in composition with Boulanger in Paris (1933–36), he taught composition at the Lisbon Cons.

WORKS: *O homem do cravo*, ballet (1941); *Fantasia sobre temas populares portugueses* for Piano and Orch. (1945); Violin Concerto (1948); Concerto for Piano and String Orch. (1951); *O terramoto de Lisboa*, symphonic poem (1962); *Suite Concertante* for Harpsichord and Chamber Orch. (1967); Violin Sonata (1946); piano pieces.

Fernândez, Oscar Lorenzo. See **Lorenzo Fernândez, Oscar.**

Ferneyhough, Brian (John Peter), English composer and teacher; b. Coventry, Jan. 16, 1943. He studied at the Birmingham School of Music (1961–63); then took courses with Lennox Berkeley and Maurice Miles at the Royal Academy of Music in London (1966–67); furthermore, received instruction in advanced composition with Ton de Leeuw in Amsterdam and Klaus Huber in Basel (1969–73). From 1971 to 1986 he was on the faculty at the Hochschule für Musik in Freiburg im Breisgau; then taught at the Royal Cons. of Music at The Hague (from 1986) and at the Univ. of Calif. at San Diego (from 1987). His output is marked by an uncompromising complexity.

WORKS: *4 Miniatures* for Flute and Piano (1965); *Coloratura* for Oboe and Piano (1966); Sonata for 2 Pianos (1966); *Prometheus* for Wind Sextet (1967); 4 string quartets (1967; 1980; 1986–87; 1990); *Epicycle* for 20 Strings (Hilversum, Sept. 7, 1969); *Firecycle Beta* for Orch. and 5 Conductors (1969–71); *Funérailles I* for String Sextet, Double Bass, and Harp (1969–77) and *II* for 7 Strings and Harp (1980); *Missa brevis* for 12 Solo Voices (1971); *7 Sterne* for Organ (1971); *Time and Motion Study I* for Bass Clarinet (1971–77), *II* for Cello and Electronics (1973–75), and *III* for 16 Solo Voices and Percussion (1974); *Transit* for 6 Amplified Voices and Chamber Orch. (1972–75; Royan, France, March 25, 1975); *Perspectivae corporum irregularum* for Oboe, Viola, and Piano (1975); *Unity Capsule* for Flute (1975–76); *La Terre est un homme* for Orch. (1976–79); *Lemma-Icon-Epigram* for Piano (1981); *Superscriptio* for Piccolo (1981); *Carceri d'invenzione I* for 16 Instruments (1981–82), *II* for Flute and Chamber Orch. (1984), and *III* for 15 Wind Instruments and 3 Percussionists (1986); *Adagissimo* for String Quartet (1983); *Études transcendantales* for Mezzo-soprano, Flute, Oboe, Cello, and Harpsichord (1982–85); *Allgebrah* for Oboe and String Orch. (1990); *Bone Alphabet* for Percussion (1991); *Terrain* for Violin and Ensemble (1992).

Fernström, John (Axel), Swedish violinist, conductor, teacher, and composer; b. Ichang, China (of Swedish parents), Dec. 6, 1897; d. Lund, Oct. 19, 1961. He was the son of a Swedish missionary in China. After settling in Sweden, he studied violin at the Malmö Cons. (1913–15); also with Max Schlüter in Copenhagen (1917–21; 1923–24), and with Issay Barmas in Berlin (1921–22); he also studied composition with Peder Gram in Copenhagen (1923–30) and pursued composition and conducting studies at the Sonderhausen Cons. (1930). After playing violin in the Hälsingborg Sym. Orch. (1916–39), he was director of the Malmö Radio (1939–41). He then settled in Lund, where he was director of the municipal music school (1948–61); he also was conductor of the Orch. Soc. and founder-conductor of the Nordic Youth Orch. In 1953 he was made a member of the Royal Academy of Music in Stockholm. In addition to his writings on music theory, he was the author of the interesting autobiography *Jubals son och blodsarvinge* (1967). Fernström was an adept composer of instrumental music. In his works, he pursued a median course between traditional idioms and avant-garde styles; he wrote both tonal and atonal scores with fine results.

WORKS: OPERAS: *Achnaton* (1931); *Isissystarnas bröllop* (1942); *Livet en dröm* (1946). **ORCH.:** 12 syms. (1920; 1924; *Exotica*, 1928; 1930; 1932; 1938; *Sinfonietta in forma di sonata de chiesa*, 1941; *Amore studiorum*, 1942; *Sinfonia breve*, 1943; *Sinfonia discrète*, 1944; *Utan mask*, 1945; 1951); *Symphonic Variations* (1930); *Chaconne* for Cello and Orch. (1936); Clarinet Concerto (1936); Viola Concerto (1937); 2 violin concertos (1938, 1952); Concertino for Flute, Women's Chorus, and Small Orch. (1941); Bassoon Concerto (1946); Cello Concertino (1949); *Ostinato* for Strings (1952). **CHAMBER:** 8 string quartets (1920, 1925, 1931, 1942, 1945, 1947, 1950, 1952). **VOCAL:** Mass for Soli, Chorus, and Orch. (1931); *Stabat Mater* for Soli, Chorus, and Strings (1943); *Den mödosamma vä gen*, profane oratorio (1947); choral pieces; songs.

Ferrani (real name, **Zanaggio), Cesira,** admired Italian soprano; b. Turin, May 8, 1863; d. Pollone, May 4, 1943. She studied with Antonietta Fricci in Turin, where she made her operatic debut in 1887 at the Teatro Carignano as Gilda. She then sang at the Teatro Regio there, where she created the roles of Manon Lescaut (Feb. 1, 1893) and Mimi (Feb. 1, 1896). From 1894 to 1909 she was a principal singer at Milan's La Scala. Among her other notable roles were Elsa, Eva, and Mélisande.

Ferrara, Franco, Italian conductor and pedagogue; b. Palermo, July 4, 1911; d. Florence, Sept. 6, 1985. He studied piano, violin, organ, and composition at the conservatories of Palermo and Bologna. He made his debut as a conductor in Florence in 1938. From 1958 poor health prompted him to devote himself to teaching.

Ferrari, Gustave, Swiss pianist, singer, conductor, and composer; b. Geneva, Sept. 28, 1872; d. there, July 29, 1948. He studied at the Geneva Cons. and in Paris. After a period as an operetta conductor, he toured as accompanist to Yvette Guilbert; later toured on his own as a singer-pianist in the folk song repertoire. He wrote dramatic music, choral pieces, and songs.

Ferrari-Fontana, Edoardo, Italian tenor; b. Rome, July 8, 1878; d. Toronto, July 4, 1936. He studied voice and gained experience singing in operetta in Argentina and Milan before making an impressive operatic debut as Tristan in Turin on Dec. 23, 1909. He sang at Milan's La Scala (1912–14), where he created the role of Avito in *L'amore dei tre re* on April 10, 1913. It was as Avito that he made his Metropolitan Opera debut in N.Y. on Jan. 2, 1914, remaining on its roster until 1915. He also sang with the Boston Opera Co. (1913–14) and the Chicago Grand Opera Co. (1915–16). In 1926 he settled in Toronto as a voice teacher. He was married for a time to **Margarete Matzenauer**. In addition to the Italian repertory, he was esteemed for his portrayals of Siegfried, Siegmund, and Tannhäuser.

Ferrari-Trecate, Luigi, Italian composer; b. Alessandria, Piedmont, Aug. 25, 1884; d. Rome, April 17, 1964. He studied with Antonio Cicognani at the Pesaro Cons., and also with Mascagni. Subsequently he was engaged as a church organist; was prof. of organ at the Liceo Musicale in Bologna (1928–31); from 1929 to 1955, was director of the Parma Cons. He wrote several operas which had considerable success: *Pierozzo* (Alessandria, Sept. 15, 1922); *La Bella e il mostro* (Milan, March 20, 1926); *Le astuzie di Bertoldo* (Genoa, Jan. 10, 1934); *Ghirlino* (Milan, Feb. 4, 1940); *Buricchio* (Bologna, Nov. 5, 1948); *L'Orso Re* (Milan, Feb. 8, 1950); *La capanna dello Zio Tom* (Parma, Jan. 17, 1953); *La fantasia tragica; Lo spaventapasseri* (1963); also music for a marionette play, *Ciottolino* (Rome, Feb. 8, 1922); *In hora calvarii,* sacred cantata (1956); *Contemplazioni* for Orch. (1950).

Ferras, Christian, outstanding French violinist and pedagogue; b. Touquet, June 17, 1933; d. Paris, Sept. 14, 1982. He was a remarkably gifted child who began to study at a very early age with Charles Bistesi at the Nice Cons. In 1942 he made his public debut as soloist with orch. in Nice. He then continued his training at the Paris Cons. with René Benedetti (violin) and Joseph Calvet (chamber music), taking premiers prix in both subjects in 1946, the year he made his Paris debut. In 1949 he had further lessons with Enesco and captured 2nd prize in the Long-Thibaud competition in Paris. Thereafter, he pursued a distinguished career as a soloist with orchs. and as a recitalist. In 1975 he became a prof. at the Paris Cons. His interpretations were notable for their stylistic fidelity to the score and virtuoso execution.

Ferrata, Giuseppe, Italian-American composer; b. Gradoli, Romagna, Jan. 1, 1865; d. New Orleans, March 28, 1928. At the age of 14, he won a scholarship to study at the Accademia di Santa Cecilia in Rome, where he took courses with Sgambati and Terziani, graduating in 1885; then had the good fortune of benefiting from the last lessons that Liszt gave; in 1892 he went to the U.S.; taught at Tulane Univ. in New Orleans. He wrote a Sym., a Piano Concerto, a String Quartet, numerous songs to Italian and English texts, and piano pieces. He also compiled a book of scales and *Esthetic Exercises of Technique.*

Ferrer, Rafael, Spanish conductor; b. St.-Celoni, near Barcelona, May 22, 1911. He studied with Luis Millet and Enrique Morera (composition) and Eduardo Toldrá (violin). He played the violin in various orchs. in Spain; then devoted himself mainly to conducting. He specialized in Spanish music, and revived many little-known works of Granados, Turina, and other Spanish composers.

Ferrero, Lorenzo, Italian composer; b. Turin, Nov. 17, 1951. He was basically self-taught in music, but received some training from Bruni and Zaffiri. He also attended the Milan Cons. and studied aesthetics with Battimo at the Univ. of Turin (graduated, 1974, with a study of the writings of John Cage). In 1974 he began working with the group Musik-Dia-Licht-Film-Galerie in Munich. In 1980–81 he was assistant to Bussotti at the Puccini Festival in Torre del Lago, where he was artistic director in 1984. In 1981 he became a prof. at the Milan Cons. In 1982–83 he worked at IRCAM in Paris. He was artistic director of the Unione Musicale concert series in Turin from 1982 to 1988, and of the Verona Arena from 1991 to 1994. In his music, Ferrero bridges the gap between traditional opera and rock and popular music.

WORKS: DRAMATIC: *Rimbaud ou Le fils de soleil,* melodrama (1978); *Marilyn,* theater piece (1980); *La figlia del mago,* children's opera (1981); *Mare nostro,* comic opera (1985); *Salvatore Giuliano,* opera (1986); *Carlotta Corday,* opera (1988). **ORCH.:** *Siglied* for Chamber Orch. (1975); *Arioso* (1977; rev. 1981); *Balletto* (1981); *Thema 44* for Small Orch. (1982); *Dance Music* (1985); *My Rock* for Small Orch. (1986). **CHAMBER:** *My Rock, My Rag, My Blues* for Piano (1984); *Ostinato* for 6 Cellos (1987). **VOCAL:** *Canzoni d'amore* for Voices and 9 Instruments (1985); *Non parto, non resto* for Chorus (1987).

Ferrero, Willy, American-born Italian conductor and composer; b. Portland, Maine, May 21, 1906; d. Rome, March 24, 1954. He appeared as a conductor at the Teatro Costanzi in Rome at 6, and then conducted with great success throughout Europe at 8. After studies at the Vienna Academy of Music (graduated, 1924), he resumed his career but never fulfilled his early promise. He wrote a symphonic poem, *Il mistero dell' aurora,* and some chamber music.

Ferretti, Dom Paolo, eminent Italian musicologist; b. Subiaco, Dec. 3, 1866; d. Bologna, May 23, 1938. He studied theology at the Benedictine College of S. Anselmo in Rome, taking his vows as a Benedictine monk in 1884 and being ordained a priest in 1890. From 1900 to 1919 he was abbot of the Benedictine monastery of S. Giovanni in Parma; in 1922 he was made director of the Scuola Pontificia by Pope Piux XI, which became the Pontificio Istituto di Musica Sacra in 1931. He was an authority on Gregorian chant.

WRITINGS: *Princippi teorici e pratici di canto gregoriano* (Rome, 1905); *El Cursus Metrico e il ritmo delle melodie del Canto Gregoriano* (Rome, 1913); *Estetica gregoriana ossia Trattato delle forme musicali del canto gregoriano* (Rome, 1934); P. Ernetti, ed., *Estetica gregoriana dei recitativi liturgici* (Venice, 1964).

Ferrier, Kathleen (Mary), remarkable English contralto; b. Higher Walton, Lancashire, April 22, 1912; d. London, Oct. 8, 1953. She grew up in Blackburn, where she studied piano and began voice lessons with Thomas Duerden. In 1937 she won 1st prizes for piano and singing at the Carlisle Competition; she then decided on a career as a singer, and subsequently studied voice with J.E. Hutchinson in Newcastle upon Tyne and with Roy Henderson in London. After an engagement as a soloist in *Messiah* at Westminster Abbey in 1943, she began her professional career in full earnest. Britten chose her to create the title role in his *Rape of Lucretia* (Glyndebourne, July 12, 1946); she also sang Orfeo in Gluck's *Orfeo ed Euridice* there in 1947 and at Covent Garden in 1953. She made her American debut with the N.Y. Phil. on Jan. 15, 1948, singing *Das Lied von der Erde,* with Bruno Walter conducting. She made her American recital debut in N.Y. on March 29, 1949. Toward the end of her brief career, she acquired in England an almost legendary reputation for vocal excellence and impeccable taste, so that her untimely death (from cancer) was greatly mourned. In 1953 she was made a Commander of the Order of the British Empire and received the Gold Medal of the Royal Phil. Soc.

BIBL.: N. Cardus, ed., *K. F., A Memoir* (London, 1955; 2nd ed., rev., 1969); W. Ferrier, *The Life of K. F.* (London, 1955); C. Rigby, *K. F.* (London, 1955); W. Ferrier, *K. F., Her Life* (London, 1959); P. Lethbridge, *K. F.* (London, 1959); M. Leonard, *K.: The Life of K. F.: 1912–1953* (London, 1988); J. Spycket, *K. F.* (Lausanne, 1990); P. Campion, *F.: A Career Recorded* (London, 1992).

Ferris, William (Edward), American organist, choral conductor, and composer; b. Chicago, Feb. 26, 1937. He studied composition with Alexander Tcherepnin at the De Paul Univ. School of Music (1955–60) and took private lessons with Sowerby in Chicago (1957–62). In 1960 he founded the William Ferris Chorale, specializing in the music of the Renaissance and that of 20th-century composers. He served as organist of Holy Name Cathedral in Chicago (1954–58; 1962–64) and as director of music at Sacred Heart Cathedral in Rochester, N.Y. (1966–71); in 1973 he joined the faculty of the American Cons. of Music in Chicago. His compositions are mostly liturgical.

WORKS: ORCH.: *Concert Piece* for Trumpet, Horn, and Strings (1960); *October-November*, symphonic movement (1962; Rochester, N.Y., Nov. 6, 1968); *Concert Piece* for Organ and Strings (1963; Worcester, Mass., Nov. 19, 1967); *Celebrations*, overture (1966); *Acclamations* for Organ and Orch. (1981–82; Chicago, Jan. 27, 1983). **CHAMBER:** Trio for Flute, Bassoon, and Piano (1957); String Trio (1958); Piano Sonata (1976). **VOCAL:** *De profundis* (Nov. 22, 1964); *Ed e subito sera*, cantata for Tenor and String Quartet (1965); *The Angelic Salutation: Glory to God in the Highest* for Chorus, Organ, and Orch. (Rochester, N.Y., Nov. 6, 1968); *Durobrivae* for Tenors, Basses, 5 Brasses, and Kettledrums (1970); *A Canticle of Celebration* for Chorus, Brasses, and Kettledrums (1971); *Make We Joy*, cantata (Chicago, Dec. 12, 1976); *A Song of Light*, cantata (Chicago, Oct. 11, 1977); numerous works for Chorus and Organ; a cappella choruses; songs.

Ferro, Gabriele, Italian conductor; b. Pescara, Nov. 15, 1937. He studied with Franco Ferrara at the Conservatorio di Santa Cecilia in Rome. In 1967 he founded the Bari Sym. Orch., and from 1974 he conducted sym. concerts with the La Scala Orch. in Milan. He made his U.S. debut as a guest conductor with the Cleveland Orch. in 1978. He was music director of the orchestra Sinfonica Siciliana in Palermo, and, from 1988, served as chief conductor of the RAI Orch. in Rome. In 1992 he became Generalmusikdirektor of the Stuttgart State Theater.

Ferroud, Pierre-Octave, French composer and music critic; b. Chasselay, near Lyons, Jan. 6, 1900; d. in an automobile accident near Debrecen, Hungary, Aug. 17, 1936. He studied harmony with Commette in Lyons and attended the Univ. there, and then pursued his training with Ropartz in Strasbourg (1920–22) and Schmitt in Lyons. In 1923 he settled in Paris as a composer and music critic. His output was influenced by Schmitt and Bartók. He publ. *Autour de Florent Schmitt* (Paris, 1927).

WORKS: DRAMATIC: OPERATIC SKETCH: *Chirurgie* (Monte Carlo, March 20, 1928). **BALLETS:** *Le Porcher* (Paris, Nov. 15, 1924); *Jeunesse* (1931; Paris, April 29, 1933); *Vénus ou L'Équipée planétaire* (1935). **ORCH.:** *Foules*, symphonic poem (1922–24; Paris, March 21, 1926); *Sérénade* (1929); Sym. (1930; Paris, March 8, 1931). **CHAMBER:** Violin Sonata (1928–29); Cello Sonata (1932); Trio for Oboe, Clarinet, and Bassoon (1933); String Quartet (1934); piano pieces. **VOCAL:** Song cycles.

BIBL.: C. Rostand, *L'oeuvre de P.-O. F.* (Paris, 1958).

Fetler, Paul, American composer and teacher; b. Philadelphia, Feb. 17, 1920. His family moved to Europe when he was a child; he had early music studies in Latvia, the Netherlands, Sweden, and Switzerland; he composed 2 dozen small works and part of a sym. that were later discarded. In 1939 he returned to the U.S. and studied briefly at the Chicago Cons. of Music; he then studied composition with David Van Vactor at Northwestern Univ. (graduated, 1943). Drafted into military service, he was sent at the end of World War II to Berlin as a liaison officer and Russian interpreter assigned to the Allied Control Council. It was during this time that he became a student of Celibidache, who arranged the premiere of his *Prelude* for Orch. with members of the Berlin Phil. (July 13, 1946, composer conducting). In 1946 he returned to the U.S. to study with Porter and Hindemith at Yale Univ. (M.M., 1948). In 1948 he was appointed to the music faculty of the Univ. of Minnesota, which became his permanent position and where he earned his Ph.D. degree in 1956. He retired in 1990. He returned to Berlin in 1953 to study with Blacher on a Guggenheim fellowship. His 2nd Guggenheim fellowship (1960) took him to Kreuth, Bavaria, where he composed his *Soundings* for Orch. (Minneapolis, Oct. 12, 1962). One of his most successful scores, *Contrasts* for Orch. (Minneapolis, Nov. 7, 1958), was widely performed. He received 3 NEA grants (1975, 1977, 1980).

WORKS: DRAMATIC: *Sturge Maclean*, opera for youth (St. Paul, Minn., Oct. 11, 1965); incidental music to plays; film scores. **ORCH.:** *Symphonic Fantasia* (1941); *Passacaglia* (1942); *Dramatic Overture* (1943); *Berlin Scherzo* (1945); *Prelude* (Berlin, July 13, 1946); 4 syms.: No. 1 (1948), No. 2 (Rochester, N.Y., Nov. 5, 1951), No. 3 (1954; Minneapolis, Nov. 25, 1955), and No. 4 (Minneapolis, May 1, 1968); *Orchestral Sketch* (Minneapolis, Aug. 15, 1949); *A Comedy Overture* (Minneapolis, March 2, 1952); *Gothic Variations*, on a theme of Machaut (Minneapolis, Nov. 13, 1953); *Contrasts* (Minneapolis, Nov. 7, 1958); *Soundings* (Minneapolis, Oct. 12, 1962); *Cantus tristis*, in memory of President John F. Kennedy (Minneapolis, Nov. 20, 1964); 2 violin concertos: No. 1 (St. Paul, Minn., March 27, 1971) and No. 2 (1980; Minneapolis, March 18, 1981); *Celebration* (1976; Indianapolis, Dec. 16, 1977); *3 Impressions* for Guitar and Orch. (1977; Minneapolis, May 31, 1978); *Serenade* (Minneapolis, July 26, 1981; rev. 1982); Piano Concerto (Minneapolis, Oct. 4, 1984); *Capriccio* for Flute, Winds, and Strings (Minneapolis, June 6, 1985); *3 Excursions*, concerto for Percussion, Piano, and Orch. (1987; Buffalo, Dec. 10, 1988); *Divertimento* for Flute and Strings (Rochester, N.Y., May 15, 1994). **CHAMBER:** Sextet for String Quartet, Clarinet, and Horn (1942); 2 string quartets (1947, 1989); 2nd Violin Sonata (Minneapolis, March 6, 1952); *Cycles* for Percussion and Piano (Washington, D.C., May 31, 1970); *Pastoral Suite* for Piano Trio (St. Paul, Minn., April 11, 1976; *Rhapsody* for Violin and Piano (1985; rev. 1987); *6 Pieces* for Flute and Guitar (1985; rev. 1987); *12 Hymn Settings* for Organ and Instruments (1994); Suite for Oboe, Clarinet, and Bassoon (1995). **VOCAL:** 3 cantatas: *Of Earth's Image* for Soprano, Chorus, and Orch. (1958), *This Was the Way* for Chorus and Orch. (St. Paul, Minn., May 7, 1969), and *The Hour Has Come* for 2 Choruses, Organ, and Brass (1981); *December Stillness* for Voices, Flutes, and Harp (Minneapolis, Dec. 3, 1994); choral pieces; songs.

Feuermann, Emanuel, greatly gifted Austrian-born American cellist; b. Kolomea, Galicia, Nov. 22, 1902; d. N.Y., May 25, 1942. As a child he was taken to Vienna, where he first studied cello with his father; subsequently studied cello with Friedrich Buxbaum and Anton Walter. He made his debut in Vienna in 1913 in a recital. He went to Leipzig in 1917 to continue his studies with Julius Klengel; his progress was so great that he was appointed to the faculty of the Gurzenich Cons. in Cologne by Abendroth at the age of 16; he also was 1st cellist in the Gurzenich Orch. and was a member of the Bram Eldering Quartet. In 1929 he was appointed prof. at the Hochschule für Musik in Berlin; as a Jew, he was forced to leave Germany after the advent of the Nazis to power; he then embarked on a world tour (1934–35). He made his American debut on Dec. 6, 1934, with the Chicago Sym. Orch.; then appeared as soloist with leading American orchs.; also played chamber music with Schnabel and Huberman, and later with Rubinstein and Heifetz.

BIBL.: S. Itzkoff, *E. F., Virtuoso: A Biography* (University, Ala., 1979).

Février, Henri, French composer; b. Paris, Oct. 2, 1875; d. there, July 6, 1957. He studied at the Paris Cons. with Fauré, Leroux, Pugno, and Massenet; also privately with Messager. He publ. a monograph on the latter (Paris, 1948).

WORKS: DRAMATIC: OPERAS: *Le Roi aveugle* (Paris, May 8, 1906); *Monna Vanna* (Paris, Jan. 13, 1909); *Gismonda* (Chicago, Jan. 14, 1919; Paris, Oct. 15, 1919); *La Damnation de Blanche-Fleur* (Monte Carlo, March 13, 1920); *La Femme nue* (Monte Carlo, March 23, 1929). **OPERETTAS:** *Agnès, dame* *galante* (1912); *Carmosine* (1913); *Ile désenchantée* (Paris, Nov. 21, 1925). **OTHER:** Chamber music; piano pieces; choral works; songs.

Fiala, George (Joseph), Russian-born Canadian composer, pianist, organist, and teacher; b. Kiev, March 31, 1922. As the son of pianists, he began his own piano lessons at 7. At 12, he became a piano student of Mikhailov, and also had training in theory and composition. Following composition studies with Groudine, Revutsky, Liatoshinsky, and Olkhovsky at the Kiev Cons. (1939–41), he went to Berlin to study composition (with Dombrowski), conducting (with Furtwängler) and musicology at the Hochschule für Musik (Ph.D., 1945); he then completed his training with L. Jongen in Brussels. In 1949 he emigrated to Canada and in 1955 became a naturalized Canadian citizen. In addition to his activities as a performer, teacher, and composer, he produced programs for the Russian section of Radio Canada International (1967–87). He composed in a tonal style until the early 1960s, and then began to utilize some serial procedures in his works while retaining traditional forms.

WORKS: ORCH.: Piano Concerto (1946); *Autumn Music* (1949); 5 syms., including Sym. in E minor (1950), No. 4, *Ukrainian* (1973; Toronto, Nov. 21, 1982), and No. 5, *Sinfonia breve* (1981); Concertino for Piano, Trumpet, Timpani, and Strings (1950); *Suite concertante* for Oboe and Strings (1956); *Introduction and Fugato* for English Horn and Strings (1961); *Capriccio* for Piano and Orch. (1962); *Shadows of Our Forgotten Ancestors* (1962); *Divertimento concertante* for Violin and Orch. (1965); *Eulogy: In Memory of President J.F. Kennedy* (1965; rev. 1985); *Montreal* (1967); *Musique concertante* for Piano and Orch. (1968); *Serenade concertante* for Cello and Strings (1968); *Sinfonietta concertata* for Accordion, Harpsichord, and Strings (1971); *Ouverture burlesque* (1972); Violin Concerto (1973); *Overtura buffa* (1981); *The Kurelek Suite* (1982); *Festive Ouverture* (1983); *Music* for Strings No. 1 (1985) and No. 2 (1989); *OVERture AND OUT* (1989); *Divertimento capriccioso* for Flute and Strings (1990). **CHAMBER:** *Chamber Music for 5 Wind Instruments* for Flute, Oboe, Clarinet, Horn, and Bassoon (1948); *Ukrainian Suite* for Cello and Piano (1948); Trio for Oboe, Cello, and Piano (1948); Wind Octet (1948); 3 saxophone quartets (1955, 1961, 1983); String Quartet (1956); Piano Quartet (1957); *3 Movements* for Violin, Viola, Cello, and Piano (1957); *Pastorale and Allegretto* for 4 Recorders (1963); 3 cello sonatas (1969, 1971, 1982); Violin Sonata (1969); Saxophone Sonata (1970); *Duo Sonata* for Violin and Harp (1971); *Sonata for 2* for Soprano Saxophone and Accordion (1971); *Concertino canadese* for 4 Harps (1972); *Sonata breve* for Clarinet and Harp (1972); *Partita da camera* for 2 Violins (1977); *Duettino concertante* for Clarinet and Harp (1981); *Terzetto concertante* for Clarinet, Cello, and Harp (1981); *Partita concertata* for Violin and Cello (1982); Piano Quintet (1982); *2 Movements* for Oboe and Piano (1984); Flute Sonata (1986); Trio Sonata for Violin, Cello, and Piano (1987); Viola Sonata (1989). **PIANO:** *Children's Suite* (1941; rev. 1975); 8 sonatas (n.d.–1970); *10 Postludes* (1947; rev. 1968); *Australian Suite* (1963); *3 Bagatelles* (1968); 3 sonatas for 2 Pianos (1970, 1983, 1989); *Piano Music Nos. 1–3* (1976–89); *Concerto da camera* for Piano, 4-hands (1978); *Concerto breve* for 2 Pianos (1979); *Ukrainian Dance* for 2 Pianos (1979); *Canadian Sketches* (1989). **VOCAL:** *Cantilena and Rondo* for Soprano, Recorder, and Piano (1963); *Canadian Credo* for Chorus and Orch. (1966); *5 Ukrainian Songs* for Soprano and Orch. (1973); *Concerto Cantata* for Chorus, Piano, and Chimes Obbligato (1984); *The Millennium Liturgy* for Chorus (1986); other songs.

Fialkowska, Janina, Canadian pianist; b. Montreal, May 7, 1951. She was born of a Polish father and a Canadian mother. At age 5, she commenced piano lessons with her mother; later she was a pupil of Yvonne Hubert at the École Vincent-d'Indy in Montreal (B.Mus., 1968; M.Mus., 1968); after studies with Yvonne Lefébure in Paris (1968), she attended Sascha Gorodnitzki's classes at the Juilliard School in N.Y. (1969); she continued to work with him until 1976, and then served as his assistant (1979–84). After taking one of the 3rd prizes at the 1st Artur Rubenstein competition in Israel in 1974, she appeared as a soloist with leading orchs. and as a recitalist in North and South America and Europe. Her fluent technique and beauty of expression have suited her well in the Romantic repertoire. She has played the complete works of Chopin and on May 3, 1990, she was soloist with the Chicago Sym. Orch. in the first performance of the newly discovered Liszt E-flat major Concerto.

Ficher, Jacobo, Russian-Argentine composer; b. Odessa, Jan. 15, 1896; d. Buenos Aires, Sept. 9, 1978. He studied violin with Stolarsky and Korguev in Odessa and composition with Kalafati and Steinberg at the St. Petersburg Cons., graduating in 1917. In 1923 he emigrated to Argentina. In 1956 he was appointed prof. of composition at the National Cons. of Music in Buenos Aires. His music is characterized by a rhapsodic fluency of development and a rich harmonic consistency. He particularly excelled in chamber music.

WORKS: DRAMATIC: CHAMBER OPERAS: *El oso* (1952); *Pedido de mano* (1955). **BALLETS:** *Colombina de Hoy* (1933); *Los Invitados* (1933); *Melchor* (1938–39); *Golondrina* (1942). **ORCH.:** *Poema heroico* (1927; rev. 1934); *Sulamita*, tone poem (1927; Buenos Aires, July 20, 1929; rev. 1960); *Obertura patética* (1928; Buenos Aires, May 17, 1930; rev. as *Exodus*, 1960); 8 syms. (1932; 1933; 1938–40; 1947; 1948; 1956; 1958–59; 1965); Violin Concerto (1942); 3 piano concertos (1945, 1954, 1960); Harp Concerto (1956); Flute Concerto (1965). **CHAMBER:** 4 string quartets (1927, 1936, 1943, 1952); 3 violin sonatas (1929, 1945, 1959); *Suite en estilo antiguo* for Woodwind Quintet (1930); Sonata for Viola, Flute, and Piano (1931); Sonatina for Saxophone, Trumpet, and Piano (1932); Piano Trio (1935); Flute Sonata (1935); Clarinet Sonata (1937); Oboe Sonata (1940); Cello Sonata (1943); Sonata for Flute and Clarinet (1949); Sonata for Flute, Oboe, and Bassoon (1950); Viola Sonata (1953); Piano Quintet (1961); Wind Quintet (1967). **PIANO:** 8 sonatas; several sets of pieces (including 2 groups of effective "fables," descriptive of animals). **VOCAL:** 3 cantatas: *Salmo de alegria* (1949), *Mi aldea* (1958), and *Kadisch* (1969).

BIBL.: B. Zipman, *J. F.* (Buenos Aires, 1966).

Fickénscher, Arthur, American pianist, teacher, and composer; b. Aurora, Ill., March 9, 1871; d. San Francisco, April 15, 1954. He studied at the Munich Cons. with Rheinberger and Thuille, graduating in 1898. He toured the U.S. as accompanist to famous singers, among them Bispham and Schumann-Heink. From 1920 to 1941 he was head of the music dept. of the Univ. of Virginia, Charlottesville. In 1947 he settled in San Francisco. An inquisitive musician, he elaborated a system of pure intonation; contrived the "Polytone," an instrument designed to play music in which the octave is subdivided into 60 tones. He publ. an article, "The Polytone and the Potentialities of a Purer Intonation," *Musical Quarterly* (July 1941). His major work was the *Evolutionary Quintet*, evolved from a violin sonata and an orch. scherzo written in the 1890s; the MSS were burned in the San Francisco earthquake and fire of 1906; the musical material was then used from memory for a Quintet for Piano and Strings, in 2 movements; the 2nd movement, entitled *The 7th Realm*, became an independent work. He also wrote *Willowwave and Wellowway* for Orch. (1925); *The Day of Judgment* for Orch. (1927; Grand Rapids, Feb. 10, 1934); *Dies irae* for Chamber Orch. (1927); *Out of the Gay Nineties* for Orch. (Richmond, Va., Dec. 4, 1934, composer conducting); *Variations on a Theme in Medieval Style* for Strings (1937); *The Chamber Blue*, mimodrama (1907–09; rev. 1935; Charlottesville, Va., April 5, 1938); *The Land East of the Sun* for Chorus and Orch. (unfinished); Piano Quintet (1939).

BIBL.: W. Jones, *Life and Works of A. F., American Composer (1871–1954)* (Memphis, Tenn., 1992).

Ficker, Rudolf von, distinguished German musicologist; b. Munich, June 11, 1886; d. Igls, near Innsbruck, Aug. 2, 1954. From 1905 to 1912 he studied at the Univ. of Vienna with Adler (musicology), and in Munich with Thuille and Courvoisier (composition); received his Ph.D. from the Univ. of Vienna in 1913 with the diss. *Die Chromatik im italienischen Madrigal des 16. Jahrhunderts.* He taught at the Univ. of Innsbruck from 1920; became a prof. there in 1923, then at the Univ. of Vienna in 1927, and in 1931 at the Univ. of Munich. He was a specialist in medieval music. In addition to articles for music journals, he also left unfinished a book entitled *Die Grundlagen der abendländischen Mehrstimmigkeit.*

Fiedler, Arthur, highly popular American conductor; b. Boston, Dec. 17, 1894; d. Brookline, Mass., July 10, 1979. Of a musical family, he studied violin with his father, Emanuel Fiedler, a member of the Boston Sym. Orch. In 1909 he was taken by his father to Berlin, where he studied violin with Willy Hess, and attended a class on chamber music with Dohnányi; he also had some instruction in conducting with Kleffel and Krasselt. In 1913 he formed the Fiedler Trio with 2 other Fiedlers. In 1915 he returned to America, and joined the 2nd violin section of the Boston Sym. Orch.; later he moved to the viola section; he also doubled on the celesta, when required. In 1924 he organized the Arthur Fiedler Sinfonietta, a professional ensemble of members of the Boston Sym. Orch. In 1929 he started a series of free open-air summer concerts at the Esplanade on the banks of the Charles River in Boston, presenting programs of popular American music intermingled with classical numbers. The series became a feature in Boston's musical life, attracting audiences of many thousands each summer. In 1930 Fiedler was engaged as conductor of the Boston Pops, which he led for nearly half a century. Adroitly combining pieces of popular appeal with classical works and occasional modern selections, he built an eager following, eventually elevating the Boston Pops to the status of a national institution via numerous tours, recordings, radio broadcasts, and television concerts. In 1977 President Gerald Ford bestowed upon him the Medal of Freedom.

BIBL.: R. Moore, *F., The Colorful Mr. Pops* (Boston, 1968); C. Wilson, *A. F., Music for the Millions* (N.Y., 1968); J. Holland, *Mr. Pops* (N.Y., 1972); H. Dickson, *A. F. and the Boston Pops* (Boston, 1981).

Fiedler, (August) Max, German conductor and composer; b. Zittau, Dec. 31, 1859; d. Stockholm, Dec. 1, 1939. He studied with his father (piano), with G. Albrecht (organ and theory), and at the Leipzig Cons. (1877–80). He then was a teacher (from 1882) and director (from 1903) of the Hamburg Cons., and was also conductor of the Hamburg Phil. (1904–08); subsequently he was conductor of the Boston Sym. Orch. (1908–12) and music director in Essen (1916–33).

WORKS: Sym; *Lustpiel* overture; Piano Quintet; String Quartet; piano pieces; songs.

BIBL.: G. Dejmek, *M.F.: Werden und Werken* (Essen, 1940).

Fiévet, Paul, French composer; b. Valenciennes, Dec. 11, 1892; d. Paris, March 15, 1980. His father, Claude Fiévet (1865–1938), was a composer. Paul Fiévet studied piano and theory at the Paris Cons., where he was a student of Xavier Leroux, Caussade, and Widor, obtaining the premier prix in harmony in 1913, and 3 premier prix in composition in 1917, 1918, and 1919. He received the Grand Prix International in Ostende in 1931 and the Grand Prix of Paris in 1932. Among his works are an operetta, *Le Joli Jeu* (Lyons, 1933), and several symphonic suites of the type of "landscape music," e.g., *Orient* (Paris, 1929), *Les Horizons dorés* (Paris, 1932), *Puerta del Sol* (Paris, 1933), and *Images de France* (Paris, 1964). He also wrote several string quartets (one of which he whimsically entitled *Sputnik*), a Brass Sextet, and numerous choruses and piano pieces.

Figner, Medea, famous Italian-Russian mezzo-soprano, later soprano; b. Florence, April 3, 1858; d. Paris, July 8, 1952. She studied voice with Bianchi, Carozzi-Zucchi, and Panofka in Florence. She made her debut as Azucena in Sinalunga, near Florence, in 1875; then sang in the opera theaters of Florence. From 1877 to 1887 she toured in Italy, Spain, and South America; she met Nikolai (Nikolaievich) Figner during her travels, and followed him to Russia; after their marriage in 1889, she appeared under the name Medea Mei-Figner; they were divorced in 1903. She became extremely successful on the Russian operatic stage, and was a member of the Maryinsky Imperial Opera Theater in St. Petersburg from 1887 until 1912. She then devoted herself mainly to voice teaching. Her voice was described by critics as engagingly soft, rich, "velvety," and "succulent." She could sing soprano roles as impressively as those in the mezzo-soprano range. She was fortunate in having been coached by Tchaikovsky in the role of Liza in his opera *The Queen of Spades*, which she sang at its premiere in St. Petersburg (Dec. 19, 1890); her husband sang the role of her lover in the same opera. Her other successful roles were Tosca, Mimi, Donna Anna, Elsa, Brünnhilde, Marguerite, Desdemona, Aida, Amneris, and Carmen. She publ. a book of memoirs (St. Petersburg, 1912).

Figuš-Bystrý, Viliam, Slovak composer; b. Banská Bystrica, Feb. 28, 1875; d. there, May 11, 1937. He spent many years collecting Slovak folk melodies, which he publ. in 5 vols. (1906–15) for voice and piano; also publ. a collection of 1,000 arranged for piano only (1925–31). He further wrote an opera, *Detvan* (1924; Bratislava, Aug. 1, 1928); a cantata, *Slovenská Piesen* (1913); an orch. suite, *From My Youth*; Piano Quartet; Piano Trio; 3 violin sonatines; other violin pieces; piano works; choruses and songs.

Filiasi, Lorenzo, Italian composer; b. Naples, March 25, 1878; d. Rome, July 30, 1963. He studied at the Conservatorio di S. Pietro a Majella in Naples with Nicola d'Arienzo. His first success came with the opera *Manuel Menendez* (Milan, May 15, 1904), which won the Sonzogno Competition Prize in 1902. His other operas included *Fior di Neve* (Milan, April 1, 1911) and *Messidoro* (1912). He also wrote a pantomime, *Pierrot e Bluette* (1895); *La preghiera del marinaio italiano* for Chorus and Orch.; *Visioni romantiche* for Orch.; violin pieces; many songs.

Filleul, Henry, French composer; b. Laval, May 11, 1877; d. Saint-Omer, May 1, 1959. He studied at the Paris Cons. with Lavignac and Casadesus. In 1908 he became director of the École Nationale de Musique at St. Omer.

WORKS: *Le Jugement de Triboulet*, comic opera (1923); 5 oratorios: *Le Christ vainqueur* (1925), *Le Miracle de Lourdes* (1927), *Les Doulces Joyes de Nostre Dame* (1928), *Jeanne d'Arc* (1929), and *Eva* (1931); *Variations symphoniques sur un thème languedocien* (1939); *Fantaisie concertante* for Piano and Orch. (1950); Cello Concerto; violin pieces, with organ; motets; men's choruses.

BIBL.: *Hommage à Henri F.* (St. Omer, 1952).

Fillmore, (James) Henry (Jr.), American bandmaster and composer; b. Cincinnati, Feb. 3, 1881; d. Miami, Fla., Dec. 7, 1956. His paternal grandfather was August Damerin Fillmore (2nd cousin of President Millard Fillmore); his father, James Henry Fillmore, and his uncles Fred A. and Charles M. Fillmore were the founders of the Cincinnati music publishing firm of Fillmore Bros. Co. He was educated at the Miami (Ohio) Military Inst., and later at the Cincinnati College of Music. As a bandmaster, he led the Syrian Shrine Band of Cincinnati to national prominence from 1920 to 1926, making several transcontinental tours; in 1915 he founded the Fillmore Band, which was one of the earliest bands to make regular radio broadcasts (1927–34). In 1938 he moved to Miami, Fla., where he conducted bands at the Orange Bowl. He is best known, however, as the composer of numerous popular marches (*Americans We, Men of Ohio, His Honor* et al.), 2nd only to Sousa's in their tuneful liveliness. He was also the leading proponent of the "trombone smear," a humorous effect of the trombone glissando. He used numerous pseudonyms in his publ. pieces (**Al Hayes, Harry Hartley, Ray Hall, Gus Beans, Henrietta Moore**, and **Harold Bennett**, under which name he publ. the popular *Military Escort March*). He was also a compiler of sacred songs and tune books. In 1956 he received an honorary D.Mus. degree from the Univ. of Miami (Fla.).

BIBL.: P. Bierley, *Hallelujah Trombone: The Story of H. F.* (Columbus, Ohio, 1982); idem, *The Music of H. F. and Will Huff* (Columbus, Ohio, 1982).

Finck, Henry T(heophilus), prominent American music critic; b. Bethel, Mo., Sept. 22, 1854; d. Rumford Falls, Maine, Oct. 1, 1926. He studied philosophy at Harvard Univ. (graduated, 1876), where he also received instruction in music from J.K. Paine. After writing for several U.S. periodicals in Europe, he was again at Harvard (1877–78), where he won the Harris fellowship, which enabled him to study philosophy and comparative psychology in Berlin, Heidelberg, and Vienna. Upon returning to the U.S., he was made music critic of the *N.Y. Evening Post* and *The Nation* in 1881, retiring in 1924. He also taught music history at the National Cons. of Music of America from 1888. In addition to his perceptive writings on music, he publ. books on psychology, anthropology, and other non-musical subjects. In 1890 he married the pianist Abbie Cushman. A fine literary stylist, she succeeded in copying his style so effectively that she wrote music reviews for him.

WRITINGS (all publ. in N.Y. unless otherwise given): *Chopin and Other Musical Essays* (1889); *Wagner and His Works: The Story of His Life, With Critical Comments* (1893); *Paderewski and His Art* (1895); ed. with others, *Anton Seidl: A Memorial by His Friends* (1899); *Songs and Song Writers* (1900; 2nd ed., 1902); *Edvard Grieg* (1906); *Grieg and His Music* (1909); *Success in Music and How It Is Won* (1909; 2nd ed., 1913); *Massenet and His Operas* (1910); *Richard Strauss: The Man and His Works* (Boston, 1917); *Musical Progress: A Series of Practical Discussions of Present Day Problems in the Tone World* (Philadelphia, 1923); *Musical Laughs: Jokes, Tittle-tattle, and Anecdotes, Mostly Humorous, About Musical Celebrities* (1924); *My Adventures in the Golden Age of Music* (1926).

Fine, Irving (Gifford), remarkable American composer and teacher; b. Boston, Dec. 3, 1914; d. there, Aug. 23, 1962. He studied piano with Frances Glover in Boston (1924–35) and pursued training in composition with Hill and Piston at Harvard Univ. (B.A., 1937; M.A., 1938) and with Boulanger in Cambridge, Mass., and Paris (1938–39). From 1939 to 1945 he was assistant conductor of the Harvard Glee Club. He taught in the music dept. at Harvard Univ. from 1939 to 1950, and also taught composition at the Berkshire Music Center at Tanglewood (summers, 1946–57). From 1950 until his death he taught theory and composition at Brandeis Univ., where he was the Walter W. Naumburg Prof. of Music and chairman of the School of Creative Arts. In 1949 he won the N.Y. Music Critics' Circle Award for his *Partita* for Wind Quintet. In 1949–50 he was in Paris on a Fulbright research fellowship. He held Guggenheim fellowships in 1951–52 and 1958–59. On Aug. 12, 1962, he conducted a performance of his *Symphony 1962* with the Boston Sym. Orch. at the Berkshire Music Center. He succumbed to a heart attack just eleven days later. Fine was at first influenced by the music of Stravinsky and Hindemith, which led him to adopt a cosmopolitan style of composition in which contrapuntal elaboration and energetic rhythms were his main concern. He later developed a distinctive personal style, marked by a lyrical flow of cohesive melody supported by lucid polyphony.

WORKS: ORCH.: *Toccata Concertante* (1947; Boston, Oct. 22, 1948); *Notturno* for Strings and Harp (1950–51; Boston, March 28, 1951); *Serious Song: A Lament* for Strings (Louisville, Nov. 16, 1955); *Blue Towers* (1959; Boston, May 31, 1960); *Diversions* (1959–60; Boston, Nov. 5, 1960); *Symphony 1962* (Boston, March 23, 1962). **CHAMBER:** Violin Sonata (1946; N.Y., Feb. 9, 1947); *Partita* for Wind Quintet (1948; N.Y., Feb. 19, 1949); String Quartet (1952; N.Y., Feb. 18, 1953); *Fantasia* for String Trio (1959); *Romanza* for Wind Quintet (1959; Washington, D.C., Feb. 1, 1963); *"One, Two, Buckle My Shoe"* for Oboe, Clarinet, Violin, and Cello (WGBH-TV, Boston, Nov. 3, 1959). **PIANO:** *Music* (1947; Boston, Nov. 19, 1948); didactic pieces: *Victory March of the Elephants* (1956), *Lullaby for a Baby Panda* (1956), and *Homage à Mozart* (1956). **VOCAL:** *3 Choruses from Alice in Wonderland* for Chorus and Piano (1942; Cambridge, Mass., March 4, 1943; also for Chorus and Orch., Worcester, Mass., Oct. 1949); *The Choral New Yorker* for Chorus and Piano Obbligato (1944; Cambridge, Mass., Jan. 25, 1945); *A Short Alleluia* for Women's Voices (1945); *Hymn "In Grato Jubilo"* for Women's Voices and Small Orch. (Boston, May 2, 1949); *The Hour-Glass* for Chorus (1949; Boston, May 1, 1952); *Mutability*, 6 songs for Mezzo-soprano and Piano (N.Y., Nov. 28, 1952); *An Old Song* for Chorus (1953; Cambridge, Mass., March 1954); *3 Choruses from Alice in Wonderland* for Women's Voices and Piano (1953; Bradford, Mass., April 1954); *Childhood Fables for Grownups* for Medium Voice and Piano (set 1, 1954, N.Y., Feb. 20, 1956; set 2, 1955); *McCord's Menagerie* for Men's Voices (1957; Cambridge, Mass., June 9, 1958).

Fine, Vivian, American composer, teacher, and pianist; b. Chicago, Sept. 28, 1913. She became a scholarship student in piano at the age of 5 at the Chicago Musical College; she studied piano with Djane Lavoie-Herz, harmony and composition with Ruth Crawford and Adolf Weidig, and composition with Cowell; in 1931 she went to N.Y., where she studied piano with Whiteside, composition with Sessions, and orchestration with Szell; she also appeared as a pianist. She held teaching positions at N.Y. Univ. (1945–48), the Juilliard School of Music in N.Y. (1948), the State Univ. of N.Y. at Potsdam (1951), the Conn. College School of Dance (1963–64), and Bennington (Vt.) College (1964–87). In 1980 she received a Guggenheim fellowship and was elected to the American Academy and Inst. of Arts and Letters. She was particularly adept at writing vocal and instrumental works in a dissonant but acceptable style. In 1935 she married the sculptor Benjamin Karp.

WORKS: DRAMATIC: THEATER: *The Race of Life* (1937; N.Y., Jan. 23, 1938); *Opus 51* (Bennington, Vt., Aug. 6, 1938); *Tragic Exodus* (N.Y., Feb. 16, 1939); *They Too Are Exiles* (1939; N.Y., Jan. 7, 1940); *Alcestis* (N.Y., April 29, 1960); *My Son, My Enemy* (New London, Conn., Aug. 15, 1965). **CHAMBER OPERA:** *The Women in the Garden* (1977; San Francisco, Feb. 12, 1978). **ORCH.:** *Elegiac Song* for Strings (1937; Lenox, Mass., Aug. 8, 1971); Concertante for Piano and Orch. (1944); *Romantic Ode* for Violin, Viola, Cello, and String Orch. (Bennington, Vt., Aug. 28, 1976); *Drama for Orchestra* (1982; San Francisco, Jan. 5, 1983); *Poetic Fires* for Piano and Orch. (1984; N.Y., Feb. 21, 1985, composer soloist); *Dancing Winds* (1987); *After the Tradition* for Chamber Orch. (1988). **CHAMBER:** String Trio (1930); *Prelude* for String Quartet (1937); *Capriccio* for Oboe and String Trio (1946); Violin Sonata (1952); String Quartet (1957); *3 Pieces* for Flute, Bassoon, and Harp (1961); *Dreamscape* for 3 Flutes, Cello, Piano, and Percussion Ensemble (1964); Chamber Concerto for Solo Cello, Oboe, Violin, Viola, Cello, Double Bass, and Piano (1966); Quintet for String Trio, Trumpet, and Harp (1967); Brass Quintet (1978); Piano Trio (1980); Quintet for Oboe, Clarinet, Violin, Cello, and Piano (1984); Cello Sonata (1986); also piano pieces; other works for solo instruments. **VOCAL:** *The Great Wall of China* for Medium Voice, 2 Violins, Viola, and Cello (1947); *Psalm 13* for Baritone, Women's Chorus, and Piano or Organ (1953); *Valedictions* for Soprano, Tenor, Chorus, and 10 Instruments (1959); *Epitaph* for Chorus and Orch. (1967; Bennington, Vt., Nov. 5, 1983); *Sounds of the Nightingale* for Soprano, Women's Chorus, and Nonet (1971); *Meeting for Equal Rights, 1866* for Soprano, Baritone, Narrator, Chorus, and Orch. (N.Y., April 23, 1976); *3 Sonnets* for Baritone and Orch. (Bennington, Vt., Dec. 12, 1976); *Ode to Purcell* for Medium Voice and String Quartet (1984).

Fink, Michael Jon, American composer, performer, and teacher; b. Los Angeles, Dec. 7, 1954. He studied composition at the Calif. Inst. of the Arts with Budd, Kraft, Childs, and Powell (B.F.A., 1976; M.F.A., 1980). He performed with the Negative Band and Stillife. In 1982 he joined the faculty of the Calif. Inst. of the Arts. In 1985 he was composer-in-residence at North Michigan Univ. His music is unusually spare and quiet and meticulously crafted, achieving a graceful sense of timelessness. Among his compositions are *2 Pieces* for Piano (1983), an untitled work for Small Orch. (1986), *Living to Be Hunted by the Moon* for Clarinet, Bass Clarinet, and Electronics (1987), *A Temperament for Angels* for Computer-controlled Electronics and 3 Electronic Keyboards (1989), *Sound Shroud Garden*, sound installation (with Jim Fox; 1989), and *Epitaph* for Bass Clarinet (1990). He publ. *Inside the Music Business: Music in Contemporary Life* (N.Y., 1989).

Finke, Fidelio F(ritz or **Friedrich),** German composer and pedagogue; b. Josefsthal, near Gablonz, Bohemia, Oct. 22, 1891; d. Dresden, June 12, 1968. He studied with his father and with his uncle, Romeo Finke, director of the German Academy of Music in Prague, and then attended Novák's master classes in composition at the Prague Cons. (1908–11). He joined its faculty as a teacher of theory and piano in 1915, becoming a prof. in 1926; he also was national inspector of the German music schools in Czechoslovakia (1920–38) and head of the master classes in composition at the German Academy of Music in Prague (1927–45). After serving as director and as a teacher of a master class in composition at the Dresden Akademie für Musik und Theater (1946–51), he was a prof. of composition at the Leipzig Hochschule für Musik (1951–59). His works evolved from German classicism to the exploration of the Second Viennese School and neo-Classicism before embracing a readily accessible style.

WORKS: DRAMATIC: OPERAS: *Die versunkene Glocke* (1915–18); *Die Jakobsfahrt* (Prague, Oct. 17, 1936); *Der schlagfertige Liebhaber* (1950–54); *Der Zauberfisch* (Dresden, June 3, 1960). **DANCE PANTOMIME:** *Lied der Zeit* (1946). **ORCH.:** *Eine Schauspiel-Ouvertüre* (1908); 8 suites: No. 1 for Strings (1911), No. 2 (1948), No. 3 (1949), No. 4 for 16 Winds and Percussion (1953), No. 5 for Winds (1955), No. 6 (1956), No. 7 (1961), and No. 8 for 5 Winds, 2 Pianos, and Strings (1961); *Pan*, sym. (1919); Piano Concerto (1930); *Concerto for Orchestra* (1931); *Divertimento* for Chamber Orch. (1964); *Festliche Musik* (1965). **CHAMBER:** Piano Quintet (1911); 5 string quartets (1914–64); Piano Trio (1923); Violin Sonata (1924); Sonata for Solo Cello (1926); Flute Sonata (1927); Sonata for 4 Recorders (1936); *100 Stücke* for Recorder (1936); Sonata for Solo Harp (1945); Horn Sonata (1946); Clarinet Sonata (1949); Viola Sonata (1954); Wind Quintet (1955); piano pieces; organ music. **VOCAL:** *Deutsche Kantate* for Soprano, Bass, Chorus, Boys' Chorus, Organ, and Orch. (1940); *Eros*, cantata for Soprano, Tenor, and Orch. (1966); songs.

BIBL.: D. Härtwig, *F.F.F.: Leben und Werk* (Habilitationsschrift, Univ. of Leipzig, 1970).

Finko, David, Russian-born American composer and teacher; b. Leningrad, May 15, 1936. He received training in piano and violin at the Rimsky-Korsakov School of Performing Arts in Leningrad (1950–55; 1956–58), and then studied composition and theory (1960–65) and conducting (with Musin, 1970–79) at the Leningrad Cons. He then emigrated to the U.S. and became a naturalized American citizen in 1986. After lecturing at the Univ. of Pa. in Philadelphia (1980–84), he was an adjunct prof. of music there (1986–92); he also was composer-in-residence at the Univ. of Texas in El Paso (1981–84) and a faculty member of the Combs College of Music in Philadelphia (1984–90). In 1981 he founded Deko Publishers in Philadelphia. He frequently appeared as a pianist, violinist, and conductor of his own works. His music reflects his Jewish heritage and is set in a modern style but not without melodic overtones.

WORKS: OPERAS: *Polinka* (1965); *That Song* (1970; rev. 1991); *The Enchanted Tailor* (1983–93); *The Klezmers* (1989); *The Kabbalists* (1990); *Abraham and Hanna* (1993); *The Woman is a Devil* (1993; Philadelphia, July 15, 1995). **ORCH.:** *The Holocaust*, tone poem (1965; rev. 1985); 2 syms. (1969, 1972); Piano Concerto (1971); Viola Concerto (1971); Concerto for Violin, Viola, and Orch. (1973); *Russia*, tone poem (1974; rev. 1990); Concerto for Viola, Double Bass, and Orch. (1975); Harp Concerto (1976); Concerto for Viola d'Amore, Guitar, and Orch. (1977); *The Wailing Wall*, tone poem (1983); Concerto for 3 Violins and Orch. (1984); Violin Concerto (1988). **CHAMBER:** *Mourning Music* for Violin, Viola, and Cello (1968); *Lamentations of Jeremiah* for Violin (1969); *Dithyramb* for Viola and Organ (1974); *Fromm Septet* for Oboe, Clarinet, Bass Clarinet, Violin, Cello, Double Bass, and Percussion (1981). **PIANO:** *Fantasia on a Medieval Russian Theme* (1961); 2 sonatas (1964, 1993); *B-88* (1973). **VOCAL:** *Hear, O Israel*, Sabbath Eve service for 2 Singers, Chorus, and Orch. (1986).

Finney, Ross Lee, distinguished American composer and teacher, brother of **Theodore M(itchell) Finney**; b. Wells, Minn., Dec. 23, 1906. He studied at the Univ. of Minnesota with Donald Ferguson and received a B.A. in 1927 from Carleton College. In 1927 he went to Paris, where he took lessons with Boulanger; returning to America, he enrolled at Harvard Univ., where he studied with Edward Burlingame Hill (1928–29); in 1935 he had instructive sessions with Sessions. From 1929 to 1949 he was on the faculty of Smith College; concurrently he taught at Mt. Holyoke College (1938–40). In 1931–32 he was in Vienna, where he took private lessons with Berg; in 1937 he studied with Malipiero in Asolo. He then taught composition at the Hartt School of Music in Hartford, Conn. (1941–42), and at Amherst College (1946–47). His professional career was facilitated by 2 Guggenheim fellowships (1937, 1947) and a Pulitzer traveling fellowship (1937). In 1948–49 he was a visiting lecturer at the Univ. of Mich. in Ann Arbor; from 1949 to 1973 he was a prof. there, and also served as chairman of the dept. of composition; furthermore, he established there an electronic music laboratory. He was the author of *Profile of a Lifetime: A Musical Autobiography* (N.Y., 1992). In 1962 he was elected a member of the National Inst. of Arts and Letters. F. Goossen ed. *Thinking About Music: The Collected Writings of Ross Lee Finney* (Tuscaloosa, 1990). Because of the wide diversification of his stylistic propensities, Finney's works represent a veritable encyclopedic inventory of styles and idioms, from innocently pure modalities to highly sophisticated serialistic formations. About 1950 he devised a sui generis dodecaphonic method of composition which he called "complementarity." In it a 12-tone row is formed by 2 mutually exclusive hexachords, often mirror images of each other; tonal oases make their welcome appearances; a curious air of euphony of theoretically dissonant combinations is created by the contrapuntal superposition of such heterophonic ingredients, and his harmonies begin to sound seductively acceptable despite their modernity.

WORKS: DRAMATIC: OPERAS: *Weep Torn Land* (1984); *Computer Marriage* (1987). **DANCE:** *Heyoka* (N.Y., Sept. 14, 1981); *The Joshua Tree* (N.Y., Oct. 10, 1984); *Ahab* (1985). **ORCH.:** 2 violin concertos: No. 1 (1933; rev. 1952) and No. 2 (1973; Dallas, March 31, 1976; rev. 1977); *Barbershop Ballad* (CBS, Feb. 6, 1940); *Overture for a Drama* (1940; Rochester, N.Y., Oct. 28, 1941); *Slow Piece* for Strings (1940; Minneapolis, April 4, 1941); 4 syms.: No. 1, *Communiqué 1943* (1942; Louisville, Dec. 8, 1964), No. 2 (1958; Philadelphia, Nov. 13, 1959), No. 3 (1960; Philadelphia, March 6, 1964), and No. 4 (1972; Baltimore, March 31, 1973); *Hymn, Fuguing, and Holiday*, based on a hymn tune of William Billings (1943; Los Angeles, May 17, 1947); 2 piano concertos: No. 1 (1948) and No. 2 (1968; Ann Arbor, Mich., Nov. 1, 1972); *Variations* (1957; Minneapolis, Dec. 30, 1965); *3 Pieces* for Chamber Orch. and Tape (1962; Toledo, Ohio, Feb. 23, 1963); Concerto for Percussion and Orch. (1965; Northfield, Minn., Nov. 17, 1966); Symphonie Concertante (1967; Kansas City, Mo., Feb. 27, 1968); *Summer in Valley City* for Band (1969; Ann Arbor, Mich., April 1, 1971); *Landscapes Remembered* (1971; Ithaca, N.Y., Nov. 5, 1972); *Spaces* (1971; Fargo, N.Dak., May 26, 1972); Concerto for Alto Saxophone and Wind Orch. (1974; Ann Arbor, Mich., April 17, 1975); *Narrative* for Cello and 14 Instruments (1976; Urbana, Ill., March 5, 1977); Concerto for Strings (N.Y., Dec. 5, 1977); *Skating on the Sheyenne* for Band (1977; N.Y., May 20, 1978). **CHAMBER:** 3 violin sonatas (1934, 1951, 1955); 8 string quartets (1935–60); 2 viola sonatas (1937, 1953); 2 piano trios (1938, 1954); Piano Quartet (1948); Cello Sonata No. 2 (1950); 2 piano quintets (1953, 1961); *Chromatic Fantasy* for Cello (1957); String Quintet (1958); *Fantasy in 2 Movements* for

Violin (Brussels, June 1, 1958); *Divertissement* for Piano, Clarinet, Violin, and Cello (1964); *3 Studies in 4* for 4 Percussionists (1965); *2 Acts for 3 Players* for Clarinet, Percussion, and Piano (1970); *2 Ballades* for Flute and Piano (1973); *Tubes I* for 1 to 5 Trombones (1974); Quartet for Oboe, Cello, Percussion, and Piano (1979); *2 Studies* for Saxophones and Piano (1981); solo pieces. **PIANO:** 5 sonatas (1933–61); *Fantasy* (1939); *Nostalgic Waltzes* (1947); *Variations on a Theme by Alban Berg* (1952); *Sonata quasi una fantasia* (1961); *Waltz* (1977); *Lost Whale Calf* (1980); *Youth's Companion* (1980); *Narrative in Retrospect* (1983). **VOCAL:** *Pilgrim Psalms* for Chorus (1945); *Spherical Madrigals* for Chorus (1947); *Immortal Autumn* for Tenor and Chorus (1952); *Edge of Shadow* for Chorus and Orch. (1959); *Earthrise: A Trilogy Concerned with the Human Dilemma: 1, Still Are New Worlds* for Baritone, Chorus, Tape, and Orch. (1962; Ann Arbor, Mich., May 10, 1963), *2, The Martyr's Elegy* for High Voice, Chorus, and Orch. (Ann Arbor, Mich., April 23, 1967), and *3, Earthrise* for Soloists, Chorus, and Orch. (1978; Ann Arbor, Mich., Dec. 11, 1979); *The Remorseless Rush of Time* for Chorus and Orch. (1969; River Falls, Wis., April 23, 1970).

BIBL.: P. Cooper, "The Music of R.L. F.," *Musical Quarterly* (Jan. 1967); D. Amman, *The Choral Music of R.L. F.* (diss., Univ. of Cincinnati, 1972); E. Borroff, *Three American Composers* (1986).

Finney, Theodore M(itchell), American music educator, brother of **Ross Lee Finney;** b. Fayette, Iowa, March 14, 1902; d. Pittsburgh, May 19, 1978. He studied with Donald Ferguson at the Univ. of Minnesota (B.A., 1924), at the American Cons. in Fontainbleau (1926), at the Stern Cons. and the Univ. of Berlin (1927–28), and at the Univ. of Pittsburgh (Litt.M., 1938). After serving as a violist in the Minneapolis Sym. Orch. (1923–25), he was an assistant prof. of music at Carleton College (1925–32) and a lecturer at the Smith College Summer School (1930–32); subsequently he was a prof. and chairman of the music dept. at the Univ. of Pittsburgh (1936–68).

WRITINGS: *A History of Music* (N.Y., 1935; 2nd ed., rev., 1947); *Hearing Music: A Guide to Music* (N.Y., 1941); *We Have Made Music* (Pittsburgh, 1955); *A Union Catalogue of Music and Books on Music Printed before 1801 in Pittsburgh Libraries* (Pittsburgh, 1959; 2nd ed., 1963; supplement, 1964).

Finnie, Linda, Scottish mezzo-soprano; b. Paisley, May 9, 1952. She was a student of Winifred Busfield at the Royal Scottish Academy of Music in Glasgow. In 1976 she made her operatic debut with Glasgow's Scottish Opera. In 1977 she won the Kathleen Ferrier Prize at the 's-Hertogenbosch Competition in the Netherlands, and then pursued successful engagements in both opera and concert. In 1979 she became a member of the Welsh National Opera in Cardiff; also appeared as a guest artist in London with the English National Opera and at Covent Garden. In 1986 she was a soloist in Mahler's 8th Sym. at the London Promenade Concerts and in Verdi's *Requiem* in Chicago; in 1988, made her first appearance at the Bayreuth Festival. In 1995 she sang in the *Ring* cycle at the Vienna State Opera. Among her prominent operatic roles are Amneris, Eboli, Ortrud, Brangäne, Fricka, and Waltraute. Her concert repertoire extends from Handel to Prokofiev.

BIBL.: B. Brand, ed., *E. F.* (Berlin, 1991).

Finnilä, Birgit, Swedish contralto; b. Falkenberg, Jan. 20, 1931. She studied with I. Linden in Göteborg and with Roy Henderson at the Royal Academy of Music in London. In 1963 she made her formal concert debut in Göteborg, and then sang regularly in her homeland. After making her London debut in 1966, she sang in Germany. In 1967 she made her operatic debut as Gluck's Orfeo in Göteborg. In 1968 she toured North America, and then appeared in many of the major European music centers. She was active principally as a concert artist, appearing as a soloist with the major orchs. and as a recitalist.

Finnissy, Michael (Peter), English composer; b. London, March 17, 1946. He studied composition with Stevens and Searle at the Royal College of Music in London (1964–66) and with Roman Vlad in Rome. In 1969 he organized the music dept. of the London School of Contemporary Dance, where he taught until 1974; later he taught at Winchester College (from 1987), the Univ. of Sussex (from 1989), and at the Royal Academy of Music in London (from 1991). He served as president of the ISCM from 1991 to 1996.

WORKS: MUSIC THEATER: *Mysteries,* in 8 parts, for Vocal and Instrumental Forces, some with Dancers and Mimes: *1, The Parting of Darkness from Light; 2, The Earthly Paradise; 3, The Great Flood; 4, The Prophecy of Daniel; 5, The Parliament of Heaven; 6, The Annunciation; 7, The Betrayal and Crucifixion of Jesus of Nazareth; 8, The Deliverance of Souls* (1972–79); *Circle, Chorus, and Formal Act* for Baritone, Women's Chorus, Percussion, Chorus, 6 Sword Dancers, 4 Mimes, and Small Ensemble (1973); *Mr. Punch* for Speaker, 5 Instruments, and Percussion (1976–77); *Vaudeville* for Mezzo-soprano, Baritone, 2 Mimes, 6 Instruments, and Percussion (1983); *The Undivine Comedy,* opera for 5 Singers and 9 Instruments (1988). **ORCH.:** *Song II* and *IV* (1963–69); *Song X* (1968–75); piano concertos: No. 1 (1975; rev. 1983–84), No. 2 (1975–76; Saintes, France, July 15, 1977), No. 3 (1978), and No. 7 (1981); *Offshore* (1975–76); *Pathways of Sun and Stars* (London, Nov. 15, 1976); *Alongside* for Small Orch. (1979); *Sea and Sky* (1979–80); *Red Earth* (London, Aug. 2, 1988); *Eph-Phatha* (1988–89; Northampton, May 2, 1989). **INSTRUMENTAL ENSEMBLE:** *As when upon a tranced summer night* for 3 Cellos, 2 Pianos, and 2 Percussion (1966–68); *Transformations of the Vampire* for Clarinet, Violin, Viola, and 3 Percussion (1968–71); *Evening* for 6 Instruments and Percussion (1974); *Long Distance* for Piano and 14 Instruments (1977–78); *Keroiylu* for Oboe, Bassoon, and Piano (1981); *Banumbirr* for Flute, Clarinet, Violin, Cello, and Piano (1982); *Australian Sea Shanties II* for Recorder Consort (1983); *Câtana* for 8 Instruments and Percussion (1984); String Quartet (1984); String Trio (1986); *Obrecht Motetten I* for 9 Instruments (1988), *II* for 3 Instruments (1989), and *IV* for Brass Quintet (1990). **VOCAL:** *From the Revelations of St. John the Divine* for Soprano, Flute, and String Sextet (1965–70); *Jeanne d'Arc* for Soprano, Tenor, Cello, and Small Orch. (1967–71); *World* for 2 Sopranos, Contralto, Tenor, Baritone, Bass, and Orch. (1968–74); Piano Concerto No. 5 for Piano, Mezzo-soprano, and Ensemble (1980); *Ngano* for Mezzo-soprano, Tenor, Chorus, Flute, and 2 Percussion (1983–84; London, June 12, 1984); *Celi* for 2 Sopranos, Flute, Oboe, Bass Trombone, and Double Bass (1984); *Haiyim* for Chorus and 2 Cellos (1984; London, March 15, 1985); *The Battle of Malden* for Baritone, Chorus, and Small Ensemble (1990–91).

BIBL.: A. Clements, "F.'s Undivine Comedy," *Musical Times* (July 1988).

Finscher, Ludwig, distinguished German musicologist; b. Kassel, March 14, 1930. He was a student of Gerber at the Univ. of Göttingen (Ph.D., 1954, with the diss. *Die Messen und Motetten Loyset Compères*; publ. as *Loyset Compère (c.1450–1518): Life and Works* in Musicological Studies and Documents, XII, 1964), completing his Habilitation at the Univ. of Saarbrücken in 1967 with his *Das klassische Streichquartett und seine Grundlegung durch Joseph Haydn* (publ. as *Studien zur Geschichte des Streichquartetts: I, Die Entstehung des klassischen Streichquartetts: Von den Vorformen zur Grundlegung durch Joseph Haydn,* Kassel, 1974). He was assistant lecturer at the inst. of musicology at the Univ. of Kiel (1960–65), and then at the Univ. of Saarbrücken (1965–68). After serving as prof. of musicology at the Univ. of Frankfurt am Main (1968–81), he held that position at the Univ. of Heidelberg (from 1981). He was ed. (1961–68) and co-ed. (1968–74) of *Die Musikforschung.* Finscher served as president of the Gesellschaft für Musikforschung (1974–77), and also was vice-president (1972–77) and president (1977–82) of the International Musicological Soc. He ed. the complete musical works of Gaffurius in the Corpus Mensurabilis Musicae series (2 vos., 1955, 1960), and a collected edition of the works of Compère in the same series (4 vols., 1958–72); with K. von Fischer, he ed. the complete works of Hindemith (Mainz, 1976 et seq.). He also ed. (with F. Blume et al.) *Geschichte der Evangelischen Kirchenmusik* (Kassel, 2nd ed., 1965; Eng. tr., aug., 1974 as *Protestant Church Music: A History*), *Quellenstudien zu Musik der Renaissance* (2 vols., Munich, 1981, Wiesbaden, 1983), *Ludwig van Beethoven* (Darmstadt, 1983), *Die Musik des 15. und 16. Jahrhunderts* (Laaber, 1989 et seq.), and *Die Mannheimer Hofkapelle im Zeitalter Carl Theodors* (Mannheim, 1992). Finscher holds the prestigious position of editor of the exhaustive revision of *Die Musik in Geschichte und Gegenwart*, which commenced publication in 1994. It is anticipated that when it is completed in 2004, it will consist of 20 vols.

Finzi, Gerald (Raphael), gifted English composer; b. London, July 14, 1901; d. Oxford, Sept. 27, 1956. After training with Ernest Farrar in Harrogate (1914–16) and Edward Bairstow in York (1917–22), he studied counterpoint with R.O. Morris in London (1925). From 1930 to 1933 he taught composition at the Royal Academy of Music in London. In 1940 he founded the Newbury String Players, which he conducted in varied programs, including music of 18th-century English composers. During World War II, he worked in the Ministry of War Transport (1941–45). He also made his home a haven for German and Czech refugees. In 1951 he was stricken with Hodgkin's disease, but he continued to pursue his activities until his death. While the influence of Parry, Elgar, and Vaughan Williams may be discerned in some of his works, he found a distinctive style which is reflected in a fine body of orch. and vocal scores. Among his most notable works are the Concerto for Clarinet and Strings, the Cello Concerto, the cantata *Dies Natalis*, the *Intimations of Immortality* for Tenor, Chorus, and Orch., and *For St. Cecilia* for Tenor Chorus, and Orch.

WORKS: DRAMATIC: *Love's Labours Lost*, incidental music to Shakespeare's play (BBC, Dec. 16, 1946; orch. suite, 1952, 1955; 1st complete perf., BBC, July 26, 1955). **ORCH.:** *Prelude* for Strings (1920s; Stockcross, Berks, April 27, 1957); *A Severn Rhapsody* for Chamber Orch. (1923; Bournemouth, June 4, 1924); *Introit* for Violin and Small Orch. (1925; 1st perf. as the 2nd movement of a Violin Concerto, later withdrawn, London, May 4, 1927; 1st perf. as a separate work, London, Jan. 31, 1933; rev. 1942); *New Year Music (Nocturne)* (1926; Bournemouth, March 16, 1932; rev. 1940s); *Eclogue* for Piano and Strings (late 1920s; rev. late 1940s; London, Jan. 27, 1957); *Fantasia* for Piano and Orch. (c.1928; rev. version as *Grand Fantasia and Toccata*, Newbury, Dec. 9, 1953); *The Fall of the Leaf (Elegy)* (1929; rev. 1939–41; orchestration completed by H. Ferguson; Manchester, Dec. 11, 1957); *Interlude* for Oboe and Strings (1932–36; also for Oboe and String Quartet); Concerto for Clarinet and Strings (1948–49; Hereford, Sept. 9, 1949); Cello Concerto (1951–52, 1954–55; Cheltenham, July 19, 1955). **CHAMBER:** *Interlude* for Oboe and String Quartet (1932–36; London, March 24, 1936; also for Oboe and String Orch.); *Prelude and Fugue* for String Trio (1938; Brimingham, May 13, 1941); *5 Bagatelles* for Clarinet and Piano (1938–43; London, Jan. 15, 1943; arranged for Symphonic Wind Band by B. Wiggins, 1984, and for Clarinet and String Orch. by L. Ashmore, 1992); *Elegy* for Violin and Piano (1940; London, Dec. 1954). **VOCAL:** (10) *Children's Songs* for Chorus and Piano (1920–21); *By Footpath and Stile*, song-cycle for Baritone and String Quartet (1921–22; London, Oct. 14, 1923; rev. 1941); *To a Poet*, 6 songs for Low Voice and Piano (1920s–56; London, Feb. 20, 1959); *Oh Fair to See*, 7 songs for High Voice and Piano (1921–56; London, Nov. 8, 1965); *Requiem da camera* for Baritone, Chorus, and Orch. (1924; London, June 7, 1990); *Farewell to Arms* for Voice and Small Orch. or Strings (c.1925, 1944; Manchester, March 30, 1945); *2 Sonnets* for Tenor or Soprano and Small Orch. (c.1925; London, Feb. 6, 1936); *Dies natalis*, cantata for Tenor or Soprano and Strings (c.1925, 1938–39; London, Jan. 26, 1940); *3 Short Elegies* for Chorus (1926; BBC, March 23, 1936); *A Young Man's Exhortation*, 10 songs for Tenor and Piano (1926–29; London, Dec. 5, 1933); *Till Earth Outwears*, 7 songs for High Voice and Piano (1927–56; London, Feb. 21, 1958); *Earth and Air and Rain*, 10 songs for Baritone and Piano (1928–32; London, July 2, 1945); *I Said to Love*, 6 songs for Baritone and Piano (1928–56; London, Jan. 27, 1957); *Let Us Garlands Bring*, 5 songs for Baritone and Piano (1929–42; London, Oct. 12, 1942; also for Baritone and Strings, BBC, Oct. 18, 1942); *Before and After Summer*, 10 songs for Baritone and Piano (1932–49); *7 Unaccompanied Part Songs* (1934–37; BBC, Dec. 29, 1938); *Intimations of Immortality*, ode for Tenor, Chorus, and Orch. (c.1938, 1949–50; Gloucester, Sept. 5, 1950); *Lo, the full, final sacrifice*, festival anthem for Chorus and Organ (Northampton, Sept. 21, 1946; also for Chorus and Orch., Gloucester, Sept. 12, 1947); *For St. Cecilia*, ceremonial ode for Tenor, Chorus, and Orch. (1946–47; London, Nov. 22, 1947); *My lovely one*, anthem for Chorus and Orch. (1947); *Muses and Graces* for Soprano or Treble Voices and Piano or Strings (Northamptonshire, June 10, 1950); *God is gone up*, anthem for Chorus and Organ (Holborn Viaduct, Nov. 22, 1951; arranged for Chorus, Organ, and Strings by W. Godfree, London, May 20, 1952); *Thou didst delight my eyes* for Men's Chorus (1951); *All this night*, motet for Chorus (London, Dec. 6, 1951); *Let us now praise famous men* for Tenors or Sopranos, Basses or Contraltos, and Strings (1951; also with piano, 1952); *Magnificat* for Chorus and Organ (Northampton, Mass., Dec. 12, 1952; also for Soloists ad libitum, Chorus, and Orch., Bromley, May 12, 1956); *White-flowering days* for Chorus (1952–53; London, June 2, 1953); *Welcome sweet and sacred feast*, anthem for Chorus and Organ (BBC, Oct. 11, 1953); *In terra pax*, Christmas scene for Soprano, Baritone, Chorus, and Orch. (1954; BBC, Feb. 27, 1955; rev. version, Gloucester, Sept. 6, 1956).

Finzi, Graciane, French composer; b. Casablanca, Morocco, July 10, 1945. She entered the Paris Cons. in 1955 and studied with Joseph Benvenuti (piano) and Barraine and Aubin (theory), taking premiers prix in harmony (1962), counterpoint and fugue (1964), and composition (1969). After organizing music festivals in Casablanca, she became a prof. at the Paris Cons. in 1979.

WORKS: DRAMATIC: *Songs* for 3 Dancers and Instruments (1975); *Avis de recherche*, music theater (1981); *3 Opéras drôles* (1984); *Pauvre Assassin*, opera (1987; Strasbourg, Jan. 1992). **ORCH.:** *Édifice*, violin concerto (1976); *De la terre à la vie* for Clarinet and Strings (1979); *Il était tant de fois*, cello concerto (1979); *Trames* for 26 Instruments (1981); Concerto for 2 Violins and Orch. (1981); *Soleil vert* (1984); *Cadenza*, bassoon concerto (1987); Concerto for Flute, Harp, and Orch. (1989); *Univers de lumière*, symphonic poem for Reciter and Orch. (1990–91; Seville, Sept. 30, 1992). **CHAMBER:** *Toujours plus* for Organ and Harpsichord (1975); *4 Études* for String Quartet (1976); Saxophone Quartet (1982); *Free-Quartet* for Piano Quartet (1984) and *II* for Oboe, English Horn, Bassoon, and Harpsichord (1988); *Phobie* for Violin (1990); *Ainsi la vie* for Viola (1991); *Engrenage* for Brass Quintet (1992); *Interférences* for String Sextet (1992). **VOCAL:** *Processus I* for Soprano, Flute, Cello, and Piano (1972) and *II* for Voice and Double Bass (1986); *Quand les étoiles* for 6 Voices (1990).

Firkušný, Rudolf, eminent Czech-born American pianist and pedagogue; b. Napajedla, Feb. 11, 1912; d. Staatsburg, N.Y., July 19, 1994. He studied composition privately with Janáček in 1919 and piano with Růzena Kurzová at the Brno Cons. (1920–27); also attended the Univ. of Brno. His further instructors were Vilém Kurz and Rudolf Karel (theory) at the Prague Cons., Suk (composition; 1929–30), and Artur Schnabel in N.Y. (1932). He made his debut as a child pianist in Prague on June 14, 1920, playing a Mozart piano concerto. He first performed in London in 1933; on Jan. 13, 1938, he made his U.S. debut in N.Y., where he settled in 1940 and became a naturalized citizen. In 1943–44 he made a tour of Latin America and in 1946 participated in the Prague Festival; in subsequent years he also toured Europe, Israel, and Australia. After an absence of 44 years, he again played in Prague in 1990 as soloist in Martinů's 2nd Piano Concerto. His interpretations of the standard piano literature were greatly esteemed. Firkušný was a champion of the music of

Janáček; he also gave the first performances of Martin's 3rd (Dallas, Nov. 20, 1949) and 4th (N.Y., Oct. 4, 1956) piano concertos. He likewise gave the first performances of piano concertos of Menotti (No. 1; Boston, Nov. 2, 1945) and Howard Hanson (Boston, Dec. 31, 1948). His technical equipment was of the highest caliber; his lyrical talent enhanced his virtuosity. He was also a composer; he wrote a Piano Concerto, a String Quartet, and a number of attractive piano études and miniatures. In 1979 he began publication, with the violinist Rafael Druian, of a complete ed. of the Mozart violin sonatas. An excellent teacher, Firkušný gave master classes at the Juilliard School of Music in N.Y. and at the Aspen Music School in Colorado.

Firsova, Elena (Olegovna), Russian composer; b. Leningrad, March 21, 1950. She was a student of Pirumov (composition) and Kholopov (analysis) at the Moscow Cons. (1970–75); also profited from further studies with Denisov. From 1979 her works were heard abroad. In 1993 she became a prof. and composer-in-residence at the Univ. of Keele in England. In 1972 she married **Dmitri Smirnov**. In her works, she has developed an intimate style notable for its poetic handling of both harmony and melody.

WORKS: OPERAS: *Feast in Plague Time*, chamber opera (1972); *The Nightingale and the Rose* (1991). **ORCH.:** *5 Pieces* (1971); *Chamber Music* for Strings (1973); 2 cello concertos: No. 1 (1973; Moscow, June 10, 1975) and No. 2, as *Chamber Concerto No. 2* (Moscow, Oct. 17, 1982); *Stanzas* (1975); 2 violin concertos (1976, 1983); *Postlude* for Harp and Orch. (1977; Moscow, Feb. 22, 1978); *Chamber Concerto No. 1* for Flute and Strings (1978; Moscow, March 10, 1980), *No. 3* for Piano and Orch. (1985), and *No. 4* (1988); *Autumn Music* for Chamber Orch. (1988); *Nostalgia* (1989); *Cassandra* (1992). **CHAMBER:** *Scherzo* for Flute, Oboe, Clarinet, Bassoon, and Piano (1967); 7 string quartets (1970, 1974, 1980, 1989, 1992, 1994, 1995); Cello Sonata (1971); 2 Piano Trios (1972, 1993); *Capriccio* for Flute and Saxophone Quartet (1976); Sonata for Solo Clarinet (1976); *3 Pieces* for Xylophone (1978); *Sphinx* for Harp (1982); *Spring Sonata* for Flute and Piano (1982); *Mysteria* for Organ and 4 Percussion (1984); *Music for 12* (1986); *Monologue* for Bassoon (1989); *Odyssey* for 7 Players (1990); *Verdehr-Terzett* for Violin, Clarinet, and Piano (1990); *Far Away* for Saxophone Quartet (1991); *Meditation in the Japanese Garden* for Flute, Viola, and Piano (1992); *You and I* for Cello and Piano (1992); *Starry Flute* for Flute (1992); *Vigilia* for Violin and Piano (1992); *Otzvuki* for Flute and Guitar (1992); *Phantom* for 4 Viols (1993); *Monologue* for Alto Saxophone (1994). **VOCAL:** *3 Poems by Osip Mandelstam* for Chorus (1970); *Petrarca's Sonnets* for Voice and 8 Instruments (1976); *The Bell* for Chorus (1976; in collaboration with D. Smirnov); *Night* for Voice and Saxophone Quartet (1978); *Tristia* for Voice and Chamber Orch. (1979); *Shakespeare's Sonnets* for Voice and Organ (1981); *The Stone* for Voice and Orch. (1983); *Earthly Life* for Soprano and 10 Instruments (1986); *Augury* for Chorus and Orch. (1988); *Stygian Song* for Soprano and Ensemble (1989); *7 Haiku* for Voice and Lyre (1991); *Sea Shell* for Voice and Ensemble (1991); *Whirlpool* for Voice, Flute, and Percussion (1991); *Silentium* for Voice and String Quartet (1991); *Secret Way* for Voice and Orch. (1992); *Distance* for Voice and Ensemble (1992).

Fischer, Ádám, Hungarian conductor, brother of **Iván Fischer**; b. Budapest, Sept. 9, 1949. He studied at the Béla Bartók Cons. in Budapest, later taking conducting courses with Swarowsky at the Vienna Academy of Music and with Ferrara in Venice and Siena (1970–71). In 1973 he won 1st prize in the Cantelli Competition in Milan. He was conductor of the Finnish National Opera in Helsinki (1974–77), first conductor at the Karlsruhe Opera (1977–78), and Generalmusikdirektor in Freiburg im Breisgau (1981–83) and in Kassel (from 1987); he also was music director of the Austro-Hungarian Haydn Festival in Eisenstadt. In 1989 he made his debut at London's Covent Garden.

Fischer, Annie (actually, **Anny**), distinguished Hungarian pianist; b. Budapest, July 5, 1914; d. there, April 11, 1995. She attended the Franz Liszt Academy of Music in Budapest and also was a pupil of Székely and Dohnányi. At the age of 8, she made her first public appearance in Budapest as soloist in Beethoven's 1st Piano Concerto. Her formal debut followed in Zürich in 1926. After winning 1st prize in the Liszt Competition in Budapest in 1933, she performed throughout Europe until World War II forced her to seek refuge in Sweden. After the War, she pursued an international career as a soloist with orchs. and as a recitalist. She was widely admired for her patrician interpretations of Mozart, Beethoven, and Schubert. In 1937 she married **Aladár Tóth.**

Fischer, Edwin, eminent Swiss pianist, conductor, and pedagogue; b. Basel, Oct. 6, 1886; d. Zürich, Jan. 24, 1960. He was a pupil of Hans Huber at the Basel Cons. (1896–1904) before pursuing his studies with Martin Krause at the Stern Cons. in Berlin (1904–05), where he subsequently was a faculty member (1905–14). He was conductor of the Lübeck Musikverein (1926–28) and the Munich Bachverein (1928–32) before founding his own chamber orch. in Berlin, which he regularly conducted from the keyboard; he also taught at the Hochschule für Musik there (from 1931). In 1942 he returned to his homeland, where he played in a noted trio with Kulenkampff (later succeeded by Schneiderhan) and Mainardi. From 1945 to 1958 he gave master classes in Lucerne. Although his interpretations were securely rooted in the Romantic tradition, he eschewed the role of the virtuoso in order to probe the intellectual content of the score at hand. He ed. works by Bach, Mozart, and Beethoven, composers he championed. Among his books were *J.S. Bach* (Potsdam, 1945), *Musikalische Betrachtungen* (Wiesbaden, 1949; Eng. tr., 1951, as *Reflections on Music*), *Ludwig van Beethovens Klaviersonaten* (Wiesbaden, 1956; Eng. tr., 1959), and *Von den Aufgaben des Musikers* (Wiesbaden, 1960).

BIBL.: B. Gavoty and R. Hauert, *E.F.* (Geneva and Monaco, 1954); H. Haid, ed., *Dank an E.F.* (Wiesbaden, 1962).

Fischer, György, Hungarian-born Austrian conductor and pianist; b. Budapest, Aug. 12, 1935. He received training at the Franz Liszt Academy of Music in Budapest and at the Salzburg Mozarteum. After working as an assistant to Karajan at the Vienna State Opera, where he conducted works by Mozart, he was active as a conductor at the Cologne Opera (from 1973). In 1973 he made his British debut conducting *Die Zauberflöte* with the Welsh National Opera in Cardiff; made his London debut conducting *Mitridate* in 1979. From 1980 he appeared as a conductor with the English Chamber Orch. in London; also conducted widely in other European music centers, as well as in North and South America, and in Australia. As a piano accompanist, he toured the world with many outstanding artists. For a time he was married to **Lucia Popp**.

Fischer, Irwin, American composer, teacher, and conductor; b. Iowa City, July 5, 1903; d. Wilmette, Ill., May 7, 1977. He graduated in 1924 from the Univ. of Chicago; studied organ with Middelschulte, piano with Robyn, and composition with Weidig at the American Cons. in Chicago (M.M., 1930); later studied composition briefly with Boulanger in Paris (1931) and Kodály in Budapest (1936); took lessons in conducting with Paumgartner and Malko at the Salzburg Mozarteum (1937). In 1928 he joined the faculty of the American Cons. in Chicago, becoming its dean in 1974; he also conducted several community orchs. As a composer, he held fast to tonal techniques. In the 1930s he developed a polytonal technique, which he described as biplanal, and from 1960 he utilized serialism.

WORKS: ORCH.: *Rhapsody of French Folk Tunes* (1933); Piano Concerto (1935; Chicago, Feb. 23, 1936); *Marco Polo*, fantasy overture (1937); *Hungarian Set* (1938); *Lament* for Cello and Orch. (1938); *Chorale Fantasy* for Organ and Orch. (1940); Sym. No. 1 (1943); *Variations on an Original Theme* (1950); *Legend* (1956); *Poem* for Violin and Orch. (1959); *Passacaglia and Fugue* (1961); *Overture on an Exuberant Tone Row* (1964–65); *Short Symphony* (1970–71; Hinsdale, April 16, 1972; orchestration of Piano Sonata); *Concerto giocoso* for Clarinet and Orch. (1971; Hinsdale, Jan. 21, 1973). **CHAMBER:** *Divertimento* for Flute, Clarinet, Bassoon, Horn, Trumpet, Violin, Cello, and Double Bass (1963); *Fanfare* for Brass and Percussion (1976). **PIANO:** *Introduction and Triple Fugue* (1929); *Rhapsody* (1940); Sonata (1960). **VOCAL:** *5 Symphonic Psalms* for Soprano, Chorus, and Orch. (1967); *Orchestral Adventures of a Little Tune* for Narrator and Orch. (1974; Chicago, Nov. 16, 1974); *Statement 1976* for Soprano, Chorus, Brass, Strings, and Percussion (New Haven, April 25, 1976); choruses; songs.

BIBL.: E. Borroff, *Three American Composers* (1986).

Fischer, Iván, Hungarian conductor, brother of **Ádám Fischer**; b. Budapest, Jan. 20, 1951. He studied cello and composition at the Béla Bartók Cons. in Budapest (1965–70); then took lessons in conducting with Swarowsky at the Vienna Academy of Music and with Harnoncourt in Salzburg. During the 1975–76 season, he conducted concerts in Milan, Florence, Vienna, and Budapest; beginning in 1976, he filled engagements with the BBC Sym. Orch. in London and the BBC regional orchs. From 1979 to 1982 he was co-conductor of the Northern Sinfonia Orch. in Newcastle upon Tyne. In 1983 he became music director of the Budapest Festival Orch. Also in 1983 he made his first appearance in the U.S. as a guest conductor with the Los Angeles Phil. He was music director of the Kent Opera (1984–88), and then its artistic director. From 1989 he was principal guest conductor of the Cincinnati Sym. Orch.

Fischer, Jan (Frank), Czech composer; b. Louny, Sept. 15, 1921. He studied at the Prague Cons. (1940–45) and took lessons in composition from Rídký at the master class there (1945–48); also attended the Charles Univ. in Prague (1945–48), where he later received his Ph.D. (1990). He won prizes from the city of Prague (1966) and the Guild of Composers (1986). His music occupies the safe ground of Central European Romanticism, not without some audacious exploits in euphonious dissonance.

WORKS: DRAMATIC: OPERAS: *Ženichové* (Bridegrooms; 1956; Brno, Oct. 13, 1957); *Romeo, Julie a tma* (Romeo, Juliet, and Darkness; 1959–61; Brno, Sept. 14, 1962); *Oh, Mr. Fogg*, comic chamber opera after Jules Verne's *Around the World in 80 Days* (1967–70; Saarbrücken, June 27, 1971); *Miracle Theater*, radio opera (1970); *Decamerone*, chamber opera (1975–76); *Copernicus* (1981); *Rites* (1990). **BALLETS:** *Eufrosyne* (1951); *Le Marionnettists* (1978). **ORCH.:** *Pastoral Sinfonietta* (1944); Viola Concerto (1946); *Essay* for Piano and Jazz Orch. (1947); *Popular Suite* for Piano and Wind Orch. (1950); *Dance Suite* (1957); *Fantasia* for Piano and Orch. (1953); Sym. No. 1, *Monothematic* (1959); Clarinet Concerto (1965); *Obrazy* (Pictures) *I* (1970), *II* (1973), and *III* (1977); Harp Concerto (1972); *Tryzna* (Commemoration; 1973); *Večerní hudba* (Night Music) for Strings (1973); *Concerto for Orchestra* (1980); *Partita* for Strings (1982). **CHAMBER:** Flute Sonata (1944); Suite for Wind Sextet (1944); Suite for English Horn and Piano (1945); *Ballada* for String Quartet and Clarinet (1949); Piano Quintet (1949); *Ut stellae* for Soprano, 2 Pianos, Flute, Bass Clarinet, Percussion, and Tape (1966); *Amoroso* for Clarinet and Piano (1970); Wind Quintet (1971); *4 Studies* for Harp (1971); *Conversation with Harp*, quintet for Flute, Violin, Viola, Cello, and Harp (1979); *A Fairy Tale* for Harp and Flute (1979); Brass Quintet (1983); *Prague Preludes* for 5 Harps (1983); Duet for 2 Harps (1986); *Lyric Rhapsody* for Viola and Piano (1987); *Hommage à Bohuslav Martinů*, suite for Flute and Harp (1988); *Monologues* for Harp (1991); *Cante Hondo* for Flute and Guitar (1992); *Due pezzi per amici* for Bass Clarinet and Piano (1992).

Fischer, Kurt von, distinguished Swiss musicologist; b. Bern, April 25, 1913. He studied piano with Hirt and Marek at the Bern Cons. and musicology with Kurth and Gurlitt at the Univ. of Bern (Ph.D., 1938, with the diss. *Griegs Harmonik und die nordländische Folklore*; publ. in Bern, 1938; Habilitationsschrift, 1948, *Die Beziehungen von Form und Motiv in Beethovens Instrumentalwerken*; publ. in Strasbourg, 1948; 2nd ed., 1972). After teaching piano at the Bern Cons. (1939–57) and musicology at the Univ. of Bern (1948–57), he was prof. of musicology at the Univ. of Zürich (1957–79). In 1965 he became co-ed. of the *Archiv für Musikwissenschaft*. From 1967 to 1972 he was president of the International Musicological Soc. He was general ed. of the series Polyphonic Music of the 14th Century from 1977 to 1992. From 1979 to 1987 he was president of the commission of the Répertoire International des Sources Musicales. He was honored with Feschriften on his 60th (1973), 70th (1983), and 80th (1993) birthdays. In 1980 he was made a corresponding member of the American Musicological Soc.

WRITINGS: *Die Variation* (Cologne, 1956; Eng. tr., 1962); *Studien zur italienischen Musik des Trecento und frühen Quattrocento* (Bern, 1956); *Der Begriff des "Neuens" in der Musik von der Ars nova bis zur Gegenwart* (N.Y., 1961); *Die Passion von ihren Anfangen bis ins 16. Jahrhundert* (Bern and Munich, 1973); *Arthur Honegger* (Zürich, 1977); T. Evans, ed., and C. Skoggard, tr., *Essays in Musicology* (N.Y., 1989); *E. Schmid* (Zürich, 1992).

Fischer, Res (actually, **Maria Theresia**), German contralto; b. Berlin, Nov. 8, 1896; d. Stuttgart, Oct. 4, 1974. She studied in Stuttgart and Prague; then took lessons in Berlin with Lilli Lehmann. She made her debut in 1927 in Basel, where she sang until 1935; then appeared with the Frankfurt am Main Opera (1935–41); in 1941 she joined the Stuttgart Opera, remaining on its roster until 1961; was made its honorary member in 1965. She also sang at the festivals of Salzburg and Bayreuth, and with the state operas in Vienna, Hamburg, and Munich. She created the title role in Orff's *Antigonae* (Salzburg, 1949) and sang in the first performance of Wagner-Régeny's *Bergwerk von Falun* (Salzburg, 1961).

Fischer, Wilhelm (Robert), eminent Austrian musicologist; b. Vienna, April 19, 1886; d. Innsbruck, Feb. 26, 1962. He studied with Guido Adler at the Univ. of Vienna, where he received his Ph.D. with the diss. *Matthias Georg Monn als Instrumentalkomponist* in 1912; he completed his Habilitation there with his *Zur Entwicklungsgeschichte des Wiener klassischen Stils* in 1915. He joined the faculty of the Univ. of Vienna in 1919; subsequently was lecturer in musicology at the Univ. of Innsbruck from 1928 until the Anschluss of 1938, when he was conscripted as a forced laborer; after World War II, he was restored to the faculty of the Univ. of Innsbruck as a prof., serving there from 1948 until his retirement in 1961. In 1951 he was elected president of the Central Inst. of Mozart Research at the Mozarteum in Salzburg. He publ. numerous essays on Mozart and other Classical composers; wrote the valuable study "Geschichte der Instrumentalmusik 1450 bis 1880" for Adler's *Handbuch der Musikgeschichte* (Frankfurt am Main, 1924; 2nd ed., rev., 1930).

Fischer-Dieskau, (Albert) Dietrich, celebrated German baritone; b. Berlin, May 28, 1925. The surname of the family was originally Fischer; his paternal grandmother's maiden surname of Dieskau was legally conjoined to it in 1937. His father, a philologist and headmaster, was self-taught in music; his mother was an amateur pianist. He began to study piano at 9, and voice at 16; he then studied voice with Hermann Weissenborn at the Berlin Hochschule für Musik (1942–43). In 1943 he was drafted into the German army. He was made a prisoner of war by the Americans while serving in Italy in 1945; upon his release in 1947, he returned to Germany and made his first professional appearance as a soloist in the Brahms *Requiem* in Müllheim. He continued his vocal training with Weissenborn in Berlin, where he soon was heard on radio broadcasts over the RIAS. On May 6, 1948, he made his operatic debut in the bass role of Colas in an RIAS broadcast of Mozart's *Bastien und Bastienne*. On Nov. 18, 1948, he made his stage debut as Rodrigo, Marquis of Posa, in *Don Carlos* at the Berlin Städtische Oper, where he remained an invaluable member for 35 years. He also pursued his operatic career with appearances at leading opera houses and festivals in Europe. It was as a lieder and concert artist, however, that Fischer-Dieskau became universally known. On April 5, 1955, he made his U.S. debut with the Cincinnati Sym. Orch.; his U.S. recital debut followed at N.Y.'s Town Hall on May 2, 1955. In subsequent years, he made tours all over the world to enormous critical acclaim. On Dec. 31, 1992, he gave his farewell stage performance in Munich. However, he made occasional appearances as a conductor. His finest operatic roles included Count Almaviva, Don Giovanni, Papageno, Macbeth, Falstaff, Hans Sachs, Mandryka, Mathis der Maler, and Wozzeck. He created the role of Mittenhofer in Henze's *Elegy for Young Lovers* (1961) and the title role in Reimann's *Lear* (1978). His honors include membership in the Berlin Akademie der Künste (1956), the Mozart Medal of Vienna (1962), Kammersänger of Berlin (1963), the Grand Cross of Merit of the Federal Republic of Germany (1978), honorary doctorates from the Univ. of Oxford (1978) and the Sorbonne in Paris (1980), and the Gold Medal of the Royal Phil. Soc. of London (1988). In 1978 he married his 4th wife, **Julia Varady**.

WRITINGS: *Texte deutscher Lieder: Ein Handbuch* (Munich, 1968; 7th ed., 1986; Eng. tr., 1976, as *The Fischer-Dieskau Book of Lieder*); *Auf den Spuren der Schubert-Lieder: Werden-Wesen-Wirkung* (Wiesbaden, 1971; Eng. tr., 1976, as *Schubert: A Biographical Study of His Songs*; U.S. ed., 1977, as *Schubert's Songs: A Biographical Study*); *Wagner und Nietzsche: Der Mystagoge und sein Abtrünniger* (Stuttgart, 1974; Eng. tr., 1976, as *Wagner and Nietzsche*); *Robert Schumann: Das Vokalwerk* (Munich, 1985); *Töne sprechen, Worte klingen: Zur Geschichte und Interpretation des Gesangs* (Stuttgart and Munich, 1985); *Nachklang: Ansichten und Erinnerungen* (Stuttgart, 1987; Eng. tr., 1989, as *Reverberations: The Memoirs of Dietrich Fisher-Dieskau*); *Wenn Musik der Liebe Nahrung ist: Künstlerschicksale im 19. Jahrhundert* (Stuttgart, 1990); *Weil nicht alle Blütenträume reiften: Johann Friedrich Reichardt, Hofkapellmeister dreier Preussenkönige: Porträt und Selbstporträt* (Stuttgart, 1992); *Fern die Klage des Fauns: Claude Debussy und seine Welt* (Stuttgart, 1993).

BIBL.: K. Whitton, *D. F.-D.—Mastersinger: A Documented Study* (London and N.Y., 1981); W.-E. von Lewinski, *D. F.-D.* (Munich and Mainz, 1988).

Fišer, Luboš, Czech composer; b. Prague, Sept. 30, 1935. He studied composition with Hlobil at the Prague Cons. (1952–56) and with Bořkovec at the Prague Academy of Music, graduating in 1960. His music is often associated with paintings, archeology, and human history; his style of composition employs effective technical devices without adhering to any particular doctrine. His *15 Prints after Dürer's Apocalypse* for Orch. (1964–65), his most successful work, received the UNESCO prize in Paris in 1967.

WORKS: DRAMATIC: *Lancelot*, chamber opera (1959–60; Prague, May 19, 1961); *Dobrý voják Švejk* (The Good Soldier Schweik), musical (Prague, 1962); *Changing Game*, ballet (1971); *Faust Eternal*, television opera (1986). **ORCH.:** *Suite* (1954); 2 syms. (1956; 1958–60); *Symphonic Fresco* (1962–63); *Chamber Concerto* for Piano and Orch. (1964; rev. 1970); *15 Prints after Dürer's Apocalypse* (1964–65; Prague, May 15, 1966); *Pietà* for Chamber Ensemble (1967); *Riff* (1968); *Double* (1969); *Report* for Wind Instruments (1971); *Kreutzer Étude* for Chamber Orch. (1974); *Labyrinth* (1977); *Serenade for Salzburg* for Chamber Orch. (1978); *Albert Einstein*, portrait for Organ and Orch. (1979); Piano Concerto (1980); *Meridian* (1980); *Romance* for Violin and Orch. (1980); *Centaures* (1983); Concerto for 2 Pianos and Orch. (1986). **CHAMBER:** *4 Compositions* for Violin and Piano (1955); String Quartet (1955); Sextet for Wind Quintet and Piano (1956); *Ruce* (Hands), violin sonata (1961); *Crux* for Violin, Kettledrums, and Bells (1970); Cello Sonata (1975); *Variations on an Unknown Theme* for String Quartet (1976); Piano Trio (1978); Sonata for 2 Cellos and Piano (1979); *Testis* for String Quartet (1980); Sonata for Solo Violin (1981). **PIANO:** 6 sonatas (1955; 1957; 1960; 1962–64; 1974; 1978). **VOCAL:** *Caprichos* for Vocalists and Chorus (1966); Requiem for Soprano, Baritone, 2 Choruses, and Orch. (Prague, Nov. 19, 1968); *Lament over the Destruction of the City of Ur* for Soprano, Baritone, 3 Narrators, Chorus, Children's and Adult's Speaking Choruses, 7 Timpani, and 7 Bells (1969; as a ballet, 1978); *Ave Imperator* for Cello, Men's Chorus, 4 Trombones, and Percussion (1977); *The Rose* for Chorus (1977); *Per Vittoria Colona* for Cello and Women's Chorus (1979); *Istanu*, melodrama for Narrator, Alto Flute, and 4 Percussionists (1980); *Znameni* (The Sign) for Soloists, Chorus, and Orch. (1981); *Address to Music*, melodrama for Narrator and String Quartet (1982).

Fisher, Avery (Robert), American pioneer in audio equipment and munificent music patron; b. N.Y., March 4, 1906; d. New Milford, Conn., Feb. 26, 1994. He was educated at N.Y. Univ. (B.S., 1929); then worked for the publishing house of Dodd, Mead as a graphic designer (1933–43). In 1937 he founded the Phil. Radio firm, later known as Fisher Radio; it became one of the foremost manufacturers of audio equipment in the world, producing high-fidelity and stereophonic components. Having amassed a substantial fortune, he sold the firm in 1969. In 1973 he gave the N.Y. Phil. $10 million to renovate the interior of Phil. Hall; in 1976 it was inaugurated at a gala concert in which it was officially renamed Avery Fisher Hall in his honor. He also created the Avery Fisher Prize, which is awarded to outstanding musicians of the day.

Fisher, Sylvia (Gwendoline Victoria), admired Australian soprano; b. Melbourne, April 18, 1910; died there, Aug. 25, 1996. She was a student of Adolf Spivakovsky at the Melbourne Cons. In 1932 she made her operatic debut as Hermione in Lully's *Cadmus et Hermione* in Melbourne. After settling in London, she made her first appearance at Covent Garden as Beethoven's Leonore in 1949; subsequently she was a leading dramatic soprano there until 1958, excelling particularly as Sieglinde, the Marschallin, and Kostelnička in *Jenůfa*. In 1958 she sang at the Chicago Lyric Opera. She was a member of the English Opera Group in London (1963–71), and also sang there with the Sadler's Wells (later the English National) Opera. She created the role of Miss Wingrave in Britten's *Owen Wingrave* (BBC-TV, London, May 16, 1971), and was notably successful as Elizabeth I in his *Gloriana*.

Fisk, Eliot (Hamilton), outstanding American guitarist; b. Philadelphia, Aug. 10, 1954. He studied with Oscar Ghiglia at the Aspen School of Music (1970–76); also studied with Ralph Kirkpatrick and Albert Fuller at Yale Univ. (B.A., 1972; M.M., 1977). In 1976 he made his recital debut at N.Y.'s Alice Tully Hall. After winning the Gargano classical guitar competition in Italy in 1980, he appeared as a soloist with orchs., as a recitalist, and as a chamber music artist. He was on the faculty at the Aspen (Colo.) School of Music (1973–82), Yale Univ. (1977–82), and the Mannes College of Music in N.Y. (1978–82); in 1982 he became a prof. at the Cologne Hochschule für Musik, and then in 1989 at the Salzburg Morzarteum. He has expanded the repertoire of his instrument by preparing his own brilliant transcriptions of works by Bach, Scarlatti, Mozart, Paganini et al.

Fiske, Roger (Elwyn), English musicologist; b. Surbiton, Sept. 11, 1910; d. London, July 22, 1987. He attended Wadham College, Oxford (B.A. in English, 1932), then received instruction in composition from Herbert Howells at the Royal College of Music in London before completing his education at the Univ. of Oxford (D.Mus., 1937). He was active as a BBC broadcaster (1939–59), and served as general ed. of the Eulenburg miniature scores (1968–75).

WRITINGS (all publ. in London): *Beethoven's Last Quartets* (1940); *Listening to Music* (1952); *Ballet Music* (1958); *Score Reading* (1958–65); *Chamber Music* (1969); *Beethoven's Concertos and Overtures* (1970); *English Theatre Music in the Eighteenth Century* (1973; 2nd ed., 1986); *Scotland in Music* (1983).

Fistoulari, Anatole, Russian-born English conductor; b. Kiev, Aug. 20, 1907; d. London, Aug. 21, 1995. He studied with his father, Gregory Fistoulari, an opera conductor. He was only 7 when he conducted Tchaikovsky's 6th Sym. in Kiev, and he subsequently conducted throughout Russia. At 12, he made his first conducting tour of Europe. In 1931 he appeared as conductor with the Grand Opera Russe in Paris, and later conducted the Ballets Russes de Monte Carlo on tours of Europe and in 1937 on a tour of the U.S. In 1939 he joined the French Army; after its defeat in 1940, he made his way to London. In 1942 he appeared as a guest conductor with the London Sym. Orch., and then served as principal conductor of the London Phil. (1943–44). He subsequently appeared as a conductor of sym. concerts and opera in England, becoming a naturalized British subject in 1948. In 1956 he toured the Soviet Union with the London Phil. In 1942 he married Mahler's daughter Anna, but their union was dissolved in 1956.

Fitelberg, Grzegorz, eminent Latvian-born Polish conductor and composer, father of **Jerzy Fitelberg;** b. Dvinsk, Oct. 18, 1879; d. Katowice, June 10, 1953. He was a student of Barcewicz (violin) and Noskowski (composition) at the Warsaw Cons. With his friend Szymanowski, he helped to found the Assn. of Young Polish Composers in Berlin in 1905. He began his career as a violinist in the Warsaw Phil., eventually serving as its concertmaster before being named its conductor in 1908. He then was a conductor at the Vienna Court Opera (1911–14) in Russia, and with Diaghilev's Ballets Russes in Paris (1921–23). After again conducting the Warsaw Phil. (1923–34), he was founder-conductor of the Polish Radio Sym. Orch. in Warsaw (1934–39). At the outbreak of World War II, he fled Europe and eventually reached Buenos Aires in 1940, later residing in the U.S. (1942–45). In 1945–46 he was a guest conductor with the London Phil. In 1947 he became conductor of the Polish Radio Sym. Orch. in Katowice. Fitelberg was a distinguished champion of Polish music. The Polish government awarded him a state prize in 1951. He composed 2 syms. (1903, 1906); Violin Concerto (1901); 2 Polish rhapsodies for Orch. (1913, 1914); *In der Meerestiefe*, symphonic poem (1913); Violin Sonata (Paderewski prize, 1896) and other chamber works.

Fitelberg, Jerzy, talented Polish composer, son of **Grzegorz Fitelberg;** b. Warsaw, May 20, 1903; d. N.Y., April 25, 1951. He studied with his father before pursuing his training with Schreker at the Berlin Hochschule für Musik (1922–26). After living in Paris (1933–39), he settled in N.Y. in 1940. His works were performed at various festivals, including those at the ISCM (1932, 1937). In 1936 he was awarded the Elizabeth Sprague Coolidge prize for his 4th String Quartet and in 1945 received a prize from the American Academy of Arts and Letters. His works were notable for their energetic rhythm and strong contrapuntal texture. A rather unconventional neo-Classical style later admitted elements of Polish melos.

WORKS: ORCH.: 3 suites (1925, 1928, 1930); 2 violin concertos: No. 1 (1928; Vienna, June 20, 1932; rev. 1947) and No. 2 (1935; Paris, June 22, 1937); 2 piano concertos (1929, 1934); *Prometeusz źle spętany* (The Badly Hobbled Prometheus), ballet suite (1929); Concerto for Strings (1930); String Quartet Concerto (1931); Cello Concerto (1931); *3 Mazurkas* (1932); *4 Studies* (1932); Suite for Violin and Orch. (1932); *Divertimento* (1934); *Konzertstück* (1937); *Złoty róg* (Golden Horn) for Strings (1942); *Epitafium* for Violin and Orch. (1942); *Nocturne* (1944; N.Y., March 28, 1946); Sinfonietta (1946); *Obrazy polskie* (Polish Pictures; 1946); Sym. for Strings (1946); Concerto for Trombone, Piano, and Strings (1947); Clarinet Concerto (1948). **CHAMBER:** Wind Octet (1925); 5 string quartets (1926, 1928, 1936, 1936, 1945); *Serenade* for 9 Instruments (1926); Wind Quintet (1929; rev. as *Capriccio*, 1947); *Divertimento* for Winds (1929); Piano Trio (1937); Violin Sonata (1938); Sonata for 2 Violins and Piano (1938); Sonata for Solo Cello (1945); piano pieces, including 3 sonatas (1926, 1929, 1936).

BIBL.: E. Elsner, "J.F.," *The Chesterian* (Sept.-Oct. 1939).

Fiume, Orazio, Italian composer and teacher; b. Monopoli, Jan. 16, 1908; d. Trieste, Dec. 21, 1976. He studied piano and theory in Palermo and Naples; was later a student of Pizzetti (composition) and Molinari (conducting) in Rome. He taught harmony at the Parma Cons. (1941–51), in Milan (1951–59), and in Pesaro (1959–60); was director of the Trieste Cons. (from 1961). His music followed the tradition of expansive Italian Romanticism. He wrote *3 Pieces* for Chamber Orch. (1937); *Ajace*, cantata (1940); 2 concertos for Orch. (1945, 1956); Sym. (1956); *Il tamburo di panno*, opera (Rome, April 12, 1962); songs.

Fizdale, Robert, American pianist; b. Chicago, April 12, 1920; d. N.Y., Dec. 6, 1995. He studied with Ernest Hutcheson at the Juilliard School of Music in N.Y. He formed a piano duo with Arthur Gold, and they made their professional debut at N.Y.'s New School for Social Research in 1944 in a program devoted entirely to John Cage's music for prepared pianos. They toured widely in the U.S., Europe, and South America; works were written specially for them by Barber, Milhaud, Poulenc, Auric, Thomson, Dello Joio, and Rorem. With Gold, Fizdale publ. a successful book, *Misia* (N.Y., 1979), on the life of Maria Godebska, a literary and musical figure in Paris early in the century. He retired in 1982.

Fjeldstad, Øivin, Norwegian conductor; b. Christiania, May 2, 1903; d. there (Oslo), Oct. 16, 1983. He was a pupil of Lange at the Christiania Cons., Davisson at the Leipzig Cons., and Krauss at the Berlin Cons. He began his career as a violinist in 1921, and then was a member of the Christiania (later Oslo) Phil. (1924–45). In 1931 he made his conducting debut with the Oslo Phil. He served as chief conductor of the Norwegian State Broadcasting Orch. in Oslo (1945–62), the Oslo Opera (1958–59), and the Oslo Phil. (1962–69). He was a persuasive advocate of Scandinavian music.

Flagello, Ezio (Domenico), American bass, brother of **Nicolas (Oreste) Flagello;** b. N.Y., Jan. 28, 1931. He was a pupil of Schorr and Brownlee at the Manhattan School of Music in N.Y. In 1952 he made his debut in a concert performance of *Boris Godunov* at N.Y.'s Carnegie Hall, followed in 1955 by his stage debut as Dulcamara at the Empire State Festival in Ellenville, N.Y. He then pursued his training in Rome on a Fulbright scholarship with Luigi Rossi, appearing as Dulcamara with the Opera there in 1956. In 1957 he won the Metropolitan Opera Auditions of the Air, which led to his debut with the company in N.Y. as the Jailer in *Tosca* on Nov. 9 of that year. He subsequently sang regularly there until 1987. In 1966 he created the role of Enobarbus in Barber's *Antony and Cleopatra* at the opening of the new Metropolitan Opera house. He also was a guest artist in Vienna, Berlin, and Milan. He was particularly known for his buffo roles, excelling in operas by Mozart and Rossini. He also was successful in operas by Verdi and Wagner.

Flagello, Nicolas (Oreste), American composer and conductor, brother of **Ezio (Domenico) Flagello**; b. N.Y., March 15, 1928; d. New Rochelle, N.Y., March 16, 1994. He began piano lessons at the incredible age of 3, and played in public at 5. At 6, he began taking violin lessons with Francesco di Giacomo. He also learned to play the oboe, and was a member of the school band, performing on these instruments according to demand. In 1945–46 he played the violin in Stokowski's All-American Youth Orch. in N.Y. In 1946 he entered the Manhattan School of Music (B.M., 1949; M.M., 1950), studying with a variety of teachers in multifarious subjects (Harold Bauer, Hugo Kortschak, Hugh Ross, and Vittorio Giannini). He also took conducting lessons with Mitropoulos. It was with Giannini that he had his most important training in composition (1935–50), and it was Giannini who influenced him most in his style of composition—melodious, harmonious, euphonious, singingly Italianate, but also dramatically modern. After obtaining his master's degree, Flagello took lessons with Pizzetti at the Accademia di Santa Cecilia in Rome (Mus.D., 1956). He taught composition and conducting at the Manhattan School of Music from 1950 to 1977. He also appeared as a guest conductor with the Chicago Lyric Opera and the N.Y. City Opera, and toured as accompanist to Tito Schipa, Richard Tucker, and other singers.

WORKS: OPERAS: *Mirra* (1953); *The Wig* (1953); *Rip Van Winkle* (1957); *The Sisters* (1958; N.Y., Feb. 23, 1961); *The Judgment of St. Francis* (1959; N.Y., March 18, 1966); *The Piper of Hamelin* (1970); *Beyond the Horizon* (1983). **ORCH.:** *Beowulf* (1949); 4 piano concertos (1950, 1956, 1962, 1975); *Symphonic Aria* (1951); *Overture giocosa* (1952); Flute Concerto (1956); *Missa sinfonica* (1957); Concerto for Strings (1959); *Capriccio* for Cello and Orch. (1962); *Lautrec* (1965); 2 syms. (1968, 1970); *Serenata* (1968); *Credendum* for Violin and Orch. (1974); *Odyssey* for Band (1981); *Concerto sinfonico* for Saxophone Quartet and Orch. (1985). **CHAMBER:** *Divertimento* for Piano and Percussion (1960); Harp Sonata (1961); *Burlesca* for Flute and Guitar (1961); Piano Sonata (1962); Concertino for Piano, Brass, and Timpani (1963); Violin Sonata (1963); Suite for Harp and String Trio (1965); *Electra* for Piano and Percussion (1966); *Declamation* for Violin and Piano (1967); *Ricercare* for Brass and Percussion (1971); *Prisma* for 7 Horns (1974); *Diptych* for 2 Trumpets and Trombone (1979). **VOCAL:** *The Land* for Bass-baritone and Orch. (1954); 5 songs for Soprano and Orch. (1955); *Tristis est anima mea* for Chorus and Orch. (1959); *Dante's Farewell* for Soprano and Orch. (1962); *Contemplazioni* for Soprano and Orch. (1964); *Te Deum for All Mankind* for Chorus and Orch. (1967); *Passion of Martin Luther King*, oratorio for Bass-baritone, Chorus, and Orch. (1968); *Remembrance* for Soprano, Flute, and String Quartet (1971); *Canto* for Soprano and Orch. (1978); *Quattro amori* for Mezzo-soprano and Piano (1983).

Flagstad, Kirsten (Malfrid), famous Norwegian soprano; b. Hamar, July 12, 1895; d. Oslo, Dec. 7, 1962. She studied voice with her mother and with Ellen Schytte-Jacobsen in Christiania, then made her operatic debut there as Nuri in d'Albert's *Tiefland* (Dec. 12, 1913). During the next 2 decades, she sang throughout Scandinavia, appearing in operas and operettas, and in concert. In 1933 she sang a number of minor roles at Bayreuth, and then scored her first major success there in 1934 when she appeared as Sieglinde. She made an auspicious Metropolitan Opera debut in N.Y. in that same role on Feb. 2, 1935, and was soon hailed as the foremost Wagnerian soprano of her time. On May 18, 1936, she made her first appearance at London's Covent Garden as Isolde. While continuing to sing at the Metropolitan Opera, she made guest appearances at the San Francisco Opera (1935–38) and the Chicago Opera (1937), and also gave concerts with major U.S. orchs. She returned to her Nazi-occupied homeland in 1941 to be with her husband, a decision that alienated many of her admirers. Nevertheless, after World War II, she resumed her career with notable success at Covent Garden. In 1951 she also returned to the Metropolitan Opera, where she sang Isolde and Leonore; made her farewell appearance there in Gluck's *Alceste* on April 1, 1952. She retired from the operatic stage in 1954, but continued to make recordings; from 1958 to 1960 she was director of the Norwegian Opera in Oslo. Among her other celebrated roles were Brünnhilde, Elisabeth, Elsa, and Kundry. She narrated an autobiography to L. Biancolli, which was publ. as *The Flagstad Manuscript* (N.Y., 1952).

BIBL.: E. McArthur, *F.: A Personal Memoir* (N.Y., 1965); T. Gunnarson, *Sannheten om K. F.: En dokumentarbiografi* (Oslo, 1985); H. Vogt, *F.* (London, 1987).

Flament, Édouard, French bassoonist, conductor, and composer; b. Douai, Aug. 27, 1880; d. Bois-Colombes, Seine, Dec. 27, 1958. He studied at the Paris Cons. with Bourdeau (bassoon), Lavignac, Caussade, and Lenepveu (composition). After graduation (1898), he played the bassoon in the Lamoureux Orch. (1898–1907) and in the Société des Instruments à Vent (1898–1923) in Paris; conducted opera and concerts in Paris (1907–12), Algiers (1912–14), and Marseilles (1919–20), and summer concerts at Fontainebleau (1920–22); then with the Diaghilev ballet in Monte Carlo, Berlin, London, and Spain (1923–29). In 1930 he became conductor at the Paris Radio.

WORKS: OPERAS: *La Fontaine de Castalie*; *Le Coeur de la rose*; *Lydéric et Rosèle*. **ORCH.:** 8 syms.; *Oceano Nox*, symphonic poem; *Variations radio-phoniques*; 5 piano concertos; *Concertstück* for Bassoon and Orch. **CHAMBER:** *Divertimento* for 6 Bassoons; Quintet for 5 Bassoons; Quartet for 4 Bassoons; 3 string quartets; Violin Sonata; Viola Sonata; 2 cello sonatas.

Flanagan, William (Jr.), American composer and music critic; b. Detroit, Aug. 14, 1923; d. of an overdose of barbiturates in N.Y., Aug. 31, 1969. He studied composition at the Eastman School of Music in Rochester, N.Y., with Phillips and Rogers; then at the Berkshire Music Center in Tanglewood with Honegger, Berger, and Copland; also, in N.Y., with Diamond. Concurrently, he became engaged in musical journalism; was a reviewer for the *N.Y. Herald Tribune* (1957–60) and later wrote for *Stereo Review*. His style of composition was characterized by an intense pursuit of an expressive melodic line, projected on polycentric but firmly tonal harmonies.

WORKS: DRAMATIC: OPERAS: *Bartleby* (1952–57; N.Y., Jan. 24, 1961); *The Ice Age* (1967; unfinished); incidental music to E. Albee's plays *The Sandbox* (1961), *The Ballad of Bessie Smith* (1961), *The Ballad of the Sad Cafe* (1963), and *Malcolm* (1966); 2 films scores. **ORCH.:** *A Concert Overture* (1948; N.Y., Dec. 4, 1959); *Divertimento* (1948; Toledo, Ohio, Jan. 9, 1960); *A Concert Ode* (1951; Detroit, Jan. 14, 1960); *Notations* (1960); *Narrative* (1964; Detroit, March 25, 1965). **CHAMBER:** *Divertimento* for String Quartet (1947); *Chaconne* for Violin and Piano (1948). **PIANO:** *Passacaglia* (1947); Sonata (1950). **VOCAL:** *The Waters of Babylon* for Voices and String Quartet (1947); *Billy in the Darbies* for Chorus and Piano or Orch. (1949); *A Woman of Valor* for Chorus (1949); *The Weeping Pleiades* for Baritone and 5 Instruments (1953); *The Lady of Tearful Regret* for Soprano, Baritone, Flute, Clarinet, String Quartet, and Piano (1959); *King Midas* for Soloists and Orch. (c.1961); *Chapter from Ecclesiastes* for Chorus and String Quintet (1962); *Another August* for Soprano, Piano, Harpsichord, and Small Orch. (1966); various songs.

BIBL.: L. Trimble, "W. F. (1923–1969), an Appreciation," *Stereo Review*, XXIII/5 (1969).

Fleischmann, Ernest (Martin), German-born English music administrator; b. Frankfurt am Main, Dec. 7, 1924. His family moved to Johannesburg, where he studied accounting at the Univ. of the Witwatersrand. He then devoted himself to music studies, obtaining a B.Mus. at the Univ. of Cape Town (1954). He was ambitious and took lessons in conducting with Coates; also acted as an organizer of musical events, including the Van Riebeeck Festival in Cape Town (1952). Furthermore, he served as director of music and drama for the Johannesburg Festival (1956). In the process he learned Afrikaans, and acquired a literary fluency in English. Seeking ever wider fields of endeavor, he went to London, becoming a naturalized British subject in 1959; he acted as general manager of the London Sym. Orch. until 1967 and also made a number of conducting appearances in England. He finally emigrated to the U.S., which became the main center of his activities; from 1969 to 1997 he was executive director of the Los Angeles Phil. as well as general manager of the Hollywood Bowl. Ever sure of his direction, he was a powerful promoter of the orch. he headed, so that the Los Angeles Phil. became actively involved in extensive national and international tours, garnering profitable recording contracts in addition to television and radio broadcasts, youth programs, and special festivals. Well-educated and fluent in several European languages, Fleischmann acquired an international reputation as a highly successful entrepreneur.

Fleisher, Edwin A(dler), American music patron; b. Philadelphia, July 11, 1877; d. there, Jan. 9, 1959. He studied at Harvard Univ. (B.A., 1899). He founded a Sym. Club in Philadelphia (1909) and engaged conductors to rehearse an amateur orch. there; at the same time he began collecting orch. scores and complete sets of parts, which became the nucleus of the great Edwin A. Fleisher Collection, presented by him to the Free Library of Philadelphia. A cumulative catalog covering the period from 1929 to 1977 was publ. in Boston in 1979.

Fleisher, Leon, distinguished American pianist, conductor, and teacher; b. San Francisco, July 23, 1928. His mother was a singing teacher. He received the rudiments of music from his mother; then studied piano with Lev Shorr. He played in public at the age of 6; then was sent to Europe for studies with Schnabel at Lake Como, Italy; continued his studies with him in N.Y. At the age of 14, he appeared as soloist in the Liszt A major Piano Concerto with the San Francisco Sym. Orch. (April 16, 1943); at 16, he was soloist with the N.Y. Phil. (Nov. 4, 1944); in 1952 he became the first American to win 1st prize at the Queen Elisabeth of Belgium International Competition in Brussels; this catapulted him into a brilliant career. He made several European tours; also gave highly successful recitals in South America. In 1964 he was stricken with repetitive stress syndrome of the right hand. Disabled, Fleisher turned to piano works written for left hand alone (Ravel, Prokofiev, and others). He also began to conduct. He had studied conducting with Monteux in San Francisco and at the conducting school established by Monteux in Hancock, Maine; he also profited from advice from Szell. In 1968 he became artistic director of the Theater Chamber Players in Washington, D.C.; in 1970 he became music director of the Annapolis Sym. Orch. as well. From 1973 to 1977 he was assoc. conductor of the Baltimore Sym. Orch.; then was its resident conductor in 1977–78. He also made guest conducting appearances with major U.S. orchs. A treatment with cortisone injections and even acupuncture and the fashionable biofeedback to control the electrophysiological motor system did not help. In 1981 he decided to undergo surgery; it was momentarily successful, and on Sept. 16, 1982, he made a spectacular comeback as a bimanual pianist, playing the *Symphonic Variations* by Franck with Comissiona and the Baltimore Sym. Orch. In 1985 he became artistic director-designate of the Berkshire Music Center at Tanglewood, and fully assumed his duties as artistic director in 1986. In 1993 he marked the 50th anniversary of his professional career with a gala concert at the San Francisco Cons. of Music. On July 23, 1994, he was soloist in the premiere of Foss's Piano Concerto for Left Hand and Orch. with Ozawa and the Boston Sym. Orch. at Tanglewood. Fleisher devoted much time to teaching; he joined the faculty of the Peabody Cons. of Music in Baltimore in 1959, and subsequently was named to the Andrew W. Mellon Chair in Piano. Among his brilliant pupils were André Watts and Lorin Hollander.

Fleming, Renée, gifted American soprano; b. Indiana, Pa., Feb. 14, 1959. She received vocal training in N.Y. After winning a Metropolitan Opera audition in 1988, she made her debut at London's Covent Garden as Dircé in Cherubini's *Médée* in 1989. In 1990 she received the Richard Tucker Award, and also took the Grand Prix in the Belgian singing competition. Following engagements as Dvořák's Rusalka at the Houston Grand Opera and the Seattle Opera, she made her Metropolitan Opera debut in N.Y. as Mozart's Countess on March 16, 1991, which role she also sang at the Teatro Colón in Buenos Aires. On Dec. 19, 1991, she appeared as Rosina in the premiere of Corigliano's *The Ghosts of Versailles* at the Metropolitan Opera, returning in subsequent seasons to sing Mozart's Countess and Pamina, and Desdemona. In 1992 she returned to Covent Garden as Rossini's Mme. de Folleville, sang Mozart's Donna Elvira at Milan's La Scala and his Fiordiligi at the Geneva Opera and the Glyndebourne Festival, and appeared as Mimi at the opening of the new Bath and Wessex Opera. She made her N.Y. recital debut at Alice Tully Hall on March 29, 1993. In Aug. 1993 she was the soloist in Barber's *Knoxville: Summer of 1915* at the opening of the new concert hall in Aspen, Colo. In Oct. 1993 she sang the title role in the revival of Floyd's *Susannah* at the Chicago Lyric Opera. She appeared as Mozart's Countess at the opening of the new opera theater at the Glyndebourne Festival on May 28, 1994. On Sept. 10, 1994, she sang Mme. de Tourvel in the premiere of Susa's *The Dangerous Liaisons* at the San Francisco Opera. In 1995 she appeared as Rusalka at the San Diego Opera. She also sang with the Opera Orch. of N.Y., the Dallas Opera, the Washington (D.C.) Opera, the Vienna State Opera, and the Opéra de la Bastille in Paris. As a concert and oratorio artist, Fleming had many engagements in North America and Europe. Among her other outstanding operatic roles are Rossini's Armida, Tatiana, the Marschallin, Salome, Jenůfa, and Ellen in *Peter Grimes*.

Fleming, Robert (James Berkeley), Canadian composer, pianist, organist, choirmaster, and teacher; b. Prince Albert, Saskatchewan, Nov. 12, 1921; d. Ottawa, Nov. 28, 1976. He was a student of Benjamin (piano) and Howells (composition) at the Royal College of Music in London (1937–39); he then studied piano with Lyell Gustin (1941–42) and attended the Toronto Cons. of Music (1941, 1945) as a student of Norman Wilks (piano), Frederick Silvester and John Weatherseed (organ), Mazzoleni (conducting), and Willan (composition). In 1945–46 he taught piano at Upper Canada College, and then was a staff composer (1946–58) and music director (1958–70) with the National Film Board; he also served as organist-choirmaster at Glebe United Church (1954–56) and at St. George's Anglican Church of Ste-Anne-de-Bellevue (1959–70) in Quebec. Settling in Ottawa, he joined the faculty of Carleton Univ. in 1970 and in 1972 he became organist-choirmaster at St. Matthias' Church. In his extensive catalogue of works, Fleming adhered to a generally tonal path.

WORKS: DRAMATIC: BALLETS: *Chapter 13* (1948); *Shadow on the Prairie* (1951); *Romance* (1954); 3 puppet plays; more than 250 film scores. **ORCH.:** 5 suites (1942–63); *Rondo* (1942); *6 Variations on a Liturgical Theme* for Strings (1946); *Red River Country* (1953); *Seaboard Sketches* (1953); *Recollections* for Violin and Strings (1954); *Ballet Introduction* (1960); *Concerto 64* for Piano and Orch. (1964); Tuba Concerto (1966); *4 Fantasias on Canadian Folk Themes* (1966); *Hexad* (1972); band pieces. **CHAMBER:** Violin Sonata (1944); *A Musician in the Family* for Trombone and Piano (1952); *A 2 Piece Suite* for 2 Clarinets and Bass Clarinet (1958); *Colours of the Rainbow* for Wind Quartet, String Quartet, and Harp (1962); *Maritime Suite* for Wind Quartet, String Quartet, and Harp (1962); *3 Miniatures* for Brass Quintet (1962); *Go for Baroque* for Flute, Oboe, and Harpsichord (1963); *3 Dialogues* for Flute or Oboe and Piano or Harpsichord (1964); Brass Quintet (1965); String Quartet (1969); *Almost Waltz* for Flute and Piano (1970); *Divertimento* for Organ, 2 Oboes, 2 Violins, Viola, Cello, and Double Bass (1970); *Explorations* for Accordion (1970); *Threo* for Soprano Saxophone and Piano (1972); many piano pieces; organ music. **VOCAL:** Choral works and songs.

Fleming, Shirley (Moragne), American music critic and editor; b. N.Y., Dec. 2, 1931. She was educated at Smith College in Northampton, Mass. (B.A., 1952; M.A., 1954). She was assistant music ed. of *Hi-fi Music at Home* (1958–60) and of *High Fidelity* (1960–64); then was ed. of *Musical America* (1964–91), and subsequently of the valuable "Music in Concert" section of the expanded *American Record Guide* (from 1992). She also wrote for other periodicals.

Flesch, Carl (actually, **Károly**), celebrated Hungarian violinist and pedagogue; b. Moson, Oct. 9, 1873; d. Lucerne, Nov. 14, 1944. He began to study the violin at the age of 6 in Moson, then continued his training with Jakob Grün at the Vienna Cons. (1886–90), and with Sauzay (1890–92) and Marsick (1892–94) at the Paris Cons., graduating with the premier prix. While still a student, he played in the Lamoureux Orch. in Paris and made his formal debut in Vienna (1895); went to Bucharest (1897), where he was active as a performer and as a prof. at the Cons. until 1902; he subsequently went to Amsterdam, where he taught at the Cons. (1903–08). In 1908 he made his home in Berlin, where he engaged in private teaching when not engaged on extensive tours. In 1913 he made his N.Y. debut; then served as head of the violin dept. at the Curtis Inst. of Music in Philadelphia (1924–28). Returning to Berlin in 1928, he joined the faculty of the Hochschule für Musik. With the advent of Hitler, he went to London (1934). He was in the

Netherlands when World War II erupted in 1939, and lived there until the Nazi invasion in 1940; then made his way to Hungary, finally settling in Lucerne in 1943 as a teacher at the Cons. He acquired an outstanding reputation as an interpreter of the German repertoire. However, his greatest legacy remains his work as a pedagogue. His *Die Kunst des Violin-Spiels* is an exhaustive treatise on violin technique and interpretation, and is duly recognized as the standard work of its kind. He also prepared eds. of the violin concertos of Beethoven, Mendelssohn, and Brahms, the violin sonatas of Mozart (with A. Schnabel), 20 études of Paganini, and the études of Kreutzer. In 1945 the Flesch Competition was organized in London to honor his memory; it later became part of the City of London International Competition for Violin and Viola, which awards the Flesch Medal.

WRITINGS: *Urstudien* (Berlin, 1911); *Die Kunst des Violin-Spiels* (vol. I, Berlin, 1923; 2nd ed., 1929; Eng. tr., Boston, 1924; vol. II, Berlin, 1928; Eng. tr., Boston, 1934); *Das Klangproblem im Geigenspiel* (Berlin, 1931; Eng. tr., N.Y., 1934); H. Keller and C.F. Flesch, eds., *The Memoirs of Carl Flesch* (London, 1957; 3rd ed., 1974; Ger. ed. as *Erinnerungen eines Geigers*, Freiburg im Breisgau, 1960); *Die hohe Schule des Fingersetzes auf der Geige* (MS; 1st publ. in Italian as *Alta scuola di diteggiature violinistica*, Milan, 1960; Eng. tr., 1966, as *Violin Fingering: Its Theory and Practice*).

BIBL.: W. Brederode, *C. F.* (Haarlem, 1938); C.F. Flesch, *"Und spielste Die auch Geige?"* (Zürich, 1990).

Fleta, Miguel, Spanish tenor, father of **Pierre Fleta**; b. Albalate, Dec. 28, 1893; d. La Coruña, May 30, 1938. He studied at the Barcelona and Madrid conservatories; also took vocal lessons in Italy with Louisa Pierrick, who became his wife. He made his debut in Trieste on Nov. 14, 1919 as Paolo in Zandonai's *Francesca da Rimini.* After several busy tours in Europe, Mexico, and South America, he made his debut at the Metropolitan Opera in N.Y. on Nov. 8, 1923, as Cavaradossi; remained on its roster until 1925; from 1923 to 1926 he sang at La Scala in Milan, where he created the role of Prince Calaf in *Turandot* (April 25, 1926). In 1926 he returned to Spain.

Fleta, Pierre, French tenor of Spanish descent, son of **Miguel Fleta;** b. Villefranche-sur-Mer, July 4, 1925. He studied with his mother, Luisa Pierrick. In 1949 he made his operatic debut in Barcelona, and then sang in Nice (1949–51) and at the Théâtre Royal de la Monnaie in Brussels (from 1952); he also toured as a concert artist.

Fletcher, (Horace) Grant, American composer and teacher; b. Hartsburg, Ill., Oct. 25, 1913. He studied composition with William Kritch, theory with Bessie Louise Smith, and conducting with Henry Lamont at Illinois Wesleyan Univ. (1932–35); took a course in conducting with Thor Johnson; for 3 summers (1937–39) attended composition classes with Krenek at the Univ. of Mich.; then took classes with Willan in Toronto; later studied at the Eastman School of Music in Rochester, N.Y., where his teachers were Rogers and Hanson (1947–49; Ph.D., 1951); also had private lessons with Elwell in Cleveland. From 1945 to 1948 he was conductor of the Akron (Ohio) Sym. Orch., and from 1952 to 1956 of the Chicago Sinfonietta; from 1949 to 1951 he was on the faculty of the Chicago Musical College; later taught at Arizona State Univ. at Tempe (1956–78). In his music, he follows the median line of modern techniques.

WORKS: DRAMATIC: *The Carrion Crow,* buffa fantasy opera (1948); *Lomotawi,* ballet-pantomime (1957); *The Sack of Calabasas,* opera (1964–66); *Cinco de Mayo,* ballet (1973); incidental music. **ORCH.:** *Rhapsody* for Flute and Strings (1935; withdrawn); *A Rhapsody of Dances* for Chamber Orch. (1935; for Wind Instruments, 1970; for Full Orch., 1972); *Nocturne* (1938); *Song of Honor,* on Yugoslav themes (1944; 1st perf. as *A Song for Warriors,* Rochester, N.Y., Oct. 25, 1945); *An American Overture* (1945; Duluth, April 23, 1948); *Panels from a Theater Wall* (Rochester, N.Y., April 27, 1949); 2 syms.: No. 1 (1950; Rochester, N.Y., April 24, 1951) and No. 2 (1982–83); *The Pocket Encyclopedia of Orchestral Instruments,* with optional Narrator (1953; also perf. as *Dictionary of Musical Instruments*); 4 concertos: No. 1 for Piano and Orch. (1953), No. 2, *Regency Concerto,* for Piano and Strings (1966), No. 3, Concerto for Winds (1969), and No. 4, Multiple Concerto for 5 Solo Winds, for 1 Soloist playing on 5 different Wind Instruments, with Wind Ensemble (1970); *Sumare and Wintare* (1956); *7 Cities of Cibola* (1961); *Retrospection (Rhapsody III)* for Flute, 9 Strings, and Tape (1965; revision of *Rhapsody* of 1935); *Dances from the Southwest* for Strings and Piano (1966); *Glyphs* for Band (1970); *Diversion III* for Strings (1971); *The 5th of May,* ballet suite (1972); *Aubade* for Wind Instruments (1974); *Celebration of Times Past* (1976); *A More Proper Burial Music for Wolfgang* for Wind Instruments (1977); *Saxson II* for Saxophone and Strings (1977); *Serenade* (1979); *Symphonic Suite* (1980); *Partita* for Chamber Orch. (1985). **CHAMBER:** *Musicke for Christening:* No. 1 for Cello and Piano (1945), No. 2 for Saxophone and Piano (1979), and No. 3 for Clarinet and Piano (1979); *Heralds* for Brass and Timpani (1949); *Tower Music* for Brass (1957); 5 sonatas: No. 1 for Clarinet and Piano (1958), No. 2, *Sōn,* for Cello and Piano (1972), No. 3 for Saxophone and Piano (1974), No. 4 for Solo Viola (1977), and No. 5 for Solo Violin (1983); *PrognosIs Nos. 1–3* for Brass Quintet (1965–67); *Uroboros* for Percussion (1967); *Octocelli* for 8 Solo Cellos or their multiples (1971); Trio for Flute, Guitar, and Piano (1973); *Toccata II* for Marimba (1979); *Quadra* for Percussion (1975); String Quartet (1975; 4 earlier quartets were withdrawn); *Zortzicos No. 2* for Double Bass and Piano (1977), *No. 3* for Bassoon and Piano (1979), *No. 4* for Cello and Piano (1979), *No. 5* for Clarinet and Piano (1980), and *No. 6* for Viola and Piano (1980; *Zortzicos No. 1* is the last movement of the piano piece *Izquierdas*); *Saxsōn I* for Saxophone (1977); *Trio Bulgarico* for Flute, Oboe, and Bassoon (1980); *Palimpsest* for Flute Choir (1980); *Madrigals* for Clarinet Choir (1981). **KEYBOARD: PIANO:** *2 Books of Nocturnes* (1935); *4 American Dance Pieces* (1944); *Openend Triptych* (1957); *Izquierdas* for Piano, Left Hand (1967); *Diversion I* and *II* (1971); *Toccata I* (1974). **ORGAN:** *Dodecachordon* (1967). **VOCAL:** *The Crisis* for Chorus and Orch. (1945; Walla Walla, Wash., Feb. 22, 1976); *House Made of Dawn* for Alto, Piano, Flute, Indian Drum, and Rattle (1957); 4 sacred cantatas: No. 1, *O Childe Swete* (1965), No. 2 (1967), No. 3, *The Branch* (1970), and No. 4, *Judas* (1978); *Who Is Sylvia?* for Baritone, Flute, Oboe, Bassoon, and Guitar (1969); *Psalm I* for Chorus and Organ (1979); choruses; songs.

WRITINGS: *Fundamental Principles of Counterpoint* (Rock Hill, S.C., 1942); *Syllabus for Advanced Integrated Theory* (Tempe, Ariz., 1962; 4th ed., rev., 1976); *Rhythm: Notation and Production* (Tempe, 1967).

Fletcher, Percy (Eastman), English conductor and composer; b. Derby, Dec. 12, 1879; d. London, Sept. 10, 1932. He went to London in 1899 as a conductor at various theaters. He composed many works in a light, melodious style, including the orch. pieces *Woodland Pictures, Sylvan Scenes, Parisian Sketches,* and *3 Frivolities,* and the overture *Vanity Fair;* also a short sacred cantata, *Passion of Christ.*

Fleury, André (Edouard Antoine Marie), French organist, pedagogue, and composer; b. Neuilly-sur-Seine, July 25, 1903; d. Le Vésinet, Aug. 6, 1995. After training with his father, he studied with Gigout and Dupré at the Paris Cons., taking a premier prix in improvisation in 1926; he also was a private student in organ of Marchal and Vierne and in composition of Vidal. He was active in Paris as organist at St. Augustin (from 1930) and as a prof. of organ at the École Normale de Musique (from 1943). After serving as organist at the Cathedral and as a prof. at the Cons. in Dijon (1949–71), he returned to Paris as co-organist at St. Éustache and as a prof. at the Schola Cantorum. He wrote 2 organ syms. (1947, 1949) and many other organ works.

Fleury, Louis (François), eminent French flutist; b. Lyons, May 24, 1878; d. Paris, June 11, 1926. He studied at the Paris

Cons. From 1905 until his death he was head of the famous Société Moderne d'Instruments à Vent; also (from 1906) of the Société des Concerts d'Autrefois, with which he gave concerts in England; made appearances with Melba and Calvé. Debussy composed *Syrinx* for Unaccompanied Flute for him. He ed. much early flute music, including sonatas and other pieces by Blavet, Naudet, Purcell, J. Stanley et al., and contributed to French and English periodicals.

Flier, Yakov (Vladimirovich), Russian pianist and pedagogue; b. Orekhovo-Zuyevo, Oct. 21, 1912; d. Moscow, Dec. 18, 1977. He was a pupil at the Moscow Cons. of Kozlovsky and Igumnov. From 1935 he made tours in Russia, and later appeared abroad. From 1937 he also taught at the Moscow Cons., numbering among his notable students Bella Davidovich and Viktoria Postnikova.

Flipse, Eduard, Dutch conductor; b. Wissekerke, Feb. 26, 1896; d. Etten-Leur, Sept. 11, 1973. He studied piano and composition in Rotterdam and conducting in Utrecht. In 1930 he became chief conductor of the Rotterdam Phil., a post he retained until 1965. In 1952 he became chief conductor of the Holland Festival, and was later chief conductor of the Antwerp Phil. (1961–70). During his long tenure in Rotterdam, he introduced works of numerous contemporary composers. He was also a passionate propagandist of the music of Mahler.

Flor, Claus Peter, German conductor; b. Leipzig, March 16, 1953. He entered the Zwickau Cons. at 10 to study violin and clarinet, and then continued his training at the Weimar Hochschule für Musik; he completed his study of the violin at the Leipzig Hochschule für Musik, and also received training in conducting with Reuter and Masur; later he continued his conducting studies with Kubelik and Kurt Sanderling. In 1979 he won the Mendelssohn-Stipendium of the Ministry of Culture and captured 1st prize in the Fitelberg Competition in Katowice; he subsequently took prizes in the Kubelik Competition in Lucerne (1982) and in the Malko Competition in Copenhagen (1983). From 1981 to 1984 he was chief conductor of the Suhler Phil. In 1984–85 he was chief conductor of the (East) Berlin Sym. Orch., and then was made its Generalmusikdirektor in 1985. That same year, he made his U.S. debut at the Hollywood Bowl. In 1988 he took the Berlin Sym. Orch. on a world tour. In 1991 he left his Berlin post to serve as principal guest conductor of the Philharmonia Orch. in London and as principal guest conductor and artistic advisor of the Tonhalle Orch. in Zürich. As a guest conductor, he has appeared with many of the world's major orchs. He has also appeared as an opera conductor.

Floros, Constantin, distinguished Greek musicologist; b. Thessalonika, Jan. 4, 1930. He studied composition with Uhl and conducting with Swarowsky and Kassowitz at the Vienna Academy of Music, graduating in 1953; he concurrently studied musicology with Schenck at the Univ. of Vienna (Ph.D., 1955, with the diss. *C.A. Campioni als Instrumentalkomponist*) and then continued his training with Husmann at the Univ. of Hamburg, where he completed his Habilitation in 1961; in 1967 he became ausserplanmässiger prof. and in 1972 prof. of musicology there. P. Petersen ed. a Festschrift in honor of his 60th birthday (Wiesbaden, 1990).

WRITINGS: *Universale Neumenkunde* (3 vols., Kassel, 1970); *Gustav Mahler* (3 vols., Wiesbaden, 1977–85); *Beethovens Eroica und Prometheus-Musik: Sujet Studien* (Wilhelmshaven, 1978); *Mozart-Studien I: Zu Mozarts Sinfonik, Opern- und Kirchenmusik* (Wiesbaden, 1979); *Brahms und Bruckner: Studien zur musikalischen Exegetik* (Wiesbaden, 1980); *Einführung in die Neumenkunde* (Wilhelmshaven, 1980); *Musik als Botschaft* (Wiesbaden, 1989); *Alban Berg: Musik als Autobiographie* (Wiesbaden, 1992).

Flosman, Oldřich, Czech composer; b. Plzeň, April 5, 1925. He studied composition with K. Janeček at the Prague Cons. (1944–46), and with Bořkovec at the Prague Academy of Music, graduating in 1950. In his music, he follows the neo-Romantic tradition of the Czech school of composition, with strong formal design and an animating rhythmic pulse; the influence of Prokofiev's lyrical dynamism is much in evidence.

WORKS: BALLETS: *Pierrot and Columbine* (1957); *The Woman Partisan* (1959); *The Taming of the Shrew* (1960); *The Salted Fairy-Tale* (1982). **ORCH.:** Double Concerto for Harp, Clarinet, and Orch. (1950); Clarinet Concerto (1954); Bassoon Concertino (1956); 2 violin concertos (1958, 1972); *Dances* for Harp and String Quartet or String Orch. (1961); *Cuban Overture* (1962); 3 syms. (1964, 1974, 1984); *3 Studies* for Piano and Strings (1965); *Concertant Music* for Wind Quintet and Chamber Orch. (1965); Flute Concerto (1969); Horn Concerto (1970); Fugues for Strings (1970); *Fires on the Hills,* overture (1973); *Visions of Michelangelo* for Viola and Orch. (1979); *Rural Partita* for Chamber Orch. (1976); *Symphonic Fugue* (1977); Sym.-Concerto for Piano and Orch. (1979); *Philharmonic Variations* (1980); *Symphonic Plays* for Bass Clarinet, Piano, and Orch. (1983); *Nuptial Dances of Charles IV* for Piano and Chamber Orch. (1984). **CHAMBER:** 2 wind quintets (1948, 1962); *Bagatelles* for Winds and Piano (1950); Clarinet Sonatina (1952); *Jesenik Suite* for Viola and Piano (1956); 3 string quartets (1956, 1963, 1966); *Dreaming about a Violin* for Violin and Piano (1962); *Romance and Scherzo* for Flute and Harp (1962); Nonet No. 2 (1967); Sonata for Wind Quintet and Piano (1970); *Chamber Music* for Flute, Oboe, Violin, Viola, and Cello (1971); Sonata for Violin, Cello, and Piano (1971); *Music* for Double Bass and String Quartet (1980); Serenade for Brass Quintet (1981); *Music* for Flute and Piano or Guitar (1984); piano pieces, including *Motýli zde nežijí* (Butterflies Don't Live Here Any Longer), sonata inspired by the film about children's drawings from a Nazi concentration camp (1961). **VOCAL:** Sonata for Soprano and Strings (1967); choral pieces; songs.

Flothuis, Marius (Hendrikus), eminent Dutch composer; b. Amsterdam, Oct. 30, 1914. He received his rudimentary musical education at home from his uncle, who taught him piano; then had piano lessons with Arend Koole and studied theory with Brandts-Buys. He took academic courses at the Univ. of Amsterdam, and musicology at the Univ. of Utrecht (1932–37). He served as assistant manager of the Concertgebouw Orch. After the occupation of the Netherlands by the Germans in 1940, he was dismissed from his job (his wife was half Jewish). On Sept. 18, 1943, he was arrested by the Nazis on the charge of hiding Jews, and transported to the concentration camp in Vught, the Netherlands, and a year later to a German labor camp. His liberation came on May 4, 1945, in a forest near Schwerin; he returned to Amsterdam and was reinstated at his managerial job at the Concertgebouw in 1953. From 1955 to 1974 he was artistic director of the Concertgebouw. In 1974 he was appointed prof. of musicology at the Univ. of Utrecht. He publ. several books, including a monograph on W.A. Mozart (The Hague, 1940) and the essay *Mozarts Bearbeitungen eigener und fremder Werke* (Kassel, 1969). In his compositions, he adopted the motivic method of melodic writing and its concomitant form of variations in freely dissonant counterpoint and largely neo-Classical format. Dissatisfied with his youthful works, he destroyed his MSS dating before 1934, including some perfectly acceptable symphonic pieces.

WORKS: ORCH.: Concertino for Small Orch. (1940); *Small Overture* for Soprano and Orch. (1942); *Dramatic Overture* (1943–46); Flute Concerto (Utrecht, Dec. 19, 1945); Concerto for Horn and Small Orch. (1945); *Valses sentimentales* for Small Orch. (1946; also for Piano, 4-hands); Concerto for Piano and Small Orch. (1946–48); *Capriccio* for Wind or String Orch. (1949); Concerto for Violin and Small Orch. (1950; Utrecht, Jan. 14, 1952); *Fantasia* for Harp and Small Orch. (1953; Amsterdam, May 26, 1955); *Sinfonietta concertante* for Clarinet, Saxophone, and Small Orch. (1954–55; Amsterdam, June 2, 1955); Concert Overture (1955); *Rondo festoso* (Amsterdam, July 7, 1956); Clarinet Concerto (1957); *Symphonic Music* (1957); *Spes patriae,* sinfonietta for Small Orch. (1962); *Espressioni cordiali,* 7 bagatelles for Strings (1963); *Canti e Giouchi* (Songs and Games) for Wind

Quintet and Strings (1964); Concertino for Oboe and Small Orch. (1968); *Per Sonare ed Ascoltare*, 5 canzonas for Flute and Orch. (1971); *Nocturne* (1977); *Cantus amoris* for Strings (1979). **CHAMBER:** Sonata for Solo Cello (1937–38); *Nocturne* for Flute, Oboe, and Clarinet (1941); Quintet for Flute, Oboe, Clarinet, Bass Clarinet, and Bassoon (1941–42); *Sonata da camera* for Flute and Piano (1943); *Aria* for Trumpet and Piano (1944); *3 Pieces* for 2 Horns (1945); *Ronde champêtre* for Flute and Harpsichord (1945); Sonata for Solo Violin (1945); *Partita* for Violin and Piano (1950); *Pour le tombeau d'Orphée* for Harp (1950); *Trio serio* for Piano Trio (1950–51); *Sonata da camera* for Flute and Harp (1951); *Small Suite* for 12 Harps (1951; in collaboration with L. van Delden); String Quartet (1951–52); *Small Suite* for Oboe, Trumpet, Clarinet or Saxophone, and Piano (1952); *Divertimento* for Clarinet, Bassoon, Horn, Violin, Viola, and Double Bass (1952); *4 invenzioni* for 4 Horns (1963); Partita for 2 Violins (1966); Concertino for Oboe, Violin, Viola, and Cello (1967); *Allegro vivace* for 2 Harps (1969); *Caprices roumains* for Oboe and Piano (1975); *Adagio* for Piano, 4-hands, and Percussion (1975); *Romeo's Lament* for Horn (1975); *Canzone* for 4 Wind Instruments (1978); *Capriccio* for 4 Saxophones (1985–86); Sonata for Oboe, Horn, and Harpsichord (1986); *Preludio e Fughetta* for 3 Trumpets (1986); Quartet for 2 Violins, Viola, and Cello (1991–92); piano pieces. **VOCAL:** *Hymnus* for Soprano and Orch. (1965); *Santa Espina* for Mezzo-soprano and Orch. (1985–86); numerous other pieces, including choral works and songs.

Flower, Sir (Walter) Newman, noted English publisher and writer on music; b. Fontmell Magna, Dorset, July 8, 1879; d. Blandford, Dorset, March 12, 1964. He joined the firm of Cassel & Co. in 1906 and purchased it in 1927. He became deeply interested in music; publ. an extensive biography, *George Frideric Handel: His Personality and His Times* (London, 1923; 2nd ed., rev., 1947); also *Sir Arthur Sullivan: His Life, Letters and Diaries* (London, 1927; 2nd ed., rev., 1950); *Franz Schubert: The Man and His Circle* (London, 1928; 2nd ed., rev., 1949); also prepared a *Catalogue of a Handel Collection Formed by Newman Flower* (Sevenoaks, 1921); publ. a vol. of memoirs, *Just As It Happened* (London, 1950). He was knighted in 1938.

BIBL.: A. Walker, *George Frideric Handel: The N. F. Collection* (Manchester, 1972).

Floyd, Carlisle (Sessions, Jr.), American composer and teacher; b. Latta, S.C., June 11, 1926. He studied at Syracuse Univ. with Ernst Bacon (Mus.B., 1946; Mus.M., 1949); also took private piano lessons with Rudolf Firkušný and Sidney Foster. In 1947 he joined the staff of the School of Music of Florida State Univ., Tallahassee; in 1976, became a prof. of music at the Univ. of Houston. His musical drama *Susannah* was premiered in Tallahassee (Feb. 24, 1955); it was later staged at the City Center in N.Y. (Sept. 27, 1956), winning the N.Y. Music Critics Circle Award. Floyd's other works include *Slow Dusk*, musical play (1949); *Fugitives*, musical drama (1951); operas: *Wuthering Heights* (Santa Fe, July 16, 1958); *The Passion of Jonathan Wade* (N.Y., Oct. 11, 1962); *The Sojourner and Mollie Sinclair* (Raleigh, N.C., Dec. 2, 1963); *Markheim* (New Orleans, March 31, 1966); *Of Mice and Men* (Seattle, Jan. 22, 1970); *Bilby's Doll* (Houston, Feb. 29, 1976); *Willie Stark* (Houston, April 24, 1981). He further wrote the ballet *Lost Eden* for 2 Pianos (1952); *Pilgrimage*, cycle of 5 songs (1955); *The Mystery (5 Songs of Motherhood)* for Soprano and Orch. (1962); *In Celebration: An Overture* (1970); other vocal and instrumental pieces.

Flummerfelt, Joseph, American conductor; b. Vincennes, Ind., Feb. 24, 1937. He studied at DePauw Univ. (B.Mus., 1958), the Philadelphia Cons. of Music (M.Mus., 1962), and the Univ. of Ill. (D.M.A., 1971); he also had private lessons with Herford in San Diego (1958) and Boulanger in Fontainebleau (1964). He was director of choral activities at DePauw Univ. (1964–68) and Florida State Univ. (1968–71); in 1971 he was appointed choral director at Westminster Choir College; in 1982 he became artistic director and principal conductor there. He served as choral director of the Spoleto Festival in Italy (from 1971) and in the U.S. (from 1976); also held the posts of director of the N.Y. Choral Artists and chorus master of the N.Y. Phil. In 1990 he became director of choral activities at the New England Cons. of Music in Boston.

Flury, Richard, Swiss composer, conductor and teacher; b. Biberist, March 26, 1896; d. there, Dec. 23, 1967. He studied musicology in Basel, Bern, and Geneva, then theory and composition with Kurth, Hubert, Lauber, and Marx. He conducted orchs. and choral societies in Switzerland; taught at the Solothurn Canton School. He wrote an autobiography, *Lebenserinnerungen* (1950; with a list of works).

WORKS: DRAMATIC: OPERAS: *Eine florentinische Tragödie* (1926); *Die helle Nacht* (1932); *Casanova e l'Albertolli* (1937). **BALLET:** *Die alte Truhe* (1945). **ORCH.:** 7 syms.: No. 1 (1923), *Fastnachts-Symphonie* (1928), *Tessiner Symphonie* (No. 2, 1936), *Waldsymphonie* (1942), *Bucheggbergische Symphonie* (No. 3, 1946), *Liechtensteinische Symphonie* (No. 4, 1951), and No. 5 (1955–56); 6 symphonic overtures; 2 piano concertos (1927, 1943); 4 violin concertos (1933, 1940, 1944, 1965); *Caprice* for Violin and Orch. (1967). **CHAMBER:** Oboe Sonata (1926); 7 string quartets (1926, 1929, 1938, 1940, 1955, 1958, 1964); 3 cello sonatas (1937, 1941, 1966); Piano Quintet (1948); 11 violin sonatas (Nos. 5–11, 1940–61). **PIANO:** Sonata (1920); *50 romantische Stücke*; 24 preludes. **OTHER:** 15 military marches and other music for Band; choruses; about 150 songs.

Flynn, George (William), American composer; b. Miles City, Mont., Jan. 21, 1937. He studied composition with Ussachevsky (1960–64), Beeson (1964–66), and Luening at Columbia Univ. (D.M.A., 1972). He was on the faculty at his alma mater (1966–73) and also taught at City College of the City Univ. of N.Y. (1973–76). In 1977 he was appointed chairman of the composition dept. at DePaul Univ. in Chicago. He was a co-founder of Chicago Soundings, a performing group for contemporary music. His own music is of a quaquaversal nature, disdaining nothing, absorbing anything of modernistic applicability.

WORKS: DRAMATIC: *Mrs. Brown*, ballet for Chamber Orch. and Tape (1965). **ORCH.:** 2 syms.: No. 1, *Music for Orchestra* (1966) and No. 2 (Chicago, May 19, 1981); *Lammy* for Strings (1973); *Javeh* (1973); *Meditations, Praises* (Chicago, June 20, 1981); *Focus* for Chamber Orch. (1983); *Coloration* for Chamber Orch. (1983); *Quietude* for Chamber Orch. (1983); *Lost and Found* for Youth Orch. (1984). **CHAMBER:** Piano Quartet (1963); *Solo and Duos* for Violin and Piano (1964); Wind Quintet (1965; rev. 1983); *4 Pieces* for Violin and Piano (1965); *Duo* for Clarinet and Piano (1966); *Duo* for Trumpet and Piano (1974); *Duo* for Viola and Piano (1974); *American Rest* for Clarinet, Viola, Cello, and Piano (1975; rev. 1982); *American Festivals and Dreams* for String Quartet (1976); *Duo* for Cello and Piano (1977); *Celebration* for Violin and Piano (1980); Saxophone Quartet (1980); *4 Fantasy-Etudes* for Violin (1981); *Diversion* for Flute, Clarinet, Violin, Cello, and Piano (1984). **KEYBOARD: PIANO:** *Fuguing* (1962); 4 Preludes (1965); *Fantasy No. 1* (1966) and *No. 2* (1980–82); *Music* for Piano, 4-hands (1966); *Wound* (1968); *Canal* (1976). **HARPSICHORD:** *Drive* (1973). **VOCAL:** *Tirades and Dreams* for Actress, Soprano, and Chamber Orch. (1972); *Songs of Destruction*, 5 duos for Soprano and Piano (1973–74); *American Songs*, 6 settings for Chorus, Horn, and Piano (1983–84); choruses.

Fodi, John, Hungarian-born Canadian composer; b. Nagyteval, March 22, 1944. He emigrated to Canada from Germany with his family in 1951, becoming a naturalized citizen in 1961. He studied theory and composition with Betts in Hamilton (1964–66), composition with Weinzweig and Beckwith and electronic music with Ciamaga at the Univ. of Toronto (B.Mus., 1970), and composition with Anhalt and electronic music with Pedersen at McGill Univ. in Montreal (1970–71); then returned to the Univ. of Toronto to complete his training in composition with Weinzweig (M.Mus., 1972). He subsequently had some lessons with Davidovsky at Johnson State College (1973) and later took his M.L.S. degree at the Univ. of Toronto (1990). In 1967 he founded the Contemporary Music Group at the Univ. of Toronto, serving as its artistic director until 1970; while at McGill Univ., he was co-founder of the New Music Group and in 1971 helped to organize ARRAY, a contemporary music group, later serving as its president and artistic director (1976–79). In 1974 he joined the staff of the Edward Johnson Music Library at the Univ. of Toronto. His compositions partake of multifarious techniques of ultramodern music, with an evident preoccupation with abstract textures and mathematical processes.

WORKS: DRAMATIC: *Music Bockxd* for 3 Actors or Dancers, 7 Music Boxes, and Tape (1969). **ORCH.:** 2 syms.: No. 1 (1964–66) and No. 2 (1987–); *Symparanekromenoi* (1969–71; Toronto, July 25, 1974); Concerto for Viola and 2 Wind Ensembles (1972); *Dragon Day* (1976); *Adagio* for Strings (1980); Concertino for Bassoon and Chamber Orch. (1983); Concerto Grosso for Chamber Ensemble (1984); *Kootenay* for Chamber Orch. (1986); Suite for Junior String Orch. (1988–89). **CHAMBER:** 7 string quartets: No. 1 (1963), No. 2, *Short* (1963), No. 3 (1965), No. 4, *Fantasia* (1967), No. 5, *Concerto a quattro* (1973), No. 6, *Aus tiefer Not* (1981), and No. 7, *Purcell* (1987–89); Piano Sonata (1964–66); Chamber Sym. for Flute, Horn, Piano, and String Quartet (1967); *Tettares* for Percussion Quartet (1968); Harpsichord Sonata (1968); *4 for 4* for Clarinet Quartet (1968); *Signals* for Soprano Saxophone, Tenor Saxophone, Trombone, Percussion, and Piano (1969); *Ch'ien* for String Quartet (1969); *Elements* for 1 to 5 Melody Instruments (1972); *Variations II* for Woodwind Quintet (1975); *In campo aperto* for Flute, Oboe, Percussion, 2 Pianos, and Cello (1976); Trio for Flute, Viola, and Harpsichord (1977); *Concerto in 4 Parts* for Accordion (1978); *Dum transisset, "sonata for 5 instruments"* for Flute, Trombone, Piano, Viola, and Cello (1978–); *Birds*, 4 pieces for Various Instruments (1978–79); *Time's fell hand defac'd* for Flute, English Horn or Clarinet, Percussion, Piano, and Cello (1978–89); *Western Wynde, "serenata for 7 instruments"* for Flute, Clarinet, Brass Instrument, Piano, Violin, Viola, and Cello (1979; rev. 1986); Wind Octet for 2 Oboes, 2 Clarinets, 2 Bassoons, and 2 Horns (1980–81); Partita for Brass Quintet (1981–82); Sonata for Double Wind Quintet (1982–83); Tuba Quartet for 2 Euphoniums and 2 Tubas (1984). **VOCAL:** Choruses; songs.

Fodor, Eugene (Nicholas, Jr.), American violinist; b. Turkey Creek, Colo., March 5, 1950. His great-great-grandfather founded the Fodor Cons. in Hungary. He studied violin with Harold Wippler in Denver; in 1967 he went to N.Y. and studied with Galamian; then with Gingold at the Indiana Univ. School of Music in Bloomington (diploma, 1970); later took lessons in the master class of Heifetz at the Univ. of Southern Calif. in Los Angeles (1970–71). In 1972 he won the Paganini Competition in Genoa, Italy. In 1974 he shared 2nd prize with 2 Soviet violinists (no 1st prize was awarded) at the Tchaikovsky Competition in Moscow. Returning to America, he was given the honors of the state of Colorado, and on Sept. 12, 1974, played at a state dinner at the White House in Washington, D.C., for the premier of Israel, Rabin. In subsequent years, he appeared as a soloist with a number of major orchs., and also was active as a recitalist. His seemingly successful career took a bizarre twist in 1989 when he was arrested and jailed for cocaine and heroin possession, cocaine trafficking, and breaking-and-entering on Martha's Vineyard in Massachusetts. However, he was able to overcome this setback and resumed his career.

Foerster, Josef Bohuslav, eminent Czech composer and teacher; b. Prague, Dec. 30, 1859; d. Nový Vestec, near Stará Boleslav, May 29, 1951. He was the son of the organist, teacher, and composer Josef Förster (b. Osojnitz, Feb. 22, 1833; d. Prague, Jan. 3, 1907). He studied at the Prague Organ School (1879–82), then was organist at St. Vojtěch (1882–88) and choirmaster of Panna Marie Sněžná (1889–94). He married the Czech soprano Berta Foerstrová-Lautererová (b. Prague, Jan. 11, 1869; d. there, April 9, 1936) in 1888; when she became a member of the Hamburg Opera in 1893, he settled there as a music critic and later became a prof. of piano at the Cons. in 1901. After his wife became a member of the Vienna Court Opera in 1903, he became a prof. of composition at the New Vienna Cons. He returned to Prague in 1918; then taught composition at the Cons. (1919–22), at its master school (1922–31), and at the Univ. of Prague (1920–36). He served as president of the Czech Academy of Sciences and Art (1931–39), and was awarded the honorary title of National Artist of the Czech government in 1945. He continued to teach privately and to compose during the last years of his long life. He taught many distinguished Czech composers of the 20th century. He publ. a detailed autobiography (Prague, 1929–47), as well as several vols. of essays and articles. Of his numerous compositions, the most important are his operas, instrumental music, and choral pieces written before World War I. His works from this period are suffused with lyric melos, and reveal characteristic national traits in Foerster's treatment of melodic and rhythmic material; his harmonic idiom represents the general style of Central European Romanticism.

WORKS: DRAMATIC: OPERAS (all 1st perf. in Prague): *Debora* (1890–91; Jan. 27, 1893); *Eva* (1895–97; Jan. 1, 1899); *Jessika* (1902–04; April 16, 1905); *Nepřemoženi* (Invincibilities; 1917; Dec. 19, 1918); *Srdce* (Hearts; 1921–22; Nov. 15, 1923); *Bloud* (The Fool; 1935–36; Feb. 28, 1936); incidental music for various plays. **ORCH.:** 5 syms.: No. 1 (1887–88), No. 2 (1892–93), No. 3 (1894), No. 4 (1905), and No. 5 (1929); *Mé mládí* (My Youth), symphonic poem (1900); *Cyrano de Bergerac*, suite (1903); *Ze Shakespeara* (From Shakespeare), suite (1908–09); *Legenda o štěstí* (Legend of Happiness), symphonic poem (1909); 2 violin concertos (1910–11; 1925–26); *Jaro a touha* (Spring and Longing), symphonic poem (1912); *Jičínská suita* (1923); Cello Concerto (1930); Capriccio for Flute and Small Orch. (1945–46). **CHAMBER:** 3 piano trios (1883; 1894; 1919–21); String Quintet (1886); 5 string quartets (1888; 1893; 1907–13; 1944; 1951); 2 cello sonatas (1898, 1926); Wind Quintet (1909); Piano Quintet (1928); Nonet (1931); Violin Sonata (1925); *Sonata quasi fantasia* for Solo Violin (1943); piano pieces. **VOCAL:** Choral works; songs.

BIBL.: Z. Nejedlý, *J.B. F.* (Prague, 1910); J. Bartoš, *J.B. F.* (Prague, 1923); J. Bartoš, P. Pražák, and J. Plavec, eds., *J.B. F.: Jeho životní pout a tvorba: 1859–1949* (on his life and work; Prague, 1949); F. Pala, *J.B. F.* (Prague, 1962).

Fogg, (Charles William) Eric, English organist and composer; b. Manchester, Feb. 21, 1903; d. London, Dec. 19, 1939. He studied organ with his father and composition with Bantock. He was active as an organist in Manchester; then was on the staff of the BBC. He wrote an overture to the *Comedy of Errors* (1922); *Poem* for Cello and Piano; Suite for Violin, Cello, and Harp; piano pieces; choral works; songs.

BIBL.: L. Foreman, "F. out of the mists . . . ," *Music and Musicians International* (Sept. 1989).

Foldes (actually, **Földes**), **Andor,** admired Hungarian-born American pianist; b. Budapest, Dec. 21, 1913; d. Herrliberg, Switzerland, Feb. 9, 1992. He began piano lessons at an early age with his mother, and was only 8 when he appeared as soloist in Mozart's 15th Piano Concerto, K.450, with the Budapest Phil. In 1922 he entered the Royal Academy of Music in Budapest and studied with Dohnányi (piano), Weiner (composition), and Ernst Unger (conducting). Upon graduating and winning the Liszt Prize in 1933, he made his first tour of Europe. In 1939 he went to N.Y., where he made his U.S. debut as an orch. soloist in a radio concert in 1940. In 1941 he made his U.S. recital debut at N.Y.'s Town Hall. He became a naturalized American citizen in 1948, but pursued a global concert career. From 1957 to 1965 he also gave master classes at the Saarbrücken Hochschule für Musik. In 1961 he settled in Switzerland. While he continued to devote himself mainly to his career as a piano virtuoso, he occasionally appeared as a conductor and was active as a composer, primarily of piano pieces. Foldes was esteemed for his performances of the Classical and early

Romantic masters, but he also displayed a special affinity for the music of Bartók. With his wife Lili Foldes, he publ. *Two on a Continent* (N.Y., 1947). He also publ. *Keys to the Keyboard* (N.Y., 1948) and *Gibt es einen zeitgenössischen Beethoven-Stil? und andere Aufsätze* (Wiesbaden, 1963). His *Erinnerungen* appeared posthumously (Frankfurt am Main, 1993).

BIBL.: W.-E. von Lewinski, *A.F.* (Berlin, 1970).

Fongaard, Björn, Norwegian composer and guitarist; b. Christiania, March 2, 1919; d. there (Oslo), Oct. 26, 1980. He took up the guitar at an early age before pursuing his musical training at the Oslo Cons. with Per Steenberg, Bjarne Brustad, and Karl Andersen. He appeared as a guitarist and also taught guitar at the Oslo Cons. His interest in the potentialities of fractional intervals led him to devise special guitars for playing microtonal music with the aid of electronic techniques which he described as "orchestra microtonalis." He composed a prolific corpus of works in every conceivable genre.

WORKS: DRAMATIC: *Skapelse II* (Creation II), church opera (1972); *Andromeda*, ballet music (1972); *Dimensions*, ballet music (1974). **ORCH.:** 2 sinfoniettas (1951, 1968); Sonata Concertante for Guitar and Orch. (1963); 12 symphonic poems (1963–71); *Orchestral Antiphonalis* (1968); *Symphony of Space I–III* (1969); *Sinfonia Geo-Paleontologica I–V* (1970); *Relativity: Symphony I–III* (1970); 23 piano concertos (1973–76); 3 flute concertos (1973–76); 7 violin concertos (1973–77); 3 horn concertos (1973–77); 2 oboe concertos (1976); 2 clarinet concertos (1976); 2 trumpet concertos (1977); 5 organ concertos (1977–78); many other concertos; 7 syms. for Strings (1980). **CHAMBER:** 2 guitar sonatas (1947, 1963); 2 microtonal guitar sonatas (1965, 1975); 2 sonatas for Solo Oboe (1967, 1968); Sonata for Electronically Metamorphosed Tam-tam (1968); Sonata for Saxophone and Microtonal Guitar (1970); Sonata for Solo Bassoon (1972); Trio for Flute, Viola, and Harp (1971); 21 string quartets (1973); 9 wind quintets (1974); 9 wind trios (1975); 6 wind quartets (1975); 12 string trios (1975); numerous other works, including 57 solo sonatas. Additional works include a vast amount of piano music, organ pieces, vocal music, and tape pieces.

Fonseca, Julio, Costa Rican composer; b. San José, May 22, 1885; d. there, June 22, 1950. He received elementary musical training at home from his father, a military band musician. A government grant enabled him to pursue serious study at the Milan Cons. and in Brussels. Returning to Costa Rica, he became active as a teacher at music schools in San Jose and as a church organist. His works consist mostly of pleasant salon music for piano and effective band pieces, much of it based on native folk rhythms.

Fontyn, Jacqueline, Belgian composer and teacher; b. Antwerp, Dec. 27, 1930. She studied piano with Ignace Bolotine in her native city, and later with Marcel Maas; took theory, orchestration, and composition lessons with Marcel Quinet in Brussels and Max Deutsch in Paris; then completed her study of composition at the Chapelle Musicale Reine Elisabeth in Brussels (graduated, 1959). She taught at the Royal Flemish Cons. in Antwerp (1963–70); then was a prof. of composition at the Brussels Cons. (1970–90). Fontyn won many prizes for her compositions, including the Koopal Prize of the Belgian Ministry of Culture (1961, 1979), the Camille Huismans Prize of Antwerp (1974), and the Arthur Honegger Prize of Paris (1987). In 1961 she married **Camille Schmitt**.

WORKS: BALLET: *Piedigrotta* (1958). **ORCH.:** *Petite suite* (1951); *Divertimento* for Strings (1953); *Danceries* (1956); *Prelude and Allegro* (1957); *Mouvements concertants* for 2 Pianos and Strings (1957); *Deux estampies* (1961); *Digressions* for Cello and Chamber Orch. (1962); *Six ébauches* (1963); *Digressions* for Chamber Orch. (1964); *Galaxie* for Chamber Orch. (1965); Piano Concerto (1967); *Colloque* for Wind Quintet and Strings (1970); *Pour II archets* (1971); *Evoluon* (1972); *Per archi* for Strings (1973); Violin Concerto (1975); *Frises I* (1975) and *II* (1976); *Halo* for Harp and 16 Instruments or Chamber Orch. (1978); *Creneaux* (1982); *Arachne* (1985); *In the Green Shade* (1988); *Reverie and Turbulence*, piano concerto (1989); *A l'orée du Songe*, viola concerto (1990); *Colinda*, cello concerto (1991); *On a Landscape by Turner* (1992). **CHAMBER:** Wind Quintet (1954); Trio for Violin, Cello, and Piano (1956); String Quartet (1958); *Musica a quattro* for Violin, Clarinet, Cello, and Piano (1966); Nonet (1969); *Strophes* for Violin and Piano (1970); *Six climats* for Violin and Piano (1972); *Horizons* for String Quartet (1977); *Zones* for Flute, Clarinet, Cello, Percussion, and Piano (1979); *Rhumbs* for 2 Trumpets, Horn, Trombone, and Tuba (1980); *Analecta* for 2 Violins (1981); *Controverse* for Bass Clarinet or Tenor Saxophone and Percussion (1983); *Either . . . or entweder . . . oder* for String Quintet or Clarinet and String Quartet (1984); *Cheminement* for 9 Instrumentalists (1986); *La Devinière* for Violin and Piano (1988); *Scurochiatro* for 7 Instrumentalists (1989); *Compagnon de la nuit* for Oboe and Piano (1989). **KEYBOARD: PIANO SOLO:** *2 Impromptus* (1950); *Capriccio* (1954); *Ballade* (1964); *Mosaici* (1964); *Le Gong* (1980); *Bulles* (1980); *Aura* (1982). **2 PIANOS:** *Spirales* (1971). **HARPSICHORD:** *Shadows* (1973). **VOCAL:** *La Trapéziste qui a perdu son coeur* for Mezzo-soprano and Chamber Orch. (1953); *Psalmus Tertius* for Baritone, Chorus, and Orch. (1959); *Ephémères* for Mezzo-soprano and 11 Instruments (1979); *Alba* for Soprano and 4 Instruments (1981); *Pro & Antiverbe(e)s* for Soprano and Cello (1984); *Blake's Mirror* for Mezzo-soprano and Symphonic Band (1993).

BIBL.: B. Brand, *J. F.* (Berlin, 1991).

Foote, Arthur (William), distinguished American composer; b. Salem, Mass., March 5, 1853; d. Boston, April 8, 1937. He studied harmony with Emery at the New England Cons. of Music in Boston (1867–70) and took courses in counterpoint and fugue with Paine at Harvard College (1870–74), where he received the first M.A. degree in music granted by an American univ. (1875). He also studied organ and piano with B.J. Lang, and later with Stephen Heller in France (1883). Returning to the U.S., he taught piano, organ, and composition in Boston; was organist at Boston's Church of the Disciples (1876–78) and at the 1st Unitarian Church (1878–1910); also frequently appeared as a pianist with the Kneisel Quartet (1890–1910), performing several of his own works. He was a founding member and president (1909–12) of the American Guild of Organists. He taught piano at the New England Cons. of Music (1921–37). Foote was elected a member of the National Inst. of Arts and Letters (1898). His music, a product of the Romantic tradition, is notable for its fine lyrical élan. His Suite in E major for Strings (1907) enjoyed numerous performances and became a standard of American orch. music. He publ. *Modern Harmony in Its Theory and Practice* (with W.R. Spalding; 1905; rev. ed., 1959; republ. as *Harmony*, 1969), *Some Practical Things in Piano-Playing* (1909), and *Modulation and Related Harmonic Questions* (1919). His autobiography was privately printed (Norwood, Mass., 1946) by his daughter, Katharine Foote Raffy.

WORKS: ORCH.: *In the Mountains*, overture (1886; Boston, Feb. 5, 1887; rev. 1910); Cello Concerto (1887–93); *Francesca da Rimini*, symphonic prologue (1890; Boston, Jan. 24, 1891); *Serenade* for Strings (1891; based on the earlier Suites, opp. 12 and 21); Suite in D minor, op. 36 (1894–95; Boston, March 7, 1896); *4 Character Pieces* after the *Rubáiyát* of Omar Khayyam (1900; based on a set of piano pieces); Suite in E major for Strings, op. 63 (1907; rev. 1908; Boston, April 16, 1909); *A Night Piece* for Flute and Strings (1922; derived from the *Nocturne and Scherzo* for Flute and String Quartet, 1918). **CHAMBER:** 2 piano trios (1882; rev. 1883; 1907–08); 3 string quartets (1883; 1893; 1907–11); Violin Sonata (1889); *Romance and Scherzo* for Cello and Piano (1890); Piano Quartet (1890); Piano Quintet (1897); Sonata for Cello or Viola and Piano (n.d.); *Nocturne and Scherzo* for Flute and String Quartet (1918; also as *A Night Piece* for Flute and Strings, 1922); also various piano pieces; organ music. **VOCAL:** *The Farewell of Hiawatha* for Men's Chorus and Orch. (1885); *The Wreck of the Hesperus* for Chorus and Orch. (1887–88); *The Skeleton in Armor* for Chorus and Orch. (1891); *O Fear the Immortals, Ye Children of Men* for Mezzo-soprano and Orch. (1900); *Lygeia* for Women's Chorus and Orch. (1906); some 100 songs, 52 part songs, and 35 anthems.

BIBL.: F. Kopp, *A. F.: American Composer and Theorist* (diss., Univ. of Rochester, 1957); D. Alviani, *The Choral Church Music of A.W. F.* (diss., Union Theological Seminary, 1962); D. Moore, *The Cello Music of A. F., 1853–1937* (diss., Catholic Univ. of America, 1977); W. Cipolla, *A Catalog of the Works of A. F. (1853–1937)* (Detroit, 1980).

Foote, George (Luther), American composer; b. Cannes, France (of American parents), Feb. 19, 1886; d. Boston, March 25, 1956. He studied with E.B. Hill at Harvard Univ.; then in Berlin with Koch and Klatte. Upon his return to the U.S., he was a member of the staff in the music dept. of Harvard Univ. (1921–23) and president of the South End Music School in Boston (until 1943).

WORKS: *98th Psalm* for Chorus and Organ (1934); *Variations on a Pious Theme* for Orch. (Boston, Feb. 11, 1935); *In Praise of Winter*, symphonic suite (Boston, Jan. 5, 1940); *We Go Forward*, sacred pantomime (1943); Trio for Flute, Harp, and Violin; other chamber music; piano pieces.

Forbes, Elliot, American choral conductor, musicologist, and music educator; b. Cambridge, Mass., Aug. 30, 1917. He studied at Harvard Univ. (B.A., 1941; M.A., 1947); also took courses at the Mozarteum in Salzburg (1937). He subsequently was on the staff of the music dept. of Princeton Univ. (1947–57). From 1958 to 1984 he was a prof. at Harvard Univ., and from 1958 to 1970 conductor of the Harvard Glee Club and Radcliffe Choral Soc.; conducted the Harvard Glee Club in a tour around the world in 1961 and the Harvard-Radcliffe Chorus in a North American tour in 1964. He was the ed. of the revision of *Thayer's Life of Beethoven* (Princeton, 1964; 2nd ed., rev., 1967), gen. ed. of *Harvard-Radcliffe Choral Music* (from 1959), and ed. of the *Harvard Song Book* (Boston, 1965); publ. *A History of Music at Harvard to 1972* (Cambridge, Mass., 1988) and *A Report of Music at Harvard 1972–1990* (Cambridge, Mass., 1993).

BIBL.: L. Lockwood and P. Benjamin, eds., *Beethoven Essays: Studies in Honor of E. F.* (Cambridge, Mass., 1984).

Forbes, Sebastian, English organist, choral conductor, and composer; b. Amersham, Buckingham, May 22, 1941. He studied with Ferguson at the Royal Academy of Music in London (1958–60) and with Radcliffe and Dart at King's College, Cambridge (1960–64). He subsequently held positions as conductor of the Aeolian Singers (1965–69), Seiriol Singers (1969–72), and Horniman Singers (1981–90), and was a univ. lecturer at Bangor (1968–72) and Surrey (from 1972).

WORKS: *Pageant of St. Paul*, suite for Orch. (1964); Piano Trio (1964); *Antiphony* for Violin and Piano (1965); *Partita* for Clarinet, Cello, and Piano (1966); *Chaconne* for Orch. (1967); *Sequence of Carols* for Chorus (1967); *2nd Sequence of Carols* for Men's Chorus, String Orch., and Organ (London, May 1, 1968); String Quartet (1969); *Essay* for Clarinet and Orch. (London, July 28, 1970); *3rd Sequence of Carols* for Chorus (1971); 3 syms. (1972, 1978, 1990); *Fantasy* for Cello (1974); Sonata for 8 Instruments (1978); String Quartet No. 3 (1982).

Fordell, Erik, Finnish composer; b. Kokkola, July 2, 1917; d. Kaarlela, Dec. 21, 1981. He studied in Helsinki at the Sibelius Academy and the Inst. of Church Music. Fordell's output was enormous.

WORKS: 45 syms. (1949–81); 2 violin concertos (1955, 1959); Horn Concerto (1956); 4 piano concertos (1961–62); 8 string suites; 4 wind quintets; 7 string quartets; Violin Sonata; Flute Sonata; piano pieces; choral music; songs.

Formichi, Cesare, Italian baritone; b. Rome, April 15, 1883; d. there, July 21, 1949. He studied in Rome. He made his debut at the Teatro Lirico in Milan in 1911; then sang at the Teatro Colón in Buenos Aires, in Madrid, in Barcelona, and at the Paris Opéra; appeared with the Chicago Opera Co. (1922–32); sang at Covent Garden in London (1924). He was particularly effective in dramatic roles, such as Rigoletto, Iago, and Scarpia.

Fornerod, Aloÿs, Swiss violinist, music critic, educator, and composer; b. Montet-Cudrefin, Nov. 16, 1890; d. Fribourg, Jan. 8, 1965. He studied violin and theory at the Lausanne Cons. and at the Schola Cantorum in Paris. He was a member of the Lausanne Sym. Orch.; in 1954 he was appointed director of the Fribourg Cons. As a composer, he followed the French modern style, in the spirit of fin-de-siècle Impressionism. He publ. *Les Tendances de la musique moderne* (Lausanne, 1924); was for 40 years a critic for *La Tribune de Lausanne*.

WORKS: COMIC OPERA: *Geneviève* (Lausanne, May 20, 1954). **ORCH.:** *Le Voyage de printemps*, suite (1943); Piano Concerto (1944). **CHAMBER:** Violin Sonata (1925); Concerto for 2 Violins and Piano (1927); Cello Sonata (1934). **VOCAL:** Te Deum for Soloists, Chorus, and Orch. (1955); *Hymne à la Très Sainte Trinité* for Chorus and Brass (1961); choruses; songs.

BIBL.: J. Viret, *A. F., ou, Le Musicien et le pays* (Lausanne, 1982).

Fornia-Labey, Rita (née **Regina Newman**), American soprano, later mezzo-soprano; b. San Francisco, July 17, 1878; d. Paris, Oct. 27, 1922. She adopted the name Fornia after California; following her marriage to J.P. Labey in 1910, she used the name Fornia-Labey. She studied with Emil Fischer and Sofia Scalchi in N.Y. and Selma Nicklass-Kempner in Berlin. After making her operatic debut in Hamburg in 1901, she completed her training with Jean de Reszke in Paris. In 1903 she made her N.Y. debut as Siebel in *Faust* at the Brooklyn Academy of Music, and then toured with H.W. Savage's Opera Co. On Dec. 6, 1907, she made her Metropolitan Opera debut in N.Y. as the Geisha in Mascagni's *Iris*, remaining on its roster for the rest of her life.

Forrest, Hamilton, American composer; b. Chicago, Jan. 8, 1901; d. London, Dec. 26, 1963. He was a student of Weidig at the American Cons. of Music in Chicago (M.M., 1926). His opera *Yzdra* (1925) received the Bispham Memorial Medal, and his opera *Camille*, with Mary Garden in the title role, was highly praised at its premiere (Chicago, Dec. 10, 1930). He prepared settings of 33 Kentucky mountain melodies and Negro folk songs, including *He's Got the Whole World in His Hands*, which were championed by Marian Anderson.

WORKS: DRAMATIC: OPERAS: *Yzdra* (1925); *Camille* (Chicago, Dec. 10, 1930); *Marie Odile* (n.d.); *Don Fortunio* (Interlochen, Mich., July 22, 1952); *Daelia* (Interlochen, July 21, 1954); *Galatea* (1957). **BALLETS:** *The Yellow Wind* and *Le Paus des Revenants*. Also incidental music. **OTHER:** 2 piano concertos; *Panorama* for Piano and Orch.; *Watercolors* for 14 Wind Instruments and Harp; piano pieces; songs.

Forrester, Maureen (Kathleen Stewart), outstanding Canadian contralto; b. Montreal, July 25, 1930. She studied piano and sang in Montreal church choirs. At 16, she began vocal training with Sally Martin in Montreal; at 19, she became a student of Frank Rowe; at 20, she found a mentor in Bernard Diamant, with whom she continued to work for over a decade; she also had lessons with Michael Raucheisen in Berlin in 1955. On Dec. 8, 1951, she made her professional debut in Elgar's *The Music Makers* with the Montreal Elgar Choir. Her recital debut followed in Montreal on March 29, 1953. On Feb. 14, 1955, she made her European debut in a recital at the Salle Gaveau in Paris, and then toured throughout Europe. She made her N.Y. debut at Town Hall on Nov. 12, 1956. Her extraordinary success as a soloist in Mahler's 2nd Sym. with Bruno Walter and the N.Y. Phil. on Feb. 17, 1957, set the course of a brilliant international career as a concert artist. In subsequent years, she appeared as a soloist with most of the principal conductors and orchs. of the world, and also gave numerous recitals. From 1965 to 1974 she was a member of the Bach Aria Group in N.Y., and also served as chairman of the voice dept. at the Philadelphia Musical Academy (1966–71). She also began to give increasing attention to opera. On May 28, 1962, she made her Toronto stage debut as Gluck's Orfeo. In 1963 she appeared as Brangäne at the Teatro Colón in Buenos Aires. She made her U.S. stage debut as Cornelia in Handel's *Julius Caesar* at the

N.Y. City Opera on Sept. 27, 1966. On Feb. 10, 1975, she made her Metropolitan Opera debut in N.Y. as Erda in *Das Rheingold.* In 1982 she appeared as Madame de la Haltière in Massenet's *Cendrillon* at the San Francisco Opera. In 1990 she made her debut at Milan's La Scala as the Countess in *The Queen of Spades.* From 1983 to 1988 she was chairperson of the Canada Council, and from 1986 to 1990 she was chancellor of Wilfrid Laurier Univ. She received over 30 honorary doctorates. In 1967 she was made a Companion of the Order of Canada and in 1990 received the Order of Ontario. With M. MacDonald, she wrote *Out of Character: A Memoir* (Toronto, 1986). In spite of her later success in opera, Forrester's reputation was first and foremost that of a remarkable interpreter of solo works with orch., oratorio, and Lieder.

Forsell, John (actually, **Carl Johan Jacob),** famous Swedish baritone and pedagogue; b. Stockholm, Nov. 6, 1868; d. there, May 30, 1941. He served as an officer in the Swedish Army before pursuing vocal training in Stockholm. On Feb. 26, 1896, he made his operatic debut as Figaro in *Il barbiere di Siviglia* at the Royal Opera in Stockholm, where he was a member until 1901, and again from 1903 to 1909. On June 26, 1909, he made his debut at London's Covent Garden as Don Giovanni, his most celebrated role. He made his Metropolitan Opera debut in N.Y. on Nov. 20, 1909, as Telramund, but remained on its roster for only that season before pursuing his career in Europe. He made guest appearances in Berlin, Vienna, Bayreuth, and other music centers. In 1938 he appeared as Don Giovanni for the last time in Copenhagen. From 1923 to 1939 he was director of the Royal Opera in Stockholm, and he also was prof. of voice at the Stockholm Cons. from 1924 to 1931. His notable students included Jussi Björling, Set Svanholm, and Aksel Schiøtz. The beauty of his voice was ably seconded by his assured vocal technique. Among his other roles were Hans Sachs, Beckmesser, Amfortas, Eugene Onegin, Germont, and Scarpia.

BIBL.: E. Ljungberger, *J.F.* (Stockholm, 1916); *Boken om J.F.* (Stockholm, 1938); K. Liliedahl, *J.F.: A Discography* (Trelleborg, 1972).

Forsyth, Cecil, English composer and writer on music; b. Greenwich, Nov. 30, 1870; d. N.Y., Dec. 7, 1941. He received his general education at the Univ. of Edinburgh; then studied at the Royal College of Music in London with Stanford and Parry. He joined the viola section in the Queen's Hall Orch.; also was connected with the Savoy Theatre, where he produced 2 of his comic operas, *Westward Ho!* and *Cinderella.* After the outbreak of World War I, he went to N.Y., where he remained for the rest of his life. He composed a Viola Concerto and *Chant celtique* for Viola and Orch.; also songs, sacred music, and instrumental pieces. He was the author of a comprehensive manual, *Orchestration* (N.Y., 1914; 2nd ed., 1935; reprinted 1948); *Choral Orchestration* (London, 1920); also a treatise on English opera, *Music and Nationalism* (London, 1911). He publ. (in collaboration with Stanford) *A History of Music* (London, 1916) and a collection of essays, *Clashpans* (N.Y., 1933).

Forsyth, Malcolm (Denis), South African-born Canadian composer, trombonist, conductor, and teacher; b. Pietermaritzburg, Dec. 8, 1936. He was educated at the Univ. of Cape Town (M.Mus., 1966; D.Mus., 1972); among his mentors were Stefans Grove, Mátyás Seiber, and Gideon Fagan (composition), George Hurst and Georg Tintner (conducting), and Hans Grin (trombone). He was co-principal trombonist in the Cape Town Municipal Orch. (1961–67) before settling in Canada; in 1974 he became a naturalized Canadian citizen. He played in the Edmonton Sym. Orch. (from 1968), serving as its principal trombone (1973–80); also was a member of the Univ. of Alberta Brass Quintet (1975–83), and founder-leader of the Malcolm Forsyth Trombone Ensemble (1976–83). He served as conductor of the St. Cecilia Orch. in Edmonton (1977–86). In 1968 he joined the faculty of the Univ. of Alberta, becoming artistic director of its music dept. in 1986. As a composer, he successfully applied both African and North American folk elements.

WORKS: ORCH.: *Erewhon,* overture (1962); *Jubilee Overture* (Cape Town, May 5, 1964; rev. 1966); *Essay for Orchestra '67* (Cape Town, Dec. 15, 1967); 3 syms.: No. 1 (1968–72; Cape Town, Sept. 5, 1972), No. 2, *". . . a host of nomads . . ."* (1976; Edmonton, March 11, 1977), and No. 3, *African Ode* (1980–87; Edmonton, Jan. 30, 1987); *Sketches from Natal* (CBC, March 23, 1970); Piano Concerto (1973–75; Edmonton, March 30, 1979); 3 concerti grossi: No. 1, *Sagittarius* (Banff, Aug. 16, 1975), No. 2, *Quinquefid* (1976–77; Edmonton, April 6, 1977), and No. 3, *The Salpinx* (1981; Edmonton, Feb. 5, 1982); *Images of Night* (1982); *Rhapsody* for 14 Strings (1982; Edmonton, April 18, 1983); *Ukuzalwa* (1983); *Springtide* (Banff, April 3, 1984); *Atayoskewin,* suite (Edmonton, Nov. 16, 1984); *Serenade* for Strings (1985–86; Toronto, May 12, 1986); Trumpet Concerto (1987; Montreal, Jan. 11, 1988); *Songs from the Qu'appelle Valley* for Brass Band (1987); *Little Suite* for Strings (1988); *Valley of a Thousand Hills* (1989). **CHAMBER:** *Quartet '61* for Brass (1961); *Pastorale and Rondo* for Flute, Clarinet, Horn, Bassoon, and Piano (1968–69); *Quartet '74* for Brass (1974); *6 Episodes after Keats* for Violin, Viola, and Piano (1979–81); *Music for Wit and Science* for Recorder, Lute, and Viola da Gamba, or for Flute, Guitar, and Cello (1982); Wind Quintet (1986); *Soliloquy, Epitaph, and Allegro* for Trombone and Organ (1988); *Zephyrus* for Brass (1989).

Forte, Allen, American music theorist; b. Portland, Oreg., Dec. 23, 1926. He was educated at Columbia Univ. (B.S., 1950; M.A., 1952), then taught at Teachers College of Columbia Univ. (1953–59), the Mannes College of Music (1957–59), and Yale Univ. (from 1959). He was ed. of the *Journal of Music Theory* (1960–67). His most important contribution to music theory is an analytic method designed for the explication of atonal music. His *Tonal Harmony in Concept and Practice* (N.Y., 1962; 3rd ed., 1979) represents an original and sophisticated approach to traditional harmony.

WRITINGS: *Contemporary Tone-structures* (N.Y., 1955); *The Compositional Matrix* (Baldwin, N.Y., 1961); *Tonal Harmony in Concept and Practice* (N.Y., 1962; 3rd ed., 1979); *The Structure of Atonal Music* (New Haven, Conn., 1973); *The Harmonic Organization of "The Rite of Spring"* (New Haven, 1978); *The American Popular Ballad of the Golden Era, 1924–1950* (Princeton, N.J., 1995).

Fortner, Wolfgang, important German composer and pedagogue; b. Leipzig, Oct. 12, 1907; d. Heidelberg, Sept. 5, 1987. He studied composition with Grabner at the Leipzig Cons., and musicology with Kroyer at the Univ. there (1927–31). Upon graduation, he was engaged for 22 years as instructor in theory at the Inst. of Sacred Music in Heidelberg; then was a prof. of composition at the North West Music Academy in Detmold (1954–57) and held a similar position at the Hochschule für Musik in Freiburg im Breisgau (1957–73). Concurrently he led the concerts of Music Viva in Heidelberg, Freiburg, and Munich; after 1954 he was also a lecturer at the Academy of the Arts in West Berlin. His music is marked by exceptional contrapuntal skills, with the basic tonality clearly present even when harmonic density reaches its utmost; in some of his works from 1947, Fortner gave a dodecaphonic treatment to melodic procedures; in his textures, he often employed a "rhythmic cell" device. He was equally adept in his works for the musical theater and purely instrumental compositions; the German tradition is maintained throughout, both in the mechanics of strong polyphony and in rational innovations.

WORKS: DRAMATIC: OPERAS: *Bluthochzeit* (1956; Cologne, June 8, 1957; rev. 1963; a reworking of a dramatic scene, *Der Wald* for Voices, Speaker, and Orch., Frankfurt am Main, June 25, 1953); *Corinna,* opera buffa (Berlin, Oct. 3, 1958); *In seinem Garten liebt Don Perlimlin Belisa* (1961–62; Schwetzingen, May 10, 1962); *Elisabeth Tudor* (1968–71; Berlin, Oct. 23, 1972); *That Time* (Baden-Baden, April 24, 1977). **BALLETS:** *Die weisse Rose* (1949; concert premiere, Baden-Baden, March 5, 1950; stage premiere, Berlin, April 28, 1951); *Die Witwe von Ephesus* (Berlin, Sept. 17, 1952); *Carmen* (1970;

Stuttgart, Feb. 28, 1971). **ORCH.:** *Suite*, on music of Sweelinck (1930); Concerto for Organ and Strings (1932; reused as a Harpsichord Concerto, 1935); Concerto for Strings (1933); Concertino for Viola and Small Orch. (1934); *Capriccio und Finale* (1939); *Ernste Musik* (1940); Piano Concerto (1942); *Streichermusik II* for Strings (1944); Violin Concerto (1946; Baden-Baden, Feb. 16, 1947); Sym. (1947; Baden-Baden, May 2, 1948); *Phantasie über die Tonfolge B-A-C-H* for 2 Pianos, 9 Solo Instruments, and Orch. (1950); Cello Concerto (Cologne, Dec. 17, 1951); *Mouvements* for Piano and Orch. (1953; Baden-Baden, Feb. 6, 1954; as a ballet, Essen, Feb. 26, 1960); *La Cecchina*, Italian overture after Piccini (1954); *Impromptus* (Donaueschingen, Oct. 20, 1957); *Ballet blanc* for 2 Solo Violins and String Orch. (1958; as a ballet, Wuppertal, Dec. 30, 1959); *Aulodie* for Oboe and Orch. (1960; rev. 1966); *Triplum* for Orch. and 3 Obbligato Pianos (1965–66; Basel, Dec. 15, 1966; as a ballet, Munich, 1969); *Immagini* for Small or Large String Orch. (1966–67; also for Large String Orch. and Soprano); *Marginalien* (1969; Kiel, Jan. 12, 1970); *Zyklus* for Cello, Winds, Harp, and Percussion (1969; orig. for Cello and Piano, 1964); *Prolegomena* (concert suite from the opera *Elisabeth Tudor*, 1973; Nuremberg, April 19, 1974); *Prismen* for Flute, Oboe, Clarinet, Harp, Percussion, and Orch. (1974; Basel, Feb. 13, 1975); *Triptychon* (1976–77; in 3 parts: *Hymnus I* for 6 Brasses, *Improvisation* for Large Orch., and *Hymnus II* for 18-voice String Orch.; 1st complete perf., Düsseldorf, April 6, 1978); *Variations* for Chamber Orch. (1979; Basel, March 27, 1980); *Madrigal* for 12 Cellos (1979); *Klangvariation* for Violin and Panel (1981). **CHAMBER:** 4 string quartets (1929, 1938, 1948, 1975); *Suite* for Cello (1932); Violin Sonata (1945); *Serenade* for Flute, Oboe, and Bassoon (1945); Flute Sonata (1947); Cello Sonata (1948); String Trio (1952); *6 Madrigals* for Violins and Cellos (1954); *New-Delhi-Musik* for Flute, Violin, Cello, and Harpsichord (1959); *5 Bagatelles* for Wind Quintet (1960); *Zyklus* for Cello and Piano (1964); *Theme and Variations* for Cello (1975); *9 Inventionen und ein Anhang* for 2 Flutes (1976); Trio for Violin, Cello, and Piano (1978); *Capricen* for Flute, Oboe, and Bassoon (1979); Trio for Violin, Viola, and Cello (1983). **KEYBOARD: PIANO:** Sonatina (1935); *Kammermusik* (1944); *7 Elegies* (1950); *Epigramme* (1964); *6 späte Stücke* (1982). **ORGAN:** *Toccata and Fugue* (1930); *Preamble and Fugue* (1935); *Intermezzi* (1962). **VOCAL:** *Fragment Maria*, chamber cantata (1930); *Grenzen der Menschheit*, cantata (1930); *Nuptiae Catulli* for Tenor, Chamber Chorus, and Chamber Orch. (1937; Basel, April 5, 1939); *An die Nachgeborenen*, cantata (1947; Baden-Baden, April 4, 1948); *2 Exerzitien* for 3 Women's Voices and 15 Instruments (1948); *Mitte des Lebens*, cantata for Soprano and 5 Instruments (1951); *Isaaks Opferung*, oratorio-scene for 3 Soloists and 40 Instruments (Donaueschingen, Oct. 12, 1952); *The Creation* for Voice and Orch. (1954; Basel, Feb. 18, 1955; Fischer-Dieskau, soloist); *Chant de naissance*, cantata for Soprano, Chorus, Violin, Strings, Winds, Percussion, and Harp (1958; Hamburg, April 12, 1959); *Berceuse royale* for Soprano, Solo Violin, and String Orch. (a section from *Chant de naissance*, 1958; rev. in 1975 for Soprano and 7 Instruments); *Prelude und Elegie* for Soprano and Orch., parergon to the *Impromptus* for Soprano and Orch. (1959); *Die Pfingstgeschichte nach Lukas* for Tenor, Chorus, 11 Instruments or Chamber Orch., and Organ (1962–63; Düsseldorf, May 7, 1964); *Der 100. Psalm* for Chorus, 3 Horns, 2 Trumpets, and 2 Trombones (1962); *"Versuch eines Agon um . . . ?"* for 7 Singers and Orch. (Hannover, Nov. 8, 1973); *Gladbacher Te Deum* for Baritone, Chorus, Tape, and Orch. (1973; Mönchengladbach, June 6, 1974); *Machaut-Balladen* for Voice and Orch. (1973; Saarbrücken, Jan. 19, 1975); choruses; songs.

BIBL.: B. Weber, *Die Opernkompositionen von W. F.* (diss., Univ. of Hannover, 1992).

Fortunato, D'Anna, American mezzo-soprano; b. Pittsburgh, Feb. 21, 1945. She studied with Frederick Jagel, Gladys Miller, and John Moriarty at the New England Cons. of Music in Boston (1965–72) and with Phyllis Curtin at the Berkshire Music Center in Tanglewood (1971, 1972). She made her European opera debut with the Boston Camerata as Dido in Purcell's *Dido and Aeneas* in Paris in 1980, and her U.S. opera debut at the N.Y. City Opera as Ruggiero in Handel's *Alcina* in 1983. From 1974 to 1982 she taught at the Longy School of Music in Cambridge, Mass. Her operatic and concert repertoire is extensive, ranging from early music to contemporary works.

Fortune, Nigel (Cameron), English musicologist; b. Birmingham, Dec. 5, 1924. He studied at the Univ. of Birmingham (B.A., 1950); received his Ph.D. in 1954 from Gonville and Caius College, Cambridge, with the diss. *Italian Secular Song from 1600 to 1635: The Origins and Development of Accompanied Monody.* He was music librarian at the Univ. of London (1956–59); in 1959 he became a lecturer at the Univ. of Birmingham; from 1969 to 1986 was a reader in music there. He was a senior consulting ed. of *The New Grove Dictionary of Music and Musicians* (1980) and joint ed. of *Music & Letters* (from 1981). With D. Arnold, he ed. *The Monteverdi Companion* (London, 1968; 2nd ed., rev., 1985, as *The New Monteverdi Companion*) and *The Beethoven Companion* (London, 1971). He also ed. *Music and Theatre: Essays in Honour of Winton Dean* (Cambridge, 1987).

Foss, Hubert J(ames), English writer on music and composer; b. Croydon, May 2, 1899; d. London, May 27, 1953. He attended Bradfield College. In 1921 he became a member of the educational dept. of the Oxford Univ. Press, and in 1924 founded the music dept., which he headed until 1941. He composed *7 Poems by Thomas Hardy* for Baritone, Men's Chorus, and Piano; instrumental pieces; songs. He was the author of *Music in My Time* (1933); *The Concertgoer's Handbook* (London, 1946); *Ralph Vaughan Williams* (London, 1950); also collected and ed. *The Heritage of Music, Essays . . .* (2 vols., London, 1927–34). His book *London Symphony: Portrait of an Orchestra* remained unfinished at his death, and was completed by Noel Goodwin (London, 1954).

Foss (real name, **Fuchs**), **Lukas,** brilliant German-born American pianist, conductor, and composer; b. Berlin, Aug. 15, 1922. He was a scion of a cultured family; his father was a prof. of philosophy; his mother, a talented painter. He studied piano and theory with Julius Goldstein-Herford in Berlin. When the dark shadow of the Nazi dominion descended upon Germany in 1933, the family prudently moved to Paris; there Foss studied piano with Lazare Lévy, composition with Noël Gallon, and orchestration with Felix Wolfes. He also took flute lessons with Louis Moÿse. In 1937 he went to the U.S. and enrolled at the Curtis Inst. of Music in Philadelphia, where he studied piano with Vengerova, composition with Scalero, and conducting with Reiner; in 1939–40 he took a course in advanced composition with Hindemith at Yale Univ., and also studied conducting with Koussevitzky at the Berkshire Music Center in Tanglewood (summers, 1939–43). He became a naturalized American citizen in 1942. He was awarded a Guggenheim fellowship in 1945; in 1960 he received his 2nd Guggenheim fellowship. His first public career was that of a concert pianist, and he elicited high praise for his appearances as soloist with the N.Y. Phil. and other orchs. He made his conducting debut with the Pittsburgh Sym. Orch. in 1939. From 1944 to 1950 he was pianist of the Boston Sym. Orch.; then traveled to Rome on a Fulbright fellowship (1950–52). From 1953 to 1962 he taught composition at the Univ. of Calif. at Los Angeles, where he also established the Improvisation Chamber Ensemble to perform music of "controlled improvisation." In 1963 he was appointed music director of the Buffalo Phil.; during his tenure ,he introduced ultramodern works, much to the annoyance of some regular subscribers; he resigned his position in 1970. In 1971 he became principal conductor of the Brooklyn Philharmonia; also established the series "Meet the Moderns" there. From 1972 to 1975 he conducted the Jerusalem Sym. Orch. He became music director of the Milwaukee Sym. Orch. in 1981; relinquished his position in 1986 after a tour of Europe, and was made its conductor laureate; continued to hold his Brooklyn post until 1990. In 1986 he was the Mellon Lecturer at the National Gallery of Art in Washington, D.C. In 1962 he was elected a member of the National Inst. of Arts and Letters. He was elected a member of the American Academy and Inst. of Arts and Letters in 1983. Throughout the years, he evolved an astounding activity as conductor, composer, and lately college instructor, offering novel ideas in education and performance. As a composer, he traversed a protean succession of changing styles, idioms, and techniques. His early compositions were marked by the spirit of Romantic lyricism, adumbrating the musical language of Mahler; some other works reflected the neo-Classical formulas of Hindemith; still others suggested the hedonistic vivacity and sophisticated stylization typical of Stravinsky's productions. But the intrinsic impetus of his music was its "pulse," which evolves the essential thematic content into the substance of original projection. His earliest piano pieces were publ. when he was 15 years old; there followed an uninterrupted flow of compositions in various genres. Foss was fortunate in being a particular protégé of Koussevitzky, who conducted many of his works with the Boston Sym. Orch.; and he had no difficulty in finding other performers. As a virtuoso pianist, he often played the piano part in his chamber music, and he conducted a number of his symphonic and choral works.

WORKS: DRAMATIC: OPERAS: *The Jumping Frog of Calaveras County* (1949; Bloomington, Ind., May 18, 1950); *Griffelkin* (1953–55; NBC-TV, Nov. 6, 1955); *Introductions and Goodbyes* (1959; N.Y., May 7, 1960). **BALLETS:** *The Heart Remembers* (1944); *Within These Walls* (1944); *Gift of the Magi* (1944; Boston, Oct. 5, 1945). **INCIDENTAL MUSIC TO:** Shakespeare's *The Tempest* (1939–40; N.Y., March 31, 1940). **ORCH.:** *2 Symphonic Pieces* (1939–40; not extant); *2 Pieces* (1941); 2 clarinet concertos: No. 1 (1941; rev. as Piano Concerto No. 1, 1943) and No. 2 (1988); 2 piano concertos: No. 1 (1943) and No. 2 (1949–51; Venice, Oct. 7, 1951; rev. version, Los Angeles, June 16, 1953); *The Prairie*, symphonic suite after the cantata (Boston, Oct. 15, 1943); 3 syms.: No. 1 (1944; Pittsburgh, Feb. 4, 1945), No. 2, *Symphony of Chorales* (1955–58; Pittsburgh, Oct. 24, 1958), and No. 3, *Symphony of Sorrows* (1991; Chicago, Feb. 19, 1992); *Ode* (1944; N.Y., March 15, 1945; rev. version, Philadelphia, Oct. 17, 1958); *Pantomime*, suite after *Gift of the Magi* (1945); *Recordare* (Boston, Dec. 31, 1948); *Elegy* for Clarinet and Orch. (1949); Concerto for Improvising Instruments and Orch. (Philadelphia, Oct. 7, 1960); *Elytres* for Chamber Orch. (Los Angeles, Dec. 8, 1964); *Stillscape*, renamed *For 24 Winds* for Wind Orch. (Caracas, May 11, 1966); *Cello Concert* for Cello and Orch. (N.Y., March 5, 1967); *Baroque Variations* (Chicago, July 7, 1967); *Geod* (1969); *Orpheus* (1972; Ojai, Calif., June 2, 1973; rev. as *Orpheus and Euridice* for 2 Violins, Chamber Orch., and Tape, 1983); *Fanfare* (Istanbul, June 28, 1973); Concerto for Solo Percussion and Orch. (1974; Camden, N.J., April 9, 1975); *Folksong* (1975–76; Baltimore, Jan. 21, 1976; rev. 1978); *Salomon Rossi Suite* (1974); *Quintets* (Cleveland, April 30, 1979); *Night Music for John Lennon* for Brass Quintet and Orch. (1980–81; N.Y., April 1, 1981); *Dissertation* (Bloomington, Ind., July 2, 1981; new version as *Exeunt*, 1982); *Renaissance Concerto* for Flute and Orch. (1985–86; Buffalo, May 9, 1986); *Griffelkin Suite*, after the opera (Oshkosh, May 3, 1986); *For Lenny (Variation on N.Y., N.Y.)* for Piano Obbligato and Orch. (1988); *Elegy for Anne Frank* for Piano Obbligato and Orch. (N.Y., June 12, 1989); Guitar Concerto, *American Landscapes* (N.Y., Nov. 29, 1989); *Celebration*, renamed *American Fanfare*, for the 50th anniversary of the Berkshire Music Center at Tanglewood (July 6, 1990); Concerto for Piano, Left-hand, and Orch. (1993; Tanglewood, July 23, 1994). **CHAMBER:** *4 Preludes* for Flute, Clarinet, and Bassoon (1940); Duo (Fantasia) for Cello and Piano (1941); *3 Pieces* for Violin and Piano (N.Y., Nov. 13, 1944; arranged as *3 Early Pieces* for Flute and Piano, 1986); 3 string quartets: No. 1 (1947), No. 2, *Divertissement pour Mica* (1973), and No. 3 (1975; N.Y., March 15, 1976); *Capriccio* for Cello and Piano (1948); *Studies in Improvisation* for Clarinet, Horn, Cello, Percussion, and Piano (1959; N.Y., March 11, 1962); *Echoi* for 4 Players (1961–63; N.Y., Nov. 11, 1963); *Non-Improvisation* for Clarinet, Cello, Piano or Electric Organ, and Percussion (N.Y., Nov. 7, 1967); *Paradigm* for Percussionist-Conductor (N.Y., Oct. 31, 1968; rev. version, Buffalo, Nov. 8, 1969); *Waves* for Instruments (Hempstead, N.Y., Jan. 17, 1969); *MAP (Musicians at Play)*, musical game for 5 Players (St. Paul de Vence, July 16, 1970; rev. version for 4 Players, Buffalo, June 14, 1977); *The Cave of Winds (La Grotte des Vents)* for Flute, Oboe, Clarinet, Bassoon, and Horn (N.Y., Dec. 14, 1972); *Ni Bruit Ni Vitesse* for 2 Pianos and 2 Percussion (Buffalo, Feb. 13, 1972); *Chamber Music* for Percussion and Electronics (Buffalo, March 22, 1975; in collaboration with J. Chadabe); *Quartet Plus* for 2 String Quartets, Narrator, and Video (N.Y., April 29, 1977; based on String Quartet No. 3); *Music for 6* for 6 Treble Clef Instruments (1977; rev. 1978); *Curriculum Vitae* for Accordion (N.Y., Nov. 1, 1977); Brass Quintet (1978); *Round a Common Center* for Piano Quartet or Quintet (1979; Lake Placid, N.Y., Jan. 30, 1980); *Percussion Quartet* (Rochester, N.Y., Nov. 5, 1983); Horn Trio (1983); Saxophone Quartet (Buffalo, Sept. 22, 1985); *Embros* for 3 Winds, 3 Brass, Percussion, Strings, and Electric Instruments (1985; N.Y., Feb. 25, 1986); *Tashi* for Clarinet, 2 Violins, Viola, Cello, and Piano (1986; Washington, D.C., Feb. 17, 1987); *Central Park Reel* for Violin and Piano (Singapore, June 17, 1987); *Chaconne* for Guitar (N.Y., Nov. 8, 1987). **KEYBOARD: PIANO:** *Fantasy Rondo* (1944); *Prelude* (1949); *Scherzo Ricercato* (1953); *Solo* (1981; Paris, March 24, 1982; new version as *Solo Observed* for Piano and 3 Instruments, Miami, June 7, 1982). **ORGAN:** *Etudes* (Mount Vernon, Iowa, Nov. 14, 1967). **VOCAL:** *Melodrama and Dramatic Song for Michelangelo* for Voice and Orch. (1940); *We Sing*, cantata for Children's Chorus and Piano (1941); *The Prairie* for Soprano, Alto, Tenor, Bass, Chorus, and Orch. (1943; N.Y., May 15, 1944); *Song of Anguish* for Baritone or Bass and Orch. (1945; Boston, March 10, 1950); *Song of Songs* for Soprano or Mezzo-soprano and Orch. (1946; Boston, March 7, 1947); *Adon Olom: A Prayer* for Cantor or Tenor, Chorus, and Organ (1948); *Behold! I Build an House* for Chorus and Organ (Boston, March 14, 1950); *A Parable of Death* for Narrator, Tenor, Chorus, and Orch. (1952; Louisville, March 11, 1953); *Psalms* for Chorus and Orch. (1955–56; N.Y., May 9, 1957); *Time Cycle* for Soprano and Orch. (1959–60; N.Y., Oct. 20, 1960; also for Soprano and Chamber Group, Tanglewood, July 10, 1961); *Fragments of Archilochos* for Countertenor, Male Speaker, Female Speaker, 4 Small Choruses, Optional Large Chorus, and Orch. (Potsdam, N.Y., May 1965); *3 Airs for Frank O'Hara's Angel* for Male Speaker, Soprano, Women's Chorus, and Instruments (N.Y., April 26, 1972); *Lamdeni* (Teach Me) for Chorus and 6 Instruments (1973); *American Cantata* for Soprano, Tenor, Speakers, Chorus, and Orch. (Interlochen, Mich., July 24, 1976; rev. version, N.Y., Dec. 1, 1977); *Then the Rocks on the Mountain Begin to Shout* for Chorus (1978; N.Y., Nov. 9, 1985); *13 Ways of Looking at a Blackbird* for Soprano or Mezzo-soprano, Instruments, and Tape (1978); *Measure for Measure* for Tenor and Chamber Orch. (1980); *De Profundis* for Chorus (1983); *With Music Strong* for Chorus and Orch. (1988; Milwaukee, April 15, 1989). **OTHER:** *For 200 Cellos (A Celebration)* (College Park, Md., June 4, 1982).

BIBL.: K. Perone, *L. F.: A Bio-Bibliography* (N.Y., 1991).

Foster, Lawrence (Thomas), noted American conductor; b. Los Angeles, Oct. 23, 1941. He studied conducting with F. Zweig in Los Angeles. He made his first conducting appearance with the Young Musicians Foundation Debut Orch. in Los Angeles in 1960. At the age of 24, he was appointed assistant conductor of the Los Angeles Phil., which post he held until 1968; in 1966, received the Koussevitzky Memorial Conducting Prize at the Berkshire Music Center at Tanglewood. From 1969 to 1974 he was chief guest conductor of the Royal Phil. in London. From 1971 to 1978 he was conductor-in-chief of the Houston Sym. Orch. From 1979 to 1990 he was chief conductor of the Opera and the Orchestre National de Monte Carlo (called

Orchestre Philharmonique de Monte Carlo from 1980). He also became Generalmusikdirektor in the city of Duisburg in 1981, remaining in that position until 1988. From 1990 to 1996 he was music director of the Aspen (Colo.) Music Festival. In 1992 he resumed the position of chief conductor of the Orchestre Philharmonique in Monte Carlo. He was also music director of the Lausanne Chamber Orch. (1985–90) and the Jerusalem Sym. Orch. (1988–92). In 1996 he became music director of the Barcelona Sym. Orch. Foster is particularly notable for his dynamic interpretations of modern works, but has also been acclaimed for his precise and intelligent presentations of the Classical and Romantic repertoire.

Foster, Sidney, esteemed American pianist and pedagogue; b. Florence, S.C., May 23, 1917; d. Boston, Feb. 7, 1977. He began piano training as a child with Walter Goldstein in New Orleans, and at the age of 10 was admitted to the Curtis Inst. of Music in Philadelphia, where he studied with Vengerova and Saperton and took his diploma in 1938. In 1940 he won the 1st Leventritt Foundation Award, which entitled him to an appearance as soloist with the N.Y. Phil. in Beethoven's 3rd Piano Concerto on March 16, 1941. This was the beginning of a fine international career. In 1964 he played 16 concerts in Russia. He taught piano at Florida State Univ. (1949–51); from 1952 to 1977 he was on the piano faculty of Indiana Univ. at Bloomington.

Fotek, Jan, Polish composer; b. Czerwinsk, Nov. 28, 1928. He studied composition with Wiechowicz at the State College of Music in Kraków and with Szeligowski at the State College of Music in Warsaw.

WORKS: *Opus concertante* for Organ, Piano, and Percussion (1959); *Gregorian Hymn* for Chorus and Orch. (1963); *A Cycle of Verses* for Children's Chorus and Orch. (1963); *Trimorphie* for 3 Flutes, Harpsichord, and Piano (1966); *Epitasis* for Orch. (1967); *Galileo*, musical drama (1969); *The Last War*, rhapsody for Narrator, Chorus, and Orch. (1971); *Cantata copernicana* (1973); *Partita* for 12 Bassoons and 3 Double Bassoons (1973); *A Forest King's Daughter*, opera-ballet (1977); *Musica chromatica* for String Chamber Orch. (1982); *Anyone*, opera-mystery (1983); Tuba Sonata (1984); *Czarnolas Suite* for String Chamber Orch. (1986); *Ecloga* for Countertenor and Ensemble of Early Instruments (1987).

Fougstedt, Nils-Eric, Finnish conductor and composer; b. Raisio, near Turku, May 24, 1910; d. Helsinki, April 12, 1961. He studied composition in Helsinki with Furuhjelm, in Italy with Carlo Felice Boghen, and in Berlin with Max Trapp. Upon returning to Finland in 1932, he lectured in theory at the Music Inst. in Helsinki; was also active as a conductor; led the Finnish Radio Orch. from 1951 until his death.

WORKS: Piano Trio (1933); Suite for Orch. (1936); *Divertimento* for Wind Quintet (1936); Violin Concertino (1937); Violin Sonata (1937); 2 syms. (1938, 1949); String Quartet (1940); Cello Concerto (1942); Piano Concerto (1944); *Tulukset* (The Tinderbox), cantata after Hans Christian Andersen (1950); *Trittico sinfonico* (1958); many choruses and songs.

Foulds, John (Herbert), significant English composer and music theorist; b. Manchester, Nov. 2, 1880; d. Calcutta, April 24, 1939. He was precocious and began to compose at a single-digit age; learned to play cello; earned a living by playing in theater orchs. In 1900 he joined the Hallé Orch. in Manchester; then moved to London in 1910, where he served as music director for the Central YMCA (1918–23); also conducted the Univ. of London Music Soc. (1921–26). In 1935 he went to India; undertook a thorough study of Indian folk music; served as director of European music for the All-India Radio at Delhi and Calcutta (1937–39); also formed an experimental "Indo-European" orch., which included both European and Asian instruments. He was the first English composer to experiment with quarter tones, and as early as 1898 wrote a string quartet with fractional intervals; he also composed semi-classical pieces using traditional Indian instruments. Unfortunately, many of his MSS are lost.

WORKS: DRAMATIC: *The Vision of Dante*, concert opera (1905–08); *Cleopatra*, miniature opera (1909; not extant); *The Tell-Tale Heart*, melodrama (1910); *Avatara*, opera (1919–30; not extant); music for the ritual play *Veils* (1926; unfinished). **ORCH.:** *Undine Suite* (c.1899); *Epithalamium* (London, Oct. 9, 1906); *Lento e scherzetto* for Cello and Orch. (c.1906); 2 cello concertos: No. 1 (1908–09; Manchester, March 16, 1911) and No. 2 (c.1910; not extant); *Apotheosis* for Violin and Orch. (1908–09); *Mirage*, symphonic poem (1910); *Suite française* (1910); *Keltic Suite* (1911); *Music Pictures (Group III)*, suite (London, Sept. 4, 1912); *Hellas* for Double String Orch., Harp, and Percussion (1915–32); *Miniature Suite* (1915); *Peace and War*, meditation (1919); *3 Mantras* (1919–30); *Le Cabaret*, overture to a French comedy (1921); *Suite fantastique* (1922); *Music Pictures (Group IV)* for Strings (c.1922); *Saint Joan Suite* (1924–25); *Henry VIII Suite* (1925–26); *April-England*, tone poem (1926–32); *Dynamic Triptych* for Piano and Orch. (1929; Edinburgh, Oct. 15, 1931); *Keltic Overture* (1930); *Indian Suite* (1932–35); *Pasquinades symphoniques*, sym. in 3 movements (1935; finale left unfinished); *Deva-Music* (1935–36; only fragments extant); *Chinese Suite* (1935); *3 Pasquinades* (c.1936); *Symphony of East and West* for European and Indian Instruments (1937–38; not extant); *Symphonic Studies* (1938; not extant). **CHAMBER:** 10 string quartets: Nos. 1–3 (before 1899; not extant), No. 4 (1899), No. 5 (not extant), No. 6, *Quartetto romantico* (1903), No. 7 (not extant), No. 8 (1907–10), No. 9, *Quartetto intimo* (1931–32), and No. 10, *Quartetto geniale* (1935; only the 3rd movement, *Lento quieto*, extant); Cello Sonata (1905; rev. 1927); *Impromptu on a Theme of Beethoven* for 4 Cellos (1905); *Music Pictures (Group I)* for Piano Trio (1910; not extant); *Ritornello con variazioni* for String Trio (1911); *Aquarelles (Music Pictures—Group II)* for String Quartet (c.1914); *Sonia* for Violin and Piano (1925). **PIANO:** *Dichterliebe*, suite (1897–98); *Essays in the Modes*, 6 studies (1920–27); *Egotistic*, modal essay (1927); *2 Landscapes* (c.1928); *Scherzo chromatico* (1927; not extant). **VOCAL:** *The Song of Honor* for Speaker, Chamber Orch., and Women's Chorus ad libitum (1918); *A World Requiem* for 4 Soloists, Small Boys' Chorus, Mixed Chorus, and Orch. (1919–21; London, Nov. 11, 1923); choruses; songs.

WRITINGS: *Music To-Day: Its Heritage from the Past, and Legacy to the Future* (London, 1934).

BIBL.: M. MacDonald, *J. F.: His Life in Music* (London, 1975); idem, *J. F., A centenary brochure from Musica Viva* (1979); idem, *J. F. and His Music* (N.Y. and London, 1990).

Fountain, Primous, III, black American composer; b. St. Petersburg, Fla., Aug. 1, 1949. He studied at De Paul Univ. and at the Berkshire Music Center at Tanglewood. In 1974 he won a Guggenheim fellowship. His music shows quaquaversal influences, in a spectrum ranging from Stravinskian neo-Classicism to hot jazz.

WORKS: BALLET: *Manifestation* (1968; Chicago, March 13, 1970). **ORCH.:** *Ritual Dances of the Amaks* (1972); *Exiled* (1974); *Osiris* (1975); Cello Concerto (1976; Minneapolis, Dec. 28, 1977); *Poème* for 17 Wind Instruments (1978); *Caprice* (1978; N.Y., May 12, 1980); Concerto for Harp and Chamber Orch. (1981). **CHAMBER:** *3 Pieces* for Flute, Violin, and Piano (1967); *Will* for Flute, Clarinet, Horn, and Piano (1967); *Meditation on a Theme* for Piano (1967); *Ricia* for Piano Trio (1977). **VOCAL:** *Evolutio quaestionis* for Soprano and Ensemble (1967).

Fourestier, Louis (Félix André), French conductor, pedagogue, and composer; b. Montpellier, May 31, 1892; d. Boulogne-Billancourt, Sept. 30, 1976. He was a student of Gédalge and Leroux at the Paris Cons., winning the Grand Prix de Rome with his cantata *La Mort d'Adonis* in 1925. After conducting in the French provinces, he returned to Paris and conducted at the Opéra-Comique (1927–32) and the Opéra (1938–45). On Nov. 11, 1946, he made his Metropolitan Opera debut in N.Y. conducting *Lakmé*, and remained on its roster until 1948. From 1945 to 1963 he was a prof. at the Paris Cons. He wrote mainly orch. works and chamber music.

Fouret, Maurice, French composer; b. St.-Quentin, Nov. 28, 1888; d. Paris, Jan. 22, 1962. He studied with Ravel, Charpentier, and Büsser. He composed several symphonic poems on exotic subjects, among them *Aladdin* (Paris, Nov. 28, 1920) and *Danse de Sita* (1922); also the ballets *Le Rustre imprudent* (1931) and *La Jeune Fille aux joues roses* (1934); a group of symphonic suites inspired by Alsatian folklore; songs.

Fournet, Jean, distinguished French conductor and pedagogue; b. Rouen, April 14, 1913. He received training in flute from M. Moyse (premier prix, 1932) and in conducting from Gaubert (1930–36) at the Paris Cons. In 1936 he made his conducting debut in Rouen, where he was active until 1940. After conducting in Marseilles (1940–44), he returned to Paris and served as music director of the Opéra-Comique (1944–57) and as a teacher of conducting at the École Normale de Musique (1944–62). From 1961 to 1968 he was principal guest conductor of the Hilversum Radio Orch. in the Netherlands, where he was also engaged in teaching conducting. In 1965 he made his debut with the Chicago Lyric Opera. After serving as music director of the Rotterdam Phil. (1968–73) and l'Orchestre de l'Ile-de-France (1973–82), he was active as a guest conductor. He made his belated Metropolitan Opera debut in N.Y. on March 28, 1987, conducting *Samson et Dalila.* Fournet was especially esteemed for his idiomatic interpretations of scores from the French symphonic and operatic repertory.

Fournier, Pierre (Léon Marie), famous French cellist; b. Paris, June 24, 1906; d. Geneva, Jan. 8, 1986. He first studied piano with his mother; stricken by polio at age 9, he turned to the cello, studying with Paul Bazelaire and André Hekking at the Paris Cons., and at the École Normale de Musique. He made his debut in 1925 and subsequently appeared both as a soloist with orchs. and as a chamber music artist; taught at the Paris Cons. (1941–49). After World War II, he made major tours throughout the world; he appeared regularly in the U.S. from 1948. He was made a Chevalier of the Legion of Honor in 1953; was promoted to Officier in 1963. In 1970 he settled in Switzerland, where he gave master classes. He was renowned for his elegant tone and impeccable musicianship; his repertoire was comprehensive, ranging from Bach to contemporary music. Several composers wrote works for him; he gave first performances of works by Roussel, Martin, Poulenc, and Martinů.

BIBL.: B. Gavoty, *P. F.* (Geneva, 1957).

Fou Ts'ong, Chinese pianist; b. Shanghai, March 10, 1934. He studied piano in his native city; then won 3rd prizes in the Bucharest Piano Competition (1953) and the Warsaw International Chopin Competition (1955); continued his studies at the Warsaw Cons. In 1958 he decided to make his home in London; appeared with many of the major orchs. of Europe and the U.S.; also gave many recitals. He was particularly noted for his expressive playing of works by Chopin and Debussy.

Fowler, Jennifer, Australian composer; b. Bunbury, Western Australia, April 14, 1939. She studied at the Univ. of Western Australia, graduating in arts (1961) and music (1968). After working at the electronic music studio at the Univ. of Utrecht on a Dutch scholarship (1968–69), she settled in London to pursue her career as a composer. In 1971 she was joint winner of England's Radcliffe Award. In 1975 she won 1st prize in the International Competition for Women Composers in Mannheim.

WORKS: ORCH.: *Sculpture in 4 Dimensions* (1969); *Look on This Oedipus* (1973); *Chant with Garlands* (1974); *Ring Out the Changes* for Strings and Bells (1978); *Plainsong* for Strings (1992). **CHAMBER:** String Quartet (1967); *Revelation* for 2 Violins, Viola, and 2 Cellos (1971); *Chimes, Fractured* for 2 Flutes, 2 Oboes, 2 Clarinets, 2 Bassoons, Organ, Bagpipes, and Percussions (1971); *The Arrows of Saint Sebastian II* for Bass Clarinet, Cello, and Tape (1981) and *II* for 13 Instruments (1982); *The Invocation to the Veiled Mysteries* for Flute, Clarinet, Bassoon, Violin, Cello, and Piano (1982); *Line Spun With Stars* for Violin or Flute, Cello, and Piano (1982); *Echoes from an Antique Land* for 5 Percussion Players (1983; also for Flute, Clarinet, Piano, and Bass, 1983, or for 5 or 10 Instruments, 1986); *Threaded Stars* for Harp (1983); *Blow Flute: Answer Echoes in Antique Lands Dying* for Flute (1983); *Between Silence and the World* for Wind Quintet (1987); *Lament* for Baroque Oboe and Bass Viol or Cello (1987); *We Call to You, Brother* for Flute, English Horn, Cello, Percussion, 2 Trombones, and Didjeridoo (1988); *Restless Dust* for Viola, Cello, and Double Bass (1988; also for Cello and Piano); *Reeds, Reflections . . . Ripples Re-sound Resound* for Oboe, Violin, Viola, and Cello (1990); *Remembering 1695* for 4 Winds (1994). **PIANO:** *Piece for an Opera House* for 2 Pianos or Piano and Tape or Solo Piano (1973); *Music for Piano: Ascending and Descending* (1981); *Piece for E.L.* (1981). **VOCAL:** *Hours of the Day* for 4 Mezzo-sopranos, 2 Oboes, and 2 Clarinets (1968); *Veni Sancte Spiritus: Veni Creator* for Chamber Chorus or 12 Solo Singers (1971); *Voice of the Shades* for Soprano, Oboe or Clarinet, and Violin or Flute (1977; also for Soprano, 2 Trumpets, and Oboe or Clarinet, and for Soprano, Clarinet, Oboe, and Violin or Flute); *Tell Out, My Soul: Magnificat* for Soprano, Cello, and Piano (1980; rev. 1984); *When David Heard . . .* for Chorus and Piano (1982); *Letter from Haworth* for Mezzo-soprano, Clarinet, Cello, and Piano (1984); *And Ever Shall Be,* 4 songs for Mezzo-soprano and Chamber Ensemble (1989); *Australia Sends Greetings to Alaska* for Soprano, Alto, and Optional Piano (1992); *Let's Stop Work!* for 2 Equal Treble Parts, 3rd Treble Part, and Optional Piano (1992).

Fox, Charles Warren, American musicologist; b. Gloversville, N.Y., July 24, 1904; d. there, Oct. 15, 1983. He took courses in psychology at Cornell Univ. (B.A., 1926; Ph.D., 1933); also studied musicology there with Kinkeldey. In 1932 he became a part-time instructor in psychology at the Eastman School of Music in Rochester, N.Y.; in 1933, began giving courses in music history and musicology; he retired in 1970. From 1952 to 1959 he was ed. of the *Journal of the American Musicological Society.* From 1954 to 1956 he served as president of the Music Library Assn.

Fox, Frederick (Alfred), American composer and teacher; b. Detroit, Jan. 17, 1931. He received training in saxophone from Laurence Teal and in theory and arranging from Ray McConnell. He then pursued studies in composition with Ruth Shaw Wylie at Wayne State Univ. in Detroit (B.M., 1953), Ross Lee Finney at the Univ. of Mich. in Ann Arbor (1953–54), and Bernhard Heiden at Indiana Univ. in Bloomington (M.M., 1957; D.Mus., 1959). After teaching at Franklin (Ind.) College (1959–61) and Sam Houston State Univ. in Huntsville, Texas (1961–62), he was composer-in-residence of the Minneapolis Public Schools (1962–63). In 1964 he joined the faculty of Calif. State Univ. at Hayward, where he was chairman of the music dept. (1970–72) and prof. of composition (1972–74). In 1974–75 he was a visiting prof. of composition at Indiana Univ, and in 1975 became prof. of composition there. He also was founder-director of its New Music Ensemble and from 1981 to 1994 was chairman of its composition dept. Fox's music reflects his interest in jazz, improvisation, and serialism.

WORKS: ORCH.: Violin Concerto (1971); *Ternion* for Oboe and Orch. (1972); *Variables 5* (1974); *Beyond Winterlock* (1977); *Night Ceremonies* (1979); *Tracings* (1981); *Januaries* (1984); Fanfare for Wind and Percussion Orch. (1984); *Now and Then* for Chamber Orch. (1985); *In the Elsewhere* (1986); *Polarities* for Symphonic Band (1987); *Mystic Dances* for Chamber Orch. (1990); *Dark Moons/Bright Shadows* (1991); *Echo Blues* (1992); *3 Epigrams* for Concert Band (1993); Concerto for Symphonic Band (1994); *Impressions* (1995). **CHAMBER:** *Quantic* for Woodwind Quintet (1969); *Variations* for Violin, Cello, and Piano (1970); *Ad Rem* for Guitar (1970); *Matrix* for Cello, Strings, and Percussion (1972); *Variables 1* for Violin and Piano (1972), *2* for Flute (1973), *3* for Flute, Clarinet, Horn, Violin, Cello, and Piano (1973), *4* for Clarinet (1973), and *6* for Flute, Clarinet, Violin, Cello, and Percussion (1975); Quartet for Violin, Piano, and Percussion (1974); *Connex* for Brass Ensemble (1974); *Tria* for Flute, Piano, and Percussion (1975); *Ambient Shadows* for 8 Instrumentalists (1978); *S.A.X.* for Alto Saxophone and Saxophone Quartet (1979); *Annexus* for Alto Saxophone and Piano (1980); *Sonaspheres 1* for 10 Instrumentalists (1980), *2: Nexus* for Flute, Viola, Cello, and Piano (1983), *3:Ensphere* for 6 Instrumentalists (1983), *4: Tromper* for Trumpet, Trombone, and Percussion (1983), and *5* for 10 Instrumentalists (1983); *Bren* for Brass Ensemble (1982); *Gaber!* for 6 Percussionists (1982); *Visitations* for 2 Saxophones (1982); *Dawnen Grey* for String Quartet (1984); *Fanfare '84* for 5 Trumpets, 4 Horns, 4 Trombones, and Tuba (1984); *Vis-a-vis* for Horn and String Quartet (1985); *Shaking the Pumpkin* for Saxophone, Piano, and 2 Percussionists (1986); *3 Diversions* for Saxophone Quartet (1987); *Silver Skeins* for 9 Flutes (1987); *Upon the Reedy Stream* for Oboe and String Quartet (1987); *Nightscenes* for Strings, Harp, Piano or Celesta, and 5 Percussionists (1988); *Time Messages* for Brass Quintet (1988); *Flight of Fantasy* for Cello and Piano (1988); *Auras* for Flute, Clarinet, Cello, Piano, and Percussion (1988); *The Avenging Spirit* for Saxophone Quartet (1989); *Fantasy* for Woodwind Quintet and Piano (1989); *Devil's Tramping Ground* for 7 Instrumentalists (1991); *Hear Again in Memory* for Saxophone (1991); *Sing Down the Moon* for Clarinet and Piano (1992); *Echoes and Shadows* for Violin and Piano (1993); *Fantasy* for Viola and Piano (1993); *Time Weaving* for Clarinet Trio (1993); *Kokopelli* for Flute and Piano (1994); *Dreamcatcher* for 13 Instrumentalists for the 175th anniversary of the founding of Indiana Univ. (1994). **VOCAL:** *A Stone, a Leaf, and Unfound Door* for Soprano, Chorus, Clarinet, and Percussion (1966–68); *The Descent* for Chorus, Piano, and 2 Percussionists (1969); *Time Excursions* for Soprano, Speaker, and 7 Instrumentalists (1976); *Nilrem's Odyssey* for Baritone/Speaker and Chorus (1980); *A Threat* for Soprano and Viola (1981).

Fox, Virgil (Keel), famous American organist; b. Princeton, Ill., May 3, 1912; d. West Palm Beach, Fla., Oct. 25, 1980. He studied piano as a child, but soon turned to the organ as his favorite instrument. He played the organ at the First Presbyterian Church in his hometown at the age of 10, and gave his first public recital in Cincinnati at 14. He then enrolled in the Peabody Cons. of Music in Baltimore, graduating in 1932. To perfect his playing he went to Paris, where he took lessons with Dupré at St. Sulpice and Vierne at Notre Dame. He returned to the U.S. in 1938 and became head of the organ dept. at the Peabody Cons. of Music. From 1946 to 1965 he was organist at the Riverside Church in N.Y., where he played on a 5-manual, 10,561-pipe organ specially designed for him. He then launched a remarkable career as an organ soloist. He was the first American to play at the Thomaskirche in Leipzig, and also played at Westminster Abbey in London. As a solo artist, he evolved an idiosyncratic type of performance in which he embellished Baroque music with Romantic extravaganza; he also took to apostrophizing his audiences in a whimsical mixture of lofty sentiment and disarming self-deprecation. This type of personalized art endeared him to the impatient, emancipated musical youth of America, and he became one of the few organists who could fill a concert hall. He also displayed a robust taste for modern music; he often played the ear-stopping, discordant arrangement of "America" by Charles Ives. Wracked by cancer, he gave his last concert in Dallas on Sept. 26, 1980.

Fox Strangways, A(rthur) H(enry), noted English writer on music and editor; b. Norwich, Sept. 14, 1859; d. Dinton, near Salisbury, May 2, 1948. He studied at Wellington College, London; received his M.A. in 1882 from Balliol College, Oxford; then was a schoolmaster at Dulwich College (1884–86) and Wellington College (1887–1910). From 1911 to 1925 he wrote music criticism for the *Times* of London; in 1925 he became music critic of the *Observer*. In 1920 he founded the quarterly journal *Music & Letters*, which he ed. until 1937. He was a specialist on Indian music and wrote several books on the subject, including *The Music of Hindostan* (Oxford, 1914); also publ. a collection of essays, *Music Observed* (London, 1936), and a biography of Cecil Sharp (with M. Karpeles; London, 1933; 2nd ed., 1955). He contributed the article "Folk-Song" to the introductory vol. of *The Oxford History of Music* (London, 1929).

BIBL.: Special issues of *Music & Letters* (Oct. 1939 and July 1948); F. Howes, "A.H. F.S.," ibid. (Jan. 1969).

Frackenpohl, Arthur (Roland), American composer and teacher; b. Irvington, N.J., April 23, 1924. He studied with Rogers at the Eastman School of Music in Rochester, N.Y. (B.A., 1947; M.A., 1949); took courses with Milhaud at the Berkshire Music Center in Tanglewood (summer, 1948) and with Boulanger in Fontainebleau (1950); completed his studies at McGill Univ. in Montreal (D.M.A., 1957). He became a teacher at the Crane School of Music at the State Univ. of N.Y. at Potsdam (1949); was a prof. there (1961–85). He publ. *Harmonization at the Piano* (1962; 6th ed., 1990).

WORKS: CHAMBER OPERA: *Domestic Relations ("To Beat or Not to Beat")*, after O. Henry (1964). **ORCH.:** *Allegro giocoso* for Band (1956); *A Jubilant Overture* (1957); *Allegro scherzando* (1957); *Overture* (1957); Sym. for Strings (1960); *Largo and Allegro* for Horn and Strings (1962); *Short Overture* (1965); Concertino for Tuba and Strings (1967); Suite for Trumpet and Strings (1970); *American Folk Song Suite* for Band (1973); *Flute Waltz* for 3 Flutes and Orch. (1979); Concerto for Brass Quintet and Strings (1986). **CHAMBER:** Brass Quartet (1950); 4 brass quintets (1963, 1972, 1986, 1994); Trombone Quartet (1967); Brass Trio (1967); String Quartet (1971); *Breviates* for Brass Ensemble (1973); Trio for Oboe, Horn, and Bassoon (1982); Tuba Sonata (1983); piano pieces. **VOCAL:** *The Natural Superiority of Men*, cantata for Women's Voices and Piano (1962); (7) *Essays on Women*, cantata for Soloists, Chorus, and Piano (1967); *Meet Job*, 3 litanies for 4 Voices and Winds (1978); *A Child This Day*, cantata for Soloists, Chorus, Narrator, Brass Quartet, and Organ (1980); Mass for Chorus and Orch. (1990); song cycles.

Fradkin, Fredric, American violinist and teacher; b. Troy, N.Y., April 2, 1892; d. N.Y., Oct. 3, 1963. At the age of 5, he became a pupil of Schradieck; later studied with Max Bendix and Sam Franko in N.Y.; then went to Paris and studied at the Cons. with Lefort, graduating in 1909 with 1st prize. He was concertmaster of the Bordeaux Opera Orch.; then took instruction with Ysaÿe in Brussels. Returning to America, he made his debut as a concert violinist in N.Y. on Jan. 10, 1911; then gave concerts in Europe; in 1918–19 he was concertmaster of the Boston Sym. Orch.; later settled in N.Y. as a teacher.

Fraenkel, Wolfgang, German composer; b. Berlin, Oct. 10, 1897; d. Los Angeles, March 8, 1983. He studied violin, piano, and theory at the Klindworth-Scharwenka Cons. in Berlin; at the same time, he took courses in jurisprudence and was a judge in Berlin until the advent of the Nazi regime in 1933; he was interned in the Sachsenhausen concentration camp, but as a 50 percent Jew (his mother was an Aryan, as was his wife), he was released in 1939, and went to China, where he enjoyed the protection of Chiang Kai-shek, who asked him to organize music education in Nanking and Shanghai. In 1947 he emigrated to the U.S. and settled in Los Angeles. He earned a living by composing background music for documentary films in Hollywood, supplementing his income by copying music (he had a calligraphic handwriting). Fraenkel's music was evolved from the standard German traditions, but at a later period he began to experiment with serial methods of composition. His 3rd string quartet (1960) won the Queen Elisabeth of Belgium Prize and his *Symphonische Aphorismen* (1965) won 1st prize at the International Competition of the City of Milan. His works, both publ. and in MS, were deposited in the Moldenhauer Archive in Spokane, Wash.

WORKS: OPERA: *Der brennende Dornbusch* (1924–27). **ORCH.:** Flute Concerto (1930); *Frescobaldi*, transcription for Orch. of 5 organ pieces by Frescobaldi (1957); *Symphonische Aphorismen* (1965). **CHAMBER:** 3 string quartets (1924, 1949, 1960); Cello Sonata (1934); Violin Sonata (1935); Sonata for Solo Violin (1954); *Variations and a Fantasy on a Theme by Schoenberg* for Piano (1954); Viola Sonata (1963); *Klavierstück* for Tape and Piano (1964); String Quintet (1976). **VOCAL:** *Der Wegweiser*, cantata (1931); *Filippo* for Speaker and Orch. (1948); *Joseph* for Baritone and Orch., to a text by Thomas Mann (1968); *Missa aphoristica* for Chorus and Orch. (1973).

Frager, Malcolm (Monroe), outstanding American pianist; b. St. Louis, Jan. 15, 1935; d. Pittsfield, Mass., June 20, 1991. He commenced piano lessons at a very early age and made his recital debut in St. Louis when he was only 6. He continued his training there with Carl Madlinger (1942–49). At 10, he appeared as soloist in Mozart's 17th Piano Concerto, K.453, with Golschmann and the St. Louis Sym. Orch. He subsequently pursued his studies with Carl Friedberg in N.Y. (1949–55), and attended the American Cons. in Fontainebleau (1951–52), where he won the Prix d'Excellence; he also majored in Russian at Columbia Univ., taking his B.A. in 1957. After capturing the highest honors at the Geneva (1955), Leventritt (N.Y., 1959), and Queen Elisabeth of Belgium (Brussels, 1960) competitions, he toured throughout the world with enormous success. Frager was an extraordinary virtuoso who tempered his brilliant technique with a profound sensitivity. His repertory ranged from Haydn to the moderns, and included such rare works as the original versions of the Schumann Piano Concerto and Tchaikovsky's 1st Piano Concerto.

Françaix, Jean, significant French composer; b. Le Mans, May 23, 1912. He first studied at the Le Mans Cons., of which his father was director, and later took courses at the Paris Cons. with Philipp (piano) and Boulanger (composition). In his music, he associated himself with the new French school of composers, pursuing the twofold aim of practical application and national tradition; his instrumental works represent a stylization of Classical French music; in this respect, he comes close to Ravel.

WORKS: DRAMATIC: OPERAS: *Le Diable boîteux*, comic chamber opera (1937; Paris, June 30, 1938); *L'Apostrophe*, musical comedy, after Balzac (1940; Amsterdam, July 1, 1951); *Paris à nous deux (ou Le Nouveau Rastignac)*, comic opera (Fontainebleau, Aug. 7, 1954); *La Princesse de Clèves* (1961–65; Rouen, Dec. 11, 1965). **BALLETS:** *Scuola de Ballo*, on themes of Boccherini (1933); *Les Malheurs de Sophie* (1935; Paris, Feb. 25, 1948); *Le Roi nu* (1935; Paris, June 15, 1936); *Le Jeu sentimental* (Brussels, July 8, 1936); *La Lutherie enchantée* (Antwerp, March 21, 1936); *Le Jugement d'un fou* (1938; London, Feb. 6, 1939); *Verreries de Venise* (1938; Paris, June 22, 1939); *Les Demoiselles de la nuit* (Paris, May 20, 1948); *Les Zigues de mars* (1950); *La Dame dans la lune* (Paris, Feb. 18, 1958); *Pierrot ou Les Secrets de la nuit* (1980). **ORCH.:** Sym. (Paris, Nov. 6, 1932); Suite for Violin and Orch. (1934); *Sérénade* for Chamber Orch. (1934); *Divertissement* for Violin, Viola, Cello, and Orch. (Paris, Dec. 22, 1935); Quadruple Concerto for Flute, Oboe, Clarinet, Bassoon, and Orch. (1935); *Au musée Grévin*, suite (1936); Piano Concerto (Berlin, Nov. 3, 1936); *Musique de cour*, duo concertante for Flute, Violin, and Orch. (1937); *Divertissement* for Bassoon and Strings (1942; Schwetzingen, May 5, 1968); *Rhapsodie* for Viola and Small Orch. (1946); *L'Heure du berger* for Piano and Strings (1947); *Symphonie d'archets* for Strings (1948); *Les Zigues de mars*, "petit ballet militaire" (Paris, Feb. 19, 1950); *Variations de Concert* for Cello and String Orch. (1950); Sym. (La Jolla, Calif., Aug. 9, 1953); Harpsichord Concerto (1959; Paris, Feb. 7, 1960); *L'Horloge de Flore* for Oboe and Orch. (1959; Philadelphia, April 1, 1961); *Le Dialogue des carmélites*, symphonic suite (1960; Paris, April 4, 1969); *Sei preludi* for String Chamber Orch. (1963; Lucerne, Sept. 3, 1964); Concerto for 2 Pianos and Orch. (Maastricht, Nov. 26, 1965); Flute Concerto (1966; Schwetzingen, May 13, 1967); Clarinet Concerto (1967; Nice, July 30, 1968); 2 violin concertos: No. 1 (1968; Quebec, Jan. 26, 1970) and No. 2 (Braunschweig, Nov. 30, 1979); *La Ville mystérieuse*, fantaisie (Nuremberg, March 15, 1974); *Thème et variations* (Bochum, Dec. 12, 1974); Double Bass Concerto (Frankfurt am Main, Nov. 1, 1974); *Le Gay Paris* for Trumpet and Winds (1974; Wiesbaden, April 6, 1975); *Cassazione* for 3 Orchs. (Salzburg, Aug. 12, 1975); Concerto grosso for Flute, Clarinet, Bassoon, Horn, String Quintet, and Orch. (1976; Mainz, Feb. 6, 1977); *Ouverture anacréontique* (1978; Recklinghausen, Feb. 22, 1981); *Tema con variazioni* for Clarinet and Strings (Florence, Sept. 14, 1978); Concerto for 2 Harps and 11 String Instruments (1978; Schwetzingen, May 11, 1979); Bassoon Concerto (1979; Frankfurt am Main, May 20, 1980); Concerto for Guitar and Strings (1983); *Pavane pour un génie vivant* (Montpellier, July 23, 1987); Concerto for 15 Soloists and Orch., *Suivi d'une surprise* (1988; Vienna, May 16, 1990); Double Concerto for Flute, Clarinet, and Orch. (1991; Schwetzingen, June 8, 1992). **CHAMBER:** Quartet for Flute, Oboe, Clarinet, and Bassoon (1933); Trio for Violin, Viola, and Cello (1933); Quintet for Flute, Violin, Viola, Cello, and Harp (1934); Quartet for 2 Violins, Viola, and Cello (1934); Quintet for Flute, Oboe, Clarinet, Bassoon, and Horn (1948); Quartet for English Horn, Violin, Viola, and Cello (1971); Trio for Flute, Harp, and Cello (1971); Octet for Clarinet, Horn, Bassoon, 2 Violins, Viola, Cello, and Double Bass (1972); *Aubade* for 12 Cellos (1975); Quintet for Clarinet and String Quartet (1977); *Danses exotiques* for 12 Instrumentalists (1981); *Dixtour* for Wind and String Quintet (1986); Wind Quintet No. 2 (1987); Quintet for Flute, 2 Violins, Cello, and Harpsichord (1988); Wind Sextet (1991); piano pieces, including a Sonata (1960); organ music. **VOCAL:** *Trois épigrammes* for Chorus and String Quintet or String Orch. (1938); *L'Apocalypse selon St. Jean*, oratorio for 4 Soli, Chorus, and 2 Orchs. (1939; Paris, June 11, 1942); *La Cantate de Méphisto* for Bass and String Orch. (1952; N.Y., Jan. 25, 1953); *Déploration de Tonton, chien fidèle*, deploring the death of "the faithful dog Tonton," humorous cantata for Mezzo-soprano and String Orch. (1956); *Les Inestimables Chroniques du bon géant Gargantua* for Speaker and String Orch. (1971); *La Promenade à Versailles*, cantata for 4 Men's Voices and 11 Strings (1976); *Trois poèmes de Paul Valéry* for Chorus (1984); other vocal works.

BIBL.: M. Lanjean, *J. F.* (Paris, 1961).

Francescatti, Zino (actually, **René-Charles),** eminent French violinist; b. Marseilles, Aug. 9, 1902; d. La Ciotat, Sept. 17, 1991. He studied with his father René, a violinist and cellist, and with his mother Erneste, a violinist. When he was only 5, he made his public debut in a recital. At age 10, he appeared as soloist in the Beethoven Violin Concerto. After making his Paris debut in 1925, he toured England in duo recitals with Ravel in 1926. He soon established himself as a virtuoso via tours of Europe and South America. On Nov. 18, 1939, he made his U.S. debut as soloist in Paganini's 1st Violin Concerto with Barbirolli and the N.Y. Phil. After the close of World War II in 1945, he pursued an outstanding international career until his retirement in 1976. He then sold his celebrated "Hart" Stradivarius of 1727 and established the Zino Francescatti Foundation in La Ciotat to assist young violinists. In 1987 an international violin competition was organized in his honor in Aix-en-Provence. Francescatti's playing was marked by a seemingly effortless technique, warmth of expression, and tonal elegance.

Francesch, Homero, Uruguayan pianist; b. Montevideo, Dec. 6, 1947. He studied piano with Santiago Baranda Reyes; then took piano lessons in Munich with Maria Hindemith-Landes and Steurer. Following concerts in West Germany, he began an international career; appeared as soloist with the Berlin Phil., London Sym., Vienna Sym., Orchestre National de France of Paris, and other leading orchs.

Franchetti, Alberto, Italian composer; b. Turin, Sept. 18, 1860; d. Viareggio, Aug. 4, 1942. He studied in Turin with Niccolò Coccon and Fortunato Magi; then with Rheinberger in Munich and with Draeseke in Dresden. He devoted his entire life to composition, with the exception of a brief tenure as director of the Cherubini Cons. in Florence (1926–28).

WORKS: OPERAS: *Asrael* (Reggio Emilia, Feb. 11, 1888); *Cristoforo Colombo* (Genoa, Oct. 6, 1892); *Fior d'Alpe* (Milan, March 15, 1894); *Il Signor di Pourceaugnac* (Milan, April 10, 1897); *Germania* (Milan, March 11, 1902); *La Figlia di Jorio*

(Milan, March 29, 1906); *Notte di leggenda* (Milan, Jan. 14, 1915); *Giove a Pompei* (Rome, June 5, 1921; in collaboration with U. Giordano); *Glauco* (Naples, April 8, 1922). **ORCH.:** Sym. (1886); 2 symphonic poems: *Loreley* and *Nella selva nera.* **OTHER:** Vocal works, including *Inno* for Soli, Chorus, and Orch. (for the 800th anniversary of the Univ. of Bologna); several pieces of chamber music; songs.

Franci, Benvenuto, Italian baritone, father of **Carlo Franci;** b. Pienza, near Siena, July 1, 1891; d. Rome, Feb. 27, 1985. He was a student of Cotogni and Rosati in Rome. In 1918 he made his operatic debut at Rome's Teatro Costanzi as Giannetto in Mascagni's *Lodoletta,* where he later sang in the premiere of that composer's *Il piccolo Marat* in 1921. In 1923 he sang Amonasro at Milan's La Scala, where he returned to sing in the premieres of Giordano's *Cena delle Beffe* in 1924 and Zandonai's *Cavalieri di Ekebù* in 1925. From 1928 to 1949 he was a principal member of the Rome Opera. He also made guest appearances at London's Covent Garden in 1925, 1931, and 1946. In 1955 he made his farewell appearance in Trieste. Among his other roles were Rigoletto, Macbeth, Gerard, Telramund, Barnaba, Barak, and Scarpia.

Franci, Carlo, Italian conductor and composer, son of **Benvenuto Franci;** b. Buenos Aires, July 18, 1927. He went to Rome and studied composition with Turchi and Petrassi at the Cons. and conducting with Previtali at the Accademia di Santa Cecilia. After conducting the Radio Eireann Sym. Orch. in Dublin (1955–57) and the RAI in Rome (1961–63), he appeared with the Rome Opera. In 1968 he conducted the Rome Opera production of Rossini's *Otello* during its visit to the Metropolitan Opera in N.Y. On Feb. 1, 1969, he made his debut at the Metropolitan Opera conducting *Lucia di Lammermoor,* and remained on its roster until 1972. As a guest conductor, he appeared with opera houses in Milan, Berlin, Budapest, Munich, Madrid, Paris, Hamburg, Zürich et al. In 1988 he appeared as a guest conductor with the PACT (Performing Arts Council, Transvaal) Opera in Pretoria, where he subsequently served as principal conductor of the Transvaal Phil. Among his compositions are *4 Studies* for Orch. (1993) and the *African Oratorio* (1994).

Franck, Richard, German pianist; b. Cologne, Jan. 3, 1858; d. Heidelberg, Jan. 22, 1938. He studied with his father, Eduard Franck (b. Breslau, Oct. 5, 1817; d. Berlin, Dec. 1, 1893) in Berlin and also attended the Leipzig Cons. (1878–80). He was in Basel from 1880 to 1883 and again from 1887 to 1900, and was active there as a pianist and teacher. He was highly regarded as an interpreter of Beethoven's sonatas. Franck publ. a book of memoirs, *Musikalische und unmusikalische Erinnerungen* (Heidelberg, 1928).

BIBL.: P. and A. Feuchte, *Die Komponisten Eduard Franck und R. F.: Leben und Werk, Dokumente, Quellen* (Stuttgart and Hamburg, 1993).

Franckenstein, Clemens von, German composer; b. Wiesentheid, July 14, 1875; d. Hechendorf, Aug. 19, 1942. He spent his youth in Vienna; then went to Munich, where he studied with Thuille; later took courses with Knorr at the Hoch Cons. in Frankfurt am Main. He traveled with an opera company in the U.S. in 1901; then was a theater conductor in London (1902–07). From 1912 to 1918 and from 1924 to 1934 he was Intendant at the Munich Opera. He wrote several operas, the most successful of which was *Des Kaisers Dichter* (on the life of the Chinese poet Li-Tai Po), premiered in Hamburg (Nov. 2, 1920). Other operas were *Griselda* (Troppau, 1898), *Fortunatus* (Budapest, 1909), and *Rahab* (Hamburg, March 25, 1911). He also wrote several orch. works.

BIBL.: A. McCredie, *C.v. F.* (Tutzing, 1992).

Franco, Johan (Henri Gustav), Dutch-born American composer; b. Zaandam, July 12, 1908; d. Virginia Beach, Va., April 14, 1988. After studies at the Amsterdam Cons. (1929–34), he emigrated to the U.S. and in 1942 became a naturalized American citizen.

WORKS: ORCH.: 5 syms. (1933, 1939, 1940, 1950, 1958); 5 "concertos liricos": No. 1 for Violin and Chamber Orch. (1937), No. 2 for Cello and Orch. (1962), No. 3 for Piano and Chamber Orch. (1967), No. 4 for Percussion and Chamber Orch. (1970), and No. 5 for Guitar and Chamber Orch. (1973); Violin Concerto (Brussels, Dec. 6, 1939); *Serenata concertante* for Piano and Chamber Orch. (N.Y., March 11, 1940); *Fantasy* for Cello and Orch. (1951). **CHAMBER:** 6 string quartets (1931–60); Violin Sonata (1965); piano pieces; numerous carillon pieces. **OTHER:** Many vocal works; incidental music.

François, Samson, admired French pianist; b. Frankfurt am Main (son of the French consul there), May 18, 1924; d. Paris, Oct. 22, 1970. He began piano studies at a very early age and was only 6 when he played a Mozart concerto under Mascagni in Italy. While still a youth, he obtained 1st prizes at the Belgrade Cons. and the Nice Cons. He continued his training in Paris with Cortot at the École Normale de Musique and then with Long at the Cons. (premier prix, 1940). In 1943 he won 1st prize at the first Long-Thibaud Competition in Paris. From 1945 he toured regularly in Europe, and in 1947 he made his first appearances in the U.S. He subsequently played all over the globe, including Communist China in 1964. In addition to his notable performances of works by such French masters as Fauré, Debussy, and Ravel, he was equally notable in his performances of Chopin and Schumann.

Frandsen, John, respected Danish conductor; b. Copenhagen, July 10, 1918. He was educated at the Royal Danish Cons. of Music in Copenhagen; then was organist at the Domkirke there (1938–53); also made appearances as a conductor. After serving as conductor with the Danish Radio Sym. Orch. in Copenhagen (1945–46), he became a conductor at the Royal Danish Theater there; also made appearances with the Royal Danish Orch. in Copenhagen. In 1958 he toured the U.S. with the Danish Radio Sym. Orch. He was also active as a teacher, at both the Royal Danish Cons. of Music and the Opera School of the Royal Danish Theater. In 1980 he was named orch. counselor of the Danish Radio. He was particularly noted for his outstanding performances of Danish music.

Frank, Alan (Clifford), English music scholar; b. London, Oct. 10, 1910; d. July 9, 1994. He studied the clarinet, conducting, and composition. At the age of 17, he joined the staff of the Oxford Univ. Press; during World War II, he was in the Royal Air Force. In 1947 he was appointed music ed. of the Oxford Univ. Press; in 1954 he became head of its music dept.; retired in 1975. In 1935 he married **Phyllis Tate**. He publ. *The Playing of Chamber Music* (with G. Stratton; London, 1935; 2nd ed., 1951) and *Modern British Composers* (London, 1953); he was also co-author (with F. Thurston) of *A Comprehensive Tutor for the Boehm Clarinet* (London, 1939).

Frank, Claude, esteemed German-born American pianist and pedagogue, father of **Pamela Frank;** b. Nuremberg, Dec. 24, 1925. After the consolidation of power by the Nazis, he went with his family to Paris in 1937; from there they fled to Lisbon and finally reached safety in the U.S. in 1940. In 1944 he became a naturalized American citizen. Following training with A. Schnabel (piano) and Dessau (theory and composition) in N.Y. (1941–44), he pursued composition studies with Lockwood (1946–48) and attended Koussevitzky's conducting course at the Berkshire Music Center in Tanglewood (summer, 1947); he also attended Columbia Univ. In 1947 he made his N.Y. recital debut. After appearing as a soloist with the NBC Sym. Orch. in 1948, he toured as a soloist with various other orchs., as a recitalist, and as a chamber music player. He also devoted time to teaching. In 1959 he married **Lilian Kallir**, with whom he appeared as a duo pianist. He also appeared in duo concerts with his daughter. Frank is highly admired for his insightful performances of the classics.

Frank, Pamela, American violinist and teacher, daughter of **Claude Frank** and **Lilian Kallir**; b. N.Y., June 20, 1967. She began violin lessons at the age of 5. Following studies with Shirley Givens, she pursued training with Szymon Goldberg and Jaime Laredo, graduating from the Curtis Inst. of Music in Philadelphia in 1989. In 1985 she made her formal debut as soloist with Alexander Schneider and the N.Y. String Orch. at N.Y.'s Carnegie Hall. In 1988 she was awarded the Avery Fisher Career Grant. In addition to engagements as a soloist with major American orchs., she was active as a recitalist and chamber music player. She frequently appears in concert with her parents, as well as with other artists, including Peter Serkin and Yo-Yo Ma.

Frankel, Benjamin, English composer; b. London, Jan. 31, 1906; d. there, Feb. 12, 1973. He worked as an apprentice watchmaker in his youth; then went to Germany to study music; returning to London, he earned his living by playing piano or violin in restaurants. It was only then that he began studying composition seriously. In the interim, he made arrangements, played in jazz bands, and wrote music for films; some of his film scores, such as that for *The Man in the White Suit,* are notable for their finesse in musical characterization. In 1946 he was appointed to the faculty of the Guildhall School of Music and Drama in London. Frankel also took great interest in political affairs; was for many years a member of the British Communist Party and followed the tenets of socialist realism in some of his compositions.

WORKS: OPERA: *Marching Son* (1972–73). **ORCH.:** Violin Concerto (1951; Stockholm, June 10, 1956); 8 syms.: No. 1 (1952), No. 2 (Cheltenham, July 13, 1962), No. 3 (1964), No. 4 (London, Dec. 18, 1966), No. 5 (1967), No. 6 (London, March 23, 1969), No. 7 (1969; London, June 4, 1970), and No. 8 (1971); *Concertante Lirico* for Strings (1953); *Serenata concertante* for Piano Trio and Orch. (1961); Viola Concerto (1966); *A Catalogue of Incidents* for Chamber Orch. (1966); *Overture for a Ceremony* (1970); *Pezzi melodici* (Stroud Festival, Oct. 19, 1972). **CHAMBER:** 5 string quartets (1944, 1945, 1947, 1948, 1965); String Trio (1944); 2 sonatas for Solo Violin (1944, 1962); *3 Poems* for Cello and Piano (1950); Quintet for Clarinet and Strings (1953); Piano Quartet (1953); *Bagatelles* for 11 Instruments (1959); *Pezzi pianissimi* for Clarinet, Cello, and Piano (1964). **VOCAL:** *The Aftermath* for Tenor, Trumpet, Harp, and Strings (1947); *8 Songs* for Medium Voice and Piano (1959).

Frankenstein, Alfred (Victor), American writer on music and art; b. Chicago, Oct. 5, 1906; d. San Francisco, June 22, 1981. He played clarinet in the Civic Orch. of Chicago before turning to writing; from 1935 to 1975 he was music critic of the *San Francisco Chronicle*; concurrently served as its principal art critic; from 1937 to 1963 he was program annotator of the San Francisco Sym. He publ., besides innumerable articles, a book of essays, *Syncopating Saxophones* (Chicago, 1925); *Modern Guide to Symphonic Music* (N.Y., 1966); and several publications dealing with modern American art. He was the first to publ. the sketches of Victor Hartmann that inspired Mussorgsky's *Pictures at an Exhibition* (*Musical Quarterly*, July 1939).

Frankl, Peter, brilliant Hungarian-born English pianist; b. Budapest, Oct. 2, 1935. He studied at the Franz Liszt Academy of Music in Budapest; his teachers included Kodály, Leo Weiner, and Lajos Hernadi. In 1957 he won 1st prize in the Long-Thibaud Competition in Paris, and also 1st prizes in competitions in Munich (1957) and Rio de Janeiro (1959), which catapulted him into an international career. He made his debut in America in a Dallas recital in 1965. Eventually he moved to London, and became a naturalized British subject in 1967. In England he formed the Frankl-Pauk-Kirshbaum Trio in 1969. His repertoire is extensive, ranging from Classical music to contemporary works.

Franko, Nahan, American violinist and conductor, brother of **Sam Franko**; b. New Orleans, July 23, 1861; d. Amityville, N.Y., June 7, 1930. As a child prodigy, he toured with Adelina Patti; then studied in Berlin with Joachim and Wilhelmj. Returning to America, he joined the orch. of the Metropolitan Opera in N.Y.; was its concertmaster from 1883 to 1905; made his debut there as a conductor on April 1, 1900; was the first native-born American to be engaged as conductor there (1904–07).

Franko, Sam, American violinist, brother of **Nahan Franko**; b. New Orleans, Jan. 20, 1857; d. N.Y., May 6, 1937. He studied in Berlin with Joachim, Heinrich de Ahna, and Eduard Rappoldi. Returning to the U.S. in 1880, he joined the Theodore Thomas Orch. in N.Y., and was its concertmaster from 1884 to 1891; in 1883 he toured the U.S. and Canada as a soloist with the Mendelssohn Quintette Club of Boston. In order to prove that prejudice against native orch. players was unfounded, he organized in 1894 the American Sym. Orch., using 65 American-born performers; this orch. was later used for his Concerts of Old Music (1900–1909). In 1910 he went to Berlin and taught at the Stern Cons.; he returned to N.Y. in 1915. He publ. for piano: *Album Leaf* (1889); *Viennese Silhouettes* (a set of 6 waltzes, 1928); etc.; several violin pieces; practical arrangements for violin and piano. His memoirs were publ. posth. under the title *Chords and Discords* (N.Y., 1938).

Frantz, Ferdinand, German bass-baritone; b. Kassel, Feb. 8, 1906; d. Munich, May 26, 1959. He made his debut at the opera in Kassel in 1927 as Ortel in *Die Meistersinger von Nürnberg*; then sang in Halle (1930–32) and Chemnitz (1932–37). He was a leading member of the Hamburg State Opera (1937–43) and the Bavarian State Opera in Munich (1943–59). He made a fine impression at his Metropolitan Opera debut in N.Y. on Dec. 12, 1949, as Wotan in *Die Walküre*; sang there until 1951 and again in 1953–54; he also appeared at Covent Garden in London in 1953–54. He was primarily known as an effective Wagnerian bass and baritone.

Frantz, Justus, German pianist, conductor, and teacher; b. Hohensalza, May 18, 1944. He studied piano with Eliza Hansen at the Hamburg Hochschule für Musik; later took private courses with Kempff. After winning a prize in the Munich Competition in 1967, he began appearing with leading European orchs. He made his U.S. debut with the N.Y. Phil. in 1975; subsequently appeared with many other American orchs. He also toured with Christoph Eschenbach in duo-piano concerts. In 1986 he founded the Schleswig-Holstein Music Festival, with which he was associated until 1994. In 1985 he became a prof. at the Hamburg Hochschule für Musik. He also was founder-director of the Schleswig-Holstein Festival (1986–94).

Franz, Paul (real name, **François Gautier**), French tenor; b. Paris, Nov. 30, 1876; d. there, April 20, 1950. After private voice studies with Louis Delaquerrière, he made his debut at the Paris Opéra in 1909 as Lohengrin; remained on its roster until 1938; also appeared at London's Covent Garden (1910–14). From 1937 he taught voice at the Paris Cons.

Fraser, Norman, Chilean-born English pianist and composer; b. Valparaiso, Nov. 26, 1904. He pursued his musical studies in Chile; in 1917 he went to England, and attended classes at the Royal Academy of Music in London; then took piano lessons with Isidor Philipp in Paris. He subsequently made several tours in South America as a representative of various British organizations. From 1954 to 1971 he was engaged as European music supervisor at the BBC. He gave numerous joint recitals with his wife, Janet Fraser, the English mezzo-soprano (b. Kirkealdy, May 22, 1911). In 1973 he settled at Seaford, England. He composed a number of attractive piano pieces and some chamber music.

Frazzi, Vito, Italian composer and teacher; b. San Secondo Parmense, Aug. 1, 1888; d. Florence, July 8, 1975. He studied organ at the Parma Cons.; also took courses in piano and theory. From 1912 to 1958 he taught at the Florence Cons.; also taught at the Accademia Chigiana in Siena (1932–63). He wrote a music drama, *Re Lear*, after Shakespeare (Florence, 1939); an opera, *Don Quixote* (Florence, April 27, 1952); several symphonic poems; chamber music; also orchestrated Monteverdi's stage works.

Freccia, Massimo, Italian conductor; b. Florence, Sept. 19, 1906. He studied at the Florence Cons. and later in Vienna with Franz Schalk. From 1933 to 1935 he conducted the Budapest Sym. Orch.; was guest conductor at the Lewisohn Stadium in N.Y. (1938–40); then was conductor of the Havana Phil. (1939–43), the New Orleans Sym. Orch. (1944–52), and the Baltimore Sym. Orch. (1952–59). He returned to Italy in 1959, and conducted the Rome Radio Orch. until 1963.

Freed, Isadore, Russian-born American composer and teacher; b. Brest-Litovsk, March 26, 1900; d. Rockville Centre, N.Y., Nov. 10, 1960. He went to the U.S. at an early age; graduated from the Univ. of Pa. in 1918 (Mus.Bac.); then studied with Bloch and with d'Indy in Paris. He returned to the U.S. in 1934; held various teaching positions; in 1944 he was appointed head of the music dept. at the Hartt College of Music in Hartford, Conn.

WORKS: DRAMATIC: OPERAS: *Homo Sum* (1930); *The Princess and the Vagabond* (Hartford, May 13, 1948). **BALLET:** *Vibrations* (Philadelphia, 1928). **ORCH.:** *Jeux de timbres* (Paris, 1933); 2 syms.: No. 1 (1941) and No. 2 for Brass (San Francisco, Feb. 8, 1951); *Appalachian Symphonic Sketches* (Chautauqua, N.Y., July 31, 1946); *Festival Overture* (San Francisco, Nov. 14, 1946); *Rhapsody* for Trombone and Orch. (radio premiere, N.Y., Jan. 7, 1951); Violin Concerto (N.Y., Nov. 13, 1951); Cello Concerto (1952); Concertino for English Horn and Orch. (1953). **CHAMBER:** 3 string quartets (1931, 1932, 1937); Trio for Flute, Viola, and Harp (1940); *Triptych* for Violin, Viola, Cello, and Piano (1943); *Passacaglia* for Cello and Piano (1947); Quintet for Woodwinds and Horn (1949); Oboe Sonatina (1954); piano pieces; organ music. **OTHER:** Vocal music.

BIBL.: E. Steinhauer, *A Jewish Composer by Choice, I. F.: His Life and Work* (N.Y., 1961).

Freed, Richard (Donald), distinguished American music critic, annotator, and broadcaster; b. Chicago, Dec. 27, 1928. He was educated at the Univ. of Chicago (graduated, 1947). After working for various newspapers, he was a contributor to the *Saturday Review* (1959–71) and a critic for the *N.Y. Times* (1965–66). He served as assistant to the director of the Eastman School of Music in Rochester, N.Y. (1966–70); was a contributing ed. to *Stereo Review* (from 1973); was also a record critic for the *Washington Star* (1972–75), the *Washington Post* (1976–84), and radio station WETA-FM in Washington, D.C. (from 1985); likewise was program annotator for the St. Louis Sym. Orch. (1973–96), the Philadelphia Orch. (1974–84), the Houston Sym. Orch. (1977–80), the National Sym. Orch. in Washington, D.C. (from 1977), and the Baltimore Sym. Orch. (1984–92). From 1974 to 1989 he was executive director of the Music Critics Assn.; was named consultant to the music director of the National Sym. Orch. in 1981. He received the ASCAP-Deems Taylor Award in 1984 for his erudite and engagingly indited program annotations, and again in 1986 for his equally stylish record annotations. He occasionally wrote under the names Paul Turner, Gregor Philipp, and Priam Clay.

Freedman, Harry, Polish-born Canadian composer; b. Łódź, April 5, 1922. He was taken to Canada as a child and became a naturalized citizen in 1931. At 13, he became a student at the Winnipeg School of Art to study painting. At 18, he took up the clarinet; he then studied oboe with Perry Bauman and composition with John Weinzweig at the Royal Cons. of Music of Toronto (1945–51); also attended Messiaen's class in composition at the Berkshire Music Center in Tanglewood (summer, 1949). He began his career performing with and composing for dance bands and jazz ensembles; played English horn in the Toronto Sym. Orch. (1946–70), then served as its composer-in-residence (1970–71); was a founder and president (1975–78) of the Canadian League of Composers. In 1985 he was made an Officer of the Order of Canada. In his works, he reveals a fine command of writing in various idioms, ranging from symphonic to jazz scores.

WORKS: DRAMATIC: OPERA: *Abracadabra* (1979). **BALLETS:** *Rose Latulippe* (Stratford, Aug. 16, 1966); *5 over 13* (1969); *The Shining People of Leonard Cohen* (1970); *Star Cross'd* (1973; rev. 1975; retitled *Romeo and Juliet*); *Oiseaux exotiques* (1984–85); *Heroes of Our Time* (1986); *Breaks* (1987). Also incidental music; film and television scores. **ORCH.:** *Nocturne I* (1949) and *II* (1975); *Matinee Suite* (1951–55); *Fantasia and Dance* for Violin and Orch. (1955; rev. 1959); *Images*, symphonic suite (1957–58); 3 syms.: No. 1 (1954–60; Washington, D.C., April 23, 1961), No. 2, *A Little Symphony* (1966), and No. 3 (1983; rev. 1985); *Chaconne* (1964); *Armana* (1967); *Tangents*, symphonic variations (Montreal, July 21, 1967); *Klee Wych* (The Laughing One [Indian name of the artist Emily Carr]; 1970); *Scenario* for Saxophone, Electric Bass Guitar, and Orch. (Toronto, May 29, 1970); *Graphic I (Out of Silence . . .)* for Orch. and Tape (Toronto, Oct. 26, 1971); *Preludes* (1971; orchestrated from Debussy); *Tapestry* for Small Orch. (1973); *Tsolum Summer* for Flute, Percussion, and Strings (1976); *Royal Flush*, concerto grosso for Brass Quintet and Orch. (1981); *Chalumeau* for Clarinet and String Orch. or String Quartet (1981); *Concerto for Orchestra* (1982); *Accord* for Violin and Orch. (1982); *The Sax Chronicles* for Saxophone and Orch. (1984); *Passacaglia* for Jazz Band and Orch. (1984); *Graphic VI (Town)*, after the painting of Harold Town (1986); *A Dance on the Earth* (1988); Sonata for Symphonic Winds (1988). **CHAMBER:** Wind Quintet (1962); *The Tokaido* for Chorus and Wind Quintet (1964); *Variations* for Oboe, Flute, and Harpsichord (1965); *Graphic II* for String Quartet (1972); Quartet for Trombones, Bassoons, or Cellos (1973); *5 Rings* for Brass Quintet (1976); *Monday Gig* for Woodwind Quintet (1978); *Opus Pocus* for Flute, Violin, Viola, and Cello (1979); *Blue* for String Quartet (1980); *A Little Girl Blew* for Bass Clarinet (1988); other chamber works. **VOCAL:** *3 poèmes de Jacques Prevert* for Soprano and String Orch. (1962); *2 Sonnets of Love and Age* for Soprano, Baritone, Woodwind Quintet, and Brass Quintet (1975); *Fragments of Alice* for Soprano, Alto, Baritone, and Chamber Orch. (1976); *Nocturne III* for Chorus and Orch. (1980); *A Time Is Coming* for Voices (1982); *Rhymes from the Nursery* for Children's Chorus (1986); other vocal works.

Freeman, Betty (née **Wishnick**), American music patron, photographer, and record producer; b. Chicago, June 2, 1921. She studied music, piano, and English literature at Wellesley College (B.A., 1942); later took piano lessons at the Juilliard School of Music in N.Y. and at the New England Cons. of Music in Boston. She also studied privately in N.Y. with Erich Itor Kahn (harmony) and Beveridge Webster (piano) and in Los Angeles with Victoria Front and Joanna Graudan. After moving to Los Angeles in 1950, she began collecting American avant-garde art. In 1960 she became a founding member of the Contemporary Art Council of the Los Angeles County Museum of Art. In the 1960s she completed books on Clyfford Still and Sam Francis. From 1964 to 1973 she was one of the leaders of the music program "Encounters" at the Pasadena Art Museum. During this time, she became the patron and promoter of the uniquely original composer Harry Partch, who became the subject of her prize-winning documentary film *The Dreamer That Remains* (1972). She also began still photography, studying with Ansel Adams, Cole Weston, Fred Picker and others, her subjects being largely the American composers and performing artists who were also her beneficiaries. Her premiere photo exhibit took place at the Otis-Parsons Gallery in Los Angeles in 1985; other shows followed in Milan (1987), the Los Angeles Phil. (1988), the Brooklyn Academy of Music (1988), the Univ. of Calif. at Irvine (1989), the Berlin Phil. (1990), four locations throughout Japan (1990), the Cologne Phil. (1991), Ace Gallery in Los Angeles (1991), Ferrara, Italy (1991), the Eastman School of Music (1991), the Univ. of Calif. at San Diego (1992), the Salzburg Festival (1992), the Théâtre Royal de la Monnaie in Brussels (1993), the Ojai Festival (1993), Budapest (1993), the Univ. of Calif. at San Diego (1995), La Fenice Theatre (1995), Royal Festival Hall in London (1996), N.Y.'s Lincoln Center

(1996), Helsinki (1996), and the Univ. of Calif. at Berkeley (1996). From 1981 to 1991 she presented monthly musicales of contemporary composers at her home in Beverly Hills with the music critic Alan Rich. From the 1960s she was an active supporter of West Coast composers, including Robert Erickson, Paul Dresher, Morton Subotnick, Terry Riley, Lou Harrison, Dane Rudhyar, Peter Garland, Daniel Lentz, and John Adams. In addition, she supported the work of Steve Reich, Philip Glass, La Monte Young, John Cage, Virgil Thomson, Conlon Nancarrow, Christopher Rouse, and Steven Mackey. Later her support extended to Europe, particularly to the composers Birtwistle, Lutowslawski, George Benjamin, and György Kurtag, and to the Salzburg Festival. She served twice on the Inter-Arts Panel of the NEA (1983–84), and received the Cunningham Dance Foundation award for "distinguished support of the arts" (1984). She further received an award from the American Music Center (1986) and the Gold Baton from the American Sym. Orch. League (1987). She has great admirers in the artists she supports; she was the dedicatee of John Cage's *Freeman Etudes* (1977) and John Adams's *Nixon in China* (1987). From 1989 to 1994 she served on the board of directors of the Los Angeles Phil. She was married to Stanley Freeman with whom she busily produced 4 children in 6 years. Divorced in 1971, she married the Italian artist Franco Assetto, with whom she divided her time between Turin and Los Angeles until his death. Her belief in and support of contemporary music resulted from her firm belief that music written since 1950 is infinitely more rewarding and convincing than anything written during the more popular 19th century with, of course, the exceptions of Beethoven and Schubert.

Freeman, Harry Lawrence, black American composer, conductor, and teacher; b. Cleveland, Oct. 9, 1869; d. N.Y., March 24, 1954. He studied theory with J.H. Beck and piano with E. Schonert and Carlos Sobrino. He taught at Wilberforce Univ. (1902–04) and the Salem School of Music (1910–13); organized and directed the Freeman School of Music (1911–22) and the Freeman School of Grand Opera (from 1923); conducted various theater orchs. and opera companies; in 1920 he organized the Negro Opera Co.; conducted a pageant, *O Sing a New Song*, at the Chicago World's Fair in 1934. He was the first black composer to conduct a sym. orch. in his own work (Minneapolis, 1907), and the first of his race to write large operatic compositions. All of his music is written in folk-song style, his settings in simple harmonies; his operas, all on Negro, oriental, and Indian themes, are constructed of songs and choruses in simple concatenation of separate numbers.

WORKS: DRAMATIC: OPERAS: *The Martyr* (Denver, 1893); *Zuluki* (1898); *African Kraal* (Chicago, June 30, 1903; rev. 1934); *The Octoroon* (1904); *Valdo* (Cleveland, May 1906); *The Tryst* (N.Y., May 1911); *The Prophecy* (N.Y., 1912); *The Plantation* (1914); *Athalia* (1916); *Vendetta* (N.Y., Nov. 12, 1923); *American Romance*, jazz opera (1927); *Voodoo* (N.Y., Sept. 10, 1928); *Leah Kleschna* (1930); *Uzziah* (1931); *Zululand*, tetralogy of music dramas: *Nada, The Lily* (1941–44), *Allah* (1947), and *The Zulu King* (1934). **BALLET:** *The Slave* for Choral Ensemble and Orch. (N.Y., Sept. 22, 1932). **OTHER:** Songs.

Freeman, Paul (Douglas), black American conductor; b. Richmond, Va., Jan. 2, 1936. He studied piano, clarinet, and cello in his youth; continued his musical training at the Eastman School of Music in Rochester, N.Y. (B.Mus., 1956; M.Mus., 1957; Ph.D., 1963); also took courses at the Berlin Hochschule für Musik (1957–59). Returning to the U.S., he took conducting lessons with Richard Lert and Pierre Monteux. He subsequently held the post of conductor with the Opera Theater of Rochester (1961–66), the San Francisco Cons. Orch. (1966–67), and the San Francisco Little Sym. Orch. (1967–68); then was assoc. conductor of the Dallas Sym. Orch. (1968–70) and resident conductor of the Detroit Sym. Orch. (1970–79); also served as principal guest conductor of the Helsinki Phil. (1974–76). From 1979 to 1988 he was music director of the Victoria (B.C.) Sym. Orch. In 1987 he became music director of the Chicago Sinfonietta.

Freeman, Robert (Schofield), American musicologist, pianist, and educator; b. Rochester, N.Y., Aug. 26, 1935. He received training in piano from Gregory Tucker, Artur Balsam, and Rudolf Serkin, and pursued his academic studies at Harvard College (A.B., *summa cum laude*, 1957) and at Princeton Univ. (M.F.A., 1960; Ph.D., 1967, with the diss. *Opera without Drama: Currents of Change in Italian Opera, 1675–1725*; publ. in Ann Arbor, 1981); he also studied at the Univ. of Vienna on a Fulbright fellowship (1960–62). He taught at Princeton Univ. (1963–68) and at the Mass. Inst. of Technology (1968–73), and also was a visiting assoc. prof. at Harvard Univ. (1972). In 1972 he became director and prof. of musicology at the Eastman School of Music in Rochester, N.Y., where he revitalized its administration and oversaw an extensive renovation of its facilities. As a musicologist and educator, he has contributed many articles to journals, as well as to *The New Grove Dictionary of Music and Musicians* (1980).

Freer, Eleanor (née **Everest**), American composer; b. Philadelphia, May 14, 1864; d. Chicago, Dec. 13, 1942. She studied singing in Paris (1883–86) with Mathilde Marchesi; then took a course in composition with Benjamin Godard. Upon her return to the U.S., she taught singing at the National Cons. of Music of America in N.Y. (1889–91); settled in Chicago, where she studied theory with Bernhard Ziehn (1902–07). She publ. some light pieces under the name Everest while still a young girl, but most of her larger works were written after 1919. She also wrote an autobiography, *Recollections and Reflections of an American Composer* (Chicago, 1929). Among her works were 9 operas, of which the following were performed: *The Legend of the Piper* (South Bend, Ind., Feb. 28, 1924); *The Court Jester* (Lincoln, Nebr., 1926); *A Christmas Tale* (Houston, Dec. 27, 1929); *Frithiof* (concert perf., Chicago, Feb. 1, 1931); *A Legend of Spain* (concert perf., Milwaukee, June 19, 1931). She also composed *Sonnets from the Portuguese*, song cycle; about 150 songs; piano pieces.

BIBL.: A. Foster, *E. F. and Her Colleagues* (Chicago, 1927).

Freire (actually, **Pinto Freire**), **Nelson (José),** Brazilian pianist; b. Boa Esperanza, Oct. 18, 1944. He began to play the piano at a very early age and made his public debut when he was only 5. After winning the Rio de Janeiro competition at 13, he went to Vienna to study with Bruno Seidlhofer; in 1964 he won the Vianna da Motta Prize in Lisbon. After making a major tour of Europe in 1968, he made his U.S. debut in N.Y. in 1969. He subsequently appeared in all the major music centers, winning particular praise for his refulgent performances of the Romantic repertory.

Freitas (Branco), Frederico (Guedes) de, Portuguese conductor and composer; b. Lisbon, Nov. 15, 1902; d. there, Jan. 12, 1980. He studied piano with Aroldo Silva, composition with A.E. da Costa Ferreira, musicology with Luis de Freitas Branco, and violin at the National Cons. in Lisbon (1919–24); won the National Composition prize (1926). He conducted the Lisbon Emissora National Orch. (from 1934), the Lisbon Choral Soc. (1940–47), the Oporto Sym. Orch. (1949–53), and the Orquesta de Concierto (from 1955). In his Violin Sonata (1923) he made the first known use of linear polyphony by a Portuguese composer.

WORKS: DRAMATIC: OPERAS: *O eremita* (1952); *A igreja do mar*, radio opera (1957; Lisbon, Feb. 5, 1960); *Don João e a máscara*, radio opera (1960). **BALLETS:** *Muro do derrete* (1940); *A dança da Menina Tonta* (1941); *Imagens da terra e do mar* (1943); *Nazaré* (1948). **ORCH.:** *A lenda dos bailarins*, symphonic poem (1926); *Quarteto concertante* for 2 Violins, 2 Cellos, and String Orch. (1945); Flute Concerto (1954); *Suite Medieval* (1958); *Os Jerónimos*, sym. (1962). **CHAMBER:** *Nocturno* for Cello and Piano (1926); Violin Sonata (1946); String Quartet (1946); Wind Quintet (1950); *3 Peças sem importância* for Violin and Piano (1959). **KEYBOARD: PIANO:** *Dança* (1923); *Ingenuidades* (1924); Sonata (1944); *Ciranda* (1944); *6 Pieces* (1946); *Bagatelles* (1953); *Variations* (1954). **ORGAN:**

Sonata (1963). **VOCAL:** *Missa solene* for 4 Soloists, Chorus, and Orch. (1940); *As sete palavras de Nossa Senhora*, cantata (1946); songs.

Freitas Branco, Luís de, eminent Portuguese composer, pedagogue, musicologist, and music critic; b. Lisbon, Oct. 12, 1890; d. there, Nov. 27, 1955. He was a student of Tomás Borba, Désiré Pâque, Augusto Machado, and Luigi Mancinelli in Lisbon, of Humperdinck in Berlin, and of Grovlez in Paris. He taught at the National Cons. in Lisbon from 1916, and also was active as a musicologist and music critic. He also held government positions, but lost these in 1939 for his outspoken criticism of the treatment of musicians in Germany and Italy; it was not until 1947 that these positions again became available to him. Freitas Branco was one of the most significant figures in Portuguese musical life. As a composer, he introduced impressionism and expressionism to Portugal.

WORKS: ORCH.: *Manfredo*, dramatic sym. for Soli, Chorus, and Orch. (1905); 5 symphonic poems: *Antero do Quental* (1908); *Os paraisos artificias* (1910); *Vathek* (1913); *Viriato* (1916); *Solemnia verba* (1952); Violin Concerto (1916); *Balada* for Piano and Orch. (1917); *Cena lirica* for Cello and Orch. (1917); *Suite alentejana* No. 1 (1919) and No. 2 (1927); 4 syms. (1924, 1926, 1943, 1952); *Variaçoes e fuga tríplice sobre um tema original* for Organ and Strings (1947); *Homenagem a Chopin: Polaca sobre um tema de Chopin* (1949). **CHAMBER:** 2 violin sonatas (1907, 1928); String Quartet (1911); Cello Sonata (1913); piano pieces; organ music. **VOCAL:** Sacred choral works; songs.

Frémaux, Louis, French conductor; b. Aire-sur-la-Lys, Aug. 13, 1921. He attended the Valenciennes Cons., but his education was interrupted by World War II. He served in the Résistance during the Nazi occupation. After the war, he studied conducting at the Paris Cons. with Fourestier, graduating in 1952 with the premier prix. From 1956 to 1965 he was chief conductor of the Orchestre National de Monte Carlo, and then music director of the Orchestre Philharmonique Rhône-Alpes in Lyons (1968–71). From 1969 to 1978 he was music director of the City of Birmingham Sym. Orch. From 1979 to 1982 he was chief conductor of the Sydney (Australia) Sym. Orch.

Fremstad, Olive, famous Swedish-born American soprano; b. Stockholm, March 14, 1871 (entered into the parish register as the daughter of an unmarried woman, Anna Peterson); d. Irvington-on-Hudson, N.Y., April 21, 1951. She was adopted by an American couple of Scandinavian origin, who took her to Minnesota; she studied piano in Minneapolis; went to N.Y. in 1890 and took singing lessons with E.F. Bristol. She then held several church positions; in 1892 she sang for the first time with an orch. (under C. Zerrahn) in Boston. In 1893 she went to Berlin to study with Lilli Lehmann; made her operatic debut in Cologne as Azucena (1895); sang contralto parts at the Bayreuth Festival in 1896; in 1897 she made her London debut; also sang in Cologne, Vienna, Amsterdam, and Antwerp. From 1900 to 1903 she was at the Munich Court Opera. She made her American debut as Sieglinde at the Metropolitan Opera in N.Y. on Nov. 25, 1903. Subsequently she sang soprano parts in Wagnerian operas; at first she was criticized in the press for her lack of true soprano tones; however, she soon triumphed over these difficulties, and became known as a soprano singer to the exclusion of contralto parts. She sang Carmen with great success at the Metropolitan (March 5, 1906) with Caruso; her performance of Isolde under Mahler (Jan. 1, 1908) produced a deep impression; until 1915 she was one of the brightest stars of the Metropolitan, specializing in Wagnerian roles, but she was also successful in *Tosca* and other Italian operas. She sang Salome at the first American performance of the Strauss opera (N.Y., Jan. 22, 1907) and in Paris (May 8, 1907). After her retirement from the Metropolitan, she appeared with the Manhattan Opera, the Boston Opera, and the Chicago Opera, and in concerts; presented her last song recital in N.Y. on Jan. 19, 1920. In 1906 she married Edson Sutphen of N.Y. (divorced in 1911); in 1916 she married her accompanist, Harry Lewis Brainard (divorced in 1925). In Willa Cather's novel *The Song of the Lark*, the principal character was modeled after Fremstad.

Freni (real name, **Fregni**), **Mirella,** noted Italian soprano; b. Modena, Feb. 27, 1935. Curiously enough, her mother and the mother of the future celebrated tenor Luciano Pavarotti worked for a living in the same cigarette factory; curiouser still, the future opera stars shared the same wet nurse. Freni studied voice with her uncle, Dante Arcelli; made her first public appearance at the age of 11; her accompanist was a child pianist named Leone Magiera, whom she married in 1955. She later studied voice with Ettore Campogalliani. Freni made her operatic debut in Modena on Feb. 3, 1955, as Micaëla; then sang in provincial Italian opera houses. In 1957 she took 1st prize in the Viotti Competition in Vercelli. In 1959 she sang with the Amsterdam Opera at the Holland Festival; then at the Glyndebourne Festival (1960), Covent Garden in London (1961), and La Scala in Milan (1962). She gained acclaim as Mimi in the film version of *La Bohème*, produced at La Scala in 1963 under Karajan's direction. When La Scala toured Russia in 1964, Freni joined the company and sang Mimi at the Bolshoi Theater in Moscow. She also chose the role of Mimi for her American debut with the Metropolitan Opera in N.Y. on Sept. 29, 1965. She subsequently sang with the Vienna State Opera, the Bavarian State Opera in Munich, the Teatro San Carlo in Naples, and the Rome Opera. In 1976 she traveled with the Paris Opéra during its first American tour. In addition to Mimi, she sang the roles of Susanna, Zerlina, Violetta, Amelia in *Simon Boccanegra*, and Manon. She won acclaim for her vivid portrayal of Tatiana, which she sang with many major opera companies, including the Metropolitan Opera in 1989. In 1990 she celebrated the 35th anniversary of her debut in Modena by returning there as Manon Lescaut.

Frešo, Tibor, Slovak conductor and composer; b. Spišský, Nov. 20, 1918; d. Bratislava, July 7, 1987. He studied composition with A. Moyzes and conducting with J. Vincourek at the Bratislava Cons., graduating in 1938; then studied with Pizzetti at the Accademia di Santa Cecilia in Rome (1939–42). Returning to Czechoslovakia, he served as conductor of the Slovak National Theater in Bratislava (1942–49) and the Košice Opera (1949–52); in 1953 he was appointed chief opera conductor of the Slovak National Opera.

WORKS: OPERAS: *Martin and the Sun*, children's opera (Bratislava, Jan. 25, 1975); *Poor François* (1982–84). **ORCH.:** *Little Suite* (1938); *Concert Overture* (1940); *Symphonic Prolog* (1943); symphonic poems: *A New Morning* (1950) and *Liberation* (1955); *Little Concerto* for Piano and Orch. (1976). **CHAMBER:** Wind Quintet (1983). **VOCAL:** 3 cantatas: *Stabat Mater* (1940), *Mother* (1959), and *Hymn to the Fatherland* (1961); *Meditation* for Soprano and Orch. (1942); *Song about Woman* for Alto, Narrator, Children's and Mixed Choruses, and Orch. (1975).

Freund, Marya, German soprano; b. Breslau, Dec. 12, 1876; d. Paris, May 21, 1966. She was a student of Sarasate (violin) and Stockhausen (voice). After making her debut in 1909, she appeared as a soloist with orchs. and as a recitalist in Europe and the U.S., gaining distinction as a champion of contemporary music. She settled in Paris and taught voice during the last 30 years of her life.

Frey, Emil, eminent Swiss pianist, teacher, and composer, brother of **Walter Frey**; b. Baden, April 8, 1889; d. Zürich, May 20, 1946. He studied with Otto Barblan at the Geneva Cons.; at the age of 15, he was accepted as a student of Diemer in piano and Widor in composition; in 1907 he went to Berlin, and later to Bucharest, where he became a court pianist. In 1910 he won the Anton Rubinstein prize for his Piano Trio in St. Petersburg; on the strength of this success, he was engaged to teach at the Moscow Cons. (1912–17). Returning to Switzerland after the Russian Revolution, he joined the faculty of the Zürich Cons.; he continued his concert career throughout Europe and also in South America. He wrote 2 syms. (the 1st with a choral finale),

Piano Concerto, Violin Concerto, Cello Concerto, *Swiss Festival Overture*, Piano Quintet, String Quartet, Piano Trio, Violin Sonata, Cello Sonata, several piano sonatas, piano suites, and sets of piano variations. He publ. a piano instruction manual, *Bewusst gewordenes Klavierspiel und seine technischen Grundlagen* (Zürich, 1933).

Frey, Walter, Swiss pianist and teacher, brother of **Emil Frey**; b. Basel, Jan. 26, 1898; d. Zürich, May 28, 1985. He studied piano with F. Niggli and theory with Andreae. From 1925 to 1958 he was an instructor in piano at the Zürich Cons.; concurrently evolved an active concert career in Germany and Scandinavia; specialized in modern piano music and gave first performances of several piano concertos by contemporary composers; later he became well known for his championship of the keyboard works of Bach. He publ. (with W. Schuh) a collection, *Schweizerische Klaviermusik aus der Zeit der Klassik und Romantik* (Zürich, 1937).

Fribec, Krešimir, Croatian composer; b. Daruvar, May 24, 1908. He studied with Zlatko Grgošević in Zagreb; later was active as music ed. of the Zagreb Radio (1943–64); also served as director of the Croatian Music Soc. Most of his large output was composed in an accessible style.

WORKS: DRAMATIC: OPERAS: *Sluga Jernej* (1951); *Krvava svadba* (Blood Wedding; 1958); *Prometej* (1960); *Jerma* (1960); *Maljiva* (1962); *Čehovljev humoristicon* (1962); *Nova Eva* (1963); *Juduška Golovljiev* (1964); *Adagio melancolico* (1965); *Dolazi revisor* (The Government Inspector; 1965); *Dunja u kovčegu* (1966); *Veliki val* (The Large Wave; 1966); *Heretik* (1971); *Ujak Vanja* (Uncle Vanya; 1972). Also many ballets. **ORCH.:** *Ritmi drammatici* for Chamber Orch. (1960); *Accenti tragici* (1961); *Kosmička kretanja* (Cosmic Movements; 1961); Piano Concerto (1964); *Canto* for Strings (1965); *Ekstaza*, symphonic suite (1965); *Simfonija* (1965); *Lamento* for Strings (1967); *Koncertantna muzika* for Violin and Orch. (1970); Cello Concerto (1971); *Covjek*, sym. (1972). **CHAMBER:** 7 string quartets (1962–72); *Musica aleatorica* for Flute, Cello, Vibraphone, and Piano (1961); Sonata for Cello (1966); Violin Sonata (1967); *Divertimento* for Viola and Percussion (1970); *Alterations*, piano trio (1971).

Frick, Gottlob, German bass; b. Olbronn, Württemberg, July 28, 1906; d. Mühlacker, near Pforzheim, Aug. 18, 1994. He studied at the Stuttgart Cons. and also took vocal lessons with Neudörfer-Opitz. After singing in the Stuttgart Opera chorus, he made his operatic debut as Daland in *Der fliegende Holländer* in Coburg (1934); then sang in Freiburg im Breisgau and Königsberg, and subsequently was a leading member of the Dresden State Opera (1941–52). He appeared at the Städtische Oper in West Berlin (from 1950), the Bavarian State Opera in Munich (from 1953), and the Vienna State Opera (from 1953); made his debut at London's Covent Garden (1951), and later sang there regularly (1957–67). On Dec. 27, 1961, he made his Metropolitan Opera debut in N.Y. as Fafner in *Das Rheingold*; also sang at Bayreuth, Milan's La Scala, and Salzburg. He gave his farewell performance in 1970, but continued to make a few stage appearances in later years. A fine Wagnerian, he excelled as Gurnemanz and Hagen; was also admired for his portrayal of Rocco in *Fidelio*.

Fricke, Heinz, German conductor; b. Halberstadt, Feb. 11, 1927. He studied in Halberstadt and with Abendroth in Weimar (1948–50). From 1950 to 1960 he was conductor at the Leipzig City Theater. In 1960–61 he was Generalmusikdirektor in Schwerin, and then held that title with the Berlin State Opera from 1961 to 1992. He also appeared as a guest conductor with many opera houses in Europe and South America. In 1992 he conducted *Parsifal* at the reopening of the Chemnitz Opera House. In 1993 he became music director of the Washington (D.C.) Opera.

Fricker, Herbert A(ustin), English-Canadian organist, conductor, teacher, and composer; b. Canterbury, Feb. 12, 1868; d. Toronto, Nov. 11, 1943. He was a pupil of William H. Longhurst, the Canterbury Cathedral organist, where he was a chorister (1877–83) and assistant organist (1884–90); he also studied with Bridge and Lemare in London, becoming a fellow of the Royal College of Organists (1888) and receiving his B.Mus. from the Univ. of Durham (1893). He was active at Trinity Church, Folkstone (1891–98) before going to Leeds as city organist; he also was founder-conductor of the Leeds Phil. (1900–1917) and the Leeds Sym. Orch. (1902–17), and served as chorusmaster of the Leeds Festivals (1904–13). In 1917 he was called to Toronto as conductor of the Mendelssohn Choir, a post he retained with distinction until 1942; he also was organist-choirmaster at Metropolitan United Church (1917–43), a teacher of organ at the Toronto Cons. of Music (1918–32), and an active recitalist. In addition to composing sacred and secular choral music and organ pieces, Fricker made numerous arrangements for organ.

Fricker, Peter Racine, distinguished English composer and pedagogue; b. London, Sept. 5, 1920; d. Santa Barbara, Calif., Feb. 1, 1990. He studied theory and composition with R.O. Morris at the Royal College of Music in London; following service in the Royal Air Force (1941–46), he completed his training with Mátyás Seiber (1946–48). He was director of music at Morley College in London (from 1952) and a prof. of composition at the Royal College of Music (from 1955). In 1964 he was a visiting prof. at the Univ. of Calif. at Santa Barbara, where he then was a full prof. (from 1965); he also was chairman of its music dept. (1970–74). In his works, Fricker utilized various techniques. His output revealed a fascination for the development of small cells, either melodically, harmonically, or rhythmically.

WORKS: DRAMATIC: RADIO OPERA: *The Death of Vivien* (1956). **BALLET:** *Canterbury Prologue* (1951). **ORCH.:** *Rondo scherzoso* (1948); 5 syms.: No. 1 (1949; Cheltenham, July 5, 1950), No. 2 (1950–51; Liverpool, July 26, 1951), No. 3 (London, Nov. 8, 1960), No. 4, "in memoriam Mátyás Seiber" (1966; Cheltenham, Feb. 14, 1967), and No. 5 (1975–76); *Prelude, Elegy, and Finale* for Strings (1949); 2 violin concertos: No. 1 (1949–50) and No. 2, *Rapsodia Concertante* (1952–54; Cheltenham, July 15, 1954); Concerto for English Horn and Strings (1950); *Concertante* for 3 Pianos, Strings, and Timpani (1951; London, Aug. 10, 1956); Viola Concerto (1952; Edinburgh, Sept. 3, 1953); Piano Concerto (1952–54; London, March 21, 1954); *Litany* for Double String Orch. (1955); *Comedy Overture* (1958); *Toccata* for Piano and Orch. (1959); *3 Scenes* (1966; Santa Barbara, Calif., Feb. 26, 1967); *7 Counterpoints* (Pasadena, Calif., Oct. 21, 1967); *Nocturne* for Chamber Orch. (1971); *Introitus* (Canterbury, June 24, 1972); *Sinfonia in memoriam Benjamin Britten* for 17 Wind Instruments (1976–77); *Laudi Concertati* for Organ and Orch. (1979); *Rondeaux* for Horn and Orch. (1982); *Concerto for Orchestra* (1986); *Walk by Quiet Waters* (1989). **CHAMBER:** Wind Quintet (1947); 3 string quartets (1947; 1952–53; 1975); 2 violin sonatas (1950, 1988); Horn Sonata (1955); Cello Sonata (1956); Octet for Wind and String Instruments (1957–58); *Serenade* No. 1 for 6 Instruments (1959), No. 2 for Flute, Oboe, and Piano (1959), and No. 3 for Saxophone Quartet (1969); *4 Dialogues* for Oboe and Piano (1965); *Fantasy* for Viola and Piano (1966); *Concertante* No. 5 for Piano and String Quartet (1971); *Spirit Puck* for Clarinet and Percussion (1974); *Aspects of Evening* for Cello and Piano (1985). **KEYBOARD: PIANO:** *Variations* (1957–58); *12 Studies* (1961); *Episodes I* (1967–68) and *II* (1969); *Anniversary* (1978); Sonata for 2 Pianos (1978). **ORGAN:** Sonata (1947); *Choral* (1956); *Ricercare* (1965); *6 Pieces* (1968); *Toccata* (1968); *Praeludium* (1970); Trio-Sonata (1974). **VOCAL:** *Madrigals* for Chorus (1947); *Night Landscape* for Soprano and String Trio (1947); *3 Sonnets by Cecco Angiolieri* for Tenor, Wind Quintet, Cello, and Double Bass (1947); *Musick's Empire* for Chorus and Small Orch. (1955); *Tomb of St. Eulalia* for Countertenor, Viola da Gamba, and Harpsichord (1955); *The Vision of Judgement*, oratorio for Soprano, Tenor, Chorus, and Orch. (1957–58; Leeds, Oct. 13, 1958); Cantata for Tenor and Chamber Orch. (1962); *O*

Longs désirs, 5 songs for Soprano and Orch. (1963); *The Day and the Spirits* for Soprano and Harp (1966–67); *Ave Maris Stella* for Chorus (1967); *Magnificat* for Soloists, Chorus, and Orch. (Santa Barbara, May 27, 1968); *Some Superior Nonsense* for Tenor, Flute, Oboe, and Harpsichord (1968); *The Roofs* for Coloratura Soprano and Percussion (1970); *Come, sleep* for Contralto, Alto Flute, and Bass Clarinet (1972); *6 Melodies de Francis Jammes* for Tenor and Piano Trio (1980); *Whispers at These Curtains*, oratorio for Baritone, Chorus, Boys' Chorus, and Orch. (1984).

Fricsay, Ferenc, distinguished Hungarian-born Austrian conductor; b. Budapest, Aug. 9, 1914; d. Basel, Feb. 20, 1963. He received his initial musical training from his father, a military bandmaster, and then was a pupil of Bartók (piano) and Kodály (composition) at the Budapest Academy of Music; he learned to play almost every orchestral instrument. He was conductor in Szeged (1933–44), and also held the post of 1st conductor at the Budapest Opera (1939–45). In 1945 he became music director of the Hungarian State Opera in Budapest. On Aug. 6, 1947, he made an impressive debut at the Salzburg Festival conducting the premiere of Gottfried von Einem's opera *Dantons Tod*, which led to engagements in Europe and South America. In 1948 he became a conductor at the Städtische Oper in West Berlin; in 1951–52 he was its artistic director but resigned after a conflict over artistic policies. In 1949 he became chief conductor of the RIAS (Radio in the American Sector) Sym. Orch. in Berlin, an esteemed position he retained until 1954. After it became the Radio Sym. Orch. of Berlin in 1955, he appeared with it regularly until 1961. On Nov. 13, 1953, he made his U.S. debut as a guest conductor of the Boston Sym. Orch. In 1954 he was engaged as conductor of the Houston Sym. Orch., but he resigned his position soon afterward following a disagreement with its management over musical policies. From 1956 to 1958 he was Generalmusikdirektor of the Bavarian State Opera in Munich. In 1959 he became a naturalized Austrian citizen. In 1961 he was invited to conduct *Don Giovanni* at the opening of the Deutsche Oper in West Berlin. Soon thereafter leukemia compelled him to abandon his career. Fricsay excelled as an interpreter of the Romantic repertory but he also displayed a special affinity for the masterworks of the 20th century. He was the author of the book *Über Mozart und Bartók* (Frankfurt am Main, 1962).

BIBL.: F. Herzfeld, *F.F.: Ein Gedenkbuch* (Berlin, 1964).

Frid, Géza, Hungarian-born Dutch composer; b. Máramarossziget, Jan. 25, 1904; d. Beverwijk, Sept. 13, 1989. He studied composition with Kodály and piano with Bartók at the Budapest Academy of Music (1912–24). He settled in Amsterdam in 1929, becoming a naturalized Dutch citizen in 1948; later taught at the Utrecht Cons. (1964–69).

WORKS: DRAMATIC: OPERA: *De zwarte bruid* (1959). **BALLETS:** *Luctor et Emergo* (1953); *Euridice* (1961). **ORCH.:** *Podium-Suite* for Violin and Orch. (1928); Violin Concerto (1930); *Tempesta d'orchestra* (1931); *Divertimento* for String Orch. or String Quintet (1932); Sym. (1933); *Romance and Allegro* for Cello and Orch. (1935); *Abel et Cain*, symphonic tableau for Low Voice and Orch. (1938); *Nocturnes* for Flute, Harp, and String Orch. or String Quintet (1946); *Paradou*, symphonic fantasy (1948); *Fête champêtre*, suite of dances for Strings and Percussion (1951); Concerto for 2 Violins and Orch. (1952); *Caecilia Ouverture* (1953); *Études symphoniques* (1954); *South African Rhapsody* for Orch. or Wind Orch. (1954); Serenade for Chamber Orch. (1956); Concerto for 2 Pianos and Orch. (1957); Concertino for Violin, Cello, Piano, and Orch. (1961); *Sinfonietta* for Strings (1963); *7 pauken en een koperorkest*, concerto for 7 Percussionists and Brass Orch. (1964); Concerto for 3 Violins and Orch. (The Hague, July 4, 1970); Concerto for 4 different Clarinets (1 Soloist) and Strings (1972); *Olifant-variaties*, double bass concerto (1977). **CHAMBER:** 5 string quartets (1926, 1939, 1949, 1956, 1984); String Trio (1926); *Serenade* for Wind Instruments (1928); Cello Sonata (1931); Sonata for Solo Violin (1936); Piano Trio (1947); Violin Sonata (1955); *12 Metamorphoses* for 2 Flutes and Percussion (1957); *Fuga* for 3 Harps (1961); Sextet for Wind Quintet and Piano (1965); *Dubbeltrio* for Wind Instruments (1967); *Chemins divers* for Flute, Bassoon, and Piano (1968; also for 2 Violins and Piano); *Paganini Variations* for 2 Violins (1969); *Caprices roumains* for Oboe and Piano (1975); *Sons roumains* for Flute, Viola, Harp, and Percussion (1975); *Music* for 2 Violins and Viola (1977); *Vice Versa* for Alto Saxophone and Marimba (1982); piano pieces. **OTHER:** Vocal works.

Fried, Alexej, Czech composer; b. Brno, Oct. 13, 1922. He studied piano and composition at the Brno Cons., and then composition with Hlobil and Bořkovec at the Prague Academy of Music (graduated, 1953). He first gained notice as an arranger for various Czech jazz groups in 1947; also led his own orchs., lectured, and composed. Many of his works are in the "3rd-stream" manner, fusing jazz with Classical styles.

WORKS: ORCH.: Triple Concerto for Flute, Clarinet, Horn, and Orch. (1971); Concerto (1974); Concerto No. 2 for Clarinet and Orch. (1976); Concerto for Horn and Chamber Orch. (1977); *Concerto di Freiberg* for Chamber Orch. (1977; rewritten 1982 as *Gothic Concerto*); Triple Concertino for Oboe, Clarinet, Bassoon, 2 Percussion, and Strings (1981); *Bread and Games*, musical picture for Flute, Soprano Saxophone, Horn, and Orch. (1982); *Cassation* for Chamber Orch. (1985). **CHAMBER:** *Sonatina drammatica* for Violin and Piano (1975); *Moravian Trio* for Flute, Marimba, and Harp (1978); *Guernica*, quintet for Soprano Saxophone and String Quartet (1978); Quintet for Flute, Violin, Viola, Cello, and Piano (1979); *Tympanum*, trio for Violin, Soprano Saxophone, and Piano (1982); Sextet for Flute, Clarinet, Bass Clarinet, Piano, Double Bass, and Percussion (1984); Sonata for Saxophone Quartet (1987); *3 Characteristic Études* for Horn (1990); Concertino for Flute, Guitar, String Quartet, and 2 Percussion (1992). **JAZZ WORKS FOR BIG BAND:** *The Act* for Trumpet, Flute, and Big Band (1968); Jazz Concerto for Clarinet and Big Band (1970); *Souvenir* (1970); *Jazz Ballet Études* for Clarinet and Big Band (1970); *Sidonia* for Trumpet and Big Band (1971); *Moravian Wedding*, sinfonietta (1972); *The Solstice*, concerto for 2 Big Bands (1973); Concertino for Clarinet and Big Band (1974); *Dialogue* for 2 Alto Saxophones and Big Band (1974); *Paraphrases to Motives of Blue Skies* for Soprano Saxophone and Big Band (1975); Concerto (1976); *Jazz Composition* for Trombone and Big Band (1977); *Polyphone* (1978); *Song* for Trumpet and Big Band (1979); *Plays* for Percussion, Tenor Saxophone, and Big Band (1980); *Silhouettes* for Baritone Saxophone and Big Band (1983); *A Picture Postcard from Moravia* for Baritone Saxophone and Big Band (1985); *The Nude* for Trumpet, Flute, and Big Band (1986); *Salute* for Soprano Saxophone, Flute, and Big Band (1987).

Fried, Miriam, Romanian-born Israeli violinist and teacher; b. Satu Mare, Sept. 9, 1946. She was taken to Israel at age 2. After studies at the Rubin Academy of Music in Tel Aviv, she pursued her training with Gingold at the Indiana Univ. School of Music in Bloomington (1966–67) and Galamian at the Juilliard School of Music in N.Y. (1967–69). In 1968 she won 1st prize in the Paganini Competition in Genoa, and in 1971 won 1st prize in the Queen Elisabeth of Belgium Competition in Brussels. Following her N.Y. debut in 1969 and her British debut at Windsor Castle in 1971, she appeared as a soloist with many of the principal world orchs., as a recitalist, and as a chamber music artist. She also was a prof. at the Indiana Univ. School of Music from 1986.

Fried, Oskar, German-born Russian conductor and composer; b. Berlin, Aug. 10, 1871; d. Moscow, July 5, 1941. He studied with Humperdinck in Frankfurt am Main and P. Scharwenka in Berlin. He played the horn in various orchs. until the performance of his choral work with orch. *Das trunkene Lied*, given by Muck in Berlin (April 15, 1904), attracted much favorable attention; he continued to compose prolifically. At the same time, he began his career as a conductor, achieving considerable renown in Europe; he was conductor of the Stern Choral

Soc. in Berlin (from 1904), of the Gesellschaft der Musikfreunde in Berlin (1907–10), and of the Berlin Sym. Orch. (1925–26). He left Berlin in 1934 and went to Russia; became a naturalized Russian citizen in 1940. For several years he was conductor of the Tbilisi Opera; later was chief conductor of the All-Union Radio Orch. in Moscow.

BIBL.: P. Bekker, *O. F.* (Berlin, 1907); P. Stefan, *O. F.* (Berlin, 1911); D. Rabinovitz, *O. F.* (Moscow, 1971).

Friedberg, Carl, noted German pianist and teacher; b. Bingen, Sept. 18, 1872; d. Merano, Italy, Sept. 8, 1955. He studied piano at the Frankfurt am Main Cons. with Kwast, Knorr, and Clara Schumann; also took a course in composition with Humperdinck. He subsequently taught piano at the Frankfurt am Main Cons. (1893–1904) and at the Cologne Cons. (1904–14). In 1914 he made his first American tour, with excellent success. He taught piano at the Inst. of Musical Art in N.Y.; was a member of the faculty of the Juilliard School of Music in N.Y. Among his pupils were Percy Grainger, Ethel Leginska, Elly Ney, and other celebrated pianists.

BIBL.: J. Smith, *Master Pianist: The Career and Teaching of C. F.* (N.Y., 1963).

Friedhofer, Hugo (William), American composer of film music; b. San Francisco, May 3, 1901; d. Los Angeles, May 17, 1981. He studied composition with Domenico Brescia. In 1929 he went to Hollywood, where he worked as an arranger and composer for early sound films. In 1935 he was engaged as an orchestrator for Warner Brothers, and received valuable instruction from Korngold and Steiner. In Los Angeles he attended Schoenberg's seminars and took additional lessons in composition with Toch and Kanitz; he also had some instruction with Boulanger during her sojourn in California. He wrote his first complete film score for *The Adventures of Marco Polo* in 1938, and in the following years composed music for about 70 films. His film music for *The Best Years of Our Lives* won the Academy Award in 1946. His other distinguished film scores included *Broken Arrow* (1950), *Vera Cruz* (1954), *The Rains of Ranchipur* (1955), *The Sun Also Rises* (1957), and *The Young Lions* (1958). Friedhofer was highly esteemed for his ability to create a congenial musical background, alternatively lyrical and dramatic, for the action on the screen, never sacrificing the purely musical quality for the sake of external effect.

BIBL.: L. Morton, "Film Music Profile: H. F.," *Film Music Notes* (1950); I. Atkins, *H. F.* (Los Angeles, 1974).

Friedlaender, Max, German music scholar; b. Brieg, Silesia, Oct. 12, 1852; d. Berlin, May 2, 1934. He studied voice with Manuel García in London and Julius Stockhausen in Frankfurt am Main, and then pursued his academic training with P. Spitta at the Univ. of Berlin before completing his studies at the Univ. of Rostock (Ph.D., 1887, with the diss. *Beiträge zur Biographie Franz Schuberts*; publ. in Berlin, 1887). In 1894 he became Privatdozent at the Univ. of Berlin, where he later was a prof. and director of music (1903–32). He discovered the MSS of over 100 lost songs by Schubert and pursued folk song research. His major work was *Das Deutsche Lied im 18. Jahrhundert* (2 vols., Stuttgart and Berlin, 1902). He also publ. *Chorschule nach Stockhausens Methode* (Leipzig, 1891), *Brahms Lieder* (Berlin, 1922; Eng. tr., 1928), and *Franz Schubert, Skizze seines Lebens und Wirkens* (Leipzig, 1928).

Friedman, Erick, American violinist and teacher; b. Newark, N.J., Aug. 16, 1939. He began his studies with his father; after lessons from Samuel Applebaum, he enrolled at age 10 as a pupil of Galamian at the Juilliard School of Music in N.Y.; he also received lessons from Milstein and later from Heifetz (1956–58). In 1953 he won the Music Education League Competition and made his formal debut as soloist with the Little Orch. Soc. of N.Y. His recital debut followed at N.Y.'s Carnegie Hall in 1956. He made tours of North and South America, Europe, and the Far East. In 1975 he became the Mischa Elman Prof. at the Manhattan School of Music in N.Y.

Friedman, Ignaz, famous Polish pianist and composer; b. Podgorze, near Kraków, Feb. 14, 1882; d. Sydney, Australia, Jan. 26, 1948. He studied theory with Riemann in Leipzig and piano with Leschetizky in Vienna. In 1904 he launched an extensive career as a concert pianist; gave about 2,800 concerts in Europe, America, Australia, Japan, China, and South Africa. In 1941 he settled in Sydney. He was renowned as an interpreter of Chopin; prepared an annotated ed. of Chopin's works in 12 vols.; also edited piano compositions of Schumann and Liszt. Among his compositions were a hundred or so pieces for piano in an effective salon manner, among them a group of *Fantasiestücke.*

Friedman, Ken, American composer; b. New London, Conn., Sept. 19, 1939. He became associated with Richard Maxfield, who initiated him into the arcana of modern music. Friedman developed feverish activities in avant-garde intellectual and musical fields. Most of his works are verbal exhortations to existentialist actions, e.g., *Scrub Piece* (scrubbing a statue in a public square), *Riverboat Brawl* (starting a brawl in a riverboat at Disneyland), *Goff Street* (a "theft event," transplanting a street sign), *Come Ze Revolution* (chanting pseudo-Greek songs), and *Watermelon* (splitting a watermelon with a karate blow). He also composed a *Quiet Sonata* (1969) for 75 Truncated Guitar Fingerboards with no strings attached and realized for Nam June Paik his alleged *Young Penis Symphony* for 10 ditto, and had it performed at a hidden retreat in San Francisco.

Friedman, Richard, American composer; b. N.Y., Jan. 6, 1944. He received training in electronics. After working with Morton Subotnick at the Intermedia Electronic Music Studio at N.Y. Univ. (1966–68), he joined the music dept. of KPFA radio in Berkeley. His output reflected his interest in avant-garde pursuits with a special emphasis on the application of electronics.

Friedrich, Götz, German opera producer and administrator; b. Naumburg, Aug. 4, 1930. He was educated in Weimar. In 1953 he was appointed an assistant to Walter Felsenstein at the East Berlin Komische Oper; became a producer there in 1959 and was chief producer from 1968 to 1972; was also active as a producer in West Germany. In 1976 he was named principal producer at Covent Garden, London. In 1981 he became Generalintendant of the Deutsche Oper in West Berlin. He also was director of the Theater des Westens there from 1984 to 1993. His productions reflected his adherence to Marxist doctrine. He publ. *Walter Felsenstein: Weg und Werk* (Berlin, 1967), *Musiktheater: Beiträge zur Methodik und zie Inszenierungs-Konzeptionen* (ed. by S. Stompor; Leipzig, 1970; 2nd ed., 1978); *Wagner-Regie* (ed. by S. Jaeger; Zürich, 1983), and *Musiktheater: Ansichten, Einsichten* (Frankfurt am Main, 1986). He was married to **Karan Armstrong**.

BIBL.: *Zeit für Oper: G. F.s Musiktheater, 1958–1990* (Frankfurt am Main, 1991).

Friedrich, Karl, Austrian tenor; b. Vienna, Jan. 15, 1905; d. there, March 8, 1981. He received his musical education at the Vienna Academy of Music. He sang operatic engagements in Düsseldorf and Hamburg; in 1938, joined the roster of the Vienna State Opera, retiring in 1969.

Friemann, Witold, Polish composer and teacher; b. Konin, Aug. 20, 1889; d. Laski, near Warsaw, March 22, 1977. He was a student of Noskowski (composition) and Michalowski (piano) at the Warsaw Cons. (graduated, 1910), and of Reger in Leipzig. After teaching at the Lwów Cons. (1921–29) and the Katowice Military School of Music (1929–33), he was head of the music division of the Polish Radio (1934–39); he later taught at a school for the blind in Laski.

WORKS: OPERAS: *Giewont* (1934); *Polski misterium narodowe* (1946); *Kain* (1952); *Bazyliszek* (1958). **ORCH.:** 3 syms.: No. 1, *Slavonic* (1948), No. 2, *Mazovian* (1950), and No. 3 (1953); also concertos: 5 for Piano (1911, 1951, 1952, 1956, 1960), 3 for Trombone (1969, 1969, 1970), 2 for Viola (1952, 1968), 2 for Clarinet (1954, 1964), and 1 for Cello (1950), Violin

(1953–54), 2 Pianos (1960), Oboe (1961), Flute (1963), Bassoon (1965–67), Horn (1966–68), Trumpet (1967), and 2 Bassoons (1968). **OTHER:** Much chamber music and vocal pieces.

Frijsh, Povla (real name, **Paula Frisch**), Danish-American soprano; b. Århus, Aug. 3, 1881; d. Blue Hill, Maine, July 10, 1960. She studied piano and theory in Copenhagen with O. Christensen, later voice in Paris with Jean Périer. She made her debut in Paris at the age of 19; appeared in concert and recital in Paris and briefly in opera in Copenhagen; made her American debut in 1915. She gave many first performances of modern vocal music and made a specialty of the modern international song literature.

Friml (actually, **Frimel**), **(Charles) Rudolf,** notable Bohemian-born American composer and pianist; b. Prague, Dec. 2, 1879; d. Los Angeles, Nov. 12, 1972. He was a student of Dvořák (composition) and Jiránek (piano) at the Prague Cons. He toured Europe as accompanist to Kubelik, with whom he visited the U.S. in 1900 and 1906, settling there in the latter year. In 1907 he appeared as soloist in his 1st Piano Concerto with Damrosch and the N.Y. Sym. Orch., and subsequently gave recitals throughout the U.S. While he continued to perform for most of his career, he also pursued his career as a composer of concert and lighter fare. His first great success in the latter came with his operetta *The Firefly* (N.Y., Dec. 2, 1912). With his musical farce *High Jinks* (N.Y., Dec. 10, 1913), he acquired global fame. His *Katinka* (N.Y., Dec. 23, 1915) proved another extraordinary success. Among a spate of succeeding N.Y. productions, the most successful were *You're in Love* (Feb. 6, 1917), *Sometime* (Oct. 4, 1918), *Glorianna* (Oct. 28, 1918), *The Little Whopper* (Oct. 13, 1919), and *The Blue Kitten* (Jan. 13, 1922). Then, in collaboration with Herbert Stothart, he brought out the enormously successful musical *Rose Marie*, which was first heard in N.Y. on Sept. 2, 1924. Its title song and the song *Indian Love Call* became celebrated. Among his subsequent scores, acclaim was accorded *The Vagabond King* (N.Y., Sept. 21, 1925) and *The 3 Musketeers* (N.Y., March 13, 1928). In 1925 Friml settled in Los Angeles. His final success as a composer came with his reworking of *Chansonette*, first heard in the *Ziegfeld Follies of 1923*, as *The Donkey Serenade* for the film version of *The Firefly* (1937). In a number of his works, Friml used the pseudonym of Roderick Freeman.

WORKS: MUSIC THEATER (all 1st perf. in N.Y. unless otherwise given): *The Firefly* (Dec. 2, 1912); *High Jinks* (Dec. 10, 1913); *The Ballet Girl* (Albany, N.Y., Nov. 12, 1914); *Katinka* (Dec. 23, 1915); *You're in Love* (Feb. 6, 1917); *Kitty Darlin'* (Nov. 7, 1917); *Sometime* (Oct. 4, 1918); *Glorianna* (Oct. 28, 1918); *Tumble In* (March 24, 1919); *The Little Whopper* (Oct. 13, 1919); *June Love* (April 25, 1921); *Ziegfeld Follies of 1921* (June 21, 1921; in collaboration with others); *The Blue Kitten* (Jan. 13, 1922); *Bibi of the Boulevards* (Providence, R.I., Feb. 12, 1922); *Cinders* (April 3, 1923); *Ziegfeld Follies of 1923* (Oct. 20, 1923; in collaboration with others); *Rose Marie* (Sept. 2, 1924; in collaboration with H. Stothart); *The Vagabond King* (Sept. 21, 1925); *No Foolin'* (June 24, 1926; in collaboration with J. Hanley); *The Wild Rose* (Oct. 20, 1926); *The White Eagle* (Dec. 26, 1927); *The 3 Musketeers* (March 13, 1928); *Luana* (Sept. 17, 1930); *Annina* or *Music Hath Charm* (Dec. 29, 1934). **FILM SCORES:** *The Lottery Bride* (1930); *Music for Madame* (1937); *Northwest Outpost* (1947). **ORCH.:** *Round the World*, sym.; 2 piano concertos; *Chinese Suite; Arabian Suite; A Day in May*, suite; *Rural Russian Scene; Escape to Hong Kong*. **OTHER:** Chamber music; many piano pieces; numerous songs.

Frischenschlager, Friedrich, Austrian composer and teacher; b. Gross Sankt Florian, Styria, Sept. 7, 1885; d. Salzburg, July 15, 1970. He studied music in Graz. In 1909 he went to Berlin, where he studied musicology with J. Wolf and Kretzschmar, and also attended Humperdinck's master classes in composition. In 1918 he was engaged as a music teacher at the Mozarteum in Salzburg, and remained there until 1945; also ed. its bulletin. An industrious composer, Fritschenschlager wrote the fairy tale operas *Der Schweinehirt*, after Hans Christian Andersen (Berlin, May 31, 1913), *Die Prinzessin und der Zwerg* (Salzburg, May 12, 1927), and *Der Kaiser und die Nachtigall*, after Andersen (Salzburg, March 27, 1937); *Symphonische Aphorismen* for Orch.; choral works; teaching materials for voice.

Friskin, James, Scottish-American pianist and composer; b. Glasgow, March 3, 1886; d. N.Y., March 16, 1967. He studied with E. Dannreuther (piano) and Stanford (composition) at the Royal College of Music in London; then taught at the Royal Normal College for the Blind (1909–14). In 1914 he went to the U.S. In 1934 he gave 2 recitals in N.Y. consisting of the complete *Wohltemperierte Clavier* of Bach. In 1944 he married **Rebecca Clarke**. Among his works were *Phantasie* for String Quartet; *Phantasie* for Piano Trio; *Phantasy* for Piano, 2 Violins, Viola, and Cello (1912); Quintet for Piano and Strings; Violin Sonata. He publ. *The Principles of Pianoforte Practice* (London, 1921; new ed., N.Y., 1937); also (with I. Freundlich) *Music for the Piano* (N.Y., 1954).

Froidebise, Pierre (Jean Marie), eminent Belgian composer, musicologist, and organist; b. Ohey, May 15, 1914; d. Liège, Oct. 28, 1962. Following training in harmony and organ with Camille Jacquemin (1932–35), he studied with Barbier at the Namur Cons.; he then was a student of Moulaert (composition), J. Jongen (fugue), Malengreau (premier prix in organ, 1939), and Absil (composition) at the Brussels Cons. He also studied composition with Gilson, and then went to Paris to complete his training in organ with Tournemire. Returning to Belgium, he won the 2nd Prix de Rome with his cantata *La navigation d'Ulysse* in 1943. In 1947 he became prof. of harmony at the Liège Cons. In 1949 he organized his so-called "Variation" group for young performers and composers, which sought to champion a broad expanse of music, ranging from the 13th to the 20th centuries. Froidebise was especially known for his championship of early organ music, and was ed. of the monumental *Anthologie de la musique d'orgue des primitifs à la renaissance* (Paris, 1958). In his own compositions, he favored an advanced idiom utilizing aleatoric and serial procedures.

WORKS: DRAMATIC: RADIO OPERAS: *La lune amère* (1956); *L'aube* (n.d.); *La bergère et le ramoneur* (n.d.). **BALLET:** *Le bal chez le voisin* (c.1953). **INCIDENTAL MUSIC TO:** Sophocles' *Antigone* (1936) and *Oedipe roi* (c.1946); A. Curvers' *Ce vieil Oedipe* (c.1946); M. Lambilliotte's *Jan van Nude* (1951); Aeschylus' *Les choéphores* (1954); Euripides' *Hippolyte* (n.d.); Calderón's *La maison a deux portes* (n.d.); etc. **FILM SCORES:** *Visite à Picasso* (1951; in collaboration with A. Souris); *Lumière des hommes* (1954). **ORCH.:** *De l'aube à la nuit* (1934–37); *La légende de St. Julien l'Hospitalier* (1941). **CHAMBER:** Violin Sonata (1938); *Petite suite monodique* for Flute or Clarinet (n.d.); *Petite suite* for Wind Quintet (n.d.). **KEYBOARD: PIANO:** *7 croquis brefs* (1934); *Hommage à Chopin* (1947). **ORGAN:** *Suite brève* (1935); *Diptyque* (1936); *Prélude et Fugue* (1936); Sonatine (1939); *Prélude et fughetta* (n.d.); *Livre de noëls belges* (n.d.); *3 pièces* (n.d.); *Hommage à J.S. Bach* (n.d.). **VOCAL:** *La lumière endormie*, cantata (1941); *3 poèmes japonais* for Soprano or Tenor and Orch. (1942); *La navigation d'Ulysse*, cantata (1943); *5 comptines* for Soprano or Tenor and 11 Instruments (1947); *Amercoeur* for Soprano and 7 Instruments (1948); *La cloche engloutie*, cantata (1956); *Stèle pour sei Shonagon* for Soprano and 19 Instruments (1958).

Froment, Louis (Georges François) de, French conductor; b. Toulouse, Dec. 5, 1921; d. Cannes, Aug. 19, 1994. He received training in violin, flute, and harmony at the Toulouse Cons., and then was a student of Fourestier, Bigot, and Cluytens at the Paris Cons. (premier prix in conducting, 1948). He was active as a conductor with the French Radio in Paris, and also was music director of the casinos in Cannes and Deauville (1950–56), and in Vichy (1953–69). In 1958–59 he was conductor of the Nice Radio Chamber Orch. From 1958 to 1980 he was chief conductor of the Luxembourg Radio Sym. Orch.

Fromm, Herbert, German-born American organist, conductor, and composer; b. Kitzingen, Feb. 23, 1905; d. Brookline, Mass., March 10, 1995. He studied piano, organ, conducting, and composition at the Munich Academy of Music (M.A.). He was conductor of the theaters in Bielefeld (1930) and Würzburg (1931–33). In 1937 the Nazis forced him out of Germany and he emigrated to the U.S. He served as organist and choirmaster at Temple Beth Zion in Buffalo (1937–41) and at Temple Israel in Boston (1941–73). In addition to his articles and essays in various journals and newspapers, he wrote the books *The Key of See: Travel Journey of a Composer, Seven Pockets*, and *On Jewish Music: A Composer's View*. He composed an extensive body of music for the synagogue, and also a number of secular works.

Fromm, Paul, prominent German-born American music patron; b. Kitzingen, Sept. 28, 1906; d. Chicago, July 4, 1987. He was born into a family of vintners; emigrated to the U.S. in 1938, becoming a naturalized American citizen in 1944. He founded the Great Lakes Wine Co. in Chicago in 1940, subsequently organizing the Fromm Music Foundation (1952), which assumed a leading role in commissioning and sponsoring performances of contemporary music, including those at the Berkshire Music Center in Tanglewood (from 1956), the annual Festival of Contemporary Music there (1964–83), and the Aspen (Colo.) Music Festival (from 1985).

Frotscher, Gotthold, German musiciologist; b. Ossa, near Leipzig, Dec. 6, 1897; d. Berlin, Sept. 30, 1967. He studied in Bonn and Leipzig; received his Ph.D. from the Univ. of Leipzig in 1922 with the diss. *Die Ästhetik des Berliner Liedes*; completed his Habilitation at the Technische Hochschule in Danzig with his *Hauptprobleme der Musikästhetik im 18. Jahrhundert* (1924; publ. in Danzig, 1924). He taught at the Univ. of Danzig (1924–32) and then was a prof. at the Univ. of Berlin (1935–45); from 1950, taught at the Pedagögische Hochschule in Berlin. He wrote the valuable *Geschichte des Orgelspiels und der Orgelkomposition* (2 vols., Berlin, 1935; 3rd ed., rev., 1966); also publ. *Aufführungspraxis alter Musik* (Wilhelmshaven, 1963; 4th ed., 1977) and *Orgeln* (Karlsruhe, 1968).

Frugoni, Orazio, Italian pianist and pedagogue; b. Davos, Switzerland, Jan. 28, 1921. After graduating as a student of Scuderi at the Milan Cons. in 1939, he attended the master classes of Casella at the Accademia Musicale Chigiana in Siena and of Lipatti at the Geneva Cons., where he was awarded the prix de virtuosité in 1945. From 1939 he played in Italy; after making his U.S. debut at N.Y.'s Town Hall in 1947, he performed throughout the U.S.; he also taught at the Eastman School of Music in Rochester, N.Y. (1951–67), and then was director of the Graduate School of Fine Arts at Villa Schifanoia in Florence (1967–75); he taught at the Cherubini Cons. in Florence (from 1972).

Frühbeck de Burgos (originally, **Frühbeck**), **Rafael,** eminent Spanish conductor; b. Burgos, Sept. 15, 1933. His father was German, his mother Spanish. He studied violin before pursuing musical training at the Bilbao Cons. and the Madrid Cons. (1950–53); then received instruction in conducting from Eichhorn at the Munich Hochschule für Musik (1956–58). He was conductor of the Bilbao Municipal Orch. (1958–62), chief conductor of the Orquesta Nacional de España in Madrid (1962–77), Generalmusikdirektor of the Düsseldorf Sym. Orch. (1966–71), and music director of the Orchestre Symphonique de Montréal (1975–76). He appeared as a guest conductor with major European and North American orchs.; served as principal guest conductor of the National Sym. Orch. in Washington, D.C. (1980–89) and of the Yomiuri Nippon Sym. Orch. in Tokyo (1980–93). He was chief conductor of the Vienna Sym. Orch. (from 1991), held the title of Generalmusikdirektor of the Deutsche Oper in Berlin (from 1992), and was chief conductor of the Berlin Radio Orch. (from 1993). His idiomatic performances of Spanish music have won him many accolades; he has also demonstrated expertise as an interpreter of the standard orch. repertoire.

Frumerie, (Per) Gunnar (Fredrik) de, esteemed Swedish composer, pianist, and teacher; b. Nacka, near Stockholm, July 20, 1908; d. Mörby, Sept. 9, 1987. He was a student of Lundberg (piano) and Ellberg (composition) at the Stockholm Cons. (1923–29); after pursuing his training with Sauer (piano) and Stein (composition) on a Jenny Lind Foundation stipend in Vienna (1929–31), he completed his studies with Cortot (piano) and Sabaneyev (composition) in Paris. He was active as a concert pianist in Sweden, and also taught piano at the Stockholm Musikhögskolan (1945–74). In 1943 he was made a member of the Royal Swedish Academy of Music. His music reflected the influence of Scandinavian Romanticism, crafted along traditional lines with a respect for folk elements.

WORKS: DRAMATIC: *En Moder*, melodrama (1932); *Singoalla*, opera (1937–40; Stockholm, March 16, 1940); *Johannesnatten*, ballet (1947). **ORCH:** 2 piano concertos (1929, 1932); *Suite in an Ancient Style* for Chamber Orch. (1930); *Variations and Fugue* for Piano and Orch. (1932); Violin Concerto (1936; rev. 1976); *Partita* for Strings (1937); *Pastoral Suite* for Flute, Harp, and Strings (1941; also for Flute and Piano, 1933); Symphonic Variations (1941); *Symphonie Ballad* for Piano and Orch. (1943–44); *Divertimento* (1951); Concerto for 2 Pianos and Orch. (1953); Concerto for Clarinet, Harp, Percussion, and Strings (1958); Trumpet Concerto (1959); Concertino for Oboe, Harp, Percussion, and Strings (1960); Flute Concerto (1969); Horn Concerto (1971–72); *Ballad* (1975); Violin Concerto (1976); Concertino for Piano and Strings (1977); Cello Concerto (1984; orchestration of the 2nd Cello Sonata, 1949; also orchestrated as a Trombone Concerto, 1986). **CHAMBER:** 2 piano trios (1932, 1952); 2 violin sonatas (1934, 1944); 2 piano quartets (1941, 1963); *Elegiac Suite* for Cello and Piano (1946); Suite for Wind Quintet (1973); String Quintet (1974); *Musica per nove*, octet (1976); piano pieces, including 2 sonatas (1968). **VOCAL:** *Fader var*, cantata (1945); 8 Psalms for Chorus and Orch. (1953–55); a cappella choruses; songs.

Fryer, George Herbert, English pianist, pedagogue, and composer; b. London, May 21, 1877; d. there, Feb. 7, 1957. He studied in London with Beringer at the Royal Academy of Music (1893–95) and with Franklin Taylor at the Royal College of Music (1895–98). After further studies with Busoni in Weimar (1898), he made his London debut on Nov. 17, 1898, and subsequently toured in Europe; in 1914 he made his first tour of North America. He taught at the Royal Academy of Music (1905–14); after teaching in N.Y. (1915–17), he was on the faculty of the Royal College of Music (1917–47). He continued to tour in Europe, and also played in Canada and the Far East. He publ. *Hints on Pianoforte Practice* (N.Y., 1914) and composed piano pieces and songs.

Fryklöf, Harald (Leonard), Swedish organist, teacher, and composer; b. Uppsala, Sept. 14, 1882; d. Stockholm, March 11, 1919. He studied organ at the Stockholm Cons. (diploma, 1903), where he also had lessons in composition and counterpoint with Lindegren (1902–05); he likewise studied piano with Richard Andersson (1904–10), and went to Berlin to study orchestration with P. Scharwenka (1905). In 1904 he became a teacher at Andersson's music school; in 1908 he was made organist at the Cathedral and a teacher at the Cons. in Stockholm. He was elected to membership in the Swedish Royal Academy of Music in 1915. Fryklöf publ. the book *Harmonisering av koraler i dur och moll jämte kyrkotonarterna* (1916). With H. Palm, O. Sandberg, and A. Hellerström, he ed. *Musica sacra: Körsånger för kyrkan och skolan* (Stockholm, 1915). His music reflected German and French tendencies.

WORKS: Concert Overture (1908); *Sonata alla leggenda* for Violin and Piano (1919); organ music, including a Fugue (1909), Doppel-Canon (1910), and Passacaglia (n.d.); piano pieces; Psalm 98 for Chorus; songs.

Fryklund, (Lars Axel) Daniel, Swedish musicologist; b. Västerås, May 4, 1879; d. Hälsingborg, Aug. 25, 1965. He studied Romanic philology at the Univ. of Uppsala (Ph.D., 1907). He taught at the Univ. of Hälsingborg (1921–44). He was a specialist in the history and etymology of musical instruments; publ. many articles and books, and also amassed a collection of over 800 musical instruments and 10,000 MSS.

Fuchs, Joseph (Philip), American violinist and teacher, brother of **Lillian Fuchs**; b. N.Y., April 26, 1900. He studied violin with Kneisel at the Inst. of Musical Art in N.Y. He was concertmaster of the Cleveland Orch. (1926–40); made his N.Y. debut in 1943; joined the faculty of the Juilliard School of Music in N.Y. in 1946; toured Europe in 1954, South America in 1957, and Russia in 1965.

Fuchs, Lillian, American violist, teacher, and composer, sister of **Joseph (Philip) Fuchs**; b. N.Y., Nov. 18, 1903; d. Englewood, N.J., Oct. 6, 1995. After taking up the piano at an early age, she studied violin with her father. She then was a student of violin of Svecenski and Kneisel and of composition of Goetschius at the Inst. of Musical Art in N.Y. (graduated, 1924). In 1926 she made her N.Y. debut as a violinist, but soon concentrated her career on the viola. She made appearances as a soloist with major American orchs. and played in various chamber music ensembles. She also appeared in concerns with her brothers, Joseph and Harry. Fuchs was the first violist to play and record Bach's 6 suites for solo cello. She taught at the Manhattan School of Music in N.Y. (1963–91), the Aspen (Colo.) Music School (1964–90), and the Juilliard School in N.Y. (1971–93). Her compositions were mainly for the viola.

BIBL.: A. Williams, *L. F.: First Lady of the Viola* (Lewiston, 1994).

Fuchs, Lukas. See **Foss, Lukas.**

Fuchs, Marta, admired German soprano; b. Stuttgart, Jan. 1, 1898; d. there, Sept. 22, 1974. She was trained in Stuttgart, Munich, and Milan. In 1928 she made her operatic debut in Aachen as a mezzo-soprano, singing there until 1930. She then was a prominent member of the Dresden State Opera (1930–45); she also was a guest artist at the Berlin State Opera, the Bayreuth Festival, and the Vienna State Opera, and toured as a concert singer. Among her notable roles were Brünnhilde, Isolde, Kundry, Donna Anna, the Marschallin, and Ariadne.

Fuerstner, Carl, German-born American pianist, conductor, teacher, and composer; b. Strasbourg, June 16, 1912; d. Bloomington, Ind., Dec. 5, 1994. He studied composition and conducting at the Cologne Hochschule für Musik (1930–34), where his teachers were Abendroth, Braunfels, Jarnach, and Klussmann. While still a student, he composed incidental music for theatrical plays. In 1939 he went to the U.S. as assistant conductor of the San Francisco Opera; he became a naturalized American citizen in 1945. From 1945 to 1950 he was head of the opera dept. at the Eastman School of Music in Rochester, N.Y.; then served on the faculty of Brigham Young Univ. in Provo, Utah (1951–61), where he was resident pianist, opera conductor, principal piano teacher, and head of the composition dept. (1955–61); also toured widely as a piano accompanist to many celebrated artists of the day and conducted an impressive repertoire of standard and modern operas in the U.S. and Europe. From 1963 to 1982 he was principal opera coach at the Indiana Univ. School of Music in Bloomington, where he also conducted operas. He also was on the faculty of the Summer Academy of the Salzburg Mozarteum (1973–82); then was active with the American Inst. of Musical Studies in Graz (1983–85); concurrently was associated with the "Festa Musica Pro" in Assisi, Italy. From 1981 to 1989 he was music director of the Bloomington (Ind.) Sym. Orch.

WORKS: *Concerto rapsodico* for Cello and Orch. (Rochester, N.Y., May 11, 1947); *Metamorphoses on a Chorale Theme* for 20 Trombones, 2 Tubas, and Percussion (Rochester, N.Y., April 5, 1949); *Symphorama* for Orch. (1960); *Overture* (1954), *Allegro ritmico* (1958), and many other pieces for Concert Band, as well as band transcriptions of Classical and Romantic works; *Divertimento* for String Quartet (1950); Clarinet Sonata (1950); *Allegro concertante* for Trombone and 10 Instruments (1966); Sonata for Bass Clarinet and Piano or Cello (1977); *Conjurations* for Soprano Saxophone and Piano (1985); piano pieces; choral works, including the *46th Psalm* for Chorus, 4 Trumpets, 4 Trombones, and Organ (1983).

Fuga, Sandro, Italian pianist, teacher, and composer; b. Mogliano Veneto, Nov. 26, 1906; d. Turin, March 1, 1994. He studied piano, organ, and composition at the Turin Cons. He was a concert pianist until 1940; became a lecturer at the Turin Cons. in 1933, and in 1966 its director, which post he held until 1977.

WORKS: DRAMATIC: *La croce deserta* (Bergamo, 1950); *Otto Schnaffs* (Turin, 1950); *Confessione* (RAI Radio, 1962). **ORCH.:** *Ode in memoria* (1945; Turin, March 5, 1948); *Passacaglia* (1950); Toccata for Piano and Orch. (1952); Trumpet Concertino (1953); *Concerto sacro III* (1954); Cello Concerto (1955); Violin Concerto (1959); Concerto for Strings and Percussion (1963); Oboe Concertino (1964); Sym. (1967); Piano Concerto (Rome, Jan. 14, 1970). **CHAMBER:** Piano Trio (1943); 4 string quartets (1943, 1945, 1948, 1965); Violin Sonata (1951); piano pieces, including 2 sonatas (1957, 1978). **VOCAL:** *Concerto sacro I* for Chorus and Orch. (1938; Turin, Feb. 3, 1939), *II* for Baritone, Men's Chorus, and Orch. (1951), and *IV* for Tenor and Double Chorus (1956).

Fugère, Lucien, remarkable French baritone; b. Paris, July 22, 1848; d. there, Jan. 15, 1935. He was a student at the Paris Cons. of Raguneau and Batiste. In 1870 he began his career singing at the Café-Concert, Ba-ta-can. In 1874 he joined the Bouffes-Parisiens. He made his debut at the Paris Opéra-Comique in 1877 as Jean in Masse's *Les noces de Jeannette*, and remained on its roster until 1910. He appeared in over 100 roles there, including the premieres of Chabrier's *Le roi malgré lui* (1887), Messager's *La Basoche* (1890), Saint-Saëns' *Phryné* (1893), Massenet's *Cendrillon* (1899), and Charpentier's *Louise* (1900). In 1897 he sang at London's Covent Garden. After appearing at the Gaîté-Lyrique in Paris (1910–19), he returned to the Opéra-Comique, where he celebrated his 50th anniversary as a singer on March 5, 1920. He continued to make appearances until he was 80, singing his farewell performance in *La Basoche* in Le Touquet in 1928, the year he was awarded the Légion d'honneur. He was particularly celebrated for his portrayals of Leporello, Papageno, Figaro, and Bartolo. Mary Garden was among his students.

BIBL.: R. Duhamel, *L.F.* (Paris, 1929).

Fujiie, Keiko, Japanese composer; b. Tokyo, July 22, 1963. She received training at the Tokyo National Univ. of Fine Arts and Music (graduated, 1987). She was awarded the Asian Cultural Counsel fund and lived in N.Y. in 1992–93.

WORKS: ORCH.: *Malposition* (Tokyo, June 6, 1985); *Panorama* (1986); Clarinet Concerto (1986; rev. 1993); *Intermezzo* for String Ensemble (1986); *Jade Sea Panorama* (1992; Amsterdam, Sept. 11, 1993); *Beber* for Chamber Orch. (1994). **CHAMBER:** *Reunion* for Flute, Violin, Cello, Piano, and 2 Percussionists (1984); 3 Pieces for Clarinet (1985); *Pas de Deux I* and *II* for Piano (1987–89); String Trio (1988–92); *Midday Island* for 6 Players (1991); *Flower Garden* for 5 Percussionists (1992); *Bodrum Sea* for Guitar (1992); *Yellow Cow* for Oboe, Accordion, and Double Bass (1993); *Sansara* for Wind Quintet (1993); *Now the Horizon Comes into View* for Guitar. **VOCAL:** *Love Song* for Soprano, Flute, Harp, Double Bass, and Percussion (1987); *Nobody, Not Even the Rain, Has Such Small Hands* for Mezzo-soprano, Prepared Piano, 4-hands, and Tape (1990).

Fujikawa, Mayumi, Japanese violinist; b. Asahigawa, July 27, 1946. She studied at the Toho School of Music in Tokyo and at the Antwerp Cons.; later took lessons with Leonid Kogan in

Nice. In 1970 she won 2nd prize in the Tchaikovsky Competition in Moscow and 1st prize in the Vieuxtemps Competition in Verviers, Belgium; then appeared as soloist with major orchs. in Europe and America and was active as a recitalist and chamber music player.

Fuleihan, Anis, Cypriot-born American pianist, conductor, and composer; b. Kyrenia, April 2, 1900; d. Palo Alto, Calif., Oct. 11, 1970. He studied at the English School in Kyrenia; went to the U.S. in 1915 and continued his study of the piano in N.Y. with Alberto Jonás; toured the U.S., also the Near East, from 1919 to 1925; then lived in Cairo, returning to the U.S. in 1928. He was on the staff of G. Schirmer, Inc. in N.Y. (1932–39); in 1947, became a prof. at Indiana Univ. in Bloomington; in 1953, director of the Beirut Cons. in Lebanon. In 1962 he went to Tunis under the auspices of the State Dept.; in 1963, organized the Orch. Classique de Tunis; remained there until 1965.

WORKS: OPERA: *Vasco* (1960). **ORCH.:** *Mediterranean Suite* (1930; Cincinnati, March 15, 1935); *Preface to a Child's Story Book* (1932); 2 syms.: No. 1 (N.Y., Dec. 31, 1936) and No. 2 (N.Y., Feb. 16, 1967); 3 piano concertos: No. 1 (Saratoga Springs, N.Y., Sept. 11, 1937), No. 2 (1938), and No. 3 (1963); *Fantasy* for Viola and Orch. (1938); 3 violin concertos (1930, 1965, 1967); *Fiesta* (Indianapolis, Dec. 1, 1939); *Symphonie concertante* for String Quartet and Orch. (N.Y., April 25, 1940); Concerto for 2 Pianos and Orch. (Hempstead, N.Y., Jan. 10, 1941); *Epithalamium* for Piano and Strings (Philadelphia, Feb. 7, 1941); Concerto for Theremin and Orch. (N.Y., Feb. 26, 1945); *Invocation to Isis* (Indianapolis, Feb. 28, 1941); Concerto for Violin, Piano, and Orch. (1943); Ondes Martenot Concerto (1944); *3 Cyprus Serenades* (Philadelphia, Dec. 13, 1946); *Rhapsody* for Cello and Strings (Saratoga Springs, Sept. 12, 1946); *The Pyramids of Giza*, symphonic poem (1952); *Toccata* for Piano and Orch. (1960); *Islands*, symphonic suite (1961); Flute Concerto (1962); Cello Concerto (1963); Viola Concerto (1963); *Le Cor anglais s'amuse* for English Horn and Strings (1969). **CHAMBER:** 5 string quartets (1940–67); 14 piano sonatas (1940–68); *Overture* for 5 Winds (N.Y., May 17, 1947); Horn Quintet (1959); Piano Quintet (1967); Piano Trio (1969); Clarinet Quintet; Violin Sonata; Viola Sonata; Cello Sonata. **VOCAL:** Choral pieces; songs.

Fulkerson, Gregory (Locke), American violinist; b. Iowa City, May 9, 1950. He studied at Oberlin College (1967–71) and with Dorothy DeLay, Robert Mann, and Ivan Galamian at the Juilliard School in N.Y. (1975–79); also played in the Cleveland Orch. (1971–74) and later was concertmaster of the Honolulu Sym. Orch. (1979–81). After winning 1st prize in the International American Music Competition in Washington, D.C., in 1980, he pursued a career as a soloist. An adventurous artist, he maintains an enormous repertoire, which includes a number of neglected works; among posthumous premieres was Roy Harris's Violin Concerto (Wilmington, N.C., March 21, 1984). Other premieres of works by contemporary composers include Richard Wernick's Violin Concerto (Philadelphia, Jan. 17, 1986).

Fulkerson, James (Orville), American composer and trombonist; b. Streator, Ill., July 2, 1945. He studied composition with Wilbur Ogdon and Abram Plum and trombone with John Silver at Illinois Wesleyan Univ. (B.A., 1966) and composition with Maritirano, Gaburo, Hiller, and Brun at the Univ. of Ill. (M.M., 1969). He was a creative assoc. of the Center for the Creative and Performing Arts at the State Univ. of N.Y. in Buffalo (1969–72); then was composer-in-residence at the Deutscher Akademischer Austauschdienst in Berlin (1973), the Victorian College of the Arts in Melbourne (1977–79), and Dartington College in Devon, England (from 1981). He is a virtuoso on the trombone, and he makes a specialty of playing the most fantastically difficult modern pieces. His own compositions are no less advanced.

WORKS: DRAMATIC: *Raucasity and the Cisco Kid . . . or, I Skate in the Sun* (1977–78); *Vicarious Thrills* (1978–79); *Cheap Imitations II: Madwomen* (1980); *Force Fields and Spaces* (1981); *Cheap Imitations IV* (1982); *Put Your Foot Charlie* (1982); *Rats Tale* (1983); *Studs*, ballet music (1992). **ORCH.:** *Globs* for Small Orch., Live Electronics, and Tape (1968); *About Time* (1969); *Something about Mobiles* (1969); *Planes* for 4 Orch. Groups (1969); *Behind Closed Doors* for Violin and Orch. (1971); *Patterns IX* (1972); *To See a Thing Clearly* (1972); *For We Don't See Anything Clearly* (1972); Guitar Concerto (1972); Trombone Concerto, with Tape (1973); *Orchestra Piece* (1974); *Stations, Regions, and Clouds* for Bass Trombone and Orch. (1977); Concerto for Amplified Cello and Large Ensemble (1978); Sym. (1980); Concerto *(. . . fierce and coming from far away)* (1981); *Pessoa I* for Large Ensemble (1992); Concerto for Electric Violin and Large Ensemble (1992). **CHAMBER:** *Co-ordinative Systems* Nos. 1–10 (1972–76); Music for Brass Instruments Nos. 1–6 (1975–78); Suite for Amplified Cello (1978–79).

Fuller, Albert, American harpsichordist and teacher; b. Washington, D.C., July 21, 1926. He studied organ with Paul Callaway at the National Cathedral in Washington, D.C.; then attended classes at the Peabody Cons. of Music and at Georgetown and Johns Hopkins Univs. He studied harpsichord with Kirkpatrick at Yale Univ. and also theory there with Hindemith, graduating with a M.Mus. in 1954. He then went to Paris on a Ditson fellowship; upon his return to the U.S., he made his N.Y. recital debut in 1957; his European debut followed in 1959. In 1964 he became a prof. of harpsichord at the Juilliard School of Music in N.Y. He also was on the faculty of Yale Univ. from 1976 to 1979. From 1972 to 1983 he was founder-artistic director of the Aston Magna Foundation.

Fulton, (Robert) Norman, English composer and teacher; b. London, Jan. 23, 1909; d. Birmingham, Aug. 5, 1980. He studied harmony and composition with Demuth at the Royal Academy of Music in London (1929–33). After serving on the staff of the BBC (1936–60), he was prof. of harmony and composition at the Royal Academy of Music (from 1966).

WORKS: DRAMATIC: *Augury*, ballet (1960); radio and film music. **ORCH.:** *Serenade* for Strings (1944); *5 Entertainments* for Small Orch. (1946); Overture (1950); 3 syms.: No. 1, *Sinfonia pastorale* (1950), No. 2 (1955), and No. 3, *Mary Stuart* (1971–73); *Curtain Wells Sketches* for Small Orch. (1959); *Waltz Rhapsody* for Piano and Orch. (1961); *Symphonic Dances* (1965). **CHAMBER:** *Sonata da camera* for Viola and Piano (1946); *Introduction, Air, and Reel* for Viola and Piano (1950); Piano Trio (1950); *3 Movements* for Clarinet and Piano (1951); *Scottish Suite* for Recorder and Piano or Harpsichord (1954); Oboe Sonatina (1962); *Night Music* for Flute and Piano (1969). **PIANO:** Sonatina (1945); *Waltz, Air, and Polka* for 2 Pianos (1947); *Prelude, Elegy, and Toccata* (1954); *Fantasy on a Ground* (1969); *3 Pieces* (1970). **VOCAL:** Choral music; songs.

Furlanetto, Ferruccio, Italian bass; b. Pordenone, Sicily, May 16, 1949. He was a student of Campogaliahi and Casagrande. After making his operatic debut as Sparafucile in Vicenza in 1974, he held engagements in Turin, Trieste, Bologna, Venice, Parma, and Aix-en-Provence. In 1978 he made his U.S. debut as Zaccaria with the New Orleans Opera. He first appeared at the San Francisco Opera as Alvise in 1979. On Feb. 26, 1980, he made his Metropolitan Opera debut in N.Y. as the Grand Inquisitor; also appeared at the Glyndebourne Festival (1980), the San Diego Opera (1985), the Paris Opéra (1985), the Salzburg Festival (1986), and the Royal Opera, Covent Garden, London (1988). In addition to such Mozart roles as Figaro, Don Alfonso, Leporello, and Don Giovanni, he has sung in many operas by Rossini and Verdi.

Fürst, Janos, Hungarian conductor; b. Budapest, Aug. 8, 1935. He received training in violin at the Franz Liszt Academy of Music in Budapest. In the aftermath of the failed Hungarian Revolution of 1956, he fled his homeland and pursued violin studies at the Brussels Cons., where he won the premier prix. He went to Dublin and was a violinist in the Irish Radio Orch. (1958–63). In 1963 he became founder-conductor of the Irish

Chamber Orch. In 1968 he was made resident conductor of the Ulster Orch. in Belfast. Following his London debut with the Royal Phil. in 1972, he appeared as a guest conductor with principal British orchs. and with various orchs. on the Continent. From 1974 to 1978 he was music director of the Malmö Sym. Orch., then music director of the Ålborg Sym. Orch. (1980–83). From 1981 to 1989 he was music director of the Opera and Phil. in Marseilles; was also principal conductor of the RTE (Radio Telefís Eireann) Orch. in Dublin (1983–89). On April 12, 1990, he made his U.S. debut as a guest conductor of the Indianapolis Sym. Orch. In 1990 he became music director of the Winterthur Stadtorchester.

Furtwängler, (Gustav Heinrich Ernst Martin) Wilhelm, great German conductor; b. Berlin, Jan. 25, 1886; d. Ebersteinburg, Nov. 30, 1954. His father, Adolf Furtwängler, was a distinguished archaeologist and director of the Berlin Museum of Antiquities, and his mother, Adelheid (née Wendt) Furtwängler, was a painter. A precocious child, he received instruction in piano at a very early age from his mother and his aunt; by the time he was 7, he had begun to compose. After his father was called to the Univ. of Munich as prof. of archaeology in 1894, he was tutored at home by the archaeologist Ludwig Curtius, the art historian and musicologist Walter Riezler, and the sculptor Adolf Hildebrand. He commenced formal training in composition with Beer-Walbrunn, and then pursued the study of advanced counterpoint with Rheinberger (1900–1901); he subsequently completed his studies with Schillings. After working as répétiteur at the Breslau Opera (1905–06), he became 3rd conductor at the Zürich Opera in 1906; that same year he scored a notable success conducting Bruckner's 9th Sym. in Munich with the Kaim Orch. From 1907 to 1909 he was an assistant conductor under Mottl at the Munich Court Opera. He then was 3rd conductor under Pfitzner at the Strasbourg Municipal Opera from 1909 to 1911. In 1911 he was appointed music director in Lübeck, a position he held until 1915 when he was called to Mannheim as Generalmusikdirektor. It was during this period that Furtwängler began to secure his reputation as a conductor of great promise. In 1915 he made his first appearance in Vienna conducting the Konzertvereinsorchester. He scored a notable success at his debut with the Berlin Phil. on Dec. 14, 1917. In 1920 he resigned his position in Mannheim to serve as Strauss' successor as music director of the Berlin State Opera orch. concerts, remaining there until 1922; concurrently he served as Mengelberg's successor as music director of the Frankfurt am Main Museumgesellschaft concerts. On Aug. 30, 1921, he made his debut with the Leipzig Gewandhaus Orch. to critical acclaim. Upon the death of Nikisch in 1922, Furtwängler was appointed his successor as music director of both the Berlin Phil. and the Leipzig Gewandhaus Orch., retaining the latter position until 1928. On March 27, 1922, he made his debut with the Vienna Phil. He made his first appearance in Milan in 1923 when he conducted the La Scala Orch. On Jan. 24, 1924, Furtwängler made his British debut with the Royal Phil. Soc. in London. His auspicious U.S. debut followed on Jan. 3, 1925, with the N.Y. Phil.; he returned to conduct there again in 1926 and 1927. Upon Weingartner's resignation as regular conductor of the Vienna Phil. in 1927, Furtwängler was elected his successor. He made his debut at the Vienna State Opera conducting *Das Rheingold* on Oct. 17, 1928. That same year he was awarded an honorary doctorate by the Univ. of Heidelberg. His debut as an opera conductor in Berlin took place on June 13, 1929, when he conducted *Le nozze di Figaro* at the Berlin Festival. In 1929 the German government awarded him the medal Pour le Mérite in recognition of his outstanding contributions to German musical culture. In 1930 he resigned his position with the Vienna Phil., having been named Generalmusikdirektor of Berlin. In 1930 he was made music director of the Bayreuth Festival. He made his first appearance there conducting *Tristan und Isolde* on July 23, 1931, but resigned his position at the close of the season. He then made his debut at the Berlin State Opera on Nov. 12, 1931, conducting the local premiere of Pfitzner's *Das Herz*, and in 1932 was appointed its music director.

After the Nazis came to power in 1933, they moved quickly to appropriate Furtwängler's stature as Germany's greatest conductor for their own propaganda purposes. He was made vice-president of the newly organized Reichsmusikkammer and then was appointed one of the newly created Prussian State Councilors, an honorary lifetime title which Furtwängler refused to use. He also refused to join the Nazi party. Early on, he began to encounter difficulties with the authorities over personal and artistic matters. He opposed the regime's policies against the Jews and others, and did all he could to assist those who sought him out, both musicians and non-musicians alike, often at great personal risk. For the 1933–34 season of the Berlin State Opera, Furtwängler scheduled the premiere of Hindemith's *Mathis der Maler*, even though the Nazis had branded the composer a "cultural Bolshevist" and a "spiritual non-Aryan" (his wife was half Jewish). The Nazis compelled Furtwängler to withdraw the work, but he attempted to defy them by conducting a symphonic version of the score with the Berlin Phil. on March 11, 1934. It elicited a prolonged ovation from the audience, but drew condemnation from the Nazi press as a contemptible example of "degenerate" music. The ensuing polemical campaign against Furtwängler led him to resign all of his positions on Dec. 4, 1934. (As a propaganda ploy, the Nazis would not accept his resignation as a Prussian State Councilor since this was a lifetime "honor" granted by the regime.) Furtwängler's devotion to what he considered to be the true (non-Nazi) Germany and his belief that it was his duty to preserve its great musical heritage compelled him to make an uneasy peace with the regime. On April 25, 1935, he returned as a conductor with the Berlin Phil. Although he appeared regularly with it in succeeding years, he refused an official position with it so as not to be beholden to the Nazis. In 1936 he was offered the position of conductor of the N.Y. Phil. in succession to Toscanini, but he declined the offer in the face of accusations in the American press that he was a Nazi collaborator. In 1937 he was invited to London to participate in the musical celebrations in honor of the coronation of King George VI, where he conducted the *Ring* cycle at Covent Garden and Beethoven's 9th Sym. On Aug. 27, 1937, he made his first appearance at the Salzburg Festival conducting Beethoven's 9th Sym. In 1939 he was honored by the French government as a Commandeur of the Légion d'honneur. After the outbreak of World War II on Sept. 1, 1939, Furtwängler confined his activities almost exclusively to Germany and Austria, principally with the Berlin Phil. and the Vienna Phil. In 1944, after learning that Himmler had placed him on the Nazi's liquidation list, Furtwängler sent his family to Switzerland for safety, while he remained behind to keep his conducting engagements for the 1944–45 season. However, after conducting the Vienna Phil. in Jan. 1945, he too fled to Switzerland. His decision to pursue his career in his homeland during the Third Reich left him open to charges by the Allies after the war of being a Nazi collaborator. Although the Vienna denazification commission cleared him on March 9, 1946, as a German citizen he was ordered to stand trial in Berlin before the Allied Denazification Tribunal for Artists. Following his trial on Dec. 11 and 17, 1946, he was acquitted of all charges; it was not until March 1947, however, that he was formally "normalized." On May 25, 1947, he conducted the Berlin Phil. for the first time since the close of World War II, leading an all-Beethoven concert to extraordinary approbation. On Aug. 10, 1947, he also resumed his association with the Vienna Phil. when he conducted it at the Salzburg Festival. He made his first postwar appearance at the Berlin State Opera on Oct. 3, 1947, conducting *Tristan und Isolde.* In Feb. 1948 he returned to England for the first time in more than a decade to conduct a series of concerts with the London Phil. He also became active as a conductor with the Philharmonia Orch. of London. When the management of the Chicago Sym. Orch. announced Furtwängler's engagement as a guest conductor for the 1949–50 season, a campaign against him as a Nazi collaborator compelled him to cancel his engagements. However, in Western Europe his appearances on tours with the Berlin Phil. and the Vienna Phil. were acclaimed. In 1950 he made his debut at Milan's La Scala conducting the *Ring* cycle. With Flagstad as soloist, he conducted the premiere of Strauss' *Vier letzte Lieder* in London on May 22, 1950. On July 29, 1951, he reopened the Bayreuth Festival conducting Beethoven's 9th Sym. In 1952 he resumed his position of music director of the Berlin Phil., but increasing ill health and growing deafness clouded his remaining days. He was scheduled to conduct the Berlin Phil. on its first tour of the U.S. in the spring of 1955, but his health further declined, leading to his death in the fall of 1954; Herbert von Karajan was elected his successor.

Furtwängler was the perfect embodiment of all that was revered in the Austro-German tradition of the art of conducting. As its foremost exponent, he divined and made manifest the spiritual essence of the great masterworks of the symphonic and operatic repertory. His often refulgent and always inspired interpretations of Mozart, Beethoven, Schubert, Schumann, Brahms, Wagner, and Bruckner, many of which have been preserved on recordings, attest to his greatness as a recreative artist of the highest order. Furtwängler was also a creative artist who composed in an expansive Romantic style. Sketches for an early sym. (1903) were utilized in a mature sym. (1937–41), premiered in Mark kreis Recklinghausen on April 27, 1991, Alfred Walter conducting. Another sym. (1943–47) had 3 of its movements premiered in Berlin on Jan. 26, 1956, Joseph Keilberth conducting. Among his other works were a *Te Deum* (1910); Piano Quintet (1935); Symphonie Concertante for Piano and Orch. (1937); 2 violin sonatas (1937, 1940).

WRITINGS: *Johannes Brahms und Anton Bruckner* (Leipzig, 1941; 2nd ed., 1952); W. Abendroth, ed., *Gespräche über Musik* (Zürich, 1948; 7th ed., 1958; Eng. tr., 1953, as *Concerning Music*); *Ton und Wort* (Wiesbaden, 1954; 8th ed., 1958); M. Hürlimann, ed., *Der Musiker und sein Publikum* (Zürich, 1955); S. Brockhaus, ed., *Vermächtnis* (Wiesbaden, 1956; 4th ed., 1958); F. Thiess, ed., *Briefe* (Wiesbaden, 1964); E. Furtwängler and G. Birkner, *Wilhelm Furtwängler Aufzeichnungen 1924–54* (Mainz, 1980; Eng. tr., 1989); R. Taylor, tr. and ed., *Furtwängler on Music: Essays and Addresses* (Aldershot and Brookfield, Vt., 1991).

BIBL.: R. Specht, *W.F.* (Vienna, 1922); O. Schrenck, *W.F.* (Berlin, 1940); F. Herzfeld, *W.F.: Weg und Wesen* (Leipzig, 1941; 3rd ed., rev., 1950); B. Geissmar, *Two Worlds of Music* (N.Y., 1946); W. Siebert, *F.: Mensch und Künstler* (Buenos Aires, 1950); C. Riess, *F.: Musik und Politik* (Bern, 1953; abridged Eng. tr., 1955); B. Gavoty and R. Hauert, *W.F.* (Geneva, 1954); M. Hürlimann, ed., *W.F.: Im Urteil seiner Zeit* (Zürich, 1955); D. Gillis, ed., *F. Recalled* (Tuckahoe, N.Y., 1966); idem, *F. and America* (Woodhaven, N.Y., 1970); E. Furtwängler, *Über W.F.* (Wiesbaden, 1979; Eng. tr., 1993); K. Hoecker, *Die nie vergessenen Klänge: Erinnerungen an W.F.* (Berlin, 1979); P. Pirie, *F. and the Art of Conducting* (London, 1980); J. Hunt, *The F. Sound* (London, 1985; 3rd ed., 1989); J. Squire and J. Hunt, *F. and Great Britain* (London, 1985); B. Wessling, *W.F.: Eine kritische Biographie* (Stuttgart, 1985); G. Gefen, *F.: Une Biographie par le Disque* (Paris, 1986); J. Matzner, *F.: Analyse, Dokument, Protokoll* (Zürich, 1986); F. Prieberg, *Kraftprobe: W.F. im Dritten Reich* (Wiesbaden, 1986; Eng. tr., 1991); H.-H. Schönzeler, *F.* (London, 1990); S. Shirakawa, *The Devil's Music Master: The Controversial Life and Career of W.F.* (Oxford, 1992).

Furuhjelm, Erik Gustaf, Finnish composer; b. Helsinki, July 6, 1883; d. there, June 13, 1964. He studied violin; then took lessons in composition with Sibelius and Wegelius; continued his studies in Vienna with Robert Fuchs. From 1909 to 1935 he lectured on theory at the Helsinki School of Music, and from 1920 to 1935 served as assistant director there. He founded the magazine *Finsk Musikrevy*; in 1916 he wrote the first book-length biography of Sibelius.

WORKS: ORCH.: 2 syms. (1906–11; 1925–26); *Romantic Overture* (1910); *Konzertstück* for Piano and Orch. (1911); *Intermezzo and Pastorale* (1920–24); *Fem bilder* (1924–25); *Phantasy* for Violin and Orch. (1925–26); *Folklig svit* (1939); *Solitude* (1940). **OTHER:** Chamber music.

Fussan, Werner, German composer and teacher; b. Plauen, Dec. 25, 1912; d. Mainz, Aug. 16, 1986. He was a pupil of Gmeindl and Höffer at the Berlin Hochschule für Musik (1937–40). After teaching at the Wiesbaden Cons. (1945–48), he joined the faculty of the Mainz Hochschule für Musik, where he later was prof. of music education (1966–78).

WORKS: ORCH.: *Musik* for Strings (1943); *Musik* (1947); *Prelude* (1947); *Capriccio* (1949); *Musik* for Strings, Piano, Timpani, and Percussion (1950); Suite for Strings (1951); Concertino for Flute and Strings (1957); *Little Suite* for Strings (1958); Concertino for Clarinet, Strings, and Trumpet (1966). **CHAMBER:** Piano Sonata (1946); *Musik* for Flute and Piano (1947); *Musik* for Violin and Piano (1949); String Trio (1953). **VOCAL:** *Heiteres Aquarium* for Chorus (1967); *Tanzlieder-Kantate* for Soloists, Choruses, and Orch. (1970); *Feier-Kantate* for Choruses and Small Orch. (1972); *Swing and Sing* for Chorus and Rhythm Group (1972). **OTHER:** Numerous educational pieces.

Fussell, Charles C(lement), American composer and conductor; b. Winston-Salem, N.C., Feb. 14, 1938. He received lessons in piano from Clemens Sandresky in Winston-Salem; in 1956 he enrolled in the Eastman School of Music in Rochester, N.Y., where he studied composition (B.M., 1960) with Thomas Canning, Wayne Barlow, and Bernard Rogers, piano with José Echaniz, and conducting with Herman Genhart; in 1962 he received a Fulbright grant and studied with Blacher at the Berlin Hochschule für Musik; attended Friedelind Wagner's Bayreuth Festival Master Class in opera production and conducting in 1963; then completed his training in composition at the Eastman School of Music (M.M., 1964). In 1966 he joined the faculty of the Univ. of Mass. in Amherst; also founded its Group for New Music in 1974 (later renamed Pro Musica Moderna). He taught composition at the North Carolina School of the Arts in Winston-Salem (1976–77) and at Boston Univ. (1981); in 1981–82 he conducted the Longy School Chamber Orch. in Cambridge, Mass. In his music, he adopts a prudent modernistic idiom and favors neo-Romantic but never overladen sonorities, without doctrinaire techniques.

WORKS: OPERA: *Caligula* (1962). **ORCH.:** 15 syms.: No. 1, *Symphony in 1 Movement* (1963), No. 2 for Soprano and Orch. (1964–67), No. 3, *Landscapes*, for Chorus and Orch. (1978–81), No. 4, *Wilde*, for Baritone and Orch. (1989); and No. 5 (1994–95); *3 Processionals* (1972–73; Springfield, Mass., April 25, 1974); *Northern Lights*, 2 portraits for Chamber Orch., portraying Leoš Janáček and Edvard Munch (1977–79); *Virgil Thomson Sleeping*, portrait for Chamber Orch. (1981); *4 Fairy Tales*, after Oscar Wilde (1980–81); *Maurice Grosser Cooking*, portrait No. 2 for Chamber Orch. (1982–83); *Jack Larson*, portrait No. 3 for Chamber Orch. (1986). **CHAMBER:** Trio for Violin, Cello, and Piano (1962); *Dance Suite* for Flute, Trumpet, Viola, and 2 Percussionists (1963); *Ballades* for Cello and Piano (1968; rev. 1976); *Greenwood Sketches: Music for String Quartet* (1976); *Free Fall* for 7 Players (N.Y., May 9, 1988); *Last Trombones* for 6 Trombones, 5 Percussion, and 2 Pianos (1990). **VOCAL:** *Saint Stephen and Herod*, drama for Speaker, Chorus, and Winds (1964); *Poems* for Voices and Chamber Orch. (1965); *Julian*, drama for Soprano, Tenor, Chorus, and Orch. (1969–71; Winston-Salem, N.C., April 15, 1972); *Voyages* for Soprano, Tenor, Women's Chorus, Piano, Winds, and Recorded Speaker (Amherst, Mass., May 4, 1970); *Eurydice* for Soprano and Chamber Ensemble (1973–75; Winston-Salem, N.C., Jan. 30, 1976); *Résumé*, cycle of 9 songs for Soprano, Clarinet, String Bass, and Piano (1975–76); *Cymbeline*, romance for Soprano, Tenor, Narrator, and Chamber Ensemble (Boston, April 2, 1984); *The Gift* for Soprano and Chorus (1986; Boston, Dec. 24, 1987); *5 Goethe Lieder* for Soprano or Tenor and Piano (1987; also for Soprano or Tenor and Orch., 1991); *A Song of Return* for Chorus and Orch. (1989); *Wilde*, 2 monologues for Baritone and Orch. (1989–90); *Specimen Days*, cantata for Baritone, Chorus, and Orch. (1993–94).

Füssl, Karl Heinz, Austrian composer, musicologist, publisher, and music critic; b. Jablonec, Czechoslovakia, March 21, 1924; d. Eisenstadt, Sept. 4, 1992. He went to Berlin and began his formal training at 15 with Konrad Friedrich Noetel (composition), Gerd Otto (piano), and Hugo Distler (choral conducting). Following World War II, he settled in Vienna and completed his studies with Alfred Uhl (composition), Erwin Ratz (analysis), and Hans Swarowsky (conducting). He was active as a music critic and served as head of production for Universal Edition. In addition to overseeing its Urtext Editions, he was associated with the publication of the works of Haydn, Mozart, Johann Strauss, and Mahler. In 1974 he became a teacher of form analysis at the Vienna Academy of Music, where he served as a prof. from 1985. In his music, Füssl demonstrated an adept handling of dodecaphonic procedures.

WORKS: DRAMATIC: *Die Maske*, ballet (1954); *Dybuk*, opera (1958–70; Karlsruhe, Sept. 26, 1970); *Celestina*, opera (1973–75); *Kain*, religious play (1984–85); *Resurrexit*, musical play (1991–92); incidental music. **ORCH.:** *Divertimento* (1952); *Szenen* for Strings (1954); *Epitaph und Antistrophe* (1956; rev. 1971); *Refrains* for Piano and Orch. (1972); *Sonate: Arkadenhof-Serenade* (1983; rev. 1988); *Moments Musicaux*, 8 pieces (1988); 7 *Haikai* for Strings and Percussion (1991). **CHAMBER:** *Kleine Kammermusik* for Flute, Oboe, Clarinet, Horn, and Bassoon (1940); Duo for Cello and Piano (1948–53; rev. 1983); Concertino I (1948) and II (1952) for Clarinet and Piano, 4-hands; *Triptychon* for Cello and Organ (1976); *2 Stücke* for Clarinet and Piano (1977); *Ragtime* for Guitar and Piano (1977); *Nachtmusik* for String Trio (1977; rev. 1988); *Improvisation* for String Quartet (1979); *Les Rondeaux*, 3 duets for 2 Violins (1980; 2nd version, 1981); *Aphorismen über Rhythmische Modelle* for Clarinet and Piano (1980); *Perpetuum Mobile* for Oboe or Trumpet and Piano (1987); *Ekloge* for Cello and Piano (1987); *Konzert zu Viert* for Clarinet and Saxophone (1989); *1 Minute* for String Quartet (1991); *Cantus I* and *II* for String Quartet (both 1991); *Ricercare* for String Quartet (1992). **KEYBOARD:** *Fünf Töne-Fünf Finger*, 6 little pieces for Piano (1941; rev. 1959); *Motetus Victimae Pascali Laudes* for Organ and Voice(s) ad libitum (1976; rev. 1988); *Fantasia for Organ* (1978–79); Concertino for Organ (1980); *Esercizi: Hommage à Domenico Scarlatti* for Harpsichord or Piano (1992). **VOCAL:** *Dialogue in Praise of the Owl and the Cuckoo* for Tenor and 7 Instruments (1947–48; rev. 1961; also for Bass and 4 Instruments, 1968); *Görög Ilona* for Chorus (1948; rev. 1971); *Concerto Rapsodico* for Alto or Mezzo-soprano and Chamber Orch. (1957); *Miorita* for High Voice, Women's Chorus ad libitum, and 5 Instruments (1963); *Missa* for Chorus and Organ (1966; 2nd version, 1986); *A Medieval Passion* for Alto, Bass, Chorus, and Orch. (1967); *Cantiunculae Amoris* for Tenor and String Quartet or String Orch. (1976); *Bilder der Jahreszeit* for High Voice and String Orch. (1981); *Suspirium ad Amorem*, 2 cantatas for Medium Voice(s), Chorus, and Chamber Orch. (1986); *3 Mediaeval Songs* for Alto or Baritone and Chamber Orch. (1987); *10 Lieder nach Hölderlin* for Medium Voice and Chamber Orch. (1987); *4 Lieder nach Hölderlin* for High Voice and Chamber Orch. (1989); *2 Kommentare zu Hölderlin* for High Voice and String Orch. (1989); various other choral works and song cycles.

Gabichvadze, Revaz (Kondratevich), Georgian composer; b. Tiflis, June 11, 1913. He was a student of Bagrinovsky, Shcherbachev, and Tuskia at the Tiflis Cons. (graduated, 1935), where he took postgraduate courses with Aranov and Ryazanov. In 1938 he joined its faculty, but he also was active as a theater conductor. He was founder-director of the State Light Orch. (1941–43), and also music ed. of the Georgian Radio. In 1967 he was named a People's Artist of the Georgian S.S.R. In his earlier compositions, Gabichvadze wrote in a traditional style which often utilized folk elements. Around 1960 he adopted an advanced style which partook of dodecaphonic and aleatoric techniques, as well as electronics and collage.

WORKS: DRAMATIC: *Nana*, opera (1949; rev. 1960); *Strekoza* (The Dragonfly), operetta (Sverdlovsk, Dec. 31, 1952); *Mï, materi mira: Vosstaniye Niobey* (We, Mothers of the World: The Revolt of Niobe), opera (1966); *Hamlet*, ballet (1971); incidental music; film scores. **ORCH.:** Sinfonietta (1935); *The Tutor*, symphonic poem (1944); Cello Concerto (1946); Violin Concerto (1947); 3 syms. (1963, 1966, 1972); 2 chamber syms. (1964, 1968). **CHAMBER:** 4 string quartets; violin pieces; Piano Sonata; Piano Preludes. **VOCAL:** *The Knight in the Tigerskin*, oratorio (1938); *3 Monologues about Lenin* for Bass, Women's Chorus, and Orch. (1970); songs.

Gabold, Ingolf, German-born Danish composer; b. Heidelberg, March 31, 1942. He studied theory and music history at the Royal Danish Cons. of Music in Copenhagen, and composition with Nørgård at the Århus Cons. His stated goal is to "combine music with Jung's depth psychology."

WORKS: DRAMATIC: *Syv scener til Orfeus* (7 Visions to Orpheus), opera for 4 Singers, Actor, Dancers, and Orch. (1969–70; Danish TV, Sept. 28, 1970); *Mod Vandmandens tegn* (Toward Aquarius), television play for Soprano, Bass, Chorus, and Organ (1971–72; Copenhagen, Nov. 11, 1973). **ORCH.:** *Atlantis* for Rock Group and Orch. (1971; Danish Radio, Feb. 4, 1972). **VOCAL:** *Visione* for 4 Soloists and Chorus (1962); *Für Louise* for Soprano and Chamber Orch. (1966; Copenhagen, Aug. 18, 1967); *Your Sister's Drown'd* for Soprano and Men's Chorus (1968); *Written in Sand* for Chorus (1973).

Gabrilowitsch, Ossip (Salomonovich), notable Russian-American pianist and conductor; b. St. Petersburg, Feb. 7, 1878; d. Detroit, Sept. 14, 1936. From 1888 to 1894 he was a pupil at the St. Petersburg Cons., studying piano with A. Rubinstein and composition with Navrátil, Liadov, and Glazunov; graduated as winner of the Rubinstein Prize, and then completed his piano training in Vienna with Leschetizky (1894–96). He subsequently toured Germany, Austria, Russia, France, and England. His first American tour (debut Carnegie Hall, N.Y., Nov. 12, 1900) was eminently successful, as were his 7 subsequent visits (1901–16). During the 1912–13 season, he gave in Europe a series of 6 historical concerts illustrating the development of the piano concerto from Bach to the present day; on his American tour in 1914–15, he repeated the entire series in several of the larger cities, meeting with an enthusiastic reception. On Oct. 6, 1909, he married the contralto Clara Clemens (daughter of Mark Twain), with whom he frequently appeared in joint recitals. He conducted his first N.Y. concert on Dec. 13, 1916; was appointed conductor of the Detroit Sym. Orch. in 1918. From 1928 he also conducted the Philadelphia Orch., sharing the baton with Leopold Stokowski, while retaining his Detroit position.

BIBL.: C. Clemens, *My Husband G.* (N.Y., 1938).

Gaburo, Kenneth (Louis), American composer and teacher; b. Somerville, N.J., July 5, 1926; d. Iowa City, Jan. 26, 1993. He studied composition, piano, and theory at the Eastman School of Music in Rochester, N.Y. (B.M., 1944; M.M., 1949), composition and conducting at the Conservatorio di Santa Cecilia in Rome (1954–55), and composition, theater, and linguistics at the Univ. of Ill., Urbana (D.M.A., 1962); he also studied composition at the Berkshire Music Center at Tanglewood (summer, 1956), and attended the Princeton Seminar in Advanced Musical Studies (summer, 1959). After teaching at Kent State Univ.

(1950), he was assoc. prof. at McNeese State Univ. (1950–54); then was a prof. at the Univ. of Ill. (1955–67) and at the Univ. of Calif. at San Diego (1967–75); also was founder-director of the Studio for Cognitive Studies in San Diego (1975–83) and a prof. at the Univ. of Iowa (from 1983). He was the recipient of a Fulbright fellowship (1954), ASCAP awards (from 1960), a Guggenheim fellowship (1967), and an NEA award (1975); in 1985 he received the Milhaud Chair fellowship at Mills College in Oakland, California. His music was quaquaversal.

WORKS: OPERAS: *The Snow Queen* (Lake Charles, La., May 5, 1952); *Blur* (Urbana, Ill., Nov. 7, 1956); *The Widow* (Urbana, Ill., Feb. 26, 1961). **ORCH.:** *3 Interludes* for Strings (Rochester, N.Y., May 27, 1948); *Concertante* for Piano and Orch. (Rochester, N.Y., April 29, 1949); *On a Quiet Theme* (1950; N.Y., Feb. 26, 1955); *Elegy* for Small Orch. (1956; N.Y., April 3, 1959); *Shapes and Sounds* (1960); *Antiphony IX (—a dot is no mere thing—)* for Orch., Children, and Tape (1984–85; Kansas City, Mo., Oct. 13, 1985). **CHAMBER:** *Music for 5 Instruments* for Flute, Clarinet, Trumpet, Trombone, and Piano (1954); *Ideas and Transformations No. 1* for Violin and Viola, *No. 2* for Violin and Cello, *No. 3* for Viola and Cello, and *No. 4* for Violin, Viola, and Cello (all 1955); String Quartet (1956); *Line Studies* for Flute, Clarinet, Viola, and Trombone (N.Y., Dec. 15, 1957). **ELECTRONIC AND TAPE:** *Antiphony I (Voices)* for 3 String Groups and Tape (1958), *II (Variations on a Poem of Cavafy)* for Soprano, Chorus, and Tape (1962), *III (Pearl-White Moments)* for Chamber Chorus and Tape (1963), *IV (Poised)* for Piccolo, Trombone, Double Bass, and Tape (1967), *V* for Piano and Tape (1968–89), *VI (Cogito)* for String Quartet, Slides, and 2- and 4-channel Tape (1971), *VII (—And)* for 4 Video Systems and 4-channel Tape (1974–89), *VIII (Revolution)* for Percussionist and Tape (1983–84), and *X (Winded)* for Organ and Tape (1985–89); numerous other works involving tape, actors, slides, film, lighting, and various acoustic instruments. **OTHER:** Vocal pieces.

Gade, Jacob, Danish conductor and composer; b. Vejle, Nov. 29, 1879; d. Copenhagen, Feb. 21, 1963. He studied violin; was a member of the N.Y. Sym. Orch. (1919–21); then returned to Copenhagen and was active as a conductor. Among his light compositions, *Jalousie* (1925) attained great popularity. He also wrote several symphonic poems.

BIBL.: K. Bjarnjof, *Tango Jalousie* (Copenhagen, 1969).

Gadzhibekov, Sultan, Azerbaijani conductor, pedagogue, and composer; b. Shusha, May 8, 1919; d. Baku, Sept. 19, 1974. He studied composition with B. Zeidman at the Baku Cons. (graduated, 1946), where he then taught instrumentation and composition, later becoming a prof. (1965) and rector (1966); also conducted the Azerbaijan Phil. (1955–62). He received state prizes for his ballet *Gulshen* (1952) and his *Concerto for Orchestra* (1970). He was named a People's Artist of the Azerbaijan S.S.R. (1960).

WORKS: DRAMATIC: *The Red Rose,* musical comedy (1940); *Iskender and the Shepherd,* children's opera (1947); *Gulshen,* ballet (1950). **ORCH.:** *Variations* (1941); 2 syms. (1944, 1946); *Caravan,* symphonic picture (1945); Violin Concerto (1945); Overture (1956); Concerto (1964); 3 suites: *Gulshen* (1953), *Bulgarian* (1957), and *Indian* (1970). **CHAMBER:** String Quartet (1943); 2 scherzos (1949). **PIANO:** Sonata (1940); *6 Preludes* (1941). **OTHER:** Vocal works.

BIBL.: D. Danilov, *S. G.* (Baku, 1956); E. Abasova, *S. G.* (Baku, 1965); A. Tagizade, *S. G.* (Baku, 1967).

Gadzhibekov, Uzeir, Azerbaijani composer; b. Agdzhabedy, near Shusha, Sept. 17, 1885; d. Baku, Nov. 23, 1948. He studied in Shusha; then lived in Baku, where he produced his first opera on a native subject, *Leyly and Medzhnun* (Jan. 25, 1908). His comic opera *Arshin Mal Alan* (Baku, Nov. 27, 1913) had numerous performances; another opera, *Kyor-Oglu* (A Blind Man's Son), was premiered at the Azerbaijan Festival in Moscow (April 30, 1937).

Gadzhiev, (Akhmed) Jevdet, Azerbaijani composer; b. Nukha, June 18, 1917. He studied with M. Rudolf and U. Gadzhibekov at the Baku Cons. (1936–38), and with Anatoli Alexandrov, S. Vasilenko, and Shostakovich at the Moscow Cons. (1938–41; graduated, 1947); then taught composition at the Baku Cons., where he later was a prof. (from 1963) and rector (until 1969). He received state prizes for his opera *Veten* (1946) and the symphonic poem *For Peace* (1952). He was made a People's Artist of the Azerbaijan S.S.R. (1960).

WORKS: DRAMATIC: *Veten,* opera (1945; in collaboration with K. Karayev); *Ghazal My Flower* (1956); *The Maiden Gathering Apples* (1957). **ORCH.:** 3 symphonic poems: *Azerbaijan* (1936), *Epistle to Siberia* (1937), and *For Peace* (1951); Sinfonietta (1938); *Azerbaijan Suite* (1941); 5 syms. (1944; 1946; 1947; *In Memory of Lenin,* 1956; *Man, Earth, Universe,* 1971). **CHAMBER:** *Fugue* (1940); *3 Fugues* (1941); String Quartet (1941); *Quartet Poem* (1961). **PIANO:** *24 Preludes* (1935); *Ballade* (1950); Sonata (1956); *Scherzo* (1957); *Children's Corner Suite* (1962). **OTHER:** Vocal works.

BIBL.: E. Muradova, *J. G.* (Baku, 1962); K. Abezgauz, *J. G.* (Baku, 1965); E. Abasova, *J. G.* (Baku, 1967).

Gage, Irwin, American pianist and teacher; b. Cleveland, Sept. 4, 1939. He studied with Eugene Bossart at the Univ. of Mich., with Ward Davenny at Yale Univ., and with Erik Werba, Hilde Langer-Rühl, Kurt Schmidek, and Klaus Vokurka at the Vienna Academy of Music. He subsequently acquired a fine reputation as an accompanist to the leading singers of the day, with whom he appeared in all the principal music centers of the globe. He also was a prof. at the Zürich Cons. and gave master classes around the world.

Gagnebin, Henri, Swiss music educator and composer; b. Liège (of Swiss parents), March 13, 1886; d. Geneva, June 2, 1977. He studied organ with Vierne and composition with d'Indy at the Paris Cons. He was organist in Paris (1910–16) and in Lausanne (1916–25). From 1925 to 1957 he was director of the Geneva Cons. In 1938 he founded the Geneva International Competition, which he served as president until 1959. He was the author of *Entretiens sur la musique* (Geneva, 1943), *Musique, mon beau souci* (Paris, 1968), and *Orgue, musette et bourbon* (Neuchâtel, 1975).

WORKS: ORCH.: 4 syms. (1911; 1918–21; 1955; 1970); Suite (1936); *3 Tableaux symphoniques d'après F. Hodler* (1942); *Suite d'orchestre sur des psaumes huguenots* (1950); Piano Concerto (1951); Clarinet Concerto (1971); Concerto for Oboe, Bassoon, and Strings (1972). **CHAMBER:** Violin Sonata (1915); 3 string quartets (1916–17; 1924; 1927); Cello Sonata (1922); Suite for Cello (1932); Trio for Piano, Flute, and Cello (1941); Quartet for Piano, Flute, Violin, and Cello (1961); String Trio (1968); Wind Octet (1970); Brass Quintet (1970); Wind Sextet (1971). **KEYBOARD: PIANO:** Suite (1936). **ORGAN:** *100 Pièces sur des psaumes huguenots* (1940–64). **VOCAL:** Choruses; songs.

Gaigerova, Varvara, Russian pianist and composer; b. Oryekhovo-Zuyevo, Oct. 17, 1903; d. Moscow, April 6, 1944. She studied piano at the Moscow Cons. with Neuhaus and composition with Miaskovsky. In most of her compositions, she cultivated folk materials of the constituent republics of the U.S.S.R., including those of the Mongol populations of Siberia and Central Asia.

WORKS: ORCH.: 3 syms. (1928, 1934, 1937); 3 suites for Domra Ensembles (1932, 1934, 1935). **CHAMBER:** 2 string quartets (1927, 1947); piano pieces. **VOCAL:** *The Sun of Socialism,* cantata (1932); some 150 songs.

Gaillard, Marius-François, French composer and conductor; b. Paris, Oct. 13, 1900; d. Evecquemont, Yvelines, July 23, 1973. He studied with Diémer and Leroux at the Paris Cons. He began his career as a pianist; then conducted concerts in Paris (1928–49). He traveled all over the world, collecting examples of primitive music. His compositions follow a neo-impressionist trend.

WORKS: BALLETS: *La Danse pendant le festin* (1924); *Détresse* (1932). **ORCH.:** 3 syms.; *Guyanes,* symphonic suite (1925); *Images d'Epinal* for Piano and Orch. (1929); *Concerto* *classique* for Cello and Orch. (1950); *Tombeau romantique* for Piano and Orch. (1954); *Concerto leggero* for Violin and Orch. (1954); *Concerto agreste* for Viola and Orch. (1957); Harp Concerto (1960). **CHAMBER:** Violin Sonata (1923); String Trio (1935); *Sonate baroque* for Violin and Piano (1950); piano pieces. **VOCAL:** Many songs.

Gaito, Constantino, Argentine composer and teacher; b. Buenos Aires, Aug. 3, 1878; d. there, Dec. 14, 1945. He studied in Naples with Platania; lived in Buenos Aires as a teacher; wrote the operas (all premiered in Buenos Aires) *Shafras* (1907), *I Doria* (1915), *I paggi di Sua Maesta* (1918), *Caio Petronio* (Sept. 2, 1919), *Flor de nieve* (Aug. 3, 1922), *Ollantay* (July 23, 1926), *Lazaro* (1929), and *La sangre de las guitarras* (Aug. 17, 1932); also *La flor del Irupe*, ballet (July 17, 1929); *San Francisco Solano*, oratorio (1940); *El ombu*, symphonic poem (1924); songs; piano pieces.

Gál, Hans, Austrian musicologist and composer; b. Brunn, near Vienna, Aug. 5, 1890; d. Edinburgh, Oct. 3, 1987. He studied with Mandyczewski and Adler at at the Univ. of Vienna, where he lectured (1919–29); then was director of the Mainz Cons. (1929–33). He returned to Vienna in 1933; after the Anschluss, he was compelled to leave Vienna in 1938, and settled in Edinburgh, where he lectured on music at the Univ. (1945–65) while continuing to compose.

WRITINGS: *Anleitung zum Partiturlesen* (Vienna, 1923; Eng. tr., 1924, as *Directions for Score-Reading*); *The Golden Age of Vienna* (London, 1948); *Johannes Brahms* (Frankfurt am Main, 1961; Eng. tr., 1964); *Richard Wagner* (Frankfurt am Main, 1963); *The Musician's World: Great Composers in Their Letters* (London, 1965; Ger. tr., 1966); *Franz Schubert, oder Die Melodie* (Frankfurt am Main, 1970; Eng. tr., 1974); *Giuseppe Verdi und die Oper* (Frankfurt am Main, 1982).

WORKS: OPERAS: *Der Arzt der Sobeide* (Breslau, 1919); *Die heilige Ente* (Düsseldorf, April 29, 1923); *Das Lied der Nacht* (Breslau, April 24, 1926); *Der Zauberspiegel* (Breslau, 1930; also as an orch. suite); *Die beiden Klaas* (1933). **ORCH.:** 4 syms. (1928, 1949, 1952, 1975); Violin Concerto (1931); *A Pickwickian Overture* (1939); Cello Concerto (1944); Piano Concerto (1947); Concertino for Organ and Strings (1948); Concertino for Cello and Strings (1965); *Idyllikon* for Small Orch. (1969); *Triptych* (1970). **CHAMBER:** Piano Quartet (1915); 4 string quartets (1916, 1929, 1969, 1971); Violin Sonata (1921); String Trio (1931); Piano Trio (1948). **VOCAL:** Numerous sacred and secular choral works.

BIBL.: W. Waldstein, *H. G.* (Vienna, 1965); *H. G. zum 100. Geburtstag* (Mainz, 1990).

Galajikian, Florence Grandland, American pianist and composer; b. Maywood, Ill., July 29, 1900; d. River Forest, Ill., Nov. 16, 1970. She studied at Northwestern Univ. and Chicago Musical College; her teachers were Oldberg, Lutkin, Rubin Goldmark, Carl Beecher, and Noelte. She toured as a pianist; composed a number of songs which enjoyed favor among sopranos; she also wrote orch. pieces. Her *Symphonic Intermezzo* was awarded NBC's 4th prize, and was performed by the NBC Sym. Orch. on May 8, 1932.

Galamian, Ivan (Alexander), eminent Armenian-born American violinist and pedagogue; b. Tabriz, Persia (of Armenian parents), Feb. 5, 1903; d. N.Y., April 14, 1981. He studied with Konstantin Mostras at the school of Moscow's Phil. Soc. (1916–22); then attended Lucien Capet's master course in Paris (1922–23), making his formal debut there (1924). He taught at the Russian Cons. (1925–39) and at the École Normale de Musique (1936–39) there. He settled in N.Y. (1939), becoming a teacher at the Henry St. Settlement School (1941); was later named to the faculty of the Curtis Inst. of Music in Philadelphia (1944) and of the Juilliard School of Music in N.Y. (1946); was also founder of the Meadowmount School for string players in Westport, N.Y. (1944). Among his numerous students were Itzhak Perlman, Michael Rabin, Kyung-Wha Chung, Erick Friedman, Miriam Fried, Pinchas Zuckerman, Young-Uck Kim, and Jaime Laredo. He publ. *Principles of Violin Playing and Teaching* (with E. Green; Englewood Cliffs, N.J., 1962; 2nd ed., rev., 1985) and *Contemporary Violin Technique* (with F. Neumann; 2 vols., N.Y., 1966, 1977).

BIBL.: R. Schmidt, "The Legacy of I. G.," *American String Teacher*, XXXV/2 (1985); E. Green et al., *Miraculous Teacher: I. G. and the Meadowmount Experience* (Ann Arbor, 1993).

Galas, Diamanda (Dimitria Angeliki Elena), remarkable American avant-garde composer and vocalist of Greek descent; b. San Diego, Aug. 29, 1955. She studied biochemistry, psychology, music, and experimental performance at the Univ. of Calif. at San Diego (1974–79); she also took private vocal lessons. In her scientific studies, she and a group of medical students began investigating extreme mental states, using themselves as subjects in a series of bizarre mind-altering experiments; her resultant understanding of psychopathology (notably schizophrenia and psychosis) became an underlying subject in most of her work. After some success as a jazz pianist, she began a vocal career, in which her remarkable precision and advanced technique attracted attention. Although she has performed such demanding works as Xenakis's microtonal *N'Shima* (Brooklyn, Jan. 15, 1981) and Globokar's *Misère* (Cologne, 1980), she is best known for her theatrical performances of her own solo vocal works, given at venues ranging from the Donaueschingen Festival to the N.Y. rock club Danceteria. Her compositions, most of which employ live electronics and/or tape, are improvised according to rigorous, complex "navigation(s) through specified mental states." Her performances have stringent requirements for lighting and sound and possess a shattering intensity. Her brother Philip Dimitri Galas, a playwright whose works were as violent as is his sister's music, died of AIDS in the late 1980s; her increasing emotional and political involvement in what she regards as this "modern plague" led to her 4-part work *Masque of the Red Death* (1986–). She publ. an aesthetic statement as "Intravenal Song" in *Perspectives of New Music*, XX (1981).

WORKS: *Medea tarantula* for Voice (1977); *Les Yeux sans sang* for Voice and Electronics (1978); *Tragouthia apo to aima exoun fonos* (Song from the Blood of Those Murdered) for Voice and Tape (1981); *Wild Women with Steak Knives* for Tape and Live Electronics (1981–83); *Litanies of Satan* for Voice, Tape, and Live Electronics (1982); *Panoptikon* for Voice, Tape, and Live Electronics (1982–83); *Masque of the Red Death* for Voice, Electronics, and Instrument (*The Divine Punishment, Saint of the Pit, You Must Be Certain of the Devil*, and a 4th work in progress; 1986–).

BIBL.: L. Morra, "D. G.: Rebellious Soprano," *East Village Eye* (March 1983); S. Holden, "D. G., Avant-garde Diva," *N.Y. Times* (July 19, 1985); J. Johnson and B. Coley, "D. G.: Tura Satana without Cleavage," *Forced Exposure*, XV (1989).

Galeffi, Carlo, esteemed Italian baritone; b. Malamocco, near Venice, June 4, 1882; d. Rome, Sept. 22, 1961. He was a student of Sbrigilia in Paris and of Cotogni in Rome. In 1903 he made his operatic debut in Rome as Enrico, and then won success in Naples as Amonasro and Rigoletto. On Nov. 29, 1910, he made his only appearance at the Metropolitan Opera in N.Y. as Germont. In 1911 he sang in the premiere of Mascagni's *Isabeau* in Buenos Aires. From 1912 to 1938 he was a leading member of Milan's La Scala, winning particular distinction in such roles as Tell, Rigoletto, Boccanegra, Nabucco, Luna, and Germont; he also created the roles of Manfredo in Montemezzi's *L'amore dei tre Re* (1913) and Fanuel in Boito's *Nerone* (1924). His operatic farewell performance took place in 1954.

BIBL.: A. Marchetti, *C.G.: Una vita per el canto* (Rome, 1973).

Gales, Weston (Spies), American organist and conductor; b. Elizabeth, N.J., Nov. 5, 1877; d. Portsmouth, N.H., Oct. 21, 1939. He studied with Horatio Parker (theory and composition), Samuel Sanford (piano), and Gaston-Marie Déthier (organ) at Yale Univ., graduating in 1898; he later pursued his organ studies in Paris with Widor (1908) and Vierne (1912). He was a church organist and choirmaster in N.Y. (1898–1908) and Boston (1908–13); then founder-conductor of the Detroit Sym. Orch. (1914–18); and later assoc. conductor of the N.Y. State Sym. Orch. (1924–28).

Galimir, Felix, Austrian-born American violinist and pedagogue; b. Vienna, May 12, 1910. He studied with Adolf Bak at the Vienna Cons. (diploma, 1928) and with Carl Flesch in Berlin and Baden-Baden (1929–30). In 1929 he founded the Galimir String Quartet in Vienna. Emigrating to the U.S. in 1938, he made his debut at N.Y.'s Town Hall, and also organized a new Galimir String Quartet, which subsequently acquired a fine reputation for its performances of contemporary music. He became a naturalized American citizen in 1944. He was 1st violinist of the NBC Sym. Orch. in N.Y. (1939–54), concertmaster of the Sym. of the Air in N.Y. (1954–56), and a performer and teacher at the Marlboro (Vt.) Festival and Music School (from 1954). He held teaching positions at the Juilliard School of Music in N.Y. (from 1962), the Curtis Inst. of Music in Philadelphia (from 1972), and the Mannes College of Music in N.Y. (from 1977), where his quartet was in residence.

Galindo (Dimas), Blas, noted Mexican composer and pedagogue; b. San Gabriel, Jalisco, Feb. 3, 1910; d. Mexico City, April 19, 1993. He was 7 when he began his musical training with Antonio Velasco; in 1931 he entered the Conservatorio Nacional de Música de México in Mexico City, where he studied with José Rolón (harmony, counterpoint, and fugue), Candelario Huizar (analysis and orchestration), César Chávez (composition), and Rodríguez Vizcarra (piano), and graduated with highest honors in 1944; he also attended Copland's composition classes at the Berkshire Music Center in Tanglewood (summers, 1941, 1942). With Daniel Ayala, Salvador Contreras, and José Pablo Moncayo, he was a founder-member of the contemporary music group El Grupo de los Cuatro (1935–40). In 1944 he became a teacher at the Conservatorio Nacional de Música de México, where he later was its director (1947–61). In 1966 he became a founder-member of the Mexican National Academy of the Arts. The Mexican government honored him with the National Award of Arts and Sciences in 1964. In his extensive output, he displayed a genuine respect for traditional forms. The folkloric element of his early works gave way to a sophisticated use of dissonance without abandoning accessibility.

WORKS: DRAMATIC: BALLETS: *Entre sombras anda el fuego* (Mexico City, March 23, 1940); *Danza de las fuerzas nuevas* (1940); *El zánate* (Mexico City, Dec. 6, 1947); *La manda* (Mexico City, March 31, 1951); *El sueño y la presencia* (Mexico City, Nov. 24, 1951); *La hija del yori* (1952); *El maleficio* (Mexico City, Oct. 28, 1954). **THEATER:** *Astucia* (1948); *Los signos del zodiaco* (1951). Also incidental music. **ORCH.:** *Obra para orquesta mexicana* (1938); *Sones de mariachi* for Small Orch. (1940; also for Large Orch., 1941); 2 piano concertos: No. 1 (Mexico City, July 24, 1942) and No. 2 (1961; Mexico City, Aug. 17, 1962); *Nocturno* (1945); *Arrullo* for Strings (1945); *Don Quijote* (1947); *Homenaje a Cervantes*, suite (1947); *Poema de Neruda* for Strings (1948); *Pequeñas variaciones* (1951); 3 syms.: No. 1, *Sinfonía breve* or *Pequeña sinfonía* for Strings (Mexico City, Aug. 22, 1952), No. 2 (Caracas, March 19, 1957), and No. 3 (Washington, D.C., April 30, 1961); *Obertura mexicana* No. 1 (1953), No. 2 (1981), and No. 3 (1982); 2 flute concertos: No. 1 with Orch. (1960, New Orleans, April 3, 1965) and No. 2 with Symphonic Band (1979); *4 Pieces* (1961; Mexico City, Nov. 15, 1963); Violin Concerto (1962; Mexico City, Sept. 13, 1970); *3 Pieces* for Clarinet and Orch. (1962); Overture for Organ and Strings (1963); *3 Pieces* for Horn and Orch. (1963); Concertino for Electric Guitar and Orch. (1973; Mexico City, June 12, 1977); *Tríptico* for Strings (1974); Concertino for Violin and Strings (1978); *Homenaje a Juan Rulfo* (1980); Cello Concerto (1984); Suite for Chamber Orch. (1985); Concerto for Guitar and Symphonic Band (1988); *Homenaje a Rodolfo Halffter* (1989); *Popocatepetl*, symphonic poem for Soprano, Tenor, and Orch. (1990). **CHAMBER:** Suite for Violin and Cello (1933); Quartet for Cellos (1936); *Bosquejos* for Oboe, Clarinet, Horn, and Bassoon (1937); *Dos preludios* for Oboe, English Horn, and Piano (1938); *Sexteto de alientos* for Flute, Clarinet, Bassoon, Horn, Trumpet, and Trombone (1941); Violin Sonata (1945); Cello Sonata (1948); Suite for Violin and Piano (1957); Quintet for Bow Instruments and Piano (1957); *Tres sonsonetes* for Wind Quintet and Tape (1967); Quartet for Bow Instruments (1970); *Titoco-tico* for Native Percussion (1971); *Invenciones* for Brass Quintet (1977); *3 Pieces* for Percussion (1980); Sonata for Solo Cello (1981); Wind Quintet (1982); Duo for Violin and Cello (1984). Also many piano pieces, including a Sonata (1976); organ music. **VOCAL:** *Primavera* for Children's Chorus and Band or Piano (1944); *Arullo* for Voices and Orch. (1945); *A la patria* for Chorus and Orch. (1946); *Homenaje a Juárez* for Soprano, Tenor, Bass, Reciter, Chorus, and Orch. (1957); *A la independencia* for Soprano, Alto, Tenor, Bass, Chorus, and Strings (1960); *Tríptico Teotihuacan* for Soprano, Baritone, Chorus, Band, and Native Instruments (1964); *Letanía erótica para La Paz* for Narrator, Alto, Tenor, Bass, Chorus, Organ, and Orch. (1965); *Homenaje a Rubén Darío* for Reciter and String Orch. (1966); *Homenaje a Rufino Tamayo* for Tenor and Orch. (1987).

BIBL.: X. Ortiz, *B. G.: Biografía, antología de textos y catálogo* (Mexico City, 1994).

Galkin, Elliott W(ashington), American conductor, music critic, and educator; b. N.Y., Feb. 22, 1921; d. Baltimore, May 24, 1990. He studied at Brooklyn College (B.A., 1943); then served with the U.S. Air Force (1943–46); was stationed in France, and received conducting diplomas from the Paris Cons. (1948) and the École Normale de Musique (1948). Returning to the U.S., he studied at Cornell Univ. (M.A., 1950; Ph.D., 1960, with the diss. *The Theory and Practice of Orchestral Conducting from 1752*). During 1955–56, he was an apprentice conductor with the Vienna State Opera; in 1956 he joined the faculty of Goucher College in Towson, Md.; served as chairman of the music dept. (1960–77) and as a prof. (1964–77). In 1957 he joined the faculty of the Peabody Cons. of Music in Baltimore as a conductor; was chairman of the music history and literature dept. (1964–77); also was director of musical activities and a prof. at Johns Hopkins Univ. (from 1968). From 1977 to 1982 he served as director of the Peabody Cons. of Music, and subsequently was director of its graduate program in music criticism. He also was active as conductor of the Baltimore Chamber Orch. (from 1960) and served as music ed. and critic of the *Baltimore Sun* (1962–77). In 1972 and 1975 he received ASCAP-Deems Taylor Awards, and in 1982 was awarded the George Foster Peabody Medal for outstanding contributions to music. He publ. the valuable study *A History of Orchestral Conducting* (Stuyvesant, N.Y., 1988).

Gall (real name, **Galle**), **Yvonne,** French soprano; b. Paris, March 6, 1885; d. there, Aug. 21, 1972. She studied at the Paris Cons. She made her operatic debut at the Paris Opéra in 1908 as Mathilde, and remained on its roster until 1935; also sang at the Opéra-Comique in Paris (1921–34). From 1918 to 1921 she was a member of the Chicago Grand Opera, then sang in San Francisco (1931). After her retirement, she taught voice at the Paris Cons. She was highly successful in the French and Italian operatic repertoire. In 1958 she married **Henri Büsser**, who, although much older, outlived her and reached the age of 101.

Galla-Rini, Anthony, American accordionist, composer, and arranger; b. Manchester, Conn., Jan. 18, 1904. He began his musical training with his father, a bandmaster; from the age of 6 he played the accordion and other instruments on tours of the U.S. and Canada. He studied harmony with John Van Broekhaven in N.Y. (1918) and theory and conducting with Gaston Usigli at the San Francisco Cons. (1933). As a champion of the accordion as a classical instrument, he was the first to give accordion recitals in the major music centers. He was also the first accordionist to appear as a soloist with a sym. orch. when he gave the premiere of his own 1st Accordion Concerto in Oklahoma City on Nov. 15, 1941. He made many technical improvements for his instrument. Among his books were a *Method for Accordion* (1931), an *Accordion Course* (1955–56), the *Galla-Rini Accordion Primer* (1958), and *A Collection of Lectures* (1981). He composed 2 accordion concertos (1941, 1976), an Accordion Sonata (1981), and solo accordion pieces; he also prepared numerous transcriptions for the accordion.

BIBL.: O. Hahn, *A. G.-R.* (Stockholm, 1986).

Galli-Curci, Amelita, brilliant Italian soprano; b. Milan, Nov. 18, 1882; d. La Jolla, Calif., Nov. 26, 1963. She studied in Milan and intended to be a pianist; graduated in 1903 from the Milan Cons., winning 1st prize. She then had a few voice lessons with Carignani and Dufes, and received advice from Mascagni and William Thorner. She made her operatic debut in Trani as Gilda (Dec. 26, 1906), then sang in various opera houses in Italy and in South America (1910). She continued her successful career as an opera singer in Europe until 1915; then made a sensationally successful U.S. debut with the Chicago Opera Co. as Gilda (Nov. 18, 1916); made her first appearance with the Metropolitan Opera in N.Y. as Violetta (Nov. 14, 1921); remained as a member of the Metropolitan until 1930, and then toured as a recitalist. She was married to the painter Luigi Curci (1910; divorced 1920) and to Homer Samuels, her accompanist.

BIBL.: C. LeMassena, *G.-C.'s Life of Song* (N.Y., 1945).

Gallico, Paolo, Italian-American pianist, teacher, and composer; b. Trieste, May 13, 1868; d. N.Y., July 6, 1955. At the age of 15, he gave a recital at Trieste; then studied at the Vienna Cons. under Julius Epstein, graduating at 18 with highest honors. After successful concerts throughout Europe, he settled in N.Y. in 1892 as a pianist and teacher; toured the U.S. frequently as pianist in recitals and as a soloist with the principal orchs. He wrote an oratorio, *The Apocalypse* (N.Y., Nov. 22, 1922); a symphonic episode, *Euphorion* (Los Angeles, April 6, 1923); an opera, *Harlekin* (1926); piano pieces; and songs. His son, Paul Gallico, was a well-known writer.

Galliera, Alceo, Italian conductor and composer; b. Milan, May 3, 1910. He studied piano, organ, and composition at the Milan Cons., and then was on its faculty. After World War II, he appeared as a conductor throughout Europe and South America; was music director of the Victorian Sym. Orch. in Melbourne (1950–51), at the Teatro Carlo Felice in Genoa (1957–60), and of the Strasbourg Phil. (1964–71). He wrote a ballet, orch. pieces, chamber music, and songs.

Gallo, Fortune, Italian-American impresario; b. Torremaggiore, May 9, 1878; d. N.Y., March 28, 1970. After piano studies, he emigrated to the U.S. in 1895. In 1909 he founded the San Carlo Opera Co., which toured throughout the U.S. until it disbanded in 1955. In 1926 he built the Gallo Theater in N.Y. He was a pioneering figure in the production of operatic sound films, *Pagliacci* being the first such effort in 1928.

Gallois-Montbrun, Raymond, French violinist, music educator, and composer; b. Saigon, Aug. 15, 1918; d. Paris, Aug. 13, 1994. He studied at the Paris Cons. (1929–39) with Firmin Touche (violin), Büsser (composition), and Jean and Noël Gallon (theory). In 1944 he won the Prix de Rome with his cantata *Louise de la miséricorde*. He made concert tours in Europe, and also played in Japan and Africa. He served as director of the Versailles Cons. (1957–62), and then of the Paris Cons. (1962–83).In 1980 he was made a member of the Académie des Beaux-Arts.

WORKS: DRAMATIC: *Le Rossignol et l'Empereur*, chamber opera (1959); *Stella ou le Piège de sable*, opera (1964). **ORCH.:** *Symphonie concertante* for Violin and Orch. (1949); *Symphonie japonaise* (1951); Violin Concerto (1957); *Le Port de Delft*, symphonic poem (1960); Cello Concerto (1961); *Les Ménines*, symphonic poem (1961); Piano Concerto (1964). **OTHER:** *Louise de la miséricorde*, cantata for 3 Soloists and Orch. (1944); *Tableaux indochinois* for String Quartet (1946) and other chamber pieces.

Gallon, Jean, French composer and pedagogue, brother of **Noël Gallon**; b. Paris, June 25, 1878; d. there, June 23, 1959. He studied piano with Diémer and theory with Lavignac and Lenepveu at the Paris Cons. He was chorus master of the Paris Société des Concerts du Conservatoire (1906–14) and at the Paris Opéra (1909–14). From 1919 to 1949 he taught harmony at the Paris Cons. Among his pupils were Robert Casadesus, Marcel Delannoy, Henri Dutilleux, Olivier Messiaen, and Jean Rivier. He publ. harmony exercises for use at the Cons.; with his brother, he composed several pieces of theater music, among them a ballet, *Hansli le Bossu* (1914); also composed some chamber music and songs.

Gallon, Noël, French composer and pedagogue, brother of **Jean Gallon**; b. Paris, Sept. 11, 1891; d. there, Dec. 26, 1966. He studied piano with Philipp and Risler, and theory with Caussade, Lenepveu, and Tabaud at the Paris Cons. In 1910 he received the 1st Prix de Rome. From 1920 he was on the faculty of the Paris Cons. as an instructor in solfège, counterpoint, and fugue. As a composer, he was influenced by his brother, his first tutor in music, with whom he wrote a ballet, *Hansli le Bossu* (1914); his own works comprise a few symphonic pieces; Suite for Flute and Piano (1921); Quintet for Horn and Strings (1953); teaching pieces.

Galpin, Francis W(illiam), English writer on music; b. Dorchester, Dorset, Dec. 25, 1858; d. Richmond, Surrey, Dec. 30, 1945. He graduated with classical honors from Trinity College, Cambridge (B.A., 1882; M.A., 1885); received his music education from Garrett and Sterndale Bennett. He held various posts as vicar and canon (1891–1921); wrote many articles on early instruments for *Music & Letters* and *Monthly Musical Record* (1930–33). A Galpin Soc. was formed in London in 1946 with the object of bringing together all those interested in the history of European instruments and to commemorate the pioneer work of Galpin; it publishes the *Galpin Society Journal* (1948–). In addition to his numerous monographs, Galpin was the editor of the revised and augmented ed. of Stainer's *Music of the Bible* (1913).

WRITINGS: *Descriptive Catalogue of the European Instruments in the Metropolitan Museum of Art, N.Y.* (1902); *The Musical Instruments of the American Indians of the North West Coast* (1903); *Notes on the Roman Hydraulus* (1904); *The Evolution of the Sackbut* (1907); *Old English Instruments of Music* (1910; 4th ed., rev., 1965, by T. Dart); *A Textbook of European Musical Instruments* (1937); *The Music of the Sumerians, Babylonians and Assyrians* (1937); *The Music of Electricity* (1938).

Galway, James, famous Irish flutist; b. Belfast, Dec. 8, 1939. He took up the tin whistle at 7 and began playing the flute in a neighborhood flute band when he was 9. He then went to London on a scholarship, where he studied with John Francis at the Royal College of Music (1956–59) and with Geoffrey Gilbert at the Guildhall School of Music and Drama (1959–60); a 2nd scholarship allowed him to proceed to Paris to continue his training with Gaston Crunelle at the Cons. and privately with Marcel Moyse and Jean-Pierre Rampal. He was a flutist in the orchs. of the Sadler's Wells Opera (1961–66) and the Royal Opera, Covent Garden (1965), in London; after playing in the London Sym. Orch. (1966–67) and the Royal Phil. of London (1967–69), he was a member of the Berlin Phil. (1969–75). Thereafter he pursued a brilliant career as a flute virtuoso, making highly successful tours all over the world. In later years, he also took up conducting. He publ. *James Galway: An Autobiography* (London, 1978) and *Flute* (London, 1982). In 1977 he was made an Officer of the Order of the British Empire and in 1987 an Officier des Arts et Lettres of France. Galway's repertory ranges over a vast expanse of music, including not only the classics and contemporary scores, but traditional Irish music and popular fare.

Gamba, Piero (actually, **Pierino**), Italian conductor; b. Rome, Sept. 16, 1936. From a musical family (his father was a professional violinist), he was trained at home; his precocity was so remarkable that he was reportedly able to read an orch. score at the age of 8, and at 9 conducted a regular sym. concert in

Rome. He also composed. Unlike the talent of so many child musicians, his gift did not evaporate with puberty; he became a professional artist. According to ecstatic press reports, he conducted in 40 countries and 300 cities, so that his name became familiar to uncounted multitudes (including a billion people in China). From 1970 to 1981 he served as music director of the Winnipeg Sym. Orch.; from 1982 to 1987 he was principal conductor of the Adelaide (Australia) Sym. Orch.

Ganche, Edouard, French physician and writer on music; b. Baulon, Ille-et-Vilaine, Oct. 13, 1880; d. Lyons, May 31, 1945. He was trained in medicine but also received instruction in music in Paris from Imbert and Expert. Although a practicing physician, he devoted much time to the study of Chopin, and was ed. of the Oxford edition of Chopin's works (3 vols., 1928–32).

WRITINGS (all publ. in Paris): *La Vie de Frédéric Chopin dans son oeuvre: Sa liaison avec George Sand* (1909); *Frédéric Chopin: Sa vie et ses oeuvres, 1810–1849* (1909; 3rd ed., 1949); *La Pologne et Frédéric Chopin* (1921); *Dans le souvenir de Frédéric Chopin* (1925); *Souffrances de Frédéric Chopin: Essai de medicine et de psychologie* (1934; 2nd ed., 1935); *Voyages avec Frédéric Chopin* (1934).

Gandini, Gerardo, Argentine composer, pianist, and teacher; b. Buenos Aires, Oct. 16, 1932. He studied with Pia Sebastini, Roberto Caamaño, and Ginastera in Buenos Aires (1956–59); completed studies in Rome with Petrassi (1966–67). He taught in Buenos Aires and N.Y. As a pianist, he specialized in contemporary music.

WORKS: CHAMBER OPERA: *La Pasión de Buster Keaton* (1978). **ORCH.:** *Variations* (1962); *Música nocturna II* for Chamber Orch. (1965); *Cadencias I* for Violin and Chamber Orch. (1966) and *II* for Chamber Orch. (1967); *Mutantes I* for Chamber Orch. (1966); *Fuggevole* for Chamber Orch. (1967); *Contrastes* for 2 Pianos and Orch. (1968); *Fases* for Clarinet and Orch. (1969); *Fantasie-Impromptu*, "imaginary portrait of Chopin" for Piano and Orch. (1970); Guitar Concerto (1975; Washington, D.C., May 18, 1976); Piano Concerto (Washington, D.C., April 25, 1980); *Soria Moria II* for Strings (1981); Concerto for Flute, Guitar, and Orch. (1986). **CHAMBER:** *Concertino I* for Clarinet, String Trio, and Percussion, *II* for Flute and Instruments, and *III* for Harpsichord and Instruments (1962–63); *Musica nocturna I* for Flute, Piano, and String Trio (1964); *L'Adieu* for Piano, Vibraphone, 3 Percussionists, and Conductor (1967); *A Cow in a Mondrian Painting* for Flute and Instruments (1967); *Soria Moria* for Variable Instrumental Ensemble (1968); *Play* for Piano and an Instrument (1969); *Piange e sospira* for Flute, Violin, Clarinet, and Piano (1970); *Il concertino* for Flute and Instruments (1971); *Lunario sentimental* for Violin, Cello, and Piano (1989).

Ganelin, Viacheslav, Russian pianist and composer; b. Kraskovo, 1944. He graduated from the Lithuanian State Cons. in Vilnius and was music director of the Russian Dramatic Theater. He wrote much theater music, film scores, an opera, *The Red-Haired Liar and the Soldier*, and a rock musical, *The Devilish Bride*. When he met the percussionist Vladimir Tarasov (b. Archangelsk, 1947) in Vilnius, the 2 formed what was to be the basis of the Ganelin Trio; after playing at the Jazz Club in Sverdlovsk in the early 1960s, they were joined by Chaksin (b. Sverdlovsk, 1947), a graduate of the Sverdlovsk Cons. The Ganelin Trio has an eclectic and ironic style, synthesizing strong formal structural ideas with improvisation and stressing constant innovation and Ganelin's conviction that the 2 most important elements of jazz are "swing and improvisation." Ganelin himself plays the piano and basset horn, providing harmony and bassline; Tarasov, on percussion, states the rhythms; Chaksin controls the melodic line, strongly influenced by Ornette Coleman and John Coltrane, on an assortment of reeds, flute, trombone, and violin. In time, the trio was widely acclaimed on its visits to European jazz festivals.

Gange, Fraser, distinguished Scottish-American baritone and pedagogue; b. Dundee, June 17, 1886; d. Baltimore, July 1, 1962. He studied with his father in Dundee and with Amy Sherwin in London. After making his debut at 16, he toured in England, Scotland, Australia, and New Zealand. On Jan. 18, 1924, he made his U.S. debut in N.Y., and subsequently toured as an oratorio and lieder artist. He also taught at the Peabody Cons. of Music in Baltimore (1931–57) and at the Juilliard School of Music in N.Y. (summers, 1932–46).

Gann, Kyle (Eugene), American music critic and composer; b. Dallas, Nov. 21, 1955. His mother was a piano teacher and his first teacher; he studied formally with Randolph Coleman at the Oberlin (Ohio) College Cons. of Music (B.Mus., 1977) and with Peter Gena at Northwestern Univ. (M.Mus., 1981; D.Mus., 1983); also privately with Ben Johnston and Morton Subotnick. He began writing free-lance music criticism for a variety of Chicago newspapers, and in 1986 joined the staff of the *Village Voice* in N.Y., where he became especially well known as a provocative and insightful reviewer of contemporary music. From 1990 he taught at Bucknell Univ. His compositions are written in a minimalistic fashion and often incorporate native American elements; he has also been influenced by astrology and Jungian psychology. He publ. *The Music of Conlon Nancarrow* (Cambridge, 1995).

WORKS: *Long Night* for 3 Pianos (1981); *Mountain Spirit* for 2 Flutes, Synthesizer, and 2 Drums (1982–83); *Baptism* for 2 Flutes, Synthesizer, and 2 Drums (1983); *The Black Hills Belong to the Sioux* for Trumpet or Saxophone, Accordion or Synthesizer, Flute, and Drum (1984); *I'itoi Variations* for 2 Pianos (1985); *Cyclic Aphorisms* for Violin and Piano (1986–88); *Paris Intermezzo* for Toy Piano (1989); *The Convent at Tepoztlan (Homage to Nancarrow)* for 2 Pianos and Tape (1989).

Ganne, (Gustave) Louis, French conductor and composer; b. Buxières-les-Mines, Allier, April 5, 1862; d. Paris, July 13, 1923. He studied at the Paris Cons. with Dubois, Massenet, and Franck. He was a conductor for the Bals de l'Opéra in Paris and in various spa towns. In 1905 he organized his own Concerts Louis Ganne series in Monte Carlo. As a composer, Ganne wrote many light scores. His circus musical *Les Saltimbanques* (Paris, Dec. 30, 1899) was notably successful, but he scored his greatest success with the operetta *Hans, le joueur de flûte* (Monte Carlo, April 14, 1906). He also composed the popular *La Marche Lorraine* and the march *Le Père de la Victoire*.

WORKS: DRAMATIC: MUSIC THEATER (all 1st perf. in Paris unless otherwise given): *Tout Paris* (June 16, 1891); *Rabelais* (Oct. 25, 1892); *Les Colles des femmes* (Sept. 29, 1893); *Les Saltimbanques* (Dec. 30, 1899); *Hans, le joueur de flûte* (Monte Carlo, April 14, 1906); *Rhodope* (Monte Carlo, Dec. 13, 1910); *Cocorico* (Nov. 29, 1913); *L'Archiduc des Folies-Bergère* (Oct. 7, 1916); *La Belle de Paris* (Oct. 22, 1921); vaudevilles; ballet music. **OTHER:** Dances; marches, including *La Marche Lorraine* and *Le Père de la Victoire*; many piano pieces; songs.

Ganz, Rudolph, distinguished Swiss-American pianist, conductor, and pedagogue; b. Zürich, Feb. 24, 1877; d. Chicago, Aug. 2, 1972. He studied music assiduously, first as a cellist (with Friedrich Hegar), then as a pianist (with Robert Freund) in Zürich; also took composition lessons with Charles Blanchet at the Lausanne Cons.; in 1897–98 he studied piano with F. Blumer in Strasbourg, and in 1899 took a course in advanced piano playing with Busoni in Berlin. He made his first public appearance at the age of 12 as a cellist, and at 16 as a pianist. In 1899 he was the soloist in Beethoven's *Emperor Concerto* and Chopin's E-minor Concerto with the Berlin Phil., and in May 1900 the Berlin Phil. performed his 1st Sym. In 1901 he went to the U.S. and was engaged as a prof. of piano at the Chicago Musical College; between 1905 and 1908 he made several tours of the U.S. and Canada, and from 1908 to 1911 toured Europe. After 1912 he toured in both Europe and America. From 1921 to 1927 he was music director of the St. Louis Sym. Orch.; from 1938 to 1949 he conducted a highly successful series of Young People's Concerts with the N.Y. Phil.; concurrently (1929–54) he served as director of the Chicago Musical College. He played first performances of many important works, including those of Busoni, Ravel, and Bartók. He was a highly successful pedagogue, and continued to teach almost to the time of his death, at the age of 95. Besides the early sym., he wrote a lively suite of 20 pieces for Orch., *Animal Pictures* (Detroit, Jan. 19, 1933, composer conducting); Piano Concerto (Chicago, Feb. 20, 1941, composer soloist); *Laughter—Yet Love, Overture to an Unwritten Comedy* (1950); solo piano pieces; and about 200 songs to German, French, English, Swiss, and Alsatian texts. He publ. *Rudolph Ganz Evaluates Modern Piano Music* (N.Y., 1968).

BIBL.: J. Collester, *R. G.: A Musical Pioneer* (Metuchen, N.J., 1995).

Ganzarolli, Wladimiro, Italian bass-baritone; b. Venice, Jan. 9, 1936. He received his training at the Venice Cons. In 1958 he made his operatic debut as Méphistophélès in *Faust* at Milan's Teatro Nuovo, and from 1959 was a member of Milan's La Scala; from 1964 he also sang at the Vienna State Opera. In 1965 he made his debut at London's Covent Garden as Figaro. His guest engagements in the U.S. took him to San Francisco, Chicago, Dallas, and N.Y. In addition to his roles in Italian operas, he was especially admired for his roles in Mozart's operas.

Garaguly, Carl von, Hungarian-born Swedish violinist and conductor; b. Budapest, Dec. 28, 1900; d. Stockholm, Oct. 8, 1984. He studied violin with Hubay at the Royal Academy of Music in Budapest (1907–09) and with Marteau at the Berlin Hochschule für Musik (1911–16). After playing in the Berlin Phil. (1917–18), he pursued violin studies with Kresz at the Stern Cons. in Berlin and privately with Marteau (1920–23). He then settled in Sweden, becoming a naturalized Swedish citizen in 1930. He was concertmaster of the Göteborg Sym. Orch. (1923–30) and the Stockholm Concert Soc. Orch. (1930–40), subsequently serving as conductor of the latter (1941–53). From 1940 he also appeared with his own string quartet. He was music director of the Bergen Phil. (1953–58), Arnhem's Het Gelders Orch. (1959–70), and the Sønderborg Sym. Orch. (1965–80).

Garant, (Albert Antonio) Serge, Canadian composer, conductor, pianist, and teacher; b. Quebec City, Sept. 22, 1929; d. Sherbrooke, Quebec, Nov. 1, 1986. He learned to play the clarinet and saxophone, and then played in the Sherbrooke Sym. Orch. and in jazz groups. He also studied piano and harmony in Sherbrooke (1946–50), and was a student of Yvonne Hubert (piano) and Champagne (composition) in Montreal (1948–50) before pursuing his training in Paris with Messiaen (musical analysis) and Vaurabourg-Honegger (counterpoint) in 1951–52; later he had lessons in conducting with Boulez in Basel (summer, 1969). He was actively engaged in contemporary music circles in Montreal. In 1966 he helped found the Société de musique contemporaine du Québec there, for which he served as conductor for the rest of his life. From 1967 he also taught at the Univ. of Montreal. In 1980 he was made a member of the Order of Canada. His output charted a thoroughly contemporary course in which serial techniques were relieved by an infusion of lyricism. His *Nucléogame* (1955) was the first score by a Canadian composer to combine the use of tape and instruments.

WORKS: DRAMATIC: Film and television scores. **ORCH.:** *Musique pour la mort d'un poète* for Piano and Strings (1954); *Ennéade* (1963); *Ouranos* (1963); *Amuya* (1968); *Phrases II* (1968); *Offrande I* (1969) and *II* (1970); *Circuits III* (1973); *Plages* (1981). **CHAMBER:** *Nucléogame: In Memoriam Anton Webern* for Flute, Oboe, Clarinet, Trumpet, Trombone, Piano, and Tape (1955); *Canon VI* for 10 Performers (1957); *Pièces pour quatuor* for String Quartet (1958–59); *Asymétries No. 2* for Clarinet and Piano (1959); *Jeu à quatre* for 4 Instrumental Groups (1968); *Offrande III* for 3 Cellos, 2 Harps, Piano, and 2 Percussion (1971); *Circuits I* for 6 Percussionists (1972) and *II* for 14 Performers (1972); Quintet for Flute, Oboe, Cello, Piano, and Percussion (1978). **PIANO:** *Pièce No. 1* (1953; rev. 1959) and *No. 2* (1962); *Musique rituelle* (1954); *Variations* (1954); *Asymétries No. 1* (1958). **VOCAL:** *Anerca* for Soprano and 8 Performers (1961); *Cage d'oiseau* for Soprano and Piano (1962); *Phrases I* for Mezzo-soprano, Piano, Celesta, and Percussion (1967); *. . . chant d'amours* for Soprano, Contralto, Baritone, and 13 Performers (1975); *Rivages* for Baritone and 8 Performers (1976).

BIBL.: M.-T. Lefebvre, *S.G. et la révolution musicale au Québec* (Montreal, 1986).

Garay Narciso, Panamanian violinist, composer, and diplomat; b. Panama, June 12, 1876; d. there, March 27, 1953. He studied at the Brussels Cons., graduating with a premier prix; later attended the Schola Cantorum in Paris. He publ. a Violin Sonata and a valuable treatise on Panamanian folk music, *Tradiciones y cantares de Panama* (1930). He also occupied diplomatic posts and was Minister of Foreign Affairs.

Garbin, Edoardo, Italian tenor; b. Padua, March 12, 1865; d. Brescia, April 12, 1943. He studied with Alberto Selva and Vittorio Orefice in Milan. In 1891 he made his operatic debut in Vicenza as Alvaro in *La forza del destino*; also sang in Milan (Teatro dal Verme), Naples, and Genoa. On Feb. 9, 1893, he created the role of Fenton in Verdi's *Falstaff* at La Scala in Milan. Garbin made guest appearances in Rome, Vienna, Berlin, London, Russia, and South America. He married **Adelina Stehle**. He was particularly distinguished in *verismo* roles.

Garbousova, Raya, greatly admired Russian-born American cellist and pedagogue; b. Tiflis, Sept. 25, 1906. She began to study piano as a very small child, and then took up playing a small cello when she was 6; when she was 7, she entered the Tiflis Cons. as a pupil of Konstantin Miniar, and soon thereafter made her first public appearance in Tiflis. After giving concerts in Moscow and Leningrad in 1924, she went to Berlin to pursue her training with Heinz Becker. Following successful concerts in Berlin in 1926 and in Paris in 1927, she had further instruction with Diran Alexanian. She appeared as a soloist with U.S. orchs., and then made her N.Y. recital debut at Town Hall in 1934. In subsequent years, she appeared with orchs. on both sides of the Atlantic and as a recitalist. She lived in Paris until her husband, a Frenchman in the Résistance, was killed in 1943. She eventually made her way to the U.S., where she married the cardiologist Kurt Biss in 1946 and became a naturalized citizen. Garbousova resumed her international career, but she also devoted increasing attention to teaching. In addition to giving master classes around the world, she taught at the Hartt School of Music at the Univ. of Hartford (1970–89) and then at Northern Illinois Univ. in DeKalb. She distinguished herself as an interpreter not only of the standard repertory, but also of contemporary music. She gave the premieres of a number of major scores, including the cello concertos of Barber (1946) and Rieti (1956).

García Mansilla, Eduardo, American-born French-Argentine composer; b. Washington, D.C., March 7, 1870; d. Paris, May 9, 1930. He studied composition with Massenet, Saint-Saëns, and d'Indy in Paris and with Rimsky-Korsakov in St. Petersburg. His opera *Ivan* was premiered in St. Petersburg in 1905, and another opera, *La angelica Manuelite*, in Buenos Aires in 1917. He also wrote choruses.

García Navarro, (Luis Antonio). See **Navarra, (Luis Antonio) García.**

Gardelli, Lamberto, distinguished Italian conductor; b. Venice, Nov. 8, 1915. He studied piano and composition at the Liceo Musicale Rossini in Pesaro, and then completed his training in Rome with Zanella, Ariani, Petrassi, and Bustini. He was an assistant to Serafin in Rome, where he made his conducting debut at the Opera with *La Traviata* in 1944; then he conducted at the Royal Opera in Stockholm (1946–55). From 1955 to 1961 he was conductor of the Danish Radio Sym. Orch., and then conducted at the Hungarian State Opera in Budapest (1961–65) and at the Glyndebourne Festivals (1964–65; 1968). In 1964 he made his first appearance in the U.S. conducting *I Capuleti e i Montecchi* at N.Y.'s Carnegie Hall. On Jan. 30, 1966, he made his Metropolitan Opera debut in N.Y. conducting *Andrea Chénier;* he remained on its roster until 1968. He made his first appearance at London's Covent Garden in 1969 conducting *Otello,* and returned for the 1970–71, 1975–76, and 1979–80 seasons. From 1970 to 1975 he was music director of the Bern City Theater. From 1973 he also conducted at the Royal Opera in Copenhagen. He later was chief conductor of the Munich Radio Orch. (1983–88) and of the Danish Radio Sym. Orch. in Copenhagen (1986–89). Gardelli has acquired a notable reputation as an interpreter of the Italian operatic repertory. He also has composed 4 operas, orch. pieces, and songs.

Garden, Mary, celebrated Scottish soprano; b. Aberdeen, Feb. 20, 1874; d. Inverurie, Jan. 3, 1967. She went to the U.S. as a child; studied violin and piano; in 1893 she began the study of singing with Mrs. Robinson Duff in Chicago; in 1895 she went to Paris, where she studied with Sbriglia, Bouhy, Trabadello, Mathilde Marchesi, and Lucien Fugere. Her funds, provided by a wealthy patron, were soon depleted, and Sybyl Sanderson introduced her to Albert Carré, director of the Opéra-Comique. Her operatic debut was made under dramatic circumstances on April 10, 1900, when the singer who performed the title role of Charpentier's *Louise* at the Opéra-Comique was taken ill during the performance, and Garden took her place. She revealed herself not only as a singer of exceptional ability, but also as a skillful actress. She subsequently sang in several operas of the general repertoire; also created the role of Diane in Pierné's *La Fille de Tabarin* (Opéra-Comique, Feb. 20, 1901). A historic turning point in her career was reached when she was selected to sing Mélisande in the premiere of Debussy's *Pelléas et Mélisande* (Opéra-Comique, April 30, 1902); she became the center of a raging controversy when Maurice Maeterlinck, the author of the drama, voiced his violent objection to her assignment (his choice for the role was Georgette Leblanc, his common-law wife) and pointedly refused to have anything to do with the production. Garden won warm praise from the critics for her musicianship, despite the handicap of her American-accented French. She remained a member of the Opéra-Comique; also sang at the Grand Opéra, and at Monte Carlo. She made her U.S. debut as Thaïs at the Manhattan Opera House, N.Y. (Nov. 25, 1907), and sang Mélisande there the first U.S. performance of *Pelléas et Mélisande* (Feb. 19, 1908). In 1910 she joined the Chicago Opera Co.; she was its general director for the 1921–22 season, during which the losses mounted to about $1,000,000. She continued to sing at the Chicago Opera until 1931, and then made sporadic operatic and concert appearances until giving her farewell performance at the Paris Opéra-Comique in 1934. In 1939 she settled in Scotland. With L. Biancolli, she publ. *Mary Garden's Story* (N.Y., 1951).

Gardiner, H(enry) Balfour, English composer, great-uncle of **John Eliot Gardiner;** b. London, Nov. 7, 1877; d. Salisbury, June 28, 1950. He was educated at Oxford and studied composition with Knorr at the Hoch Cons. in Frankfurt am Main (1894–96). He was music master at Winchester College. From 1910 to 1920 he promoted concerts of contemporary British music. He also was active as a folk song collector.

WORKS: ORCH.: *English Dance* (1904); *Overture to a Comedy* (1906); Sym. (1908; not extant); *Fantasy* (1908; not extant); *Shepherd Fennel's Dance* (1911); *A Berkshire Idyll* (1913). **CHAMBER:** String Sextet; String Quartet; piano pieces. **VOCAL:** Many choral pieces, including *Evening Hymn* (1908), *News from Wydah,* with orch. (1912), *April* (1912–13), and *Philomeda* (1923); songs.

BIBL.: S. Lloyd, *H.B.G.* (Cambridge, 1984).

Gardiner, John Eliot, outstanding English conductor, great-nephew of **H(enry) Balfour Gardiner;** b. Fontmell Magna, Dorset, April 20, 1943. As a child, he attended the Bryanston Summer School of Music and later played in the National Youth Orch. He studied history at King's College, Cambridge (M.A., 1965) and pursued advanced training in music with Dart at King's College, London (1966); a French government scholarship enabled him to study with Boulanger in Paris and Fontainebleau (1966–68). In 1964 he founded the Monteverdi Choir, followed by its complement, the Monteverdi Orch., in 1968. In the latter year, he conducted his own performing edition of Monteverdi's *Vespers* at the London Promenade Concerts. He made his first appearance at the Sadler's Wells Opera in London in 1969 conducting *Die Zauberflöte.* In 1971 he discovered in Paris the MS of Rameau's opera *Abaris, ou Les Boréades,* which he conducted in its concert premiere in London on April 19, 1975, and in its stage premiere at the Aix-en-Provence Festival on July 21, 1982. In 1973 he made his debut at London's Covent Garden conducting Gluck's *Iphigénie en Tauride.* He founded the English Baroque Soloists in 1977, which he conducted in performances utilizing original instruments of the Baroque era. From 1980 to 1983 he was principal conductor of the CBC Orch. in Vancouver. He served as artistic director of the Göttingen Handel Festivals from 1981 to 1990. From 1983 to 1988 he was music director of the Lyons Opera. In 1990 he organized the Orchestre Révolutionaire et romantique, an orch. devoted to performing scores on instruments of the period. He conducted it in Beethoven's 9th Sym. at its U.S. debut in N.Y. in 1996. From 1991 to 1994 he was chief conductor of the North German Radio Sym. Orch. in Hamburg. As a guest conductor, Gardiner has appeared in many of the principal music centers of the world. In 1990 he was made a Commander of the Order of the British Empire. His repertoire is immense, ranging from the pre-Baroque to modern eras. His interpretations reflect his penchant for meticulous scholarship while maintaining stimulating performance standards.

Gardner, John (Linton), English composer and teacher; b. Manchester, March 2, 1917. He studied organ with Sir Hugh Allen, Ernest Walker, and Thomas Armstrong, and composition with R.O. Morris at Exeter College, Oxford (Mus.B., 1939). He pursued his career in London, where he was a tutor (1952–76) and director of music (1965–69) at Morley College; he also taught at the Royal Academy of Music (1956–86) and was director of music at St. Paul's Girls' School (1962–75). In 1976 he was made a Commander of the Order of the British Empire. His extensive catalogue of works reveals a fine craftsmanship in an eclectic style.

WORKS: DRAMATIC: OPERAS: *A Nativity Opera* (1950); *The Moon and Sixpence* (1956; London, May 24, 1957); *The Visitors* (1971; Aldeburge, June 10, 1972); *Bel and the Dragon* (1973); *Tobermory* (1976). **MUSICAL:** *Vile Bodies* (1960). **MASQUE:** *The Entertainment of the Senses* (1973; London, Feb. 2, 1974). **BALLETS:** *Reflection* (1952); *Dress Rehearsal* (1958). Also incidental music. **ORCH.:** 3 syms.: No. 1 (1950; Cheltenham, July 5, 1951), No. 2 (1985), and No. 3 (1989); *A Scots Overture* (London, Aug. 16, 1954); Piano Concerto No. 1 (1957); *Suite of 5 Rhythms* (1960); *Sinfonia piccola* for Strings (1960); Concerto for Trumpet and Strings (1963); *Occasional Suite* (1968); *An English Ballad* (1969); *3 Ridings Suite* (1970); Sonatina for Strings (1974); *English Suite* for Concert Band (1977); Oboe Concerto (1990). **CHAMBER:** 3 string quartets (1938, 1979, 1986); 2 oboe sonatas (1953, 1986); *Concerto da camera* for Recorder, Violin, Cello, and Harpsichord (1967); Chamber Concerto for Organ and 11 Instruments (1969); *Sonata secolare* for Organ and Brass Quintet (1973); *Sonata da chiesa* for 2 Trumpets and Organ (1977); *Sonatina lirica* for Brass Quintet (1983); Saxophone Quartet (1985); *Pentad* for Recorder Octet (1986); *French Suite* for Saxophone Quartet (1986); *Chanson triste* for Oboe and Piano (1989). Also piano pieces and organ music. **VOCAL:** *Cantiones Sacrae* for Soprano, Chorus, and Orch. (1952); *Jubilate Deo* for Chorus (1957); *The Ballad of the White Horse* for Chorus and Orch. (1958); *Herrick Cantata* for Tenor, Chorus, and Orch. (1960); *A*

Latter Day Athenian Speaks for Chorus (1961); *The Noble Heart* for Soprano, Bass, Chorus, and Orch. (1964); *Mass* for Chorus (1965); *Mass* for Mezzo-soprano, Chorus, and Orch. (1983); numerous choral pieces; many songs.

Gardner, Samuel, Russian-American violinist and composer; b. Elizavetgrad, Aug. 25, 1891; d. N.Y., Jan. 23, 1984. He went early to the U.S. and studied violin with Felix Winternitz and Franz Kneisel; also studied composition with Goetschius, and later with Loeffler in Boston. He was a member of the Kneisel String Quartet (1914–15); also played in American orchs. From 1924 to 1941 he taught violin at the Inst. of Musical Art in N.Y. Among his works were a tone poem, *Broadway* (Boston, April 18, 1930), and *Country Moods* for String Orch. (N.Y., Dec. 10, 1946). He publ. *Essays for Advanced Solo Violin* (1960).

Garland, Peter, American composer, publisher, and writer on music; b. Portland, Maine, Jan. 27, 1952. He studied with Tenney and Budd at the Calif. Inst. of the Arts (B.F.A., 1972), then began editing and publishing *Soundings*, a journal comprising scores and writings by a variety of American composers. During the 1970s he lived in Mexico, where he made field recordings; from 1980 he lived in Santa Fe, N.Mex., where he directed his own performing ensemble. In 1984 he was guest composer at the Darmstadt Ferienkurse. As a composer, Garland is influenced by native American and Mexican cultures and by his teacher Budd; his works are spare and lyrical, often using exotic instruments.

WRITINGS (all publ. in Santa Fe): *Music Is Dangerous* (1973); *Magic Animals* (1975); *Americas: Essays on American Music and Culture* (1982).

WORKS: *Apple Blossom* for 2 to 4 Marimbas (1972); *Dreaming of Immortality in a Thatched Cottage* for Voices, Angklung, Marimba, Harpsichord, and Percussion (1977); *The Conquest of Mexico*, theater work for Dancers, Shadow Puppets, Soloists, Recorder, Harp, Harpsichord, and Percussion (1977–80); *Matachin Dances* for 2 Violins and Gourd Rattles (1980–81); *Another Sunrise* for Chamber Ensemble (N.Y., Dec. 1, 1995).

Garrido, Pablo, Chilean composer and ethnomusicologist; b. Valparaiso, March 26, 1905; d. Santiago, Sept. 14, 1982. He studied in Santiago; conducted concerts of Chilean music and gave lectures; publ. a valuable monograph, *Biografía de la Cueca Chilena* (Santiago, 1942). He composed an opera, *La sugestión* (Santiago, Oct. 18, 1961); a ballet, *El Guerrillero* (1963); *Rapsodía chilena* for Piano and Orch. (1938); Piano Concerto (1950); *Fantasía antillana* for Cello and Orch. (1950); *13 & 13* for String Quartet (1951); piano pieces and songs based on Chilean folklore.

Garrido-Lecca, Celso, Peruvian composer; b. Piura, March 9, 1926. He studied theory with Andrés Sas and Rodolfo Holzmann in Lima; then went to Santiago, Chile, where he took courses in composition with Domingo Santa Cruz. In 1964 he received a Guggenheim fellowship. In 1967 he was appointed to the faculty of the Univ. of Chile.

WORKS: ORCH.: Sinfonia (Washington, D.C., April 22, 1961); *Laudes* (1963); *Elegía a Machu Picchu* (1965; N.Y., March 23, 1967). **CHAMBER:** *Música* for 6 Instruments and Percussion (1957); *Divertimento* for Wind Quintet (1965); String Quartet (1963); *Antaras* for String Nonet (1969); piano pieces. **VOCAL:** Choruses; songs.

Garrison, Mabel, American soprano; b. Baltimore, April 24, 1886; d. N.Y., Aug. 20, 1963. She attended Western Maryland College and then pursued vocal training with Heinendahl and Minetti at the Peabody Cons. of Music in Baltimore (1909–11), and in N.Y. with Saenger (1912–14) and Witherspoon (1916). In 1908 she married the composer George Siemonn. On April 18, 1912, she made her operatic debut under her married name as Philine in *Mignon* with the Aborn Opera Co. in Boston. On Feb. 15, 1914, she first sang at the Metropolitan Opera in a concert; her stage debut there followed as a Flower Maiden in *Parsifal* on Nov. 26, 1914, with her formal debut coming the next day as Frasquita. She continued to sing at the Metropolitan Opera until her farewell as Lucia on Jan. 22, 1921. In 1921 she made guest appearances at the Berlin State Opera, the Vienna State Opera, and the Cologne Opera, and then launched a concert tour of the globe. After singing with the Chicago Opera (1925–26), she taught at Smith College (1933–39). Among her finest roles were the Queen of the Night, Rosina, Gilda, Urbain, Martha, and the Queen of Shemakha. In her recitals, she often included songs by her husband, who frequently appeared as her accompanist.

Gasdia, Cecilia, Italian soprano; b. Verona, Aug. 14, 1960. She studied in Verona. After winning the Maria Callas competition of the RAI in 1981, she made her operatic debut as Bellini's Giulietta in Florence. In 1982 she made her first appearance at Milan's La Scala as Anna Bolena, and also sang in Perugia and Naples. She made her debut at the Paris Opéra in 1983 as Anais in Rossini's *Moïse*. In 1985 she made her U.S. debut as Gilda in a concert performance of *Rigoletto* in Philadelphia. In 1986 she sang for the first time at the Chicago Lyric Opera and at the Metropolitan Opera in N.Y. In subsequent years, she sang at leading opera houses and festivals on both sides of the Atlantic, winning particular notice for her Rossini, Verdi, and Puccini roles.

Gasperini, Guido, Italian musicologist; b. Florence, June 7, 1865; d. Naples, Feb. 20, 1942. He was a pupil of Tacchinardi (composition) and Sbolci (cello). From 1902 to 1924 he was librarian and a teacher of music history at the Parma Cons.; later, librarian at the Naples Cons. (1924–35); in 1908 he founded the Associazione dei Musicologi Italiani, one of the main purposes of which was the examination and cataloguing of all books on music and musical MSS in the Italian libraries.

WRITINGS: *Storia della musica* (1899); *Dell' arte d'interpretare la scrittura della musica vocale del Cinquecento* (1902); *Storia della Semiografia musicale* (1905); *I caratteri peculiari del Melodramma italiano* (1913); *Musicisti alla Corte dei Farnesi; Noterelle su due liutiste al servizio di Casa Farnese* (1923).

Gaston, E(verett) Thayer, American music educator and music therapist; b. Woodward, Okla., July 4, 1901; d. Springfield, Mo., June 3, 1970. He took premed courses at Sterling (Kansas) College (B.A., 1923), then studied music there (B.M., 1936) and at the Univ. of Kansas (M.A. in music education, 1938; Ph.D. in educational psychology, 1940). He was a prominent figure in the fields of music education and music therapy in the U.S.; was founder of the National Assn. for Music Therapy, serving as its president (1952–53). He prepared the *Gaston Test of Musicality* (1941; 4th ed., 1957) and ed. the textbook *Music in Therapy* (1968).

BIBL.: R. Johnson, *E.T. G.: Contributions to Music Therapy and Music Education* (diss., Univ. of Mich., 1973); idem, "E.T. G.: Leader in Scientific Thought on Music in Therapy and Education," *Journal of Research in Music Education*, XXIX (1981).

Gastoué, Amédée (-Henri-Gustave-Noël), French organist and music scholar; b. Paris, March 19, 1873; d. there, June 1, 1943. He studied piano and harmony with A. Deslandres (1890), harmony with Lavignac (1891), then organ with Guilmant and counterpoint and composition with Magnard. From 1896 to 1905 he was ed. of *Revue du Chant Grégorien*; in 1897 he began to contribute to the *Tribune de St.-Gervais*; became its ed. in 1904 and, in 1909, ed.-in-chief and director. He was prof. of Gregorian chant at the Schola Cantorum from its foundation (1896); also music critic of *La Semaine Littéraire* (from 1905). He was organist and maître de chapelle at St.-Jean-Baptiste-de-Belleville, Paris, where he also gave concerts; was a lecturer at the Catholic Univ. and the École des Hautes Études Sociales; in 1925 he became a member of the Académie des Beaux Arts.

WRITINGS: *Cours théorique et pratique de plain-chant romain grégorien* (1904); *Histoire du chant liturgique à Paris* (vol. I: *Des Origines à la fin des temps carolingiens*, 1904; 2nd ed., 1917); *Les Origines du chant romain, l'antiphonaire grégorien* (1907); *Catalogue des manuscrits de musique byzantine* *de la Bibliothèque Nationale de Paris et des bibliothèques publiques de France* (1907); *Nouvelle méthode pratique de chant grégorien* (1908); *Traité d'harmonisation du chant grégorien* (1910); *L'Art grégorien* (1911; 3rd ed., 1920); *La Musique de l'eglise* (1911); *Variations sur la musique d'église* (1912); *Musique et liturgie: Le Graduel et l'Antiphonaire romain* (1913); *L'Orgue en France de l'antiquité au début de la période classique* (1921); *Les Primitifs de la musique française* (1922); *Le Cantique populaire en France: Ses sources, son histoire* (1924); *La Vie musicale de l'église* (1929); *La Liturgie et la musique* (1931); *Le Manuscrit de musique polyphonique du trésor d'Apt, XIVe–XVe siècles* (1936); *L'Église et la musique* (Paris, 1936).

Gatti, Daniele, Italian conductor; b. Milan, Nov. 6, 1961. He received training in conducting and composition at the Milan Cons. After making his debut as an opera conductor in Milan with *Giovanni d'Arco* in 1982, he appeared with opera houses and orchs. throughout Italy, including the orchs. of the RAI. In 1986 he became founder-conductor of the Stradivari Chamber Orch. He made his first appearance at Milan's La Scala in 1988 conducting Rossini's *L'Occasion fa il Ladro.* In 1991 he made his U.S. debut conducting *Madama Butterfly* in Chicago. In 1992 he became music director of the Orch. Sinfonica dell'Accademia Nazionale di Santa Cecilia in Rome, and also made his debut at the Royal Opera in London conducting *I Puritani.* During the 1993–94 season, he appeared as a guest conductor with the Chicago Sym. Orch., the Cincinnati Sym. Orch., the London Phil., the London Sym. Orch., the Philadelphia Orch., and the San Francisco Sym.; also toured Germany and South America with his Rome orch. In 1994 he was appointed principal guest conductor of the Royal Opera in London, and also made his debut as guest conductor with the Royal Phil. in the British capital. On Dec. 1, 1994, he made his first appearance at the Metropolitan Opera in N.Y. conducting *Madama Butterfly.* In 1996 he became music director of the Royal Phil. in London.

Gatti, Guido M(aggiorino), eminent Italian writer on music, critic, and editor; b. Chieti, May 30, 1892; d. Grottaferrata, May 10, 1973. He took up violin training at 6 and piano studies at 12, and later studied engineering at the Univ. of Turin (1909–14). He was ed.-in-chief of *Riforma musicale* (1913–15; 1918). In 1920 he founded *Il pianoforte,* which was renamed the *Rassegna musicale* in 1928. He ed. it until it ceased publication in 1944, and then again from 1947 when it resumed publication in Rome. In 1962 it was renamed again as *Quaderni della Rassegna.* He also was director-general of the Teatro di Torino (1925–31), administrator of Lux films (1934–66), music critic of *Tempo* (1951–69), and ed. of *Studi musicali* (1972–73). In addition, he was ed. of several series, was music ed. of the *Dizionario Bompiani delle opere e dei personaggi* (1946–49) and the *Dizionario degli autori* (1956), and was a contributor of numerous articles to European and U.S. journals. Gatti was particularly influential in contemporary music circles.

WRITINGS: *I "Lieder" di Schumann* (Turin, 1914); *Figure di musicisti francesi* (Turin, 1915); *Giorgio Bizet* (Turin, 1915); *Musicisti moderni d'Italia e di fuori* (Bologna, 1920; 2nd ed., enl., 1925); *Débora e Jaèle di I. Pizzetti* (Milan, 1922); ed. with A. della Corte, *Dizionario di musica* (Turin, 1925; 6th ed., 1959); *Le barbier de Séville de Rossini* (Paris, 1925); *Ildebrando Pizzetti* (Turin, 1934; 2nd ed., 1955; Eng. tr., 1951); ed. with L. Dallapiccola, *F.B. Busoni: Scritti e pensieri sulla musica* (Florence, 1941; 2nd ed., rev., 1954); ed. with others, *L'opera di Gian Francesco Malipiero* (Treviso, 1952); *Cinquanta anni di opera a balletto in Italia* (Rome, 1954); with F. D'Amico, *Alfredo Casella* (Milan, 1958); *V. de Sabata* (Milan, 1958); ed. with A. Basso, *La musica: enciclopedia storica* (Turin, 1966) and *La musica: Dizionario* (Turin, 1968–71); ed. with B. Marziano, *Riccardo Gualino e la cultura torinese: Le manifestazioni del Teatro di Torino* (Turin, 1971).

BIBL.: A. Basso, "G.M.G. (1892–1973)," *Studi musicali,* II (1973).

Gatti-Casazza, Giulio, distinguished Italian operatic administrator; b. Udine, Feb. 3, 1868; d. Ferrara, Sept. 2, 1940. He was educated at the Univs. of Ferrara and Bologna, and graduated from the Naval Engineering School at Genoa; abandoned his career as engineer and became director of the opera in Ferrara in 1893. His ability attracted the attention of the Viscount di Modrone and A. Boito, who, in 1898, offered him the directorship of La Scala at Milan. During the 10 years of his administration, the institution came to occupy 1st place among the opera houses of Italy. From 1908 to 1935 he was general director of the Metropolitan Opera in N.Y., a tenure of notable distinction. During his administration, he engaged many celebrated musicians, produced over 175 works, including premieres by American as well as foreign composers, and expanded audiences through major tours and regular nationwide broadcasts. On April 3, 1910, Gatti-Casazza married **Frances Alda**; they were divorced in 1929; in 1930 he married Rosina Galli, premiere danseuse and ballet mistress. Gatti-Casazza's *Memories of the Opera* was posth. publ. in Eng. in 1941.

Gaubert, Philippe, French conductor and composer; b. Cahors, July 3, 1879; d. Paris, July 8, 1941. He studied flute with Taffanel at the Paris Cons.; in 1905, won the 2nd Prix de Rome. From 1919 to 1938 he was conductor of the Paris Cons. concerts; from 1920 to 1941, was also principal conductor at the Paris Opéra. He publ. a *Méthode complète de flûte* (8 parts, 1923).

WORKS: DRAMATIC: OPERAS: *Sonia* (Nantes, 1913); *Naila* (Paris, April 7, 1927). **BALLET:** *Philotis* (Paris, 1914). **ORCH.:** *Rhapsodie sur des thèmes populaires* (1909); *Poème pastoral* (1911); *Le Cortège d'Amphitrite* (Paris, April 9, 1911); *Fresques,* symphonic suite (Paris, Nov. 12, 1923); *Les Chants de la mer,* 3 symphonic pictures (Paris, Oct. 12, 1929); Violin Concerto (Paris, Feb. 16, 1930); *Les Chants de la terre* (Paris, Dec. 20, 1931); *Poème romanesque* for Cello and Orch. (Paris, Jan. 30, 1932); *Inscriptions sur les portes de la ville,* 4 symphonic tableaux (Paris, Nov. 18, 1934); Sym. (Paris, Nov. 8, 1936); *Poème des champs et des villages* (Paris, Feb. 4, 1939). **CHAMBER:** *Médailles antiques* for Flute, Violin, and Piano; *Divertissement grec* for Flute and Harp; *Sur l'eau* for Flute and Piano; *Intermède champêtre* for Oboe and Piano; Violin Sonata. **VOCAL:** *Josiane,* oratorio (Paris, Dec. 17, 1921); songs. **OTHER:** Many transcriptions for flute.

Gauk, Alexander, Russian conductor, teacher, and composer; b. Odessa, Aug. 15, 1893; d. Moscow, March 30, 1963. He studied composition with Kalafati and Vitols, and conducting with N. Tcherepnin, at the Petrograd Cons. (graduated, 1917); then conducted at the State Opera and Ballet Theater there (1920–31). He was chief conductor of the Leningrad Phil. (1930–34), the U.S.S.R. State Sym. Orch. of Moscow (1936–41), and the All-Union Radio Sym. Orch. of Moscow (1953–63). He also taught conducting at the conservatories of Leningrad (1927–33), Tbilisi (1941–43), and Moscow (1939–63). His pupils included such distinguished conductors as Mravinsky, Melik-Pashayev, Simeonov, and Svetlanov. He championed the music of Russian composers; restored Rachmaninoff's 1st Sym. to the active Russian repertoire from orch. parts found in the archives of the Moscow Cons. He wrote a Sym., a Harp Concerto, a Piano Concerto, and songs.

Gaul, Harvey B(artlett), American organist, conductor, music critic, and composer; b. N.Y., April 11, 1881; d. Pittsburgh, Dec. 1, 1945. He studied organ, harmony, and composition with George LeJeune in N.Y., then with Dudley Buck (1895); after further studies with Alfred R. Gaul in Birmingham and Philip Ames in Durham (1906), he went to Paris to complete his training with Widor, Guilmant, and Decaux (organ) at the Cons. and with d'Indy (composition and orchestration) at the Schola Cantorum (1909–10). He was assistant organist at St. John's Chapel in N.Y. (1899–1901), and then organist and choirmaster at the Emmanuel Church in Cleveland (1901–09); also wrote music criticism for the *Cleveland News.* In 1910 he settled in Pittsburgh as organist of Calvary Church; served as music critic (1914–34) and arts ed. (1929–34) of the *Post-Gazette*; then conducted the Pittsburgh Civic String Orch. (1936–45) and the Savoyard Opera Co. (1939–45) and taught at the Univ. of Pittsburgh and the Carnegie Inst. of Technology. Gaul wrote more than 500 works, becoming best known for his church and organ music. He was also the author of a study of Stephen Foster, *The Minstrel of the Alleghenies* (Pittsburgh, 1952).

Gauthier, (Ida Josêphine Phoebe) Eva, notable Canadian mezzo-soprano and teacher; b. Ottawa, Sept. 20, 1885; d. N.Y., Dec. 26, 1958. She began her training in Ottawa, where she had lessons in piano and harmony with J. Edgar Birch, and then in voice with Frank Buels. She gained experience as soloist at St. Patrick Church in Ottawa, and then made her professional debut at the Ottawa Basilica at the commemoration service for Queen Victoria in 1902. After pursuing her studies in Paris with Auguste-Jean Dubulle, and then with Jacques Bouhy, Emma Albani invited her to tour the British Isles with her in 1905. In 1906 she accompanied Albani on her farewell tour of Canada. In 1907 she was soloist in C. Harriss' *Coronation Mass for Edward VII* at the Queen's Hall in London. During this time, she also had vocal lessons with William Shakespeare in London. Following further studies with Giuseppe Oxilia in Milan (1907–08), she made her only stage appearance as Micaëla in Pavia in 1909. From 1910 to 1914 she toured extensively as a recitalist in Southeast Asia. After making her N.Y. recital debut in 1915, she appeared regularly there in imaginative programs, which included works by Stravinsky, Schoenberg, Ravel, Bartók, Hindemith, Kern, Berlin, and Gershwin, not to mention works by lesser-known composers of the past and even non-Occidental works. From 1936 she devoted herself principally to teaching.

BIBL.: I. Kolodin, "The Art of E.G," *Saturday Review* (May 28, 1966); N. Turbide, *Biographical Study of E.G. (1885–1958): First French-Canadian Singer of the Avant-garde* (diss., Univ. of Montreal, 1986).

Gavazzeni, Gianandrea, Italian conductor, writer on music, and composer; b. Bergamo, July 27, 1909. He studied at the Accademia di Santa Cecilia in Rome (1921–25), and then took courses in piano with Renzo Lorenzoni and in composition with Ildebrando Pizzetti and Mario Pilati at the Milan Cons. (1925–31). While he devoted much time to musical journalism, he also pursued a conducting career from 1940. In 1948 he became a regular conductor at Milan's La Scala, where he served as artistic director from 1966 to 1968. He took La Scala companies on visits to the Edinburgh Festival (1957), to Moscow (1964), and to Montreal (1967). In 1957 he conducted *La Bohème* at the Lyric Opera of Chicago and in 1965 *Anna Bolena* at the Glyndebourne Festival. On Oct. 11, 1976, he made his Metropolitan Opera debut in N.Y. conducting *Il Trovatore*. He then pursued his career in Europe, where he was especially admired for his interpretations of the Italian operatic repertory. Among his numerous writings were *Donizetti* (Milan, 1937); *Musorgskij e la musica russa dell'800* (Florence, 1943); *Le feste musicali* (Milan, 1944); *Il suono è stanco* (Bergamo, 1950); *Quaderno del musicista* (Bergamo, 1952); *Musicisti d'Europa* (Milan, 1954); *La musica e il teatro* (Pisa, 1954); *La morte dell'opera* (Milan, 1954); *La casa di Arlecchino* (Milan, 1957); *Trent'anni di musica* (Milan, 1958); *Diario di Edimburgo e d'America* (Milan, 1960); *La campane di Bergamo* (Milan, 1963); *I nemici della musica* (Milan, 1965); *Carta da musica* (Milan, 1968); *Non eseguire Beethoven e altri scritti* (Milan, 1974).

WORKS: DRAMATIC: OPERA: *Paolo e Virginia* (1932; Bergamo, 1935). **BALLET:** *Il furioso all'isola di S. Domingo* (1940). **ORCH.:** *Preludio sinfonico* (1928); *Concerto bergamasco* (1931); *Tre Episodi* (1935); *Canti di operai lombardi* (1936); Cello Concerto (1936); Violin Concerto (1937); *Ritmi e paesaggi di atleti* (1938); *Piccolo Concerto* for Flute, Horn, and Strings (1940); 3 *Concerti di Cinquandò* (1941; 1942; for Strings, 1949). **CHAMBER:** Violin Sonata (1930); Cello Sonata (1930); Trio for Violin, Cello, and Piano (1931); Flute Sonata (1944); *Sonata da casa* for Violin, Piano, and Strings (1944); piano pieces, including a Sonata (1933). **VOCAL:** Choral pieces; songs.

Gavoty, Bernard (Georges Marie), French writer on music and organist; b. Paris, April 2, 1908; d. there, Oct. 24, 1981. He studied philosophy and literature at the Sorbonne, and organ and composition at the Cons. in Paris. In 1942 he became organist at Saint-Louis des Invalides in Paris. Under the nom de plume Clarendon, he was music critic of the Paris newspaper *Le Figaro* from 1945 until his death. He publ. a series of lavishly illustrated monographs on contemporary celebrated musicians under the general title of *Les Grands Interprètes* (Geneva, 1953–55), and also made documentary films on famous musicians.

WRITINGS (all publ. in Paris unless otherwise given): *Louis Vierne: Vie et l'oeuvre* (1943); *Jehan Alain, musicien français (1911–1940)* (1945); *Les Français sont-ils musiciens?* (1948); *Souvenirs de Georges Enesco* (1955); with J.-Y. Daniel-Lesur, *Pour ou contre la musique moderne?* (1957); *La Musique adoucit les moeurs* (1959); with É. Vuillermoz, *Chopin amoureux* (1960); *Dix grands musiciens* (1963); *Vingt grand interprètes* (Lausanne, 1967); *L'Arme à gauche* (1971); *Parler, parler!* (1972); *Chopin* (1974); *Reynaldo Hahn: Le Musicien de la belle époque* (1976); *Alfred Cortot* (1977); *Anicroches* (1979); *Liszt: Le Virtuose, 1811–1848* (1980).

Gavrilov, Andrei, outstanding Russian pianist; b. Moscow, Sept. 21, 1955. He studied piano with his mother, then entered the Central Music School in Moscow when he was 6 and studied with Tatiana Kestner; subsequently trained with Lev Naumov at the Moscow Cons. He won 1st prize at the Tchaikovsky Competition in Moscow in 1972, and thereafter pursued a distinguished career, making an impressive N.Y. recital debut in 1985. His superlative technique and interpretive insights are revealed in his remarkable performances of a comprehensive repertoire, ranging from the Baroque to the avant-garde.

Gay, Maria (née **Pitchot**), Spanish contralto; b. Barcelona, June 13, 1879; d. N.Y., July 29, 1943. She studied sculpture and the violin; became a singer almost by chance, when Pugno, traveling in Spain, heard her sing and was impressed by the natural beauty of her voice. She sang in some of his concerts; also with Ysaÿe in Brussels; made her operatic debut there as Carmen (1902), a role that became her finest. She then studied in Paris with Ada Adiny, and when she returned to the operatic stage, made an international reputation. After tours in Europe, including appearances at London's Covent Garden (1906) and Milan's La Scala (1906–07), she made her American debut at the Metropolitan Opera in N.Y. as Carmen on Dec. 3, 1908, with Toscanini conducting. She sang with the Boston Opera Co. from 1910 to 1912 and with the Chicago Opera Co. from 1913 to 1927, when she retired from the stage. She and her husband, **Giovanni Zenatello**, whom she married in 1913, settled in N.Y. as teachers (1927).

Gayer (Ashkenasi), Catherine, American soprano; b. Los Angeles, Feb. 11, 1937. She studied at the Univ. of Calif. at Los Angeles and in Berlin. She made her operatic debut in Venice in the premiere of *Intolleranza* as the Companion on April 13, 1961; then joined the Deutsche Oper in West Berlin, and was made a Kammersängerin in 1970; also appeared at the East Berlin Komische Oper. She made guest appearances in Vienna, Salzburg, and Milan. She excelled in the modern operatic repertoire, but also was admired for her Queen of the Night, Constanze, Sophie, Gilda, Mélisande, and Zerbinetta.

Gazzelloni, Severino, outstanding Italian flutist and teacher; b. Roccasecca, Frosinone, Jan. 5, 1919; d. Cassino, near Rome, Nov. 21, 1992. He studied with Giambattista Creati and at the Accademia di Santa Cecilia in Rome, graduating in 1942. In 1945 he made his formal debut in Rome, and then was 1st flutist in the RAI Orch. there for some 3 decades. He also pursued an international career as a soloist and recitalist of the first magnitude, excelling in an expansive repertoire ranging from the Baroque masters to the most demanding exponents of the contemporary avant-garde. Many composers wrote works especially for him. He taught at the Accademia di Santa Cecilia and at the Accademia Musicale Chigiana in Siena, as well as abroad.

BIBL.: G.-L. Petrucci and M. Benedetti, *S. G.: Il flauto del Novecento* (Naples, 1993).

Gebhard, Heinrich, German-American pianist, composer, and teacher; b. Sobernheim, July 25, 1878; d. North Arlington, N.J., May 5, 1963. As a boy of 8, he went with his parents to Boston, where he studied with Clayton Johns; after a concert debut in Boston (April 24, 1896), he went to Vienna to study with Leschetizky. He gave first American performances of works by d'Indy; his most notable interpretation was Loeffler's work for Piano and Orch., *A Pagan Poem*, which he played nearly 100 times with U.S. orchs.; also arranged the work for 2 Pianos. His own works are in an impressionistic vein: *Fantasy* for Piano and Orch. (N.Y. Phil., Nov. 12, 1925, composer soloist); *Across the Hills*, symphonic poem (1940); *Divertimento* for Piano and Chamber Orch. (Boston, Dec. 20, 1927); String Quartet; *Waltz Suite* for 2 Pianos; *The Sun, Cloud and the Flower*, song cycle; and many piano pieces. His book *The Art of Pedaling* was publ. posth. with an introduction by Leonard Bernstein, who was one of his students (N.Y., 1963).

Geck, Martin, German musicologist; b. Witten, March 19, 1936. He was educated at the Univ. of Kiel (Ph.D., 1962, with the diss. *Die Vokalmusik Dietrich Buxtehude und der frühe Pietismus*; publ. in Kassel, 1965). In 1976 he became a prof. at the Dortmund Pädagogische Hochschule. He was prof. of musicology at the Univ. of Dortmund from 1980.

WRITINGS: *Die Wiederentdeckung der Matthäuspassion im 19. Jahrhundert* (Regensburg, 1967); *Nicolaus Bruhns: Leben und Werk* (Cologne, 1968); *Die Bildnisse Richard Wagners* (Munich, 1970); *Deutsche Oratorien 1800 bis 1840: Verzeichnis der Quellen und Aufführungen* (Wilhelmshaven, 1971); *Musiktherapie als Problem der Gesellschaft* (Stuttgart, 1973; Swedish tr., Stockholm, 1977; Danish tr., Copenhagen, 1978); with J. Deathridge and E. Voss, *Wagner-Werk-Verzeichnis* (Mainz, 1986); with P. Schleuning, *"Geschrieben auf Bonaparte." Beethovens "Eroica": Revolution, Reaktion, Rezeption* (Reinbek bei Hamburg, 1989); *Johann Sebastian Bach* (Reinbek bei Hamburg, 1993); *Von Beethoven bis Mahler: Die Musik des deutsche Idealismus* (Stuttgart, 1993); with U. Tadday, *W. Feldmanns Versuch einer Geschichte des Dortmunder Conzerts aus dem Jahre 1830* (Hildesheim, 1994).

Gédalge, André, eminent French pedagogue and composer; b. Paris, Dec. 27, 1856; d. Chessy, Feb. 5, 1926. He began to study music rather late in life, and entered the Paris Cons. at the age of 28. However, he made rapid progress, and obtained the 2nd Prix de Rome after a year of study (with Guiraud). He then elaborated a system of counterpoint, later publ. as *Traité de la fugue* (Paris, 1901; Eng. tr., 1964), which became a standard work. In 1905 he became a prof. of counterpoint and fugue at the Paris Cons.; among his students were Ravel, Enesco, Koechlin, Roger-Ducasse, Milhaud, and Honegger. He also publ. *Les Gloires musicales du monde* (1898) and other pedagogic works. As a composer, he was less significant. Among his works are a pantomime, *Le Petit Savoyard* (Paris, 1891); an opera, *Pris au piège* (Paris, 1895); and 3 operas that were not performed: *Sita, La Farce du Cadi*, and *Hélène*; he also wrote 3 syms., several concertos, some chamber music, and songs.

BIBL.: "Hommage à G.," *Revue Musicale* (March 1, 1926).

Gedda (real name, **Ustinov**), **Nicolai (Harry Gustav),** noted Swedish tenor; b. Stockholm, July 11, 1925. Gedda was his mother's name, which he assumed in his professional life. His father was a Russian who went to Sweden after the Civil War. He studied at the opera school at the Stockholm Cons. On April 8, 1952, he made his operatic debut as Chapelou in *Le Postillon de Longjumeau* at the Royal Opera in Stockholm. In 1953 he made his debut at La Scala in Milan; in 1954 he sang Faust at the Paris Opera and the Duke of Mantua at Covent Garden in London; in 1957 he sang Don José in *Carmen* at the Vienna State Opera. He made his U.S. debut as Faust with the Pittsburgh Opera on April 4, 1957; his Metropolitan Opera debut followed in N.Y. on Nov. 1, 1957, in that same role; he created the role of Anatol in Barber's *Vanessa* at the Metropolitan on Jan. 15, 1958. Because of his natural fluency in Russian and his acquired knowledge of German, French, Italian, and English, he was able to sing with total freedom the entire standard operatic repertoire. In 1980 and 1981 he made highly successful appearances in Russia, both in opera and on the concert stage. In 1986 he made his London recital debut. In 1991 he appeared as Christian II in a revival of Naumann's *Gustaf Wasa* in Stockholm. His memoirs were publ. as *Gåvan är inte gratis* (Stockholm, 1978).

Gedike, Alexander. See **Goedike, Alexander.**

Gedzhadze, Irakly, Russian composer; b. Mtskheta, Oct. 26, 1925. He studied with Matchavariani at the Tbilisi Cons.; graduated in 1957. His works include the opera *Sunrise* (Tbilisi, Nov. 23, 1961); *Lake Palestomi*, symphonic poem (1956); piano pieces.

Geehl, Henry Ernest, English composer and teacher; b. London, Sept. 28, 1881; d. Beaconsfield, Buckinghamshire, Jan. 14, 1961. A pupil of R.O. Morgan, he was appointed a prof. at Trinity College of Music, London, in 1919. He wrote a Sym.; Violin Concerto; Piano Concerto; pieces for brass band, including *Cornwall* and *Cornish Rhapsody*; pedagogic piano pieces; songs.

Gefors, Hans, Swedish composer; b. Stockholm, Dec. 8, 1952. He studied composition with Per-Gunnar Alldahl and Maurice Karkoff, with Ingvar Lidholm at the Stockholm Musikhögskolan (1972), and with Nørgård at the Århus Cons.; also wrote music criticism and worked as an ed. In 1988 he joined the faculty at the Univ. of Lund.

WORKS: *Aprahishtita* for Cello, Piano, and Tape (1970–71); *Matutino* for Flute, Violin, Viola, Cello, and Piano (1973); *Visviter* for String Orch. (1973); *Reveille* for Voice and 5 Instruments (1974–75); *Orpheus singt*, cantata for Chorus and Orch. (1976–77); *Poeten och glasmästaren*, chamber opera (1979; Århus, April 26, 1980); *Me morire en Paris* for Baritone and 4 Instruments (1979); *Syndabocken*, theater music (1979); Trio for Voice, Guitar, and Violin (1981); *Slits* for Orch. (1981; Hälsingborg, Feb. 18, 1982); *Galjonsfiguren* for Soprano, Electric Guitar, and Tape (1983); *Christina*, opera (1983–86; Stockholm, Oct. 18, 1986); *Der Park*, opera (1986–91); *Twine* for Orch. (1988; Nörrkoping, May 11, 1989); *Die Erscheinung im Park* for Orch. (1990; Malmö, March 14, 1991); *Botho Strauss* for Orch. (1991; Wiesbaden, April 25, 1992); Concerto for 5 Percussion and Sinfonietta (1993).

Gehlhaar, Rolf (Rainer), German-born American composer; b. Breslau, Dec. 30, 1943. He emigrated to the U.S. in 1953 and in 1958 became a naturalized American citizen. He took courses in philosophy, science, and music at Yale Univ. (B.A., 1965) and in music at the Univ. of Calif. at Berkeley (1965–67). From 1967 to 1970 he was the personal assistant to Stockhausen. In 1976 he settled in London. He founded the electronic music studio at Dartington College in 1976, and that same year he served as director of the composition course in Darmstadt. In 1977 he was composer-in-residence at the New South Wales State Conservatorium of Music in Sydney. In 1978 he returned as director of the composition course in Darmstadt. He worked at IRCAM in Paris in 1979. In 1981 he worked there again and created the first composition utilizing digitally generated "3-dimensional" sounds, *Pas à pas . . . music for ears in motion*. In 1984 he commenced research on a computer-controlled interactive musical environment which resulted in his Sound=Space series. In 1995 he opened the Sound=Space Centre in London, the first permanent installation devoted to his creative workshops.

WORKS: *Cello Solo* (1966); *Klavierstück 1–1* for Piano

(1967); *Helix* for Quintet (1967); *Der, die oder das Klavier* for Piano and Film (1967); *Beckenstück* for 6 Amplified Cymbals (1969); *Klavierstück 2–2* for 2 Pianos (1970); *Wege* for Amplified Piano and 2 Strings (1971); *Cybernet I* and *II*, interactive electronic environment (1971); *Phase* for Orch. (1972); *Musi-Ken* for String Quartet (1972); *Protoypen* for 4 Orch. Groups (1973); *Liebeslied* for Alto and Orch. (1974); *Solipse* for Cello and Tape Delay (1974); *Spektra* for 4 Trumpets and 4 Trombones (1974); *5 Deutsche Tänze* for Tape (1975); *Rondell* for Trombone and Tape Delay (1975); *Resonanzen* for 8 Orch. Groups (1976); *Lamina* for Trombone and Orch. (1977); *Isotrope* for Chorus (1977); *Particles* for Soprano, Chamber Orch., and Electronics (1977–78); *Polymorph* for Bass Clarinet or Clarinet and Tape Delay (1978); *Linear A* for Marimbaphone (1978); *Camera oscura* for Brass Quintet (1978); *Strangeness, Charm, and Colour* for Piano and 3 Brass (1978); *Worldline* for 4 Voices and Live Electronics (1980); *Fluid* for Clarinet, Violin, Cello, and Piano (1980); *Sub Rosa* for Tape (1980); *Pas à pas . . . music for ears in motion* for Live Electronics (1981); *Pixels* for 8 Instruments (1981); *Tokamak* for Piano and Orch. (1982; rev. 1988); *Das Mädchen aus der Ferne* for Soprano, Flute, and Piano (1983); *Nairi* for Amplified Violin or Viola (1983); *Sound=Space*, interactive musical environment (1985); *Infra* for 10 Amplified Instruments (1985); *Copernic Opera* for 15 Dancers in a Sound=Space (1986); *Eichung* for 3 Instruments in a Sound=Space (1986); *Origo* for 5 Amplified Instruments (1987); *Sudden Adventures* for 2 Dancers in a Sound=Space (1988); *Head Pieces* for 2 Heads in a Sound=Space (1988); *Diagonal Flying* for Keyboards and Electronics (1989); Suite for Piano (1990); *Strange Attractor* for Computer-controlled Piano (1991); *Chronik* for 2 Pianos, 2 Percussionists, and Electronics (1991); *Maree* for 6 Percussionists and Live Electronics (1991); *Cusps, Swallowtails, and Butterflies* for Tape, Amplified Cymbals, and Live Electronics (1992); *Grand Unified Theory of Everything (GUTE)* for Flute, Bass Clarinet, Alto Clarinet, and Piano (1992); *Angaghoutiun* for Piano Quartet (1994); *Amor* for Flute (1994); *Quantum Leap* for Piano (1994).

Gehrkens, Karl (Wilson), American music educator; b. Kelleys Island, Ohio, April 19, 1882; d. Elk Rapids, Mich., Feb. 28, 1975. After graduation from Oberlin (Ohio) College (B.A., 1905; M.A., 1912), he became a prof. of school music at the Oberlin Cons. of Music in 1907; retired in 1942. He was ed. of *School Music* from 1925 to 1934 and author or co-author of 9 books on music education. During his tenure as president of the Music Supervisors National Conference (1923), he coined the slogan "Music for every child, and every child for music."

BIBL.: F. Lendrim, *Music for Every Child: The Story of K.W. G.* (diss., Univ. of Mich., 1972).

Geiringer, Karl (Johannes), eminent Austrian-American musicologist; b. Vienna, April 26, 1899; d. Santa Barbara, Calif., Jan. 10, 1989. He studied composition with Gál and Stohr, and musicology with Adler and Fischer in Vienna; continued his musicological studies with Sachs and Johannes Wolf in Berlin; received his Ph.D. from the Univ. of Vienna with the diss. *Die Flankenwirbelinstrumente in der bildenden Kunst* (1300–1550) in 1923 (publ. in Tutzing, 1979). In 1930 he became librarian and museum curator of the Gesellschaft der Musikfreunde in Vienna. He left Austria in 1938 and went to London, where he worked for the BBC; also taught at the Royal College of Music (1939–40). He then emigrated to the U.S.; was a visiting prof. at Hamilton College, Clinton, N.Y. (1940–41); in 1941 he became a prof. at Boston Univ. and head of graduate studies in music; in 1962 he was made a prof. at the Univ. of Calif., Santa Barbara; he retired in 1972. In 1955–56 he was president of the American Musicological Soc. In 1959 he was elected a Fellow of the American Academy of Arts and Sciences; also was an honorary member of the Österreichische Gesellschaft für Musikwissenschaft and of the American chapter of the Neue Bach-Gesellschaft; in addition, was a member of the Joseph Haydn Inst. of Cologne. A music scholar and writer of great erudition, he contributed valuable publications on the Bach family, Haydn, and Brahms. He was general ed. of the Harbrace History of Musical Forms and of the Univ. of Calif., Santa Barbara, Series of Early Music.

WRITINGS: With H. Kraus, *Führer durch die Joseph Haydn Kollektion im Museum der Gesellschaft der Musikfreunde in Wien* (Vienna, 1930); *Joseph Haydn* (Potsdam, 1932); *Johannes Brahms: Leben und Schaffen eines deutschen Meisters* (Vienna, 1935; Eng. tr., 1936; rev. and enl. ed., 1981); *Musical Instruments: Their History in Western Culture from the Stone Age to the Present Day* (London, 1943; 3rd ed., rev. and enl., 1978, as *Instruments in the History of Western Music*); *Haydn: A Creative Life in Music* (N.Y., 1946; 3rd ed., 1983); *A Thematic Catalogue of Haydn's Settings of Folksongs from the British Isles* (Superior, Wis., 1953); *The Bach Family: Seven Generations of Creative Genius* (N.Y., 1954); *Music of the Bach Family: An Anthology* (Cambridge, Mass., 1955); *Johann Sebastian Bach: The Culmination of an Era* (N.Y., 1966); *This I Remember* (Santa Barbara, Calif., 1993).

BIBL.: A. Silver, ed., *K. G.: A Checklist of His Publications in Musicology* (Santa Barbara, Calif., 1969); H.C. Robbins Landon and R. Chapman, *Studies in Eighteenth-Century Music: A Tribute to K. G. on His 70th Birthday* (N.Y. and London, 1970).

Geiser, Walther, Swiss violist, conductor, pedagogue, and composer; b. Zofingen, May 16, 1897; d. Oberwil, near Basel, March 6, 1993. He was a student of Hirt (violin) and Suter (composition) at the Basel Cons. (1917–20), of Eldering (violin) in Cologne, and of Busoni (composition) at the Prussian Academy of Arts in Berlin (1921–23). From 1924 to 1963 he taught at the Basel Cons.; he also was active as a violist and conductor, and was conductor of the Basel Bach Choir (1954–72). He generally followed a late Romantic path as a composer.

WORKS: 2 flute concertos (1921, 1963); Violin Concerto (1930); Horn Concerto (1934); *Konzertstück* for Organ and Chamber Orch. (1941); 4 orch. fantasies (1942, 1945, 1949, 1963); 2 syms. (1953, 1967); *Concerto da camera* for 2 Violins, Harpsichord, and String Orch. (1957); Piano Concerto (1959); chamber music; piano pieces; *Stabat Mater* for Baritone, Chorus, Orch., and Organ (1936); *Te Deum* for 4 Soloists, Chorus, Orch., and Organ (1960); choral music.

Geissler, Fritz, German composer; b. Wurzen, near Leipzig, Sept. 16, 1921; d. Bad Saarow, Jan. 11, 1984. He studied at the Leipzig Hochschule für Musik with Max Dehnert and Wilhelm Weismann (1948–50); later taught there (1962–70); then joined the faculty of the Dresden Cons.; was named a prof. there in 1974. His music is dialectical and almost Hegelian in its syllogistic development and climactic synthesis; the ground themes are carefully adumbrated before their integration in a final catharsis; formal dissonances are emancipated by a freely modified application of 12-tone writing.

WORKS: DRAMATIC: OPERAS: *Der Schatten*, fantastic opera (1975); *Die Stadtpfeifer* (1977); *Das Chagrinleder* (1978). **BALLETS:** *Pigment* (1960); *Sommernachtstraum* (1965); *Der Doppelgänger* (1969). Also *Der verrückte Jourdain*, a "Rossiniada" (1971). **ORCH.:** 2 chamber syms. (1954, 1970); *Italienische Lustspielouverture*, after Rossini (1958); *November 1918*, suite (1958); 9 syms.: No. 1 (1961), No. 2 (1963), No. 3 (1965–66), No. 4 for Strings (1968), No. 5 (1969), No. 6, *Sinfonia concertante*, for Wind Quintet and Strings (1971), No. 7 (1973), No. 8 for Soloists, Chorus, and Orch. (1974), and No. 9 (1978); *Sinfonietta giocosa* (1963); *The Adventures of the Good Soldier Schweik*, symphonic burlesque (1963); *Essay* (1969); *2 Symphonic Scenes* (1970); Piano Concerto (1970); *Beethoven-Variationen* (1971); Cello Concerto (1974); *Offenbach-Metamorphosen* (1977); Concerto for Flute, Strings, Harpsichord, and Percussion (1977); Concerto for Organ, Percussion, and Strings (1979). **CHAMBER:** String Quartet (1951); Suite for Wind Quintet (1957); Chamber Concerto for Harpsichord, Flute, and 10 Instruments (1967); *Ode to a Nightingale* for Nonet (1967–68); Viola Sonata (1969); Piano Trio (1970); piano pieces. **VOCAL:** *Gesang vom Menschen*, oratorio (1968); *Nachtelegien*, romance for High Voice and Instruments (1969); *Die Liebenden*, romance for Tenor and 2 Instrumental Groups (1969); *Schöpfer Mensch*, oratorio (1973); *Die Glocke von Buchenwald*, cantata (1974); *Die Flamme von Mansfeld*, oratorio (1978); choruses; songs.

Gelber, Bruno-Leonardo, esteemed Argentine pianist of Austrian and French-Italian descent; b. Buenos Aires, March 19, 1941. His parents were musicians and he took up the piano at a very early age; he was only 5 when he made his first public appearance, and at 6 became a pupil of Vincenzo Scaramuzza. When he was 7 he was stricken with poliomyelitis; while confined to his bed for a year, he continued to practice with his bed slid under the piano. At age 8, he made his formal recital debut; when he was 15 he attracted wide notice when he appeared as soloist in the Schumann Concerto under Lorin Maazel's direction in Buenos Aires. In 1960 he was awarded a French government grant and pursued his training in Paris with Marguerite Long. In 1961 he won 3rd prize in the Long-Thibaud competition. In subsequent years he toured all over the world, appearing as a soloist with the great orchs. and as a recitalist in the major music centers. He has won deserved accolades for his compelling performances of the Classical and Romantic repertory.

Gelbrun, Artur, Polish-born Israeli composer and teacher; b. Warsaw, July 11, 1913; d. Tel Aviv, Dec. 24, 1985. He studied at the Warsaw Cons.; then took courses with Molinari and Casella at the Accademia di Santa Cecilia in Rome; later studied composition with W. Burkhard and conducting with Scherchen in Zürich. He was an orch. and solo violinist in Warsaw, Lausanne, and Zürich (1936–47). In 1949 he emigrated to Israel and joined the staff of the Tel Aviv Academy of Music as prof. of conducting and composition.

WORKS: DRAMATIC: RADIOPHONIC ORATORIO: *Le Livre du Feu* (1964; Jerusalem, 1966). **BALLETS:** *Hedva* (1951; concert premiere, Ein-Gev, May 27, 1951; stage premiere, St. Gallen, 1958); *Miadoux* (1966–67); *Prologue to the Decameron* (1968); *King Solomon and the Hoopoes* (1976). **ORCH.:** Suite (1947); *Prelude, Passacaglia and Fugue* (1954); *Variations* for Piano and Orch. (1955); *Prologue Symphonique* (1956); *5 Capriccios* (1957); 3 syms. (1957–58; 1961; *Jubilee*, 1973); Cello Concerto (1962); *Piccolo Divertimento* for Youth Orch. (1963; also perf. as a ballet); *4 Pieces* for Strings (1963); *Concerto-Fantasia* for Flute, Harp, and Strings (1963); Concertino for Chamber Orch. (1974); *Adagio* for Strings (1974); *Hommage à Rodin* (1979–81); Concerto for Oboe and Strings (1985; rev. and orchestrated by L. Biriotti, 1986). **CHAMBER:** String Trio (1945); String Quartet (1969); Wind Quintet (1971); Trio for Trumpet, Horn, and Trombone (1972); Piano Trio (1977); Septet for Harp, Flute, Clarinet, and String Quartet (1984); solo pieces; piano music. **VOCAL:** *Lieder der Mädchen* for Voice and Orch. (1945); *Song of the River* for Soprano and Orch. (1959); *Salmo e Alelujah* for Soprano and Orch. (1968); *Holocaust and Revival*, cantata for Narrator, Chorus, and Orch. (1977–78); songs.

Gelineau, Joseph, French composer and editor; b. Champsur-Layon, Maine-et-Loire, Oct. 31, 1920. At the age of 21, he entered the Order of the Jesuits; studied organ and composition at the École César Franck in Paris; also obtained a doctorate in theology. He publ. *Chant et musique dans le culte chrétien* (Paris, 1962); composed *Missa plebs sancta* (1960), Psalms, etc.; tr. and set to music the Psalmody of the Bible of Jerusalem.

Gellman, Steven (David), Canadian composer and teacher; b. Toronto, Sept. 16, 1947. He studied composition with Dolin at the Royal Cons. of Music of Toronto; then studied with Berio, Sessions, and Persichetti at the Juilliard School of Music in N.Y. (1965–68), with Milhaud at Aspen, Colo. (summers, 1965–66), and with Messiaen at the Paris Cons. (1974–76; premiers prix in analysis, 1975, and in composition, 1976). In 1976 he joined the faculty of the Univ. of Ottawa. He adopted an uncompromisingly modernistic idiom in most of his music, while safeguarding the formal design of Classical tradition.

WORKS: ORCH.: 2 piano concertos (1962, 1989); *Andante* for Strings (1963); *Mural* (1965); *Andante-Agitato* for Violin and Orch. (1966); *Movement* for Violin and Orch. (1967); *Symphony in 2 Movements* (Ottawa, July 15, 1971); *Odyssey* for Rock Group, Piano, and Orch. (Hamilton, Ontario, March 9, 1971); *Symphony II* (Toronto, Dec. 2, 1972); *Encore (Mythos I Revisited)* (1972); *Overture for Ottawa* (1972); *Chori* (1974; rev. 1976); *Animus-Anima* (Paris, April 28, 1976); *Awakening* (1982); *The Bride's Reception: A Symphonic Contemplation* (1981–83); *Universe Symphony* (1985; Toronto, Jan. 8, 1986); *Burnt Offerings* for Strings (1990); *Child-Play* for Chamber Orch. (1992). **CHAMBER:** *2 Movements* for String Quartet (1963); *Soliloquy* for Cello (1966; rev. 1982); *After Bethlehem* for String Quartet (1966); *Quartets: Poems of G.M. Hopkins* for Voice, Flute, Cello, and Harp (1966–67); *Mythos II* for Flute and String Quartet (1968); *Sonate pour sept* for Flute, Clarinet, Cello, Guitar, Piano, and 2 Percussionists (1975); *Wind Music* for 2 Trumpets, Horn, Trombone, and Bass Tuba (1978); *Dialogue I* for Horn (1978) and *II* for Flute and Piano (1979); *Transformation* for Flute and Piano (1980); *Trikâya* for Violin, Clarinet, Percussion, and Piano (1981); *Chiaroscuro* for Flute, Clarinet, Violin, Viola, Cello, Piano, and Percussion (1988); Concertino for Guitar and String Quartet (1988); *Musica Eterna* for String Quartet (1991); Cello Sonata (1995). **PIANO:** 2 sonatas (1964, 1973); *Fantasy* (1967); *Melodic Suite* (1971–72); *Veils* (1974); *Poème* (1977); *Waves and Ripples* (1979); *Fantasia on a Theme by Robert Schumann* (1983); *Keyboard Triptych* (Montreal, Oct. 19, 1986). **VOCAL:** *Love's Garden* for Soprano and Orch. (1988); *Canticles* for Chorus and Orch. (1989).

Gelmetti, Gianluigi, Italian conductor; b. Rome, Sept. 11, 1945. He studied conducting at the Accademia di Santa Cecilia in Rome (diploma, 1965); his principal mentor was Ferrara (1962–67), but he also studied with Celibidache and in Vienna with Swarowsky. After serving as music director of the Orch. of the Pomeriggi Musicale in Milan (until 1980), he was chief conductor of the RAI Orch. in Rome (1980–84) and music director of the Rome Opera (1984–85). He was chief conductor of the Stuttgart Radio Sym. Orch. (from 1989) and music director of the Orchestre Philharmonique de Monte Carlo (1990–92).

Gencer, Leyla, Turkish soprano; b. Constantinople, Oct. 10, 1924. She studied at the Ankara Cons. with Elvira de Hidalgo; she also studied with Arangi-Lombardi in Istanbul. After making her operatic debut as Santuzza in Ankara in 1950, she completed her training in Italy with Apollo Granforte. In 1953 she sang in Naples, and then joined Milan's La Scala in 1956; she also appeared at the San Francisco Opera (1956–58). Her career was mainly concentrated in Europe, where she first sang at the Spoleto Festival (1959), the Salzburg Festival (1961), London's Covent Garden (1962), the Glyndebourne Festival (1962), and the Edinburgh Festival (1969). Among her admired roles were Donna Anna, Countess Almaviva, Anna Bolena, Norma, Elisabeth de Valois, and Maria Stuarda.

Gendron, Maurice, French cellist, conductor, and pedagogue; b. Nice, Dec. 26, 1920; d. Grez-sur-Loing, Aug. 20, 1990. He studied cello with Stéphane Odero in Cannes, Jean Mangot at the Nice Cons. (premier prix, 1935), and Gérard Hekking at the Paris Cons. (premier prix, 1938); later he found mentors in conducting in Désormiere, Scherchen, and Mengelberg. In 1945 he acquired a following as a cello virtuoso when he appeared as soloist in Prokofiev's Cello Concerto in London; thereafter he played with major European orchs. He also was active as a conductor in France, and later was conductor with the Bournemouth Sinfonietta (1971–73). He served as a prof. at the Saarbrücken Hochschule für Musik (1953–70), and then at the Paris Cons. (1970–87).

Gennrich, Friedrich, respected German musicologist; b. Colmar, March 27, 1883; d. Langen, Sept. 22, 1967. He studied Roman philology at the Univ. of Strasbourg; took courses in musicology with F. Ludwig. In 1921 he went to Frankfurt am Main, where he taught musicology at the Univ. until 1964. He was a leading authority on music of the troubadours, trouvères, and Minnesinger.

WRITINGS: *Musikwissenschaft und romanische Philologie*

(Halle, 1918); *Der musikalische Vortrag der altfranzösischen Chansons de geste* (Halle, 1923); *Die altfranzösiche Rotrouenge* (Halle, 1925); *Das Formproblem des Minnesangs* (Halle, 1931); *Grundriss einer Formenlehre des mittelalterlichen Liedes* (Halle, 1932); *Die Strassburger Schule für Musikwissenschaft* (Würzburg, 1940); *Abriss der frankonischen Mensuralnotation* (Nieder-Modau, 1946; 2nd ed., Darmstadt, 1956); *Abriss der Mensuralnotation des XIV. und der 1. Hälfte des XV. Jahrhunderts* (Nieder-Modau, 1948); *Melodien altdeutscher Lieder* (Darmstadt, 1954); *Franco von Köln, Ars Cantus Mensurabilis* (Darmstadt, 1955); *Die Wimpfener Fragmente der Hessischen Landesbibliothek* (Darmstadt, 1958); *Der musikalische Nachlass der Troubadours* (Darmstadt, 1960).

Gentele, Goeran, brilliant Swedish opera manager; b. Stockholm, Sept. 20, 1917; d. in an automobile accident near Olbia, Sardinia, July 18, 1972. He studied political science in Stockholm, and art at the Sorbonne in Paris. He was first engaged as an actor, then was stage director at the Royal Drama Theater (1941–52) and at the Royal Opera (1952–63) in Stockholm, where he was appointed director in 1963. In 1970 he was appointed general manager of the Metropolitan Opera in N.Y., effective June 1972; great expectations for his innovative directorship in America were thwarted by his untimely death during a vacation in Italy.

Genzmer, Harald, German composer and pedagogue; b. Blumenthal, Feb. 9, 1909. After piano and organ lessons in Marburg, he studied with Hindemith at the Berlin Hochschule für Musik. He taught at the Berlin Volksmusikschule (1938–45), and then was a prof. of composition at the Freiburg im Breisgau Hochschule für Musik (1946–57) and the Munich Hochschule für Musik (1957–74). Hindemith proved a major influence on his music, which is especially notable for its display of skillful craftsmanship in a utilitarian manner.

WORKS: BALLETS: *Kokua* (1951); *Der Zauberspiegel* (1965). **ORCH.:** *Bremer Sinfonie* (1942); 3 numbered syms. (1957, 1958, 1986); 3 piano concertos (1948–74); Cello Concerto (1950); Flute Concerto (1954); Violin Concerto (1959); Concerto for Harp and Strings (1965); Viola Concerto (1967); 2 concertos for Trumpet and Strings (1968, 1985); Concerto for Cello and Winds (1969); *Sinfonia da camera* (1970); 2 organ concertos (1970, 1980); Concerto for Trumpet and Large Wind Orch. (1971–72); Chamber Concerto for Viola and Strings (1973); *Musik* (1977–78); *Sinfonia per Giovani* (1979); Concerto for 2 Clarinets and Strings (1983); *Lyrisches Konzert* for Cello and Orch. (1984); Concerto for 4 Horns and Orch. (1984); Concerto for Cello, Double Bass, and Strings (1985); *Cassation* for Strings (1987); Saxophone Concerto (1992). **CHAMBER:** Trio for Violin, Cello, and Piano (1944); Trio for Flute, Viola, and Harp (1947); Quintet for Flute, Oboe, Clarinet, Horn, and Bassoon (1956–57); Sonata for Solo Violin (1957); Sonata for Cello and Harp (1963); Trio for Piano, Violin, and Cello (1964); Sextet for 2 Clarinets, 2 Horns, and 2 Bassoons (1966); Quartet for Violin, Viola, Cello, and Double Bass (1967); Quintet for 2 Trumpets, Horn, Trombone, and Tuba (1970); Sonata for Trumpet and Organ (1971); Trombone Sonata (1971); Trio for Flute, Horn or Cello, and Harpsichord or Piano (1973); Bassoon Sonata (1974); Sonata for Solo Flute (1975); Sonata for Trombone and Organ (1977); Sonata for Cello and Organ (1979); Sonata for 2 Flutes (1981); Vibraphone Sonata (1981); Sonata for Solo Cello (1982); *Mallet/Spiele* for Marimbaphone/Vibraphone (1966); Guitar Sonata (1986); *Konzert 1994* for Trumpet, Trombone, and Organ (1994); piano pieces; organ music. **VOCAL:** *Jiménez-Kantate* for Soprano, Chorus, and Orch. (1962); *Mistral-Kantate* for Soprano and Orch. (1969–70); *Deutsche Messe* for Chorus and Organ (1973); *Oswald von Wolkenstein*, cantata for Soprano, Baritone, Chorus, and Orch. (1975–76); *The Mystic Trumpeter*, cantata for Soprano or Tenor, Trumpet, and Strings (1978); *Geistliche Kantate* for Soprano, Men's Chorus, Organ, and Percussion (1979); *Kantate 1981 nach engl. Barockgedichten* for Soprano, Chorus, and Orch. (1981).

BIBL.: M. Brück and R. Münster, *H.G.: Ausstellung zum 80. Geburtstag: Musiklesesaal, 8. September–17. November 1989* (Munich, 1989).

George, Earl, American composer, conductor, teacher, and music critic; b. Milwaukee, May 1, 1924. He studied composition with Hanson and Rogers and conducting with Paul White and Herman Genhart at the Eastman School of Music in Rochester, N.Y. (B.M., 1946; M.M., 1947; Ph.D., 1958); he also attended courses of Lopatnikoff and Martinů at the Berkshire Music Center in Tanglewood (summer, 1946), and continued his studies with the latter in N.Y. (1947). In 1947 he received the Gershwin Prize and in 1957 held a Guggenheim followship. From 1948 to 1956 he taught theory and composition at the Univ. of Minnesota, and in 1955–56 was a Fulbright lecturer at the Univ. of Oslo. He then was prof. of theory and composition at Syracuse Univ. (1959–88), where he was founder-conductor of the Univ. Singers (1963–69) and conductor of the Univ. Sym. Orch. (1971–80). He also was music critic of the Syracuse *Herald-Journal* from 1961. His works follow an astute median course of prudent American modernism.

WORKS: OPERAS: *Birthdays*, 2 operas individually titled *Pursuing Happiness* and *Another 4th of July* (Syracuse, April 23, 1976); *Genevieve* (Berea, Ohio, Feb. 10, 1984). **ORCH.:** *Passacaglia* (1944); *Adagietto* (1946); *Introduction and Allegro* (1946); Concerto for Strings (1948); *A Thanksgiving Overture* (1949); *A Currier and Ives Set* for Chamber Orch. (1953); Violin Concerto (1953); *Introduction, Variations, and Finale* (1957); *Some Night Music* for Strings (1957); Piano Concerto (1958); *Declamation* for Wind Ensemble (1965). **CHAMBER:** *Arioso* for Cello and Piano (1947); *3 Pieces* for Violin, Cello, and Piano (1949); String Quartet (1961); *Tuckets and Sennets* for Trumpet and Piano (1973); piano pieces, including a Sonata (1948). **VOCAL:** *Missa brevis* for Soloists, Chorus, and Orch. (1948); *Abraham Lincoln Walks at Midnight* for Soprano, Chorus, and Orch. (1949); *3 Poems of William Wordsworth* for Narrator, Chorus, and Piano (1960); *War is Kind* for Men's Chorus, Trumpet, Percussion, and Piano (1966); *Voyages* for Soprano, Speaker, Chorus, and 5 Instrumentalists (1967); *Voices* for Soprano, Chorus, 2 Pianos, and Percussion (1974); *Hum-drum Heaven* for Soprano, Speaker, Chorus, and Piano (1978); choruses; song cycles.

Georgescu, Dan Corneliu, Romanian composer; b. Craiova, Jan. 1, 1938. He studied at the Popular School for the Arts (1952–56) and with Ion Dumitrescu, Ciortea, Olah, and Mendelsohn at the Bucharest Cons. (1956–61). From 1962 to 1983 he was head of research at the Ethnography and Folklore Inst. of the Romanian Academy; then pursued research at the Inst. for the History of Art (from 1984). In 1987 he went to Berlin, and then was active in ethnomusicological pursuits at the Free Univ. from 1991. His output extends from traditional to electronic scores.

WORKS: OPERA-BALLET: *Model mioritic* (1973; Cluj, Oct. 1, 1975). **ORCH.:** *3 Pieces* (1959); *Motive maramureşene*, suite (1963); *4 pieces: I: Jocuri* (1963), *II: Dialogue rythmique* (1964), *III: Danses solennelles* (1965), and *IV: Collages* (1966); *Partita* (1966); cycle of 4 pieces for various orch. groupings: *Alb-negru* (1967), *Zig-Zag* (1967), *Continuo* (1968), and *Rubato* (1969); 3 syms.: No. 1, *Armoniile simple* (1976), No. 2, *Orizontale* (1980), and No. 3, *Privirile culorilor* (1985). **CHAMBER:** Piano Sonata (1958); Trio for Flute, Clarinet, and Bassoon (1959); *Chorals I, II*, and *III* for Flute, Violin, Viola, Cello, and Piano (1970); 3 string quartets (1982; 1983–84; 1985); 2 *Contemplative Preludes* for Organ (1991). **VOCAL:** *Schite pentru o fresca*, cantata (1976). **ELECTRONIC:** *Crystal Silence* (1989).

Georgescu, George, Romanian conductor; b. Sulina, Sept. 12, 1887; d. Bucharest, Sept. 1, 1964. After initial training in Bucharest, he went to Berlin and studied cello with H. Becker and conducting with Nikisch and Strauss. He began his conducting career in Berlin in 1918, and then returned to Bucharest as music director of the Phil. (1920–49) and the Opera (1922–26; 1932–34); from 1954 until his death he was music director of the George Enesco State Phil. He also made guest appearances throughout Europe.

BIBL.: T. Georgescu, *G.G.* (Bucharest, 1971).

Georgiades, Thrasybulos, Greek musicologist; b. Athens, Jan. 4, 1907; d. Munich, March 15, 1977. He studied piano in Athens; then studied musicology with Rudolf von Ficker at the Univ. of Munich, where he received his Ph.D. in 1935 with the diss. *Englische Diskanttraktate aus der ersten Hälfte des 15. Jahrhunderts* (publ. in Würzburg, 1937); he also studied composition with Orff. In 1938 he became a prof. at the Athens Odeon; was its director from 1939 to 1941. He completed his Habilitation at the Univ. of Munich in 1947 with his *Bemerkungen zur antiken Quantitätsmetrik* (publ. in Hamburg, 1949, as *Der griechische Rhythmus. Musik, Reigen, Vers und Sprache*; 2nd ed., 1977; Eng. tr., N.Y., 1956). In 1948 he joined the faculty of the Univ. of Heidelberg; in 1956 he became a prof. at the Univ. of Munich, retiring in 1972. He contributed valuable papers to German music journals on ancient Greek, Byzantine, and medieval music. His other writings include *Volkslied als Bekenntnis* (Regensburg, 1947); *Musik und Sprache* (Berlin, 1954; Eng. tr., Cambridge, 1983); *Musik und Rhythmus bei den Griechen* (Hamburg, 1958); *Zum Ursprung der abendländischen Musik* (Hamburg, 1958); *Musik und Schrift* (Munich, 1962); *Das musikalische Theater* (Munich, 1965); *Schubert, Musik und Lyrik* (Göttingen, 1967).

Georgiadis, Georges, Greek pianist and composer; b. Salonika, Sept. 8, 1912; d. Athens, May 8, 1986. He studied piano and composition at the Athens Cons. In 1943 he was appointed prof. of piano there. His music, cast in a traditional mold, was inspired chiefly by Greek folk resources. Among his compositions were a Concertino for Piano and Orch. (1959); *De la paix*, sym. (1960); 2 violin sonatas; songs; many piano pieces; incidental music.

Georgii, Walter, German pianist and pedagogue; b. Stuttgart, Nov. 23, 1887; d. Tübingen, Feb. 23, 1967. He studied piano in Stuttgart and theory in Leipzig, Berlin, and Halle. From 1914 to 1945 he taught piano in Cologne. He publ. *Weber als Klavierkomponist* (Leipzig, 1914), *Geschichte der Musik für Klavier zu 2 Hände* (Zürich, 1941; rev. ed., 1950), and *Klavierspielerbuchlein* (Zürich, 1953), as well as an anthology of piano music, *400 Jahre europaïscher Klavier Musik* (Cologne, 1950).

Gérardy, Jean, Belgian cellist; b. Spa, Dec. 6, 1877; d. there, July 4, 1929. At the age of 5, he began to study cello with R. Bellmann; was a pupil of Alfred Massau at the Liège Cons. from 1885 to 1889. In 1888 he played as a student in a trio with Ysaÿe and Paderewski; he became noted as an ensemble player; with Ysaÿe and Godowsky, he formed a trio and toured the U.S. in 1913–14. Gérardy's instrument was a 1710 Stradivari.

Gerber, René, Swiss composer and teacher; b. Travers, June 29, 1908. He attended the Univ. of Zürich (1929) and studied with Andreae and Müller at the Zürich Cons. (1931–33) before completing his training in Paris (1934) with Dukas, Boulanger, Siohan, and Dupont. After serving as prof. of music at the Latin College in Neuchâtel (1940–47), he was director of the Neuchâtel Cons. (1947–51). His works were marked by tonal and modal writing.

WORKS: OPERAS: *Roméo et Juliette* (1957–61); *Le Songe d'une nuit d'été* (1978–81). **ORCH.:** 2 concertos for Harp and Chamber Orch. (1931, 1969); Clarinet Concerto (1932); *Hommage à Ronsard* (1933); 2 piano concertos: No. 1 for Piano and Chamber Orch. (1933) and No. 2 for Piano and Orch. (1966–70); *Suite française I* (1933), *II* (1934), and *III* (1945) for Chamber Orch.; Concerto for Flute and Chamber Orch. (1934); Concerto for Bassoon and Chamber Orch. (1935–39); *Les Heures de France* (1937); Concerto for Trumpet and Chamber Orch. (1939); Violin Concerto (1941); *Trois Paysages de Breughel* (1942); *Le Terroir animé* (1944); *Trois Danses espagnoles* for Chamber Orch. (1944); 2 sinfoniettas for Strings (1949, 1968); *L'Imagier médiéval* (1952–74); *Lais Corinthiaca* (1957); *Suite brévinière* (1960); *Le Moulin de la Galette* (1970); Concerto for English Horn and Chamber Orch. (1976); *L'École de Fontainebleau* (1978–79); Concerto for Trumpet, Strings, and Percussion (1983); *The Old Farmer's Almanac* (1986). **CHAMBER:** Sonata for Solo Harp (1932); 4 string quartets (1933, 1934, 1941, 1947); Concertino for Winds, Piano, and Percussion (1935); *Ballet* for Flute and Piano (1943); Violin Sonata (1943); Trio for Violin, Cello, and Piano (1944); Flute Sonata (1945); Cello Sonata (1945); Trumpet Sonata (1948); Saxophone Sonata (1948); Suite for Flute, Oboe, and Piano (1948); Sonatine for Cor de chasse and Piano (1965); Trio for 2 Clarinets and Bassoon (1982; also for 3 Clarinets); *A Terpsychore* for Clarinet Ensemble (1993). **VOCAL:** *5 Impressions* for Voice, Wind Orch., 2 Harps, and Percussion (1942); *Le Tombeau de Botticelli* for Chorus and 11 Instruments (1967); *Trois Visions espagnoles* for Voice, 5 Winds, Piano, and 2 Percussion (1973); *3 Poèmes de la Renaissance* for Contralto or Baritone, Violin, Cello, and Piano (1977); *3 Poèmes* for Soprano, Violin, Cello, and Piano (1988); other songs; noëls, etc.

Gerber, Rudolf, learned German musicologist; b. Flehingen, Baden, April 15, 1899; d. Göttingen, May 6, 1957. He studied at the Univ. of Halle, and then at the Univ. of Leipzig (Ph.D., 1922, with the diss. *Die Arie in den Opern Johann Adolf Hasses*; publ. as *Der Operntypus Johann Adolf Hasses und seine textlichen Grundlagen*, Leipzig, 1925). In 1923 he became Abert's assistant at the Univ. of Berlin. He completed his Habilitation in 1928 at the Univ. of Giessen with his *Das Passionsrezitativ bei Heinrich Schütz und seine stilgeschichtlichen Grundlagen* (publ. in Gütersloh, 1929). In 1928 he joined its faculty, where he later was a prof. and head of its Music-Historical Inst. (1937–43). In 1943 he became a prof. at the Univ. of Göttingen. Among his other writings were *Johannes Brahms* (Potsdam, 1938), *Christoph Willibald Ritter von Gluck* (Potsdam, 1941; 2nd. ed., rev., 1950); and *Bachs Brandenburgische Konzerte* (Kassel, 1951). He also ed. works by Schütz, J.S. Bach, and Gluck.

Gerelli, Ennio, Italian conductor and composer; b. Cremona, Feb. 12, 1907; d. there, Oct. 5, 1970. He studied at the Bologna Cons. He conducted ballet and opera in Italy; was on the staff of La Scala in Milan (1935–40); in 1961 he founded the Camerata di Cremona. He also wrote some chamber music.

Gergiev, Valery (Abissalovich), notable Russian conductor; b. Moscow, May 2, 1953. He received training in piano and conducting at the Ordzhonikidze College of Music, then pursued conducting studies with Ilya Musin at the Leningrad Cons. (graduated, 1977). In 1975 he won 1st prize in the All-Union Conductors' Competition in Moscow. In 1977 he captured 2nd prize in the Karajan competition in Berlin and was named assistant conductor at the Kirov Opera in Leningrad, where he made his debut conducting *War and Peace* in 1978; in 1979, was made permanent conductor there. He also served as chief conductor of the Armenian State Sym. Orch. in Yerevan (1981–85). In 1988 he was appointed artistic director and principal conductor of the Kirov Opera. From 1989 to 1992 he also was principal guest conductor of the Rotterdam Phil. He conducted the Kirov Opera on many tours abroad, including its first visit to the U.S. in 1992 when it appeared at the Metropolitan Opera in N.Y. On March 21, 1994, he made his Metropolitan Opera debut conducting *Otello*. In the autumn of 1994 he made a concert tour of the U.S. conducting the Kirov Orch. In 1995 he became music director of the Rotterdam Phil. Gergiev's interpretative insights, backed by an assured conducting technique, made him one of the most admired conductors of his generation. While his idiomatic performances of the Russian repertoire are particularly compelling, he has demonstrated skills in a broad operatic and symphonic repertoire well beyond the Russian tradition.

Gerhard, Roberto, eminent Catalonian-born English composer and teacher of Swiss-German and Alsatian descent; b. Valls, Sept. 25, 1896; d. Cambridge, Jan. 5, 1970. After training in piano from Granados (1915–16) and in composition from Pedrell (1916–20) in Barcelona, he pursued advanced studies in composition with Schoenberg in Vienna (1922–25) and Berlin (1925–28). Returning to Barcelona, he was made a prof. of music at the Ecola Normal de la Generalitat in 1931 and head of the music dept. of the Catalan Library in 1932, positions he held until the defeat of the Republic in the Spanish Civil War in 1939. He settled in Cambridge, where he held a research scholarship at King's College. In 1956 he taught at the Dartington Summer School of Music. In 1960 he was a visiting prof. of composition at the Univ. of Mich. in Ann Arbor. He taught at the Berkshire Music Center at Tanglewood in the summer of 1961. In 1960 he became a naturalized British subject. Gerhard was made a Commander of the Order of the British Empire in 1967 and was awarded an honorary doctor of music degree by the Univ. of Cambridge in 1968. In his early works, Gerhard followed traditional Spanish melodic and rhythmic patterns. The influence of Schoenberg is felt in his serial usage in the Wind Quintet (1928), but it was not until he settled in England that he began to reassess Schoenberg's 12-tone method with a detailed study of Hauer's and A. Hába's serial procedures. In 1952 he turned to the athematic procedures of Hába, which led to his composition of scores of great originality and merit. Among his finest works were the opera *The Duenna*, the ballet *Don Quixote*, and the 1st Sym.

WORKS: DRAMATIC: OPERA: *The Duenna* (1945–47; BBC, 1947; rev. 1950; concert perf., Wiesbaden, June 27, 1951; stage perf., Madrid, Jan. 21, 1992; also *Interlude and Arias from The Duenna* for Mezzo-soprano and Orch., London, Sept. 18, 1961). **BALLETS:** *Ariel* (1934; concert perf., Barcelona, May 18, 1936); *Soirées de Barcelone* (1936–38; unfinished; orch. suite, 1936–38; also for Piano, c.1958; London, Jan. 12, 1985); *Don Quixote* (1940–41; 1947–49; London, Feb. 20, 1950; also *Dances from Don Quixote* for Piano, BBC, London, Nov. 26, 1947, and for Orch., 1958); *Alegrías* (1942; Birmingham, July 16, 1943; orch. suite, BBC, April 4, 1944); *Pandora* (1943–44; Cambridge, Jan. 26, 1944; orchestrated 1945; orch. suite, BBC, London, Feb. 1950). Also incidental music to plays, and film, radio, and television scores. **ORCH.:** *Albada, Interludi i Danza* (1936; London, June 24, 1938); *Pedrelliana* (1941; final movement of subsequent work); 1 unnumbered sym.: *Homenage a Pedrell* (1941; BBC, London, 1954); 5 numbered syms.: No. 1 (1952–53; Baden-Baden, June 21, 1955), No. 2 (1957–59; London, Oct. 28, 1959; rev. 1967–68 as *Metamorphoses*), No. 3, *Collages* (1960; London, Feb. 8, 1961), No. 4, *New York* (N.Y., Dec. 14, 1967), and No. 5 (1969; unfinished); Violin Concerto (1942–43; rev. 1945, 1949; Florence, June 16, 1950); *Cadiz*, fantasia on a zarzuela by Chueca and Valverde (1943); *Gigantes y Cabezudos* (Giants and Dwarfs), fantasia on a zarzuela by Fernández Caballero (c.1943); *La Viejecita*, fantasia on a zarzuela by Fernández Caballero (c.1943); Concerto for Piano and Strings (1950); Concerto for Harpsichord, Strings, and Percussion (1955–56); *Lamparilla Overture*, after a zarzuela by Barbieri (1956); *Concerto for Orchestra* (Boston, April 25, 1965); *Epithalamion* (Valdagno, Sept. 17, 1966). **CHAMBER:** Piano Trio (1918); *2 Sardanas* for 11 Instruments (1928); Wind Quintet (1928); *Capriccio* for Flute (1949); 2 string quartets: No. 1 (1950–55; Dartington, Aug. 18, 1955) and No. 2 (1960–62); Cello Sonata (1956); Nonet for Wind Quintet, Trumpet, Trombone, Tuba, and Accordion (1956–57; BBC, London, Sept. 4, 1957); *Fantasia* for Guitar (1957); *Chaconne* for Violin (1959); *Concert for 8* for Flute, Clarinet, Mandolin, Guitar, Accordion, Percussion, Piano, and Double Bass (London, May 17, 1962); *Hymnody* for Flute, Oboe, Clarinet, Horn, Trumpet, Trombone, Tuba, 2 Percussion, and 2 Pianos (London, May 23, 1963); *Gemini* for Violin and Piano (1966); *Libra* for Flute, Clarinet, Guitar, Percussion, Piano, and Violin (1968); *Leo* for Flute, Clarinet, Horn, Trumpet, Trombone, 2 Percussion, Piano, Violin, and Cello (Hanover, N.H., Aug. 23, 1969). **PIANO:** *Dos apunts* (2 sketches; 1921–22); *3 Impromptus* (1950). **VOCAL:** *L'Infantament Meravellos de Shahrazada*, song cycle for Soprano or Tenor and Piano (1917); *7 Haiku* for Soprano or Tenor, Flute, Oboe, Clarinet, Bassoon, and Piano (1922; rev. 1958); *14 Cançons Populars Catalanes* for Soprano or Tenor and Piano (1928; 6 orchestrated 1931; Vienna, June 16, 1932); *L'Alta Naixença del Rei en Jaume*, cantata for Soprano, Baritone, Chorus, and Orch. (1932; 1st complete perf., Barcelona, Nov. 17, 1984); *Cançons y Arietes* for Voice and Piano (1936); *Cancionero de Pedrell* for Soprano or Tenor and Piano (1941; also for Soprano or Tenor and 13 Instruments, 1941); *Por do Pasaré la Sierra* for Soprano or Tenor and Piano (1942); *7 Canciones de Vihuela* for High Voice and Piano (1942); *6 Tonadillas* for Soprano or Tenor and Piano (1942); *Sevillanas* for Soprano or Tenor and Piano (1943); *3 Toreras* for Medium Voice and Orch. (c.1943; also for Voice and Piano); *Engheno Novo* for Voice and Orch. (c.1943); *The Akond of Swat* for Mezzo-soprano or Baritone and 2 Percussion (1954; London, Feb. 7, 1956); *6 French Folksongs* for High Voice and Piano (1956); *Cantares* for Soprano or Tenor and Guitar (1956); *The Plague* for Speaker, Chorus, and Orch. (1963–64; London, April 1, 1964). **TAPE:** *Audiomobiles I–IV* (1958–59); *Lament for the Death of a Bullfighter* for Speaker and Tape (1959); 10 pieces (c.1961); *Sculptures I–V* (1963).

BIBL.: Special issue of *The Score* (Sept. 1956); K. Potter, *The Life and Works of R.G.* (diss., Univ. of Birmingham, 1972); R. Paine, *Hispanic Traditions in Twentieth-Century Catalan Music with Particular Reference to G., Mompou, and Montsalvatge* (N.Y. and London, 1989); J. Homs, *R.G. i la seva obra* (Barcelona, 1991).

Gerhardt, Elena, celebrated German-born English mezzo-soprano; b. Leipzig, Nov. 11, 1883; d. London, Jan. 11, 1961. She studied at the Leipzig Cons. (1899–1903) with Marie Hedmont. She made her public debut on her 20th birthday in a recital, accompanied by Nikisch; after appearing at the Leipzig Opera (1903–04), she toured Europe as a lieder artist with great success; made her English debut in London in 1906, and her American debut in N.Y., Jan. 9, 1912. In 1933 she settled in London, making appearances as a singer, and teaching. She compiled *My Favorite German Songs* (1915), ed. a selection of Hugo Wolf's songs (1932), and wrote an autobiography, *Recital* (London, 1953).

Gerle, Robert, Hungarian-born American violinist, conductor, and teacher; b. Abbazia, Italy, April 1, 1924. He was educated at the Franz Liszt Academy of Music and the National Cons. in Budapest; received the Hubay Prize in 1942; played in recital and with major orchs. in Europe. He eventually settled in the U.S.; headed the string dept. of the Univ. of Okla. (1950–54); then was on the staff of the Peabody Cons. of Music in Baltimore (1955–68), the Mannes College of Music in N.Y. (1959–70), the Manhattan School of Music (1967–70), and Ohio State Univ. (1968–72). In 1972 he was named head of the Instrumental Program of the Univ. of Maryland, Baltimore County; was active as a conductor there and also continued his career as a violinist. He publ. *The Art of Practicing the Violin* (London, 1983) and *The Art of Bowing Practice: The Expressive Bow Technique* (London, 1991).

German, Sir Edward (real name, **German Edward Jones**), admired English composer; b. Whitchurch, Salop, Feb. 17, 1862; d. London, Nov. 11, 1936. After studies with W.C. Hay in Shrewsbury (1880), he pursued his training at the Royal Academy of Music in London (1880–87) with Steggall (organ), Weist-Hill and Burnett (violin), Banister (theory), and Prout (composition and orchestration). He played violin in theater orchs., and soon began conducting them. From 1888 he was active with various London theaters, establishing his reputation as a composer with his incidental music. German scored his most notable stage success with the comic opera *Merrie England* (London, April 2, 1902). In 1928 he was knighted and in 1934 was awarded the Gold Medal of the Royal Phil. Soc. of London.

WORKS: DRAMATIC: OPERAS: *The Rival Poets* (1883–86); *The Emerald Isle* (London, April 27, 1901; completion of an unfinished work by Sullivan); *Merrie England* (London, April 2,

1902); *A Princess of Kensington* (London, Jan. 22, 1903); *Tom Jones* (1907; London, April 17, 1908); *Fallen Fairies* or *Moon Fairies* (London, Dec. 15, 1909). **INCIDENTAL MUSIC TO:** *Richard III* (1889); *Henry VIII* (1892); *The Tempter* (1893); *Romeo and Juliet* (1895); *As You Like It* (1896); *Much Ado About Nothing* (1898); *Nell Gwyn* (1900); *The Conqueror* (1905). **ORCH.:** 2 syms. (1890; *Norwich*, 1893); *Marche Solonnelle* (1891); *Gypsy Suite* (1892); *The Leeds*, suite (1895); *English Fantasia: In Commemoration* (1897); *Hamlet*, symphonic poem (1897); *The Seasons*, suite (1899); *March Rhapsody* or *Rhapsody on March Themes* (1902); *Welsh Rhapsody* (1904); *The Irish Guards* for Military Band (1918); *Theme and 6 Diversions* (1919); *The Willow Song*, tone picture (1922); *Cloverely Suite* (1934). **OTHER:** Chamber music, many piano pieces, organ works, choral music, and songs.

BIBL.: W. Scott, *Sir E.G.: An Intimate Biography* (London, 1932); B. Rees, *A Musical Peacemaker: The Life and Works of Sir E.G.* (Bourne End, Buckinghamshire, 1987).

Germani, Fernando, Italian organist; b. Rome, April 5, 1906. He studied with Bajardi (piano), Dobici (theory), Respighi (composition), and Manari (organ) at the Accademia di Santa Cecilia in Rome. He taught organ at the Curtis Inst. of Music in Philadelphia (1936–38), and at various institutions in Italy, including the Rome Cons. (1935–76). He served as 1st organist at St. Peter's Cathedral in Rome (1948–59); also made numerous tours of Europe and North America. He ed. *Frescobaldi's Opere per organo e cembalo* (3 vols., Rome, 1964).

Gérold, (Jean) Théodore, eminent Alsatian music scholar; b. Strasbourg, Oct. 26, 1866; d. Allenwiller, Feb. 15, 1956. He studied voice, violin, and theory at the Strasbourg Cons.. From 1888 to 1906 he was solo bass singer at St. Guillaume in Strasbourg, during which time he pursued vocal training with Romaine Bussine and Charles Bordes in Paris and with Julius Stockhausen in Frankfurt am Main; he also studied music history with Gustaf Jacobsthal and took courses in theology at the German Univ. of Strasbourg (Ph.D., 1910, with the diss. *Zur Geschichte der französischen Gesangkunst*, publ. in Leipzig, 1910). He lectured on music at the Univ. of Basel (1914–18), and then at the new French Univ. in Strasbourg (1919–37), where he received his Dr. ès lettres in 1921 with the diss. *L'Art du chant en France au XVIIe siècle* (publ. in Strasbourg, 1921; subsidiary diss., *Le manuscrit de Bayeux, Chanson du XVe siècle;* publ. in Strasbourg and Paris, 1921), and his doctorat d'État in theology in 1931. From 1922 until his death he was pastor of the Lutheran parish in Allenwiller.

WRITINGS: *Kleine Sänger-Fiebel: Sprachliche Übungen für Sänger* (Mainz, 1908; 2nd ed., 1911); *Das Liederbuch einer französischen Provinzdame um 1620* (Frankfurt am Main, 1912); *Chansons populaires des XVe et XVIe siècles avec leurs mélodies* (Strasbourg, 1913); *Clément Marot: Les Psaumes avec leurs mélodies* (Strasbourg, 1919); *La Musicologie médiévale* (Paris, 1921); *François Schubert* (Paris, 1923); *Jean Sébastien Bach* (Paris, 1925); *Les Pères de l'église et la musique* (Paris, 1931); *La Musique au moyen âge* (Paris, 1932); *Histoire de la musique des origines à la fin du XIVe siècle* (Paris, 1936); *Marie-Joseph Erb: Sa vie, son oeuvre* (Strasbourg and Paris, 1948).

BIBL.: F. Münch, "In memoriam T. G. (1866–1956)," *Revue d'histoire et de philosophie religieuses*, XXXVII (1956).

Gerschefski, Edwin, American composer, pianist, and teacher; b. Meriden, Conn., June 10, 1909; d. Athens, Ga., Dec. 17, 1992. He studied piano with Bruce Simonds and composition at Yale Univ. (1926–31); following further training in piano at the Matthay school in London (1931–33) and with Schnabel in Como (1935), he completed his studies in composition with Schillinger in N.Y. (1936–38). In 1940 he joined the faculty of Converse College in Spartanburg, S.C., where he was dean of its music school (1945–59); he then was head of the music depts. at the Univs. of New Mexico (1959–60) and Georgia (1960–72), continuing on the faculty of the latter until 1976. In some of his works, he employed the Schillinger system of composition. He attracted particular notice for his settings of exact texts from newspapers, magazines, and business letters in several of his vocal scores.

WORKS: ORCH.: *Classic Symphony* (1931); Piano Concerto (1931); *Discharge in E* and *Streamline* for Band (1935); Violin Concerto (1951–52); *Toccata and Fugue* (1954); *Celebration* for Violin and Orch. (1964). **CHAMBER:** *Workout* for 2 Violins and 2 Violas (1933); Piano Quintet (1935); *8 Variations* for String Quartet (1937); Brass Septet (1938); *America*, variations for Winds (1962); *Rhapsody* for Violin, Cello, and Piano (1963); *The Alexander Suite* for 2 Cellos (1971); *Poem* for Cello and Piano (1973); various piano pieces, including 2 sonatas (1936, 1968). **VOCAL:** *Half Moon Mountain*, cantata for Baritone, Women's Chorus, and Orch., after a *Time* magazine article (1947–48; Spartanburg, S.C., April 30, 1948); *The Lord's Controversy with His People*, cantata for Soloist, Women's Chorus, and Small Orch. or Piano (1949); *Psalm C* for Soprano, Baritone, Chorus, Percussion, and Piano (1965); *Border Patrol* for Chorus and Piano, after a *Time* magazine article (1966); *Letter from BMI* for Chorus and Small Orch. (1981); songs. **OTHER:** Film music.

Gershfeld, David, Moldavian composer; b. Bobrinets, Aug. 28, 1911. After studying horn and theory in Odessa, he moved to Kishinev, where he produced 2 operas on Moldavian subjects: *Grozovan* (June 9, 1956) and *Aurelia* (April 26, 1959); also a Violin Concerto (1951) and *26 Commissars of Baku*, ballad for Chorus (commemorating the Bolshevik representatives in Azerbaijan killed by the British expeditionary force). In 1966 he moved to Sochi in the Caucasus.

Gershwin, George (real name, **Jacob Gershvin**), immensely gifted American composer, brother of **Ira Gershwin**; b. N.Y., Sept. 26, 1898; d. Los Angeles, July 11, 1937. His father was an immigrant from Russia whose original name was Gershovitz. Gershwin's extraordinary career began when he was 16, playing the piano in music stores to demonstrate new popular songs. His studies were desultory; he took piano lessons with Ernest Hutcheson and Charles Hambitzer in N.Y.; studied harmony with Edward Kilenyi and Rubin Goldmark; later on, when he was already a famous composer of popular music, he continued to take private lessons; he studied counterpoint with Cowell and Riegger and, during the last years of his life, applied himself with great earnestness to his studies with Joseph Schillinger in an attempt to organize his technique in a scientific manner; some of Schillinger's methods he applied in *Porgy and Bess.* But it was his melodic talent and his genius for rhythmic invention, rather than any studies, that made Gershwin a genuinely important American composer. As far as worldly success was concerned, there was no period of struggle in Gershwin's life; one of his earliest songs, *Swanee*, written at the age of 19, became enormously popular, selling more than a million copies of sheet music and some 2,250,000 recordings. He also took time to write a lyrical *Lullaby* for String Quartet (1920). Possessing phenomenal energy, he produced musical comedies in close succession, using fashionable jazz formulas in original and ingenious ways. A milestone in his career was *Rhapsody in Blue* for Piano and Jazz Orch., in which he applied the jazz idiom to an essentially classical form. He played the solo part at a special concert of the work conducted by Paul Whiteman at Aeolian Hall in N.Y. on Feb. 12, 1924. The orchestration was by Ferde Grofé, a circumstance that generated rumors of Gershwin's inability to score for instruments; these rumors, however, were quickly refuted by his production of several orch. works, scored by himself in a brilliant fashion. He played the solo part of his Piano Concerto in F, with Walter Damrosch and the N.Y. Sym. Orch. (Dec. 3, 1925); this work had a certain vogue, but its popularity never equaled that of the *Rhapsody in Blue.* Reverting again to a more popular idiom, Gershwin wrote a symphonic work, *An American in Paris* (N.Y., Dec. 13, 1928, Damrosch conducting). His *Rhapsody No. 2* was performed by Koussevitzky and the Boston Sym. Orch. on Jan. 29, 1932, but was unsuccessful; there followed a *Cuban Overture* (N.Y., Aug. 16, 1932) and

Variations for Piano and Orch. on his song *I Got Rhythm* (Boston, Jan. 14, 1934, composer soloist). In the meantime, Gershwin composed his *Of Thee I Sing* (Dec. 26, 1931), an engaging and political satire; he also became engaged in his most ambitious and, what would be in time, his most important, undertaking: the composition of *Porgy and Bess*, an American opera in a folk manner, for black singers, after the book by Dubose Heyward. It was first staged in Boston on Sept. 30, 1935, and in N.Y. on Oct. 10, 1935. Its reception by the press was not uniformly favorable, but its songs, and especially *Summertime, I Got Plenty o' Nuthin', It Ain't Neccessarily So*, and *Bess, You Is My Woman Now*, rapidly attained great popularity. Gershwin's death (of a gliomatous cyst in the right temporal lobe of the brain) at the age of 38 was mourned as a great loss to American music. The 50th anniversary of his death brought forth a number of special tributes in 1987, including a major joint broadcast of his music by the PBS and BBC television networks. His stage works (all musical comedies with 1st N.Y. perf. unless otherwise given) comprised: *Half Past 8*, revue (Dec. 9, 1918); *La la Lucille* (May 26, 1919); *George White's Scandals of 1920*, revue (June 7, 1920); *A Dangerous Maid* (Atlantic City, N.J., March 21, 1921); *George White's Scandals of 1921*, revue (July 11, 1921); *Blue Monday*, opera (Aug. 28, 1922; retitled *135th Street*); *George White's Scandals of 1922*, revue (Aug. 28, 1922); *Our Nell* (Dec. 4, 1922); *The Rainbow*, revue (London, April 3, 1923); *George White's Scandals of 1923*, revue (June 18, 1923); *Sweet Little Devil* (Jan. 21, 1924); *George White's Scandals of 1924*, revue (June 30, 1924); *Primrose* (London, Sept. 11, 1924); *Lady, Be Good!* (Dec. 1, 1924); *Tell me More* (April 13, 1925); *Tip-toes* (Dec. 28, 1925); *Song of the Flame*, operetta (Dec. 30, 1925); *Oh, Kay!* (Nov. 8, 1926); *Strike Up the Band* (Philadelphia, Sept. 5, 1927; rev. version, N.Y., Jan. 14, 1930); *Funny Face* (Nov. 22, 1927); *Rosalie* (Jan. 10, 1928); *Treasure Girl* (Nov. 8, 1928); *Show Girl* (July 2, 1929); *Girl Crazy* (Oct. 14, 1930); *Of Thee I Sing* (Dec. 26, 1931); *Pardon My English* (Jan. 20, 1933); *Let 'em Eat Cake* (Oct. 21, 1933); *Porgy and Bess*, folk opera (Boston, Sept. 30, 1935). He also wrote the film scores for *Delicious* (1931), *Shall We Dance?* (1937), *A Damsel in Distress* (1937), and *The Goldwyn Follies* (1938; completed by V. Duke), as well as many songs.

BIBL.: I. Goldberg, *G. G., A Study in American Music* (N.Y., 1931; 2nd ed., rev., 1958); V. Thomson, "G. G.," *Modern Music* (Nov. 1935); M. Armitage, ed., *G. G.* (N.Y., 1938); O. Levant, *A Smattering of Ignorance* (N.Y., 1938); D. Ewen, *A Journey to Greatness; G. G.* (N.Y., 1956; 2nd ed., rev., 1970, as *G. G., His Journey to Greatness*); E. Jablonski and L. Stewart, *The G. Years* (Garden City, N.Y., 1958; 2nd ed., rev., 1973); C. Schwartz, *G.: His Life and Music* (Indianapolis, 1973); idem, *G. G.: A Selective Bibliography and Discography* (Detroit, 1974); C. Hamm, "The Theatre Guild Production of *Porgy and Bess*," *Journal of the American Musicological Society* (Fall 1987); E. Jablonski; *G.: A Biography* (Garden City, N.Y., 1987); A. Kendall, *G. G.: A Biography* (N.Y., 1987); P. Kresh, *An American Rhapsody: The Story of G. G.* (N.Y., 1988); R. Wyatt, "The Seven Jazz Preludes of G. G.: A Historical Narrative," *American Music* (Spring 1989); H. Alpert, *The Life and Times of Porgy and Bess: The Story of an American Classic* (N.Y., 1990); E. Jablonski, *G.* (Boston, 1990); D. Rosenberg, *Fascinating Rhythm: The Collaboration of G. and Ira G.* (N.Y., 1991); J. Peyser, *The Memory of All That: The Life of G. G.* (N.Y., 1993).

Gershwin (real name, **Gershvin**), **Ira,** greatly talented American librettist and lyricist, brother of **George Gershwin**; b. N.Y., Dec. 6, 1896; d. Beverly Hills, Aug. 17, 1983. He attended night classes at the College of the City of N.Y., wrote verses and humorous pieces for the school paper, and served as cashier in a Turkish bath of which his father was part owner. He began writing lyrics for shows in 1918, using the pseudonym Arthur Francis. His first full-fledged libretto was for the musical comedy *Be Yourself*, for which he used his own name for the first time. He achieved fame when he wrote the lyrics for his brother's musical comedy, *Lady, Be Good!* (1924). He remained his brother's collaborator until George Gershwin's death in 1937, and his lyrics became an inalienable part of the whole, so that the brothers became artistic twins, like Gilbert and Sullivan, indissolubly united in some of the greatest productions of the musical theater in America: *Strike Up the Band* (1927), *Of Thee I Sing* (1931), and the culminating product of their brotherly genius, the folk opera *Porgy and Bess* (1935). Ira Gerschwin also wrote lyrics for other composers, among them Vernon Duke (*The Ziegfeld Follies of 1936*), Kurt Weill (*Lady in the Dark*, and several films), and Jerome Kern (the enormously successful song *Long Ago and Far Away* for the film *Cover Girl*). R. Kimball ed. *The Complete Lyrics of Ira Gershwin* (N.Y., 1993).

BIBL.: D. Rosenberg, *Fascinating Rhythm: The Collaboration of George and I. G.* (N.Y., 1991); P. Furia, *I. G.: The Art of the Lyricist* (Oxford, 1995).

Gerson-Kiwi, (Esther) Edith, German-born Israeli musicologist; b. Berlin, May 13, 1908; d. Jerusalem, July 15, 1992. She attended the Stern Cons. in Berlin (1918–25) and took a pianist's diploma at the Leipzig Hochschule für Musik (1930); she also studied harpsichord with Ramin in Leipzig and Landowska in Paris. She studied musicology with W. Gurlitt at the Univ. of Freiburg, Kroyer at the Univ. of Leipzig, and Besseler at the Univ. of Heidelberg (Ph.D., 1933, with the diss. *Studien zur Geschichte des italienischen Liedmadrigals im 16. Jahrhundert*; publ. in Würzburg, 1938). In 1935 she went to Palestine, where she was active in research and teaching; in 1969 she joined the faculty of the Univ. of Tel Aviv. She is a prolific and versatile writer; her subjects included Renaissance, Classical, Romantic, and contemporary music, and the ethnic music of the Middle East, on which she was an outstanding authority. Her books included *The Persian Doctrine of Dastgah Composition: A Phenomenological Study in the Musical Modes* (Tel Aviv, 1963), *The Legacy of Jewish Music through the Ages of Dispersion* (Jerusalem, 1963–64), and *Migrations and Mutations of the Music in East and West* (Tel Aviv, 1980).

BIBL.: S. Burstyn, ed., *Essays in Honor of E. G.-K.* (Tel Aviv, 1986).

Gerstenberg, Walter, German musicologist; b. Hildesheim, Dec. 26, 1904; d. Tübingen, Oct. 26, 1988. He studied at the Univs. of Berlin and Leipzig (Ph.D., 1929, with the diss. *Die Klavierkompositionen Domenico Scarlattis*; publ. in Regensburg, 1933; new ed., 1969), and then completed his Habilitation at the Univ. of Cologne in 1935 with his *Beiträge zur Problemgeschichte der evangelischen Kirchenmusik*. He taught at the Univs. of Leipzig (1929–32) and Cologne (1932–38), and then was prof. of musicology at the Univs. of Rostock (1941–48), Berlin (Free Univ., 1948–52), Tübingen (1952–58; 1959–70), and Heidelberg (1958). G. van Dadelsen and A. Holschneider ed. a Festschrift for his 60th birthday (Wolfenbüttel, 1964).

WRITINGS: *Die Zeitmasse und ihre Ordnungen in Bachs Musik* (Einbeck, 1951); *Zur Erkenntnis der Bachsen Musik* (Berlin, 1951); *Musikerhandschriften von Palestrina bis Beethoven* (Zürich, 1960); *Über Mozarts Klangwelt* (Tübingen, 1966).

Gerster, Ottmar, German violinist, composer, and pedagogue; b. Braunfels, June 29, 1897; d. Leipzig, Aug. 31, 1969. He studied theory with Sekles at the Frankfurt am Main Cons. (1913–16); then studied violin with Adolf Rebner (1919–21). He played viola in string quartets (1923–27), and concurrently was concertmaster of the Frankfurt am Main Museumgesellschaft Orch. From 1927 to 1939 he taught violin and theory at the Folkwang-Schule in Essen; then was on the faculty of the Hochschule für Musik in Weimar (1947–52) and in Leipzig (1952–62). His music is marked by melodious polyphony in a neo-Classical vein; in his operas, he used folklike thematic material.

WORKS: DRAMATIC: OPERAS: *Madame Liselotte* (Essen, 1933); *Enoch Arden* (Düsseldorf, 1936); *Die Hexe von Passau* (Düsseldorf, 1941); *Das Verzauberte Ich* (Wuppertal, 1949); *Der* *fröhliche Sünder* (Weimar, 1963). **BALLET:** *Der ewige Kreis* (Duisburg, 1939). **ORCH.:** 3 syms.: *Kleine Sinfonie* (1931), *Thüringer Sinfonie* (1952), and *Leipziger Sinfonie* (1965); *Oberhessische Bauerntänze* (1937); Cello Concerto (1946); Piano Concerto (1956); Horn Concerto (1962). **CHAMBER:** 2 string quartets (1923, 1954); String Trio (1957). **VOCAL:** *Ballade vom Manne Karl Marx (und der Veränderung der Welt)* for Baritone, Chorus, and Orch. (1961); many other choruses, some to words of political significance; songs.

BIBL.: O. Goldhammer, *O. G.* (Berlin, 1953); R. Malth, *O. G.: Leben und Werk* (Leipzig, 1988).

Gerstman, Blanche, South African pianist and composer of English descent; b. Cape Town, April 2, 1910; d. there, Aug. 11, 1973. She adopted the family name of her adoptive parents. She studied theory with Hely-Hutchinson and later with William Henry Bell at the South African College of Music. She was subsequently active as a radio pianist; in 1950 she went to London, where she took additional courses at the Royal College of Music with Howard Ferguson. Returning to South Africa in 1952, she taught at the College of Music in Cape Town. She composed pleasurable piano pieces, singable choruses, and some playable chamber music.

Gertler, André, Hungarian violinist and pedagogue; b. Budapest, July 26, 1907. He studied violin with Hubay and composition with Kodály at the Budapest Academy of Music (diploma, 1925). He toured as a soloist; also appeared in recitals with Bartók (1925–38) and was violinist in his own Quatuor Gertler in Brussels (1931–51); was a prof. at the Brussels Cons. (1940–54), the Cologne Hochschule für Musik (1954–59), and the Hannover Hochschule für Musik (1964–78). He became well known as a sympathetic interpreter of contemporary music.

Gesensway, Louis, Latvian-American violinist and composer; b. Dvinsk, Feb. 19, 1906; d. Philadelphia, March 11, 1976. The family moved to Canada when he was a child; he studied violin. In 1926 he joined the Philadelphia Orch., remaining with it until 1971. He was a prolific composer of some originality; he developed a system of "color harmony" by expanding and contracting the intervals of the diatonic scale into fractions, establishing a difference between enharmonically equal tones; such a scale in his projection contained 41 degrees.

WORKS: ORCH.: Flute Concerto (Philadelphia, Nov. 1, 1946); *The 4 Squares of Philadelphia* for Narrator and Orch. (Philadelphia, Feb. 25, 1955); *Ode to Peace* (Philadelphia, April 15, 1960); *Commemoration Symphony* (1966–68; Philadelphia, Feb. 25, 1971); *A Pennsylvania Overture* (1972); Cello Concerto (1973). **CHAMBER:** Concerto for 13 Brass Instruments (1942); Quartet for Clarinet and Strings (1950); Quartet for Oboe, Bassoon, Violin, and Viola (1951); Sonata for Solo Bassoon; Duo for Oboe and Guitar (1959); Duo for Viola and Bassoon (1960); Duo for Violin and Cello (1970).

Geszty (real name, **Witkowsky**), **Sylvia,** Hungarian soprano; b. Budapest, Feb. 28, 1934. She studied at the Budapest Cons. In 1959 she made her operatic debut at the Hungarian State Opera in Budapest; was a member of the Berlin State Opera (1961–70), the Berlin Komische Oper (1963–70), the Hamburg State Opera (1966–72; 1973), and the Württemberg State Theater in Stuttgart (from 1970). She sang the Queen of the Night at London's Covent Garden in 1966, and repeated the role at the Salzburg Festival in 1967; at the Munich Opera Festival she also sang Zerbinetta, a favorite soubrette role, which she chose for her Glyndebourne Festival debut in 1971. She made her North American debut as Sophie in *Der Rosenkavalier* with the N.Y. City Opera during its visit to Los Angeles on Nov. 19, 1973; she also appeared with the Berlin Städtische Oper, the Paris Opera, La Scala in Milan, and the Teatro Colón in Buenos Aires, and in concerts and recitals.

Getty, Gordon, American composer; b. Los Angeles, Dec. 20, 1933. He was the scion of the billionaire oil executive and art collector Jean Paul Getty. In 1945 he was taken to San Francisco, where he studied English literature at San Francisco State College (graduated, 1956) and took courses at the San Francisco Cons. of Music. From his earliest attempts at composition, he proclaimed faith in the primacy of consonance and a revival of Romantic ideals. His preference lay with vocal music, and he possessed a natural gift for writing a fetching melodic line. For his songs and choruses, he selected the poems of Housman, Tennyson, Poe, and Dickinson. He also produced an opera, *Plump Jack,* based on the character of Shakespeare's Falstaff (excerpts only; San Francisco, March 13, 1985). The inevitable headline in one of several newspaper reviews was "Billionaire Has a Hit in Plump Jack!" Every critic's writing about Getty must deal with the inescapable suspicion that his music is the accidental outgrowth of his material for tune, and must conquer conscious or subliminal prejudice in favor or disfavor of a work. Getty deserves full credit for braving this test/ courageously, ignoring bouquets and brickbats and persevering in writing his kind of music. Among his other works are the piano pieces *Homework Suite, 3 Diatonic Waltzes,* and *Tiefer und Tiefer* (all 1986), and a vocal work, *The White Election for Soprano and Piano,* to poems by Emily Dickinson (1986).

Geyer, Stefi, Hungarian-born Swiss violinist and teacher; b. Budapest, Jan. 28, 1888; d. Zürich, Dec. 11, 1956. She studied with Hubay at the Royal Academy of Music in Budapest; toured in Europe and the U.S. at an early age. In 1919 she settled in Zürich and married **Walter Schulthess**. She taught at the Zürich Cons. (1923–53). She was an object of passion on the part of Bartók, who wrote a violin concerto for her (1907).

Ghedini, Giorgio Federico, Italian composer and pedagogue; b. Cuneo, July 11, 1892; d. Nervi, March 25, 1965. He studied piano and organ with Evasio Lovazzano, cello with S. Grossi, and composition with G. Cravero at the Turin Cons.; then composition at the Liceo Musicale in Bologna with M.E. Bossi, graduating in 1911. He was prof. of harmony and composition at the conservatories in Turin (1918–37), Parma (1938–41), and Milan (from 1941), serving as director of the latter (1951–62). His works evolved from neo-Classicism to more advanced contemporary techniques.

WORKS: DRAMATIC: OPERAS: *Gringoire* (1915); *Maria d'Alessandria* (Bergamo, Sept. 9, 1937); *Re Hassan* (Venice, Jan. 26, 1939); *La pulce d'oro* (Genoa, Feb. 15, 1940); *Le Baccanti* (Milan, Feb. 21, 1948); *Billy Budd,* after Melville (Venice, Sept. 7, 1949); *Lord Inferno,* "harmonious comedy" for radio, after Beerbohm's *The Happy Hypocrite* (RAI, Oct. 22, 1952; rev. version as *L'Ipocrita felice,* Milan, March 10, 1956); *La Via della Croce* (Venice, April 9, 1961). **BALLET:** *Girotondo,* mime play for children (Venice, 1959). **ORCH.:** *Partita* (1926); *Concerto grosso* for Wind Quintet and Strings (1927); *Pezzo concertante* for 2 Violins, Viola obbligato, and Orch. (1931); *Marinaresca e baccanale* (1933; Rome, Feb. 2, 1936); Sym. (1938); *Architetture* (1940; Rome, Jan. 19, 1941); *Invenzioni* for Cello, Strings, Kettledrums, and Cymbals (1940); Piano Concerto (1946); *Musica Notturna* for Chamber Orch. (1947); Concerto for 2 Pianos and Chamber Orch. (1947; Milan, Jan. 24, 1948); *Il Belprato* for Violin and Strings (1947); *Canzoni* (1948); *L'Alderina* for Flute, Violin, and Orch. (1951); *L'Olmeneta* for 2 Cellos and Orch. (1951); *Musica da concerto* for Viola and Strings (1953); *Concentus Basiliensis* for Violin and Chamber Orch. (1954); *Vocalizzo da concerto* for Cello or Baritone and Orch. (1957); *Fantasie* for Piano and Strings (1958); *Sonata da concerto* for Flute, Strings, and Percussion (1958); *Divertimento* for Violin and Orch. (1960); *Studi per un affresco di battaglia* (1962); *Contrappunti* for Violin, Viola, Cello, and Strings (1962); *Musica concertante* for Cello and Strings (1962); *Appunti per un credo* for Chamber Orch. (1962); *Concert Overture* (1963). **CHAMBER:** Wind Quintet (1910); Piano Quartet (1917); Double Quartet for 5 Winds, 5 Strings, Harp, and Piano (1921); Violin Sonata (1922); Cello Sonata (1924); 2 string quartets (1927, 1959); *Adagio e allegro da Concerto* for Flute, Clarinet, Horn,

Viola, Cello, and Harp (1936); *Concertato* for Flute, Viola, and Harp (1942); *7 Ricercari* for Piano Trio (1943); *Canons* for Violin and Cello (1946); *Concentus* for String Quartet (1948); *Music* for Flute, Cello, and Piano (1963); piano pieces. **VOCAL:** *Le messa del Venerdi santo*, oratorio (1929; Perugia, Sept. 27, 1949); masses; cantatas; motets; choral pieces; songs.

BIBL.: N. Castiglioni, *G.F. G* (Milan, 1955).

Ghent, Emmanuel (Robert), Canadian-born American composer; b. Montreal, May 15, 1925. He studied medicine at McGill Univ. in Montreal (B.S., 1946; M.D., 1950), where he also received instruction in piano and bassoon. In 1951 he settled in the U.S. and completed his training in music with Shapey. In 1967 he held a Guggenheim fellowship. From 1969 he was active at the Bell Telephone Laboratories, where he prepared computer-generated works. His other works include mixed media scores and tape pieces. He also invented electronic devices capable of transmitting synchronization signals to musicians.

Gheorghiu, Valentin, Romanian composer; b. Galaţi, March 21, 1928. He studied composition with Jora and Andricu at the Bucharest Cons.; then studied piano with Lazare Lévy and harmony at the Paris Cons. (1937–39). His works include 2 syms. (1949; 1953, rev. 1974); Piano Concerto (1959); *Imagini din copilarie* (Images of Youth), suite for Orch. (1961); *Burlesca* for Piano and Orch. (1964); String Quartet (1946); Piano Sonata (1946); Cello Sonata (1950); Piano Trio (1950); songs.

Ghezzo, Dinu, Romanian-born American composer, conductor, and teacher; b. Tuzla, July 2, 1941. He took courses in music education and conducting (diploma, 1964), and in composition (diploma, 1966), at the Bucharest Cons., and then completed his training at the Univ. of Calif. at Los Angeles (Ph.D. in composition, 1973). In 1978 he became a naturalized American citizen. From 1974 to 1976 he was an assistant prof. at Queens College of the City Univ. of N.Y. He served as director of the New Repertory Ensemble of N.Y. from 1975 to 1988. In 1977 he became a prof. of music at N.Y. Univ. He also was composer-in-residence at the Univ. of Wisc. in Madison in 1995. His music is in a thoroughly contemporary style.

WORKS: ORCH.: *Thalla* for Piano and 17 Players (1974); Concertino for Clarinet and Symphonic Wind Ensemble (1975); *Celebrations* for Chamber Orch. and Tape (1980); *7 Short Pieces* for Chamber Orch. (1981); *Sketches* for Clarinet and Chamber Orch. (1981); *Echoes of Romania* for Strings (1990). **CHAMBER:** Clarinet Sonata (1967); String Quartet (1967); *Kanones II* for 6 Players (1978); *Aphorisms* for Clarinet and Piano (1981); Nonetto (1982); *Structures* for Cello and Piano (1982); *Sound Shapes I*, 5 studies for Wind Player (1984) and *II*, 5 pieces for Brass Player (1985); *From Here to . . . There* for 6 Players (1986); *Elegies* for Violin and Cello (1989); *Freedom* for Clarinet, Piano, Chamber Ensemble, and Tape (1990); *Ostrom I* for Quartet, Slides, and Tape (1990) and *II* for 6 to 18 Players (1990). **VOCAL:** *Letters to Walt Whitman* for Soprano, Clarinet, and Piano (1983); *2 Prayers* for Soprano and Tape (1988); *A Book of Songs* for Soprano, Chamber Group, and Tape (1989).

Ghiaurov, Nicolai, outstanding Bulgarian bass; b. Lydjene, near Velingrad, Sept. 13, 1929. He was a student of Brambarov at the Sofia Cons., and then pursued his training at the Moscow Cons. (1950–55). After making his operatic debut as Don Basilio at the Moscow Opera Studio in 1955, he reprised that role for his Sofia debut in 1956. In 1957 he sang for the first time at the Paris Opéra, the Vienna State Opera, and at the Bolshoi Theater in Moscow, where he quickly established his reputation. In 1959 he made an impressive debut as Varlaam at Milan's La Scala, and in 1962 sang for the first time at London's Covent Garden as the Padre Guardino. In 1964 he made his first appearance at the Lyric Opera of Chicago as Gounod's Méphistophélès, which role he also chose for his Metropolitan Opera debut in N.Y. on Nov. 8, 1965. In subsequent years, he appeared with most of the principal opera houses of Europe and North America, as well as at many of the leading festivals. Ghiaurov's remarkable vocal and dramatic gifts placed him among the foremost bassos of his day. His other roles included Don Giovanni, Pimen, Ramfis, Boris Godunov, Philip II, Massenet's Don Quichotte, and Boito's Mefistofele. In 1981 he married **Mirella Freni.**

Ghiglia, Oscar, Italian guitarist; b. Livorno, Aug. 13, 1938. He studied at the Accademia di Santa Cecilia in Rome (graduated, 1962); then took lessons with Segovia at the Accademia Musicale Chigiana in Siena. After winning a guitar competition in Paris in 1963, he received a scholarship to the Schola Cantorum, where he studied music history with Jacques Chailley (1963–64). He made his American and British debuts in 1966; subsequently toured in America and in Europe.

Ghisi, Federico, Italian musicologist and composer; b. Shanghai, Feb. 25, 1901; d. Luzerna San Giovanni, July 18, 1975. His father was in the diplomatic corps in China. After the family settled in Italy in 1908, he studied harmony and counterpoint at the Milan Cons., and also piano privately with Faggioni; later he pursued training in chemistry at the Univ. of Pavia (graduated, 1923). While employed as a chemist, he took courses in composition with Ghedini at the Turin Cons. and in music history with Torrefranca at the Univ. of Florence (libera docenza, 1936). He then taught at the latter (1937–40), at the Università per Stranieri in Perugia (1945–74), and at the Univ. of Pisa (1963–70). Ghisi wrote many articles on Florence during the Renaissance era. Among his compositions were the operas *Il dono dei Re Magi* (1959) and *Il Vagabondo e la guardia* (1960), and the oratorio *L'ultima visione* (1967–72).

WRITINGS: *I canti carnascialeschi nelle fonti musicali del XV e XVI secolo* (Florence, 1937); *Le feste musicali della Firenze Medicea* (Florence, 1939); *Alle Fonti della Monodia: Nuovi brani della "Dafne" di J. Peri e "Il fuggilotio musicale" di G. Caccini* (Milan, 1940).

Ghitalla, Armando, distinguished American trumpeter and teacher; b. Alfa, Ill., June 1, 1925. He studied at the Juilliard School of Music in N.Y. with William Vacchiano (1946–49). In 1949 he joined the Houston Sym. Orch.; in 1951 he was engaged by the Boston Sym. Orch., serving as its 1st trumpeter from 1965 to 1979. In 1979 he became prof. of trumpet at the Univ. of Mich. at Ann Arbor.

Gianneo, Luis, Argentine composer, conductor, and teacher; b. Buenos Aires, Jan. 9, 1897; d. there, Aug. 15, 1968. He studied harmony with Gaito and counterpoint and composition with Fornarini. From 1923 to 1943 he taught at the Inst. Musical in Tucumán; then was a prof. of music at various schools in Buenos Aires. He was especially interested in the problems of musical education of the very young; in 1945 he organized and conducted the Orquesta Sinfónica Juvenil Argentina; from 1955 to 1960 he was director of the Buenos Aires Cons.

WORKS: BALLET: *Blanca nieves* (1939). **ORCH.:** *Turay-Turay*, symphonic poem (Buenos Aires, Sept. 21, 1929); 3 syms. (1938, 1945, 1963); *Obertura para una comedia infantil* (1939); Piano Concerto (1941); Sinfonietta (Buenos Aires, Sept. 20, 1943); Violin Concerto (Buenos Aires, April 13, 1944); *Variaciones sobre tema de tango* (1953). **CHAMBER:** 4 string quartets (1936, 1944, 1952, 1958); 2 piano trios; String Trio; Violin Sonata; Cello Sonata; 3 piano sonatas (1917, 1943, 1957). **VOCAL:** *Cantica Dianae* for Chorus and Orch. (1949); *Angor Dei* for Soprano and Orch. (1962); *Poema de la Saeta* for Soprano and Orch. (1966); solo songs.

Giannini, Dusolina, American soprano, daughter of **Ferruccio** and sister of **Vittorio Giannini**; b. Philadelphia, Dec. 19, 1900; d. Zürich, June 26, 1986. She received early musical training at home, then studied voice with Sembrich in N.Y., where she made her concert debut on March 14, 1920. She made her operatic debut as Aida with the Hamburg Opera on Sept. 12, 1925, then sang in Berlin, Vienna, and London. She made her Metropolitan Opera debut in N.Y. as Aida on Feb. 12, 1936, and remained on its roster until 1941; she also appeared with other

American opera houses. She sang again in Europe (1947–50), then taught voice. Giannini created the role of Hester in her brother's *The Scarlet Letter* (Hamburg, June 2, 1938).

Giannini, Ferruccio, Italian-American tenor, father of **Dusolina** and **Vittorio Giannini**; b. Ponte d'Arnia, Nov. 15, 1868; d. Philadelphia, Sept. 17, 1948. He emigrated to the U.S. in 1885; studied with Eleodoro De Campi in Detroit. He made his debut in Boston in 1891, then toured the U.S. with the Mapleson Opera Co. (1892–94); made the first operatic recordings, which were issued by Emile Berliner in 1896. He later settled in Philadelphia, where he presented operas, concerts, and plays in his own theater.

Giannini, Vittorio, American composer and teacher, son of **Ferruccio** and brother of **Dusolina Giannini**; b. Philadelphia, Oct. 19, 1903; d. N.Y., Nov. 28, 1966. Brought up in a musical family, he showed a precocious talent. He was sent to Italy at the age of 10, and studied at the Milan Cons. (1913–17). After returning to the U.S., he took private lessons with Martini and Trucco in N.Y.; in 1925 he entered the Juilliard graduate school, where he was a pupil of Rubin Goldmark in composition and Hans Letz in violin; in 1932 he won the American Prix de Rome; was in Rome for a period of 4 years. Upon his return to N.Y., he was appointed to the faculty of the Juilliard School of Music in 1939 as a teacher of composition and orchestration; in 1941 he also became an instructor in theory; furthermore, he was appointed prof. of composition at the Curtis Inst. of Music in Philadelphia in 1956. In 1965 became the first director of the North Carolina School of the Arts in Winston-Salem. As a composer, Giannini was at his best in opera, writing music of fine emotional éclat, excelling in the art of bel canto and avoiding extreme modernistic usages; in his symphonic works, he also continued the rich Italian tradition; these qualities endeared him to opera singers, but at the same time left his music out of the mainstream of contemporary music making.

WORKS: OPERAS: *Lucedia* (Munich, Oct. 20, 1934); *Not all Prima Donnas are Ladies* (n.d.); *The Scarlet Letter* (1937; Hamburg, June 2, 1938); *Flora* (1937); *Beauty and the Beast* (CBS, Nov. 24, 1938; stage premiere, Hartford, Conn., Feb. 14, 1946); *Blennerhasset* (CBS, Nov. 22, 1939); *Casanova* (n.d.); *The Taming of the Shrew* (1952; concert premiere, Cincinnati, Jan. 31, 1953; television premiere, NBC, March 13, 1954); *Christus* (1956); *The Harvest* (Chicago, Nov. 25, 1961); *Rehearsal Call* (1961; N.Y., Feb. 15, 1962); *The Servant of 2 Masters* (1966; N.Y., March 9, 1967); *Edipus Rex* (unfinished). **ORCH.:** Concerto Grosso for Strings (1931); Suite (1931); Piano Concerto (1935); Sym., *In Memoriam Theodore Roosevelt* (1935; N.Y., Jan. 19, 1936, composer conducting); Sym., *I.B.M.* (1939); 5 numbered syms.: No. 1, *Sinfonia* (1950; Cincinnati, April 6, 1951), No. 2 (1955; St. Louis, April 16, 1956), No. 3 for Band (1958), No. 4 (N.Y., May 26, 1960), and No. 5 (1965); Organ Concerto (1937); *Prelude, Chorale, and Fugue* (1939); Violin Concerto (1944); Trumpet Concerto (1945); *Frescobaldiana* (1948); 3 divertimentos (1953, 1961, 1964); *Prelude and Fugue* for Strings (1955); *Love's Labour Lost*, suite for Chamber Orch. (1958); *Psalm CXXX* for Double Bass or Cello and Chamber Orch. (1963). **CHAMBER:** 2 violin sonatas (1926, 1945); String Quartet (1930); Piano Quintet (1931); Piano Trio (1931); Woodwind Quintet (1933); Sonata for Solo Violin (1945); piano pieces. **VOCAL:** Stabat mater for Chorus and Orch. (1920); Madrigal for 4 Solo Voices and String Quartet (1931); *Primavera*, cantata (1933); Requiem for Chorus and Orch. (1937); *Lament for Adonis*, cantata (1940); *Canticle of Christmas* for Baritone, Chorus, and Orch. (1951); *Canticle of the Martyrs* for Chorus and Orch. for the 500th anniversary of the Moravian Church (1956); *The Medead* for Soprano and Orch. (1960); *Antigone* for Soprano and Orch. (1962); numerous songs.

BIBL.: M. Mark, *The Life and Works of V. G. (1903–1966)* (diss., Catholic Univ. of America, 1970).

Giazotto, Remo, Italian musicologist; b. Rome, Sept. 4, 1910. He studied piano and composition at the Milan Cons. (1931–33), his principal mentors being Torrefranca, Pizzetti, and Paribeni; he also took courses in literature and philosophy at the Univ. of Genoa. In 1932 he joined the staff of the *Rivista Musicale Italiana*, serving as its ed. (1945–49), and later as co-ed. of the *Nuova Rivista Musicale Italiana* (from 1967); he also was a prof. of music history at the Univ. of Florence (1957–69). The popular *Adagio* for Strings and Organ frequently attributed to Albinoni is almost totally the work of Giazotto.

WRITINGS: *Il melodramma a Genova nel XVII e XVIII secolo* (Genoa, 1942); *Tomaso Albinoni, musico di violino, dilettante veneto* (Milan, 1945); *Busoni: La vita nell'opera* (Milan, 1948); *Poesia melodrammatica e pensiero critico nel Settecento* (Milan, 1952); *La musica a Genova nella vita pubblica e privata dal XIII al XVIII secolo* (Genoa, 1952); *La musica italiana a Londra negli anni di Purcell* (Rome, 1955); *Giovanni Battista Viotti* (Milan, 1956); *Musurgia nova* (Milan, 1959); *Vita di A. Stradella: Un "Orfeo assassinato"* (2 vols., Milan, 1962); *Vivaldi* (Milan, 1965); *Quattro secoli di storia dell'Accademia di Santa Cecilia* (2 vols., Milan, 1970); *Le due patri di Giulio Caccini, musico mediceo (1551–1618)* (Florence, 1984); *Puccini in Casa Puccini* (Lucca, 1992).

Gibbs, Cecil Armstrong, English composer; b. Great Braddow, near Chelmsford, Aug. 10, 1889; d. Chelmsford, May 12, 1960. He studied at Trinity College, Cambridge (B.A., 1911; Mus.B., 1913); took courses in composition with Charles Wood and Vaughan Williams and in conducting with Boult at the Royal College of Music in London, where he also taught (1921–39). In 1934 he received the Cobbett Gold Medal for his services to British chamber music. His style adhered to the Romantic school; he was best known for his songs, many to texts by Walter De la Mare.

WORKS: DRAMATIC: *The Blue Peter*, comic opera (London, 1923); *The Sting of Love*, comic opera (1926); *When One Isn't There*, operetta (1927); *Twelfth Night*, opera (1946–47); *The Great Bell of Burley*, children's opera (1952); also incidental music. **ORCH.:** 3 syms.; Oboe Concerto; *Essex Suite* for String Quartet and Strings; *The Enchanted Wood*, dance phantasy for Piano and Strings (1919); *Fancy Dress*, dance suite (1935); *A Spring Garland*, suite for Strings (1937); Concertino for Piano and Strings (1942); *Prelude, Andante, and Finale* for Strings (1946); *Dale and Fell*, suite for Strings (1954); *A Simple Concerto* for Piano and Strings (1955); *Threnody for Walter De la Mare* for String Quartet and Strings (1956); *A Simple Suite* for Strings (1957); *Shade and Shine*, suite for Strings (1958); *Suite* for Strings (1958–59); *Suite of Songs from the British Isles* (1959); *4 Orch. Dances* (1959). **CHAMBER:** 11 string quartets; 2 sonatas for Cello and Piano; *Country Magic*, piano trio (1922); *Lyric Sonata* for Violin and Piano (1928); Piano Trio (1940); Suite for Violin and Piano (1943); piano pieces. **CHORAL:** *La Belle Dame sans merci* for Chorus and Orch. (1928); *The Birth of Christ* for Soloists, Chorus, and Orch. (1929); *The Highwayman* for Chorus and Orch. (1932); *The Ballad of Gil Morrice* for Chorus and Orch. (1934); *Deborah and Barak* for Soloists, Chorus, and Orch. (1936); *Odysseus* for Soloists, Chorus, and Orch. (1937–38); *The Passion According to St. Luke* for Chorus and Organ (1945); *Pastoral Suite* for Baritone, Chorus, and Orch. (1948–49); also anthems, motets, Psalms, part songs, carols, and about 150 songs.

BIBL.: D. Brown, "A. G. and His 'Odysseus' Symphony," *Music and Musicians International* (Oct. 1987); idem, "A Paradoxical Figure: A. G. (1889–1960)," ibid. (Aug. 1989).

Gibson, Sir Alexander (Drummond), distinguished Scottish conductor; b. Motherwell, Feb. 11, 1926; d. London, Jan. 14, 1995. He studied piano at the Royal Scottish Academy of Music in Glasgow, and also was a student in music at the Univ. of Glasgow; he then held a piano scholarship at the Royal College of Music in London, where he first studied conducting; he later received additional training in conducting from Markevitch at the Salzburg Mozarteum and from Kempen at the Accademia Musicale Chigiana in Siena. In 1951 he became a répétiteur and in 1952 a conductor at the Sadler's Wells Opera in London. After serving as assoc. conductor of the BBC Scottish Sym. Orch. in Glasgow (1952–54), he again conducted at the Sadler's Wells Opera (from 1954), where he later was music director (1957–59). In 1959 he made his first appearance at London's Covent Garden. From 1959 to 1984 he was principal conductor and artistic director of the Scottish National Orch. in Glasgow. In 1962 he founded Glasgow's Scottish Opera and was its artistic director until 1987. He also was principal guest conductor of the Houston Sym. Orch. (1981–83). In 1991 he became president of the Scottish Academy of Music and Drama in Glasgow. In 1967 he was made a Commander of the Order of the British Empire. He was knighted in 1977. Gibson was equally admired as an interpreter of the orch. and operatic repertoire.

Gideon, Miriam, American composer and teacher; b. Greeley, Colo., Oct. 23, 1906; d. N.Y., June 18, 1996. She studied piano in N.Y. with Hans Barth and in Boston with Felix Fox, and pursued her education at Boston Univ. (B.A., 1926); later she took courses in musicology at Columbia Univ. (M.A., 1946) and in composition at the Jewish Theological Seminary of America (D.S.M., 1970), and also studied with Saminsky and Sessions. She taught at Brooklyn College (1944–54) and the City College of the City Univ. of N.Y. (1947–55; 1971–76); she also was an assoc. prof. of music at the Jewish Theological Seminary (from 1955) and a teacher at the Manhattan School of Music (from 1967). In 1975 she was elected to the National Inst. of Arts and Letters. Her music was distinguished by its attractive modernism.

WORKS: OPERA: *Fortunato* (1958). **ORCH.:** *Epigrams*, suite for Chamber Orch. (1941); *Lyric Piece* for Strings (1941; London, April 9, 1944); *Symphonia brevis (Two Movements for Orchestra)* (N.Y., May 16, 1953). **CHAMBER:** *Incantation on an Indian Theme* for Viola and Piano (1939); Flute Sonata (1943); String Quartet (1946); *Divertimento* for Woodwind Quartet (1948); *Fantasy on a Javanese Motive* for Cello and Piano (1948); Viola Sonata (1948); *Biblical Masks* for Violin and Piano or Solo Organ (1960); Suite for Clarinet or Bassoon and Piano (1972); *Fantasy on Irish Folk Motives* for Oboe, Bassoon, Vibraphone, Glockenspiel, Tam-tam, and Viola (1975); Trio for Clarinet, Cello, and Piano (1978); *Eclogue* for Flute and Piano (1988); piano pieces, including a Sonata (1977). **VOCAL:** *Sonnets from Shakespeare* for High or Low Voice, Trumpet, and String Orch. or Quartet (1950; N.Y., April 1, 1951); *Songs of Youth and Madness* for High Voice and Orch. (N.Y., Dec. 5, 1977); choral pieces; many song cycles; solo songs.

Giebel, Agnes, Dutch soprano of German descent; b. Heerlen, Aug. 10, 1921. She studied with Hilde Weselmann at the Folkwangschule in Essen. She began a career as a concert singer in 1947. She gained wide recognition for her radio broadcasts of the Bach cantatas over the RIAS in Berlin in 1950. At a later period, she promoted modern music; her performances of works by Schoenberg, Berg, Hindemith, and Henze were praised. She made several tours as a concert artist in the U.S.

Gieburowski, Waclaw, eminent Polish musicologist; b. Bydgoszcz, Feb. 6, 1876; d. Warsaw, Sept. 17, 1943. He was a student of theology in Regensburg, where he also took courses in church music with Haberl; then studied at the Univ. of Berlin with Wolf and Kretzschmar and at the Univ. of Breslau with Kinkeldey, where he took his Ph.D. with the diss. *Die Musica Magistri Szydlowitae, Ein polnischer Choraltraktat des 15. Jahrhunderts und seine Stellung in der Choraltheorie des Mittelalters* (1913; publ. Posen, 1915). He settled in Posen as choirmaster at the Cathedral in 1916; was a prof. of church music at the Univ. (1925–39). From 1928 to 1939 he publ. the valuable series Cantica Selecta Musices Sacrae in Polonia; restored to use many sacred works by Polish composers of the Renaissance; publ. several treatises on this subject; also composed several sacred choral works.

Giegling, Franz, Swiss musicologist; b. Buchs, near Aarau, Feb. 27, 1921. He studied piano and theory at the Zürich Cons. with Cherbuliez; received his Ph.D. from the Univ. of Zürich in 1947 with the valuable diss. *Giuseppe Torelli, Ein Beitrag zur Entwicklungsgeschichte des italienischen Konzerts* (publ. in Kassel, 1949). He was music critic of the *Neue Zürcher Zeitung* (1947–53); subsequently worked for Radio Zürich and Radio Basel. Giegling was one of the eds. of the 6th edition of the Köchel catalogue of Mozart's works; he also contributed articles to *Die Musik in Geschichte und Gegenwart.*

Gielen, Michael (Andreas), noted German conductor; b. Dresden, July 20, 1927. His father, Josef Gielen, was an opera director who settled in Buenos Aires in 1939; his uncle was **Eduard Steuermann**. Gielen studied piano and composition with Erwin Leuchter in Buenos Aires (1942–49). He was on the staff of the Teatro Colón there (1947–50), then continued his training with Polnauer in Vienna (1950–53). In 1951 he became a répétiteur at the Vienna State Opera, and later was its resident conductor (1954–60). He was principal conductor of the Royal Opera in Stockholm (1960–65), a regular conductor with the Cologne Radio Sym. Orch. (1965–69), and chief conductor of the Orchestre National de Belgique in Brussels (1968–73) and the Netherlands Opera in Amsterdam (1973–75). From 1977 to 1987 he was artistic director of the Frankfurt am Main Opera and chief conductor of its Museumgesellschaft concerts; also was chief guest conductor of the BBC Sym. Orch. in London (1979–82) and music director of the Cincinnati Sym. Orch. (1980–86). In 1986 he became chief conductor of the South-West Radio Sym. Orch. in Baden-Baden; he also was prof. of conducting at the Salzburg Mozarteum (from 1987). Gielen has acquired a fine reputation as an interpreter of contemporary music; he has also composed a number of works of his own, including a Violin Sonata (1946); a Trio for Clarinet, Viola, and Bassoon (1948); *Variations* for String Quartet (1949); *Music* for Baritone, Strings, Piano, Trombone, and Percussion (1954); *4 Songs of Stefan George* for Chorus and Instruments (1955); *Variations* for 40 Instruments (1959); *Pentaphonie* for Piano, 5 Soloists, and 5 Quintets (1960–63); String Quartet (1983); *Pflicht und Neigung* for 22 Players (1988); *Rückblick*, trio for 3 Cellos (1989); and *Weitblick*, sonata for Solo Cello (1991).

Gieseking, Walter (Wilhelm), celebrated German pianist; b. Lyons, Nov. 5, 1895; d. London, Oct. 26, 1956. He studied with Karl Leimer at the Hannover Cons., graduating in 1916. In 1912 he made his debut in Hannover, and from 1921 he made tours of Europe. In 1923 he made his British debut in London, He made his American debut at Aeolian Hall in N.Y. on Feb. 22, 1926, and after that appeared regularly in the U.S. and Europe with orchs. and in solo recitals. He became the center of a political controversy when he arrived in the U.S. in 1949 for a concert tour; he was accused of cultural collaboration with the Nazi regime, and public protests forced the cancellation of his scheduled performances at Carnegie Hall in N.Y. However, he was later cleared by an Allied court in Germany and was able to resume his career in America. He appeared again at a Carnegie Hall recital on April 22, 1953, and until his death continued to give numerous performances in both hemispheres. He was one of the most extraordinary pianists of his time. A superb musician capable of profound interpretations of both Classical and modern scores, his dual German-French background enabled him to project with the utmost authenticity the masterpieces of both cultures. He particularly excelled in the music of Mozart, Beethoven, Schubert, and Brahms; his playing of Debussy and Ravel was also remarkable; he was also an excellent performer of works by Prokofiev and other modernists. He composed some chamber music and made piano transcriptions of songs by Richard Strauss. His autobiography, *So Wurde ich Pianist*, was publ. posth. in Wiesbaden (1963).

BIBL.: B. Gavoty, *G.* (Geneva, 1955).

Gifford, Helen (Margaret), Australian composer; b. Hawthorn, Victoria, Sept, 5, 1935. She studied with Roy Shepherd (piano) and Dorian Le Gallienne (harmony) at the Univ. of Melbourne Conservatorium of Music (Mus.Bac., 1958). From

1970 to 1982 she was active as a composer for the Melbourne Theatre Co.; in 1974 was also composer-in-residence of the Australian Opera in Sydney.

WORKS: DRAMATIC: OPERAS: *Jo Being* (1974); *Regarding Faustus* (1983); *Iphigenia in Exile* (1985); incidental music to plays. **ORCH.:** *Phantasma* for Strings (1963); *Chimaera* (1967); *Canzone: Hommage to Stravinsky* for Chamber Orch. (1968); *Imperium* (1969); *On Reflection* for 2 Violins and String Orch. (1972). **CHAMBER:** *Fantasy* for Flute and Piano (1958); Septet for Flute, Oboe, Bassoon, Harpsichord, Violin, Viola, and Cello (1962); *Skiagram* for Flute, Viola, and Vibraphone (1963); *Lyric* for Flute, Clarinet, and Cello (1964); String Quartet (1965); *Sonnet* for Flute, Guitar, and Harpsichord (1969); *Of Old Angkor* for Horn and Marimba (1970); *Company of Brass* for 9 Brass Instruments (1972); *Play* for 10 Instruments (1979); *Time and Time Again* for 6 Instruments (1981); *Going South* for 2 Trumpets, Horn, and 2 Trombones (1987); *A Plaint for Lost Worlds* for Piccolo, Clarinet, and Piano (1994). **PIANO:** Sonata (1960); *Catalysis* (1964); *Cantillation* (1966); *The Spell* (1966); *Souvenence* (1973); *Toccato attacco* (1990). **VOCAL:** *The Wanderer* for Male Speaker and Ensemble (1962); *The Glass Castle* for Soprano and Women's Chorus (1968); *Bird Calls from an Old Land* for 5 Sopranos and Women's Chorus (1971); *Images for Christmas* for Speaker and Ensemble (1973); *Foretold at Delphi* for Soprano, Piccolo, Oboe, Arab Drum, and Pre-recorded Crumhorn (1978); *Music for the Adonia* for Soprano and 8 Instruments (1993); *Point of Ignition* for Voice and Orch. (1995).

Gigli, Beniamino, celebrated Italian tenor; b. Recanati, March 20, 1890; d. Rome, Nov. 30, 1957. He was a chorister at Recanati Cathedral; commenced serious vocal studies with Agnese Bonucci in Rome, and continued his training with Cotogni and Rosati as a scholarship student at the Liceo Musicale there. After winning 1st prize in the Parma competition in 1914, he made his operatic debut as Enzo in *La Gioconda* in Rovigo on Oct. 14, 1914; subsequently sang in various Italian theaters, including Milan's La Scala in 1918 as Boito's Faust, a role he repeated in his Metropolitan Opera debut in N.Y. on Nov. 16, 1920. He remained on the Metropolitan roster as one of its leading singers until 1932, then returned for the 1938–39 season. He made his Covent Garden debut in London as Andrea Chénier on May 27, 1930; sang there again in 1931, 1938, and 1946. He spent the years during World War II in Italy; then resumed his operatic appearances, making his farewell to the stage in 1953; however, he continued to give concerts, making a final, impressive tour of the U.S. in 1955. Gigli's voice, with its great beauty and expressivity, made him one of the foremost tenors of his era; he was famous for such roles as the Duke of Mantua, Nemorino, Lionel, Des Grieux, Nadir, and Gounod's Faust, as well as for the leading roles in Puccini's operas. His memoirs were publ. in an Eng. tr. in London in 1957.

BIBL.: R. Rosner, *B. G.* (Vienna, 1929); D. Silvestrini, *B. G.* (Bologna, 1937); R. Gigli, *B. G. mio padre: A cura di Celso Minestroni* (Parma, 1986).

Gil-Marchex, Henri, French pianist; b. St. Georges d'Ésperance, Isère, Dec. 16, 1894; d. Paris, Nov. 22, 1970. He studied at the Paris Cons., then with Capet and Cortot. He toured Europe, Russia, and Japan, and performed modern works at various festivals in Europe. From 1956 he was director of the Poitiers Cons.

Gilardi, Gilardo, Argentine composer; b. San Fernando, May 25, 1889; d. Buenos Aires, Jan. 16, 1963. He studied with Pablo Berutti, then devoted himself to teaching and composing. Two of his operas were premiered at the Teatro Colón in Buenos Aires: *Ilse* (July 13, 1923) and *La leyenda de Urutau* (Oct. 25, 1934). He also wrote *Sinfonia cíclico* (1961), 3 piano trios, 2 string quartets, *Sonata Popular Argentina* for Violin and Piano (1939), and many dances and songs based on native melodies.

Gilbert, Anthony (John), English composer and teacher; b. London, July 26, 1934. He studied composition with Milner, Goehr, and Seiber in London both privately and at Morley College (1958–63); studied conducting at Morley with Del Mar (1967–69) and received training in composition from Nono and Berio at the Dartington Summer School (1961, 1962) and from Schuller, Shifrin, Carter, and Sessions at the Berkshire Music Center in Tanglewood (summer, 1967); studied piano with Denis Holloway at London's Trinity College of Music; completed his training at the Univ. of Leeds (M.A., 1984; Mus.D., 1990). He taught at Goldsmiths' College, Univ. of London (1968–73); served as composer-in-residence (1970–71) and visiting lecturer (1971–72) at the Univ. of Lancaster; then taught at Morley College (1971–74). In 1973 he joined the faculty of the Royal Northern College of Music in Manchester; in 1978–79 he also was senior lecturer in composition at the New South Wales State Conservatorium of Music in Sydney, and in 1981 was composer-in-the-community of Bendigo, Australia. A modernist by nature, Gilbert nevertheless writes music in Classical forms and is not averse to representational music; on the purely structural side, he adopts various attenuated forms of serial music, and in thematic development uses disparate agglutinative blocks.

WORKS: OPERAS: *The Scene Machine* (1970; Kassel, April 1, 1971); *The Chakravaka-bird*, radio opera (1977; BBC, Jan. 1982). **ORCH.:** *Sinfonia* for Chamber Orch. (London, March 30, 1965); *Regions* for 2 Orchs. (1966); *Peal II* for Big Band (1968); Sym. (Cheltenham, July 12, 1973); *Ghost and Dream Dancing* (Birmingham, Sept. 19, 1974); *Crow-cry* for Chamber Orch. (1976; London, March 16, 1977); *Welkin* for Student Orch. (1976); *Towards Asavari* for Piano and Chamber Orch. (1978; Manchester, Jan. 26, 1979); *Koonapippi* for Youth Orch. (1981); *Little Fantasia on Gold-Digger Tunes* for Chamber Orch. (1981); *Dream Carousels* for Wind Band (1988; London, Feb. 26, 1989); *Tree of Singing Names* for Chamber Orch. (1989; rev. 1993); *Mozart Sampler with Ground* (1991); *Igorochki* for Concertini Recorders and Chamber Orch. (1992). **CHAMBER:** *Brighton Piece* for Clarinet, Horn, Trumpet, Trombone, Cello, and 3 Percussion (1967); *9 or 10 Osannas* for Clarinet, Horn, Violin, Cello, and Piano (1967); *The Incredible Flute Music* for Flute and Piano (1968); *O'Grady Music* for Clarinet, Cello, and Toy Instruments (1971); String Quartet with Piano Pieces (1972); *Canticle I: Rock-song* for 2 Clarinets, Bass Clarinet, 2 Horns, 2 Trumpets, and Trombone (1973); *Vasanta with Dancing* for Flute or Alto Flute, Oboe or English Horn, Violin, Viola, Harp, Percussion, and Optional Dancer (1981); *Fanfarings* 1 and 2 (1983), 3 and 4 (1986–87), 5 (1988), and 6 (1992) for Brass; *Quartet of Beasts* for Flute, Oboe, Bassoon, and Piano (1984); *6 of the Bestiary* for Saxophone Quartet (1985); String Quartet II (1987) and III (1987); *Ziggurat* for Brass and Marimba (1994). **PIANO:** 2 sonatas (1962, 1966). **VOCAL:** *Love Poems* for Soprano, Clarinet, Cello, Accordion or Soprano, Bass Clarinet, and Chamber Organ (1970); *Inscapes* for Soprano, Speaker, and Small Ensemble (1975); *Chant of Cockeye Bob* for Children's Voices and Instruments (1981); *Beastly Jingles* for Soprano and Instrumental Ensemble (1984); *Certain Lights Reflecting* for Soprano and Orch. (Cheltenham, July 14, 1989); *Upstream River Rewa* for Narrator and Indo-European Ensemble (1991); also choruses.

Gilbert, Henry F(ranklin Belknap), remarkable American composer; b. Somerville, Mass., Sept. 26, 1868; d. Cambridge, Mass., May 19, 1928. He studied at the New England Cons. of Music in Boston and with E. Mollenhauer; from 1889 to 1892 he was a pupil of MacDowell (composition) in Boston. Rather than do routine music work to earn his livelihood (he had previously been a violinist in theaters, etc.), he took jobs of many descriptions, becoming, in turn, a real estate agent, a factory foreman, a collector of butterflies in Florida, etc., and composed when opportunity afforded. In 1893, at the Chicago World's Fair, he met a Russian prince who knew Rimsky-Korsakov and gave him many details of contemporary Russian composers whose work, as well as that of Bohemian and Scandinavian composers which was based on folk song, influenced Gilbert greatly in his later composition. In 1894 he made his first trip abroad and stayed in

Paris, subsequently returning to the U.S.; when he heard of the premiere of Charpentier's Louise, he became intensely interested in the work because of its popular character, and, in order to hear it, earned his passage to Paris, in 1901, by working on a cattle boat; the opera impressed him so much that he decided to devote his entire time thereafter to composition. In 1902 he became associated with Arthur Farwell, whose Wa-Wan Press publ. Gilbert's early compositions. From 1903 he employed Negro tunes and rhythms extensively in his works. The compositions of his mature period (from 1915) reveal an original style, not founded on any particular native American material but infused with elements from many sources, and are an attempt at "un-European" music, expressing the spirit of America and its national characteristics.

WORKS: DRAMATIC: OPERAS: *Uncle Remus* (c.1906; unfinished); *Fantasy in Delft* (1915–20). **INCIDENTAL MUSIC TO:** *Cathleen ni Houlihan* (1903); *Pot of Broth* (1903); *Riders to the Sea* (1904; rev. 1913; symphonic prologue, Peterboro, N.H., Aug. 20, 1914); *The Twisting of the Rope* (1904); *The Redskin, or The Last of his Race* (1906; not extant). **PAGEANT:** *Pilgrim Tercentenary Pageant* for Band (1921; orch. suite, 1921; Boston, March 31, 1922). **ORCH.:** *2 Episodes* (c.1895; Boston, Jan. 13, 1896); *Orlamonde*, symphonic poem (c.1896; not extant); *Summer-day Fantasie* (c.1899); *Gavotte* (n.d.); *Americanesque* (1902–08; Boston, May 24, 1911; retitled *Humoresque on Negro-Minstrel Tunes*); *Comedy Overture on Negro Themes* (1906; N.Y., Aug. 17, 1910); (3) *American Dances* (c.1906); *The Dance in Place Congo*, symphonic poem (c.1908; rev. 1916; as a ballet, N.Y., March 23, 1918); *Strife* (1910–25); (6) *Indian Sketches* (1911; rev. 1914; Boston, March 4, 1921); *Negro Rhapsody* (1912; Norfolk, Conn., June 5, 1913, composer conducting); *To Thee, America* for Chorus and Orch. (1914; Peterboro, N.H., Jan. 25, 1915); *The Island of the Fay*, symphonic poem (1923); *Dance* for Jazz Band (1924); *Symphonic Piece* (1925); *Nocturne* (1925–26; Philadelphia, March 16, 1928); Suite for Chamber Orch. (1926–27; Boston, April 28, 1928). **CHAMBER:** *Gavotte* for String Quartet; *Scherzino* for Piano Trio; Quartette; Waltz for String Quartet; *Tempo di rag* for Flute, Oboe, Cornet, Piano, 2 Violins, and Cello; String Quartet (1920); piano pieces. **VOCAL:** Many songs, including *Pirate Song*, after Stevenson, *Celtic Studies*, 4 songs after Irish poets, and *The Lament of Deirdre.*

BIBL.: A. Farwell, "Wanderjahre of a Revolutionist," *Musical America* (April 10, 1909); "An American Composer's Triumph in Russia," *Current Opinion* (May 1916); E. Ranck, "The Mark Twain of American Music," *Theatre Magazine* (Sept. 1917); O. Downes, "An American Composer," *Musical Quarterly* (Jan. 1918); E. Carter, "American Figure, with Landscape" *Modern Music*, XX (1942–43); O. Downes, "H. G.: Nonconformist," in *A Birthday Greeting to Carl Engel* (N.Y., 1943); H. Sear, "H.F. G.," *Music Review*, V (1944); K. Longyear, *H.F. G.: His Life and Works* (diss., Univ. of Rochester, 1968).

Gilbert, Jean (real name, **Max Winterfeld**), German composer; b. Hamburg, Feb. 11, 1879; d. Buenos Aires, Dec. 20, 1942. He was trained in Kiel, Sondershausen, Weimar, and Berlin. In 1897 he began his career as a conductor at the Bremerhaven City Theater. Soon after, he went to Hamburg as conductor at the Carl-Schultze Theater. In 1900 he became conductor at the Centralhallen-Theater, where he brought out his first stage work, *Das Jungfernstift* or *Comtesse* (Feb. 8, 1901). After conducting in provincial music centers, he devoted himself to composing for the theater. He attained his first notable success with the musical comedy *Polnische Wirtschaft* (Cottbus, Dec. 26, 1909). Then followed an even greater success with *Die keusche Susanne* (Magdeburg, Feb. 26, 1910), which was subsequently performed throughout Germany, France, England, and Spain. In 1910 he went to Berlin, where he brought out *Autoliebchen* (March 16, 1912), *Puppchen* (Dec. 19, 1912), *Die Kino-Königen* (March 8, 1913; rev. version of *Die elfte Muse*, Hamburg, Nov. 22, 1912), and *Die Tango-Prinzessin* (Oct. 4, 1913). He also had success with *Fräulein Tralala* (Königsberg, Nov. 15, 1913). During World War I, he continued to compose numerous stage works, including the Berlin favorites *Die Fräulein von Amt* (Sept. 2, 1915), *Blondinchen* (March 4, 1916), *Die Fahrt ins Glück* (Sept. 2, 1916), *Das Vagabundenmädel* (Dec. 2, 1916), and *Die Dose seiner Majestät* (Sept. 1, 1917). Also notable were *Arizonda* (Vienna, Feb. 1, 1916) and *Eheurlaub* (Breslau, Aug. 1, 1918). With the War over, Gilbert had a tremendous success with *Die Frau im Hermelin* (Berlin, Aug. 23, 1919) and *Katja, die Tänzerin* (Vienna, Jan. 5, 1922). Subsequent works included *Dorine und der Zufall* (Berlin, Sept. 15, 1922), *Die kleine Sünderin* (Berlin, Oct. 1, 1922), *Das Weib im Purpur* (Vienna, Dec. 21, 1923), *Geliebte seiner Hoheit* (Berlin, Sept. 24, 1924), *Uschi* (Hamburg, Jan. 24, 1925; later used in the pasticcio *Yvonne*, London, May 22, 1926), *Annemarie* (Berlin, July 2, 1915), and *Hotel Stadt Lemberg* (Hamburg, July 1, 1929). After the Nazis came to power in Germany in 1933, Gilbert lived in several European cities before emigrating to Buenos Aires in 1939. His son, Robert Gilbert (real name, David Robert Winterfeld; b. Berlin, Sept. 29, 1899; d. Minusio, March 20, 1978), was a librettist, lyricist, and composer. He collaborated with his father on several scores and also wrote many of his own. However, he became best known for his German-language adaptations of such American musicals as *Annie Get Your Gun* (1956), *My Fair Lady* (1961), *Hello, Dolly!* (1966), and *The Man of La Mancha* (1968).

Gilbert, Kenneth, esteemed Canadian harpsichordist, organist, musicologist, and pedagogue; b. Montreal, Dec. 16, 1931. He received training in organ from Conrad Letendre in Montreal, where he also studied at the Cons. with Yvonne Hubert (piano) and Gabriel Cusson (harmony and counterpoint). After winning the Prix de Europe for organ in 1953, he pursued his training in Europe with Boulanger (composition), Litaize and Duruflé (organ), and Sylvia Spicket and Ruggero Gerlin (harpsichord) until 1955. From 1952 to 1967 he was organist and music director of Queen Mary Road United Church in Montreal. He devoted himself almost exclusively to harpsichord performances from 1965. After making his London recital debut in 1968, he pursued a global career. He also taught at the Montreal Cons. (1957–74), McGill Univ. (1964–72), and Laval Univ. (1969–76). In 1969–70 he was artist-in-residence at the Univ. of Ottawa. From 1971 to 1974 he was a guest prof. at the Royal Flemish Cons. of Music in Antwerp. He gave master classes in various European and American cities. In 1988 he became a teacher at the Salzburg Mozarteum. He also served as prof. of harpsichord at the Paris Cons. from 1988, the first Canadian to hold such a position there. Gilbert ed. the complete harpsichord works of François Couperin (4 vols., 1969–72), all 555 sonatas of Domenico Scarlatti (11 vols., 1971–84), and the complete harpsichord works of Rameau (1979). In 1986 he was made an Officer of the Order of Canada. He was elected to membership in the Royal Soc. of Canada in 1988.

Gilbert, Pia, spirited German-born American composer and pedagogue; b. Kippenheim, June 1, 1921. She began her career as a dance accompanist in the N.Y. studios of Lotte Goslar, Doris Humphreys, and Martha Graham; then found her niche as a composer for dance and theater. She served in various capacities during her lengthy tenure as prof. in the dance dept. at the Univ. of Calif., Los Angeles (1947–85), including resident composer and music director of its dance company; in 1986 she joined the music faculty at the Juilliard School in N.Y. As a teacher, Gilbert is distinguished by her commitment to the musical literacy of dancers, as well as for her interdisciplinary approach. Her compositions, whether for dance, theater, or simply "music per se," are always subtly dramatic, and a certain sly humor invades several of her vocal works; *Vociano*, first performed by Jan DeGaetani at the 1978 Aspen (Colo.) Music Festival, is pleasing for its use of imaginary languages, and her later chamber opera, *Dialects* (1990–91; Bonn, May 21, 1991), is a modern-day recreation of the most playful of Futurist ideals. With A. Lockhart, she publ. *Music for the Modern Dance* (1961).

WORKS: DRAMATIC: CHAMBER OPERA: *Dialects* (1990–91; Bonn, May 21, 1991). **DANCE:** *In 2s It's Love* (1949); *Songs of Innocence and Experience* (1952); *Trio* for Piano, Dancer, and Lights (1956); *Valse* for Lotte Goslar (1959); *Bridge of the 7th Moon* (1960); *Freke-Phreec-Freake-Phreaque-Freak* (1969); *Irving, the Terrific* (1971); *Requiem for Jimmy Dean* (1972); *Legend* (1985). **THEATER** (all 1st perf. by the Mark Taper Forum Theatre Group, Los Angeles): *The Deputy*, after R. Hochhuth (1966); *Murderous Angels*, after C.C. O'Brien (1970); *Tales from Hollywood*, after C. Hampton (1982). **ORCH.:** *Gestures* (1988). **CHAMBER:** *Transmutations* for Organ and Percussion (1975); *Spirals and Interpolations* for Small Ensemble (1976); *Interrupted Suite* for Clarinet and 3 Pianos (1978); *Tri, dispute, dialogue, diatribe* for Cello and Piano (1978); *Volatile* for Piano (1987). **VOCAL:** *Vociano* for Mezzo-soprano and Piano (1978); *Food* for Soprano, Baritone, Trumpet, Piano, and Snare Drum, to texts by John Cage (1981); *Bells* for Soprano and Piano (1983); *Das Lied der Gefallenen* for Voice and Piano, after L. Feuchtwanger (1984); *Quotations and Interludes* for Soprano, Clarinet, Violin, Piano, and Balloons (1990).

Gilboa, Jacob, Czech-born Israeli composer; b. Košice, May 2, 1920. He grew up in Vienna and went to Palestine in 1938. He studied composition with Tal in Jerusalem and Ben-Haim in Tel Aviv (1944–47); then traveled to Germany and attended courses of new music with Stockhausen, Pousseur, Alois Kontarsky, and Caskel. His music represents a blend of oriental and Eastern Mediterranean idioms, basically lyrical, but technically ultramodern.

WORKS: *7 Little Insects*, piano pieces for children (1955); *Wild Flowers*, 4 lyrical pieces for Woman's Voice, Horn, Harp, and String Orch. (1957); *Passing Clouds* for Woman's Voice, Clarinet, Cello, and Piano (1958); Violin Sonata (1960); *The 12 Jerusalem Chagall Windows* for Voices and Instruments (1966); *Crystals* for Flute, Viola, Cello, Piano, and Percussion (1967); *Horizons in Violet and Blue*, ballet scene for 6 Players (1970); *Pastels* for 2 Prepared Pianos (1970); *Thistles*, theater piece for Singing and Speaking Voices, Horn, Cello, Piano, and Percussion (1970); *Cedars* for Orch. (1971); *From the Dead Sea Scrolls* for Chorus, Children's Chorus, 2 Organs, Tape, and Orch. (1971; Hamburg, Jan. 11, 1972); *14 Epigrams for Oscar Wilde* for Woman's Voice, Piano, and Tape (1973); *Bedu*, metamorphoses on a Bedouin call, for Man's Voice, Cello, Flute, and Piano (1975); *The Beth Alpha Mosaic* for Woman's Voice, Chamber Ensemble, and Tape (1975; Chicago, Jan. 24, 1976); *3 Red Sea Impressions* for Violin, Piano, Harp, Electric Guitar, Organ, and Tape (1976); *3 Vocalises for Peter Breughel* for Mezzo-soprano, Tape, and 13 Instruments (1979); *Gittit* for Chamber Orch. (1980); *7 Ornaments on a Theme of Ben-Haim* for Piano and Orch. (1981); Cello Sonata (1981); String Quartet (1984); *3 Lyric Pieces in the Mediterranean Style* for Chamber Orch. (1984); *3 Strange Visions of Hieronymus Bosch* for Organ (1987); *The Gray Colors of Käthe Kollwitz* for Woman's Voice, Synthesizer, Tape, and Chamber Ensemble (1990); *Blossoms in the Desert* for Flute and Piano (1991); *Lyric Triptych* for Alto, Girl's Chorus, Synthesizer, and Chamber Ensemble (1993).

Gilels, Elizabeta, Russian violinist, sister of **Emil (Grigorievich) Gilels**; b. Odessa, Sept. 30, 1919. She studied with Stoliarsky at his school for gifted youths in Odessa and later graduated from the Moscow Cons., where she took lessons from A. Yampolsky. She received 3rd place in the Ysaÿe Competition (Brussels, 1937); taught at the Moscow Cons. (from 1967). She played duets with her husband, **Leonid Kogan**; their son, Pavel Kogan, was also a talented violinist.

Gilels, Emil (Grigorievich), eminent Russian pianist, brother of **Elizabeta Gilels**; b. Odessa, Oct. 19, 1916; d. Moscow, Oct. 14, 1985. He entered the Odessa Cons. at the age of 5 to study with Yakov Tkatch, making his first public appearance at 9, followed by his formal debut at 13; after further studies with Bertha Ringbald at the Cons., he went to Moscow for advanced studies with Heinrich Neuhaus (1935–38). He won 1st prize at the Moscow Competition in 1933; after taking 2nd prize at the Vienna Competition in 1936, he won 1st prize at the Brussels Competition in 1938; that same year, he became a prof. at the Moscow Cons. Following World War II, he embarked upon an esteemed international career. He was the first Soviet musician to appear in the U.S. during the Cold War era, making his debut in Tchaikovsky's 1st Piano Concerto with Ormandy and the Philadelphia Orch. (Oct. 3, 1955). He subsequently made 13 tours of the U.S., the last in 1983. A member of the Communist party from 1942, he received various honors from the Soviet government. Gilels was one of the foremost pianists of his time. He was especially renowned for his performances of Beethoven, Schubert, Schumann, Chopin, Liszt, Tchaikovsky, and Brahms.

BIBL.: V. Delson, *E. G.* (Moscow, 1959); S. Hentova, *E. G.* (Moscow, 1967).

Gillis, Don, American composer; b. Cameron, Mo., June 17, 1912; d. Columbia, S.C., Jan. 10, 1978. He was educated at Texas Christian Univ. (graduated, 1936) and at North Texas State Univ. (M.M., 1943). In 1943 he joined NBC in Chicago, and then worked for the network in N.Y. (1944–54), mainly as a producer. In 1967–68 he was chairman of the music dept. at Southern Methodist Univ.; after serving as chairman of fine arts and director of media instruction at Dallas Baptist College (1968–72), he was composer-in-residence and director of the inst. for media arts at the Univ. of South Carolina (from 1973). His compositions, clothed in a conservative garb, were often enlivened by a whimsical bent.

WORKS: DRAMATIC: OPERAS: *The Park Avenue Kids* (Elkhart, Ind., May 12, 1957); *Pep Rally* (Interlochen, Mich., Aug. 15, 1957); *The Libretto* (1958; Norman, Okla., Dec. 1, 1961); *The Legend of Star Valley Junction* (1961–62; N.Y., Jan. 7, 1969); *The Gift of the Magi* (Forth Worth, Texas, Dec. 7, 1965); *World Premiere* (1966–67); *The Nazarene* (1967–68); *Behold the Man* (1973); also ballets. **ORCH.:** *The Woolyworm* (1937); *Thoughts Provoked on Becoming a Prospective Papa*, suite (1937); 10 syms. (1939–67), including Sym. No. 5 1/2, the "Symphony for Fun" (1947); *The Panhandle*, suite (1937); *Intermission—10 Minutes* (1940); *Prairie Poem* (1943); *The Alamo* (1944); *A Short Overture to an Unwritten Opera* (1944); *To an Unknown Soldier* (1945); Rhapsody for Harp and Orch. (1946); *Tulsa: A Symphonic Portrait in Oil* (1950); *Dude Ranch*, suite (1967); 2 piano concertos; also band music. **CHAMBER:** 6 string quartets (1936–47); 3 suites for Woodwind Quintet (1938, 1939, 1939). **OTHER:** Vocal works; instrumental pieces.

Gilly, Dinh, French baritone; b. Algiers, July 19, 1877; d. London, May 19, 1940. He studied at the Toulouse Cons. and with Cotogni in Rome; after completing his studies at the Paris Cons., he made his debut as the Priest in *Sigurd* at the Paris Opéra in 1899; continued to sing there until 1908. On Nov. 16, 1909, he made his debut with the Metropolitan Opera in N.Y. at the New Theatre as Albert in *Werther*; his formal debut at the Metropolitan Opera was as Alfio in *Cavalleria rusticana* on Nov. 24, 1909, and he remained on its roster until 1914; he first appeared at London's Covent Garden as Amonasro in Aida on May 15, 1911; sang there until 1914 and again from 1919 to 1924. He also made appearances with the Beecham, Carl Rosa, and British National Opera companies. He made London his home and was active in later years as a teacher; among his pupils was John Brownlee.

Gilman, Lawrence, American music critic; b. Flushing, N.Y., July 5, 1878; d. Franconia, N.H., Sept. 8, 1939. He was self-taught in music. From 1901 to 1913 he was music critic of *Harper's Weekly*; from 1915 to 1923, music, dramatic, and literary critic of the *North American Review*; from 1921 to 1939, author of the program notes of the N.Y. Phil. and Philadelphia Orch. concerts; from 1923 to 1939 he was music critic of the *N.Y. Herald Tribune*. He was a member of the National Inst. of Arts and Letters.

WRITINGS: *Phases of Modern Music* (1904); *Edward Mac-*

Dowell (1905; 2nd ed., rev. and enl., 1909, as *Edward MacDowell: A Study*); *The Music of To-Morrow* (1906); *Stories of Symphonic Music* (1907); *Aspects of Modern Opera* (1909); *Nature in Music* (1914); *A Christmas Meditation* (1916); *Music and the Cultivated Man* (1929); *Wagner's Operas* (1937); *Toscanini and Great Music* (1938).

BIBL.: C. Engel, "L. G.," *Musical Quarterly* (Jan. 1940).

Gilse, Jan van, Dutch conductor and composer; b. Rotterdam, May 11, 1881; d. Oegstgeest, near Leiden, Sept. 8, 1944. He studied with Wüllner at the Cologne Cons. (1897–1902) and with Humperdinck in Berlin (1902–3). He was a conductor of the Bremen Opera (1905–8) and of the Dutch Opera at Amsterdam (1908–09); was music director of the City of Utrecht (1917–22). He lived again in Berlin (1922–33); then was director of the Utrecht Cons. (1933–37). His music is heavily imbued with German Romanticism.

WORKS: OPERAS: *Frau Helga von Stavern* (1911); Thijl (1938–40; 1st complete perf., Amsterdam, Sept. 21, 1976; also a symphonic extract, *Funeral Music*, 1940). **ORCH.:** 5 syms.: No. 1 (1900–1901), No. 2 (1902–03), No. 3, *Erhebung* for Soprano and Orch. (1903; rev. 1928), No. 4 (1914), and No. 5 (1922–23; unfinished sketch only); Concert Overture (1900); *Variaties over een St. Nicolaasliedje* (Variations on a St. Nicholas Song; 1909; also for Piano); *3 Tanzskizzen* (Dance Sketches) for Piano and Small Orch. (1926); *Prologus brevis* (1928); *Kleine Vals* for Small Orch. (1936). **CHAMBER:** Nonet (1916); Trio for Flute, Violin, and Viola (1927). **VOCAL:** *Eine Lebensmesse*, oratorio (1904); 6 Songs for Soprano and Orch. (3 songs, 1915; 3 songs, 1923); *Der Kreis des Lebens*, oratorio (1928); other songs.

Gilson, Paul, notable Belgian composer, pedagogue, and writer on music; b. Brussels, June 15, 1865; d. there, April 3, 1942. He studied with Auguste Cantillon (theory) and Charles Duyck (harmony) before pursuing his training at the Brussels Cons. (1887–89) with Gevaert (composition), where he won the Belgian Prix de Rome with his cantata *Sinai* (1889). His orch. work *La mer* (1892) placed him in the forefront of Belgian musical life. During the following decade, he composed his finest scores before concentrating on teaching and writing. He was prof. of harmony at the Brussels Cons. (1899–1909) and the Antwerp Cons. (1904–09), and then was inspector of music education in the Belgian schools (1909–30). He was music critic of *Le Soir* (1906–14), *Le Diapson* (1910–14), and of *Midi*. In 1925 a group of his students formed the Synthetistes to carry on his ideals, which led to the founding of the journal *Revue Musicale Belge*. Gilson's compositions reflect the considerable gifts of a traditionalist.

WRITINGS (all publ. in Brussels unless otherwise given): *Le tutti orchestral* (1913); *Traité d'harmonie* (1919); *Quintes, octaves, secondes et polytonie* (1921); *Manuel de musique militaire* (Antwerp, 1926); *Notes de musique et souvenirs* (1942).

WORKS: DRAMATIC: OPERAS: *Le démon* (1890; Mons, April 9, 1893); *Prinses Zonneschijn* (Antwerp, Oct. 10, 1903; as *La princesse Rayon de Soleil*, Brussels, Sept. 9, 1905); *Gens de mer* (Antwerp, Oct. 15, 1904; in French, Brussels, Dec. 16, 1929); *Rooversliefde* (Antwerp, Jan. 30, 1910). **BALLETS:** *La captive* (1896–1900); *Les deux bossus* (1910–21). **ORCH.:** Concertino for Flute and Orch. (1882–1920); Suite (1885); *3 Pieces* (1885–92); *3 mélodies populaires flamandes* for Strings (1891–92); *Mélodies écossaises* for Strings (1891–92); Suites (1891–1941); *La mer* (Brussels, March 20, 1892); *Overture dramatique* (1900; Brussels, Jan. 13, 1901); 2 saxophone concertos (1902); *Thème et variations* or *Variations symphoniques* (1903; Brussels, Nov. 8, 1908); *Romance-fantaisie* for Violin and Orch. (1903); *Troisieme ouverture symphonique* (1903–04); Concertstück for Trumpet and Orch. (1905–06); *Andante et scherzo* for Cello and Orch. (1906); *Prélude symphonique:Le chant du coq* (1906); *Prélude pour le drame "Henry VIII" de Shakespeare* (1906–16; Brussels, May 26, 1918); *Symphonie inaugurale* (1909–10); *Suite à la manière ancienne* for Strings (1913–14); *Cavatina* (1921); *Epithalame* (1925); *Cinq paraphrases sur des chansons populaires flamanade* (1929); *Préludes hébraïques* (1934); *Caledonia* (1939); *Scherzando* for Piano and Orch. (1941); numerous pieces for Wind or Brass Band. **CHAMBER:** 2 string quartets (1907; 1918–19); Trio for Oboe, Clarinet, and Bassoon (1934); suites; many piano pieces. **VOCAL:** cantatas: *Au bois des elfes* (1887), *Sinai* (1889), *Et la lumière descend sur tous* (1896), *Hymne à l'art* (1897), *Ludus pro patria* (1905), and *La voix de la forêt* (1934); oratorio: *Francesca da Rimini* (1892).

BIBL.: Special issue of *Review Musicale Belge*, X (1935); G. Brenta, *P.G.* (Brussels, 1965).

Giltay, Berend, Dutch composer; b. Hilversum, June 15, 1910; d. Utrecht, March 21, 1975. He studied violin and viola with Dick Waleson and composition with Badings. He was a violinist with the Hilversum Radio Phil. and with various other Dutch orchs. From 1963 to 1966 he attended courses in electronic music at the Univ. of Utrecht and worked in Bilthoven at the Gaudeamus electronic studio.

WORKS; ORCH.: Violin Concerto (1950); Concerto for Viola and Chamber Orch. (1955); Oboe Concerto (1956–57); *Sinfonia* (1956–57); Horn Concerto (c.1958); *Concerto for Orchestra* (1960); *Kurucz Valtozatok Zenekarra*, variations (1966–67); Concerto for 2 Violins and Orch. (1966–67); *Gossauer Symphonie* (Utrecht, Oct. 3, 1972); *Kosmochromie I* for 4 Loudspeakers and Orch. (Utrecht, Feb. 22, 1974) and *II* for String Quartet, Chamber Orch., and Tape (1974). **CHAMBER:** *4 Miniatures* for Viola and Piano (1952); *Sonata a tre* for Oboe, Clarinet, and Bassoon (1953); Wind Quintet (1956); String Quintet (1957); 2 duos for 2 Violins (1962, 1966); *Divertimento* for 5 Flutes (1963); *Scherzo* for 2 Violins (1963); *6 studi concertante* for Viola (1963); *Phonolieten* for Tape (1965); *Polychromie I* for Tape (1966) and *II* for Piccolo, Flute and Alto Flute, 4 Flutes or other Instruments, and Tape (1972); *Elegy* for Alto Flute and 4 Flutes (1969); Trio for 2 Violins and Cello (1971).

Gimenez, Raul, Argentine tenor; b. Santa Fe, Sept. 14, 1950. He received training in Buenos Aires. Following his operatic debut there in 1980 at the Teatro Colón as Ernesto, he appeared in concert and opera in various South American music centers. In 1984 he made his European debut at the Wexford Festival as Filandro in Cimarosa's *La astuzie femminili*, and subsequently sang in Paris, Venice, Pesaro, Amsterdam, Rome, Aix-en-Provence, Zürich, and Geneva. He made his U.S. debut as Ernesto in Dallas in 1989, choosing that role for his first appearance at London's Covent Garden in 1990. He sang Rossini's Count Almaviva at his debut at the Vienna State Opera in 1990. In 1993 he sang for the first time at Milan's La Scala as Tancredi. Gimenez is highly regarded for his roles in Rossini operas, among them Almaviva, Argiro, Rodrigo, Count Alberto, Giocondo, and Florville.

Gimpel, Bronislav, distinguished Austrian-born American violinist and teacher, brother of **Jakob Gimpel;** b. Lemberg, Jan. 29, 1911; d. Los Angeles, May 1, 1979. He was a pupil of Pollack at the Vienna Cons. (1922–26) and of Flesch at the Berlin Hochschule für Musik (1928–29). In 1925 he appeared as soloist with the Vienna Sym. Orch. He was a laureate in the Wieniawski Competition in 1935. He was concertmaster of the Königsberg Radio Orch. (1929–31), the Göteborg Sym. Orch. (1931–37), and the Los Angeles Phil. (1937–42), and later was 1st violin in the American Artist Quartet; he also played in the New Friends of Music Piano Quartet and the Mannes Piano Trio (1950–56). Following tours of Europe as a soloist, where he also gave master classes in Karlsruhe (1959–61), he was 1st violin in the Warsaw Quintet (1962–67) and the New England Quartet (1967–73); he also was a prof. at the Univ. of Conn. (1967–73). Gimpel's remarkable technique made him a notable soloist, recitalist, and chamber music player.

Gimpel, Jakob, esteemed Austrian-born American pianist and pedagogue, brother of **Bronislav Gimpel;** b. Lemberg, April 16, 1906; d. Los Angeles, March 12, 1989. He studied at the Lemberg Cons. before pursuing his training in Vienna with Steuermann (piano) and Berg (theory). After making his debut in Vienna in 1923, he gave concerts with extraordinary success in Germany until the advent of the Nazi regime forced him to go to Palestine. In 1938 he settled in the U.S. After World War II, he gave concerts on both sides of the Atlantic. He also devoted much time to teaching, and in 1971 he was made Distinguished Professor-in-Residence at Calif. State Univ. at Northridge. Gimpel was especially admired for his interpretations of the Romantic repertory.

Ginastera, Alberto (Evaristo), greatly talented Argentine composer; b. Buenos Aires, April 11, 1916; d. Geneva, June 25, 1983. He was of Catalan-Italian descent. He took private lessons in music as a child; then entered the National Cons. of Music in Buenos Aires, where he studied composition with José Gil, Athos Palma, and José André; also took piano lessons with Argenziani. He began to compose in his early youth; in 1934 he won 1st prize of the musical society El Únisono for his *Piezas infantiles* for Piano. His next piece of importance was *Impresiones de la Puna* for Flute and String Quartet, in which he made use of native Argentine melodies and rhythms; he discarded it, however, as immature; he withdrew a number of his other works, some of them of certain value, for instance, his *Concierto argentino*, which he wrote in 1935, and *Sinfonia Porteña*, his 1st Sym. (which may be identical in its musical material with *Estancia*). Also withdrawn was his 2nd Sym., the *Sinfonía elegíaca*, written in 1944, even though it was successfully performed. In 1946–47 Ginastera traveled to the U.S. on a Guggenheim fellowship. Returning to Argentina, he served as director of the Cons. of the province of Buenos Aires in La Plata (1948–52; 1956–58); he then taught at the Argentine Catholic Univ. and also was a prof. at the Univ. of La Plata. In 1968 he left Argentina and lived mostly in Geneva. From his earliest steps in composition, Ginastera had an almost amorous attachment for the melodic and rhythmic resources of Argentine folk music, and he evolved a fine harmonic and contrapuntal setting congenial with native patterns. His first significant work in the Argentine national idiom was *Panambí*, a ballet, composed in 1935 and performed at the Teatro Colón in Buenos Aires on July 12, 1940. There followed a group of *Danzas argentinas* for Piano, written in 1937; in 1938 he wrote 3 songs; the first one, *Canción al árbol del olvido*, is a fine evocation of youthful love; it became quite popular. In 1941 he was commissioned to write a ballet for the American Ballet Caravan, to be called *Estancia*; the music was inspired by the rustic scenes of the pampas; a suite from the score was performed at the Teatro Colón on May 12, 1943, and the complete work was brought out there on Aug. 19, 1952. A series of works inspired by native scenes and written for various instrumental combinations followed, all infused with Ginastera's poetic imagination and brought to realization with excellent technical skill. Soon, however, he began to search for new methods of musical expression, marked by modern and sometimes strikingly dissonant combinations of sound, fermented by asymmetrical rhythms. Of these works, one of the most remarkable is *Cantata para América Mágica*, scored for dramatic soprano and percussion instruments, to apocryphal pre-Columbian texts, freely arranged by Ginastera; it was first performed in Washington, D.C., on April 30, 1961, with excellent success. An entirely new development in Ginastera's evolution as composer came with his first opera, *Don Rodrigo* (1964), produced on July 24, 1964, at the Teatro Colón. In it he followed the general formula of Berg's *Wozzeck* in its use of classical instrumental forms, such as rondo, suite, scherzo, and canonic progressions; he also introduced *Sprechstimme*. In 1964 he wrote the *Cantata Bomarzo* on a commission from the Elizabeth Sprague Coolidge Foundation in Washington, D.C. He used the same libretto by Manuel Mujica Láinez in his opera *Bomarzo*, which created a sensation at its production in Washington, D. C., on May 19, 1967, by its unrestrained spectacle of sexual violence. It was announced for performance at the Teatro Colón on Aug. 9, 1967, but was canceled at the order of the Argentine government because of its alleged immoral nature. The score of *Bomarzo* reveals extraordinary innovations in serial techniques, with thematical employment not only of different chromatic sounds, but also of serial progressions of different intervals. His last opera, *Beatrix Cenci*, commissioned by the Opera Soc. of Washington, D.C., and produced there on Sept. 10, 1971, concluded his operatic trilogy. Among instrumental works of Ginastera's last period, the most remarkable was his 2nd Piano Concerto (1972), based on a tone-row derived from the famous dissonant opening of the finale of Beethoven's 9th Sym.; the 2nd movement of the concerto is written for the left hand alone. He was married to the pianist Mercedes de Toro in 1941. After their divorce in 1965, Ginastera married the Argentine cellist Aurora Natola, for whom he wrote the Cello Sonata, which she played in N.Y. on Dec. 13, 1979, and his 2nd Cello Concerto, which she performed in Buenos Aires on July 6, 1981.

WORKS: DRAMATIC: OPERAS: *Don Rodrigo* (1963–64; Buenos Aires, July 24, 1964); *Bomarzo* (1966–67; Washington, D.C., May 19, 1967); *Beatrix Cenci* (Washington, D.C., Sept. 10, 1971). **BALLETS:** *Panambí* (1935; suite, Buenos Aires, Nov. 27, 1937; 1st complete perf., Buenos Aires, July 12, 1940); *Estancia* (1941; Buenos Aires, Aug. 19, 1952). Also film music. **ORCH.:** *Primer concierto argentino* (Montevideo, July 18, 1941; withdrawn); *Primera sinfonía (Porteña)* (1942; withdrawn); *Obertra para el "Fausto" Criollo* (1943; Santiago, Chile, May 12, 1944); *Sinfonía elegíaca* (2nd Sym.; Buenos Aires, May 31, 1946; withdrawn); *Ollantay*, 3 symphonic movements after an Inca poem (1947; Buenos Aires, Oct. 29, 1949); *Variaciones concertantes* for Chamber Orch. (Buenos Aires, June 2, 1953); *Pampeana No. 3*, symphonic pastoral (Louisville, Ky., Oct. 20, 1954); Harp Concerto (1956; Philadelphia, Feb. 18, 1965); 2 piano concertos: No. 1 (Washington, D.C., April 22, 1961) and No. 2 (1972; Indianapolis, March 22, 1973); Violin Concerto (N.Y., Oct. 3, 1963); Concerto for Strings (1965; Caracas, May 14, 1966); *Estudios sinfónicos* (1967; Vancouver, March 31, 1968); 2 cello concertos: No. 1 (Hanover, N.H., July 7, 1968; rev. 1971–72 and 1977) and No. 2 (Buenos Aires, July 6, 1981); *Popul Vuh* (1975–83; unfinished; St. Louis, April 7, 1989); *Glosses sobre temes de Pau Casals* for String Orch. and String Quintet "in lontano" (San Juan, Puerto Rico, June 14, 1976; rev. for Full Orch. and 1st perf. in Washington, D.C., Jan. 24, 1978); *Iubilum* (1979–80; Buenos Aires, April 12, 1980). **CHAMBER:** *Impresiones de la Puna* for Flute and String Quartet (1942; withdrawn); *Dúo* for Flute and Oboe (1945); *Pampeana No. 1* for Violin and Piano (1947) and *No. 2* for Cello and Piano (1950); 4 string quartets: No. 1 (1948), No. 2 (1958), No. 3, with Soprano (1973), and No. 4, with Baritone, to the text of Beethoven's Heiligenstadt Testament (1974; unfinished); Piano Quintet (1963); *Puneña No. 2* for Cello (1976); Guitar Sonata (1976); Cello Sonata (N.Y., Dec. 13, 1979); *Fanfare* for 4 Trumpets in C (from *Iubilum*, 1980); *Serenade* for Cello, Flute, Oboe, Clarinet, Bassoon, Horn, Double Bass, Harp, and Percussion (1980). **KEYBOARD: PIANO:** *Piezas infantiles* (1934); *Danzas argentinas* (1937); *3 piezas* (1940); *Malambo* (1940); *12 Preludios americanos* (1944); *Suite de Danzas criollas* (1946); *Rondó sobre temas infantiles argentinos* (1947); 3 sonatas (1952, 1981, 1982); *Pequeña danza* from *Estancia* (1955); *Toccata*, arranged from *Toccata per organo* by Domenico Zipoli (1972). **ORGAN:** *Toccata, Villancico y Fuga* (1947); *Variazioni e Toccata* (1980). **VOCAL:** *2 Canciones*: No. 1, *Canción al árbol del ovido*, and No. 2, *Canción a la luna lunanca* (1938); *Cantos del Tucumán* for Voice, Flute, Violin, Harp, and 2 Indian Drums (1938); *Psalm 150* for Chorus, Boys' Chorus, and Orch. (1938; Buenos Aires, April 7, 1945); *5 Canciones populares argentinas* for Voice and Piano (1943); *Las horas de una estancia* for Voice and Piano (1943); *Hieremiae prophetae lamentatiónes* for Chorus (1946); *Cantata para América Mágica* for Dramatic Soprano and Percussion, to an apocryphal pre-Columbian text (1960; Washington, D.C., April 30, 1961); *Sinfonía Don Rodrigo* for Soprano and Orch. (Madrid, Oct. 31, 1964); *Cantata Bomarzo* for Speaker, Baritone, and Chamber Orch. (Washington, D.C., Nov. 1, 1964); *Milena*, cantata for Soprano and Orch., to texts from Kafka's letters (1971; Denver, April 16, 1973); *Serenata* for Cello, Baritone, and Chamber Ensemble, to texts of Pablo Neruda (1973;

N.Y., Jan. 18, 1974); *Turbae ad Passionem Gregorianam* for Tenor, Baritone, Bass, Boys' Chorus, Mixed Chorus, and Orch. (1974; Philadelphia, March 20, 1975).

BIBL.: P. Suárez Urtubey, *A. G.* (Buenos Aires, 1967); *A. G.: A Catalogue of His Published Works* (London, 1976); F. Spangemacher, ed., *A. G.* (Bonn, 1984); L. Tan, "An Interview with A. G.," *American Music Teacher* (Jan. 1984).

Gingold, Josef, distinguished Russian-born American violinist and pedagogue; b. Brest-Litovsk, Oct. 28, 1909; d. Bloomington, Ind., Jan. 11, 1995. He went to the U.S. in 1920. He studied violin in N.Y. with Vladimir Graffman, and later in Brussels with Eugène Ysaÿe. He then served as 1st violinist in the NBC Sym. Orch. in N.Y. (1937–43); later was concertmaster of the Detroit Sym. Orch. (1943–46) and the Cleveland Orch. (1947–60). He taught at Case Western Reserve Univ. (1950–60) and was prof. of chamber music at the Meadowmount School of Music (1955–81). In 1960 he was appointed to the faculty of the Indiana Univ. School of Music in Bloomington; was made a distinguished prof. of music there in 1965. He also gave master classes at the Paris Cons. (1970–81), in Tokyo (1970), in Copenhagen (1979), and in Montreal (1980); held the Mischa Elman Chair at the Manhattan School of Music in N.Y. (1980–81). He was a guiding force in establishing the International Violin Competition of Indianapolis; was its first honorary chairman and president of the jury in 1982, positions he held again in 1986 and 1990.

Ginsburg, Lev (Solomonovich), Russian cellist, music scholar, and pedagogue; b. Mogilev, Jan. 28, 1907; d. Moscow, Nov. 21, 1981. He studied cello, chamber music, and music history at the Moscow Cons. (graduated, 1931; kandidat degree, 1938, with the diss. *Luidzhi Bokkerini i evo rol' v razvitii violonchel'novo iskusstva* [Luigi Boccherini and his role in the development of the art of cello playing]; publ. in Moscow, 1938; Ph.D., 1947, with the diss. *Violonchel'noye iskusstvo ot evo istok ov do kontsa XVIII stoletiya* [The art of cello playing from its origin to the end of the XVIII century]). In 1936 he joined the faculty of the Moscow Cons., where he served as a prof. from 1950. He publ. the valuable *Istoriya violonchel'novo iskusstva* (History of the art of cello playing; vols. I and II, Moscow and Leningrad, 1950, 1957; vol. III, Moscow, 1965). His other works included monographs on Casals (Moscow, 1958; 2nd ed., enl., 1966), Ysaÿe (Moscow, 1959), Rostropovich (Moscow, 1963), and Tartini (Moscow, 1969), and collections of articles and essays.

Ginsburg, Semion, Russian musicologist; b. Kiev, May 23, 1901. He studied art history and musicology in Petrograd. In 1925 he was appointed to the faculty of the Leningrad Cons. In his scientific pursuits, he explored the sociological foundation of national musical resources. He publ. books on the fundamentals of musical culture (Leningrad, 1935) and on Russian music on the threshold of the 20th century (Moscow, 1966).

Giordano, Umberto, noted Italian composer; b. Foggia, Aug. 28, 1867; d. Milan, Nov. 12, 1948. He studied with Gaetano Briganti at Foggia, and then with Paolo Serrao at the Naples Cons. (1881–90). His first composition performed in public was a symphonic poem, *Delizia* (1886); he then wrote some instrumental music. In 1888 he submitted a short opera, *Marina,* for the competition established by the publisher Sonzogno; Mascagni's *Cavalleria rusticana* received 1st prize, but *Marina* was cited for distinction. Giordano then wrote the opera *Mala vita,* which was performed in Rome, Feb. 21, 1892; it was only partly successful; it was then revised and presented under the title *Il voto in Milan* (Nov. 10, 1897). There followed the opera *Regina Diaz* (Rome, Feb. 21, 1894), which obtained a moderate success. Then he set to work on a grand opera, *Andrea Chénier,* its premiere at La Scala in Milan (March 28, 1896) was a spectacular success and established Giordano as one of the best composers of Italian opera of the day. The dramatic subject gave Giordano a fine opportunity to display his theatrical talent, but the score also revealed his gift for lyric expression. Almost as successful was his next opera, *Fedora* (Teatro Lirico, Milan, Nov. 17, 1898), but it failed to hold a place in the world repertoire after the initial acclaim; there followed *Siberia* (La Scala, Dec. 19, 1903; rev. 1921; La Scala, Dec. 5, 1927). Two short operas, *Marcella* (Milan, Nov. 9, 1907) and *Mese Mariano* (Palermo, March 17, 1910), were hardly noticed and seemed to mark a decline in Giordano's dramatic gift; however, he recaptured public attention with *Madame Sans-Gêne,* produced at a gala premiere at the Metropolitan Opera in N.Y. on Jan. 25, 1915, conducted by Toscanini, with Geraldine Farrar singing the title role. With Franchetti, he wrote *Giove a Pompeii* (Rome, July 5, 1921); he then produced *La cena delle beffe,* which was his last signal accomplishment; it was staged at La Scala, Dec. 20, 1924. He wrote 1 more opera, *Il Re* (La Scala, Jan. 10, 1929). During his lifetime, Giordano received many honors, and was elected a member of the Accademia Luigi Cherubini in Florence and of several other institutions. Although not measuring up to Puccini in musical qualities or to Mascagni in dramatic skill, Giordano was a distinguished figure in the Italian opera field for some 4 decades.

BIBL.: G. Paribeni, *Madame Sans-Gêne di U. G.* (Milan, 1923); D. Cellamare, *U. G.: La vita e le opere* (Milan, 1949); R. Giazotto, *U. G.* (Milan, 1949); G. Confalonieri, *U. G.* (Milan, 1958); D. Cellamare, *U. G.* (Rome, 1967); M. Morini, ed., *U. G.* (Milan, 1968).

Giorni, Aurelio, Italian-American pianist, teacher, and composer; b. Perugia, Sept. 15, 1895; d. (suicide) Pittsfield, Mass., Sept. 23, 1938. He studied piano with Sgambati at the Accademia di Santa Cecilia in Rome (1909–11) and composition with Humperdinck in Berlin (1911–13). He emigrated to the U.S. in 1914 and was active mainly as a teacher; he was on the faculty at Smith College, the Philadelphia Cons. of Music, and the Hartford School of Music. He was also a fairly prolific composer; his Sym. in D minor was performed in N.Y. on April 25, 1937, but had such exceedingly bad reviews that he sank into a profound state of depression; several months later, he threw himself into the Housatonic River. Among his other works were *Orlando furioso,* symphonic poem (1926); Sinfonia concertante (1931); 3 trios; 2 string quartets; Cello Sonata; Violin Sonata; Piano Quartet; Piano Quintet; Flute Sonata; Clarinet Sonata; 24 concert études for Piano; songs.

BIBL.: E. Giorni Burns (his daughter), *The Broken Pedal* (Whittier, Calif., 1986).

Gipps, Ruth (Dorothy Louisa), English conductor and composer; b. Bexhill-on-Sea, Sussex, Feb. 20, 1921. She studied oboe with Leon Goossens, piano with Kendall Taylor, and composition with Vaughan Williams at the Royal College of Music in London (1937–42), and attended the Matthay Piano School (1942–43); obtained a B.Mus. in 1941 and a D.Mus. in 1948. She began her performing career as a pianist and oboist; after serving as director of the City of Birmingham Choir (1948–50), she was conductor of the London Repertoire Orch. (1955–86); also was founder-conductor of the London Chanticleer Orch. (from 1961), and music director of the Rondel Ensemble, a wind group. She taught at Trinity College, London (1959–66), the Royal College of Music (1967–77), and Kingston Polytechnic (1977–79). In 1981 she was made a Member of the Order of the British Empire.

WORKS: ORCH.: Clarinet Concerto (1940); Oboe Concerto (1941; London, June 13, 1942); 5 syms.: No. 1 (1942; Birmingham, March 25, 1945), No. 2 (1945; Birmingham, Oct. 3, 1946), No. 3 (1965; London, March 19, 1966), No. 4 (1972; London, May 28, 1973), and No. 5 (1982; London, March 6, 1983); Violin Concerto (1943; London, Feb. 5, 1944); *Death on the Pale Horse* (Birmingham, Nov. 14, 1943); *Chanticleer,* overture (1944); *Song for Orchestra* (1948; Sutton Coldfield, Jan. 10, 1949); Piano Concerto (1948; Birmingham, March 21, 1949); *Cringlemire Garden* for Strings (Birmingham, Feb. 20, 1952); *Coronation Procession* (1953; Melbourne, Sept. 27, 1954); *The Rainbow,* pageant overture (1954; Birmingham, Oct. 6, 1964); Concerto for Violin, Viola, and Orch. (1957; London, Jan. 30,

1962); Horn Concerto (1968; London, Nov. 15, 1969); *Leviathan* for Double Bassoon and Chamber Orch. (1969; London, Feb. 13, 1971); *Ambarvalia* (1988); *Introduction and Carol: The Ox and the Ass* for Double Bass and Chamber Orch. (1988). **CHAMBER:** 2 oboe sonatas (1939, 1985); Trio for Oboe, Clarinet, and Piano (1940); *Sabrina,* string quartet (1940); Quintet for Oboe, Clarinet, Violin, Viola, and Cello (1941); *Brocade,* piano quartet (1941); *Rhapsody* for Clarinet and String Quartet (1942); Violin Sonata (1954); Clarinet Sonata (1955); String Quartet (1956); Horn Sonatina (1960); *Triton* for Horn and Piano (1970); Cello Sonata (1978); Wind Octet (1983); *The Riders of Rohan* for Tenor Trombone and Piano (1987). **OTHER:** Various vocal works.

Giraldoni, Eugenio, notable Italian baritone; b. Marseilles, May 20, 1871; d. Helsinki, June 23, 1924. He was the son of the baritone Leone Giraldoni (b. Paris, 1824; d. Moscow, Oct. 1, 1897) and the soprano Carolina Ferni-Geraldoni (b. Como, Aug. 20, 1839; d. Milan, June 4, 1926). He received his training from his mother. In 1891 he made his operatic debut as Escamillo in Barcelona, and then sang in various Italian music centers, including Milan's La Scala and Rome's Teatro Costanzi; at the latter he created the role of Scarpia on Jan. 14, 1900. On Nov. 28, 1904, he made his Metropolitan Opera debut in N.Y. as Barnaba, singing there for a season; he then pursued his career in Europe and South America. Among his other roles of distinction were Amonasro, Valentin, Boris Godunov, Rigoletto, and Gérard.

Giraud, Fiorello, Italian tenor; b. Parma, Oct. 22, 1870; d. there, March 29, 1928. He was the son of the tenor Lodovico Giraud (1846–82). He studied with Babacini in Parma. He made his debut as Lohengrin in 1891 in Vercelli; then sang in Barcelona, Lisbon, and South America, and at La Scala in Milan. He created the role of Canio in Leoncavallo's *Pagliacci* (Milan, May 21, 1892). He was a fine interpreter of other verismo roles.

Girdlestone, Cuthbert (Morton), English music scholar; b. Bovey-Tracey, Sept. 17, 1895; d. St. Cloud, France, Dec. 10, 1975. He was educated at the Sorbonne (licence ès lettres, 1915) and the Schola Cantorum in Paris; then entered Trinity College, Cambridge. He became a lecturer at Cambridge in 1922; from 1926 to 1960 he was prof. of French at the Univ. of Durham, Newcastle division (later the Univ. of Newcastle upon Tyne). He publ. a valuable analysis of Mozart's piano concertos, *Mozart et ses concertos pour piano* (Paris, 1939; Eng. tr., 1948; 2nd ed., 1964); also the important monograph *Jean-Philippe Rameau: His Life and Work* (London, 1957; 2nd ed., rev., 1969). He further wrote *La Tragédie en musique (1673–1750) considérée comme genre littéraire* (Paris, 1972).

BIBL.: N. Suckling, ed., *Essays Presented to C.M. G.* (Newcastle upon Tyne, 1960).

Gistelinck, Elias, Belgian composer; b. Beveren Leie, May 27, 1935. He received his training at the Brussels Cons. and the Paris Cons., then served as a producer for the Belgian Radio and Television (from 1961). He received the Italia Prize (1969) and a prize from the Fondation de France (1984).

WORKS: BALLETS: *Terpsychore en Euterpe* (1971); *De Bijen* (1972). **ORCH.:** *Ad Maiorem Limburgiae Fodientium Gloriam* for Alto Saxophone, Bass Clarinet, and Strings (1970); *Drie Middelheimsculpturen* for Trumpet, Bass, Drums, Brass, and Winds (1972); *Weest gelukkig* for Tenor Saxophone, Trombone, Vibraphone, and Jazz Orch. (1974); *Muziek* for 3 Brass Groups and Percussion (1975); *Elegie voor Jan* (1976); *Drie bewigingen* for Jazz Quintet and Orch. (1985); Violin Concerto (1986); *Music for Halloween* (1988); Sinfonietta for Chamber Orch. (1988). **CHAMBER:** Trio for Oboe, Clarinet, and Bassoon (1962); Suite for Flute, Oboe, Clarinet, Horn, and Bassoon (1962); *5 Portraits* for Clarinet (1965); *Antieke alchemie* for String Quartet (1967); *Koan* for Clarinet Quartet (1971); *Cantus* for Oboe (1973); *Kleine treurmuziek voor "Che"* for Flute and Piano (1974); *Treurmuziek voor Ptak IV* for Violin, Cello, and Piano (1975); *So What, Brother* for Alto Saxophone (1981); *Lullaby for Nathaly* for Violin and Piano (1984); *Music for RGIP* for Violin and Piano (1987); *Memories of Childhood* for Trumpet and 4 Groups of Trumpets (1988); piano pieces. **OTHER:** Vocal works.

Giteck, Janice, American composer and pianist; b. N.Y., June 27, 1946. She studied with Milhaud and Subotnick at Mills College in Oakland, California (B.A., 1968; M.A., 1969), and with Messiaen at the Paris Cons. (1969–70). She also studied electronic music with Lowell Cross and Anthony Gnazzo, Javanese gamelan with Daniel Schmidt, and West African drumming with Obo Addy. From 1979 she taught at the Cornish Inst. in Seattle. Her compositions, variously scored, reflect interest in the language and lore of American Indians; her best-known work is the ceremonial opera *A'agita* (orig. and sacrilegiously entitled *Wi'igita*), based on the legends and mythologies of the Pima and Papago, a native American tribe living in southwestern Arizona and Mexico.

WORKS: String Quartet No. 1 (1963); Quintet for Piano and Strings (1965); *How to Invoke a Garden/How to Invoke the Same Garden,* cantata for Soloists and 10 Instruments (1969); *Messalina,* mini-opera for Man's Voice, Cello, and Piano (1973); *Helixes* for Flute, Trombone, Violin, Cello, Guitar, Piano, and Percussion (1974); *Wi'igita,* later renamed *A'agita,* ceremonial opera for 3 Singing Actors, Dancing Actor, and 8 Instrumentalists/Actors (1976); *8 Sandbars on the Takano River* for 5 Women's Voices, Flute, Bassoon, and Guitar (1976); *Thunder, Like a White Bear Dancing,* ritual performance for Soprano, Flute, Piano, Hand Percussion, and Slide Projections, after the *Mide Picture Songs of the Ojibwa Indians* (1977); *Callin' Home Coyote,* burlesque for Tenor, Steel Drums, and String Bass (1977); *Far North Beast Ghosts the Clearing* for Chorus, after Swampy Creek Indians (1978); *Peter and the Wolves* for Trombonist/Actor and Prepared Tape (1978); *Breathing Songs from a Turning Sky* for Flute, Clarinet, Bassoon, Cello, Piano, and Percussion (1979–80; rev. 1984); *When the Crones Stop Counting* for 60 Flutes (1980); *Tree,* chamber sym. (1982); *Loo-wit* for Viola and Orch. (1983); *Hopi: Songs of the 4th World,* film score (1983); *Pictures of the Floating World* for Chorus and 10 Instruments (1987); *Hearts and Hands,* film score (1987); *Tapasya* for Viola and Percussion (1987).

Gitlis, Ivry, Israeli violinist; b. Haifa, Aug. 22, 1922. He began violin lessons at 6 and made his debut at 8; after training at the École Normale de Musique in Paris (1932–35), he completed his studies with Enesco, Thibaud, and Flesch. During World War II, he played for British troops, and then appeared as a soloist with British orchs. In 1951 he won 5th prize in the Long-Thibaud Competition and made his Paris debut. In 1955 he played for the first time in the U.S. Thereafter he toured widely as a soloist with orchs. and as a recitalist, acquiring particular distinction as a champion of contemporary music.

Giulini, Carlo Maria, eminent Italian conductor; b. Barletta, May 9, 1914. He began to study the violin as a boy; at 16 he entered the Conservatorio di Musica di Santa Cecilia in Rome, where he studied violin and viola with Remy Principe, composition with Alessandro Bustini, and conducting with Bernardino Molinari; also received instruction in conducting from Casella at the Accademia Musicale Chigiana in Siena. He then joined the Augusteo Orch. in Rome in the viola section. He was drafted into the Italian army during World War II, but went into hiding as a convinced anti-Fascist; after the liberation of Rome by the Allied troops in 1944, he was engaged to conduct the Augusteo Orch. in a special concert celebrating the occasion. He then became assistant conductor of the RAI Orch. in Rome, and was made its chief conductor in 1946. In 1950 he helped to organize the RAI Orch. in Milan; in 1952 he conducted at Milan's La Scala as an assistant to Victor de Sabata; in 1954 he became principal conductor there; his performance of *La Traviata,* with Maria Callas in the title role, was particularly notable. In 1955 he conducted Verdi's *Falstaff* at the Edinburgh Festival, earning great praise. On Nov. 3, 1955, he was a guest conductor with the Chicago Sym. Orch. and later was its principal guest conductor (1969–72); during its European tour of 1971, he was joint conductor with Sir Georg Solti. From 1973 to 1976 he was principal conductor of the Vienna Sym. Orch., and in 1975 he took it on a world tour. On Oct. 24, 1975, he led it at a televised concert from the United Nations in N.Y. In 1978 he succeeded Zubin Mehta as music director of the Los Angeles Phil., and succeeded in maintaining it at a zenith of orchestral brilliance until 1984. His conducting style embodies the best traditions of the Italian school as exemplified by Toscanini, but is free from explosive displays of temper. He is above all a Romantic conductor who can identify his musical *Weltanschauung* with the musical essence of Mozart, Beethoven, Schubert, Schumann, Brahms, Bruckner, Verdi, and Mahler; he leads the classics with an almost abstract contemplation. In the music of the 20th century, he gives congenial interpretations of works by Debussy, Ravel, and Stravinsky; the expressionist school of composers lies outside of his deeply felt musicality, and he does not actively promote the experimental school of modern music. His behavior on the podium is free from self-assertive theatrics, and he treats the orch. as comrades-in-arms, associates in the cause of music, rather than subordinate performers of the task assigned to them. Yet his personal feeling for music is not disguised; often he closes his eyes in fervent self-absorption when conducting without score the great Classical and Romantic works.

BIBL.: *Le Grand Baton* (Sept. 1977; includes articles and discography).

Glanville-Hicks, Peggy, Australian-born American composer; b. Melbourne, Dec. 29, 1912; d. Sydney, June 25, 1990. She entered the Melbourne Cons. in 1927 as a composition student of Hart; in 1931 she went to London and studied with Benjamin (piano), Morris and Kitson (theory), Vaughan Williams (composition), Jacob (orchestration), and Lambert and Sargent (conducting); she then pursued further training with Boulanger in Paris and with Wellesz (musicology and advanced composition) in Vienna (1936–38). In 1938 she married **Stanley Bate,** but they divorced in 1948. In 1939 she went to the U.S. and in 1948 became a naturalized American citizen. From 1948 to 1958 she wrote music criticism for the *N.Y. Herald Tribune*, and also was active in contemporary music circles. In 1956 and 1958 she held Guggenheim fellowships. After living in Athens (1959–76), she returned to Australia. She utilized serial techniques in her music but not without explorations of early and non-Western modalities.

WORKS: DRAMATIC: OPERAS: *Caedmon* (1933); *The Transposed Heads* (1952–53; Louisville, April 3, 1954); *The Glittering Gate* (1957; N.Y., May 14, 1959); *Nausicaa* (1959–60; Athens, Aug. 19, 1961); *Carlos Among the Candles* (1962); *Sappho* (1963); *Beckett* (1989–90). **BALLETS:** *Hylas and the Nymphs* (1935); *Postman's Knock* (1938); *Killer-of-Enemies* (1946); *The Masque of the Wild Man* (Spoleto, June 10, 1958); *Triad* (Spoleto, June 10, 1958); *Saul and the Witch of Endor* (CBS-TV, June 7, 1959; also for Orch. as *Drama*); *A Season in Hell* (1965; N.Y., Nov. 15, 1967); *Tragic Celebration: Jephthah's Daughter* (CBS-TV, Nov. 6, 1966). Also film scores. **ORCH.:** *Meditation* (1933); 2 sinfoniettas (1934, 1938); Piano Concerto (1936); Flute Concerto (1937); *Prelude and Scherzo* (1937); *Sinfonia da Pacifica* (1952–53; Melbourne, June 25, 1954); *3 Gymnopédies* (1953); *Estruscan Concerto* for Piano and Chamber Orch. (1954; N.Y., Jan. 25, 1956); *Concerto Romantico* for Viola and Orch. (1956; N.Y., Feb. 19, 1957); *Tapestry* (1958). **CHAMBER:** String Quartet (1937); Sonatina for Alto Recorder or Flute and Piano (1939); *Concerto da Camera* for Flute, Clarinet, Bassoon, and Piano (1946; Amsterdam, June 10, 1948); Sonata for Harp, Flute, and Horn (1950); Sonata for Solo Harp (1950–51); Sonata for Piano and Percussion (1951; N.Y., May 6, 1952); *Concertino Antico* for Harp and String Quartet (1955; Washington, D.C., Jan. 17, 1958); *Musica Antiqua* for 2 Flutes, Harp, Marimba, Timpani, and 2 Percussion (1957; Sydney, Jan. 21, 1982); *Prelude and Presto for Ancient American Instruments* (1957); *Girondelle for Giraffes* for 6 Instruments (1978). **VOCAL:** *Pastoral* for Women's Chorus and Clarinet or English Horn (1932–33); *Poem* for Chorus and Orch. (1933); *In Midwood Silence* for Soprano, Oboe, and String Quartet (1935); *Song in Summer* for Chorus and Orch. (1935); *Choral Suite* for Women's Chorus, Oboe, and Strings (1937); *Aria Concertante* for Tenor, Women's Chorus, Oboe, Piano, and Gong (1945); *Dance Cantata* for Tenor, Narrator, Speaking Chorus, and Orch. (1947); *Thomsoniana* for Tenor or Soprano, Flute, Horn, Piano, and String Quartet (1949); *Letters from Morocco* for Tenor and Orch. (1952; N.Y., Feb. 22, 1953); songs.

BIBL.: D. Hayes, *P.G.-H.: A Bio-Bibliography* (Westport, Conn., 1990).

Glaser, Werner Wolf, German-born Swedish pianist, conductor, teacher, and composer; b. Cologne, April 14, 1910. He studied composition with Jarnach at the Cologne Hochschule für Musik, where he also received training in piano and conducting; later studied composition with Hindemith at the Berlin Hochschule für Musik, art history at the Univ. of Bonn, and psychology at the Univ. of Berlin, receiving a Ph.D. After conducting the Chemnitz Opera orch. (1929–31) and serving as chorus master in Cologne (1931–33), he went to Copenhagen as a teacher at the Fredriksberg Cons. (1936–43); with I. Skovgaard, he founded the Lyngby School of Music in 1939. He settled in Sweden, becoming a naturalized citizen in 1951; was conductor of the Södra Västmanland Orch. Soc. (1944–59) and was active as a music critic. With I. Andrén and G. Axén, he founded the Västerås School of Music in 1945, and was its director of studies from 1954 until his retirement in 1975. A man of wide interests, he studied modern art and literature and wrote poetry; he also investigated the potentialities of music therapy. A prolific composer, he followed the neo-Classical line.

WORKS: DRAMATIC: OPERAS: *Kagekiyo*, chamber opera (1961); *Encounters*, chamber opera (Vasterås, Dec. 13, 1970); *A Naked King* (1971; Göteborg, April 6, 1973); *Cercatori*, chamber opera (1972); *The Boy and the Voice*, children's opera (1973); *Freedom Bells* (1980). **BALLETS:** *Persefone* (1960); *Les Cinq Pas de l'homme* (1973). **ORCH.:** 13 syms. (1934; 1936; 1936; 1943; 1949; 1957; 1961; 1964; 1976; 1974–80; 1983; 1989; 1990); Flute Concerto (1934); Concertino for Alto Saxophone and Strings (1935); *Trilogia I* (1939) and *II* (1981); *3 Pieces* for Strings (1947); *Idyll, Elegy, and Fanfare* (1954); Concerto No. 2 (1957); *Music* for Strings (1957); *Concerto della Capella* for Winds, Percussion, and Piano (1960); *Le tre gradi* for Strings (1961); *Capriccio No. 3* for Piano and Orch. (1962); Concertino for Clarinet and Small Orch. (1962); Concerto for Violin, Winds, and Percussion (1962); Violin Concerto (1964); *4 Dance Scenes* (1964); *3 pezzi* for Oboe d'Amore and Chamber Orch. (1964); *Conflitti* (1966); Oboe Concerto (1966); *Transformations* for Piano and Orch. (1966); *Modi gestus* for Strings (1966); *Syringa* for 3 Flutes and Strings (1966); Concerto for 20 Wind Instruments and Percussion (1966); *Paradosso* for 2 String Orchs. (1967); Concerto for Flute and Strings (1967); Horn Concerto (1969); *Arioso e Toccata No. 2* for Piano and Orch. (1969); *Canto* for Soprano Saxophone and Strings (1970); *3 Symphonic Dances* (1975); Cello Concerto (1976); *Adagio* for Strings (1977); *Divertimento No. 2* for Wind Quintet and Strings (1979) and *No. 3* (1983); Concerto for Soprano Saxophone and Strings (1980); Concerto for Tenor Saxophone and Strings (1981); *5 Serious Short Songs* for Strings (1984); *Concerto breve* for Violin, Strings, and Percussion (1986); *Nigeria* (1986); *5 Choreographic Scenes* for Chamber Orch. (1987); *Theme and Variations* (1987); Piano Concerto (1988); *Konzertstück* for Baritone Saxophone and Strings (1992). **CHAMBER:** 13 string quartets (1934; 1937; 1946; 1947; 1948; 1948; 1954; 1967; 1967; 1978; 1980; 1988; 1992–93); *Quartetto piccolo* for Strings (1938); Trio for 2 Violins and Cello (1947); Trio for Clarinet, Violin, and Cello (1948); Quartet for Saxophone, Violin, Viola, and Cello (1950); *Chamber Music* for Clarinet, Cello, and Piano (1952); Trio for Clarinet, Bassoon, and Piano (1953); Quartet for Flute, Clarinet, Cello, and Piano (1960); *Musica sacra* for Flute, Clarinet,

Organ, and Strings (1960); *Intrada* for String Quartet (1964); Sonata for Solo Flute (1966); *Music* for Clarinet, Violin, and Double Bass (1967); 2 string trios (1969, 1975); 2 wind quintets (1970, 1970); Sonata for Solo Violin (1971); *Paysages sonores* for Piano Trio (1973); *Variations and Interlude* for 8 Cellos (1978); Trio for Flute, Oboe, and Cello (1978); Trio for Flute, Guitar, and Viola (1979); *3 Pieces* for 11 Saxophones (1982); 3 piano quintets (1984; 1991; 1993–94); Saxophone Quartet (1984); *Linda Quartet* for Baritone Saxophone and String Trio (1985); 2 trios for Flute, Cello, and Piano (1985, 1991); Oboe Sonata (1986); Baritone Saxophone Sonata (1986); *Trezze* for Oboe and String Quartet (1987); *Fantasia all antico* for Violin (1988); *Concerto da camera* for 6 Instruments (1990); Trio for Flute, Clarinet, and Cello (1992); Quartet for Oboe, Bassoon, Horn, and Piano (1993); piano pieces; organ music. **VOCAL:** *Concerto lirico* for Soprano, Piano, Timpani, and Strings (1971); cantatas; choruses; songs.

Glass, Louis (Christian August), Danish pianist, conductor, pedagogue, and composer; b. Copenhagen, March 23, 1864; d. there, Jan. 22, 1936. He began his training with his father, Christian Hendrik Glass (1821–93), a piano teacher and composer. He also studied with Gade before pursuing his training in piano with J. de Zarembski and J. Wieniawski and in cello with J. Servais at the Brussels Cons. (1884–85). From 1893 to 1932 he was director of the piano cons. in Copenhagen founded by his father. He also was active as a pianist, and later as a conductor. In 1898 he organized the Dansk Musikpaedagogisk Forening. He served as director of the Dansk Koncertforening from 1915 to 1918. He was a skillful composer of symphonic and chamber music in a late Romantic style.

WORKS: BALLET: *Artemis* (1915). **ORCH.:** 6 syms.: No. 1 (1893), No. 2 (1898–99), No. 3, *Skovsymfoni* (Wood Sym.; 1901), No. 4 (1910–11), No. 5, *Svastica* (1919), and No. 6, *Skjoldungeaet* (Birth of the Scyldings; 1926); overtures: *Der Volksfeind* and *Dänemark*, 2 suites; Oboe Concerto; Violin Concerto; *Foraarssang* for Cello and Orch.; *Fantasie* for Piano and Orch. **CHAMBER:** Cello Sonata (1889); 2 violin sonatas; 4 string quartets (c.1890; 1893; 1896; 1901–06); String Sextet (1892); Piano Trio (c.1895); Piano Quintet (1896); many piano pieces, including 2 sonatas (c.1890; 1898–99). **OTHER:** Various songs.

Glass, Philip, remarkable American composer; b. Baltimore, Jan. 31, 1937. He entered the Peabody Cons. of Music in Baltimore as a flute student when he was 8; then took courses in piano, mathematics, and philosophy at the Univ. of Chicago (1952–56); subsequently studied composition with Persichetti at the Juilliard School of Music in N.Y. (M.S., 1962). He received a Fulbright fellowship in 1964 and went to Paris to study with Boulanger; much more important to his future development was his meeting with Ravi Shankar, who introduced him to Hindu rāgas. During a visit to Morocco, Glass absorbed the modalities of North African melo-rhythms, which taught him the art of melodic repetition. When he returned to N.Y. in 1967, his style of composition became an alternately concave and convex mirror image of Eastern modes, undergoing melodic phases of stationary harmonies in lieu of modulations. He formed associations with modern painters and sculptors who strove to obtain maximum effects with a minimum of means. He began to practice a similar method in music, which soon acquired the factitious sobriquet of Minimalism. Other Americans and some Europeans followed this practice, which was basically Eastern in its catatonic homophony; Steve Reich was a close companion in minimalistic pursuits of maximalistic effects. Glass formed his own phonograph company, Chatham Square, which recorded most of his works. He also organized an ensemble of electrically amplified instruments, which became the chief medium of his compositions. On April 13, 1968, he presented the first concert of the Philip Glass Ensemble at Queens College in N.Y. He subsequently toured widely with it, making visits abroad as well as traveling throughout the U.S. His productions, both in America and in Europe, became extremely successful among young audiences, who were mesmerized by his mixture of rock realism and alluring mysticism; undeterred by the indeterminability and interminability of his productions, some lasting several hours, these young people accepted him as a true representative of earthly and unearthly art. The mind-boggling titles of his works added to the tantalizing incomprehensibility of the subjects that he selected for his inspiration. The high point of his productions was the opera *Einstein on the Beach* (in collaboration with Robert Wilson), which involved a surrealistic comminution of thematic ingredients and hypnotic repetition of harmonic subjects. It was premiered at the Avignon Festival on July 25, 1976, and was subsequently performed throughout Europe. It was given on Nov. 21, 1976, at the Metropolitan Opera in N.Y., where it proved something of a sensation of the season; however, it was not produced as part of the regular subscription series. In Rotterdam on Sept. 5, 1980, he produced his opera *Satyagraha*, a work based on Gandhi's years in South Africa ("Satyagraha" was Gandhi's slogan, composed of 2 Hindu words: satya [truth] and āgraha [firmness])). Another significant production were the film scores, *Koyaanisqatsi* (a Hopi Indian word meaning "life out of balance;" 1983) and *Powaqqatsi* (a Hopi Indian word meaning "life in transformation," 1990). The music represented the ultimate condensation of the basic elements of Glass's compositional style; here the ritualistic repetition of chords arranged in symmetrical sequences becomes hypnotic, particularly since the screen action is devoid of narrative; the effect in the first film score is enhanced particularly by the opening deep bass notes of an Indian chant. His mixed media piece *The Photographer: Far from the Truth*, based on the life of the photographer Eadweard Muybridge, received its first U.S. performance in N.Y. on Oct. 6, 1983. It was followed by the exotic opera *Akhnaton*, set in ancient Egypt, with a libretto in ancient Akkadian, Egyptian, and Hebrew, with an explanatory narration in English; it was produced in Stuttgart on March 24, 1984. In collaboration with Robert Moran, he produced the opera *Juniper Tree* (Cambridge, Mass., Dec. 11, 1985). After bringing out the dance-theater piece *A Descent into the Maelstrom* (1986) and the dance piece *In the Upper Room* (1986), he wrote a Violin Concerto (1987). His symphonic score *The Light* was first performed in Cleveland on Oct. 29, 1987. It was followed by his opera *The Making of the Representative for Planet 8* (to a text by Doris Lessing), which received its premiere in Houston on July 8, 1988. His next opera, *The Fall of the House of Usher*, was first performed in Cambridge, Mass., on May 18, 1988. The music theater piece *1000 Airplanes on the Roof* was produced in Vienna in 1988. On Nov. 2, 1989, his *Itaipu* for Chorus and Orch. was premiered in Atlanta. His opera *Voyages*, celebrating the voyages of discovery of Christopher Columbus, was performed for the first time at the Metropolitan Opera in N.Y. on Oct. 12, 1992. On Nov. 13, 1992, his *Low Symphony*, based on music of David Bowie and Brian Eno, was given its premiere in N.Y. His opera *Orphée*, after Jean Cocteau's film, was first presented in Cambridge, Mass., on May 14, 1993. Glass's 2nd Sym. was performed for the first time in N.Y. on Oct. 14, 1994. On Dec. 7, 1994, his opera *La Belle et la Bête* was premiered in N.Y. Among his other works are *Music with Changing Parts* (N.Y., Nov. 10, 1972), *Music in 12 Parts* (N.Y., June 1, 1974), and *North Star* for 2 Voices and Instruments (1975). With R. Jones, he publ. *Music by Philip Glass* (N.Y., 1987; new ed., with supplement, 1988, as *Opera on the Beach: On His New World of Music Theatre*).

BIBL.: W. Mertens, *American Minimal Music: La Monte Young, Terry Riley, Steve Reich, P. G.* (London, 1991).

Glaz, Herta, Austrian-American contralto; b. Vienna, Sept. 16, 1908. She was trained in Vienna and made her operatic debut at the Breslau Opera in 1931, presaging a successful career, but in 1933 was forced to leave Germany. She toured Austria and Scandinavia as a concert singer; sang at the German Theater in Prague in 1935–36; in 1936 she took part in the American tour of the Salzburg Opera Guild; subsequently sang at the Chicago

Opera (1940–42); on Dec. 25, 1942, she made her debut with the Metropolitan Opera in N.Y. as Amneris, and remained on its roster until 1956; then taught voice at the Manhattan School of Music, retiring in 1977. Her husband was **Joseph Rosenstock**.

Glazer, David, American clarinetist and teacher; b. Milwaukee, May 7, 1913. He studied at Milwaukee State Teachers College (B.Ed., 1935) and the Berkshire Music Center in Tanglewood (summers, 1940–42). After teaching at the Longy School of Music in Cambridge, Mass. (1937–42), he played in the Cleveland Orch. (1946–51); then toured as a soloist with orchs. and as a chamber music artist; was active with the N.Y. Woodwind Quintet (1951–85). He also taught at the Mannes College of Music, the N.Y. College of Music, N.Y. Univ., and the State Univ. of N.Y. at Stony Brook.

Glazunov, Alexander (Konstantinovich), eminent Russian composer and teacher; b. St. Petersburg, Aug. 10, 1865; d. Neuilly-sur-Seine, March 21, 1936. Of a well-to-do family (his father was a book publisher), he studied at a technical high school in St. Petersburg, and also took lessons in music with N. Elenkovsky. At 15, he was introduced to Rimsky-Korsakov, who gave him weekly lessons in harmony, counterpoint, and orchestration. He made rapid progress, and at the age of 16 completed his 1st Sym., which was conducted by Balakirev on March 29, 1882, in St. Petersburg. So mature was this score that Glazunov was hailed by Stasov, Cui, and others as a rightful heir to the masters of the Russian national school. The music publisher Belaiev arranged for publication of his works, and took him to Weimar, where he met Liszt. From that time Glazunov composed assiduously in all genres except opera. He was invited to conduct his syms. in Paris (1889) and London (1896–97). Returning to St. Petersburg, he conducted concerts of Russian music. In 1899 he was engaged as an instructor in composition and orchestration at the St. Petersburg Cons. He resigned temporarily during the revolutionary turmoil of 1905 in protest against the dismissal of Rimsky-Korsakov by the government authorities, but returned to the staff after full autonomy was granted to the Cons. by the administration. In 1905 Glazunov was elected director and retained this post until 1928, when he went to Paris. In 1929 he made several appearances as conductor in the U.S. He was the recipient of honorary degrees of Mus.D. from the univs. of Cambridge and Oxford (1907). Although he wrote no textbook on composition, his pedagogical methods left a lasting impression on Russian musicians through his many students who preserved his traditions. His music is often regarded as academic, yet there is a flow of rhapsodic eloquence that places Glazunov in the Romantic school. He was for a time greatly swayed by Wagnerian harmonies, but resisted this influence successfully; Lisztian characteristics are more pronounced in his works. Glazunov was one of the greatest masters of counterpoint among Russian composers, but he avoided extreme polyphonic complexity. The national spirit of his music is unmistakable; in many of his descriptive works, the programmatic design is explicitly Russian. His most popular score is the ballet *Raymonda.* The major portion of his music was written before 1906, when he completed his 8th Sym.; after that he wrote mostly for special occasions. He also completed and orchestrated the overture to Borodin's *Prince Igor* from memory, having heard Borodin play it on the piano.

WORKS (all 1st perf. in St. Petersburg [Petrograd] unless otherwise given): **DRAMATIC: BALLETS:** *Raymonda* (1896; Jan. 19, 1898); *The Ruses of Love* (1898; 1900); *The Seasons* (1899; Feb. 20, 1900). Also Introduction and Dance of Salome for *Salome* by O. Wilde (1912); incidental music to *The King of the Jews* by K. Romanov (Jan. 9, 1914). **ORCH.:** 9 syms.: No. 1, in E major (1881; March 29, 1882; rev. 1885, 1929), No. 2, in F-sharp minor (1886; Paris, June 29, 1889), No. 3, in D major (Dec. 20, 1890), No. 4, in E-flat major (1893; Feb. 3, 1894), No. 5, in B-flat major (1895; London, Jan. 28, 1897), No. 6, in C minor (1896; Feb. 21, 1897), No. 7, in F major (1902; Jan. 3, 1903), No. 8, in E-flat major (Dec. 22, 1906), and No. 9, in D major (1910; completed by G. Yudin, 1948); *2 Overtures on Greek Themes* (1881, 1883); *2 Serenades* (1883, 1884); *Lyric Poem* (1884); *Stenka Razin,* symphonic poem (1885); *To the Memory of a Hero* (1885); *Characteristic Suite* (1885); *Idyll and Oriental Reverie* (1886); *The Forest,* symphonic poem (1887); *Mazurka* (1888); *Melody* and *Spanish Serenade* for Cello and Orch. (1888); *Slavonic Festival* (1888; from String Quartet No. 3); *Wedding March* (1889); *The Sea,* symphonic fantasy (1889); *Oriental Rhapsody* (1890); *The Kremlin,* musical picture (1891); *Spring,* musical picture (1891); *Chopiniana,* suite on themes by Chopin (1893); *Carnaval,* overture (1893); *2 Concert Waltzes* (1894); *2 Solemn Processionals* (1894, 1910); *Ballet Suite* (1894); *From Darkness to Light,* fantasy (1894); *Fantasy* (1895); *Suite* (1898) and *Characteristic Dance* (1900) from *Raymonda*; *Romantic Intermezzo* (1900); *Festival Overture* (1900); *Song of a Minstrel* for Cello and Orch. (1900; also for Cello, Piano, and Orch.); *March on a Russian Theme* (1901); *Ballade* (1902); *From the Middle Ages,* suite (1902; Jan. 3, 1903); *Ballet Scene* (1904); Violin Concerto (1904; March 4, 1905, L. Auer soloist); *Russian Fantasy* for Balalaika Orch. (March 11, 1906); *2 Preludes: No. 1, In Memory of V. Stasov* (1906) and *No. 2, In Memory of Rimsky-Korsakov* (1908); *The Song of Destiny,* overture (1908); *In Memory of N. Gogol* (1909); *Finnish Fantasy* (1909; March 27, 1910); 2 piano concertos (1910; Nov. 11, 1917); *Finnish Sketches* (1912); *Karelian Legend,* musical picture (1914); *Paraphrase on National Anthems of the Allies* (1915); *Mazurka-Oberek* for Violin and Orch. (1917; orchestration by I. Yampolsky of work for Violin, Piano, and Orch.); *Variations* for Strings (1918); *Concerto-Ballata* for Cello and Orch. (1931; Paris, Oct. 14, 1933, Maurice Eisenberg soloist); Saxophone Concerto (1931; Nykoping, Nov. 25, 1934, Sigurd Rascher soloist); *Epic Poem* (1934). **CHAMBER:** 7 string quartets: No. 1, in D major (1882), No. 2, in F major (1884), No. 3, *Quatuor Slave,* in G major (1888), No. 4, in A minor (1894), No. 5, in D minor (1898), No. 6, in B-flat major (1921), and No. 7, in C major (1930); *5 Novelettes* for String Quartet (1886); *Elegy to the Memory of F. Liszt* for Cello and Piano (1886); *Reverie* for Horn and Piano (1890); Suite for String Quartet (1891); String Quintet (1895); *Meditation* for Violin and Piano (1891); *In modo religioso* for Brass Quartet (1892); *Elegy* for Viola and Piano (1893); *Mazurka-Oberek* for Violin and Piano (1917); *Elegy* for String Quartet (1928); Saxophone Quartet (1932). **PIANO:** *Suite on the Theme "Sacha"* (1883); *Barcarolle and Novelette* (1889); *Prelude* and *2 Mazurkas* (1889); *Nocturne* (1889); *3 Études* (1890); *Little Waltz* (1892); *Grand Concert Waltz* (1893); *3 Miniatures* (1893); *Salon Waltz* (1893); *3 Pieces* (1894); *2 Impromptus* (1895); *Prelude and Fugue* (1899); *Theme and Variations* (1900); 2 sonatas (both 1901); *4 Preludes and Fugues* (1918–23); *Idylle* (1926); *Prelude and Fugue* (1926); *Suite* for 2 Pianos (1920). **VOCAL:** *Triumphal March* for Chorus and Orch. for the Chicago Columbian Exposition (1893); Coronation Cantata (1894); *Cantata in Memory of Pushkin's 100th Birthday* (1899); *Hymn to Pushkin* for Women's Chorus and Piano (1899); *Love* for Chorus (1907); *Prelude-Cantata for the 50th Anniversary of the St. Petersburg Cons.* (1912); 21 songs.

BIBL.: A. Ossovsky, *G.: His Life and Works* (St. Petersburg, 1907); V. Belaiev, *G.* (vol. 1, Petrograd, 1922); V. Derzhanovsky, *A. G.* (Moscow, 1922); I. Glebov, *G.* (Leningrad, 1924); G. Fedorova, *G.* (Moscow, 1947; 2nd ed., 1961); H. Gunther, *A. G.* (Bonn, 1956); M. Ganina, *G.: Life and Works* (Leningrad, 1961); D. Gojowy, *A. G.: Sein Leben in Bildern und Dokumenten: Unter Ein beziehung des biographischen Fragments von G.s Schwiegersohn Herbert Günther* (Munich, 1986); D. Venturini, *A. G., 1865–1936: His Life and Works* (Delos, Ohio, 1992).

Gleason, Harold, American organist, musicologist, and teacher; b. Jefferson, Ohio, April 26, 1892; d. La Jolla, Calif., June 28, 1980. He studied music privately and took courses in civil engineering at the Calif. Inst. of Technology (1910–12); he then studied organ with Farnam in Boston (1917–18) and Bonnet in Paris (1922–23), and composition with Inch at the Eastman School of Music in Rochester, N.Y. After serving as a church organist in California (1910–17), he was director of

Boston's Music School Settlement (1917–18) and organist and choirmaster of N.Y.'s Fifth Ave. Presbyterian Church (1918–19). He then went to Rochester, N.Y., as George Eastman's personal organist and music director; he also was founder-director of the David Hochstein Memorial Music School (1919–29). From 1921 to 1953 he was head of the organ dept. at the Eastman School of Music, where he also was prof. of musicology (1932–50) and of music literature (1939–55), and director of graduate studies (1953–55). His wife was **Catharine Crozier.** He publ. *Method of Organ Playing* (1937; 7th ed., 1987), *Examples of Music before 1400* (1942; rev. ed., 1945), *Music Literature Outlines* (1949–55; rev. with W. Becker, 1979–81), and, with W. Marrocco, *Music in America* (1964).

Glebov, Evgeny, Russian composer; b. Roslavl, near Smolensk, Sept. 10, 1929. He studied at the Belorussian Cons. in Minsk with Bogatyrev; later was appointed to its faculty. Several of his compositions reflect the events of World War II, which devastated Belorussia in 1941.

WORKS: *Partisan Symphony* (1958); *A Vision,* ballet (1961); *Our Spring,* opera (1963); Concerto for Voice and Orch. (1965); pieces for Belorussian instruments; cantatas.

BIBL.: L. Mukharinskaya, *E. G.* (Moscow, 1959); E. Rakova, *E. G.* (Minsk, 1971).

Glenn, Carroll, American violinist and teacher; b. Richmond, Va., Oct. 28, 1918; d. N.Y., April 25, 1983. She was only 4 years old when she began studies with her mother; after lessons with Felice de Horvath in Columbia, S.C., she entered the Juilliard School of Music in N.Y. at age 11 to study with Edouard Déthier, graduating when she was 15. In 1938 she won the Naumburg Award, which led to her N.Y. debut at Town Hall on Nov. 7 of that year. From 1941 she appeared as a soloist with many U.S. orchs. In 1943 she married **Eugene List**, with whom she frequently appeared in duo concerts. She also taught at the Eastman School of Music in Rochester, N.Y. (1964–75), the Manhattan School of Music (from 1975), and Queens College of the City Univ. of N.Y. (from 1975). She actively sought rarely-heard works for performance at her concerts.

Glennie, Evelyn (Elizabeth Ann), remarkable Scottish timpanist and percussionist; b. Aberdeen, July 19, 1965. Although she was born deaf, she nonetheless determined on a career in music; took up percussion training as a youth with Ron Forbes in Aberdeen, then studied at the Royal Academy of Music in London and with Keiko Abe in Japan. After playing in the National Youth Orch. of Scotland, she made her debut as a solo performer at London's Wigmore Hall in 1986. Her extraordinary talent brought her engagements with principal orchs. and festivals in Great Britain; subsequently toured extensively worldwide. In 1994 she appeared as soloist with Andrew Davis and the BBC Sym. Orch. at the traditional last night at the Proms in London, marking the close of its 100th anniversary season. She publ. the autobiography *Good Vibrations* (1990). In 1993 she was made a member of the Order of the British Empire. Glennie has done much to elevate the status of the timpanist and percussionist, and has also commissioned many new works.

Glick, Srul Irving, Canadian composer, radio producer, conductor, and teacher; b. Toronto, Sept. 8, 1934. He studied composition with Weinzweig at the Univ. of Toronto (B.Mus., 1955; M.Mus., 1958), with Milhaud in Aspen, Colo. (summers, 1956–57), and with Louis Saguer and Max Deutsch in Paris (1959–60). From 1962 to 1986 he was a music producer for the CBC radio; he also taught theory and composition at the Royal Cons. of Music of Toronto (1963–69) and at York Univ. (1985–86). He served as conductor of the choir at the Beth Tikvah Synagogue in Toronto from 1969, and also led it on tours of Canada, Israel, and the U.S. After composing scores marked by a lyrical penchant with polytonal writing, he turned to a more contemporary idiom only to find his anchor later by combining classical and Jewish traditions of musical expression in a thoroughly personal idiom.

WORKS: BALLET: *Heritage* (1967). **ORCH.:** *2 Essays* (1957); Sonata for Strings (1957); Sinfonietta (1958); *Sinfonia Concertante No. 1* for Strings (1961) and *No. 2, Lamentations,* for String Quartet and Orch. (1972); *Suite Hébraïque No. 1* (1961; also arranged for various forces); *Danse Concertante No. 1* for Small Orch. (1963); *Elegy* (1964); *Symphonic Dialogues* for Piano and Orch. (Toronto, Dec. 20, 1964); *Pan* (1966); 2 syms.: No. 1 for Chamber Orch. (Toronto, April 24, 1966) and No. 2 (1967; Toronto, Jan. 24, 1969); *Gathering In* for Strings (Montreal, March 26, 1970); *Psalm* (Hamilton, Oct. 17, 1971); *Symphonic Elegy, with Line Drawing and Funeral March* for Strings (Toronto, April 20, 1974); Violin Concerto, *Shir Hamaalot—Song of Ascension* (Victoria, British Columbia, Nov. 14, 1976); *Romance—Song of Joy* for Piano and Orch. (1978); Concerto for Viola and Strings (1981); *Devequt,* sonata (1982); *Lament and Cantorial Chant* for Viola and Strings (1985); *The Vision of Ezekiel,* fantasy for Violin and Orch. (1986); *Divertimento* for Strings (1987); *The Reawakening,* symphonic poem (1991). **CHAMBER:** *Divertimento Sextet* for Flute, Clarinet, Bassoon, and String Trio (1958); Trio for Clarinet, Piano, and Cello (1958–59); *Petite Suite* for Flute (1960); String Trio (1963); *Danse Concertante No. 2* for Flute, Clarinet, Trumpet, Cello, and Piano (1964); Sonata for Jazz Quintet (1964); Sonatina for Jazz Sextet (1965); *Divertissement* for 7 Instruments and Conductor (1968); *Suite Hébraïque No. 2* for Clarinet, String Trio, and Piano (1969), *No. 3* for String Quartet (1975), *No. 4* for Alto Saxophone or Clarinet or Viola and Piano (1979), *No. 5* for Flute, Clarinet, Violin, and Cello (1980), and *No. 6* for Violin and Piano (1984); *Prayer and Dance* for Cello and Piano (1975); Flute Sonata (1983); String Quartet No. 1 (Toronto, June 25, 1984); *Dance Suite* for 2 Guitars (1986); *. . . from out of the depths; mourning music for the 6 million . . .* for String Quartet (1986); Oboe Sonata (1987); Trio for Flute, Viola, and Harp (1988); Cello Sonata (1989); Trio for Violin, Cello, and Piano (1990). **PIANO:** *4 Preludes* (1958); *7 Preludes* (1959); *Ballade* (1959); *Song and Caprice* (1960); *Nistar (Secret),* fantaisie elegiaque (1979). **VOCAL:** *Music for Passover* for Chorus and String Quartet or String Orch. (1963); *. . . i never saw another butterfly . . .* for Alto and Chamber Orch., after children's poems written in the Theresienstadt concentration camp (1968); *Hashiriam asher L'Yisrael,* liturgical synagogal music for Chorus (1969–88; also for Chorus, Flute, Clarinet, and String Quartet); *Halleluyah* for Chorus (1970); *4 Songs* for Tenor and Orch. (1972); *Yiddish Suite No. 1* for Chorus and Cello or String Quartet (1979) and *No. 2, Time Cycle,* for Chorus, Flute, Clarinet, Harp, and String Quartet (1984); *I Breathe a New Song* for Cantor and Chorus (1981); *Northern Sketches* for Chorus, Piano, Violin, and Cello (1982); *The Hour Has Come,* sym. for Chorus and Orch. (1984; Toronto, Feb. 25, 1985); *Sing unto the Lord a New Song* for Chorus and Harp or Orch. (1986; Toronto, Jan. 25, 1987); *Canticle of Peace* for Chorus (1987); *If We Would But Listen,* cantata for Narrator, Tenor, Chorus, Flute, Clarinet, and String Quartet (1988); *Visions through Darkness: An Oratorio of Our Time* for Narrator, Mezzo-soprano, Tenor, Chorus, and Instruments (1988); *Songs of Creation* for Chorus, Brass Quintet, 4 Percussion, and Organ (1989); *The Flame Is Not Extinguished* for Tenor, Mezzo-soprano, Women's Chorus, and Piano (1990); many other sacred and secular vocal works.

Glière, Reinhold (Moritsovich), eminent Russian composer and pedagogue; b. Kiev, Jan. 11, 1875; d. Moscow, June 23, 1956. Following training in Kiev (1891–94), he studied violin with Hrimaly at the Moscow Cons., where he also took courses with Arensky, Taneyev, and Ippolitov-Ivanov (1894–1900), graduating with a gold medal. He completed his studies in Berlin (1905–07). Returning to Russia, he became active as a teacher; was appointed prof. of composition at the Kiev Cons., and was its director from 1914 to 1920; then was appointed to the faculty of the Moscow Cons., a post he retained until 1941. He traveled extensively in European and Asiatic Russia, collecting folk melodies; he also conducted many concerts of his own works. He was a prolific composer, and was particularly distinguished in symphonic works, in which he revealed himself as a successor of the Russian national school. He never transgressed the natural borderline of traditional harmony, but he was able to achieve effective results. His most impressive work is his 3rd Sym., subtitled *Ilya Muromets*, an epic description of the exploits of a legendary Russian hero. In his numerous songs, Glière showed a fine lyrical talent. He wrote relatively few works of chamber music, most of them early in his career. In his opera *Shah-Senem*, he made use of native Caucasian songs. Glière was the teacher of 2 generations of Russian composers; among his students were Prokofiev and Miaskovsky. He received Stalin prizes for the String Quartet No. 4 (1948) and the ballet The Bronze Knight (1950).

WORKS: DRAMATIC: OPERAS: *Zemlya i nebo* (Earth and Sky; 1900); *Shah-Senem* (1923; Baku, 1926; rev. 1934); *Gyulsara*, music drama (1936; Moscow, 1937; in collaboration with Sadikov; rev. version as an opera, Tashkent, Dec. 25, 1949); *Leyli i Mejnun* (Tashkent, July 18, 1940); *Rashel*, after Maupassant's *Mademoiselle Fifi* (1942; Moscow, April 19, 1947). **BALLETS:** *Khirzis* (Moscow, Nov. 30, 1912); *Ovechiy istochnik* (Sheep's Spring; 1922; rev. as *Komedianti* [The Comedians], 1930; Moscow, April 5, 1931); *Kleopatra* (1925; Moscow, Jan. 11, 1926); *Krasnïy mak* (The Red Poppy; 1926–27; Moscow, June 14, 1927; rev. as *Krasniy tsvetok* [The Red Flower], 1949); *Mednïy vsadnik* (The Bronze Horseman; 1948–49; Leningrad, March 14, 1949); *Taras Bulba* (1951–52); *Dog Kastilii* (1955). Also incidental music to plays. **ORCH.:** 3 syms.: No. 1 (1899–1900; Moscow, Jan. 3, 1903), No. 2 (1907–08; Berlin, Jan. 23, 1908, Koussevitzky conducting), and No. 3, *Ilya Muromets* (1909–11; Moscow, March 23, 1912); 3 symphonic poems: *The Sirens* (1908), *The Cossacks of Zaporozh* (1938), and *Zapovit* (1938); Concertos for Harp (Moscow, Nov. 23, 1938), Coloratura Soprano (Moscow, May 12, 1943), Cello (1946; Moscow, Feb. 18, 1947), Horn (1950; Moscow, Jan. 26, 1952), and Violin (1956; completed and orchestrated by Liatoshinsky); 7 overtures: *Holiday at Ferghana* (1940); *The Friendship of the Peoples* (1941); *Overture on Slav Themes* (1941); *For the Happiness of the Fatherland* (1942); *25 Years of the Red Army* (1943); *War Overture* (1943); *Victory* (1945). **BAND:** *Fantasy for the Festival of the Comintern* (1924); *Red Army March* (1924); *Heroic March for the Buryiat-Mongolian A.S.S.R.* (1936); *Solemn Overture for the 20th Anniversary of the October Revolution* (1937). **CHAMBER:** 2 string sextets (1900, 1902); 4 string quartets (1900, 1905, 1928, 1948); String Octet (1900); 8 pieces for Violin and Cello (1909); 12 pieces for Cello and Piano (1910); 10 duos for 2 Cellos (1911); numerous piano pieces. **VOCAL:** *Imitation of Ezekiel* for Narrator and Orch. (1919); 2 Poems for Soprano and Orch. (1924); *A Toast* for Voice and Orch. (1939); numerous songs.

BIBL.: I. Boelza, *R.M. G.* (Moscow, 1955; 2nd ed., 1962); N. Petrova, *R.M. G.* (Leningrad, 1962).

Gliński, Mateusz, Polish conductor, musicologist, and composer; b. Warsaw, April 6, 1892; d. Welland, Ontario, Jan. 3, 1976. He studied at the Warsaw Cons. with Barcewicz (violin) and Statkowski (composition); then took courses in Leipzig with Reger (composition), Riemann and Schering (musicology), and Nikisch (conducting). He went to St. Petersburg in 1914; studied composition with Glazunov and Steinberg, and conducting with Nikolai Tcherepnin. In 1918 he went to Warsaw; from 1924 to 1939 was ed. of the periodical *Muzyka*. At the outbreak of World War II in 1939, he went to Rome, where he engaged in various activities as music critic and ed. In 1949 he established in Rome the Istituto Internazionale Federico Chopin. From 1959 to 1965 he taught at Assumption Univ. in Windsor, Ontario. In 1965 he established the Niagara Sym. Orch., which he conducted. His works include an opera, *Orlotko*, after Rostand's play *L'Aiglon* (1918–27); symphonic poem, *Wagram* (1932); choral works; songs; piano pieces. He publ. a monograph on *Scriabin* (Warsaw, 1933); *Chopin's Letters to Delfina Potocka* (Windsor, 1961), in which he subscribes to the generally refuted belief that these letters, which came to light in 1945, are indeed genuine; and *Chopin the Unknown* (Windsor, 1963).

Globokar, Vinko, French composer, trombonist, and teacher of Slovenian descent; b. Anderny, July 7, 1934. He studied trombone at the Ljubljana Academy of Music (1949–54), and then with André Lafosse at the Paris Cons. (1955–59), where he received the premier prix; subsequently he took private composition and conducting lessons with Leibowitz (1960–63) before completing his composition studies with Berio (1965). In 1965–66 he was a member of the Center for Creative and Performing Arts at the State Univ. of N.Y. in Buffalo. After teaching at the Cologne Hochschule für Musik (1968–76), he was head of vocal and instrumental research at IRCAM in Paris (1976–79); subsequently he was a prof. at the Scuola di musica di Fiesole in Florence (1984–90). Globokar's mastery of improvisation as a trombonist has been reflected in his output as a composer. He has embraced a utilitarian view in which nothing is off limits in the compositional process or the means of expression.

WORKS: ORCH.: *Étude pour Folklora II* (Frankfurt am Main, Aug. 26, 1968); Concerto grosso (1969–75; Cologne, Nov. 6, 1970); *La tromba e mobile* for 1 or More Wind Orchs. and Percussion (1970; Zagreb, May 17, 1979); *Ausstrahlungen* for Small Orch. (Royan, April 8, 1971); *Das Orchester* (Bonn, Dec. 1, 1974); *Der Käfig* for Improvising Soloist and Chamber Orch. (Lugano, Feb. 7, 1980); *Labour* (1993). **CHAMBER:** *Fluide* for 12 Instruments (1967); *Discours I* for Trombone and 4 Percussion (1967), *II* for 5 Trombones or Trombone and Tape (1967–68), *III* for 5 Oboes or Oboe and Tape (1969), *IV* for 3 Clarinets (1973–74), *V* for 4 Saxophones (1981), *VI* for String Quartet (1982), *VII* for Brass Quintet (1987), *VIII* for Wind Quintet (1989), and *IX* for 2 Pianos (1993); *Correspondences* for 4 Instruments (1969); *Drama* for Piano, Percussion, and Electronics (1971); *Vendre le vent* for 11 Instruments (1972); *Laboratorium* (1973–85); *Koexistenz* for 1 or 2 Cellos (1976); *Pre-Occupation* for Organ and Tape (1980); *Tribadabum extensif sur rythme fantôme* for Percussionists (1981); *Introspection d'un tubiste* for Tuba, Electronics, Tape, Lights, and Scenery (1983); *Freu(n)de* for 6 Cellos (1987); *Ombre* for Percussionist and Rhythm Machine (1989); *Kvadrat* for Percussion Quartet (1989). **VOCAL:** *Voie* for Speaker, 3 Choruses, and Orch. (1966; Zagreb, May 16, 1967); *Traumdeutung* for 4 Choruses and 4 Instruments (1967; Rotterdam, Oct. 7, 1968); *Airs de voyages vers l'intérieur* for 8 Voices, Clarinet, Trombone, and Electronics (1972); *Un Jour comme un autre* for Soprano and 5 Instruments (1975); *Carrousel* for 4 Voices and Chamber Orch. (1976); *Standpunkte* for Soloists, Chorus, and Orch. (Donaueschingen, Oct. 22, 1977); *Les Emigrés*, triptych for Singers, Narrators, Orch., Tape, Film, Slide Projection, and Puppets (1982–87; 1st complete perf., Bonn, Oct. 27, 1987); *Hallo, Do You Hear Me?* for Chorus, Jazz Quintet, and Orch. (1986; 1st perf. simultaneously in Helsinki, Oslo, and Stockholm, March 9, 1987); *Kolo* for Chorus and Trombone (1988).

Glock, Sir William (Frederick), English music critic and broadcasting administrator; b. London, May 3, 1908. He was an organ scholar at Gonville and Caius College, Cambridge (1919–26); then took piano lessons with Artur Schnabel in Berlin (1930–33). He made some appearances as a concert pianist, but devoted most of his time and effort to criticism. In 1934 he joined the staff of the *Observer*, served as its chief music critic from 1939 to 1945. In 1949 he founded the magazine the *Score*, and ed. it until 1961. In 1948 he established the Summer School of Music at Bryanston, Dorset, which relocated to Dartington Hall, Devon, in 1953; he continued as its director until 1979. In 1959 he assumed the important post of controller of music of the BBC, retaining it until 1973. From 1976 to 1984 he was artistic director of the Bath Festival. He publ. *Notes in Advance: An Autobiography in Music* (Oxford, 1991). In 1964 he was made a Commander of the Order of the British Empire; he was knighted in 1970.

Glodeanu, Liviu, Romanian composer; b. Dârja, Aug. 6, 1938; d. Bucharest, March 31, 1978. He studied at the Cluj Cons. and the Bucharest Cons., his principal teachers being Comes,

Negrea, and Mendelsohn. In his music, he respected Romanian musical tradition while subtly employing modern means of expression.

WORKS: OPERAS: *Ulysse* (1967–72; Cluj, April 25, 1973); *Zamolxe* (1968–69; Cluj, April 25, 1973). **ORCH.:** Concerto for Strings and Percussion (1959); Piano Concerto (1960; Cluj, April 7, 1962); Symphonic Movement (1961); Flute Concerto (1962; Cluj, Jan. 6, 1965); Violin Concerto (1964–66; Cluj, Feb. 5, 1972); *Studii* (1967; Bucharest, Feb. 14, 1968); *Ricercare* (Cluj, April 15, 1971); Symphonies for Winds (1971; Bucharest, Feb. 18, 1972); *Pintea Viteazul* (Pintea the Brave), symphonic poem (1976; Cluj, April 1, 1978); Organ Concerto (Bucharest, April 20, 1978). **CHAMBER:** Clarinet Sonata (1959); 2 string quartets (1959, 1970); Violin Sonatina (1961–63); Inventions for Wind Quintet and Percussion (1963); *Mélopée* for Flute, Clarinet, Cello, and Tape (1971). **PIANO:** 2 sonatas (1958, 1963). **VOCAL:** 4 cantatas (1958, 1959, 1960, 1961); *Ulysse* for Soprano or Tenor and Orch. (1967); *Un pămînt numit România*, oratorio for Baritone, Reciter, Chorus, and Orch. (Bucharest, May 21, 1977).

Glorieux, François, Belgian pianist, composer, teacher, and conductor; b. Courtrai, Aug. 27, 1932. He studied at the Royal Cons. in Ghent (graduated, 1953), then toured as a pianist; he taught chamber music at the Royal Cons. in Ghent, and was head of the summer courses in piano at the Royal Cons. in Antwerp. He became especially successful in presenting entertaining improvisational recitals in 5 languages; also conducted his own 25-member orch. from 1979. His compositions run the gamut from serious works to popular scores and arrangements, the last including pieces by Stan Kenton and Michael Jackson. He also prepared a new version of the Belgian national anthem (1981).

WORKS: DRAMATIC: TELEVISION MUSICAL: *Rip van Winkel* (1969). **BALLETS:** *L'Énigme* (1964); *Ritus paganus* (1972); *The Dream* (1982). **OTHER:** *Manhattan* for Piano and Orch. (1973–74; Antwerp, March 28, 1974); *Walking on the Street* for Big Band (1975); *Evolution* for African Percussion Instruments, Piano, Electric Guitar, and Drums (1975); *Tribute to Stan Kenton* for Piano, Flute, Brass, Bass Guitar, and Percussion (1976); *Fanfare for Europe* for Brass and Percussion Ensemble (1977–78); *In memoriam Stan Kenton* for Piano, Flute, Brass, Bass Guitar, and Percussion (1979); *Hello Mister Joplin* for Synthesizers (1982); *Tribute to Michael Jackson*, instrumental suite in 8 parts (1984–88); *The Legend of Bruce Lee* for Flute, Synthesizers, Brass, and Percussion (1986); *Glorieux Hymn* for Organ or Synthesizer, Brass, Percussion, and Chorus ad libitum (1988); *6 Pieces* for 8 Trumpets (1988); *Contrasts* for Tenor Trombone and Orch. (1988); other chamber works; film scores.

Glossop, Peter, English baritone; b. Sheffield, July 6, 1928. He was a student of Mosley, Rich, and Hislop. In 1952 he joined the chorus of the Sadler's Wells Opera in London, where he then was a principal member of the company (1953–62). In 1961 he won the Sofia Competition and made his debut at London's Covent Garden as Demetrius in *A Midsummer Night's Dream*, appearing there regularly until 1966. On Aug. 18, 1967, he made his Metropolitan Opera debut as Rigoletto during the company's visit to Newport, R.I. His formal debut at the Metropolitan Opera in N.Y. took place as Scarpia on June 5, 1971. He also sang with other opera houses in Europe and North America. Among his other roles were Nabucco, Iago, Simone Boccanegra, Falstaff, Wozzeck, and Billy Budd.

Glover, Jane (Alison), English conductor and musicologist; b. Helmsley, Yorkshire, May 13, 1949. She was educated at St. Hugh's College, Oxford (Ph.D., 1978, with a diss. on Cavalli). She made her professional conducting debut at the Wexford Festival in 1975 with her own performing ed. of Cavalli's *Eritrea*, which she later presented in London (1982); in 1980 she became chorus master at the Glyndebourne Festival, and from 1982 to 1985 served as music director of the Glyndebourne Touring Opera; she also served as music director of the London Choral Soc. (from 1983) and the Huddersfield Choral Soc. (1989–96), and was artistic director of the London Mozart Players (1984–92). She appeared as a guest conductor in England and on the Continent; in 1988 she made her Covent Garden debut in London conducting *Die Entführung aus dem Serail*. She also engaged in research and teaching; was a research fellow (1973–75) and lecturer in music (1976–84) at St. Hugh's College, Oxford; likewise lectured at St. Anne's College (1976–80) and Pembroke College (1979–84) there; in 1979 she was elected to the music faculty of the Univ. of Oxford. In her performing eds., she endeavors to preserve the authenticity of the original scores.

Gluck, Alma (née **Reba Fiersohn**), famous Romanian-born American soprano; b. Iaşi, May 11, 1884; d. N.Y., Oct. 27, 1938. She was taken to the U.S. as an infant and was educated in N.Y. In 1902 she married Bernard Gluck; although they were divorced in 1912, she used the name Alma Gluck throughout her professional career. After vocal training with Arturo Buzzi-Peccia in N.Y. (1906–09), she made her first appearance with the Metropolitan Opera as Massenet's Sophie during the company's visit to the New Theatre on Nov. 16, 1909. Her formal debut at the Metropolitan Opera took place as the Spirit in Gluck's *Orfeo ed Euridice* on Dec. 23, 1909. She remained on its roster until 1912, winning acclaim in such roles as Mimi, Nedda, and Gilda. After additional training with Sembrich in Berlin, she devoted herself to a distinguished concert career. During the 1913–15 and 1916–18 seasons, she was engaged to sing at the Sunday Concerts at the Metropolitan Opera. She became one of the leading recording artists of her day, excelling in both serious and popular genres. She had a daughter with Bernard Gluck, (Abigail) Marcia Davenport, who became a noted novelist and writer on music. In 1914 she married **Efrem Zimbalist.** Their son, Efrem Zimbalist, Jr., became a well-known actor. His daughter, Stefanie Zimbalist, also followed a thespian bent.

Glyn, Margaret H(enrietta), English musicologist and composer; b. Ewell, Surrey, Feb. 28, 1865; d. there, June 3, 1946. She studied in London under C.J. Frost and Yorke Trotter. Glyn became an authority on keyboard music of the Tudor period. She ed. organ and virginal music by Byrd, Orlando Gibbons, John Bull, and other composers, and publ. *The Rhythmic Conception of Music* (1907), *Analysis of the Evolution of Musical Form* (1909), *About Elizabethan Virginal Music and Its Composers* (1924; 2nd ed., 1934), and *Theory of Musical Evolution* (1924). She also composed a number of works for organ.

Glynne, Howell, Welsh bass; b. Swansea, Jan. 24, 1906; d. in an automobile accident in Toronto, Nov. 24, 1969. He labored as a miner while pursuing vocal training with Davies and Warlich. He gained a place in the chorus of the Carl Rosa Opera Co., and in 1931 made his operatic debut with it as Sparafucile. He was a member of the Sadler's Wells Opera in London (1946–50; 1956–63); from 1947 he also appeared at London's Covent Garden, and was active as a concert artist. In 1964 he joined the faculty of the Univ. of Toronto. Among his best roles were Bartolo, Varlaam, and Baron Ochs.

Gnattali, Radamés, Brazilian pianist, conductor, arranger, and composer; b. Pôrto Alegre, Jan. 27, 1906; d. Rio de Janeiro, Feb. 3, 1988. He was a pupil of Fontainha at the Pôrto Alegre Cons.; after obtaining his degree from the Instituto de Belas-Artes in Pôrto Alegre (1924), he studied harmony with França at the Escola Nacional de Música in Rio de Janeiro. For some years he was director of the Rádio Nacional in Rio de Janeiro, and then was active as a performer, arranger, and composer. From 1967 to 1970 he worked for TV Globo in São Paulo as an arranger and conductor. In 1945 he was made a member of the Academia Brasiliera de Música. From his earliest years as a composer he wrote works in which jazz and indigenous rhythms and harmonies predominated.

WORKS: *Rapsódia Brasileira* for Orch. (1931); 4 piano concertos (1934, 1936, 1960, 1967); Cello Concerto (1941); 14

Brasilianas for Various Instruments or Orch. (1944 et seq.); 3 violin concertos (1947, 1962, 1969); *Variações* for Piano, Violin, and Orch. (1949); *Concêrto romântico* No. 1 (1949) and No. 2 (1964) for Piano and Orch.; 3 *Concêrtos cariocas* for Soloists and Orch. (1950–70); 3 *Sinfonias populares* (1955, 1962, 1969); Harp Concerto (1958); 2 string quartets; piano pieces, including 2 sonatas.

Gnazzo, Anthony J(oseph), American composer; b. Plainville, Conn., April 21, 1936. He studied theory at the Hartt School of Music in Hartford, Conn. (B.A., 1957), mathematics at the Univ. of Hartford (B.A., 1963), and theory with Krenek, Berger, and Shapero at Brandeis Univ. (M.F.A., 1965; Ph.D., 1970). He was an instructor in electronic system design at the Univ. of Toronto (1965–66), and director of the tape-music center at Mills College in Oakland, California (1967–69); in 1974 he became an audio technician at the electronic music studio at Calif. State Univ. at Hayward. His compositions include text-sound pieces, electronic scores, environmental pieces, and kinetic sculpture.

WORKS: INSTRUMENTAL: *Music* for 2 Pianos and Electronic Sound (1964); *Chamber Music* for 13 Instruments (1965); *Cross-cut for Paul Hertelendy* for 3 Electric Saws and String Orch. (1969); *Tighten Up* for 4 Rock Groups (1970); *Music* for Cello and Tape I (1971) and II (1974); *Music* for Piano and Instruments (1974); *Riding the Thorny Shrub of Hearing* for Piano (1992). **VOCAL:** *Eden* for Narrator and 7 Instruments (1964); *Music* for Large Vocal Groups (1966; rev. 1969); *The Question*, oratorio for Chorus (1969); *Prime Source Nos. 1–23* (1971–79); *End Sheets* for Mixed Voices (1986); *A:10* for Mixed Voices (1991). **TAPE:** *Stereo Radio I* and *II* (1970), *III* (1971), *IV* and *V* (1972); *The Art of Canning Music* (1976); *Image/Delusion* (1980); *2-Pulse* (1983); *Museum Piece 1* (1990). **MIXED MEDIA:** *Theater Piece I–XXVI* (1967–71); *10 Pieces for Pauline Oliveros* (1969); *Compound Skull Fracture* for Actor, Tape, and Slides (1975; in collaboration with J. Cuno); *Waiting for JB* (1980); *Lontano* for Narrator, Tape, and Slides (1982); *Visionary Romp* (1986); *Terra, Terra, Terra* (1991). **OTHER:** Incidental music; dance scores; film and television music.

Gnecchi, Vittorio, Italian composer; b. Milan, July 17, 1876; d. there, Feb. 1, 1954. He studied at the Milan Cons. His opera *Cassandra* was performed at Bologna on Dec. 5, 1905; some years later, after the premiere of Strauss's *Elektra*, there was considerable discussion when Giovanni Tebaldini pointed out the identity of some 50 themes in the two works ("Telepatia Musicale," *Rivista Musicale Italiana*, XVII, 1909). Gnecchi also wrote the operas *Virtù d'amore* (1896) and *La rosiera*, after a comedy by Alfred de Musset (in German, Gera, Feb. 12, 1927; in Italian, Trieste, Jan. 24, 1931).

Gnessin, Mikhail (Fabianovich), Russian composer and pedagogue; b. Rostov-na-Donu, Feb. 2, 1882; d. Moscow, May 5, 1957. After lessons with O. Fritch in Rostov, he studied with Rimsky-Korsakov and Liadov at the St. Petersburg Cons. (1901–05; 1906–09). He later went to Moscow, where he was a prof. of composition at the Gnessin Academy (from 1923) and at the Cons. (from 1925); after serving as a prof. at the Leningrad Cons. (1935–44), he returned to Moscow and was head of the Gnessin State Inst. for Musical Education (1944–51). Most of his works composed after 1914 reflect his interest in Jewish themes. He publ. his reflections and reminiscences of Rimsky-Korsakov in Moscow in 1956.

WORKS: DRAMATIC: *Yunost Avraama* (Abraham's Youth), opera (1921–23); incidental music; film scores. **ORCH.:** *Iz Shelli* (1908); *Mourning Dances from "Elegy to Adonais"* (1917); Symphonic Fantasy (1919); *The Jewish Orchestra at the Ball in Nothingtown* (1926). **CHAMBER:** *Requiem* for Piano Quintet (1914); *Variations on a Jewish Theme* for String Quartet (1917); *Songs of a Knight Errant* for String Quartet and Harp (1917); Violin Sonata (1928); *Adïgeya* for Clarinet, Horn, and Piano Quartet (1933); *Elegia-pastoral* for Piano Trio (1940); Piano Trio (1943); Sonata-Fantasia for Piano Quartet (1945); *Theme with Variations* for Cello and Piano (1953); piano pieces. **VOCAL:** *Vrubel* for Voice and Orch. (1911); *The Conqueror Worm* for Voice and Orch. (1913); *1905–1917* for Chorus and Orch. (1926); choruses; about 50 songs; folk song arrangements.

Gobbi, Tito, famous Italian baritone; b. Bassano del Grappa, near Venice, Oct. 24, 1913; d. Rome, March 5, 1984. He received vocal lessons from Barone Zanchetta in Bassano del Grappa before going to Rome to train with Giulio Crimi; made his operatic debut as Count Rodolfo in *La Sonnambula* in Gubbio (1935); during the 1935–36 season, he was an understudy at Milan's La Scala, where he made a fleeting stage appearance as the Herald in Pizzetti's *Oreseolo* (1935). In 1936 he won 1st prize in the male vocal section of the Vienna International Competition; then went to Rome, where he sang Germont *père* at the Teatro Adriano (1937); that same year he made his first appearance at the Teatro Reale, in the role of Lelio in Wolf-Ferrari's *Le Donne curiose*; after singing secondary roles there (1937–39), he became a principal member of the company; appeared as Ford in *Falstaff* during its visit to Berlin in 1941. He also sang on the Italian radio and made guest appearances with other Italian opera houses; in Rieti in 1940 he first essayed the role of Scarpia, which was to become his most celebrated characterization. In 1942 he made his formal debut at La Scala as Belcore in *L'elisir d'amore.* In 1947 he appeared as Rigoletto in Stockholm, and in 1948 he sang in concerts in London and also made his U.S. debut as Figaro in *Il Barbiere di Siviglia* at the San Francisco Opera. In 1950 he made his Covent Garden debut in London as Renato in *Un ballo in maschera.* He made his first appearance at the Chicago Opera as Rossini's Figaro in 1954. On Jan. 13, 1956, he made his Metropolitan Opera debut in N.Y. as Scarpia. In subsequent years, his engagements took him to most of the principal music centers of the world. He was also active as an opera producer from 1965. In 1979 he bade farewell to the operatic stage. He was the brother-in-law of **Boris Christoff**. Gobbi was acclaimed as an actor as well as a singer; his mastery extended to some 100 roles. He publ. *Tito Gobbi: My Life* (1979) and *Tito Gobbi and His World of Italian Opera* (1984).

Godfrey, Sir Dan(iel Eyers), English conductor; b. London, June 20, 1868; d. Bournemouth, July 20, 1939. He was the son of the bandmaster Dan(iel) Godfrey (b. Westminster, Sept. 4, 1831; d. Beeston, Nottinghamshire, June 30, 1903). He studied at the Royal College of Music in London. He was conductor of the London Military Band (a civilian group in reality) from 1889 to 1891. In 1893 he settled in Bournemouth as conductor of the Winter Gardens orch.; founded the Sym. Concerts there in 1894; directed them until his retirement in 1934; he brought the concerts to a high level, and used all his efforts to promote the works of British composers. He was knighted in 1922 for his services to orch. music. He wrote his memoirs, *Memories and Music* (London, 1924).

Godfrey, Isidore, English conductor; b. London, Sept. 27, 1900; d. Sussex, Sept. 12, 1977. He was educated at the Guildhall School of Music in London. In 1925 he joined the D'Oyly Carte Opera Co. as a conductor; from 1929 to 1968 he served as its music director. In 1965 he was named an Officer of the Order of the British Empire.

Godowsky, Leopold, famous Polish-born American pianist and pedagogue; b. Soshly, near Vilnius, Feb. 13, 1870; d. N.Y., Nov. 21, 1938. He played in public as a child in Russia; at 14, was sent to Berlin to study at the Hochschule für Musik, but after a few months there, proceeded to the U.S.; gave his first American concert in Boston on Dec. 7, 1884; in 1885, played engagements at the N.Y. Casino; in 1886, toured Canada with Ovide Musin. He then played in society salons in London and Paris, and became a protégé of Saint-Saëns. In 1890 he joined the faculty of the N.Y. College of Music; in 1891 he became a naturalized American citizen. He taught at the Broad St. Cons. in Philadelphia (1894–95) and was head of the piano dept. of the Chicago Cons. (1895–1900). He then embarked on a European tour, giving a highly successful concert in Berlin (Dec. 6, 1900), where he remained as a teacher; from 1909 to 1914 he conducted a master class at the Vienna Academy of Music; made tours in the U.S. from 1912 to 1914, and settled permanently in the U.S. at the outbreak of World War I. After the war, he toured in Europe, South America, and Asia. In 1930 he suffered a stroke during a recording session. His subsequent career was greatly restricted. Godowsky was one of the outstanding masters of the piano; possessing a scientifically inclined mind, he developed a method of "weight and relaxation"; applying it to his own playing, he became an outstanding technician of his instrument, extending the potentialities of piano technique to the utmost, with particular attention to the left hand. He wrote numerous piano compositions of transcendental difficulty, yet entirely pianistic in style; also arranged works by Weber, Brahms, and Johann Strauss. Particularly remarkable are his 53 studies on Chopin's études, combining Chopin's themes in ingenious counterpoint; among his original works, the most interesting are *Triakontameron* (30 pieces; 1920; no. 11 is the well-known *Alt Wien*) and *Java Suite* (12 pieces; 1924–25). He also wrote simple pedagogical pieces, e.g., a set of *46 Miniatures* for Piano, 4-hands, in which the pupil is given a part within the compass of 5 notes only (1918); ed. piano studies by Czerny, Heller, Köhler et al.; composed music for the left hand alone (*6 Waltz Poems, Prelude and Fugue*, etc.); and publ. an essay, "Piano Music for the Left Hand," *Musical Quarterly* (July 1935).

BIBL.: L. Saxe, "The Published Music of L. G.," *Notes* (March 1957; with an annotated list of original works, arrangements, and eds.); C. Hopkins, "G's 'Phonoramas': A 20th-century 'Wanderlust'," *Musical Times* (July 1989); J. Nicholas, *G.—The Pianists' Pianist: A Biography of L. G.* (Hexham, 1989).

Godron, Hugo, Dutch composer; b. Amsterdam, Nov. 22, 1900; d. Zoelmond, Dec. 6, 1971. He studied violin at the music school in Bussum, and composition with Sem Dresden in Amsterdam (1921–22). He taught composition and harmony at music schools in Bussum, Hilversum, and Utrecht; from 1939 to 1969 he was active as a sound engineer in Hilversum and Amsterdam. His music is generally joyful, almost playful, in character.

WORKS: RADIO FAIRY TALE: *Assepoes* (Cinderella; 1946–47). **ORCH.:** Sinfonietta for Small Orch. (1932–33); *7 Miniatures* for Piano and Strings (1933); Piano Concerto (1938–39); *Sérénade occidentale* (1942–48); *Amabile Suite* for Clarinet, Piano, and Strings (1943); Concerto Grosso for Clarinet and Small Orch. (1944–45); *Concert Suite* for Piano and Strings (1945–47); *Miniatuur symphonie* (1949–50; orchestration of *Gardenia Suite* for Piano); *2 Polkas* (1950–51; 1957–58); Suite for Harpsichord and Strings (1950); *Hommage à Chabrier* (1950–51); *Hommages classiques* for Flute, Piano, and Strings (1950); *Concerto for Orchestra* (1953–54); *Variations traditionnelles* for Small Orch. (1954); *Promenades*, suite (1954–55); *4 impressies* for Chamber Orch. (1956–57); *Aubade Gaudeamus*, suite for Piano, Strings, and Percussion (1966–68); *Hommage à Bizet* for Small Orch. (1971). **CHAMBER:** String Trio (1937); *Serenade* for Piano and Wind Quintet (1947); Sonatina for Flute, Violin, Viola, and Piano (1948); Piano Trio (1948); *Sonata facile* for Cello and Piano (1950); *Divertimento* for 2 Violins and Piano (1956); *Nouvelles* for Piano Trio (1963); *Quatuor bohémien* for Piano Quartet (1970); piano pieces.

Godwin, Joscelyn, English-born American musicologist, composer, and painter; b. Kelmscott, Jan. 16, 1945. He was educated at Christ Church Cathedral Choir School, Oxford (1952–58); Radley College (1958–62); and Magdalene College, Cambridge (B.A., 1965; M.A., 1968). He became a Fellow of the Royal College of Organists in 1965. He also studied at Cornell Univ. (Ph.D., 1969, with a diss. on the music of Henry Cowell). He was an instructor in music at Cleveland State Univ. (1969–71); then joined the faculty of Colgate Univ. (1982). He has lectured widely in the U.S. and the United Kingdom; he became a naturalized U.S. citizen in 1980. While his compositions are occasionally performed, and he himself performs frequently as a conductor and an instrumentalist, he is best known as the author of numerous books, articles, and trs. dealing with mysticism and ancient philosophies in relation to music.

WRITINGS: *Music, Mysticism and Magic: A Sourcebook* (London, 1986); *Harmonies of Heaven and Earth* (London, 1987); *The Mystery of the Seven Vowels in Theory and Practice* (Grand Rapids, Mich., 1991).

Goeb, Roger (John), American composer; b. Cherokee, Iowa, Oct. 9, 1914. He studied agriculture at the Univ. of Wisc., graduating in 1936; in 1938 went to Paris, where he took lessons with Boulanger at the École Normale de Musique. Returning to America in 1939, he was a pupil of Luening, pursued graduate work at N.Y. Univ., was a pupil of Elwell at the Cleveland Inst. of Music (M.Mus., 1942), and obtained his Ph.D. at the Univ. of Iowa (1945). He occupied teaching posts at the Univ. of Okla. (1942–44), Iowa State Univ. (1944–45), and the Juilliard School of Music (1947–50). He held 2 Guggenheim fellowships (1950, 1952); taught music at Stanford Univ. (1954–55); then was executive secretary of the American Composers' Alliance (1956–62). Personal misfortunes (both his wife and his son died of multiple sclerosis) caused him to interrupt his professional activities in 1964; but he resumed composition in 1979.

WORKS: ORCH.: 6 syms.: No. 1 (1941; withdrawn), No. 2 (1945), No. 3 (1950; N.Y., April 3, 1952, Stokowski conducting), No. 4 (1955; Pittsburgh, Feb. 24, 1956), No. 5 (1981), and No. 6 (1987); *Lyric Piece* for Trumpet and Orch. (1942); *Prairie Songs* for Small Orch. (1947); *Fantasy* for Oboe and Strings (1947); *4 Concertantes*: No. 1 for Flute, Oboe, Clarinet, and Strings (1948), No. 2 for Bassoon or Cello and Strings (1950), No. 3 for Viola and Orch. (1951), and No. 4 for Clarinet, Timpani, 2 Percussion, Piano, and Strings (1951); *Romanza* for Strings (1948); 2 concertinos: No. 1 (1949) and No. 2 (Louisville, Nov. 28, 1956); *5 American Dances* (1952; 1–3 for Strings; 4 and 5 for Orch.); Violin Concerto (1953; N.Y., Feb. 1954); Piano Concerto (1954); *2 Sinfonias* (1957, 1962); *Enconium* (1958); *Iowa Concerto* for Small Orch. (1959); *Divertissement* for Strings (1982); *Memorial* (1982); *Caprice* (1982); *Fantasia* (1983); *Essay* (1984); *Gambol* (1984). **CHAMBER:** 4 string quartets (1942, withdrawn; 1948; 1954; 1980); Sonata for Solo Viola (1942); Suite for Woodwind Trio (1946); Brass Septet (1949); Quintet for Trombone and String Quartet (1949); 4 wind quintets (1949, 1955, 1980, 1982); *2 Divertimenti* for Flute (1950); *3 Processionals* for Organ and Brass Quintet (1951); Piano Quintet (1955); Sonata for Solo Violin (1957); *Running Colors* for String Quartet (1961); Quartet for Oboe and String Trio (1964); Trio for Horn, Trumpet, and Trombone (1979); Quintet for Cello and String Quartet (1980); Octet for Clarinet, Bassoon, Horn, and Strings (1980); Flute Quartet (1983); *Black on White* for Clarinet and Strings (1985); *Nuances* for Clarinet and Viola (1986).

Goebel, Reinhard, esteemed German violinist and conductor; b. Siegen, Westphalia, July 31, 1952. He commenced violin lessons in his youth, receiving principal training in Cologne and Amsterdam from Maier, Gawriloff, and Leonhardt. In 1973 a passion for early music led him to organize the Musica Antiqua Köln, an ensemble dedicated to performing works on original instruments or modern replicas; after a major tour of Europe in 1978, the ensemble toured widely in North and South America, the Far East, and Australia, acquiring an international reputation through its exacting but spirited performances. Goebel plays a Jacobus Stainer violin built in 1665.

Goedike, Alexander, Russian pianist, pedagogue, and composer of German descent; b. Moscow, March 4, 1877; d. there, July 9, 1957. He studied with Safonov and G. Pabst (piano) and Arensky (composition) at the Moscow Cons. (graduated, 1898), where he was a prof. of piano from 1909.

WORKS: OPERAS: *Virineya* (1915); *At the Crossing* (1933); *Jacquerie* (1937); *Macbeth* (1944). **ORCH.:** Piano Concerto

(1900); 3 syms. (1903, 1905, 1922); Organ Concerto (1929); Horn Concerto (1929); Trumpet Concerto (1930); Violin Concerto (1951). **CHAMBER:** Piano Quintet; 2 piano trios; String Quartet. **OTHER:** Pedagogic pieces for Piano.

BIBL.: V. Yakovlev, *A.G.* (Moscow, 1927); K. Adzhemov, *A.G.* (Moscow, 1960).

Goehr, (Peter) Alexander, prominent German-born English composer and teacher, son of **Walter Goehr;** b. Berlin, Aug. 10, 1932. He was a student of Richard Hall at the Royal Manchester College of Music (1952–55), and then of Messiaen and Loriod in Paris (1955–56). After lecturing at Morely College in London (1955–57), he was a music assistant at the BBC (1960–68). In 1968–69 he served as composer-in-residence at the New England Cons. of Music in Boston, and then was an assoc. prof. of music at Yale Univ. in 1969–70. From 1971 to 1976 he was the West Riding prof. of music at the Univ. of Leeds, and in 1975 he also was artistic director of the Leeds Festival. He subsequently was prof. of music at the Univ. of Cambridge from 1976. In 1980 he was a visiting prof. at the Beijing Cons. of Music. In 1989 he was made an honorary member of the American Academy and Inst. of Arts and Letters. Goehr's oeuvre has been notably influenced by Schoenberg, although he has succeeded in developing an individual mode of expression utilizing serial, tonal, and modal means.

WORKS: DRAMATIC: *La belle dame sans merci*, ballet (1958); *Arden muss sterben* or *Arden must die*, opera (1966; Hamburg, March 5, 1967); *Triptych*, theater piece consisting of *Naboth's Vineyard* (London, July 16, 1968), *Shadowplay* (London, July 8, 1970), and *Sonata about Jerusalem* (1970; Tel Aviv, Jan. 1971); *Behold the Sun* or *Die Wiedertäufer*, opera (1981–84; Duisburg, April 19, 1985); *Arianna*, opera (1994–95; London, Sept. 15, 1995). **ORCH.:** *Fantasia* (1954; rev. 1959); *Hecuba's Lament* (1959–61); Violin Concerto (1961–62); *Little Symphony* (1963); *Little Music* for Strings (1963); *Pastorale* (1965); *Romanza* for Cello and Orch. (1968); *Konzertstück* for Piano and Small Orch. (1969); *Symphony in 1 Movement* (1969; London, May 9, 1970; rev. 1981); Piano Concerto (Brighton, May 14, 1972); *Metamorphosis/Dance* (1973–74; London, Nov. 17, 1974); *Fugue on the Notes of the 4th Psalm* for Strings (London, July 8, 1976); Sinfonia for Chamber Orch. (1979; London, Nov. 20, 1980); *Duex Études* (1980–81; Glasgow, Sept. 17, 1981); *Symphony with Chaconne* (1985–86; Manchester, Jan. 13, 1987); *Still Lands* for Small Orch. (1988–90); *Colossos or Panic* (1991–92); *Cambridge Hockett* for 4 Horns and Orch. (1993). **CHAMBER:** *Fantasias* for Clarinet and Piano (1954); 4 string quartets (1956–57, rev. 1988; 1967; 1975–76; 1990); *Variations* for Flute and Piano (1959); Suite for Flute, Clarinet, Horn, Harp, Violin or Viola, and Cello (1961); Piano Trio (1966); *Paraphrase on the Dramatic Madrigal "Il Combattimento di Tancredi e Clorinda" by Monteverdi* for Clarinet (1969); Concerto for 11 Instruments (1970; Brussels, Jan. 25, 1971); *Chaconne* for Winds (Leeds, Nov. 3, 1974); *Lyric Pieces* for 8 Instruments (London, Nov. 15, 1974); *Prelude and Fugue* for 3 Clarinets (1978); Cello Sonata (1984); *. . . A Musical Offering (J.S.B. 1985) . . .* for 14 Instruments (Edinburgh, Aug. 19, 1985); *Variations on Bach's Sarabande from the English Suite in E minor* for 10 Instruments (1990). **PIANO:** Sonata (1951–52); *Capriccio* (1957); *3 Pieces* (1964); *Nonomiya* (1969). **VOCAL:** *The Deluge* for Soprano, Contralto, and 8 Instruments (1957–58); *4 Songs from the Japanese* for High Voice and Piano or Orch. (1959); *Sutter's Gold* for Bass, Chorus, and Orch. (1959–60); *2 Choruses* (1962); *A Little Cantata of Proverbs* (1962); *Virtutes* for Speaker, Chorus, and Instruments (1963); *5 Poems and an Epigram of William Blake* for Chorus and Trumpet (1964); *Warngedichte* for Low Voice and Piano (1966–67); *Psalm 4* for Soprano, Alto, Women's Chorus, Viola, and Organ (London, July 8, 1976); *Babylon the Great is Fallen* for Chorus and Orch. (London, Dec. 12, 1979); *Das Gesetz der Quadrille* or *The Law of the Quadrille* for Low Voice and Piano (1979); *Behold the Sun*, concert aria for Soprano and Instruments (1981); *2 Imitations of Baudelaire* for Chorus (1985); *Eve Dreams in Paradise* for Mezzo-soprano, Tenor, and Orch. (1987–88; Birmingham, March 14, 1989); *Carol for St. Steven* for Chorus (Cambridge, Dec. 24, 1989); *Sing, Ariel* for Mezzo-soprano, 2 Sopranos, and 5 Instruments (1989–90; Aldeburgh, June 23, 1990); *The Mouse Metamorphosed Into a Maid* for Chorus (1991); *The Death of Moses* for Soprano, Contralto or Male Alto, Tenor, Baritone, Bass, Chorus, Children's Chorus or Semi-chorus of Women's Voices, and 13 Instruments (1991–92); *Psalm 39* for Chamber Chorus and Wind Ensemble (1992–93).

BIBL.: B. Northcott, ed., *The Music of A.G.: Interviews and Articles* (London, 1980).

Goehr, Walter, German-born English conductor and composer, father of **(Peter) Alexander Goehr**; b. Berlin, May 28, 1903; d. Sheffield, Dec. 4, 1960. He studied theory with Schoenberg in Berlin; then was a conductor with the Berlin Radio (1925–31). In 1933 he went to England and was music director of the Columbia Graphophone Co. until 1939; from 1945 to 1948 he was conductor of the BBC Theatre Orch.; also was conductor of the Morley College concerts from 1943 until his death. He composed theater, radio, and film scores.

Goepp, Philip H(enry), American organist, writer on music, teacher, and composer; b. N.Y., June 23, 1864; d. Philadelphia, Aug. 25, 1936. He studied in Germany (1872–77) and with J.K. Paine at Harvard Univ. (B.A., 1884); he then studied law at the Univ. of Pa. (graduated, 1888) and completed his musical training with David D. Wood. He was organist at Philadelphia's 1st Unitarian Church and a teacher of theory at Temple Univ.; he was also program annotator of the Philadelphia Orch. (1900–1921). He publ. *Annals of Music in Philadelphia* (1896) and *Symphonies and Their Meaning* (3 vols., 1898, 1902, 1913). Among his works were orch. music, chamber pieces, piano music, organ pieces, choral works, and songs.

Goethals, Lucien (Gustave Georges), Belgian composer and teacher; b. Ghent, June 26, 1931. He studied with Rosseau at the Royal Cons. in Ghent (1947–56) and took courses at the Ghent Inst. for Psycho-Acoustics and Electronic Music at the Univ. of Ghent; he also worked in an electronic studio in Germany. In 1963 he organized the Belgian contemporary music group Spectra. From 1971 to 1991 he taught at the Ghent Cons. In 1981 he was awarded the Culture Prize of the City of Ghent. His compositions explore the problems of modernistic constructivism.

WORKS: DRAMATIC: *Vensters*, audio-visual play for 2 Narrators, Cello, Piano, Percussion, Recorded Sounds, and Film Projections (Brussels, Sept. 16, 1967); *Hé*, audio-visual production for 10 Instruments, Tapes, and Film Projections (1971; in collaboration with H. Sabbe and K. Goeyvaerts). **ORCH.:** *5 Impromptus* for Chamber Orch. (1959); *Dialogos* for Strings, Wind Quintet, 2 String Quintets, Percussion, and Tape (1963); *Dialogos Suite* for Chamber Orch. (1963); *Sinfonia in Gris Mayor* for 2 Orchs., Percussion, and Tape (Brussels, June 14, 1966); *Enteuxis* for Strings, Oboe, and Flute (1968); *Concerto for Orchestra* (1972); *4 Pieces* (1976); Concerto for 2 Clarinets and Orch. (1980–83). **CHAMBER:** Violin Sonata (1959); *Rituele Suite* for Wind Quintet (1959); *Endomorfie I* for Violin, Piano, and Tape (1964) and *II* for Flute, Oboe, Clarinet, Bassoon, 2 Trumpets, Trombone, and Tuba (1964); *Cellotape* for Cello, Piano, Tape, and Contact Microphone (1965); *Movimientos y acciones* for Flute, Clarinet, String Quartet, Chromatic Harp, and Percussion (1965); *Mouvement* for String Quartet (1967); *Quebraduras* for Piano Quartet (1969); *Ensimismamientos* for Violin, Cello, Bassoon, Piano, and Tape (1969); *Superposiciones* for Violin, Cello, Bassoon, and Piano (1970); *Suma* for an undefined number of Instruments, and Tape (1971); *3 paisajes sonores* for Flute, Oboe, Cello, Trombone, Double Bass, and Harpsichord (1973); *Diferencias* for 10 Instruments (1974); *Musica con cantus firmus triste* for Flute, Violin, Viola, and Cello (1978); *Ritueel* for Cheng, Percussion, and Tape (1979); Trio for Flute, Bass Clarinet, and Piano (1980); *Beweging* for Clarinet Quartet (1981); *Duelos* for Xylorimba and Percussion

(1984); piano pieces; organ music. **OTHER:** Vocal pieces; solo tape works.

Goetschius, Percy, American music pedagogue; b. Paterson, N.J., Aug. 30, 1853; d. Manchester, N.H., Oct. 29, 1943. He studied at the Stuttgart Cons., and taught various classes there; then was on the faculty of Syracuse Univ. (1890–92) and at the New England Cons. of Music in Boston (1892–96). In 1905 he was appointed head of the dept. of music at the N.Y. Inst. of Musical Art; he retired in 1925.

WRITINGS: *The Material Used in Musical Composition* (Stuttgart, 1882; 14th ed., 1913); *The Theory and Practice of Tone-relations* (Boston, 1892; 17th ed., 1917); *Models of Principal Musical Forms* (Boston, 1895); *Syllabus of Music History* (1895); *The Homophonic Forms of Musical Composition* (N.Y., 1898; 10th ed., 1921); *Exercises in Melody Writing* (N.Y., 1900; 9th ed., 1923); *Applied Counterpoint* (N.Y., 1902); *Lessons in Music Form* (Boston, 1904); *Exercises in Elementary Counterpoint* (N.Y., 1910); with T. Tapper, *Essentials in Music History* (N.Y., 1914); *The Larger Forms of Musical Composition* (N.Y., 1915); *Masters of the Symphony* (Boston, 1929); *The Structure of Music* (Philadelphia, 1934).

BIBL.: A. Shepherd, "'Papa' G. in Retrospect," *Musical Quarterly* (July 1944).

Goetze, Walter W(ilhelm), German composer; b. Berlin, April 17, 1883; d. there, March 24, 1961. He was trained in Berlin. After working as a bassoonist and theater conductor, he had his first success as a theater composer with his *Parkettsitz Nr. 10* (Hamburg, Sept. 24, 1911). After bringing out such scores as *Zwischen zwölf und eins* (Leipzig, Feb. 9, 1913), *Der liebe Pepi* or *Der Bundesbruder* (Berlin, Dec. 23, 1914), and *Am Brunnen vor dem Tore* (Hannover, May 26, 1918), he had his finest success with *Ihre Hoheit die Tänzerin* (Stettin, May 8, 1919). Among the best of his subsequent works were *Adrienne* (Hamburg, April 24, 1926), *Henriette Sontag* (Altenberg, Jan. 20, 1929; rev. version as *Die göttliche Jette*, Berlin, Dec. 31, 1931), *Der goldene Pierrot* (Berlin, March 31, 1934), *Schach dem König!* (Berlin, May 16, 1935), and *Liebe im Dreiklang* (Heidelberg, Nov. 15, 1950; in collaboration with E. Malkowsky).

Goeyvaerts, Karel (August), significant Belgian composer; b. Antwerp, June 8, 1923; d. there, Feb. 3, 1993. He studied at the Royal Flemish Cons. of Music in Antwerp (1943–47), with Milhaud and Messiaen at the Paris Cons. (1947–51), and at the summer courses in new music in Darmstadt (1951). In 1964 he joined the Inst. for Psycho-Acoustics and Electronic Music (IPEM) at the Univ. of Ghent. He worked as an ed. for electronic music at the Flemish Radio in Antwerp (1970–74) and for contemporary music at the Belgian Radio and TV in Brussels (1974–87). Goeyvaerts was one of the pioneers in Belgium of serialism, spatial music, and electronic techniques.

WORKS: BALLET: *Cataclysme* (1963). **ORCH.:** 5 Pieces for Strings (1944); *Preludium, Fuga en Koraal* for Strings (1945); 2 violin concertos (1947, 1951); *Diafonie* (1957); *Jeux d'Été* for 3 Orchs. (1962); *De Passie* (1962); *Al naar gelang . . .* for 5 Orch. Groups and Tape ad libitum (1971); *. . . erst das Gesicht . . . dann die Hände . . . und zuletzt erst das Haar . . .* for Chamber Orch. (1975); *Litanie III* (1981). **CHAMBER:** Trio for Violin, Clarinet, and Cello (1946); 2 string quartets (1947, 1992); Violin Sonata (1948); *Tre Lieder per sonare a venti-sei* for Various Instrumental Combinations (1949); *Opus 2* for 13 Instruments (1951); *Opus 3 met gestreken en geslagen tonen* (with striking and rubbing sounds) for 9 Instruments (1952); *Pièce pour trois* for Flute, Violin, and Piano (1960); *Parcours* for 2 to 6 Violins (1967); *Actief—Reactief* for 2 Oboes, 2 Trumpets, and Piano (1968); Piano Quartet with Tape ad libitum (1971); *You'll Never Be Alone Any More* for Bass Clarinet and Tape (1974); *Voor tsjeng* for Cheng (Chinese Zither) (1974); *Ach Golgatha!* for Positive Organ, Harp, and 3 Percussion (1975); *Pour que les fruits mûrissent cet été* for 14 Renaissance Instruments (1975); *Litanie II* for 3 Percussion (1980) and *V* for Harpsichord and Tape (1982); *After Shave* for Recorder, Violin, and Harpsichord (1982); *Instant OXO* for 3 Percussion (1982); *Zum Wassermann* for 14 Instruments (1985); *Avontuur* for Piano and 10 Winds (1985); *Aemstel-Kwartet* for Flute, Violin, Cello, and Harp (1985); *De zeven zegels* for String Quartet (1986); *De heilige stad* for 12 Instrumentalists (1986); *Veertien heilige kwinten met aureool* for Cheng (Chinese Zither) and Percussion (1986); *Ambachtelijk weefsel* for Shakuhachi and 2 Kōtōs (1989); *Chivas Regal* for Harpsichord and Percussion (1989); *Voor Harrie, Harry en René* for Flute, Bass Clarinet, and Piano (1990); *. . . das Haar* for 10 Instruments (1990). **PIANO:** *Nummer 1*, sonata for 2 Pianos (1951); *Stuk* for Piano and Tape (1964); *De schampere pianist* (1976); *Litanie I* (1979); *Pas à Pas* (1985). **VOCAL:** *Elegische Muziek* for Alto, Piano, and Orch. (1950); *Improperia*, cantata for Alto, 2 Choruses, Flute, Oboe, Clarinet, Viola, and Percussion (1959); *Goathemala* for Mezzo-soprano and Flute (1966); *Mass*, in memory of Pope John XXIII, for Chorus, 2 Oboes, English Horn, 2 Bassoons, 2 Trumpets, and 3 Trombones (1968); *". . . Bélise dans un jardin"* for Chorus, Clarinet, Bass Clarinet, Bassoon, Violin, Viola, and Cello (1971); *Het dagelijks leven van de Azteken* for Speaker and Percussion (1978); *Claus-ule* for Speaker and 8 Instruments (1979); *Litanie IV* for Soprano, Flute, Clarinet, Violin, Cello, and Piano (1981); *De dunne bomen* for Soprano and Dance Group (1985); *Ode* for Counter-tenor, Baritone, Flute, and Bass Clarinet (1988); *. . . want de tijd is nabij* for Men's Chorus and String Orch. (1989); *Aquarius*, scenic cantata for 8 Sopranos, 16 Instrumentalists, and 5 Dancers (1990; also for 8 Sopranos, 8 Baritones, and Orch., 1991); choral pieces; songs. **OTHER:** *Nummer 4 net dode tonen* for Tape (1952); *Nummer 5 met zuivere tonen* for Tape (1953); *Nummer 6* for 180 Sound Objects (1954); *Nummer 7 met convergerende en divergerende klankniveaus* for Electronics (1955); *HE . . . !*, audiovisual manipulation for Pantomime, Projection, Tape, and 10 Instruments (1971; in collaboration with L. Goethals and H. Sabbe); *Nachklänge aus dem Theater I/II* for Tape (1971); *Op acht paarden wedden* for Tape (1973); *Partiduur* for Tape (1974); *Honneurs funèbres a la tete musicale d'Orphée* for 6 Ondes Martenots (1976); *Muziek voor een koninklijk vuurwerk* for Tape (1976).

BIBL.: H. Sabbe, "K.G. (1923–1993): Aesthetic Radicalism and Ideology," *Neue Musik, Ästhetik und Ideologie* (Wilhelmshaven, 1994).

Gogorza, Emilio (Edoardo) de, American baritone and teacher; b. Brooklyn, May 29, 1874; d. N.Y., May 10, 1949. After singing as a boy soprano in England, he returned to the U.S. and studied with C. Moderati and E. Agramonte in N.Y. He made his debut in 1897 with Marcella Sembrich in a concert; sang throughout the country in concerts and with leading orchs. Beginning in 1925, he was an instructor of voice at the Curtis Inst. of Music in Philadelphia. He married **Emma Eames** in 1911.

Goh, Taijiro, Japanese composer; b. Dairen, Manchuria, Feb. 15, 1907; d. Shizuoka, July 1, 1970. He studied in Tokyo. He organized the Soc. of Japanese Composers, and created the Japan Women's Sym. Orch. (1963). His music follows the European academic type of harmonic and contrapuntal structure.

WORKS: DRAMATIC: OPERAS: *Madame Rosaria* (1943); *Tsubaki saku koro* (When Camellias Blossom; 1949; unfinished); *Tais* (1959; unfinished). **BALLET:** Oni-Daiko (Devil Drummers; 1956). **CHOREOGRAPHIC PLAYS:** *Koku-sei-Ya* (1954); *Rashômon* (1954)). **ORCH.:** 8 syms.: No. 1 (1925), No. 2 (1930), No. 3, *Kumo* (Clouds; 1938), No. 4 (1938), No. 5, *Nippon* (1939), No. 6, *Asia* (1939), No. 7, *Sokoku* (Motherland; 1942), and No. 8, *Chô jô Banri* (The Long Wall; 1945; only the 1st movement was completed); 3 violin concertos (1935, 1937, 1962); 2 piano concertos (1936, 1940); *Movement* for Cello, Temple Blocks, and Orch. (1937); *Theme and Variations* (1938); 2 overtures: *Otakebi* (War Cry; 1939) and *Over the Tan-Shan Southern Path* (1941); 3 symphonic marches: *Eiyû* (Hero; 1940), *Taiiku* (Gymnastics; 1940), and *Akeyuku Azia* (Asia Dawning; 1942); *Shimpi-shu* (Mysteries), ballet suite (1942);

Seija to Eiyû (The Saint and the Hero), symphonic dance piece (1961); *Brasil*, symphonic poem for Narrator, Chorus, and Orch. (1967). **CHAMBER:** *Theme and Variations* for String Trio (1933); 2 string quartets (1935, 1938); *Imayo* for Cello and Piano (1954). **PIANO:** 5 sonatas (1915, 1919, 1920, 1927, 1927); *November in Manchuria*, rhapsody (1926); *Fantasy* (1927); *Variations* (1931); *8 Chinese Dances* (1941); *Katyusha*, choreographic poem (1954). **VOCAL:** *Nemuri no Serenâde* (Serenade for Slumber) for Voice and Orch. (1944); *The Flow of the River Dalny* for Chorus and Orch. (1950); other vocal works, including over 100 songs.

Göhler, (Karl) Georg, German conductor and composer; b. Zwickau, June 29, 1874; d. Lübeck, March 4, 1954. He was a pupil of Vollhardt in Zwickau; then studied at the Cons. and the Univ. of Leipzig (Ph.D., 1897, with a diss. on Cornelius Freundt). He then pursued a career as a conductor, becoming best known as a champion of Bruckner and Mahler. He wrote an opera, *Prinz Nachtwächter* (1922); several syms.; Piano Concerto; Clarinet Concerto; 2 violin concertos; Cello Concerto; *Quartetto enimmatico* for Piano and Strings; String Trio; choral works; songs; piano pieces.

Gold, Arthur, Canadian pianist; b. Toronto, Feb. 6, 1917; d. N.Y., Jan. 3, 1990. He studied with Josef and Rosina Lhévinne at the Juilliard School of Music in N.Y. Upon graduation, he formed a piano duo with Robert Fizdale with whom he gave numerous concerts in Europe and America, in programs of modern music, including works specially written for them by such celebrated composers as Barber, Milhaud, Poulenc, Auric, and Thomson. They also pioneered performances of works by Cage for prepared piano. With Fizdale, he publ. a successful book, *Misia* (N.Y., 1979), on the life of Maria Godebska, a literary and musical figure in Paris early in the century. Gold retired in 1982, and in a spirit of innocent but practical amusement he publ., with Fizdale, *The Gold and Fizdale Cookbook* (1983).

Gold (real name, **Goldner**), **Ernest,** Austrian-born American composer and conductor; b. Vienna, July 13, 1921. He studied piano and violin at home, and later piano, conducting, and composition at the Vienna Academy of Music (1937–38); he went to the U.S. in 1938 and became a naturalized American citizen in 1946; studied harmony with Otto Cesana and conducting with Leon Barzin in N.Y. Moving to Hollywood, he worked as an arranger and took lessons with Antheil (1946–48); he became particularly successful as a composer for films, winning an Academy Award for his score for *Exodus* (1960). He was music director of the Santa Barbara Sym. Orch. (1958–60) and founder-conductor of Los Angeles's Senior Citizens' Orch.

WORKS: Many film scores, including: *The Defiant Ones* (1958); *On the Beach* (1959); *Exodus* (1960); *Inherit the Wind* (1960); *Judgment at Nuremberg* (1961); *It's a Mad, Mad, Mad, Mad World* (1963); *Ship of Fools* (1965); *The Secret of Santa Vittoria* (1969); also 2 musicals: *Too Warm for Furs* (1956) and *I'm Solomon* (1968); 2 syms.: No. 1, *Pan American* (1941) and No. 2 (1947); Piano Concerto (1943); *Ballad* for Orch. (1944); *Symphonic Preludes* (1944); *Allegorical Overture* (1947); *Band in Hand* for Narrator and Band (1966); *Boston Pops March* (1966); chamber music; piano pieces; songs.

Goldberg, Reiner, noted German tenor; b. Crostau, Oct. 17, 1939. He was a student of Arno Schellenberg at the Dresden Hochschule für Musik. In 1966 he began his career in Radebeul, and that same year made his Dresden debut as Luigi in *Il Tabarro*. In 1973 he became a member of the Dresden State Opera, and in 1977 of the (East) Berlin State Opera; he toured with both companies in Europe and abroad. In 1982 he made his debut at London's Covent Garden as Walther von Stolzing, in Paris as Midas in a concert perf. of *Die Liebe der Danae*, at the Salzburg Easter Festival as Erik, and at the Salzburg Summer Festival as Florestan. He also sang Parsifal on the soundtrack for the Syberberg film version of Wagner's opera. In 1983 he made his N.Y. debut as Guntram in a concert perf. of Strauss' opera. He sang for the first time at Milan's La Scala as Tannhäuser in 1984. In 1987 he first appeared at the Bayreuth Festival as Walther von Stolzing. He made his Metropolitan Opera debut in N.Y. on Jan. 27, 1992, as Florestan. As one of the leading Heldentenors of his day, Goldberg has won considerable distinction for his portrayals of Siegmund, Tannhäuser, Siegfried, Erik, and Parsifal. His versatile repertoire also includes Bacchus, Max, Hermann in *The Queen of Spades*, Faust, the Drum Major in *Wozzeck*, and Sergei in *Lady Macbeth of the District of Mtzensk*.

Goldberg, Szymon, eminent Polish-born American violinist and conductor; b. Włocławek, June 1, 1909; d. Ôyama-machi, Japan, July 19, 1993. He played violin as a child in Warsaw. In 1917 he went to Berlin and took violin lessons with Carl Flesch. After a recital in Warsaw in 1921, he was engaged as concertmaster of the Dresden Phil. (1925–29); in 1929 he was appointed concertmaster of the Berlin Phil., but was forced to leave in 1934 despite Furtwängler's vigorous attempts to safeguard the Jewish members of the orch.; he then toured Europe. He made his American debut in N.Y. in 1938; while on a tour of Asia, he was interned in Java by the Japanese from 1942 to 1945; eventually he went to the U.S. and became a naturalized American citizen in 1953. From 1951 to 1965 he taught at the Aspen Music School; concurrently was active as a conductor. In 1955 he founded the Netherlands Chamber Orch. in Amsterdam, which he led with notable distinction for 22 years; he also took the ensemble on tours. From 1977 to 1979 he was conductor of the Manchester Camerata. He taught at Yale Univ. (1978–82), the Juilliard School in N.Y. (from 1978), the Curtis Inst. of Music in Philadelphia (from 1980), and the Manhattan School of Music in N.Y. (from 1981). From 1990 until his death he conducted the New Japan Phil. in Tokyo.

BIBL.: B. Gavoty, *S. G.* (Geneva, 1961).

Goldberg, Theo, German-born Canadian composer and teacher; b. Chemnitz, Sept. 29, 1921. He received training in composition from Blacher at the Berlin Hochschule für Musik (1945–50). In 1954 he emigrated to Canada and in 1973 became a naturalized Canadian citizen. He taught school in Vancouver but pursued his education at Washington State Univ. in Pullman (M.A., 1969) and the Univ. of Toronto (D.Mus., 1972). From 1970 to 1987 he taught music education at the Univ. of British Columbia in Vancouver. In his output from 1975, he placed special emphasis on mixed media, tape, and computers.

WORKS: DRAMATIC: *Nacht mit Kleopatra*, opera-ballet (1950; Karlsruhe, Jan. 20, 1952); *Robinson und Freitag*, radio opera (1951); *Engel-Étude*, chamber opera (Berlin, Sept. 20, 1952); *Galatea Elettronica*, chamber opera (1969); *The Concrete Rose*, rock opera (1970); *Orphée aux enfers*, "opéra son et lumières" (1975); *Daedalus*, "opéra son et lumières" (1977); *Orion*, sound images (1978); incidental music for stage, radio, and television; various multimedia pieces, among them *Variations of a Mandala* (1973), *The Magic Carpet* (1982), and *The Hoard of the Nibelungen, as performed by a company of Baenkelsaengers* (1988). **ORCH.:** *Liebesliederwalzer Variations*, on a theme by Strauss (1952); Sinfonia Concertante for Flute, Clarinet, Trumpet, Violin, Cello, and Orch. (1967); *Canadiana: Suite für Piano und Orchester nach Canadischen Volksweisen* (1971); *Songs of the Loon and the Raven* for Orch. and Tape (1975); *The Beaux' Stratagem* (1978); Flügelhorn Concerto, *Il Caro Sassone* (1981). **CHAMBER:** *Samogonski-Trio* for Baritone, Clarinet, Cello, and Piano (1951); Clarinet Quintet (1951); *3 Movements* for Bassoon and Buchla (1971); *Antithesis* for Saxophone and Tape (1974); *St. Francis' Sermon to the Birds* for Bassoon and Tape (1975).

Golde, Walter, American pianist, vocal teacher, and composer; b. Brooklyn, Jan. 4, 1887; d. Chapel Hill, N.C., Sept. 4, 1963. After piano training with Hugo Troetschel in Brooklyn, he studied at Dartmouth College, graduating in 1910; then went to Vienna, where he took vocal lessons and studied counterpoint and composition with Robert Fuchs at the Cons. Returning to the U.S., he was accompanist to many famous musicians of the day. From 1944 to 1948 he headed the voice dept. of Columbia Univ.; in 1953 he was appointed director of the Inst. of Opera at the Univ. of North Carolina. He composed a number of attractive songs and piano pieces.

Goldenweiser, Alexander (Borisovich), Russian piano pedagogue and composer; b. Kishinev, March 10, 1875; d. Moscow, Nov. 26, 1961. He studied piano with Siloti and P. Pabst and composition with Arensky, Ippolitov-Ivanov, and Taneyev at the Moscow Cons. In 1896 he made his debut as a pianist in Moscow. After teaching at the Moscow Phil. School (1904–06), he was a prof. at the Moscow Cons. from 1906 until his death; he also served as its rector (1922–24; 1939–42). Two generations of Russian pianists were his pupils, among them Kabalevsky and Berman. As a pedagogue, he continued the traditions of the Russian school of piano playing, seeking the inner meaning of the music while achieving technical brilliance. He was a frequent visitor at Tolstoy's house near Moscow, and wrote reminiscences of Tolstoy (Moscow, 1922); publ. several essays on piano teaching; also composed chamber music and piano pieces.

Goldman, Edwin Franko, eminent American bandmaster and composer, father of **Richard Franko Goldman;** b. Louisville, Jan. 1, 1878; d. N.Y., Feb. 21, 1956. He studied composition with Dvořák, and cornet with J. Levy and C. Sohst in N.Y. He became solo cornetist of the Metropolitan Opera orch. when he was 21, remaining there for 10 years. For the next 13 years, he taught cornet and trumpet. He formed his first band in 1911. In 1918 the Goldman Band outdoor concerts were inaugurated. His band was noted not only for its skill and musicianship but for its unusual repertoire, including modern works especially commissioned for the band. Goldman was a founder and first president of the American Bandmasters' Assn.; he received honorary D.Mus. degrees from Phillips Univ. and Boston Univ., and medals and other honors from governments and associations throughout the world. He wrote more than 100 brilliant marches, of which the best known is *On the Mall*; also other band music; solos for various wind instruments; studies and methods for cornet and other brass instruments; several songs. He was the author of *Foundation to Cornet or Trumpet Playing* (1914), *Band Betterment* (1934), and *The Goldman Band System* (1936).

Goldman, Richard Franko, distinguished American bandmaster, writer on music, teacher, and composer, son of **Edwin Franko Goldman**; b. N.Y., Dec. 7, 1910; d. Baltimore, Jan. 19, 1980. He graduated from Columbia Univ. in 1931; later studied composition with Boulanger in Paris. He became an assistant of his father in conducting the Goldman Band in 1937; on his father's death in 1956, he succeeded him as conductor; continued to conduct the band into the summer of 1979, when ill health forced him to retire and allow the band to dissolve. He taught at the Juilliard School of Music (1947–60); was a visiting prof. at Princeton Univ. (1952–56); in 1968 he was appointed director of the Peabody Cons. of Music in Baltimore, serving as its president from 1969 to 1977. He was the N.Y. critic for the *Musical Quarterly* (1948–68) and ed. of the *Juilliard Review* (1953–58). He wrote many works for various ensembles: *A Sentimental Journey for Band* (1941); 3 duets for Clarinets (1944); Sonatina for 2 Clarinets (1945); Duo for Tubas (1948); Violin Sonata (1952); etc.; many arrangements for band. A progressive musician, Goldman experimented with modern techniques, and his music combined highly advanced harmony with simple procedures accessible to amateurs.

WRITINGS (all publ. in N.Y. unless otherwise given): *The Band's Music* (1938); *Landmarks of Early American Music, 1760–1800* (1943); *The Concert Band* (1946); *The Wind Band: Its Literature and Technique* (Boston, 1961); *Harmony in Western Music* (1965); D. Klotzman, ed., *Richard Franko Goldman: Selected Essays and Reviews, 1948–1968* (1980).

Goldmann, Friedrich, German conductor, teacher, and composer; b. Siegmar-Schönau, April 27, 1941. After attending Stockhausen's seminar in Darmstadt (summer, 1959), he studied composition with Thilman at the Dresden Hochschule für Musik (1959–62); then attended the master classes of Wagner-Régeny at the Akademie der Künste in East Berlin (1962–64); subsequently took courses in musicology with Knepler and Meyer at Humboldt Univ. in East Berlin (1964–68). In 1973 he received the Hanns Eisler Prize, and later the German Democratic Republic's Arts Prize (1977) and the National Prize (1987). In 1978 he became a member of the Akademie der Künste in East Berlin, and in 1990 was made president of the German section of the ISCM. In 1988 he became conductor at the Berlin Hochschule der Künste, where he was prof. of composition and conducting from 1991.

WORKS: OPERA-FANTASY: *R. Hot bzw. die Hitze* (1976). **ORCH.:** *Essay I–III* (1963–64; 1968; 1971); 4 syms. (1972–73; 1976; 1986; 1988–89); *Musik für Kammerorchester* (1973); Concerto for Trombone and 3 Instrumental Groups (1977); Violin Concerto (1977); Oboe Concerto (1978); Piano Concerto (1979); *Inclinatio temporum* (1981); *Exkursion: Musica per Orchestra con Henrico Sagittario* (1984); *Spannungen aingegrentz* (1988); *Klangszenen I* (1990) and *II* (1994). **CHAMBER:** Trio for Flute, Percussion, and Piano (1966–67); String Trio (1967); Sonata for Wind Quintet and Piano (1969–70); So und So for English Horn, Trombone, and Double Bass (1972); *Cellomusik* (1974); String Quartet (1975); *Zusammenstellung* for Wind Instruments (1976); Piano Trio (1978); *Für P.D. for 15 Strings* (1975); Oboe Sonata (1980); 2 ensemble concertos (1982, 1985); *Sonata a quattro* for 16 Players (1989); *zerbrechlich schwebend*, octet (1990). **VOCAL:** *Odipus Tyrann: Kommentar* for Chorus and Orch. (1968–69); *Sing' Lessing* for Baritone, Flute, Oboe, Clarinet, Horn, Bassoon, and Piano (1978).

Goldmark, Rubin, American pianist, pedagogue, and composer; b. N.Y., Aug. 15, 1872; d. there, March 6, 1936. He was the nephew of the eminent Hungarian composer, Karl (Karoly) Goldmark (b. Keszthely, May 18, 1830; d. Vienna, Jan. 2, 1915). He studied at the College of the City of N.Y. (1889–91), with Door (piano) and R. Fuchs (composition) at the Vienna Cons. (1891), and with Joseffy (piano) and Dvořák (composition) at the National Cons. of Music in America in N.Y. (1891–93). After serving as director of the Colorado Springs College Cons. (1895–1901), he returned to N.Y. to teach privately before being named head of the composition dept. at the Juilliard Graduate School in 1924. He toured as a recitalist in the U.S. and Canada. His compositions were reflective of European traditions, although in several of his works he was inspired by American subjects.

WORKS: ORCH.: *Hiawatha*, overture (1899; Boston, Jan. 13, 1900); *Samson*, tone poem (Boston, March 14, 1914); Requiem, suggested by Lincoln's Gettysburg Address (1918; N.Y., Jan. 30, 1919); *A Negro Rhapsody* (1922; N.Y., Jan. 18, 1923); *The Call of the Plains* (1925; also for Violin and Piano, 1915). **CHAMBER:** Piano Trio (1896); Piano Quintet (1909); Piano Quartet (1910); Violin Sonata; piano pieces, including a sonata. **VOCAL:** Songs and part songs.

BIBL.: A. Copland, "R.G.: A Tribute," *Juilliard Review*, III/3 (1956); D. Tomatz, *R.G., Postromantic: Trial Balances in American Music* (diss., Catholic Univ. of America, 1966).

Goldovsky, Boris, Russian-American pianist, conductor, opera producer, lecturer, and broadcaster, son of **Lea** and nephew of **Pierre Luboshutz**; b. Moscow, June 7, 1908. He studied piano with his uncle and took courses at the Moscow Cons. (1918–21); in 1921 he made his debut as a pianist with the Berlin Phil., and continued his studies with Schnabel and Kreutzer at the Berlin Academy of Music (1921–23); after attending Dohnányi's master class at the Budapest Academy of Music (graduated, 1930), he received training in conducting from Reiner at the Curtis Inst. of Music in Philadelphia (1932). He served as head of the opera depts. at the New England Cons. of Music in Boston (1942–64), the Berkshire Music Center at Tanglewood (1946–61), and the Curtis Inst. of Music (from 1977). In 1946 he founded the New England Opera Theater in

Boston, which became the Goldovsky Opera Inst. in 1963; he also toured with his own opera company until 1984. He was a frequent commentator for the Metropolitan Opera radio broadcasts (from 1946) and also lectured extensively; he prepared Eng. trs. of various operas.

WRITINGS: *Accents on Opera* (1953); *Bringing Opera to Life* (1968); with A. Schoep, *Bringing Soprano Arias to Life* (1973); with T. Wolf, *Manual of Operatic Touring* (1975); with C. Cate, *My Road to Opera* (1979); *Good Afternoon, Ladies and Gentlemen!: Intermission Scripts from the Met Broadcasts* (1984); *Adult Mozart: A Personal Perspective* (4 vols., 1991–93).

Goldsand, Robert, Austrian-American pianist and pedagogue; b. Vienna, March 17, 1911; d. Danbury, Conn., Sept. 16, 1991. He studied piano with Moriz Rosenthal and Emil von Sauer, and theory and composition with Camillo Horn and Joseph Marx in Vienna. After making his debut at age 10 in Vienna, he toured throughout Europe and Latin America; at 16, he made his U.S. debut in a recital at N.Y.'s Town Hall (March 21, 1927). In 1940 he settled in the U.S. and became a teacher at the Cincinnati Cons. while pursuing his concert career. From 1953 to 1990 he taught at the Manhattan School of Music in N.Y. He was best known for his judicious readings of the 19th-century repertory.

Goldsbrough, Arnold (Wainwright), English organist, harpsichordist, and conductor; b. Gomersal, Oct. 26, 1892; d. Tenbury Wells, Dec. 14, 1964. After studies in Bradford, he took courses in double bass, conducting, and composition at the Royal College of Music in London (1920–22). In 1923 he joined its faculty, and concurrently held various posts as an organist. In 1948 he founded his own orch. in London, with which he devoted himself to the performance of early music. In 1960 the orch. became the English Chamber Orch., which subsequently gained a distinguished reputation.

Goldschmidt, Berthold, German-born English composer and conductor; b. Hamburg, Jan. 18, 1903; d. London, Oct. 17, 1996. He studied at the Univ. of Hamburg (1918–22) and took courses in composition (with Schreker) and in conducting at the Berlin State Academy of Music (1922–24). He participated as a répétiteur and celesta player in the premiere of Berg's opera *Wozzeck* in Berlin in 1925. After working as an assistant conductor at the Darmstadt Opera (1927–29), he was a conductor in Berlin with the Radio and the Städtische Oper (from 1931). With the Nazi takeover in 1933, he was dismissed. In 1935 he fled to England and in 1947 became a naturalized British subject. He made numerous appearances as a guest conductor in England. In 1959 he conducted the first complete British performance of Mahler's 3rd Sym. That same year he was consulted by Deryck Cooke on the latter's performing version of Mahler's 10th Sym. Goldschmidt conducted Cooke's first though incomplete reconstruction of the sym. in a London recording studio on Dec. 19, 1960. He conducted the first complete performance of the sym. at a London Promenade Concert on Aug. 13, 1964. Goldschmidt's inability to secure a performance of his opera *Beatrice Cenci* led him to cease composing in 1958. It was nearly 25 years before he broke his silence with his Clarinet Quartet of 1983. By the end of the 1980s he had been "discovered," and was composing again with renewed vigor. Several of his works were either lost during World War II (*Passacalia* for Orch. and *Requiem* for Chorus and Orch.) or were withdrawn by the composer (Sym. and Harp Concerto).

WORKS: DRAMATIC: OPERAS: *Der gewaltige Hahnrei* (1929–30; Mannheim, Feb. 14, 1932); *Beatrice Cenci* (1949; concert version, London, April 16, 1988; stage version, Magdeburg, Sept. 10, 1994). **BALLET:** *Chronica* for 2 Pianos (1938; orch. suite, 1958). **ORCH.:** Overture to Shakespeare's *Comedy of Errors* (1925); *Ciaccona Sinfonica* (1936); *Greek Suite* (1940–41); Sinfonietta (1945–46); Violin Concerto (1951–55; expansion of a Concertino, 1933); Cello Concerto (1952; expansion of a Concertino, 1933); Clarinet Concerto (1954); *Intrada* for Wind or Sym. Orch. (1985–86). **CHAMBER:** 4 string quartets (1926; 1936; 1988–89; 1992); Clarinet Quartet (1983); Piano Trio (1985); *Retrospective*, string trio (1991); *Fantasy* for Oboe, Cello, and Harp (1991); *Capriccio* for Violin (1992). **PIANO:** 2 sonatas (1921, not extant; 1926); *Variations on a Palestine Shepherd's Song* (1934); *Scherzo* and *From the Ballet*, 2 pieces (1957–58). **VOCAL:** *Zwei Betrachtungen* for Chamber Chorus, Speaker, Piano, and Percussion (1931; renamed *Letzte Kapitel*, 1984); *Mediterranean Songs* for Voice and Orch. (1958); choruses; solo songs.

BIBL.: D. Matthews, "B.G.: A Biographical Sketch," *Tempo* (March 1983); M. Struck, "Evidence from a Fragmented Musical History; Notes on B.G.'s Chamber Music," ibid. (Sept. 1990); S. Hilger and W. Jacobs, eds., *B. G.* (Bonn, 1993).

Goldschmidt, Harry, Swiss-born German musicologist; b. Basel, June 17, 1910; d. Dresden, Nov. 19, 1986. He was educated in Basel at the Cons. and the Univ. After working as a music critic in Basel (1933–49), he settled in East Berlin, where he received his Ph.D. in 1958 from the Humboldt Univ. In 1949–50 he was head of the music dept. of the East Berlin Radio, and then taught music history at the Hochschule für Musik (1950–55). From 1956 to 1965 he was director of the Central Inst. of Musicology. He publ. *Franz Schubert* (Berlin, 1954; 6th ed., 1976) and *Um die Sache der Musik: Vorträge und Aufsätze* (Leipzig, 1970; 2nd ed., aug., 1976). He also ed. *Beethoven-Studien* (Leipzig, I, 1974, II, 1977, and III, 1975), *Zu Beethoven: Aufsätze und Annotationen* (Berlin, 1979), and *Zu Beethoven, 2: Aufsätze und Dokumente* (Berlin, 1984).

Goldstein, Mikhail, Russian violinist, musicologist, teacher, and composer; b. Odessa, Nov. 8, 1917; d. Hamburg, Sept. 7, 1989. While still an infant, he took violin lessons with Stoliarsky in Odessa, where he made his debut at 5; at 13, he became a pupil of Yampolsky (violin) at the Moscow Cons., where he also studied with Miaskovsky (composition) and Saradzhev (conducting). After he married a German woman, the Soviet authorities discriminated against him. In witty retaliation, he claimed to have found a sym. written in 1810 by one Ovsianiko-Kulikovsky. The sym. was hailed as a major find. When Goldstein admitted that it was actually a work of his own, he was denounced as an imposter attempting to appropriate a Russian treasure. With his career in eclipse, he went to East Berlin in 1967. After teaching violin in Jerusalem (1967–69), he became a prof. at the Hamburg Hochschule für Musik in 1969. He also was active as a concert artist. Goldstein pursued legitimate research in Russian and German musical biography of the 18th and 19th centuries.

WORKS: ORCH.: 4 syms. (1934, 1936, 1944, 1945); 2 violin concertos (1936, 1939); Piano Concerto (1940); *Niccòlo Paganini*, symphonic poem (1963); *Ukrainian Rhapsody* (1965); *Kinderszenen* (1966); *Hamburger Konzert* for Chamber Orch. (1975). **CHAMBER:** 3 string quartets (1932, 1940, 1975); Piano Trio (1933); 4 violin sonatas (1935, 1940, 1950, 1975); *Ukrainian Suite* for Violin and Piano (1952); Duo for Violin and Double Bass (1979); Quartet for 4 Violas (1982).

Goléa, Antoine, Austrian-born French writer on music of Romanian descent; b. Vienna, Aug. 30, 1906; d. Paris, Oct. 12, 1980. He studied at the Bucharest Cons. (1920–28). After further training at the Sorbonne in Paris (1928–31), he settled in that city as a journalist. His wife was the soprano Colette Herzog (1923–86).

WRITINGS (all publ. in Paris unless otherwise given): *Pelléas et Mélisande, analyse poétique et musicale* (1952); *Esthétique de la musique contemporaine* (1954); *L'Avénement de la musique classique, de Bach à Mozart* (1955); *Recontres avec Pierre Boulez* (1958); *Georges Auric* (1958); *Recontres avec Olivier Messiaen* (1959); *La Musique dans la société européenne depuis le moyen âge jusqu'a nos jours* (1960); *L'Aventure de la musique au XXe siècle* (1961); with A. Hodier and C. Samuel, *Panorma de l'art musical contemporaine* (1962); *Vingt ans de musique contemporaine* (1962); *J.-S. Bach* (1963); *Claude Debussy: L'homme et son oeuvre* (1965); *Richard Strauss* (1965);

Entretiens avec Wieland Wagner (1967; German tr., 1968); *Histoire du ballet* (Lausanne, 1967); *Marcel Landowski: L'homme et son oeuvre* (1969); *Je suis un violoniste raté* (1973); *La Musique de la nuit des temps aux aurores nouvelles* (1977).

Goleminov, Marin, Bulgarian composer and pedagogue; b. Kjustendil, Sept. 28, 1908. He studied at the Bulgarian State Academy of Music in Sofia (graduated, 1931), in Paris with d'Indy (composition) and Labé (conducting) at the Schola Cantorum, with Dukas (composition) at the École Normale de Musique, and aesthetics and music history at the Sorbonne (1931–34), and with J. Haas (composition) and H. Knappe and E. Erenberg (conducting) at the Munich Akademie der Tonkunst (1938–39). From 1943 he taught at the Bulgarian State Academy of Music, where he was a prof. of orchestration, composition, and conducting, and its rector. From 1965 to 1967 he was director of the National Opera. He received various honors from the Bulgarian government. In 1976 he was awarded the Gottfried von Herder Prize of the Univ. of Vienna. In 1991 he became a member of the Bulgarian Academy of Sciences. He publ. books in Sofia on the sources of Bulgarian musical composition (1937), instrumentation (1947), orchestration (2 vols., 1953; 3rd ed., 1966), and on the creative process (1971). In his music, he utilized folk elements, particularly the asymmetrical rhythms of Bulgarian folk motifs, in a fairly modern but still quite accessible idiom.

WORKS: DRAMATIC: OPERAS: *Ivailo* (1958; Sofia, Feb. 13, 1959); *Zlatnata ptica* (The Golden Bird; Sofia, Dec. 20, 1961); *Zahari the Icon Painter* (1971; Sofia, Oct. 17, 1972); *Thracian Idols* (1981). **BALLETS:** *Nestinarka* (1940; Sofia, Jan. 4, 1942); *The Daughter of Kaloyan* (Sofia, Dec. 23, 1973). **ORCH.:** *The Night*, symphonic poem (1932); *Prelude, Aria and Toccata* for Piano and Orch. (1947–53); 2 cello concertos (1949–50; 1992); *Poem* (1959); Concerto for String Quartet and String Orch. (1963; Moscow, Feb. 11, 1964); 4 syms.: No. 1, *Children's Symphony* (1963), No. 2 (1967; Sofia, March 6, 1968), No. 3, *Peace in the World* (1970; Sofia, April 21, 1971), and No. 4, *Shopophonia* (1978); Violin Concerto (1968); *Aquarelles* for Strings (1973); Piano Concerto (1975); *Diptyque* for Flute and Orch. (1982); Oboe Concerto (1983); *Concert* for Strings (1993). **CHAMBER:** 8 string quartets (1934; 1938; 1944; *Micro-quartet*, 1967; 1969; 1975; 1977; 1983); 2 wind quintets (1936, 1946); Trio for Oboe, Clarinet, and Bassoon (1964); Sonata for Solo Cello (1969); *Concert* for Brass Quintet (1978). **VOCAL:** *Father Paissy*, cantata (1966); *The Titan*, oratorio (Sofia, June 25, 1972); *Ballad of the April Insurrection* for Soloists, Chorus, and Orch. (1976); *Symphonic Impressions on the Picture of a Master* for Voice and Orch. (1982); Sym.-Cantata for Soloist, Chorus, and Orch. (1993); choruses; songs.

BIBL.: B. Arnaudova, *M. G.* (Sofia, 1968); S. Lazarov, *M. G.* (Sofia, 1971); R. Apostolova, *M. G.* (Sofia, 1988); L. Braschowanowa and M. Miladinova, *M. G.: Biobibliografski ocherk* (Sofia, 1990).

Golestan, Stan, Romanian-born French composer and music critic; b. Vaslui, June 7, 1875; d. Paris, April 21, 1956. He settled in Paris and studied composition and orchestration with d'Indy, Roussel, and Dukas at the Schola Cantorum (1895–1903); he then was a music critic for *Le Figaro*. In 1915 he won the Enesco Prize for composition.

WORKS: ORCH.: *La Dembovitza* (1902); *Lăutarul şi Cobzarul* (1902); Sym. (1910); *Rapsodie roumaine* (1912); *Rapsodie concertante* for Violin and Orch. (1920); *Concerto roumain* for Violin and Orch. (1933); *Concerto moldave* for Cello and Orch. (1936); Piano Concerto, *Sur les cîmes des Carpathiques* (1938). **CHAMBER:** Sonata for Piano and Violin (1906–08); 2 string quartets (1927, 1938); Sonatina for Flute and Piano (1932); *Ballade roumaine* for Harp (1932); *Arioso et Allegro de concert* for Viola and Piano (1933); *Eglogue* for Clarinet and Piano (1933); *Elégie et Danse rustique* for Oboe and Piano (1938). **PIANO:** *Poèmes et paysages* (1922); *Thème, Variations et Danses* (1927). **VOCAL:** Songs.

Golovanov, Nikolai (Semyonovich), Russian conductor, composer, and pedagogue; b. Moscow, Jan. 21, 1891; d. there, Aug. 28, 1953. He studied choral conducting with Kastalsky at the Synodal School in Moscow, graduating in 1909; then entered the composition classes of Ippolitov-Ivanov and Vassilenko at the Moscow Cons. After graduation in 1914, he was engaged as assistant chorus master at the Bolshoi Theater in Moscow; was its chief conductor (1919–28; 1948–53); was also chief conductor of the Moscow Phil. (1926–29), the U.S.S.R. All-Union Radio Sym. Orch. (1937–53), and the Stanislavsky Opera Theater (1938–53). He was awarded the Order of the Red Banner in 1935, and was 4 times recipient of the 1st Stalin Prize (1946, 1948, 1950, 1951). He wrote an opera, *Princess Yurata*; Sym.; symphonic poem, *Salome*, after Oscar Wilde; numerous piano pieces; songs. He was married to **Antonina Nezhdanova**.

BIBL.: N. Anosov, "N. G.," *Sovetskaya Musyka* (May 1951).

Golschmann, Vladimir, notable French-born American conductor of Russian descent; b. Paris, Dec. 16, 1893; d. N.Y., March 1, 1972. He studied violin and piano, and received training at the Paris Schola Cantorum in harmony, counterpoint, and composition. He played violin in orchs. in Paris, where he founded the Concerts Golschmann in 1919, at which he conducted many premieres of contemporary works; he also conducted opera and from 1920 was a conductor of ballet for Diaghilev. In 1923 he conducted in the U.S. for the first time with Les Ballets Suédois, and returned in 1924 as a guest conductor of the N.Y. Sym. Orch. A successful engagement as a guest conductor of the St. Louis Sym. Orch. in 1931 led to his appointment that year as its music director, a position he held with distinction for 27 years. In 1947 he became a naturalized American citizen. He later was music director of the Tulsa Phil. (1958–61) and the Denver Sym. Orch. (1964–70). Throughout his long career, he appeared as a guest conductor in North America and Europe. In addition to the 20th-century repertory, Golschmann's brilliance as an interpreter was at its best in the colorful works of the Romantic era.

BIBL.: J. Titzler, "V.G., Conductor," *Le Grand Baton* (Sept.–Dec. 1979).

Goltz, Christel, German soprano; b. Dortmund, July 8, 1912. She studied in Munich with Ornelli-Leeb. In 1935 she joined the chorus of the Fürth Opera, where she soon made her operatic debut as Agathe; from 1936 to 1950 she was a member of the Dresden State Opera; also sang with the Berlin State Opera and the Berlin City Opera. In 1951 she sang Salome at her debut at London's Covent Garden. From 1951 to 1970 she made many appearances with the Vienna State Opera; in 1952 she was named a Kammersängerin. On Dec. 15, 1954, she made her Metropolitan Opera debut in N.Y. as Salome, remaining on its roster for the season. She sang in many productions of modern operas.

Golubev, Evgeny, Russian composer and pedagogue; b. Moscow, Feb. 16, 1910; d. there, Dec. 25, 1988. He studied composition with Miaskovsky at the Moscow Cons., graduating in 1936. He joined the faculty of his alma mater upon graduation and taught special courses in polyphonic composition. Several well-known Soviet composers were his students, among them Khrennikov, Eshpai, and Schnittke.

WORKS: BALLET: *Odysseus* (1965). **ORCH.:** 7 syms. (1933, 1937, 1942, 1947, 1960, 1966, 1972); 3 piano concertos (1944, 1948, 1956); Cello Concerto (1958); Viola Concerto (1962); Violin Concerto (1970). **CHAMBER:** 19 string quartets; 2 string quintets; 10 piano sonatas. **VOCAL:** 2 oratorios: *Return of the Sun* (1936) and *Heroes Are Immortal* (1946); many choruses.

Golyscheff, Jefim, Russian composer and painter; b. Kherson, Sept. 20, 1897; d. Paris, Sept. 25, 1970. He studied violin in Odessa; in 1909, in the wake of anti-Jewish pogroms, he went to Berlin, where he studied chemistry as well as music theory; at the same time, he began to paint in the manner of Abstract

Expressionism. He played a historic role in the development of the serial methods of composition; his String Trio, written about 1914 and publ. in 1925, contains passages described by him as "Zwölftondauer-Komplexen," in which 12 different tones are given 12 different durations in the main theme. As both a painter and a musician, he was close to the Dada circles in Berlin, and participated in futuristic experiments. On April 30, 1919, he presented at a Dada exhibition his *Anti-Symphonie*, subtitled *Musikalische Kreisguillotine*, with characteristic titles of its movements: 1, *Provocational Injections*; 2, *Chaotic Oral Cavity, or Submarine Aircraft*; and 3, *Clapping in Hyper F-sharp Major*. On May 24, 1919, he appeared at a Dada soirée with a piece entitled *Keuchmaneuver*. All this activity ceased with the advent of the Nazis in 1933. Golyscheff fled to Paris, but after the fall of France in 1940 he was interned by the Vichy authorities. His life was probably spared because of his expertise as a chemist; he was conscripted as a cement laborer. In 1956 he went to Brazil, where he devoted himself exclusively to painting. In 1966 he returned to Paris.

BIBL.: D. Gojowy, "J. G., der unbequeme Vorläufer," *Melos* (May–June 1975).

Gombosi, Otto (János), eminent Hungarian musicologist; b. Budapest, Oct. 23, 1902; d. Natick, Mass., Feb. 17, 1955. He studied piano with Kovács and composition with Weiner and Siklós at the Budapest Academy of Music; then musicology with Hornbostel, Sachs, and Wolf at the Univ. of Berlin (Ph.D., 1925, with the diss. *Jacob Obrecht: Eine stilkritische Studie*; publ. in Leipzig, 1925). From 1926 to 1928 he ed. the progressive Hungarian music periodical *Crescendo*. In 1939 he went to the U.S.; was a lecturer in music at the Univ. of Wash., Seattle (1940–46); then taught at Michigan State Univ. and the Univ. of Chicago (1949–51); from 1951 to 1955, was a prof. at Harvard Univ. He contributed numerous valuable papers to various periodicals, in Hungarian, German, Italian, and English; among his most important writings were *Bakfark Bálint élete és müvei (Der Lautenist Valentine Bakfark)* (in Hungarian and German; Budapest, 1935) and *Tonarten und Stimmungen der antiken Musik* (Copenhagen, 1939).

Gomez, Jill, British Guianan soprano; b. New Amsterdam, Sept. 21, 1942. She studied in London at the Royal Academy of Music and the Guildhall School of Music. After her operatic debut in a minor role in *Oberon* with the Cambridge Univ. Opera in 1967, she sang Adina with the Glyndebourne Touring Opera in 1968. In 1969 she made her first appearance at the Glyndebourne Festival as Mélisande. On Dec. 2, 1970, she created the role of Flora in Tippett's *The Knot Garden* at London's Covent Garden. She appeared as the Countess in Musgrave's *The Voice of Ariadne* with the English Opera Group in 1974. In 1977 she sang Tatiana at the Kent Opera. On March 25, 1979, she created the title role in the posthumous premiere of Prokofiev's *Maddalena* on the BBC. She appeared as the Governess in Britten's *The Turn of the Screw* at the English National Opera in London in 1984. She also sang opera in Glasgow, Cardiff, Zürich, Geneva, Frankfurt am Main, Lyons, and other cities. Among her other roles were Fiordiligi, Donna Anna, Handel's Cleopatra, Berlioz's Teresa, Bizet's Leïla, and Britten's Helena. As a concert artist, she was engaged for many appearances in Europe and North America.

Gomezanda, Antonio, Mexican pianist and composer; b. Lagos, Jalisco, Sept. 3, 1894; d. Mexico City, March 26, 1961. He studied composition in Berlin. Returning to Mexico, he taught piano at the National Cons. (1921–29) and at the Univ. of Mexico (1929–32). Among his works was an "Aztec ballet," *Xiuhtzitzquilo* (Berlin, Feb. 19, 1928).

Gomez Martínez, Miguel Angel, Spanish conductor; b. Granada, Sept. 17, 1949. After piano studies with his mother, he enrolled at the Granada Cons.; also studied composition, piano, and violin at the Madrid Cons.; later attended the conducting classes of Boult and Leinsdorf the Berkshire Music Center at Tanglewood; then studied with Markevitch in Madrid and Swarowsky in Vienna. He was music director of the St. Pölten Stadttheater (1971–72) and principal conductor of the Lucerne Stadttheater (1972–74); in 1973 he conducted at the Deutsche Oper in Berlin; was subsequently its resident conductor (1974–77). In 1976 he was made resident conductor at the Vienna State Opera; also conducted in Berlin, Munich, Hamburg, London (at Covent Garden), Geneva, and Paris; in 1980 he made his U.S. debut, conducting at the Houston Grand Opera. From 1984 to 1987 he was principal conductor of the Orquestra Sinfónica de Radiotelevisión Española in Madrid. He was artistic director and chief conductor of the Teatro Lérico Nacional in Madrid from 1985 to 1991. In 1990 he became Generalmusikdirektor in Mannheim. He then served as chief conductor of the National Opera in Helsinki (from 1993), and of the Hamburg Sym. Orch. (from 1993).

Gondek, Juliana (Kathleen), American soprano; b. Pasadena, Calif., May 20, 1953. She studied at the Univ. of Southern Calif. in Los Angeles (B.M., 1975; M.M., 1977), and also attended the Britten-Pears School of Advanced Musical Studies in Aldeburgh. After singing with the San Diego Opera (1979–81), she appeared in 1983 with the Baltimore Opera and sang Giovanna d'Arco with the N.Y. Grand Opera. She won the gold medals at the Geneva (1983) and Francisco Viñas (Barcelona, 1984) competitions; then appeared as Mozart's Countess with the Netherlands Opera in Amsterdam (1986). In 1987 she sang Alcina with the Opera Theatre of St. Louis and Bianca with the Greater Miami Opera. She made her Metropolitan Opera debut in N.Y. as Marianne in *Der Rosenkavalier* on Sept. 25, 1990. In 1991 she appeared as Vitellia with Glasgow's Scottish Opera and as Elvira with the Seattle Opera. Gondek also pursued wide-ranging concert engagements with major orchs. in North America and Europe; also appeared at leading festivals and as a recitalist.

Gönnenwein, Wolfgang, German conductor, pedagogue, and operatic administrator; b. Schwäbisch-Hall, Jan. 29, 1933. He was educated at the Stuttgart Hochschule für Musik and at the Univs. of Heidelberg and Tübingen. In 1959 he became conductor of the South German Madrigal Choir of Stuttgart, with which he toured Germany and Europe. In 1968 he was made prof. of choral conducting at the Stuttgart Hochschule für Musik, and in 1973 was named its director. He also was conductor of the Bach Choir of Cologne (1969–73) and later Intendant of the Württemberg State Theater in Stuttgart (1985–92).

González-Avila, Jorge, Mexican composer; b. Mérida, Yucatán, Dec. 10, 1925. He studied with Francisco Agea Hermosa (piano), R. Halffter (composition), Galindo (harmony), and Hernández Moncada (theory) at the National Cons. in Mexico City (1949–53), with Bal y Gay (1952), and with Chávez (1953). He then devoted himself mainly to teaching and composing. While his output included some orch., chamber, and vocal pieces, he concentrated his compositional skills on producing an extensive catalogue of solo piano music.

Good, Daniel (Seinfel), American clarinetist, composer, teacher, and writer on music; b. N.Y., Jan. 24, 1936. After studies in philosophy at the Oberlin (Ohio) Cons. of Music (B.A., 1957), he studied with Cowell and Luening at Columbia Univ. in N.Y. (M.A., 1962) and with Gaburo and Oliveros at the Univ. of Calif. at San Diego (1968–70). In 1983 he co-founded the DownTown Ensemble in N.Y.; also was a founding member of Gamelan Son of Lion. In 1971 he became an assistant prof. at Livingston College, Rutgers Univ.; in 1981, became a prof at its Mason Gross School of the Arts. As a composer, Good combines the techniques of process music with improvisation. His *Clarinet Songs* (1979–91), an evening-length suite comprised of 16 independent settings, explores non-traditional notations, circular breathing, and alternate, microtonal fingerings, all of which conspire to produce unusual, often striking timbres. A collection of his writings was publ. as *From Notebooks 1968–* (Lebanon, N.H., 1984).

WORKS: *Orbits* for 6 Moving Bodies and 2 Instrumentalists (1970); *Circular Thoughts* for Clarinet (1974); *Phrases of the*

Hermit Thrush for Clarinet (1974; also for Clarinet and Orch., 1979); *The Thrush from Upper Dunakyn* for Bass Recorder (1974); *Cage's DREAM dreamed* for Piano (1977); *Stamping in the Dark* for an unspecified number of stamping individuals (1977); *Circular Thoughts* for Gamelan Ensemble (1978); *Clarinet Songs* for Clarinet (1979–91); *Eine Kleine Gamelan Music* for Gamelan Ensemble (1980); *40 Random Numbered Clangs* for Gamelan Ensemble (1980); *Wind Symphony* for Wind Band (1980); *Fiddle Studies* for Woodwind Quartet (1981); *Semaphores* for Gamelan Ensemble (1981); *Cape Breton Concerto* for 6 Traditional Fiddlers, Traditional (Scottish) Piano, and Symphonic Band (1982); *The Red and White Cows* for unspecified instrumentation (1985; also for Violin, Viola, and Piano); *Shaking Music* for an unspecified number of moving instrumentalists (1986); *The Shouting Opera*, intermedia piece with slides, video, dance, music, computer speech, and audience participation (1986); *Diet Polka* for Accordion and Instruments obbligato (1987); *Tunnel-Funnel* for 15 Instruments (1988); *Flower Forms I, II, III* for Wind Ensemble (1988–90); *Clothesline* for Soprano and 8 Instruments (1992); *UFOs Made Me Do It* for Computer Voice (1992); *Nod Drama* for (unspecified) Mixed Ensemble (1993); *Pornography Made Me Do It Again* for Computer Voices (1993); *Eight Thrushes, Accordion and Bagpipe* for 10 Mixed Winds and Strings (1994).

Goodall, Sir Reginald, notable English conductor; b. Lincoln, July 13, 1901; d. Barham, May 5, 1990. He studied piano, violin, and conducting at the Royal College of Music in London, and later pursued his training in Munich and Vienna. In 1936 he made his debut conducting *Carmen* in London, and became a répétiteur at Covent Garden there. From 1936 to 1939 he was assistant conductor of the Royal Choral Soc. in London. His decision to join the British Union of Fascists just 5 days after Hitler invaded Poland in 1939 undoubtedly played a role in delaying his career opportunities. From 1944 to 1946 he was a conductor at the Sadler's Wells Opera in London, where he was chosen to conduct the premiere of Britten's *Peter Grimes* on June 7, 1945. From 1946 to 1961 he was on the conducting staff at Covent Garden, but then was relegated to the position of a répétiteur there from 1961 to 1971. Thereafter he again had the opportunity to conduct there. In 1968 he emerged as a major operatic conductor when he conducted a remarkable performance of *Die Meistersinger von Nürnberg* in English at the Sadler's Wells Opera. In 1973 he conducted an acclaimed traversal of the *Ring* cycle there in English. In subsequent years, he was ranked among the leading Wagnerian interpreters of the day. In 1975 he was made a Commander of the Order of the British Empire. He was knighted in 1985.

BIBL.: J. Lucas, *Reggie: The Life of R.G.* (London, 1993).

Goode, Richard (Stephen), American pianist; b. N.Y., June 1, 1943. He was a pupil of Elvira Szigeti (1949–52) and Claude Frank (1952–54); subsequently was an extension student at the Mannes College of Music in N.Y. (1954–56), where he trained with Nadia Reisenberg (piano), Carl Schachter (theory), and Carl Bamberger (conducting). He studied with Serkin in Marlboro, Vt., and then privately (1960) and at the Curtis Inst. of Music in Philadelphia (1961–64), where he also studied with Horszowski. After attending the City College of the City Univ. of N.Y. (1964–67), he completed his training at the Mannes College of Music (1967–69; B.S., 1969). On Feb. 12, 1962, he made his formal debut in N.Y.; his European debut followed at the Festival of Two Worlds in Spoleto, Italy, in 1964. In 1967 he became a member of the Boston Sym. Chamber Players; from 1969 to 1979 he was a member of the Chamber Music Soc. of Lincoln Center in N.Y. His career as a solo artist was enhanced with his capture of the 1st prize at the Clara Haskil competition in 1973; in 1980 he was awarded the Avery Fisher Prize. He made various appearances as a soloist with orchs. and as a recitalist; also appeared with the Chamber Music Soc. of Lincoln Center again from 1983 to 1989. A non-specialist, he won praise as a virtuoso soloist, compelling recitalist, committed chamber music performer, and sensitive accompanist. His repertoire ranges from the standard literature to contemporary scores.

Goodman (real name, **Guttmann**), **Alfred,** German-American composer; b. Berlin, March 1, 1920. After training in Berlin, he went to England in 1939 and then to the U.S. in 1940, and subsequently served in the U.S. Army. Following studies with Cowell and Luening at Columbia Univ. (B.S., 1952; M.A., 1953), he returned to Germany in 1960 and was a composer and broadcaster with the Bavarian Radio in Munich; he later was its music adviser (1971–85). In 1973 he received his Ph.D. from the Free Univ. of Berlin, and then taught at the Munich Hochschule für Musik (from 1976). He publ. *Musik von A–Z* (Munich, 1971) and *Sachwörterbuch der Musik* (Munich, 1982).

WORKS: OPERAS: *The Audition* (1948–54; Athens, Ohio, July 27, 1954); *Der Läufer* (1969); *The Lady and the Maid* (1984). **ORCH.:** 2 syms. (1949, 1962); *Prelude '51* (1951); Sinfonietta (1952); *Uptown-Downtown* (1954); Clarinet Concerto (1959); *Mayfair Overture* (1961); *Capriccio Transatlantique* (1968); *Balkan Panorama* (1969); *A Yankee in Schwabing* (1969); *3 Essays* for Harpsichord and Strings (1972); *Pro Memoria* (1974). **CHAMBER:** 2 string quartets (1950, 1959); Trumpet Sonata (1950); Violin Sonata (1960); *Brass Quintet in 7 Rounds* (1963); *5 Sequences* for Woodwind Quartet (1969); *2 Soliloquies* for Double Bass (1976); *Across the Board* for Brass Ensemble (1978); *Brassology for 11* (1984–85); *Direction L.A.* for 4 Trumpets and 4 Trombones (1985); piano pieces; organ music. **VOCAL:** Choral pieces; songs.

Goodman, Benny (actually, **Benjamin David**), famous American clarinetist and bandleader; b. Chicago, May 30, 1909; d. N.Y., June 13, 1986. He was 10 when he commenced musical studies at Chicago's Kehelah Jacob Synagogue. At 11, he became a member of the boys club band at Jane Addams' Hull House, where he took lessons with James Sylvester, its director. He also pursued classical clarinet training with Franz Schoepp. He was only 12 when he made his professional debut at Chicago's Central Park Theatre. During his high school years, he made appearances with the so-called Austin High School Gang. In 1925 he went to Los Angeles to join Ben Pollock's band, returning with it to Chicago in 1926 to make his first recording. In 1928 he proceeded to N.Y. with the band, which he left in 1929 to pursue work as a freelance artist in radio and on recordings. In 1934 he formed his first big band, which won success on the NBC radio show "Let's Dance" in 1934–35. He also formed the Benny Goodman Trio in 1935 with Teddy Wilson and Gene Krupa, which soon proved a success. On Aug. 21, 1935, Goodman appeared with his big band at the Palomar Ballroom in Los Angeles, an engagement broadcast on nationwide radio. Goodman became an overnight sensation and soon acquired acclaim as the "King of Swing." In 1936 he expanded his trio to a quartet by engaging Lionel Hampton, which added to his success. Goodman also regularly employed black musicians in his big band, being one of the first noted white musicians to break the color line. He and his band appeared in films for the first time in *The Big Broadcast of 1937.* On Jan. 16, 1938, he made history when he presented the first jazz concert at N.Y.'s Carnegie Hall. In the meantime, he also pursued his interest in the classical clarinet. On Nov. 4, 1938, he made his public recital debut at N.Y.'s Town Hall. Following studies with Reginald Kell, he devoted part of his time to engagements as a soloist with the major U.S. orchs. He also commissioned scores from several composers, including Bartók's *Contrasts* (1938) and the clarinet concertos of Copland (1947) and Hindemith (1947). Goodman continued to lead various bands and small groups in later years. He made his first tour of Europe in 1950. In 1956–57 he played throughout the Far East. He later toured South America (1961), the Soviet Union (1962), and Japan (1964). On Jan. 17, 1978, he appeared with a specially formed big band at Carnegie Hall to celebrate the 40th anniversary of his first engagement there. With I. Kolodin, he publ. *The Kingdom of Swing* (N.Y., 1939). In addition to his many jazz and classical recordings, he also recorded the sound track for the film *The Benny Goodman Story* (1955). Goodman was the premier jazz clarinetist of his era, excelling as a master of improvisational virtuosity. He also distinguished himself as a classical musician of fine taste.

BIBL.: D. Connor and W. Hicks, *B.G. on the Record* (New Rochelle, N.Y., 1969); S. Baron, *King of Swing: A Pictorial Biography* (N.Y., 1979); F. Kappler and G. Simon, *Giants of Jazz: B.G.* (Alexandria, Va., 1979); D. Connor, *The Record of a Legend: B.G.* (N.Y., 1984); idem, *B.G.: Listen to his Legacy* (Metuchen, N.J., 1988); J. Collier, *B.G. and the Swing Era* (N.Y., 1989); R. Firestone, *Swing, Swing, Swing: The Life and Times of B.G.* (N.Y., 1993).

Goodrich, (John) Wallace, American organist, conductor, and writer on music; b. Newton, Mass., May 27, 1871; d. Boston, June 6, 1952. He studied at the New England Cons. of Music in Boston (organ with Dunham, composition with Chadwick); then in Munich with Rheinberger (1894–95) and with Widor in Paris. In 1897 he returned to Boston and became an instructor at the New England Cons. of Music; was appointed dean in 1907, and in 1931 director, a post he held until 1942. He was organist of the Boston Sym. Orch. from 1897 to 1909. He founded the Choral Art Soc. in 1902, and was its conductor until 1907; was also conductor of the Cecilia Soc., the Boston Opera Co., and the Worcester County Choral Assn. He composed an *Ave Maria* for Chorus and Orch. (Munich, 1895) and other choral music; wrote *The Organ in France* (Boston, 1917).

Goodson, Katharine, English pianist; b. Watford, Hertfordshire, June 18, 1872; d. London, April 14, 1958. From 1886 to 1892 she was a pupil of O. Beringer at the Royal Academy of Music in London, and from 1892 to 1896 of Leschetizky in Vienna. She made her debut in London at a Saturday Popular Concert, Jan. 16, 1897, with signal success; then made tours of England, France, Austria, and Germany, which established her reputation; her American debut, with the Boston Sym. Orch., took place on Jan. 18, 1907; she subsequently made many tours of the U.S., the Netherlands, Belgium, and Italy. In 1903 she married **Arthur Hinton**.

Goossens, prominent family of English musicians of Belgian descent:

(1) Eugène Goossens, conductor; b. Bruges, Feb. 25, 1845; d. Liverpool, Dec. 30, 1906. He studied violin at the Bruges Cons. and violin and composition at the Brussels Cons.; in 1873 he went to London, where he appeared as an operetta conductor; was 2nd conductor (1883–89) and principal conductor (1889–93) of the Carl Rosa Opera Co., then settled in Liverpool, where he was founder-conductor of the Goossens Male Voice Choir (from 1894).

(2) Eugène Goossens, violinist and conductor, son of the preceding; b. Bordeaux, Jan. 28, 1867; d. London, July 31, 1958. He studied in Bruges and at the Brussels Cons. (1883–86); then went to England, where he worked as a violinist, répétiteur, and assistant conductor under his father with the Carl Rosa Opera Co.; also continued his studies at London's Royal Academy of Music (1891–92). After conducting various traveling opera companies, he served as principal conductor of the Carl Rosa Opera Co. (1899–1915); later was a conductor with the British National Opera Co. He had the following 4 children, who became musicians:

(3) Sir (Aynsley) Eugene Goossens, distinguished conductor and composer; b. London, May 26, 1893; d. there, June 13, 1962. He first studied at the Bruges Cons. (1903–04), then at the Liverpool College of Music. After winning a scholarship to the Royal College of Music in London in 1907, he studied there with Rivarde (violin), Dykes (piano), and C. Wood and Stanford (composition). He was a violinist in the Queen's Hall Orch. (1912–15), then was assistant conductor to Beecham (1915–20). In 1921 he founded his own London orch.; conducted opera and ballet at Covent Garden (1921–23). After serving as conductor of the Rochester (N.Y.) Phil. (1923–31), he greatly distinguished himself as conductor of the Cincinnati Sym. Orch. from 1931 to 1947. He then was conductor of the Sydney (Australia) Sym. Orch. and director of the New South Wales Conservatorium (1947–56). In 1955 he was knighted. He was a discriminating interpreter of the late 19th- and early 20th-century repertoire of the Romantic and Impressionist schools. As a composer, he wrote in all genres; his style became a blend of impressionistic harmonies and neo-Classical polyphony; while retaining a clear tonal outline, he often resorted to expressive chromatic melos bordering on atonality. He publ. *Overture and Beginners: A Musical Autobiography* (London, 1951).

WORKS: DRAMATIC: *L'École en crinoline*, ballet (1921); *East of Suez*, incidental music to Maugham's play (1922); *Judith*, opera (1925; London, June 25, 1929); *Don Juan de Mañana*, opera (1934; London, June 24, 1937). **ORCH.:** *Variations on a Chinese Theme* (1911); *Miniature Fantasy* for Strings (1911); *Perseus*, symphonic poem (1914); *Ossian*, symphonic prelude (1915); *The Eternal Rhythm* (London, Oct. 19, 1920); *Sinfonietta* (London, Feb. 19, 1923); *Rhythmic Dance* (Rochester, N.Y., March 12, 1927); Concertino for Double String Orch. (1928); Oboe Concerto (London, Oct. 2, 1930, L. Goossens soloist); 2 syms.: No. 1 (Cincinnati, April 12, 1940) and No. 2 (BBC, Nov. 10, 1946); *Fantasy-Concerto* for Piano and Orch. (Cincinnati, Feb. 25, 1944, José Iturbi soloist, composer conducting). **CHAMBER:** Suite for Flute, Violin, and Harp (1914); *5 Impressions of a Holiday* for Flute, Cello, and Piano (1914); *Phantasy Quartet* for Strings (1915); 2 string quartets (1916, 1942); *By the Tarn* and *Jack o' Lantern*, 2 sketches for String Quartet (1916); 2 violin sonatas (1918, 1930); Piano Quintet (1919); *Lyric Poem* for Violin and Piano (1921; also for Violin and Orch.); String Sextet (1923); *Pastoral and Harlequinade* for Flute, Oboe, and Piano (1924); *Fantasy* for Wind Instruments (1924). **PIANO:** *Kaleidoscope*, suite (1917–18); *4 Conceits* (1918). **VOCAL:** *Silence* for Chorus and Piano (1922); *Apocalypse*, oratorio (1951; Sydney, Nov. 22, 1954, composer conducting).

(4) Marie (Henriette) Goossens, harpist; b. London, Aug. 11, 1894; d. Dorking, Surrey, Dec. 18, 1991. She studied at the Royal College of Music in London. She made her debut in Liverpool in 1910, then was principal harpist at Covent Garden, the Diaghilev Ballet, the Queen's Hall Orch. (1920–30), the London Phil. (1932–39), the London Sym. Orch. (1940–59), and the London Mozart Players (from 1972). She was also prof. of harp at the Royal College of Music (1954–67). In 1984 she was made an Officer of the Order of the British Empire. Her autobiography was publ. as *Life on a Harp String* (1987).

(5) Leon Goossens, eminent oboist; b. Liverpool, June 12, 1897; d. Tunbridge Wells, Feb. 13, 1988. He studied at the Royal College of Music in London (1911–14). He played in the Queen's Hall Orch. (1914–24), and later in the orchs. of Covent Garden and the Royal Phil. Soc.; subsequently was principal oboe of the London Phil. (1932–39); was also prof. of oboe at the Royal Academy of Music (1924–35) and the Royal College of Music (1924–39). In succeeding years, he appeared as a soloist with major orchs. and as a chamber music artist; in 1962 he suffered injuries to his lips and teeth as a result of an automobile accident, but after extensive therapy he was able to resume his virtuoso career. He commissioned works from several English composers, among them Elgar and Vaughan Williams. In 1950 he was made a Commander of the Order of the British Empire.

(6) Sidonie Goossens, harpist; b. Liscard, Cheshire, Oct. 19, 1899. She studied at the Royal College of Music in London. She made her orch. debut in 1921; was principal harpist of the BBC Sym. Orch. in London (1930–80); served as prof. of harp at the Guildhall School of Music there (from 1960). She was made a Member of the Order of the British Empire in 1974 and an Officer of the Order of the British Empire in 1981.

BIBL.: C. Rosen, *The G.* (London, 1993).

Gorchakov (real name, **Zweifel**), **Sergei,** Russian conductor, teacher, arranger, and composer; b. Moscow, Feb. 10, 1905; d. there, July 4, 1976. He studied conducting with Saradzhev at the Moscow Cons., graduating in 1929. From 1939 to 1952 he conducted the orch. of the All-Union Soviet Radio; from 1960 he taught orchestration at the Inst. of Military Band Conducting. He became particularly interested in the problem of orch. arrangements; in 1959 he submitted a diss. on specific problems of transcribing piano music for wind orchestra, for which he received the degree of candidate of arts and sciences. He also publ. a practical manual of orchestration for wind orch. (Moscow, 1962). He made numerous orch. arrangements of piano music; of these, particularly notable was his orchestration of Mussorgsky's *Pictures at an Exhibition*.

Gorchakova, Galina, compelling Russian soprano; b. Novokuznetsk, March 1, 1962. She was born into a musical family, her father being a baritone and her mother a soprano. She studied at the Novokuznetsk Academy of Music and Cons. From 1988 to 1990 she sang with the Sverdlovsk Opera. During this time, she also appeared as a guest artist throughout Russia. In 1990 she made her debut at the Kirov Opera in St. Petersburg as Yaroslavna in *Prince Igor.* She secured her position as one of the company's leading artists shortly thereafter with her stunning portrayal of Renata in *The Fiery Angel.* In 1991 she sang Renata again in a concert performance in London, and again in 1992 with the visiting Kirov Opera at the Metropolitan Opera in N.Y. On Jan. 4, 1995, she made her debut with the Metropolitan Opera as Cio-Cio San. Later that year she sang in Rome, Los Angeles, Edinburgh, and London, and appeared as Tosca at the Opéra de la Bastille in Paris. In 1996 she was engaged as Cio-Cio San at Milan's La Scala and as Tosca at London's Covent Garden. She also pursued a highly successful career as a recitalist. In addition to her compelling interpretations of the Russian operatic repertoire, Gorchakova has won distinction in operas by Verdi and Puccini.

Gordeli, Otar, Russian composer; b. Tiflis, Nov. 18, 1928. He studied composition with Andrei Balanchivadze; later took courses at the Moscow Cons., graduating in 1955. In 1959 he was appointed instructor at the Tbilisi Cons. In his music, he applied resources of native folk songs; his polyphonic structure was considerably advanced.

WORKS: Piano Concerto (1952); *The Seasons*, cantata for Narrator, Boys' Chorus, and Chamber Orch. (1955); Concertino for Flute and Orch. (1958); *Festive Overture* (1959); *Georgian Dance* for Orch. (1961); Sym. (1964); film music; jazz pieces.

Gordon, Jacques, Russian-American violinist and teacher; b. Odessa, March 7, 1899; d. Hartford, Conn., Sept. 15, 1948. He made his debut in Odessa at age 7; after graduating from the Odessa Cons. (1913), he emigrated to the U.S., where he studied with Kneisel (violin) and Goetschius (theory) at N.Y.'s Inst. of Musical Art. He played in the Russian Sym. Orch. in N.Y. and then was concertmaster of the Chicago Sym. Orch. (1921–31); also played in the Berkshire String Quartet (1917–20). He founded the Gordon String Quartet (1930), and led it until 1947; also was conductor of the Hartford (Conn.) Sym. Orch. (1936–39). He taught at the American Cons. of Music in Chicago (from 1921) and at the Eastman School of Music in Rochester, N.Y. (from 1942).

Górecki, Henryk (Mikołaj), celebrated Polish composer; b. Czernica, Dec. 6, 1933. He received training in music in Rybnik (1952–55), and then was a composition student of Szabelski at the Katowice Cons. (1955–60). While a student there, he was honored with an all-Górecki concert on Feb. 27, 1958, which included premieres of five of his works; in 1960 his *Monologhi* for Soprano and 3 Instrumental Groups won 1st prize in the Polish Composers' Union competition. His *Scontri* for Orch. created a great stir at its premiere at the Warsaw Autumn Festival on Sept. 21, 1960. In 1961 he was active in Paris, where his 1st Sym. won 1st prize in the 2nd Biennale. He also met Boulez there and Stockhausen in Cologne. Until 1963 Górecki followed a confirmed modernist course as a composer. With his *3 Pieces in Old Style* for String Orch. (Warsaw, April 30, 1964), he instituted a "white note" modal idiom, inspired by medieval Polish music, which which was to become prominent in all of his later vocal scores. His *Ad Matrem* for Soprano, Chorus, and Orch. (Warsaw, Sept. 24, 1972) consoliated this modal idiom for the ensuing decade; the work won 1st prize at the International Composers' Forum in Paris in 1973. In 1973–74 Górecki was in Berlin under the auspices of the Deutscher Akademischer Austauschdienst. In 1975 he became rector of the Katowice Cons. He then composed what would later become his most famous score, the 3rd Sym., *Symphony of Lamentation Songs* for Soprano and Orch. (Royan, April 4, 1977). The three movements of the work (1, a Lamentation of the Holy Cross Monastery of the 15th century; 2, the prayer of 18-year-old Helena Wanda Blazusiakowna inscribed on her Gestapo cell wall in Zakopane during World War II; 3, a folk song of the Opole region) made a profound impression upon auditors in the waning years of an unlamented century marked by man's inhumanity to man. For Pope John Paul II's first visit as Pope to his Polish homeland in 1979, Górecki composed his *Beatus Vir* for Baritone, Chorus, and Orch., which was premiered in the presence of the Pope in Kraków on June 9 of that year. Later that year, Górecki was compelled to resign his post as rector of the Katowice Cons. in the face of pressure from the Communist government. In the wake of the Communist regime's attempts to destroy the Solidarity movement, Górecki was moved to compose his *Miserere* for Chorus in 1981, a work finally premiered in Włocławek on Sept. 10, 1987. With the end of Communist rule in 1989, Górecki was free to pursue his career unfettered as one of Poland's foremost composers in a style notable both for its uniqueness and for its highly refined spirituality.

WORKS: ORCH.: *Pieśni o radości i rytmie* (Songs of Joy and Rhythm) for 2 Pianos and Chamber Orch. (1956; Katowice, Feb. 27, 1958; rev. 1960; London, July 8, 1990); 3 syms.: No. 1, *1959*, for Strings and Percussion (Warsaw, Sept. 14, 1959), No. 2, *Copernican*, for Soprano, Baritone, Chorus, and Orch. (1972; Warsaw, June 22, 1973), and No. 3, *Symfonia pieśni żalosnych* (Symphony of Lamentation Songs), for Soprano and Orch. (1976; Royan, April 4, 1977); *Scontri* (Collisions; Warsaw, Sept. 21, 1960); *Trzy utwory w dawnym stylu* (Three Pieces in Old Style) for Strings (1963; Warsaw, April 30, 1964); *Choros I* for Strings (Warsaw, Sept. 22, 1964); *Refren* (Refrain; Geneva, Oct. 27, 1965); *Muzyka staropolska* (Old Polish Music) for Brass and Strings (1967–69; Warsaw, Sept. 24, 1969); *Canticum Graduum* (Düsseldorf, Dec. 11, 1969); *3 Dances* (Rybnik, Nov. 24, 1973); Concerto for Harpsichord or Piano and Strings (harpsichord version, Katowice, March 2, 1980); *Concerto-Cantata* for Flute and Orch. (Amsterdam, Nov. 28, 1992). **CHAMBER:** *Variations* for Violin and Piano (1956; Katowice, Feb. 27, 1958); *Quartettino* for 2 Flutes, Oboe, and Violin (1956; Katowice, Feb. 27, 1958); *Sonatina in 1 Movement* for Violin and Piano (1956); Sonata for 2 Violins (1957; Katowice, Feb. 27, 1958); Concerto for 5 Instruments and String Quartet (1957; Katowice, Feb. 27, 1958); *3 Diagrams* for Flute (1959; Warsaw, Sept. 21, 1961); *Diagram IV* for Flute (1961); *Genesis I: Elementi* for String Trio (Kraków, May 29, 1962) and *II: Canti Strumentali* for 15 Players (Warsaw, Sept. 16, 1962); *Muzyczka* (Musiquette) *I* for 2 Trumpets and Guitar (1967), *II* for 4 Trumpets, 4 Trombones, 2 Pianos, and Percussion (Warsaw, Sept. 23, 1967), *III* for Violas (Katowice, Oct. 20, 1967), and *IV* for Trombone, Clarinet, Cello, and Piano (Wieden, April 15, 1970); *3 Little Pieces* for Violin and Piano (1977; Katowice, Jan. 5, 1978); *Lullabies and Dances* for Violin and Piano (1982); *Recitatives and Ariosos: Lerchenmusik* for Clarinet, Cello, and Piano (1984–85; Warsaw, Sept. 25, 1985); *For You, Anne-Lill* for Flute and Piano (1986–90; Lerchenborg, Aug. 4, 1990); *Aria* for Tuba, Piano, Tam-tam, and Bass Drum (1987); 2 string quartets: No. 1, *Already it is Dusk* (1988; Minneapolis, Jan. 21, 1989) and No. 2, *Quasi una Fantasia* (1990–91; Cleveland, Oct. 27, 1991); *Kleines Requiem für eine Polka* for Piano and 13 Instruments (Amsterdam, June 12, 1993); Piece for String Quartet (1993; N.Y., Jan. 20, 1994). **KEYBOARD: PIANO:** *4 Preludes* (1955; Katowice, Jan. 30, 1970); *Toccata* for 2 Pianos (1955; Katowice, Feb. 27, 1958); Sonata (1956–90; Helsinki, March 17, 1991); *Lullaby* (1956); *Z ptasiego gniazda* (From the Bird's

Nest), 5 little preludes (1956); (4) *Sundry Pieces* (1956–90); *Mazurkas* (1980); *Intermezzo* (1990). **ORGAN:** *Cantata* (1968; Kamień Pomorski, July 18, 1969). **VOCAL:** *3 Songs* for Medium Voice and Piano (1956); *2 Songs of Lorca* for Medium Voice and Piano (1956, 1980); *Epitafium* for Chorus and Instruments (Warsaw, Oct. 3, 1958); *Monologhi* for Soprano and 3 Instrumental Groups (1960; Berlin, April 26, 1968); *Genesis III: Monodrama* for Soprano, Metal Percussion, and 6 Double Basses (1963); *Do Matki* (Ad Matrem) for Soprano, Chorus, and Orch. (1971; Warsaw, Sept. 24, 1972); *2 Sacred Songs* for Baritone and Orch. (1971; Poznań, April 6, 1976; also for Baritone and Piano); *Euntes Ibant et Flebant* for Chorus (1972; Wroclaw, Aug. 31, 1975); *2 Little Songs of Tuwim* for Chorus of 4 Equal Voices (1972); *Amen* for Chorus (1975); *Beatus Vir* for Baritone, Chorus, and Orch. (Kraków, June 9, 1979); *Szeroka woda* (Broad waters), 5 folk songs for Chorus (1979); *Blogoslawione Pieśni Malinowe* (Blessed Raspberry Songs) for Voice and Piano (1980); *Miserere* for Chorus (1981; Włocławek, Sept. 11, 1987); *Wieczor ciemny się uniża* (Dark evening is falling), folk songs for Chorus (1981); *Wisło moja, Wisło szara* (My Vistula, Grey Vistula), folk song for Chorus (1981; Poznań, April 28, 1987); *2 Songs of Słowacki* for Voice and Piano (1983; Zakopane, Sept. 14, 1985); *3 Lullabies* for Chorus (1984; rev. version, Lerchenborg, Aug. 2, 1991); *Ach, mój wianku lewandowy* (O my little garland of lavender), folk song for Chorus (1984); *Idzie chmura, pada deszcz* (Cloud comes, rain falls), folk song for Chorus (1984); *Zdrowaś bądź Maryja* (5 Marian Songs) for Chorus (1985); *O Domina Nostra*, meditation on the Black Madonna, for Soprano and Organ (Poznań, March 31, 1985; rev. version, London, July 7, 1990); *Under Your Protection*, Marian song for Chorus (1985); *Angelus Domini* for Chorus (1985); *Totus Tuus* for Chorus (Warsaw, July 19, 1987); *Come Holy Spirit*, church song for Chorus (1988); *Dobra Noc* (Good Night), "in memoriam Michael Vyner," for Soprano, Alto Flute, Piano, and 3 Tam-tams (London, Nov. 4, 1990).

Gorini, Gino (actually, **Luigino**), Italian pianist, teacher, and composer; b. Venice, June 22, 1914; d. there, Jan. 27, 1989. He studied with Tagliapietra (piano diploma, 1931) and Agostini (composition diploma, 1933) at the Venice Cons., and also had composition lessons with Malipiero. He was a prof. of piano at the Venice Cons. from 1940, and also made tours as a pianist in Italy and abroad. He publ. *La musica pianistica di G. Francesco Malipiero* (Florence, 1977).

WORKS: DRAMATIC: Film scores. **ORCH.:** *Maschere* for Small Orch. (1934); *Tre omaggi* (1934); Suite for Violin and Orch. (1934); *Due studi da concerto* for Piano and Orch. (1935); Flute Concerto (1935); Sym. (1936); *Introduzione e arioso* (1937); *Due Invenzioni* for Piano and Orch. (1937); Violin Concerto (1943); Piano Concerto (1948); *Serenata* for Strings, Harpsichord, and Percussion (1966); Concerto for Viola, Piano, and Orch. (1974). **CHAMBER:** *Contrasti* for 5 Instruments (1934); *Divertimento* for 8 Instruments (1935); Concertino for Chamber Group (1935); *Tempo di sonata* for Violin and Piano (1935); String Quartet (1937); Cello Sonata (1939); *Canto notturno* for Cello and Piano (1945); Piano Quintet (1948); Sonata for Solo Violin (1982). **PIANO:** Sonata (1936); 10 *Preludi brevi* (1941); *Ricercare e Toccata* (1960).

Goritz, Otto, German baritone; b. Berlin, June 8, 1873; d. Hamburg, April 11, 1929. He received his musical education from his mother, Olga Nielitz. He made his debut on Oct. 1, 1895, as Matteo (*Fra Diavolo*) at Neustrelitz; his success led to an immediate engagement for 3 years; from 1898 to 1900 he was in Breslau; from 1900 to 1903, in Hamburg. On Dec. 24, 1903, he made his American debut at the Metropolitan Opera in N.Y. as Klingsor in the first production of *Parsifal* outside Bayreuth; remained there until 1917. In 1924 he returned to Germany, where he sang in Berlin and Hamburg.

Gorney, Jay, Polish-American composer; b. Bialystok, Dec. 12, 1896; d. N.Y., June 14, 1990. He emigrated to the U.S. as a child; studied music at the Univ. of Mich. in Ann Arbor. Beginning in 1924 he wrote a number of scores and separate songs for Broadway. His N.Y. revue *Americana* (1932) featured the celebrated Depression-era song *Brother, Can You Spare a Dime?*

Gorodnitzki, Sascha, Russian-born American pianist and pedagogue; b. Kiev, May 24, 1904; d. N.Y., April 4, 1986. He was taken to the U.S. at an early age. After piano lessons with his mother, he studied with Edwin Hughes at N.Y.'s Inst. of Musical Art; he then was a pupil of J. Lhévinne (piano) and Goldmark (composition) at N.Y.'s Juilliard Graduate School (1926–32). In 1931 he made his formal debut as soloist with the N.Y. Phil., and then made tours throughout North America and Latin America. He also taught at the Juilliard Summer School from 1932, and then was a member of the piano faculty at the Juilliard School of Music from 1948 until his death. Among his outstanding students were Eugene Istomin and Garrick Ohlsson.

Gorr, Rita (real name, **Marguerite Geirnaert**), noted Belgian mezzo-soprano; b. Zelzaete, Feb. 18, 1926. She was a student in Ghent of Poelfiet and in Brussels of Pacquot-d'Assy. After winning 1st prize in the Verviers Competition in 1946, she made her formal operatic debut as Fricka in Antwerp in 1949, and then sang in Strasbourg (1949–52). In 1952 she won 1st prize in the Lausanne Competition, which led to engagements at the Opéra-Comique and the Opéra in Paris that same year. In 1958 she appeared at the Bayreuth Festival for the first time. In 1959 she made her debut at London's Covent Garden as Amneris, where she sang regularly with notable success until 1971. In 1960 she sang at Milan's La Scala for the first time as Kundry. She made her Metropolitan Opera debut in N.Y. as Amneris on Oct. 17, 1962, and remained on its roster until 1967. Gorr was a remarkably versatile artist, excelling in the works of Wagner and Verdi as well as in the French repertory. Among her memorable roles were Fricka, Kundry, Ortrud, Azucena, Eboli, Amneris, Ulrica, Charlotte, Dalila, and Berlioz's Dido.

Gossett, Philip, esteemed American musicologist; b. N.Y., Sept. 27, 1941. He was educated at Amherst College (B.A., 1963), Columbia Univ. (1961–62), and Princeton Univ. (M.F.A., 1965; Ph.D., 1970, with the diss. *The Operas of Rossini: Problems of Textual Criticism in Nineteenth-Century Opera*); held a Fulbright fellowship (1965–66) and a Guggenheim fellowship (1971–72). He joined the faculty at the Univ. of Chicago in 1968, where he was a prof. (from 1977) and chairman of the music dept. (1978–84). From 1995 to 1996 he was president of the American Musicological Soc. He ed. and tr. Rameau's *Traité de l'harmonie* as *Treatise on Harmony by Jean-Philippe Rameau* (N.Y., 1971); with C. Rosen, he ed. *Early Romantic Opera* (44 vols., N.Y., 1977–83); also ed. *Italian Opera 1810–1840* (58 vols., N.Y., 1984–); also served as general ed. of *The Works of Giuseppe Verdi*. He publ. *The Tragic Finale of Tancredi* (Pesaro, 1977), *Le Sinfonie di Rossini* (Pesaro, 1981), and *Anna Bolena and the Artistic Maturity of Gaetano Donizetti* (Oxford, 1985), for which he received the ASCAP-Deems Taylor Award in 1986.

Gostuški, Dragutin, Serbian composer and musicologist; b. Belgrade, Jan. 3, 1923. He studied art history at the Univ. of Belgrade (Ph.D., 1965); also took courses in composition and conducting at the Belgrade Academy of Music; subsequently was active as a music critic. In 1952 he was engaged as a member of the staff of the Musicological Inst. of the Serbian Academy of Arts and Sciences; in 1974 he became its director. His works include a symphonic poem, *Belgrade* (Belgrade, June 11, 1951); *Concerto accelerato* for Violin and Orch. (Belgrade, Nov. 14, 1961); a fantastic ballet, *Remis* (1955; 1st stage perf., Zagreb, May 15, 1963); chamber music; piano pieces; songs.

Gotovac, Jakov, Croatian conductor and composer; b. Split, Oct. 11, 1895; d. Zagreb, Oct. 16, 1982. He studied law at the Univ. of Zagreb, and music with Antun Dobronić in Zagreb and with Joseph Marx in Vienna. In 1923 he was appointed conductor of the Croatian National Opera in Zagreb, retaining this post until 1958. He composed mostly for the theater; his instrumental music is imbued with the folkways of Croatia, enhancing the simple native materials by carefully proportioned modernistic mutations while preserving the impulsive asymmetrical patterns of the original songs.

WORKS: OPERAS: *Dubravka* (1928); *Morana* (Brno, Nov. 29, 1930); *Ero s onoga svijeta* (A Rogue from the World Beyond; Zagreb, Nov. 2, 1935; in Ger. as *Ero der Schelm*, Karlsruhe, April 3, 1938); *Kamenik* (The Quarry; Zagreb, Dec. 17, 1946); *Mila Gojsalica* (Zagreb, May 18, 1952); *Stanac* (Zagreb, Dec. 6, 1959); *Dalmaro* (Zagreb, Dec. 20, 1964); *Petar Svačiç*, opera-oratorio (1969). **ORCH.:** *Simfonijsko kolo* (Zagreb, Feb. 6, 1927); *Orači* (Ploughmen; 1937); *Pjesme i ples za Balkana* (Balkan Song and Dance) for Strings (1939); *Guslar* (Gusla Player; Zagreb, Oct. 7, 1940); *Bunjevačka igra* (1960); *Dalmatinsko pastirče* (Dalmatian Shepherd) for Recorders (1962). **OTHER:** Choral pieces; songs.

Gottlieb, Jack, American composer; b. New Rochelle, N.Y., Oct. 12, 1930. He was a student of Rathaus at Queens College in N.Y. (B.A., 1953), of Fine at Brandeis Univ. (M.F.A., 1955), of Copland and Blacher at the Berkshire Music Center in Tanglewood (summers, 1954–55), and of Phillips and Palmer at the Univ. of Ill. (D.M.A., 1964, with the diss. *The Music of Leonard Bernstein: A Study of Melodic Manipulations*). From 1958 to 1966 he was Bernstein's assistant at the N.Y. Phil. After serving as music director of Temple Israel in St. Louis (1970–73), he returned to N.Y. and was composer-in-residence (1973–75) and assistant prof. (1975–77) at the School of Music at Hebrew Union College-Jewish Inst. of Religion. From 1977 he worked for Amberson Enterprises, the company responsible for Bernstein's musical activities. After Bernstein's death, he served as an archivist-consultant for the Bernstein Estate. He also was president of the American Soc. for Jewish Music from 1991. In both his secular and sacred music, Gottlieb has followed a generally contemporary course.

WORKS: DRAMATIC: *Tea Party*, opera (1955; Athens, Ohio, Aug. 4, 1957); *Public Dance*, opera (1964); *The Song of Songs, Which is Solomon's*, operatorio (1968–76); *The Movie Opera* (1982; rev. 1994); *Death of a Ghost*, opera (N.Y., Dec. 13, 1988); *After the Flood*, musical fable (1990–91; rev. 1995); *Monkey Biz'nis*, musical diversion (1991–93); *Love, Divorce, and Other Considerations*, theater piece (1994–95). **ORCH.:** *Pieces of 7*, overture (Jacksonville, Fla., Oct. 23, 1962); *Articles of Faith* (1965; Detroit, April 14, 1966). **CHAMBER:** Clarinet Quartet (1952); *Pastorale and Dance* for Violin and Piano (1953); String Quartet (1954); *Twilight Crane* for Woodwind Quintet (1961; N.Y., March 24, 1962); piano pieces, including a Sonata (1960; N.Y., Feb. 9, 1963) and *The Silent Flickers*, 12 diversions for Piano, 4-hands (1968; rev. as *13 Diversions* for Piano and Piccolo-Flute Obbligato, 1981); organ music. **VOCAL:** *Hoofprints*, 3 songs for Soprano and Piano (1954; rev. 1963; N.Y., March 8, 1964); *Kid's Calls* for Chorus and Piano (1957; Urbana, Ill., Feb. 23, 1958); *In Memory of . . .* , cantata for Tenor, Chorus, and Organ (N.Y., March 18, 1960); *Love Songs for Sabbath*, Friday Evening Service for Cantor, Chorus, and Organ (N.Y., May 7, 1965; also with Optional Reader and Dancer, White Plains, N.Y., May 12, 1966); *Downtown Blues for Uptown Halls*, 3 songs for Woman's Voice, Clarinet, and Piano (1967; rev. 1977; N.Y., March 26, 1978); *Shout for Joy*, Psalms for Mostly Unison Chorus, Piano, 2 Flutes, and 3 Drums (1967; N.Y., Jan. 19, 1969); *New Year's Service for Young People* for Chorus (St. Louis, Oct. 1, 1970); *Verses from Psalm 118* for Chorus and Organ (St. Louis, June 6, 1973); *Sharing the Prophets* for Soloists, Chorus, Piano, Double Bass, and Percussion (1975; N.Y., March 14, 1976); *Psalmistry* for Soli, Chorus, and 11 Players (1978–79; N.Y., Oct. 12, 1980); *Presidential Suite*, 7 pieces for Chorus (1989; N.Y., Oct. 27, 1990); *Solitaire*, song cycle for Tenor and Piano (1988–91; N.Y., Feb. 25, 1992); *Scrapbook*, cabaret song cycle for Tenor and Piano (1988–91; N.Y., March 31, 1992); *The English Lesson* for Soprano, Mezzo-soprano or Alto, and Piano (1993); *If* for Voice and Piano or Organ (1994).

Gottwald, Clytus, German choral conductor, musicologist, and composer; b. Bad Salzbrunn, Silesia, Nov. 25, 1925. He received training in voice, choral conducting, and musicology at the Univ. of Tübingen, and also took courses in sociology, theology, and folklore. He completed his education at the Univ. of Frankfurt am Main (Ph.D., 1961, with the diss. *Johannes Ghiselen—Johannes Verbonnet: Stilkritische Untersuchung zum Problem ihrer Identität*; publ. in Wiesbaden, 1962). In 1960 he founded the Schola Cantorum Stuttgart, a polyphonic vocal ensemble he conducted in enterprising concerts until 1990. In addition to works of the 15th and 16th ceturies, he also conducted contemporary avant-garde scores. From 1969 to 1989 he was an ed. for new music for the South German Radio in Stuttgart. He contributed valuable articles to many journals and other publications on subjects ranging from early music to the avant-garde, from Josquin to John Cage. He ed. the complete works of Ghiselen in Corpus Mensurabilis Musicae, XXIII/1–4 (1961–68) and publ. *Codices musici* (series 1, *Die Handschriften der Württembergischen Landesbibliothek Stuttgart*, Wiesbaden, 1964; series 2, *Die Handschriften der ehemals Königlichen Hofbibliothek*, Wiesbaden, 1965) and *Katalog der Musikalien in der Schermar-Bibliothek Ulm* (Wiesbaden, 1993). As a composer, he tended toward the experimental, producing a number of advanced vocal works.

Goudoever, Henri Daniel van, Dutch cellist, conductor, and composer; b. Utrecht, Nov. 12, 1898; d. The Hague, March 3, 1977. He studied cello privately, then attended classes in composition with Johan Wagenaar at the Utrecht Cons. (1913–16); completed his cello studies with Charles van Isterdael in Utrecht (1916–18) and Gérard Hekking in Paris (1918–21). He appeared as soloist in some of his own works with the N.Y. Phil. (1921–22); was then 1st cellist of the Amsterdam Concertgebouw Orch. (1922–24); then served as conductor in Coburg, Bavaria, at the behest of the exiled King Ferdinand of Bulgaria (1924–32); subsequently conducted the Utrecht Municipal Orch. (1932–37). In 1937 he abandoned music and became a disciple of Rudolf Steiner, founder of the Anthroposophical Soc.; traveled as a speaker and monitor of anthroposophy until his death. He composed *La Fête bleue*, symphonic poem for Cello and Orch. (1917); *Sphynx*, nocturne for Orch. (1919); pieces for cello.

Gould, Glenn (Herbert), remarkable and individualistic Canadian pianist; b. Toronto, Sept. 25, 1932; d. there, Oct. 4, 1982. His parents were musically gifted and fostered his precocious development; he began to play piano, and even compose, in his childhood. At the age of 10, he entered the Royal Cons. of Music in Toronto, where he studied piano with Alberto Guerrero, organ with Frederick C. Silvester, and theory with Leo Smith, graduating in 1945 at the age of 13. He made his debut in Toronto on May 8, 1946. As he began practicing with total concentration on the mechanism of the keyboard, he developed mannerisms that were to become his artistic signature. He reduced the use of the pedal to a minimum in order to avoid harmonic "haze"; he cultivated "horizontality" in his piano posture, bringing his head down almost to the level of the keys. He regarded music as a linear art; this naturally led him to an intense examination of Baroque structures; Bach was the subject of his close study rather than Chopin; he also cultivated performances of Sweelinck, Gibbons, and other early keyboard masters. He played Mozart with emphasis on the early pianoforte techniques; he largely omitted the Romantic composers Chopin, Schumann, and Liszt from his repertoire, although he favored an early sonata by Richard Strauss. He found the late sonatas of Beethoven more congenial to his temperament, as well as the piano works of the modern Vienna school—Schoenberg, Berg, and Webern—perhaps because of their classical avoidance of purely decorative tonal formations. Actually, his selective but challenging repertoire ranged widely, from the 16th century to jazz. Following his U.S. debut in Washington, D.C., on Jan. 2, 1955, he evoked unequivocal praise at his concerts, but in 1964 he abruptly terminated his stage career and devoted himself exclusively to recording. This enabled him to perform unfettered by the presence of an audience and to select the best portions of the music he played in the studio, forming a mosaic unblemished by accidental mishaps. Certainly part of the interest he aroused with the public at large was due to mannerisms that marked his behavior on the stage. He used a 14-inch-high chair that placed his eyes almost at the level of the keyboard; he adopted informal dress; he had a rug put under the piano and a glass of distilled water within easy reach. He was in constant fear of bodily injury; he avoided shaking hands with the conductor after playing a concerto (he actually sued the Steinway piano company for a large sum of money when an enthusiastic representative shook his hand too vigorously). He also had an unshakable habit of singing along with his performance, even allowing his voice to be audible on his carefully wrought, lapidary recordings. Nonetheless, Gould acquired a devoted following, and a small coterie of friends, despite the fact that he was quite reclusive; he found release from his self-imposed isolation in editing a series of radio documentaries for the CBC, entitled "The Idea of North," three of which aired as "solitude tragedies." Symbolically, they were devoted to the natural isolation of the Canadian Arctic, the insular life of Newfoundland, and the religious hermetism of the Mennonite sect. Fittingly, upon his death in 1982, 7 days after a stroke from which he never recovered, it was learned that Gould had bequeathed his estate in equal portions to the A.S.P.C.A. (Assn. for the Prevention of Cruelty to Animals) and to the Salvation Army. In 1994 his life became the subject of a successful film, *Thirty-Two Short Films About Glenn Gould.* He was also made the invisible protagonist of Thomas Bernhart's immensely entertaining novel, *The Loser.* A selection of his writings is contained in T. Page, ed., *The Glenn Gould Reader* (N.Y., 1985). J. Roberts and G. Guertin ed. a selection of his letters (Oxford, 1992).

BIBL.: G. Paysant, *G. G.: Music and Mind* (Toronto, 1978; rev. ed., 1984); J. Cott, *Conversations with G. G.* (Boston, 1984); W. Matheis, *G. G.: Der Unheilige am Klavier* (Munich, 1987); O. Friedrich, *G. G.: A Life and Variations* (N.Y., 1989); A. Kazdin, *G. G. at Work: Creative Lying* (N.Y., 1989); J. Hagestedt, *Wie spielt G. G.?: Zu einer Theorie der Interpretation* (Munich, 1991); E. Angilette, *Philosopher at the Keyboard: G. G.* (Metuchen, N.J., 1992); M. Stegemann, *G. G.: Leben und Werk* (Munich, 1992).

Gould, Morton, extraordinarily talented American composer and conductor; b. N.Y., Dec. 10, 1913. He composed his first work when he was only 6. At 8, he received a scholarship to the Inst. of Musical Art in N.Y. At 13, he also commenced piano lessons with Abby Whiteside, and later studied harmony and counterpoint with Vincent Jones. With the coming of the Great Depression, Gould was compelled to quit high school and earn his keep playing piano on the vaudeville circuit. He also played in movie theaters and toured in the Gould and Shefter piano duo. He worked as an arranger, composer, and conductor for WOR Radio (1934–42) and for CBS (1942–45) in N.Y. Gould secured his reputation as a composer with his *Spirituals* for orch., which he conducted in its premiere in N.Y. on Feb. 9, 1941. Several of his eminently accessible scores became notably popular via the radio, and many of his works were taken up by the leading American orchs. He toured widely as a guest conductor throughout North America and abroad, leading programs not only of his own works but also by other composers with aplomb. In 1986 he was elected a member of the American Academy and Inst. of Arts and Letters. From 1986 to 1994 he served as president of ASCAP. In 1994 he received a Kennedy Center Honor. He was awarded the Pulitzer Prize in Music in 1995 for his *String Music.* Gould's remarkable versatility as a composer was admirably revealed in various genres. While he was notably successful in producing works of broad appeal in a popular vein, he also wrote a number of scores in a more serious mode. He was especially masterful in creating works for the orch.

WORKS: DRAMATIC: MUSICALS: *Billion Dollar Baby* (N.Y., Dec. 21, 1945); *Arms and the Girl* (N.Y., Feb. 2, 1950). **BALLETS:** *Interplay* (N.Y., Oct. 17, 1945); *Fall River Legend* (N.Y., April 22, 1947; orch. suite, San Francisco, Jan. 6, 1949); *Fiesta* (Cannes, March 17, 1957); *Clarinade* (1964); *I'm Old Fashioned, Astaire Variations* (N.Y., June 16, 1983). **FILM SCORES:** *Delightfully Dangerous* (1945); *Cinerama Holiday* (1955); *Windjammer* (1958). **TELEVISION SCORES:** *World War I* (1964–65); *Holocaust* (1978; orch. suite, NBC-TV, April 1978; band suite, Tempe, Ariz., May 29, 1980, composer conducting); *Celebration '81* (1981). **ORCH.:** *3 American Symphonettes* (1933, 1935, 1937); *Chorale and Fugue in Jazz* for 2 Pianos and Orch. (1934; N.Y., Jan. 2, 1936); Piano Concerto (1934; WOR Radio, N.Y., June 16, 1938); Violin Concerto (1938); *Foster Gallery* (1939; Pittsburgh, Jan. 12, 1940); *A Homespun Overture* (1939); *Latin-American Symphonette* (N.Y., Feb. 22, 1941); *Spirituals* (N.Y., Feb. 9, 1941); *Lincoln Legend* (N.Y., Nov. 1, 1942); *Cowboy Rhapsody* (1942); *American Salute* (1943); 6 syms.: No. 1 (Pittsburgh, March 5, 1943), No. 2, *On Marching Tunes* (N.Y., June 2, 1944), No. 3 (Dallas, Feb. 16, 1947, composer conducting; rev. version, N.Y., Oct. 28, 1948), No. 4, *West Point Symphony* for Band (West Point, N.Y., April 13, 1952, composer conducting), No. 5, *Symphony of Spirituals* (Detroit, April 1, 1976), and No. 6, *Centennial Symphony: Gala* for Band (Austin, Texas, April 9, 1983, composer conducting); Viola Concerto (1943); *Concerto for Orchestra* (Cleveland, Feb. 1, 1945); *Harvest* for Vibraphone, Harp, and Strings (St. Louis, Oct. 27, 1945); *Minstrel Show* (Indianapolis, Dec. 21, 1946); *Holiday Music* (1947); *Philharmonic Waltzes* (N.Y., Nov. 16, 1948); *Guajira* for Clarinet and Orch. (1949); *Serenade of Carols* (1949); *Big City Blues* (1950; also for Band); *Family Album,* suite (1951); *Tap Dance Concerto* (Rochester, N.Y., Nov. 16, 1952, composer conducting); *Inventions* for Piano Quartet and Orch. (N.Y., Oct. 19, 1953); *Dance Variations* for 2 Pianos and Orch. (N.Y., Oct. 24, 1953); *Showpiece* (Philadelphia, May 7, 1954); *Hoofer Suite* for Tap Dancer and Orch. (1956); *Jekyll and Hyde Variations* (1956; N.Y., Feb. 2, 1957); *Cafe Rio* (1957); *Dialogues* for Piano and Strings (N.Y., Nov. 3, 1958); *Spirituals* for Harp and Strings (1961); *Calypso Souvenir* (1964); *Festive Music* (1964; Rock Island, Ill., Jan. 16, 1965, composer conducting); *Columbia: Broadsides* (Washington, D.C., July 14, 1967); *Venice* for Double Orch. and Brass Choirs (Seattle, May 2, 1967); *Vivaldi Gallery* for String Quartet and Divided Orch. (Seattle, March 25, 1968); *Soundings* (Atlanta, Sept. 18, 1969); *Concerto Grosso* (1969; N.Y., Dec. 4, 1988); *Troubadour Music* for 4 Guitars and Orch. (San Diego, March 1969); *Fire Music: Toccata* (1970); *Indian Attack* (1970); *Night Music* (1970); *Serenade* (1970); *American Ballads* (N.Y., April 24, 1976, composer conducting); *Chorales and Rags: Finale* (1977–82; N.Y., Nov. 13, 1988); *Cheers!,* celebration march (Boston, May 1, 1979; also for Band); *Burchfield Gallery* (Cleveland, April 9, 1981); *Celebration Strut* (NBC-TV, April 27, 1981); *Housewarming* (Baltimore, Sept. 16, 1982); *Apple Waltzes* (N.Y., Dec. 11, 1983, composer conducting); *Flourishes and Galop* (Louisville, Nov. 19, 1983); Flute Concerto (1983–84; Chicago, April 18, 1985); *Classical Variations on Colonial Themes* (1984–85; Pittsburgh, Sept. 11, 1986); *Flares and Declamations* (N.Y., Oct. 18, 1987); *Notes of a Remembrance* (1989; Washington, D.C., June 13, 1990); *Minute + Waltz Rag* (Baltimore, Oct. 25, 1990); *Diversions* for Tenor Saxophone and Orch. (N.Y., Nov. 28, 1990, composer conducting); *String Music* (Washington, D.C., March 10, 1994). **BAND:** *Jericho Rhapsody* (1940); *Concertette* for Viola and Band (1943); *Fanfare for Freedom* (1943); *Ballad* (1946); *Big City Blues* (1950; also for Orch.); *Derivations* for Clarinet and Dance Band (1955; Washington, D.C., July 14, 1956; also for Clarinet and Piano); *Santa Fe Saga* (1956); *St. Lawrence Suite* (Massena, N.Y., Sept. 5, 1958, composer conducting); *Prisms* (Chicago, Dec. 17, 1962, composer conducting); *Formations* (1964); *Mini-Suite* (1968); *Cheers!,* celebration march (1979; also for Orch.). **CHAMBER:** Suite for Violin and Piano (1945); *Derivations* for Clarinet and Piano (1955; also for Clarinet and Dance Band); *Parade* for Percussion Trio (1956); *Benny's Gig,* 8 duos for Clarinet and Double Bass (1962); *Columbian Fanfares* for 3 Trumpets, 3 Trombones, and Tuba (1967); Tuba Suite for Tuba and 3 Horns (1967); Suite for Cello and Piano (1981; Miami, June 21, 1982); *Concerto Concertante* for Violin, Wind Quintet, and Piano (1981–82; Washington, D.C., Oct. 29, 1983); Duo for Flute and Clarinet (1982); *Cellos* for 8 Cellos or Multiples (Tempe, Ariz., June 9, 1984); *Recovery Music* for Clarinet (1984); *Festive Fanfare* for 2 Trumpets, 2 Trombones, Tuba, Timpani, and Percussion (1991); *Hail to a First Lady* for 2 Trumpets, 2 or 3 Trombones, Tuba, Timpani, and Percussion (1991). **PIANO:** *Boogie Woogie Étude* (1943); *Dance Gallery* (1952); *Abby Variations* (1964); *At the Piano* (2 vols., 1964); *10 for Deborah* (1965); *Patterns* (1984; Madrid, May 14, 1985); *Pieces of China* (1985); *2 Pianos* for Piano Duet (1987); *Ghost Waltzes* (1991). **VOCAL:** *Of Time and the River* for Chorus (Princeton, N.J., Oct. 8, 1945); *Declaration* for 2 Narrators, Speaking Men's Chorus, and Orch. (1956; Washington, D.C., Jan. 20, 1957; orch. suite, Washington, D.C., Jan. 22, 1957); *Rhythm Gallery* for Narrator and Orch. (1959); *Come Up From the Valley, Children* for Voice and Piano (1964); *Salutations* for Narrator and Orch. (N.Y., April 27, 1966); *2* for Chorus (1966); *Something to Do*, labor cantata for Soli, Narrator, Chorus, and Orch. (Washington, D.C., Sept. 4, 1976); *Quotations* for 2 Choruses and Wind Orch. (1983; N.Y., Jan. 28, 1984); *American Sing* for Soprano, Mezzo-soprano, Tenor, Bass, and Orch. (1984); *The Jogger and the Dinosaur* for Rapper and Orch. (Pittsburgh, April 4, 1993).

BIBL.: L. Evans, *M.G.: His Life and Music* (diss., Columbia Univ. Teachers College, 1978); H. Phillips, "M.G.-Musical Citizen," *Instrumentalist*, v/41 (1987); S. Flatow, "M.G.," *Musical America* (Jan. 1989).

Grabner, Hermann, Austrian composer and music theorist; b. Graz, May 12, 1886; d. Bolzano, Italy, July 3, 1969. He took his degree in law at the Univ. of Graz. in 1909; then studied music with Reger and Sitt at the Leipzig Cons. He became a lecturer in theory at the Strasbourg Cons. in 1913; served in the German army in World War I; after the Armistice, taught at the Mannheim Cons.; from 1924 to 1938 he was prof. of composition at the Leipzig Cons.; then taught at the Hochschule für Musik (1938–45) and Cons. (1950–51) in Berlin. He wrote an opera, *Die Richterin* (Barmen, May 7, 1930); *Perkeo Suite* and *Burgmusik* for Wind Orch.; Concerto for 3 Violins; organ pieces; songs; etc.

WRITINGS: *Die Funktionstheorie Hugo Riemanns und ihre Bedeutung für die praktische Analyse* (Munich, 1923); *Allgemeine Musiklehre* (Stuttgart, 1924; 5th ed., 1949); *Lehrbuch der musikalischen Analyse* (Leipzig, 1925); *Der lineare Satz; Ein Lehrbuch des Kontrapunktes* (Stuttgart, 1930; rev. ed., 1950); *Handbuch der Harmonielehre* (Berlin, 1944).

Grabovsky, Leonid, Ukrainian composer; b. Kiev, Jan. 28, 1935. He studied at the Univ. of Kiev (1951–56) and took courses in composition with Revutsky and Liatoshinsky at the Kiev Cons. (1954–62; diploma, 1962). After teaching at the latter (1961–63; 1966–68), he was active as a composer, editor, and translator. He was one of the earliest composers in the Soviet Union to espouse minimalism. His works also reveal Asian influences.

WORKS: CHAMBER OPERAS: *The Bear* (1963); *The Marriage Proposal* (1964). **ORCH.:** *Intermezzo* (1958); *Symphonic Frescoes on a Theme of Boris Prorokov* (1961); *Little Chamber Music No. 1* for 16 String Players (1966) and *No. 2* for Oboe, Harp, and 12 String Players (1971); *Homöomorphie IV* (1970); *Meditation and Pathetic Recitative* for Strings (1972); *On St. John's Eve*, symphonic legend (1976). **CHAMBER:** Sonata for Solo Violin (1959); Trio for Violin, Double Bass, and Piano (1964; rev. 1975); *Microstructures* for Oboe (1964; rev. 1975); *Constants* for Violin, 4 Pianos, and 6 Percussion Groups (1964); *Ornament* for Oboe, Harp or Guitar, and Viola (1969); *Concorsuono* for Horn (1977); *Concerto misterioso* for Flute, Clarinet, Bassoon, Antique Cymbals, Harpsichord, Harp, Violin, Viola, and Cello (1977). **PIANO:** 4 2-part inventions (1962); *5 Character Studies* (1962); *Homöomorphie I–II* (1968) and *III* for 2 Pianos (1969); *Für Elise* (1988). **VOCAL:** *4 Ukrainian Songs* for Chorus and Orch. (1959); *Pastelle* for Mezzo-soprano, Violin, Viola, Cello, and Double Bass (1964; rev. 1975); *An Epitaph for Rainer Maria Rilke* for Soprano, Harp, Celesta, Guitar, and Bells (1965; rev. 1975); *La Mer* for Speaker, Chorus, Organ, and Orch. (1966–70); *Marginalia on Heisenbüttel* for Speaker, 2 Trumpets, Trombone, and Percussion (1967; rev. 1975); *Kogda* for Soprano, Violin, Clarinet, Piano, and Strings dd libitum (1987).

Grace, Harvey, English organist and writer on music; b. Romsey, Jan. 25, 1874; d. Bromley, Kent, Feb. 15, 1944. He studied with M. Richardson at Southwark Cathedral, London; was organist at various churches in London; from 1918 to his death, he was editor of the *Musical Times* and wrote editorials for it under the name "Feste"; also ed. the *New Musical Educator* (London, 1934). He wrote organ music and prepared transcriptions for organ.

WRITINGS: *Music in Parish Churches* (London, 1917; 3rd ed., 1944); *French Organ Music, Past and Present* (N.Y., 1919); *The Complete Organist* (London, 1920; 4th ed., 1956); *The Organ Works of Bach* (London, 1922); *The Organ Works of Rheinberger* (London, 1925); *Ludwig van Beethoven* (London, 1927); *A Musician at Large* (collection of articles from the *Musical Times*; London, 1928); *A Handbook for Choralists* (London, 1928); with Sir W. Davies, *Music and Worship* (London, 1935; 2nd ed., 1948); *The Training and Conducting of Choral Societies* (London, 1938); *The Organ Works of Cesar Franck* (London, 1948).

Gracis, Ettore, Italian conductor; b. La Spezia, Sept. 24, 1915; d. Treviso, April 12, 1992. He studied violin at the Parma Cons. and piano and composition at the Venice Cons.; also took courses in composition with Malipiero and Guarnieri at the Accademia Musicale Chigiana in Siena. He made his conducting debut in 1942; from that time, appeared with many opera houses of Italy. He also conducted sym. concerts. He was active in bringing out contemporary scores; conducted a number of works by Malipiero and other leading Italian composers.

Grad, Gabriel, Lithuanian composer; b. Retovo, near Kovno, July 9, 1890; d. Tel Aviv, Dec. 9, 1950. He studied in Ekaterinoslav and in Berlin. He was founder-director of a Jewish music school in Kovno (1920–22); went to Palestine in 1924; then was founder-director of the Benhetov Cons. in Tel Aviv (from 1925). He wrote an opera, *Judith and Holofernes*, and about 250 other works, including chamber music, piano pieces, choruses, and songs, many based on Jewish folk melodies.

Gradenwitz, Peter (Werner Emanuel), German-born Israeli musicologist and composer; b. Berlin, Jan. 24, 1910. He took courses in musicology, literature, and philosophy at the Univs. of Berlin and Freiburg im Breisgau (1928–33); also studied at the Berlin Hochschule für Musik and was a pupil in composition of Eisler and Rufer in Berlin, Weismann in Freiburg im Breisgau, and Milhaud in Paris (1934); completed his training in musicology at the German Univ. in Prague (Ph.D., 1936, with the diss. *Johann Stamitz: Das Leben*; publ. in Brno, 1936; 2nd ed., greatly aug., as *Johann Stamitz: Leben, Umwelt, Werke*, 2 vols., Wilhelmshaven, 1984). In 1936 he settled in Palestine, and was active as a writer, lecturer, and concert organizer; was founder, ed., and director of Israeli Music Publications, Ltd. (1949–82); also taught at the Univ. of Tel Aviv (1968–77). He lectured in Europe and the U.S.; in 1980 he was made an honorary prof. at the Univ. of Freiburg im Breisgau, where he subsequently led annual seminars. He contributed numerous articles to various journals and other publications. He composed, numbering among his works a Sym.; *Serenade* for Violin and Orch.; String Quartet; Trio for Flute, Viola, and Cello; *Palestinian* (later *Biblical*) *Landscapes* for Oboe and Piano; and songs.

WRITINGS: *Toldot hamusika* (Jerusalem, 1939; 8th ed., 1969); *The Music of Israel* (N.Y., 1949; new ed., enl., 1995); *Olam hasimofonia* (Tel Aviv, 1945; 9th ed., 1974); *Olaf hapsantran* (Tel Aviv, 1952); *Die Musikgeschichte Israels* (Kassel,

1961); *Wege zur Musik der Gegenwart* (Stuttgart, 1963; 2nd ed., rev., 1974); *Wege zur Musik der Zeit* (Wilhelmshaven, 1974); *Musik zwischen Orient und Okzident: Eine Geschichte der Wechselbeziehungen* (Wilhelmshaven, 1977); *Das Heilige Land in Augenzeugenberichten* (Munich, 1984); *Leonard Bernstein: Eine Biographie* (Zürich, 1984; 4th ed., 1995; Eng. tr., Oxford, 1986; new ed., 1995); *Kleine Kulturgeschichte der Klaviermusik* (Munich, 1986); *Literatur und Musik im Geselligen Kreis* (Stuttgart, 1991).

Gradstein, Alfred, Polish composer; b. Czestochowa, Oct. 30, 1904; d. Warsaw, Sept. 9, 1954. He studied with Statkowski (composition) and Melcer (conducting) at the Warsaw Cons. (1922–25) and with Marx (composition) and Krauss (conducting) at the Vienna Academy of Music. From 1928 to 1947 he lived in Paris; then returned to Poland. He wrote a Piano Concerto (1932), chamber music, piano pieces, and many songs.

Graener, Paul, significant German composer; b. Berlin, Jan. 11, 1872; d. Salzburg, Nov. 13, 1944. He studied composition with Albert Becker at the Veit Cons. in Berlin. He traveled in Germany as a theater conductor; in 1896 he went to London, where he taught at the Royal Academy of Music (1897–1902). He was then in Vienna as a teacher at the Neues Konservatorium; subsequently directed the Mozarteum in Salzburg (1910–13); after serving as prof. of composition at the Leipzig Cons. (1920–25), he was director of the Stern Cons. in Berlin (1930–33); thereafter he was vice-president of the Reichsmusikkammer (1933–41). His many songs reveal a penchant for folk-like melodies. His other works follow along traditional Romantic lines with some neo-Baroque aspects.

WORKS: OPERAS: *Don Juans letztes Abenteuer* (Leipzig, June 11, 1914); *Theophano* (Munich, June 5, 1918); *Schirin und Gertraude* (Dresden, April 28, 1920); *Hanneles Himmelfahrt* (Dresden, Feb. 17, 1927); *Friedemann Bach* (Schwerin, Nov. 13, 1931); *Der Prinz von Homburg* (Berlin, March 14, 1935); *Schwanhild* (Cologne, Jan. 4, 1941). **ORCH.:** Sym.; *Romantische Phantasie*; *Waldmusik*; *Gothische Suite*; Piano Concerto; Cello Concerto. **CHAMBER:** 6 string quartets; Piano Quintet; 3 violin sonatas.

BIBL.: G. Graener, *P. G.* (Leipzig, 1922); P. Grümmer, *Verzeichnis der Werke P. G.s* (Berlin, 1937).

Graeser, Wolfgang, Swiss composer; b. Zürich, Sept. 7, 1906; d. (suicide) Nikolassee, June 13, 1928. He went to Berlin in 1921, where he studied violin with Karl Klingler and quickly acquired erudition in theory; he also made a serious study of various unrelated arts and sciences (mathematics, Oriental languages, and painting). His signal achievement was an orchestration of Bach's *Kunst der Fuge* (Leipzig Thomaskirche, June 26, 1927). He publ. *Körpersinn* (Munich, 1927).

BIBL.: H. Zurlinden, *W. G.* (Munich, 1935).

Graetzer, Guillermo, Austrian-Argentine composer; b. Vienna, Sept. 5, 1914; d. Jan. 22, 1993. He was a pupil of Pisk in Vienna. In 1930 he settled in Buenos Aires. He was engaged in educational work and composed a number of orch. works and made arrangements of folk music.

Graf, Hans, Austrian conductor; b. Linz, Feb. 15, 1949. He studied piano at the Bruckner Cons. in Linz (1957–59) and later took diplomas in piano and conducting at the Graz Hochschule für Musik (1971); also pursued training in conducting with Ferrara in Siena (1970, 1971) and Hilversum (1972), Celibidache in Bologna (1972), and Yansons in Weimar (1972) and Leningrad (1972–73). In 1975–76 he was music director of the Iraqi National Sym. Orch. in Baghdad. In 1979 he won 1st prize in the Karl Böhm conducting competition in Salzburg. He subsequently made appearances as a guest conductor with the Vienna Sym. Orch. (from 1980), the Vienna State Opera (from 1981), and at the Salzburg Festival (from 1983). In 1984 he became music director of the Mozarteum Orch. and the Landestheater in Salzburg. In 1985 he made his first tour of the U.S. and Japan with the Mozarteum Orch. In 1987 he made his British debut as a guest conductor with the Royal Liverpool Phil. In 1995 he became principal conductor of the Calgary (Alberta) Phil. He retained his position with the Mozarteum Orch., but resigned his duties with the Landestheater in Salzburg.

Graf, Herbert, Austrian-born American opera producer and director, son of **Max Graf**; b. Vienna, April 10, 1903; d. Geneva, April 5, 1973. He studied at the Univ. of Vienna with Adler; received his Ph.D. in 1925. He then was a producer at the opera houses in Münster, Breslau, Frankfurt am Main, and Basel. In 1934 he went to the U.S.; was associated with the Philadelphia Opera in 1934–35; in 1936 he was appointed producer of the Metropolitan Opera in N.Y.; in 1949 he also became head of the opera dept. at the Curtis Inst. of Music in Philadelphia. He later returned to Europe, where he was director of the Zürich Opera (1960–62) and the Grand Theatre in Geneva (1965–73). He publ. *The Opera and Its Future in America* (N.Y., 1941), *Opera for the People* (Minneapolis, 1951), and *Producing Opera for America* (Zürich, 1961).

Graf, Max, Austrian music critic, teacher, and musicologist, father of **Herbert Graf**; b. Vienna, Oct. 1, 1873; d. there, June 24, 1958. He studied music history with Hanslick at the Univ. of Vienna (Ph.D., 1896, with the diss. *Die Musik der Frau in der Renaissancezeit*; publ. in Vienna, 1905), and also had lessons in theory with Bruckner. From 1900 to 1938 he wrote music criticism for the *Wiener Allgemeine Zeitung*; he lectured on musicology and aesthetics at the Cons. of the Gesellschaft der Musikfreunde (1902–09); then was on the staff of the Academy of Music (1909–38). In 1938, when Austria was incorporated into the Greater German Reich, he went to the U.S. He returned to Vienna in 1947. A brilliant writer in his homeland, he lapsed into speculative journalism in his books publ. in America, which are rendered worthless because of blatant inaccuracies.

WRITINGS: *Deutsche Musik im 19. Jahrhundert* (Berlin, 1898); *Wagner-Probleme und andere Studien* (Vienna, 1900); *Die innere Werkstatt des Musikers* (Stuttgart, 1910); *Richard Wagner im "Fliegenden Holländer"* (Vienna and Leipzig, 1911); *Vier Gespräche über deutsche Musik* (Regensburg, 1931); *Legend of a Musical City* (N.Y., 1945; 2nd ed., 1969); *Composer and Critic* (N.Y., 1946; 2nd ed., 1969); *Modern Music* (N.Y., 1946; 2nd ed., 1969; Ger. ed., 1953, as *Geschichte und Geist der modernen Musik*); *From Beethoven to Shostakovich* (N.Y., 1947; 2nd ed., 1969); *Die Wiener Oper* (Vienna, 1955); *Jede Stunde war erfüllt: Ein Halbes Jahrhundert Musik und Theaterleben* (Vienna and Frankfurt am Main, 1957).

Graf, Walter, Austrian ethnomusicologist; b. St. Pölten, June 20, 1903; d. Vienna, April 11, 1982. He studied musicology with Lach, Adler, and Wellesz, as well as anthropology, philosophy, psychology, and phonetics, at the Univ. of Vienna (Ph.D., 1932, with a diss. on German influences on Estonian folk song; Habilitation, 1952, with a study of the music of New Guinea; publ. in Vienna, 1950). He became lecturer (1958) and then assistant prof. (1962) at the Univ. of Vienna; from 1957 to 1963 he also was head of the Austrian Academy of Sciences recording archive, which he greatly expanded. In his articles, he continued Lach's anthropological concept of music; he also attempted to define the characteristics of sound that are important in the hearing and understanding of music. Among his writings are "Die ältesten deutschen Überlieferungen estnischer Volkslieder," *Musik des Ostens*, I (1962), *Die musikalische Klangforschung: Wege zur Erfassung der musikalischen Bedeutung der Klangfarbe* (Karlsruhe, 1969), and "Zur Rolle der Teiltonreihe in der Gestaltung klingend tradierter Musik," *Festschrift Kurt Blaukopf* (Vienna, 1975).

BIBL.: E. Schenk, ed., *Musik als Gestalt und Erlebnis: Festschrift W. G. zum 65. Geburtstag* (Vienna, 1970).

Graffman, Gary, outstanding American pianist; b. N.Y., Oct. 14, 1928. He won a scholarship to the Curtis Inst. of Music in Philadelphia when he was 8, and studied with Isabelle Vengerova. He was only 10 when he gave a piano recital at

Town Hall in N.Y. After graduating in 1946, he was a scholarship student at Columbia Univ. (1946–47). In 1946 he won the 1st regional Rachmaninoff competition, which secured for him his debut with the Philadelphia Orch. in 1947. In 1949 he was honored with the Leventritt Award. Subsequently he received a Fulbright grant to go to Europe (1950–51). Returning to the U.S., he had lessons with Horowitz in N.Y. and Serkin in Marlboro, Vt. From 1955 he pursued an international career as a soloist with the foremost orchs. and as a recitalist. In 1979 his distinguished career was tragically imperiled when he was stricken with carpal-tunnel syndrome in his right hand. He was appointed to the faculty of the Curtis Inst. of Music in 1980; was made its artistic director in 1986. Graffman also made some appearances in the left-hand piano literature. On Feb. 4, 1993, he was soloist in the premiere of Rorem's 4th Piano Concerto for Left Hand and Orch. He brought out an autobiography under the title *I Really Should Be Practicing* (Garden City, N.Y., 1981).

Graham, Colin, English opera director and librettist; b. Hove, Sussex, Sept. 22, 1931. He attended the Royal Academy of Dramatic Art in London (1951–52). After working as a stage manager, he directed his first opera, Britten's *Noye's Fludde*, at the Aldeburgh Festival in 1958. In subsequent years, he worked closely with Britten, becoming an artistic director at the Aldeburgh Festival in 1968. He worked with the English Opera Group, serving as its director of productions from 1963 to 1975; from 1961 he was active at the Sadler's Wells (later English National) Opera in London, where he was director of productions from 1977 to 1982. He was also associated with London's Covent Garden (1961–73). In 1975 he created the English Music Theatre Co., with which he was active until 1978. In 1978 he was named director of production at the Opera Theatre of St. Louis, serving as its artistic director from 1985. Graham also pursued theological studies at the New Covenant School of Ministry in St. Louis, and was ordained in 1988. He staged the first British productions of *The Cunning Little Vixen* (1961), *From the House of the Dead* (1965), and *War and Peace* (1972). Among the 47 world premieres he directed were Britten's *Curlew River* (1964), *The Burning Fiery Furnace* (1966), *The Golden Vanity* (1967), *The Prodigal Son* (1968), *Owen Wingrave* (1972), and *Death in Venice* (1973), Bennett's *Mines of Sulphur* (1963) and *A Penny for a Song* (1967; librettist), Paulus's *The Postman Always Rings Twice* (1982; librettist), and Minoru Miki's *Joruri* (1985; librettist). Graham's early training in the dramatic arts, combined with his extraordinary command of every aspect of the music theater, have placed him among the leading masters of his craft.

Graham, Susan, admired American mezzo-soprano; b. Roswell, N.Mex., July 23, 1960. She studied with Cynthia Hoffman at the Manhattan School of Music in N.Y. (M.M., 1987). While still a student there, she attracted critical notice as Massenet's Chérubin, and then appeared with the operas in St. Louis and Seattle. During the 1989–90 season, she sang Annius in *La clemenza di Tito* at the Chicago Lyric Opera, Sonia in Argento's *The Aspern Papers* in Washington, D.C., Dorabella and Strauss's Composer in Santa Fe, and as soloist in *Das Knaben Wunderhorn* at N.Y.'s Carnegie Hall. In 1990–91 she appeared as Minerva in Monteverdi's *Il ritorno d'Ulisse in patria* at the San Francisco Opera and as Berlioz's Beatrice in Lyons. Her success in the Metropolitan Opera National Auditions led to her debut with the company in N.Y. during the 1991–92 season as the 2nd Lady in *Die Zauberflöte*, where she subsequently was engaged to sing Cherubino, Tebaldo in *Don Carlos*, Meg Page, Octavian, Ascanio, and Dorabella. From 1993 she sang at the Salzburg Festivals as well. During the 1993–94 season, she made her debut at London's Covent Garden as Chérubin. In 1995 she sang for the first time at Milan's La Scala as Berlioz's Marguerite and at the Vienna State Opera as Octavian, and on Sept. 15 of that year she created the title role in Goehr's *Arianna* at Covent Garden. Her engagements as a concert artist have taken her to principal North American and European music centers, where she has appeared with many notable orchs.

Grahn, Ulf, Swedish composer; b. Solna, Jan. 17, 1942. He studied piano, violin, and composition with Hans Eklund at the Stockholm Citizen's School (1962–66); then took various courses at the Stockholm Musikhögskolan (1966–70). In 1972 he and his wife, the pianist Barbro Dahlman, went to America; he enrolled at the Catholic Univ. of America (M.M., 1973). With Dahlman, he founded the Contemporary Music Forum (1974), presenting programs of modern music by American and European composers; he served as its program director until 1984. After teaching at Northern Virginia Community College (1975–80), he joined the faculty of George Washington Univ. in Washington, D.C. (1983); he also served as artistic and managing director of the Lake Siljan Music Festival in Sweden (1988–89). In his music, Grahn maintains the golden mean of contemporary idioms, without doctrinaire deviations, scrupulously serving the tastes of the general audience.

WORKS: BALLET: *Lux* (1972; Stockholm, April 6, 1972). **ORCH.:** *Musica da camera* for Chamber Orch. (1964); *Fancy* (1965); *Lamento* for Strings (1967); 2 syms.: No. 1 (1967) and No. 2 (1983; Stockholm, June 20, 1984); *Hommage à Charles Ives* for Strings (1968; Trondheim, Feb. 13, 1969); Concerto for Double Bass and Chamber Orch. (1968; Santa Barbara, Calif., Feb. 7, 1973); *Joy* for Symphonic Band (1969; Stockholm, Feb. 2, 1970); *Ancient Music* for Piano and Chamber Orch. (1970; Copenhagen, March 20, 1972); *A Dream of a Lost Century* for Chamber Orch. (1971; Stockholm, June 1, 1972); *Concerto for Orchestra* (1973; Philadelphia, April 10, 1981); Concertino for Piano and Strings (1979); *Rondeau* for Chamber Orch. (1980); Guitar Concerto (Reston, Va., June 15, 1985); *As Time Passes By* (1993); *Pezzo* (1993); *A Tale* (1993). **CHAMBER:** Trio for Flute, Oboe, and Clarinet (1967); *This Reminds Me of . . .* for Flute, Clarinet, Horn, Trombone, and Percussion (1972; Washington, D.C., Dec. 15, 1975); *Soundscapes I* for Flute, Bass Clarinet, English Horn, and Percussion (Washington, D.C., Oct. 28, 1973), *II* for Instruments (1974), and *III* for Flute, Clarinet, Percussion, and Tape (1975); Chamber Concerto for Viola d'Amore and 10 Instruments (1975; Washington, D.C., Jan. 17, 1977); *Order-Fragments-Mirror* for Flute, Bass Clarinet, Percussion, and Piano (1975); Flute Sonata (1976); *Magnolias in Snow* for Flute and Piano (1976); String Quartet No. 2 (1979); *Floating Landscape* for 8 Flutes (1979); Piano Quartet (1980); *Summer Deviation* for Flute, Violin, Viola, Cello, and Piano (1981); *Images* for Bass Clarinet and Marimba (1981); *Eldorado* for Flute, Violin, Clarinet, Piano, and Baryton (1982); Violin Sonata (1983); *Nocturne* for Piano Trio and Tape (1987; Washington, D.C., March 7, 1988); *3 Dances with Interludes* for 6 Percussionists (1990); *Madrigal* for 4 Trombones (1991); *3 Water Colors* for Horn and Piano (1991). **PIANO:** Sonata (1980). **VOCAL:** *Soundscapes IV* for Soprano, Flute, Bass Clarinet, Percussion, and Piano (1975); *Un Coup de dés* for Soprano and Chamber Ensemble (Washington, D.C., April 20, 1987).

Grainger, (George) Percy (Aldridge), celebrated Australian-born American pianist, composer, and folk song collector; b. Melbourne, July 8, 1882; d. White Plains, N.Y., Feb. 20, 1961. He studied with his mother and received piano lessons from Louis Pabst in Melbourne; he then was a pupil of Kwast (piano) and Knorr (composition) at the Hoch Cons. in Frankfurt am Main (1895–99); later he had additional piano lessons with Busoni in Berlin (1903). In 1901 he appeared as a pianist in London, and then played throughout Great Britain, Europe, Australia, New Zealand, and South Africa. In 1905 he joined the English Folk Song Soc. and became an ardent collector of folk songs. In 1914 he went to N.Y., where he made a sensational debut on Feb. 11, 1915. During service as an oboist in the U.S. Army Band (1917–19), he became a naturalized American citizen in 1918. He taught piano at the Chicago Musical College during several summers between 1919 and 1928. In 1926 he toured Australia again. He married the Swedish poet and artist Ella Viola Ström in 1928 in a spectacular ceremony at the Hollywood Bowl, at which he conducted his *To a Nordic Princess,* written for his bride. In 1932–33 he was chairman of the music dept. at N.Y. Univ. In 1934–35 he again toured Australia, during which time he began organizing the Grainger Museum at the Univ. of Melbourne to house his MSS and personal effects and to serve as an ethnomusicological research center. He dedicated the museum in 1938. During World War II, he made numerous concert appearances for the Allied cause. After the War, he made his home in White Plains. Although Grainger was honored by election to the National Inst. of Arts and Letters in 1950, his last years were embittered by his belief that his work as a composer had been unjustly neglected. Always the eccentric, he directed that his skeleton be placed on display at the Grainger Museum, but his request was denied and he was buried in the ordinary manner. He prepared an autobiographical sketch as *The Aldridge-Grainger-Ström Saga* (1933), publ. the vol. *Music: A Commonsense View of All Types* (Sydney, 1934), and ed. 12 collections of music. Grainger's philosophy of life and art called for the widest communion of peoples. His profound study of folk music underlies the melodic and rhythmic structure of his own music. He made a determined effort to re-create in art music the free flow of instinctive songs of the people. He experimented with "gliding" intervals within the traditional scales and polyrhythmic combinations with independent strong beats in the component parts. In a modest way, he was a pioneer of electronic music. As early as 1937, he wrote a quartet for electronic instruments, notating the pitch by zigzags and curves. He introduced individual forms of notation and orch. scoring, rejecting the common Italian designations of tempi and dynamics in favor of colloquial English expressions.

WORKS: ORCH.: *English Dance* for Organ and Orch. (1899–1909; 1924–25); *Youthful Suite* (1899–1945); *Colonial Song* (1905–12; rev. c.1928); *In a Nutshell,* suite (1905–16); *Mock Morris* for Strings (1910; also for Orch., 1914); *The Warriors* for 3 Pianos and Orch. (1912–16); *The Power of Rome and the Christian Heart* for Organ and Orch. (1918–43); *To a Nordic Princess* (1927–28); *Handel in the Strand* for Strings (1932); *Harvest Hymn* (1932); *The Immovable Do* (c.1939). **LARGE WIND ENSEMBLE:** *The Lads of Wamphray March* for Band (1906–07; rev. 1937–38); *Hill Song No. 2* for Band (1907; rev. 1911 and 1940–46); *Over the Hills and Far Away* for Piano and Band (1916–19); *Colonial Song* for Band (1918); *Marching Song of Democracy* for Band (1948). **CHAMBER:** *Walking Tune* for Wind Quartet (1900–1905); *Youthful Rapture* for Cello and Piano or Piano Trio, with 9 Instruments ad libitum (1901; 1929); *Hill Song No. 1* for 21 Instruments (1901–02; also for 22 or 23 Instruments, 1921; rev. 1923) and *No. 2* for 22 or 23 Wind Instruments and Cymbal (1907; rev. 1911 and 1940–46); *Free Music* for String Quartet (1907; also for Theremins, 1935–36); *Arrival Platform Humlet* for Viola (1908–12); *Mock Morris* for 3 Violins, Viola, and 2 Cellos (1910; also for Violin and Piano, 1910); *Handel in the Strand* for Piano Trio and Viola ad libitum (1911–12); *The Lonely Desert Man Sees the Tents of the Happy Tribes* for Various Instrumental Combinations (1911–14; 1949); *Colonial Song* for Piano Trio (1912); *Echo Song Trials* for Various Instrumental Combinations (1945); many keyboard pieces. **OTHER:** Choral works, pieces for Solo Voice and Piano or Other Instruments, and numerous folk song settings.

BIBL.: D. Parker, *P.A. G.: A Study* (N.Y., 1918); C. Scott, *P.G.: A Course in Contemporary Musical Biography* (N.Y., 1919); R. Goldman, "P.G.'s 'Free Music'," *Juilliard Review,* II (1955); R. Watanabe, "The P.G. Manuscripts," *University of Rochester Library Bulletin,* XIX (1963–64); P. Willetts, "The P.G. Collection," *British Museum Quarterly,* XXVII (1963–64); T. Slattery, *The Wind Music of P.A.G.* (diss., Univ. of Iowa, 1967); M. Tan, *The Free Music of P.G.* (diss., Juilliard School, 1971); T. Slattery, *P.G.: The Inveterate Innovator* (Evanston, Ill., 1974); T. Balough, *A Complete Catalogue of the Works of P.G.* (Nedlands, 1975); J. Bird, *P.G.: The Man and the Music* (London, 1976); L. Foreman, ed., *The P.G. Companion* (London, 1981); T. Balough, ed., *A Musical Genius from Australia: Selected Writings by and about P.G.* (Nedlands, 1982); D. Tall, ed., *P.G.: A Catalogue of the Music* (London, 1982); R. Simon, *P.G.: The Pictorial Biography* (N.Y., 1984); K. Dreyfus, ed., *The Farthest North of Human Kindness: Letters of P.G. 1901–14* (London, 1985); J. Blacking, *"A Commonsense View of All Music": Reflections on P.G.'s Contribution to Ethnomusicology and Music Education* (Cambridge, 1987); T. Lewis, *Source Guide to the Music of P.G.* (White Plains, N.Y., 1991); W. Mellers, *P.G.* (Oxford, 1992); M. Gillies, ed., *The All-Round Man: Selected Letters of P.G., 1914–1961* (Oxford, 1994).

Gram, Peder, Danish conductor and composer; b. Copenhagen, Nov. 25, 1881; d. there, Feb. 4, 1956. After graduation from the Univ. of Copenhagen, he studied theory at the Leipzig Cons. with Sitt and Krehl and conducting with Nikisch (1904–07). Returning to Copenhagen, he was chief conductor of the Danish Concert Soc. (1918–32) and head of the music dept. of the Danish Radio (1937–51). He publ. *Musikens formlaere i grundtraek* (1916), *Moderne musik* (1934), and *Analytisk harmonilaere* (1947), all in Copenhagen.

WORKS: ORCH.: *Romance* for Violin and Orch. (1909); *Symfonik fantasi* (1908); *Poème lyrique* (1911); 3 syms. (1913, 1925, 1954); Violin Concerto (1919); Overture (1921); *Festouverture* (1927); *Prolog til et drama af Shakespeare* (1928); *Intrada seria* (1946). **CHAMBER:** 3 string quartets (1907, 1928, 1941); Piano Trio (1914); Cello Sonata (1914); Oboe Sonatina (1935); Wind Quintet (1943); piano pieces. **VOCAL:** *Avalon* for Soprano and Orch. (1916); *Min ungdoms drøm* for Tenor and Orch. (1921); songs.

Gramatges, Harold, Cuban composer, pianist, and teacher; b. Santiago de Cuba, Sept. 26, 1918. He was a student of Ardévol and Roldan in Havana, and then of Copland (composition) and Koussevitzky (conducting) at the Berkshire Music Center in Tanglewood (summer, 1942). Returning to Havana, he was active in contemporary music circles. He also devoted time to teaching. After serving in the Cuban Embassy in Paris (1961–64), he returned to Havana and was director of the music dept. of the Casa de las Américas (1965–70). In 1970 he joined the music section of the Consejo Nacional de Cultura, and in 1976 the composition dept. of the music faculty of the Instituto Superior de Arte. His output represents an enlightened functionalist approach to composition in an effective modern style.

WORKS: DRAMATIC: *Icaro,* ballet (1943); *Mensaje al futuro,* ballet (1944); *Cantata a la paz,* theater piece (1987); incidental music. **ORCH.:** Sym. (1945); *Dos danzas cubanas* (1950); Sinfonietta (1955); *In memoriam (homenaje a Frank País)* (1961); *Para la dama duende* for Guitar and Orch. (1973). **CHAMBER:** Duo for Flute and Piano (1943); Trio for Clarinet, Cello, and Piano (1944); Concertino for Piano and Winds (1945); Quintet for Flute, Clarinet, Bassoon, Viola, and Double Bass (1950); Quintet for Flute, Oboe, Clarinet, Bassoon, and Trumpet (1957); *Movil II* for 7 Instruments (1970); *Diseños,* quintet for Winds and Percussion (1976); *Guirigay,* quintet (1985); piano pieces; guitar music. **VOCAL:** *La muerte del guerrillero* for Reciter and Orch. (1968–69); *Oda martiana* for Baritone and Orch. (1980); choral pieces; songs.

Gramm (real name, **Grambasch**), **Donald (John),** American bass-baritone; b. Milwaukee, Feb. 26, 1927; d. N.Y., June 2, 1983. He studied piano and organ at the Wisconsin College-Cons. of Music (1935–44); also studied voice with George Graham. He made his professional debut in Chicago at the age of 17 when he sang the role of Raimondo in *Lucia di Lammermoor,* he continued his vocal studies at the Chicago Musical College and at the Music Academy of the West in Santa Barbara, where he was a student of Martial Singher. On Sept. 26, 1952, he made his debut at the N.Y. City Opera as Colline in *La Bohème,* and continued to appear with the company for the rest of his life. On Jan. 10, 1964 he made his Metropolitan Opera debut in N.Y. as Truffaldino in *Ariadne auf Naxos,* and then sang major roles there until his death. He was extremely versatile in his roles; he sang Méphistophélès, Leporello,

Mozart's Figaro, Falstaff in Verdi's opera, Baron Ochs, and Scarpia. He also distinguished himself as an interpreter of such difficult parts as Dr. Schön in Berg's *Lulu* and as Moses in Schoenberg's *Moses und Aron*.

Granados (y Campiña), Eduardo, Spanish conductor and composer, son of **Enrique Granados (y Campiña)**; b. Barcelona, July 28, 1894; d. Madrid, Oct. 2, 1928. He studied in Barcelona with his father; then at the Madrid Cons. with Conrado del Campo. He taught at the Granados Academy in Barcelona; was also active as a conductor; presented many works by his father. He wrote several zarzuelas, of which the first, *Bufon y Hostelero*, was performed with some success in Barcelona (Dec. 7, 1917); other stage works were *Los Fanfarrones*, comic opera; *La ciudad eterna*, mystery play; *Los Cigarrales*, operatic sketch; and musical comedies.

Granados (y Campiña), Enrique, distinguished Spanish composer, pianist, and teacher, father of **Eduardo Granados (y Campiña);** b. Lérida, July 27, 1867; d. in the aftermath of the torpedoing of the S.S. *Sussex* by a German submarine in the English Channel, March 24, 1916. He went to Barcelona and studied piano with Francisco Jurnet at the Escolania de la Marcé and privately with Joan Baptista Pujol, and from 1883 took private composition lessons with Pedrell. In 1887 he went to Paris to pursue his training in piano with Charles de Bériot. In 1889 he returned to Barcelona, and in 1890 made his recital debut there. He continued to make successful appearances as a pianist in subsequent years while pursuing his interest in composing. On Nov. 12, 1898, he scored a notable success as a composer with the premiere of his zarzuela *María del Carmen* in Madrid. In 1900 he organized the Sociedad de Conciertos Clasicos in Barcelona, and from 1901 taught there at his own Academia Granados. He secured his reputation as a composer with his imaginative and effective piano suite *Goyescas* (1911). He subsequently utilized music from the suite and from some of his vocal tonadillas to produce the opera *Goyescas*, which received its premiere at the Metropolitan Opera in N.Y. on Jan. 28, 1916, with the composer in attendance. It was on his voyage home that Granados perished. Although he was picked up by a lifeboat after the attack on the S.S. *Sussex*, he dove into the sea to save his drowning wife and both were lost. Granados' output reflected the influence of the Spanish and Romantic traditions, and the Castilian tonadilla. His finest scores are notable for their distinctive use of melody, rhythm, harmony, and color.

WORKS: DRAMATIC: *María del Carmen*, zarzuela (Madrid, Nov. 12, 1898); *Blancaflor* (Barcelona, Jan. 30, 1899); *Petrarca*, lyric drama (n.d.); *Picarol*, lyric drama (Barcelona, Feb. 23, 1901); *Follet*, lyric drama (Barcelona, April 4, 1903); *Gaziel*, lyric drama (Barcelona, Oct. 27, 1906); *Liliana*, lyric drama (Barcelona, July 9, 1911); *La cieguecita de Belén* or *El portalico de Belén* (1914); *Goyescas*, opera (1915; N.Y., Jan. 28, 1916); also *Miel de la Alcarria*, incidental music (n.d.) and *Ovillejos o La gallina ciega*, Sainte lírico (n.d.; unfinished). **ORCH.:** *Marcha de los vencidos* (Barcelona, Oct. 31, 1899); *Suite on Gallician Themes* (Barcelona, Oct. 31, 1899); *Dante*, or *La Divina Commedia* for Mezzo-soprano and Orch. (private perf., Barcelona, June 1908; rev. version, Barcelona, May 25, 1915); *Navidad* (1914; Madrid, May 31, 1916); undated scores: *Boires baixes: Suite árabe u oriental; Torrijos*. **CHAMBER:** Trio for Violin, Cello, and Piano (1894; Madrid, Feb. 15, 1895); Piano Quintet (Madrid, Feb. 15, 1895); Violin Sonata (c.1910); *Serenade* for 2 Violins and Piano (Paris, April 4, 1914); *Madrigal* for Cello and Piano (Barcelona, May 2, 1915); undated scores: *Romanza* for Violin and Piano; Cello Sonata; *3 Preludes* for Violin and Piano. **PIANO:** *Danzas españolas* (1892–1900); *Goyescas*, 2 books (Book 1, Barcelona, March 11, 1911); numerous solo pieces. **VOCAL:** *Cant de les estrelles* for Chorus, Piano, and Organ (1910; Barcelona, March 11, 1911); *Elisenda* for Voice, Piano, Harp, String Quintet, Flute, Oboe, and Clarinet (1910; Barcelona, July 7, 1912); *L'Herba de amor* for Chorus and Organ (1914); songs.

BIBL.: G. Boladeres Ibern, *E.G.: Recuerdos de su vid y estudio critico de su obra por su antiguo discipulo* (Barcelona, 1921); H. Collet, *Albéniz et G.* (Paris, 1925; 2nd ed., 1948); J. Subirá, *E.G.: Su producción musical, su madrileñismo, su personalidad artística* (Madrid, 1926); A. Fernández-Cid, *G.* (Madrid, 1956); P. Vila San-Juan, *Papeles intimos de E.G.* (Barcelona, 1966); J. Riera, *E.G.: Estudio* (Lérida, 1967); A. Tarazona, *E.G.: El último romántico* (Madrid, 1975); A. Carreras i Granados, *G.* (Barcelona, 1988); M. Larrad, *The Goyescas of G.* (thesis, Univ. of Liverpool, 1988); C. Hess, *E.G.: A Bio-Bibliography* (N.Y., 1991); M. Larrad, *The Catalan Theater Works of E.G.* (diss., Univ. of Liverpool, 1991); C. Hess, "E.G. i la vida musical barcelonina entre 1891–1916," in A. Pacheco and K. Kobbervig, eds., *Actes del Sisè Colloqui d'Estudis Catalans a Nord-América (Vancouver, 1990)* (Montserrat, 1992).

Grandert, Johnny, Swedish composer; b. Stockholm, July 11, 1939. He studied under Lidholm at the Stockholm Musikhögskolan (1959–64); also took music courses in Germany, Italy, and America; was mainly antodidact in music; also was active as a painter. In 1972 he became principal and in 1986 director of music at the Norrtalje School of Music. The titles of his compositions betray a desire to puzzle and tantalize, but the music itself is not forbidding, despite the application of startling effects (as in his *Mirror 25* for Chorus and Orch. [1966], in which a machine gun is included in the orchestra and in which the chorus is invited to belch at certain points).

WORKS: OPERA: *Gyllene jord* (1984). **ORCH.:** *The D. of B.* (1967); *Barypet*, concerto for Trumpet and Baritone Saxophone, with 16 Flutes, Percussion, and Strings (1968); *Skorogovorka* (Tongue Twister) for Wind Orch. and Percussion (1971); 6 syms.: No. 1 (1971), No. 2 (1973), No. 3, *Sinfonia Calamagrostis* (1972), No. 4 (1974; Stockholm, Nov. 29, 1975), No. 5 (1976; Swedish Radio, Feb. 22, 1977), and No. 6 (1982; Helsinki, March 3, 1983); *Jerikos murar* for Flute, Slide Flute, 3 Bass Recorders, 3 Clarinets, 15 Trombones, Percussion, Organ, and Strings (1972); *Rodensiana* (1984); *Staccato* for Strings (1990). **CHAMBER:** *Chamber Music* for Chamber Ensemble (1961); 7 string quartets (1963–92); Nonet for Winds, Euphonium, and Cello (1964); *86 T* for Chamber Ensemble (1965); *10 an' 30* for Chamber Ensemble (1966); Octet for 3 Voices, Flute, Trombone, Viola, Double Bass, and Harp (1966); *Prego I* for Cello and Horn (1968); *Non omesso* for Chamber Ensemble (1969); *Non lo so* for Flute, Cello, and Piano (1970); *Pour Philippe*, wind quintet (1970); Quartet for Recorders (1972); Saxophone Quintet (1975); *Temptation*, essay for String Quartet (1979); *Midtwedt*, canon for 8 Violins (1986); *Isola Sale* for Chamber Ensemble (1989); Brass Quintet (1989); *Boureause* for Chamber Ensemble (1991). **VOCAL:** *Mirror 25* for Chorus and Orch. (1966); *Pour Pjotr* for Voice, Piano, Cello, Clarinet, and Percussion (1971).

Grandi, Margherita (née **Margaret Garde**), Australian soprano; b. Hobart, Oct. 4, 1894; d. Milan, 1972. She studied at the Royal College of Music in London, with Calvé in Paris, and with Russ in Milan. In 1919 she made her operatic debut under the stage name of Djema Vécla (an anagram of Calvé) at the Paris Opéra-Comique in *Werther*. In 1922 she created the title role in Massenet's *Amadis* in Monte Carlo. After marrying the scenic designer Giovanni Grandi, she sang under her married name. In 1932 she appeared as Aida at Milan's Teatro Carcano, and returned to that city to sing Elena in *Mefistofele* at La Scala in 1934. She sang at the Glyndebourne Festivals in 1939, 1947, and 1949. In 1946 she appeared at the Verona Arena. In 1947 she sang Tosca and Donna Anna at London's Cambridge Theatre. In 1949 she returned to London to create the role of Diana in Bliss's *The Olympians* at Covent Garden. She also made guest appearances in South America. In 1951 she retired from the operatic stage. Grandi's most acclaimed roles were Lady Macbeth and Tosca, which she projected in the grand manner.

Grandjany, Marcel (Georges Lucien), distinguished French-born American harpist, pedagogue, and composer; b. Paris,

Sept. 3, 1891; d. N.Y., Feb. 24, 1975. He was a student of Henriette Renié, taking the premier prix at the Paris Cons. in 1905. At age 17, he made his formal debut as soloist with the Lamoureux Orch. in Paris. In 1922 he made his first appearance in London and in 1924 made his debut in N.Y. From 1921 to 1935 he taught at the Fontainebleau Cons. In 1936 he settled in N.Y. and in 1945 became a naturalized American citizen. He taught at the Juilliard School of Music in N.Y. (1938–75), and also at the Montreal Cons. (1943–63). Among his works were a *Poème symphonique* for Harp, Horn, and Orch., other harp pieces, and songs. He publ. *First Grade Harp Pieces* (N.Y., 1964).

Granichstaedten, Bruno, Austrian composer; b. Vienna, Sept. 1, 1879; d. N.Y., May 20, 1944. He was a student of Jadassohn at the Leipzig Cons. Returning to Vienna, he began his career as a songwriter and singer. He scored a notabale success as a composer for the theater with his first operetta, *Bub oder Mädel?* (Vienna, Nov. 13, 1908), which was later heard in N.Y. as *The Rose Maid.* He then had success with such scores as *Majestät Mimi* (Vienna, Feb. 17, 1911), *Madame Serafin* (Hamburg, Sept. 1, 1911), *Casimirs Himmelfahrt* (Vienna, Dec. 25, 1911), *Die verbotene Stadt* (Berlin, Dec. 23, 1913; in collaboration with C. Lindau), *Auf Befehl der Kaiserin* or *Auf Befehl der Herzogin* (Vienna, March 20, 1915), *Walzerliebe* (Vienna, Feb. 16, 1918; in collaboration with R. Bodanzky), *Indische Nächte* (Vienna, Nov. 25, 1921), and *Die Bacchusnacht* (Vienna, May 18, 1923; in collaboration with E. Marischka). Following the remarkable success of *Der Orlow* (Vienna, April 3, 1925; in collaboration with Marischka), he went on to compose such popular scores as *Das Schwalbennest* (Vienna, Sept. 2, 1926; in collaboration with Marischka), *Die Königin* (Vienna, Feb. 4, 1927; in collaboration with O. Straus and Marischka), *Evelyne* or *Die Milliardärin* (Berlin, Dec. 23, 1927; in collaboration with P. Hertz and A. Schutz), and *Reklame* (Vienna, Feb. 28, 1930; in collaboration with Marischka). With the Nazi assumption of power in Germany in 1933, his career was derailed. After the Anschluss in Austria in 1938, he made his way to N.Y., where he was compelled to make ends meet playing piano in bars.

Grant, Clifford (Scantlebury), Australian bass; b. Randwick, Sept. 11, 1930. He studied at the New South Wales State Conservatorium of Music in Sydney and with Otakar Kraus in London. In 1951 he made his operatic debut with the New South Wales Opera as Raimondo in *Lucia di Lammermoor.* After further appearances in Australia, he made his debut at the Sadler's Wells Opera in London in 1966 as Silva in *Ernani,* where he later sang Pogner, Sarastro, Hunding, the Commendatore, and Hagen. He also made his U.S. debut in 1966 at the San Francisco Opera as Lord Walton in *I Puritani,* and returned there to sing such roles as the King in *Aida,* Monterone, and Oroveso. He first sang at the Glyndebourne Festival as Nettuno in *Il Ritorno d'Ulisse* in 1972. His Covent Garden debut followed in London in 1974 as Mozart's Bartolo. On Nov. 19, 1976, he made his debut at the Metropolitan Opera in N.Y. as Phorcas in *Esclarmonde.* From 1976 to 1990 he pursued his operatic career in Australia. In 1993 he appeared as Alvise with England's Opera North.

Grant, (William) Parks, American composer; b. Cleveland, Jan. 4, 1910. He studied at Capital Univ. in Columbus, Ohio, graduating with a B.Mus. (1932); received a Ph.D. from the Eastman School of Music in Rochester, N.Y. (1948). He retired in 1974, culminating a 40-year teaching career at various institutions. He was an ed. for the International Gustav Mahler Soc. in Vienna (1965–66; 1970; 1972–73), for whose Critical Collected Edition he corrected the new editions of Mahler's 2nd, 3rd, 8th, and 9th syms. and *Das klagende Lied.*

WORKS: *The Dream of the Ballet-Master,* ballet for Piano Quintet (1934); 3 syms. (1936, 1947, 1961); *The Masque of the Red Death,* symphonic poem (1938); Horn Concerto (1940); 6 overtures; Clarinet Concerto (1944); *Integrated Concerto* for Double Bass and Orch. (1946); *Scherzo* for Flute and Small Orch. (1950); 3 suites for String Orch.; 2 string quartets; *Essay* for Horn and Organ (1948); 3 suites for Brass Quintet (1949, 1951, 1953); *Varied Obstinacy* for 2 Saxophones (1974); *Pensive Monologue* for Cello (1976); choruses; songs.

WRITINGS: *Music for Elementary Teachers* (N.Y., 1951; rev. ed., 1960); *Handbook of Music Terms* (Metuchen, N.J., 1967).

Grantham, Donald, American composer; b. Duncan, Okla., Nov. 9, 1947. He studied composition at the Univ. of Okla. (B.Mus., 1970) and then entered the Univ. of So. Calif. in Los Angeles in the composition classes of Robert Linn and Halsey Stevens (M.M., 1974; D.M.A., 1980). In the summers of 1973 and 1974 he studied with Boulanger at the American Cons. in Fontainebleau. After lecturing at the Univ. of Southern Calif. in Los Angeles (1974–75), he joined the faculty of the Univ. of Texas at Austin in 1975, where he became a prof. in 1991. With K. Kennan, he was co-author of the 4th ed. of *The Technique of Orchestration* (Englewood Cliffs, N.J., 1990).

WORKS: OPERA: *The Boor* (1989). **ORCH.:** *Música para "Los desastres de la guerra"* (1974); *5 Variations and Double Fugue on "L'Homme armé"* (1970); *El album de los duendecitos* (1983); *To the Wind's 12 Quarters* (1993); *Fantasy on Mr. Hyde's Song* (1993). **CHAMBER:** Brass Quintet (1970); Piano Trio (1971); *Intrada* for Trumpet, Horn, and Trombone (1973); Chamber Concerto for Harpsichord and String Quartet (1974); *4 caprichos de Francisco Goya* for Violin (1976); *Fanfare festiva* for 2 Trumpets, 2 Trombones, Timpani, and Organ (1978); *Sonata in 1 Movement* for Bass Trombone and Piano (1979); Concerto for Bass Trombone and Wind Ensemble (1979); *Caprichos II* for Cello (1979) and *III* for Double Bass (1982); *3 Epigrams* for Clarinet, Bassoon, and Piano (1980); *Duendecitos!* for Flute and Piano (1981). **VOCAL:** *The War Prayer* for Baritone and Orch. or Piano, after Mark Twain (1974); *La noche en la isla* for Baritone and Chamber Orch. or Piano, after Pablo Neruda (1980); *To the King Celestial* for Soprano and Chamber Orch., after a 14th-century Eng. text (1981); *7 Choral Settings of Poems by Emily Dickinson* (1983); *A Collect for the Renewal of Life* for Chorus and Organ (1986); *3 Choral Settings of Poems by William Butler Yeats* (1986); *You Shall Go Out in Joy* for Chorus and Organ (1989); *On This Day,* Christmas cantata for Soprano, Chorus, Children's Chorus, Percussion, and Harp (1993).

Grappelli (actually, **Grappelly**), **Stêphane,** outstanding French jazz violinist; b. Paris, Jan. 26, 1908. He was trained as a classical musician, but turned to jazz in the late 1920s. He organized the Quintette du Hot Club de France with the guitarist Django Reinhardt in 1934; subsequently toured widely and made recordings; made his U.S. debut at the Newport (R.I.) Jazz Festival in 1969. He appeared regularly in concert with Yehudi Menuhin from 1973, and later with Nigel Kennedy. In 1974 he made his Carnegie Hall debut in N.Y.; played there for a special 80th-birthday concert in 1988. He was the foremost jazz violinist in the European style of "Le Jazz hot."

BIBL.: R. Horricks, *S. G., or the Violin with Wings: A Profile* (N.Y., 1983); G. Smith, *S. G.: A Biography* (London, 1987).

Gräsbeck, Gottfrid (Gustaf Unosson), Finnish conductor, musicologist, and composer; b. Turku, Feb. 15, 1927. He graduated with a philosophy degree from the Turku Academy; traveled on study trips to West Germany and America. Upon his return to Finland, he taught in Turku; also founded his own concert agency. Among his works were *Toccata dodecafonica* for Orch. (1959); Concerto for Orch. and Tape (1964); *Visan från molnet* (Song about the Cloud), cantata for Women's Chorus and Orch. (1967); *Sinfonia da camera* (1969); *Lucia musik* for Solo Voices, Chorus, Organ, and Orch. (1971); Guitar Sonata (1974).

Grasse, Edwin, American violinist and composer; b. N.Y., Aug. 13, 1884; d. there, April 8, 1954. Blind from infancy, he dictated his compositions to an accompanist. He studied violin with Hauser in N.Y.; then went to Brussels for study with Thomson at the Cons., where he won 1st prize in 1900, and diplôme de capacité in 1901. He toured Europe and America. His works included *American Fantasie* for Violin and Orch.; Violin Sonata and other violin pieces; organ pieces.

Grassi, Eugène, French composer; b. Bangkok (of French parents), July 5, 1881; d. Paris, June 8, 1941. He went to France as a youth and studied with d'Indy; he revisited Siam from 1910 to 1913 to collect materials on indigenous music. His works reflect this study as well as, in harmonic idiom, the influence of Debussy. Among his compositions, all with oriental flavor, were *Le Réveil de Bouddha*, symphonic poem (Paris, Feb. 20, 1920); *Poème de l'univers* for Orch. (Paris, April 9, 1922); *Les Sanctuaires* (Paris, March 25, 1926); also songs in the impressionist manner.

Graudan, Nikolai, esteemed Russian-American cellist and teacher; b. Libau, Latvia, Sept. 5, 1896; d. Moscow, Aug. 9, 1964. He was a pupil of L. Abbiate at the St. Petersburg Cons. (1913–18), and joined its faculty in 1919. In 1922 he went to Düsseldorf as 1st cellist, and then held that post with the Berlin Phil. (1926–35). After a sojourn in London (1936–38), he went to the U.S. and was 1st cellist with the Minneapolis Sym. Orch. (1939–44). In subsequent years, he toured with his wife, the pianist Joanna Freudberg Graudan. He taught at Black Mountain College (1944), at Kenyon College (1945), at the Music Academy of the West at Santa Barbara (1949–50), and at the Aspen (Colo.) Music School (1951–60), where he was a member of the Festival Quartet (1954–62). Graudan died while on a visit to Russia.

Graunke, Kurt (Karl Wilhelm), German violinist, conductor, and composer; b. Stettin, Sept. 30, 1915. He studied violin with Gustav Havemann at the Berlin Hochschule für Musik, composition with Adolf Lessle and Hermann Grabner, violin with Hanns Weisse and Hans Dunschede, and conducting with Felix Husadel. During World War II, he studied in Vienna with Wolfgang Schneiderhan and played violin in the radio orch. In Munich in 1945 he founded his own orch., which he conducted for over 40 years and which made many recordings of scores for movies and television; it also gave several concerts each year, playing the world premieres of many works. His compositions are firmly rooted in Germanic modern Romanticism.

WORKS (all 1st perf. in Munich): 8 syms.: No. 1 (May 14, 1969), No. 2 (Sept. 9, 1972), No. 3 for Strings (Nov. 7, 1975; also for Orch., May 12, 1976), No. 4 (Jan. 25, 1978), No. 5 (May 13, 1981), No. 6 (May 12, 1982), No. 7 (May 11, 1983), and No. 8 (Sept. 11, 1985); Violin Concerto (Sept. 17, 1959); *Air* for Harp and Orch.; *2 Symphonic Dances; Novelette; Perpetuum mobile; Valse Anastasia.*

Graveure, Louis (real name, **Wilfred Douthitt**), English baritone; b. London, March 18, 1888; d. Los Angeles, April 27, 1965. He studied voice with Clara Novello-Davies. He sang in the operetta *The Lilac Domino* in N.Y. on Oct. 28, 1914. In 1915 he reappeared in N.Y. as Louis Graveure (after his mother's maiden name) and became a popular concert artist, singing all types of music. On Feb. 5, 1928, he gave a concert in N.Y. as a tenor; from 1931 to 1938 he was in Germany; from 1938 to 1940, in France; from 1940 to 1947, in England. In 1947 he returned to the U.S. and taught in various music schools.

BIBL.: "The Case of a Beardless Baritone," N. Slonimsky, *A Thing or Two about Music* (N.Y., 1948).

Gray, Alan, English organist and composer; b. York, Dec. 23, 1855; d. Cambridge, Sept. 27, 1935. He took degrees in law and music from Trinity College, Cambridge (Mus.D., 1889). He was music director of Wellington College (1883–92) and conductor of the Cambridge Univ. Musical Soc. (1892–1912); also organist at Trinity College (1892–1930). He wrote 5 cantatas; *Coronation March*; chamber music; many organ works. Vaughan Williams was one of his students.

Gray, Anne, English-born American musicologist; b. Vienna, Oct. 26, 1941. She was smuggled to London, where she was reared. In 1947 she was taken to N.Y. and in 1948 became a naturalized American citizen. Following training in music, speech, and drama at Hunter College (B.A., 1963), she pursued studies in English and education at San Diego State Univ. (M.A., 1968). After a hiatus for marriage and motherhood, she took her Ph.D. in human behavior at La Jolla Univ. (1982). Her tomes, *The Popular Guide to Classical Music* (1994; rev. ed., 1996) and *The Popular Guide to Women in Classical Music* (1996), received critical praise.

Gray, Cecil, Scottish writer on music and composer; b. Edinburgh, May 19, 1895; d. Worthing, Sept. 9, 1951. He studied at the Univ. of Edinburgh and with Bantock in Birmingham. He was co-ed. with P. Heseltine of the periodical *The Sackbut* from 1920; was music critic for the *Nation and Athenaeum* (1925–30), the *Daily Telegraph* (1928–33), and the *Manchester Guardian* (1932). He wrote the operas (to his own texts) *Deirdre, Temptation of St. Anthony*, and *The Trojan Women*; also other works.

WRITINGS: *A Survey of Contemporary Music* (1924; 2nd ed., 1927); with P. Heseltine, *Carlo Gesualdo, Prince of Venosa: Musician and Murderer* (1926); *The History of Music* (1928); *Sibelius* (1931; 2nd ed., 1934); *Peter Warlock* (1934); *Sibelius: The Symphonies* (1935); *Predicaments, or Music and the Future* (1936); *The 48 Preludes and Fugues of Bach* (1938); *Contingencies and Other Essays* (1947); *Musical Chairs or Between Two Stools* (memoirs; 1948).

BIBL.: R. Gorer, "The Music of C. G.," *Musical Review* (Aug. 1947); H. Davies, "Bernard van Dieren, Philip Heseltine and C. G.: A Significant Affiliation," *Music & Letters* (Jan. 1988); P. Gray, *C. G.: His Life and Notebooks* (London, 1989).

Gray, Linda Esther, Scottish soprano; b. Greenock, May 29, 1948. After training at the Royal Scottish Academy of Music in Glasgow, she went to London to pursue her studies at the Opera Centre and with Dame Eva Turner. During her student days, she made her first appearances in opera at the Sadler's Wells Theatre in London (1970). In 1972 she sang Mimi with the Glyndebourne Touring Opera Co., and then made her first appearance at the Glyndebourne Festival in 1973 as Mozart's 1st Lady. She then sang with the Scottish Opera in Glasgow. In 1978 she made her debut as Micaëla at the English National Opera in London, and in 1979 sang for the first time at the Welsh National Opera in Cardiff as Isolde. She made her debut at London's Covent Garden in 1980 as Gutrune, followed by her U.S. debut in Dallas in 1981 as Sieglinde. Although highly admired for her talent, she inextricably ceased singing in 1983. Among her other roles were Donna Elvira, Countess Almaviva, Leonore, Kundry, Aida, Tosca, and Ariadne.

Greef, Arthur de, Belgian pianist, teacher, and composer; b. Louvain, Oct. 10, 1862; d. Brussels, Aug. 29, 1940. He studied at the Brussels Cons. with L. Brassin (piano) and Gevaert (composition); then traveled as a pianist in Europe. In 1885 he became a prof. of piano at the Brussels Cons., retaining that post until 1930.

WORKS: *De Marketenster*, opera (Louvain, 1879); Sym.; *Ballad* for Strings; 2 piano concertos; 2 violin sonatas; *4 vieilles chansons flamandes* for Piano; piano études; songs.

BIBL.: F. Rasse, "Notice sur A. d.G.," *Annuaire de l'Académie Royale de Belgique* (1949).

Green, Adolph, notable American librettist, lyricist, and musician; b. N.Y., Dec. 2, 1915. Following his graduation from high school, he became active in the N.Y. nightclub act the Revuers, where he first worked with Betty Comden. They established their reputation as co-authors of the Broadway musical *On the Town* (1945), based on Leonard Bernstein's ballet *Fancy Free.* In 1951 they collaborated with Jule Styne on *Two on the Aisle.* After writing the accomplished screenplays for *Singin' in the Rain* (1952) and *The Band Wagon* (1953), they returned to Broadway to work with Bernstein on the notable *Wonderful Town* (1953). They subsequently worked again with Styne on such outstanding works as *Peter Pan* (1954), *Bells Are Ringing* (1956), *Do Re Mi* (1960), and *Hallelujah Baby!* (1967). Their collaboration with Charles Strouse on *Applause* (1970) won a Tony Award. Their success continued with the collaboration with Cy Coleman on the Tony Award winning *On the Twentieth*

Century (1978). They then worked again with Coleman on *The Will Rogers Follies* (1991), which also won a Tony Award. The brilliant collaborative efforts of Comden and Green became the longest in the annals of the American theater. In 1991 they received Kennedy Center Honors.

BIBL.: A. Robinson, *Betty Comden and A. G.: A Bio-Bibliography* (Westport, Conn., 1993).

Green, Elizabeth A(dine) H(erkimer), American string and conducting pedagogue; b. Mobile, Ala., Aug. 21, 1906. She began violin lessons at age 4 with her father, Albert Wingate Green, then studied at Wheaton (Ill.) College (Mus.B., 1924; B.S., 1928). She had advanced training with Clarence Evans (viola) in Chicago and Jacques Gordon (violin) in Falls Village, Conn., and then pursued her education at Northwestern Univ. (M.Mus., 1939). She later received instruction in conducting from Malko in Chicago (1940–42), and completed violin studies with Galamian at the Meadowmount School in N.Y. (summers, 1948–53; 1955–56); still later she studied at Eastern Michigan Univ. (B.F.A., 1978). She taught at East High School in Waterloo, Iowa (1928–42), and also played in the Waterloo Sym. Orch. From 1942 to 1954 she taught in the Ann Arbor (Mich.) public schools, then at the Univ. of Mich., retiring in 1974. She became well known as a teacher of string instruments and of conducting, and appeared as a conductor of various ensembles in the U.S. She publ. the widely consulted textbook *The Modern Conductor* (1961; 5th ed., 1992).

WRITINGS: *Orchestral Bowings and Routines* (1949; 2nd ed., 1957); *The Modern Conductor* (1961; 5th ed., 1992); *Teaching Stringed Instruments in Classes* (1966); with N. Malko, *The Conductor and His Score* (1975; 2nd ed., 1985, as *The Conductor's Score*); *The Dynamic Orchestra: Principles of Orchestral Performance for Instrumentalists, Conductors and Audiences* (1987); with others, *Miraculous Teacher: Ivan Galamian and the Meadowmount Experience* (1993).

BIBL.: D. Smith, *E.A.H. G.: A Biography* (diss., Univ. of Mich., 1986).

Green, John (Waldo), American pianist, conductor, arranger, and composer; b. N.Y., Oct. 10, 1908; d. Beverly Hills, May 15, 1989. He studied economics at Harvard Univ. (B.A., 1928), where he also received instruction in theory from W.R. Spalding; later studied piano with Hilsberg, orchestration with Deutsch, and conducting with Tours. Working as an arranger for Guy Lombardo, he produced his first hit song, *Coquette* (1928); while working as accompanist to Gertrude Lawrence, he wrote the popular *Body and Soul* (1930). He became an arranger for Paramount Pictures in Hollywood (1930); made recordings with his own dance band and performed on the radio. He settled in Hollywood as a member of the music staff of MGM Studios (1942), serving as head of its music dept. (1949–58). He prepared award-winning adaptations of the original scores for film versions of *Easter Parade* (1948), *An American in Paris* (1951), *West Side Story* (1961), and *Oliver!* (1968); he also wrote the score for the film *Raintree County* (1957). He was assoc. conductor of the Los Angeles Phil. (1959–61); also appeared as a guest conductor with several of the major U.S. orchs.

Green, Ray (Burns), American composer; b. Cavendish, Mo., Sept. 13, 1909. He began piano study at 14, winning a composition scholarship to the San Francisco Cons., where he studied with Bloch (1927–33); after further studies with Elkus and Stricklen at the Univ. of Calif. at Berkeley (1933–35), he won a scholarship to Paris to study with Milhaud (composition) and Monteux (conducting). He returned to the U.S. (1937); was active with the WPA and served as director of the Federal Music Project of Northern California (1939–41); then was chief of music for the Veterans Administration in Washington, D.C. (1946–48); subsequently was executive director of the American Music Center in N.Y. (1948–61). He also founded his own music publishing company, American Music Editions (1951). His works are often modal in harmonic settings; rhythmic animation is much in evidence in his pieces based on American rural songs.

WORKS: DRAMATIC: Incidental music; dance scores. **ORCH.:** Piano Concertino (1937); *Prelude and Fugue* (1937); *Sunday Sing Symphony* for Flute, Clarinet, Bassoon, and Orch. (1939–40); *3 Short Symphonies* (1945–53; 1970; 1974); *3 Pieces for a Concert* for Chamber Orch. (1947); *Jig Theme and 3 Changes* for Piano and Strings (1948); Violin Concerto (1952); *Rhapsody* for Harp and Orch. (1953); band music. **CHAMBER:** Suite for Violin and Piano (1929); Suite for Viola and Piano (1930); *5 Epigrammic Portraits* for String Quartet (1933; rev. 1950–52); *5 Epigrammic Romances* for String Quartet (1933); String Quartet (1933); Wind Quintet (1933); *Holiday for 4* for Viola, Violin, Bassoon, and Piano (1936; rev. 1939); *Concertante* for Viola or Clarinet and Piano (1940; also for Viola and Orch., 1946); *Concert Set* for Trumpet, Piano, and Drums (1941). **PIANO:** Sonata (1933); *12 Short Sonatas* (1948–62); other works. **VOCAL:** Choral pieces.

BIBL.: S. Vise, *R. G.: His Life and Stylistic Elements of His Music from 1938–1962* (diss., Univ. of Missouri, 1976).

Greenawald, Sheri (Kay), American soprano; b. Iowa City, Nov. 12, 1947. She studied with Charles Matheson at the Univ. of Northern Iowa (B.A., 1968), with Maria DeVarady, Hans Heinz, and Daniel Ferro in N.Y., and with Audrey Langford in London. In 1974 she made her professional debut in Poulenc's *Les Mamelles de Tirésias* at N.Y.'s Manhattan Theater Club, and then sang with the San Francisco Opera, the Houston Grand Opera, the Santa Fe Opera, the Washington (D.C.) Opera et al. In 1980 she made her European debut as Mozart's Susanna with the Netherlands Opera. She toured extensively as a concert artist. Among her many roles were Zerlina, Despina, Massenet's Sophie, Violetta, Mimi, and Britten's Ellen Orford. She also created roles in Pasatieri's *Signor Deluso* (1974) and *Washington Square* (1976), Floyd's *Bilby's Doll* (1976), and Bernstein's *A Quiet Place* (1983).

Greenberg, Noah, American conductor; b. N.Y., April 9, 1919; d. there, Jan. 9, 1966. He studied music privately, and then organized choruses in N.Y. In 1952 he founded the N.Y. Pro Musica Antiqua, an organization specializing in Renaissance and medieval music, performed in authentic styles and on copies of early instruments; he revived the medieval liturgical music dramas *The Play of Daniel* (1958) and *The Play of Herod* (1963); traveled with his ensemble in Europe in 1960 and 1963. It was primarily through the efforts of this group (later known as the N.Y. Pro Musica) that early music, in the U.S., became a viable idiom available to modern audiences. He held a Guggenheim fellowship in 1955 and Ford fellowships in 1960 and 1962.

Greene, (Harry) Plunket, Irish bass-baritone and teacher; b. Old Connaught House, County Wicklow, June 24, 1865; d. London, Aug. 19, 1936. He was a student of Hromada in Stuttgart, Vannuccini in Florence, and J.B. Welsh and A. Blume in London. On Jan. 21, 1888, he made his debut as a soloist in Handel's *Messiah* in Stepney. In 1890 he appeared at London's Covent Garden, but soon became a successful concert artist; from 1893 he appeared in recitals with Leonard Borwick, and that same year made his first tour of the U.S. In 1899 he married Parry's daughter, Gwendolen. Greene devoted his later years to vocal pedagogy. He publ. the manual *Interpretation in Song* (London, 1912) and a book of reminiscences, *From the Blue Danube to Shannon* (London, 1934); also a biography of Stanford (London, 1935). He was a fine interpreter of Schumann and Brahms, and also sang in the premieres of works by Parry, Stanford, Elgar, and Vaughan Williams.

Greenhouse, Bernard, esteemed American cellist and pedagogue; b. Newark, N.J., Jan. 3, 1916. He began his training with William Berce; in 1933 he entered the Juilliard School of Music in N.Y. as a pupil of Salmond; after receiving a diploma from its graduate school in 1938, he pursued his studies with Feuermann (1940–41), Alexanian (1944–46), and Casals (1946–47). He was 1st cellist in the CBS Sym. Orch. in N.Y. (1938–42), and also was a member of the Dorian String Quartet (1939–42). During his military service, he was solo cellist with the U.S. Navy Sym. Orch. and a member of the Navy String Quartet (1942–45). On Feb. 11, 1946, he made his recital debut at N.Y.'s Town Hall, where he gave annual recitals until 1957. He was a member of the Harpsichord Quartet (1947–51) and of the Bach Aria Group (1948–76), but it was as a founder-member of the Beaux Arts Trio (1955–87) that he won his greatest distinction. He taught at the Manhattan School of Music in N.Y. (1950–82), the Juilliard School of Music (1951–61), the Hartt School of Music in Hartford, Conn. (1956–65), the Indiana Univ. School of Music in Bloomington (summers, 1956–65), the State Univ. of N.Y. at Stony Brook (1960–85), the New England Cons. of Music in Boston (from 1986), and at Rutgers, the State Univ. of New Jersey (from 1987). He also gave master classes around the globe. Greenhouse served as president of the Cello Soc. (1955–59; from 1987). In addition to the standard repertory, he performed much contemporary American music.

BIBL.: N. Delbanco, *The Beaux Arts Trio: A Portrait* (N.Y. and London, 1985).

Gregor, Bohumil, Czech conductor; b. Prague, July 14, 1926. He studied at the Prague Cons. with Alois Klima. After conducting at the 5th of May Theater in Prague (1947–49) and in Brno (1949–51), he served as music director in Ostrava (1958–62). From 1962 he was a regular guest conductor at the National Theater in Prague; he also appeared as a guest conductor throughout Europe; in 1969 he made his U.S. debut with the San Francisco Opera conducting *Jenůfa*. He was closely associated with the music of Janáček and other Czech composers.

Gregor, Čestmír, Czech composer; b. Brno, May 14, 1926. He began his training with his father, Josef Gregor, who had been a student of Novák; later he studied with Kvapil (1950–54) and Kapr (1965–70) at the Janáček Academy of Music in Brno. From 1959 to 1972 he was director of music for the Czech Radio in Ostrava. In his works, he pursued an atonal style of composition.

WORKS: DRAMATIC: OPERA: *Profesionální žena* (A Professional Woman; 1983). **BALLETS:** *Závrat* (Vertigo; 1963; ballet version of the *Choreographic Symphony); Horko* (Heat; 1978). **ORCH.:** *Joyous Overture* (1951); *If All Girls of the World*, symphonic poem (1953); 3 syms. (*Country and People*, 1953; *Choreographic*, 1963; *Symphony of My City*, 1971; rev. 1973); *Once in Spring Evening*, suite for Chamber Orch. (1954); *No One is Alone*, piano concerto (1955); *May I Speak?*, overture (1956); *Tragic Suite* for Small Orch. (1957); *Concerto semplice* for Piano and Orch. (1958); Suite for Strings (1959); *Polyfonietta* (1961); *Daedalus's Children*, symphonic poem (1961); *If All Men of the World*, overture (1963); Violin Concerto (1965; rev. 1968); Cello Concerto, *Complimento à la musica di ogni giorno* (1974); Sinfonietta (1976); *Concerto da camera* for Clarinet and Strings (1977); *I've Joined the Army*, variations (1978); Piano Concerto (1979); *Symphonic Metamorphoses on a Blues Theme* (1986; rev. 1990). **CHAMBER:** Trio for Flute, Viola, and Bass Clarinet (1959); String Quartet (1965); *Amenities* for Violin and Piano (1987); 2 violin sonatas (1989); *Dolce Vita* for Violin and Piano (1990); *3 Generations* for String Quartet (1991); *Auspicious Word*, bass clarinet sonata (1993). **PIANO:** *Experiment* (1946); *Sonata brevis* (1946); *Ash Wednesday* (1962); *3 Movements* (1966); *Sonata in 3 Tempi* (1966). **VOCAL:** *2 Capricious Ballads* for Soprano and Piano (1975); *The Sea's Children*, choral cantata (1975).

Gregson, Edward, English conductor, teacher, and composer; b. Sunderland, July 23, 1945. He was a pupil in composition of Alan Bush at the Royal Academy of Music in London (1963–67). In 1976 he became a lecturer, in 1989 a reader, and in 1993 a prof. of music at Goldsmiths' College, Univ. of London. As a conductor, he was an advocate of contemporary scores.

WORKS: ORCH.: *Music* for Chamber Orch. (1968); Concerto for Horn and Brass Band (1971; also for Horn and Orch.); Concerto for Tuba and Brass Band (Manchester, April 24, 1976; also for Tuba and Orch., 1978; Edinburgh, June 11, 1983); *Flourish* (1978; rev. 1986); *Metamorphoses* (1979); Trombone Concerto (London, July 25, 1979); Trumpet Concerto (London, April 20, 1983); *Contrasts* (1st perf. as *Greenwich Dances*, London, May 7, 1983); *Celebration* (1991); *Blazon* (1992); Clarinet Concerto (1993); Concerto for Piano and Winds (1995). **BRASS BAND:** *Essay* (1970); Concerto Grosso (1973); *Connotations* (1976); *Dances and Arias* (1984); *Occasion* (1986). **WIND BAND:** *Festivo* (1985). **CHAMBER:** Oboe Sonata (1965); *Divertimento* for Trombone and Piano (1967); Quintet for 2 Trumpets, Horn, Trombone, and Tuba (1967); *Prelude and Capriccio* for Trumpet and Piano (1972); *Equale Dances* for Brass Quintet (1983). **VOCAL:** *In the Beginning* for Chorus and Piano (1966; rev. 1981); *Missa Brevis Pacem* for Baritone, Treble Voices, and Large Symphonic Wind Ensemble (1988).

Greindl, Josef, German bass; b. Munich, Dec. 23, 1912; d. Vienna, April 16, 1993. He was a student in Munich of Paul Bender and Anna Bahr-Mildenburg. In 1936 he made his formal operatic debut as Hunding in Krefeld. After singing in Düsseldorf (1938–42), he was a member of the Berlin State Opera (from 1942); in 1949 he became a member of the Berlin Städtische (later Deutsche) Oper. In 1943 he made his first appearance at the Bayreuth Festival as Pogner, and returned to sing there regularly from 1951 to 1969. On Nov. 15, 1952, he made his Metropolitan Opera debut in N.Y. as Wagner's Heinrich, but remained on the roster for only a season. From 1956 to 1969 he sang at the Vienna State Opera. In 1963 he appeared at London's Covent Garden. In 1961 he was made a prof. at the Saarbrücken Hochschule für Musik, and in 1973 at the Vienna Hochschule für Musik. Greindl was equally convincing in dramatic and buffo roles. Among his other roles were Sarastro, Don Alfonso, Hans Sachs, and the Wanderer in *Siegfried*.

Grešák, Jozef, Slovak composer; b. Bardejov, Dec. 30, 1907; d. Piešt'any, April 17, 1987. He studied piano and organ, but was mainly autodidact as a composer.

WORKS: DRAMATIC: *Prichod Slovákov* (The Arrival of the Slovaks), opera (1925); *Radúz and Mahuliena*, ballet (1954–55); *With Rosary*, opera (1970–73); *Zuzanka Hrašovie*, monodrama (1973; Bratislava, Jan. 15, 1975). **ORCH.:** Piano Concerto (1963); *Concertino-Pastorale* for Oboe, English Horn, Horn, and Orch. (1965); *Morceau I* for Violin and Orch. (1968); *Rotors II* (1969); *Concertant Symfonietta* (1975; Košice, May 5, 1976). **OTHER:** Chamber works; *The Emigrant Songs* for Soloists, Men's Chorus, and Orch. (1961) and other vocal pieces; piano music.

Gretchaninoff, Alexander (Tikhonovich), Russian-born American composer; b. Moscow, Oct. 25, 1864; d. N.Y., Jan. 3, 1956. He studied at the Moscow Cons. (1881–91) with Safonov (piano) and Arensky (composition); then studied composition at the St. Petersburg Cons. as a pupil of Rimsky-Korsakov (1891–1903). He was a prof. of composition at the Moscow Inst. from 1891 to 1922; then lived in Paris. He visited the U.S., where he appeared with considerable success as a guest conductor of his own works (1929–31); went to the U.S. again in 1939, settling in N.Y. He became a naturalized American citizen on July 25, 1946. He continued to compose until the end of his long life. A concert of his works was presented in his presence on the occasion of his 90th birthday at Town Hall in N.Y. (Oct. 25, 1954). Gretchaninoff's music is rooted in the Russian national tradition; influences of both Tchaikovsky and Rimsky-Korsakov are in evidence in his early works; toward 1910 he attempted to inject some impressionistic elements into his vocal compositions, but without signal success. His masterly sacred works are of historical importance, for he introduced a reform into Russian church singing by using nationally colored melodic patterns; in several of his masses, he employed instrumental accompaniment contrary to the prescriptions of the Russian Orthodox faith, a circumstance that precluded the use of these works in Russian churches. His *Missa oecumenica* represents a further expansion toward ecclesiastical universality; in this work, he makes use of elements pertaining to other religious music, including non-Christian. His instrumental works are competently written, but show less originality. His early *Lullaby* (1887) and the song *Over the Steppes* long retained their popularity, and were publ. in numerous arrangements. After the Revolution, Gretchaninov wrote a new Russian national anthem, *Hymn of Free Russia* (sung in N.Y. at a concert for the benefit of Siberian exiles, May 22, 1917), but it was never adopted by any political Russian faction. He publ. a book of reminiscences as *My Life* (Paris, in Russian, 1934; Eng. tr., 1951, with a complete catalogue of works as well as additions and an introduction by N. Slonimsky).

WORKS: DRAMATIC: OPERAS: *Dobrinya Nikititch* (Moscow, Oct. 27, 1903); *Sister Beatrice* (Moscow, Oct. 25, 1912; suppressed after 3 perfs. as being irreverent); *The Dream of a Little Christmas Tree*, children's opera (1911); *The Cat, the Fox, and the Rooster*, children's opera (1919); *The Castle Mouse*, children's opera (1921); *Marriage*, comic opera after Gogol (1945–46; Tanglewood, Aug. 1, 1948). **BALLET DIVERTISSEMENT:** *Idylle forestière* (N.Y., 1925). **INCIDENTAL MUSIC TO:** Ostrovsky's *Snegoruchka* (Moscow, Nov. 6, 1900); Tolstoy's *Tsar Feodor* (Moscow, Oct. 26, 1898) and *Death of Ivan the Terrible* (1899). **ORCH.:** Concert Overture in D minor (1892; St. Petersburg, March 1893); *Elegy in Memory of Tchaikovsky* (1893; St. Petersburg, Dec. 31, 1898, Rimsky-Korsakov conducting); 5 syms: No. 1 (1893; St. Petersburg, Jan. 26, 1895), No. 2 (1909; Moscow, March 14, 1909), No. 3 (1920–23; Kiev, May 29, 1924), No. 4 (1923–24; N.Y., April 9, 1942), and No. 5 (1936; Philadelphia, April 5, 1939); *Poème élégiaque* (Boston, March 29, 1946); *Festival Overture* (Indianapolis, Nov. 15, 1946); *Poème lyrique* (1948). **CHAMBER:** 4 string quartets; 2 trios; Violin Sonata; Cello Sonata; 2 clarinet sonatas; 2 *Miniatures* for Saxophone and Piano. **PIANO:** 2 sonatas (n.d., 1944); *Petits tableaux musicaux* (1947); other works. **VOCAL:** *Liturgy of St. John Chrysostom* (Moscow, Oct. 19, 1898); *Laudate Deum* (Moscow, Nov. 24, 1915); *Liturgia domestica* (Moscow, March 30, 1918); *Missa oecumenica* for Soli, Chorus, and Orch. (Boston, Feb. 25, 1944); 84 choruses; 14 vocal quartets; 8 duets; 258 songs.

BIBL.: J. Yasser, "G.'s 'Heterodox' Compositions," *Musical Quarterly* (July 1942).

Grevillius, Nils, Swedish conductor; b. Stockholm, March 7, 1893; d. Mariefred, Aug. 15, 1970. He was a violin student of Book at the Stockholm Cons. (1905–11), where he received 1st prize and the Prix Marteau, and later was a conducting student in Sondershausen and London. He began his career as concertmaster of the Royal Theater Orch. in Stockholm (1911–14). After serving as assistant conductor of the Stockholm Concert Soc. (1914–20), he conducted the Ballet Suédois in Paris (1922–23) and the Vienna Tonkünstlerverein (1923). Upon his return to Stockholm, he was conductor of the Royal Orch. (1924–53) and the Radio Orch. (1927–39), and also was court music director (1931–53).

Grey, Madeleine (real name, **Madeleine Nathalie Grumberg**), French mezzo-soprano; b. Villaines-la-Juhel, Mayenne, June 11, 1896; d. Paris, March 13, 1979. She was a student of Cortot (piano) and Hettich (voice) at the Paris Cons., and then devoted herself to a concert career. Fauré wrote his *Mirages* for her, and served as her accompanist at the cycle's premiere in Paris in 1919. Grey became particularly associated with the music of Ravel, who accompanied her in recordings of his *Chansons hébraïques* and *Chansons madécasses* in 1932. Canteloube dedicated his *Chants d'Auvergne* to her. Grey made many tours abroad, winning success in Italy, the U.S., and South America. She retired in 1952. While her command of diction and clarity of vocal timbre were especially suited to the French repertoire, she also championed works by Respighi, Malipiero, Villa Lobos, and other composers of her era.

Griebling, Karen (Jean), American violist, violinist, conductor, teacher, and composer; b. Akron, Ohio, Dec. 31, 1957. She was trained at the Eastman School of Music in Rochester, N.Y. (B.M., 1980), the Univ. of Houston (M.M., 1982), and the Univ. of Texas at Austin (D.M.A., 1986). She played in the Texas Chamber Orch. (1980–81), the Houston Ballet Orch. (1980–82), the Corpus Christi Sym. Orch. (1985–86), and the Albany (N.Y.) Sym. Orch. (1986–87). In 1987 she joined the faculty of Hendrix College in Conway, Ark., became a member of the Fort Smith Sym. Orch., and was made co-director of the Conway Civic Orch.; she also was a member of the Arkansas String Quartet (from 1988). In 1990 she founded and became conductor of the Conway Chamber Orch.

WORKS: 6 string quartets (1970–92); Trio for 2 Violins and Viola (1973); Trio for Flute, Clarinet, and Bassoon (1976); 2 viola sonatas (1976, 1987); Oboe d'Amore Sonata (1980); *Johnny Appleseed*, ballet (1983); *Homage* for Winds (1983); Concerto Grosso (1985); *The House of Bernarda Alba*, opera (1986); *Gloria* for Chorus and Instrumental Ensemble (1988); *Sonata a Due* for Viola and Bass Trombone (1992); piano music; songs.

Griffes, Charles Tomlinson, outstanding American composer; b. Elmira, N.Y., Sept. 17, 1884; d. N.Y., April 8, 1920. He began piano lessons at an early age with his sister; about 1899 he became a piano student of Mary Selena Broughton, an instructor at Elmira College. Thanks to Broughton's financial assistance, Griffes was able to go to Berlin in 1903 to pursue his training at the Stern Cons. with Ernst Jedliczka and Gottfried Galston (piano), Philippe Rufer and Humperdinck (composition), and Max Lowengard and Klatte (counterpoint). After private composition lessons with Humperdinck (1905–06), he again studied piano with Galston (1906–07). Upon his return to the U.S. in 1907, he was made director of music at the Hackley School in Tarrytown, N.Y. Until about 1911 Griffes' works followed along the path of German Romanticism. He then pursued his fascination with impressionism in a number of piano pieces and songs. His subsequent interest in the potentialities of the oriental scale resulted in such scores as his Japanese pantomime *Sho-jo* (1917) and the orch. version of his remarkable piano piece *The Pleasure-Dome of Kubla Khan* (1917). In his last works, such as his Piano Sonata (1917–18), he revealed a strong individual style tending toward extreme dissonance.

WORKS: DRAMATIC: *The Kairn of Koridwen*, dance drama (1916; N.Y., Feb. 10, 1917); *Sho-jo*, Japanese pantomime (Atlantic City, N.J., Aug. 5, 1917); *The White Peacock*, ballet (N.Y., June 22, 1919; arrangement of the piano piece, 1915); *Salut au monde*, festival drama (1919; N.Y., April 22, 1922). **ORCH.:** Overture (c.1905); *Symphonische Phantasie* (1907); *The Pleasure-Dome of Kubla Khan* (1917; Boston, Nov. 28, 1919; arrangement of the piano piece, 1912); *Notturno für Orchester* (c.1918; Philadelphia, Dec. 19, 1919); *Poem* for Flute and Orch. (1918; N.Y., Nov. 16, 1919); *Bacchanale* (Philadelphia, Dec. 19, 1919; arrangement of the *Scherzo* for Piano, 1913); *Clouds* (Philadelphia, Dec. 19, 1919; arrangement of the piano piece, 1916); *The White Peacock* (Philadelphia, Dec. 19, 1919; arrangement of the piano piece, 1915); *Nocturne* (1919; arrangement of the 2nd movement of the Piano Sonata, 1917–18). **CHAMBER:** Movement for String Quartet (1903); *3 Tone-Pictures: The Lake at Evening, The Vale of Dreams,* and *The Night Winds* for Woodwind and Harp (1915; also for Wind Quintet, String Quintet, and Piano, 1919; arrangements of the piano pieces, 1910–12); *Vivace (Allegro assai quasi presto)* for String Quartet (1917); *2 Sketches Based on Indian Themes: Lento e mesto* and *Allegro giocoso* for String Quartet (1918–19); *Allegro energico ma maestoso* for String Quartet (1919). **PIANO:** *6 Variations* (1898); *Mazurka* (1898–1900); *4 Preludes* (1899–1900); 5 sonatas (c.1904; c.1910; c.1911; c.1912; 1917–18, N.Y., Feb. 26, 1918, 2nd movement orchestrated as *Nocturne*, 1919); *3 Tone-Pictures* (1910–12); (8) *Fantasy Pieces* (1912–15), including *Scherzo* (1913; orchestrated as *Bacchanale*, 1919); (4) *Roman Sketches: The White Peacock* (1915; orchestrated 1919), *Nightfall* (1916), *The Fountain of the Acqua Paola* (1916), and *Clouds* (1916; orchestrated 1919); *3 Preludes* (1919). **SONGS:** (3) *Tone-Images* (1912–14); *2 Rondels* (c.1914); *4 Impressions* (1914–16); *3 Poems* (1916); *5 Poems of Ancient China and Japan* (1916–17; N.Y., Nov. 1, 1917); *2*

Poems (1917–18); *3 Poems of Fiona MacLeod* (1918; N.Y., March 22, 1919; orchestrated 1918; Wilmington, Del., March 24, 1919).

BIBL.: J. Howard, *C.T.G.* (N.Y., 1923); W. Upton, "The Songs of C.T.G.," *Musical Quarterly* (July 1923); M. Bauer, "C.T.G. as I Remember Him," ibid. (July 1943); E. Maisel, *C.T.G.: The Life of an American Composer* (N.Y., 1943); G. Conrey, *The Published Songs of C.T.G.: A Stylistic Examination* (diss., Chicago Musical College, 1955); D. Boda, *The Music of C.G.* (diss., Florida State Univ., 1962); H. Pratt, *The Complete Piano Works of C.T.G.* (diss., Boston Univ., 1975); D. Anderson, *C.T.G.: An Annotated Bibliography-Discography* (Detroit, 1977); idem, *The Works of C.T.G.: A Descriptive Catalogue* (Ann Arbor, 1984); idem, *C.T.G.: A Life in Music* (Washington, D.C., 1993).

Griffes, Elliot, American pianist, teacher, and composer; b. Boston, Jan. 28, 1893; d. Los Angeles, June 8, 1967. He studied at Ithaca College (graduated, 1913), then with Horatio Parker at the Yale Univ. School of Music (1915–16), and with Chadwick, Stuart Mason, and Pattison at the New England Cons. of Music in Boston (1917–18); won a Juilliard scholarship (1922) and a Pulitzer scholarship (1931). He was active as a recitalist; also taught in various institutions, including Grinnell College in Iowa (1920–22), the Brooklyn Settlement School (1923–24), the St. Louis School of Music (head of theory dept., 1935–36), and the Westchester Cons. in White Plains, N.Y. (director, 1942–43); settled in Los Angeles as a composer of film scores. He wrote works in ingratiatingly Romantic colors.

WORKS: DRAMATIC: *The Blue Scarab*, operetta (1934); *Port of Pleasure*, opera (Los Angeles, June 29, 1963). **ORCH.:** *A Persian Fable* (1925); *Paul Bunyan, Colossus*, symphonic poem (1926–34); 2 syms.: No. 1 (1931) and No. 2, *Fantastic Pursuit*, for Strings (1941); *Yon Green Mountain*, suite (1943); *Montevallo*, concerto grosso for Organ, Piano, and Strings (1945). **CHAMBER:** 3 string quartets (1926, 1930, 1937); Violin Sonata (1931); *To the Sun*, symphonic fragment for Piano Trio (1940); Suite for Piano Trio (1941); *The Aztec Flute* for Flute and Piano Trio (1942); *The Fox and the Crow* for Chamber Ensemble (1950); piano pieces. **VOCAL:** Song cycles and solo songs.

Griffiths, Paul, English music critic and writer on music; b. Bridgend, Glamorgan, Wales, Nov. 24, 1947. He received his education at Lincoln College, Oxford. From 1971 he wrote music criticism for many publications. He was chief music critic of *The Times* of London from 1982 to 1992, and then of the *New Yorker* from 1992. He served as area ed. for 20th-century music for the *New Grove Dictionary of Music and Musicians* (1980) and the *New Oxford Companion to Music* (1983). Among his books are *A Concise History of Modern Music* (1978), *Modern Music: The Avant-Garde since 1945* (1981), *The Rake's Progress* (1982), *The String Quartet* (1983), *Bartók* (1984), *New Sounds, New Personalities: British Composers of the 1980s* (1985), *An Encyclopedia of 20th Century Music* (1986), and *Stravinsky* (1992).

Grigoriu, Theodor, Romanian composer; b. Galaţi, July 25, 1926. He studied violin with Enacovici at the Bucharest Cons. (1935–36); after private composition lessons with Jora (1949–54), he studied composition at the Moscow Cons. with Khatchaturian and Golubev (1954–55). In 1943 he won the George Enesco Prize for Composition, in 1975 the prize of the Romanian Academy, and in 1969, 1974, and 1985 prizes of the Romanian Composers's Union.

WORKS: DRAMATIC: Film scores. **ORCH.:** *Sinfonia cantabile* (1950; rev. 1966); *Dans tătar* (1953); *Theatrical Suite in the Classical Style* for Chamber Orch. (1956); *Symphonic Variations*, on a melody by Anton Pann (1955; Bucharest, Jan. 21, 1956); Concerto for Double Chamber Orch. and Solo Oboe (1957); *Hommage to Enesco* for 4 Groups of Violins (1960); *Melodic infinită* for Chamber String Orch. (1969); *Tristia* (1974); *Pastorale şi idile transilvane* (1984; 2nd version, 1986); Violin Concerto (1993; Indianapolis, May 1, 1994). **CHAMBER:** String Quartet (1943); Piano Trio (1943); *The River Arges Flows On*, suite for String Quartet (1953). **VOCAL:** 2 cantatas: *Cantata pentru 23 August* (1951) and *Oda orasului meu* (Ode to My City; 1963; rev. 1971); *Vis cosmic* (Cosmic Dream), symphonic poem for Vocalizing Tenor or Electronic Instrument and Orch. (1959; Bucharest, Oct. 28, 1965); *Elegie pontică* for Bass-Baritone, Women's Chorus, and Chamber Orch., after Ovid (Bucharest, June 24, 1969); *Vocalizele mării*, choral sym. (1984); songs.

Grimm, Carl Hugo, American organist and composer; b. Zanesville, Ohio, Oct. 31, 1890; d. Cincinnati, Oct. 25, 1978. He studied music with his father, then held positions as organist in Cincinnati, where he also taught composition at the Cons. (1907–31).

WORKS: ORCH.: *Erotic Poem* (1927); *Thanatopsis* (1928); *Abraham Lincoln*, "character portrait" (1930); *Montana*, symphonic poem (Cincinnati, March 26, 1943); *An American Overture* (Cincinnati, Feb. 15, 1946); Trumpet Concerto (1948); Sym. (1950); *Pennsylvania Overture* (1954). **CHAMBER:** *Byzantine Suite* for 10 Instruments (1930); *Little Serenade* for Wind Quintet (1934); Cello Sonata (1945); many organ pieces; works for ensembles of multiple flutes. **VOCAL:** *Gothic Mass* (1970); many anthems; songs.

Grinblat, Romuald, Russian composer; b. Tver, April 11, 1930. He studied at the Latvian Cons. in Riga. Upon graduation in 1955, he devoted himself to composition and teaching. His compositions included dramatic works, orch. scores, chamber music, and vocal pieces.

Grishkat, Hans (Adolf Karl Willy), German conductor and pedagogue; b. Hamburg, Aug. 29, 1903; d. Stuttgart, Jan. 10, 1977. He studied at the Univ. of Tübingen and at the Hochschule für Musik in Stuttgart. In 1924 he organized the Reutlingen Chorale; in 1931 he formed the Swabian Chorale, and in 1936 the Grishkat Chorale in Stuttgart; gained a fine reputation as a choral conductor in Germany. From 1945 to 1950 he led the Swabian Sym. Orch. in Reutlingen. In 1946 he was appointed instructor of choral conducting at the Hochschule für Musik in Stuttgart; from 1968 until his death he led the orch. conducting classes there.

Grist, Reri, black American soprano; b. N.Y., Feb. 29, 1934. While still a child, she appeared as a dancer and singer in musicals. She was educated at N.Y.'s High School of Music and Art, and then at Queens College; her voice teacher was Claire Gelda. In 1957 she sang Consuelo in the Broadway staging of *West Side Story*. In 1959 she made her operatic debut as Blöndchen at the Sante Fe Opera, and then sang with the N.Y. City Opera. In 1960 she made her European debut in Cologne as the Queen of the Night, and then sang in Zürich as Zerbinetta. She appeared as Despina at the Glyndebourne Festival in 1962, the year she also made her debut at London's Covent Garden as the Queen of Shemakha. In 1965 she sang Blöndchen at the Salzburg Festival. On Feb. 25, 1966, she made her Metropolitan Opera debut in N.Y. as Rossini's Rosina, returning for the 1968–73 and 1977–78 seasons. Her operatic engagements also took her to many other music centers in North America and Europe. She also sang widely as a soloist with orchs. and as a recitalist. Among her other roles were Susanna, Adina, Norina, Gilda, Oscar, and Sophie.

Griswold, Putnam, American bass-baritone; b. Minneapolis, Dec. 23, 1875; d. N.Y., Feb. 26, 1914. He went to London to study at the Royal College of Music and with A. Randegger. After making his operatic debut at Covent Garden as Leonato in Stanford's *Much Ado About Nothing* (1901), he pursued his training in Paris with Bouhy, in Frankfurt am Main with Stockhausen, and in Berlin with Emerich. In 1904 he sang at the Berlin Royal Opera; after touring the U.S. with Savage's opera company as Gurnemanz in an English language production of *Parsifal* (1904–05), he returned to Berlin to sing with fine success at the Royal Opera (1906–11). On Nov. 23, 1911, he made his Metropolitan Opera debut in N.Y. as Hagen, and sang there until his death. He was highly admired as a Wagnerian, being notably successful as Wotan, King Marke, Pogner, and Daland.

Grob-Prandl, Gertrud, Austrian soprano; b. Vienna, Nov. 11, 1917; d. there, May 16, 1995. She was a student of Burian in Vienna. In 1938 she made her operatic debut as Santuzza at the Vienna Volksoper; after singing at the Zürich Opera (1946–47), she was a valued member of the Vienna State Opera (1947–64); she also appeared at London's Covent Garden (from 1951), in Milan, Berlin, and South America. She was known for her Wagnerian roles, most notably Ortrud, Brünnhilde, and Isolde.

Grobe, Donald (Roth), American tenor; b. Ottawa, Ill., Dec. 16, 1929; d. Berlin, April 1, 1986. He attended the Mannes College of Music in N.Y. and also received vocal coaching from Robert Long, Martial Singher, Robert Weede, and Marguerite von Winterfeldt. In 1952 he made his operatic debut as Borsa in *Rigoletto* in Chicago, and then sang in musicals, on television, and in concerts in N.Y. After singing opera in Krefeld/Mönchengladbach (1956–57) and Hannover (1957–60), he was a member of the Berlin Deutsche Oper, where he created the roles of Wilhelm in Henze's *Der Junge Lord* (1965) and Arundel in Fortner's *Elisabeth Tudor* (1972); in 1970, was made a Kammersänger. He also appeared at the Hamburg State Opera (1958–61; 1966–75) and the Bavarian State Opera in Munich (from 1967). On Nov. 22, 1968, he made his Metropolitan Opera debut in N.Y. as Froh in *Das Rheingold.* His other roles included Ferrando, Eisenstein, Hoffmann, Alwa in *Lulu,* and Flamand in *Capriccio.*

Grofé, Ferde (actually, **Ferdinand Rudolph von**), American composer, arranger, and pianist; b. N.Y., March 27, 1892; d. Santa Monica, Calif., April 3, 1972. He studied with Pietro Floridia. He was a violist in the Los Angeles Sym. Orch. (1909–19); he also played piano in film theaters, ragtime bands, and vaudeville. In 1917 he became an arranger and pianist for Paul Whiteman, for whom he prepared highly successful arrangements of *Avalon, Japanese Sandman,* and *Whispering.* His arrangement of Gershwin's *Rhapsody in Blue* for Whiteman in 1924 established Grofé's reputation. After his association with Whiteman ended in 1933, he conducted on the radio (1933–34) and taught at the Juilliard Graduate School in N.Y. (1939–42). In 1944 he won an Academy Award for his score for the film *Minstrel Man.* Of his many light orch. works, he remains best known for his *Grand Canyon Suite* (1931).

WORKS: ORCH.: *Mississippi: A Tone Journey* (1926); *Grand Canyon Suite* (Chicago, Nov. 22, 1931); *Tabloid Suite* (1933); *Killarney: An Irish Fantasy* (1934); *Hollywood Ballet* (1935); *Symphony in Steel* (1935; N.Y., Jan. 19, 1937); *Tin Pan Alley: The Melodic Decades* (1938); *Biography of an American* (1943); *Atlantic Crossing* (1950); *Lincoln's Gettysburg Address* (1954); *Hudson River Suite* (1956); *Niagara Falls Suite* (1960); *World's Fair Suite* (1963; N.Y., April 22, 1964); *Virginia City: Requiem for a Ghost Town* (Virginia City, Nev., Aug. 10, 1968); Piano Concerto (n.d.); pieces for Jazz Band and Brass Band. **OTHER:** Film scores, including *The King of Jazz* (1930), *Yankee Doodle Rhapsody* (1936), *Minstrel Man* (1944), and *Time out of Mind* (1946); piano pieces; songs; arrangements.

Grondahl, Launy, Danish conductor and composer; b. Ordrup, near Copenhagen, June 30, 1886; d. Copenhagen, Jan. 21, 1960. He studied violin with Anton Bloch and Axel Gade, and theory with Ludolf Nielsen; later took music courses in Paris, Italy, Vienna, and elsewhere. Returning to Denmark, he became president of the Soc. of Young Musicians; from 1925 he conducted the Danish Radio Sym. Orch., serving as its chief conductor from 1931 to 1956. Among his compositions were a Violin Concerto (1917); Sym. (1919); Trombone Concerto (1924); Bassoon Concerto (1943); 2 string quartets; Violin Sonata; numerous piano pieces; and songs.

Groot, Cor de, Dutch pianist and composer; b. Amsterdam, July 7, 1914. He studied composition with Sem Dresden at the Amsterdam Cons. In 1936 he won the international piano contest in Vienna; then gave concerts in Europe and America. He taught piano in The Hague; also served as librarian and archivist in Hilversum.

WORKS: ORCH.: Piano Concerto (1931); *Concerto classico* for Piano and Orch. (1932); Concerto for 2 Pianos and Orch. (1939); Concerto for 2 Oboes and Orch. (1939); Piano Concertino (1939); Clarinet Concerto (1940); Flute Concerto (1940); Violin Concerto (1940); *Divertimento* (1949); *Wilhelmus ouverture* (1950); *Minuten Concerto* for Piano and Orch. (1950); *Ouverture energico* (1951); *Capriccio* for Piano and Orch. (1955); *Variations imaginaires* for Piano, Left-hand and Orch. (1960–62); Concertino for Clarinet and Small Orch. (1971); *"Bis" (Evocation)* for Piano and Orch. (1972); *Les Chatons de Paris* for Accordion and Orch. (1978). **CHAMBER:** String Quartet (1947); *Serenade* for Oboe and Bassoon (1949); *Apparition* for Violin and Piano (1960); *2 Figures* for Oboe and Piano (1968); *Solitude* for Cello and Piano (1968); *Cloches dans le matin* for 1 or 2 Pianos (1972); *Invocation* for Cello and Piano (1974); *Satie-re* for 4 Pianos (1974); *Zit-liedjes en spring-dansjes* for Irish Harp (1982); *Music for the Party* for 2 Harps (1983).

Grosskopf, Erhard, German composer; b. Berlin, March 17, 1934. He studied in Berlin with Pepping at the School for Church Music (1957–59) and with Blacher at the Hochschule für Musik (1959–64), and later worked at the Inst. for Electronic Music at the Univ. of Utrecht (1970–71). From 1968 he was active in avant-garde music circles in Berlin.

WORKS: *Sonata concertante No. 1* for Small Orch. (1966) and *No. 2* for Violin and Orch. (1967); *Konzertante Aspekte II* for Flute, Cello, Piano, and Orch. (1967); *Hörmusik* for Cello, 5 Orch. Groups, and Live Electronics (Berlin, Sept. 30, 1971); *Sun Music* for 3 Instrumental Groups (1972); *Quintett über den Herbstanfang* for Orch. (1982); String Quartet No. 1 (1983); Octet (1985); *Lichtknall: Eine apokalyptische Odyssee,* ballet (1987); *Lenzmusik I* for Violin, Clarinet, and Piano (1992); *Zeit der Windstille,* sym. (1993).

Grossmann, Ferdinand, Austrian conductor, teacher, and composer; b. Tulln, July 4, 1887; d. Vienna, Dec. 5, 1970. He studied music in Linz; later took a course in conducting with Weingartner in Vienna. In 1923 he founded a Volkskonservatorium in Vienna; in 1946 he organized the Chamber Chorus of the Vienna Academy of Music and toured with it in Europe and America. He composed a *German Mass* for Chorus (1952).

Grosz, Wilhelm, Austrian composer; b. Vienna, Aug. 11, 1894; d. N.Y., Dec. 10, 1939. He studied in Vienna with Richard Robert (piano), at the Cons. with Heuberger, Fuchs, and Schreker (theory and composition), and at the Univ. with Adler (musicology; Ph.D., 1920, with the diss. *Die Fugenarbeit in W.A. Mozarts Vokal- und Instrumentalwerken*). He was active mainly in Vienna, where he was conductor of the Kammerspiele in 1933–34. As a Jew, he sought refuge in London before emigrating to the U.S. in 1938.

WORKS: DRAMATIC: *Sganarell,* opera (Dessau, Nov. 21, 1925); *Der arme Reinhold,* dance fable (Berlin, Dec. 22, 1928); *Achtung, Aufnahme!,* musical comedy (Frankfurt am Main, March 23, 1930); incidental music for plays, films, and radio. **ORCH.:** 2 *Phantastische Stücke: Serenade* (1916) and *Tanz* (1917); *Overture to an Opera Buffa* (n.d.); *Symphonischer Tanz* for Piano and Orch. (1930); *Española,* jazz rhapsody (1937). **CHAMBER:** String Quartet (1915); *Jazzband* for Violin and Piano (1924); Violin Sonata (1925); piano pieces. **VOCAL:** Serious and light songs.

Grout, Donald J(ay), eminent American musicologist; b. Rock Rapids, Iowa, Sept. 28, 1902; d. Skaneateles, N.Y., March 9, 1987. He studied philosophy at Syracuse Univ. (A.B., 1923) and musicology at Harvard Univ. (A.M., 1932; Ph.D., 1939); he also received piano instruction in Boston, and took a course in French music in Strasbourg and in the history of opera in Vienna. After serving as a visiting lecturer at Mills College in Oakland, California (1935–36), he was on the faculties of Harvard Univ. (1936–42) and the Univ. of Texas at Austin (1942–45); subsequently was a prof. of musicology at Cornell Univ. (1945–70). He held a Guggenheim Foundation grant in 1951. He served as president of the American Musicological Soc. (1952–54; 1960–62); in 1966 he became curator of the Accademia Monteverdiana in N.Y.

WRITINGS: *A Short History of Opera* (2 vols., N.Y., 1948; 3rd ed., 1988); *A History of Western Music* (N.Y., 1960; 4th ed., 1988); *Mozart in the History of Opera* (Washington, D.C., 1972); *Alessandro Scarlatti: An Introduction to His Operas* (Berkeley, 1979).

BIBL.: W. Austin, ed., *New Looks at Italian Opera: Essays in Honor of D.J. G.* (Ithaca, N.Y., 1968).

Grové, Stefans, South African composer and teacher; b. Bethlehem, Orange Free State, July 23, 1922. He studied with his mother and his uncle, David Roode, and learned to play the piano and organ. He continued his piano training in Cape Town at the South African College of Music (diploma, 1948) and was a student in composition of W.H. Bell (1945–46). In 1953 he went to the U.S. on a Fulbright scholarship and pursued his studies at Harvard Univ., taking the M.A. in musicology and the M.Mus. under Piston in 1955; he also studied composition with Copland at the Berkshire Music Center in Tanglewood (summer, 1954). After teaching at Bard College in Annandale-on-Hudson, N.Y. (1956–57), he was on the faculty of the Peabody Cons. of Music in Baltimore (1957–71). In 1972 he was a lecturer at the South African College of Music, and then taught theory and composition at the Univ. of Pretoria from 1974. With the composition of his Violin Sonata on African motives (1984), he has pursued a style which is characterized by the incorporation of African elements in his music. These ethnic elements consist mainly of rhythmic and melodic procedures, resulting in complex rhythmic patterns with constant metric changes, as well as ostinato figures with constant changes.

WORKS: DRAMATIC: OPERA: *Die bose Wind* (1983). **BALLETS:** *Waratha* (1977); *Pinocchio* (1983). **ORCH.:** *Elegy* for Strings (1948); Overture (1953); Sinfonia concertante (1956); Violin Concerto (1959); Sym. (1962); *Partita* (1964); Concerto grosso for Violin, Cello, Piano, and Orch. (1974); *Maya*, concerto grosso for Violin, Piano, and Strings (1977); *Kettingrye* for Instrumentalists and Orch. (1978); *Vladimir's Round Table*, symphonic poem (1982); *Suite Concertato* for Harpsichord and Strings (1985); *Dance Rhapsody—An African City* (1985); *Concertato Overture on 2 Zulu Themes* (1988); *Overture Itubi*, festival dance for Youth Orch. (1992). **CHAMBER:** 2 string quartets (1946, 1955); String Trio (1948); Clarinet Sonata (1949); Trio for Violin, Cello, and Piano (1952); *Serenade* for Flute, Oboe, Viola, Bass Clarinet, and Harp (1952); Trio for Oboe, Clarinet, and Bassoon (1952); Cello Sonata (1953); Quintet for Harp and Strings (1954); *Divertimento* for Recorders (1955); Flute Sonata (1955); *Daarstelling* for Flute, Harpsichord, and Strings (1972); *Die nag van 3 April* for Flute and Harpsichord (1975); *Vir 'n winterdag* for Bassoon and Piano (1977); *Gesprek vir drie* for Oboe, Clarinet, and Percussion (1978); *Symphonia quattuor cordis* for Violin (1980); *Suite Juventuti* for Winds and Percussion (1982); *Jeu de Timbres* for Percussion (1983); Violin Sonata (1984); *Quintet—A City Serenade* for Flute or Alto Flute, Clarinet or Bass Clarinet, Viola, Cello, and Harp (1985); Trio for Violin, Horn, and Piano (1988); *Song of the African Spirits* for String Quartet (1993). **KEYBOARD: PIANO:** *3 Inventions* (1951); *Stylistic Experiment*, 12 pieces (1971); *Tweespalt* for Piano, Left-hand (1975); *Songs and Dances from Africa*, 7 études (1988); *The Blus Dream Valley*, 4 fantasy pieces (1992). **ORGAN:** *Ritual* (1969); *Chorale Prelude on Psalm 42* (1974); *Rhapsodic Toccata* (1977); *Afrika Hymnus*, concert fantasy (1991). **VOCAL:** *Cantata profana* for 2 Voices, Flute, Oboe, Harpsichord, and Cello (1959); Sym. for Chorus and Orch. (1975); *5 Ingrid Jonker Songs* for Soprano and Piano (1982); *Omnis Caterva Fidelium* for Children's Chorus and Piano (1985); *7 Songs on Bushman Poems* for Soprano, String Quartet, and Piano (1990); *Zulu Horizons* for Baritone and Orch. (1992).

Groven, Eivind, Norwegian composer and musicologist; b. Lårdal, Telemark, Oct. 8, 1901; d. Oslo, Feb. 8, 1977. He studied at the Christiania Cons. (1923–25) and in Berlin. In 1931 he was appointed a consultant on folk music for Norwegian Radio; remained there until 1946; in 1940 he received a state composer's pension. His many theoretical studies include *Naturskalaen* (The Natural Scale; Skein, 1927); *Temperering og renstemning* (Temperament and Non-tempered Tuning; Oslo, 1948; Eng. tr., 1970); *Eskimomelodier fra Alaska* (Eskimo Melodies from Alaska; Oslo, 1955). He collected about 1,800 Norwegian folk tunes, several of which he used as thematic foundation for his own compositions. In 1965 he patented an electronic organ, with special attachments for the production of non-tempered intervals.

WORKS: ORCH.: 5 symphonic poems: *Renaissance* (1935), *Historiske syner* (Historical Visions; 1936), *Fjelltonar* (Tunes from the Hills; 1938), *Skjebner* (The Fates; 1938), and *Bryllup i skogen* (Wedding in the Wood; 1939); 2 syms.: No. 1, *Innover viddene* (Toward the Mountains; 1937; rev. 1951) and No. 2, *Midnattstimen* (The Midnight Hour; 1946); *Hjalarljod*, overture (1950); Piano Concerto (1950); *Symfoniske slåtter* (Norwegian Folk Dances), 2 sets: No. 1 (1956) and No. 2, *Faldafeykir* (1967). **CHAMBER:** *Solstemning* (Sun Mood) for Flute or Flute and Piano (1946); *Balladetone* for 2 Hardanger Fiddles (1962); *Regnbogen* (The Rainbow) for 2 Hardanger Fiddles (1962). **VOCAL:** *Brudgommen* (The Bridegroom) for Soprano, 2 Altos, Tenor, Chorus, and Orch. (1928–31); *Naturens tempel* (The Temple of Nature) for Chorus and Orch. (1945); *Ivar Aasen*, suite for Soprano, Bass, Chorus, and Orch. (1946); *Soga om ein by* (The Story of a Town) for Soprano, Tenor, Bass, Chorus, and Orch. (1956); *Margjit Hjukse* for Chorus and Hardanger Fiddle (1963); *Draumkaede* for Soprano, Tenor, Baritone, Chorus, and Orch. (1965); *Ved foss og fjord* (By Falls and Fjord) for Men's Chorus and Orch. (1966); many songs.

Groves, Sir Charles (Barnard), distinguished English conductor; b. London, March 10, 1915; d. there, June 20, 1992. He received training in piano and organ at the Royal College of Music in London. In 1938 he joined the BBC as a chorus master, and then was assoc. conductor of the BBC Theatre Orch. (1942–44) and subsequently conductor of the BBC Northern Orch. in Manchester (1944–51). In 1951 he became conductor of the Bournemouth Municipal Orch.; after it was renamed the Bournemouth Sym. Orch. in 1954, he continued as its conductor until 1961. After serving as music director of the Welsh National Opera in Cardiff (1961–63), he was principal conductor of the Royal Liverpool Phil. from 1963 to 1977. He launched the career of several conductors through his sponsorship of the Liverpool International Conductors' Competition. In 1978–79 he was music director of the English National Opera in London, and later was principal conductor of the Guildford Phil. (from 1986). In 1958 he was made an Officer and in 1968 a Commander of the Order of the British Empire, and in 1973 he was knighted. Groves acquitted himself admirably as a conductor of the orch., operatic, and choral repertory.

Grovlez, Gabriel (Marie), French conductor and composer; b. Lille, April 4, 1879; d. Paris, Oct. 20, 1944. He studied at the Paris Cons. with Descombes, Diémer, Fauré, Gédalge, and Lavignac, taking a premier prix in piano in 1899. He toured Europe as accompanist to Marteau. He concentrated his activities on Paris, where he was prof. of piano at the Schola Cantorum (1899–1909), and also choirmaster and conductor at the Opéra-Comique (1905–08). After serving as music director of the Théâtre des Arts (1911–13), he was director of the Opéra (1914–34); he also conducted opera abroad. In 1939 he became prof. of chamber music at the Cons. His works reflect the finest qualities of the Gallic tradition.

WORKS: DRAMATIC: OPERAS: *Coeur de rubis* (1906; Nice, 1922); *Le marquis do Carabas* (1926). **BALLETS:** *La princesse au jardin* (1914; Paris, 1941); *Maïmouna* (1916; Paris, 1921); *Le vrai arbre de Robinson* (1921; N.Y., 1922). **ORCH.:** *Dans le jardin*, symphonic poem for Soprano, Women's Voices, and Orch. (1907); *La vengeance des fleurs*, symphonic poem (1910); *Madrigal lyrique* for Soprano and Orch. (1910); *Le reposoir des* *amants,* symphonic poem (1914); *Fantasia iberica* for Piano and Orch. (1941). **OTHER:** Piano pieces; many songs.

Grozăvescu, Trajan, Romanian tenor; b. Lugoj, Nov. 21, 1895; d. (murdered) Vienna, Feb. 15, 1927. He studied in Bucharest and Cluj. After making his debut in Cluj as Pinkerton in 1920, he continued his vocal studies in Vienna with F. Steiner. He made appearances with the Vienna Volksoper, the Prague National Theater, and the Vienna State Opera. He was shot to death by his wife.

BIBL.: M. Demeter-Grozăvescu and I. Voledi, *T. G.* (Bucharest, 1965).

Gruber, Georg, Austrian conductor; b. Vienna, July 27, 1904. He studied music at the Univ. of Vienna; received his Ph.D. in 1928. In 1930 he became conductor of the famous Vienna Choirboys, and toured with them throughout Europe, South America, and the U.S. He also arranged for his choir folk songs and choral works of the Renaissance period. In 1953 he was appointed prof. of music at Rhodes Univ. in Grahamstown, South Africa.

Gruber, H(einz) K(arl) "Nali," Austrian composer and double bass player; b. Vienna, Jan. 3, 1943. He was the great-great-grandson of Austrian composer Franz Xaver Gruber (b. Unterweizburg, near Hochburg, Nov. 25, 1787; d. Hallein, near Salzburg, June 7, 1863). After singing in the Vienna Boys' Choir (1953–57), he studied double bass with Planyavsky and Streicher, composition with Uhl and Ratz, and serial techniques with Jelinek at the Vienna Academy of Music (1957–63). In 1963–64 he attended a master class in composition there with Einem. He pursued his career in Vienna, where he joined the die reihe ensemble as a double bass player in 1961. From 1963 to 1969 he was principal double bass in the Niederösterreiches Tonkünstler Orch. In 1968 he co-founded with Schwertsik and Zykan the avant-garde group MOB art & tone ART, with which he was active until 1971. He played double bass in the Austrian Radio Sym. Orch. from 1969. In 1979 he was awarded the music prize of the Austrian Ministry of Culture and Education. While Gruber's works are basically tonal in nature, he has developed an unbuttoned personal style in which serious and lighter elements are given free reign as the mood strikes him. His self-described "pan-demonium" *Frankenstein!!* (1976–77) brought him international recognition. Among his later significant works were his 2 violin concertos (1977–78; 1988) and his Cello Concerto (1989).

WORKS: DRAMATIC: *Die Vertreibung aus dem Paradies,* melodrama (1966; ORF, Vienna, Feb. 11, 1969; rev. 1979); *Gomorra,* musical spectacle (1970–72; withdrawn; new version, 1984–91; Vienna, Jan. 18, 1993); *Reportage aus Gomorra* for 5 Singers and 8 Players (1975–76); *Frankenstein!!,* "pan-demonium" for Baritone Channsonier and Orch. (1976–77; Liverpool, Nov. 25, 1978; also for Baritone Channsonier and 12 Instruments, Berlin, Sept. 30, 1979); *Bring me the head of Amadeus,* music for the television series *Not Mozart* (BBC2-TV, London, Nov. 17, 1991); *Gloria von Jaxtberg,* music theater (1992–93). **ORCH.:** *Concerto for Orchestra* (1960–64); *Manhattan Broadcasts* for Light Orch. (1962–64); *fürbass,* double bass concerto (1965); *Revue* for Chamber Orch. (1968); *Vergrösserung* (1970); *Arien* for Violin and Orch. (1974–75; withdrawn); 2 violin concertos: No. 1, *. . . aus Schatten duft gewebt* (1977–78; Berlin, Sept. 29, 1979; rev. 1992) and No. 2, *Nebelsteinmusik* (St. Florian, July 19, 1988); *Entmilitarisierte Zonen,* march paraphrases for Brass Band (Zagreb, May 17, 1979); *Charivari: An Austrian Journal* (1981; London, Aug. 23, 1983; rev. 1984); *Rough Music,* percussion concerto (1982–83; ORF, Vienna, Oct. 30, 1983); Concerto for Cello and Ensemble or Small Orch. (Tanglewood, Aug. 3, 1989). **CHAMBER:** Suite for 2 Pianos, Winds, and Percussion (1960); *Improvisationen* for Wind Quintet (1961); Concerto No. 1 for Flute, Vibraphone, Xylophone, and Percussion (1961) and No. 2 for Tenor Saxophone, Double Bass, and Percussion (1961); *4 Pieces* for Violin (1963; Vienna, May 20, 1966); *Gioco a Tre* for Violin, Cello, and Piano (1963); *2 Rhapsodies* for Cello and Piano (1964); *Spiel* for Wind Quintet (1967); *3 MOB Pieces* for 7 Interchangeable Instruments and Percussion (1968; rev. 1977; Graz, Oct. 14, 1979); *Bossa Nova* for Ensemble (1968); *Die wirkliche Wut über den verlorenen Groschen* for 5 Players (1972); *Festmusik* for Chamber Ensemble (1972); *Phantom-Bilder auf der Spur eines verdächtigten Themas* for 12 or 13 Players or Small Orch. (1977; London, March 7, 1979); *Anagramm* for 6 Cellos (ORF, Graz, Oct. 22, 1987). **PIANO:** *Episoden* for 2 Pianos (1961); *Sechs Episoden aus einer unterbrochenen Chronik* (1967; Vienna, Feb. 20, 1968); *Luftschlösser* (Schloss Grafenegg, May 9, 1981). **VOCAL:** *Mass* for Chorus, 2 Trumpets, English Horn, Double Bass, and Percussion (1960); *Drei Lieder* for Baritone, Ensemble, and Tape (1961); *5 Kinderlieder* for Women's Chorus (1965; rev. 1980); other choruses and songs. **TAPE:** *Konjugationen* (1963).

Gruberová, Edita, Czech soprano; b. Bratislava, Dec. 23, 1946. She was a student in Prague of Maria Medvecká and in Vienna of Ruthilde Boesch. In 1968 she made her operatic debut as Rossini's Rosina at the Slovak National Theater in Bratislava. In 1970 she made her first appearance at the Vienna State Opera as the Queen of the Night, and subsequently sang there regularly. In 1973 she sang at the Glyndebourne Festival and in 1974 at the Salzburg Festival. On Jan. 5, 1977, she made her Metropolitan Opera debut in N.Y. as the Queen of the Night. She appeared as Giulietta in *I Capuleti e i Montecchi* at London's Covent Garden in 1984. In subsequent years, she appeared with many of the leading opera houses of the world. She also toured widely as a concert singer. Among her other admired roles were Zerbinetta, Donna Anna, Lucia, Gilda, Violetta, and Ariadne.

Gruenberg, Erich, Austrian-born English violinist; b. Vienna, Oct. 12, 1924. After studying in Vienna, he was awarded a scholarship to the Jerusalem Cons. in 1938; subsequently was engaged as concertmaster of the radio orch. there. In 1946 he went to London; became a naturalized British subject in 1950. He served as concertmaster of the Boyd Neel Orch.; then of the Stockholm Phil. (1956–58), the London Sym. Orch. (1962–65), and the Royal Phil. (1972–76); also made appearances as a soloist and as a chamber music player. In 1994 he was made an Officer of the Order of the British Empire.

Gruenberg, Louis, Russian-born American composer; b. near Brest Litovsk, Aug. 3, 1884; d. Los Angeles, June 9, 1964. He went with his family to the U.S. when he was 2; after piano lessons with Adele Margulies in N.Y., he went to Berlin in 1903 to study piano and composition with Busoni and Friedrich Koch. In 1912 he made his debut as a soloist with the Berlin Phil. under Busoni's direction, and then toured Europe and the U.S.; he also became an instructor at the Vienna Cons. that year. Upon winning the Flagler Prize in 1920 for his orch. piece *The Hill of Dreams,* he decided to settle in the U.S. and devote himself to composition. In 1923 he helped found the League of Composers and became a champion of contemporary music. The influence of jazz and spirituals resulted in one of his most successful scores, *The Daniel Jazz* for Tenor, Clarinet, Trumpet, and String Quartet (1924). In 1930 he was awarded the RCA Victor Prize for his 1st Sym. He then composed his most successful stage work, the opera *The Emperor Jones,* which was premiered at the Metropolitan Opera in N.Y. on Jan. 7, 1933. It received the David Bispham Medal. After serving as head of the composition dept. at the Chicago Musical College (1933–36), Gruenberg settled in California. His film scores for *The Fight for Life* (1940), *So Ends our Night* (1941), and *Commandos Strike at Dawn* (1942) won him Academy Awards. He was elected a member of the National Inst. of Arts and Letters in 1947.

WORKS: DRAMATIC: *Signor Formica,* operetta (1910); *The Witch of Brocken,* operetta (1912); *Piccadillymädel,* operetta (1913); *The Bride of the Gods,* opera (1913); *Roly-boly Eyes,* musical (1919; in collaboration with E. Brown); *The Dumb Wife,* chamber opera (1923); *Hallo! Tommy!,* operetta (1920s); *Lady X,* operetta (c.1927); *Jack and the Beanstalk,* opera (N.Y.,

Nov. 19, 1931); *The Emperor Jones*, opera (1931; N.Y., Jan. 7, 1933); *Helena's Husband*, opera (1936); *Green Mansions*, radio opera (CBS, Oct. 17, 1937); *Volpone*, opera (1945); *One Night of Cleopatra*, opera (n.d.); *The Miracle of Flanders*, musical legend (1954); *The Delicate King*, opera (1955); *Antony and Cleopatra*, opera (1955; rev. 1958 and 1961); ballets; pantomimes; incidental music; film scores: *The Fight for Life* (1940; orch. suite, 1954); *So Ends our Night* (1941); *Commandos Strike at Dawn* (1942); *An American Romance* (1944); *Counterattack* (1945); *Gangster* (1947); *Arch of Triumph* (1948); *Smart Women* (1948); *All the King's Men* (1949); *Quicksand* (1950). **ORCH.:** 2 piano concertos (1915; 1938, rev. 1963); *The Hill of Dreams*, symphonic poem (1920; N.Y., Oct. 23, 1921); *The Enchanted Isle*, symphonic poem (c.1920; rev. 1928; Worcester, Mass., Oct. 3, 1929); 6 syms.: No. 1 (1919; rev. 1928; Boston, Feb. 10, 1934), No. 2 (1941; rev. 1959 and 1963), No. 3 (1941–42; rev. 1964), No. 4 (1946; rev. 1964), and Nos. 5–6 (unfinished); *Vagabondia*, symphonic poem (1921–30; rev. 1957); *Jazz Suite* (1925; Cincinnati, March 22, 1929); *Moods* (c.1929); *Prairie Song* (c.1930; rev. 1954); *Serenade to a Beauteous Lady* (1934; Chicago, April 4, 1935); *Music to an Imaginary Legend* (1945); *Music to an Imaginary Ballet* (1945; rev. 1946); Violin Concerto (Philadelphia, Dec. 1, 1944); *Americana Suite* (1945; rev. 1964); *Dance Rhapsody* for Violin and Orch. (c.1946); *Variations on a Pastoral Theme* (1947); *5 Country Sketches* (c.1948); Cello Concerto (1949; rev. 1963); *Poem* for Viola and Orch. (c.1951); *Harlem Rhapsody* (1953); Concerto for Strings and Piano (c.1953; rev. 1955). **CHAMBER:** 3 violin sonatas (c.1912, c.1919, c.1950); Suite for Violin and Piano (c.1914); 2 string quartets (1914, 1937); 4 Bagatelles for Cello and Piano (1922); *4 Indiscretions* for String Quartet (c.1924); *Poem* for Cello and Piano (c.1925); *Jazzettes* for Violin and Piano (c.1925); *4 Diversions* for String Quartet (c.1930); 2 divertimentos: No. 1 for 2 Pianos and Percussion (c.1930) and No. 2 for Violin, Horn, Cello, and Piano (1955); Piano Quintet (1937); *Poem* for Viola and Piano (c.1951); Piano Trio (n.d.). **PIANO:** *Jazzberries* (c.1925); *Jazz Masks* (1929–31); *Jazz Epigrams* (1929); *3 Jazz Dances* (1931); etc. **VOCAL:** *The Daniel Jazz* for Tenor, Clarinet, Trumpet, and String Quartet (1924; N.Y., Feb. 22, 1925); *The Creation* for Baritone and 8 Instruments (1925; N.Y., Nov. 27, 1926); *An American Hymn* for Soloist, Men's Voices, and Orch. (1940s); *A Song of Faith*, oratorio for Speaker, Soloists, Chorus, Dancers, and Orch. (1952–62; Los Angeles, Nov. 1, 1981); solo songs; arrangements of spirituals.

BIBL.: R. Nisbett, *L.G.: His Life and Work* (diss., Ohio State Univ., 1979); idem, "L.G.'s American Idiom," *American Music* (Spring 1985).

Gruhn (originally, **Grunebaum**), **Nora,** English soprano of German descent; b. London, March 6, 1905. She studied at the Royal College of Music in London and with Hermine Bosetti in Munich. She made her operatic debut in Kaiserslautern in 1928; sang with the Cologne Opera (1929–30); appeared at Covent Garden (1929–33; 1936–37) and Sadler's Wells (1946–48) in London. She sang the part of Gretel in an English production of Humperdinck's *Hansel und Gretel* reportedly more than 400 times.

Grumiaux, Arthur, eminent Belgian violinist; b. Villers-Perwin, March 21, 1921; d. Brussels, Oct. 16, 1986. He studied violin and piano with Fernand Quinet at the Charleroi Cons. and violin with Alfred Dubois at the Royal Cons. in Brussels; also took private lessons in composition with Enesco in Paris. In 1940 he was awarded the Prix de Virtuosité from the Belgian government. In 1949 he was appointed prof. of violin at the Royal Cons. In 1973 he was knighted by King Baudouin for his services to music; he thus shared the title of baron with Paganini. His performances were characterized by a studied fidelity to the composer's intentions, assured technical command, and a discerning delineation of the inner structures of music.

Grümmer, Elisabeth, distinguished German soprano; b. Niederjeutz, near Diedenhofen, Alsace-Lorraine, March 31, 1911; d. Berlin, Nov. 6, 1986. She began her career as an actress; after being persuaded to study voice by Karajan, she had lessons with Schlender in Aachen. In 1940 she made her operatic debut in Aachen as the 1st Flowermaiden in *Parsifal*, and then sang her first major role there in 1941 as Octavian. After appearances in Duisburg (1942–44), she was a member of the Berlin Städtische Oper (from 1946). On June 29, 1951, she made her first appearance at London's Covent Garden as Eva in *Die Meistersinger von Nürnberg*. She then made debuts at the Vienna State Opera and the Salzburg Festival in 1953, at the Glyndebourne Festival in 1956, and at the Bayreuth Festival in 1957. On Feb. 17, 1967, she made her debut at the N.Y. City Opera as the Marschallin, followed by her Metropolitan Opera debut in N.Y. as Elsa in *Lohengrin* on April 20, 1967. She then continued her career in Europe until retiring in 1972. In addition to opera, she toured extensively as a concert artist. From 1959 she was a prof. of voice at the (West) Berlin Hochschule für Musik. Grümmer's exquisite voice and admirable dramatic gifts made her an exemplary interpreter of the music of Mozart and Richard Strauss. Among her other outstanding roles were Pamina, Donna Anna, Ilia, and the Mozart and Strauss Countess.

Grümmer, Paul, eminent German cellist, viola da gambist, and pedagogue; b. Gera, Feb. 26, 1879; d. Zug, Oct. 30, 1965. He studied with Klengel at the Leipzig Cons. and with Becker in Frankfurt am Main. He began his career as a cellist in 1898, appearing regularly in London from 1902. He became solo cellist of the Vienna Opera and Konzertverein (1905), and was a founding member of the Busch Quartet (1913); also toured with his own chamber orch. He taught at the Vienna Academy of Music (1907–13; 1940–46), the Cologne Hochschule für Musik (1926–33), and the Berlin Hochschule für Musik (1933–40). He publ. pedagogical works, including a *Viola da Gamba Schule* (Leipzig, 1928), and ed. Bach's unaccompanied cello suites (Vienna, 1944). His autobiography was publ. as *Begegnungen* (Munich, 1963).

Grunenwald, Jean-Jacques, distinguished French organist and composer; b. Cran-Gevrier, near Annecy (of Swiss parents), Feb. 2, 1911; d. Paris, Dec. 19, 1982. He studied with Dupré (organ; premier prix, 1935) and Büsser (composition; premier prix, 1937) at the Paris Cons. From 1936 to 1945 he was Dupré's assistant at St.-Sulpice in Paris; from 1955 to 1970 he was organist at St.-Pierre-de-Montrouge. He was a prof. at the Schola Cantorum in Paris from 1958 to 1961, and from 1961 to 1966 was on the faculty of the Geneva Cons. Through the years, he played more than 1,500 concerts, presenting the complete organ works of Bach, Franck et al. He also became famous for the excellence of his masterly improvisations, which rivaled those of Dupré. His compositions include *Fêtes de la lumière* for Orch. (1937); Piano Concerto (1940); *Concert d'été* for Piano and String Orch. (1944); *Sardanapale*, lyric drama (1945–50); *Ouverture pour un Drame sacre* for Orch. (1954); *Cantate pour le Vendredi Saint* (1955); *Psalm 129 (De profundis)* for Chorus and Orch. (1959); *Fantaisie en dialogue* for Organ and Orch. (1964); Organ Sonata (1964); piano pieces.

Grüner-Hegge, Odd, Norwegian conductor and composer; b. Christiania, Sept. 23, 1899; d. there (Oslo), May 11, 1973. He studied piano and composition at the Christiania Cons. and conducting with Weingartner. In 1927 he began his conducting career; from 1931 he was a conductor with the Oslo Phil., subsequently serving as its chief conductor from 1945 to 1961; he then was manager of the Norwegian Opera in Oslo from 1961 to 1969. He also appeared as a guest conductor with many of the leading European orchs. Among his works were orch. scores, chamber music, and piano pieces.

Guadagno, Anton, Italian-born American conductor; b. Castellammare del Golfo, May 2, 1925. He studied at the Palermo Cons.; after obtaining degrees in conducting and composition at the Accademia di Santa Cecilia in Rome, he took 1st prize in conducting at the Salzburg Mozarteum; his principal conducting mentors were Ferrara, Molinari, C. Zecchi, and Karajan. Following engagements in Italy and South America, he emigrated to the U.S. and became a naturalized American citizen. In 1952 he made his U.S. debut conducting at a Carnegie Hall concert in N.Y. In 1958–59 he was an assistant conductor at the Metropolitan Opera in N.Y. From 1966 to 1972 he was music administrator of the Philadelphia Lyric Opera. In 1970 he made his London debut conducting *Andrea Chénier* at Drury Lane, and returned to London in 1971 to make his debut at Covent Garden conducting *Un Ballo in Maschera*. On Nov. 9, 1982, he made his formal debut at the Metropolitan Opera in N.Y. conducting the latter opera. He was artistic director of the Palm Beach (Fla.) Opera from 1984.

Guarino, Carmine, Italian composer; b. Rovigo, Oct. 1, 1893; d. Genoa, June 5, 1965. He studied violin and composition at the Naples Cons. His first opera, *Madama di Challant*, set in the tradition of Verdi, was premiered there on March 9, 1927, attracting favorable comments. He was also the composer of the first Italian radio opera, *Cuore di Wanda* (Radio Italiano, Dec. 20, 1931). Other works for the stage were an operetta, *Gaby* (San Remo, March 20, 1924); *Tabarano alla Corte di Nonesiste*, musical fable (1931); 2 operas: *Balilla* (Rome, March 7, 1935) and *Sogno di un mattino d'autunno* (Cluj, March 30, 1936); and a ballet, *El Samet, il silenzioso* (1958).

Guarino, Piero, Italian pianist, conductor, pedagogue, and composer; b. Alexandria, Egypt, June 20, 1919; d. Rovereto, May 23, 1991. He studied piano and composition at the Athens Cons. (1936–39) before pursuing his training at the Accademia di Santa Cecilia in Rome; he completed advanced studies with Casella and Bonucci. From 1939 he was active as a pianist and conductor. After serving as director of the Alexandria Cons. (1950–60), he was director of the chamber orch. of the Accademia Musicale Napoletana (1962–73); he also taught at the Salzburg Mozarteum (1963–67) and the Perugia Cons. (1965–66). He then was director of the Sassari Cons. (1969–75) and the Parma Cons. (1975–89).

WORKS: CHAMBER OPERA: *Vettura-letto* (1969). **ORCH.:** Sym. for Strings (1946); Piano Concerto (1947); *Jeu parti* for Chamber Orch. (1966); *Omaggio a Clementi* for Student Orch. (1972). **CHAMBER:** *Gagliarda, Sarabanda e Giga* for Viola and Piano (1941); *Sonata da camera* for Cello and Piano (1943); *Introduzione, aria e finale* for Violin and Piano (1944); *12 Pezzi* for 10 Instruments (1945); Trio for Violin, Cello, and Piano (1945); *Divertimento su un Capriccio di Piatti* for 4 Cellos or 4 Groups of Cellos (1974); various piano pieces. **VOCAL:** *De Profundis* for 2 Women's Voices and String Orch. (1965); *Salve Regina* for Chorus (1977); *Schlaflied* for Women's Chorus (1978); *Quattro Haiku* for Soprano and Piano (1987).

Guarnieri, Antonio, distinguished Italian conductor; b. Venice, Feb. 1, 1880; d. Milan, Nov. 25, 1952. He studied cello, piano, and composition in Venice. He began his career as a cellist in the Martucci Quartet. After making his conducting debut in Siena in 1904, he conducted in various Italian theaters. Following an engagement at the Vienna Court Opera (1912–13), he returned to Italy and founded the Società Sinfonica Italiana in Milan in 1915. In 1922 he made his first appearance at Milan's La Scala, where he subsequently was one of its principal conductors from 1929 until shortly before his death. Guarnieri was highly esteemed for his interpretations of the Italian operatic repertory.

Guarnieri, (Mozart) Camargo, esteemed Brazilian composer, conductor, and teacher; b. Tietê, Feb. 1, 1907; d. São Paulo, Jan. 13, 1993. His father was an Italian emigrant, his mother a Brazilian. After musical instruction from his parents, he went to São Paulo in 1922 and studied with Lamberto Baldi and Mário de Andrade; later he pursued his training with Koechlin (composition) and Rühlmann (conducting) in Paris (1938–39). Upon returning to São Paulo, he served as resident conductor of the Municipal Sym. Orch. and, from 1975, was conductor of the Univ.'s Sym. Orch.; he also was engaged in teaching. Between 1941 and 1981 he made a number of visits to the U.S., occasionally appearing as a conductor of his own works. His extensive catalogue of music, skillfully crafted in a tonal style, is basically reflective of Brazilian national elements.

WORKS: DRAMATIC: *Pedro Malazarte*, comic opera (1931); *O Homen Só*, opera (1960). **ORCH.:** *Suite Infantil* (1929); *Curuçá* (1930); 5 piano concertos (1931, 1946, 1964, 1968, 1970); 2 violin concertos (1940, 1953); *Encantamento* (1941); *Abertura Concertante* (1942); 7 syms. (1944, 1944, 1954, 1963, 1977, 1981, 1985); *Prólogo e Fuga* (1947); *Suite Brasiliana* (1950); *Chôro* for Violin and Orch. (1952), for Clarinet and Orch. (1956), for Piano and Orch. (1956), for Cello and Orch. (1961), for Flute and Orch. (1974), for Viola and Orch. (1975), and for Bassoon and Orch. (1990); *Variações sobre a Tema de Nordeste* for Piano and Orch. (1953); *Suite IV Centenário* (1954); *Suite Vila Rica* (1957); Piano Concertino (1961); *Seresta* for Piano and Chamber Orch. (1965); *Homenagem á Villa-Lobos* for Wind Orch. (1966); *Sequência: Coral e Ricercare* for Chamber Orch. (1966); *Abertura Festiva* (1971); *Saratí* for Piano and Orch. (1987); Sonatina for Violin and Chamber Orch. (1988). **CHAMBER:** 7 violin sonatas (1930, 1933, 1950, 1956, 1959, 1963, 1978); 3 string quartets (1932, 1944, 1962); 3 cello sonatas (1939, 1955, 1977); Viola Sonata (1950); Trio for Piano, Violin, and Cello (1989); numerous piano pieces. **VOCAL:** Cantatas; choral pieces; more than 300 songs.

Guarrera, Frank, American baritone; b. Philadelphia, Dec. 3, 1923. He studied voice with Richard Bonelli in Philadelphia. On Dec. 14, 1948, he made his Metropolitan Opera debut in N.Y. as Escamillo in *Carmen*, where he remained on its roster until 1976. He was invited by Toscanini to sing at La Scala in Milan; also made guest appearances in San Francisco, Chicago, Paris, and London. He was best known for his performances of Italian roles.

Guastavino, Carlos, Argentine composer; b. Santa Fe, April 5, 1912. He studied chemistry; then took a course in composition with Athos Palma. He cultivated miniature forms, mostly for piano; of these, the suites *10 cantilenas argentinas* (1958) and *Las presencias* (1961) radiated a certain melorhythmic charm. He also wrote a ballet, *Fué una vez* (1942); *Romance de Santa Fé* for Piano and Orch. (1952); Violin Sonata (1952); choruses on Argentine themes; many songs.

Guba, Vladimir, Russian composer; b. Kiev, Dec. 22, 1938. He studied at the Kiev Cons. with Liatoshinsky. He became interested in modern techniques of composition; applied the 12-tone method in his piano pieces *Deformation and Echo* (1961); he also wrote a series of 30 piano pieces, *In the World of Childhood*, and a cycle of 24 piano pieces, *Sonorous Exhibits*.

Gubaidulina, Sofia (Asgatovna), remarkable Russian composer; b. Chistopol, Oct. 24, 1931. She received training in piano from Maria Piatnitskaya and in theory from Nazib Zhiganov at the Academy of Music (1946–49), and in piano from Leopold Lukomsky and Grigory Kogan, and in composition from Albert Leman at the Cons. (1949–54) in Kazan; she then studied composition with Nikolai Peiko and Vissarion Shebalin at the Moscow Cons. (1954–63), and later pursued research at the Moscow Electronic Music Studio (from 1968). In 1991 she settled in Germany. Gubaidulina's heritage—her grandfather was a mullah, her father was a Tatar, and her mother was of Russian, Polish, and Jewish descent—has played a significant role in her development as a composer. Claiming that "I am the place where East meets West," the spiritual quality of her works is reflected in the influence of the Muslim, Orthodox, Jewish, and Roman Catholic faiths. While she has pursued advanced compositional methods along avant-garde lines, she has done so in victorially divergent paths which have allowed her to retain a unique individuality.

WORKS: DRAMATIC: OPERA-BALLET-ORATORIO: *Ora-*

tion for the Age of Aquarius (1991). **BALLETS:** *Volshebnaya svirel* (1960); *Flute of Tania* (1961); *Begushchaya po volnam* (1962). Film scores. **ORCH.:** 2 syms.: No. 1 (1958) and No. 2, *Stimmen . . . Verstummen* (Berlin, Sept. 4, 1986); Piano Concerto (1959); *Adagio and Fugue* for Violin and String Orch. (1960); *Intermezzo* for 8 Trumpets, 16 Harps, and Percussion (1961); *Triumph*, overture (1963); *Fairy Tale Poem* (1971); *Detto II* for Cello and Orch. (1972; Moscow, May 5, 1973); Concerto for Bassoon and Low Strings (1975; Moscow, May 6, 1976); Concerto for Orch. and Jazz Band (1976; Moscow, Jan. 16, 1978); *Te salutant* for Large Light Orch. (1978); *Introitus* for Piano and Chamber Orch. (Moscow, Feb. 22, 1978); *Offertorium* for Violin and Orch. (1980; Vienna, May 30, 1981; rev. version, Berlin, Sept. 24, 1982; final version, London, Nov. 2, 1986); *(Last) 7 Words* for Cello, Bayan, and Strings (Moscow, Oct. 20, 1982); *Antwort ohne Frage* for 3 Orchs. (1988); *Pro et Contra* (Louisville, Nov. 24, 1989); *Und: Das Feste ist in vollem Gange*, cello concerto (1993; La Palmas, Canary Islands, Jan. 31, 1994); *Zeitgestalten* (Birmingham, Nov. 29, 1994); Flute Concerto (1994–95). **CHAMBER:** *Variations* for String Quartet (1956); Piano Quintet (1957); *Allegro rustico* for Flute and Piano (1963); *5 Études* for Harp, Double Bass, and Percussion (1965); Percussion Sonata (1966); *Pantomime* for Double Bass and Piano (1966); *Concordanza* for 10 Instruments (Prague, May 23, 1971); 4 string quartets: No. 1 (1971; Cologne, March 24, 1979), No. 2 (Kuhmo, Finland, July 23, 1987), No. 3 (Edinburgh, Aug. 22, 1987), and No. 4 (1990); *Music* for Harpsichord and Percussion (Leningrad, April 5, 1972); *10 Preludes* for Cello (1974); *Quattro* for 2 Trumpets and 2 Trombones (1974); *Rumore e silenzio* for Percussion and Harpsichord or Celesta (1974); Double Bass Sonata (1975); *2 Ballads* for 2 Trumpets and Piano (1976); Trio for 3 Trumpets (1976); *Dots, Line and Zigzag* for Bass Clarinet and Piano (1976); *On Tatar Folk Themes* for Domra and Piano (1977); Duo Sonata for 2 Bassoons (1977); *Misterioso* for 7 Percussion (1977); Quartet for 4 Flutes (1977); *Lamento* for Tuba and Piano (1977); *Muzika* for Harpsichord and Percussion (1977); *Song Without Words* for Trumpet and Piano (1977); *Detto I* for Organ and Percussion (1978); *Sounds of the Forest* for Flute and Piano (1978); Flute Sonatina (1978); *De Profundis* for Bayan (1978); *2 Pieces* for Horn and Piano (1979); *Jubilatio* for 4 Percussion (1979); *In croce* for Cello and Organ (1979); *Garten von Freuden und Traurigkeiten* for Flute, Harp, Viola, and Speaker ad libitum (1980); *Sonata: Rejoice!* for Violin and Cello (1981); *Descensio* for 9 Instruments (Paris, April 30, 1981); *Quasi Hoquetus* for Viola, Bassoon, and Piano (1984); Bayan Sonata (1985); *Silenzio*, 5 pieces for Accordion, Violin, and Cello (1991); *Der Seiltänzer*, violin sonata (Washington, D.C., Feb. 24, 1994); *In Erwartung* for Saxophone Quartet and 6 Percussionists (1994). **KEYBOARD: PIANO:** Sonatina (1952); *8 Preludes* (1955); *Chaconne* (1962); Sonata (1965); *Musical Toys*, 14 children's pieces (1969); *Toccata-troncata* (1971); *Invention* (1974). **ORGAN:** *Light and Darkness* (1976). **VOCAL:** *Fazelija* for Soprano and Orch. (1956); *Night in Memphis* for Mezzo-soprano, Men's Chorus, and Orch. (1968); *Rubâiyât* for Baritone and Chamber Orch. (1969; Moscow, Dec. 24, 1976); *Stufen* for Speaking Chorus and Orch. (1972); *Laudatio Pacis* for Soprano, Alto, Tenor, Bass, Speaker, 2 Choruses, and Orch. (1975; in collaboration with M. Kopelent and P.-H. Dittrich); *Perception* for Soprano, Baritone, 2 Violins, 2 Violas, 3 Cellos, Double Bass, and Tape (1983; Lockenhaus, June 11, 1986); *Hommage à Marina Tsvetayeva* for Chorus (1984); *Hommage à T.S. Eliot* for Soprano and 8 Instruments (Cologne, March 25, 1987); *Witty Waltzing in the Style of Johann Strauss* for Soprano and 8 Instruments (Cologne, March 25, 1987); *Jauchzt vor Gott* for Chorus and Organ (1989); *Alleluia* for Boy Soprano, Chorus, and Orch. (1990); *Aus dem Stundenbuch* for Men's Chorus, Cello, and Orch. (1991); *Jetzt Immer Schnee* for Chamber Chorus and Chamber Ensemble (Amsterdam, June 12, 1993).

Gubrud, Irene (Ann), American soprano; b. Canby, Minn., Jan. 4, 1947. She studied at St. Olaf College in Northfield, Minn. (B.M., 1969), and with Marion Freschel at the Juilliard School of Music in N.Y. She won the Naumburg International Voice Competition (1980), and made her operatic debut as Mimi in St. Paul, Minn., in 1981; also toured widely as a recitalist. She was successful in a comprehensive repertoire, extending from early music to the avant-garde.

Gudmundsen-Holmgreen, Pelle, noted Danish composer; b. Copenhagen, Nov. 21, 1932. He received training in violin; after private theory and composition lessons with Høffding (1951–53), he continued his training at the Royal Danish Cons. of Music in Copenhagen (1953–58), where he studied theory, composition, and music history with Høffding and Westergaard, and instrumentation with Holmboe. From 1967 to 1973 he taught composition at the Royal Cons. of Music in Århus, and then devoted himself fully to composition. In 1973 he received the Carl Nielsen Prize. In 1980 he was awarded the Nordic Council Music Prize for his Sym. No. 3, *Antifoni*. After utilizing serial techniques, he developed an individual means of expression, a minimalist simplicity achieved through persistent repetition of notes and patterns.

WORKS: BALLETS: *Den gamle mand* (1976); *Rituelle danse* (1976); *Flight* (1981). **ORCH.:** *Ouverture* for Strings (1955); *Lamento* for Chamber Orch. (1957); *Chronos* for Chamber Orch. (1962); 3 syms.: No. 1 (1962–65), No. 2, *På Rygmarven* (1966), and No. 3, *Antifoni* (1974–77); *Collegium Musicum Koncert* for Chamber Orch. (1964); *Mester Jakob/Frère Jacques* for Chamber Orch. (1964); *Repriser* for Chamber Orch. (1965); *5 Pieces* (1966); *Tricolore I* (1966), *II* (1966), *III* (1966), and *IV* (1969); *Segnali* for Wind Orch. (1966); *Rerepriser* for Chamber Orch. (1967); *Stykke for stykke* for Chamber Orch. (1968); *Kvartet for 18* for Wind Orch. (1968); *Spejl II* (1973); *Oktober* for Chamber Orch. (1977); *Mosaik* for Chamber Orch. (1979); *Triptykon*, percussion concerto (1985); *Naer og fjern* for Chamber Orch. (1987); *Concord* for Chamber Orch. (1988); Concerto Grosso for String Quartet and Orch. (1990); *Traffic* (1994). **CHAMBER:** *Variationer* for Cello (1954); Nonet for Woodwind Quintet, 2 Percussion, and Piano (1958); 8 string quartets: No. 1 (1959), No. 2, *Quartetto facile* (1959), No. 3, *5 små studier* (1959), No. 4 (1967), No. 5, *Step by Step* (1982), No. 6, *Parting* (1983), No. 7, *Parted* (1984), and No. 8, *Ground* (1986); *In Terra Pax* for Clarinet, 2 Percussion, and Piano (1961); *Kanon* for 9 Instruments (1967); *Plateaux pour deux* for Percussion and Cello (1970); *Terrasse* for Woodwind Quintet (1970); *Solo* for Electric Guitar (1971–72); *So Long* for Electric Guitar (1972); *Re-Cycling* for 7 Instruments (1975); *Kysset*, ritual dance for 5 Percussion and Electric Guitar (1976; also for 6 Percussion); *Passacaglia* for Clarinet, Piano, Percussion, Violin, and Cello (1977); Trio, *Møder og drømme* (1979); *Spejlstykker* for Clarinet, Cello, and Piano (1980); *reTurning* for Flute, Clarinet, Percussion, Harp, and Piano (1987); *Naer og fjern* for Wind Quintet, String Quartet, and Double Bass (1987). **KEYBOARD: PIANO:** *Variations* (1959); *3 Epigrams* (1962); *Pictures at an Exhibition* (1968); *For Piano* (1992). **ORGAN:** *Mirror III* (1974). **VOCAL:** *Wandering* for Chorus (1956); *Je ne me tairai jamais. Jamais* for 12 Voices or Chorus, Narrator, and Chamber Ensemble (1966); *Statements* for Children's Chorus or Equal Voices (1969); *Examples* for Chorus (1970); *Yes-No* for Double Chorus (1973); *Light* for 5 Solo Voices or Chorus and Organ (1976); *Songs Without* for Mezzo-soprano or Contralto and Piano (1976); *Turn* for Soprano, Bass Flute, Guitar, and Harp (1993).

Gueden, Hilde, noted Austrian soprano; b. Vienna, Sept. 15, 1917; d. Klosterneuburg, Sept. 17, 1988. She studied with Wetzelsberger at the Vienna Cons., then made her debut in operetta at the age of 16. She made her operatic debut as Cherubino in 1939 in Zürich, where she sang until 1941. After appearing in Munich (1941–42) and Rome (1942–46), she sang at the Salzburg Festival (1946); subsequently was a leading member of the Vienna State Opera until 1973. She first appeared at London's Covent Garden with the visiting Vienna State Opera in 1947; her Metropolitan Opera debut followed in

N.Y. on Nov. 15, 1951, when she appeared as Gilda; she continued to sing there until 1960. In 1951 she was made an Austrian Kammersängerin. She maintained a wide-ranging repertoire, singing roles from Mozart to contemporary composers such as Britten and Blacher; she also was a fine operetta singer. She particularly excelled as Despina, Sophie, Zerbinetta, and Daphne.

Guelfi, Giangiacomo, Italian baritone; b. Rome, Dec. 21, 1924. He studied law in Florence and received vocal training from Ruffo. In 1950 he made his operatic debut as Rigoletto in Spoleto, and then sang at Milan's La Scala (from 1952); he also made appearances in Chicago (from 1954) and in London (from 1958). On Feb. 5, 1970, he made his Metropolitan Opera debut in N.Y. as Scarpia, remaining on its roster for only that season. In 1975 he sang Scarpia at London's Covent Garden.

Guerra Peixe, César, Brazilian composer, violinist, and conductor; b. Petrópolis, March 18, 1914; d. Rio de Janeiro, Nov. 23, 1993. Following training in violin and theory locally (1925–30), he went to Rio de Janeiro and studied violin and theory (1932–37) and then composition with Newton Pádua at the Cons. Brasileiro (1934–43) and privately with Koellreuther (1944). He played violin in theater orchs. and in the National Sym. Orch. In 1946–47 he appeared as a conductor of his own works with the BBC in England. He taught composition privately, conducted many Brazilian orchs., and was director and music arranger for Tupi-TV in Rio de Janeiro. As a composer, he plunged headlong into the torrent of dodecaphony, but about 1949 he changed his orientation and reclaimed his Brazilian roots, nurtured by melorhythmic folksong resources.

WORKS: ORCH.: 2 syms.: No. 1 (1946) and No. 2, *Brasília*, for Narrator, Chorus, and Orch. (1960); *Instantâneos Sinfônicos* 1 and 2 (1947); 2 divertimentos for Strings (1947); Suite for Strings (1949); *Abertura Solene* (1950); *Suite Sinfónica 1: Paulista* (1955) and *2: Pernambucana* (1955); *Ponteado* (1955); *Pequeño concerto* for Piano and Orch. (1956); *Museu de Inconfidência* (1972); Violin Concertino (1975); *Tribute to Portinari* (Rio de Janeiro, Oct. 15, 1993). **CHAMBER:** *Music* for Flute and Piano (1944); Nonet (1945); *Cuarto Mixto* for Flute, Clarinet, Violin, and Cello (1945); 2 string quartets (1947, 1958); 2 wind trios (1948, 1951); Violin Sonata (1950); Piano Trio (1960); Guitar Sonata (1969); *Dueto característico* for Violin and Guitar (1970); Duo for Clarinet and Bassoon (1970); *Variações Opcionais* for Violin and Accordion (1977). **PIANO:** *Música No. 1* (1945); 3 suites (1949, 1954, 1954); 2 sonatas (1950, 1967); 2 sonatinas (1950, 1969).

Guerrini, Guido, Italian composer and pedagogue; b. Faenza, Sept. 12, 1890; d. Rome, June 13, 1965. He studied with Torchi and Busoni at the Bologna Liceo Musicale. After teaching on its faculty (1920–24), he taught at the Parma Cons. (1925–28); he then was director of the Florence Cons. (1928–47), the Bologna Cons. (1947–49), and the Cons. di Santa Cecilia in Rome (1950–60). In addition to books on harmony and orchestration, he publ. *Ferrucio Busoni: La vita, la figura e l'opera* (Florence, 1941) and *Antonio Vivaldi: La vita e l'opera* (Florence, 1951). He was especially effective in composing orch., sacred, and chamber pieces.

WORKS: OPERAS: *Zalebi* (1915); *Nemici* (Bologna, Jan. 19, 1921); *La vigna* (1923–25; Rome, March 7, 1935); *L'arcangelo* (1930; Bologna, Nov. 26, 1949); *Enea* (Rome, Feb. 11, 1953). **ORCH.:** *Visioni dell'antico Egitto*, symphonic poem (1919); *L'ultimo viaggio d'Odisseo*, symphonic poem (1921); *Poemetto* for Cello and Orch. (1924); *Preludio a corale* for Organ and Orch. (1930); 3 Pieces for Piano, Percussion, and Strings (1931); *Danza degli spiriti* (1932); *7 Variations on a Sarabande by Corelli* for Piano and Strings (1940); *Canzone e ballo forlivese* for Chamber Orch. (1952); *7 Variations on an Allemande by John Bull* (1962–63). **CHAMBER:** 3 string quartets (1920, 1922, 1959); 2 piano trios (1920, 1926); Violin Sonata (1921); Piano Quintet (1927); String Quintet (1950); piano pieces. **VOCAL:** *Bacco ubbriaco* for Bass and Orch. (1938); *Il lamento di Job* for Bass, Piano, Tam-tam, and Strings (1938); *Missa pro defunctis* "alla memoria di G. Marconi" for Solo Voices, Chorus, and Orch. (1938–39); *La città beata, La città perduta* for Solo Voice or Voices, Chorus, and Orch. (1942); *Nativitas Cristi* for Solo Voices, Chorus, and Orch. (1952); *Vigiliae Sulamitis* for Mezzo-soprano and Orch. (1953); 4 Masses; many songs.

BIBL.: A. Damerini, *Profilo critico di G.G.: Biografia e bibliografia* (Milan, 1928); P. Fragapane, *G.G. e i suoi poemi sinfonici* (Florence, 1932); *Catalogo delle opere di G.G. al suo settantesimo anno di età e curriculum della sua vita e cura dell'interessato, come saluto e ricordo agli amici* (Rome, 1961).

Guerrini, Paolo (Antigono), Italian music historian; b. Bagnolo Mella, Brescia, Nov. 18, 1880; d. Brescia, Nov. 19, 1960. He specialized in Italian sacred music; ed. the periodical *Brixia Sacra* (1910–25); in 1930 he began publication of the historical studies *Memorie storiche della Diocesi di Brescia*; served further as archivist and librarian in Brescia. In 1936 he was appointed canon of the Brescia Cathedral. He revived and tr. into Italian the music books of Cardinal Katschthaler as *Storia della musica sacra* (Turin, 1910; 3rd ed., 1936).

Guest, George (Hywel), esteemed Welsh organist, conductor, and teacher; b. Bangor, Feb. 9, 1924. He studied organ with Boyle in Chester and then was an organ scholar under Orr at St. John's College, Cambridge (Mus.B., 1951). From 1951 to 1991 he was organist and choirmaster at St. John's College. He led the choir on various tours, and also appeared as an organ recitalist. He served as assistant lecturer (1953–56) and then as lecturer (1956–82) at the Univ. of Cambridge, and in 1960–61 he was a prof. at the Royal Academy of Music in London. From 1974 to 1991 he was organist at the Univ. of Cambridge. He served as president of the Royal College of Organists (1978–80), the Cathedral Organists' Assn. (1980–82), and the Incorporated Assn. of Organists (1987–89). In 1987 he was made a Commander of the Order of the British Empire. His discriminating repertory as a choral conductor ranged from Palestrina to Britten. His years at Cambridge are highlighted in his book *A Guest at Cambridge* (Orleans, Mass., 1994).

Guézec, Jean-Pierre, French composer; b. Dijon, Aug. 29, 1934; d. Paris, March 9, 1971. He enrolled at the Paris Cons., where he attended classes of Messiaen, Milhaud, and Rivier; received the premier prix in 1963; joined the faculty of the Paris Cons. in 1969.

WORKS: Concerto for Violin and 14 Instruments (1960); *Concert en trois parties* for 11 Instruments (1961); *Suite pour Mondrian* for Orch. (1962); *Architectures colorées* for 15 Instruments (1964); *Ensemble multicolore 65* for 18 Instruments (1965); *Formes* for Orch. (1966); *Textures enchaînées* for 13 Wind Instruments (1967); *Assemblages* for 28 Instruments (1967); String Trio (1968); *Reliefs polychromés* for Chorus (1969); *Couleurs juxtaposées* for 2 Percussion Groups (1969); *Onze pour cinq* for Percussionists (1970).

Gui, Vittorio, eminent Italian conductor; b. Rome, Sept. 14, 1885; d. Florence, Oct. 16, 1975. He studied composition with Falchi at the Liceo Musicale di Santa Cecilia in Rome, and also attended the Univ. of Rome. On Dec. 7, 1907, he made his debut conducting *La Gioconda* at Rome's Teatro Adriano. After conducting in Naples, he appeared at Milan's La Scala (1923–25; 1932–34). In 1925 he was a founder and conductor of the Teatro di Torino. In 1928 he organized the Orch. Stabile in Florence, which served as the foundation of the famous Maggio Musicale Fiorentino, which he instituted in 1933; he also was a conductor at the Teatro Comunale there. In 1938–39 he conducted at London's Covent Garden, and returned there in 1952. He was chief conductor of the Glyndebourne Festivals from 1952 to 1960, and then was its artistic counsellor from 1960 to 1965. Gui continued to conduct in Italy until the close of his long life, making his final appearance only a few weeks before his death at the age of 90. He was one of the leading Italian conductors of his day, excelling not only in opera but also in symphonic music. He also composed the operas *David* (Rome, 1907) and *Fata Malerba* (Turin, May 15, 1927); the orch. works *Giulietta e Romeo* (1902), *Il tempo che fu* (1910), *Scherzo fantastico* (1913), *Fantasia bianca* (1919), and *Giornata di festa* (1921); chamber music; songs. Gui publ. the study *Nerone di Arrigo Boito* (Milan, 1924) and a vol. of critical essays *Battute d'aspetto* (Florence, 1944).

Guillou, Jean, prominent French organist, pianist, teacher, and composer; b. Angers, April 18, 1930. He began to study the piano at 5 and the organ at 10. When he was 12, he became organist at the church of St.-Serge in Angers. He then was a student at the Paris Cons. (1945–53) of Dupré, Duruflé, and Messiaen, where he took premiers prix in organ, harmony, counterpoint, and fugue. After serving as prof. of organ at the Istituto de Alta Cultura in Lisbon (1953–57), he went to Berlin to puruse his career. In 1963 he was named organist at St.-Eustache in Paris. He also pursued an international career as a recitalist, principally as an organist. In addition to teaching master classes in organ, he publ. a book on organ theory and design, *L'Orgue, Souvenir et Avenir* (Paris, 1978; 2nd ed., aug., 1989). Guillou's vast repertoire ranges from the Baroque to the contemporary periods. As a virtuoso organist, he has acquired a reputation for daring registration and rhythms, and for a mastery of improvisation.

WORKS: ORCH.: 5 organ concertos (1960, 1963, 1965, 1978, 1979); 2 piano concertos (1969, 1986); 3 syms.: No. 1 for Mezzo-soprano and Orch., *Judith-Symphonie* (1970), No. 2 for Strings (1974), and No. 3, *La Foule* (1977); *Concerto Heroïque* for Organ and Orch. (1985); Trombone Concerto (1990). **CHAMBER:** *Colloque* No. 1 for Flute, Oboe, Violin, and Piano (1956), No. 2 for Piano and Orch. (1964), No. 3 for Oboe, Harp, Celesta, Percussion, 4 Cellos, and 2 Double Basses (1964), No. 4 for Piano, Organ, and 2 Percussion (1966), and No. 5 for Piano and Organ (1969); Oboe Quartet (1971); Sonata for Trumpet and Organ (1972); Concerto for Violin and Organ (1982); *Fantaisie Concertante* for Cello and Organ (1991). **KEYBOARD: PIANO:** 2 sonatas (1958, 1978). **ORGAN:** *Fantaisie* (1954); 18 Variations (1956); Sinfonietta (1958); *Toccata* (1963); *Symphonie Initiatique* for 2 Organs (1969); 7 *Sagas* (1970–83); *Scènes d'Enfants* (1974); *Jeux d'Orgue* (1978); *Sonate en Trio* (1984); *Hyperion* (1988); many transcriptions. **VOCAL:** *Andromede* for Soprano and Organ (1984); *Peace* for Chorus and Organ (1985); *Aube* for Chorus and Organ (1988).

Guion, David (Wendell Fentress), American composer and teacher; b. Ballinger, Texas, Dec. 15, 1892; d. Dallas, Oct. 17, 1981. He studied piano with Godowsky in Vienna, but was autodidact in composition. He then held various teaching posts in Texas, and was active in collecting and arranging American folk songs. His best known work was his version of *Home on the Range* (1930). Among his other works were the African ballet suite, *Shingandi* (1929); several orch. suites, including *Texas* (1952); piano pieces; songs.

Gulbranson, Ellen (née **Norgren**), Swedish soprano; b. Stockholm, March 4, 1863; d. Oslo, Jan. 2, 1947. She studied at the Stockholm Cons. and with M. and B. Marchesi in Paris. In 1886 she made her concert debut in Stockholm, and in 1889 her operatic debut at that city's Royal Opera as Amneris. She gained distinction as a Wagnerian, singing Brünnhilde at every Bayreuth Festival from 1896 to 1914; she also appeared as Kundry. She sang in Berlin from 1895 and in Vienna from 1896; in 1900 she appeared as Brünnhilde at London's Covent Garden, returning there in 1907–08. She also sang in other major music centers until her retirement in 1915.

Gulda, Friedrich, remarkable Austrian pianist; b. Vienna, May 16, 1930. He began his training at the Grossmann Cons. After piano lessons with Felix Pazofsky (1938–42), he studied with Bruno Seidlhofer (piano) and Joseph Marx (composition) at the Vienna Academy of Music. At 14, he made his formal debut and at 16 won 1st prize at the Geneva Competition. Thereafter he pursued an outstanding international career. On Oct. 11, 1950, he made a brilliant U.S. debut at N.Y.'s Carnegie Hall. He was praised for his intellectual penetration of the music of Bach, Beethoven, and Mozart. About 1955 he became intensely fascinated by jazz, particularly in its improvisatory aspect, which he construed as corresponding to the freedom of melodic ornamentation in Baroque music. He often included jazz numbers (with drums and slap bass) at the end of his recitals; he learned to play the saxophone, began to compose for jazz, and organized the Eurojazz Orch. As a further symptom of his estrangement from musical puritanism, he returned the 1970 Beethoven Bicentennial ring given to him by the Vienna Academy of Music in appreciation of his excellence in playing Beethoven's music, and gave a speech explaining the reasons for his action. He composed and performed jazz pieces, among them *Music Nos. 1* and *2* for Piano and Big Band (1962, 1963); *Music* for 3 Jazz Soloists and Band (1962); Sym. in F for Jazz Band and Orch.; *The Veiled Old Land* for Jazz Band (1964); *The Excursion* for Jazz Orch., celebrating the flight of the American spaceship Gemini 4 (1965); and Concertino for Players and Singers (1972). He made a bold arrangement of Vienna waltzes in the manner of the blues; also composed a jazz musical, *Drop-out oder Gustav der Letzte* (1970), freely after Shakespeare's *Measure for Measure.* He publ. a book of essays, *Worte zur Musik* (Munich, 1971).

BIBL.: E. Jantsch, *F. G.: Die Verantwortung des Interpreten* (Vienna, 1953); K. Geitel, *Fragen an F. G.* (Berlin, 1973).

Gülke, Peter, German conductor and musicologist; b. Weimar, April 29, 1934. He was educated at the Franz Liszt Hochschule für Musik in Weimar, the Friedrich Schiller Univ. in Jena, and the Karl Marx Univ. in Leipzig (Ph.D., 1958, with the diss. *Liedprinzip und Polyphonie in der burgundischen Chanson des 15. Jahrhundert*), where he taught (1957–59). In 1959 he made his conducting debut in Rudolstadt, and then was music director of the theaters in Stendal (1964–65), Potsdam (1966–69), and Stralsund (1972–76). After conducting at the Dresden State Opera (1976–81), he was Generalmusikdirektor of the Mannheim National Theater (1981–83). In 1984 he became a lecturer in musicology at the Technical Univ. in Berlin. He was Generalmusikdirektor in Wuppertal from 1986. In 1978 he brought out a performing edition of Schubert's Sym. in D major, D.936a, a work sometimes listed as that composer's Sym. No. 10. With D. Gülke, he ed. *Jean Jacques Rousseau: Ausgewählte Schriften zur Musik* (Leipzig, 1981). He also publ. *Brahms—Bruckner: Zwei Studien* (Kassel, 1989), *Franz Schubert und seine Zeit* (Laaber, 1991), and *Fluchtpunkt Musik: Reflexionen eines Dirigenten zwischen Ost und West* (Kassel and Stuttgart, 1994).

Gulli, Franco, distinguished Italian violinist; b. Trieste, Sept. 1, 1926. He studied violin with his father, making his debut in 1933; then went to the Trieste Cons.; also studied in Siena and Paris; his teachers included Arrigo Serato and Joseph Szigeti. He married the pianist Enrica Cavallo; in 1947 they formed the noted Gulli-Cavallo Duo, which made several successful tours. In 1968 he was soloist with the Dallas Sym. Orch.; subsequently played with several American orchs. In 1972 he was appointed prof. at the Indiana Univ. School of Music in Bloomington. An artist of integrity, Gulli secures fine performances of Classical and modern music faithful to the style of the period.

Gundry, Inglis, English composer; b. London, May 8, 1905. He studied law at Balliol College, Oxford (M.A, 1927) and at the Middle Temple (1927–29) before pursuing his musical training with Vaughan Williams, Gordon Jacob, and R.O. Morris at the Royal College of Music in London (1935–38). In 1936 he won the Cobbett Prize. From 1946 he lectured on music, and later was founder-music director of the Sacred Music Drama Soc. (1960–86). He publ. *Opera in a Nutshell* (1945), *The Nature of Opera as a Composite Art* (1947), and *Composers by the Grace of God: A Study of Music and Religion* (1989).

WORKS: OPERAS: *Naaman: The Leprosy of War* (1936–37); *The Return of Odysseus* (1938); *The Partisans* (London, May 28,

1946); *Avon* (London, April 11, 1949); *The Tinners of Cornwall* (London, Sept. 30, 1953); *The Logan Rock* (Porthcurno, Aug. 15, 1956); *The Prince of Coxcombs* (London, Feb. 3, 1965); *The 3 Wise Men* (Kings Langley, Hertfordshire, Jan. 7, 1967); *The Prisoner Paul* (London, Oct. 16, 1970); *A Will of her Own* (1971–73; London, May 31, 1985); *The Rubicon* (1981–83); *Lindisfarne* (1984–86); *Claudia's Dream* (1986–89); *Galileo* (1992–93). **OTHER:** *Variations on an Indian Theme* for Orch. (1940); *5 Bells Suite* for Chorus and Orch. (1942); Harp Concerto; orch. suites; *Phantasy* for String Quartet; solo harp pieces, including a Solo Harp Concerto; *The Daytime of Christ*, oratorio; song cycles.

Gunn, Glenn Dillard, American pianist, conductor, and music critic; b. Topeka, Kansas, Oct. 2, 1874; d. Washington, D.C., Nov. 22, 1963. He studied at the Leipzig Cons. and in Chicago with Ziehn (theory). He taught at the Chicago Musical College (1901–5). In 1915 he founded the American Sym. Orch., whose object was the performance of American works and the engagement of American soloists; in 1922 he founded the Glenn Dillard Gunn School of Music and Dramatic Art; in 1932 he became artistic director of the Chicago Cons. of Music. He was music critic for the *Chicago Tribune* (1910–15), the *Chicago Herald and Examiner* (1922–36), and the *Washington Times-Herald* (1940–54). He publ. *A Course of Lessons on the History and Aesthetics of Music* (Chicago, 1912) and *Music, Its History and Enjoyment* (N.Y., 1930).

Günther, Mizzi, greatly talented Austrian soprano; b. Warnsdorf, Feb. 8, 1879; d. Vienna, March 18, 1961. After appearances in provincial theaters, she settled in Vienna and first gained attention as O Mimosa San in *Die Geisha* in 1901. Later that year she had her first starring role as Lotti in *Die drei Wünsche* at the Carltheater, then had her first great success as Lola Winter there in *Das süsse Mädel*. She joined the Theater an der Wien in 1905 singing Jessie in *Vergeltsgott*. On Dec. 30, 1905, she created the role of Hanna Glawari in Lehár's *Die lustige Witwe*, and thereafter was recognized as one of the leading operetta stars of her era. She went on to appear to great acclaim as Alice in *Die Dollarprinzessin* (1907) and as Lori in *Der Mann mit den drei Frauen* (1908). In 1909 she became a member of the Johann Strauss-Theater, where she created the role of Mary Ann in Lehár's *Das Fürstenkind*. In 1911 she rejoined the Theater an der Wien and created the title role in Lehár's *Eva*. After again appearing at the Johann Strauss-Theater (from 1915), she once more sang at the Theater an der Wien (from 1919), where she created the role of Katja in *Katja, die Tänzerin* (1923). In subsequent years, she concentrated on character roles. She later appeared at the Raimundtheater and the Volksoper. As late as 1948 she was seen on the Vienna stage, marking some 50 years in the musical theater.

Gunzenhauser, Stephen (Charles), American conductor; b. N.Y., April 8, 1942. He studied at the Oberlin (Ohio) College Cons. of Music (B.Mus., 1963) and at the Salzburg Mozarteum (diploma, 1962); following further training at the New England Cons. of Music in Boston (M.Mus., 1965), he held 3 Fulbright grants and completed his education at the Cologne Hochschule für Musik (artist diploma, 1968). In 1967 he took 1st prize in the Santiago, Spain, conducting competition, and then was an assistant conductor to Markevitch and l'Orchestre National de l'Opéra de Monte Carlo (1968–69) and to Stokowski and the American Sym. Orch. in N.Y. (1969–70). He was music director of the Brooklyn Center Chamber Orch. (1970–72); then was artistic (1974–82) and administrative (1982–87) director of the Wilmington (Del.) Music School. In 1978 he became music director of the Delaware Sym. Orch. in Wilmington; concurrently, was principal conductor (1978–81) and music director (from 1981) of the Lancaster (Pa.) Sym. Orch.

Gura, Hermann, German baritone; b. Breslau, April 5, 1870; d. Bad Wiessee, Bavaria, Sept. 13, 1944. He studied with Hasselbeck and Zenger in Munich, making his debut as the Dutchman in Weimar in 1890; then sang in Riga (1890–91), Berlin (Kroll Opera, 1891–92), Aachen (1892–93), Zürich (1893–94), Basel (1894–95), and Munich (1895–96). He subsequently was a singer and producer at the Schwerin Hoftheater in Munich (1896–1908), then director of the Berlin Komische Opera (from 1911); also worked at London's Covent Garden as a producer in 1913. After producing opera in Helsinki from 1920 to 1927, he taught voice in Berlin.

Guridi (Bidaola), Jésus, Spanish organist, teacher, and composer; b. Vitoria, Álava province, Sept. 25, 1886; d. Madrid, April 7, 1961. He studied harmony with Valentín Arín, and then with José Sainz Besabé in Bilbao; took courses in piano with Grovlez, organ with Decaux, composition with Sérieyx, and counterpoint and fugue with d'Indy at the Paris Schola Cantorum; studied organ and composition with Jongen in Liège; finally took a course in instrumentation with Neitzel in Cologne. He was an organist in Bilbao (1909–29); also conducted the Bilbao Choral Soc. (1911–26). In 1939 he settled in Madrid, where he became prof. of organ at the Cons. in 1944. During his years in Bilbao, he promoted the cause of Basque folk music; publ. an album of 22 Basque songs. His zarzuelas make frequent use of Basque folk music; of these, *El caserio* (Madrid, 1926) attained enormous success in Spain. Other stage works include *Mirentxu*, idyll (Madrid, 1915), *Amaya*, lyric drama (Bilbao, 1920), and *La Meiga* (Madrid, 1928). He also wrote a symphonic poem, *Una aventura de Don Quijote* (1916); *Sinfonia pirenáica*; *Basque Sketches* for Chorus and Orch.; an orch. suite, *10 Basque Melodies*; a number of a cappella choral works on Basque themes; 4 string quartets; piano pieces; and songs.

BIBL.: J. de Arozamena, *J. G.* (Madrid, 1967).

Gurlitt, Manfred, German conductor, teacher, and composer, cousin of **Wilibald Gurlitt;** b. Berlin, Sept. 6, 1890; d. Tokyo, April 29, 1972. He was a student in Berlin of Mayer-Mahr and Breithaupt (piano), Kaun (theory and composition), and Humperdinck (composition). In 1911 he became an assistant at the Bayreuth Festivals, and also conducted opera in Essen and Augsburg. After serving as 1st conductor and opera director at the Bremen City Theater (1914–24), he returned to Berlin and was granted the title of Generalmusikdirektor, appeared as a guest conductor at the State Opera and on the radio, and taught at the Hochschule für Musik. After the Nazis proscribed his activities, he settled in Tokyo in 1939 as a conductor and teacher. He conducted his own opera company there from 1953.

WORKS: OPERAS: *Die Heilige* (Bremen, Jan. 27, 1920); *Wozzeck* (Bremen, April 22, 1926); *Soldaten* (Düsseldorf, Nov. 1930); *Nana* (Dortmund, 1933); *Nächtlicher Spuk* (1937); *Warum?* (1940); *Nordische Ballade* (1944); *Wir schreiten aus* (1958). **ORCH.:** *Symphonische Musik* (1922); *Orchester-Gesänge* (1925); Chamber Concerto No. 1 for Piano and Chamber Orch. (1927) and No. 2 for Violin and Chamber Orch. (1929); Cello Concerto (1937); 2 syms.: No. 1, *Goya-Symphonie* (1938) and No. 2, *Shakespeare-Symphonie* for 5 Voices and Orch. (1954). **VOCAL:** *5 Gesänge* for Soprano and Chamber Orch. (1923); *Drei politische Reden aus der Französischen Revolution* for Baritone, Men's Chorus, and Orch. (1944); songs. **OTHER:** Chamber music and piano pieces.

Gurlitt, Wilibald, eminent German musicologist and editor, cousin of **Manfred Gurlitt**; b. Dresden, March 1, 1889; d. Freiburg im Breisgau, Dec. 15, 1963. He studied musicology at the Univ. of Heidelberg with Philipp Wolfrum; also with Riemann and Schering at the Univ. of Leipzig, where he received his Ph.D. in 1914 with the diss. *Michael Praetorius (Creuzbergensis): Sein Leben und seine Werke* (publ. in Leipzig, 1915); subsequently was an assistant to Riemann. He served in World War I, and was taken prisoner in France. After the Armistice, he became a lecturer at the Univ. of Freiburg im Breisgau in 1919; directed its dept. of musicology from 1920; was made a full prof. in 1929, but was removed from his position by the Nazi regime in 1937; resumed his professorship in 1945; retired in

1958. Gurlitt's investigations of the organ music of Praetorius led him to construct (in collaboration with O. Walcker) a "Praetorius organ," which was to reproduce the tuning of the period. This gave impetus in Germany to performance of historic works on authentic or reconstructed instruments. Gurlitt's other interests included the problem of musical terminology, resulting in the publication of his *Handwörterbuch der musikalischen Terminologie.* In 1952 he revived the moribund *Archiv für Musikwissenschaft.* He edited the 1st 2 vols. of the 12th ed. of *Riemann's Musik-Lexikon* (Mainz, 1959 and 1961). He also publ. *Johann Sebastian Bach: Der Meister und sein Werk* (Berlin, 1936; 4th ed., 1959; Eng. tr., St. Louis, 1957).

BIBL.: A. Schmitz, "W. G.," *Jahrbuch der Akademie der Wissenschaften und der Literatur* (Mainz, 1964).

Gurney, Ivor (Bertie), English poet and composer; b. Gloucester, Aug. 28, 1890; d. Dartford, Kent, Dec. 26, 1937. He became a chorister at Gloucester Cathedral in 1900, where he studied with Brewer. After serving as assistant organist there (1906–11), he continued his studies as a scholarship student in composition with Stanford at the Royal College of Music in London (1911–15). He then served in the British Army during World War I, and in 1917 was wounded and gassed at Passchendaele. Although he never recovered his mental and physical health, he resumed his studies at the Royal College of Music in 1919 as a student of Vaughan Williams. In 1922 he was declared insane and spent the rest of his life in mental hospitals. Gurney was a gifted composer of songs, being principally influenced by Parry and German lieder. He set some of his own poems, as well as others, to music. In all, he publ. some 40 songs (4 vols., 1917–22). Among his other works were piano pieces and violin pieces.

BIBL.: C. Moore, *Maker and Lover of Beauty: I.G., Poet and Songwriter* (Rickmansworth, 1976); M. Hurd, *The Ordeal of I.G.* (Oxford, 1978); A. Boden, ed., *Stars in a Dark Night: The Letters of I.G. to the Chapman Family* (Gloucester, 1986); M. Pilkington, *G., Ireland, Quilter and Warlock* (London, 1989); T. Hold, "I.G.: Poet and Composer," *Musical Times* (Aug. 1990).

Guschlbauer, Theodor, Austrian conductor; b. Vienna, April 14, 1939. He was educated at the Vienna Academy of Music and in Salzburg. He was conductor of the Vienna Baroque Ensemble (1961–69); subsequently served as chief conductor of the Salzburg Landestheater (1966–68); then went to Lyons as conductor of the Opera. In 1975 he was appointed chief conductor of the Landestheater in Linz; concurrently assumed the post of chief conductor of the Linz-Bruckner Sym. Orch. and director of the annual Bruckner Festival. In 1983 he became chief conductor of the Strasbourg Phil. From 1983 to 1988 he was also chief conductor of the Deutsche Oper am Rhein in Düsseldorf.

Gusikoff, Michel, American violinist and composer, b. N.Y., May 15, 1893; d. there, July 10, 1978. He was the great-grandson of the Polish xylophonist and composer Michał Józef Guzikov (1806–1837). He studied violin with Mark Fonaroff and Kneisel, and composition with Goetschius. He was concertmaster of the St. Louis Sym. Orch., Russian Sym. Orch. in N.Y., N.Y. Sym. Orch., Philadelphia Orch., NBC Sym. Orch. in N.Y., Pittsburgh Sym. Orch., and Bell Telephone Hour Orch. Among his works were *American Concerto* or *Jazz Fantasy* for Violin and Orch. (1931); *Oh! Susanna* for String Quartet or String Orch. (1942); violin pieces; violin arrangements of Gershwin's songs.

Gutchë, Gene (real name, **Romeo Maximilian Eugene Ludwig Gutsche**), German-born American composer; b. Berlin, July 3, 1907. He studied in Germany, Italy, and Switzerland; in 1925 he went to the U.S., where he later undertook additional academic work at the Univ. of Minnesota with Donald Ferguson and at the Univ. of Iowa with Philip Greeley Clapp (Ph.D., 1953). He held 2 Guggenheim fellowships (1961, 1964). His music is marked by a fairly advanced idiom and a neo-Romantic treatment of programmatic subject matter. In some of his orch. works, he applies fractional tones by dividing the strings into 2 groups tuned at slightly differing pitches.

WORKS: ORCH.: 6 syms.: No. 1 (Minneapolis, April 11, 1950), No. 2 (1950–54), No. 3 (1952), No. 4 (1960; Albuquerque, March 8, 1962), No. 5 for Strings (Chautauqua, N.Y., July 29, 1962), and No. 6 (1968); *Rondo capriccioso* (1953; N.Y., Feb. 19, 1960); Piano Concerto (Minneapolis, June 19, 1956); Cello Concerto (1957); *Bongo Divertimento* for Solo Percussionist and Orch. (1962); *Timpani Concertante* (Oakland, Calif., Feb. 14, 1962); Violin Concerto (1962); *Genghis Khan,* symphonic poem (Minneapolis, Dec. 6, 1963); *Rites in Tenochtitlan* for Small Orch. (St. Paul, Jan. 26, 1965); *Gemini* (Minneapolis, July 26, 1966); *Classic Concerto* (St. Paul, Nov. 11, 1967); *Epimetheus USA* (Detroit, Nov. 13, 1969); *Icarus,* suite (1975); *Bi-Centurion* (1975; Rochester, N.Y., Jan. 8, 1976); *Perseus and Andromeda XX* (1976; Cincinnati, Feb. 25, 1977). **CHAMBER:** 4 string quartets; 3 piano sonatas.**VOCAL:** *Akhenaten* for Chorus and Orch. (St. Louis, Sept. 23, 1983); choruses.

Gutheil-Schoder, Marie, prominent German mezzo-soprano; b. Weimar, Feb. 16, 1874; d. Bad Ilmenau, Oct. 4, 1935. She was largely self-taught, although she received some coaching from Richard Strauss in Weimar, where she made her operatic debut as the 1st Lady in *Die Zauberflöte* in 1891. After singing in Berlin and Leipzig, she was engaged by Mahler for the Vienna Court Opera (debut as Nedda, Feb. 16, 1900). In her early performances, she was criticized for her small voice; Mahler made note of her "disagreeable middle register," but he also declared that she was a musical genius; her strong dramatic characterizations made her a favorite there until 1926. She was successful as Carmen, Elektra, Eva, and the 3 principal soprano roles in *Les Contes d'Hoffmann*; her Mozart roles included Pamina, Elvira, Susanna, and Cherubino. Her only London appearance was at Covent Garden as Octavian in 1913; 3 years later she sang the role of the Composer, under Strauss's direction, in a Zürich production of the revised version of *Ariadne aux Naxos.* She was closely associated with the music of Schoenberg; she took part in the premiere of his 2nd String Quartet (Vienna, Feb. 5, 1907), and later frequently performed in his *Pierrot Lunaire*; Schoenberg conceived the part of The Woman in his monodrama *Erwartung* as a "Gutheil part"; she appeared in its first performance (Prague, June 6, 1924). After her retirement, she was active as a teacher and producer in Vienna and Salzburg. She was successively married to the violinist and composer Gustav Gutheil and the Viennese photographer Franz Setzer.

Gutiérrez, Horacio, brilliant Cuban-born American pianist; b. Havana, Aug. 28, 1948. He studied in Havana, where he made his debut as soloist with the local orch. at age 11. In 1962 his family went to Los Angeles and in 1967 he became a naturalized American citizen. He completed his training at the Juilliard School of Music in N.Y. (1967–70). In 1970 he won 2nd prize at the Tchaikovsky Competition in Moscow, and then made successful debuts in N.Y. in 1972 and in London in 1974. In 1982 he was awarded the Avery Fisher Prize. He toured regularly throughout the world, appearing as a soloist with the foremost orchs., as a recitalist, and as a chamber music player.

Gutiérrez Heras, Joaquín, Mexican composer; b. Tehuacán, Sept. 28, 1927. He attended classes in architecture at the National Univ. of Mexico and then studied composition with Blas Galindo and Rodolfo Halffter at the National Cons. of Mexico (1950–52). A scholarship from the French Inst. of Mexico enabled him to go to Paris, where he took courses in composition with Messiaen, Rivier, and Dandelot at the Paris Cons. (1952–53); on a Rockefeller Foundation scholarship, he studied composition with Bergsma and Persichetti at the Juilliard School of Music in N.Y. (1960–61). Upon his return to Mexico, he gave radio lectures and taught theory. As a composer, he professed a "voluntary lack of complexity."

WORKS: *Divertimento* for Piano and Orch. (1949); *El*

deportista, satirical ballet (1957); *Variations on a French Song* for Piano or Harpsichord (1958–60); *Chamber Cantata on Poems by Emilio Prados* for Soprano, 2 Flutes, Harp, and 4 Strings (1961); *Los Cazadores* (The Hunters), symphonic scene (1962); Duo for Alto Flute and Cello (1964); *Sonata simple* for Flute and Piano (1965); Trio for Oboe, Clarinet, and Bassoon (1965); *2 Pieces for 3 Brasses* (1967); *Night and Day Music* for Wind Sym. Orch. (1973); *De profundis* for Chorus (1977); several scores for theater and film.

Gutman, Natalia, Russian cellist; b. Moscow, June 14, 1942. At the age of 5, she became a pupil of Saposhnikov at the Gnessin Music School, later pursuing training with Rostropovich at the Moscow Cons. She made her first public appearance at the age of 9. After winning a medal at the Tchaikovsky Competition in Moscow in 1962, she took 1st prize in the German Radio Competition in Munich in 1967. She subsequently pursued a far-ranging career as a soloist with principal orchs. of Europe, North America, and Japan; also was active as a recitalist and chamber music player, frequently appearing in duo concerts with her husband **Oleg Kagan**. In addition to the standard cello repertory, Gutman acquired a fine reputation for her championship of contemporary music.

Güttler, Ludwig, noted German trumpeter, conductor, and pedagogue; b. Sosa, June 13, 1943. He commenced music studies when he was 5, and began playing the trumpet at 14; after obtaining a degree in architecture, he studied trumpet with Armin Mennel at the Leipzig Hochschule für Musik (1961–65). From 1965 he was solo trumpeter of the Handel Festival Orch. in Halle, and later, of the Dresden Phil. (1969–81). In 1976 he founded the Leipziger Bach-Collegium, in 1978 the Blechbläserensemble Ludwig Güttler, and in 1985 the Virtuosi Saxoniae; made many tours with these groups, appearing as a trumpeter and conductor. In 1972 he joined the faculty of the Dresden Hochschule für Musik, taking charge of its master classes in wind instruments in 1982; also served as a guest teacher at the Weimar International Music Seminar (from 1977) and in Austria, Japan, and the U.S. Güttler discovered many scores for his instrument in various German archives, libraries, and castles, and made a special effort to bring them before the public. He won renown for his performances of Baroque and Classical works on period instruments. In 1978 he won the National Prize of the German Democratic Republic and in 1989 was awarded the Music Prize of the City of Frankfurt am Main.

Guyonnet, Jacques, Swiss composer; b. Geneva, March 20, 1933. He studied at the Geneva Cons. (1950–58) and had courses in new music with Boulez at the summer sessions held in Darmstadt (1958–61). In 1959 he founded the Studio de Musique Contemporaine in Geneva; from 1976 to 1981 was president of the ISCM.

WORKS: DRAMATIC: *Entremonde,* ballet for Flute, Piano, 4 Percussionists, and Tape (1967); *Electric Sorcerers,* rock opera (1980–81). **ORCH.:** *Monades II* and *III* (1960, 1961); *En 3 éclats!* for Piano and Chamber Orch. (1964); *Stele in memoriam J.F. Kennedy* for Chamber Orch. and Tape (1964); *7 portes du temps* (1966–69); *A Single R* for Viola and Chamber Orch. (1971); *Die Wandlung* (1973); *Les Enfants du désert* for Strings (1974); *Zornagore* (1976); *Les profondeurs de la terre* (1977); *Ombre* (1979); *Les Dernières Demeures* (1979); *Harmonique-Souffle* for Chamber Orch. (1980). **CHAMBER:** *Monades I* for Chamber Ensemble (1958); *Polyphonie I* for Flute and Piano (1961) and *III* for Flute, Viola, and 2 Pianos (1964); *The Approach to the Hidden Man I* for Solo Cello and 6 Instruments (1966); *Let There Be Events!* for 17 Instrumental Soloists (1968–71); *Modèles I–II* for any number of Instrumental Soloists (1970); *Mémorial* for 4 Trumpets and 4 Trombones (1974); *Un soupir pour Aurore* for Cello and Piano (1990). **PIANO:** *Polyphonie II* for 2 Pianos (1959); *Chronicles* (1964–71). **VOCAL:** *The Approach to the Hidden Man II* for Mezzo-soprano, Chamber Orch., and Electronic Sound (1967); *Good Grief Jerry!* for Soprano and Chamber Orch. (1970–71); *Le Chant remémoré* for 4 Vocal Soloists and Orch. (1972).

Gysi, Fritz, Swiss music critic and musicologist; b. Zofingen, Feb. 18, 1888; d. Zürich, March 5, 1967. He studied at the Basel Cons., and then took courses in musicology and art history at the Univs. of Zürich, Berlin, and Bern (Ph.D., 1913, with the diss. *Die Entwicklung der kirchlichen Architektur in der deutschen Schweiz im 17. und 18. Jahrhundert;* publ. in Zürich, 1914); subsequently completed his Habilitation in music history at the Univ. of Zürich in 1921, where he was made a titular prof. in 1931. He was also a music critic for the *Basler Nachrichten* and the Basel *National-Zeitung* (from 1915) and the Zürich *Tagesanzeiger* (from 1928).

WRITINGS: *Mozart in seinen Briefen* (Zürich, 1919–21); *Max Bruch* (Zürich, 1922); *Claude Debussy* (Zürich, 1926); *Richard Wagner und die Schweiz* (Frauenfeld, 1929); *Richard Wagner und Zürich* (Zürich, 1933); *Richard Strauss* (Potsdam, 1934); *Hans Georg Nägeli* (Zürich, 1936).

H

Haapanen, Toivo (Elias), Finnish musicologist and conductor; b. Karvia, May 15, 1889; d. Asikkala, July 22, 1950. He studied violin and theory in Helsinki, Berlin, and Paris and musicology with I. Krohn at the Univ. of Helsinki (M.A., 1918; Ph.D., 1925, with the diss. *Die Neumenfragmente der Universitätsbibliothek Helsingfors*). In 1925 he became a lecturer at the Univ. of Helsinki; was a prof. there from 1946. From 1929 to 1946 he was head of the music division of the Finnish Broadcasting Co.; was chief conductor of its Radio Sym. Orch. from 1929 until his death. He publ. a valuable *Verzeichnis der mittelalterlichen Handschriftenfragmente in der Universitätsbibliothek zu Helsingfors* (3 vols., Helsinki, 1922, 1925, 1932). He further publ. *Suomen säveltaide* (The Art of Music in Finland; Helsinki, 1940) and ed. a dictionary of music (Helsinki, 1948).

Haar, James, American musicologist; b. St. Louis, July 4, 1929. He studied at Harvard Univ. (B.A., 1950) and the Univ. of North Carolina (M.A., 1954); then returned to Harvard to complete his training under John Ward and Nino Pirrotta (Ph.D., 1961, with the diss. *Musica mundana: Variations on a Pythagorean Theme*); served on its faculty (1960–67). He taught at the Univ. of Pa. (1967–69), N.Y. Univ. (1969–78), and the Univ. of North Carolina (from 1978); was general ed. of the *Journal of the American Musicological Society* (1966–69), later serving as the society's president (1976–78). With L. Bernstein, he ed. *The Duos of Jhan Gero* (1977); publ. *The Tugendsterne of Harsdorffer and Staden* (1965) and *Essays on Italian Poetry and Music in the Renaissance, 1350–1600* (1986). With I. Fenlon, he publ. *The Italian Madrigal in the Early Sixteenth Century: Sources and Interpretation* (1989).

Haas, Joseph, eminent German composer and pedagogue; b. Maihigen, March 19, 1879; d. Munich, March 30, 1960. He was a pupil of Reger (composition) in Munich and Leipzig, and also in the latter city of Straube (organ) and Ruthardt (piano). In 1911 he became a teacher and in 1916 a prof. of composition at the Stuttgart Cons. In 1921 he settled in Munich as a prof. in the Catholic church music dept. of the Akademie der Tonkunst, and later was president of the Hochschule für Musik (1945–50). In 1949 a Joseph Haas Soc. was formed to promote his music, which is written in a well-crafted and accessible style. He publ. a biography of Reger (Bonn, 1949), and a collection of his speeches and articles appeared as *Reden und Aufsätze* (Mainz, 1964).

WORKS: OPERAS: *Die Bergkönigin* (1927); *Tobias Wunderlich* (Kassel, Nov. 24, 1937); *Die Hochzeit des Jobs* (Dresden, July 2, 1944). **ORCH.:** *Variationensuite über ein altes Rokokothema* for Small Orch. (1924); *Ouvertüre zu einem frohen Spiel* (1943). **CHAMBER:** 2 string quartets (1905, 1919); Violin Sonata (1908); Horn Sonata (1910); Trio for 2 Violins and Piano (1912); 2 church sonatas for Violin and Organ (1926); piano pieces, including 3 sonatas (1918, 1923, 1923); organ music, including a Sonata (1907) and 31 *Variationen über ein eigenes Thema* (1911). **VOCAL: ORATORIOS:** *Die Heilige Elisabeth* (1931); *Das Lebensbuch Gottes* (1934); *Das Lied von Mutter* (1939); *Das Jahr im Lied* (1952); *Die Seligen* (1956). **OTHER:** *Christnacht*, Weihnachtsliederspiel for Soli, Speaker, Chorus, and Orch. (1932); *Christ-König-Messe* (1935); *Münchner Liebfrauen-Messe* (1944); *Te Deum* (1945); *Totenmesse* (1945); *Deutsche Weihnachtsmesse* (1954); *Schiller-Hymne* for Baritone, Chorus, and Orch. (1957); *Deutsche Kindermesse* (1958); choruses; songs.

BIBL.: K. Laux, *J.H.* (Mainz, 1931); *Festgabe J.H.* (Mainz, 1939); K. Laux, *J.H.* (Hamburg, 1940); idem, *J.H.* (Berlin and Düsseldorf, 1954); S. Gmeinwieser, W. Haas, H.-M. Palm-Beulich, and F. Schieri, *J.H.* (Tutzing, 1994).

Haas, Karl (Wilhelm Jacob), German conductor and musicologist; b. Karlsruhe, Dec. 27, 1900; d. London, July 7, 1970. He studied at the Univs. of Munich and Heidelberg; then worked for the Karlsruhe and Stuttgart radios; was active as a collector of valuable early instruments. He made microfilms of early music. In 1939 he emigrated to England; in 1943 he organized the London Baroque Ensemble; led it until 1966 in performances of little-known Baroque music. He also ed. works by Haydn, Boccherini, and Cherubini.

Haas, Monique, French pianist; b. Paris, Oct. 20, 1906; d. there, June 9, 1987. She studied at the Paris Cons. with Lazare-Lévy (piano; premier prix, 1927), Tournemire (chamber music), Demarquez (harmony), and Emmanuel (music history), and also received private instruction from R. Casadesus, Serkin, and Enesco. Following her debut in 1927, she toured as a soloist with orchs. and as a recitalist; she also appeared in duo recitals with Enesco and Fournier. In 1968–69 she was a prof. at the Paris Cons. While her repertory included works from the Classical and Romantic eras, she became known primarily for her performances of music of the 20th century. Her interpretations of Debussy and Ravel were particularly notable. She was married to **Marcel Mihalovici.**

Haas, Pavel, Czech composer; b. Brünn, June 21, 1899; d. in the concentration camp in Auschwitz, Oct. 17, 1944. He studied piano and composition in Brünn; was a soldier in the Austrian army in World War I; after the Armistice, continued his study with Petrželka at the Brno Cons. (1919–21) and at the master class there with Janáček (1920–22). He tried to leave Czechoslovakia after its occupation by the Nazi hordes, but the outbreak of World War II made this impossible; in 1941 he was deported to the Jewish ghetto camp in Theresienstadt, where he continued to compose until, in Oct. 1944, he was sent to Auschwitz and put to death. His extant MSS are preserved in the Moravian Museum in Brno.

WORKS: OPERA: *Šarlatán* (The Charlatan), to his own libretto (1934–37; Brno, April 2, 1938). **ORCH.:** *Zesmutnělé Scherzo* (Mournful Scherzo) (1921); *Předehra pro rozhlas* (Overture for Radio) for Narrator, Men's Chorus, and Orch. (1930); Sym. (1941; unfinished); *Studie* for Strings (1943; Theresienstadt camp, Sept. 13, 1944); *Variations* for Piano and Orch. (1944). **CHAMBER:** 3 string quartets (1920, 1925, 1938); *Fata morgana*, piano quintet, with Tenor Solo (1923); Wind Quintet (1929); Suite for Piano (1935); Suite for Oboe and Piano (1939). **VOCAL:** *Introduction and Psalm XXIX*, cantata (1931); songs.

BIBL.: L. Peduzi, *P. H.: Života dilo skladatele* (Brno, 1993).

Haas, Robert (Maria), distinguished Austrian musicologist; b. Prague, Aug. 15, 1886; d. Vienna, Oct. 4, 1960. He received his primary education in Prague; then studied music history at the Univs. of Prague, Berlin, and Vienna; obtained his Ph.D. in 1908 from the Univ. of Prague with his diss. *Das Wiener Singspiel.* He then was an assistant to Guido Adler at the Inst. for Music History in Vienna (1908–09). During World War I he was in the Austrian army; then joined the staff of the Nationalbibliothek in Vienna, becoming chief of the music division in 1920. He completed his Habilitation at the Univ. of Vienna in 1923 with his *Eberlins Schuldramen und Oratorien*; then became a lecturer there; also devoted much of his time to the music of the Baroque and Classical eras. After the founding of the International Bruckner Soc., he became ed. of the critical edition of Bruckner's works; he also edited works for Denkmäler der Tonkunst in Österreich. He retired in 1945.

WRITINGS: *Gluck und Durazzo im Burgtheater* (Vienna, 1925); *Die estensischen Musikalien: Thematisches Verzeichnis mit Einleitung* (Regensburg, 1925); *Die Wiener Oper* (Vienna, 1926); *Wiener Musiker vor und um Beethoven* (Vienna, 1927); *Die Musik des Barocks* (Potsdam, 1928); *Aufführungspraxis der Musik* (Potsdam, 1931); *W.A. Mozart* (Potsdam, 1933; 2nd ed., 1950); *Anton Bruckner* (Potsdam, 1934); *Bach und Mozart in Wien* (Vienna, 1951); *Ein unbekanntes Mozart-Bildnis* (Vienna, 1955).

BIBL.: G. Reichert, "R. H.," *Österreichische Musikzeitschrift*, XIII (1958); H. Federhofer, "In memoriam R. H.," *Acta Musicologica*, XXXII (1960).

Haas, Werner, German pianist; b. Stuttgart, March 3, 1931; d. in an automobile accident in Nancy, Oct. 11, 1976. He studied with Lili Kroebec-Asche at the Stuttgart Hochschule für Musik (1947–54) and in Gieseking's master classes at the Saarbrücken Staatlichen Konservatorium (1954–56). After making his public debut in Stuttgart in 1955, he toured widely in Europe. He was especially admired for his perceptive interpretations of Debussy and Ravel.

Haase, Hans, German musicologist; b. Neumunster, Schleswig-Holstein, May 12, 1929. He studied with Blume and Albrecht at the Univ. of Kiel (1950–55). From 1954 to 1958 he was an editorial contributor to *Die Musik in Geschichte und Gegenwart*; also wrote music criticism for newspapers. He publ. the monographs *Jobst vom Brandt* (Kassel, 1967) and *Heinrich Schütz* (Wolfenbüttel, 1972), and numerous valuable articles on German composers of the Reformation. He also became interested in applied psychology and lectured on this subject in Zürich and Vienna. He publ. *Die harmonikalen Wurzeln der Musik* (Vienna, 1969) and *Aufsätze zur harmonikalen Naturphilosophie* (Graz, 1974).

Hába, Alois, notable Czech composer and pedagogue, brother of **Karel Hába**; b. Vizovice, Moravia, June 21, 1893; d. Prague, Nov. 18, 1973. He studied with Novák at the Prague Cons. (1914–15); then privately with Schreker in Berlin (1918–20), continuing as his student at the Hochschule für Musik (1920–22). He became interested in the folk music of the Orient, which led him to consider writing in smaller intervals than the semitone. His first work in the quarter-tone system was the 2nd String Quartet (1920); in his 5th String Quartet (1923), he first applied sixth-tones; in his 16th String Quartet (1967), he introduced fifth-tones. He notated these fractional intervals by signs in modified or inverted sharps and flats. The piano manufacturing firm of A. Förster constructed for him 3 types of quarter-tone pianos (1924–31), a quarter-tone (1928) and a sixth-tone (1936) harmonium, and a quarter-tone guitar (1943); other firms manufactured at his request a quarter-tone clarinet (1924) and trumpet (1931). From 1924 to 1951 (World War II excepted) he led a class of composition in fractional tones at the Prague Cons., attracting a large number of students, among them his brother, Karel, the conductors Ančerl and Susskind, and the composers Dobiáš, Ježek, Kowalski, Kubín, Lucký, Ponc, Reiner (who, along with E. Schulhoff, specialized in quarter-tone piano playing and premiered 10 of Hába's works), Seidel and Srnka, as well as such foreigners as Iliev, Osterc, and Akses. Hába publ. an important manual of modern harmony, *Neue Harmonielehre des diatonischen, chromatischen, Viertel-, Drittel-, Sechstel-, und Zwölfteltonsystems* (New Principles of Harmony of the Diatonic, Chromatic, Fourth-, Third-, Sixth-, and Twelfth-Tone Systems; Leipzig, 1927), detailing new usages introduced by him in his classes; he further publ. *Harmonicke základy čtvrttónove soustavy* (Harmonic Foundation of the Quarter-Tone System; Prague, 1922), *Von der Psychologie der musikalischen Gestaltung, Gesetzmässigkeit der Tonbewegung und Grundlagen eines neuen Musikstils* (On the Psychology of Musical Composition; Rules of Tonal Structure and Foundation of New Musical Style; Vienna, 1925), and *Mein Weg zur Viertel- und Sechstetonmusik* (Düsseldorf, 1971). As a composer, he cultivated a "non-thematic" method of writing, without repetition of patterns and devoid of development. In 1963 he was made an Artist of Merit and in 1968 he received the Order of the Republic in recognition of his contributions to Czech music.

WORKS: OPERAS: *Matka* (Mother; 1927–29; in quarter tones, 1st perf. in German as *Die Mutter*, Munich, May 17, 1931; 1st perf. in Czech, Prague, May 27, 1947); *Nová Země* (The New Land; 1934–36; only overture perf., Prague, April 8, 1936); *Přijd královstvi Tvé* (Thy Kingdom Come; 1937–40; in fractional tones). **ORCH.:** Overture (Berlin, Dec. 9, 1920); *Symphonic Fantasy* for Piano and Orch. (1921); *Cesta života* (The Path of Life; Winterthur, March 15, 1934); *Valašská suita* (Prague, Oct. 29, 1953); Violin Concerto (1955; Prague, Feb. 17, 1963); Viola Concerto (1955–57). **CHAMBER:** Violin Sonata (1951); string quartets Nos. 1, 7, 8, 9, 13, and 15 (1919; 1951; 1951; 1952;

Astronautic, 1961; 1964); *Fantasy* for Flute or Violin and Piano (1928; also for Bass Clarinet and Piano, 1967); 4 nonets for Wind and String Instruments (1931, based on a 12-tone row; 1932, based on a 7-tone row; 1953; 1963); Sonata for Solo Guitar (1943); Sonata for Chromatic Harp (1944); Sonata for Diatonic Harp (1944); *Intermezzo and Preludium* for Diatonic Harp (1945); Suite for Bassoon (1950; also for Bass Clarinet, 1968); Suite, quartet for Bassoons (1951); Sonata for Solo Clarinet (1952); suites for Solo Violin (1955), Cello (1955), Cymbalom (1960), Bass Clarinet (1964), and Saxophone (1968); Suite for Bass Clarinet and Piano (1969); *Observations from a Journal* for Narrator and String Quartet (1970); Suite for Violin and Piano (1972). **KEYBOARD: PIANO:** *2 morceaux* (1917–18; arranged for String Orch. by R. Kubin, 1930); Sonata (1918); *Fugue Suite* (1918); *Variations on a Canon by Schumann* (1918); *6 Pieces* (1920); *4 Modern Dances* (1927); *Toccata quasi una Fantasia* (1931); *6 Moods* (1971). **ORGAN:** *Fantasy* (1951); *Fugue* (1951). **OTHER: WORKS IN QUARTER TONES:** String quartets Nos. 2, 3, 4, 6, 12, and 14 (1920, 1922, 1922, 1950, 1960, 1963); *Fantasy* for Violin (1921); *Music* for Violin (1922); *Fantasy* for Cello (1924); *Fantasy* for Violin and Piano (1925); Suite No. 1 for Clarinet and Piano (1925); *Fantasy* for Viola and Piano (1926); Fantasy for Cello and Piano (1927); 2 suites for Guitar (1943, 1947); Suite No. 2 for Clarinet (1943–44); Suite for Trumpet and Trombone (1944); Suite for 4 Trombones (1950); Suite for Violin (1961–62); 6 suites for Piano (1922, rev. 1932; 1922, rev. 1932; 1923; 1924; 1925; 1959); 11 fantasies for Piano (Nos. 1–10, 1923–26; No. 11, 1959); Piano Sonata (1947). **WORKS IN FIFTH-TONES:** String Quartet No. 16 (1967). **WORKS IN SIXTH-TONES:** String quartets Nos. 5, 10, and 11 (1923, 1952, 1958); Duo for 2 Violins (1937); Suite for Violin (1955); Suite for Cello (1955); *6 Pieces* for Harmonium (1928). He also wrote songs and choral pieces, many of them in the quarter-tone system.

BIBL.: J. Vysloužil, *A. H.: Život a dílo* (Prague, 1974).

Hába, Karel, Czech composer and music educator, brother of **Alois Hába;** b. Vizovice, Moravia, May 21, 1898; d. Prague, Nov. 21, 1972. He spent his entire life in Prague, where he studied violin with Karel Hoffmann and Jan Mařák, and theory with Novák, Křicka, and Foerster at the Cons.; he also attended his brother's class in quarter-tone music there (1925–27). After playing violin in the Czech Radio Orch. (1929–36), he was head of the music education dept. of the Czech Radio (1936–50); he then lectured on music education at the Charles Univ. (1951–63); he also was active as a music critic. Hába faithfully followed the athematic method of composition espoused by his brother.

WORKS: OPERAS: *Jánošík* (1929–32; Prague, Feb. 23, 1934); *Stará historia* (The Old Story; 1934–37); *Smolíček*, children's opera (Prague, Sept. 28, 1950); *Kalibův zločin* (Kaliba's Crime; 1957–61; Košice, May 16, 1968). **ORCH.:** Overture (1922); Violin Concerto (Prague, March 6, 1927); *Scherzo* (1928); Cello Concerto (Prague, Sept. 1, 1935); 2 syms. (1947–48; 1953–54); *Brigand's Suite* (1955); Suite (1963). **CHAMBER:** 4 string quartets (1922, 1924, 1943, 1969); Trio for Violin, Cello, and Quarter Tone Piano (1926); *3 Pieces* for Violin and Piano in quarter tones (1927); Flute Sonatina (1927); Septet for Violin, Clarinet, Viola, Horn, Cello, Bassoon, and Piano (1928–29); Duo for Violin and Cello (1935); Piano Trio (1940); Wind Quintet (1944); *3 Inventions* for Harp (1945); Nonet (1950); Trio for 2 Violins and Viola (1952); *15 Concert Études* for Violin (1956); Sonatina for 2 Violins (1960); Sonatina for 3 Clarinets (1960); *3 Instructive Duos* for 2 Violins (1968). **PIANO:** 2 suites (1920, 1929); Suite for Quarter Tone Piano (1925); Sonata (1942). **VOCAL:** Cantata; choruses; songs.

Habich, Eduard, German baritone; b. Kassel, Sept. 3, 1880; d. Berlin, March 15, 1960. He studied in Frankfurt am Main with Max Fleisch. He made his operatic debut in Koblenz in 1904; then sang in Posen, Halle, and Düsseldorf, at the Berlin Royal (later State) Opera (1910–30), at the Bayreuth Festival (1911–31), at London's Covent Garden (1924–36; 1938), and at the Chicago Civic Opera (1930–32). He made his Metropolitan Opera debut in N.Y. on Dec. 20, 1935, as Peter in *Hänsel und Gretel*, and remained on its roster until 1937; later taught voice in Berlin. Among his admired roles were Beckmesser, Faninal, Alberich, Telramund, and Klingsor.

Hacker, Alan (Ray), English clarinetist, conductor, and pedagogue; b. Dorking, Sept. 30, 1938. He studied at Dulwich College and the Royal Academy of Music in London; continued his training in Paris, Vienna, and Bayreuth. He played clarinet in the London Phil. (1959–66), and in 1965 was a founding member of the Pierrot Players, which became the Fires of London in 1970. In 1971 he founded his own group, Matrix, and in 1977, the Classical Orch. As a guest conductor, he appeared in various European music centers. He taught at the Royal Academy of Music (1960–76) and the Univ. of York (1976–85). In 1988 he was made an Officer of the Order of the British Empire. His extensive repertoire ranges from early music to contemporary scores.

Hackett, Charles, American tenor; b. Worcester, Mass., Nov. 4, 1889; d. N.Y., Jan. 1, 1942. He was a student of Arthur J. Hubbard at the New England Cons. of Music in Boston and of Vincenzo Lombardi in Florence. After making his operatic debut in Genoa as Thomas' Wilhelm Meister in 1914, he sang throughout Italy, including Milan (La Scala, 1916); he also sang at the Teatro Colón in Buenos Aires. On Jan. 31, 1919, he made his Metropolitan Opera debut in N.Y. as Count Almaviva, remaining on the roster until 1921; after singing with the Chicago Civic Opera (1923–32), he was again on the roster of the Metropolitan Opera (1933–39). His other roles included the Duke of Mantua, Alfredo, Roméo, Rodolfo, Lindoro, and Pinkerton.

Hadley, Henry (Kimball), noted American conductor and composer; b. Somerville, Mass., Dec. 20, 1871; d. N.Y., Sept. 6, 1937. He received training in piano, violin, and conducting from his father, and then studied harmony with Emery and counterpoint and composition with Chadwick in Somerville and at the New England Cons. of Music in Boston; he then took lessons in counterpoint with Mandyczewski in Vienna (1894–95) and in composition with Thuille in Munich (1905–07). After teaching at St. Paul's School in Garden City, N.Y. (1895–1902), he devoted himself fully to conducting and composing. He was conductor of the Mainz Stadttheater (1907–09) and of the Seattle Sym. Orch. (1909–11). In 1911 he became conductor of the newly organized San Francisco Sym. Orch., which he conducted until 1915. After serving as assoc. conductor of the N.Y. Phil. (1920–27), he was founder-conductor of the Manhattan Sym. Orch. (1929–32). In 1934 he founded the Berkshire Music Festival in Stockbridge, Mass., which he conducted for 2 seasons. In 1924 he was elected a member of the American Academy of Arts and Letters. In 1933 he organized the National Assn. for American Composers and Conductors, which subsequently endowed the Henry Hadley Memorial Library at the N.Y. Public Library. In 1938 the Henry Hadley Foundation was organized in N.Y. to further Hadley's championship of American music. In his own compositions, Hadley wrote well-crafted scores in a late Romantic vein. His 2nd Sym. received the Paderewski Prize in 1901.

WORKS: DRAMATIC: *Happy Jack*, operetta (1897); *Nancy Brown*, operetta (1903); *Safie*, opera (Mainz, April 4, 1909); *The Atonement of Pan*, incidental music (1912; also an orch. suite, 1912); *The Pearl Girl*, operetta (n.d.); *Azora, Daughter of Montezuma*, opera (1914; Chicago, Dec. 26, 1917); *The Masque of Newark*, pageant (1916); *Bianca*, opera (1917; N.Y., Oct. 15, 1918); *The Fire Prince*, operetta (1917); *Cleopatra's Night*, opera (1918; N.Y., Jan. 31, 1920); *Semper virens*, music drama (1923); *A Night in Old Paris*, opera (1924); *The Legend of Hani*, incidental music (1933; also an orch. suite, 1933); *The Red Flame*, musical (n.d.). **ORCH.:** Ballet Suite (1895); *Festival March* (1897); 5 syms.: No. 1, *Youth and Life* (N.Y., Dec. 2, 1897), No. 2, *The 4 Seasons* (N.Y., Dec. 20, 1901), No. 3 (1906; Berlin, Dec. 27, 1907), No. 4, *North, East, South, and West* (Norfolk, Conn., Jan. 6, 1911), and No. 5, *Connecticut* (Norfolk, Conn., 1935);

Herod, overture (1901); *In Bohemia*, overture (Boson, Dec. 16, 1901); *Oriental Suite* (1903); *Symphonic Fantasia* (1904); *Salome*, tone poem (1905–06; Boston, April 12, 1907); *Konzertstück* for Cello and Orch. (1907); *The Culprit Fay*, rhapsody (1908; Grand Rapids, Mich., May 28, 1909); *Lucifer*, tone poem (1910; Norfolk, Conn., June 2, 1914); *Silhouettes*, suite (1918; Philadelphia, July 17, 1932); *Othello*, overture (Philadelphia, Dec. 26, 1919); *The Ocean*, tone poem (1920–21; N.Y., Nov. 17, 1921); *Suite ancienne* (1924); *Streets of Pekin*, suite (Tokyo, Sept. 24, 1930); *San Francisco*, suite (1931); *Youth Triumphant*, overture for Band (1931); *Alma mater*, overture (1932); *Scherzo diabolique* (Chicago, Aug. 1934). **CHAMBER:** Violin Sonata (1895); 2 string quartets (c.1896, 1934); 2 piano trios (c. 1896, 1933); Piano Quintet (1919); piano pieces. **VOCAL:** Cantatas: *In Music's Praise* for Soloists, Chorus, and Orch. (1898); *The Princess of Ys* for Women's or Mixed Voices and Orch. (1903); *A Legend of Granada* for Soloists and Women's Chorus (1904); *The Fate of Princess Kiyo* for Soloists, Women's Chorus, and Orch. (1907); *The Nightingale and the Rose* for Soloist, Women's Chorus, and Orch. (1911); *The Golden Prince* for Soloists, Women's Chorus, and Orch. (1914); *The Fairy Thorn* for Soloists, Women's Voices, and Piano or Orch. (1917); *Prophecy and Fulfillment* for Soloists, Chorus, and Orch. (1922); *The Admiral of the Seas* for Soloist, Chorus, and Orch. (1928); *Belshazzar* for Soloists, Chorus, and Orch. (1932); Other: *The Fairies* for Soprano, Chorus, and Orch. or Piano (1894); *Lelawala* for Chorus and Orch. (1898); *Merlin and Vivian*, lyric drama for Soloists, Chorus, and Orch. (1906); *Music: An Ode* for Soloists, Chorus, and Orch. (1915); *In Arcady*, idyll for Chorus and Orch. (c.1918); *The New Earth*, ode for Soloists, Chorus, and Orch. (1919); *Resurgam*, oratorio for Soloists, Chorus, and Orch. (1922); *Mirtil in Arcadia*, pastoral for Soloists, Narrator, Chorus, Children's Chorus, and Orch. (1926); anthems; choruses; more than 200 songs.

BIBL.: H. Boardman, *H.H., Ambassador of Harmony* (Atlanta, 1932); P. Berthoud, ed., *The Musical Works of Dr. H.H.* (N.Y., 1942); J. Canfield, *H.K.H. (1871–1937): His Life and Works* (diss., Florida State Univ., 1960).

Hadley, Jerry, American tenor; b. Princeton, Ill., June 12, 1952. He studied music education at Bradley Univ. (B.A., 1974) and voice at the Univ. of Ill. (M.A., 1977), where he found a mentor in David Lloyd; then studied with Thomas LoMonaco in N.Y. In 1976 he made his professional operatic debut as Ferrando at the Lake George (N.Y.) Opera Festival. On Sept. 14, 1979, he made his first appearance at the N.Y. City Opera as Lord Arturo Bucklaw in *Lucia di Lammermoor*, remaining with the company until 1985; also appeared regularly with the Washington (D.C.) Opera (from 1980). He made his debut at the Vienna State Opera in 1982 as Nemorino, and in 1983 he sang for the first time at the Bavarian State Opera in Munich, the Glyndebourne Festival, and the Netherlands Opera in Amsterdam. In 1984 he made his debut at London's Covent Garden as Fenton and his Carnegie Hall recital debut in N.Y.; his Metropolitan Opera debut in N.Y. followed on March 7, 1987, as Massenet's Des Grieux; he sang there regularly from 1990. In 1991 he sang in the premiere of McCartney's *Liverpool Oratorio*. He also toured extensively as a concert artist. In addition to his Mozart and *bel canto* roles, Hadley has found success as Berlioz's and Gounod's Faust, Offenbach's Hoffmann, Verdi's Alfredo, and Stravinsky's Tom Rakewell. His performances in works by Weill, Kern, Rodgers and Hammerstein, Bernstein, and Lerner and Lowe have added further luster to his success.

Hadley, Patrick (Arthur Sheldon), English composer and teacher; b. Cambridge, March 5, 1899; d. King's Lynn, Norfolk, Dec. 17, 1973. He studied at the Royal College of Music in London with Vaughan Williams and others (1922–25); then taught there (1925–62); from 1938 to 1946 he held a fellowship at Gonville and Caius College, Cambridge; subsequently was prof. of music there from 1946 to 1962. He composed mostly vocal music; among his works are the cantatas *The Trees So High* (1931); *La Belle Dame sans merci* (1935); *Travelers* (1940); *The Hills* (1944); *Fen and Flood* (1954); *Connemara* (1958); *Cantata for Lent* (1960); many songs.

BIBL.: W. Todds, *P. H.; A Memoir* (London, 1974; with catalog of works).

Hadow, Sir W(illiam) H(enry), English music educator, writer on music, and composer; b. Ebrington, Gloucestershire, Dec. 27, 1859; d. London, April 8, 1937. He studied at Malvern College (1871–78) and Worcester College, Oxford (1878–82); received the degrees of M.A. (1885) and Mus.B. (1890). He was a lecturer at Worcester College (1885–1909). After serving as principal of Armstrong College in Newcastle upon Tyne (1909–18), he was vice-chancellor of the Univ. of Sheffield (1919–30). In 1918 he was knighted. He wrote a cantata, *The Soul's Pilgrimage*; String Quartet; 2 violin sonatas; Viola Sonata; and a number of anthems. Hadow's importance, however, lies in his books, written in a lively journalistic style. His book *A Croatian Composer: Notes toward the Study of Joseph Haydn* (London, 1897), claiming that Haydn was of Slavonic origin, aroused considerable controversy; later research disproved this theory. Of more solid substance are his other writings: *Studies in Modern Music* (2 vols., 1892–95; 10th ed., 1921); *Sonata Form* (1896; 2nd ed., 1915); *The Viennese Period* (vol. 5 of the *Oxford History of Music*, 1904; 2nd ed., 1931); *William Byrd* (1923); *Music* (1924; 3rd ed., rev., 1949, by G. Dyson); *Church Music* (1926); *A Comparison of Poetry and Music* (1926); *Collected Essays* (1928); *English Music* (1931); *The Place of Music among the Arts* (1933); *Richard Wagner* (1934). He also ed. songs of the British Isles (1903) and was ed.-in-chief of the *Oxford History of Music* (1901–05 and 1929).

Hadzidakis, Manos, Greek composer; b. Xanthi, Macedonia, Oct. 23, 1925; d. Athens, June 15, 1994. He wrote piano pieces in an advanced idiom, recalling Prokofiev; then turned to film music. He became best known for his theme song composed for the film released in America under the title *Never on Sunday* (1960).

Haebler, Ingrid, esteemed Austrian pianist; b. Vienna, June 20, 1929. She began her musical training with her mother, and then pursued her studies with Scholz at the Salzburg Mozarteum (1940–42; 1948–49) and with Weingarten (1943–47) and Hauser (1952–53) at the Vienna Academy of Music; she also attended the master classes of Magaloff at the Geneva Cons. (1950–51; Prix de Virtuosité, 1951) and of Long at the Paris Cons. (1953). In 1952 she was co-winner of the 2nd prize at the Geneva Competition (no 1st prize was awarded), and in 1954 she took 1st prize in both the Munich Competition and the Geneva Schubert Competition. She then appeared with many of the leading orchs. of the day and at the principal festivals. In 1959 she made her U.S. debut as soloist with the Minneapolis Sym. Orch. She also appeared as a recitalist and chamber music player. As a duo recitalist, she often performed with Szeryng. From 1969 to 1971 she was a prof. at the Salzburg Mozarteum. She was awarded the Mozart medals of Vienna in 1971 and of the Salzburg Mozarteum in 1980, and in 1986 she received the Medal of Honor of Vienna. In addition to her admired interpretations of Mozart, she has won distinction for her performances of J.C. Bach (on the fortepiano), Haydn, Beethoven, Schubert, Schumann, and Chopin.

Haefliger, Ernst, noted Swiss tenor; b. Davos, July 6, 1919. He studied at the Zürich Cons., with Fernando Carpi in Geneva, and with Julius Patzak in Vienna. After making his debut as the Evangelist in Bach's *St. John Passion* in 1942, he sang at the Zürich Opera (1943–52). He gained wide recognition when he created the role of Tiresias in Orff's *Antigonae* at the Salzburg Festival on Aug. 9, 1949. From 1952 to 1974 he was a member of the Berlin Städtische (later Deutsche) Oper, but he also appeared as a guest artist with many of the principal European opera houses. His roles in Mozart's operas were particularly esteemed. He pursued a distinguished career as a concert singer and lieder artist. His appearances as the Evangelist in Bach's passions and his lieder recitals were notable. He was a prof. at the Munich Hochschule für Musik (from 1971). Haefliger publ. the book *Die Singstimme* (Bern, 1983).

Haenchen, Hartmut, German conductor; b. Dresden, March 21, 1943. He was a student of Matschke, Neuhaus, and Förster at the Dresden Hochschule für Musik (1960–66), and of Koch and Höft in Berlin; in 1971 he won 1st prize in the Carl Maria von Weber competition in Dresden. After serving as director of the Robert-Franz-Singakadamie and the Halle orch. (1966–72), he was chief conductor of the Zwickau Theater (1972–73). From 1973 to 1976 he was permanent conductor of the Dresden Phil., and, from 1974 to 1976, of the Phil. Choir of Dresden; he then was chief conductor of the Mecklenburg State Theater (1976–79). He was a prof. of conducting at the Dresden Hochschule für Musik (1980–86), and also music director of the C.P.E. Bach Chamber Orch. in Berlin (from 1980). In 1986 he became music director of the Netherlands Opera in Amsterdam. Haenchen has appeared as a guest conductor with major opera houses throughout Europe, North America, and Japan.

Haendel, Ida, Polish-born English violinist; b. Chelm, Dec. 15, 1923. She was a child prodigy. At 4, she began formal studies with Miecyzslaw Michalowicz at the Warsaw Cons., where she won its gold medal in 1933; she then pursued her training in Paris and London with Flesch and Enesco. In 1935 she won the Polish prize offered at the 1st Wieniawski Competition in Warsaw. At 14, she attacted notice in London when she appeared as soloist in the Brahms Concerto under Sir Henry Wood's direction at a Proms concert. During World War II, she gave many concerts for Allied troops. In 1940 she became a naturalized British subject. In 1946–47 she made her first tour of the U.S. Although she lived in Montreal from 1952 to 1989, she made annual tours of Europe, and also appeared regularly in South America and Asia, including a tour of China in 1973 as soloist with John Pritchard and the London Phil. From 1991 she was also active as a teacher. In 1982 she was awarded the Sibelius Medal. Her career was the subject of the CBC-TV documentary "Ida Haendel: A Voyage of Music" in 1988. In 1991 she was made a Commander of the Order of the British Empire. She publ. the autobiographical vol. *Woman with Violin* (London, 1970). Haendel's virtuoso technique, ably complemented by a thoroughgoing musicianship, has won her admirers in both the concerto and recital repertoires. Her extensive concerto repertoire embraces scores from Bach to Walton.

Hafez (Shabana), Abdel Halim, renowned Egyptian singer; b. Zakazik, Sharkia, 1929; d. London, March 30, 1977. He rose to prominence in Egypt, and the Arab world in general, as the foremost interpreter of romantic and nationalistic songs; won renown for his renditions of *Safini Marra* and *Ala Kad el Shouk*. He used Western instruments in his performances, and even utilized the Moog synthesizer. So widespread was his fame at the time of his death that 100,000 Egyptians lined the streets of the funeral procession in Cairo.

Hafgren, Lily (Johana Maria), Swedish soprano; b. Stockholm, Oct. 7, 1884; d. Berlin, Feb. 27, 1965. She was educated in Frankfurt am Main; began her career as a pianist; Siegfried Wagner encouraged her to consider an operatic career, and she studied voice in Stuttgart with Max Fleisch. In 1908 she made her operatic debut as Freia at the Bayreuth Festival, where she sang again in 1911, 1912, and 1924; also sang in Mannheim (1908–12) and at the Royal (later State) Opera in Berlin (1912–21); also appeared in Paris, Rome, Milan, Dresden, Stockholm, Prague, and other operatic centers. She retired in 1934. In later years, she used her married names, Hafgren-Waag and Hafgren-Dinkela. Among her finest roles were Brünnhilde, Eva, and Isolde.

Hagegård, Håkan, outstanding Swedish baritone; b. Karlstad, Nov. 25, 1945. After initial training in Karlstad, he studied at the Stockholm Musikhögskolan and with Erik Werba and Gerald Moore in Salzburg. He made his operatic debut at the Royal Theater in Stockholm as Papageno (1968); after further study with Tito Gobbi, he made his first venture outside his homeland at the Glyndebourne Festival in 1973. He gained wide recognition through his notable portrayal of Papageno in Ingmar Bergman's film version of *Die Zauberflöte* (1975); subsequently appeared throughout Europe in opera and concert. On Dec. 7, 1978, he made his Metropolitan Opera debut in N.Y. as Dr. Malatesta. He appeared as Wolfram at his debut at London's Covent Garden in 1987. On Dec. 19, 1991, he created the role of Beaumarchais in the premiere of Corigliano's *The Ghosts of Versailles* at the Metropolitan Opera in N.Y. He is married to **Barbara Bonney.** He particularly distinguished himself in operas by Mozart, Rossini, Donizetti, and Verdi.

Hageman, Richard, distinguished Dutch-American pianist, conductor, and composer, son of **Maurits (Leonard) Hageman**; b. Leeuwarden, July 9, 1882; d. Beverly Hills, March 6, 1966. He studied music with his father, then took courses at the Brussels Cons. with Gevaert and Arthur de Greef. He held an auxiliary position as conductor at the Royal Opera in Amsterdam (1899–1903). After playing accompaniments for Mathilde Marchesi in Paris (1904–05), he went to the U.S. as accompanist for Yvette Guilbert in 1906; was on the conducting roster of the Metropolitan Opera in N.Y. (1908–10; 1911–21; 1935–37), the Chicago Civic Opera (1922–23), and the Los Angeles Grand Opera (1923). In 1938 he settled in Hollywood, where he was engaged as a composer of film music. He wrote 2 operas: *Caponsacchi* (1931; 1st perf. as *Tragödie in Arezzo*, Freiburg im Breisgau, Feb. 18, 1932; received the David Bispham Memorial Medal) and *The Crucible* (Los Angeles, Feb. 4, 1943). He achieved a lasting reputation mainly through his solo songs, of which *Do Not Go My Love* (to words by Rabindranath Tagore; 1917) and *At the Well* (1919) became extremely popular.

Hagen-Groll, Walter, German choral conductor; b. Chemnitz, April 15, 1927. He studied at the Stuttgart Hochschule für Musik (1947–52) and with J. Pembaur, Jr. (piano) in Munich. After serving as a répétiteur and conductor at the Stuttgart Opera (1952–57), he was chorus master at the Heidelberg Opera (1957–61). In 1961 he became chorus master of the Berlin Deutsche Oper and conductor of the chorus of the Berlin Phil.; he also was chorus master at the Salzburg Festival (from 1965) and conductor of the New Philharmonia Orch. Chorus in London (1971–74). In 1984 he became chorus master of the Vienna State Opera. He was named choral director at the Salzburg Mozarteum in 1986. He also was director of the Vienna Singakademie from 1987.

Hager, Leopold, Austrian conductor; b. Salzburg, Oct. 6, 1935. He took courses in piano, organ, harpsichord, conducting, and composition at the Salzburg Mozarteum (1949–57); his principal teachers were Paumgartner, Wimberger, Bresgen, J.N. David, and Kornauth. He was assistant conductor at the Mainz City Theater (1957–62); after conducting the Linz Landestheater (1962–64), he held the post of 1st conductor of the Cologne Opera (1964–65). After serving as Generalmusikdirektor in Freiburg im Breisgau (1965–69), he was chief conductor of the Mozarteum Orch. and of the Landestheater in Salzburg (1969–81). On Oct. 14, 1976, he made his Metropolitan Opera debut in N.Y. conducting *Le Nozze di Figaro*, and remained on its roster until 1978. He also appeared as a guest conductor with other opera houses as well as orchs. in Europe and the U.S. In 1981 he became chief conductor of the Orchestre Symphonique de Radio-Télé Luxembourg.

Hagerup Bull, Edvard, Norwegian composer; b. Bergen, June 10, 1922. He was an organ student of Sandvold at the Oslo Cons. (graduated, 1947); he also received training in piano from Erling Westher and Reimar Riefling, and in composition from Brustad and Irgens Jensen; after further studies at the Paris Cons. with Milhaud, Koechlin, and Rivier (Prix de composition, 1952), he completed his training with Blacher and Rufer at the Berlin Hochschule für Musik. Hie early neo-Classical style tended later toward free tonality.

WORKS: DRAMATIC: OPERAS: *Fyrtøjet* (1973–74); *Den Grimme Aelling* (1972–77). **BALLET:** *Munchhausen* (1961). **ORCH.:** *Le Soldat de plomb*, ballet suite (1948–49); *Serenade* (1950); *Morceaux rapsodiques*, divertimento (1950); 2 trumpet concertos (1950, 1960); *Sinfonia di teatro*, symphonic prelude (1950–51); *Petite suite symphonique* for Small Orch. (1951); *Escapades*, suite (1952); *Divertimento* for Piano and Orch. (1954); 6 syms.: No. 1, *3 mouvements symphoniques* (1955), No. 2, *In modo d'una sinfonia* (1958–59), No. 3, *Sinfonia espressiva* (1964), No. 4, *Sinfonia humana* (1968), No. 5, *Sinfonia in memoriam* (1971–72), and No. 6, *Lamentazione, Sinfonia da camera pour la Pologne, Solidarité et Lech Walesa* (1981–82); *3 morceaux brefs* for Saxophone and Orch. (1955); *Cassation* for Chamber Orch. (1959); *Epilogue* for Strings (1961); *Undecim Sumus* for Chamber Orch. of Soloists (1962); *Dialogue* for Flute, Strings, and Piano (1965); *6 épigrammes* for Chamber Ensemble (1969); Concerto for Flute and Chamber Orch. (1969); *Air solennel*, symphonic movement (1972); *Chant d'Hommage à Jean Rivier*, symphonic movement (1975); Alto Saxophone Concerto (1980); *Movimenti* (1985); *Piece héroique pour le centenaire d'un géant* (1991); *Hymne joyeux pour un jubilé de fête* (1992); *Giocoso bucolico*, tuba concertino (1992). **CHAMBER:** Clarinet Sonata (1950); *3 bucoliques* for Oboe, Clarinet, and Bassoon (1953); 2 duos for Violin and Piano (1956, 1973); *Ad usum amicorum* for Flute, Violin, Cello, and Piano (1957); *Marionnettes sérieuses* for Wind Quintet (1960); *Quadrige* for 4 Clarinets (1964); Sextet for Flute, Oboe, Clarinet, Horn, Bassoon, and Alto Saxophone or Clarinet (1965); *Sonata cantabile* for Flute, Violin, Cello, and Piano (1966); *Concert* for Trumpet, Horn, and Trombone (1966; also for 2 Trumpets, Horn, Trombone, and Tuba); Wind Quintet No. 2 (1973); *Posthumes* for 8 Wind Instruments and Double Bass (1978); *Profils pour un Drame Rustique* for Piano, Flute, Oboe, Clarinet, and Bassoon (1978); *Sonata con Moto* for Violin, Cello, and Piano (1982); *Sonata a Quatro* for String Quartet (1983); Sextet for Flute, Clarinet, Violin, Cello, Piano, and Percussion (1985); *Musique* for 4 Strings (1988); piano pieces. **VOCAL:** Songs.

Haggin, B(ernard) H., American music critic; b. N.Y., Dec. 29, 1900; d. there, May 29, 1987. He was a music critic for the *Brooklyn Daily Eagle* (1934–37) and the *Nation* (1936–57), and also wrote record reviews for the *Yale Quarterly*. Haggin pursued a polemical style of personal journalism.

WRITINGS (all publ. in N.Y. unless otherwise given): *A Book of the Symphony* (1937); *Music on Records* (1938; 4th ed., 1945); *Music for the Man who Enjoys Hamlet* (1944; 2nd ed., rev., 1960); *Music in The Nation* (1949); *The Listener's Musical Companion* (New Brunswick, N.J., 1956; new ed., 1991, by T. Hathaway); *Conversations with Toscanini* (Garden City, N.J., 1959; 2nd ed., 1979); *Music Observed* (1964); *The New Listener's Companion and Record Guide* (1967; 5th ed., 1978); *The Toscanini Musicians Knew* (1967); *A Decade of Music* (1973); *Music and Ballet, 1973–1983* (1984).

Hahn, Reynaldo, Venezuelan-born French conductor, music critic, and composer; b. Caracas, Aug. 9, 1874; d. Paris, Jan. 28, 1947. His father, a merchant from Hamburg, settled in Venezuela c.1850; the family moved to Paris when Reynaldo was 5 years old. He studied singing and apparently had an excellent voice; a professional recording he made in 1910 testifies to that. He studied theory with Dubois and Lavignac and composition with Massenet at the Paris Cons., who exercised the most important influence on Hahn's own music. He also studied conducting, achieving a high professional standard as an opera conductor. In 1934 he became music critic of *Le Figaro*. He remained in France during the Nazi occupation at a considerable risk to his life, since he was Jewish on his father's side. In 1945 he was named a member of the Institut de France and in 1945–46 was music director of the Paris Opéra. Hahn's music is distinguished by a facile, melodious flow and a fine Romantic flair. Socially, he was known in Paris for his brilliant wit. He maintained a passionate youthful friendship with Marcel Proust, who portrayed him as a poetic genius in his novel *Jean Santeuil*; their intimate correspondence was publ. in 1946. He was a brilliant journalist; his articles were publ. as *Du Chant* (Paris, 1920; 2nd ed., 1957), *Notes. Journal d'un musicien* (Paris, 1933), *L'Oreille au guet* (Paris, 1937), and *Thèmes variés* (Paris, 1946). A series of his letters dating from 1913–14 were publ. in an Eng. tr. by L. Simoneau as *On Singers and Singing* (Portland, Oreg., 1990).

WORKS: DRAMATIC: *Fin d'amour*, ballet-pantomime (1892); *L'île du reve*, opera (Paris, March 23, 1898); *La carmélite*, opéra comique (Paris, Dec. 16, 1902); *La pastorale de Noël*, Christmas mystery (1908); *Le bal de Béatrice d'Este*, ballet (1909); *La fête chez Thérèse*, ballet (1909); *Le bois sacré*, ballet-pantomime (1912); *Le dieu bleu*, ballet (Paris, May 14, 1912); *Fête triomphale*, opera (Paris, July 14, 1919); *Nausicaa*, opéra comique (Monte Carlo, April 10, 1919); *La colombe de Bouddah*, conte lyrique (Cannes, March 21, 1921); *Ciboulette*, operetta (Paris, April 7, 1923); *Mozart*, musical comedy (Paris, Dec. 2, 1925); *La reine de Sheba*, scène lyrique (1926); *Une revue* (1926); *Le temps d'aimer*, musical comedy (Paris, Nov. 6, 1926); *Brummel*, operetta (1930; Paris, Jan. 20, 1931); *O mon bel inconnu!*, musical comedy (Paris, Oct. 5, 1933); *Malvina*, operetta (Paris, March 23, 1935); *Le marchand de Venise*, opera (Paris, March 25, 1935); *Beaucoup de bruit pour rien*, musical comedy (1936); *Aux bosquets d'Idalie*, ballet (1937); *Le oui des jeunes filles*, opera (orchestrated by H. Büsser; Paris, June 21, 1949); also incidental music to Daudet's *L'obstacle* (1890), Croisset's *Les deux courtisanes* (1902), Hugo's *Angelo* (1905), Racine's *Esther* (1905), Mendès's *Scarron* (1905), Hugo's *Lucrèce Borgia* (1911), and Magre's *Méduse* (1911). **ORCH.:** *Nuit d'amour bergamasque*, symphonic poem (1897); Violin Concerto (1927; Paris, Feb. 26, 1928); Piano Concerto (1930; Paris, Feb. 4, 1931); *Concerto provençal* (n.d.); *Strasbourg reconquise* (n.d.). **CHAMBER:** Violin Sonata (1927); 2 string quartets (n.d., 1943); Piano Quintet (n.d.); piano pieces, including *Portraits de peintres* (1894). **VOCAL:** *Prométhée triomphant* for Solo Voices, Chorus, and Orch. (1908); several song cycles.

BIBL.: D. Bendahan, *R. H. Su vida y su obra* (Caracas, 1973); B. Gavoty, *R. H.: Le Musicien de la belle époque* (Paris, 1976); M. Milanca Guzmán, *R. H., caraqueño: Contribución a la biografía caraqueña de R. H. Echenagucia* (Caracas, 1989).

Haieff, Alexei (Vasilievich), Russian-American composer; b. Blagoveshchensk, Siberia, Aug. 25, 1914; d. Rome, March 1, 1994. He received his primary education at Harbin, Manchuria; in 1931 he went to the U.S.; studied with Goldmark and Jacobi at the Juilliard School of Music in N.Y. (1934–38); during 1938–39, he studied with Boulanger in Paris and in Cambridge, Mass. He held a Guggenheim fellowship in 1946 and again in 1949; was a Fellow at the American Academy in Rome (1947–48), a prof. at the Univ. of Buffalo (1962–68), and composer-in-residence at the Univ. of Utah (1968–70). His Piano Concerto won the N.Y. Music Critics' Circle Award and his 2nd Sym. the American International Music Fund Award. In his music, Haieff followed Stravinsky's neo-Classicism, observing an austere economy of means, but achieving modernistic effects by a display of rhythmic agitation, often with jazzy undertones.

WORKS: BALLETS: *The Princess Zondilda and Her Entourage* (1946); *Beauty and the Beast* (1947). **ORCH.:** 3 syms.: No. 1 (1942), No. 2 (Boston, April 11, 1958), and No. 3 (New Haven, Conn., April 11, 1961); Divertimento (N.Y., April 5, 1946); Violin Concerto (1948); Piano Concerto (N.Y., April 27, 1952); *Éloge* for Chamber Orch. (1967). **CHAMBER:** Sonatina for String Quartet (1937); *3 Bagatelles* for Oboe and Bassoon (1939); *Serenade* for Oboe, Clarinet, Bassoon, and Piano (1942); *Eclogue* for Cello and Piano (1947); *La Nouvelle Héloïse* for Harp and String Quartet (1963); Cello Sonata (1963); *Rhapsodies* for Guitar and Harpsichord (1980); Wind Quintet (1983). **PIANO:** Sonata for 2 Pianos (1945); Sonata (1955). **VOCAL:** *Caligula* for Baritone and Orch., after Robert Lowell (N.Y., Nov. 5, 1971); songs.

Hailstork, Adolphus (Cunningham), black American composer and teacher; b. Rochester, N.Y., April 17, 1941. He studied composition with Mark Fax at Howard Univ. in Washington, D.C. (B.Mus., 1963), Boulanger at the American Cons. in Fontainebleau (summer, 1963), Ludmila Ulehla, Flagello, Giannini, and Diamond at the Manhattan School of Music in N.Y. (B.Mus., 1965; M.Mus., 1966), and H. Owen Reed at Michigan State Univ. in East Lansing (Ph.D., 1971). He also attended sessions on synthesizer and computer music given by John Appleton and Herbert Howe at the New Hampshire Electronic Music Inst. (summer, 1972), and on contemporary music at the State Univ. of N.Y. at Buffalo (summer, 1978). In 1987 he held a Fulbright fellowship for study in Guyana. He taught at Michigan State Univ. (1969–71), Youngstown (Ohio) State Univ. (1971–76), and Norfolk (Va.) State Univ. (from 1977). Several of his works reflect his Afro-American experience. He has received various commissions, and a number of his works have been performed by major U.S. orchs.

WORKS: OPERA: *Paul Laurence Dunbar: Common Ground* (1994). **ORCH.:** *Phaedra*, tone poem (1966); *SA-1* for Jazz Ensemble (1971); *Bellevue* (1974); *Celebration* for Orch. or Concert Band (1974); Concerto for Violin, Horn, and Orch. (1975); *American Landscape No. 1* for Concert Band (1977) and *No. 3* (1982); *Epitaph: In Memoriam: Martin Luther King, Jr.* (1979); *Norfolk Pride*, march for Concert Band (1980); *Sport of Strings* for Strings (1982); *American Guernica* for Piano and Concert Band (1983); *An American Port of Call* (1984); *2 Struts with Blues* for Strings, Flute, Horn, and Jazz Quartet (1985); Sym. No. 1 (1988); *My Lord What a Mourning* for Chamber Orch. (1989); *Sonata da Chiesa* for Strings (1991); *Intrada* (1991); Piano Concerto (1992); *Festival Music* (1992); *And Deliver Us From Evil* for Band (1994). **CHAMBER:** Horn Sonata (1966); *Capriccio for a Departed Brother: Scott Joplin* for Strings (1969); *From the Dark Side of the Sun* for 3 Flutes, Soprano Saxophone, Strings, and Percussion (1971); String Sextet (1971); Violin Sonata (1971); *Spiritual* for Brass Octet (1975); *American Landscape No. 2* for Violin and Cello (1978); *Variations* for Trumpet (1981); *Music* for 10 Players (1982); Trio for Violin, Cello, and Piano (1985); *3 Preludes* for Guitar (1989); *Arabesques* for Flute and Percussion (1991); *2 Impromptus* for Harp (1993); Consort Piece for Chamber Ensemble (1993). **PIANO:** *Ignis Fatuus* (1976); *5 Friends* (1978); 2 sonatas (1980, 1989); *Reflections* (1981); Sonata for 2 Pianos (1987); Trio Sonata (1991). **VOCAL:** *My Name is Toil* for Chorus, Brass, and Timpani (1973); *Oracle* for Tenor, Women's Chorus, 3 Flutes, 2 Percussion, and Tape (1977); *Psalm 72* for Chorus, Brass, and Organ (1981); *Look to this Day* for Chorus and Concert Band (1982); *Songs of Isaiah* for Chorus and Orch. (1987); *Break Forth* for Chorus, Organ, Brass, and Timpani (1990); *Hodie (Christus Natus Este)* for Chorus (1994); other choruses and songs.

Haimovitz, Matt, Israeli-born American cellist; b. Tel Aviv, Dec. 3, 1970. His family emigrated to California when he was 5. After taking lessons with Gabor Rejto, he studied with Leonard Rose and Channing Robbins at the Juilliard School in N.Y. (1982–87); also received private lessons with Yo-Yo Ma. He pursued his education at Princeton (1989–91) and Harvard (from 1993) Univs. After winning the Avery Fisher Career Grant in 1985, he was engaged as a soloist with majors orchs. and as a recitalist in the U.S., Europe, and Israel. In 1988 he made his first tour of Japan. In 1989 he made a major recital tour of Europe, then of the U.S. in 1990. In 1991 he played the solo cello repertoire in N.Y. and Paris recitals, and also made his first tour of Australia. In addition to his appearances with orchs. and as a recitalist, Haimovitz has played in many chamber music settings. His adventuresome repertoire embraces masters from Bach to Ligeti.

Haitink, Bernard (Johann Herman), eminent Dutch conductor; b. Amsterdam, March 4, 1929. He studied violin as a child, and later at the Amsterdam Cons., where he took a conducting course with Felix Hupka. He then played in the Radio Phil. in Hilversum. In 1954–55 he attended the conducting course of Ferdinand Leitner, sponsored by the Netherlands Radio; in 1955 he was appointed to the post of 2nd conductor of the Radio Phil. in Hilversum, becoming its principal conductor in 1957. In 1956 he made his first appearance as a guest conductor with the Concertgebouw Orch. of Amsterdam. He made his U.S. debut with the Los Angeles Phil. in 1958. In 1959 he conducted the Concertgebouw Orch. in England. In 1961 he became co-principal conductor of the Concertgebouw Orch., sharing his duties with Eugen Jochum; that same year he led it on a tour of the U.S., followed by one to Japan in 1962. In 1964 he became chief conductor of the Concertgebouw Orch., a position he held with great distinction until 1988. In 1982 he led it on an acclaimed transcontinental tour of the U.S. In 1967 he also assumed the post of principal conductor and artistic adviser of the London Phil., becoming its artistic director in 1969; he resigned from this post in 1978. He made his first appearance at the Glyndebourne Festival in 1972, and from 1978 to 1988 was its music director. In 1977 he made his Covent Garden debut in London conducting *Don Giovanni.* On March 29, 1982, he made his debut at the Metropolitan Opera in N.Y. conducting *Fidelio.* From 1987 to 1997 he was music director of the Royal Opera House at London's Covent Garden. He likewise served as music director of the European Union Youth Orch. (from 1994) and as principal guest conductor of the Boston Sym. Orch. (from 1995). In his interpretations, Haitink avoids personal rhetoric, allowing the music to speak for itself. Yet he achieves eloquent and colorful effect; especially fine are his performances of the syms. of Bruckner and Mahler; equally congenial are his projections of the Classical repertoire. He has received numerous international honors, including the Netherlands' Royal Order of Orange-Nassau (1969), the Medal of Honor of the Bruckner Soc. of America (1970), and the Gustav Mahler Soc. Gold Medal (1971); he was named a Chevalier de l'Ordre des Arts et des Lettres of France (1972). He received the rare distinction of being made an Honorary Knight Commander of the Order of the British Empire by Queen Elizabeth II in 1977. In 1991 he was awarded the Erasmus Prize of the Netherlands.

BIBL.: S. Mundy, *B. H.: A Working Life* (London, 1987).

Hajdu, André, Hungarian-born Israeli composer and teacher; b. Budapest, March 5, 1932. He studied with Kodály, Szabó, Szervánsky, and Kosá at the Budapest Academy of Music (1947–56) and with Milhaud and Messiaen at the Paris Cons. (1957–59). He taught at the Tunis Cons. (1959–61); emigrated to Israel in 1966, and in 1967 became a teacher at the Tel Aviv Academy of Music. His music is folkloristic in its sources of inspiration, while the harmonic idiom is fairly advanced.

WORKS: DRAMATIC: *Jonah*, children's opera (1986). **ORCH.:** *A Little Hell* (1960); *Babeliana* (1964); 2 piano concertos (1968; 1988–90); *Terouath Melech*, Jewish rhapsody for Clarinet and Strings (1973); *Stories about Mischievous Boys* (1976); *Concerto for 10 Little Pianists and Grand Orchestra* (1978; also arranged for 2 Pianos); *Of Light and Depth: Preludes and Interludes* for Chamber Orch. (1983–84); *Overture in the Form of a Kite* (1985); *Little Sym.* for Winds (1988); *Symphonie Concertante* for 5 Soloists and String Orch. (1993; Tel Aviv, May 18, 1994). **CHAMBER:** *Military Diary (The Art of the Canon)*, 50 canons for different instrumental combinations (1976); *5 Sketches in a Sentimental Mood* for Piano Quartet (1976); *Plasmas* for 10 Players (1982); String Quartet (1985); Octet (1989); *Black Upon White* for Piano (1989). **VOCAL:** *Gypsy Cantata* (1956); *Ludus Paschalis* for 8 Soloists, Children's Chorus, and 9 Instruments (1970); *The Prophet of Truth and the Prophet of Deceit* for Narrator and String Orch. (1977); *Psalms* for Bass, Children's Choruses, and Orch. (1982); *Sueños en España*, cantata (1991); Jerusalem, Jan. 13, 1992); *Jacob and His Comforters*, oratorio (1992); *Ecclesiastes* for Narrator, Solo Cello, and Cello Ensemble (1994).

Hajdu, Mihály, Hungarian composer and teacher; b. Orosháza, Jan. 30, 1909. He settled in Budapest and studied composition with Kodály and piano with Thomán and Székely at the Academy of Music (1929–33). After teaching in a private music school (1933–40), he taught at the Upper Music School (1941–49) and the Béla Bartók Music School (1949–60); subsequently he was prof. of theory at the Academy of Music (1960–77). In 1957 he received the Erkel Prize.

WORKS: OPERA: *Kádár Kata* (1957). **ORCH.:** 2 suites (1934, 1958); *Serenade* (1941); *A munka dícsérete* (In Praise of Work), symphonic poem (1958); Piano Concertino (1962); *Capriccio all'ongarese* for Clarinet and Orch. (1969); *8 Etudes* for Youth String Orch. (1970); *Herendi porcelánok* (Herend Porcelain), suite (1976); *Divertimento* for Chamber Orch. (1978). **CHAMBER:** 2 string quartets (1936, 1970); Clarinet Duets (1951); *Magyar pásztordalok* (Hungarian Shepherd Songs) for Flute and Piano (1953); 2 violin sonatas (1953, 1977); *Variations and Rondo* for Cello and Piano (1955); *3 Clarinet Pieces* for Clarinet and Piano (1956); Piano Trio (1957); Wind Trio (1958); Cello Sonatina (1969); *30 Little Pieces* for Cello and Piano (1973; also for 2 Cellos); *2 Concert Études* for Harp (1978); *4 Movements* for Wind Quintet (1979). **PIANO:** *3 Scherzos* (1931); *Elegy* (1932); Sonata (1940); Sonatina (1952); *5 Piano Pieces* (1955); *3 Pieces* for 2 Pianos (1971); *6 Bagatelles* (1987). **VOCAL:** Choruses; song cycles; solo songs; folk song arrangements.

Håkanson, Knut (Algot), Swedish composer, pianist, conductor, teacher, and music critic; b. Kinna, Nov. 4, 1887; d. Göteborg, Dec. 13, 1929. He studied composition and counterpoint with Johan Lindegren in Stockholm (1906–08) and piano with Knut Bäck (1909–10); he also took courses in languages and philosophy at the Univ. of Uppsala (1906–13) before completing his musical training with Ruben Liljefors (1913–15) and on the Continent. He settled in Borås, where he was director of the orch. soc. (1916–25); he also was founder-director of the Borås Music Inst. (1922–25) and was music critic of the *Göteborgs Handels- och sjöfarts-tidning* (from 1927). His most important compositions were classically inclined and often incorporated folk tunes he had collected.

WORKS: BALLET: *Mylitta* (1918). **ORCH.:** *Sérénade dramatique* for Violin and Orch. (1914); *Festmarsch* (1914; arranged as *Bröllopsmarsch* [Wedding March] for Organ or Piano); *Från skogstemplet* (From the Forest Temple; 1921–22; also for Piano); *Svensk svit* No. 1 for Piano and Orch. (1923; also for Piano and String Trio) and No. 2 (1925); *Marbolåtar* (Marbo Melodies; 1923; also for Piano); *Variationer och final över ett tema av Lomjansguten* (Variations and Finale on a Theme by Lomjansguten; 1926–28); *Divertimento* (1927). **CHAMBER:** 2 string trios; 2 string quartets; *Midsommarkransen* (Midsummer Wreath) for Clarinet Quintet (1921; also for Piano); *Prelude and Fugue* for String Trio (1928; also for Piano); piano pieces, including *10 variationer och fuga över en svensk folkvisa* (10 Variations and Fugue on a Swedish Folksong; 1929). **VOCAL:** *Skåne* for Solo Voices, Chorus, and Orch. (1928); *4 madrigaler* for Chorus (1929); *3 Karlfeldtskörer* for Chorus (1929); other choral pieces; about 120 solo songs; folk song arrangements.

Hakim, Talib Rasul (Stephen Alexander Chambers), black American composer; b. Asheville, N.C., Feb. 8, 1940; d. New Haven, Conn., March 31, 1988. He studied at the Manhattan School of Music in N.Y. (1958–59), the N.Y. College of Music (1959–63), and Adelphi Univ. (1978). He taught at Pace Univ. (1970–72), Nassau Community College (1971–81), Adelphi Univ. (1972–79), and Morgan State Univ. (1978–79). After converting to Sufism, he took the name Talib Rasul Hakim in 1973. His output followed a dissonant path.

WORKS: ORCH.: *Shapes* (1965); *Visions of Ishwara* (1970); *Re/Currences* (1974); *Concepts* (1976); *Arkan-5* for Orch. and Tape (1980); jazz band pieces. **CHAMBER:** *Peace-Mobile* for Wind Quintet (1964); *Encounter* for Wind Quintet, Trumpet, and Trombone (1965); *Portraits* for Flute, Bass Clarinet, Piano, and 3 Percussion (1965); *Currents* for String Quartet (1967); *Placements* for Piano and 5 Percussion (1970); *On Being Still-on the 8th Wind* for 4 Winds, Cello, Double Bass, Piano, and Percussion (1978); *Fragments from Other Places—Other Times* for 5 Percussion (1978); piano pieces. **VOCAL:** *Sound-Image* for Women's Voices, Brass, Strings, and Percussion (1969); *Tone-Prayers* for Chorus and Percussion (1973); *Music* for Soprano and 9 Players (1977); *Psalm of Akhnaton: ca. 1365–1348* for Mezzo-soprano, Piccolo or Flute or Alto Flute, and Piano (1978); *Quote-unquote* for Tenor, Oboe, Trumpet, and Percussion (1983); *Spiritual and Other Fragments from Another Time and Other Places* for Chorus, Winds, Brass, Piano, and Strings (1983); solo songs.

Halász, László, Hungarian-born American conductor; b. Debrecen, June 6, 1905. He studied piano and conducting at the Budapest Cons., graduating in 1929. He toured Europe as a pianist and conductor until emigrating to the U.S. in 1936; became a naturalized American citizen in 1943. He was music director of the St. Louis Grand Opera (1937–42); in 1944 he was appointed music director of the N.Y. City Opera, where he established an audacious policy of producing modern operas, but became embroiled in personal difficulties with the management, and resigned in 1951. From 1949 to 1952 he conducted opera in Chicago, and from 1955 to 1959 was conductor of the German repertoire at the Barcelona Opera; served as artistic director of N.Y.'s Empire State Music Festival (1957–65) and the National Grand Opera (from 1983). He was head of the conducting dept. at the Eastman School of Music in Rochester, N.Y. (1965–67); then was on the faculty of the State Univ. of N.Y. College at Old Westbury (1968–71) and at Stony Brook (1971–75).

Hale, Philip, eminent American music critic; b. Norwich, Vt., March 5, 1854; d. Boston, Nov. 30, 1934. He took music lessons in his early youth, and as a boy played the organ in the Unitarian Church at Northampton, Mass. He went to Yale Univ. to study law, and was admitted to the bar in 1880. He then took organ lessons with Dudley Buck; subsequently went to Europe (1882–87), where he studied organ with Haupt in Berlin, and composition with Rheinberger in Munich and with Guilmant in Paris. Returning to America, he served as a church organist in Albany and Troy, N.Y., and in Boston, but soon abandoned this employment for his true vocation, that of drama and music critic. Hale was music critic for the *Boston Home Journal* (1889–91), the *Boston Post* (1890–91), the *Boston Journal* (1891–1903), and the *Boston Herald*, of which he was also drama ed. (1904–33). He was also ed. of the *Boston Musical Record* (1897–1901). From 1901 to 1933 he compiled the program books of the Boston Sym. Orch., setting a standard of erudition and informative annotation. He was joint author, with L. Elson, of *Famous Composers and Their Works* (1900), and was ed. of the collection *Modern French Songs* (2 vols., 1904). J. Burk ed. *Philip Hale's Boston Symphony Programme Notes* (Garden City, N.Y., 1935; 2nd ed., rev., 1939). Hale was a forceful and brilliant writer; his articles were often tinged with caustic wit directed against incompetent performers and, regrettably, against many modern composers; he also disliked Brahms, and was credited with the celebrated but possibly apocryphal quip that the exits in the newly opened Sym. Hall in Boston should have been marked not "Exit in Case of Fire," but "Exit in Case of Brahms." Another verbal dart attributed to Hale was his dismissal of a singer with the concluding sentence, "Valuable time was consumed."

Halffter (Jiménez-Encina), Cristóbal, prominent Spanish composer and conductor, nephew of **Ernesto** and **Rodolfo Halffter (Escriche);** b. Madrid, March 24, 1930. He studied composition with Conrado del Campo at the Madrid Cons. (1947–51) and with Tansman in Paris (1959). From 1953 he was active as a conductor in Spain, and later conducted abroad. After serving as a teacher of composition (1961–66) and as director (1964–66) at the Madrid Cons., he lectured at the Univ. of Navarra (1970–78). He was president of the Spanish section of the ISCM (1976–78). In 1979 he was artistic director of the electronic music studio of the Heinrich Strobel-Stiftung in Freiburg im Breisgau. He was made a member of the Royal Academy of Fine Arts of San Fernando in 1983, of the Berlin Academy of Arts in 1985, and of the Swedish Royal Academy in Stockholm in

1988. As a composer, Halffter has perfected a highly personal style which makes use of the full range of contemporary means of expression, from dodecaphony to electronics.

WORKS: DRAMATIC: *Saeta*, ballet (Madrid, Oct. 28, 1955); *El pastor y la estrella*, children's television chamber opera (Madrid, Dec. 28, 1959); *Don Quichotte*, opera (1969). **ORCH.:** *Scherzo* (1951); 2 piano concertos (1952–53, rev. 1956; 1987); Concertino for Strings (1956; also as String Quartet No. 1, *Tres piezas*, 1955); *Dos movimientos* for Timpani and Strings (1956); *Partita* for Cello and Orch. (1957–58; also for Guitar and Orch., 1973); *Cinco Microformas* (1959–60); *Rapsodia española* for Piano and Orch. (1959–60); *Sinfonía* for 3 Instrumental Groups (1961–63); *Secuencias* (1964); *Líneas y puntos* for 20 Winds and Electronics (1966); *Anillos* (1967–68; rev. 1969); *Fibonaciana* for Fluteand Orch. (1969); *Requiem por la libertad imaginada* (1971); *Pinturas negras* for Orch. and Concertante Organ (1972); 2 cello concertos (1974; . . . *No queda más que el silencio* . . . , 1985); *Tiempo para espacios* for Harpsichord and Strings (1974); *Elegías a la muerte de tres poetas españoles* (1975); 2 violin concertos: No. 1 (1979) and No. 2 for Violin and Strings (1990–91); *Tiento* (1980–81); *Fantasía über einen Klang von G.F. Händel* for 4, 8, or 12 Cellos and String Orch. (1981); *Sinfonía ricercata* for Organ and Orch. (1982); *Versus* (1983); Double Concerto for Violin, Viola, and Orch. (1984); *Paráfrasis über die Fantasía über einen Klang von G.F. Händel* (1984); *Tiento del primer tono y batalla imperial* (1986); *Dortmunder Variationen* (1986–87); *Preludio à Nemesis* (1988–89); Saxophone Quartet Concerto (1989–90; also as *Fractal* for Saxophone Quartet, 1991); *Pasacalle escurialense* for Strings (1992); *Mural Sonante* (1993–94). **CHAMBER:** 3 string quartets: No. 1, *Tres piezas* (1955; also as the Concertino for String Orch., 1956), No. 2, *Mémoires 1970* (1970; also as *Pourquoi* for 12 Strings, 1974), and No. 3 (1978); *Tres piezas* for Flute (1959; also as the Sonata for Solo Violin, 1959); *Epitafio a Ramón Gómez de la Serna* for 3 Percussion and Tape (1963; also as *Espejos* for 4 Percussion and Tape, 1963); *Codex* for Guitar (1963); *Antiphonismoi* for Flute, Oboe, Clarinet, Violin, Viola, Cello, and Piano (1967); *Oda para felicitar a un amigo* for Flute, Bass Clarinet, Viola, Cello, and Percussion (1969); *Planto por las víctimas de la violencia* for Chamber Ensemble and Electronics (1970–71); *Noche activa del espíritu* for 2 Pianos and Ring Modulators (1972–73); *Procesional* for 2 Pianos, Winds, and Percussion (1973–74); *Variation über das Thema eSACHERe* for Cello (1975); *Variaciones sobre la resonancia de un grito* for 11 Instruments, Tape, and Electronics (1976–77); *Mizar I* for 2 Flutes, 3 Percussion, and Strings (1977; also as *Mizar II* for 2 Flutes and Electronics, 1979); *Adieu* for Harpsichord (1978); *Debla* for Flute (1980); Concerto for Flute and String Sextet (1982); *Canción callada* for Violin, Cello, and Piano (1988); *Fandango* for 8 or More Cellos (1988–89); *Con bravura y sentimiento* for String Quartet (1991); *Fractal* for Saxophone Quartet (1991; also as the Saxophone Quartet Concerto, 1989–90). **KEYBOARD: PIANO:** Sonata (1951); *Introducción, fuga y final* (1957); *Formantes* for 2 Pianos (1960–61); *Cadencia* (1983); *El ser humano muere solamente cuando lo olvidan* (1987). **ORGAN:** *Ricercare* (1981). **VOCAL:** *Antífona Pascual* for Soloists, Chorus, and Orch. (1952); *Dos canciones* for Soprano and Guitar (1952; also for Soprano and Chamber Orch., 1955); *Misa Ducal* for Chorus and Organ or Orch. (1955–56); *In Exspectatione Resurrectionis Domini*, cantata for Baritone, Men's Chorus, Mixed Chorus ad libitum, and Orch. (1961; rev. 1964–65); *Drei Brechtlieder* for Medium Voice and 2 Pianos (1964–65; also for Medium Voice and Orch., 1967); *Misa da la juventud* for Chorus and Orch. (1965); *Symposion* for Baritone, Chorus, and Orch. (1965–66; rev. 1972); *In Memoriam Anaïck* for Child Speaker, Chorus, Winds, and Percussion (1966); *Yes, speak out, yes* for Soprano, Baritone, 2 Choruses, 2 Orchs., and 2 Conductors (1968; rev. 1969); *Noche pasiva del sentido* for Soprano, 2 Percussion, and Electronics (1969–70); *Faudium et Spes—Beunza* for 2 Choruses and Tape (1971–73); *Oración a Platero* for Speaker, Children's Chorus, Mixed Chorus, and 5 Percussion (1974); *Officium Defunctorum* for Soloists, Chorus, Children's Voices, and Orch. (1977–78); *Jarchas del dolor de ausencia* for 12 Voices (1978–79); *Himno a Santa Teresa* for Soprano, Chorus, Winds, Percussion, and Organ (1981); *Leyendo a Jorge Guillén* for Speaker, Viola, and Cello (1982); *Dona nobis pacem* for Chorus and Instruments (1983–84); *Tres poemas de la lírica española* for Baritone and Orch. (1985–86); *Canciones de Al Andalus* for Mezzo-soprano and String Quartet (1987–88); *Dos motetes* for 3 Choruses (1988; also as *Dos corales litúrgicos* for 3 Choruses and Instrumental Ensemble, 1990); *Muerte, mudanza y locura* for Voice and Electronics (1989); *Preludio para Madrid '92* for Chorus and Orch. (1991); *Siete cantos de España* for Soprano, Baritone, and Orch. (1991–92); *Veni creator spiritus* for 2 Choruses and Instrumental Ensemble (1992). **OTHER:** *Nocturno (30 de Mayo de 1972)*, tape collage (1972); . . . *La soledad sonora/La música callada* . . . , audio-visual environment (1982–83).

BIBL.: T. Marco, *C.H.* (Madrid, 1972); E. Casares Rodicio, *C.H.* (Oviedo, 1980); U. Mosch, "Vom Neoklassizismus zur Avantgarde—C.H.s Weg zur Neuen Musik," *Neue Zürcher Zeitung*, no. 231 (1991).

Halffter (Escriche), Ernesto, esteemed Spanish composer and conductor, brother of **Rodolfo Halffter (Escriche)** and uncle of **Cristóbal Halffter (Jiménez-Encina);** b. Madrid, Jan. 16, 1905; d. there, July 5, 1989. He was trained in composition by Manuel de Falla and Adolfo Salazar. At the outbreak of the Spanish Civil War in 1936, he went to Lisbon. In 1960 he returned to Madrid. In addition to Falla, his output reflects the influence of such French masters as Ravel and Poulenc. He completed and orchestrated Falla's scenic cantata *Atlántida* (Milan, June 18, 1962; later rev. and perf. in concert form, Lucerne, Sept. 9, 1976).

WORKS: DRAMATIC: CHAMBER OPERA: *Entr'acte* (1964). **BALLETS:** *Sonatina* (1928); *Dulcinea* (1940); *Cojo enamorado* (1954); *Fantasía galaica* (1955). **ORCH.:** Sinfonietta (Oxford, July 23, 1931); *Fantaisie portugaise* (Paris, March 23, 1941); *Rapsodia portuguesa* for Piano and Orch. (1962); Guitar Concerto (1968). **VOCAL:** *Canticum in memoriam P.P. Johannem XXIII* for Soprano, Baritone, Chorus, and Orch. (1964); *Psalmen* for Soloist, Chorus, and Orch. (1967).

Halffter (Escriche), Rodolfo, eminent Spanish-born Mexican composer and pedagogue, brother of **Ernesto Halffter (Escriche)** and uncle of **Cristóbal Halffter (Jiménez-Encina);** b. Madrid, Oct. 30, 1900; d. Mexico City, Oct. 14, 1987. He was mainly autodidact although he received some instruction from Falla in Granada (1929). Halffter became a prominent figure in the promotion of modern Spanish music, and was made chief of the music section of the Ministry of Propaganda (1936) and then a member of the Central Music Council (1937) of the Spanish Republic. Following the defeat of the regime in the Spanish Civil War, Halffter fled in 1939 to France and then to Mexico, where he became a naturalized Mexican citizen. In 1940 he founded the contemporary ballet ensemble La Paloma Azul. From 1941 to 1970 he taught at the Conservatorio Nacional de México in Mexico City. In 1946 he founded the publishing firm Ediciones Mexicanas de Música and the journal *Nuestra Música*, which he ed. until 1952. In 1969 he was made a member of the Academia de Artes de Mexico and in 1984 he was made an honorary member of the Real Academia de Bellas Artes in Madrid. In his early works, Halffter followed in the path of Falla but he later explored contemporary techniques, including 12-tone writing. His *Tres Hojas de Álbum* (1953) was the earliest 12-tone music publ. in Mexico.

WORKS: DRAMATIC: *Clavileño*, opera buffa (1934–36; not extant); *Don Lindo de Almería*, ballet (1935; Mexico City, Jan. 9, 1940; orch. suite, 1936); *La madrugada del panadero*, ballet (Mexico City, Sept. 20, 1940; orch. suite, 1940); *Lluvia de toros*, ballet (1940); *Elena la traicionera*, ballet (Mexico City, Nov. 23, 1945); *Tonanzintla*, ballet (1951; also as *Tres Sonatas de Fray Antonio* for Orch.); much film music. **ORCH.:** *Tres piezas* (1924–25; rev. as an orch. suite, 1924–28; rev. 1930; Madrid, Nov. 5, 1930); *Diferencias sobre La Gallarda Milanesa de Félix*

Antonio de Cabezón (1930); *Obertura concertante* for Piano and Orch. (1932; rev. version, Valencia, May 23, 1937); *Impromptu* (1932; not extant); *Preludio atonal: Homenaje a Arbós* (1933); Violin Concerto (1939–40; Mexico City, June 26, 1942; rev. 1952); *Tres Sonatas de Fray Antonio Soler* (1951; also as the ballet *Tonanzintla*); *Obertura festiva* (1952; Mexico City, May 25, 1953); *Tres piezas* for Strings (1954; Mexico City, Aug. 10, 1955); *Tripartita* or *Tres piezas* (1959; Mexico City, July 15, 1960); *Diferencias* (Mexico City, Sept. 13, 1970; rev. 1975 and 1985); *Alborada* (1975; Mexico City, May 9, 1976; incorporated in *Dos ambientes sonoros*, 1975–79); *Dos ambientes sonoros* (1975–79; incorporates *Alborada*, 1975); *Elegía: In memoriam Carlos Chávez* for Strings (1978). **CHAMBER:** *Giga* for Guitar (1930); *Divertimento* for String Quartet (1930; not extant); *Pastorale* for Violin and Piano (1940); *Tres piezas breves* for Harp (1951); Quartet for String Instruments (1957–58); Cello Sonata (1959–60); *Tres movimientos* for String Quartet (1962); *Ocho tientos* for String Quartet (1973); *Capricho* for Violin (1978); *Epinicio* for Flute (1979); *. . . huésped de las nieblas . . . Rimas sin palabras* for Flute and Piano (1981); *Egloga* for Oboe and Piano (1982); *Paquiliztli* for 7 Percussion (1983). **PIANO:** *Naturaleza muerta* (1922); *Dos Sonatas de El Escorial* (1928; rev. 1929); *Preludio y fuga* (1932); *Danza de Avila: En lo alto de aquella montaña* (1936); *Perpetuum mobile: Homenage a Francis Poulenc* (1936); *Para la tumba de Lenin: Variaciones elegíacas* (1937); *Muñieira des vellas* (1938); *Homenaje a Antonio Machado* (1944); 3 sonatas (1947, 1951, 1967); *Once bagatelas* (1949); *Al sol puesto* (1952); *Copla* (1952); *Tonada* (1952); *Tres hojas de álbum* (1953); *Música* for 2 Pianos (1965); *Laberinto: Cuatro intentos de acertar con la salida* (1971–72); *Nocturno: Homenaje a Arturo Rubinstein* (1973); *Facetas* (1976); *Secuencias* (1977); *Escolio* (1980); *Una vez y otra, con coda: Cantilena variada* (1982). **VOCAL:** *Marinero en Tierra* for Voice and Piano (1925–60); *Canciones de la Guerra Civil Española* for Soloists, Chorus, and Orch. (1937–38); *Dos Sonetos* for Voice and Piano (1940–46); *La nuez* for Children's Chorus (1944); *Tres Epitafios* for Chorus (1947–53); *Desterro* for Voice and Piano (1967); *Pregón para una pascua pobre* for Chorus, Trumpets, Trombones, and Percussion (1968).

BIBL.: J. Alcaraz, *R. H.* (Madrid, 1987); X. Ruiz Ortiz, *R. H.: Antología, Introducción y Catálogos* (Mexico City, 1990); A. Iglesias, *R. H.: Tema, Nueve décadas y Final* (Madrid, 1991).

Hall, David, American writer on music; b. New Rochelle, N.Y., Dec. 16, 1916. He was educated at Yale Univ. (B.A., 1939) and Columbia Univ. (graduate study in psychology, 1939–40). He worked for Columbia Records and NBC (1942–48); from 1948 to 1956 he was music director of the classics division of the Mercury Record Corp., where he pioneered in the development of high-fidelity recordings; then was music ed. of *Stereo Review* (1957–62); later was president of Composers Recordings, Inc. (1963–66). From 1967 to 1980 he was head of the Rodgers and Hammerstein Archives of Recorded Sound at the N.Y. Public Library, and from 1980 its curator. He publ. several annotated guides to recordings; also contributed countless articles and record reviews to leading publications.

Hall, Frederick Douglass, black American music educator and composer; b. Atlanta, Dec. 14, 1898; d. there, Dec. 28, 1982. He studied at Morehouse College in Atlanta (B.A., 1921), Chicago Musical College (B.Mus., 1924), Columbia Univ. Teachers College (M.A., 1929; D.Mus. Ed., 1952), Royal Academy of Music in London (licentiate), and Univ. of London (1933–35). He taught at various institutions, including Dillard Univ. in New Orleans (1936–41; 1960–74), where he led a male quartet, and Alabama State College in Montgomery (1941–55). His compositions include an oratorio, *Deliverance* (1938); a song-cycle, *Afro-American Religious Work Songs* (1952); and some 20 art songs; he also prepared choral arrangements of spirituals (6 vols., 1929–55).

Hall, Marie (actually, **Mary Paulina**), English violinist; b. Newcastle upon Tyne, April 8, 1884; d. Cheltenham, Nov. 11, 1956. As a small child, she gave performances in the homes of music-lovers in Newcastle, Malvern, and Bristol with her father, an amateur harp player, her uncle (violin), her brother (violin), and her sister (harp). Elgar heard her, and was impressed by her talent; he sent her to Wilhelmj in London for regular study; she also studied with Johann Kruse. At the age of 15, she won the 1st Wessely Exhibition at the Royal Academy of Music. She was recommended by Jan Kubelik to Ševčik in Prague (1901), from whom she received a rigorous training; she made her professional debut in Prague (1902); then played in Vienna. After a highly successful London concert (Feb. 16, 1903), she made her American debut as soloist with the N.Y. Sym. Orch., Walter Damrosch conducting (Nov. 8, 1905); toured Australia (1907) and India (1913). On Jan. 27, 1911, she married her manager, Edward Baring, and settled in Cheltenham; she continued to appear in concerts in England until 1955, with her daughter, Pauline Baring, as her accompanist.

Hall, Pauline (Margarete), Norwegian composer; b. Hamar, Aug. 2, 1890; d. Oslo, Jan. 24, 1969. She studied piano with Johan Backer Lunde (1908–10) and theory and composition with Catharinus Elling (1910–12) in Christiania; completed her studies in Paris and Dresden (1912–14). She was the Berlin music and drama correspondent for the Norwegian newspaper *Dagbladet* (1926–32), then was its music critic in Oslo (1934–42; 1945–64). In her early works, she was greatly influenced by French Impressionism; she later evolved a neo-Classical style seasoned by disturbing dissonance.

WORKS: DRAMATIC: *Markisen* (The Marquise), ballet (1950); incidental music. **ORCH.:** *Poème élégiaque* (1920); *Verlaine Suite* (1929); *Cirkusbilder* (1939). **CHAMBER:** Suite for Wind Quintet (1945); *Little Dance Suite* for Oboe, Clarinet, and Bassoon (1958); *4 tosserier* for Soprano, Clarinet, Bassoon, Horn, and Trumpet (1961); *Variations on a Classical Theme* for Flute (1961); piano pieces. **VOCAL:** Choral works; songs.

Hall, Sir Peter (Reginald Frederick), noted English theater and opera producer; b. Bury St. Edmunds, Nov. 22, 1930. He was educated at St. Catharine's College, Cambridge. In 1955–56 he was director of the Arts Theatre, London. He was managing director of the Royal Shakespeare Theatre from 1960 to 1968; from 1973 to 1988 he was director of the National Theatre; worked also at the Royal Opera House, Covent Garden. In 1970 he began a long and fruitful association as an opera producer at Glyndebourne, serving as its artistic director from 1984 to 1990. He was head of his own Peter Hall Production Co. (from 1988). For several years he was married to **Maria Ewing**. He was made a Commander of the Order of the British Empire in 1963 and was knighted in 1977. He is known for his versatility, having produced operas by Cavalli, Mozart, Wagner, Tchaikovsky, Schoenberg, and Tippett. In 1983 he produced the new *Ring* cycle at Bayreuth for the 100th anniversary of Wagner's death, with Solti conducting.

Hallberg, Björn Wilho, Norwegian-born Swedish composer; b. Oslo, July 9, 1938. After training with Brustad and Mortensen at the Oslo Cons., he settled in Stockholm in 1962 and completed his studies at the Musikhögskolan with Blomdahl, Wallner, and Linholm. In 1968 he became a naturalized Swedish citizen.

WORKS: DRAMATIC: OPERAS: *Evakueringen* (Stockholm, Dec. 9, 1969); *Josef* (1976–79); *Förföraren* (Stockholm, Dec. 22, 1981); *Regina* (1985); *Majdagar* (Stockholm, Dec. 16, 1989). Ballet music. **ORCH.:** *Aspiration* (Östersund, July 11, 1971); *Novelletten* (1973). **CHAMBER:** *Felder* for Flute and Percussion (Vienna, June 17, 1961); String Quartet (1963); *Ur dagboken* for Percussion Ensemble (1964); *Études* for Chamber Ensemble (1966); piano pieces. **VOCAL:** *Missa pro defunctis* for Soprano, Chorus, Tape, and Orch. (1967; Stockholm, May 17, 1968); *Conversation/Vide* for 5 Voices, 5 Winds, Tape, and Loudspeakers (1968); *Etats* for Soprano, Flute, Double Bass, Piano, and Percussion (1970); solo songs.

Hallgrímsson, Haflidi (Magnus), Icelandic cellist and composer; b. Akureyri, Sept. 18, 1941. He studied cello at the Reykjavík College of Music (1958–62), and then with Mainardi at the Accademia de Santa Cecilia in Rome (1962–63); he pursued training in composition with Simpson at the Royal Academy of Music in London (1964–67), and then privately with Bush and Maxwell Davies (1968–72). After playing in the Haydn String Trio (1967–70) and the English Chamber Orch. (1968–74) in London, he was principal cellist of the Scottish Chamber Orch. in Glasgow (1977–83). He then was a member of the Mondrian Piano Trio in Edinburgh (1984–88) and principal cellist of the London Festival Orch. (from 1984). His *Poemi* for Violin and Strings won the Nordic Council Prize in 1986.

WORKS: ORCH.: *Poemi* for Violin and Strings (1984); *Mystery Play* for Strings (1985); *Daydreams in Numbers* for Strings (1986); Cello Concerto (Glasgow, March 15, 1995). **CHAMBER:** *Venetian Quartet* (1963); *Solitaire* for Cello (1969; rev. 1979); *Hoa-Haka-Hana-Ia* for Clarinet, Marimba, Harp, Strings, and Percussion (1972; rev. 1976); Duo for Viola and Cello (1972); *7 Icelandic Folksongs* for Cello and Piano (1973); *Divertimento* for Harpsichord and String Trio (1974); *Verse I* for Flute and Cello (1975) and *II* for Flute, Amplified Clavichord, Cello, and Piano (1975); *Fimma* for Cello and Piano (1976); *Origami* for Piano Trio (1977); *Polar* for Chamber Ensemble (1978); *Jacob's Ladder* for Guitar (1984); *Tristia* for Guitar and Cello (1984); *7 Folksongs from Iceland* for Cello and Piano (1985); String Quartet, *From Memory* (1989); *4 Pieces: In memorium Bryn Turley* for String Quartet (1990); *The Flight of Icarus* for Flute (1990); *The Flight of Time* for Violin (1990); Wind Quintet (1991). **VOCAL:** *Elegy* for Mezzo-soprano, Flute, 2 Cellos, Piano, and Celesta (1971); *You Will Hear Thunder* for Soprano and Cello (1982); *Triptych* for Voices (1986); *Words in Winter* for Soprano and Orch. (1987); *Syrpa* for Soprano, Clarinet, Cello, and Piano (1993).

Hallnäs, (Johan) Hilding, distinguished Swedish composer, organist, and teacher; b. Halmstad, May 24, 1903; d. Stockholm, Sept. 11, 1984. He was a pupil of Gustaf Hägg and Otto Olsson at the Stockholm Cons. (1924–29), where he took diplomas as an organist and music teacher; he then studied organ with Cellier in Paris and composition with Grabner in Leipzig. After serving as an organist in Strömstad and Jönköping, he went to Göteborg and was organist of the Johanneberg parish from 1933 to 1968; he also taught theory at the Orchestral Assn. (until 1951) and was active in contemporary music circles, serving as chairman of the Göteborg Composers Assn. (1957–72). In 1974 he settled in Stockholm. In 1952 he was made a member of the Royal Academy of Music in Stockholm. In his early music, Hallnäs followed a neo-Classical path. After World War II, he embraced the 12-tone method of composition albeit in a manner which allowed him to develop a personal style all his own.

WORKS: BALLETS: *Kärlekens ringdans* (1955–56); *Ifigenia* (1961–63). **ORCH.:** 9 syms., but 2 withdrawn: No. 1, *Sinfonia pastorale* (1944; Göteborg, March 22, 1945), No. 2, *Sinfonia notturna* (Göteborg, March 4, 1948), No. 3, *Little Symphony* (Göteborg, Oct. 3, 1948), No. 4, *Metamorfose sinfonische* (Göteborg, April 17, 1952; rev. 1960), No. 5, *Sinfonia aforistica* (1962; Göteborg, Jan. 24, 1963), No. 6, *Musica intima* (Malmö, Nov. 7, 1967), and No. 7, *A Quite Small Symphony,* for Chamber Orch. (Minneapolis, June 12, 1974); *Divertimento* (1937); 2 violin concertos (1945, 1965); Piano Concerto (1956); 2 concertos for Flute, Strings, and Percussion (1957, 1962); Concerto for Strings and Percussion (1959); *Epitaph* for Strings (1963); *En grekisk saga* (1967–68); *Momenti bucolichi* for Oboe and Orch. (1969); *Horisont och linjespel* for Strings (1969); Triple Concerto for Violin, Clarinet, Piano, and Orch. (1972–73); Viola Concerto (1976–78); Cello Concerto (1981). **CHAMBER:** 4 string quartets (1949; 1967; with soprano, 1976; 1980); Quintet for Flute, Oboe, Viola, Cello, and Piano (1954); 2 violin sonatas (1957, 1975); Piano Trio, *Stanze sensitive* (1959); *24 Preludes* for Guitar (1967); *3 momenti musicali* for Violin, Horn, and Piano (1971); Trio for Clarinet, Cello, and Piano, *Confessio* (1973); *Triptykon* for Violin, Clarinet, and Piano (1973); *4 Monologues* for Clarinet (1974); *Legend* for Clarinet and Organ (1974); *Trauma* for 4 Strings and Piano (1979); *Musikaliska aforismer* for String Trio (1982). **KEYBOARD: PIANO:** 4 sonatas (1963–83). **ORGAN:** 2 sonatas (*De Profundis,* 1965; 1977); *Passionmusik,* 15 pieces (1968). **VOCAL:** Cantata for Soprano, Flute, Clarinet, Cello, and Piano (1955); *Cantica lyrica* for Tenor, Chorus, and Orch. (1957); *Rapsodie* for Soprano and Chamber Orch. (1963); *Invocatio* for Chorus and String Quartet (1971).

Halpern, Steven, American composer, performer, and producer; b. N.Y., April 18, 1947. He played trumpet and guitar in jazz and rock bands as a youth, and in the late 1960s began to explore the effects of music on the listener. He studied at the State Univ. of N.Y. at Buffalo (B.A., 1969), Lone Mountain College in San Francisco (M.A., 1973), and Sierra Nevada Univ. in Barcelona (Ph.D., 1977). He became absorbed in musical therapy, and developed a study curriculum of healing through music. In 1976 he began distributing his music to bookshops and health food stores, creating what has become Sound Rx Productions, a distribution company, which promotes therapeutic methods in music. He is a pioneer of New Age music, particularly the variety that is intended to be therapeutic; many of his recordings include subliminal suggestions for physical and mental improvement. Among his many solo and collaborative recordings, both audio and video, are *Spectrum Suite* (1975), *Dawn* (1981), and *Radiance* (1988). From 1986 to 1988 he ed. *New Frontier Magazine*; he also publ. *Tuning the Human Instrument* (Belmont, Calif., 1978) and *Sound Health* (N.Y., 1985).

Halvorsen, Johan, notable Norwegian conductor and composer; b. Drammen, March 15, 1864; d. Oslo, Dec. 4, 1935. He began violin lessons at 7 and, while still a youth, played several instruments in the local civil defense band. He pursued his musical training with Lindberg and Nordquist at the Stockholm Cons. In 1885 he made his debut as a soloist in the Beethoven Violin Concerto in Bergen, where he served as concertmaster of the Harmonien Music Soc. He then was a violinist in the Gewandhaus Orch. in Leipzig, where he studied violin with Brodsky. After serving as concertmaster of the Aberdeen Musical Soc., he taught at the Helsinki Cons. (1889–92). He also completed his studies in St. Petersburg, Berlin (composition with Becker), and Liège (violin with Thomson). Upon returning to Bergen in 1893, he became conductor of the orch. of the theater and of the Harmonien Music Soc. In 1899 he was called to Christiania (Oslo) as conductor of the orch. of the newly opened National Theater, where he led symphonic as well as theater scores until his retirement in 1929. He was married to a niece of Grieg. Halvorsen's compositions were influenced by Grieg, Svendsen, and the folk melodies of his native land. Outside of Norway he is best known for his celebrated orch. march *Entry of the Boyars* (1893), as well as the Passacaglia for Violin and Viola, after a Handel keyboard suite (1897), the *Andante religioso* for Violin and Orch. (1903), and *Bergensiana, Rococo Variations on an Old Melody from Bergen* for Orch. (1913). Among his other works were 3 syms.: No. 1 (Christiania, 1923), No. 2, *Fatum* (1923; Christiania, March 15, 1924; rev. 1928), and No. 3 (1928; Oslo, March 15, 1929); Violin Concerto; *Norwegian Festival Overture* (1899); several orch. suites, including *Nordraakiana,* after 5 works of R. Nordraak; 2 Norwegian rhapsodies (1919–20); incidental music to more than 30 plays; *Reisen til Julestjernen* (Journey to the Christmas Star), a popular children's Christmas play (1924).

BIBL.: J. Eriksen, "J. H.: En biografi," *Norsk musikktidsskrijt,* VII/2 (1970); H. Rossiné, "J. H.: Beyond the Transitory," *Listen to Norway,* III/2 (1994).

Hamari, Julia, Hungarian mezzo-soprano; b. Budapest, Nov. 21, 1942. She studied with Fatime Martin; after further training at the Budapest Academy of Music, she won the Erkel competition in 1964, and then completed her studies at the Stuttgart Hochschule für Musik. In 1966 she made her debut as a soloist in the *St. Matthew Passion* in Vienna, and subsequently was notably successful as a concert and lieder artist in Europe. In 1967 she made her stage debut in Salzburg. In 1972 she made her U.S. debut as a soloist with the Chicago Sym. Orch. As an opera singer, she appeared with the opera houses in Düsseldorf and Stuttgart. On April 24, 1982, she made her Metropolitan Opera debut in N.Y. as Rossini's Rosina. Her concert and lieder repertoire extends from Monteverdi to Verdi. Among her other operatic roles are Cherubino, Dorabella, Cenerentola, Carmen, and Octavian.

Hambourg, noted family of Russian-born musicians:

(1) Michael (Mikhail) Hambourg, pianist and teacher; b. Yaroslavl, July 12, 1855; d. Toronto, June 18, 1916. He studied with N. Rubinstein and Taneyev in St. Petersburg and at the Moscow Cons.; was prof. at the latter (1880–90), and then at the Guildhall School of Music in London (1890–1910). He went to Toronto in 1911 and founded the Hambourg Cons. of Music with his son Boris. All of his sons were musicians:

(2) Mark Hambourg, pianist; b. Bogutchar, June 12, 1879; d. Cambridge, Aug. 26, 1960. He studied with his father, making his debut in Moscow at age 9; then studied with Leschetizky in Vienna. After international tours, he settled in England and became a naturalized British subject. He publ. *How to Play the Piano* (Philadelphia, 1922), *From Piano to Forte: A Thousand and One Notes* (London, 1931), and *The Eighth Octave* (London, 1951).

(3) Jan Hambourg, violinist; b. Voronezh, Aug. 27, 1882; d. Tours, Sept. 29, 1947. He studied with Sauret and Wilhelmj in London, Sevčik in Prague, and Ysaÿe in Brussels; played in a trio with his brothers. He died during a concert tour in France.

(4) Boris Hambourg, cellist; b. Voronezh, Jan. 8, 1885; d. Toronto, Nov. 24, 1954. He studied with his father and with H. Walenn in London, H. Becker at the Frankfurt am Main Cons. (1898–1903), and Ysaÿe (1904); played in a trio with his brothers. He went to Toronto in 1911 and founded the Hambourg Cons. of Music with his father, serving as its director until 1951; he also played in the Hart House Quartet (1924–46).

Hambraeus, Bengt, prominent Swedish composer, organist, musicologist, and pedagogue; b. Stockholm, Jan. 29, 1928. He studied organ with Alf Linder (1944–48), and also pursued training in musicology at the Univ. of Uppsala (1947–56; M.A., 1950; Fil.Lic., 1956) and attended the summer courses in new music in Darmstadt (1951–55). After service with the Inst. of Musicology at the Univ. of Uppsala (1948–56), he joined the music dept. of the Swedish Broadcasting Corp. in Stockholm in 1957, where he later was head of its chamber music section (1965–68) and production manager (1968–72). He subsequently was a prof. at McGill Univ. in Montreal from 1972 to 1995. In 1967 he was made a member of the Swedish Royal Academy of Music in Stockholm. In addition to his numerous articles and essays, he publ. *Codex Carminum Gallicorum* (Uppsala, 1961), *Portrait av Bach* (with others; Stockholm, 1968), and *Om Notskrifter* (Stockholm, 1970). Hambraeus is one of the pioneering figures of the Swedish avant-garde. His *Doppelrohr* for Tape (1955) was one of the earliest electronic pieces by a Scandinavian composer. While he has found inspiration in both the Western and non-Western musical traditions, he has pursued an adventuresome course in his oeuvre.

WORKS: OPERAS: *Experiment X*, church opera (1968–69; Stockholm, March 9, 1971); *Se människen*, church opera (1970; Stockholm, May 15, 1972); *Sagan*, radio opera (1978–79; Swedish Radio, Aug. 31, 1980); *L'Oui-dire* (1984–86). **ORCH.:** Concerto for Organ and Strings (1948); *Kleine Musik* for Oboe, Strings and Timpani (1949); *Rota* for 3 Orchestral Groups, Percussion, and Tape (1956–62; Stockholm, May 27, 1964); *Transfiguration* (1962–63; Swedish Radio, Feb. 20, 1965); *Rencontres* (1968–71; Swedish Radio, Sept. 8, 1971); *Pianissimo in due tempe* for 20 Strings (1970–72; Uppsala, April 16, 1972); *Invocation* (Ames, Iowa, Nov. 11, 1971); *Continuo a partire de Pachelbel* for Organ and Orch. (1974–75; Nuremberg, June 15, 1976); *Ricordanza* (1975–76; Norrköping, April 29, 1977); *Parade* for Wind Orch. (1977); *That Harmony* for Brass Band (1983); *Quodlibet re BACH* (1984; Toronto, March 15, 1985); *Litanies* (1988–89; Stockholm, May 13, 1990); Piano Concerto (1992); Piano Concerto (1992); Horn Concerto (1995–96). **CHAMBER:** Concerto for Organ and Harpsichord (1947–51); *Music for Ancient Strings* for String Ensemble and Harpsichord (1948); 3 string quartets (1948–67); *Musique* for Trumpet (1949); *Kammarmusik* for Flute, Oboe, Clarinet, Alto Saxophone, Viola, and Harpsichord (1950); *Recitativ och Koral* for Violin and Piano (1950); *Giuco del Cambio* for Flute, English Horn, Bass Clarinet, Vibraphone, Harpsichord, Piano, and 3 Percussion (1952–54; Stockholm, Jan. 29, 1955); *Komposition for Studio II* for Vibraphone, Chimes, 3 Percussion, Piano, Harpsichord, and Organ (1955); *Introduzione—Sequenze—Coda* for 3 Flutes and 6 Percussion (1958–59; Stockholm, Dec. 11, 1959); *Segnali* for Electric Guitar, Harp, Violin, Viola, Cello, and Double Bass (1959–60; Swedish Radio, April 8, 1962); *Mikrogram: 7 Aphorisms* for Alto Flute, Viola, Vibraphone, and Harp (Stockholm, Dec. 4, 1961); *Notazioni* for Harpsichord, 3 Flutes, English Horn, Bass Clarinet, 3 Trumpets, 3 Trombones, Celesta, and 6 Percussion (1961; Stockholm, March 17, 1965); *Notturno de vecchi strumenti* for Soprano Recorder, Crumhorn, Alto Bassoon, Viola d'amore, Bass Gamba, Clavichord, 2 Glockenspiels, and Tambourine (1961; Stockholm, Nov. 17, 1963); *Transit II* for Horn, Trombone, Electric Guitar, and Piano (Malmö, Nov. 30, 1963); *Advent: Veni redemptor gentium* for Organ, 4 Trumpets, 4 Trombones, and Percussion (1975); *Jeu de cinq* for Wind Quintet (1976; Toronto, Feb. 24, 1977); *Relief—haut et bas* for 2 Flutes, 3 Horns, Trombone, 2 Percussion, and 2 Double Basses (1979; Montreal, April 10, 1980); *Strata* for 2 Oboes, 2 Clarinets, 2 Basset Horns, 2 Bassoons, 2 Horns, and Double Bass (1979–80; Stockholm, Sept. 20, 1980); *Sheng* for Oboe and Organ (1983; Toronto, Sept. 12, 1984); *Monologo* for Flute (1984); Trio Sonata for Free Bass Accordion, Trombone, and Prepared Piano (1985); *Mirrors* for Oboe and Tape (1986–87); *Night Music* for Guitar and Percussion (1988); *Dos recercadas* for Guitar and Cello (1988); *Cinque studi canonici* for 2 Flutes (1988); *Nazdar M J* for 3 Trumpets, 4 Horns, 3 Trombones, Tuba, Timpani, and Chimes (1989). **KEYBOARD: PIANO:** *Toccata* (1947–49); *Cercles* (1948); *Klockspel* (1968); *Carillon: Le Recital oublié* for 2 Pianos (1972–74); *Tre intermezzi* (1984); *Vortex* for 2 Pianos (1986). **ORGAN:** *Koralforspel* (1948); *Toccata pro tempore pentecostes* (1948); *Introitus et Triptychon* (1949–50); *Musik* (1950); *Liturgia* (1951–52); *Permutations and Hymn: Nocte surgentes* (1953); *Constellations I* (1958), *II* with Tape (1959), *III* with Tape (1961), and *IV* with Percussion (1978); *Interferenzen* (1961–62); *Tre pezzi* (1966–67); *Nebulosa* (1969); *Toccata pro organo: Monumentum per Max Reger* (1973); *Ricercare* (1974); *Icons* (1974–75); *Extempore* (1975); *Antiphonie* (1977); *Livre d'orgue* (4 vols., 1981); *Voluntary on a Swedish Hymn Tune from Dalecarlia* (1981); *Variations sur un thème de Gilles Vigneault* (1984); *La Passacaille errante—autour Haendel 1985* (1984); *Pedalexercitium* (1985); *Après-Sheng* (1988); *Cadenza* (1988). **VOCAL:** *Cantigas de Santa Maria* for Soprano, Alto, Baritone, and 3 Instrumental Groups (Stockholm, Dec. 17, 1949; also for Chorus and Organ, 1950); *Spectrogram* for Soprano, Flute, Vibraphone, and Percussion (1953); *Antiphonies en rondes* for Soprano and Orch. (1953); *Psalmus CXXI* and *CXXII* for Soprano and Organ (1953); *Gacelas y casidas de Federico García Lorca* for Tenor, Flute, English Horn, Bass Clarinet, Vibraphone, Bells, and Percussion (Stockholm, Jan. 23, 1953); *Crystal Sequence* for Soprano Chorus, 2 Trumpets, Vibraphone, Bells, Percussion, and 12 Violins (1954); *Responsorier* for Tenor, Chorus, Congregation, and 2 Organs (1964; Uppsala, June 16, 1966); *Praeludium, Kyrie, Sanctus* for 2 Choruses, Soloist, 2 Organs, and Congregation (Stockholm, Aug. 13, 1966); *Motectum archangeli Michaelis* for Chorus and Organ (Stockholm, Oct. 15, 1967); *Nonsens* for Chorus (1970); *Inductio* for Soprano, Alto Mixed Chorus, 3 Trumpets, and 3 Trombones (1979; Montreal, Feb. 8, 1980); *Alpha—Omega* for Chorus and Organ (1982); *Constellations V* for 2 Amplified Sopranos, Chorus, and Organ (1982–83; Nuremberg, Sept. 16, 1983); *Symphonia sacra in tempore passionis* for Soloists, Chorus, Winds, and Percussion (1986; Montreal, March 6, 1987); *Apocalipsis cum figuris secundum Duerer 1498* for

Bass, Chorus, and Organ (1987; Nuremberg, Oct. 7, 1988); *5 Psalms* for Chorus (1987); *Echoes of Loneliness* for 4 Choruses (1988). **ELECTRONIC:** *Doppelrohr* (1955; Cologne, May 30, 1956); *Fresque sonore* (1956–57); *Visioner over en svensk folkvisa* (Swedish Radio, Nov. 13, 1959); *Intrada* (1976).

Hämeenniemi, Eero (Olavi), Finnish composer; b. Valkeakoski, April 29, 1951. He studied with Heininen at the Sibelius Academy in Helsinki (1973–78), Schaeffer in Kraków, Donatoni in Italy (1979), and Schwantner and Warren Benson at the Eastman School of Music in Rochester, N.Y. (1980–81). In 1975 he became active with Korvat Auki, the Finnish society for the promotion of contemporary music; served as its chairman (until 1979; 1981–82). He also taught at the Sibelius Academy (from 1977).

WORKS: DRAMATIC: *Loviisa,* ballet (1985–86; Helsinki, March 19, 1987); *The Bird and the Wind* for Soprano, 2 Indian Dancers and Orch. (1994). **ORCH.:** *. . . Only the Earth and Mountains* (1981); 2 syms.: No. 1 (1982–83) and No. 2 (Helsinki, Aug. 31, 1988); *Soitto* (1984); *Dialogi* for Piano and Orch. (1985). **CHAMBER:** *Duo I* for Flute and Cello (1976); *Dedicato . . .* for 12 Instruments (1978); *Aria* for Horn (1978); Piano Sonata (1979); Clarinet Sonata (1983); *Efisaes* for Piano and 12 Solo Strings (1983); *Canterai . . .* for Flute (1983); 2 String Quartets (1989, 1994).

Hamel, Fred, German musicologist; b. Paris, Feb. 19, 1903; d. Hamburg, Dec. 9, 1957. He studied chemistry in Bonn and Berlin and musicology in Berlin and Giessen; in 1930 he received his Ph.D. from the Univ. of Giessen with the diss. *Form- und Stilprinzipien in der Vokalmusik Johann Rosenmüllers.* He publ. a monograph on J.S. Bach, *Geistige Welt* (Göttingen, 1951), and contributed numerous articles to German music journals. From 1948 he served as production manager for Deutsche Grammophon Gesellschaft; founded its prestigious Archiv-Produktion of recordings of early music in authentic performances.

Hamelin, Marc-André, Canadian pianist; b. Montreal, Sept. 5, 1961. He began piano lessons at the age of 5, and at 9 became a pupil of Yvonne Hubert and Sister Rita-de-la-Croix at the École Vincent-d'Indy in Montreal; completed his training with Harvey Wedeen and Russell Sherman at Temple Univ. in Philadelphia (B.Mus., 1983; M.Mus., 1985). After placing 1st in both the International Stepping Stones of the Canadian Music Competition and the Pretoria, South Africa competition (1982), he won 1st prize at the International Competition of American Music at N.Y.'s Carnegie Hall in 1985. Thereafter he appeared as soloist with various North American orchs., as a recitalist, and as a chamber music player. In 1987 he was a soloist with the Montreal Sym. Orch. on its tour of Europe. From 1989 he toured in a duo with the cellist Sophie Rolland. Hamelin's repertoire includes not only standard works but rarely performed pieces from all eras.

Hamerik (real name, **Hammerich**), **Ebbe,** Danish conductor and composer; b. Copenhagen, Sept. 5, 1898; d. there (drowned in the Kattegat), Aug. 11, 1951. His father was the Danish composer Asger Hamerik (b. Frederiksberg, April 8, 1843; d. there, July 13, 1923) and his uncle the Danish musicologist Angul Hammerich (b. Copenhagen, Nov. 25, 1848; d. Frederiksberg, April 26, 1931). He studied with his father and with Frank van der Stucken. He was active mainly as a conductor; held the post of 2nd conductor at the Royal Danish Theater in Copenhagen (1919–22) and conductor of the Copenhagen music society (1927–31) and the State Radio Sym. Orch.

WORKS: OPERAS: *Stepan* (Mainz, Nov. 30, 1924); *Leonardo da Vinci* (Antwerp, March 28, 1939); *Marie Grubbe* (Copenhagen, May 17, 1940); *Rejsekammeraten,* after Andersen (Copenhagen, Jan. 5, 1946); *Drømmerne* (posthumous; Århus, Sept. 9, 1974). **ORCH.:** 5 syms., *Ur cantus firmus I–V* (1937; 1947; 1947–48; 1949; 1949). **CHAMBER:** Wind Quintet (1942); 2 string quartets (1917, 1917); piano pieces. **VOCAL:** Songs.

Hamilton, David (Peter), American music critic; b. N.Y., Jan. 18, 1935. He was educated at Princeton Univ. (1952–56; A.B., 1956; M.F.A., music history, 1960). He was music and record librarian there (1961–65); in 1965 he became assistant music ed. of W.W. Norton & Co. in N.Y.; was music ed. from 1968 to 1974. In 1967 he became a contributing ed. of *High Fidelity,* and in 1968, music critic of the *Nation;* he also served as N.Y. music correspondent for the *Financial Times* of London (1969–74) and assoc. ed. of the *Musical Newsletter* (1971–77). He wrote *The Listener's Guide to Great Instrumentalists* (N.Y., 1981) and *The Metropolitan Opera Encyclopedia: A Comprehensive Guide to the World of Opera* (N.Y., 1987); also publ. *The Music Game: An Autobiography* (London, 1986).

Hamilton, Iain (Ellis), remarkable Scottish composer; b. Glasgow, June 6, 1922. He was taken to London at the age of 7, and attended Mill Hill School; after graduation, he became an apprentice engineer, but studied music in his leisure time. He was 25 years old when he decidedly turned to music; won a scholarship to the Royal Academy of Music, where he studied piano with Harold Craxton and composition with William Alwyn; concurrently studied at the Univ. of London (B.Mus., 1950). He made astonishing progress as a composer, and upon graduation from the Royal Academy of Music received the prestigious Dove Prize (1950); other awards included the Royal Phil. Soc. Prize for his Clarinet Concerto (1951), the Koussevitzky Foundation Award for his 2nd Sym. (1951), the Edwin Evans Prize (1951), the Arnold Bax Gold Medal (1957), and the Vaughan Williams Award (1974). From 1951 to 1960 he was a lecturer at Morley College in London; he also lectured at the Univ. of London (1952–60). He served as Mary Duke Biddle Prof. of Music at Duke Univ. in Durham, N.C. (1961–78), where he was chairman of its music dept. (1966–67); also was composer-in-residence at the Berkshire Music Center at Tanglewood, Mass. (summer, 1962). In 1970 he received an honorary D.Mus. from the Univ. of Glasgow. His style of composition is marked by terse melodic lines animated by a vibrant rhythmic pulse, creating the impression of kinetic lyricism; his harmonies are built on a set of peculiarly euphonious dissonances, which repose on emphatic tonal centers. For several years he pursued a sui generis serial method, but soon abandoned it in favor of a free modern manner; in his operas, he makes use of thematic chords depicting specific dramatic situations.

WORKS: DRAMATIC: *Clerk Saunders,* ballet (1951); *The Royal Hunt of the Sun,* opera (1966–68; 1975; London, Feb. 2, 1977); *Agamemnon,* dramatic narrative (1967–69); *Pharsalia,* dramatic commentary (1968); *The Cataline Conspiracy,* opera (1972–73; Stirling, Scotland, March 16, 1974); *Tamburlaine,* lyric drama (1976; BBC, London, Feb. 14, 1977); *Anna Karenina,* opera (1977–78; London, May 7, 1981); *Dick Whittington,* lyric comedy (1980–81); *Lancelot,* opera (1982–83; Arundel, England, Aug. 24, 1985); *Raleigh's Dream,* opera (1983; Durham, N.C., June 3, 1984); *The Tragedy of Macbeth,* opera (1990); *London's Fair,* opera (1992). **ORCH.:** 4 syms.: No. 1 (1948), No. 2 (1951), No. 3, *Spring* (1981; London, July 24, 1982), and No. 4 (1981; Edinburgh, Jan. 21, 1983); *Variations on an Original Theme* for Strings (1948); 2 piano concertos: No. 1 (1949) and No. 2 (1960; rev. 1967, 1987; BBC, Glasgow, May 1989); Clarinet Concerto (1950); Sinfonia Concertante for Violin, Viola, and Chamber Orch. (1950); 2 violin concertos: No. 1 (1952) and No. 2, *Amphion* (1971); *Scottish Dances* (1956); *Sonata per orchestra da camera* (1956); *Overture: 1812* (1957); Concerto for Jazz Trumpet and Orch. (1957); *Sinfonia* for 2 Orchestras (1958); *Ecossaise* (1959); *Arias* for Small Orch. (1962); *The Chaining of Prometheus* for Wind Instruments and Percussion (1963); *Cantos* (1964); Concerto for Organ and Small Orch. (1964); *Circus* for 2 Trumpets and Orch. (1969); *Alastor* (1970); *Voyage* for Horn and Chamber Orch. (1970); *Commedia,* concerto (London, May 4, 1973); *Aurora* (N.Y., Nov. 21, 1975); *The Alexandrian Sequence* for Chamber Orch. (1976). **CHAMBER:** 2 quintets for Clarinet and String Quartet: No. 1 (1948) and No. 2, *Sea Music* (1974); 4 string quartets

(1949, 1965, 1984, 1984); Quartet for Flute and String Trio (1951); *3 Nocturnes* for Clarinet and Piano (1951); Viola Sonata (1951); *Capriccio* for Trumpet and Piano (1951); Clarinet Sonata (1954); Piano Trio (1954); 2 octets: No. 1 for Strings (1954) and No. 2 for Winds (1983); *Serenata* for Violin and Clarinet (1955); 2 cello sonatas (1958, 1974); Sextet for Flute, 2 Clarinets, Violin, Cello, and Piano (1962); *Sonatas and Variants* for 10 Wind Instruments (1963); Brass Quintet (1964); *Sonata notturna* for Horn and Piano (1965); Flute Sonata (1966); Violin Sonata (1974); *Hyperion* for Clarinet, Horn, Violin, Cello, and Piano (1977); *Spirits of the Air* for Bass Trombone (1977). **KEYBOARD: PIANO:** 3 sonatas (1951, rev. 1971; 1973; 1978); *3 Pieces* (1955); *Nocturnes with Cadenzas* (1963); *Palinodes* (1972); *Le Jardin de Monet* (1986). **ORGAN:** *Fanfares and Variants* (1960); *Aubade* (1965); *Threnos—In Time of War* (1966); *Paraphrase of the Music for Organs in Epitaph for this World and Time* (1970); *Roman Music* (1973); *A Vision of Canopus* (1975); *Le Tombeau de Bach* (1986). **VOCAL:** *The Bermudas* for Baritone, Chorus, and Orch. (1956); *Cinque canzone d'amore* for Tenor and Orch. (1957); *Nocturnal* for 11 Solo Voices (1959); *A Testament of War* for Baritone and Small Instrumental Ensemble (1961); *Dialogues* for Coloratura Soprano and Small Instrumental Ensemble (1965); *Epitaph for This World and Time* for 3 Choruses and 3 Organs (1970); *The Golden Sequence* for Chorus, Congregation, and Organ (1973); *Te Deum* for Chorus, Winds, Brass, and Percussion (1973–74); *Cleopatra*, dramatic scene for Soprano and Orch. (1977); *Requiem* for Chorus (1979; BBC, Glasgow, May 1980); *Mass* for Chorus (1980; London, April 4, 1981); *Vespers* for Chorus, 2 Pianos, Harp, and Percussion (1980); *The Morning Watch* for Chorus and 10 Wind Instruments (1981); *The Passion of Our Lord According to St. Mark* for Soprano, Alto, Tenor, Bass, Chorus, and Orch. (1982; London, May 6, 1983); *The Bright Heavens Sounding* for Soprano, Alto, Tenor, Bass, Chorus, and Instrumental Ensemble (1985; London, June 27, 1986); *Prometheus* for Soprano, Mezzo-soprano, Tenor, Baritone, Chorus, and Orch. (1986); *Paris de Crépuscule à l'aube* for Voice and Orch. or Piano (1986); *La Mort de Phèdre* for Voice and Orch. (1987).

Hamm, Charles (Edward), American musicologist; b. Charlottesville, Va., April 21, 1925. He studied at the Univ. of Virginia (B.A., 1947) and Princeton Univ. (M.F.A., 1950; Ph.D., 1960, with the diss. *A Chronology of the Works of Guillaume Dufay;* publ. in Princeton, 1964). He taught at Princeton Univ. (1948–50; 1958), at the Cincinnati Cons. of Music (1950–57), and at Tulane Univ. (1959–63). In 1963 he was appointed prof. of musicology at the Univ. of Ill.; in 1976 he joined the faculty of Dartmouth College. He served as president of the American Musicological Soc. from 1973 to 1974, and in 1993 he was made an honorary member. A versatile scholar, Hamm publ. books on a variety of subjects, including *Opera* (Boston, 1966); *Yesterdays: Popular Song in America* (N.Y., 1979); *Music in the New World* (N.Y., 1983); *Afro-American Music, South Africa, and Apartheid* (N.Y., 1988).

Hammerstein, Oscar (Greeley Clendenning), II, outstanding American lyricist; b. N.Y., July 12, 1895; d. Highland Farms, Doylestown, Pa., Aug. 23, 1960. His grandfather was the celebrated German-American impresario Oscar Hammerstein (b. Stettin, May 8, 1846; d. N.Y., Aug. 1, 1919). He studied law at Columbia Univ., graduating in 1917; then became interested in the theater. He collaborated on the librettos for Friml's *Rose Marie* (1924), Romberg's *The Desert Song* (1926), and Kern's *Show Boat* (1927; included the celebrated song *Ol' Man River*). In 1943 he joined forces with the composer Richard Rodgers, and together they produced some of the most brilliant and successful musical comedies in American theater: *Oklahoma!* (1943; Pulitzer Prize); *Carousel* (1945); *Allegro* (1947); *South Pacific* (1949; Pulitzer Prize); *The King and I* (1951); *Me and Juliet* (1953); *Pipe Dream* (1955); *The Flower Drum Song* (1958); *The Sound of Music* (1959). His lyrics are characterized by appealing sentiment and sophisticated nostalgia, making them particularly well suited to the modern theater.

BIBL.: D. Taylor, *Some Enchanted Evenings: The Story of Rodgers and H.* (N.Y., 1953); M. Wilk, *They're Playing Our Song* (N.Y., 1973); H. Fordin, *Getting to Know Him, A Biography of O. H. II* (N.Y., 1977); S. Citron, *The Wordsmiths: O. H. II and Alan Jay Lerner* (Oxford, 1995).

Hammond, Frederick (Fisher), American musicologist and harpsichordist; b. Binghamton, N.Y., Aug. 7, 1937. He received his B.A. and Ph.D. from Yale Univ., where he studied harpsichord with Kirkpatrick. He taught at the Univ. of Chicago (1962–65) and at Queens College (1966–68), then joined the faculty at the Univ. of Calif. at Los Angeles (1968). In 1989 he became Irma Brandeis Prof. of Romance Studies at Bard College. He made his N.Y. recital debut in 1969. He was assistant music director of the Castelfranco Veneto Festival (1975–80), assistant music director of the Clarion Music Soc. (from 1978), and director of the Nakamichi Festival of Baroque Music (from 1986). His research focuses on Italian harpsichord composers; his *Girolamo Frescobaldi* (Cambridge, Mass., 1983) is the definitive biography. He also publ. *Girolamo Frescobaldi: A Guide to Research* (N.Y., 1988). His honors include a Rome Prize fellowship (1965–66) and the Cavaliere al merito della Repubblica (1986).

Hammond, Dame Joan (Hood), prominent New Zealand soprano; b. Christchurch, May 24, 1912. She studied at the Sydney Cons., in Vienna, and with Borgioli in London. In 1929 she made her operatic debut in Sydney as Siebel. In 1938 she made her London debut in a recital, and then sang in Vienna. From 1942 to 1945 she appeared with the Carl Rosa Opera Co. in London. On Oct. 6, 1948, she made her debut at London's Covent Garden as Verdi's Leonora, and continued to sing there until 1951; she appeared there again in 1953. She made her N.Y. City Opera debut as Cio-Cio-San on Oct. 16, 1949, and remained on its roster for the season. She also pursued an active concert career. After her retirement in 1965, she taught voice in Wellington at Victoria Univ. Her autobiography was publ. as *A Voice, a Life* (London, 1970). She was made an Officer (1953), a Commander (1963), and a Dame Commander (1974) of the Order of the British Empire. Among her finest operatic roles were Beethoven's Leonore, Violetta, Marguerite, Tatiana, Rusalka, Salome, and Tosca.

Hammond, Laurens, American manufacturer of keyboard instruments; b. Evanston, Ill., Jan. 11, 1895; d. Cornwall, Conn., July 1, 1973. He studied engineering at Cornell Univ.; then went to Detroit to work on the synchronization of electrical motor impulses, a principle which he later applied to the Hammond Organ (1933), an electronic keyboard instrument, resembling a spinet piano, which suggests the sound of the pipe organ. Still later, he developed a newfangled electrical device which he called the Novachord and which was designed to simulate the sound of any known or hypothetical musical instrument; he gave the first demonstration of the Novachord in the Commerce Dept. auditorium in Washington, D.C., on Feb. 2, 1939. In 1940 he introduced the Solovox, an attachment to the piano keyboard which enables an amateur player to project the melody in organlike tones. A further invention was the "chord organ," which he introduced in 1950, and which is capable of supplying basic harmonies when a special button is pressed by the performer.

Hammond-Stroud, Derek, English baritone; b. London, Jan. 10, 1929. He was a student of Elena Gerhardt in London and of Gerhard Hüsch in Vienna and Munich. In 1954 he made his London recital debut, followed by his operatic debut there in 1955 as Creon in Haydn's *L'anima del filosofo ossia Orfeo ed Euridice* at St. Pancras Town Hall. From 1961 to 1971 he was a principal member of the Sadler's Wells Opera in London, and then sang at London's Covent Garden from 1971. In 1973 he made his first appearance at the Glyndebourne Festival. He made his U.S. debut with the Houston Grand Opera in 1975. On Dec. 5, 1977, he made his first appearance at the Metropolitan Opera in N.Y. as Faninal. In addition to his operatic appearances, he also pursued an active concert career. In 1987 he was made an Officer of the Order of the British Empire. His successful operatic roles included Papageno, Bartolo, Don Magnifico, Melitone, Alberich, and Beckmesser.

Hampson, Thomas, admired American baritone; b. Elkhart, Ind., June 28, 1955. He studied at Eastern Washington Univ. (B.A., 1977), Fort Wright College (B.F.A., 1979), the Univ. of Southern Calif., and the Music Academy of the West at Santa Barbara, where he won the Lotte Lehmann award (1978). In 1980 he took 2nd prize at the 's Hertogenbosch International Vocal Competition, and in 1981 1st place in the Metropolitan Opera Auditions. In 1981 he appeared with the Deutsche Oper am Rhein in Düsseldorf, and in 1982 attracted wide notice as Guglielmo in *Così fan tutte* with the Opera Theatre of St. Louis. In subsequent seasons, he appeared with opera companies in Santa Fe, Cologne, Lyons, and Zürich. In 1985 he made his N.Y. recital debut. On Oct. 9, 1986, he made his Metropolitan Opera debut in N.Y. as Mozart's Count Almaviva. During the 1986–87 season, he sang for the first time with the Bavarian State Opera in Munich and the Vienna State Opera. In 1988 he appeared at the Salzburg Festival as Mozart's Count Almaviva. In 1989 he made his debut at the Berlin Deutsche Oper as Don Giovanni. He appeared for the first time at the San Francisco Opera as Ulisse in *Il Ritorno d'Ulisse* in 1990. In 1992 he made his Carnegie Hall recital debut in N.Y. In 1993 he made his debut at London's Covent Garden as Rossini's Figaro. He has won particular success for roles in operas by Mozart, Rossini, Donizetti, Verdi, and Puccini. As a concert artist, Hampson has appeared as a soloist with orchs. and as a recitalist in principal music centers of the world. His concert repertoire embraces works from Bach to Cole Porter and beyond.

Hampton, Calvin, esteemed American organist, choirmaster, and composer; b. Kittanning, Pa., Dec. 31, 1938; d. Port Charlotte, Fla., Aug. 5, 1984. He studied organ and composition at the Oberlin (Ohio) College Cons. of Music (B.M., 1960), and then at Syracuse Univ. (M.M., 1962). He was organist-choirmaster at N.Y.'s Calvary Episcopal Church (later combined with Holy Communion and St. George's; 1963–83). Hampton was a brilliant recitalist who played his own notable transcriptions of works by Chopin and Mussorgsky. On March 2, 1980, at St. George's, he conducted what is thought to be the first complete U.S. performance, in French, of Franck's oratorio *Les Béatitudes*. His compositions fuse popular and classical influences with striking effect, producing a lyrical and romantic underpinning that belies the modernity of their instrumentation. Some of his anthems are found in supplements to the Episcopal hymnal.

WORKS: *Prisms* for Piano (1963); *Catch-Up* for Tape and 2 Quarter Tone Pianos (1967); *Triple Play* for Ondes Martenot and 2 Quarter Tone Pianos (1967); *Prelude and Variations on Old 100th* for Organ (1970); *Transformation and Despair* for Organ (1971); *God Plays Hide and Seek* for Synthesizer and Organ (1971); *The Road to Leprachaunia* for Soprano, Synthesizer, and Organ (1973); Concerto for Saxophone Quartet, Strings, and Percussion (1973); *Labyrinth* for Soprano and Saxophone Quartet (1973); *O Lord, Support Us* for Chorus and Prerecorded Synthesizer (1974); *Pentecost Cantata* for Soli, Chorus, and Percussion (1977); *Candlelight Carol Service* for Soli, Chorus, Dancers, Pantomime, Organ, and Orch. (1978); Concerto for Organ and Strings (St. Paul, June 18, 1980); Concerto for Solo Organ (1981); *Cantata for Palm Sunday* for Tenor, Chorus, and Organ (1981); *In Praise of Humanity* for Organ (1981); *Dances* for Organ (1982); *It Happened in Jerusalem*, music drama for Soli, Speakers, Actors, Dancers, Chorus, Organ, Percussion, and Tape (1982); *Variations on "Amazing Grace"* for English Horn and Organ (1983); songs and anthems.

BIBL.: L. King, "C. H.: A Twenty-Year Ministry," *American Organist* (Oct. 1983).

Handford, Maurice, English conductor; b. Salisbury, April 29, 1929; d. Warminster, Dec. 16, 1986. He studied horn at the Royal Academy of Music in London. He was principal horn in the Hallé Orch. in Manchester (1949–61); in 1960 he made his conducting debut with it, and then served as its assistant (1964–66) and assoc. (1966–71) conductor. In 1961 he became conductor of the Royal Academy of Music First Orch.; he also was conductor with the City of Birmingham Sym. Orch. (1970–74) and music director of the Calgary (Alberta) Phil. (1971–75).

Handley, Vernon (George), English conductor; b. London, Nov. 11, 1930. He was educated at Balliol College, Oxford, and the Guildhall School of Music in London. He made his debut with the Bournemouth Sym. Orch. in 1961. From 1962 to 1983 he was principal conductor of the Guildford Phil.; was also a prof. at the Royal College of Music in London (1966–72). In 1982 he was appointed assoc. conductor of the London Phil. In 1983 he became principal guest conductor of the BBC Scottish Sym. Orch. in Glasgow. He was also principal conductor of the Ulster Orch. in Belfast (1985–89) and the Malmö Sym. Orch. (1985–91); in 1988 he was named principal guest conductor of the Royal Liverpool Phil. In 1994 he became chief conductor of the West Australian Sym. Orch. in Perth.

Handschin, Jacques (Samuel), eminent Swiss organist and musicologist; b. Moscow, April 5, 1886; d. Basel, Nov. 25, 1955. He studied organ in Moscow; in 1905 he studied mathematics and history at the Univ. of Basel; then went to Munich to pursue his academic studies; also studied organ and theory with Reger; he later attended some of the lectures in musicology given in Leipzig by Riemann and in Berlin by Hornbostel; took additional courses in organ with Straube in Leipzig and with Widor in Paris. Returning to Russia, he taught organ at the St. Petersburg Cons. (1909–20); gave numerous organ recitals in Russia, and promoted contemporary organ works by Russian composers, among them Glazunov and Taneyev; included these works in his anthology *Les Maîtres contemporains de l'orgue* (Paris, 1913–14). In 1920 he returned to Switzerland; in 1921 he received his Ph.D. from the Univ. of Basel with the diss. *Choralbearbeitungen und Kompositionen mit rhythmischem Text in der mehrstimmigen Musik des 13. Jahrhunderts*; completed his Habilitation there in 1924 with his *Über die mehrstimmige Musik der St. Martial-Epoche sowie die Zusammenhänge zwischen Notre Dame und St. Martial und die Zusammenhänge zwischen einem dritten Stil und Notre Dame und St. Martial*. In 1924 he became Privatdozent at the Univ. of Basel; later was a prof. of musicology there (1935–55). He also served as a church organist in Zürich and Basel. He was greatly esteemed for his erudition and the soundness of his analytical theories; he evolved philosophical principles of musical aesthetics seeking the rational foundations of the art. His most important work is *Der Toncharakter: Eine Einführung in die Tonpsychologie* (Zürich, 1948), which sets down his principles of musical aesthetics; other works include *La Musique de l'antiquité* (Paris, 1946) and *Musikgeschichte im Überblick* (Lucerne, 1948).

BIBL.: H. Oesch, *Gedenkschrift J. H.: Aufsätze und Bibliographie* (Bern and Stuttgart, 1957); H. Anglés et al., eds., *In memoriam J. H.* (Strasbourg, 1962); M. Maier, *J. H.s "Toncharakter": Zu den Bedingungen seiner Entstehung* (Stuttgart, 1991).

Handt, Herbert, American tenor and conductor; b. Philadelphia, May 26, 1926. He studied at the Juilliard School of Music in N.Y. and the Vienna Academy of Music, making his operatic debut at the Vienna State Opera (1949). After making his conducting debut in Rome (1960), he prepared performing eds. of rarely-heard Italian scores; he later settled in Lucca, where he was founder-director of the Associazione Musicale Lucchese, the Lucca Chamber Orch., and the Marlia International Festival.

Hann, Georg, Austrian bass-baritone; b. Vienna, Jan. 30, 1897; d. Munich, Dec. 9, 1950. He was a student of Lierhammer at the Vienna Academy of Music. From 1927 until his death he was a member of the Bavarian State Opera in Munich; he also made guest appearances in Vienna, Berlin, Salzburg, London, Milan, and Paris. He was noted for such buffo portrayals as Leporello, Nicolai's Falstaff, Kecal, Baron Ochs, and La Roche, which he created (Munich, Oct. 28, 1942); his admired dramatic roles included Sarastro, Pizarro, Amfortas, Gunther, and Rigoletto.

Hannan, Michael (Francis), Australian composer, pianist, teacher, and writer on music; b. Newcastle, New South Wales, Nov. 19, 1949. Endowed by nature and intellectual inheritance (his father was a mathematician), he easily obtained the requisite degrees at the Univ. of Sydney (B.A., 1972; Ph.D., 1979). He plunged headlong into the wilderness of ultramodern music, absorbing the novel tonal, metric, and rhythmic innovations with easy penetration, adorning his own works with engaging titles, such as *Riff Madness* for Jazz Piano, borrowing concepts from oriental philosophy as in *Zen Variations*, or geometric art forms as in *Improvisatory Mobiles* and occasionally indulging in iconoclastic fantasies as in *Beethoven Deranged*. Yet advanced logic reigns in all of his creations and recreations. An excellent pianist, he is able to give a full account of modern pieces in his repertoire. As an instructor, he held positions at the Univ. of Sydney, the New South Wales and Queensland Cons. of Music, and the Northern Rivers College of Advanced Education (later Southern Cross Univ.) in Lismore, New South Wales (from 1986), where he became head of the Performing Arts and Music Divisions (1987). He traveled to California in 1983 on a Fulbright fellowship, and was a visiting prof. at the Univ. of Southern Calif. in 1990. Exceptionally gifted for the exploration of tonal, polytonal, and atonal techniques of composition, Hannan also possesses a saving grace of humor, as revealed in such works, recorded on electronic tape, as *Alphabeat* [sic] and *Slonimsky Variations*. In his purely scholarly pursuits, he compiled the section on musical terms to the *Macquarie Dictionary* (1981). He also contributed essays on Australian music to various publications and compiled the critical biography *Peter Sculthorpe: His Music and Ideas, 1929–79* (1982).

WORKS: CHAMBER: *Eliza Survivor* for Speaker, Piano, Flute, and Live Electronics (1978); *Garland Piece* for Large Ensemble (1979); *Occasional Medley* for String Quartet (1981); *Island Song* for Large Recorder Ensemble, Percussion, and Organ (1983); *Interaction I* for Ensemble (1987). **PIANO:** *Piano Collage I* (1978) and *II* (1979) for Piano and Tapes; *7 Studies for Single Hands* (1981); *Riff Madness* for Jazz Pianist (1981); *3 Improvisatory Mobiles* (1981); *Zen Variations* (1982); *3 Meditations for Dane Rudhyar* (1983–84); *Resonances I* (1986–87), *II* (1989), *III* (1992), and *IV* (1994–95); *Beethoven Deranged* (1987); *Mysterious Flowers* (1990); *Minimal Study I* (1990); *Homage to Chopin* (1990–91); *Mood Variations* (1991). **OTHER:** *Bracefell's Story* for Voice and Piano (1990); *Haka I* for Vocal Ensemble (1992); numerous works with dancers.

Hannay, Roger D(urham), talented American composer; b. Plattsburg, N.Y., Sept. 22, 1930. He studied composition with F. Morris and D. Newlin at Syracuse Univ. (1948–52), H. Norden at Boston Univ. (1952–53), Rogers and Hanson at the Eastman School of Music in Rochester, N.Y. (1954–56; Ph.D., 1956), and Foss and Copland at the Berkshire Music Center at Tanglewood (summer, 1959); had sessions with Sessions and attended lectures by Carter at the Princeton Seminar for Advanced Studies (1960). He taught at various colleges; in 1966, joined the music faculty of the Univ. of North Carolina at Chapel Hill; was founder and director of the New Music Ensemble (1967–82), and also served as chairman of the Division of Fine Arts there (1979–82). An unprejudiced and liberal music-maker, Hannay makes use of varied functional resources, from neo-Classical pandiatonism to dodecaphony; resorts also to the device of "objets trouvés," borrowing thematic materials from other composers.

WORKS: DRAMATIC: *2 Tickets to Omaha, The Swindlers*, chamber opera (1960); *The Fortune of St. Macabre*, chamber opera (1964); *Marshall's Medium Message* for Mod Girl Announcer, Percussion Quartet, 2 Action Painters, Tape, Films, and Slides (1967); *Live and in Color!* for Mod Girl Announcer, Percussion Quartet, 2 Action Painters, Tape, Films, and Slides (1967); *The Inter-Planetary Aleatoric Serial Factory* for Soprano, String Quartet, Rock Band, Actors, Dancers, Tapes, Film, and Slides (1969); *The Journey of Edith Wharton*, opera (1982); *The Nightingale and the Rose*, theater piece (1986); *Dates and Names*, monodrama for Soprano and Piano, after original and adapted texts from *Baker's Biographical Dictionary of Musicians* (1991). **ORCH.:** 7 syms.: No. 1 (1953; rev. 1973), No. 2 (1956), No. 3, *The Great American Novel*, with Chorus and Tape-recorded Sound (1976–77), No. 4, *American Classic* (1977), No. 5 (1987–88), No. 6 (1992), and No. 7 (1994–95); *Dramatic Overture*, homage to Schoenberg (1955); *Lament* for Oboe and Strings (1957); Sym. for Band (1963); *Sonorous Image* (1968); *Fragmentation* for Orch. or Chamber Orch. (1969); *Listen* (1971; Greensboro, N.C., July 7, 1973); *Celebration* for Tape and Orch. (N.Y., May 19, 1975); *Suite-Billings* for Youth Orch. (1975); *American Colonial* for Concert Band (1979); *Introduction and Allegro* for Symphonic Band (1981); *Pastorale*, "from Olana," for Horn and Strings (1982); *The Age of Innocence*, suite arranged from *The Journey of Edith Wharton* (1983); *A Farewell to Leonard Bernstein* for Chamber Ensemble (1990); *Vikingrwest*, tone poem (1993). **CHAMBER:** Sonata for Brass Ensemble (1957); *Divertimento* for Wind Quintet (1958); *Concerto da camera* for Recorder, Violin, Viola, Cello, Harpsichord, and Soprano (1958; rev. 1975); 4 string quartets: No. 1 (1962), No. 2, *Lyric* (1962), No. 3, *Designs* (1963), and No. 4, *Quartet of Solos* (1974; comprising the simultaneous perfs. of the 4 solo pieces *Grande Concerte, 2nd Fiddle, O Solo Viola*, and *Concert Music*); *Spectrum* for Brass Quintet (1964); *Structure* for Percussion Ensemble (1965; rev. 1974); *Squeeze Me* for Chamber Ensemble and Film (1970); *4 for 5* for Brass Quintet (1973); *Oh Friends!* for Chamber Wind Ensemble and Pitched Percussion (1976); *Festival Trumpets* for 10 Trumpets and Conductor (1978); Duo for Percussion and Electronic Tape (1978); *Nocturnes*, woodwind quintet (1979); Trumpet Sonata (1980); *La Ronde* for Flute, Clarinet, Cello, and Piano (1980); *Ode for an Election Evening Concert* for Flute and Piano (1980); Suite for Flute, Clarinet, Cello, and Piano (1981); *Masquerade* for Synthesizer (1982); *Posthaste* for Clarinet (1982); *Addendum* for Oboe and Piano (1982); *Souvenir* for Flute, Clarinet, Violin, Cello, Percussion, Piano, and Conductor (1984); *Trio-Rhapsody* for Flute, Cello, and Piano (1984); *Sic Transit Spiritus* for Wind Ensemble (1985); *Ye Musick for the Globe Theatre* for Brass and Percussion (1985); *Pavane* for Flute, Oboe, and Guitar (1986); *Consorting Together* for Viola da Gamba Consort (1986); *Souvenir II* for Flute, Clarinet, Violin, Cello, and Piano (1986); *Modes of Discourse* for Flute, Violin, and Cello (1988). **PIANO:** Suite (1954); *Abstractions* (1962); Sonata (1964); *Sonorities* (1966); *The Episodic Refraction* for Tape and Piano (1971); *Mere Bagatelle* for Piano, 4-hands, and Synthesizer (1978); *Serenade* for Piano and Synthesizer (1979); *Dream Sequence* for Piano and Electronic Tape (1980); *Luminere* (1988). **VOCAL:** *Cantata* (1952); *Requiem*, after Whitman's *When Lilacs Last in the Dooryard Bloom'd* (1961); *The Fruit of Love* for Soprano and Piano or Chamber Orch., after Edna St. Vincent Millay (1964–69); *Sayings for Our Time* for Chorus and Orch., after a text from the "current news media" (Winston-Salem, N.C., Aug. 2, 1968); *Tuonelan Joutsen* for Soprano, English Horn, and Film, after Silbelius's *Swan of Tuonela* (1972); choruses; songs.

Hannikainen, distinguished family of Finnish musicians:

(1) Pekka (or **Pietari) (Juhani),** conductor and composer; b. Nurmes, Dec. 9, 1854; d. Helsinki, Sept. 13, 1924. He was self-taught; was active as a choral conductor and teacher of choral singing in Helsinki; wrote a number of choral works and songs that became popular in his native country. His wife, Alli (née Laura Alfhild; b. Helsinki, June 21, 1867; d. there, April 12, 1949), was a teacher of singing and conductor of a women's choir. Their sons also became prominent musicians:

(2) (Toivo) Ilmari, pianist and composer; b. Jyväskylä, Oct. 19, 1892; d. Kuhmoinen, July 25, 1955. He studied piano and composition at the Helsinki music school (1911–13); then with Schreker in Vienna (1913–14) and Siloti and Steinberg in Petrograd (1916–17). He made his debut in Helsinki in 1914 and later toured with his brothers Tauno (Heikki) and Arvo (Sakari) in a trio; also taught piano at his alma mater and then at the Sibelius Academy (1939–55). He wrote a folk play, *Talkoottanssit* (1930); a Piano Concerto; a Piano Quartet; and many pieces for solo piano.

(3) Tauno (Heikki), cellist and conductor; b. Jyväskylä, Feb. 26, 1896; d. Helsinki, Oct. 12, 1968. He studied cello with O. Forström in Helsinki, making his debut there as a soloist in 1920; then took lessons with Casals in Paris (1921). After making his conducting debut in 1921, he served as conductor of the Finnish Opera in Helsinki until 1927; also played in a trio with his brothers (Toivo) Ilmari and Arvo (Sakari). He was conductor of the Turku Sym. Orch. (1929–39); then went to the U.S., where he was music director of the Duluth (Minn.) Sym. Orch. (1942–46). Subsequently he was conductor of the Chicago Civic Orch. (1947–50), as well as assistant conductor (1947–49) and assoc. conductor (1949–50) of the Chicago Sym. Orch. From 1950 to 1963 he was conductor of the Helsinki Phil.

(4) Arvo (Sakari), violinist and conductor; b. Jyväskylä, Oct. 11, 1897; d. Helsinki, Jan. 8, 1942. He studied violin in Helsinki (1915–17), in Berlin and Weimar (1920–23), with Thibaud and Ysaÿe in Paris, and with Jacobsen in Berlin (1931). In 1917 he became a member of the Helsinki orch., then 1st violinist in 1923; he also played in a trio with his brothers (Toivo) Ilmari and Tauno (Heikki). He taught at the Sibelius Academy, and was conductor of its student orch.

(5) Väinö (Aatos), harpist and composer; b. Jyväskylä, Jan. 12, 1900; d. Kuhmoinen, Aug. 7, 1960. He studied in Helsinki and Berlin. He was 1st harpist in the Helsinki orch. (1923–57). He wrote several symphonic poems, a Harp Concerto, a Harp Sonata, and songs.

Hanson, Howard (Harold), eminent American composer, music educator, and conductor; b. Wahoo, Nebr., Oct. 28, 1896; d. Rochester, N.Y., Feb. 26, 1981. After obtaining a diploma from Luther College in Wahoo (1911), he studied with Goetschius at the Inst. of Musical Art in N.Y. (1914) and with Oldberg and Lutkin at Northwestern Univ. in Evanston, Ill. (B.A., 1916). In 1915–16 he was an assistant teacher at Northwestern Univ. In 1916 he became a teacher of theory and composition at the College of the Pacific in San Jose, California, where he was made dean of its Cons. of Fine Arts in 1919. In 1921 he received the Rome Prize for his *California Forest Play of 1920.* During his stay at the American Academy in Rome, he received training in orchestration from Respighi and composed his first major work, the Sym. No. 1, *Nordic,* which he conducted in its premiere on May 17, 1923. Returning to the U.S., he conducted the premiere of his "symbolic" poem *North and West* with the N.Y. Sym. Orch. in Jan. 1924. In subsequent years, Hanson appeared often as a guest conductor throughout the U.S. and Europe championing not only his own music but numerous scores by other American composers. In 1924 he was appointed director of the Eastman School of Music in Rochester, N.Y., which he molded into one of the outstanding music schools of the U.S. As both a music educator and conductor, he proved profoundly influential. He promoted the cause of music education through his energetic work with many national organizations, among them the Music Teachers National Assn., of which he was president (1930–31), the Music Educators National Conference, the National Assn. of Schools of Music, and the National Music Council, of which he was founder-president. From 1925 to 1935 he conducted a series of American Composers' Concerts, and from 1935 to 1971 he was director of the Festivals of American Music. For the 50th anniversary of the Boston Sym. Orch., Hanson was commissioned to compose his Sym. No. 2, *Romantic.* Koussevitzky conducted its premiere on Nov. 28, 1930, and the score remains Hanson's most famous orch. work. His opera *Merry Mount* was first heard in a concert performance under the composer's direction in Ann Arbor on May 20, 1933. It received its stage premiere at the Metropolitan Opera in N.Y. on Feb. 10, 1934. While it failed to find a place in the operatic repertoire, an orch. suite (1936) won favor. Hanson's Sym. No. 4, *The Requiem,* was composed in memory of his father. The composer conducted its first performance with the Boston Sym. Orch. on Dec. 3, 1943. In 1944 it was awarded the Pulitzer Prize in Music. Hanson remained as director of the Eastman School of Music until 1964, the year he founded the Inst. of American Music. In 1935 he was elected a member of the National Inst. of Arts and Letters. In 1979 he was elected a member of the Academy of the American Academy and Inst. of Arts and Letters. He also received many other notable honors, including various awards and numerous honorary doctorates. As a composer, Hanson eschewed serialism and other modern techniques to pursue a neo-Romantic course. While much has been made of the influence of Grieg and especially of Sibelius on his works, his compositions remain basically true to the American spirit. At his most inspired, Hanson's oeuvre displays an array of sonorous harmonies, bold asymmetrical rhythms, and an overall mastery of orchestration one would expect of a remarkable compositional craftsman.

WORKS: DRAMATIC: *California Forest Play of 1920* (1919; Calif. State Redwood Park, July 1920, composer conducting); *Merry Mount,* opera (1933; concert perf., Ann Arbor, May 20, 1933, composer conducting; stage perf., N.Y., Feb. 10, 1934, Serafin conducting; suite, N.Y., March 23, 1936, Iturbi conducting); *Nymphs and Satyr,* ballet (Chautauqua, N.Y., Aug. 9, 1979). **ORCH.:** *Symphonic Prelude* (1916); *Concerto da camera* for Piano and Strings (1916–17; Rome, April 1922; also for Piano and String Quartet); *Symphonic Legend* (1917; incorporated with *Symphonic Rhapsody* to form *Legend and Rhapsody*); *Symphonic Rhapsody* (1919; Los Angeles, May 26, 1921, composer conducting; incorporated with *Symphonic Legend* to form *Legend and Rhapsody); Before the Dawn* (1919–20); *March Carillon* (1920; arranged from *2 Yuletide Pieces* for Piano); *Exaltation* (1920; also for 2 Pianos and Small Ensemble); 7 syms.: No. 1, *Nordic* (1922; Rome, May 17, 1923, composer conducting), No. 2, *Romantic* (1928–30; Boston, Nov. 28, 1930, Koussevitzky conducting), No. 3 (1937–38; NBC, N.Y., March 15, 1938, composer conducting; rev. with wordless choral finale, 1957), No. 4, *The Requiem* (1940–43; Boston, Dec. 3, 1943, composer conducting), No. 5, *Sinfonia Sacra* (1954; Philadelphia, Feb. 18, 1955, Ormandy conducting), No. 6 (N.Y., Feb. 28, 1968, composer conducting), and No. 7, *A Sea Symphony* for Chorus and Orch., after Whitman (Interlochen, Mich., Aug. 7, 1977, composer conducting); *North and West,* "symbolic" poem with chorus obbligato (1923; N.Y., Jan. 1924, composer conducting); Concerto for Organ, Strings, and Harp (1923; CBS, Aug. 29, 1943; based on *North and West*); *Lux Aeterna,* symphonic poem with viola obbligato (1923; also for Viola and String Quartet); *Pan and Priest,* symphonic poem with piano obbligato (1925–26; London, Oct. 26, 1926); Organ Concerto (1926; Rochester, N.Y., Gleason organist, composer conducting; based on the Concerto for Organ, Strings, and Harp); *Fantasy* for Strings (1939–43; also as Quartet in 1 Movement); *Variations on a Theme by Eugene Goossens* (1944; Cincinnati, March 23, 1945, Goossens conducting; with 9 other composers); *Serenade* for Flute, Harp, and Strings (Boston, Oct. 25, 1945, Koussevitzky conducting); Piano Concerto (Boston, Dec. 31, 1948, Firkušný pianist, Koussevitzky conducting); *Pastorale* for Oboe, Strings, and Harp (1948–49; Philadelphia, Oct. 20, 1950, Ormandy conducting; also for Oboe and Piano); *Symphony of Freedom* (Cleveland, April 1, 1949, composer conducting); *Fantasy Variations on a Theme of Youth* for Piano and Strings (Evanston, Ill., Feb. 18, 1951); *Elegy* or *Elegy in Memory of Serge Koussevitzky* (1955; Boston, Jan. 20, 1956, Munch conducting); *Mosaics* (Cleveland, Jan. 23, 1958, Szell conducting); *Summer Seascape* (1958–59; New Orleans, March 10, 1959, composer conducting; incorporated in *Bold Island Suite*); *Bold Island Suite* (1961; Cleveland, Jan. 25, 1962, Szell conducting; incorporates *Summer Seascape*); *For the First Time* (1962; Rochester, N.Y., May 16, 1963, composer conducting; also for Piano); *Summer Seascape II* for Viola and Strings (1965; Raleigh, N.C., April 20, 1966; also for Viola and String Quartet); *Dies Natalis* (1967; Omaha, May 1968); *Fanfare and Chorale* (Cincinnati, Feb. 20, 1976; also for Concert Band);

Rhythmic Variations on 2 Ancient Hymn Tunes for Strings (Interlochen, Mich., Aug. 7, 1977). **CONCERT BAND:** *Chorale and Alleluia* (West Point, N.Y., Feb. 26, 1954); *Centennial March* (Columbus, Ohio, Jan. 6, 1967); *Dies Natalis II* (Rochester, N.Y., April 7, 1972, Hunsberger conducting); *Young People's Guide to the 6-tone Scale* for Piano and Concert Band (Rochester, N.Y., Nov. 17, 1972, Hunsberger conducting); *4 French Songs* (c.1972); *Laude* (San Francisco, Feb. 7, 1975); *Fanfare and Chorale* (1976; also for Orch.); *Variations on an Ancient Hymn* (1977; also known as *Chorale Variations* for Wind Ensemble). **CHAMBER:** Piano Quintet (1916); *Concerto da camera* for Piano and String Quartet (1916–17; Pacific May Festival, May 1917; also for Piano and String Orch.); *Exaltation* for 2 Pianos and Small Ensemble (1920; also for Orch. with piano obbligato); Quartet in 1 Movement (1923; Washington, D.C., Oct. 30, 1925; also for *Fantasy* for String Orch.); *Lux Aeterna* for Viola and String Quartet (1923; also for Viola and Orch.); *Festival Fanfare* for 4 Horns, 3 Trumpets, 3 Trombones, Tuba, and Timpani (1937–38; Rochester, N.Y., April 28, 1938, composer conducting); *Fanfare for the Signal Corps* for 4 Horns, 3 Trumpets, 3 Trombones, Tuba, Timpani, and Percussion (1942); *Pastorale* for Oboe and Piano (1948–49; also for Oboe, Strings, and Harp); *Summer Seascape II* for Viola and String Quartet (1965; Washington, D.C., April 7, 1966; also for Viola and String Orch.); *Elegy* for Viola and String Quartet (1966). **PIANO:** *Prelude and Double Fugue* for 2 Pianos (1915); *4 Poems* (1917); Sonata (1917; San Jose, Calif., April 7, 1919); *Scandinavian Suite* (1918–19); *Clog Dance* (1919); *3 Miniatures* (1918–19); *3 Etudes* (1919); *2 Yuletide Pieces* (1919); *Enchantment* (1935); *Dance of the Warriors* (1935); *The Bell* (1942); *For the First Time* (1962; also for Orch.); *The Big Bell and the Little Bell* (1964); *Horn Calls in the Forest* (1964); *Tricks or Treats* (1964). **VOCAL:** *The Lament for Beowulf* for Chorus and Orch. (1925; Ann Arbor, 1926); *Heroic Elegy* for Chorus and Orch. (1927); (3) *Songs from "Drum Taps,"* after Whitman, for Baritone, Chorus, and Orch. (Ann Arbor, May 15, 1935, composer conducting); *Hymn for the Pioneers (Banbrytarhymn)* for Men's Chorus (Wilmington, Del., June 10, 1938); *The Cherubic Hymn* for Chorus and Orch. (1949; Rochester, N.Y., May 11, 1950, composer conducting); *Centennial Ode* for Baritone, Speaker, Chorus, and Orch. (Rochester, N.Y., June 10, 1950, composer conducting); *How Excellent Thy Name* for Women's Chorus and Piano (1952); *The Song of Democracy* for Chorus and Orch. (Washington, D.C., April 9, 1957, composer conducting); *Creator of Infinities Beyond Our Earth* for Chorus (Rochester, N.Y., Oct. 23, 1960); *Song of Human Rights* for Chorus and Orch. (Washington, D.C., Dec. 10, 1963); *4 Psalms* for Baritone, Cello, and String Quartet (Washington, D.C., Oct. 31, 1964); *One Hundred Fiftieth Psalm* for Men's Chorus (1965; also for Mixed Chorus and Piano or Organ; incorporated in *2 Psalms*); *One Hundred Twenty-first Psalm* for Alto or Baritone and Chorus (1968; incorporated in *2 Psalms*); *2 Psalms* for Alto or Baritone, Chorus, and Orch. (1968); *Streams in the Desert* for Chorus and Orch. (Lubbock, Texas, May 18, 1969, composer conducting); *The Mystic Trumpeter* for Chorus, Narrator, and Orch. (Kansas City, Mo., April 22, 1970); *Lumen in Christo* for Chorus and Orch. (Rochester, N.Y., Oct. 15, 1974; also for Women's Chorus and Orch.); *A Prayer of the Middle Ages* for Chorus (1976; also as *Hymn of the Middle Ages*); *New Land, New Covenant* for Soprano, Baritone, Narrator, Chorus, Optional Children's Chorus, Organ, and Small Orch. (Bryn Mawr, Pa., May 2, 1976); songs.

WRITINGS: *Harmonic Materials of Modern Music: Resources of the Tempered Scale* (N.Y., 1960).

BIBL.: E. Royce, "H. H.," in H. Cowell, *American Composers on American Music* (Stanford, 1933); B. Tuthill, "H. H.," *Musical Quarterly* (April 1936); M. Alter, "H. H.," *Modern Music* (Jan.–Feb. 1941); R. Watanabe, "H. H.'s Manuscript Scores," *University of Rochester Library Bulletin* (Winter 1950); idem, *Music of H. H.* (Rochester, N.Y., 1966); R. Monroe, *H. H.: American Music Educator* (diss., Florida State Univ., 1970); A. Caruine, *The Choral Music of H. H.* (diss., Univ. of Texas, 1977); B. Wehrung, "A Life in American Music," *Le Grand Baton* (March 1981; with discography by N. Brown); J. Perone, *H. H.: A Bio-Bibliography* (Westport, Conn., 1993).

Hanson-Dyer, Louise (née **Dyer**), Australian music publisher and recording executive; b. Melbourne, July 16, 1884; d. Monaco, Nov. 9, 1962. She went to Paris, where she founded the publishing firm L'Oiseau-Lyre (Lyrebird Press) in 1932. It became well known for publishing limited editions of music ranging from the medieval period to Couperin. About 1938 she also began to make recordings devoted to medieval, Renaissance, and Baroque music. Later her recording enterprise became part of the British Decca recording company, which in turn became a part of the Polygram group.

BIBL.: J. Davidson, *Lyrebird Rising: L. H.-D. of L'Oiseau-Lyre, 1884–1962* (Portland, Oreg., 1994).

Hanuš, Jan, Czech composer; b. Prague, May 2, 1915. He became a composition student of Jeremiáš in 1934; he also studied conducting at the Prague Cons. with Dědeček (1935–37; 1939–41). He worked as an ed. in music publishing houses and was active in Czech music organizations. His music is marked by a lyrical Romanticism tinged by stringent dissonant textures. Hanuš completed the instrumentations of the unfinished operas *Tkalci* by Nejedlý and *Balada o lásce* by Doubrava.

WORKS: DRAMATIC: OPERAS: *Plameny* (Flames; 1942–44); *Sluha dvou pánů* (Servant of 2 Masters; 1958); *Pochodeň Prométheova* (Torch of Prometheus; 1961–63); *Pohádka jedné noci* (Story of 1 Night; 1961–68). **BALLETS;** *Sůl nad zlato* (Salt is Worth More than Gold; 1953); *Othello* (1955–56); *Labyrint* (1981). **ORCH.:** 7 syms. (1942, 1951, 1957, 1960, 1965, 1978, 1990); *The Eulogy*, sinfonietta for Soprano and Orch. (1945); Concertante Symphony for Organ, Harp, Timpani, and Strings (1953–54); *Petr a Lucie*, fantasy (1955); Overture after Whitman's *The Bugler's Secret* (1961); Double Concerto for Oboe, Harp, and Orch. (1965); *Relay Race* (1968); *Musica Concertante* for Cello, Piano, Winds, and Percussion (1969–70); Concerto Grosso for Large Wind Orch. (1971); *Pražská nokturna* for Chamber Orch. (1972–73); *3 Essays* (1975–76); *Variations and Collage* (1982–83); *Concerto-fantasia* for Cello and Orch. (1990–91). **CHAMBER:** *Fantasy* for String Quartet (1939); Sonata-Rhapsody for Cello and Piano (1941); Suite to Paintings by Manes for Violin and Piano (1948); *Serenata semplice* for Nonet (1953; rev. 1970); *Suita dramatica* for String Quartet (1959); Piano Trio, *Frescoes* (1961); *Suita domestica* for Wind Quintet (1964); Concertino for 2 Percussionists and Tape (1972); *Sonata Seria* for Violin and Percussion (1974); *Sonata Variata* for Clarinet (1976); *Tower Music* for Brass Quintet (1976); *In Praise of Chamber Music*, sextet for Flute, Oboe, Violin, Viola, Cello, and Harpsichord (1979); *Lyric Triptych* for String Quartet (1987–88); piano pieces; organ music. **VOCAL:** 7 masses (1943; 1950; 1954; 1959; 1966; 1972–73; 1985); *The Message* for Baritone, Chorus, 2 Prepared Pianos, Electric Guitar, Percussion, and Tape (1969); *The Swallows*, concerto piccolo for Chorus, Flute, and Cello (1973); *The Passion According to Matthew* for Solo Voices and Chorus (1977–78); *Ecce Homo*, oratorio (1980); *The Passion According to John* for Solo Voices and Chorus (1982); cantatas; choruses; songs.

Hanuszewska-Schaeffer, Mieczyslawa Janina, Polish writer on music; b. Borszów, Oct. 1, 1929. She studied musicology with Jachimecki at the Jagiello Univ. in Kraków (1948–52). In 1963 she joined the staff of Kraków's *Zycie Literackie*, producing a weekly chronicle on the world's music. She has written extensively on modern music, including detailed studies on Ives, Messiaen, and the early works of Boulez. She was a contributor to *Wielka Encyklopedia Muzyczna* and *The New Grove Dictionary of Music and Musicians* (1980). With her husband, **Boguslaw Schaeffer**, she ed. *Almanach współszesnych kompozytorów polskich* (Almanac of Modern Polish Composers; Kraków, 1966; new ed., 1989); she also ed. *1000 kompozytorów* (1,000 Composers; 5th ed., Kraków, 1986).

Haquinius, (Johan) Algot, Swedish pianist, teacher, and composer; b. Stockholm, July 30, 1886; d. there, Feb. 6, 1966. He studied piano with Hilda Thegerstrom and Lennart Lundberg and composition with Ernst Ellberg at the Stockholm Cons. (1898–1906); then pursued training in composition with Johan Lindegren and piano with Moszkowski in Paris and Friedman in Berlin. He had a distinguished career as a pianist in Sweden; also taught. In 1941 he became a member of the Swedish Royal Academy of Music. His works, which include orch. pieces, chamber music, piano pieces, and songs, effectively combine Romantic and expressionist elements.

Harasowski, Adam, Polish pianist and writer on music; b. Delatyn, Sept. 16, 1904. He was brought up in a musical family. He studied at the Lwów Cons. with Adam Soltys (1923–29); also took private lessons in composition with Szymanowski during his frequent visits at Lwów. Concurrently he studied mechanical engineering, graduating from the Lwów Polytechnic in 1931, and subsequently earned his living mainly as an engineering draftsman. At the outbreak of World War II, he went to England with the Polish Air Force, and remained with the Royal Air Force of Great Britain as a flight lieutenant (1943–58); then devoted himself to journalism, both in Polish and in English. He publ. *The Skein of Legends around Chopin* (Glasgow, 1967); also compiled collections of Polish songs.

Harašta, Milan, Czech composer; b. Brno, Sept. 16, 1919; d. there, Aug. 29, 1946. He studied musicology at the Univ. of Brno before taking a course in composition with Kaprál at the Brno Cons. (1938–42). His music, written in a forward-looking, post-Janáček style, included the opera *Nikola Šuhaj* (1941–44), 3 syms. (the last unfinished), vocal music, and piano pieces.

BIBL.: M. Barík, *M. H.* (Prague, 1956).

Harászti, Emil, Hungarian musicologist; b. Nagyvárad, Nov. 1, 1885; d. Paris, Dec. 27, 1958. He was a pupil of Albert Geiger (piano) and Edmund Farkas (composition), and also pursued his academic education at the Univ. of Budapest (Ph.D., 1907; Habilitation, 1917), where he taught musicology from 1917; he also was director of the Budapest Cons. (1918–27). In 1945 he settled in Paris.

WRITINGS: *Hubay Jenő élete és munkái* (Jenő Hubay: His Life and Works; Budapest, 1913); *Wagner Rikárd és Magyarország* (Richard Wagner and Hungary; Budapest, 1916); *Schallnachahmung und Bedeutungswandel in der Instrumentenkunde mit Rücksicht auf die ungarische Organographie* (Budapest, 1928); *A zenei formák története* (The History of Musical Structure; Budapest, 1930); *Bartók Béla* (Béla Bartók; Budapest, 1930); *La musique hongroise* (Paris, 1933); *Béla Bartók: His Life and Works* (Paris, 1938); *Un Centenaire romantique: Berlioz et la Marche Hongroise d'après des documents inédits* (Paris, 1946); *Franz Liszt* (Paris, 1967).

Harbison, John (Harris), esteemed American composer, conductor, and teacher; b. Orange, N.J., Dec. 20, 1938. He studied violin, viola, piano, tuba, and voice while attending Princeton (N.J.) High School. During this time, he also profited from advice from Sessions and developed a facility as a jazz pianist. At 16, he won an award in a BMI composition contest. He pursued his education with Piston at Harvard Univ. (B.A., 1960), Blacher at the Berlin Hochschule für Musik (1961), and Sessions and Kim at Princeton Univ. (M.F.A., 1963). He also attended the conducting courses of Carvalho at the Berkshire Music Center in Tanglewood and of Dean Dixon in Salzburg. In 1968–69 he was composer-in-residence at Reed College in Portland, Oreg. In 1969 he joined the faculty of the Mass. Inst. of Technology. He also conducted the Cantata Singers and Ensemble (1969–73; 1980–82), and then the new music group Collage (from 1984). He was composer-in-residence of the Pittsburgh Sym. Orch. (1982–84) and of the Berkshire Music Center in Tanglewood (summer, 1984). After serving as new music advisor of the Los Angeles Phil. (1985–86), he was its composer-in-residence (1986–88). In 1992 he returned to Tanglewood as composer-in-residence, and also served as director of its contemporary music festival. In 1978 he received a Guggenheim fellowship. In 1980 he won the Kennedy Center Friedheim Award for his Piano Concerto. He was awarded the Pulitzer Prize in Music in 1986 for his sacred ricercar *The Flight Into Egypt*. In 1989 he received a MacArthur fellowship. In 1992 he was elected to membership in the American Academy and Inst. of Arts and Letters. Harbison's works are distinguished by their outstanding craftsmanship, rhythmic intensity, and lyricism. His experience as a conductor has made him a master of orchestral resources. He has also demonstrated a rare sensitivity in setting vocal texts.

WORKS: DRAMATIC: *The Merchant of Venice*, incidental music to Shakespeare's play (1971; Francestown, N.H., Aug. 12, 1973); *Winter's Tale*, opera (1974; San Francisco, Aug. 20, 1979; rev. 1991); *Full Moon in March*, opera (1977; Cambridge, Mass., April 30, 1979); *Ulysses*, ballet (1983). **ORCH.:** Sinfonia for Violin and Double Orch. (1963; Cambridge, Mass., March 10, 1964); *Diotima* (1976; Boston, March 10, 1977); *Descant-Nocturne* (1976; New Hampshire Festival, July 14, 1980); Piano Concerto (1978; N.Y., May 12, 1980); Violin Concerto (1980; Boston, Jan. 24, 1981; rev. 1987); 3 syms.: No. 1 (1981; Boston, March 22, 1984), No. 2 (San Francisco, May 13, 1987), and No. 3 (1990; Baltimore, Feb. 28, 1991); *Ulysses' Bow* (1983; Pittsburgh, May 11, 1984); *Ulysses' Raft* (1983; New Haven, March 6, 1984); Concerto for Oboe, Clarinet, and Strings (Sarasota, Fla., June 14, 1985); *Remembering Gatsby: Foxtrot* (1985; Atlanta, Sept. 11, 1986); *Music* for 18 Winds (Cambridge, Mass., April 18, 1986, composer conducting); *Fanfare for Foley's* (Houston, Oct. 11, 1986); Concerto for Double Brass Choir and Orch. (1988; Los Angeles, April 26, 1990); Viola Concerto (1989; Bridgewater, N.J., May 18, 1990); *David's Fascinating Rhythm Method* (1990; Baltimore, Feb. 14, 1991); Oboe Concerto (1991; San Francisco, Dec. 3, 1992); *3 City Blocks* (1992; Fort Smith, Ark., Aug. 2, 1993); *The Most Often Used Chords: Gli accordi più usati* for Chamber Orch. (Los Angeles, Oct. 22, 1993); Cello Concerto (1993; Boston, April 7, 1994); *I, II, III, IV, V: Fantasia on a Ground* (Weston, Mass., April 3, 1993); Flute Concerto (1994; N.Y., Oct. 29, 1995). **CHAMBER:** Duo for Flute and Piano (N.Y., Aug. 20, 1961); Sonata for Solo Viola (1961); *Confinement* for Chamber Ensemble (1965; N.Y., Feb. 1967); *4 Preludes* for 3 Oboes or for Flute, Clarinet, Violin or Flute, Oboe, and Clarinet (1967; Cambridge, Mass., April 1969); *Serenade* for Flute, Clarinet, Bass Clarinet, Violin, Viola, and Cello (1968; Portland, Oreg., May 1969); Piano Trio (Cambridge, Mass., April 1969); *Bermuda Triangle* for Amplified Cello, Tenor Saxophone, and Electric Organ (1970; N.Y., April 1973); *Die Kürze* for Flute, Clarinet, Piano, Violin, and Cello (N.Y., Feb. 1970); *Amazing Grace* for Oboe (1972; N.Y., Jan. 1973); *Snow Country* for Oboe and String Quintet (1979; Boston, March 1981); Wind Quintet (Boston, April 15, 1979); *Organum for Paul Fromm* for Glockenspiel, Marimba, Vibraphone, Harp, and Piano (1981; Chicago, Jan. 1982); Piano Quintet (Santa Fe, Aug. 7, 1981); *Variations* for Clarinet, Violin, and Piano (Sante Fe, July 23, 1982); *Exequiem for Calvin Simmons* for Alto Flute, Bass Clarinet, Vibraphone, Piano, 2 Violas, and Cello (1982; Williamstown, Mass., Feb. 15, 1983); *Overture: Michael Kohlhaas* for Brass Ensemble (Madison, Wisc., Nov. 1982); 3 string quartets: No. 1 (Washington, D.C., Oct. 11, 1985), No. 2 (Boston, Nov. 20, 1987), and No. 3 (1993; Waltham, Mass., April 30, 1994); *Twilight Music* for Horn, Violin, and Piano (N.Y., March 22, 1985); *4 Songs of Solitude* for Violin (Cambridge, Mass., Dec. 11, 1985); *Magnum Mysterium* for Brass Quintet (Rochester, N.Y., Dec. 21, 1987); *2 Chorale Preludes for Advent* for Brass Quintet (1987; Rochester, N.Y., Dec. 24, 1989); *Fantasy Duo* for Violin and Piano (Washington, D.C., Dec. 2, 1988); *November 19, 1828* for Piano Quartet (1988; Atlanta, Nov. 30, 1989); *Little Fantasy on the 12 Days of Christmas* for Brass Quintet (1988; Rochester, N.Y., Dec. 24, 1989); *Nocturne* for Brass Quintet (N.Y., Dec. 1, 1989); *Fanfares and Reflection* for 2 Violins (1990; N.Y., March 26, 1992); *Variations (in first position)* for String Quartet (1992; Weston, Mass., April 3, 1993); *14 Fabled Folksongs* f or Violin and Marimba (1992); *Inventions for a Young Percussionist* (1992; Weston, Mass., April 3, 1993); Suite for Cello (1993). **PIANO:** *Parody Fantasia* (1968; N.Y., Jan. 1973); Sonata: *In Memoriam Roger Sessions* (1987;

Amherst, Mass., July 15, 1988); *3 Occasional Pieces* (1978; Cambridge, Mass., Oct. 3, 1987, composer pianist); *4 More Occasional Pieces* (1987–90; Boston, Nov. 17, 1991); *Inventions for a Young Pianist* (1992; Weston, Mass., April 3, 1993). **VOCAL:** *He Shall Not Cry* for Women's Chorus and Organ (1959; Princeton, N.J., Dec. 18, 1962); *Ave Maria* for Women's Chorus (1959; Boston, May 1960); *Autumnal* for Mezzo-soprano and Piano (1965); *Shakespeare Series*, sonnets for Mezzo-soprano and Piano (1965); *Music When Soft Voices Die* for Chorus and Harpsichord or Organ (1966); *5 Songs of Experience on Poems of William Blake* for Chorus, 2 Percussion, 2 Violins, Viola, and Cello (1971; Cambridge, Mass., Feb. 28, 1973, composer conducting); *Elegiac Songs* for Mezzo-soprano and Chamber Orch. (1974; N.Y., Jan. 12, 1975); *Book of Hours and Seasons* for Mezzo-soprano or Tenor, Flute, Cello, and Piano (1975; Cambridge, Mass., March 1976); *Moments of Vision* for Soprano, Tenor, and Renaissance Consort (1975; Amherst, Mass., Feb. 12, 1988); *3 Harp Songs* for Tenor and Harp (1975; Cambridge, Mass., Nov. 18, 1976); *Nunc Dimittis* for Men's Chorus (1975; Cambridge, Mass., Dec. 12, 1981); *The Flower-Fed Buffaloes* for Baritone, Chorus, and 7 Instrumentalists (1976; Boston, Feb. 27, 1978); *Samuel Chapter* for Soprano or Tenor and 6 Instrumentalists (Cambridge, Mass., Nov. 7, 1978, composer conducting); *Motetti di Montale* for Soprano and Piano (1980; Sante Fe, Aug. 4, 1981); *Mirabai Songs* for Soprano and Piano (1982; Boston, Nov. 15, 1983; also for Soprano and Chamber Ensemble, Cambridge, Mass., Feb. 1, 1984); *The Flight into Egypt*, sacred ricercar for Soprano, Baritone, Chorus, and Orch. (Boston, Nov. 21, 1986); *The Natural World* for Soprano or Mezzo-soprano and 5 Instrumentalists (1987; Los Angeles, Nov. 13, 1989, composer conducting); *Rot und Weiss* for Voice and 4 Instrumentalists (1987; Los Angeles, Feb. 1, 1988); *Christmas Vespers* for Reader and Brass Quintet (1988; Rochester, N.Y., Dec. 24, 1989); *The 3 Wise Men* for Reader and Brass Quintet (1988; Rochester, N.Y., Dec. 24, 1989); *Im Spiegel* for Voice, Violin, and Piano (Los Angeles, Nov. 7, 1988); *Simple Daylight* for Soprano and Piano (1988; San Francisco, May 22, 1990); *Words from Paterson* for Baritone and Chamber Ensemble (1989; Washington, D.C., May 9, 1990); *2 Emmanuel Motets* for Chorus (Boston, Dec. 17, 1990); *Ave Verum Corpus* for Chorus (1990; Boston, Jan. 3, 1991; also for Chorus and String Orch., Ojai, Calif., June 2, 1991, composer conducting); *O Magnum Mysterium* for Chorus (1991; Weston, Mass., April 3, 1993; expanded setting, Boston, Dec. 13, 1992); *Between 2 Worlds* for Soprano, 2 Pianos, and 2 Cellos (Chicago, July 27, 1991); *The Flute of Interior Time* for Baritone and Piano (1991; Berlin, Jan. 11, 1992); *The Rewaking* for Soprano and String Quartet (Pittsburgh, Oct. 14, 1991); *Communion Words* for Chorus (1993; Boston, Jan. 16, 1994); *Concerning Them Which Are Asleep* for Chorus (Boston, April 17, 1994).

d'Harcourt, Marguerite (née **Béclard**), French folk-song collector and composer; b. Paris, Feb. 24, 1884; d. there, Aug. 2, 1964. She studied composition with d'Indy and Emmanuel. She composed 2 syms., *Rapsodie péruvienne* for Oboe, Clarinet, and Bassoon, and many songs. With her husband, Raoul d'Harcourt, she publ. a valuable treatise, *Musique des Incas et ses survivances* (2 vols., Paris, 1925), based on materials gathered during their journeys in Peru; another valuable publication was her compilation of 240 songs, *Chansons folkloriques françaises au Canada* (Quebec, 1956).

Hardenberger, Håkan, Swedish trumpeter; b. Malmö, Oct. 27, 1961. He began trumpet lessons at the age of 8 with Bo Nilsson in Malmö; later pursued more extensive training with Pierre Thibaud at the Paris Cons. and with Thomas Stevens in Los Angeles; also received instruction from Dokshitscher in Moscow, Herseth in Chicago, and Tarr in Basel. He began performing while still a youth, making his solo debut with orch. when he was 15. After winning prizes in competitions in Paris, Munich, Toulon, and Geneva, he toured extensively in Europe and North and South America. His repertoire includes both standard and contemporary works.

Harding, A(lbert) A(ustin), American bandmaster; b. Georgetown, Ill., Feb. 10, 1880; d. Champaign, Ill., Dec. 3, 1958. At 14 he began to play cornet, then trombone and other wind instruments. After graduation from high school in Paris, Ill., he conducted the local concert band. In 1902 he enrolled as an engineering student at the Univ. of Ill. (B.A., 1906). At the same time, he developed many campus music contacts, and in 1905 was made acting leader of the Univ. Band; in 1907 he was appointed director, a post he held until 1948. Harding was the first to succeed in raising college bands to a "symphonic" level in which oboes, saxophones, and other reed instruments supplied variety to the common brass-heavy contingent; thanks to this sonic enhancement, he was able to arrange orch. works of the general repertoire and perform them in a satisfactory musical manner; he was credited with 147 such transcriptions. John Philip Sousa, who greatly admired Harding, bequeathed to him and his band his own entire music library. Harding was a charter founder of the American Bandmasters' Assn. in 1929 and was its president in 1937–38; was honorary life president from 1956 until his death. He also was active in founding the College Band Directors' Assn., of which he was honorary life president from its founding in 1941.

BIBL.: C. Weber, "A.A. H.: Pioneer College Bandmaster," *Journal of Band Research* (Autumn 1966).

Harewood, Sir George (Henry Hubert Lascelles), 7th Earl of, distinguished English arts administrator, music critic, and music editor; b. London, Feb. 7, 1923. He was educated at Eton and King's College, Cambridge. In 1950 he founded the journal *Opera*, of which he was ed. until 1953. He was on the board of directors of the Royal Opera at Covent Garden (1951–53; 1969–72), serving as its administrative executive (1953–60); was general-director of the Leeds Festival (1958–74), later serving as its chairman (1988–90); also was director of the Edinburgh Festivals (1961–65), and chancellor of the Univ. of York (1962–67). In 1972 he was appointed managing director of the Sadler's Wells Opera (known after 1974 as the English National Opera) in London; retained this position until 1985, and then was its chairman from 1986 to 1995. In 1988 he was artistic director of the Adelaide Festival. He was knighted in 1987. He ed. *Kobbé's Complete Opera Book* in 1954, 1963, and 1972; it was publ. as *The New Kobbé's Complete Opera Book* in 1976, then as *The Definitive Kobbé's Opera Book* (1987). His autobiography was publ. as *The Tongs and the Bones* (1982).

Harich-Schneider, Eta (Margarete), German musicologist and harpsichordist; b. Oranienburg, Nov. 16, 1897; d. Vienna, Oct. 16, 1986. She studied piano and musicology in Berlin, making her debut in 1924 with the first performance of Hindemith's *1922 Suite*. She then studied harpsichord with Landowska (1929–35), subsequently forming an early-music ensemble; then became a prof. at the Berlin Hochschule für Musik, but was dismissed in 1940 when she refused to join the Nazi party. She then fled to Tokyo, where she directed the music dept. of the U.S. Army College and also taught Western music at the imperial court (1947–49). After her move to N.Y. in 1949, she pursued Japanese studies at Columbia Univ.; she also took courses in sociology at the New School for Social Research (M.A., 1955). From 1955 to 1961 she taught harpsichord at the Vienna Academy of Music. She wrote important books on harpsichord technique and repertoire and on Japanese art music; also made notable recordings of works by the Baroque masters and of collections of Japanese music. She received a Guggenheim fellowship in 1955.

WRITINGS: *Die Kunst des Cembalospiels* (Kassel, 1939; 3rd ed., 1970); *Gendai ongaku to Nippon no sakkyokusha* (Contemporary Music and Japanese Composers; Tokyo, 1950); *The Harpsichord: An Introduction to Technique, Style and the Historical Sources* (Kassel, 1954; 3rd ed., 1973); *A History of Japanese Music* (London, 1973).

Harling, William Franke, English-American composer; b. London, Jan. 18, 1887; d. Sierra Madre, Calif., Nov. 22, 1958. He was taken to the U.S. in his infancy. He filled various jobs as a church organist. Eventually he settled in Hollywood. He wrote an opera, *A Light from St. Agnes* (Chicago, Dec. 26, 1925); *Deep River*, a "native opera with jazz" (Lancaster, Pa., Sept. 18, 1926); instrumental music; more than 100 songs. He was also the composer of the march *West Point Forever.*

Harman, Carter, American music critic, recording-firm executive, and composer; b. N.Y., June 14, 1918. He studied with Sessions at Princeton Univ. (B.A., 1940) and continued his studies at Columbia Univ. (M.A., 1949). He was a music critic for the *N.Y. Times* (1947–52) and later music ed. of *Time* magazine (1952–57); from 1958 to 1967 he lived in Puerto Rico, where he became president of the West Indies Recording Corp. In 1967 Harman became producer and executive vice-president of Composers Recordings, Inc., in N.Y., devoted mainly to recording contemporary American music; was its executive director from 1976 to 1984. He publ. *A Popular History of Music from Gregorian Chant to Jazz* (N.Y., 1956; rev. 1968). Among his compositions are the ballet *Blackface* (N.Y., May 18, 1947); 2 children's operas: *Circus at the Opera* (1951) and *Castles in the Sand* (1952); children's songs; and *Alex and the Singing Synthesizer*, an entertainment of electronically-synthesized nursery rhymes (1974–77).

Harmat, Artur, Hungarian composer; b. Nyitrabajna, June 27, 1885; d. Budapest, April 20, 1962. He studied at the Budapest Academy of Music and later took courses in Prague and Berlin. From 1920 to 1946 he was an inspector of singing in the Budapest schools; from 1924 to 1959 he was a prof. of religious music at the Budapest Academy of Music. He wrote 2 valuable manuals on counterpoint (1947, 1956) and composed a great quantity of church music, based on the lines of Palestrina's polyphony.

WORKS: *Te Deum* for Chorus and Organ (1912–29); *Tu es Petrus* for Chorus and Orch. (1929); *Psalm 150* for Chorus and Instruments (1929); *De Profundis* for Chorus (1932); *Szep Ilonka* (Fair Helen), cantata (1954); Organ Sonata (1956).

Harmati, Sândor, Hungarian-born American violinist, conductor, and composer; b. Budapest, July 9, 1892; d. Flemington, N.J., April 4, 1936. He studied at the Royal Academy of Music in Budapest. After serving as concertmaster of the Budapest Sym. Orch., he emigrated to the U.S. in 1914 and became a naturalized American citizen in 1920. He was a violinist in the Letz (1917–21) and Lenox (1922–25) string quartets, conductor of the Omaha Sym. Orch. (1925–30) and the Musicians' Sym. Orch. for the Unemployed in N.Y., and prof. of music at Bard College in Annandale-on-Hudson, N.Y. (1934–36). He wrote the opera *Prelude to a Melodrama* (1928); incidental music to *The Jeweled Tree* (1926); symphonic poem *Folio* (1922); String Quartet (1925); solo violin pieces; many songs, including *The Bluebird of Happiness* (1934), his best-known piece.

Harnoncourt, Nikolaus (in full, **Johann Nikolaus de la Fontaine und d'Harnoncourt-Unverzagt**), eminent Austrian cellist, conductor, and musicologist; b. Berlin, Dec. 6, 1929. His father, an engineer, also played the piano and composed; the family settled in Graz. He began to study the cello at the age of 9, later training with Paul Grümmer and at the Vienna Academy of Music with Emanuel Brabec. He was a cellist in the Vienna Sym. Orch. (1952–69); founded the Vienna Concentus Musicus (1953), which began giving concerts in 1957, playing on period instruments or modern copies. The group made its first tour of England, the U.S., and Canada in 1966. From the mid-1970s he also appeared internationally as a guest conductor, expanding his repertoire to include music of later eras. His writings include *Musik als Klangrede: Wege zu einem neuen Musikverständnis* (Salzburg and Vienna, 1982; Eng. tr., 1988, as *Baroque Music Today: Music as Speech; Ways to a New Understanding of Music*), *Der musikalische Dialog: Gedanken zu Monteverdi, Bach und Mozart* (Salzburg, 1984; Eng. tr., 1989, as *The Musical Dialogue: Thoughts on Monteverdi, Bach, and Mozart*), and *Die Macht der Musik: Zwei Reden* (Salzburg, 1993). His wife, Alice Harnoncourt (b. Vienna, Sept. 26, 1930), studied violin with Feist and Moraves in Vienna and with Thibaud in Paris; she became concertmistress of the Vienna Concentus Musicus at its founding.

Harnoy, Ofra, Israeli-born Canadian cellist; b. Hadera, Jan. 31, 1965. She began cello lessons at age 6 under her parents' guidance. After the family emigrated to Canada in 1972, she studied with Vladimir Orloff in Toronto; she also received instruction from William Pleeth in London and attended the master classes of Rostropovich, Fournier, and Du Pré. At age 10, she made her professional debut as soloist in a C. Stamitz concerto with Boyd Neel and his orch. in Toronto. In 1978 she won 1st prize in the Montreal Sym. Orch. competition, in 1979 the Canadian Music Competition, and in 1982 the Concert Artists Guild Award of N.Y. In 1981 she made her European debut in a London recital; her U.S. debut followed in 1982 as soloist in the Tchaikovsky *Rococo Variations* with the Shreveport (La.) Sym. Orch. That same year, she also made her Carnegie Recital Hall debut in N.Y. In 1983 she was soloist in the world premiere of a long-lost Cello Concerto by Offenbach in N.Y. Thereafter she appeared as a soloist with various orchs., as a recitalist, and as a chamber music artist.

Harper, Edward (James), English composer, pianist, and teacher; b. Taunton, March 17, 1941. After studies at Christ Church, Oxford (1959–63), he received instruction in composition from Gordon Jacob at the Royal College of Music in London (1963–64) and with Donatoni in Milan (1968). From 1964 he lectured on music at the Univ. of Edinburgh. He also was director of the New Music Group of Scotland (1973–91).

WORKS: OPERAS: *Fanny Robin* (1974; Edinburgh, Feb. 5, 1975); *Hedda Gabler* (1984–85; Glasgow, June 5, 1985); *The Mellstock Quire* (1987–88; Edinburgh, Feb. 10, 1988). **ORCH.:** Piano Concerto (1969; Edinburgh, Jan. 29, 1970); Sonata for Chamber Orch. (1971; Edinburgh, Feb. 25, 1973); *Bartók Games* (Edinburgh, Nov. 26, 1972); *Fantasia I* for Chamber Orch. (Edinburgh, March 27, 1976), *IV* for Violin, Piano, and Small Orch. (1980; St. Andrews, Feb. 26, 1981), and *V*, passacaglia for Chamber Orch. (St. Magnus Festival, June 24, 1985); *Fern Hill* for Chamber Orch. (1976; St. Andrews, Feb. 23, 1977); Sym. (1978–79; Edinburgh, March 1979); Clarinet Concerto (1981–82; Llandaff, June 3, 1982); *Intrada after Monteverdi* for Chamber Orch. (1982; Edinburgh, Oct. 6, 1983); Double Variations for Oboe, Bassoon, and Winds (Manchester, Aug. 12, 1989). **CHAMBER:** Quintet for Flute, Clarinet, Violin, Cello, and Piano (Glasgow, May 1974); *Ricercari in Memoriam Luigi Dallapiccola* for Chamber Group (Edinburgh, Aug. 30, 1975); *Fantasia II* for 11 Solo Strings (Dundee, April 21, 1976) and *III* for Brass Quintet (Edinburgh, Nov. 3, 1977); String Quartet No. 2 (London, Dec. 17, 1986); *In memoriam (Kenneth Leighton)* for Cello and Piano (Edinburgh, May 8, 1990). **VOCAL:** *7 Poems by e.e. cummings* for Soprano and Orch. (Glasgow, Nov. 1, 1977); *Chester Mass* for Mixed Voices and Orch. (Chester Cathedral, Oct. 20, 1979); *The Universe* for Chorus (1979); *Mass: Qui creavit coelum* for Double Chorus (1986; Oxford, May 28, 1987); *Homage to Thomas Hardy* for Baritone and Chamber Orch. (1989); *The Lamb* for Soprano, Chorus, and Orch. (Glasgow, Dec. 9, 1990).

Harper, Heather (Mary), distinguished Irish soprano; b. Belfast, May 8, 1930. She studied at Trinity College of Music in London and also took voice lessons with Helene Isepp and Frederic Husler. She made her debut as Lady Macbeth with the Oxford Univ. Opera in 1954. She was a member of the English Opera Group (1956–75); first sang at the Glyndebourne Festival in 1957, at Covent Garden as Helena in *A Midsummer Night's Dream* in 1962, and at the Bayreuth Festival as Elsa in 1967; also sang in the U.S. and South America. Although she formally retired as a singer in 1990, she sang with Rattle and the City of Birmingham Sym. Orch. at the London Proms in 1994. From 1985 she was a prof. at the Royal College of Music in London; she also was director of singing studies at the Britten-Pears

School in Snape (from 1986) and the first visiting lecturer-in-residence at the Royal Scottish Academy of Music in Glasgow (from 1987). Her notable roles included Arabella, Marguerite, Antonia, Gutrune, Hecuba, Anne Trulove in *The Rake's Progress*, The Woman in *Erwartung*, and Ellen Orford in *Peter Grimes*; she also created the role of Nadia in Tippett's *The Ice Break* (1977). An esteemed concert artist, she sang in the premieres of Britten's *War Requiem* (1962) and Tippett's 3rd Sym. (1972). In 1965 she was made a Commander of the Order of the British Empire.

Harrell, Lynn, outstanding American cellist and teacher, son of **Mack Harrell**; b. N.Y., Jan. 30, 1944. He studied at the Juilliard School of Music in N.Y. with Leonard Rose and at the Curtis Inst. of Music in Philadelphia with Orlando Cole; also attended master classes with Piatigorsky in Dallas (1962) and Casals in Marlboro, Vt. (1963). He made his debut at a young people's concert of the N.Y. Phil. in 1961; then was 1st cellist of the Cleveland Orch. (1965–71). In 1975 he was named co-recipient (with the pianist Murray Perahia) of the 1st Avery Fisher Prize. In succeeding years, he toured throughout the globe as a soloist with orchs., as a recitalist, and as a chamber music artist. He taught at the Univ. of Cincinnati College-Cons. of Music from 1971 to 1976; then joined the faculty of the Juilliard School in N.Y.; subsequently was appointed to the newly established Gregor Piatigorsky Chair at the Univ. of Southern Calif. in Los Angeles and to the International Chair of Cello Studies at the Royal Academy of Music in London in 1986, positions he retained until 1993 when he became principal of the latter. In 1995 he resigned his London position. His playing is marked by ingratiating tonal mellowness and a facile, unforced technical display.

Harrell, Mack, distinguished American baritone, father of **Lynn Harrell;** b. Celeste, Texas, Oct. 8,1909; d. Dallas, Jan. 29, 1960. He studied violin and voice at the Juilliard School of Music in N.Y. In 1938 he made his concert debut at N.Y.'s Town Hall. After winning the Metropolitan Opera Auditions in 1938, he made his debut with the company in N.Y. on Dec. 16, 1939, as Biterolf; he remained on the roster until 1948, and returned there for the 1949–50, 1952–54, and 1957–58 seasons. On May 18, 1944, he made his first appearance at the N.Y. City Opera as Germont, and returned there in 1948, 1951–52, and 1959. He also pursued a notably successful concert career. From 1945 to 1956 he taught voice at the Juilliard School of Music. He publ. *The Sacred Hour of Song* (N.Y., 1938). Harrell's voice was one of remarkable lyrical beauty. Among his operatic roles were Papageno, Kothner, Amfortas, Jochanaan, Wozzeck, and Nick Shadow in *The Rake's Progress*, which role he created in its U.S. premiere at the Metropolitan Opera on Feb. 14, 1953.

Harris, Donald, American composer and music educator; b. St. Paul, Minn., April 7, 1931. He was a student of Paul Wilkinson in St. Paul, of Ross Lee Finney at the Univ. of Mich. at Ann Arbor (B.Mus., 1952; M.Mus., 1952), and of Max Deutsch in Paris. He also studied with Boulanger in Paris, Blacher and Foss at the Berkshire Music Center in Tanglewood (summers, 1954–55), and Jolivet at the Centre Français d'Humanisme Musical in Aix-en-Provence (1960). From 1968 to 1977 he held administrative posts at the New England Cons. of Music in Boston. In 1977 he became prof. of music at the Hartt School of Music at the Univ. of Hartford, where he was chairman of the composition and theory dept. (1977–80) and then dean of the school (1980–88). In 1988 he became dean of the College of the Arts at Ohio State Univ. in Columbus, where he also was a prof. (from 1988) and acting director (1989–91) of the School of Music. From 1994 to 1996 he also served as president of the International Council of Fine Arts Deans. With C. Hailey and J. Brand, he ed. *The Berg-Schoenberg Correspondence* (N.Y., 1987), which won the ASCAP/Deems Taylor Award in 1989. In 1956 he received a Fulbright scholarship. In 1962 he won the Prince Rainier III of Monaco Composition Award. He held a Gugggenheim fellowship in 1966. From 1973 he received annual ASCAP awards. In 1974 he received an NEA fellowship grant. He received an award from the American Academy and Inst. of Arts and Letters in 1991. As a composer, he follows the trends of the cosmopolitan avant-garde.

WORKS: DRAMATIC: *The Legend of John Henry*, ballet (1954; rev. 1979); *The Golden Deer*, ballet (1955); *Intervals*, dance piece (1959); *The Little Mermaid*, opera (1985–95); *Twelfth Night*, incidental music to Shakespeare's play (1989). **ORCH.:** *Symphony in 2 Movements* (1958–61); *On Variations* for Chamber Orch. (1976); *Prelude to a Concert in Connecticut* (1981); *Mermaid Variations* for Chamber Orch. (1992). **BAND:** *A Fanfare for the Seventies*, march (1978). **CHAMBER:** *Fantasy* for Violin and Piano (1957); String Quartet (1965); *Ludus I* for 10 Instruments (1966) and *II* for 5 Instruments (1973); *3 Fanfares* for 4 Horns (1984); *A Birthday Card for Gunther* [Schuller] for Violin (1985); *Canzona and Carol* for Double Brass Quintet and Timpani (1986). **KEYBOARD: PIANO:** Sonata (1957); *Balladen* (1979). **ORGAN:** Improvisation themes for Marie-Claire Alain (1980); *Meditations* (1984). **VOCAL:** *Charms* for Soprano and Orch. (1971–80); *For the Night to Wear* for Mezzo-soprano and Chamber Ensemble (1978); *Pierrot Lieder* for Soprano and Chamber Ensemble (1988).

Harris, Roy (actually, **Leroy Ellsworth**), significant American composer; b. Chandler, Okla., Feb. 12, 1898; d. Santa Monica, Calif., Oct. 1, 1979. His parents, of Irish and Scottish descent, settled in Oklahoma; in 1903 the family moved to California, where Harris had private music lessons with Henry Schoenfeld and Arthur Farwell. In 1926 he went to Paris, where he studied composition with Boulanger; continued his stay in Paris thanks to two consecutive Guggenheim fellowships (1927, 1928). Upon his return to the U.S., he lived in California and in N.Y.; several of his works were performed and attracted favorable attention; Farwell publ. an article in the *Musical Quarterly* (Jan. 1932) in which he enthusiastically welcomed Harris as an American genius. In his compositions, Harris showed a talent of great originality, with a strong melodic and rhythmic speech that was indigenously American. He developed a type of modal symbolism akin to Greek ethos,, with each particular mode related to a certain emotional state. Instrumental music is the genre in which he particularly excelled. His Sym. No. 3 (Boston, Feb. 24, 1939) became his best-known and most frequently perf. work; it was the first American sym. to be played in China, during the 1973 tour of the Philadelphia Orch. under the direction of Eugene Ormandy. Harris never wrote an opera or an oratorio, but made astute use of choral masses in some of his works. He held the following teaching positions: Westminster Choir School, Princeton (1934–35); Cornell Univ. (1941–43); Colorado College (1943–48); Utah State Agricultural College in Logan (1948–49); Peabody College for Teachers at Nashville (1949–51); Sewanee, Tenn. (1951); Pa. College for Women (1951–56); Univ. of Southern Ill. (1956–57); Indiana Univ. (1957–60); Inter-American Univ., San Germán, Puerto Rico (1960–61); Univ. of Calif., Los Angeles (1961–73). In 1973 he was appointed composer-in-residence at Calif. State Univ., Los Angeles, a post he held until his death. He received honorary D.Mus. degrees from Rutgers Univ. and the Univ. of Rochester in N.Y.; in 1942 he was awarded the Elizabeth Sprague Coolidge Medal "for eminent services to chamber music." In 1936 he married the pianist and teacher Johana Harris (née Beula Duffey; b. Ottawa, Ontario, Jan. 1, 1913; d. Los Angeles, June 5, 1995); she assumed her professional name Johana in honor of J.S. Bach; the single n was used owing to some esoteric numerologic considerations to which Harris was partial. After his death, she married, on Dec. 18, 1982, her 21-year-old piano student John Heggie.

WORKS: BALLETS: *From This Earth* (Colorado Springs, Aug. 7, 1941); *Namesake* (Colorado Springs, Aug. 8, 1942); *What So Proudly We Hail* (Colorado Springs, Aug. 8, 1942).

ORCH.: *Andante* (1925); *American Portrait 1929*, sym. (1929; withdrawn); 13 other syms.: No. 1, *Symphony 1933* (1933; Boston, Jan. 26, 1934), No. 2 (1934; Boston, Feb. 28, 1936), No. 3 (Boston, Feb. 24, 1939), No. 4, *Folksong Symphony*, for Chorus and Orch. (Cleveland, Dec. 26, 1940; rev. version, N.Y., Dec. 31, 1942), No. 5 (1942; Boston, Feb. 26, 1943), No. 6, *Gettysburg* (Boston, April 14, 1944), No. 7 (Chicago, Nov. 20, 1952; rev. 1955), No. 8, *San Francisco* (1961; San Francisco, Jan. 17, 1962), No. 9 (1962; Philadelphia, Jan. 18, 1963), No. 10, *Abraham Lincoln*, for Speaker, Chorus, Brass, 2 Pianos, and Percussion (Long Beach, Calif., April 14, 1965), No. 11 (1967; N.Y., Feb. 8, 1968), No. 12, *Pere Marquette*, for Tenor/Speaker and Orch. (1968–69; Milwaukee, Nov. 8, 1969), and No. 13, *Bicentennial Symphony*, for Chorus and Orch. (1975–76; 1st perf. as Sym. No. 14, Washington, D.C., Feb. 10, 1976); *Concert Piece* (1930); *Andantino* (1931; rev. 1932); *Toccata* (1931); *From the Gayety and Sadness of the American Scene*, overture (Los Angeles, Dec. 29, 1932); *When Johnny Comes Marching Home: An American Overture* (1934; Minneapolis, Jan. 13, 1935); *Farewell to Pioneers: A Symphonic Elegy* (1935; Philadelphia, Feb. 28, 1936); *Prelude and Fugue* for Strings (1935; Philadelphia, March 27, 1936); Concerto for Piano and Strings (1936; arranged from the Piano Quintet); *Time Suite* (ABC, N.Y., Aug. 8, 1937); 2 violin concertos: No. 1 (1938; withdrawn) and No. 2 (1949; Wilmington, N.C., March 21, 1984); *Prelude and Fugue* for Strings and 4 Trumpets (1939; arranged from the String Quartet No. 3); *American Creed* (Chicago, Oct. 30, 1940); *Acceleration* (Washington, D.C., Nov. 2, 1941; rev. 1942); *Evening Piece* (1941; 2nd movement of *3 Pieces*); *Mirage* (c.1941); *Ode to Truth* (San Francisco, March 9, 1941); *3 Pieces* (N.Y., April 9, 1941; nos. 1 and 3 from the *Folksong Symphony*); *Fanfare for the Forces* (c.1942); *Folk Rhythms of Today* (1942; Minneapolis, Jan. 29, 1943); Concerto for Piano and Band (Ann Arbor, April 7, 1942); *March in Time of War* (N.Y., Dec. 30, 1942; rev. 1943); Chorale for Organ and Brass (Cambridge, Mass., Sept. 26, 1943); *Fantasia* for Piano and Band (1943); *Children's Hour* (1943–44); *Chorale* (London, July 22, 1944); 2 piano concertos: No. 1 (Colorado Springs, Aug. 1944) and No. 2 (Louisville, Dec. 9, 1953); *Toccata* for Organ and Brass (Cambridge, Mass., Sept. 24, 1944); *Ode to Friendship* (N.Y., Nov. 16, 1944); *Memories of a Child's Sunday* (1945; N.Y., Feb. 21, 1946); *Variation* [No. 7] *on a Theme by Goossens* (Cincinnati, March 23, 1945; with 9 other composers); *Celebration Variations on a Timpani Theme from Howard Hanson's Third Symphony* (Boston, Oct. 25, 1946); *Melody* (N.Y., May 12, 1946); *Radio Piece* for Piano and Orch. (Rochester, N.Y., May 18, 1946); Concerto for 2 Pianos and Orch. (1946; Denver, Jan. 21, 1947); *The Quest* (1947; Indianapolis, Jan. 29, 1948); *Theme and Variations* for Accordion and Orch. (Chicago, June 1, 1947); *Elegy and Paean* for Violin and Orch. (Houston, Dec. 14, 1948); *Kentucky Spring* (Louisville, April 5, 1949); *Cumberland Concerto for Orchestra* (Cincinnati, Oct. 19, 1951); *Fantasy* for Piano and Pops Orch. (1951); *Symphonic Fantasy* (1953; Pittsburgh, Jan. 30, 1954); *Symphonic Epigram* (N.Y., Nov. 14, 1954); *Fantasy* for Piano and Orch. (Hartford, Conn., Nov. 17, 1954); *Ode to Consonance* (1956); *Elegy and Dance* (Portland, Oreg., April 19, 1958); *These Times* for Piano and Small Orch. (La Jolla, Calif., Aug. 14, 1963); *Epilogue to Profiles in Courage JFK* (Los Angeles, May 10, 1964); *Horn of Plenty* (Beverly Hills, June 14, 1964); *Salute to Youth* (1964; Santa Barbara, Calif., Feb. 28, 1965); *Fantasy* for Organ, Brass, and Timpani (1964); *Rhythms and Spaces* (N.Y., April 7, 1965; arranged from the String Quartet No. 2); Concerto for Amplified Piano, Brass, String Basses, and Percussion (Los Angeles, Dec. 9, 1968); *Folksong Suite* for Harp and Orch. (1973).

BAND: *Sad Song* for Jazz Band (1938); *Cimarron*, overture (Enid, Okla., April 18, 1941); *When Johnny Comes Marching Home* (1941; Ann Arbor, Jan. 24, 1942); *Rhythms of Today* (1943); *Conflict* (1944); *Sun and Stars* (1944); *The Sun from Dawn to Dusk* (1944); *Take the Sun and Keep the Stars* (1944); *Fruit of Gold* (Westwood, Calif., May 10, 1949); *Dark Devotion* (1950); *Kentucky Jazz Piece* (1950); Sym., *West Point* (West Point, N.Y., May 30, 1952); *Ad majorem gloriam Universitatis Illinorum*, tone poem (1958); *Bicentennial Aspirations* (San Diego, July 4, 1976).

CHAMBER: *Impressions on a Rainy Day* for String Quartet (1925); Concerto for Piano, Clarinet, and String Quartet (1926; Paris, May 8, 1928); 3 string quartets: No. 1 (1929), No. 2, *Variations on a Theme* (1933), and No. 3, *4 Preludes and Fugues* (1937); Concerto for String Sextet (1932); *Fantasy* for Winds, Horn, and Piano (Pasadena, Calif., April 10, 1932); *4 Minutes—20 Seconds* for Flute and String Quartet (1934); Piano Trio (1934); *Poem* for Violin and Piano (1935); Piano Quintet (1936); *Soliloquy and Dance* for Viola and Piano (1938); String Quintet (1940); Violin Sonata (1942); *Lyric Studies* for Woodwind and Piano (1950); Cello Sonata (1964; rev. 1968); *Childhood Memories of Ocean Moods* for Piano, String Quartet, and Double Bass (1966).

KEYBOARD: PIANO: Sonata (1928); *Little Suite* (1939); *Toccata* (1939); *Suite in 3 Movements* (1939–43); *American Ballads* (2 vols., 1942–45). **ORGAN:** *Études for Pedals* (1964; rev. 1972).

VOCAL: *Challenge 1940* for Bass, Chorus, and Orch. (N.Y., June 25, 1940); *Railroad Man's Ballad* for Chorus and Orch. (1940; N.Y., Feb. 22, 1941); *Freedom's Land* for Baritone, Chorus, and Orch. (Pittsburgh, Nov. 11, 1941); *Rock of Ages* for Chorus and Orch. (N.Y., Sept. 19, 1944); *Blow the Man Down* for Countertenor, Baritone, Chorus, and Orch. (Cleveland, May 12, 1946); *The Brotherhood of Man* for Chorus and Orch. (1966); numerous other choral works.

BIBL.: A. Farwell, "R. H.," *Musical Quarterly* (Jan. 1932); H. Cowell, "R. H.," *American Composers on American Music* (Stanford, Calif., 1933); W. Piston, "R. H.," *Modern Music* (Jan.–Feb. 1934); N. Slonimsky, "R. H.," *Musical Quarterly* (Jan. 1947); D. Stehman and C. Gibbs, "R. H.," *Ovation* (July 1984); D. Stehman, *R. H.: An American Musical Pioneer* (Boston, 1984); idem, *R. H.: A Bio-Bibliography* (N.Y., 1991).

Harris, (William) Victor, American pianist, organist, conductor, teacher, and composer; b. N.Y., April 27, 1869; d. there, Feb. 15, 1943. He was a student of Charles Blum (piano), William Courtney (voice), Frederick Schilling (composition), and Anton Seidl (conducting). He was first active as a church organist in N.Y.; later he was conductor of the Utica Choral Union (1893–94) and the St. Cecilia Club in N.Y. (1902–36); he also was active as an accompanist and teacher. He wrote some orch. music, piano pieces, a cantata, and quartets for Men's and Women's Voices, but became best known for his numerous solo songs.

Harrison, Beatrice, English cellist, sister of **May Harrison**; b. Roorkee, India, Dec. 9, 1892; d. Smallfield, Surrey, March 10, 1965. She was taken to England in infancy; entered the Royal College of Music in London; won a prize at the age of 10. She was 14 when she made her first public appearance as a soloist with an orch. (London, May 29, 1907); then went to Berlin, where she took lessons with Hugo Becker; was the winner of the prestigious Mendelssohn Prize. She made several European tours, most of them in company with her sister; toured the U.S. in 1913 and 1932. Delius wrote his Double Concerto for her and her sister.

Harrison, Frank (Francis) Ll(ewellyn), Irish musicologist; b. Dublin, Sept. 29, 1905; d. Tunbridge Wells, Dec. 31, 1987. He studied in Dublin at the Royal Irish Academy of Music and at Trinity College (Mus.B., 1926; Mus.D., 1929); later was a postdoctoral fellow under Schrade and Hindemith at Yale Univ. (1946). He taught at Queen's Univ., Kingston, Ontario (1935–46), Colgate Univ. (1946–47), Washington Univ. in St. Louis (1947–52), the Univ. of Oxford (1952–70), and the Univ. of Amsterdam (1970–76). He helped launch the Early English Church Music series, serving as its general ed. from 1961 to 1972; held a similar position with the Polyphonic Music of the Fourteenth Century series from 1962 to 1974. In 1981 he was made a corresponding member of the American Musicological Soc.

WRITINGS: *Music in Medieval Britain* (1958; 2nd ed., 1963); with J. Westrup, ed. *Collins Music Encyclopedia* (1959; U.S. edition, 1960, as *The New College Encyclopedia of Music*); with M. Hood and C. Palisca, *Musicology* (1963); with J. Rimmer, *European Musical Instruments* (1964); *Time, Place and Music: An Anthology of Ethnomusicological Observations c. 1550–c. 1800* (1973); with E. Dobson, *Medieval English Songs* (1979).

Harrison, Guy Fraser, English-American conductor; b. Guildford, Surrey, Nov. 6, 1894; d. San Miguel de Allende, Mexico, Feb. 20, 1986. He studied at the Royal College of Music, where he won an organ scholarship. He served as an organist of the Episcopal Cathedral in Manila (1914–20); was organist of St. Paul's Cathedral in Rochester, N.Y. (1920–24); then was conductor of the Eastman Theater Orch. in Rochester (1924–29) and the Rochester Civic Orch. (1930–51); also was assoc. conductor of the Rochester Phil. (1930–51). From 1951 to 1973 he was conductor of the Oklahoma City Sym. Orch.

Harrison, Julius (Allan Greenway), English conductor, composer, and teacher; b. Stourport, Worcestershire, March 26, 1885; d. Harpenden, Hertfordshire, April 5, 1963. He studied with Bantock in Birmingham and at the Midland Inst. In 1913 he conducted for the first time at London's Covent Garden; after serving as conductor of the Scottish Orch. in Glasgow (1920–23), he was a conductor with the Beecham Opera Co. and the British National Opera Co. in London (1922–27); he subsequently was conductor of the Hastings Municipal Orch. (1930–40) and a prof. of composition at the Royal Academy of Music in London. His music was principally influenced by Elgar.

WORKS: *The Canterbury Pilgrims*, opera; *Worcestershire Pieces*, orch. suite; *Bredon Hill* for Violin and Orch.; *Cornish Sketches* for Strings; *Troubadour Suite* for Strings, Harp, and 2 Horns; String Quartet; sonatas; piano pieces; Mass; Requiem; *Cleopatra*, cantata; songs.

BIBL.: G. Self, *J. H. and the Importunate Muse* (Brookfield, 1993).

Harrison, Lou (Silver), inventive American composer and performer; b. Portland, Oreg., May 14, 1917. He studied with Cowell in San Francisco (1934–35) and with Schoenberg at the Univ. of Calif. at Los Angeles (1941). From 1945 to 1948 he was a music critic for the *N.Y. Herald-Tribune*; he was also an active promoter of contemporary music, including the works of Ives, Ruggles, Varèse, and Cowell; he prepared for publication Ives' 3rd Sym., and conducted its premiere (N.Y., April 5, 1946). He taught at Reed College in Portland, Oreg. (1949–50) and at Black Mountain College in North Carolina (1951–52). In 1952 and 1954 he held Guggenheim fellowships. In 1961 he visited the Far East. In 1963 he served as the senior scholar at the East-West Center of the Univ. of Hawaii. From 1967 to 1980 he taught at San Jose State Univ., and from 1980 to 1985 at Mills College in Oakland, California. In 1983 he was a senior Fulbright scholar in New Zealand. Harrison's extensive output reflects his belief that the entire sound world is open to the creative musician. He has made use of both Western and non-Western musical traditions. He has demonstrated a preoccupation with pitch relations, most notably just intonation. In some of his works, he has utilized non-Western instruments or folk instruments, and he has also constructed various instruments of his own invention. He has even been bold enough to explore the use of unconventional "instruments," such as flowerpots, washtubs, and packing cases. Whatever the resources used, Harrison molds them into his own eclectic style in which melody and rhythm predominate.

WORKS: DRAMATIC: OPERAS: *Rapunzel* (Rome, 1954); *Young Caesar*, puppet opera (Aptos, Calif., Aug. 21, 1971). **THEATER PIECE:** *Jeptha's Daughter* (1940–63; Aptos, Calif., March 9, 1963). **DANCE SCORES:** *Changing World* (1936); *Green Mansions* (1939); *Something to Please Everybody* (1939); *Johnny Appleseed* (1940); *Omnipotent Chair* (1940); *Orpheus* (1941–69); *Perilous Chapel* (1948); *Western Dance* (1948); *The Marriage at the Eiffel Tower* (1949); *The Only Jealousy of Emer* (1949); *Solstice* (1949); *Almanac of the Seasons* (1950); *Io and Prometheus* (1951); *Praises for Hummingbirds and Hawks* (1951). Also incidental music to plays and film scores. **ORCH.:** Suite for Symphonic Strings (1936–60); Sym. No. 3 (1937–82); Concerto for Violin and Percussion Orch. (1940–59); *Elegiac Symphony* (1941–75); *Alleluia* (1944); 2 suites for Strings (1947, 1948); *Symphony on G* (1948–54; rev. 1966); Suite for Violin, Piano, and Small Orch. (1951); *Moogunkwha, se tang ak* for Korean Court Orch. (1961); *Pacifika rondo* for Chamber Orch. (1963); Concerto for Organ, Percussion, and Orch. (1972–73); *Simfony in Free Style* (1980); Double Concerto for Violin, Cello, and Large Javanese Gamelan (1981–82); Piano Concerto (N.Y., Oct. 20, 1985); *Last Symphony* (N.Y., Nov. 2, 1990); *A Parade for M.T.T.* (San Francisco, Sept. 6, 1995). **CHAMBER:** Concerto No. 1 for Flute and Percussion (1939); *Canticle No. 1* for 5 Percussion (1940) and *No. 3* for Flute or Ocarina, Guitar, and Percussion (1941; rev. 1989); *Song of Queztecoatl* for Percussion Quartet (1940); *Double Music* for Percussion Quartet (1941; in collaboration with J. Cage); *Fugue* for Percussion Quartet (1941); *Labyrinth* for 11 Players of 91 Percussion Instruments (1941); *Schoenbergiana* for 6 Woodwinds (1945); *Siciliana* for Wind Quintet (1945); *Motet for the Day of Ascension* for 7 Strings (1946); String Trio (1946); Suite for Cello and Harp (1949); Suite No. 2 for String Quartet (1949–50); *7 Pastorales* for 4 Woodwinds, Harp, and Strings (1952); *Koncherto* for Violin and 5 Percussion (1959); *Concerto in slendro* for Violin, Celesta, 2 Tack Pianos, and Strings (1961); *Quintal taryung* for 2 Flutes and Changgo (1961); *Prelude* for P'iri and Harmonium (1962); *Majestic Fanfare* for Trumpets and Percussion (1963); *At the Tomb of Charles Ives* for Chamber Group (1964); *Avalokiteshvara* for Harp and Jaltarang (1965); *Music* for Violin and Other Instruments (1967–69); *Beverly's Troubadour Piece* for Harp and 2 Percussion (1968); *In Memory of Victor Jowers* for Clarinet and Piano (1968); Suite for Violin and American Gamelan (1972–73; in collaboration with R. Dee); *Arion's Leap* for Justly Tuned Instruments and Percussion (1974); *Main bersama-sama* for Horn and Sundanese Gamelan Degung (1978); *Serenade for Betty Freeman and Franco Asseto* for Sundanese Gamelan Degung and Suling (1978); *String Quartet Set* (1978–79); Suite for Guitar and Percussion (1978–79); *Threnody for Carlos Châvez* for Sundanese Gamelan Degung and Violin (1979); *Ariadne* for Flute and Percussion (1987); *Varied Trio* for Violin, Piano, and Percussion (1987); many Javanese gamelan pieces; piano music. **VOCAL:** Mass for Chorus, Trumpet, Harp, and Strings (1939–54); *Easter Cantata* for Soloists, Chorus, and Orch. (1943–46); *Alma redemptoris mater* for Baritone, Violin, Trombone, and Tack Piano (1949); *A Political Primer* for Soloists, Chorus, and Orch. (1951); *Holly and Ivy* for Voice, Harp, and Strings (1951); *Peace Piece 3* for Voice, Violin, Harp, and Strings (1953); *4 Strict Songs* for 8 Baritones and Orch. (1955); *A Joyous Procession and a Solemn Procession* for Chorus, Trombones, and Percussion (1962); *Nova odo* for Chorus and Orch. (1962); *Haiku* for Unison Voices, Xiao, Harp, and Percussion (1968); *Peace Piece 2* for Tenor, 3 Percussion, 2 Harps, and String Quintet (1968); *Peace Piece 1* for Unison Voices, Trombone, 3 Percussion, 2 Harps, Organ, and String Quintet (1968); *La koro sutro* for Chorus, American Gamelan, and Percussion Orch. (1972); *Scenes from Cavafy* for Baritone, Men's Voices, and Large Javanese Gamelan (1979–80); *The Foreman's Song Tune* for Chorus and Gamelan (1983).

WRITINGS: *About Carl Ruggles* (N.Y., 1946); *Music Primer: Various Items About Music to 1970* (N.Y., 1971); with others, *Soundings: Ives, Ruggles, Varèse* (Santa Fe, N.M., 1974); P. Garland, ed., *A Lou Harrison Reader* (Santa Fe, N.M., 1987).

BIBL.: V. Rathbun, *L.H. and his Music* (thesis, San Jose State Univ., 1976); C. Rutman, *The Solo Piano Works of L.H.* (diss., Peabody Cons. of Music, 1983).

Harrison, May, English violinist, sister of **Beatrice Harrison;** b. Roorkee, India, March 1891; d. South Nutfield, Surrey, June 8, 1959. She was a pupil of Arbos and Rivarde at the Royal College of Music in London, winning its gold medal at age 10. In 1904 she made her debut in London. After completing her training with Auer in St. Petersburg, she pursued her career mainly in England, often appearing in concerts with her sister. Delius composed his Double Concerto for the Harrison sisters, and also dedicated his 3rd Violin Sonata to May.

Harsanyi, Janice (née **Morris**), American soprano and teacher; b. Arlington, Mass., July 15, 1929. She studied at Westminster

Choir College in Princeton, N.J. (B.Mus., 1951) and at the Philadelphia Academy of Vocal Arts (1952–54). In 1954 she launched her career, concentrating on appearances as a soloist with orchs. and as a recitalist; she also sang in opera, becoming especially well known for her championship of contemporary music. She taught voice (1951–63) and was chairman of the voice dept. (1963–65) at Westminster Choir College; also lectured on music at the Princeton Theological Seminary (1956–63). After serving as artist-in-residence at the Interlochen (Mich.) Arts Academy (1967–70), she taught voice at the North Carolina School of the Arts in Winston-Salem (1971–78) and at Salem College (1973–76). She was prof. of voice at Florida State Univ. in Tallahassee from 1979. In 1952 she married **Nicholas Harsanyi**.

Harsanyi, Nicholas, Hungarian-born American conductor and teacher; b. Budapest, Dec. 17, 1913; d. Tallahassee, July 19, 1987. He was a pupil of Hubay, Bartók, Dohnányi, Kodály, and Weiner at the Budapest Academy of Music (M.M., 1936). In 1938 he emigrated to the U.S. and in 1943 became a naturalized American citizen. He played in the Lener (1945–47) and Roth (1948–50) string quartets; also taught at Westminster Choir College in Princeton, N.J. (1948–69) and at Princeton Univ. (1953–68). He was conductor of the Princeton (N.J.) Sym. Orch. (1950–65), the Philadelphia Chamber Orch. (1955–58), the Colonial Sym. Orch. in Madison, N.J. (1955–65), the Trenton (N.J.) Sym. Orch. (1958–65), the Princeton (N.J.) Chamber Orch. (1964–70), and the Interlochen (Mich.) Arts Academy Orch. (1968–70). From 1970 to 1979 he was dean of the North Carolina School of the Arts in Winston-Salem, where he conducted its orch. as well as the Piedmont Chamber Orch. In 1980 he founded the Tallahassee Sym. Orch., which he served as music director until his death. In 1952 he married **Janice** (née **Morris**) **Harsanyi**.

Harsányi, Tibor, Hungarian composer; b. Magyarkanizsa, June 27, 1898; d. Paris, Sept. 19, 1954. He studied at the Budapest Academy of Music with Kodály; in 1923 he settled in Paris, where he devoted himself to composition. The melodic material of his music stems from Hungarian folk melos; his harmonic idiom is largely polytonal; the rhythms are sharp, often with jazzlike syncopation; the form remains classical.

WORKS: DRAMATIC: OPERAS: *Les Invités*, chamber opera (Gera, Germany, 1930); *Illusion*, radio opera (Paris, June 28, 1949). **BALLETS:** *Le Dernier Songe* (Budapest, Jan. 27, 1920); *Pantins* (Paris, 1938); *Chota Roustaveli* (Monte Carlo, 1945; in collaboration with A. Honegger and A. Tcherepnin); *L'Amour et la vie* (1951). **OTHER:** *L'Histoire du petit tailleur*, puppet show for 7 Instruments and Percussion (1939). **ORCH.:** *La Joie de vivre* (Paris, March 11, 1934, composer conducting); 2 divertissements (1940–41; 1943); Violin Concerto (Paris Radio, Jan. 16, 1947); *Figures et rythmes* (Geneva, Nov. 19, 1947, composer conducting); *Danses variées* (Basel, Feb. 14, 1950, composer conducting); Sym. (Salzburg Festival, June 26, 1952). **CHAMBER:** Violin Sonatina (1918); 2 string quartets (1918, 1935); Cello Sonata (1928); *3 Pieces* for Flute and Piano (1924); Nonet for String and Wind Instruments (Vienna, June 21, 1932); *Rhapsody* for Cello and Piano (1939); *Picnic* for 2 Violins, Cello, Double Bass, and Percussion (1951); many piano pieces, among them *5 études rythmiques* (1934), *3 pièces lyriques*, and albums for children. **VOCAL:** Choral works, including *Cantate de Noël* for Voices, Flute, and Strings (Paris, Dec. 24, 1945).

Harshaw, Margaret, outstanding American mezzo-soprano, later soprano; b. Narberth, Pa., May 12, 1909. She studied in Philadelphia and then was a scholarship student at the Juilliard Graduate School of Music in N.Y., where she studied voice with Anna Schoen-René, graduating in 1942. Shortly after graduation, she won the Metropolitan Opera Auditions of the Air and made her debut with the company in N.Y. as a mezzo-soprano in the role of the 2nd Norn in *Götterdämmerung* on Nov. 25, 1942; subsequently sang contralto and mezzo-soprano roles in German, Italian, and French operas; she also acquitted herself brilliantly as a dramatic soprano in her debut appearance in that capacity as Senta at the Metropolitan Opera on Nov. 22, 1950; was particularly successful in Wagnerian roles; she sang Isolde, Sieglinde, Kundry, Elisabeth, and all 3 parts of Brünnhilde. She also excelled as Donna Anna in *Don Giovanni* and Leonore in Beethoven's *Fidelio.* She was a guest soloist with the opera companies of Philadelphia, Cincinnati, San Francisco, and Covent Garden in London, and at the Glyndebourne Festivals. On March 10, 1964, she made her farewell appearance at the Metropolitan Opera as Ortrud. In 1962 she joined the faculty of the Indiana Univ. School of Music in Bloomington, where she taught voice until retiring in 1993.

Hart, Fritz (Bennicke), English conductor and composer; b. Brockley, Kent, Feb. 11, 1874; d. Honolulu, July 9, 1949. He studied at the Royal College of Music in London (1893–96). In 1908 he went to Australia and in 1915 became director of the Melbourne Cons.; in 1927 was appointed joint artistic director of the Melbourne Sym. Orch.; conducted the Honolulu Sym. Orch. (1932 until his death); settled in Honolulu in 1936 when appointed prof. of music at the Univ. of Hawaii; retired in 1942. He wrote operas, operettas, orch. works, chamber music, choruses, and over 500 songs.

Hart, Lorenz (Milton), American lyricist; b. N.Y., May 2, 1895; d. there, Nov. 22, 1943. He began as a student of journalism at Columbia Univ. (1914–17); then turned to highly successful theatrical writing. During his 24-year collaboration with Richard Rodgers, he wrote the lyrics for *Connecticut Yankee* (1927); *On Your Toes* (1936); *Babes in Arms* (1937); *The Boys from Syracuse* (1938); *I Married an Angel* (1938); *Too Many Girls* (1939); *Pal Joey* (1940); *By Jupiter* (1942). Some of their best songs (*Manhattan, Here in My Arms, My Heart Stood Still, Small Hotel, Blue Moon, Where or When, I Married an Angel*) are publ. in the album *Rodgers & Hart Songs* (N.Y., 1951).

BIBL.: S. Marx and J. Clayton, *Rodgers and H.* (N.Y., 1976); D. Hart, *Thou Swell, Thou Witty: The Life and Lyrics of L. H.* (N.Y., 1976); F. Nolan, *L. H.: A Poet on Broadway* (Oxford, 1994).

Hart, Weldon, American composer; b. Place-Bear Spring, Tenn., Sept. 19, 1911; d. (suicide) East Lansing, Mich., Nov. 20, 1957. He studied in Nashville, at the Univ. of Mich., and at the Eastman School of Music in Rochester, N.Y., with Hanson and Rogers, receiving his Ph.D. in 1946. He was head of the music dept. of Western Kentucky State College (1946–49) and director of the School of Music of the Univ. of West Virginia (1949–57). In 1957 he was engaged as head of the music dept. of Michigan State Univ. at East Lansing; upon arrival there, he became despondent over his inability to produce an impression with a concert of his works, and killed himself with carbon monoxide exhaust in his car. Yet his music, although not innovative, was well crafted. He wrote *The Dark Hills*, symphonic poem (1939); *Sinfonietta* (1944); Sym. (1945); Violin Concerto (1951); *3 West Virginia Folk Songs* for Chorus and Orch. (1954); several violin pieces and choruses.

Harth, Sidney, American violinist, conductor, and pedagogue; b. Cleveland, Oct. 5, 1925. He studied at the Cleveland Inst. of Music (Mus.B., 1947); then took lessons with Joseph Fuchs and Georges Enesco. He was a recipient of the Naumburg prize in 1948 and made his debut at Carnegie Hall in N.Y. in 1949. He served as concertmaster and assistant conductor of the Louisville Orch. (1953–58); he was concertmaster of the Chicago Sym. Orch. (1959–62) and of the Casals Festival Orch. in San Juan (1959–65; 1972). From 1963 to 1973 he was a prof. of music and chairman of the music dept. at Carnegie-Mellon Univ. in Pittsburgh. He served as concertmaster and assoc. conductor of the Los Angeles Phil. (1973–79); was interim concertmaster of the N.Y. Phil. in 1980; also served as music director of the Puerto Rico Sym. Orch. (1977–79). He was director of orch. studies at the Mannes College of Music in N.Y. (1981–84), prof. of violin at the State Univ. of N.Y. at Stony Brook (1981–82) and at the Yale Univ. School of Music (from 1982), and director of orch. studies at Carnegie-Mellon Univ. (1989–90). From 1990 to 1993 he was music director of the Northwest Chamber Orch.

He also was director of orch. activities at the Hartt School of Music in Hartford, Conn. (1991–93). With his wife, Teresa Testa Harth, he gave duo-violin concerts.

Hartig, Heinz (Friedrich), German composer; b. Kassel, Sept. 10, 1907; d. Berlin, Sept. 16, 1969. He studied piano at the Kassel Cons., and musicology at the Univ. of Vienna. Unable to hold a teaching post under the Nazi regime, he occupied himself with performances as a harpsichord player; in 1948 he joined the Hochschule für Musik in Berlin. In his compositions, he applied varied techniques of modern music, from neo-Classicism to serialism, with formal unity achieved by the principle of free variations. He wrote a ballet, *Schwarze Sonne* (1958); chamber opera, *Escorial* (1961); Violin Concerto (1952); *Concertante Suite* for Guitar and Orch. (1954); Piano Concerto (1959); *Mass after a Holocaust*, after Dylan Thomas, for Baritone, Chorus, and Orch. (1960); *Wohin*, oratorio (1965); *Immediate* for Flute, Clarinet, Piano, and 2 Cellos (1966); *Concerto strumentale* for Violin and Orch. (1969); *Komposition in 5 Phasen* for Cello, Orch., Chorus, and Tape (1969).

BIBL.: W. Burde, *H. H.* (Berlin, 1967).

Hartke, Stephen (Paul), American composer and teacher; b. Orange, N.J., July 6, 1952. He studied with Drew at Yale Univ. (B.A., 1973), Rochberg at the Univ. of Pa. (M.A., 1976), and Applebaum at the Univ. of Calif. at Santa Barbara (Ph.D., 1982), where he also lectured (1981–83; 1985–87); was also a Fulbright prof. of composition at the Univ. of São Paulo in Brazil (1984–85). In 1987 he joined the faculty of the Univ. of Southern Calif. in Los Angeles. From 1988 to 1992 he also was composer-in-residence of the Los Angeles Chamber Orch. In addition to several commissions, his honors include a Kennedy Center Friedheim Award (1985), several NEA grants (1988; 1989–90; 1991–92), the American Academy in Rome Prize Fellowship (1991–92), and an American Academy of Arts and Letters Award (1993).

WORKS: ORCH.: *Alvorada*, madrigals for Strings (Pasadena, Calif., March 8, 1983); *Maltese Cat Blues* (1986); *Pacific Rim* (Los Angeles, Sept. 16, 1988); Sym. No. 2 (1990; Los Angeles, Feb. 8, 1991); Violin Concerto (1992; Troy, N.Y., March 12, 1993); *The Ascent of the Equestrian in a Balloon* (Washington, D.C., Nov. 2, 1995). **CHAMBER:** *Caoine* for Violin (1980; Santa Barbara, Calif., May 5, 1981); *Sonata-Variations* for Violin and Piano (1984; Los Angeles, Feb. 26, 1985); *Oh Them Rats is Mean in My Kitchen* for 2 Violins (1985; Ojai, Calif., May 1986); *Precession* for 13 Instruments (1986; Los Angeles, March 10, 1987); *The King of the Sun* for Violin, Viola, Cello, and Piano (Los Angeles, Nov. 15, 1988); *Night Rubrics* for Cello (1990; Lausanne, June 1991); *Wir küssen Ihnen tausendmal die Hände*, homage to Mozart for Clarinet, Horn, Violin, Viola, Cello, and Fortepiano (Los Angeles, Oct. 31, 1991); *Un tout petit trompe-l'oreille* for Guitar (1992); *Wulfstan at the Millennium* for 10 Instruments (Cambridge, Mass., April 13, 1995). **PIANO:** *Post-Modern Homages*, 2 sets (1984–92; first complete perf., Los Angeles, Feb. 25, 1993); *The Piano Dreams of Empire* (Los Angeles, July 4, 1994). **VOCAL:** *2 Songs for an Uncertain Age* for Soprano and Orch. (1981; São Paulo, Aug. 24, 1987); *4 Madrigals on Old Portuguese Texts* for Soloists and Chorus or Chamber Chorus (1981; Santa Fe, N.M., Oct. 15, 1988); *Canções modernistas* for High Voice, Clarinet, Bass Clarinet, and Viola (1982); *Iglesia abandonada* for Soprano and Violin (Santa Barbara, Calif., May 10, 1982).

Hartley, Walter S(inclair), American composer, pianist, and teacher; b. Washington, D.C., Feb. 21, 1927. He studied with Phillips, Rogers, and Hanson at the Eastman School of Music in Rochester, N.Y. (B.M., 1950; M.M., 1951; Ph.D., 1953). He taught at the National Music Camp in Interlochen, Mich. (1956–64), and at Davis and Elkins College in W.Va. (1958–69); then was prof. of music at the State Univ. of N.Y. College at Fredonia (1969–91); was also active as a pianist, especially in chamber music settings. His works for brass and saxophones have been widely performed.

WORKS: ORCH.: Sinfonietta (1950); *3 Patterns* for Small Orch. (1951); *Triptych* (1951); *Elegy* for Strings (1952); Sonatina for Trumpet and Small Orch. (1952); Piano Concerto (1952); *Concert Overture* (1954); Chamber Sym. (1954); *Scenes from Lorca's Blood Wedding* (1956); *Elizabethan Dances* (1962); *Festive Music* (1963); *Psalm* for Strings (1964); *Partita* for Chamber Orch. (1964); *Variations* (1973); Sym. No. 3 (1983); Sinfonia No. 7 (1986); Concerto No. 2 for Alto Saxophone and Small Orch. (1989); *Fantasia* for Tuba and Chamber Orch. (1989); Concerto No. 2 for Piano and Wind Ensemble (1991); *Bagatelles* (1992); Concerto for Saxophone Quartet and Orch. or Wind Ensemble (1992). **BAND:** Concerto for 23 Winds (1957); 4 sinfonias (1961, 1963, 1965, 1977); Alto Saxophone Concerto (1966); 2 syms. for Winds (1970, 1978); *Southern Tier Suite* (1972); *Bacchanalia* (1975); *Coast Guard Overture* (1981); *Catskill Suite* (1982); Sinfonia No. 9 (1991); *Lyric Symphony* (1993). **CHAMBER:** 2 string quartets (1950, 1962); Woodwind Quartet (1950); Violin Sonata (1951); Viola Sonata (1952); Trio for Violin, Viola, and Cello (1953); Divertimento for Cello and Woodwind Quintet (1956); *Sonata concertante* for Trombone and Piano (1958); Trio for Piano, Violin, and Cello (1960); *Serenade* for Woodwind Quintet and String Bass (1963); Tuba Sonata (1967); Suite for Saxophone Quartet (1972); Concerto for Tuba and 6 Percussion Players (1974); Baritone Saxophone Sonata (1976); Quintet No. 2 for Brass (1977); Quintet for Saxophones (1981); Trio for Saxophones (1984); *Sonata Elegiaca* for Alto Saxophone and Piano (1987); Sinfonia No. 8 for 5 Percussion Players (1987); Quartet for 4 Guitars (1987); Trio for Reeds and Piano (1987); Chamber Concerto for Baritone Saxophone and Wind Octet (1988); Sextet for Euphonium and Woodwind Quintet (1993); Double Quartet for Saxophones and Brass (1994); Concertino for Piano and Saxophone Quartet (1994); *Concertino da camera* for Soprano Saxophone and Brass Quintet (1994); Sonata for Oboe or Soprano Saxophone and Piano (1994. **VOCAL:** Various works.

Hartmann, Arthur (Martinus), American violinist, teacher, and composer; b. Philadelphia, July 22, 1881; d. N.Y., March 30, 1956. He studied violin with Martinus Van Gelder in Philadelphia, making his debut there at 6; he then studied violin with Loeffler and composition with Homer Norris in Boston. From the age of 12 he made concert tours. After garnering critical accolades as a soloist with the Philadelphia Orch. (1906) and the N.Y. Phil. (1908), he went to Paris and gave recitals with Debussy, who became his close friend. At the outbreak of World War I in 1914, he returned to the U.S. and made a transcontinental tour in 1916–17; in subsequent years, he was active in N.Y. as a performer, teacher, and composer until 1954. He prepared numerous transcriptions and arrangements.

Hartmann, Carl, German tenor; b. Solingen, May 2, 1895; d. Munich, May 30, 1969. He was a student in Düsseldorf of Senff. In 1928 he made his operatic debut as Tannhäuser in Elberfeld, and then toured the U.S. as a member of Gadski's opera company in 1930. After appearing with the Cologne Opera (1933–35), he sang in Berlin and Vienna, and also made guest appearances in Italy, France, and Switzerland. On Dec. 3, 1937, he made his Metropolitan Opera debut in N.Y. as Siegfried, and remained on its roster until 1940; in 1938 he sang Tristan at the Bayreuth Festival. He was principally known as a Wagnerian.

Hartmann, Karl Amadeus, outstanding German composer; b. Munich, Aug. 2, 1905; d. there, Dec. 5, 1963. He was a student of Haas at the Munich Academy of Music (1923–27) and later of Scherchen. His first major composition was his Trumpet Concerto of 1933. During the Third Reich, he withdrew from public life and forbade the performance of his music. His defiance of the Nazi regime was manifested in his *Concerto funebre* for Violin and String Orch. (1939), composed in tribute to Czechoslovakia in the wake of its dismemberment; the score is notable for its metamorphosis, in the minor, of the famous Hussite chorale *Ye Who are God's Warriors*. In 1941–42 Hartmann pursued advanced training in composition and analysis with

Webern in Vienna. After the defeat of the Third Reich in 1945, he organized the Musica Viva concerts for new music in Munich. In 1948 he received a prize from the city of Munich and in 1952 was elected to membership in the German Academy of Fine Arts. Despite his acceptance of a highly chromatic, atonal idiom and his experimentation in the domain of rhythm (patterned after Blacher's "variable meters"), Hartmann retained the orthodox form and structural cohesion of basic Classicism. He was excessively critical of his early works, and discarded many of them, some of which were retrieved and performed after his death.

WORKS: DRAMATIC: 5 small operas under the collective title of *Wachsfigurenkabinett* (1929–30; 1, *Leben und Sterben des heiligen Teufels;* 2, *Der Mann, der vom Tode auferstand,* completed by G. Bialas and H.W. Henze; 3, *Chaplin-Ford-Trott,* completed by W. Hiller; 4, *Fürwahr . . . ?!,* completed by H.W. Henze; 5, *Die Witwe von Ephesus)*; chamber opera, *Des Simplicius Simplicissimus Jugend* (1934–35; Cologne, Oct. 20, 1949; rev. 1955 as *Simplicius Simplicissimus).* **ORCH.:** Trumpet Concerto (Strasbourg, 1933); *Miserae* (Prague, Sept. 1, 1935); 9 syms.: No. 1, *Versuch eines Requiems,* after Whitman, for Alto and Orch. (1936–40; Vienna, June 22, 1957), *Sinfonia tragica* (1940–43; Munich, May 20, 1989), No. 2, *Adagio* (1941–46; Donaueschingen, Sept. 10, 1950), No. 3 (1948–49; Munich, Feb. 10, 1950), No. 4 for Strings (1946–47; Munich, April 2, 1948), No. 5, Symphonie concertante, for Winds, Cellos, and Double Basses (1950; Stuttgart, April 21, 1951), No. 6 (1951–53; Munich, April 24, 1953), No. 7 (1958; Hamburg, March 15, 1959), and No. 8 (1960–62; Cologne, Jan. 25, 1963); *Concerto funebre* for Violin and String Orch. (1939; rev. version, Braunschweig, Nov. 12, 1959); *Symphonischen Hymnen* (1942; Munich, Oct. 9, 1975); *China kämpft,* overture (1942; Darmstadt, July 1947); Concerto for Piano, Winds, and Percussion (Donaueschingen, Oct. 10, 1953); Concerto for Viola, Piano, Winds, and Percussion (1955; Frankfurt am Main, May 25, 1956); *Kammerkonzert* for Clarinet, String Quartet, and String Orch. (n.d.; Zürich, June 17, 1969); *Kleines Konzert* for Strings and Percussion (n.d.; Braunschweig, Nov. 29, 1974; also for String Quartet and Percussion). **CHAMBER:** 2 suites for Violin (1927); 2 sonatas for Solo Violin (1927); *Tanzsuite* for Wind Quintet (1931; Frankfurt am Main, April 20, 1975); 2 string quartets (*Carillon,* 1933; 1945–46); *Burleske Musik* for 6 Winds, Percussion, and Piano (c.1933; Rotterdam, June 30, 1967). **PIANO:** *Jazz-Toccata und-Fugue* (1928); Sonatina (1931); Sonata, *27 April 1945* (1945). **VOCAL:** *Friede Anno 48* for Soprano, Chorus, and Piano, after Gryphius (1937; Cologne, Oct. 22, 1968; also as the cantata *Lamento* for Soprano and Piano); *Ghetto* for Alto, Baritone, and Chamber Orch. (1960; in collaboration with B. Blacher, P. Dessau, H.W. Henze, and R. Wagner-Régeny); *Gesangsszene* for Baritone and Orch., after Giraudoux (1962–63; unfinished; Frankfurt am Main, Nov. 12, 1964).

BIBL.: J. Distefano, *The Symphonies of K.A..H.* (diss., Florida State Univ., 1972); A. McCredie, *K.A.H.* (Wilhelmshaven, 1980); R. Wagner, ed., *K.A.H. und die Musica Viva* (Mainz, 1980); A. Jaschinski, *K.A.H.: Symphonische Tradition und ihre Auflösung* (Munich, 1982); A. McCredie, ed., *K.A.H.: Thematic Catalogue of His Works* (Wilhelmshaven, 1982).

Hartmann, Rudolf, German opera director and administrator; b. Ingolstadt, Oct. 11, 1900; d. Munich, Aug. 26, 1988. He was trained in stage design in Munich and was a student of Berg-Ehlert in Bamberg. He was an opera director in Altenburg (1924–27), Nuremberg (1928–34; 1946–52), the Berlin State Opera (1934–37), and the Bavarian State Opera in Munich (1937–44); from 1952 to 1967 he was the Bavarian Staatsintendant. He was especially known for his staging of works by Richard Strauss, and was chosen to stage the premieres of Strauss' *Friedenstag* (Munich, 1938) and *Capriccio* (Munich, 1942); he also directed the official premiere ot Strauss' *Der Liebe der Danae* (Salzburg, 1952). In his stagings, he fused the best of traditional elements with contemporary stage practices. He publ. an autobiography as *Das geliebte Haus: Mein Leben mit der Oper* (Munich, 1975). His other writings included *Oper: Regie und Bühnenbild heute* (Stuttgart, 1977) and *Richard Strauss: Die Bühnenwerke von der Uraufführung bis heute* (Munich and Fribourg, 1980; Eng. tr., 1982, as *Richard Strauss: The Staging of His Operas and Ballets).* His correspondence with Strauss was ed. by R. Schlötterer as *Richard Strauss—Rudolf Hartmann: Ein Briefwechsel* (Tutzing, 1984).

Hartmann, Thomas (Alexandrovich de), Russian composer; b. Khoruzhevka, Ukraine, Sept. 21, 1885; d. Princeton, N.J., March 26, 1956. He studied piano with Essipova and composition with Taneyev and Arensky at the St. Petersburg Cons. His first important work, the ballet *The Little Crimson Flower,* was premiered at the Imperial Theater in St. Petersburg in 1907 with Pavlova, Karsavina, Nijinsky, and Fokine. After the Revolution, he went to the Caucasus; taught at the Tiflis Cons. (1919); then went to Paris, where he remained until 1951, when he settled in N.Y. His early music is in the Russian national style, influenced particularly by Mussorgsky; from about 1925, he made a radical change in his style of composition, adopting many devices of outspoken modernism.

WORKS: DRAMATIC: OPERA: *Esther* (not perf.). **BALLETS:** *The Little Crimson Flower* (St. Petersburg, Dec. 16, 1907); *Babette* (Nice, March 10, 1935). **ORCH.:** 4 syms. (1915; 1944; 1953; 1955, unfinished); Cello Concerto (1935; Boston, April 14, 1938); Piano Concerto (1940; Paris, Nov. 8, 1942); Double Bass Concerto (1943; Paris, Jan. 26, 1945); Harp Concerto (1944); Violin Concerto (Paris, March 16, 1947); Flute Concerto (Paris, Sept. 27, 1950); *12 Russian Fairy Tales* (Houston, April 4, 1955). **CHAMBER:** Violin Sonata (1937); Cello Sonata (1942); Trio for Flute, Violin, and Piano (1946); piano pieces. **VOCAL:** 3 song cycles to words by Verlaine, Proust, and James Joyce; other songs. **OTHER:** Music to Kandinsky's *The Yellow Sound* (arranged by G. Schuller; N.Y., Feb. 9, 1982).

Härtwig, Dieter, distinguished German musicologist; b. Dresden, July 18, 1934. He was a student of Besseler, Serauky, Wolff, and Eller at the Univ. of Leipzig (Ph.D., 1963, with the diss. *Der Opernkomponist Rudolf Wagner-Régeny: Leben und Werk*; publ. in Berlin, enl. ed., 1965 as *Rudolf Wagner-Régeny: Der Opernkomponist*; Habilitation, 1970, with his *Fidelio F. Finke: Leben und Werk).* He was a dramaturg at the theaters in Schwerin (1959–60) and Dresden-Radebeul (1960–65), and then was chief dramaturg of the Dresden Phil. (from 1965). He also was a lecturer (1960–62; 1973–80), Dozent (1980–84), and prof. (1984–91) of music history at the Dresden Hochschule für Musik.

WRITINGS: *Die Dresdner Philharmonie: Eine Chronik des Orchesters 1870 bis 1970* (Leipzig, 1970); *Kurt Masur* (Leipzig, 1975); *Die Dresdner Philharmonie* (Leipzig, 1985; 2nd ed., 1989; new ed., Berlin, 1992); *Carl Maria von Weber* (Leipzig, 1986; 2nd ed., 1989).

Harty, Sir (Herbert) Hamilton, eminent Irish conductor, pianist, and composer; b. Hillsborough, County Down, Dec. 4, 1879; d. Brighton, Feb. 19, 1941. He received most of his musical training from his father, William Harty, the parish organist and a music teacher. He learned to play the piano, organ, and viola, and began composing while still a youth. In 1894 he was made organist at Magheragall Church in County Antrim, and then was a church organist in Belfast (1895–96) and Bray in County Wicklow (1896–1901). During the latter period, he profited from the guidance of Michele Esposito and established himself as a piano accompanist in Dublin. In 1901 he went to London. For the Feis Ceoil, Dublin's competitive music festival, he composed *An Irish Symphony* and won a special prize. On May 18, 1904, he made his conducting debut in Dublin leading its first performance. From 1904 he also appeared as a conductor in London, the year he married **Agnes Nicholls.** He composed several works for his wife and appeared as her accompanist. In 1913 he made his debut at London's Covent Garden, and subsequently devoted most of his time to conducting. From 1920 to 1933 he was conductor of the Hallé Orch. in Manchester, which he brought to a high level of performance. In 1931 he made his first conducting tour of the U.S. From 1932 to 1934 he was artistic adviser and conductor-in-chief of the London Sym. Orch. Although stricken with a brain tumor in 1936 which cost him his right eye, he continued to make occasional appearances as a conductor until Dec. 1940. In 1925 he was knighted and in 1934 he was awarded the Gold Medal of the Royal Phil. Soc. of London. Harty's well-crafted compositions follow along traditional lines with an infusion of Irish inflections. While none of his compositions entered the standard repertoire, his effective suites for large orch. arranged from Handel's *Water Music* (1920) and *Music for the Royal Fireworks* (1923) were popular concert staples for many years. As a conductor, he was highly esteemed as a consummate podium figure.

WORKS: ORCH.: *The Exile*, overture (c.1900); *An Irish Symphony* (Dublin, May 18, 1904; rev. 1915 and 1924); *A Comedy Overture* (1906; rev. 1908); Violin Concerto (1908); *With the Wild Geese*, poem (1910); *Variations on a Dublin Air* or *Irish Variations* for Violin and Orch. (1912); *Fantasy Scenes* (1919); Piano Concerto (1922); *À la campagne* for Oboe and Orch. (c.1931; also for Oboe and Piano, 1911); *Orientale* for Oboe and Orch. (c.1931; also for Oboe and Piano, 1911); *In Ireland*, fantasy for Flute, Harp, and Orch. (1935; also for Flute and Piano, 1915); *The Children of Lir*, poem (1938; London, March 1, 1939). **CHAMBER:** 3 string quartets (1898, c.1900, c.1902); *2 Fantasiestücke* for Piano, Violin, and Cello (c.1901); *Romance and Scherzo* for Cello and Piano (1903); Quintet for Piano, 2 Violins, Viola, and Cello (c.1904); *2 Pieces* for Cello and Piano; *Waldesstille* and *Der Schmetterling* (1907); *Chansonette* for Oboe and Piano (1911); *Irish Fantasy* for Violin and Piano (1912); *Spring Fancies*, 2 preludes for Harp (1915); *Fanfare* for 4 Trumpets and Side Drum (1921); Suite for Cello and Piano (1928); *A Little Fantasy and Fugue* for Carillon (1934); piano pieces. **VOCAL:** *Ode to a Nightingale* for Soprano or Tenor and Orch. (1907); *The Mystic Trumpeter* for Baritone, Chorus, and Orch. (1913); choruses; many songs.

BIBL.: D. Greer, ed., *H. H.: His Life and Music* (Belfast, 1978); special issue of *Le Grand Baton* (May 1990).

Hartzell, Eugene, American-born Austrian composer; b. Cincinnati, May 21, 1932. He studied at Kent State Univ. (B.S., 1953) and Yale Univ. (B.M., 1954; M.M., 1955), and with H.E. Apostel in Vienna (1956–58). He then lived in Vienna, working in various positions only peripherally connected with music. He adopted the 12-tone method of composition; his works in this idiom include *14 Monologues* for Assorted Instruments (1957–84) and *10 Workpoints* (1977–82), inspired by the English writer Lawrence Durrell, for every binary combination, from the Woodwind Quintet.

WORKS: ORCH.: *2 Pieces* (1962); 2 syms.: No. 1 for Strings (1965) and No. 2 for Wind Quintet and Strings (1968); *Synopsis for Symphony* (1970); Sinfonietta for Strings (1980). **CHAMBER:** *14 Monologues* (1957–84); Trio for Flute, Bass Clarinet or Bassoon, and Piano (1969); *Projections* for Wind Quintet (1970); *Companion Pieces to a Wind Quintet* (1973); *Outgrowths of a Wind Quintet* (1973); *10 Workpoints* (1977–82); String Quartet (1979); Clarinet Sonata (1981). **PIANO:** *Suite for a Young Pianist* (1963); *9 Uncritical Pieces* (1968). **VOCAL:** *Psalm 130* for Chorus and Organ (1973); *3 Latin Lyrics* for Chorus (1976); *A Keats Songbook* for Tenor and Guitar (1978); *9 Haikus* for Baritone and Clarinet (1978); *3 American Folksongs* for Voice and Piano (1979); *Grounds for John Donne* for Tenor and Harp (1979); *4 Latin Lyrics* for Tenor and Orch. (1981).

Harvey, Jonathan (Dean), significant English composer; b. Sutton Coldfield, Warwickshire, May 3, 1939. He was a scholarship student at St. John's College, Cambridge, and also received private instruction from Erwin Stein and Hans Keller; after obtaining his Ph.D. from the Univ. of Glasgow (1964), he attended the Darmstadt summer courses in new music (1966) and studied with Babbitt at Princeton Univ. He taught at the Univ. of Southampton (1964–77), and then at the Univ. of Sussex (1977–80), where he was a prof. of music (1980–95). In 1995 he became a prof. of music at Stanford Univ. In 1985 he received the Koussevitzky Foundation Award. In his ultimate style of composition, he astutely synthesized a number of quaquaversal idioms and techniques ranging from medieval modalities to ultramodern procedures.

WORKS: OPERAS: *Passion and Resurrection*, church opera (Winchester Cathedral, March 21, 1981); *Inquest of Love* (1992). **ORCH.:** Sym. (1966); Chaconne on *Iam dulcis amaica* (1967); *Benedictus* (1970); *Persephone's Dream* (1972; London, Jan. 18, 1973); *Smiling Immortal* for Chamber Ensemble and Tape (London, July 11, 1977); *Whom Ye Adore* (Glasgow, Sept. 19, 1981); *Bhakti* for Chamber Orch. and Tape (Paris, Dec. 3, 1982); *Easter Orisons* for Chamber Orch. (1983; Newcastle upon Tyne, Jan. 15, 1984); *Gong-Ring* for Chamber Ensemble and Electronics (Edinburgh, Sept. 1, 1984); *Madonna of Winter and Spring* Orch., Synthesizers, and Electronics (London, Aug. 27, 1986); *Lightness and Weight* for Tuba and Orch. (Poole, Feb. 18, 1987); *Timepieces* (1987; Saarbrücken, Sept. 23, 1988); Cello Concerto (1990). **CHAMBER:** *Dialogue* for Cello and Piano (1965); *Variations* for Violin and Piano (1965); *Transformation of "Love Bade Me Welcome"* for Clarinet and Piano (1968); *Studies* for 2 Clarinets (1970); Trio for Violin, Cello, and Piano (1971); *Quantumplation* for Flute, Clarinet, Violin, Cello, Percussion, and Piano (1973); *Inner Light I* for Flute or Piccolo, Clarinet, Violin, Viola, Cello, Percussion, Piano, and Tape (1973); *Smiling Immortal* for Chamber Group and Tape (1977); 2 string quartets (1977, 1988); *Concelebration* for Flute, Clarinet, Cello, Piano, and Percussion (1979; rev. 1981); *Be(coming)* for Clarinet and Piano (1981); *Modernsky Music* for 2 Oboes, Bassoon, and Harpsichord (1981); *Curve with Plateaux* for Cello (1982); *Nataraja* for Flute and Piano (1983); *Flight-Elegy* for Violin and Piano (1984); *Ricercare una melodie* for Trumpet or Flute or Oboe and Tape Delay (1985); *Tendril* for Chamber Group (1987); *The Valley of Aosta* for Chamber Group (1988); *Serenade in Homage to Mozart* for 10 Winds (1991); *Lotuses* for Flute Quartet (1992); *Scena* for Violin and Chamber Group (1992); *Chant* for Viola (1992). **VOCAL:** Cantatas: *I* for Soprano, Baritone, Chorus, Organ, and Strings (1965), *II: 3 Lovescapes* for Soprano and Piano (1967), *III* for Soprano and 7 Instruments (1968), *IV: Ludus amoris* for Soprano, Tenor, Speaker, Chorus, and Orch. (1969), *V: Black Sonnet* for Soprano, Mezzo-soprano, Baritone, Bass, and Wind Quintet (1970), *VI: On Faith* for Small Chorus and Small String Orch. (1970), and *VII: On Vision* for Soprano, Tenor, Chorus, and Chamber Group (1972); *Iam dulcis amica* for 2 Soprano, 2 Tenors, and 2 Basses (1967; also for Chorus); *In memoriam* for Soprano, Flute, Clarinet, Violin, and Cello (1969); *Angel Eros* for High Voice and String Quartet (1973); *Spirit Music* for Soprano, 3 Clarinets, and Piano (1975); *Inner Light II* for 2 Sopranos, Alto, Tenor, Bass, Chamber Group, and Tape (1977); *Magnificat and Nunc Dimittis* for Chorus and Organ (1978); *Hymn* for Chorus and Orch. for the 900th anniversary of Winchester Cathedral (Winchester Cathedral, July 12, 1979); *Resurrection* for Double Chorus and Organ (1981); *The Path of Devotion* for Chorus and Small Orch. (1983); *Come, Holy Ghost* for Double Chorus (1984); *Nachtlied* for Soprano, Piano, and Tape (1984); *Song Offerings* for Soprano and 8 Instruments (1985); *God Is Our Refuge* for Chorus and Organ (1986); *Lauds* for Chorus and Cello (1987); *From Silence* for Soprano, Violin, Viola, Percussion, 3 Synthesizers, and Tape (1988); *You* for Soprano, Clarinet, Viola, Cello, and Double Bass (1992); *One Evening* for Voices, Instruments, and Electronics (1994). **OTHER:** *Time-points* for Tape (1970); *Mortuos plango, vivos voco* for Computer-manipulated Concrete Sounds on Tape (1980); *Ritual Melodies* for Tape (1990).

Harwood, Basil, English organist and composer; b. Woodhouse, Gloucestershire, April 11, 1859; d. London, April 3, 1949. He studied piano with J.L. Roeckel and organ with George Risely; then studied with Reinecke and Jadassohn at the Leipzig Cons.; also studied theology with Corfe at Trinity College, Oxford. He was organist at St. Barnabas Church, Pimlico

(1883–87), Ely Cathedral (1887–92), and Christ Church, Oxford (1892–1909); also was the 1st conductor of Oxford's Bach Choir (1896–1900). He ed. the *Oxford Hymn Book* (1908); wrote a number of sacred works for chorus; organ pieces (2 sonatas, Organ Concerto, *Christmastide, Dithyramb*, etc.); a cantata, *Ode on May Morning*, after Milton (Leeds Festival, 1913).

Harwood, Elizabeth (Jean), English soprano; b. Barton Seagrave, May 27, 1938; d. Ingatestone, June 21, 1990. She studied at the Royal Manchester College of Music (1955–60). In 1960 she won the Kathleen Ferrier Memorial Prize and in 1963 the Verdi Prize of Busseto. She made her operatic debut in 1960 as the 2nd boy in *Die Zauberflöte* at the Glyndebourne Festival, and returned there to sing Fiordiligi, Countess Almaviva, and the Marschallin. In 1961 she became a member of the Sadler's Wells Opera in London, where she appeared as Susanna, Zerbinetta, and Massenet's Manon. In 1967 she made her first appearance at London's Covent Garden as Fiakermilli, and returned there to sing such roles as Marzelline, Gilda, Norina, and Donna Elvira; she also sang at Glasgow's Scottish Opera (1967–74). In 1970 she sang for the first time at the Salzburg Festival and in 1972 at Milan's La Scala. On Oct. 15, 1975, she made her Metropolitan Opera debut in N.Y. as Fiordiligi, remaining on the roster for that season; she returned for the 1977–78 season. In 1986 she made a tour of Australia. Among her other roles were Constanze, Lucia, Musetta, Sophie, and Hanna Glawari.

Haselböck, Hans, Austrian organist, pedagogue, and composer, father of **Martin Haselböck;** b. Nesselstauden, July 26, 1928. He received training in literature and musicology at the Univ. of Vienna (1947–52) and in organ with Walter Pach at the Vienna Academy of Music (1948–53). From 1953 he served as titular organist at the Dominikanerkirche in Vienna. He took 1st prize in the Haarlem organ competitions in 1958, 1959, and 1960. In 1961 he became prof. of organ and improvisation at the Vienna Hochschule für Musik, where he was head of its department of sacred music from 1964. He publ. the study *Barocker Orgelschatz in Niederösterreich* (Vienna, 1972). Among his compositions are sacred vocal pieces and various organ works.

Haselböck, Martin, Austrian organist, harpsichordist, conductor, and teacher, son of **Hans Haselböck;** b. Vienna, Nov. 23, 1954. He received training in organ, harpsichord, composition, and church music, his principal mentors being his father, Michael Radulescu, and Anton Heiller at the Vienna Hochschule für Musik and Jean Langlais at the Paris Schola Cantorum. In 1972 he won 1st prize in the Vienna-Melk International Improvisation Competition. He commenced his career as a keyboard player in 1970, and subsequently toured all over the world as a recitalist and as a soloist with leading orchs. He also held titular positions as director of music at the Augustinerkirche and as organist at the former Court Chapel in Vienna. In 1979 he became a prof. at the Vienna Hochschule für Musik, and in 1986 at the Lübeck Hochschule für Musik. He also gave master classes in keyboard playing in various locales. In 1985 he founded the Wiener Akademie, a period-instrument ensemble which he conducted at home and abroad. He also appeared as a guest conductor with many European orchs. In 1993 he became principal guest conductor of the Estonian State Sym. Orch. in Tallinn. As both a keyboard player and conductor, Haselböck maintains a catholic repertoire extending from the early to modern masters.

Haskil, Clara, eminent Romanian-born Swiss pianist; b. Bucharest, Jan. 7, 1895; d. Brussels, Dec. 7, 1960. A precocious child, she entered the Bucharest Cons. when she was 6; at 7, she was sent to Vienna and profited from the tutelage of Richard Robert; she was only 7 when she made her public debut there. At 10, she was sent to Paris to continue her training with Morpain, and, at 12, entered the Cons. as a pupil of Cortot. In 1909 she took 1st prize in the Concours de l'Union Française de la Jeunesse of Paris, and also 2nd prix at the Cons.; in 1910 she won the premier prix at the Cons. From 1920 she toured in Europe, and also made some appearances in the U.S. However, she became best known in France and Switzerland. In 1942 she sought refuge in the latter country and in 1949 she became a naturalized Swiss citizen. From 1950 she pursued an international career as a soloist with the foremost orchs. and as a recitalist. She also appeared in duo recitals with Arthur Grumiaux. In spite of the fact that illness hampered her throughout her career, she succeeded in becoming a keyboard artist of consummate musicianship. Her interpretations of the Classical and Romantic masters, especially Mozart, Beethoven, Schubert, Schumann, and Chopin, were greatly admired.

BIBL.: R. Wolfensberger, *C. H.* (Bern, 1961); J. Spycket, *C. H.* (Paris, 1975).

Hasse, Karl, German musicologist and composer; b. Dohna, near Dresden, March 20, 1883; d. Cologne, July 31, 1960. He studied with Kretzschmar and Riemann at the Univ., and with Straube, Nikisch, and Ruthhardt at the Cons. in Leipzig, and then with Reger and Mottl in Munich. In 1907 he became Wolfran's assistant at the Univ. of Heidelberg; in 1909 he became organist and Kantor at the Chemnitz Johanneskirche; in 1910 he was made music director in Osnabrück, where he also founded a cons. In 1919 he became music director and prof. extraordinary at the Univ. of Tübingen; in 1923 he took his Ph.D. there and was responsible for founding its music inst. and music dept. From 1935 to 1945 he was director of the Cologne Staatliche Hochschule für Musik. His compositions include a Sym.; Piano Concerto; Violin Concerto; Cello Concerto; orch. suites; chamber music; piano pieces; organ music; choral works.

WRITINGS: *Max Reger* (Leipzig, 1921; 2nd ed., 1930); *Johann Sebastian Bach* (Leipzig, 1925); *Musikstil und Musikkultur* (Kassel, 1927); *Von deutscher Kirchenmusik* (Regensburg, 1935); *Max Reger: Mensch und Werk* (Berlin, 1936); *Johann Sebastian Bach* (Cologne and Krefeld, 1938; 2nd ed., 1941); *Johann Sebastian Bach* (Leipzig, 1949); *Max Reger* (Leipzig, 1949); *Max Reger* (Dortmund, 1951).

Hassell, Jon, American composer; b. Memphis, Tenn., March 22, 1937. He was trained as a trumpet player; then studied composition with Bernard Rogers at the Eastman School of Music in Rochester, N.Y. (B.M., 1969; M.M., 1970). Progressing away from traditional arts, he also took courses in advanced electronic techniques with Stockhausen and Pousseur in Cologne (1965–67). He was composer-in-residence and a performer at the Center for Creative and Performing Arts in Buffalo (1967–69). In 1969 he moved to N.Y., where he pursued independent activities in music and in sculpture. Among his compositions from this period are *Goodbye Music* for Mixed Media (Buffalo, May 4, 1969), *Superball* for 4 Players with Hand-held Magnetic Tape Heads (Ithaca, Oct. 29, 1969), and *Map 1* and *2* for Hand-held Magnetic Playback Heads (exhibited in Buffalo as sculptures, 1969). In the 1970s he studied Indian music with Pandit Pran Nath, and developed a vocal style of trumpet playing; he combined this with avant-garde and jazz backgrounds to create a series of works marked by their remarkable syntheses of African, Asian, and Western music. His popular works in this style appear on the recordings *Earthquake Island* (1978), the synthetically sampled *Aka/Darbari/Java-Magic Realism* (1983), *Power Spot* (1986), and *The Surgeon of the Nightsky Restores Dead Things by the Power of Sound* (1987). On the recording *Flash of the Spirit* (1989), he performs with the West African group Farafina.

Hasselmans, Louis, French cellist and conductor; b. Paris, July 15, 1878; d. San Juan, Puerto Rico, Dec. 27, 1957. His father was the Belgian-born French harpist and composer Alphonse (Jean) Hasselmans (b. Liège, March 5, 1845; d. Paris, May 19, 1912). He studied with Godard, Lavignac, and Massenet; also studied cello with Jules Delsart at the Paris Cons., winning the premier prix in 1893. He was a member of the Capet Quartet (1904–09); made his conducting debut with the Lamoureux Orch. (1905); then conducted at the Opéra-Comique (1909–11; 1919–22), the Montreal Opera and Marseilles Concerts Classiques (1911–13), and the Chicago Civic Opera (1918–19); later was a conductor at the Metropolitan Opera in N.Y. (1922–36). From 1936 to 1948 he taught at the Louisiana State Univ. School of Music.

Hatrík, Juraj, Slovak composer and teacher; b. Orkučany, May 1, 1941. He was a student of A. Moyzes at the Bratislava Academy of Music (1958–63), where he pursued his postgraduate training (1965–68). After teaching at the Košice Cons. (1963–65) and the Bratislava Academy of Music (1968–71), he was a specialist with the Slovak Music Fund (1972–90); he then served as assoc. prof. of composition at the Bratislava Academy of Music (from 1990). His output is replete with traditional and modern elements.

WORKS: DRAMATIC: *Janko Polienko* (1976); *Šťastný princ* (The Happy Prince; 1977–78); *Mechúrik Koščúrik*, musical fairy tale (1980); *Turčan Poničan* (1985); *Adamove deti* (Adam's Children), tragifarce (1990); *The Brave Tin Soldier*, musical (1994). **ORCH.:** Sinfonietta (1962); *Monumento malinconico* for Organ and Orch. (1964); *Concerto grosso facile* for Violin, Cello, Piano, and String Orch. (1966); *Concertino in modo classico* for Piano and Orch. (1967); *Double Portrait: Sancho Panza and Don Quixote* (1970); *De capo al fine: Song of a Human Life*, poem (1972); *Choral Fantasia* for Accordion and Chamber Orch. (1975); 2 syms.: No. 1, *Sans Souci* (1979) and No. 2, *VICTOR*, for Tenor, Chorus, and Orch. (1986–87); *Still Life with Violin* for Violin and String Orch. (1987). **CHAMBER:** *Contrasts* for Violin and Piano (1963); *Monologues* for Accordion (1965–67); *Dreams for My Son* for 2 Violins and Piano (1966); *Dispute Over a Plastered Dwarf*, anti-duet for 2 Accordions (1969); *Metamorphoses after Gogol* for Guitar (1972–80); Sonatina for Violin and Cello (1979–80); Sonatina for Solo Guitar (1981); *Vox memoriae* for Oboe, Bassoon, Harpsichord, Cello, and Easily-mastered Instruments (1983); *Looking for a Song* for Violin and Piano (1985); Sonata for Solo Accordion (1987); *Diptych* for Violin, Cello, and Piano (1988); *Partita giocosa* for Accordion (1992). **PIANO:** Sonata (1961); *Sonata ciaccona* (1971). **VOCAL:** *Expectation* for Reciter, Flute, Harp, Percussion, and String Quartet (1966); *Home Are the Hands You May Weep On*, cantata for Reciter, Tenor, Chorus, and Orch. (1967); *Introspection to Latin Texts* for Soprano and Chamber Orch. (1967); *3 Nocturnes* for Soprano, Viola, and 2 Pianists (1971); *A Bird Flew Up*, cantata profana for Soloists, Chorus, and Chamber Orch. (1976); *The Diary of Tanya Savichevova*, monodrama for Soprano and Wind Quintet (1976); *Organ Music* for Bass, 2 Organists, and Chorus (1982); *Submerged Music*, sonata for Soprano, Violin, and 12 Strings (1982); *Canzona in memoriam A. Moyzes* for Alto, Viola, and Organ (1984); *Moment musical avec J.S. Bach*, chamber cantata for Soprano, Flute, Horn, Violin, Double Bass, and Piano (1985); *Schola ridicula*, cantata for Children's Chorus and Small Orch. (1989); *The Lost Children* for Bass and String Quartet (1993).

Haubenstock-Ramati, Roman, Polish composer; b. Kraków, Feb. 27, 1919; d. Vienna, March 3, 1994. He studied with J. Koffler at the Lwów Academy of Music (1939–41); also took courses in philosophy at the Univs. of Kraków and Lwów. From 1947 to 1950 he was music director of Radio Kraków; then was director of the State Music Library in Tel Aviv (1950–56). In 1957 he settled in Vienna, where he worked for Universal Edition until 1968; then was a prof. of composition at the Vienna Academy of Music (from 1973); in 1981 he was awarded the Austrian State Prize. In 1959 he organized in Donaueschingen the first exhibition of musical scores in graphic notation; he evolved an imaginative type of modern particella in which the right-hand page gives the outline of musical action for the conductor while the left-hand page is devoted to instrumental and vocal details. This type of notation combined the most advanced type of visual guidance with an aide-memoire of traditional theater arrangements. Several of his works bear the subtitle "Mobile" to indicate the flexibility of their architectonics.

WORKS: *Ricercari* for String Trio (1950); *Blessings* for Voice and 9 Players (1952); *Recitativo ed Aria* for Harpsichord and Orch. (1954); *Papageno's Pocket-Size Concerto* for Glockenspiel and Orch. (1955); *Les Symphonies des timbres* for Orch. (1957); *Chants et Prismes* for Orch. (1957; rev. 1967); *Séquences* for Violin and Orch. in 4 groups (1957–58); *Interpolation*, "mobile" for Flute (1958); *Liaisons*, "mobile" for Vibraphone and Marimbaphone (1958); *Petite musique de nuit*, "mobile" for Orch. (1958); *Mobile for Shakespeare* for Voice and 6 Players (1960); *Credentials or "Think, Think Lucky"* for Speech-voice and 8 Players, after Beckett (1960); *Jeux 6*, "mobile" for 6 Percussionists (1960); *Decisions*, 10 pieces of musical graphics for Variable Instrumentation (1960–68); *Amerika*, opera after Kafka's novel (1962–64; Berlin, Oct. 8, 1966); *Vermutungen über ein dunkles Haus*, 3 pieces for 3 Orchs., 2 of which are on tape (1963); *Klavierstücke I* for Piano (1963–65); *Jeux 2* and *4*, "mobiles" for 2 and 4 Percussionists (1965, 1966); *Hotel Occidental* for Speech-chorus, after Kafka (in 3 versions, 1967); *Tableau I, II*, and *III* for Orch. (1967, 1968, 1970); *Symphonie "K"* (1967; material from the opera *Amerika*); *Psalm* for Orch. (1967); *Divertimento*, text collage for Actors, Dancer, and/or Mime, and 2 Percussionists (1968; after *Jeux 2*); *La Comédie*, "anti-opera," after Beckett, for 1 Male and 2 Female Speech-singers and 3 Percussionists (St. Paul-de-Vence, Alpes-Maritimes, France, July 21, 1969; German version as *Spiel*, Munich, 1970; Eng. version as *Play*); *Catch I* for Harpsichord (1969), *II* for 1 or 2 Pianos (1970), and *III* for Organ (1971); *Multiple I–VI* for Various Instrumental Combinations (1969); *Alone* for Trombone and Mime (1969); *Describe* for Voice and Piano (1969); *Hexachord I* and *II* for 2 Guitars (1972); *Concerto a tre* for Piano, Trombone, and Percussion (1973); 2 string quartets (1973, 1978); *Shapes (in Memory of Stravinsky) I* for Organ and Tape, and *II* for Organ, Piano, Harpsichord, and Celesta (both 1973); *Endless*, endless "mobile" for 7 Players and Conductor (1974); Sonata for Solo Cello (1975); *Musik* for 12 Instruments (1976); *Ulysses*, ballet (1977); *Concerto per archi* (Graz, Oct. 11, 1977); *Symphonien* (1977; Baden-Baden, May 10, 1978); *Song* for Percussion (1978); *Self I* for Bass Clarinet or Clarinet (1978) and *II* for Saxophone (1978); *3 Nocturnes* for Orch. (1981, 1982, 1985); *Mirrors/Miroirs I*, "mobile" for 16 Pianos (1984), *II*, "mobile" for 8 Pianos (1984), and *III*, "mobile" for 6 Pianos (1984); *Cantando* for 6 Players (1984); Piano Sonata (1984); String Trio No. 2 (1985); *Enchaîné* for Saxophone Quartet (1985); *Sotto voce* for Chamber Orch. (1986).

Haubiel (real name, **Pratt**), **Charles Trowbridge,** American composer; b. Delta, Ohio, Jan. 30, 1892; d. Los Angeles, Aug. 26, 1978. His father's last name was Pratt, but he adopted his mother's maiden name, Haubiel, as his own. He had piano lessons with his sister Florence Pratt, an accomplished pianist. In 1911 he went to Europe, where he studied piano with Rudolph Ganz in Berlin; also took composition lessons with Alexander von Fielitz in Leipzig. Returning to the U.S. in 1913, he taught music at various schools in Oklahoma. When the U.S. entered World War I in 1917, he enlisted in the field artillery and served in France. After the Armistice, he resumed serious study of composition with Rosario Scalero at the David Mannes Music School in N.Y. (1919–24), while continuing piano lessons with Rosina and Josef Lhévinne (1920–26). In 1928 he won 1st prize in the Schubert Centennial Contest with his symphonic variations *Karma*. Intermittently he taught musical subjects at the Inst. of Musical Art in N.Y. (1921–31) and at N.Y. Univ. (1923–47). In 1935 he organized the Composers Press, Inc., with the purpose of promoting the publication of American music, and served as its president until 1966. His compositions reveal an excellent theoretical and practical grasp of harmony, counterpoint, instrumentation, and formal design. In his idiom, he followed the models of the Romantic school of composition, but he embroidered the basic patterns of traditional music with winsome coloristic touches, approaching the usage of French Impressionism. He was extremely prolific; many of his works underwent multiple transformations from a modest original, usually for solo piano or a chamber group, to a piece for full orch.; in all these forms, his compositions remain eminently playable.

WORKS: DRAMATIC: *Brigands Preferred*, comic opera (1929–46); *Passionate Pilgrim*, incidental music (c.1937); *The Witch's Curse*, fairy tale opera (1940); *The Birthday Cake*, operetta (c.1942); *Sunday Costs 5 Pesos*, folk opera (1947; Charlotte, N.C., Nov. 6, 1950); *The Enchanted Princess* (c.1955); *Adventures on Sunbonnet Hill*, children's operetta (c.1971). **ORCH.:** *Mars Ascending* (1923); *Karma*, symphonic variations (1928; rev. 1968 as *Of Human Destiny*); *Vox Cathedralis* (1934; N.Y., May 6, 1938); *Portraits: 3 ritratti caratteristici* (Chicago, Dec. 12, 1935); *Solari* (1935–36); *Suite Passacaille* (Los Angeles, Jan. 31, 1936); *Symphony in Variation Form* (1937); *Miniatures* for Strings (1938–39; N.Y., April 23, 1939); *Passacaglia Triptych* (1939–40); *1865 A.D.* (1945; rev. 1958 as *Mississippi Story*; Los Angeles, April 24, 1959); *Pioneers: A Symphonic Saga of Ohio* (1946; rev. 1956; Los Angeles, Feb. 19, 1960); *American Rhapsody* (1948); *A Kennedy Memorial* (1965); *Heroic Elegy* (1970); also many transcriptions of chamber and instrumental pieces. **CHAMBER:** *Ecchi classici* for String Quartet (1924); *Duoforms* for Piano Trio (1929–33); *Lodando la danza* for Oboe, Violin, Cello, and Piano (1932); *Romanza* for Piano Trio (1932); Piano Trio (1932); *Cryptics* for Bassoon and Piano (1932); *Nuances* for Flute and Piano (1938); *En saga* for Violin and Piano (1938); *In the French Manner* for Flute, Cello, and Piano (1942); Trio for Flute, Cello, and Piano (1942); String Trio (1943); *Shadows* for Violin or Cello and Piano (1947); *Pastoral Trio* for Flute, Cello, and Piano (1949); *Epochs* for Violin and Piano (1954–55); Trio for Clarinet, Cello, and Piano (1969); *Cryptics* for Cello and Piano (1973); many piano pieces. **VOCAL:** *Portals*, symphonic song cycle for High Voice and Orch. (1963); *Threnody for Love* for Alto, Flute, Clarinet, Violin, Cello, and Piano (1965); 3 cantatas; choral pieces with orch.; solo songs.

Hauer, Josef Matthias, significant Austrian composer and music theorist; b. Wiener-Neustadt, near Vienna, March 19, 1883; d. Vienna, Sept. 22, 1959. After attending a college for teachers, he became a public-school instructor; at the same time, he studied music. An experimenter by nature, with a penchant for mathematical constructions, he developed a system of composition based on "tropes," or patterns, which aggregated to thematic formations of 12 different notes. As early as 1912, he publ. a piano piece, entitled *Nomos* (Law), which contained the germinal principles of 12-tone music; in his theoretical publications, he elaborated his system in greater detail. These were *Über die Klangfarbe*, op. 13 (Vienna, 1918; aug. as *Vom Wesen des Musikalischen*, Leipzig and Vienna, 1920; 3rd ed., rev. and aug., 1966); *Deutung des Melos: Eine Frage an die Künstler und Denker unserer Zeit* (Leipzig, Vienna, and Zürich, 1923); *Vom Melos zur Pauke: Eine Einführung in die Zwölftonmusik* (Vienna, 1925; 2nd ed., 1967); *Zwölftontechnik: Die Lehre von den Tropen* (Vienna, 1926; 2nd ed., 1953); *Zwölftonspiel-Neujahr 1947* (Vienna, 1962). Hauer vehemently asserted his priority in 12-tone composition; he even used a rubber stamp on his personal stationery proclaiming himself the true founder of the 12-tone method. This claim was countered, with equal vehemence but with more justification, by Schoenberg; indeed, the functional basis of 12-tone composition in which the contrapuntal and harmonic structures are derived from the unifying tone row did not appear until Schoenberg formulated it and put it into practice in 1924. Hauer lived his entire life in Vienna, working as a composer, conductor, and teacher. Despite its forbidding character, his music attracted much attention.

WORKS: 2 operas: *Salambo* (1930; Austrian Radio, Vienna, March 19, 1983) and *Die schwarze Spinne* (1932; Vienna, May 23, 1966); *Lateinische Messe* for Chorus, Chamber Orch., and Organ (1926; unfinished; Vienna, June 18, 1972); *Wandlungen*, oratorio for 6 Soloists, Chorus, and Chamber Orch. (1927; Baden-Baden, April 16, 1928); 2 cantatas: *Emilie vor ihrem Brauttag* for Alto and Orch. (1928) and *Der Menschen Weg* for 4 Soloists, Chorus, and Orch., after Hölderlin (1934; Vienna, June 1953); *Vom Leben*, after Holderlin, for Narrator, Small Chorus, and Small Orch. (1928). **OTHER WORKS:** *Nomos* (Sym. No. 1) for 1 or 2 Pianos or Orch. (1912–13; version for 2 Pianos, Sankt Pölten, June 7, 1913); *Nomos* (Sym. No. 2) for Piano or Small Orch. (1913); *Nomos*, 7 little piano pieces (1913); *Apokalyptische Phantasie* (Sym. No. 3) for 2 Pianos or Orch. (1913; version for 2 Pianos, Wiener-Neustadt, May 9, 1914; version for Orch., Graz, Oct. 21, 1969); *Oriental Tale* for Piano (1916); *Nomos* for Piano and String Ensemble (1919); Quintet for Clarinet, Violin, Viola, Cello, and Piano (1924); 6 string quartets (1924–26); 8 suites for Orch. (1924; 1924; 1925, with Baritone; 1926; 1926; 1926, also for String Quartet; 1926; 1927); *Romantische Fantasie* for Small Orch. (1925); *7 Variations* for Flute, Clarinet, Violin, Viola, Cello, and Double Bass (1925); *Symphonische Stücke (Kammerstücke)* for Strings, Piano, and Harmonium (1926); Sinfonietta (1927; Berlin, Dec. 13, 1928); Violin Concerto (1928; Berlin, Nov. 12, 1929); Piano Concerto (1928); *Divertimento* for Small Orch. (1930); *Konzertstücke* for Orch. (1932; from the opera *Die schwarze Spinne*); *Tanzphantasien Nos. 1* and *2* for 4 Soloists and Orch. (1933) and *Nos. 3–7* for Chamber Orch. (1934); *2 Tanzsuiten* for 9 Solo Instruments (1936); *Labyrinthischer Tanz* for Piano, 4-hands (1952); *Langsamer Walzer* for Orch. (1953); *Chinesisches Streichquartet* (1953); *Hausmusik* for Piano, 4-hands (1958). Also a series of pieces begun in 1940, each ostentatiously bearing the subtitle *Zwölftonspiel*, for orch. and chamber combinations of all descriptions—their total number exceeding 100—with each one designated by the month and year composed.

BIBL.: W. Reich, "J.M. H.," *Die Musik* (May 1931); H. Picht, *J.M. H., Ein Vorkämpfer geistiger Musikauffassung* (Stuttgart, 1934); M. Lichtenfeld, *Untersuchungen zur Theorie der Zwölftontechnik bei J.M. H.* (Regensburg, 1964); W. Szmolyan, *J.M. H.* (Vienna, 1965); J. Sengstschmid, "Anatomie eines Zwölftonspiels, Ein Blick in die Werkstatt J.M. Hs.," *Zeitschrift für Musiktheorie* (April 1971); H. Schony, "Die Vorfahren des Komponisten J.M. H.," *Genealogie* (Aug. 1971); M. Keyton, *A Mathematical Construction of the "Tropen" Occurring in H.'s Musical System* (thesis, Louisiana State Univ., 1976); R. Gustafson, "J.M. H.," *Tempo* (Sept. 1979); idem, "J.M. H.: A List of Works," ibid. (Sept. 1987); H. Götte, *Die Kompositionstechniken J.M. H.s: Unter besonderer Berücksichtigung deterministischer Verfahren* (Kassel, 1989).

Haufrecht, Herbert, American composer; b. N.Y., Nov. 3, 1909. He studied piano with Severin Eisenberger at the Cleveland Music School Settlement and composition with Herbert Elwell and Quincy Porter at the Cleveland Inst. of Music; then completed his training in composition with Rubin Goldmark at the Juilliard Graduate School in N.Y (1930–34). He was a composer and arranger for the WPA Federal Theater in N.Y. (1937–39), national music director of Young Audiences, Inc. (1961–68), and an ed. and arranger for several N.Y. music publishers (1968–77). He also was active as a collector of folk music and publ. such vols. as *Folk Sing* (1960), *'Round the World Folk Sing* (1964), *Travelin' on with the Weavers* (1966), *The Judy Collins Songbook* (1969), *Folk Songs in Settings by Master Composers* (1970), and, with N. Cazden and N. Studer, *Folk Songs of the Catskills* (1982).

WORKS: OPERAS: *Boney Quillen*, folk opera (1951); *A Pot of Broth* (1961–63). **ORCH.:** Suite for Strings (1934); *3 Fantastic Marches* (1939); *Square Set* for Strings (1942); *When Dad was a Fireman*, suite (1946); Sym. for Brass and Timpani (1956); *Ballad and Country Dance* for Violin and String Orch. (1967); *Divertimento* for Chamber Orch. (1983); *Suite on Catskill Folk Tunes* for Chamber Orch. (1986); band music. **CHAMBER:** Violin Sonata (1932); 2 string quartets (1933, 1989); *Blues Prelude and Fugue* for Viola and Piano (1941); *Caprice* for Clarinet and Piano (1950); *A Woodland Serenade* for Woodwind Quintet (1954); *From Washington's Time*, suite for Flute and Piano or Harpsichord (1959); Suite for Brass Quintet (1960); *Divertimento* for Plectrum Trio (1966); *Fantasy on Haitian Themes* for Clarinet, Viola or Cello, Piano, and Percussion (1974); *Sonata for 6* for Flute, Clarinet, and String Quartet (1983; also as a

Cello Sonata, 1984); Trio for Clarinet, Cello, and Piano (1985); Trio for Flute, Oboe, and Piano (1987); Trio for Violin, Cello, and Piano (1989). **PIANO:** *Sicilian Suite* (1944); *Etudes in Blues* (1954); Sonata (1956); *Toccata on Newsboy Cries* (1958); *Toccata on Familiar Tunes* (1969); *Inventions* (1980); *Blues Nocturnes* (1991). **VOCAL:** Cantatas; choral pieces; numerous songs; folk-song arrangements.

Haug, Hans, Swiss conductor, teacher, and composer; b. Basel, July 27, 1900; d. Lausanne, Sept. 15, 1967. He studied with Petri and Levy at the Basel Cons., with Busoni, and with Courvoisier and J. Pembaur, Jr., at the Munich Academy of Music. He served as music director in Grandson and Solothurn; after working as choirmaster and assistant conductor at the Basel City Theater (1928–34), he conducted at the Interlaken Kursaal and at the Swiss Radio in Lausanne (1935–38) and in Zürich (1938–43). He subsequently devoted himself mainly to teaching and composing. His works were in an eminently appealing style.

WORKS: DRAMATIC: OPERAS: *Don Juan in der Fremde* (1929; Basel, Jan. 15, 1930); *Madrisa* (1933; Basel, Jan. 15, 1934); *Tartuffe* (Basel, May 24, 1937); *Der unsterbliche* (1946; Zürich, Feb. 8, 1947); *La colombe égarée* (Basel Radio, 1951); *Le miroir d'Agrippine* (1953–54); *Les fous* (1957; Geneva Radio, Nov. 1959); *Le souper de Venise* (1966); *Le gardien vigilant* (1966). **OPÉRA-BALLET:** *Orfée* (RTF, Paris, Sept. 24, 1954; 1st stage perf., Lausanne, June 12, 1955). **OPERETTAS:** *Liederlig Kleeblatt* (1938); *Gilberte de Courgenay* (1940); *Annely us der Linde* (1940); *Barbara* (1942); *Leute von der Strasse* (1944); *La mère Michel* (1945). Other stage pieces and incidental music. **ORCH.:** *Charlie Chaplin,* symphonic poem (1930); 2 piano concertos (1938, 1962); Sym. (1948); Guitar Concerto (1952); Double Concerto for Oboe, Viola, and Orch. (1953). **CHAMBER:** 3 string quartets; Wind Quartet; Wind Quintet. **VOCAL:** *Michelangelo,* oratorio (1942; Solothurn, Feb. 28, 1943); many cantatas.

BIBL.: J.-L. Matthey, eds., *H. H. Werkverzeichnis* (Lausanne, 1971).

Haugland, Aage, Danish bass-baritone; b. Copenhagen, Feb. 1, 1944. He studied with Mogens Wöldike and Kristian Riis in Copenhagen, making his operatic debut as the Brewer in Martinů's *Veselohra na mostě* at the Norwegian Opera in Oslo in 1968; then sang with the Royal Opera in Copenhagen (from 1973); also made guest appearances with other major European opera houses, including London's Covent Garden as Hunding (1975), Milan's La Scala as the King in *Lohengrin* (1981), in Salzburg as Rocco (1982), and in Bayreuth as Hagen (1983). In 1979 he made his U.S. debut as Boris Godunov in St. Louis, as well as his Metropolitan Opera debut in N.Y. (Dec. 13, 1979) as Baron Ochs. He continued to sing at the Metropolitan Opera with success in operas by Wagner, Mussorgsky, Tchaikovsky, Strauss, and Janáček. His other roles include Leporello, Sarastro, Gounod's Méphistophélès, and the Grand Inquisitor.

Hausegger, Siegmund von, esteemed Austrian conductor and composer; b. Graz, Aug. 16, 1872; d. Munich, Oct. 10, 1948. He studied with his father, the Austrian musicologist Friedrich von Hausegger (b. St. Andrä, Carinthia, April 26, 1837; d. Graz, Feb. 23, 1899) and with Karl Pohlig. At the age of 16, he composed a grand Mass, which he himself conducted; at 18 he brought out in Graz an opera, *Helfrid.* Richard Strauss thought well enough of Hausegger as a composer to accept for performance his comic opera *Zinnober,* which he conducted in Munich on June 19, 1898. In 1895–96 Hausegger conducted at the Graz City Theater; in 1897 he was an assistant conductor in Bayreuth. He was the conductor of the Volk-Symphonie-Konzerte in Munich (1899–1902), the Museum Concerts in Frankfurt am Main (1903–06), and the Phil. Concerts in Hamburg (1910–20). From 1918 to 1934 he was director of the Academy of Musical Art in Munich; in 1920 he was named Generalmusikdirektor of the Munich Konzertverein, which became the Munich Phil. in 1928; remained there until his retirement in 1938. He acquired a fine reputation as a conductor in Germany, becoming a champion of Bruckner's syms. in their original versions. As a composer, he wrote in a late German Romantic style. He publ. a monograph, *Alexander Ritter, Ein Bild seines Charakters und Schaffens* (Berlin, 1907), and his father's correspondence with Peter Rosegger (Leipzig, 1924). His collected articles appeared under the title *Betrachtungen zur Kunst* (Leipzig, 1921).

WORKS: OPERAS: *Helfrid* (Graz, 1890); *Zinnober* (Munich, June 19, 1898, R. Strauss conducting). **ORCH.:** *Dionysische Fantasie* (1899); 2 symphonic poems: *Barbarossa* (1900) and *Wieland der Schmied* (1904); *Natursymphonie* for Chorus and Orch. (1911); *Aufklänge,* symphonic variations on a children's song (1919). **VOCAL:** Pieces for Men's Chorus and Orch.

Haussermann, John (William, Jr.), American composer; b. Manila, Philippines, Aug. 21, 1909; d. Denver, May 5, 1986. He was taken to New Richmond, Ohio, as a child and studied piano with local teachers; in 1924 he enrolled in the Cincinnati Cons. of Music, studying organ with Parvin Titus and theory with George Leighton. In 1930 he went to Paris, where he studied organ with Dupré and composition with Le Flem. Upon returning to the U.S., he was mainly active as a composer. His music is marked by a pragmatic sense of formal cohesion, which does not exclude a flair for innovation, as exemplified by his Concerto for Voice and Orch.

WORKS: ORCH.: 3 syms.: No. 1 (1938; partial perf., N.Y., May 28, 1939), No. 2 (1941; Cincinnati, March 31, 1944), and No. 3 (1947; Cincinnati, April 1, 1949); *The After Christmas Suite* (Cincinnati, March 22, 1938); Concerto for Voice and Orch. (Cincinnati, April 24, 1942); *Ronde carnavalesque* (N.Y., Feb. 6, 1949); *Stanza* for Violin and Orch. (Mallorca, Spain, Feb. 22, 1956); Concerto for Organ and Strings (1985). **CHAMBER:** Quintet for Flute, Oboe, Clarinet, Bassoon, and Harpsichord (1935); String Quartet (1937); *Suite rustique* for Flute, Cello, and Piano (1937); *Divertissements* for String Quartet (1940); *Poème et Clair de lune* for Violin and Piano (1940); Violin Sonata (1941); *Serenade* for Theremin and Strings (1945). **KEYBOARD: PIANO:** *24 préludes symphoniques* (1932–33); *Sonatine fantastique* (1932); *Pastoral fantasie* for 2 Pianos, 4-hands (1933); *Ballade, Burlesque, et Légende* (1936); *7 Bagatelles* (1948); *9 Impromptus* (1958); *5 Harmonic Études* (1968). **ORGAN:** Numerous pieces. **VOCAL:** *Sacred Cantata* for Baritone and Orch. (Cincinnati, Jan. 31, 1965); many songs.

Hausswald, Günter, distinguished German musicologist; b. Rochlitz an der Mülde, March 11, 1908; d. Stuttgart, April 23, 1974. He studied piano with Max Pauer and composition with Karg-Elert in Leipzig, theory with Grabner at the Leipzig Hochschule für Musik, and musicology with Kroyer and others at the Univ. of Leipzig, where he took his Ph.D. in 1937 with the diss. *Johann David Heinichens Instrumentalwerke* (publ. in Wolfenbüttel and Berlin, 1937); he completed his Habilitation in 1949 at the Dresden Technical College with his *Mozarts Serenaden* (publ. in Leipzig, 1951). From 1933 to 1945 he taught school in Dresden; then was dramaturge at the Dresden State Opera (1947–53); he also lectured at the Dresden Hochschule für Musik and at the Univ. of Jena from 1950 to 1953. He then settled in West Germany, where he ed. the monthly *Musica* (1958–70); was also program director for the South German Radio at Stuttgart (1960–68). His important monographs include *Heinrich Marschner* (Dresden, 1938); *Die deutsche Oper* (Cologne, 1941); *Die Bauten des Staatstheater Dresden* (Dresden, 1948); *Das neue Opernbuch* (Dresden, 1951; 5th ed., 1956); *Richard Strauss* (Dresden, 1953); *Dirigenten: Bild und Schrift* (Berlin, 1966). He also contributed exemplary eds. to the complete works of Telemann, Gluck, Bach, and Mozart.

Hautzig, Walter, Austrian-born American pianist and teacher; b. Vienna, Sept. 28, 1921. He studied at the Vienna Academy of Music; left Austria after the rise of the Nazis to power, and went to Jerusalem and studied at the Cons. there. He continued his musical education at the Curtis Inst. of Music in Philadelphia with Harry Kaufmann and Mieczyslaw Munz; also in N.Y. with Artur Schnabel. On Oct. 31, 1943, he made his debut at N.Y.'s

Town Hall. He became a naturalized American citizen in 1945. After World War II, he made tours all over the world. In 1979 he represented the U.S. in the first visit of an American pianist to the People's Republic of China since the Cultural Revolution. He taught at the Peabody Cons. in Baltimore from 1960 to 1987.

Havelka, Svatopluk, Czech composer; b. Vrbice, May 2, 1925. He studied in Prague with Jirák (1945–47) and at the Charles Univ. there with Hutter, Sychra, and Leibich (graduated, 1949). He worked in the music dept. of the Czech Radio in Ostrava (1949–50), and concurrently was founder-artistic director of the NOTA Ensemble; after working as an instructor and composer with the Army Art Ensemble (1950–54), he devoted himself fully to composition. He was a prof. of composition at the Prague Academy of Performing Arts from 1990. In 1961 and 1989 he was awarded the State Prize, and in 1987 he was made a Merited Artist of his nation. After composing in the nationalist tradition with infusions of Moravian modalities, he turned to a progressive style which embraced various modern techniques.

WORKS: DRAMATIC: Music for over 70 full-length and 150 short films; incidental music to plays; *Pyrrhos,* ballet (1970). **ORCH.:** *Night Music* (1944); Suite for Small Orch. (1947); *Pastorale* Nos. 1 (1948) and 2 (1951); Sym. (Prague, Nov. 5, 1956); *Foam,* symphonic poem (1965; Olomouc, Feb. 9, 1966); *Ernesto Ché Guevara,* symphonic poem (1969); *Hommage à Hieronymus Bosch,* symphonic fantasy (1974); *Children's Suite* (1982). **CHAMBER:** Nonet (1976); *Percussionata,* suite for Percussion (1978); *Quiet Joy* for Viola (1985); *Disegno* for Flute (1986); *Hommage to Fra Angelica* for Guitar (1987); *Soliloquia animae ad Deum* for Clarinet and Piano (1991); *The Hidden Manna and a White Stone* for 2 Percussionists (1992). **VOCAL:** *4 Baroque Songs* for Medium Voice and Piano (1944; rev. as *Rose of Wounds* for Medium Voice and Orch., 1974); *4 Musical-Dramatic Suites* for Solo Voice, Narrator, Chorus, and Chamber Orch., after Moravian folk poetry (1948, 1949, 1949, 1951); *Spring,* vocal rhapsody for 3 Solo Voices, Chorus, Children's Chorus, and Orch. (1949); *In Praise of Light,* cantata for Soprano, Alto, Bass, Chorus, and Orch. (1959); *Heptameron: Poem on Nature and Love* for Soprano, Alto, Tenor, Bass, Narrator, and Orch. (1964); *Epistle of Poggio Bracciolini to Leonardo Bruni of Arrezo on the Condemnation of Master Jeroným of Prague,* oratorio for Soprano, Alto, Tenor, Bass, 3 Choruses, Orch., and Organ (1984); *Profeteia* for Children's Chorus, Orch., and Organ (1988).

Havemann, Gustav, German violinist and teacher; b. Güstrow, March 15, 1882; d. Schöneiche, near Berlin, Jan. 2, 1960. He was a pupil of Joachim at the Berlin Hochschule für Musik and, while still a youth, played in the Schwerin Court Orch. He was concertmaster in Lübeck, Darmstadt (1903–09), and of the Hamburg Phil. (from 1909). In 1911 he became a teacher at the Leipzig Cons.; after serving as concertmaster of the Dresden Court (later State) Opera Orch. (1915–20), he was a prof. at the Berlin Hochschule für Musik (1920–45); he also was founder and 1st violinist of the Havemann Quartet, which played much modern music. He publ. *Die Violintechnik bis zur Vollendung* (2 vols., Cologne, 1928).

Hawel, Jan Wincenty, Polish composer and conductor; b. Pszów, July 10, 1936. He studied composition and conducting at the Katowice State College of Music, graduating in 1967; then became a member of its faculty; also conducted the Silesian Chamber Orch. (from 1981).

WORKS: *Profiles* for Men's Chorus and Orch. (1962); 4 syms. (1962–77); *Contrasts* for Orch. (1964); *Constructions* for Orch. (1965); *Divertimento* for Trombone, Piano, and Percussion (1968); *Woodland Impressions* for Narrator, Chorus, and Orch. (1969); *Sinfonia concertante* for Organ and Orch. (1972); 4 string quartets (1971–82); *Stained Glass Windows* for Piano (1972); *Polish Oratorio* for Soloists, Narrator, 2 Choruses, and Orch. (Katowice, April 29, 1983); *Magnificat* for Vocal Ensemble and Orch. (Poznań, March 30, 1989).

Hawkins, John, Canadian composer, pianist, and teacher; b. Montreal, July 26, 1944. He studied piano with Lubka Kolessa at the Montreal Cons. (premier prix, 1967); he also studied piano and composition (with Anhalt) at McGill Univ. in Montreal (B.Mus., 1967; Concert Diploma, 1968; M.M.A., 1970), and attended Boulez's conducting class in Basel (1969). In 1970 he became a teacher at the Univ. of Toronto. In 1983 he won the Jules Léger Prize for his *Breaking Through* for Voice, Piano, and Percussion. His works primarily reflect the examples set by Stravinsky and Webern, with an individualistic streak notable for their lyrical qualities.

WORKS: *8 Movements* for Flute and Clarinet (1966); *5 Pieces* for Piano (1967); *3 Cavatinas* for Soprano and Chamber Ensemble (1967); *Remembrances* for Chamber Ensemble (1969); *2 Pieces* for Orch. (1970); *Waves* for Soprano and Piano (1971); *Spring Song* for Chorus (1974); *Études* for 2 Pianos (1974); Trio for Flute, Cello, and Xylophone (1975); Wind Quintet (1977); *Prelude and Prayer* for Tenor and Orch. (1980); *Dance, Improvisation and Song* for Clarinet and Piano (1981; rev. 1982); *Breaking Through* for Voice, Piano, and Percussion (1982); *Dance Variations* for Percussion Quartet (1983; rev. 1986); *3 Archetypes* for String Quartet (1984; rev. 1986); *substance-of-we-feeling* for 2 Percussion (1985); *2 Popular Pieces* for 2 Guitars (1986); *The Cicada's Song to the Sun* for Soprano, Oboe, and Guitar (1987); *Light to Dark* for Soprano, Clarinet, and Piano (1987); *The 1st Fable,* children's entertainment for Mezzo-soprano, Soprano, Dancers/Mimes, Narrator, Oboe, Cello, Percussion, and Piano (1988).

Hayasaka, Fumio, Japanese composer, b. Sendai-City, Aug. 19, 1914; d. Tokyo, Oct. 15, 1955. He studied in Tokyo with A. Tcherepnin; won the Weingartner Prize (1938). He was particularly successful in writing for Japanese films; wrote the score for the film *Rashomon,* which received 1st prize at the International Festival in Venice (1952). Among his other works were *The Ancient Dance* (Tokyo, May 15, 1939); Overture (Tokyo, March 17, 1940); Piano Concerto (Tokyo, June 22, 1948); and *Yukara,* suite (Tokyo, June 9, 1955).

Hayashi, Hikaru, Japanese composer; b. Tokyo, Oct. 22, 1931. He was a student of Otaka and Ikenouchi at the Tokyo Academy of Music.

WORKS: DRAMATIC: OPERAS: *The Naked King,* radio opera (1955); *Amanjaku and Urikohime,* television opera (1958); *The Wife in the Picture* (1961); *The Chalk Circle* (1978; orch. suite, 1982); *Legend of White Beasts* (1979); *Gorsh, the Cellist* (1986); *Joan of Arc Wearing a Skirt* (1987); *12th Night* (1989); *Hamlet's Hour* (1990); *12 Months and a Girl* (1992); ballet music. **ORCH.:** *Movement* (1953); 2 syms.: No. 1 (1953) and No. 2, *Canciones* (Tokyo, May 18, 1985); *Allegro* for Strings (1954); *Variations* (1955); *The Humid Area* (1960); *Music* (1965); *Carnival: A Wind-born Premonition* (1985); *Awakening* (1991). **CHAMBER:** *Rhapsody I* (1965) and *II: Winter on 72nd Street* (1968) for Violin and Piano; *Contrasts* for 2 Marimbas (1965); Flute Sonata (1967); *AYA I* for Flute and Harp (1970) and *II* for Harp (1972); *Play I* for 10 Players (1971) and *II* for Voice, Violin, and Piano (1971–72); *Shirabe* for 3 Flutes (1974); *America Suite* for Flute, Clarinet, Cello, Piano, and Percussion (1983); *Legende* for String Quartet (1989–90); piano pieces. **VOCAL:** *Beggar's Song,* oratorio (1962); *Children of War* for Soloists, Narrator, Chorus, and Chamber Orch. (1984); *At Noon, the August Sun* for Soprano and Orch. (1990); choruses; solo songs.

Hayashi (Nagaya), Kenzō, Japanese musicologist; b. Osaka, May 1, 1899; d. Nara, June 9, 1976. He graduated from the Tokyo Arts School in 1924, and became a moderately successful sculptor. He also wrote some music for brass instruments. In 1928 he met the Chinese scholar Kuo Mo-jo, who encouraged him to write about his findings in the field of ancient Asian music. His first book, on music of the Sui and T'ang dynasties, was tr. into Chinese by Kuo (Shanghai, 1936). In 1948 he was commissioned to begin what became his life's work, research on early Chinese instruments kept in the imperial storehouse in Hara dating as far back as the 8th century. He publ. some theoretical findings, among them *Ming yüen pa-tiao yen-chiu* (8 Musical Modes of the Ming Dynasty; Shanghai, 1957), *T'un-huang p'i-pa pu ti chieh-tu yen-chiu* (An Attempt to Interpret the T'un-huang Pipa Notation; Shanghai, 1957), and *Higashi Ajia gakki kō* (Musical Instruments of East Asia; Tokyo, 1973).

Haydon, Glen, eminent American musicologist; b. Inman, Kansas, Dec. 9, 1896; d. Chapel Hill, N.C., May 8, 1966. He studied at the Univ. of Calif., Berkeley (B.A., 1918; M.A., 1921); he then went to Paris, where he studied clarinet and composition; then enrolled at the Univ. of Vienna, where he obtained his Ph.D. in 1932 with the diss. *Zur Entwicklungsgeschichte des Quartsextakkordes; The Evolution of the Six-Four Chord: A Chapter in the History of Dissonance Treatment* (publ. in Berkeley, 1933). Returning to America, he became head of the dept. of music at the Univ. of North Carolina at Chapel Hill (1934), and held this post until his death. He was the author of the valuable textbook *Introduction to Musicology* (N.Y., 1941).

BIBL.: J. Pruett, ed., *Studies in Musicology: Essays in the History, Style and Bibliography of Music in Memory of G. H.* (Chapel Hill, 1969).

Hayes, Roland, outstanding black American tenor; b. Curryville, Ga., June 3, 1887; d. Boston, Jan. 1, 1977. He was born to former slaves. After vocal studies with A. Calhoun in Chattanooga, he attended Fisk Univ. He then pursued his vocal training with Arthur J. Hubbard in Boston. On Nov. 15, 1917, he made his recital debut there, and then made a successful concert tour of the U.S. In 1920 he went to Europe to complete his studies, finding mentors in Ira Aldridge, Victor Beigel, Sir George Henschel, and Theodor Lierhammer. After singing with leading orchs. in London, Paris, Berlin, Vienna, and Amsterdam, and giving recitals, he returned to the U.S. and made his first appearance at N.Y.'s Carnegie Hall in recital in 1923. In subsequent years, he made numerous appearances in the U.S. until retiring from the concert stage in 1973. Hayes was greatly esteemed for his compelling interpretations of German lieder and French songs, as well as for his unforgettable and poignant performances of black spirituals. He publ. expert arrangements of 30 black spirituals as *My Songs* (1948).

BIBL.: M. Helm, *Angel Mo' and Her Son, R. H.* (Boston, 1942); A. Knight, "R. H.," *Record Collector,* X (1955–56; with discography); W. Marr, II, "R. H.," *Black Perspective in Music,* II (1974); F. Woolsey, "Conversation with R. H.," ibid.; M. Carter, "In Retrospect: R. H.—Expressor of the Soul in Song," ibid., V (1977).

Hayman, Cynthia, black American soprano; b. Jacksonville, Fla., Sept. 6, 1958. She was educated at Northwestern Univ. In 1984 she made her operatic debut at the Santa Fe Opera in the U.S. premiere of Henze's *We Come to the River,* returning there to sing Xanthe in the U.S. premiere of Strauss's *Die Liebe der Danae* in 1985. That same year, she created the title role in Musgrave's *Harriet, the Woman Called Moses* at the Norfolk (Va.) Opera. In 1986 she made her European debut as Gershwin's Bess at the Glyndebourne Festival. In subsequent years, she was engaged with opera companies on both sides of the Atlantic, including London's Covent Garden, the Hamburg State Opera, the Bavarian State Opera in Munich, the Deutsche Oper in Berlin, the Canadian Opera, the Baltimore Opera, the San Francisco Opera, and the Opéra de la Bastille in Paris. She also appeared as a soloist with notable orchs. Among her other roles are Gluck's Amor, Mozart's Pamina and Susanna, Bizet's Micaëla, and Puccini's Li and Mimi.

Hayman, Richard, American composer; b. Sandia, N. Mex., July 29, 1951. He studied humanities and philosophy at Columbia Univ., where he attended Ussachevsky's classes in electronic music; he also studied flute with Eleanor Laurence at the Manhattan School of Music, Indian vocal music with Ravi Shankar, and conducting with Boulez at the Juilliard School of Music. He then descended into the avant-garde maelstrom and produced a series of "works" ranging from graffiti exhibitions to *Dali* for Orch. (1974), notated on a toothpick, with instructions to "ascend chromatically in slow pulse."

Hayman, Richard (Warren Joseph), American conductor, harmonica player, arranger, and composer; b. Cambridge, Mass., March 27, 1920. He received training in composition from Alfred Newman and Max Steiner, and in conducting from Arthur Fiedler. In 1938 he launched his career as a harmonica player, and soon began working as a composer and arranger for Hollywood film studios. After serving as arranger and director of the Vaughan Monroe Orch. (1945–50), he was director of music and of artists and repertoire of Mercury Records (1950–65) and music director of Time-Mainstream Records (1960–70); from 1950 to 1990 he also was chief arranger for the Boston Pops. As a guest conductor, he found his niche as a purveyor of light musical fare with various North American orchs.

Hays, Sorrel (actually, **Doris Ernestine**), American composer, pianist, and mixed-media artist; b. Memphis, Tenn., Aug. 6, 1941. She was educated at the Univ. of Chattanooga (B.M., 1963), the Munich Hochschule für Musik (piano and harpsichord diploma, 1966), the Univ. of Wisc. (M.M., 1968), and the Univ. of Iowa (composition and electronic music, 1969). In 1971 she won 1st prize in the International Competition for Interpreters of New Music in Rotterdam, and subsequently toured as a performer of contemporary music; was prof. of theory at Queens College of the City Univ. of N.Y. (1974–75), and a guest lecturer and performer at various institutions. In 1984 she adopted Sorrel as her first name.

WORKS: DRAMATIC: *Love in Space,* radio opera/music theater (1986); *The Glass Woman,* opera (1989–95); *Touch of Touch,* video opera (1989); *Dream in Her Mind,* opera (1994–95; West German Radio, Cologne, April 14, 1995); film scores; various works for radio. **INSTRUMENTAL:** *Scheveningen Beach* for Flute Quintet (1972); *Pieces from Last Year* for 16 Instruments (1976); *SensEvents* for 6 Instruments and Tape (1970–77); *Characters,* concerto for Harpsichord, String Quartet, and 3 Woodwinds (1978); *Segment/Junctures* for Viola, Clarinet, and Piano (1978); *Tunings* for Double Bass (1978), for Flute, Clarinet, and Bassoon (1979), for Flute, Clarinet, Violin, and Soprano (1979), for Clarinet, Piano, and Soprano (1979), for String Quartet (1980), for Viola (1980), for 2 Violins (1980), and for Violin, Cello, Piano, and Soprano (1981); *UNI,* dance suite for String Quartet, Flute, Chorus, and Tape (1978); *Lullabye* for Flute, Violin, and Piano (1979); *Tommy's Trumpet* for 2 Trumpets (1979); *Fanfare Study* for Horn, Trumpet, and Trombone (1980); *Southern Voices* for Orch. and Soprano (1982); *Harmony* for Strings (1983); *Rocking* for Flute, Violin, and Viola (1983); *After Glass* for 10 Percussionists (1984); *Juncture Dance III* for 7 Percussionists (1989); *It All Sounds Like Music to Me* for Percussionist (1994); other chamber works; piano pieces. **VOCAL:** *Star Music* for Chorus, Tape, and Bells (1974); *Hands Full* for 2-part Chorus, Drums, and Tape (1977); *In-de-pen-dance* for Chanter and Nylon String (1979); *Hush* for Voice, Reco-reco, and Sand Block (1981); *Rest Song* for Chorus and Optional Flute (1981); *Something (to Do) Doing* for Scat Singer, 15 Chanters, and 2 Actors (1984); *Hei-Ber-Ny-Pa-To-Sy-Bei-Mos* for Soprano, Flute, and Percussion (1989); *The Clearing Way: A Chant for the Nineties* for Contralto, Chorus, and Orch. (1991); other vocal works. **ELECTRONIC AND MIXED MEDIA:** *Hands and Lights* for Piano and Lights (1971); *Duet* for Pianist and Audience (1971); *Certain: Change* for Piccolo, Bass Flute, and Tape (1978); *Reading Richie's Paintings* for Synthesizer, Flute, and Slides (1979); *Exploitation* for Soprano or Chanter and Tape (1981); *The Gorilla and the Girl* for Tape (1981); *Only* for Piano, 2 Tapes, Slides, and Film (1981); *Water Music* for Soprano, Tape, Water Pump, Slides, Optional Violin, and Optional Baby Pool (1981); *Celebration of No* for Tape, Film, and Optional Violin or Soprano or Piano Trio (1983); *The Needy Sound* for Tape (1983); *M.O.M. 'n P.O.P.* for 3 Pianos, Tape, Film, Slides, and Mime (1984); *Weaving (Interviews)* for

Optional Soprano, Piano, Film, and Slides (1984); *Sound Shadows* for Oboe, Didjeridu, Saxophone, Synthesizer, Percussion, Dancer, Video, and Tape (1990); *Take a Back Country Road* for Oboe, Didjeridu with Digital Delay, Keyboard, Drum Machine, and Saxophone (1990–91); other tape pieces; sound structures.

Head, Michael (Dewar), English singer, pianist, and composer; b. Eastbourne, Jan. 28, 1900; d. Cape Town, South Africa, Aug. 24, 1976. He studied composition with Frederick Corder at the Royal Academy of Music in London, and in 1927 joined its faculty as a piano instructor. In 1947 he made a grand tour through Asia, Canada, and Australia, performing both as singer and pianist. He publ. several collections of English songs; also wrote 2 children's operas, *The Bachelor Mouse* (1954) and *Key Money* (1966); Trio for Oboe, Bassoon, and Piano (1966); Suite for Recorders (1968); cantata, *Daphne and Apollo* (1964).

Headington, Christopher (John Magenis), English pianist, writer on music, and composer; b. London, April 28, 1930; d. March 19, 1996. He studied piano with Percy Waller and composition with Lennox Berkeley at the Royal Academy of Music in London; also received private instruction in composition from Britten (1947–54) and studied piano with Lefebure and composition with Lutoslawski at the Dartington International Summer School (1963). He then devoted much time to teaching; was also active with the BBC in London (1964–65); toured as a pianist in Europe, the Middle East, and the Far East; also was active as a broadcaster.

WRITINGS: *The Orchestra and Its Instruments* (1965); *The Bodley Head History of Western Music* (1974; 2nd ed., rev., 1980); *Illustrated Dictionary of Musical Terms* (1980); *The Performing World of the Musician* (1981); *Britten* (1981); *Listener's Guide to Chamber Music* (1982); *Opera: A History* (1987); *Sweet Sleep* (lullaby anthology; 1990); *Peter Pears: A Biography* (1993); *Bach* (1994).

WORKS: *Variations* for Piano and Orch. (1950); *Introduction and Allegro* for Chamber Orch. (1951); Cello Sonata (1953); 3 string quartets (1953, 1972, 1982); 3 piano sonatas (1955, 1974, 1985); *Chanson de l'éternelle tristesse*, ballet (1957); Violin Concerto (1959); *Towards a Pindaric Ode* for Soprano, Mezzo-soprano, and Piano (1965); *A Bradfield Mass* for Chorus, Congregation, and Organ (1977); Piano Quartet (1978); *The Healing Fountain: In memoriam Benjamin Britten* for Medium Voice and Orch. (1978); Sinfonietta for Chamber Orch. (1985); Bassoon Sonata (1988); Piano Concerto (1990); *Serenade* for Cello and Strings (1993).

Healey, Derek, English composer and pedagogue; b. Wargrave, May 2, 1936. He was a student of Darke (organ) and Howells (composition) at the Univ. of Durham (B.Mus., 1961), and received training in piano, organ, and flute at the Royal College of Music in London; he then continued his composition studies with Petrassi and Berio in Italy, principally with Porena in Rome (1962–66). He also studied conducting with Celibidache at the Accademia Musical Chigiana in Siena (summers, 1961–63 and 1966). He taught at the Univ. of Victoria, British Columbia (1969–71) and at the Univ. of Toronto (1971–72); he concurrently taught at the Univ. of Waterloo. After teaching at the Univ. of Guelph (1972–78), he was prof. of theory and composition at the Univ. of Oregon in Eugene from 1979 to 1988. In 1980 he was awarded the International Composition Prize of the Univ. of Louisville.

WORKS: DRAMATIC: *Il Carcerato,* ballet (1965); *The 3 Thieves*, ballet (1967); *Mr. Punch*, children's opera (1969); *Seabird Island*, opera (Guelph, May 7, 1977). **ORCH.:** *The Willow Pattern Plate* (1957); Concerto for Organ, Strings, and Timpani (1960); *Ruba'i* (1968); *Arctic Images* (1971); *Noh*, triple concerto for Flute, Piano, Synthesizer, and Orch. (1974); *Primrose in Paradise* for Chamber Orch. (1975); *Tribulation* (1977); Sym. No. 3, *Music for a Small Planet* (1984); Sym. No. 2, *Mountain Music*, for Large Wind Ensemble and Percussion (1985). **CHAMBER:** String Quartet (1961); Cello Sonata (1961); *Partita bizzara* for Oboe and Piano (1962); *Divisions* for Brass Quintet (1963); *Mobile* for Flute, Vibraphone, Celesta, Harp, 2 Percussionists, and Cello (1963); *Movement* for Flute, Oboe, Clarinet, and String Trio (1965); *Laudes* for Flute, Horn, Percussion, Harp, 2 Violins, and Cello (1966); *Stinging* for Alto Recorder, Cello, Harpsichord, and Tape (1971); *Solana Grove* for Wind Quintet (1982); piano pieces; organ music. **VOCAL:** *Butterflies* for Mezzo-soprano and Small Orch. (1970); *Wood II* for Soprano and String Quartet (1978; rev. 1981); songs.

Heartz, Daniel (Leonard), American musicologist; b. Exeter, N.H., Oct. 5, 1928. He studied at the Univ. of New Hampshire in Durham (A.B., 1950) and at Harvard Univ. (A.M., 1951; Ph.D., 1957, with the diss. *Sources and Forms of the French Instrumental Dance in the Sixteenth Century*). From 1957 to 1960 he was on the faculty of the Univ. of Chicago; in 1960 he was appointed to the music faculty of the Univ. of Calif., Berkeley. In 1967–68 and 1978–79 he held Guggenheim fellowships. He publ. *Pierre Attaingnant, Royal Printer of Music: A Historical Study and Bibliographical Catalogue* (Berkeley, 1969), *Mozart's Operas* (Berkeley, 1990), and *Haydn, Mozart, and the Viennese School, 1740–1780* (N.Y., 1995); ed. *Preludes, Chansons, and Dances for Lute, Published by P. Attaingnant, Paris (1529–1530)* (Neuilly-sur-Seine, 1964) and *Keyboard Dances of the Earlier Sixteenth Century*, in Corpus of Early Keyboard Music, VIII (1965); also contributed numerous articles on Renaissance music to various music journals.

Hedges, Anthony (John), English composer and teacher; b. Bicester, March 5, 1931. He studied at Keble College, Oxford (M.A., B.Mus.) and at the Royal Academy of Music in London. After teaching at the Royal Scottish Academy of Music in Glasgow (1957–63), he was on the faculty of the Univ. of Hull from 1963 to 1995. He publ. the book *Basic Tonal Harmony* (1987).

WORKS: DRAMATIC: *The Birth of Freedom*, ballet (1961); *Shadows in the Sun*, opera (1976); *Minotaur*, musical (1978); music for films and television. **ORCH.:** Sinfonietta (1955); *Comedy Overture* (1962; rev. 1967); *Sinfonia Semplice* (1963); *Expressions* (1964); *Prelude, Romance, and Rondo* for Strings (1965); *Concertante Music* for Piano and Orch. (1965); *Variations on a Theme of Rameau* (1969); *An Ayrshire Serenade* (1969); *4 Diversions* for Strings (1971); Sym. (1972–73); *Celebrations* (1973); *Festival Dances* (1976); *Heigham Sound*, overture (1978); *4 Breton Sketches* (1980); *Scenes from the Humber* (1980); Sinfonia Concertante (1981); *A Cleveland Overture* (1984); Concertino for Horn and Strings (1987). **CHAMBER:** *Rondo Concertante* for Clarinet, Horn, Violin, and Cello (1967); Sonata for Violin and Harpsichord (1967); String Quartet (1970); Piano Trio (1977); *Fantasy* for Violin and Cello (1981); Cello Sonata (1983); *Variations on a Tyneside Air* for Wind Quintet (1984); Trio for Flute, Clarinet, and Piano (1985); Clarinet Quintet (1987); Piano Quartet (1992). **VOCAL:** *A Manchester Mass* for Chorus, Brass Band, and Orch. (1974); many pieces for Chorus and Orch., including *Cantiones Festivals* (1960), *Epithalamium* (1969), *To Music* (1972), *Songs of David* (1977), *The Jackdaw of Rheims* (1980), *I Sing the Birth* (1985), *I'll Make Me a World* (1990), etc.; anthems; part songs.

Hedley, Arthur, English musicologist; b. Dudley, Northumberland, Nov. 12, 1905; d. Birmingham, Nov. 8, 1969. He studied French literature at the Federal Univ. of Durham (1923–27), and music with W.G. Whittaker at Newcastle. An ardent Chopinist, he learned the Polish language to be able to study Chopin documentation in the original. He publ. a biography, *Chopin* (London, 1947; 3rd ed., rev., 1974, by M.J.E. Brown), and edited and tr. *Selected Correspondence of Fryderyk Chopin* (London, 1962).

Hedwall, Lennart, Swedish pianist, organist, conductor, teacher, writer on music, and composer; b. Göteborg, Sept. 16, 1932. He received training in organ and piano; he was a composition student of Bäck and Blomdahl at the Stockholm Musikhögskolan (1951–59), and also studied conducting with Mann and in Vienna with Swarowsky; he also pursued his composition studies abroad with Fortner, Krenek, and Jelinek. He conducted at the Riksteatern (1958–60), the Stora Teatern in Göteborg (1962–65), the Drottningsholmteatern (1966–70) and the Royal Theater (1967–68) in Stockholm, and with the Örebro Orchestral Foundation (1968–74). After teaching at the Göteborg College of Speech and Drama (1963–67), he taught at the school of the Royal Theater in Stockholm (1968–70; 1974–80; from 1985); he also served as director of the Swedish National Music Museum in Stockholm (1981–83). As a performing musician, he was very active as an accompanist. His writings include 2 books on Alfvén (monograph, 1973; pictorial biography, 1990), a study of the Swedish symphony (1983), and a pictorial biography of Peterson-Berger (1983). The idiom of his music ranges from the traditional to the audaciously modern.

WORKS: OPERAS: *Herr Sleeman kommer* (1976–78; Örebro, March 16, 1979); *Amerika, Amerika* (1980–81). **ORCH.:** 4 pieces for Strings (1950–69); Oboe Concerto (1956; Swedish Radio, Dec. 21, 1961); *Variazioni piccoli* (1958); *Canzona* for Strings (1965); Concerto for Cello and String Orch. (1970); *Fantasia on Veni redemptor gentium* for Strings (1972); *Uvetyr till Fortunios visa* (1980); *Sagan*, symphonic fantasy (Örebro, Sept. 13, 1986); *Jul igen en liten tid: En lätt säsongsbetonad rapsodi* (1992). **CHAMBER:** 2 string trios (1952, 1960); 2 sonatas for Solo Flute (1954; 1989–90); Trio for Flute, Viola, and Cello (1955); Sonata for Solo Violin (1957); *Partita* for 13 Winds (1961); Trio for Flute, Clarinet, and Bassoon (1962); Wind Quintet (1965); String Quartet (1965); 2 sonatas for Solo Bassoon (1977, 1992); *Circuli II* for Cello (1980); *Arioso* for Flute and Organ (1982); *Une petite musique de soir*, wind sextet (1984); Sonata for Solo Oboe (1990); Sonata for Solo Clarinet (1991). **KEYBOARD: PIANO:** Sonata (1960). **ORGAN:** 2 suites (1958–59; 1970); Sonata (1971); *Triptyk* (1984). **VOCAL:** *Lyric Music* for Soprano and Orch. (1959); cantatas; choral pieces; songs.

Heermann, Hugo, distinguished German violinist and teacher; b. Heilbronn, Württemberg, March 3, 1844; d. Merano, Italy, Nov. 6, 1935. As a boy, he was taken to Rossini in Paris for advice; then studied with Bériot and Meerts at the Brussels Cons., graduating in 1861; subsequently took lessons with Joachim. In 1865 he became 1st violinist of the Frankfurt String Quartet; also taught at the Hoch Cons. In 1904 he founded his own violin school; made extended tours as a concert violinist in Europe, the U.S., and Australia; from 1906 to 1909 he taught violin at the Chicago Musical College, and then taught at the Stern Cons. in Berlin and the Geneva Cons. (1911–22). He had the distinction of having been the first to play the Violin Concerto of Brahms in Paris, N.Y., and Australia. He publ. a book of memoirs, *Meine Lebenserinnerungen* (Leipzig, 1935).

Heger, Robert, German conductor and composer; b. Strasbourg, Aug. 19, 1886; d. Munich, Jan. 14, 1978. He studied in Strasbourg, with Kempter in Zürich, and with Schillings in Berlin. After conducting opera in Strasbourg (1907–08), Ulm/Donau (1908–11), and Barmen (1911), he conducted at the Vienna Volksoper (1911–13). From 1913 to 1921 he was conductor of the Nuremberg Opera, and then conducted at the Bavarian State Opera in Munich. He conducted at the Vienna State Opera from 1925 to 1933; concurrently he conducted the concerts of Vienna's Gesellschaft der Musikfreunde and conducted opera at London's Covent Garden. From 1933 to 1945 he conducted at the Berlin State Opera; he also was music director of the Kassel State Theater (1935–41) and of the Zoppot Waldoper. After conducting at the Berlin Städtische Oper (1945–50), he settled in Munich as a regular conductor at the Bavarian State Opera. He also served as president of the Munich Hochschule für Musik (1950–54). Heger acquired a respectable position among opera conductors in Germany. While his compositions failed to maintain themselves in the repertoire, his orchestrations of several of Richard Strauss' songs have become well known.

WORKS: OPERAS: *Ein Fest auf Haderslev* (Nuremberg, Nov. 12, 1919; rev. 1943); *Der Bettler Namenlos* (1931; Munich, April 8, 1932); *Der verlorene Sohn* (1935; Dresden, March 11, 1936; rev. 1942); *Lady Hamilton* (1941; Nuremberg, Feb. 11, 1951); *Das ewige Reich* (n.d.; rev. 1972 as *Trägodie der Zweitracht*). **ORCH.:** 3 syms.; *Hero und Leander*, symphonic poem; Violin Concerto; Cello Concerto. **OTHER:** Chamber music; *Te Deum* for 2 Soloists, Chorus, and Orch. (1971); choral pieces; songs.

Heiden, Bernhard, German-born American composer and pedagogue; b. Frankfurt am Main, Aug. 24, 1910. He studied piano, clarinet, violin, theory, and harmony; from 1929 to 1933 he studied at the Hochschule für Musik in Berlin, where his principal teacher was Hindemith. In 1935 he emigrated to the U.S. and became a naturalized American citizen in 1941. He taught at the Art Center Music School in Detroit; was also conductor of the Detroit Chamber Orch., as well as pianist, harpsichordist, and chamber music artist. He served in the U.S. Army (1943–45); then studied musicology with Grout at Cornell Univ. (A.M., 1946). In 1946 he joined the faculty of the Indiana Univ. School of Music in Bloomington; he retired in 1981. His music is neo-Classical in its formal structure, and strongly polyphonic in texture; it is distinguished also by its impeccable sonorous balance and effective instrumentation.

WORKS: DRAMATIC: Incidental music to *Henry IV* (1940) and *The Tempest* (1942); *Dreamers on a Slack Wire*, dance drama for 2 Pianos and Percussion (1953); *The Darkened City*, opera (1962; Bloomington, Ind., Feb. 23, 1963). **ORCH.:** 2 syms. (1933, 1954); *Euphorion: Scene for Orchestra* (1949); Concerto for Small Orch. (1949); *Memorial* (1955); Concerto for Piano, Violin, Cello, and Orch. (1956); *Philharmonic Fanfare* (1958); *Variations* (1960); *Envoy* (1963); Cello Concerto (1967); Concerto for Strings (1967); Horn Concerto (1969); *Partita* (1970); Tuba Concerto (1976); Concerto for Trumpet and Wind Orch. (1981); *Recitative and Aria* for Cello and Orch. (1985; Pittsburgh, May 8, 1986); *Fantasia concertante* for Alto Saxophone, Winds, and Percussion (1987); Concerto for Recorder and Chamber Orch. (1987); *Salute* (1989); Concerto for Bassoon and Chamber Orch. (1990); *Voyage* for Symphonic Band (1991; Bloomington, Ind., Feb. 25, 1992). **CHAMBER:** Alto Saxophone Sonata (1937); Horn Sonata (1939); 2 string quartets (1947, 1951); Sinfonia for Woodwind Quintet (1949); Quintet for Horn and String Quartet (1952); Violin Sonata (1954); Quintet for Clarinet and Strings (1955); Serenade for Bassoon, Violin, Viola, and Cello (1955); Trio for Violin, Cello, and Piano (1956); Cello Sonata (1958); Viola Sonata (1959); Quintet for Oboe and Strings (1962); *Intrada* for String Quartet (1962); 7 Pieces for String Quartet (1964); Woodwind Quintet (1965); 4 Dances for Brass Quintet (1967); *Intrada* for Woodwind Quintet and Saxophone (1970); 5 Canons for 2 Horns (1971); Variations for Tuba and 9 Horns (1974); Quintet for Flute, Violin, Viola, Bassoon, and Contrabass (1975); 4 Movements for Saxophone Quartet and Timpani (1976); Variations on *Lilliburlero* for Cello (1976); Terzetto for 2 Flutes and Cello (1979); Quartet for Horns (1981); Sextet for Brass Quintet and Piano (1983); Quartet for Piano, Violin, Cello, and Horn (1985); Trio Serenade for Violin, Clarinet, and Piano (1987); *Préludes* for Flute, Bass, and Harp (1988); Trio for Oboe, Bassoon, and Piano (1992); *Divertimento* for Tuba and 8 Solo Instruments (1992); *Serenata* for 4 Cellos (1993); *Prelude, Theme, and Variations* for Alto Recorder (1994). **KEYBOARD: PIANO:** 2 sonatas (1941, 1952); Sonata for Piano, 4-hands (1946); *Variations* (1959); *Fantasia* for 2 Pianos (1971); *Hommage à Scarlatti* (1971). **ORGAN:** Variations on *The Cruel Ship's Carpenter* (1950). **VOCAL:** *2 Songs of Spring* for Women's Chorus (1947); *4 Songs from the Song of Songs* for Soprano and Orch. or Piano (1948); *Divine Poems* for Chorus, after John Donne (1949); *In Memoriam* for Chorus (1964); *Advent Song* for Chorus (1965); *Riddles of Jonathan Swift* for Women's Chorus (1975); *Sonnets of Louise Labe* for Soprano and String Quartet (1977); *Triptych* for Baritone and Orch. (1983); *A Bestiary* for Soprano, Tenor, and Chamber Orch. (1986).

Heifetz, Daniel (Alan), American violinist and teacher; b. Kansas City, Mo., Nov. 20, 1948. He studied with several teachers in Los Angeles; then went to Philadelphia, where he had advanced training with Zimbalist, Galamian, and Jascha Brodsky at the Curtis Inst. of Music (1966–71). In 1969 he won 1st prize in the Merriweather Post Competition in Washington, D.C. On Jan. 20, 1970, he made his debut in Tchaikovsky's Violin Concerto with the National Sym. Orch. of Washington, D.C., on tour in N.Y. He then entered the Tchaikovsky Competition in Moscow, winning 4th prize (1978). He concertized in Europe and throughout the Americas; from 1980 he taught at the Peabody Cons. of Music in Baltimore.

Heifetz, Jascha (Iossif Robertovich), great Russian-born American violinist; b. Vilnius, Feb. 2, 1899; d. Los Angeles, Dec. 10, 1987. His father, Ruben Heifetz, an able musician, taught him the rudiments of violin playing at a very early age; he then studied with Ilya Malkin at the Vilnius Music School, and played in public before he was 5 years old; at the age of 6, he played Mendelssohn's Concerto in Kovno. In 1910 he was taken by his father to St. Petersburg, and entered the Cons. there in the class of Nalbandian; after a few months, he was accepted as a pupil by Leopold Auer. He gave his first public concert in St. Petersburg on April 30, 1911. The following year, with a letter of recommendation from Auer, he went to Berlin; his first concert there (May 24, 1912), in the large hall of the Hochschule für Musik, attracted great attention: Artur Nikisch engaged him to play the Tchaikovsky Concerto with the Berlin Phil. (Oct. 28, 1912), but his appearance proved uneventful. He then decided to continue his studies with Auer in St. Petersburg and in Germany. While visiting Auer in Norway in 1916, he played in a joint concert with Toscha Seidel before the king and queen of Norway. After the Russian Revolution of 1917, he went to America, by way of Siberia and the Orient. His debut at Carnegie Hall in N.Y. (Oct. 27, 1917) won for him the highest expression of enthusiasm from the public and in the press. Mischa Elman, the prime violinist of an older generation, attended the concert in the company of the pianist Leopold Godowsky. When Elman complained that it was too hot in the hall, Godowsky retorted, "Not for pianists." Veritable triumphs followed during Heifetz's tour of the U.S., and soon his fame spread all over the world. He made his first London appearance on May 5, 1920; toured Australia (1921), the Orient (1923), Palestine (1926), and South America. He revisited Russia in 1934, and was welcomed enthusiastically. He became a naturalized American citizen in 1925, and made his home in Beverly Hills, California. Heifetz made regular tours throughout the world, appearing not only with the foremost orchs. but as a recitalist. As a chamber music artist, he played in trios with Rubinstein and Feuermann, and later with Pennario and Piatigorsky. He taught classes of exceptionally talented pupils at the Univ. of Southern Calif. in Los Angeles (1962–72). In 1974 he made his last public appearance and thereby brought to a close one of the most extraordinary violin careers in history.

The Olympian quality of Heifetz's playing was unique in luminous transparency of texture, tonal perfection, and formal equilibrium of phrasing; he never allowed his artistic temperament to superimpose extraneous elements on the music; this inspired tranquillity led some critics to characterize his interpretations as impersonal and detached. Heifetz made numerous arrangements for violin of works by Bach, Vivaldi, and contemporary composers; his most famous transcription is *Hora Staccato* by Grigoraş Dinicu, made into a virtuoso piece by adroit ornamentation and rhythmic elaboration. In his desire to promote modern music, he commissioned a number of composers (Walton, Gruenberg, Castelnuovo-Tedesco, and others) to write violin concertos for him, and performed several of them.

BIBL.: H. Axelrod, ed., *H.* (Neptune City, N.J., 1976; 2nd ed., aug., 1981); A. Weschler-Vered, *J. H.* (London, 1986); D. Soria, "H.: Aloof, Awe-inspiring," *Musical America* (May 1988); I. Stern, "Remembering J. H.," *Ovation* (March 1988).

Heiller, Anton, esteemed Austrian organist, conductor, pedagogue, and composer; b. Vienna, Sept. 15, 1923; d. there, March 25, 1979. He received training in piano, organ, harpsichord, and composition at the Vienna Academy of Music (1941–42). After winning the Haarlem competition for organ improvisation in 1952, he was notably successful as an organ virtuoso, excelling especially in the music of Bach. In 1945 he joined the faculty of the Vienna Academy of Music; after it became the Vienna Hochschule für Musik, he was made a prof. there in 1971. In 1969 he was awarded the Austrian State Prize for Music. In his compositions, he displayed an adept handling of polyphonic writing; in some of his music, he utilized the 12-tone method.

WORKS: *Toccata* for 2 Pianos (1945); 2 organ sonatas (1946, 1953); *Tentatio Jesu,* chamber oratorio for Tenor, Bass, Chorus, and 2 Pianos (1952); *In festo corporis Christi* for Organ (1957); *Missa super modos duodecimales* for Chorus and 7 Instruments (1960); Organ Concerto (1963); *In principio erat verbum* for Tenor, Chorus, Orch., and Organ (1965); *Stabat mater* for Chorus and Orch. (1968); *Adventsmusik* for Chorus and Organ (1971); *Passionsmusik* for Children's Chorus and Organ (1975); other masses; cantatas.

Heininen, Paavo (Johannes), significant Finnish composer and teacher; b. Helsinki, Jan. 13, 1938. After studying privately with Merilainen, he took courses with Merikanto, Rautavaara, Englund, and Kokkonen at the Sibelius Academy in Helsinki (composition diploma, 1960); later took courses with Zimmermann in Cologne (1960–61), and with Persichetti and Steuermann at the Juilliard School of Music in N.Y. (1961–62); also worked with Lutoslawski in Poland, and attended theory classes at the Univ. of Helsinki. In 1962–63 he was on the faculty of the Sibelius Academy; taught in Turku (1963–66) before resuming his position at the Sibelius Academy, where he was mentor to a generation of Finnish composers. He was also active as a pianist, conductor, and program annotator. He developed a highly complex compositional style, employing styles and techniques ranging from neo-Classicism to dodecaphonic and serial procedures culminating in a stream-of-consciousness modality.

WORKS: DRAMATIC: *Silkkirumpu* (The Silken Drum), concerto for Singers, Players, Words, Images, and Movements (1981–83; Helsinki, April 5, 1984); *Veitsi* (The Knife), opera (1985–88; Helsinki, July 3, 1989). **ORCH.:** 4 syms.: No. 1 (1958; rev. 1960; Helsinki, March 24, 1964), No. 2, *Petite symphonie joyeuse* (Helsinki, Dec. 7, 1962), No. 3 (1969; rev. 1977; Helsinki, Jan. 24, 1978), and No. 4 (1971; Oslo, Sept. 4, 1972); *Preambolo* (1959); *Tripartita* (1959; Helsinki, Nov. 11, 1960); Concerto for Strings (1959; Helsinki, April 19, 1960; rev. 1963; Turku, May 30, 1963); *Soggetto* (1963; Helsinki, Jan. 12, 1965); *Adagio . . . concerto per orchestra in forma di variazioni . . .* (1963; Helsinki, Jan. 24, 1964; rev. 1966; Camden Festival, Feb. 19, 1967); 3 piano concertos: No. 1 (1964; Turku, Jan. 23, 1965), No. 2 (Turku, Dec. 1, 1966), and No. 3 (1981; Helsinki, March 13, 1982); *Arioso* for Strings (Helsinki, May 21, 1967); *Deux chansons* for Cello and Orch. (1976; Tampere, Feb. 25, 1977); *Tritopos* (1977; Helsinki, March 7, 1978); *Dia* (Helsinki, Sept. 12, 1979); *Attitude* (Helsinki, Dec. 10, 1980); *. . . floral view with maidens singing . . .* for Chamber Orch. (1982; Kokkola, April 8, 1983); *Dicta, "Nonette avec milieu"* for 9 plus 14 Players in the Audience (Helsinki, March 25, 1983); Saxophone Concerto (Helsinki, Aug. 29, 1983); *KauToKei* for Double String Orch. (1985; Helsinki, Feb. 12, 1986); Cello Concerto (1985; Helsinki, Feb. 26, 1986). **CHAMBER:** Quintet for Flute, Saxophone, Piano, Vibraphone, and Percussion (1961); *Musique d'été* for Flute, Clarinet, Violin, Cello, Harpsichord, Vibraphone, and Percussion (1963; rev. version, Tampere, Oct. 11, 1967); *Discantus I* for Alto Flute (1965), *II* for Clarinet (1969), and *III* for Alto Saxophone (1976); *Poesie des pensées* for Cello (1970); *Cantilena I* for Viola or Violin or Cello (1970), *II* for Cello (1970), and *III* for Violin (1976); Violin Sonata (1970; Helsinki, Feb. 18, 1973); *Deux chansons* for Cello and Piano (1974); String Quartet (1974; Helsinki, Jan. 21, 1976); *Gymel* for Bassoon and Tape (1978); *Touching* for Guitar (1978); *Jeu I* for Flute and Piano (1980) and *II* for Violin and Piano (1980); *Beateth* for Percussion (1982). **KEYBOARD: PIANO:** *Toccata*

(1956); Sonatine (1957); *Libretto della primavera* (1971); Sonata, *Poesia squillante ed incandescente* (1974); *Préludes-études-poèmes* (1974); *Poesies-periphrases* (1975); *Triple aperçu d'une amie qui fût* (1984); *Cinq moments de jour* (1984). **ORGAN:** *Oculus aquilae-trittico* (1968); *. . . irdisch gewesen zu sein . . .* (1972); *. . . des Säglichen Zeit . . .* (1972). **VOCAL:** *Canto di Natale* for Soprano and Piano (1961); *Cantico delle creature* for Baritone and Orch. (1968); *Love's Philosophy* for Tenor and Piano (1968–73); *The Autumn* for Chorus (1970); *Schatten der Erde* for Mezzo-soprano and Piano (1973); *. . . cor meum . . .* for Chorus (1976–79); *Reality* for Soprano and 10 Instruments (1978); *Virsi-81* (Hymn-81) for Chorus and Organ (1981); *4 Lullabies* for Men's Voices (1986). **ELECTRO-ACOUSTIC:** *Maiandros* (1977).

Heiniö, Mikko, Finnish composer and musicologist; b. Tampere, May 5, 1948. He was a student in piano of Liisa Pohjola and in composition of Kokkonen at the Sibelius Academy in Helsinki (1971–75; composition diploma, 1977). He also studied composition with Szalonek on a Deutscher Akademischer Austauschdienst scholarship in Berlin (1975–77). From 1977 to 1985 he taught at the Univ. of Helsinki, where he took his Ph.D. in musicology in 1984 with a diss. on the idea of innovation and tradition in the musical philosophy of contemporary Finnish composers. In 1986 he became prof. of musicology at the Univ. of Turku. He publ. several monographs and journal articles on various aspects of contemporary Finnish music. In his compositions, he is a modernist who draws upon the varied resources offered by serialism, aleatory, minimalism, and the popular genres.

WORKS: DRAMATIC: *Hermes*, dance pictures for Piano, Soprano, and Strings (1994; Turku, Aug. 11, 1995). **ORCH.:** 5 piano concertos: No. 1 (1972), No. 2 (1973; Helsinki, Feb. 26, 1975), No. 3 (1981; Tampere, Feb. 23, 1984), No. 4, *Genom kvällen* (Through the Evening), for Piano, Chorus, and Strings (1986; Espoo, May 21, 1989), and No. 5 (1989; Turku, April 5, 1990); Concerto grosso for Strings and Harpsichord (1975; Oslo, April 22, 1977); *Tredica* (1976; Helsinki, Dec. 13, 1978); Bassoon Concerto (1977; Bergen, March 2, 1978); Horn Concerto (1978; Pori, March 5, 1980); *Concerto for Orchestra* (Turku, Nov. 11, 1982); *Possible Worlds*, sym. (Turku, Dec. 10, 1987); *Dall'ombra all'ombra* for Orch. and Synthesizer (Turku, Nov. 28, 1992); *Trias* (Turku, May 26, 1995). **CHAMBER:** Suite for Flute and 2 Guitars (Helsinki, May 10, 1974); *Lindgreniana* for Oboe (1975; Helsinki, March 10, 1980); Trio for Oboe, Bassoon, and Harpsichord (Helsinki, July 29, 1976); Suite for Bassoon (1976); *Diberlimento* for 4 Flutes, 4 Trombones, and 3 Percussionists (1976; Berlin, Feb. 2, 1977); *Canto caotico* for 4 Cellos (1976; Berlin, Feb. 16, 1977); *Ākāśa* for 6 Trombones (Jyväskylä, July 7, 1977); *Notturno di fiordo* for Flute or Piccolo and Harp (1978); *Brass Mass* for 4 Trumpets, 4 Trombones, and Tuba ad libitum (1979; Helsinki, April 15, 1980); Duo for Violin and Piano (1979; Finnish Radio, May 5, 1980); *Champignons à l'herméneutique* for Flute and Guitar (1979; Helsinki, Dec. 16, 1980); *Minimba 1* for 4 or 3 Guitars (1982; Espoo, May 3, 1984); *. . . in spe* for Saxophone and Marimba or Vibraphone (1984); Trio for Violin, Cello, and Piano (1988); *In G* for Cello and Piano (1988); *Aurora*, fanfare for 11 Brass Instruments (1989; Turku, May 9, 1990); *Wintertime* for Vibraphone or Marimba and Harp (1990; Stockholm, Nov. 8, 1991); Piano Quintet (1993; Kuhmo, July 20, 1994). **PIANO:** *Deductions 1* (Helsinki, Nov. 23, 1979); *3 Repetitive Dreams* (1982; Jyväskylä, July 4, 1983); *Into Sleep* (1986); *Ritornelli* (1991; Helsinki, April 28, 1992). **VOCAL:** *4 Night Songs* for Baritone or Contralto and Piano or Orch. (1972); *Agnus Dei* for Children's Chorus, Flute, Guitar, and String Orch. (1974; Helsinki, Oct. 30, 1979; also for Children's Chorus and Organ); *Kinerva* for Tenor and Men's Chorus (1978; Helsinki, May 14, 1980); *The Land That is Not* for Children's or Women's Chorus and Piano (1980; Helsinki, May 12, 1981); *The Shadow of the Future* for Soprano, 4 Trumpets, 4 Trombones, and Tuba (1980; Helsinki, March 14, 1981); *Vuelo de alambre* for Soprano and Orch. (1983; Helsinki, April 3, 1985); *Continent Cantata* for Soprano, Baritone, Chorus, and Orch. (1985); *La* for Soprano, Mezzo-soprano or Contralto, Tenor, Bass, and Piano (1985; Helsinki, March 9, 1986); *Minimba 2* for Men's Chorus (1988); *Wind Pictures* for Chorus and Orch. (1991; Turku, Nov. 26, 1992); *Leceat* for Chorus (Helsinki, Dec. 6, 1992).

Heinitz, Wilhelm, German musicologist; b. Hamburg-Altona, Dec. 9, 1883; d. Hamburg, March 31, 1963. He studied the bassoon, and played in various orchs.; then became interested in phonetics. He studied primitive music and the languages of Africa and Polynesia; took a Ph.D. in psychology at the Univ. of Kiel (1920), and completed his Habilitation at the Univ. of Hamburg (1931) with his *Strukturprobleme in primitiver Musik* (publ. in Hamburg, 1931). In 1915 he became an assistant in the phonetics laboratory at the Univ. of Hamburg; was founder-director of its dept. of research for comparative musicology (1931–49). He wrote a number of valuable papers on the structural problems of speech, which he publ. in specialized journals; also the books *Klangprobleme im Rundfunk* (Berlin, 1926), *Instrumentenkunde* (Potsdam, 1929), *Neue Wege der Volksmusikforschung* (Hamburg, 1937), *Erforschung rassischer Merkmale aus der Volksmusik* (Hamburg, 1938), and *Physiologische Reaktion und Pulsationsmessung* (Hamburg, 1958).

Heinsheimer, Hans (Walter), German-born American publishing executive and writer on music; b. Karlsruhe, Sept. 25, 1900; d. N.Y., Oct. 12, 1993. He studied law in Heidelberg, Munich, and Freiburg im Breisgau (Juris Dr., 1923); then joined Universal Edition in Vienna, where he was in charge of its opera dept. (1924–38), and supervised the publication of such important stage works as Berg's *Wozzeck*, Krenek's *Jonny spielt auf*, Weinberger's *Schwanda*, Weill's *Aufstieg und Fall der Stadt Mahagonny*, and Antheil's *Transatlantic*. He went to the U.S. in 1938 and was associated with the N.Y. branch of Boosey & Hawkes. In 1947 he was appointed director of the symphonic and operatic repertoire of G. Schirmer, Inc.; in 1957 he became director of publications and in 1972 vice-president of the firm; in these capacities, he promoted the works of Barber, Menotti, Bernstein, and Carter. He retired in 1974 and devoted himself mainly to writing. A brilliant stylist in both German and English, he contributed numerous informative articles to *Melos*, *Musical Quarterly*, *Holiday*, *Reader's Digest*, etc. He publ. the entertaining books *Menagerie in F-sharp* (N.Y., 1947) and *Fanfare for Two Pigeons* (1952); the 2 works were publ. in German in a single vol. entitled *Menagerie in Fis-dur* (Zürich, 1953); he also wrote *Best Regards to Aida* (publ. in Ger. as *Schönste Grüsse an Aida*; Munich, 1968).

Heintze, Gustaf (Hjalmar), Swedish pianist, organist, pedagogue, and composer; b. Jönköping, July 22, 1879; d. Saltsjöbaden, March 4, 1946. His grandfather, Gustav Wilhelm Heintze (1825–1909), and father, Georg Wilhelm Heintze (1849–95), were well-known organists. He studied organ in Lund and Stockholm; also studied composition and instrumentation with Joseph Dente (1897–1900) and piano with Richard Andersson (1901) in Stockholm; then taught piano at Andersson's school (1901–18). He subsequently founded his own piano school, and was also organist at the Maria Magdalena Church. He wrote 2 piano concertos (1917, 1926), 2 violin concertos (1921, 1932), a Concerto for 2 Pianos and Orch. (1933), 3 cantatas (1923, 1934, 1940), and piano pieces.

Heinze, Sir Bernard (Thomas), eminent Australian conductor; b. Shepparton, near Melbourne, July 1, 1894; d. Sydney, June 9, 1982. He studied at the Univ. of Melbourne, the Royal College of Music in London, with d'Indy at the Schola Cantorum in Paris, and with Willy Hess (violin) in Berlin. In 1924 he joined the faculty of the Melbourne Conservatorium, where he was a prof. from 1925 to 1956. In 1924 he also became conductor of the Univ. of Melbourne Orch. After it merged with the Melbourne Sym. Orch. in 1932, Heinze served as conductor of the latter until 1949. He also was conductor of the Royal Phil. Soc.

in Melbourne (1927–53) and with the Australian Broadcasting Co. (1929–32), and its successor, the Australian Broadcasting Commission (from 1932), as well as adviser to the Sydney Sym. Orch. (1934–43). From 1956 to 1966 he was director of the New South Wales State Conservatorium in Sydney. He was knighted in 1949 and was made a Companion of the Order of Australia in 1976 for his manifold contributions to Australian music.

BIBL.: T. Radic, *B. H.: A Biography* (South Melbourne, 1986).

Heiss, Hermann, German composer and teacher; b. Darmstadt, Dec. 29, 1897; d. there, Dec. 6, 1966. He studied with Bernhard Sekles in Frankfurt am Main (1921); then took a course in 12-tone music with Hauer (1925). He was active as a teacher in Frankfurt am Main and Vienna; from 1946 he taught at the Darmstadt summer courses for new music. In his compositions, he adopted ultra-modern techniques.

WORKS: BALLETS: *Herz auf bürgerliche Art* (1953); *Der Manager* (1954). **ORCH.:** *Sinfonia atematica* (1950); *Sinfonia giocosa* (1954); *Configurationen I–II* (1956–59); *Polychromatica* (1959); *Bewegungsspiele* (1959). **OTHER:** Chamber music; electronic pieces.

BIBL.: B. Reichenbach, *H. H.* (Mainz, 1975).

Heiss, John, American flutist, conductor, teacher, and composer; b. N.Y., Oct. 23, 1938. He studied mathematics at Lehigh Univ. (B.A., 1960) before pursuing graduate studies in music with Leuning at Columbia Univ. (1960–65). He also took courses in composition (with Milhaud) and in flute at the Aspen (Colo.) Music School (summers, 1962–63). His training in composition was completed under Babbitt and Kim at Princeton Univ. (M.F.A., 1967). From 1969 to 1974 he was principal flute with Boston Musica Viva. He also played flute with other ensembles and made occasional appearances as a conductor. After teaching at Columbia Univ. (1963–65) and Barnard College (1964–65), he taught at the New England Cons. of Music in Boston (from 1967), where he was director of its Contemporary Ensemble. Among his honors were a Guggenheim fellowship, 4 NEA grants, and annual ASCAP awards.

WORKS: ORCH.: *4 Short Pieces* (1962); *Music* (1968); *Inventions, Contours, and Colors* for Chamber Orch. (1973); Concerto for Flute and Chamber Orch. (1977; recomposed as the Chamber Concerto for Flute, Clarinet, Piano, and Percussion); *Festival Prelude* (1983); *Mosaics I* for Flute Orch. (1986), *II* for Cello Choir (1987), *III* for Trombone Choir (1989), and *IV* for Clarinet Choir (1991). **CHAMBER:** *4 Lyric Pieces* for Flute (1962); Flute Sonatina (1962); *5 Pieces* for Flute and Cello (1963); *4 Movements* for 3 Flutes (1969); Quartet for Flute, Clarinet, Cello, and Piano (1971); *Capriccio* for Flute, Clarinet, and Percussion (1976); Chamber Concerto for Flute, Clarinet, Piano, and Percussion (1977; recomposition of the Concerto for Flute and Chamber Orch.); *Eloquy* for Flute, Oboe, Clarinet, and Bassoon (1978); *Études* for Flute (1979–80); *Episode I* for Violin (1980), *II: Elegia* for Double Bass (1992), and *III: Arietta* for Viola (1993); *So-nar-ity* for Piano, 4-hands, Harp, Percussion, Flute, and Clarinet (1982); *A Place in New England* for Brass Quartet or Choir and Organ (1982); *Epigrams* for Flute and Percussion (1985); Fanfare for 4 Trombones (1992); *Fantasia Appassionata* for Flute (1994). **VOCAL:** *3 Songs from Sandburg* for Treble Chorus, Piano, and Bassoon (1963); *Rejoice in the Lord* for Treble or Mixed Chorus and Keyboard (1964); *Songs of Nature* for Mezzo-soprano, Flute, Clarinet, Violin, Cello, and Piano (1975); *From Infinity Full Circle*, chamber cantata for Treble Chorus and Piano (1979); *Duple Play* for Soprano Vocalise, String Quartet, and Woodwind Quartet (1984); *Songs from James Joyce* for Mezzo-soprano, Flute, Clarinet, Violin, Cello, and Piano (1986).

Heitmann, Fritz, German organist and pedagogue; b. Ochsenwerder, near Hamburg, May 9, 1891; d. Berlin, Sept. 7, 1953. He studied organ with Straube and Pembaur and composition with Reger. In 1912 he became organist at Schleswig Cathedral. Upon settling in Berlin, he was organist at the Kaiser Wilhelm Gedächtniskirche (from 1918) and of the Singakademie (from 1920); in 1925, became prof. at the Staatlichen Akademie für Kirchen- und Schulmusik; from 1930, was organist at the Cathedral, and from 1945 prof. at the Hochschule für Musik. Heitmann won distinction as both a virtuoso organist and as a teacher.

BIBL.: R. Voge, *F. H.: Das Leben eines deutschen Organisten* (Berlin, 1963).

Hekking, André, French cellist of Dutch descent, brother of **Anton** and cousin of **Gérard Hekking**; b. Bordeaux, July 30, 1866; d. Paris, Dec. 14, 1925. He was the son of the Dutch-born French cellist Robert Gérard Hekking (1820–75), who settled in France and from whom he received his training. From 1909 he lived in Paris; in 1919, was appointed prof. at the Paris Cons.; also taught at the American Cons. in Fontainebleau. He publ. *Violoncelle, Exercices quotidiens* (Paris, 1927).

Hekking, Anton, Dutch cellist, brother of **André** and cousin of **Gérard Hekking**; b. The Hague, Sept. 7, 1856; d. Berlin, Nov. 18, 1935. He was the son of the Dutch-born French cellist Robert Gérard Hekking (1820–75). He studied at the Paris Cons. with Joseph Giese; then undertook an American tour with the pianist Essipova. Returning to Europe, he was 1st cellist of the Berlin Phil. (1884–88; 1898–1902). After another American tour, he was 1st cellist of the Boston Sym. Orch. (1889–91) and later of the N.Y. Sym. Orch. (1895–98). He returned to Berlin in 1898; taught at the Stern Cons. there, and became a member of a trio with Schnabel and Wittenberg (1902).

Hekking, Gérard, French cellist and teacher, cousin of **André** and **Anton Hekking**; b. Nancy, Aug. 22, 1879; d. Paris, June 5, 1942. He studied at the Paris Cons., winning 1st prize (1899). He was 1st cellist of the Concertgebouw Orch. in Amsterdam (1903–14) and taught at the Amsterdam Cons.; also made tours in Russia, Spain, Germany, and France. In 1927 he became a prof. at the Paris Cons. He wrote several cello pieces; also revised *Principes de la technique du violoncelle* of François Gervais (Paris, 1930).

Hekster, Walter, Dutch clarinetist, teacher, and composer; b. Amsterdam, March 29, 1937. He studied clarinet and composition at the Amsterdam Cons. (graduated, 1961). After playing clarinet in the Connecticut Sym. Orch. (1962–65), he studied with Sessions at the Berkshire Music Center in Tanglewood (summer, 1966). He taught clarinet and composition at Brandon Univ. in Canada (1965–71), and then at the conservatories in Utrecht and Arnhem.

WORKS: CHAMBER OPERA: *The Fog* (1987). **ORCH.:** *Epitaphium (In Memoriam Eduard van Beinum)* for Strings (1959); *Foci* for Violin and Chamber Ensemble (1965–66); *Facets* (1967–68); *Branches* for 15 Strings (1969; rev. 1979); *Nocturnal Conversation* (1970–71); *Early One Morning* for 15 Winds (1972); *Mobiles* (1973); *The Auroras of Autumn* for Oboes and Orch. (1975); *Parts of a World* for Viola and Orch. (1976); *Sunday* (1976); *Transport to Summer* for Clarinet and Orch. (1977); *Between 2 Worlds* for Saxophone and Orch. (1977); *Sea Surface Full of Clouds* for Strings (1978); *Primavera*, "Spring Concerto" for Piano and Orch. (1979); Guitar Concerto (1981); Clarinet Concerto (1982); Oboe Concerto (1984); Cello Concerto (1985); *Sonant* (1986); *Toward the Edge of Night* for Flute and Orch. (1989). **CHAMBER:** *Pentagram* for Wind Quintet (1961); *Reflections* for Clarinet, Horn, Cello, Vibraphone, Celesta, and Percussion (1964); Sonata for Solo Cello (1967); *Fresco* for Clarinet and String Trio (1970); *Ambage* for String Quartet (1970); *Tropos* for Flute, Oboe, Violin, Viola, Cello, and Piano (1974–75); *Graffiti* for Ondes Martenot, Percussion, and Piano (1975); *Pulsations* for Wind Quintet (1976); *Ideas of Order* for Wind Quintet (1980); Quintet (1982); *Setting No. 1* for Flute and Harp (1982), *No. 2* for Flute (1982), *No. 4* for Guitar (1984), *No. 5* for English Horn, Clarinet, Saxophone, and Bassoon (1985), *No. 6* for Clarinet, Cello, and Piano (1985), *No. 7* for Baritone Saxophone and Percussion (1985), and *No. 8* for 4 Saxophones (1986); *Shadows in a Landscape* for Wind Quintet

(1987); *Nara* for Clarinet, Violin, Cello, and Piano (1993); piano pieces. **VOCAL:** Various works.

Heldy, Fanny (real name, **Marguerite Virginia Emma Clémentine Deceuninck**), Belgian-born French soprano; b. Ath, near Liège, Feb. 29, 1888; d. Paris, Dec. 13, 1973. She studied in Liège and Brussels. She made her operatic debut as Elena in Gunsbourg's *Ivan le Terrible* at the Théâtre Royal de la Monnaie in Brussels, where she sang regularly while accepting guest engagements in Monte Carlo, Warsaw, and St. Petersburg. In 1917 she made her Paris debut as Violetta at the Opéra-Comique, and sang there until 1920; then was a member of the Paris Opéra (1920–39). In 1926 and 1928 she sang at London's Covent Garden. Among her admired portrayals were Marguerite, Nedda, Mélisande, Louise, Manon, Concepción, and Thaïs.

Helfer, Walter, American composer; b. Lawrence, Mass., Sept. 30, 1896; d. New Rochelle, N.Y., April 16, 1959. He studied at Harvard Univ.; then took courses in composition with Caussade in Paris and with Respighi in Rome. Returning to the U.S., he joined the staff of Hunter College in N.Y. He wrote an orch. *Fantasy on Children's Tunes* (1935); *Symphony on Canadian Airs* (1937); Concertino for Piano and Chamber Orch. (1947); *Soliloquy* for Cello and Piano; String Quartet; String Trio; *Elegiac Sonata* for Piano; minor piano pieces; songs.

Helfert, Vladimír, distinguished Czech musicologist; b. Plánice, near Klatovy, March 24, 1886; d. Prague, May 18, 1945. He took courses in history and geography at the Univ. of Prague, and then studied musicology with Kretzschmar, Stumpf, and Wolf at the Univ. of Berlin (1906–07); completed his studies with Hostinský at the Univ. of Prague (Ph.D., 1908, with the diss. *Jiři Benda a Jean Rousseau*). He was active as a history and geography teacher in Prague until 1919; then moved to Brno, where he became a lecturer (1921), docent (1926), and prof. of musicology (1931) at the Univ. He was founder-ed. of the Musica Antiqua Bohemica series, as well as ed. of several journals; founded the Baroque, Classical, and Janáček collections at the Moravian Museum; also conducted the amateur Brno Orchestrálni Sdružení. He was arrested by the Nazis in 1940 and held in Breslau until 1943; then was rearrested in 1945 and taken to the Terezín concentration camp, where he contracted typhus; he died a few days after his liberation.

WRITINGS (all publ. in Prague unless otherwise given): *Smetanismus a wagnerismus* (1911); *Hudební barok na českých zámcích* (The Musical Baroque in Czech Castles; 1916); *Smetanovské kapitoly* (Chapters on Smetana; 1917; 2nd ed., 1954); *Naše hudba a český stát* (Our Music and the Czech State; 1918; 2nd ed., 1970); *Hudba na Jaroměřickém zámku: František Miča 1696–1745* (Music in the Jaromerice Castle: František Miča 1696–1745; 1924); *Tvůrči rozvoj Bedřicha Smetany, I* (Bedrich Smetana's Creative Development; 1924; 2nd ed., 1953; Ger. tr., 1956); *Jiři Benda* (Brno, 1929–34); ed. with G. Černušák, *Pazdírkův hudební slovnik naučný* (Pazdírek's Scientific Music Dictionary; Brno, 1929; 1933–41); *Základy hudební výchovy na nehudebnich školách* (Principles of Musical Education in Secondary Schools; 1930); *Česka moderní hudba* (Czech Modern Music; Olomouc, 1936; Fr. and Ger. trs., 1938); with E. Steinhard, *Histoire de la musique dans la république Tchecoslovaque* (1936; Ger. tr., 1936; 2nd ed., rev., 1938, as *Die Musik in der tschechoslovakischen Republik*); *Útok na Českou moderní hudbu* (The Attack on *Česká moderní hudba*; Olomouc, 1937); *Leoš Janáček*, I (Brno, 1939); *Státní hudebně historický ústav* (The State Inst. of Music History; ed. by G. Černušák; 1945); *O Janáčkovi* (ed. by B. Štědroň; 1949); *O Smetanovi* (ed. by B. Štědroň; 1950); *O české hudbě* (On Czech Music; ed. by B. Štědroň and I. Poledňák; 1957); *Vybrané studie, I: O hudební tvořivosti* (Selected Studies, I: On Musical Creativity; ed. by F. Hrabal; 1970).

BIBL.: Special issue of *Index*, VIII/3 (1936); B. Štědroň, *Dr. V. H.* (Prague, 1940); I. Poledňák, "K některým otázkám H. ovy estetiky" (Some Questions concerning H.'s Aesthetics), *Hudební Rozhledy*, V (1957); A. Sychra, "V. H. a smysl české hudby" (V. H. and the Meaning of Czech Music), ibid., XIV (1961); M. Černý, "Hudebně historickě dílo V. H.'s" (V. H.'s Works on Music History), *Hudební Věda*, III (1966); R. Pečman and J. Vysloužil, eds., *V. H.: Pokrokový vedec a člověk* (V. H.: Progressive Scholar and Man; Brno, 1975); special issue of *Opus Musicum*, VII, no. 10 (1975).

Helffer, Claude, French pianist; b. Paris, June 18, 1922. He studied piano with Robert Casadesus; following classical studies at the École Polytechnique (1939–42), he studied harmony, counterpoint, and composition with Leibowitz. In 1948 he made his debut in Paris and subsequently made tours of Europe; in 1966 he made his first tour of the U.S.; also appeared in South America, Australia, and Japan. While a master of the standard repertory, he became best known for his championship of 20th century music. In addition to Debussy, Ravel, Bartók, and Schoenberg, he was a convincing interpreter of Boulez, Barraqué, Xenakis, Amy, and others.

Helfman, Max, Polish-born American choral conductor and composer; b. Radzin, May 25, 1901; d. Dallas, Aug. 9, 1963. He was taken to the U.S. in 1909; studied at the David Mannes School of Music in N.Y. and at the Curtis Inst. of Music in Philadelphia, where his teachers were Scalero in composition and Reiner in conducting. He subsequently was active mainly as a conductor of Jewish choral groups; was in charge of choral singing at Temple Emanuel in Paterson, N.J. (1926–39), Temple B'nai Abraham in Newark (1940–53), and Temple Sinai in Los Angeles (1954–57); was music director at the Brandeis Inst. in Santa Susanna, California, and dean of the arts at the Univ. of Judaism in Los Angeles (1958–62). He wrote a dramatic cantata, *New Hagadah* (1949), and several pieces of Jewish liturgical music; ed. a series of choral works for the Jewish Music Alliance.

BIBL.: P. Moddel, *M. H.* (Berkeley, 1974).

Helfritz, Hans, German ethnomusicologist and composer; b. Hilbersdorf, July 25, 1902. He studied with Hindemith at the Hochschule für Musik in Berlin, and with Wellesz in Vienna. In 1936 he went to South America; lived mostly in Chile, where he worked on problems of musical folklore. In 1956 he undertook a journey along the west coast of Africa and made recordings of native songs. In 1962 he settled in Ibiza in the Balearic Islands. He composed orch. works and chamber music; in some of them, he makes use of South American and African motifs.

WRITINGS: *Amerika, Land der Inka, Maya und Azteken* (Vienna, 1965); *Die Götterburgen Mexikos* (Cologne, 1968); *Mexiko, Land der drei Kulturen* (Berlin, 1968).

Heller, Hans Ewald, German-American composer; b. Vienna, April 17, 1894; d. N.Y., Oct. 1, 1966. He studied with J.B. Foerster and Camillo Horn; was engaged in Vienna as a music critic and teacher. In 1938 he settled in the U.S. Among his compositions were the light operas *Satan* (Vienna, 1927), *Messalina* (Prague, 1928), and *Der Liebling von London* (Vienna, 1930); an overture, *Carnival in New Orleans* (1940); a cantata, *Ode to Our Women* (1942); 2 string quartets; Suite for Clarinet and Piano; about 150 songs.

Heller, James G., American composer; b. New Orleans, Jan. 4, 1892; d. Cincinnati, Dec. 19, 1971. He studied at Tulane Univ. in New Orleans (B.A., 1912), the Univ. of Cincinnati (M.A., 1914), the Hebrew Union College (Rabbi, 1916), and the Cincinnati Cons. (Mus.D., 1934). For 12 years, he wrote the program notes for the Cincinnati Sym. Orch.; then taught musicology at the Cincinnati Cons. of Music. Among his works were *Elegy and Pastorale* for Voice and String Orch. (Cincinnati, Dec. 30, 1934); String Quartet; Violin Sonata; Jewish services (New Union Hymnal, 1930–32).

Hellermann, William (David), American composer and guitarist; b. Milwaukee, July 15, 1939. He studied mechanical engineering at the Univ. of Wisc. (B.S., 1962) and composition at Columbia Univ. (M.A., 1965; D.M.A., 1969), his principal mentors being Wolpe, Chou Wen-chung, Luening, and Ussachevsky. From 1966 to 1972 he was on the music faculty at Columbia Univ. He also held a composer's fellowship to the Berkshire Music Center at Tanglewood (summer, 1967) and the Prix de Rome fellowship to the American Academy in Rome (1972). In 1977 he was composer-in-residence at the Center for the Creative and Performing Arts at the State Univ. of N.Y. at Buffalo. As a guitarist, he has been especially active as a proponent of contemporary music. His compositions are thoroughly modern in range and utilization of resources. He has become particularly well known for his creations in the realm of music sculpture.

WORKS: DRAMATIC: *Parts Sequences 1 for an Open Space* for 4 Musicians, 4 Actors, 4 Dancers, and 4 Sets (N.Y., March 24, 1972); *Extraordinary Histories*, experimental opera (N.Y., April 28, 1982); *3 Sisters Who Art Not Sisters*, theater piece (1984; Barcelona, Oct. 23, 1985); *Blood on the Dining Room Floor*, theater piece (N.Y., Nov. 21, 1991). **ORCH.:** *Time and Again* (1969; Utrecht, Sept. 14, 1970); *"anyway . . ."* (Greenwich, Conn., March 22, 1977). **CHAMBER:** *Formata* for Trombone and 4 Instruments (1967); *Ek-stasis II* for Timpani, Piano, and Tape (1970); *Round and About* for 2 or More Instruments (1970); *Circle Music 1* for 4 Instruments, *2* for 2 or More Instruments, and *3* for 6 Performers (all 1971); *Passages 13: The Fire* for Trumpet and Tape (1971); *Distances/Embraces* for Guitar (1972); *On the Vanishing Point* for Piano and Tape Delay (1973); *Stop/Start* for 2 Soloists and 6 Players (1973); *Long Island Sound* for 4 Instruments (1974); *To the Last Drop* for 6 Vibraphones (1974); *"But, the moon . . ."* for Guitar and 13 Instruments (Paris, March 13, 1975); *Still and All* for Guitar (1975); *Experimental Music* for Variable Instruments (1975); *To Brush Up On* for 6 Cellos (1976); *2 Vibraphones* for 2 Vibraphones (1976); *Squeek* for Soloist (1977); *Tremble* for Guitar (1978); *3 Weeks in Cincinnati in December* for Flute (1979); *The Violin between Us* for Violin (1981); *Tremble II* for Double Bass (1981); *On the Vanishing Point* for 4 Instruments (1989); *Post/Pone* for Guitar, Clarinet, Viola, Trombine, and Piano (1990). **PIANO:** *Row Music (Tip of the Iceberg)* (1973); *For Otto (A Line in Return)* (1974); *At Sea* (1976). **VOCAL:** *En-trances* for Chorus (1976); *Local Exits* for Soprano and Chamber Ensemble (1976); *Nests* for Soloist and Chorus (1976); *City Games* for 3 Vocalists, Tape, and Sculpture (1978); *Sheet Music* for Soloist and Synthesizer (1984). **OTHER:** *Ariel* for Tape (1967); *Juicy Music* for Tape and Sculpture (1982); *El Ropo* for Keyboard, Tape, and Sculpture (1984); *1 Bar Blues* for Tape and Sculpture (1984).

Helm, Anny, Austrian soprano; b. Vienna, July 20, 1903. She was a student of Gutheil-Schoder and Gertrude Förstel in Vienna, and of Grenzebach in Berlin. In 1924 she made her operatic debut in Magdeburg, and then appeared at the Berlin State Opera (1926–33) and at the Bayreuth Festivals (1927–31). In 1933 she settled in Italy, where she sang under the name Anny Helm-Sbisa (her husband, Giuseppe Sbisa, was director of the Teatro Giuseppe Verdi in Trieste). In 1939 she appeared at London's Covent Garden. She devoted herself mainly to teaching from 1941. Her finest roles included Donna Anna, Brangäne, Isolde, Brünnhilde, Turandot, and Elektra.

Helm, E(rnest) Eugene, American musicologist; b. New Orleans, Jan. 23, 1928. He was educated at Southeastern Louisiana College (B.M.E., 1950), Louisiana State Univ. (M.M.E., 1955), and North Texas State Univ. (Ph.D., 1958, with the diss. *The Musical Patronage of Frederick the Great*). He taught at Louisiana College (1953–55), Wayne (Nebr.) State College (1958–59), the Univ. of Iowa (1960–68), and the Univ. of Maryland (from 1968), where he was also chairman of the musicology division (1971–87). He served as coordinating ed. of the Carl Philipp Emanuel Bach Edition (from 1982).

WRITINGS: *Music at the Court of Frederick the Great* (1960); with A. Luper, *Words and Music* (1971; 2nd ed., 1982); *Thematic Catalogue of the Works of Carl Philipp Emanuel Bach* (1989); *The Canon and the Curricula: A Study of Musicology and Ethnomusicology Programs in America* (1994).

Helm, Everett (Burton), American composer and musicologist; b. Minneapolis, July 17, 1913. He studied at Harvard Univ. (M.A., 1936; Ph.D., 1939); also studied in Europe (1936–38) with Malipiero, Vaughan Williams, and Alfred Einstein. Returning to the U.S., he taught at Western College in Oxford, Ohio (1943–44). From 1948 to 1950 he was a music officer under the U.S. military government in Germany. He was ed. of *Musical America* (1961–63). A linguist, he contributed articles to various music magazines in several languages; he made a specialty of the music of Yugoslavia and was a guest lecturer at the Univ. of Ljubljana (1966–68).

WRITINGS: *Béla Bartók in Selbstzeugnissen und Biddokumenten* (Reinbek-bei-Hamburg, 1965; reduction and Eng. tr., N.Y., 1972); *Composer, Performer, Public: A Study in Communication* (Florence, 1970); *Franz Liszt* (Hamburg, 1972); *Music and Tomorrow's Public* (Wilhelmshaven, 1981).

WORKS: *Adam and Eve*, an adaptation of a medieval mystery play (Wiesbaden, Oct. 28, 1951); Concerto for 5 Instruments, Percussion, and Strings (Donaueschingen, Oct. 10, 1953); 2 piano concertos: No. 1 (N.Y., April 24, 1954) and No. 2 (Louisville, Feb. 25, 1956); *The Siege of Tottenburg*, radio opera (1956); *Le Roy fait battre tambour*, ballet (1956); *500 Dragon-Thalers*, Singspiel (1956); *Divertimento* for Flutes (1957); *Sinfonia da camera* (1961); Concerto for Double Bass and String Orch. (1968); 2 string quartets; Woodwind Quintet (1967); numerous piano pieces and songs.

Helps, Robert (Eugene), American composer, pianist, and teacher; b. Passaic, N.J., Sept. 23, 1928. He attended the preparatory dept. of the Juilliard School of Music in N.Y. (1936–43), and then studied piano with Abby Whiteside and composition with Roger Sessions; he also took courses at Columbia Univ. (1947–49) and at the Univ. of Calif. at Berkeley (1949–51). After teaching piano at Stanford Univ. (1968–69), the San Francisco Cons. of Music (1968–70), the Univ. of Calif. at Berkeley (1969–70), the New England Cons. of Music in Boston (1970–72), the Manhattan School of Music (1972–78), and at Princeton Univ. (1972–78), he served as prof. of music at the Univ. of South Florida in Tampa (from 1980). As a pianist, he acquired a fine reputation as an interpreter of modern music. He received various awards and commissions, and in 1966 held a Guggenheim fellowship. He developed a personal style of expression while utilizing 12-tone procedures.

WORKS: ORCH.: Sym. (1955); *Cortège* (1963); 2 piano concertos (1969, 1976). **CHAMBER:** String Quartet (1951); Piano Trio (1957); *Serenade* in 3 parts: 1, *Fantasy* for Violin and Piano (1963), 2, *Nocturne* for String Quartet (1966), and 3, *Postlude* for Horn, Violin, and Piano (1965); Quintet for Flute, Clarinet, Violin, Cello, and Piano (1976); *Second Thoughts* for Flute (1978). **PIANO:** *Fantasy* (1952); 3 études (1956); *Images* (1957); *Starscape* (1958); *Recollections* (1959); *Portrait* (1960); *Solo* (1960); *Saccade* for 4-hands (1967); *Quartet* (1971); *3 Homages* (1973); *Nocturne* (1973); *Music for the Left Hand* (1974); *Valse mirage* (1977). **VOCAL:** 2 songs for Soprano and Piano (1950); *The Running Sun* for Soprano and Piano (1972); *Gossamer Noons* for Soprano and Orch. (1977).

Hely-Hutchinson, (Christian) Victor, South African-born English pianist, conductor, administrator, and composer; b. Cape Town, Dec. 26, 1901; d. London, March 11, 1947. He studied at Balliol College, Oxford, at the Royal College of Music, London, and with Tovey before returning to Oxford to take his D.Mus. in 1940. In 1922 he became a lecturer in music at the South African College of Music in Cape Town; in 1926 he joined the staff of the BBC in London, and later was head of its Midlands Region in Birmingham (1933–44); also was a prof. of music at the Univ. of Birmingham (1934–44) before serving as director of music of the BBC in London (1944–47). Among his compositions are *A Carol Symphony*, a Piano Quintet, a String Quintet, a Viola Sonata, choral pieces, songs, and film scores.

Hemberg, (Bengt Sven) Eskil, Swedish composer, administrator, and conductor; b. Stockholm, Jan. 19, 1938. He studied organ and was a student of Blomstedt (conducting) at the Stockholm Musikhögskolan (1957–64). From 1959 to 1964 he conducted the Stockholm Academic Choir, and then was its artistic director from 1964 to 1984. He was executive producer for the Swedish Broadcasting Corp., serving as head of its choral section (1963–70); he then was head of planning of the Inst. for National Concerts (1970–83) and president of the Swedish Soc. of Composers (1971–83). After serving as artistic director of the Stora Teatern in Göteborg (1984–87), he held that title with the Royal Theater in Stockholm from 1987. In 1974 he was elected a member of the Royal Academy of Music in Stockholm. He has written much vocal music, ranging from operas to sacred scores, in which traditional procedures are enhanced by ventures into contemporary harmony.

WORKS: DRAMATIC: OPERAS: *Love, love, love* (1973–80); *The Pirates in the Deep Green Sea* (1975–77); *St. Erik's Crown,* church opera (1979); *Herr Apfelstädt wird Kunstler,* chamber opera (1989); film music. **ORCH.:** *Migraine* (1973); *Thulegräs* for Strings (1987). **CHAMBER:** *Zona rosa* for String Quartet (1973); *Les Adieu* for String Quartet (1982); Trio for Violin, Viola, and Cello (1984; also for Flute, Violin, and Cello, 1986); *Rondo festivo* for Violin and Piano (1993); piano pieces; organ music. **VOCAL:** *18 Movements* for Chorus (1967); *Messa d'oggi* for 5 Soloists and Chorus (1968–70); Passion after St. Mark for Soloists, Chorus, and Orch. (1972–84); *Cantica* for Soloists, Chorus, and Orch. (1973); *Songbook from Österbotten* for Men's Voices, English Horn, Clarinet, Small Drum, and Double Bass (1975); *With God and his Friendship,* "a Mass about belief and politics" for Priest, Congregation, Chorus, Trumpet, and Organ (1976); *Women,* scenic cantata for Soloists, Women's Chorus, and Orch. (1978–79); *Concerning My Negotiations with Myself and with God* for Solo Quartet, Double Chorus, and Organ (1980); *Love Fancies* for Baritone, Bassoon, and String Orch. (1980); *Canticles I–III* for Soloists and Instruments (1981); *Lützener Te Deum* for Double Chorus and 3 Trombones (1982); *Canti di luce e di stelle* for Soprano and 7 Instruments (1982–91); *Magnificat* for Double Chorus (1982); *To the Light,* cantata for Soloists, Men's Chorus, and Chamber Orch. (1984); *Psalm 150* for Chorus, Viola d'Amore, and Cello (1985); *Requiem Aeternam* for Chorus (1987); *San Francisco Peace Cantata* for Soloists, Chorus, Trumpet, and Crotales (1989); *Psalm 96* for Chorus (1992); Suite for Soprano, Wind Quintet, and String Quartet (1992); *Requiem* for Chorus (1994); various other choral pieces; songs.

Hemel, Oscar van, Dutch composer; b. Antwerp, Aug. 3, 1892; d. Hilversum, July 9, 1981. He was a student of L. Mortelmans and de Boeck at the Royal Flemish Cons. in Antwerp; in 1914 he settled in the Netherlands, and later pursued his training with Pijper in Rotterdam (1931–33). The style of his works oscillated between Austro-German Romantic trends and the more complex technical structures of the Dutch modernists.

WORKS: RADIO OPERA: *Viviane* (Hilversum Radio, 1950). **ORCH.:** 5 syms.: No. 1 (1935), No. 2 (1948), No. 3, Sinfonietta for Small Orch. (1952), No. 4 (1962), and No. 5 (1963–64; rev. 1980); Suite for Chamber Orch. (1936); Suite for Flute and Chamber Orch. (1937; also for Flute and Piano); Piano Concerto (1941–42); *Ballade* (1942); 3 violin concertos (1945, 1968, 1977); *De stad,* symphonic poem (1949); Viola Concerto (1951); *Feestelijke ouverture* (1952); *Olof Suite* (1953); *Entrada festante* (1953); *Tema con variazioni* (1953); Oboe Concerto (1955); Concerto for Wind Orch. (1960); *Concerto da camera* for Flute and Strings (1962); Cello Concerto (1963); *Divertimento* for Strings (1964); *Entrada* (1964); *Serenade* for 3 Solo Winds and Strings (1965); *Polonaise* (1966); Concerto for 2 Violins and String Orch. (1970–71); *Divertimento* for Piano and Orch. (1974). **CHAMBER:** 6 string quartets (1931, 1936, 1947, 1953, 1956, 1961); 2 violin sonatas (1933, 1945); Piano Trio (1937); Piano Quartet (1938); Viola Sonata (1942); String Trio (1951); Clarinet Quintet (1958); Trio for Flute, Oboe, and Bassoon (1959); Sextet for Piano and Winds (1962); *Donquichotterie* for 4 Trombones (1962); *About Commedia dell'arte* for Oboe Quartet (1967); Wind Quintet (1972). **VOCAL:** *Maria Magdalena,* sacred cantata for Contralto, Tenor, and Orch. (1941); *Ballade van Kapitein Joos de Decker* for Contralto, Bass, Chorus, and Orch. (1943; rev. 1959); *De bruid* for Soprano, Men's Chorus, and Orch. (1946); *Da liet van Alianora* for Soprano, Men's Chorus, and Orch. (1946); *Ballade van Brabant* for Baritone/Reciter, Boy's Chorus, Men's Chorus, and Orch. (1952); *Krans der middeleeuwen* for Baritone, Chorus, and 7 Instruments (1952); *Canticum psalmorum* for Contralto, Men's Chorus, 2 Pianos, and Timpani (1954); *Le Tombeau de Kathleen Ferrier* for Contralto and Orch. (1954); *Herdenkingshymne 1940–1945* for Chorus, Children's Chorus, Brass, and Percussion (1955; with full Orch., 1970); *Les Mystères du Christ,* symphonic hymn for Contralto, Baritone, Men's Chorus, and Orch. (1958); *Te Deum* for Soprano, Contralto, Tenor, Bass, Chorus, and Orch. (1958); *Tuin van Holland* for Soprano, Baritone, Chorus, and Orch. (1958); *Trittico liturgico* for Soprano and Organ or Strings (1959); *Huwellijkscantate Beatrix* for Soprano, Tenor, Chorus, and Orch. (1966); *Song of Freedom* for Chorus and Orch. (1968–69; rev. 1981).

Heming, Percy, English baritone; b. Bristol, Sept. 6, 1883; d. London, Jan. 11, 1956. He studied in London at the Royal Academy of Music and with Henschel and Thomas Blackburn; also with Grose in Dresden. In 1915 he made his operatic debut as Paris in *Roméo et Juliette* with the Beecham Opera Co. in London, with which he appeared until 1919. In 1920 he made a tour of the U.S. in *The Beggar's Opera.* In 1922 he joined the British National Opera Co. in London, and also appeared there at Sadler's Wells (1933–35; 1940–42); also served as artistic director of London's Covent Garden English Co. (1937–39) and as artistic advisor at Covent Garden (1946–48). He was greatly admired as one of England's finest baritones. His repertory was extensive, but he excelled particularly as Mozart's Dr. Bartolo, Ford, Amfortas, Macheath, and Scarpia.

Hemke, Frederick (LeRoy), American saxophonist and teacher; b. Milwaukee, July 11, 1935. He studied at the Univ. of Wisc. (1953–55); then with Marcel Mule at the Paris Cons., becoming the first American to win a premier prix for saxophone (1956). He then continued his studies with Joseph Mariano and Robert Sprenkle at the Eastman School of Music in Rochester, N.Y., and at the Univ. of Wisc. (D.M.A., 1975). He taught at Northwestern Univ. (from 1962), serving as chairman of the dept. of wind and percussion instruments (from 1964); was also a member of the Chicago Sym. Orch. (1962–82). He publ. *The Early History of the Saxophone* (1975) and *The Teacher's Guide to the Saxophone* (1977). He commissioned Pettersson's Sym. No. 16 for Alto Saxophone and Orch., and played in its premiere (Stockholm, Feb. 24, 1983).

Hempel, Frieda, brilliant German soprano; b. Leipzig, June 26, 1885; d. Berlin, Oct. 7, 1955. She studied piano at the Leipzig Cons. (1900–1902) before pursuing vocal training with Selma Nicklass-Kempner at the Stern Cons. in Berlin (1902–05). After making her operatic debut in Breslau in 1905, she appeared with the Berlin Royal Opera for the first time on Aug. 22, 1905, as Frau Fluth in Nicolai's *Die lustigen Weiber von Windsor.* Following appearances with the Schwerin Court Opera (1905–07), she returned to Berlin and was a leading member of the Royal Opera until 1912. On May 2, 1907, she made her debut at London's Covent Garden as Bastienne in Mozart's opera and as Gretel in Humperdinck's opera in a double bill. She made her first appearance at the Metropolitan Opera in N.Y. on Dec. 27, 1912, as the Queen in *Les Huguenots.* She remained on its roster until 1919, gaining renown for her portrayals of such roles as the Queen of the Night, Susanna, Rosina, Lucia, Offenbach's Olympia, Eva, and Violetta. In 1914 and again in 1920–21 she sang with the Chicago Grand Opera. Thereafter she devoted herself to concert appearances in which she impersonated Jenny Lind in period costume. Her memoirs were publ. as *Mein Leben dem Gesang* (Berlin, 1955). Hempel possessed a remarkable coloratura voice. Her repertoire extended from Mozart to Richard Strauss, including the latter's Marschallin.

Hemsi (Chicurel), Alberto, Italian conductor, ethnomusicologist, and composer of Jewish descent; b. Cassaba, Turkey, Dec. 23, 1896; d. Aubervilliers, near Paris, Oct. 7, 1975. He studied music in Izmir, and later took courses in piano, theory, and composition at the Milan Cons. He was music director of the Grand Synagogue in Alexandria, Egypt (1927–57), and founder-conductor of the Alexandria Phil. (1928–40); also founded the Édition Orientale de Musique (1929) and was active as a teacher. In 1957 he settled in Paris as prof. at the Jewish Seminary. He was particularly interested in Sephardic Jewry. His compositions were of an oriental flavor, the most characteristic being the symphonic suite *Croquis égyptiens* (1930); other works include *Poème biblique* for Voice and Orch., *Suite Séfardie* for Violin and Piano, *6 danses turques* for Piano, and a number of songs.

Hemsley, Thomas (Jeffery), English baritone; b. Coalville, April 12, 1927. He studied at Brasenose College, Oxford, and received private vocal training from Lucie Manén. In 1951 he made his operatic debut as Purcell's Aeneas at London's Mermaid Theatre; he then sang regularly at the Glyndebourne Festivals (1953–71). He also sang at the Aachen City Theater (1953–56), the Deutsche Oper am Rhein in Düsseldorf (1957–63), the Zürich Opera (1963–67), the Bayreuth Festivals (1968–70), and at London's Covent Garden (from 1970). He likewise pursued a career as a concert singer. In later years, he was active as an opera director and as a teacher. Prominent among his roles were such portrayals as Don Fernando, Count Almaviva, Dr. Malatesta, Beckmesser, and Massetto.

Henderson, Alva, American composer; b. San Luis Obispo, Calif., April 8, 1940. He studied voice and theory at San Francisco State College. He wrote mainly vocal works, including the operas *Medea* (San Diego, Nov. 29, 1972), *The Tempest* (n.d.), and *The Last of the Mohicans* (Wilmington, Del., June 12, 1976).

Henderson, Roy (Galbraith), Scottish baritone, conductor, and pedagogue; b. Edinburgh, July 4, 1899. He studied at the Royal Academy of Music in London (1920–25). He made his London debut as Zarathustra in *A Mass of Life* by Delius in 1925; his operatic debut followed in 1928 as Donner in Wagner's *Das Rheingold* at Covent Garden; he also sang at the Glyndebourne Festivals (1934–39). He was founder and conductor of the Nottingham Oriana Choir (1936–52); was a prof. of singing at the Royal Academy of Music (1940–74). He was made a Commander of the Order of the British Empire in 1970. Henderson was especially esteemed as a concert singer, becoming well known for his championship of music by English composers. As a teacher, he numbered Kathleen Ferrier among his gifted students.

Henderson, Skitch (actually, **Lyle Russell Cedric**), English-born American pianist, conductor, composer, and arranger; b. Birmingham, Jan. 27, 1918. He settled in the U.S. as a youth and pursued his training at the Univ. of Calif. at Los Angeles and at the Juilliard School of Music in N.Y.; among his mentors were Schoenberg (theory and harmony) and Reiner (conducting). He worked in film studios and on the radio. While in military service during World War II, he became a naturalized American citizen. In 1949 he joined the staff of NBC. He became well known as a conductor, composer, and arranger for various television programs, particularly on Steve Allen's show (1954–56) and Johnny Carson's "Tonight Show" (1962–66). In subsequent years, he toured as a conductor in the U.S. and Europe, leading concerts of both classical and popular scores. After serving as music director of the Tulsa Phil. (1971–74), he founded the N.Y. Pops Orch. which gave its inaugural concert at Carnegie Hall in 1983.

Henderson, W(illiam) J(ames), noted American music critic; b. Newark, N.J., Dec. 4, 1855; d. (suicide) N.Y., June 5, 1937. He was a graduate of Princeton Univ. (B.A., 1876; M.A., 1886); also studied piano with Carl Langlotz (1868–73) and voice with Torriani (1876–77); was chiefly self-taught in theory. He was first a reporter (1883–87), then music critic of the *N.Y. Times* (1887–1902) and the *N.Y. Sun* (1902–37); lectured on music history at the N.Y. College of Music (1889–95; 1899–1902); from 1904, lectured on the development of vocal art at the Inst. of Musical Art in N.Y. A brilliant writer, Henderson was an irreconcilable and often venomous critic of modern music; he loved Wagner, but savagely attacked Debussy and Richard Strauss. Henderson, in turn, was the butt of some of Charles Ives's caustic wit.

WRITINGS (all publ. in N.Y.): *The Story of Music* (1889; 2nd ed., enl., 1912); *Preludes and Studies* (1891); *How Music Developed* (1898); *What Is Good Music?* (1898; 6th ed., 1935); *The Orchestra and Orchestral Music* (1899); *Richard Wagner, His Life and His Dramas* (1901; 2nd ed., 1923); *Modern Musical Drift* (1904); *The Art of the Singer* (1906; 2nd ed., aug., 1938, as *The Art of Singing*); *Some Forerunners of Italian Opera* (1911); *Early History of Singing* (1921).

BIBL.: O. Thompson, "An American School of Criticism: The Legacy Left by W.J. H., R. Aldrich and Their Colleagues of the Old Guard," *Musical Quarterly* (Oct. 1937).

Hendl, Walter, American conductor; b. West New York, N.J., Jan. 12, 1917. He began piano lessons in childhood; after further piano training with Clarence Adler (1934–37), he was a scholarship student of Saperton (piano, 1938) and Reiner (conducting, 1939) at the Curtis Inst. of Music in Philadelphia; during the summers of 1941–42, he attended Koussevitzky's conducting courses at the Berkshire Music Center in Tanglewood. He was assistant conductor of the N.Y. Phil. (1945–49) and a faculty member of the Juilliard School of Music in N.Y. (1947–50). From 1949 to 1958 he was music director of the Dallas Sym. Orch., and also of the Chautauqua (N.Y.) Sym. Orch. (1953–72). He was assoc. conductor of the Chicago Sym. Orch. (1958–64) and music director of its Ravinia Festival (1959–63). From 1964 to 1972 he was director of the Eastman School of Music in Rochester, N.Y. He was music director of the Erie (Pa.) Phil. from 1976 to 1990.

Hendricks, Barbara, greatly admired black American soprano; b. Stephens, Ark., Nov. 20, 1948. She sang in church and school choirs before majoring in chemistry and mathematics at the Univ. of Nebraska (graduated, 1969); during the summer of 1968 she began vocal training with Tourel at the Aspen (Colo.) Music School, continuing under her guidance at the Juilliard School in N.Y. (1969–71); she also attended Callas's master class there. In 1971 she won the Geneva International Competition, and in 1972 both the International Concours de Paris and the Kosciuszko Foundation Vocal Competition. On Feb. 20, 1973, she made her debut in Thomson's *4 Saints in 3 Acts* in the Mini-Metropolitan Opera production presented at the Lincoln Center Forum Theatre in N.Y.; later that year, she made her first concert tour of Europe. In 1974 she appeared as Erisbe in Cavalli's *Ormindo* at the San Francisco Spring Opera, and in the title role of Cavalli's *La Calisto* at the Glyndebourne Festival. On Feb. 26, 1975, she made her formal N.Y. debut as Inez in a concert performance of *La Favorite* at Carnegie Hall. In 1976 she sang Amor in Gluck's *Orfeo ed Euridice* with the Netherlands Opera at the Holland Festival, and on Nov. 14 of that year made her N.Y. recital debut at Town Hall. At the Berlin Deutsche Oper in 1978 she appeared as Mozart's Susanna, a role she quickly made her own. In 1980 she sang Gilda and in 1981 Pamina at the Orange Festival in France; in 1982 she appeared as Gounod's Juliet at both the Paris Opéra and London's Covent Garden. On Oct. 30, 1986, she made her Metropolitan Opera debut in N.Y. as Strauss's Sophie. In 1988 she sang at the 70th-birthday celebration for Leonard Bernstein at the Tanglewood Festival, and also starred as Mimi in Luigi Comencini's film version of *La Bohème*. In 1989 she appeared at the Bolshoi Theater in Moscow. In addition to her operatic career, she has won notable distinction as a recitalist. Her interpretations of the German and French lieder repertoire, as well as of Negro spirituals, have won accolades. In 1986 she was made a Commandeur des Arts et des Lettres of France. Her unswerving commitment to social justice led the High Commissioner for Refugees at the United Nations to name her a goodwill ambassador of the world body in 1987.

BIBL.: L. Marum, "B. H.: A Singular Soprano," *Ovation* (April 1989).

Hengeveld, Gerard, Dutch pianist and composer; b. Kampen, Dec. 7, 1910. He studied piano with Carl Friedberg. He appeared as a soloist with European orchs. and in recitals; also was on the piano faculty at the Royal Cons. of Music at The Hague. He composed a Violin Sonata (1944); Concertino for Piano and Orch. (1946); Piano Concerto (1947); Cello Sonata (1965); *Musica concertante* for Oboe and Chamber Orch. (1968); numerous teaching pieces for piano.

Henkemans, Hans, Dutch pianist, composer, physician, and psychiatrist; b. The Hague, Dec. 23, 1913; d. Dec. 29, 1995. He studied piano and composition with Sigtenhorst-Meyer (1926–31), and then composition with Pijper (1933–38); he also took courses in medicine at the Univ. of Utrecht (from 1931) and later took his doctorate at the Univ. of Amsterdam (1981). After making his debut as a pianist in his own Piano Concerto at 19, he pursued a successful concert career until 1969 when he decided to practice medicine and psychiatry. In his compositions, he succeeded in developing an original voice while utilizing traditional forms.

WORKS: OPERA: *Winter Cruise* (1977). **ORCH.:** 3 piano concertos (1932, 1936, 1992); Sym. (1934); *Voorspel* (1935–36); *Passacaglia and Gigue* for Piano and Orch. (1941–42); Flute Concerto (1945–46); Violin Concerto (1948–50); Viola Concerto (1954); Harp Concerto (1955); *Partita* (1960); *Barcarola fantastica* (1962); *Dona montana* (1964); *Elégies* for 4 Flutes and Orch. (1967); Horn Concerto (1981); *Villanelle* for Horn and Orch., after Dukas (1984); *Riflessioni* for Strings (1985–86); Cello Concerto (1988). **CHAMBER:** 2 wind quintets (1934, 1962); 3 string quartets; Cello Sonata (1936); *Primavera* for 12 Instruments (1944; rev. 1959); Violin Sonata (1944); *Epilogue* for Flute and Piano (1947); *4 Pieces* for Harp and Flute (1963); *Aere festivo* for 3 Trumpets and 2 Trombones (1965). **PIANO:** 2 études (1937); Sonata for 2 Pianos (1943); Sonata (1958). **VOCAL:** *Driehonderd waren wij* for Chorus and Orch. (1933; rev. 1941); *Ballade* for Contralto and Chamber Orch. (1936); *Bericht aan de levenden* for Chorus, Reciter, and Orch. (1964); *Villonnerie* for Baritone and Orch. (1965); *Tre aspetti d'amore* for Chorus and Orch. (1967–68); *Canzoni amorose del duecento* for Soprano, Baritone, and Orch. (1972–73).

Henneberg, (Carl) Albert (Theodor), Swedish composer;b. Stockholm, March 27, 1901; d. Sollentuna, April 14, 1991. His father was the German conductor and composer Richard Henneberg (b. Berlin, Aug. 5, 1853; d. Malmö, Oct. 19, 1925). He studied composition with Ellberg at the Stockholm Cons. (1920–24) and later in Vienna and Paris (1926–30). Returning to Stockholm in 1931, he became active as a conductor; later he served as secretary (1945–49) and treasurer (1947–63) of the Soc. of Swedish Composers. His compositions were conceived in a late Romantic style.

WORKS: OPERAS: *Inka* (1935–36); *Det jäser i Småland* (1937–38); *Den lyckliga staden* (1940–41); *Bolla och Badin* (1942–44); *I madonnans skugga* (1946). **ORCH.:** 6 syms.: No. 1, *På ledungsfärd* (1925), No. 2 for Baritone and Orch. (1927), No. 3, *Vårvindar* (1927), No. 4, *Pathétique* (1930–31), No. 5 (1935), and No. 6, *Vinterskärgård* (1953–54); Piano Concerto (1925); Chamber Sym. (1927); *Valborgsmässonatt*, symphonic poem (1928); *Serenade* for Strings (1931; also for String Quartet); *Sommar*, suite (1932); *Det ljusa landet* for Soloists, Chorus, and Orch. (1933); Trumpet Concerto (1934); Trombone Concerto (1935); *I brytningstider*, symphonic suite (1943); *Gustavianska kapriser* (1943); Concertino for Flute and Strings (1944); Cello Concerto (1948); Concertino for Bassoon and Strings (1956); Concertino for Clarinet, Strings, Piano, and Percussion (1960). **CHAMBER:** 2 string quartets (1931); *Little Quartet* for Flute, Oboe, Bassoon, and Horn; Violin Sonata.

Henning, Ervin Arthur, American composer; b. Marion, S.Dak., Nov. 22, 1910; d. Boston, July 27, 1982. He studied music in Chicago with **Roslyn Brogue**, whom he subsequently married. In 1944 he entered the New England Cons. of Music in Boston, graduating in 1946. He wrote mostly for chamber music combinations; in his later works, he adopted the 12-tone method of composition.

WORKS: Quintet for Flute, Horn, Violin, Viola, and Cello (1946); Partita for String Quartet (1948); Suite for Viola Concertante, 2 Violins, and Cello (1950); *Divertimento* for Bassoon (1950); Trio for Clarinet, Viola, and Piano (1959); Piano Sonata (1959); pieces for recorders; arrangements of Bach for various woodwind ensembles.

Henriot-Schweitzer, Nicole, French pianist; b. Paris, Nov. 25, 1925. She was a student at the Paris Cons. of Marguerite Long, taking the premier prix when she was 14. Following the close of World War II, she began to tour extensively; in 1948 she made her first visit to the U.S. In later years, she was active as a teacher and served as a prof. at the Liège Cons. (1970–73). Her interpretations of the French repertory were highly regarded.

Henriques, Fini (Valdemar), Danish violinist, conductor, and composer; b. Copenhagen, Dec. 20, 1867; d. there, Oct. 27, 1940. He studied violin with Valdemar Tofte in Copenhagen, and with Joachim at the Hochschule für Musik in Berlin; studied composition with Svendsen. Returning to Copenhagen, he was a violinist in the Court Orch. (1892–96); also appeared as a soloist. He organized his own string quartet, and traveled with it in Europe; also conducted orchs. As a composer, he followed the Romantic school; he possessed a facile gift of melody; his *Danish Lullaby* became a celebrated song in Denmark. He also wrote an opera, *Staerstikkeren* (Copenhagen, May 20, 1922); several ballets (*The Little Mermaid*, after Hans Andersen; *Tata*; etc.); *Hans Andersen Overture*; 2 syms.; String Quartet; Quartet for Flute, Violin, Cello, and Piano; Violin Sonata; piano pieces.

BIBL.: S. Berg, *F. V. H.* (Copenhagen, 1943).

Henry, Leigh Vaughan, English conductor, writer on music, and composer; b. Liverpool, Sept. 23, 1889; d. London, March 8, 1958. He received his earliest training from his father, John Henry, a singer and composer; then studied with Bantock in London, Viñes in France, and Buonamici in Italy. He taught music at Gordon Craig's Theatrical School in Florence (1912); then was in Germany, where he was interned during World War I. Returning to England, he ed. a modern-music journal, *Fanfare* (1921–22); also was active in various organizations promoting modern music. He was music director of the Shakespeare Festival Week in London in 1938, 1945, and 1946; organized and conducted orch. concerts of British music, and the National Welsh Festival Concerts; also conducted at the BBC. Among his compositions were *The Moon Robber*, opera; *Llyn-y-Fan*, symphonic poem; various pieces on Welsh themes.

WRITINGS: *Music: What It Means and How to Understand It* (1920); *The Growth of Music in Form and Significance* (1921); *The Story of Music* (1935); *Dr. John Bull* (largely fictional; London, 1937); with R. Hale, *My Surging World*, autobiography (1937).

Henry, Pierre, influential French composer and acoustician; b. Paris, Dec. 9, 1927. He studied with Messiaen (composition) and Boulanger (piano) at the Paris Cons. (1938–48). In 1950 he was a founder of the Groupe de Recherche de Musique Concrète with Pierre Schaeffer, but in 1958 separated from the group to experiment on his own projects in the field of electroacoustical music and electronic synthesis of musical sounds. In virtually all of his independent works, he applied electronic effects, often with the insertion of prerecorded patches of concrete music and sometimes "objets trouvés" borrowed partially or in their entirety from pre-existent compositions. In collaboration with Schaeffer, he wrote *Symphonie pour un homme seul* (1950) and the experimental opera *Orphée 53* (1953); independently, he wrote *Microphone bien tempéré* (1952); *Musique sans* *titre* (1951); *Concerto des ambiguités* (1951); *Astrologie* (1953); *Spatiodynamisme* (1955); 4 ballets: *Haut voltage* (1956), *Coexistence* (1959), *Investigations* (1959), and *Le Voyage* (1962); *Messe de Liverpool* (1967); *Ceremony* (1970); *2e Symphonie pour 16 groupes de haut-parleur* (1972); *Futuristie 1*, "electro-acoustical musical spectacle," with the reconstruction of the "bruiteurs" introduced by the Italian futurist Luigi Russolo in 1909 (Paris, Oct. 16, 1975); *Parcours-Cosmogonie* (1976); *La 10e symphonie* (1979); *Les noces chymiques* (1980); *Le paradis perdu* (1982); film music.

BIBL.: M. Chion, *P. H.* (Paris, 1980).

Henschel, Sir (Isidor) George (actually, **Georg**), esteemed German-born English baritone, pianist, conductor, teacher, and composer; b. Breslau, Feb. 18, 1850; d. Aviemore, Scotland, Sept. 10, 1934. His parents were of Polish-Jewish descent but he converted to Christianity when young. He was a student of Julius Shäffer in Breslau, of Moscheles (piano), Götze (voice), Papperitz (organ), and Reinecke (theory) at the Leipzig Cons. (1867–70), and of Kiel (composition) and Adolf Schulze (voice) at the Berlin Cons. He gave concerts as a tenor before making his debut as a pianist in Berlin in 1862. In 1866 he first appeared as a bass in Hirschberg, and then as a baritone as Hans Sachs in a concert performance in Leipzig in 1868. He subsequently sang throughout Europe. In 1881 he was selected as the first conductor of the Boston Sym. Orch., which post he held until 1884; he also appeared as a concert singer in Boston and N.Y. He then settled in England, where he was founder-conductor of the London Sym. Concerts (1886–97). He taught voice at the Royal College of Music in London (1886–88) and was conductor of the Scottish Orch. in Glasgow (1891–95); later he taught voice at the Inst. of Musical Art in N.Y. (1905–08). In 1928, at the age of 78, he sang Schubert lieder in London in commemoration of the 100th anniversary of the composer's death. In 1931 he was invited to conduct the 50th anniversary concert of the Boston Sym. Orch. In 1881 he married the American soprano, Lillian June (née Bailey) Henschel (b. Columbus, Ohio, Jan. 17, 1860; d. London, Nov. 4, 1901). In 1890 he became a naturalized British subject and in 1914 he was knighted. He publ. *Personal Recollections of Johannes Brahms* (1907), *Musings and Memories of a Musician* (1918), and *Articulation in Singing* (1926). His compositions were in the German Romantic tradition. They included the opera *Nubia* (Dresden, Dec. 9, 1899); *Stabat Mater* (Birmingham, Oct. 4, 1894); *Requiem* (Boston, Dec. 2, 1902); Mass (London, June 1, 1916); String Quartet; about 200 songs.

Hensel, Heinrich, German tenor; b. Neustadt, Oct. 29, 1874; d. Hamburg, Feb. 23, 1935. He studied with Gustav Walter in Vienna and with Eduard Bellwidt in Frankfurt am Main. He sang in Freiburg im Breisgau (1897–1900), Frankfurt am Main (1900–1906), and then at Wiesbaden (1906–11), where Siegfried Wagner heard him and engaged him to create the chief tenor part in his opera *Banadietrich* (Karlsruhe, 1910) and also to sing Parsifal at the Bayreuth Festival. He obtained excellent success; subsequently sang at Covent Garden, London (1911–14). He made his American debut at the Metropolitan Opera in N.Y. as Lohengrin (Dec. 22, 1911) and was hailed by the press as one of the finest Wagnerian tenors; he also appeared with the Chicago Opera (1911–12); he then was a leading Heldentenor at the Hamburg Opera (1912–29). He was married to the soprano Elsa Hensel-Schweitzer (1878–1937), who sang in Dessau (1898–1901) and then in Frankfurt am Main (from 1901).

Hensel, Walther (real name, **Julius Janiczek**), Bohemian-born music educator; b. Moravska Trebova, Sept. 8, 1887; d. Munich, Sept. 5, 1956. He studied in Vienna, Prague, and Freibourg, where he obtained his Ph.D. (1911). He taught languages in Prague (1912–18). He traveled in Europe (1918–25) as an organizer of folk-song activities, with the aim of raising the standards of choral music for the young. From 1925 to 1929 he was head of the Jugendmusik School at the Dortmund Cons. In 1930 he went to Stuttgart, where he organized an educational program for the promotion of folk music. In 1938 he returned to Prague; taught at the German Univ. there. After 1945 he went to Munich. He ed. a number of folk-song collections; publ. *Lied und Volk, Eine Streitschrift wider das falsche deutsche Lied* (1921); *Im Zeichen des Volksliedes* (1922; 2nd ed., 1936); *Musikalische Grundlehre* (1937); *Auf den Spuren des Volksliedes* (1944).

Henze, Hans Werner, outstanding German composer; b. Gütersloh, Westphalia, July 1, 1926. His early studies at the Braunschweig School of Music (1942–44) were interrupted by military service during World War II, and for a year he was in the German army on the Russian front. In 1946 he took music courses at the Kirchenmusikalisches Inst. in Heidelberg; he also studied privately with Fortner (1946–48). He became fascinated with the disciplinary aspects of Schoenberg's method of composition with 12 tones, and attended the seminars on the subject given by Leibowitz at Darmstadt. A musician of restless temperament, he joined a radical political group and proclaimed the necessity of writing music without stylistic restrictions in order to serve the masses. In 1953 he moved to Italy, and later joined the Italian Communist Party. From 1961 to 1967 he taught composition at the Salzburg Mozarteum, in 1969–70 in Havana, and in 1980 at the Cologne Hochschule für Musik. He successfully integrated musical idioms and mannerisms of seemingly incompatible techniques; in his vocal works, he freely adopted such humanoid effects as screaming, bellowing, and snorting; he even specified that long sustained tones were to be sung by inhaling as well as exhaling. Nonetheless, Henze managed to compose music that was feasible for human performance. But political considerations continued to play a decisive role in his career. In 1967 he withdrew from the membership of the Academy of the Arts of West Berlin, in a gesture of protest against its artistic policies. His political stance did not preclude his acceptance in "bourgeois" musical centers, for his works were performed widely in Europe. He held the International Chair of Composition Studies at the Royal Academy of Music in London from 1986. In 1989 he helped found the Munich Biennale. In 1990 he served as the first composer-in-residence of the Berlin Phil.

WORKS: DRAMATIC: *Das Wundertheater*, opera for Actors, after Cervantes (1948; Heidelberg, May 7, 1949; rev. for Singers, 1964; Frankfurt am Main, Nov. 30, 1965); *Ballet Variations* (concert premiere, Düsseldorf, Oct. 3, 1949; stage premiere, Wuppertal, Dec. 21, 1958); *Jack Pudding*, ballet (1949; Wiesbaden, Jan. 1, 1951); *Rosa Silber*, ballet (1950; concert premiere, Berlin, May 8, 1951; stage premiere, Cologne, Oct. 15, 1958); *Labyrinth*, choreographic fantasy (1951; concert premiere, Darmstadt, May 29, 1952); *Die schlafende Prinzessin*, ballet, after Tchaikovsky (1951; Essen, June 5, 1954); *Ein Landarzt*, radio opera, after Kafka (Hamburg, Nov. 19, 1951; broadcast, Nov. 29, 1951; rev. as a monodrama for Baritone and Orch., 1964; Berlin, Oct. 12, 1965; Fischer-Dieskau soloist; radio opera rev. for the stage, 1964; Frankfurt am Main, Nov. 30, 1965); *Boulevard Solitude*, opera (1951; Hannover, Feb. 17, 1952); *Der Idiot*, ballet pantomime, after Dostoyevsky (Berlin, Sept. 1, 1952); *Pas d'action*, ballet (Munich, 1952; withdrawn by the composer and rev. as *Tancredi*, 1964; Vienna, May 14, 1966); *König Hirsch*, opera (1952–55; Berlin, Sept. 23, 1956; rev. as *Il Re cervo*, 1962; Kassel, March 10, 1963); *Das Ende einer Welt*, radio opera (Hamburg, Dec. 4, 1953; rev. for the stage, 1964; Frankfurt am Main, Nov. 30, 1965); *Maratona*, ballet (1956; Berlin, Sept. 24, 1957); *Ondine*, ballet (1956–57; London, Oct. 27, 1958); *Der Prinz von Homburg*, opera (1958; Hamburg, May 22, 1960); *L'Usignolo dell'Imperatore*, pantomime, after Andersen (Venice, Sept. 16, 1959); *Elegy for Young Lovers*, chamber opera (1959–61; in German, Schwetzingen, May 20, 1961; 1st perf. to Auden's original Eng. libretto, Glyndebourne, July 13, 1961); *Der junge Lord*, comic opera (1964; Berlin, April 7, 1965); *The Bassarids*, opera seria (1965; in German, Salzburg, Aug. 6, 1966; 1st perf. to the original Eng. libretto by Auden and Kallman, Santa Fe, N. Mex., Aug. 7, 1968); *Moralities*, scenic cantatas, after Aesop, to texts by Auden (1967; Cincinnati, May 18, 1968); *Der langwierige Weg in die Wohnung der Natascha Ungeheuer*, show (RAI, Rome, May 17, 1971); *La cubana, oder Ein Leben für die Kunst*, vaudeville (1973; NET Opera Theater, N.Y., March 4, 1974; stage premiere, Munich, May 28, 1975); *We Come to the River*, actions for music (1974–76; London, July 12, 1976); *Don Chisciotte*, opera, arrangement of Paisiello (Montepulciano, Aug. 1, 1976); *Orpheus*, ballet (1978; Stuttgart, March 17, 1979); *Pollicino*, fairy-tale opera (1979–80; Montepulciano, Aug. 2, 1980); *The English Cat*, chamber opera (1980–83; Schwetzingen, June 2, 1983); *Il ritorno d'Ulisse in patria*, realization of Monteverdi's opera (1981; Salzburg, Aug. 18, 1985); *Ödipus der Tyrann oder Der Vater vertreibt seinem Sohn und Schickt die Tochter in die Küche* (Kindberg, Oct. 30, 1983); *Das verratene Meer*, opera (1989; Berlin, May 5, 1990).

ORCH.: Chamber Concerto for Piano, Flute, and Strings (Darmstadt, Sept. 27, 1946); Concertino for Piano and Winds, with Percussion (Baden-Baden, Oct. 5, 1947, Egk conducting); 8 syms.: No. 1 (Bad Pyrmont, Aug. 25, 1948, Fortner conducting; rev. version, Berlin, April 9, 1964, composer conducting), No. 2 (Stuttgart, Dec. 1, 1949), No. 3 (Donaueschingen, Oct. 7, 1951), No. 4 (1955; Berlin, Oct. 9, 1963, composer conducting), No. 5 (1962; N.Y., May 16, 1963, Bernstein conducting), No. 6 (Havana, Nov. 24, 1969), No. 7 (1983–84; Berlin, Dec. 1, 1984), and No. 8 (Boston, Oct. 1, 1993); Violin Concerto (Baden-Baden, Dec. 12, 1948); Symphonic Variations (1950); 2 piano concertos: No. 1 (1950; Düsseldorf, Sept. 14, 1952, composer conducting) and No. 2 (1967; Bielefeld, Sept. 29, 1968); *Ode to the West Wind* for Cello and Orch. (Bielefeld, April 30, 1954); *4 poemi* (Frankfurt am Main, May 31, 1955, Stokowski conducting); *3 Symphonic Studies* (1955–64; 1st version as *Symphonic Studies*, Hamburg, Feb. 14, 1956); *In Memoriam: Die weisse Rose* for Chamber Orch. (1956); Sonata for Strings (Zürich, March 21, 1958, Sacher conducting); *3 Dithyrambs* for Chamber Orch. (Cologne, Nov. 27, 1958); *Jeux des Tritons*, divertimento from the ballet *Ondine*, for Piano and Orch. (Zürich, March 28, 1960); *Antifone* (1960; Berlin, Jan. 20, 1962, Karajan conducting); *Los Caprichos*, fantasia (1963; Duisburg, April 6, 1967); *Doppio Concerto* for Oboe, Harp, and Strings (Zürich, Dec. 2, 1966, Sacher conducting); *Telemanniana* (Berlin, April 4, 1967); *Fantasia* for Strings, from the film *Junge Torless* (Berlin, April 1, 1967); Double Bass Concerto (Chicago, Nov. 2, 1967); *Compases para Preguntas Ensimismadas* (Basel, Feb. 11, 1971, Sacher conducting); *Heliogabalus Imperator*, "allegoria per musica" (Chicago, Nov. 16, 1972, Solti conducting); *Tristan* for Piano, Tape, and Mixed Orch. (1973; London, Oct. 20, 1974, C. Davis conducting); *Ragtimes and Habaneras* for Brass Instruments (London, Sept. 13, 1975); Concert Suite from the film *Katharina Blum* (Brighton, May 6, 1976, composer conducting); *Aria de la folia española* for Chamber Orch. (St. Paul, Sept. 17, 1977); *Il Vitalino raddoppiato* for Violin Concertante and Chamber Orch. (Salzburg, Aug. 2, 1978); *Barcarola* (1979; Zürich, April 22, 1980); *Apollo trionfante*, suite from *Orpheus* (1979; Gelsenkirchen, Sept. 1, 1980); dramatic scenes from *Orpheus* (1979; Zürich, Jan. 6, 1981, composer conducting); *I sentimenti di Carl Philip Emmanuel Bach*, transcriptions for Flute, Harp, and Strings (Rome, April 14, 1982); *Le Miracle de la rose* for Clarinet and 13 Players (1981; London, May 26, 1982); *Cinque piccoli concerti* (1980–82; Cabrillo Music Festival, Aug. 26, 1983); *Sieben Liebeslieder* for Cello and Orch. (1984–85; Cologne, Dec. 12, 1986); *Fandango* (1985; Paris, Feb. 5, 1986); *12 kleine Elegien* for Renaissance Instruments (Cologne, Dec. 13, 1986); *Allegro brillante* (Dallas, Sept. 14, 1989); *Requiem (9 Spiritual Concertos)* for Piano, Trumpet, and Large Chamber Orch. (1990–92).

CHAMBER: Violin Sonata (1946); Flute Sonatina (1947); 5 string quartets: No. 1 (1947), No. 2 (Baden-Baden, Dec. 16, 1952), No. 3 (Berlin, Sept. 12, 1976), No. 4 (1976; Schwetzingen, May 25, 1977), and No. 5 (1976; Schwetzingen, May 25, 1977); Serenade for Cello (1949); Variations for Piano (1949); Chamber Sonata for Piano, Violin, and Cello (1948; Cologne, March 16, 1950; rev. 1963); *Apollo et Hyazinthus* for Harpsichord, Alto, and 8 Instruments (Frankfurt am Main, June 26, 1949); Wind Quintet (1952; Bremen, Feb. 15, 1953); *Concerto per il Marigny* for Piano and 7 Instruments (Paris, March 9, 1956); Piano Sonata (1959); *Chamber Music 1958* for Tenor, Guitar, and 8 Instruments (Hamburg, Nov. 26, 1958); *Lucy Escott Variations* for Piano (1963; Berlin, March 21, 1965); *Divertimento* for 2 Pianos (N.Y., Nov. 30, 1964); *Royal Winter Music*, 2 sonatas on Shakespearean characters, for Guitar (1975–79); *Amicizia* for Clarinet, Cello, and Percussion Instruments (Montepulciano, Aug. 6, 1976); Sonata for Solo Violin (Montepulciano, Aug. 10, 1977); *L'autunno* for Wind Instruments (London, Feb. 28, 1979); Viola Sonata (Witten, April 20, 1980); *Canzona* for 7 Instruments (1982); Sonata for Wind Ensemble (Berlin, Sept. 17, 1983); Sonata for 6 Players (London, Sept. 26, 1984); *Selbst- und Zwiegespräche*, trio for Viola, Guitar, and Small Organ (1984–85); *Serenade* for Violin (1986); *5 Night Pieces* for Violin and Piano (1990); Piano Quintet (Los Angeles, March 23, 1993).

VOCAL: 5 madrigals for Chorus and 2 Solo Instruments, after Villon (1947; Frankfurt am Main, April 25, 1950); *Chorus of the Captured Trojans*, from *Faust*, Part 2, for Chorus and Orch. (1948; Bielefeld, Feb. 6, 1949; rev. 1964); *Whispers from Heavenly Death*, cantata for High Voice and 8 Solo Instruments, after Whitman (1948); *Der Vorwurf*, concert aria for Baritone, Trumpet, and Strings, after Werfel (Darmstadt, July 29, 1948); 5 Neapolitan songs for Baritone and Orch. (Frankfurt am Main, May 26, 1956; Fischer-Dieskau soloist); *Nocturnes and Arias* for Soprano and Orch. (Donaueschingen, Oct. 20, 1957); *Novae de Infinito Laudes*, cantata, after Giordano Bruno (1962; Venice, April 24, 1963); *Ariosi* for Soprano, Violin, and Orch., after Tasso (1963; Edinburgh Festival, Aug. 23, 1964); *Being Beauteous*, cantata for Soprano, Harp, and 4 Cellos, after Rimbaud (1963; Berlin, April 12, 1964); *Cantata della Fiaba Estrema* for Soprano, Small Chorus, and 13 Instruments (1963; Zürich, Feb. 26, 1965); *Choral Fantasy* for Small Chorus, 5 Instruments, and Percussion (1964; Berlin, Jan. 23, 1967); *Muses of Sicily* for Chorus, 2 Pianos, Winds, and Timpani (Berlin, Sept. 20, 1966); *Versuch über Schweine* for Baritone and Chamber Orch. (London, Feb. 14, 1969; the title is an ironic reference to certain revolting students, active during the 1960s); *Das Floss der Medusa*, oratorio to the memory of Ché Guevara (1968; concert premiere, Vienna, Jan. 29, 1971; stage premiere, Nuremberg, April 15, 1972); *El Cimarron* for Baritone, Flute, Guitar, and Percussion, after *The Autobiography of a Runaway Slave* by Esteban Montejo (Aldeburgh Festival, June 22, 1970); *Voices* for Mezzo-soprano, Tenor, and Instrumental Group, to 22 revolutionary texts (London, Jan. 4, 1974, composer conducting); *Jephtha*, realization of Carissimi's oratorio (London, July 14, 1976, composer conducting); *The King of Harlem* for Mezzo-soprano and Instrumental Ensemble, after García Lorca (Witten, April 20, 1980); *3 Auden Pieces* for Voice and Piano (Aldeburgh, June 15, 1983).

WRITINGS: *Musik und Politik: Schriften und Gespräche, 1955–1975* (Munich, 1976; in Eng. as *Music and Politics: Collected Writings, 1953–81*, London and Ithaca, N.Y., 1982).

BIBL.: K. Geitel, *H.W. H.* (Berlin, 1968); H.H. Stuckenschmidt, "H.W. H. und die Musik unserer Zeit," *Universitas*, XXVII/2 (1972); E. Restagno, ed., *H.* (Turin, 1986); D. Rexroth, ed., *Der Komponist H.W. H.: Ein Buch der Alten Oper Frankfurt, Frankfurt Feste '86* (Mainz and N.Y., 1986); P. Petersen, *H.W. H., ein politischer Musiker: Zwölf Vorlesungen* (Hamburg, 1988); W. Schottler, *"Die Bassariden" von H.W. H.: Der Weg eines Mythos von der antiken Tragödie zur modernen Oper: Eine Analyse von Stoff, Libretto und Musik* (Trier, 1992).

Heppener, Robert, Dutch composer and teacher; b. Amsterdam, Aug. 9, 1925. He studied piano with Jan Öde and Johan van den Boogert at the Amsterdam Cons., and composition with Bertus van Lier; he then taught at the Cons. of the Music Lyceum Soc. in Amsterdam.

WORKS: ORCH.: Sym. (1957); *Derivazioni* for Strings (1958; rev. 1980); Sinfonietta (1961); *Cavalcade* (1963); *Eglogues* (1963); *Scherzi* for Strings (1965); *Air et sonneries* (1969); *Hymns and Conversations* for 28 Harps (1969); *Music for Streets and Squares* (1970); *Sweelinck Fanfare* (1978) Viola Concerto (1979); *Boog* (1988). **CHAMBER:** Septet (1958); *Arcadian Sonatina* for 2 Recorders and Violin (1959); *A fond de fleurettes* for String Quartet (1961); Quartet for Alto Flute, Violin, Viola, and Cello (1967); *Canzona* for Saxophone Quartet (1969); *Trail* for 11 Instruments (1993). **PIANO:** *Nocturne* (1953); *Pas de quatre-mains* for Piano, 4-hands (1975); *Spinsel* (1986). **VOCAL:** *Cantico delle creture di S. Francesco d'Assisi* for Soprano, Harp, and Strings (1952; rev. 1954); *The 3rd Country* for Chorus and Chamber Orch. (1962); *Carnival Songs* for Chorus (1966); *Fanfare trionfale* for Chorus, Winds, Timpani, and Piano (1967); *Del iubilo del core che esce in voce* for Chorus (1974); *Nachklänge* for Chamber Chorus (1977); *Memento* for Soprano and 8 Instruments (1984).

Heppner, Ben, Canadian tenor; b. Murrayville, British Columbia, Jan. 14, 1956. He received training at the Univs. of British Columbia and Toronto. In 1979 he took 1st prize in the CBC Talent Festival. In 1987 he sang Strauss's Bacchus at the Victoria State Opera in Sydney. He made his European operatic debut as Lohengrin at the Royal Opera in Stockholm in 1988; that same year, he also won the Metropolitan Opera Auditions and the Birgit Nilsson Prize, which led to his U.S. debut at a state concert for the King and Queen of Sweden at N.Y.'s Carnegie Hall. In 1989 he appeared as Lohengrin at the San Francisco Opera. He sang Bacchus at the Vienna State Opera in 1990. He made his Metropolitan Opera debut in N.Y. as Idomeneo in 1991, and in 1992 he sang Dvořák's Dimitrij in Munich and Mozart's Titus in Salzburg. In 1994 he appeared as Lohengrin in Seattle. In addition to his activities on the operatic stage, Heppner has also been extensively engaged as a soloist with orchs. and as a concert artist.

Herbage, Julian (Livingston), English musicologist; b. Woking, Sept. 4, 1904; d. London, Jan. 15, 1976. He studied harmony and counterpoint with Charles Wood at St. John's College, Cambridge. In 1927 he became a member of the music staff of the BBC; from 1940 to 1946 he was assistant director of music there. With his wife, Anna Instone, he ed. the BBC "Music Magazine" radio program from 1944 to 1973. He also made appearances as a conductor of music by Baroque composers. He wrote the book *Handel's Messiah* (London, 1948).

Herberigs, Robert, Belgian composer and novelist; b. Ghent, June 19, 1886; d. Oudenaarde, Sept. 20, 1974. He studied voice at the Ghent Cons. In 1908 he made his operatic debut as a baritone at the Flemish Opera in Antwerp, but then abandoned his operatic aspirations to study composition. In 1909 he won the Belgian Grand Prix with his cantata *La Legénde de St. Hubert*, and subsequently composed prolifically. He also publ. several novels. His compositions followed along Romantic lines.

WORKS: DRAMATIC: *Le Mariage de Rosine*, comic opera (1919; Ghent, Feb. 13, 1925); *L'Amour médecin*, comic opera (1920); *Lam Godsspel* or *Jeu de l'Agneau Mystique*, open-air play (1948); *Antoine et Cleopatra*, radio play (1949); *Le Château des comtes de Gand*, light and sound play (1960). **ORCH.:** 2 piano concertos (1932, 1952); *Sinfonia breve* (1947); Organ Concerto (1957); numerous symphonic poems and suites, including *Cyrano de Bergerac* (1912), *Le Chant d'Hiawatha* (1921), *Vlaanderen, O Welig Huis* (1949), *Rapsodia alla Zingara* (1952), *La Petite Sirène* (1955), *4 saisons* (1956), *4 odes a Botticelli* (1958), *Hamlet* (1962), *Roméo et Juliette* (1963), and *Reinaut et Armida* (1967). **CHAMBER:** String Quartet (1921); *Poème* for Piano Trio (1923); Violin Sonata (1932); *Concert champêtre* for Wind Quintet (1938); Piano Quartet (1939); *Suite Miniature* and Sonatine for Flute and String Trio (both 1954). **PIANO:** 21 sonatas and sonatinas (1941–45); other pieces. **VOCAL:** *La Legénde de St. Hubert* (1909) and other cantatas; *Te Deum laudamus* (1912); masses; song cycles and solo songs.

Herbert, Victor (August), famous Irish-born American composer, cellist, and conductor; b. Dublin, Feb. 1, 1859; d. N.Y., May 26, 1924. He was a grandson of Samuel Lover, the Irish novelist; his father died when he was an infant; his mother married a German physician and the family moved to Stuttgart in 1867. He entered the Stuttgart high school, but did not graduate; his musical ability was definitely pronounced by then, and he selected the cello as his instrument, taking lessons from Bernhard Cossmann in Baden-Baden (1874–76). He soon acquired a degree of technical proficiency that enabled him to take a position as cellist in various orchs. in Germany, France, Italy, and Switzerland; in 1880 he became a cellist of the Eduard Strauss waltz band in Vienna; in 1881, he returned to Stuttgart, where he joined the Court Orch., and studied composition with Max Seifritz at the Cons. His earliest works were for cello with orch.; he performed his Suite with the Stuttgart orch. on Oct. 23, 1883, and his 1st Cello Concerto on Dec. 8, 1885. On Aug. 14, 1886, he married the Viennese opera singer Therese Förster (1861–1927); in the same year, she received an offer to join the Metropolitan Opera in N.Y., and Herbert was engaged as an orch. cellist there, appearing in N.Y. also as a soloist (played his own Cello Concerto with the N.Y. Phil., Dec. 10, 1887). In his early years in N.Y., Herbert was overshadowed by the celebrity of his wife, but soon he developed energetic activities on his own, forming an entertainment orch. which he conducted in a repertoire of light music; he also participated in chamber music concerts; was a soloist with the Theodore Thomas and Seidl orchs. He was the conductor of the Boston Festival Orch. in 1891; Tchaikovsky conducted this orch. in Philadelphia in a miscellaneous program, and Herbert played a solo. He was assoc. conductor of the Worcester Festival (1889–91), for which he wrote a dramatic cantata, *The Captive* (Sept. 24, 1891). In 1893 he became bandmaster of the 22nd Regiment Band, succeeding P.S. Gilmore. On March 10, 1894, he was soloist with the N.Y. Phil. in his 2nd Cello Concerto. In the same year, at the suggestion of William MacDonald, the manager of the Boston Ideal Opera Co., Herbert wrote his first operetta, *Prince Ananias*, which was premiered with encouraging success in N.Y. (Nov. 20, 1894). He quickly established himself as a leading composer in the genre, winning enduring success with such scores as *The Serenade* (1897), *Babes in Toyland* (1903), *Mlle. Modiste* (1905), *Naughty Marietta* (1910), *Sweethearts* (1913), and *The Only Girl* (1914). In 1900 he directed at Madison Square Garden, N.Y., an orch. of 420 performers for the benefit of the sufferers in the Galveston flood. On April 29, 1906, he led a similar monster concert at the Hippodrome for the victims of the San Francisco earthquake. In 1904 he organized the Victor Herbert Orch. in N.Y. In 1908 he was elected to the National Inst. of Arts and Letters.

In his finest operettas, Herbert united spontaneous melody, sparkling rhythm, and simple but tasteful harmony; his experience as a symphonic composer and conductor imparted a solidity of texture to his writing that placed him far above the many gifted amateurs in this field. Furthermore, his music possessed a natural communicative power, which made his operettas spectacularly successful with the public. In the domain of grand opera, he was not so fortunate. When the premiere of his first grand opera, *Natoma*, took place in Philadelphia on Feb. 25, 1911, it aroused great expectations; but the opera failed to sustain lasting interest. Still less effective was his second opera, *Madeleine*, staged by the Metropolitan Opera in N.Y. on Jan. 24, 1914. Herbert was one of the founders of ASCAP in 1914, and was vice-president from that date until his death. In 1916 he wrote a special score for the film *The Fall of a Nation*, in synchronization with the screenplay. He also wrote a film score for *Indian Summer* (1919).

WORKS: DRAMATIC: OPERETTAS: *Prince Ananias* (N.Y., Nov. 20, 1894); *The Wizard of the Nile* (Wilkes Barre, Pa., Sept. 26, 1895); *The Gold Bug* (N.Y., Sept. 21, 1896); *The Serenade* (Cleveland, Feb. 17, 1897); *The Idol's Eye* (Troy, N.Y., Sept. 20, 1897); *The Fortune Teller* (Toronto, Sept. 14, 1898); *Cyrano de Bergerac* (Montreal, Sept. 11, 1899); *The Singing Girl* (Montreal,

Oct. 2, 1899); *The Ameer* (Scranton, Pa., Oct. 9, 1899); *The Viceroy* (San Francisco, Feb. 12, 1900); *Babes in Toyland* (Chicago, June 17, 1903); *Babette* (Washington, D.C., Nov. 9, 1903); *It Happened in Nordland* (Harrisburg, Pa., Nov. 21, 1904); *Miss Dolly Dollars* (Rochester, N.Y., Aug. 30, 1905); *Wonderland* (Buffalo, Sept. 14, 1905); *Mlle. Modiste* (Trenton, Oct. 7, 1905); *The Red Mill* (Buffalo, Sept. 3, 1906); *Dream City* (N.Y., Dec. 25, 1906); *The Magic Knight* (N.Y., Dec. 25, 1906); *The Tattooed Man* (Baltimore, Feb. 11, 1907); *Algeria* (Atlantic City, Aug. 24, 1908; rev. as *The Rose of Algeria*, Wilkes Barre, Pa., Sept. 11, 1909); *Little Nemo* (Philadelphia, Sept. 28, 1908); *The Prima Donna* (Chicago, Oct. 5, 1908); *Old Dutch* (Wilkes Barre, Pa., Nov. 6, 1909); *Naughty Marietta* (Syracuse, Oct. 24, 1910); *When Sweet 16* (Springfield, Mass., Dec. 5, 1910); *Mlle. Rosita* (later called *The Duchess*; Boston, March 27, 1911); *The Enchantress* (Washington, D.C., Oct. 9, 1911); *The Lady of the Slipper* (Philadelphia, Oct. 8, 1912); *Sweethearts* (Baltimore, March 24, 1913); *The Madcap Duchess* (Rochester, N.Y., Oct. 13, 1913); *The Débutante* (Atlantic City, Sept. 21, 1914); *The Only Girl* (Atlantic City, Oct. 1, 1914); *The Princess Pat* (Atlantic City, Aug. 23, 1915); *Eileen* (Cleveland, Jan. 1, 1917, as *Hearts of Erin*); *Her Regiment* (Springfield, Mass., Oct. 22, 1917); *The Velvet Lady* (Philadelphia, Dec. 23, 1918); *Angel Face* (Chicago, June 8, 1919); *My Golden Girl* (Stamford, Conn., Dec. 19, 1919); *Oui Madame* (Philadelphia, March 22, 1920); *The Girl in the Spotlight* (Stamford, Conn., July 7, 1920); *Orange Blossoms* (Philadelphia, Sept. 4, 1922); *The Dream Girl* (New Haven, April 22, 1924). **OPERAS:** *Natoma* (Philadelphia, Feb. 25, 1911); *Madeleine* (1913; N.Y., Jan. 24, 1914). **OTHER:** *Miss Camille*, burlesque (1907); *The Song Birds*, musical skit (1907); *The Century Girl*, revue (N.Y., Nov. 6, 1916; in collaboration with I. Berlin); music for the films *The Fall of a Nation* (1916) and *Indian Summer* (1919), and for Ziegfeld's Follies. **ORCH.:** Suite for Cello and Orch. (Stuttgart, Oct. 23, 1883); 2 cello concertos: No. 1 (1884; Stuttgart, Dec. 8, 1885) and No. 2 (N.Y. March 10, 1894); *Serenade* for Strings (1888); *Irish Rhapsody* (1892); *American Fantasia* (1898); *Hero and Leander*, symphonic poem (1900; Pittsburgh, Jan. 18, 1901); *Suite romantique* (1901); *Soixante-neuf* for Strings (1902); *Columbus*, suite (1902; Pittsburgh, Jan. 2, 1903); *L'encore* for Flute, Clarinet, and Orch. (1910); *Whispering Willows* (1915); *Little Old N.Y.*, overture (1923); *Under the Red Robe*, overture (1923). **BAND:** *The Gold Bug*, march (1896); *The Serenade*, march (1897); *McKinley Inauguration March* (1897); *March of the 22nd Regiment* (1898). **OTHER:** Over 20 chamber pieces; about 25 piano works; several choral works, including the dramatic cantata *The Captive* (Worcester Festival, Sept. 24, 1891); about 80 songs; around 70 arrangements of scores by other composers.

BIBL.: J. Kaye, *V. H.* (N.Y., 1931); C. Purdy, *V. H.—American Music Master* (N.Y., 1944); E. Waters, *V. H.: A Life in Music* (N.Y., 1955).

Herbig, Günther, noted German conductor; b. Ústí-nad-Labem, Czechoslovakia, Nov. 30, 1931. He studied conducting with Abendroth at the Weimar Hochschule für Musik, and received further training from Scherchen, Yansons, and Karajan. He was conductor of the German National Theater in Weimar (1957–62), music director of the Hans Otto Theater in Potsdam (1962–66), and conductor of the (East) Berlin Sym. Orch. (1966–72). He was Generalmusikdirektor (1970–72) and chief conductor (1972–77) of the Dresden Phil.; then was chief conductor of the (East) Berlin Sym. Orch. (1977–83), and principal guest conductor of the Dallas Sym. Orch. (1979–81) and BBC Northern Sym. Orch. in Manchester (1981–83). From 1984 to 1990 he was music director of the Detroit Sym. Orch., and from 1990 to 1994 of the Toronto Sym. He then was artistic director of the Yale Philharmonia Orch. in New Haven, Conn.

Herford (real name, **Goldstein**), **Julius,** German-American pianist, choral conductor, and pedagogue; b. Anklam, Feb. 22, 1901; d. Bloomington, Ind., Sept. 17, 1981. He studied piano with Kwast and composition with Klatte and Willner at the Stern Cons. in Berlin (1917–23). After touring Europe as a pianist (1923–25), he returned to Berlin as a teacher. In 1939 he emigrated to the U.S. He taught at Teachers College of Columbia Univ. (1939–41), the Juilliard School of Music in N.Y. (from 1946), the Berkshire Music Center in Tanglewood (from 1946), the Union Theological Seminary in N.Y. (from 1949), the Manhattan School of Music in N.Y. (1949), and Westminster Choir College in Princeton, N.J.; he also was director of graduate studies in choral conducting at the Indiana Univ. School of Music in Bloomington (1964–80). With H. Decker, he ed. the vol. *Choral Conducting* (1973; 2nd ed., rev., 1988 as *Choral Conducting Symposium*).

Herincx, Raimund (Fridrik), English bass-baritone of Belgian descent; b. London, Aug. 23, 1927. He received his training from Van Dyck in Belgium and from Valli in Italy. In 1950 he made his operatic debut as Mozart's Figaro with the Welsh National Opera. In 1956 he joined the Sadler's Wells Opera in London, where his roles included Count Almaviva, Pizzaro, Germont, Rigoletto, and Stravinsky's Nick Shadow and Creon. In 1966 he was a soloist in Delius' *A Mass of Life* in N.Y., and in 1967 he sang in opera in Boston. From 1968 he appeared at London's Covent Garden, winning success as the King Fisher in the *Midsummer Marriage*, Macbeth, and Escamillo, and creating roles in the premieres of *The Knot Garden* (1970) and *Taverner* (1972). In 1973–74 he sang at the Salzburg East Festivals, and then in the *Ring* cycles at the English National Opera in London (1974–76). On Jan. 18, 1977, he made his debut as Mathiesen in *Le Prophète* at the Metropolitan Opera in N.Y., and then sang with the Seattle (1977–81) and San Francisco (1983) operas. In 1986 he returned to Boston to sing in the U.S. premiere of *Taverner*.

Herman, Vasile, Romanian composer; b. Satu-Mare, June 10, 1929. He studied piano in his hometown, and composition with Demian, Toduţă, and Comes at the Cluj Cons. (1949–57); subsequently was appointed to its staff. His music is cautiously modernistic, with occasional overflow into aleatoric indeterminacy.

WORKS: ORCH.: *Variante* for 2 Clarinets, Piano, and Percussion (1963–64); *4 Ritornele* (1964); *Cantilaşii* (1967); *Polifonie* for 7 Instrumental Groups (1968); *Episoade* (1968); *Postludiu* (1971); *Syntagma I* for 14 Instruments and Piano (1971); Double Concerto for Flute, Oboe, and Orch. (1973); *Simfonii şi fantezzi* (1974–75); 3 syms.: No. 1 (1976), No. 2, *Memorandum* (1980), and No. 3, *Metamorfoze* (1982); Unison (1977–78); Concerto for Strings (1979); Concertino for Trombone, Double Bass, and Orch. (1981). **CHAMBER:** *Sonata-Baladă* for Oboe and Piano (1961); *Triptic* for Violin (1964); *Melopee* for Flute (1965); Flute Sonata (1965–66); *Aforisme* for Oboe and Piano (1970); 2 string quartets: No. 1, *Omagiu lui Enescu* (1971) and No. 2, *Refrene* (1977); *3 Pieces* for Violin and Piano (1974); *Syntagma II* for Chamber Ensemble (1975); *Monofonii* for Oboe (1975); Trio for Violin, Cello, and Piano (1979); *Neanes* for Chamber Ensemble (1979); *Sonata de camera* for Flute, Oboe, Cello, and Harpsichord (1981); *Panrhytmicon* for 5 Percussion Groups (1982). **PIANO:** 2 sonatas: No. 1, *Sonata da ricercar* (1958) and No. 2 (1967); *Partita* (1961); *Microforme* (1965); *Grafică* for 1 or 2 Pianos (1969); other works. **VOCAL:** 6 cantatas (1969, 1970, 1974, 1977, 1980, 1983); songs.

Herman, Woody (actually, **Woodrow Charles**), noted American jazz bandleader, clarinetist, alto saxophonist, and singer; b. Milwaukee, May 16, 1913; d. Los Angeles, Oct. 29, 1987. He began his career as a performer in vaudeville when he was a child. While still in his youth, he learned to play the saxophone and the clarinet. After a term as a music student at Marquette Univ. in Milwaukee, he gained experience playing in several bands, including those of Tom Gerun (1929–34) and Isham Jones (from 1934). When Jones's band was dissolved in 1936, Herman selected its best players to form his own band, which he dubbed the "Band That Plays the Blues." In 1939 he and his band gained fame with their best-selling recording of *Woodchopper's Ball*. In subsequent years, his band went through several transformations, being dubbed the Thundering Herd, the First Herd, the Second Herd, etc. In addition to his recordings, he appeared on his own radio show and in films. Stravinsky composed his *Ebony Concerto* for Herman, who gave its premiere at N.Y.'s Carnegie Hall on March 25, 1946. It was during this period that Herman developed the famous 4 Brothers arrangement by showcasing the sound of 3 tenor saxophones and a baritone saxophone. With the passing of the big band era, he turned to amplified sound with the traditional elements of the big band. He continued to tour widely during the last 2 decades of his life, and in 1986 brought out the album *Woody Herman and His Big Band 50th Anniversary Tour.* His last years were marked by financial reversals which prompted his colleagues to organize a fund to aid him. His autobiography, written in collaboration with S. Troup, was publ. posthumously as *The Woodchopper's Ball: The Autobiography of Woody Herman* (N.Y., 1990).

BIBL.: E. Edwards, *W. H. and the Swinging Herd, 1959–1966* (Los Angeles, 1966); J. Treichel, *W. H.: The Second Herd* (Spottswood, N.J., 1980); D. Morrill, *W. H.: A Guide to the Big Band Recordings, 1936–1987* (N.Y., 1990); W. Clancy and A. Kenton, *W. H.: Chronicles of the Herds* (N.Y., 1995).

Hermann, Roland, German baritone; b. Bochum, Sept. 17, 1936. He attended the Univs. of Freiburg im Bresgau, Mainz, and Frankfurt am Main, and received his vocal training from Margarete von Winterfeldt, Paul Lohmann, and Flaminio Contini. In 1961 he took 1st prize in the competition of the German radio stations. In 1967 he made his operatic debut as Mozart's Figaro in Trier, then joined the Zürich Opera in 1968. He also sang opera in Munich, Cologne, Buenos Aires, Paris, Berlin, and other cities. His engagements as a soloist with orchs. and as a recitalist took him to many of the major music centers of Europe, the U.S. (debut with the N.Y. Phil., 1983), and the Far East. In addition to such operatic roles as Don Giovanni, Wolfram, Germont, and Amfortas, he sang in such rarely-performed works as Schumann's *Genoveva*, Marschner's *Der Vampyr*, Busoni's *Doktor Faust*, and Schoenberg's *Moses und Aron.* He also sang in several premieres, among them Keltenborn's *Der Kirschgarten* (Zürich, 1984) and Holler's *Der Meister und Margarita* (Paris, 1989).

Hermanson, Åke (Oscar Werner), Swedish composer; b. Mollosund, June 16, 1923. After training from Knut Bäck and Herman Asplöf in Göteborg, he went to Stockholm and studied organ with Alf Linder and Henry Lindroth, and composition with Rosenberg (1949–52). From 1969 to 1971 he was chairman of the Soc. of Swedish Composers. In 1973 he was elected a member of the Royal Academy of Music in Stockholm. In 1982 he received the Nordic Council Prize and in 1986 the Rosenberg Prize. In his music, he pursued a concentrated brevity marked by an alternation of short contrasting motifs, a usage he defined as "pendulum dynamics."

WORKS: ORCH.: *Invoco* for String (1958–60; Norrköping, May 24, 1961); *In nuce* (In a Nutshell; 1962–63; Stockholm, Oct. 9, 1964); 4 syms.: No. 1 (1964–67; Stockholm, Oct. 29, 1967), No. 2 (1973–75; Stockholm, Sept. 26, 1976), No. 3 (1980), and No. 4, *Oceanus* (1981–84; Stockholm, Dec. 19, 1984); *Appel I–IV* (1968–69; Swedish Radio, Dec. 12, 1970); *Ultima* (1971–72; Swedish Radio, Nov. 18, 1972); *Utopia* (1977–78). **CHAMBER:** *Lyrical Metamorphoses* for String Quartet (1954–57); *A due voci* for Flute and Viola (1957–58); *Suoni d'un flauto* for Alto Flute (1961); *Alarme* for Horn (1969); *In sono* for Flute, Oboe or English Horn, Viola, and Cello (1970); *Flauto d'inverno* for Bass Flute (1976); *Ars lineae* for 6 Winds (1976); *Thrice* for Oboe, Clarinet, and Trombone (1976–79); *La Strada* for Horn and Organ (1979–80); String Quartet (1982–83). **VOCAL:** *Stadier* for Soprano, Flute, Bass Clarinet, Viola, and Percussion (1960–61); *Bild* for Tenor and Trombone (1978–79); *Äggjakten* for Narrator, Tenor Saxophone, Guitar, and Percussion (1979); choruses.

Hernández, Hermilio, Mexican composer; b. Autlán, Jalisco, Feb. 2, 1931. He studied music with José Valadez and Domingo Lobato at the Escuela Superior Diocesana de Música Sagrada in Guadalajara, graduating in 1956; then studied in Italy and Paris.

WORKS: ORCH.: *5 Pieces* (1955); Violin Concerto (1960); Sonata for Chamber Orch. (1964). **CHAMBER:** Suite for Violin and Piano (1952); String Quartet (1954); Piano Trio (1955); Cello Sonata (1962); Wind Quintet (1965); *Poliédros* for Oboe, Bassoon, and Piano (1969); *Music for 4 Instruments* for Flute, Violin, Cello, and Piano (1970). **KEYBOARD: PIANO:** 2 sonatinas (1955, 1971); *Tema transfigurado* (1962); *6 Inventions* (1968); Sonata (1970); *Diálogos* for 2 Pianos (1970). **ORGAN:** *Fantasia* (1970). **VOCAL:** *Cantata Adviento* (1953); songs.

Hernández-López, Rhazés, Venezuelan composer and musicologist; b. Petare, June 30, 1918. He studied in Caracas with Vicente Emilio Sojo and Juan Bautista Plaza. Apart from composition, he engaged in teaching and radio work. In his series of piano pieces *Casualismo*, he applies the 12-tone method of composition. Other works include *Las Torres desprevenidas*, symphonic poem (1951); *Sonorritmo* for Orch. (1953); *Mérida, geografía celeste*, symphonic suite (1958); *Expansión tres* for Orch. (1965); *Tres dimensiones* for Strings (1967); *Cuadros* for Flute, Violin, Viola, Cello, and Harp (1950); Viola Sonata (1952); *Tres espacios* for Violin, Cello, and Piano (1965); *Horizontal* for Flute and Strings (1966); piano pieces; songs.

Hernández Moncada, Eduardo, Mexican conductor and composer; b. Jalapa, Sept. 24, 1899. He studied with Rafael Tello at the National Cons. in Mexico City. He conducted theater orchs.; in 1933 he became assistant conductor of the Orquesta Sinfónica in Mexico; then was conductor of the Sym. Orch. of the National Cons. (1947–49). Among his compositions were a Sym. (Mexico City, July 31, 1942) and a ballet, *Ixtepec* (1945).

Hernried, Robert (Franz Richard), Austrian-American musicologist and composer; b. Vienna, Sept. 22, 1883; d. Detroit, Sept. 3, 1951. He was trained in Vienna at the Cons. and the Univ. He taught theory at the Mannheim Academy of Music (1919–22), the Heidelberg Cons. (1923), in Erfurt (1924–26), and in Berlin at the Stern Cons. (1926–28) and the Staatliche Akademie für Kirchen- und Schulmusik (1927–34). In 1939 he went to the U.S. and taught at St. Ambrose College in Davenport, Iowa (1940–42), the State Teachers College in Dickinson, N. Dak. (1942–43), and St. Francis College in Fort Wayne, Ind. (1943–46); he then was prof. of theory and composition at the Detroit Inst. of Musical Art (1946–51). He publ. studies on Jaques-Dalcroze (Geneva, 1929) and Brahms (Leipzig, 1934), as well as *Allgemeine Musiklehre* (Berlin, 1932) and *Systematische Modulationslehre* (Berlin, 1935; 2nd ed., 1948). Among his compositions were the operas *Francesca da Rimini* and *Die Bäuerin*, orch. works, and much choral music.

Herold, Vilhelm (Kristoffer), Danish tenor; b. Hasle, March 19, 1865; d. Copenhagen, Dec. 15, 1937. He studied in Copenhagen, and then with Devillier and Sbriglia in Paris. He made his debut at the Royal Danish Theater in Copenhagen in 1893 as Faust; was a member of the Royal Theater in Stockholm (1901–03; 1907–09); also made guest appearances in London, Berlin, Dresden, and Hamburg. In 1915 he retired from the operatic stage. He served as director of Copenhagen's Royal Theater (1922–24). Herold was best known for his Wagnerian roles.

Herrera de la Fuente, Luis, Mexican conductor and composer; b. Mexico City, April 26, 1916. He took lessons in piano and violin before pursuing training in composition with Rodolfo Halffter. He composed some stage works but devoted himself principally to conducting. After establishing himself as a conductor in Mexico City with the Fine Arts Chamber Orch., he was music director of that city's Orquesta Sinfónica Nacional (1955–72); he also served in that capacity with the Orquesta Sinfónica Nacional of Peru in Lima (1965–71). As a guest conductor, he appeared with orchs. in North America and Europe. After serving as music director of the Oklahoma City Sym. Orch. (1978–88), he returned to Mexico City and was music director of the Filarmónica de la Ciudad de México from 1990.

Herreweghe, Philippe, esteemed Belgian conductor; b. Ghent, May 2, 1947. He studied piano with Marcel Gazelle at the Ghent Cons. He also pursued training in medicine and psychiatry at the Univ. of Ghent, graduating in 1975. His musical training continued at the Ghent Cons. with Gabriel Verschraegen (organ) and Johan Huys (harpsichord), where he took a prize in 1975. In 1969 he founded the Collegium Vocale in Ghent, which soon acquired distinction as one of Europe's finest early music groups. He organized the Ensemble Vocal La Chapelle Royale in Paris in 1977, which won acclaim for its performances of a vast repertoire ranging from the Renaissance to the contemporary era. From 1982 he also served as artistic director of the Saintes early music festival. In 1989 he founded the Ensemble Vocal Européen, which also won distinction. He organized the Orchestre des Champs-Elysées in Paris in 1991, which he conducted in performances of Classical and Romantic scores on original instruments. As a guest conductor, he appeared with many early music ensembles as well as with traditional orchs.

Herrmann, Bernard, American conductor and composer; b. N.Y., June 29, 1911; d. Los Angeles, Dec. 24, 1975. He studied violin and began to compose as a child. At 16, he commenced formal training in composition with Gustav Heine, and then attended N.Y. Univ. (1929–30) where he studied with James (composition) and Stoessel (conducting); he subsequently continued his studies with the latter as a fellowship student at the Juilliard School of Music in N.Y. (1930–32), where he also studied with Wagenaar (composition and harmony). In 1932–33 he attended Grainger's lectures at N.Y. Univ. In 1933 he organized the New Chamber Orch. in N.Y, and then in 1934 joined the staff of CBS in N.Y. working as an arranger, composer, and rehearsal conductor. In 1935 he became a staff conductor at CBS. As a composer, he found success with the various scores he wrote for such CBS programs as the "Columbia Workshop" (1937) and the "Mercury Theatre on the Air" (1938–39), where he was closely associated with Orson Welles. It was Welles who chose Herrmann to compose the score for his film *Citizen Kane* (1941), and thereafter Herrmann devoted much of his creative efforts to writing for films, with outstanding success. His score for the film *All That Money Can Buy* (1941) won him an Academy Award. From 1943 to 1951 Herrmann was chief conductor of the CBS Sym. Orch., with which he pursued a bold approach to programming. In addition to conducting broadcasts of early and rarely-heard works, he also led programs of much contemporary music, ranging from Ives and Schoenberg to Elgar and Vaughan Williams. After leaving CBS, he made occasional guest conducting appearances but devoted most of his time to composing film scores and for television. Particularly outstanding were his film scores for Hitchcock's *Vertigo* (1958) and *Psycho* (1960), and Truffaut's *Fahrenheit 451* (1966). Throughout his career, Herrmann also composed serious works, generally along neo-Romantic lines.

WORKS: FILM SCORES: *Citizen Kane* (1941); *All That Money Can Buy* (1941; also known as *The Devil and Daniel Webster*); *The Magnificent Ambersons* (1942); *Jane Eyre* (1943); *Hangover Square* (1945); *Anna and the King of Siam* (1946); *The Ghost and Mrs. Muir* (1947); *Portrait of Jennie* (1948; theme music only); *The Day the Earth Stood Still* (1951); *On Dangerous Ground* (1951); *5 Fingers* (1952); *The Snows of Kilimanjaro* (1952); *White Witch Doctor* (1953); *Beneath the 12-Mile Reef* (1953); *King of the Khyber Rifles* (1953); *Garden of Evil* (1954); *The Egyptian* (1954; in collaboration with A. Newman); *Prince of Players* (1954); *The Trouble with Harry* (1955); *The Kentuckian* (1955); *The Man Who Knew Too Much* (1956); *The Man in the Gray Flannel Suit* (1956); *The Wrong Man* (1956); *Williamsburg: The Story of a Patriot* (1956); *A Hatful of Rain* (1957); *Vertigo* (1958); *The Naked and the Dead* (1958); *The 7th Voyage of Sinbad* (1958); *North by Northwest* (1959); *Blue Denim* (1959); *Journey to the Center of the Earth* (1959); *Psycho* (1960); *The 3 Worlds of Gulliver* (1960); *Mysterious Island* (1961); *Tender Is the Night* (1962); *Cape Fear* (1962); *Jason and the Argonauts* (1963); *The Birds* (1963); *Marnie* (1964); *Joy in the Morning* (1965); *Torn Curtain* (1966); *Fahrenheit 451* (1966); *The Bride Wore Black* (1968); *Twisted Nerve* (1968); *The Night Digger* (1971); *The Battle of Neretva* (1971); *Endless Night* (1971); *Sisters* (1972); *It's Alive* (1974); *Obsession* (1976); *Taxi Driver* (1976). **OTHER:** Ballet music for *Americana Revue* (1932); *The Skating Rink*, ballet (1934); ballet music for the play *The Body Beautiful* (1935); *Wuthering Heights*, opera (1943–51; recorded 1966; stage premiere in a drastically cut version, Portland, Oreg., Nov. 6, 1982); *The King of Schnorrers*, musical comedy (1968; East Haddam, Conn., April 17, 1970). Also many radio scores; television music, including the operas *A Christmas Carol* (CBS-TV, Dec. 23, 1954) and *A Child Is Born* (CBS-TV, Dec. 23, 1955). **ORCH.:** *The Forest*, tone poem (1929); *November Dusk*, tone poem (1929; also known as *Late Autumn*); *Marche Militaire* for Chamber Orch. (1932); *Orchestral Variations on "Deep River" and "Water Boy"* (1933); *Prelude to "Anathema"* for Chamber Orch. (1933); *Aubade* for Chamber Orch. (1933; also known as *Silent Noon*); *The City of Brass*, symphonic poem (1934); *Nocturne and Scherzo* (1935); Sinfonietta for Strings (1935); *Currier and Ives*, suite (1935); Violin Concerto (1937; unfinished); Sym. (1939–41; CBS, July 27, 1941); *The Devil and Daniel Webster*, suite after the film *All That Money Can Buy* (1942); *For the Fallen* (N.Y., Dec. 16, 1943); *Welles Raises Kane*, suite (1943). **CHAMBER:** *Twilight*, pastoral for Violin and Piano (1929); *Aria* for Flute and Harp (1932); String Quartet (1932); *Echoes* for String Quartet (1965; also as the ballet *Ante Room*, 1971); *Souvenirs de Voyage*, clarinet quintet (1967). **VOCAL:** *Moby Dick*, cantata for Soloists, Men's Chorus, and Orch. (1937–38; N.Y., April 11, 1940); *Johnny Appleseed*, cantata for Soloists, Chorus, and Orch. (1940; unfinished); *The Fantasticks*, song cycle for Soprano, Alto, Tenor, Bass, Chorus, and Orch. (1942); songs.

BIBL.: E. Johnson, *B. H.: Hollywood's Music Dramatist* (London, 1977); G. Bruce, *B. H.: Film Music and Narrative* (Ann Arbor, 1985); S. Smith, *A Heart at Fire's Center: The Life and Music of B. H.* (Berkeley, 1991).

Herrmann, Hugo, German composer, teacher, and organist; b. Ravensburg, April 19, 1896; d. Stuttgart, Sept. 7, 1967. He studied at the Stuttgart Cons., and then with Gmeindl and Schreker at the Berlin Hochschule für Musik. He was organist and choirmaster in Balingen and Ludwigsburg (1919–23), and then at the Church of the Holy Redeemer in Detroit (1923–25). After working in Reutlingen (1925–29; 1932–35) and Wiesbaden (1929–32), he served as director of the Trossingen Städtische Musikschule (1935–62), where he was a prof. (from 1950). Herrmann was an advocate of Gebrauchsmusik, of which he left many examples. He wrote significant pieces for the accordion and also composed for the harmonica.

WORKS: OPERAS: *Gazellenhorn* (1929); *Vasantasena* (1930); *Das Wunder* (1937); *Paracelsus* (1943); etc. **ORCH.:** *Vorspiel zu einer hohen Feier* (1925); Chamber Sym. (1926); 2 organ concertos (both 1928); *Symphonik Musik* (1928); 5 syms. (1928, 1929, 1950, 1951, 1955); Violin Concerto (1930); Harpsichord Concerto (1931); Viola da Gamba Concerto (1931); 2 accordion concertos (1941, 1944); Concerto for Accordion, Harp, and Orch. (1951); *Symphonik Metamorphosen* (1953). **CHAMBER:** 4 string quartets; Violin Sonata; Piano Trio; *7 neue Spielmusiken* for Accordion. **VOCAL:** *Galgenlieder*, chamber cantata for Chorus (1928); *Jesus und seine Jünger*, oratorio for Chorus (1931); *Apokalypse 1945* for 2 Solo Voices and Strings (1945); *Cantata primavera* for Chorus (1956); masses; choruses.

BIBL.: A. Fett, *H. H. zum 60. Geburtstag* (Trossingen, 1956).

Herseth, Adolph, outstanding American trumpeter; b. Lake Park, Minn., July 25, 1921. He studied with Marcel LaFosse and Georges Mager at the New England Cons. of Music in Boston (1946–48). In 1948 he was appointed 1st trumpeter of the Chicago Sym. Orch., a position he held with distinction for more than 45 years. He also made many appearances as a soloist, as in the premiere of Husa's Trumpet Concerto (Chicago, Feb. 11, 1988), and was active as a teacher.

Hertog, Johannes den, Dutch conductor and composer; b. Amsterdam, Jan. 20, 1904; d. there, Oct. 18, 1982. He studied with his father, Herman Johannes den Hertog; then with Cornelis Dopper. He was director and conductor of the Wagner Soc. in Amsterdam; from 1938 to 1941 he was assistant conductor of the Concertgebouw Orch. there; in 1948 he was appointed conductor of the Flemish Opera in Antwerp, and from 1960 to 1965 was artistic director of the Netherlands Opera in Amsterdam. He wrote an opera, *Pygmalion* (1957); a musical play, *Pandora* (1968); orch. music; chamber pieces; choral works; songs.

Hertz, Alfred, eminent German-born American conductor; b. Frankfurt am Main, July 15, 1872; d. San Francisco, April 17, 1942. After completing his academic studies, he entered the Hoch Cons. in Frankfurt am Main, where he studied with Anton Urspruch; then held positions as an opera conductor in Halle (1891–92), Altenburg (1892–95), Barmen-Elberfeld (1895–99), and Breslau (1899–1902). On Nov. 28, 1902, he made his first appearance at the Metropolitan Opera in N.Y. conducting *Lohengrin*; conducted the first American performance of *Parsifal* there (Dec. 24, 1903), which took place against the wishes of the Wagner family; consequently, Hertz could no longer obtain permission to conduct Wagner in Germany. He made his Covent Garden debut in London in 1910. From 1915 to 1930 he led the San Francisco Sym. Orch.; also founded the summer series of concerts at the Hollywood Bowl (1922), and conducted more than 100 concerts there; he was affectionately known as the "Father of the Hollywood Bowl." From 1930 he was director of the Federal Music Project for Northern California and conductor of the San Francisco Federal Sym. Orch. His autobiography was publ. in the *San Francisco Chronicle* (May 3–14, 1942).

BIBL.: J. Toczek, "A. H.," *Le Grand Baton* (June 1981).

Hertzka, Emil, Austrian music publisher; b. Budapest, Aug. 3, 1869; d. Vienna, May 9, 1932. He studied chemistry at the Univ. of Vienna and received training in music. In 1893 he joined the firm of the music publisher Weinberger and then in 1901 of Universal Edition, of which he served as director from 1907. He purchased the catalogs of the Wiener Philharmonischer Verlag and the Albert J. Gutmann Co. (which publ. Bruckner and Mahler), and acquired the publication rights to works by many celebrated modern composers (Bartók, Schoenberg, Berg, Weill, and Krenek); also represented Soviet composers. An impassioned believer in the eventual worth of experimental music, he encouraged young composers, and took active part in the organization of concerts of modern music. An Emil Hertzka Foundation was established by his family after his death, for the purpose of helping unknown composers secure performances and publication of their works.

Hertzmann, Erich, German-American musicologist; b. Krefeld, Dec. 14, 1902; d. Berkeley, Calif., March 3, 1963. He studied at the Hoch Cons. in Frankfurt am Main and with Abert, Blume, Hornbostel, Sachs, Schering, and Wolf at the Univ. of Berlin (Ph.D., 1931, with the diss. *Adrian Willaert in der weltlichen Vokalmusik seiner Zeit*; publ in Leipzig, 1931). In 1938 he emigrated to the U.S. and taught at Columbia Univ. until his death; he also lectured at Princeton Univ. (1946–49) and in 1949 held a Guggenheim fellowship. His major field of research was in Renaissance music and the creative process in the music of Mozart and Beethoven, subjects he treated in many articles in German and American music journals.

Hervig, Richard (Bilderback), American composer and teacher; b. Story City, Iowa, Nov. 24, 1917. He studied English at Augustana College in Sioux Falls (B.A., 1939) and composition with Clapp at the Univ. of Iowa in Iowa City (M.A., 1941; Ph.D., 1947), where he then was on its faculty (1947–52). After serving as assoc. prof. of composition and theory at Long Beach (Calif.) State College (1952–55), he returned to the Univ. of Iowa as a prof. in 1955; he also headed its composition dept., and later was co-director of its Center for New Music (1966–84).

WORKS: ORCH.: 2 syms. (1947, 1950); *Music for a Concert* (1959); *A Diversion* (1962); *President's Fanfare* for Band (1964). **CHAMBER:** 2 clarinet sonatas (1953, 1971); String Quartet (1955); *Music* for Wind and Percussion (1960); *Diversion* for Trombone and Percussion (1969); *Chamber Music for 6 Players* for Flute, Clarinet, Violin, Double Bass, Piano, and Percussion (1976); *An Entertainment* for Clarinet and Vibraphone or Marimba (1978); Violin Sonata (1979); *Lyric Piece* for Trumpet and Harp (1981); Suite for Vibraphone or Marimba (1981); *Airs and Roulades* for Clarinet and Winds (1983); *"As I drew near . . ."* for Viola and Piano (1984); *The Tree* for 9 Instruments (1984). **VOCAL:** *Ubi sunt?* for Chorus and Brass Quartet (1964); *Quid est musica?* for Chamber Chorus and 12 Instruments (1972); *5 Romantic Songs* for Medium Voice and Piano (1982); *3 Modern Parables* for Chorus (1983); *Epitaph* for Chorus (1985).

Herz, Joachim, German opera director; b. Dresden, June 15, 1924. After training in piano, clarinet, and theory, he studied at the Dresden Hochschule für Musik (1945–49) and took courses in musicology at the Humboldt Univ. in Berlin (1949–51). In 1950 he began his career as an opera director at the Dresden State Opera, and worked with its touring company (1951–53). After serving as an assistant to Felsenstein at the Berlin Komische Oper (1953–56), he worked at the Cologne Opera (1956–57). In 1957 he became principal stage director of the Leipzig Opera, and later served as its opera director (1959–76). During his Leipzig years, he staged *Die Meistersinger von Nürnberg* for the inauguration of the new opera house in 1960, and later staged a *Ring* cycle replete with social significance (1973–76). From 1976 to 1980 he was Intendant of the Berlin Komische Oper. He was principal opera director at the Dresden State Opera from 1981 to 1991. In 1985 he staged *Der Freischütz* at the inauguration of the restored Semper Oper in Dresden. His productions have been staged in various European and North American opera centers. Herz has lectured widely at home and abroad.

WRITINGS: With W. Felsenstein, *Musiktheater: Beiträge zur Methodik und su Inszenierungskonzeptionen* (Leipzig, 1970; 2nd ed., 1976); *Joachim Herz über Musiktheater* (Berlin, 1974); *Und Figaro lässt sich scheiden: Oper als Idee und Interpretation* (Munich, 1985); *Joachim Herz: Theater, Kunst des erfüllten Augenblicks: Briefe, Vorträge, Notate, Gespräche, Essays* (Berlin, 1989).

BIBL.: H.-J. Irmer and W. Stein, *J. H.: Regisseur im Musiktheater* (Berlin, 1977); U. and U. Müller, eds., *Opern und Opernfiguren: Festschrift für J. H.* (Anif, 1989); I. Kobán, ed., *J. H.: Interviews* (Berlin, 1990).

Herzog, George (actually, **György**), Hungarian-born American ethnomusicologist; b. Budapest, Dec. 11, 1901; d. Indianapolis, Nov. 4, 1983. He studied musicology and anthropology in Budapest and Berlin. In 1925 he went to America; became a research assoc. in anthropology at the Univ. of Chicago in 1929; was a member (1930–31) of its expedition to Liberia, where he made a thorough study of West African music; then was on the faculty of Yale Univ. (1932–35). He was a visiting lecturer at Columbia Univ. in 1936–37, and took his Ph.D. there in 1937 with the diss. *A Comparison of Pueblo and Pima Musical Styles*, which was publ. in the *Journal of American Folklore*, XLIX, 1936; subsequently was a visiting assistant prof. there (1937–38), and then an assistant prof. of anthropology (1939–48). In 1948 he was appointed prof. of anthropology and folk music at Indiana Univ. in Bloomington; was made prof. emeritus in 1962. In 1962 he was made an honorary member of the American Musicological Soc. He publ. *Jabo Proverbs from Liberia: Maxims in the Life of a Native Tribe* (with C. Blooah; Oxford, 1936) and *Research in Primitive and Folk Music in the United States: A Survey* (Washington, D.C., 1936).

BIBL.: B. Krader, "G. H.: A Bibliography," *Ethnomusicology* Newsletter, 1 (1956).

Heseltine, Philip (Arnold), brilliant English composer and writer on music who used the pen name Peter Warlock; b. London, Oct. 30, 1894; d. (suicide) there, Dec. 17, 1930. He studied at Eton with Colin Taylor (1908–10), in Germany, and at Oxford. A meeting with Delius in France in 1910 influenced him profoundly in the direction of composition; he adopted a style that was intimately connected with English traditions of the Elizabethan period and yet revealed impressionistic undertones in harmonic writing. Another influence was that of Bernard van Dieren, from whom he absorbed an austerely contrapuntal technique. He publ. all his musical works under his pen name. He was a conscientious objector during World War I; in 1917–18 he was in Ireland; after the Armistice, he returned to London. In 1920 he founded the progressive journal of musical opinion the *Sackbut*; wrote criticism; made transcriptions of early English music. Suffering from depression, he committed suicide by gas in his London flat. He ed. (with P. Wilson) 300 early songs; was co-editor of Oxford Choral Songs and the Oxford Orchestral Series, a collection of early English and Italian dances.

WRITINGS (all publ. in London): *Frederick Delius* (1923); *Songs of the Garden* (1925); *The English Ayre* (1926); with C. Gray, *Carlo Gesualdo, Prince of Venosa: Musician and Murderer* (1926); ed. with J. Lindsay, *J. Harrington: The Metamorphosis of Ajax* (1927); *Thomas Whythorne* (1929); *Merry-go-down* (1929); *English Ayres, Elisabethan and Jacobean: A Discourse* (1932); *Giles Earle his Books* (1932).

WORKS: ORCH.: *An Old Song* (1917); *Serenade for Delius on his 60th Birthday* for Strings (1921–22); *Capriol*, suite for Strings (1926; for Orch., 1928). **OTHER:** *Corpus Christi* for Soprano, Baritone, and String Quartet (1919–23); *The Curlew*, song cycle for Tenor, Flute, English Horn, and String Quartet (1920–21; rev. 1922); *3 Carols* for Chorus and Orch. (1923); *Sorrow's Lullaby* for Soprano, Baritone, and String Quartet (1927); other choral works and solo songs.

BIBL.: C. Gray, *Peter Warlock: A Memoir of P. H.* (London, 1934); K. Avery, "The Chronology of Warlock's Songs," *Music & Letters* (Oct. 1948); F. Tomlinson, *A Peter Warlock Handbook* (2 vols., Rickmansworth, 1974, 1977); I. Copley, *The Music of Peter Warlock: A Critical Survey* (London, 1979); M. Pilkington, *Gurney, Ireland, Quilter, and Warlock* (London, 1989); D. Cox and J. Bishops, eds., *Peter Warlock: A Centenary Celebration: The Man-his Music-his World* (London, 1994); I. Parrott, *The Crying Curlew: Peter Warlock: Family & Influences: Centenary 1994* (Llandysul, Dyfed, 1994); B. Smith, *Peter Warlock, The Life of P. H.* (Oxford, 1994).

Hess, Ludwig, German tenor and composer; b. Marburg, March 23, 1877; d. Berlin, Feb. 5, 1944. He studied singing with Vidal in Milan. He gave concerts of German lieder throughout Europe, specializing in the modern repertoire; made a successful tour of the U.S. and Canada in 1911; conducted a choral society in Königsberg (1917–20); then settled in Berlin. He wrote the operas *Abu und Nu* (Danzig, 1919), *Vor Edens Pforte*, after Byron (n.d.), and *Kranion* (Erfurt, 1933); Sym.; *Himmelskönig mit musizierenden Engeln*, symphonic poem; *Ariadne*, cantata; many choral works; numerous songs. He publ. *Die Behandlung der Stimme vor, während und nach der Mutation* (Marburg, 1927).

Hess, Dame Myra, eminent English pianist; b. London, Feb. 25, 1890; d. there, Nov. 25, 1965. She was a student of Julian Pascal and Orlando Morgan at the Guildhall School of Music in London; when she was 12, she won a scholarship to the Royal Academy of Music in London, where she completed her studies with Tobias Matthay. On Nov. 14, 1907, she made her debut as soloist in Beethoven's 4th Piano Concerto under Beecham's direction in London, and then performed throughout England. In 1922 she made her U.S. debut in N.Y. Thereafter she toured widely in Europe and the U.S. In 1936 she was made a Commander of the Order of the British Empire. In 1939 she organized the National Gallery Concerts in London, and performed there regularly throughout the course of World War II. Her perseverance in the face of the blitz did much to bolster morale during England's "finest hour," and in 1941 a grateful King George VI made her a Dame Commander of the Order of the British Empire. After the War, Hess commenced touring again and continued her notable career until her farewell concert in 1962. In addition to her solo engagements, she also played in duo concerts with her cousin Irene Scharrer. Hess was greatly admired for her interpretations of Mozart, Beethoven, and Schumann. In 1926 she publ. her own piano transcription of Bach's *Jesu, Joy of Man's Desiring* (from the Cantata No. 147), which became a great favorite with her audiences.

BIBL.: D. Lassimonne and H. Ferguson, eds., *M. H., By Her Friends* (London, 1966); M. McKenna, *M. H.: A Portrait* (London, 1976).

Hess, Willy, German violinist and teacher; b. Mannheim, July 14, 1859; d. Berlin, Feb. 17, 1939. His first teacher was his father, who was a pupil of Spohr. As a child of 6, he was taken to the U.S.; at the age of 9, he played with the Thomas Orch.; then studied with Joachim in Berlin (1876). He was concertmaster in Frankfurt am Main (1878–86), in Rotterdam, where he taught at the Cons. (1886–88), and in Manchester, England, with the Hallé Orch. (1888–95). From 1895 to 1903 he was a prof. of violin at the Cologne Cons.; then taught at the Royal Academy of Music in London (1903–04); in 1904 he was engaged as concertmaster of the Boston Sym. Orch., and remained in that position until 1910; also organized the Hess Quartet in Boston. From 1910 to 1928 he taught at the Hochschule für Musik in Berlin.

BIBL.: F. Bonavia, "W. H. as Teacher," *Monthly Musical Record*, LXI (1931).

Hess, Willy, noted Swiss musicologist; b. Winterthur, Oct. 12, 1906. He studied piano and theory at the Zürich Cons. and musicology at the Univ. of Zürich. He played bassoon in the Winterthur Stadtorchester (1942–71). As a musicologist, he devoted most of his effort to the compilation of a Beethoven catalog. He ed. a valuable *Verzeichnis der nicht in der Gesamtausgabe veröffentlichten Werke Ludwig van Beethovens* (Wiesbaden, 1957); also ed. the extensive supplement *Ludwig van Beethoven: Sämtliche Werke: Supplement zur Gesamtausgabe* (14 vols., Wiesbaden, 1959–71). His other important writings include *Ludwig van Beethoven* (Geneva, 1946); *Beethovens Oper Fidelio und ihre drei Fassungen* (Zürich, 1953); *Beethoven* (Zürich, 1956; 2nd ed., rev., 1976); *Die Harmonie der Künste* (Vienna, 1960); *Die Dynamik der musikalischen Formbildung* (2 vols., Vienna, 1960; 1964); *Vom Doppelantlitz des Bösen in der Künste, dargestellt am Beispiel der Musik* (Munich, 1963); *Vom Metaphysischen im Künstlerischen* (Winterthur, 1963); *Parteilose Kunst, parteilose Wissenschaft* (Tutzing, 1967); *Beethoven-Studien* (Munich, 1972); also an autobiography, *Aus meinem Leben: Erlebnisse, Bekenntnisse, Betrachtungen* (Zürich, 1976). He was also a prolific composer; wrote several fairy-tale operas, a Sym., a Sonata for Bassoon and Small Orch., a Horn Concerto, and numerous pieces of chamber music, including a curious work for double bassoon and string quartet.

Hesse-Bukowska, Barbara, Polish pianist; b. Łódź, June 1, 1930. She studied piano with Margerita Trombini-Kazuro; continued her musical education at the Warsaw Academy of Music. In 1949 she won 2nd prize in the Chopin Competition in Warsaw; in 1953 she was awarded the Chopin Prize at the Long-Thibaud Competition in Paris. From that time she made regular appearances in London, Paris, Moscow, Vienna, and Rome; also made extensive tours of India, Egypt, and Japan. In 1963 she became a member of the faculty of the Academy of Music in Wroclaw; in 1973 she joined the Academy of Music in Warsaw. She is regarded as a fine interpreter of Chopin and also a leading champion of contemporary Polish music.

Hessenberg, Kurt, German composer; b. Frankfurt am Main, Aug. 17, 1908; d. there, June 17, 1994. He studied in Leipzig with Raphael (composition) and Teichmüller (piano). In 1933 he was appointed to the faculty of the Hoch Cons. in Frankfurt am Main. Possessing great facility in composition, Hessenberg evolved an effective idiom, fundamentally Classical, but containing Wagnerian elements in dramatic passages, with occasional infusion of prudential modernistic devices. His most successful work was *Struwwelpeter* (1933), a suite for Small Orch. based on a well-known German children's tale. He further wrote 3 syms. (1936, 1943, 1954); Piano Concerto (1940); Concerto for 2 Pianos and Orch. (1950); *Concerto for Orchestra* (1958); 2 flute sonatas (1932); 5 string quartets (1934–67); Cello Sonata (1941); Violin Sonata (1942); String Trio (1949); Piano Trio (1950); numerous piano pieces; a number of cantatas; a multitude of lieder.

BIBL.: K. Laux, *K. H.* (Essen, 1949).

Hétu, Jacques (Joseph Robert), Canadian composer and teacher; b. Trois-Rivières, Quebec, Aug. 8, 1938. He studied piano, harmony, and Gregorian chant at the Univ. of Ottawa (1955–56); then took courses in composition and counterpoint with Clermont Pépin, in harmony with Isabelle Delorme, and in fugue with Jean Papineau-Couture at the Montreal Cons. (1956–61; premier prix in composition, 1961); also received instruction in composition from Foss at the Berkshire Music Center in Tanglewood, Mass. (summer, 1959); completed his training in Paris with Dutilleux (composition diploma, 1963) at the École Normale de Musique and with Messiaen (analysis) at the Cons. (1962–63). He taught at Laval Univ. in Quebec (1963–77) and at the Univ. of Montreal (1972–73; 1978–79); then was a prof. at the Univ. of Quebec in Montreal (from 1979). In his music, he makes use of permissible modern devices, while hewing to Classical formal conventions.

WORKS: ORCH.: 3 syms.: No. 1 for Strings (1959), No. 2 (1961), and No. 3 (1971); *Adagio et Rondo* for String Orch. or String Quartet (1960); *Rondo* for Cello and String Orch. (1965); Double Concerto for Violin, Piano, and Chamber Orch. (1967); *L'Apocalypse* (1967); Piano Concerto (1969); *Passacaille* (1970); *Fantaisie* for Piano and Orch. (1973); *Antinomie* (1977); Bassoon Concerto (1979); *Mirages* (1981); *Symphonie concertante* for Flute, Oboe, Clarinet, Bassoon, Horn, and Strings (1986); Clarinet Concerto (1987); Trumpet Concerto (1987); *Images de la Révolution* for the bicentennial of the French Revolution (1988); *Poème* for Strings (1989); Flute Concerto (1991; Ottawa, Feb. 26, 1992). **CHAMBER:** Trio for Flute, Oboe, and Harpsichord (1960); 4 Pieces for Flute and Piano (1965); Wind Quintet (1967); *Variations* for Violin or Viola or Cello (1967); String Quartet (1972); *Aria* for Flute and Piano (1977); *Incantation* for Oboe and Piano (1978); Suite for Guitar (1986); *Sérénade* for Flute and String Quartet (1988); piano pieces; organ music. **VOCAL:** *Les Clartés de la Nuit* for Soprano and Piano (1972; also for Soprano and Orch., 1987); *Les Djinns* for Chorus, 6 Percussion, and Piano (1975); *Les Abîmes du Rêve* for Bass and Orch. (1982); *Missa pro trecentesimo anno* for Chorus and Orch. (1985); *Les Illusions fanées* for Chorus (1988).

Heuss, Alfred (Valentin), Swiss-born German musicologist, music critic, and composer; b. Chur, Jan. 27, 1877; d. Gaschwitz, July 9, 1934. He studied at the Stuttgart Cons. (1896–98), then at the Akademie der Tonkunst in Munich, attending the Univ. of Munich simultaneously (1898–99); from 1899 to 1902 he studied musicology with Kretzschmar at the Univ. of Leipzig (Ph.D., 1903, with the diss. *Die Instrumentalstücke des "Orfeo" und die venezianischen Opernsinfonien*; publ. in the *Sammelbände der Insternationalen Musik-Gesellschaft*, IV, 1902–03). He was music critic of the *Signale* (1902–05), *Leipziger Volkszeitung* (1905–12), and *Leipziger Zeitung* (1912–18); ed. of the *Zeitschrift der Internationalen Musik-Gesellschaft* (1904–14), to which he contributed valuable articles; ed.-in-chief of the *Zeitschrift für Musik* (1921–29). As a composer, he wrote mainly songs.

WRITINGS (all publ. in Leipzig): *Anton Bruckner: Te Deum* (1908); *Johann Sebastian Bachs Matthäuspassion* (1909); *Franz Liszt: Missa solemnis* (c.1910); *Erläuterungen zu Franz Liszts Sinfonien und sinfonischen Dichtungen* (1912); *Kammermusikabende: Erläuterungen von Werken der Kammermusik-Literatur* (1919); *Beethoven* (1921).

Heward, Leslie (Hays), esteemed English conductor; b. Littletown, Liversedge, Yorkshire, Dec. 8, 1897; d. Birmingham, May 3, 1943. He studied with his father, an organist; then continued his training at the Manchester Cathedral Choir School, where he served as assistant cathedral organist; was made organist of St. Andrew's, Ancoats (1914); then won a scholarship in composition to the Royal College of Music in London (1917), where he studied with Stanford and Vaughan Williams. After appearing as a conductor with the British National Opera Co., he was music director of the South African Broadcasting Corp. and conductor of the Cape Town Orch. (1924–27); then was conductor of the City of Birmingham Orch. (from 1930). He was acknowledged as one of England's finest conductors. He was also a composer, but he destroyed many of his MSS; his works included 2 unfinished operas, a symphonic poem, several orch. suites, choral works, chamber music, and songs.

BIBL.: E. Blom, ed., *L. H.: A Memorial Volume* (London, 1944); W. Holmes, "L. H. Discography," *Le Grand Baton* (Dec. 1980).

Hewitt, Harry Donald, unimaginably fecund American composer; b. Detroit, March 4, 1921. His paternal grandmother was a Winnebago Indian. He was completely autodidact in music, and achieved such mastery of composition in quaquaversal directions without stylistic prejudice, that in some 40 years of writing music he produced 3,300 works in every conceivable manner, using every speculative idiom, from jazz to pop, couched in every available tonal, atonal, polytonal, and incommensurate oriental scale. Entirely free from supercilious elitism, he was not ashamed to admit the authorship of a *Hymn to Mickey Mouse* or an *Homage to Bugs Bunny.* None of his 30 syms. were ever performed. The brute weight of his collected MSS is 1 1/2 tons.

WORKS: 8 operas: *The Shadowy Waters, Moby Dick, The Song of Kawas, The Happy Hymadrayad, Doctor Too-Big, Clara's Friend, Remember George,* and *Pierre*; 30 syms., 2 of which, *Amerindian Symphony* and *War Symphony,* are unnumbered; over 300 works for Orch., including 19 symphonic poems: *Kabir, The Manchild, The Night, Fairyland, The Mysterious Sea, The Seasons, In the Shade of the Upas Tree, New Year's Eclogue, The House of Sleep, Raggedy Ann, Wa-Kon-Da, The Happy Garden, In a Green Shade, 7, Selene, The Wheel, Aldebaran, Angkor,* and *Anglesley Abbey*; 2 piano concertos; Trombone Concerto; Guitar Concerto; 18 piano sonatas; 23 string quartets; and more than 100 other works for diverse chamber ensembles, e.g., *Preludes* for Flute and Marimba, *Fantasia* for Flute and Horn, *Leaf in the Stream* for Oboe and Tuba, etc.; uncountable songs and choruses.

Hewitt, Helen (Margaret), American musicologist; b. Granville, N.Y., May 2, 1900; d. Denton, Texas, March 19, 1977. She studied at Vassar College (B.A., 1921) and the Eastman School of Music in Rochester, N.Y. (B.M., 1925); she then took lessons in organ with Widor, in harmony with Boulanger at the American Cons. in Fontainebleau (1926), and in organ with Farnam at the Curtis Inst. of Music in Philadelphia (1928–30). After taking her Master of Sacred Music degree at Union Theological Seminary (1932), she pursued training in musicology with Lang at Columbia Univ. (M.A., 1933) and Besseler at the Univ. of Heidelberg; she then completed her education at Radcliffe College (Ph.D., 1938, with the diss. *O. Petrucci: Harmonice Musices Odhecaton A*; publ. in Cambridge, Mass., 1942; 2nd ed., 1946). In 1947 she received a Guggenheim fellowship. She taught at the State Normal School in Potsdam, N.Y. (1925–28), Florida State College for Women (1938–39), Hunter College (1942), and North Texas State Univ. in Denton (1942–69). She ed. the valuable compilation *Doctoral Dissertations in Musicology* (Denton, 1952; 4th ed., rev., 1965) and contributed important articles on Renaissance music to various journals.

Hewitt, Maurice, French violinist, conductor, and teacher; b. Asnières, Oct. 6, 1884; d. Paris, Nov. 7, 1971. He was trained at the Paris Cons. In 1904 he began his career as a violinist as a chamber music player; after serving as 2nd violinist in the Capet Quartet (1909–14; 1919–28), he was founder-1st violinist of his own quartet in Paris (1928–30). After teaching and playing in a quartet at the Cleveland Inst. of Music (1930–34), he became a prof. at the American Cons. in Fontainebleau in 1934; he also was founder-1st violinist of his own Quatuor Hewitt (1935–39; 1946–48) and founder-conductor of the Orchestre de Chambre Hewitt (from 1939). From 1942 to 1955 he was a prof. of chamber music at the Paris Cons.

Heyman, Katherine Ruth Willoughby, American pianist and composer; b. Sacramento, Calif., 1877; d. Sharon, Conn., Sept. 28, 1944. She made her debut as soloist with the Boston Sym. Orch. in 1899; from 1905 to 1915 she toured the U.S. and Europe with Schumann-Heink, Marcella Sembrich, and others. She became greatly interested in the works of Scriabin, and played recitals of his works in Europe and America; also publ. many articles on Scriabin's theosophic ideas. In 1928 she founded in Paris the Groupe Estival pour la Musique Moderne. She publ. *The Relation of Ultra-Modern to Archaic Music* (Boston, 1921). Among her compositions were *Studies in Modern Idiom* for Piano and songs.

Hickmann, Hans (Robert Hermann), German musicologist; b. Rosslau bei Dessau, May 19, 1908; d. Blandford Forum, Dorset, England, Sept. 4, 1968. He studied musicology in Halle and with Blume, Hornbostel, Sachs, Schering, Schünemann, and Wolf at the Univ. of Berlin (Ph.D., 1934, with the diss. *Das Portativ*; publ. in Kassel, 1936). He then was active in Cairo, where he pursued research in Egyptian music and worked as an organist, conductor, teacher, and broadcaster. In 1957 he became director of the German Cultural Inst. in Cairo, but that same year he was made prof. of ethnomusicology at the Univ. of Hamburg; he also was director of the Archiv Produktion division of the Deutsche Grammophon Gesellschaft (from 1958) and first president of the Deutsche Gesellschaft für Musik des Orients (from 1959). Hickmann wrote many articles on ancient Egyptian music for various learned journals.

WRITINGS: *Catalogue général des antiquités égyptiennes du Musée du Caire: Instruments de musique* (Cairo, 1949); *45 siècles de musique dans l'Egypte ancienne à travers la sculpture, la peinture, l'instrument* (Paris, 1956); *Ägypten* in Musikgeschichte in Bildern, ii/1 (Leipzig, 1961).

BIBL.: K. Neumann, "Special Bibliography: H. H.," *Ethnomusicology*, IX (1965); J. Gillis, F. Bose, and J. Elrod, "Supplementary Bibliography: H. H.," ibid., XIII (1969).

Hickox, Richard (Sidney), English conductor; b. Stokenchurch, Buckinghamshire, March 5, 1948. He studied at the Royal Academy of Music in London (1966–67), and was an organ scholar at Queen's College, Cambridge (1967–70). In 1971 he founded in London the Richard Hickox Singers and Orch., with which he gave programs of works ranging from the 14th century to the present era; also was music director of the City of London Sinfonia (from 1971) and organist and master of music at St. Margarets, Westminster (1972–82). He likewise served as conductor of the London Sym. Orch. Chorus (from 1976), artistic director of the Northern Sinfonia in Newcastle upon Tyne (1982–90), and assoc. conductor of the San Diego Sym. Orch. (1983–85) and the London Sym. Orch. (from 1985). In 1990 he founded, together with Simon Standage, the Collegium Musicum 90 of London. He also was principal guest conductor of the Bournemouth Sym. Orch. from 1992. As a guest conductor, he appeared with all the principal British orchs., opera houses, and festivals.

Hidalgo, Elvira de, Spanish soprano and teacher; b. Aragón, Dec. 27, 1892; d. Milan, Jan. 21, 1980. She studied with Bordalba in Barcelona and Vidal in Milan. In 1908 she made her operatic debut as Rossini's Rosina in Naples. On March 7, 1910, she sang that role in her Metropolitan Opera debut in N.Y., returning there for the 1924–26 seasons. She also appeared at Milan's La Scala (1916), in Rome (1919), at Buenos Aires's Teatro Colón (1922), and at London's Covent Garden (1924). From 1932 she devoted herself to teaching, being the mentor of Maria Callas in Athens. She later taught in Ankara (1949–59) and then in Milan. In addition to Rosina, she was greatly admired for her portrayals of Gilda, Linda, Philine, Elvira, Musetta, and Lakmé.

Hidas, Frigyes, Hungarian composer; b. Budapest, May 25, 1928. He was a student of Viski at the Budapest Academy of Music. He served as music director of the National Theater in Budapest (1951–66), and then at the Municipal Operetta Theater in Budapest (1974–79). In subsequent years, he devoted himself solely to composition. In 1959 and 1980 he was awarded the Erkel Prize. In 1986 the Hungarian government made him a Merited Artist.

WORKS: DRAMATIC: *Színek* (Colors), ballet (1960); *Riviera*, operetta (1963); *Az Asszony és az igazság* (The Woman and the Truth), chamber opera (1965); *Tökéletes alattvaló* (The Perfect Subject), opera (1973); *Cédrus* (Cedar), ballet (1975); *Bösendorfer*, opera (1977); *Dunakanyar* (Danube Bend), opera (1984); *Álmodj Bachot* (Dream Bach), musical play (1991; Budapest, May 25, 1993). **ORCH.:** Oboe Concerto (1951); Violin Concertino (1957); 2 clarinet concertos (1958, 1977); Viola Concerto (1959); Sym. (1960); Flute Concerto (1967); 2 horn concertos (1968, 1989); Concertino for 4 Flutes, 4 Clarinets, and Strings (1969); Piano Concerto (1972); Trombone Concerto (1979); Harp Concerto (1979); Bassoon Concerto (1980); *Ballad* for Cello and Orch. (1982); *Cymbog* for Cimbalom, Oboe, and Strings (1982); *Baroque Concerto* for Alto Trombone and Strings (1983); Trumpet Concerto No. 2 (1983); *Széchenyi Concerto* (1984); *Preludium, Passacaglia, and Fugue* for 2 Cimbaloms and Strings (1984); *Quintetto Concertante* for Brass Quintet and Orch. (1986); *3 Movements* (1987); Double Concerto for Tenor and Bass Trombones and Orch. (1988); *The Undanced Ballet* (1989); *Brussels Concerto* for Violin and Orch. (1992); String Fantasy (1992); Suite for Small String Orch. (1993). **CONCERT BAND:** Trumpet Concerto No. 1 (1956); *Ballet Music* (1980); Suite (1981); *Rhapsody* for Bass Trombone and Concert Band (1982); Concerto No. 2 for Flute and Wind Ensemble (1983); *Circus Suite* (1985); 2 folksong suites (1985, 1985); *4 Movements* (1991); *Almost B.A.C.H.* (1993); *Musica Solenne* (1993). **CHAMBER:** 3 string quartets (1954, 1963, 1978); Oboe Sonata (1955); 3 wind quintets (1961, 1969, 1979); *Chamber Music* for 4 Horns (1974); *5 Movements* for 3 Trumpets, 2 Trombones, and Tuba (1978); Brass Quintet (1978); *7 Bagatelles* for 12 Trombones (1979); Sextet for 3 Trumpets, Horn, 2 Trombones, and Tuba (1982); *Music for Brass* for 5 Trumpets and 5 Trombones (1983); *Divertimento* for Wind Octet (1985); *Music for 6* for String Quartet, Double Bass, and Piano (1985); *Alteba Trio* for Alto, Tenor, and Bass Trombones (1986); *1 + 5*, sextet for Bass Trombone and Wind Quintet (1989); Saxophone Quartet (1990); Tuba Quartet (1990); *Domine, Dona Nobis Pacem* for Trombone and Organ (1991); Suite for 4 Trombones (1991); *Tale* for Violin and Harp (1991); *Music* for Harp and Violin (1992); *Triga* for Trumpet, Horn, and Trombone (1992). **VOCAL:** *Missa Brevis* for Chorus and Organ (1956); *Cantate de Minoribus* for Narrator, Men's Chorus, and Orch. (1959); *From Dawn to Evening* for Children's Chorus and Chamber Orch. (1967); *Requiem for an Army* for Tenor, Baritone, Bass, Chorus, and Orch. (1973); *Missa in Honorem Reginae Pacis* for Soprano, Alto, Tenor, Bass, Chorus, and Organ (1991).

Hier, Ethel Glenn, American composer, teacher, and pianist; b. Cincinnati, June 25, 1889; d. Winter Park, Fla., Jan. 14, 1971. She studied piano at the Cincinnati Cons. of Music (diploma, 1908); in 1911 she resumed piano studies there and also received instruction in composition from Kelley. During the summer of 1912, she pursued training in composition from Kaun in Germany. In 1917 she went to N.Y. and studied composition with Goetschius and Bloch at the Inst. of Musical Art; after further training with Berg, Wellesz, and Malipiero in Europe, she completed her piano studies with Friedberg (1923). In subsequent years, she was mainly active as a teacher, composer, and promoter of women in American musical life. In

1926 she helped to found the Assn. of American Women Composers. In 1948 she founded the Composers Concerts in N.Y. In her music, she leavened impressionistic elements with infusions of popular and jazz styles. Among her works were *Asolo Bells* for Orch. (Rochester, N.Y., Oct. 25, 1939); *Mountain Preacher*, cantata (N.Y., Dec. 5, 1941); 2 string quartets; 3 quintets; piano pieces; songs.

Higgins, Dick (actually, **Richard Carter**), English-born American composer, performer, music publisher, and writer; b. Cambridge, March 15, 1938. He was taken to the U.S. as a child. He studied piano in Worcester, Mass.; after training in composition and orchestration with Harry Levenson (1953), he studied with Cowell at Columbia Univ., where he took a B.S. in English (1960), and with Cage at the New School for Social Research (1958–59). Caught up in the avant-garde movement, he became a proponent of the intermedia group who advocated the union of music with other allied arts. In 1958 he became active in the first "happenings," and from 1961 he worked in the Fluxus movement. He was founder-director of the Something Else Press (1964–73). In 1972 he founded Unpublished Editions, which became Printed Editions in 1978. He taught at the Calif. Inst. of the Arts (1970–71) and was a research assoc. in the visual arts dept. of the State Univ. of N.Y. at Purchase (from 1983). He wrote widely on music and the arts. In his compositions, he pursued the objective of total involvement, in which music is verbalized in conceptual designs without reification or expressed in physical action. He also utilized graphic notation. Among his works are *Graphis*, a series of pieces for Varying Groups (from 1958); *Danger Music*, a series of pieces for Varying Groups (1961–64); *Hrušalk*, opera (1965); *The 1000 Symphonies*, a series for Orch. (from 1968); *Piano Album, 1962–84* (1980); *26 Mountains for Viewing the Sunset From* for Singers, Dancers, and Chamber Orch. (1980); *Trinity* for Piano and Percussion (1981); *Variations on a Natural Theme* for Orch. (1981); *St. Columbia* for String Quartet, Orch. or 4 Voices, Chorus, and Tubular Chimes (1983); numerous vocal works; tape pieces; many performance works with music; film scores. Among his many books are *Foew&ombuhnw* (N.Y., 1969); *Computers for the Arts* (Somerville, Mass., 1970); *A Dialectic of Centuries: Notes Towards a Theory of the New Arts* (N.Y., 1978; 2nd ed., rev., 1979); *Horizons: The Poetics and Theory of the Intermedia* (Carbondale, Ill., 1983).

Higginson, Henry Lee, American music patron; b. N.Y., Nov. 18, 1834; d. Boston, Nov. 14, 1919. He attended Harvard Univ. (1851) and studied music in Vienna (1856–60). In 1868 he became a partner in his father's Boston brokerage firm of Lee, Higginson and Co. His great love for music prompted him to found the Boston Sym. Orch. in 1881, which he subsequently nurtured as its munificent patron. In 1885 he founded the Boston Music Hall Promenade Concerts, a summer series of lighter fare which became celebrated as the Boston Pops.

BIBL.: B. Perry, *Life and Letters of H. L. H.* (Boston, 1921); P. Hart, "H. L. H.—Patron," *Orpheus in the New World* (N.Y., 1973).

Hijman, Julius, Dutch-American pianist, teacher, and composer; b. Almelo, Jan. 25, 1901; d. N.Y., Jan. 6, 1969. He studied piano privately with Dirk Schaefer, then with Paul Weingartner in Vienna; subsequently theory and composition with Sem Dresden in the Netherlands. He went to the U.S. in 1940; was an instructor at the Houston Cons. (1940–42) and at the Kansas City Cons. (1945–49); then taught composition at the Philadelphia Musical Academy and the N.Y. College of Music. He composed mostly chamber music; sonatas for violin, cello, saxophone, oboe, and flute, with piano; 4 string quartets; Sonata for 2 Violins and Piano.

Hill, Alfred (Francis), noted Australian composer; b. Melbourne, Nov. 16, 1870; d. Sydney, Oct. 30, 1960. He played violin in traveling theater orchs.; then studied with Paul, Schreck, and Sitt at the Leipzig Cons. (1887–91); subsequently was active in New Zealand and Australia as a conductor, and later as a prof. at the New South Wales State Conservatorium (1916–34). He was made an Officer of the Order of the British Empire in 1953 and a Companion of the Order of St. Michael and St. George in 1960. He wrote over 500 works, some of which employ Maori and Australian Aboriginal materials. He publ. *Harmony and Melody* (London, 1927).

WORKS: OPERAS: *Whipping Boy* (1893); *Lady Dolly* (1898; Sydney, 1900); *Tapu* (1902–03); *A Moorish Maid or Queen of the Riffs* (Auckland, 1905); *Teora—The Weird Flute* (1913; Sydney, 1928); *Giovanni, the Sculptor* (1913–14; Melbourne, 1914); *Rajah of Shivapore* (Sydney, 1914); *Auster* (1919; Sydney, 1922); *The Ship of Heaven* (1923; 1st complete perf., Sydney, 1933). **ORCH.:** 13 syms., including No. 1, *Maori* (1896–1900), No. 2, *Joy of Life* (1941), No. 3, *Australia* (1951), No. 4, *Pursuit of Happiness* (1955), No. 5, *Carnival* (1955), No. 6, *Celtic* (1956), No. 7 (1956), No. 8, *The Mind of Man* (1957), No. 9, *Melodious* (1958), and No. 10 (1958), all transcribed from chamber pieces except No. 1. **CHAMBER:** 17 string quartets; 6 violin sonatas; Wind Septet (1950); piano pieces. **VOCAL: CHORAL:** *The New Jerusalem* (1892); *Hinemoa, a Maori Legend* (1895); *Tawhaki* (1897); Mass (1931); also *Life* for 8 Solo Voices and Piano Quintet (1912); part songs; songs.

BIBL.: A. McCredie, "A. H. (1870–1960): Some Backgrounds and Perspectives for an Historical Edition," *Miscellanea Musicologica*, III (1968); J. Thomson, *A Distant Music: The Life and Times of A. H., 1870–1960* (Oxford, 1982).

Hill, Edward Burlingame, eminent American composer and teacher; b. Cambridge, Mass., Sept. 9, 1872; d. Francestown, N.H., July 9, 1960. A member of a distinguished family of educators (his father was a prof. of chemistry at Harvard, and his grandfather, president of Harvard), he pursued regular courses at Harvard Univ.; studied music with J.K. Paine; graduated in 1894 summa cum laude; took lessons in piano with B.J. Lang and A. Whiting, in composition with Chadwick and Bullard; also (for 1 summer) studied with Widor in Paris. He became greatly interested in the new tonal resources of the impressionist school of composers; wrote articles in the *Boston Evening Transcript* and other publications dealing with French music; publ. a book, *Modern French Music* (Boston, 1924). In 1908 he joined the faculty of Harvard Univ. as an instructor in music; became assoc. prof. in 1918, prof. in 1928, and then was the James E. Ditson Prof. (1937–40). He was a member of the National Inst. of Arts and Letters and of the American Academy of Arts and Sciences; also was a Chevalier of the Legion d'Honneur. In his music, Hill reveals himself as a follower of the French school; clarity of design and elegance of expression are his chief characteristics. His best works are for orch., but he also composed some fine chamber and choral music.

WORKS: BALLET-PANTOMIME: *Jack Frost in Midsummer* (1908). **ORCH.:** *The Parting of Lancelot and Guinevere*, tone poem (St. Louis, Dec. 31, 1915); *Stevensoniana Suite No. 1* (1916–17; N.Y., Jan. 27, 1918) and *No. 2* (1921–22; N.Y., March 25, 1923); *The Fall of the House of Usher*, tone poem (Boston, Oct. 29, 1920); *Prelude to the Trojan Women* (1920); *Waltzes* (Boston, Feb. 24, 1922); *Scherzo* for 2 Pianos and Orch. (Boston, Dec. 19, 1924); *Lilacs*, tone poem (Cambridge, Mass., March 31, 1927); 3 syms.: No. 1 (1927; Boston, March 30, 1928), No. 2 (1929; Boston, Feb. 27, 1931), and No. 3 (1936; Boston, Dec. 3, 1937); *Ode for the 50th Anniversary of the Boston Symphony Orchestra* for Chorus and Orch. (Boston, Oct. 17, 1930); Piano Concertino (1931; Boston, April 25, 1932); Sinfonietta for Strings (1932; N.Y., April 3, 1936); Violin Concerto (1933–34; rev. 1937; Boston, Nov. 11, 1938); Concertino for Strings (Boston, April 19, 1940); *Music* for English Horn and Orch. (1943; Boston, March 2, 1945); Concerto for 2 Flutes and Small Orch. (1947); *4 Pieces* for Small Orch. (1948); *Prelude* (N.Y., March 29, 1953). **CHAMBER:** Flute Sonata (1926); Clarinet Sonata (1927); Sextet for Flute, Oboe, Clarinet, Bassoon, Horn, and Piano (1934); String Quartet (1935); Piano Quartet (1937); Sonata for 2 Clarinets (1938); Quintet for Clarinet and String Quartet (1945); *Diversion* for Chamber Ensemble (1946); Bassoon Sonata (1948); Cello Sonatina (1949); Violin Sonatina (1951). **PIANO:** *Poetical*

Sketches (1902); *Country Idyls*, 6 pieces; *Jazz Study* for 2 Pianos (1924). **VOCAL:** *Nuns of the Perpetual Adoration*, cantata for Women's Voices and Orch. or Piano (1908); *Autumn Twilight* for Soprano and Orch.; *The Wilderness Shall Rejoice*, anthem for Chorus (1915).

BIBL.: G. Smith, "E.B. H.," *Modern Music*, XVI (1939); L. Tyler, *E.B. H.: A Bio-Bibliography* (N.Y., 1989).

Hill, Ralph, English writer on music; b. Watford, Oct. 8, 1900; d. London, Oct. 19, 1950. He studied cello with his father at the Guildhall School of Music in London. He was active in music publishing (1920–29); was music ed. of the *Radio Times* (1933–45); also was assistant music critic (1933–39) and later chief music critic (1945–50) of the *Daily Mail*. He publ. the following works, all in London: *An Outline of Musical History* (1929); *Brahms: A Study in Musical Biography* (1933); *Liszt* (1936; 2nd ed., 1949); *Challenges: A Series of Controversial Essays on Music* (1943); *Music without Fears* (1945); *Prelude to Music* (1951); also ed. *The Symphony* (1949) and *The Concerto* (1952).

Hill, Richard S(ynyer), American music librarian; b. Chicago, Sept. 25, 1901; d. Naples, Fla., Feb. 7, 1961. He was educated at Phillips Exeter Academy; then studied at Cornell Univ. (B.A., 1924) and did post-graduate work at the Univ. of Oxford (1924–26); held a research fellowship in psychology with Kurt Koffka at Smith College (1927–29); returned to Cornell Univ. for further study in psychology and musicology, the latter under Otto Kinkeldey. He joined the staff of the Music Division of the Library of Congress in Washington, D.C., in 1939; served as ed. of *Notes*, the quarterly journal of the Music Library Assn., from 1943 to the time of his death; was president of the International Assn. of Music Libraries (1951–55). He contributed articles and reviews to various journals, one of the most notable being his "Schoenberg's Tone Rows and the Tonal System of the Future," *Musical Quarterly* (Jan. 1936).

BIBL.: C. Bradley and J. Coover, eds., *R.S. H.: Tributes from Friends* (Detroit, 1987).

Hillborg, Anders, Swedish composer and teacher; b. Stockholm, May 31, 1954. He received training in counterpoint (1976–78) and in composition (from Bucht, 1978–82) at the Stockholm Musikhögskolan; also had lessons from Feldman in Buffalo (1980). He was a prof. of composition at the Malmö Musikhögskolan (from 1989). He has pursued an inventive road as a composer, utilizing both traditional and non-traditional styles.

WORKS: ORCH.: *Worlds* (1979); *Lamento* for Clarinet and Strings (Stockholm, May 13, 1982); *Himmelsmekanik* (Celestial Mechanic) for Strings (1983–85; Stockholm, Oct. 31, 1986); *Clang and Fury* (1985–89); Violin Concerto (1990–92); *Strange Singing* for Trombone and Orch. (1993–94). **CHAMBER:** *Hyacintrummet* for Harp (1982); *Musik* for 10 Cellos (Stockholm, Dec. 18, 1987); *Hauptosaune* for Trombone and Drum Machine or Tape (London, Oct. 6, 1990); *Fanfare* for Brass Quintet (1991); *Tampare raw* for Clarinet and Piano (1991); *Un-Tangia-Na* for Trombone and Organ (1991); *Close Ups* for Flute (1991). **VOCAL:** *Lilla Sus Grav* for Chorus (1978); *Stella Maris* for Chorus (1983); *Hosianna I–II* for Chorus (1989); *Variations* for Soprano, Mezzo-soprano, Flute, Saxophone, Percussion, Viola, and Double Bass (1991); *Psaltarpsalm* for Chorus, Brass Quintet, and Organ (1993). **ELECTRONIC:** *Mental Hygien III* (1979); *Rite of Passage* (1981); *Spöksonaten* (1982; Stockholm, Jan. 8, 1983); *Living-room* (1983); *Kamaloka* (Berlin, Feb. 14, 1984); *Musik till Friends* (1987); *Hudbason* (1990); *Strange Dances and Singing Water* (1994).

Hillebrecht, Hildegard, German soprano; b. Hannover, Nov. 26, 1927. She made her operatic debut as Leonora in *Il Trovatore* in Freiburg im Breisgau (1951); then sang in Zürich (1952–54), Düsseldorf (1954–59), Cologne (1956–61), Munich (from 1961), and again in Zürich (from 1972). She also made guest appearances in Vienna, Hamburg, Berlin, Salzburg, Paris, and Rome. In 1967 she made her Covent Garden debut in London as the Empress in *Die Frau ohne Schatten*; on Nov. 8, 1968, she made her Metropolitan Opera debut in N.Y. as Sieglinde in *Die Walküre*. She was best known for her roles in operas by Mozart, Wagner, Puccini, Strauss, and Verdi; she also sang in the premiere of Dallapiccola's *Ulisse* in Berlin (1968).

Hiller, Lejaren (Arthur, Jr.), American composer and teacher; b. N.Y., Feb. 23, 1924; d. Buffalo, Jan. 26, 1994. He studied chemistry at Princeton Univ. (B.A., 1944; M.A., 1946; Ph.D., 1947), where he also took courses in composition with Babbitt and Sessions; later he studied at the Univ. of Ill. (M.Mus., 1958). After working as a research chemist (1947–52), he taught chemistry at the Univ. of Ill. (1952–58), where he subsequently was prof. of music and director of its experimental music studio (1958–68). In 1968 he became the Frederick B. Slee Prof. of Composition at the State Univ. of N.Y. at Buffalo, where he also was co-director of its Center of the Creative and Performing Arts (1968–74); from 1980 to 1989 he was the Birge-Cary Prof. of Music there. Hiller's scientific bent led him to explore the application of electronics and computers to composition. With Leonard Isaacson, he collaborated on the *Illiac Suite*, his 4th string quartet (1955–56), which was the first composition composed with the aid of a computer. With Isaacson, he publ. *Experimental Music: Composition with an Electronic Computer* (N.Y., 1959).

WORKS: MELODRAMA: *John Italus* (unfinished). **ORCH.:** Piano Concerto (1949); Suite for Small Orch. (1951); 3 syms. (1953, 1960, unfinished); *Time of the Heathen*, suite for Chamber Orch. (1961); *A Preview of Coming Attractions* (1975); *The Fox Trots Again* for Chamber Ensemble (1985). **CHAMBER:** 7 string quartets (1949; 1951; 1953; 1957, *Illiac Suite*, in collaboration with L. Isaacson; 1962; 1972; 1979); 3 violin sonatas (1949, 1955, 1970); *Persiflage* for Flute, Oboe, and Percussion (1977); *Minuet and Trio* for 6 Performers (1980); *Fast and Slow* for Saxophone Quartet (1984); *Metaphors* for Guitar Quartet (1986). **PIANO:** 6 sonatas (1946, rev. 1968; 1947; 1950; 1950; 1961; 1972). **VOCAL:** *Computer Cantata* for Soprano, Chamber Ensemble, and Tape (1963; in collaboration with R. Baker); songs. **OTHER:** *Nightmare Music* for Tape (1961); *7 Electronic Studies* for Tape (1963; in collaboration with R. Baker); *Machine Music* for Piano, Percussion, and Tape (1964); *A Triptych for Hieronymus* for Actors, Dancers, Projections, Tape, and Orch. (1966); *An Avalanche* for Pitchman, Prima Donna, Player Piano, Percussionist, and Pre-recorded Playback (1968); *HPSCHD* for 1 to 7 Harpsichords and 1 to 51 Tapes (1968; in collaboration with J. Cage); *Algorithms I* for 9 Instruments and Tape (1968), *II* for 9 Instruments and Tape (1972; in collaboration with R. Kumra), and *III* for 9 Instruments and Tape (1984); *A Portfolio* for Diverse Performers and Tape (1974); *Electronic Sonata* for Tape (1976); *Midnight Carnival* for a Principal Tape, an Indeterminate Number of Subsidiary Tapes, and other events in an urban environment (1976); *Expo '85* for Multiple Synthesizers (1985; in collaboration with C. Ames and J. Myhill).

Hillier, Paul (Douglas), English baritone and conductor; b. Dorchester, Feb. 9, 1949. He trained at the Guildhall School of Music in London, and then served as vicar-choral at St. Paul's Cathedral (1973–74). In 1974 he made his formal concert debut at London's Purcell Room and also founded the Hilliard Ensemble, which he directed in performances of early music until 1990. In 1989 he founded the Theatre of Voices. He also was a prof. of music at the Univ. of Calif. at Davis from 1990. He also gave master classes in early music performance. He publ. *300 Years of English Partsongs* (1983), *Romantic English Partsongs* (1986), *The Catch Book* (1987), and *The Music of Arvo Pärt* (1996).

Hillis, Margaret (Eleanor), American conductor; b. Kokomo, Ind., Oct 1, 1921. She studied piano as a child and played the tuba and double bass in school bands. After taking her B.A. at Indiana Univ. (1947), she studied choral conducting at the Juilliard School of Music in N.Y. (1947–49) and with Robert Shaw, who engaged her as his assistant (1952–53). In 1950 she became music director of the American Concert Choir and

Orch. in N.Y. From 1952 to 1968 she was conductor of the chorus of the American Opera Soc. there, and also was choral director of the N.Y. City Opera (1955–56). From 1956 to 1960 she was music director of the N.Y. Chamber Soloists. In 1957 Fritz Reiner, music director of the Chicago Sym. Orch., asked Hillis to organize its chorus. She conducted it with great distinction until her retirement in 1994. She also was choral director of the Santa Fe (N.M.) Opera (1958–59), music director of the Kenosha (Wis.) Sym. Orch. (1961–68), resident conductor of the Chicago Civic Orch. (1967–90), conductor of the Cleveland Orch. Chorus (1969–71), music director of the Elgin (Ill.) Sym. Orch. (1971–85), and conductor of the San Francisco Sym. Chorus (1982–83). From 1950 to 1960 she taught at the Union Theological Seminary in N.Y., and also at the Juilliard School of Music (1951–53). After serving as director of choral activities at Northwestern Univ. (1970–77), she was a visiting prof. at the Indiana Univ. School of Music in Bloomington (from 1978). She also led various master classes in choral conducting. In 1954 she founded and became director of the American Choral Union. In 1994 she was honored with the Theodore Thomas Award in recognition of her long and distinguished career.

Hilsberg (real name, **Hillersberg**), **Alexander,** Polish-born American violinist, conductor, and teacher; b. Warsaw, April 24, 1897; d. Camden, Maine, Aug. 10, 1961. He studied violin with Auer at the St. Petersburg Cons. In 1923 he emigrated to the U.S. and became a naturalized citizen. He was made a violinist (1926), concertmaster (1931), and assoc. conductor (1945) of the Philadelphia Orch.; he also taught at the Curtis Inst. of Music (1927–53). From 1952 to 1960 he was conductor of the New Orleans Phil., and then was head of the orch. dept. at the New School of Music in Philadelphia.

Hindemith, Paul, eminent German-born American composer and teacher; b. Hanau, near Frankfurt am Main, Nov. 16, 1895; d. Frankfurt am Main, Dec. 28, 1963. He began studying violin at the age of 9; at 14, he entered the Hoch Cons. in Frankfurt am Main, where he studied violin with A. Rebner, and composition with Arnold Mendelssohn and Sekles. His father was killed in World War I, and Hindemith was compelled to rely on his own resources to make a living. He was concertmaster of the orch. of the Frankfurt am Main Opera (1915–23), and later played the viola in the string quartet of his teacher Rebner; from 1922 to 1929 he was violist in the Amar String Quartet; also appeared as a soloist on the viola and viola d'amore; later was engaged as a conductor, mainly of his own works. As a composer, he joined the modern movement and was an active participant in the contemporary music concerts at Donaueschingen, and later in Baden-Baden. In 1927 he was appointed instructor in composition at the Berlin Hochschule für Musik. With the advent of the Hitler regime in 1933, Hindemith began to experience increasing difficulties, both artistically and politically. Although his own ethnic purity was never questioned, he was married to Gertrud Rottenberg, daughter of the Jewish conductor Ludwig Rottenberg, and he stubbornly refused to cease ensemble playing with undeniable Jews. Hitler's propaganda minister, Goebbels, accused Hindemith of cultural Bolshevism, and his music fell into an official desuetude. Unwilling to compromise with the barbarous regime, Hindemith accepted engagements abroad. Beginning in 1934, he made 3 visits to Ankara at the invitation of the Turkish government, and helped to organize the music curriculum at the Ankara Cons. He made his first American appearance at the Coolidge Festival at the Library of Congress in Washington, D.C., in a performance of his Unaccompanied Viola Sonata (April 10, 1937). Hindemith was an instructor at the Berkshire Music Center at Tanglewood in the summer of 1940; from 1940 to 1953 he was a prof. at Yale Univ.; during the academic year 1950–51, he was the Charles Eliot Norton Lecturer at Harvard Univ. He became a naturalized American citizen in 1946. In 1953 he went to Switzerland and gave courses at the Univ. of Zürich. He also was active as a guest conductor in Europe and the U.S.

Hindemith's early music reflects rebellious opposition to all tradition; this is noted in such works as the opera *Mörder, Hoffnung der Frauen* (1919) and *Suite 1922* for Piano (1922); at the same time, he cultivated the techniques of constructivism, evident in his theatrical sketch *Hin und Zurück* (1927), in which *Krebsgang* (retrograde movement) is applied to the action on the stage, so that events are reversed; in a work of a much later period, *Ludus Tonalis* (1943), the postlude is the upside-down version of the prelude. Along constructive lines is Hindemith's cultivation of *Gebrauchsmusik*, that is, music for use; he was also an ardent champion of *Hausmusik*, to be played or sung by amateurs at home; the score of his *Frau Musica* (as revised in 1944) has an obbligato part for the audience to sing. A neo-Classical trend is shown in a series of works, entitled *Kammermusik*, for various instrumental combinations, polyphonically conceived, and Baroque in style. Although he made free use of atonal melodies, he was never tempted to adopt an integral 12-tone method, which he opposed on aesthetic grounds. Having made a thorough study of early music, he artfully assimilated its polyphony in his works; his masterpiece of this genre was the opera *Mathis der Maler*. A prolific composer, Hindemith wrote music of all types for all instrumental combinations, including a series of sonatas for each orch. instrument with piano. His style may be described as a synthesis of modern, Romantic, Classical, Baroque, and other styles, a combination saved from the stigma of eclecticism only by Hindemith's superlative mastery of technical means. As a theorist and pedagogue, he developed a self-consistent method of presentation derived from the acoustical nature of harmonies.

WORKS: DRAMATIC: OPERAS: *Mörder, Hoffnung der Frauen*, op. 12 (1919; Stuttgart, June 4, 1921); *Das Nusch-Nuschi*, op. 20, marionette opera (1920; Stuttgart, June 4, 1921; rev. version, Königsberg, Jan. 22, 1931); *Sancta Susanna*, op. 21 (1921; Frankfurt am Main, March 26, 1922); *Cardillac*, op. 39 (Dresden, Nov. 9, 1926; rev. version, Zürich, June 20, 1952); *Hin und Zurück*, op. 45a, 1-act sketch (Baden-Baden, July 17, 1927); *Neues vom Tage* (1928–29; Berlin, June 8, 1929; rev. 1953; Naples, April 7, 1954, composer conducting); *Mathis der Maler* (1934–35; Zürich, May 28, 1938); *Orfeo*, realization of Monteverdi's opera (1943); *Die Harmonie der Welt* (1950–57; Munich, Aug. 11, 1957, composer conducting); *Das lange Weihnachtsmahl* (1960; Mannheim, Dec. 17, 1961). **INCIDENTAL MUSIC:** *Tuttifantchen* (Darmstadt, Dec. 13, 1922). **BALLETS:** *Der Dämon*, op. 28, pantomime (1922; Darmstadt, Dec. 1, 1923); *Nobilissima visione*, dance legend in 6 scenes (perf. as *St. Francis* by the Ballets Russes de Monte Carlo, London, July 21, 1938, composer conducting); *Theme and Variations: The 4 Temperaments* for String Orch. and Piano (1940; N.Y., Nov. 20, 1946); *Hérodiade*, after Mallarmé (perf. as *Mirror before Me* by the Martha Graham Dance Co., Washington, D.C., Oct. 30, 1944).

ORCH.: Cello Concerto, op. 3 (1916); *Lustige Sinfonietta*, op. 4 (1916); Piano Concerto, op. 29 (1924); Concerto for Oboe, Bassoon, Violin, and Orch., op. 38 (Duisburg, July 25, 1925); *Konzertmusik* for Wind Orch., op. 41 (Donaueschingen, July 1926); *Konzertmusik* for Viola and Orch., op. 48 (Hamburg, March 28, 1930, composer soloist); *Konzertmusik* for Piano, Brass, and 2 Harps, op. 49 (Chicago, Oct. 12, 1930); *Konzertmusik* for Strings and Brass, op. 50 (for 50th anniversary of the Boston Sym. Orch.; Boston, April 3, 1931); *Konzertstück* for Trautonium and Strings (1931); *Philharmonisches Konzert*, variations (Berlin, April 15, 1932); *Mathis der Maler*, sym. from the opera (Berlin, March 11, 1934, Furtwängler conducting); *Der Schwanendreher*, concerto for Viola and Small Orch. (Amsterdam, Nov. 14, 1935, composer soloist); *Trauermusik* for Solo Viola or Violin or Cello and String Orch. (written for a memorial broadcast for King George V, who died on Jan. 20, 1936; London, Jan. 22, 1936, composer soloist); *Symphonic Dances* (London, Dec. 5, 1937); *Nobilissima visione*, suite from the ballet (Venice, Sept. 13, 1938); Violin Concerto (1939; Amsterdam, March 14, 1940); Cello Concerto (1940; Boston, Feb. 7, 1941; Piatigorsky soloist); Sym. in E-flat (1940; Minneapolis, Nov. 21,

1941); *Cupid and Psyche*, overture for a ballet (Philadelphia, Oct. 29, 1943); *Symphonic Metamorphosis on Themes of Carl Maria von Weber* (1943; N.Y., Jan. 20, 1944); *Theme and Variations: The 4 Temperaments* for String Orch. and Piano (Boston, Sept. 3, 1944, Foss soloist); Piano Concerto (1945; Cleveland, Feb. 27, 1947, Sanroma soloist); *Symphonia Serena* (1946; Dallas, Feb. 2, 1947); Clarinet Concerto (1947; Philadelphia, Dec. 11, 1950, Benny Goodman soloist); Concerto for 4 Winds, Harp, and Small Orch. (N.Y., May 15, 1949); Concerto for Trumpet, Bassoon, and Strings (New Haven, Conn., Nov. 4, 1949; 3rd movement added in 1952); Sinfonietta (1949; Louisville, March 1, 1950, composer conducting); Horn Concerto (1949; Baden-Baden, June 8, 1950, Dennis Brain soloist); Sym. in B-flat for Concert Band (Washington, D.C., April 5, 1951, composer conducting); *Die Harmonie der Welt*, sym. from the opera (1951; Basel, Jan. 24, 1952); *Pittsburgh Symphony* (1958; Pittsburgh, Jan. 30, 1959, composer conducting); Organ Concerto (1962–63; N.Y., April 25, 1963, Heiller soloist, composer conducting).

CHAMBER: *Andante and Scherzo*, op. 1, trio for Clarinet, Horn, and Piano (1914); unnumbered String Quartet in C, op. 2 (1915); Piano Quintet, op. 7 (1917); *3 Stücke* for Cello and Piano, op. 8 (1917); 6 numbered string quartets: No. 1, op. 10 (Frankfurt am Main, June 2, 1919), No. 2, op. 16 (Donaueschingen, Aug. 1, 1922), No. 3, op. 22 (Donaueschingen, Nov. 4, 1922), No. 4, op. 32 (Vienna, Nov. 5, 1923), No. 5 (Washington, D.C., Nov. 7, 1943), and No. 6 (Washington, D.C., March 21, 1946); set of 6 sonatas, opp. 11/1–6: 2 for Violin and Piano (1918), 1 for Cello and Piano (1919), 1 for Viola and Piano (1919), 1 for Solo Viola (1919), and 1 for Solo Violin (1919); *Kleine Kammermusik*, op. 24/2, for Wind Quintet (1922); set of 4 sonatas, opp. 25/1–4: 1 for Solo Viola (1922), 1 for Viola d'Amore and Piano (1923), 1 for Solo Cello (1923), and 1 for Viola and Piano (1924); *"Minimax"—Reportorium für Militärmusik*, parody for String Quartet (1923); Quintet for Clarinet and String Quartet, op. 30 (Salzburg Festival, Aug. 7, 1923); set of 4 sonatas, opp. 31/1–4: 2 for Solo Violin (1924), 1, *Canonic Sonatina*, for 2 Flutes (1924), and 1 for Solo Viola (1924); 2 trios for Violin, Viola, and Cello (op. 34, Salzburg, Aug. 6, 1924; Antwerp, March 17, 1933); *Rondo* for 3 Guitars (1925); *3 Stücke* for 5 Instruments (1925); 7 numbered pieces titled *Kammermusik*: No. 1, op. 24/1 (Donaueschingen Festival, July 31, 1922), No. 2, op. 36/1, for Piano and 12 Instruments (Frankfurt am Main, Oct. 31, 1924), No. 3, op. 36/2, for Cello and 10 Instruments (Bochum, April 30, 1925; composer's brother, Rudolf, soloist), No. 4, op. 36/3, for Violin and Large Chamber Orch. (Dessau, Sept. 25, 1925), No. 5, op. 36/4, for Viola and Large Chamber Orch. (Berlin, Nov. 3, 1927), No. 6, op. 46/1, for Viola d'Amore and Chamber Orch. (1927; Cologne, March 29, 1928), and No. 7, op. 46/2, for Organ and Chamber Ensemble (1927; Frankfurt am Main, Jan. 8, 1928); *8 Pieces* for Flute (1927); Trio for Viola, Heckelphone or Saxophone, and Piano, op. 47 (1928); *2 Canonic Duets* for 2 Violins (1929); *14 Easy Duets* for 2 Violins (1931); *Konzertstück* for 2 Saxophones (1933); *Duet* for Viola and Cello (1934); 2 violin sonatas (1935, 1939); Flute Sonata (1936); Sonata for Solo Viola (1937); *Meditation* for Violin or Viola or Cello and Piano (1938); Quartet for Clarinet, Violin, Cello, and Piano (1938); Oboe Sonata (1938); Bassoon Sonata (1938; transcribed for Bass Clarinet in 1959 for Josef Horák); Clarinet Sonata (1939); Horn Sonata (1939); Trumpet Sonata (1939); Sonata for Solo Harp (1939); Viola Sonata (1939); English Horn Sonata (1941); Trombone Sonata (1941); *A Frog He Went a-Courting*, variations for Cello and Piano (1941); *Echo* for Flute and Piano (1942); Sonata for Saxophone or Alto Horn or Horn and Piano (1943); Septet for Winds (1948); Double Bass Sonata (1949); Sonata for 4 Horns (1952); Tuba Sonata (1955); Octet for Clarinet, Bassoon, Horn, and String Quintet (Berlin, Sept. 23, 1958).

PIANO: 7 *Waltzes*, op. 6, for 4-hands (1916); *In einer Nacht*, op. 15, a set of 14 pieces (1920); Sonata, op. 17 (1917); *Tanzstücke*, op. 19 (1922); *Suite "1922,"* op. 26 (1922); *Klaviermusik*, op. 37, incorporating *Übung in drei Stücken*, op. 37/1 (1925) and *Reihe kleiner Stücke*, op. 37/2 (1927); 3 numbered sonatas (1936); Sonata for 4-hands (1938); Sonata for 2 Pianos (1942); *Ludus Tonalis*, studies (Chicago, Feb. 15, 1943).

VOCAL: *3 Songs* for Soprano and Orch., op. 9 (1917); *Melancholie* for Contralto and String Quartet, op. 13 (1918); *Des Todes Tod*, op. 23/1, 3 songs for Woman's Voice, 2 Violas, and 2 Cellos (1922); *Die junge Magd*, op. 23/2, 6 poems for Contralto, Flute, Clarinet, and String Quartet (1922); *Lieder nach alten Texten*, op. 33, for Chorus (1923); *Die Serenaden*, op. 35, little cantata for Soprano, Oboe, Viola, and Cello (1925); *Der Lindenbergflug* for Soloists and Orch. (1929); *Das Unaufhörliche*, oratorio (Berlin, Nov. 21, 1931); *5 Songs on Old Texts* for Chorus (c.1938); *6 Chansons* for Chorus, after Rilke (1939); *3 Choruses* for Men's Chorus (1939); *The Demon of the Gibbet* for Men's Chorus (1939); *When Lilacs Last in the Dooryard Bloom'd*, an American Requiem after Whitman, for Mezzo-soprano, Baritone, Chorus, and Orch. (N.Y., May 14, 1946); *Apparebit Repentina Dies* for Chorus and Brass (Cambridge, Mass., May 2, 1947); *Das Marienleben* for Soprano and Orch., after Rilke (1938–48; rev., shortened, and orchestrated version of songs orig. for Voice and Piano, 1923); *Ite, angeli veloces*, cantata trilogy: *Chant de triomphe du roi David, Custos quid de nocte*, and *Cantique de l'espérance* (1953–55; 1st complete perf., Wuppertal, June 4, 1955); *12 Madrigals* for 5-part Chorus (1958); *Der Mainzer Umzug* for Soprano, Tenor, Baritone, Chorus, and Orch. (Mainz, June 23, 1962); Mass for Chorus (Vienna, Nov. 12, 1963). **VOICE AND PIANO:** *3 Hymnen*, op. 14, after Whitman (1919); *8 Songs* for Soprano, op. 18 (1920); *Das Marienleben*, op. 27, after Rilke (Donaueschingen, June 17, 1923; rev. radically and perf. in Hannover, Nov. 3, 1948); *6 Lieder* for Tenor and Piano (1933–35); *13 Motets* (1941–60); *9 English Songs* (1942–44).

GEBRAUCHSMUSIK: Music for Mechanical Instruments, op. 40: Toccata for Player Piano, and Music for Mechanical Organ (both 1926–27); music for the film *Felix the Cat* for Mechanical Organ, op. 42 (1927); *Spielmusik* for Strings, Flutes, and Oboes, op. 43/1 (1927); *Lieder für Singkreise* for Voices, op. 43/2 (1927); *Schulwerk fur Instrumental-Zusammenspiel*, op. 44, (1927); *Sing- und Spielmusiken für Liebhaber und Musikfreunde*, including: *Frau Musica* for Soli, Chorus, and Strings, op. 45/1 (1928; rev. as *In Praise of Music*, 1943), *8 Canons* for 2 Voices and Instruments, op. 45/2 (1928), *Ein Jäger aus Kurpfalz* for Strings and Winds, op. 45/3 (1928), *Kleine Klaviermusik*, op. 45/4 (1929), and *Martinslied* for Unison Chorus and 3 Instruments, op. 45/5 (1929); *Lehrstück* for Male Soloists, Narrator, Chorus, Orch., Dance Group, Clowns, and Community Singing, after Brecht (Baden-Baden, July 28, 1929); *Wir bauen eine Stadt*, play for Children's Soli and Chorus, and Instruments (Berlin, June 21, 1930); *Ploner Musiktag*, in 4 sections: *Morgenmusik* for Brass Quintet, *Tafelmusik* for Strings and Brass, *Kantate* for Soli, Children's Chorus, Narrator, Strings, Winds, and Percussion, and *Abendkonzert*, 6 individual pieces for Chamber and Orch. Grouping (all 1932; Plon, June 1932); *Wer sich die Musik erkiest* for Voices and Instruments (1952).

The Auftrag der Hindemith-Stiftung began issuing a collected ed. in 1975. Thematic indexes have been compiled by K. Stone (N.Y., 1954; verified by the composer) and H. Rösner, *Paul Hindemith—Katalog seiner Werke, Diskographie, Bibliographie, Einführung in das Schaffen* (Frankfurt am Main, 1970).

WRITINGS: *Unterweisung im Tonsatz* (2 vols., 1937, 1939; Eng. ed. as *The Craft of Musical Composition*, N.Y., 1941; rev., 1945); *A Concentrated Course in Traditional Harmony* (2 vols., N.Y., 1943, 1953); *Elementary Training for Musicians* (N.Y., 1946); *J.S. Bach: Heritage and Obligation* (New Haven, Conn., 1952; Ger. ed., *J.S. Bach: Ein verpflichtendes Erbe*, Wiesbaden, 1953); *A Composer's World: Horizons and Limitations* (Cambridge, Mass., 1952).

BIBL.: The *H.-Jahrbuch* began publication in 1971. See also the following: F. Willms, "P. H.," *Von neuer Musik* (Cologne, 1925); W. Altmann, "P. H.," ibid.; H. Kleemann, "Das Kompositionsprinzip P. H.s," *Gedenkschrift für Hermann Abert* (Halle, 1928); H. Strobel, *P. H.* (Mainz, 1928; 3rd ed., aug., 1948); W.

Reich, "P. H.," *Musical Quarterly* (Oct. 1931); P. Rosenfeld, "Neo-Classicism and H.," *Discoveries of a Music Critic* (N.Y., 1936); H.H. Stuckenschmidt, "H. Today," *Modern Music* (1937); F. Muser, "The Recent Works of P. H.," *Musical Quarterly* (Jan. 1944); N. Cazden, "H. and Nature," *Music Review* (Nov. 1954); R. Stephan, "H.'s Marienleben, An Assessment of Its Two Versions," *Zeugnis in Bildern* (Mainz, 1955; updated ed., 1965, as *P. H.: Die letzten Jahre; Ein Zeugnis in Bildern*); H. Schilling, *P. H.'s Cardillac* (Würzburg, 1962); H. Boatwright, "P. H. as a Teacher," *Musical Quarterly* (July 1964); H. Tischler, "Remarks on H.'s Contrapuntal Technique," *Essays in Musicology: A Birthday Offering for Willi Apel* (Bloomington, Ind., 1968); A. Briner, *P. H.* (Zürich, 1970; Eng. tr., 1987); I. Kemp, *H.* (London, 1970); E. Zwink, *P. H.s Unterweisung im Tonsatz* (Göppingen, 1974); G. Skelton, *P. H.: The Man behind the Music* (London, 1975); G. Metz, *Melodische Polyphonie in der Zwölftonordnung: Studien zum Kontrapunkt P. H.s* (Baden-Baden, 1976); D. Rexroth, *Erprobungen und Erfahrungen: Zu P. H.s Schaffen in den Zwanziger Jahren* (Frankfurt am Main, 1978); G. Schubert, *H.* (Hamburg, 1981); D. Rexroth, *P. H. Briefe* (Frankfurt am Main, 1982); E. Preussner, *P. H.: Ein Lebensbild* (Innsbruck, 1984); D. Neumeyer, *The Music of P. H.* (New Haven, 1986); S. Cook, *Opera During the Weimar Republic: The Zeitopern of Ernst Krenek, Kurt Weill, and P. H.* (Ann Arbor, 1987); A. Briner, D. Rexroth, and G. Schubert, *P. H.: Leben und Werk in Bild und Text* (Zürich, 1988); S. Hinton, *The Idea of Gebrauchsmusik: A Study of Musical Aesthetics in the Weimar Republic (1919–1933) with Particular Reference to the Works of P. H.* (N.Y. and London, 1989); L. Noss, *P. H. in the United States* (Urbana, 1989).

Hinderas (real name, **Henderson**), **Natalie,** black American pianist; b. Oberlin, Ohio, June 15, 1927; d. Elkins Park, Pa., July 22, 1987. Her father was a jazz musician, and her mother was a music teacher. She was a child prodigy and was accepted at the Oberlin School of Music at the age of 8; graduated at 18 (B.Mus., 1945). She subsequently took lessons with Olga Samaroff at the Juilliard School of Music in N.Y.; then studied piano with Eduard Steuermann and composition with Vincent Persichetti. She made her N.Y. debut in 1954; later toured in Europe and the Far East. In addition to the standard piano repertoire, she included in her concert programs pieces by black composers.

Hines (real name, **Heinz**), **Jerome (Albert Link),** distinguished American bass; b. Los Angeles, Nov. 8, 1921. He received training in mathematics, chemistry, and physics at the Univ. of Calif. at Los Angeles (B.A., 1943), and concurrently took vocal lessons with Gennaro Curci in Los Angeles; he later studied voice with Samuel Margolis in N.Y. In 1940 he made his stage debut as Bill Bobstay in *H.M.S. Pinafore* with the Los Angeles Civic Light Opera. On Oct. 19, 1941, he made his San Francisco Opera debut as Monterone. He then made appearances as a soloist with American orchs., and also sang with the New Orleans Opera (1944–46). After winning the Caruso Award in 1946, he made his debut at the Metropolitan Opera in N.Y. as the Sergeant in *Boris Godunov* on Nov. 21, 1946; he first sang its title role there on Feb. 18, 1954, making a memorable impression. In the meantime, he sang in South America and Europe. He appeared at the Glyndebourne and Edinburgh Festivals in 1953, at the Bavarian State Opera in Munich in 1954, and at La Scala in Milan and the Bayreuth Festival in 1958. On Sept. 23, 1962, he made a dramatic debut at the Bolshoi Theater in Moscow when he sang Boris Godunov in Russian. He continued to sing regularly at the Metropolitan Opera, where he remained on the roster for over 45 years. In addition to his commanding portrayal of Boris Godunov, he also won distinction for such roles as Don Giovanni, Sarastro, Wotan, Philip II, Don Basilio, and King Marke. His deep religious faith was revealed in his choice of Christ as the subject of his opera *I Am the Way*, and in the title of his autobiography *This is My Story, This is My Song* (1968). He also publ. a book of interviews as *Great Singers on Great Singing* (1982).

Hinrichs, Gustav, German-American conductor, teacher, and composer; b. Ludwigslust, Dec. 10, 1850; d. Mountain Lake, N.J., March 26, 1942. He studied violin and piano with his father, and received training in composition in Hamburg from Marxsen. He began conducting at 15, and at 20 went to San Francisco, where he conducted the Fabbri Opera. In 1885 he went to N.Y. as assistant conductor to Theodore Thomas and the American Opera Co. In 1888 he founded his own opera company in Philadelphia, where he conducted the U.S. premieres of *Cavalleria rusticana* (Sept. 9, 1891) and *Manon Lescaut* (Aug. 29, 1894); he also conducted the U.S. premiere of *Pagliacci* in N.Y. (June 15, 1893). On Oct. 14, 1899, he conducted *Il Barbiere di Siviglia* with the Metropolitan Opera Co. during its visit to Syracuse, N.Y.; on Oct. 19, 1899, he conducted *Faust* at the Metropolitan Opera in N.Y., remaining on its roster for the season; he returned there for the 1903–04 season. He taught at the National Cons. and at Columbia Univ. (1895–1906). Among his works were the opera *Onti-Ora* (Philadelphia, July 28, 1890, composer conducting), a symphonic suite, and some vocal pieces.

Hinshaw, William Wade, American baritone, pedagogue, and operatic impresario; b. near Union, Iowa, Nov. 3, 1867; d. Washington, D.C., Nov. 27, 1947. He studied civil engineering (B.S., 1888), music (Mus.B., 1890), and law (LL.B., 1897) at Valparaiso (Ind.) Univ.; he also pursued vocal training with Arturo Marescalchi and Alfred Hertz. In 1893 he made his debut at a concert at the World's Columbian Exposition in Chicago. From 1895 to 1899 he was head of the music dept. at Valparaiso Univ. On Nov. 6, 1899, he made his operatic debut as Gounod's Méphistophélès with Henry Savage's opera company in St. Louis. Returning to Chicago, he became secretary of the Hinshaw School of Opera and Drama; when it merged with the Chicago Cons. in 1903, he became president of the new institution; subsequently he was director of the Hinshaw Cons. (1907–10). With the tenor James Sheehan, he organized the Metropolitan Grand Opera Co. to stage operas in English at the International Theatre; Hinshaw sang Telramund in the company's first production in 1908. On Nov. 16, 1910, he made his debut at the Metropolitan Opera in N.Y. at Biterolf, and subsequently remained on its roster as a distinguished Wagnerian until 1913; he also appeared at the Wagner Festivals in Graz (1912) and Berlin (1914). In 1916 he offered a prize of $1,000 for the best 1-act opera by an American composer, which was won by Hadley with his opera *Bianca*. After serving as president of the Soc. of American Singers in N.Y. (1918–20), he toured the U.S., Canada, and Cuba with his own opera company (1920–26). He spent his remaining years compiling the *Encyclopedia of American Quaker Genealogy* (6 vols., 1936–47).

Hirai, Kozaburo, Japanese composer; b. Kochi, Sept. 10, 1910. He studied violin with Robert Pollak and composition and conducting with Klaus Pringsheim at the Tokyo Imperial Academy of Music (1929–34); taught at the Academy (1937–47); in 1966 he organized the Assn. of Composers and Authors (ACA).

WORKS: DRAMATIC: OPERETTA: *Taketori-Monogatari* (1949). **BALLET:** *Spirit of the Snow* (1942; rev. 1968). **ORCH.:** *Festival of Insects*, suite (Tokyo, Sept. 15, 1941); *Pastoral* for Clarinet and Strings (1943); *On the Grass*, suite (1947); Koto Concerto (Tokyo, Nov. 12, 1950); *Festival*, concerto grosso for 3 Koto Soli and Koto Orch. (1962); *Symphonic Ballad* (1963); *Seaside Sketch* for Chamber Orch. (1967); *Marriage of the Whale*, symphonic chorus for 3 Voices, Chorus, and Orch. (Tokyo, Nov. 27, 1969); *Hakusan* for Shakuhachi, Solo Koto, Chorus, Percussion, and Koto Ensemble (1970); *Tosa Fudoki*, symphonic poem (1981); *Echoes from the Ancient Capital of Mars* (1983); *Divertimento* for Strings (1985). **CHAMBER:** Trio for Flute, Viola, and Guitar (1942); String Quartet No. 1, *Japanese Suite* (1943); String Trio (1946); *Fantasy* for Strings (1954); Cello Sonata (1956; rev. 1989); Sonata for Koto and Oboe (1956); *Duet* for Violin and Trombone (1966); *3 Capriccios* for Violin (1971); *Sakura Sakura*, fantasy for Piano (1971); *Varia-*

tions on "Sakura, Sakura" for Viola and Cello (1987); *Andante* for Viola and Piano (1988); *Concert Études* for Koto (1990).

Hirao, Kishio, Japanese composer; b. Tokyo, July 8, 1907; d. there, Dec. 15, 1953. He graduated from Keio Univ. in 1930; studied composition with Guy de Lioncourt at the Schola Cantorum in Paris (1931–34); became a prof. at the Tokyo Music Academy.

WORKS: CHOREOGRAPHIC DRAMA: *Histoire de Wanasa—Otome* (1943). **ORCH.:** *Cantilène antique* (1937); *Variations on a Japanese Theme* (1938); *Suite* for Flute and Orch. (1940); *Kinuta*, symphonic poem (1942); *La Paix*, overture (1951). **CHAMBER:** String Quartet (1940); Flute Sonatina (1941); Octet (1944); Piano Quintet (1945); Violin Sonata (1947); Piano Sonata (1948); Trio for Flute, Violin, and Piano (1949); Wind Quintet (1950); Oboe Sonata (1951).

Hirayoshi, Takekuni, Japanese composer; b. Kobe, July 10, 1936. He studied with Yoshio Hasegawa at the Tokyo Univ. of Arts (1955–61); later attended the graduate school there (1963–67). His Symphonic Variations was awarded the 1969 Odaka Prize.

WORKS: ORCH.: *Composition* (1962); *Ballade* (1966); Symphonic Variations (Tokyo, Oct. 23, 1969); *Ballade* for Organ and Orch. (1974); *Requiem* for Violin and Orch. (1975); Guitar Concerto (1980); *A Landscape of the Sea* for Timpani and Orch. (1981); *Poem of Kobe* for Orch. (1989). **CHAMBER:** String Quartet (1960); *Dialog* for Marimba, Flute, Clarinet, and Cello (1968); Prelude and Fantasia for Guitar (1970); *Monodrama* for Piano (1970); *Impromptu* for Flute, Violin, and Piano (1970); *Epitaph* for Cello (1971); Octet for 4 Japanese Instruments and String Quartet (1972); *Epitaph* for 2 Flutes (1973); *Song of the Wind* for 2 Marimbas (1973); *The Carnival Has Come* for Piano, 4-hands (1985); *Elegia* for Viola (1990); *El vent de Catalyuna* for Guitar and String Quartet (1991); *Rhapsody* for Brass Octet (1992); *Stars Party* for 5 Players (1992).

Hirsch, Paul (Adolf), German-English music collector and bibliographer; b. Frankfurt am Main, Feb. 24, 1881; d. Cambridge, Nov. 23, 1951. He began collecting rare musical eds. in 1896, and publ. successive catalogs of his rapidly growing library. In 1936 he left Germany and was able to transport his entire collection to England; it was purchased by the British Museum in 1946; the total number of items was about 20,000. In 1922 he began the publication of new eds. (several in facsimile, and with commentaries) of rare works. See the *Music Review*, XII (1951).

Hirst, Grayson, American tenor; b. Ojai, Calif., Dec. 27, 1939. He studied at the Music Academy of the West in Santa Barbara, California, with Singher at the Univ. of Calif. at Los Angeles, and with Tourel at the Juilliard School of Music in N.Y. (1963–72), making his professional debut as Cavalli's Ormindo with the Opera Soc. of Washington, D.C. (1969). His first appearance in N.Y. was as Tonio in a concert performance of *La Fille du régiment* at Carnegie Hall (1970); after singing Quint in *The Turn of the Screw* at the N.Y. City Opera (1972), he appeared in opera throughout the U.S. and Europe while also pursuing an extensive concert career. In 1986 he joined the faculty at the Univ. of Arizona. His operatic repertoire includes over 70 roles, ranging from Mozart to contemporary roles.

Hirt, Franz Josef, Swiss pianist and teacher; b. Lucerne, Feb. 7, 1899; d. Bern, May 20, 1985. He studied with Hans Huber and Ernst Lévy at the Basel Cons.; later took lessons with Petri and Cortot. In 1919 he became a teacher at the Bern Cons.; also gave numerous piano recitals in Europe. He publ. *Meisterwerke des Klavierbaues* (1955; Eng. tr., 1968, as *Stringed Keyboard Instruments, 1440–1880*).

Hislop, Joseph, Scottish tenor; b. Edinburgh, April 5, 1884; d. Upper Largo, Fife, May 6, 1977. He studied in Stockholm with Gillis Bratt. On Sept. 12, 1914, he made his operatic debut at the Royal Opera in Stockholm as Faust, and subsequently was active in Scandinavia before singing at the Teatro San Carlo in Naples (1919–20). On May 14, 1920, he made his first appearance at London's Covent Garden as Rodolfo; that same year, he made his U.S. debut in Chicago, then appeared in N.Y. in 1921 before touring the country with Scotti's company. In 1923 he sang in Venice and Turin, and was the first British tenor to sing a leading role at Milan's La Scala when he appeared as Edgardo. In 1925 he appeared at the Teatro Colón in Buenos Aires. After retiring in 1937, he taught voice in Stockholm, where his most gifted students were Jussi Björling and Birgit Nilsson. In 1947 he went to London, where he was artistic advisor at Covent Garden and subsequently at the Sadler's Wells Opera. In later years, he was active as a teacher at the Guildhall School of Music. He was admired for his roles in operas by Verdi and Puccini, the latter praising him as the ideal Rodolfo. His French roles were also noteworthy.

BIBL.: M. Turnbull, *J. H.: Gran Tenore* (Aldershot, 1992).

Hitchcock, H(ugh) Wiley, eminent American musicologist and editor; b. Detroit, Sept. 28, 1923. He was educated at Dartmouth College (A.B., 1943) and the Univ. of Mich. (M.Mus., 1948; Ph.D., 1954, with the diss. *The Latin Oratorios of Marc-Antoine Charpentier*). He taught music at the Univ. of Mich. (1947–61); then was prof. of music at Hunter College (1961–71); in 1971 he became prof. of music at Brooklyn College (named Distinguished Prof. of Music in 1980), where he also served as director of the Inst. for Studies in American Music. A recipient of numerous grants, including Fulbright senior research fellowships in 1954–55 (Italy) and 1968–69 (France), and a Guggenheim fellowship in 1968–69, Hitchcock also served on the boards of numerous organizations; in 1991–92 he was president of the American Musicological Soc., and in 1994 was made an honorary member. He was also ed. of The Prentice-Hall History of Music Series (Englewood Cliffs, N.J., 1965–), *Earlier American Music* (reprints of music; N.Y., 1972–), and *Recent Researches in American Music* (Madison, Wis., 1976–). He was co-ed. of *The New Grove Dictionary of American Music* (4 vols., N.Y., 1986). His research interests are wide and meritorious, covering French Baroque and American music; his editorial contributions include the works of Caccini, Leonardo Leo, Charpentier, and Lully.

WRITINGS: *Music in the United States: A Historical Introduction* (Englewood Cliffs, N.J., 1969; 2nd ed., rev. and enl., 1974; 3rd ed., 1988); *Charles Ives Centennial Festival-Conference 1974* (program book; N.Y., 1974); *Ives* (London, 1977; rev. 1983); co-ed., with V. Perlis, *An Ives Celebration: Papers and Panels of the Charles Ives Centennial Festival-Conference* (Urbana, Ill., 1977); *The Phonograph and Our Musical Life* (Brooklyn, 1980); with L. Inserra, *The Music of Ainsworth's Psalter (1612)* (Brooklyn, 1981); *The Works of Marc-Antoine Charpentier: A Catalogue Raisonné* (Paris, 1982); *Ives: A Survey of the Music* (N.Y., 1983); *Marc-Antoine Charpentier* (Oxford, 1990).

BIBL.: R. Crawford, R. Lott, and C. Oja, eds., *A Celebration of American Music: Words and Music in Honor of H. W. H.* (Ann Arbor, 1989).

Hlobil, Emil, Czech composer and teacher; b. Veselí nad Lužnici, Oct. 11, 1901; d. Prague, Jan. 25, 1987. He studied with Křička at the Prague Cons. (1920–23) and in the master classes of Suk there (1924–25; 1927–30). After teaching at the Prague Women Teachers' Inst. (1930–41), he taught at the Cons. (1941–58) and afterward at the Academy of Music and Dramatic Arts in Prague. He was made an Artist of Merit (1972) and a National Artist (1981) for his services to Czech music. He followed the national tradition of the modern Czech school, and also cautiously experimented with serial methods of composition.

WORKS: OPERAS: *Anna Karenina* (1962; České Budějovice, April 16, 1972); *Le Bourgeois gentilhomme* (1965); *Král Václav IV* (1981). **ORCH.:** 7 syms.: No. 1 (1949), No. 2, *The Day of Victory* (1951), No. 3 (1957), No. 4 (1959), No. 5 (1969), No. 6 for Strings (1972), and No. 7 (1973); 4 symphonic suites: *Summer in the Giant Mountains* (1950), *Folk Merry-Mak-*

ing (1950), *Spring in the Gardens of Prague* (1951–53), and *In the Valachian Village* (1952); Violin Concerto (1955); Accordion Concerto (1956); *Labor Holiday* (1960); Organ Concerto (1963); *Concerto filharmonico* (1965); *Invocazioni* (1967); Double Bass Concerto (1968); *The Path of the Living* (1974); *Jubilace* (1977); Marimba Concerto (1979); Cello Concerto (1983). **CHAMBER:** String Quintet (1925); 4 string quartets (1931, 1936, 1955, 1969); Piano Trio (1938); Wind Quintet (1940); Horn Sonata (1942; rev. 1948); Quartet for Harpsichord, Violin, Viola, and Cello (1943); Nonet (1946); Wind Octet (1956); Violin Sonata (1959); Quartet for Flute, Oboe, Clarinet, and Bassoon (1964); Flute Sonata (1966); Trumpet Sonata (1967); Bass Clarinet Sonata (1970); Trombone Sonata (1973); Sonata for 2 Cellos (1973); Trio for Violin, Guitar, and Accordion (1976); Clarinet Sonata (1978); *Canto pensieroso* for Saxophone (1983); piano pieces, including Sonata for 2 Pianos (1958) and 2 sonatas (both 1968); organ music. **VOCAL:** Choral works; songs.

BIBL.: J. Bajer, *E. Hlovil: Hudební putování stoletím* (Prague, 1984).

Hoboken, Anthony van, eminent Dutch music collector and bibliographer; b. Rotterdam, March 23, 1887; d. Zürich, Nov. 1, 1983. He studied with Anton Verhey in Delft; after studies with Knorr (composition) and Sekles (harmony) at the Hoch Cons. in Frankfurt am Main, he completed his training with Schenker in Vienna (1925–34). In 1919 he began to build a private collection of first and early eds. of music and literature associated with music. His collection on Haydn proved invaluable, and amassed to more than 1,000 items. In 1927 he founded the Archiv für Photogramme musikalischer Meister-Handschriften in the music section of the Austrian National Library in Vienna. He publ. *Joseph Haydn: Thematisch-bibliographisches Werkverzeichnis* (2 vols., Mainz, 1957, 1971), designating Haydn's works by H. or Hob. numbers. In 1974 the Austrian government purchased his private collection, which was officially opened at the Austrian National Library on Hoboken's 90th birthday (March 23, 1977). J. Schmidt-Görg ed. a Festschrift for his 75th birthday (Mainz, 1962).

Hobson, Ian, English pianist, conductor, and teacher; b. Wolverhampton, Aug. 7, 1952. He studied piano and organ at the Royal Academy of Music in London; then pursued academic studies at Magdalene College, Cambridge (B.A., 1972); subsequently studied piano with Claude Frank and harpsichord with Ralph Kirkpatrick at Yale Univ. (D.M.A., 1978). He made his London debut in 1979. In 1981 he won 1st prize in the Leeds International Pianoforte Competition. He made his U.S. debut in N.Y. in 1983. He has appeared as soloist with major orchs. of Europe and North America. In 1975 he joined the faculty of the Univ. of Ill.

Hoddinott, Alun, prominent Welsh composer and teacher; b. Bargoed, Aug. 11, 1929. He studied at Univ. College in Cardiff (B.A., 1949; Ph.D., 1960), and also had private instruction from Arthur Benjamin. After teaching at the Cardiff College of Music and Drama (1951–59), he was a lecturer (1959–65), reader (1965–67), and prof. (1967–87) of music at Univ. College. From 1966 to 1989 he served as artistic director of the Cardiff Festival of Twentieth Century Music. In 1957 he was awarded the Arnold Bax Medal and in 1983 he was made a Commander of the Order of the British Empire. Hoddinott's extensive output displays a notable command of various styles, ranging from the traditional to serial and aleatoric techniques.

WORKS: OPERAS: *The Beach of Falesá* (1973; Cardiff, March 26, 1974); *Murder, the Magician* (1975; Welsh TV, Feb. 11, 1976; stage version as *The Magician*, Cardiff, April 1976); *What the Old Man Does is Always Right* (1975; Fishguard, July 27, 1977); *The Rajah's Diamond* (television premiere, Nov. 24, 1979); *The Trumpet Major* (Manchester, April 1, 1981). **ORCH.:** 2 clarinet concertos: No. 1 for Clarinet and Strings (1950; BBC, March 15, 1951) and No. 2 for Clarinet and Orch. (Manchester, Feb. 20, 1987); *Fugal Overture* (1952; BBC, April 20, 1953); *Nocturne* (1952; BBC, Sept. 22, 1953); 9 syms.: No. 1 (1954–55; Pwillheli, Aug. 5, 1955), No. 2 (Cheltenham, July 11, 1962), No. 3 (Manchester, Dec. 5, 1968), No. 4 (Manchester, Dec. 4, 1969), No. 5 (1972; London, March 6, 1973), No. 6 (Cardiff, June 15, 1984), No. 7 for Organ and Orch. (Swansea, Oct. 17, 1989), No. 8 for Brass and Percussion (1992), and No. 9, *A Vision of Eternity,* for Brass and Orch, (1993); Concerto for Oboe and Strings (1955; Sheffield, Oct. 13, 1957); Harp Concerto (1957); Cheltenham, July 16, 1958); Concertino for Viola and Small Orch. (Llandaff, June 25, 1958); *4 Welsh Dances* (London, June 28, 1958), *Welsh Dances: 2nd Suite* (Merthyr, April 16, 1969), and *Welsh Dances: 3rd Suite* (1985); *2 Welsh Nursery Tunes* (1959; BBC, Jan. 22, 1961); *Nocturne and Dance* for Harp and Orch. (1959); 3 piano concertos: No. 1 for Piano, Winds, and Percussion (London, Feb. 22, 1960), No. 2 for Piano and Orch. (Cardiff, Aug. 5, 1960), and No. 3 for Piano and Orch. (Cheltenham, July 12, 1966); *Entry* (London, Nov. 22, 1960); Violin Concerto (Birmingham, March 30, 1961); *Folksong Suite* (1962); *Variations* (Newtown, Aug. 4, 1963; rev. 1964); *Sinfonia* for Strings (Birmingham, April 19, 1964); *Jack Straw*, overture (Aberystwyth, May 1, 1964); 2 concerti grossi: No. 1 (Caerphilly, June 11, 1965) and No. 2 (Ammanford, July 28, 1966); *Aubade and Scherzo* for Horn and Strings (1965; Cardiff, Oct. 24, 1966); *Pantomime*, overture (Croydon, July 16, 1966); *Variants* (London, Nov. 2, 1966); *Night Music* (1966; Aberystwyth, Jan. 30, 1967); Organ Concerto (Llandaff, June 19, 1967); 4 sinfoniettas: No. 1 (Cardiff, April 29, 1968), No. 2 (Cheltenham, July 4, 1969), No. 3 (Swansea, March 10, 1970), and No. 4 (Rhos, July 30, 1971); *Fioriture* (Aberdeen, Nov. 24, 1968); *Nocturnes and Cadenzas* for Cello and Orch. (Cardiff, Feb. 27, 1969); Horn Concerto (Llandaff, June 3, 1969); *Investiture Dances* (London, June 22, 1969); *Divertimento* for Small Orch. (Llandaff, Nov. 14, 1969); Suite (Southampton, April 16, 1970); *The Sun, the Great Luminary of the Universe* (Swansea, Oct. 8, 1970); Concertino for Trumpet, Horn, and Orch. (Llangefni, April 8, 1971); *The Hawk is Set Free* (Abergavenny, Sept. 21, 1972); *The Floore of Heav'n* (London, April 30, 1973); *Landscapes* (Criccieth, Aug. 8, 1975; rev. version, Cardiff, March 9, 1976); *Welsh Airs and Dances* for Symphonic Wind Band (Cardiff, Aug. 21, 1975); *French Suite* for Small Orch. (Cardiff, March 13, 1977); *Passagio* (Cheltenham, July 6, 1977); *The Heaventree of Stars* for Violin and Orch. (Cardiff, March 3, 1980); *Lanterne des Morts* (Cardiff, Sept. 21, 1981); *Quodlibet on Welsh Nursery Tunes* (1982; Cardiff, Jan. 9, 1983); *Doubles*, concertante for Oboe, Harpsichord, and Strings (St. David's Cathedral, June 3, 1982); *Hommage à Chopin* (1984); *Scenes and Interludes*, concertante for Trumpet, Harpsichord, and Strings (St. David's Cathedral, June 2, 1984); Concerto for Violin, Cello, Piano, and Orch. (Cheltenham, July 5, 1986); *Divisions*, concertante for Horn, Harpsichord, and Strings (Cardiff, July 2, 1986); *Concerto for Orchestra* (Cardiff, July 22, 1986); *Star Children* (London, Sept. 7, 1989); *Noctis Equi* for Cello and Orch. (London, Oct. 27, 1989). **CHAMBER:** String Trio (1949); Septet for Clarinet, Horn, Bassoon, Piano, Violin, Viola, and Cello (BBC, Dec. 8, 1956; rev. 1973); *Rondo scherzoso* for Trumpet or Trombone and Piano (1957); Sextet for Flute, Clarinet, Bassoon, Violin, Viola, and Cello (Llandaff, April 28, 1960); *Variations* for Flute, Harp, Clarinet, and String Quartet (1962); Fanfare for 3 Trumpets, 3 Trombones, and Drums (1963); *Divertimento* for Oboe, Clarinet, Horn, and Bassoon (1963); Harp Sonata (1964); 3 string quartets (1965, 1984, 1988); *Arabesque* for Violin and Piano (1966); Clarinet Sonata (1967); Suite for Harp (1967); 5 violin sonatas (1969, 1970, 1971, 1976, 1991); 2 cello sonatas (1970, 1977); 2 piano trios (1970, 1983); Horn Sonata (1971); Piano Quintet (1972); *Ritornelli* for Trombone, Winds, and Percussion (1974); *Indian Suite* for Recorder and Guitar (1977); *Scena* for String Quartet (1979); *Masks* for Oboe, Bassoon, and Piano (1983); *Bagatelles* for Oboe and Harp (1984); Sonata for 4 Clarinets (1985); *Chorales, Variants, and Fanfares* for Organ and Brass Quintet (1992); Quintet for Flute, Oboe, Clarinet, Horn, and Bassoon (1992). **KEYBOARD: PIANO:** 2 nocturnes (1956, 1959); 7 sonatas (1959, 1962, 1965, 1966, 1968, 1972, 1984). **ORGAN:** *Toccata alla giga* (1964); *Intrada* (1966); *Sarum Fanfare* (1970); *Passacaglia and Fugue*

(1985). **VOCAL:** *The Race of Adam*, masque for Soloists, Chorus, Boys' Voices, Orch., and Organ (Llandaff, June 23, 1961); *Job* for Bass, Chorus, and Orch. (Swansea, May 18, 1962; rev. 1977); *Dives and Lazarus*, cantata for Soloists, Chorus, and Orch. or Organ (Farnham, May 20, 1965); *Eryi* for Soloists, Chorus, and Orch. (Caernarvon, July 1, 1969); *Voyagers* for Baritone, Men's Voices, and Orch. (1970); *The Tree of Life*, oratorio for Soprano, Tenor, Chorus, and Orch. (Gloucester, Aug. 25, 1971); *St. Paul at Malta*, cantata for Tenor, Chorus, and Orch. (Stroud, Oct. 14, 1971); *Sinfonia fidei* for Soprano, Tenor, Chorus, and Orch. (Llandaff, June 18, 1977); *Te Deum* for Mixed Voices and Organ (Fishguard, July 29, 1981); *Bells of Paradise*, Christmas cantata for Baritone, Chorus, and Orch. (1984); *The Legend of St. Julian* for Narrator, Chorus, and Orch. (1987); *Emynau Pantycelyn* for Baritone, Chorus, and Orch. (1989); *Lines from Marlowe's Dr. Faustus* for Chorus and Brass (1989); *Songs of Exile* for Tenor and Orch. (1989); *May Song* for Children's Chorus and Orch. (1992); *Paradwys Mai* for Soprano, Piano, and String Quintet (1992); choruses; other songs.

BIBL.: B. Deane, *A. H.* (Cardiff, 1977); G. Lewis, "H. and the Symphony," *Musical Times* (Aug. 1989); S. Craggs, *A. H.: A Bio-Bibliography* (Westport, Conn., 1993).

Hodgson, Alfreda (Rose), English contralto; b. Morecombe, June 7, 1940; d. there, April 16, 1992. She received training at the Northern School of Music in Manchester. In 1961 she made her concert debut in Liverpool, followed by her first appearance in London (in 1963). In subsequent years, she appeared as a soloist with all of the principal British orchs.; her concert engagements abroad took her to Israel, the U.S., and Canada. She also appeared in opera, singing for the first time in London at the English National Opera in 1974 and at Covent Garden in 1983. Her concert repertoire ranged from Bach to Britten.

Hodkinson, Sydney P(hillip), Canadian-born American conductor, teacher, and composer; b. Winnipeg, Jan. 17, 1934. He studied composition with Louis Mennini and Bernard Rogers, and conducting with Paul White and Frederick Fennell at the Eastman School of Music in Rochester, N.Y. (M.Mus., 1958); after attending the Seminar in Advanced Musical Studies given by Carter, Sessions, and Babbitt at Princeton Univ. (1960), he studied conducting with Max Rudolf; completed his training in composition with Bassett, Castiglioni, Finney, and George B. Wilson at the Univ. of Mich. (D.M.A., 1968). From 1970 to 1972 he was music director of the St. Paul (Minn.) Chamber Orch.; concurrently served as artist-in-residence in Minneapolis-St. Paul. He taught at the Univ. of Virginia (1958–63), Ohio Univ. (1963–66), and the Univ. of Mich. (1968–73), where he conducted its Contemporary Directions Ensemble. In 1973 he joined the faculty of the Eastman School of Music, where he was also conductor of its Musica Nova Ensemble. From 1984 to 1986 he was a visiting prof. at Southern Methodist Univ. in Dallas. In 1971 he received an award from the American Academy and National Inst. of Arts and Letters; was granted 4 awards from the NEA (1976, 1978, 1980, 1984); in 1978–79 he held a Guggenheim fellowship. In his compositions, he explores modern techniques with pragmatic coherence.

WORKS: DRAMATIC: OPERAS: *The Swinish Cult* (1969–75); *The Wall* (1980); *In the Gallery* (1981); *Catsman* (1985). **OTHER:** *Lament*, fable with music for Guitar and 2 Lovers (1962); *Taiwa*, myth for Actors, Dancers, and Musicians (1965); *Vox Populous*, active oratorio for 2 Actors, Electronics Technician, 4 Vocal Soloists, and Chorus (1971–72). **ORCH.:** *Diversions* for Strings (1964); 6 syms., including: No. 1, *Fresco*, mural in 5 panels (1965–68; Buffalo, April 26, 1974), No. 3, *The Celestial Omnibus* (1975), No. 4, *Horae Canonica* for Soprano, Baritone, Narrator, 2 Choruses, and Orch. (1977–83), No. 5, *Sinfonia Concertante*, for Chamber Orch. (1980), and No. 6, *Sonata quasi una fantasia* (1982–83); *Caricatures* (1966; Dallas, April 5, 1969); *Stabile* (1970; Milwaukee, Feb. 6, 1972); *Valence* for Chamber Orch. (1970); *Epigrams* (1971); *Celestial Calendar* for Strings (1976); *The Edge of the Olde One*, chamber concerto (N.Y., May 13, 1977); *Bumberboom*, scherzo diabolique (Montreal, Nov. 9, 1982); *Burning Bell*, symphonic poem for Youth Orch. (1985). **WIND ENSEMBLE OR BAND:** *Litigo* for Winds and Percussion (1959); *Blocks* for Concert Band (1972); *Monolith: Megalith VI* for Wind Ensemble (1974); *Tower* for Concert Band (1974; Buffalo, N.Y., Dec. 12, 1976); *Cortège: Dirge-Canons* for Wind, Brass, and Percussion (1975); *Palisade: Megalith VIII* for Brass Ensemble and Percussion (1975); *Bach Variations* for Winds and Percussion (1977; Ann Arbor, Feb. 16, 1979); *Echo Preludes* for Brass Choir and Cello Obbligato (1983). **CHAMBER:** *Drawings: Set No. 1* for 4 Percussion (1960), *Set No. 3* for Clarinet and Drums (1961), *Set No. 4* for 3 Percussion (1961), *Set No. 6* for Violin, 2 Clarinets, and Bass Clarinet (1965), *Set No. 9* for 3 Percussion (1977), and *Set No. 10, Cerberus*, for 4 Tubas (1977); *Mosaic* for Brass Quintet (1964); *Armistice*, truce for Dancers and Musicians (1966); *Interplay*, histrionic controversy for 4 Musicians (1966; Montreal, July 17, 1967); String Quartet No. 1 for 5 Players (1967); *Dissolution of the Serial* for Piano and 1 Instrument, with Tape Excerpt (1967); *1 Man's Meat* for Double Bass and Electronic Tape (1970; Los Angeles, Feb. 9, 1972); Double Bass Sonata (1980); Sym. No. 2, *Symphonie fantastique*, for Organ, Brass, and Percussion (1974–82); String Trio, *Alla marcia* (1983); Sonata, *Das Lebewohl*, for Piano Trio (1984); *The Steps of Time*, elegy for Cello or Trombone, String Quartet, and Percussion (1984); *Trauermusik* for Trombone or Cello, Piano, and Percussion (1984); keyboard music. **VOCAL:** *Lengeren: Megalith V* for Medium Voice and Double Quintet (1973); *Daydream* for Chorus, Speaker, and Orch. (1974); *November Voices* for Voice, Speaker, and Small Instrumental Ensemble (1975); *Chansons de jadis: 6 Songs of Loneliness* for Voice and Orch. (1978–79); choruses; song cycles.

Hoelscher, Ludwig, noted German cellist; b. Solingen, Aug. 23, 1907; d. Tutzing, May 7, 1996. He studied cello in Leipzig with Julius Klengel and in Berlin with Hugo Becker. In 1930 he won the Mendelssohn Prize. In 1936 he became a prof. at the Berlin Hochschule für Musik; later gave master classes at the Mozarteum in Salzburg; subsequently was a prof. at the Stuttgart Hochschule für Musik from 1954. From 1931 he engaged in far-flung tours in Europe and in the Far East; gave duo-recitals with the pianist Elly Ney. A musician of great culture, Hoelscher arranged his programs covering both the classical and the modern literature, ranging from Bach to the works of Pfitzner, Krenek, Fortner, and Henze.

BIBL.: E. Valentin, *Cello, Das Instrument und sein Meister L. H.* (Pfullingen, 1955); M. Kaindl-Hönig, *L. H.* (Geneva, 1962); W.-E. von Lewinski, *L. H.* (Tutzing, 1967).

Hoelscher, Ulf, talented German violinist; b. Kitzingen, Jan. 17, 1942. After study with Bruno Masurat at the Heidelberg Cons., he received a grant which enabled him to go to America and enroll in the classes of Galamian at the Curtis Inst. of Music in Philadelphia and of Gingold at the Indiana Univ. School of Music in Bloomington. He then developed an international career, touring Europe, Australia, and the Far East, as well as the U.S. In 1981 he became a prof. at the Karlsruhe Hochschule für Musik. In 1987 he was appointed a prof. at the Berlin Hochschule der Künste. His repertoire is commendably large, encompassing works of the Baroque era, the Romantic school, and the contemporary avant-garde.

Hoerburger, Felix, German musicologist; b. Munich, Dec. 9, 1916. He studied composition at the Munich Academy of Music and musicology at the Univ. of Munich (Ph.D., 1941, with a diss. on the music of the Ungoni in East Africa), completing his Habilitation at the Univ. of Erlangen (1963, with a study of dance among Albanian Yugoslavs). He was organist and research assistant at the Music Research Inst. in Regensburg (1947–68) and at the Musicology Research Inst. of the Univ. of Erlangen (1968), where he later became lecturer (1970). He then was a prof. at the Univ. of Regensburg (from 1971). His extensive publications on folk music include studies of the music and dance of Bavaria, Turkey, the Balkans, Nepal, and Afghanistan.

WRITINGS: *Volkstanzkunde* (Kassel, 1961–64); *Musica vulgaris: Legengesetze der instrumentalen Volksmusik* (Erlangen, 1966); *Studien zur Musik in Nepal* (Regensburg, 1975).

Hoérée, Arthur (Charles Ernest), Belgian-French music critic, musicologist, and composer; b. St. Gilles, near Brussels, April 16, 1897; d. Paris, June 3, 1986. He received training in organ and theory at the Brussels Cons. (1908–12) and the Institut Musical in Anderlecht (1914–16); he pursued his education at the École Polytechnique in Brussels (1916–19), and concurrently studied with Henner (piano), De Bondt (organ), Moulaert (harmony and counterpoint), and Closson (music history). He subsequently completed his training in Paris with Gigout (organ), d'Indy (conducting), and Vidal (fugue and composition). He settled in Paris as a music critic; in 1950 he became a prof. at the École Normale Supérieure de Musique, in 1958 a prof. at the Centre de Formation Professionelle of the French Radio and Television, and in 1972 a prof. of musicology at the Sorbonne. He publ. the monograph *Albert Roussel* (Paris, 1938), the major biography *Roussel* (Paris, 1969), and *La Musique française au XXe siècle* (Paris, 1974). Among his works were ballets; various film and radio scores; *Pastorale et danse* for String Quartet (1923); Septet (1923); piano music; *Crève-Coeur, le Magicien* for Soloists, Chorus, and Orch. (1961).

Hoesslin, Franz von, German conductor and composer; b. Munich, Dec. 31, 1885; d. in an airplane crash in southern France, Sept. 28, 1946. He studied at the Univ. of Munich and with Mottl (conducting) and Reger (composition). He conducted in St. Gallen (1908–11), Riga (1912–14), Lübeck (1919–20), Mannheim (1920–22), and at the Berlin Volksoper (1922–23). After serving as Generalmusikdirektor in Dessau (1923–26), he conducted in Barmen-Elberfeld (1926–27), Bayreuth (1927–28), and Breslau (1932–35). After his wife, the singer Erna Liebenthal, was forced out of Nazi Germany, they settled in Switzerland. He composed orch. works, a Clarinet Quintet, and choral pieces.

Høffding, (Niels) Finn, Danish composer and pedagogue; b. Copenhagen, March 10, 1899. He studied violin with K. Sandby (1911–21), composition and harmony with Jeppesen (1918–21), organ with R. Rung-Keller (1919–21), and music history with Laub (1920–23) in Copenhagen; he also studied with Marx in Vienna (1921–22). He taught at the Royal Danish Cons. of Music in Copenhagen (1931–69), where he was its director (1954–69). His large output followed along post-Nielsen lines.

WORKS: OPERAS: *Kejserens nye Klaeder* (The Emperor's New Clothes; 1926; Copenhagen, Dec. 29, 1928); *Kilderejsen* (The Healing Spring; 1931; Copenhagen, Jan. 13, 1942); *Pasteur*, school opera (1935; Copenhagen, March 9, 1938). **ORCH.:** 4 syms.: No. 1, *Sinfonia impetuosa* (1923; Copenhagen, Aug. 22, 1925), No. 2, *Il Canto de Liberato*, for Soprano, Chorus, and Orch. (1924), No. 3 for 2 Pianos and Orch. (1928), and No. 4, *Sinfonia concertante*, for Chamber Orch. (1934); *Overture* for Small Orch. (1930); Concerto for Oboe and Strings (1933); *Fanfare* (1939); 4 symphonic fantasies: No. 1, *Evolution* (1939; Copenhagen, Sept. 4, 1940), No. 2, *Det er ganske vist* (It is Perfectly True; 1940; Copenhagen, March 6, 1944; as a pantomime, Copenhagen, July 1, 1948), No. 3, *Vår-Höst* (Spring-Autumn) for Baritone and Orch. (1944; Danish Radio, Jan. 24, 1946), and No. 4, *The Arsenal at Springfield*, for 3 Soloists, Chorus, and Orch. (1953; Danish Radio, Sept. 22, 1955); *Fire Minespil*, suite (1944); *Majfest* (1945); *Fantasia concertante* (Danish Radio, Copenhagen, April 1, 1965). **CHAMBER:** 2 string quartets (1920, 1925); 2 wind quintets (1940, 1954); Oboe Sonata (1943); piano pieces. **OTHER:** Various choral works, songs, and pieces for school performance.

BIBL.: S. Bruhns and D. Fog, *F. H.s Kompositionen* (Copenhagen, 1969).

Höffer, Paul, German composer and teacher; b. Barmen, Dec. 21, 1895; d. Berlin, Aug. 31, 1949. He studied with Georgii, Bölsche, and Abendroth at the Cologne Cons., and with Schreker at the Berlin Hochschule für Musik, where he joined the faculty as a piano instructor in 1923. From 1930 he taught composition and theory, and was made a prof. in 1933; in 1948 he became its director. He made use of polytonality and atonality in his compositions.

WORKS: DRAMATIC: OPERAS: *Borgia* (1931); *Der falsche Waldemar* (1934). **BALLET:** *Tanz um Liebe und Tod* (1939). **ORCH.:** *Sinfonische Ouvertüre* (1922); *Sinfonische Musik* (1922); Sym. (1926–27); *Sinfonie der grossen Stadt* (1937); *Symphonische Variationen über einen Bass von Bach* (1940); *Serenade* for Strings (1944); 2 piano concertos; Violin Concerto; Cello Concerto; Concerto for Oboe and Strings. **CHAMBER:** Wind Sextet; Piano Quintet; Wind Quintet; 3 string quartets; 2 piano trios; String Trio; Trio Sonata for Flute, Viola, and Piano; 2 sonatas for Solo Violin; much piano music. **VOCAL:** 4 oratorios: *Der reiche Tag* (1938), *Vom edlen Leben* (1942), *Mysterium Liebe* (1943), and *Die letzte Stunde* (1945–47); cantatas; choruses; songs.

BIBL.: H. Tiessen, "Erinnerung an P. H.," *Musica*, X (1956).

Höffgen, Marga, German contralto; b. Mülheim an der Ruhr, April 26, 1921; d. Müllheim, Baden, July 7, 1995. She studied at the Berlin Hochschule für Musik and with Hermann Weissenborn. She made her concert debut in Berlin in 1952; in 1953 she made a highly successful appearance in Vienna as a soloist in the *St. Matthew Passion* conducted by Karajan; she then was active as a concert singer in Europe; also appeared in opera at Covent Garden in London, at the Vienna State Opera, and at the Bayreuth Festival.

Hoffman, Grace (actually, **Goldie**), American mezzo-soprano; b. Cleveland, Jan. 14, 1925. She was educated at Western Reserve Univ. in Cleveland; then studied voice with Schorr in N.Y. and Basiola in Milan. After appearances in the U.S., she sang in Florence and Zürich; in 1955 she became a member of the Württemberg State Theater in Stuttgart. On March 27, 1958, she made her Metropolitan Opera debut in N.Y. as Brangäne in *Tristan und Isolde*. She made many appearances at La Scala in Milan, Covent Garden in London, Bayreuth, and the Vienna State Opera. In 1978 she became a prof. of voice at the Hochschule für Musik in Stuttgart. She was noted for her performances of the music of Wagner and Verdi, particularly for her roles of Brangäne, Kundry, and Eboli; also sang widely in concerts.

Hoffman, Irwin, American conductor; b. N.Y., Nov. 26, 1924. He studied violin at the Juilliard School of Music in N.Y. From 1952 to 1964 he was music director of the Vancouver (B.C.) Sym. Orch. He was assoc. conductor of the Chicago Sym. Orch. (1964–70), serving as its acting music director (1968–69). In 1968 he was made music director of the Florida Gulf Coast Sym. Orch., which post he retained when it became the Florida Orch. in 1984; after stepping down in 1987, he was made its music director laureate. From 1972 to 1976 he was also chief conductor of the Orchestre Symphonique de la RTBF (Belgian Radio and Television) in Brussels. In 1987 he was appointed music director of the Orquesta Sinfónica Nacional of Costa Rica in San José.

Hoffmann, Bruno, German glass harmonica player and composer; b. Stuttgart, Sept. 15, 1913; d. there, April 11, 1991. He studied piano, organ, and voice. In 1929 he became interested in building a modern "glass harp" and eventually expanded its range to 4 octaves, covering a full chromatic scale. With this instrument, he gave concert tours in Europe (from 1949), Asia (from 1962), the U.S. and Canada (from 1964), and South America (from 1969); he also composed a number of works for the glass harp.

Hoffmann, Hans, German conductor and musicologist; b. Neustadt, Silesia, Jan. 26, 1902; d. Bielefeld, Aug. 8, 1949. He studied musicology at the Univ. of Breslau, and later in Leipzig, Berlin, and Kiel. Concurrently he took instruction in singing and for several years sang in oratorio performances in Germany. In 1933 he became a choral conductor in Hamburg, and taught theory at the Univ. of Hamburg. He was also active as a sym. and opera conductor, and in 1940 was appointed music director of the Bielefeld Opera. Among his publications were *Heinrich Schütz und Johann Sebastian Bach: Zwei Tonsprachen und ihre Bedeutung für die Aufführungspraxis* (Kassel, 1940) and *Vom Wesen der zeitgenössischen Kirchenmusik* (Kassel, 1949).

Hoffmann, Richard, Austrian-born American composer and teacher; b. Vienna, April 20, 1925. He studied at the Univ. of New Zealand (B.Mus.) before emigrating to the U.S. in 1947 and becoming a naturalized American citizen in 1964; he studied musicology at the Univ. of Calif. at Los Angeles (1949–51) and composition with Schoenberg, serving as his assistant and secretary (1948–51). In 1951–52 he taught at the Univ. of Calif. at Los Angeles, and then at Oberlin (Ohio) College (from 1954). He was an ed. of the complete works of Schoenberg. In 1970 and 1977 he held Guggenheim fellowships. He developed a sui generis serial technique, in which intervals, meters, rhythms, timbres, and dynamics are systematically organized, while the tone row is not necessarily dodecaphonic; he also utilized computer-generated sounds in some of his works.

WORKS: ORCH.: *Prelude and Double Fugue* for Strings (1944); Violin Concerto (1948); 2 pieces (1952, 1961); Piano Concerto (1953–54); Cello Concerto (1956–59); *Music* for Strings (1970–71); *Souffler* (1975–76); *Intravolatura* for Strings and Percussion (1980). **CHAMBER:** 4 string quartets (1947; 1950; 1972–74; 1977, with computer-generated sounds); Trio for Piano, Violin, and Bass Clarinet (1948); Duo for Piano and Violin (1949; rev. 1965); Duo for Violin and Cello (1949); Tripartita for Violin (1950); Piano Quartet (1950); String Trio (1963); *Decadanse* for 10 Players (1972); *Changes* for 2 Chimes (1974). **KEYBOARD: PIANO:** Sonata (1945–46); *3 Small Pieces* (1947); 2 sets of variations (1951, 1957); Sonatina (1952). **ORGAN:** *Fantasy and Fugue* (1951). **COMPUTER-GENERATED TAPE:** *In memorium patris* (1976).

Hoffmeister, Karel, Czech pianist, pedagogue, and writer on music; b. Liblice, Sept. 26, 1868; d. Hluboká, Sept. 23, 1952. He studied piano with Jindřich Kàan, and later attended Hostinský's lectures at the Univ. of Prague and graduated from the Prague Organ School. After teaching piano in Laibach (1891–98), he was made assistant lecturer (1898) and then prof. (1902) at the Prague Cons.; from 1919, gave master classes there. With K. Stecker, he was co-ed. of *Hudební revue* (1908–18). As a pianist, Hoffmeister was a fine chamber music player, being the founder of the Czech Trio.

WRITINGS (all publ. in Prague): *Bedrich Smetana* (1915; 2nd ed., abr., 1917); *Klavir* (1923; 2nd ed., 1939); *Antonín Dvořák* (1924; Eng. tr., 1928); *Josef Klička* (1944); *Tvorba Vitězslava Nováka z let 1941–8* (The Works of Vitězslav Novák Between 1941–8; 1949); *50 let s Vitězslavem Novákem* (50 Years with Vitězslav Novák; 1949); *Vývoj klavirní virtuosity* (The Development of Piano Virtuosity; n.d.).

BIBL.: O. Kredba, *K. H.: Obraz života a dila* (K. H.: A Picture of Life and Works; Prague, 1948); idem, "Za K. H.," *Hudební Rozhledy*, V (1952).

Hofman, Shlomo, Polish-Israeli composer and musicologist; b. Warsaw, April 24, 1909. He studied at the Warsaw Cons., graduating in 1934; then went to Paris, where he studied composition with Roger-Ducasse, Koechlin, and Milhaud (1937–38). He subsequently settled in Palestine; in 1954 he became a lecturer in musicology at the Academy of Music in Tel Aviv. Among his works were an Oboe Concerto (1950), Hebrew cantata, *Tawashih* (1960), and Quintet for Clarinet and Strings (1945). He publ. a valuable thesis, *L'Oeuvre de clavecin de François Couperin le Grand* (Paris, 1961); also a polyglot *Dictionary of Musical Terms* (Jerusalem, 1955), *The Music of Israel* (1959), and *La Musique arabe en Israel* (1963).

Hofmann, Josef (Casimir) (actually, **Józef Kazimierz**), celebrated Polish-born American pianist; b. Podgorze, near Kraków, Jan. 20, 1876; d. Los Angeles, Feb. 16, 1957. His father was the Polish pianist, conductor, and composer Casimir (Kazimierz) Hofmann (b. Kraków, 1842; d. Berlin, July 6, 1911). At the age of 4, he began to play the piano, tutored by an older sister and an aunt; at 5, he began taking regular lessons from his father. He was barely 6 when he first appeared in public in Ciechocinek; at the age of 10, he played Beethoven's Concerto No. 1 with the Berlin Phil. under Hans von Bülow. He also made a tour of Scandinavia; played in France and England; his concerts as a child prodigy became a European sensation; soon an American offer of a concert tour came from the impresarios Abbey, Schoeffel & Grau. On Nov. 29, 1887, Hofmann appeared at the Metropolitan Opera House as soloist in Beethoven's Concerto No. 1; he also played works by Chopin and some of his own little pieces. He electrified the audience, and hardheaded critics hailed his performance as a marvel. He appeared throughout the U.S., giving 42 concerts in all; then agitation was started by the Soc. for the Prevention of Cruelty to Children against the exploitation of his talent. Alfred Corning Clark of N.Y. offered $50,000 to the family for his continued education. The offer was accepted, and he began serious study with Moszkowski (piano) and Urban (composition) in Berlin. Then Anton Rubinstein accepted him as a pupil in Dresden, where Hofmann traveled twice a week for piano lessons. At the age of 18, he resumed his career, giving recitals in Dresden and elsewhere in Germany with enormous success; made his first tour of Russia in 1896, attaining huge popularity there; he reappeared in Russia frequently. In 1898 he again played in the U.S.; from then on, he appeared in American cities almost every year. At the peak of his career, he came to be regarded as one of the greatest pianists of the century. He possessed the secret of the singing tone, which enabled him to interpret Chopin with extraordinary delicacy and intimacy. He was also capable of summoning tremendous power playing Liszt and other works of the virtuoso school. His technique knew no difficulties; but in his interpretations, he subordinated technical effects to the larger design of the work. When the Curtis Inst. of Music was founded in Philadelphia (1924), Hofmann was engaged to head the piano dept.; he was director from 1926 to 1938. He became a naturalized American citizen in 1926. On Nov. 28, 1937, his golden jubilee in the U.S. was celebrated with a concert at the Metropolitan Opera in N.Y. He performed the D-minor Concerto of Anton Rubinstein, and his own *Chromaticon* for Piano and Orch. From 1938 to his death he lived mostly in California, his concert career coming sadly to a close in 1945 owing to alcoholism. Hofmann was also a composer, under the pen name Michel Dvorsky (a transliteration of the literal translation into Polish of his German name, meaning "courtyard man"). Among his works are several piano concertos; some symphonic works; *Chromaticon* for Piano and Orch. (Cincinnati, Nov. 24, 1916, composer soloist); numerous piano pieces. He also publ. a practical manual, *Piano-Playing with Piano-Questions Answered* (1915).

Hofmann, Peter, outstanding German tenor; b. Marienbad, Aug. 12, 1944. He studied at the Hochschule für Musik in Karlsruhe. He made his operatic debut in 1972 in Lübeck as Tamino; in 1973 he joined the Württemberg State Theater in Stuttgart. He came to prominence in his performance of the role of Siegmund in the centennial Bayreuth productions of *Der Ring des Nibelungen* (1976); that same year, he made his first appearance at London's Covent Garden in the same role. He made his U.S. debut as Siegmund with the San Francisco Opera in 1977; sang Lohengrin on Jan. 24, 1980, at his Metropolitan Opera debut in N.Y. In 1986 he sang Tristan at the Bayreuth Festival. His other roles included Max, Florestan, Alfred in *Die Fledermaus*, Loge, and Bacchus.

BIBL.: M. Müller, *P. H.: Singen ist wie Fliegen* (Bonn, 1983).

Hogwood, Christopher (Jarvis Haley), prominent English harpsichordist, conductor, and musicologist; b. Nottingham, Sept. 10, 1941. He studied classics as well as music at Pembroke College, Cambridge (B.A., 1964); received instruction in harpsichord from Puyana and Leonhardt, and also took courses at the Charles Univ. and the Academy of Music in Prague. In

1967 he joined David Munrow in organizing the Early Music Consort, an ensemble devoted to the performance of medieval music. In 1973 he founded the Academy of Ancient Music with the aim of performing music of the Baroque and early Classical periods on original instruments; he toured widely with the ensemble and made many recordings with it, including a complete set of Mozart's syms. utilizing instruments of Mozart's time. He also served as artistic director of the Handel and Haydn Soc. of Boston (from 1986) and music director of the St. Paul (Minn.) Chamber Orch. (1988–92), subsequently serving as principal guest conductor of the latter (from 1992). He also was the International Prof. of Early Music Performance at the Royal Academy of Music in London (from 1992) and a visiting prof. at King's College, London (from 1992). His guest conducting engagements took him all over Europe and North America. In 1989 he was made a Commander of the Order of the British Empire. He ed. works by J.C. Bach, Purcell, and Croft; was a contributor to *The New Grove Dictionary of Music and Musicians* (1980). He publ., in London, *Music at Court* (1977), *The Trio Sonata* (1979), and *Handel* (1984).

Hoiby, Lee, talented American composer and pianist; b. Madison, Wis., Feb. 17, 1926. He began piano study at age 5, and while attending high school received instruction from Gunnar Johansen; then studied at the Univ. of Wisc. (B.A., 1947); attended Petri's master class in Ithaca, N.Y. (1944), and at Mills College in Oakland, California (M.A., 1952), where he also studied composition with Milhaud; he also received instruction in composition from Menotti at the Curtis Inst. of Music in Philadelphia. He received a Fulbright fellowship (1953), an award from the National Inst. of Arts and Letters (1957), and a Guggenheim fellowship (1958). In addition to his career as a composer, he appeared as a concert pianist; made his N.Y. recital debut on Jan. 17, 1978. He has composed a number of highly successful vocal and instrumental works, being particularly adept in writing operas in a manner reminiscent of Menotti—concise, dramatic, and aurally pleasing, and sometimes stimulating.

WORKS: DRAMATIC: OPERAS: *The Scarf*, after Chekhov (Spoleto, June 20, 1958); *Beatrice*, after Maeterlinck (Louisville, Oct. 23, 1959; withdrawn); *Natalia Petrovna*, after Turgenev (N.Y., Oct. 8, 1964; rev. version as *A Month in the Country*, Boston, Jan. 1981); *Summer and Smoke*, after Tennessee Williams (1970; St. Paul, Minn., June 19, 1971); *Something New for the Zoo* (1979; Cheverly, Md., May 17, 1982); *The Tempest*, after Shakespeare (1982–86; Indianola, Iowa, June 21, 1986); *This is the Rill Speaking* (1993); also *The Italian Lesson*, monodrama for Mezzo-soprano and Chamber Orch. (1980; Newport, R.I., 1982); incidental music to various plays. **BALLETS:** *Hearts, Meadows, and Flags* (1950); *After Eden* (1966); *Landscape* (1968). **ORCH.:** *Pastoral Dances* for Flute and Small Orch. (New Orleans, Nov. 6, 1956); 2nd Suite (1953); 2 piano concertos (1958, 1979); *Design* for Strings (1965); *Music for a Celebration*, overture (1975). **CHAMBER:** Violin Sonata (1951; rev. 1980); *Diversions* for Woodwind Quartet (1953); Piano Quintet (1974); *Serenade* for Violin and Piano (Washington, D.C., Nov. 4, 1988); piano pieces. **VOCAL:** *A Hymn of the Nativity* for Soprano, Baritone, Chorus, and Orch. (1960); *The Tides of Sleep*, symphonic song for Low Voice and Orch., after Thomas Wolfe (1961); *Galileo Galilei*, oratorio for Soloists, Chorus, and Orch. (1975); *Psalm 93* for Large Chorus, Organ, Brass, and Percussion (Cathedral of St. John the Divine, N.Y., May 17, 1985); *I Was There*, 5 songs for Baritone and Orch., after Whitman (1995).

Hokanson, Leonard (Ray), American pianist and teacher; b. Vinalhaven, Maine, Aug. 13, 1931. He received training in piano from Hedwig Rosenthal (1947–48), Artur Schnabel (1948–51), Karl Ulrich Schnabel (1951–53), and Claude Frank (1952–55); pursued his academic studies at Clark College (B.A., 1952) and Bennington College (M.A., 1954). In 1949 he made his debut as soloist with the Philadelphia Orch., and subsequently toured internationally as a soloist with orchs., as a recitalist, as a chamber music player, and as an accompanist. He was a prof. at the Frankfurt am Main Hochschule für Musik (1976–78) and at the Indiana Univ. School of Music in Bloomington (from 1986).

Holbrooke, Joseph (actually, **Josef Charles**), English composer; b. Croydon, July 5, 1878; d. London, Aug. 5, 1958. He was a student of Corder (composition) and Westlake (piano) at the Royal Academy of Music in London. He then worked as a conductor and pianist. The success of his symphonic poem *The Raven* (1900) encouraged him to write a large body of music along Romantic lines. His most ambitious work was the operatic trilogy *The Cauldron of Annwn* (1909–29). Holbrooke's initial success as a composer was not sustained. Especially in his early years he was a trenchant critic of the musical establishment. He was the author of *Contemporary British Composers* (London, 1925).

WORKS: DRAMATIC: *Pierrot and Pierrette*, lyric drama (London, Nov. 11, 1909; rev. version as *The Stranger*, Liverpool, Oct. 1924); *The Cauldron of Annwn*, operatic trilogy: 1, *The Children of Don* (London, June 15, 1912); 2, *Dylan: Son of the Wave* (1909; London, July 4, 1914); and 3, *Bronwen* (Huddersfield, Feb. 1, 1929); *The Red Mask*, ballet ; *The Moth and the Flame*, ballet; *The Enchanter*, opera-ballet (Chicago, 1915); *Coromanthe*, ballet; *The Sailor's Arms*, comic opera; *The Snob*, comic opera; *Aucassin et Nicolette*, ballet. **ORCH.:** 4 symphonic poems: *The Raven* (1900), *Ulalume* (1901–03), *The Viking* (1904), and *The Birds of Rhiannon* (1925); 1 unnumbered Piano Concerto (1896–1900); 2 numbered piano concertos: No. 1, *The Song of Gwynn ap Nudd* (1907) and No. 2, *L'orient* (1928); *The New Renaissance*, overture (1903); *Apollo and the Seaman* (1907); Violin Concerto, *The Grasshopper* (1917); 8 syms., including No. 3, *Ships* (1925), and No. 4, *Homage to Schubert* (1929); Cello Concerto, *Cambrian* (1936); *Tamerlaine*, concerto for Clarinet or Saxophone, Bassoon, and Orch. (1939); Sinfonietta for Chamber Orch.; military band music. **CHAMBER:** 6 string quartets (1896; *Belgium-Russia*, 1915; *The Pickwick Club*, 1916; nos. 4–6, 1918–19); Piano Quartet, *Byron* (1902); String Sextet, *Al Aaraaf* (1902); 2 clarinet quintets (c.1903; *Fate, or Ligeia*, 1910); Fantasie Sonata for Cello and Piano (1904); Piano Quintet (1904); Quartet for Violin, Viola, Clarinet, and Piano (1905); 2 sextets for Piano and Strings (*In memoriam*, 1905; 1906); Fantasie String Quartet (1906); Sextet, *Israfel*, for Piano and Winds (1906); 3 violin sonatas; Woodwind Quartet; Saxophone Sonata; Quartet for Flute, Viola, Cello, and Harp; Quintet for Winds and Piano; Quintet for Flute, Oboe, Violin, Cello, and Harp; piano pieces, including 2 sonatas. **VOCAL:** Chorus and Orch.: *Ode to Victory* (1901); *Queen Mab* (1902); *The Bells* (1903); *Byron* (1906); also *Homage to E.A. Poe*, dramatic choral sym. (1908), and numerous songs.

BIBL.: G. Lowe, *J. H. and his Work* (London, 1920); *J. H.: Various Appreciations by Many Authors* (London, 1937); P. Washtell, "The Operas of J. H.," *British Opera in Retrospect* (n.p., 1986).

Holde, Artur, German-American choral conductor and music critic; b. Rendsburg, Oct. 16, 1885; d. N.Y., June 23, 1962. He studied musicology at the Univ. of Berlin. From 1910 to 1936 he was music director of the Frankfurt am Main Synagogue; also was active as a music critic. In 1937 he emigrated to the U.S.; was choirmaster at the Hebrew Tabernacle in N.Y. (1937–43) and music critic of the German periodical *Aufbau* in N.Y. He publ. *Jews in Music* (N.Y., 1959) and *A Treasury of Great Operas* (N.Y., 1965); also contributed articles to the *Musical Quarterly* and other American publications.

Holewa, Hans, Austrian-born Swedish composer; b. Vienna, May 26, 1905; d. Bromma, April 24, 1991. He studied conducting at the New Cons. of Music in Vienna, and piano and theory with J. Heinz. In 1937 he settled in Stockholm as a pianist and pedagogue; there he introduced Schoenberg's 12-tone technique. From 1949 to 1970 he worked in the music library of the Swedish Broadcasting Corp.

WORKS: OPERA: *Apollos förvandling* (1967–71). **ORCH.:**

Vier kleine Märsche (1940); *Variations* for Piano and Orch. (1943); 6 syms.: No. 1 (1948), No. 2 (1976; Stockholm, April 28, 1978), No. 3 for Textless Soprano and Orch. (1977; Stockholm, Oct. 17, 1979), No. 4 (1980; Stockholm, June 7, 1984), No. 5 (1983; Västerås, Nov. 15, 1984), and No. 6 (1985–86; Stockholm, April 8, 1988); Violin Concerto (1963; Swedish Radio, Feb. 7, 1965); *Komposition* (1965–66; Swedish Radio, Oct. 8, 1966); *Quattro cadenze* for Cello and Orch. (1968; Swedish Radio, April 12, 1970); *Movimento espressivo* (Stockholm, April 17, 1971); 3 piano concertos: No. 1 (1972; Swedish Radio, April 28, 1973), No. 2 (1980–81; Swedish Radio, Feb. 11, 1983), and No. 3 (1984–85; Swedish Radio, Jan. 30, 1987); Concerto for 2 Pianos and Strings (1975; Uppsala, April 8, 1976). **CHAMBER:** 2 string quartets (1939, 1965); Sonata for Solo Cello (1952); Trio for Violin, Viola, and Cello (1959); 9 concertinos (1960–87); Sonata for Solo Violin (1960); Quintet for Clarinet, Trombone, Cello, Percussion, and Piano (1962); *Chamber Music* No. 1 (1964), No. 2 (1973), and No. 3 (1981) for Cello and Piano; Chamber Concerto for Viola and 11 Strings (1966); *Lamenti*, 3 pieces for Horn, Alto Saxophone, and Bassoon (1976); Quartet for Oboe, Violin, Viola, and Cello (1979); Octet for Clarinet, Horn, Bassoon, 2 Violins, Viola, Cello, and Double Bass (1982); Wind Quintet (1982); *Sonata Movement* for String Quartet (1984); Trio for Clarinet, Cello, and Piano (1984); Violin Sonata (1985); Trio for Violin, Viola, and Cello (1986); Quartet for Flute, Oboe, Cello, and Piano (1988); also numerous piano pieces. **VOCAL:** Choral works; songs.

Holguín, Guillermo. See **Uribe-Holguín, Guillermo.**

Hollaender, Gustav, German violinist, pedagogue, and composer, brother of **Viktor Hollaender;** b. Leobschütz, Silesia, Feb. 15, 1855; d. Berlin, Dec. 4, 1915. He studied violin with his father, and then with David at the Leipzig Cons.; later he was a student of Joachim (violin) and Kiel (composition) at the Berlin Hochschule für Musik. He began his concert career at age 20; after serving as concertmaster of the Gürzenich Orch. and as a teacher at the Cons. in Cologne (1881–84), he settled in Berlin as a royal chamber musician of the court opera orch. in 1884; he was head of the violin dept. at the Kullak Academy (from 1885), and then was director of the Stern Cons. (from 1894). He wrote principally solo violin pieces, in an effective virtuoso style. Among his other works were 3 violin concertos, cello pieces, and vocal duets.

Hollaender, Viktor, German conductor and composer, brother of **Gustav Hollaender;** b. Leobschütz, Silesia, April 20, 1866; d. Los Angeles, Oct. 24, 1940. After training in Berlin with Kullak, he was a theater conductor in Hamburg, Milwaukee (1890), Berlin, Chicago, and London (1894–1901). Returning to Berlin, he was musical director at the Metropoltheater (1901–08) and the Thalia-Theater (1908–09), where he brought out various revues. His more ambitious light theater scores included *San Lin* (Breslau, Jan 28, 1898), *Der rote Kosak* (Berlin, Dec. 21, 1901), *Der Sonnenvogel* or *Der Phönix* (St. Petersburg, Aug. 22, 1903), *Die schöne vom Strand* (Berlin, Feb. 5, 1915), and *Die Prinzessin vom Nil* (Berlin, Sept. 18, 1915). He had his finest success with the incidental music he composed for the pantomime *Sumurun* (Berlin, 1910). In 1934 he emigrated to the U.S. His son, Friedrich Hollaender (b. London, Oct. 18, 1896; d. Munich, Jan. 18, 1976), was a composer. He was a student at the Berlin Hochschule für Musik and of Humperdinck. After composing revues, operettas, and other light theater scores, he became best known as a composer of film scores. Among his finest film scores were *Der blaue Engel* (1930), *Die grosse Sehnsucht* (1930), *One Hundred Men and a Girl* (1937), *Destry Rides Again* (1939), *The Man Who Came to Dinner* (1942), and *Das Spukschloss im Spessart* (1962). His autobiography appeared as *Von Kopf bis Fuss, mein Leben mit Text und Musik* (Munich, 1965).

Holland, Charles, black American tenor; b. Norfolk, Va., Dec. 27, 1909; d. Amsterdam, Nov. 7, 1987. He studied with May Hamaker Henley, Georges Le Pyre in Los Angeles, and Clyde Burrows in N.Y. He sang with the bands of Benny Carter and Fletcher Henderson, appeared in the film *Hullabaloo* (1941), and had his own concert program on NBC radio. In 1949 he settled in France, where he appeared on radio and television; made his European operatic debut in *Die Zauberflöte* at the Paris Opéra in 1954, and in 1955 he became the first black artist to sing at the Paris Opéra-Comique. He later sang throughout Europe, Australia, New Zealand, and Canada, making his N.Y. debut in a recital at Carnegie Hall in 1982.

Holland, Dulcie (Sybil), Australian pianist and composer; b. Sydney, Jan. 5, 1913. She studied at the Sydney Cons. with Alfred Hill, Frank Hutchens, and Roy Agnew. She then went to London, where she took courses with John Ireland at the Royal College of Music. Returning to Australia, she was active as a pianist and composer. Among her works were a *Symphony for Pleasure* (1974), some theater music, and songs for children. She also publ. several school manuals.

Holland, Theodore (Samuel), English composer and teacher; b. London, April 25, 1878; d. there, Oct. 29, 1947. He studied with F. Corder at the Royal Academy of Music in London and with Joachim at the Hochschule für Musik in Berlin. In 1927 he became prof. of composition at the Royal Academy of Music. He was an estimable composer, particularly proficient in writing for the theater. Among his works were a children's operetta, *King Goldemar*, a musical play, *Santa Claus*; *Evening on a Lake* for Chamber Orch. (1924); *Cortège* for an Ensemble of Cellos (1939); *Spring Sinfonietta* (1943); 2 string quartets; 2 piano trios; Suite for Viola and Piano; several song cycles.

Hollander, Lorin, talented American pianist; b. N.Y., July 19, 1944. He began his training with his father, a violinist; he then was a student of Steuermann (piano) and Giannini (composition) at the Juilliard School of Music in N.Y., and he also had instruction from Max Rudolf, Leon Fleisher, and Olga Stroumillo. He was only 11 when he made his Carnegie Hall debut in N.Y., and soon began appearing throughout the U.S. After his first tour of Europe in 1965, he performed with many of the leading orchs. around the world. As an advocate of musical outreach, he also played in such non-traditional settings as hospitals, nursing homes, and prisons. Hollander's extraordinary technique has been displayed in a virtuoso repertoire ranging from the masters of the past to the contemporary era.

Höller, Karl, German composer and teacher; b. Bamberg, July 25, 1907; d. Hausham, April 14, 1987. He received training in piano, organ, and cello in Bamberg; he then was a student of Zilcher (composition) at the Würzburg Cons. and of Haas and Waltershausen (composition), Gatscher (organ), and Hausegger (conducting) at the Munich Academy of Music; he also took courses with Sandberger at the Univ. of Munich. After teaching at the Munich Academy of Music (1933–37) and the Frankfurt am Main Hochschule für Musik (1937–46), he taught a master class in composition at the Munich Hochschule für Musik (1949–72), where he also served as its president (1954–72). His compositional style owed much to late Romanticism.

WORKS: ORCH.: Organ Concerto (1930; rev. 1966); *Hymnen über gregorianische Choral-melodien* (1932–34); Chamber Concerto for Harpsichord and Small Orch. (1934; rev. 1958); *Symphonische Phantasie über Thema von Frescobaldi* (1935; rev. 1965); 2 violin concertos (1938, rev. 1964; 1947–48); *Passacaglia und Fuge* (1939); *Heroische Musik* (1940); 2 cello concertos (1940–41; 1949); 2 syms. (1942–46; 1973); *Sweelinck-Variationen "Mein junges Lebe hat ein End"* (1950–51); Piano Concerto (1973). **CHAMBER:** 8 violin sonatas (1929, rev. 1968; 1942; 1943; 1944; 1945; 1946; 1947; 1949); Piano Quartet (1930; rev. 1955); 6 string quartets (1938, rev. 1966; 1945; 1947; 1947; 1948; 1949); Cello Sonata (1943; also for Viola and Clarinet, 1967); Piano Trio (1944; also for Harp, Violin, and Cello, 1966); Trio Sonata (1946; also as Concerto Grosso for 2 Violins and Piano, 1965); 2 flute sonatas (1947, 1948); Viola Sonata, *"in memoriam Paul Hindemith"* (1967). **PIANO:** *Zwei leine Sonaten* for Piano, 4 Hands (1943); 3 small sonatas (1946);

Tessiner Klavierbuch (1961). **VOCAL:** *Missa brevis* (1929); *Weihnachts- und Passionmusik* (1932); *Requiem* (1932); *Tenebrae factae*, Good Friday motet (1937).

Höller, York (Georg), German composer; b. Leverkusen, Jan. 11, 1944. He studied composition with Zimmermann and Eimert, piano with Alfons Kontarsky, conducting, and music education (diploma, 1967) at the Cologne Hochschule für Musik. He also took courses in musicology and philosophy at the Univ. of Cologne, and attended Boulez's analysis sessions at the summer course in new music in Darmstadt (1965). In 1971–72 he was active at the WDR Electronic Music Studio in Cologne. In 1974–75 he was in residence at the Cité Internationale des Arts in Paris. From 1976 to 1989 he taught analysis and theory at the Cologne Hochschule für Musik. His *Antiphon* for String Quartet was commissioned for the opening of the Centre Pompidou in Paris in 1977. In 1978 he realized his *Arcus* at IRCAM in Paris, which was commissioned for the opening of its Espace de Projection. The score was subsequently performed on both sides of the Atlantic by the Ensemble Inter-Contemporain. In 1979 he received the Bernd Alois Zimmermann Prize of Cologne. In 1984–85 he was in residence at the Villa Massimo in Rome. He was named Chevalier dans l'Ordre des Arts et des Lettres of France in 1986. The International Composer's Forum of UNESCO awarded him its prize for his 2nd Piano Concerto in 1987. In 1990 he became director of the WDR Electronic Music Studio. In his oeuvre, Höller has effectively utilized both traditional and electronic modes of expression.

WORKS: OPERAS: *Der Meister und Margarita* (1984–89; Paris, May 20, 1989); *Caligula* (1992). **ORCH.:** *Topic* (1967); 2 pianos concertos: No. 1 (1970) and No. 2 (1983–84; London, Dec. 3, 1985); *Chroma* for Orch., Organ, and Live Electronics (1972–74); *Arcus* for Chamber Orch. and Tape (1978); *Mythos* for Chamber Orch. and Electronic Tape (1979); *Umbra* for Orch. and Tape (1979–80); *Résonance* for Orch. and Computer Sounds on Tape (1981); *Schwarze Halbinseln* for Orch. and Electronic Tape (1982); *Magische Klanggestalt* (1984; Hamburg, March 16, 1986); *Improvisation sur le nom de Pierre Boulez* for 16 Instruments (1984–85; Baden-Baden, March 31, 1985); *Fanal* for Trumpet and Orch. (1989–90; Paris, June 17, 1991); *Pensées*, Requiem for Piano, Orch., and Electronics (1990–91; Cologne, June 11, 1993); *Aura* (1991–92). **CHAMBER:** *Drei Stücke* for String Quartet (1966); Sonata for Solo Cello (1968–69); *Epitaph (for Jan Palach)* for Violin and Piano (1969); *Tangens* for Cello, Electric Guitar, Electric Organ or Piano, and 2 Synthesizers (1973); *Klanggitter* for Cello, Piano, Synthesizer, and Tape (1975–76); *Antiphon* for String Quartet and Tape (1976–77); *Moments musicaux* for Flute and Piano (1979); *Pas de trois* for Violin, Cello, and Double Bass (1982); *Pas de deux* for Cello and Piano (Cologne, June 19, 1993); *Tagträume* for Piano Trio (1994). **PIANO:** *Fünf Klavierstücke* (1964); *Diaphonie: Hommage à Béla Bartók* for 2 Pianos (1965; rev. 1974; Cologne, Feb. 26, 1984); 2 sonatas: No. 1, *Sonate informelle* (1968), and No. 2, *Hommage à Franz Liszt* (1987). **VOCAL:** *Herr, es ist Zeit* for Soprano and 8 Instruments (1966); *Traumspiel* for Soprano, Orch., and Electronic Tape (Metz, Nov. 18, 1983). **ELECTRONIC:** *Horizont* (1972).

Holliger, Heinz, outstanding Swiss oboist, pedagogue, and composer; b. Langenthal, May 21, 1939. He commenced playing the recorder at 4 and the piano at 6; later studied oboe with Cassagnaud and composition with Veress at the Bern Cons., then oboe with Pierlot and piano with Lefébure at the Paris Cons. In 1959 he won 1st prize in the Geneva competition, and then played in the Basel Sym. Orch.; also attended Boulez's master classes in composition in Basel (1961–63). After winning 1st prize in the Munich competition in 1961, he embarked upon a brilliant international career; toured in Europe and the U.S. as soloist with the Lucerne Festival Strings in 1962. He also gave concerts with his wife, the harpist Ursula Hanggi, and his own Holliger Ensemble. In addition to giving master classes, he was a prof. at the Freiburg im Breisgau Hochschule für Musik (from 1965). He is generally recognized as the foremost oboist of his era, his mastery extending from early music to the commissioned works of such modern composers as Penderecki, Henze, Stockhausen, Krenek, Berio, Jolivet, and Lutosławski. In his own works, he is an uncompromising avant-gardist.

WORKS: DRAMATIC: *Der magische Tänzer* for 2 Singers, 2 Dancers, 2 Actors, Chorus, Orch., and Tape (1963–65; Basel, April 26, 1970); *Come and Go/Va et vient/Kommen und Gehen*, chamber opera, after Samuel Beckett (1976–77; Hamburg, Feb. 16, 1978); *Not I*, monodrama for Soprano and Tape, after Beckett (1978–80; Avignon, July 15, 1980); *What Where*, chamber opera, after Beckett (1988; Frankfurt am Main, May 19, 1989). **ORCH.:** *Elis—Drei Nachtstücke* (1963; rev. 1973; Basel, May 3, 1973); *Siebengesang* for Oboe, Orch., Voices, and Loudspeakers (1966–67; Rotterdam, June 17, 1968); *Pneuma* for Winds, Percussion, Organ, and Radios (Donaueschingen, Oct. 18, 1970); *Atembogen* (1974–75; Basel, June 6, 1975); *Scardanelli-Zyklus III: Übungen zu Scardanelli* for Small Orch. and Tape (1978–85) and *IV: Ostinato funèbre* for Small Orch. (1991); *Ad marginem* for Chamber Orch. and Tape (1983; Baden-Baden, March 8, 1985); *Engführung* for Chamber Orch. (1983–84; Donaueschingen, Oct. 18, 1985); *Der ferne Klang* for Chamber Orch. and Tape (1983–84; Donaueschingen, Oct. 18, 1985); *Schaufelrad* for Chamber Orch. and 4 to 5 Women's Voices ad libitum (1983–84; Donaueschingen, Oct. 18, 1985); *Turm-Musik* for Flute, Small Orch., and Tape (1984; Basel, Jan. 17, 1985); *Tonscherben*, "Orchester-Fragmente in memoriam David Rokeah" (Geneva, Sept. 26, 1985); *Zwei Liszt-Transkriptionen* (1986; Basel, Feb. 12, 1987); *Ostinato funèbre* for Small Orch. (1991); *(S)irato: Monodie* (1993). **CHAMBER:** *Mobile* for Oboe and Harp (1962); Trio for Oboe or English Horn, Viola, and Harp (1966); *h* for Wind Quintet (1968); *Cardiophone* for Oboe and 3 Magnetophones (1971); String Quartet (1973); *Chaconne* for Cello (1975); *Scardanelli-Zyklus II: (t)air(e)* for Flute (1980–83); *Studie II* for Oboe (1981); *Trema* for Viola or Cello (1981; also for Violin, 1983); Duo for Violin and Cello (1982); *Vier Lieder ohne Worte* for Violin and Piano (1982–83); *Praeludium, Arioso und Passacaglia* for Harp (1987); *Felicity's Shake-Wag* for Violin and Cello (1988); Quintet for Piano and Winds (1989); piano pieces; organ music. **VOCAL:** *Glühende Rätsel* for Alto and 10 Instrumentalists (1964); *Dona Nobis Pacem* for 12 Voices (1968–69); *Psalm* for Chorus (1971); *Scardanelli-Zyklus I: Die Jahreszeiten* for Chorus (1975); *Gesänge der Frühe* for Chorus, Orch., and Tape (1987; Cologne, March 4, 1988).

BIBL.: H. Waleson, "H. H.: Musical Renaissance Man," *Ovation* (Feb. 1989).

Hollingsworth, Stanley, American composer and teacher; b. Berkeley, Calif., Aug. 27, 1924. He studied at San Jose State College; then with Milhaud at Mills College and with Menotti at the Curtis Inst. of Music in Philadelphia; subsequently was at the American Academy in Rome (1955–56). He received a Guggenheim fellowship in 1958; also was awarded several NEA grants. From 1961 to 1963 he taught at San Jose State College; in 1963 he joined the faculty of Oakland Univ. in Rochester, Mich. His music follows the principles of practical modernism; in this respect, he emulates Menotti. He used the pseudonym Stanley Hollier in some of his works.

WORKS: OPERAS: *The Mother*, after Andersen (1949; Philadelphia, March 29, 1954); *La Grande Bretèche*, after Balzac (1954; NBC-TV, Feb. 10, 1957); *The Selfish Giant* (1981); *Harrison Loved His Umbrella* (1981). **ORCH.:** Piano Concerto (1980); *Divertimento* (1982); *3 Ladies beside the Sea* for Narrator and Orch. (1983). **CHAMBER:** Oboe Sonata; *3 impromptus* for Flute and Piano (1975); *Ricordanza* for Oboe and String Trio (in memory of Samuel Barber; 1981); *Reflections and Diversions* for Clarinet and Piano (1984). **VOCAL:** *Dumbarton Oaks Mass* for Chorus and String Orch.; *Stabat Mater* for Chorus and Orch. (San Jose, May 1, 1957); *Psalm of David* for Tenor, Chorus, and Orch. (1962).

Holloway, Robin (Greville), English composer, teacher, and writer on music; b. Leamington Spa, Oct. 19, 1943. He studied privately with Goehr (1959–63), and also attended King's College, Cambridge (1961–64); completed his education at New College, Oxford (1965–67; Ph.D., 1971, with a diss. on Debussy and Wagner; publ. in London, 1979). He was a lecturer at the Univ. of Cambridge (from 1975); also contributed various articles to periodicals and anthologies. His output is notable for its remarkable command of various styles and genres. While he has tended along tonal paths, he is not averse to non-tonal and constructivist techniques. He has also made much use of "objets trouvés."

WORKS: OPERA: *Clarissa* (1976; also *Clarissa Symphony* for Soprano, Tenor, and Orch., Birmingham, Dec. 9, 1982). **ORCH.:** 2 concertinos for Small Orch.: No. 1 (1964; rev. 1968–69; London, March 14, 1969) and No. 2 (1967, 1974; London, Jan. 8, 1975); Concerto for Organ and Wind Orch. (1965–66; St. Albans, July 1, 1967); 3 concertos for Orch.: No. 1 (1966–69; Glasgow, April 25, 1973), No. 2 (1978–79; Glasgow, Sept. 22, 1979), and No. 3 (1993); *Divertimento No. 1* for Amateur or Youth Orch., with Piano Obbligato (Cambridge, June 9, 1968); *Scenes from Schumann*, 7 paraphrases (Cheltenham, July 10, 1970); *Domination of Black*, symphonic poem (1973–74; London, Aug. 8, 1974); *Romanza* for Violin and Small Orch. (1976; London, Aug. 8, 1978); *Idyll* for Small Orch. (1979–80; Cheltenham, July 17, 1981); Horn Concerto (1979–80); *Ode* for 4 Winds and Strings (London, June 4, 1980); *Serenata notturna* for 4 Horns, 2 Trumpets, and Strings (1982; London, Dec. 9, 1984); *2nd Idyll* for Small Orch. (1982–83; London, Oct. 10, 1983); *Seascape and Harvest*, 2 pictures (1983–84; Birmingham, April 29, 1986); Viola Concerto (1983–84; London, Sept. 7, 1985); *Romanza* for Oboe and Strings (1984; Peterborough, N.H., Aug. 30, 1986); *Ballad* for Harp and Small Orch. (1984–85; Cheltenham, July 28, 1985); Bassoon Concerto (1984–85; Newcastle upon Tyne, Jan. 8, 1986); *Inquietus* for Small Orch. (1986; London, April 3, 1987); Double Concerto for Clarinet, Saxophone, and 2 Chamber Orchs. (1987–88); Violin Concerto (1990); *Entrance; Carousing; Embarkation* for Symphonic Wind Band (1990); *Serenade* for Strings (1990); *Frost at Midnight* for Chamber Orch. (1994). **CHAMBER:** *Garden Music* for 9 Players (1962; rev. 1967, 1982); *Fantasy-Pieces* on Schumann's *Liederkreis* for Piano and 12 Instruments (Oxford, Dec. 11, 1971); *Evening with Angels* for 16 Players (1972; London, Jan. 1, 1973; rev. 1983); *Divertimento No. 2* for Wind Nonet (1972; London, May 31, 1975); Concertino No. 3: *Homage to Weill* for 11 Players (1975; Aldeburgh, Jan. 23, 1977); *The Rivers of Hell*, concertante for 7 Players (London, Nov. 1, 1977); *Serenade* for Octet (1978–79); *Aria* for 14 Players (1979–80; London, July 14, 1980); Sonata for Solo Violin (1981); *Showpiece*: Concertino No. 4 for 14 Players (1982–83; London, May 23, 1983); *Serenade* for Wind Quintet and String Quintet (1983; London, June 26, 1985); *Serenade* for String Sextet and Double Bass (1986; Keele, May 14, 1987; also for String Orch.); Brass Quintet (1987); works for solo instruments. **VOCAL:** *Melodrama* for Speaker, Men's Chorus, and Ensemble (1967); *The Wind Shifts* for High Voice and Strings (1970); *Cantata on the Death of God* for Soloists, Chorus, and Orch. (1972–73); *Sea Surface Full of Clouds* for Soloists, Small Chorus, and Chamber Orch. (1974–75); *Conundrums* for Soprano and Wind Quintet (1977–79); *Brand*, dramatic ballad for Soloists, Chorus, and Orch. (1981); *On Hope* for Soprano, Mezzo-soprano, and String Quartet (1984); *The Spacious Firmament* for Chorus and Orch. (1990); choruses; song cycles.

Hollreiser, Heinrich, German conductor; b. Munich, June 24, 1913. He studied at the Munich Academy of Music; took lessons in conducting with Elmendorff. He subsequently was engaged as an opera conductor in Wiesbaden (1932), Darmstadt (1935–38), Mannheim (1938–39), Duisburg (1939–42), and Munich (1942–45). From 1945 to 1952 he was Generalmusikdirektor in Düsseldorf. He then was a conductor at the Vienna State Opera (1952–61) and chief conductor of the Deutsche Oper in West Berlin (1961–64); also served as a regular conductor at Bayreuth for several seasons. In 1978 he made his U.S. debut with the Cleveland Orch. In subsequent years, he appeared as a guest conductor with various European orchs. and opera houses. In 1993 he became permanent guest conductor of the Deutsche Oper in Berlin.

Hollweg, Ilse, German soprano; b. Solingen, Feb. 23, 1922; d. there, Feb. 9, 1990. She studied with Gertrude Förstel at the Cologne Hochschule für Musik. In 1942 she made her operatic debut as Blöndchen in Saarbrücken. From 1946 to 1951 she sang in Düsseldorf, and also appeared as Constanze at the Glyndebourne Festival (1950) and then as Zerbinetta at the Edinburgh Festival. In 1951 she made her debut at London's Covent Garden as Gilda. Her guest engagements also took her to Berlin, Hamburg, Vienna, Salzburg, and Bayreuth. From 1955 to 1970 she was a member of the Deutsche Oper am Rhein in Düsseldorf. She also sang in works by Schoenberg, Krenek, Karl Amadeus Hartmann, Boulez, and Nono to great effect.

BIBL.: K. Ruhrberg, *I. H.* (Duisburg, 1971).

Hollweg, Werner (Friedrich), German tenor; b. Solingen, Sept. 13, 1936. He received his training in Detmold, Lugano, and Munich. After making his debut with the Vienna Chamber Opera in 1962, he sang in Bonn (1963–67) and Gelsenkirchen (1967–68). His success as Belmonte in Florence in 1969 and as a soloist in Beethoven's 9th Sym. under Karajan in Osaka in 1970 led to engagements with the Hamburg State Opera, the Bavarian State Opera in Munich, the Deutsche Oper in Berlin, the Deutsche Oper am Rhein in Düsseldorf, and the Vienna State Opera. He also appeared in Rome, Paris, N.Y., Los Angeles, and at London's Covent Garden (debut as Titus, 1976). He won particular distinction in such Mozart portrayals as Don Ottavio, Idomeneo, Tamino, Basilio, and Ferrando. He also sang in contemporary operas, creating the role of Matthew Levi in Höller's *Der Meister und Margarita* (Paris, 1989). His concert repertoire ranged from Haydn to Kodály. His interpretations of the songs of Schubert, Schumann, and Loewe were especially esteemed.

Holm, Mogens Winkel, Danish composer; b. Copenhagen, Oct. 1, 1936. He was a student of Jørgen Jersild (theory and composition) and Mogens Andreassen (oboe) at the Royal Danish Cons. of Music in Copenhagen (1955–61). He then was an oboist in several Copenhagen orchs.; he was a music critic for the Copenhagen newspapers *Ekstra Bladet* and *Politiken* (1965–71), and subsequently served as chairman of the Danish Composers' Soc. (1971–75; from 1982).

WORKS: DRAMATIC: OPERAS: *Aslak*, chamber opera (1962; Copenhagen, Jan. 27, 1963); *Sonata for 4 Opera Singers*, textless chamber opera (Copenhagen, April 19, 1968). **BALLETS:** *Tropismer II* (Copenhagen, May 24, 1964); *Kontradans* (Danish Radio, July 16, 1965); *Bikt* (Swedish Radio, May 5, 1969; rev. as *Krønike* [Chronicle]); *Galgarien* (Malmö, Nov. 27, 1970); *Rapport* (Report; Danish Radio, March 19, 1972); *Tarantel* (1975); *Eurydike tøver* (Eurydice Hesitates; 1977); *Gaerdesanger under kunstig stjerneheimmel* (Whitethroat Under an Artificial Firmament; 1979–80); *Til Blåskaeg* (To Bluebeard; 1982). **ORCH.:** *Chamber Concertante* for Bassoon, String Quartet, and String Orch. (1959); *Concerto piccolo* (1961); *Cumulus* (1965); *Aiolos*, sym. (Danish Radio, March 24, 1972; symphonic version of the ballet *Rapport*); *Glasskoven* (The Glass Forest) for Glass Players and Strings (1974); *Cries* (1983–84). **CHAMBER:** Trio for Oboe, Clarinet, and Bassoon (1956); Wind Quintet (1957); *Little Chamber Concerto* for 5 Winds, Violin, and Cello (1958); String Quartet (1959); *ABRACADABRA* for Flute, Trumpet, Cello, and 4 Timpani (1960); *Tropismer I* for Oboe, Bassoon, Horn, and Piano (1961); Sonata for Woodwind Quintet (1965); *Overtoninger II* for Flute, Piano, and Cello (1972); *Syv breve til stilheden* (7 Letters to Silence) for Flute, Oboe, Guitar, Piano, Vibraphone, and Viola (1976); *Adieu* for Flute, Violin, Cello, Harp, and Percussion (1982); *Note-book* for Oboe, Clarinet, and Bassoon (1983). **VOCAL:** *A Ghost Story* for Soloists, Chorus, and Orch. (1964); *Annonce* for Soprano and Chamber Group (1965); *Overtoninger I* for Soprano, Cimbalom, and

Cello (1971); *Konungens sorg* for 3 Sopranos, Harp, and 3 Oboes (1989); choruses; songs.

Holm, Peder, Danish composer; b. Copenhagen, Sept. 30, 1926. He studied violin with Thorval Nielsen and counterpoint with Jeppesen at the Royal Danish Cons. of Music in Copenhagen (1945–47). He became a lecturer at the Esbjerg Cons. in 1949 and in 1964 was named its director.

WORKS: OPERA: *Ingen mad i dag, men i morgen* (No Food Today but Tomorrow; 1962). **ORCH.:** Violin Concerto (1952); Piano Concerto (1953); *Fantasy* for Viola and Orch. (1954); *Concerto for Orchestra* (1955); Sym. No. 1 (1955); *Preludio, Scherzo, and Fantasia* (1956); *Symphonic Dance* (1957); *Capriccio* (1959); 2 concertos for Piano and Strings (1963, 1967); *Pezzo concertante* (1964); *2 Sketches* for Trumpet, Trombone, and Orch. (1966); *3 Pieces* (1966); *VYL* (1967; Esbjerg, May 2, 1968); *KHEBEB* for 2 Pianos and Orch. (1968); Trumpet Concertino (1970); Clarinet Concertino (1970). **CHAMBER:** String Quartet (1967); *2 Pieces* for Wind Quintet (1968). **VOCAL:** *Moerlille* for Chorus and Ensemble (1987).

Holm, Renate, German soprano; b. Berlin, Aug. 10, 1931. After winning 1st prize in a vocal competition sponsored at the RIAS in Berlin in 1952, she embarked upon a career as a pop singer; she also pursued vocal training with Maria Ivogün in Vienna. In 1958 she made her debut in Oscar Straus' *Ein Walzertraum* at the Vienna Volksoper, where she subsequently sang with fine success. In 1961 she joined the Vienna State Opera. Her guest engagements took her to the Salzburg Festival, Covent Garden in London, the Bolshoi Theater in Moscow, and the Teatro Colón in Buenos Aires. She was notably successful as Blöndchen, Papagena, Rosina in *Il barbiere di Siviglia*, Marie in *Zar und Zimmermann*, and Musetta, as well as in Viennese operettas. She was the author of *Ein Leben nach Spielplan: Stationen einer ungewöhnlichen Karriere* (Berlin, 1991).

Holm, Richard, German tenor; b. Stuttgart, Aug. 3, 1912; d. Munich, July 20, 1988. He studied in Stuttgart with Rudolf Ritter. In 1937 he made his operatic debut in Kiel; became a member of the Kiel Opera; also made guest appearances at other German opera houses; in 1948 he joined the Bavarian State Opera in Munich. On March 15, 1952, he made his Metropolitan Opera debut in N.Y. as David in *Die Meistersinger von Nürnberg*; was on its roster until 1953. He also made successful appearances in London, Vienna, Salzburg, and Bayreuth. In 1967 he became a prof. of voice at the Hochschule für Musik in Munich. Among his roles were Xerxes, Titus, Belmonte, Tamino, Loge, Flamand, Novagerio in *Palestrina*, Robespierre in *Dantons Tod*, and Aschenbach in *Death in Venice*.

Holmboe, Vagn, eminent Danish composer and pedagogue; b. Horsens, Jutland, Dec. 20, 1909; d. Ramløse, Sept. 1, 1996. He was a student of Høffding and Jeppesen at the Copenhagen Cons. (1925–29), and then of Toch at the Berlin Hochschule für Musik (1930). After pursuing ethnomusicological research in Romania (1933–34), he returned to Copenhagen as a private teacher. He taught at the Royal Danish Inst. for the Blind (1940–49), and also was a music critic for the newspaper *Politiken* (1947–55). In 1950 he became a teacher at the Royal Danish Cons. of Music in Copenhagen, where he subsequently was a prof. of theory and composition from 1955 to 1965. He held a lifetime government grant to pursue composition. He publ. *Mellemspil* (Interlude; Copenhagen, 1961) and *Det Uforklarlige* (Copenhagen, 1981; Eng. tr., 1991, as *Experiencing Music: A Composer's Notes*). As the leading Danish composer in the post-Nielsen era, Holmboe pursued a neo-Classical style in which he displayed a thorough command of counterpoint and instrumentation. His symphonic compositions are notable for their development of "germ themes" which grow metamorphically. In addition to his important contribution to the symphony, he also composed an outstanding series of string quartets.

WORKS: DRAMATIC: *Fanden og borgemesteren* (The Devil and the Mayor), symphonic fairy play (1940); *Den galsindede tyrk*, ballet (1942–44); *Lave og Jon*, opera (1946–48); *Kniven* (The Knife), chamber opera (1959–60; Copenhagen, Dec. 2, 1963); music for plays, films, and radio. **ORCH.:** *Concerto for Orchestra* (1929); Concerto for Chamber Orch. (1931; Copenhagen, April 3, 1933); *Chamber Music No. 1* for Small Orch. (1931) and *No. 2* for Strings (1932); *Divertimento No. 1* (Copenhagen, March 29, 1933) and *No. 2* for Strings (1933; Copenhagen, Jan. 31, 1944); Concerto for Strings (1933); 3 suites for Chamber Orch.: No. 1 (1935; Copenhagen, March 30, 1936), No. 2 (1935–36; Copenhagen, April 20, 1939), and No. 3 (1936; Copenhagen, Nov. 23, 1938); Chamber Sonata No. 1 (1935); 13 numbered syms.: No. 1 (1935; Århus, Feb. 21, 1938), No. 2 (1938–39; Copenhagen, Dec. 5, 1939), No. 3, *Sinfonia Rustica* (1941; Copenhagen, June 12, 1948), No. 4, *Sinfonia Sacra* (1941; rev. version, Copenhagen, Sept. 11, 1945), No. 5 (1944; Copenhagen, June 16, 1945), No. 6 (1947; Copenhagen, Jan. 8, 1948), No. 7 (1950; Copenhagen, Oct. 18, 1951), No. 8, *Sinfonia Boreale* (1951–52; Copenhagen, March 5, 1953), No. 9 (Copenhagen, Dec. 19, 1968), No. 10 (1970–71; Detroit, Jan. 27, 1972), No. 11 (1980; Copenhagen, Feb. 17, 1983), No. 12 (1988; Cardiff, Oct. 21, 1989), and No. 13 (1994); *Romanian Suite* for Piano and Chamber Orch. (1935) and *Romanian Suite* for Chamber Orch. (1938); *Rhapsody* for Flute and Chamber Orch. (1935); *Little Overture* (1936; Copenhagen, March 16, 1938); *Serenade* (1936; Copenhagen, Oct. 21, 1939); Concerto Sym. for Violin and Orch. (1937); 2 violin concertos (1938, 1979); 2 unnumbered concertinos (1938, Copenhagen, June 6, 1941; 1957, Copenhagen, Sept. 28, 1958); 13 chamber concertos: No. 1 for Piano, Strings, and Percussion (1939; Copenhagen, March 5, 1941), No. 2 for Flute, Violin, Celesta, Percussion, and Strings (1940; Copenhagen, April 21, 1942), No. 3 for Clarinet, 2 Trumpets, 2 Horns, and Strings (1940), No. 4, *Triple Concerto*, for Violin, Cello, Piano, and Chamber Orch. (1942; Copenhagen, March 22, 1943), No. 5 for Viola and Chamber Orch. (1943; Copenhagen, Feb. 14, 1946), No. 6 for Violin and Chamber Orch. (1943; Copenhagen, Dec. 12, 1944), No. 7 for Oboe and Chamber Orch. (1944–45; Copenhagen, Jan. 29, 1948), No. 8, *Sinfonia Concertante*, for Chamber Orch. (1945; Copenhagen, July 26, 1947), No. 9 for Violin, Viola, and Chamber Orch. (1945–46; Copenhagen, Oct. 26, 1954), No. 10, *Trae-messing-tarm*, for Chamber Orch. (1945–46; Randers, April 26, 1946), No. 11 for Trumpet, 2 Horns, and Strings (1948; Copenhagen, April 8, 1949), No. 12 for Trombone and Chamber Orch. (1951; Copenhagen, May 23, 1952), and No. 13, *Collegium musicum concerto No. 2*, for Oboe, Viola, and Chamber Orch. (1955–56; Randers, Nov. 6, 1958); 2 numbered concertinos: No. 1 for Violin, Viola, and Strings (1940; Copenhagen, Sept. 16, 1963) and No. 2 for Violin and Strings (1940; Copenhagen, June 12, 1948); Symphonic Overture (1941; Copenhagen, April 13, 1943); 3 chamber syms: No. 1 (Copenhagen, March 9, 1951), No. 2 (1968; Copenhagen, Jan. 20, 1969), and No. 3 (1969–70; Ålborg, Oct. 14, 1970); 2 unnumbered sinfonias: *Sinfonia in memoriam* (1954–55; Copenhagen, May 5, 1955) and *Sinfonia Sielariana* (1964); 4 symphonic metamorphoses: *Epitaph* (London, Dec. 28, 1956); *Monolith* (Århus, Sept. 9, 1960); *Epilogue* (1961–62; Göteborg, Nov. 23, 1962); and *Tempo Variable* (1971–72; Bergen, May 24, 1972); 4 sinfonias for Strings: No. 1 (1957; Copenhagen, July 3, 1958), No. 2 (1957; Århus, Nov. 20, 1958), No. 3 (1958–59; Århus, Jan. 22, 1962), and No. 4 (1962; Århus, Jan. 27, 1964); *Skoven* (1960; Randers, May 2, 1961); Cello Concerto (1974); Recorder Concerto (1974); 2 flute concertos (1975, 1981); Tuba Concerto (1976); Concerto for Brass (1984); *Intermezzo Concertante* for Tuba and Strings (1987); *Prelude: To the Victoria Embankment* for Chamber Orch. (1990). **CHAMBER:** Trio for Flute and 2 Violins (1926; also for 3 Violins); String Quintet (1928); Quartet for Flute, Oboe, Viola, and Cello (1930); *Allegro sostenuto* for Piano and Violin (1931); *5 Duets* for Flute and Viola (1932); *7 Duos* for Flute and Horn (1932); *4 Duos* for Flute and Trombone (1932); Trio for Oboe, Bassoon, and Horn (1932–39); Quintet for Flute, Oboe, Clarinet, Bassoon, and Horn (Copenhagen, Oct. 30, 1933); 3 violin sonatas: No. 1 (Lund, Nov. 13, 1935), No. 2 (1939; Copenhagen, Jan. 16, 1942), and No. 3 (Brussels, May 4, 1965); *Serenade* for Flute,

Clarinet, and Bassoon (1935); *Rhapsody* for Clarinet and Violin (1936); Quartet for Flute, Violin, Cello, and Piano (1936; Paris, July 1937); Quintet for Flute, Oboe, Clarinet, Violin, and Viola (1936; Copenhagen, July 24, 1939); *Rhapsodic Interlude* for Clarinet, Piano, and Violin (1938); *Serenade* for Flute, Piano, Violin, and Cello (1940; Vienna, March 25, 1949); *Notturno* for Flute, Oboe, Clarinet, Bassoon, and Horn (Copenhagen, Nov. 2, 1940); 20 string quartets: No. 1 (1941–44; rev. 1949), No. 2 (1948–49; Copenhagen, Jan. 31, 1950), No. 3 (1949–50; Copenhagen, Nov. 18, 1950), No. 4 (1953–54; Copenhagen, Jan. 8, 1955; rev. 1956), No. 5 (1955; Kolding, Feb. 20, 1956), No. 6 (1961; Hindsgavl, Aug. 1962), No. 7 (1964–65; Birkerod, Sept. 27, 1965), No. 8 (Frederiksberg, Dec. 14, 1965), No. 9 (1965–66; Horsens, Aug. 23, 1967; rev. 1969), No. 10 (1969; Göteborg, April 7, 1970), No. 11, *Quartetto rustico* (Soro, March 8, 1972), No. 12 (Hillerod, Nov. 19, 1973), No. 13 (1975), No. 14 (1975), No. 15 (1976–77), No. 16 (1981), No. 17, *Mattinata* (1982), No. 18, *Giornata* (1982), No. 19, *Serata* (1985), and No. 20, *Notturno* (1985); *Isomeric duo concertante* for 2 Violins and Piano (Copenhagen, July 20, 1950); *Primavera* for Flute, Piano, Violin, and Cello (1951; Copenhagen, Oct. 24, 1952); Sonata for Solo Violin (1953); Trio for Piano, Violin, and Cello (1954; Copenhagen, Oct. 24, 1956); *Quartetto medico* for Flute, Oboe, Clarinet, and Piano (1956); Sonata for Solo Flute (1957); *Aspekter* for Flute, Oboe, Clarinet, Bassoon, and Horn (1957; Copenhagen, April 9, 1958); *Tropos* for 2 Violins, 2 Violas, and Cello (Kongens Lyngby, Oct. 9, 1960); Quintet for Horn, 2 Trumpets, Trombone, and Tuba (1961); Sonata for Solo Double Bass (1962); Sonata for Violin and Viola (1963); Quartet for Flute, Violin, Viola, and Cello (Hindsgavl, July 15, 1966); Oboe Sonatina (1966); Trio for Flute, Cello, and Percussion (Kongens Lyngby, Oct. 8, 1968); Sonata for Solo Cello (1968–69); *Musik til Morten* for Oboe and String Quartet (Humlebaek, Nov. 17, 1970); *Fanden los i vildmosen* for Clarinet, 2 Violins, and Double Bass (Vra, July 30, 1971); *Ondata* for Tuned Gongs (1972); Sextet for Flute, Clarinet, Bassoon, Violin, Viola, and Cello (1972–73; Odense, Nov. 13, 1973); *Diafora* for 4 Strings (1973); *Nuigen* for Piano, Violin, and Cello (1976); *Firefir* for 4 Flutes (1976–77); Trio for Clarinet, Cello, and Piano (1978); *Notes* for 3 Trombones and Tuba (1979); 2 guitar sonatas (1979, 1979); Sonata for Recorder and Harpsichord (1980); *Gioco* for Violin, Viola, and Cello (1983); *Ballata* for Violin, Viola, Cello, and Piano (1984); Tuba Sonata (1986); *Prelude: To a Pine Tree* for Chamber Ensemble (1986); Quintet for 2 Violins, Viola, Cello, and Double Bass (1986); *Prelude: To a Dolphin* for Chamber Ensemble (1986); Duo concertante for Violin and Guitar (1986); *Prelude: To a Maple Tree* for Chamber Ensemble (1986); *Prelude: To a Willow Tree* for Chamber Ensemble (1987); Trombone Sonata (1987); *Translation* for Violin, Viola, Cello, Double Bass, and Piano (1987; rev. 1989); *Capriccio* for Clarinet and Piano (1988); Sonata for Solo Viola (1988); *Prelude: To the Pollution of Nature* for Chamber Ensemble (1989); *Epos* for 2 Pianos and Percussion (1990); *Eco* for Clarinet, Cello, and Piano (1991); *Prelude: To the Unsettled Weather* for Chamber Ensemble (1993). **KEYBOARD: PIANO:** *Scherzo* (1928); *12 Little Pieces* (1928–29); *Chorale Fantasy* (1929); Sonata (1929); *4 Pieces* (1930); *Symphony for Piano* (1930); *5 Pieces* (1930); *5 1- and 2-part Pieces* (1930); *Allegro affetuoso* (1931); *Little Pieces* (1931; also for Recorders); *Pieces* (1931); *1-, 2-, and 3-part Pieces* (1931); *Julen* (1931); *Concerto for Piano* (1931); *Suites and Dances* (1931); *7 Preludes* (1932); *Capriccio* (1932); *6 Pieces* (1933); *6 Sketches* (1934); *10 Romanian Dances* (1934); *Suite* (1937); *New Pieces* (1937); *Danish Suite* (1937; also for Orch.); *6 Pieces* (1939); *Étude* (1939); *Sonatina briosa* (1941); *5 Epigrams* (1942); *Suona da bardo*, suite (1949–50); *Moto austero* (1965); *Moto austero* (1972); *I venti* (1972). **ORGAN:** *Fabula I* (1972) and *II* (1973); *Contrasti* (1972). **VOCAL:** *Requiem* for Soloists, Chorus, and Orch. (1931); *Provinsen* for Soloists, Chorus, Flute, Oboe, Violin, and Cello (1931); 12 cantatas, including: No. 2 for Chorus and Orch. (Horsens, Dec. 19, 1941), No. 3 for Voices and Strings (Horsens, June 28, 1942), No. 4 for Voices and Orch. (1942–45; Copenhagen, Nov. 26, 1945), No. 6 for Chorus and Orch. (1947), No. 7 for Sopranos, Women's Voices, and Orch. or 2 Pianos (Copenhagen, Oct. 27, 1949), No. 8 for Baritones, Bass, Reciter, and Strings (1951; Falster, May 1, 1952), No. 9 for Women's Voices, Violin, Cello, Flute, and 2 Pianos (Randers, April 28, 1955), No. 10 for Mixed Voices (1957; Copenhagen, July 2, 1958), No. 11 for Baritone, Mezzo-soprano, Chorus, and Orch. (1958), and No. 12 for Mezzo-soprano, Contralto, Baritone, Chorus, and Orch. (1958–59; Århus, Sept. 11, 1959); *Arhundredstjernen* for Baritone, Chorus, and Orch. (1946; Copenhagen, March 18, 1947); *Liber canticorum I–IV* for Mixed Voices (1951–53); *Traeet* for Chorus and Chamber Orch. (1953); *Requiem for Nietzsche* for Alto, Tenor, Baritone, Chorus, and Orch. (1963; Copenhagen, Nov. 26, 1964); *Zeit* for Alto and String Quartet (1966); *Beatus Vir: Liber canticorum V* for Mixed Voices (1968); *Cantata profana Frise* for Mixed Voices (1970); *Edward* for Baritone and Orch. (1971); *The Wee, Wee Man* for Tenor and Orch. or Mixed Voices (1971–72); *Beatus parvo* for Mixed Voices and Orch. (1973); *Biblical Cantata* for Soloists, Chorus, and Orch. (1982); *Ode to the Soul* for Chorus and Brass (1985); *Winter* for Soprano and Chorus (1989); *Die Erfullung* for Soprano, Baritone, 2 Choruses, and 9 Winds (1990); many choruses and solo songs.

BIBL.: P. Rapoport, *V. H.: A Catalogue of His Music, Discography, Bibliography, Essays* (London, 1974; 2nd. ed., rev. and enl., Copenhagen, 1979); idem, *V. H.'s Symphonic Metamorphoses* (diss., Univ. of Ill., 1975); R. Layton, "V. H.: An Eightieth Birthday Salute," *Nordic Sounds* (Dec. 1989).

Holmes, Ralph, English violinist; b. Penge, April 1, 1937; d. Beckenham, Sept. 4, 1984. He studied with David Martin at the Royal Academy of Music in London, and later with Enesco in Paris and Galamian in N.Y. He made his London debut at a children's concert of the Royal Phil. (1951); then won prizes at international competitions in Paris (1957) and Bucharest (1958). He pursued a successful career in England before making his U.S. debut with Barbirolli and the Houston Sym. Orch. at N.Y.'s Carnegie Hall in 1966; in subsequent years, he toured widely; with Anthony Goldstone and Moray Welsh, he formed his own piano trio in 1972. He was a prof. at the Royal Academy of Music from 1964. His repertoire included all the major 20th-century concertos written for his instrument.

Holmes, Reed K., American composer; b. Oak Ridge, Tenn., Aug. 20, 1952. He studied at the Univ. of Tenn. (B.M., 1974; M.M., 1976) and the Univ. of Texas at Austin (Ph.D., 1981, with the diss. *Relational Systems and Process in Recent Works of Luciano Berio*), where he taught (from 1985) and was director of its Electronic Music Studio. He was a founding member of the Texas Composers Forum (1985); received an ASCAP Award in Composition (1989) and an NEA grant (1990–91). His spirited compositions are often minimalist in design, motivated by rhythmic and timbral processes.

WORKS: MULTIMEDIA: *Moiré* for Dancers and Computer-generated Sound (1981); *Nova* for Dissolve Slide Projections and Quadraphonic Sound (1982–83); *Around the Waves* for Dissolve Slide Projections and Quadraphonic Sound (1983); *Drumfire* for Dancers and Computer (1986); *Electric Symphonies* for Dancers and Computer (1988). **CHAMBER:** *Sound Streams* for Flute Choir (1979); *Patterns* for Any Group of Homogeneous Wind Instruments (1982); *Kaleidoscope* for 23 Musicians (1984); *Pocket Hocket* for 4 Synthesizers (or for Any 4 Parts) (1985); *Circle Sonata* for 5 Percussionists and Tape (1986); *Variations* for 6 Parts Performed by Any Homogeneous Group of Instruments (1988); *Nonet* for Soprano, English Horn or Oboe, Saxophone, Trumpet, Violin, Viola, Cello, Piano, and Mallet Percussion (1991). **SOLO, WITH TAPE:** *Dream Quest* for Percussion (1975); *Chalumeau Rain* for Clarinet (1980); *Song and Fantasy* for Trombone (1982); *With Wings They Came* for Saxophone (1983); *Cat's Cradle 4* for Cello (1990).

Holoman, D(allas) Kern, American musicologist and conductor; b. Raleigh, N.C., Sept. 8, 1947. He pursued his academic training at Duke Univ. (B.A., 1969) and Princeton Univ. (M.F.A.,

1971; Ph.D., 1974, with the diss. *Autograph Musical Documents of Hector Berlioz, c.1818–1840*; publ. in a rev. and corrected ed. as *The Creative Process in the Autograph Musical Documents of Hector Berlioz, c.1818–1840*, Ann Arbor, 1980), receiving a Fulbright fellowship (1972–73). In 1973 he joined the faculty of the Univ. of Calif. at Davis, where he was founder-director of its Early Music Ensemble (1973–77; 1979), conductor of its sym. orch. (from 1978), and chairman of the music dept. (1980–88). With J. Kerman and R. Winter, he was founding ed. of the distinguished journal *19th Century Music* (1977), subsequently serving as its managing ed. In 1989 he became general ed. of the series Recent Researches in the Music of the Nineteenth and Twentieth Centuries. His writings are notable for their accessible prose style and engaging, dry wit. An authority on Berlioz, he publ. the first thematic catalog of that composer's output and ed. his *Romeo et Juliette* for the New Berlioz Edition.

WRITINGS: Ed., with C. Palisca, *Musicology in the 1980s* (N.Y., 1982); *Dr. Holoman's Handy Guide to Concert-Going* (Sacramento and Davis, 1983); *Catalogue of the Works of Hector Berlioz* (Kassel, 1987); *Writing about Music: A Style-Sheet from the Editors of 19th Century Music* (Berkeley and Los Angeles, 1988); *Berlioz* (Cambridge, Mass., 1989); *Evenings with the Orchestra: A Norton Companion for Concertgoers* (N.Y., 1992).

Holoubek, Ladislav, Slovak conductor and composer; b. Prague, Aug. 13, 1913. He studied composition with Moyzes at the Bratislava Academy of Music (1926–33) and with Novák at the Prague Cons. (1934–36). He conducted at the Slovak National Theater in Bratislava (1933–52; 1959–66) and at the State Theater in Košice (1955–58; from 1966). His operas have contributed significantly to the advancement of modern Slovak opera.

WORKS: OPERAS (all 1st perf. in Bratislava unless otherwise given): *Stella* (March 18, 1939; rev. 1948–49 and 1954–55); *Svitanie* (Dawn; March 12, 1941); *Tužba* (Yearning; Feb. 12, 1944; rev. 1963 and 1969); *Rodina* (The Family; Nov. 12, 1960); *Professor Mamlock* (May 21, 1966); *Bačovské žarty* (Shepherds' Games; 1975; Košice, Jan. 16, 1981). **ORCH.:** Sym. (1946); Sinfonietta (1950); *10 Variations on an Original Theme* (1950); *Defiances and Hopes*, symphonic poem (1973). **CHAMBER:** Violin Sonata (1933); 3 string quartets (1936, 1948, 1962); Wind Quintet (1938); Trio for Flute, Violin, and Harp (1939); 2 piano sonatas (1931, 1937). **VOCAL:** Cantatas and songs.

Holst, Gustav(us Theodore von), significant English composer, father of **Imogen (Clare) Holst**; b. Cheltenham, Sept. 21, 1874; d. London, May 25, 1934. He was of Swedish descent. He received his primary musical training from his parents. In 1892 he became organist and choirmaster in Wyck Rissington, Gloucestershire; in 1893 he entered the Royal College of Music in London, where he studied composition with Stanford and Rockstro, organ with Hoyte, and piano with Sharpe; also learned to play the trombone. After graduating in 1898, he was a trombonist in the orch. of the Carl Rosa Opera Co. (until 1900) and the Scottish Orch. in Glasgow (1900–1903). His interest in Hindu philosophy, religion, and music during this period led to the composition of his settings from the Sanskrit of *Hymns from the Rig Veda* (1907–08). He worked as a music teacher in a Dulwich girls' school (1903–20); was director of music at St. Paul's Girls' School, Hammersmith (1905–34), and of London's Morley College (1907–24). He became a teacher of composition at the Royal College of Music (1919); was also prof. of music at Univ. College, Reading (1919–23). Plagued by suspicions of his German sympathies at the outbreak of World War I in 1914, he removed the Germanic-looking (actually Swedish) nobiliary particle "von" from his surname; his early works had been publ. under the name Gustav von Holst. He was deemed unfit for military service, but served as YMCA musical organizer among the British troops in the Near East in 1918. After the war, he visited the U.S. as a lecturer and conductor in 1923 and 1932. However, his deteriorating health limited his activities; his daughter described his mind in the last years of his life as "closed in gray isolation." Holst's most celebrated work, the large-scale orch. suite *The Planets*, was inspired by the astrological significance of the planets. It consists of 7 movements, each bearing a mythological subtitle: *Mars, the Bringer of War; Venus, the Bringer of Peace; Mercury, the Winged Messenger; Jupiter, the Bringer of Jollity; Saturn, the Bringer of Old Age; Uranus, the Magician; Neptune, the Mystic*, with an epilogue of female voices singing wordless syllables. It was first performed privately in London (Sept. 29, 1918); 5 movements were played in public (Feb. 15, 1920); the first complete performance followed (Nov. 15, 1920). The melodic and harmonic style of the work epitomizes Holst's musical convictions, in which lyrical, dramatic, and triumphant motifs are alternately presented in coruscatingly effective orch. dress. His music in general reflects the influence of English folk songs and the madrigal. He was a master of choral writing; one of his notable works utilizing choral forces was *The Hymn of Jesus* (1917). His writings were ed. by S. Lloyd and E. Rubbra as *Gustav Holst: Collected Essays* (London, 1974).

WORKS: DRAMATIC: OPERAS: *The Revoke*, op. 1 (1895); *The Youth's Choice*, op. 11 (1902); *Sita*, op. 23 (1899–1906); *Savitri*, chamber opera, op. 25 (1908; London, Dec. 5, 1916); *The Perfect Fool*, op. 39 (1918–22; London, May 14, 1923); *At the Boar's Head*, op. 42 (1924; Manchester, April 3, 1925); *The Wandering Scholar*, chamber opera, op. 50 (1929–30; Liverpool, Jan. 31, 1934). **OTHER:** *Lansdown Castle*, operetta (Cheltenham, Feb. 7, 1893); *The Idea*, children's operetta (c.1898); *The Vision of Dame Christian*, masque, op. 27a (London, July 22, 1909). **BALLETS:** *The Lure* (1921); *The Golden Goose*, choral ballet, op. 45/1 (BBC, London, Sept. 21, 1926); *The Morning of the Year*, choral ballet, op. 45/2 (1926–27; London, March 17, 1927). **INCIDENTAL MUSIC:** *The Sneezing Charm* (1918); 7 choruses from *Alcestis* (1920); *The Coming of Christ* (1927; Canterbury, May 28, 1928).

ORCH.: *A Winter Idyll* (1897); *Walt Whitman*, overture, op. 7 (1899); Sym. in F major, op. 8, *The Cotswolds* (1899–1900; Bournemouth, April 24, 1902); *Suite de ballet* in E-flat major, op. 10 (1899; London, May 20, 1904; rev. 1912); *Indra*, symphonic poem, op. 13 (1903); *A Song of the Night* for Violin and Orch., op. 19/1 (1905); *Invocation* for Cello and Orch., op. 19/2 (1911); *Songs of the West*, op. 21/1 (1906–07); *A Somerset Rhapsody*, op. 21/2 (1906–7; London, April 6, 1910); *2 Songs without Words: Country Song* and *Marching Song* for Chamber Orch., op. 22 (1906); 2 suites for Military Band: No. 1, in E-flat major, op. 28/1 (1909) and No. 2, in F major, op. 28/2 (1911); *Beni Mora*, oriental suite, op. 29/1 (1909–10; London, May 1, 1912); *Phantastes*, suite in F major (1911); *St. Paul's Suite* for Strings, op. 29/2 (1912–13); *The Planets*, op. 32 (1914–16; private perf., London, Sept. 29, 1918; 1st complete public perf., London, Nov. 15, 1920); *Japanese Suite*, op. 33 (1915); *A Fugal Overture*, op. 40/1 (1922; as the overture to *The Perfect Fool*, London, May 14, 1923); *A Fugal Concerto* for Flute, Oboe, and Strings, op. 40/2 (London, Oct. 11, 1923); *Egdon Heath: Homage to Hardy*, op. 47 (1927; N.Y., Feb. 12, 1928); *A Moorside Suite* for Brass Band (London, Sept. 29, 1928); Double Concerto for 2 Violins and Orch., op. 49 (1929; London, April 3, 1930); *Hammersmith: Prelude and Scherzo* for Military Band, op. 52 (1930; 2nd version for Orch., 1931; London, Nov. 25, 1931); Jazz-band Piece (1932; ed. by I. Holst as *Capriccio*, 1967; London, Jan. 10, 1968); *Brook Green Suite* for Strings (1933); *Lyric Movement* for Viola and Chamber Orch. (1933; BBC, London, March 18, 1934); *Scherzo* (1933–34; London, Feb. 6, 1935).

CHAMBER: *Fantasiestücke* for Oboe and String Quartet, op. 2 (1896; rev. 1910); Quintet in A minor for Piano, Oboe, Clarinet, Horn, and Bassoon, op. 3 (1896); Wind Quintet in A-flat major, op. 14 (1903; London, Sept. 15, 1982); *Terzetto* for Flute, Oboe, and Viola (1925). **PIANO:** *Toccata* (1924); *Chrissemas Day in the Morning*, op. 46/1 (1926); 2 folk-song fragments: *O I hae seen the roses blaw* and *The Shoemaker*, op. 46/2 (1927); *Nocturne* (1930); *Jig* (1932).

VOCAL: *Light Leaves Whisper* for Chorus (c.1896); *Clear and Cool* for Chorus and Orch., op. 5 (1897); *Clouds o'er the Sum-*

mer Sky for Women's Chorus and Piano (c.1898); *Ornulf's Drapa* for Baritone and Orch., op. 6 (1898); 5 Part Songs, op. 9a (1897–1900); *Ave Maria* for 8-part Women's Chorus, op. 9b (1900); *I Love Thee* for Chorus (n.d.); 5 Part Songs, op. 12 (1902–03); *King Estmere* for Chorus and Orch., op. 17 (1903; London, April 4, 1908); *Thou Didst Delight My Eyes* for Chorus (c.1903); *In Youth Is Pleasure* for Chorus (n.d.); *The Mystic Trumpeter* for Soprano and Orch., op. 18 (1904; London, June 29, 1905; rev. 1912); *Songs from the Princess* for Women's Chorus, op. 20a (1905); *4 Old English Carols* for Chorus or Women's Chorus and Piano, op. 20b (1907); 2 carols for Chorus, Oboe, and Cello (1908, 1916); *Pastoral* for Women's Chorus (c.1908); *Choral Hymns from the Rig Veda* for Chorus and Orch. or Ensemble, op. 26 (1908–10); *O England My Country* for Chorus and Orch. (1909); *The Cloud Messenger* for Chorus and Orch., op. 30 (1909–10); *Christmas Day* for Chorus and Orch. (1910); 4 Part Songs for Women's Chorus and Piano (1910); *2 Eastern Pictures* for Women's Chorus and Harp (1911); *Hecuba's Lament* for Alto, Women's Chorus, and Orch., op. 31/1 (1911); 2 Psalms for Tenor, Chorus, Strings, and Organ (1912); *The Swallow Leaves Her Nest* for Women's Chorus (c.1912); *The Homecoming* for Men's Chorus (1913); *Hymn to Dionysus* for Women's Chorus and Orch., op. 31/2 (1913); *A Dirge for 2 Veterans* for Men's Chorus, Brass, and Percussion (1914); *Nunc dimittis* (1915); *This I Have Done for My True Love*, op. 34/1 (1916); *Lullay My Liking* for Soprano and Chorus, op. 34/2 (1916); *Of One That Is So Fair* for Soprano, Alto, Tenor, Bass, and Chorus, op. 34/3 (1916); *Bring Us in Good Ale*, op. 34/4 (1916); 3 carols for Chorus and Orch. (1916–17); 3 Festival Choruses with Orch., op. 36a (1916); 6 Choral Folk Songs, op. 36b (1916); *Diverus and Lazarus* for Chorus (1917); 2 Part Songs for Women's Chorus and Piano (1917); *A Dream of Christmas* for Women's Chorus, and Strings or Piano (1917); *The Hymn of Jesus* for 2 Choruses, Women's Semi-chorus, and Orch., op. 37 (1917; London, March 25, 1920); *Ode to Death* for Chorus and Orch., op. 38 (1919; Leeds Festival, Oct. 6, 1922); *Short Festival Te Deum* for Chorus and Orch. (1919); *I Vow to Thee, My Country* for Chorus and Orch. (1921; arranged from *The Planets*, no. 4); *1st Choral Symphony* for Soprano, Chorus, and Orch., op. 41 (1923–24; Leeds Festival, Oct. 7, 1925); *The Evening-watch* for Chorus, op. 43/1 (1924); *Sing Me the Men* for Chorus, op. 43/2 (1925); 7 Part Songs for Soprano, Women's Chorus, and Strings, op. 44 (1925–26); 2 anthems (1927); *Wassail Song* for Chorus (1928–30); *A Choral Fantasia* for Soprano, Chorus, Organ, Strings, Brass, and Percussion, op. 51 (1930; Gloucester Festival, Sept. 8, 1931); 12 Welsh Folk Songs for Chorus (1930–31); 6 choruses, some with accompaniment, op. 53 (1931–32); 8 canons (1932). **SONGS:** 4 Songs, op. 4 (1896–98); 6 Songs, op. 15 (1902–03); 6 Songs for Soprano and Piano, op. 16 (1903–04); *Hymns from the Rig Veda*, op. 24 (1907–08); *The Heart Worships* (1907); 4 Songs for Soprano or Tenor, and Violin, op. 35 (1916–17); 12 Songs, op. 48 (1929).

See I. Holst and C. Matthews, eds., *Gustav Holst: Collected Facsimile Edition of Autograph Manuscripts of the Published Works* (4 vols., London, 1974–83).

BIBL.: L. Dyer, *G. H.* (London, 1931); A. Bliss, "G. H.: A Lonely Figure in Music," *Radio Times* (June 15, 1934); A. Boult, "G. H.: The Man and His Work," ibid.; E. Evans, "G. H.," *Musical Times* (July 1934); A. Foster, "G. H.—An Appreciation," *Monthly Musical Record*, LXIV (1934); G. Jacob, "H. the Composer," *R.C.M. Magazine*, XXX (1934); I. Holst, *G. H.: A Biography* (London, 1938; 2nd ed., 1969); E. Rubbra, *G. H.* (Monaco, 1947); I. Holst, *The Music of G. H.* (London, 1951; 3rd ed., rev., 1986, including *H.'s Music Reconsidered*); M. Tippett, "H.—Figure of Our Time," *Listener*, LX (Nov. 13, 1958); U. Vaughan Williams and I. Holst, eds., *Heirs and Rebels* (London, 1959); J. Warrack, "A New Look at G. H.," *Musical Times* (Feb. 1963); A. Boult, "Interpreting The Planets," ibid. (March 1970); idem, "G. H.," *R.C.M. Magazine*, LXX (1974); I. Holst, *H.* (London, 1974; 2nd ed., 1981); idem, "H. and the Royal College of Music," *R.C.M. Magazine*, LXX (1974); idem, *A Thematic Catalogue of G. H.'s Music* (London, 1974); H. Ottaway, "H. as an Opera Composer," *Musical Times* (June 1974); M. Short, ed., *G. H. (1874–1934): A Centenary Documentation* (London, 1974); J. Warrack, "H. and the Linear Principle," *Musical Times* (June 1974); D. Boyer, "H.'s The Hymn of Jesus: An Investigation into Mysticism in Music," *Music Review*, XXXVI (1975); I. Holst, ed., *A Scrapbook for the H. Birthplace Museum* (Cheltenham, 1978); idem, "H.'s At the Boar's Head," *Musical Times* (May 1982); idem, "H. in the 1980s," ibid. (May 1984); C. Matthews, "Some Unknown H.," ibid.; J. Mitchell, *From Kneller Hall to Hammersmith: The Band Works of G. H.* (Tutzing, 1990); M. Short, *G. H.: The Man and His Music* (Oxford, 1990); R. Greene, *G. H. and a Rhetoric of Musical Character: Language and Method in Selected Orchestral Works* (N.Y., 1994).

Holst, Henry, Danish violinist of English descent; b. Copenhagen, July 25, 1899; d. there, Oct. 15, 1991. He was a pupil of Telmanyi at Copenhagen Cons. and of Hess in Berlin. In 1919 he made his debut in Copenhagen. After serving as concertmaster of the Berlin Phil. (1923–31), he was active as a soloist and chamber music player. He also taught at the Royal Manchester College of Music (1931–46; 1950–53), the Royal College of Music in London (1946–54), the Royal Danish Cons. of Music in Copenhagen (from 1953), and the Tokyo Univ. of the Arts (1961–63).

Holst, Imogen (Clare), English conductor and writer on music, daughter of **Gustav(us Theodore von) Holst**; b. Richmond, Surrey, April 12, 1907; d. Aldeburgh, March 9, 1984. She studied at the St. Paul's Girls' School and the Royal College of Music in London. From 1943 to 1951 she was music director of the Dartington Hall arts center. From 1952 to 1964 she was musical assistant to Britten; she also conducted the Purcell Singers (1953–67) and served as artistic director of the Aldeburgh Festival (from 1956). In 1975 she was made a Commander of the Order of the British Empire. Her most important writings include *Gustav Holst: A Biography* (London, 1938; 2nd ed., 1969), *The Music of Gustav Holst* (London, 1951; 3rd ed., rev., 1986, including *Holst's Music Reconsidered*), and *A Thematic Catalogue of Gustav Holst's Music* (London, 1974). With C. Matthews, she ed. *Gustav Holst: Collected Facsimile Edition of Autograph Manuscripts of the Published Works* (London, 1974–83).

BIBL.: P. Cox and J. Dobbs, eds., *I. H. at Dartington* (Dartington, 1988).

Holt, Simeon ten, Dutch composer; b. Bergen, North Holland, Jan. 24, 1923. He studied with Honegger in Paris. After working at the Inst. for Sonology at the Univ. of Utrecht (1960–70), he was active with his own electronic music studio.

WORKS: ORCH.: *Diagonal Music* for Strings (1956); *Epigenese* (1964); *Centrifuga* (1979); *Une musique blanche* (1982). **CHAMBER:** Suite for String Quartet (1954); *Divertimento* for 3 Flutes (1957); *Triptichon* for 6 Percussionists (1965); String Quartet (1965); *Differenties* for 3 Clarinets, Piano, and Vibraphone (1969); *Scenario X* for Brass Quintet (1970); *Canto ostinato* for Instruments (1979); *Horizon* for Keyboard Instruments (1983–85). **PIANO:** *Compositions I–IV* (1942–45); Suite (1953); 2 sonatas (1953, 1959); *20 Bagatelles* (1954); *Allegro ex machina* (1955); *Diagonal Suite* (1957); *20 Epigrams* (1959); *Soloduiveldans I* (1959) and *II* (1986); *5 Etudes* (1961); *Natalon in E* (1980). **VOCAL:** *Atalon* for Mezzo-soprano and 36 Playing and Talking Instrumentalists (1967–68). **ELECTRONIC:** *Sevenplay* (1970); *Inferno I* (1970) and *II* (1971); *Modules I–VI* (1971); *I am Sylvia* (1973); *Recital I* and *II* (1972–74).

Holten, Bo, Danish conductor and composer; b. Copenhagen, Oct. 22, 1948. He studied at the Univ. of Copenhagen but was principally autodidact. He acquired a fine reputation as a conductor with his own vocal ensemble, Ars Nova, in Copenhagen; in 1990 he became a guest conductor of the BBC Singers in London. He has frequently led challenging concerts in which works from various eras and nations have appeared on the same program. As a composer, Holton has been particularly noted for his inventive counterpoint and melodic writing.

WORKS: DRAMATIC: *The Bond*, opera (1978–79); film scores. **ORCH.:** *Mahler-Impromptu* (1972–73); *Venetian Rhapsody* for Chamber Orch. (1974); *Caccia* (1979); 2 syms.: No. 1 for Chorus and Orch. (1981–82) and No. 2, *Sønderjysk Sommer Symfoni* for Soprano, Baritone, Chorus, and Orch. (1993); *Sinfonia Concertante* for Cello and Orch. (1985–86); Clarinet Concerto (1987); *Plainsongs* for Trumpet and Orch. (1989); *Le jardin magique de Ravel* (1991); Oboe Concerto (1992–93). **CHAMBER:** *Cut* for 6 Percussion (1980); *Pillows and Fragments* for 2 Trumpets, Horn, Trombone, and Tuba (1981); *Czerny Goes Mad* for 6 Percussion (1983); *Ancher Erectum* for 2 Percussion (1984); *Sarabande à trois* for Oboe, Cello, and Harpsichord (1984); *Waltz Ache I* for Vibraphone (1984); *Chaconne* for String Quartet (1987); *La marcia alla follia* for Flute, Violin, Viola, Cello, and Piano (1990). **VOCAL:** *Little Kirstin at the Stake* for Soprano and Chorus (1972); *Pavane Fantasia* for Soloists and Chorus (1974); Sonata for Soprano, Violin, and Cello (1976); *Tallis Variations* for Chorus and 9 Solo Strings (1976); *La douce nuit* for Chorus and Bells (1976); *The Garden of Love* for Tenor, Oboe, Clarinet, and String Quartet (1979); *Wave and Cut* for Chorus and 6 Percussion (1979); *Lumbago* for Chorus, Chamber Ensemble, and Synthesizer (1981); *The Clod and the Pebble* for 2 Choruses, 3 Clarinets, and Percussion (1982); *The Flame and the Coal* for Mezzo-soprano, Flute, Violin, Viola, Cello, and Piano (1983); *5 Motets* for Chorus and Organ (1983); *Imperia* for Chorus and Orch. (1983); *The Hours of Folly* for Medium or High Voice, Flute, Clarinet, and String Quartet (1984); *Tertia Die* for Chorus and Orch. (1985); *Waltz Ache II* for Chorus and Vibraphone (1985); *Pastell-Bilder* for Medium Voice, Flute, Clarinet, Guitar, and Percussion (1985–86); *Songs of Dusk* for Soprano, Bassoon, and Orch. (1987); *A Time for Everything* for Chorus (1990); *Rain and Rush and Rosy Bush* for Chorus (1991); *Night* for Chorus (1992).

Holter, Iver (Paul Fredrik), Norwegian conductor and composer; b. Gausdal, Dec. 13, 1850; d. Oslo, Jan. 25, 1941. He entered the Univ. of Christiania as a student of medicine, but devoted much more time to music, which he studied under Svendsen; then was a pupil of Jadassohn, Richter, and Reinecke at the Leipzig Cons. (1876–78). He became Grieg's successor as conductor of the Harmonien in Bergen (1882); from 1886 to 1911 he was conductor of the Musikföreningen in Christiania, and from 1890 to 1905, of the Handvaerkersångföreningen; in 1907 he founded (and conducted until 1921) Holters Korforening. In 1919 the Norwegian government granted him an artist's stipend. He was ed. of the *Nordisk Musik Revue* (1900–1906). His compositions include a Sym. (1885); a Violin Concerto; chamber music; several cantatas, as for the 300-year jubilee of Christiania (1924) and for the 900-year Olavs-jubilee (1930); choruses; songs.

Holý, Alfred, Portuguese harpist; b. Oporto, Aug. 5, 1866; d. Vienna, May 8, 1948. He studied violin and piano; then took harp lessons with Stank at the Prague Cons. (1882–85). He subsequently was 1st harpist in the orchs. of the German Opera in Prague (1885–96), the Berlin Royal Opera (1896–1903), and the Vienna Court Opera (1903–13). In 1913 he became 1st harpist of the Boston Sym. Orch.; retired in 1928. He publ. various harp transcriptions.

Holzmair, Wolfgang (Friedrich), esteemed Austrian baritone; b. Vöcklabruck, April 24, 1952. He graduated from the Vienna Univ. of Economics but pursued training in voice with Rössl-Madjan and in lieder interpretation with Werba at the Vienna Academy of Music. After taking a prize at the 1982 International Song Competition of the Vienna Musikverein, he appeared in opera in Bern and Gelsenkirchen; also sang at the Bavarian State Opera in Munich, the Zürich Opera, and the Vienna State Opera. In 1989 he made his London debut in a recital at the Wigmore Hall. His U.S. debut followed in 1992 as soloist in Mahler's *Rückert-Lieder* with Dohnányi and the Cleveland Orch. He made his N.Y. debut in 1993 in a recital at the Frick Museum, and that same year made his debut at London's Covent Garden as Papageno; also appeared at the Salzburg Festival. Holzmair's operatic repertoire includes Gluck's Orfeo, Don Giovanni, Rossini's Figaro, Eugene Onegin, Wolfram, Pélleas, and Wozzeck. His repertoire is expansive, including works from all periods since the Baroque era, but he has become especially well known for his interpretations of Schubert and Mahler.

Homer, Louise (Dilworth née **Beatty**), esteemed American contralto; b. Shadyside, near Pittsburgh, April 30, 1871; d. Winter Park, Fla., May 6, 1947. She studied in Philadelphia and at the New England Cons. of Music in Boston, where she received instruction in harmony from **Sidney Homer**, who later became her husband (1895); then went to Paris to study voice with Fidèle Koenig and dramatic acting with Paul Lhérie, making her operatic debut as Leonora in *La Favorite* in Vichy (June 5, 1898). She made her first appearance at London's Covent Garden as Lola in *Cavalleria rusticana* on May 9, 1899, and appeared there again in 1900; was also on the roster of the Théâtre Royal de la Monnaie in Brussels (1899–1900). On Nov. 14, 1900, she made her U.S. debut as Amneris with the touring Metropolitan Opera in San Francisco, which role she sang at her formal debut on Dec. 22, 1900, with the company in N.Y. She remained on its roster until 1919, the 1914–15 season excepted. She was acclaimed for her interpretation of Gluck's Orfeo in Paris in 1909, a role she repeated later that year at the Metropolitan Opera under Toscanini; she also created the roles of the Witch in Humperdinck's *Königskinder* (Dec. 28, 1910) and of Mona in Parker's opera (March 14, 1912) there. After singing with opera companies in Chicago (1920–25) and in San Francisco and Los Angeles (1926), she returned to the Metropolitan (1927), continuing on its roster until her farewell performance as Azucena on Nov. 28, 1929. She subsequently appeared in recitals with her daughter, the soprano Louise Homer Stires. In addition to Italian and French roles, she sang with great success such Wagernian roles as Brangäne, Erda, Fricka, Ortrud, and Waltraute. Her nephew was **Samuel Barber**.

BIBL.: S. Homer, *My Wife and I* (N.Y., 1939); A. Homer, *L. H. and the Golden Age of Opera* (N.Y., 1973).

Homer, Sidney, American composer; b. Boston, Dec. 9, 1864; d. Winter Park, Fla., July 10, 1953. He studied in Boston with Chadwick; then in Leipzig and Munich. In 1895 he married **Louise (Dilworth** née **Beatty) Homer**, his pupil, and went with her to Paris. He publ. a book of memoirs, *My Wife and I* (N.Y., 1939). He publ. about 100 songs, many of which won great favor, particularly *A Banjo Song*; also *Dearest, Requiem, Prospice, Bandanna Ballads, It was the time of roses, General William Booth Enters into Heaven, The Song of the Shirt, Sheep and Lambs, Sing me a song of a lad that is gone*, and *The Pauper's Drive.* He also composed a Sonata for Organ (1922); Quintet for Piano and Strings (1932); Violin Sonata (1936); String Quartet (1937); Piano Trio (1937).

BIBL.: H. Thorpe, "The Songs of S. H.," *Musical Quarterly* (Jan. 1931).

Homs (Oller), Joaquín, Catalan composer; b. Barcelona, Aug. 22, 1906. He studied cello and later took lessons in theory with Roberto Gerhard (1931–37). He formed a constructivist style with thematic contents derived from Catalan melos.

WORKS: 7 string quartets (1938–68); Duo for Flute and Clarinet (1936); Wind Quintet (1940); Concertino for Piano and Strings (1946); Sextet (1959); String Trio (1968); *Impromptu for 10* (1970).

Honegger, Arthur (Oscar), remarkable French composer; b. Le Havre (of Swiss parents), March 10, 1892; d. Paris, Nov. 27, 1955. He studied violin in Paris with Capet; then took courses with Kempter and Hegar at the Zürich Cons. (1909–11). Returning to France in 1912, he entered the Paris Cons., in the classes of Gédalge and Widor; also took lessons with d'Indy. His name first attracted attention when he took part in a concert of Les Nouveaux Jeunes in Paris on Jan. 15, 1918. In 1920 Henri Collet publ. an article in *Comoedia* in which he drew a fortuitous parallel between the Russian Five and a group of young French composers whom he designated as Les Six. These Six were Honegger, Milhaud, Poulenc, Auric, Durey, and Tailleferre. The label persisted, even though the 6 composers went their separate ways and rarely gave concerts together. In the early years of his career, Honegger embraced the fashionable type of urban music, with an emphasis on machine-like rhythms and curt, pert melodies. In 1921 he wrote a sport ballet, *Skating Rink*, and a mock-militaristic ballet, *Sousmarine*. In 1923 he composed the most famous of such machine pieces, *Mouvement symphonique No. 1*, subtitled *Pacific 231*. The score was intended to be a realistic tonal portrayal of a powerful American locomotive, bearing the serial number 231. The music progressed in accelerating rhythmic pulses toward a powerful climax, then gradually slackened its pace until the final abrupt stop; there was a simulacrum of a lyrical song in the middle section of the piece. *Pacific 231* enjoyed great popularity and became in the minds of modern-minded listeners a perfect symbol of the machine age. Honegger's 2nd *Mouvement symphonique*, composed in 1928, was a musical rendering of the popular British sport rugby. His *Mouvement symphonique No. 3*, however, bore no identifying subtitle. This abandonment of allusion to urban life coincided chronologically with a general trend away from literal representation and toward absolute music in classical forms, often of historical or religious character. Among his most important works in that genre were *Le Roi David*, to a biblical subject, and *Jeanne d'Arc au bücher*, glorifying the French patriot saint on the semimillennium of her martyrdom. Honegger's syms. were equally free from contemporary allusions; the first 2 lacked descriptive titles; his 3rd was entitled Liturgique, with a clear reference to an ecclesiastical ritual; the 4th was named Deliciae Basilienses, because it was written to honor the city of Basel; the somewhat mysterious title of the 5th, *Di tre re*, signified nothing more arcane than the fact that each of its movements ended on the thrice-repeated note D. Honegger spent almost all of his life in France, but he retained his dual Swiss citizenship, a fact that caused some biographers to refer to him as a Swiss composer. In 1926 he married the pianist-composer Andrée Vaurabourg (1894–1980), who often played piano parts in his works. In 1929 he paid a visit to the U.S.; he returned in 1947 to teach summer classes at the Berkshire Music Center at Tanglewood, but soon after his arrival was stricken with a heart ailment and was unable to complete his term; he returned to Paris and remained there until his death. He publ. a book, *Je suis compositeur* (Paris, 1951; Eng. tr., London, 1966).

WORKS: DRAMATIC: *Le Roi David*, dramatic Psalm for Narrator, Soloists, Chorus, and 15 Instruments (Mézières, June 11, 1921; rev. as an oratorio with Full Orch., 1923; Winterthur, Dec. 2, 1923); *Antigone*, opera (1924–27; Brussels, Dec. 28, 1927); *Judith*, biblical drama (Mézières, June 11, 1925; expanded as an opera, Monte Carlo, Feb. 13, 1926); *Amphion*, melodrama (1929; Paris, June 23, 1931); *Les Aventures du Roi Pausole*, operetta (1929–30; Paris, Dec. 12, 1930); *Cris du Monde*, stage oratorio for Soprano, Contralto, Baritone, Chorus, and Orch. (1930; Solothurn, May 3, 1931); *La Belle de Moudon*, operetta (Mézières, May 30, 1931); *Jeanne d'Arc au bûcher*, dramatic oratorio (1934–35; concert version, without Prologue, Basel, May 12, 1938; stage premiere, in German, Zürich, June 13, 1942); *L'Aiglon*, opera (1935; Monte Carlo, March 11, 1937; in collaboration with J. Ibert); *Les Mille et Une Nuits*, spectacle for Soprano, Tenor, Chorus, and Orch. (Paris Exhibition, 1937); *Les Petites Cardinal*, operetta (1937; Paris, Feb. 20, 1938; in collaboration with J. Ibert); *Nicolas de Flue*, dramatic legend for Narrator, Chorus, Children's Chorus, and Orch. (1939; concert premiere, Solothurn, Oct. 26, 1940; stage premiere, Neuchâtel, May 31, 1941). **BALLETS:** *Vérité-Mensonge*, marionette ballet (Paris, Nov. 1920); *Skating Rink* (1921; Paris, Jan. 20, 1922); *Sousmarine* (1924; Paris, June 27, 1925); *Roses de métal* (Paris, 1928); *Semiramis*, ballet-melodrama (1931; Paris, May 11, 1934); *Un Oiseau blanc s'est envolé* (Paris, June 1937); *Le Cantique des cantiques* (1937; Paris, Feb. 2, 1938); *La Naissance des couleurs* (1940; Paris, 1949); *Le Mangeur de rêves* (Paris, 1941); *L'Appel de la montagne* (1943; Paris, July 9, 1945); *Chota Roustaveli* or *L'Homme à la peau de léopard* (1945; Monte Carlo, May 5, 1946; scenes 2 and 3 by Harsányi and A. Tcherepnin); *De la musique* (1950). **INCIDENTAL MUSIC:** *Les Dit des jeux du monde* for Flute, Trumpet, Percussion, and Strings (1918; as a ballet, Paris, Dec. 2, 1918); *La Mort de Sainte Alméenne* (1918); *La Danse macabre* (1919); *Saül* (Paris, June 16, 1922); *Fantasio* (1922); *Antigone* (1922); *La Tempête* (1923); *Liluli* (1923); *Le Miracle de Notre-Dame* (1925); *L'Impératrice aux rochers* (1925; Paris, Feb. 17, 1927); *Phèdre* (1926); *800 mètres* (1941); *Le Soulier de satin* for Soprano, Baritone, and Orch. (Paris, Nov. 17, 1943); *Charles le Téméraire* for Chorus, 2 Trumpets, 2 Trombones, and Percussion (1943–44; Mézières, May 27, 1944); *Hamlet* for Narrator, Chorus, and Orch. (Paris, Oct. 17, 1946); *Prométhée* (1946); *L'État de siège* (Paris, Oct. 27, 1948); *Tête d'or* (1948); *Oedipe-Roi* (1948). **RADIO MUSIC:** *Les Douze Coups de minuit*, "radio-mystère" for Chorus and Chamber Orch. (Paris Radio, Dec. 27, 1933); *Radio panoramique* for Tenor, Soprano, Organ, String Quintet, Wind Instruments, and Percussion (Geneva Radio, March 4, 1935; concert premiere, Paris, Oct. 19, 1935); *Christophe Colomb*, radio oratorio for 2 Tenors, Chorus, and Orch. (Lausanne Radio, April 17, 1940); *Les Battements du monde* for Woman's Voice, Child's Voice, Chorus, and Orch. (Lausanne Radio, May 18, 1944); *Saint François d'Assise* for Narrator, Baritone, Chorus, and Orch. (Lausanne Radio, Dec. 3, 1949). **FILM MUSIC:** *Les Misérables* (1934); *Mayerling* (1935); *Regain* (1937); *Mlle. Doctor* (1937); *Pygmalion*, after G.B. Shaw's play (1938); *Mermoz* (1943); *Bourdelle* (1950); 36 others.

ORCH.: *Prélude pour "Aglavaine et Sélysette,"* after Maeterlinck (1916–17; Paris Cons. orch. class, April 3, 1917, composer conducting); *Le Chant de Nigamon* (1917; Paris, Jan. 3, 1920); *Entrée, Nocturne et Berceuse* for Piano and Chamber Orch. (Paris, 1919); *Pastorale d'été* (1920; Paris, Feb. 12, 1921); *Horace Victorieux*, "mimed sym." (1920–21; concert premiere, Lausanne, Oct. 30, 1921; mimed premiere, Essen, Dec. 28, 1927); *Marche funèbre* (1 section of *Les Mariés de la Tour Eiffel*, with other individual sections by Auric, Milhaud, Poulenc, and Tailleferre; Paris, June 18, 1921); *Chant de joie* (Paris, April 7, 1923); *Prélude pour "La Tempête,"* after Shakespeare (Paris, May 1, 1923); *Pacific 231* (*Mouvement symphonique No. 1*; 1923; Paris, May 8, 1924); Piano Concertino (1924; Paris, May 23, 1925; A. Vaurabourg soloist); Suite from incidental music to *L'Impératrice aux rochers* (1925); Suite from incidental music to *Phèdre* (1926); *Rugby* (*Mouvement symphonique No. 2*; Paris, Oct. 19, 1928, Ansermet conducting); *Prélude, Fugue et Postlude*, from the melodrama *Amphion* (1929; Geneva, Nov. 3, 1948); Cello Concerto (1929; Boston, Feb. 17, 1930); 5 syms.: No. 1 (1929–30; Boston, Feb. 13, 1931), No. 2 for Strings and optional Trumpet (1941; Zürich, May 18, 1942), No. 3, *Liturgique* (1945–46; Zürich, Aug. 17, 1946), No. 4, *Deliciae Basilienses* (1946; Basel, Jan. 21, 1947), and No. 5, *Di tre re* (1950; Boston, March, 9, 1951); *Mouvement symphonique No. 3* (1932–33; Berlin, March 26, 1933); Suite from the film *Les Misérables* (1934; Paris, Jan. 19, 1935); *Prélude, Arioso et Fughetta sur le nom de BACH* for Strings (arranged by A. Hoérée from the piano version, 1936; Paris, Dec. 5, 1936); *Nocturne* (Brussels, April 30, 1936); *La Marche sur la Bastille* for Band, from incidental music for Romain Rolland's pageant *Le Quatorze Juillet* (Paris, July 14, 1936); *La Grande Barrage*, "image musicale" (1942); *Jour de fête suisse*, suite from the ballet *L'Appel de la montagne* (1943; Winterthur, Nov. 14, 1945); 2 extracts from the film *Mermoz* (1943); *Sérénade à Angélique* for Small Orch. (Zürich Radio, Nov. 19, 1945); *Concerto da camera* for Flute, English Horn, and Strings (Zürich, May 6, 1949); *Toccata* (1 section of *La Guirlande de Campra*, with other individual sections by Lesur, Manuel, Tailleferre, Poulenc, Sauguet, and Auric, 1950; complete work, Aix-en-Provence Festival, July 31, 1952); *Suite archaïque* (1950–51; Louisville, Feb. 28, 1951); *Monopartita* (Zürich, June 12, 1951).

CHAMBER: 2 violin sonatas (1916–18; 1919); 3 string quartets (1916–17; 1934–36; 1936–37); *Rapsodie* for 2 Flutes, Clarinet (or 2 Violins, Viola), and Piano (1917); *Danse de la chèvre* for Flute (1919); Sonatina for 2 Violins (1920); Viola Sonata (1920); Cello Sonata (1920); *Hymn* for 10 String Instruments (1920); Sonatina for Clarinet or Cello and Piano (1921–22); *3 contrepoints* for Flute, English Horn, Violin, and Cello (1923); *Prélude et Blues* for Quartet of Chromatic Harps (1925); Sonatina for Violin and Cello (1932); *Petite suite* for any 2 Treble Instruments and Piano (1934); Sonata for Solo Violin (1940); *Sortilèges* for Ondes Martenot (1946); *Intrada* for Trumpet and Piano (1947); *Romance* for Flute and Piano (1953). **PIANO:** *3 pièces* (*Scherzo, Humoresque,* and *Adagio espressivo*; 1910); *3 pièces: Hommage à Ravel* (1915); *Prélude et Danse* (1919); *Toccata et Variations* (1916); *7 pièces brèves* (1919–20); *Sarabande* (1920); *Le Cahier Romand,* 5 pieces (1921–23); *Hommage à Albert Roussel* (1928); Suite for 2 Pianos (1928); *Prélude, Arioso et Fughetta sur le nom de BACH* (1932; arranged for Strings by A. Hoérée in 1936); *Scenic-Railway* (1937); *Partita* for 2 Pianos (1940; arranged from *3 contrepoints*); *2 esquisses,* in Obouhov's simplified notation (1943–44); *Souvenir de Chopin* (1947).

VOCAL: *Cantique de Pâques* for 3 Women's Voices, Women's Chorus, and Orch. (1918; Toulouse, March 27, 1923); *Pâques à New York* for Voice and String Quartet (1920); *Chanson de Ronsard* for Voice, Flute, and String Quartet (1924); *3 chansons de la petite sirène* for Voice, Flute, and Strings or String Quartet (1926); *La Danse des morts,* oratorio for Narrator, Soloists, Chorus, Organ, and Orch. (1938; Basel, March 1, 1940); *Chant de libération* for Baritone, Unison Chorus, and Orch. (1942; Paris, Oct. 22, 1944); *Une Cantate de Noël* for Baritone, Chorus, Children's Chorus, Organ, and Orch. (sketched 1941, completed 1953; Basel, Dec. 18, 1953). **SONGS:** *4 poèmes* (1914–16); *6 poèmes de Apollinaire* (1915–17; Nos. 1 and 3–6 orchestrated as *5 poèmes de Apollinaire,* 1916–17); *3 poèmes de Paul Fort* (1916); *6 poésies de Jean Cocteau* (1920–23); *2 chants d'Ariel* (1923; also arranged for Orch.); *3 poèmes de Claudel* (1939–40); *3 Psalms* (1940–41); *5 mélodies-minute* (1941); *4 Songs* for Low Voice and Piano (1944–45).

BIBL.: Roland-Manuel, *A. H.* (Paris, 1925); A. George, *A. H.* (Paris, 1926); W. Tappolet, *A. H.* (in German, Zürich, 1933; 2nd Ger. ed., Zürich, 1954; French ed., Neuchâtel, 1938; 2nd Fr. ed., Neuchâtel, 1957); C. Gérard, *A. H.: Catalogue succinct des oeuvres* (Brussels, 1945); J. Bruyr, *H. et son oeuvre* (Paris, 1947); J. Matter, *H. ou La Quête de joie* (Lausanne, 1956); A. Gauthier, *A. H.* (London, 1957); M. Landowski, *H.* (Paris, 1957); W. Reich, ed., *A. H., Nachklang: Schriften, Photos, Dokumente* (Zürich, 1957); J. Feschotte, *A. H.: L'Homme et son oeuvre* (Paris, 1966); P. Meylan, *A. H., Humanitäre Botschaft der Musik* (Frauenfeld, 1970); J. Mailliard and J. Nahoum, *Les Symphonies d'A. H.* (Paris, 1974); G. Spratt, *The Music of A. H.* (Cork, 1987); H. Ehrler, *Untersuchungen zur Klaviermusik von Francis Poulenc, A. H. und Darius Milhaud* (Tutzing, 1990); H. Halbreich, *A. H., un musicien dans la cité des hommes* (Paris, 1992); J. Roy, *Le groupe des six: Poulenc, Milhaud, H., Auric, Tailleferre, Durey* (Paris, 1994).

Honegger, Henri (Charles), Swiss cellist; b. Geneva, June 10, 1904; d. Conches, Aug. 4, 1992. He studied with Ami Briquet in Geneva, Klengel at the Leipzig Cons., and Casals and Alexanian in Paris. He was 1st cellist in the Orchestre de la Suisse Romande in Geneva until 1964; he also appeared as a soloist with orchs. throughout Europe, North and South America, and Japan, and also appeared as a recitalist.

Honegger, Marc, French musicologist; b. Paris, June 17, 1926. He was educated in Paris, where he studied with Chailley and Masson (music history and theory) at the Sorbonne (1947–50), Santiago Riera (piano), Ion Constantinesco and Bigot (conducting), and Migot (composition) at the École Supérieure de Musique, and at the Univ. (docteur-ès-lettres, 1970, with 2 diss., *Les chansons spirituelle de Didier Lupi Second et les débuts de la musique protestante en France au XVIe siècle,* publ. in Lille, 1971, and *Les messes de Josquin des Pres dans la tablature de Diego Pisador (Salamanque 1552): Contribution a l'étude des alterations au XVIe siècle*). After working at the Inst. of Musicology at the Univ. of Paris (1954–58), he taught at the Univ. of Strasbourg (1958–91). He was secretary general (1973–77) and president (1977–80) of the Société française de musicologie, and vice-president of the International Musicological Soc. (1982–92).

WRITINGS: *La musique française de 1830 à 1914* (1962); ed. *Dictionnaire de la musique* (2 vols., Strasbourg, 1970; 4th ed., rev., 1993); ed. *Science de la musique* (4 vols., Paris, 1976); *Georges Migot humaniste* (Strasbourg, 1977); *Catalogue des oeuvres musicale de Georges Migot* (Strasbourg, 1977); ed. *Dictionnaire des oeuvres de la musique vocale* (3 vols., Paris, 1991–92).

Höngen, Elisabeth, esteemed German mezzo-soprano; b. Gevelsberg, Dec. 7, 1906. She studied voice with Hermann Weissenborn and Ludwig Horth in Berlin. In 1933 she made her operatic debut as Lady Macbeth at the Wuppertal Opera, where she was a member until 1935. She then sang with the Düsseldorf Opera (1935–40) and the Dresden State Opera (1940–43). In 1943 she joined the Vienna State Opera, where she remained one of its principal artists during the next 2 decades. In 1947 she was honored as an Austrian Kammersängerin. She first sang at London's Covent Garden in 1947 as a member of the visiting Vienna State Opera, returning there in 1959–60. From 1948 to 1950, and again in 1959, she appeared at the Salzburg Festivals. In 1951 she was a soloist in Beethoven's 9th Sym. under Furtwängler at the reopening of the Bayreuth Festival. On Jan. 10, 1952, she made her Metropolitan Opera debut in N.Y. as Hérodias, returning there that season as Waltraute and Klytemnestra. She also was a guest artist in Berlin, Munich, Paris, Milan, Buenos Aires, and other operatic centers. From 1957 to 1960 she was a prof. at the Vienna Academy of Music. Among her other notable portrayals were Dorabella, Marcellina, Ortrud, Eboli, and Fricka.

Hood, Mantle, American ethnomusicologist and composer; b. Springfield, Ill., June 24, 1918. He studied composition privately with Toch (1945–50); was enrolled at the Univ. of Calif., Los Angeles (B.A., 1951; M.A. in composition, 1951); continued his studies at the Univ. of Amsterdam (Ph.D., 1954, with the diss. *The Nuclear Theme as a Determinant of Patet in Javanese Music*; publ. in Groningen, 1954). In 1954 he joined the faculty at the Univ. of Calif., Los Angeles, becoming a full prof. there in 1962 and in 1961 was appointed director of its Inst. of Ethnomusicology. In 1956–57 he traveled to Indonesia on a Ford Foundation fellowship, and in 1976 received a Fulbright fellowship for study in India. In 1976 he became an adjunct prof. at the Univ. of Maryland; in 1977 was a visiting prof. at Yale Univ. and at Wesleyan Univ. He publ. *The Ethnomusicologist* (N.Y., 1971; 2nd ed., rev., 1982) and *The Paragon of the Roaring Sea* (Wilhelmshaven and N.Y., 1988); also contributed valuable articles on Oriental music to learned journals and musical encyclopedias. His compositions include a symphonic poem, *Vernal Equinox* (1955); Woodwind Trio (1950); 6 duets for Soprano and Alto Recorder (1954); piano pieces.

Hoof, Jef van, Belgian composer; b. Antwerp, May 8, 1886; d. there, April 24, 1959. He studied composition at the Antwerp Cons. with Gilson, Mortelmas, and Huybrechts. He composed 3 operas: *Tycho-Brahe* (1911), *Meivuur* (1916), and *Jonker Lichthart* (1928); 5 syms. (1938, 1941, 1945, 1951, 1956); choruses; lieder; piano pieces. His style of composition is neo-Romantic, with a penchant for expansive sonorities.

Hoogstraten, Willem van, Dutch conductor; b. Utrecht, March 18, 1884; d. Tutzing, Sept. 11, 1965. He studied violin with Alexander Schmuller; then with Bram Eldering at the Cologne Cons. and with Ševčik in Prague. He played concerts with **Elly Ney**, whom he married in 1911 (divorced in 1927). From 1914 to 1918 he conducted the Krefeld orch.; in 1922 he was engaged as conductor of the summer concerts of the N.Y. Phil. (until 1938); was its assoc. conductor (1923–25). He was conductor of the Portland (Oreg.) Sym. Orch. from 1925 to 1938. After conducting the Salzburg Mozarteum Orch. (1939–45), he was a guest conductor in Europe.

Hopekirk, Helen, Scottish-born American pianist, teacher, and composer; b. Edinburgh, May 20, 1856; d. Cambridge, Mass., Nov. 19, 1945. Following training with A.C. Mackenzie, she attended the Leipzig Cons. (1876–78). On Nov. 28, 1878, she made her debut as soloist with the Gewandhaus Orch. in Leipzig, and then toured the Continent and Great Britain. In 1882 she married the businessman, music critic, and landscape painter William A. Wilson, who subsequently served as her manager. On Dec. 7, 1883, she made her U.S. debut as soloist with the Boston Sym. Orch., and then toured the country until 1887. After piano lessons with Leschetizky in Vienna (1887–89), she pursued training in composition in Paris (1892–94). From 1897 to 1901 she taught at the New England Cons. of Music in Boston, and thereafter privately. She continued to pursue her career as a pianist, making her farewell appearance in 1939 in a concert devoted entirely to her own compositions. In 1918 she became a naturalized American citizen. As a performer, she gave the first U.S. performances of several works by Debussy and other French composers. In her own works, she gave primary concern to producing scores notable for their modal melodies and harmonies. She arranged and ed. *Seventy Scottish Songs* (Boston, 1905).

WORKS: Concertstück for Piano and Orch. (1894); Piano Concerto (Boston, Dec. 27, 1900, composer soloist); 2 violin sonatas (n.d., 1891); many piano pieces; choral works; 91 songs.

BIBL.: C. Hall and H. Tetlow, *H. H. 1856–1945* (Cambridge, Mass., 1954).

Hopf, Hans, German tenor; b. Nuremberg, Aug. 2, 1916; d. Munich, June 25, 1993. He studied in Munich with Paul Bender and in Oslo with Ragnvald Bjärne. In 1936 he made his operatic debut as Pinkerton at the Bavarian Landesbühnen in Munich, and then sang with the Augsburg Opera (1939–42), the Dresden State Opera (1942–43), the Oslo Opera (1943–44), and the Berlin State Opera (1946–49). In 1949 he joined the Bavarian State Opera in Munich, and sang there regularly until his retirement in 1988. In 1951 he was a soloist in Beethoven's 9th Sym. under Furtwängler at the reopening of the Bayreuth Festival, where he later sang from 1961 to 1966. From 1951 to 1953 he appeared at London's Covent Garden, returning there in 1963. On March 15, 1952, he made his Metropolitan Opera debut in N.Y. as Walther von Stolzing, remaining on the roster until 1953; he was again on its roster for the 1954–55, 1960–62, and 1963–64 seasons. He also sang at the Salzburg Festivals from 1954, and was a guest artist in Milan, Moscow, Zürich, San Francisco, Chicago, and Buenos Aires. Among his prominent roles were Florestan, Max in *Der Freischütz*, Siegfried, Parsifal, Tristan, Tannhäuser, Otello, and the Kaiser in *Die Frau ohne Schatten*.

Hopkins (real name, **Reynolds**), **Antony,** English pianist, conductor, broadcaster, writer on music, and composer; b. London, March 21, 1921. He was a pupil of Cyril Scott and Gordon Jacob at the Royal College of Music in London (1939–42). He then served as music director of the Intimate Opera Co. (1952–64), for which he composed several scores. He also wrote music for films, radio, and the theater, and was active as a radio broadcaster, hosting the series "Talking about Music" (1954–92). His books include *Understanding Music* (1979), *The Nine Symphonies of Beethoven* (1980), *The Concertgoer's Companion* (2 vols., 1984, 1986), and *Sounds of the Orchestra* (1993). In 1976 he was made a Commander of the Order of the British Empire.

Hoppin, Richard H(allowell), American musicologist; b. Northfield, Minn., Feb. 22, 1913; d. Columbus, Ohio, Nov. 1, 1991. He studied piano at the École Normale de Musique in Paris (1933–35), and musicology at Harvard Univ. (M.A., 1938; Ph.D., 1952). He was on the music faculty of the Univ. of Texas, Austin (1949–61); in 1961 he was appointed prof. of music at Ohio State Univ. In 1959–60 he was the recipient of a Guggenheim fellowship. He ed. the important collection *The Cypriot-French Repertory of the Manuscript Torino, Biblioteca Nazionale, J. II. 9.*, Corpus Mensurabilis Musicae, XXI (1960–63); also publ. the invaluable *An Introduction to Medieval Music* (N.Y., 1978).

Horák, Josef, Czech bass clarinetist; b. Znojmo, March 24, 1931. He attended the Brno Cons. (1945–51). He was a clarinetist in the Brno State Phil. and Prague Radio Sym. Orch. On Oct. 20, 1955, he made his debut as a performer on the bass clarinet, and began a career as a virtuoso on that instrument; along with the Dutch bass clarinetist Harry Sparnaay, Horák is responsible for the revival of interest in the bass clarinet. In 1963 he and the pianist Emma Kovárnová formed the chamber duo Due Boemi di Praga, and performed numerous specially commissioned works by Alois Hába, Jolivet, Martin, Messiaen, Stockhausen, and many, many others. In 1972 he was appointed to the faculty of the Prague Cons.

Horenstein, Jascha, distinguished Russian-born American conductor; b. Kiev, May 6, 1898; d. London, April 2, 1973. He began his musical training in Königsberg as a piano student of his mother, and he also studied with Max Brode. In 1911 he went to Vienna, where he studied philosophy at the Univ. and was a pupil of A. Busch (violin), Marx (theory), and Schreker (composition) at the Academy of Music; he then continued his training with Schreker at the Berlin Hochschule für Musik (1920). He served as an assistant to Furtwängler and began his career conducting the Schubert Choir in Berlin. In 1923 he was a guest conductor with the Vienna Sym. Orch. Returning to Berlin, he conducted the Blüthner Concerts (1924) and was conductor of the Berlin Sym. Orch. (1925–28); he also appeared as a guest conductor with the Berlin Phil. In 1929 he became music director of the Düsseldorf Opera, but was removed from that position in 1933 by the Nazi regime because he was a Jew. After conducting in Europe, Australia, New Zealand, and Palestine, he went to the U.S. in 1940 and became a naturalized American citizen. Following the end of World War II, he resumed his career in Europe. He became especially admired in England, where he appeared as a guest conductor with the London Sym. Orch. In 1961 he made his debut at London's Covent Garden conducting *Fidelio*. While Horenstein's repertoire ranged widely from the Baroque era to the 20th century, he acquired his greatest renown as an interpreter of Bruckner and Mahler.

BIBL.: *Le Grand Baton* (June 1976).

Horký, Karel, Czech composer; b. Štěmechy, near Třebíč, Sept. 4, 1909; d. Brno, Nov. 27, 1988. He played in a military band as a boy; studied bassoon; took lessons in composition with V. Polivka and Pavel Haas; then entered the Prague Cons. as a student of Křička, graduating in 1944. He taught harmony (1945–52) and was director (1964–71) at the Brno Cons.

WORKS: DRAMATIC: OPERAS: *Jan Hus* (Brno, May 27, 1950); *Hejtman Šarovec* (Brno, 1953); *Jed z Elsinoru* (The Poison from Elsinor), freely after Shakespeare's *Hamlet* (Brno, Nov. 11, 1969); *Dawn* (Brno, July 4, 1975); *Atlantida* (1980). **BALLETS:** *Lastura* (The Shell; Brno, Oct. 23, 1945); *Král Ječmínek* (King Ječmínek; Brno, Sept. 21, 1951). **ORCH.:** *Klythia*, symphonic poem (1941); *Romantic Sinfonietta* (1944); Cello Concerto (1953); Violin Concerto (1955); 5 syms. (1959, 1964, 1971, 1974, 1977); *Serenade* for Strings (1963); Bassoon Concerto (1966); Horn Concerto (1971); *Fateful Preludes* for Piano and Orch. (1972); *Dimitrov*, symphonic poem, in memory of the chairman of the Bulgarian Communist Party (1972). **CHAMBER:** 4 string quartets (1938, 1954, 1955, 1963); Violin Sonata (1943); Suite for Wind Quintet (1943); Nonet (1958); Clarinet Quintet (1960); piano pieces. **VOCAL:** Choruses; songs.

Hornbostel, Erich Moritz von, eminent Austrian musicologist; b. Vienna, Feb. 25, 1877; d. Cambridge, England, Nov. 28, 1935. He studied philosophy in Vienna and Heidelberg; received a Ph.D. in chemistry from the Univ. of Vienna (1900). In 1905–06 he was the assistant of Stumpf in Berlin; in 1906 he went to the U.S. to record and study Indian music (Pawnee); from 1906 to 1933, was director of the Phonogramm-Archiv in

Berlin, and concurrently a prof. at the Univ. of Berlin (1917–33); then went again to the U.S. In 1934 he went to England. He was a specialist in Asian, African, and other non-European music; also investigated the problems of tone psychology; contributed hundreds of articles to scholarly publications on these subjects. He ed. a collection of records, *Musik des Orients* (Lindstrom, 1932); from 1922 until his death, was co-ed., with C. Stumpf, of the *Sammelbände für vergleichende Musikwissenschaft.* Hornbostel's writings were prepared for reissue, ed. by K. Wachsmann et al. (The Hague, 1975 et seq.).

Horne, Marilyn (Bernice), outstanding American mezzo-soprano; b. Bradford, Pa., Jan. 16, 1934. She studied with William Vennard at the Univ. of Southern Calif. in Los Angeles; also attended Lotte Lehmann's master classes. She then went to Europe, where she made her professional operatic debut as Giulietta at the Gelsenkirchen Opera in 1957; remained on its roster until 1960, appearing in such roles as Mimi, Tatiana, Minnie, Fulvia in *Ezio,* and Marie in *Wozzeck,* the role she repeated in her U.S. debut at the San Francisco Opera on Oct. 4, 1960. She married **Henry Lewis** in 1960, and subsequently made a number of appearances under his direction; they were separated in 1976. In 1965 she made her debut at London's Covent Garden, again as Marie. She appeared at Milan's La Scala in 1969, and on March 3, 1970, made her Metropolitan Opera debut in N.Y. as Adalgisa; subsequently became one of the Metropolitan's principal singers. Her notable performances there included Rosina in *Il Barbiere di Siviglia* (Jan. 23, 1971), Carmen (Sept. 19, 1972), Fides in *Le Prophète* (Jan. 18, 1977), Rinaldo (the first Handel opera to be staged there, Jan. 19, 1984), Isabella in *L'Italiana in Algeri* (telecast live by PBS, Jan. 11, 1986), and Samira in the premiere of Corigliano's *The Ghosts of Versailles* (Dec. 19, 1991). In 1992 President Bush awarded her the National Medal of Arts. On Jan. 20, 1993, she sang at the inauguration of President Clinton in Washington, D.C. That same year, she founded the Marilyn Horne Foundation with the goal of encouraging young singers as art song recitalists. In 1994 she began teaching at the Music Academy of the West in Santa Barbara, where she was artist-in-residence and director of the voice program from 1995. In 1995 she received a Kennedy Center Honor. Acclaimed for her brilliant portrayals in roles by Handel, Rossini, and Meyerbeer, she won equal praise as an outstanding concert artist. She publ. an autobiography (with J. Scovell; N.Y., 1983).

Horovitz, Joseph, Austrian-born English composer, conductor, and teacher; b. Vienna, May 26, 1926. He went to England in 1938 and studied music (with Westrup) and literature at New College, Oxford (M.A. and B.Mus., 1948), with Jacob at the Royal College of Music in London, and with Boulanger in Paris. In 1950–51 he was music director of the Bristol Old Vic Co. From 1952 to 1963 he was assoc. director of the Intimate Opera Co. He was prof. of composition at the Royal College of Music from 1961. From 1981 to 1989 he served as president of the International Council of Composers and Lyricists. In 1959 he received the Commonwealth Medal for Composition and in 1961 the Leverhulme Music Research Award. His facility as a composer is evident in both his handling of serious and light scores.

WORKS: DRAMATIC: *Gentleman's Island,* opera (Cheltenham, July 9, 1959); *The Dumb Wife,* opera (Antwerp, Jan. 10, 1972); 16 ballets, including *Alice in Wonderland* (1953), *Les Femmes d'Alger, Miss Carter Wore Pink,* and *Concerto for Dancers*; theater, radio, and television scores. **ORCH.:** *Fantasia on a Theme of Couperin* for Strings (London, July 29, 1962); Trumpet Concerto (1963); Jazz Harpsichord Concerto (1965); *Horizon Overture* (1972); *Toy Symphony* for 17 Toy Instruments, Piano, and Strings (1977). **BRASS BAND:** *Ballet for Band; Sinfonietta; Concertino Classico,* double trumpet concerto; *Theme and Co-Operation* (1994). **WIND ORCH.:** *Bacchus on Blue Ridge; Wind-Harp; Ad Astra; Dance Suite; Fête Galante; Commedia dell'Arte.* **CHAMBER:** 5 string quartets; Oboe Quartet (1956); *Music Hall Suite* for Brass Quintet (1964); *Adam-Blues* for Trombone and Piano (1968); Clarinet Sonatina (1981). **VOCAL:** *Horrortorio,* nuptial cantata for Soli, Chorus, and Orch. (1959); *Captain Noah and his Floating Zoo* for Chorus (1970); *Samson,* oratorio for Chorus and Brass Band (London, Oct. 8, 1977); choruses; songs.

Horowitz, Richard, American composer and instrumentalist; b. Buffalo, Jan. 6, 1949. In 1968 he became a pianist with Alan Sylvia's Orch., playing at European festivals. He returned to America in 1969 to study at Antioch College, but difficulties with the selective service led to a decade-long exodus to Europe and North Africa. From 1970 to 1980 he studied electronic music in Paris, and microtonal modulation and the ney (reed flute) in Morocco with Kasmi Nacquisabundi. He composed for the Mabou Mines and choreographer Alice Farley; he performed with Anthony Braxton, Jon Hassell, and David Byrne. His recordings include *Oblique Sequences/Solo Ney Improvisations No. 1* (1979) and *Solo Ney Improvisations No. 3*; he also collaborated with Daniel Kobialka on the album *Memoire* (1982). His film scores include Bertolucci's *The Sheltering Sky* (1990; screenplay by Paul Bowles). In 1981 he began a remarkable collaboration with the Iranian-born American vocalist, dancer, and composer Sussan Deiheim (b. Teheran, Dec. 14, 1956); their works are based on a dense tangle of Middle Eastern, jazz, and avant-garde styles, and involve improvisation, electronics, and computer processing. The works themselves are hypnotically intense but highly formal, with structures and titles based on complex puns and paradoxes; among their stage works are *Desert Equations* (1984), *Azax/Attra* (1985), *Ibn Sabbah, Ghost of the Assassin* (N.Y., 1988), and *X-Isle Isle X* (1989). They also collaborated on a recording, *Abstract Quotients* (1984).

Horowitz, Vladimir (Samoliovich), legendary Russian-born American pianist; b. Berdichev, Oct. 1, 1903; d. N.Y., Nov. 5, 1989. Reared in a musically inclined Jewish family, he began playing piano in his early childhood under the direction of his mother, a professional pianist. His other teachers were Vladimir Puchalsky, Sergei Tarnowsky, and Felix Blumenfeld. He made his first public appearance in a recital in Kiev on May 30, 1920, which marked the opening of a fantastically successful career. The revolutionary events in Russia did not prevent him from giving concerts in and around Kiev until he decided to leave Russia; his first official concert abroad took place in Berlin on Jan. 2, 1926. Arriving in Paris in 1928, he took brief instruction with Alfred Cortot, and on Jan. 12 of that same year, he made his American debut in Tchaikovsky's 1st Piano Concerto with the N.Y. Phil. under the direction of Sir Thomas Beecham; he subsequently appeared as soloist with several other American orchs., earning the reputation of a piano virtuoso of the highest caliber, so that his very name became synonymous with pianistic excellence. In 1933 he married Wanda Toscanini, daughter of Arturo Toscanini. In 1942 he became a naturalized American citizen.

Horowitz seemed to possess every gift of public success; he was universally admired, and his concerts sold out whenever and wherever he chose to appear. His natural affinity was with the Russian repertoire; he formed a sincere friendship with Rachmaninoff, despite the disparity in their ages; Rachmaninoff himself regarded Horowitz as the greatest pianist of the century; Horowitz's performance of Rachmaninoff's 3rd Piano Concerto, which he played numerous times, was his proudest accomplishment. His performances of works by Chopin, Liszt, Schumann, and Tchaikovsky were equally incomparable. During World War II, he appeared with Toscanini in numerous patriotic concerts; it was for such a celebration in N.Y.'s Central Park that he made a vertiginous transcription for piano of Sousa's *Stars and Stripes Forever,* a veritable tour de force of pianistic pyrotechnics, which he performed for years as an encore, to the delight of his audiences. On Dec. 9, 1949, he gave the premiere of Samuel Barber's Piano Sonata in Havana. On Feb. 25, 1953, the 25th anniversary of his American debut, he gave a recital in Carnegie Hall in N.Y. After this recital, he withdrew from the stage, not to return for nearly 12 years. However, he enjoyed making recordings when he was free to change his successive versions in the sanctuary of a studio. He also accepted a few private pupils. He then announced a definite date for a concert in Carnegie Hall: May 9, 1965. Tickets went on sale 2 weeks in advance, and a line formed whose excitement and agitation would equal and surpass that of a queue of fans for a baseball game. Horowitz himself was so touched by this testimony of devotion that he sent hundreds of cups of coffee to the crowd to make the waiting more endurable on a rainy day.

On Feb. 26, 1978, he played at the White House at the invitation of President Carter, a performance that coincided with the 50th anniversary of Horowitz's American debut. On May 22, 1982, at the behest of the Prince of Wales, he gave a recital in the Royal Festival Hall in London, marking his first appearance in Europe in 31 years. Through his recordings, he formed a large following in Japan; to respond to his popularity there, he gave a series of concerts in Tokyo and other Japanese cities (June 1983). The climax of his career, which became a political event as well, was his decision to accept an invitation to revisit Russia in 1986, where he played for the first time after an absence of 61 years to enormous acclaim. His Steinway grand piano was shipped to Moscow. Horowitz himself was accompanied by his wife, a piano tuner, and his cook (to prepare the special foods consisting of fresh sole and other delicacies that were airmailed to Moscow each day). Horowitz made a short introductory speech in Russian before he played his program of works by Rachmaninoff, Tchaikovsky, and Scriabin, and also pieces by Scarlatti and Chopin.

Returning to N.Y., Horowitz resumed his concert and recording career. He was awarded the U.S. Medal of Freedom by President Reagan in 1986, and the National Medal of Arts in 1989. He made his last recording on Nov. 1 of that year; 4 days later, in the afternoon, he suddenly collapsed and died of a heart attack. His passing created a universal feeling of loss the world over. His body lay in state in N.Y. and was then flown by his wife to Italy, where it was interred in the Toscanini family plot in Milan.

BIBL.: G. Plaskin, *H.: A Biography* (N.Y., 1983); D. Dubal, *Evenings with H.: A Personal Portrait* (Secaucus, N.J., 1991); H. Schonberg, *H.: His Life and Music* (N.Y., 1992).

Horst, Anthon van der, Dutch organist, conductor, pedagogue, and composer; b. Amsterdam, June 20, 1899; d. Hilversum, March 7, 1965. He studied with de Pauw (piano; Prix d'Excellence for Organ, 1919) and Zweers (composition) at the Amsterdam Cons. He was organist of Amsterdam's Grande Eglise Wallonne (1915–18) and English Reformed Church (1918–41), Hilversum's Netherland's Protestant League (1944–55), and Naarden's Grote Kerk (1955–64). Horst taught at the Amsterdam Muzieklyceum (1922–27) and Cons. (1935–65). He conducted various choral groups and was conductor of the Netherlands Bach Soc. of Amsterdam from 1931. In some of his organ and piano pieces, he adopted Pijper's scales, which he called "modus conjunctus."

WORKS: ORCH.: 3 syms. (1935–37; *Divertimento pittorale,* 1954; 1959); *Nocturne funèbre* (1950–51); Organ Concerto, *Concerto per organo romantico* (1952); Violin Concerto, *Concerto Spagnuolo* (1953); *3 études symphoniques* (1954); *Concerto in Baroque Style* for Organ and Strings (1960); *Reflexions sonores* (1962); *Ricercar svelato* for Brass, Organ, and Strings (1963); *Salutatio joyeuse* (1964). **CHAMBER:** Cello Suite (1941); *Theme, Variations, and Fugue* for Flute, Violin, and Viola (1957). **KEYBOARD: PIANO:** *Tema con variazioni in modo conjuncto* (1950); *Sonata in modo conjuncto* for 2 Pianos (1951). **ORGAN:** *Suite in modo conjuncto* (1943); *Partita diverse sopra Psalm 8* (1947); Suite for 31-tone Organ (1953). **VOCAL:** *Choros I–VIII* for Soloists, Chorus, and Orch. (1931–58); *Rembrandt Cantata* (1956); choruses; songs.

BIBL.: G. Oost, *A.v.d. H., 1899–1965: Leven en Werken* (Alphen aan den Rijn, 1992).

Horst, Louis, American composer; b. Kansas City, Mo., Jan. 12, 1884; d. N.Y., Jan. 23, 1964. He studied violin and piano in San Francisco, and composition with Richard Stöhr in Vienna, as well as with Max Persin and Riegger in N.Y. (1925). From 1915 to 1925 he was music director of the Denishawn Dance Co., and from 1926 to 1948, of Martha Graham's dance company, for which he wrote a number of works that played a crucial role in the development of modern dance. He wrote extensively on the subject of music and dance; founded and ed. the journal *Dance Observer* (1934), and publ. the books *Pre-classic Dance Forms* (1940) and *Modern Dance Forms* (with C. Russell; 1961). He was also active as a teacher at Bennington (Vt.) College (1934–45), Columbia Univ. Teachers College (1938–41), and the Juilliard School of Music in N.Y. (1958–63).

BIBL.: E. Pease, *L. H.: His Theories on Modern Dance Composition* (diss., Univ. of Mich., 1953); J. Soares, *L. H.: Musician in a Dancer's World* (Durham, N.C., 1992).

Horszowski, Mieczyslaw, remarkable Polish-born American pianist and pedagogue; b. Lemberg, June 23, 1892; d. Philadelphia, May 22, 1993. A child prodigy, he began to study the piano at a very early age with his mother. At age 5, he played and transposed Bach inventions. After further training with Melcér and Soltys in Lemberg, he went to Vienna in 1899, where his own *Marche Solennelle* was performed for Emperor Franz Josef II. He had lessons with Kistler (1899) and pursued his studies with Leschetizky (until 1904); later he was a pupil of Heuberger and Mouquet (harmony and counterpoint). Following his Warsaw debut as soloist in Beethoven's 1st Piano Concerto in 1902, debuts followed in Vienna and Berlin in 1903, and then in Paris in 1905. In 1906 he played in London before Queen Alexandra, at the Vatican before Pope Pius X, and in N.Y. at Carnegie Hall. After tours of Europe and the Americas (1907–11), he took courses in philosophy, literature, and art at the Sorbonne in Paris (1911–13). He then resumed his career and distinguished himself as an interpreter not only of Bach, Mozart, Beethoven, and Chopin, but also of contemporary composers. From 1914 to 1939 he lived in Milan. In 1942 he settled in the U.S. and in 1948 became a naturalized American citizen. He joined the faculty of the Curtis Inst. of Music in Philadelphia in 1942, where he remained an eminent member of the faculty for the rest of his life. In 1954–55 he played all of Beethoven's solo piano music in a series of N.Y. recitals, and in 1960 all of Mozart's sonatas. In 1961 he appeared at the White House in Washington, D.C., with Pablo Casals and Alexander Schneider, and in 1978 he played there again. In 1981 he married the Italian pianist Beatrice Costa. About this time his eyesight began to fail rapidly, which precluded him from playing concertos and appearing in chamber-music settings. All the same, he continued to give critically acclaimed recitals from memory. In 1987 he performed at the opening of the Casals Hall in Tokyo. On Oct. 31, 1991, at the astounding age of 99, he gave his last recital in Philadelphia, thus bringing to a close one of the most outstanding performing and teaching careers of the 20th century.

Horton, Austin Asadata Dafora, Nigerian composer; b. Freetown, Sierra Leone, West Africa, Aug. 4, 1890; d. N.Y., March 4, 1965. As a youth, he became deeply interested in African folk dance festivals and studied the culture of many African tribes. He then organized a dance group in Germany. He settled in the U.S. in 1921, devoting himself to the propagation of African art, coaching singers, dancers, and drummers for performance of African dances. He utilized authentic African melorhythms in several of his stage spectacles, for which he also arranged the musical scores. Of these, *Kykunkor, the Witch,* produced at the Unity Theater Studio in N.Y. on May 7, 1934, attracted considerable attention. He also produced a dance drama, *Tunguru.*

Horvat, Milan, Yugoslav conductor; b. Pakrac, July 28, 1919. He was educated in Zagreb, studying law at the Univ. and taking courses with Svetislav Stančić (piano), Fritz Zaun (conducting), and Zlatko Grgošević (composition) at the Academy of Music (1939–46). In 1945 he became conductor of the Zagreb Radio Chorus, and from 1946 he conducted the Zagreb Radio

Orch. From 1953 to 1958 he conducted the Radio Telefís Eireann Sym. Orch. in Dublin. He was music director of the Phil. (1956–70) and Opera (1958–65) in Zagreb. After serving as chief conductor of the Austrian Radio Sym. Orch. in Vienna (1969–75), he held that title with the Zagreb Radio Orch. (from 1975). As a guest conductor, he appeared widely in Europe.

Horvat, Stanko, Croatian composer; b. Zagreb, March 12, 1930. He studied composition with Šulek at the Zagreb Academy of Music, graduating in 1956; then took a course with Aubin at the Paris Cons. and private composition lessons with Leibowitz (1958–59); returning to Yugoslavia, he was appointed to the music faculty of the Zagreb Academy of Music in 1961. In his style of composition, he traversed successively a period of neo-Classical mannerisms, serialism in its dodecaphonic aspect, aleatory expressionism, and sonorism; eventually he returned to a median technique of pragmatic modernism.

WORKS: DRAMATIC: *Izabranik* (The Chosen One), ballet (1961); *3 Legends*, television opera (Salzburg, 1971). **ORCH.:** Sinfonietta (1954); Sym. (1956); *Concerto rustico* for Strings (1958); Piano Concerto (1966; Zagreb, April 3, 1967); *Choral* for Strings (1967); *Taches* for Piano and Chamber Orch. (Graz, Sept. 26, 1968); *Hymnus* (1969); *Perpetuum mobile* for Strings (Zagreb, May 9, 1971); *Krik* (The Cry) for Mezzo-soprano and Orch., after García Lorca (1968; Zagreb, March 19, 1969). **CHAMBER:** *Choral Variations* for String Quartet (1953); *Contrasts* for String Quartet (1963); *Rondo* for String Quartet (1967). **PIANO:** *Variants* (1965); *Sonnant* (1970). **VOCAL:** *Jama* (The Pit), cantata (Zagreb, Dec. 18, 1971).

Horvath, Josef Maria, Austrian composer of Hungarian descent; b. Pécs, Dec. 20, 1931. He studied piano and composition at the Franz Liszt Academy of Music in Budapest; in 1956 he went to Salzburg, where he studied composition and took instruction in electronic music. Subsequently he became a composition teacher at the Salzburg Mozarteum. Among his compositions were *Entropia*, sym. (1961); Trio for Violin, Horn, and Piano (1963); a group of works under the generic title *Redundance* for Wind Octet and/or String Quartet (1970); *Origines* for Chamber Group (1975).

Hotter, Hans, greatly esteemed German bass-baritone; b. Offenbach am Main, Jan. 19, 1909. He studied voice with Matthäus Roemer, making his debut as the Speaker in *Die Zauberflöte* in Opava in 1929; was a member of the opera there from 1930, and also sang at the German Theater in Prague (1932–34). He then sang at the Hamburg State Opera (1934–45), Bavarian State Opera in Munich (1937–72), Berlin State Opera (1939–42), and Vienna State Opera (1939–72). He made his first appearance at London's Covent Garden with the visiting Vienna State Opera in 1947; made appearances regularly at Covent Garden until 1967; was a principal singer at the Bayreuth Festivals (1952–64), where he became renowned for his portrayal of Wotan; he also distinguished himself in such roles as Kurwenal, Hans Sachs, Amfortas, Gurnemanz, Marke, and Pogner. He made his Metropolitan Opera debut in N.Y. as the Dutchman in *Der fliegende Holländer* on Nov. 9, 1950, remaining on its roster until 1954; also sang at La Scala in Milan, the Paris Opéra, the Salzburg Festival, the Chicago Opera, and the Teatro Colón in Buenos Aires. He became a member of the faculty of the Vienna Hochschule für Musik in 1977. In addition to his Wagnerian roles, Hotter also sang in several first performances of operas by Richard Strauss; created the roles of the Kommandant in *Friedenstag* (Munich, July 24, 1938), of Olivier in *Capriccio* (Munich, Oct. 28, 1942), and of Jupiter in *Die Liebe der Danae* (public dress rehearsal, Salzburg, Aug. 16, 1944).

BIBL.: B. Wessling, *H. H.* (Bremen, 1966); P. Turing, *H. H.: Man and Artist* (London, 1983).

Hough, Stephen (Andrew Gill), English pianist; b. Heswall, Cheshire, Nov. 22, 1961. He began piano lessons at age 6, later becoming a pupil of Gordon Green and Derrick Wyndham at the Royal Northern College of Music in Manchester and of Adele Marcus at the Juilliard School in N.Y. In 1982 he won the 1st Terence Judd Award and made his London debut; in 1983 he won the Naumburg International Piano Competition in N.Y. He made his N.Y. debut in 1984; in subsequent seasons, he appeared as a soloist with many of the world's leading orchs. and toured widely as a recitalist. His vast repertoire ranges from early keyboard works to contemporary scores.

Houtmann, Jacques, French conductor; b. Mirecourt, March 27, 1935. He studied at the Nancy Cons., and at the École Normale de Musique in Paris with Jean Fournet and Henri Dutilleux; then took courses in conducting with Franco Ferrara in Rome. He won 1st prize in the conductors' competition in Besançon (1961) and the Mitropoulos Competition in N.Y. (1964); was an assistant conductor of the N.Y. Phil. (1965–66). He served as conductor with the Rhône-Alpes Phil. in Lyons (1967–71). In 1971 he went again to the U.S., and was music director of the Richmond (Va.) Sym. Orch. (until 1986); then was music director of the Lorraine Phil. in Metz (from 1986).

Hovhaness (real name, **Chakmakjian**), **Alan (Vaness Scott),** prolific American composer of Armenian-Scottish descent; b. Somerville, Mass., March 8, 1911. He took piano lessons with Adelaide Proctor and Heinrich Gebhard in Boston; his academic studies were at Tufts Univ.; in 1932 he enrolled in the New England Cons. of Music in Boston as a student of Frederick Converse; then was a scholarship student of Martinů at the Berkshire Music Center at Tanglewood in the summer of 1942. He served on the faculty of the New England Cons. of Music (1948–51); then moved to N.Y. He was awarded 2 Guggenheim fellowships (1954 and 1958). In 1959 he received a Fulbright fellowship and traveled to India and Japan, where he collected native folk songs for future use and presented his own works, as pianist and conductor, receiving acclaim. In 1962 he was engaged as composer-in-residence at the Univ. of Hawaii; then traveled to Korea. In 1967 he was composer-in-residence of the Seattle Sym. Orch. From his earliest attempts at composition, he took great interest in the musical roots of his paternal ancestry, studying the folk songs assembled by Komitas. He gradually came to believe that music must reflect the natural monody embodied in national songs and ancient church hymns. In his music, he adopted modal melodies and triadic harmonies. This *parti pris* had the dual effect of alienating him from the milieu of modern composers while exercising great attraction for the music consumer at large. By dint of ceaseless repetition of melodic patterns and relentless dynamic tension, he succeeded in creating a sui generis type of impressionistic monody, flowing on the shimmering surfaces of euphony, free from the upsetting intrusion of heterogeneous dissonance; an air of mysticism pervaded his music, aided by the programmatic titles which he often assigned to his compositions. A composer of relentless fecundity, he produced over 60 syms.; several operas, quasi-operas, and pseudo-operas; and an enormous amount of choral music. The totality of his output is in excess of 370 opus numbers. In a laudable spirit of self-criticism, he destroyed 7 of his early syms. and began numbering them anew so that his 1st numbered sym. (subtitled *Exile*) was chronologically his 8th. He performed a similar auto-da-fé on other dispensable pieces. Among his more original compositions is a symphonic score *And God Created Great Whales*, in which the voices of humpback whales recorded on tape were used as a solo with the orch.; the work was performed to great effect in the campaign to save the whale from destruction by human (and inhuman) predators.

WORKS: DRAMATIC: OPERAS: *Etchmiadzin* (1946); *The Blue Flame* (San Antonio, Dec. 13, 1959); *Spirit of the Avalanche* (Tokyo, Feb. 15, 1963); *Wind Drum* and *The Burning House* (both at Gatlinburg, Tenn., Aug. 23, 1964); *Pilate* (Los Angeles, June 26, 1966); *The Travelers* (Los Altos Hills, Calif., April 22, 1967); *Pericles* (1975); *Tale of the Sun Goddess Going into the Stone House* (1979). **OPERETTA:** *Afton Water*, after William Saroyan (1951). **BALLETS:** *Killer of Enemies* (1983); *God the Revenger* (1986).

ORCH.: SYMS. (the numbering does not always coincide with the chronological order of composition): No. 1, *Exile* (BBC, London, May 26, 1939), No. 2, *Mysterious Mountain* (Houston, Oct. 31, 1955, Stokowski conducting), No. 3 (N.Y., Oct. 14, 1956), No. 4 for Concert Band (Pittsburgh, June 28, 1959), No. 5, *Short Symphony* (1959), No. 6, *Celestial Gate* (1959), No. 7, *Nanga Parvat*, for Band (1959), No. 8, *Arjuna* (1947; Madras, India, Feb. 1, 1960), No. 9, *St. Vartan* (N.Y., March 11, 1951), No. 10 (1959), No. 11, *All Men Are Brothers* (1960; New Orleans, March 21, 1961; rev. version, New Orleans, March 31, 1970), No. 12 for Chorus and Orch. (1960), No. 13 (1953), No. 14, *Ararat* (1960); No. 15, *Silver Pilgrimage* (N.Y., March 28, 1963), No. 16, *Korean Kayageum*, for Strings and Korean Percussion Instruments (Seoul, Jan. 26, 1963), No. 17 for Metal Orch., commissioned by the American Metallurgical Congress (Cleveland, Oct. 23, 1963), No. 18, *Circe* (1964), No. 19, *Vishnu* (N.Y., June 2, 1967), No. 20, *3 Journeys to a Holy Mountain*, for Concert Band (1968), No. 21, *Etchmiadzin* (1968), No. 22, *City of Light* (1970), No. 23, *Ani*, for Band (1972), No. 24, *Majnun*, for Chorus and Orch. (1973; Lubbock, Texas, Jan. 25, 1974), No. 25, *Odysseus*, for Chamber Orch. (1973; London, April 10, 1974), No. 26, *Consolation* (San Jose, Calif., Oct. 24, 1975), No. 27 (1975), No. 28 (1976), No. 29 for Horn and Orch. (Minneapolis, May 4, 1977), No. 30 (1976), No. 31 for Strings (Seattle, Dec. 7, 1977), No. 32 for Chamber Orch. (1977), No. 33 for Chamber Orch. (1978), No. 34 (1977), No. 35 for Korean Instruments and Orch. (Seoul, June 9, 1978), No. 36 for Flute and Orch. (Washington, D.C., Jan. 16, 1979; Rampal soloist; Rostropovich conducting), No. 37 (1978), No. 38 for Soprano and Orch. (1978), No. 39 for Guitar and Orch. (1978), No. 40 for Brass, Timpani, and Orch. (1979; Interlochen, April 9, 1982), No. 41, *Mountain Sunset* (1979), No. 42 (1979), No. 43 (1979; Aptos, Calif., Aug. 20, 1981), No. 44 (1980), No. 45 (1979), No. 46, *To the Green Mountains* (Burlington, Vt., May 2, 1981), No. 47, *Walla Walla, Land of Many Waters*, for Soprano and Orch. (Walla Walla, Wash., Nov. 24, 1981), No. 48, *Vision of Andromeda* (Miami, Fla., June 21, 1982), No. 49, *Christmas*, for Strings (1981), No. 50, *Mount St. Helens* (1982), No. 51 for Trumpet and Strings (1982), No. 52, *Journey to Vega* (1983), No. 53, *Star Dawn*, for Band (1983), No. 54 (1983), No. 55 (1983), No. 56 (1983), No. 57, *Cold Mountain*, for Tenor, Soprano, Clarinet, and Strings (1983), No. 58, *Sacra*, for Soprano, Baritone, Chorus, and Orch. (Valparaiso, Ind., Nov. 10, 1985), No. 59 (Bellevue, Wash., Jan. 28, 1985), No. 60, *To the Appalachian Mountains* (Knoxville, Tenn., April 24, 1985), No. 61 (Boise, Idaho, Oct. 4, 1986). No. 62, *Let Not Man Forget*, for Baritone and Strings (1987), No. 63, *Loon Lake* (1988), No. 64 (1989), and No. 65, *Artsakh* (N.Y., Oct. 6, 1991). **CONCERTOS:** Cello Concerto (1936); *Lousadzak* (Coming of Light) for Piano and Strings (1944; Boston, Feb. 4, 1945); *Return and Rebuild the Desolate Places*, concerto for Trumpet and Strings (N.Y., June 17, 1945); *Asori*, concerto for Flute, Cornet, Bassoon, Trumpet, Timpani, and Strings (1946); *Sosi*, concerto for Violin, Piano, Percussion, and Strings (1948; N.Y., March 6, 1949); *Artik*, horn concerto (1948; Rochester, N.Y., May 7, 1954); *Zertik Parkim*, concerto for Piano and Chamber Orch. (1948); *Elibris* (God of Dawn), concerto for Flute and Strings (1949; San Francisco, Jan. 26, 1950); *Khaldis*, concerto for 4 Trumpets, Piano, and Percussion (1951); *Talin*, concerto for Viola and String Orch. (1952); Accordion Concerto (1959); Concerto for Harp and Strings (1973); Euphonium Concerto (1977); 2 guitar concertos (1977, 1985); Soprano Saxophone Concerto (1980). Also 8 numbered concertos: No. 1, *Arevakal* (Season of the Sun), for Orch. (1951; N.Y., Feb. 18, 1952), No. 2 for Violin and Strings (1951–57), No. 3, *Diran*, for Baritone Horn or Trombone and Strings (1948), No. 4 for Orch. (1952; Louisville, Ky., Feb. 20, 1954), No. 5 for Piano and Strings (1952), No. 6 for Harmonica and Strings (1953), No. 7 for Orch. (1953), and No. 8 for Orch. (1953). **OTHER:** *Storm on Mt. Wildcat* (1931); *Celestial Fantasy* (1944); *3 Armenian Rhapsodies* (1944); *Khiriam Hairis* for Trumpet and Strings (1944); *Tzaikerk* (Evening Song; 1945); *Kohar* (1946); *Forest of Prophetic Sounds* (1948); Overture for Trombone and Strings (1948); *Janabar*, 5 hymns for Violin, Trumpet, Piano, and Strings (1949; N.Y., March 11, 1951); *Prelude and Quadruple Fugue* (1955); *Meditation on Orpheus* (1957–58); *Copernicus*, tone poem (1960); *Mountain of Prophecy* (1960); *Meditation on Zeami*, symphonic poem (1963; N.Y., Oct. 5, 1964); *Ukiyo, Floating World*, tone poem (1964; Salt Lake City, Jan. 30, 1965); *Fantasy on Japanese Wood Prints* for Xylophone and Orch. (Chicago, July 4, 1964); *The Holy City* (Portland, Oreg., April 11, 1967); *Fra Angelico*, symphonic poem (Detroit, March 21, 1968); *Mountain and Rivers without End* for 10 Instruments (1968); *And God Created Great Whales* for Orch., with Voices of Humpback Whales recorded on Tape (1969; N.Y., June 11, 1970); *A Rose for Emily*, ballet (1970); *Dawn on Mt. Tahoma* (1973); *Fanfare to the New Atlantis* (1975); *Ode to Freedom* for Violin and Orch. (Vienna, Va., July 3, 1976, Yehudi Menuhin soloist); *Rubaiyat* for Narrator, Accordion, and Orch. (1975; N.Y., May 20, 1977).

CHAMBER: 2 piano quintets (1926, rev. 1962; 1964); Piano Trio (1935); 5 string quartets (1936, 1950, 1968, 1970, 1976); Violin Sonata (1937); Suite for English Horn and Bassoon (1938); *Varak* for Violin and Piano (1944); *Anahid* for Flute, English Horn, Trumpet, Timpani, Percussion, and Strings (1944); *Saris* for Violin and Piano (1946); *Haroutiun* (Resurrection), aria and fugue for Trumpet and Strings (1948); *Sosi* (Forest of Prophetic Sounds) for Violin, Piano, Horn, Timpani, Giant Tam-tam, and Strings (1948); *Khirgiz Suite* for Violin and Piano (1951); *Orbit No. 1* for Flute, Harp, Celesta, and Tam-tam (1952) and *No. 2* for Alto Recorder and Piano (1952); *koke no kiwa* (Moss Garden) for English Horn, Clarinet, Harp, and Percussion (1954); Wind Quintet (1960); *Nagooran* for Ensemble of South Indian Instruments (1962); String Trio (1962); Sextet for Violin and 5 Percussionists (1966); *6 Dances* for Brass Quintet (1967); *Spirit of Ink*, 9 pieces for 3 Flutes (1968); *Vibration Painting* for 13 String Instruments (1969); *The Garden of Adonis* for Flute and Harp (1971); Sonata for 2 Bassoons (1973); Clarinet Quartet (1973); *Night of a White Cat* for Clarinet and Piano (1973); *Fantasy* for Double Bass and Piano (1974); Suite for 4 Trumpets and Trombone (1976); Suite for Alto Saxophone and Guitar (1976); Septet for Flute, Clarinet, Bass Clarinet, Trumpet, Trombone, Double Bass, and Percussion (1976); Sonata for 2 Clarinets (1977); *Sunset on Mt. Tahoma* for 2 Trumpets, Trombone, and Organ (1978); Sonata for Clarinet and Harpsichord (1978); Saxophone Trio (1979); 2 sonatas for 3 Trumpets and 2 Trombones (1979); *Lake Winnipesaukee*, sextet (1982); *Capuan Sonata* for Viola and Piano (1982); *Prelude and Fugue* for Brass Quartet (1983); *Spirit of Trees*, sonata for Harp and Guitar (1983); Clarinet Sonata (1983); *Starry Night* for Flute, Xylophone, and Harp (1984); Sonata for Alto Recorder and Harpsichord (1984); *Mountain under the Sea* for Alto Saxophone, Timpani, Vibraphone, Tam-tam, and Harp (1984). **KEYBOARD** (for Piano Solo unless otherwise given): *Mountain Lullaby* (1931); *3 Preludes and Fugues* (1935); *Sonata Ricercare* (1935); *Macedonian Mountain Dance* (1937); *Do you remember the last silence?* (1957); *Poseidon Sonata* (1957); *Child of the Garden* for Piano, 4-hands (1958); *Madras Sonata* (1947; final rev., 1959); *Bardo Sonata* (1959); *Love Song Vanishing into Sounds of Crickets* (1979); *Sonata Catamount* (1980); Sonata, *Journey to Arcturus* (1981); *Hiroshige's Cat* (1982); Sonata No. 5 for Harpsichord (1982); *Sonata on the Long Total Eclipse of the Moon, July 6, 1982* (1982); *Tsugouharu Fujita's Cat* (1982); *Lake Sammamish* (1983); Organ Sonata No. 2, *Invisible Sun* (1984); *Lilydale* (1986); *Cougar Mountain*, sonata (1985); Sonata (1986).

VOCAL: *Ad Lyram* for Solo Voices, Double Chorus, and Chamber Orch. (Houston, March 12, 1957); *To the God Who Is in the Fire*, cantata (Urbana, Ill., April 13, 1957); *Magnificat* for Solo Voices, Chorus, and Chamber Orch. (1957); *Fuji*, cantata for Women's Voices, Flute, Harp, and String Orch. (1960); *In the Beginning Was the Word* for Vocal Soloists, Chorus, and Orch. (1963); *Lady of Light* for Solo Voices, Chorus, and Chamber Orch. (1969); *Saturn*, 12 pieces for Soprano, Clarinet, and Piano (1971); *The Way of Jesus*, folk oratorio (N.Y., Feb. 23, 1975); *Revelations of St. Paul*, cantata (1980; N.Y., Jan. 28,

1981); *The Waves Unbuild the Wasting Shore*, cantata for Tenor, Chorus, and Organ (1983); *Cantata Domino* for Chorus and Organ (1984); innumerable hymns, anthems, sacred and secular choruses; songs.

Hovland, Egil, Norwegian organist, music critic, and composer; b. Mysen, Oct. 18, 1924. He studied organ and composition at the Oslo Cons. (1946–49), later studying privately with Brustad (1951–52, in Oslo), Holmboe (1954, in Copenhagen), Copland (1957, at Tanglewood), and Dallapiccola (1959, in Florence). He then was active as an organist, music critic, and composer. In 1983 he was made a Knight of the Royal Order of St. Olav for his services to Norwegian music. He cultivates a peculiarly Scandinavian type of neo-Classical polyphony, but is apt to use serial techniques.

WORKS: DRAMATIC: OPERAS: *Brunnen*, church opera (1971–72; Oslo, March 17, 1982); *Fange og fri* (1990). **BALLETS:** *Dona Nobis Pacem* (1982); *Den Heliga Dansen* (1982); *Veni Creator Spiritus* (1984); *Danses de la Mort* (Bergen, June 8, 1983). **ORCH.:** *Passacaglia and Fugue* for Strings (1949); *Festival Overture* (1951); 3 syms.: No. 1, *Symphonia Veris* (Sym. of Spring; 1952–53; Oslo, Dec. 10, 1954), No. 2 (1954–55; Bergen, Nov. 8, 1956), and No. 3 for Narrator, Chorus, and Orch. (1969–70; Oslo, April 9, 1970); Suite (1954); Concertino for 3 Trumpets and Strings (1954–55); *Music* for 10 Instruments (1957); Suite for Flute and Strings (1959); *Festival Overture* for Wind Orch. (1962); *Lamenti* (Oslo, April 24, 1964); *Rorate* for 5 Sopranos, Organ, Chamber Orch., and Tape (1966–67); *Rapsodi 69* (1969); Trombone Concerto (1972); Violin Concerto (1974); *Noël-Variations* (1975); Piano Concerto (1976–77; Oslo, Dec. 1, 1977); *Tombeau de Bach* (1977–78); Concerto for Piccolo, Flute, and Strings (1986; Oslo, April 20, 1989). **CHAMBER:** Suite for Flute and Piano (1950); *Motus* for Flute (1961); *Varianti* for 2 Pianos (1964); Piano Trio (1965); 2 wind quintets (1965, 1980); *Elemento* for Organist and 2 Assistants (1965; rev. 1966); Variations for Oboe and Piano (1968–69); String Quartet (1981); organ pieces. **VOCAL:** *Song of Songs* for Soprano, Violin, Percussion, and Piano (1962–63); *Magnificat* for Alto, Flute, and Harp (1964); *Missa vigilate* for Soprano, Baritone, Chorus, 2 Female Dancers, Organ, and Tape (1967); *Mass to the Risen Christ* for Chorus and Instruments (1968); *All Saints' Mass* for Soprano, Chorus, Organ, and Instruments (1970); *Den vakreste rosen* (The Most Beautiful Rose) for Narrator, 4 Sopranos, Organ, and Orch., after Hans Christian Andersen (1970); *Missa verbi* for Chorus, Organ, and Instruments (1972–73); *Pilgrim's Mass* for Chorus, Organ, 9 Brasses, and Congregation (1982).

Howard, Ann (real name, **Pauline Swadling**), English mezzo-soprano; b. London, July 22, 1936. She was a student of Topliss Green and Rodolfa Lhombino; after singing in musical theater, she joined the chorus of the Royal Opera House, Covent Garden, London, and was awarded a grant to pursue her training with Modesti in Paris. In 1964 she made her operatic debut as Azucena with the Welsh National Opera in Cardiff; that same year, she made her first appearance at the Sadler's Wells Opera in London as Czipra in *Der Zigeunerbaron*, and subsequently appeared there regularly, and later with its successor, the English National Opera. In 1973 she made her Covent Garden debut as Amneris. As a guest artist, she sang in Europe, the U.S. (debut as Carmen in New Orleans, 1971), Canada, Mexico, and South Africa. Among her many roles were Fricka, Brangäne, Ortrud, Eboli, Clytemnestra, Dalila, Carmen, Offenbach's Hélène, Herodiade, and Jocasta. She also sang in operetta and in contemporary operas.

Howard, John Tasker, eminent American writer on music; b. Brooklyn, Nov. 30, 1890; d. West Orange, N.Y., Nov. 20, 1964. He attended Williams College in Williamstown, Mass.; then studied composition with Howard Brockway and Mortimer Wilson. He was managing editor of the *Musician* (1919–22); served as educational director of the Ampico Corp. (1922–28); ed. the music section of *McCall's Magazine* (1928–30) and *Cue* (1936–38); taught at Columbia Univ. (1950–54). From 1940 to 1956 he was the curator of the Americana Music Collection at the N.Y. Public Library, which he enriched to a great extent. His major achievement was the publication of several books and monographs on American music and musicians. He was also a composer of modest, but respectable, attainments. He wrote a piece for Piano and Orch., *Fantasy on a Choral Theme* (Orange, N.J., Feb. 20, 1929); also *Foster Sonatina* for Violin and Piano; piano pieces; some songs.

WRITINGS (all publ. in N.Y.): *Our American Music* (1931; 4th ed., rev., 1965); *Stephen Foster, America's Troubadour* (1934; 2nd ed., rev., 1953); *Ethelbert Nevin* (1935); *Our Contemporary Composers, American Music in the 20th Century* (1941); *This Modern Music* (1942; new ed. by J. Lyons, 1957, as *Modern Music*); *The World's Great Operas* (1948); with G. Bellows, *A Short History of Music in America* (1957).

BIBL.: G. Bellows, "J.T. H.," *Notes* (Sept. 1957; with complete list of his publ. writings).

Howard, Kathleen, Canadian-American contralto; b. Niagara Falls, Ontario, July 17, 1884; d. Los Angeles, Aug. 15, 1956. She studied in N.Y. with Bouhy and in Paris with Jean de Reszke. She appeared at the Metz Opera (1907–09), at Darmstadt (1909–12), at Covent Garden in London (1913), and with the Century Opera in N.Y. (1914–15). After appearing as the nurse in *Boris Godunov* with the Metropolitan Opera in Brooklyn on Nov. 14, 1916, she amde her formal debut with the company in N.Y. as the 3rd Lady in *Die Zauberflöte* on Nov. 20, 1916, remaining on its roster until 1928. After her retirement from the stage, she was engaged in magazine work and was fashion ed. of *Harper's Bazaar* (1928–33). She publ. an autobiography, *Confessions of an Opera Singer* (N.Y., 1918).

Howard, Leslie (John), Australian pianist, organist, conductor, musicologist, and composer; b. Melbourne, April 29, 1948. He was educated at Monash Univ., Victoria (B.A., 1969; M.A., 1972), the Univ. of Melbourne (1966–71), and the Accademia Musicale Chigiana in Siena (1972–75); also received private instruction from Guido Agosti (piano), Donald Britton (organ and harpsichord), Fritz Rieger (conducting), and Franco Donatoni (composition). After making his formal debut as a pianist in Melbourne in 1967, he appeared as a soloist with orchs., as a recitalist, and as a chamber music artist in Australia, Europe, North and South America, and Asia. He also taught at Monash Univ. (1970–72) and was a prof. of piano at the Guildhall School of Music and Drama in London (1987–92). While Howard's keyboard repertoire extends from classical masterpieces to contemporary scores, he has become particularly associated with the music of Liszt, both as a performer and a researcher. In 1988 he became president of the Liszt Soc. in England. Among his honors are the Liszt Medal of Honor of the Hungarian government (1986) and the Medal of Honor of the Liszt Soc. of America (1993). His writings have appeared in various publications.

WORKS: DRAMATIC: *Fruits of the Earth*, ballet (1971); *Hreidar the Fool*, opera (1973–74). **ORCH.:** *Canzona Sinfonica* for Symphonic Wind Band (1977–78). **CHAMBER:** String Quartet (1966); Trio for Piano, Violin, and Cello (1968); Violin Sonata (1968); Sonata for Percussion and Piano (1968); *Quattro Riflessioni* for Violin, Clarinet, and Piano (1969); *Pavane* for Clarinet, 2 Violins, and Piano (1970); Horn Sonata (1970); *Ramble on a Russian Theme* for Domra or Mandolin or Violin and Piano (1972); *Romance* for Flute and Piano (1980); Cello Sonata (1983); Trio for Piano, Violin, and Viola or Clarinet (1987); *Grand Galop drolatique* for Organ and Piano (1993). **KEYBOARD: PIANO:** *Capriccio* for 2 Pianos (1967); Sonata (1970); *2 Album-Leaves* (1972); *Variations on a Theme by Bartók* for Piano Duet (1973); *24 Classical Preludes* (1989). **ORGAN:** *Moto di gioia—Postludium* (1993); *Mr. Haydn's Clock—Ein Orgelstück für einer Uhr?* (1993). **VOCAL:** *Choral Song* for Solo Treble Voices, Chorus, and Orch. (1970); *Recitation* for Speaker, Guitar, Cello, and Double Bass (1972); *A Festival Mass* for Chorus and Organ (1973); *Missa Sancti Petri* for Double Chorus and Organ (1992–93); songs.

Howarth, Elgar, English trumpeter and conductor; b. Cannock, Staffordshire, Nov. 4, 1935. He studied at the Univ. of Manchester and the Royal Manchester College of Music; then played trumpet in the orch. of the Royal Opera House, Covent Garden (1958–63), with the Royal Phil. (1963–69), and with other London ensembles. In 1969 he began his career as a conductor with the London Sinfonietta; became its director in 1973. From 1985 to 1988 he was principal guest conductor of Opera North. He also composed music for brass band. With Patrick Howarth, he publ. *What a Performance! The Brass Band Plays . . .* (London, 1988).

Howe, Mary (Carlisle), American pianist and composer; b. Richmond, Va., April 4, 1882; d. Washington, D.C., Sept. 14, 1964. She received training in piano from Richard Burmeister in Germany and with Ernest Hutcheson and Harold Randolph at the Peabody Cons. of Music in Baltimore, where she also studied composition with Gustav Strube; she also had lessons with Boulanger. She toured as a duo-pianist with Anne Hull from 1920 to 1935; with her 3 children, she appeared with the "4 Howes" singing madrigals and early music. In 1926 she helped to organize the Assn. of American Women Composers. She was an accomplished composer of works in a tonal idiom.

WORKS: BALLETS: *Cards* (1936); *Le jongleur de Notre Dame* (1959). **ORCH.:** *Fugue* for Strings (1922); *Poèma* (1924); *Sand* (1926); *Castellana* for 2 Pianos and Orch. (1930); *Dirge* (1931); *Free Passacaglia with Fugue* for Chamber Orch. (1932); *American Piece: What Price Glory* (1935); *Coulennes* (1936; also for Chamber Orch.); *Stars* (1937); *Paean* (1940); *Potomac* (1940); *Polka, Waltz, and Finale* (1946); *Agreeable Overture* for Chamber Orch. (1949); *Rock* (1955); *Stars and Sand* (1963). **OTHER:** 3 string quartets; piano pieces; choral works; numerous songs.

Howell, Gwynne (Richard), Welsh bass; b. Gorseinon, June 13, 1938. He was educated at the Univ. of Wales in Swansea (B.Sc.) and pursued training in town planning at the Univ. of Manchester; he also studied voice with Redvers Llewellyn, at the Royal Manchester College of Music with Gwilym Jones, and in London with Otakar Kraus (1968–72). While in Manchester, he gained experience singing Hunding, Fasolt, and Pogner. In 1968 he made his first appearance at the Sadler's Wells Opera in London as Monterone, where he became a principal artist, and with its successor, the English National Opera. In 1970 he made his debut at Covent Garden in London as the 1st Nazarene in *Salome*, where he later created the title role in Maxwell Davies' *Taverner* (July 12, 1972) and sang various Italian, German, and French roles. On Jan. 21, 1985, he made his Metropolitan Opera debut in N.Y. as Lodovico. Among his finest roles were the Commendatore, Sarastro, Pimen, Timur, Gurnemanz, the Landgrave, Philip II, and Hans Sachs. He also sang widely in concert.

Howells, Anne (Elizabeth), English mezzo-soprano; b. Southport, Jan. 12, 1941. She was a student of Frederick Cox at the Royal Manchester College of Music, where she sang Eros in the first English production of Gluck's *Paride ed Elena* (1963). Following further training with Vera Rosza, she made her professional operatic debut as Flora in *La Traviata* with the Welsh National Opera in Cardiff in 1966. From 1966 she appeared regularly at the Glyndebourne Festivals. In 1967 she made her first appearance at London's Covent Garden as Flora, returning there in subsequent years as Rosina, Cherubino, Siébel, Ascanio, Mélisande, Meg Page, Despina, and Giulietta. In 1972 she made her U.S. debut as Dorabella with the Chicago Lyric Opera, which role she also sang at her debuts at the Metropolitan Opera in N.Y. (Oct. 15, 1975), and the San Francisco Opera (1979). She also had guest engagements in Geneva, Salzburg, Berlin, and Paris. In 1966 she married **Ryland Davies.** After their divorce in 1981, she married **Stafford Dean.**

Howells, Herbert (Norman), distinguished English composer; b. Lydney, Gloucestershire, Oct. 17, 1892; d. Oxford, Feb. 24, 1983. In 1912 he entered the Royal College of Music in London, where he studied composition with Stanford and counterpoint with Charles Wood; in 1920 he was appointed an instructor in composition there, a position he held for more than 40 years. In 1936 he succeeded Holst as music director at St. Paul's Girls' School, remaining there until 1962; he also was a prof. of music at the Univ. of London (1954–64). In 1953 he was made a Commander of the Order of the British Empire and in 1972 a Companion of Honour. The music Howells wrote during his long life was nobly British, in its national references, its melodic outspokenness, and its harmonic opulence; in this it was a worthy continuation of the fine tradition of Elgar and Vaughan Williams. In 1987 the Herbert Howells Soc. was founded to further the cause of his music.

WORKS: ORCH.: 2 piano concertos (1913, London, July 10, 1914; 1924); 3 dances for Violin and Orch. (1915); *The B's*, suite (1915); *Puck's Minuet and Merry-eye* (1917–20); *Procession* (1922); *Pastoral Rhapsody* (1923); *Paradise Rondel* (1925); *Pageantry* for Brass Band (1934); *Fantasia* for Cello and Orch. (1937); Concerto for Strings (1939); Suite for Strings (1944); *Music for a Prince*, suite (1949); *Triptych* for Brass Band (1960). **CHAMBER:** Piano Quartet (1916); *Rhapsodic Quintet* for Clarinet and Strings (1917); 2 string quartets (*Phantasy*, 1918; *In Gloucestershire*, 1923); 3 violin sonatas (1918, 1918, 1923); Oboe Sonata (1943); Clarinet Sonata (1949). **KEYBOARD: PIANO:** Sonatina (1971). **ORGAN:** 2 sonatas (1911, 1933); *Prelude—De profundis* (1958); *Partita* (1971). **CLAVICHORD:** *Lambert's Clavichord* (1926–27); *Howells' Clavichord* (1951–56). **CHORAL:** *Sine nomine* for 2 Soloists, Chorus, and Orch. (1922); *A Kent Yeoman's Wooing Song* for Soloists, Chorus, and Orch. (1933); *Requiem* for Chorus (1936); *Hymnus Paradisi* for Soprano, Tenor, Chorus, and Orch. (1938); *A Maid Peerless* for Women's Voices and Strings or Piano (1949); *Missa Sabrinensis* for Soloists, Chorus, and Orch. (Worcester Festival, Sept. 7, 1954); *An English Mass* (1956); *Stabat Mater* for Tenor, Chorus, and Orch. (1963); *Take him, earth, for cherishing (Motet on the Death of President Kennedy)* (1964); *The Coventry Mass* for Chorus and Organ (1968).

BIBL.: R. Spearing, *H. H.: A Tribute to H. H. on His Eightieth Birthday* (London, 1972); C. Palmer, *H. H.: A Study* (London, 1978); M. Dreyer, "H. H. at 90: The Cello Fantasia and Its Orchestral Predecessors," *Musical Times* (Oct. 1982); N. Webber, "H. H. 1892–1983," *American Organist* (June 1983); R. Wells, "H.'s Unpublished Organ Works," *Musical Times* (Aug. 1987); C. Palmer, *H. H.: A Centenary Celebration* (London, 1993).

Howes, Frank (Stewart), English music critic, writer, and editor; b. Oxford, April 2, 1891; d. Standlake, Oxfordshire, Sept. 28, 1974. He studied at St. John's College, Oxford. In 1925 he joined the staff of the *Times* of London as music critic, and from 1943 to 1960 was its chief music critic. He was also ed. of the *Folk Song Journal* (later known as the *Journal of the English Folk Dance and Song Society*) from 1927 to 1945; taught music history and appreciation at the Royal College of Music in London (1938–70); was Cramb Lecturer at the Univ. of Glasgow (1947 and 1952). In 1954 he was made a Commander of the Order of the British Empire.

WRITINGS (all publ. in London unless otherwise given): *The Borderland of Music and Psychology* (1926); *The Appreciation of Music* (1928); *William Byrd* (1928); *A Key to the Art of Music* (1935); with P. Hope-Wallace, *A Key to Opera* (1939); *Full Orchestra* (1942; 2nd ed., rev. and enl., 1976); *The Music of William Walton* (2 vols., 1942–43; new ed., 1965); *Man, Mind and Music* (1948); *Music: 1945–50* (1951); *The Music of Ralph Vaughan Williams* (1954); *Music and Its Meanings* (1958); *The Cheltenham Festival* (1965); *The English Musical Renaissance* (1966); *Oxford Concerts: A Jubilee Record* (Oxford, 1969); *Folk Music of Britain—and Beyond* (1970).

Hoyland, Vic(tor), English composer; b. Wombwell, Yorkshire, Dec. 11, 1945. He studied at the Univ. of Hull and with Robert Sherlaw Johnson and Bernard Rands at the Univ. of York, where he served as a visiting lecturer in 1984; then was a lecturer at the Univ. of Birmingham (from 1985).

WORKS: *Em* for 24 Voices (1970); *Es* for Voices and Ensemble (1971); *Jeux-Theme* for Mezzo-soprano and Ensemble (1972); *Ariel* for Voice and Ensemble (1975); *Esem* for Double Bass and Ensemble (1975); Serenade for 14 Players (1979); *Xingu*, music theater piece (1979); *Reed* for Double Reed Instruments (1980); *Fox* for Chamber Ensemble (1983); *Quintet of Brass* (1985); 3 string quartets (1985, n.d., 1994); *In Transit* for Orch. (1987); *Of Fantasy, Of Dreams, and Ceremonies* for 13 Strings (1989); Trio for Piano, Violin, and Cello (1989); Quintet for Piano and String Quartet (1990); *Le Madre*, opera (1990).

Hřimalý, Otakar, Czech violinist, conductor, and composer; b. Czernowitz, Bukovina, Dec. 20, 1883; d. Prague, July 10, 1945. He was the son of the Czech violinist, conductor, and composer Adalbert (Vojtěch) Hřimalý (b. Pilsen, July 30, 1842; d. Vienna, June 15, 1908) and the nephew of the Czech violinist and teacher Johann Hřimalý (b. Pilsen, April 13, 1844; d. Moscow, Jan. 24, 1915). He was trained in Vienna at the Cons. and the Univ. He went to Moscow, where he was conductor of the Cons. opera dept. (1910–16) and at the Opera (1919–22); he then lived in Czernowitz until the Russian occupation forced him to flee to Prague, where he joined the Cons. in 1940. He wrote an opera; 2 ballets; 7 syms.; Piano Concerto; Violin Concerto; chamber music; piano pieces.

Hrisanide, Alexandru, Romanian composer; b. Petrila, June 15, 1936. He studied with P. Constantinescu, Ciortea, Vancea, Jora, and Mendelsohn at the Bucharest Cons. (1953–64), with Boulanger at the American Cons. in Fontainebleau (1965), and in Darmstadt (1966–67). After teaching at the Academy of Music (1959–62) and Cons. (1962–72) in Bucharest, he was a visiting prof. at the Univ. of Oregon (1972–73); he then went to the Netherlands. His output followed along constructivist lines with the application of modified serial techniques.

WORKS: ORCH.: *Poem* (1958); *Passacaglia* (1959); *"Vers-Antiqua": Hommage à Euripide* for Chamber Orch. (1960); *Concerto for Orchestra* (1964); *Ad perpetuam rei memoriam* (1966); *RO* (1968); *Sonnets*, harpsichord concerto (1973). **CHAMBER:** 3 flute sonatas (1956; 1956; 1960–62); Violin Sonata (1957); Trio for Violin, Viola, and Bassoon (1958); String Quartet (1958); Clarinet Sonata (1960–62); *Volumes-Inventions* for Cello and Piano (1963); *M. P. 5 (Musique pour 5)* for Violin, Viola, Cello, Saxophone or Clarinet, and Piano (1966); *Directions* for Wind Quintet (1967–69); *Première musique pour RA* for Piano and Tape (1968–69); *Seconde musique pour RA* for Piano and Tape (1969); *Troisième musique pour RA* for Piano, Percussion, and Tape (1970); *Quatrième musique pour RA* for Piano and Tape (1970); *Sixième musique pour RA* for Piano, Varying Instruments, and Tape (1970); *Soliloquium × 11* for String Quartet (1970); *Cinquième musique pour RA* for Piano, Celesta, Harpsichord, and Tape (1973); piano pieces, including 3 sonatas (1955–56; *Sonata piccola*, 1959; *Picasso Sonata*, 1956–64). **VOCAL:** *I-RO-LA-HAI* for Voice and Orch. (1971); cantatas; songs.

Hristič, Stevan, Serbian conductor, teacher, and composer; b. Belgrade, June 19, 1885; d. there, Aug. 21, 1958. He studied with Nikisch (conducting) and Krehl and Hofmann at the Leipzig Cons., and then pursued studies in Moscow, Rome, and Paris. Returning to Belgrade, he was conductor of the National Opera Theater (1912–14); then was chief conductor of the Belgrade Phil. (1923–34) and Opera (1924–34); then was a prof. of composition at the Academy of Music (1937–50). He composed a music drama, *Suton* (Sunset, 1925; rev. 1954); a ballet, *Legend of Okhrid* (1933; rev. 1958); many choral works.

Hrušovský, Ivan, Slovak composer and musicologist; b. Bratislava, Feb. 23, 1927. After training at the Žilina Music School, he studied composition with A. Moyzes at the Bratislava Cons. (1947–52), continuing under his tutelage at the Bratislava Academy of Music (graduated, 1957); he also pursued training in musicology, philosophy, and aesthetics at Comenius Univ. in Bratislava (1947–52). He later completed postgraduate studies with his thesis on the genesis of Cikker's musical thinking (1965–66), and his Habilitation with his thesis on the development of Slovak music, 1939–48 (1967). After working at the Inst. of Musicology at the Slovak Academy of Sciences in Bratislava (1952–53), he taught at the Bratislava Academy of Music from 1953, becoming assoc. prof. of musicology in 1968 and prof. of composition in 1984. In 1976 and 1986 he won the Unioin of Slovak Composers Prize, and in 1988 was made a Meritorious Artist of Slovakia. Among his writings are *Úvod do štúdia teórie harmónie* (Introduction to the Study of Harmony; Bratislava, 1960; 2nd ed., 1972), *Slovenská hudba v profiloch a rozboroch* (Slovak Music in Portraits and Analyses; Bratislava, 1964), and *Antonín Dvořák* (Bratislava, 1964). In his compositions, he makes effective utilization of the entire gamut of contemporary musical expression.

WORKS: ORCH.: *Pastoral Suite* for Small Orch. (1955); Piano Concerto (1957); *Tatra Poem* (1960); *Concertante Overture* for Strings (1963); *Passacaglia* (1966); *Musica nocturna per archi* (1970); *Confrontations* (1979); *Suita quasi una fantasia* for Chamber String Orch. (1980); *Little Romance* for Chamber String Orch. (1986); *Music for V. Hložník*, symphonic fresco (1986); *Noble Dances of Levoca*, suite for Chamber String Orch. (1987); Sym. (1988). **CHAMBER:** *Suita piccola* for Cello and Piano (1963); *Combinazioni sonoriche per 9*, nonet for Flute, Oboe, Bass Clarinet, Trumpet, Vibraphone, Piano, Violin, Viola, and Cello (1963); Sonata for Solo Violin (1969); *3 Canons* for Violin and Harpsichord (1980); *Dialoghi in ritmo* for Organ and Percussion (1982); 2 string quartets (1983, 1990); *Musica rustica* for Flute (1984); Septetino for Flute, Clarinet, Bassoon, Horn, Violin, Viola, and Cello (1987). **KEYBOARD: PIANO:** 2 sonatas (1965, 1968); *Toccata chromatica* (1970); *Fantasia, Introduction, and Fugue in the Old Style* for Piano, 4-hands (1986); Suite for 2 Pianos (1986; also for Piano, 4-hands). **HARPSICHORD:** *Sonata in modo classico* (1977); *Suite of Old Dances from the Levoča Collection* (1978). **VOCAL:** *Against Death*, cantata trilogy: 1, *Hiroshima* for Reciter, Soprano, Baritone, Chorus, and Orch. (1961–65); 2, *White Birch, Sister of Mine . . .* for Mezzo-soprano and Women's Chorus (1961); and 3, *Dream about a Man* for Reciter, Soprano, Chorus, and Orch. (1964); *Madrigal Sonata* for Chorus (1974); *Odes* for 3 Choruses (1975); *Canti* for Chamber Choruses (1978); *That Love*, cantata for Mezzo-soprano and Chorus (1984); *Canticum pro pace*, oratorio for Reciter, Mezzo-soprano, Bass, Chorus, and Orch. (1985); *Cantus de caritate* for Chorus and Piano or Organ (1990); other choral works; many song cycles. **ELECTRO-ACOUSTIC:** *Invocation* (1973); *Idée fixe* (1976).

Hsu, John (Tseng-Hsin), Chinese-born American cellist, viola da gambist, baryton player, and teacher; b. Shantou, April 21, 1931. He emigrated to the U.S. (1949) and became a naturalized American citizen (1961); he studied at Carroll College, the Berkshire Music Center in Tanglewood, and the New England Cons. of Music in Boston (B.Mus., 1953; M.Mus., 1955); his teachers included Josef Schroetter, Alfred Zinghera, and Samuel Mayes for cello, and Eugene Lehner and William Kroll for chamber music performance. From 1955 he taught at Cornell Univ., and toured widely as a recitalist. He was a founding member of the Amadé Trio (1972), dedicated to performing early music on original instruments; also in 1972 he joined the Aston Magna Foundation for Music, serving as its artistic director from 1987 to 1990. He was music director of the Apollo Ensemble from 1991. In 1981 he organized the Haydn Baryton Trio for the purpose of playing Haydn's rarely heard baryton trios. He also ed. the collected works of Marais (1980) and wrote *A Handbook of French Baroque Viol Technique* (1981).

Hsu, Tsang-houei, Chinese composer, musicologist, and teacher; b. Changhau, Taiwan, Sept. 6, 1929. He studied violin in Tokyo from the age of 11, remaining in Japan until 1945, when he returned to Taiwan. He studied violin and composition at the National Univ. (1949–53); in 1954 he went to Paris to study violin at the École César Franck and music history and analysis at the Sorbonne (1956–58). He also studied with Jolivet and Messiaen at the Paris Cons. In 1959 he returned to Taiwan;

his first concert (1960), which introduced avant-garde ideas to Taiwan audiences, met with both censure and enthusiasm. He taught advanced composition techniques and founded several organizations to promote contemporary music, including the Chinese Composers' Forum (1961) and the Chinese Soc. for Contemporary Music (1969); he also was active in the League of Asian Composers. Hsu made extensive study of Taiwanese folk music, elements of which are integrated into his compositions. He co-founded the Centre for Chinese Folk Music Research (1967), and was appointed examiner in charge of folk-music research by the Taiwanese provincial government (1976). He held professorships at the National Academy of Arts, Soochow Univ., and the College of Chinese Culture, and lectured throughout East Asia and the U.S. His early compositions show a variety of influences, including aspects of impressionism, atonality, and serialism, along with traditional Chinese and Taiwanese elements; his later works are less aggressively modern, but have a distinctive identity and unified style. His writings reflect his interest in folk music research.

WORKS: DRAMATIC: OPERA: *The Legend of White Horse* (1979–87). **BALLETS:** *Chang-o Flies to the Moon* (1968); *The Peach Blossom* (1977); *Peach Blossom Girl* (1983); *Chen San and the 5th Madame* (1985). **ORCH.:** *Chinese Festival Overture* (1965–80); *2 Movements* for Strings (1970); *White Sand Bay*, sym. (1974); *Spring for All* for Piano and Traditional Chinese Orch. (1981). **CHAMBER:** Violin Sonata (1958–59); Quintet for Flute, Clarinet, Violin, Cello, and Piano (1960–87); *5 Preludes* for Violin (1965–66); *The Blind* for Flute (1966–76); *The Reminiscence of Childhood* for Chinese Ocarina (1967); Clarinet Sonata (1973–83); *Taiwan* for Violin, Clarinet, and Piano (1973); *3 Pieces* for Hugin (1977); *Dou-o's Lament* for Cello or Viola and Piano (1988); piano pieces. **VOCAL:** Choral pieces; songs.

Huang, Cham-Ber, Chinese-American harmonica player and manufacturer; b. Shanghai, Oct. 17, 1925. He commenced playing the harmonica when he was 6; later studied violin, theory, and composition at the Shanghai School of Music (1945–49) and St. John's Univ. in Shanghai (B.A., 1949). He went to the U.S., where he taught at N.Y.'s Turtle Bay Music School (1958–76) and at the Grand Teton Music Festival in Teton Village, Wyo. (1975–79). He also toured widely as a harmonica virtuoso, from 1979 making regular tours of China, where he helped to make his instrument popular. In 1983 he formed Huang Harmonics, a manufacturing firm in Farmingdale, N.Y.

Hubay, Jenő, celebrated Hungarian violinist, pedagogue, and composer; b. Budapest, Sept. 15, 1858; d. Vienna, March 12, 1937. He received his initial training from his father, Karl Hubay, prof. of violin at the Budapest Cons.; gave his first public concert at the age of 11; then studied with Joachim in Berlin (1873–76). His appearance in Paris, at a Pasdeloup concert, attracted the attention of Vieuxtemps, of whom he became a favorite pupil; in 1882 he succeeded Vieuxtemps as prof. at the Brussels Cons. In 1886 he became a prof. at the Budapest Cons. (succeeding his father); from 1919 to 1934 he was its director. In Budapest he formed the celebrated Hubay String Quartet. In 1894 he married the Countess Rosa Cebrain. Among his pupils were Vecsey, Szigeti, Telmanyi, Eddy Brown, and other renowned violinists. He ed. the violin études of Kreutzer (1908), Rode, Mayseder, and Saint Lubin (1910).

WORKS: OPERAS (all 1st perf. in Budapest): *Alienor* (Dec. 5, 1891); *Le Luthier de Crémone* (Nov. 10, 1894); *A Falu Rossza* (The Village Vagabond; March 20, 1896); *Moosröschen* (Feb. 21, 1903); *Anna Karenina* (Nov. 10, 1923); *Az álarc* (The Mask; Feb. 26, 1931). **ORCH.:** 4 syms.: No. 1 (1885), No. 2, *1914–15* (1915), No. 3, *Vita nuova*, for Soli, Chorus, and Organ (1921), and No. 4, *Petőfi-Sinfonie*, for Soli, Chorus, and Orch. (1925); *Biedermeyer Suite* (1913); 4 violin concertos; *Scènes de la Csárda*, 14 pieces for Violin and Orch. **CHAMBER:** *Sonate romantique* for Violin and Piano.

Hubeau, Jean, French pianist and composer; b. Paris, June 22, 1917; d. there, Aug. 19, 1992. He entered the Paris Cons. at the age of 9; studied piano with Lévy, and composition with J. and N. Gallon and Dukas. He won the premier prix for piano at age 13, and for composition at 16; in 1934, at the age of 17, he received the 2nd Grand Prix de Rome with his cantata *La Légende de Roukmani.* He made several European tours as a pianist; from 1942 to 1957 he was director of the Versailles Cons.; then joined the staff of the Paris Cons.

WORKS: BALLETS: *Trois fables de La Fontaine* (Paris, March 2, 1945); *La Fiancée du diable* (Paris, Dec. 8, 1945); *Un Coeur de diamant ou L'Infante* (Monte Carlo, April 7, 1949). **ORCH.:** *Tableaux hindous* (Paris, Oct. 18, 1936); Violin Concerto (Paris, March 30, 1941); Cello Concerto (Paris, Nov. 28, 1942); *Concerto heroïque* for Piano and Orch. (Paris, Dec. 22, 1946). **CHAMBER:** Violin Sonata (1941); *Sonatine-Humoresque* for Horn, Flute, Clarinet, and Piano (1942); Trumpet Sonata (1943); *Sonate-Caprice* for 2 Violins (1944); *Air varié* for Clarinet and Piano (1961); *Idylle* for Flute and Piano (1966); piano pieces. **VOCAL:** Choruses; songs.

Huber, Klaus, Swiss composer and pedagogue; b. Bern, Nov. 30, 1924. He studied violin with Geyer (1947–49) and theory and composition with his godfather Burkhard (1947–55) at the Zürich Cons., and then completed his training with Blacher at the Berlin Hochschule für Musik (1955–56). He taught violin at the Zürich Cons. (1950–60) and music history at the Lucerne Cons. (1960–63). From 1961 to 1972 he taught at the Basel Academy of Music, where he was director of the composition and instrumentation classes (1964–68) and then of the master composition class (1968–72). In 1969 he founded the international composers' seminar in Boswil, with which he was active until 1980. In 1973 he held the Deutscher Akademischer Austauschienest scholarship in Berlin. From 1973 to 1990 he taught composition and was head of the inst. for contemporary music at the Freiburg im Breisgau Hochschule für Musik. He served as president of the Swiss Composers' Assn. from 1979 to 1982. In 1975 he won the Composers' Prize of the Swiss Composers' Assn. and in 1978 was awarded the arts prize of the City of Basel. He was a member of the Bayerische Akademie der Schönen Künste of Munich and the Akademie der Künste of Berlin. He publ. *Klaus Huber: Gesammelte Schriften* (Cologne, 1995). In his music, Huber has written a large body of works notable for their exquisite craftsmanship in a highly personal style evocative of contemporary means of expression.

WORKS: OPERAS: *Jot, oder wann kommt der Herr zurück* (1972–73; Berlin, Sept. 27, 1973); *Im Paradies oder Der Alte vom Berge* (1973–75). **ORCH.:** *Inventionen und Choral* (1956); *Litania instrumentalis* (1957); *Terzen-Studie* (1958); *Cantio-Moteti-Inventione* for Strings (1963; also for String Quartet, 1962–63); *Tenebrae* (1966–67); *James Joyce Chamber Music* for Harp, Horn, and Chamber Orch. (1966–67); *Alveare vernat* for Flute and Strings (1967; also for Flute and 12 Solo Strings, 1965); *Tempora*, violin concerto (1969–70); *Erinnere dich an G . . .* for Double Bass and Chamber Orch. (1976–77); *. . . ohne Grenze und Rand . . .* for Viola and Small Orch. (1976–77); *Zwei Sätze für Ensemble* (1978–79; 1983); *Beati Pauperes II* for Small Orch. (1979; also for 7 Solo Voices and Small Orch.); *Protuberanzen* (1985–86); *Plainte-die umgepflügte Zeit I* for Viola d'Amore and Chamber Orch. (1990; *II* for Mezzo-soprano, Tenor, Viola d'amore, and Chamber Orch.); *Intarsi*, chamber concerto for Piano and Ensemble (1993–94; Lucerne, Aug. 22, 1994); *Lamentationes de fine vicesimi saeculi* for 4 Orch. Groups and Sufi Singer ad libitum (1992–94; Frankfurt am Main, Dec. 11, 1994). **CHAMBER:** *Sonata da chiesa* for Violin and Organ (1953); *Partita* for Cello and Harpsichord (1954); *Concerto per la Camerata* for 6 Instruments (1954–55; rev. 1965); *2 Movements* for 2 Winds (1957–58); *3 Movements in 2 Parts* for Wind Quintet (1958–59); *Noctes intelligibilis lucis* for Oboe and Harpsichord (1961); 2 string quartets: No. 1, *Moteti-Cantiones* (1962–63; also for String Orch., 1963) and No. 2, *. . . von Zeit zu Zeit . . .* (1984–85); *Sabeth* for Flute, English Horn or Viola, and Harp (1966–67); *Ascensus* for Flute, Cello, and Piano (1969); *Ein Hauch von Unzeit III* for 2 to 7 Players (1972); *Schattenblätter* for Bass Clarinet, Cello, and Piano (1975); *Lazarus I–II* for Cello and Piano (1978); *Beati Pauperes I* for Flute, Viola, Piano, and Percussion (1979); *2 Movements* for Chamber Ensemble (1983); *Des Dichters Pflug,* trio for Violin, Viola, and Cello (1989); *Agnus Dei in umgepflügter Zeit* for 8 Instruments (1990–91); *Plainte-lieber spaltet mein Herz . . .* for Viola d'amore or Viola, Guitar, and Percussion (1990–92); String Quintet (1993–94); piano pieces; organ music. **VOCAL:** *Das Te Deum laudamus deutsch* for Soloists and Chorus (1955–56); *Antiphonische Kantate* for Chorus and Orch. (1956); *Oratio Mechtildis,* chamber sym. for Alto and Chamber Orch. (1956–57); *Des Engels Anredung an die Seele,* chamber cantata for Tenor, Flute, Clarinet, Horn, and Harp (1957); *Auf die ruhige Nacht-Zeit* for Soprano, Flute, Viola, and Cello (1958); *Soliloquia,* oratorio for Soloists, 2 Choruses, and Orch. (1959–64); *Psalm of Christ* for Baritone and 8 Instruments (1967); *Kleine deutsche Messe* for Chorus, Congregation, Organ, String Trio, and Harp (1969); *. . . inwendig voller Figur . . .* for Chorus, Orch., Loudspeaker, and Tape (1970–71); *. . . ausgespannt . . .* for Baritone, 5 Instrumental Groups, Loudspeaker, Tape, and Organ (1972); *Erniedrigt-Geknechtet-Verlassen-Verachtet* for 4 Soloists, 2 Choruses, and Orch. (1975–78; 1981–82); *Beati Pauperes II* for 7 Voices and Small Orch. (1979); *Ñudo que ansí juntáis* for 16 Solo Voices (1984); *Cantiones de circulo gyrante* for Soloists, Chorus, and Chamber Orch. (1985; reworked as *Kleines Requiem für Heinrich Böll* for Chorus and Bass Baritone ad libitum, 1994); *Spes contra Spem* for Soloists and Orch. (1986; 1988–89); *La terre des hommes* for Mezzosoprano, Countertenor/Speaker, and Chamber Orch. (1987–89); *Die umgepflügte Zeit* for Soloists, Speaker, Choruses, and Orch. (1990); *Agnus Dei cum recordatione,* "Hommage à Jehan Okeghem" for Countertenor, 2 Tenors, Bass Baritone, Renaissance Lute, and 2 Fiddles or Guitar and 2 Violas (1990–91); *Die Erde bewegt sich auf den Hörnern eines Ochsen* for Sufi Singer and Arab and European Instruments (1992–93).

Huber, Kurt, eminent German musicologist of Swiss descent; b. Chur, Oct. 24, 1893; d. (executed by the Gestapo) Munich, July 13, 1943. He studied philosophy and psychology with Becher and Külpe and musicology with Kroyer and Sandberger at the Univ. of Munich (Ph.D., 1917, with the diss. *Ivo de Vento: Ein Beitrag zur Musikgeschichte des 16. Jahrhunderts,* 1; publ. in Lindenberg, 1918); then completed his Habilitation in psychology (1920). He became assistant lecturer at the Univ. of Munich's Inst. of Psychology in 1920; was made a Dozent there in 1926. From 1925 he devoted himself to collecting and recording early Bavarian folk songs, which he publ. with Paul Kiem. He actively opposed the Nazi regime, and was imprisoned and executed for his participation in student protests. In addition to his book *Die Doppelmeister des 16. Jahrhunderts* (Munich, 1920), the following vols. have been publ.: O. Ursprung ed. his *Ästhetik* (Ettal, 1954) and *Musikästhetik* (Ettal, 1954), J. Hanslmeier his *Grundbegriffe der Seelenkunde: Einführung in die allgemeine Psychologie* (Ettal, 1955), and C. Huber and O. von Müller his *Volkslied und Volkstanz: Aufsätze zur Volksliedkunde des bajuwarischen Raumes* (Ettal, 1960).

BIBL.: W. Rubsamen, "K. H. of Munich," *Musical Quarterly* (April 1944); C. Huber, ed., *K. H. zum Gedächtnis: Bildnis eines Menschen, Denkers und Forchers* (Regensburg, 1947); E. Grave, *Die ästhetischen Kategorien in K. H.s Ästhetik* (diss., Univ. of Munich, 1957).

Huberman, Bronislaw, famous Polish violinist; b. Częstochowa, Dec. 19, 1882; d. Corsier-sur-Vevey, Switzerland, June 15, 1947. He began to study violin with Michalowicz at age 6, making his debut when he was 7 as soloist in Spohr's 2nd Violin Concerto; then studied with Izydor Lotto. When he was 9 he was taken to Berlin, where he studied with Joachim's assistant Markees; he then studied privately with Carl Grigorovich, his most influential mentor; later took some lessons with Heermann in Frankfurt am Main and Marsick in Paris. He played in the Netherlands and Belgium in 1893, then in Paris and London in 1894. Adelina Patti heard him in London and engaged him for her farewell appearance in Vienna (Jan. 12, 1895), where he scored a brilliant success. He then played the Brahms Violin Concerto there in the presence of the composer (Jan. 29, 1896), who commended him warmly. He made his first tour of the U.S. in 1896–97; subsequently made world tours and was active as a teacher in Vienna. He went to Palestine in 1936 and founded the Palestine Sym. Orch., an ensemble composed mainly of Jewish musicians who had lost their positions in the wake of Nazism in Europe. The orch. prospered and became the Israel Phil. Orch. in 1948. He went to the U.S. in 1940, but returned to Europe at the end of World War II (1945). He publ. *Aus der Werkstatt des Virtuosen* (1912) and *Mein Weg zu Paneuropa* (1925).

BIBL.: H. Goetz, *B. H. and the Unity of Europe* (Rome, 1967); I. Ibbeken and T. Avni, eds., *An Orchestra Is Born: The Founding of the Palestine Orchestra as Reflected in B. H.'s Letters, Speeches, and Articles* (Tel Aviv, 1969).

Hübler, Klaus K(arl), German composer; b. Munich, July 12, 1956. He studied composition with Peter Kiesewetter (1975–76) and Brian Ferneyhough (1980–82), and also studied musicology at the Univ. of Munich. He received several fellowships and prizes; visited the U.S. as a participant in the Pittsburgh International Music Festival (1986). After being stricken with a serious illness in 1989, he ceased to compose. His compositions are extremely complex, demanding an intricate system of notation.

WORKS: ORCH.: *Wer die Schönheit Angeschaut mit Augen* for Cello and Chamber Orch. (1979); *Arie dissolute* for Viola and Chamber Ensemble (1986–87); *Epiphyt* for Flute and Chamber Orch. (1987–88). **CHAMBER:** *MUSICA MENSURABILIS* for 2 Violins and Viola (1975–76); 3 string quartets: No. 1, *Hommage à Alban Berg* (1977), No. 2, *sur le premier prélude* (1979–80), and No. 3, *Dialektische Fantasie* (1982–84); *Chanson sans paroles, Kafkastudie I* for Clarinet, Cello, and Piano (1978); Sonata for Solo Violin (1978); *Riflessi* for Flute, Violin, Viola, Cello, and Harp (1979); *Notturno* for 10 Instruments (1980); String Trio No. 1, *Konzertparaphrase* (1980–81); *"Feuerzauber" auch Augenmusik: Studie in/über Phantasmagorie* for 3 Flutes, Cello, and Harp (1981); *Am Ende des Kanons: Musica con(tro)versa* for Trumpet and Organ (1983); *CERCAR* for Trumpet (1983); *Grave e sfrenato* for Oboe (1985); *sklEros* for Flute, Oboe d'Amore, Clarinet, Bassoon, and Horn Obbligato (1985–86); *Sonetto LXXXIII del Michelangelo* for Piano (1986); *Opus breve* for Cello (1987); *Reisswerck* for Guitar (1987); *Kryptogramm* for 9 Musicians (1989).

Hudson, Frederick, English organist and musicologist; b. Gateshead, Durham, Jan. 16, 1913. He studied with Edward Bairstow (1939–46) and with Gordon Slater at Lincoln Cathedral; received the degree of B.Mus. at the Univ. of Durham in 1941, and of D.Mus. in 1950. He served as organist and choirmaster at Alnwick (1941–48); was a lecturer in music at King's College, Univ. of Durham (1949–70), and then a reader in music at the Univ. of Newcastle upon Tyne (from 1970). He ed. works by Bach, Handel, Giovanni Gabrieli, William Byrd, and others for the new editions of their works; contributed important papers dealing with watermarks of undated MSS and prints, making use of beta-radiography with carbon-14 sources; also compiled a catalog of the works of Charles Villiers Stanford (*Music Review,* XXXVII, 1976).

Hüe, Georges (Adolphe), French composer and teacher; b. Versailles, May 6, 1858; d. Paris, June 7, 1948. After piano lessons with his mother, he studied counterpoint and fugue with Paladilhe and organ and composition with Franck and Reber at the Paris Cons. In 1879 he won the Prix de Rome with his cantata *Médée* and in 1881 he received the Prix Crescent with his comic opera *Les pantins.* He devoted himself to composing and teaching in Paris. In 1922 he succeeded to Saint-Saëns' seat in the Académie des Beaux-Arts.

WORKS: DRAMATIC (all 1st perf. in Paris): *Les pantins,* opéra comique (Dec. 18, 1881); *Le roi de Paris,* opera (April 26, 1901); *Titania,* opera (1902; Jan. 20, 1903); *Le miracle,* opera (Dec. 14, 1910); *Dans l'ombre de la cathédrale,* opera (Dec. 7,

1921); *Siang-Sin*, ballet-pantomime (March 12, 1924); *Riquet à la houppe*, comédie-musicale (Dec. 17, 1928). **ORCH.:** *Rübezahl*, symphonic legend (1886); *Le Berger* for Violin and Orch. (1893); Sym. (n.d.); etc. **VOCAL:** *Médée*, cantata (1879); choral pieces; songs.

Huehn, Julius, American baritone; b. Revere, Mass., Jan. 12, 1904; d. Rochester, N.Y., June 8, 1971. He studied engineering at the Carnegie Inst. of Technology; later took voice lessons with Anna Schoen-René at the Juilliard School of Music in N.Y. He made his operatic debut with the Metropolitan Opera in N.Y. as the Herald in *Lohengrin* on Dec. 21, 1935, singing there until 1944; then served in the U.S. Air Force and carried out missions in Europe as a bombardier. He sang again at the Metropolitan after the war (1945–46). He was particularly noted for his performances of heroic baritone parts in Wagner's operas.

Huggler, John, American composer; b. Rochester, N.Y., Aug. 30, 1928. He studied at the Eastman School of Music in his hometown (graduated, 1950), and with Charles Warren Fox (musicology) and Dante Fiorillo (composition). He received 2 Guggenheim fellowships (1962, 1969); also served as composer-in-residence of the Boston Sym. Orch. (1964–65).

WORKS: ORCH.: *Elegy to the Memory of Federico García Lorca* (1952); Horn Concerto (1957); *Ecce Homo* (1959); *Divertimento* for Viola and Orch. (1961); *Music in 2 Parts* (1966); Flute Concerto (1967); Trumpet Concerto (1968); Sym. in 3 Movements (1980); *Continuum* (1985). **CHAMBER:** 9 string quartets (1951–67); 4 brass quintets (1957, 1962, 1973, 1982); 3 string quintets (1958); *Outdoor Piece for Tanglewood* for Brass and Percussion (1966); *Sinfonia* for 13 Players (1974); *Poem* for Violin and Piano (1985); *Capriccio Sregolato* for Flute, Clarinet, Violin, Viola, and Cello (1986). **PIANO:** 7 Bagatelles (1953); Sonata (1957). **VOCAL:** *Sculptures* for Soprano and Orch. (1964); *7 Songs on Poems of E.J. Leavenworth* for Soprano and Orch. (1974).

Hughes, Dom Anselm, eminent English musicologist; b. London, April 15, 1889; d. Nashdom Abbey, Burnham, Buckinghamshire, Oct. 8, 1974. He studied at Keble College, Oxford (B.A., 1911; M.A., 1915), and at Ely Theological College (1911–12); was ordained a priest (1913). He was a curate and choirmaster in several London churches (1912–22) before joining the Anglican Benedictine community at Pershore Abbey; was professed there (1923) and served as its director of music (1922–45) and prior (1936–45), continuing after its 1926 move to Nashdom Abbey. He was a leading authority on medieval and Renaissance music; contributed articles to the 3rd, 4th, and 5th eds. of *Grove's Dictionary of Music and Musicians* and to the 2nd ed. of *The Oxford History of Music*; edited the 2nd and 3rd (with G. Abraham) vols. of *The New Oxford History of Music*; also edited the *Old Hall Manuscript* (with H. Collins). He composed *Missa Sancti Benedicti* (1918) and other sacred pieces.

WRITINGS: *Latin Hymnody: An Enquiry into the Underlying Principles of the Hymnarium* (London, 1922); *The House of My Pilgrimage* (London, 1929); *Index to the Facsimile Edition of MS Wolfenbüttel 677* (Oxford, 1939); *Liturgical Terms for Music Students* (Boston, 1940); *Medieval Polyphony in the Bodleian Library* (Oxford, 1951); *Catalogue of the Musical Manuscripts at Peterhouse, Cambridge* (Cambridge, 1953); *Septuagesima: Reminiscences of the Plainsong and Mediaeval Music Society* (London, 1959); *Plainsong for English Choirs* (Leighton Buzzard, 1966).

Hughes, Arwel, Welsh conductor and composer, father of **Owain Arwel Hughes**; b. Rhosllanerchrugog, Aug. 25, 1909; d. Cardiff, Sept. 23, 1988. He studied with Kitson and Vaughan Williams at the Royal College of Music in London; then returned to Wales, where he became a member of the music dept. of the BBC in 1935; from 1965 to 1971 he was head of music there. He was made an Officer of the Order of the British Empire in 1969. He wrote the operas *Menna* (1950–51) and *Serch yw'r doctor* (Love's the Doctor), after Molière (1959); Sym. (1971); choral works; chamber music.

Hughes, Edwin, American pianist and teacher; b. Washington, D.C., Aug. 15, 1884; d. N.Y., July 17, 1965. He studied with S.M. Fabian in Washington, D.C., with Joseffy in N.Y. (1906–07), and with Leschetizky in Vienna (1907–10). He taught at the Ganapol School of Musical Art in Detroit (1910–12), the Volpe Inst. of Music in N.Y. (1916–17), and the Inst. of Musical Art in N.Y. (1918–23); lectured at various schools. From 1920 to 1926 he was special ed. of piano music for G. Schirmer, Inc. He toured widely in the U.S. and Europe after the close of World War I; performed duo-recitals with his wife, the pianist Jewel Bethany Hughes, and also gave master classes.

Hughes, Herbert, Irish music critic and composer; b. Belfast, March 16, 1882; d. Bristol, May 1, 1937. He studied at the Royal College of Music in London. From 1911 to 1932 he was music critic of the *Daily Telegraph*. He collected and arranged numerous folk songs. His own works include incidental music, chamber pieces, piano music, and vocal works.

Hughes, Owain Arwel, Welsh conductor, son of **Arwel Hughes**; b. Cardiff, March 21, 1942. He first studied at Univ. College in Cardiff; then (1964–66) at the Royal College of Music in London, where his teachers included Boult and Harvey Philips; subsequently studied with Kempe in London and Haitink in Amsterdam. He made his London debut in 1968; then appeared as a guest conductor with leading English orchs.; also conducted at the Welsh National Opera and the English National Opera. In 1977 he became music director of the Royal National Eisteddfod of Wales; also was assoc. conductor of the BBC Welsh Sym. Orch. (from 1980) and music director of the Huddersfield Choral Soc. (1980–86); then was assoc. conductor of the Philharmonia Orch. of London (from 1987).

Hughes, Robert Watson, Scottish-born Australian composer; b. Leven, Fyfeshire, March 27, 1912. He emigrated to Australia in 1930 and studied with A.E.H. Nickson at the Univ. of Melbourne Conservatorium of Music (1938–40). He worked as a music librarian at the Australian Broadcasting Commission in Melbourne; was chairman of the Australian Performing Right Assn. (1977–85). In 1978 he was made a Member of the Order of the British Empire. He withdrew most of his early compositions.

WORKS: DRAMATIC: OPERA: *The Intriguers* (1975). **BALLETS:** *Xanadu* (1954); *The Forbidden Rite* (1962). **ORCH.:** *Festival Overture* (1948); *Farrago*, suite (1949); *Serenade* for Small Orch. (1952); Sym. (1952); *Essay I* (1953) and *II* (1982); *Masquerade Overture* (1956); Sinfonietta (1957) *Synthesis* (1969); *Sea Spell* (1973). **VOCAL:** *5 Indian Poems* for Chorus, Woodwinds, and Percussion (1971); *2 Indian Poems* for Soprano and Chamber Orch. (1979).

Hughes, Rupert, American novelist, writer on music, and composer; b. Lancaster, Mo., Jan. 31, 1872; d. Los Angeles, Sept. 9, 1956. He studied with W.G. Smith in Cleveland (1890–92), E.S. Kelley in N.Y. (1899), and C. Pearce in London (1900–1901). His publications include *American Composers* (Boston, 1900; rev. 1914); *The Musical Guide* (2 vols., N.Y., 1903; republ. as *Music Lovers' Encyclopedia*, in 1 vol., 1912; rev. and newly ed. by D. Taylor and R. Kerr as *Music Lover's Encyclopedia*, 1939; rev. 1954); ed. *Thirty Songs by American Composers* (1904). He also composed a dramatic monologue for Baritone and Piano, *Cain* (1919); piano pieces; songs. He was principally known, however, as a novelist.

Hugon, Georges, French composer and teacher; b. Paris, July 23, 1904; d. Blauvac, Vaucluse, July 19, 1980. He studied at the Paris Cons.; received the Prix Bizet (1926). He was director of the Boulogne-sur-Mer Cons. (1934–41); in 1941 he became a prof. at the Paris Cons. His compositions include an oratorio, *Chants de deuil et d'espérance* (1947); 2 syms. (1941, 1949); 2 symphonic poems: *Au nord* (1930) and *La Reine de Saba* (1933); Piano Concerto (1962); Flute Sonata (1965); Piano Trio; String Quartet; piano pieces; songs.

Huízar (García de la Cadena), Candelario, Mexican composer; b. Jerez, Feb. 2, 1883; d. Mexico City, May 3, 1970. He studied violin and composition before training with Gustavo Campa at the Mexico City Cons. He played horn (1929–37) and was librarian (1929–48) with the Orquesta Sinfónica de Mexico. His output reflected Mexican folk modalities with an infusion of authentic Mexican themes.

WORKS: ORCH. (all 1st perf. in Mexico City): 3 symphonic poems: *Imágenes* (Dec. 13, 1929), *Pueblerinas* (Nov. 6, 1931), and *Surco* (Oct. 25, 1935); 4 syms. (Nov. 14, 1930; Sept. 4, 1936; July 29, 1938; Aug. 7, 1942). **CHAMBER:** Sonata for Clarinet and Bassoon (1931); String Quartet (1938).

Hull, Anne, American pianist, teacher, and composer; b. Brookland, Pa., Jan. 25, 1888; d. Westport, Conn., Jan. 31, 1984. She studied piano at the Peabody Cons. of Music in Baltimore (teacher's certificate, 1907; artist's diploma, 1913). After touring as a duo-pianist with Mary Howe (1920–35), she taught at the Inst. of Musical Art (1942–46) and the Juilliard Graduate School (1946–68) in N.Y. Her best-known work was *Ancient Ballad* for 2 Pianos.

Hull, Arthur Eaglefield, English writer on music; b. Market Harborough, March 10, 1876; d. (suicide) London, Nov. 4, 1928. He was a student of Matthay and C. Pearce. In 1912 he became ed. of the *Monthly Musical Record.* In 1918 he organized the British Music Soc. He publ. the pioneering *Dictionary of Modern Music and Musicians* (1924), a vol. flawed by many egregious errors and misconceptions; A. Einstein publ. a corrected German tr. (1926). Hull's *Music: Classical, Romantic and Modern* (1927) proved to be a pasticcio of borrowings from various English and American writers. When he was exposed, the book was withdrawn by the publisher in 1928 and Hull threw himself under a train at the Huddersfield Railway Station, dying a few weeks later. He also publ. *Organ Playing, Its Technique and Expression* (1911); *Modern Harmony: Its Explanation and Application* (1914; 3rd ed., 1923); *The Sonata in Music* (1916); *Scriabin* (1916); *Modern Musical Styles* (1916); *Design or Construction in Music* (1917); *Cyril Scott* (1918).

Humble, (Leslie) Keith, Australian pianist, conductor, teacher, and composer; b. Geelong, Victoria, Sept. 6, 1927; d. May 23, 1995. After obtaining his diploma at the Melbourne Cons. (1949), he studied with Vivian Langrish (piano) and Howard Ferguson (composition) at the Royal Academy of Music in London (1950–51). He then went to Paris and studied with Cortot (piano) at the École Normale de Musique (1951–52), and then privately with Leibowitz (composition and conducting, 1952–54). In 1959 he founded Le Centre de Musique in Paris, which he led as musical director until 1968. In 1966 he became senior lecturer in composition at the Melbourne Cons., and also founded its electronic music studio. From 1971 to 1974 he was a prof. at the Univ. of Calif. at San Diego. In 1974 he became the Foundation Prof. in the music dept. of La Trobe Univ. in Victoria, Australia, which position he held until 1989 when he became prof. emeritus. From 1975 to 1978 he was music director of the Australia Contemporary Music Ensemble. He was a visiting prof. at the Univ. of Calif. at San Diego from 1982 to 1990, where he made appearances as a soloist and conductor with the Ensemble Sonor. In 1982 he was made a Member of the Order of Australia. A confirmed avant-gardist, Humble early on developed a personal 12-tone method. He later experimented with improvisation in a series of works he called *Nuniques.* Still later he explored the realm of temporal composition.

WORKS: String Trio (1953); 4 piano sonatas (1959; 1977, rev. 1980; 1985; 1990); *Ainsi s'acheve* for Chamber Ensemble (1967); *Music for Monuments* for Instruments and/or Voices and Prepared Tape (1967); *Materials for Larountala* for 22 Solo Strings (1968); *Solfege I* for Diverse Instruments and Electronics ad libitum (1968) and *II* for Performer and Electronics (1969); *Nunique I–IX*, improvisation pieces (1968–84); *Arcade I–V* for Solo Instrument, Chamber Ensemble, Orch., or Tape (all 1969); *Apres La Legende* for Piano and Orch. (1969); *La Legende*, cantata for Voice, Chorus, Electronics, and Instruments (1970); *Statico I* for Organ and 2 Synthesizers (1971) and *III* for Orch. (1972–73); *A Music for Baroque Ensemble* for Harpsichord, Flute, Oboe, and Double Bass (1971); *Now V*, opera (1971); *Prime Riff* for Percussion Ensemble and Tape (1974); *A.C.F.* for Chamber Ensemble (1980); Trio No. 2 for Violin, Clarinet, and Piano (1982); *Ways, By-Ways* for Chamber Ensemble (1983); Trio No. 3 for Flute, Percussion, and Piano (1985); Percussion Sonata (1986); *Soundscapes* for Chorus and Instrumental Ensemble (1987; also for Instrumental Ensemble and Prerecorded Tape); *Etchings* for Percussion Quartet (1988); *4 All Seasons* for Strings (1989); Flute Sonata (1990); *Concert No. 1* for Flute and Strings (1991) and *No. 2* for Trombone and String Sextet or String Orch. or Chamber Music Ensemble (1992); *A Symphony (of Sorrows)* for Orch. (1994); Trio No. 5 for Organ, Trumpet, and Trombone (1995).

Hume, Paul (Chandler), American music critic; b. Chicago, Dec. 13, 1915. He studied at the Univ. of Chicago; took private lessons in piano, organ, and voice; was organist, choirmaster, and baritone soloist at various churches in Chicago and Washington, D.C.; also gave song recitals. From 1946 to 1982 he was music ed. and critic of the *Washington Post;* was an instructor in music history at Georgetown Univ. (1950–77); was active as a lecturer and radio commentator on music. He publ. *Catholic Church Music* (1956), *Our Music, Our Schools, and Our Culture* (1957), *The Lion of Poland* (1962), *King of Song* (1964), and *Verdi* (1977). Hume leaped to national fame in 1950, when President Truman, outraged by his unenthusiastic review of Margaret Truman's song recital, wrote him a personal letter threatening him with bodily injury. Hume sold the letter to a Connecticut industrialist for an undisclosed sum of money.

Humel, Gerald, American composer; b. Cleveland, Nov. 7, 1931. He studied at Hofstra Univ. in N.Y. (B.A., 1954), the Royal College of Music in London (A.R.C.M., 1956), the Oberlin (Ohio) College Cons. of Music (M.M., 1958), and the Univ. of Mich. in Ann Arbor (1958–60); in 1960 he went to Berlin, where he took private lessons with Blacher and Rufer. His music at first maintained a median line of cosmopolitan modernism, in a neo-Classical direction, but gradually he became oriented toward dodecaphonic techniques.

WORKS: DRAMATIC: OPERAS: *The Proposal* (1949); *The Triangle* (Oberlin, Nov. 14, 1958). **BALLETS:** *Devil's Dice* (1957); *1st Love* (1965); *Herodias* (1967). **ORCH.:** Flute Concerto (1964); Chamber Concerto for Horn, Piano, and Strings (1966); Concerto for Wind Orch. (1968); *Flashes* for Chamber Ensemble (1968); *Fantasie* for 2 Flutes, Cello, and Piano (1968); *Lepini* (1977). **CHAMBER:** *Duo* for Viola and Cello (1964); Cello Sonata (1967); 2 sonatas for Solo Viola (1967, 1968); Clarinet Sonata (1968).

Humpert, Hans, German composer; b. Paderborn, April 19, 1901; d. in battle in Salerno, Sept. 15, 1943. He studied at the Frankfurt am Main Cons. and in Berlin; then taught at Paderborn until he was called into the army. His music is marked by a neo-Romantic quality, with a strong contrapuntal structure; these include 2 syms. (1937, 1942); 3 string quartets; String Trio; Violin Sonata; Viola Sonata; Sonata for Solo Flute; 5 cantatas; 4 masses; 3 motets; 7 Psalms; choral and organ works.

BIBL.: G. Hoffmann, "H. H.," *Musica* (Sept. 1953).

Hungerford, Bruce, Australian pianist; b. Korumburra, Victoria, Nov. 24, 1922; d. in an automobile accident in N.Y., Jan. 26, 1977. He received his initial education in Melbourne; studied piano with Ignaz Friedman in Sydney (1944), and later with Ernest Hutcheson at the Juilliard School of Music in N.Y. (1945–47); took private lessons with Myra Hess in N.Y. (1948–58) and also with Carl Friedberg (1948–55). He gave his first piano recital in N.Y. in 1951; from then until 1965 he appeared under the name Leonard Hungerford. Apart from his virtuoso technique, he possessed an extraordinary mastery of dynamic gradations and self-consistent musical phraseology. He also gained recognition as a color photographer and archeologist, specializing in Egyptology; he recorded a 17-part audiovisual lecture entitled "The Heritage of Ancient Egypt" (1971).

Hüni-Mihacsek, Felice, Hungarian soprano; b. Pecs, April 3, 1891; d. Munich, March 26, 1976. She studied in Vienna with Rosa Papier. She made her operatic debut as the 1st Lady in *Die Zauberflöte* with the Vienna State Opera in 1919, remaining there until 1926; was then a member of the Bavarian State Opera in Munich (1926–44); she retired from the stage in 1953. She particularly excelled in Mozart's operas, winning distinction as the Queen of the Night, Constanze, Fiordiligi, and Donna Anna. Among her other admired roles were Elsa and Eva.

Hunt, Jerry (Edward), American pianist and composer; b. Waco, Texas, Nov. 30, 1943; d. Canton, Texas, Nov. 27, 1993. He studied piano and composition at North Texas State Univ. in Denton (1960–61). As a pianist, he championed the cause of contemporary music. After teaching at Southern Methodist Univ. (1967–73), he was artist-in-residence at the Video Research Center in Dallas (1974–77). Hunt was enamored of multimedia works in which he could utilize the most varied elements, ranging from live performers and performance spaces to video and microwave detection systems.

WORKS: *Helix* for Instrument(s) (1963); *Sur Dr. John Dee* for 0 to 11 Performers (1963); *Infrasolo* for Instrument(s) (1970); *Haramand Plane: Parallel/Regenerative* for Audio and Video (1973); *Cantegral Segment(s)* for Various Instruments and Electronics (1973–78); *Volta* for Voice and Electronics (1977); *Phalba (Working): Kernel* for Electronics (1980); *Volta (Stream)* for Voice(s) and Electronics (1980); *Ground: Field (Still-core-Set)* and *Ground: Field (Transform de Chelly)* for Performers and Electronics (both 1981); tape pieces.

Hunter, Rita (Nellie), distinguished English soprano; b. Wallasey, Aug. 15, 1933. She studied with Edwin Francis in Liverpool and with Clive Carey and Redvers Llewellyn in London; sang in the Sadler's Wells chorus (1954–56) before touring with the Carl Rosa Opera Co. (1956–58); after further studies with Dame Eva Turner, she joined the Sadler's Wells Opera (1959), singing leading roles there from 1965, including Brünnhilde in the English-language version of *Die Walküre* (June 29, 1970); later sang Brünnhilde in the first complete English-language version of the *Ring* (July–Aug. 1973). On Dec. 19, 1972, she made her Metropolitan Opera debut in N.Y. as Brünnhilde; appeared as Norma at the San Francisco Opera in 1975. Her other notable roles included Donna Anna, Aida, Senta, and Santuzza. In 1980 she was made a Commander of the Order of the British Empire. She publ. an autobiography, *Wait Till the Sun Shines, Nellie* (London, 1986).

Hupperts, Paul (Henri Franciscus Marie), Dutch conductor; b. Gulpen, Jan. 1, 1919. He studied music in Utrecht; then appeared as a guest conductor in the Netherlands. In 1947 he was appointed conductor of the Limburg Orch. From 1949 to 1977 he was chief conductor of the Utrecht Sym. Orch.. In his programs, he often included works by modern Dutch composers.

Hurd, Michael (John), English composer, conductor, broadcaster, and writer on music; b. Gloucester, Dec. 19, 1928. He was a pupil of Thomas Armstrong and Bernard Rose at Pembroke College, Oxford (1950–53), and of Lennox Berkeley (1954–56). He taught at the Royal Marines School of Music (1953–59), and from 1956 was a broadcaster with the BBC. His compositions are written in an accessible style; among his lighter scores, the "pop" cantatas have been particularly successful.

WORKS: DRAMATIC: *Little Billy*, children's opera (1964); *Mr. Punch*, operatic entertainment for young people (1970); *The Widow of Ephesus*, chamber opera (Stroud, Oct. 23, 1971); *The Aspern Papers*, opera (1993). **ORCH.:** *Concerto to an Unwritten Comedy* (1970); *Dance Diversions* (1972); *Sinfonia Concertante* for Violin and String Orch. (1973); *Concerto da Camera* for Oboe and Small Orch. (1979); *A Little Suite* for Strings (1985); *Overture to an Unwritten Comedy* (1987). **CHAMBER:** Flute Sonatina (1964); Violin Sonata (1970; rev. 1986); *Harlequin Suite* for Brass (1971; rev. 1982). **VOCAL:** 12 "pop" cantatas: *Jonah-man Jazz* (1966; rev. 1967), *Swingin' Samson* (1972), *Hip-Hip Horatio* (1974), *Rooster Rag* (1975), *Pilgrim* (1978), *Adam-in-Eden* (1981), *Mrs. Beeton's Book* (1982), *A New Nowell* (1986), *Captain Coram's Kids* (1988), *Prodigal* (1989), *The Liberty Tree* (1989), and *King and Conscience* (1990); also *Shepherd's Calender*, sym. for Baritone, Chorus, and Orch. (1975); choral works; songs.

WRITINGS: *Immortal Hour: The Life and Period of Rutland Boughton* (1962; rev. and enl. ed, 1993, as *Rutland Boughton and the Glastonbury Festivals*); *The Composer* (1968); *An Outline of European Music* (1968; 2nd ed., rev., 1988); *Elgar* (1969); *Vaughan Williams* (1970); *Mendelssohn* (1970); *The Ordeal of Ivor Gurney* (1978); *The Oxford Junior Companion to Music* (1979); *Vincent Novello and Company* (1981); *The Orchestra* (1981).

Huré, Jean, French pianist, organist, composer, and writer on music; b. Gien, Loiret, Sept. 17, 1877; d. Paris, Jan. 27, 1930. He received his musical education at a monastery in Angers. He went to Paris in 1895, where he founded the École Normale de Musique (1910), the École Normale pour Pianistes (1912), and the monthly magazine *L'Orgue et les Organistes* (1923). In 1925 he became church organist at St. Augustin; in 1926 he won the Prix Chartier for composition. His ballet, *Le Bois sacré*, was produced at the Opéra-Comique in Paris on June 28, 1921; he further wrote incidental music to Musset's *Fantasio*; 3 syms.; Violin Concerto; *Andante* for Saxophone and Orch.; 2 string quartets; Piano Quintet; Violin Sonata; 3 cello sonatas; etc. He publ. the manuals *La Technique du piano* (1908); *La Technique de l'orgue* (1918); also *L'Esthétique de l'orgue* (1923) and *Saint Augustin, musicien* (1924).

BIBL.: G. Migot, *J. H.* (Paris, 1926).

Hurford, Peter (John), noted English organist; b. Minehead, Somerset, Nov. 22, 1930. He studied law and music at Jesus College, Cambridge; later took organ lessons with Marchal in Paris. In 1958 he was named Master of the Music at St. Albans Abbey; in 1963 he founded the International Organ Festival there. He left St. Albans in 1979 to pursue his international career as a leading interpreter of the music of the Baroque period. He publ. the study *Making Music on the Organ* (Oxford, 1988; rev. ed., 1990). In 1984 he was made an Officer of the Order of the British Empire.

Hurley, Laurel, American soprano; b. Allentown, Pa., Feb. 14, 1927. Of a musical family, she studied with her mother, a church organist; at 16, she appeared on Broadway (Aug. 21, 1943) as Kathie in Romberg's operetta *The Student Prince*; then toured with the company that produced it. In 1952 she made her N.Y. City Opera debut as Zerlina. She was the winner of the Walter W. Naumburg Foundation Award, which enabled her to give a song recital in N.Y. (Nov. 6, 1952). She made her debut at the Metropolitan Opera in N.Y. on Feb. 8, 1955, as Oscar; she remained at the Metropolitan until 1967, singing such roles as Musetta, Susanna, Périchole, Adele, Mimi, and Despina.

Hurník, Ilja, Czech pianist and composer; b. Poruba, near Svinov, Nov. 25, 1922. He moved to Prague in 1938 and had piano lessons with Kurz (1939–45); studied composition with Řídký and was the last pupil of Novák (1941–44); later studied piano with Štěpánová at the Cons. (1945–48) before completing his training at the Academy of Music (1948–52). He then made several concert tours in Czechoslovakia. He taught at the Prague Cons. (from 1970) and at the Bratislava Academy of Music. His works are marked with modernistic tendencies.

WORKS: DRAMATIC: OPERAS: *Dámá a lupiči* (The Lady and the Gangster), after the film *The Ladykillers* (1966); *Mudrci a bloudi* (The Wise and the Foolish; 1968); *Diogenes* (1974). **BALLET:** *Ondráš* (1950). **ORCH.:** Flute Concerto (1953); *Serenade* for Strings (1954); Concerto for Winds and Percussion

(1956); Concerto for Oboe, Strings, and Piano (1959); *Musikanti* (The Musicians) for 20 Instruments (1962); *Chamber Music* for Strings (1962); *Kyklopes* (Prague, June 4, 1965); Concerto for Piano and Small Orch. (1972); *Věci*, divertimento for Chamber Orch. (1977); *Overture to a Comedy* (1985); Concertino for Organ and Chamber Ensemble (1990). **CHAMBER:** 2 wind quintets (1944, 1985); 2 string quartets (1949; 2nd, with Baritone, to Old Testament texts, 1961); Viola Sonata (1952); *Die vier Jahreszeiten* for 12 Solo Instruments (1952); *Sonata da camera* for Flute, Oboe, Cello, and Harpsichord (1953); Piano Quintet (1953); *Ballet* for 9 Instruments (1954); *Esercizi* for Flute, Oboe, Clarinet, and Bassoon (1958); *Moments musicaux* for 11 Winds (1962); *Gloria di flauti* for 2 Flutes (1973). **KEYBOARD: PIANO:** *Preludes* (1943); Sonatina (1952); *Étude* (1972); *Variations on a Theme of Pergolesi* for Piano, 4-hands (1983; also for Chamber Ensemble); *Innocenza* for Piano, 4-hands (1992). **ORGAN:** 3 sonatas (1956). **VOCAL:** *Maryka*, cantata (1948; rev. 1955); *Noe* (Noah), oratorio (1959); *Ezop* (Aesop), cantata (1964); *Sulamit*, song cycle for Woman's Voice and Orch., after the Old Testament (1963); *Ozěvna*, chamber cantata (1981); *Madrigal* for Voices (1982); *Ancient Portrait* for Children's Chorus and Orch. (1988); *Missa Vinea Crucis* for Children's Chorus and Orch. or Organ (1991).

Hurok, Sol(omon Israelovich), famous Russian-born American impresario; b. Pogar, April 9, 1888; d. N.Y., March 5, 1974. He emigrated to the U.S. in 1906 and became a naturalized American citizen in 1914. After organizing concerts for labor groups, he attracted notice with his star performers at N.Y.'s Hippodrome in 1913. He subsequently became one of the most colorful and successful impresarios of his era, managing such celebrated artists as Chaliapin, Rubinstein, Segovia, Elman, Stern, Piatigorsky, and Marian Anderson. After World War II, he played a significant role in bringing Soviet artists and organizations to the U.S. His extraordinary career inspired the film *Tonight We Sing*. In 1973 he received the Diamond Jubilee Medal at the Metropolitan Opera in N.Y. for his services to music. He likewise was honored in death by a public funeral at Carnegie Hall in N.Y.

BIBL.: H. Robinson, *The Last Impresario: The Life, Times, and Legacy of S. H.* (N.Y., 1994).

Hurst, George, English conductor; b. Edinburgh, May 20, 1926. He first studied piano with Isserlis, then took courses in conducting and composition at the Royal Cons. of Music of Toronto; also studied conducting with Monteux. He was a teacher and conductor at the Peabody Cons. of Music in Baltimore (1947–55), and also was conductor of the York (Pa.) Sym. Orch. (1950–55); then was assistant conductor of the London Phil. (1955–57) and of the BBC Northern Sym. Orch. at Manchester (1958–68); subsequently conducted the Bournemouth Sym. Orch. (1969–71), and also was artistic advisor of the Bournemouth Sinfonietta until 1978. From 1986 to 1989 he was principal guest conductor of the BBC Scottish Sym. Orch. in Glasgow. In 1990–91 he was principal conductor of the National Sym. Orch. of Ireland in Dublin.

Hurum, Alf (Thorvald), Norwegian pianist, conductor, composer, and painter; b. Christiania, Sept. 21, 1882; d. Honolulu, Aug. 15, 1972. He studied with Max Bruch and Robert Kahn at the Hochschule für Musik in Berlin (1905–09); later took additional courses in Paris and in Russia. He was a co-founder of the Soc. of Norwegian Composers in 1917. After touring as a concert pianist, he settled in Hawaii, where he established the Honolulu Sym. Orch. and was its conductor (1924–26). His 2nd career was that of a silk painter in the Japanese manner, which preoccupied him during his later years. In his music, he cultivated coloristic harmonies, somewhat in an impressionist mode.

WORKS: 2 violin sonatas (1911, 1916); *3 Aquarelles* for Piano (1912); String Quartet (1913); *Exotic Suite* for Violin and Piano (1916); *Pastels*, 4 pieces for Piano (1916); *Eventyrland* (Fairy Land), suite for Orch. or Piano (1920); *Gotiske bilder*, 6 pieces for Piano (1920); *Norse Suite* for Orch. (1920); *Bendikt and Aarolilja*, symphonic poem (1923); Sym. (1927); songs; motets.

Hurwitz, Emanuel (Henry), English violinist and conductor; b. London, May 7, 1919. He received a scholarship from Bronislaw Huberman which allowed him to study at the Royal Academy of Music in London. In 1948 he became concertmaster of the Goldsborough (later English) Chamber Orch., a position he held until 1968; was then concertmaster of the New Philharmonia Orch. (1969–71). He was also active as a chamber music artist; was 1st violinist of the Hurwitz String Quartet (1946–51), the Melos Ensemble (1956–72), and the Aeolian Quartet (from 1970). In 1968 he founded the Hurwitz Chamber Orch. (from 1972 known as the Serenata of London), a conductorless ensemble. He was made a Commander of the Order of the British Empire in 1978.

Husa, Karel, distinguished Czech-born American composer, conductor, and pedagogue; b. Prague, Aug. 7, 1921. He studied violin and piano in his youth; concurrently took courses in engineering; in 1941 he entered the Prague Cons., studying composition with Řídký; in 1945–46 he attended the Academy of Music; in 1946 he was awarded a French government grant to continue his studies in Paris at the École Normale de Musique and the Cons.; his teachers included Honegger and Boulanger; he also studied conducting with Fournet and Cluytens. In 1954 he emigrated to the U.S., and joined the music dept. of Cornell Univ. as teacher of composition and conductor of the student orch., remaining there until his retirement in 1992. He also taught at Ithaca College (1967–86). He became a naturalized American citizen in 1959. He appeared widely as a guest conductor, frequently including his own music in his programs. In his early works, he followed the modern Czech school of composition, making thematic use of folk tunes; later he enlarged his musical resources to include atonal, polytonal, microtonal, and even occasional aleatory procedures, without following doctrinaire prescriptions to the letter. His music is oxygenated by humanistic Romanticism; as a result, it gains numerous performances. In 1969 Husa received the Pulitzer Prize in Music for his 3rd String Quartet. In 1974 he was elected to membership in the Royal Belgian Academy of the Arts and Sciences. In 1986 he received an honorary Doctor of Music degree from Ithaca College. In 1993 he received the Grawemeyer Award of the Univ. of Louisville for his Cello Concerto. He became a member of the American Academy of Arts and Letters in 1994. In 1995 President Havel of the Czech Republic bestowed upon him the State Medal Award of Merit, 1st Class.

WORKS: BALLETS: *Monodrama* (Indianapolis, March 26, 1976); *The Trojan Women* (Louisville, March 28, 1981). **ORCH.:** Overture (1st public perf., Prague, June 18, 1946); Sinfonietta (Prague, April 25, 1947); *3 fresques* (Prague, April 27, 1949; rev. as *Fresque*, Syracuse, N.Y., May 5, 1963); *Divertimento* for Strings (Paris, Oct. 30, 1949); Piano Concertino (Brussels, June 6, 1952); *Musique d'amateurs*, 4 Easy Pieces for Oboe, Trumpet, Percussion, and Strings (1953); *Portrait* for Strings (Donaueschingen, Oct. 10, 1953); 2 syms.: No. 1 (Brussels, March 4, 1954) and No. 2, *Reflections* (Greensboro, N.C., July 16, 1983); *4 Little Pieces* for Strings (Fürsteneck, March 17, 1957); *Fantasies* (Ithaca, N.Y., April 28, 1957); *Divertimento* for Brass and Percussion (Ithaca, N.Y., Feb. 17, 1960); *Poem* for Viola and Chamber Orch. (Cologne, June 12, 1960); *Mosaïques* (Hamburg, Nov. 7, 1961); *Elégie et Rondeau* for Alto Saxophone and Orch. (Ithaca, N.Y., May 6, 1962); *Serenade* for Woodwind Quintet Solo with Strings, Xylophone, and Harp (Baltimore, Jan. 7, 1964); Concerto for Brass Quintet and Strings (Buffalo, Feb. 15, 1970); Concerto for Alto Saxophone and Concert Band (Ithaca, N.Y., March 17, 1968); *Music for Prague 1968* (2 versions; for Band: Washington, D.C., Jan. 31, 1969; for Orch., Munich, Jan. 31, 1970; 1st Czech perf. of orch. version, Prague, Feb. 13, 1990, composer conducting); Concerto for Percussion and Wind Instruments (Waco, Texas, Feb. 7, 1972); *Apotheosis* *of This Earth* for Wind Instruments (Ann Arbor, April 1, 1971; 2nd version for Chorus and Orch.: Ithaca, N.Y., April 12, 1973); *2 Sonnets from Michelangelo* (Evanston, Ill., April 28, 1972); Trumpet Concerto (Storrs, Conn., Aug. 9, 1974); *Fanfare* for Brass Ensemble (1980); *Pastoral* for Strings (Miami Beach, April 12, 1980); Concerto for Wind Ensemble (Lansing, Mich., Dec. 3, 1982); *Smetana Fanfare* for Wind Ensemble (San Diego, April 3, 1984); *Symphonic Suite* (Athens, Ga., Oct. 1, 1984); *Concerto for Orchestra* (N.Y., Sept. 25, 1986); Organ Concerto, *The Sunlights* (Cleveland, Oct. 28, 1987); Trumpet Concerto (Chicago, Feb. 11, 1988); Cello Concerto (1988; Los Angeles, March 2, 1989); *Overture: Youth* (Seattle, Dec. 1, 1991); *Cayuga Lake: Memories* for Chamber Orch. (1992); Violin Concerto (N.Y., May 27, 1993). **CHAMBER:** String Quartet (1942–43); 4 numbered string quartets: No. 1 (Prague, May 23, 1948), No. 2 (Paris, Oct. 23, 1954), No. 3 (Chicago, Oct. 14, 1968), and No. 4 (1989–90); Suite for Viola and Piano (1945); *Evocations of Slovakia* for Clarinet, Viola, and Cello (Paris, May 4, 1952); *2 Preludes* for Flute, Clarinet, and Bassoon (Ithaca, N.Y., April 21, 1966); *Divertimento* for Brass Quintet (Ithaca, N.Y., Nov. 20, 1968); *Studies* for Percussion (1968); Violin Sonata (N.Y., March 31, 1974); *Landscapes* for Brass Quintet (Kalamazoo, Mich., Oct. 17, 1977); *3 Dance Sketches* for Percussion (Miami Beach, April 12, 1980); *Intradas and Interludes* for 7 Trumpets and Timpani (Columbus, Ohio, June 20, 1980); *Sonata a tre* for Violin, Clarinet, and Piano (Hong Kong, March 23, 1982); *Recollections* for Woodwind Quintet and Piano (Washington, D.C., Oct. 28, 1982); *Variations* for Violin, Viola, Cello, and Piano (Atlanta, May 20, 1984); *Intrada* for Brass Quintet (Baltimore, Nov. 15, 1984); *5 Poems* for Woodwind Quintet (1994; N.Y., Feb. 10, 1995). **PIANO:** 2 sonatas (1950, 1975). **VOCAL:** *12 Moravian Songs* for Voice and Piano (1956); *Festive Ode* for Chorus and Orch. (1965); *The Steadfast Tin Soldier* for Narrator and Orch. (Boulder, Colo., May 10, 1975); *An American Te Deum* for Baritone, Chorus, and Wind Ensemble (Cedar Rapids, Iowa, Dec. 4, 1976; 2nd version for Baritone, Chorus, and Orch., Washington, D.C., May 10, 1978); *3 Moravian Songs* for Chorus (1981); *Every Day* for Chorus (1981); Cantata for Men's Chorus and Brass Quintet (Crawfordsville, Ind., April 20, 1983).

BIBL.: L. Hartzell, "K. H.: The Man and the Music," *Musical Quarterly* (May 1976); S. Hitchens, *K. H.: A Bio-Bibliography* (N.Y., 1991).

Hüsch, Gerhard (Heinrich Wilhelm Fritz), esteemed German baritone and pedagogue; b. Hannover, Feb. 2, 1901; d. Munich, Nov. 23, 1984. He received his training from Hans Emge in Hannover. In 1923 he made his operatic debut as Lieberau in Lortzing's *Der Waffenschmied* in Osnabrück. After singing in Bremen, he was a member of the Cologne Opera (1927–30). He then went to Berlin and sang with the City and State Operas (1930–42); he also appeared in Dresden, Hamburg, Munich, Vienna, Milan, Bayreuth (1930–31), and London (Covent Garden debut as Falke, 1930; returned there, 1931 and 1938). In later years, Hüsch became well known as an exponent of lieder. He also taught voice in Munich.

Husmann, Heinrich, distinguished German musicologist; b. Cologne, Dec. 16, 1908; d. Brussels, Nov. 8, 1983. He studied musicology with Ludwig at the Univ. of Göttingen, and with Hornbostel, Schering, Wolf, and Blume at the Humboldt Univ. in Berlin; received his Ph.D. there in 1932. In 1933 he was appointed assistant lecturer at the musicological inst. at the Univ. of Leipzig; completed his Habilitation there in 1941, and then was made its acting director in 1944. He completed a 2nd Habilitation at the Univ. of Hamburg in 1948; organized its musicological inst. in 1949; was a reader there from 1956 and a prof. from 1958. In 1960 he became a prof. of musicology at the Univ. of Göttingen. His books include *Fünf- und siebenstellige Centstafeln zur Berechnung musikalischer Intervalle* (Leiden, 1951); *Vom Wesen der Konsonanz* (Heidelberg, 1953); *Einführung in die Musikwissenschaft* (Heidelberg, 1958); *Grundlagen der antiken und orientalischen Musikkultur* (Berlin, 1961).

BIBL.: H. Becker and R. Gerlach, eds., *Speculum musicae artis: Festgabe für H. H.* (Munich, 1970).

Huss, Henry Holden, American pianist and composer; b. Newark, N.J., June 21, 1862; d. N.Y., Sept. 17, 1953. He was a descendant of Jan Huss, the Bohemian martyr. His mother, Sophia Ruckle Holden Huss, was a granddaughter of Levi Holden, a member of George Washington's staff. Huss studied piano and theory with his father and with O. Boise. In 1882 he went to Germany, and studied organ and composition with Rheinberger at the Munich Cons.; graduated with a *Rhapsody* for Piano and Orch. (1885), which he subsequently performed with several American orchs., as well as his Piano Concerto (1894). In 1904 he married Hildegard Hoffmann, a concert singer; they appeared frequently in joint recitals.

WORKS: *Rhapsody* for Piano and Orch. (1885); *Romance and Polonaise* for Orch. (1889); Piano Concerto (1894); Violin Concerto (1906); 2 symphonic poems: *Life's Conflicts* (1921) and *La Nuit* (orig. for Piano Solo, 1902; orchestrated 1939; Washington, D.C., March 12, 1942); 4 string quartets; Violin Sonata; Cello Sonata; Viola Sonata; choral works.

BIBL.: G. Greene, *H.H. H.: An American Composer's Life* (Metruchen, 1995).

Huston, (Thomas) Scott (, Jr.), American composer and pedagogue; b. Tacoma, Wash., Oct. 10, 1916; d. Cincinnati, March 1, 1991. After attending the Univ. of Puget Sound (1934–35), he studied with Phillips, Rogers, and Hanson at the Eastman School of Music in Rochester, N.Y. (B.M., 1941; M.M., 1942; Ph.D., 1952). He taught at several schools of higher learning before joining the Cincinnati Cons. of Music in 1952; after it merged with the College of Music in 1955, he was dean until 1956; he then taught there until 1988. His output was marked by a fine command of tonal and atonal writing.

WORKS: OPERA: *Blind Girl* (1981; concert perf., Lake George, N.Y., May 1984). **ORCH.:** *Toccata* for Piano and Orch. (1951); *Abstract* (1955); Concerto for Trumpet, Harp, and Orch. (1963); 6 syms., including No. 3, *Phantasms* (1967; Cincinnati, Feb. 2, 1968), No. 4 for Strings (Cincinnati, Aug. 10, 1972), No. 5 (1975), and No. 6, *The Human Condition* (1981); *2 Images* for Strings (1964); *Fanfare for the 200th* (1975); *Impressions from Life* for Small Chamber Orch. (1977). **CHAMBER:** Flute Sonata (1959); Viola Sonata (1960); *Intensity I* (1962) and *II* (1975) for Winds; Timpani Suite (1963); *Pro vita* for Piano and Brass Quintet (1965); *Phenomena* for Flute, Oboe, Harpsichord, and Double Bass (1966); Violin Sonata, *Mercury and Venus* (1967); *Life-Styles I–IV* for Piano Trio or Clarinet, Cello, and Piano (1972); *Cool to Hot* for Jazz Quartet (1973); *For Our Times*, suite for 6 Brass (1974); *Eleatron* for Viola and Piano (1975); *Fragments, Disputes, Mirrors* for 2 Oboes (1977); *Shadowy Waters* for Clarinet, Cello, and Piano (1977); *Variables* for 4 Saxophones (1979); *In Memoriam Norman Dinerstein* for Piano and Chamber Group (1983); *Optimism: A Way of Life* for Brass Quintet (1986); *The Glass Children* for Violin (1988). **KEYBOARD: PIANO:** *Penta-Tholoi* (1966); *5 Notes for Ada* for 2 Pianos (1984). **ORGAN:** Sonata (1960). **VOCAL:** *Ante mortem* for Men's Chorus, Brass, and Organ (1965); *The Oratorio of Understanding* (1969); *Divinely Superfluous Beauty and Natural Music* for Soprano and Chamber Ensemble (1971); *Tamar*, monodrama for Soprano and Prepared Piano (1974); *Ecstasies of Janus* for Countertenor and Chamber Ensemble (1978); *Time/Reflections* for Chorus and Chamber Orch. (1978); *Songs of the Courtesans* for Voice and Chamber Ensemble (1985); *An Ecumenical Mosaic of Cincinnati* for Chorus, Organ, and Double String Quartet (1987); choruses; songs.

Huszka, Jenő, Hungarian composer; b. Szeged, April 24, 1875; d. Budapest, Feb. 2, 1960. He was a student of Hubay (violin) and Koessler (composition) at the Royal Academy of Music in Budapest. At age 24, he launched a career as a composer for the theater in Budapest. His first operetta, *Bob herceg* (Dec. 12, 1902), was followed by such successful scores as *Aranyvirág* (Nov. 6, 1903), *Gül Baba* (Dec. 9, 1905), *Rébusz báró* (Nov. 20,

1909), *Nemtudomka* (Jan. 14, 1914), *Lili bárónő* (March 7, 1919), *Mária főhadnagy* (Sept. 23, 1942), and *Szabadság, szerelem* (April 1, 1955).

Hutchens, Frank, New Zealand pianist, teacher, and composer; b. Christchurch, Jan. 15, 1892; d. Sydney, Australia, Oct. 18, 1965. He studied at the Royal Academy of Music in London with Matthay (piano) and Corder (composition); taught there from 1908 to 1914; in 1915 he was appointed a prof. at the New South Wales State Conservatorium in Sydney. In 1962 he was made an Officer of the Order of the British Empire. His compositions include *Ballade* for Orch. (1938); Concerto for 2 Pianos and Orch. (1940); *Air Mail Palestine* for Voice and Orch. (1942); also piano pieces.

Hutcheson, Ernest, Australian pianist, writer on music, teacher, and composer; b. Melbourne, July 20, 1871; d. N.Y., Feb. 9, 1951. He studied piano in Australia with Max Vogrich; played concerts as a very young child; then was sent to the Leipzig Cons. to study with Reinecke and Jadassohn, graduating in 1890. In 1898 he performed his own Piano Concerto with the Berlin Phil. He was head of the piano dept. at the Peabody Cons. of Music in Baltimore (1900–1912). In 1915 he created a sensation in N.Y. by playing 3 concertos (Tchaikovsky, Liszt, and MacDowell) in a single evening; in 1919 he repeated his feat, playing 3 Beethoven concertos in one evening. From 1924 to 1945 he was variously associated with the Juilliard School in N.Y., including serving as its dean (1927–37) and its president (1937–45). Among his compositions are several symphonic works and numerous piano pieces. He publ. *The Elements of Piano Technique* (N.Y., 1907); *Elektra by Richard Strauss: A Guide to the Opera* (N.Y., 1910); *A Musical Guide to the Richard Wagner Ring of the Nibelung* (N.Y., 1940); *The Literature of the Piano* (N.Y., 1948; 2nd ed., rev., 1964).

Hutchings, Arthur (James Bramwell), English musicologist; b. Sunbury-on-Thames, July 14, 1906; d. Colyton, Devon, Nov. 13, 1989. He studied violin and piano; later received his Ph.D. from the Univ. of Durham (1953), where he was prof. of music (1947–68) and then at the Univ. of Exeter (1968–71). His books, all publ. in London, include *Schubert* (1945; 4th ed., 1973); *Delius* (1948); *A Companion to Mozart's Piano Concertos* (1948; 3rd ed., 1980); *The Invention and Composition of Music* (1958); *The Baroque Concerto* (1961; 3rd ed., rev., 1973); *Church Music in the Nineteenth Century* (1967); *Mozart: The Man, the Musician* (1976); *Purcell* (1982).

Hutschenruyter, Wouter, noted Dutch conductor, musicologist, and composer; b. Rotterdam, Aug. 15, 1859; d. The Hague, Nov. 14, 1943. His grandfather was the noted Dutch conductor and composer Wouter Hutschenruyter (1796–1878) and his father the noted Dutch horn player and conductor Willem Jacob Hutschenruyter (1828–1889). He studied in Rotterdam, where he began his career as a choral conductor and teacher; then was 2nd conductor of the Concertgebouw Orch. in Amsterdam (1890–92); subsequently was conductor of the Utrecht municipal orch. (1892–1917), which he developed into a respected Dutch ensemble; later was director of the music school of Rotterdam's Maatschappij tot Bevordering der Toonkunst (1917–25). He composed a Piano Concerto, a *Nocturne* for Horn and Orch., various other orch. pieces, chamber music, piano pieces, and songs.

WRITINGS: *Richard Strauss* (Haarlem, 1898); *Orkest en orkestspel na 1600* (Utrecht, 1903); *Felix Weingartner* (Haarlem, 1906); *Het muziekleven in de 17e eeuw* (Baarn, 1909); *Wolfgang Amadeus Mozart* (Rotterdam, 1909; abridged ed., 1927, as *Mozart*; 2nd ed., 1943); *De geschiedenis der toonkunst* (Amsterdam, 1920); *De programma muziek* (Bussum, 1922); *De geschiedenis van het orkest en van zijn instrumenten* (Amsterdam, 1926); *Mahler* (The Hague, 1927); *De symphonieën van Beethoven en toegelicht* (The Hague, 1928; 2nd ed., 1943); *Wagner* (The Hague, 1928); *Brahms* (The Hague, 1929); with J. Kruseman, *Richard Strauss* (The Hague, 1929); *Een en ander uit de geschiedenis der militaire muziek* (Hilversum, 1930); *Grepen uit geschiedenis van de piano en vat het pianospel* (Hilversum, 1930); *De sonates van Beethoven geanalyseerd en toegelicht* (The Hague, 1930); *De dirigent* (Hilversum, 1931; 3rd ed., 1955); *De ontwikkeling der symphonie door Haydn, Mozart en Beethoven* (Hilversum, 1935); with J. Kruseman, *Musiciana* (The Hague, 1938); *Frédéric Chopin* (The Hague, 1939; 3rd ed., 1949); *Bijdrage tot de bibliographie der muziekliteratur* (Leiden, 1941–43); *Grepen uit de geschiedenis van de snaarinstrumenten en van het snarenspel* (Hilversum, 1942); *Franz Schubert* (The Hague, 1944).

Hüttel, Josef, Czech conductor and composer; b. Mělník, July 18, 1893; d. Plzeň, July 6, 1951. He studied with Černý (piano), Štěpán Suchý (violin), and Novák (composition) at the Prague Cons. (1908–12). After further instruction with Taneyev (composition) in Moscow (1912–13), he was active as a choirmaster there; then conducted opera in Voronezh (1918–20). In 1921 he went to Egypt, where he was conductor of the Alexandria Phil. (1929–34) and head of European music for Cairo Radio (1934–44). In 1946 he returned to Czechoslovakia and was an ed. and archivist for the Czech Radio music dept. (until 1950).Among his compositions were a *Sinfonietta* (1923); *Images égyptiennes* for Orch. (1928); *Amon Raa*, symphonic poem (1931); Sym. (1935; won the Smetana jubilee prize); String Quartet (1927); *Divertissement grotesque* for Wind Quintet and Piano (1929; won the Coolidge prize); *Ragtime* for Violin and Piano (1929).

Huybrechts, Albert, Belgian composer; b. Dinant, Feb. 12, 1899; d. Woluwe-St.-Pierre, near Brussels, Feb. 21, 1938. He studied at the Brussels Cons. with Martin Lunssens, Paulin Marchand, Léon Dubois, and Joseph Jongen. In 1926 he gained international recognition by winning 2 U.S. prizes, the Elizabeth Sprague Coolidge Prize of the Library of Congress in Washington, D.C., for his Violin Sonata, and the Ojai Valley Prize in California for his String Quartet. In 1937 he was appointed a prof. at the Brussels Cons., but a severe attack of uremia led to his premature death. He wrote in a judiciously modern idiom, seasoned with prudential dissonance.

WORKS: ORCH.: 2 symphonic poems: *David* (1923) and *Poème féerique* (1923); *Chant funèbre* for Cello and Orch. (1926); *Sérénade* (1929); *Chant d'angoisse* (1930); *Nocturne* (1931); *Divertissement* for Brass and Percussion (1931); Cello Concertino (1932). **CHAMBER:** 2 string quartets (1924, 1927); Violin Sonata (1925); Trio for Flute, Viola, and Piano (1926); Sextet for Wind Quintet, with 2nd Flute (1927); Suite for Flute, Oboe, Clarinet, Bassoon, and Piano (1929); *Choral* for Organ (1930); *Sicilienne* for Piano (1934); *Pastourelle* for Cello and Piano (1934); Sonatine for Flute and Viola (1934); String Trio (1935); Wind Quintet (1936). **VOCAL:** Songs, including *Horoscopes* (1926).

Hvorostovsky, Dmitri, Russian baritone; b. Krasnoyarsk, Oct. 16, 1962. He was a student of Ekaterina Yofel at the Krasnoyarsk School of the Arts (1982–86). In 1986 he joined the Krasnoyarsk Opera. In 1987 he won the Glinka Prize, and in 1989 the BBC Cardiff Singer of the World Competition, which resulted in an appearance on BBC-TV; that same year, he made his London recital debut at the Wigmore Hall, and sang Tchaikovsky's Yeletsky in Nice. On March 4, 1990, he made an acclaimed U.S. debut in recital at N.Y.'s Alice Tully Hall. In 1991 he appeared in *War and Peace* at the San Francisco Opera. In 1992 he was engaged to sing in *I Puritani* at London's Covent Garden and appeared as Posa at Milan's La Scala. In 1993 he made his U.S. operatic debut as Germont at the Lyric Opera of Chicago.

Hvoslef (real name, **Saeverud**), **Ketil,** Norwegian composer, son of **Harald Saeverud**; b. Fana, near Bergen, July 19, 1939. He took his mother's maiden name in 1980. He studied piano with Thomas Rayna in London (1961) and took an organ diploma at the Bergen Cons. (1962); he then studied composition with Blomdahl and Lidholm in Stockholm, Jersild in Copenhagen, and Lazaroff in London. From 1963 to 1979 he was on the faculty of the Bergen Cons. After a period of hesitant serialism, he evolved a "motivic assimilation technique," wherein a central motif influences all the other thematic material in the manner of a theme with variations.

WORKS: DRAMATIC: OPERAS: *The Ballad of Narcissus and Echo* (1981); *Dode Sardiner* (1986–87); *Trio for Tretten; Acotral* (1987); much incidental music. **ORCH.:** Sinfonietta (1963); Piano Concertino (1964); Trumpet Concerto (1968–69; Bergen, April 22, 1972); *Mi-Fi-Li*, symphonic poem (Oslo, Sept. 4, 1972); Double Bass Concerto (1973); 2 cello concertos (1976–87; 1990–91); *Variations* for Chamber Orch. (1976); Double Concerto for Flute, Guitar, and Strings (1977); Concertino (Trondheim, Sept. 20, 1979); Concerto for Bassoon and Strings (1979); Suite for School Orch. (1980); *Antigone*, symphonic variations (1981–82); *Air* (1983); *Il Compleanno* (Bergen, Oct. 8, 1985); Violin Concerto (1988–89). **CHAMBER:** Clarinet Quartet (1962); Wind Quintet (1964); *Suite* for Guitar (1966); *Ariseturo*, concerto for Percussion and 8 Wind Instruments (1966); *Duets* for Bassoons (1966); 2 string quartets (1969, 1973); *Flauto Solo* (1970); *Tromba Solo* (1971); *Kim* for 4 Crumhorns, 4 Recorders, Bass Gamba, and Percussion (1975); Trio for Oboe, Violin, and Percussion (1978); Octet for Flutes (1978); *Brass* for 13 Brass Instruments (1978); *Violino Solo* (1980); *Post*, sextet (1980); *Duodu* for Violin and Viola (1982); *Erkejubel* for 2 Trumpets, 2 Trombones, Synthesizer, and Percussion (1982); Quintet for Clarinet and String Quartet (1983); *Rikstrio* for Flute, Violin, and Synthesizer (1984); *Scheherazade Carries on With Her Story* for Violin and Harp (1986); Sextet for Flute and 5 Percussion (1988); *Framenti di Roma* for Oboe, Clarinet, and Bassoon (1988); *Kirkeduo* for Guitar and Organ (1988). **KEYBOARD: PIANO:** *Rondo con variazioni* (1970); *Beethoven Fantasy* (1982). **ORGAN:** *Variations* (1972); *Organo Solo* (1974); *Easter Variations* (1986); *Toccata: Fontana dell'Organo, Villa d'Este* (1988). **VOCAL:** *So einsam ist der Mensch* for Chorus or Vocal Quartet, after Nelly Sachs (1970); *Or "Havamal"* (Sayings of the High One), cantata for Chorus and Orch. (1971; rev. 1974); *Kvartoni* for Voice, Recorder, Guitar, and Piano (1974); Trio for Soprano, Alto, and Piano (1974); *Collage in Black/White with Red* for Baritone Narration, Violin, Guitar, Clarinet, and Percussion (1975); Concerto for Chorus and Orch. (1977); *Spillemaend* (Fiddlers) for Chorus, Hardanger Fiddle, and Organ (1980); *Dano Tiore*, quintet for Soprano, Violin, Viola, Cello, and Harpsichord (1985); *Entrata Bergensis* for Chorus, Tape, and Orch. (1989).

BIBL.: L. Reitan, "K. H.—the Champion of Intuition," *Nordic Sounds* (Sept. 1985).

Hwang, Byung-Ki, Korean composer, virtuoso kayagum performer, and pedagogue; b. Seoul, May 31, 1936. He studied traditional Korean music and the kayagum (a 12-stringed Korean zither with movable bridges, dating from the turn of the 7th century) at the National Classical Music Inst. in Seoul (1951–58), his principal teachers being Yong-yun Kim, Yun-dok Kim, and Sang-gon Sim. He received 1st prize at the National Competition of Traditional Music (1954, 1956), a National Music Prize (1965), and the Korean Cinema Music Award (1973). From 1974 he was prof. of Korean traditional music at the College of Music, Ewha Women's Univ., in Seoul; in 1985–86 he was a visiting scholar at Harvard Univ. Hwang is noted as the first Korean composer to write modern works for the kayagum; he is also a distinguished kayagum player, and has appeared in recital in the U.S., West Germany, France, and Austria. His U.S. debut took place in N.Y.'s Carnegie Hall on April 20, 1986, in a program which included a number of his own compositions. His works are translucent and elegant in their structures, and impressionistic in harmonic and melodic design.

WORKS: KAYAGUM: *The Forest* (1963); *The Pomegranate House* (1965); *Kara Town* (1967); *Chimhyangmu* (1974); *The Silk Road* (1977); *Sounds of the Night* (1985); *Southern Fantasy* (1989). **OTHER INSTRUMENTS:** *Pungyo* for Piri (Korean oboe; 1972); *Mandaeyop-haetan* for Korean Orch. (1976); *Chasi* for Taegum (Korean bamboo flute; 1978); *Unbak* for Korean Orch. (1979); *Harim Castle* for Taegum (1982); *Soyopsanbang* for Komungo (Korean 6-stringed plucked zither with 16 frets; 1989). **VOCAL:** *Beside a Chrysanthemum* for Voice, Komungo, and Changgu (Korean hour-glass drum with 2 heads; 1962); *Chongsando and Kanggangsullae* for Chorus (1974); *The Labyrinth* for Voice and Kayagum (1975); *Nolbujon*, narrative song (1976); *The Evening Chant* for Chorus and Percussion (1983); also dance music; film scores.

Hyde, Walter, English tenor; b. Birmingham, Feb. 6, 1875; d. London, Nov. 11, 1951. He studied with Gustave Garcia at the Royal College of Music in London, where he sang in student performances. He then sang in light opera before he undertook Wagnerian roles, which became his specialty. He sang Siegmund in the English-language production of the *Ring* cycle at Covent Garden in London in 1908; his other roles included Walther von Stolzing and Parsifal. He made his Metropolitan Opera debut in N.Y. on March 28, 1910, as Siegmund in *Die Walküre*; then returned to England and made regular appearances at Covent Garden until 1924; later sang with the Beecham Opera Co. and the British National Opera Co., serving as a director of the latter. He was a frequent participant at many musical festivals in England.

Hye-Knudsen, Johan, Danish conductor and composer; b. Nyborg, May 24, 1896; d. Copenhagen, Sept. 28, 1975. He studied cello at the Copenhagen Cons. with Rudinger; also in Paris with André Hekking; studied conducting in Dresden with Fritz Busch. In 1925 he was named a conductor of the Royal Danish Theater in Copenhagen; concurrently led concerts of the Royal Danish Orch. He wrote a number of orch. works and 2 operas: *Orfeus i underverdenen* (Copenhagen, Jan. 1, 1934) and *Kirke og orgel* (Copenhagen, Nov. 8, 1947).

Hykes, David (Bond), distinctive American composer and vocalist; b. Taos, N.Mex., March 2, 1953. He studied filmmaking at Antioch College in Ohio (1970–74), and arts administration at Columbia Univ. (M.F.A., 1984). He also studied classical Azerbaijani and Armenian music with Zevulon Avshalomov (1975–77) and north Indian rāga singing with S. Dahr (1982). In 1975 he founded the Harmonic Choir, whose members employ vocal techniques borrowed from Tibetan and Mongolian music in which strongly resonated upper partials are produced in addition to the fundamental tone. From 1979 the ensemble was in residence at the ideal location of the Cathedral of St. John the Divine in N.Y., and from 1980 made tours of the U.S. and Europe. In 1981 Hykes traveled to Mongolia under the auspices of the Asian Cultural Council. His compositions for voice use harmonics to produce rich waves of slowly changing sounds over diatonic melodies; the result resembles a sort of modernized chant with an ethereal haze of overtones. Among such compositions are *Hearing Solar Winds* (1977–83), *Current Circulation* (1983–84), and *Harmonic Meetings* (1986). He has also written several film and television scores and a number of instrumental works.

BIBL.: N. Kenyon, "Tuning the Skies," *New Yorker*, LVIII (1982); J. Reinhard, "An Interview with D. H.," *Ear Magazine East*, VII/5 (1982–83); R. Palmer, "Get Ready for the Music of Harmonics," *N.Y. Times* (July 17, 1983).

Hynninen, Jorma, distinguished Finnish baritone and operatic administrator; b. Leppävirta, April 3, 1941. He studied at the Sibelius Academy in Helsinki (1966–70); also took courses in Rome with Luigi Ricci and in Salzburg with Kurt Overhoff. He won 1st prize at the singing competition in Lappeenranta in 1969, and in the Finnish division of the Scandinavian singing competition in Helsinki in 1971. In 1970 he made his concert debut in Helsinki, as well as his operatic debut as Silvio in *Pagliacci* with the Finnish National Opera there, and subsequently sang leading roles with the company. He also made first appearances at La Scala in Milan (1977), the Vienna State Opera (1977), the Hamburg State Opera (1977), the Bavarian State Opera in Munich (1979), and the Paris Opéra (1980); gave recitals throughout Europe and the U.S. He made his N.Y.

debut in a recital in 1980; his operatic debut followed in 1983, when he sang with the Finnish National Opera during its visit to America; made his Metropolitan Opera debut in N.Y. as Rodrigo in *Don Carlo* on March 30, 1984. He was artistic director of the Finnish National Opera from 1984 to 1990, and then of the Savonlinna Festival from 1992. In addition to such traditional operatic roles as Pelleas, Wolfram, Orpheus, Valentin in *Faust*, and Macbeth, he has sung parts in contemporary Finnish operas; he created the role of the King in *The King Goes Forth to France* by Aulis Sallinen, first performed at the Savonlinna Festival on July 7, 1984; also created the title role in Rautawaura's *Thomas*, performed in Joensuu on June 21, 1985.

I

Iannaccone, Anthony (Joseph), American composer and teacher; b. N.Y., Oct. 14, 1943. While still in high school, he had lessons in composition with Copland and Giannini; then continued his training in composition with Giannini, Diamond, and Flagello at the Manhattan School of Music in N.Y. (M.M., 1968), and with Adler and Benson at the Eastman School of Music in Rochester, N.Y. (Ph.D., 1971). In 1971 he became prof. of composition at Eastern Michigan Univ., where he founded an Electronic Music Studio. In his music, he applies serial methods with a certain liberality toward unintentional occurrences of tonal, and even explicitly triadic, elements. In his band music, he openly exploits pop devices.

WORKS: ORCH.: Suite (1962); 3 syms. (1965; 1966; *Night Rivers*, 1992); Violin Concertino (1967); *Lysistrata*, overture (1968); *Variations* for Violin and Orch. (1969); *Interlude* for Wind Instruments (1970); *Antiphonies* for Wind Instruments (1973); *Scherzo* for Band (1976); *Of Fire and Ice* for Band (1977); *After a Gentle Rain* for Band (1980); *Images of Songs & Dance*: No. 1, *Orpheus* (1982) and No. 2, *Terpsichore*, (1981), for Wind Instruments; *Plymouth Trilogy* for Wind Instruments (1981); *Divertimento* (1983); *Apparitions* for Wind Ensemble or Band (1986); *Sinfonia concertante* for Flute, Violin, Viola, Cello, Piano, and Orch. (1988; rev. 1989); *Whispers of Heavenly Death* (1989); *Sea Drift* for Band or Wind Ensemble (1993); Concertante for Clarinet and Orch. (1994). **CHAMBER:** Piano Trio (1959); Viola Sonata (1961); 2 violin sonatas (1964, 1971); String Quartet (1965); *Remembrance* for Viola and Piano (1968); *Hades* for Brass Quartet (1968); *3 Mythical Sketches* for Brass Quintet (1971); *Anamorphoses* for 2 Trumpets, Trombone, and Percussion (1972); *Rituals* for Violin and Piano (1973); *Parodies* for Wind Quintet (1974); *Bicinia* for Flute and Saxophone (1975); Sonatina for Trumpet and Tuba (1975); *Night Song* for Bassoon and Piano (1975); *Aria concertante* for Cello and Piano (1976); *Invention* for 2 Saxophones (1978); Trio for Flute, Clarinet, and Piano (1979); *Toccata-Fanfares* for Brass Sextet or Brass Choir (2 vols., 1986); *Mobiles* for 3 Brass and 2 Percussion Players (1988). **PIANO:** *Retail Rags* (1959); *Partita* (1967); *Keyboard Essays* (1972); *Inventions* for 2 Pianos (1985). **VOCAL:** *Magnificat* for Double Chorus and Orch. (1963); *The Prince of Peace* for Soprano, Mezzo-soprano, Baritone, Bass, Chorus, and Chamber or Wind Orch. (1970); *Music Strong I Come* for Chorus and Chamber Ensemble or 2 Pianos (1974); *Walt Whitman Song No. 2* for Solo Voices, Chorus, and Winds (1980); *Whitman Madrigals* for Chorus and Piano (1984); *Chautauqua Psalms* for Chorus and Piano (1987). **OTHER:** Tape pieces.

Ibert, Jacques (François Antoine), distinguished French composer; b. Paris, Aug. 15, 1890; d. there, Feb. 5, 1962. He studied at the Paris Cons. with Gédalge and Fauré (1911–14); during World War I, he served in the French navy; then returned to the Paris Cons. after the Armistice and studied with Vidal, and received the Prix de Rome in 1919 for his cantata *Le Poète et la fée*. While in Rome, he wrote his most successful work, the symphonic suite *Escales* (Ports of Call), inspired by a Mediterranean cruise while serving in the navy. In 1937 he was appointed director of the Académie de France of Rome, and held this post until 1960; was also administrator of the Réunion des Théâtres Lyriques Nationaux in Paris (1955–56). He was elected a member of the Institut de France (1956). In his music, Ibert combined the most felicitous moods and techniques of Impressionism and neo-Classicism; his harmonies were opulent; his instrumentation was coloristic; there was an element of humor in lighter works, such as his popular orch. *Divertissement* and an even more popular piece, *Le Petit Ane blanc*, from the piano suite *Histoires*. His craftsmanship was excellent; an experimenter in tested values, he never fails to produce the intended effect.

WORKS: DRAMATIC: OPERAS: *Angélique* (Paris, Jan. 28, 1927); *Persée et Andromède, ou Le Plus Heureux des trois* (1921; Paris, May 15, 1929); *Le Roi d'Yvetot* (Paris, Jan. 15, 1930); *Gonzague* (Monte Carlo, Dec. 7, 1931); *L'Aiglon* (Monte Carlo, March 11, 1937; in collaboration with A. Honegger); *Les Petites Cardinal* (Paris, 1938; in collaboration with A. Honegger); *Barbebleue*, radio opera (Lausanne Radio, Oct. 10, 1943). **BALLETS**

(all 1st perf. in Paris): *Les Rencontres* (Nov. 21, 1925); *Diane de Poitiers* (April 30, 1934); *Les Amours de Jupiter* (March 9, 1946); *Le Chevalier errant* (May 5, 1950); *Tropismes pour des Amours Imaginaires* (1957). **ORCH.:** *Noël en Picardie*, symphonic poem (1914); *Ballade de la geôle de Reading*, after Oscar Wilde (Paris, Oct. 22, 1922); *Escales*, 3 symphonic pictures (Paris, Jan. 6, 1924); *Féerique*, symphonic scherzo (Paris, Dec. 12, 1925); Concerto for Cello and Wind Instruments (Paris, Feb. 28, 1926); *Divertissement*, suite (Paris, Nov. 30, 1930; from incidental music to *Le Chapeau de paille d'Italie*); *Paris*, suite for Chamber Orch. (Venice, Sept. 15, 1932; from incidental music to *Donogoo*); Flute Concerto (Paris, Feb. 25, 1934); *Concertino da camera* for Saxophone and Chamber Orch. (Paris, May 2, 1935); *Capriccio* (1938); *Ouverture de fête* (Paris, Jan. 18, 1942); *Suite élisabéthaine* (1944); *Symphonie concertante* for Oboe and Strings (Basel, Feb. 11, 1949); *Louisville Concerto* (Louisville, Ky., Feb. 17, 1954); *Bostoniana* (1956–61); *Hommage à Mozart* (1957); *Bacchanale* (1958). **CHAMBER:** 6 pieces for Harp (1917); *2 mouvements* for 2 Flutes, Clarinet, and Bassoon (1923); *Jeux*, flute sonatina (1924); *3 pièces brèves* for Flute, Oboe, Clarinet, Horn, and Bassoon (1930); *Pastoral* for 4 Fifes (in *Pipeaux*, by various composers, 1934); *Entr'acte* for Flute and Guitar (1935); piece for Flute (1936); String Quartet (1944); Trio for Violin, Cello, and Harp (1944); *2 Interludes* for Violin and Harpsichord (1949). **PIANO:** *Histoires* (10 pieces); *Les Rencontres*, arranged from the ballet (5 pieces); *Petite suite en 15 images* (1943). **VOCAL:** *Le Poète et la fée*, cantata (1919); *3 chansons de C. Vidrac* for Voice and Orch. or Piano (1923); *Chant de folie* for Solo Voices, Chorus, and Orch. (1923–24; Boston, April 23, 1926); *La Verdure dorée* for Voice and Piano (1924); *4 chansons de Don Quichotte* for Bass and Orch. or Piano (1932); *Chanson du rien* for Voice and Piano; *Quintette de la peur* for Chorus and Piano (1946).

BIBL.: A. Hoerée, "J. I.," *Revue Musicale* (July 1929); J. Feschotte, *J. I.* (Paris, 1959); G. Michel, *J. I., L'Homme et son oeuvre* (Paris, 1968).

Ichiyanagi, Toshi, Japanese composer; b. Kobe, Feb. 4, 1933. He studied composition with Kishio Hirao and piano with Chieko Hara, and then pursued training in N.Y. at the Juilliard School of Music and the New School for Social Research (1954–58), receiving instruction in composition from Cage and in piano from Beveridge Webster. He worked at the NHK electronic music studio in Tokyo, and also received a Rockefeller Foundation grant in 1967. In 1976 he was the Deutscher Akademischer Austauschdienst composer-in-residence in Berlin. In addition to various composition prizes, he was made a member of the Ordre des Arts et des Lettres of France in 1985. Ichiyanagi's output reflects his penchant for experimentation in the best avant-garde tradition, and includes the utilization of unusual performance techniques, chance, electronics, and graphic notation.

WORKS: ORCH.: *Life Music* for Orch. and Tape (1962); *The Field* (1966); *Activities* for Electric Ensemble and Orch. (1967); *Up-to-Date Applause* for Pop Group, Orch., and Tape (1968); *In the Relection of Lighting Image* for Percussion and Orch. (1980); 3 piano concertos: No. 1, *Reminiscence of Space* (1981), No. 2, *Winter Portrait* (1987), and No. 3, *Cross Water Road* (1991); *Engen* for Koto and Orch. (1982); Violin Concerto, *Circulating Scenery* (1983); *Time Surrounding* (1984); *Paganini Personal* for Marimba and Orch. (1984–86; also for Marimba and Piano or Marimba, Piano, and Orch.); 4 syms.: *Reingaku Symphony: The Shadows Appearing Through the Darkness* for Chanting Shōmyō Buddhist, Ancient Instruments, and Gagaku Orch. (1987), *Berlin Renshi Symphony* for Soprano, Tenor, and Orch. (1988), *Reigaku Symphony No. 2: Kokai* for Shōmyō, Gagaku, and Reigaku Orch. (1989), and *Recollection of Reminiscence Beyond* (Osaka, Sept. 17, 1994); *Interspace* for Strings (1987); *Existence* for Organ and Orch. (1989); *Voices from the Environment* (1989); *The Origin*, concerto for Koto and Chamber Orch. (1989); *Kyoto* (1989); *Luminous Space* for Shō, Ondes Martenot, and Orch. (1991). **CHAMBER:** Violin Sonata (1954); String Quartet (1957); 3 numbered string quartets: No. 1, *Nagaoka* (1964; in graphic notation), No. 2, *Interspace* (1986), and No. 3, *Innder Landscape* (1994); *Sapporo* for Any Number of Players and Conductor (1962); *Appearances* for 3 Instruments, 2 Oscillators, and 2 Ring Modulators (1967); *Arrangements* for Percussion (1972); *Music for Living Process* for Instruments and 2 Dancers (1973); *Trichrome* for Instruments (1975); *Scenes I* for Violin and Piano (1978), *II* for Violin (1979), *III* for Violin (1980), *IV* for Violin and Piano (1981), and *V* for Violin and Piano (1982); *Recurrence* for 7 Instruments (1979); *Distance* for 7 Instruments (1979); *Ogenraku* for Gagaku Ensemble (1980); *Wa* for 2 Kotos, Piano, and Percussion (1981); *Time in Tree, Time in Water* for Percussion and Piano (1981); *Flowers Blooming in Summer* for Harp and Piano (1982); *Enenraku* for Gagaku Ensemble (1982); *Wind Trace* for Marimba, Vibraphone, and Antique Cymbal (1984); *Cloud Shore, Wind Roots* for Ancient Instruments and Gagaku Ensemble (1984); *Cloud Figures* for Oboe (1984); Piano Quintet, *Prana* (1985); *Presage* for 6 Ondes Martenot (1986); *Transstream* for 18 Percussionists (1987); *Wind Gradation* for Ryateki and Piano (1989); *The Way* for 2 Shō, 2 Hichiriki, O-Hichiriki, Shakuhachi, Koto, Biwa, and 2 Percussion (1990); *Troposphere* for Ondes Martenot and Marimba (1990); *Trio Interlink* for Violin, Piano, and Percussion (1990); *Interrelations* for Cello and Piano (1991); *Cosmos of Coexistence* for Marimba and Piano (1992). **KEYBOARD: PIANO:** *Music for Piano Nos. 1–7* (1959–61); *Time Sequence* (1976); *2 Existence* for 2 Pianos (1980); *Cloud Atlas I, II,* and *III* (1985), *IV, V,* and *VI* (1987), and *VII, VIII,* and *IX* (1989); *Inter Konzert* (1987); *Piano Nature* (1989); *Inexhaustible Fountain* (1990). **ORGAN:** *Dimensions* (1990). **OTHER:** Choruses; songs; electronic pieces.

Idelsohn, Abraham Zevi, eminent Latvian musicologist; b. Pfilsburg, near Libau, July 13, 1882; d. Johannesburg, Aug. 14, 1938. He began his training as a Jewish cantor in Libau; after attending the Stern Cons. in Berlin, he studied at the Leipzig Cons. with Jadassohn (harmony), Krehl (counterpoint), Zoellner (composition), and Kretzschmar (music history). He was a cantor of the Regensburg Synagogue (1903–05), and then was active in Jerusalem (1906–21), where he founded the Inst. for Jewish Music (1910) and a Jewish music school (1919). From 1924 until suffering a paralytic stroke in 1934 he was a lecturer at the Hebrew Union College in Cincinnati. Idelsohn was a leading authority on Jewish music. His most important work was the monumental *Hebräisch-Orientalischer Melodienschatz* (10 vols., Leipzig, 1914–32; Eng. tr. as *Thesaurus of Hebrew-Oriental Melodies*, and Hebrew tr. as *Otzar Negionoth Ysrael*). He also ed. *Sefer ha-Shirim* (A New Collection of Hebrew Songs; Berlin, 1922), *Tzelilé ha-Aretz* (Love and Folk-Songs; Berlin, 1922), and a *Jewish Song Book for the Synagogue, Home and School* (Cincinnati, 1928). Among his own compositions were the music drama *Jephtah* (1922), syngogue services, and Hebrew songs.

WRITINGS: *Phonographierte Gesänge und Aussprachsproben des Hebräischen der jemenitischen, persischen und syrischen Juden* (Vienna, 1917); *Manual of Musical Illustrations . . . on Jewish Music* (Cincinnati, 1926); *The Ceremonies of Judaism* (Cincinnati, 1929); *Jewish Music in its Historical Development* (N.Y., 1929); *Jewish Liturgy and Its Development* (N.Y., 1932).

Ifukube, Akira, Japanese composer; b. Kushiro, March 7, 1914. As a young man, he was trained in forestry; then took lessons from Alexander Tcherepnin. His music is rooted in Japanese modalities, but he adorns them with impressionistic harmonies.

WORKS: BALLETS: *Salome* (1948); *Enchanted Citadel* (Tokyo, Dec. 20, 1949); *Fire of Prometheus* (1950); *Drums of Japan* (Tokyo, Dec. 29, 1951); *The Martyrs of Japan* (Tokyo, March 30, 1972). **ORCH.:** *Japanese Rhapsody* (1935; Boston, April 5, 1936); *Triptyque aborigène* (1937); Piano Concerto (1941; Tokyo, March 3, 1942; MS destroyed in an air raid); *Ballade symphonique* (Tokyo, Nov. 20, 1943); *Arctic Forest* (Changchun, Manchuria, April 26, 1944); 2 violin concertos: No.

1 (Tokyo, June 22, 1948) and No. 2 (1978); *Bascana* (1949); *Rapsodia concertante* for Violin and Orch. (1951); *Buddha* (1953); *Sinfonia Tapkaara* (1954; Indianapolis, Jan. 21, 1955; rev. 1979; Tokyo, April 6, 1980); *Ritmica ostinata* for Piano and Orch. (1961); *Rondo in Burlesque* for Concert Band (1972); *Lauda concertata* for Marimba and Orch. (1976; rev. 1979); *Eglogue symphonique* for Orch. and Japanese Instruments (1982); *Gotama, the Buddha*, symphonic ode for Chorus and Orch. (1989); *Tomo no Oto*, orch. paraphrase (1990); *Japanese Suite* (1991). **OTHER:** *Okhotsk*, choral ode for Chorus and Orch. (1958); guitar pieces.

Igumnov, Konstantin (Nikolaievich), distinguished Russian pianist and pedagogue; b. Lebedyan, near Tambov, May 1, 1873; d. Moscow, March 24, 1948. He studied piano with Zverev and Siloti, and theory with Taneyev, Arensky, and Ippolitov-Ivanov at the Moscow Cons., graduating as a pianist in the class of Pabst (1894). He gave numerous concerts, specializing in Romantic music, and was regarded as an artist of impeccable taste who worked out every detail of the music to the utmost perfection. But great as his artistic reputation was in Russia (he rarely, if ever, played abroad), his main accomplishment was as a piano pedagogue. He was appointed a prof. of the Moscow Cons. in 1899, and remained on its staff until his death. Among his students were Nikolai Orlov, Dobrowen, and Oborin. In 1946 he was made a People's Artist of the U.S.S.R.

BIBL.: Y. Milstein, *K.N. I.* (Moscow, 1975).

Ikebe, Shin-Ichiro, Japanese composer and teacher; b. Mito City, Sept. 15, 1943. He studied with Ikenouchi, Yashiro, and Miyoshi at the Tokyo Univ. of Fine Arts and Music (graduated, 1967), where he later was an assistant (1971–77). Subsequently he served as a prof. at the Tokyo College of Music. He won the Prix Italia in 1976, the music prize of the Japanese Academy in 1980, 1984, and 1992, and the Otaka Prize in 1991.

WORKS: DRAMATIC: *The Death Goddess*, opera (NHK-TV, July 25, 1971); *The Whistling of the Wind*, television musical fantasy (1976); *The Silence*, radiophonic music drama (1977); *The Adventures of Pinocchio*, musical comedy (1981); *Hoichi, the Earless*, opera (1982); *Cleopatra, Her Love and Death*, ballet (1983); *Mobile et Immobile*, ballet (1984); *The Window*, musical drama (1986); *Chichibu-Bansho*, opera (1988); *Taro's Tree*, choral opera (1991–92). **ORCH.:** *Movement* (1965); *Construction* (1966); 2 piano concertos: No. 1 (1966–67) and No. 2, *Tu M'* (1987); 6 numbered syms.: No. 1 (1967; Tokyo, March 30, 1968), No. 2, *Trias* (1979), No. 3, *Ego Phano* (1984), No. 4 (1990), No. 5, *Simplex* (1990), and No. 6, *On the Individual Coordinates* (1993); 2 unnumbered syms.: *Petite symphonie pour enfants* for Small Orch. (1969) and *Symphony for Green and Friendship* (1987); *Lion* for Brass Ensemble (1969); *Energia* for 60 Players (1970); *Dimorphism* for Organ and Orch. (1974); *Quadrants* for Japanese Instruments and Orch. (1974); *"Haru-no-umi"* (1980); Violin Concerto (1981); *Imagine* (1983); *Overture for the Time of Flying Star* (1984); *Overture for the Coming of the New Spring* (1986); *Overture for the Nile* (1988); *Spontaneous Ignition* (1989); *Hokkai Swells*, symphonic study (1992). **CHAMBER:** Violin Sonata (1965); *Crepa in sette capitoli* for Violin, 3 Violas, Cello, and Double Bass (1966); Trio for Oboe, Clarinet, and Bassoon (1966); *Raccontino* for Violin and Piano (1967); *Un-en* for 2 Kotos, Ju-shichi-gen, Violin, Viola, Cello, and Double Bass (1970); *Clipper by 9* for Nonet (1971); *Trivalence I* for Flute, Violin, and Piano or Organ (1971) and *II* for Harpsichord, Clarinet, and Cello (1973); *Flash!* for Flute Ensemble (1972); *Monovalence I* for Marimba (1972); *Spirals* for 9 Horns (1979); *Black Blank Blaze* for 9 Clarinets (1982); *Strata I* for String Quartet (1988), *II* for Flute (1988), and *III* for Clarinet and Cello (1989); *Safari I* and *II* for Percussion (1990); *Quinquévalence* for Violin, Viola, Cello, Double Bass, and Piano (1991). **PIANO:** *Hitches in the Stories* (1988). **VOCAL:** *Kusabi* for Women's Chorus, 11 Players, and Dancers (1972); *Mizu Kuguru Monogatari* for Soprano, Baritone, Women's Chorus, and Chamber Orch. (1984); *Oedipus's Pilgrimage* for Joruri, Men's Chorus, and 10 Players (1984); *Himeji*, symphonic poem for Chorus and Orch. (1989); *For a Beautiful Star*, cantata (1990); choruses; songs.

Ikenouchi, Tomojirô, Japanese composer and pedagogue; b. Tokyo, Oct. 21, 1906; d. there, March 9, 1991. He was the first Japanese student at the Paris Cons. (1926–36), where he studied with Fauchet (harmony), Caussade (fugue), and Büsser (composition), and took the premier prix in harmony. In 1936 he joined the faculty of Nihon Univ. in Tokyo, and then was prof. of composition at the Tokyo National Univ. of Fine Arts and Music from 1947. Ikenouchi was highly esteemed as a teacher. His small but well-crafted output reflects the influence of his Western training.

WORKS: DRAMATIC: *Yuya* (1942; Tokyo, Feb. 1, 1943). **ORCH.:** *3 Pieces* (1937); *4 Seasons* (1938); *Umaki-Uta* (1938); Sym. (Tokyo, Nov. 4, 1951). **CHAMBER:** 3 string quartets (1937, 1945, 1946); *Fantasy* for Cello and Piano (1940); Flute Sonata (1946); Violin Sonata (1946); Cello Sonatina (1946). **PIANO:** Sonatina (1946); *Ceremonial Music*, duet (1958). **VOCAL:** *Koi no omoni* (Burden of Love) for Baritone, Chorus, and Timpani (1974).

Ikonen, Lauri, Finnish musicologist and composer; b. Mikkeli, Aug. 10, 1888; d. Helsinki, March 21, 1966. He studied at the Univ. of Helsinki and with Paul Juon in Berlin (1910–13); was ed. of the Finnish music magazine *Suomen Musikkilehti* (1923–29). His music followed the Romantic tradition of Sibelius.

WORKS: 6 syms.: No 1, *Sinfonia inornata* (1922), No. 2 (1937), No. 3, *Lemmin poika* (Son of Lemmi; 1941; rev. 1959), No. 4, *Sinfonia concentrata* (1942), No. 5, *Sinfonia aperta* (1943), and No. 6 (1956); *Koulemaantuomitun mielialoja* (Thoughts of a Condemned Man) for Baritone and Orch. (1936); Violin Concerto (1939); Piano Trio (1941); *Concerto meditativo* for Cello and Orch. (1942); *Concerto intimo* for Piano (1956); *Elaman lahja* (The Gift of Life) for Soloists, Chorus, and Orch. (1956); 2 violin sonatas; Piano Sonata; choral works; songs.

Ikonomov, Boyan Georgiev, Bulgarian composer; b. Nikopol, Dec. 14, 1900; d. Sofia, March 27, 1973. He studied in Sofia (1920–26); then went to Paris, where he attended classes of d'Indy and Lioncourt at the Schola Cantorum (1928–32); also studied with Boulanger and Roussel, and then took a course in conducting with Weingartner in Basel (1934). Returning to Bulgaria, he was music director of Sofia Radio (1937–48) and of the Bulgarian film center (1948–56); then was head of the music dept. of Sofia Radio (1957–60). His music was rooted in Bulgarian folk songs, with an emphasis on modal melodic progressions and asymmetric rhythms.

WORKS: DRAMATIC: OPERA: *Indje Voivoda* (1960). **BALLETS:** *The 7 Mortal Sins* (1933); *The Tragedy of Othello* (1946); *The Light Floods Everything* (1967). **ORCH.:** *Haidouk Rhapsody* (1932); Sinfonietta (1934); *Kaliakra*, symphonic poem (1935); *Pastorale* for Chamber Orch. (1937); 4 syms. (1937, 1947, 1955, 1971); *Pastorale and Dance* (1939); *Shar Planina*, symphonic poem (1942); Violin Concerto (1951); *Divertimento* for String Quartet and Orch. (1956); Piano Concertino (1958). **CHAMBER:** 6 string quartets (1933, 1937, 1941, 1944, 1945, 1949); 2 trios for Oboe, Clarinet, and Bassoon (1935, 1968); Cello Sonata. **VOCAL:** 2 cantatas: *George Dimitrov* (1954) and *Poem about Lenin* (1969); 2 oratorios: *The Legend of Shipka* (1968) and *Vassil Levsky* (1972); choruses; songs.

Iliev, Konstantin, Bulgarian conductor, teacher, and composer; b. Sofia, March 9, 1924; d. there, March 6, 1988. He studied composition with Khadzhiev and Vladigerov, and conducting with Goleminov, at the Bulgarian State Cons. in Sofia (1942–46); later took courses in composition with Řídký and A. Hába, and in conducting with Talich, at the Prague Cons. (1946–47). He conducted at the Sofia Opera (1948–49); after serving as chief conductor of the Ruse Opera and Sym. Orch. (1949–52), and then of the Varna Sym. Orch. (1952–56), he was principal conductor of the Sofia Phil. (1956–85). From 1964 to 1985 he was on the faculty of the Bulgarian State Cons. in Sofia. As a composer, he evolved a rather stimulating idiom, adroitly exploring the asymmetric Balkan rhythms and oriental melismas to create an aura of folkloric authenticity; in non-ethnic pieces he often applied serial principles of melodic formations.

WORKS: OPERAS: *The Master of Boyana* (Sofia, Oct. 3, 1962); *The Kingdom of the Deer* (1975). **ORCH.:** 5 syms. (1947, 1951, 1954, 1958, 1959); *Concerto grosso* for Strings, Piano, and Percussion (1949); *Symphonic Variations* (1951); *Tempi concertanti I* for Strings (1967) and *II* for Flute, Harpsichord, and 12 Instruments (1969); Violin Concerto (1971). **CHAMBER:** 4 string quartets (1949, 1952, 1953, 1956); Piano Trio (1976); 7 *Bagatelles* for Clarinet and Cello (1987). **VOCAL:** *Eulogy to Constantin the Philosopher*, oratorio (1971); choruses.

Ilitsch, Daniza, Serbian soprano; b. Belgrade, Feb. 21, 1914; d. Vienna, Jan. 15, 1965. She studied at the Stankovic Cons. in Belgrade, then in Berlin. She made her operatic debut as Nedda in *Pagliacci* with the Berlin State Opera (Nov. 6, 1936); was on its roster for 2 seasons; then was a member of the Vienna State Opera (1938–41). The German army of occupation put her in a concentration camp in 1944, and she spent 4 months there until the liberation of Vienna. She made her debut with the Metropolitan Opera in N.Y. as Desdemona (March 12, 1947), remaining on its roster until 1948. Thereafter she pursued her career in Europe and South America. In 1959 she settled in Vienna. She was principally known for her roles in Italian opera, including Aida, Desdemona, Gioconda, Amelia, and Cio-Cio-San.

Imai, Nobuko, Japanese violist; b. Tokyo, March 18, 1943. She was a student of Toshiya Eto and Hideo Saito at the Toho School of Music in Tokyo (B.A., 1965), of David Schwartz and Broadus Erle at Yale Univ. Graduate School (1965–66), and of Walter Trampler at the Juilliard School of Music in N.Y. (1966–68). She took 1st prize at both the Munich (1967) and Geneva (1968) international viola competitions. In 1967 she made her U.S. debut in N.Y., and in 1969 she made her British debut. From 1974 to 1979 she was a member of the Vermeer Quartet. She also appeared as a soloist with leading European and American orchs., and performed at various festivals. She was a member of the Casals Hall Quartet in Tokyo from 1990. Imai was a prof. at the Detmold Hochschule für Musik from 1985. Her repertoire encompasses scores from Haydn to Schnittke. She was a soloist in the premieres of Tippett's Triple Concerto (1980) and Takemitsu's Viola Concerto (1989).

Imbrie, Andrew (Welsh), distinguished American composer and pedagogue; b. N.Y., April 6, 1921. He studied piano and composition with Ornstein (until 1942), and also received instruction in composition from Boulanger (1937) and in piano with R. Casadesus (1941). From 1937 he pursued composition studies with Sessions, graduating from Princeton Univ. with a B.A. in 1942. After serving in the U.S. Army during World War II, he completed his studies with Sessions at the Univ. of Calif. at Berkeley, where he took his M.A. in 1947. In the latter year he joined its faculty as an instructor in music, becoming an assistant prof. in 1951, assoc. prof. in 1957, and prof. in 1960, a position he held until 1991. He also taught at the San Francisco Cons. of Music, serving as chairman of its composition dept. from 1970. In 1991 he was the composer-in-residence at the Tanglewood Festival of Contemporary Music. In 1982 he was the Jacob Ziskind Visiting Professor at Brandeis Univ. He was a fellow at the American Academy in Rome (1947–49), returning there on a Guggenheim fellowship (1953–54) and as its composer-in-residence (1967–68). In 1959–60 he was in Tokyo on a 2nd Guggenheim fellowship. In addition to various commissions, he won the N.Y. Music Critics' Circle Award for his 1st String Quartet (1944), the Alice M. Ditson Award (1947), and the Naumburg Award for his Violin Concerto (1954). In 1969 he was elected a member of the National Inst. of Arts and Letters, and in 1980 of the American Academy of Arts and Sciences. Imbrie's style of composition is marked by a sharp and expressive melodic line, while the polyphony is vigorously motile; harmonic confluence is dissonant but euphoniously tonal. His natural propensity is toward instrumental writing, although his mastery is displayed in other genres, including dramatic.

WORKS: OPERAS: *3 Against Christmas* or *Christmas in Peebles Town* (1960; Berkeley, Dec. 3, 1964); *Angle of Repose* (San Francisco, Nov. 6, 1976). **ORCH.:** *Ballad* (1947; Rome, June 20, 1949); Violin Concerto (1954; Berkeley, April 22, 1958); *Little Concerto* for Piano, 4-hands, and Orch. (1956; Oakland, Nov. 14, 1961); *Legend* (San Francisco, Dec. 9, 1959); 3 syms.: No. 1 (1965; San Francisco, May 11, 1966), No. 2 (San Francisco, May 20, 1970), and No. 3 (Manchester, England, Dec. 4, 1970); Chamber Sym. (Hanover, N.H., Aug. 11, 1968); Cello Concerto (1972; Oakland, April 30, 1973); 3 piano concertos: No. 1 (Saratoga, Calif., Aug. 4, 1973), No. 2 (1974; Terre Haute, Ind., Jan. 2, 1976), and No. 3 (1992; N.Y., April 21, 1993); Flute Concerto (N.Y., Oct. 13, 1977). **CHAMBER:** 5 string quartets (1942, 1953, 1957, 1969, 1987); 2 trios for Violin, Cello, and Piano (1946, 1989); *Divertimento* for Flute, Bassoon, Trumpet, Violin, Cello, and Piano (1948); *Serenade* for Flute, Viola, and Piano (1952); *Impromptu* for Violin and Piano (1960); Cello Sonata (1966); *3 Sketches* for Trombone and Piano (1967); *Dandelion Wine* for Oboe, Clarinet, String Quartet, and Piano (1967); *To A Traveler* for Clarinet, Violin, and Piano (1971); *Pilgrimage* for Flute, Clarinet, Violin, Cello, Piano, and Percussion (1983); *Dream Sequence* for Flute, Oboe, Clarinet, Violin, Viola, Cello, Piano, and Percussion (1986); *3 Piece Suite* for Harp and Piano (1987). **KEYBOARD: PIANO:** Sonata (1947); *Short Story* (1982); *Eulogy* (1986). **ORGAN:** *Prelude* (1987). **VOCAL:** *On the Beach at Night* for Chorus and String Orch., after Walt Whitman (1949); *Drum-Taps* for Chorus and Orch., after Walt Whitman (1960); *Prometheus Bound* for 3 Soloists, Double Chorus, Orch., and Dance (1979); *5 Roethke Songs* for Soprano and Piano (1980); *3 Campion Songs* for Soprano, Alto, Tenor, Bass, and Piano (1981); *Song for St. Cecilia's Day* for Chorus, Brass, Percussion, 2 Pianos, Flute, and 2 Violins (1981); *Requiem: In memoriam John Imbrie* for Soprano, Chorus, and Orch. (1984).

Inbal, Eliahu, prominent Israeli-English conductor; b. Jerusalem, Feb. 16, 1936. He received training in violin and theory at the Jerusalem Academy of Music (diploma, 1956). In 1956 he made his debut conducting the Youth Sym. Orch. of Israel. During military service, he was active with a combined army and youth orch. A recommendation from Bernstein in 1958 resulted in his receiving a scholarship from the Israel-America Foundation to pursue conducting studies with Fourestier at the Paris Cons. (1960–62); he also studied with Ferrara and Celibidache. After winning 1st prize in the Cantelli Competition in 1963, he appeared as a guest conductor with leading orchs. in Europe and the U.S.; he also was active as an opera conductor from 1969. From 1974 to 1990 he was chief conductor of the Frankfurt Radio Sym. Orch., which he led on its first tour of the U.S. in 1980. He also was artistic director of the Teatro La Fenice in Venice from 1983 to 1986. During his tenure in Frankfurt am Main, Inbal conducted the premieres of many scores. He also became particularly well known for his performances of cycles of works by Schumann, Bruckner, Mahler, and Scriabin.

Inch, Herbert Reynolds, American composer and teacher; b. Missoula, Mont., Nov. 25, 1904; d. La Jolla, Calif., April 14, 1988. He was a student of Josephine Swenson and A.H. Weisberg at the Univ. of Montana in Missoula, and then of Hanson and Edward Royce at the Eastman School of Music in Rochester, N.Y. (B.M., 1925; M.M., 1928); later took his Ph.D. at the Univ. of Rochester (1941). In 1931 he received a fellowship to the American Academy in Rome. After teaching at the Eastman School of Musc (1925–28; 1930–31), he taught at Hunter College in N.Y. (1937–65). Inch's works display a fine feel for lyrical and contrapuntal writing.

WORKS: ORCH.: *Variations on a Modal Theme* (Rochester, N.Y., April 29, 1927); *3 Pieces* for Small Orch. (Rochester, N.Y., Oct. 24, 1930); Sym. (Rochester, N.Y., May 5, 1932); *Serenade* for Small Orch. (Rochester, N.Y., Oct. 24, 1939); Piano Concerto (1940); *Answers to a Questionnaire* (1942); *Northwest Overture* (1943); Violin Concerto (1946–47; Rochester, N.Y., May 1, 1947); 3 symphoniettas (1948, 1950, 1955). **CHAMBER:** Piano Quintet (1930); 2 string quartets (1933, 1936); *Divertimento* for Brass (1934); 3 piano sonatas (1935, 1946, 1966); Cello Sonata (1941); Piano Trio (1963). **VOCAL:** *Return to Zion* for Women's Chorus and Piano (1945); choruses.

d'Indy, (Paul-Marie-Théodore-) Vincent, eminent French composer and pedagogue; b. Paris, March 27, 1851; d. there, Dec. 2, 1931. Owing to the death of his mother at his birth, his education was directed entirely by his grandmother, Countess Rézia d'Indy, a woman of culture and refinement who had known Grétry and Monsigny, and who had shown a remarkable appreciation of the works of Beethoven when that master was still living. From 1862 to 1865 he studied piano with Diémer and Marmontel; in 1865 he studied harmony with Lavignac. In 1869 he made the acquaintance of Duparc, and with him spent much time studying the masterpieces of Bach, Beethoven, Berlioz, and Wagner; at that time, he wrote his opp. 1 and 2, and contemplated an opera on Hugo's *Les Burgraves* (1869–72; unfinished). During the Franco-Prussian War, he served in the Garde Mobile, and wrote of his experiences in *Histoire du 105e bataillon de la Garde nationale de Paris en l'année 1870–71* (1872). He then began to study composition with Franck (1872); when the latter was appointed prof. of organ at the Paris Cons. (1873), d'Indy joined the class, winning a 2nd *accessit* in 1874 and the 1st the following year. On his first visit to Germany in 1873, he met Liszt and Wagner, and was introduced to Brahms; in 1876 he heard the first performances of the *Ring* dramas at Bayreuth, and for several years thereafter made regular trips to Munich to hear all the works of Wagner; he also attended the premiere of *Parsifal* in 1882. From 1872 to 1876 he was organist at St. Leu-la-Forêt; from 1873 to 1878, chorus master and timpanist with the Colonne Orch.; for the Paris premiere of *Lohengrin* in 1887, he drilled the chorus and was Lamoureux's assistant. In 1871 he joined the Société Nationale de Musique as a junior member, and was its secretary from 1876 to 1890, when, after Franck's death, he became president. In 1894 he founded, with Bordes and Guilmant, the famous Schola Cantorum (opened 1896), primarily as a school for plainchant and the Palestrina style. Gradually the scope of instruction was enlarged to include all musical disciplines, and the inst. became one of the world's foremost music schools. D'Indy's fame as a composer began with the performance of his *Le Chant de la cloche* at a Lamoureux concert in 1886; the work itself had won the City of Paris Prize in the competition of the preceding year. As early as 1874, Pasdeloup had played the overture *Les Piccolomini* (later embodied as the 2nd part in the Wallenstein trilogy), and in 1882 the 1-act opera *Attendez-moi sous l'orme* had been produced at the Paris Opéra-Comique; but the prize work attracted general attention, and d'Indy was recognized as one of the most important French composers of his day. Although he never held an official position as a conductor, he frequently, and with marked success, appeared in that capacity (chiefly upon invitation to direct his own works); thus, he visited Spain in 1897, Russia in 1903 and 1907, and the U.S. in 1905, when he conducted the Boston Sym. Orch. In 1892 he was a member of the commission appointed to revise the curriculum of the Cons., and refused a proffered professorship of composition; but in 1912 he accepted an appointment as prof. of the ensemble class. Besides his other duties, he was, from 1899, inspector of musical instruction in Paris. He was made a Chevalier of the Legion of Honor in 1892, an Officer in 1912. Both as teacher and creative artist, d'Indy continued the traditions of Franck. Although he cultivated almost every form of composition, his special talent was in the field of the larger instrumental forms. Some French critics assign to him a position in French music analogous to that of Brahms in German music. His style rests on Bach and Beethoven; however, his deep study of Gregorian chant and the early contrapuntal style added an element of severity, and not rarely of complexity, that renders his approach somewhat difficult, and has prompted the charge that his music is lacking in emotional force. He wrote numerous articles for various journals, which are remarkable for their critical acumen and literary finish.

WRITINGS: *Cours de Composition musicale* (Book I, 1903; Book II: Part 1, 1909, Part 2, 1933); *César Franck* (1906; Eng. tr., 1910); *Beethoven: Biographie critique* (1911; Eng. tr., 1913); *La Schola Cantorum en 1925* (1927); *Wagner et son influence sur l'art musical français* (1930); *Introduction à l'étude de Parsifal* (1937).

WORKS: DRAMATIC: *Les Burgraves*, opera (1869–72; unfinished); *Attendez-moi sous l'orme*, comic opera (Paris, Feb. 11, 1882); *Karadec*, incidental music (Paris, May 2, 1891); *Le Chant de la cloche*, dramatic legend (Brussels, Nov. 21, 1912); *Fervaal*, lyric drama (Brussels, March 12, 1897); *Medée*, incidental music (1898); *L'Étranger*, lyric drama (Brussels, Jan. 7, 1903); *La Légende de Saint-Christophe*, lyric drama (Paris, June 9, 1920); *Le Rêve de Cynias*, lyric comedy (Paris, June 10, 1927).

ORCH.: 3 syms.: No. 1, *Jean Hunyade* (Paris, May 15, 1875), No. 2 (Paris, Feb. 28, 1904), and No. 3, *Sinfonia brevis de bello Gallico* (1916–18; Paris, Dec. 14, 1919); 2 other syms.:

Symphonie Cévenole sur un chant montagnard français (1886; Paris, March 20, 1887) and *La Queste de Dieu*, after *La Légende de Saint-Christophe* (1917); *Antoine et Cléopâtre*, overture (Paris, Feb. 4, 1877); *La Forêt enchantée*, symphonic legend (Paris, March 24, 1878); *Wallenstein*, symphonic trilogy: *Le Camp de Wallenstein* (April 12, 1880), *Max et Thécla* (Jan. 25, 1874; orig. *Les Piccolomini*), and *La Mort de Wallenstein* (April 11, 1884); *Lied* for Cello and Orch. (Paris, April 18, 1885); *Saugefleurie*, legend (Paris, Jan. 25, 1885); Suite for Trumpet, 2 Flutes, and Strings (Paris, March 5, 1887); *Sérénade et Valse* for Small Orch. (1887); *Fantaisie* for Oboe and Orch. (Paris, Dec. 23, 1888); *Tableaux de voyage* (Le Havre, Jan. 17, 1892); *Istar*, symphonic variations (Brussels, Jan. 10, 1897); *Choral varié* for Saxophone and Orch. (Paris, May 17, 1904); *Jour d'été à la montagne* (Paris, Feb. 18, 1906); *Souvenirs*, tone poem (Paris, April 20, 1907); *Le Poème des rivages* (N.Y., Dec. 1, 1921); *Diptyque méditerranéen* (Paris, Dec. 5, 1926); Concerto for Piano, Flute, Cello, and Strings (Paris, April 2, 1927). **CHAMBER:** Piano Quartet (1878); Trio for Piano, Clarinet, and Cello (1888); 3 string quartets (1891, 1898, 1929); *Chansons et Danses*, divertissement for 7 Wind Instruments (Paris, March 7, 1899); Violin Sonata (1905); Piano Quintet (1925); Cello Sonata (1926); *Suite en 4 parties* for Flute, Strings, and Harp (Paris, May 17, 1930); String Sextet (1928); Trio for Piano, Violin, and Cello (1929). **KEYBOARD: PIANO:** *3 romances sans paroles* (1870); *Petite sonate* (1880); *Poème des montagnes: Le Chant des bruyères, Danses rythmiques*, and *Plein-air* (1881); *4 pièces* (1882); *Helvetia*, 3 waltzes (1882); *Saugefleurie* (1884; also arranged for Orch.); Nocturne (1886); *Promenade* (1887); *Schumanniana*, 3 pieces (1887); *Tableaux de voyage*, 13 pieces (1889); *Petite chanson grégorienne* for Piano, 4-hands (1904); Sonata (1907); *Menuet sur le nom de Haydn* (1909); *13 Short Pieces*; *12 petites pièces faciles*; *7 chants de terroir* for Piano, 4-hands; *Pour les enfants de tous les âges*, 24 pieces; *Thème varié, fugue et chanson*; *Conte de fées*, suite (1926); 6 paraphrases on French children's songs; *Fantaisie sur un vieil air de ronde française* (1931). **ORGAN:** *Prélude et Petit Canon* (1893); *Vêpres du Commun d'un Martyr* (1889); *Prélude* (1913).

VOCAL: *Chanson des aventuriers de la mer* for Baritone and Men's Chorus (1870); *La Chevauchée du Cid* for Baritone, Chorus, and Orch. (1879); *Cantate Domino* (1885); *Ste. Marie-Magdeleine*, cantata (1885); *Sur la mer* for Women's Voices and Piano (1888); *Pour l'inauguration d'une statue*, cantata (1893); *L'Art et le peuple* for Men's Chorus (1894); *Deus Israël*, motet (1896); *Ode à Valence* for Soprano and Chorus (1897); *Les Noces d'or du sacerdoce* (1898); *Sancta Maria*, motet (1898); *6 Chants populaires français* for Chorus (1928, 1931); *Le Bouquet de printemps* Women's Chorus (1929); *La Vengeance du mari* for 3 Soloists, Chorus, and Orch. (1931); songs.

BIBL.: E. Deniau, *V. d'I.* (Toulouse, 1903); F. Starczewski, *La Schola Cantorum de Paris, ou V. d'I. considéré comme professeur* (Warsaw, 1905); L. Borgex, *V. d'I.: Sa vie et son oeuvre* (Paris, 1913); A. Sérieyx, *V. d'I.* (Paris, 1913); E. Hill, "V. d'I., An Estimate," *Musical Quarterly* (April 1915); P. Landormy, "V. d'I.," ibid. (July 1932); M. de Fraguier, *V. d'I.* (Paris, 1933); L. Vallas, "The Discovery of Musical Germany by V. d'I. in 1873," *Musical Quarterly* (April 1939); idem, *V. d'I.: I. La Jeunesse, II. La Maturité, La Vieillesse* (Paris, I, 1946; II, 1950); J. Canteloube, *V. d'I.* (Paris, 1949); N. Demuth, *V. d'I.* (London, 1951); J. Guy-Ropartz, ed., *Le Centenaire de V. d'I., 1851–1951* (Paris, 1952); L. Davies, *César Franck and His Circle* (Boston, 1970); C. Paul, "Rameau, d'I., and French Nationalism," *Musical Quarterly* (Jan. 1972).

Ingarden, Roman (Witold), important Polish music theorist and aesthetician; b. Kraków, Feb. 5, 1893; d. there, June 14, 1970. He studied philosophy with Husserl and mathematics with Hilbert at the Univs. of Göttingen and Freiburg im Breisgau (Ph.D., 1918). After completing his Habilitation (1921), he joined the faculty at the Univ. of Lwów. In 1945 he became chairman of the philosophy dept. at the Jagellonian Univ. in Kraków, only to be barred from teaching in 1950 by the Communist government because of his adherence to "idealism"; during his forced sabbatical, he tr. Kant's *Critique of Pure Reason.* He regained his academic post in 1956, retiring in 1963. Ingarden is regarded as the ablest of Husserl's students, preserving the cognitive core of Husserl's phenomenology that was lost in Heidegger's and Sartre's emotional reduction of it to existentialism. His *The Work of Music and the Problem of Its Identity* (Berkeley, 1986), an excerpt from his *Studia z estetyki* (Studies in Aesthetics; Warsaw, 1957–70), is an important consideration of ontology and epistemology in musical aesthetics. His other publications include *Spór o istnienie świata* (Controversy over the Existence of the World; Kraków, 1947–48); *Untersuchungen zur Ontologie der Kunst: Musikwerk, Bild, Architektur, Film* (Tübingen, 1962); *The Literary Work of Art: An Investigation on the Borderlines of Ontology, Logic, and Theory of Literature, with an Appendix on the Functions of Language in the Theater* (Evanston, Ill., 1973); and *Selected Papers in Aesthetics* (Washington, D.C., 1985).

Ingenhoven, Jan, Dutch composer; b. Breda, May 29, 1876; d. Hoenderlo, May 20, 1951. He studied with L. Brandts-Buys in Rotterdam and Mottl in Munich, where he conducted the noted Madrigal Soc. (1909–12); then devoted himself mainly to composition. His works are influenced by Debussy, but he preserved an element of peculiarly native melos. Among his works are *Symphonische Fantasie über Zarathustras* for Orch. (1906); *Brabant and Holland,* symphonic fantasy; 3 symphonic poems (*Lyric; Dramatic; Romantic*); 3 string quartets (1907–08; 1911; 1912); Woodwind Quintet (1911); Clarinet Sonata (1916–17); 2 violin sonatas (1919–20; 1921); 2 cello sonatas (1919, 1922); choral works; songs.

BIBL.: D. Ruyneman, *De componist J. I.* (Amsterdam, 1938).

Inghelbrecht, D(ésiré)-É(mile), noted French conductor and composer; b. Paris, Sept. 17, 1880; d. there, Feb. 14, 1965. He began violin lessons as a child, and later studied solfège and harmony with Taudou at the Paris Cons. only to be expelled as musically unpromising. After working as an orch. player, he became conductor of the Théâtre des Arts in Paris in 1908. In 1912 he organized l'Association Chorale Professionnelle. After serving as music director at the Théâtre des Champs-Elysées in Paris, he founded the Concerts Ignace Pleyel in 1919 to promote the music of the 17th and 18th centuries. From 1920 to 1923 he toured Europe as conductor of the Ballets Suédois, and then returned to Paris as music director of the Opéra-Comique in 1924–25; then held the post of 2nd conductor of the Concerts Pasdeloup (1928–32). After serving as director of the Algiers Opera (1929–30), he was again music director of the Opéra-Comique (1932–33). In 1934 he founded l'Orchestre National de la Radio Française, serving as its director until 1944. From 1945 to 1950 he was chief conductor of the Paris Opéra, and subsequently appeared as a conductor with Radio Française. Inghelbrecht was greatly admired for his interpretations of French music, particularly the works of Debussy, Ravel, and Roussel. He was also an accomplished composer in his own right. He was the author of *Comment on ne doit pas interpréter Carmen, Faust et Pelléas* (1933); *Diabolus in musica* (1933); *Mouvement contraire: Souvenirs d'un musicien* (1947); *Le Chef d'orchestre et son équipe* (1948; Eng. tr., 1953, as *The Conductor's World*); *Claude Debussy* (1953); *Le Chef d'orchestre parle au public* (1957).

WORKS: DRAMATIC: OPERA: *La nuit vénitienne* (1908). **OPERETTA:** *Virage sur l'aile* (1947). **OPERA-BALLET:** *Le chêne et le tilleul* (1960). **BALLETS:** *El Greco* (Paris, Nov. 18, 1920); *Le diable dans le beffroi* (1921; Paris, June 1, 1927); *La métamorphose d'Eve* (1928); *Jeux de Couleurs* (Paris, Feb. 21, 1933). **ORCH.:** *Marine* (1903); *La serre aux nénuphars* (1903); *Automne* (1905); *Pour le jour de la première neige au vieux Japon* (1908); *Rapsodie de printemps* (1910); *3 poèmes dansés* (1923); *6 danses suédoises* (1929); *Sinfonia breve da camera* (1930); *La valse retrouvée* (1937); *Ballade dans le goût irlandais* for Harp and Orch. (1939); *Pastourelles sur des noëls anciens* (1943); *Ibériana* for Violin and Orch. (1948); *Vézelay* (1952). **CHAMBER:** *2 esquisses antiques* for Flute and Harp (1903); *Poème sylvestre* for Winds (1905); *Prélude et saltarelle* for Viola and Piano (1905); *Nocturne* for Cello and Piano (1905); Quintet for Harp and Strings (1918); Sonatine for Flute and Harp (1919); *Impromptu* for Viola and Piano (1922); *4 Fanfares* for Winds (1932); String Quartet (1956). **PIANO:** *2 esquisses* (1903); *La nursery* (5 vols., 1905–11; also orcestrated); *Suite Petite russienne* (1908); *Paysages* (1918); *Dernières nurseries* (1932); *Pastourelles* (1949). **VOCAL:** *Cantique des créatures* for Voice and Piano (1910); *4 chansons populaires françaises* for Chorus (1915); *Vocalise-étude* for Voice and Piano (1929); *La légende du grand St. Nicolas* for Voice and Piano (1932); *Requiem* for Soprano, Tenor, Baritone, Chorus, and Orch. (1941); *Tant que noël durera* for Voice and Orch. (1943); *Chantons jeunesse* for Chorus (1946).

Inghilleri, Giovanni, Italian baritone and composer; b. Porto Empedocle, March 9, 1894; d. Milan, Dec. 10, 1959. He made his operatic debut as Valentine at the Teatro Carcano in Milan in 1919, and then sang throughout Italy; was a member of La Scala in Milan from 1945. He also sang at London's Covent Garden (1928–30; 1935) and at the Chicago Civic Opera (1929–30). After his retirement in 1953, he taught voice in Pesaro and Milan. Among his best known roles were Amonasro, Amfortas, Gérard, and Scarpia. He composed an opera, *La burla,* a ballet, and songs.

Ingólfsdóttir, Thorgerdur, Icelandic choral conductor and teacher; b. Reykjavík, Nov. 5, 1943. She was a student at the Reykjavík College of Music (teacher's diploma, 1965); also studied theology at the Univ. of Iceland and choral conducting and musicology with Robert Ottósson (1963–65). In 1966–67 she held a graduate fellowship at the Univ. of Ill., and then continued her studies with Ottósson in her homeland (1968–74). She also studied choral conducting in England, N.Y., Switzerland, Israel, Norway, and Vienna. In 1967 she founded the Hamrahlíd Choir in Reykjavík, which she molded into one of Iceland's most important performing groups. She conducted it throughout Europe and in Israel and Japan. As a teacher, she served on the faculties of the Reykjavík College of Music (from 1967) and of Hamrahlíd College (from 1967). In 1985 the president of Iceland made her a Knight of the Order of the Falcon for her services to Icelandic music; in 1992 the king of Norway named her a Commander of the Royal Order of Merit.

Ioannidis, Yannis, Greek composer; b. Athens, June 8, 1930. He studied piano at the Athens Cons. (1946–55), then organ, composition, and harpsichord at the Vienna Academy of Music (1955–63). He taught at Pierce College in Athens (1963–68); in 1968 went to Caracas (his family was from Venezuela), where he served as artistic director of the chamber orch. of the National

Inst. of Culture and Fine Arts; he was a prof. there from 1969, and at the Caracas Cons. and Univ. from 1971. He returned to Athens in 1976. As a composer, he followed the precepts of the 2nd Vienna School, with a firm foundation of classical forms.

WORKS: ORCH.: *Triptych* (1962); *Tropic* (1968); *Metaplassis A* and *B* (1969, 1970); *Transiciones* (1971); *Orbis* for Piano and Orch. (1975–76). **CHAMBER:** *Arioso* for String Nonet (1960); 2 string quartets (1961, 1971); Duo for Violin and Piano (1962); *Peristrophe* for String Octet (1964); *Versi* for Clarinet (1967); *Schemata (Figures)* for String Ensemble (1968); *Projections for Strings, Winds, and Piano* (1968); *Fragments I* for Cello and Piano (1969) and *II* for Flute (1970); *Actinia* for Wind Quintet (1969); *Estudio I, II,* and *III* for Piano (1971–73); *Fancy for 6* for 4 Winds, Cello, and Percussion (1972); *Nocturno* for Piano Quartet (1972); *Dance Vision* for Trombone, Clarinet, Cello, and Piano (1980). **VOCAL:** Transcriptions of Greek folk songs for chorus.

Iokeles, Alexander, Russian pianist and teacher; b. Moscow, March 11, 1912; d. there, June 14, 1978. He was a student of Igumnov at the Moscow Cons. In 1934 he made his first appearance as a soloist with the Moscow Phil., and later played in a trio with Tsomik and Zatulovsky (1943–58). He taught at the Moscow Cons. (1931–42), the Tbilisi Cons. (1946–52), and the Gnessin Inst. in Moscow (from 1952), where he was head of its piano dept. (from 1964). Iokeles gave premiere performances of many works, including concertos by Dolukhanian, Gordeli, Makarov-Rakitin, and Taktakishvili, and also first Russian performances of many works by non-Russian composers.

Ippolitov-Ivanov (real name, **Ivanov**), **Mikhail (Mikhailovich),** important Russian composer and pedagogue; b. Gatchina, Nov. 19, 1859; d. Moscow, Jan. 28, 1935. He assumed his mother's name to distinguish himself from Michael Ivanov, the music critic. He studied composition with Rimsky-Korsakov at the St. Petersburg Cons., graduating in 1882. He then received the post of teacher and director of the Music School in Tiflis, where he remained until 1893; he became deeply interested in Caucasian folk music; many of his works were colored by the semi-oriental melodic and rhythmic inflections of that region. Upon Tchaikovsky's recommendation, he was appointed prof. of composition at the Moscow Cons. in 1893; in 1906 he became its director, retiring in 1922; then taught at the Tiflis Cons. (1924–25). Among his pupils were Glière and Vasilenko. He was also active as a conductor in Moscow, where he led the Russian Choral Soc. (1895–1901), the Mamontov Opera (1898–1906), and the Bolshoi Theater (from 1925). Outside Russia, he is known mainly for his effective symphonic suite *Caucasian Sketches* (1895). He publ. his memoirs (Moscow, 1934; Eng. tr. in the *Musical Mercury*, N.Y., 1937).

WORKS: OPERAS: *Ruf* (Ruth; 1883–86; Tiflis, Feb. 4, 1887); *Azra* (Tiflis, Dec. 4, 1890); *Asya* (Moscow, Oct. 11, 1900); *Izmena* (Treason; 1908–09; Moscow, Dec. 17, 1910); *Ole iz Nordlands* (Ole from the Northland; Moscow, Nov. 21, 1916); *Poslednyaya barrikada* (The Last Barricade; 1933); also completed Mussorgsky's unfinished opera *Zhenitba* (Marriage; Moscow, Oct. 18, 1931). **ORCH.:** *Symphonic Scherzo* (St. Petersburg, May 20, 1882); *Yar-Khmel*, spring overture (1882; St. Petersburg, Jan. 23, 1883); *Caucasian Sketches* (1894; Moscow, Feb. 5, 1895); *Armenian Rhapsody* (1895); *Iveria* (1896); Sym. (1908); *Mtzyri*, symphonic poem (1922); *From the Songs of Ossian* (1925); *In the Steppes of Turkmenistan* (1935); *Musical Scenes of Uzbekistan* (c.1935); *Karelia*, suite (1935); marches. **CHAMBER:** Violin Sonata; Piano Quintet; 2 string quartets (1894, c.1934); piano pieces. **VOCAL:** *Hymn of the Pythagoreans to the Rising Sun* for Chorus, 10 Flutes, Tuba, 2 Harps, and Organ ad libitum (1904); *Hymn to Labor* for Chorus and Orch. (1934); mass songs; choruses.

BIBL.: S. Chemodanov, *M.M. I.-I.* (Moscow, 1933); S. Boguslavsky, *I.-I.* (Moscow, 1936); L. Podzemskaya, *M.M. I.-I. i gruzinskaya muzikalnaya kultura* (Tbilisi, 1963); N. Sokolov, ed., *M.M. I.-I.: Pisma, stati, vospominaniya* (M.M. I.-I.: Letters, Articles, Reminiscences; Moscow, 1986).

Ipuche-Riva, Pedro, Uruguayan composer; b. Montevideo, Oct. 26, 1924. He studied at the Montevideo Cons., and later in Paris with Rivier and N. Gallon. Returning to Uruguay, he unfolded energetic activities as a music critic, lecturer, teacher, and radio commentator. Among his compositions are a symphonic poem, *El Arbol solo* (1961); 3 syms. (1962, 1965, 1968); Cello Concerto (1962); *Fantasía concertante* for Trumpet and Strings (1963); String Quartet (1962); Quartet for Flute, Violin, Cello, and Piano (1963); *Espejo roto* for Violin, Horn, and Piano (1966); Concerto for Small Orch. (1966); *Sinfonietta-Concertino* for Piano and Orch. (1967); *Animales ilustres*, suite for Wind Quintet (1967); *Pieza* for Oboe and Piano (1969); piano pieces; choruses; songs.

Ireland, John (Nicholson), eminent English composer and teacher; b. Inglewood, Bowdon, Cheshire, Aug. 13, 1879; d. Rock Mill, Washington, Sussex, June 12, 1962. A member of a literary family (both his parents were writers), he received a fine general education. As his musical inclinations became evident, he entered the Royal College of Music in London in 1893, studying piano with Frederick Cliffe (until 1897) and composition with Stanford (1897–1901). He obtained positions as organist in various churches; the longest of these was at St. Luke's, Chelsea (1904–26). In 1905 he received the degree of Bac.Mus. at the Univ. of Durham; was awarded an honorary Mus.Doc. there in 1932. He taught at the Royal College of Music (1923–39); Benjamin Britten, Alan Bush, E.J. Moeran, and other British composers were his pupils. He began to compose early in life; during his student years, he wrote a number of works for orch., chamber groups, and voices, but destroyed most of them; 2 string quartets (1895, 1897) came to light after his death. His early compositions were influenced by the German Romantic school; soon he adopted many devices of the French impressionist school; his rhythmic concepts were enlivened by the new Russian music presented by the Diaghilev Ballet. At the same time, he never wavered in his dedication to the English spirit of simple melody; his music re-creates the plainsong and the usages of Tudor music in terms of plagal modalities and freely modulating triadic harmonies.

WORKS: DRAMATIC: *Julius Caesar*, incidental music to Shakespeare's play (BBC, London, Sept. 28, 1942); *The Vagabonds*, ballet (London, Oct. 29, 1946; based on *Mai-Dun* and the *Concertino pastorale*); *The Overlanders*, film music (1946–47). **ORCH.:** *Tritons*, symphonic prelude (1899; London, March 21, 1901); *Orchestral Poem* (1903–04); *The Forgotten Rite*, prelude (1913; London, Sept. 13, 1917); *Mai-Dun* (1920–21; London, Dec. 12, 1921); Piano Concerto (London, Oct. 2, 1930); *Legend* for Piano and Orch. (1933; London, Jan. 12, 1934); *Concertino pastorale* for Strings (Canterbury, June 14, 1939); *Epic March* (1941–42; London, June 27, 1942); *Satyricon*, overture (1944–46; London, Sept. 11, 1946). **BRASS BAND:** *A Downland Suite* (London, Oct. 1, 1932); *Comedy Overture* (London, Sept. 29, 1934; reworked version as *A London Overture* for Orch., London, Sept. 23, 1936). **CHAMBER:** 2 string quartets (1897, 1897); Sextet for Clarinet, Horn, 2 Violins, Viola, and Cello (1898; London, March 25, 1960); *Berceuse* for Violin and Piano (1902); 3 trios for Violin, Cello, and Piano: No. 1, *Phantasie-Trio* (1906; London, Jan. 26, 1909), No. 2 (London, June 12, 1917), and No. 3 (BBC, London, April 4, 1938); 2 violin sonatas: No. 1 (1908–09; London, March 7, 1913; rev. 1917 and 1944) and No. 2 (1915–17; London, March 6, 1917); *Bagatelle* for Violin and Piano (1911); Trio for Clarinet, Cello, and Piano (1912–14; London, June 9, 1914); Cello Sonata (1923; London, April 4, 1924; arranged as a Viola Sonata by L. Tertis, 1941; BBC, Bedford, Dec. 14, 1942); *Fantasy Sonata* for Clarinet and Piano (1943; London, Feb. 5, 1944). **PIANO:** *In Those Days* (1895); *Sea Idyll* (1899–1900); *Rhapsody* No. 1 (1905–06) and No. 2 (1915); *Decorations* (1912–13); *The Almond Trees* (1913); *3 Dances* (1913); [4] *Preludes* (1913–15; No. 3, *The Holy Boy*, arranged for String Orch., 1941); [3] *London Pieces* (1917–20); *Leaves from a Child's Sketchbook* (1918); *Merry Andrew* (1918); *The Towing Path* (1918); Sonata (1918–20; London, June 12,

1920); *Summer Evening* (1919); *The Darkened Valley* (1920); *2 Pieces* (1921); *On a Birthday Morning* (1922); *Soliloquy* (1922); *Equinox* (1922); *Prelude* (1924); *2 Pieces* (1925); Sonatina (1926–27; BBC, London, April 19, 1928); *Ballade* (1929); *2 Pieces* (1929–30); *Ballade of London Nights* (1930); *Indian Summer* (1932); *Month's Mind* (1932); *Green Ways: 3 Lyric Pieces* (1937); *Sarnia: An Island Sequence* (1940–41; London, Nov. 29, 1941); *3 Pastels* (1941; BBC, Bedford, March 8, 1942); *Columbine* (1949; rev. 1951). **VOCAL:** *Vexilla Regis*, hymn for Passion Sunday for Soloists, Chorus, Brass, and Organ (1898); [5] *Songs of a Wayfarer* for Voice and Piano (1903–11); *Te Deum* for Chorus and Organ (1907); *Psalm 42* for Soloists, Chorus, and String Orch. (1908); *Greater love hath no man*, motet for Treble and Baritone Soli, Chorus, and Organ (1911; also with Orch., 1922); *Communion Service* for Chorus and Organ (1913); *Sea Fever* for Voice and Piano (1913); *The Land of Lost Content*, 6 songs for Voice and Piano (1920–21); *3 Songs to Poems by Thomas Hardy* for Voice and Piano (1925); *5 Poems by Thomas Hardy* for Baritone and Piano (1926); [6] *Songs Sacred and Profane* for Voice and Piano (1929–31); *These things shall be*, cantata for Baritone or Tenor, Chorus, and Orch. (1936–37; BBC, London, May 13, 1937); many other sacred works, choral pieces, and songs.

BIBL.: N. Townshend, "The Achievement of J. I.," *Music & Letters* (April 1943); J. Longmire, *J. I.: Portrait of a Friend* (London, 1969); M. Searle, *J. I.: The Man and His Music* (Tunbridge Wells, 1979); M. Pilkington, *Gurney, I., Quilter and Warlock* (London, 1989); S. Craggs, *J. I.: A Catalogue, Discography, and Bibliography* (Oxford, 1993).

Irgens-Jensen, Ludvig (Paul), Norwegian composer; b. Christiania, April 13, 1894; d. Piazza Armerina, Sicily, April 11, 1969. He received training in philosophy, music theory, and piano in Christiania, but was mainly self-taught in composition. In 1946 he received the Norwegian guaranteed income for art. His works were mainly influenced by late German Romanticism.

WORKS: ORCH.: *Tema con variazioni* (1925); Passacaglia (1926); *Partita sinfonica* (1937); Sym. (1942); *Canto d'omaggio*, festival overture (1950). **CHAMBER:** Violin Sonata (1924); Piano Quintet (1927). **VOCAL:** *Japanischer Frühling* for Voice and Piano (1918–19); *Der Gott und die Bajadere*, cantata (1921–32); *Heimferd* (The Journey Home), oratorio for Soloists, Chorus, and Orch. for the 900th anniversary of the death of St. Olav (1929; Oslo, 1930; also as an opera, Oslo, Aug. 27, 1947); choruses; songs.

BIBL.: H. Irgens, *L. I.-J.: His Life and His Songs* (thesis, Univ. of Iowa, 1994); A. Vollsnes, "L. I.-J.: A Quest for Heights," *Listen to Norway*, III/2 (1994).

Irino, Yoshirō, Japanese composer and pedagogue; b. Vladivostok, Nov. 13, 1921; d. Tokyo, June 28, 1980. Although of pure Japanese ancestry, he was baptized in the Greek Orthodox faith, which he retained throughout his life. His family took him to Tokyo when he was 6. He studied economics at the Univ. of Tokyo; at the same time, he took composition lessons with Saburo Moroi. He became a teacher at the Tōhō Gakuen School of Music in 1952; was its director (1960–70); then was prof. at the Tokyo Music College (from 1973). A prolific composer, he wrote music of all categories, adopting a style decidedly modern in character, marked by fine instrumental coloration, with a complete mastery of contemporary techniques. Most of his vocal and stage music is imbued with a pronounced Japanese sensibility, with touches that are almost calligraphic in their rhythmic precision.

WORKS: DRAMATIC: *Kamisama ni shikarareta otoko* (The Man in Fear of God), radio operetta (NHK, May 25, 1954); *Fuefuki to Ryuo no musumetachi* (The Piper and the Dragon King's Daughters), radio opera (1959); *Sarudon no mukoiri* (The Marriage of Mr. Monkey), radio opera (NHK, Nov. 26, 1961; 1st stage perf., Tokyo, March 15, 1962; in collaboration with Moroi and Shimizu); *Aya no tsuzumi* (The Damask Drum), television opera (NHK, Aug. 9, 1962; 1st stage perf., Tokyo, March 26, 1975); *Sonezaki shinju* (The Lover's Suicide at Sonezaki), chamber opera (Osaka, April 10, 1980). **ORCH.:** *Adagietto and Allegro vivace* (1949); Sinfonietta for Chamber Orch. (1953); Ricercari for Chamber Orch. (1954); Double Concerto for Violin, Piano, and Orch. (1955); *Concerto grosso* (1957); Sinfonia (1959); Concerto for Strings (1960); Suite for Jazz Ensemble (1960); *Music* for Harpsichord, Percussion, and 19 Strings (1963); Sym. No. 2 (1964); *2 Fantasies* for 17 and 20 Kotos (1969); *Sai-un* (Colorful Clouds) for 15 Strings (1972); *Wandlungen* for 2 Shakuhachi and Orch. (1973). **CHAMBER:** 2 string quartets (1945, 1957); Piano Trio (1948); String Sextet (1950); *Chamber Concerto* for 7 Instruments (1951); Quintet for Clarinet, Saxophone, Trumpet, Cello, and Piano (1958); *Divertimento* for 7 Winds (1958); *Music* for Violin and Cello (1959); *Music* for Vibraphone and Piano (1961); *Partita* for Wind Quintet (1962); String Trio (1965); *3 Movements* for 2 Kotos and Jushichi-gen (1966); *7 Inventions* for Guitar and 6 Players (1967); Violin Sonata (1967); *3 Movements* for Cello (1969); Sonata for Piano, Violin, Clarinet, and Percussion (1970); Trio for Flute, Violin, and Piano (1970); *Globus I* for Horn and Percussion (1970), *II* for Marimba, Double Bass, and Percussion (1971), and *III* for Violin, Cello, Piano, Harp, Shō, and 2 Dancers (1975); Suite for Viola (1971); *Cloudscape* for String Ensemble (1972); *3 Scenes* for 3 Kotos (1972); *Strömung* for Flute, Harp, and Percussion (1973); *Shō-yō* for Japanese Instruments (1973); *Gafu* for Flute, Shō, and Double Bass (1976); *Movements* for Marimba (1977); Cosmos for Shakuhachi, Violin, Piano, 2 Kotos, and Percussion (1978); *Shi-dai* for Shakuhachi, 20-gen, 17-gen, and Shamisen (1979); *Duo Concertante* for Alto Saxophone and Koto (1979). **VOCAL:** Various works, including *A Demon's Bride* for Chorus, Oboe, Horn, Piano, and Percussion (1970).

Irving, Robert (Augustine), English conductor; b. Winchester, Aug. 28, 1913; d. there, Sept. 13, 1991. He studied at Winchester College (1926–32), at New College, Oxford (B.A., 1935), and with Sargent and Lambert at the Royal College of Music in London (1934–36). He was assoc. conductor of the BBC Scottish Orch. in Glasgow (1945–48); after serving as principal conductor of the Sadler's Wells (later Royal) Ballet in London, (1948–58), he was music director of the N.Y. City Ballet (1958–89); he also conducted for the Martha Graham Dance Co. in N.Y. (1960–65; 1974–77). Although he appeared as a guest conductor with various orchs. in England and the U.S., it was as an exemplary conductor of ballet that he secured his reputation. He also wrote music for the theater and for films.

Isamitt, Carlos, Chilean composer; b. Rengo, Colchagua, March 13, 1887; d. Santiago, July 2, 1974. He studied both music and painting in Chile; then in Italy, Spain, France, and the Netherlands. As a composer, he became interested in the folk music of the Araucanian Indians, and made use of these authentic materials in several of his works: Sonata for Solo Flute (1954); Harp Concerto (1957); *Te kuduam mapuche* for Voice, Bassoon, and the Araucanian Drum Kultrún (1958); *4 movimientos sinfónicos* (1960).

Isbin, Sharon, American guitarist and teacher; b. Minneapolis, Aug. 7, 1956. She studied with Jeffrey Van in Minneapolis, then took courses at Yale Univ. (B.A., 1978; M.A., 1979); she also received instruction from Rosalyn Tureck, from Oscar Ghiglia at the Aspen (Colo.) Music School (1971–75), and from Alirio Diaz at the Banff Music Festival (1972). She won 1st prizes in the Toronto International Guitar Competition (1975), the Munich International Guitar Competition (1976), and the Queen Sofia Competition in Madrid (1979), subsequently appearing throughout the world as a soloist with orchs. and as a recitalist. She taught at N.Y.'s Manhattan School of Music (from 1979) and Mannes College of Music (from 1984). In 1989 she became head of the guitar dept. at N.Y.'s Juilliard School. Her repertoire ranges from the Classical period to jazz, folk, and beyond. She has commissioned works from a variety of composers, including Leo Brouwer, Joan Tower, and Joseph Schwanter.

BIBL.: H. Waleson, "Magnificent Obsession: S. I.'s—with the Guitar—Opens New Horizons," *Musical America* (Jan. 1988).

Iseler, Elmer (Walter), prominent Canadian choral conductor; b. Port Colborne, near Niagara Falls, Ontario, Oct. 14, 1927. He studied piano and organ; then studied church music at Waterloo Lutheran Univ.; subsequently completed his education at the Univ. of Toronto (B.Mus., 1950). He taught music in high schools in Toronto (1952–64); in 1964 he became conductor of the Toronto Mendelssohn Choir; he also taught choral music at the Univ. of Toronto (1965–68) and founded the Elmer Iseler Singers in 1978. He ed. the Festival Singers of Canada Choral Series. Iseler is generally acknowledged as one of Canada's leading choral conductors. In 1975 he was made an Officer of the Order of Canada.

Isepp, Martin (Johannes Sebastian), Austrian pianist and harpsichordist; b. Vienna, Sept. 30, 1930. He studied at Lincoln College, Oxford, and at the Royal Academy of Music in London. In 1957 he joined the music staff of the Glyndebourne Festival, serving as head of its music staff from 1978 to 1993. From 1973 to 1976 he was head of opera training at Juilliard School in N.Y.; also was head of music studies at the National Opera Studio in London (1978–95) and head of the academy of singing at the Banff Centre School of Fine Arts in Canada (1981–93). He became best known as an accompanist to many of the foremost singers of the day, including Dame Janet Baker, Hans Hotter, Elisabeth Schwarzkopf, and John Shirley-Quirk.

Isham, Mark, American composer and instrumentalist; b. N.Y., Sept. 7, 1951. His mother was a violinist, and his father taught music and art; he studied piano, violin, and trumpet from an early age. After his family moved to California, he played trumpet in the Oakland and San Francisco Syms. and in the San Francisco Opera Orch.; also played in various jazz and rock bands, including the Beach Boys. He became a synthesizer programmer in the early 1970s, and in 1979 he formed (with Peter Maunu, Patrick O'Hearn, and Terry Bozzio) the groundbreaking art-rock Group 87, which produced 2 albums before its demise in 1986. His first solo album (1983) was the first electronic release by the New Age label Windham Hill. Among his film scores is the important documentary *The Times of Harvey Milk* (1985); also *The Moderns* (1988). His music is slow and delicate, overlapping harmonies and rhythms in a haze of electronics; it is distinct from other New Age music in its nobility, a hieratic effect created by his special use of brass instruments. Among his compositions are *Vapor Drawings* (1983), *Castalia* (1988), and *Tibet* (1989).

Ishii, Kan, Japanese composer, brother of **Maki Ishii**; b. Tokyo, March 30, 1921. He is one of two sons of Baku Ishii, a renowned scholar of modern dance. He studied in Tokyo at the Musashino Music School with Goh, Ikenouchi, and Odaka (1939–43); in 1952 he took lessons with Orff at the Hochschule für Musik in Munich. Returning to Japan, he taught at the Tōhō Gakuen School of Music in Tokyo (1954–66), the Aichi-Prefectural Arts Univ. in Nagoya (1966–86), and the Showa Music College (from 1986).

WORKS: DRAMATIC: OPERAS: *Mermaid and Red Candle* (1961); *Kaguyahime* (Prince Kaguya; 1963); *En-no-Gyojia* (Tokyo, 1964); *Lady Kesa and Morito* (Tokyo, Nov. 24, 1968); *Women are Wonderful* (1978); *Kantomi* (1981). **OPERETTA:** *Blue Lion* (1989). **BALLETS:** *God and the Bayadere* (Tokyo, Nov. 6, 1950); *Birth of a Human* (Tokyo, Nov. 27, 1954); *Frökln Julie* (1955); *Shakuntara* (1961); *Marimo* (Tokyo, 1963); *Biruma no tategoto* (Harp of Burma; 1963); *Haniwa* (1963); *Hakai* (1965); *Ichiyo Higuchi* (1966). **ORCH.:** *Yama* (Mountain), symphonic poem (Tokyo, Oct. 7, 1954); *Kappa's Penny* for Youth Orch. (1956). **CHAMBER:** *Music* for 8 Percussionists (1970); Viola Sonata (1960); *Music* for Flute (1972). **VOCAL:** *Sinfonia Ainu* for Soprano, Chorus, and Orch. (1958–59); *The Reef*, cantata for Baritone, Chorus, 4 Pianos, and Percussion (1967); *Akita the Great* for Chorus and Brass (1968); *Foot steps to Tomorrow*, cantata for Solo Soprano (1972); folk songs; choruses.

Ishii, Maki, Japanese composer and conductor, brother of **Kan Ishii**; b. Tokyo, May 28, 1936. His father, Baku Ishii, was a celebrated scholar of modern dance. As a child, he was introduced to traditional Japanese instruments. Later he studied piano, violin, and theory. After receiving instruction in conducting from Watanabe (1952–54), he studied theory and composition with Ifukube and Ikenouchi (from 1956) in Tokyo. In 1958 he went to Berlin to study composition with Blacher, counterpoint with Pepping, and 12-tone technique with Rufer. Upon returning to Tokyo in 1961, he was active with the electronic music studio at the NHK. In 1969 he was again in Berlin on a scholarship from the Deutscher Akademischer Austauschdienst. He subsequently was active as a composer and conductor in contemporary music circles in Europe, the U.S., and Asia. From 1978 to 1984 he was host and conductor of the TBS-TV program "Here Comes the Orchestra" in Japan. After serving as artistic director of the Tokyo Summer Festival from 1985 to 1989, he founded the Asian Music Festival there in 1990. In his works, Ishii attempts to combine the coloristic effects of Japanese instruments with European techniques of serial music and electronic sounds.

WORKS: *Prelude and Variations* for 9 Players (1959–60); 7 *Stücke* for Small Orch. (1960–61); *Transitions* for Small Orch. (1962); *Aphorismen I* for String Trio, Percussion, and Piano (1963) and *II* for Piano (1972); *Galgenlieder* for Baritone, Men's Chorus, and 13 Players (1964); *Characters* for Flute, Oboe, Piano, and Guitar (1965); *Hamon* for Violin, Chamber Ensemble, and Tape (1965); *Expressions* for Strings (1967); *5 Elements* for Guitar and 6 Players (1967); *Piano Piece* for Pianist and Percussionist (1968); *Kyō-ō* for Piano, Orch., and Tape (1968); *Kyō-sō* for Percussion and Orch. (1969); *La-sen I* for 7 Players and Tape (1969) and *II* for Cello (1970); *Sō-gū I* for Shakuhachi and Piano (1970) and *II* for Gagaku and Orch. (1971; work resulting from simultaneous perf. of *Music* for Gagaku and *Dipol*); *Music* for Gagaku (1970); *Dipol* for Orch. (1971); *Sen-ten* for Percussion Player and Tape (1971); *Chō-etsu* for Chamber Group and Tape (1973); *Polaritäten* for Soloists and Orch. (1973; work exists in 3 versions, each having different soloists: *I* for Biwa and Harp, *II* for Shakuhachi and Flute, and *III* for Biwa, Harp, Shakuhachi, and Flute); *Synkretismen* for Marimba, 7 Soloists, Strings, and 3 Percussionists (1973); *Anime Amare* for Harp and Tape (1974); *Jō* for Orch. (1975); *Lost Sounds III*, violin concerto (1978); *Translucent Vision* for Orch. (1981–82); *Afro-Concerto* for Percussion and Orch. (1982); *Kaguya-Hime*, symphonic suite for Percussion Group (1984); *Gioh*, symphonic poem for Yokobue (Japanese Flute) and Orch. (1984); *Gedatsu*, concerto for Yokobue and Orch. (1985); *Herbst Variante* for Orch. (1986); *Intrada* for Orch. (1986); *Concertante* for Marimba and 6 Percussionists (1988); *Fū Shi I* for Orch. (1989) and *II* for Nō-kan and Small Orch. (1989); *Suien Densetsu/Legend of the Water Flame* for Yokobue, Percussion, Reciter, and Dance (1990); *Weisser Nachtklang*, ode to Tchaikovsky for Strings (1990); *Strange Tales: Urashima Tarō/A Fiction: Relativity Theory*, "iconological performance" for Gagaku, Syōmyō, Percussion, Bugaku, and Modern Dance (1991); *South—Fire—Summer*, percussion concerto (1992); *Floating Wind*, symphonic triptych (1992); *West—Gold—Autumn* for String Quartet (1992).

Isler, Ernst, Swiss organist and music critic; b. Zürich, Sept. 30, 1879; d. there, Sept. 26, 1944. He studied at the Zürich Music School (1895–99) and with Rudorff at the Berlin Hochschule für Musik (1899–1901). He was organist at Zürich's Reformed Church (1901–19) and of the Fraumünster (1919–42), and also taught at the Cons. He became music critic of the influential daily newspaper *Neue Zürcher Zeitung* in 1902, and held this position until his death; from 1910 to 1927 he was also ed. of the *Schweizerische Musikzeitung*. He publ. *Das Züricherische Musikleben seit der Eröffnung der neuen Tonhalle (1895)* (2 vols., Zürich, 1935–36).

BIBL.: H. Grossmann et al., eds., *E. I. zum Gedächtnis* (Zürich, 1944).

Isoir, André, French organist; b. St.-Dizier, July 20, 1935. He studied in Paris at the École Cesar Franck with Souberbielle and at the Cons. with Falcinelli, where he received the premier prix in 1960. In 1965 he took 1st prize in the St. Alban's Competition in England, then won 3 consecutive annual prizes in the Haarlem Competition in the Netherlands (1966–68). He served as organist at St.-Médard (1952–67), St.-Séverin (1967–73), and St.-Germain-des-Prés (from 1973). As a recitalist, he became particularly well known for his performances of the works of J.S. Bach.

Ísólfsson, Páll, distinguished Icelandic organist, administrator, and composer; b. Stokkseyri, Oct. 12, 1893; d. Reykjavík, Nov. 23, 1974. He was an organ student of Straube in Leipzig (1913–18), where he was an assistant organist at the Thomaskirche (1917–19). Following further training with Bonnet in Paris (1925), he settled in Reykjavík. He was founding director of the College of Music (1930–57), head of the music dept. of the Icelandic State Broadcasting Service (1930–59), and organist at the Cathedral (1939–68). He also made tours as a recitalist. In 1945 the Univ. of Oslo awarded him an honorary doctorate and in 1956 he was elected a member of the Royal Swedish Academy in Stockholm. He publ. an autobiography (2 vols., 1963–64). Among his compositions were a few orch. works; much vocal music, including a cantata for the 1,000th anniversary of the Icelandic Althing (Parliament; 1930), a university cantata, and a cantata for the 900th anniversary of the bishopric of Skálholt (1956), as well as mixed and men's choruses and numerous songs for voice and piano; several organ works, including preludes, chorale preludes, *Introduction and Passacaglia*, and a chaconne; piano pieces.

BIBL.: J. Thorarinsson, *P. I.* (Reykjavík, 1963).

Isoz, Kálmán, Hungarian musicologist; b. Budapest, Dec. 7, 1878; d. there, June 6, 1956. He studied piano and theory at the Budapest Cons. (1895–99); later completed his training at the Univ. of Budapest (Ph.D., 1921, with the diss. *Latin zenei paleográfia és a Pray-kódex zenei hangjelzései* [Latin Musical Paleography and the Musical Notation of the Pray Manuscript]; publ. in Budapest, 1922). In 1897 he joined the staff of the Hungarian National Museum in Budapest, where he was its general secretary (from 1920); from 1908 he also taught at the Univ. of Budapest. From 1924 to 1934 he was chief librarian of the Széchényi Library in Budapest, and then served as secretary of the Hungarian Royal Academy of Music from 1934 to 1943. With D. Bartha, he ed. Musicologica Hungaria. His writings on Hungarian music and musicians remain valuable sources.

WRITINGS (all publ. in Budapest): With I. Mészáros, *A filharmóniai társaság multja és jelene, 1853–1903* (Past and Present of the Philharmonic Society, 1853–1903; 1903); *Arnold György* (1908); *Erkel és a szimfónikus zene; Erkel emlékek és levelezés* (Erkel and Symphonic Music; Erkel Documents and Correspondence; 1910); *Erkel Ferenc* (1910); *Doppler Ferenc levelei Erkelhez* (Ferenc Doppler's Letters to Erkel; 1911); *Buda és Pest zenei müvelődése, I: 1686–1873* (The Musical Culture of Buda and Pest, I: 1686–1873; 1926); *Magyar zeneművek könyvészete: Petőfi dalok* (Hungarian Bibliography of Music: Petőfi Songs; 1931); *A Pest-Budai Hangászegyesület es nyilvános hangversenyei, 1836–1851* (The Musical Society of Pest-Buda and its Public Concerts, 1836–1851; 1934); *Erkel Ferenc "Bátori Máriá"-ja* (1944).

Israel, Brian M., American composer, pianist, and teacher; b. N.Y., Feb. 5, 1951; d. Syracuse, N.Y., May 8, 1986. He wrote an opera before he was 8, and received BMI student composer awards in 1966 and 1968; he pursued training in composition with Kay at Lehman College in N.Y. (B.A., 1971) and with Palmer, Phillips, and Husa at Cornell Univ. (M.F.A., 1974; D.M.A., 1975), where he was on the faculty (1972–75). In 1975 he began teaching at Syracuse Univ., and in 1984 was made a prof. there. As a pianist, he performed much contemporary music. At the time of his death from leukemia, he was at the height of his compositional creativity. His works form an eclectic traversal from Baroque contrapuntal devices to serialism, juxtaposing humor and grotesqueries. He wrote extensively for concert band and frequently featured lesser-used instruments in solos.

WORKS: OPERAS: *Ladies' Voices*, mini-opera (1970); *The Obtaining of Portia*, chamber opera (Bloomington, Ind., April 13, 1976); *Love and Other Important Nonsense* (1977); *Winnie the Pooh*, children's opera (Syracuse, June 1, 1979). **ORCH.:** *Contrasts* for Cello and Orch. (1967); Sym. No. 2 (1974), No. 4 for Women's Chorus and Orch. (1984), and No. 6 for Soprano, Bass, and Orch. (Syracuse, N.Y., May 4, 1986); Viola Concerto (1974); *Dorian Variations* for Strings (1981); 2 sinfoniettas (1983, 1985); Mandolin Concerto (1985). **BAND:** Sym. No. 1 (1972–74), No. 3 (1981), and No. 5 for Men's Chorus, Organ, and Band (1983–84); *Concerto Sacra* (1974); Piano Concerto (1979; Ithaca, N.Y., March 2, 1980); *Concerto Buffo* for 9 Soloists and Band (1980); Baritone Saxophone Concerto (1982); Trumpet Concerto (1982); *Rhapsody* for Baritone Horn and Band (1983); *Winter Evening Song* (1983); Clarinet Concerto (1984); Double Concerto for Sopranino and Bass Saxophones and Band (1984). **CHAMBER:** Sonata for Cello and Percussion (1969); Clarinet Sonata (1969); 3 string quartets: No. 1, *Canonic Variations* (1971), No. 2, *Musik für den nachsten toten* (1976; rev. 1983), and No. 3 (1978); *Pastoral* for Oboe, Strings, and Piano (1971); Oboe Sonata (1972); Wind Quartet (1973); Piano Quintet (1973); *Dance Variations* for Trumpet and Tape (1974); 2 sonatas for 2 Tubas (1976, 1977); Sonata for 2 Trombones (1977); *Characteristic Variations* for Trumpet (1978); Concertino for Clarinet and String Quartet (1978); *Serenade* for 3 Trumpets (1978); Piano Trio, "in memoriam Ernest Bloch" (1980); Sonata for 2 Horns (1980); Concerto for Tuba Ensemble (1980); Alto Saxophone Sonata (1980); *Sonata di Chiesa* for 4 Trumpets (1983); *Serenata* for Flute, Cello, and Harpsichord (1983); Concertino for Saxophone Ensemble (1985); *Sonatinetta* for Mandolin and Guitar (1984); *Arioso and Canzona* for Saxophone Ensemble (1985); *Surrealistic Serenade* for Mandolin and Euphonium (1985); Piano Quartet, *Variations on a Hymn Tune* (1985); *Trois Grotesques* for Clarinet or Soprano Saxophone and Piano (1985). **PIANO:** *Night Variations* (1973); *6 Miniatures* (1982); *12 Bagatelles* (1985). **VOCAL:** *Madrigal on Nudity* for Chorus (1971); *. . . Where Night Gathers* for Tenor and 2 Pianos (1974); *M'bevrashua*, after Burma Shave road signs, for Chorus and Percussion (1974); *Lovesongs, Lions, and Lullabyes (Barcarolles)* for Soprano, Clarinet, and Piano (1979); *In Praise of Practically Nothing* for Tenor and 9 Instruments (1980); *Psalm 117* for Chorus, Organ, and Trumpet (1981); *The Song of Moses*, canticle for Chorus, Organ, and Brass Quartet (1985).

Isserlis, Julius, Russian pianist; b. Kishinev, Nov. 7, 1888; d. London, July 23, 1968. He studied with Puchalsky at the Kiev Cons.; then with Safonov and Taneyev at the Moscow Cons. He taught at the Moscow Phil. Inst. of Music (1913–23), then in Vienna (1923–28); in 1928 he settled in London. In addition to Russian composers, he was known for his performances of Chopin. He wrote a number of character pieces for piano.

Isserlis, Steven, English cellist; b. London, Dec. 19, 1958. He received his training at the International Cello Centre in London (1969–76) and at the Oberlin (Ohio) College-Cons. of Music (1976–78). In 1977 he made his London debut at Wigmore Hall, and then performed throughout England. His tours abroad have taken him all over Europe, North America, and Israel; in addition to his solo engagements with orchs., was also active as a recitalist and chamber music performer. In 1993 he received the Gregor Piatigorsky Artist Award. His repertoire embraces the traditional cello repertoire, including early music played on original instruments, and also includes much contemporary music. In 1989 he was soloist in the premiere of Tavener's *The Protecting Veil* at the London Promenade Concerts.

Istel, Edgar, eminent German musicologist; b. Mainz, Feb. 23, 1880; d. Miami, Fla., Dec. 17, 1948. He studied composition with Volbach in Mainz, and then took courses with Thuille at the Munich Hochschule für Musik and Sandberger at the Univ. of Munich (Ph.D., 1900, with the diss. *J.J. Rousseau als Komponist seiner lyrischen Scene "Pygmalion"*; publ. in *Publikatio-*

nen der International Musikgesellschaft, I/i, Leipzig, 1901). He was active as a lecturer, critic, and writer on music in Munich (1900–1913), and then taught at Berlin's Humboldt Academy (1913–19) and Lessing Hochschule (1919–20). In 1920 he moved to Madrid, where he remained until the outbreak of the civil war in 1936; then went to England, and eventually to the U.S. (1938). He was also a composer; wrote 5 operas, oratorios, and smaller pieces.

WRITINGS: *Das deutsche Weihnachtsspiel und seine Wiedergeburt aus dem Geiste der Musik* (1901); *Richard Wagner im Lichte eines zeitgenössischen Briefwechsels* (1902); *Peter Cornelius* (1906); *Die Entstehung des deutschen Melodramas* (1906); *Die komische Oper* (1906); *Die Blützeit der musikalischen Romantik in Deutschland* (1909); *Das Kunstwerk Richard Wagners* (1910); *Das Libretto* (1914; Eng. tr., 1922, as *The Art of Writing Opera Librettos*); *Die moderne Oper vom Tode Wagners bis zum Weltkrieg* (1915); *Niccolo Paganini* (1919); *Revolution und Oper* (1919); *Das Buch der Oper* (1919); *Die deutschen Meister von Gluck bis Wagner* (1919); *Bizet und Carmen* (1927).

Istomin, Eugene (George), distinguished American pianist; b. N.Y., Nov. 26, 1925. He began piano lessons as a child with Kiriena Siloti, and then studied at the Mannes College of Music in N.Y.; at 12, he entered the Curtis Inst. of Music in Philadelphia, where he was a student of Serkin and Horszowski. After winning the Philadelphia Orch. youth competition, he appeared with that orch. under Ormandy's direction as soloist in Chopin's 2nd Piano Concerto on Nov. 17, 1943. He also won the Leventritt Award, which led to his first appearance as soloist with the N.Y. Phil. under Rodzinski's direction in Brahms's 2nd Piano Concerto on Nov. 21, 1943. In succeeding years, he was engaged as a soloist with principal American orchs. and was active as a recitalist. From 1956 he made regular tours abroad. He also played in the renowned Stern-Rose-Istomin Trio from 1961 until Rose's death in 1984. In 1975 he married Casals's widow Martita. Istomin was one of the leading pianists of his generation.

Istrate, Mircea, Romanian pianist and composer; b. Cluj, Sept. 27, 1929. He studied piano and composition at the Cluj Cons. (1945–53) and in Bucharest (1954–57), where he subsequently taught piano.

WORKS: ORCH.: *Muzică stereofonică* for 2 String Orchs. (1955–57); *Algoritm* (1964); *Interferente* (Interferences) for Orch. and Electronics (1965); *Pulsations* (1973). **CHAMBER:** Flute Sonata (1954); *Burlesca* for Violin, Oboe, Clarinet, Bassoon, and Double Bass (1955); Oboe Sonata (1962); *Evenimente I–II–III,* etc., for Prepared Piano, Percussion within a Piano, Electric Guitar, Double Bass, Vibraphone, Horn, Marimba, and Tape (1966). **VOCAL:** *Evocare* for Mezzo-soprano, Women's Chorus, and Orch. (1960); *Pe o plajă japoneză* (On a Japanese Beach), sequences for Women's Chorus, Orch., and Tape (1961); songs.

Ištvan, Miloslav, Czech composer and teacher; b. Olomouc, Sept. 2, 1928; d. Brno, Jan. 20, 1990. He was a student of Kvapil at the Brno Academy of Music and Dramatic Arts (1948–52), and then completed his postgraduate studies there (1953–56). In 1956 he joined its faculty as an assistant lecturer, becoming a lecturer there in 1966. He was also active with the avant-garde Group A and Group B, and worked in the electronic music studios of Brno Radio. In 1961 he won the Janáček Prize, and in 1982 and 1988 he was awarded prizes of the Union of Czech Composers. After following nationalist trends in his works, he adopted contemporary techniques, including serialism and electronics.

WORKS: ORCH.: Concerto for Horn, Strings, and Piano (1949); Sym. (1952); *Winter Suite* for Strings, Piano, and Percussion (1956); Concerto-Sym. for Piano and Orch. (1957); *Ballad of the South,* 3 symphonic frescoes after Lewis Allan's satirical view of the American South (1960); Concertino for Violin and Chamber Orch. (1961); *6 Studies* for Chamber Orch. (1964); Sonata for Violin and Chamber Orch. (1970); *In Memoriam Josef Berg* (1971); *Shakespearean Variations* (1975); *The Games* (1977); *Partita* for 16 Strings (1980); *Tempus Ire* (1983); *Solitude* for Strings (1988). **CHAMBER:** Trio for Clarinet, Cello, and Piano (1950); Clarinet Sonata (1954); Piano Trio (1958); *Dodekameron* for 12 Players (1962–64); 2 string quartets (1963, 1986); *Ritmi ed antiritmi* for 2 Pianos and 2 Percussionists (1966); Cello Sonata (1970); *Omaggio à J.S. Bach* for Wind Quintet (1971); *Psalmus niger* for 6 Percussionists (1971); *Blacked-out Landscape,* in memory of those fallen in World War II, for String Quartet (1975); *The Micro-Worlds Diptych: Summer Micro-Worlds* for Flute, Harp, and Harpsichord, and *Micro-Worlds of My Town* for 2 Violas, Oboe, and Clarinet (1977); *Capriccio* for Vibraphone, Marimba, and Percussion (1978); *Canto I* for Viola (1979), *II* for Prepared Violas and Woman's Voice (1980), and *III* for Flute (1983); Trio for Clarinet, Piano, and Percussion (1987); *Rotations and Returns* for Horn, Viola, and Cello (1988). **PIANO:** 3 sonatas (1954, 1959, 1978); *Odyssey of a Child from Lidice* (1963); *Variations* for 2 Pianos (1972). **VOCAL:** *Conjuration of Time* for 2 Narrators and Orch. (1967); *I, Jacob* for Soprano, Pop Tenor, Speaker, Instrumental Ensemble, and Tape (1968); *Love, Defiance, and Death* for Mezzo-soprano and Chamber Ensemble (1984); Vocal Sym. (1986); *Variations on a Renaissance Theme* for Chorus and Chamber Orch. (1988).

Ito, Ryûta, Japanese composer; b. Kure, March 4, 1922. He graduated from the faculty of medicine of the Univ. of Tokyo in 1946 (Doctor of Medical Science, 1955); then studied composition with Takata, Moroi, Ikenouchi, and Fukai. Subsequently he divided his interests between music and medicine and became a prof. of pharmacy at the school of medicine of Toho Univ.; also served as secretary and a member of the committee of the Japanese Soc. for Contemporary Music (1952–61).

WORKS: CHAMBER OPERA: *The Court of Judgment* (1954). **ORCH.:** *Allemand and Aria* (1945; Tokyo, May 19, 1950); *2 Moments* (Tokyo, Oct. 29, 1947); *Divertissement* (1950); *Festival Music* (1953); Suite for Strings (1954); *Ostinato concertanto* for Piano and Orch. (Tokyo, Oct. 18, 1957); *Temariuta* (Handball Song; 1958); Concerto for Japanese Flute and Orch. (Tokyo, Nov. 28, 1958); *Suzuka,* suite (1959); *Suite* for Chamber Orch. (1959); *Suite* (1961); *Les Cloches,* symphonic suite for Japanese Instruments, Celesta, Percussion, Men's Chorus, Viola, Cello, and Double Bass (Tokyo, Nov. 9, 1971); *Movement* for String Ensemble (1983); Concerto for Shakuhachi, Jūshichi-gen, and Orch. (1989); *Fantasia alla Yoshizawa* (1990). **OTHER:** *Abrasion of a Life,* suite for Chorus (1984); several works for Japanese instruments, including 3 duets for Shakuhachi and Jūshichi-gen (1987–90).

Iturbi, José, celebrated Spanish pianist and conductor; b. Valencia, Nov. 28, 1895; d. Los Angeles, June 28, 1980. He began playing the piano at the incredible age of 3, and by the time he was 7 he was earning a living by appearing in street cafes. Following training at the Valencia Cons. (1st prize, 1908), he studied with Maláts, at the Paris Cons. with Staub (premier prix, 1912), and in Barcelona. After serving as head of the piano dept. at the Geneva Cons. (1919–23), he embarked on a brilliant career as a virtuoso. In 1923 he made a highly successful London debut, and then toured Europe and South America. On Oct. 10, 1929, he made his U.S. debut in Philadelphia, and subsequently appeared widely in America. In 1933 he made his debut as a conductor in Mexico City, and therefter pursued a dual career as a pianist and conductor, sometimes conducting from the keyboard. From 1936 to 1944 he was conductor of the Rochester (N.Y.) Phil. Iturbi was one of the most popular classical artists of his day, a popularity enhanced by his film appearances and recordings. While he had his detractors as an interpreter of the classics, there was no denying his idiomatic mastery of Spanish music. He also composed a number of piano pieces in the Spanish vein. His sister, Amparo Iturbi (b. Valencia, March 12, 1898; d. Beverly Hills, April 21, 1969), was also a talented pianist. She frequently appeared in duo concerts with her brother in the U.S. and Europe.

Ivanov, Georgi, Bulgarian conductor and composer; b. Sofia, Aug. 23, 1924. He studied with Lubomir Pipkov and Veselin Stoyanov in Sofia; then went to Moscow, where he studied with Shaporin (1946–50). Returning to Bulgaria, he became conductor of the National Youth Theater in Sofia. Among his works are 2 symphonic poems: *Legend of the Lopian Forest* (Sofia, Feb. 15, 1951) and *The Mutiny on the S.S. Nadezhda* (1955); Sym. (Sofia, June 22, 1960); *Divertimento* for Clarinet, Violin, Harpsichord, and Chamber Orch. (1962); *Metamorphosis* for Strings (1967); *Timbres in Rhythm* for Orch. (1968); *Variations* for Orch. (1969); *Musica concertante* for Orch. (1970).

Ivanov, Konstantin, Russian conductor and composer; b. Efremov, May 21, 1907; d. Moscow, April 15, 1984. He played trumpet in Soviet cavalry orchs.; then enrolled in the conducting class at the Moscow Cons.; after graduation in 1937, he served as assistant conductor at various operatic and sym. posts. From 1941 to 1946 he was conductor of the Bolshoi Radio Orch.; from 1946 to 1975 he was conductor of the State Sym. Orch. of the U.S.S.R.; made world tours with it, which included the U.S. and Japan, as well as countries of Western Europe. He wrote several symphonic poems and a Double Bass Concerto.

Ivanov-Boretzky, Mikhail Vladimirovich, Russian musicologist and composer; b. Moscow, June 16, 1874; d. there, April 1, 1936. He studied jurisprudence at the Univ. of Moscow, graduating in 1896; at the same time, he took music lessons; in 1898 he went to St. Petersburg and became a student of composition of Rimsky-Korsakov. From 1921 to 1936 he taught at the Moscow Cons. His music was mainly imitative of Rimsky-Korsakov's works. He wrote the operas *Adolfina* (Moscow, Dec. 10, 1908) and *The Witch* (Moscow, Aug. 14, 1918); Sym.; piano music; choruses; songs. His importance to Russian music, however, lies in his writings. He publ. monographs on Palestrina, Handel, Schumann, Mendelssohn, and Beethoven; also a useful anthology of music history, with a synoptic table of 18th-century music (Moscow, 1934). A collection of his articles was publ. in Moscow in 1972.

Ivanov-Radkevitch, Nikolai, Russian composer and teacher; b. Krasnoyarsk, Siberia, Feb. 10, 1904; d. Moscow, Feb. 4, 1962. He studied composition with Glière and orchestration with Vasilenko at the Moscow Cons., graduating in 1928; subsequently was on its faculty (1929–48). In 1952 he was appointed instructor in orchestration at the Inst. of Military Bandleaders of the Soviet Army. He was particularly successful in writing popular marches for band, of which *Our Own Moscow* and *Victory March* received the State Prize. He also composed 4 syms. (1928, 1932, 1937, 1945); 12 symphonic suites on folk motifs; Violin Sonata; various pieces for other instruments; film music.

Ivanovs, Janis, Latvian composer and teacher; b. Preili, Oct. 9, 1906; d. Riga, March 27, 1983. He studied composition with Wihtol, piano with Dauge, and conducting with Schneevoigt at the Riga Cons., graduating in 1931; then worked at the Latvian Radio; in 1944 he was appointed to the composition faculty at the Riga Cons. An exceptionally fecund composer, he wrote 20 syms., several of a programmatic nature descriptive of the Latvian countryside, including No. 1, *Symphonie-Poème* (1933), No. 2, *Atlantida* (1941), No. 6, *Latgales* (Latvian; 1949), No. 12, *Sinfonia energica* (1967), and No. 13, *Symphonia humana* (1969). His symphonic poems also reflect nature scenes; e.g., *Varaviksne* (Rainbow; 1938) and *Padebešu Kalns* (Mountain under the Sky; 1939). He further wrote 3 string quartets (1933, 1946, 1961); Cello Concerto (1938); Violin Concerto (1951); Piano Concerto (1959); choruses; songs; piano pieces; film music.

BIBL.: N. Grünfeld, *J. I.* (Moscow, 1959); V. Berzina, *Dzives simfonija Jana I.* (Riga, 1964).

Ives, Charles (Edward), one of the most remarkable American composers, whose individual genius created music so original, so universal, and yet so deeply national in its sources of inspiration that it profoundly changed the direction of American music; b. Danbury, Conn., Oct. 20, 1874; d. N.Y., May 19, 1954. His father, George Ives, was a bandmaster of the 1st Conn. Heavy Artillery during the Civil War, and the early development of Ives was, according to his own testimony, deeply influenced by his father. At the age of 12, he played the drums in the band and also received from his father rudimentary musical training in piano and cornet playing. At the age of 13, he played organ at the Danbury Church; soon he began to improvise freely at the piano, without any dependence on school rules; as a result of his experimentation in melody and harmony, encouraged by his father, he began to combine several keys, partly as a spoof, but eventually as a legitimate alternative to traditional music; at 13, he also wrote the *Holiday Quick Step*, which was first performed in Danbury on Jan. 16, 1888; at 17, he composed his *Variations on America* for organ in a polytonal setting. In 1894 he entered Yale Univ., where he took regular academic courses and studied organ with Buck and composition with Parker; from Parker he received a fine classical training; while still in college, he composed 2 full-fledged syms., written in an entirely traditional manner demonstrating great skill in formal structure, fluent melodic development, and smooth harmonic modulations. After his graduation in 1898, Ives joined an insurance company; he also played organ at the Central Presbyterian Church in N.Y. (1899–1902). In 1907 he formed an insurance partnership with Julian Myrick of N.Y.; he proved himself to be an exceptionally able businessman; the firm of Ives & Myrick prospered, and Ives continued to compose music as an avocation. In 1908 he married Harmony Twichell. In 1918 he suffered a massive heart attack, complicated by a diabetic condition, and was compelled to curtail his work both in business and in music because his illness made it difficult to handle a pen. He retired from business in 1930, and by that time had virtually stopped composing. In 1919 Ives publ. at his own expense his great masterpiece, the *Concord Sonata*, for piano, inspired by the writings of Emerson, Hawthorne, the Alcotts, and Thoreau. Although written early in the century, its idiom is so extraordinary, and its technical difficulties so formidable, that the work did not receive a performance in its entirety until John Kirkpatrick played it in N.Y. in 1939. In 1922 Ives brought out, also at his expense, a vol. of *114 Songs*, written between 1888 and 1921 and marked by great diversity of style, ranging from lyrical Romanticism to powerful and dissonant modern invocations. Both the *Concord Sonata* and the *114 Songs* were distributed gratis by Ives to anyone wishing to receive copies. His orch. masterpiece, *3 Places in New England*, also had to wait nearly 2 decades before its first performance; of the monumental 4th Sym., only the 2nd movement was performed in 1927, and its complete performance was given posthumously in 1965. In 1947 Ives received the Pulitzer Prize in Music for his 3rd Sym., written in 1911.

The slow realization of the greatness of Ives and the belated triumphant recognition of his music were phenomena with little precedence in music history. Because of his chronic ailment, and also on account of his personal disposition, Ives lived as a recluse, away from the mainstream of American musical life; he never went to concerts and did not own a record player or a radio; while he was well versed in the musical classics, and studied the scores of Beethoven, Schumann, and Brahms, he took little interest in sanctioned works of modern composers; yet he anticipated many technical innovations, such as polytonality, atonality, and even 12-tone formations, as well as polymetric and polyrhythmic configurations, which were prophetic for his time. In the 2nd movement of the *Concord Sonata*, he specified the application of a strip of wood on the white and the black keys of the piano to produce an echo-like sonority; in his unfinished *Universe Symphony* he planned an antiphonal representation of the heavens in chordal counterpoint and the earth in contrasting orch. groups. He also composed pieces of quarter-tone piano music. A unique quality of his music was the combination of simple motifs, often derived from American church hymns and popular ballads, with an extremely complex dissonant counterpoint which formed the supporting network for the melodic lines. A curious idiosyncrasy is the frequent quotation of the "fate motive" of Beethoven's 5th Sym. in many of his works. Materials of his instrumental and vocal works often overlap, and the titles are often changed during the process of composition. In his orchestrations, he often indicated interchangeable and optional parts, as in the last movement of the *Concord Sonata*, which has a part for flute obbligato; thus he reworked the original score for large orch. of his *3 Places in New England* for a smaller ensemble to fit the requirements of Slonimsky's Chamber Orch. of Boston, which gave its first performance, and it was in this version that the work was first publ. and widely performed until the restoration of the large score was made in 1974.

Ives also possessed an uncommon gift for literary expression; his annotations to his works are both trenchant and humorous; he publ. in 1920 *Essays before a Sonata* as a literary companion vol. to the *Concord Sonata*; his *Memos* in the form of a diary, publ. after his death, reveal an extraordinary power of aphoristic utterance. He was acutely conscious of his civic duties as an American, and once circulated a proposal to have federal laws enacted by popular referendum. His centennial in 1974 was celebrated by a series of conferences at his alma mater, Yale Univ.; in N.Y., Miami, and many other American cities; and in Europe, including Russia. While during his lifetime he and a small group of devoted friends and admirers had great difficulties in having his works performed, recorded, or publ., a veritable Ives cult emerged after his death; eminent conductors gave repeated performances of his orch. works, and modern pianists were willing to cope with the forbidding difficulties of his works. The influence of his music on the new generation of composers reached a high mark, so that the adjective "Ivesian" became common in music criticism to describe certain acoustical and coloristic effects characteristic of his music. All of the Ives MSS and his correspondence were deposited by his widow at Yale Univ., forming a basic Ives archive. The Charles Ives Soc., in N.Y., promotes research and publications. Letters from Ives to N. Slonimsky are reproduced in the latter's book *Music Since 1900* (5th ed., N.Y., 1993). The film *A Good Dissonance Like a Man* (1977) depicts the life of Ives with fine dramatic impact.

WORKS: ORCH.: March No. 2 (1892); March No. 3 (1892); Postlude (1895); Overture (1895?); 4 numbered syms.: No. 1 (1896–98; Washington, D.C., April 26, 1953, R. Bales conducting), No. 2 (1900–1902; N.Y., Feb. 22, 1951, Bernstein conducting), No. 3, *The Camp Meeting* (1904; N.Y., April 5, 1946, L. Harrison conducting), and No. 4 (1909–16; 1st complete perf., N.Y., April 26, 1965, Stokowski conducting); *Universe Symphony* (1911–28; unfinished; Los Angeles, Dec. 13, 1984); *Fugue in 4 Keys, on The Shining Shore* for Flute, Cornet, and Strings (1897); *Yale-Princeton Football Game* (1898?); *Cartoons (Take-offs)* for Small Orch. (1898?–1916); *Ragtime Dances* Nos. 1–4 for Small Orch. (1902–04; unfinished); *Overture and March "1776"* for Small Orch. (1903); *Country Band March* for Small Orch. (1903); *The General Slocum* (1904; unfinished); *Thanksgiving and/or Forefathers' Day* (1904; N.Y., April 9, 1954, Dorati conducting); *Autumn Landscapes from Pine Mountains* for Small Orch. (1904; not extant); *The Pond* for Small Orch. (1906); *[2 Contemplations]: The Unanswered Question* and *Central Park in the Dark* for Small Orch. (1906); *Set* for Theatre or Chamber Orch. (1906–11; Danbury, Conn., Feb. 1932); *Over the Pavements* for Small Orch. (1906–13); *Emerson Overture* (1907; unfinished; also as a Piano Concerto); *Set No. 1* (1907–11), *No. 2* (1911–12), and *No. 3* (1912?–18; N.Y., Dec. 6, 1962, Schuller conducting) for Small Orch.; *Robert Browning Overture* (1908–12; N.Y., Oct. 1963, Stokowski conducting); *First Orchestral Set (A New England Symphony* or *3 Places in New England)* (1908–14?; N.Y., Jan. 10, 1931, Slonimsky conducting); *Second Orchestral Set* (1909–15); *Third Orchestral Set* for Small Orch. (1919–26); *Washington's Birthday* for Small Orch. (1909; San Francisco, Sept. 3, 1931, Slonimsky conducting); *The Gong on the Hook and Ladder* or *Firemen's Parade on Main Street* for Small Orch. (1911?; N.Y., Jan. 21, 1967, Bernstein conducting); *The Fourth of July* (1911–13; Paris, Feb. 21, 1932, Slonimsky conducting); *Tone Roads* (1911–15); *Decoration Day* (1912; Havana, Dec. 27, 1931, A. Roldán conducting); *Matthew Arnold Overture* (1912; unfinished); *Holidays* (1912?; Minneapolis, April 9, 1954, Dorati conducting); Quarter-tone Chorale for Strings (1913–14; not extant); *The Rainbow* or *So May It Be!* for Small Orch. (1914); *Chrômatimelôdtune* for Small Orch. (1919?; arranged by Schuller; N.Y., Dec. 6, 1962, Schuller conducting). **BAND:** *Intercollegiate March* (1892); March (1896); *Runaway Horse on Main Street* (1905?; unfinished).

CHAMBER: *Holiday Quickstep* for Piccolo, 2 Cornets, 2 Violins, and Piano (1887); 2 string quartets: No. 1, *From the Salvation Army* (1896; N.Y., April 24, 1957) and No. 2 (1907–13; Saratoga Springs, N.Y., Sept. 15, 1946); Pre-First Violin Sonata (1899–1903?); *From the Steeples and the Mountains* for Trumpet, Trombone, and 4 Sets of Bells (1901–02?); 4 violin sonatas: No. 1 (1902–08; N.Y., March 31, 1946), No. 2 (1907–10; N.Y., March 18, 1924), No. 3 (1913–14?; Los Angeles, March 16, 1942), and No. 4, *Children's Day at the Camp Meeting* (1906–16?; N.Y., Jan. 14, 1940); *Largo* for Violin, Clarinet, and Piano (1902?); Trio for Violin, Clarinet, and Piano (1902–03?; Berea, Ohio, May 24, 1948); *An Old Song Deranged* for Clarinet or English Horn, Harp, and String Quartet (1903?); *A Set of 3 Short Pieces*: 1, *Hymn* for String Quartet and Double Bass (1904), 2, *Holding Your Own* for String Quartet (1903–14), and 3, *The Innate* for String Quartet, Double Bass, and Piano (1908); Pre-Second String Quartet (1904–05; not extant); Trio for Violin, Cello, and Piano (1904–11); *Take-off No. 3, "Rube Trying to Walk 2 to 3!!"* for Clarinet, Bassoon, Trumpet, and Piano (1906); *Hallowe'en* for String Quartet and Piano (1906; San Francisco, May 28, 1934); *Largo risoluto* No. 1, *"as to the Law of Diminishing Returns"* (1906; N.Y., Feb. 19, 1965) and No. 2, *"a shadow made—a silhouette"* (1906) for String Quartet and Piano; *All the Way Around and Back* for Clarinet, Bugle, Violin, Bells, and Piano (1906); *Decoration Day* for Violin and Piano (1912); *In re con moto et al* for String Quartet and Piano (1913). **PIANO:** 7 marches (c.1890–97); 2 sonatas: No. 1 (1901–09; N.Y., Feb. 17, 1949, Masselos pianist) and No. 2, *Concord, Mass., 1840–60* (1910–15; N.Y., Jan. 20, 1939, J. Kirkpatrick pianist); *Ragtime Dances* (1902–04); *3-page Sonata* (1905); *5 Take-offs* (1906–07); *Studies* (1907–08); *Waltz-Rondo* (1911); *4 Transcriptions from Emerson* (c.1917–22); *Varied Air and Variations* (1923?); *3 Quarter-tone Pieces* for 2 Pianos (1923–24); *The Celestial Railroad* (c.1924); *3 Improvisations* (n.d.). **VOCAL:** Choral pieces; part songs; numerous solo songs.

BIBL.: H. Bellamann, "C. I., The Man and His Music," *Musical Quarterly* (Jan. 1933); H. Cowell, "C. I.," in *American Composers on American Music* (Stanford, 1933); P. Rosenfeld, "I.' Concord Sonata," *Modern Music* (Jan.–Feb. 1939); N. Slonimsky, "C. I., America's Musical Prophet," *Musical America* (Feb. 15, 1954); H. and S. Cowell, *C. I. and His Music* (N.Y., 1955; reprinted with additional material, 1969); J. Kirkpatrick, *A Temporary Mimeographed Catalogue of the Music Manuscripts and Related Materials of C.E. I.* (New Haven, 1960); S. Charles, "The Use of Borrowed Materials in I.' Second Symphony," *Music Review* (May 1967); D. Marshall, "C. I.' Quotations: Manner or Substance?," *Perspectives of New Music* (Spring–Summer 1968); J. Bernlef and R. de Leeuw, *C. I.* (Amsterdam, 1969); D.-R. de Lerma, *C.E. I., 1874–1954: A Bibliography of His Music* (Kent, Ohio, 1970); V. Perlis, *C. I. Remembered: An Oral History* (New Haven, 1974); R. Perry, *C. I. and the American Mind* (Kent, Ohio, 1974); D. Wooldridge, *From the Steeples and Mountains: A Study of C. I.* (N.Y., 1974); F. Rossiter, *C. I. and His America* (N.Y., 1975); H. Wiley Hitchcock, *C. I.* (London, 1977); H. Wiley Hitchcock and V. Perlis, *An I. Celebration: Papers and Panels of the C. I. Centennial Festival-Conference* (Urbana, Ill., 1977); H. Sive, *Music's Connecticut Yankee* (N.Y., 1977); B. Chmaj, *Sonata for American Studies: Perspectives on C. I.* (Sacramento, 1978); H. Wiley Hitchcock, *I.: A Survey of the Music* (N.Y., 1983); J. Burkholder, *C. I.: The Ideas behind the Music* (New Haven, 1985); M. Solomon, "C. I.: Some Questions of Veracity," *Journal of the American Musicological Society* (Fall 1987); G. Block, *C. I.: A Bio-Bibliography* (Westport, Conn., 1988); M.

Alexander, *The Evolving Keyboard Style of C. I.* (N.Y., 1989); W. Rathert, *C. I.* (Darmstadt, 1989); C. Henderson, *The C. I. Tunebook* (Warren, Mich., 1990); K. Niemöller, ed., *Internationale Symposion "C. I. und die amerikanische Musiktradition bis zur Gegenwart" (1988: Cologne, Germany)* (Regensburg, 1990); W. Rathert, *The Seen and the Unseen: Studien zum Werk von C. I.* (Munich, 1991); S. Feder, *C. I., "My Father's Song:" A Psychoanalytic Biography* (New Haven, Conn., 1992); L. Starr, *A Union of Diversities: Style in the Music of C. I.* (N.Y., 1992).

Ivogün, Maria (real name, **Ilse Kempner**), esteemed Hungarian soprano; b. Budapest, Nov. 18, 1891; d. Beatenberg, Switzerland, Oct. 2, 1987. Her mother was the singer Ida von Günther. She studied voice with Schlemmer-Ambros in Vienna, then with Schöner in Munich, where she made her debut as Mimi at the Bavarian Court Opera (1913). She became renowned there for her portrayal of Zerbinetta, and also created the role of Ighino in Pfitzner's *Palestrina* (1917). In 1925 she joined the Berlin Stadtische Oper; also made guest appearances with the touring German Opera Co. in the U.S. (1923), at the Chicago Opera (1923), at London's Covent Garden (1924, 1927), and at the Salzburg Festivals (1925, 1930). She gave her farewell performance as Zerbinetta at the Berlin Städtische Oper (1934); subsequently was active as a teacher, later serving on the faculties of the Vienna Academy of Music (1948–50) and the Berlin Hochschule für Musik (1950–58); her most celebrated pupil was Elisabeth Schwarzkopf. She was married to **Karl Erb** (1921–32), then to her accompanist Michael Raucheisen (from 1933). Among her other notable roles were Constanze, the Queen of the Night, Norina, Gilda, and Oscar.

Iwaki, Hiroyuki, Japanese conductor; b. Tokyo, Sept. 6, 1932. He received training in percussion at the Academy of Music and in conducting from Saito and Watanabe (1951–54) at the Univ. of Arts in Tokyo. In 1954 he became assistant conductor of the NHK (Japanese Broadcasting Corp.) Sym. Orch. in Tokyo, serving as its principal resident conductor from 1969. From 1965 to 1967 he was also music director of the Fujiwara Opera Co., and from 1974 chief conductor of the Melbourne Sym. Orch. In 1988 he was named music director of the new Orchestra-Ensemble Kanazawa, but continued to hold his post with the NHK Sym. Orch. As a guest conductor, he appeared throughout the Far East, Europe, and North America.

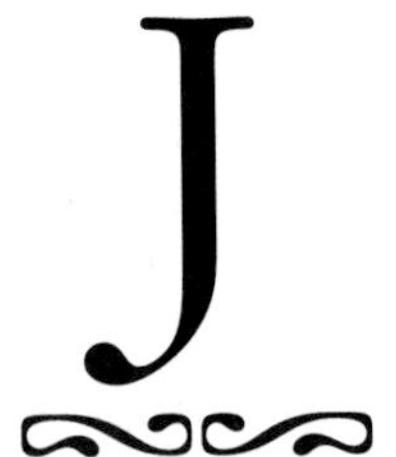

Jachimecki, Zdzislaw, eminent Polish musicologist; b. Lemberg, July 7, 1882; d. Kraków, Oct. 27, 1953. He studied music with Niewiadomski and Jarecki in Lemberg; then musicology with Adler at the Univ. of Vienna (Ph.D., 1906, with the diss. *Psalmy Mikolaja Gomólki*; publ. in an abr. ed., Kraków, 1907); also studied composition with Grädener and Schoenberg in Vienna and completed his Habilitation at the Univ. of Kraków in 1911 with his *Wplywy wloskie w muzyce polskiej cześč I. 1540–1560* (Italian Influence on Polish Music, Part 1, 1540–1560; publ. in Kraków, 1911); then was a lecturer in music history there, later being made a reader (1917) and a prof. (1921); was also a guest lecturer at many European univs. He conducted sym. concerts in Kraków (1908–24), and composed a number of orch. pieces and songs.

WRITINGS: *Ryszard Wagner: Zycie i twórczośč* (Richard Wagner: Life and Works; Lemberg, 1911; 2nd ed., aug., 1922; 4th ed., 1973); *Tabulatura organowa z biblioteki klasztoru Św. Ducha w Krakówie z roku 1548* (Organ Tablature from the Library of the Monastery of the Holy Spirit in Kraków, 1548; Kraków, 1913); *Muzyka na dworze krota Wladyslawa Jagielly 1424–1430* (Music at the Court of Wladyslaw Jagiello 1424–1430; Kraków, 1916); *Pieśń rokoszan z roku 1606* (A Rebel Song from 1606; Kraków, 1916); *Historia muzyki polskiej w zarysie* (The History of Polish Music in Outline; Warsaw, 1920); *Fryderyk Chopin: Zarys zycia i twórczości* (Frédéric Chopin: An Outline of His Life and Work; Kraków, 1927; 4th ed., aug., 1957); *Mikolaj Gomólka i jego poprzednicy we historii muzyki polskiej* (Mikolaj Gomolka and His Predecessors in the History of Polish Music; Warsaw, 1946); *Bartlomiej Pekiel* (Warsaw, 1948); *Muzyka polska w rozwoju historycznym od czasów najdawniejszych do doby obecnej* (The Historical Evolution of Polish Music from the Earliest Times to the Present Day; Kraków, 1948–51); *Muzykologia i piśmiennictwo muzyczne w Polsce* (Musicology and Writing on Music in Poland; Kraków, 1948).

Jachino, Carlo, Italian composer; b. San Remo, Feb. 3, 1887; d. Rome, Dec. 23, 1971. He studied with Luporini in Lucca and then with Riemann in Leipzig (1909–10). He taught in Parma (1928–33), Naples (1933–38), and Rome (1938–51). After serving as director of the conservatories in Naples (1951–53) and Bogotá, Colombia (1953–56), he was artistic director of the Teatro San Carlo in Naples (1961–69). He publ. *Tecnica dodecafonica* (Milan, 1948) and *Gli strumenti d'orchestra* (Milan, 1950). In his early compositions, he followed the Romantic Italian style; after adopting a modified 12-tone method, he finally returned to tonality in his last years.

WORKS: DRAMATIC: OPERA: *Giocondo e il suo re* (1915–21; Milan, June 24, 1924). Film scores. **ORCH.:** *Sonata drammatica* for Violin and Orch. (1930); *Pastorale di Natale* (1932); *Fantasia del rosso e nero* (1935); *Pagine di Ramon* (1937); 2 piano concertos (1952, 1957); *L'ora inquieta* for Strings (1953); Cello Concerto (1960); *Variazioni su un tema car a Napoleone I* (1966). **CHAMBER:** Sonata for 9 Instruments (1922); 3 string quartets (1925, 1927, 1930); Trio for Flute, Cello, and Piano (1954); *Quintetto dell'alba* for Clarinet, Horn, and String Trio (1956); keyboard music. **VOCAL:** Choral pieces; songs.

Jackson, Francis (Alan), English organist, conductor, and composer; b. Malton, Yorkshire, Oct. 2, 1917. He studied with Bairstow in York, then was made a Fellow of the Royal College of Organists (1937) and later studied at Durham Univ. (D.Mus., 1957). He was organist of Malton Parish Church (1933–40), Master of the Music at York Minster (1946–82), and also conductor of the York Sym. Orch. (1947–80); made numerous tours of Europe and North America as an organist. He was made an Officer of the Order of the British Empire (1978). He wrote a Sym., choral works, and much music for the organ.

Jackson, George Pullen, American folklorist; b. Monson, Maine, Aug. 20, 1874; d. Nashville, Tenn., Jan. 19, 1953. He studied philology in Dresden and at the Univ. of Chicago (Ph.B., 1904; Ph.D., 1911). He was a teacher of German at Vanderbilt Univ. (1918–43), founder of the Tennessee State Sacred

Harp Singing Assn., and president of the Tennessee Folklore Soc. (1942).

WRITINGS: *The Rhythmic Form of the German Folk Songs* (1917); *White Spirituals in the Southern Uplands* (1933); *Spiritual Folksongs of Early America* (1937; 3rd ed., 1965); *Down-East Spirituals* (1943; 2nd ed., 1953); *White and Negro Spirituals* (1943); *Story of the Sacred Harp* (1944); *Another Sheaf of White Spirituals* (1952).

Jackson, Isaiah (Allen), black American conductor; b. Richmond, Va., Jan. 22, 1945. He majored in Russian studies at Harvard Univ. (B.A., 1966), then studied conducting at Stanford Univ. (M.A., 1967), and composition with Boulanger at the American Cons. in Fontainebleau; completed his training at the Juilliard School in N.Y. (M.S., 1969; D.M.A., 1973). He was founder-conductor of the Juilliard String Ensemble (1970–71), and also assistant conductor of the American Sym. Orch. in N.Y. (1970–71). After serving as assistant conductor of the Baltimore Sym. Orch. (1971–73), he was assoc. conductor of the Rochester (N.Y.) Phil. (1973–87) and music director of the Flint (Mich.) Sym. Orch. (1982–87). He was music director of the Royal Ballet at London's Covent Garden (1987–90) and of the Dayton (Ohio) Phil. (1987–95), and principal guest conductor of the Queensland Sym. Orch. in Brisbane (from 1993). In 1996 he became music director of the Youngstown (Ohio) Sym. Orch.

Jackson, Judge, black American composer and tunebook compiler; b. Ozark, Ala., March 12, 1883; d. there, April 7, 1958. He learned shape-note hymn singing from the blacks of southeastern Alabama. He was active as a singing-school teacher. He wrote shape-note religious songs and also compiled *The Colored Sacred Harp* (1934), which proved influential as a tunebook among blacks.

BIBL.: J. Work, "Plantation Meistersinger," *Musical Quarterly* (Jan. 1941); J. Boyd, "J. J.: Black Giant of White Spirituals," *Journal of American Folklore,* LXXXIII (1970).

Jacob, Gordon (Percival Septimus), distinguished English composer and pedagogue; b. London, July 5, 1895; d. Saffron Walden, June 8, 1984. He studied at Dulwich College and took courses in composition with Stanford, Howells, and Wood at the Royal College of Music in London (D.Mus., 1935). He taught at the Royal College of Music from 1926 to 1966; among his notable students were Malcolm Arnold, Imogen Holst, Elizabeth Maconchy, and Bernard Stevens. In 1968 he was made a Commander of the Order of the British Empire. Jacob produced a significant output of instrumental music, and also publ. several important books.

WRITINGS (all publ. in London): *Orchestral Technique: A Manual for Students* (1931; 3rd ed., 1983); *How to Read a Score* (1944); *The Composer and His Art* (1954); *The Elements of Orchestration* (1962).

WORKS: ORCH.: 2 viola concertos (1925, 1979); 2 piano concertos (1927, 1957); 2 syms. (1928–29; 1943–44); *Denbigh Suite* for Strings (1929); *Variations on an Air by Purcell* for Strings (1930); *Passacaglia on a Well-known Theme* (1931); 2 oboe concertos (1933, 1956); *Variations on an Original Theme* (1936); *Divertimento* (1938); 3 suites (1941; 1948–49; 1949); 3 sinfoniettas (1942, 1951, 1953); Sym. for Strings (1943); Concerto for Bassoon, Strings, and Percussion (1947); *Rhapsody* for English Horn and Strings (1948); Concerto for Horn and Strings (1951); Flute Concerto (1951); Trombone Concerto (1952); Concerto for Violin and Strings (1953); Violin Concerto (1954); *Divertimento* for Harmonica and Strings (1954); Cello Concerto (1955); *Prelude and Toccata* (1955); Sym. for Small Orch. (1958); 2 overtures (1965); Concerto for Piano Duet, 3-hands, and Orch. (1969); Concerto for Band (1970); *A York Symphony* for Woodwinds (1971); Suite for Tuba and Strings (1972). **CHAMBER:** String Quartet (1928); Quartet for Oboe and Strings (1938); Quintet for Clarinet and Strings (1942); *Serenade* for 8 Woodwind Instruments (1950); Piano Trio (1955); Cello Sonata (1957); Sextet for Wind Quintet and Piano (1962); Suite for 4 Trombones (1968); *Divertimento* for 8 Wind Instruments (1969); Suite for Bassoon and String Quartet (1969); Trio for Clarinet, Viola, and Piano (1969); *Introduction and Rondo* for Clarinet Choir (1972); Piano Quartet (1971); Suite for 8 Violas (1976); Viola Sonata (1978); piano pieces. **VOCAL:** Sacred and secular choral works; songs.

Jacob, Maxime, French composer; b. Bordeaux, Jan. 13, 1906; d. in the Benedictine Abbey in En-Calcat, Tarn, Feb. 26, 1977. He studied with Gédalge, Koechlin, Milhaud, and Nat in Paris. Pursuing a whimsical mode, he became associated with the École d'Arcueil, named after a modest Paris suburb where Satie presided over his group of disciples; then made a 180° turn toward established religion, and in 1929 took holy orders; he adopted the name Clément as a Benedictine novice, and served mainly as an organist; also served as a soldier (1939–40) and army chaplain (1944–45) during World War II. He wrote a Piano Concerto (1961); 8 string quartets (1961–69); 3 violin sonatas; 2 cello sonatas; 15 piano sonatas; a curious *Messe syncopée* (1968); and over 500 songs. He wrote the books *L'Art et la grâce* (Paris, 1939) and *Souvenirs à deux voix* (Toulouse, 1969).

BIBL.: R. Chalupt, *M. J.* (Paris, 1927); J. Roy, "M. J.," *La Revue Musicale* (July 1939).

Jacobi, Erwin R(euben), Swiss musicologist; b. Strasbourg, Sept. 21, 1909; d. Zürich, Feb. 27, 1979. He studied economics in Berlin, obtaining a diploma of engineering in 1933. From 1934 to 1952 he lived in Israel, where he studied harpsichord with Pelleg and composition with Ben-Haim; in 1952 he went to the U.S. to study with Landowska (harpsichord), Hindemith (composition), and Sachs (music history); completed his studies at the Univ. of Zürich (Ph.D., 1957, with the diss. *Die Entwicklung der Musiktheorie in England nach der Zeit von Jean-Philippe Rameau*; publ. in Strasbourg, 1957–60; 2nd ed., rev. and aug., Baden-Baden, 1971). He was an assistant lecturer there (from 1961); also was a visiting prof. at the Univ. of Iowa (1970) and at Indiana Univ. (1971–72). He wrote a number of valuable articles on Baroque composers for various music journals; ed. *J.-P. Rameau: Complete Theoretical Writings* (Rome, 1967–72); publ. *Albert Schweitzer und die Musik* (Wiesbaden, 1975) and served as ed. of his writings.

Jacobi, Frederick, American composer, conductor, and teacher; b. San Francisco, May 4, 1891; d. N.Y., Oct. 24, 1952. He was a student of Gallico, Joseffy, Goldmark, and Bloch in N.Y., and of Juon at the Berlin Hochschule für Musik. After studying the music of the Pueblo Indians in New Mexico and Arizona, he returned to N.Y. and taught harmony at the Master School of the United Arts (1924–36) and composition at the Juilliard Graduate School (1936–50). He also served as director of the American section of the ISCM, and actively promoted the cause of contemporary American music. In 1945 he received the David Bispham Award for his opera *The Prodigal Son.* In some of his works, he made use of native American Indian themes. However, his music as a whole was characterized by an assured usage of Classical and Romantic idioms.

WORKS: OPERA: *The Prodigal Son* (1943–44). **ORCH.:** *The Pied Piper,* symphonic poem (1915); *A California Suite* (San Francisco, Dec. 6, 1917); *The Eve of St. Agnes,* symphonic poem (1919); 2 syms.: No. 1, *Assyrian* (1922; San Francisco, Nov. 14, 1924) and No. 2 (1947; San Francisco, April 1, 1948); *Indian Dances* (1927–28); *3 Psalms* for Cello and Orch. (1932); Piano Concerto (1934–35); Violin Concerto (1936–37); *Ave Rota: 3 Pieces in Multiple Style* for Piano and Orch. (1939); *Rhapsody* for Harp and Strings (1940); *Night Piece* for Flute and Small Orch. (1940); *Ode* (1941); Concertino for Piano and Strings (Saratoga Springs, N.Y., Sept. 3, 1946); *2 Pieces in Sabbath Mood* (1946); *Music Hall,* overture (1948). **CHAMBER:** *Nocturne* for String Quartet (n.d.); *3 Preludes* for Violin and Piano (1921); 3 string quartets ("on Indian Themes," 1924; 1933; 1945); *Scherzo* for Flute, Oboe, Clarinet, Bassoon, and Horn (1936); *Swing Boy* for Violin and Piano (1937); *Hagiographia: 3 Biblical Narratives* for String Quartet and Piano (1938); *Fantasy* for Viola and Piano (1941); *Ballade* for Violin and Piano (1942);

Impressions from the Odyssey for Violin and Piano (1945); *Music for Monticello* for Flute, Cello, and Piano (1945); *Meditation* for Trombone and Piano (1947); Cello Sonata (1950); *Night Piece and Dance* for Flute and Piano (1952). **KEYBOARD: PIANO:** *6 Pieces* (1921); *Pieces for Children* (1935); *Fantasy Sonata* (1945); *Moods* (1946); *Prelude* (1946); *Toccata* (1946); *Introduction and Toccata* (1946); *Suite fantasque* (1948). **ORGAN:** *6 Pieces for Use in the Synagogue* (1933); *3 Quiet Preludes* (1950). **VOCAL:** *The Poet in the Desert* for Baritone, Chorus, and Orch. (1925); *Sabbath Evening Service* for Baritone and Chorus (1930–31); *Sadia*, hymn for Men's Voices (1942); *Ahavas Olom* for Tenor, Chorus, and Organ (1945); *Contemplation* for Chorus and Piano (1947); *Ode to Zion* for Chorus and 2 Harps (1948); *Arvit I'shabbat: Friday Evening Service No. 2* for Cantor, Chorus, and Organ (1952); songs.

BIBL.: D. Diamond, "F. J.," *Modern Music* (March–April 1937).

Jacobs, Arthur (David), English music critic, editor, writer on music, and translator; b. Manchester, June 14, 1922. He studied at Merton College, Oxford. He was music critic for the *Daily Express* (1947–52) and deputy ed. of the journal *Opera* (1960–71). He was a prof. at the Royal Academy of Music in London (1964–79) and head of the music dept. at Huddersfield Polytechnic (1979–84); also ed. the British Music Yearbook (1971–80). An accomplished linguist, he prepared admirable trs. of some 20 operas into English; he also wrote the libretto for Maw's opera *One Man Show* (1964).

WRITINGS: *Gilbert and Sullivan* (London, 1951); *A New Dictionary of Music* (Harmondsworth, 1958; new ed., rev., 1978 as *The New Penguin Dictionary of Music;* 6th ed., rev., 1996); with S. Sadie, *The Pan Book of Opera* (London, 1964; rev. ed., 1972, as *Opera: A Modern Guide*; new ed., 1984); *A Short History of Western Music* (Harmondsworth, 1972); *Arthur Sullivan: A Victorian Musician* (Oxford, 1984; 2nd ed., rev. and enl., 1992); *The Pan Book of Orchestral Music* (London, 1988); *The Penguin Dictionary of Musical Performers* (Harmondsworth, 1990); *Henry J. Wood: Maker of the Proms* (London, 1994).

Jacobs, Paul, American pianist, harpsichordist, and teacher; b. N.Y., June 22, 1930; d. there, Sept. 25, 1983. He was a student of Hutcheson and a graduate student at the Juilliard School of Music in N.Y. (1951). He began his career performing with the Composers Forum and Robert Craft's Chamber Arts Soc. in N.Y. After making his formal debut in N.Y. in 1951, he was active in Europe in avant-garde circles. In 1956 he gave an unprecedented recital in Paris of the complete piano works of Schoenberg. Returning to the U.S. in 1960, he taught at the Mannes School of Music, the Manhattan School of Music, the Berkshire Music Center at Tanglewood, and Brooklyn College. In 1962 he was named the official pianist of the N.Y. Phil., and also was its official harpsichordist from 1974. While he played much Baroque music, Jacobs acquired a fine reputation as a champion of contemporary music, most notably of scores by Stravinsky, Schoenberg, Copland, Messiaen, Cage, Boulez, and Stockhausen. Jacobs was one of the first musicians of prominence to succumb to the plague of AIDS.

Jacobs, René, Belgian countertenor and conductor; b. Ghent, Oct. 30, 1946. He pursued training in philology at the Univ. of Ghent, then studied voice with Louis Devos in Brussels and Lucie Frateur in The Hague; subsequently pursued an international career as a performer with various early-music groups, as an opera singer, and as a recitalist; also taught at the Schola Cantorum Basiliensis in Basel. He has been particularly successful in works by Cavalli, Monteverdi, Charpentier, Gluck, and Handel. As a conductor, he was active with his own Collegium Vocale. He conducted his own eds. of Cavalli's *Giasone* at the Innsbruck Festival in 1988 and of Monteverdi's *L'Orfeo* at the Salzburg Festival in 1993. He is the author of *La Controverse sur le timbre de contre-ténor* (1985).

Jacobs-Bond, Carrie. See **Bond, Carrie Jacobs.**

Jacobson, Maurice, English composer and music publisher; b. London, Jan. 1, 1896; d. Brighton, Feb. 1, 1976. He studied piano at the Modern School of Music (1913–16) and composition with Stanford and Holst at the Royal College of Music in London. In 1923 he joined the music publ. firm of J. Curwen & Sons as a music reader; in 1933, was made its director and later its chairman (1950–72). In 1971 he was made an Officer of the Order of the British Empire. He composed a ballet, *David* (1935); also the cantatas *The Lady of Shalott* (1940) and *The Hound of Heaven* (1953), many short instrumental pieces, chamber music, and songs.

Jacoby, Hanoch (actually **Heinrich**), German-born Israeli violist and composer; b. Königsberg, March 2, 1909. He studied composition with Hindemith, Bihnke, Mahlke, and Wolfsthal at the Berlin Hochschule für Musik (1927–30). He played in Fischer's chamber orch. (1929–30) and the Frankfurt am Main Radio Orch. (1930–33). He emigrated to Jerusalem in 1934, where he taught at the Academy of Music until 1958; also played in the Palestine (later Israel) Broadcasting Sym. Orch. (1936–58) and then in the Israel Phil.

WORKS: ORCH.: Viola Concerto (1939); 3 syms. (1940, 1951, 1960); Violin Concerto (1942); *7 Miniatures* for Small Orch. (1945); *King David's Lyre* for Small Orch. (1948); *Capriccio israélien* (1951); Sinfonietta (1960); *Serio giocoso* (1964); *Partita concertata* (1970–71); *Mutatio* (1975); *Variations* (1976); *Jewish Oriental Folklore*, suite for Strings (1977). **CHAMBER:** Concertino for String Trio (1932); 2 string quartets (1937, 1938); *Theme, Variations, and Finale* for Piano Trio (1940); Wind Quintet (1946); *Canzona* for Harp (1960); *2 Suites of Jewish Oriental Folklore* for Brass Quintet (1975); *Mutatio II* for Oboe, Bassoon, 2 Trumpets, 2 Trombones, 2 Violas, and Double Bass (1976).

Jacques, (Thomas) Reginald, respected English organist and conductor; b. Ashby de la Zouch, Jan. 13, 1894; d. Stowmarket, June 2, 1969. He was educated at Queen's College, Oxford, where he became organist and director of music in 1926; was also conductor of the Oxford Orchestral Soc. (1930–36). From 1931 to 1960 he was conductor of the Bach Choir in London. In 1936 he founded his own Jacques Orch., which he conducted until 1960. In 1954 he was made a Commander of the Order of the British Empire.

Jacquillat, Jean-Pierre, French conductor; b. Versailles, July 13, 1935; d. in an automobile accident in Chambo-sur-Lignon, Aug. 6, 1986. He was educated at the Paris Cons., winning premiers prix in harmony, percussion, and piano; also studied conducting with Munch, Cluytens, and Dervaux. He was assistant conductor (1967) and assoc. conductor (1968) of the Orch. de Paris; toured with it in the Soviet Union, North America, and Mexico. In 1970 he was named resident conductor and music director of the Angers Phil.; in 1971 he became permanent conductor of the Lyons Opera and the Rhône-Alpes Phil.; then was resident conductor and music adviser to the Lamoureux Orch. in Paris (1975–78); subsequently was chief conductor of the Iceland Sym. Orch. in Reykjavík (1980–86).

Jadlowker, Hermann, distinguished Latvian tenor; b. Riga, July 17, 1877; d. Tel Aviv, May 13, 1953. He studied with J. Gänsbacher at the Vienna Cons. He made his operatic debut as Gomez in *Nachtlager von Granada* in Cologne (1897); after appearances in Königsberg, Stettin, Rostock, and Riga, he sang in Karlsruhe (1906–10) and at Berlin's Kroll Opera (from 1907). He made his Metropolitan Opera debut in N.Y. as Gounod's Faust (Jan. 22, 1910), and sang there until 1912; also sang in Boston (1910–12), and at the Berlin Royal Opera (1911–12). He created the role of Bacchus in Richard Strauss's *Ariadne auf Naxos* (Stuttgart, Oct. 25, 1912). After guest appearances in Europe and a period with the Berlin State Opera (1922–23), he served as chief cantor of the Riga synagogue (1929–38) and taught at the Riga Cons. (1936–38); then settled in Tel Aviv as a teacher.

Jaffee, Michael, American early-music performer and instrument builder; b. N.Y., April 21, 1938. He studied music at N.Y.

Univ. (B.A., 1959; M.A., 1963), and learned to play the guitar. While still a student, he married Kay Cross (b. Lansing, Mich., Dec. 31, 1937), a keyboard player, in 1961. Their interest in early music led Michael to master the lute and Kay the recorder; they subsequently organized the Waverly Consort, a group dedicated to performances of music from the medieval and Renaissance eras using period instruments and costumes; the group made its formal debut at N.Y.'s Carnegie Hall in 1966. The two founders became highly proficient on a variety of instruments or copies, many of which they built themselves. The Waverly Consort toured extensively, becoming one of the most successful early-music groups in the U.S.

BIBL.: H. Waleson, "The Waverly Consort: New Masters of an Ancient Repertoire," *Ovation* (Nov. 1983).

Jagel, Frederick, American tenor and teacher; b. Brooklyn, June 10, 1897; d. San Francisco, July 5, 1982. He sang in local choirs as a youth and later appeared as a tenor soloist. After training from William Brady in N.Y., he completed his studies in Milan. In 1924 he made his operatic debut under the name Federico Jeghelli in Livorno as Rodolfo, and then appeared throughout Italy and with an Italian opera company in the Netherlands. On Nov. 8, 1927, he made his Metropolitan Opera debut in N.Y. as Radamès, and remained on its roster until 1950. Among his prominent roles there were Alfredo, the Duke of Mantua, Cavaradossi, Turiddu, Pinkerton, Pollione, and Peter Grimes. He also appeared in Buenos Aires (1928; 1939–41), San Francisco (debut as Jack Rance, 1930), Chicago (debut as Lohengrin, 1934), and at the N.Y. City Opera (debut as Herod, 1947). From 1949 to 1970 he taught voice at the New England Cons. of Music in Boston.

Jairazbhoy, Nazir (Ali), English ethnomusicologist and instrumentalist of Indian descent; b. Clifton, Oct. 31, 1927. After schooling in England and India, he studied at the Univ. of Wash. (B.A., 1951) and at the School of Oriental and African Studies in London (Ph.D., 1971, with the diss. *The Rāgas of North Indian Music: Their Structure and Evolution*; publ. in London, 1971), where he lectured on Indian music (1962–69). He was assoc. prof. of Asian studies at the Univ. of Windsor, Ontario (1969–75), and prof. of ethnomusicology at the Univ. of Calif., Los Angeles (from 1975), where he later became the chairman of its Department of Ethnomusicology and Systematic Musicology (1988). His study of the evolution of different rāgas and scales contributed greatly to knowledge about North Indian music.

Jalas (real name, **Blomstedt**), **Jussi,** Finnish conductor; b. Jyväskylä, June 23, 1908. He studied at the Helsinki Cons. and with Ilmari Krohn at the Univ. of Helsinki; later studied in Paris with Rhené-Baton and Monteux. He was active as a theater conductor in Helsinki (1930–45); subsequently conducted at the Finnish National Opera there, serving as its music director until 1973; also made guest conducting appearances throughout Europe, the U.S., and Japan. He was highly regarded as an interpreter of the music of Sibelius, his father-in-law; he also excelled in performances of 20th-century works, ranging from Puccini to Shostakovich.

James, Dorothy, American composer and teacher; b. Chicago, Dec. 1, 1898; d. St. Petersburg, Fla., Dec. 1, 1982. She was a student of Gruenberg and Weidig at the Chicago Musical College and the American Cons. of Music in Chicago (M.M., 1927), of Hanson at the Eastman School of Music in Rochester, N.Y., of Willan in Toronto, and of Krenek at the Univ. of Mich. In 1927 she joined the faculty of Eastern Michigan Univ. in Ypsilanti, where she was later a prof. (1962–68); she also was music critic of the *Ypsilanti Press*. She was the author of *Music of Living Women Composers* (1976). Her compositions display fine craftsmanship, particularly her choral works.

WORKS: OPERA: *Paola and Francesca* (partial concert perf., Rochester, N.Y., April 2, 1931). **ORCH.:** *3 Symphonic Fragments* (Rochester, N.Y., April 2, 1931); *Elegy for the Lately Dead* (1938); Suite for Small Orch. (1940). **CHAMBER:** *3 Pastorales* for Clarinet, Strings, and Celesta (1933); *Recitative and Aria* for Viola, 2 Violins, and 2 Cellos (1944); *Morning Music* for Flute and Piano (1967); *Motif* for Oboe and Organ (1970); *Patterns* for Harp (1977). **KEYBOARD: PIANO:** *2 Satirical Dances* (1934); *Dirge* (1962); *Impressionistic Study* (1962); *Tone Row Suite* (1962); *2 in 1* (1962). **ORGAN:** *Autumnal* (1934); *Dedication* (1958). **VOCAL:** *Tears* for Chorus and Orch. (1930); *4 Preludes from the Chinese* for Alto or Bass and Piano Quintet (1930); *The Jumblies* for Women's Voices and Orch. (1935); *Paul Bunyan* for Baritone, Women's Voices, and Orch. (1937); *Niobe* for Women's Voices and Chamber Orch. (1941); *The Golden Years* for Chorus and Orch. (1953); *The Nativity Hymn* for Chorus (1957); *Mutability* for Women's Voices and Ensemble (1967); songs.

James, (Mary) Frances, Canadian soprano and teacher; b. Saint John, New Brunswick, Feb. 3, 1903; d. Victoria, British Columbia, Aug. 22, 1988. She studied with Walter Clapperton at the McGill Cons. in Montreal, and with Emmy Hein at the Toronto Cons. of Music (1934); then was a student of Jeanne Dusseau (1936), had lessons with Enrico Rosati and Maria Kurenko in N.Y., and worked with Roland Hayes in Boston. She became well known to Canadian audiences via radio, and as a soloist and recitalist; in 1940 she made her first appearance in the U.S. From 1952 to 1973 she taught at the Univ. of Saskatchewan, and then in Victoria at the Cons. of Music and at the Univ. In 1931 she married **Murray Adaskin**. She was especially admired for her championship of the 20th-century vocal repertoire.

BIB.: G. Lazarevich, *The Musical World of F. J. and Murray Adaskin* (Toronto, 1987).

James, Philip (Frederick Wright), American organist, conductor, composer, and teacher; b. Jersey City, N.J., May 17, 1890; d. Southampton, N.Y., Nov. 1, 1975. He received rudimentary instruction in music from his sister; later studied composition with Rubin Goldmark, Homer Norris, Elliot Schenck, and Rosario Scalero; also studied organ with J. Warren Andrews, and later with Joseph Bonnet and Alexandre Guilmant in Paris. He served in the U.S. Army during World War I; in 1918–19 he served as bandmaster of the American Expeditionary Force General Headquarters Band. Returning to the U.S., he held various posts as organist and choirmaster in several churches in N.Y., and also conducted the Victor Herbert Opera Co. (1919–22). He then was founder-conductor of the New Jersey Sym. Orch. (1922–29); also conducted the Brooklyn Orch. Soc. (1927–30) and the Bamberger Little Sym. (WOR Radio, N.Y., 1929–36). In 1923 he joined the faculty of N.Y. Univ., becoming chairman of its music dept. in 1933; retired in 1955. In 1933 he was elected a member of the National Inst. of Arts and Letters. His compositions generally followed along late Romantic lines.

WORKS: ORCH.: 3 *Bret Harte* overtures (n.d.; 1924; 1934, rev. 1938); Kammersymphonie (1926); *Overture in Olden Style on French Noëls* for Small Orch. (1926; rev. for Large Orch., 1929; N.Y., Feb. 23, 1930); *Judith* for Reciter and Chamber Orch. (1927; N.Y., Feb. 18, 1930; also for Reciter and Piano); *Sea Symphony* for Baritone and Orch. (1928; Frankfurt am Main, July 14, 1960); *Station WGZBX*, suite (1931; N.Y., May 1, 1932); *Song of the Night*, symphonic poem (1931; N.Y., March 15, 1938); Suite for Strings (1933; N.Y., April 28, 1934); *Gwalia, Welsh Rhapsody* for Small Orch. (N.Y., Nov. 14, 1935; rev. for Large Orch., 1937); Sinfonietta for Chamber Orch. (1938; N.Y., Nov. 10, 1941; rev. 1943); *Brennan on the Moor* for Small Orch. (N.Y., Nov. 28, 1939; also for Large Orch., 1940); 2 syms.: No. 1 (1943; rev. 1961) and No. 2 (1946; Rochester, N.Y., May 7, 1966); *Miniver Cheevy and Richard Cory* for Reciter and Orch. (Saratoga Springs, N.Y., Sept. 9, 1947); *Chaumont*, symphonic poem for Small Orch. (1948; N.Y., May 2, 1951). **BAND:** *Perstare et Praestare* (N.Y., June 10, 1942; also for Orch., 1946); *E.F.G.*, overture (1944; N.Y., June 13, 1945); *Fanfare and Ceremonial* (1955; N.Y., June 20, 1956; rev. 1962). **CHAMBER:** String Quartet (1924; rev. 1939); Suite for Woodwind Quintet

(1936); Piano Quartet (1938; rev. 1948). **KEYBOARD: PIANO:** *Our Town*, suite (1945); *12 Preludes* (1946–51). **ORGAN:** *Méditation à Ste. Clotilde* (1915); *Dithyramb* (1921); *Fête* (1921); Sonata (1929); *Pantomime* (1941); *Galarnad* (1946); *Novelette* (1946); *Solemn Prelude* (1948); *Alleluia-Toccata* (1949); *Pastorale* (1949); *Requiescat in pace* (1949; rev. 1955); *Passacaglia on an Old Cambrian Bass* (1951; also for Orch., 1956, and for Band, 1957); *Sortie* (1973). **VOCAL:** *Magnificat* for Soloists, Chorus, and Organ (1910); *Te Deum* for Chorus and Organ (1910); *The Victory Riders* for Baritone and Orch. (1919–25); *Stabat mater speciosa* for Chorus and Orch. (1921; rev. 1930); *Missa imaginum* for Chorus and Orch. (1929); *Chorus of Shepherds and Angels* for Women's Voices and Strings (1959); *Missa brevis* for Chorus (1963; rev. as *Mass in Honor of St. Mark*, 1966); about 13 cantatas (1916–66); motets; anthems; Psalms; part songs; songs.

BIBL.: H. James, *A Catalog of the Musical Works of P. J. (1890–1975)* (N.Y., 1980; supplement, 1984).

Janáček, Leoš, greatly significant Czech composer; b. Hukvaldy, Moravia, July 3, 1854; d. Moravská Ostrava, Aug. 12, 1928. At the age of 11, he was sent to Brno to serve as a chorister at the Augustinian Queen's Monastery, where he was schooled under its choirmaster, Křízkovský. After studies at the German College, he was a scholarship student at the teacher's training college (1869–72). He then began his teaching career while serving as choirmaster at the monastery; he also served as choirmaster of the men's chorus, Svatopluk (1873–77), taking an opportunity to study organ with Skuherský at the Prague Organ School (1874–75). He conducted the Beseda Choral Soc. in Brno (1876–88), and also pursued studies at the Leipzig Cons., where he took music history courses with Oskar Paul and composition courses with Leo Grill (1879–80). He continued his composition studies with Franz Krenn at the Vienna Cons. (1880). Returning to Brno, he was appointed the first director of the new organ school (1881). His social position in Brno was enhanced by his marriage to Zdenka Schulzová, the daughter of the director of the teachers' training college. He also engaged in scholarly activities; from 1884 to 1886 he was ed. of the music journal *Hudební Listy* (Music Bulletins); he further became associated with František Bartoš in collecting Moravian folk songs. From 1886 to 1902 he taught music at the Brno Gymnasium. In 1919 he retired from his directorship of the Brno Organ School, and then taught master classes in Brno (1920–25). Throughout all these busy years, he worked diligently on his compositions, showing particular preference for operas.

Janáček's style of composition underwent numerous transformations, from Romantic techniques of established formulas to bold dissonant combinations. He was greatly influenced by the Russian musical nationalism exemplified by the "realistic" speech inflections in vocal writing. He visited St. Petersburg and Moscow in 1896 and 1902, and publ. his impressions of the tour in the Brno press. From 1894 to 1903 he worked assiduously on his most important opera, *Její pastorkyňa* (Her Foster Daughter), to a highly dramatic libretto set in Moravia in the mid-19th century, involving a jealous contest between 2 brothers for the hand of Jenůfa (the innocent heroine), and infanticide at the hands of a foster mother, with an amazing outcome absolving Jenůfa and her suitors. The opera encountered great difficulty in securing production in Prague because of its grisly subject, but was eventually produced on various European stages, mostly in the German text, and under the title *Jenůfa*. Another opera by Janáček that attracted attention was *Výlet pana Broučka do XV stoleti* (Mr. Brouček's Excursion to the 15th Century), depicting the imaginary travel of a Czech patriot to the time of the religious struggle mounted by the followers of the nationalist leader Hus against the established church. There followed an operatic fairy tale, *Příhody Lišky Bystroušky* (The Adventures of the Vixen Bystrouška, or The Cunning Little Vixen), and a mystery play, *Věc Makropulos* (The Makropulos Affair). Janáček's great interest in Russian literature was reflected in his opera *Kát'a Kabanová*, after the drama *The Storm* by the Russian playwright Ostrovsky, and one after Dostoyevsky, *Z mrtvého domu* (From the House of the Dead). He further composed a symphonic poem, *Taras Bulba* (the fictional name of a Ukrainian patriot, after a story by Gogol). In 1917 Janáček became enamored of Kamila Stösslová, the 26 year-old wife of an antique dealer. His unconsummated love for her proved an inspiration and led to the composition of several major works by an aging composer. Like most artists, writers, and composers of Slavic origin in the old Austro-Hungarian Empire, Janáček had a natural interest in the Pan-Slavic movement, with an emphasis on the common origins of Russian, Czech, Slovak, and other kindred cultures; his *Glagolitic Mass*, to a Latin text tr. into the Czech language, is an example. Janáček lived to witness the fall of the old Austrian regime and the national rise of the Slavic populations. He also showed great interest in the emerging Soviet school of composition, even though he refrained from any attempt to join that movement. Inevitably, he followed the striking innovations of the modern school of composition as set forth in the works of Stravinsky and Schoenberg, but he was never tempted to experiment along those revolutionary lines. He remained faithful to his own well-defined style, and it was as the foremost composer of modern Czech music that he secured for himself his unique place in history.

WORKS: DRAMATIC: OPERAS: *Šárka* (1887–88; rev. 1918–19, with Act 3 orchestrated by O. Chlubna; rev. 1924–25; Brno, Nov. 11, 1925); *Počátek romanu* (The Beginning of a Romance; 1891; Brno, Feb. 10, 1894); *Její pastorkyňa* (Her Foster Daughter; generally known by its German title, *Jenůfa*; 1894–1903; Brno, Jan. 21, 1904; several subsequent revisions, including final version by K. Kovařovic, 1916; Prague, May 26, 1916); *Osud* (Fate; 1903–05; rev. 1906–07; 1st complete perf., Brno Radio, Sept. 18, 1934; 1st stage perf., National Theater, Brno, Oct. 25, 1958); *Výlet pana Broučka do měsíce* (Mr. Brouček's Excursion to the Moon; 1908–17; National Theater, Prague, April 23, 1920); a sequel to the preceding, *Výlet pana Broučka do XV stoleti* (Mr. Brouček's Excursion to the 15th Century; 1917; National Theater, Prague, April 23, 1920); *Kát'a Kabanová* (1919–21; Brno, Nov. 23, 1921); *Příhody Lišky Bystroušky* (The Adventures of the Vixen Bystrouška; The Cunning Little Vixen; 1921–23; Brno, Nov. 6, 1924); *Věc Makropulos* (The Makropulos Affair; 1923–25; Brno, Dec. 18, 1926); *Z mrtvého domu* (From the House of the Dead; 1927–28; rev. and reorchestrated by O. Chlubna and B. Bakala, 1930; Brno, April 12, 1930). **FOLK BALLET:** *Rákos Rákoczy* (National Theater, Prague, July 24, 1891).

ORCH.: *Suite* for Strings (Brno, Dec. 2, 1877); *Idyll* for Strings (Brno, Dec. 15, 1878); *Suite (Serenade)*, op. 3 (1891; Brno, Sept. 23, 1928); *Adagio* (1891); *Žárlivost* (Jealousy), overture (1894; 1st concert perf., Prague, Nov. 10, 1906); *Šumařovo dítě* (The Fiddler's Child), ballad (1912; Prague, Nov. 14, 1917); *Taras Bulba*, rhapsody after Gogol (1915–18; Brno, Oct. 9, 1921); *Balada blanická* (The Ballad of Blanik), symphonic poem (Brno, March 21, 1920); *Sinfonietta* (Prague, June 29, 1926); *Dunaj* (The Danube), symphonic poem (1923–28; unfinished; completed by O. Chlubna, 1948); Violin Concerto: *Putování dušičky* (Pilgrimage of the Soul; 1926; Brno, Sept. 29, 1988).

CHAMBER: *Znělka* (Fanfare) for 4 Violins (1875); *Zvuky ku památce Förchgotta-Tovačovského* (Sounds in Memory of Forchgotta-Tovacovskeho) for 3 Violins, Viola, Cello, and Double Bass (c.1875); *Romance* for Violin and Piano (1879); *Dumka* for Violin and Piano (1880); *Prohádka* (Fairy Tale) for Cello and Piano (1910; rev. 1923); *Presto* for Cello and Piano (c.1910); Violin Sonata (1914–21; Balada only); 2 string quartets: No. 1 (1923–24; Prague, Sept. 17, 1924; based on the lost Piano Trio of 1908–9) and No. 2, *Listy důvěrné* (Intimate Letters; Brno, Sept. 11, 1928; rev. 1947 by O. Šourek); *Mládí* (Youth), suite for Wind Sextet (Brno, Oct. 21, 1924); *Pochod Modráčků* (March of the Blue Boys) for Piccolo and Piano (1924); Concertino for Piano, 2 Violins, Viola, Clarinet, Horn, and Bassoon (1925; Brno, Feb. 16, 1926); *Capriccio Vzdor* (Defiance) for Piano,

Left-hand, and Chamber Ensemble (1926; Prague, March 2, 1928). **PIANO:** *Thema con variazioni* (*Zdenciny variace*: Zdenka Variations; 1880); *Na památku* (In Memoriam; c.1886); *Po zarostlém chodníčku* (On the Overgrown Path), 15 pieces (1901–8; 7 originally for Harmonium); Sonata *1.X.1905 Z ulice* (From the Street; 1905; only 2 movements extant; inspired by the abortive but sanguine Russian revolt); *V mlhách* (In the Mists; 1912; rev. 1949, by B. Štědroń); *Vzpomínka* (Reminiscence; 1928).

VOCAL: CHORAL: SACRED: *Fidelis servus* for Mixed Voices (c.1870); *Graduale in festo purificationis B.V.M.* for Mixed Voices (c.1870; rev. 1887); Mass (c.1870; not extant); *Graduale (Speciosus forma)* for Mixed Voices and Organ (1874); *Introitus (in festo Ss. Nominis Jesu)* for Mixed Voices and Organ (c.1874); *Benedictus* for Soprano, Mixed Voices, and Organ (1875); *Communio* for Mixed Voices (1875); *Exaudi Deus* for Mixed Voices and Organ (1875); *Exaudi Deus* for Mixed Voices (1875); *Odpočin si* (Take Your Rest) for Men's Voices (c.1875); *Regnum mundi* for Mixed Voices (c.1878); *Sanctus* for Mixed Voices (1879); *Deset českých církevních zpěvo z Lehnerova mešního kancinonálu* (10 Czech Hymns from the Lehner Hymnbook for Mass) with Organ (1881); *Ave Maria* (1883); *Hospodine!* (Lord Have Mercy) for Soprano, Alto, Tenor, Bass, Double Chorus, Organ, Harp, 4 Trombones, and Tuba (1896); *Slavnostní sbor* (Festival Chorus) for Men's Voices (1897); *Svatý Václave!* (St. Wenceslas; 1902); *Constitues* for Men's Voices and Organ (c.1902); *Zdrávas Maria* for Tenor, Mixed Voices, and Organ (1904); (7) *Církevni zpěvy české vicehlasné z příborského kancionálu* (Czech Hymns for Several Voices from the Pribor Hymnbook; c.1904); Mass in E-flat major for Voices and Organ (1907–08; left incomplete; finished and orchestrated by V. Petrželka; Brno, March 7, 1943); *Veni sancte spiritus* for Men's Voices (1910). **SECULAR** (all for Men's Voices unless otherwise given): *Srbská lidová piseň* (Serbian Folk Song) for Mixed Voices (1873); *Orání* (Ploughing; 1873); *Válečná* (War Song; 1873); *Nestálost lásky* (The Fickleness of Love; 1873); *Osámělá bez techy* (Alone without Comfort; 1874; rev. 1898 and 1925); *Divim se milému* (I Wonder at My Beloved; c.1875); *Vínek stonulý* (A Drowned Wreath; c.1875); *Láska opradivá* (True Love; 1876); *Když mne nechceš coz je víc* (If You Don't Want Me, What Else Is There?; 1876); *Zpěvná duma* (Choral Elegy; 1876); *Slavnostní sbor* (Festival Chorus) for Soloists and Voices (1877); *Osudu neujdeš* (You Cannot Escape Your Fate; 1878); *Na košatej jedli dva holubi sed'á* (On the Bushy Fir Tree 2 Pigeons Are Perched; c.1878); *Píseň v jeseni* (Autumn Song) for Mixed Voices (1880); *Na prievoze* (c.1883); *Mužské sbory* (Men's Voice Choruses; 1885); *Kačena divoká* (The Wild Duck) for Mixed Voices (c.1885); *Tři mužské sbory* (3 Men's Voice Choruses; 1888); *Naše píseň* (Our Song) for Mixed Voices and Orch. (1890); *Zelené sem sela* (I Have Sown Green) for Mixed Voices and Orch. (1892); *Což ta naše bříza* (Our Birch Tree; 1893); *Vinek* (The Garland; 1893); *Už je slúnko z tej hory ven* (The Sun Has Risen above That Hill) for Baritone, Mixed Voices, and Piano (1894); *Čtvero mužských sborů moravských* (4 Moravian Men's Voice Choruses; 1904); *Kantor Halfar* (1906); *Maryčka Magdónova* (1906–07); *Sedmdesát tisíc* (The 70,000; 1909); *Perina* (The Eiderdown; c.1914); *Vlčí stopa* (The Wolf's Trail) for Soprano, Women's Voices, and Piano (1916); *Hradčanské pisničky* (Songs of Hradcany) for Women's Voices (1916); *Kaspar Rucký* for Soprano and Women's Voices (1916); *Česká legie* (The Czech Legion; 1918); *Potulný šílenec* (The Wandering Madman) for Soprano and Men's Voices (1922); *Naše vlajka* (Our Flag) for 2 Sopranos and Men's Voices (1925–26); *Sbor při kladenízakladního kamene Masarykovy university v Brne* (Chorus for Laying the Foundation Stone of Masaryk University in Brno; 1928). **CANTATAS:** *Amarus* for Soprano, Tenor, Baritone, Chorus, and Orch. (1897; Kroměříž, Dec. 2, 1900; rev. 1901 and 1906); *Otče náš* (Our Father) for Tenor, Chorus, and Piano or Harmonium (Brno, June 15, 1901; rev. 1906); *Elegie na smrt dcery Olgy* (Elegy on the Death of My Daughter Olga) for Tenor, Chorus, and Piano (1903; rev. 1904; Brno Radio, Dec. 20, 1930); *Na Soláni Čarták* (Cartak on the Solan) for Tenor, Men's Voices, and Orch. (1911; Brno, March 13, 1912); *Věčné evangelium* (The Eternal Gospel) for Soprano, Tenor, Chorus, and Orch. (1914; Prague, Feb. 5, 1917; rev. 1924); *Glagolská mše* (Glagolitic Mass) for Soprano, Alto, Tenor, Bass, Chorus, Orch., and Organ (1926; Brno, Dec. 5, 1927). **CHAMBER VOCAL:** *Zapisnik zmizeleho* (The Diary of One Who Disappeared), song cycle for Tenor, Alto, 3 Women's Voices, and Piano (1917–19; Brno, April 18, 1921); *Říkadla* (Nursery Rhymes), 8 pieces for 3 Women's Voices, Clarinet, and Piano (Brno, Oct. 26, 1925; rev. version, 1927, as 18 pieces and an introduction for 2 Sopranos, 2 Altos, 3 Tenors, 2 Basses, 9 Instruments, and Children's Drum).

Janáček made many arrangements of folk music and prepared the following eds. of folk songs: with F. Bartoš, *Kytice z národních písní moravských* (A Bouquet of Moravian Folk Songs; Telč, 1890; 3rd ed., rev., 1901; 4th ed., 1953, edited by A. Gregor and B. Štědroň); 53 songs (Telč, 1892–1901; 2nd ed., 1908, as *Moravaská lidová poesie v pisnich*; Moravian Folk Poetry in Songs; 4th ed., 1947, edited by B. Štědroň); with F. Bartoš, *Národní pisne moravské v nově nasbírané* (Moravian Folk Songs Newly Collected; 1899); with P. Váša, *Moravské písně milostné* (Moravian Love Songs; 1928). A complete critical ed. of the works of Janáček began publication in Prague in 1978.

WRITINGS: J. Vysloužil, ed., *O lidové písni a lidové hudbě* (Folk Song and Folk Music; Prague, 1955); Z. Blažek, ed., *Hudebně teoretické dilo* (Music Theory Works; 2 vols., Prague, 1968, 1974); M. Boyars, ed., *J.'s Uncollected Essays on Music* (London and N.Y., 1989).

BIBL.: SOURCE MATERIAL: His correspondence was ed. by A. Rektorys and J. Racek (9 vols., Prague, 1934–53); J. Racek, ed., *L. J.: Obraz života a dila* (L. J.: A Picture of His Life and Works; Brno, 1948); B. Štědroň, *L. J. v obrazech* (L. J. in Pictures; Prague, 1958); idem, *Dilo Leoše Janáčka: Abecedni seznam Janáčkových skladeb a úprav* (L. J.'s Works: An Alphabetical Catalog of J.'s Compositions and Arrangements; Prague, 1959; Eng. tr., 1959, as *The Work of L. J.*); T. Strakova, ed., *Iconographia janáčkiana* (Brno, 1975); N. Simeone, *The First Editions of L. J.: A Bibliographical Catalogue, with Reproductions of Title Pages* (Tutzing, 1991); M. Beckerman and G. Bauer, eds., *Proceedings of the International Conference on J. and Czech Music* (Stuyvesant, N.Y., 1993); J. Tyrrell, ed. and tr., *Intimate Letters: L. J. to Kamila Stösslová* (Princeton, N.J., 1994). **BIOGRAPHICAL:** M. Brod, *L. J.: Život a dilo* (L. J.: Life and Works; Prague, 1924; Ger. ed., 1925; 2nd ed., rev., 1956); D. Muller, *L. J.* (Paris, 1930); A. Vašek, *Po stopách dra Leoše Janáčka* (On the Track of Dr. L. J.; Brno, 1930); H. Kašlik, *L. J. dirigent* (Prague, 1936); O. Jeremiáš, *L. J.* (Prague, 1938); V. Helfert, *L. J.* (Brno, 1939); idem, *O Janáčkovi* (About J.; ed. by B. Štědroň, Prague, 1949); H. Richter, *L. J.* (Leipzig, 1958); J. Vogel, *L. J.: Leben und Werk* (Kassel, 1958; Eng. tr., 1962; 2nd ed., rev., 1980); J. Šeda, *L. J.* (Prague, 1961); J. Racek, *L. J.: Mensch und Künstler* (Leipzig, 1962; 2nd ed., 1971; Czech ed., 1963); H. Hollander, *L. J.* (London, 1963; Ger. ed., 1964); M. Černohorská, *L. J.* (in Eng.; Prague, 1966); B. Štědroň, *L. J.: K jeho lidskému a uměleckému profilu* (L. J.'s Image as Man and Artist; Brno, 1976); J. Vysloužil, *L. J.* (Brno, 1978); I. Horsbrugh, *L. J.* (Newton Abbot, 1981); K. Honolka, *L. J.: Sein Leben, sein Werk, seine Zeit* (Stuttgart, 1982); S. Přibáňová, *L. J.* (Prague, 1984); C. Susskind, *J. and Brod* (London, 1986); F. Pulcini, *J.: Vita, opere, scritti* (Florence, 1993). **CRITICAL, ANALYTICAL:** L. Firkušný, *Odkaz Leoše Janáčka české opeře* (L. J.'s Legacy to Czech Opera; Brno, 1939); L. Kundera, *Janáčkova varhanická škola* (J.'s Organ School; Olomouc, 1948); J. Burghauser, "Janáčkova tvorba komorni a symfonická" (J.'s Chamber and Symphonic Works), *Musikologie*, III (1955); Č. Gardavský, "Chrámové a varhanní skladby Leoše Janáčka" (L. J.'s Church and Organ Works), ibid.; L. Kundera, "Janáčkova tvorba klavírni" (J.'s Piano Works), ibid.; F. Pala, "Jevistni dilo Leoše Janáčka" (L. J.'s Stage Works), ibid.; T. Straková, "Janáčkova opera Osud" (J.'s Opera *Fate*), *Časopis Moravského Musea*, XLI (1956); D. Shawe-Taylor, "The Operas of L. J.," *Proceedings of the Royal Musical Association*, LXXXV (1958–59); J.

Vysloužil, "Janáčkova tvorba ve světle jeho hudebně folkloristické teorie" (J.'s Works in the Light of His Folk-Music Theories), *Sbornik Janáčkovy akademie múzických umění*, II (1960); Z. Sádecký, "Celotónový charakter hudební řeči v Janáčkově 'Lišce Bystroušce'" (The Whole-Tone Character of the Musical Language of J.'s *Cunning Little Vixen*), *Živá hudba*, II (1962); J. Tyrrell, "The Musical Prehistory of J.'s Počátek románu and Its Importance in Shaping the Composer's Dramatic Style," *Časopis Moravského Musea*, LII (1967); Z. Sádecký, "Výstava dialogu a monologu v Janáčkov Její pastorkyňi" (Dialogue and Monologue Structure in J.'s *Její pastorkyňa*), *Živá hudba*, IV (1968); B. Štědroň, *Zur Genesis von L. J.s Oper Jenůfa* (Brno, 1968; 2nd ed., 1971); A. Tučapský, *Mužské sbory Leoše Janáčka a jejich interpretační tradice* (L. J.'s Male Voice Choruses and Their Performance Tradition; Ostrava, 1968); J. Tyrrell, "Mr. Brouček's Excursion to the Moon," *Časopic Moravského Musea*, LIII–LIV (1968–69); J. Blatný, "J. učitel a teoretik" (J. as Teacher and Theorist), *Opus Musicum*, I (1969); J. Tyrrell, "J. and the Speech-Melody Myth," *Musical Times* (Aug. 1970); E. Chisholm, *The Operas of L. J.* (Oxford, 1971); O. Chlubna, "O kompozičním myšlení Leoše Janáčka" (L. J.'s Compositional Thought Processes), *Hudební Rozhledy*, XXIV (1971); T. Kneif, *Die Bühnenwerke von L. J.* (Vienna, 1974); A. Geck, *Das Volksliedmaterial L. J.s: Analysen der Strukturen unter Einbeziehung von J.s Randbemerkungen und Volkstudien* (Regensburg, 1975); D. Ströbel, *Motiv und Figur in den Kompositionen der Jenufa-Werkgruppe* (Freiburg, 1975); M. Ewans, *J.'s Tragic Operas* (London, 1977); J. Vysloužil, "L. J. 1854–1928," *Acta Janáčkiana*, II (Brno, 1985); P. Wingfield, "J.'s 'Lost' Kreutzer Sonata," *Journal of the Royal Musical Association*, 112/2 (1987); J. Vysloužil, "The Style and Musical Poetics of L. J.," *Acta Janáčkiana*, III (Brno, 1988); Z. Skoumal, *Structure in the Late Instrumental Music of L. J.* (diss., City Univ. of N.Y., 1992); J. Tyrrell, ed., *J.'s Operas: A Documentary Account* (Princeton, N.J., 1992); P. Wingfield, *J.: Glagolithic Mass* (Cambridge, 1992); M. Beckerman, *J. as Theorist* (Stuyvesant, N.Y., 1993).

Jander, Owen (Hughes), American musicologist; b. Mount Kisco, N.Y., June 4, 1930. He was educated at the Univ. of Virginia (B.A., 1951) and Harvard Univ. (M.A., 1952; Ph.D., 1962, with the diss. *The Works of Alessandro Stradella Related to the Cantata and the Opera*). In 1960 he joined the dept. of music at Wellesley College, where he later became the Catherine Mills Davis Prof. in Music History; was founder of its Collegium Musicum for the performance of early music and also initiated the project to construct the outstanding Fisk Organ there for the performance of the pre-Bach repertoire; also served as ed. of The Wellesley Edition and The Wellesley Edition Cantata Index Series (1962–74). In 1966–67 he held a Guggenheim fellowship, and in 1985 he received an NEH Fellowship for Senior Scholars. He initially devoted himself to 17th-century Italian music, but later turned to Beethoven. He contributed numerous articles to *The New Grove Dictionary of Music and Musicians* (1980), and also served as co-ed. of *Charles Benton Fisk: Organ Builder* (2 vols., 1986).

Jandó, Jenő, Hungarian pianist and teacher; b. Pecs, Feb. 1, 1952. He began piano lessons at the age of 7 with his mother; in 1968, entered the Franz Liszt Academy of Music in Budapest, where he was a student of Katalin Nemes and Kodosa, graduating in 1974. After taking prizes in Hungarian competitions, as well as in the György Cziffra (2nd, 1972), Dino Ciani (2nd, 1975), and Sydney Chamber Music (1st, 1977) competitions, he pursued a global career as a soloist with orchs., recitalist, and chamber music artist. He also taught at the Franz Liszt Academy of Music. Jandó has won particular distinction for his sensitive interpretations of the Classical and Romantic masters. His repertoire includes all the Mozart piano concerti and sonatas, as well as all the piano sonatas of Haydn, Beethoven, and Schubert. He is also noted for his performances of Liszt and Bartók.

Janeček, Karel, Czech composer and music theorist; b. Czestochowa, Poland, Feb. 20, 1903; d. Prague, Jan. 4, 1974. He spent his boyhood in Kiev. After completing his secondary education at an industrial school, he went to Prague, where he took courses in composition with Křička (1921–24) and Novák (1924–27). From 1929 to 1941 he taught at the Plzeň Music School; then was prof. of composition at the Prague Cons. (1941–46); subsequently helped to found the Prague Academy of Music (1947), where he taught; was a prof. there (from 1961). In his early works, Janeček adopted a traditional national style; later he occasionally employed a personalized dodecaphonic scheme.

WORKS: ORCH.: *Overture* (1926–27); 2 syms. (1935–40; 1954–55); *Lenin*, symphonic triptych (1953); *Legend of Prague*, overture for Strings (1956); *Fantasy* (1962–63); Sinfonietta (1967); *Large Symposium* for 15 Soloists (1967). **CHAMBER:** 3 string quartets (1924, 1927, 1934); *Divertimento* for 8 Instruments (1925–26); String Trio (1930); Trio for Flute, Clarinet, and Bassoon (1931); Duo for Violin and Viola (1938); Violin Sonata (1939); *Divertimento* for Oboe, Clarinet, and Bassoon (1949); Cello Sonata (1958); *Little Symposium*, suite for Flute, Clarinet, Bassoon, and Piano (1959); Duo for Violin and Cello (1960); *Chamber Overture* for Nonet (1960); Quartet for Flute, Oboe, Clarinet, and Bassoon (1966). **PIANO:** *Trifles and Abbreviations* (1926); *Tema con variazioni*, inspired by the Nazi destruction of the village of Lidice (1942). **VOCAL:** Choral works, including *To the Fallen* (1950–51), *To the Living* (1951), and *My Dream* (1972); songs.

WRITINGS (all publ. in Prague): *Otakar Šin* (1944); *Hudební formy* (Musical Forms; 1955); *Melodika* (1956); *Vyjádření souzvukv* (The Writing of Chords; 1958); *Harmonie rozborem* (Harmony Through Analysis; 1963); *Základy moderni harmonie* (The Basis of Modern Harmony; 1965); *Tektonika* (Structure; 1968); *Tvorba a tvůrci* (Creativity and Creations; 1968); *Skladatelská práce v oblasti klasické harmonie* (Composition Based on Classical Harmony; 1973).

Janigro, Antonio, esteemed Italian cellist, conductor, and pedagogue; b. Milan, Jan. 21, 1918; d. there, May 1, 1989. He enrolled at the Milan Cons. at 11, where he studied cello with Gilberto Crepax; he also received advice from Casals and was a student of Alexanian at the École Normale de Musique in Paris. In 1934 he made his formal recital debut in Pavia, and then pursued an active career as a cello virtuoso. From 1939 to 1953 he was prof. of cello at the Zagreb Cons. In 1948 he launched a 2nd career as a conductor in Zagreb, where he later conducted the Radio and Television Sym. Orch from 1954 to 1964. In 1954 he founded the chamber ensemble I Solisti di Zagreb, which he conducted on extensive tours until 1967. He also was conductor of the Angelicum Orch. in Milan from 1965 to 1967. From 1968 to 1971 he was conductor of the Saarland Radio Chamber Orch. in Saarbrücken. As a guest conductor, Janigro appeared widely in Europe and North America. He also continued throughout the years to tour as a cellist. From 1965 to 1974 he was prof. of the master class in cello at the Düsseldorf Cons. His repertoire as both a cellist and conductor was remarkably comprehensive, ranging from early music to contemporary scores.

BIBL.: B. Gavoty and R. Hauert, *A. J.* (Geneva, 1962).

Janis (real name, **Yanks**, abbreviated from **Yankelevitch**), **Byron,** outstanding American pianist; b. McKeesport, Pa., March 24, 1928. He began to study piano with a local teacher; at the age of 7, he was taken to N.Y., where he became a pupil of Adele Marcus. Progressing rapidly, he made his professional debut in 1943, playing Rachmaninoff's 2nd Piano Concerto with the NBC Sym. Orch.; he played it again with the Pittsburgh Sym. Orch. on Feb. 20, 1944, with the 13-year-old Lorin Maazel on the podium; Vladimir Horowitz happened to be present at the concert and told Janis that he would be willing to take him as a private pupil; these private lessons continued for several years. In 1948 he toured South America; that same year he played in Carnegie Hall, N.Y., to critical acclaim. In 1952 he made a tour of Europe. In 1960 he made his first tour of Russia, under the auspices of the U.S. State Dept.; played there again in 1962. During a visit to France in 1967, he discovered the autograph MSS of 2 waltzes by Chopin, the G-flat major, op. 70, no. 1, and the E-flat major, op. 18; in 1973 he located 2 variants of these waltzes in the library of Yale Univ. In 1975 he made the film *Frédéric Chopin: A Voyage with Byron Janis*, which was produced by the Public Broadcasting Service. In 1953 he married June Dickinson Wright; they were divorced in 1965; in 1966 he married Maria Veronica Cooper, the daughter of the movie star Gary Cooper. At the climax of his career, Janis was stricken with crippling psoriatic arthritis in his hands and wrists. In spite of the attendant physical and emotional distress, he persevered in his international career. On Feb. 25, 1985, he gave a special concert at the White House in Washington, D.C., at which time his illness was publicly disclosed. He was named Ambassador for the Arts of the National Arthritis Foundation, and subsequently gave concerts on its behalf.

Jankélévitch, Vladimir, French philosopher and writer on music; b. Bourges, Aug. 31, 1903; d. Paris, June 6, 1985. He was educated in Paris at the School of Oriental Languages and at the École Normale Supérieure; received a degree in philosophy in 1925 and the doctorat ès lettres in 1933. He was a prof. of philosophy at the Institut de Prague (1927–33); then at the univs. of Lille (1933–39; 1945–52) and Toulouse (1939–45); was a prof. of ethics and moral philosophy at the Sorbonne in Paris (1952–78). His writings on music reflect his philosophical bent; these include *Gabriel Fauré et ses mélodies* (Paris, 1938; 2nd ed., aug., 1951, as *Gabriel Fauré, Ses mélodies, son esthétique*); *Maurice Ravel* (Paris, 1939; 2nd ed., aug., 1956, as *Ravel*); *Debussy et le mystère* (Neuchâtel, 1949); *La Rhapsodie, verve et improvisation musicale* (Paris, 1955); *Le Nocturne: Fauré: Chopin et la nuit: Satie et le matin* (Paris, 1957); *La Musique et l'ineffable* (Paris, 1961; 2nd ed., 1983); *La Vie et la mort dans la musique de Debussy* (Neuchâtel, 1968); *Fauré et l'inexprimable* (Paris, 1974); *Debussy et le mystère de l'instant* (Paris, 1976); with B. Berlowitz, *Quelque part dans l'inachevé, Moussorgsky, Liszt, Bartók, Chopin . . .* (Paris, 1978); *Liszt et la rhapsodie: Essai sur la virtuosité* (Paris, 1979); *La Présence lointaine, Albéniz, Severac, Mompou* (Paris, 1983).

BIBL.: L. Jerphagnon, *J.* (Paris, 1969).

Janků, Hana, Czech soprano; b. Brno, Oct. 25, 1940; d. Vienna, April 28, 1995. She studied with Jaroslav Kvapil in Brno, making her operatic debut there as the Countess in Novák's *Lucerna* in 1959; later sang with the Prague National Theater Opera. She made her first appearance at Milan's La Scala in 1967 as Turandot; appeared regularly at the Deutsche Oper am Rhein in Düsseldorf and the Deutsche Oper in West Berlin (from 1970). In 1973 she sang Tosca at her Covent Garden debut in London. She also made guest appearances at the Vienna State Opera, the Bavarian State Opera in Munich, the Hamburg State Opera, the San Francisco Opera, and the Teatro Colón in Buenos Aires. In addition to the Czech repertory, she was also known for such roles as Gioconda, Elsa, Kundry, Desdemona, and Ariadne.

Janowitz, Gundula, esteemed German soprano; b. Berlin, Aug. 2, 1937. She studied with Herbert Thöny at the Graz Cons. She made her formal operatic debut as Barbarina at the Vienna State Opera (1959), and later became one of its leading members; also sang at the Bayreuth Festivals (1960–63) and the Salzburg Festivals (from 1963); was a member of the Frankfurt am Main Opera (1963–66); then joined the Deutsche Oper in West Berlin. She appeared at the Glyndebourne Festival (1964); sang at Karajan's Salzburg Easter Festivals (1967–68). She made her Metropolitan Opera debut in N.Y. as Sieglinde on Nov. 21, 1967. She was chosen to sing the role of Mozart's Countess at the reopening of the Paris Opéra in 1973; subsequently made her debut at London's Covent Garden as Donna Anna (1976). She was made an Austrian Kammersängerin in 1970. In 1990–91 she was director of the Graz-Steiermark Theater. Her other notable roles included Fiordiligi, Agathe, Eva, Aida, Elisabeth, Desdemona, and Ariadne. She was also well known as a concert and lieder artist.

Janowski, Marek, Polish-born German conductor; b. Warsaw, Feb. 18, 1939. He was taken to Germany while young; studied mathematics and music at the Univ. of Cologne; continued his musical studies in Vienna and at the Accademia Chigiana in Siena. He conducted sym. concerts in Italy, and then opera in Aachen and Cologne; subsequently held the post of 1st conductor at the Deutsche Oper am Rhein in Düsseldorf (1964–69) and at the Hamburg State Opera (1969–74); also made guest appearances in Stuttgart, Cologne, and Munich. In 1969 he made his English debut conducting the visiting Cologne Opera in the British premiere of Henze's *Der junge Lord*. From 1973 to 1975 he was chief conductor in Freiburg im Breisgau, and from 1975 to 1979 Generalmusikdirektor in Dortmund. He made his U.S. debut conducting *Lohengrin* at the Chicago Lyric Opera in 1980. He was principal guest conductor (1980–83) and artistic advisor (1983–86) of the Royal Liverpool Phil.; was also chief conductor of the Nouvel Orch. Philharmonique de Radio France in Paris (from 1984) and of the Gürzenich Orch. in Cologne (1986–91).

Janson, Alfred, Norwegian composer and pianist; b. Oslo, March 10, 1937. His mother, a piano teacher, oversaw his early music instruction. He also learned to play the accordion and began appearing in Oslo restaurants when he was 12. He later received some instruction in composition from Finn Mortensen. In 1962 he made his debut as a pianist in Oslo, and subsequently was frequently engaged in jazz settings. After composing in a decidedly contemporary idiom, his works took on more tonal leanings. His interest in jazz and electronics also played a role in his path as a composer.

WORKS: DRAMATIC: *Mot solen* (Towards the Sun), ballet (1969); *Et Fjelleventyret* (A Mountain Adventure), opera (1970–73; Oslo, April 9, 1973); music for theater, films, and television. **ORCH.:** *Construction and Hymn* (1963); *Canon* for Chamber Orch. and 2 Tape Recorders (1965); *Prelude* for Violin and Orch. (1973–75); *Mellomspill* (1985); *National Anthem* (1988); *Fragment* for Cello and Orch. (1991). **CHAMBER:** String Quartet (1978); *Tarantella* for Chamber Ensemble (1989). **PIANO:** *November 1962* (1962); *Senza pedales* (1992). **VOCAL:** *Lullaby* for Soprano and String Orch. (1963); *Theme* for Chorus, Organ, Percussion, and Piano (1966); *Nocturne* for Chorus, 2 Cellos, 2 Percussionists, and Harp, after Nietzsche (1967); *Valse triste* for Voice, Jazz Quintet, and Tape (1970); *3 Poems by Ebba Lindqvist* for Chorus (1975–80); *Hymn to Josef* for Voice and Piano (1977); *Errotikk og Pollitikk* for Chorus, Organ, and Rhythmbox (1983); *Wings* for Chorus and Jazz Ensemble (1983). **OTHER:** *Diaphony* for 4 Wind Band Groups, Bugle Corps, 4 Percussionists, Dancers/Actors/Musicians, and Tape (1990; in collaboration with K. Kolberg and R. Wallin).

Jansons, Arvid. See **Yansons, Arvid.**

Jansons, Mariss, prominent Latvian conductor, son of **Arvid Yansons**; b. Riga, Jan. 14, 1943. He studied at the Leningrad Cons., where he took courses in violin, viola, piano, and conducting. He profited from initial conducting studies with his father; then studied with Swarowsky in Vienna, Karajan in Salzburg, and Mravinsky in Leningrad. In 1971 he won 2nd prize in the Karajan Competition in West Berlin; then made appearances with major orchs. and opera houses in the Soviet Union and Eastern Europe; also conducted in Western Europe and America. In 1979 he was named chief conductor of the Oslo Phil., with which he toured Europe; also toured the U.S. with it in 1987. He likewise was closely associated with the St. Petersburg Phil., and from 1992 he was principal guest conductor of the London Phil. In 1994 he took the Oslo Phil. on a major tour of Europe and North America in celebration of its 75th anniversary. In 1996–97 he was music director designate and from 1997 music director of the Pittsburgh Sym. Orch.

Janssen, Herbert, noted German-born American baritone; b. Cologne, Sept. 22, 1892; d. N.Y., June 3, 1965. He studied in Cologne, and then with Oskar Daniel in Berlin, making his operatic debut in Schreker's *Der Schatzgräber* at the State Opera there (May 5, 1922), and remaining on its roster until 1938; he also made regular appearances at London's Covent Garden (1926–39) and at the Bayreuth Festivals (1930–37), where he excelled in such roles as Amfortas, the Dutchman, Gunther, Kurwenal, and Wolfram. He made his Metropolitan Opera debut as Wotan during the company's visit to Philadelphia (Jan. 24, 1939); his formal debut with the company followed in N.Y. as Wolfram (Jan. 28, 1939); he continued as a prominent member on its roster until 1952. He became a naturalized American citizen in 1946. In later years, he was active as a voice teacher. He was also well known for his portrayal of Kothner.

Janssen, Werner, American conductor and composer; b. N.Y., June 1, 1899; d. Stony Brook, N.Y., Sept. 19, 1990. He studied with Clapp at Dartmouth College (B.Mus., 1921) and with Converse, Friedheim, and Chadwick at the New England Cons. of Music in Boston; then studied conducting with Weingartner in Basel (1920–21) and Scherchen in Strasbourg (1921–25); won the Prix de Rome of the American Academy (1930) and studied orchestration with Respighi at the Accademia di Santa Cecilia in Rome (1930–33). In 1930 he made his debut as a conductor in Rome; he gave a concert of music by Sibelius in Helsinki in 1934 and was praised by Sibelius himself; received the Finnish Order of the White Rose. He made his American debut with the N.Y. Phil. on Nov. 8, 1934; served as conductor of the Baltimore Sym. Orch. (1937–39); then went to Los Angeles, where he organized the Janssen Sym. Orch. (1940–52) and commissioned American composers to write special works. He was conductor of the Utah Sym. Orch. in Salt Lake City (1946–47), of the Portland (Ore.) Sym. Orch. (1947–49), and of the San Diego Phil. (1952–54). In 1937 he married the famous film actress Ann Harding; they were divorced in 1963. As a composer, Janssen cultivated the art of literal pictorialism; his most successful work of this nature was *New Year's Eve in New York* (Rochester, N.Y., May 9, 1929), a symphonic poem for Large Orch. and Jazz Instruments; the orch. players were instructed to shout at the end "Happy New Year!" Other works were: *Obsequies of a Saxophone* for 6 Wind Instruments and a Snare Drum (Washington, D.C., Oct. 17, 1929); *Louisiana Suite* for Orch. (1930); *Dixie Fugue* (extracted from the *Louisiana Suite*; Rome, Nov. 27, 1932); *Foster Suite* for Orch., on Stephen Foster's tunes (1937); 2 string quartets (1934, 1935); Quintet for 10 Instruments (1968); piano music; many film scores; popular songs.

Jaques-Dalcroze, Emile, Swiss music educator and composer, creator of "Eurhythmics"; b. Vienna (of French parents), July 6, 1865; d. Geneva, July 1, 1950. In 1873 his parents moved to Geneva; having completed his courses at the Univ. and at the Cons. there, he went to Vienna for further study under Fuchs and Bruckner; then to Paris, where he studied with Delibes and Fauré; he returned to Geneva as instructor of theory at the Cons. (1892). Since he laid special stress on rhythm, he insisted that all his pupils beat time with their hands, and this led him, step by step, to devise a series of movements affecting the entire body. Together with the French psychologist Edouard Claparide, he worked out a special terminology and reduced his practice to a regular system, which he called "Eurhythmics." When his application to have his method introduced as a regular course at the Cons. was refused, he resigned, and in 1910 established his own school at Hellerau, near Dresden. As a result of World War I, the school was closed in 1914; he then returned to Geneva and founded the Institut Jaques-Dalcroze. Interest in his system led to the opening of similar schools in London, Berlin, Vienna, Paris, N.Y., Chicago, and other cities. Aside from his rhythmical innovations, he also commanded respect as a composer of marked originality and fecundity of invention; many of his works show how thoroughly he was imbued with the spirit of Swiss folk music.

WRITINGS: *Le coeur chante: Impressions d'un musicien* (Geneva, 1900); *Vorschläge zur Reform des musikalischen Schulunterrichts* (Zürich, 1905); *La respiration et l'innervation musculaire* (Paris, 1906); *Méthode Jaques-Dalcroze* (Paris, 1906–17); *La rythmique* (Lausanne, 1916–17); *La portée musicale* (Lausanne, n.d.); *Introduction à l'étude de l'harmonie* (Geneva, n.d.); *Le rhythme, la musique et l'education* (Paris, 1919; 2nd ed., 1965; Eng. tr., 1921; 2nd ed., 1967); C. Cox, ed., *Eurhythmics, Art and Education* (London, 1930); *Rhythmics Movement* (London, 1931); *Métrique et rythmique* (Paris, 1937–38); *Souvenirs, notes et critiques* (Neuchâtel, 1942); *La musique et nous: Notes de notre double vie* (Geneva, 1945); *Notes bariolées* (Geneva, 1948).

WORKS: DRAMATIC: OPERETTA: *Riquet à la houppe* (1883). **OPÉRAS COMIQUES:** *Onkel Dazumal* (Cologne, 1905; as *Le Bonhomme Jadis*, Paris, 1906); *Les jumeaux de Bergame* (Brussels, 1908). **COMÉDIE LYRIQUE:** *Sancho Pança* (Geneva, 1897). **OTHER:** Numerous orch. works, including 2 violin concertos (1902, 1911); chamber music; piano pieces; choruses; songs.

BIBL.: P. Boepple, *Der Rhythmus als Erziehungsmittle für das Leben und die Kunst: Sechs Vorträge von E. J.-D. zur Begründung seiner Methode der rhythmischen Gymnastik* (Basel, 1907); W. Dohrn, *Die Bildungsanstalt E. J.-D.* (Dresden, 1912); M. Sadler, *The Eurhythmics of J.-D.* (London, 1912; 3rd ed., rev., 1920); K. Storck, *E. J.-D.: Seine Stellung und Aufgabe in unserer Zeit* (Stuttgart, 1912); H. Brunet-Lecomte, *J.-D., sa vie, son oeuvre* (Geneva, 1950); F. Martin et al., *E. J.-D.: L'Homme, le compositeur, le créateur de la rhythmique* (Neuchâtel, 1965); M.-L. Bachmann, *Le Rhythmique J.-D.: Une éducation par la musique et pour la musique* (Neuchâtel, 1984; Eng. tr., 1991, as *D. Today: An Education Through and Into Music*); I. Spector, *Rhythm and Life: The Work of E. J.-D.* (Stuyvesant, N.Y., 1990).

Járdányi, Pál, Hungarian composer, ethnomusicologist, and music critic; b. Budapest, Jan. 30, 1920; d. there, July 27, 1966. He studied piano and violin as a child; in 1938, became a composition student of Kodály and Siklós at the Budapest Academy of Music (until 1942); concurrently studied at the Univ. of Budapest (Ph.D., 1943, with the diss. *A kidei magyarság világi zenéje*; [The Secular Music of the Kide Magyars]; publ. in Kolozsvar, 1943). He was active as a music critic (1943–49) and as a teacher at the Budapest Academy of Music (1946–59); then was a member of the folk music research commission of the Hungarian Academy. He was awarded the Erkel Prize in 1952 and in 1954 received the Kossuth Prize for his *Vörösmarty Symphony*. His works follow the style of modern Hungarian music, based on national folk songs. He publ. the vol. *Magyar népdaltípusok* (Budapest, 1961).

WORKS: ORCH.: Sinfonietta (1940); *Divertimento concertante* (1942–49); *Dance Music* (1950); *Tisza mentén* (Along the Tisza), symphonic poem (1951); *Vörösmarty Symphony* (1953); *Rhapsody from Borsod* (1953); *Symphonic March* (1953); Harp Concerto (1959); *Vivente e moriente* (1963); Concertino for Violin and String Orch. (1964); *Székely rapszódia* (1965). **CHAMBER:** Violin duets (1934–37); 2 string quartets (1947; 1953–54); Flute Sonata (1952); *Fantasy and Variations on a Hungarian Folk Song* for Wind Quintet (1955); Quartet for 3 Violins and Cello (1958); String Trio (1959). **PIANO:** Rondo (1939); Sonata (1940); Sonata for 2 Pianos (1942); *Bulgarian Rhythm* for Piano Duet (1956).

Jarecki, Tadeusz, Polish conductor and composer; b. Lemberg, Dec. 31, 1888; d. N.Y., April 29, 1955. He studied with his father, the Polish conductor and composer Henryk Jarecki (b. Warsaw, Dec. 6, 1846; d. Lwów, Dec. 18, 1918), then with Niewiadomski in Lemberg; subsequently went to Moscow, where he studied with Taneyev at the Cons., graduating in 1913; also studied with Jaques-Dalcroze in Geneva (1912–13). In 1917–18 he lived in the U.S.; then returned to Poland and conducted opera in Stanislawow (1932–37); after a sojourn in Paris and London, he returned to the U.S. in 1946. In 1921 he married the American soprano Louise Llewellyn (b. N.Y., Dec. 10, 1889; d. there, March 6, 1954). He publ. the book *The Most Polish of Polish Composers: Frédéric Chopin 1810–1849* (N.Y., 1949). Among his compositions are 5 syms.; *Chimère*, symphonic suite (1926); *Sinfonia breve* (Lwów, Jan. 15, 1932); 3 string quartets; numerous songs.

Jarnach, Philipp, French-born German composer and pedagogue of Catalonia-Flemish descent; b. Noisy, July 26, 1892; d. Bornsen, near Bergedorf, Dec. 17, 1982. He was a son of a Catalonian sculptor and a Flemish mother. He studied with Risler (piano) and Lavignac (theory) at the Paris Cons. (1912–14). At the outbreak of World War I, he went to Zürich, where he met Busoni and taught at the Cons. (1915–21); this meeting was a decisive influence on his musical development; he became an ardent disciple of Busoni, and after his death completed Busoni's last opera, *Doktor Faust,* which was produced in Jarnach's version in Dresden on May 21, 1925. During the years 1922–27, Jarnach wrote music criticism for Berlin's *Börsen-Kurier.* In 1931 he became a naturalized German citizen. From 1927 to 1949 he was prof. of composition at the Cologne Hochschule für Musik, and from 1949 to 1970 at the Hamburg Cons. Jarnach's music is determined by his devotion to Busoni's ideals; it is distinguished by impeccable craftsmanship, but it lacks individuality. He participated in the modern movement in Germany between the two world wars, and many of his works were performed at music festivals during that period. He wrote *Prolog zu einem Ritterspiel* for Orch. (1917); *Sinfonia brevis* (1923); *Musik mit Mozart* for Orch. (1935); String Quintet (1920); String Quartet (1924); *Musik zum Gedächtnis des Einsamen* for String Quartet (1952; also for Orch.); piano pieces; songs.

BIBL.: E. Klussmann, *Der Künstler P. J. und das Gesetz* (Hamburg, 1952).

Järnefelt, (Edvard) Armas, distinguished Finnish-born Swedish conductor and composer; b. Vyborg, Aug. 14, 1869; d. Stockholm, June 23, 1958. He studied with Wegelius and Busoni at the Helsinki Cons. (1887–90), with Becker in Berlin (1890), and with Massenet in Paris (1893–94); then was conductor of the Vyborg Municipal Orch. (1898–1903) and director of the Helsinki Music Inst. (1906–07). He became a conductor at the Royal Opera in Stockholm in 1907; was named court conductor in 1910, the same year he became a naturalized Swedish citizen; later was chief conductor of the Royal Opera (1923–32). He subsequently was chief conductor of the Finnish National Opera (1932–36) and the Helsinki Phil. (1942–43). He married the soprano Maikki Pakarinen (b. Joensuu, Aug. 26, 1871; d. Turku, July 4, 1929) in 1893; they were divorced in 1908; in 1910 he married the soprano Liva Edström (b. Vänersborg, March 18, 1876; d. Stockholm, June 24, 1971). Jarnefelt was the brother-in-law of Sibelius. His compositions, which included the symphonic poem *Korsholma* (1894), a Symphonic Fantasy for Orch. (1895), and *Berceuse* for Small Orch. (1904), were written in the Finnish national style.

Jarno, Georg (real name, **György Kohner**), Hungarian conductor and composer; b. Budapest, June 3, 1868; d. Breslau, May 20, 1920. He worked as a theater conductor in Bremen, Halle, Metz, Chemnitz, Magdeburg, and other cities before concentrating on composing light theater scores. After bringing out such pieces as *Die schwarze Kaschka* (Breslau, May 27, 1895) and *Der Richter von Zalamea* (1899), he produced his first operetta, *Der zerbrochene Krug* (Hamburg, Jan. 15, 1903). The respectable staging of his *Der Goldfisch* (Breslau, Jan. 20, 1907) led to the notable Viennese premieres of his *Die Förster-Christl* (Dec. 17, 1907), *Das Musikantenmädel* (Feb. 18, 1910), and *Die Marinen-Gustl* (March 22, 1912). He went on to score further successes with *Das Farmermädchen* (Berlin, March 22, 1913), *Mein Annerl* (Vienna, Oct. 7, 1916), *Jungfer Sonnenschein* (Hamburg, Feb. 16, 1918), and *Die Csikós-Baroness* (Hamburg, Oct. 28, 1919).

Jaroch, Jiří, Czech composer; b. Smilkov, Sept. 23, 1920; d. Prague, Dec. 30, 1986. He studied composition with Řídký at the Prague Cons. (1940–46). He was a manager and producer for Prague's Czech Radio (from 1947). As a composer, he took a median line in Central European music, within the pragmatic limits of modernistic permissiveness.

WORKS: ORCH.: *Scherzo* (1947); *Burlesque* (1951); *Symphonic Dance* (1953); *Smuteční fantasie* (Mourning Fantasy; 1954); 4 syms.: No. 1 (1954–56), No. 2 (1958–60), No. 3, *Concertante,* for Violin and Orch. (1968–69), and No. 4 (1975); *Shakuntala,* suite (1957); *Stařec a moře* (The Old Man and the Sea), symphonic poem, after Ernest Hemingway (1961); *Summer Festival,* tarantella (1964); *Fantasy* for Viola and Orch. (1966). **CHAMBER:** 2 string quartets (1949–50; 1970); *Children's Suite* for Nonet (1952); Nonet No. 2 (1963); *Metamorphosis* for 12 Winds (1967–68); Sonata for Solo Violin (1973).

Jaroff, Sergei, Russian choral conductor; b. Moscow, March 20, 1896; d. Lakewood, N.J., Oct. 5, 1985. He studied at the Academy for Church Singing at the Imperial Synod; then became a Cossack officer. After the Revolution and the defeat of the White Army, he left Russia and established the Don Cossack Chorus, with which he made successful tours in Europe; eventually settled in America. The repertoire of his chorus included popular Russian songs in artful arrangements, emphasizing dynamic contrasts, and also sacred works by Russian composers.

Jarre, Maurice (Alexis), French composer; b. Lyons, Sept. 13, 1924. He studied electrical engineering before entering the Paris Cons. in 1943, where he was a student of La Presle (harmony) and Aubert (orchestration). He also profited from advice from Honegger. After working with Radiodiffusion Française (1946–50), he served as director of music at the Théâtre National Populaire in Paris (1951–63). In 1955 and 1962 he won the Prix Italia. He became especially successful as a film composer, winning Academy Awards for *Lawrence of Arabia* (1963), *Dr. Zhivago* (1965), and *A Passage to India* (1985). Among his other film scores were *The Longest Day* (1962), *Ryan's Daughter* (1970), *Shogun* (1980), and *Dead Poets Society* (1990). His other compositions include *Armida,* opéra-ballet (1954); *Fâcheuse rencontre,* ballet (1958); *Loin de Rueil,* musical comedy (1961); *Notre-Dame de Paris,* ballet (1966); *Mouvements en relief* for Orch. (1953); *Passacaille* in memory of Honegger for Orch. (Strasbourg, June 15, 1956); *Polyphonies concertantes* for Piano, Trumpet, Percussion, and Orch. (1959); and *Mobiles* for Violin and Orch. (Strasbourg, June 20, 1961).

Jarrett, Keith, versatile American pianist; b. Allentown, Pa., May 8, 1945. He began playing piano as a young child and made his first recital appearance at the age of 7. He received training in classical piano, but soon began to spike his youthful concert appearances with improvisations and his own works, which led him to pursue his interest in jazz. After studying at the Berklee School of Music in Boston, he plunged into the N.Y. jazz scene, coming to prominence as a member of the Charles Lloyd quartet (1966–70); he then worked with Miles Davis (1970–71) and toured with his own trio and as a solo artist. In 1975 he made a sensationally popular recording of solo improvisations, *The Köln Concert,* which established his reputation as a jazz virtuoso. From the early 1980s he made appearances as a classical pianist, specializing in modern works and especially those of Bartók; in 1987 he gave a particularly spirited performance in N.Y. of Lou Harrison's Piano Concerto, a performance he repeated in Tokyo which served as the basis for the critically acclaimed 1988 recording. He later became an exponent of Baroque music as well.

BIBL.: I. Carr, *K. J.: The Man and His Music* (London, 1991).

Järvi, Neeme, prominent Estonian conductor; b. Tallinn, June 7, 1937. He graduated with degrees in percussion and choral conducting from the Tallinn Music School, then studied conducting with Mravinsky and Rabinovich at the Leningrad Cons. (1955–60); he pursued postgraduate studies in 1968, and in 1971 captured 1st prize in the Accademia di Santa Cecilia conducting competition in Rome. He was active in Tallinn as music director of the Estonian State Sym. Orch. (1960–80) and of the Estonian Opera Theater (1964–77). He subsequently served as principal guest conductor of the City of Birmingham Sym. Orch. in England (1981–84). In 1982 he became music director of the Göteborg Sym. Orch. in Sweden; also was principal conductor of the Scottish National Orch. in Glasgow (1984–88). In 1990 he became music director of the Detroit Sym. Orch. His guest conducting engagements have taken him to most of the principal music centers of the world. He has won particular notice in concert settings and on recordings for his efforts in championing such rarely performed composers as Berwald, Gade, Svendsen, Stenhammar, and Tubin.

Jaubert, Maurice, French composer; b. Nice, Jan. 3, 1900; d. in battle in Azerailles, Meurthe-et-Moselle, June 19, 1940. He studied piano and composition at the Nice Cons., receiving 1st prize for piano in 1916; then studied harmony and counterpoint with Albert Groz in Paris (1923). He wrote the successful score for the film *Carnet de bal* (1937); other works included *Suite française* for Orch. (St. Louis, Nov. 10, 1933), *Jeanne d'Arc*, symphonic poem (1937), and *Sonata a due* for Violin, Cello, and String Orch. (Boston, Dec. 27, 1946).

Jeanneret, Albert, Swiss violinist, educator, and composer; b. La Chaux-de-Fonds, Feb. 7, 1886; d. Montreux, April 25, 1973. He studied violin with Andreas Moser at the Berlin Hochschule für Musik and with Henri Marteau at the Geneva Cons., graduating with the Premier Prix de Virtuosité (1909); then joined the staff of the Jaques-Dalcroze Inst. of Eurhythmics in Hellerau. He went to Paris in 1919, where he founded a school of rhythmic gymnastics and a children's orch. In 1939 he returned to Switzerland and settled in Vevey, where he also led a children's orch. About the same time, he became a follower of the Moral Rearmament Movement. On July 21, 1968, he purportedly received (and subsequently publ.) a telepathic message from his brother, the architect Le Corbusier (Charles Édouard Jeanneret), who had died 3 years before, urging him to continue his pursuits of functional art. In accordance with these ideas, which he shared with his brother, Jeanneret wrote some 25 "symphonies enfantines" for children's orch., employing "bruits humanisés" produced by graduated bottles partially filled with water at different levels, metal pipes, wooden boxes, etc.; he also composed a *Suite pittoresque* for 3 Violins and a number of choruses for Moral Rearmament meetings.

BIBL.: P. Meylan, "A. J. et les 'bruits humanisés'," *Revue Musicale de la Suisse Romande* (March 1971).

Jedlička, Dalibor, Czech bass-baritone; b. Svojanov, May 23, 1929. He received his training from Rudolf Vašek in Ostrává. In 1953 he made his operatic debut as Mumalal in Smetana's *The 2 Widows* in Opava. In 1957 he became a member of the National Theater in Prague, where his extensive repertoire included not only standard German, Italian, and French roles but various Czech roles. He toured with the company abroad, including its visit to Edinburgh in 1970 when he sang in the first British performance of Janáček's *The Excursions of Mr. Brouček*; also appeared as a guest artist in Amsterdam, Zürich, Warsaw, Venice, Bologna, and other cities. In 1993 he made his U.S. debut at the San Francisco Opera as Kolenaty in Janáček's *The Makropoulos Affair.*

Jelinek, Hanns, Austrian composer; b. Vienna, Dec. 5, 1901; d. there, Jan. 27, 1969. He studied harmony and counterpoint with Schoenberg (1918–19) and piano, harmony, and counterpoint with F. Schmidt (1920–22) at the Vienna Academy of Music. Jelinek's output ranged from light music to works utilizing serial techniques. He made a living by playing piano in bars, leading his own band, and composing for films under the name Hanns Elin. He became a lecturer (1955) and a prof. (1965) at the Vienna Academy of Music. He publ. the manual *Anleitung zur Zwölftonkomposition* (2 vols., Vienna, 1952 and 1958; 2nd ed., 1967).

WORKS: OPERETTA: *Bubi Caligula* (1947). **ORCH.:** *Praeludium, Passacaglia und Fuge* for Flute, Clarinet, Bassoon, Horn, and Strings (1922; Wuppertal, March 12, 1954); 6 syms.: No. 1 (1926–30; Breslau, June 13, 1932; rev., 1940 and 1945–46), No. 2, *Sinfonia ritmica*, for Jazz Band and Orch. (1929; Vienna, March 14, 1931; rev. 1949), No. 3, *Heitere Symphonie*, for Brass and Percussion (1930–31; Vienna, June 20, 1932), No. 4, *Sinfonia concertante*, for String Quartet and Orch. (1931; rev. 1953; Vienna, May 2, 1958), No. 5, *Symphonie brevis* (1948–50; Vienna, Dec. 19, 1950), and No. 6, *Sinfonia concertante* (Venice, Sept. 15, 1953; rev. 1957); *Sonata ritmica* for Jazz Band and Orch. (1928; rev. 1960; Vienna, Nov. 26, 1960); *Rather Fast*, rondo for Jazz Band and Orch. (1929); Suite for Strings (1931); Concertino for String Quartet and String Orch. (1951); *Phantasie* for Clarinet, Piano, and Orch. (1951; Salzburg, June 21, 1952); *Preludio solenne* (1956); *Rai buba*, étude for Piano and Orch. (1956–61); *Perergon* for Small Orch. (1957). **CHAMBER:** *6 Aphorismen* for 2 Clarinets and Bassoon (1923–30); Suite for Cello (1930); 2 string quartets (1931, 1935); *Das Zwölftonwerk*, a collection of 9 individually titled chamber pieces in 2 series: *Series 1* of 6 works for Piano (1947–49) and *Series 2* of 3 works for Various Instruments (1950–52); *3 Blue Sketches* for 9 Jazz Soloists (1956); Sonata for Solo Violin (1956); *Ollapotrida*, suite for Flute and Guitar (1957); *2 Blue O's* for 7 Jazz Performers (1959); *10 Zahme Xenien* for Violin and Piano (1960). **PIANO:** *4 Structuren* (1952); *Zwölftonfibel* (1953–54). **VOCAL:** *Prometheus* for Baritone and Orch., after Goethe (1936); *Die Heimkehr*, radio cantata for Soloists, Chorus, Orch., and Tape (1954); *Unterwegs*, chamber cantata for Soprano, Vibraphone, and Double Bass (1957); *Begegnung*, dance scene for Chorus and Orch. (1965); songs.

Jellinek, George, Hungarian-born American writer on music and broadcaster; b. Budapest, Dec. 22, 1919. He studied violin in Hungary (1925–37). In 1941 he went to the U.S. and became a naturalized American citizen in 1943; served in the U.S. Army. He was active in broadcasting; in 1968, was named music director of radio station WQXR in N.Y., where he produced such popular programs as "The Vocal Scene" and "Music at First Hearing." From 1958 he was a contributing ed. of *Stereo Review*; also wrote articles for the *Saturday Review, Opera News*, and other publs. In 1976 he became an adjunct assistant prof. of music at N.Y. Univ. He received an honorary doctorate from Long Island Univ. in 1984. He wrote librettos for Eugene Zador's operas *The Magic Chair* and *The Scarlett Mill.* His study of *Maria Callas, Portrait of a Prima Donna*, was publ. in 1960.

Jemnitz, Sándor (Alexander), Hungarian conductor, composer, and music critic; b. Budapest, Aug. 9, 1890; d. Balatonföldvár, Aug. 8, 1963. He studied with Koessler at the Budapest Royal Academy of Music (1906–08); then briefly with Nikisch (conducting), Reger (composition), Straube (organ), and Sitt (violin) at the Leipzig Cons. After conducting in various German opera houses (1911–13), he studied with Schoenberg in Berlin; returned to Budapest (1916) and was music critic of *Népszava* (1924–50); subsequently taught at the Budapest Cons. (from 1951). He publ. monographs on Mendelssohn (1958), Schumann (1958), Beethoven (1960), Chopin (1960), and Mozart (1961). As a composer, he followed the median line of Middle European modernism of the period between the 2 world wars, representing a curious compromise between the intricate contrapuntal idiom of Reger and the radical language of atonality modeled after Schoenberg's early works. He wrote mostly instrumental music.

WORKS: BALLET: *Divertimento* (1921; Budapest, April 23, 1947). **ORCH.:** Concerto for Chamber Orch. (1931); *Prelude and Fugue* (1933); *7 Miniatures* (1948); *Overture for a Peace Festival* (1951); Concerto for Strings (1954); *Fantasy* (1956). **CHAMBER:** 3 violin sonatas (1921, 1923, 1925); Cello Sonata (1922); 3 Sonatas for Solo Violin (1922, 1932, 1938); Flute Trio (1924); 2 wind trios (1925); Trumpet Quartet (1925); 2 string trios (1925, 1929); Flute Sonata (1931); *Partita* for 2 Violins (1932); Guitar Trio (1932); Sonata for Solo Cello (1933); Sonata for Solo Harp (1933); Duet Sonata for Saxophone and Banjo (1934); Sonata for Solo Double Bass (1935); Sonata for Solo Trumpet (1938); Sonata for Solo Flute (1941); Sonata for Solo Viola (1941); String Quartet (1950); 2 suites for Violin and Piano (1952, 1953); Trio for Flute, Oboe, and Clarinet (1958). **KEYBOARD: PIANO:** 5 sonatas (1914, 1927, 1929, 1933, 1954); *3 Pieces* (1915); 2 sonatinas (1919); *17 Bagatelles* (1919); *Recueil*

(1938–45); *8 Pieces* (1951). **ORGAN:** 3 sonatas (1941, 1959, 1959). **VOCAL:** Songs.

Jencks, Gardner, American pianist and composer; b. N.Y., Jan. 7, 1907; d. Cambridge, Mass., Aug. 6, 1989. He studied piano with Heinrich Gebhard in Boston (1923) and with Josef and Rosina Lhévinne in N.Y. (from 1927); later took courses at the Diller-Quaile School (1930–34); concurrently took private lessons in composition with Franklin Robinson, and then with Gustav Strube at the Peabody Cons. of Music in Baltimore (artist's diploma, 1940). On Feb. 24, 1941, he made his debut in N.Y. as a pianist; while pursuing his career, he also studied composition with Goeb and Cowell at Columbia Univ. (1956). He wrote numerous works for piano. His idiom of composition was derived from the considerations of relative sonorous masses in chordal structures and interactive rhythmic patterns; the general effect may be likened to neo-Classical concepts; tonality and atonality are applied without prejudice in his melodic lines, as are concords and discords in contrapuntal combinations.

Jeney, Zoltán, Hungarian composer; b. Szolnok, March 4, 1943. He was a student of Pongrácz in Debrecen, Farkas at the Budapest Academy of Music (1961–66), and Petrassi at the Accademia di Santa Cecilia in Rome (1967–68). In 1970 he helped to organize the Budapest New Music Studio, where he was active as a composer, keyboard player, and percussionist. In 1986 he joined the faculty of the Academy of Music. In 1988–89 he was in Berlin under the sponsorship of the Deutscher Akademischer Austauschdienst. Among his honors are the Erkel Prize (1982) and the Bartók-Pásztory Award (1988).

WORKS: ORCH.: *Laude* (1967–77); *Rimembranze* (1968); *Alef—Hommage à Schoenberg* (1971–72); *Quemadmodum* for Strings (1975); *Something Round* for 25 Strings (1975); *Sostenuto* (1979); *Something Like* for 25 Strings (1980). **CHAMBER:** *Soliloquium No. 1* for Flute (1967) and *No. 2* for Violin (1974–78); *Wei wu wei* for Chamber Ensemble (1968); *Round* for Piano, Harp, and Harpsichord (1972); *Movements of the Eye IV* for 1 or 3 Chamber Ensembles (1973); *4 Quartet* for 1 or More String Quartets (1973); *Orpheus's Garden* for 8 Instruments (1974); *A Leaf Falls—Brackets to e.e. cummings* for Violin or Viola, Contact Microphone, and Prepared Piano (1975); *Tropi* for 2 Trumpets (1975); *Arthur Rimbaud in the Desert* for Optional Keyboard Instruments (1976); *Complements* for Cimbalom (1976); *2 Mushrooms* for Chamber Ensemble (1977); *Impho 102/6* for 6 Antique Cymbals (1978); *Pontpoint* for 6 Percussionists (1978); *Being-Time I* (1979), *II* (1979), *V* (1985), *VI* (1985), and *IV* (1991) for 4 Optional Players; *Interlude with Sounds* for 1 Player (1979); *The End of a Game* for 6 Instruments (1980); *Arupa* for 6 to 8 Chimes and Drum (1981); *Something Found* for Piano, Harmonium or Organ, and Optional Chamber Ensemble (1981); *Etwas getragen* for String Quartet (1988); *Ouverture Étrusque* for Oboe, Synthesizer or Tape, and Antique Cymbals (1989); *Self-Quotations* for 5 Instruments (1991); *Fungi-Epitaphium John Cage* for Alto Flute (1992). **KEYBOARD: PIANO:** *5 Pieces* (1962); *Soliloquium No. 3* (1980); *Endgame* (1973); *Movements of the Eye I* (1973), *II* for 2 Pianos (1973), and *III* for 3 Pianos (1973); *Desert Plants* for 2 Prepared or Unprepared Pianos or 2 Pianos and Tape (1975); *Something Lost* for Prepared Piano (1975); *Transcriptions Automatiques* (1975); *Kalah* (1983); *Meditazione su una tema di Goffredo Petrassi* (1984); *Ricercare* (1992); *A Mounderin Tongue in a Pounderin Jowl* (1993). **ORGAN:** *Soliloquium No. 4* (1980); *OM* for 2 Electric Organs or Electric Organ and Tape (1979); *Ricercare in variazioni sopra il motto dal Rito Funebre* (1988). **VOCAL:** *Omaggio* for Soprano and Orch. (1966); *12 Songs* for Soprano, Violin, and Piano (1975–83); *Monody (in memoriam Igor Stravinsky)* for Soprano and Piano (1977); *To Apollon*, cantata for Chamber Chorus, English Horn, Organ, and 12 Antique Cymbals (1978); *The Eternal Corridor* for Chorus and Optional Chamber Ensemble (1983); *Spaziosa calma . . .* for Woman's Voice and Chamber Ensemble (1984; rev. 1987); *El Silencio* for Woman's Voice and String Quartet (1986); *Movements from the Funeral Rite* for Soloists, Chorus, and Chamber Orch. (1987); *Psalmus 5* for Woman's Voice and Chamber Ensemble (1989), *102* for Chorus and 5 Instruments (1989), and *50* for Woman's Voice and String Quartet (1991); *Funeral Rite* for Soloists, Chorus, and Orch. (1994). **OTHER:** Electronic, live electronic, and tape pieces; film music; collaborative scores.

Jenkins, Graeme (James Ewers), English conductor; b. London, Dec. 31, 1958. He was a chorister at Dulwich College, attended the Univ. of Cambridge, where he conducted the British premiere of *Stiffelio*, and studied conducting with Del Mar and Willcocks at the Royal College of Music in London, where he conducted student performances of *Albert Herring* and *The Turn of the Screw*. In 1982 he made his professional conducting debut with the Kent Opera with *The Beggar's Opera*. In 1986 he became music director of the Glyndebourne Touring Opera, a position he retained until 1991. He made his first appearance at the Glyndebourne Festival in 1987 conducting *Carmen*, the same year that he made his debut on the Continent in Geneva conducting *Hänsel und Gretel*. In 1988 he made his first appearance at the English National Opera in London conducting *Così fan tutte*. As a guest conductor, Jenkins has appeared with opera companies and orchs. at home and abroad. In 1994 he became music director of the Dallas Opera.

Jenkins, Leroy, black American jazz violinist, bandleader, and composer; b. Chicago, March 11, 1932. He played violin in a local Baptist church and picking up the rudiments of theory while teaching in a local ghetto school; later he was a scholarship student of Bruce Hayden at Florida A. & M. Univ. He played with the Assn. for the Advancement of Creative Musicians and the Creative Construction Co. in Chicago (1965–69). After helping to found the Revolutionary Ensemble in 1971, he led his own groups from 1978. In 1980 he appeared at N.Y.'s Carnegie Recital Hall and Town Hall. In addition to his tours of North America, he also performed in Europe. Jenkins is a master of improvisation, and particularly of the atonal variety. Among his many recordings are *Manhattan Cycles* (1972), *For Players Only* (1975), *Solo Concerto* (1977), *Legend of Ai Glatson* (1978), *Space Minds, New Worlds, Survival of America* (1978), and *Urban Blues* (1984).

BIBL.: L. Birnbaum, "L. J.," *Ear Magazine* (Nov. 1989).

Jenkins, Newell (Owen), American conductor and musicologist; b. New Haven, Conn., Feb. 8, 1915. He studied at the Orchesterschule der Sachsischen Staatskapelle in Dresden, and later in Freiburg im Breisgau at the Städtische Musikseminar; also took courses with Wilibald Gurlitt in Freiburg im Breisgau and with Carl Orff in Munich. Upon his return to the U.S., he worked with Leon Barzin at the National Orch. Assn. in N.Y. Following army service in World War II, he received a Fulbright grant to study in Italy. In 1957 he founded the Clarion Music Soc. of N.Y., with which he presented a stimulating series of annual concerts of rarely performed works of the Baroque period. He also appeared as a guest conductor in London, Hilversum, Milan, Naples, Turin, Florence, Stuttgart, and Stockholm. In 1975 he founded the Festival of Venetian Music of the 17th and 18th Centuries at Castelfranco Veneto. From 1964 to 1974 he taught at N.Y. Univ.; from 1971 to 1979 he was a lecturer at the Univ. of Calif. at Irvine. He ed. (with B. Churgin) *Thematic Catalogue of the Works of G.B. Sammartini* (1976); also ed. 9 syms. of Brunetti (1979).

Jensen, Thomas, admired Danish conductor; b. Copenhagen, Oct. 25, 1898; d. there, Nov. 13, 1963. He studied organ and cello at the Copenhagen Cons. He was a cellist in various Swedish and Danish orchs. (1917–27). After conducting studies in Paris and Dresden (1925–26), he went to Århus as conductor of the Phil. Soc. in 1927; founded that city's first permanent sym. orch. in 1935; also conducted the Tivoli summer concerts in Copenhagen (1936–48) and founded the Jutland Opera in Århus (1947); subsequently was conductor of the Danish Radio Sym. Orch. in Copenhagen (from 1957), with which he toured in Europe and the U.S. He was known especially as a champion of the music of Nielsen.

Jenson, Dylana (Ruth), American violinist; b. Los Angeles, May 14, 1961. Her mother gave her early instruction in violin playing; also had lessons in childhood with Manuel Compinsky and, later, with Heifetz and Gingold. She made her formal debut as soloist in the Mendelssohn Concerto with Kostelanetz and the N.Y. Phil. at the age of 12; at 13, she made her European debut with Zürich's Tonhalle Orch. After further instruction in Milstein's master classes in Zürich (1973–76), she won 2nd prize in the Tchaikovsky Competition in Moscow in 1978. Thereafter she appeared as a soloist with major orchs. and as a recitalist in North and South America, Europe, and the Far East.

Jeppesen, Knud (Christian), eminent Danish musicologist and composer; b. Copenhagen, Aug. 15, 1892; d. Risskov, June 14, 1974. He began his career as an opera conductor, using the name Per Buch, in Elbing and Liegnitz (1912–14); then studied organ at the Royal Danish Cons. of Music (diploma, 1916) and musicology with Angul Hammerich at the Univ. of Copenhagen (M.A., 1918); he also received instruction from Carl Nielsen and Thomas Laub. He prepared his Ph.D. diss., *Die Dissonanzbehandlung bei Palestrina*, at the Univ. of Copenhagen; however, the retirement of Hammerich made it necessary for the diss. to be approved by and completed under Guido Adler at the Univ. of Vienna (1922; publ., in an aug. ed., in Copenhagen in 1923 as *Palestrinastil med saerligt henblik paa dissonansbehandlingen*; Eng. tr. by M. Hamerik as *The Style of Palestrina and the Dissonance*, Copenhagen, 1927; 2nd ed., 1946). Jeppesen served as organist of Copenhagen's St. Stephen's (1917–32) and of the Holmens Church (1932–47); also taught theory at the Royal Danish Cons. of Music (1920–46). He became the first prof. of musicology at the Univ. of Århus (1946), where he founded its musicological inst. in 1950, retiring in 1957. He was ed.-in-chief of *Acta Musicologica* (1931–54) and president of the International Musicological Soc. (1949–52). Jeppesen was an authority on Palestrina and the music of the Italian Renaissance. As a composer, he demonstrates his erudition in his music: precise in its counterpoint, unfailingly lucid in its harmonic structure, and set in impeccable classical forms.

WRITINGS: *Kontrapunkt (vokalpolyfoni)* (Copenhagen, 1930; German tr., 1935; 5th ed., 1970; Eng. tr., 1939; new ed., 1992; 3rd Danish ed., 1962); *La frottola* (Copenhagen, 1968–70).

EDITIONS: With V. Brøndal, *Der Kopenhagener Chansonnier* (Copenhagen and Leipzig, 1927; 2nd ed., rev., 1965); *Vaerker af Mogens Pedersøn* (Copenhagen, 1933); with V. Brøndal, *Die mehrstimmige italienische Laude um 1500* (Copenhagen and Leipzig, 1935); *Die italienische Orgelmusik am Anfang des Cinquecento* (Copenhagen, 1943; 2nd ed., rev. and aug., 1960); *La flora, arie &c antiche italiane* (Copenhagen, 1949); *Antichi balli veneziani per cembalo* (Copenhagen, 1962); *Italia sacra musica: Musiche corali italiane sconosciute della prima metà del cinquecento* (Copenhagen, 1962).

WORKS: OPERA: *Rosaura, eller Kaerlighed besejrer alt* (1946; Copenhagen, Sept. 20, 1950). **ORCH.:** *Sjaellandsfar*, sym. (1938–39); *Waldhorn Concerto* (1942). **VOCAL:** *Dronning Dagmar messe* (1945); *Te Deum danicum* for Soloists, 2 Choruses, Organ, and Orch. (1945); *Tvesang: Grundtvig-Kierkegaard* for Chorus and Orch. (1965; Danish Radio, Copenhagen, Jan. 12, 1967); cantatas; motets; songs. **OTHER:** Chamber music; organ pieces.

BIBL.: B. Hjelmborg and S. Sørenson, eds., *Natalicia musicologica K. J. septuagenario collegis oblata* (Copenhagen, 1962).

Jepson, Helen, American soprano; b. Titusville, Pa., Nov. 28, 1904. She studied in Philadelphia with Queena Mario at the Curtis Inst. of Music (B.Mus., 1934); in 1936, went to Paris to study with Mary Garden. She sang with the Philadelphia Grand Opera (1928–30), then made her Metropolitan Opera debut in N.Y. as Helene in Seymour's *In the Pasha's Garden* on Jan. 24, 1935, remaining on its roster until 1943; also sang with the Chicago Opera (1935–42). Her roles of note included Eva in *Die Meistersinger von Nürnberg*, Marguerite in *Faust*, Desdemona in *Otello*, and Nedda in *Pagliacci*.

Jeremiáš, Jaroslav, Czech pianist and composer, brother of **Otakar Jeremiáš**; b. Pisek, Aug. 14, 1889; d. České Budějovice, Jan. 16, 1919. His father was the well-known Czech conductor, composer, and teacher Bohuslav Jeremiáš (b. Řestorky, Chrudim district, May 1, 1859; d. Česke Budjovicé, Jan. 18, 1918). He studied at his father's music school in Pisek; then studied piano with A. Miks at the Prague Cons. and privately with Novák (1909–10). Although he died at the age of 29, he left several significant works: the opera *Starý král* (The Old King; 1911–12; Prague, April 13, 1919); the oratorio *Mistr Jan Hus* (1914–15; Prague, June 13, 1919); Viola Sonata; songs.

BIBL.: B. Bělohlávek, *J. J.* (Prague, 1935).

Jeremiáš, Otakar, Czech conductor and composer, brother of **Jaroslav Jeremiáš**; b. Pisek, Oct. 17, 1892; d. Prague, March 5, 1962. His father was the well-known Czech conductor, composer, and teacher Bohuslav Jeremiáš (b. Řestorky, Chrudim district, May 1, 1859; d. Česke Budjovicé, Jan. 18, 1918). He began his musical training with his parents; then studied composition at the Prague Cons. (1907) and privately with Novák (1909–10); also took cello lessons with Jan Burian. He was a cellist in the Czech Phil. (1911–13); took over his father's music school (1919). He then was conductor of the Prague Radio orch. (1929–45); subsequently was director of the Prague National Theater (1945–47); was also the first chairman of the Union of Czech Composers. He was made a National Artist (1950) and received the Order of the Republic (1960). His music continues the traditions of the Czech national school, with a pronounced affinity to the style of Smetana, Foerster, and Ostrčil.

WORKS: DRAMATIC: *Romance o Karlu IV*, melodrama (1917); *Bratři Karamazovi* (The Brothers Karamazov), opera, after Dostoyevsky (1922–27; Prague, Oct. 8, 1928); *Enšpígl* (Til Eulenspiegel), opera (1940–44; Prague, May 13, 1949); film scores. **ORCH.:** *Písně jara* (Song of Spring; 1907–08); *Podzimní suita* (Autumn Suite; 1907–08); 2 syms. (1910–11; 1914–15). **CHAMBER:** Piano Trio (1909–10); String Quartet (1910); Piano Quartet (1911); String Quintet (1911); *Fantasie na staročeské choraly* (Fantasy on Old Czech Chorales) for Nonet (1938). **PIANO:** 2 sonatas (1909, 1913). **VOCAL:** *Fantasie* for 2 Choruses and Orch. (1915; Prague Radio, Oct. 27, 1942); 2 cantatas: *Mohamedův zpěv* (1932) and *Písně o rodné zemi* (Song of the Native Land; 1940–41); songs.

BIBL.: J. Plavec, *O. J.* (Prague, 1943); idem, *Národni umělec: O. J.* (National Artist: O. J.; Prague, 1964; includes list of works).

Jerger, Alfred, noted Austrian bass-baritone; b. Brünn, June 9, 1889; d. Vienna, Nov. 18, 1976. He studied at the Vienna Academy of Music, where his teachers included Fuchs, Grädener, and Gutheil; then became an operetta conductor at the Zürich Opera (1913). He began his vocal career in 1915, appearing as Lothario in *Mignon* at the Zürich Opera in 1917; then sang at the Bavarian State Opera in Munich (1919–21). He was a leading member of the Vienna State Opera (1921–53); also sang at the Salzburg Festivals, at London's Covent Garden, and other major music centers of Europe. In 1947 he joined the faculty of the Vienna Academy of Music; was also a producer at the Vienna Volksoper. He created the role of the Man in Schoenberg's *Die Glückliche Hand* (Vienna, Oct. 14, 1924) and the role of Mandryka in Strauss's *Arabella* (Dresden, July 1, 1933). His other outstanding Strauss roles included Baron Ochs, Orestes, John the Baptist, and Barak. He also was a fine Leporello, Don Giovanni, Pizzaro, Hans Sachs, Beckmesser, Grand Inquisitor, and King Philip.

Jeritza (real name, **Jedlitzková**), **Maria,** celebrated Moravian-born American soprano; b. Brünn, Oct. 6, 1887; d. Orange, N.J., July 10, 1982. She studied in Brünn and sang in the Stadttheater chorus there; after completing her training in Prague, she made her formal operatic debut as Elsa in *Lohengrin* in Olomouc

(1910); then became a member of the Vienna Volksoper. In 1912 Emperor Franz Josef heard her sing in Bad Ischl, after which he decreed that she should be engaged at the Vienna Court Opera, where she made her first appearance as Oberleitner's Aphrodite. Strauss then chose her to create the title role in his opera *Ariadne auf Naxos* (Stuttgart, Oct. 25, 1912), and also in its revised version (Vienna, Oct. 4, 1916); she likewise created the role of the Empress in his *Die Frau ohne Schatten* (Vienna, Oct. 10, 1919). On Nov. 19, 1921, she made her U.S. debut at the Metropolitan Opera in N.Y. in the first U.S. production of Korngold's opera *Die tote Stadt.* Her compelling portrayals of Tosca and Turandot quickly secured her place as the prima donna assoluta there, and she remained on its roster until 1932. She made her debut at London's Covent Garden as Tosca on June 16, 1926. Throughout the years, she remained a leading singer in Vienna as well, continuing to appear there until 1935. In 1943 she became a naturalized American citizen. She again sang in Vienna (1949–52); also appeared as Rosalinda in a Metropolitan Opera benefit performance of *Die Fledermaus* in N.Y. (Feb. 22, 1951). At the zenith of her career in the years between the 2 world wars, she won extraordinary acclaim in such roles as Sieglinde, Elisabeth, Santuzza, Fedora, Thaïs, Carmen, Salome, Octavian, Tosca, and Turandot. She led a colorful life, both on and off the operatic stage: she married 3 times, had many romantic affairs, and her spats with fellow artists became legendary. She publ. an autobiography, *Sunlight and Song* (N.Y., 1924).

BIBL.: E. Decsey, *M. J.* (Vienna, 1931); R. Werba, *M. J.: Primadonna des Verismo* (Vienna, 1981).

Jersild, Jørgen, Danish composer and teacher; b. Copenhagen, Sept. 17, 1913. He received training in composition and theory from Schierbeck and in piano from Stoffregen in Copenhagen; he continued his studies with Roussel in Paris (1936) and studied musicology at the Univ. of Copenhagen (M.A., 1940). After working in the music dept. of the Danish Radio in Copenhagen (1939–43), he became a teacher at the Copenhagen Cons. in 1943; later he was a prof. of theory there (1953–75). Among his pedagogical books were *Ear Training* (1966), *Advanced Rhythmical Studies* (1980), and *Analytisk Harmonilaere* (1989). He also publ. a study of Romantic harmony à la the music of César Franck (1970). His compositions are cast in a thoroughly cosmopolitan style while retaining essential Danish qualities.

WORKS: DRAMATIC: *Lunefulde Lucinda* (Capricious Lucinda), ballet (1954); *Alice in Wonderland,* musical fairy tale (1958); *Gertrude,* film music (1964); music for plays. **ORCH.:** *The Birthday Concert* (1945; rev. 1962); *Pastoral* for Strings (1946); *Little Suite* for Strings (1950); Harp Concerto (1971–72; Aldeburgh, June 9, 1972). **CHAMBER:** *Music Making in the Forest,* serenade for Wind Quintet (1947); *Pezzo Elegiaco* for Harp (1968); *Fantasia e Canto Affettuoso* for Harp, Flute, Clarinet, and Cello (1969); *Fantasia* for Harp (1977); String Quartet (1980); *Für Gefühlvolle Spieler* for 2 Harps (1982); *Lento* for 4 Cellos and Double Bass (1985); *10 Impromptus* for Violin and Guitar (1987). **KEYBOARD: PIANO:** *Trois pieces en concert* (1945); Duo Concertante for Piano, 3- and 4-hands (1956); *30 Polyrhythmic Études* (1976); *15 Piano Pieces for Julie* (1985); *Fantasia* (1989); *Jeu polyrythmique,* 3 études (1990); *2 Impromptus* (1993). **ORGAN:** *Fantasia* (1985). **VOCAL:** Numerous choruses, including *3 Madrigali* (1958), *3 Danish Love Songs* (1968), *3 Romantic Choral Songs* (1971), *3 Latin Madrigals* (1987), and *Il Cantico della Creature* (1991); pieces for Solo Voice and Piano.

Jerusalem, Siegfried, prominent German tenor; b. Oberhausen, April 17, 1940. He received training in violin and piano at the Essen Folkwangschule, where he played principal bassoon in its orch. He began his career as an orchestral bassoonist in 1961; was a member of the Stuttgart Radio Sym. Orch. (1972–77). He began serious vocal study in Stuttgart with Hertha Kalcher in 1972, appearing in minor roles at the Württemberg State Theater from 1975. He sang Lohengrin in Darmstadt and Aachen in 1976, and then at the Hamburg State Opera in 1977; that same year he made his debut at the Bayreuth Festival as Froh, returning in later seasons as Lohengrin, Walther, Parsifal, and Loge in the Solti-Hall mounting of the *Ring* cycle in 1983. After making his first appearance at the Berlin Deutsche Oper as Tamino in 1978, he became a leading member of the company. He made his U.S. debut with the Metropolitan Opera in N.Y. as Lohengrin on Jan. 10, 1980, his British debut at London's Coliseum as Parsifal on March 16, 1986, and his Covent Garden debut in London on March 18, 1986, singing Erik; he also appeared at the Vienna State Opera, Milan's La Scala, and the Paris Opéra. His later appearances at Bayreuth were highlighted by his portrayals of Siegfried (1988, 1990, 1992) and Tristan (1993).

Jessel, Leon, German composer; b. Stettin, Jan. 22, 1871; d. Berlin, Jan. 4, 1942. At age 20, he began working as a theater conductor, appearing in Gelsenkirchen, Mülheim, Celle, Freiburg-im-Breisgau, Stettin, Chemnitz, and Lübeck. As a composer, he first attracted notice with his piano and instrumental pieces. His *Die Parade der Zinnsoldaten* (1905) became internationally celebrated. In 1911 he settled in Berlin, where he first won success as an operetta composer with his *Die beiden Husaren* (Feb. 6, 1913). He scored a signal triumph with his *Das Schwarzwaldmädel* (Aug. 25, 1917). Of his subsequent scores, the most successful were *Die närrische Liebe* Nov. 28, 1919), *Die Postmeisterin* (Feb. 3, 1921), *Das Detektivmädel* (Oct. 28, 1921), *Des Königs Nachbarin* (April 15, 1923), and the Viennese premiered *Meine Tochter Otto* (May 5, 1927). As a Jew, Jessel's works were banned after the Nazis came to power in 1933. His last operetta, *Die goldene Mühle,* received its premiere in Olten, Switzerland (Oct. 29, 1936). Jessel died as a result of manhandling by the Gestapo.

Ježek, Jaroslav, Czech composer; b. Prague, Sept. 25, 1906; d. N.Y., Jan. 1, 1942. He studied composition with Jirák and Suk; also experimented with quarter-tone techniques under the direction of Alois Hába. In 1928 he became resident composer for the "Liberated Theater," a Prague satirical revue; produced the scenic music for 20 of its plays. In 1939, shortly before the occupation of Czechoslovakia by the Nazis, he emigrated to the U.S.

WORKS: BALLET: *Nerves* (1928). **ORCH.:** Piano Concerto (Prague, June 23, 1927); *Fantasy* for Piano and Orch. (Prague, June 24, 1930); Concerto for Violin and Wind Orch. (Prague, Sept. 26, 1930); *Symphonic Poem* (Prague, March 25, 1936). **CHAMBER:** Wind Quartet (1929); Wind Quintet (1931); 2 string quartets (1932, 1941); Violin Sonata (1933); Duo for 2 Violins (1934). **PIANO:** Suite for Quarter Tone Piano (1927); *Capriccio* (1932); *Bagatelles* (1933); *Rhapsody* (1938); *Toccata* (1939); Sonata (1941).

Jílek, František, Czech conductor; b. Brünn, May 22, 1913; d. there (Brno), Sept. 16, 1993. He took courses with Balatka, Chalabala, and Kvapil at the Brno Cons. and with Novák at the Prague Cons.; then was répétiteur and conductor at the Brno Opera (1936–39). After serving as assistant conductor at the Ostrava Opera (1939–48), he returned to Brno as conductor (1948–52) and chief conductor (1952–78) at the Opera; also taught at the Janáček Academy of Music there; was chief conductor of the Brno State Phil. (1978–83). He acquired a fine reputation through his championship of the music of his homeland, most notably of works by Smetana and Janáček.

Jiménez-Mabarak, Carlos, Mexican composer and pedagogue; b. Tacuba, Jan. 31, 1916; d. Cuautla, Morelos, June 21, 1994. He studied piano with Jesús Castillo in Guatemala (1923–27); he continued his piano training at the Cons. in Santiago, Chile (1928–29), where he then attended the Liceo de Aplicación (1930–33); in 1933 he went to Brussels, where he received instruction in piano and harmony at the Inst. of Advanced Studies in Music and Drama, in harmony, counterpoint, and analysis with Wouters at the Cons., and in musicology with Van den Borren at the Univ.; returning to his homeland, he studied orchestration with Revueltas at the Cons. (1938); still later (1953–56), he studied composition with Turchi at the Accademia di Santa Cecilia in Rome and dodecaphonic techniques with Leibowitz in Paris. From 1942 to 1965 he was prof. of music education, harmony, and composition at the National Cons. of Music in Mexico City. After serving as a prof. at the Villahermosa School of the Arts in Tabasco (1965–68), he was the cultural attaché of the Mexican Embassy in Vienna (1972–74). He first composed in a neo-Classical style but later became an accomplished dodecaphonist. He was one of the first Mexican composers to utilize electronics and to experiment with "musique concrète."

WORKS: DRAMATIC: OPERAS: *Misa de seis* (1960; Mexico City, June 21, 1962); *La guerra* (1980; Mexico City, Sept. 26, 1982). **BALLETS:** *Perifonema* (Mexico City, March 9, 1940); *El amor del agua* (1945); *Balada del pájaro y las doncellas* (1947); *Balada del venado y la luna* (1948); *Danza fúnebre* (1949); *Recuerdo a zapata*, ballet-cantata (1950); *Balada mágico o danza de las cuatro estaciones* (1951); *Retablo de la annunciación* (1951); *El nanual herido* (1952); *La maestra rural* (1952); *Balada de los quetzales* (1953); *El paraíso de los Ahogados* (1960); *La llorona* (1961); *La portentosa vida de la muerte* (1964); *Pitágoras dijo . . .* (1966); *Balada de los rios de Tabasco* (1990). **OTHER:** Incidental music to several plays, including Camus's *Caligula* (1947), and various film scores. **ORCH.:** 2 syms.: No. 1 (Mexico City, July 6, 1945) and No. 2, *Symphony in 1 Movement* (Mexico City, Aug. 1962); Concerto for Piano and Chamber Orch. (1945; Mexico City, Nov. 8, 1946); *Obertura para orquesta de arcos* (Mexico City, Sept. 2, 1963); Sinfonia concertante for Piano and Orch. (1968; Mexico City, March 11, 1977). **CHAMBER:** *Preludio y fuga* for Clarinet and Piano (1937); *Concierto del abuelo* for Piano and String Quartet (1938); Quartet (1947); *El retrato de lupe* for Violin and Piano (1953); Concerto for Piano, Timpani, Bells, Xylophone, and Percussion (1961); *5 Pieces* for Flute and Piano (1965); *La ronda junto a la fuente* for Flute, Oboe, Violin, Viola, and Cello (1965); *2 Pieces* for Cello and Piano (1966); *Invention* for Clarinet and Trumpet (1970); *Invention* for Oboe, Tenor Trombone, and Piano (1971). **PIANO:** *Allegro romántico* (1935); *Pequeño preludio* (1935); *Danza española I* and *II* (1936); *Sonata del majo enamorado* (1936); *Retrato de Mariana Sánchez* (1952); *Variaciones sobre la alegría* for 2 Pianos (1952); *La fuente armoniosa* (1957). **VOCAL:** *Los niños heroes* for Chorus and Orch. (1947); *Traspié entre dos estrellas* for Reciter and 6 Instruments (1957); *Homenaje a Juarez* for Soloists, Chorus, and Orch. (1958); *Simón Bolivar* for Soloists, Chorus, and Orch. (1983); many choruses; songs.

Jirák, K(arel) B(oleslav), distinguished Czech conductor and composer; b. Prague, Jan. 28, 1891; d. Chicago, Jan. 30, 1972. He received training in law and philosophy at the Univ. of Prague, and studied composition privately with Novák (1909–11) and J.B. Foerster (1911–12). He was a répétiteur and conductor at the Hamburg Opera (1916–19); also conducted opera in Brno and Moravska Ostrava (1918–20). He then was conductor of Prague's Hlahol choir and 2nd conductor of the Czech Phil. (1920–21); was prof. of composition at the Prague Cons. (1920–30). From 1930 to 1945 he was music director of the Czech Radio. From 1935 to 1946 he was married to **Marta Krásová**. In 1947 he went to the U.S.; in 1948 he became chairman of the theory dept. at Roosevelt College (later Univ.) in Chicago; held the same position also at Chicago Cons. College from 1967 to 1971. His music represents the finest traditions of Middle European 20th-century Romanticism. His 5th Sym. won the Edinburgh International Festival prize in 1951. He publ. a textbook on musical form (Prague, 1922; 5th ed., 1946); also biographies of Fibich (Ostrava, 1947), Mozart (Ostrava, 1948), and Dvořák (N.Y., 1961).

WORKS: OPERA: *Žena a bůh* (The Woman and God; 1911–14; Brno, March 10, 1928). **ORCH.:** 6 syms.: No. 1 (1915–16), No. 2 (1924), No. 3 (1929–38; Prague, March 8, 1939), No. 4, *Episode from an Artist's Life* (1945; Prague, April 16, 1947), No. 5 (1949; Edinburgh, Aug. 26, 1951), and No. 6 (1957–70; Prague, Feb. 17, 1972); *Overture to a Shakespearean Comedy* (1917–21; Prague, Feb. 24, 1927); *Serenade* for Strings (1939); *Symphonic Variations* (Prague, March 26, 1941); *Overture "The Youth"* (1940–41); *Rhapsody* for Violin and Orch. (1942); *Symphonietta* for Small Orch. (1943–44); Piano Concerto (1946; Prague, Dec. 12, 1968); *Symphonic Scherzo* for Band or Orch. (1950; orch. version, Chicago, April 25, 1953); *Serenade* for Small Orch. (1952; Santa Barbara, Calif., March 24, 1965); *Legend* for Small Orch. (1954; Chicago, March 20, 1962); Concertino for Violin and Chamber Orch. (1957; Chicago, May 18, 1963). **CHAMBER:** 7 string quartets (1915; 1927; 1937–40; 1949; 1951; 1957–58; 1960); String Sextet, with Alto Voice (1916–17); Cello Sonata (1918); Violin Sonata (1919); Viola Sonata (1925); *Divertimento* for String Trio (1925); Flute Sonata (1927); Wind Quintet (1928); *Variations, Scherzo and Finale*, nonet (1943); *Serenade* for Winds (1944); Piano Quintet (1945); *Mourning Music* for Viola and Organ (1946; also for Orch.); Clarinet Sonata (1947); *Introduction and Rondo* for Horn and Piano (1951); *3 Pieces* for Cello and Piano (1952); Horn Sonata (1952); Oboe Sonata (1953); Trio for Oboe, Clarinet, and Bassoon (1956); Suite for Solo Violin (1964); Piano Trio (1966–67). **KEYBOARD: PIANO:** *Summer Nights*, 4 pieces (1914); *Suite in Olden Style* (1920); *The Turning Point* (1923); 2 sonatas (1926, 1950); *Epigrams and Epitaphs* (1928–29); *4 Caprices in Polka Form* (1945); *5 Miniatures* (1954); *4 Pieces for the Right Hand* (1968–69). **ORGAN:** Suite (1958–64); Passacaglia and Fugue (1971). **VOCAL:** *Psalm 23* for Chorus and Orch. (1919); *Requiem* for Solo Quartet, Chorus, Organ, and Orch. (1952; Prague, Nov. 17, 1971); works for male chorus; song cycles (many with orch.), including *Lyric Intermezzo* (1913), *Tragicomedy*, 5 songs (1913), *Fugitive Happiness*, 7 songs (1915–16), *13 Simple Songs* (1917), *3 Songs of the Homeland* (1919), *Evening and Soul* (1921), *Awakening* (1925), *The Rainbow* (1925–26), *The Year* (1941), *7 Songs of Loneliness* (1945–46), *Pilgrim's Songs* (1962–63), and *The Spring* (1965).

BIBL.: M. Očadlík, *K.B. J.* (Prague, 1941); A. Tischler, *K.B. J.: A Catalog of his Works* (Detroit, 1975).

Jirásek, Ivo, Czech composer; b. Prague, July 16, 1920. He studied composition with Šin in Prague and was a student at the Prague Cons. (1938–45) of Krejčí and A. Hába (composition) and Dědeček (conducting). After working as assistant to Kubelik and the Czech Phil. in Prague (1945–46), he conducted at the Zdeněk Nejedlý Theater in Opava (1946–53), where he then was director of its opera company (until 1956). From 1969 to 1978 he was active with the copyright union in Prague. In 1980 he was made a Merited Artist by the Czech government. His output was greatly influenced by French music, but it also owed much to Stravinsky and Berg.

WORKS: DRAMATIC: OPERAS: *Pan Johanes* (Mr. Johanes; 1951–52; Opava, March 24, 1956); *Svítání nad vodami* (Daybreak Over the Waters; 1960–61; Plzeň, Nov. 23, 1963); *Medvěd* (The Bear), after Chekhov (1962–64; Prague, Jan. 25, 1965); *Klíč* (The Key; 1967–68; Prague, March 15, 1971); *Danse macabre* (1970–71; Prague, Sept. 27, 1972); *Mistr Jeroným* (Master Jerome; 1979–80; Prague, March 26, 1992); *Zázrak* (Miracle; 1981). **BALLET:** *Faust* (1982–85). **ORCH.:** *Ciaconna* (1944); Concertante Sym. for Violin and Orch. (1958); *Small Suite* (1964); *Variations* (1965); *Festive Overture* (1971); *Mother Hope Symphony* (1973–74; Prague, March 16, 1974); *Mozartiana*, concertino for Chamber Orch. (1978); *4 Dramatic Studies* (1985); *Evening Music* for English Horn and Strings (1985); Concertino for Harpsichord and 11 Strings (1985); *Little Concert Music* for Synthesizer and Orch. (1988). **CHAMBER:** Violin Sonata (1946); 3 string quartets (*4 Studies*, 1963–66; *Ludi con tre toni*, 1977–78; *Meditation on a Theme by Bohuslav Martinů*, 1989); *Sonata da camera* for 13 Strings (1966); *Serenades* for Flute, Bass Clarinet, and Percussion (1967); *3 Pieces* for 4 Instruments (1971); Partita for Winds (1972); *Prague with Fingers of Rain*, suite for Dulcimer (1974); *Spectra* for Bass Clarinet and Piano (1975); Sonata for Viola and Percussion (1976); Trio for Violin, Cello, and Piano (1979); *Permutazione* for Flute, Cello, and Piano (1981); *Carnival in Rio* for Flute, Clarinet, Piano, Double Bass, and Percussion (1986); *Preludium, Fugue, and Chorale on a Theme by Domenico Scarlatti* for Flute, Clarinet, Piano, Double Bass, and Percussion (1987); *Oh, quels beaux jours!*, sonata for Solo Cello (1991); *Soirée dansante*, wind quintet (1993). **VOCAL:** *A Hospital Ballad*, cantata for Soloists, Chorus, and Orch. (1944; rev. 1957); *You, My Home*, song cycle for Baritone and Orch. (1960); *Love*, cantata for Bass, Women's Chorus, and Chamber Orch. (1960); *Year in a Rusty-Colored Forest*, 8 songs for Men's Chorus and Chamber Ensemble or Piano (1966); *Music* for Soprano, Flute, and Harp (1967); *Stabat Mater*, oratorio for Soloists, Chorus, Organ, and Wind Orch. (1968; Prague, March 3, 1969); *Song of the Planet Named Earth*, cantata for Soloists, Chorus, and Orch. (1975–76; Prague, April 2, 1977); *Portrait of a Woman* for Soprano, Flute, Bass Clarinet, Vibraphone, and Piano (1975–76); *4 Psalms* for Men's Chorus (1991); *Time*, 3 songs for Soprano and String Quartet (1992).

Jirko, Ivan, Czech composer; b. Prague, Oct. 7, 1926; d. there, Aug. 20, 1978. He studied medicine at the Univ. of Prague (graduated, 1951), and also studied composition with K. Janeček (1944–49) and Bořkovec (1949–52) at the Prague Cons.; then pursued a dual career as a psychiatrist and a composer.

WORKS: OPERAS: *The Twelfth Night*, after Shakespeare (1963–64; Liberec, Feb. 25, 1967); *The Strange Story of Arthur Rowe*, after Graham Greene's novel *Ministry of Fear* (1967–68; Liberec, Oct. 25, 1969); *The Millionairess*, operatic divertimento (1969–71); *The Strumpet* (1970; Olomouc, June 23, 1974); *The Way Back* (1974). **ORCH.:** 4 piano concertos (1949, 1951, 1958, 1966); *Serenade* for Small Orch. (1951); Clarinet Concerto (1955); 3 syms.: No. 1 (1957), No. 2, *The Year 1945* (1962; withdrawn), and No. 3 (1977); *Macbeth*, symphonic fantasy (1962); *Elegy on the Death of a Friend* (1965); *Divertimento* for Horn and Orch. (1965); *Symphonic Variations* (1966); *Serenata giocosa* for Chamber String Orch. (1967; also for Violin and Guitar); Sonata for 14 Winds and Kettledrums (1967); *Capriccio all'antico* (1971); *Prague Seconds*, symphonic sketches (1972); Trumpet Concerto (1972); Flute Concerto (1973); *Prague Annals*, symphonic triptych (1973); *At the Turning Point*, symphonic fantasy (1972–73; uses material from the 2nd sym.); Double Concerto for Violin, Piano, and Orch. (Charleroi, Nov. 18, 1976). **CHAMBER:** Wind Quintet (1947); 6 string quartets (1954, 1962, 1966, 1969, 1972, 1974); Cello Sonata (1954–55); Suite for Wind Quintet (1956); Violin Sonata (1959); *Kaleidoscope* for Violin and Piano (1965); *Serenata in due tempi* for Nonet or Oboe Quartet (1970); *Guiocchi per tre* for String Trio (1972); *Partita* for Solo Violin (1974); Piano Quintet (1977–78). **PIANO:** 2 sonatas (1956; *Elégie disharmonique*, 1970); *Preludio, Canzone e Toccata* (1977). **VOCAL:** *Requiem* (1971); *Štěsí* (Happiness), musical panorama for Narrator, Soprano, Baritone, and Orch. (1975–76); songs.

Jo, Sumi, Korean soprano; b. Seoul, Nov. 22, 1962. She received her training in Seoul and at the Accademia di Santa Cecilia in Rome (1983–86). In 1986 she made her operatic debut as Gilda in Trieste. After engagements in Lyons, Nice, and Marseilles (1987–88), she won particular distinction as Barbarina at the Salzburg Festival in 1988, the year in which she also made her first appearance in Munich and her debut at Milan's La Scala as Thetis/Fortune in Jommelli's *Fetonte*. In 1989 she made her Metropolitan Opera debut in N.Y. as Gilda, and also sang in Vienna. She appeared at the Chicago Lyric Opera in 1990 as the Queen of the Night. In 1991 she made her debut at London's Covent Garden as Olympia in *Les Contes d'Hoffmann*. In 1992 she sang Matilde in Rossini's *Elisabetta regina d'Inghilterra* in Naples. Among her other roles are Fiorilla in *Il Turco in Italia*, Elvira in *I Puritani*, Adèle in *Le Comte Ory*, Zerlina in *Fra Diavolo*, and Oscar in *Un Ballo in Maschera*.

Joachim, Otto, German-born Canadian composer, violinist, violist, and teacher; b. Düsseldorf, Oct. 13, 1910. He took violin lessons with his father, then studied at the Buths-Neitzel Konservatorium in Düsseldorf (1916–28) and at the Rheinische Musik Schule in Cologne (1928–31). He fled Germany in 1934 and spent the succeeding 15 years in the Far East, mainly in Singapore and Shanghai; constructed electronic string instruments of the entire violin family (1944–45). In 1949 he emigrated to Canada, becoming a naturalized citizen in 1957. He was a member (1952–57) and later principal violist (1961–65) of the Montreal Sym. Orch.; also was a co-founder-member of the Montreal String Quartet (1957–58) and was associated with Glenn Gould. In 1956 he organized his own electronic music studio; was founder-director of the Montreal Consort of Ancient Instruments (1958–68). He taught at McGill Univ. (1956–64) and at the Cons. de Musique de Montreal et Quebec (1956–76). His music is quaquaversal, but its favorite direction is asymptotic.

WORKS: ORCH.: *Asia*, symphonic poem (1928–39); Concertante No. 1 for Violin, String Orch., and Percussion (1955–57; Paris, Sept. 9, 1958) and No. 2 for String Quartet and String Orch. (1961; Montreal, March 12, 1962); *Contrastes* (Montreal, May 6, 1967). **CHAMBER:** *Music* for Violin and Viola (1953); Cello Sonata (1954); String Quartet (1956); *Interlude*, saxophone quartet (1960); Nonet for Wind Quartet, String Quartet, and Piano (1960); *Divertimento* for Wind Quintet (1962); *Expansion* for Flute and Piano (1962); *Dialogue* for Viola and Piano (1964); *Illumination I* for Speaker, Chamber Ensemble, and Projectors (1965); *Kinderspiel* for Narrator, Violin, Cello, and Piano (1969); *12 12-Tone Pieces for the Young* for Violin and Piano (1970); 6 Pieces for Guitar (1971); *Requiem* for Violin or Viola or Cello (1977); *4 Intermezzi* for Flute and Guitar (1978); *Night Music* for Flute and Guitar (1978); *Tribute to St. Romanus* for Organ, 4 Horns, and 4 Percussion (1981); *Paean* for Cello (1989). **KEYBOARD: PIANO:** *Bagatelles* (1939); *L'Eclosion* (1954). **ORGAN:** *Fantasia* (1961). **ELECTROACOUSTIC AND MIXED MEDIA:** *Katimavik* for Tape (1967); *Illumination II* for Instruments, 4-track Tape, and Projectors (1969); *5.9* for 4-track Tape (1971); *6 1/2* for 4-track Tape (1971); *Mankind* for 4 Speakers, 4 Synthesizers, Organ, Timpani, Incense, Slides, and Projectors (1972); *Stimulus à Goad* for Guitar and Synthesizer (1973); *Uraufführung* for Guitar, 14 Instruments, and Electronics (1977); *7 Electronic Sketches* for Tape (1984); *Mobile für Johann Sebastian Bach* for 4 Woodwinds, Celesta, Organ, 4 Strings, and Tape (1985).

Jochum, Eugen, eminent German conductor, brother of **Georg Ludwig** and **Otto**, and father of **(Maria) Veronica Jochum**; b. Babenhausen, Nov. 1, 1902; d. Munich, March 26, 1987. He began playing the piano at 4 and the organ at 7; after attending the Augsburg Cons. (1914–22), he studied composition with Waltershausen and conducting with Hausegger at the Munich Academy of Music (1922–25). He commenced his career as a répétiteur at the Bavarian State Opera in Munich and in Mönchengladbach; appeared as a guest conductor with the Munich Phil. in 1926; then was a conductor at the Kiel Opera (1926–29) and conducted the Lübeck sym. concerts. After conducting at the Mannheim National Theater (1929–30), he served as Generalmusikdirektor in Duisburg (1930–32); then was music director of the Berlin Radio and a frequent guest conductor with the Berlin Phil. From 1934 to 1945 he was Generalmusikdirektor of the Hamburg State Opera. Although his tenure coincided with the Nazi era, Jochum successfully preserved his artistic independence; he avoided joining the Nazi party, assisted a number of his Jewish players, and programmed several works by officially unapproved composers. From 1934 to 1949 he also was Generalmusikdirektor of the Hamburg State Phil. In 1949 he was appointed chief conductor of the Bavarian Radio Sym. Orch. in Munich, a position he held with great distinction until 1960. He also appeared as a guest conductor throughout Europe. In 1953 he made his first appearance at the Bayreuth Festival, conducting *Tristan und Isolde*. He made his U.S. debut as a guest conductor with the Los Angeles Phil. in 1958. From 1961 to 1964 he was co-principal conductor of the Concertgebouw Orch. of Amsterdam, sharing his duties with Bernard

Haitink. From 1969 to 1973 he was artistic director of the Bamberg Sym. Orch.; he also served as laureate conductor of the London Sym. Orch. (1977–79). His many honors included the Brahms Medal (1936), the Bruckner Medal (1954), the Bülow Medal of the Berlin Phil. (1978), and the Bruckner Ring of the Vienna Sym. Orch. (1980); he was also made an honorary prof. by the senate of the city of Hamburg (1949). Jochum became known as an outstanding interpreter of the music of Bruckner; he also gained renown for his performances of Bach, Haydn, Mozart, Beethoven, Schubert, Brahms, and Richard Strauss.

Jochum, Georg Ludwig, German conductor, brother of **Eugen** and **Otto Jochum**; b. Babenhausen, Dec. 10, 1909; d. Mülheim an der Ruhr, Nov. 1, 1970. He studied at the Augsburg Cons. and then with Haas (composition) and Hausegger (conducting) at the Munich Academy of Music. He was music director in Münster (1932–34); then was a conductor at the Frankfurt am Main Opera and Museumgesellschaft concerts (1934–37); subsequently was Generalmusikdirektor in Linz (1940–45) and Duisburg (1946–58); was also director of the Duisburg Cons. (1946–58). He appeared as a guest conductor in Europe, South America, and Japan.

Jochum, Otto, German composer, brother of **Eugen** and **Georg Ludwig Jochum**; b. Babenhausen, March 18, 1898; d. Bad Reichenhall, Oct. 24, 1969. He studied at the Augsburg Cons. and at the Munich Academy of Music with Heinrich Kasper Schmid, Gustav Geierhaas, and Joseph Haas (1922–31). From 1932 to 1951 he served as director of the Augsburg Municipal Singing School.

WORKS: *Goethe-Sinfonie* (1941); *Florianer-Sinfonie* (1946); 2 oratorios: *Der jungste Tag* and *Ein Weihnachtssingen*; 12 masses; many choral works; arrangements of folk songs; songs.

Jochum, (Maria) Veronica, gifted German pianist, daughter of **Eugen Jochum**; b. Berlin, Dec. 6, 1932. She studied piano with Eliza Hansen and then with Maria Landes-Hindemith at the Munich Staatliche Hochschule für Musik (M.A., 1955; concert diploma, 1957); after additional studies with Edwin Fischer in Lucerne (1958–59), she completed her training with Rudolf Serkin in Philadelphia (1959–61). She commenced her career in Germany in 1954; made tours of Europe from 1961. Following her successful N.Y. debut as soloist in Beethoven's 1st Piano Concerto with Gerard Schwarz and the Y Chamber Sym. (March 21, 1981), she made appearances throughout the U.S. She maintained an intriguing repertoire, ranging from Mozart and Beethoven to Bartók and Schoenberg; she also championed lesser-known scores by such diverse composers as Clara Schumann and Ernst Krenek; likewise performed new works, including the premiere of Gunther Schuller's 2nd Piano Concerto (1982).

Jodál, Gábor, Romanian composer of Hungarian parentage; b. Odorhei, April 25, 1913. He received a doctorate in jurisprudence at the Univ. of Cluj (1937), then studied composition with Kodály, Kósa, and J. Adám at the Budapest Academy of Music (1939–42). He was a répétiteur at the Cluj National Theater (1942–44); then was a lecturer at the Hungarian Inst. of Art (1948–50) and a lecturer (from 1950) and director (1965–73) of the Cons. As a composer, he continues an amiable but rhythmically incisive tradition of the ethnically variegated music of Transylvania.

WORKS: BALLET: *Meseorszag kapujaban* (At the Gate of the Land of Story; 1952). **ORCH.:** Sinfonietta (1957); *Divertimento* (1964); *Nocturne* for Chamber Orch. (1976); *Scherzo* for Chamber Orch. (1978); *Sinfonia brevis* (1981). **CHAMBER:** 2 violin sonatas (1946, 1953); *3 Pieces* for Viola and Piano (1946); Suite for Flute and Piano (1955); String Quartet (1955); *3 Pieces* for Wind Quintet (1959); *Introduction and Scherzo* for Bassoon and Piano (1964); Suite for Wind Quintet (1966); *3 Nocturnes* for Flute, Clarinet, Viola, Cello, and Piano (1967); Viola Sonata (1974); Piano Sonata (1977). **VOCAL:** 2 cantatas: *Revolutia* (1964) and *Treptele împlinirii* (1977); choruses; songs.

Jöde, (Wilhelm August Ferdinand) Fritz, prominent German music educator; b. Hamburg, Aug. 2, 1887; d. there, Oct. 19, 1970. He studied at the Hamburg teachers' training college and then began his career as a provincial school teacher; after service in the German army during World War I, he studied musicology with Abert at the Univ. of Leipzig (1920–21). In 1923 he was made prof. of choral conducting and folk music education at Berlin's Staatliche Akademie für Kirchen- und Schulmusik. He organized societies for the propagation of folk music, and was very active in various youth movements in Germany until the Nazis removed him from his positions in 1935. He joined the faculty of the Salzburg Mozarteum in 1939, but was compelled to give up that position as well in 1943. After the fall of the Third Reich, he resumed his various activities; was made director of the youth music program of Hamburg's Hochschule für Musik (1947) and also director of the Internationales Institut für Jugend- und Volksmusik. He ed. several periodicals and many song collections.

WRITINGS: Ed. *Musikalische Jugendkultur* (Hamburg, 1918); *Musik und Erziehung* (Wolfenbüttel, 1919); *Pädagogik deines Wesens* (Hamburg, 1920); *Musikmanifest* (Rudolstadt, 1921); *Die Lebensfragen der neuen Schule* (Hamburg, 1921); *Unser Musikleben* (Wolfenbüttel, 1923; 2nd ed., 1925); *Musikschulen für Jugend und Volk* (Wolfenbüttel, 1924; 2nd ed., 1928); *Das schaffende Kind in der Musik* (Wolfenbüttel, 1928; 2nd ed., 1962); ed. *Musik in der Volksschule* (Berlin, 1928); *Kind und Musik* (Berlin, 1930; reprint, 1966); *Vom Wesen und Werden der Jugendmusik* (Mainz, 1954); *Die Herzberger Bachwochen* (Trossingen and Wolfenbüttel, 1959).

BIBL.: R. Stapelberg, *F. J.: Leben und Werk* (Trossingen and Wolfenbüttel, 1957); G. Trautner, *Die Musikerziehung bei F. J.: Quellen und Grundlagen* (Wolfenbüttel, 1968).

Johannesen, Grant, eminent American pianist and pedagogue; b. Salt Lake City, July 30, 1921. He studied piano with Robert Casadesus at Princeton Univ. (1941–46) and with Egon Petri at Cornell Univ.; also took courses in composition with Sessions and Boulanger. He made his concert debut in N.Y. in 1944. In 1949 he won 1st prize at the Ostend Concours Internationale, which was the beginning of his international career. He toured Europe with Mitropoulos and the N.Y. Phil. in 1956 and 1957; made another European tour with Szell and the Cleveland Orch. in 1968. From 1960 to 1966 he taught at the Aspen (Colo.) Music School; in 1973 he became music consultant and adviser of the Cleveland Inst. of Music; subsequently was its music director (1974–77), and finally its president (1977–85). He also taught at the Mannes College of Music in N.Y. and at the Salzburg Mozarteum. Johannesen acquired a reputation as a pianist of fine musicianly stature, subordinating his virtuoso technique to the higher considerations of intellectual fidelity to the composer's intentions; he was particularly esteemed for his performances of French and American music. He also composed some piano works. He was married to **Zara Nelsova** from 1963 to 1973.

Jóhannesson, Einar, Icelandic clarinetist; b. Reykjavík, Aug. 16, 1950. He entered the Children's Music School in Reykjavík when he was 6; while still attending elementary school, took up the clarinet. After training at the Reykjavík College of Music (1963–69), where he studied with Gunnar Egilsson, he went to London to pursue training at the Royal College of Music (1969–74) under Bernard Walton and John McCaw. In 1979 he was awarded the Sonning Prize for young Nordic soloists, which enabled him to complete his study with Walter Boeykens in Nice. Returning to Reykjavík, he became first clarinetist in the Iceland Sym. Orch. He also pursued a career as a soloist, recitalist, and chamber music player, touring throughout Europe. He has won particular distinction for his performances of contemporary scores.

Jóhannsson, Magnús Blöndal, Icelandic conductor and composer; b. Skálar, Sept. 8, 1925. He was taken to Reykjavík as an infant, and showed a precocious musical talent; at the age of

10, he was admitted to the Reykjavík School of Music, where he studied under F. Mixa and V. Urbantschitsch (1935–37; 1939–45); then took courses at the Juilliard School of Music in N.Y. (1947–53). He returned to Iceland in 1954 and was a staff member of the Iceland State Broadcasting Service (1956–76); was also a conductor at the National Theater in Reykjavík (1965–72). As a composer, he was attracted to the novel resources of electronic music; his *Study* for Magnetic Tape and Wind Quintet (1957) was the first Icelandic work employing electronic sound. His other works include *4 Abstractions* for Piano (1955); *Ionization* for Organ (1956); *Samstirni* for Tape (1960); *Punktar* (Points) for Tape and Small Orch. (1961); *15 Minigrams* for Flute, Oboe, Clarinet, and Double Bass (1961); *Dimensions* for Violin (1961); *Sonorities I–III* for Piano (1961–68); *Birth of an Island*, tape music for the film depicting the volcanic creation of an island near Iceland (1964); *Sequence*, ballet for Dancers, Instruments, and Lights (1968); *The Other Iceland*, music from the film (1973); *Adagio* for Percussion, Celesta, and Strings (1980); *Solitude* for Flute (1983).

Johanos, Donald, American conductor; b. Cedar Rapids, Iowa, Feb. 10, 1928. He studied violin and conducting at the Eastman School of Music in Rochester, N.Y. (Mus.B., 1950; Mus.M., 1952); received grants from the American Sym. Orch. League and the Rockefeller Foundation for conducting studies with Ormandy, Szell, Beecham, Beinum, Karajan, and Klemperer (1955–58). He won the Netherlands Radio Union conducting competition in 1957. From 1953 to 1956 he was music director of the Altoona (Pa.) Sym. Orch., and also of the Johnstown (Pa.) Sym. Orch. in 1955–56. In 1957 he became assoc. conductor of the Dallas Sym. Orch., and then its resident conductor in 1961, and subsequently its music director in 1962, achieving estimable results. He was assoc. conductor of the Pittsburgh Sym. Orch. and director of its chamber orch. (1970–80); was music director of the Honolulu Sym. Orch. (1979–94) and artistic director of the Hawaii Opera Theatre (1979–83).

Johansen, David Monrad, Norwegian pianist, music critic, and composer, father of **(David) Johan Kvandal (Johansen)**; b. Vefsn, Nov. 8, 1888; d. Sandvika, Feb. 20, 1974. He studied piano with Winge and Johnson (1904–09); then theory with Elling and Holter, as well as piano with Nissen at the Christiania Cons. (1909–15); in 1915 he went to Berlin, where he took lessons with Humperdinck and Kahn; by this time in middle age, he continued his studies in composition in Paris (1927) and in Leipzig (1933, 1935), where he took a special course in counterpoint with Grabner. In the meantime, he pursued an active career as a concert pianist and composer; made his debut in Christiania in 1910. He was ed. of *Norsk musikerblad* (1917–18); was music critic of *Norske intelligenss edler* (1916–18) and of *Aftenposten* (1925–45). He wrote a monograph on Grieg (Oslo, 1934; 3rd ed., 1956; Eng. tr., 1938). His music continued the national Norwegian tradition, in the lyric manner of Grieg; as time went by, Johansen experienced a mild influence of Russian and French music, gradually forming an innocuous modern style with sporadic audacious incursions into the domain of sharp dissonance.

WORKS: ORCH.: *Symphonic Fantasy* (1936); *Pan*, symphonic poem (1939); Piano Concerto (1955). **CHAMBER:** Violin Sonata (1912); Piano Quartet (1947); Quintet for Flute and String Quartet (1967); String Quartet (1969); piano pieces. **VOCAL:** *Voluspa*, oratorio (1926); *Sigvat Skald* for Baritone and Orch. (1928); several choruses; songs.

BIBL.: O. Sandvik and O. Gaukstad, *D.M. J. i skrift og tate* (Oslo, 1968).

Johansen, Gunnar, remarkable Danish-American pianist, composer, and teacher; b. Copenhagen, Jan. 21, 1906; d. Blue Mounds, Wis., May 25, 1991. He made his public debut at the age of 12 in Copenhagen, where he studied with Schioler; then went to Berlin when he was 14, becoming a member of the Busoni circle; after further piano studies with Lamond and Fischer, he completed his training with Petri at the Hochschule für Musik (1922–24). He toured Europe (1924–29) and then settled in the U.S., where he pursued an active concert career, gaining particular distinction for his series of 12 historical piano recitals encompassing works from Frescobaldi to Stravinsky, which he presented in San Francisco, Chicago, and N.Y. in the late 1930s; then held the specially created position of artist-in-residence at the Univ. of Wisc. at Madison (1939–76). Johansen produced a sensation when he substituted on short notice for a colleague as soloist in the piano version of Beethoven's Violin Concerto with Ormandy and the Philadelphia Orch. in N.Y. (Jan. 14, 1969). He excelled in works of transcendental difficulty; he played and recorded the complete solo piano works of Liszt and Busoni, including the latter's Bach transcriptions, as well as the complete solo clavier works of Bach. In 1986 he appeared at the Indianapolis Romantic Music Festival playing works of Liszt in commemoration of the composer's death a century before. He was a composer of fantastic fecundity; among his compositions are 3 piano concertos (1930, 1970, 1981), 31 piano sonatas (1941–51), and 515 piano sonatas improvised directly on the keyboard and recorded on tape (1952–82).

BIBL.: A. Corleonis, "A Birthday Greeting to G. J. on His 80th," *Fanfare* (Feb. 1986).

Johanson, Sven-Eric (Emanuel), Swedish composer, organist, and pedagogue; b. Västervik, Dec. 10, 1919. He studied at the Ingesund School of Music (1938), then obtained diplomas as a music teacher (1943) and organist and choirmaster (1946) at the Stockholm Musikhögskolan; also studied composition with Melchers, and later with Valen (1951) and finally with Dallapiccola in Florence (1957). After serving as organist and choirmaster at the Uppsala Missionary Church (1944–50), he settled in Göteborg in 1952 and was organist at the Alvsborg Church (until 1977); was also active as a teacher. In 1971 he was made a member of the Royal Swedish Academy of Music in Stockholm. His output ranges from electro-acoustic compositions to popular scores.

WORKS: DRAMATIC: OPERAS: *Borthbytingarna* (1954–55); *Kunskapens vin* (Göteborg, May 21, 1959); *Sagan om ringen* (1972); *Reliken* (1974; Borås, Jan. 18, 1975); *Skandal, Ers Majestät* (Umeå, May 8, 1978); *Du människa* (1980); *Pojken med flöjten* (Göteborg, Dec. 3, 1980); *Tjuvens pekfinger*, opera-buffa (1968–82; Göteborg, Jan. 14, 1983). **OTHER:** Radio operas; incidental music; *Rivalerna*, micro-drama (1967; Swedish Radio, March 16, 1969); *Kassandras omvändelse*, monodrama (1977); *Slottet*, ballet (1983). **ORCH.:** Syms.: No. 1, *Sinfonia ostinata* (1949–54), No. 2, *Duinoelegi*, for Tenor, Chorus, and Orch. (1954; also for String Orch. as *Sinfonia elegiaca*, 1954–55; Göteborg, Feb. 8, 1956), No. 3 (1956; Göteborg, Sept. 23, 1959), No. 5, *Elementsymfonin* (1965–68), No. 6, *Sinfonietta pastorella* (1972; Abo, April 5, 1973), No. 7, *Spelmanssymfoni*, for Strings (1974), No. 8, *En Frödingsymfoni* (1983–84; Swedish Radio, March 11, 1984), No. 9, *Sinfonia d'estate* (Malmö, May 6, 1987), No. 10, *Chez nous* (1990; Göteborg, Feb. 7, 1991), No. 11, *Sinfonia d'autunno* (1991), and No. 12, *Sinfonia da camera: Arnold Schönberg in memoriam* (1992); Concerto for Organ and Strings (1946); *Sinfonietta concertante* for Violin, Balalaika, and Chamber Orch. (1951–81); *Concerto da camera* for Cello and Orch. (1958; Swedish Radio, June 25, 1959); *Maskarad-Divertissement* (1958); *Variations on a Värmland Folk Tune* (1963; Göteborg, March 8, 1964); *Vagues* (1965; Göteborg, Jan. 28, 1966); *Fotia* (Uppsala, Oct. 6, 1966); *Vientos* (1967; Swedish Radio, March 7, 1968); *Terra* for Orch. and Tape (Göteborg, Sept. 12, 1968); *Fantyr* (Göteborg, Aug. 31, 1969); *Concerto Götenburghese* for Piano and Orch. (1970; Göteborg, Aug. 19, 1971); Concerto for Nyckel Harp (keyed fiddle) and Strings (1971); *Astrofonia* for Strings (Uppsala, July 11, 1974); *Nalle Puh*, symphonic saga (1979; Göteborg, Jan. 3, 1980); *Festuvertyr Gränna-Brahe* (1993). **CHAMBER:** 8 string quartets (1947; 1948; 1950; 1961, *Séquences variables*; 1964; 1976; 1980; 1981); Sonata for Solo Violin (1948); 4 piano sonatas (1949; 1956; 1959; 1982–83, *Sonata flexa*); Wind Quintet (1964); Trio for Clarinet, Violin, and Cello (1974); *Slag i slag* for Percussion and Tape (1979); *Sonatina per Marika* for Violin and Piano (1982); *Sagan om ringen: Ringmotivet* for Clarinet and Piano (1989); *A la recherche* for Flute (1992). **VOCAL:** *Aff Sancto Christofforo*, chamber oratorio (1948); *Anadyomene* for Soprano and Orch. (1950); Sym. No. 4, *Sånger i Förvandlingens Natt,* for Chorus (1958; Stockholm, April 3, 1959); *The Hazetrees* for Soprano, Clarinet, Violin, Cello, Piano, and Tape (1961); *Ave crax, ave crux* for Baritone, Chorus, Organ, and Tape (1967); *Concerto de chiesa: Den förlorade sonen* for Narrator, Chorus, Wind Quintet, Percussion, and Organ (1980); *Det stora ljuset*, Advent cantata for Narrator, Soprano, Alto, Chorus, and Strings (1983); *Cantata concertante* for Chorus, Brass Quintet, and Organ (1984); various sacred works; choruses.

BIBL.: P.-G. Bergfors, *Mitt hjärtas melodi: En Bok om S.-E. J.* (1994).

Johansson, Bengt (Viktor), Finnish composer; b. Helsinki, Oct. 2, 1914; d. Visuvesi, June 22, 1989. He studied composition with Sulho Ranta and Selim Palmgren; also cello at the Sibelius Academy in Helsinki, graduating in 1947; made study trips to Europe, Italy, and America. Returning to Finland, he served as director of music broadcasting for the Finnish Radio (1952–74); was a teacher (from 1960) and a lecturer in music history (from 1965) at the Sibelius Academy. His music makes use of a wide variety of resources, including electronic sound.

WORKS: OPERA: *Linna* (1975). **ORCH.:** *Serenade* for Strings (1945); *Petite suite de ballet* (1948); *Aquarelles* (1948); Piano Concerto (1951); Suite for Violin, Strings, Piano, and Timpani (1952); *Festivo*, overture (1952); *Expressions* for Strings (1954); *Tema con 7 variazioni in modo antico* for Cello and Orch. (1954); *Dialogeja* for Cello and Orch. (1970). **CHAMBER:** *Sonata piccola* for Cello and Piano (1945); *Dialogues* for Cello and String Quintet (1970); violin pieces. **VOCAL:** *Stabat Mater* for Chorus (1951); *It's Perfectly True*, "musical fairy tale" for Narrator, Solo Voices, Women's Chorus, and Orch. (1957); *Missa Sacra* for Tenor, Chorus, and Orch. (1960); *12 Passages from the Bible* for Men's Chorus and Organ (1960); *The Tomb at Akr Çaar* for Baritone and Chamber Chorus, after Ezra Pound (1964); *Triptych* for Soprano, Baritone, and Chorus (1965); *Requiem* for Baritone, 2 Choruses, 2 String Orchs., and Timpani (1966); *3 Classic Madrigals* for Chorus (1967); *Cantata humana* for Baritone, 4 Narrators on Tape, Chorus, and Orch., after Dag Hammarskjöld (Helsinki, April 9, 1970); *The Song of the Bride* for Soprano and Orch. (1972); *Venus and Adonis I–V* for Chorus (1972–74); *Songs of the Psyche* for Soprano and Piano (1978). **ELECTRONIC:** *3 Études* (1960).

Johner, Dominicus (actually, **Franz-Xaver Karl**), distinguished German music scholar; b. Waldsee, Dec. 1, 1874; d. Beuron, Jan. 4, 1955. He studied theology and music at the Benedictine abbeys in Prague, Seckau, and Beuron, his teachers at the latter being the cantor Ambrosius Kienle and the organist Raphael Molitor; after taking his vows in 1894, he studied theology at the Cucujães Monastery in Portugal (1896–1900), being ordained in 1898. In 1900 he returned to Beuron, where he was cantor of the abbey (1905–49); was also prior there (1913–33), and taught at the church music school of Gregoriushaus, near Beuron (1906–14). He was a lecturer at the Hochschule für Musik in Cologne (from 1925). He was a leading authority on ecclesiastical music. He also composed a cycle, *Neue Marienlieder* for Chorus and Organ (2 books, 1916, 1918), and *Neue Kommunionslieder* (1916).

WRITINGS: *Neue Schule des gregorianischen Choralgesanges* (Regensburg, 1906; 7th ed., 1937, as *Grosse Choralschule*; 8th ed., 1956, as *Choralschule*); *Der gregorianische Choral: Sein Wesen, Werden, Wert und Vortrag* (Stuttgart, 1924); *Die Sonn- und Festtagslieder des vatikanischen Graduale, nach Text und Melodie erklärt* (Regensburg, 1928; 2nd ed., 1933); *Erklärung des Kyriae nach Text und Melodie* (Regensburg, 1933); *Wort und Ton im Choral: Ein Beitrag zur Aesthetik des gregorianischen Gesanges* (Leipzig, 1940; 2nd ed., 1953).

BIBL.: F. Tack, ed., *Der kultische Gesang der abendländischen Kirche: In gregorianisches Werkheftaus Anlass des 75. Geburtstages von D. J.* (Cologne, 1950).

Johnsen, Hallvard Olav, Norwegian flutist and composer; b. Hamburg (of Norwegian parents), June 27, 1916. He went to Norway as a youth; studied flute with Stenseth and Wang, conducting with Fjeldstad, harmony and counterpoint with Steenberg, and composition with Brustad at the Oslo Cons. (1930–41); then studied composition with Karl Andersen in Oslo (1942–45), and later with Holmboe in Copenhagen (1956). He was a flutist in the orch. of the National Theater in Oslo (1945–47) and played in military bands (1947–73). His style of composition evolved from late Romanticism to free tonal techniques.

WORKS: OPERAS: *The Legend of Svein and Maria* (1971; Oslo, Sept. 9, 1973); *Det Kjempende Menneske* (1982); *Nattergalen* (1991). **ORCH.:** 2 suites for Chamber Orch. (1939, 1947); *Fantasia (Serenade)* for Chamber Orch. (1947); 19 syms. (1949; *Pastorale*, 1954; 1957; 1959; 1960; 1961; 1962; 1964; 1968; 1973; 1975; 1976; 1983; 1985; 1987; 1989; 1991; 1993; *Oceano*, 1994); *Ouverture Festivo* (1954); Concerto for Flute and Strings (1955); Concerto for Violin and Chamber Orch. (1959); Trumpet Concerto (1966); Violin Concerto (1968); *Ouverture Festoso* (1971); Cello Concerto (1977); *Norvegese alla Marcia* for Symphonic Band (1986). **CHAMBER:** Trio for Flute, Violin, and Viola (1938); Quartet No. 1 for Flute and String Trio (1945); 3 string quartets (1962, 1966, 1972); *Serenade* for Wind Quintet (1962); Suite for Flute and Horn (1964); Wind Quintet with Vibraphone (1965); Sextet for Flute, Horn, Vibraphone, Violin, Viola, and Cello (1974); *Serenade* for Flute, Viola, and Cello (1974); Saxophone Quartet (1974); *Divertimento* for Brass Quintet (1974); 3 brass quintets (1978–86); Trio for Trumpet, Trombone, and Vibraphone (1980); *Pastorale* for Flute, Violin, and Vibraphone (1981); *Canzona* for Trombone and Organ (1988); piano pieces. **VOCAL:** *Norsk Natur* (Norwegian Nature) for Chorus and Orch. (1952); 2 motets for Chorus (1959, 1965); *Krosspåske*, cantata for Baritone, Chorus, and Orch. (1963); *Der Ligger et Land*, cantata for Tenor, Men's Chorus, and Orch. (1966); *Fra Salmenes Bok*, cantata for Chorus and Organ (1977); *Logos*, oratorio for 8 Solo Voices, Chorus, Organ, and Orch. (1979); *10 Psalms* for Man's Voice and Organ (1979); *Bergammen*, melodrama for Man's Voice and Orch. (1980); Cantata for Voice and Orch. (1984); *Såkornet* for Narrator, 2 Violins, Viola, and Cello (1993).

Johnson, Bengt-Emil, Swedish composer and poet; b. Ludvika, Dec. 12, 1936. He studied piano and composition with Knut Wiggen (1956–62), at the same time pursuing his abiding interest in modernistic poetry. In 1966 he joined the staff of the Swedish Radio in Stockholm, where he later was named director of the music dept. (1979) and program director (1984). He publ. 14 collections of poetry (1963–86). Many of his compositions take the form of text-sound scores.

WORKS: *Disappearances* for Piano and Tape (1974); *Alpha* for Chorus (1975); *Escaping (Memories 1961–1977)* for 5 or More Performers (Swedish Radio, April 6, 1978); *Night Chants I*, radio piece (Swedish Radio, Aug. 19, 1981) and *II* for Voice and Tape (1985); *Döden sopran*, radio opera (Swedish Radio, Sept. 7, 1986); various text-sound scores.

Johnson, Edward, distinguished Canadian-born American tenor and operatic administrator; b. Guelph, Ontario, Aug. 22, 1878; d. there, April 20, 1959. He sang in concert and oratorio performances before going to N.Y. in 1899 to study with Mme. von Feilitsch; after appearing in the U.S. premiere of Oscar Straus's *A Waltz Dream* in 1907, he continued his studies with Richard Barthélemy in Paris (1908) and Vincenzo Lombardi in Florence (1909). He made his operatic debut as Andrea Chénier at the Teatro Verdi in Padua on Jan. 10, 1912, using the stage name of Edoardo Di Giovanni; he subsequently appeared in Milan at La Scala, where he sang the title role in *Parsifal* at its first complete stage production in Italy, on Jan. 4, 1914. He made his U.S. debut as Loris in *Fedora* at the Chicago Grand Opera on Nov. 20, 1919, remaining on its roster until 1922; then made his Metropolitan Opera debut in N.Y. as Avito in

L'amore dei tre Re on Nov. 16, 1922, continuing to sing there until 1935, when he became its general manager, guiding its fortunes through the difficult years of World War II and the postwar era; he retired in 1950. Although he became a naturalized American citizen in 1922, he maintained a close connection with Canada; returned there after his retirement. He was particularly esteemed for such roles as Romeo, Tannhäuser, Don José, Siegfried, Canio, and Pelléas; he also created leading roles in Deems Taylor's *The King's Henchman* (1927) and *Peter Ibbetson* (1931) at the Metropolitan.

BIBL.: R. Mercer, *The Tenor of His Time: E. J. of the Met* (Toronto, 1976).

Johnson, (Francis) Hall, black American choral conductor, composer, and arranger; b. Athens, Ga., June 2, 1887; d. N.Y., April 30, 1970. He studied at the Univ. of Pa. (B.A., 1910), where he took a course in composition with Hugh A. Clark; later studied with Goetschius at the Inst. of Musical Art in N.Y. (1923–24). In 1925 he formed the Hall Johnson Choir, with which he gave numerous concerts; from 1938 to 1946 he conducted the Festival Choir of Los Angeles, and then settled in N.Y. as conductor of the Festival Negro Chorus, with which he toured Germany and Austria under the auspices of the U.S. State Dept. (1951). He composed a folk opera, *Run Littl' Chillun* (1933), a cantata, *Son of Man* (1946), choral music, songs, and arrangements for film and television.

Johnson, Hunter, American composer and teacher; b. Benson, N.C., April 14, 1906. He studied at the Univ. of North Carolina (1924–26), and at the Eastman School of Music in Rochester, N.Y., graduating in 1929. In 1933 he received the Rome Prize. He taught at the Univ. of Mich. (1929–33), the Univ. of Manitoba (1944–47), Cornell Univ. (1948–53), the Univ. of Ill. (1959–65), and the Univ. of Texas (1966–71). In 1941 and 1954 he held Guggenheim fellowships. His output follows in the tradition of Ives and Copland.

WORKS: BALLETS: *In Time of Armament* (1939); *Letter to the World* (1940); *Deaths and Entrances* (1942); *The Scarlet Letter* (1975). **ORCH.:** *Prelude* (1930); Sym. (1931); Concerto for Piano and Chamber Orch. (1935); *Elegy* for Clarinet and Strings (1937); *Concerto for Orchestra* (1944); *Music* for Strings (1949–54); *North State*, to commemorate the tricentennial of the Carolina Charter (1963); *Past the Evening Sun* (1964). **CHAMBER:** Piano Sonata (1934; rev., 1936 and 1947–48); *Elegy for Hart Crane* for Clarinet Quintet (1936); *Serenade* for Flute and Clarinet (1937); Violin Sonatina (1937); Trio for Flute, Oboe, and Piano (1954). **VOCAL:** Songs.

BIBL.: R. Monaco, *The Music of H. J.* (diss., Cornell Univ., 1960).

Johnson, James Weldon, black American man of letters, brother of **J(ohn) Rosamond Johnson**; b. Jacksonville, Fla., June 17, 1871; d. in an automobile accident in Wiscasset, Maine, June 26, 1938. He studied literature at Atlanta Univ. (B.A., 1894; M.A., 1904); also passed the Florida bar examination to practice law (1897). As a poet, he began writing texts to his brother's compositions; their song *Lift Every Voice and Sing* (1900) proved popular, becoming known as "the Negro National Anthem." The brothers settled in N.Y. in 1902, where they joined Bob Cole in the enormously successful songwriting team of Cole and Johnson Bros.; among their hit songs, mostly in black dialect, were *Under the Bamboo Tree* (1902), which was parodied by T. S. Eliot in "Fragment of the Agon," and *Congo Love Song* (1903). Under the pseudonym Will Handy, they produced *Oh, Didn't He Ramble* (1902), which became a jazz standard; the team's success was such that they became known as "Those Ebony Offenbachs." Johnson was then active as a diplomat (1906–14), serving as consul to Venezuela and, later, to Nicaragua. His tr. of Granados's *Goyescas* was used for the Metropolitan Opera's first performance of this work. He publ. anonymously the novel *The Autobiography of an Ex-Colored Man* (Boston, 1912), which includes vivid descriptions of the ragtime era in N.Y. He collaborated with his brother in compiling 2 books of American Negro spirituals (N.Y., 1926 and 1927); wrote *Black Manhattan* (N.Y., 1930), a history of blacks in N.Y. which includes valuable information on black musical life; also publ. an autobiography, *Along This Way* (1931). His papers are on deposit at Yale Univ.

BIBL.: E. Levy, *J. W. J.* (Chicago, 1973).

Johnson, J(ohn) Rosamond, black American composer and bass, brother of **James Weldon Johnson**; b. Jacksonville, Fla., Aug. 11, 1873; d. N.Y., Nov. 11, 1954. He studied at Atlanta Univ. and at the New England Cons. of Music in Boston; took voice lessons with David Bispham. He set his brother's poem *Lift Every Voice and Sing* (1900) to music, which later became known as "the Negro National Anthem." The brothers collaborated on many other songs, selling them to various musical reviews in N.Y.; in 1902 they formed, with Bob Cole, the songwriting team of Cole and Johnson Bros.; Johnson also wrote some songs that were accepted on the concert stage, among them *Li'l Gal* and *Since You Went Away*. In 1911–12 he was music director of Hammerstein's Opera House in London; also sang in opera, and later toured the U.S. and Europe in programs of Negro spirituals. With his brother, he compiled 2 vols. of Negro spirituals (1926, 1927), adding piano accompaniments; wrote a ballet, *African Drum Dance*, and many vocal works; also *Rolling Along in Song* (a history of black music with 85 song arrangements). He sang the role of Lawyer Frazier in the early performances of Gershwin's *Porgy and Bess*.

Johnson, Lockrem, American pianist, music publisher, and composer; b. Davenport, Iowa, March 15, 1924; d. Seattle, March 5, 1977. He studied at the Cornish School of Music in Seattle (1931–38) and at the Univ. of Wash. (1938–42); subsequently was a member of its faculty (1947–49); concurrently served as music director of the Eleanor King Dance Co. (1947–50) and pianist in the Seattle Sym. Orch. (1948–51). In 1952 he held a Guggenheim fellowship; lived in N.Y., where he served as education director for Mercury Music (1951–54), head of the orch. dept. of C.F. Peters (1954–58), and president of Dow Publishers (1957–62); subsequently returned to Seattle as head of the music dept. at the Cornish School of Music (1962–69); also founded Puget Music Publications (1970), which was devoted to publishing works by composers of the Northwest. His works reveal a fine lyrical gift of expression.

WORKS: DRAMATIC: *She*, ballet (1948; rev. 1950); *A Letter to Emily*, chamber opera (1951; N.Y., Jan. 25, 1955). **ORCH.:** *Lyric Prelude* (1948; rev. 1949); Sym. (Seattle, Dec. 2, 1966). **CHAMBER:** 3 violin sonatas (1942; 1948, rev. 1949; 1953); 2 cello sonatas (1949, 1953); Trumpet Sonatina (1950). **PIANO:** 3 sonatas (1947, rev. 1983; 1949; 1954); 24 Preludes; many other pieces. **VOCAL:** *Suite of Noels*, cantata for Chorus and Keyboard (1954); songs.

Johnson, Robert Sherlaw, English pianist and composer; b. Sunderland, May 21, 1932. He was educated at King's College, Univ. of Durham (1950–53), and at the Royal Academy of Music in London (1953–57); then studied piano with Fevrier and composition with Boulanger in Paris (1957–58), where he also attended Messiaen's classes at the Cons.; returning to England, he gave piano recitals in programs of 20th-century music. He lectured at the univs. of Leeds (1961–63) and York (1965–70). In 1970 he was appointed to the faculty of the Univ. of Oxford; was a visiting prof. at the Eastman School of Music in Rochester, N.Y. (1985). He wrote a study on Messiaen (1974). In his music, he re-creates Renaissance forms and mannerisms in a modern modal idiom. He composes mainly for chamber ensembles and vocal groups.

WORKS: OPERA: *The Lambton Worm* (1976). **ORCH.:** Piano Concerto (1983). **CHAMBER:** 2 string quartets (1966, 1969); *Triptych* for Flute, Clarinet, Violin, Cello, Piano, and Percussion (1973); Quintet for Clarinet, Violin, Viola, Cello, and Piano (1974); Sonata for Alto Flute and Cello (1976). **PIANO:** 3 sonatas (1963, 1967, 1976); *Asterogenesis* for 8-octave (Bösendorfer) Piano (1973); *Nymphaea ("Projections")* (1976).

VOCAL: *The Praises of Heaven and Earth* for Soprano, Tape, and Piano (1969); *Incarnatio* for Chorus (1970); *Green Whispers of Gold* for Voice, Tape, and Piano (1971); *Carmina vernalia* for Soprano and Instruments (1972); *Christus resurgens* for Chorus (1972); *Festival Mass of the Resurrection* for Chorus and Chamber Orch. (1974); *Anglorum feriae* for Soprano, Tenor, Chorus, and Orch. (1976); *Veritas veritatus* for 6 Voices (1980).

Johnson, Thor, American conductor; b. Wisconsin Rapids, Wis., June 10, 1913; d. Nashville, Tenn., Jan. 16, 1975. He studied at the Univ. of North Carolina and later at the Univ. of Mich. (M.A., 1935), where he was founder and conductor of its Little Sym. Orch. (1934–36; 1938–42); also took courses in conducting with Malko, Abendroth, Weingartner, and Walter in Europe (1936–37), and with Koussevitzky at the Berkshire Music Center in Tanglewood (summers, 1940–41). He was conductor of the Grand Rapids (Mich.) Sym. Orch. (1940–42); subsequently enlisted in the U.S. Army (1942), and conducted the 1st Army Sym. Orch. in Fort Myers, Va.; subsequently conducted the Juilliard School of Music orch. in N.Y. (1946–47). From 1947 to 1958 he was music director of the Cincinnati Sym. Orch., one of the first native-born Americans to hold such a position with a major U.S. orch. From 1958 to 1964 he was a prof. and director of orchestral activities at Northwestern Univ. in Chicago, and from 1964 to 1967 was director of the Interlochen Arts Academy. He was music director of the Nashville (Tenn.) Sym. Orch. from 1967 until his death.

Johnson, Tom, American composer; b. Greeley, Colo., Nov. 18, 1939. He was educated at Yale Univ. (B.A., 1961; M.Mus., 1967) and studied with Morton Feldman in N.Y. After writing music criticism for N.Y.'s *Village Voice* newspaper (1972–82), he settled in Paris to pursue his career as a composer. An anthology of his articles from the *Village Voice* appeared as *The Voice of New Music* (Eindhoven, 1991). In his music, Johnson has made use of minimalist resources while steering his own independent course made refreshing by his wit and penchant for ironical expression.

WORKS: DRAMATIC: OPERAS: *The 4-Note Opera* (1972); *The Masque of Clouds* (1975); *Window* (1978); *Dryer* (1978); *Drawers* (1978); *Door* (1978); *Sopranos Only* (1984); *Riemannoper* (1988); *Deux cents ans* (1989); *Una opera Italiana* (1991). **RADIO SCORE:** *Cling Clang* (1993). **ORCH.:** *The Secret of the River* (1966); *Dragons in A* (1979). **CHAMBER:** *Action Music IV* for Violist (1968); *Failing, a very difficult piece for solo string bass* (1975); *60-note Fanfares* for 4 Trumpets (1976); *Monologue* for Tuba (1978); *8 Patterns* for 8 Instruments (1979); *9 Bells* for Suspended Bells (1979); *Movements* for Wind Quintet (1980); *Doublings* for Double Bass (1980); *Rational Melodies* for Melodic Instrument (1982); *Harpiano* for Harp and Piano (1982); *Self-Portrait* for Box Mover/Composer and 2 to 10 Musicians (1983); *Predictables* for Violin, Cello, and Piano (1984); *Bedtime Stories* for Clarinet and Narrator (1985); *Infinite Melodies* for Any Melodic Instrument (1986); *Chord Catalogue* for Any Keyboard Instrument (1986); *6-note Melody* for Organ (1986); *Eggs and Baskets* for 2 Instruments and Narrator (1987); *Music and Questions* for Bells or Glockenspiel and Questions for the Audience (1988); *Alexandrins pour guitare* (1989); *Narayana's Cows* for Instruments and Narrator (1989); *Quatour pour Flutes* (1989); *Maximum Efficiency* for 3 Instruments (1991); *Einstimmiger Polyrhythmus* for Tenor Saxophone, Guitar, and Bass (1992); *Sequenza Minimalista* for Trombone (1992); *Composition with Descending Chromatic Scales in 8-voice Canon Played in 3 Ways, Separated by 2 Piano Interludes, Which Bring the Music Back Up to its Starting Position* (1993); *Composition with Ascending Chromatic Scales in 11 Tempos, all Beginning Simultaneously, the Piano Playing the Low Notes, the Clarinet the Middle Notes, and the Violin the High Notes* (1993); *Formulas* for String Quartet (1994). **PIANO:** *Spaces* (1969); *Scene* for Piano and Tape (1969); *An Hour for Piano* (1971); *Septapede* (1973; rev. 1993); *Private Pieces* (1976); *Triple Threat* (1979); *Symmetries* for Piano, 4-hands (1981–90); *Counting Keys* (1982); *Tango* (1984); *Music for 88* (1988); *Cosinus* (1994). **VOCAL:** *Trinity* for 4 Choruses (1978); *Bonhoeffer Oratorio* for 4 Soloists, 2 Choruses, and Orch. (1990); *Le choeur* for Children's Chorus (1994).

BIBL.: G. Grönemeyer, "Lust am Zahlen: T. J.—ein Portrat," *MusikTexte* (July–Aug. 1988).

Johnston, Ben(jamin Burwell), American composer and pedagogue; b. Macon, Ga., March 15, 1926. He studied at the College of William and Mary in Williamsburg, Va. (A.B., 1949), the Cincinnati Cons. of Music (M.Mus., 1950), and Mills College in Oakland, California (M.A., 1953); held a Guggenheim fellowship (1959–60). He taught at the Univ. of Ill. in Urbana (1951–83).

WORKS: DRAMATIC: OPERAS: *Gertrude, or Would She Be Pleased to Receive It?* (1965); *Carmilla* (1970). **BALLETS:** *St. Joan* (1955); *Gambit* for Dancers and Orch. (1959; also concert version entitled *Ludes* for 12 Instruments). **ORCH.:** Concerto for Brass (1951); *Passacaglia and Epilogue* (1955–60); Quintet for Groups (1966); Sym. (Rocky Mount, N.C., Oct. 29, 1988); also 2 pieces for Jazz Band: *Ivesberg Revisited* and *Newcastle Troppo* (both 1960). **CHAMBER:** Septet for Wind Quintet, Cello, and Bass (1956–58); *9 Variations* for String Quartet (1959); *Knocking Piece* for 2 Percussionists and Piano (1962); Duo for Flute and String Bass (1963); string quartets (beginning with No. 2: 1964, 1966–73, 1973, 1980, 1980, 1985, 1986, 1988); Trio for Clarinet, Violin, and Cello (1982); *The Demon Lover's Double* for Trumpet and Microtonal Piano (1985); piano pieces. **VOCAL:** *Night*, cantata (1955); choral music; songs.

BIBL.: H. Von Gunden, *The Music of B. J.* (Metuchen, N.J., and London, 1986).

Jokinen, Erkki, Finnish composer and teacher; b. Janakkala, Oct. 16, 1941. He entered the Sibelius Academy in Helsinki in 1960, where he was a composition student of Kokkonen (from 1965) and then of Bergman, taking his degree in 1970. After further training with Ton de Leeuw in Bilthoven, the Netherlands (1971), he returned to Helsinki and later taught theory and composition at the Sibelius Academy. In 1987 he served as the composer of the year at the Helsinki Festival. In his music, Jokinen places emphasis upon tonal effects and structure with a utilization of occasional pointillistic and minimalistic infusions.

WORKS: ORCH.: Cello Concerto (1969–70; Helsinki, Oct. 21, 1971); Concerto for Accordion and Chamber Orch. (Helsinki, July 16, 1987); *Voyage No. 1*, Concerto for Violin and Chamber Orch. (Helsinki, Aug. 28, 1990) and *No. 2* for Chamber Orch. (Hämeenlinna, Aug. 29, 1991). **CHAMBER:** *Taksis* for Flute and Piano (Hämeenlinna, April 28, 1968); *Contrasts* for Flute, Clarinet, Violin, Cello, and Piano (Helsinki, May 17, 1968); *Music* for 4 Brass Instruments (1968; Hämeenlinna, May 25, 1969); *CeGeda* for Cello (1969); 4 string quartets: No. 1 (1971; Helsinki, Feb. 28, 1973), No. 2 (Hämeenlinna, Nov. 28, 1976), No. 3 (1988; Oulu, Feb. 16, 1989), and No. 4 (1994); *Do der Sumer komen was* for Clarinet, Horn, Flugelhorn, Piano, and Percussion (Hämeenlinna, June 9, 1978); *Distances* for Clarinet and Piano (Hämeenlinna, Aug. 17, 1978); *Air* for Bass Clarinet (1979); *Alone* for Accordion (1979); *Songs* for Bass Clarinet, Trombone, Piano, Percussion, and Double Bass (Hämeenlinna, June 8, 1980); *Face* for Flute, Harp, Harpsichord, Violin, Viola, and Cello (Helsinki, March 24, 1983); *Pillars* for Cello and Double Bass (1983); *Reflections* for 2 Accordions (1983); *Frieze* for Oboe, Horn, Piano, Violin, and Double Bass (1984); *Hommage à Marc Chagall* for Organ (1985; Helsinki, April 9, 1986); *Rise No. 1* for 4 Pianists (1989; Hämeenlinna, Nov. 22, 1990), *No. 2* for Flute, Clarinet, and Percussion (1992), and *No. 3* for Percussionist (1992); *. . . pressentir . . .* for Accordion and Double Bass (1989; Helsinki, Aug. 10, 1990); *Aspis* for Alto Flute, Accordion, Guitar, and Percussion (Tampere, April 22, 1990); *Pros* for Clarinet and Cello (1990; Helsinki, March 16, 1991). **VOCAL:** *Psalmus* for Chorus (1971); *Tempora per omnia* for Men's Chorus (1980; Hämeenlinna, Nov. 6, 1982); *Floating Leaves* for Soprano and Piano (Hämeenlinna, July 29, 1982); *Oh, Let the Heart Be Filled* for Chorus (1985); *Do You Remember the Time* for Chorus (1986); *That Time of Year* for Women's Chorus (1988).

Jolas, Betsy (real name, **Elizabeth Illouz**), American composer and teacher; b. Paris (of American parents), Aug. 5, 1926. She went to the U.S. in 1940 and studied with Boepple (composition), Helen Schnabel (piano), and Weinrich (organ) at Bennington (Vt.) College (B.A., 1946). Returning to Paris, she completed her training with Milhaud (composition), Plé-Caussade (fugue), and Messiaen (analysis) at the Cons. From 1971 to 1974 she taught Messiaen's course at the Cons., and then served on its faculty from 1975 to 1991. She won the Grand Prix National de la Musique (1974), the Grand Prix de la Ville de Paris (1981), the Grand Prix de la SACEM (1982), the Maurice Ravel Prix International (1992), and the Prix SACEM (1994). In 1983 she was elected a member of the American Academy of Arts and Letters. In 1985 she was made a Commandeur des Arts et des Lettres. Her Franco-American training is reflected in her music, which is particularly notable for its imaginative handling of form and structure with judicious infusions of color and lyricism.

WORKS: OPERAS: *Le Pavillon au bord de la rivière*, chamber opera after a medieval Chinese play (Avignon, July 25, 1975); *Le Cyclope*, chamber opera (Avignon, July 27, 1986); *Schliemann* (1988; concert perf., Paris, April 4, 1990; stage perf., Lyons, May 1995). **ORCH.:** Sym. (1957); *Quatre Plages* for Strings (1967); *D'un opéra de voyage* for Chamber Orch. (Royan, April 1967); *Musique d'hiver* for Organ and Small Orch. (1972); *Trois Rencontres* (Strasbourg, June 1973); *Tales of a Summer Sea* (1977); *Onze Lieder* for Trumpet and Chamber Orch. (Paris, Oct. 1977); *Stances* for Piano and Orch. (Radio France, Paris, April 1978); *Cinq Pièces pour Boulogne* for Small Orch. (1982); *Préludes-Fanfares-Interludes-Sonneries* for Winds and Percussion (1983; Paris, Jan. 28, 1984); Viola Concerto (1990–91); Saxophone Concerto (1996). **CHAMBER:** *Sonate à trois* for String Trio (1955); Viola Sonata (1955); 5 string quartets: No. 1 (1956), No. 2, with Soprano (Paris, March 1966), No. 3 (1973; Washington, D.C., Jan. 1974), No. 4 (1989; Paris, June 1990), and No. 5 (1994; Paris, Feb. 16, 1995); *Figures* for 9 Instruments (1956–65; Evreux, March 20, 1984); *J.D.E.* for 14 Instruments (1966); *Points d'Aube* for Viola and 13 Winds (Havre, Dec. 1968); *Etats* for Violin and 6 Percussionists (Persépolis, Sept. 1969); *Lassus Ricercare* for 10 Instruments (1970); *How Now* for 8 Instruments (1973; Paris, June 1974); *Well Met* for 12 Instruments (1973; Paris, June 1976); *O Wall* for Wind Quintet (N.Y., Nov. 5, 1976); *Quatre duos* for Viola and Piano (1979; Radio France, April 1980); *Points d'or* for Saxophone and 15 Instruments (1982); *Trois duos* for Tuba and Piano (1983; Lugano, March 23, 1984); *Music for Joan* for Vibraphone and Piano (1988); Trio for Piano, Violin, and Cello (1988); *Les heures* for String Trio (1990; Paris, May 14, 1991); *Études aperçues* for Violin and 5 Bells (1992); *Musique for Delphine* for Violin and Cello (1992); *Music for Here* for Bassoon, Viola, and Cello (1994); *Quoth the Raven* for Clarinet and Piano (1994); pieces for solo instruments, including a Piano Sonata (1973; N.Y., Jan. 1974) and organ music. **VOCAL:** *L'oeil égaré*, radiophonic cantata for Soloists, Chorus, and Chamber Orch. (1961); *Dans la chaleur vacante*, radiophonic cantata for Soloists, Chorus, and Chamber Orch. (1963); *Mots* for 5 Soloists and 7 Instruments (1963; Geneva, March 1964); *Motet II* for Chorus (1965; Angers, Oct. 1986); *Diurnes* for Chorus (1970); *Sonate à 12* for 3 Sopranos, 3 Altos, 3 Tenors, and 3 Basses (1970; Royan, April 1971); *Caprice à deux voix* for Soprano and Countertenor or Alto (1978; Radio France, Paris, March 1979); *Liring balade* for Baritone and Orch. (1980); *Plupart du temps II* for Tenor, Tenor Saxophone, and Cello (1989; Zagreb, Nov. 1990); *Frauenleben* for Alto and Orch. (1992); *Perriault le Deluné* for 12 Solo Voices (1993).

Jolivet, André, prominent French composer; b. Paris, Aug. 8, 1905; d. there, Dec. 20, 1974. A son of artistically inclined parents, he took an interest in the fine arts, wrote poetry, and improvised at the piano; studied cello with Louis Feuillard and theory with Aimé Théodas at Notre Dame de Clignancourt. At the age of 15, he wrote a ballet and designed a set for it; then undertook a prolonged study of musical techniques with Le Flem (1928–33). Of decisive importance to the maturation of his creative consciousness was his meeting in 1930 with Varèse, then living in Paris, who gave him a sense of direction in composition. In 1935 he organized in Paris the progressive group La Spirale. In 1936, in association with Baudrier, Messiaen, and Daniel-Lesur, he founded La Jeune France, dedicated to the promotion of new music in a national French style. He served as conductor and music director of the Comédie Française (1943–59); was technical adviser of the Direction Générale des Arts et des Lettres (1959–62), and president of the Concerts Lamoureux (1963–68); he also was prof. of composition at the Paris Cons. (1965–70). He toured throughout the world as a conductor of his own music. Jolivet injected an empiric spirit into his music, making free use of modernistic technical resources, including the electronic sounds of the Ondes Martenot. Despite these esoteric preoccupations, and even a peripheral deployment of serialism, his music was designed mainly to provide aural stimulation and aesthetic satisfaction.

WORKS: DRAMATIC: OPERA-BUFFA: *Dolorès, Le Miracle de la femme laide* (1942; Paris Radio, May 4, 1947). **BALLETS:** *Guignol et Pandore* (1943; Paris, April 29, 1944); *L'Inconnue* (Paris, April 19, 1950); *Ariadne* (1964; Paris, March 12, 1965). **OTHER:** Incidental music. **ORCH.:** *Andante* for Strings (1935); *Danse incantatoire* for Orch. and 2 Ondes Martenot (1936); *Cosmogonie* (1938; Paris, Nov. 17, 1947; also for Piano); *5 danses rituelles* (1939; Paris, June 15, 1942); *Symphonie de danses* (1940; Paris, Nov. 24, 1943); *Psyché* (1946; Paris, March 5, 1947); Ondes Martenot Concerto (1947; Vienna, April 23, 1948); 2 trumpet concertos (1948, 1954); 2 flute concertos (1949, 1965); Piano Concerto (1949–50; Strasbourg, June 19, 1951); Concerto for Harp and Chamber Orch. (1952); 3 numbered syms.: No. 1 (1953; Haifa, May 30, 1954), No. 2 (Berlin, Oct. 3, 1959), and No. 3 (Mexico City, Aug. 7, 1964, composer conducting); Concerto for Bassoon, Harp, Piano, and Strings (Paris Radio, Nov. 30, 1954); *Suite transocéane* (Louisville, Ky., Sept. 24, 1955); *Suite française* (1957); Percussion Concerto (1958; Paris, Feb. 17, 1959); *Adagio* for Strings (1960); *Les Amants magnifiques* (Lyons, April 24, 1961); Sym. for Strings (1961; Paris, Jan. 9, 1962); 2 cello concertos: No. 1 (Paris, Nov. 20, 1962) and No. 2 (1966; Moscow, Jan. 6, 1967); Violin Concerto (1972; Paris, Feb. 28, 1973); *La Flèche du temps* for 12 Solo Strings (1973); *Yin-Yang* for 11 Solo Strings (1974). **CHAMBER:** Suite for String Trio (1930); String Quartet (1934); *3 poèmes* for Ondes Martenot and Piano (1935); *5 incantations* for Flute (1936); *Ballet des étoiles* for 9 Instruments (1941); *Suite delphique* for Winds, Harp, Ondes Martenot, and Percussion (1943; Vienna, Oct. 22, 1948); *Nocturne* for Cello and Piano (1943); *Pastorales de Noël* for Flute or Violin, Bassoon or Viola, and Harp (1943); *Chant des Linos* for Flute and Piano, or Flute, Violin, Viola, Cello, and Harp (1944); *Sérénade* for Oboe and Piano, or Wind Quintet (1945); *Sérénade* for 2 Guitars (1956); *Rhapsodie à 7* for Clarinet, Bassoon, Trumpet, Trombone, Percussion, Violin, and Double Bass (1957); Flute Sonata (1958); Sonatina for Flute and Clarinet (1961); Sonatina for Oboe and Bassoon (1963); *Alla rustica* for Flute and Harp (1963); *Suite rhapsodique* for Violin (1965); *Suite en concert* for Cello (1965); *5 églogues* for Viola (1967); *Ascèses* for Flute or Clarinet (1967); *Cérémonial en hommage à Varèse* for 6 Percussionists (1968); *Controversia* for Oboe and Harp (1968); *Arioso barocco* for Trumpet and Organ (1969); *Heptade* for Trumpet and Percussion (1971–72). **KEYBOARD: PIANO:** *3 Temps* (1930); *Mana* (1935); 2 sonatas (1945, 1957); *Hopi Snake Dance* for 2 Pianos (1948); *Patchinko* for 2 Pianos (1970). **ORGAN:** *Hymne à l'univers* (1961); *Mandala* (1969). **VOCAL:** *3 chants des hommes* for Baritone and Orch. (1937); *Poèmes pour l'enfant* for Voice and 11 Instruments (1937; Paris, May 12, 1938); *3 complaintes du soldat* for Voice and Orch. or Piano (1940); *Messe pour le jour de la paix* for Voice, Organ, and Tambourine (1940); *Suite liturgique* for Voice, Oboe, Cello, and Harp (1942); *Epithalame* for 12-part Vocal "Orch." (1953; Venice, Sept. 16, 1956); *Messe "Uxor tua"* for 5 Voices and 5 Instruments or Organ (1962);

Madrigal for 4 Voices and 4 Instruments (1963); *Songe à nouveau rêvé* for Soprano and Orch. (1970).

BIBL.: V. Fédorov and P. Guinard, compilers, *A. J.: Catalogue des oeuvres* (Paris, 1969); H. Jolivet, *Avec A. J.* (Paris, 1978).

Jonák, Zdeněk, Czech composer; b. Prague, Feb. 25, 1917. He studied composition with Řídký at the Prague Cons. (graduated, 1941), continuing his study with Řídký and Křička at its master school (graduated, 1947). He subsequently devoted himself mainly to pragmatic musical tasks, such as making arrangements of folk songs and writing music for the theater.

WORKS: ORCH.: *Prelude* (1939); *Passacaglia* (1940); *Suite* (1951); Chamber Sym. (1964); Trumpet Concerto (1972). **CHAMBER:** 3 string quartets (1941, 1947, 1980); Cello Sonata (1955). **VOCAL:** *Epigrams*, song cycle for Chorus (1975).

Jonas, Maryla, Polish pianist; b. Warsaw, May 31, 1911; d. N.Y., July 3, 1959. She was a precocious child pianist, and appeared in public at the age of 8; took lessons with Turczynski and was commended by Paderewski. She began her professional career as a concert pianist at the age of 15; after the invasion of Poland in 1939, she made her way to Rio de Janeiro, and gave a series of concerts in South America; then went to N.Y., where she made an exceptionally successful debut in Carnegie Hall (Feb. 25, 1946); her auspicious career was thwarted by an irremediable illness.

Jonas, Oswald, Austrian-American musicologist; b. Vienna, Jan. 10, 1897; d. Riverside, Calif., March 19, 1978. He studied musicology with Schenker (1915–22); also studied law at the Univ. of Vienna (Ph.D., 1921). He taught at Berlin's Stern Cons. (1930–34); then worked at the Schenker Inst. at the New Vienna Cons. (1935–38). After the annexation of Austria by the Nazis in 1938, he went to the U.S., where he taught at Roosevelt Univ. in Chicago and associated schools (1941–64); after a sojourn as a teacher at the Vienna Academy of Music (1964–65), he became a prof. at the Univ. of Calif. at Riverside (1966). He publ. *Das Wesen des musikalischen Kunstwerks* (Vienna, 1934; 2nd ed., rev., 1973 as *Einführung in die Lehre Heinrich Schenkers*); also wrote numerous articles on Schenker's theories and ed. several of his works.

Jones, Alton, American pianist and teacher; b. Fairfield, Nebr., Aug. 3, 1899; d. N.Y., Jan. 2, 1971. He studied at Drake Univ. (B.M., 1919) and at the Inst. of Musical Art in N.Y., where his teachers were Edwin Hughes and Richard Buhlig; he graduated in 1921. He made his concert debut in N.Y. in 1924; was a soloist with the N.Y. Phil. in 1949; gave his last N.Y. recital in 1955. He taught at the Juilliard School of Music in N.Y. from 1921 until his death; his reputation as a pedagogue was high; many American pianists were his pupils.

Jones, Charles, Canadian-born American composer and teacher; b. Tamworth, June 21, 1910. He settled in the U.S. in 1928, where he studied violin at the Inst. of Musical Art (diploma, 1932) and composition with Wagenaar at the Juilliard School of Music (diploma, 1939) in N.Y. He taught at Mills College in Oakland, California (1939–44), then at the Juilliard School of Music (1954–60; 1973), and at the Mannes College of Music (from 1972); also taught at the Aspen (Colo.) School of Music. After composing in a neo-Classical style, he developed a complex mode of expression notable for its chromaticism.

WORKS: BALLET: *Down with Drink* for Women's Voices, Piano, and Percussion (1943). **ORCH.:** Suite for Strings (1937); 4 syms.: No. 1 (1939), No. 2 (1957), No. 3 (1962), and No. 4 (1965); *Little Symphony for the New Year* (1953); *Galop* (1940); *Pastorale* for Chamber Orch. (1940); *Cowboy Song* for Oboe and Strings (1941); *Overture* (1942); *5 Melodies* (1945); *Cassation* (1948); *Introduction and Rondo* for Strings (1957); *Suite after a Notebook of 1762* for Chamber Orch. (1957); Concerto for 4 Violins and Orch. (1963); *Allegory* (1970). **CHAMBER:** 10 string quartets (1936–94); Sonatina for Solo Violin (1938); Violin Sonatina (1942); Suite for Violin and Piano (1945); Duo for Violin and Piano (1947); *Threnody for* Viola (1947); *Lyric Waltz Suite* for Wind Quartet (1948); *Sonata a tre* for Piano Trio (1952); Duo for Violin and Viola (1956); Violin Sonata (1958); *Sonata piccola* for Piccolo and Harpsichord (1961); Sonata for Oboe and Harpsichord (1965); *Music for 2 Violinists* (1966); String Trio (1968); *In Nomine* for Violin and Piano (1972); *Serenade* for Flute, Violin, Cello, and Harpsichord (1973); *Triptychon I* for Violin, Viola, and Piano (1975) and *II* for Violin and Piano (1981); Trio for Violin, Cello, and Piano (1982); *Meditation* for Bass Clarinet and Piano (1982); *Capriccio* for Cello and Piano (1983); *Ballade* for Violin and Piano (1986); *Serena* for 9 Instruments (1986). **KEYBOARD: PIANO:** 2 sonatas (1946, 1950); Sonata for 2 Pianos (1947); *Toccata* (1955); *Psalm* (1976); *Book of the Hours* (1979–81); Sonata for Piano, 4-hands (1983). **HARPSICHORD:** *Keyboard Book* (1953); Suite (1993). **ORGAN:** *Noël* (1983); *Emblemata* (1994). **VOCAL:** *The Seasons*, cantata (1959); *I Am a Mynstrel* for Tenor, Violin, Harpsichord, Piano, and Percussion (1967); *Masque* for Speaker and 12 Players, after Pope's *Rape of the Lock* (1968); 4 scenes for Voice and Piano, after Pope (1982); *Poemata* for Voice, Violin, and Cello (1987); songs.

Jones, Daniel (Jenkyn), remarkable Welsh composer; b. Pembroke, Dec. 7, 1912; d. Swansea, April 23, 1993. Both his parents were musicians, and he absorbed the natural rudiments of music instinctively at home. He studied English literature at Univ. College of Wales, Swansea (B.A., 1934; M.A., 1939), and also attended the Royal Academy of Music in London (1935–38), where he studied composition with Farjeon, conducting with Wood, viola with Lockyear, and horn with Aubrey Brain; later completed his education at Univ. College of Wales (D.Mus., 1951). He retained interest in literature; was ed. of the collected poems of Dylan Thomas (1971) and the author of *My Friend Dylan Thomas* (1973). He was made an Officer of the Order of the British Empire (1968). In 1936 he promulgated a system of "complex metres," in which the numerator in the time signature indicates the succession of changing meters in a clear numerical progression, e.g. 32–322–3222–322–32, followed by 332–3332–332, etc.; his other innovation is a category of "continuous modes," with the final note of the mode (non-octaval) serving as the initial note of a transposed mode. He authored numerous articles expounding his philosophy of music, some of which were incorporated in the book *Music and Esthetic* (1954).

WORKS: OPERAS: *The Knife* (1961; London, Dec. 2, 1963); *Orestes* (1967). **ORCH.:** *The Flute Player* (1942); *Comedy Overture* (1942); 12 syms.: No. 1 (1944; Liverpool, Aug. 6, 1948), No. 2 (1950), No. 3 (1951), No. 4, *In memoriam Dylan Thomas* (1954), No. 5 (1958), No. 6 (1964), No. 7 (1971), No. 8 (1972), No. 9 (1974), No. 10 (1981), No. 11 (1983), and No. 12 (1985); *Cloud Messenger* (1945); *Miscellany* (1946); *Dobra Niva*, suite (1956); *Ieuenctid* (Youth), overture (1956); *Salute to Dylan Thomas* (1956); *Capriccio* for Flute, Harp, and Strings (1965); Violin Concerto (1966); *Investiture Processional Music* for the Prince of Wales (1969); 2 sinfoniettas (1972, 1991); Oboe Concerto (1982); Cello Concerto (Swansea, Oct. 4, 1986); *Orpheus and Bacchus*, overture (Guildford, Surrey, Sept. 24, 1989). **CHAMBER:** 2 string trios (1946, 1970); 7 string quartets (1948, 1957, 1975, 1978, 1980, 1982, 1988); Cello Sonata (1973); Suite for Flute and Harpsichord (1979); Divertimento for Wind Quintet (1990). **VOCAL:** *Kyrie* for Chorus (1949); *The 3 Hermits* for Chorus and Piano or Organ (1969); *Triptych* for Chorus and Piano (1969); *The Witnesses* for Men's Chorus and Orch. (1971); *Hear the Voice of the Ancient Bard* for Chorus and Orch. (1977); *To Night* for Chorus and Piano (1978); *Come My Way, My Truth, My Life* for Tenor, Chorus, and Orch. (1987); songs.

Jones, Della, Welsh mezzo-soprano; b. Neath, April 13, 1946. She was educated at the Royal College of Music in London and in Geneva, where, in 1970, she made her operatic debut as Fyodor in *Boris Godunov.* Returning to London, she sang at the Sadler's Wells Opera in 1973. From 1977 she made regular appearances at the English National Opera. In 1983 she sang for the first time at Covent Garden. She also was a guest artist at the Welsh National Opera in Cardiff and the Scottish Opera in Glasgow, and in Paris, N.Y., Los Angeles, Venice, Geneva, and other opera centers. She also was engaged at many leading festivals. As a soloist, she appeared with orchs. and in recital throughout Europe, North America, and the Far East. The great versatility of her vocal and dramatic gifts have made her equally at home in the early, standard, and contemporary operatic and concert repertoires.

Jones, Geraint (Iwan), Welsh organist, harpsichordist, and conductor; b. Porth, May 16, 1917. He studied at the Royal Academy of Music in London. He made his debut as harpsichordist at the National Gallery in 1940; subsequently gave numerous recitals as an organist, often on historical instruments of Europe; in 1951 he founded the Geraint Jones Singers and Orch., which he led in many performances of Baroque music. He also was music director of the Lake District Festival (1960–78) and the Kirckman Concert Soc. (from 1963), and artistic director of the Salisbury Festival of the Arts (1972–77) and the Manchester International Organ Festival (from 1977).

Jones, Dame Gwyneth, prominent Welsh soprano; b. Pontnewyndd, Nov. 7, 1936. She studied at the Royal College of Music in London, and in Siena, Geneva, and Zürich, where she made her operatic debut as Gluck's Orfeo (1962). In 1963 she first appeared at the Welsh National Opera in Cardiff and at London's Covent Garden; she also sang at the Vienna State Opera and at the Bayreuth Festivals from 1966. In 1966 she made her U.S. debut in N.Y. in a concert version of Cherubini's *Médée*; her Metropolitan Opera debut followed there as Sieglinde in *Die Walküre* on Nov. 24, 1972. She also sang at the San Francisco Opera, Milan's La Scala, Munich's Bavarian State Opera, and the Rome Opera; appeared as Brünnhilde in the centenary performances of the *Ring* cycle at Bayreuth in 1976. In 1976 she was made a Commander of the Order of the British Empire and in 1986 a Dame Commander of the Order of the British Empire. On Sept. 12, 1988, she celebrated the 25th anniversary of her Covent Garden debut by opening its season as Turandot. In 1992 she celebrated the 30th anniversary of her operatic debut. In addition to Wagner and Verdi roles, she also won praise for her portrayals of Donna Anna, Medea, Leonore, the Marschallin, Tosca, and Salome.

BIBL.: T. Haberfeld, *G. J.: Pictures of Her Life and Career* (Zürich, 1991).

Jones, (Herbert) Kelsey, American-born Canadian composer, harpsichordist, and teacher; b. South Norwalk, Conn., June 17, 1922. He went to Canada in 1939; became a naturalized Canadian citizen in 1956. He studied with Harold Hamer at Mount Allison Univ. (B.Mus., 1945), then with Sir Ernest MacMillan, Healey Willan, and Leo Smith at the Univ. of Toronto (B.Mus., 1946; D.Mus., 1951), and with Boulanger in Paris (1949–50). He was founder-conductor of the St. John (New Brunswick) Sym. Orch. (1950–54). From 1954 to 1984 he taught at McGill Univ. in Montreal. His output is traditional in nature but not without effective utilization of dissonant writing.

WORKS: CHAMBER OPERA: *Sam Slick* (Halifax, Sept. 5, 1967). **ORCH.:** *Miramichi Ballad* (1954); Suite for Flute and Strings (1954); *Adagio, Presto, and Fugue* for String Quartet and String Orch. (1973); *Fantasy on a Theme* (1976). **JAZZ BAND:** *Jazzum Opus Unum* (1978). **CHAMBER:** *4 Pieces* for Recorder Quartet (1955); *Mosaic* for Flute, Viola, and Harp (1956); *Sonata da camera* for Flute, Oboe, and Harpsichord (1957); *Introduction and Fugue* for Violin and Piano (1959); *Rondo* for Flute (1963); *Sonata da chiesa* for Flute, Oboe, and Harpsichord (1967); Wind Quintet (1968); *Passacaglia and Fugue* for Brass Quintet (1978); *Musica d'Occasione* for Brass Quintet (1982). **VOCAL:** *Nonsense Songs* for Chorus (1955); *Songs of Time* for Chorus and Piano, 4-hands (1955); *To Music*, song cycle for Alto and Piano (1957); *Songs of Experience* for Chorus (1958); *Prophecy of Micah* for Chorus and Instrumental Ensemble (1963); *Songs of Winter* for Soprano, Alto, and Piano (1973); *De Musica, con Amore* for Chorus and Brass Quintet (1977); *3 Preludes and a Fugue: A Little Offering* for Chorus and Saxophone (1982).

Jones, Mason, American horn player, conductor, and teacher; b. Hamilton, N.Y., June 16, 1919. He was a pupil of Tabuteau and Reiner at the Curtis Inst. of Music in Philadelphia (1936–38). In 1938 he joined the Philadelphia Orch., where he was 1st horn (1940–78), personnel manager (1963–86), and conductor of the school concerts (1972–82); also was conductor of the Episcopal Academy Orch. (1958–60) and assistant conductor of the Philadelphia Chamber Orch. (1961–64). He was a founding member of the Philadelphia Woodwind Quintet (1950–80) and of the Philadelphia Brass Ensemble (from 1957); taught at the Curtis Inst. of Music (from 1946) and at Temple Univ. College of Music (1976–83); in 1986–87 he was president of the International Horn Soc. He ed. *Solos for the Horn Player* (1962) and *20th Century Orchestral Studies* (1971).

Jones, Parry, Welsh tenor; b. Blaina, Monmouthshire, Feb. 14, 1891; d. London, Dec. 26, 1963. He studied at the Royal College of Music in London; also with Colli in Italy, Scheidemantel in Dresden, and John Coates in England. He made his debut in London in 1914; then sang in the U.S. He survived the German submarine attack on the *S.S. Lusitania* on his return trip to England in 1915, and then sang with the Beecham and D'Oyly Carte opera companies. He was a leading member of the Carl Rosa Opera Co. (1919–22) and the British National Opera Co. (1922–28); made his Covent Garden debut in London in 1921 as Turiddu; sang there again (1925–26; 1930–32; 1935; 1937), serving as a principal tenor there from 1949 to 1955, the 1953–54 season excepted. He then taught voice at the Guildhall School of Music in London. In 1962 he was made an Officer of the Order of the British Empire. He sang in the first British performances of *Wozzeck*, *Mathis der Maler*, and *Doktor Faust* in concert broadcasts by the BBC; was also active as an oratorio singer.

Jones, Philip (Mark), outstanding English trumpeter; b. Bath, March 12, 1928. He studied at the Royal College of Music in London with Ernest Hall; then served as principal trumpet player in the Royal Phil. (1956–60), Philharmonia Orch. (1960–64), London Phil. (1964–65), New Philharmonia Orch. (1965–67), and BBC Sym. Orch. (1968–71). In 1951 he founded the Philip Jones Brass Ensemble, commissioning many composers to write works for his ensemble; remained its director until 1986. He was head of the wind and percussion dept. at the Royal Northern College of Music in Manchester (1975–77) and then at the Guildhall School of Music in London (1983–88). From 1989 to 1994 he was principal of Trinity College of Music in London. He was made an Officer of the Order of the British Empire in 1977 and in 1986 a Commander of the Order of the British Empire.

Jones, (James) Sidney, English composer and conductor; b. London, June 17, 1861; d. there, Jan. 29, 1946. He was the son of Sidney James, the conductor of the Leeds Grand Theatre and municipal band. He learned to play the clarinet and served as a musician under his father before setting out on his own as a touring theater conductor. In 1891 he toured the U.S. and Australia as conductor of London's Gaiety Theater company. Returning to England, he composed his first operetta, *Our Family Legend* (Brighton, Oct. 8, 1892). He made London the center of his activities, where he conducted at several theaters and had his first major success as a composer with *A Gaiety Girl* (Oct. 14, 1893). After bringing out *An Artist's Model* (Feb. 2, 1895), Jones scored a triumphant success with *The Geisha* (April 25, 1896). It subsequently was given around the globe and remained a staple in the repertoire of light theater works for decades. Following the premiere of *A Greek Slave* (June 8, 1898), he scored another outstanding success with *San Toy* (Oct. 21, 1899). Success also attended *My Lady Molly* (Brighton, Aug. 11, 1902). His London efforts resumed with the unsuccessful *The Medal and the Maid* (April 25, 1903), but he had better luck with *See See* (June 20, 1906). While his *King of Caledonia* (Sept. 3, 1908) met with public favor, *A Persian Princess* (April 27, 1909) did not. After an unsuccessful collaboration with Paul Rubens on *The Girl from Utah* (Oct. 18, 1913) and *The Happy Day* (May 13, 1916), Jones abandoned the musical theater.

Jong, Marinus de, Dutch-born Belgian composer, pianist, and pedagogue; b. Osterhout, Aug. 14, 1891; d. Ekeren, June 13, 1984. He was a student of Bosquet (piano) and Mortelmans (composition) at the Antwerp Cons. After touring Europe and the U.S. as a pianist, he settled in Belgium in 1926; was made a prof. of piano (1931) and of counterpoint and fugue (1948) at the Antwerp Cons. His works were in a neo-impressionistic style, with polytonal counterpoint as its mainstay.

WORKS: DRAMATIC: OPERAS: *Mitsanoboe* (1962); *Die häslichen Mädchen von Bagdad* (1966; Antwerp, Jan. 7, 1967); *Esmoreit* (Antwerp, Sept. 11, 1970). **BALLETS:** *De vrouwen van Zalongo* (1951); *De kleine haven* (1952); *De kringloop* (1955); *Carrefour* (1956); *De Reiskameraad* (1959). **ORCH.:** 3 piano concertos (1924; 1952; 1956–57); 3 syms. (1932; 1965–66; 1976); concertos for Trumpet (1937), Cello (1946; rev. 1969), Violin (1954), Viola (1958), Oboe (1966–67), Horn (1966–67), Bassoon (1967), Flute (1967), Clarinet (1967), and Organ (1974); *Heidestemmingen (Impressions de Bruyère)* (1937); *Hiawatha*, symphonic poem (1945); *Aphoristische tryptiek* (1952; also for Wind Quintet); *Flemish Rhapsody No. 1* (1955), *No. 2* (1971), and *No. 3* (1971); *Boublitschky Suite* (1956); *Ruimteraket, Atlas (Fusée interplanétaire)*, symphonic poem (1964). **CHAMBER:** 6 string quartets (1923, 1926, 1947, 1956, 1956, 1962); *Pacis, Doloris et Amoris*, violin sonata (1927); Quartet for 4 Cellos (1936); Nonet (1939); 3 wind quintets (1952, 1965, 1971); Trio for Oboe, Clarinet, and Bassoon (1961); Wind Quartet (1968); Piano Quartet (1971); Sextet for Piano and Winds (1972). **KEYBOARD: PIANO:** 3 sonatas (1926, 1933, 1934); *Fantaisie-Walsen* (1960); *12 Preludes* (1975); also organ music. **VOCAL:** 4 oratorios: *Hiawatha's Lied* (1947), *Imitatio Christi* (1956), *Kerkhofblommen* (1957), and *Proverbia Bruegeliana* (1961); pieces for Soloists, Chorus, and Orch.; choruses; songs.

Jongen, (Marie-Alphonse-Nicolas-) Joseph, eminent Belgian composer and teacher, brother of **Léon (Marie-Victor-Justin) Jongen**; b. Liège, Dec. 14, 1873; d. Sart-lez-Spa, July 12, 1953. He studied at the Liège Cons.; received a premier prix for each of the academic subjects and also for piano and organ. In 1891 he joined the faculty of the Liège Cons. as a teacher of harmony and counterpoint. In 1894 he gained attention as a composer when he won 2 national prizes; in 1897 he won the Belgian Prix de Rome. He then received advice from Strauss in Berlin and d'Indy in Paris. After returning to Brussels, he taught at a music academy; from 1898, also held the position of professeur adjoint at the Liège Cons., where he became a prof. in 1911. After the outbreak of World War I in 1914, he went to London; made appearances as a pianist and organist; with Defauw, Tertis, and Doehaerd, organized a piano quartet, which became known as the Belgian Quartet. In 1919 he returned to Belgium; in 1920 he became a prof. of counterpoint and fugue at the Brussels Cons.; from 1925 to 1939 he was its director; was succeeded by his brother, Léon. During World War II, he lived in France; then returned to his country estate at Sart-lez-Spa. While not pursuing extreme modern effects, Jongen succeeded in imparting an original touch to his harmonic style.

WORKS: ORCH.: Sym. (1899); Violin Concerto (1899); Cello Concerto (1900); *Fantasie sur deux Noëls populaires wallons* (1902); *Lalla-Roukh*, symphonic poem after Thomas Moore (1904); *Prélude et Danse* (1907); *2 Rondes wallones* (1912; also for Piano); Trumpet Concertino (1913); *Impressions d'Ardennes* (1913); Suite for Violin and Orch. (1915); *Épithalame et Scherzo* for 3 Violins and Orch. or Piano (1917); *Tableaux pittoresques* (1917); *Poème heroïque* for Violin and Orch. (1919); *Prélude élégiaque et Scherzo* (1920); *Fantasie rhapsodique* for Cello and Orch. (1924); *Hymne* for Organ and Strings (1924); *Symphonie concertante* for Organ and Orch. (1926); *Pièce symphonique* for Piano and Orch. (1928); *Passacaille et Gigue* (1929); *Suite No. 3, dans le style ancien* (1930); *10 Pièces* (1932); *Triptyque* (1935); *Ouverture Fanfare* (1939); *Alleluia* for Organ and Orch. (1940); *Ouverture de fête* (1941); Piano Concerto (1943); *Bourrée* (1944); Harp Concerto (1944); *In memoriam* (1947); *Ballade, Hommage à Chopin* (1949); *3 Mouvements symphoniques* (1951). **CHAMBER:** 3 string quartets (1893, 1916, 1921); Piano Trio (1897); Piano Quartet (1901); 2 violin sonatas (1902, 1909); Trio for Piano, Violin, and Viola (1907); Cello Sonata (1912); *2 Serenades* for String Quartet (1918); *2 Pièces* for Flute, Cello, and Harp (1924); *2 Pièces* for 4 Cellos (1929); *Sonata eroica* for Organ (1930); Wind Quintet (1933); Quintet for Harp, Flute, Violin, Viola, and Cello (1940); Concerto for Wind Quintet (1942); Quartet for 4 Saxophones (1942); String Trio (1948); a number of piano pieces, including 24 preludes in all keys (1941); solo pieces for various instruments with piano. **VOCAL:** *Mass* for Chorus, Organ, and Orch. (1946); choral pieces; songs. A catalog of his works was publ. by the Centre Belge de Documentation Musicale (Brussels, 1954).

BIBL.: J. Whiteley, "J. and His Organ Music," *Musical Times* (March 1983; includes a biographical profile).

Jongen, Léon (Marie-Victor-Justin), respected Belgian composer and pedagogue, brother of **(Marie-Alphonse-Nicolas-) Joseph Jongen**; b. Liège, March 2, 1884; d. Brussels, Nov. 18, 1969. He was trained at the Liège Cons. From 1898 to 1904 he was organist at St. Jacques in Liège. In 1913 he won the Belgian Grand Prix de Rome with his cantata *Les Fiancés de Noël* (1913). From 1927 to 1929 he was conductor of the Tonkin Opera in Hanoi. He was his brother's successor as director of the Brussels Cons. (1939–49). His Violin Concerto (1962) was the compulsory work for the 12 finalists of the 1963 Queen Elisabeth violin competition held in Brussels.

WORKS: DRAMATIC: *L'Ardennaise*, opera (1909); *Le Rêve d'une nuit de Noël*, musical fairy tale (1917; Paris, March 18, 1918); *Thomas l'Agnelet*, opera (1922–23; Brussels, Feb. 14, 1924); *Le Masque de la Mort rouge*, ballet, after Poe (1956). **ORCH.:** *Campéador* (1932); *Malaisie*, suite (1935); *In Memoriam Regis* (1935); *Prélude, Divertissement et Final* for Piano and Orch. (1937); *Rhapsodia belgica* for Violin and Orch. (1948); *Divertissement en forme de variations sur un thème de Haydn* (1956); Violin Concerto (1962). **CHAMBER:** String Quartet (1919); *Divertissement* for 4 Saxophones (1937); Trio for Oboe, Clarinet, and Bassoon (1937); Trio for Flute, Violin, and Viola (1937); Piano Quartet (1955); Quintet for Piano, Flute, Clarinet, Horn, and Bassoon (1958). **VOCAL:** *Geneviève de Brabant* for Chorus and Orch. (1907); *La Légende de St. Hubert* for Chorus and Orch. (1909; St. Hubert, July 21, 1968); *Les Fiancés de Noël*, cantata (1913); *Trilogie de Psaumes* for Chorus and Orch. (1937–39); songs.

Jonsson, Josef Petrus, Swedish composer, music critic, and teacher; b. Enköping, June 21, 1887; d. Norrköping, May 9, 1969. He studied piano, and later received instruction in orchestration from Ivar Hellman in Norrköping. From 1922 to 1966 he was music critic of the newspaper *Östergötlands Folkblad*. His works reveal a fine command of classical forms in a late Romantic style. He wrote 3 syms. (*Nordland*, 1919–22; 1931; 1947); Chamber Symphony (1949); several orch. overtures and suites; Violin Concerto (Norrköping, April 10, 1960); *Festival Prelude* for Orch. (1961); *Korallrevet*, symphonic poem for Baritone, Chorus, and Orch. (1916); *Missa solemnis* for Chorus, Orch., and Organ (1934); Cantata for Speaking Chorus, Women's Chorus, Soli, 2 Flutes, and Piano (Norrköping, May 5, 1962); chamber music; piano pieces; songs.

Joó, Arpád, Hungarian-born American conductor; b. Budapest, June 8, 1948. He pursued private musical instruction with Kodály (1954–65) and Ferencsik (1954–68). From 1958 to 1964 he was a piano student at the Béla Bartók Cons. in Budapest; was a private pupil of Carlo Zecchi (piano and conducting, 1963–65) and of Magaloff (piano, 1964–65); studied piano with Joseph Gat and Kadosa at the Franz Liszt Academy of Music in Budapest (1964–68). After further piano lessons with Irwin Freundlich at the Juilliard School in N.Y. (1968–69), he concentrated on conducting studies with Rozsnyai in San Diego (1969), Wolfgang Vacano and Tibor Kozma at Indiana Univ. (1970–73), Markevitch (1972–73), and Giulini (1979). In 1975 he became a naturalized American citizen. He was music director of the Knoxville (Tenn.) Sym. Orch. (1973–78) and the Calgary (Alberta) Phil. (1978–81), subsequently serving as music adviser and principal conductor of the latter (1981–83). In 1985 he was principal guest conductor of the European Community Chamber Orch. in Eindhoven; from 1985 to 1987 he was music director of the Nyirbator Festival in Hungary. In 1986 he was appointed principal guest conductor of the Budapest Sym. Orch., and in 1987, music director of the sym. orch. and chorus of Spanish Radio and Television in Madrid, which position he held until 1991; also was prof. of conducting at the master classes in Assisi (from 1987) and music adviser and principal guest conductor of the Brabant Orch. in Eindhoven (1989–91). He has won critical accolades for his idiomatic performances of Liszt, Bartók, and Kodály.

Joplin, Scott, remarkable black American pianist and composer; b. probably near Marshall, Texas, Nov. 24, 1868; d. N.Y., April 1, 1917. He learned to play the piano at home in Texarkana, and later studied music seriously with a local German musician. He left home at 17 and went to St. Louis, earning his living by playing piano in local emporia. In 1893 he moved to Chicago (drawn by the prospect of the music-making and other gaiety of the World's Fair), and in 1896 went to Sedalia, Mo., where he took music courses at George Smith College, a segregated school for blacks. His first music publications were in 1895, of genteel, maudlin songs and marches, typical of the period. His success as a ragtime composer came with the *Maple Leaf Rag* (1899; the most famous of all piano rags), which he named after a local dance hall, the Maple Leaf Club. The sheet-music ed. sold so well that Joplin was able to settle in St. Louis and devote himself exclusively to composition; he even attempted a ragtime ballet, *The Ragtime Dance* (1902) and a ragtime opera, *A Guest of Honor* (copyright 1903, but the music is lost; newspaper notices indicate it was probably perf. by the Scott Joplin Opera Co. in 1903). In 1907 he went to N.Y., where he continued his career as a composer and teacher. Still intent on ambitious plans, he wrote an opera, *Treemonisha*, to his own libretto (the title deals with a black baby girl found under a tree by a woman named Monisha); he completed the score in 1911 and produced it in concert form in 1915 without success. Interest in the opera was revived almost 60 years later; T. J. Anderson orchestrated it from the piano score, and it received its first complete performance in Atlanta on Jan. 28, 1972. Despite Joplin's ambitious attempts to make ragtime "respectable" by applying its principles to European forms, it was with the small, indigenous dance form of the piano rag that he achieved his greatest artistic success. Altogether, he wrote about 50 piano rags, in addition to the 2 operas, and a few songs, waltzes, and marches. The titles of some of these rags reflect his desire to transcend the trivial and create music on a more serious plane: *Sycamore*, "A Concert Rag" (1904); *Chrysanthemum*, "An Afro-American Intermezzo" (1904); *Sugar Cane*, "A Ragtime Classic 2 Step" (1908); *Fig Leaf Rag*, "A High Class Rag" (1908); and *Reflection Rag*, "Syncopated Musings" (1917). In his last years, he lamented at having failed to achieve the recognition he felt his music merited. Suffering from syphilis, he became insane and died shortly afterward in a state hospital. More than 50 years later, an extraordinary sequence of events—new recordings of his music and its use in an award-winning film, *The Sting* (1974)—brought Joplin unprecedented popularity and acclaim: among pop recordings, *The Entertainer* (1902) was one of the best-selling discs for 1974; among classical recordings, Joplin albums represented 74 percent of the best-sellers of the year. In 1976 he was awarded exceptional posthumous recognition by the Pulitzer Prize Committee. See V. Lawrence, ed., *The Collected Works of Scott Joplin* (2 vols., N.Y., 1971; 2nd ed., rev., 1981 as *The Complete Works of Scott Joplin*).

BIBL.: K. Preston and N. Huggins, *S. J.* (N.Y., 1988); E. Berlin, *S. J.* (Oxford, 1994); S. Curtis, *Dancing to a Black Man's Tune: A Life of S. J.* (Columbia, Mo., 1994).

Jora, Mihail, distinguished Romanian composer and pedagogue; b. Roman, Aug. 14, 1891; d. Bucharest, May 10, 1971. He received training in piano in Iaşi (1901–12), where he also studied theory at the Cons. (1909–11); after studies with Teichmüller (piano) and Krell and Reger (counterpoint and composition) at the Leipzig Cons. (1912–14), he completed his training with Schmitt in Paris (1919–20). Settling in Bucharest, he helped to organize the Soc. of Romanian Composers in 1920, serving as its vice-president. From 1939 to 1962 he was prof. of harmony, counterpoint, and composition at the Bucharest Cons. He was the author of *Momente muzicale* (Bucharest, 1968). Jora was notably influential as a teacher. In his compositions, he made effective use of Romanian folk music. He excelled as a composer of ballets and songs.

WORKS: BALLETS: *La piaţă* (At the Market Place; 1928; Bucharest, March 17, 1932); *Demoazela Măriuţa* (1940; Bucharest, Oct. 5, 1942); *Curtea veche* (The Old Court; 1948); *Cînd strugurii se coc* (When the Grapes Ripen; 1953; Bucharest, 1954); *Întoarcerea din adîncuri* (Return to the Abyss; 1959; Bucharest, 1965); *Hanul Dulcinea* (The Inn Dulcinea; 1966; Bucharest, 1967). **ORCH.:** Suite (1914; Iaşi, Jan. 28, 1918); *Poveste indică* (Hindu Tale), symphonic poem (Bucharest, Dec. 15, 1920); *Privelişti moldoveneşti* (Moldavian Landscapes), suite (Bucharest, May 5, 1924); *Cortegiu* (1926; Bucharest, March 3, 1929; also for Piano, 1925); *Şase cîntece şio rumbă* (6 Songs and a Rumba; 1932); Sym. (Bucharest, Nov. 28, 1937); *Burlesca* (1949). **CHAMBER:** *Small Suite* for Violin and Piano (1917); 2 string quartets (1926, 1966); Viola Sonata (1951); Violin Sonata (1962). **PIANO:** *Joujoux pour ma Dame* (1925); Sonata (1942); *Variations and Fugue on a Theme of Schumann* (1943); *Portraits and Jokes* (3 sets, 1948, 1959, 1963); *13 Preludes* (1960); Sonatina (1961). **VOCAL:** *Baladă* for Baritone, Chorus, and Orch. (1955); choruses; numerous songs.

Jordá, Enrique, Spanish-born American conductor and composer; b. San Sebastian, March 24, 1911; d. Brussels, March 22, 1996. After training at the Colegio Católico Santa Maria in San Sebastian and at the Univ. of Madrid, he went to Paris to continue his education at the Sorbonne, and also was a student of Dupré (organ), Rühlmann (conducting), and Le Flem (composition). He conducted the Basque Ballet (1937–39), the Madrid Sym. Orch. (1940–45), and the Cape Town Sym. Orch. (1948–54). In 1952 he made his U.S. debut as a guest conductor with the San Francisco Sym. Orch., and then was its conductor from 1954 to 1963; later he was conductor of the Antwerp Phil. (1970–76) and the Euskadi Sym. Orch. in San Sebastian (1982–84). Among his compositions were ballets and choral pieces. He was the author of *El director de orquesta ante la partitura* (1969) and *De canciones, denzas y musicos del Pais Vasco* (1978).

Jordan, Armin, Swiss conductor; b. Lucerne, April 9, 1932. He received his musical training in Lucerne and Geneva. After holding the post of 1st conductor at the Zürich Opera (1963–68), he was conductor in St. Gallen (1968–71) and at the Basel Opera (1968–89). From 1973 to 1985 he was music director of the Lausanne Chamber Orch., with which he toured the U.S. in 1983. In 1985 he became chief conductor of l'Orchestre de la Suisse Romande in Geneva, while concurrently serving as principal guest conductor of the Ensemble Orchestral de Paris from 1986 to 1993. He conducted the soundtrack and also portrayed the role of Amfortas, with the vocal part dubbed in by Wolfgang Schöne, for the Syberberg film version of *Parsifal*. Jordan has appeared as a guest conductor with various opera houses and orchs., and has won particular distinction for his performances of the French repertoire.

Jordan, Irene, American soprano; b. Birmingham, Ala., April 25, 1919. She studied at Judson College in Marion, Ala. (A.B., 1939) and with Clytie Mundy in N.Y. On Nov. 11, 1946, she made her Metropolitan Opera debut in N.Y. in the mezzo-soprano role of Mallika in *Lakmé,* and remained on its roster until 1948. After training as a soprano (1949–52), she sang opera in Chicago (1954), at the Metropolitan Opera (1957), and at the N.Y. City Opera (1957); she also appeared as a soloist with various American orchs. Among her admired roles were Donna Elvira, the Queen of the Night, Leonore, Lady Macbeth, and Aida.

Jordan, Sverre, Norwegian pianist, conductor, and composer; b. Bergen, May 25, 1889; d. there, Jan. 10, 1972. He studied piano in Bergen; then took courses in piano and composition with Da Motta, Ansorge, Klatte, and Gortatowski in Berlin (1907–14). He made his debut as a pianist in Bergen (1911); was music critic of the *Morgenavisen* there (1917–31); also conducted the Bergen Harmonien choir (1922–32) and was director of Den Nasjonale Scene, Bergen's major theater (1931–57). In his works, he made liberal use of national folk songs, which met the tastes of the general public. Typical of these nationally oriented works are *Suite in Old Style* for Small Orch. (1911); *Norvegiani* for Orch. (1921); *Smeden* (The Smith) for Baritone, Chorus, and Orch. (1924); *Norge i vare hjerter,* cantata for the opening of the Bergen Exhibition (1928); *Suite on Norwegian Folk Tunes* and Dances for Orch. (1936); *Holberg-silhuetter* for Orch. (1938); *Norwegian Rhapsody* for Orch. (1950); *Suite in Old Style on Holberg Themes* for Orch. (1954); *Concerto romantico* for Horn and Orch. (1956); and *Kongen* (The King), orch. melodrama with narration and choral finale (1957). Other works are a Piano Concerto (1945); Cello Concerto (1947); *Concerto piccolo* for Piano and Orch. (1963); Violin Concerto (1966); 2 violin sonatas (1917, 1943); 2 piano trios (1958, 1963); Piano Sonata (1963); incidental music for plays; over 200 songs, often with orch. accompaniment.

Jørgensen, Erik, Danish composer and teacher; b. Copenhagen, May 10, 1912. He received lessons in theory from Jeppesen, in organ from Rung-Keller, and in piano from Anders Rachlew. Following training in composition with Høffding at the Copenhagen Cons. (from 1931), he took a course in conducting with Scherchen in Geneva (1936). From 1947 to 1982 he taught at the Copenhagen Inst. for the Blind. In his music, Jørgensen developed a personal style which utilized 12-tone procedures and aleatory.

WORKS: DRAMATIC: *Skyggen af en drøm* (Shadow of a Dream), chamber opera (1969); *Eventyret* (Fairytale), madrigal comedy (1973–74). **ORCH.:** Concerto grosso for Flute, Clarinet, Bassoon, and Strings (1933–34); Concerto for Violin, Strings, and Piano (1935); *Modello per archi* for Strings (1957); *Notturno* for 24 Solo Instruments (1965–66); *Confrontations* (1967–68); *A Piece of Life,* sym. (1981); *Dialogue* for Oboe, Horn, and Small Orch. (1984). **CHAMBER:** *Introduction and Theme with Variations* for Flute, Violin, Cello, and Piano (1937); Concertino for Flute, Clarinet, Violin, and Piano (1937); *Rhapsody* for Violin and Piano (1939–40); Sonatine for Clarinet and Bassoon (1942); *Figure in Tempo* for Cello and Percussion (1960–61); Quintet for 2 Pianos, 2 Percussionists, and Double Bass (1962); *Astrolabium* for 11 Instruments (1964); Piece for String Quartet (1964–65); *Improvisations* for Wind Quintet (1971); *Stemninger og tilstande* for Flute, Violin, Cello, and Horn (1973); Recorder Quartet (1975); Percussion Quintet (1982); *Symbiose* for Violin and Cello (1987); *Dobbeltspil* for Double Bass and Piano (1988); *Music* for Harp (1988); Concerto for Percussion Trio (1990); *Pastorale* for Oboe d'Amore and Chamber Ensemble (1990). **VOCAL:** *Tre vekselsange* for Soprano, Tenor, and Chamber Orch. (1934); *Havet* for Chorus (1936); *Modello 2* for Soli, Chorus, and Ensemble (1963); *Fragmenter af Hojsangen* for Soprano and 7 Instruments (1978); *Ode to a Grecian Urn* for Chorus (1979–80); *3 Gurresange* for Chorus (1990); other choral pieces and solo songs.

Jørgensen, Poul, Danish conductor; b. Copenhagen, Oct. 26, 1934. He was educated at the Univ. of Copenhagen and the Royal Danish Cons. of Music in Copenhagen. In 1961 he became a conductor at the Royal Theater in Copenhagen; in 1966, was appointed Royal Conductor; was also active in Sweden as a conductor of the Radio Sym. Orch. in Stockholm. In his concert programs, he steadfastly cultivated symphonic works by Danish, Norwegian, Swedish, and Finnish composers.

Jörn, Karl, Latvian tenor of German descent; b. Riga, Jan. 5, 1873; d. Denver, Dec. 19, 1947. He studied with Schütte-Harmsen, Jacobs, and Ress in Berlin. He made his operatic debut as Lyonel in Martha in Freiburg im Breisgau (1896); then sang in Zürich (1898–99) and Hamburg (1899–1902). He was a member of Berlin's Royal Opera (1902–08). On Jan. 22, 1909, he made his Metropolitan Opera debut in N.Y. as Walther von Stolzing, remaining on its roster until 1914; after further appearances in Berlin (1914), he returned to the U.S.; toured with Gadski's German opera company (1929–31) and then taught voice in N.Y. and later in Denver, where he settled. He was best known for his Wagnerian roles.

Joselson, Tedd, American pianist; b. Antwerp (of American parents), Oct. 4, 1954. He studied piano with Adele Marcus at the Juilliard School of Music in N.Y. In 1974 he was a soloist with the Philadelphia Orch.; then made a coast-to-coast recital tour of the U.S. in 1976–77; subsequently appeared as soloist with many of the major orchs. His forte is Russian music, but he also has a natural affinity with the masters of the Classical period.

Josephs, Wilfred, esteemed English composer; b. Newcastle upon Tyne, July 24, 1927. He studied music with Arthur Milner (1947) and took a degree in dental surgery in 1951 from the Univ. of Durham Sutherland Dental School; then was an orthodontist in the British army. In 1954 he entered the Guildhall School of Music in London, where he studied with Alfred Nieman until 1956; then had private lessons with Max Deutsch in Paris (1958–59). In 1956 he won the Cobbett Prize, in 1957 the Harriett Cohen Medal, and in 1963 the first City of Milan and La Scala international composition competition for his *Requiem* set to the Hebrew Kaddish. He was a visiting prof. at the Univ. of Wisc. in Milwaukee (1970), Roosevelt Univ. in Chicago (1972), and Ohio State Univ. (1992). In 1988 he became a musical consultant to the London International Film School. He developed an individualistic style based on dodecaphony but not without exploiting his mastery of melodic invention.

WORKS: DRAMATIC: *The Magic Being,* ballet (1961; Newcastle upon Tyne, May 31, 1963); *The Nottingham Captain,* music theater (Wellingborough, Sept. 11, 1962); *The King of the Coast,* children's musical (1962–67); *Pathelin,* theater piece (1963); *La Répétition de Phèdre,* ballet (Newcastle upon Tyne, June 22, 1964); *The Appointment,* television opera (1968); *A Child of the Universe,* theater piece (1971); *Through the Looking Glass and What Alice Found There,* children's opera (1977–78; Harrogate, Aug. 3, 1978); *Equus,* ballet (Baltimore, March 21, 1980); *Rebecca,* opera (1981–83; Leeds, Oct. 15, 1983); *Alice in Wonderland,* children's opera (1985–88); *Cyrano de Bergerac,* ballet (1990–91); also numerous film and television scores. **ORCH.:** *The Ants,* comedy overture (1955; BBC, Feb. 6, 1961); 10 syms.: No. 1 (London, Dec. 17, 1955; rev. 1957–58 and 1974–75), No. 2 (1963–64; Cheltenham, July 5, 1965), No. 3, *Philadelphia,* for Small Orch. (1967; London, April 15, 1969), No. 4 (1967–70; BBC, May 26, 1983), No. 5, *Pastoral* (1970–71; Kingston-upon-Hull, Nov. 25, 1971), No. 6 for Soprano, Baritone, Chorus, and Orch. (1974), No. 7, *Winter,* for Small Orch. (1976; Bournemouth, Dec. 14, 1978), No. 8, *The 4 Elements,* for Wind Orch. or Symphonic Band (1975–77; Harrogate, Aug. 13, 1977), No. 9, *Sinfonia Concertante,* for Small Orch. (1979–80; Warrington, Feb. 11, 1981), and No. 10, *Circadian Rhythms* (Norwich, Oct. 19, 1985); *Elegy* for Strings (London, May 25, 1957); *Concerto a Dodici* (1959; BBC, March 18, 1967); *A Tyneside Overture* (1960); *Concerto da Camera* for Violin and Strings (1959–60; Maastricht, Dec. 20, 1961); *Meditatio de Boernmundo* for Viola and Strings (1960–61; Birmingham, May 7, 1961); *Aelian Dances* (1961; BBC, Dec. 1, 1962); *Monkchester Dances* (1961); *Cantus natalis,* cello concerto (1961–62; BBC,

Jan. 16, 1971); *Canzonas on a Theme of Rameau* for Strings (1965; London, Feb. 13, 1966); 2 piano concertos: No. 1 (1965; London, March 5, 1967) and No. 2 (1971; Dudley, May 19, 1972); Concerto for Light Orch. (1966; Munich, Oct. 1, 1967); *Polemic* for Strings (Harrogate, Aug. 14, 1967); *Spirit of the Waltz* (1967); *Rail,* symphonic picture for Strings (Newcastle upon Tyne, June 15, 1967); Oboe Concerto (Hemel Hempstead, Sept. 25, 1967; rev. 1968); *Serenade* for Small Orch. (1968); *Variations on a Theme of Beethoven* (1969; N.Y., Jan. 23, 1970); Concerto for 2 Violins and String Orch. (London, Sept. 19, 1969); *The Last Last Post* (1971); *Saratoga Concerto* for Guitar, Harp, Harpsichord, and Chamber Orch. (1972; Manchester, April 16, 1978); Concerto for Brass Band (1972–73; Hanley, Aug. 9, 1974); *The 4 Horsemen of the Apocalypse,* overture (1973–74; Gloucester, Aug. 18, 1974); Clarinet Concerto (1975; Edinburgh, June 12, 1976); *Symphonic Poem Eve (d'après Rodin)* (1977–78); *Concerto d'Amore* for Violin(s) and Orch. (1979; 's-Hertogenbosch, Feb. 12, 1980); *Consort Music* (London, Dec. 21, 1980); Double Bass Concerto (1980; Chester, Aug. 1, 1981); *The Brontës,* overture (1981; Halifax, May 1, 1982); *High Spirits,* overture (1981–82; Sevenoaks, April 2, 1983); Percussion Concerto (1982; London, Jan. 15, 1983); Concerto for Viola and Small Orch. (1983; Adelaide, Feb. 21, 1987); *The Heaving Bagpipe,* overture (1984); *Feu de joie* (London, June 18, 1984); *Caen Wood,* "celebratory" overture (London, June 8, 1985); *Disconcerto* for Piano and Orch. (1985; Freiburg im Breisgau, May 25, 1986); *Festival Overture (on Brabant Themes)* (1987); *In the North—Hommage à Sibelius* (1990); *Wordless Song* for Strings (1990). **CHAMBER:** 4 string quartets: No. 1 (1954; London, Dec. 17, 1955), No. 2 (1957–58; Belgian Radio, Sept. 1959; rev. 1960), No. 3 (1971; Milwaukee, March 3, 1974), and No. 4 (1981; London, Sept. 8, 1982); *Siesta* for Violin and Piano (1955); Sonata for Solo Violin (1957); *Wry Rumba* for Wind Quintet (1957–60); *An Old English Suite* for 5 Clarinets and Basset Horn (1961); *Requiescant pro defunctis fundaeis,* string quintet (1961; London, Sept. 24, 1965); *Chacony* (1962–63; N.Y., Oct. 23, 1963); Octet (1964; London, March 18, 1966); 3 violin sonatas: No. 1 (N.Y., Oct. 22, 1965), No. 2 (1975; BBC, Nov. 29, 1976), and No. 3 (1986–87); Trio for Flute, Violin, and Cello (1965–66; London, May 11, 1969); String Trio (1966; Birmingham, April 15, 1967); Sonata for Solo Cello (1970; BBC, Dec. 17, 1971); *Doubles* (1970–73); Trio for Horn, Violin, and Piano (Newport, Wales, Nov. 7, 1971); Piano Trio (1974; Newcastle upon Tyne, Feb. 21, 1979; rev. 1981); 2 sonatas for Brass Quintet: No. 1 (1974; Nottingham, Nov. 16, 1981) and No. 2 (1989); Piano Quintet (1974–76; Newcastle upon Tyne, Sept. 15, 1978); Flute Sonata (1976–77); Wind Quintet (London, March 5, 1978); Concerto for 4 Pianos and 6 Percussion (1978; Manchester, March 15, 1979); *Thoughts on a Spanish Guitar* (1979); Oboe Quartet (1979); Double Bass Sonata (1980); *8 Aphorisms* for Trombone Octet (1981; Bristol, July 26, 1982); *Arcadian Rhapsody* for Flute, String Trio, and Harp (Newcastle upon Tyne, Oct. 7, 1984); Clarinet Quintet (1984–85; Arundel, Sussex, Aug. 25, 1985); *Northumbrian Dances* for Soprano Saxophone and Piano (1986); *William's Fancye* for 5 Players (1986); Clarinet Sonata (1987–88); Oboe Sonata (1988); *Papageno Variations* for Wind Sextet (1989; Letchworth, Feb. 3, 1990). **KEYBOARD: PIANO:** Sonata No. 2 (1963); *14 Studies* (1966); *29 Preludes* (1969); *Sonata Duo* for Piano Duet (1976); *Arabesques* (1985–88). **ORGAN:** *Fantasia on 3 Notes* (1978); *Tombeaux* (1980); *Testimony,* toccata (1981). **VOCAL:** *12 Letters,* "entertainment" for Narrator, Clarinet, String Trio, and Piano, after Belloc (1957; London, Jan. 19, 1964); *Requiem* for Bass, Baritone or Bass-Baritone, 2 Cellos, and Chorus (1962–63; Milan, Oct. 28, 1965); *Protégez-moi* for Children's or Women's Voices, Piano, Optional Recorders, Percussion, and School Orch. (1964; London, March 11, 1968); *Mortales* for Soloists and Choruses (1967–69; Cincinnati, May 23, 1970); *Adam and Eve,* "entertainment" for Narrator and Chamber Ensemble (1967–68; London, Feb. 4, 1968); *Nightmusic* for Voice and Orch. (1969–70; Liverpool, Oct. 23, 1974); *Aeroplanes and Angels* for Chorus and Piano Duet, after Günter Grass (1977–78; London, April 12, 1978); *Tenebrae* for Chorus, Piano Duet, Optional Flute, Optional Percussion, and Strings (1989); *William and the Bomb* for Narrator and Orch. (Cardiff, Sept. 25, 1993); choruses; song cycles; solo songs.

Josif, Enriko, Serbian composer and teacher; b. Belgrade, May 1, 1924. He studied theory with Milenko Živkovič at the Belgrade Academy of Music (1947–54) and later was a student of Petrassi at the Accademia di Santa Cecilia in Rome (1961–62). He was a prof. of composition at the Belgrade Academy of Music from 1957.

WORKS: BALLET: *Ptico, ne sklapaj svoja krila* (Bird, Don't Break Your Wings; Belgrade, Oct. 7, 1970). **ORCH.:** Sinfonietta (1954); *Sonata antica* (1955); *Lyrical Symphony* (1956); Piano Concerto (1959); *Symphony in One Movement* (1964; Belgrade, Jan. 24, 1966); *Sinfonietta di tre re* (1968). **CHAMBER:** *Improvisations on a Folk Theme* for 14 Winds (1949); String Quartet (1953); *Dream Visions* for Flute, Harp, and Piano (1964); *Divertimento* for Wind Quintet (1964); *Epigram I* for Chamber Ensemble (1967) and *II* for Piano Trio (1967); *Chronicles* for Wind Quintet (1971); *Vatrenja* for Piano Trio (1972); piano pieces. **VOCAL:** *Oratorio profano da camera* for Narrator, Soprano, Celesta, Piano, and Percussion (1956); *The Death of Stefan of Decane,* chamber motets for Narrator, Soloists, Chorus, and 16 Instruments (1956; enl. and orchestrated as a dramatic epic, Belgrade, Oct. 7, 1970); *Rustikon,* cantata (1962).

Josten, Werner (Erich), German-born American conductor, teacher, and composer; b. Elberfeld, June 12, 1885; d. N.Y., Feb. 6, 1963. He studied with Siegel in Munich; then with Jaques-Dalcroze in Geneva; later was made assistant conductor at the Bavarian State Opera in Munich (1918). In 1920 he went to the U.S.; became a naturalized American citizen in 1933. He taught at Smith College in Northampton, Mass. (1923–49); also conducted its orch. His compositions are couched in the lyrical manner of German Romantic music, with a strong undercurrent of euphonious counterpoint within the network of luscious harmonies. During his American period, he became interested in exotic art, and introduced impressionistic devices in his works.

WORKS: BALLETS: *Batouala* (1930–31; symphonic suite as *Suite nègre,* Northampton, Mass., Nov. 10, 1963); *Joseph and His Brethren* (1932; N.Y., March 9, 1936; symphonic suite, Philadelphia, May 15, 1939); *Endymion* (1933; symphonic suite, N.Y., Oct. 28, 1936). **ORCH.:** *Concerto sacro I–II* (1925; N.Y., March 27, 1929); *Jungle,* symphonic movement inspired by Henri Rousseau's painting *Forêt exotique* (1928; Boston, Oct. 25, 1929); *Serenade* for Small Orch. (1934); 2 syms.: No. 1 for Strings (1935; Saratoga Springs, N.Y., Sept. 3, 1946) and No. 2 (Boston, Nov. 13, 1936); *Rhapsody* for Violin and Orch. (1959). **CHAMBER:** String Quartet (1934); Violin Sonata (1936); Sonata for Violin, Cello, and Piano (1938); Cello Sonata (1938); Concertante for 4 Bassoons (1939; also for 4 Cellos, 1941); Violin Sonatina (1940); Trio for Flute, Clarinet, and Bassoon (1941); Trio for Violin, Viola, and Cello (1942); Trio for Flute, Cello, and Piano (1943); Horn Sonata (1944); *Canzona seria* for Flute, Oboe, Clarinet, Bassoon, and Piano (N.Y., Nov. 23, 1957); piano pieces, including a sonata (1937). **VOCAL:** *Crucifixion* for Chorus (1915); *3 Songs* for Tenor and Orch. (1918–29); *Hymnus to the Quene of Paradys* for Chorus (1922); *Ode for St. Cecilia's Day* for Chorus (1925); *Fragments from the Brome Play "Abraham and Isaac"* for Solo Voices, Chorus, and Orch. (1926).

BIBL.: *W. J., 1885–1963. A Summary of His Compositions with Press Reviews* (N.Y., 1964).

Joteyko, Tadeusz, Polish conductor and composer; b. Poczujki, near Kiev, April 1, 1872; d. Cieszyn, Silesia, Aug. 19, 1932. He studied at the Brussels Cons. with Jacobs (cello) and Gevaert (composition) and with Noskowski (composition) and Cinke (cello) at the Warsaw Cons. He conducted the Warsaw Phil. (1914–18) and taught at the Warsaw Cons. He wrote the operas *Grajek* (The Player; Warsaw, Nov. 23, 1919), *Zygmunt August* (Warsaw, Aug. 29, 1925), and *Królowa Jadwiga* (Queen

Jadwiga; Warsaw, Sept. 7, 1928), but is best remembered for his choral music. He also composed a Sym. (1895), chamber music, songs, and piano pieces. He publ. *Zasady muzyki* (Principles of Music; Warsaw, 1914) and *Historia muzyki polskiej i powszechnej w zarysie* (Warsaw, 1916).

Joubert, John (Pierre Herman), prominent South African-born English composer; b. Cape Town, March 20, 1927. After attending the Diocesan College in Rondebosch (1934–44), he studied composition with Bell at the South African College of Music in Cape Town (1944–46); subsequently he completed his training in London with Holland and Ferguson at the Royal Academy of Music (B.Mus., 1950). In 1949 he won the Royal Phil. Soc. Prize. He taught at the univs. of Hull (1950–62) and Birmingham (1962–86). In 1991 he was awarded an Hon. Doc. in Music from the Univ. of Durham. Joubert has succeeded in developing an effective means of expression within the tonal tradition.

WORKS: DRAMATIC: *Legend of Princess Vlei*, ballet (Cape Town, Feb. 21, 1952); *Antigone*, radio opera (BBC, London, July 21, 1954); *In the Drought*, chamber opera (1955; Johannesburg, Oct. 20, 1956); *Silas Marner*, opera, after George Eliot (Cape Town, May 20, 1961); *The Quarry*, opera for young players (1964; London, March 25, 1965); *Under Western Eyes*, opera, after Joseph Conrad (1968; London, May 20, 1969); *The Prisoner*, school opera (London, March 14, 1973); *The Wayfarers*, opera for young people (1983; Huntington, April 4, 1984). **ORCH.:** Overture (1951; Cheltenham, June 12, 1953); *Symphonic Prelude* (1953; Durban, May 15, 1954); Violin Concerto (York, June 17, 1954); 2 syms.: No. 1 (1955; Hull, April 12, 1956) and No. 2 (1970; London, March 24, 1971); Piano Concerto (1958; Manchester, Jan. 11, 1959); *A North Country Overture* (1958); Sinfonietta (1962); *In Memoriam 1820* (1962); Bassoon Concerto (1974; Carlisle, March 12, 1975); *Threnos* for Harpsichord and 12 Solo Strings (London, March 30, 1974); *Déploration* (Birmingham, Dec. 28, 1978); *Temps Perdu* for Strings (London, Oct. 1, 1984). **CHAMBER:** 4 string quartets: No. 1 (1950), No. 2 (1977; Birmingham, Feb. 18, 1978), No. 3 (1986; Birmingham, March 13, 1987), and No. 4, *Quartetto Classico* (1988; Birmingham, Oct. 19, 1989); Viola Sonata (1951); *Miniature String Quartet* (1953); Trio for Violin, Viola, and Cello (1958); Octet for Clarinet, Bassoon, Horn, String Quartet, and Double Bass (1961); *Sonata à cinque* for Recorder or Flute, 2 Violins, Cello, and Harpsichord (1963); Duo for Violin and Cello (1971); *Kontaktion* for Cello and Piano (1971); *Chamber Music* for Brass Quintet (1985); Piano Trio (1986; Hereford, March 19, 1987). **KEYBOARD: PIANO:** *Divertimento* for 2 Pianos (1950); *Dance Suite* (1956); 2 sonatas (1957, 1972). **ORGAN:** *Passacaglia and Fugue* (1961); *6 Short Preludes on English Hymn Tunes* (1990). **VOCAL:** *Torches* for Chorus and Orch. (1951); *The Burghers of Calais* for Soloists, Chorus, and Chamber Orch. (1953); *Urbs beata* for Tenor, Baritone, Chorus, and Orch. (1963); *Te Deum* for Soprano, Chorus, and Organ (1964); *The Choir Invisible* for Baritone, Chorus, and Orch. (Halifax, Yorkshire, May 18, 1968); *The Martyrdom of St. Alban* for Speaker, Tenor, Bass, Chorus, and Chamber Orch. (1968); *The Raising of Lazarus* for Mezzo-soprano, Tenor, Chorus, and Orch. (1970; Birmingham, Sept. 30, 1971); *The Magus* for Tenor, 2 Baritones, Chorus, and Orch. (1976; Sheffield, Oct. 29, 1977); *Herefordshire Canticles* for Soprano, Baritone, Chorus, Boy's Chorus, and Orch. (Hereford, Aug. 23, 1979); *Gong-Tormented Sea* for Baritone, Chorus, and Orch. (1981; Birmingham, April 29, 1982); *South of the Line* for Soprano, Baritone, Chorus, 2 Pianos, Timpani, and Percussion (1985; Birmingham, March 1, 1986); *The Instant Moment* for Baritone and String Orch. (1986; Birmingham, March 21, 1987); *Missa brevis* for Soloists, Chorus, and Chamber Orch. (Birmingham, Oct. 16, 1988); *For the Beauty of the Earth* for Soprano, Baritone, Chorus, and Orch. (Birmingham, Nov. 25, 1989); choruses; anthems; hymns; carols; songs.

Journet, Marcel, distinguished French bass; b. Grasse, Alpes Maritimes, July 25, 1867; d. Vittel, Sept. 5, 1933. He studied at the Paris Cons. with Obin and Seghettini. He made his operatic debut in *La Favorite* in Montpellier (1891); then sang at the Théâtre Royal de la Monnaie in Brussels (1894–1900). On July 10, 1897, he made his debut at London's Covent Garden as the Duke of Mendoza in d'Erlanger's *Inez Mendo*; appeared there regularly until 1907, and returned in 1927–28. He made his Metropolitan Opera debut in N.Y. on Dec. 22, 1900, as Ramfis, and remained on its roster until 1908; then was a member of the Paris Opéra (1908–32); also sang at the Chicago Grand Opera (1915–17; 1918–19) and at Milan's La Scala (1917; 1922–27), where he created the role of Simon Mago in Boito's *Nerone* (May 1, 1924). Among his finest roles were Hans Sachs, Gurnemanz, Wotan, Méphistophélès, Golaud, and Scarpia.

Joy, Geneviève, French pianist; b. Bernaville, Oct. 4, 1919. She studied at the Paris Cons. with Yves Nat (piano) and Jean and Noël Gallon (theory); received the Premier Prix in piano in 1941. In 1945 she married **Henri Dutilleux**. She specialized in modern music; gave numerous first performances of piano works by French composers, some of them written especially for her.

Juch, Emma (Antonia Joanna), noted American soprano; b. Vienna (of Austrian-born American parents), July 4, 1863; d. N.Y., March 6, 1939. She was taken at the age of 4 to the U.S., where she studied with her father and with Murio Celli in Detroit. She made her recital debut in N.Y.'s Chickering Hall (1881), then her stage debut as Philine in *Mignon* at London's Her Majesty's Theatre (1881); that same year she appeared at N.Y.'s Academy of Music. She was a leading member of the American (later National) Opera Co. (1884–89), subsequently touring the U.S., Canada, and Mexico with her own Emma Juch Grand Opera Co. (1889–91); she retired from the operatic stage upon her marriage (1894). She was a great advocate of opera in English. Her voice was admired for its extensive range, which enabled her to sing a wide repertoire.

Juchelka, Miroslav, Czech composer; b. Velká Polom, March 29, 1922. He studied composition with Řídký and Hlobil at the Prague Cons. (1939–43) and then with Albín Šíma at the Master School there (1943–47). He was music director of the Czech Radio in Prague (1953–78).

WORKS: ORCH.: *Symphonic Fantasy* (1952); Accordion Concerto (1954); *Burlesque* for Piano and Orch. (1958); Suite for Strings (1961); *Burlesque* for Clarinet and Promenade Orch. (1970); *From the Beskyds*, suite (1972); Clarinet Concerto (1974); Piano Concerto (1979); *Tarantela festiva* (1980). **CHAMBER:** *Miniatures* for Cello and Piano (1951); Suite for Nonet (1962); Clarinet Sonatina (1964); *5 Compositions for Due Boemi* for Bass Clarinet and Piano (1972); Violin Sonatina (1982).

Judd, James, English conductor; b. Hertford, Oct. 30, 1949. He studied piano with Alfred Kitchin and conducting with Bernard Keefe at Trinity College of Music in London (1967–71), then was active with the London Opera Centre; subsequently was assistant conductor of the Cleveland Orch. (1973–75). He was co-founder and conductor of the Chamber Orch. of Europe in 1981; toured with it in the U.S. (1984–85). He also appeared widely as a guest conductor in England, on the Continent, and in the U.S. In 1987 he became music director of the Phil. Orch. of Florida in Fort Lauderdale. He also was artistic director of the Greater Miami Opera from 1993.

Judson, Arthur (Leon), influential American concert manager; b. Dayton, Ohio, Feb. 17, 1881; d. Rye, N.Y., Jan. 28, 1975. He took violin lessons with Max Bendix and Leopold Lichtenberg in N.Y. He was dean of the music dept. at Denison Univ., Granville, Ohio (1900–1907); subsequently was manager of the Philadelphia Orch. (1915–35) and the N.Y. Phil. (1922–56); also devoted much time to artist representation, organizing the Judson Radio Program Corp. (1926) in order to showcase his artists; also organized Columbia Concerts Corp. (1932), which grew into one of the most powerful management agencies in the U.S.; it later became Columbia Artists Management, Inc. He later formed the Judson, O'Neill, Beall and Steinway (JOBS) Agency (1962), which was renamed Arthur Judson Management (1969); upon his retirement in 1972, it became Harry Beall Management, Inc.

Jung, Manfred, German tenor; b. Oberhausen, July 9, 1945. He studied with Hilde Wesselmann at the Essen Folkwangschule. After singing in the Bayreuth Festival chorus (1970–73), he made his operatic debut in Dortmund in 1974, and then sang in Kaiserslautern, Saarbrücken, and Karlsruhe. In 1977 he became a member of the Deutsche Oper am Rhein in Düsseldorf; made his debut at the Bayreuth Festival as Siegfried in *Götterdämmerung* (1977), and then appeared in the televised version of that role in the *Ring* cycle. He made his Metropolitan Opera debut in N.Y. in the title role of *Siegfried* on Sept. 24, 1981, and subsequently sang other Wagnerian roles there. He returned to the Bayreuth Festival in 1983 to sing Siegfried in the Solti-Hall production, commemorating the 100th anniversary of Wagner's death; also appeared in concert throughout Europe, North America, and the Far East.

Jungwirth, Manfred, Austrian bass; b. St. Pölten, June 4, 1919. He studied voice in St. Pölten, Vienna, Bucharest, Munich, and Berlin; entered the Univ. of Vienna to study medicine in 1937, but passed the examinations in voice, piano, and conducting instead (1940). He sang for German troops in Romania and Bulgaria (1941–45); made his operatic debut as Gounod's Méphistophélès at the Bucharest Opera (1942), and then sang at the Innsbruck Landestheater (1945–47). In 1948 he was awarded his Ph.D. in musicology in Vienna and also won 1st prize in the Geneva voice competition; then sang in Zürich, Berlin, Hamburg, Paris, and London; he made regular appearances at the Frankfurt am Main Opera (1960–67) and the Vienna State Opera (from 1967). On Feb. 16, 1974, he made his debut at the Metropolitan Opera in N.Y. as Baron Ochs, which became his most famous role.

Juon, Paul (actually, **Pavel Fedorovich**), Russian composer of Swiss and German descent; b. Moscow, March 6, 1872; d. Vevey, Aug. 21, 1940. He was a pupil of Hřímaly (violin) and of Taneyev and Arensky (composition) at the Moscow Cons.; then studied with Bargiel at the Berlin Hochschule für Musik (1894–95), where he won the Mendelssohn Prize; subsequently became a teacher (1906) and a prof. (1911) there. He was elected a member of the Prussian Academy of Arts in 1919; retired to Vevey in 1934. His works display pronounced Romantic inclinations.

WORKS: ORCH.: Sym. (1903); *Vaegtervise* (1906); *Aus einem Tagebuch*, suite (c.1906); Chamber Sym. (1907); *Eine Serenadenmusik* (1909); 3 violin concertos (1909, 1913, 1931); *Episodes concertantes* for Piano Trio and Orch. (1912); *Mysterien*, symphonic poem for Cello and Orch. (1928); *Serenade* for Strings (1929); *Little Symphony* for Strings (1930); *Divertimento* for Strings (1933); *Anmut und Wurde*, suite (1937); *Rhapsodische Sinfonie* (1939); *Tanz-Capricen* (1941); *Burletta* for Violin and Orch. (1940); *Sinfonietta capricciosa* (1940). **CHAMBER:** 3 string quartets (1898, 1904, 1920); Piano Trios: No. 1 (1901), *Trio-Caprice* (1908), Trio (1915), *Litaniae* (1920; rev. 1929), *Legende* (1930), and *Suite* (1932); Sextet (1902); 2 piano quintets (1906, 1909); *Divertimento* for Wind Quintet and Piano (1913); Wind Quintet (1930); *Arabesken* for Oboe, Clarinet, and Bassoon (1941); various sonatas and piano pieces. **VOCAL:** *Psyche* for Tenor, Chorus, and Orch. (1906).

Juozapaitis, Jurgis, Lithuanian composer; b. near Šiauliai, June 29, 1942. He studied with Juzeliunas at the Lithuanian State Cons. in Vilnius, graduating in 1968. His music is rooted in native folk modes, which are enhanced by a modernistic harmonic investiture and a rich employment of polyrhythmic percussion.

WORKS: OPERA: *Sea Bird* (1976). **ORCH.:** Concerto for Organ, Strings, and Kettledrums (1970); *Vitrages*, symphonic poem (1971); *Rex*, sym. in memory of M.K. Čiurlionis (1973); *Festive Poem* (1976); *Zodiacus*, sym. (1977). **CHAMBER:** Wind Quintet (1970); *Music* for Flute, Percussion, Piano, Viola, and Cello (1970); Concerto for 4 Percussionists (1971); Sonata for Solo Violin (1972); *Jūrate and Kastytis*, chamber sym. for Flute, Oboe, Viola, Cello, Piano, Percussion, and Electronic Tape (1974); *Diptych* for Wind Quintet (1977); 2 string quartets (1978, 1980); organ pieces. **VOCAL:** Songs; choruses.

Jürgens, Jürgen, German conductor and teacher; b. Frankfurt am Main, Oct. 5, 1925; d. Hamburg, Aug. 4, 1994. He studied with Kurt Thomas at the Frankfurt am Main Musisches Gymnasium and with Konrad Lechner at the Freiberg im Breisgau Staatliche Hochschule für Musik. In 1955 he became conductor of the Hamburg Monteverdi Choir; toured with it throughout Europe, America, and the Far East. He became a lecturer (1960) and a prof. (1977) at the Univ. of Hamburg; was made its music director in 1966. He ed. works of Monteverdi and A. Scarlatti. As a conductor, he cultivated works of the Baroque period, while not neglecting modern music of a polyphonic nature.

Jurinac, Sena (actually, **Srebrenka**), famous Yugoslav soprano; b. Travnik, Oct. 24, 1921. She studied at the Zagreb Academy of Music, and also with Milka Kostrenčić, making her operatic debut as the 1st Flower Maiden at the Zagreb Opera (1942); her first major role there was Mimi that same year. In 1945 she made her Vienna State Opera debut as Cherubino, and soon established herself as one of its outstanding members; she accompanied it on its visit to London's Covent Garden in 1947, where she sang Dorabella; that same year, she made her debut at the Salzburg Festival. She also appeared at the Glyndebourne Festivals (1949–56). She made her U.S. debut at the San Francisco Opera (1959); sang regularly at Covent Garden (1959–63; 1965; 1973). In 1953 she married **Sesto Bruscantini**. A distinguished interpreter of Mozart, she excelled as Fiordiligi, Cherubino, Pamina, and Donna Elvira, and later mastered the more demanding roles of Donna Anna and the Countess. She was also renowned for her portrayals of Octavian, the Composer, Elektra, and the Marschallin in the operas of Richard Strauss.

BIBL.: U. Tamussino, *S. J.* (Augsburg, 1971).

Jurovský, Šimon, Slovak composer; b. Ulmanka, Feb. 8, 1912; d. Prague, Nov. 8, 1963. He attended the Bratislava Academy of Music (1931–36); then took courses in composition with Joseph Marx at the Vienna Academy of Music (1943–44). He was manager of the Bratislava Opera and director of the Slovak Folk Art Ensemble. In his music, he followed the broad tenets of national Romanticism, with frequent references to folk themes.

WORKS: DRAMATIC: OPERA: *Dcery Abelovy* (The Daughters of Abel, 1961). **BALLET:** *Rytierska balada* (The Song of Chivalry; Bratislava, 1960). Also much film music. **ORCH.:** 2 suites (1939, 1943); *Serenade* for Strings (1940); *Začatá cesta* (The Journey Begun), symphonic poem (1948); *Radostné súženie* (A Joyous Competition), symphonic scherzo (1949); 2 syms.: No. 1, *Mírová* (Peace), for Piano and Strings (1950), and No. 2, *Heroická* (Heroic), for Organ and Orch. (1960); Cello Concerto (1953); Concertino for Piano and Strings (1962). **CHAMBER:** Quartet for Winds (1936); *Melodies and Dialogues*, string quartet (1944); String Trio (1948); *Concert Dance* for Piano (1960). **VOCAL:** *3 uspávanky* (Lullabies) for Soprano, Piano, Harp, and Strings (1947); choral pieces; folk song arrangements; songs.

BIBL.: Z. Bokesová, *Š. J.* (Bratislava, 1955).

Juzeliūnas, Julius, Lithuanian composer; b. Čepole, Feb. 20, 1916. He studied with Gruodis at the Kaunas Cons. (graduated, 1948); then entered the Leningrad Cons., in the class of Voloshinov (graduated, 1952). Returning to Lithuania, he taught at the State Cons. in Vilnius (from 1952). His compositions follow the spirit of socialist realism, treating heroic themes in stage productions and romantic subjects in instrumental music; on occasion, he uses modern techniques, including dodecaphony.

WORKS: OPERAS: *Sukilėliai* (The Rebels; 1957; Vilnius, 1960); *Žaidimas* (The Game; 1968). **ORCH.:** 5 syms.: No. 1 (1948), No. 2 (1949), No. 3, *Žmogaus lyra* (Man's Lyre) for Baritone, Chorus, and Orch. (1965), No. 4 (1974), and No. 5, *Hymn of the Plains*, for Women's Chorus and String Orch. (1982);

Heroic Poem (1950); *African Sketches*, suite (1961); *Poem-Concerto* for Strings (1961); *Passacaglia-Poem* (1962); Concerto for Organ, Violin, and Strings (1963); *Concerto Grosso* for Strings, Wind Quintet, and Piano (1966); Concerto for Clarinet and Strings (1985; also for Clarinet and String Quartet). **CHAMBER:** 2 piano sonatas (1947, 1986); 4 string quartets (1962, 1966, 1969, 1980); Sonata for Oboe and Clarinet (1971); Violin Sonata (1972); Sonata for Solo Horn (1975); Sonata for Violin and Cello (1977); *Diptych* for Violin and Organ (1981); *Ragamalika* for Wind Quintet (1982); Sym. for Solo Organ (1984); *Flobo-Clavio*, quartet for Flute, Oboe, Harpsichord, and Cello (1987). **VOCAL:** Concerto for Tenor and Orch. (1955); *Pelenu lopšine* (Lullaby to the Ashes), symphonic poem for Mezzo-soprano, Chorus, and Orch. (1963); *Melika*, sonata for Voice and Organ (1973); *Cantus magnificat*, sym.-oratorio for 2 Soloists, 2 Choruses, Organ, and Orch. (1979); *The Language of Flowers*, cantata for Soprano and String Orch. or Organ (1985).

Jyrkiäinen, Reijo (Einari), Finnish composer; b. Suistamo, April 6, 1934. He studied composition with Fougstedt and Kokkonen at the Sibelius Academy in Helsinki (1956–63), and theory at the Univ. of Helsinki (1958–63); attended modern music courses at Darmstadt (summers, 1962–63) and the electronic sessions at the Bilthoven Radio Studio in the Netherlands (1963). He was head of music programming for the Finnish Radio and TV in Helsinki (1967–71), then managing director of the Helsinki Phil. (1971–90). He also was vice-chairman of the Helsinki Concert Center (1980–87), later serving as its project chief for music (from 1990). In his works, he has pursued advanced experimentation, ranging from classical Schoenbergian dodecaphony to electronics.

WORKS: *5 Dodecaphonic Etudes* for Piano (1961); *Frammenti per il septetto d'archi* for 3 Violins, 2 Violas, Cello, and Double Bass (1962); *Sounds I, II*, and *III*, concrete music on Tape (1963–66); *Mesto* for Flute, Clarinet, Guitar, and Percussion (1963); *For 4* for Violin, Clarinet, Guitar, and Percussion (1963); *Contradictions* for Flute, Clarinet, Piano, Guitar, and String Quartet (1965); *5 Piano Pieces for Children* (1966); *Idiopostic I* and *II*, electronic music (1963, 1966); *Varianti* for Viola and Piano (1967).

K

Kabaivanska, Raina (Yakimova), Bulgarian soprano; b. Burgas, Dec. 15, 1934. She studied at the Bulgarian State Cons. in Sofia. In 1957 she made her operatic debut at the National Opera as Tatiana. She then studied with Zita Fumagalli-Riva in Milan and with Giulia Tess in Vercelli; then made her first appearance at La Scala as Agnese in *Beatrice di Tenda* (1961), and subsequently sang there regularly. In 1962 she made her debut at London's Covent Garden as Desdemona; made her American debut at the Metropolitan Opera in N.Y. as Nedda on Oct. 27, 1962; first sang at the Paris Opéra as Leonora in *La forza del destino* in 1975. She also made guest appearances in Chicago, San Francisco, Dallas, Vienna, and Buenos Aires. She was best known for her Verdi and Puccini roles.

Kabalevsky, Dmitri (Borisovich), noted Russian composer and pedagogue; b. St. Petersburg, Dec. 30, 1904; d. Moscow, Feb. 14, 1987. When he was 14 years old, his family moved to Moscow; he received his primary music education at the Scriabin Music School (1919–25); also studied theory privately with Gregory Catoire; in 1925 he entered the Cons. as a student of Miaskovsky in composition and Goldenweiser in piano. In 1932 he was appointed instructor in composition there; in 1939, became a full prof. As a pedagogue, he developed effective methods of musical education; in 1962, was elected head of the Commission of Musical Esthetic Education of Children; in 1969, became president of the Scientific Council of Educational Aesthetics in the Academy of Pedagogical Sciences of the U.S.S.R.; in 1972, received the honorary degree of president of the International Soc. of Musical Education. As a pianist, composer, and conductor, he made guest appearances in Europe and the U.S. Kabalevsky's music represents a paradigm of the Russian school of composition in its Soviet period; his melodic writing is marked by broad diatonic lines invigorated by an energetic rhythmic pulse; while adhering to basic tonality, his harmony is apt to be rich in euphonious dissonances. In his operas, he successfully reflected both the lyrical and the dramatic aspects of the librettos, several of which are based on Soviet subjects faithful to the tenets of socialist realism. His instrumental writing was functional, taking into consideration the idiomatic capacities of the instruments.

WORKS: DRAMATIC: OPERAS: *Kola Bryunon: Master iz Klamsi* (Colas Breugnon: The Master of Klamsi), after Romain Rolland (1936–38; Leningrad, Feb. 22, 1938; rev. version, Leningrad, April 16, 1970); *V ogne: Pod Moskvoi* (Into the Fire: Near Moscow; 1942; Moscow, Sept. 19, 1943; rev. version, Moscow, Nov. 7, 1947); *Semya Tarasa* (The Family of Taras; Moscow, Nov. 2, 1947; rev. version, Leningrad, Nov. 7, 1950; 2nd rev. version, Moscow, Nov. 17, 1967); *Nikita Vershinin* (1954–55; Moscow, Nov. 26, 1955). **OPERETTAS:** *Vesna poyot* (Spring Sings; Moscow, Nov. 4, 1957); *Syostrï* (The Sisters; 1967; Perm, May 31, 1969). Also incidental music for plays and film scores. **ORCH.:** 3 piano concertos: No. 1 (1928; Moscow, Dec. 11, 1931, composer soloist), No. 2 (1935; Moscow, May 12, 1936), and No. 3 (1952; Moscow, Feb. 1, 1953, Ashkenazy soloist, composer conducting); 4 syms.: No. 1 (Moscow, Nov. 9, 1932), No. 2 (Moscow, Dec. 25, 1934), No. 3, *Requiem for Lenin*, for Chorus and Orch. (1933; Moscow, Jan. 21, 1934), and No. 4 (1954; Moscow, Oct. 17, 1956); *The Comedians*, suite for Small Orch. (1940); Suite for Jazz Orch. (1940); Violin Concerto (Leningrad, Oct. 29, 1948); 2 cello concertos: No. 1 (1948–49; Moscow, March 15, 1949) and No. 2 (1964); *Pathétique Overture* (1960); *Spring*, symphonic poem (1960); *Rhapsody* for Piano and Orch. (1963); *In Memory of the Heroes of Gorlovka*, symphonic poem (1965). **CHAMBER:** *2 Pieces* for Cello and Piano (1927); 2 string quartets (1928, 1945); *Improvisation* for Violin and Piano (1934); *Rondo* for Volin and Piano (1961); Cello Sonata (1962); *20 Simple Pieces* for Violin and Piano (1965). **PIANO:** 3 sonatas (1927, 1945, 1946); 2 sonatinas (1930, 1933); *24 Préludes* (1943–44); *6 Préludes and Fugues* (1958–59); many children's pieces. **VOCAL:** *Poem of Struggle* for Chorus and Orch. (1930); *The Mighty Homeland*, cantata for Voices and Orch. (1941–42); *The People's Avengers* for Chorus and Orch. (1942); *Song of Morning, Spring, and Peace*, cantata for Children's Chorus and Orch. (1957–58); *Leninists* for Youth and Adult Choruses (1959); *Requiem* for Voices and Orch. (1962; Moscow, Feb. 9, 1963); *Of the Homeland*, cantata for Voices and Orch. (1965); *Letter to the 30th Century*, oratorio for Voices and Orch. (1972); numerous choral pieces.

BIBL.: L. Danilevich, *D. K.* (Moscow, 1954); G. Abramovsky, *D. K.* (Moscow, 1960); R. Glezer, *K.* (Moscow, 1969); P. Nazarevsky, ed., *D.B. K.: Notograficheskiy i bibliografischeskiy spravochnik* (D.B. K.: Worklist and Bibliography; Moscow, 1969); Y. Korev, *K.* (Moscow, 1970).

Kabasta, Oswald, prominent Austrian conductor; b. Mistelbach, Dec. 29, 1896; d. (suicide) Kufstein, Feb. 6, 1946. He studied at the Vienna Academy of Music. After conducting in Wiener-Neustadt and Baden bei Wien, he was Generalmusikdirektor in Graz (1926–31). He became music director of the Vienna Radio (1931), and took its orch. on tours of Europe; concurrently taught conducting at the Vienna Academy of Music; was also conductor of the Gesellschaft der Musikfreunde and the Vienna Sym. Orch. (from 1935); then was Generalmusikdirektor of the Munich Phil. (1938–45). Having compromised himself by a close association with the Austrian Nazis, he committed suicide a few months after the conclusion of World War II. He championed the music of the late Austro-German Romantic school; was particularly known for his performances of the works of Bruckner.

Kabeláč, Miloslav, Czech conductor and composer; b. Prague, Aug. 1, 1908; d. there, Sept. 17, 1979. He studied composition with Jirák and conducting with Pavel Dědeček (1928–31) and piano with Kurz (1931–34) at the Prague Cons. He served as conductor and music director at the Czech Radio in Prague (1932–39; 1945–54); taught composition at the Prague Cons. (1958–62) and lectured on electronic music at the Czech Radio in Plzeň (1968–70). In his music, he followed a fairly advanced modern idiom, occasionally applying dodecaphonic devices, but hewing closely to the fundamentals of tonality.

WORKS: ORCH.: *Sinfonietta* (1931); *Fantasy* for Piano and Orch. (1934); 2 overtures (1939, 1947); 8 syms.: No. 1 for Strings and Percussion (1941–42), No. 2 (1942–46), No. 3 for Organ, Brass, and Timpani (1948–57), No. 4 for Chamber Orch. (1954–58), No. 5, *Dramatica*, for Soprano and Orch. (1959–60), No. 6, *Concertante*, for Clarinet and Orch. (1961–62), No. 7 for Narrator and Orch., on Old Testament texts (1967–68), and No. 8, *Antiphonies*, for Soprano, Chorus, Percussion, and Organ (1970); *Dětem* (For Children), suite (1955); *Mysterium času* (Mystery of Time; Prague, Oct. 23, 1957); *Hamletovská improvizace* (Hamlet Improvisations), commemorating the Shakespeare quadricentennial (1962–63; Prague, May 26, 1964); *Zrcadlení* (Reflections), 9 miniatures (1963–64; Prague, Feb. 2, 1965); Variations on the chorale *Hospodine, pomiluj ny* (Our Lord, Forgive Us) *II* for Piano and Orch. (1978). **CHAMBER:** Wind Sextet (1940); *3 Pieces* for Cello and Piano (1941); *Ballade* for Violin and Piano (1956); *Suite* for Saxophone and Piano (1959); *8 Inventions* for Percussion (1963; as a ballet, Strasbourg, April 22, 1965); *8 Ricercari* for Percussion (1966–67; rev. 1971); *Laments and Smiles*, 8 bagatelles for Flute and Harp (1969; rev. 1976). **KEYBOARD: PIANO:** *8 Préludes* (1955–56); *Motifs*, cycle (1959); *Small Suite* for Piano, 4-hands (1960). **ORGAN:** *Fantasy* (1957); *4 Préludes* (1963). **VOCAL:** *Little Christmas Cantata* for Soprano, Men's Chorus, and Chamber Ensemble (1937); *Neustupujte* (Do Not Yield), resistance cantata (against the Nazi occupation of Czechoslovakia) for Men's Chorus, Band, and Percussion (1939; Prague, Oct. 28, 1945); *Moravian Lullabies* for Soprano and Chamber Orch. (1951); 6 lullabies for Alto, Women's Chorus, and Orch. (1955); *3 Melodramas* for Narrators and Orch. (1957); *Tajemství ticha* (Euphemias Mysterion) for Soprano and Chamber Orch. (1964–65; Warsaw, Sept. 30, 1965); Variations on the chorale *Hospodine, pomiluj ny* (Our Lord, Forgive Us) *I* for Female Speaker, Baritone, Men's Chorus, and Mixed Chorus (1977).

Kabos, Ilona, Hungarian pianist; b. Budapest, Dec. 7, 1893; d. London, May 28, 1973. She studied with Arpád Szendy, Kodály, and Leo Weiner at the Budapest Academy of Music, winning the Liszt Prize when she was 15; then made her debut in Budapest at 16 and subsequently toured throughout Europe, eventually gaining a fine reputation as an interpreter of contemporary music. In later years, she made her home in London, where she was active as a teacher; also gave master classes in Europe and North America, numbering among her outstanding students Peter Frankl, John Ogdon, and Joseph Kalichstein. From 1931 to 1945 she was married to **Louis Kentner**.

Kačinskas, Jerome, Lithuanian-born American conductor and composer; b. Viduklé, April 17, 1907. He studied with his father, a church organist; then at the State Music School in Klaipeda and at the Prague Cons. with Jaroslav Křička and Alois Hába. Returning to Lithuania, he was conductor of the Klaipeda Sym. Orch. (1932–38); in 1938, was appointed music director for the Lithuanian Radio in Kaunas; during World War II, conducted the Vilnius Phil. In 1944 he left Lithuania, and from 1945 to 1949 lived in a displaced-persons camp in Augsburg; in 1949 he settled in the U.S., and in 1954 became a naturalized American citizen. His music reflects the influences of Scriabin and French Impressionists. Among his works are a Trumpet Concerto; 2 string quartets; sacred choruses; piano pieces.

Kadosa, Pál, esteemed Hungarian composer and pedagogue; b. Léva, Sept. 6, 1903; d. Budapest, March 30, 1983. He studied piano with Arnold Székely and Kodály at the Budapest Academy of Music (1921–27); had a brief career as a concert pianist, then taught at Budapest's Fodor Music School (1927–43) and Goldmark Music School (1943–44); then at the Academy of Music (from 1945). He won the Kossuth Prize (1950) and the Erkel Prize (1955, 1962); was made a Merited Artist (1953) and an Honored Artist (1963) of the Hungarian People's Republic. In his music, he combined the elements of the cosmopolitan modern idiom with strong Hungarian rhythms and folklike melodies; in his treatment of these materials, and particularly in the energetic asymmetrical passages, he was closer to the idiom of Bartók than to that of Kodály. The lyrical element in modal interludes adds to the Hungarian charm of his music.

WORKS: OPERA: *A huszti kaland* (The Adventure of Huszt; 1949–50; Budapest, Dec. 22, 1951). **ORCH.:** Chamber Sym. (1926); 4 piano concertos: No. 1 (1931; Amsterdam, June 9, 1933, composer soloist), No. 2 (1938), No. 3 (1953), and No. 4 (1966); 2 violin concertos (1932, rev. 1969–70; 1940–41, rev. 1956); 2 divertimentos (1933; 1933–34, rev. 1960); Concerto for String Quartet and Chamber Orch. (1936); Viola Concertino (1937); 8 syms.: No. 1 (1941–42; Budapest, 1965), No. 2, *Capriccio* (Budapest, 1948), No. 3 (1953–55; Budapest, 1957), No. 4 for Strings (1958–59; Budapest, 1961), No. 5 (1960–61; Hungarian Radio, 1962), No. 6 (Hungarian Radio, Aug. 19, 1966), No. 7 (1967; Budapest, 1968), and No. 8 (1968; Hungarian Radio, 1969); *Partita* (1943–44); *Morning Ode* (1945); *March*, overture (1945); *Honor and Glory*, suite (1951); Suite (1954); *Pian e forte*, sonata (1962); Suite for Small Orch. (1962); *Sinfonietta* (1974). **CHAMBER:** solo sonatinas for Violin (1923) and Cello (1924); Sonatina for Violin and Cello (1923); 2 violin sonatas (1925, rev. 1969–70; 1963); Suite for Violin and Piano (1926; rev. 1970); 2 string trios (1929–30; 1955); *Partita* for Violin and Piano (1931); Suite for Violin (1931); 3 string quartets (1934–35; 1936; 1957); Wind Quintet (1954); Piano Trio (1956); *Improvisation* for Cello and Piano (1957); Flute Sonatina (1961); Violin Sonatina (1962); *Serenade* for 10 Instruments (1967). **PIANO:** 3 suites (1921; 1921–23; 1923, rev. 1970); cycles: *7 Bagatelles* (1923), *8 Epigrams* (1923–24), *5 Sketches* (1931), *6 Hungarian Folksongs* (1934–35), *6 Little Preludes* (1944), *10 Bagatelles* (1956–57), *4 Caprichos* (1961), *Kaleidoscope* (8 pieces, 1966), and *Snapshots* (1971); 4 sonatas (1926, rev. 1970; 1926–27; 1930; 1959–60); Sonatina (1927); Sonata for 2 Pianos

(1947); Suite for Piano Duet (1955); also albums for children. **VOCAL:** Cantatas; songs, including *3 Radnoti Songs* (1961) and *7 Attila Jozsef Songs* (1964); folk-song arrangements.

BIBL.: F. Bónis, *K. P.* (Budapest, 1965).

Kafenda, Frico, significant Slovak pedagogue and composer; b. Mošovcé, Nov. 2, 1883; d. Bratislava, Sept. 3, 1963. He studied conducting with Nikisch and composition with Jadassohn at the Leipzig Cons. (1901–05). In 1920 he became a piano instructor at the Bratislava Cons., where he served as its director from 1922 to 1949; then taught at the Bratislava Academy of Music and at the Univ. of Bratislava. As a teacher of composition, he had great influence upon Slovak music; among his students were R. Berger, M. Novák, and E. Suchoň. His wife, Anna Kafendová-Zochová, taught piano at the Cons. and the Academy in Bratislava. His compositions are permeated with the spirit of mid-European Romanticism; among them are Cello Sonata (1905), String Quartet (1916), Violin Sonata (1918), choral music, and songs.

Kagan, Oleg, Russian violinist; b. Sakhalin, Nov. 22, 1946; d. Munich, July 15, 1990. He was a pupil at the Latvian State Cons. in Riga before going to Moscow, where he studied with Boris Kuznetsov and David Oistrakh at the Central Music School; then completed his training at the Cons. After taking prizes in the Enesco (Bucharest, 4th, 1964), Sibelius (Helsinki, 1st, 1965), Tchaikovsky (Moscow, 2nd, 1966), and Bach (Leipzig, 1st, 1968) competitions, he toured as a soloist with orchs., a recitalist, and a chamber music artist. Kagan often appeared in duo concerts with his wife, **Natalia Gutman**.

Kagel, Mauricio (Raúl), notable Argentine composer and pedagogue; b. Buenos Aires, Dec. 24, 1931. He studied in Buenos Aires, taking courses in theory with Juan Carlos Paz and in piano, cello, organ, conducting, and voice with Alfredo Schiuma et al.; he also studed philosophy and literary history at the Univ. there. In 1949 he became active with the Agrupacion Nueva Musica and joined the staff of the Teatro Colón in Buenos Aires. In 1957 he went to Cologne on a stipend from the Deutscher Akademischer Austauschdienst. He taught at the courses for new music in Darmstadt from 1960, and was founder-director of the Cologne Ensemble for New Music from 1961. After serving as the Slee Prof. of Composition at the State Univ. of N.Y. in Buffalo (1964–65), he was director of the Inst. for New Music at the Rheinische Musikschule in Cologne (from 1969). In 1974 he became a prof. at the Cologne Hochscule für Musik. In 1989 he was composer-in-residence at the Cologne Philharmonie. In 1977 he became a member of the Akademie der Künste in Berlin. He was awarded the Mozart Medal of Frankfurt am Main in 1983 and was made a Commandeur de L'Ordre des Arts et des Lettres of France in 1985. He is the author of *Worte über Musik: Gespräche, Aufsätze, Reden, Hörspiele* (Munich, 1991). Kagel has developed an extremely complex system of composition in which a fantastically intricate and yet wholly rational serial organization of notes, intervals, and durations is supplemented by aleatory techniques. Some of these techniques are derived from linguistic permutations, random patterns of light and shadows on exposed photographic film, and other processes. In his hyper-serial constructions, he endeavors to unite all elements of human expression, ultimately aiming at the creation of a universe of theatrical arts in their aural, visual, and societal aspects.

WORKS: DRAMATIC: *Sur Scène*, chamber-music theater piece (1959–60); *Antithese* for 1 or 2 Performers and Electronics (1962); *Tremens*, scenic montage (1963–65); *Die Himmelsmechanik*, piece with theater scenery (1965); *Pas de cing*, variable scene for 5 Performers (1965); *Staatstheater*, scenic piece (1967–70); *Con voce* for 3 Mimes and Instruments ad libitum (1972); *Mare nostrum*, scenic piece (1973–75); *Présentation* for Speaker, Piano, and Tape (1976–77); *Variété*, concert spectacle for Artists and Musicians (1976–77); *Die Erschöpfung der Welt*, scenic illusion (1976–78); *Umzug* for Mime (1977); *Die Rhythmusmaschinen*, action for 10 Gymnasts and Instruments (1977–78); *Ex-Position*, action for Vocal Ensemble and Instruments (1977–78); *Aus Deutschland*, lieder opera (1977–80); *Der Tribun* for Political Orator, Marching Band, and Loudspeaker (1978–79); *Der mündliche Verrat* or *La Trahison orale*, musical epic on the Devil for 1 Female Performer, 2 Male Singers, Tuba, Viola or Violin, Double Bass, Piano or Electric Organ, 3 Percussion, and Tape (1981–83); *. . . nach einer Lektüre von Orwell*, theater picture or scenic environment (1982–83); *Tantz-Schul*, ballet d'action (1985–87); *Zwei Akte* for 2 Actors, Saxophone, and Harp (1988–89). **ORCH.:** *Heterophonie* (1959–61); *Sonant* for Electric Guitar, Harp, Double Bass, and Small Orch. (1960); *Diaphonie II* for Orch. and 2 Slide Projectors (1964); *Music for Renaissance Instruments* for 23 Performers (1965–66); *Klangwehr I* for Military Marching Band (1969–70; *II* for Military Marching Band and Chorus); *Musi* for Strings (1971); *Variationen ohne Fuge* (1971–72); *10 Märsche, um den Sieg zu verfehlen* for Wind and Percussion Orch. (1978–79); *Finale* for Chamber Orch. (1980–81); *Rrrrrr . . .* (1980–82); *Szenario* for Strings and Tape (1981–82); *Musik* (1987–88); *Les idées fixes* (1988–89); *Die Stücke der Windrose* for Salon Orch. (1988–93); *Les idées fixes* (1988–89); *Opus 1.991* (1990); *Konzertstück* for Kettle Drum and Orch. (1990–92). **CHAMBER:** *Variationen* for Flute, Piano, Violin, and Cello (1951); String Sextet (1953; rev. 1957); *Transicion II* for Piano, Percussion, and 2 Tapes (1958–59); *Schlag auf Schlag* for 4 Music Saws and Percussion (1963–64); *Match* for 2 Cellos and Percussion (1964); 4 string quartets (1965, 1967, 1988, 1993); *Phantasie* for Organist, Assistants, and 2 Tapes (1967); *Der Schall* for 5 Performers (1968); *Acustica III* for 2 to 5 Instrumentalists or Tape (1968–70); *Unter Strom* for 3 Performers (1969); *Tactil* for Piano, 2 Guitars, and Electronics (1970); *Charakterstuck* for Zither Quartet (1971); *Exotica* for 6 Performers (1971–72); *Aus Zungen Stimmen* for Accordion Quintet (1972); *Dressur*, percussion trio (1976–77); *Blue's Blue* for 4 Performers (1978–79); *Klangwölfe* for Violin and Piano (1978–79); *Aus dem Nachlass* for Violin, Cello, and Double Bass (1981–86); Trio for Violin, Cello, and Piano (1984–85); *Pan* for Piccolo and String Quartet (1985); *For us: Happy birthday to you!* for 4 Cellos (1987); *Phantasiestück* for Flute and Piano (1987–88; also for Flute, Piano, Clarinet, Bass Clarinet, Violin, Viola, and Cello); *Zwei Akte* for Saxophone and Harp (1988–89). **VOCAL:** *Anagrama* for 4 Soloists, Speaking Chorus, and Chamber Ensemble (1957–58); *Diaphonie I* for Chorus, Orch., and Slide Projectors (1964) and *III* for Chorus and 2 or More Slide Projectors (1964); *Musik aus Diaphonie* for Voices and Instruments (1964); *Hallelujah* for Voices (1967–68); *Abend* for Double Vocal Quartet, Trombone Quintet, Electric Organ, and Piano (1972); *Kantrimiusik* for Voices and Instruments (1975); *Chorbuch* for Vocal Ensemble, Piano, and Harmonium or Electric Organ (1975–78); *Tango Alemán* for Voice, Violin, Bandoneon or Accordion, and Piano (1977–78); *Vox humana?*, cantata for Women's Voices, Orch., and Loudspeaker (1978–79); *Mitternachtsstük* for 4 Soloists, Speaking Chorus, and 9 Instruments (1980–81; 1986); *Sankt-Bach-Passion* for Mezzo-soprano, Tenor, Baritone, Speaker, Chorus, Speaking Chorus, Boy's Chorus, and Orch. (1981–85); *Fürst Igor, Strawinsky* for Bass and 6 Instruments (1982); *Intermezzo* for Speaker, Chorus, and Orch. (1983); *Ein Brief* for Mezzo-soprano and Orch. (1985–86); *Quodlibet* for Woman's Voice and Orch. (1986–88); *Fragende Ode* for Double Chorus, Winds, and Percussion (1988–89); *. . . den 24, XII. 31* for Baritone and Instruments (1988–91); *Liturgien* for Tenor, Baritone, Bass, Double Chorus, and Orch. (1989–90). **OTHER:** Film-collage; tape piece; electronic scores.

Kagen, Sergius, Russian-born American pianist, teacher, and composer; b. St. Petersburg, Aug. 22, 1909; d. N.Y., March 1, 1964. He went to Berlin in 1921 and studied with Leonid Kreutzer and Paul Juon at the Hochschule für Musik; emigrated to the U.S. in 1925 and became a naturalized American citizen in 1930; studied with Carl Friedberg, Rubin Goldmark, and Marcella Sembrich at the Juilliard School of Music in N.Y. (diploma, 1930); later joined its faculty (1940), and also taught at the Union Theological Seminary (1957–64). He wrote the books

Music for the Voice (N.Y., 1949; 2nd ed., rev., 1968) and *On Studying Singing* (N.Y., 1950). He composed an opera, *Hamlet* (Baltimore, Nov. 9, 1962), more than 70 songs, and various piano pieces.

BIBL.: B. Woods, *S. K.: His Life and Works* (diss., George Peabody College for Teachers, 1969); idem, "The Songs of S. K.," *NATS Bulletin*, XXVII/3 (1971).

Kahane, Jeffrey (Alan), American pianist; b. Los Angeles, Sept. 12, 1956. He studied at the San Francisco Cons. (graduated, 1977) and with Howard Wiesel, Jakob Gimpel, and John Perry at the Juilliard School in N.Y. In 1978 he made his debut in San Francisco; won 2nd prize in the Clara Haskil Competition in 1977, 4th prize in the Van Cliburn Competition in 1981, and 1st prize in the Arthur Rubinstein Competition in 1983. He made his Carnegie Hall debut in N.Y. in 1983 and his London debut in 1985. He made numerous appearances as soloist with various orchs., as a recitalist, and as a chamber music player. In 1988 he joined the faculty of the Eastman School of Music in Rochester, N.Y.

Kahl, Willi, German musicologist; b. Zabern, Alsace, July 18, 1893; d. Cologne, Oct. 3, 1962. He first studied in Freiburg im Breisgau and Munich, and then received his Ph.D. in 1919 from the Univ. of Bonn with the diss. *Das lyrische Klavierstück zu Beginn des 19. Jahrhunderts (1800 bis 1830) und seine Vorgeschichte im 17. und 18. Jahrhundert*; subsequently completed his Habilitation in 1923 at the Univ. of Cologne with his *Studien zur Geschichte der Klaviermusik des 18. Jahrhunderts.* In 1928 he became Bibliotheksrat of the Univ. of Cologne and of the city library; was also a reader at the Univ. from 1928; he retired in 1958. His writings include *Musik und Musikleben im Rheinland* (Cologne, 1923), *Herbart als Musiker* (Langensalza, 1936), and *Verzeichnis des Schrifttums über Franz Schubert, 1828–1928* (Regensburg, 1938). He also ed. various works and compiled the important documentary vol. *Selbstbiographien deutscher Musiker des XVIII. Jahrhunderts* (Cologne, 1948).

Kahn, Erich Itor, German-American pianist and composer; b. Rimbach, July 23, 1905; d. N.Y., March 5, 1956. He studied at the Hoch Cons. in Frankfurt am Main. From 1928 to 1933 he was co-director of the Frankfurt am Main Radio; went to France in 1933; in 1938–39, toured as accompanist to Casals in France and North Africa. He emigrated in 1941 to the U.S., where he organized the Albeneri Trio in 1944 (the name being derived from assorted syllables of the first names of the participants: Alexander Schneider, violin; Benar Heifetz, cello; and Erich Kahn, piano). He became the pianist of the Bach Aria Group in 1951. In 1948 he was awarded the Coolidge Medal for eminent service to chamber music. He was held in high esteem as a composer of inventive intellect.

WORKS: *Präludien zur Nacht*, suite for Chamber Orch. (1927); Suite for Violin and Piano (1937; rev. as Suite concertante for Violin and Orch., 1937; orchestration completed by R. Leibowitz, 1964); *3 chansons populaires* for Mezzo-soprano and Piano (1938); *3 caprices de Paganini* for Violin and Piano (1942); *Ciaccona dei tempi di guerra* for Piano (1943); *Actus tragicus* for 10 Instruments (1946; Baden-Baden, June 18, 1955); *4 Nocturnes* for Soprano and Piano (1954); String Quartet (1954); *Les symphonies bretonnes* for Orch. (1955).

BIBL.: D. Newlin, "In Memoriam: E.I. K., Retrospect and Prospect," *American Composers Alliance Bulletin*, 3 (1957); R. Leibowitz and K. Wolff, *E.I. K., un grand representant de la musique contemporaine* (Paris, 1958); H.-K. Metzger and R. Riehn, eds., *E.I. K.* (Munich, 1994).

Kahn, Otto Hermann, German-American music patron, brother of **Robert Kahn**; b. Mannheim, Feb. 21, 1867; d. N.Y., March 29, 1934. He was engaged in the banking profession in London (1888–93); settled in N.Y. in 1893; was a member of the firm Kahn, Loeb & Co. He became interested in the musical affairs of N.Y. City, and from 1907 to his death was on the board of the Metropolitan Opera; also was vice-president of the N.Y. Phil.

BIBL.: M. Matz, *The Many Lives of O. K.* (N.Y., 1963); J. Kobler, *O. the Magnificent: The Life of O. K.* (N.Y., 1989).

Kahn, Robert, German pianist and composer, brother of **Otto Hermann Kahn**; b. Mannheim, July 21, 1865; d. Biddenden, Kent, May 29, 1951. He studied music with Lachner in Mannheim and with Rheinberger in Munich. In 1885 he went to Berlin, and in 1890 moved to Leipzig, where he organized a Ladies' Choral Union, which he conducted; in 1893 he was appointed instructor of piano at the Berlin Hochschule für Musik, retiring in 1931. After the advent of the Nazi government in Germany, he emigrated to England. He composed a considerable amount of respectable chamber music and choral works.

BIBL.: E. Radecke, *R. K.* (Leipzig, 1894); B. Laugwitz, "R. K. and Brahms," *Musical Quarterly*, no. 4 (1990).

Kahowez, Günter, Austrian composer; b. Vöcklabruck, Dec. 4, 1940. He studied at the Bruckner Cons. in Linz and at the Vienna Academy of Music with Schiske. With neo-Classical precepts as points of departure, he rapidly progressed in the direction of modern serialism. Among his compositions were a Wind Quintet (1959); String Quartet (1960); *Klangrhythmen* for Piano (1962); *Flachengitter* for Flute (1962); *Megalyse* for Electronic Instruments (1962); *Duale* for Clarinet and Guitar (1963); *Schichtungen* for Orch. (1963); *Ouverture & Pantomime* for Orch. (1964); *Elementalichemie* for Cello and Percussion (1975).

Kaim, Franz, German literary historian and music patron; b. Kirchheim unter Tech, near Stuttgart, May 13, 1856; d. Munich, Nov. 17, 1935. After settling in Munich, he built a concert hall and organized the "Kaim-Konzerte" in 1891; then in 1893 organized an orch., which had such notable permanent conductors as Löwe (1897–98) and Weingartner (1898–1905). With the end of the Kaim Orch. in 1908, the Konzertverein was formed with Löwe as conductor (1908–14); later conductors included Pfitzner (1919–20) and Hausegger (from 1920); when the Konzertverein orch. officially became the Munich Phil. in 1928, Hausegger continued as conductor until 1938; his eminent successors included Rosbaud (1945–48), Kempe (1967–76), and Celibidache (1979–96).

BIBL.: E. Faehndrich and A. Ott, *Die Münchner Philharmoniker, 1893–1968: Ein Kapitel Kulturgeschichte* (Munich, 1968).

Kaipainen, Jouni (Ilari), Finnish composer; b. Helsinki, Nov. 24, 1956. He studied with Sallinen (1973–76) and Heininen (1976–82) at the Sibelius Academy in Helsinki. From 1991 to 1993 he was artistic director of the Helsinki Festival. His style of composition is typical of the modern school of Finnish music, drawing away from the nationalistic trends of Sibelius, creating a thoroughly individual style.

WORKS: TELEVISION OPERA: *Konstanzin Ihme* (The Miracle of Konstanz; 1987). **ORCH.:** *Concerto grosso per orchestra di camera* (1974); *Apotheosis* for Chamber Orch. (1975); 2 syms. (1980–85; 1992–94); *Carpe diem!*, clarinet concerto (1990); Oboe Concerto (1994). **CHAMBER:** 4 string quartets (1973, 1974, 1984, 1994); *Aspetti* for Clarinet and Piano (1975); *". . . la chimère de l'humidité de la nuit?"* for Alto Saxophone (1978); *Trois morceaux de l'aube* for Cello and Piano (1980–81); *Far from Home* for Flute, Alto Saxophone, Guitar, and Percussion (1981); *Altaforte* for Electric Trumpet and Tape (1982); *Trio No. 1* for Clarinet, Cello, and Piano (1983); *Elegia* for Cello and Piano (1983); *Parcours* for Flute and Harpsichord (1983); *Piping Down the Valleys Wild* for Bass Clarinet and Piano (1984); *Andamento: Trio No. 2* for Flute, Bassoon, and Piano (1986); *Trio No. 3* for Violin, Cello, and Piano (1986–87); *Gena* for Accordion (1987); *L'annello di Aurora* for Violin (1988). **PIANO:** Sonatina (1976); *Ladders to Fire* for 2 Pianos (1979); *Je chante la chaleur désespérée* (1981); *Conte* (1985). **VOCAL:** *Yölaujuja* (Nocturnal Songs) for Soprano and Chamber Ensemble (1978); *Cinq poèmes de René Char* for Soprano and Orch. (1978–80); *Pitkän kesän poikki iltaan* (Through the Long Summer to the Evening) for Soprano, Flute, Horn, Percussion, and

Cello (1979); *Stjarnenatten* (Star Night) for Soprano and Ensemble (1989); *Lachrymosa* for Chorus (1989).

Kaiser, Henry, innovative American improvisational guitarist and keyboardist; b. Oakland, Calif., Sept. 19, 1952. He took up the guitar at 12, developing a unique and eclectic style that shows influences as varied as East Asian, classical North Indian, and Hawaiian music, free jazz and improvisation, and American steel-string guitar; he also draws freely from other abiding interests, which include information theory, experimental cinema and literature, mathematics, and scuba diving. He has performed extensively with such groups as Crazy-Backwards Alphabet, Invite the Spirit, the Henry Kaiser Band, the Obsequious Cheeselog, French-Frith-Kaiser-Thompson, and the Henry Kaiser Quartet. His list of collaborators is extensive; he also has assisted various composers and performers in their compositional and recording endeavors through his elaborate recording studio in Oakland, California. He is senior instructor in Underwater Scientific Research at the Univ. of Calif. at Berkeley. Among his solo recordings or recordings in which he is a featured artist are *Those Who Know History Are Doomed to Repeat It, Re-Marrying for Money,* and *Alternate Visions*; he also produced an instructional video, *Eclectric Electric, Exploring New Horizons of Guitar and Improvisation* (1990).

Kajanus, Robert, outstanding Finnish conductor; b. Helsinki, Dec. 2, 1856; d. there, July 6, 1933. He studied with R. Faltin and G. Niemann at the Helsinki Cons., and later at the Leipzig Cons. with Reinecke, Richter, and Jadassohn (1877–79); then went to Paris, where he studied with Svendsen (1879–80). After returning to Helsinki in 1882, he founded an orch. society that sponsored concerts by the newly organized Helsinki Phil., which he led until his death; from 1897 to 1926 he was music director at the Univ. of Helsinki. He was an early champion of the music of Sibelius; made the first recordings of the 1st and 2nd syms. with the London Sym. Orch. He composed the symphonic poems *Kullervo* (1881) and *Aino* (1885); 2 Finnish rhapsodies (1882, 1889); an orch. suite, *Sommarminnen* (Summer Memories; 1896); piano pieces; songs.

BIBL.: Y. Suomalainen, *R. K.: Hänen elämänsä ja toimintansa* (R. K.: His Life and Work; Helsinki, 1952).

Kakinuma, Toshie, significant Japanese musicologist and music critic; b. Shizuoka Prefecture, July 31, 1953. She was educated in Tokyo at the Kunitachi College of Music (B.M., 1977) and Ochanomizu Univ. (M.A., 1981); then took her Ph.D. at the Univ. of Calif., San Diego in 1989 with the diss. *The Musical Instruments of Harry Partch as an Apparatus of Production in Musical Theatre.* She taught at the Yoshiro Irino Music Inst. (from 1990), Nippon Electronics College (from 1992), and Takushoku Univ. (from 1995); also was a guest lecturer at Nippon Univ. (1995). Kakinuma has been an important figure in the organization of new music festivals in Japan, including "Music History of Quotation" (1983) and "Sound Culture Festival" (1993); also was curator of Betty Freeman's photographic exhibitions at the B (NTT Shinuya) and Studio 200 in Tokyo. Her important writings, primarily on contemporary Japanese, American, and English composers, have appeared widely in publs. in both Japan and the U.S.; she is a regular writer/reviewer to *Ongakugeijutsu* (from 1980), *On-Stage* (from 1989), and *inTune* and the *Asahi Evening News* (from 1994); from 1981 to 1991 she was a regular contributor to *Philharmony,* the program guide for the NHK Sym. Orch. (1982–91). She also publ., with others, a number of music reference works (1982, 1983, 1993), and prepared a Japanese tr. of John Cage's *Silence* (Tokyo, 1995).

Kalabis, Viktor, Czech composer; b. Červený Kostelec, Feb. 27, 1923. He studied with Hlobil at the Prague Cons. (1945–48) and with Řídký at the Prague Academy of Music (1948–52); also took courses in philosophy and musicology at the Univ. of Prague. He was an ed. and music producer with the Czech Radio in Prague (1953–72); then devoted himself totally to composition. In 1967 he received the Czech Music Critics' Prize and in 1969 the Klement Gottwald State Prize; in 1983 he was made an Artist of Merit by the Czech government. In 1952 he married **Zuzana Růžičková**. His early works adhered to traditional methods, but he later adopted modified serial procedures.

WORKS: ORCH.: Concerto for Chamber Orch., *Hommage à Stravinsky* (1948); Overture (1950); Cello Concerto (1951); *Strážnice Suite* (1953); 2 piano concertos (1954, 1985); 5 syms.: No. 1 (1957), No. 2, *Sinfonia Pacis* (1961), No. 3 (1971), No. 4 (1972), and No. 5 (1976); 2 violin concertos (1959, 1978); *Chamber Music* for Strings (1963); *Symphonic Variations* (1964); *Concerto for Orchestra* (1966); Trumpet Concerto (1973); Concerto for Harpsichord and Strings (1975); *Fable* for Chamber Orch. (1983); Concertino for Bassoon and Wind Instruments (1983); *Diptych* for Strings (1987); *Meantatioas* for 13 Wind Instruments (1988). **CHAMBER:** 6 string quartets (1949, 1962, 1977, 1984, 1984, 1987); *Divertimento* for Wind Quintet (1952); *Bagpiper,* suite for Oboe and Piano (1953); 2 nonets (*Classical,* 1956; *Homage to Nature,* 1975); Sonata for Violin and Harpsichord (1967); Small Chamber Music for Wind Quintet (1967); Cello Sonata (1968); Clarinet Sonata (1969); *Variations* for Horn and Piano (1969); Trombone Sonata (1970); Trio for Violin, Cello, and Piano (1974); *Spring Whistles,* octet for Winds (1979); Suite for Clarinet and Piano (1981); Violin Sonata (1982); Duettino for Violin and Cello (1987). **PIANO:** 3 sonatas (1947, 1948, 1982). **VOCAL:** *The War,* chamber cantata for Chorus, Dulcimer, and Flute (1977); *Canticum Canticorum,* cantata for Contralto, Tenor, Chorus, and Chamber Orch. (1986); choruses; songs.

Kalafati, Vasili (Pavlovich), Russian composer and pedagogue of Greek descent; b. Eupatoria, Feb. 10, 1869; d. Leningrad, Jan. 30, 1942. He studied at the St. Petersburg Cons. with Rimsky-Korsakov, graduating in 1899; subsequently was on its teaching staff (1907–29). A musician of thorough knowledge, he was held in great esteem by his colleagues and students; Rimsky-Korsakov sent Stravinsky to him for additional training in harmony. As a composer, Kalafati faithfully continued the traditions of the Russian national school; his works include an opera, *Zygany* (The Gypsies; 1939–41), a Sym., a Piano Quintet, 2 piano sonatas, piano pieces, and a number of songs, all set in impeccably euphonious harmonies.

Kalaš, Julius, Czech composer; b. Prague, Aug. 18, 1902; d. there, May 12, 1967. He studied composition with Foerster and Křička at the Prague Cons. (1921–24), then attended Suk's master classes there (1924–28). He was pianist and artistic director of the satirical male sextet the Teachers of Gotham (1925–53), for which he wrote numerous witty ballads and songs. He was a prof. in the film dept. of the Prague Academy of Musical Arts from 1948; was its dean (1949–50) and vice-dean (1955–57). He wrote 6 operas, the most notable being *Nepokoření* (The Proud Ones; 1960); 6 operettas, including the popular *Mlynárka z Granady* (The Miller's Wife of Granada; 1954); 2 ballets; Cello Concerto (1949); Viola Concerto (1950); cantatas; chamber music; film scores.

Kalenberg, Josef, German tenor; b. Cologne, Jan. 7, 1886; d. Vienna, Nov. 8, 1962. He received his training at the Cologne Cons. In 1911 he made his operatic debut as Turiddu at the Cologne Opera. After singing in Krefeld (1912–16), Barmen (1919–21), Düsseldorf (1921–25), and Cologne (1925–27), he made his first appearance at the Vienna State Opera as Parsifal in 1927, remaining on its roster until 1942. He also sang at the Salzburg Festivals (1928–36) and made guest appearances in France, Italy, and England before retiring in 1949.

Kalichstein, Joseph, Israeli-American pianist; b. Tel Aviv, Jan. 15, 1946. He studied at the Juilliard School of Music in N.Y. with Kabos and Steuermann (M.S., 1969). He made his N.Y. recital debut and won the Young Concert Artists' Award (1967), then appeared as soloist in Beethoven's 4th Piano Concerto with Bernstein and the N.Y. Phil. on national television (1968). After winning 1st prize in the Leventritt Competition (1969), he pursued an active concert career; toured widely in a trio with the violinist Jaime Laredo and the cellist Sharon Robinson (from 1976).

Kálik, Václav, Czech pianist, conductor, and composer; b. Opava, Oct. 18, 1891; d. Prague, Nov. 18, 1951. He studied with Novák at the Univ. of Prague (1911–13); later attended Suk's master classes at the Prague Cons. (1924–26). He was mainly active as a pianist and conductor.

WORKS: OPERAS: *Jarní jitro* (A Spring Morning; 1933; Olomouc, 1943); *Lásky div* (Love's Miracle; 1942–43; Liberec, Nov. 20, 1950); *Posvěcení mládí* (Consecration of Youth; 1946–48). **ORCH.:** *Fantazie* (1915); *Moře* (The Sea), symphonic poem (1924); 2 syms.: No. 1, *Mírová* (Peace), for Soprano and Orch. (1927) and No. 2 (1941–43); *Prelude* (1931); *Venezia* for Strings (1932). **OTHER:** Chamber music; vocal pieces, including *Intermezzo* for Tenor, Violin, and Piano (1913), *Zlá láska* (Evil Love) for Soprano, Violin, and Piano (1919), and *Pražské obrazy* (Prague Pictures) for Men's Chorus (1949–50).

BIBL.: J. Vratislavský, *V. K.* (Ostrava, 1961).

Kalisch, Paul, German tenor; b. Berlin, Nov. 6, 1855; d. St. Lorenz am Mondsee, Austria, Jan. 27, 1946. He studied architecture; then went to Milan, where he took voice lessons with Leoni and Lamperti. He made his operatic debut under the name Paolo Alberti in Rome as Edgardo (1879); subsequently sang in Milan's La Scala (1882) and other Italian opera houses. After appearing in Munich (1883), he was a member of Berlin's Royal Opera (1884–87); made his first appearance in London at Her Majesty's Theatre (1887). In 1888 he married **Lilli Lehmann**, with whom he frequently appeared in operatic performances. On Jan. 30, 1889, he sang Tannhäuser in his Metropolitan Opera debut in N.Y.; sang there again in 1890 and 1891. He later separated from Lehmann, although they never legally divorced; after her death in 1929, he settled on her estate.

Kalischer, Alfred, German writer on music; b. Thorn, March 4, 1842; d. Berlin, Oct. 8, 1909. After obtaining his Ph.D. at the Univ. of Leipzig, he took music courses with Burgel and Bohmer in Berlin; he ed. the *Neue Berliner Musikzeitung* (from 1873). He was best known for his writings on Beethoven. He ed. *Neue Beethovenbriefe* (1902) and *Beethovens sämtliche Briefe* (5 vols., 1906–08; in Eng., 1909).

WRITINGS: *Lessing als Musikasthetiker* (1889); *Die "Unsterbliche Geliebte" Beethovens* (1891); *Die Macht Beethovens* (1903); *Beethoven und seine Zeitgenossen* (4 vols., 1908: I, *Beethoven und Berlin*; II and III, *Beethovens Frauenkreis*; IV, *Beethoven und Wien*).

Kalish, Gilbert, American pianist and teacher; b. N.Y., July 2, 1935. He studied at Columbia College (B.A., 1956) and the Columbia Univ. Graduate School of Arts and Sciences (1956–58). In addition, he took piano lessons with Isabelle Vengerova, Leonard Shure, and Julius Herford. He made his N.Y. recital debut and his European debut in London in 1962; then made tours as a soloist in the U.S., Europe, and Australia; also was active with the Contemporary Chamber Ensemble and the Boston Sym. Chamber Players. He also was a regular accompanist to Jan DeGaetani. He was artist-in-residence at Rutgers, the State Univ. of New Jersey (1965–67), and Swarthmore (Pa.) College (1966–72); was head of keyboard activities at the Berkshire Music Center in Tanglewood, and also taught at the State Univ. of N.Y. at Stony Brook (from 1970).

Kallenberg, Siegfried Garibaldi, German composer; b. Bad Schachen, near Lindau, Nov. 3, 1867; d. Munich, Feb. 9, 1944. He studied with Faisst at the Stuttgart Cons. and at the Munich Academy of Music. He became director of the Stettin Cons. (1892), and later taught in Konigsberg, Hannover, and Munich (from 1910). He publ. *Musikalische Kompositionsformen* (Leipzig, 1913) and monographs on R. Strauss (Leipzig, 1926) and Reger (Leipzig, 1930). As a composer, he was inspired by neo-Romanticism; in some of his works there are touches of Impressionism; in others, his absorption in symbolic subjects brought him into a kinship with the Expressionist school in Germany. Apart from works on exotic subjects, he wrote music in a traditional style; he was particularly strong in choral polyphony.

WORKS: 3 operas: *Sun Liao*, *Das goldene Tor*, and *Die lustigen Musikanten*; 3 syms.; *Impressionen* for Orch.; *Konzertante Fantasie* for Piano and Orch.; about 10 chamber works; 3 piano sonatas; a set of *Miniaturen* for Piano; choral works: *90th Psalm*, *Germania an ihre Kinder*, *Requiem*, *Den Gefallenen*, *Eine kleine Passionmusik*, and *Eine Pfingstmusik*; some 300 songs.

Kallir, Lilian, Czech-born American pianist and teacher; b. Prague, May 6, 1931. She was taken as a child to the U.S., where she studied with Isabelle Vengerova and Herman de Grab at the Mannes College of Music in N.Y. (1946–49). She won the National Music League Award and the American Artists Award of the Brooklyn Inst. of Arts and Sciences at 16. She made her debut as soloist with the N.Y. Phil. at 17; her recital debut followed at N.Y.'s Town Hall at 18; thereafter she toured widely in the U.S., South America, Europe, and Israel, appearing as soloist with orchs. and as a recitalist. She married **Claude Frank** in 1959, and subsequently appeared in duo recitals with him. She has also given concerts with her daughter, **Pamela Frank.** In 1975 she joined the faculty of the Mannes College of Music.

Kallmann, Helmut (Max), German-born Canadian librarian, musicologist, and editor; b. Berlin, Aug. 7, 1922. He studied music with his father; left Germany in 1939 for London, where he was interned as a German citizen in 1940; then was interned in Canada (1940–43); after his release, he became a naturalized Canadian citizen (1946). He took music courses at the Univ. of Toronto (B.Mus., 1949), and then became a music librarian for the CBC in 1950; was supervisor of its music collection from 1962. From 1970 to 1987 he served as chief of the music division of the National Library of Canada in Ottawa. He publ. a number of useful books, including a *Catalogue of Canadian Composers* (Toronto, 1952) and *A History of Music in Canada 1534–1914* (Toronto, 1960); with G. Potvin and K. Winters, he ed. the authoritative *Encyclopedia of Music in Canada* (Toronto, 1981; 2nd ed., rev., 1992).

BIBL.: J. Beckwith and F. Hall, eds., *Musical Canada: Words and Music Honouring H. K.* (Toronto, 1988).

Kallstenius, Edvin, Swedish composer; b. Filipstad, Aug. 29, 1881; d. Danderyd, Nov. 22, 1967. He studied science at the Univ. of Lund (1898–1903) and music at the Leipzig Cons. (1903–07); then was active as a music critic in Stockholm. He also was a music librarian for the Swedish Radio (1928–46). In his early works, he followed the Romantic traditions of Scandinavian music; later turned to advanced modern techniques, including explicit application of dodecaphonic configurations.

WORKS: ORCH.: *Scherzo fugato* for Small Orch. (1907; rev. 1923); *Sista Striden*, dramatic overture (1908); *En serenad i sommarnatten* (A Serenade in the Summer Night; 1918); *Sinfonia concertata* for Piano and Orch. (1922); 4 sinfoniettas (1923; 1946; *Dodicitonica*, 1956; *Semi-seriale*, 1958); 5 syms. (1926, rev. 1941; 1935; 1948; 1954; *Sinfonia su temi 12-tonici*, 1960); *Dalarapsodi* (1931); *Dalslandsrapsodi* (1936); *Romantico*, overture (1938); *Högtid och fest*, trilogy (1940); *Musica gioconda* for Strings (1942); *Cavatina* for Viola and Orch. (1943); *Passacaglia enarmonica* (1943); *Kraus-variationer* (1947); *Sonata concertate* for Cello and Orch. (1951); *Musica sinfonica* for Strings (1953; full orch. version, 1959); *Nytt vin i gamla läglar* (New Wine in Old Bottles) for Small Orch. (1954); *Choreographic Suite* (1957); *Prologo seriale* (1966). **CHAMBER:** 8 string quartets (1904; 1905; 1913; *Divertimento alla serenata*, 1925; 1945; 1953; *Dodecatonica*, 1957; 1961); Cello Sonata (1908); Violin Sonata (1909); Clarinet Quintet (1930); Suite for Winds and Percussion (1938); Wind Quintet (1943); *Trio divertente* for Flute, Violin, and Viola (1950); *Piccolo trio seriale* for Flute, English Horn, and Clarinet (1956); *Trio svagante* for Clarinet, Horn, and Cello (1959); solo sonatas for Cello (1961), Flute (1962), and Violin (1965); *Lyric Suite* for Flute, Saxophone, and Cello (1962); String Trio (1965). **VOCAL:** *När vi do* (When Mankind Perishes), Requiem for Chorus and Orch. (1919); *Sångoffer* (Song Offering), cantata for Baritone and Orch. (1944); *Stjärntändningen* for Chorus and Orch. (1949); *Hymen, o, Hymenaios* for Soli, Chorus, and Orch. (1955).

Kálmán, Emmerich (actually, **Imre**), remarkable Hungarian composer; b. Siófolk, Oct. 24, 1882; d. Paris, Oct. 30, 1953. He went to Budapest, where he studied law at the Univ. and theory and composition with Koessler at the Royal Academy of Music. From 1904 to 1908 he was a répétiteur at the Vigszinhás, and also wrote music criticism. Although he attracted notice as a composer with his symphonic poem *Saturnalia* (1904) and a song cycle, which was awarded the Franz-Josef Prize (1907), he soon concentrated his activities on the musical theater. His first operetta, *Tatárjárás* (The Happy Hussars; Feb. 22, 1908), was so successful that it was subsequently performed throughout Europe and eventually made its way to N.Y. His next score, *Az obsitos* (March 16, 1910), assured his reputation when it was subsequently staged in Vienna as *Der gute Kamerad* (Oct. 10, 1911; rev. version as *Gold gab ich für Eisen*, Oct. 16, 1914). Its unqualified success led Kálmán to settle in Vienna, where he brought out the highly successful *Der Zigeunerprimás* (Oct. 11, 1912), which subsequently triumphed on various European stages and as *Sari* on Broadway. After producing *The Blue House* (London, Oct. 28, 1912), *Der kleine König* (Vienna, Nov. 27, 1912), and *Kivándorlók* (Budapest, Sept. 26, 1913), Kálmán had a notable success with *Zsuzsi kisasszony* (Budapest, Feb. 23, 1915), which later became a Broadway favorite as *Miss Springtime*. With Vienna again the center of his activities, he scored a triumph with his *Die Csárdásfürstin* (Nov. 17, 1915), which ran for almost 600 performances and became a beloved repertoire piece. The success of *Die Faschingsfee* (Sept. 21, 1917) was followed by the popular *Das Hollandweibchen* (Jan. 31, 1920). Kálmán then composed 2 outstanding scores, *Die Bajadere* (Dec. 23, 1921) and *Gräfin Mariza* (Feb. 28, 1924), which were heard throughout Europe to great acclaim. The latter was so successful that it also became a repertoire work. After further success with *Die Zirkusprinzessin* (March 26, 1926), Kálmán attempted to transfer his golden touch to Broadway with *Golden Dawn* (Nov. 30, 1927) but without success. Back in Vienna, success was his again with *Die Herzogin von Chicago* (April 5, 1928), although *Das Veilchen vom Montmartre* (March 21, 1930) and *Der Teufelsreiter* (March 10, 1932) elicited little interest. He also wrote the film score for *Ronny* (1931). After composing *Kaiserin Josephine* (Zürich, Jan. 18, 1936), the ominous clouds of Nazism led Kálmán to go to Paris in 1939. In 1940 he emigrated to the U.S. and in 1942 became a naturalized American citizen. During his American sojourn, he had some success with the musical *Marinka* (N.Y., July 18, 1945). With World War II over, Kálmán returned to Europe. His last stage work, *Arizona Lady*, was premiered posthumously in Bern on Feb. 14, 1954.

BIBL.: J. Bistron, *E. K.* (Vienna, 1932); R. Oesterreicher, *E. K.: Der Weg eines Komponisten* (Vienna, 1954); V. Kálmán, *Gruss' mir die süssen, die reizenden Frauen: Mein Leben mit E. K.* (Bayreuth, 1966); R. Oesterreicher, *E. K.: Das Leben eines Operettenfürsten* (Vienna, 1988).

Kálmán, Oszkár, Hungarian bass; b. Kis-Szent-Péter, June 18, 1887; d. Budapest, Sept. 18, 1971. He was a student at the Budapest Academy of Music of József Sík. In 1913 he made his debut as Sarastro at the Budapest Opera, where, in 1918, he created Bartók's Duke Bluebeard. After appearances in Hamburg (1926), at the Berlin Kroll Opera (1927), and in Vienna and Barcelona (1927–29), he again sang at the Budapest Opera (1929–54); also made appearances as a concert artist. Kálmán was particularly admired for his Wagnerian roles.

Kalmár, László, Hungarian composer; b. Budapest, Oct. 19, 1931. He received training in composition from Major at the Bela Bartók Music School and later from Farkas privately. In 1957 he joined the staff of Editio Musica Budapest, where he became ed.-in-chief in 1970 and then head of music in 1987. In 1985 he was awarded the Erkel Prize.

WORKS: ORCH.: *Toccata concertante* for Piano and Strings (1968–70); *Cycles* for Strings (1971–74); *Notturno* No. 1 for 15 Instruments (1973); *Horae* (1982); *Lectiones* for Chamber Ensemble (1982); *Hermes* (1983–84); Piano Concerto No. 2 (1984–85); *Ballet des fleurs blanches* for Strings (1984–85); *Ballet des amphores* (1985–86); Chamber Concerto (1986); *3 Symphonic Pictures* (1986–87); *At Janus's Gate* (1988). **CHAMBER:** *Divertimento* for 2 Violins and Cello (1961); Trio for Flute, Marimba, and Guitar (1968); *Monologo* for Guitar (1968), Violin (1973), Flute (1974), Cello (1975), Clarinet (1977), Saxophone (1978), and Horn (1983); Flute Sonata (1970–71); *Triangoli* for Clarinet, Horn, Harp, Violin, and Cello (1970–71); *Distichon* for Piano, Harp, and Percussion (1970–71); Quartet for English Horn, Viola, Vibraphone, and Harpsichord (1972); String Trio (1972); *Sotto voce* for Organ, Vibraphone, and Harp (1973); *La stanza quarta* for 3 Horns (1976); *Terzina* for Violin, Viola, and Harp (1976); *Morfeo* for String Quartet (1977); *Chorale* for 3 Clarinets (1979); *Serioso* for 2 Cimbaloms (1979); Trio Sonata for Clarinet, Horn, and Cello (1981); *Ad Blasium* for Brass Quintet (1984). **VOCAL:** Choral pieces; motets; songs.

Kalninš, Alfreds, Latvian organist and composer, father of **Janis Kalninš**; b. Zehsis, Aug. 23, 1879; d. Riga, Dec. 23, 1951. He studied at the St. Petersburg Cons. (1897–1901) with Homilius (organ) and Liadov (composition); then was organist in various Lutheran churches in Dorpat, Libau, and Riga; gave recitals in Russia, and was also active as a teacher in Riga. From 1927 to 1933 he lived in N.Y.; then returned to Riga, where he taught at the Latvian Cons.; was its rector (1944–48). He wrote the first national Latvian opera, *Banuta* (Riga, May 29, 1920); also the operas *Salinieki* (The Islanders; Riga, 1925) and *Dzimtenes atmoda* (The Nation's Awakening; Riga, Sept. 9, 1933); other works include a symphonic poem, *Latvia*; some 100 choruses; piano pieces; about 200 songs; arrangements of Latvian folk songs.

BIBL.: J. Vitolinš, *A. K.* (Riga, 1968).

Kalninš, Imants, significant Latvian composer; b. Riga, May 26, 1941. He studied composition with A. Skulte at the Latvian Cons. in Riga, graduating in 1964. In 1959 he directed the choral organization Lachplesis in Lielvarde, then was pianist for a pantomime group in Riga (1962–64) and taught music in Liepaja and later at the Latvian Cons. (1973–80). About 1980 he turned his attention mostly to rock music. His output is innovative, fusing a diversity of styles; his 4th Sym. is scored for jazz ensemble and orch.

WORKS: DRAMATIC: OPERAS: *Is There Anyone Here?* (1971); *I Play, I Dance* (1977). **OPERETTA:** *Quo Vadis My Guitar?* (1971). **ORCH.:** Cello Concerto (1963); 4 syms. (1964, 1965, 1968, 1972); Concerto (1966). **CHAMBER:** *Toccata* for Cello and Piano (1962); Viola Sonata (1962); Piano Sonata (1962). **VOCAL: ORATORIOS:** *In October* (1967); *The Poet and the Mermaid* (1973); *Morning Drudgery* (1977).

Kalninš, Janis, Latvian-born Canadian organist, conductor, pedagogue, and composer, son of **Alfreds Kalninš**; b. Pernu, Estonia (of Latvian parents), Nov. 3, 1904. He studied piano and organ with his father; then composition with Vitols at the Latvian State Cons. in Riga (1920–24); also studied conducting with Kleiber in Salzburg, Abendroth in Leipzig, and Blech in Berlin. Returning to Riga, he served as music director of the Latvian National Theater (1923–33) and the Latvian National Opera (1933–44). In 1948 he emigrated to Canada, becoming a naturalized citizen in 1954. From 1948 to 1989 he was organist and choirmaster at St. Paul's United Church in Fredericton, New Brunswick; he served as prof. of music at the Fredericton Teachers' College (1951–71), and was conductor of the Fredericton Civic Orch. (1951–58), the St. John Sym. Orch. (1958–61), and the New Brunswick Sym. Orch. (1961–67).

WORKS: DRAMATIC: OPERAS: *Lolita's Magic Bird* (1933); *Unguni* (1933); *In the Fire* (1934); *Hamlet* (1935; Riga, Feb. 17, 1936). **BALLETS:** *Autumn* (1936); *The Nightingale and the Rose* (1936). **ORCH.:** *2 Latvian Peasant Dances* (1936); 5 syms.: No. 1 (1939–44), No. 2, *Symphony of the Beatitudes*, for Chorus and Orch. (1953), No. 3 (1972–73), No. 4 (1979), and No. 5 (1990); Violin Concerto (1945–46); *Marching Through Fredericton* (1963); *Theme and Variations* for Clarinet, Horn, and Orch. (1963); *Music* for Strings (1965); *New Brunswick Rhapsody* (1967); *Festival Overture* (1969); *Latvian Rhapsody* (1975); Concerto for Piano and Chamber Orch. (1985). **CHAMBER:** String Quartet (1948); Oboe Sonata (1963); Trio for Violin, Cello, and Piano (1966); *Klusa Stunda* for Violin and Piano (1968); Violin Sonata (1982); *Larghetto Serioso* for Violin and Organ or Piano (1975); Trio for Violin, Viola, and Cello (1979); Sonata for Solo Violin (1975); Piano Quartet (1987); piano pieces, including 2 piano sonatas; organ music. **VOCAL:** Cantata for Men's Chorus and Orch. (1965); *Spring Song*, cantata for Chorus and Orch. (1981); *Requiem* for Soprano, Baritone, Chorus, and Piano or Organ or Orch. (1988–89); choral pieces; songs.

Kalomiris, Manolis, distinguished Greek composer and pedagogue; b. Smyrna, Dec. 26, 1883; d. Athens, April 3, 1962. He studied piano with Bauch and Sturm, theory and composition with Grädener, and music history with Mandyczewski at the cons. of the Gesellschaft der Musikfreunde in Vienna (1901–06); then went to Russia, where he taught piano at a private school in Kharkov. He settled in Athens, where he taught at the Cons. (1911–19); was founder-director of the Hellenic Cons. (1919–26) and of the National Cons. (1926–48). He was greatly esteemed as a teacher; publ. several textbooks on harmony, counterpoint, and orchestration. Kalomiris was the protagonist of Greek nationalism in music; almost all his works are based on Greek folk-song patterns, and many are inspired by Hellenic subjects. In his harmonies and instrumentation, he followed the Russian school of composition, with a considerable influx of lush Wagnerian sonorities.

WORKS: OPERAS: *O Protomastoras* (The Master-Builder), after Kazantzakis (Athens, March 24, 1916; rev. 1929 and 1940); *To dachtylidi tis manas* (The Mother's Ring; 1917; rev. 1939); *Anatoli* (Sunrise), musical fairy tale, to a libretto by the composer after Cambyssis (1945; rev. 1948); *Ta xotika nera* (The Shadowy Waters), after Yeats (1950; rev. 1952); *Constantinos o Palaeologus*, music legend after Kazantzakis (Athens, Aug. 12, 1962). **ORCH.:** *Greek Suite* (1907); *Iambs and Anapests*, suite (1914); *Greek Rhapsody* for Piano and Orch. (orchestrated by G. Pierné and conducted by him, Paris, April 3, 1926); *Island Pictures* for Violin and Orch. (1928); *3 Greek Dances* (1934); Piano Concerto (1935); *Triptych* (1940); *Minas the Rebel*, tone poem (1940); *The Death of the Courageous Woman*, tone poem (1945); Violin Concertino (1955). **CHAMBER:** Piano Quintet, with Soprano (1912); String Trio (1921); Quartet quasi fantasia for Harp, Flute, English Horn, and Viola (1921); Violin Sonata (1948). **PIANO:** *Sunrise* (1902); *3 Ballads* (1906); *For Greek Children* (1910); *2 Rhapsodies* (1921); 5 preludes (1939). **VOCAL:** *The Olive Tree* for Women's Chorus and Orch. (1909); *Valor Symphony* for Chorus and Orch. (1920); *Symphony of the Kind People* for Mezzo-soprano, Chorus, and Orch. (1931); *At the Ossios Loukas Monastery* for Narrator and Orch. (1937); *Palamas Symphony* for Chorus and Orch., after Palamas (Athens, Jan. 22, 1956); choruses; songs.

Kalter (real name, **Aufrichtig**), **Sabine,** noted Hungarian mezzo-soprano; b. Jaroslaw, March 28, 1889; d. London, Sept. 1, 1957. She studied at the Vienna Academy of Music; made her debut at the Vienna Volksoper in 1911; then was a principal member of the Hamburg Opera (1915–35). After being compelled to leave Germany by the Nazis, she settled in London, where she sang at Covent Garden (1935–39); in later years she devoted herself to a concert career, making her last appearance with the Hamburg Radio in 1950. She was also active as a teacher. Her finest roles were Ortrud, Brangäne, and Fricka.

Kamensky, Alexander, Russian pianist and teacher; b. Geneva (of Russian parents), Dec. 12, 1900; d. Leningrad, Nov. 7, 1952. He studied piano at the Petrograd Cons. (graduated, 1923), then developed an energetic career as a concert pianist; did not interrupt his activities even during the siege of Leningrad in 1941–42, when he played almost 500 recitals under the most dangerous conditions. In 1934 he was appointed prof. of piano of the Leningrad Cons. In his programs, he featured many works by Soviet composers and also by modern Western music masters, including Schoenberg and Stravinsky.

Kamieński, Lucian, Polish composer and pedagogue; b. Gniezno, Jan. 7, 1885; d. Thorn, July 27, 1964. He studied composition with Bruch and musicology with Kretzschmar and Wolf at the Univ. of Berlin (Ph.D., 1910, with the diss. *Die Oratorien von Johann Adolf Hasse*; publ. in Leipzig, 1912); then was a music critic in Königsberg (until 1919). He taught at the Poznań Academy of Music (1920–39); also taught musicology at the Univ. of Poznań. After World War II, he taught privately.

WORKS: 2 comic operas: *Tabu* (Königsberg, April 9, 1917) and *Dami i huzary* (Poznan, Oct. 2, 1938); *Sinfonia paschalis* (1928); *Silesia Sings*, symphonic sketch (1929); Violin Sonata; several piano suites on Polish themes; an album of 60 workers' songs to his own words (Berlin, 1905–10), which he issued under the name Dolega-Kamieński.

Kaminski, Heinrich, eminent German composer; b. Tiengen, Baden, July 4, 1886; d. Ried, Bavaria, June 21, 1946. He studied at the Univ. of Heidelberg with Wolfrum and in Berlin with Kaun, Klatte, and Juon; settled in Ried (1914); taught a master class at the Prussian Academy of the Arts in Berlin (1930–33) and then returned to Ried. His writing is strictly polyphonic and almost rigid in form; the religious and mystic character of his sacred music stems from his family origins (he was the son of a clergyman); the chief influences in his work were Bach and Bruckner. The Heinrich-Kaminski-Gesellschaft was organized in 1987.

WORKS: DRAMATIC: Passionspiel (1920); *Jürg Jenatsch*, opera (Dresden, April 27, 1929); *Das Spiel vom König Aphelius*, music drama (1946; Göttingen, Jan. 29, 1950). **ORCH.:** Concerto Grosso for 2 Orchs. (1922); *Dorische Musik* (1933); *Concerto for Orchestra* (1936); Piano Concerto (1937); *Tanzdrama* (1942). **CHAMBER:** Quartet for Clarinet, Viola, Cello, and Piano (1912); 2 string quartets (1913, 1916); Quintet for Clarinet, Horn, Violin, Viola, and Cello (1924); *Musik* for 2 Violins and Harpsichord (1931); *Hauskonzert* for Violin and Piano (1941); *Ballade* for Horn and Piano (1943). **KEYBOARD: PIANO:** *Klavierbuch* (1934); *10 kleine Übungen für das polyphone Klavierspiel* (1935). **ORGAN:** *Wie schön leucht' uns der Morgenstern*, toccata (1923); *Chorale-Sonata* (1926); 3 chorale preludes (1928); *Toccata and Fugue* (1939). **VOCAL:** *O Herre Gott*, motet for Chorus and Organ (1918); Magnificat for Soprano, Viola, Chorus, and Orch. (1925); *Der Mensch*, motet for Alto, Chorus, and Orch. (1926); *Die Erde*, motet for Chorus (1928); *Triptychon* for Alto or Baritone and Organ (1926–29); *Die deutsch Messe* for Chorus (1934); *In memoriam Gabrielae* Alto, Violin, and Orch. (1940); other songs; folk-song arrangements.

BIBL.: K. Schleifer, *H. K.* (Kassel, 1945); K. Schleifer and R. Schwarz-Stilling, *H. K.: Werkverzeichnis* (Kassel, 1947); I. Samson, *Das Vokalschaffen von H. K., mit Ausnahme der Opern* (Frankfurt am Main, 1956); A. Suder, ed., *H. K.* (Tutzing, 1986); H. Hartog, *H. K.* (Tutzing, 1987).

Kaminski, Joseph, Russian-born Israeli violinist and composer; b. Odessa, Nov. 17, 1903; d. Gedera, Oct. 14, 1972. He studied composition with Friedrich Koch in Berlin and Hans Gál in Vienna. He was concertmaster of the Warsaw Radio Orch., then emigrated to Tel Aviv, where he was concertmaster of the Palestine (later Israel Phil.) Orch. (1937–69).

WORKS: ORCH.: Trumpet Concertino (1940–41; Tel Aviv, May 5, 1941); *Ha'Alijah*, variations (1942); *Comedy Overture* (1944); *Ballade* for Harp and Chamber Orch. (Tel Aviv, Feb. 2, 1946); Violin Concerto (1947–49; Tel Aviv, 1954); *3 Israeli Sketches* (1955); *Variations* for English Horn and Strings (1958);

Symphonic Overture (1960). **CHAMBER:** String Quartet (1945); *Triptych* for Piano (1958).

Kamu, Okko (Tapani), prominent Finnish conductor; b. Helsinki, March 7, 1946. He studied violin at the Sibelius Academy in Helsinki under Onni Suhonen (graduated, 1967). He played in the Helsinki Youth Orch.; founded the Suhonen Quartet (1964); was a member of the Helsinki Phil. (1965–66) and concertmaster of the orch. of the Finnish National Opera (1966–68); then was its 3rd conductor (1968–69). After winning 1st prize in the Karajan Competition for conductors (1969), he appeared as a guest conductor with the Royal Opera in Stockholm (1969–70); then was a conductor with the Finnish Radio Sym. Orch. (1970–71), and subsequently its chief conductor (1971–77). He was chief conductor of the Oslo Phil. (1975–79) and of the Helsinki Phil. (1979–90). In 1988 he became principal conductor of the Sjaelland Sym. Orch. in Copenhagen. He also was chief conductor of the Helsingborg Sym. Orch. from 1991.

Kancheli, Giya (Alexandrovich), Georgian composer; b. Tbilisi, Aug. 10, 1935. He was a student of Tuskiya at the Tbilisi Cons. (1959–63), where he became a member of the faculty in 1970. From 1984 to 1989 he was first secretary of the Union of Georgian Composers. In 1991 he settled in Berlin. His compositions were honored with prizes by the Soviet (1976) and Georgian (1981) governments. Kancheli's music has been significantly influenced by Georgian melos, and yet he has managed to pursue an eclectic path which is modernistic and accessible at the same time.

WORKS: DRAMATIC: *The Pranks of Hanum,* musical comedy (1973); *Music for the Living,* opera (1984; in collaboration with R. Strua); incidental music for plays; film scores. **ORCH.:** *Concerto for Orchestra* (1962; Tbilisi, Feb. 2, 1963); *Largo and Allegro* (1963); 7 syms.: No. 1 (1967; Tbilisi, May 12, 1968), No. 2, *Chants* (Tbilisi, Oct. 31, 1970), No. 3 (Tbilisi, Oct. 11, 1973), No. 4, *In memoriam Michelangelo* (1974; Tbilisi, Jan. 23, 1975), No. 5 (1977; Tbilisi, Feb. 27, 1978), No. 6 (1979; Tbilisi, April 7, 1980; rev. 1981), and No. 7, *Epilogue* (1985; Prague, 1986); *Mourned by the Wind,* liturgy for Viola and Orch. (1989; Berlin, Sept. 9, 1990); *Abii ne viderem* for Strings, Flute, Piano, and Bass Guitar (Amsterdam, June 10, 1992); *Noch einen Schritt . . .* for Orch. and Tape (1992; Donaueschingen, Oct. 15, 1993); *Flügellos* (Saarbrücken, May 23, 1993); *Trauerfarbenes Land* (Bonn, Dec. 9, 1994). **CHAMBER:** *Magnum Ignotum* for 10 Instruments and Tape (1994). **VOCAL:** *Bright Sorrow* for 2 Boy Soloists, Boy's Chorus, and Orch. (1985). **OTHER:** *Life Without Christmas,* cycle of 4 works: *Morning Prayers* for Chamber Orch. and Tape (1990), *Midday Prayers* for Chamber Orch., Child Soprano, and Clarinet (1990; Salzau, Aug. 8, 1991), *Evening Prayers* for Chamber Orch. and 8 Voices (1991), and *Night Prayers* for String Quartet and Tape (1992).

Kang, Sukhi, Korean composer; b. Seoul, Oct. 22, 1934. He studied at the College of Music at the Seoul National Univ. (graduated, 1960), the Hannover Hochschule für Musik (1970), and with Blacher and Yun at the Berlin Hochschule für Musik (1971–75). He subsequently taught at the Seoul National Univ. (1975–80; from 1982), and was named chairman of its composition dept. in 1987, which position he held until 1991. Kang has actively promoted contemporary music in South Korea; he served as founding director of the annual Pan-Music-Festival in Seoul in 1969. In 1972 he became president of the Korean section of the ISCM, and from 1984 to 1990 he was vice-president of the ISCM of UNESCO in Paris. His compositions have won various awards. He received the composer's prize of the Korean Ministry of Culture in 1978 and of the Korean president in 1979, and was named best musician of the year by the Assn. of Korean Musicians in 1989. His compositions are meticulously crafted, utilizing densely stratified materials to create complex musical structures, including electronic sonorities. Many of these were presented in Berlin, securing for him international attention. His *The Feast of Id* (1966) was the first Korean composition to use electronically manipulated sounds.

WORKS: DRAMATIC: *Penthesilea,* music theater (1985; Berlin, March 2, 1986). **ORCH.:** *Generation '69* (Seoul, March 24, 1969); *Reflexionen* (Seoul, Sept. 9, 1975); *Catena* (Solingen, May 31, 1975); *Dal-ha* (Seoul, Sept. 14, 1978); *Mega-Melos* (Berlin, Sept. 14, 1980); *Man-pa* for Solo Flute and Flute Orch. (Berlin, March 31, 1982); *Symphonic Requiem* (Seoul, Nov. 7, 1983); *Successions* (Berlin, June 15, 1985); *Ch'uit'ahyang* for Traditional Korean Orch. (Seoul, June 23, 1987); *Prometheus kommt* (The Olympic Torch Music of the Seoul Olympiad; Seoul, Sept. 15, 1988). **CHAMBER:** *Nirmanakaya* for Cello, Piano, and Percussion (Seoul, Sept. 5, 1969); *Roundtone* for Flute, Oboe, Clarinet, Viola, Cello, Vibraphone, and Percussion (1969); *Parodie* for Flute and Organ (1972); *Nong* for Flute and Piano (1973); *Kleines Stück* for Oboe, Cello, and Harp (1973); *Strukturen* for 4 Cellos (1973); *Banya* for Flute, Oboe, Clarinet, Tuba, Violin, Cello, Piano, and Percussion (Berlin, March 6, 1974); *Metamorphosen* for Flute and String Quartet (Tokyo, July 17, 1974); *Dialog* for Viola and Piano (1976); *Myung* for 4 Huns, Taekum, Kayagŭm, and Tam-tam (1976); *Dala (Parodie Waltz)* for Clarinet, Trombone, Cello, Piano, and Tape (Warsaw, Sept. 22, 1980); *Bronzenzeit* for Percussion and Tape (Cologne, Aug. 5, 1980); *Manpa* for Flute Ensemble (Berlin, March 31, 1982); *Thal* for Contrabass Flute (1983); String Quartet (1983; Saarbrücken, May 29, 1986); *Aniri IV* for Harp (1987). **VOCAL:** *Lyebul* for Man's Voice, Men's Chorus, and 30 Percussionists (Seoul, Nov. 20, 1969); *Buro* for Woman's Voice, Flute, Clarinet, Piano, and 2 Percussionists (Berlin, Oct. 7, 1976); *Yong-Bi,* cantata for 3 Soloists, 2 Choruses, and Orch. (Seoul, April 21, 1978); *Vision* for Woman's Voice, Guitar, and Tape (1978); *Aniri II* for Woman's Voice and Tape (1983) and *III* for Woman's Voice (1984); *The Rite of Sun,* cantata for Soloists, Chorus, and Orch. (Seoul, Oct. 3, 1985). **ELECTRONIC:** *The Feast of Id* (Seoul, Dec. 9, 1966); *Mosaico* (Berlin, April 7, 1981); *Klanspuren* (Berlin, April 7, 1981).

Kanitz, Ernest (actually, **Ernst**), Austrian-American composer and teacher; b. Vienna, April 9, 1894; d. Menlo Park, Calif., April 7, 1978. He changed his first name to Ernest in order to distinguish himself from a homonymous concert manager in Vienna. He studied with Heuberger (1912–14) and Schreker (1914–20) in Vienna; then taught at the Neues Konservatorium there (1922–38). After the Anschluss (1938), he emigrated to the U.S.; taught theory at various colleges, including the Univ. of Southern Calif. in Los Angeles (1945–59) and Marymount College in Palos Verdes, California (1960–64). He publ. *A Counterpoint Manual: Fundamental Techniques of Polyphonic Music Writing* (Boston, 1948).

WORKS: OPERAS: *Kumana* (1953); *Room No. 12* (1957; Los Angeles, Feb. 26, 1958); *Royal Auction* (1957; Los Angeles, Feb. 26, 1958); *The Lucky Dollar* (1959); *Perpetual* (Los Angeles, April 26, 1961); *Visions at Midnight* (1963; Los Angeles, Feb. 26, 1964). **ORCH.:** *Heitere Ouvertüre* (1918); Theremin Concertino (1938); *Intermezzo concertante* for Saxophone and Orch. (1948); Concerto Grosso (1949); Bassoon Concerto (San Francisco, April 8, 1964); 2 syms.: No. 1, *Sinfonia seria* (St. Louis, Oct. 17, 1964) and No. 2 (1965; San Francisco, Dec. 11, 1968). **CHAMBER:** *Dance Sonata* for Flute, Clarinet, Trumpet, Bassoon, and Piano (1932); Quintettino for Piano and Winds (1945); Sonata for Violin and Cello (1947); *Divertimento* for Viola and Cello (1949); *Notturno* for Flute, Violin, and Viola (1950); String Trio (1951); *Sonata breve* for Violin, Cello, and Piano (1952); *Sonata Californiana* for Alto Saxophone and Piano (1952); Sonata for Solo Cello (1956); Viola Sonatina (1958); Suite for Brass Quintet (1960); *Little Concerto* for Saxophone (1970). **VOCAL:** *Das Hohelied,* oratorio (1921); *Zeitmusik,* radio cantata (1931); *Cantata 1961* for Chorus and 2 Pianos (1961).

Kann, Hans, respected Austrian pianist, pedagogue, and composer; b. Vienna, Feb. 14, 1927. He studied piano with A. Bloch, A. Göllner, and F. Wührer, chamber music with O. Schulhoff, composition with J. Lechthaler, and analysis with J. Polnauer in

Vienna, where he made his debut (1946). After winning the Silver Medal at the Geneva International Competition in 1948, he pursued an international career. Beginning in 1955, he made regular tours of Japan; he toured South America and Russia in 1966; gave concerts in China in 1980, 1982, and 1985; and played in the U.S. in 1981 and 1984. In 1987–88 he gave in Vienna the first complete performance of the Haydn sonatas; in 1988–89 he presented a "Biedermeier" cycle there, consisting of works by Beethoven and Schubert and their lesser-known contemporaries; in 1989–90 he performed the complete piano works of Mozart there, including Mozart's pieces for children and his didactic works. Among other places, Kann taught at the Vienna Academy of Music (1950–52), the Univ. of Arts in Tokyo (1955–58), and the Vienna Hochschule für Musik (from 1977). He also gave master classes at the Darmstadt Academy of Music (1961–67). He wrote a book on piano playing that was publ. in Japanese. His compositions include a ballet, theater and film scores, chamber music, lieder, works for synthesizer, and various pieces for solo piano, including a curious album entitled *10 Klavierstücke ohne Bassschlüssel*, and *12 Alt-Wiener Walzer*, as well as didactic pieces, exemplified by *33 Spezialstudien*, *Tägliche Fingerübungen*, and *Models*.

Kanner-Rosenthal, Hedwig, Hungarian-American pianist and pedagogue; b. Budapest, June 3, 1882; d. Asheville, N.C., Sept. 5, 1959. She studied with Leschetizky and **Moriz Rosenthal**, whom she married; appeared with him in duo recitals. She settled in N.Y. as a teacher (1939), numbering among her students Charles Rosen and Robert Goldsand.

Kantorow, Jean-Jacques, French conductor and violinist; b. Cannes, Oct. 3, 1945. Following training at the Nice Cons., he pursued studies at the Paris Cons. (premier prix in violin, 1960, and in chamber music, 1963). In 1962 he won the medal of the Carl Flesch competition in London, and also prizes in the Genoa (Paganini), Brussels (Queen Elisabeth of Belgium), Helsinki (Sibelius), Montreal, and Geneva (1965) violin competitions. He began his career as an orch. player, but soon emerged as a solo artist and chamber music player. Eventually he gave increasing attention to a conducting career. In 1985 he became music director of l'Orchestre d'Auvergne in Clermont-Ferrand, and in 1993 of l'Ensemble Orchestral de Paris.

Kapell, William, brilliant American pianist; b. N.Y., Sept. 20, 1922; d. in an airplane crash at King's Mountain, near San Francisco, Oct. 29, 1953. He studied with Dorothea La Follette in N.Y., and later with Olga Samaroff at the Philadelphia Cons. of Music and at the Juilliard School of Music in N.Y. After winning the Philadelphia Orch.'s youth competition and the Naumburg Award (1941), he made his N.Y. debut on Oct. 28, 1941; subsequently appeared as a soloist with the major American orchs. and in Europe. He died on a return flight from Australia, where he had been touring. Kapell was an outstanding technician who was also capable of the most refined playing.

BIBL.: T. Page, *W. K.: A Documentary Life History of the American Pianist* (College Park, Md., 1992).

Kaplan, Mark, American violinist; b. Cambridge, Mass., Dec. 30, 1953. He was brought up in Syracuse, N.Y.; began violin lessons as a small child; at the age of 8, he won a local violin competition, and enrolled as a student of Dorothy DeLay at the Juilliard School of Music in N.Y.; received its Fritz Kreisler Memorial Award. In 1973 he was awarded the prestigious Award of Special Distinction at the Leventritt Competition in N.Y.; subsequently was a soloist with many of the major orchs. of North America and Europe, meriting praise for his fine musicianship and virtuoso technique.

Kapp, Artur, significant Estonian composer, father of **Eugen (Arturovich)** and uncle of **Villem Kapp**; b. Suure-Jaani, Feb. 28, 1878; d. there, Jan. 14, 1952. He began his music training with his father, an organist and choral conductor; then continued his studies at the St. Petersburg Cons., where he received degrees in organ (1898) and composition (1900), studying the latter with Rimsky-Korsakov and Liadov. From 1903 to 1920 he was director of the Astrakhan Cons.; returning to Estonia, he was prof. of composition at the Tallinn Cons. (1924–43). He was the first Estonian composer to use native folk material, which he utilized in his first orch. suite (1906). His 4th Sym. was awarded the State Prize (1949) and the 1st Stalin Prize (1950).

WORKS: ORCH.: *Don Carlos*, symphonic poem (1900); 4 suites (1906, 1930, 1936, 1947); 5 syms. (1924–49); 5 concertos (1934–46). **CHAMBER:** Violin Sonata (1897); String Quintet (1918); Trio for Violin, Cello, and Organ (1936); String Sextet (1951). **VOCAL:** *Hiob*, oratorio (1929); 4 cantatas, including *For Peace* (1951); choral works; numerous songs.

BIBL.: P. Anton, *A. K.* (Tallinn, 1968).

Kapp, Eugen (Arturovich), important Estonian composer, son of **Artur Kapp**; b. Astrakhan, May 26, 1908. He graduated from his father's composition class at the Tallinn Cons. (1931), then became a teacher of composition there (1935); after serving as founder-director of the Estonian State Ensemble in Yaroslavl (1941–44), he became a prof. at the Estonian Cons. (1947) and was its director (1952–64). He received the Order of Lenin (1950) and was made a People's Artist of the Estonian S.S.R. (1950) and of the U.S.S.R. (1956). His operas *Tasuleegid* and *Vabaduse laulik* won Stalin Prizes in 1946 and 1950, respectively, as well as his ballet *Kalevipoeg* in 1952.

WORKS: DRAMATIC: OPERAS: *Tasuleegid* (Flames of Vengeance; Tallinn, July 21, 1945); *Vabaduse laulik* (Freedom's Singer; Tallinn, July 20, 1950); *Talvemuinasjutt* (Winter Fairy Tale; Tartu, Oct. 28, 1958); *Tabamatu* (Elusive Marta; 1960; Tartu, March 19, 1961); *Rembrandt* (March 30, 1975); *Enneolematu ime* (Unheard of Wonder), children's opera (Tallinn, May 8, 1983). **OPERETTA:** *Assol* (1965). **BALLETS:** *Kalevipoeg* (1947); *Kullaketrajad* (Goldspinners; 1956). **ORCH.:** *The Avenger*, symphonic poem (1931); 6 suites (1933–57); 4 overtures (1938–69); 3 syms. (1942, 1954, 1964); Piano Concerto (1969); Flute Concerto (1975); Concerto-Fantasy for Violin and Chamber Orch. (1978; also for Violin and Orch., 1980); *Theme and Variations on Ukrainian Folk Music* for Strings (1982). **CHAMBER:** Piano Trio (1930); 2 string quartets (1935, 1956); 2 violin sonatas (1936, 1943); Cello Sonata (1948); *Meditations* for Cello (1969); *4 Estonian Dances* for Violin and Piano (1973); *4 Pieces* for Flute and Piano (1974); *Starling's Song to the Sun* for Violin (1983). **PIANO:** Sonatina (1945); *Little Sonatina* (1975). **VOCAL:** Oratorios; cantatas; songs.

BIBL.: G. Polyanovsky, *E. K.* (Moscow, 1957).; H. Kyrvits, *E. K.* (Tallinn, 1964).

Kapp, Julius, German writer on music; b. Seelbach, Baden, Oct. 1, 1883; d. Sonthofen, March 18, 1962. He studied in Marburg, Munich, and Berlin (Ph.D. in chemistry, 1907). From 1904 to 1907 he ed. Berlin's *Literarischer Anzeiger*, which he founded; then was adviser on productions at the Berlin State Opera and ed. of its *Blätter der Staatsoper* (1921–45); subsequently was an adviser on productions at the Berlin Städtische Oper (1948–54). He wrote significant biographies of Liszt and Wagner.

WRITINGS: *Richard Wagner und Franz Liszt: Eine Freundschaft* (Berlin and Leipzig, 1908); *Arthur Schnitzler* (Berlin, 1909); *Franz Liszt: Eine Biographie* (Berlin and Leipzig, 1909; 20th ed., 1924); *Franz Liszt: Gesammelte Schriften (allgemeine Inhaltsübersicht)* (Leipzig, 1910); *Franz Liszt und die Frauen* (Leipzig, 1910); *Liszt-Brevier* (Leipzig, 1910); *Richard Wagner: Eine Biographie* (Berlin, 1910; 32nd ed., 1929); ed. *Der junge Wagner: Dichtungen, Aufsätze, Entwürfe, 1832–1849* (Berlin, 1910); ed. *Franz Liszt: Gesammelte Schriften* (Leipzig, 1910); *Liszt-Brevier* (Leipzig, 1910); *Richard Wagner und die Frauen: Eine erotische Biographie* (Berlin, 1912; 16th ed., 1929; rev. 1951; Eng. tr., 1951, as *The Loves of Richard Wagner*); *Niccolò Paganini: Eine Biographie* (Berlin and Leipzig, 1913; 18th ed., 1954); ed. *Richard Wagner: Gesammelte Schriften und Dichtungen* (Leipzig, 1914); ed. *Richard Wagners gesammelte Briefe, I–II* (Leipzig, 1914–33); ed. *Richard Wagner an Mathilde und Otto Wesendonk* (Leipzig, 1915; 2nd ed., 1936); *Berlioz: Eine Biographie* (Berlin and Leipzig, 1917; 2nd ed., rev., 1922); *Das*

Dreigestirn: Berlioz, Liszt, Wagner (Berlin, 1920); *Giacomo Meyerbeer: Eine Biographie* (Berlin, 1920; 8th ed., rev., 1932); *Franz Schreker: Der Mann und sein Werk* (Munich, 1921); *Das Opernbuch* (Leipzig, 1922; 18th ed., 1928; rev. 1939); *Die Oper der Gegenwart* (Berlin, 1922); *Carl Maria von Weber* (Stuttgart and Berlin, 1922; 15th ed., 1944); ed. *Ludwig van Beethovens sämtliche Briefe* (Leipzig, 1923; rev. ed. of Kastner); ed. *Richard Strauss und die Berliner Oper* (Berlin, 1934); *Geschichte der Staatsoper Berlin* (Berlin, 1937).

Kapp, Richard, American conductor; b. Chicago, Oct. 9, 1936. He studied at Johns Hopkins Univ. (B.A., 1957); then took courses in conducting, composition, and piano at the Staatliche Hochschule für Musik in Stuttgart. Returning to the U.S., he studied jurisprudence at N.Y. Univ. (J.D., 1966) and had private lessons with Rosbaud and Halasz in conducting, Simon in piano, and Marlowe in harpsichord. He began his musical career as a répétiteur at the Basel Stadttheater (1960–62); then was music director of the Opera Theater of the Manhattan School of Music in N.Y. (1963–65). In 1968 he led a concert in N.Y. with a specially assembled group billed as the Philharmonia Virtuosi; later toured with it in programs of varied repertoire, from Baroque to jazz.

Kapp, Villem, Estonian composer, nephew of **Artur Kapp**; b. Suure-Jaani, Sept. 7, 1913; d. Tallinn, March 24, 1964. He began his training with his uncle, then studied with Eller at the Tallinn Cons. (1939–44); from 1945 to 1964, was a prof. of composition there. He wrote in an expansive Romantic style rooted in folk song; his opera, *Lembitu* (Tallinn, Aug. 23, 1961), glorifies Estes Lembitu, the leader of the Estonian struggle against the invading Teutonic crusaders in 1217. He also wrote 2 syms. (1947, 1955), 4 cantatas (1949–63), Piano Sonata (1940), Piano Trio (1946), Wind Quintet (1957), and songs.

BIBL.: H. Tönson, *V. K.* (Tallinn, 1967).

Kappel, Gertrude, noted German soprano; b. Halle, Sept. 1, 1884; d. Pullach, April 3, 1971. She studied with Nikisch and Noe at the Leipzig Cons. She made her debut in 1903 at the Hannover Opera, where she was a regular member (until 1924); also sang at London's Covent Garden (1912–14; 1924–26) and the Vienna State Opera (1924–29). She was a principal member of the Bavarian State Opera in Munich (1927–31). She made her Metropolitan Opera debut in N.Y. as Isolde on Jan. 16, 1928, and remained a member until 1936; also sang with the San Francisco Opera; she returned to Germany, retiring in 1937. Her finest roles were Isolde and Brünnhilde, but she also was admired for her Senta, Sieglinde, Marschallin, and Elektra.

Kapr, Jan, Czech composer; b. Prague, March 12, 1914; d. there, April 29, 1988. He studied with his father, a musician, then composition with Řídký and later with Křička in his master class at the Prague Cons. (1933–40). He was a music producer for the Czech Radio in Prague (1939–46), a music critic (1946–49), and an ed. in music publishing (1950–54); from 1961 to 1970 he taught at the Janáček Academy of Music and Dramatic Arts in Brno. His style of composition is derived from the Czech national school; in his later works, he audaciously introduced modernistic serial procedures. He publ. a vol. on contemporary music entitled *Konstanty* (The Constants; Prague, 1967).

WORKS: OPERA: *Muzikantská pohádka* (Musicians' Fairy Tale; 1962). **ORCH.:** 3 piano concertos (1938, 1953, 1986); *Marathon,* symphonic scherzo (1939); Sinfonietta for Small Orch. (1940); 10 syms.: No. 1 (1943), No. 2 (1946), No. 3 for Small Orch. (1946), No. 4 (1957), No. 5, *Olympijská* (Olympic; 1959), No. 6 (1960; rev. 1964), No. 7, *Krajina dětství* (Country of Childhood), for Children's Chorus and Orch. (1968), No. 8, *Campanae Pragenses* (The Bells of Prague), for Chorus, Orch., and Bell Sounds on Tape (1970), No. 9 (1982), and No. 10, *Lanžhotská,* for 2 Vocal Soloists and Orch. (1985); *Harvested,* symphonic rhapsody (1950); *Zitra* (Tomorrow), symphonic picture (1953); *Léto* (Summer) for Chamber Orch. (1954); *Allegretto* for Violin and Orch. (1955); Violin Concerto (1955); *Variations* for Flute and Strings (1958); Concertino for Viola and Wind Orch. (1965); *Omaggio alla tromba* for 2 Solo Trumpets, Wind Orch., Piano, and Timpani (1967–68); *Anachron* for Chamber Orch. (1974); Concertino for Clarinet and Chamber Ensemble (1975). **CHAMBER:** 8 string quartets (1937; 1941; 1954; 1957; 1961; with Baritone, 1963; 1965; 1976); Nonet (1943); *Fantasy* for Violin and Piano (1958); *4 Moods* for Nonet (1959); *Šifry* (Ciphers) for Piano, Percussion, and Tape (1966); *Oscilace* (Oscillation) for Violin, Clarinet, Trumpet, Piano, Cello, and Percussion (1965); *Rotation 9* for Piano Quartet (1967); *Shadow Play and Dreambook* for Soprano, Flute, and Harp (1968); Sonata for Solo Cimbalom (1968); *Testimonies* for Cello, Bass Clarinet, Piano, and Light Source (1969); *Woodcuts* for 8 Brass (1973); *Colors of Silence* for 8 Instruments (1973); *Circuli* for Violin and Accordion (1974); Sonata for Flute, Horn, and Piano (1976); *Claricello* for Clarinet and Cello (1981); *Miniatures* for Winds and Cello (1985). **PIANO:** 4 sonatas (1945, 1947, 1958, 1980). **OTHER:** Cantatas; choruses; film music.

Kaprál, Václav, Czech composer, father of **Vítězslava Kaprálová**; b. Určice u Prostějova, March 26, 1889; d. Brno, April 6, 1947. He studied with Janáček at the Brno Organ School (1908–10), Novák in Prague (1919–20), and Cortot in Paris (1923–24). He established his own music school in Brno in 1911; lectured at the Univ. of Brno (1927–36); then taught at the Brno Cons. from 1936 until his 3-year internment in a concentration camp in Svatobořice during World War II; in 1946 he became a prof. at the Janáček Academy of Music in Brno. In his works, he shows a fine eclectic talent, enhanced by refulgent lyricism.

WORKS: CHAMBER: 2 string quartets (1925; 1927, with Baritone); *Ballad* for Cello and Piano (1946). **PIANO:** 4 sonatas (1912, 1921, 1924, 1939); *Miniatury* (Miniatures; 1922); *Con duolo* for Piano, Left-hand (1926); 3 sonatinas (1930, 1936, 1943); Fantasie (1934). **VOCAL:** *Pro ni* (For Her) for Voice and Piano Quartet (1927); *Pízeň podzimu* (Song of Autumn) for Voice and String Quartet (1929); *Uspavánsky* (Lullabies) for Voice and Chamber Orch. (1932; Barcelona, April 20, 1936).

BIBL.: E. Štaudová, *V. K., 1889–1947: Personální bibliografie* (Brno, 1989).

Kaprálová, Vitězslava, Czech composer, daughter of **Václav Kaprál**; b. Brünn, Jan. 24, 1915; d. Montpellier, June 16, 1940. She received her early education from her father, then studied with Petrželka (composition) and Chalabala (conducting) at the Brno Cons. (1930–35); subsequently took master classes with Novák (composition) and Talich (conducting) at the Prague Cons. (1935–37). In 1937 she received a scholarship to Paris, where she took lessons in conducting with Munch and composition with Martinů. She appeared as a guest conductor with the BBC Sym. Orch. at the ISCM Festival in London in 1938. She returned to France in 1939, her promising career being cut tragically short by miliary tuberculosis.

WORKS: ORCH.: *Suite en miniature* (1932–35); Piano Concerto (Brno, June 17, 1935); *Military Sinfonietta* (Prague, Nov. 26, 1937); *Suita rustica* (Brno, April 16, 1939); *Partita* for Piano and Strings (Brno, Nov. 12, 1941); *Christmas Prelude* for Chamber Orch. (1939); Concertino for Violin, Clarinet, and Orch. (1940; unfinished). **CHAMBER:** *Legenda a Burleska* for Violin and Piano (1932); String Quartet (1936); *2 Ritournelles* for Cello and Piano (1940). **PIANO:** *Sonata appassionata* (1933); *6 Variations on the Bells of the Church of Saint Etienne in Paris* (1938).

BIBL.: J. Macek, *V. K.* (Prague, 1958).

Karabtchewsky, Isaac, Brazilian conductor; b. São Paulo, Dec. 27, 1934. He studied in Brazil; then at the Hochschule für Musik in Freiburg im Breisgau. Upon his return to Brazil in 1969, he became music director of the Brazil Sym. Orch. in Rio de Janeiro; also was a guest conductor in the U.S. From 1987 to 1994 he was chief conductor of the Vienna Niederösterreichisches Tonkünstler Orch. His conducting is marked by an expansively Romantic quality, much in the vein of the old Russian school of interpretation.

Karajan, Herbert (actually, **Heribert) von,** great Austrian conductor; b. Salzburg, April 5, 1908; d. Anif, near Salzburg, July 16, 1989. He was a scion of a cultured family of Greek-Macedonian extraction whose original name was Karajannis. His great-grandfather was Theodor Georg von Karajan (b. Vienna, Jan. 22, 1810; d. there, April 28, 1873), a writer on music; his father was a medical officer who played the clarinet and his brother was a professional organist. Karajan himself began his musical training as a pianist; he took lessons with Franz Ledwinka at the Salzburg Mozarteum. He further attended the conducting classes of the Mozarteum's director, Bernhard Paumgartner. Eventually he went to Vienna, where he pursued academic training at a technical college and took piano lessons from one J. Hofmann; then entered the Vienna Academy of Music as a conducting student in the classes of Clemens Krauss and Alexander Wunderer. On Dec. 17, 1928, he made his conducting debut with a student orch. at the Vienna Academy of Music; shortly afterward, on Jan. 23, 1929, he made his professional conducting debut with the Salzburg Orch. He then received an engagement as conductor of the Ulm Stadttheater (1929–34). From Ulm he went to Aachen, where he was made conductor of the Stadttheater; he subsequently served as the Generalmusikdirektor there (1935–42). On April 9, 1938, he conducted his first performance with the Berlin Phil., the orch. that became the chosen medium of his art. On Sept. 30, 1938, he conducted *Fidelio* at his debut with the Berlin State Opera. After his performance of *Tristan und Isolde* there on Oct. 21, 1938, he was hailed by the *Berliner Tageblatt* as "das Wunder Karajan." His capacity of absorbing and interpreting the music at hand and transmitting its essence to the audience became his most signal characteristic; he also conducted all of his scores from memory, including the entire *Ring des Nibelungen.* His burgeoning fame as a master of both opera and sym. led to engagements elsewhere in Europe. In 1938 he conducted opera at La Scala in Milan and also made guest appearances in Belgium, the Netherlands, and Scandinavia. In 1939 he became conductor of the sym. concerts of the Berlin State Opera Orch.

There was a dark side to Karajan's character, revealing his lack of human sensitivity and even a failure to act in his own interests. He became fascinated by the ruthless organizing solidity of the National Socialist party; on April 8, 1933, he registered in the Salzburg office of the Austrian Nazi party, where his party number was 1 607 525; barely a month later he joined the German Nazi party in Ulm, as No. 3 430 914. He lived to regret these actions after the collapse of the Nazi empire, but he managed to obtain various posts, and in 1947 he was officially denazified by the Allies' army of occupation. His personal affairs also began to interfere with his career. He married the operetta singer Elmy Holgerloef in 1938, but divorced her in 1942 to marry Anita Gütermann. Trouble came when the suspicious Nazi genealogists discovered that she was one-quarter Jewish and suggested that he divorce her. But World War II was soon to end, and so was Nazi hegemony. He finally divorced Gütermann in 1958 to marry the French fashion model Eliette Mouret.

Karajan was characteristically self-assertive and unflinching in his personal relationships and in his numerous conflicts with managers and players. Although he began a close relationship with the Vienna Sym. Orch. in 1948, he left it in 1958. His association as conductor of the Philharmonia Orch. of London from 1948 to 1954 did more than anything to re-establish his career after World War II, but in later years he disdained his relationship with that ensemble. When Wilhelm Furtwängler, the longtime conductor of the Berlin Phil., died in 1954, Karajan was chosen to lead the orch. on its first tour of the U.S. However, he insisted that he would lead the tour only on the condition that he be duly elected Furtwängler's successor. Protesters were in evidence for his appearance at N.Y.'s Carnegie Hall with the orch. on March 1, 1955, but his Nazi past did not prevent the musicians of the orch. from electing him their conductor during their visit to Pittsburgh on March 3. After their return to Germany, the West Berlin Senate ratified the musicians' vote on April 5, 1955.

Karajan soon came to dominate the musical life of Europe as no other conductor had ever done. In addition to his prestigious Berlin post, he served as artistic director of the Vienna State Opera from 1956 until he resigned in a bitter dispute with its general manager in 1964. He concurrently was artistic director of the Salzburg Festival (1957–60), and thereafter remained closely associated with it. From 1969 to 1971 he held the title of artistic adviser of the Orchestre de Paris. In the meantime, he consolidated his positions in Berlin and Salzburg. On Oct. 15, 1963, he conducted the Berlin Phil. in a performance of Beethoven's 9th Sym. at the gala concert inaugurating the orch.'s magnificent new concert hall, the Philharmonie. In 1967 he organized his own Salzburg Easter Festival, which became one of the world's leading musical events. In 1967 he re-negotiated his contract and was named conductor-for-life of the Berlin Phil. He made a belated Metropolitan Opera debut in N.Y. on Nov. 21, 1967, conducting *Die Walküre.* He went on frequent tours of Europe and Japan with the Berlin Phil., and also took the orch. to the Soviet Union (1969) and China (1979).

In 1982 Karajan personally selected the 23-year-old clarinetist Sabine Meyer as a member of the Berlin Phil. (any romantic reasons for his insistence were not apparent). The musicians of the orch. rejected her because of their standing rule to exclude women, but also because the majority of the musicians had less appreciation of Fräulein Meyer as an artist than Karajan himself did. A compromise was reached, however, and in 1983 she was allowed to join the orch. on probation. She resigned in 1984 after a year of uneasy co-existence.

In 1985 Karajan celebrated his 30th anniversary as conductor of the Berlin Phil., and in 1988 his 60th anniversary as a conductor. In 1987 he conducted the New Year's Day Concert of the Vienna Phil., which was televised to millions on both sides of the Atlantic. In Feb. 1989 he made his last appearance in the U.S., conducting the Vienna Phil. at N.Y.'s Carnegie Hall. In April 1989 he announced his retirement from his Berlin post, citing failing health. Shortly before his death, he dictated an autobiographical book to Franz Endler; it was publ. in an English tr. in 1989.

Through his superlative musical endowments, charismatic and glamorous personality, extraordinary capacity for systematic work, and phenomenal command of every aspect of the great masterworks of the symphonic and operatic repertoire fully committed to memory, Karajan attained legendary stature in his own time. A renowned orchestral technician, he molded the Berlin Phil. into the most glorious musical ensemble of its kind. His interpretations of Beethoven, Wagner, Brahms, Bruckner, Mahler, and Richard Strauss placed him among the foremost conductors in the history of his chosen profession.

BIBL.: E. Haeusserman, *H. v.K. Biographie* (Gütersloh, 1968; new ed., Vienna, 1978); C. Spiel, ed., *Anekdoten um H. v.K.* (Munich, 1968); P. Robinson, *K.* (Toronto, 1975); W. Stresemann, *The Berlin Philharmonic from Bülow to K.* (in Ger. and Eng.; Berlin, 1979); R. Bachmann, *K.: Anmerkungen zu einer Karriere* (Düsseldorf, 1983); H. Kröber, *H. v.K.: Der Magier mit dem Taktstock* (Munich, 1986); R. Vaughan, *H. v.K.: A Biographical Portrait* (N.Y. and London, 1986); H. Götze and W. Simon, eds., *Wo sprache aufhört . . . H. v.K. zum 5. April 1988* (Berlin, 1988); H. Goldsmith, "K.'s Early Years Reappraised," *Musical Times* (May 1989); H. Grünewald, *H.v. K. zum Gedenken 1908–1989* (Berlin, 1989); R. Osborne, *Conversations with K.* (Oxford, 1989); R. Bachmann, *K.: Notes on a Career* (N.Y., 1991); W. Stresemann, *Ein seltsamer Mann: Erinnerungen am H. v.K.* (Frankfurt am Main, 1991); F. Endler, *K.: Eine Biographie* (Hamburg, 1992); K. Lang, *The K. Dossier* (London and Boston, 1992); B. Wessling, *H. v.K.: Eine kritische Biographie* (Munich, 1994).

Karastoyanov, Assen, Bulgarian composer and teacher; b. Samokov, June 3, 1893; d. Sofia, Sept. 8, 1976. He studied flute at the Sofia Music School (1914–18); subsequently took courses with Juon (harmony) at the Berlin Hochschule für Musik (1921–22), Dukas (composition) at the École Normale de

Musique in Paris (1930–31), and Raphael (composition) at the Leipzig Cons. (1931–32). He taught in Sofia at the Bulgarian State Academy of Music (1933–44), where he was a prof. (1944–58).

WORKS: DRAMATIC: 7 operettas, including *Michel Strogoff*, after Jules Verne (1937–40). **ORCH.:** *A Balkan Suite* (1928); 4 syms.: No. 1, *Miner's Symphony* (1940), No. 2, *Danubian*, for Brass Orch. (1960), No. 3, *Rhodopean* (1973), and No. 4, *Proto-Bulgarian* (1975); Flute Concerto (1959); *A Bogomil Legend* for Strings (1973). **CHAMBER:** 2 string quartets (1937, 1970); 2 suites for Flute and Piano (1955, 1968); *Capriccio* for Violin and Piano (1970). **PIANO:** *Scherzino* (1933); Sonata (1938). **VOCAL:** Cantatas; songs.

Karatygin, Viacheslav (Gavrilovich), Russian writer on music; b. Pavlovsk, Sept. 17, 1875; d. Leningrad, Oct. 23, 1925. He learned to play the piano from his mother, who was a professional pianist, then took courses in physics and mathematics at the Univ. of St. Petersburg (graduated, 1897); subsequently was a chemist in the naval dept. (until 1907); also studied composition with Sokolov at the St. Petersburg Cons. (1897–1902). From 1907 to 1917 he was active as a music critic; also taught aesthetics and music history at the Petrograd Cons. (from 1916), being made a prof. (1919). As a critic, he welcomed the music of Scriabin, Stravinsky, and Prokofiev at a time when most Russian critics regarded them as unacceptable, and he enunciated the idea of a "musical revolution." He publ. monographs on Mussorgsky, Chaliapin, and Scriabin, and also composed some piano pieces and songs.

BIBL.: A. Rimsky-Korsakov et al., eds., *V.G. K.: Zhizn, deyatelnost, stati i materiali* (V.G. K.: Life, Work, Articles, and Materials; Leningrad, 1927).

Karayev, Kara (Abulfazogli), Russian composer; b. Baku, Feb. 5, 1918; d. Moscow, May 13, 1982. He studied piano with Sharoyev at the Baku Music Technical School (1930–35) and then composition with Rudolf at the Azerbaijani Cons.; later took courses in composition with Alexandrov and Shostakovich and instrumentation with Vasilenko at the Moscow Cons. (graduated, 1946). He taught at the Azerbaijani Cons. (from 1946), serving as its director (1949–52). His music is derived mainly from his semi-oriental environment, comprising not only the native Tartar motifs, but also other Asian resources; particularly effective are his theatrical spectacles featuring native dances and choral ensembles.

WORKS: DRAMATIC: OPERA: *Fatherland* (1945). **BALLETS:** *7 Beauties* (1952); *On the Track of Thunder* (1958). **ORCH.:** *Poem of Joy* for Piano and Orch. (1937); 3 syms. (1944, 1946, 1965); *Leyly and Medzhnun*, symphonic poem (1947); *Albanian Rhapsody* (1952); *Don Quixote*, symphonic sketches (1960); Violin Concerto (1967). **OTHER:** Chamber music; piano pieces; oratorio; cantatas; film scores.

BIBL.: L. Karagicheva, *K. K.* (Baku, 1956).

Kardoš, Dezider, Slovak composer; b. Nadlice, Dec. 23, 1914; d. Bratislava, March 18, 1991. He studied composition with Moyzes at the Bratislava Academy of Music (graduated, 1937) and with Novák at the Prague Cons. (1937–39). He worked for the Czech Radio in Prešov (1939–45) and Košice (1945–51); then became a teacher at the Bratislava Academy of Music (1963), being made a prof. in 1968. The thematic sources of his musical inspiration are found in eastern Slovak folklore.

WORKS: ORCH.: 7 syms.: No. 1 (1942), No. 2, *Of Native Land* (1955), No. 3 (1961), No. 4, *Piccola* (1962), No. 5 (1965), No. 6 (1974–75), and No. 7, *Ballade vom Traum*, for Baritone, Chorus, and Orch. (1983–84); 3 overtures: *My Home* (1946), *East Slovak* (1950), and *Res philharmonica* (1970); *Concerto for Orchestra* (1957); *Heroic Ballad* for Strings (1959); Concerto for Strings (1963); Piano Concerto (1969); *Partita* for 12 Strings (1972); *Slovakophonia*, variations on a folk theme (1975–76); Violin Concerto (1980); *Symphonietta* (1988). **CHAMBER:** 4 string quartets (1935, 1966, 1978, 1985); Wind Quintet (1938); *3 Compositions* for Violin and Piano (1966). **KEYBOARD: PIANO:** 2 suites (both 1937); *Bagatelles* (1948). **ORGAN:** *Preludium quasi una fantasia* (1940); *Elevazioni* (1967). **VOCAL:** *Peace Cantata* (1951); *Songs about Life*, cycle of 4 microdramas for Soprano, Tenor, and Orch. (1973–74); choruses; songs.

Kardos, István, Hungarian conductor and composer; b. Debrecen, June 6, 1891; d. Budapest, Dec. 22, 1975. He studied composition with Herzfeld at the Budapest Academy of Music; then was a theater conductor in Hungary, Germany, and Switzerland (1917–46). From 1948 to 1959 he taught at the Budapest Academy of Music.

WORKS: ORCH.: *Dance* (1918); 4 syms. (1919, 1958, 1967, 1968); *Hungarian Scherzo* (1936); Violin Concertino (1947); *Janus* (1950); 2 piano concertos (1956, 1963); Double Bass Concertino (1959); Double Concerto for Viola, Double Bass, and Orch. (1964); *Alliage* for Violin and Chamber Orch. (1966); *Intrada* (1968); *Visitation* (1969). **CHAMBER:** 6 string quartets (1917, 1925, 1951, 1960, 1967, 1971); Viola Sonata (1942); Double Bass Sonata (1949); Flute Sonata (1957); Wind Quintet (1959); String Trio (1960); *Bipartitum* for Bassoon and Piano (1963); Sonata for Solo Clarinet (1965); *Poem and Burlesque* for Double Bass and Piano (1969); 2 sextets for Clarinet, String Quartet, and Piano (1971); *Grotesque* for Octave Flute, Cello, and Double Bass (1971); *Notturno* for Horn, Flute, Violin, and Harp (1971). **PIANO:** Sonata (1916); *Dickens Suite* (1957); *Toccata* (1960); *Variations and Fugue* (1969). **VOCAL:** *Áprilisi hajnal* (Dawn in April), cantata (1950); songs.

Karel, Rudolf, Czech composer; b. Pilsen, Nov. 9, 1880; d. in the concentration camp in Terezín, March 6, 1945. He was the last student of Dvořák, with whom he studied in Prague for 1 year during his term at the Prague Cons. (1901–04). In 1914 he went to Russia as a teacher. After the Revolution, he made his way to Irkutsk, Siberia; during the Russian civil war, he became a member of the Czechoslovak Legion and conducted an orch. organized by the legionnaires. He returned to Prague in 1920; from 1923 to 1941, taught at the Prague Cons. As a member of the Czech resistance in World War II, he was arrested by the Nazis in March 1943; was transferred to Terezín in Feb. 1945, and died there of dysentery shortly before liberation. His music reflects Romantic concepts. He had a predilection for programmatic writing; the national element is manifested by his treatment of old modal progressions; his instrumental writing is rich in sonority and the polyphonic structure is equally strong.

WORKS: DRAMATIC: *Ilseino srdce* (Ilsea's Heart), lyric comedy (1906–09; Prague, Oct. 11, 1924); *Smrt Kmotříčka* (Godmother Death), musical fairy tale (1928–33; Brno, Feb. 3, 1933); *Tři vlasy děda Vševěda* (3 Hairs of the Wise Old Man), musical fairy tale (1944–45; arranged by Z. Vostřak; Prague, Oct. 28, 1948); incidental music. **ORCH.:** Suite (1903–04); *Comedy Overture* (1904–05); *Fantasy* (1905); *The Ideals* (1906–09); 2 syms. (*Renaissance*, 1910–11; *Spring*, 1935–38); *4 Slavonic Dance Moods* (1912); *The Demon* (1918–20); *Capriccio* for Violin and Orch. (1924); *Revolutionary Overture* (1938–41). **CHAMBER:** 3 string quartets (1902–03; 1907–13; 1935–36); Piano Trio (1903–04); Violin Sonata (1912); Nonet for Wind Quintet and String Quartet (1945; completed by F. Hertl). **PIANO:** *5 Pieces* (1902); *Notturno* (1906–07); Sonata (1910); *Thema con variazioni* (1910); *3 Waltzes* (1913); *Burlesques* (1913–14). **VOCAL:** *Vzkříšení* (Resurrection), sym. for Soloists, Chorus, and Orch. (1923–27; Prague, April 9, 1928); *Sladká balada dětská* (Sweet Ballad for a Child) for Soprano, Chorus, and Orch. (1928–30); *Černoch* (A Negro) for Baritone and Orch. or Piano (1934); choruses; songs.

BIBL.: O. Šourek, *R. K.* (Prague, 1947).

Karetnikov, Nikolai, Russian composer; b. Moscow, June 28, 1930; d. there, Oct. 10, 1994. He was a student of Shebalin at the Moscow Cons. (1948–53). He embraced contemporary means of expression in his works, including 12-tone techniques. His advanced scores were not welcomed in official circles, although some of his music was performed abroad. His opera *Til Ulenshpigel* (Till Eulenspiegel; 1985) had to be recorded in secret, which prompted Gerard McBurney on BBC Radio 3 to dub it the first *samizdat* opera. It was finally performed in public in Bielefeld in 1993. He also composed the opera-oratorio *Misteriya apostola Pavla* (The Mystery of St. Paul; 1972–87); ballet music; film scores; 4 syms.; much chamber music; piano pieces.

Karg-Elert (real name, **Karg**), **Sigfrid,** distinguished German organist, pedagogue, and composer; b. Oberndorf am Neckar, Nov. 21, 1877; d. Leipzig, April 9, 1933. (His real name, which means "avaricious," sounded unattractive to his audiences, so he changed it to Karg-Elert.) He was a chorister at St. John in Leipzig, where he received instruction in music from the cantor Rothig. He studied with Homeyer, Jadassohn, Reinecke, and Teichmüller at the Leipzig Cons.; in 1919, joined its faculty. He gave organ recitals, becoming known as a great virtuoso; he also played the Kunstharmonium, for which he wrote many compositions. In 1931–32 he made a concert tour of the U.S. As a composer, he developed a brilliant style, inspired by the music of the Baroque, but he embellished this austere and ornamental idiom with impressionistic devices; the result was an ingratiating type of music with an aura of originality. He publ. *Akustische Ton-, Klang-, und Funktionsbestimmung* (1930) and *Polaristiche Klang- und Tonalitätslehre* (1931). In 1984 the Karg-Elert-Gesellschaft was organized in Heidelberg.

WORKS: KUNSTHARMONIUM: Sets of pieces: *Skizzen* (1903); *Aquarellen* (1906); *Miniaturen* (1908); *Intarsien* (1911); *Impressions* (1914); *Idyllen* (1915); *Innere Stimmen* (1918). **FUNDAMENTAL TECHNICAL WORKS:** *Die Kunst des Registrierens; Die ersten grundlegenden Studien; Hohe Schule des Legatospiels; Die Harmoniumtechnik* (*Gradus ad Parnassum*); *Theoretische-praktische Elementarschule.* **ORGAN:** 66 chorale improvisations (1908–10); 20 chorale preludes and postludes (1912); *10 Poetic Tone Pictures; 3 Pastels, Cathedral Windows* (on Gregorian themes). **OTHER:** Wind Quintet; 2 clarinet sonatas; Sonata for Solo Flute; *Trio bucolico* for Violin, Flute, and Piano; lieder.

BIBL.: A. Eaglefield Hull, "K.-E.," *Musical Times* (Feb.–March 1913); H. Gaul, "Bonnet, Bossi, K.-E.," *Musical Quarterly* (July 1918); P. Schenk, *S. K.-E.* (Berlin, 1927); H. Avril, *S. K.-E.: Kompositions-verzeichnis mit einer monographischen Skizze* (Berlin, 1928); G. Sceats, *The Organ Works of K.-E.* (Orpington, 1940; rev. ed., London, 1950); W. Kwasnik, *S. K.-E.: Sein Leben und Werk in Heutiger Sicht* (Westerwald, 1971); S. Gerlach, *S. K.-E.: Verzeichnis sämtlicher Werke* (Frankfurt am Main, 1984); G. Hartmann, *Die Orgelwerke von S. K.- E.* (Bonn, 1985); A. Hayden, "K.-E. and the Art of Registration," *Musical Times* (Nov. 1987); A. Wollinger, *Die Flötenkompositionen von S. K.-E. (1877–1933)* (Frankfurt am Main, 1991).

Karjalainen, Ahti, Finnish conductor and composer; b. Oulu, March 20, 1907; d. Jyväskylä, Oct. 2, 1986. He studied composition at the Helsinki Cons., the Viipuri Inst., and the Sibelius Academy in Helsinki. After playing violin and trombone in various orchs., he conducted the Jyväskylä City Orch.

WORKS: ORCH.: *Polonaise* for Trombone and Orch. (1935); *Scherzo* for Trumpet, Trombone, and Orch. (1940); Trombone Concerto (1942); *Summer Scenes* for Oboe and Orch. (1944); *Winter Scenes* (1948); Sym. (1948); Concert Suite for Bassoon and Orch. (1949); Duo for 2 Trumpets and Orch. (1950); Violin Concerto (1952); *Ostinato* for Cello and Orch. (1954); 2 cello concertos (1956, 1966). **CHAMBER:** 6 partitas for Various Instrumental Combinations (1936, 1940, 1945, 1961, 1964, 1965); Wind Sextet (1945); solo pieces. **VOCAL:** *The Eagle's Way* for Chorus and Orch. (1965); *Setting Out* for Narrator, Baritone, Mixed Chorus, Men's Chorus, and Orch. (1968); *The Song of Wood,* cantata (1971).

Karkoff, Maurice (Ingvar), prominent Swedish composer and teacher; b. Stockholm, March 17, 1927. He began his training in theory with Blomdahl (1944–47), concurrently studying piano at the Stockholm Musikhögskolan (1945–51) and theory with Larsson (1948–53); later pursued composition studies with Koch in Stockholm, Holmboe in Copenhagen, Jolivet in Paris, and Vogel in Switzerland. He was music critic of the Stockholm daily *Tidningen* (1962–66); in 1965 he became a teacher of theory and composition at the Stockholm Municipal Music Inst. In 1976 he was awarded the City of Stockholm Prize of Honor, and in 1977 was elected a member of the Royal Swedish Academy of Music in Stockholm. In his music, he absorbed many cultures; these are reflected in his compositions, many of which may be described as romantically modernistic and thematically sensitive to exotic resources and coloristic instrumental timbres.

WORKS: CHAMBER OPERA: *Grandskibbutzen* (The Frontier Kibbutz; 1971–72). **ORCH.:** Sinfonietta (1954); Saxophone Concertino (1955); syms.: No. 1 (Bergen, Oct. 22, 1956), No. 2 (1957; Swedish Radio, Jan. 5, 1959), No. 3, *Sinfonia breve* (1958–59; Gavle, Jan. 10, 1960), No. 4 (1963; Stockholm, April 4, 1964), No. 5, *Sinfonia da camera* (Gavle, Nov. 11, 1965), No. 6 (1972–73; Stockholm, Oct. 12, 1974), No. 7, *Sinfonia da camera* (1975), No. 8 (1979–80), *Short Symphony* for Symphonic Band (1980–81; Stockholm, Sept. 27, 1982), *Dolorous Symphony* for Strings (1981–82); *Sinfonia piccola* (1982–83), No. 10 (1984–85); *Little Symphony* (1987), and No. 11, *Sinfonia della vita* (1993–94); Violin Concerto (1956); Piano Concerto (1957); Cello Concerto (1957–58); Trombone Concerto (1958); Horn Concerto (1959); *9 Aphoristic Variations* (1959); Clarinet Concerto (1959); Variations (1961); *Serenata* for Chamber Orch. (1961); *Suite* for Harpsichord and Strings (1962); *Concerto da camera* for Balalaika and Orch. (1962–63); *Concerto for Orchestra* (1963); *Oriental Pictures* (1965–66; also for Piano); *Transfigurate mutate* (1966); *Tripartita* (1966–67); *Textum* for Strings (1967); *Metamorphoses* (1967); *Sinfonietta grave* (1968–69); *Epitaphium* for Small Chamber Orch. (1968; also for Nonet); *5 Summer Scenes* (1969); *Triptyk* (1970); *Partes caracteris* (1971); *Symphonic Reflexions* (1971); *Passacaglia* for Strings (1971); Trumpet Concerto (1977); *Tre colori* for Strings (1978); *Textur* (1978); *Tre schizzi da Capri* for Small Orch. (1979–80); *Musica seria* for Flute, Harpsichord, and Strings (1980); *Fantasia* (1988); *4 Sketches* for Strings (1990); Concerto for Bassoon and Strings (1990); Concerto for Tuba and Strings (1991); *Concertino lirico* for Flute and Strings (1992). **CHAMBER:** Flute Sonata (1953); Cello Sonata (1954–55); Violin Sonata (1956); Wind Quintet (1956–57); 2 string quartets (1957, 1984); Quartet for 2 Trumpets, Horn, and Trombone (1958); Trio for Violin, Viola, and Cello (1960); *Chamber Concerto* for 14 Winds, Timpani, Percussion, and String Basses (1961); *Metamorphoses* for 4 Horns (1966); *Terzetto* for Flute, Cello, and Piano (1967); *Epitafium* for Flute, Oboe, Clarinet, Bassoon, Horn, and String Quartet (1968); *4 parte* for 13 Brasses and Percussion (1968); *Epitafium* for Accordion, Electric Guitar, and Percussion (1970); *Characters* for Wind Quintet, Trombone, Euphonium, and Percussion (1973–74); *Quasi una marcia* for 2 Wind Quintets and Percussion (1974); *Serenata* for Flute or Alto Flute and Piano (1975–76); *Ernst und Spass* for Saxophone Quartet (1984); *Profilen* for Alto and Baritone Saxophones (1984); *Reflexionen* for Saxophone Quartet (1986); *Ballata quasi una fantasia* for Baritone Saxophone and Piano (1988); *Poem* for Clarinet, Viola, Alto Saxophone, and Piano (1988); *5 Poems* for English Horn and Piano (1991). **PIANO:** Sonata (1956); *Partita piccola* (1958); *Capriccio on Football* (1961; a musical report on a football game); *Monopartita* (1969); *3 Expressions* for 2 Pianos (1971); *3 Nocturnes* (1974); *Femton albumblad* (1988–89); *Fantasia* for Piano, Left-hand (1992). **VOCAL:** *6 Serious Songs* for Low Voice and Orch. (1955); *6 Allvarliga Songs* for High Voice and Orch. (1955); *Det Svenska Landet,* cantata for Baritone, Men's Chorus, and Orch. (1956); *Livet* (Life) for Alto and Orch. (1959); *10 Japanese Songs* for High Voice and Piano or Orch. (1959); *Gesang des Abgeschiedenen,* 5 romances for Baritone and Piano or Orch. (1959); *Himmel och Jord,* cantata (1960); *6 Nocturnes* for Soprano, Flute, Violin, Viola, and Guitar (1963); *Sju rosor senare* for Reciter, Speaking Chorus, Mixed Chorus, and Orch. (1964); *Jeremiah* for Reciter, Baritone, Speaking Chorus, Men's Chorus, and Orch. (1965); *Das ist sein Erlauten,* cantata (1965);

Landschaft aus Schreien for Soprano, Reciter, Oboe or Oboe d'amore or English Horn, 2 Clarinets, Double Bass, and Harp, after Nelly Sachs (1967); *6 Chinese Impressions* for Soprano, Flute, Oboe, Clarinet, Cello, and Percussion (1973); *Varsel och aningar* for High Voice, Winds, and Percussion (1975); *Voices from the Past: Songs to 7 Korean Poems* for Contralto or Baritone and Small String Orch. (1981); *Karlak och var i japan* for 5 Women's Voices, Flute or Alto Flute or Piccolo, Clarinet or Bass Clarinet, Guitar, and 2 Percussion (1986–87); *Ljus och mörker*, cantata (1991); *Herren är min herde*, cantata for Reciter, Soloists, Chorus, 4 Winds, and 3 Percussion (1992–93); choruses; many other songs.

Karkoschka, Erhard, German composer, conductor, and pedagogue; b. Moravská Ostrava, Czechoslovakia, March 6, 1923. He studied composition with Marx at the Stuttgart Hochschule für Musik (1946–53) and musicology with Gerstenberg and Reichert at the Univ. of Tübingen (Ph.D., 1959, with a diss. on Webern's early compositional techniques). He was conductor of the orch. and choir at the Univ. of Hohenheim (1948–68), and in 1958 joined the faculty of the Stuttgart Hochschule für Musik, where he became a prof. in 1964 and director of its electronic music studio in 1973; he retired in 1987. He also founded its Ensemble for New Music (1962), which became an independent ensemble in 1976 under the name Contact-Ensemble. From 1974 to 1980 he was president of the Gesellschaft für Neue Musik. In 1987 he was elected a member of the Free Academy of the Arts in Mannheim. He adoped Webern's serial method of composition, often incorporating electronics and also occasionally resorting to graphic notation in order to achieve greater freedom of resulting sonorities; in his desire to unite the arts, he created various pieces of music sculpture.

WRITINGS: *Das Schriftbild der neuen Musik* (1965; Eng. tr., 1972, as *Notations of New Music*); *Analyse neuer Musik* (1976); *Neue Musik-Hören-Verstehen* (1978); with H. Haas, *Hörererziehung mit neuer Musik* (1982).

WORKS: CHAMBER OPERA: *Orpheus? Oder Hadeshöhe* (1990–92). **ORCH.:** Concertino for Chamber Orch. (1952); *Symphonische Evolution aus zwei eigenen Themen* (1953); *Streichersonate* (1954); Little Concerto for Violin and Chamber Orch. (1955); *Polphone Studie* for Orch. and Piano obbligato (1956); *Symphonia choralis über "Veni Sancte Spiritus"* for Wind Orch. (1957); *Undarum continuum* (1960); *vier stufen* (1965); *Variationen zu keinem Originalthema und aus diesem heraus* (1974); *Teleologies* (1978); *Entfalten* for Clarinet, Cello, Percussion, Piano, and Orch. (1982–83); *Kammermusik* (1983–84). **CHAMBER:** String Quartet (1952); *Divertimento* for Wind Quintet (1952); *Festmusik* for 6 Winds (1954); *quattrologe* for String Quartet (1966); *antinomie* for Wind Quintet (1969); *tempora mutantur* for String Quartet (1971); *kammerkitsch* for Soprano, Tenor, Bass, 3 Instruments, and Tape (1974); *CHRONOS II: Komposition-Improvisation* for 4 Instruments (1975); *im dreieck* for 3 Flutes or Flute and Stereo Sound System (1975); *links und rechts*, march for Flute, 2 Microphones, Amplifier, and Loudspeaker (1976); *Spiralend I* and *II* for 15 Flutes or 3 Flutes and Tape (1980); *Aus einer Figur* for 3 Flutes or 3 Flutes and Tape (1982); *Bläsergedichte* for Woodwind Quintet (1987); *Nach Paul Celan* for Speaker, Guitar, Flute, Clarinet, Marimba, Viola, and Cello (1988); *Klangzeitspektakel* for String Quartet, Computer, and Projection (1988); *Zeitvariation* for Cello (1993); keyboard music. **ELECTRONIC:** *Drei Bilder aus der Offenbarung des Johannes* (1960); *LSD* (1973); *Improvisation* (1974); *CHRONOS I* (1975) and *V* (1976); *Gag-Montagen* (1977); *Meditationsmühle I* and *II* (both 1982); *Zeitmosaik I* (1985); *Skulpturmusik* (1985); multimedia creations; *Geburtztaxtextelein*, word-music score (1989); etc.

Karlins, M(artin) William, American composer and teacher; b. N.Y., Feb. 25, 1932. He studied in N.Y. with Frederick Piket (1954–57), Gianinni at the Manhattan School of Music (1958–61), and with Wolpe (1960–61) before completing his training with Bezanson and Hervig at the Univ. of Iowa (1963–65; Ph.D., 1965). He taught at Western Illinois Univ. in Macomb (1965–67), and then was a teacher (1967–73) and later (from 1973) a prof. at Northwestern Univ. in Evanston.

WORKS: ORCH.: *Concert Music I* (1959), *III* (1963–64), *IV* (1964), and *V* (1972–73); *Reflux*, concerto for Amplified Double Bass and Solo Wind Ensemble, Piano, and Percussion (1971–72); Sym. No. 1 (1979–80); *Catena I* for Little Orch. and Clarinet Obbligato (1980–81) and *III*, horn concerto (1983); Alto Saxophone Concerto (1981–82); *Elegy* (1992). **BAND:** *Passacaglia and Rounds* (1970). **CHAMBER:** Concerto grosso I for 9 Instruments (1959–60) and II for 7 Instruments (1961); String Quartet (1960); *Birthday Music I* for Flute, Bass Clarinet, and Double Bass (1962) and *II* for Flute and Double Bass (1963); String Trio (1962–63); *Little Pieces* for 4 Double Basses (1962); *4 Inventions and a Fugue* for Bassoon, Piano, and Optional Woman's Voice (1962); *Solo Piece with Passacaglia* for Clarinet (1964); *Variations on "Obiter dictum"* for Cello, Piano, and Percussion (1965); *Blues* for Saxophone Quartet (1965); *Music* for Oboe, Bass Clarinet, and Piano (1966); *Music for Cello Alone I* (1966) and *II* (1969); 3 saxophone quartets (1966–67; 1975; 1992–93); *Music* for English Horn and Piano (1968); *Music* for Alto Saxophone and Piano (1968); *Music* for Tenor Saxophone and Piano (1969); *Graphic Mobile* for Any 3 or Multiples of 3 Instruments (1969); 2 woodwind quintets (1970; 1977–78); *Celebration* for Flute, Oboe, and Harpsichord (1970); *Fantasia on My Mother's Name* for Flute (1971); Quintet for Alto Saxophone and String Quartet (1973–74); *Infinity* for Oboe d'Amore, Clarinet, Viola, and Woman's Voice (1978); *Fantasia* for Tenor Saxophone and Percussion (1978–79); *Fanfare with Fugato* for Cello, 2 Trumpets, and 2 Trombones (1981); *Catena II* for Soprano Saxophone and Brass Quintet (1982); *Chameleon* for Harpsichord (1984); *Impromptu* for Alto Saxophone and Organ or Electric Keyboard or Piano (1985–86); *Seasons* for Saxophone (1987); *Saxtuper* for Alto or Soprano Saxophone, Tuba, and Percussion (1989); *Introduction and Passacaglia* for 2 Saxophones and Piano (1990); *Nostalgie* for Saxophone Ensemble (1991); *Under and Over* for Flute or Alto Flute and Contrabass (1994). **KEYBOARD: PIANO:** 3 sonatas (1959, 1962, 1965); *Outgrowths-Variations* (1961); *Suite of Preludes* (1988). **ORGAN:** *Obiter dictum* (1964). **VOCAL:** *Children's Bedtime Songs* for Chorus (1955); *3 Love Songs* for Men's Chorus (1957); *Concert Music II* for Chorus and Orch. (1960); Song for Soprano, Alto Flute, and Cello (1963); *3 Poems* for Chorus (1966); *3 Songs* for Soprano, Flute, and Piano (1967); *Lamentations: In Memoriam* for Speaker and Chamber Ensemble (1968); *Returning the Scroll to the Arc* for Cantor and Organ (1985); *Looking Out My Window* for Treble Chorus and Viola (1990).

Karpath, Ludwig, Austrian singer and music critic; b. Budapest, April 27, 1866; d. Vienna, Sept. 8, 1936. He was a pupil at the Budapest Cons.; studied singing in Vienna; was a member of the National Opera Co. in the U.S. (singing minor bass roles; 1886–88). Returning to Vienna, he became an influential music critic; wrote for the *Neues Wiener Tageblatt* (1894–1921). He publ. *Siegfried Wagner als Mensch und Künstler* (1902) and *Richard Wagner, der Schuldenmacher* (1914).

Kárpáti, János, distinguished Hungarian musicologist; b. Budapest, July 11, 1932. He studied musicology with Kodály, Szabolcsi, and Bartha at the Franz Liszt Academy of Music in Budapest, then was an ed. with the music dept. of the Hungarian Radio (1957–59) and music producer with the Hungaroton Record Co. (1959–61). In 1961 he was named chief librarian of the Liszt Academy. He obtained his degree of Candidate of Sciences in 1968 and his Ph.D. in 1969 with the diss. *Bartók vonósnegyesi* (publ. in Budapest, 1967; rev. ed., 1976, as *Bartók' kamarazenéje*; Eng. tr., 1975, as *Bartók's String Quartets*; rev. and aug. ed., 1993, as *Bartók's Chamber Music*). His books include *Domenico Scarlatti* (Budapest, 1959); *Arnold Schönberg* (Budapest, 1963); *Kelet zenéje* (Music of the Orient; Budapest, 1981). He compiled the 2nd and 4th vols. for an encyclopedic ed., *Muzsikáló zenetörténet* (History of Music). In 1981 he was guest lecturer at Harvard Univ.; in 1982 he was a delegate at the Bartók Memorial Conference in Bloomington, Ind., and in 1983 was a guest lecturer at the Univ. of Calif. at Los Angeles, at North Texas State Univ. in Denton, and at the Univ. of Texas in Austin.

Karpeles, Maud, English ethnomusicologist; b. London, Nov. 12, 1885; d. there, Oct. 1, 1976. She was educated in England and Germany. She was associated with Cecil Sharp in collecting and organizing English folk songs (from 1909); in 1914 she visited the U.S., where she assembled American songs of English origin. She founded the International Folk Music Council (1947), and ed. its journal (1949–63). She was made an Officer of the Order of the British Empire in 1961. With Sharp, she publ. the collections *English Folk Songs from the Southern Appalachians* (London, 1917; 3rd ed., 1960) and *The Country Dance Book*, V (London, 1918); her own collections included *The Lancashire Morris Dance Tunes* (London, 1930), *Folk Songs from Newfoundland* (London, 1934; 2nd ed., aug., 1971), and *Cecil Sharp's Collection of English Folk Songs* (London, 1973). She also publ. *Cecil Sharp* (with A.H. Fox Strangways; London, 1932; 2nd ed., 1955; rev. ed., 1967, as *Cecil Sharp: His Life and Work*), *Folk Songs of Europe* (London, 1956), and *An Introduction to English Folk Song* (London, 1973).

BIBL.: W. Rhodes, "Memorial Obituary: M. K. 1885–1976," *Ethnomusicology* (May 1977).

Karpman, Laura, American composer; b. Los Angeles, March 1, 1959. She studied with Bolcom and Bassett at the Univ. of Mich. (B.M., 1983), Harbison at Tanglewood (1984), and Babbitt at the Juilliard School in N.Y. (M.M., 1983; D.M., 1985). She taught at the Manhattan School of Music (1985–87), the New School for Social Research (1986–87), and Whittier (Calif.) College (from 1989). Her compositions are vaguely surrealistic, and include *Matisse and Jazz* for Soprano, Piano, Percussion, and Saxophone (1987), *Portrait of Jaco* for Violin, Viola, Cello, Double Bass, and Piano (1988), and *Caprices* for String Trio (1990).

Karr, Gary (Michael), outstanding American double bass player; b. Los Angeles, Nov. 20, 1941. He was born into a family of double bass players, and at 8 began formal lessons with Uda Demonstein. He gained experience by playing in local synagogues; subsequently took cello lessons with Herman Reinshagen, Gabor Rejto at the Univ. of Southern Calif. in Los Angeles, and Stuart Sankey at the Juilliard School of Music in N.Y.; he also was a scholarship student at the Aspen (Colo.) Music School. In 1962 he made his N.Y. recital debut and in 1964 he toured Europe. He founded the International Inst. for the String Bass in 1967 and subsequently taught in the U.S. and Canada. His instrument, the 1611 Amati, was once owned by Koussevitzky and was given to Karr by Koussevitzky's widow. Karr's career was the subject of the BBC-TV documentary "Amazing Bass" (1985). In addition to performing the Classical repertoire, he has done much to enlarge the literature for his instrument by commissioning works from Henze, Schuller, Wilder, Arnold, and other composers; he also includes in his repertoire folk-inspired pieces, as well as modern rock and dance forms.

BIBL.: A. Angarano, "Romancing the Doublebass with G. K.," *Musical America* (Nov. 1987); H. Waleson, "Virtuoso Bassist G. K.," *Ovation* (March 1988).

Kars, Jean-Rodolphe, Austrian pianist; b. Calcutta, March 15, 1947. He studied with Jeanne Manchon-Theist and Katchen at the Paris Cons. (1958–64); made his London recital debut in 1967, and subsequently pursued an international career as a soloist. He champions the music of Messiaen, and excels as an interpreter of Mozart, Schubert, Liszt, Debussy, and Ravel.

Karyotakis, Theodore, Greek composer; b. Argos, July 21, 1903; d. Athens, June 14, 1978. He studied with Mitropoulos (composition) and Varvoglis (counterpoint and orchestration) in Athens; concurrently was enrolled in the law dept. of the Univ. of Athens. He wrote music in a neo-Romantic vein, permeated with euphonious dissonances; several of his works are inspired by Greek folk modes.

WORKS: OPERA: *Tou fengariou louloudi* (Flower of the Moon; 1953–55). **ORCH.:** *Rhapsody* for Violin and Orch. (1940); *Epic Song* (1944); *Concerto for Orchestra* (1967); Sym. (1974). **CHAMBER:** 2 violin sonatas (1945, 1955); String Trio (1949); String Quartet, with Voice (1963); *11 Sketches* for Flute and Viola (1963); *9 Inventions* for Violin and Piano (1966); Trio for Clarinet, Viola, and Piano (1969); Duo for Flute and Clarinet (1969); *Music* for Flute, Clarinet, Horn, and Bassoon (1973); numerous piano pieces. **VOCAL:** *6 Erotic Songs* for Voice, Flute, and Harp (1948); *Serenities*, 10 songs for Voice, Clarinet, Celesta, Strings, and Percussion (1962); songs.

Kasemets, Udo, Estonian-born Canadian conductor, composer, and teacher; b. Tallinn, Nov. 16, 1919. He studied at the Tallinn Cons., the Stuttgart Staatliche Hochschule für Musik, and the Darmstadt Kranichstein Institut; also took conducting courses with Scherchen. He emigrated to Canada in 1951, becoming a naturalized Canadian citizen in 1957. In addition to his work as a conductor and composer, he was music critic for the *Toronto Daily Star* (1959–63); was on the faculty of the dept. of experimental art at the Ontario College of Art (1971–87). His early music is set in peaceful Romantic modalities with Estonian undertones, but soon he espoused serialism and the pantheatricalism of the most uninhibited avant-garde.

WORKS: *Estonian Suite* for Chamber Orch. (1950); *Sonata da camera* for Solo Cello (1955); Violin Concerto (1956); String Quartet (1957); *Logos* for Flute and Piano (1960); *Haiku* for Voice, Flute, Cello, and Piano (1961); *Squares* for Piano, 4-hands (1962); $\sqrt{5}$ for 2 Performers on 2 Pianos and Percussion (1962–63); *Trigon* for 1, 3, 9, or 27 Performers, a multidimensional score with thematic information provided by a deoxyribonucleic matrix (1963; 11 subsequent versions, 1964–66); *Communications*, noncomposition to words by e.e. cummings, a cybernetic manifestation for Singular or Plural Singers, Speakers, Instrumentalists, or Dancers, of an indeterminate duration (1963); *Cumulus* for Any Solo Instrument or Ensemble, and 2 Tape Recorders, the score consisting of 9 segments to be played in any order (1963–64; 2 later versions, 1966, 1968); *Calceolaria*, time/space variations on a floral theme, for Any Number of Performers (1966; version for 4-channel Tape, 1967); *Contactics*, choreography for Musicians and Audience (1966); *Variations on Variations on Variations* for Singers, Instrumentalists, and 4 Loudspeakers (1966); *Quartets of Quartets*, 4 separate works for varying ensembles of Readers, Tape, Calibrators, Wind-bells, Wind Generators, Opaque Projectors, and Any Other Sound-producing Media: *Music for Nothing, Music for Anything (Wordmusic), Music for Something (Windmusic)*, and *Music for Everything* (all 1971–72); *Music(s) for John Cage*, incorporating *Guitarmusic for John Cage* for Any Number of Guitars, Projections, and Dimmers, *Voicemusic for John Cage* for Any Number of Voices, *Saladmusic for John Cage* for Any Number of Salad Makers, and *Walking/Talking* for Any Number of Walkers/Talkers (all 1972); *Time-Space Interface* for Any Number of Participants and Any Media, in both indoor and outdoor versions (1971–73); *Quadraphony (Music of the Quarter of the Moon of the Lunar Year)*, an acoustical/architectural time/space exploration project (1972–73); *La Crasse du tympan* for Record/Tape Mix (1973); *WATEARTHUNDAIR: Music of the 10th Moon of the Year of the Dragon*, a nature-sound-mix with verbal and visual commentary (1976); *KANADANAK*, a "celebration of our land and its people . . ." for Readers, Drummers, and Audience participation (1976–77); *Counterbomb Renga*, spectacle by about 100 poets and musicians, protesting against the proliferation of nuclear weapons, conceived and coordinated by Kasemets (CBC, April 3, 1983); *Yi Jing Jitterbug: 50 Hz Octet* for 8 Winds and/or Bowed Strings (1984); *Duchampera*, music theater for Singers, Speakers, Actors, Glass Orch., Piano, Sound-playback, and Lighting Systems (1987); *Vertical Music: In Remembrance of Morton Feldman* for Any 7 Instruments (1987); a series entitled *Portrait: Music of the 12 Moons of the I Ching* for Various Instruments (1988).

Kashkashian, Kim, American violist of Armenian descent; b. Detroit, Aug. 31, 1952. She studied with Trampler (1969–70) and Karen Tuttle (1970–75) at the Peabody Cons. of Music in Baltimore; after winning several competitions, she was a soloist with major American and European orchs. She taught at the New School of Music in Philadelphia (1981–86), the Mannes College of Music in N.Y. (1983–86), the Indiana Univ. School of Music in Bloomington (1985–87), and the Freiburg im Breisgau Hochschule für Musik (from 1989). She has done much to promote contemporary music, commissioning many works for viola.

Kasianov, Alexander, Russian composer; b. Bolobonovo, near Nizhny-Novgorod, Aug. 29, 1891; d. there (Gorky), Feb. 13, 1982. He studied composition with Sokolov at the Petrograd Cons. (graduated, 1917); also studied piano with Liapunov. In 1918 he went to Nizhny-Novgorod, where he organized radio broadcasts; in 1951 he joined the faculty of the Cons. In his compositions, he continued the tradition of early Russian music; his many choral works are quite effective.

WORKS: OPERAS: *Stepan Razin* (Gorky, Oct. 29, 1939; rev. version, Gorky, Nov. 14, 1953); *A Partisan Girl* (1941); *On Far North* (1947); *Ermak* (1957). **ORCH.:** *Overture on Russian Themes* (1943). **PIANO:** 7 sonatas; 24 preludes. **VOCAL:** Numerous choruses and songs.

BIBL.: N. Ugrumov, *A. K.* (Moscow, 1957).

Kašlík, Václav, Czech conductor, opera producer, and composer; b. Polička, Sept. 28, 1917; d. Prague, June 4, 1989. He took courses in theory and aesthetics at the Charles Univ. in Prague (1936–39); received training in composition with Karel and A. Hába and in conducting with Doležil and Dědeček at the Prague Cons. (1936–40), completing his studies in conducting in Talich's master classes there (1940–42). From 1941 to 1944 he was assistant director of the National Theater in Prague. He was principal conductor and opera producer in Brno (1944–45). Upon returning to Prague, he was director of the 5th of May Theater (1945–48); subsequently was an opera producer and conductor with the National Theater; also conducted at the Smetana Theater (1952–62). In addition to his long association with the National Theater, he was a guest producer in Leningrad, Moscow, Milan, Vienna, London, Geneva, Verona, and Houston. In 1956 he was awarded the Klement Gottwald State Prize and in 1958 was made an Honored Artist by the Czech government. His productions were noteworthy for their use of film, experimental lighting, stereophonic sound, and other modern innovations.

WORKS: DRAMATIC: OPERAS: *Zbojnická balada* (The Brigand's Ballad; 1939–42; Prague, June 17, 1948; rev. 1978; Prague, Oct. 2, 1986); *Křížova cesta* (The Way of the Cross; 1941–45; unfinished); *Krakatit* (Czech TV, March 5, 1961); *La strada* (1980; Prague, Jan. 13, 1982); *Krysar* (Pied Piper; 1983; Plzeň, Oct. 27, 1984). **BALLETS:** *Don Juan* (1940); *Janošík* (1950); *Pražský karneval* (1954). Also film scores. **ORCH.:** *Vesnicka symfonie* (1955); *Slavnostic*, symphonic triptych (1981). **CHAMBER:** String Quartet (1938). **VOCAL:** *Dramatic Cantata* (1944).

Kasparov, Yuri, Armenian composer; b. Moscow, June 8, 1955. He began his music training in childhood. He studied at the Moscow Power Inst. (1972–78), qualifying as an engineer. After further training at a music college (1978–80), he studied with Tchulaki at the Moscow Cons. (1980–84), where he later pursued postgraduate studies with Denisov (1989–91). In 1984 he joined the Central Studio of Documentary Films in Moscow, where he was ed.-in-chief from 1985 to 1989; was also founder-artistic director of the Moscow Contemporary Music Ensemble from 1990, with which he presented many modern works. In 1985 his first Sym., *Guernica*, won 1st prize in the All-Union Composers Competition. In 1989 his *Ave Maria* for 12 Voices, Violin, Vibraphone, and Organ received 1st prize in the Guido d'Arezzo International Composers Competition in Italy. In his works, Kasparov follows an advanced course reflective of contemporary trends.

WORKS: MONOOPERA: *Nevermore* (1991). **ORCH.:** 2 syms.: No. 1, *Guernica* (1984; Moscow, June 29, 1994) and No. 2, *Kreutzer* (Yaroslavl, Jan. 30, 1987); *Lincos* (1988; Norrköping, April 3, 1990); Oboe Concerto (1988; Moscow, Nov. 30, 1991); *Diffusion* (1988; Cheliabinsk, May 22, 1989); *Silencium*, chamber sym. (1989; Moscow, April 27, 1990); *Devil's Trills* for Chamber Orch. (Moscow, Dec. 14, 1990); *Over Eternal Peace*, chamber concerto for Bassoon and 14 Players (Zürich, Nov. 14, 1992); *Concerto for Orchestra* (1993). **CHAMBER:** *Epitaph in Memory of Alban Berg* for Oboe, Violin, Harp, and Percussion (1988); *Invention* for String Quartet (Moscow, Oct. 19, 1989); *Notturno* for Clarinet, Violin, and Piano (1989; Cologne, Sept. 15, 1991); *Sonata-Infernale* for Bassoon (1989; Frankfurt am Main, Aug. 14, 1992); *Sketch of Picture with Collage* for Violin, Trumpet, and Piano (1990); *Variations* for Clarinet and Piano (1990); *Cantus firmus* for Violin (1990); *Credo* for Organ (1990); *Postludio* for Harp (1990); *Landscape Fading Into Infinity* for Clarinet, Violin, Cello, and Piano (1991; Frankfurt am Main, Sept. 24, 1992); *Goat's Song* for Bassoon, Double Bass, and Percussion (1991; Valencia, May 8, 1994); *Chaconne* for Bassoon, Cello, and Electronics (1992; Paris, Feb. 15, 1993); *Schoenberg's Space* for Violin, Cello, and Piano (Hamburg, Nov. 14, 1993); *Game of Gale* for Tenor Saxophone, Marimba, and Piano (1994); *Briefly About Serious Matters* for Trombone and Organ (1994). **VOCAL:** *Ave Maria* for 12 Soloists, Violin, Organ, and Vibraphone (1989; Moscow, Nov. 18, 1990); *Stabat Mater* for Soprano and String Quartet (1991).

Kassern, Tadeusz (Zygfrid), Polish-born American composer; b. Lemberg, March 19, 1904; d. N.Y., May 2, 1957. He studied composition with Soltys and piano with Lalewicz at the Lwow Cons.; later with Opienski and Brzostowski at the Poznań Cons. (1922–26); also studied law. He went to Paris (1931), then was made cultural attaché at the Polish Consulate in N.Y. (1945). He broke with the Communist government in Poland, and remained in N.Y.; became a naturalized American citizen in 1956. As a composer, he pursued a cosmopolitan trend; although many of his works are inspired by Polish folk music, the idiom and the method are of a general European modern character.

WORKS: OPERAS: *The Anointed* (1949–51); *Sun-Up* (1952; N.Y., Nov. 10, 1954); *Comedy of the Dumb Wife* (1953); *Eros and Psyche* (1954; unfinished). **ORCH.:** Flute Concerto (1934); *Dies irae*, symphonic poem in memory of Marshal Pilsudski (1935; not extant); Concertino for Oboe and Strings (1936–37; rev. 1946); Double Bass Concerto (1937); Concerto for Strings (1944); Concertino for Flute, Strings, Xylophone, and Celesta (1948); *Teen-Age Concerto* for Piano and Orch. (1952; N.Y., May 1956). **OTHER:** Chamber music; piano pieces; choruses; songs.

Kastalsky, Alexander (Dmitrievich), Russian choral conductor and composer; b. Moscow, Nov. 28, 1856; d. there, Dec. 17, 1926. He was a pupil of Tchaikovsky, Taneyev, and Hubert at the Moscow Cons. (1875–81). In 1887 he joined the faculty of Moscow's Synodal School; in 1910 he was appointed director of the school and principal conductor of the choir. In 1911 he took the choir on an extended European tour. In 1918 the Synodal School became a choral academy; in 1923 it merged with the Moscow Cons. Kastalsky was also a teacher of conducting at the Moscow Phil. Inst. (1912–22); in 1923, was appointed prof. of choral singing at the Moscow Cons. He wrote *Osobennosti narodno-russkoy muzikalnoy sistemï* (Peculiarities of the Russian Folk Music System; Moscow and Petrograd, 1923; 2nd ed., 1961); V. Belaiev ed. his *Osnovï narodnovo mnogogolosiya* (Principles of Folk Polyphony; Moscow and Leningrad, 1948). He also wrote the article "My Musical Career and My Thoughts on Church Music," *Musical Quarterly* (April 1925). He was a notable composer of Russian sacred music, into which he introduced modern elements, combining them with the ancient church modes.

WORKS: DRAMATIC: *Clara Militch*, opera (1907); incidental music. **ORCH.:** *Pictures of Russian Festivities* (1912); *A Marketplace in Ancient Russia* (1924); *Rustic Symphony* (Moscow, Dec. 13, 1925). **VOCAL:** *Brotherly Prayer for the Dead* for Soloist, Chorus, and 17 Instruments (1916); *To Lenin: At His*

Graveside for Reciter, Chorus, and Orch. (1924; perf. at Lenin's funeral); cantatas; numerous choral pieces. **OTHER:** Various editions and arrangements, folk-song collections, etc.

BIBL.: W. Print, "K. and Russian Folk Polyphony," *Music & Letters* (Oct. 1929).

Kastle, Leonard (Gregory), American composer and pianist; b. N.Y., Feb. 11, 1929. After attending the Juilliard School of Music in N.Y. (1938–40), he received training in piano from Sheridan and in composition from Szell at the Mannes College of Music in N.Y. (1940–42); then studied piano with Wittgenstein and Vengerova; also held scholarships in composition with Scalero, Menotti, and Barber at the Curtis Inst. of Music in Philadelphia (1944–50; B.A., 1950); he further attended Columbia Univ. (1947–50), and was a student in conducting with Bamberger in N.Y. (1950–52). He was a visiting prof. of humanities and fine arts at the State Univ. of N.Y. at Albany (1978–88).

WORKS: DRAMATIC: OPERAS: *The Swing* (1954; NBC-TV, June 11, 1956); *Deseret* (1960; NBC-TV, Jan. 1, 1961; rev. for Voices, Piano, and Organ, 1978); *The Pariahs* (1962–66); *The Calling of Mother Ann* (Hancock Shaker Village, Mass., June 21, 1985); *The Journey of Mother Ann* (1986–87; Albany, N.Y., Jan. 22, 1987); *Professor Lookalike and the Children* (1988; Albany, N.Y., May 8, 1989); *The Countess Cathleen* (1995). **PLAY WITH MUSIC:** *The Birdwatchers* (1980–81). **ORCH.:** Piano Concerto (Albany, N.Y., Feb. 14, 1981, composer soloist). **CHAMBER:** Piano Sonata (1950); Violin Sonata (1955; rev. version, Albany, N.Y., March 17, 1986); Piano Suite (1957). **VOCAL:** *From a Whitman Reader* for Voice and Orch. (1954); *3 Walt Whitman Songs* for Chorus (1956); *Acquainted with the Night*, song cycle, after Robert Frost (1957); *3 Songs from Moby Dick* for Chorus (1963); *Pontoosuc* for Baritone and Orch. (1974–75; Tanglewood, July 4, 1976); *Mass* for Chorus, Organ, and Piano (PBS, Dec. 25, 1977; rev. version, Albany, N.Y., May 30, 1978).

Kastner, Alfred, Austrian harpist, composer, and teacher; b. Vienna, March 10, 1870; d. Los Angeles, May 24, 1948. He studied harp with Antonio Zamara at the Vienna Cons. (1882–88), then was 1st harp in the orchs. of the Warsaw Opera (1890) and the Budapest Opera (from 1893); was also active as a teacher. He was 1st harp in the Philadelphia Orch. (1901–02; 1903–04); also toured Europe as a soloist. After playing in the Queen's Hall Orch. (1904–14) and teaching at the Royal Academy of Music (1909–13) in London, he joined the N.Y. Phil.; then was 1st harp in the Los Angeles Phil. (1919–36). He wrote several works for harp and made various arrangements.

BIBL.: M. Cambern, "A. K., Man, Musician, Pedagogue," *Harp News*, 1/10 (1954); A. Stockton, "A. K.," *American Harp Journal*, 1/4 (1968).

Kastner, (Macario) Santiago, distinguished English pianist, harpsichordist, and musicologist; b. London, Oct. 15, 1908; d. Lisbon, May 12, 1992. He studied in London and Amsterdam, then took courses with Hans Beltz (piano), Ramin (harpsichord), Hans Prüfner (musicology), and Friedrich Högner (theory) in Leipzig; completed his studies with Juan Gilbert Camins (harpsichord and clavichord) and Anglès (musicology) in Barcelona. He settled in Lisbon in 1933; taught at the Cons. there (from 1947). He was an authority on Hispanic keyboard music; in addition to writing several important books, he ed. works by Portuguese and Spanish composers.

WRITINGS: *Música hispanica: O estilo do P.M. Rodrigues Coelho: A interpretação de música hispanica para tecla desde 1450 ate 1650* (Lisbon, 1936); *Contribución al estudio de la música española y portuguesa* (Lisbon, 1941); *Carlos Seixas* (Coimbra, 1947); *Federico Mompou* (Madrid, 1947); *Antonio und Hernando de Cabezón: Eine Chronik dargestellt am Leben zweier Generationen von Organisten* (Tutzing, 1977); *The Interpretation of 16th- and 17th-century Iberian Keyboard Music* (Stuyvesant, N.Y., 1987).

Kastorsky, Vladimir (Ivanovich), Russian bass; b. Bolshive Soly, March 14, 1871; d. Leningrad, July 2, 1948. He studied with Cotogni and Gabel. He made his debut with Champagner's touring opera company (1894); became a member of the Maryinsky Theater in St. Petersburg (1899) and later sang with Zimin's opera company in Moscow; also appeared in Diaghilev's Russian Seasons in Paris and London (1907–08); concurrently formed a vocal quartet specializing in Russian folk songs, with which he toured abroad. He remained on the operatic stage for nearly 45 years, and appeared in concerts to the end of his life. In addition to his Russian operatic roles, he also was admired as King Marke, Hagen, and Wotan.

Katchen, Julius, admired American pianist; b. Long Branch, N.J., Aug. 15, 1926; d. Paris, April 29, 1969. He studied in N.Y. with Saperton. When he was 11, he made his debut in a national radio broadcast and then was soloist in Mozart's D Minor Concerto with Ormandy and the Philadelphia Orch. on Oct. 21, 1937. He studied academic subjects at Haverford College (graduated, 1945); after a period of study on a French scholarship, he settled in Paris. In subsequent years, he toured as a soloist with orchs., as a recitalist, and as a chamber music artist. His career was entering its most promising phase when he was fatally stricken with cancer. He maintained a broad repertoire extending from the Classical era to contemporary music.

Kates, Stephen (Edward), American cellist and teacher; b. N.Y., May 7, 1943. He studied at the Meadowmount School of Music (1961–62), with Piatigorsky at the Univ. of Southern Calif. in Los Angeles (1964–67), and with Leonard Rose and Claus Adam at the Juilliard School of Music in N.Y. (diploma, 1969). He made his N.Y. debut in 1963; after winning 2nd prize in the Tchaikovsky Competition in Moscow (1966), he appeared as soloist with leading orchs. in the U.S.; also was active as a chamber music artist and recitalist. He taught at Ohio State Univ. in Columbus (1969–72); then was a member of the cello and chamber music depts. of the Peabody Cons. in Baltimore (from 1974); also conducted master classes, and was president of the Violoncello Soc. (1983–87). His repertoire extends from Bach to contemporary music; he commissioned and gave the first performance of Claus Adam's Cello Concerto (1973).

Katims, Milton, American violist and conductor; b. N.Y., June 24, 1909. He attended Columbia Univ., studying violin with Herbert Dittler and conducting with Barzin (1931–35). From 1935 to 1943 he was solo violist and assistant conductor for WOR Radio in N.Y.; from 1943 to 1954, was 1st violist in the NBC Sym. Orch. in N.Y.; was its assistant conductor under Toscanini from 1947; also taught at the Juilliard School of Music in N.Y. (1947–54). From 1954 to 1976 he was music director of the Seattle Sym. Orch.; from 1976 to 1984, artistic director of the Univ. of Houston School of Music; then was a prof. at the Shanghai Cons. of Music (from 1985). He prepared various eds. of compositions for viola. In 1964 he received the Alice M. Ditson Award for conductors and in 1986 the Arturo Toscanini Artistic Achievement award.

Katin, Peter (Roy), English-born Canadian pianist and teacher; b. London, Nov. 14, 1930. He studied with Harold Craxton at the Royal Academy of Music in London (1943–48), making his debut at London's Wigmore Hall in 1948. In subsequent years, he toured globally. He taught at the Royal Academy of Music (1956–69) and at the Univ. of Western Ontario in Canada (1978–84); became a naturalized Canadian citizen. He is best known for his performances of works from the Romantic and Impressionist periods, most especially of Chopin.

Katsaris, Cyprien, French pianist, teacher, and composer; b. Marseilles, May 5, 1951. He began piano lessons as a child; later pursued his studies with Aline von Barentzen, Monique de la Bruchollerie, and Jean Hubeau at the Paris Cons., where he won a premier prix for piano (1969) and for chamber music (1970). In 1970 he received the Albert Roussel Prize and in 1977 captured 1st prize in the Cziffra Competition; subsequently appeared as a soloist with the world's major orchs., and also gave recitals and played in chamber music concerts.

On May 23, 1986, he made his N.Y. recital debut at Alice Tully Hall with notable success. He also was active as a teacher and composer. His repertoire is catholic, ranging from works of Bach to those of Boulez; he won particular acclaim for his virtuoso performances of Liszt's piano transcriptions of the 9 Beethoven syms.

Kattnigg, Rudolf, Austrian composer and conductor; b. Oberdorf bei Treffen, April 9, 1895; d. Klagenfurt, Sept. 2, 1955. He went to Vienna and studied law at the Univ. before pursuing training in music at the Academy of Music with Mandyczewski, Löwe, J. Marx, and Krauss (1918–22). From 1928 to 1934 he was director of the Innsbruck Music School. He also was active as a theater conductor, settling in Vienna in 1939. He became best known as an operetta composer, his finest score being *Balkanliebe* or *Die Gräfin von Durazzo* (1937).

WORKS: DRAMATIC: OPERA: *Donna Miranda* (1953). **MUSIC THEATER:** *Der Prinz von Thule* (Basel, Dec. 13, 1936); *Kaiserin Katharina* (Berlin, Feb. 3, 1937); *Balkanliebe* or *Die Gräfin von Durazzo* (Leipzig, Dec. 22, 1937); *Mädels vom Rhein* (Bremen, 1938); *Die Mädel von St. Goar* (Bremen, Feb. 4, 1939); *Hansi fliegt zum Negerkral* (Vienna, Dec. 16, 1942); *Ben Ami* (Vienna, Jan. 18, 1949); *Rendezvouz um Mitternacht* (Vienna, May 20, 1956). **BALLET:** *Tarantella* (1942). Also film scores. **OTHER:** 2 syms. (1925, 1930); Piano Concerto (1934); chamber music.

Katulskaya, Elena, Russian soprano; b. Odessa, June 2, 1888; d. Moscow, Nov. 20, 1966. She studied privately in Odessa (1904) and St. Petersburg (1905–07) before training with Natalia Iretskaya at the St. Petersburg Cons. (1907–09). She then made her operatic debut as Lakmé at the Maryinsky Theater in St. Petersburg, where she sang until 1911. From 1913 to 1945 she was a principal member of the Bolshoi Theater in Moscow. In 1948 she became a teacher at the Moscow Cons. In 1965 she was made a People's Artist of the U.S.S.R. While Katulskaya was particularly esteemed for her roles in Russian operas, she also had success in the Italian and French repertoires.

Katwijk, Paul van, Dutch-American pianist, conductor, teacher, and composer; b. Delfshaters, Dec. 7, 1885; d. Dallas, Dec. 11, 1974. He studied at The Hague Cons., then in Berlin with Klatte and in Vienna with Godowsky. In 1912 he settled in the U.S.; taught at Drake Univ. in Des Moines (1914–18) and also conducted the Des Moines Sym. Orch.; in 1918 he was appointed dean of music at Southern Methodist Univ. in Dallas; resigned in 1949, but continued to teach piano there until 1955. He was conductor of the Dallas Municipal Opera (1922–25) and the Dallas Sym. Orch. (1925–36). He composed several symphonic works, including the suite *Hollandia* (Dallas, March 15, 1931).

Katz, Israel J(oseph), American ethnomusicologist; b. N.Y., July 21, 1930. He studied at the Univ. of Calif. at Los Angeles with Klaus Wachsmann and Boris Kremenliev (B.A., 1956; Ph.D., 1967, with the diss. *Judeo-Spanish Traditional Ballads from Jerusalem: An Ethnomusicological Study*; publ. in 2 vols., N.Y., 1972, 1975). He taught at McGill Univ. in Montreal (1968–69) and at Columbia Univ. (1969–75); then at York College and the Graduate Center of the City Univ. of N.Y. (from 1977). He was ed. of *Ethnomusicology* (1971–72) and co-ed. of *Musica Judaica* (from 1975).

Katz, Martin, American pianist and teacher; b. Los Angeles, Nov. 27, 1945. He began piano lessons at age 5; later, was a scholarship student at the Univ. of Southern Calif. in Los Angeles, where he received instruction in the art of accompaniment from Gwendolyn Koldofsky; while still a student there, he served as an accompanist in the master classes of Lehmann, Heifetz, Piatigorsky, and Bernac. After completing his education, Katz pursued a distinguished career as an accompanist, making tours throughout the world with many celebrated artists. He also taught at Westminster Choir College in Princeton, N.J. (from 1976) and at the Univ. of Mich. in Ann Arbor (from 1983).

Katz, Mindru, Romanian-born Israeli pianist and teacher; b. Bucharest, June 3, 1925; d. during a recital in Istanbul, Jan. 30, 1978. He studied with Floria Musicescu at the Royal Academy of Music in Bucharest. Katz made his debut with the Bucharest Phil. in 1947, and then played throughout Eastern Europe. He made his Western European debut in Paris in 1957, then settled in Israel (1959) but continued to make extensive tours. He joined the faculty of the Rubin Academy of Music in Tel Aviv in 1962, becoming a prof. of piano there in 1972.

Katzer, Georg, German composer; b. Habelschwerdt, Silesia, Jan. 10, 1935. He studied with Wagner-Régeny and Zechlin at the Hochschule für Musik in East Berlin (1954–59); then entered the classes of Eisler and Spies at the Akademie der Künste there (1960–63), where he was elected to membership (1979) and became artistic director of its electronic music studio. He served as president of the national section of the International Soc. for Electroacoustic Music (from 1989). In 1981 he received the National Prize for Art of the German Democratic Republic. In his music, Katzer is a universalist, applying constructivist principles with lapidary precision. Under the influence of Eisler, he adopted a broad variety of methods, including 12-tone techniques, using his materials for specific purposes accessible to mass audiences.

WORKS: DRAMATIC: *Das Land Bum-Bum,* children's opera (1974); *Schwarze Vögel,* ballet (1974); *Ein neuer Sommernachtstraum,* ballet (1979–80); *Gastmahl oder über die Liebe,* opera (1987; Berlin, April 30, 1988); *Antigone oder die Stadt,* opera (1989). **ORCH.:** 3 sonatas: No. 1 (1968), No. 2 (1969), and No. 3, *Homage à Jules Verne,* for Chamber Orch. (1970); *Baukasten* (1972); *Die D-Dur Musikmaschine* (1973); *Concerto for Orchestra No. 1* (1973), *No. 2* (1985), and *No. 3* (1988; Berlin, Sept. 22, 1989); Concerto for Jazz Group and Orch. (1975); *Empfindsame Musik* for 58 Strings and 3 Percussionists (1976; Leipzig, June 2, 1977); *Dramatische Musik* (1977); *Sound-House* for Orch., 3 Orch. Groups, Organ, and Tape (1979); Piano Concerto (1980); Double Concerto for Cello, Harp, and Orch. (1980); Cello Concerto (1985; Karl-Marx-Stadt, Oct. 24, 1989); Flute Concerto (1985–86; Berlin, Feb. 25, 1986); Oboe Concerto (Leipzig, Sept. 21, 1989); *Offene Landschaft mit Obligatem Ton e* (1990); *Gloria* (1991–92; Berlin, Sept. 20, 1992); *Recit* for Chamber Orch. (1992); Triple Concerto for Saxophone, Percussion, Accordion, and Orch. (1994). **CHAMBER:** 3 string quartet (1966; with Soprano, 1967; 1987); *Streichmusik I* for 14 Solo Strings (1971) and *II* for 18 Solo Strings (1972); Piano Quintet (1972); *Scene* for Chamber Ensemble (1975); Concerto for Harpsichord and Wind Quintet (1977); Trio for Oboe, Cello, Piano, and Tape (1979); Concerto for Violin, 14 Strings, and Harpsichord (1980–81); *Ballade* for Clarinet and Percussion (1982); *Kommen und gehen* for Wind Quintet and Piano (1982); *La Mettrie I* (1985) and *II* (1987) for Wind Quintet and Piano; *Hex* for 6 Instruments (1988); *Zungen und Saiten* for String Trio and Accordion (1988); *Strahlung/Brechung* for String Quintet (1991); Saxophone Quartet (1992); String Trio (1992); *Odd and Even* for Flute, Percussion, and Piano (1993); piano pieces. **VOCAL:** *Dialog imaginär 6* for Tenor, Saxophone, and Tape (1994); choruses; song cycles.

Kauder, Hugo, Austrian-born American violonist and composer; b. Tobitschau, Moravia, June 9, 1888; d. Bussum, the Netherlands, July 22, 1972. He was a member of the Konzertverein Orch. in Vienna (1910–19), then went to the U.S. (1938), where he became a naturalized American citizen (1944). His music is contrapuntal, with canonic devices much used in free and often asymmetric rhythm, while the harmonies are conservative. He wrote 4 syms., a Cello Concerto, and a great number of works for chamber music combinations. He publ. *Entwurf einer neuen Melodie- und Harmonielehre* (Vienna, 1932) and *Counterpoint: An Introduction to Polyphonic Composition* (N.Y., 1960).

Kauffmann, Leo Justinus, German composer; b. Dammerkirch, Sept. 20, 1901; d. in an air raid in Strasbourg,

Sept. 25, 1944. He studied with Erb in Strasbourg and with Jarnach and Abendroth in Cologne. He taught at Cologne's Rheinische Musikschule (1929–32) and worked for the Cologne Radio (1932–33); later taught at the Strasbourg Cons., serving as its director until his death. He wrote the operas *Die Geschichte vom schönen Annerl* (Strasbourg, June 20, 1942) and *Das Perlenhem* (Strasbourg, 1944); Sym.; Concertino for Double Bass and Chamber Orch.; Mass.

Kaufman, Harry, American pianist and teacher; b. N.Y., Sept. 6, 1894; d. Beverly Hills, Aug. 22, 1961. He studied at the Inst. of Musical Art with Stojowski in N.Y.; later was a pupil of Josef Hofmann. In 1924 he was appointed teacher of the art of accompanying at the Curtis Inst. of Music in Philadelphia. Though principally known as an excellent accompanist, he also appeared as soloist with the N.Y. Phil., the Philadelphia Orch. et al. and as a member of several chamber music groups.

Kaufman, Louis, distinguished American violinist; b. Portland, Oreg., May 10, 1905; d. Los Angeles, Feb. 9, 1994. He studied with Kneisel. He won the Loeb Prize in 1927 and the Naumburg Award in 1928; subsequently toured widely. He gave numerous first performances of works by contemporary composers, among them a violin concerto by Dag Wiren (Stockholm, Oct. 25, 1953), and first American performances of violin works by Milhaud, Knipper, Martinů, and others; also played American works in Europe; gave the first performance in England of Walter Piston's Violin Concerto (London, April 6, 1956). He ed. 6 sonatas for Violin by G.P. Telemann and *Sonata concertante* by L. Spohr; publ. *Warming Up Scales and Arpeggios* (1957).

BIBL.: J. Yoell, "In Conversation with L. K.," *Fanfare* 9, no. 4 (March–April 1986).

Kaufmann, Armin, Romanian-born Austrian composer; b. Itzkany, Bukovina, Oct. 30, 1902; d. Vienna, June 30, 1980. In 1914 his family settled in Vienna, where he enrolled at the Academy of Music, studying theory with Joseph Marx. From 1938 to 1966 he played the viola in the Vienna Sym. Orch.

WORKS: ORCH.: 4 syms. (1929, 1962, 1966, 1968); Tárogató Concerto (1967); Piano Concerto (1970). **CHAMBER:** 7 string quartets; Trio for Violin, Zither, and Guitar (1962); Quintet for Piano, Violin, Viola, Cello, and Double Bass (1965); Trio for Flute, Viola, and Harp (1967); *Rhapsody* for Guitar (1970).

Kaufmann, Helen, American writer on music; b. N.Y., Feb. 2, 1887; d. there, Sept. 17, 1978. She was educated at Barnard College; upon graduation, she devoted herself to educational work. She publ. a number of popular books on music appreciation, among them *Home Book of Music Appreciation* (1942); *Little Guide of Music Appreciation* (1948); *The Story of Music through the Ages* (1949); also concise biographies of Mozart, Prokofiev, and other composers.

Kaufmann, Walter, German-born American conductor, composer, and musicologist; b. Karlsbad, April 1, 1907; d. Bloomington, Ind., Sept. 9, 1984. He studied composition with Schreker in Berlin; also studied musicology in Prague. In 1935 he traveled to India, where he remained for 10 years; devoted much time to the study of the Hindu systems of composition; also appeared as conductor, serving as music director of the Bombay Radio. In 1947 he moved to Nova Scotia and taught piano at the Halifax Cons.; from 1948 to 1957 he was music director of the Winnipeg Sym. Orch. In 1957 he settled in the U.S., where he joined the faculty of the Indiana Univ. School of Music in Bloomington. He became a naturalized American citizen in 1964. He wrote *Musical Notations of the Orient* (Bloomington, 1967); *The Ragas of North India* (Bloomington, 1968); *Tibetan Buddhist Chant* (tr. by T. Norbu; Bloomington, 1975); *Involvement with Music: The Music of India* (N.Y., 1976); *Musical References in the Chinese Classics* (Detroit, 1976); *The Ragas of South India* (Bloomington, 1976); *Altinden* (Leipzig, 1981); also valuable articles on Eastern music for American music journals.

WORKS: DRAMATIC: OPERAS: *Der grosse Dorin* (1932); *Der Hammel bringt es an den Tag* (1932); *Esther* (1931–32); *Die weisse Gottin* (1933); *Anasuya*, radio opera (Bombay, Oct. 1, 1938); *The Cloak*, after Gogol (1933–50); *A Parfait for Irene* (Bloomington, Feb. 21, 1952); *The Research* (1951); *The Golden Touch*, children's opera (1953); *Christmas Slippers*, television opera (1955); *Sganarelle* (1955); *George from Paradise* (1958); *Paracelsus* (1958); *The Scarlet Letter*, after Hawthorne (Bloomington, May 6, 1961); *A Hoosier Tale* (Bloomington, July 30, 1966); *Rip van Winkle*, children's opera (1966). **BALLETS:** *Visages* (1950); *The Rose and the Ring* (1950); *Wang* (1956). **ORCH.:** 6 syms. (1931, 1935, 1936, 1938, 1949, 1956); *Prag*, suite (1932); 2 piano concertos (1934, 1949); *2 Bohemian Dances* (1942); *Andhera* for Piano and Orch. (1942–49); 2 violin concertos (1943, 1944); *6 Indian Miniatures* (1943); *Navaratnam*, suite for Piano and Chamber Orch. (1945); *Phantasmagoria* (1946); *Variations* for Strings (1947); Concertino for Piano and Strings (1947); *Dirge* (1947); *Madras Express* (Boston, June 23, 1948); *Fleet Street Overture* (1948); *Strange Town at Night* (1948); *Faces in the Dark* (1948); *Divertimento* for Strings (1949); Cello Concerto (1950); *Chivaree Overture* (1950); *Main Street* for Strings (1950); *Kalif Storch*, fairy tale for Speaker and Orch. (1951); *Arabesques* for 2 Pianos and Orch. (1952); *Vaudeville Overture* (1952); *Sewanee River Variations* (1952); *Short Suite* for Small Orch. (1953); *Nocturne* (1953); *Pembina Highway* (1953); *4 Skies* (1953); *3 Dances to an Indian Play* (1956); *4 Essays* for Small Orch. (1956); *Sinfonietta No. 2* (1959); Timpani Concerto (1963); *Festival Overture* (1968); Violin Concertino (1977). **CHAMBER:** 10 string quartets (1935–46); 3 piano trios (1942–46); 6 Pieces for Piano Trio (1957); String Quartet (1961); *Partita* for Woodwind Quintet (1963); *Arabesques* for Flute, Oboe, Harpsichord, and Bass (1963); 8 Pieces for 12 Instruments (1967); *Passacaglia and Capriccio* for Brass Sextet (1967); Sonatina for Solo Piccolo or Flute (1968). **PIANO:** Concertino (1932); 2 sonatinas (1948, 1956); Sonata (1948–51); *Arabesques* for 2 Pianos (1952); Suite (1957). **VOCAL:** 3 cantatas: *Galizische Baume* for Chorus and Orch. (1932), *Coronation Cantata* for Soloists, Chorus, and Orch. (1953), and *Rubayyat* for Soloist and Orch. (1954); songs.

BIBL.: T. Noblitt, ed., *Music East and West: Essays in Honor of W. K.* (N.Y., 1981).

Kaul, Oskar, German musicologist; b. Heufeld, Oct. 11, 1885; d. Unterwössen, July 17, 1968. He studied at the Cologne Cons. (1905–08), then took courses in musicology with Sandberger and Kroyer at the Univ. of Munich (Ph.D., 1911, with the diss. *Anton Rosetti: Sein Leben und seine Werke*). He joined the faculty of the Würzburg Cons. (1913); was its deputy director (1924–45); was also a Privatdozent (1922–28) and reader (1928–45) at the Univ. of Würzburg. He ed. 5 syms. and chamber music of Rosetti for the Denkmäler der Tonkunst in Bayern, XXII, Jg. XII/1 (1912; 2nd ed., rev., 1968) and XXXIII, Jg. XXV (1925). His writings include *Die Vokalwerke Anton Rosettis* (Cologne, 1911), *Geschichte der Würzburger Hofmusik im 18. Jahrhundert* (Würzburg, 1924), and *Zur Musikgeschichte der ehemaligen Reichsstadt Schweinfurt* (Würzburg, 1935).

Kaun, Hugo, German composer; b. Berlin, March 21, 1863; d. there, April 2, 1932. He studied at the Berlin Hochschule für Musik (1879–80); then with Oskar Raif (piano) and at the Prussian Academy of Arts with Friedrich Kiel (composition). He was active as a teacher and conductor of the Liederkranz in Milwaukee (1887–1901), then returned to Berlin, becoming a prof. at the Klindworth-Scharwenka Cons. (1922). He publ. *Harmonie- und Modulationslehre* (Leipzig, 1915; 2nd ed., 1921); also an autobiography, *Aus meinem Leben* (Berlin, 1932). A cultured composer, he incorporated in his well-crafted works elements of both Brahmsian and Wagnerian idioms.

WORKS: OPERAS: *Sappho* (Leipzig, Oct. 27, 1917); *Der Fremde* (Dresden, Feb. 23, 1920); *Menandra* (staged in Kiel and several other German opera houses simultaneously, Oct. 29, 1925). **ORCH.:** 3 syms.; 2 piano concertos; *Der Sternenbanner*, festival march on the *Star-Spangled Banner*; *Der Maler von Antwerpen*, overture (Chicago, Feb. 3, 1899); *Im Urwald*, 2 symphonic poems, after Longfellow's *Minnehaha* and *Hiawatha* (Chicago, Feb. 7, 1903). **OTHER:** Chamber music; many piano pieces; choral works; songs.

BIBL.: W. Altmann, *H. K.* (Leipzig, 1906); G. Kruse, "H. K.," *Die Musik*, IX/24 (1909–10); R. Schaal, *H. K., 1863–1932, Leben und Werk: Ein Beitrag zur Musik der Jahrhundertwende* (Regensburg, 1946).

Kavafian, Ani, gifted Turkish-born American violinist of Armenian descent, sister of **Ida Kavafian**; b. Istanbul, May 10, 1948. In 1956 she went with her family to the U.S., where she took violin lessons with Ara Zerounian (1957–62) and Mischakoff (1962–66) in Detroit; then entered the Juilliard School of Music in N.Y., where she received instruction in violin from Galamian and in chamber music performance from Galimir and members of the Juilliard Quartet (M.A., 1972). In 1969 she made her debut at Carnegie Recital Hall in N.Y.; her European debut followed in Paris in 1973. In 1976 she received the Avery Fisher Prize. She appeared as soloist with the leading orchs.; also played chamber music concerts, serving as an artist-member of the Chamber Music Soc. of Lincoln Center (from 1980); likewise gave duo performances with her sister. She taught at the Mannes College of Music (from 1982), and at the Manhattan School of Music and Queens College of the City Univ. of N.Y. (from 1983). On Sept. 24, 1993, she was soloist in the premiere of Machover's *Forever and Ever*, a concerto for Hyperviolin and Chamber Orch., with Hugh Wolff and the St. Paul (Minn.) Chamber Orch.

Kavafian, Ida, talented Turkish-born American violinist of Armenian descent, sister of **Ani Kavafian**; b. Istanbul, Oct. 29, 1952. She went with her family to the U.S. (1956), where she took up violin studies with Ara Zerounian in Detroit at the age of 6, and later received instruction from Mischakoff there; entered the Juilliard School in N.Y. (1969), where she continued her training with Shumsky and Galamian (M.A., 1975); she won the Vianna da Motta International Violin Competition in Lisbon (1973) and the silver medal at the International Violin Competition of Indianapolis (1982). She helped to found the chamber group Tashi (1973), and subsequently toured with it; made her N.Y. recital debut (1978) and her European debut in London (1982); also played in duo concerts with her sister. In 1988 she was awarded the Avery Fisher Career Grant. In 1993 she became a member of the Beaux Arts Trio.

Kay, Hershy, American composer, arranger, and orchestrator; b. Philadelphia, Nov. 17, 1919; d. Danbury, Conn., Dec. 2, 1981. He studied cello with Salmond and orchestration with Thompson at the Curtis Inst. of Music in Philadelphia (1936–40); then went to N.Y., and began a fruitful career as an arranger of Broadway musicals and ballets. He orchestrated a number of Leonard Bernstein's theater works: *On the Town* (1944), *Peter Pan* (incidental music; 1951), *Candide* (1956; revival, 1973), *Mass* (1971), and the Bicentennial pageant *1600 Pennsylvania Avenue* (1976). His last arrangement for Bernstein was *Olympic Hymn* (Baden-Baden, Sept. 23, 1981). His other orchestrations for Broadway include *A Flag Is Born* (1947), *The Golden Apple* (1954), *Once upon a Mattress* (1958), *Juno* (1958), *Sand Hog* (1958), *Livin' the Life* (1958), *Milk and Honey* (1961), *The Happiest Girl in the World* (1961), *110 in the Shade* (1963), *Coco* (1969), *A Chorus Line* (1975), *American Musical Jubilee* (1976), *Music Is* (1976), *On the Twentieth Century* (1977), *Evita* (1979), *Carmelina* (1979), and *Barnum* (1980). He made numerous arrangements for the N.Y. City Ballet, among them *Cakewalk* (1951, after Gottschalk), *Western Symphony* (1954, after cowboy songs and fiddle tunes), *The Concert* (1956, after Chopin), *Stars and Stripes* (1958, after Sousa's marches), *Who Cares?* (1970, after Gershwin), and *Union Jack* (1976, after popular British music). His ballet arrangements for other companies include *The Thief Who Loved a Ghost* (1950, after Weber), *L'Inconnue* (1965), *The Clowns* (1968; a rare 12-tone arrangement), *Meadowlark and Cortège Burlesque* (1969), *Grand Tour* (1971, after Noel Coward), and *Winter's Court* (1972). He also orchestrated a Gottschalk piano piece, *Grand Tarantella*, for Piano and Orch. (1957) and completed the orchestration of Robert Kurka's opera *The Good Soldier Schweik* (N.Y., April 23, 1958).

Kay, Ulysses Simpson, eminent black American composer and teacher; b. Tucson, Ariz., Jan. 7, 1917; d. Englewood, N.J., May 20, 1995. He received his early music training at home; on the advice of his uncle "King" Oliver, a leading jazz cornetist and bandleader, he studied piano. In 1934 he enrolled at the Univ. of Arizona at Tucson (Mus.B., 1938); he then went to study at the Eastman School of Music in Rochester, N.Y., where he was a student of Rogers and Hanson (M.M., 1940); later attended the classes of Hindemith at the Berkshire Music Center in Tanglewood (1941–42). He served in the U.S. Navy (1942–45); then studied composition with Luening at Columbia Univ. (1946–49); went to Rome as winner of the American Rome Prize, and was attached there to the American Academy (1949–52). From 1953 to 1968 he was employed as a consultant by Broadcast Music Inc. in N.Y.; was on the faculty of Boston Univ. (1965) and of the Univ. of Calif., Los Angeles (1966–67); in 1968, was appointed prof. of music at the Herbert H. Lehman College in N.Y.; was made Distinguished Prof. there in 1972, retiring in 1988. He received honorary doctorates from several American univs. His music followed a distinctly American idiom, particularly in its rhythmic intensity, while avoiding ostentatious ethnic elements; in harmony and counterpoint, he pursued a moderately advanced idiom, marked by prudentially euphonious dissonances; his instrumentation was masterly.

WORKS: DRAMATIC: OPERAS: *The Boor*, after Chekhov (1955; Lexington, Ky., April 3, 1968); *The Juggler of Our Lady* (1956; New Orleans, Feb. 3, 1962); *The Capitoline Venus* (1970; Urbana, Ill., March 12, 1971); *Jubilee* (Jackson, Miss., April 12, 1976); *Frederick Douglass* (1980–85; Newark, April 14, 1991). **BALLET:** *Dance Calinda* (Rochester, N.Y., April 23, 1941). **FILM SCORE:** *The Quiet One* (1988). **ORCH.:** Oboe Concerto (Rochester, N.Y., April 16, 1940); *5 Mosaics* for Chamber Orch. (Cleveland, Dec. 28, 1940); *Of New Horizons*, overture (N.Y., July 29, 1944); *Suite in 5 Movements* (1945; N.Y., May 21, 1950); *A Short Overture* (N.Y., March 31, 1947); *Portrait Suite* (1948; Erie, Pa., April 21, 1964); Suite for Strings (Baltimore, April 8, 1949); Sinfonia in E major (Rochester, N.Y., May 2, 1951); 6 Dances for Strings (1954); *Concerto for Orchestra* (N.Y., Feb. 1954); *Serenade* (Louisville, Sept. 18, 1954); *Fantasy Variations* (Portland, Maine, Nov. 19, 1963); *Umbrian Scene* (New Orleans, March 31, 1964); *Markings*, symphonic essay, dedicated to the memory of Dag Hammarskjöld (Rochester, Mich., Aug. 8, 1966); Sym. (1967; for the Illinois Sesquicentennial, Macomb, Ill., March 28, 1968); *Theater Set* (Atlanta, Sept. 26, 1968); *Scherzi musicali* for Chamber Orch. (Detroit, Feb. 13, 1969); *Aulos* for Flute and Chamber Orch. (Bloomington, Ind., Feb. 21, 1971); Quintet Concerto for 5 Brass Soli and Orch. (N.Y., March 14, 1975); *Southern Harmony* (Raleigh, N.C., Feb. 10, 1976); *Chariots*, rhapsody (Saratoga, N.Y., Aug. 8, 1979, composer conducting); *String Triptych* (1987); band music. **CHAMBER:** Quintet for Flute and Strings (1947); Piano Quintet (1949); 3 string quartets (1953, 1956, 1961); *5 Portraits* for Violin and Piano (1972); *Guitarra*, guitar suite (1973; rev. 1985); *Tromba* for Trumpet and Piano (1983); *5 Winds*, divertimento for Woodwind Quintet (1984); *Pantomime*, fantasy for Clarinet (1986); *Everett Suite* for Bass Trombone (1988). **PIANO:** Sonata (1940); *2 Nocturnes* (1973); *2 Impromptus* (1986). **VOCAL:** *Song of Jeremiah*, cantata (Nashville, Tenn., April 23, 1954); *3 Pieces after Blake* for Soprano and Orch. (N.Y., March 27, 1955); *The Western Paradise* for Female Narrator and Orch. (Washington, D.C., Oct. 12, 1976); many choral pieces; songs.

BIBL.: N. Slonimsky, "U. K.," *American Composers Alliance Bulletin* (Fall 1957); L. Hayes, *The Music of U. K., 1939–1963* (diss., Univ. of Wisc., 1971); C. Dower, "U. K.: Distinguished American Composer," *Musart* (Jan.–Feb. 1972); R. Hadley, *The Published Choral Music of U.S. K., 1943–1968* (diss., Univ. of Iowa, 1972); L. Wyatt, "U. K.'s *Fantasy Variations*: An Analysis,"

Black Perspective in Music (Spring 1977); C. Hobson and D. Richardson, *U. K.: A Bio-Bibliography* (Westport, Conn., 1994).

Kayser, Leif, Danish composer, pianist, and organist; b. Copenhagen, June 13, 1919. He studied at the Copenhagen Cons., and later took courses with Rosenberg in Stockholm; then went to Rome, where he studied theology (1942–49), and was ordained a Catholic priest; later studied with Boulanger in Paris (1955). He served as chaplain at St. Ansgar church in Copenhagen (1949–64); in 1964, was appointed to the faculty of the Royal Danish Cons. of Music in Copenhagen. He wrote 4 syms. (1939, 1940, 1956, 1963); *Christmas Oratorio* (1943); *Sinfonietta* for Amateur Orch. (1967); *Divertimento* for 4 Recorders (1968); Organ Sonata; sacred choruses; etc.

Kazandjiev, Vasil, Bulgarian conductor and composer; b. Marten, near Ruse, Sept. 10, 1934. He studied composition privately with Iliev, then composition with Vladigerov and conducting with Simeonov at the Bulgarian State Cons. in Sofia, graduating in 1957; in 1964, was appointed to its faculty. In 1979 he became principal conductor of the Bulgarian Radio and Television Sym. Orch. In his music, he applies modern techniques, including modified serialism, to modalities of Bulgarian folk music.

WORKS: ORCH.: Concerto for Strings (1951); *Sinfonietta* (1954); Trumpet Concerto (1955); *Divertimento* (1957); Concerto for Piano, Saxophone, and Orch. (1957–60); Violin Concerto (1961); *Complexi sonori* for Strings (1965); *Symphony of Timbres* (1968); *The Living Icons* for Chamber Orch. (1970); *Pictures from Bulgaria* for Strings and Percussion (1971); *Festive Music* (1972); *Capriccio* (1974); *Apocalypse* (1978); *Illuminations* (1980); Sym. No. 3 (1981). **CHAMBER:** Wind Quintet (1951); *Variations* for Oboe, Clarinet, Violin, Viola, Cello, and Piano (1954); Horn Sonata (1955); Clarinet Sonata (1956); Sonata for Solo Violin (1957); 2 string quartets (1965, 1970); *Concert Improvisations* for Flute, Viola, Harp, and Harpsichord (1974); *Poco a poco* for Percussion and Organ (1979); Piano Quintet (1981). **PIANO:** Sonata (1957); *The Triumph of the Bells* (1974). **VOCAL:** Choruses; songs.

Kazarnovskaya, Ljuba, admired Russian soprano; b. Moscow, July 18, 1960. She was 16 when she began vocal training with Nadezhda Malysheva in Moscow; at 19, she enrolled at the Moscow Cons., where she continued her studies with Elena Shumilova. In 1982 she made her formal operatic debut as Tatiana at the Stanislavsky Theater in Moscow. She first sang at the Bolshoi Theater in Moscow in 1983. In 1986 she scored a fine success as Leonora in *La Forza del Destino* at the Kirov Theater in Leningrad, where she remained as a principal artist until 1989. She also toured with the company abroad, notably as Tatiana at the Paris Opéra and at London's Covent Garden in 1987. In 1989 she was engaged as a soloist in the Verdi *Requiem* at the Salzburg Festival, and subsequently she pursued a successful operatic and concert career in the West. In 1992 she made her North American debut as soloist in the Shostakovich 14th Sym. with the Boston Sym. Orch. Her Metropolitan Opera debut in N.Y. followed later that year, as Tatiana, to critical acclaim. After singing Desdemona there in 1993, she returned there to outstanding acclaim in 1994. In 1995 she sang Rimsky-Korsakov's Fevronia during the Kirov company's visit to the Brooklyn Academy of Music. Her engagements also took her to Milan's La Scala, the Vienna State Opera, the Bavarian State Opera in Munich, the Hamburg State Opera, the Teatro Colón in Buenos Aires, and Chicago's Lyric Opera. As a concert artist, she appeared with leading orchs. and at principal festivals. In addition to her esteemed Russian repertoire, she has won notable success as Donna Anna, Vitellia, Marguerite, Amelia, Violetta, Mimi, and Salome.

Kazuro, Stanislaw, Polish composer; b. Teklinapol, near Vilnius, Aug. 1, 1881; d. Warsaw, Nov. 30, 1961. He studied in Warsaw, Paris, and Rome. He was active mainly in Warsaw as a pedagogue and choral conductor; he also publ. several school manuals. His compositions, in an academic style, were chiefly designed for pedagogic purposes; among them are 2 folk operas, orch. music, choral works, and piano pieces.

Keats, Donald (Howard), significant American composer; b. N.Y., May 27, 1929. He studied piano at the Manhattan School of Music in N.Y.; then enrolled in Yale Univ., where he attended classes with Porter and Hindemith in composition (Mus.B., 1949) and musicology with Einstein and Schrade; then attended classes in composition at Columbia Univ. with Luening, Moore, and Cowell (M.A., 1953), and took a course in musicology with Lang. Subsequently he entered the Graduate School of Music at the Univ. of Minnesota, where he studied composition with Fetler and Argento and musicology with Riedel (Ph.D., 1962). In 1954 he received a Fulbright traveling grant and went to Germany, where he became a student of Jarnach at the Hochschule für Musik in Hamburg. In 1964–65 he received his first Guggenheim fellowship to continue his studies in Paris, Florence, and Vienna; in 1972–73 he obtained a 2nd Guggenheim fellowship and traveled to France and England. Other awards and prizes were from the NEA, Yale Univ., the Rockefeller Foundation, and the Ford Foundation. In 1948–49 he served as a teaching fellow at the Yale Univ. School of Music; was then called to military service and was an instructor at the U.S. Naval School of Music in Washington, D.C. (1953–54); later was a member of the faculty of Antioch College in Yellow Springs, Ohio (1957–76); in 1969–70 he was visiting prof. of music at the School of Music, Univ. of Wash., in Seattle. In 1976 he was appointed prof. of music and composer-in-residence at the Univ. of Denver School of Music. In the meantime, he gave guest performances in various parts of the world as a pianist in his own works. In his compositions, Keats appears as a classical lyricist; his music is sparse in texture but opulent in sonorous substance, frugal in diction but expansive in elaborate developments; its expressive power is a musical equivalent of "Occam's razor," a medieval law of parsimony which proclaims the principle of multa paucis, multitude by paucity, abundance in concision. The titles of his works often indicate this economic precision of design: *Musica instrumentalis; Polarities; Diptych; Branchings.* In *An Elegiac Symphony,* he gives full expression to the lyric nature of his talent; it is an outgrowth of an orchestral *Elegy* inspired by the sadness upon the death of his infant son.

WORKS: BALLET: *The New Work* (1967). **ORCH.:** *Concert Piece* (1952; Columbus, Ohio, Feb. 3, 1968); 2 syms.: No. 1 (1955–57) and No. 2, *An Elegiac Symphony* (1959; Dayton, Ohio, Jan. 20, 1960; rev. 1973); *Branchings* (1976); Piano Concerto (1981–85). **CHAMBER:** Clarinet Sonata (1948); Piano Trio (1948); *Divertimento* for Wind and String Instruments (1949); 2 string quartets (1951, 1965); String Trio (1951); *Polarities* for Violin and Piano (1968); *Dialogue* for Piano and Wind Instruments (1973); *Diptych* for Cello and Piano (1973); *Epithalamium* for Violin, Cello, and Piano (1977); *Musica instrumentalis* for 10 Instruments (1980); *Revisitations* for Violin, Cello, and Piano (1992). **PIANO:** *Theme and Variations* (1954); Sonata (1960). **VOCAL:** *The Naming of Cats* for Vocal Quartet and Piano, after T.S. Eliot (1951); *The Hollow Men* for Chorus, Clarinet, 3 Trombones, and Piano, after T.S. Eliot (1952; Hamburg, July 12, 1955); *A Love Triptych,* song cycle for Soprano and Piano, after Yeats (1970); *Tierras del alma* for Soprano, Flute, and Guitar (Denver, May 23, 1979).

Kee, Cornelis, distinguished Dutch organist, pedagogue, and composer, father of **Piet(er Willem) Kee**; b. Zaandam, Nov. 24, 1900. He studied organ and piano with de Pauw, composition with Dresden, and voice with Denijs at the Amsterdam Cons. He was active as a church and concert organist, becoming widely known as a master of improvisation. In 1951 he became a prof. at the Haarlem International Summer Academy. In 1976 he was made a Knight of the Order of Oranje-Nassau. He publ. 3 collections of Psalms for organ, which treat old Psalm tunes contrapuntally. In some of his own compositions (almost exclusively for organ), he applies polyphonic devices of the classical Flemish school in a modern way, including serial procedures.

WORKS: *Reeksveranderingen* (Serial Permutations; 1966); *Phases* for Organ (1966); *Phases* for Organ (1969); *Blijde incomste* (Joyful Entry), variations on a traditional song, for Brass, Percussion, and Piano (1969); *Sweelinck Variations* for Horn, 2 Trumpets, 2 Trombones, and Organ (1973); Suite for Harpsichord or Organ (1974); *Homopoly*, 4 pieces for Piano (1979); numerous teaching pieces for organ.

Kee, Piet(er Willem), noted Dutch organist, teacher, and composer, son of Cornelis Kee; b. Zaandam, Aug. 30, 1927. He studied organ with his father, and then with Anthon van de Horst at the Amsterdam Cons., graduating in 1948; won the International Organ Improvisation Competition for 3 consecutive years (1953–55). In 1941 he made his debut as an organist in Zaandam. From 1952 to 1987 he was organist at St. Laurens, Alkmar; from 1956 to 1989, municipal organist at St. Bavo, Haarlem; from 1954 to 1987, prof. of organ at the Sweelinck Cons. in Amsterdam. In 1972 he was made a Knight of the Order of Oranje-Nassau; in 1987 he was elected an honorary fellow of the Royal College of Organists in London. Among his compositions are many organ pieces, including *Variations on a Carol* (1954), *Triptych on Psalm 86* (1960), *Music and Space* for 2 Organs, 3 Trumpets, and 2 Trombones (1969), *Confrontation* for 3 Street Organs and Church Organ (1979), and *Integration* for Chorus, Flageolet, Mechanical Birds, Barrel Organs, and Church Organ (1980); chamber music; choral pieces; arrangements of hymns and folk songs.

Keene, Christopher, prominent American conductor and music administrator; b. Berkeley, Calif., Dec. 21, 1946; d. N.Y., Oct. 8, 1995. He studied piano as a child, and during his high school years conducted several groups; then attended the Univ. of Calif. at Berkeley (1963–67). In 1965 he made his public debut conducting Britten's *The Rape of Lucretia* in Berkeley; in 1966 he became an assistant conductor at the San Francisco Opera, and in 1967 at the San Diego Opera. In 1968 he made his European debut conducting Menotti's *The Saint of Bleecker Street* at the Spoleto (Italy) Festival. He was music director of the American Ballet Co. (1969–70). On Oct. 18, 1970, he made his N.Y. City Opera debut conducting Ginastera's *Don Ridrigo*, and, on Sept. 24, 1971, his Metropolitan Opera debut in N.Y. conducting *Cavalleria rusticana*. He served as co-music director (1971–73), general manager (1973–75), and music director (1975–76) of the Spoleto Festival; was music director (from 1974) and president (1975–89) of Artpark, the Lewiston, N.Y., summer festival. From 1975 to 1984 he was music director of the Syracuse (N.Y.) Sym. Orch.; also held that title with the Spoleto Festival U.S.A. in Charleston, S.C. (1977–80), and with the Long Island (N.Y.) Phil. (1979–90). He was artistic supervisor (1982–83) and music director (1983–86) of the N.Y. City Opera, returning there in 1989 as general director. Keene became well known for his championship of rarely heard operas during his years at the N.Y. City Opera. His career was cut short by AIDS-induced lymphoma.

Keene, Constance, American pianist and pedagogue; b. N.Y., Feb. 9, 1921. She studied with **Abram Chasins** (1938–49), whom she married in 1949 and with whom she subsequently performed. She was an early teacher of Arthur Rubinstein's children; also taught at the Mannes School of Music in N.Y., numbering among her students Minoru Nojima, Peter Nero, and David Bar-Illan. Her 1964 recordings of the preludes of Rachmaninoff were critically acclaimed. As a soloist, she appeared with major orchs. in the U.S. and abroad; also gave master classes.

Kegel, Herbert, distinguished German conductor; b. Dresden, July 29, 1920; d. there, Nov. 20, 1990. He studied at the Dresden Staatskapelle's orch. school, where his mentors included Böhm and Blacher (1935–40). In 1946 he became conductor of the Rostock Opera; in 1949, was engaged as conductor of the Leipzig Radio Choir and Orch.; was made conductor (1953), Generalmusikdirektor (1958), and chief conductor (1960) of the Leipzig Radio Sym. Orch. From 1975 to 1978 he was a prof. at the Leipzig Hochschule für Musik, and in 1978 became a prof. at the Dresden Hochschule für Musik. From 1977 to 1985 he served as chief conductor of the Dresden Phil. He was regarded as one of the most competent conductors of East Germany, combining a thorough knowledge of his repertoire with a fine sense of effective presentation of the music.

Kehr, Günter, German violinist and conductor; b. Darmstadt, March 16, 1920; d. Mainz, Sept. 22, 1989. He studied violin in Frankfurt am Main and Cologne; then took univ. courses in Berlin and Cologne, receiving a Ph.D. with the diss. *Untersuchungen zur Violintechnik um die Wende des 18. Jahrhunderts* (1941). As a violinist, he gave the first German performances of the concertos of Hindemith and Bartók; also played in a string trio. He then pursued a career as a conductor; in 1955 he founded the Mainz Chamber Orch., with which he made numerous tours. From 1953 to 1961 he was director of the Peter-Cornelius-Konservatorium in Mainz; from 1959 he taught at the Hochschule für Musik in Cologne, becoming a prof. there in 1961; remained there until 1987. He ed. Urtext editions of the violin sonatas of Bach and Brahms; also supervised new editions of the orch. works of Albinoni, Rameau, Telemann, and other composers.

Keilberth, Joseph, distinguished German conductor; b. Karlsruhe, April 19, 1908; d. while conducting a performance of *Tristan und Isolde* at the Nationaltheater in Munich, July 20, 1968. He studied in Karlsruhe, where he became a répétiteur (1925), then Generalmusikdirektor (1935–40) at the State Opera. He was chief conductor of the German Phil. Orch. of Prague (1940–45), and then Generalmusikdirektor of the Dresden Staatskapelle (1945–50). He was chief conductor of the Bamberg Sym. Orch. (1949–68), with which he toured Europe in 1951 and the U.S. and Latin America in 1954; was also a conductor at the Bayreuth Festivals (1952–56) and concurrently Generalmusikdirektor of the Hamburg State Phil. Orch. (1950–59); then of the Bavarian State Opera in Munich (1959–68). He was particularly esteemed for his performances of works from the Classical and Romantic Austro-German repertoire.

BIBL.: W.-E. von Lewinski, *J. K.* (Berlin, 1968).

Kelberine, Alexander, Russian-American pianist; b. Kiev, Feb. 22, 1903; d. (suicide) N.Y., Jan. 30, 1940. He studied at the Kiev Cons., then at the Univ. of Vienna; took lessons from Busoni in Berlin; in 1923, went to America and studied at the Juilliard Graduate School in N.Y. with Siloti (piano) and Goldmark (composition); later also studied with Toch. A victim of acute depression, he programmed his last recital for pieces in minor keys and of funereal connotations, concluding with Liszt's *Todtentanz*; he then went home and took an overdose of sleeping pills. He was married to **Jeanne Behrend**, but was estranged from her.

Keldorfer, Robert, Austrian composer, son of **Viktor (Josef) Keldorfer**; b. Vienna, Aug. 10, 1901; d. Klagenfurt, Sept. 13, 1980. He received his early musical training from his father, then took courses at the Vienna Academy of Music with Prohaska, Springer, and Stöhr (1917–19). From 1930 to 1939 he was director of the Linz Cons., and from 1941 to 1966 director of the Klagenfurt Cons. Among his works are an opera, *Verena* (1951); Oboe Concerto (1965); *Sonata ritmica* for Alto Recorder and Piano (1964); Viola Sonata (1964); Sonata for Recorder and Guitar (1967); choral works; songs.

Keldorfer, Viktor (Josef), Austrian conductor and composer, father of **Robert Keldorfer**; b. Salzburg, April 14, 1873; d. Vienna, Jan. 28, 1959. He was a student at the Salzburg Mozarteum. He was chief conductor of the Vienna Männergesang-Verein (1909–21). From 1922 to 1938, and again from 1945 to 1954, he was director of the Vienna Schubertbund; also conducted the Ostdeutscher Sängerbund, which became a model for many Austrian men's choruses. His works include a *Missa solemnis*, 2 vols. of *Lieder für grosse und kleine Kinder*, many men's choruses, and arrangements of Strauss waltzes for men's chorus and orch. He also ed. a complete collection of Schubert's men's choruses.

BIBL.: O. Dobrowolny, *V. K.: Leben und Wirken eines österreichischen Künstlers* (Vienna, 1947).

Keldysh, Yuri (Vsevolodovich), eminent Russian musicologist; b. St. Petersburg, Aug. 29, 1907. He was a student in music history of Ivanov-Boretsky at the Moscow Cons. (graduated, 1930; candidate degree, 1940; Ph.D., 1947, with the diss. *Khudozhestvennoye mirovozzreniye V.V. Stasova* [The Artistic Views of V.V. Stasov]). From 1930 to 1950 he taught at the Moscow Cons., where he became a prof. in 1948. He again served on its faculty from 1957. From 1950 to 1956 he was a teacher at the Cons. and from 1955 to 1957 was director of the Inst. of Music and Theater in Leningrad. He was ed. of the journal *Sovetskaya muzika* (1957–60) and of the valuable *Muzikalnaya Entsiklopediya* (6 vols., 1973–82). Keldysh was one of the foremost Russian musicologists of the Soviet era, and was the author of numerous articles and books.

WRITINGS (all publ. in Moscow unless otherwise given): *Romansovaya lirika Musorgskovo* (Mussorgsky's Lyrical Songs; 1933); *Russkaya klassicheskaya muzïka* (1945; 2nd ed., enl., 1960); *Istoriya russkoy muzïki* (History of Russian Music; 3 vols., 1947–54); ed. with M. Druskin, *Ocherki po istoril russkoy muzïki 1790–1825* (Essays on the History of Russian Music 1790–1825; Leningrad, 1956); *La musique russen en XIXe siècle* (Neuchâtel, 1958); *Russkaya sovetskaya muzïka* (1958); ed. *Voprosï muzïkoznaniya* (Questions of Musicology; 1960); *Kritika i zhurnalistika: Sbornik statey* (Criticism and Journalism: Collection of Articles; 1963); *Russkaya muzïka XVIII veka* (Russian Music of the XVIII Century; 1965); *100 let Moskovskoy konservatorii* (100 Years of the Moscow Conservatory; 1966); *Rakhmaninov i evo vremya* (Rachmaninoff and his Time; 1973).

Kelemen, Milko, significant Croatian composer; b. Podrawska Slatina, March 30, 1924. He was taught to play piano by his grandmother; in 1945, entered the Zagreb Academy of Music, where he studied theory with Šulek; then went to Paris, where he took courses with Messiaen and Aubin at the Cons. (1954–55); supplemented his studies at Freiburg im Breisgau with Fortner (1958–60); then worked on electronic music at the Siemens studio in Munich (1966–68). He taught composition at the Zagreb Cons. (1955–58; 1960–65), the Schumann Cons. in Düsseldorf (1969–73), and the Stuttgart Hochschule für Musik (1973–91). He publ. *Klanglabyrinthe: Reflexionen eines Komponisten über die Neue Musik* (Munich, 1981). As a composer, Kelemen began his career following the trend of European modernism well within academically acceptable lines, but changed his style radically about 1956 in the direction of the cosmopolitan avant-garde, adopting successively or concurrently the techniques of serialism, abstract expressionism, constructivism, and sonorism, making use of electronic sound; he also wrote alternatively valid versions for a single piece.

WORKS: DRAMATIC: *Der Spiegel*, ballet (Paris, Aug. 18, 1960); *Abbandonate*, ballet (Lübeck, Sept. 1, 1964); *Der neue Mieter*, musical scene, after Ionesco (Münster, Sept. 15, 1964); *Der Belagerungszustant*, opera, after Camus (1969–70; Hamburg, Jan. 13, 1970); *Yebell*, action for Soloists and Chamber Ensemble (Munich, Sept. 1, 1972); *Apocalyptica*, multimedia ballet-opera (concert perf., Graz, Oct. 10, 1979). **ORCH.:** *Preludio, Aria e Finale* for Strings (Zagreb, May 20, 1948); *Sinfonietta* for Chamber Orch. (Zagreb, May 4, 1950); Sym. (Zagreb, Feb. 18, 1952); Piano Concerto (Zagreb, Feb. 22, 1953); Violin Concerto (Zagreb, June 20, 1957); *Koncertantne improvizacije* for Strings (Zagreb, Oct. 10, 1955); *Adagio ed Allegro* for Strings (Zagreb, Feb. 16, 1956); Concerto for Bassoon and Strings (Zagreb, May 13, 1957); *Concerto giocoso* for Chamber Orch. (Zagreb, Jan. 10, 1957); Concertino for Double Bass or Cello and Strings (Zagreb, April 20, 1957); *Skolion* (Cologne, June 12, 1960); *Transfigurationen* for Piano and Orch. (Hamburg, April 6, 1962); *Équilibres* for 2 Orchs. (Bonn, March 19, 1962); *Sub Rosa* (Zagreb, May 12, 1965); *Surprise* for Strings (Zagreb, May 12, 1967); *Composé* for 2 Pianos and Orch. Groups (Donaueschingen, Oct. 23, 1967); *Changeant* for Cello and Orch. (Cologne, Nov. 8, 1968); *Floreal* (Washington, D.C., Oct. 30, 1970); *Olifant* for 5 Winds and 2 Orch. Groups (Royan, April 8, 1971); *Passionato* for Flute and 3 Orch. Groups (Berlin, Oct. 18, 1972); *Abecedarium* for Strings (Graz, Oct. 13, 1974); *Mirabilia* for Piano, Ring Modulator, and 2 Orch. Groups (Paris, April 21, 1975); *Mageia* (Augsburg, June 12, 1978); *Infinity* (Zagreb, May 18, 1979); *Grand Jeu Classique* for Violin and Orch. (Metz, Nov. 21, 1982); *Drammatico* for Cello and Orch. (Stuttgart, March 2, 1985); *Phantasmes* for Viola and Orch. (Stuttgart, Dec. 16, 1985); *Archetypon* (Hannover, Jan. 10, 1986); *Antiphony* for Organ and Orch. (1987). **CHAMBER:** *Musika* for Violin (Zagreb, April 4, 1958); *Études contrapuntiques* for Wind Quintet (Paris, Nov. 14, 1959); *Studie* for Flute (Darmstadt, Sept. 5, 1959); Oboe Sonata (Darmstadt, July 7, 1960); *Radiant* for Chamber Ensemble (Darmstadt, July 16, 1963); *Entrances* for Wind Quintet (Hanover, N.H., June 10, 1966); *Motion* for String Quartet (Madrid, March 4, 1969); *Fabliau I* for Flute (Stockholm, Oct. 20, 1972), *II* for Organ (Düsseldorf, May 10, 1972), and *III* for Flute and Harpsichord (Siena, Aug. 10, 1980); *Varia melodia* for String Quartet (Düsseldorf, Sept. 21, 1972); *Tantana*, improvisations for 10 to 20 Performers (Opatija, Nov. 12, 1975); *Splintery* for String Quartet (Paris, Dec. 5, 1977); *Rontondo I* for Wind Trio (Cologne, April 27, 1977) and *II* for Harmonica and Wind Trio (Stuttgart, Oct. 3, 1980); *Love Song* for Saxophone Quartet (Stuttgart, Sept. 6, 1985); *Memories* for String Trio (1986; Zagreb, Jan. 30, 1987); *Sonette* for String Quartet (Bomberg, May 22, 1987). **VOCAL:** *Die Spiele*, song cycle for Baritone and Strings (Strasbourg, May 13, 1958); *Epitaph* for Mezzo-soprano, Viola, and Percussion (Darmstadt, Sept. 8, 1961); *Hommage à Heinrich Schütz* for Solo Voices and Chorus (Berlin, May 12, 1965); *O Primavera*, cantata for Tenor and Strings (Zagreb, May 19, 1965); *Die Wörter*, cantata for Mezzo-soprano and Orch. (Lübeck, May 9, 1966); *Musik für Heinssenbüttel* for Mezzo-soprano, Violin, Cello, and Clarinet (Rome, Feb. 24, 1968); *Gasho* for 4 Choral Groups (Tokyo, April 20, 1974); *Die sieben Plagen* for Mezzo-soprano (Vienna, Nov. 19, 1975); *Drei irische Volkslieder* (Cork, Ireland, May 10, 1980); *Landschaftbilder* for Mezzo-soprano and String Quartet (1985; Graz, Oct. 24, 1986); Requiem for Speaker and Ensemble (1994); *Salut au Monde*, oratorio for Soloists, 2 Choruses, Orch., Projections, and Light Actions (1995).

Kelemen, Zoltán, Hungarian bass; b. Budapest, March 12, 1926; d. Zürich, May 9, 1979. He was educated at the Budapest Academy of Music and at the Accademia di Santa Cecilia in Rome. He made his operatic debut in Augsburg (1959). After singing in Wuppertal, he joined the Cologne Opera (1961); also appeared at Bayreuth (from 1962) and Salzburg (from 1966). On Nov. 22, 1968, he made his Metropolitan Opera debut in N.Y. as Alberich in *Das Rheingold*, a role he repeated for his debut performance at London's Covent Garden (1970). Among his best roles were Osmin, Leporello, the Grand Inquisitor, Dulcamara, Falstaff, and Gianni Schicchi.

Kell, Reginald (Clifford), noted English clarinetist and pedagogue; b. York, June 8, 1906; d. Frankfort, Ky., Aug. 5, 1981. He studied violin at an early age, but later took up the clarinet, and earned a living by playing in silent-movie houses. He received a scholarship to the Royal Academy of Music in London (1929–32), where he studied with Haydn Draper. From 1931 he played in various London orchs., serving as principal clarinet in the London Phil. (1932–36), the London Sym. Orch. (1936–39), and the Philharmonia Orch. (1945–48). He taught at the Royal Academy of Music (1935–39; 1958–59) and at the Aspen (Colo.) Music School (1951–57).

Keller, Hans (Heinrich), Austrian-born English writer on music; b. Vienna, March 11, 1919; d. London, Nov. 6, 1985. He received training in violin in Vienna, and then settled in England in 1938 and became a naturalized British subject in 1948. He played in orchs. and string quartets. Keller mastered the English language to an extraordinary degree, and soon began pointing out solecisms and other infractions on the purity of the tongue to native journalists; wrote articles on film music, and boldly invaded the sports columns in British newspapers, flaunting his mastery of the lingo. In 1947 he founded (with D. Mitchell) the periodical *Music Survey* and was its co-ed. (1949–52); joined the music division of the BBC in 1959, retiring in 1979. He originated a system of functional analysis for radio, in which verbal communication was replaced solely by musical examples to demonstrate a composition's structure and thematic development. He publ. several articles expounding the virtues of his ratiocination, among them the fundamental essay "Functional Analysis: Its Pure Application," *Music Review*, XVIII (1957).

WRITINGS (all publ. in London): *Albert Herring* (1947); *Benjamin Britten: The Rape of Lucretia* (1947); *The Need for Competent Film Music Criticism* (1947); ed. with D. Mitchell, *Benjamin Britten: A Commentary on His Works from a Group of Specialists* (1952); *1975 (1984 minus nine)* (1977); *The Great Haydn Quartets: Their Interpretation* (1986); *Criticism* (1987).

Keller, Hermann, German organist and musicologist; b. Stuttgart, Nov. 20, 1885; d. in an automobile accident in Freiburg im Breisgau, Aug. 17, 1967. He studied with Reger (composition), Straube (organ), and Teichmüller (piano), then musicology at the Univ. of Tübingen (Ph.D., 1924, with the diss. *Die musikalische Artikulation insbesondere bei Joh. Seb. Bach*; publ. in Stuttgart, 1925). He held various posts as organist; from 1919, taught at the Stuttgart Hochschule für Musik; was director of its church and school music dept. (from 1928) and then director (1946–52).

WRITINGS: *Reger und die Orgel* (Munich, 1923); *Schule des Klassichen Triospiels* (Kassel, 1928; 4th ed., 1955); *Schule des Generalbass-Spiels* (Kassel, 1931; 4th ed., rev., 1956; Eng. tr., 1965); *Schule der Choralimprovisation* (Leipzig, 1939); *Die Kunst des Orgelspiels* (Leipzig, 1941); *Die Orgelwerke Bachs* (Leipzig, 1948; Eng. tr., 1967); *Die Klavierwerke Bachs* (Leipzig, 1950); *Phrasierung und Artikulation* (Kassel, 1955; Eng. tr., 1965); *Domenico Scarlatti: Ein Meister des Klaviers* (Leipzig, 1957); *Das Wohltemperierte Klavier von Johann Sebastian Bach* (Kassel, 1965).

Keller, Homer, American composer; b. Oxnard, Calif., Feb. 17, 1915. He studied at the Eastman School of Music in Rochester, N.Y., with Hanson and Rogers (B.M., 1937; M.M., 1938), then in Paris, on a Fulbright grant, with Honegger and Boulanger (1950–51). He taught at the Univ. of Mich. (1947–54) and the Univ. of Oregon (1958–77).

WORKS: ORCH.: 3 syms.: No. 1 (N.Y. Nov. 2, 1940), No. 2 (Ann Arbor, Mich., April 1, 1948), and No. 3 (Honolulu, Dec. 9, 1950); Piano Concerto (Ojai, Calif., May 29, 1949); *Sonorities* (Eugene, Oreg., Feb. 23, 1971). **OTHER:** Chamber music; vocal works.

Kelley, Edgar Stillman, American composer and teacher; b. Sparta, Wis., April 14, 1857; d. N.Y., Nov. 12, 1944. He studied with F. Merriam (1870–74), then with Clarence Eddy and N. Ledochowsky in Chicago (1874–76); subsequently took courses at the Stuttgart Cons. with Seifritz (composition), Krüger and Speidel (piano), and Friedrich Finck (organ). Returning to the U.S., he served as an organist in San Francisco; taught piano and theory at various schools and at the N.Y. College of Music (1891–92). He was music critic for the *San Francisco Examiner* (1893–95); lecturer on music for the Univ. Extension of N.Y. Univ. (1896–97) and then acting prof. at Yale Univ. (1901–02). In 1902 he went to Berlin, where he taught piano and theory. From 1910 to 1934 he was dean of the composition dept. of the Cincinnati Cons. He publ. *Chopin the Composer* (N.Y., 1913) and *Musical Instruments* (Boston, 1925). With his wife, Jessie (née Gregg) Stillman Kelley (b. Chippewa Falls, Wis., 1865; d. Dallas, April 3, 1949), a pianist and teacher, he founded the Kelley Stillman Publishing Co., which brought out several of his scores. Although his stage and symphonic works were quite successful when first performed (some critics described him as a natural successor to MacDowell in American creative work), little of his music survived the test of time.

WORKS: DRAMATIC: *Music to Macbeth*, incidental music for Chorus and Orch. (1882–84; San Francisco, Feb. 12, 1885; rev. as the orch. suite *Gaelic March*); *Pompeiian Picnic*, operetta (1887); *Prometheus Bound*, incidental music (1891); *Puritania*, operetta (Boston, June 9, 1892); *Ben Hur*, incidental music for Solo Voices, Chorus, and Orch. (1899; N.Y., Oct. 1, 1900); *The Pilgrim's Progress*, musical miracle play (1917; Cincinnati May Festival, May 10, 1918). **ORCH.:** *Confluentia* for Strings (1882; arranged from No. 2 of the *3 Pieces* for Piano); *Aladdin: A Chinese Suite* (1887–93; San Francisco, April 1894); 2 syms.: No. 1, *Gulliver: His Voyage to Lilliput* (1900; Cincinnati, April 9, 1937) and No. 2, *New England* (Norfolk, Conn., June 3, 1913, composer conducting); *Alice in Wonderland*, suite (Norfolk, Conn., June 5, 1919, composer conducting); *The Pit and the Pendulum*, suite, after Poe (1925). **CHAMBER:** *Theme and Variations* for String Quartet (c.1880); Piano Quintet (1898–1901). **PIANO:** *3 Pieces* (1891); *Lyric Opera Sketches* (1894). **VOCAL:** *A Wedding Ode* for Men's Chorus and Orch. (1882); *Phases of Love*, 6 songs for Soprano and Piano (1888); 2 songs (1901); *O Captain! My Captain!* for Chorus and Orch. (n.d.); *A California Idyll* for Soprano and Orch. (N.Y., Nov. 14, 1918); *America's Creed* for Chorus and Orch. (1919).

BIBL.: M. King, *E.S. K.: American Composer, Teacher, and Author* (diss., Florida State Univ., 1970).

Kelly, Bryan, English composer; b. Oxford, Jan. 30, 1934. He studied with Jacob and Howells at the Royal College of Music in London (1951–55); then with Boulanger in Paris. After teaching at the Royal Scottish Academy of Music in Glasgow, he was prof. of composition at his alma mater (1962–84).

WORKS: ORCH.: *Latin Quarter Overture* (1955); *Music for Ballet* (1957); *The Tempest Suite* for Strings (1964); *Cookham Concertino* (1969); Oboe Concerto (1972); Guitar Concerto (1978); 2 syms. (1983, 1986). **BRASS BAND:** *Divertimento* (1969); *Edinburgh Dances* (1973); *Andalucia* (1976); *Concertante Music* (1979). **CHAMBER:** *3 Pieces* for Violin and Piano (1959); *2 Concert Pieces* for Clarinet and Piano (1964); *Zodiac* for Clarinet and Piano (1978); *Suite parisienne* for Brass Quintet (1979); *Umbrian Variations* for 8 Cellos (1984). **KEYBOARD: PIANO:** Sonata (1971). **ORGAN:** *Prelude and Fugue* (1960); *Pastorale and Paean* (1973). **VOCAL:** *Tenebrae Nocturnes* for Tenor, Chorus, and Orch. (1965); *The Shell of Achilles* for Tenor and Orch. (1966); *Stabat Mater* for Soprano, Bass, Chorus, and Orch. (1970); *At the Round Earth's Imagined Corners* for Tenor, Chorus, and Strings (1972); *Let There be Light* for Soprano, Narrator, Chorus, and Orch. (1972–73); *Latin Magnificat* for Chorus and Winds (1979); *St. Francis of Assisi*, cantata for Soloists, Chorus, and Orch. (1983); *Proud Music of the Storm* for Tenor, Chorus, and Orch. (1983).

Kelly, Robert, American composer and teacher; b. Clarksburg, W.Va., Sept. 26, 1916. He studied violin with Gardner at the Juilliard School of Music in N.Y. (1935–36); after further violin training at the Cincinnati College of Music (1937–38), he studied composition with Scalero at the Curtis Inst. of Music in Philadelphia (B.M., 1942) and with Elwell at the Eastman School of Music in Rochester, N.Y. (M.M., 1952). From 1946 to 1976 he taught at the Univ. of Ill. at Urbana. His music, while experimental in nature, is skillfully written to utilize traditional forms and structures.

WORKS: DRAMATIC: *Paiyatuma*, ballet (1946); *Tod's Gal*, folk opera (1950; Norfolk, Va., Jan. 8, 1971); *The White Gods*, opera (Urbana, Ill., July 3, 1966). **ORCH.:** *Adirondack Suite* (Philadelphia, April 9, 1941); *Rounds* for Strings (1947; Urbana, Ill., Nov. 17, 1957); 3 syms.: No. 1, *A Miniature Symphony* (Austin, Texas, Oct. 15, 1950), No. 2 (1958), and No. 3, *Emancipation Symphony* (Washington, D.C., Feb. 5, 1963); Concerto for Violin, Cello, and Orch. (Urbana, Ill., March 8, 1961); *An American Diptych* (Austin, Texas, April 26, 1963); *Colloquy* for Chamber Orch. (Chicago, April 17, 1965); Violin Concerto (Urbana, Ill., Oct. 17, 1968); Cello Concerto (1974; Urbana, Ill., March 2,

1975); Viola Concerto (1976; Urbana, Ill., Feb. 5, 1978); Concertino for Chamber Orch. (1977; Ft. Worth, Texas, Oct. 30, 1979); Concerto for Violin, Viola, and Orch. (Urbana, Ill., Feb. 5, 1978); *Garden of Peace: A Meditation* for Strings (1979; Aspen, July 24, 1980); *Tubulations*, concerto for Tuba, Winds, and Percussion (1979); *The Celestial Trumpet*, "trinity" for Trumpet, Symphonic Brass Ensemble, and Percussion (1982). **CHAMBER:** 4 string quartets (1944, 1952, 1963, 1982); Viola Sonata (1950); Violin Sonata (1952); Trombone Sonata (1952); Sonata for Oboe and Harp (1952); Quintet for Clarinet and Strings (1956); Cello Sonata (1958); *Triptych* for Cello and Piano (1962); *Variant* for Violin, Cello, and Piano (1967); *3 Expressions* for Violin and Cello or Viola (1971); *Fantasia* for Harp, Alto Flute, Oboe, and String Quartet (1984). **VOCAL:** *Patterns* for Soprano and Orch. (1953; Urbana, Ill., March 1954); *Walden Pond* for Narrator, Soprano, Chorus, Percussion Ensemble, Flute, and Piano (1975; Urbana, Ill., April 4, 1976); *Rural Songs* for Soprano and Orch. (1980; Urbana, Ill., Nov. 9, 1984); choruses.

Kelterborn, Rudolf, prominent Swiss composer and pedagogue; b. Basel, Sept. 3, 1931. He studied at the Basel Academy of Music with Gustav Güldenstein and Walther Geiser (composition) and Alexander Krannhals (conducting); subsequently took lessons in conducting with Markevitch and in composition with Burkhard in Zürich (1952), Blacher in Salzburg (1953), and Fortner and Bialas at the North-West German Music Academy in Detmold (1955). He taught at the Basel Academy of Music (1955–60) and at the North-West German Music Academy (1960–68); then was on the faculty of the Zürich Cons. and Musikhochschule (1968–75; 1980–83). He was ed.-in-chief of the *Schweizerische Musikzeitung* (1969–75) and director of the music division of the Radio D(eutschen und) R(ätoromanischen) S(schweiz) (1974–80); subsequently was a prof. at the Staatlichen Hochschule für Musik in Karlsruhe (1980–83) and director of (1983–94) and teacher at (1983–96) the Basel Academy of Music. Kelterborn appeared as a guest conductor in performances of his own works; he also lectured in the U.S., England, and Japan. He was awarded the composer's prize of the Assn. of Swiss Musicians and the Kunstpreis of the City of Basel in 1984. He publ. *Zum Beispiel Mozart: Ein Beitrag zur musikalischen Analyse* (Basel, 1980; Japanese tr., Tokyo, 1986). In his music, he applies a precisely coordinated serial organization wherein quantitative values of duration form a recurrent series; changes of tempo are also subjected to serialization. Both melody and harmony are derived from a tone row in which the dissonant intervals of the major seventh and minor second are the mainstays.

WORKS: DRAMATIC: OPERAS: *Die Errettung Thebens* (1960–62; Zürich, June 23, 1963); *Kaiser Jovian* (1964–66; Karlsruhe, March 4, 1967); *Ein Engel kommt nach Babylon* (1975–76; Zürich, June 5, 1977); *Der Kirschgarten*, after Chekhov (1979–81; Zürich, Dec. 4, 1984); *Ophelia* (1982–83; Schwetzingen, May 2, 1984); *Die schwarze Spinne*, musical drama (1984). **BALLET:** *Relations* (1973–74; Bern, Feb. 16, 1975). **ORCH.:** Suite for Brass, Percussion, and Strings (1954); Sonata for 16 Solo Strings (1955); *Mouvements* (1957; Winterthur, May 23, 1959); *Canto appassionato* (1958; Darmstadt, July 6, 1960); Concertino for Piano, 2 Percussion, and Strings (1958–59; Lausanne, Sept. 3, 1960); *Kammersinfonie I* for Violin, 10 Winds, Percussion, Harp, and Strings (Kassel, Oct. 9, 1960) and *II* for Strings (Zürich, Aug. 21, 1964); *Variationen* for Oboe and Strings (1960; Lisbon, March 2, 1961); *Metamorphosen* (Basel, Nov. 7, 1960); *Lamentationes* for Strings (1961; Stuttgart, April 1, 1962); *Scènes fugitives* for Alto and Sopranino Recorders and Orch. (1961; Braunschweig, Nov. 9, 1962); *Vier Nachtstücke* for Chamber Orch. (Zürich, Dec. 11, 1963); *Musik* for Clarinet and Strings (1965–66; Lucerne, Aug. 28, 1966); *Phantasmen* (1965–66; Hannover, Jan. 28, 1967); *Sonata sacra* for Brass (1965–66; Basel, Jan. 18, 1968); 4 syms.: No. 1 (1966–67; Zürich, Jan. 5, 1968), No. 2 (1969–70; Munich, Oct. 22, 1970), No. 3, *Espansioni*, for Baritone, Orch. and Tape (1974–75; Basel, Sept. 29, 1976), and No. 4 (1985–86; Bamberg, Feb. 3, 1987); *Miroirs* (1966; Detmold, May 3, 1968); *Traummusik* for Small Orch. (1971; Zürich, Jan. 28, 1972); *Kommunikationen* for 6 Orch. Groups (1971–72; Lucerne, Aug. 15, 1973); *Changements* (1972–73; Montreux, Sept. 19, 1973); *Nuovi canti* for Flute and Chamber Orch. (1973; Munich, April 24, 1974); *Tableaux encadrés* for 13 Solo Strings (1974; Zürich, June 15, 1975); *Szene* for 12 Solo Cellos (1977; Lucerne, Aug. 30, 1980); *Erinnerungen an Orpheus* (1977–78; Bern, Jan. 18, 1979); *Visions sonorés* (1979; Basel, June 4, 1980); *Chiaroscuro: Canzoni* (1979–80; Salzburg, Aug. 29, 1980); *Musica luminosa* (1983–84; Locarno, Sept. 13, 1985); *Sonatas* for Winds (1986; Zürich, Feb. 24, 1987); *Musik* for Double Bass and Orch. (1986–87); *Rencontres* for Piano and Orch. (1991–92; Duisburg, Nov. 25, 1992). **CHAMBER:** 5 string quartets: No. 1 (1954), No. 2 (1956; Munich, Oct. 27, 1959), No. 3 (1962; Hannover, Oct. 23, 1963), No. 4 (1968–70; Zagreb, May 12, 1971), and No. 5 (Basel, Oct. 25, 1989); *Kammermusik* for Flute, Violin, and Piano (1957); *Fünf Fantasien* for Transverse Flute, Cello, and Harpsichord (1958); *Sieben Bagatellen* for Wind Quintet (1958); *Lyrische Kammermusik* for Clarinet, Violin, and Viola (1959); *Varianti* for 6 Instruments (1959); Sonata for Oboe and Harpsichord (1960); *Esquisses* for Harpsichord and Percussion (1962); *Meditationen* for 6 Winds (1963); *Musik* for Violin and Guitar (1964); *Vier Miniaturen* for Oboe and Violin (1964); *Fantasia à tre* for Piano Trio (1967); *Moments musicaux* for Bassoon and Piano (1967); *Incontri brevi* for Flute and Clarinet (1967); Octet for Clarinet, Horn, Bassoon, 2 Violins, Viola, Cello, and Double Bass (1969; Zürich, Jan. 29, 1970); *Vier Stücke* for Clarinet and Piano (1969); *Inventionen und Intermezzi* for 2 Gambens and Harpsichord (1969); *Neuen Momente* for Viola and Piano (1973); *Reaktionen* for Violin and Piano (1973–74); *Kammermusik* for Flute or Piccolo, Oboe, Clarinet, Horn, and Bassoon (1974); *Consort-Music* for Flute or Piccolo or Alto Flute, Clarinet or Bass Clarinet, Trumpet, and String Quartet (1975; Hamburg, June 15, 1976); *7 Minute Play* for Flute and Piano (1976); *Monodie I* for Flute and Harp (1977); Trio for Flute, Oboe, and Bassoon (1980); *Notturni* for Cello and Double Bass (1981); *Musik* for 6 Percussionists (1983–84); *6 Short Pieces* for Flute, Viola, and Guitar (1984); Cello Sonata (1985); *Escursioni* for Flute, Cello, and Harpsichord (1988–89). **VOCAL:** *Elegie* for Alto, Oboe, Viola, Percussion, and Harpsichord (1955); *Missa* for Soprano, Tenor, Chorus, and Orch. (1958; Basel, Dec. 1, 1961); *Canta profana* for Baritone, Chorus, and 13 Instruments (1959–60); *Die Flut* for Speaker, Soprano, Alto, Tenor, Baritone, Chorus, and Orch. (1963–64; Basel, May 14, 1965); *Kana/Auferstehung* for Baritone, 2 Violins, and Organ (1964); *Der Traum meines Lebens verdämmert* for Mezzo-soprano, Flute, 2 Clarinets or Bass Clarinet, Harp, and String Quartet (1964); *Tres cantiones sacrae* for Chorus (1967; Kassel, April 12, 1969); *Fünf Madrigale* for Soprano, Tenor, and Orch. (1967–68; Lucerne, Aug. 20, 1969); *Dies unus* for Soprano, Men's Chorus, and Orch. (1971–72; Zürich, May 26, 1973); *Drei Fragmente* for Chorus (1973; Stuttgart, Feb. 10, 1974); *Gesänge zur Nacht* for Soprano and Chamber Orch. (1978; Zürich, March 2, 1979); *Fünf Gesänge* for Chorus, Clarinet, Horn, Trumpet, and Trombone (1980–81; Basel, Feb. 5, 1982); *Schlag an mit deiner Sichel* for 4 Voices and Renaissance Instruments (1981–82); *Lux et tenebrae* for Soprano, Baritone, Men's Chorus, and Orch. (1986–87); *Gesänge der Liebe* for Baritone and Orch. (1987–88).

BIBL.: D. Larese and F. Goebels, *R. K.* (Amriswiler, 1970); M. Weber, *Die Orchesterwerke R. K.s* (Regensburg, 1980); K. von Fischer, "R. K.," *Dissonanz*, no. 4 (1985).

Kemp, Barbara, German soprano; b. Kochem an der Mosel, Dec. 12, 1881; d. Berlin, April 17, 1959. She studied at the Strasbourg Cons. (1902–05). In 1903 she made her operatic debut as the Priestess in *Aida* in Strasbourg. She then sang in Rostock (1906–08) and Breslau (1908–13) before being engaged as a member of the Berlin Royal (later State) Opera (1913–31); made her first appearance at the Bayreuth Festival as Senta (1914), and returned there as Kundry (1924–27). She made her Metropolitan Opera debut in N.Y. as Mona Fiordalisa and the Wife in

Max von Schilling's *Mona Lisa* (March 1, 1923), and married the composer that same year; sang there until 1924, and then continued her career in Europe. She later taught voice in Berlin.

BIBL.: O. Bie, *B. K.* (Berlin, 1921).

Kempe, Rudolf, eminent German conductor; b. Niederpoyritz, near Dresden, June 14, 1910; d. Zürich, May 11, 1976. He studied oboe at the Orchestral School of the Dresden Staatskapelle. In 1929 he became 1st oboist of the Gewandhaus Orch. in Leipzig. He made his conducting debut at the Leipzig Opera in 1936. He served in the German army during World War II; then conducted in Chemnitz; was director of the Opera there (1945–48) and at the Weimar National Theater (1948–49). From 1949 to 1953 he was Generalmusikdirektor of the Dresden Staatskapelle; then served in an identical capacity with the Bavarian State Opera in Munich (1952–54); also made appearances in opera in Vienna, in London (Covent Garden), and at the Metropolitan in N.Y. In 1960 Sir Thomas Beecham named him assoc. conductor of the Royal Phil. of London; upon Beecham's death in 1961, he became its principal conductor; from 1963 to 1975, was artistic director as well. He was chief conductor of the Tonhalle Orch. in Zürich (1965–72) and of the Munich Phil. (from 1967); from 1975 he conducted the BBC Sym. Orch. in London. He was a distinguished interpreter of Beethoven, Brahms, Wagner, Bruckner, and Richard Strauss; also conducted lighter scores with equal aplomb.

BIBL.: C. Kempe-Oettinger, *R. K.: Pictures of a Life* (Munich, 1977; Eng. tr., London, 1979); K. memorial issue of *Le Grand Baton* (March/June 1978).

Kempen, Paul van, prominent Dutch-born German conductor; b. Zoeterwoude, near Leiden, May 16, 1893; d. Hilversum, Dec. 8, 1955. He studied violin in Amsterdam, then was a violinist in the Concertgebouw Orch. there (1913–15). In 1916 he went to Germany and served as concertmaster with several orchs. before embarking upon a conducting career, becoming music director in Oberhausen in 1932. He also became a naturalized German citizen. From 1934 to 1942 he was chief conductor of the Dresden Phil.; although he was obliged to conduct concerts for the German army, he refused to join the Nazi party. After serving as Generalmusikdirektor in Aachen (1942–43), he returned to the Netherlands. Following World War II, he made guest conducting appearances with the Rotterdam Phil. and the Residentie Orch. in The Hague; was chief conductor of the Radio Phil. in Hilversum (from 1949) and also taught conducting there and at the Accademia Chigiana in Siena. He proved himself a discriminating interpreter of the Austro-German repertoire.

BIBL.: N. Steffen, "P. v.K. in the Netherlands," *Le Grand Baton* (Sept./Dec. 1979).

Kempff, Wilhelm (Walter Friedrich), distinguished German pianist, pedagogue, and composer; b. Juterbog, Nov. 25, 1895; d. Positano, Italy, May 23, 1991. He studied piano with his father, also named Wilhelm Kempff; at the age of 9, he entered the Berlin Hochschule für Musik, where he studied composition with Robert Kahn and piano with Heinrich Barth; also attended the Univ. of Berlin. He began his concert career in 1916; in 1918 he made the first of many appearances with the Berlin Phil.; from that time he toured throughout Europe, South America, and Japan, featuring improvisation as part of his programs. From 1924 to 1929 he was director of the Stuttgart Hochschule für Musik; from 1957 he gave annual courses in Positano, Italy. He made his London debut in 1951 and his American debut in N.Y. in 1964. He continued to appear in concerts well past his octogenarian milestone; in 1979 he was a soloist with the Berlin Phil., after having had an association with it for more than 60 years. Kempff epitomized the classic tradition of German pianism; he eschewed flamboyance in his performances of Mozart, Beethoven, Schubert, and other masters. He publ. a book of memoirs, *Unter dem Zimbelstern* (Stuttgart, 1951).

WORKS: OPERAS: *König Midas* (Königsberg, 1930); *Familie Gozzi* (Stettin, 1934); *Die Fasnacht von Rottweil* (Hannover, 1937). **ORCH.:** 2 piano concertos (1915, 1931); 2 syms. (1923, 1926); Violin Concerto (1932); *Arkadische Suite* for Chamber Orch. (1939); *Epitaph* for Strings (1946); *Legende* for Piano and Orch. (1947). **CHAMBER:** 2 string quartets (1942); piano pieces. **OTHER:** *Von der Geburt des Herrn*, scenic mystery (1925); *Te Deum* (1926).

BIBL.: B. Gavoty and R. Hauert, *K.* (Monaco and Geneva, 1954).

Keneman, Feodor, Russian pianist and composer of German descent; b. Moscow, April 20, 1873; d. there, March 29, 1937. He studied with Safonov (piano; graduated, 1895) and Ippolitov-Ivanov (composition; graduated, 1897) at the Moscow Cons.; also with Taneyev (counterpoint) there. From 1899 to 1932 he taught theory at the Moscow Cons. He gave recitals and was the favorite accompanist of Chaliapin, for whom he composed the popular Russian ballad *As the King Went to War* and arranged the folk song *Ei ukhnem!* He toured the U.S. with Chaliapin (1923–24). He also composed military marches and band pieces.

Kenessey, Jenö, Hungarian conductor and composer; b. Budapest, Sept. 23, 1905; d. there, Aug. 19, 1976. He studied with Lajtha (composition) and Sugár (organ) at the Budapest Cons., Siklós (composition) at the Budapest Academy of Music, and Shalk (conducting) in Salzburg. He was a conductor at the Budapest Opera (1932–65), where he conducted his opera *Arany meg az asszony* (Gold and the Woman; 1942; May 8, 1943) and his ballet *May Festival* (Nov. 29, 1948). His other works included the ballets *Montmartre* (1930), *Johnny in Boots* (1935), *Mine Is the Bridegroom* (1938), *Perhaps Tomorrow* (1938), *Miraggio* (1938), *The Kerchief* (1951), and *Bihari's Song* (1954); *Dance Impressions* for Orch. (1933); *Divertimento* for Soprano and Orch. (1945); *Dances from Sarköz* for Orch. (1953); *Beams of Light*, cantata (1960); *Canzonetta* for Flute and Chamber Orch. (1970); *Dawn at Balaton*, symphonic poem, with Narrator and Women's Voices (1972); Piano Quartet (1928–29); Sonata for Flute and Harp (1940); 2 harp trios (1940, 1972), Sonata Flute, Viola, and Piano (1940); *Divertimento* for Viola and Harp (1963); *Elegy and Scherzo* for Piano (1973); songs and choruses.

Kenins, Talivaldis, distinguished Latvian-born Canadian composer, teacher, pianist, organist, and choirmaster; b. Liepāja, April 23, 1919. He took up piano at 5 and composition at 8. While preparing for a diplomatic career at the Lycée Champollion (B.Litt., 1939) in Grenoble, he continued to pursue training in piano. He then was a student of piano and composition of Wihtol at the Latvian State Cons. in Riga (1940–44). With the Soviet occupation of his homeland, he went to Paris and studied at the Cons. (1945–51) with Plé-Caussade (counterpoint and fugue), Messiaen (analysis and aesthetics), and Aubin (composition; premier prix, 1950). In 1951 he emigrated to Canada and in 1956 became a naturalized Canadian citizen. He was organist and choirmaster at Toronto's St. Andrew's Lutheran Church from 1951, serving as founder-conductor of its noted St. Andrew's Latvian Choir (1951–58). From 1952 to 1984 he taught at the Univ. of Toronto. In 1973–74 he served as president of the Canadian League of Composers. In 1989 he was named an honorary prof. of the Latvian Academy of Music and in 1990 his life was the subject of a Latvian film documentary. In 1994 his 75th birthday was celebrated in Latvia by concerts of his music, where his music had been virtually forbidden during the 50-year Soviet occupation. Ottawa honored him with the naming of a street, only the 2nd living Canadian to receive such a distinction. With G. Ridout, he ed. the vol. *Celebration* (Toronto, 1984). His French training proved crucial in his compositional development. While his music retains its adherence to formal design, he has effectively applied the resources of the cosmopolitan contemporary school to his extensive output.

WORKS: ORCH.: Piano Concerto (1946); Duo for Piano and Orch. (1951); *Scherzo Concertante* (1953); 8 syms.: No. 1 (1959), No. 2, *Sinfonia Concertante* (1967), No. 3 (1970), No. 4 (1972), No. 5 (1975), No. 6, *Sinfonia ad Fugam* (1978), No. 7

(1980), and No. 8, *Sinfonia Concertata,* for Organ and Orch. (1986); *Folk Dance and Fugue No. 1* (1964) and *No. 2* (1986); Concerto for Violin, Cello, and Strings (1964); *Nocturne and Dance* for Strings (1969); *Fantaisies Concertantes* for Piano and Orch. (1971); Violin Concerto (1974); *Naačnaača,* symphonic poem (1975); Sinfonietta (1976); *Beatae voces tenebrae* (1977); *Concerto da Camera No. 1* for Piano, Flute, Clarinet, and Strings (1981) and *No. 2* for Flute and Ensemble (1983); Concerto for 14 Instruments (1982); *Partita for Strings on Lutheran Chorales* (1983); Concerto for 5 Percussionists and Orch. (1983); *Aria per corde* for Strings (1984); Concerto for Flute, Guitar, Strings, and Percussion (1985); *Canzona-Sonate* for Viola and String Orch. (1986); Double Concerto for Violin, Piano, and Orch. (1987); Concerto for Piano, Strings, and Percussion (1990); *Honour and Freedom* (1991). **CHAMBER:** String Quartet (1948); Septet for Clarinet, Horn, Bassoon, Violin, Viola, Cello, and Double Bass (1949); Cello Sonata (1950); Trio for Violin, Cello, and Piano (1952); Suite Concertante for Cello and Piano (1955); 2 violin sonatas (1955, 1979); 2 quartets for Piano and Strings (1958, 1979); *Diversions for Cello and Piano on a Gipsy Song* (1958); *Divertimento* for Clarinet and Piano (1960); Concertante for Flute and Piano (1966); *Fantasy-Variations* for Flute and Viola (1967); *Concertino à Cinque* for Flute, Oboe, Viola, Cello, and Piano (1968); *Serenade* for Oboe and Cello (1973); Sextet for Bassoon and Strings (1978); *Chaconne on a Latvian Folk Theme* for Violin (1978); Sonata for Solo Cello (1982); Quintet for Piano and Winds (1984); *Variations on a Theme by Schubert* for Woodwind Quintet (1984); *Adagio and Fugue* for Viola, Cello, and Organ (1985); *Concertino Barocco* for 2 Violins (1985); *Suite en Concert* for 2 Guitars and String Quartet (1987); Trio for Violin, Viola, and Cello (1989); *Die Zauberklarinette* for Clarinet (1991); Nonet, *L'Ultima Sinfonia,* for Oboe, Clarinet, Horn, String Quintet, and Piano (1993); Quintet for Piano and Strings (1994). **KEYBOARD: PIANO:** Concertino for 2 Pianos (1956); 3 sonatas (1961–85); Sonata for 2 Pianos (1988); *Schumann Paraphrases and Fugue* (1995). **ORGAN:** Suite (1967); *Sinfonia Notturna* (1978); *Introduction, Pastorale, and Toccata* (1983); *Scherzo-Fantasy* (1989); *Ex Mari* (1992). **VOCAL:** *To a Soldier,* cantata for Soloists, Chorus, and Organ (1953); *Bonhomme, bonhomme* for Chorus (1964); *The Carrion Crow* for Men's Voices (1967); *Land of the Silver Birch* for Men's Voices (1967); *The Maiden's Lament* for Men's Voices (1967); *Chants of Glory and Mercy (Gloria)* for Soloists, Chorus, and Orch. (1970); *Cantata Baltica* for Chorus, 2 Trumpets, Timpani, and Organ (1974); *Songs to the Almighty* for Mezzo-soprano and Orch. (1986); *Cantata of Chorales on Themes by J.S. Bach* for Soprano, Chorus, Horn, Trumpet, and Organ (1992); numerous other works, including original or folk songs on Latvian texts.

BIBL.: I. Zemzare, *T. K.: Starp Divām Pasaulēm* (T. K.: Between Two Worlds; Riga, 1994; with summaries in Eng. and French).

Kennan, Kent Wheeler, American composer and teacher; b. Milwaukee, April 18, 1913. He studied composition with Hunter Johnson at the Univ. of Mich. (1930–32); then with Hanson and Rogers at the Eastman School of Music in Rochester, N.Y. (M.B., 1934; M.M., 1936); won the American Prix de Rome, and took some lessons with Pizzetti in Rome. Returning to the U.S., he taught at Kent State Univ. (1939–40) and at the Univ. of Texas in Austin (1940–42); during World War II, served as bandleader in the U.S. Army (1942–45), then taught again at the Univ. of Texas (1945–46) and at Ohio State Univ. (1947–49). In 1949 he joined the staff of the Univ. of Texas on a permanent basis, retiring in 1983. He publ. *The Technique of Orchestration* (N.Y., 1952; 4th ed., rev., 1990 with D. Grantham); *Counterpoint Based on 18th-Century Practice* (N.Y., 1959; 3rd ed., 1987); 2 workbooks on orchestration (1952, 1969); a counterpoint workbook (1959; 3rd ed., 1987). Toscanini chose one of Kennan's innocent little symphonic pieces, *Night Soliloquy* for Flute and Orch. (1936), for performance by the NBC Sym. Orch. (N.Y., Feb. 26, 1943), a rare distinction at that time for an American composer.

WORKS: ORCH.: *Night Soliloquy* for Flute and Orch. (1936); *Il campo dei fiori* for Trumpet and Orch. (1937); *Nocturne* for Viola and Orch. (1937); *Dance Divertimento* (1938; also for 2 Pianos); *Promenade* (1938); Sym. (1938); *Andante* for Oboe and Orch. (1939); Piano Concertino (1946; also for Piano and Winds, 1963). **CHAMBER:** *Sea Sonata* for Violin and Piano (1939); *Scherzo, Aria, and Fugue* for Oboe and Piano (1948); Trumpet Sonata (1956). **PIANO:** *3 Preludes* (1939); Sonatina (1945); *2 Preludes* (1951). **VOCAL:** *Blessed Are They That Mourn* for Chorus and Orch. (1939); *The Unknown Warrior Speaks* for Men's Chorus (1944); songs.

Kennedy, (George) Michael (Sinclair), esteemed English music critic and writer on music; b. Manchester, Feb. 19, 1926. He was educated at the Berkhamsted School. In 1941 he joined the staff of the London *Daily Telegraph,* where he was its northern music critic (from 1950), northern ed. (1960–86), and joint chief music critic (1986–89). From 1989 he was music critic of the *Sunday Telegraph.* In 1981 he was made an officer of the Order of the British Empire. In addition to his perceptive music criticism, he has published a number of valuable biographies and reference works.

WRITINGS: *The Hallé Tradition: A Century of Music* (Manchester, 1960); *The Works of Ralph Vaughan Williams* (London, 1964; rev. 1980); *Portrait of Elgar* (London, 1968; rev. 1982; 3rd ed., 1987); *Elgar: Orchestral Music* (London, 1969) *Portrait of Manchester* (Manchester, 1970); *A History of the Royal Manchester College of Music* (Manchester, 1971); *Barbirolli: Conductor Laureate* (London, 1971); *Mahler* (London, 1974; rev. 1990); ed. *The Autobiography of Charles Hallé, with Correspondence and Diaries* (London, 1976); *Richard Strauss* (London, 1976; rev. 1983; rev. and aug., 1995); ed. *The Concise Oxford Dictionary of Music* (Oxford, 3rd ed., 1980; rev. 1995); *Britten* (London, 1981; rev. 1993); *The Hallé 1858–1983* (Manchester, 1983); *Strauss: Tone Poems* (London, 1984); *The Oxford Dictionary of Music* (Oxford, 1985; 2nd ed., rev., 1994); *Portrait of Walton* (London, 1989); *Music Enriches All: 21 Years of the Royal Northern College of Music, Manchester* (Manchester, 1994).

Kennedy, Nigel (Paul), versatile English violinist; b. Brighton, Dec. 28, 1956. He was born into a family of cellists; at 7, he won a piano scholarship to the Yehudi Menuhin School, but soon became a prize violin student there; in 1972 he became a student of Dorothy DeLay at the Juilliard School in N.Y. In 1977 he made his London debut as soloist with the Philharmonia Orch., and subsequently performed throughout his homeland and on the Continent; in 1985 he made his first tour of the U.S. His interests range over the fields of serious, jazz, rock, and pop music; he has been closely associated with jazz notable Stephane Grappelli and has led his own rock group.

Kennedy-Fraser, Marjorie (née **Kennedy**), Scottish singer, pianist, and folk-song collector; b. Perth, Oct. 1, 1857; d. Edinburgh, Nov. 22, 1930. She was the daughter of the Scottish tenor David Kennedy (b. Perth, April 15, 1825; d. Stratford, Ontario, Oct. 12, 1856). From the age of 12 she traveled with her father as his accompanist. She then studied voice with Mathilde Marchesi in Milan and Paris; also took courses in piano with Matthay and in music history with Niecks. Inspired by the example of her father, she became a dedicated collector of folk songs. In 1905 she went to the Outer Hebrides, after which she made a specialty of research in Celtic music. She publ. the eds. *Songs of the Hebrides* (with K. Macleod; 3 vols., London, 1909, 1917, 1921); *From the Hebrides* (Glasgow and London, 1925); *More Songs of the Hebrides* (London and N.Y., 1929); also the handbook *Hebridean Song and the Laws of Interpretation* (Glasgow, 1922). She wrote the libretto for and sang the title role in Bantock's opera *The Seal Woman* (1924). She also publ. the autobiography *A Life of Song* (London, 1928).

Kenny, Yvonne, Australian soprano; b. Sydney, Nov. 25, 1950. She received her training at the New South Wales State Conservatorium of Music in Sydney and at the La Scala Opera School in Milan (1973–74). In 1975 she made her debut in London in a concert perf. as Donizetti's Rosamunda d'Inghilterra. On July 12, 1976, she made her first appearance at London's Covent Garden in the premiere of Henze's *We Come to the River*, and returned there in subsequent years to sing such roles as Mozart's Susanna, Pamina, and Ilia, Verdi's Oscar, Bizet's Micaëla, Handel's Semele, and Puccini's Liù. In 1977 she made her debut at London's English National Opera as Strauss' Sophie. In 1985 she made her first appearance at the Glyndebourne Festival as Ilia. In 1993 she sang Strauss' Madeleine at the Berlin State Opera. Her guest engagements also took her to Paris, Vienna, Hamburg, Munich, Salzburg, Edinburgh, and other music centers. She was also very active as a concert artist. In 1989 she was made a Member of the Order of Australia.

Kentner, Louis (actually, **Lajos Philip**), admired Hungarian-born English pianist; b. Karwin, July 19, 1905; d. London, Sept. 22, 1987. He studied piano with Székely and Weiner and composition with Koessler and Kodály at the Royal Academy of Music in Budapest. He made his formal debut in Budapest in 1920, then toured throughout Europe. In 1935 he settled in England, becoming a naturalized British subject in 1946. On Nov. 28, 1956, he made his U.S. debut in N.Y. In 1978 he was made a Commander of the Order of the British Empire. In 1931 he married **Ilona Kabos**; they divorced in 1945. He was praised for his interpretations of works by Mozart, Beethoven, Schubert, Chopin, and Liszt, as well as those by Bartók and various contemporary English composers.

BIBL.: H. Taylor, ed., *K.: A Symposium* (N.Y., 1987).

Kenton (real name, **Kornstein**), **Egon,** Hungarian violinist, musicologist, and music librarian; b. Nagyszalonta, May 22, 1891; d. Paris, Dec. 3, 1987. He studied violin with Hubay at the Budapest Royal Academy of Music, graduating in 1911. He was violist in the Hungarian String Quartet (1911–23); then emigrated to the U.S.; in 1947, received his M.A. in musicology from N.Y. Univ.; subsequently taught musicology at the Univ. of Conn. in Storrs (1950–61); from 1961 to 1971, served as librarian of the Mannes College of Music in N.Y. He wrote the first English-language study of the life and music of Giovanni Gabrieli (Rome, 1967).

Kerman, Joseph (Wilfred), eminent American musicologist; b. London (of American parents), April 3, 1924. He studied at Univ. College School, London, then at N.Y. Univ. (A.B., 1943), subsequently taking courses with Strunk, Thompson, and Weinrich at Princeton Univ. (Ph.D., 1950, with the diss. *The Elizabethan Madrigal: A Comparative Study*; publ. in N.Y., 1962); also taught at Westminster Choir College in Princeton, N.J. (1949–51). In 1951 he joined the faculty at the Univ. of Calif. at Berkeley, being made a prof. in 1960; also was chairman of its music dept. (1960–63). After serving as Heather Prof. of Music at the Univ. of Oxford (1971–74), he resumed his professorship at Berkeley. He retired in 1994. In 1977 he became a founding ed. of the journal *19th Century Music*, serving as its co-ed. until 1989. His various honors included his being made an Honorary Fellow of the Royal Academy of Music in London (1972) and a Fellow of the American Academy of Arts and Sciences (1973). An erudite scholar and provocative critic, Kerman holds an influential position among American musicologists of his generation.

WRITINGS: *Opera as Drama* (N.Y., 1956; rev. 1988); *The Beethoven Quartets* (N.Y. and London, 1967); with H. Janson, *History of Art & Music* (N.Y. and Englewood Cliffs, N.J., 1968); ed. *L. van Beethoven: Autograph Miscellany ("Kafka Sketchbook")* (London, 1970); ed. *W.A. Mozart: Concerto in C, K. 503* (N.Y., 1970; Norton Critical Score); with V. Kerman, *Listen* (N.Y., 1972); *The Music of William Byrd: Vol. I, The Masses and Motets of William Byrd* (London, 1981); *Contemplating Music* (Cambridge, Mass., 1985; publ. in England as *Musicology*, London, 1985); ed. *Music at the Turn of the Century: A "19th-Century Music" Reader* (Berkeley and Oxford, 1990); *Write All These Down: Essays on Music* (Berkeley, 1994).

Kern, Adele, German soprano; b. Munich, Nov. 25, 1901; d. there, May 6, 1980. She was trained in Munich. In 1924 she made her operatic debut there as Olympia in *Les contes d'Hoffmann* at the Bavarian State Opera, and sang there until 1926 when she became a member of the Frankfurt am Main Opera. In 1927–28 she toured South America. From 1927 to 1935 she appeared at the Salzburg Festivals. She also sang in Munich, as well as at the Vienna State Opera (1929–30) and the Berlin State Opera (1935–37). She subsequently sang at the Bavarian State Opera (1937–43; 1945–46). As a guest artist, she appeared at London's Covent Garden (1931, 1934), Milan's La Scala, the Rome Opera, and at other European operatic centers. She was admired for her Mozart and Richard Strauss roles, among them Despina, Susanna, Zerbinetta, Marzelline, and Sophie.

Kern, Jerome (David), famous American composer; b. N.Y., Jan. 27, 1885; d. there, Nov. 11, 1945. He was educated in N.Y. public schools; studied music with his mother, then with Paolo Gallico and Alexander Lambert (piano) and Austin Pearce and Albert von Doenhoff (theory) at the N.Y. College of Music (1902–03); subsequently theory and composition in Heidelberg (1903–04). He then returned to N.Y., where he became a pianist and salesman for a publishing firm in 1905; publ. his first song, *How'd You Like to Spoon with Me*, which became famous; in 1906 he was in London, where he was connected with a theatrical production. He obtained his first success as a composer for the stage with his musical comedy *The Red Petticoat* (N.Y., Nov. 13, 1912). After that he produced musical comedies in rapid succession, bringing out more than 40 works; also wrote several film scores. Kern's greatest success was *Show Boat* (Washington, D.C., Nov. 15, 1927); a most remarkable score, and one of the finest of its kind in the genre, it contains the famous song "Ol' Man River." On Jan. 23, 1985, Kern was immortalized in the first 22-cent American postage stamp, designed by James Sharpe of Westport, Conn., commemorated in a ceremony held in the main gallery of the New York Public Library for the Performing Arts at N.Y.'s Lincoln Center; in attendance were Hal David, president of ASCAP, as well as Kern's daughter, Betty Kern Miller, who traveled from her home in Danville, Ky.

WORKS (all perf. in N.Y. unless otherwise given): *La Belle Paree* (March 20, 1911; in collaboration with F. Tours); *The Red Petticoat* (Nov. 13, 1912); *Oh, I Say!* (Oct. 30, 1913); *90 in the Shade* (Jan. 15, 1915); *Nobody Home* (April 20, 1915); *Cousin Lucy* (Aug. 27, 1915); *Miss Information* (Oct. 5, 1915); *Very Good, Eddie* (Dec. 23, 1915); *Have a Heart* (Jan. 11, 1917); *Love o' Mike* (Jan. 15, 1917); *Oh Boy!* (Feb. 20, 1917); *Leave It to Jane* (Aug. 28, 1917); *Miss 1917* (revue; Nov. 5, 1917; in collaboration with V. Herbert); *Oh Lady! Lady!* (Feb. 1, 1918); *Toot, Toot* (March 11, 1918); *Head over Heels* (April 29, 1918); *Rock-a-bye-Baby* (May 22, 1918); *She's a Good Fellow* (May 5, 1919); *Night Boat* (Feb. 2, 1920); *Hitchy Koo of 1920* (revue; Oct. 19, 1920); *Sally* (Dec. 21, 1920; ballet music by V. Herbert; also a film, 1929); *Good Morning, Dearie* (Nov. 1, 1921); *The Cabaret Girl* (London, Sept. 19, 1922); *The Bunch and Judy* (Nov. 28, 1922); *The Beauty Prize* (London, Sept. 5, 1923); *Stepping Stones* (Nov. 6, 1923); *Sitting Pretty* (April 8, 1924); *Dear Sir* (Sept. 23, 1924); *Sunny* (Sept. 22, 1925; also films, 1930 and 1941); *The City Chap* (Oct. 26, 1925); *Criss Cross* (Oct. 12, 1926); *Lucky* (March 22, 1927); *Show Boat* (Washington, D.C., Nov. 15, 1927); *Blue Eyes* (London, April 27, 1928); *Sweet Adeline* (musical romance; Sept. 2, 1929; also a film, 1935); *The Cat and the Fiddle* (Oct. 15, 1931; also a film, 1933); *Music in the Air* (Nov. 8, 1932; also a film, 1934); *Roberta* (Nov. 18, 1933; also films, 1935 and 1952); *3 Sisters* (London, April 9, 1934); *Gentlemen Unafraid* (St. Louis, June 3, 1938); *Very Warm for May* (Nov. 17, 1939). *Show Boat* was also filmed in 1929, 1936, and 1951; his other films were *I Dream Too Much* (1935); *Swing Time* (1936); *High, Wide and Handsome* (1937); *When You're in Love* (1937); *Joy of Living* (1938); *One Night in the Tropics* (1940); *You Were Never Lovelier* (1942); *Can't Help Singing* (1944); *Cover Girl* (1944); *Centennial Summer* (1946); *Till the Clouds Roll By* (1946; a film biography after a song from *Oh Boy!*). He also wrote songs for various other musicals and films; among the most popular were *They Didn't Believe Me* for *The Girl from Utah* (1914) and *The Last Time I Saw Paris* for *Lady Be Good* (1941). His other works include *Scenario* for Orch. (based on themes from *Show Boat*; 1941) and *Mark Twain Suite* for Orch. (Cincinnati, May 14, 1942). For information on his songs, see *The Jerome Kern Song Book* (N.Y., 1955).

BIBL.: D. Ewen, *The Story of J. K.* (N.Y., 1953); idem, *The World of J. K.* (N.Y., 1960); H. Fordin, *J. K.: The Man and His Music* (Santa Monica, Calif., 1975); A. Lamb, *J. K. in Edwardian London* (N.Y., 1981; 2nd ed., rev., 1985); G. Bordman, "J. K.: Innovator/Traditionalist," *Musical Quarterly*, no. 4 (1985); M. Kreuger, *Show Boat: The Story of a Classic American Musical* (N.Y., 1990); S. Suskind, *Berlin, K., Rodgers, Hart, and Hammerstein: A Complete Song Catalogue* (Jefferson, N.C., 1990); L. Davis, *Bolton and Wodehouse and K.: The Men Who Made Musical Comedy* (N.Y., 1994).

Kern, Patricia, Welsh mezzo-soprano; b. Swansea, July 4, 1927. She was a student at the Guildhall School of Music in London of Parry Jones (1949–52). In 1952 she made her operatic debut in *Cenerentola* with London's Opera for All group, remaining with it until 1955. In 1959 she made her first appearance with the Sadler's Wells Opera in London as Rusalka, singing there regularly for 10 seasons. In 1967 she made her debut at London's Covent Garden as Zerlina. She made her first appearance in the U.S. in 1969 in Washington, D.C. She also made guest appearances in Glyndebourne, Stockholm, Spoleto, N.Y., Chicago, Dallas, and other operatic centers. Among her esteemed roles were Cherubino, Marcellina, Dorabella, Rosina, Ottone, and Isabella.

Kernis, Aaron Jay, American composer; b. Philadelphia, Jan. 15, 1960. He was a student of John Adams at the San Francisco Cons. of Music (1977–78), of Wuorinen and Elias Tanenbaum at the Manhattan School of Music in N.Y. (B.Mus., 1981), and of Druckman, Amy, Rands, and Subotnick at the Yale Univ. School of Music (1981–83). He won the Rome Prize and was in residence at the American Academy in Rome in 1984–85. In 1985 he received the Joseph N. Bearns Prize of Columbia Univ. In 1985–86 he held a Guggenheim fellowship. In 1988 he received the N.Y. Foundation for the Arts fellowship. The early influence of traditional music, impressionism, and minimalism on his output eventually led to a more personal style, noted for its accessible but still modern means of expression.

WORKS: ORCH.: *Mirror of Heat and Light* (1985); *Invisible Mosaic III* (1988); 2 syms.: No. 1, *Symphony in Waves* (1989; 1st complete perf., N.Y., Nov. 9, 1991) and No. 2 (1991; N.Y., Jan. 15, 1992); *New Era Dances* (1992); *Colored Field*, English horn Concerto (San Francisco, April 21, 1994). **CHAMBER:** *Meditation*, in memory of John Lennon, for Cello and Piano (1981); *Music for Trio: Cycle IV* for Flute, Cello, and Piano (1982); *Suite in 3 Parts* for Guitar or Organ (1982); *Passacaglia-Variations* for Viola and Piano (1985); *Invisible Mosaic I* for Clarinet, Violin, Cello, and Piano (1986) and *II* for Chamber Ensemble (1988); *Phantom Polka* for Accordion (1987); *Delicate Songs* for Flute, Violin, and Cello (1988); String Quartet, *musica celestis* (1990); *Mozart en Route: "a little traveling music"* for Violin, Viola, and Cello (1991); *100 Greatest Dance Hits* for Guitar and String Quartet (1993); *Harlem River Reveille* for Brass Quintet (1993); *Still Movement with Hymn* for Piano Quartet (1993); *Hymn* for Accordion (1993); *Air* for Violin and Piano (1995). **PIANO:** *Cycle II* for Piano Duo (1979); *Before Sleep and Dreams* (1987–90); *Superstar Etude No. 1* (1992). **VOCAL:** *Stein Times 7* for Chorus and Piano (1980); *Cycle III* for Soprano, Baritone, and Chamber Ensemble (1981); *Dream of the Morning Sky: Cycle V* for Soprano and Orch. (1982); *Morningsongs* for Baritone and Orch. (1982–83); *America(n) (Day) Dreams* for Mezzo-soprano and Chamber Ensemble (1984); *Love Scenes* for Soprano and Cello (1987); *Barbara Allen* for Soprano and Orch. (1988); *Songs of Innocents* for High Voice and Piano (2 books, 1989); *Brilliant Sky, Infinite Sky* for Baritone, Violin, Percussion, and Piano (1991); *La quattro stagioni dalla cucina futurismo* for Narrator, Violin, Cello, and Piano (1991); *Simple Songs* for Soprano or Tenor and Orch. (1991); *Goblin Market* for Narrator and Ensemble (1995).

Kerr, Harrison, American composer; b. Cleveland, Oct. 13, 1897; d. Norman, Okla., Aug. 16, 1978. He studied composition with James H. Rogers and Claus Wolfram in Cleveland, and then continued his training in France with Boulanger (composition) and Philipp (piano) at the American Cons. in Fontainebleau, and with Vidal (composition) and Wolff (conducting). In 1927–28 he was director of music of Greenbriar College in Lewisburg, W.Va., and then was director of music and art at the Chase School in N.Y. (1929–35). In subsequent years, he was active with the American Composers' Alliance and the American Music Center, serving as executive secretary for both organizations. From 1949 to 1960 he was dean of the College of Fine Arts at the Univ. of Okla., where he continued on its faculty as composer-in-residence until 1968. He utilized traditional forms in his works, enfusing them with linear chromatic writing and judicious dissonances.

WORKS: DRAMATIC: OPERA: *The Tower of Kel* (1958–60). **BALLET:** *Dance Sonata* (1938). **ORCH.:** 3 syms. (1927–29, rev. 1938; 1943–45; 1953–54); *Movement* for Strings (1936); *Dance Suite* (1939–40); Violin Concerto (1950–51; rev. 1956); *Variations on a Ground Bass* (1966); *Sinfonietta da Camera* (1967–68); *Episodes from The Tower of Kel* (1971–72). **CHAMBER:** 3 string quartets (1935, 1937, 1973); Trio for Clarinet, Cello, and Piano (1936); *Study* for Cello (1937); Piano Trio (1938); Suite for Flute and Piano (1940–41); *Overture, Arioso, and Finale* for Cello and Piano (1941–51; also for Cello and Orch., 1966–67); Sonata for Solo Violin (1954); Violin Sonata (1956); *Quasi Quodlibet* for 8 Trombones (1974); 3 Duos for 2 Flutes (1976). **PIANO:** *Poem* (1929); 2 sonatas (1929, 1943); *4 Preludes* (1943); *Frontier Day* (1956). **VOCAL:** *3 Songs* for Voice and Piano or Chamber Orch. (1924–28); *Notations on a Sensitized Plate* for High or Medium Voice, Clarinet, Piano, and String Quartet (1935); *Wink of Eternity* for Chorus and Orch. (1937); *In Cabin'd Ships at Sea* for Chorus and Orch. (1971); other songs.

BIBL.: A. Ringer, "H. K.: Composer and Educator," *American Composers Alliance Bulletin*, VIII/2 (1959); R. Kohlenberg, *H. K.: Portrait of a Twentieth-century American Composer* (diss., Univ. of Okla., 1978).

Kersjes, Anton (Frans Jan), Dutch conductor; b. Arnhem, Aug. 17, 1923. He studied conducting with Felix Hupka in Amsterdam and Eugène Bigot in Paris. In 1953 he became co-founder and conductor of the Kunstmaand Chamber Orch. in Amsterdam, which became the Kunstmaand Orch. in 1955 and the Amsterdam Phil. in 1969; was its principal conductor until 1983. He took this orch. to the Soviet Union in 1972, making it the first Dutch ensemble to give concerts there. From 1969 to 1979 he led the conducting class at the Sweelinck Cons. in Amsterdam.

Kersters, Willem, Belgian composer and teacher; b. Antwerp, Feb. 9, 1929. He studied at the Royal Flemish Cons. of Music in Antwerp, and with Louël (counterpoint), Absil and Quinet (fugue), Poot (composition), and Defossez (conducting) at the Royal Cons. of Music in Brussels. From 1962 to 1994 he taught at the Royal Flemish Cons. of Music. He also taught at the Maastricht Cons. in the Netherlands from 1967 to 1994. In his music, Kersters has made imaginative use of both tonal and atonal resources.

WORKS: DRAMATIC: OPERA: *Gansendonk* (1979–82; Antwerp, Sept. 29, 1984). **BALLETS:** *Parwati* (1956); *Triomf van de Geest* (1959); *Halewyn* (1973; Brussels, Jan. 25, 1974); *Ulenspiegel de Geus* (1975–76). **ORCH.:** Concertino for Oboe and Strings (1953); Sinfonietta for Chamber Orch. (1955); Sinfonia concertante for Flute, Clarinet, Bassoon, and Strings (1957); *Sinfonia piccola* (1958); *Divertimento* for Strings (1958); 5 syms. (1962; 1963; 1967; *Gezelle*, 1979; 1987); *Plechtige Overture* (1963); Sinfonietta for Wind Orch. (1967); *Anaglyphos* for Percussion Orch. (1969); *Capriccio* (1972); *Serenade* for Chamber Orch. (1976); Piano Concerto (1977); *Valerius*, overture for Wind Orch. (1983); *Incantations* for Brass Band (1983); Violin Concerto (1989). **CHAMBER:** Wind Quintet (1954); Viola Sonata (1954); *Partita* for Violin and Piano (1956); 2 string quartets (1962, 1964); *Concert Music* for Strings, Piano, Percussion, and Timpani (1964); Suite for Clarinet and Strings (1964); Sonata for Solo Violin (1965); *De drie tamboers*, septet for 4 Clarinets, Percussion, Timpani, and Piano (1966); *Variations on a Theme of Giles Farnaby* for 4 Clarinets (1967); *Meditation on the Name of BACH* for Trumpet, Piano, and Strings (1968); *3 Rondos* for Brass Quintet (1969); *Contrasts* for Percussion and Piano (1969); Quartet for Violin, Viola, Cello, and Piano (1970); Quartet for Clarinet, Violin, Viola, and Cello (1971); *Laudes* for Brass and Percussion (1973); *Diagram* for Violin and Cello (1974); *Coincidences* for 9 Percussionists (1974); *Aveniana* for Oboe, Clarinet, and Bassoon (1984); Nonetto for 9 Instruments (1985); *Ballade* for Alto Saxophone and Strings (1987); Sextet for Piano and Strings (1990); *Idyll* for Harp and Strings (1992); Violin Sonata (1993); piano pieces, including a sonata (1985); organ music. **VOCAL:** *De geestelikje bruiloft* for Soprano, English Horn, Clarinet, Piano, and String Quintet (1955); *La chanson d'Eve* for Soprano and String Quartet (1959); *Psalms* for Alto, Men's Chorus, Winds, Organ, and Timpani (1962); *A Gospel Song* for 4 Soloists, Chorus, and Orch. (1965); *A Hymn of Praise,* oratorio for Soloists, Chorus, and Orch. (1966); *Barbaarse dans* for Soloists, Chorus, and Instrumental Ensemble (1970); *Angst . . . een dans* for Tenor, Reciter, Chorus, Harp, Piano, and Percussion Orch. (1970); *Kinderwereld* for Choruses and Orch. (1988); *De Feesten van Angst en Pijn* for Tenor, Alto, Reciter, Chorus, Harp, Piano, Percussion, and Strings (1995).

Kertész, István, noted Hungarian-born German conductor; b. Budapest, Aug. 28, 1929; d. (drowned while swimming in the Mediterranean) Kfar Saba, Israel, April 16, 1973. He studied violin and composition at the Franz Liszt Academy of Music in Budapest, where his principal teachers were Kodály and Weiner; also received instruction in conducting from Somogyi. He conducted in Györ (1953–55) and at the Hungarian State Opera in Budapest (1955–56); after the unsuccessful Hungarian revolution (1956), he settled in West Germany and became a naturalized citizen; he completed his conducting studies with Previtali at the Accademia di Santa Cecilia in Rome (1958). He was Generalmusikdirektor in Augsburg (1958–63); made his first appearances as a guest conductor in England in 1960 and in the U.S. in 1961. In 1964 he became Generalmusikdirektor of the Cologne Opera, a post he retained until his death; he was also principal conductor of the London Sym. Orch. (1965–68), which he led on a world tour (1965). His readings of the Romantic repertoire were especially admired for their warmth and lyricism.

BIBL.: K. Richter, *I. K.* (Augsburg, 1976).

Kes, Willem, Dutch conductor and composer; b. Dordrecht, Feb. 16, 1856; d. Munich, Feb. 21, 1934. He studied violin with various teachers in the Netherlands, then with Ferdinand David at the Leipzig Cons. (1871), Wieniawski in Brussels (1873), and Joachim in Berlin (1875); also composition with Reinecke, Bargiel, and Kiel in Berlin. In 1876 he was made 1st concertmaster of Amsterdam's Park-Orkest; was its conductor in 1883 and also conductor of Dordrecht's orch., choir, and music school (1877–88). He became the first conductor of Amsterdam's Concertgebouw Orch., leading its inaugural concert on Nov. 3, 1888, and remaining with it until 1895. In 1895 he succeeded Henschel as conductor of the Scottish Orch. in Glasgow. In 1898 he went to Russia, where he conducted the Moscow Phil. Soc. (1901–05); subsequently was conductor of the Koblenz Orch. and director of the music school there (1905–26). Among his works are a Sym.; overtures; Violin Concerto; Cello Concerto; *Der Taucher* for Chorus and Orch.; chamber music; piano pieces; songs.

Kessler, Thomas, Swiss composer and teacher; b. Zürich, Sept. 25, 1937. He received training in German and Romance philology at the Univs. of Zürich and Paris, and in composition with Hartig, Blacher, and Pepping at the Berlin Hochschule für Musik. In 1965 he organized his own electronic music studio in Berlin, and then served as director of the Electronic Beat Studio there and of the Centre Universitaire International de Formation et de Recherches Dramatiques in Nancy. In 1972 he beccame a teacher of theory and composition at the Basel Academy of Music. He also served as director of the Basel electronic music studio from 1987. Kessler has also made appearances as a synthesizer performer. In his works, he has pursued an advanced course which has prompted him to utilize electronics and tape.

WORKS: *Konstellationen I* for Flute, Trombone, Cello, and Piano (1965) and *II* for Flute, Piano, Violin, and Cello (1967); *4 Stücke* for String Quartet (1965); *Countdown for Orpheus* for Variable Performers (1966); *Musik* for Flute, Piano, and Tape (1966); *Musik* for Double Bass, Piano, and Tape (1966); *Revolutionsmusik* for Ensemble and Tape (1968); Trio for Violin, Viola, and Cello (1968); *Nationale Feiertage,* opera (1969); *Smog* for Trombone and Orch. (1970); *Portrait* for Ensemble (1971); *Aufbruch* for Instruments (1973); *Loop* for Tape and Instruments (1973); *Piano Control* for Piano and Synthesizer (1974); *Lost Paradise* for Harp, Piano, Alto Flute, English Horn, Viola, and 2 Synthesizers (1975); *Klangumkehr* for Orch. (1975); *Dialoge* for 4 Performers and Vocoder (1977); *Violin Control* for Violin and Synthesizer (1978); *Unisono* for 3 Clarinets (1978); *Schallarchiv,* radiophonic piece (1979); *Pujaparwata* for Gamelan Ensemble (1980); *Traumklang* for Ensemble and Live Electronics (1981); *Drumphony* for Percussion, Computer, and Orch. (1981); *Aufbruch* for Orch. and 5 Computers (1990).

Kessner, Daniel (Aaron), American composer; b. Los Angeles, June 3, 1946. He studied composition with Lazarof at the Univ. of Calif. at Los Angeles (B.A., 1967; M.A., 1968; Ph.D., 1971). In 1970 he was appointed to the faculty of the Calif. State Univ. in Northridge, where he also conducted its New Music Ensemble; was prof. there from 1980. In 1970 and 1971 he received BMI awards; won the Queen Marie-José International Composition Prize in Geneva in 1972, and in 1974 and 1977 he received NEA grants.

WORKS: DRAMATIC: *The Telltale Heart,* monodrama for Tenor and Chamber Orch. (1975–78); *The Masque of the Red Death,* tale in music, dance, and light for Dancer, Conductor, and 7 Players (1979); *Texts for Nothing,* musical-literary-theatrical stream for Soprano, Flute, Trombone, Viola, Cello, and Conductor (1980–82). **ORCH.:** *Strata* (1971); *Mobile* (1973); *Romance: Orchestral Prelude No. 1* (1979) and *Raging: Orchestral Prelude No. 2* (1981); Piano Concerto (1984–86); *Breath* for Cello and Orch. (1991); *Lyric Piece* for Piano and Orch. (1994). **SYMPHONIC BAND:** *Wind Sculptures* (1973); *Variations* (1977); *Sky Caves* (1984–85). **CHAMBER:** *Equali I* for 4 Flutes, Violin, Viola, Cello, and Double Bass (1968–69), *II* for Piano or Celesta and 3 Percussionists (1970), *III (Nebulae)* for String Trio, 2 Guitars, and Harpsichord (1972), *IV* for Brass Quintet (1977), *V* for 6 Horns (1977–82), and *VI* for Marimba Ensemble (1978); 5 chamber concertos: *No. 1* for Recorder, High Voice, Oboe, String Quartet, Piano, and Percussion (1972), *No. 2* for Marimba and Percussion Ensemble (1978), *No. 3* for Piano, Alto Flute, English Horn, Bass Clarinet, Bassoon, and String Quintet (1980; also for String Orch.), *No. 4* for Woodwind Quartet and String Quintet (1989), and *No. 5* for Clarinet, Horn, Bassoon, and String Quintet (1992); *Array,* pieces for 2, 3, and 4 Guitars (1973); *6 Aphorisms* for Clarinet and Guitar (1975); Trio for Violin, Guitar, and Cello (1976); *The Bells of Poe* for Percussion Quartet (1978); *Ancient Song* for Alto Recorder, Viola, and Prepared Guitar (1980); *Continuum* for Marimba (1981–82); *Arabesque* for Alto Saxophone and Vibraphone (1983); *Incantations* for Trombone and Percussion (1984); *Circle Music I* for Piano and Solo Instrument (1985) and *II* for Flute and Guitar (1985); *Intersonata* for Guitar (1987); *2 Old English Songs* for Soprano, Flute, Viola, and Guitar (1988); *Droning* for Clarinet and Viola (1988); String Quartet (1990); *Studies in Melodic*

Expression for Various Solo Instruments (1990–91); *2 Visions* for Flute, Clarinet, Violin, Cello, and Piano (1991); *Lament* for Clarinet and Tape (1991–92); *One Voice, Alone* for Flute, English Horn, Clarinet, Horn, and Bassoon (1993); *Shades of Pastel* for Alto Flute and Prepared Guitar (1993).

Kestenberg, Leo, eminent Hungarian-born Israeli music educator; b. Rosenberg, Nov. 27, 1882; d. Tel Aviv, Jan. 14, 1962. He studied piano with Franz Kullak and Busoni and composition with Draeseke in Berlin; then taught at the Stern Cons. and at the Klindworth-Scharwenka Cons. He became music adviser to the Prussian Ministry of Science, Culture, and Education (1918); was made director of the Central Inst. for Education and Training (1922), and subsequently devoted himself to reorganizing the system of music education in Prussia. After the Nazis came to power (1933), he went to Prague; was founder-director of the International Soc. for Music Education; then settled in Tel Aviv, where he was general manager of the Palestine Sym. Orch. (1939–45); subsequently founded Israel's first training college for music teachers there. He publ. his memoirs as *Bewegte Zeiten: Musisch-musikantische Lebenserinnerungen* (Zürich, 1961).

WRITINGS: *Musikerziehung und Musikpflege* (Leipzig, 1921; 2nd ed., 1927); *Schulmusikunterricht in Preussen* (Berlin, 1927); ed. *Musik im Volk, Schule und Kirche* (Leipzig, 1927); ed. with W. Günther, *Der Musiklehrer* (Berlin, 3rd ed., 1928); ed. *Musikpädagogische Gegenswartsfragen* (Leipzig, 1928); *Musikpflege im Kindergarten* (Leipzig, 1929); *Schulmusik und Chorgesang* (Leipzig, 1930); *Jahrbuch der deutschen Musikorganisation 1931* (Berlin, 1931); *Der Privatunterricht in der Musik* (Berlin, 5th ed., 1932).

BIBL.: G. Braun, *Die Schulmusikerziehung in Preussen von den Falkschen Bestimmungen bis zur K.-Reform* (Kassel, 1957); U. Günther, *Die Schulmusikerziehung von der K.-Reform bis zum Ende des Dritten Reiches* (Neuwied, 1967).

Ketèlbey, Albert (William), English conductor and composer; b. Birmingham, Aug. 9, 1875; d. Cowes, Isle of Wight, Nov. 26, 1959. Precociously gifted in music, he wrote a piano sonata at the age of 11, and played it at the Worcester Town Hall; Elgar heard it and praised it. At the age of 13, he competed for a Trinity College scholarship in London, and was installed as Queen Victoria Scholar; at 16, he obtained the post of organist at St. John's Church at Wimbledon; at 20, began tours as the conductor of a musical comedy troupe, then was a theater conductor in London. He became best known for such light orch. pieces as *In a Monastery Garden* (1915), *In a Persian Market* (1920), *In a Chinese Temple Garden* (1923), *Sanctuary of the Heart* (1924), and *In the Mystic Land of Egypt* (1931); also wrote many smaller pieces under various pseudonyms. His other works include the comic opera *The Wonder Worker* (1900) and chamber music.

Ketting, Otto, Dutch composer, son of **Piet Ketting**; b. Amsterdam, Sept. 3, 1935. He studied composition at the Royal Cons. in The Hague (1952–58); played trumpet in the Residentie Orch., The Hague (1955–60); taught composition at the Rotterdam Cons. (1967–71) and at the Royal Cons. in The Hague (1971–74). His music represents a valiant effort to adapt Classical modalities to the aesthetics of contemporary musical expression.

WORKS: DRAMATIC: OPERAS: *Dummies* (The Hague, Nov. 14, 1974); *O, Thou Rhinoceros* (Holland Festival, June 2, 1977); *Ithaka* (Amsterdam, Sept. 23, 1986). **BALLETS:** *Het laatste bericht* (The Last Message; 1962); *Intérieur* (1963); *Barrière* (1963); *The Golden Key* (1964); *Choreostruction* (1963); *Theater Piece* (1973). **ORCH.:** *Sinfonietta* (1954); *2 canzoni* (1957); *Passacaglia* (1957); 3 syms. (1957–59; 1978; 1990); Concertino for 2 Solo Trumpets, Strings, 3 Horns, and Piano (1958); Concertino for Jazz Quintet and Orch. (1960); *Variations* for Wind Orch., Harp, and Percussion (1960); *Pas de deux*, choreographic commentary (1961); a series of "collages," among which the most uninhibited is *Collage No. 9* for 22 Musicians (Conductor, 16 Brass, and 5 Percussionists; 1963; Amsterdam, Jan. 26, 1966; audience reaction, hopefully that of outrage, is part of the perf.: the conductor is instructed to treat his environment with disdain and contempt, to arrive late, leave early, and refuse to acknowledge social amenities); *In Memoriam Igor Stravinsky* (1971); *Time Machine* for Winds and Percussion (Rotterdam, May 5, 1972); *For Moonlight Nights* for Flutist (alternating on Piccolo and Alto Flute) and 26 Players (1973; Hilversum, April 17, 1975); *Adagio* for Chamber Orch. (1977); *Monumentum* (1983). **CHAMBER:** Concerto for Solo Organ (1953); Sonata for Brass Quartet (1955); Piano Sonatina (1956); *Serenade* for Cello and Piano (1957); *A Set of Pieces* for Flute and Piano (1967); *A Set of Pieces* for Wind Quintet (1968); *Minimal Music* for 28 Toy Instruments (1970); *Quodlibet* for Percussion and Various Instruments (1979); *Mars* for Saxophone Ensemble (1979); *Autumn* for Horn and Piano (1980); *Musik zu einem Tonfilm* for Percussion and Various Instruments (1982); *Summer* for Piano, Flute, and Bass Clarinet (1985). **VOCAL:** *Kerstliederen* (Christmas Songs) for Chorus and Small Orch. (1953); *The Light of the Sun* for Soprano and Orch., after poems of ancient Egypt (1978; rev. 1983).

Ketting, Piet, Dutch pianist, conductor, and composer, father of **Otto Ketting**; b. Haarlem, Nov. 29, 1904; d. Rotterdam, May 25, 1984. He studied with Averkamp in Utrecht, then took composition lessons with Pijper (1926–32). As a pianist, he formed a duo with the flutist Johan Feltkamp (1927), and a trio with Feltkamp and oboist Jaap Stotijn (1935). From 1930 to 1956 he taught at the Rotterdam Cons.; also served as director of the Amsterdam Music Lyceum (1946–49). He was founder-conductor of the Rotterdam Chamber Choir (1937–60) and Orch. (1949–60). From 1960 to 1974 he immersed himself in the numerical symbolism of J.S. Bach's works. In his own works, he pursued a modern Baroque system of composition, with a discreet application of euphonious dissonance.

WORKS: ORCH.: 2 syms. (1929, 1975); *Sinfonia* for Cello and Orch. (1963; radio perf., Dec. 1, 1965); Bassoon Concertino (1968); Clarinet Concertino (1973); *Tema con 6 variazioni, in modo cabalistico*, for Flute and Orch. (1976); *Concertone 1980* for Viola, Winds, and Percussion (1980). **CHAMBER:** String Trio (1925); 3 string quartets (1927–28); Cello Sonata (1928); Trio for Flute, Clarinet, and Bassoon (1929); Flute Sonata (1930); Sonata for Flute, Oboe, and Piano (1936); *Partita* for 2 Flutes (1936); *Fantasia No. 1* for Harpsichord, Descant, and Treble Recorders and Flute (1969) and *No. 2* for Harpsichord (1972); *Preludium e Fughetta* for Alto Flute and Piano (1969). **PIANO:** 4 sonatinas (1926, 1926, 1927, 1929); *Prelude, Interlude and Postlude* for 2 Pianos (1971). **VOCAL:** *De minnedeuntjes* (The Love Songs) for Chorus and Orch. (1966–67; Dutch Radio, May 9, 1968); *Jazon and Medea*, dramatic scene for Chorus, Piano, Flute, and Clarinet (1975).

Keuris, Tristan, Dutch composer and teacher; b. Amersfoort, Oct. 3, 1946. He was a student of Jan van Vlijmen at the Amersfoort Music School, and then of Ton de Leeuw at the Utrecht Cons. (1963–69; graduated with a composition prize, 1969). After teaching at the Utrecht Cons., he joined the faculty of the Hilversum Cons. In 1975 he was awarded the Matthijs Vermeulen Prize for his *Sinfonia*. His music has evolved along postserial lines, and is marked by an emotive quality ably complemented by an assured command of technique, form, and structure.

WORKS: ORCH.: *Kwartet* (1967); *Choral Music* (1969); *Soundings* (1970); Alto Saxophone Concerto (1971); *Sinfonia* (1972–74; Amsterdam, Jan. 31, 1976); *Serenade* for Oboe and Orch. (1974–76); Piano Concerto (1979–80); *Movements* (1981); *7 Pieces* for Bass Clarinet and Orch. (1983); Violin Concerto (1984); *Variations* for Strings (1985); Saxophone Quartet Concerto (1986; Amsterdam, June 21, 1987); *Aria* for Flute and Orch. (1987; Scheveningen, April 21, 1988); *Symphonic Transformations* (Houston, Sept. 18, 1987); *Catena: Refrains and Variations* for 31 Winds, Percussion, and Celesta (1988; London, Nov. 2, 1989); *3 Sonnets* for Alto Saxophone and Orch. (Amsterdam, Sept. 8, 1989); Double Concerto for 2 Cellos and

Orch. (1992); Organ Concerto (1993). **CHAMBER:** *Play* for Clarinet and Piano (1967); Saxophone Quartet (1970); *Concertante Muziek* for 9 Instruments (1973); *Muziek* for Clarinet, Violin, and Piano (1973); *Fantasia* for Flute (1976); Concertino for Clarinet and String Quartet (1977; rev. 1979); Violin Sonata (1977); *Capriccio* for Chamber Ensemble (1978); *8 Miniatures* for 6 Instruments (1980); *Divertimento* for 8 Instruments (1982); 2 string quartets (1982, 1985); Clarinet Quartet (1983); Piano Trio (1984); *Music* for Saxophone Quartet (1986; London, March 3, 1987); *5 Pieces* for Brass Quintet (1988; Rotterdam, April 1, 1989); Clarinet Quintet (1988; Amsterdam, Jan. 20, 1989); *Intermezzi* for Chamber Ensemble (Manchester, Nov. 5, 1989); *Canzone* for Clarinet (1990). **PIANO:** Sonata (1970). **VOCAL:** *To Brooklyn Bridge* for 24 Voices and 15 Instruments (1988; Utrecht, Dec. 17, 1989); *3 Michelangelo Songs* for Mezzo-soprano and Orch. (1989; Arnhem, March 21, 1990); *L'Infinito* for Soprano, Mezzo-soprano, Alto, Tenor, Bass, and Chamber Ensemble (1990; Utrecht, Feb. 28, 1991); *Laudi* for Mezzo-soprano, Baritone, Chorus, and Orch. (1993).

Keussler, Gerhard von, German conductor and composer; b. Schwanenburg, Livonia, July 5, 1874; d. Niederwartha bei Dresden, Aug. 21, 1949. He studied with Reinecke and Jadassohn at the Leipzig Cons., and musicology with Riemann and Kretzschmar at the Univ. of Leipzig (Ph.D., 1902, with the diss. *Die Grenzen der Aesthetik*). From 1906 to 1910 he was a choral conductor in Prague; then went to Hamburg, where he conducted the Phil. concerts until 1920 and led the Singakademie. In 1931 he toured in Australia as a conductor; returning to Germany, he taught at the Prussian Academy of Arts in Berlin (1934–41). He publ. the books *Das deutsche Volkslied und Herder* (Prague, 1915), *Händels Kulturdienst und unsere Zeit* (Hamburg, 1919), *Die Berufsehre des Musikers* (Leipzig, 1927), and *Paul Bucaenus* (Riga, 1931). He composed several symphonic dramas, including *Wandlungen* (1903), *Gefängnisse* (Prague, April 22, 1914), and *Die Gesselfahrt* (Hamburg, 1923); also 2 syms. (1925, 1928), the symphonic fantasy *Australia* (1935), and many songs.

Khachaturian, Aram (Ilich), brilliant Russian composer of Armenian descent, uncle of **Karen (Surenovich) Khachaturian**; b. Tiflis, June 6, 1903; d. Moscow, May 1, 1978. He played tuba in the school band, and also studied biology. He then went to Moscow and entered the Gnessin Music School (1922–25); later studied composition with Gnessin (1925–29). In 1929 he became a student at the Moscow Cons., graduating in 1934 in the class of Miaskovsky; finished his postgraduate studies there (1937). He commenced composing at the age of 21, and soon progressed to the first rank of Soviet composers of his generation. His music was in the tradition of Russian Orientalism; he applied the characteristic scale progressions of Caucasian melos, without quoting actual folk songs. His *Sabre Dance* from his ballet *Gayane* became popular all over the world. In 1948 he was severely criticized by the Central Committee of the Communist party, along with Prokofiev, Shostakovich, and others, for modernistic tendencies; although he admitted his deviations in this respect, he continued to compose essentially in his typical manner, not shunning highly dissonant harmonic combinations. He was made a People's Artist of the U.S.S.R. in 1954. He appeared as a conductor of his own works throughout Europe and in Japan. He made his American debut in Washington, D.C., on Jan. 23, 1968, conducting the National Sym. Orch. in a program of his works. A critical ed. of his works was publ. in Moscow (1982 et seq.). In 1933 he married **Nina Makarova**.

WORKS: DRAMATIC: BALLETS: *Shchastye* (Happiness; Yerevan, 1939; Moscow, Oct. 24, 1939); *Gayane* (1940–42; Perm, Dec. 9, 1942; rev. 1952 and 1957; 3 symphonic suites, 1943; includes the immensely popular *Sabre Dance*); *Spartak* (Spartacus; 1950–56; Leningrad, Dec. 26, 1956; rev. 1957–58; 4 symphonic suites: Nos. 1–3, 1955, and No. 4, 1966). **INCIDENTAL MUSIC:** *The Widow of Valencia* (1939–40; orch. suite, 1953); *Masquerade* (1940; orch. suite, 1944). **FILM MUSIC:** *The Battle of Stalingrad* (Moscow, Dec. 9, 1949). **ORCH.:** *Dance Suite* (1932–33); 3 syms.: No. 1 (1932–33; Moscow, April 23, 1935), No. 2 (Moscow, Dec. 30, 1943; rev., Moscow, March 6, 1944), and No. 3 for 15 Solo Trumpets, Orch., and Organ (Leningrad, Dec. 13, 1947); Piano Concerto (1936; Leningrad, July 5, 1937); Violin Concerto (Moscow, Nov. 16, 1940; transcribed for Flute by J.-P. Rampal, 1968); *2 Armenian Dances* for Cavalry Band (1943); *Solemn Overture* (1945); *Russian Fantasy* (1946); Cello Concerto (1945–46; Moscow, Oct. 30, 1946); *Ode in Memory of Lenin* (Moscow, Dec. 26, 1948); *Concerto-Rhapsody* for Piano and Orch. (1955–68); *Salutation*, overture (1958–59); *Concerto-Rhapsody* for Violin and Orch. (1961–62; Yaroslavl, Oct. 7, 1962; Moscow, Nov. 3, 1962); *Concerto-Rhapsody* for Cello and Orch. (1963; Gorky, Jan. 4, 1964). **CHAMBER:** *Song-Poem* for Violin and Piano (1929); Violin Sonata (1932); String Quartet (1932); Trio for Clarinet, Violin, and Piano (1932); *Jazz Composition* for Clarinet (1966; written for Benny Goodman); *Sonata-Monologue* for Solo Cello (1974); *Sonata-Fantasia* for Solo Violin (1975). **PIANO:** 2 albums of children's pieces (1926–47; 1965); *Poem* (1927); *7 Fugues with Recitatives* (1928–66); *Suite* (1932); *Toccata* (1932); *Suite*, 3 pieces for 2 Pianos (1945); Sonatina (1952); Sonata (1961). **VOCAL:** *Poem about Stalin* for Chorus and Orch. (Moscow, Nov. 29, 1938); *3 Concert Arias* for Soprano and Orch. (1946); *Ode to Joy* for Mezzo-soprano, Chorus, 10 Harps, Unison Violins, Band, and Orch. (1955); *Ballade about the Fatherland* for Bass and Orch. (1961); *In Memory of the Heroes*, cantata for Soprano, Men's Chorus, and Orch. (1976; a reworking of *The Battle of Stalingrad*); songs.

BIBL.: I. Martynov, *A. K.* (Moscow, 1956); G. Schneerson, *A. K.* (Moscow, 1960); G. Khubov, *A. K.* (Moscow, 1962; 2nd ed., 1966); V. Tigranov, *A.I. K.* (Leningrad, 1978; new ed., 1987); V. Iuzefovich, *A. K.* (N.Y., 1985; Russian tr., Moscow, 1990).

Khachaturian, Karen (Surenovich), Russian composer, nephew of **Aram (Ilich) Khachaturian**; b. Moscow, Sept. 19, 1920. He studied at the Moscow Cons. with Litinsky; during World War II, he served in the entertainment division of the Red Army. He resumed studies in 1945 at the Moscow Cons. with Shebalin, Shostakovich, and Miaskovsky, graduating in 1949; then joined its faculty in 1952. His music follows the general line of socialist realism, nationalist or ethnic in thematic resources and realistic in harmonic and contrapuntal treatment. He wrote a number of effective scores for films.

WORKS: DRAMATIC: *An Ordinary Girl*, operetta (1959); *Cipollino*, ballet, after Rodari's fairy tale (Kiev, Nov. 8, 1974). **ORCH.:** Sinfonietta (1949); Overture (1949); *New-Year Tree*, suite (1951); *Youth Overture* (Moscow, Dec. 10, 1951); *In Mongolia*, suite (1951); *Oriental Suite* (1952); *Sports Suite* (1954); 3 syms.: No. 1 (Moscow, March 12, 1955), No. 2 (Moscow, Nov. 27, 1968), and No. 3 (Moscow, Oct. 15, 1982); *Friendship Overture* (1959); *At the Circus*, suite (1968); Cello Concerto (1983). **CHAMBER:** Violin Sonata (1947); Cello Sonata (1966); String Quartet (1969); Trio for Horn, Violin, and Piano (1981). **VOCAL:** *Glory to Consomol* for Chorus and Orch. (Moscow, Oct. 29, 1948); *At the Lone Willow*, cantata (1950); *A Moment of History*, oratorio to documented texts of the Soviet Revolution of 1917 (Moscow, April 26, 1971); choruses; songs.

BIBL.: M. Uspenskaya, *K. K.* (Moscow, 1956); E. Dolinskaya, *K. K.* (Moscow, 1975).

Khadzhiev, Parashkev, Bulgarian composer; b. Sofia, April 14, 1912. He studied composition with Vladigerov and piano with Stoyanov at the Sofia Cons., graduating in 1936; then went to Vienna, where he studied composition with Marx (1937), and to Berlin, where he took a course in composition with Thiessen at the Hochschule für Musik (1938–40). Returning to Bulgaria, he occupied various teaching positions.

WORKS: DRAMATIC: OPERAS: *Imalo edno vreme* (Once upon a Time; Sofia, April 11, 1957); *Lud gidiya* (Madcap; Sofia, Nov. 15, 1959); *Albena* (Varna, Nov. 2, 1962); *Jukka nosht* (July Night; 1964; Plovdiv, Feb. 16, 1965); *The Millionaire* (1964; Sofia, March 14, 1965); *Master Woodcarvers* (Sofia, Oct. 9,

1966); *The Knight* (Varna, 1969); *The 3 Brothers and the Golden Apple* (1970; Sofia, Jan. 28, 1971); *The Year 893* (1972; Ruse, March 26, 1973). **OPERETTAS:** *Delyana* (1952); *Aika* (1955); *Madame Sans-Gêne* (1958); *King Midas Has Ass's Ears* (1976). **MUSICAL:** *Job Hunters* (1972). **BALLET:** *Srebarnite pantofki* (The Silver Slippers; 1961; Varna, March 20, 1962). **ORCH.:** *Skici* (Sketches; 1940); Violin Concertino (1941); Flute Concertino (1945); *Capriccio* (1951); *Small Dance Suite* (1952); *Rondino* (1969). **CHAMBER:** 2 violin sonatas (1940, 1946); *3 Pieces* for Wind Quintet (1942); 2 string quartets (1948, 1953); piano pieces. **VOCAL:** Choruses; folk-song arrangements.

Khaikin, Boris (Emmanuilovich), prominent Russian conductor; b. Minsk, Oct. 26, 1904; d. Moscow, May 10, 1978. He studied piano with Goedicke and conducting with Saradzhev and Malko at the Moscow Cons. He was a conductor at the Stanislavsky Theater in Moscow (1928–35). From 1936 to 1943 he served as principal conductor of the Maly Theater in Leningrad; from 1943 to 1954, at the Kirov Theater in Moscow, and from 1954 to 1978, at Moscow's Bolshoi Theater. He taught at the Leningrad Cons. (1935–53); then was prof. of conducting at the Moscow Cons. (1954–78). His most famous student was Kirill Kondrashin. He was made a People's Artist of the U.S.S.R. in 1972. He conducted the premieres of a number of Soviet operas.

Khodzha-Einatov, Leon, Russian composer; b. Tiflis, March 23, 1904; d. Leningrad, Nov. 1, 1954. He studied with Spendiarov. In 1927 he went to Leningrad, where he wrote music for the stage. He wrote the opera *Rebellion* (Leningrad, May 16, 1938); also 3 Armenian operas: *Arshak* (1945), *David Bek* (1951), and *Namus* (1952); *Symphonic Dances*; Sym. (1953).

Khrennikov, Tikhon (Nikolaievich), important Russian music administrator and composer; b. Elets, June 10, 1913. He was the 10th child in the musical family of a provincial clerk; his parents and siblings played the Russian guitar and the mandolin and sang peasant songs. He took piano lessons with a local musician; in 1927 he went to Moscow, where he was introduced to Gnessin, who accepted him as a student in his newly founded musical technicum; there he studied counterpoint with Litinsky and piano with Ephraim Hellman. After graduation, he entered the Moscow Cons., where he studied composition with Shebalin and piano with Neuhaus (1932–36); later continued postgraduate work with Shebalin. He developed a mildly modernistic, and technically idiomatic, type of composition which remained his recognizable style throughout his career as a composer. In 1961 he joined the faculty of the Moscow Cons., and was named a prof. in 1966. In the meantime, he became engaged in the political life of the country. He was attached to the music corps of the Red Army and accompanied it during the last months of World War II; in 1947 he joined the Communist party, and also became a deputy of the Supreme Soviet. In 1948 he was named personally by Stalin as secretary-general of the Union of Soviet Composers, and in 1949 became president of the music section of the All-Union Soc. for Cultural Exchange with Europe and America. He further served as head of the organizing committee for the International Festivals and the Tchaikovsky Competitions in Moscow. He received numerous honors; was a member of the Soviet delegation to the U.S. in 1959, was named a Hero of Socialist Labor in 1973, and in 1974 received the Lenin Prize. Amid all this work, he never slackened the tempo of his main preoccupation, that of composition. During his entire career, he was a stout spokesman for Soviet musical policy along the lines of socialist realism. He compromised himself, however, by his vehement condemnation of "formalist" directions in modern music, specifically attacking Stravinsky, Prokofiev, Shostakovich, and, later, also Schnittke and Gubaidulina. But as Soviet aesthetical directions underwent a liberal change, Khrennikov himself became the target of sharp criticism. He defended himself by claiming that he had protected a number of young musicians from attacks by entrenched functionaries of the Soviet musical establishment, and he succeeded in retaining his position as secretary-general of the Union of Soviet Composers until 1991. His compositions express forcefully the desirable qualities of erstwhile Soviet music, a flowing melody suggesting the broad modalities of Russian folk songs, a vibrant and expressive lyricism, and effective instrumental formation.

WORKS: DRAMATIC: *V buryu* (Into the Storm), opera (Moscow, May 31, 1939; rev. version, Moscow, Oct. 12, 1952); *Frol Skobeyev*, comic opera (Moscow, Feb. 24, 1950; rev. as *Bezrodnïy zyat* [The Unrelated Son-in-Law], after the novel by Gorky, Novosibirsk, Dec. 29, 1966); *Mat* (Mother), opera (Moscow, Oct. 26, 1957); *100 Chertey i odna devushka* (100 Devils and a Single Girl), operetta (Moscow, May 16, 1963); *Belaya noch* (White Night), operetta (Moscow, May 23, 1967); *Malchik-velikan* (Boy Giant), children's fairy-tale opera (Moscow, Dec. 19, 1969); *Mnogo shuma . . . iz-za serdets* (Much Ado about . . . Hearts), comic opera (Moscow, March 11, 1972); *Doroteya*, comic opera (Moscow, May 26, 1983); *Zolotoy telyonok* (The Golden Calf), comic opera (Moscow, March 9, 1985); *Golïy korol* (The Naked King), comic opera (Leningrad, May 1988); ballets; incidental music to plays; film scores. **ORCH.:** 3 piano concertos (1933, 1970, 1982); 3 syms.: No. 1 (1935; Moscow, Oct. 10, 1955), No. 2, expressing "the irresistible will to defeat the Fascist foe" (1940–43; Moscow, Jan. 10, 1943), and No. 3 (1973); 2 violin concertos (1959, 1975); 2 cello concertos: No. 1 (Moscow, May 13, 1964) and No. 2 (1986). **OTHER:** Chamber music, including a String Quartet (1967); piano pieces; choruses; many songs.

BIBL.: L. Kaltat, *T. K.* (Moscow, 1946); V. Kukharsky, *T. K.* (Moscow, 1957); Y. Kremlev, *T. K.* (Moscow, 1963); I. Martinov, *T.N. K.* (Moscow, 1987).

Khristov, Dobri, Bulgarian choral conductor, pedagogue, and composer; b. Varna, Dec. 14, 1875; d. Sofia, Jan. 23, 1941. He began to teach himself music in his youth. While attending secondary school in Varna, he began to compose. He founded its choir and gained experience as a conductor before being invited to serve as conductor of the choir of Gusla, the town's music soc. After teaching school, he pursued training with Dvořák at the Prague Cons. (1900–1903). Following further work as a conductor and teacher in Varna, he settled in Sofia as a teacher in 1907. In 1908 he became chorus master of the Opera. In 1922 he became a teacher at the State Academy of Music, where he later was a prof. (1926–33) and director. In 1935 he was made choirmaster of the Alexander Nevsky Memorial Church. In 1928 Khristov was made a member of the Bulgarian Academy of Sciences, the first Bulgarian musician to be so honored. He was the author of *Tekhnicheskiyat stroezh na balgarskata narodna muzika* (The Technical Structure of Bulgarian Folk Music; Sofia, 1928; 2nd ed., 1956). His works were principally inspired by Bulgarian folk music. He was especially esteemed for his choral output.

WORKS: ORCH.: 2 Balkan suites (1903, 1914); *Ivailo*, festive overture (1907); *Tutrakan epopoeya* (1917). **VOCAL:** Numerous choral pieces; hundreds of songs; sacred music; many folk-song arrangements.

BIBL.: I. Kamburov, *D. K.* (Sofia, 1942); V. Krastev, *D. K.* (Sofia, 1954); idem, ed., *Muzikalno-teoretichno i publitsistichno nasledstvo na D. K.* (Sofia, 1971).

Kielland, Olav, Norwegian conductor and composer; b. Trondheim, Aug. 16, 1901; d. Bø, Telemark, Aug. 5, 1985. He studied with Lhose (conducting) and Krehl (composition) at the Leipzig Cons. (1921–23) and took Weingartner's conducting class in Basel (1929). He was conductor of the Oslo Phil. (1931–45) and the Bergen Phil. (1952–55); also appeared as a guest conductor abroad. His music followed the tradition of Norwegian national trends.

WORKS: 4 sinfonias (1935, 1961, 1966, 1976); Violin Concerto (1939–40); *Overtura tragica* (1941); *Mot blåsnøhøgdom* (The White-capped Mountains), symphonic suite for High Voice and Orch. (1945–46); *Concerto grosso norvegese* for 2 Horns and Strings (1952); *Tvileikar* for 4 Instruments (1954); String Quartet (1964); *Marcia del Coraggio* for Orch. (1968); *Ouverture solenne* (1974); Piano Concerto (1977).

Kienzl, Wilhelm, Austrian composer; b. Waizenkirchen, Jan. 17, 1857; d. Vienna, Oct. 3, 1941. He studied in Graz with Johann Buwart and Mortier de Fontaine (piano) and with Ignaz Uhl (violin); also with Mayer-Rémy (composition) at the Univ. there, and then with Krejči at the Univ. of Prague (1876), at the Univ. of Leipzig (1877), with Rheinberger in Munich, with Liszt in Weimar, and at the Univ. of Vienna (Ph.D., 1879, with the diss. *Die musikalische Deklamation*; publ. in Leipzig, 1880). He was director of Amsterdam's German Opera (1883); conducted in Krefeld before returning to Graz (1884); then was director of the Steiermärkischer Musikverein there until 1886. He held the post of 1st conductor of the Hamburg Opera (1890–92), then was court conductor in Munich (1892–94). His most successful work was the opera *Der Evangelimann* (Berlin, May 4, 1895). After World War I, he wrote the new national anthem of Austria (1918), replacing Haydn's; it was adopted on June 6, 1920, but was dropped on Dec. 13, 1929, in favor of Haydn's melody. He also completed Adolf Jensen's opera *Turandot*. He publ. several books, including an autobiography (1926).

WORKS: DRAMATIC: OPERAS: *Urvasi* (1884; Dresden, Feb. 20, 1886; rewritten 1909); *Heilmar, der Narr* (Munich, March 8, 1892); *Der Evangelimann* (Berlin, May 4, 1895); *Don Quichote*, "musical tragi-comedy" (Berlin, Nov. 18, 1898); *In Knecht Rupprechts Werkstatt*, Weihnachtsmärchenspiel (Graz, Dec. 25, 1907); *Der Kuhreigen (Ranz des Vaches)* (Vienna, Nov. 23, 1911); *Das Testament* (Vienna, Dec. 6, 1916); *Hassan der Schwarmer* (Chemnitz, Feb. 27, 1925); *Sanctissimum* (Vienna, Feb. 14, 1925). **SINGSPIEL:** *Hans Kipfel* (Vienna, 1926). Also incidental music. **OTHER:** Chamber music; piano pieces; choral works; songs.

BIBL.: M. Morold, *W. K.* (Leipzig, 1909); H. Hagen, ed., *Festschrift zum 60. Geburtstag von W. K.* (Graz, 1917); *Festschrift zum 80. Geburtstag von W. K.* (Vienna, 1937); H. Sittner, *K.—Rosegger: Eine Künstlerfreundschaft* (Zürich, 1953); I. Samlick-Hagen, *Lehr- und Wanderjahre W. K.s (1874–1897)* (diss., Univ. of Vienna, 1979).

Kiepura, Jan, Polish-American tenor; b. Sosnowiec, May 16, 1902; d. Rye, N.Y., Aug. 15, 1966. He studied in Warsaw and Milan. He made his operatic debut as Faust in Lwów (1924), then appeared in Vienna, Berlin, Milan, Paris, Buenos Aires, and other opera centers. He made his U.S. debut with the Chicago Opera in 1931; first appeared with the Metropolitan Opera in N.Y. as Rodolfo (Feb. 10, 1938); sang there until 1939 and again in 1942. He was admired for such roles as Des Grieux and Faust; also was successful as a film artist and as an operetta singer. He was married to **Martha Eggerth**.

Kiesewetter, Tomasz, Polish composer; b. Sosnowka, Sept. 8, 1911. He studied composition with Rytel and conducting with Bierdiajew at the Warsaw Cons.; during the German occupation in World War II, he was active in resistance groups; after the war, he taught at the Łódź State College of Music.

WORKS: DRAMATIC: *King's Jester*, ballet (1954); *The Lonely Ones*, operetta (1963). **ORCH.:** *Polish Dances* (1947, 1950); 3 syms. (1949, 1952, 1958); Viola Concerto (1950).

Kijima, Kiyohiko, Japanese composer; b. Tokyo, Feb. 19, 1917. He studied composition with Ikenouchi at Nihon Univ.; later joined its faculty. He received 2 prizes given by the Tokyo newspaper *Mainichi* (1938, 1948).

WORKS: ORCH.: *Symphonic Overture* (1942); *Prelude and Fugue* (1948); *5 Meditations* (1956); *Divertimento* (1963). **CHAMBER:** String Quartet (1950); Violin Sonata (1951); Trio for Flute, Violin, and Piano (1958; rev. 1970); Piano Quintet (1965); *2 Legends* for Piano (1969). **VOCAL:** *Satsukino*, poem for Soprano and Small Orch. (1940); *Mi-Chi-No-Ku* for Chorus, Flute, Piano, and Percussion (1963); songs.

Kiladze, Grigori, Russian composer; b. Batum, Oct. 25, 1902; d. Tbilisi, April 3, 1962. He studied at the Tiflis Cons. with Ippolitov-Ivanov (1924–27); then at the Leningrad Cons. with Shcherbachev (1927–29). He was an active proponent of ethnic Georgian music in a modern idiom derived thematically from folk melorhythms. He wrote 2 operas on subjects from Caucasian revolutionary history: *Bakhtrioni* (1936) and *Lado Ketzkhoveli* (1941); *Sinatle*, ballet (1947); *Poem about Stalin* for Chorus and Orch. (1935); *Heroic Symphony* (1944); *Childhood and Adolescence of the Leader*, oratorio (1951); *Triumph*, overture (1957).

Kilar, Wojciech, Polish composer; b. Lwów, July 17, 1932. He studied piano and composition with Woytowica and theory with Malawski at the Katowice State College of Music (1950–55); later took courses at the Kraków State College of Music (1955–58); then went to Paris, where he took private lessons with Boulanger (1959–60). Returning to Poland, he became a teacher at the Katowice State College of Music. Of an experimental turn of mind, he makes use of a variety of modern techniques while retaining essential Classical forms.

WORKS: DRAMATIC: BALLET: *The Mask of the Red Death*, after Poe (1962). Incidental music to plays and film scores. **ORCH.:** 2 syms. (1955, 1956); *Béla Bartók in Memoriam* for Violin, Winds, and 2 Percussion Groups (1957); Concerto for 2 Pianos and Percussion (1958); *Riff 62* (1962); *Générique* (1963); *Springfield Sonnet* (1965); *Prelude and a Carol* for 4 Oboes and Strings (1972); *Koscielec 1909*, symphonic poem (1976); *Orawa* for 15 String Instruments (1986). **VOCAL:** *Herbsttag* for Soprano and String Quartet, after Rilke (1960); *Diphthongs* for Chorus, 6 Percussionists, 2 Pianos, and Strings (1964); *Solenne* for Soprano, Strings, and Brasses (1967); *Upstairs-Downstairs* for 2 Children's Choruses and Orch. (1971); *Mother of God* for Chorus and Orch. (1975); *Exodus* for Chorus and Orch. (1981); *Angelus* for Soprano, Chorus, and Orch. (1984).

Kilenyi, Edward, Jr., American pianist and teacher, son of **Edward Kilenyi, Sr.**; b. Philadelphia, May 7, 1910. He was 12 when he began private training with Dohnányi, and then continued to study under that mentor at the Budapest Academy of Music (1927–30; diploma, 1930). In 1929 he made his professional debut in Amsterdam, and then gave concerts throughout Europe. On Oct. 21, 1940, he made his N.Y. recital debut. From 1953 to 1983 he taught at Florida State Univ. in Tallahassee, and then was adjunct prof. there. In addition to his championship of the works of Dohnányi, he performed the music of other Hungarian composers. His repertoire of the classics ranged from Bach to Debussy.

Kilenyi, Edward, Sr., Hungarian-American composer, father of **Edward Kilenyi, Jr.**; b. Békésszentràndrás, Jan. 25, 1884; d. Tallahassee, Fla., Aug. 15, 1968. He studied in Budapest, in Szarvas, with Mascagni at Rome's Scuola Nazionale Musicale, and at the Cologne Cons.; then settled in the U.S. (1908), where he completed his training at Columbia Univ. with Rybner and Daniel Gregory Mason (M.A., 1915). He was a teacher of George Gershwin (1919–21). In 1930 he went to Hollywood, where he wrote film scores; he also wrote an opera, *The Cry of the Wolf* (1916), a String Quartet (1912), and other chamber music.

Killebrew, Gwendolyn, black American mezzo-soprano; b. Philadelphia, Aug. 26, 1939. She studied at Temple Univ. in Philadelphia, and then in N.Y. at the Juilliard School of Music and at the Metropolitan Opera Studio. After winning 1st prize in the Belgian International Vocal Competition, she won a Metropolitan Opera audition and made her operatic debut with the company in N.Y. as Waltraute in *Die Walküre* on Nov. 21, 1967; made her first appearance at the N.Y. City Opera as Ulrica in *Un ballo in maschera* (Sept. 11, 1971). She was a member of the Deutsche Oper am Rhein in Düsseldorf (from 1976); also appeared in Munich, Geneva, Salzburg, Bayreuth, and other European opera centers. She made numerous concert, oratorio, and lieder appearances on both sides of the Atlantic. Among her notable operatic roles are Gluck's Orfeo, Azucena, Mistress Quickly, Amneris, Fricka, and Baba the Turk in *The Rake's Progress*.

Killmayer, Wilhelm, German composer; b. Munich, Aug. 21, 1927. He studied conducting and composition with Waltershausen (1945–50); then musicology with Ficker at the Univ. of Munich (1950–53), and composition with Orff (1953). He taught at the Trapp Cons. in Frankfurt am Main (1955–58); then was ballet conductor at the Bavarian State Opera in Munich (1961–64), and later a prof. at Munich's Staatliche Hochschule für Musik (1973–91).

WORKS: DRAMATIC: OPERAS: *La Buffonata*, ballet-opera (1959–60; concert perf., South German Radio, Stuttgart, Oct. 21, 1960; stage perf., Heidelberg, April 30, 1961); *La Tragedia di Orfeo* (1960–61; Munich, June 9, 1961); *Yolimba oder Die Grenzen der Magie* (1962–63; Wiesbaden, March 15, 1964; rev. version, Munich, May 9, 1970); *Une leçon de français* or *Die Französischstunde* (1964; concert perf., South German Radio, Stuttgart, Oct. 20, 1964; stage perf., Stuttgart, Oct. 19, 1966). **BALLETS:** *Pas de deux classique* (1964; Munich, May 12, 1965); *Encores*, 2 ballet pieces (Munich, May 9, 1970); *Paradies* (1974). **ORCH.:** Piano Concerto (1955; Munich, April 21, 1956); *Divertissement* (1957); 3 syms.: No. 1, *Fogli* (1968; Hannover, Feb. 9, 1971), No. 2, *Ricordanze* (1968–69; Berlin, May 14, 1969), and No. 3, *Menschen-Los* (1972–73; Nuremberg, April 19, 1974); *Pezzi e Intermezzi* for Piano, Cello, and Orch. (1968); *Fin al punto* for Strings (1970); *Nachtgedanken* (Salzburg, Aug. 7, 1973); *Jugendzeit*, symphonic poem (1977; Freiburg im Breisgau, Jan. 16, 1978); *The Broken Farewell* for Trumpet and Small Orch. (Braunschweig, Nov. 28, 1977); *Verschüttete Zeichen*, symphonic essay (1978; Munich, March 20, 1981); *Überstehen und Hoffen*, symphonic poem (1977–78; Munich, May 6, 1978); *Im Freien*, symphonic poem (1980); *Grande Sarabande* for Strings (Zürich, May 2, 1980); *Sostenuto* for Cello and Strings (1984); *Capriccio* for Piano and Orch. (1988). **CHAMBER:** *Kammermusik* for Jazz Instruments (1957); *Per nove strumenti* for 9 Instruments (1968); 2 string quartets (1969, 1975); *The Woods so Wilde: Kammermusik No. 1* for Percussion, Flute, Viola, and Guitar (1970); *Schumann in Endenich: Kammermusik No. 2* for Piano, Electric Organ or Harmonium, and Percussion (1972); *Kindertage: Kammermusik No. 3* for Flute, Viola, Electric Organ, Piano, Accordion, Zither, Guitar, and Percussion (1973); *Brahms-Bilder*, trio for Violin, Cello, and Piano (1976); Trio for 2 Violins and Cello (1984); *Romanze* for Violin and Piano (1987); *Bagatellen* for Cello and Piano (1991); *Die Schönheit des Morgens*, 5 romances for Viola and Piano (1994); piano pieces. **VOCAL:** Choral works; song cycles; solo songs.

BIBL.: S. Mauser, ed., *Der Komponist W. K.* (Mainz and N.Y., 1992).

Kilpatrick, Jack (Frederick), American composer; b. Stillwater, Okla., Sept. 23, 1915; d. Muskogee, Okla., Feb. 22, 1967. He studied at the Univ. of Redlands, Calif., and at the Catholic Univ. of America in Washington, D.C. Of Cherokee origin, he derived virtually all of his music from Indian folklore, with the pentatonic scale as its foundation. He wrote more than 200 works.

WORKS: MUSIC DRAMAS: *Unto These Hills* (Cherokee, N.C., July 1, 1950); *The Golden Crucible* (Pittsburgh, 1959); *The Blessed Wilderness* (Dallas, April 18, 1959). **ORCH.:** 8 syms., including No. 4 for Voices and Orch. (Dallas, Jan. 17, 1951), No. 5 (Honolulu, Feb. 19, 1957), No. 6 (San Antonio, March 2, 1957), No. 7, *The Republic of Texas* (San Antonio, March 2, 1957), and No. 8, *Oklahoma*, for Narrator, Dancers, and Orch. (Oklahoma City, Nov. 17, 1957); numerous other instrumental works.

Kilpinen, Yrjö (Henrik), Finnish music critic and composer; b. Helsinki, Feb. 4, 1892; d. there, March 2, 1959. He studied with Furuhjelm at the Helsinki Music Inst. (1908–09; 1911–12; 1916–17), Hofmann and Heuberger in Vienna (1910–11), and Juon and Taubmann in Berlin (1913–14). He wrote music criticism in Helsinki (1919–31) and also taught at the Helsinki Cons.; he was elected a member of the Finnish Academy (1948). He was best known as a composer of songs, of which he wrote more than 750; many were popular in Germany as well as in Finland. He also wrote *Pastoral Suite* for Orch. (1944), *Totentanz* for Orch. (1945), more than 30 men's choruses, chamber music, 6 piano sonatas and other piano pieces.

BIBL.: W. Legge, *The Songs of Y. K.* (London, 1936); T. Karila, *Y. K.* (Borga, 1964); F. Pullano, *A Study of the Published German Songs of Y. K.* (diss., Univ. of Ill., 1970); B. Middaugh, "The Lieder of Y. K.," *National Association of Teachers of Singing Bulletin*, XXVII/2 (1970); M. Pulkinen, *Y. K.* (Helsinki, 1982).

Kim, Byong-kon, prominent Korean-born American composer, conductor, and teacher; b. Taegu, May 28, 1929. He studied with Heiden, Tibor Kozma, Wolfgang Vacano, Apel, and Kaufmann at Indiana Univ. in Bloomington (M.M., 1964; D.M.A., 1968), then was on the faculty of Calif. State Univ., Los Angeles (from 1968). He was a guest conductor with the Seoul Phil. (1978–84), the Osaka Phil. (1980), the Korea Phil. (1984), and the Taegu Sym. Orch. (1981, 1985). In 1986 he founded and became the first director of the Pacific Contemporary Music Center; also served as adviser to the Hong Kong-based Asian Youth Sym. Orch. He became a naturalized American citizen in 1974. His orch. compositions are boldly dramatic, making particularly effective use of brass and string instruments.

WORKS: ORCH.: *Nak-Dong-Kang*, symphonic poem (1964); Sym. (1967); *Sori* (1978); *Symphony of 3 Metaphors* (1983); *Festival Symphony* (1984); *Choyop* (1985). **BAND:** *Essay* for Brass and Percussion (1962); *Seoul Fanfare* (1986). **CHAMBER:** *Theme and Variations* for Violin and Viola (1962); Suite for Clarinet, Flute, and Bassoon (1962); String Quartet (1964); Concertino for Percussion (1965); *Epitaph* for Flute, Cello, and Percussion (1985); *The 7 Last Words of Christ* for Organ and Percussion (1986); Sinfonietta for 15 Strings and Harpsichord (1987); also works for solo instruments. **VOCAL:** *Flower Seed*, song cycle for High Voice (1964); *A Sunday Hymn* for Chorus (1965); *i am a little church* for Chorus and Organ (1970).

Kim, Earl (actually, **Eul**), American composer and pedagogue of Korean descent; b. Dinuba, Calif., Jan. 6, 1920. He commenced piano training at 9, and then studied with Homer Grun; subsequently studied with Schoenberg (composition and theory) at the Univ. of Calif. at Los Angeles (1939); then became a student of Bloch at the Univ. of Calif. at Berkeley (1940). His studies were interrupted by service in the U.S. Army Intelligence Service during World War II, after which he returned to Berkeley to study with Sessions (M.A., 1952). After serving as a prof. at Princeton Univ. (1952–67), he was James Edward Ditson Prof. of Music at Harvard Univ. (1967–90). In addition to his activities as a composer and teacher, he has made appearances as a pianist and conductor. Among his many honors are the Prix de Paris, a National Inst. of Arts and Letters award, the Brandeis Univ. Creative Arts Award, a Guggenheim fellowship, and an NEA fellowship.

WORKS: OPERA: *Footfalls* (1981). **ORCH.:** *Dialogues* for Piano and Orch. (1959); Violin Concerto (N.Y., Oct. 25, 1979). **CHAMBER:** *2 Bagatelles* for Piano (1952); *12 Caprices* for Violin (1980); *Scenes from Childhood* for Brass Quintet (1984). **VOCAL:** *Letters Found near a Suicide*, song cycle (1954); *Exercises en Route* for Soprano, Flute, Oboe, Clarinet, Violin, Cello, and 2 Percussion (1961–71); *Narratives* for High Soprano, Woman's Voice, Actor, 2 Violins, Cello, 2 Trumpets, Trombone, Piano, Television, and Lights (1973–76); *Now and Then* for Soprano, Flute, Harp, and Viola (1981); *Where Grief Slumbers* for Soprano, Harp, and String Orch. (1982); *Cornet* for Narrator and Orch. (1983); *The 7th Dream* for Soprano, Baritone, Violin, Cello, and Piano (1986); *The 11th Dream* for Soprano, Baritone, Violin, Cello, and Piano (1988); *3 Poems in French* for Soprano and String Quartet (1989); *4 Lines from Mallarmé* for Voice, Flute, Vibraphone, and Percussion (1989); *Some Thoughts on Keats and Coleridge*, "in memoriam Roger Sessions," for Chorus (1990); *The 26th Dream* for Baritone, Chorus, and String Orch. (1991–92); *Dear Linda* for Woman's Voice, Flute or Piccolo, Piano, Marimba, Percussion, and Cello (1992).

Kim, Jin Hi, talented South Korean composer and komungo player; b. Inchon, Feb. 6, 1958. She studied in Seoul at the National Univ. (1976–80), then went to the U.S., where she studied composition with Adams at the San Francisco Cons. of

Music (1980–81) and electronic and ethnic music at Mills College in Oakland, California (M.F.A., 1985); she also had private lessons on the Indian bansun (bamboo flute) and the Chineze gu-chin (7-string zither), and studied gagaku noh kabuji (South Eastern Asian mask dance theater). Kim attemps to integrate the "living tones" concept of traditional Korean music within a contemporary perspective in her bi-cultural compositions, frequently combining native Korean and Western instruments; notable among these works are *Nong Rock* for Komungo (a 6-stringed Korean zither) and String Quartet (1992), *Piri Quartet* for 3 Piri (a Koream double reed instrument) and Oboe or English Horn (1993), *Tchong* for Daegum (a Korean membrane bamboo flute; 1993), and *Yoeum* for Korean Male Kagok Singer and Western Male Voice (1993); the precariously hovering and often luminous sonorities that emanate from her juxtaposed atonal and microtonal structures blend the best of the East and the New West. Kim has internationally pioneered in performance on the komungo; her solo and collaborative improvisations on the komungo are spare, gestural, and formal, ever respectful of the meditative origins of the instrument. Kim also co-built the first electric komungo and electric changgo, both interractive with computer systems. She has received awards and commissions from numerous organizations, including the NEA (1991), the New York State Council on the Arts (1994), and the Rockefeller Foundation (1995), among many others. In 1995 she was composer-in-residence at the Djerassi Resident Artists program in Woodside, California. In 1995 she began work on her first multicultural music and dance theater piece, *Dragon Bond Rite*, based on Japanese Noh theatre, which will feature Korean, Japanese, Indian, Indonesian, and Mongolian artists at its 1996 premiere at New York's Japan Society.

WORKS: *The Spider's Web* for Kayagum, Yangkum, Daegum, Ajang, Piri, and Percussion (1978); *Yopo* for Flute, Ajang, Yangkum, and 2 Daegums (1980); *Kee Maek No. 1* for Bamboo Flutes and Percussion (1980), *No. 2* for Violin (N.Y., April 22, 1986), *No. 3* for Violin and Cello (Los Angeles, Nov. 29, 1989), *No. 4* for Viola and Cello (N.Y., March 9, 1988), and *No. 5* for Cello (1995); *Woon* for Chamber Ensemble (1981); *Movement and Resonance* for Dancer with 10 Asian Gongs (Oakland, Calif., Feb. 22, 1985); *x4 for solo violin* (San Francisco, Sept. 18, 1985); *Jinyang Delay*, Kayagum improvisation with Electronics (N.Y., April 22, 1986); *Bamboo Permutations No. 1* for Prerecorded Bamboo Flutes and Digital Sampling Keyboard (San Francisco, Nov. 16, 1985); *Su Wol Yong Yul* for Computer-generated Tape, Harpsichord, and Cello (Oakland, Calif., Feb. 22, 1985; based on a 15th-century treatise about Korean music); *x5 for solo flute* for Alto and Soprano Flutes and Piccolos and Prerecorded Tape (N.Y., Oct. 7, 1986); *Tehjoo Goong* for Komungo and Alto Flute (N.Y., Nov. 18, 1986); *Linking* for String Quartet (1986); *Komungo Permutations No. 1* for Synthesizer (1988); *Tchong No. 1* for Komungo and Flute (N.Y., March 9, 1988), *No. 2* for Prepared Flute (Los Angeles, June 22, 1989), and *No. 3* for Korean Mabrain Bamboo Flute and Western Flutes (Los Angeles, April 11, 1995); *Dasrum* for Komungo, Clarinet, and Cello (N.Y., Oct. 17, 1988); *Liquid Migration* for Viola, Cello, and Piano (Middletown, Conn., March 28, 1990); *Refracted Confluence* for Komungo and Computer (San Francisco, Feb. 3, 1991); *Nong Rock* for Komungo and String Quartet (N.Y., Feb. 15, 1992); *Piri Quartet* for 3 Piri and English Horn/Oboe (1993); *Electric Changgo Permutations* for MAX Computer System (N.Y., March 1994); *Yoeum* for Korean Male Kagok Singer and Western Male Voice (N.Y., April 1995); *Dragon Bond Rite*, multicultural music and mask dance theater piece (1995–96).

Kim, Young-Uck, outstanding South Korean violinist; b. Seoul, Sept. 1, 1947. He began piano studies at 5 but turned to the violin at 6. While still a child, he performed with the Seoul Sym. Orch. At 11, he was sent to the U.S., where he continued his studies with Galamian at the Curtis Inst. of Music in Philadelphia; he also attended the Marlboro (Vt.) Music School. After making an auspicious appearance with Ormandy and the Philadelphia Orch. in a nationally televised concert on May 10, 1963, he toured with them in South America. In subsequent years, he appeared as a soloist with many of the principal North American, European, and Far Eastern orchs. On Feb. 13, 1976, he made his N.Y. recital debut at Alice Tully Hall. From 1979 he toured extensively in a trio with Emanuel Ax and Yo-Yo Ma. In addition to the standard repertoire, Kim has applied his brilliant virtuoso technique and interpretive insights to many contemporary works.

Kincaid, Bradley, American folk-song collector and singer; b. Point Leavell, Ky., July 13, 1895; d. Springfield, Ohio, Sept. 23, 1989. He began to sing and play the guitar as a child; after serving in the U.S. Army in World War I, he went to Chicago and studied at the YMCA College. He made his first appearances as a singer on the "National Barn Dance" radio program; subsequently sang on the "Grand Ole Opry" in Nashville, Tenn.; he also owned his own radio station in Springfield, Ohio (1949–53). As a folk-song collector, he publ. 13 songbooks containing material from traditional sources, as well as some compositions of his own.

BIBL.: L. Jones, *Radio's Kentucky Mountain Boy, B. K.* (Berea, Ky., 1980).

Kincaid, William, outstanding American flutist and pedagogue; b. Minneapolis, April 26, 1895; d. Philadelphia, March 27, 1967. He studied flute with Georges Barrère at the Inst. of Musical Art in N.Y.; then played in the N.Y. Sym. Orch. (1914–18). In 1921 Stokowski engaged him as 1st flutist of the Philadelphia Orch., a position he held with great distinction until his retirement in 1960; he also was a distinguished teacher at the Curtis Inst. of Music, where he taught a number of noted flutists. He maintained a valuable collection of historic flutes; his own instrument was a specially made platinum flute.

BIBL.: J. Krell, *K.iana: A Flute Player's Notebook* (Culver City, Calif., 1973).

Kindler, Hans, Dutch-born American cellist and conductor; b. Rotterdam, Jan. 8, 1892; d. Watch Hill, R.I., Aug. 30, 1949. He studied at the Rotterdam Cons., receiving 1st prize for piano and cello in 1906; also had lessons with Casals. In 1911 he was appointed prof. at Berlin's Klindworth-Scharwenka Cons., and 1st cellist of Berlin's Deutsches Opernhaus Orch. In 1912–13 he made a successful tour of Europe; from 1914 to 1920, was 1st cellist of the Philadelphia Orch. In 1927 he made his debut as a conductor in Philadelphia. Kindler organized the National Sym. Orch. in Washington, D.C., in 1931, and was permanent conductor until his resignation in 1948.

King, Alec (actually, **Alexander**) **Hyatt,** esteemed English bibliographer and musicologist; b. Beckenham, Kent, July 18, 1911; d. March 10, 1995. He was educated at Dulwich College and King's College, Cambridge (B.A., 1933). In 1934 he joined the Dept. of Printed Books of the British Museum; became superintendent of its music room in 1944, retiring in 1976. He publ. a number of valuable textual and bibliographical studies.

WRITINGS (all publ. in London unless otherwise given): *Chamber Music* (1948); *Handel's Messiah* (exhibition catalog of the British Museum; 1951); *Mozart in Retrospect: Studies in Criticism and Bibliography* (1955; 3rd ed., 1970); *Mozart in the British Museum* (1956; 2nd ed., 1966); *Henry Purcell 1659?–1695*; *George Frideric Handel 1685–1759* (exhibition catalog of the British Museum; 1959); *Some British Collectors of Music c.1600–1960* (Cambridge, 1963); *Four Hundred Years of Music Printing* (1964; 2nd ed., 1968); *Handel and His Autographs* (1967); *Mozart Chamber Music* (1968; 2nd ed., 1969); *Mozart: A Biography, with a Survey of Books, Editions and Recordings* (1970); *Mozart Wind and String Concertos* (1978); *Printed Music in the British Museum: An Account of the Collections, the Catalogues, and Their Formation, up to 1920* (1979); *A Wealth of Music in the Collection of the British Library (Reference Section) and the British Museum* (1983); *A Mozart Legacy: Aspects of the British Library Collections* (1984); *Musical Pursuits: Selected Essays* (1987).

BIBL.: O. Neighbour, ed., *Music and Bibliography: Essays in Honour of A.H. K.* (London, 1980).

King, Harold Charles, Swiss-born Dutch composer; b. Winterthur, Dec. 30, 1895; d. Amsterdam, June 12, 1984. He went to the Netherlands to study engineering at the Delft Technical Univ.; served as a management consultant with a municipal corporation in Amsterdam; while thus occupied, he took composition lessons with Dopper and Badings.

WORKS: ORCH.: *Serenade* for Strings (1934); *Per Ardua*, symphonic suite (1946–49); *Concerto da camera* for Flute and Strings (1962); *Triptyque symphonique* (1964); *Sinfonietta* (1965); Organ Concerto (1966). **CHAMBER:** Cello Sonata (1940); *Trio patetico* for Violin, Viola, and Cello (1942); *3 Impressions* for Cello (1948); Wind Quintet (1949); 2 string quartets (1953, 1962); *A fleur d'eau* for Flute, Violin, Spinet, and Viola da Gamba (1964); Sonata for Solo Cello (1966); Duo for 2 Cellos (1966); *Piccolo quartetto* for String Quartet (1976). **KEYBOARD:** *Little Laddie*, piano sonatina (1966); *King David's Dance* for 4-octave Carillon (1975). **VOCAL:** *Cornet* for Chorus and Instruments (1977); *Missa 1978* for Chorus and Organ (1978); *3 chansons d'amour et une epigramme* for Voice and Instruments (1981); *Tres orationes* for Voice, Recorder, and Lute (1982); *O Leben, Leben, wunderliche Zeit* for Middle Voice and Orch. (1983).

King, James, American tenor; b. Dodge City, Kansas, May 22, 1925. He studied at the Univ. of Kansas City; also received vocal training from Martial Singher and Max Lorenz. He then went to Europe and made his professional debut as Cavaradossi in Florence (1961); subsequently sang at the San Francisco Opera (1961), the Berlin Deutsche Oper (1962), the Salzburg Festival (1962), the Bayreuth Festival (1965), the Metropolitan Opera in N.Y. (debut as Florestan, Jan. 8, 1966), London's Covent Garden (1966), and Milan's La Scala (1968). He taught voice at the Indiana Univ. School of Music in Bloomington (from 1984). Among his prominent roles were Lohengrin, Walther von Stolzing, Parsifal, Siegmund, Verdi's Otello, and Pfitzner's Palestrina.

King, Karl L(awrence), American bandmaster and composer; b. Painterville, Ohio, Feb. 21, 1891; d. Fort Dodge, Iowa, March 31, 1971. After 8 grades of public schools in Cleveland and Canton, Ohio, during which he began to play brass instruments (primarily the baritone horn) under the tutelage of local musicians, he quit school to learn the printing trade, but soon began to play in and compose for local bands. In 1910 he initiated his short career as a circus bandsman, bandmaster, and composer, ending it in 1917–18 as bandmaster of the Barnum & Bailey Circus Band (for which he had already written what was to remain his most famous march, *Barnum & Bailey's Favorite*). In 1920 he conducted his first concert with the Fort Dodge Military Band, with which he was to be associated for half a century. In 1922 the band began to receive municipal tax support under the Iowa Band Law (for which one of King's marches is named), and its name was changed to the Fort Dodge Municipal Band, although it was known commonly as Karl L. King's Band. For 40 years it toured widely over its region. He was one of the founders, in 1930, of the American Bandmasters Assn.; he served as president of that group in 1939, and in 1967 was named honorary life president. Among his 260-odd works for band are concert works, novelties, waltzes, and all manner of dance forms; but marches predominate, from the circus marches of his early days to sophisticated marches for univ. bands (such as *Pride of the Illini* for Illinois and *Purple Pageant* for Northwestern) and especially to easy but tuneful and well-written marches for the less accomplished school bands. The musical *The Music Man* (1957) was inspired in part by King's music, according to its composer and fellow Iowan, Meredith Willson.

BIBL.: T. Hatton, *K.L. K., An American Bandmaster* (Evanston, Ill., 1975).

King, Robert (John Stephen), English conductor and harpsichordist; b. Wombourne, June 27, 1960. He received an M.A. degree from St. John's College, Cambridge. In 1979 he founded the King's Consort, with which he presented many enterprising programs. He became particularly well known for his championship of the music of Purcell. In 1986 he also served as music director of the European Baroque Orch., and from 1987 of the National Youth Music Theatre. As a guest conductor, he appeared with various European orchs. He publ. the valuable biography *Henry Purcell* (London, 1994).

King, Thea, English clarinetist and teacher; b. Hitchin, Hertfordshire, Dec. 26, 1925. She studied clarinet at the Royal College of Music in London (1943–47) with **Frederick Thurston**, whom she married in 1953. She played in the Sadler's Wells Orch. (1950–52), Portia Wind Ensemble (1955–68), London Mozart Players (1956–84), English Chamber Orch. (from 1964), Melos Ensemble (from 1974), and Robles Ensemble (from 1983); also made appearances as a soloist and recitalist. From 1961 to 1987 she was a prof. at the Royal College of Music, and from 1988 at the Guildhall School of Music in London. In 1985 she was made an Officer of the Order of the British Empire. She has performed many works by contemporary British composers and has also resuscitated numerous scores of the past.

Kinkeldey, Otto, eminent American musicologist; b. N.Y., Nov. 27, 1878; d. Orange, N.J., Sept. 19, 1966. He graduated from the College of the City of N.Y. in 1898 (B.A.) and from N.Y. Univ. in 1900 (M.A.); then took lessons with MacDowell at Columbia Univ. (until 1902). He went to Berlin (1902), where he undertook a course of study with Radecke, Egidi, and Thiel at the Königlisches Akademisches Institut für Kirchenmusik; then studied musicology at the Univ. of Berlin with Fleischer, Friedlaender, Kretzschmar, and Wolf (Ph.D., 1909, with the diss. *Orgel und Klavier in der Musik des 16. Jahrhunderts*; publ. in Leipzig, 1910). He taught at the Univ. of Breslau (1909–14); returning to the U.S., he was chief of the music division of the N.Y. Public Library (1915–23; 1927–30); was prof. of music at Cornell Univ. (1923–27), subsequently prof. of musicology and a librarian there (1930–46). He was a guest prof. at various American univs.; was president of the American Musicological Soc. (1934–36; 1940–42). He contributed numerous articles to scholarly journals; also publ. *What We Know about Music* (Ann Arbor, 1946).

BIBL.: E. Dent, "O. K.," *Musical Quarterly* (Oct. 1938); G. Dickinson, "O. K.: An Appreciation," ibid.; special issue of *Notes* (Dec. 1948); "A Musicological Offering to O. K. upon the Occasion of His 80th Birthday," *Journal of the American Musicological Society* (Spring–Fall 1960).

Kinsky, Georg Ludwig, distinguished German musicologist; b. Marienwerder, Sept. 29, 1882; d. Berlin, April 7, 1951. He was self-taught in music; after working under Klopfermann at the Prussian Royal Library in Berlin (1908–09), he was curator of the private museum of W. Heyer in Cologne from 1909 until it was closed in 1927; also was a lecturer in musicology at the Univ. of Cologne (1921–32), where he received his Ph.D. in 1925 with the diss. *Doppelrohrblatt-Instrumente mit Windkapsel* (publ. in the *Archiv für Musikwissenschaft*, VII, 1925). In 1944 his home and his private library and collection were confiscated by the Nazi government; he then served a year at hard labor until the Allied victory in 1945. Although his health was shattered by this ordeal, he spent his last years in Berlin preparing a thematic catalog of Beethoven's works, a task completed by Hans Halm.

WRITINGS: *Musikhistorisches Museum von Wilhelm Heyer in Cöln: Katalog* (Cologne, Vol. I, 1910; Vol. II, 1912, and Vol. IV, 1916; Vol. III not publ.; greater portion of the MS not extant); ed. *Glucks Briefe an Franz Kruthoffer* (Vienna, 1927); with R. Haas and H. Schnoor, *Geschichte der Musik in Bildern* (Leipzig, 1929; Eng. tr., 1930; 2nd ed., 1951); *Erstlingsdrucke der deutschen Tonmeister der Klassik und Romantik* (Vienna, 1934); *Philobiblon*, VII (1934); *Die Originalausgaben der Werke Johann Sebastian Bachs* (Vienna, 1937); *Manuskripte, Briefe, Dokumente von Scarlatti bis Stravinsky, Katalog der Musik-*

autographen-Sammlung Louis Koch (Stuttgart, 1951; ed. by M.-A. Souchay); *Das Werk Beethovens: Thematisch-Bibliographisches Verzeichnis seiner sämtlichen vollendeten Kompositionen* (Munich and Duisburg, 1955; completed by H. Halm).

Kipnis, Alexander, eminent Russian-born American bass, father of **Igor Kipnis**; b. Zhitomir, Feb. 13, 1891; d. Westport, Conn., May 14, 1978. He studied conducting at the Warsaw Cons. (graduated, 1912); later took voice lessons with Ernst Grenzebach at Berlin's Klindworth-Scharwenka Cons. In 1913 he sang at Monti's Operetten Theater and in 1914 at the Filmzauber operetta theater in Berlin. At the outbreak of World War I, he was interned as an enemy alien, but was soon released and made his operatic debut as the hermit in *Der Freischütz* at the Hamburg Opera in 1915; sang there until 1917, then was a member of the Wiesbaden Opera (1917–22). He made his U.S. debut as Pogner with the visiting German Opera Co. in Baltimore on Jan. 31, 1923; he then was a member of the Chicago Civic Opera (1923–32). He also sang regularly at the Berlin Städtische Oper (1922–30), the Berlin State Opera (1932–35), and the Vienna State Opera (1935–38). In 1927 he made his first appearance at London's Covent Garden as Marcel in *Les Huguenots*, and sang there again from 1929 to 1935. He became a naturalized American citizen in 1931. During these years, he made guest appearances at the Bayreuth, Salzburg, and Glyndebourne festivals, as well as at the Teatro Colón in Buenos Aires. On Jan. 5, 1940, he made his belated Metropolitan Opera debut in N.Y. as Gurnemanz, and continued to sing there until 1946; he then devoted himself mainly to teaching. Through the years he appeared as a distinguished concert artist. In addition to his remarkable portrayal of Gurnemanz, he was greatly esteemed for such roles as Sarastro, Rocco, King Marke, Hagen, and Boris Godunov.

Kipnis, Igor, distinguished American harpsichordist and fortepianist, son of **Alexander Kipnis**; b. Berlin, Sept. 27, 1930. In 1938 the family moved to the U.S., where he took piano lessons with his maternal grandfather, **Heniot Levy**; after attending the Westport (Conn.) School of Music, he studied with Thompson and Dart at Harvard Univ. (B.A., 1952). He also took harpsichord lessons with Valenti. He made his concert debut as a harpsichordist in a N.Y. radio broadcast in 1959; his formal concert debut followed there in 1962. He taught at the Berkshire Music Center in Tanglewood (summers, 1964–67); in 1967 he made his first European tour, and subsequently toured throughout the world. He served as an assoc. prof. of fine arts (1971–75) and artist-in-residence (1975–77) at Fairfield Univ. in Conn.; also taught and played at the Festival Music Soc. concerts in Indianapolis and taught at its Early-Music Inst. In 1981 he made his debut as a fortepianist in Indianapolis. He did much to revive the fortepiano. He also promoted interest in modern music. Several contemporary composers, among them Rorem, Rochberg, Richard Rodney Bennett, Kolb, and John McCabe, have written works for him.

Király, Ernö, Hungarian composer and ethnomusicologist; b. Subotica, Yugoslavia, March 16, 1919. He studied trumpet at the Subotica School of Music (1939). In 1953 he became Hungarian folk music ed. for Novi Sad Broadcasting; in 1958, head of the folk music dept. at the Vojvodina Museum in Novi Sad. He publ. several books and articles on Hungarian folk music and instruments. As a composer, he was interested in folk music and experimented with new intonational and interpretive structures. Among his works are a children's opera, *A kis torkos* (The Little Glutton; 1962), *Vocalizzazioni* for Chorus (1969), and *Indications* for 3 Performers and Tape (1973).

Kirby, Percival Robson, Scottish-born South African musicologist, conductor, and composer; b. Aberdeen, April 17, 1887; d. Grahamstown, South Africa, Feb. 7, 1970. He studied with Terry at the Univ. of Aberdeen (degree, 1910) and with Stanford at the Royal College of Music in London. In 1914 he emigrated to South Africa and became music organizer of the Natal Education Dept.; from 1921 to 1952 he was prof. of music at Univ. College in Johannesburg (later the Univ. of the Witwatersrand). He founded and conducted the Johannesburg Sym. Orch. (1927) and the Univ. Orch. (1930). He is best known for his scholarly work on South African music; much of his field research resulted in *The Musical Instruments of the Native Races of South Africa* (London, 1934). An expedition to the Kalahari Desert in 1936 led to important studies of Bushman music. He composed numerous songs.

Kirchhoff, Walter, German tenor; b. Berlin, March 17, 1879; d. Wiesbaden, March 26, 1951. He studied in Berlin with Eugen Weiss and Lilli Lehmann. He made his operatic debut at the Berlin Royal Opera in 1906 as Faust; continued on its roster until 1920 after it became the Berlin State Opera in 1918; sang there again in 1923–24, 1928–29, and 1932; also appeared at the Bayreuth Festivals (1911–14) and at Covent Garden in London in 1913 and 1924. He made an acclaimed Metropolitan Opera debut in N.Y. as Loge in *Das Rheingold* on Jan. 28, 1927; remained on its roster until 1931. He was particularly successful in Wagnerian roles.

Kirchner, Leon, distinguished American composer, pedagogue, conductor, and pianist; b. N.Y., Jan. 24, 1919. He began piano lessons when he was 4. In 1928 the family moved to Los Angeles, where he continued his piano training. While attending Los Angeles City College, he began to compose. He studied composition with Schoenberg at the Univ. of Calif. at Los Angeles (1938–39), and then theory with Albert Elkus and Edward Strickland at the Univ. of Calif. at Berkeley (B.A., 1940). In 1942 he had private lessons with Sessions in N.Y. Following service in the U.S. Army (1943–46), he pursued postgraduate studies with Bloch and Sessions at the Univ. of Calif. at Berkeley (1946; M.A., 1949). In 1946–47 he taught there. He also taught at the San Francisco Cons. of Music. From 1950 to 1954 he was on the faculty of the Univ. of Southern Calif. at Los Angeles. In 1954 he became the first Luther Brusie Marchant Prof. at Mills College in Oakland, California. In 1961 he joined the faculty of Harvard Univ., where he served as the Walter Bigelow Rosen Prof. of Music from 1966 until his retirement in 1989. He also conducted the Harvard Chamber Players (from 1973) and the Harvard Chamber Orch. (from 1978), and was engaged as a guest conductor and as a pianist with orchs. in the U.S. and overseas. Kirchner received a Guggenheim fellowship in 1948–49, and again in 1949–50. He won the N.Y. Music Critics Circle Award for his 1st (1950) and 2nd (1960) string quartets, and the Pulitzer Prize in Music for his 3rd string quartet (1967). In 1962 he was made a member of both the National Inst. of Arts and Letters and the American Academy of Arts and Sciences. In 1994 he received a Kennedy Center Friedheim Award. Kirchner has followed a thoroughly contemporary but independent course as a composer. His finely crafted scores are notable for their linear chromaticism, asymmetric rhythms, and lyricism.

WORKS: OPERA: *Lily* (1973–76; N.Y., April 14, 1977, composer conducting; also as *Lily* for Soprano, Chamber Orch., and Tape, N.Y., March 11, 1973). **ORCH.:** *Piece* for Piano and Orch. (1946); Sinfonia (1951; N.Y., Jan. 31, 1952); 2 piano concertos: No. 1 (1953; N.Y., Feb. 23, 1956, composer soloist) and No. 2 (Seattle, Oct. 28, 1963, composer conducting); *Toccata* for Strings, Solo Winds, and Percussion (1955; San Francisco, Feb. 16, 1956); Concerto for Violin, Cello, 10 Winds, and Percussion (Baltimore, Oct. 16, 1960, composer conducting); *Music* (N.Y., Oct. 16, 1969, composer conducting); *Music* for Flute and Orch. (Indianapolis, Oct. 20, 1978); *Music II* (1990); *Music* for Cello and Orch. (Philadelphia, Oct. 16, 1992). **CHAMBER:** Duo for Violin and Piano (1947); 3 string quartets: No. 1 (1949; N.Y., March 1950), No. 2 (1958), and No. 3, with Tape (1966; N.Y., Jan. 27, 1967); *Sonata Concertante* for Violin and Piano (N.Y., Nov. 30, 1952); Trio for Violin, Cello, and Piano (Pasadena, Calif., Nov. 30, 1954); Fanfare for Brass Trio (1965; also for Flute and Optional Percussion, 1977, and as Fanfare II for 7 Instruments, 1985); *Music for 12* for Chamber Ensemble (Boston, Feb. 17, 1985, composer conducting); *Illuminations*, fanfare for 9 Instruments for the 350th anniversary of Harvard Univ. (1986);

For Cello Solo (1986; Charleston, S.C., May 28, 1988); 2 pieces for Violin: No. 1 (Indianapolis, Sept. 13, 1986) and No. 2 (1988; Washington, D.C., Jan. 22, 1989); *2 Duos* for Violin and Cello (1988); *Triptych* for Violin and Cello (Tanglewood, Aug. 17, 1988; comprised of *For Cello Solo* and *2 Duos* for Violin and Cello); Trio for Violin, Flute, and Piano (N.Y., Dec. 14, 1993). **PIANO:** Sonata (1948; N.Y., March 1949); *Little Suite* (1949); *A Moment for Roger* (1978); *5 Pieces* (Boston, March 7, 1987); *Interlude* (1989). **VOCAL:** *Dawn* for Chorus and Organ (1943–46; N.Y., Feb. 1946); *Words from Wordsworth* for Chorus (1966); *Lily* for Soprano, Chamber Orch., and Tape (N.Y., March 11, 1973; based on the opera); *The Twilight Stood,* song cycle for Soprano and Piano (Charleston, S.C., June 1, 1982).

Kiriac-Georgescu, Dumitru, Romanian conductor, composer, and teacher; b. Bucharest, March 18, 1866; d. there, Jan. 8, 1928. He studied with Gheorghe Brătianu and Eduard Wachmann at the Bucharest Cons.; then with Dubois, Widor, and Bourgault-Ducoudray at the Paris Cons. (1892–99); also with d'Indy at the Schola Cantorum. He became a prof. at the Bucharest Cons. (1900). He founded the Choral Soc. Carmen (1901); was active as a folklorist. He composed a large output of sacred choruses.

BIBL.: G. Breazul, *D. K.-G.* (Bucharest, 1973).

Kirigin, Ivo, Croatian conductor and composer; b. Zadar, Feb. 2, 1914; d. Zagreb, Oct. 21, 1964. He studied in Italy with Pizzetti. He was active as a theater conductor in Zagreb. Among his works were Concertino for Piano and Orch.; Sym. (1950); *Pjesma o zemliji,* cantata (Song of the Land; 1952); *Kameni horizonti* (Stone Horizons; Zagreb, March 16, 1955); *5 Movements* for Strings (1958); numerous songs.

Kirkby, (Carolyn) Emma, English soprano; b. Camberley, Feb. 26, 1949. She studied classics at Oxford and received vocal training from Jessica Cash. She made her debut in London in 1974 and then specialized in early music; was a member of the Academy of Ancient Music, the London Baroque, and the Consort of Musicke. In 1978 she toured the U.S.; then gave concerts in the Middle East with the lutenist Anthony Rooley (1980–83). In subsequent years, she toured widely in England and abroad. Her repertoire ranges from the Italian quattrocento to arias by Handel, Mozart, and Haydn. The careful attention she pays to the purity of intonation free from intrusive vibrato has been praised.

Kirkby-Lunn, Louise, English mezzo-soprano; b. Manchester, Nov. 8, 1873; d. London, Feb. 17, 1930. She was a student of J.H. Greenwood in Manchester and of Albert Visetti at the Royal College of Music in London. While still a student, she made her debut as Margaret in Schumann's *Genoveva* at London's Drury Lane Theatre in 1893. After singing minor roles at London's Covent Garden in 1896, she sang with the Carl Rosa Opera Co. until 1899. She then gave concerts until returning to Covent Garden in 1901, where she was a leading singer until 1914, winning particular success as Ortrud, Fricka, Brangäne, Carmen, Amneris, Dalila, and Hérodiade. On Dec. 26, 1902, she made her Metropolitan Opera debut in N.Y. as Ortrud, remaining on its roster for the season; she returned for the 1906–08 seasons, appearing principally as a Wagnerian. After appearing with the British National Opera Co. in London (1919–22), she pursued her concert career.

Kirkendale, (John) Warren, American musicologist; b. Toronto, Aug. 14, 1932. He was educated at the Univs. of Toronto (B.A., 1955) and Vienna (Ph.D., 1961, with the diss. *Fuge und Fugato in der Kammermusik des Rokoko und der Klassik*; publ. in Tuzing, 1966; Eng. tr., 1979). After teaching at the Univ. of Southern Calif. in Los Angeles (1963–67), he was an assoc. prof. (1967–75) and a prof. (1975–83) at Duke Univ. From 1983 to 1992 he was prof. ordinarius of musicology at the Univ. of Regensburg. In 1986 he was made an honorary prof. of the Univ. of Bologna and a member of the Accademico filarmonico of Bologna in 1987. He publ. the books *L'Aria di Fiorenza, id est Il Ballo del Gran Duca* (Florence, 1972) and *The Court Musicians in Florence During the Principate of the Medici, With a Reconstruction of the Artistic Establishment* (Florence, 1993), and also contributed articles to various publications. In 1959 he married the German musicologist, Ursula (née Schottler) Kirkendale (b. Dortmund, Sept. 6, 1932). She was educated at the Univ. of Bonn (Ph.D., 1961). In addition to articles in journals and other publications, she publ. the study *Antonio Caldara: Sein Leben und seine venezianische-römischen Oratorien* (Graz, 1966).

BIBL.: *Musicologia Humana: Studies in Honor of W. and U. K.* (Florence, 1994).

Kirkpatrick, John, eminent American pianist and pedagogue; b. N.Y., March 18, 1905; d. Ithaca, N.Y., Nov. 8, 1991. He was educated at Princeton Univ. (graduated, 1926) and took courses with Boulanger in Fontainebleau (summers, 1925–28) and at the École Normale de Musique in Paris (1926–27); he also studied with I. Philipp and C. Decreus, completing his piano studies with Louta Nouneberg (1928–31). He specialized in the interpretation of 17th- and 18th-century chamber music, but gained extraordinary attention when he gave from memory the premiere of Ives' difficult *Concord Sonata* in N.Y. on Jan. 20, 1939. This premiere played an important role in the public recognition of Ives. Kirkpatrick gave many recitals and lecture-recitals in succeeding years. He served as chairman of the music dept. at Monticello College (1942–43); he then taught at Mount Holyoke College (1943–46), Cornell Univ. (1946–68), where he also was director of the Chapel Choir (1953–57), and Yale Univ. (1968–73), where he also was curator of the Charles Ives Collection. He ed. *A Temporary Mimeographed Catalogue of the Music Manuscripts and Related Materials of Charles Edward Ives* (1960), *Charles E. Ives: Memos* (1972), and various compositions by Ives.

Kirkpatrick, Ralph (Leonard), eminent American harpsichordist, clavichordist, pianist, music scholar, and pedagogue; b. Leominster, Mass., June 10, 1911; d. Guildford, Conn., April 13, 1984. He commenced piano studies when he was 6. He pursued his academic education at Harvard Univ. (A.B., 1931), where he received the Paine Traveling Scholarship. After making his public debut as a harpsichordist in Cambridge, Mass., in 1930, he went to Paris to pursue research at the Bibliothèque Nationale; he also had further instruction from Boulanger (theory) and Landowska (harpsichord) before continuing his training with Dolmetsch in Haslemere and with Ramin and Tiessen in Berlin. In 1933 he made his European debut as a harpsichordist. In 1933–34 he taught at the Salzburg Mozarteum. He was awarded a Guggenheim fellowship in 1937, which enabled him to study 17th- and 18th-century performing practices in chamber music in Europe. His findings in Spain were later utilized in his valuable biography *Domenico Scarlatti* (Princeton, N.J., and London, 1953; 3rd ed., rev., 1968). In 1940 he joined the faculty of Yale Univ., where he served as a prof. of music from 1965 to 1976. In 1964 he also served as the first Ernest Bloch Prof. of Music at the Univ. of Calif. at Berkeley. Kirkpatrick greatly distinguished himself as an interpreter of Baroque keyboard music, excelling particularly in the works of Bach and Domenico Scarlatti. He prepared a chronological catalogue of the latter's sonatas, and his "K." numbers became widely accepted. He also ed. 60 of the sonatas (N.Y., 1953) and a complete collection of the keyboard works in facsimile (N.Y., 1971 et seq.) of Scarlatti. Kirkpatrick was the author of *Interpreting Bach's "Well-tempered Clavier": A Performer's Discourse of Method* (New Haven and London, 1984) and of the memoir *Early Years* (N.Y., 1984).

Kirshbaum, Ralph (Henry), American cellist; b. Denton, Texas, March 4, 1946. He studied with Lev Aronson in Dallas; made his formal debut with the Dallas Sym. Orch. in 1959; subsequently studied with Parisot at Yale Univ. (B.A., 1968). He won the Cassadó Competition in Florence in 1969 and the Tchaikovsky Competition in Moscow in 1970; thereafter pursued a fine career as a soloist in the major music centers; also joined the pianist Peter Frankl and the violinist György Pauk in organizing a trio in London in 1972, with which he appeared frequently. He was a soloist in the premiere of Tippett's Triple Concerto (London, Aug. 22, 1980). In 1987 he played Bach's 6 cello suites in London, repeating the feat there in 1993 as well as in Sydney and N.Y. with notable success. In 1988 he founded the Manchester International Cello Festival.

Kirsten, Dorothy, noted American soprano; b. Montclair, N.J., July 6, 1910; d. Los Angeles, Nov. 18, 1992. She studied at the Juilliard School of Music in N.Y.; Grace Moore took an interest in her and enabled her to study with Astolfo Pescia in Rome. With the outbreak of World War II in 1939, she returned to the U.S. She became a member of the Chicago Opera Co. (debut as Pousette in *Manon*, Nov. 9, 1940); made her first appearance in N.Y. as Mimi with the San Carlo Opera Co. (May 10, 1942); appeared with the Metropolitan Opera in N.Y. in the same role on Dec. 1, 1945; sang there until 1952, from 1954 to 1957, and from 1960 until her official farewell performance as Tosca (Dec. 31, 1975). Among her finest roles were Manon Lescaut, Cio-Cio-San, Marguerite, Louise (coached by the composer), and Nedda in *Pagliacci*; also sang in several films, including *The Great Caruso*. She publ. an autobiography, *A Time to Sing* (Garden City, N.Y., 1982).

Kishibe, Shigeo, Japanese ethnomusicologist; b. Tokyo, June 16, 1912. He studied at the Univ. of Tokyo (B.A. in oriental history, 1936; Ph.D. in literature, 1961), where he was a prof. (1949–73); also lectured (from 1952) at the Tokyo National Univ. of Fine Arts and Music and at various American univs., including the Univ. of Calif. at Los Angeles, Harvard Univ., and Stanford Univ. He is a founding member of the Soc. for Research in Asiatic Music. His research has focused particularly on the music of China and Japan, but he has also done fieldwork in Korea, India, Iran, and the Philippines. Among his numerous publications is *The Traditional Music of Japan* (Tokyo, 1966).

Kisielewski, Stefan, Polish composer, journalist, and novelist; b. Warsaw, March 7, 1911; d. there, Sept. 27, 1991. He received training in philology at the Univ. of Warsaw (1929–33) and pursued studies in piano with Lefeld (diploma, 1934) and in theory and composition with Sikorski (diplomas in both, 1937) at the Warsaw Cons., completing his training in Paris (1938–39). In 1935 he began writing on music and politics; during the Nazi occupation of Poland, he was an official of the cultural dept. of the Underground. After the liberation in 1945, he was a prof. at the Kraków College of Music (until 1950); also served as ed.-in-chief of the music weekly *Puch Muzyczny* (1945–48) and was a columnist for the Catholic opposition weekly *Sygodnih Powysechny* (1945–83) in Kraków. In addition to his writings on music, he publ. novels and books on politics, some of which have appeared abroad in translations. For his musical efforts, he received awards from the City of Kraków (1956) and the Union of Polish Composers (1982). His compositions generally follow along neo-Classical lines.

WORKS: DRAMATIC: BALLETS: *Diably polski* (Polish Devils; 1957; Warsaw, 1958); *System doktora Smoly i doktora Pierza* (The System of Dr. Pitch and Dr. Feathers; 1962); *Wesole miasteckzko* (Amusement Grounds; 1966; Gdansk, 1967); scores for theater and films. **ORCH.:** syms.: No. 1 (1939; not extant), No. 2 (1951), Chamber Sym. (1956), Sym. for 15 Performers (1961), and *Symphony in a Square* (1974–78); Concerto for Chamber Orch. (1948); *Rustic Rhapsody* (1950); *Perpetuum Mobile* (1953); *Little Overture* (1953); *Divertimento* for Flute and Chamber Orch. (1964); *Journey in Time* for Strings (1965); *Sport Signals*, overture (1966); *Cosmos I* (1970); *The Merry Kaleidoscope* (1970); *Voyage dans le temps* (1975); Piano Concerto (1980–91; Warsaw, Sept. 24, 1991). **CHAMBER:** Violin Sonata (1932); String Quartet (1935); Sonata for Solo Clarinet (1944); *Intermezzo* for Clarinet and Piano (1953); Suite for Oboe and Piano (1954); *Capriccio energico* for Violin and Piano (1956); Suite for Flute and Piano (1961); *Meetings in the Desert* for 10 Performers (1969); *Dialogues* for 14 Instruments (1970); Clarinet Sonata (1973); *Capricious Impressions* for Woodwinds (1982); *Scherzo* for Bassoon and Piano (1988). **PIANO:** 2 sonatas (1936, not extant; 1945); *Toccata* (1944); *Fantasia* (1949); Suite (1955); *3 Stormy Scenes* (1983). **VOCAL:** Choral music; songs.

Kiss, Janos, Hungarian-born American composer; b. Hosszupalyi, March 21, 1920. He studied at the Budapest Academy of Music (teaching diploma, 1954). In the wake of the Soviet invasion of Hungary (1956), he emigrated to the U.S., becoming a naturalized American citizen in 1973. He took courses in music education at Case Western Reserve Univ. in Cleveland. He subsequently taught at the Cleveland Music School Settlement (1964–79), Western Reserve Academy in Hudson, Ohio (1967–72), Holy Family School in Parma, Ohio (1974–80), and other institutions. In 1982 he became choir director and composer-in-residence at Cleveland's West Side Hungarian Reformed Church. A prolific composer, he wrote numerous orch. and choral works which are distinguished by a facility of execution reflecting his experience as a teacher.

WORKS: ORCH.: Flute Concerto (1970); Trombone Concerto (1972); Cello Concerto (1975); *Divertimento* for Violin, Viola, Double Bass, Harp, and Chamber Ensemble (1977); *Suite in stilo antico* (1978); *Via Lactea*, symphonic fantasy (1978); *Sinfonia Atlantis* (1979); *Las Vegas* for Cimbalom and Orch. (1980); *Mount of Atlantis* for Clarinet, Synthesizer, and Orch. (1981); *Quo Vadis*, symphonic poem (1982); *Rainbow at the Sea* for Flute and Chamber Orch. (1982). **CHAMBER:** *Spring at Last!* for Harp Ensemble (1970); *Josepha* for 5 Alto Recorders, Violin, Viola, Cello, and Harp (1973); *Episode* for Horn, Oboe, Bassoon, and Harp (1978); *Benedictus Dominus* for Chorus and Orch. (1981).

Kissin, Evgeny, amazingly gifted Russian pianist; b. Moscow, Oct. 10, 1971. He enrolled at the Gnessin Music School for Gifted Children in Moscow at the age of 6 as a student of Anna Kantor, who remained his only teacher even after he began his rise toward the musical stratosphere. At the age of 12, he gave performances of both Chopin piano concertos with the Moscow Phil. International reputation came to him when he was engaged in 1987 to perform Tchaikovsky's 1st Piano Concerto with Karajan and the Berlin Phil. On Sept. 20, 1990, he made his U.S. debut playing Chopin's 1st Piano Concerto with the N.Y. Phil., conducted by Zubin Mehta. Ten days later there followed his appearance at Carnegie Hall on Sept. 30, which astonished audience and critics alike by a digital velocity and propulsive dexterity sensational enough to capture the imagination of the most seasoned and experienced listeners. Subsequently he pursued a remarkably brilliant career as a soloist with the foremost orchs. of the world, as a recitalist, and as a chamber music artist.

Kitaenko, Dmitri, Russian conductor; b. Leningrad, Aug. 18, 1940. He studied choral conducting at the Leningrad Cons. and the Moscow Cons. He then went to Vienna to study conducting at the Academy of Music (1966–67). Upon his return to Moscow, he became a conductor at the Nemirovich-Danchenko Music Theater; in 1970, became chief conductor there. He also appeared as a guest conductor in Western Europe, usually in programs of Russian music; in 1975 he served as assistant conductor during the U.S. tour of the Moscow Phil. (1975). In 1976 he was appointed its chief conductor. In 1990 he became music director of the Bergen Phil. He was concurrently chief conductor of the Frankfurt am Main Radio Sym. Orch. (1990–95) and the Bern Sym. Orch. (from 1991), and music director of the Bern City Theater (from 1994).

Kitson, Charles Herbert, English organist, pedagogue, and music theorist; b. Leyburn, Yorkshire, Nov. 13, 1874; d. London, May 13, 1944. He studied for an ecclesiastical career, and was an organ scholar at Selwyn College, Cambridge, before taking an external D.Mus. degree at Oxford (1902). He was organist of

Christ Church Cathedral in Dublin (1913–20); was prof. of music at Univ. College in Dublin (1915–20) and prof. of harmony and counterpoint at the Royal College of Music in London (from 1920); also held a non-resident post as prof. of music at Dublin's Trinity College (1920–35). He publ. a number of theoretical books.

Kittel, Bruno, German violinist and conductor; b. Entenbruch, near Posen, May 26, 1870; d. Wasserberg, near Cologne, March 10, 1948. He studied in Berlin and played in theater orchs. there. From 1901 till 1907 he was conductor of the Royal Theater Orch. in Brandenburg; also was director of the Brandenburg Cons. (until 1914). In 1902 he established the Kittelsche Chor, which quickly developed into one of the finest choral societies of Europe, and with which he made many tours. He was director of the Stern Cons. in Berlin (1935–45).

Kittel, Hermine, Austrian contralto; b. Vienna, Dec. 2, 1879; d. there, April 7, 1948. She was an actress before making her operatic debut in Lemberg in 1897. Following vocal training with Materna in Vienna, she sang in Graz (1899–1900). In 1901 she returned to Vienna as a member of the Court (later State) Opera, where she sang until 1931 and again in 1936. She also appeared at the Bayreuth Festivals (1902, 1908), the Salzburg Festivals (1922, 1925), the Vienna Volksoper (1933–34), Paris, Budapest, Prague, and other European operatic centers. In later years, she devoted herself to teaching voice in Vienna. She was particularly known for her Mozart and Wagner roles.

Kiurina, Berta, Austrian soprano; b. Linz, Feb. 19, 1882; d. Vienna, May 3, 1933. She studied voice with Geiringer at the Vienna Cons. She made her operatic debut in Linz in 1904; then sang at the Vienna Court (later State) Opera (1905–22; 1926–27); made guest appearances in Salzburg, Berlin, and Buenos Aires. A fine coloratura, she excelled in such roles as the Queen of the Night, Desdemona, Gilda, Eva, and the Empress in *Die Frau ohne Schatten.*

Kiurkchiysky, Krasimir, Bulgarian composer; b. Troyan, June 22, 1936. He studied composition with Vladigerov at the Bulgarian State Cons. in Sofia (graduated, 1962); went to Moscow and took some lessons with Shostakovich. His music reflects Shostakovich's influence in its rhapsodic compactness.

WORKS: OPERA: *Yula* (Zagora, 1969). **ORCH.:** Piano Concerto (1958); *Adagio* for Strings (1959); *Symphony Concertante* for Cello and Orch. (1960); *Symphony-Requiem* (1966); *Diaphonous Study* (1967); *Concerto for Orchestra* (1975). **CHAMBER:** Trio for Violin, Clarinet, and Piano (1959); String Quartet (1959); Cello Sonata (1960); Violin Sonata (1961).

Kivy, Peter, American musical philosopher; b. N.Y., Oct. 22, 1934. He studied philosophy at the Univ. of Mich. (B.A., 1956; M.A., 1958), music history at Yale Univ. (M.A., 1960), and philosophy at Columbia Univ. (Ph.D., 1966). He joined the faculty of Rutgers Univ. in 1967. His importance to the field of music is in his writings on aesthetics, in which he has revitalized the complex and long-ignored problems of musical analysis as applied to external associations.

WRITINGS: *The Corded Shell: Reflections on Musical Expression* (Princeton, N.J., 1980); *Sound and Semblance: Reflections on Musical Representation* (Princeton, N.J., 1984); *Osmin's Rage: Philosophical Reflections on Opera, Drama and Text* (Princeton, N.J., 1988); *Sound Sentiment: An Essay on the Musical Emotions* (Philadelphia, 1989); *Music Alone: Philosophical Reflections on the Purely Musical Experience* (Ithaca, N.Y., 1990); *The Fine Art of Repetition: Essays on the Philosophy of Music* (Cambridge, 1993).

Kiyose, Yasuji, Japanese composer; b. Yokkaichi, Jan. 13, 1900; d. Tokyo, Sept. 14, 1981. He studied with Yamada, Komatsu, Pringsheim, and A. Tcherepnin. He was president of the Japanese section of the ISCM (1951–56).

WORKS: ORCH.: *Nihon sairei bukyoku* (Japanese Festival Dances; 1940); Piano Concerto (Tokyo, March 10, 1955); *Nihon no sobyo* (A Sketch of Japan; 1963). **CHAMBER:** 2 piano trios (1938, 1955); 3 violin sonatas (1941, 1948, 1950); String Trio (1949); String Quartet (1951); Quintet for Harp and Woodwinds (1957); *2 Movements* for Violin and Piano (1960); Quartet for 4 Recorders (1969); Duet for Flute and Clarinet (1970); *2 Movements* for Cello (1973). **VOCAL:** *Bokura wa umi ni yuku* (We Are Going on the Ocean, or Unknown Soldiers) for Soprano, Tenor, Chorus, and Orch. (1962).

Kjellsby, Erling, Norwegian organist, choral conductor, and composer; b. Christiania, July 7, 1901; d. there (Oslo), Feb. 18, 1976. He studied composition with Brustad and Valen. He lectured on music at Oslo's Teacher's College (1934–70) and was organist at Oslo's Uranienborg Church (1936–71). His early works, in a late Romantic style, eventually gave way to neo-Classical influences. He wrote *Norsk rapsodi* for Small Orch. (1937); choral works; 4 string quartets (1940–57); piano pieces.

Kjellström, Sven, Swedish violinist and pedagogue and folk song collector; b. Lulea, March 30, 1875; d. Stockholm, Dec. 5, 1950. He studied in Stockholm and later in Paris. Returning to Sweden in 1909, he was active in chamber music societies; was director of the Stockholm Cons. (1929–40). He also formed a string quartet, with which he traveled to remote communities in Scandinavia, including Lapland; he was an ardent collector of Swedish folk songs.

BIBL.: O. Ottelin, *S. K. och folkets musikliv* (1945).

Klami, Uuno (Kalervo), Finnish composer and music critic; b. Virolahti, Sept. 20, 1900; d. Helsinki, May 29, 1961. He studied with Melartin at the Helsinki College of Music (1915–24), Ravel in Paris (1924–25), and Willner in Vienna (1928–29). He was music critic of the *Helsingin Sanomat* (1932–59) and held a Finnish state pension (1938–59). Klami was elected a member of the Finnish Academy (1959). His music was influenced by the folk modalities of the Karelian region, which was his birthplace; the impact of the profundities of the idiom of Sibelius was considerable, but Klami ornamented it with impressionistic detail.

WORKS: ORCH.: 2 piano concertos (*Night in Montmartre,* 1924; 1950); *Sérénades espagnoles* (1924; rev. 1944); *Karelian Rhapsody* (1927); *Rhapsody* (1927); *Merikuvia* (Sea Pictures; 1928–30); 3 syms.: *Symphonie enfantine* (1928), No. 1 (1937) and No. 2 (1944); *Opernredoute* (1929); *Kuvia maalaiselämasta* (Rustic Scenes; 1930); *Helsinki March* (1930); *4 Folk Songs* for Piano and Strings (1930); *Cheremissian Fantasy* for Cello and Orch. (1930); *Fantaisie tschérémisse* for Cello and Orch. (1931); *Kalevala Suite* (1932; rev. 1943); *Sérénades joyeuses* (1933); *Lemminkäinen* (1934); *Karelian Dances* (1935); *Suomenlinna* (Fortress of Finland; 1940); Violin Concerto (1942; rev. 1954); *Revontulet* (Aurora Borealis; 1946); *Pyőrailija* (The Cyclist), rondo (1946); *Karjalainen tori* (Karelian Market Place; 1947); *Theme and Variations* for Cello and Orch. (1950). **CHAMBER:** *Nain tragédie,* string quartet (1920); Piano Quartet (1921); Piano Quintet (1923). **VOCAL:** *Psalmus* for Soloists, Chorus, and Orch. (1935–36); *Vipusessa käynti* (In the Belly of Vipunen) for Baritone, Men's Chorus, and Orch. (1938); *Laulu Kuujärvestä* (The Song of Kuujarvi) for Baritone and Orch. (1956); *Kultasauvalliset* (The People with the Golden Staffs), festive cantata (1961).

Klatzow, Peter (James Leonard), South African composer and teacher; b. Springs, Transvaal, July 14, 1945. After training with Richard Cheery and Aïda Lovell, he obtained a scholarship which allowed him to pursue his training in London at the Royal College of Music (1964–65), where he took courses in piano with Kathleen Long, Angus Morrison, and Frank Merrick, in composition with Bernard Stevens, in orchestration with Gordon Jacob, and in conducting with Sir Adrian Boult; he subsequently completed his studies in Paris with Nadia Boulanger (1965–66). He taught at the Rhodesian College of Music in Salisbury (1966–68) and then was active with the music dept. of the South African Broadcasting Corp. (1968–72). In 1973 he became a prof. of composition at the Univ. of Cape Town. With Robert Grishkoff, he founded the music publishing concern

Musications in 1981. He ed. the vol. *Composers in South Africa Today* (Cape Town, 1987). In his compositions, Klatzow generally follows the tonal path but he has not been adverse to utilizing serial and aleatoric procedures in some of his works.

WORKS: DRAMATIC: OPERA: *The Begger's Opera* (1986). **BALLETS:** *Drie Diere* (1980); *Vespers* (1986); *Hamlet* (1993). **ORCH.:** *Variations* (1964; London, Feb. 10, 1966); *Interactions* for Piano, Percussion, and Chamber Orch. (1971); *The Temptation of St. Anthony after Hieronymus Bosch* for Cello and Orch. (1972; Barcelona, May 14, 1977); *Symphony 1972, Phoenix* (1972; 1st public perf., Cape Town, Oct. 21, 1975); *Time Structure II* (1974); *Still Life, with Moonbeams* (1975); Horn Concerto (Cape Town, June 16, 1978); Organ Concerto (1981); *Incantations* (1984); Concerto for Marimba and Strings (1985); *Figures in a Landscape* (1985); *Citiscape* (1986); *A Chrysalis in Flames* (1988); Concerto for Clarinet and Chamber Orch. (1991). **CHAMBER:** *The Garden of Memories and Discoveries* for 2 Pianos, 2 Guitars, 2 Percussion, Harpsichord, and Electric Organ (1975); *The World of Paul Klee* for Flute and Piano (1977); *Night Magic* for Violin, Horn, and Piano (1978); *Chamber Concerto for 7* for Flute, Clarinet, Horn, Guitar, Percussion, and Electric Organ (1979); *Cythera Among the Lynxes* for Flute and Harp (1982); *Figures in a Landscape I* for Flute and Marimba (1985); String Quartet (1987). **PIANO:** *Moments of Night* (1969); *Piano Piece I* (1970); *Time Structure I* (1973); *3 Movements* (1980); *Murmurs of Tiger and Flame* (1982); *A Branch of Dreams* (1986). **VOCAL:** *In Memoriam N.P. van Wyk Louw* for Soprano and Strings (1970); *Charms and Incantations* for Soprano, Tenor, Horn, and Guitar (1979); *Mass* for Chorus, Horn, Marimba, and Strings (1988; rev. 1990); *Congregational Eucharist* for Chorus and Organ (1990); *Praise the Lord, O My Soul* for Chorus and Organ (1990).

Klaus, Kenneth Blanchard, American composer; b. Earlville, Iowa, Nov. 11, 1923; d. Baton Rouge, La., Aug. 4, 1980. He studied violin with Burleigh and Krasner, and composition with Philip Greeley Clapp at the Univ. of Iowa (Ph.D., 1950); also studied meteorology at the Univ. of Chicago and served as a meteorologist in the Army Air Corps during World War II; in 1950, joined the faculty at Louisiana State Univ. In his works, he applied a sui generis synthesis of expanded tonality verging on serialism. In his vocal compositions, he modernized the medieval device of "sogetto cavato" by deriving a theme from the vowels of letter names. He publ. *The Romantic Period in Music* (Boston, 1970).

WORKS: DRAMATIC: OPERAS: *Tennis Anyone?* (1957); *Crimson Stones.* Also incidental music to *Death of a Salesman* (1954). **ORCH.:** 6 syms.; several symphonic poems; 2 violin concertos; Flute Concerto; Cello Concerto; Clarinet Concerto; *Concerto brevis* for Percussion and Orch. (1955); Concerto for Piano, Right-hand, and Orch. **CHAMBER:** 4 string quartets (1947, 1951, 1957, 1963); Woodwind Quintet; Woodwind Sextet; sonatas.

Klebanov, Dmitri, outstanding Ukrainian composer; b. Kharkov, July 25, 1907; d. there, June 6, 1987. He studied with Bogatyrev at the Kharkov Inst. for Music and Drama, graduating in 1926. After playing viola in Leningrad (1927–28), he returned to Kharkov as director for several musical comedy theaters and as a teacher at the Cons. (1934–73; prof., 1960; emeritus, 1973). He wrote the Ukrainian State Hymn. Klebanov was president of the local Composer's Union (1945–49).

WORKS: DRAMATIC: OPERAS: *Aistenok*, children's opera (1934); *Single Life* (1947); *Vasily Gubanov* (1966; rev. as *Communist*, 1967); *Red Cossacks* (1971). **BALLETS:** *Aistenok* (Moscow, 1936); *Svetlana* (Moscow, 1939). **OTHER:** Musical comedies; film scores. **ORCH.:** 5 syms. (1945, 1952, 1957, 1959, 1962); *Ukrainian Concertino* (1938); 2 violin concertos (1940, 1951); *Welcoming Overture* (1945); *Ukrainian Suite* (1946); 2 cello concertos (1950, 1973); Domra Concerto (1953; rev. for Orch. of Native Instruments, 1973); *4 Preludes and Fugue* (1975). **CHAMBER:** 6 string quartets (1925, 1926, 1933, 1946, 1966, 1968); String Quintet (1953); Woodwind Quartet (1957); Piano Trio (1958); many piano works. **VOCAL:** Choruses; songs.

BIBL.: M. Cherkashina, *D. K.* (1968).

Klebe, Giselher (Wolfgang), German composer and teacher; b. Mannheim, June 28, 1925. He went to Berlin and studied violin, viola, and composition with Kurt von Wolfurt at the Cons. (1940–43) before pursuing his composition studies with Rufer at the Internationales Musikinstitut (1946) and with Blacher (1946–51). He worked in the music division of the Berlin Radio (1946–49), and then taught composition and theory at the Nordwestdeutsche Musikakademie in Detmold from 1957. In 1962–63 he held a fellowship at the Deutsche Akademie in Rome. He was made a member of the Freie Akademie der Künste in Hamburg (1963), the Akademie der Künste in Berlin (1964; president, 1986–89), and the Bayerische Akademie der Schönen Künste in Munich (1978). Klebe has developed an expressive style of composition in which melody, harmony, timbre, and rhythm are complemented by a judicious handling of 12-tone writing.

WORKS: DRAMATIC: *Die Räuber*, opera (1951–56; Düsseldorf, June 3, 1957; rev. 1962); *Die tödlichen Wünsche*, opera (1957–59; Düsseldorf, June 14, 1959); *Die Ermordung Cäsars*, opera (1958–59; Essen, Sept. 20, 1959); *Alkmene*, opera (Berlin, Sept. 25, 1961); *Figaro lässt sich scheiden*, opera buffa (1962–63; Hamburg, June 28, 1963); *Jakobowsky und der Oberst*, comic opera (Hamburg, Nov. 2, 1965); *Das Märchen von der schönen Lilie*, opera (1967–68; Schwetzingen, May 15, 1969); *Das Testament*, ballet-sym. (1970–71; Wiesbaden, April 30, 1971; as Sym. No. 4, Bochum, Jan. 27, 1972); *Ein wahrer Held*, opera (1972–73; Zürich, Jan. 18, 1975); *Das Mädchen aus Domrémy*, opera (1975; Stuttgart, June 19, 1976); *Das Rendezvous*, opera (Hannover, Oct. 7, 1977); *Der jüngste Tag*, opera (1978–79; Mannheim, July 12, 1980); *Die Fastnachtsbeichte*, opera (Darmstadt, Dec. 20, 1983). **ORCH.:** *Con moto* (1948; Bremen, Feb. 23, 1953); *Divertissement joyeux* for Chamber Orch. (Darmstadt, July 8, 1949); *Die Zwitschermaschine* (Donaueschingen, Sept. 10, 1950); *2 Nocturnes* (1951; Darmstadt, July 20, 1952); 5 syms.: No. 1 for 42 Strings (1951; Hamburg, Jan. 7, 1953), No. 2 (1953), No. 3 (1966; WDR, Cologne, Oct. 6, 1967), No. 4, *Das Testament*, ballet-sym. (1970–71; Bochum, Jan. 27, 1972; as a ballet, Wiesbaden, April 30, 1971), and No. 5 (Duisburg, Sept. 13, 1977); *Rhapsody* (1953); Double Concerto for Violin, Cello, and Orch. (Frankfurt am Main, June 19, 1954); *Moments musicaux* (1955); Cello Concerto (1957); *Omaggio* (1960); *Adagio and Fugue* (1962); *Scene und Arie* (Detmold, May 8, 1968); *Herzschläge: Furcht, Bitte und Hoffnung* for Beat Band and Orch. (1969; Gelsenkirchen, June 1, 1970); Concerto for Electronically Altered Harpsichord and Small Orch. (1971; Schwetzingen, May 12, 1972); *Orpheus* (Zagreb, Oct. 22, 1976); *La Tomba di Igor Strawinsky* for Oboe, 14 Strings, and Piano (1978; Cologne, April 25, 1979); Organ Concerto (Duisburg, Nov. 19, 1980); *Begrussung* (Lüdenscheid, Nov. 6, 1981); *Boogie agitato* (Stuttgart, Oct. 24, 1981); Clarinet Concerto (1984; Marl, May 24, 1985); *Umbria verde* (1984); *Lied* (Ludwigshafen, Sept. 30, 1985); *Notturno* (1987; Salzburg, Jan. 30, 1988); Harp Concerto (1988; Münster, Oct. 25, 1989); Cello Concerto (1989; Berlin, May 19, 1990). **CHAMBER:** Wind Quintet (1948); 3 string quartets (1949, 1963, 1981); Viola Sonata (1949); 2 sonatas for Solo Violin (1952, 1955); 2 violin sonatas (1953, 1972); *Elegia appassionata*, piano trio (1955); *Dithyrambe* for String Quartet (1957); *Missa "Miserere nobis"* for 18 Winds (1965); *Concerto à cinque* for Piano, Harpsichord, Harp, Percussion, and Double Bass (1965); *Quasi una fantasia*, piano quintet (1966); *Variationen über ein Thema von Hector Berlioz* for Organ and 3 Percussionists (1970); Double Bass Sonata (1971); *Tennen No Bi* for Flute, Oboe, Clarinet, Harp, Piano, Cello, and Double Bass (1971–72); *Al Rovescio* for Flute, Harp, Piano, and Metallidiophone (1972); 6 Pieces for Double Bass (1973); *Nenia* for Cello (1974); *Alborada* for Harp (1977); *Cinq chants sans paroles* for Harpsichord and Percussionist (1978); *Der dunkle Gedanke* for Clarinet or Bassett Horn and Piano

(1979); *Quattrofonia* for 2 Pianos and 2 Percussionists (1981–82); *Soirée* for Trombone and Chamber Ensemble (1987). **KEYBOARD: PIANO:** *Nocturnes* (1949); Sonata for 2 Pianos (1949); *4 Inventions* (1956); *Neun Klavierstücke für Sonja* (1973, 1974, and 1977); *Feuersturz* (1983); *Glockentürme* for Piano, 4-hands (1990); *Widmungen*, 5 pieces (1993). **ORGAN:** *Passacaglia* (1968); *Fantasie und Lobpreisung* (1970); *Surge aquilo: et veni, auster* (1970); *Orgelfanfare* (1989). **VOCAL:** *Geschichte vom lustigen Musikanten* for Tenor, Chorus, and 5 Instruments (1946–47); *5 Römische Elegien* for Narrator, Piano, Harpsichord, and Double Bass (1952); *Raskolnikows Traum* for Soprano, Clarinet, and Orch. (1956); *5 Lieder* for Alto and Orch. (1962); *Stabat Mater* for Soprano, Mezzo-soprano, Alto, Chorus, and Orch. (1964); *Gebet einer armen Seele*, Mass for Chorus and Organ (Kassel, Oct. 8, 1966); *Beuge dich, du Menschenseele* for Medium Voices and Organ (1975–77); *3 Lieder* for High Voice and Piano (1975–76); *Choral und Te Deum* for Soprano, Chorus, and Orch. (1977–78; Braunschweig, Sept. 24, 1978); *Weihnachtsoratorium* for Mezzo-soprano, Baritone, Speaker, Chorus, and Orch. (Bonn, Dec. 7, 1989).

BIBL.: M. Rentzsch, *G. K.: Werkverzeichnis und einführende Darstellung seines Opernschaffens* (diss., Univ. of Münster, 1990).

Klecki, Pawel. See **Kletzki, Paul.**

Klee, Bernhard, respected German conductor: b. Schleiz, April 19, 1936. He studied piano and conducting at the Cologne Hochschule für Musik; then became répétiteur at the Cologne Opera (1957) and the Bern City Theater (1958); later was an assistant to Sawallisch and a conductor at the Cologne Opera. He was 1st conductor at the opera houses in Salzburg (1962–63), Oberhausen (1963–65), and Hannover (1965–66); then was Generalmusikdirektor in Lübeck (1966–77) and chief conductor of the Hannover Radio Orch. (1976–79). From 1977 to 1987 he was Generalmusikdirektor of the Düsseldorf Sym. Orch.; served as principal guest conductor of the BBC Phil. in Manchester (1985–89). In 1991 he returned as chief conductor to the Hannover Radio Orch., which became the Hannover Radio Phil. in 1992. He also served as chief conductor of the Rheinland-Pfalz State Phil. in Ludwigshafen from 1992. In 1995 he was made honorary conductor of the Hannover Radio Orch. and chief conductor of the Staatsphilharmonie Rheinland-Pfalz in Ludwigshafen. Married to **Edith Mathis**, he served as her accompanist in recitals. As a conductor, Klee is particularly admired for his insightful performances of the Austro-German repertoire.

Klega, Miroslav, Slovak composer; b. Ostrava, March 6, 1929. He studied composition with Kříčka at the Prague Cons. (1942–44) and with Suchoň and Cikker at the Bratislava Cons. (1946–50). He taught at the Ostrava Cons. (1955–73); was its director (1967–73); then worked with the Czech Radio there.

WORKS: *Suite Bagatelle* for Piano (1948); *Černa země* (Black Soil), symphonic variations (1951); Sym. (1959); Concertino for 4 String Instruments (1961); *Pantomima*, suite for Orch. (1963); *Concerto-Partita* for Violin and Orch. (1965); *Výpověď' osamělého pěšáka* (The Confession of a Lone Pedestrian) for Narrator and Orch. (1968); *Příběhy z zazraky*, sym.-ballet (1981).

Kleiber, Carlos, outstanding German-born Austrian conductor, son of **Erich Kleiber**; b. Berlin, July 3, 1930. He left Nazi Germany with his parents in 1935, eventually settling in South America in 1940. He evinced an early interest in music, but his father opposed it as a career; after studying chemistry in Zürich (1949–50), he turned decisively to music and completed his training in Buenos Aires. In 1952 he became a répétiteur and stage assistant at the Theater am Gärtnerplatz in Munich, making his conducting debut in 1954 with Millöcker's *Gasparone* in Potsdam, where he was active until becoming a répétiteur (1956) and conductor (1958) at the Deutsche Oper am Rhein in Düsseldorf. After conducting at the Zürich Opera (1964–66), he served as 1st conductor at the Württemberg State Theater in Stuttgart (1966–68). From 1968 to 1978 he conducted at the Bavarian State Opera in Munich. In 1966 he made his British debut conducting *Wozzeck* at the Edinburgh Festival; he led performances of *Tristan und Isolde* for his first appearances at the Vienna State Opera in 1973 and at the Bayreuth Festival in 1974, the year in which he made his first appearances at London's Covent Garden and Milan's La Scala with *Der Rosenkavalier.* On Sept. 8, 1977, he made his U.S. debut conducting *Otello* at the San Francisco Opera. His first appearance with a U.S. orch. came in 1978, when he conducted the Chicago Sym. Orch. In 1979 he conducted the Vienna Phil. and in 1982 the Berlin Phil. On Jan. 22, 1988, he made his Metropolitan Opera debut in N.Y. conducting *La Bohème.* In 1989 and 1992 he conducted the New Year's Day Concert of the Vienna Phil. with noteworthy elan. He became a naturalized Austrian citizen in 1980. Kleiber has been accorded accolades from critics, audiences, and his fellow musicians. His brilliant performances reflect his unreserved commitment to the score at hand, his authority, and his mastery of technique. His infrequent appearances, combined with his passion for perfection, have made him a legendary figure among the world's contemporary podium celebrities.

BIBL.: W. Flowers, "C. K.—A Legend at 50," *Le Grand Baton* (March 1982); J. von Rhein, "The Unpredictable C. K.," *Ovation* (Sept. 1983).

Kleiber, Erich, eminent Austrian conductor, father of **Carlos Kleiber**; b. Vienna, Aug. 5, 1890; d. Zürich, Jan. 27, 1956. He studied at the Prague Cons. and the Univ. of Prague. He made his debut at the Prague National Theater in 1911; then conducted opera in Darmstadt (1912–19), Barmen-Elberfeld (1919–21), Düsseldorf (1921–22), and Mannheim (1922–23). In 1923 he was appointed Generalmusikdirektor of the Berlin State Opera. His tenure was outstanding, both for the brilliant performances of the standard repertoire and for the exciting programming of contemporary works. He conducted the world premiere of Berg's *Wozzeck* (Dec. 14, 1925). In 1934, in protest against the Nazi government, he resigned his post and emigrated to South America. He conducted regularly at the Teatro Colón in Buenos Aires from 1936 to 1949. Having first conducted at London's Covent Garden in 1937, he returned there from 1950 to 1953. He then was appointed Generalmusikdirektor once more of the Berlin State Opera in 1954, but resigned in March 1955, before the opening of the season, because of difficulties with the Communist regime. He was renowned for his performances of the music of Mozart and Beethoven. He also composed; among his works are a Violin Concerto, Piano Concerto, orch. variations, *Capriccio* for Orch., numerous chamber music works, piano pieces, and songs.

BIBL.: J. Russell, *E. K.: A Memoir* (London, 1957); C. Dillon, *E. K.: A Discogaphy* (Buenos Aires, 1990).

Klein, Elisabeth, Hungarian-born Danish pianist; b. Trenčin, July 23, 1911. She studied at the Budapest Academy of Music (graduated, 1934); then had private lessons with Bartók. She settled in Denmark, becoming a naturalized Danish citizen; made her debut in Copenhagen (1946). She toured extensively and was also active as a teacher. Klein championed the music of Bartók and contemporary Scandinavian composers.

Klein, Fritz Heinrich, Austrian music theorist and composer; b. Budapest, Feb. 2, 1892; d. Linz, July 11, 1977. He took piano lessons with his father; then went to Vienna, where he studied composition with Schoenberg and Berg, and became their devoted disciple. From 1932 to 1957 he taught theory at the Bruckner Cons. in Linz. His most ingenious composition was *Die Maschine* (1921; N.Y., Nov. 24, 1924), subtitled "Eine extonale Selbstsatire" and publ. under the pseudonym "Heautontimorumenos" (i.e., self-tormentor); this work features instances of all kinds of tonal combinations, including a "Mutterakkord," which consists of all 12 different chromatic tones and all 11 different intervals, the first time such an arrangement was proposed. He also publ. an important essay bearing on serial techniques then still in the process of formulation, "Die Grenze der Halbtonwelt," in *Die Musik* (Jan. 1925). He made the vocal score of Berg's opera *Wozzeck*. His other works include *Partita* for 6 Instruments (1953); *Divertimento* for Strings (1954); *Ein musikalisches Fliessband* for Orch. (1960); *Musikalisches Tagebuch* for Orch. (1970); also several stage works, among them the opera *Nostradamus*.

Klein, Gideon, gifted Czech composer and pianist; b. Přerov, Dec. 6, 1919; d. in the concentration camp at Fürstengrube, Silesia, probably on Jan. 27, 1945. He was reared in a Jewish family of culture, and at age 11 began piano studies with Růžena Kurzová. In 1938 he entered the piano master class of Vilém Kurz at the Prague Cons., where he also received instruction in composition from Alois Hába; also pursued the study of theory at the Charles Univ. in Prague. His education was cut short by the Nazi occupation of his homeland in 1939; nonetheless, he persevered under the most daunting conditions, producing works under a pseudonym, which he presented in private concert settings. In 1941 he was deported to the concentration camp in Terezín, where he continued his activities as both composer and pianist. In late 1944 he was transported to the concentration camp in Auschwitz, and then on to the concentration camp in Fürstengrube, where he died a few months before the Allied victory. Although he perished at the age of 25, he succeeded in composing a significant number of works of enduring value. His early interest in Moravian folk modalities gave way to the influence of Janáček, Novák, and Schoenberg, which, in turn, prompted him to find his own compositional path, which included the use of microintervals and free tonality. All of his extant works were publ. in a collaborative ed. by the Czech Music Fund in Prague and by Bote & Bote in Berlin in 1993.

WORKS: *4 Movements* for String Quartet (1936–38); Duo for Violin and Viola in Quarter Tones (1940); *Divertimento* for 8 Winds (1940); 3 songs for High Voice and Piano, after Klag, Hölderlin, and Goethe (1940); String Quartet (1941); Duo for Violin and Cello (1941; unfinished); 2 madrigals for 2 Sopranos, Alto, Tenor, and Bass (1942, 1943); *The First Sin* for Men's Chorus (1942); *Fantasy and Fugue* for String Quartet (1942–43); Piano Sonata (1943); Trio for Violin, Viola, and Cello (1944; arr. by V. Saudek as *Partita* for Chamber Orch.).

Klein, John, American organist, pianist, and composer; b. Rahns, Pa., Feb. 21, 1915; d. there, April 30, 1981. He studied at the Philadelphia Musical Academy; then went to Salzburg, where he took courses at the Mozarteum, and later to Paris, where he had lessons with Boulanger in composition and with Dupré in organ. Returning to America, he was organist at the Presbyterian Church in Columbus, Ohio (1937–42); then was engaged in radio shows as a pianist (1944–57); played carillon in recitals and at carillon festivals in Cobb, Ireland, and at the World's Fair in Brussels. He publ. *The Art of Playing the Modern Carillon* and *The First 4 Centuries of Music*; composed a Violin Concerto and a number of songs and marches, including the U.S. Army radio show theme, *Sound Off*.

Klein, Kenneth, American conductor; b. Los Angeles, Sept. 5, 1939. He studied violin at the Univ. of Southern Calif. School of Music in Los Angeles with Eudice Shapiro, Vera Barstow, and Peter Meremblum; took piano lessons with Gerhard Albersheim; studied conducting with Fritz Zweig in Los Angeles, Izler Solomon at the Aspen (Colo.) School of Music, and Richard Lert in Asilomar, California; received instruction in theory from Boulanger in Paris. He was a violinist in the Pasadena Sym. Orch.; then was founder-conductor of the Westside Sym. Orch. in Los Angeles (1963–68). He was music director of the Guadalajara Sym. Orch. (1969–78), the Nassau (L.I.) Sym. Orch. (from 1980), the Santa Cruz (Calif.) Sym. Orch. (1981–85), the N.Y. Virtuosi (from 1982), and the South Dakota Sym. Orch. (1983–85). He also appeared widely as a guest conductor in Europe. He taught at the Univ. of Guadalajara (1968–69; 1973) and the Univ. of Calif. at Santa Cruz (1981–83).

Klein, Lothar, German-born Canadian composer; b. Hannover, Jan. 27, 1932. He went to England in 1939 and to the U.S. in 1941; studied composition with Fetler at the Univ. of Minnesota (B.A., 1954); then composition with Petrassi at the Berkshire Music Center in Tanglewood (summer, 1956) and orchestration with Dorati in Minneapolis (1956–58). After winning a Fulbright fellowship, he went to Berlin to study composition with Rufer at the Free Univ. and with Blacher at the Hochschule für Musik (1958–60); also with Nono in Darmstadt; subsequently completed his studies at the Univ. of Minnesota (Ph.D., 1961), serving on its faculty (1962–64). He later taught at the Univ. of Texas at Austin (1964–68); in 1968, joined the faculty of the Univ. of Toronto, where he was chairman of its graduate music dept. (1971–76). His early music is essentially tonal, aesthetically derived from neo-Romantic procedures; he then experimented with various branches of serialism; also wrote collage pieces embodying elements of all historical periods through linkage of stylistic similarities.

WORKS: DRAMATIC: *Lost Love*, ballet (1950–56); *The Prodigal Son*, dance drama (1966); *Tale of a Father and Son*, opera (1983). **ORCH.:** *The Bluebird*, suite (1952); *Eclogues* for Horn and Strings (1954); 3 syms. (1955; 1966; *Symphonic Etudes*, 1972); Concerto for Winds, Timpani, and Strings (1956); *Appassionato* (1958); *Symmetries* (1958); *Trio concertante* for String Trio and Orch. (1961); *Epitaphs* (1963); *Rondo Giocoso* (1964); *Charivari: Music for an Imaginary Comedy* (1966); *Musique à Go-Go: A Symphonic Mêlée* (1966); *Paganini Collage* for Violin and Orch. (1967); *Le Trésor des dieux* for Guitar and Orch. (1969); *Janizary Music* for Military Orch. (1970); *Design* for Percussion and Orch. (1970); *Passacaglia of the Zodiac* for 14 Strings (1971); *Music* for Violin and Orch. (1972); *Slices of Time* for Trumpet and Orch. (1973; also for Trumpet and String Quartet); *Invention, Blues, and Chase* for Free Bass Accordion and Strings (1975); *Musica Antiqua* for Consort and Orch. (1975); *Boccherini Collage* for Cello and Orch. (1978); *Scenes* for Timpani and Strings (1979); *Concerto Sacro* for Viola and Orch. (1984); *Landscape with Pipers* for Chamber Orch. (1984); *Festival Partita* (1990); *Columbus Music* (1992); *Homage à Toulous-Latrec* (1994). **CHAMBER:** *Suite on 12th Night* for 7 Instruments (1951); Wind Quintet (1952); Piano Quintet (1954); *Partita I* for Flute, Clarinet, and Harp (1955) and *II* for Trumpet, Tuba, and Piano (1980); *3 Greek Rites* for 8 Percussion (1964); *Incantations* for 7 Percussion (1965); *Arias* for String Quartet (1966); Trio Sonata for Clarinet, Cello, Piano or Harpsichord, and Drum Set (1968); *Vaudeville*, "acrobatics" for Soprano Saxophone and Wind Quintet (1979); *Grand Duo Concertante* for Clarinet and Timpani (1979); *Cancioneros* for Violin and Piano (1980); *Meditation* "for John Lennon, Dec. 9, 1980" for Violin and Piano (1980); *Variations on 2 Well-known Airs* for 9 Instruments (1981); *Tombeau* for 2 Guitars (1981); *Choreagos* for Oboe, Percussion, and Optional Reciter (1982); *Virtuoso Music* for Viola, Cello, and Double Bass (1987); String Quartet, *Quartets of the Sounds* (1991); *Vice-Versa*, suite for 2 Trombones (1995). **PIANO:** Sonata (1968); *Canadiana* for 2 Pianos (1980). **VOCAL:** *The Masque of Orianna* for 2 Sopranos, Chorus, and Orch. (1973); *The Philosopher in the Kitchen*, "gastronomic meditations" for Contralto and Orch. (1974); *Orpheus* for Soprano, Tenor, Narrator, Chorus, and Instruments (1976); *Voices of Earth* for Soprano, Children's Chorus, and Orch. (1976); *Hachcava: Memorial Meditations* for Bass and 5 Instruments (1979); *The Jabberwock in Ogden Nash's Dining Room* for Women's Chorus and Percussion Ensemble (1991); choruses; solo songs.

Klein, Peter, German tenor; b. Zündorf, near Cologne, Jan. 25, 1907; d. Vienna, Oct. 4, 1992. He studied at the Cologne Cons. He made appearances in Düsseldorf, Kaiserslautern, and Zürich; was a member of the Hamburg State Opera (1937–41), then at the Vienna State Opera; also appeared at Bayreuth (from 1946). In 1947 he first appeared at London's Covent Garden as Jacquino with the visiting Vienna State Opera; he returned there regularly until 1960. He made his Metropolitan

Opera debut in N.Y. on Nov. 21, 1949, as Valzacchi in *Der Rosenkavalier*, remaining on its roster until 1951. From 1956 to 1977 he was head of the opera dept. at the Vienna Cons. His other roles included Basilio, Mime in the *Ring* cycle, the Captain in *Wozzeck*, and Monsieur Taupe in *Capriccio*.

Kleinsinger, George, American composer; b. San Bernardino, Calif., Feb. 13, 1914; d. N.Y., July 28, 1982. He studied with Bauer, Haubiel, and James at N.Y. Univ. (B.A., 1937) and with Jacobi and Wagenaar at the Juilliard Graduate School in N.Y. (1938–40). In 1942 he composed the first of a series of popular melodramas, *Tubby the Tuba*. Also notable was his chamber opera *Shinbone Alley* (N.Y., Dec. 6, 1954), which was based on Don Marquis' popular comic strip *Archy and Mehitabel*.

WORKS: DRAMATIC: MELODRAMAS: *Farewell to a Hero* (1941); *Tubby the Tuba* (1942); *Peewee the Piccolo* (1945); *Pan the Piper* (1946); *The Story of Celeste* (1947); *The Tree that Found Christmas* (1955). **CHAMBER OPERA:** *Shinbone Alley* (N.Y., Dec. 6, 1954). Also film scores and television music. **ORCH.:** Sym. (1942); Cello Concerto (1946); Harmonica Concerto (1947); Violin Concerto (1953). **CHAMBER:** String Quartet (1940); Clarinet Quintet (1949); Trio for Clarinet, Cello, and Piano (1955); piano pieces. **VOCAL:** *I Hear America Singing*, cantata (1940); *Brooklyn Baseball Cantata* (1942); songs.

Klemetti, Heikki, Finnish composer and choral conductor; b. Kuortane, Feb. 14, 1876; d. Helsinki, Aug. 26, 1953. He studied philosophy; then music at the Stern Cons. in Berlin. In 1900 he founded the famous men's choir Suomen Laulu (became a mixed choir in 1907), with which he toured Scandinavia and Europe (1901–25); also the U.S. (1939); led it until 1942. He publ. a history of music (several vols. from 1916), a textbook of choral singing (1917), and a textbook of voice production (1920); composed numerous choruses, masses, and antiphons (collected and officially approved as the hymnal of the State Church of Finland in 1924); also arranged songs for school and home (3 vols., 1927–28) and some early church music.

Klemperer, Otto, celebrated German conductor; b. Breslau, May 14, 1885; d. Zürich, July 6, 1973. After early musical training from his mother, he entered the Hoch Cons. in Frankfurt am Main (1901), where he studied piano with Kwast and theory with Knorr; he later received instruction in composition and conducting from Pfitzner in Berlin. He made his debut conducting Max Reinhardt's production of *Orpheus in the Underworld* in Berlin in 1906; on Mahler's recommendation, he then was appointed chorus master and subsequently conductor of the German Theater in Prague; he assisted Mahler in the latter's preparations for the Munich premiere of the *Symphony of a Thousand* in 1910. He became a conductor at the Hamburg Opera in 1910, but was obliged to leave in 1912 as the result of a scandalous liaison with the recently married soprano Elisabeth Schumann. After minor appointments at Barmen (1913–14) and Strasbourg (1914–17), where he was Pfitzner's deputy, he was appointed music director of the Cologne Opera in 1917. While in Cologne, he conducted the German premiere of Janáček's *Káťa Kabanová*. In 1924 he was named music director of the Wiesbaden Opera. He made his U.S. debut as guest conductor with the N.Y. Sym. Orch. on Jan. 24, 1926. In 1927 he became music director of Berlin's Kroll Opera, where he was given a mandate to perform new works and present repertoire pieces in an enlightened manner. He conducted the world premiere of Hindemith's *Neues vom Tage* (June 8, 1929), as well as the first Berlin performances of Hindemith's *Cardillac*, Stravinsky's *Oedipus Rex*, and Schoenberg's *Die glückliche Hand*; he also conducted the premiere performance of Schoenberg's *Begleitungsmusik* as part of the Kroll concerts. When political and economic pressures forced the Kroll Opera to close in 1931, Klemperer became a conductor at the Berlin State Opera. When the Nazis came to power in 1933, he was compelled to emigrate to the U.S. That same year, he became music director of the Los Angeles Phil.; he also appeared as a guest conductor in N.Y., Philadelphia, and Pittsburgh. His career was disrupted in 1939 when he underwent an operation for a brain tumor. In 1947 he was engaged as conductor at the Budapest State Opera, where he remained until 1950. He made his first appearance as a guest conductor with the Philharmonia Orch. of London in 1951; was appointed its principal conductor in 1959, and retained that position when the orch.'s manager, Walter Legge, unsuccessfully attempted to disband it in 1964.

Klemperer was accident-prone and a manic-depressive all his life. The two sides of his nature were reflected in his conducting styles on either side of World War II. He had earlier been noted for his energetic and hard-driven interpretations, but during his late London years he won great renown for his measured performances of the Viennese classics. He particularly distinguished himself by conducting a memorable series of the Beethoven syms. at the Royal Festival Hall. In the early 1960s he conducted new productions of *Fidelio, Die Zauberflöte*, and *Lohengrin* at Covent Garden. His serious and unsentimental readings of Mahler's syms. were largely responsible for the modern critical and popular interest shown in that composer's music. In 1970 he conducted in Jerusalem and accepted Israeli citizenship. He retired in 1972. He was also a composer. He studied with Schoenberg during the latter's American sojourn, but his compositional style had more in common with that of Pfitzner. He wrote an opera, *Das Ziel* (1915; rev. 1970), a *Missa sacra* (1916), 6 syms. (from 1960), 17 pieces for Voice and Orch. (1967–70), 9 string quartets (1968–70), and about 100 lieder. He publ. *Meine Erinnerungen an Gustav Mahler* (Zürich, 1960; Eng. tr., 1964, as *Minor Recollections*).

BIBL.: P. Heyworth, *Conversations with K.* (London, 1973); C. Osborne and K. Thomson, eds., *K. Stories: Anecdotes, Sayings and Impressions of O. K.* (London, 1980); P. Heyworth, *O. K.: His Life and Times*, vol. I, 1885–1933 (London, 1983); M. Anderson, ed., *K. on Music: Shavings from a Musician's Workbench* (London, 1986).

Klenau, Paul (August) von, Danish conductor and composer; b. Copenhagen, Feb. 11, 1883; d. there, Aug. 31, 1946. He studied violin with Hillmer and composition with Malling in Copenhagen; then took lessons in violin with Halíř and in composition with Bruch at the Berlin Hochschule für Musik (1902–04). In 1904 he went to Munich, where he studied composition privately with Thuille; in 1908, moved to Stuttgart, where he became a student of Schillings. He began his conducting career at the Freiburg im Breisgau Opera during the season of 1907–08; from 1909 to 1912, was conductor at the Stuttgart Court Opera; in 1912, was conductor of the Bach Soc. in Frankfurt am Main; then returned to the Freiburg im Breisgau Opera (1913). After World War I, he studied with Schoenberg. From 1920 to 1926 he was conductor of the Danish Phil. Soc. in Copenhagen; concurrently conducted the Vienna Konzerthausgesellschaft (1922–30). He returned to Copenhagen in 1940.

WORKS: DRAMATIC: OPERAS: *Sulamith*, after the Song of Songs (Munich, Nov. 16, 1913); *Kjartan und Gudrun* (Mannheim, April 4, 1918; rev. version as *Gudrun auf Island*, Hagen, Nov. 27, 1924); *Die Lästerschule*, after Sheridan (Frankfurt am Main, Dec. 25, 1926); *Michael Kolhaas*, after Kleist (Stuttgart, Nov. 4, 1933; new version, Berlin, March 7, 1934); *Rembrandt van Rijn*, libretto by the composer (Berlin and Stuttgart, Jan. 23, 1937); *Elisabeth von England* (Kassel, March 29, 1939; title changed to *Die Königin* after the outbreak of World War II to avoid mentioning England). **BALLETS:** *Kleine Idas Blumen*, after Hans Christian Andersen (Stuttgart, 1916); *Marion* (Copenhagen, 1920). **ORCH.:** 7 syms. (1908, 1911, 1913, 1913, 1939, 1940, 1941); *Inferno*, 3 fantasies. **OTHER:** Chamber music; piano pieces; songs.

Klenovsky, Paul. See **Wood, Sir Henry J(oseph).**

Klerk, Albert de, Dutch organist, choral conductor, pedagogue, and composer; b. Haarlem, Oct. 4, 1917. He was a student of A. van der Horst (organ) and H. Andriessen (analysis) at the Amsterdam Cons. (1934–39; graduated, 1939), receiving the Prix d'Excellence in 1941. In 1934 he became organist at the St. Joseph Church in Haarlem, a post he retained for 60 years. He also served as conductor of the Catholic Choir (1946–91) and city organist (1956–83) in Haarlem. He was prof. of organ at the Inst. for Catholic Church Music in Utrecht (1946–64), and then at the Amsterdam Cons. (1965–85). As an organist, he toured as a recitalist, being particularly admired for his improvisational skills. His repertoire was an extensive one, and included the complete organ works of Franck and H. Andriessen.

WORKS: ORCH.: 2 organ concertos (1941, 1964); *Cantabile* (1952); *Suite Concertante* for Organ and Strings (1976). **CHAMBER:** Sonatine for Violin and Cello (1937); *Fantasie* for Violin and Piano (1950); Concerto for Organ, 2 Horns, 2 Trumpets, and 2 Trombones (1967). **ORGAN:** Sonata (1940); Prelude and Fugue (1940); Inventions (1945); 10 Pieces (2 parts, 1946); Ricercare (1950); *Octo Fantasiae super themata Gregoriana* (1953); *12 Images* (1969); *Tres Meditationes Sacra* (1992–93). **VOCAL:** *Jam lucis orto sidere* for High Voice and Orch. (1942–43); *Stabat Mater* for Alto, Tenor, Chorus, and Chamber Orch. (1952); *Mater Sanctus Laelitiae* for Women's Chorus, Flute, English Horn, and Bassoon (1957); *Super omnia*, cantata for Alto, Chorus, and Organ (1960); *5 noëls français* for Alto and 10 Winds (1963); *Laudate Dominum (Psalm 150)* for Chorus and Organ (1968); *Te Deum* for Chorus and Orch. (1979); *In Honorem Sancti Bavonis* for Youth Chorus and Orch. (1983); 10 masses; many motets.

Kletzki, Paul (originally, **Pawel Klecki**), distinguished Polish-born Swiss conductor; b. Łódź, March 21, 1900; d. while rehearsing the Royal Liverpool Phil. in Liverpool, March 5, 1973. He studied composition at the Warsaw Cons., where he also received instruction in violin from Mlynarski; after further studies at the Berlin Academy of Music, he played in the Łódź Phil. (1914–19). He was active as a conductor and composer in Berlin (1921–33); then taught composition at Milan's Scuola Superiora di Musica; at the outbreak of World War II (1939), he settled in Switzerland, becoming a naturalized Swiss citizen in 1947. After the war, he pursued a notable conducting career, appearing as a guest conductor with many of the major European orchs.; he also conducted in North and South America, and maintained a close association with the Israel Phil. He was music director of the Dallas Sym. Orch. (1958–62), the Bern Sym. Orch. (1964–66), and l'Orchestre de la Suisse Romande in Geneva (1968–70). He was a fine interpreter of the Romantic orch. repertoire, excelling in both the Austro-German and the Slavic schools. He composed 4 syms., a Piano Concerto, a Violin Concerto, chamber music, and songs, but most of his works were destroyed by the havoc wreaked during World War II.

Kleven, Arvid, Norwegian composer; b. Drontheim, Nov. 29, 1899; d. Oslo, Nov. 23, 1929. He studied in Oslo, Paris, and Berlin; from 1919, played flute in the National Theater Orch. in Christiania, and in the Phil. Orch. there. His early neo-Romantic style developed along expressionist lines. Among his works are *Sinfonia libera in due parte* (1927); *Symfonisk fantasi* for Orch.; 2 symphonic poems: *Lotusland* (1922) and *Skogens sovn* (The Sleeping Forest); songs with orch.; Violin Sonata; Cello Sonata; piano pieces.

Klička, Josef, Bohemian organist, choral conductor, and composer, father of **Václav Klička**; b. Klattau, Dec. 15, 1855; d. there, March 28, 1937. He studied with Skuherský in Prague; then conducted various choral societies there; was prof. of organ at the Prague Cons. (1885–1924) and inspector of music in Bohemia (1906–20). He wrote an opera, *Spanilá mylnářka* (Die Schöne Müllerin; Prague, 1886), 9 masses, 2 oratorios, chamber works, and many organ pieces.

BIL.: K. Hoffmeister, *J. K.* (Prague, 1944).

Klička, Václav, Czech harpist, teacher, and composer, son of **Josef Klička**; b. Prague, Aug. 1, 1882; d. there, May 22, 1953. He studied harp with Hanuš Trneček and theory and composition with Karel Knittl and Karel Stecker at the Prague Cons. After playing in the Pilsen theater orch. (1903–10), he made tours of Europe as a soloist with orchs. and as a recitalist. From 1922 until the Nazi occupation of his homeland he was a prof. of harp at the Prague Cons. Following the liberation of his country in 1945, he resumed his activities. He composed much harp music and also prepared various arrangements for the harp.

Klien, Walter, admired Austrian pianist; b. Graz, Nov. 27, 1928; d. Vienna, Feb. 9, 1991. He studied in Frankfurt am Main (1939–45), Graz (1946–49), and with Josef Dichler at the Vienna Academy of Music (1950–53); he also was a student of Michelangeli (piano) and Hindemith (composition). In 1951 and 1952 he took the Busoni prize in Bolzano, and in 1953 the Bösendorfer prize in Vienna. Subsequently he made extensive tours as a soloist with the leading orchs. and as a recitalist. He also toured in duo concerts with Wolfgang Schneiderhan from 1963. Klien displayed a special affinity for the music of Haydn, Mozart, Schubert, Schumann, and Brahms.

Klima, Alois, Czech conductor; b. Klatovy, Dec. 21, 1905; d. Prague, June 11, 1980. He began his musical training with his father; after taking courses in mathematics and physics at the Univ. of Prague, he studied with Dědeček and Doležil (conducting) and Křička and Řídký (composition) at the Prague Cons. He conducted the radio orchs. in Košice (1936) and Ostrava (1936–38), and then was chief conductor of the Prague Opera Studio (1939–46) and the Prague Radio Sym. Orch. (1950–70); he also was a teacher at the Prague Cons. and Academy of Music.

Klimov, Mikhail (Georgievich [originally, **Egorovich**]), Russian choral conductor and pedagogue; b. Moscow, Oct. 21, 1881; d. Zavidovo, near Tver, Feb. 20, 1937. He studied composition with Rimsky-Korsakov and conducting with Nikolai Tcherepnin at the St. Petersburg Cons., graduating in 1908. In 1919 he was called upon to reorganize the former Imperial Church Choir as a secular group, which he then conducted until 1935. In 1908 he joined the faculty of the St. Petersburg Cons., becoming a prof. in 1916 and artistic director of its opera studio in 1921.

BIBL.: V. Muzalevsky, *M.G. K.* (Leningrad, 1960).

Klimov, Valery (Alexandrovich), Russian violinist; b. Kiev, Oct. 16, 1931. His father was a professional conductor and a pedagogue. Klimov studied in Odessa and with D. Oistrakh at the Moscow Cons., graduating in 1956; won 1st prize in the Prague and Paris competitions (1956) and then at the Tchaikovsky Competition in Moscow (1958), which opened for him great opportunities for world tours; he played with much success in Europe, the U.S., and Australia.

Klobučar, Berislav, Yugoslav conductor; b. Zagreb, Aug. 28, 1924. He was educated at the Zagreb Academy of Music; studied conducting with Lovro von Matačić and Clemens Krauss. He was conductor at the Zagreb National Theater (1941–51); in 1953 he appeared at the Vienna State Opera; became a regular conductor there. He was chief conductor of the Graz Phil. and Opera (1961–72); after serving as principal conductor at Stockholm's Royal Theater (1972–81), he was music director of the Orchestre Philharmonique de Nice (1982–88). He also appeared as a guest conductor with the major European and U.S. opera houses.

Klose, Friedrich (Karl Wilhelm), Swiss composer; b. Karlsruhe (of Swiss parents), Nov. 29, 1862; d. Ruvigliana, near Lugano, Dec. 24, 1942. He studied with V. Lachner in Karlsruhe and Ruthardt in Geneva; then with Bruckner in Vienna (1886–91). He taught in Switzerland, Austria, and Germany before joining the faculty at Munich's Akademie der Tonkunst (1907–19). He publ. *Meine Lehrjahre bei Bruckner* (Regensburg, 1927) and *Bayreuth* (Regensburg, 1929).

WORKS: ORCH.: 3 symphonic poems: *Elfenreigen* (1892), *Das Leben ein Traum* (1896), and *Festzug* (1913); *Ilsebill*, dramatic sym. (Munich, Oct. 29, 1905). **CHAMBER:** String Quartet (1911); organ works. **VOCAL:** Mass (1889); *Der Sonne-Geist*, oratorio (Basel, 1918); songs.

BIBL.: H. Knappe, *F. K.: Eine Studie* (Munich, 1921); idem, ed., *F. K. zum 80. Geburtstag* (Lugano, 1942).

Klose, Margarete, esteemed German contralto; b. Berlin, Aug. 6, 1902; d. there, Dec. 14, 1968. She studied at the Klindworth-Scharwenka Cons. in Berlin and received vocal training from Bültemann and Marschalk. She made her operatic debut in Ulm in 1927, then sang in Kassel (1928–29) and Mannheim (1929–31). She was a leading member of the Berlin State Opera (1931–49; 1955–61); also sang at the Bayreuth Festivals (1936–42) and London's Covent Garden (1935, 1937), and was a member of the Berlin Städtische Oper (1949–58). She was particularly praised for her Wagner and Verdi portrayals.

Klucevsek, Guy, American composer and accordionist; b. N.Y., Feb. 26, 1947. He grew up in a Slovenian community in Pennsylvania, where he learned to play polkas. He studied theory and composition at the Indiana Univ. of Pennsylvania (B.A., 1969) and with Subotnick at the Univ. of Pittsburgh (M.A., 1971) and the Calif. Inst. of the Arts (1971–72). In 1980 he discovered the polkas of Cajun and Texan/Mexican origin, and in 1986 he invited a number of composers to contribute to his recording *Polkas from the Fringe* (1987). He also encouraged and created virtuoso accordion music in other styles, and premiered various works by composers including Henry Cowell, Lois Vierk, and John Zorn. Among his compositions are *Sea Chandeliers* for Gamelan (1985), *Scenes from a Mirage* for Accordion (1986), and *Flying Vegetables of the Apocalypse* for Violin, Cello, and Accordion (1988).

Klusák, Jan, Czech composer; b. Prague, April 18, 1934. He studied theory with Řídký and Bořkovec at the Prague Academy of Music (1953–57). He wrote a number of works in a neo-Baroque idiom, set in tolerably dissonant counterpoint; also paid tribute to the ethnic resources of Czech music. He soon succumbed, however, to the Circean lure of cosmopolitan formalism and total serialism, with a well-nigh monastic exercise of tonal egalitarianism.

WORKS: DRAMATIC: OPERAS: *Proces* (The Trial), after Kafka (1966); *Viola* (1984–85). **BALLET:** *Stories from Tapestries* (1988). **FILM MUSIC:** *The Count of Monte Cristo* (1993; for H. Fescourt's silent film of 1928); *Eoritkon* (1994). **ORCH.:** Concertino for Flute and Strings (1955); *Partita* for Strings (1955); 3 syms. (1956, 1959, 1960); Concerto Grosso for Wind Quintet and Strings (1957); *Variations on a Theme of Mahler*, after the latter's 5th Sym. (1960–62); *Inventions I* (1961), *II* (1962), *III* (1962), *IV* (1964), *VII* (1973), and *VIII*, *Quadratura orbis* (Squaring of the Circle; 1973) for Chamber Orch.; *2 Czech Dances* for Wind Orch. (1964); *Lyric Fantasy, Hommage à Grieg* (1965); *Le Forgeron harmonieux*, after Handel's so-called *Harmonious Blacksmith* (1966); *Pasticcio olandese per orchestra, A Friesland Friday* (1969–70); *Hamburger Doppelinvention* (1974); *Kleine Farbenlehre, Hommage à Goethe* (1974–75); *6 Small Preludes* (1984); *Missing Mozart*, fantasy for Chamber Orch. (1991); Concertino for Oboe and Small Orch. (1991); *Tetragrammaton sive Nomina Eius* (1992). **CHAMBER:** *Music to the Fountain* for Wind Quintet (1954); 5 string quartets (1956; 1961–62; 1975; 1990; 1994); *Obrazy* (Pictures) for 12 Wind Instruments (1960); *Monoinvention* for Cello (1962); *Risposte* for Violin (1963); Sonata for Violin and Wind Instruments (1964–65); *Invention V, Hra v šachy* (Game of Chess) for Wind Quintet (1965); *1-4-3-2-5-6-7-10-9-8-11* (invertible all-interval 12-tone series) for Flute (1965); *Invention VI* for Wind Quintet and String Quartet (1969); *Contrapunto fiorito* for 8 Instruments (1966); *Short John* for Cimbalom (1971); *Jupiter-Duo* for Clarinet and Cello (1973); Percussion Sonata (1974); *Solo* for Trumpet (1975–76); *Die heilige Zahl*, duo for Violin and Percussion (1975–76); *Tango-Polka* for Clarinet, Trumpet, Cello, and Piano (1980); *Variations* for 2 Harps (1982); *Diario* for Cello (1982); *Once There Were 3 Goddesses* for Brass Quintet and Harp (1983); *Fantasia on Adam Michna of Otradovice* for Brass Quintet and Harp (1983); *Šmidři suita* for 4 Saxophones (1983); *Trigon* for Flute, Marimba, and Guitar (1983); *The Art of Harmony* for 13 Winds and Double Bass (1992); piano pieces. **VOCAL:** *Prislovi* (Proverbs) for Low Voice and Wind Instruments (1959); *4 Small Vocal Exercises* for Narrator and 11 Wind Instruments, after Kafka (1960); *Radix nativitatis I. S.* (memorial for Igor Stravinsky) for Voice, Flute, Clarinet, Viola, and Piano (1972); *Bridal Cantata 1979* for Men's Chorus and Orch. (1979); *The Moon in Zenith* for Mezzo-soprano, Clarinet, Viola, and Piano, after Anna Akhmatova (1981); solo songs.

Kmentt, Waldemar, Austrian tenor; b. Vienna, Feb. 2, 1929. He was a student at the Vienna Academy of Music of Adolf Vogel, Elisabeth Rado, and Hans Duhan; while still a student, he toured the Netherlands and Belgium with a student ensemble of the Academy. In 1950 he made his formal debut as a soloist in Beethoven's 9th Sym. in Vienna, and then appeared as the Prince in *The Love for 3 Oranges* at the Vienna Volksoper in 1951. In the latter year, he became a member of the Vienna State Opera, where he appeared as Jaquino at the reopening of the opera house in 1955. He also sang regularly in Salzburg (from 1955) and Düsseldorf (from 1958), and made guest appearances in Milan, Paris, Rome, Bayreuth, Munich, and other operatic centers. As a concert artist, he sang widely in Europe as well. He acquired a fine reputation for his performances of works from the Austro-German repertoire.

Knab, Armin, German composer; b. Neu-Schleichach, Feb. 19, 1881; d. Bad Wörishofen, June 23, 1951. He studied piano in Würzburg. From 1934 to 1943 he taught at the Hochschule für Musik-Erziehung in Berlin. He was particularly esteemed for his lieder. He followed the Romantic tradition, but tended toward a more severe modal style in his larger works.

WORKS: Sacred cantatas: *Mariae Geburt* (1928); *Vanitas mundi* (1946); *Engelsgruss* (1950); musical fairy tale: *Sneewittchen and Rumpelstilzchen*; folk-song cantatas: *Singt und klingt* (1934); *Gruss Gott, du schöner Maien* (1935); *Glück auf, ihr Bergleute* (1946); a great number of choral works; many instrumental pieces for school use.

BIBL.: O. Lang, *A. K., Ein Meister deutscher Liedkunst* (Munich, 1937; 2nd ed., rev., 1981).

Knaifel, Alexander (Aronovich), Russian composer; b. Tashkent, Nov. 28, 1943. He began his training in the special music school at the Leningrad Cons. (1950–61); after attending the Moscow Cons. (1961–63), he studied composition with Arapov at the Leningrad Cons. (1963–67). In his works, Knaifel employs a variety of modern compositional techniques.

WORKS: DRAMATIC: *Kentervilskoe prividenie* (The Canterville Ghost), chamber opera (1965–66); ballets; film scores. **ORCH.:** *Burleska* for Trombone and Strings (1963); *Dream*, fantasia for Chamber Orch. (1963); *131* for Viola, Double Bass, Winds, and Percussion (1964); *Onrush*, ballet-sym. (1964); *Seekers of the Future City* for Strings, Percussion, and Organ (1965); *Magdalene Repentant*, choreographic scene (1967); *Medea*, choreographic sym. (1968); *Joan*, passion for 13 Instrumental Groups (1970–78); *Early Cranes* (1979); *Vera* for Strings (1980); *Madness* for Chamber Orch. (1987); *Litania* (1988). **CHAMBER:** *Dyad*, 2 pieces for Flute, Viola, Piano, and Percussion (1963); *Ostinati* for Violin and Cello (1964); *Disarmament*, choreographical striptease for Ensemble (1966); *Lamento* for Cello (1967); *Tournament Music* for Horn and Piano (1967); *A prima vista* for 4 Percussionists (1972); *Rafferti* for Jazz Ensemble (1980); *Yes* for Soloist and Ensemble (1980); *Nika* for 17 Players (1983–84); *Agnus Dei* for 4 Instrumentalists (1987). **VOCAL:** *Chuck it into My Garden* for Chorus and Orch. (1962); *Confession* for Reader and Percussion Ensemble (1963); *Petrograd Sparrows*, suite-phantasmagoria for Boy's Chorus and Chamber Orch. (1967); *150,000,000*, dithyrambe for Chorus and Chamber Orch. (1968); *Monodia* for Woman's Voice (1968); *Lenin's Letter to the Members of the Central Committee* for Unison Bass Chorus (1969); *Anna Akhmatova: Midnight Poems* for 4 Performers (1972–73); *Status Nascendi* for 3 Performing Groups (1975); *Ainana* for Chamber Chorus, Percussion, and Tape (1978); *Stupid Horse*, 15 stories for Singer and Piano (1981);

Accidental for Girl Soloist, Chorus, String Orch., and Organ (1982); *Pagan Rock* for Bass Chorus, Percussion, and Rock Group (1982); *Opposition* for Bass Chorus and Orch. (1984); *God* for 2 Choruses (1985); *The Wings of a Lackey*, vocal/choreographic fresco (1986); *Through the Rainbow of Unwilling Tears* for Singer and Cello (1988).

Knap, Rolf, Dutch composer; b. Amsterdam, Oct. 17, 1937. He studied oboe at the Amsterdam Cons.; took private composition lessons with Karel Mengelberg; then studied electronic music at the Inst. of Sonology of the Univ. of Utrecht. He was an orch. oboist (1960–67); then taught oboe.

WORKS: *(Sym)phonic Piece* for Orch. (1971); *Le Couple(t)* for Voice, Piano, and Electronics (1971); *Dilemmaniana for Marrie* for Narrator, Cello, and Live Electronics (1972); *Zelomanniana* for Oboe and Piano (1974); 2 song cycles: *Liederen van Doofstommen* (Songs of Deaf-Mutes; 1974, 1976); *Harmonische reflecties* for Piano (1976; rev. 1984); *De boetseerder* for Soprano and Piano (1978).

Knape, Walter, German musicologist, conductor, and composer; b. Bernburg, Jan. 14, 1906. He studied at the Univ. of Leipzig, receiving his Ph.D. in 1934 with the diss. *Die Sinfonien von Karl Friedrich Abel*; then joined its faculty. From 1948 to 1957 he was conductor of the Leipzig Sing-Akademie and the Phil. Choir; he also taught at the Berlin Hochschule für Musik (1954–57), and subsequently at the Univs. of Hamburg, Hannover, and Cuxhaven. He devoted much time to the study of the life and works of Abel; ed. a complete edition of his works (16 vols., Cuxhaven, 1958–74) and a bibliographic-thematic catalog (Cuxhaven, 1971); also wrote *Karl Friedrich Abel: Leben und Werk eines frühklassischen Komponisten* (Bremen, 1973). He composed several symphonic and choral works, chamber music, and many piano pieces.

Knappertsbusch, Hans, eminent German conductor; b. Elberfeld, March 12, 1888; d. Munich, Oct. 25, 1965. He studied philosophy at the Univ. of Bonn before pursuing musical training with Steinbach and Lohse at the Cologne Cons. (1908–12). He was conductor in Mülheim and served as assistant conductor at the Bayreuth Festivals (1910–12), then conducted in Bochum (1912–13). He was director of opera in Elberfeld (1913–18); subsequently conducted opera in Leipzig (1918–19) and Dessau (1919–22). In 1922 he became Generalmusikdirektor of the Bavarian State Opera in Munich, a post he held with great distinction until resigning in the face of Nazi pressure in 1936; then conducted at the Vienna State Opera (1936–45); was also a conductor with the Vienna Phil. (1937–44). After World War II, he returned to Germany and made his home in Munich. He conducted at the Salzburg Festivals (1947–50; 1954–55); was a regular guest conductor with the Vienna Phil. (1947–64) and at the Bayreuth Festivals (from 1951). He was one of the great interpreters of the operas of Wagner and Richard Strauss. The authority and spontaneity he brought to such masterworks as *Götterdämmerung* and *Parsifal* were extraordinary.

BIBL.: R. Betz and W. Panofsky, *K.* (Ingolstadt, 1958).

Knipper, Lev (Konstantinovich), important Russian composer; b. Tiflis, Dec. 3, 1898; d. Moscow, July 30, 1974. He studied piano with Gnesina and composition with Glière and Zhilyaev at Moscow's Gnessin School; also took private lessons with Jarnach in Berlin and Julius Weissmann in Freiburg im Breisgau. Under the influence of western European trends, he wrote music in a fairly advanced style of composition, but soon abandoned these experiments and devoted himself to the study of folk music of different nationalities of the Soviet Union.

WORKS: DRAMATIC: OPERAS: *Severniy veter* (The North Wind; 1929–30; Moscow, March 30, 1930); *Marya* (1936–38); *Aktrisa* (The Actress; 1942); *Na Baykale* (On the Baikal Lake; 1946–48); *Korenzhizni* (The Source of Life; 1948–49); also ballets. **ORCH.:** 14 syms. (1929–54); orch. suites on ethnic motifs; overtures; 3 violin concertos (1944, 1965, 1967); 2 cello concertos (1962, 1972); Clarinet Concerto (1966); Oboe Concerto (1967); Bassoon Concerto (1969). **CHAMBER:** 3 string quartets; other chamber music; piano pieces. **VOCAL:** Songs.

Knorr, Ernst-Lothar von, German conductor and composer; b. Eitorf, near Cologne, Jan. 2, 1896; d. Heidelberg, Oct. 30, 1973. He studied at the Cologne Cons. with Bram Eldering (violin), Franz Bölsche (composition), and Fritz Steinbach (conducting). After graduation, he played violin in various provincial orchs. In 1925 he moved to Berlin and taught violin at the Hochschule für Musik. He served as director of the Hannover Hochschule für Musik (1952–61) and the Heidelberg Hochschule für Musik (1961–69). Most of his MSS perished in an air raid on Frankfurt am Main in 1944; his extant works include Concerto for 2 Orchs.; Chamber Concerto for Piano, Saxophone, Chorus, and Small Orch.; cantatas; choral works; chamber music.

BIBL.: O. Riemer, ed., *E.-L. v.K. zum 75. Geburtstag* (Cologne, 1971).

Knote, Heinrich, distinguished German tenor; b. Munich, Nov. 26, 1870; d. Garmisch, Jan. 12, 1953. He studied with Kirschner in Munich. On May 7, 1892, he made his operatic debut as Georg in Lortzing's *Der Waggenschmied* at the Munich Court Opera, where he soon became a principal singer, continuing on its roster when it became the Bavarian State Opera (1918); also sang at London's Covent Garden (1901; 1903; 1907–08; 1913). He made his Metropolitan Opera debut in N.Y. as Walther von Stolzing (Dec. 3, 1904), singing there until 1906 and again in 1907–08; later toured the U.S. with the German Opera Co. (1923–24). His remarkable Munich career spanned almost half a century; made his farewell appearance there as Siegfried (Dec. 15, 1931); subsequently taught voice. He was a greatly esteemed Heldentenor, excelling in such roles as Tannhäuser, Lohengrin, Tristan, and Siegfried.

BIBL.: J. Wagenmann, *Der sechzigjährige deutsche Meistersinger H. K. in seiner stimmbildnerischen Bedeutung und im Vergleich mit anderen Sängern* (Munich, 1930).

Knüpfer, Paul, German bass; b. Halle, June 21, 1865; d. Berlin, Nov. 4, 1920. After attending the Sondershausen Cons., he received vocal lessons from Bernhard Gunzburger. In 1885 he made his operatic debut in Sondershausen, and then was a member of the Leipzig Opera (1887–98) and the Berlin Royal (later State) Opera (1898–1920). Following additional vocal studies with J. Kniese in Bayreuth (1900), he appeared at the Festivals there until 1912. He also sang at London's Covent Garden (1904; 1907–14). Among his finest portrayals were Osmin, Daland, Pogner, Gurnemanz, King Marke, and Baron Ochs.

Knushevitsky, Sviatoslav (Nikolaievich), Russian cellist and teacher; b. Petrovsk, Jan. 6, 1908; d. Moscow, Feb. 19, 1963. He was a pupil at the Moscow Cons. of Kozolupov. From 1929 to 1943 he was first cellist in the orch. of the Bolshoi Theater in Moscow. After taking 1st prize in the All-Union competition in Moscow in 1933, he also pursued a solo career. From 1942 to 1963 he taught at the Moscow Cons., where he was head of the cello and double bass dept. (1954–59). Glière, Miaskovsky, and A. Khachaturian wrote concertos for him.

Knussen, (Stuart) Oliver, English composer and conductor; b. Glasgow, June 12, 1952. Remarkably precocious, he began playing piano as a small boy and showed unusual diligence also in his composition studies, mostly with John Lambert (1963–69) while attending the Central Tutorial School for Young Musicians (1964–67). On April 7, 1968, he made musical headlines when, at the age of 15, he conducted the London Sym. Orch. in the premiere performance of his own 1st Sym., written in an eclectic, but astoundingly effective, modern style. He was awarded fellowships for advanced study with Schuller at the Berkshire Music Center in Tanglewood (1970–73). From 1977 to 1982 he taught composition at the Royal College of Music in London. He served as an artistic director of the Aldeburgh Festivals (from 1983) and as coordinator of contemporary music activities at Tanglewood (1986–93). He served as composer-in-residence of the Philharmonia Orch. in London from 1984. With Steuart Bedford, he served as co-artistic director of the Aldeburgh Festival from 1989. In 1994 he was made a Commander of the Order of the British Empire. In his mature works, Knussen has revealed a penchant for experimentation with various styles and for revising scores without surcease, resulting in compositions of great refinement and lucidity.

WORKS: OPERAS: *Where the Wild Things Are* (1979–80; Bussels, Nov. 28, 1980; rev. 1980–83; London, Jan. 9, 1984); *Higglety Pigglety Pop!* (1983–85; Glyndebourne, Aug. 5, 1985). **ORCH.:** 3 syms.: No. 1 (1966–67; London, April 7, 1968), No. 2 for Soprano and Small Orch. (Windsor, Oct. 3, 1970; rev. 1970–71; Tanglewood, Aug. 18, 1971), and No. 3 (1973–79; London, Sept. 6, 1979); *Concerto for Orchestra* (1968–69; London, Feb. 1, 1970; rev. 1974); *Choral* for Wind Orch. (1970–72; Boston, Nov. 8, 1973); *Music for a Puppet Court* for 2 Chamber Orchs., after John Lloyd (1972, 1983; London, Aug. 23, 1983); *Coursing* for Chamber Orch. (1979); *The Wild Rumpus* from the opera *Where the Wild Things Are* (1983; London, July 21, 1987); *Fanfares for Tanglewood* for Brass and Percussion (Tanglewood, Aug. 2, 1986); *Flourish with Fireworks*, overture (1988). **CHAMBER:** *Processionals* for Wind Quintet and String Quartet (1968, 1978; Bristol, Dec. 15, 1978); *Masks* for Flute (1969); *3 Little Fantasies* for Wind Quintet (1970; rev. version, Kingston-upon-Thames, June 1, 1983); *Turba* for Double Bass (1971); *Ophelia Dances, Book I*, for Flute, English Horn, Clarinet, Horn, Piano, Celesta, Violin, Viola, and Cello (N.Y., May 9, 1975); *Triptych: I, Autumnal*, for Violin and Piano (1976–77; London, July 10, 1980), *II, Sonya's Lullaby*, for Piano (1977–78; Amsterdam, Jan. 6, 1979), and *III, Cantata*, for Oboe and String Trio (1977; Athens, Sept. 17, 1979); Piano Variations (1989); *Secret Song* for Violin (1990); *Songs Without Voices* for 8 Instruments (N.Y., April 26, 1992). **VOCAL:** *Hums and Songs of Winnie-the-Pooh* for High Soprano, Flute, English Horn, Clarinet or Contrabass Clarinet, Percussion, and Cello (1970, 1983; Aldeburgh, June 14, 1983); *Rosary Songs* for Soprano, Clarinet, Viola, and Piano (London, Aug. 21, 1972); *Océan de terre* for Soprano, Flute or Alto Flute, Clarinet or Bass Clarinet, Percussion, Piano or Celesta, Violin, Cello, and Double Bass (1972–73; rev. version, London, July 29, 1976); *Trumpets* for Soprano and 3 Clarinets (London, Feb. 27, 1975); *Frammenti da "Chiara"* for 2 Women's Choruses (1975, 1986; London, June 23, 1986); *Songs and a Sea Interlude* for Soprano and Orch. from the opera *Where the Wild Things Are* (1979–81; BBC, Feb. 14, 1981); *4 Late Poems and an Epigram of Rainer Maria Rilke* for Soprano (1988); *Whitman Settings* for Soprano and Orch. or Piano (1991–92).

Kobayashi, Ken-Ichiro, Japanese conductor; b. Iwaki, April 13, 1940. He studied composition with Mareo Ishiketa and piano with Atsuko Ohhori, then took courses in composition and conducting at the Tokyo Univ. of Fine Arts and Music, where his principal mentors were Akeo Watanabe and Kazuo Yamada. In 1970 he became assistant conductor of the Tokyo Sym. Orch. After winning the Budapest conducting competition (1974), he appeared widely in Europe as well as in his homeland, and was a conductor with the Amsterdam Phil. (from 1976). He was chief conductor of the Kyoto Sym. Orch. (from 1985), and principal conductor of the Hungarian State Orch. in Budapest (from 1987).

Koch, Caspar (Petrus), German-American organist, pedagogue, and composer; b. Karnap, Nov. 25, 1872; d. Pittsburgh, April 3, 1970. He was taken to the U.S. by his parents (1881); graduated from St. Francis College in Joliet, Ill., and later took courses with Heinrich Reimann and Franz Kullak in Berlin and at the Regensburg Kirchenmusikschule. He was Pittsburgh city organist (1904–54) and also organist at the Holy Trinity Catholic Church there; taught at the Carnegie Inst. of Technology (1914–41). He wrote the valuable *Book of Scales for the Organ* (1918) and the *Organ Student's Gradus ad Parnassum* (1945); also composed organ music.

Koch, (Sigurd Christian) Erland von, Swedish composer, son of **(Richert) Sigurd (Valdemar) von Koch**; b. Stockholm, April 26, 1910. He studied music with his father, then at the Stockholm Cons. (1931–35); went to Germany, where he studied composition with Paul Höffer and conducting with Clemens Krauss and Gmeindl (1936–38); also had piano lessons with Arrau. He subsequently taught at Wohlfart's Music School in Stockholm (1939–53); also was a sound technician with the Swedish Radio (1943–45); in 1953, joined the faculty of the Stockholm Musikhögskolan, becoming a prof. in 1968. In 1957 he became a member of the Royal Swedish Academy of Music in Stockholm. In some of his later works, he endeavored to create a curious amalgam of folk motifs with 12-tone rows ("12-tone and folk-tone").

WORKS: DRAMATIC: CHILDREN'S OPERA: *Pelle svanslös* (Tailless Peter; 1948; Göteborg, Jan. 7, 1949; rev. 1966). **BALLETS:** *Askungen* (Cinderella; 1942; also an orch. suite); *Samson and Delila* (1963; orch. suite, 1964; rev. 1972). Also incidental music for the radio play *Bjälbojarlen*, after Strindberg (Swedish Radio, Jan. 25, 1968). **ORCH.:** *Little Suite* for Chamber or String Orch. (1933); 3 piano concertos: No. 1 (1936), No. 2 (1962), and No. 3 for Wind Orch. (1970; for Full Orch., 1972); 2 violin concertos (1937; 1979–80); 6 syms.: No. 1 (1938), No. 2, *Sinfonia Dalecarlia* (1944), No. 3 (1948), No. 4, *Sinfonia seria* (1952–53; rev. 1962), No. 5, *Lapponia* (1976–77; Stockholm, Oct. 30, 1977), and No. 6, *Salvare la terra* (1991–92); *Nordic Capriccio* (1943); *Rural Suite* for Strings (1945); Viola Concerto (1945; rev. 1966); *Sinfonietta* (1949); *Triptychon* for Violin and Orch. (1949); *Arkipelag* (1950); *Musica intima* for Strings (1950; rev. 1965); Cello Concerto (1951); *Musica malinconica* for Strings (1952); *Concert Music* (1955); Concerto for Small Orch. (1955); the Oxberg trilogy: *Oxberg Variations* (1956), *Lapland Metamorphoses* (1957), and *Dance-Rhapsody* (1957); Concerto for Saxophone and Strings (1958); *Concerto lirico* for Strings (1959; rev. of 4th String Quartet); *Concerto piccolo* for Soprano and Alto Saxophones and Strings (1962); *Fantasia concertante* for Violin and Orch. (1964); the Impulsi trilogy: *Impulsi* (1964), *Echi* (1965), and *Ritmi* (1966); *Arioso e Furioso* for Strings (1967); *Polska svedese* (1968); *Musica concertante* for 8 Winds, Strings, and Percussion (1969); Double Concerto for Flute, Clarinet, and Strings (1971); *A Swede in New York* (1973); Concerto for Oboe and Strings (1978); Tuba Concerto (1978); *4 Symphonic Myths* (Stockholm, Oct. 9, 1982); Guitar Concerto (Göteborg, Feb. 3, 1983); *Svenska danser 1–6* (1982–83); *Trombonia* for Trombone and Strings (1983); *Romanza* for Violin and Orch. (1984); *Serenade* for Double Bass and Strings (1985); *Midvinterblot-Sommarsolstånd*, 2 Nordic frescoes (1986–87); *Presto* for Violin and Strings (1990); *Whirl Dance* (1991); *Dalarondo* (1993). **CHAMBER:** 6 string quartets: No. 1 (1934), No. 2 (1944), No. 3, *Musica intima* (1950), No. 4 (1956; rev. 1959), No. 5 (1961), and No. 6, *Serenata espressiva* (1963); *Larghetto* for Cello or Viola and Piano (1937; rev. 1965); *Berceuse* for Violin and Piano (1953); *Sonatina semplice* for Violin and Piano (1960); *Varianti virtuosi II* for Violin and Piano (1968); *Quattro tempi* for Wind Quintet (1968); *Miniatures* for Saxophone Quartet (1970); *Canto e danza* for Flute and Guitar (1975); *Karaktarer* for Violin and Piano (1980: *Auda* for Brass Quintet (1981); *Polysaxo* for Saxophone Ensemble (1981); *Tubania* for Tuba and Piano (1983); Alto Saxophone Sonata (1985); *Fantasia melodica* for Guitar and Wind Quintet (1986–89); *Capricietto* for Flute and Piano (1992); *Suonata per tre* for Piano Trio (1993); piano pieces; organ music. **VOCAL:** *Midsommardalen* for Baritone, Chorus, and Orch. (1960–61); *Sängarkvall* for Baritone, Men's Chorus, and Wind Orch. (1972); *Te Deum* for Chorus and Orch. or Organ (1994–95); songs.

BIBL.: B. Huldt, "A Portrait of E. v.K.," *Nordic Sounds* (Dec. 1988).

Koch, Helmut, German conductor; b. Wuppertal-Barmen, April 5, 1908; d. Berlin, Jan. 26, 1975. He studied conducting with Fiedler, Lehmann, and Scherchen. He led workers' choruses for many years; after World War II, was active in East Germany; was founder-conductor of the Berlin Chamber Orch. (1945), conductor of the Berlin Radio Choir (from 1948), and director of the Berlin Singakademie (from 1963); was also a guest conductor at the Berlin State Opera (from 1960). He was widely known in East Germany for his performances of the music of Handel. He made numerous arrangements of German folk songs.

Koch, Karl, Austrian organist, choral conductor, and composer; b. Biberwier, Tyrol, Jan. 29, 1887; d. Innsbruck, Sept. 20, 1971. He studied religion and music at a Brixen seminary (1905–09); took courses in conducting with Max Springer and composition with Joseph Marx at the Vienna Academy of Music (1920–21). In 1924 he settled in Innsbruck as a choral conductor, retiring in 1967. He publ. *Harmonielehre* (Vienna, 1948) and *Erganzungsbuch zur Harmonielehre* (Vienna, 1957).

WORKS: *Jubilate Deo* for Chorus and Orch. (1916); *Festmesse zu Ehren der Geburt unseres Herren Jesu Christi* for Soloists, Chorus, and Orch. (1916; Bozen, Jan. 6, 1917); *Requiem* for Chorus and Organ (1916); *Missa "In medio vitae"* for Soloists, Chorus, and Orch. (1925); *Missa "Super flumina Babylonis"* for Soloists, Chorus, and Orch. (Innsbruck, Nov. 20, 1932); *Sinfonie "Aus den Bergen"* (1942; Innsbruck, Feb. 17, 1947); *Missa in honorem Papae Pii X* (2 versions, 1953); *Requiem* for Soloists, Chorus, and Orch. (1955–58; Innsbruck, Feb. 20, 1960); *Psalm-kantate*, vocal sym. for Solo, Vocal Quartet, Women's Chorus, Mixed Chorus, and Orch. (Wattens, Austria, Oct. 26, 1958); *Brixner Dom Messe* for Soloists, Boys' Chorus, Mixed Chorus, Organ, and Orch. (Brixen, Sept. 10, 1958); *Hubertus-Messe* for Unison Chorus and Wind Septet or Organ (1967); also String Quartet (1948); 2 piano sonatas; sacred choruses; much organ music.

BIBL.: W. Isser, *K. K.: Das Bild eines zeitgenössischen Komponisten* (Innsbruck, 1969).

Kochan, Günter, German composer and teacher; b. Luckau, Oct. 2, 1930. He studied composition with Blacher, Noetel, and Wunsch at the (West) Berlin Hochschule für Musik (1946–50); then attended Eisler's master classes at the (East) Berlin Akademie der Künste of the German Democratic Republic (1950–53). From 1950 to 1991 he taught at the (East) Berlin Hochschule für Musik. In 1965 he was elected to the Akademie der Künste. His music is eminently functional, and in it the formal design is paramount; main subjects are stated repeatedly with utmost clarity; the rhythmic formulas are explicit; there is a distinct affinity with the symphonic processes used by Eisler; polymodal themes abound within starkly dissonant harmonies.

WORKS: DRAMATIC: *Karin Lenz*, opera (1968–70); *Luther*, melodrama (1981). **ORCH.:** 2 violin concertos (1951–52; 1980); *Kleine Suite* (1956); Piano Concerto (1958); *Sinfonietta* (1960); *Fröhliche Ouvertüre* for Chamber Orch. (1960); 2 concertos for orchestra (1961–62; 1988–90); 5 syms.: No. 1 for Chorus and Orch. (1963–64), No. 2 (1968), No. 3 for Soprano and Orch. (1972), No. 4 (1983–84), and No. 5 (1985–87); *Divertimento*, variations on a theme of C.M. von Weber (1964); *Variationen über eine venezianische Canzonetta* for Piano and Chamber Orch. (1966); *4 Movements* for Strings (1966); 2 cello concertos (1967, 1976); *Mendelssohn-Variationen* for Piano and Orch. (1972); Viola Concerto (1974); Concerto for Wind Quintet and 2 String Groups (1975–77); *7 Orchesterstücke* (1976–77); *Passacaglia und Hymne* (1979); *Und ich lächle im Dunkeln dem Leben* (1987); *Herbstbilder*, metamorphosen for 28 Strings (1990–91); *In Memoriam* (1982); *Praludium* (1985). **CHAMBER:** Piano Trio (1953–54); *Divertimento* for Flute, Clarinet, and Bassoon (1956); Cello Sonata (1960); *5 Movements* for String Quartet (1961); *Short String Quartet* (1965); String Quartet (1973–74); *7 Miniaturen* for 4 Tubas (1977); String Trio (1979–80); Violin Sonata (1984–85); *5 Bagatelles* for 4 Trombones (1987); Piano Quintet (1992–93); *7 Szenen* for Flute, Viola, and Guitar (1993); *7 Deutsche Volkslieder* for 4 Trombones and Tuba (1993); Duo for Clarinet and Piano (1994–95). **PIANO:** *Suite* (1952); *Praludien, Intermezzi und Fugen* (1954); *11 Short Pieces* for Piano, 4-hands (1958); *5 Piano Pieces* (1971); *7 Short Piano Pieces* (1971); Sonata (1981). **VOCAL:** *Die Welt ist jung*, cantata (1952); *Ernst Thälmann*, cantata in memory of the leader of the German Communist party who died in a concentration camp (1959); *3 Shakespeare-Lieder* for Alto, Flute, and Strings (1964); *Asche von Birkenau*, cantata for Alto and Orch. (1965); *Aurora* for Women's Voices, Chorus, and Orch. (1966; a tribute to the sailors of the Russian ship *Aurora*, which bombarded the Winter Palace in Petrograd on the day of the Soviet Revolution in 1917); *Wir, unaufhaltsam*, "symphonic demonstration" for Baritone, Speaker, Chorus, and Orch. (1970); *Das Testament von Ho Chi-Minh* for Speaker, Chamber Orch., and 9 Solo Instruments (1971); *Die Hände der Genössen*, cantata for Baritone and Orch. (1974); *3 Epitaphe* for Baritone and Instruments (1975); *Das Friedensfest oder Die Teilhabe*, oratorio (1978); *Tryptichon* for Mezzo-soprano, Alto Flute, Bass Clarinet, Viola, and Cello (1991); choruses; songs.

Kochánski, Paul (actually, **Pawel**), noted Polish violinist; b. Orel, Sept. 14, 1887; d. N.Y., Jan. 12, 1934. He studied with Mlynarski in Warsaw. At 14, he joined the Warsaw Phil., becoming its concertmaster in 1901; in 1903, went to Brussels to study with César Thomson at the Cons., where he took the premier prix that same year. In 1907 he was appointed prof. at the Warsaw Cons., and in 1913 at the St. Petersburg Cons. From 1917 to 1919 he taught at the Kiev Cons., then went to the U.S., making his debut with the N.Y. Sym. Orch. on Feb. 14, 1921. From 1924 he taught at the Juilliard School of Music in N.Y. He excelled in the performance of modern works; did a great service in promoting the violin music of Szymanowski, inspiring him to write his *Mity* (Myths; 1915) and 1st Violin Concerto (1916) for him. He made many transcriptions for violin and piano.

BIBL.: H. Roth, "Refined Colourist," *Strad* (Sept. 1987).

Kocián, Jaroslav, noted Czech violinist and pedagogue; b. Ústí nad Orlicí, Feb. 22, 1883; d. Prague, March 9, 1950. He studied violin with Sevcik at the Prague Cons. (1896–1901), and also took lessons in composition with Dvořák. After his graduation, he traveled widely as a concert violinist, almost rivaling the success of his famous compatriot Jan Kubelik. He made 4 American tours; also appeared in Asia and Africa. He also served as a prof. at the Odessa Cons. (1907–09). In 1928 he abandoned his concert career. He was a prof. at the Master School of the Prague Cons. (1924–43), and also its rector (1939–40). He composed several effective violin pieces, as well as choruses and songs.

BIBL.: B. Urban, *Mistr J. K.* (Kolín, 1926); V. Polívka, *S K.em kolem světa* (With K. Round the World; Prague, 1945); C. Sychra, ed., *J. K.: Sborník statí a vzpomínek* (J. K.: Collections of Articles and Recollections; Prague, 1953); A. Šlajs, *J. K.* (Pardubice, 1958).

Kocsár, Miklós, Hungarian composer; b. Debrecen, Dec. 21, 1933. He studied with Farkas at the Budapest Academy of Music (1954–59). He taught at the Béla Bartók Cons. in Budapest (from 1972); was also on the staff of the music dept. of the Hungarian Radio (from 1974), serving as its deputy head (from 1983). He won the Erkel Prize in 1973 and again in 1980. In 1987 he was made a Merited Artist by the Hungarian government.

WORKS: ORCH.: Horn Concerto (1957); *Serenata per archi* (1959; rev. 1971); *Capriccio* (1961); *5 Movements* for Clarinet, Strings, and Harpsichord (1976); *Variations* (1977); *Capricorn Concerto* for Flute and Chamber Ensemble (1978); *Metamorphoses* (1979); *Sequenze per archi* (1980); *Dances from Pozsony* for Youth String Orch. (1980); *Episodi* for Oboe and Strings (1982); *Concerto—In Memoriam ZH* for Horn and Chamber Orch. (1983); *Elégia* for Bassoon and Chamber Orch. (1985); *Formazioni* (1986); Suite for Youth String Orch. (1986). **CHAMBER:** *Duo Serenade* for Violin and Viola (1955); *Divertimento* for Oboe, Clarinet, and Bassoon (1956); 3 wind quintets (1956, rev. 1959; 1968; 1984); *3 Duos* for Oboe and Clarinet (1956);

Violin Sonata (1957); Trio for 2 Trombones and Trumpet (1958); *Dialoghi* for Bassoon and Piano (1964–65); *Ungaresca* for Oboe and Clarinet, or 2 Clarinets, or Flute and Clarinet (1968); *Saltus hungaricus* for Flute or Oboe or Violin and Piano (1970); *Repliche I* for Flute and Cimbalom or Harpsichord (1971), *II* for Horn and Cimbalom (1976), and *III* for Cimbalom (1983); *7 Variations* for Viola (1983); *Echos* for Horn (1984); *Quintetto d'ottoni* (1986). **VOCAL:** *Hegyi legények* (Mountain Lads), cantata for Men's Chorus, Brass, and Percussion (1957); *Magyanos enek* (Solitary Song) for Soprano and Chamber Ensemble (1969); *Az éjszaka képei* (Pictures of the Night), oratorio for Mezzo-soprano, Baritone, Chorus, and Orch. (1987); many choral pieces; songs.

Kocsis, Zoltan (György), brilliant Hungarian pianist; b. Budapest, May 30, 1952. He began his studies at the Béla Bartók Cons. (1963–68), then trained with Pál Kadosa, Ferenc Rados, and György Kurtág at the Franz Liszt Academy of Music (graduated, 1973) in Budapest. In 1970 he won the Hungarian Radio Beethoven competition; after appearing as soloist with the Dresden Phil. in 1971, he made his first tour of the U.S. as soloist with the Hungarian Radio and Television Sym. Orch. In 1973 he won the Liszt Prize and soon launched an acclaimed international career. With the conductor Ivan Fischer, he founded in 1983 the Budapest Festival Orch., with which he frequently appeared as a soloist and for which he served as artistic director. A performer of extraordinary versatility, he includes in his repertoire works ranging from Bach to the avant-garde. He has made numerous transcriptions for piano; has also composed orch. music, including the topical *Memento (Chernobyl '86)*. In 1978 he was awarded the Kossuth Prize, and in 1984 he was named a Merited Artist by the Hungarian government.

Koczalski, Raoul (actually, **Raul Armand Georg**), Polish pianist and composer; b. Warsaw, Jan. 3, 1884; d. Poznań, Nov. 24, 1948. He was trained by his parents; at the age of 4, he played at a charity concert in Warsaw and was at once proclaimed an "infant phenomenon." He studied with Mikuli in Lemberg, and then with Anton Rubinstein. He performed in Vienna (1892), Russia, Paris, and London (1893); made nearly 1,000 public appearances before he was 12. His sensational success diminished to some extent as he grew out of the prodigy age, but he was appreciated as a mature pianist, and particularly for his sensitive playing of Chopin. He lived mostly in France, Germany, and Sweden; after World War II, he returned to Poland and taught in Poznań and Warsaw. He publ. *Frédéric Chopin: Betrachtungen, Skizzen, Analysen* (Cologne, 1936). His precocity extended to composition as well; he wrote some 50 works before he was 10; he later wrote the operas *Rymond* (Elberfeld, Oct. 14, 1902) and *Die Suhne* (Muhlhausen, 1909), as well as many piano pieces.

BIBL.: B. Vogel, *R. K.* (Leipzig and Warsaw, 1896); M. Paruszewska, *Biographical Sketch and the Artistic Career of R. K.* (Poznań, 1936).

Koczirz, Adolf, Austrian musicologist; b. Wierowan, Moravia, April 2, 1870; d. Vienna, Feb. 22, 1941. He studied law, and also musicology with Adler, at the Univ. of Vienna (Ph.D., 1903, with the diss. *Der Lautenist Hans Judenkünig*). He was employed in the Ministry of Finance (1891–1935). He distinguished himself as an authority on the lute and guitar; ed. 2 vols. of 16th- and 17th-century lute music in Denkmaler der Tonkunst in Österreich, XXXVII, Jg. XVIII/2 (1911) and I, Jg. XXV/2 (1918).

BIBL.: R. Haas and J. Zuth, eds., *Festschrift A. K. zum 60. Geburtstag* (Vienna, 1930).

Kodalli, Nevit, Turkish conductor and composer; b. Mersin, Jan. 12, 1924. He studied with Necil Kazim Akses at the Ankara Cons., graduating in 1947; then went to Paris, where he took lessons with Honegger and Boulanger (1948–53). After teaching at the Ankara Cons. (1953–55), he conducted at the Ankara Opera (from 1955). He was a composer at the Ankara State Theater (from 1962). His music preserves the traits of Turkish folk melos, but the harmonic and contrapuntal treatment is in the manner of the French modern school. Among his works are 2 operas (1955, 1963), a Sym. (Ankara, May 20, 1950), an oratorio, *Ataturk* (Ankara, Nov. 9, 1953), and 2 string quartets (1947, 1966).

Kodály, Zoltán, renowned Hungarian composer, ethnomusicologist, and music educator; b. Kecskemét, Dec. 16, 1882; d. Budapest, March 6, 1967. He was brought up in a musical family; received his general education at the Archiepiscopal Grammar School in Nagyszombat; at the same time, he took lessons in piano, violin, viola, and cello. He soon began to compose, producing an overture when he was 15; it was performed in Nagyszombat in 1898. He then went to Budapest (1900), where he entered the Univ. as a student of Hungarian and German; also studied composition with Koessler at the Royal Academy of Music (diplomas in composition, 1904, and teaching, 1905; Ph.D., 1906, with a diss. on the stanzaic structure of Hungarian folk song). He became associated with Bartók, collecting, organizing, and editing the vast wealth of national folk songs; he made use of these melodies in his own compositions. In 1906 he went to Berlin, and in 1907 proceeded to Paris, where he took some lessons with Widor, but it was the music of Debussy which most profoundly influenced him in his subsequent development as a composer. He was appointed a prof. at the Royal Academy of Music in Budapest in 1907. In collaboration with Bartók, he prepared the detailed paper "Az uj egyetemes népdalgyüjtemény tervezete" (A Project for a New Universal Collection of Folk Songs) in 1913. They continued their collecting expeditions until World War I intervened. Kodály wrote music criticism in Budapest (1917–19). In 1919 he was appointed deputy director of the Budapest Academy of Music, but lost his position that same year for political reasons; however, he resumed his teaching there in 1922. In 1923 he was commissioned to write a commemorative work in celebration of the half-century anniversary of the union of Buda, Pest, and Obuda into Budapest. The resulting work, the oratorio *Psalmus hungaricus* (1923), brought him wide recognition. The initial performance in Budapest was followed by numerous productions all over Europe, and also in America. Another major success was his opera *Háry János* (1926); an orch. suite from this work became highly popular in Hungary and throughout the world. His orch. works *Marosszéki táncok* (Dances of Marosszék; 1930; based on a piano work) and *Galántai táncok* (Dances of Galanta; for the 80th anniversary of the Budapest Phil. Soc., 1933) were also very successful. His reputation as one of the most significant national composers was firmly established with the repeated performances of these works. Among his most important subsequent works were the orch. pieces *Variations on a Hungarian Folk Song* "Felszállott a páva," the *Peacock Variations* (for the 50th anniversary of the Amsterdam Concertgebouw Orch., 1939), and the *Concerto for Orchestra* (for the 50th anniversary of the Chicago Sym. Orch., 1941). His great interest in music education is reflected in his numerous choral works, which he wrote for both adults and children during the last 30 years of his life. He also pursued his ethnomusicological studies; from 1940 he was associated with the Hungarian Academy of Sciences, serving as its president (1946–49). He continued to teach at the Academy of Music until 1940, and then gave instruction in Hungarian folk music until 1942; even after his retirement, he taught the latter course there. He toured as a conductor of his own music in England, the U.S., and the Soviet Union (1946–47); then throughout Western Europe. In succeeding years, he held a foremost place in the musical life of his country, receiving many honors; was awarded 3 Kossuth Prizes (1948, 1952, 1957). He also received foreign honors, being made an honorary member of the Moscow Cons. (1963) and the American Academy of Arts and Sciences (1963); was also awarded the Gold Medal of the Royal Phil. Soc. of London (1967). An International Kodály Soc. was organized in Budapest in 1975.

As a composer, Kodály's musical style was not as radical as that of Bartók; he never departed from basic tonality, nor did his experiments in rhythm reach the primitivistic power of Bartók's percussive idiom. He preferred a Romantic treatment of his melodic and harmonic materials, with an infusion of Impressionistic elements. All the same, he succeeded in producing a substantial body of music of notable distinction. He was married twice; his first wife, Emma, whom he married in 1910, died in 1958; on Dec. 18, 1959, he married Sarolta Péczely, a student (b. 1940).

WRITINGS: With B. Bartók, *Erdelyi magyarsag: Nepdalok* (The Hungarians of Transylvania: Folk Songs; Budapest, 1923); *A magyar népzene* (Hungarian Folk Music; Budapest, 1937; 2nd ed., aug., 1943; 3rd ed., aug., 1952 by L. Vargyas; Eng. tr., 1960); with A. Gyulai, *Arany János népdalgyüjteménye* (The Folk Song Collection of János Arany; Budapest, 1953); A. Szöllöy, ed., *A zene mindenkie* (Budapest, 1954; 2nd ed., 1975); F. Bónis, ed., *Visszatekintés* (In Retrospect: Budapest, 1964; 2nd ed., aug., 1974); *The Selected Writings of Zoltán Kodály* (Budapest, 1974).

WORKS: DRAMATIC: *Notre Dame de Paris*, incidental music for a parody (Budapest, Feb. 1902); *Le Cid*, incidental music for a parody (Budapest, Feb. 1903); *A nagybácsi* (The Uncle), incidental music (Budapest, Feb. 1904); *Pacsirtaszó* (Lark Song), incidental music for Voice and Small Orch. (Budapest, Sept. 14, 1917); *Háry János*, Singspiel (Budapest, Oct. 16, 1926); *Székely fonó* (The Transylvanian Spinning Room), lyrical play (1924–32; Budapest, April 24, 1932); *Czinka Panna*, Singspiel (1946–48; Budapest, March 15, 1948).

ORCH.: Overture in D minor (1897; Nagyszombat, Feb. 1898); *Nyári este* (Summer Evening; Budapest, Oct. 22, 1906; rev. 1929–30; N.Y., April 3, 1930); *Régi magyar katonadalok* (Old Hungarian Soldiers' Songs; 1917; Vienna, Jan. 12, 1918; also arranged for Cello and Piano as *Magyar Rondo*); *Ballet Music* (1925; Budapest, Oct. 16, 1926; originally for *Háry János*); *Háry János Suite* (version for Brass Band, not by Kodály, Barcelona, March 24, 1927; version for Orch., N.Y., Dec. 15, 1927); *Szinházi nyitány* (Theater Overture; 1927; Budapest, Jan. 10, 1928; originally for *Háry János*); *Marosszéki táncok* (Dances of Marosszék; Dresden, Nov. 28, 1930; based on a piano work; also arranged as a ballet); *Galántai táncok* (Dances of Galanta; Budapest, Oct. 23, 1933); Sym. in C major (1930s–1961; Lucerne, Aug. 16, 1961); *Variations on a Hungarian Folk Song* "Felszállott a páva," the *Peacock Variations* (Amsterdam, Nov. 23, 1939); *Concerto for Orchestra* (1939–40; Chicago, Feb. 6, 1941); *Honvéd Parad March* for Brass Band (1948; from *Háry János*); *Minuetto serio* (1948–53; aug. from *Czinka Panna*).

CHAMBER: *Romance lyrique* for Cello and Piano (1898); Trio in E-flat major for 2 Violins and Viola (1899); *Adagio* for Violin, Viola or Cello, and Piano (1905); 2 string quartets (1908–9; 1916–18); Cello Sonata (1909–10); *Duo* for Violin and Cello (1914); Sonata for Solo Cello (1915); *Capriccio* for Cello (1915); *Magyar Rondo* for Cello and Piano (1917); *Serenade* for 2 Violins and Viola (1919–20); Cello Sonatina (1921–22); *Hivogató tábortüzhöz* (Calling to Camp Fire) for Clarinet (1930); Exercise for Violin (1942); *Feigin* for Violin and Piano (1958; arrangement of *Kállai kettös*); Wind Quartet (c.1960). **PIANO:** *Valsette* (1907); *Méditation sur un motif de Claude Debussy* (1907); *Zongoramuzsika* (Piano Music; 9 pieces; 1909); 7 pieces (1910–18); *Ballet Music* (1925; arrangement of orch. work); *Marosszéki táncok* (Dances of Marosszék; 1927; also arranged for orch. and as a ballet); *Gyermektancok* (Children's Dances; 1945).

VOCAL: CHORUS AND ORCH.: *Offertorium (Assumpta est)* for Baritone, Chorus, and Orch. (1901); *Psalmus hungaricus* for Tenor, Chorus, Organ, Orch., and Children's Chorus ad libitum (Budapest, Nov. 19, 1923); *Budavári Te Deum* for 4 Soloists, Chorus, Organ, and Orch. (Budapest Cathedral, Sept. 12, 1936); *Missa brevis* for Chorus and Organ or 3 Sopranos, Alto, Tenor, Bass, Chorus, Orch., and Organ ad libitum (1942–44; Budapest, Feb. 11, 1945); *Vértanúk sírjánál* (At the Martyr's Grave) for Chorus and Orch. (1945); *Kállai kettös* (Kallo Double Dance) for Chorus and Small Orch. (1950; Budapest, April 4, 1951); *The Music Makers: An Ode* for Chorus and Orch., after A. O'Shaughnessy (1964). **CHORUS AND INSTRUMENT(S):** *Mass* for Chorus and Organ (c.1896; unfinished); *Ave Maria* for Chorus and Organ (c.1899); *5 Tantum ergo* for Children's Chorus and Organ (1928); *Pange lingua* for Chorus or Children's Chorus and Organ (1929); *Kantonadal* (Soldier's Song) for Men's Chorus, Trumpet, and Side Drum (1934); *Karácsonyi pásztortánc* (Shepherds' Christmas Dance) for Children's Chorus and Recorder (1935); *Ének Szent István királyhoz* (Hymn to St. Stephen) for Chorus and Organ (1938); *Vejnemöjnen muzsikál* (Vejnemöjnen Makes Music) for High Voices and Harp or Piano (1944); *A 114. genfi zsoltár* (Geneva Psalm CXIV) for Chorus and Organ (1952); *Intermezzo* for Chorus and Piano (1956; from *Háry János*); *Magyar mise* (Hungarian Mass) for Unison Chorus and Organ (1966); *Laudes organi* for Chorus and Organ (1966). Also many choral works for mixed voices a cappella, children's choruses, and songs.

OTHER: Organ music; numerous educational works; Bach arrangements.

BIBL.: B. Bartók, "K. Z.," *Nyugat*, XIV (1921); M.D. Calvocoressi, "Choral Music of K.," *Listener*, XV (1936); A. Molnár, *K. Z.* (Budapest, 1936); B. Szabolcsi and D. Bartha, eds., *Emlékkönyv K. Z. 70. születésnapjára* (Budapest, 1953); L. Eősze, *K. Z. élete és munkassaga* (Z. K.'s Life and Work; Budapest, 1956; Eng. tr., 1962); idem, *K. Z. élete képekben* (Z. K.'s Life in Pictures; Budapest, 1957; 2nd ed., 1958; Eng. tr., 1971); P. Young, *Z. K.: A Hungarian Musician* (London, 1964); H. Stevens, "The Choral Music of Z. K.," *Musical Quarterly* (April 1968); H. Szabó, *The K. Concept of Music Education* (London, 1969); E. Hegyi, *Solfege According to the K. Concept* (Kecskemet, 1975); L. Eősze, *K. Z. életének krónikája* (Z. K.: Chronicle of His Life; Budapest, 1977); J. Breuer, *K.-kalauz* (Budapest, 1982; Eng. tr., 1990, as *A Guide to K.*); E. Lendvai, *The Workshop of Bartók and K.* (Budapest, 1983); E. Szőnyi, *K. Z. nevelési eszméi* (Budapest, 1984); I. Kecskeméti, *K., the Composer: Brief Studies on the First Half of K.'s Oeuvre* (Kecskemét, 1986); G. Ránki, *Bartók and K. Revisited* (Budapest, 1987); B. Reuer, *Z. K.s Bühnenwerk "Háry János": Beiträge zu seinen volksmusikalischen und literarischen Quellen* (Munich, 1991).

Koechlin, Charles (Louis Eugène), noted French composer, pedagogue, and writer on music; b. Paris, Nov. 27, 1867; d. Le Canadel, Var, Dec. 31, 1950. He studied for a military career, but was compelled to change his plans when stricken with tuberculosis; while recuperating in Algeria, he took up serious music studies; then entered the Paris Cons. (1890), where he studied with Gédalge, Massenet, Tadou, and Fauré, graduating in 1897. He lived mostly in Paris, where he was active as a composer, teacher, and lecturer; with Ravel and Schmitt, he organized the Société Musicale Indépendante (1909) to advance the cause of contemporary music; with Satie, Roussel, Milhaud, and others, he was a member of the group Les Nouveaux Jeunes (1918–20), a precursor to Les Six. Although he composed prolifically in all genres, he became best known as a writer on music and as a lecturer. He made 3 lecture tours of the U.S. (1918, 1928, 1937). He became president of the Fédération Musicale Populaire (1937). His pro-Communist leanings caused him to promote music for the proletariat during the 1930s; he wrote a number of works "for the people" and also film scores. In spite of the fact that such works as his *Symphonie d'hymnes* (Prix Cressent, 1936) and Sym. No. 1 (Prix Halphan, 1937) won honors, his music made no real impact. Taking Fauré as his model, he strove to preserve the best elements in the French Classical tradition. A skillful craftsman, he produced works of clarity and taste, marked by advanced harmonic and polyphonic attributes.

WRITINGS: *Étude sur les notes de passage* (Paris, 1922); *Précis des règles du contrepoint* (Paris, 1926; Eng. tr., 1927); *Gabriel Fauré* (Paris, 1927; Eng. tr., 1946); *Claude Debussy* (Paris, 1927); *Traité de l'harmonie* (3 vols., Paris, 1927–30); *Étude sur* *le choral d'école* (Paris, 1929); *Théorie de la musique* (Paris, 1934); *Étude sur l'écriture de la fugue d'école* (Paris, 1934); *Pierre Maurice, musicien* (Geneva, 1938); *Les instruments à vent* (Paris, 1948); *Traité de l'orchestration* (4 vols., Paris, 1954–59).

WORKS (Koechlin orchestrated many of his works well after their original completion. Dates given are those of original, often unorchestrated, versions): **DRAMATIC: PASTORALE BIBLIQUE:** *Jacob chez Laban* for Soprano, Tenor, Chorus, and Orch. (1896–1908; Paris, May 19, 1925). **BALLETS:** *La Forêt païenne* (1911–16; Paris, June 17, 1925); *La Divine Vesprée* (1917); *L'Âme heureuse* (1945–47); *Voyages: Film danse* (1947). **ORCH.:** Sym. (1895–1900; unfinished); *L'Automne*, symphonic suite (1896–1906); *La Forêt*, symphonic poem in 2 parts: No. 1, *Le Jour* (1897–1904) and No. 2, *La Nuit* (1896–1907); 2 symphonic poems: *Soleil et danses dans la forêt* and *Vers la plage lointaine* (1898–1909); *En mer, la nuit*, symphonic poem, after Heine (1899–1904); *Nuit de walpurgis classique (Ronde nocturne)*, symphonic poem, after Verlaine (1901–07; rev. 1915–16); 2 symphonic poems: *(L'Été): Nuit de juin* and *Midi en août* (1908–11); *Suite légendaire (La Nuit féerique)* (1901–15); *Études antiques (Suite païenne; Poèmes antiques)*, symphonic suite (1908–14); *La Course de printemps*, symphonic poem, after Kipling (1908–25); 2 symphonic poems: *Le Printemps* and *L'Hiver* (1908–16); *Ballade* for Piano and Orch. (1911–15); 2 syms: No. 1 (1911–16; arranged from the String Quartet No. 2) and No. 2 (1943–44; arranged from several other works); *Rapsodie sur des chansons françaises* (1911–16); *The Bride of a God*, symphonic poem (1929; in collaboration with C. Urner); Symphonic Fugue (1932); *Choral fugué* (1933); *Choral fugué du style modal* for Organ and Orch. (1933); *Sur les flots lointaines*, symphonic poem (1933); *Hymne à la jeunesse*, after Gide (1934); *Symphonie d'hymnes* (1936; arranged from several other works); *La Méditation de Purun Bhagat*, symphonic poem, after Kipling (1936); *La Cité nouvelle, rêve d'avenir*, symphonic poem, after Wells (1938); *Le Buisson ardent*, symphonic poem, after Rolland (1938); *La Loi de la jungle*, symphonic poem, after Kipling (1939); *Les Bandar-log*, symphonic poem, after Kipling (1939); *Le Docteur Fabricius*, symphonic poem, after C. Dollfus (1941–44); *Offrande musical sur le nom de BACH* (1942); *Silhouettes de comédie* for Bassoon and Orch. (1942–43); *Partita* for Chamber Orch. (1945); *Introduction et 4 interludes de style atonal-sériel* (1947). **CHAMBER:** Viola Sonata (1902–15); Piano Quintet (1908; 1911; 1917–21); 3 string quartets (1911–13; 1911–16; 1917–21); Flute Sonata (1911–13); *Suite en quatuor* for Flute, Violin, Viola, and Piano (1911–15); Oboe Sonata (1911–16); Violin Sonata (1915–16); Cello Sonata (1917); Bassoon Sonata (1918–19; also for Horn and Piano); Sonata for 2 Flutes (1918–20); 2 clarinet sonatas (1923, 1923); Trio for Strings or Woodwinds (1924); *Quintet Primavera* for Flute, Harp, Violin, Viola, and Cello (1936); Wind Septet (1937); Trio for Oboe, Clarinet, and Bassoon (1945); Quintet for Flute, Harp, Violin, Viola, and Cello (1949); also many works for piano, including *Paysages et marines* (12 pieces; 1915–16), *Les Heures persanes* (16 pieces; 1916–19), and *L'Ancienne Maison de campagne* (12 pieces; 1932–33). **OTHER:** Choral works, music for band, film scores, organ music, and songs.

BIBL.: R. Orledge, "C. K. and the Early Sound Film 1933–38," *Proceedings of the Royal Musical Association*, XCVIII (1971–72); idem, *A Study of the Composer C. K. (1867–1950)* (diss., Univ. of Cambridge, 1973); J. Woodward, *The Theoretical Writings of C. K.* (diss., Univ. of Rochester, 1974); H. Sauget, ed., *Oeuvres de C. K.* (Paris, 1975; a catalog); E. Kirk, *The Chamber Music of C. K.* (diss., Catholic Univ. of America, Washington, D.C., 1977); R. Orledge, "Satie, K. and the Ballet 'Uspud'," *Music & Letters* (Jan. 1987); idem, *C. K. (1867–1950): His Life and Works* (Vol. I, N.Y., 1989).

Koellreutter, Hans Joachim, German conductor, composer, and teacher; b. Freiburg im Breisgau, Sept. 2, 1915. He studied with Martienssen (piano), Scheck (flute), Thomas and Scherchen (conducting), Schunemann and Seifert (musicology), and Hindemith (composition) at the Berlin Academy of Music (1934–36), and then with Moyse (flute) at the Geneva Cons. (1937–38). He went to Rio de Janeiro, where he taught at the Brazilian Cons. (1937–52) and at the São Paulo Inst. of Music (1942–44). He was director of the São Paulo Free Academy of Music (1952–55) and the music dept. of Bahia Univ. (1952–62); was also chief conductor of the Bahia Sym. Orch. (1952–62). He then was in charge of the music programs of the Goethe Inst. in Munich (1963–65); was its regional representative in New Delhi (1965–69), where he also was head of the Delhi School of Music (1966–69). From 1970 to 1975 he was director of the Goethe Inst. in Tokyo, where he also was prof. at the Inst. of Christian Music and conductor of the Heinrich Schütz Chorale; then returned to Brazil (1975) and taught at the Goethe Inst. in Rio de Janeiro (until 1980). After serving as director of the Tatui Cons. (1983–84), he was a prof. at the Univ. in Minas Gerais (1984–88) and at the São Paulo Cons. (1988–90). His music follows Classical forms, while the thematic materials are modeled after the 12-tone method of composition; in several of his works, he makes use of exotic motifs of South America, India, and Japan.

WRITINGS: *Attitudes of Consciousness in Indian and Western Music* (New Delhi, 1966); *Three Lectures on Music* (Mysore, 1968); *Jazz Harmonia* (São Paulo, 1969); *Ten Lectures on Music* (New Delhi, 1969); *History of Western Music* (New Delhi, 1970).

WORKS: ORCH.: *4 Pieces* (1937); *Variations* (1945); *Música* (1947); *Sinfonia de camara* for 11 Instruments (1948); *Mutacoes* (1953); *Concretion* for Orch. or Chamber Orch. (1960); *Constructio ad synesin* for Chamber Orch. (1962); *Advaita* for Sitar and Orch. or Chamber Orch. (1968); *Sunyata* for Flute, Chamber Orch. of Western and Indian Instruments, and Tape (1968); *Acronon* (1978–79); *Wu-Li* (1988). **CHAMBER:** 2 flute sonatas (1937, 1939); Violin Sonata (1939); *Inventions* for Oboe, Clarinet, and Bassoon (1940); *Variations* for Flute, English Horn, Clarinet, and Bassoon (1941); *Música 1947* for String Quartet (1947); *Diaton 8* for Flute, English Horn, Bassoon, Harp, and Xylophone (1955); *Tanka I–VII* for Voice and Instrument (1970–82). **VOCAL:** *Noturnos de Oneyda Alvarenga* for Mezzo-soprano and String Quartet (1945); *O cafe*, choral drama (1956); *8 Haikai de Pedro Xisto* for Baritone, Flute, Electric Guitar, Piano, and Percussion (1963); *Cantos de Kulka* for Soprano and Orch. (1964); *Indian Report*, cantata for Soprano, Speaker, Chamber Chorus, Speaking Chorus, and Chamber Orch. of Western and Indian Instruments (1967); *Yū* for Soprano and Japanese Instruments (1970); *Mu-dai* for Voice (1972); *O cafe* for Chorus (1975).

Koenemann, Theodore. See **Keneman, Feodor.**

Koenen, Tilly (actually, **Mathilde Caroline**), Dutch mezzo-soprano; b. Salatiga, Java, Dec. 25, 1873; d. The Hague, Jan. 4, 1941. She studied piano, on which she became a proficient performer, then voice with Cornelia van Zanten. She toured Germany and Austria from 1900 with excellent success; visited the U.S. in 1909–10 and 1915–16. She was particularly impressive in her interpretations of German Romantic songs; also performed some songs by her compatriots.

Koenig, Gottfried Michael, German composer; b. Magdeburg, Oct. 5, 1926. He attended the Braunschweig Staatsmusikschule (1946–47), and then was a student of Bialas (composition) and Maler (analysis) at the North West German Music Academy in Detmold (1947–50); later he studied at the Cologne Hochschule für Musik (1953–54) and at the Univ. of Bonn (1963–64). After working in the electronic music studios of the West German Radio in Cologne (1954–64), he was artistic and scientific director of the Instituut voor Sonologie at the Univ. of Utrecht (1964–86). In 1987 he was awarded the Matthijs Vermeulen Prize of the City of Amsterdam. Koenig was one of the leading figures in the development of electronic music, being particularly influential in the application of the computer to the creation of musical works. As an important theorist on serial music, he has written extensively. Among his most significant works is the study on serial and aleatory music publ. as *Musik in ihrer technischen Rationalität* (Bilthoven, 1963).

WORKS: ORCH.: Harpsichord Concerto (1948–49); *Horae* (1951); *Beitrag* (1985–86). **CHAMBER:** Woodwind Quintet (1958–59); 2 string quartets (1959; 1987–88); *Project I* for 14 Instruments (1965–66; also 2 other versions); *Segmente 99–105* for Violin and Piano (1982); *Drei ASKO Stücke* for 14 Instruments (1982); *Segmente 92–98* for Violin and Cello (1983); *Segmente 85–91* for Flute or Piccolo, Bass Clarinet, and Cello (1984); *Intermezzo* for Flute or Piccolo or Bass Flute, Bass Clarinet or E-flat Clarinet, and Piano (1987). **PIANO:** *2 Pieces* (1957); *Übung* (1969–70); *Segmente 1–7* (1982). **ELECTRONIC:** *Klangfiguren I* (1955) and *II* (1955–56); *Essay* (1957–58); *Materialien zu einem Ballett* (1961); Suite (1961); *Terminus I* (1962), *2* (1966–67), and *10* (1967); *Funktion Grün* (1967); *Funktion Gelb* (1968); *Funktion Orange* (1968); *Funktion Rot* (1968); *Funktion Blau* (1969); *Funktion Indigo* (1969); *Funktion Violett* (1969); *Funktion Grau* (1969). **COMPUTER:** *Output* (1979).

Koering, René, French composer; b. Andlau, Alsace, May 27, 1940. He studied piano; in 1960, went to Darmstadt, where he absorbed some modernistic notions through his attendance at courses given by Boulez, Stockhausen, and Maderna; subsequently taught at the École des Beaux Arts in Paris (from 1969). He composed experimentally in every conceivable classical and popular genre. His denouement came with his decision to write understandable music with a minimum of feasible modernities. Among his compositions were *Triple et trajectoires* for Piano and 2 Orchs. (1963), *Combat T 3 N* for Piano and Orch. (1970), and Sym. No. 1 (Royan, March 23, 1974).

Koetsier, Jan, Dutch conductor and composer; b. Amsterdam, Aug. 14, 1911. He studied in Berlin at the Stern Cons. (1924–26) and at the Hochschule für Musik (1927–34). He was a conductor in Lübeck and Berlin, and then in The Hague (1941–42); was 2nd conductor of the Concertgebouw Orch. in Amsterdam (1942–49), then again conducted in The Hague (1949–50). He thereafter was a conductor with the Bavarian Radio Sym. Orch. in Munich (1950–66); subsequently he was a prof. at the Munich Staatliche Hochschule für Musik (1966–76). In his music, he explores the modern applications of Baroque techniques.

WORKS: DRAMATIC: *Demeter*, ballet (1943); *Frans Hals*, opera (1949). **ORCH.:** *Concerto capriccioso* for Piano and Orch. (1935; rev. 1975); *Adagietto e Scherzino* (1936; rev. 1952); *Barocksuite* (1936; rev. 1953); Oboe Concertino (1936; rev. 1953); *Serenata Serna* for Strings (1937; rev. 1953); Duo concertante for Flute, Violin, and Orch. (1937; rev. 1956); *Vision pastorale* for English Horn and Strings (1937; rev. 1954); *Symhonische Musik* (1939); *Valerius Overture* (1942; rev. 1966); *Music* for 2 String Orchs., 3 Trumpets, 3 Trombones, and Timpani (1943); *Sinfonietta* (1943; rev. 1960); *Divertimento* (1943); *Music* for 4 Orchs. (1944); 3 syms. (1945, rev. 1968; 1946; 1954); *Kreisleriana* for 2 Pianos and Orch. (1965); *Valeriussuite* (1966); *Sinfonietta Concertante* for Oboe, Clarinet, Horn, Bassoon, and Strings (1968); *Concertino lirico* for Violin, Cello, and Strings (1968); *Homage to Gershwin* (1969); *Intrada classica* for Wind Instruments, Timpani, and Harp (1971); *Hymnus monaciensis* (1971); *Concertino drammatico* for Violin, Viola, and Strings (1981); Concertino for Trombone and Strings (1983); Concerto for 4 Horns and Orch. (1983); *Französisches Concerto*, suite for 2 Flutes and Strings (1984); *Dance Suite* (1985); *Burg-Serenade* (1987). **CHAMBER:** Quintet for Flute, Oboe, Violin, Viola, and Cello (1932; rev. 1965); Septet (1932; rev. 1959); 2 divertimentos for Wind Quintet (1937, 1947); Trio for Flute, Oboe, and Piano (1938); English Horn Quintet (1955); String Quintet (1959); Octet for 2 Oboes, 2 Clarinets, 2 Horns, and 2 Bassoons (1968); Clarinet Quintet (1968); sonatinas for Trumpet, for Trombone, and for Tuba (all 1970); Trio for Alto Flute, Viola da Gamba, and Harpsichord (1971); Sonata for Cello and Harp (1972); Piano Trio (1975); *Serenade* for String Trio (1977); Trio for Flute, Bassoon, and Piano (1978); *Fantasie*, trio for Cello, Bassoon, and Piano (1981); Quartet for 4 Cellos (1981); Sonata for Horn and Harp (1984); String Quartet (1985); *Petit Concert pour Violin et Contrebasse* for Violin, Double Bass, Clarinet, Bassoon, Cornet, Trombone, and Percussion (1987); organ music; piano pieces. **VOCAL:** *Von Gottes und des Menschen Wesen*, 7 madrigals for Chorus and 7 Instruments (1940; rev. 1969); *Gesang der Geister über Wassern* for Chorus and 7 Instruments (1940; rev. 1973); *Der Mann Lot* for Baritone, Speaker, Men's Chorus, and Orch. (1940; rev. 1962); *Antonius Mass* (1984); songs.

BIBL.: H. Beermann et al., *J. K.* (Tutzing, 1988).

Koffler, Józef, Polish composer; b. Stryj, Nov. 28, 1896; d. with his wife and child during a Nazi roundup of Jews in Wieliczka, near Kraków, 1943. He was a student in Vienna of Grädener (1914–16), Schoenberg (1920–24), and at the Univ. with Adler (Ph.D., 1925, with the diss. *Über orchestrale Koloristik in den symphonischen Werken von Mendelssohn-Barthold*y). He went to Lwów, where he taught at the Cons. (1929–41) and ed. the periodicals *Orkiestra* (1930–38) and *Echo* (1936–37). Koffler was the first Polish composer to embrace Schoenberg's 12-tone system.

WORKS: ORCH.: *Hanifa*, overture (1925); *Suite orientale* (1925); *Sielanka: Capriccio pastorale* for Chamber Orch. (1925); *Variations sur une succession de douze tons* for Strings (1927; based on *15 Variations d'après une suite de douze tons* for Piano); 4 syms.: No. 1 for Small Orch. (1931), No. 2 (1933), No. 3 for Winds (1935; London, June 17, 1938), and No. 4 (1940); Piano Concerto (1931); *Prelude and Fugue* (1936); *Polish Suite* for Small Orch. (1936); *Little Suite after J.S. Bach* (1937); *Joyful Overture* (1940); *Haendeliana*, 30 variations (1940). **CHAMBER:** String Trio (1928; Oxford, July 23, 1931); *Little Serenade* for Oboe, Clarinet, and Bassoon (1931); String Quartet (1934); *Capriccio* for Violin and Piano (1936); *Ukrainian Sketches* for String Quartet (1941). **PIANO:** *40 Polish Folk Songs* (1925); *Musique de ballet* (1926); *Musique quasi una sonata* (1927); *15 Variations d'après une suite de douze tons* (1927; also as *Variations sur une succession de douze tons* for String Orch.); Sonatine (1930); Sonata (1935); *Variations sur une Valse de Johann Strauss* (1935). **VOCAL:** *Love*, cantata for Mezzo-soprano, Clarinet, Viola, and Cello (1931); songs.

BIBL.: M. Gołąb, "Zwölftontechnik bei J. K.: Ein polnischer Beitrag zur Geschichte der Dodekaphonie in der ersten Hälfte des 20. Jahrhunderts," *Musik des Ostens*, X (1986).

Kogan, Leonid (Borisovich), outstanding Russian violinist and pedagogue, father of **Pavel Kogan**; b. Dnepropetrovsk, Nov. 14, 1924; d. on the train at the Mytishcha railroad station, Dec. 17, 1982. His father was a photographer who played the violin; when Kogan was 10 years old, the family moved to Moscow, where he became a pupil of Abram Yampolsky, first at the Central Music School and later at the Cons. (1943–48); subsequently pursued postgraduate studies with him (1948–51). In 1947 he was a co-winner of the 1st prize at the World Festival of Democratic Youth in Prague; then won 1st prize in the Queen Elisabeth of Belgium Competition in Brussels in 1951. His career was instantly assured; he played in Europe to unanimous acclaim. He made an auspicious American debut playing the Brahms Violin Concerto with Monteux and the Boston Sym. Orch. on Jan. 10, 1958. In 1952 he joined the faculty of the Moscow Cons.; was named prof. in 1963 and head of the violin dept. in 1969. In 1965 he received the Lenin Prize. His playing exemplified the finest qualities of the Russian School: an emotionally romantic elan and melodious filigree of technical detail. In addition to the standard repertoire, in which he excelled, he also played modern violin works, particularly those by Soviet composers. He was married to **Elizabeth Gilels**.

BIBL.: M. Zazovsky, *L. K.* (Moscow, 1956).

Kogan, Pavel, Russian violinist and conductor, son of **Leonid (Borisovich) Kogan;** b. Moscow, June 6, 1952. He enrolled at Moscow's Central Music School when he was 6, and later pursued his training at the Moscow Cons. with Jankelevitch. After taking 1st prize in the Sibelius Competition in Helsinki in 1970, he toured extensively as a violin virtuoso. In later years, he took up a career as a conductor. In 1988 he became a conductor at the Bolshoi Theater in Moscow. He also conducted the Moscow State Sym. Orch. from 1989.

Kogoj, Marij, Slovenian composer; b. Trieste, May 27, 1895; d. Ljubljana, Feb. 25, 1956. He was a student of Schreker and Schoenberg in Vienna (1914–18); then was active as a conductor at the Ljubljana Opera and as a music critic. Although Kogoj's promising career was thwarted in 1932 when he became mentally ill, he was one of the earliest Slovenian composers to experiment with expressionism, as evinced in his opera *Črne maske* (Black Masks; Ljubljana, May 7, 1929). Among his other works were choral pieces, chamber music, and piano pieces.

Köhler, Siegfried, German conductor; b. Freiburg im Breisgau, July 30, 1923. He studied at the local Hochschule für Musik. After conducting opera in provincial German cities, he conducted in Cologne; in 1964 he was named Generalmusikdirektor in Saarbrucken, and in 1974 in Wiesbaden. From 1990 to 1995 he was principal conductor of the Royal Opera in Stockholm. In 1992 he was named Royal Court Conductor of Sweden.

Köhler, Siegfried, German composer, teacher, and administrator; b. Meissen, March 2, 1927; d. Berlin, July 14, 1984. He studied with MacGregor (piano), Hintze (conducting), and Finke (composition) at the Dresden Hochschule für Musik (1946–50) and with Serauky (musicology) and Jahn (art history) at the Univ. of Leipzig (Ph.D., 1955, with the diss. *Die Instrumentation als Mittel musikalischer Ausdrucksgestaltung*). In 1957 he became director of the Berlin International Music Library. After serving as artistic director of the Deutsche Schallplaten (1963–68), he was director of the Dresden Hochschule für Musik (1968–80), where he also was prof. of composition (from 1969). In 1982 he became president of the Assn. of Composers and Music Scholars of the German Democratic Republic. In 1983 he became Intendant of the Dresden State Opera.

WORKS: OPERA: *Der Richter von Hohenburg* (1963). **ORCH.:** *Fröhliche Suite* (1956); 5 syms. (1965–84); Concertino for Clarinet and Strings (1968); Piano Concerto (1972). **VOCAL:** *Reich des Menschen*, oratorio (1962); cantatas; choruses; various songs.

BIBL.: G. Schönfelder, *S. K. für Sie porträtiert* (Leipzig, 1984).

Kohn, Karl (Georg), Austrian-born American pianist, conductor, teacher, and composer; b. Vienna, Aug. 1, 1926. After the Anschluss in 1938, he emigrated with his family to the U.S., becoming a naturalized American citizen in 1945. He studied piano with C. Werschinger and conducting with Prüwer at the N.Y. College of Music (graduated, 1944), then studied composition with Piston, Ballantine, Fine, and Thompson at Harvard Univ. (B.A., 1950; M.A., 1955), where he was a teaching fellow (1954–55); also taught at the Berkshire Music Center in Tanglewood (summers, 1954, 1955, 1957). In 1950 he joined the music faculty at Pomona College in Claremont, California, where he served as a prof. from 1965 to 1994. With his wife, Margaret, he performed the contemporary 2-piano repertoire in the U.S. and Europe; he also made appearances as a conductor. He held a Fulbright scholarship for study in Finland (1955–56), a Guggenheim fellowship (1961–62), and 4 grants from the NEA (1975, 1976, 1979, 1986). In his compositions, Kohn tends toward prudent serialism but also explores diatonic modalities, applying the power of pervicacious iteration of pandiatonic chordal complexes; he successfully adapts to contemporary usages medieval polyphonic devices such as the integration of precomposed thematic fragments, a technique anciently known as "centone" (literally, "patchwork quilt"). He makes use of topological rearrangements of Classical pieces, as in *Son of Prophet Bird*, dislocated and paraphrased from Schumann's *Bird as a Prophet*.

WORKS: ORCH.: *Sinfonia concertante* for Piano and Orch. (1951); *Overture* for Strings (1953); *Castles and Kings*, symphonic suite for children (1958); *Concerto mutabile* for Piano and Orch. (1962); *Episodes* for Piano and Orch. (1966); *Intermezzo I* for Flute and Strings (1969); *Centone per orchestra* (Claremont Music Festival, June 27, 1973); Concerto for Horn and Small Orch. (1974); *Innocent Psaltery*, "colonial music" (1976); *The Prophet Bird I* (metamorphosis of Schumann's *Bird as a Prophet*; 1976) and *II* for Piano and Chamber Orch. (Los Angeles, March 9, 1982); *Waldmusik*, clarinet concerto (1979; also for Clarinet, Piano, and Wind Ensemble, 1983); *Time Irretrievable* (1983); *An Amiable Piece* for 2 Pianos, Winds, and Percussion (1987); *Return*, symphonic essay for Brass, Percussion, and Strings (1990); *Ode* for Strings (1991); *Concert Music* for Strings (1993). **BAND:** *Serenade II* (1977); *Wind Chamber* (1981); *Rückgabe* (1990). **CHAMBER:** String Trio (1950); *Concert Music* for 12 Winds (1956); Violin Sonata (1956); *Capriccios I* for Flute, Clarinet, Cello, Harp, and Bassoon (1962) and *II* for Chamber Ensemble (1983); *Serenade* for Wind Quintet and Piano (1962); *Kaleidoscope* for String Quartet (1964); *Encounters I* for Flute, Piccolo, and Piano (1965), *II* for Horn and Piano (1967), *III* for Violin and Piano (1971), *IV* for Oboe and Piano (1972), *V* for Bassoon and Piano (1973), and *VI* for Cello and Piano (1977); *Introductions and Parodies* for Clarinet, Horn, Bassoon, String Quartet, and Piano (1967); *Rhapsodies* for Marimba, Vibraphone, and Percussion (1968); *Impromptus* for 8 Winds (1969); Trio for Violin, Horn, and Piano (1972); Brass Quintet (1976); *Son of Prophet Bird* for Harp (1977); *San Gabriel Set* for Clarinet, Violin, Viola, Cello, and Piano (1984); *Entr'acte* for String Quartet (1985); *Senza Sordino* for Horn and Viola (1985); *Choice Wood, Precious Metals* for Flute, Trumpet, Marimba, and Glockenspiel (1986); *Before Beethoven* for Clarinet, Cello, and Piano (1989); *Cassation* for Wind Quintet (1990); *End Piece* for Flute, Viola, Cello, Vibraphone, and Piano (1993); *Ternaries* for Flute and Piano (1993); *Middle Piece* for Flute, Viola, Cello, Marimba, and Piano (1994); *Ensemble Wiener Collage* for 10 Players (1995); piano pieces; organ music. **VOCAL:** Choral works; songs.

Kohoutek, Ctirad, prominent Czech composer, pedagogue, music theorist, and administrator; b. Zábřeh na Moravě, March 18, 1929. He studied at the Brno Cons. with Vilám Petrželka, and with Jaroslav Kvapil at the Janáček Academy of Music there (1949–53); later attended Lutosławski's lectures at the Dartington Summer School of Music (1963) and sessions given by Boulez and Ligeti at the Darmstadt summer courses in new music; obtained his Ph.D. from Palacký Univ. in Olomouc (1973) and his C.Sc. from J.E. Purkyně Univ. in Brno (1980). In 1953 he joined the faculty of the Janáček Academy of Music in Brno (assoc. prof., 1965–80). In 1980 he became assoc. prof. of composition at the Prague Academy of Music, and later that year prof. of composition, which position he retained until 1990. He also served as artistic director of the Czech Phil. (1980–87). In 1988 he was made an Artist of Merit by the Czech government. His music follows the traditions of Central European modernism, well contained within Classical forms but diversified by serial procedures and glamorized by electronic sounds. He is the brother of the astronomer Luboš Kohoutek.

WORKS: OPERA: *O Kohoutkovi a Slepičce* (About the Cock and Hen; 1988–89). **ORCH.:** *Mnichov* (Munich), symphonic poem (1952–53); *Festivalová předehra* (Festival Overture; 1955–56); Violin Concerto (1958); *Velký přelom* (Great Turning Point; 1960–62); *Symfonické tance* (Symphonic Dances; 1961); Symfonieta (1962–63); Concertino for Cello and Chamber Orch. (1964; also for Cello and Piano, 1966); *Preludia* for Chamber Orch. (1965); *Teatro del mondo*, symphonic rotation in 4 scenes (1968–69); *Panteon*, sound image (1970); *Slavonstní prolog* (Ceremonial Prologue; 1971); *Slavností světla* (Feast of Light), cycle of symphonic pictures (1975); *Symfonické aktuality* (Symphonic Newsreel), concert frescoes (1976–78); *Pocta životu* (Homage to Life; 1988–89; Brno, March 26, 1992). **CHAMBER:** *Sonatina semplice* for Oboe and Piano (1950); *Suita romantica* for Viola and Piano (1957); Suite for Wind Quintet (1958–59); String Quartet

(1959); *Memento 1967*, concerto for Percussion and Winds (1966); *Panychida: Hudba o dvou zvukových vrstvách* (Prayer for the Dead: Music in 2 Sound Layers) for 2 Violas, 2 Pianos, Percussion, and Tape (1968); *Tkaniny doby* (Fabrics of Time), sound fantasies for Bass Clarinet or Cello, Piano, and Percussion (1977); *Minuty jara* (Minutes of Spring), impressions for Wind Quintet (1980); *3 Variations of Folk Dances* for 2 Accordions or Accordion Ensemble (1986); *Motivy léta* (Motifs of Summer) for Violin, Cello, and Piano (1990); *Žerty a úsměvy* (The Fun and the Smiles, or Funny Smiles) for Oboe, Clarinet, and Bassoon (1991); *V zahradách chrámu Kyota* (In the Gardens of Kyoto's Temples) for English Horn, Bass Clarinet, and Percussion (1992); *Zimní ticha* (Winter Silences) for Brass and Percussion (1992–93); *Oživené zátiší* (The Revived Still Life) for Horn (1994). **VOCAL:** *Za všechny děti: Ukolébavka černošské mamy* (For All Children: Black Mama's Lullaby), cantata for Contralto, Chorus, and Orch. (1951–52); *Balady z povstání* (Ballads from the Uprising), 2 cantatas (1960); *Pátý živel* (The 5th Element), melodrama for Reciter and Small Orch. (1964); *The Birth of Man*, monologues for Man's and Woman's Voice and Orch. or Piano (1981); *Broskvička* (The Little Peach) for Chorus, Piano, and Percussion (1993); choruses; songs.

Kohs, Ellis (Bonoff), noted American composer and teacher; b. Chicago, May 12, 1916. His mother was a good violinist, and when Kohs learned to play the piano he often accompanied her at home. In 1928 the family moved from San Francisco (following his early musical studies there at the Cons.) to N.Y., where he studied with Adelaide Belser at the Inst. of Musical Art. In 1933 he enrolled at the Univ. of Chicago as a student in composition with Carl Bricken (M.A., 1938). Upon graduation, he proceeded to N.Y., where he entered the Juilliard School of Music, studying composition with Wagenaar and musical pedagogy with Samaroff. He continued his musical studies at Harvard Univ., with Piston in composition and Leichtentritt and Apel in musicology (1939–41); also attended a seminar given by Stravinsky at Harvard Univ. in 1940–41. During the summer of 1940, he was a lecturer in music at the Univ. of Wisc. in Madison. From 1941 to 1946 he served in the U.S. Army as a chaplain's assistant and organist, and in the U.S. Air Force as a bandleader. After his discharge from service, he engaged in pedagogical work and in active composition; his teaching posts included Wesleyan Univ. (1946–48), the Kansas City Cons. of Music (1946–47), the College of the Pacific in Stockton, California (1948–50), Stanford Univ. (1950), and the Univ. of Southern Calif. in Los Angeles (1950–85). In his music, he pursues the aim of classical clarity; he is particularly adept in variation structures; the rhythmic patterns in his works are often asymmetrical, and the contrapuntal fabric highly dissonant; in some of his works, he makes use of a unifying 12-tone row, subjecting it to ingenious metamorphoses, as revealed in his opera *Amerika*, after the novel by Kafka. A humorous streak is shown in his choral piece *The Automatic Pistol*, to words from the U.S. Army weapons manual, which he composed during his military service. He publ. the useful manuals *Music Theory, a Syllabus for Teacher and Student* (2 vols., N.Y., 1961), *Musical Form: Studies in Analysis and Synthesis* (Boston, 1976), and *Musical Composition: Projects in Ways and Means* (Metuchen, N.J., 1980).

WORKS: DRAMATIC: *Amerika*, opera, after Kafka (1969; abridged concert version, Los Angeles, May 19, 1970; 2 orch. suites, 1986, 1987); *Lohiau and Hiiaka*, Hawaiian legend for Narrators, Flute, Cello, Percussion, and Dancers (1987; also as a suite for Flute, Cello, and Percussion, 1988); incidental music. **ORCH.:** *Concerto for Orchestra* (Berkeley, Calif., Aug. 9, 1942); *Passacaglia* for Organ and Strings (1946); *Legend* for Oboe and Strings (Columbus, Ohio, Feb. 27, 1947); Cello Concerto (1947); Chamber Concerto for Viola and String Nonet (1949); 2 syms.: No. 1 (1950) and No. 2 for Chorus and Orch. (Urbana, Ill., April 13, 1957); Violin Concerto (1980; Los Angeles, April 24, 1981). **CHAMBER:** 3 string quartets (1940–84); *Night Watch* for Flute, Horn, and Timpani (1943); Bassoon Sonatina (1944); *Short Concert* for String Quartet (1948); Clarinet Sonata (1951); *Variations* for Recorder (1956); Brass Trio (1957); *Studies in Variation* in 4 parts: for Woodwind Quintet, for Piano Quartet, for Piano, for Violin (1962); Snare Drum Sonata (1966); *Duo* for Violin and Cello, after Kafka's *Amerika* (1971); Concerto for Percussion Quartet (1979); Trio for Strings (1983); *Fantasies, Intermezzi, and Canonic Etudes on the Name EuDiCe SHApiro* for Violin (1985). **KEYBOARD: PIANO:** *Étude in Memory of Bartók* (1946); *Variations* (1946); *Variations on L'Homme armé* (1947); *Toccata* for Harpsichord or Piano (1948); *Fantasy on La, Sol, Fa, Re, Mi* (1949); *10 Inventions* (1950). **ORGAN:** *Capriccio* (1948); *3 Chorale-Variations on Hebrew Hymns* (1952). **VOCAL:** *The Automatic Pistol* for Men's Voices (Washington, D.C., Sept. 5, 1943); *25th Psalm* (1947); *Fatal Interview*, song cycle, Edna St. Vincent Millay (1951); *Lord of the Ascendant* for Chorus, Soloists, Dancers, and Orch., after the Gilgamesh (1956); *3 Songs from the Navajo* for Chorus (1957); *3 Greek Choruses* for Women's Chorus (1957); *23rd Psalm* for Soloists and Chorus (1957); *Men* for Narrator and 3 Percussionists (1982; Los Angeles, March 15, 1984); *Subject Cases* for Narrator and Percussionist, after Gertrude Stein (Los Angeles, Feb. 14, 1983).

Koizumi, Fumio, Japanese ethnomusicologist; b. Tokyo, April 4, 1927. He studied aesthetics at the Univ. of Tokyo (degree, 1951); also took courses in music with Eishi Kikkawa. In 1960 he was appointed to the faculty of the Tokyo National Univ. of Fine Arts and Music; in 1969 and 1970 he lectured at Wesleyan Univ. in the U.S. His primary field of study is Japanese music, but he has also worked on the problems of national music in India, Iran, the Near East, Eastern Europe, and Spain. Among his publications is *Nihon dentō ongaku no kenkyū* (Study of Japanese Traditional Music; Tokyo, 1958).

Koizumi, Kazuhiro, Japanese conductor; b. Kyoto, Oct. 16, 1949. He studied at the Tokyo Univ. of the Arts, and later at the Berlin Hochschule für Musik; also worked with Ozawa. In 1970 he won 1st prize in the Min-Ono conducting competition in Japan, and in 1972, 1st prize in the Karajan Competition in Berlin. After serving as assistant conductor of the Japan Phil. in Tokyo (1970–72), he was music director of the New Japan Phil. there (1975–80) and of the Winnipeg Sym. Orch. (1983–89); also was chief conductor of the Tokyo Metropolitan Sym. Orch. (1984–87). He was principal conductor of the Kyūshū Sym. Orch. in Fukuoka from 1988.

Kojian, Varujan (Haig), Armenian-born American conductor; b. Beirut (of Armenian parents), March 12, 1935; d. Carpinteria, Calif., March 4, 1993. He studied violin at the Paris Cons. (1953–56), winning a premier prix, with Galamian at the Curtis Inst. of Music in Philadelphia, and with Heifetz in Los Angeles (1960). He became assistant concertmaster of the Los Angeles Phil. (1965); after conducting studies with Sasha Popov, he was made Mehta's assistant at the Los Angeles Phil. (1970); then went to Vienna for additional conducting studies with Swarowsky (1971), taking 1st prize in the Sorrento competition (1972). From 1973 to 1976 he was assistant conductor of the Seattle Sym. Orch., and from 1973 to 1980, principal guest conductor of the Royal Opera in Stockholm; then was music director of the Utah Sym. Orch. in Salt Lake City (1980–83), the Chautauqua (N.Y.) Sym. Orch. (1981–86), Ballet West in Salt Lake City (from 1984), and the Santa Barbara Sym. orch. (from 1985). In 1967 he became a naturalized American citizen.

Kókai, Rezső, Hungarian composer and teacher; b. Budapest, Jan. 15, 1906; d. there, March 6, 1962. He was a student of Koessler (composition) and Emánuel Hegyi (piano) at the Budapest Academy of Music (1925–26), and of W. Gurlitt at the Univ. of Freiburg im Breisgau (Ph.D., 1933, with a diss. on Liszt's early piano music). He taught in Budapest at the National Cons. (1926–34) and at the Academy of Music (from 1929); he also was head of the music dept. of the Hungarian Radio (1945–48). In 1952, 1955, and 1956 he received the Erkel Prize.

WORKS: DRAMATIC: *István király* (King Stephen), scenic oratorio (1942); *A rossz feleség* (The Shrew), dance ballad (1942–45); *Lészen ágyú* (There Shall be Cannons), radio opera

(1951); music for radio plays and films. **ORCH.:** *2 Rondos* for Small Orch. (1947); *Verbunkos szvit* (Recruiting Suite; 1950); Violin Concerto (1952); *Széki táncok* (Dances from Szék; 1952); *Rhapsody* for Clarinet and Folk Orch. (1952); *Kis magyar verbunk* (Little Hungarian Recruiting Dance) for Youth Orch. (1954); *Concerto all'ungherese* (1957); *Magyar táncok* (Hungarian Dances) for Youth Orch. (1960). **CHAMBER:** *Serenade* for String Trio (1949–50); *2 Dances* for Cello and Piano (1950); *4 Hungarian Dances* for Clarinet and Piano (1951); Quartettino for Clarinet and String Trio (1952); *Verbunkos rapszódia* (Recruiting Rhapsody) for Violin and Piano (1952); *Capriccio* for Violin and Piano (1952); *Aria seria: Burla ostinata* for Violin and Piano (1953). **PIANO:** *Toccata* (1927); Sonata for 2 Pianos (1949); *Quattro improvvisazioni* (1949–50). **VOCAL:** Songs.

Kokkonen, Joonas, prominent Finnish composer, pianist, pedagogue, and administrator; b. Iisalmi, Nov. 13, 1921; d. Jarvenpaa, Oct. 1, 1996. He was educated at the Univ. (M.A., 1948) and the Sibelius Academy (piano diploma, 1949) in Helsinki. In addition to appearances as a pianist, he was active as a music critic. He also was a teacher (1950–59) and a prof. (1959–63) of composition at the Sibelius Academy. He served as chairman of the Assn. of Finnish Composers (1965–71), the Nordic Composers Council (1968–71), and of TEOSTO, the Finnish copyright bureau (1968–88). In 1963 he became a member of the Academy of Finland, in 1968 he was awarded the Nordic Council Music Prize, and in 1973 he received the Sibelius Prize of the Wihuri Foundation. After composing in a highly personal dodecaphonic style, Kokkonen developed a compositional idiom marked by an intensive motivic technique and economy of expression tending toward the ascetic in his later works.

WORKS: OPERA: *Viimeiset Kiusaukset* (The Last Temptations; 1973–75; Helsinki, Sept. 2, 1975). **ORCH.:** *Music* for Strings (Helsinki, March 5, 1957); 4 syms.: No. 1 (Helsinki, March 15, 1960), No. 2 (Helsinki, April 18, 1961), No. 3 (Helsinki, Sept. 12, 1967), and No. 4 (Helsinki, Nov. 16, 1971); *Sinfonia da camera* for 12 Strings (Lucerne, Aug. 31, 1962); *Opus sonorum* (1964; Helsinki, Feb. 16, 1965); *Symphonic Sketches* (Helsinki, May 16, 1968); Cello Concerto (Helsinki, Oct. 16, 1969); *Inauguratio* (Helsinki, Sept. 5, 1971); *Interludes From the Opera The Last Temptations* (Helsinki, Sept. 27, 1977); *". . . durch einen Spiegel . . ."* for 12 Strings and Harpsichord (Lucerne, Aug. 25, 1977); *Il Paesaggio* for Chamber Orch. (1986–87; Järvenpää, Feb. 13, 1987). **CHAMBER:** Piano Trio (Oslo, Oct. 12, 1948); Piano Quintet (Helsinki, Oct. 26, 1953); Duo for Violin and Piano (Helsinki, Nov. 6, 1955); 3 string quartets: No. 1 (Helsinki, May 3, 1959), No. 2 (Helsinki, Oct. 17, 1966), and No. 3 (Helsinki, Aug. 24, 1976); Wind Quintet (1973; Oslo, April 15, 1975); Cello Sonata (1976; Basel, April 3, 1986); *Improvvisazione* for Violin and Piano (Indianapolis, Sept. 12, 1982). **KEYBOARD: PIANO:** Sonatina (Helsinki, Oct. 26, 1953); *Religioso* (1956); *5 Bagatelles* (Göteburg, April 21, 1969). **ORGAN:** *Wedding March* (Tapiola, Aug. 17, 1968); *Funeral March* (Tuusula, June 14, 1969); *Lux aeterna* (Helsinki, Aug. 9, 1974); *Iuxta crucem* (Lahti, Aug. 5, 1979). **VOCAL:** *3 Songs of Einari* for High Voice and Piano (1941, 1947; Helsinki, Nov. 11, 1991); *The Evenings*, song cycle for Soprano and Piano (1955); *Christmas Songs* for Children for Medium Voice and Piano (1956, 1958, 1966); *The Hades of the Birds*, song cycle for Mezzo-soprano and Orch. (1958–59; Helsinki, April 7, 1959); *Psalm of the Frog in the Rain* for Men's Chorus (Helsinki, Nov. 30, 1963); *Missa a cappella* for Chorus (Helsinki, Aug. 7, 1963); *Laudatio domini* for Soprano and Chorus (1966; London, Feb. 1, 1967); *Erekhteion*, cantata for Soprano, Baritone, Chorus, and Orch. (1969; Turku, Feb. 28, 1970); *Sub rosa*, song cycle for Mezzo-soprano and Piano (Helsinki, March 25, 1973); *2 Monologues From the Opera The Last Temptations* for Bass and Orch. (1975; Helsinki, Aug. 26, 1977); *Requiem: In memoriam Maija Kokkonen*, the composer's wife, for Soprano, Baritone, Chorus, and Orch. (Helsinki, Sept. 17, 1981); *Väinämöinen Plucked the Strings* for Men's Chorus (1985; Helsinki, May 13, 1986).

Kolar, Victor, Bohemian-American violinist, conductor, and composer; b. Budapest (of Bohemian parents), Feb. 12, 1888; d. Detroit, June 16, 1957. After initial violin training with Jan Kubelik, he studied violin with Ševčik and composition with Dvořák at the Prague Cons. (graduated, 1904). He then settled in the U.S.; was a violinist in the Chicago Sym. Orch. (1904–05), the Pittsburgh Sym. Orch. (1905–08), and the N.Y. Sym. Orch. (1908–20), serving the latter as assistant conductor as well (1914–20). He subsequently became a violinist in the Detroit Sym. Orch., and also held various conducting posts with it until 1942. After teaching at the Arthur Jordan Cons. of Music in Indianapolis, he returned to Detroit to conduct its Scandinavian Sym. Orch. (1950–53) and Women's Sym. Orch. (1950–57); also taught at the Inst. of Musical Arts (1950–56). He wrote a Sym. (N.Y., Jan. 28, 1916); *Hiawatha*, symphonic poem (Pittsburgh, Jan. 31, 1908); *Americana*, symphonic suite (1912); *Slovakia*, rhapsody for Orch. (1922); many songs.

Kolb, Barbara, talented American composer; b. Hartford, Conn., Feb. 10, 1939. She received training in clarinet and composition at the Hartt School of Music in Hartford (1957–61; B.Mus., 1961), where she continued her composition studies with Arnold Franchetti (1961–64; M.Mus., 1965); she also taught there and played clarinet in the Hartford Sym. Orch. During the summer of 1964, she attended the composition courses of Schuller and Foss at the Berkshire Music Center at Tanglewood, and returned in the summer of 1968 to study again with Schuller. In 1966 she studied in Vienna on a Fulbright scholarship. In 1968 she held a MacDowell Colony fellowship, and returned there in 1969, 1971–72, 1980, 1983, and 1987–89. In 1969 she became the first American woman to receive the U.S. Prix de Rome, and was then active at the American Academy in Rome until 1971. In 1971–72 and 1976–77 she held Guggenheim followships. She was composer-in-residence at the Marlboro (Vt.) Music Festival in 1973 and at the American Academy in Rome in 1974–75. After teaching at Brooklyn College of the City Univ. of N.Y. (1973–75), she was artistic director of the "Music New to N.Y." series at the Third Street Music School Settlement (1979–82). In 1983–84 she was active at IRCAM in Paris. She was a visiting prof. at the Eastman School of Music in Rochester, N.Y., in 1984–85. In 1987 she received a Kennedy Center Friedheim Award for her *Millefoglie*. Her music is marked by a sui generis melodic, harmonic, and rhythmic environment in which atonal writing is occasionally complemented by elements à la American jazz and French impressionism.

WORKS: DRAMATIC: *Cantico*, tape collage score for J. Herbert's film on St. Francis of Assisi (N.Y., Dec. 5, 1982); dance score (N.Y., April 18, 1995). **ORCH.:** *Crosswinds* for Wind Ensemble and Percussion (1969; Rome, Sept. 24, 1970); *Trobar Clus* for Chamber Ensemble (Tanglewood, Aug. 17, 1970); *Soundings* for Chamber Ensemble and Tape (1971–72; N.Y., Oct. 27, 1972; rev. version for Orch., N.Y., Dec. 11, 1975; 2nd rev. version, Boston, Feb. 16, 1978); *Grisaille* (1978–79; Portland, Maine, Feb. 13, 1979); *Yet That Things Go Round* for Chamber Orch. (1986–87; N.Y., May 2, 1987; rev. 1988); *The Enchanted Loom* (1988–89; Atlanta, Feb. 15, 1990; rev. 1992); *Voyants* for Piano and Chamber Orch. (Paris, Feb. 22, 1991). **CHAMBER:** *Rebuttal* for 2 Clarinets (1964); *Figments* for Flute and Piano (1967; rev. 1969); *Solitaire* for Piano and Tape (1971; N.Y., Oct. 27, 1972); *Toccata* for Harpsichord and Tape (1971; San Marcos, Texas, Sept. 12, 1973); *Spring River Floers Moon Night* for 2 Pianos and Tape (1974–75; N.Y., Jan. 12, 1976); *Looking for Claudio* for Guitar and Tape (Belgian Radio and TV, Brussels, May 22, 1975); *Homage to Keith Jarrett and Gary Burton* for Flute and Vibraphone (Dallas, March 31, 1976; rev. 1977); *Appello* for Piano (Washington, D.C., Oct. 20, 1976); *3 Lullabies* for Guitar (Paris, March 27, 1980); *Related Characters* for Clarinet or Trumpet and Piano (1980; also for Viola and Piano, Los Angeles, Nov. 7, 1982, and for Alto Saxophone and Piano); *The Point That Divides the Wind* for Organ, Percussion, and 3 Men's Voices (1981–82; N.Y., March 7, 1983); *Cavatina* for Violin (Washington, D.C., May 21, 1983; rev. 1985); *Millefoglie* for 9 Instrumentalists and Computer-generated Tape (1984–85; Paris, June 5, 1985; rev. 1987); *Time . . . and Again* for Oboe, String Quartet, and Computer Tape (Washington, D.C., Nov. 22, 1985); *Umbrian Colors* for Violin and Guitar (Marlboro, Vt., Aug. 13, 1986); *Introduction and Allegra* for Guitar (Washington, D.C., Feb. 19, 1992); *Extremes* for Flute and Cello (N.Y., March 15, 1989); *Cloudspin* for Organ and Tape (Cleveland, Oct. 23, 1991; also for Brass Quintet and Organ). **VOCAL:** *Chansons bas* for Soprano, Harp, and 2 Percussionists (1966); *3 Place Settings* for Narrator, Clarinet, Violin, Double Bass, and Percussion (1968); *Songs Before an Adieu* for Soprano, Flute or Alto Flute, and Guitar (1976–79; WFMT-FM, Chicago, May 23, 1979); *Chromatic Fantasy* for Narrator and 6 Instruments (Minneapolis, Nov. 4, 1979); *The Sundays of My Life*, popular song (1982).

Kolessa, Filaret (Mikhailovich), significant Ukrainian ethnomusicologist; b. Chodowitschi, July 17, 1871; d. Lwów, March 3, 1947. He studied in Lemberg (Lwów); later took a course in musicology with Adler at the Univ. of Vienna (Ph.D., 1918). He taught at the state high school in Lemberg (from 1898); became a prof. at the Univ. of Lwów and director of the Ethnographic Museum there (1939). He laid the foundation for the comparative study of Slavonic and East European folk music.

WRITINGS: *Rytmika ukrayinskykh narodnykh pisen* (Rhythm in Ukrainian Folk Songs; Lemberg, 1906–07); "Pro muzychnu formu dum" (On the Musical Form of Historical Chants), *Melodiyi ukrayinskykh narodnykh dum* (Lemberg, 1910; 2nd ed., rev., 1969); *Varianty melodiy ukrainskykh narodnykh dum, ikh kharakterystyka i grupovannya* (Variations in Melody of Ukrainian Folk Historical Chants, Their Characteristics and Classification; Lemberg, 1913); *Pro genezu ukrayinskykh narodnykh dum (ukrainksi narodni dumy u vidnoshenni do pisen, virshiv i pokhoronnykh holosin)* (On the Origin of Ukrainian Folk Historical Chants in Relation to Songs, Religious Songs, and Folk Laments; Lwów, 1920–22). **COLLECTIONS:** *Melodii haivok, skhopleni na fonograf Y. Rozdolskym* (Easter Song Melodies Recorded by Rozdolsky; Lemberg, 1909); *Melodiyi ukrayinskykh narodnykh dum* (Tunes of Ukrainian Historical Chants; Lemberg, 1910–13; 2nd ed., rev., 1969); "Narodni pisni z pivdennoho Pidkarpattya" (Folk Songs from Southern Subcarpathia), *Naukoviy zbirnyk tovarystva "Prosvita" v Uzhhorodi* (1923); *Narodni pisni z halytskoyi Lemkivshchyny: Teksty i melodiyi* (Folk Songs from West Galicia, Lemky Country: Texts and Melodies; Lwów, 1929); "Narodni pisni z pidkarpatskoy Rusi, melodii i teksty" (Folk Songs from Subcarpathian Ruthenia, Melodies and Texts), *Naukovyy zbirnyk tovarystva "Prosvita" v Uzhhorodi*, XIII–XIV (1938).

BIBL.: K. Kvitka, "F. K.," *Muzyka*, 11–12 (Kiev, 1925); S. Hrytsa, *F.M. K.* (Kiev, 1962); O. Palamarchuk, *M. K.* (Kiev, 1989).

Kolinski, Mieczyslaw, Polish-born Canadian ethnomusicologist, music theorist, and composer; b. Warsaw, Sept. 5, 1901; d. Toronto, May 7, 1981. He began his musical training in Hamburg, and then studied piano and composition at the Berlin Hochschule für Musik; took courses in musicology, psychology, and anthropology at the Univ. of Berlin (Ph.D., 1930, with the diss. *Die Musik der Primitivstämme auf Malaka und ihre Beziehungen zur samoanischen Musik*, publ. in *Anthropos*, XXV, 1930). He assisted Hornbostel at the Berlin Staatliches Phonogramm-Archiv (1926–33); then moved to Prague, where he remained until 1938, when he went to Belgium to avoid the Nazis; during much of the German occupation, he was in hiding. He settled in N.Y. in 1951; was co-founder (1955) and president (1958–59) of the Soc. for Ethnomusicology; taught at the Univ. of Toronto (1966–76); became a naturalized Canadian citizen in 1974. He transcribed more than 2,000 works from all over the world; publ. *Konsonanz als Grundlage einer neuen Akkordlehre* (Prague, 1936).

WORKS: 2 piano sonatas (1919; 1946, rev. 1966); Violin Sonata (1924); Cello Sonata (1926); *Lyric Sextet* for Soprano, Flute, and String Quartet (1929); 4 piano suites (1929–46); String Quartet (1931); *Expresszug-Phantasie*, ballet (Salzburg, 1935); Concertino for Soprano, String Quartet, and Piano (1951); *Dahomey Suite* for Flute or Oboe and Piano or String Orch. (1951); *Hatikvah Variations* for String Quartet (1960); *Dance Fantasy* for Strings (1968); *Encounterpoint* for Organ and String Quartet (1973); Concertino for Soprano, Clarinet, and Piano (1974); music for recorder ensemble; songs; folk-song arrangements.

BIBL.: R. Kennedy, "A Bibliography of the Writings of M. K.," *Current Musicology*, 3 (1966).

Kolisch, Rudolf, Austrian-born American violinist; b. Klamm am Semmering, July 20, 1896; d. Watertown, Mass., Aug. 1, 1978. He began training in childhood; after sustaining an injury to his left hand, he learned to hold his violin with his right hand and the bow with his left. He continued his studies at the Vienna Academy of Music and the Univ. of Vienna (graduated, 1913); took courses with Ševčik (violin) and Schreker and Schoenberg (theory and composition). In 1922 he organized the Kolisch Quartet, which systematically presented works by modern composers. It was the first string quartet to perform works from the standard repertoire from memory. In 1935 he went to the U.S.; after his quartet disbanded (1939), he became 1st violin of the Pro Arte Quartet (1942). He taught at the Univ. of Wisc. (1944–67), and served as artist-in-residence and head of the chamber music dept. of the New England Cons. of Music in Boston.

Kollo (real name, **Kollodziejski**), **René,** esteemed German tenor, grandson of **(Elimar) Walter Kollo (Kollodziejski)**; b. Berlin, Nov. 20, 1937. He studied with Elsa Varena in Berlin. He made his operatic debut as Oedipus Rex in Braunschweig (1965). He sang in Düsseldorf (1967–71); then with the Vienna State Opera. In 1969 he first appeared at Bayreuth as the Steersman; sang in the centenary *Ring* performances there (1976); made his Covent Garden debut in London that same year as Siegmund. He made his Metropolitan Opera debut in N.Y. as Lohengrin on Nov. 4, 1976. As a guest artist, he sang in Berlin, Munich, Hamburg, Milan, Salzburg, and other music centers. Among his other roles were Walther von Stolzing, Parsifal, Tamino, and Lensky. From 1996 he was Intendant of the Berlin Metropol-Theater

BIBL.: I. Fábián, *I. Fábián im Gesprach mit R. K.* (Zürich, 1982).

Kollo (real name, **Kollodziejski**), **(Elimar) Walter,** noted German composer, grandfather of **René Kollo;** b. Neidenburg, Jan. 28, 1878; d. Berlin, Sept. 30, 1940. He studied at the Sondershausen Cons. He began his career writing songs and cabaret music, and also was active as a theater conductor. After working in Königsberg and Stettin, he settled in Berlin and composed several theater pieces before attaining notable success with his musical comedy, *Filmzauber* (Oct. 19, 1912). It soon was performed internationally with great success. Then followed another outstanding score, *Wie einst im Mai!* (Oct. 4, 1913; in collaboration with W. Bredschneider). After composing *Der Juxbaron* (Hamburg, Nov. 14, 1913), Kollo produced a series of remarkably successful Berlin scores, including *Extrablätter* (Oct. 24, 1914; in collaboration with Bredschneider), *Immer feste druff!* or *Gloria Viktoria* (Oct. 1, 1914), *Wenn zwei Hochzeit machen* (Oct. 23, 1915; in collaboration with Bredschneider), *Auf Flügeln des Gesanges* (Sept. 9, 1916; in collaboration with Bredschneider), *Der selige Balduin* (March 31, 1916), *Die tolle Komtess* (Feb. 21, 1917), *Die Gulaschkanone* (Feb. 23, 1917), *Drei alte Schachteln* (Nov. 6, 1917), *Blitzblaues Blut* (Feb. 9, 1918), and *Sterne, die wieder leuchtet* (Nov. 6, 1918). Following the success of *Fräulein Puck* (Munich, June 25, 1919), Kollo resumed composing for the Berlin theaters, producing such successful scores as *Marietta* (Dec. 22, 1923) and *Drei arme kleine Mädels* (April 22, 1927). During this same period, he also composed the music for several highly popular revues, among them *Drunter und Drüber* (1923), which included the hit song *Solang noch Untern Linden.* While Kollo continued to compose until his death, he never succeeded in attaining the success of his earlier years.

Kolman, Peter, Slovak-born Austrian composer; b. Bratislava, May 29, 1937. In 1944 the Nazis imprisoned him at the Theresienstadt concentration camp, from which he was liberated in 1945. Returning to Bratislava, he pursued his composition studies at the Cons. (1951–56) and the Academy of Music (1956–60). In 1961 he became a music ed. in the division of serious music of the Czech Radio in Bratislava, where he was director of its experimental studio (studio for electronic music) from 1965 to 1977. After the Soviet-bloc invasion of his homeland in 1968, he was expelled from the Slovak Composers Soc. as a result of a performance ban on his music. In 1977 he emigrated to Austria and in 1979 became a naturalized Austrian citizen. He worked as an ed. at Universal Edition in Vienna. As a composer, Kolman followed in the paths of the 2nd Viennese School and the post-World War II avant-garde.

WORKS: ORCH.: *Funeral Music* (1958); Violin Concerto (1960); *4 Pieces* (1963); *Monumento per 6,000,000* (1964–66). **CHAMBER:** *Partecipazioni* for 12 Instruments (1962); *Sonata canonica* for Clarinet and Bass Clarinet (1963); *Panegyrikos* for 4 Oboes, 4 Trumpets, 4 Percussion, and 4 Cellos (1964); *Molisation*, mobile for Flute and Vibraphone (1965); String Quartet (1970); *Movement* for Winds and Percussion (1971); *". . . wie ein Hauch von Glückseligkeit"* for Violin and Piano (1978); *Music* for 14 Strings (1978). **KEYBOARD: PIANO:** *3 Piano Pieces in Memory of Arnold Schönberg* (1960); *Note bene* (1978). **ORGAN:** *Laudatio* (1982); *Interludium* (1984); *Jeu de touches* (1986). **ELECTRONIC:** *Omaggio a Gesualdo* (1970); *Lentement mais pas trop* (1972); *Poliritmica* (1974); *E 15* (1974); *9½* (1976).

Kolneder, Walter, noted Austrian musicologist; b. Wels, July 1, 1910; d. Karlsruhe, Jan. 30, 1994. He studied composition privately with Johann Nepomuk David (1927–29); also studied with Paumgartner (conducting) and Strub (viola) at the Salzburg Mozarteum (1925–35); took courses in musicology at the Univ. of Vienna (1934–35) and with W. Fischer at the Univ. of Innsbruck (Ph.D., 1949, with the diss. *Die vokale Mehrstimmigkeit in der Volksmusik der österreichischen Alpenländer*); completed his Habilitation at the Univ. of Saarbrücken with his *Antonio Vivaldi: Neue Studien zur Biographie und Stilistik seiner Werke* (extracts in *Aufführungspraxis bei Vivaldi*, Leipzig, 1955; 2nd ed., 1973). He taught at the Graz Cons. (1936–39) and the Staatliche Hochschule für Musikerziehung in Graz-Eggenberg (1936–45); was director of the Luxembourg Cons. (1953–59); also was a Privatdozent at the Univ. of Saarbrücken (from 1956). He was director of the Darmstadt Academy from 1959 to 1965 and of the Karlsruhe Hochschule für Musik from 1966 to 1972; was made ausserplanmässiger prof. of musicology at the Univ. of Karlsruhe (1966). His writings included *Anton Webern: Einführung in Werk und Stil* (Rodenkirchen, 1961; Eng. tr., 1968, as *Anton Webern: An Introduction to His Works*); *Geschichte der Musik: Ein Studien- und Prüfungshelfer* (Heidelberg, 1961; 5th ed., 1973); *Musikinstrumentenkunde: Ein Studien- und Prüfungshelfer* (Heidelberg, 1963; 3rd ed., 1972); *Singen, Hören, Schreiben: Eine praktische Musiklehre in vier Lehr- und vier Übungsheften* (Mainz, 1963–67); *Antonio Vivaldi: Leben und Werk* (Wiesbaden, 1965; Eng. tr., 1970); *Das Buch der Violine* (Zürich, 1972); *Anton Webern: Genesis und Metamorphosen eines Stils* (Vienna, 1973); *Melodietypen bei Vivaldi* (Zürich, 1973); *Schule des Generalbassspiels* (2 vols., Wilhelmshaven, 1983–84); *Johann Sebastian Bach (1685–1750): Leben, Werk, und Nachwirken in zeitgenössischen Dokumenten* (Wilhelmshaven, 1991).

Kolodin, Irving, prominent American music critic and writer on music; b. N.Y., Feb. 22, 1908; d. there, April 29, 1988. He studied at the Inst. of Musical Art in N.Y. (1930–31). He was music critic for the *N.Y. Sun* (1932–50) and the *Saturday Review* (1947–82); served as program annotator for the N.Y. Phil. (1953–58); also taught at N.Y.'s Juilliard School (from 1968).

WRITINGS (all publ. in N.Y. unless otherwise given): *The Metropolitan Opera . . .* (1936; 4th ed., rev., 1966); with Benny Goodman, *The Kingdom of Swing* (1939); ed. *The Critical Composer* (1940); *A Guide to Recorded Music* (Garden City, N.Y., 1941; 2nd ed., rev., 1946 as *New Guide to Recorded Music*; 3rd ed., rev., 1950); *Mozart on Records* (1942); with C. Burke and E. Canby, *The Saturday Review Home Book of Recorded Music and Sound Reproduction* (1952; 2nd ed., 1956); *Orchestral Music* (1955); *The Musical Life* (1958); ed. *The Composer as Listener: A Guide to Music* (1958); *The Continuity of Music: A History of Influence* (1969); *The Interior Beethoven: A Biography of the Music* (1975); *The Opera Omnibus: Four Centuries of Critical Give and Take* (1976); *In Quest of Music* (1980).

Komitas (real name, **Sogomonian**), Armenian ethnomusicologist and composer; b. Kutina, Turkey, Oct. 8, 1869; d. Paris, Oct. 22, 1935. He studied at the Gevorkian Theological Seminary in Vagharshapat; was made a vardapet (archimandrite) in 1894, taking the name Komitas, after a 7th-century Armenian hymn writer. In 1895 he went to Tiflis, where he studied theory; then lived in Berlin (1896–99), where he took courses at Richard Schmidt's private cons. and with Bellermann, Fleischer, and Friedlaender at the Univ. He studiously collected materials on Armenian folk music, publishing articles on the subject and also composing works utilizing Armenian motifs. In 1910 he moved to Constantinople; the Armenian massacre of 1915 so affected him that he became incurably psychotic, and lived from 1919 in a Paris hospital. His body was reburied in the Pantheon of Armenian Artists in Yerevan in 1936. His collected compositions were ed. by R. Atayan (3 vols., Yerevan, 1960–69).

BIBL.: A. Shaverdian, *K. i armyanskaya musikalmaya kultura* (K. and Armenian Music; Yerevan, 1956); H. Begian, *Gomidas Vartabed: His Life and Importance to Armenian Music* (diss., Univ. of Mich., 1964); G. Geodakian, *K.* (Yerevan, 1969).

Komorous, Rudolf, Czech-born Canadian composer, bassoonist, and teacher; b. Prague, Dec. 8, 1931. He studied bassoon at the Prague Cons. (1946–52) before pursuing his training with Karel Pivoňka (bassoon) and Bořkovec (composition) at the Prague Academy of Music (1952–56); later he studied electronic music in Warsaw (1959). After teaching at the Beijing Cons. (1959–61), he returned to Prague as 1st bassoonist in the orch. of the National Theater. In 1961 he was co-founder of Musica Viva Pragensis. In 1969 he emigrated to Canada and in 1974 became a naturalized Canadian citizen. He was a visiting prof. at Macalester College in St. Paul, Minn. (1969–71). In 1971 he joined the faculty of the Univ. of Victoria to teach composition and advanced theory, and also organized its electronic music studio; he then was acting chairman (1975–76) and director (from 1976) of its school of music. He was director of the School for the Contemporary Arts at Simon Fraser Univ. from 1989 to 1994, remaining on the Univ. faculty until his retirement in 1996. In his music, Komorous has explored various contemporary paths and byways. In some of his scores, he has made use of musical quotations by other composers. His *Sinfony No. 1, Stardust*, makes use of Hoagy Carmichael's famous song.

WORKS: OPERAS: *Lady Whiterose* (1966); *No no miya*, chamber opera (Vancouver, Sept. 30, 1988). **ORCH.:** *Chamber Music* for Bassoon and Small Orch. (1959); *The Gloomy Grace* for Small Orch. (1968); *Bare and Dainty* (1970); *Rossi* for Chamber Orch. (1974; rev. 1975); *Sinfony No. 1, Stardust* (Toronto, Nov. 20, 1988), *No 2, Canadian* (1990; Vancouver, March 17, 1991), and *No. 3, Ex c*, for Strings (1994–95); *Demure Charm* for Bassoon, Flute, and Strings (Toronto, Oct. 17, 1990); Bassoon Concerto (1994–95; Rotterdam, Aug. 31, 1995). **CHAMBER:** *Duettino* for Clarinet and Bassoon (1954); *The Sweet Queen* for Mouth Harmonica, Bass Drum, and Piano (1962); *Olympia* for Flexatone, Mouth Harmonica, Nightingale, Acolyte Bells, Sleigh Bells, and Rattle (1964); *Mignon* for 4 String Bowed Instruments (1965); *Chanson* for Guitar, Clock Spiral, and Viola (1965); *York* for Flute, Oboe or Trumpet, Bassoon, Triangle, Piano, Mandolin, and Double Bass (1967); *Preludes* for 13 Early Instruments (1974); *The Midnight Narcissus* for Alto Flute, Piccolo, Horn, Oboe, Cello, Piano, and Triangle (1977); String Trio (1981; rev. as *Serenade* for String Orch., 1982);

Fumon Manga for Flute, Oboe, Clarinet, Bassoon, and Horn (1981; rev. 1983); *Quartettino: Les Amours Jaunes* for Bassoon, Violin, Viola, and Cello (1983); *The Necklace of Clear Understanding* for Baroque Flute (1986); *Ritratto di Laura Battiferri* for 2 Violins, 2 Violas, and 2 Cellos (1989); *Aokigahara* for Bass Flute and Thing-spa (Tibetan Cymbals) (1989); *Dame's Rocket* for Clarinet, Cornet, Vibraphone, Marimba, Piano, and Contrabass (1991); *Hermione Dreaming* for Baroque Flute, Baroque Bassoon, Conga, Harpsichord, Baroque Viola, and Baroque Cello (1992). **VOCAL:** *23 Poems About Horses* for Narrator and 9 Instruments (1978; rev. 1985); *Vermilion Dust* for Baritone, Chorus, and Small Orch. (1980; rev. 1984); choral pieces; songs. **ELECTRONIC:** *The Tomb of Malevich* (1965); *Anatomy of Melancholy* (1974); *Listening to Rain* (1986).

Komorzynski, Egon, Austrian musicologist; b. Vienna, May 7, 1878; d. there, March 16, 1963. He took courses at various univs., including those of Berlin, Leipzig, Munich, and Vienna (graduated, 1900). He was a prof. of German language studies and literature at Vienna's Handelsakademie (1904–34); was also music critic of the *Österreichische Volkszeitung* for 40 years.

WRITINGS: *Emanuel Schikaneder: Ein Beitrag zur Geschichte des deutschen Theaters* (Berlin, 1901; 2nd ed., rev., 1951); *Mozarts Kunst der Instrumentation* (Stuttgart, 1906); *Mozart: Sendung und Schicksal eines deutschen Künstlers* (Berlin, 1941; 2nd ed., rev., 1955); *Der Vater der Zauberflöte: Emanuel Schikaneders Leben* (Vienna, 1948).

Kondorossy, Leslie, Hungarian-American composer; b. Pressburg, June 25, 1915. He studied at the Academy of Music in Budapest. After World War II, he settled in Cleveland; continued his studies at Western Reserve Univ., and later studied Japanese music and theater at Tokyo's Sophia Univ.; was active as a teacher, conductor, and composer. He was especially proficient in producing short operas.

WORKS: DRAMATIC: OPERAS: *Night in the Puszta* (Cleveland, June 28, 1953); *The Voice* (Cleveland, May 15, 1954); *The Pumpkin* (Cleveland, May 15, 1954); *The Midnight Duel*, radio opera (Cleveland, March 20, 1955); *The String Quartet*, radio opera (Cleveland, May 8, 1955); *Unexpected Visitor* (Cleveland, Oct. 21, 1956); *The 2 Imposters* (Cleveland, Oct. 21, 1956); *The Fox* (Cleveland, Jan. 28, 1961); *The Baksis* (1964); *Nathan the Wise* (1964); *The Poorest Suitor*, children's opera (Cleveland, May 24, 1967); *Shizuka's Dance*, children's opera (Cleveland, April 22, 1969); *Kalamona and the 4 Winds*, children's opera (Cleveland, Sept. 12, 1971); *Ruth and Naomi*, church opera (Cleveland, April 28, 1974). **BALLETS:** *Magic Dance* (1948); *The Ideal* (1950); *King Solomon* (1952). **ORCH.:** *Serenade* for English Horn and Chamber Orch. or Piano (Bavarian Radio, Munich, Feb. 2, 1948); Trombone Concerto (1958); Trumpet Concerto (1959); Harp Concerto (1961); *Prelude and Fugue* (1966); Harpsichord Concerto (1972); *Music* (1973). **CHAMBER:** 2 piano sonatas (No. 1, Cleveland, May 17, 1966; No. 2, 1955); Harpsichord Sonata (1958); Trio for Violin, Viola, and Cello (1958); String Quartet No. 1 (Cleveland, Dec. 9, 1960); *Music* for Flute and Piano (1961); Suite for Violin and Piano (1964); Harpsichord Trio (Cleveland, Dec. 8, 1972); Suite for Brass Sextet (Cleveland, July 9, 1977); *Music* for Organ and Trumpet (1981). **VOCAL:** *Kossuth Cantata* (Cleveland, March 16, 1952); *New Dreams for Old*, cantata for Soloists, Chorus, and Chamber Orch. (Cleveland, Nov. 19, 1959); *David, a Son of Jesse*, oratorio (Cleveland, June 4, 1967); *Jazz Mass* for Voices and Jazz Band (1968); *Ode to the Loyalty of the First*, cantata for Soloists, Chorus, and Chamber Orch. (Cleveland, Sept. 19, 1971); *Sacred Fire*, oratorio (1979).

Kondracki, Michal, Russian-American composer; b. Poltava, Oct. 5, 1902. He studied with Statkowski, Melcer, and Szymanowski at the Warsaw Cons. (graduated, 1926); then with Dukas and Boulanger at the Paris École Normale de Musique (until 1931). He was a music critic in Warsaw (1933–39); with the outbreak of World War II (1939), he went to Brazil; then settled in the U.S. in 1943

WORKS: DRAMATIC: OPERA: *Popiliny* (Warsaw, May 4, 1934; not extant). **BALLET:** *Metropolis* (1929; not extant). **ORCH.:** *Partita* for Chamber Orch. (1928; not extant); *Concerto for Orchestra* (1936); Sym. (1942); *Brazilian Dances* (1944); Concertino for Piano and Chamber Orch. (1944); *Pastorale* (1953); *Afrodite* for Strings (1957). **VOCAL:** *Cantata ecclesiastica* (1937).

Kondrashin, Kirill (Petrovich), noted Russian conductor; b. Moscow, March 6, 1914; d. Amsterdam, March 7, 1981. He studied piano and theory at the Musical Technicum in Moscow; then took a course in conducting with Khaikin at the Moscow Cons. (1932–36). While still a student, he conducted light opera (1934–37); then conducted at the Malyi Opera Theater in Leningrad (1937–41). In 1943 he received an appointment to the staff of the Bolshoi Theater in Moscow, where he conducted a wide repertoire emphasizing Russian operas (until 1956). He received Stalin prizes in 1948 and 1949. In 1969 he was named People's Artist of the U.S.S.R. Kondrashin was the first Soviet conductor to appear in the U.S. (1958), and held numerous subsequent engagements in America, the last being a concert he conducted at the Hollywood Bowl in Feb. 1981. In 1960 he was appointed chief conductor of the Moscow Phil., with which he performed numerous new Soviet works, including Shostakovich's controversial 13th Sym. He also taught at the Moscow Cons. (1950–53; 1972–75). After 1975 he increased his guest engagements outside Russia, and in 1978 decided to emigrate; in 1979 he assumed the post of permanent conductor of the Concertgebouw Orch. in Amsterdam. His conducting style was marked by an effective blend of lyrical melodiousness and dramatic romanticism, without deviating from the prevalent Russian traditions. He publ. a book on the art of conducting (Leningrad, 1970).

BIBL.: D. McIntire, "K. K. (1914–1981)," *Le Grand Baton* (Sept./Dec. 1981).

Konetzni, Anny, esteemed Austrian soprano, sister of **Hilde Konetzni**; b. Ungarisch-Weisskirchen, Feb. 12, 1902; d. Vienna, Sept. 6, 1968. She studied with Erik Schmedes at the Vienna Cons. and later in Berlin with Jacques Stuckgold. She made her operatic debut as a contralto at the Vienna Volksoper in 1925; soon turned to soprano roles. She sang in Augsburg, Elberfeld, and Chemnitz; sang with the Berlin State Opera (1931–34) and also appeared with the Vienna State Opera, La Scala in Milan, the Paris Opéra, and London's Covent Garden. She made her Metropolitan Opera debut in N.Y. as Brünnhilde in *Die Walküre* on Dec. 26, 1934; remained on its roster until the close of the season. After her retirement in 1955, she taught voice in Vienna. She was particularly notable in Wagner and Strauss roles.

Konetzni, Hilde, famous Austrian soprano, sister of **Anny Konetzni**; b. Vienna, March 21, 1905; d. there, April 20, 1980. She studied at the Vienna Cons., and later in Prague with Prochaska-Neumann. She made her operatic debut as Sieglinde in *Die Walküre* in Chemnitz in 1929; then sang at the German Theater in Prague (1932–36). In 1936 she became a member of the Vienna State Opera; also appeared at Salzburg, La Scala in Milan, Covent Garden in London, South America, and the U.S. In 1954 she joined the faculty of the Vienna Academy of Music. She was an outstanding interpreter of Wagner and Strauss.

König, Klaus, German tenor; b. Beuthen, May 26, 1934. He was a student in Dresden of Johannes Kemter. In 1970 he joined the Cottbus City Theater, and in 1973 became a member of the Dessau Landestheater. After singing with the Leipzig City Theater (1978–82), he was a member of the Dresden State Opera (from 1982). In 1984 he made debuts at Milan's La Scala and London's Covent Garden as Tannhäuser, one of his most striking roles. In 1985 he appeared as Tristan at the Théâtre Royal de la Monnaie in Brussels and as Weber's Max at the first performance of the restored Semper Opera House in Dresden. In 1988 he made his U.S. debut as Tannhäuser with the Houston Grand Opera. He also sang opera in Paris, Strasbourg, Madrid, Barcelona, Cologne, Munich, Vienna, and elsewhere in

Europe. Among his other roles are Parsifal, Walther von Stolzing, Lohengrin, Don Alvaro, Florestan, Don José, Radames, and Don Carlos. He also appeared throughout Europe as a concert and oratorio artist.

Konjović, Petar, Serbian composer; b. Sombor, May 6, 1882; d. Belgrade, Oct. 1, 1970. He studied at the Prague Cons. with Novák and Stecker. He was director of the Zagreb Opera (1921–26), the national theaters in Osijek, Split, and Novi Sad (1927–33), and again at the Zagreb Opera (1933–39); then was prof. at the Belgrade Academy of Music (1939–50), where he also served twice as rector.

WORKS: OPERAS: *Vilin Veo* or *Ženidba Miloševa* (The Wedding of Milos; Zagreb, April 25, 1917); *Knez od Zete* (The Duke of Zeta; Belgrade, May 25, 1929); *Koštana* (Zagreb, April 16, 1931); *Sel jaci* (The Peasants; Belgrade, March 3, 1952); *Otadžbina* (Homeland; 1960). **ORCH.:** *Serbia liberata*, symphonic poem (1906); Sym. (1907; rev. by D. Jakšič, 1955); *Na selu* (In the Country), symphonic variations (1915; rev. 1935); *Jadranski capriccio* (Adriatic Capriccio) for Violin and Orch. (1920); *Makar Čudra*, symphonic poem (1944). **CHAMBER:** 3 string quartets; solo pieces for violin, cello, and piano. **VOCAL:** *Moja zemlja* (My Country), 100 folk songs, of which 25 are arranged for Voice and Small Orch.; songs.

Kono, Kristo, Albanian composer; b. Korçë, July 17, 1907; d. Tirana, Jan. 22, 1991. After training at the Milan Cons., he returned to Albania and became a prominent figure in the development of a national music. He eventually championed the cause of socialist realism. Kono composed the first Albanian operetta *Agimi* (The Dawn; Korçë, Nov. 22, 1954). Among his other works were the opera *Lulja e kujtimit* (The Flowers of Remembrance; Tirana, Nov. 5, 1961), orch. pieces, and choral works.

Konoye, Hidemarō, Japanese conductor and composer; b. Tokyo, Nov. 18, 1898; d. there, June 2, 1973. A member of an aristocratic Japanese family, he received his education in Japan and in Europe; attended classes in composition of d'Indy at the Schola Cantorum in Paris; then took courses with Franz Schreker and Georg Schumann at the Berlin Cons. He made his European debut as a conductor with the Berlin Phil. on Jan. 18, 1924. Returning to Japan, he was principal conductor of the New Sym. Orch. in Tokyo (1926–34), specializing in new works of Japanese, European, and American composers. He conducted in the U.S. in 1937 and 1957. He was the composer of several orch. pieces based on Japanese subjects; also orchestrated early Japanese court music for the modern Western orch.; arranged the music of *Madama Butterfly* for the films (inserting many Japanese folk melodies).

BIBL.: B. Flowers, "Viscount H. K. 1898–1973," *Le Grand Baton* (Dec. 1984).

Kont, Paul, Austrian composer and teacher; b. Vienna, Aug. 19, 1920. He studied violin with Vittorio Borri and piano with Hans Nast at the Vienna Cons. (1939–40), then took a course in conducting with Josef Krips and Swarowsky (diploma, 1947) and in composition with Josef Lechthaler (diploma, 1948) at the Vienna Academy of Music; also studied analysis with Josef Polnauer. After attending Fortner's class in Darmstadt (1951), he completed his training with Messiaen, Milhaud, and Honegger in Paris (1952). In 1969 he joined the faculty of the Vienna Academy of Music, where he was a prof. of composition (1980–86). His honors included the Austrian State Prize (1964), the prize of the City of Vienna (1975), the Gold Medal of the City of Vienna (1986), and the Great Honorary Citation of the Austrian Republic (1987). He adopted a serial method applying the statistical principles of valid recurrences of all musical parameters, including pitch, rhythm, and dynamics. He publ. *Antianorganikum* (Vienna, 1967).

WORKS: DRAMATIC: OPERAS: *Indische Legende* (1950); *Peter und Susanne* (Vienna, June 26, 1959); *Inzwischen* (1953–66; Vienna, Jan. 5, 1967); *Lysistrate* (1957–60); *Plutos* (1975–76; Klagenfurt, Feb. 7, 1977); *Die Paare* (1985–86). **BALLETS:** *Italia passata* (1967); *Komodie der Unart* (Vienna, Dec. 12, 1978); *Il ballo del mondo* (1980–82); *Arkadien* (1984); *K* (1984; Klagenfurt, Feb. 2, 1985); *Und der Engel sprach . . .* (1991; Vienna, July 9, 1992); *Daphnis und Chloe* (1993; Dresden, Dec. 11, 1994). **OTHER:** *Traumleben*, musical fairy tale (1958; Salzburg, Dec. 22, 1963); *Celestina*, musical play (1966); other works. **ORCH.:** *Drei Tanzskizzen* (1946–51); *Konzertantes Triptychon* (1950–69); *Komplex E* (1956; Vienna, Sept. 12, 1957); *Concerto des Infants* for Piano and Small Orch. (1956); *Streichersymphonie mit Quodlibet* (1956–65); Cello Concerto (1960; Vienna, May 2, 1966); Concerto for Winds and Strings (1964; Vienna, Nov. 27, 1970); *Divertimento* for Trumpet and Small Orch. (1966–73; Vienna, Feb. 1, 1976); Suite (1971; Vienna, Aug. 14, 1980); *Partita* for Strings (1971–72; Vienna, April 8, 1973); *Kurzkonzert* for Clarinet and Orch. (1973; Vienna, Jan. 25, 1974); *Der Raucher* for Cello and Strings (1973; Vienna, Jan. 22, 1975); *La Symphonie* (1974–80); *Mediterrane Harmonien* for Double Bass and Orch. (1976–77; Vienna, Feb. 28, 1983); *Konzert 1977* for Piano and Orch. (1977; Bregenz, Aug. 13, 1979); *Vivaldi-Monument* (1978; Vienna, Feb. 10, 1980); 5 syms.: No. 1 (1979), No. 2, *Der Toten*, for Soprano, Chorus, and Orch. (1983), No. 3 (1981), No. 4, *Den Liebenden*, for Tenor, Women's Chorus, and Orch. (1983), and No. 5 (1980; Vienna, March 11, 1982); *Sinfonia und Sinfonina* (1979; Vienna, Oct. 4, 1989); Percussion Concerto (1983; Vienna, May 11, 1986); Concerto (1984); *Sache für Musikanten* (1985); *Regeriana* (1987); *Miss Lyss Nausick* (1988); *Serenade* for Strings (1989); *Sequenzen* (1991); *Konzertante Symphonie* for Baritone Saxophone and Strings (Linz, April 30, 1991); *Barock Suite* (1992); *Der grosse Marsch* (1992). **CHAMBER:** *Sonate und Sonatine* for String Quartet (1944–81); Quartet for Oboe, Clarinet, Bass Clarinet, and Bassoon (1947); Quartet for Oboe, Clarinet, Horn, and Bassoon (1956); *Meditationes Beatae Virginis Mariae* for 7 Instruments (1956–61); *Holzmusik I* for Oboe, Clarinet, Bassoon, and Flute (1956–82) and *II* for 6 Instruments (1980–82); Piano Trio (1964); *Triptychon in progressiver Besetzung: I, Serenata a tre* for Flute, Violin, and Viola (1965), *II, Concerto lirico* for Flute, Clarinet, Violin, Viola, and Cello (1963), and *III, Septett* for Flute, Clarinet, Bassoon, Violin, Viola, Cello, and Double Bass (1961); *Blechmusik I:* 1, Trio for Trumpet, Horn, and Trombone (1966), 2, Quartettino for Trumpet, 2 Horns, and Trombone (1966), and 3, Quartet for Trumpet, Horn, Trombone, and Tuba (1968) and *II:* 1, *Blechmusik* for 2 Trumpets, Horn, Trombone, and Tuba (1971), and 2, Harmonien for 2 Trumpets, 2 Horns, 2 Trombones, and Tuba (1973); *Finis austriae* for String Quartet (1973–76); *Musica marina* for 2 Violins, Viola, and Cello (1978); Viola Sonata (1979); *Kammertanz Suite* for Saxophone Quartet (1988); *5 Sketches* for Saxophone Quartet (1989); *En rose et noir* for Piano Trio (1989); *Quadrum I* and *III* for Piano (1992), *II* for Viola (1992), and *IV* for String Quartet (1992); *4 and Half Very Old Dances* for Bassoon Quartet (1992); *Eine Sinfonie* for 4 Harpsichords (1994); *Stück-Werk*, 19 pieces for Alto Saxophone and Accordion (1994); *Toccata-Cantata-Sonata* for Violin and Piano (1994). **VOCAL:** *Bruchstücke zu Franz Grillparzers Trauerspiel "Sappho"* for Alto and Orch. (1993); choral works; songs.

Kontarsky, Alfons, German pianist and teacher, brother of **Aloys** and **Bernhard Kontarsky**; b. Iserlohn, Westphalia, Oct. 9, 1932. He studied piano with Else Schmitz-Gohr and Maurits Frank at the Cologne Hochschule für Musik (1953–55) and with Eduard Erdmann in Hamburg (1955–57). With his brother Aloys, he won 1st prize for duo-piano playing in the Bavarian Radio Competition in Munich (1955); they subsequently toured throughout the world, giving performances of many modern scores. He taught at the Cologne Hochschule für Musik (from 1967). He publ. *Pro musica nova: Studien zum Spielen neuer Musik für Klavier* (Cologne, 1973).

Kontarsky, Aloys, German pianist and pedagogue, brother of **Alfons** and **Bernhard Kontarsky**; b. Iserlohn, Westphalia, May 14, 1931. He studied piano with Else Schmitz-Gohr and

Maurits Frank at the Cologne Hochschule für Musik (1952–55) and with Eduard Erdmann in Hamburg (1955–57). With his brother Alfons, he won 1st prize for duo-piano playing at the Bavarian Radio Competition in Munich (1955); thereafter they made tours throughout the world, specializing in contemporary music. He taught master classes at the Cologne Hochschule für Musik (from 1969).

Kontarsky, Bernhard, German pianist and conductor, brother of **Alfons** and **Aloys Kontarsky**; b. Iserlohn, Westphalia, April 26, 1937. He studied at the Cologne Hochschule für Musik and at the Univ. of Cologne. In 1964 he received the Mendelssohn Prize in Chamber Music. He was a conductor at the Wurttemberg State Theater in Stuttgart; also appeared as a pianist, both as a soloist and in ensemble with his brothers.

Konwitschny, Franz, esteemed German conductor; b. Fulnek, northern Moravia, Aug. 14, 1901; d. Belgrade, July 28, 1962. He studied violin at the German Musikverein School in Brünn and at the Leipzig Cons. (1923–25); while a student, he played viola and violin in the theater orch. and the Gewandhaus Orch. in Leipzig, subsequently becoming a violist in the Fitzner Quartet in Vienna (1925), and also a teacher at the Volkskonservatorium there. He became répétiteur at the Stuttgart Opera in 1927, rising to chief conductor in 1930; after serving as Generalmusikdirektor in Freiburg im Breisgau (1933–38), he assumed that position with the Frankfurt am Main Opera and Museumgesellschaft concerts in 1938, and then with the Hannover Opera in 1945. He was appointed chief conductor of the Gewandhaus Orch. in 1949; was also Generalmusikdirektor of the Dresden State Opera (1953–55) and the (East) Berlin State Opera (1955–62). Although he held posts under both the Nazi and Communist regimes, he successfully avoided political encounters. He died while on tour and was given a state funeral by the German Democratic Republic; his request for a Requiem Mass was honored, much to the chagrin of the authorities.

BIBL.: H. Sanders, ed., *Vermächtnis und Verpflichtung: Festschrift für F. K.* (Leipzig, 1961).

Konya, Sándor, Hungarian tenor; b. Sarkad, Sept. 23, 1923. He was educated at the Budapest Academy of Music; also studied in Detmold, Rome, and Milan. He made his first professional appearance as Turiddu in Bielefeld in 1951, singing there until 1954; after appearing in Darmstadt (1954–55), he joined the Berlin Städtische Oper in 1955; in 1958, sang for the first time at the Bayreuth Festival as Lohengrin; also sang at Milan's La Scala (1960) and the San Francisco Opera (1960–65). On Oct. 28, 1961, he made his Metropolitan Opera debut in N.Y. as Lohengrin; sang there regularly until 1973. He first appeared at London's Covent Garden in the same role (1963). His most notable roles included Walther von Stolzing, Parsifal, Max, and Don Carlos.

Koole, Arend (Johannes Christiaan), Dutch musicologist; b. Amsterdam, April 22, 1908. He studied at the Amsterdam Cons. (1925–30) and with Smijers (musicology; 1933–37) at the Univ. of Utrecht (Ph.D., 1949, with the diss. *Leven en werken van Pietro Antonio Locatelli da Bergamo;* publ. in Amsterdam, 1949; 2nd ed., rev., 1970). He taught at the Cons. in Rotterdam (1938–41), Utrecht (1933–37; 1941–44), and Amsterdam (1946–49); also made appearances as a pianist and conductor. In 1949 he went to South Africa, where he served as senior lecturer in musicology at the Univ. of Bloemfontein; from 1964 to 1973 he was a prof. of music history at the Univ. of Southern Calif. in Los Angeles; in 1974 he returned to South Africa. He publ. a monograph on Mendelssohn (Haarlem, 1953; 2nd ed., 1958).

Koopman, Ton, remarkable Dutch organist, harpsichordist, and conductor; b. Zwolle, Oct. 12, 1944. He studied organ with Simon Jansen and harpsichord with Gustav Leonhardt in Amsterdam, and also took courses in musicology; obtained doctorates in all 3 (1968–70), then won the Prix d'excellence for organ (1972) and harpsichord (1974). After serving as director of Musica Antiqua and as a teacher at the Sweelinck Cons. in Amsterdam, he founded the Amsterdam Baroque Orch. (1979). He toured widely in subsequent years as a conductor, organist, and harpsichordist, excelling in early music performances. In 1992 he founded the Amsterdam Baroque Choir. In 1994 he became co-principal conductor (with Peter Eötvös) of the Netherlands Radio Chamber Orch. in Hilversum.

Kopecký, Pavel, Czech composer; b. Prague, April 5, 1949. He studied with Dobiáš at the Prague Academy of Arts and Music (1972–77) and with Donatoni in Siena (1976); after pursuing postgraduate studies with Sidelnikov at the Moscow Cons. (1977–79), he joined the faculty of the film academy at the Prague Academy of Arts. His music explores the dynamics of modern compositional trends.

WORKS: *3 Studies* for 2 Cellos (1974); 2 piano sonatas (1975, 1979); *Cesty* (The Roads), variations for String Orch. (1976); *Syntéza* for Piano and Tape (1976); Piano Concerto (1977); Quartet for Flute and Strings (1978); *4 Symphonic Preludes—Moscow* (1979); *Bláznovy zápisky* (Madman's Diary), piano suite, after Gogol (1980); Piano Trio (1981); *On a oni* (He and They), concerto for Clarinet and Strings (1982).

Kopelent, Marek, Czech composer; b. Prague, April 28, 1932. He was a student of Řídký at the Prague Academy of Music (1951–55). From 1956 to 1971 he worked as a music ed. for Supraphon, and from 1965 to 1973 he served as artistic director of the Musica viva Pragensis ensemble. In 1969–70 he was active in Berlin on a Deutscher Akademischer Austauschdienst scholarship. In 1991 he became a prof. of composition at the Prague Academy of Music. In his works, Kopelent has made use of the resources of the multimedia avant-garde.

WORKS: DRAMATIC: *Bludný hlas* (The Wandering Voice) for Actress, Chamber Ensemble, and Film and Light Projection ad libitum (1969–70); *Musica*, comic opera for Soprano, 2 Actors, Flute, Oboe, and Harpsichord (1979); *Lament of Women*, melodrama-monologue for Actress, 7 Brass, 4 Women's Voices, and Children's Chorus (1980). **ORCH.:** *3 Movements* for Strings (1958); *Contemplation* for Chamber Orch. (1966); *Quarrels* for 12 Solo Instruments and Orch. (1967–68; Prague, March 7, 1969); *Seclusion* for Viola and Chamber Orch. (1968); *Appassionato* for Piano and Orch. (1970–71); *A Few Minutes with an Oboist* for Oboe and Chamber Orch. (1972); *Veronika's Veil* for 11 Strings (1972–73); *A Cozy Chat* for Saxophone and Orch. (1974–75); Sym. (1982–83; Basel, Feb. 17, 1983); Concertino for English Horn and Small Orch. (1984); *Musique concertante* for Solo Cello, 12 Cellos, and Orch. (1991–92). **CHAMBER:** 5 string quartets (1954, 1955, 1963, 1967, 1980); Trio for Flute, Clarinet, and Bassoon (1962); Trio for Flute, Bass Clarinet, and Piano (1962); *Reflexe* for Flute, Violin, Viola, and Cello (1962); *Music for 5* for Oboe, Clarinet, Bassoon, Viola, and Piano (1964); *Intimissimo* for Chamber Group (1972); *Musique piquante* for Violin and Cimbalom (1971); Wind Quintet (1972); *Rondo* for 5 Percussionists (1973); *Taps* for Harp, Harpsichord, Cimbalom, and Guitar (1974); *Capriccio* for Trumpet (1976); *Etres fins en mouvement* for 6 Percussionists (1989). **VOCAL:** *Bread and Birds*, oratorio (1957–62); *Nenie with Flute* for 9 Women's Voices, Flute, and Chamber Ensemble (1961); *Prayer of Stones* for Narrator, 2 Small Choruses, 3 Gongs, and Tam-tam (1965); *Love* for Soprano and Chamber Ensemble (1967); *Complaints* for 2 Choruses, Trumpet, Percussion, and Tape ad libitum (1969); *Il Canto degli Augei* for Soprano and Orch. (1978); *The Legend*, oratorio (1981); *Agnus Dei* for Soprano and Chamber Ensemble (1982–83); *Messaggio della povertà* for Soprano, Baritone, Children's Chorus, Chorus, and Orch. (1988).

Koppel, Herman D(avid), Danish pianist, teacher, and composer of Polish parentage, father of **Thomas Herman Koppel**; b. Copenhagen, Oct. 1, 1908. He was a student of Simonson (piano), Bangert (theory), and Hansen (orchestration) at the Copenhagen Cons. (1926–29). He made his debut in 1930 as a concert pianist; toured widely in Europe. He taught at the Royal Inst. of Music for the Blind in Copenhagen (1940–43; 1945–49);

lived in Örebro, Sweden (1943–45), to avoid the Nazi occupation. In 1949 he joined the faculty of the Royal Danish Cons. of Music in Copenhagen; was a prof. there (from 1955). As a pianist, he performed the music of Nielsen and other 20th-century Danish composers. His early compositions were influenced by Nielsen, Stravinsky, and Bartók, but he eventually developed an individualistic style, marked by rhythmic intensity and melodic expressivity.

WORKS: DRAMATIC: *Macbeth*, opera (1968; Copenhagen, 1970); also incidental music; music to 29 films. **ORCH.:** Violin Concerto (1929); 7 syms.: No. 1 (1930), No. 2 (1943), No. 3 (1944–45), No. 4 (1946), No. 5 (1955), No. 6, *Sinfonia breve* (1957), and No. 7 (1960–61; Copenhagen, May 16, 1961); *Music* for Strings (1930); 4 piano concertos (1931–32; 1936–37; 1948; 1960–63); *Music* for Jazz Orchestra (1932); *Capriccio* for Violin and Orch. (1934); *Variations* for Small Orch. (1935); 2 concertinos for Strings (1937–38; 1957); Clarinet Concerto (1941); *Sinfonietta* (1945); Concerto for Violin, Viola, and Orch. (1947); Cello Concerto (1952); Oboe Concerto (1970); Chamber Concerto for Violin and Strings (1970); Flute Concerto (1971); *Concerto for Orchestra* (1977–78); *Intrada* (1979); Concerto for Violin, Viola, Cello, and Small Orch. (1984); Bassoon Concerto (1989); *Memory* for the 50th anniversary of the liberation of Denmark (Århus, May 5, 1995). **CHAMBER:** 6 string quartets (1928–29; 1939; 1944–45; 1964; 1975; 1979); Trio for Clarinet, Violin, and Piano (1931); Sextet for Winds and Piano (1942); *Fantasy* for Clarinet (1947); Piano Sonata (1950); *Ternio I* for Cello or Violin and Piano (1951) and *II* for Saxophone (1973); Piano Quintet (1953); Cello Sonata (1956); *Variations* for Clarinet and Piano (1961); *9 Variations* for Piano Trio (1969); Suite for Cello (1971); Piano Trio (1971); *8 Variations and Epilogue* for Piano and 13 Players (1972); *Divertimento* for String Trio (1972); *Pastorale Variations* for Flute, Violin, Viola, and Cello (1975); Piano Quartet (1985); Trio for Clarinet, Cello, and Piano (1986); *Cantilena* for Violin and Cello (1988); *Music* for Wind Octet (1991); *Music* for Violin and Piano (1991). **VOCAL:** *3 Psalms of David* for Tenor, Chorus, and Orch. (1949); *Immortalis mortalium* for Baritone, Boy's Chorus, and Orch. (1954); *2 Biblical Songs* for Soprano and Orch. or Piano (1955); *The Song of the Sun* for Children's Chorus, Strings, and Piano (1958); *Moses*, oratorio (1963–64; Copenhagen, Oct. 21, 1965); Requiem (1965–66); *Hymns of Thanksgiving* for Soli, Chorus, and Orch. (1974).

Koppel, Thomas Herman, Danish composer, son of **Herman D(avid) Koppel**; b. Örebro, Sweden, April 27, 1944. He studied piano and theory with his father at the Royal Danish Cons. of Music in Copenhagen (1963–67). In 1968 he organized in Copenhagen the pop group Savage Rose, and joined the Danish avant-garde in other venturesome activities.

WORKS: DRAMATIC: OPERAS: *Historien om en moder* (The Story of a Mother), after H.C. Andersen (Copenhagen, Oct. 17, 1965); *Bérénice* (1968). **BALLETS:** *Triumph of Death* (1971); *The Emperor's New Clothes*, music for ice ballet (1985–86). **ORCH.:** *Visions fugitives* for Piano and Orch. (1965); *Overture solennelle* (1967); Recorder Concerto (1991). **CHAMBER:** 3 string quartets (1963, 1964, 1966); *Impressions lyriques* for Percussion (1968); *Skipper Klement* for 2 Violins, Viola, Guitar, and Double Bass (1984). **VOCAL:** *Cloches* for Voice and 6 Players (1964); *Phrases*, cantata for 2 Sopranos, 12 Mezzo-sopranos, 4 Solo Instruments, and Orch. (1966; Danish Radio, April 6, 1967); *Concert heroïque* for 3 Pianos, Orch., Chorus, and Wind Machine (Copenhagen, Jan. 9, 1967); *Petit air* for Soprano and 4 Instruments (1966); *Nocturne from a Long Gray Street* for Mezzo-soprano and String Trio (1983); *Carmen* for Voices, Piano, and Drums (1989); *Bella Vita* for Voice and Small Orch. (1993).

Kopytman, Mark, Russian-born Israeli composer, b. Kamenets-Podolski, Dec. 6, 1929. He began his musical training at the music college (graduated, 1950) and pursued medical studies in Chernovtsy (M.D., 1952); he then studied with Simovitz at the Lwów Academy of Music (M.A., 1955) and with S. Bogatyrev at the Moscow Cons. (Ph.D., 1958). He taught in various Russian music institutes (1955–72), then emigrated to Israel, where he joined the faculty of the Rubin Academy of Music in Jerusalem in 1974, serving as its deputy director (from 1985). He also was a guest prof. at the Hebrew Univ. in Jerusalem (from 1979). In 1985 he was a visiting prof. at the Univ. of Pa. and composer-in-residence at the Canberra School of Music. In 1989 he again was at the Univ. of Pa.

WORKS: OPERAS: *Casa mare* (1966); *Chamber Scenes from the Life of Susskind von Trinberg* (1983). **ORCH.:** Sym. (1955); Violin Concertino (1963); *6 Moldavian Tunes* (1965); Piano Concerto (1971); Concerto (1976); *Rotations for Vocalise* (1979); *Kaddish* for Cello and Strings (1982); *Cantus III* for Bass Clarinet and Orch. (1984) and *V* for Viola and Orch. (1990); *Ornaments* for Harpsichord and Orch. (1987). **CHAMBER:** *2 Miniatures on Kazakh Folk Tunes* for String Quartet (1961); String Quartet No. 2 (1965); String Quartet No. 3 (1969); *For Percussion* (1975); *Monodrama* for Sextet (1975); *For Harp* (1976); *For Harpsichord* (1976); *About an Old Tune* for Piano Quartet (1977); *For Organ* (1978); *2 Poems* for Flute, Violin, and Viola (1978); *And a Time for Every Purpose* for Flute, Trumpet, Trombone, and Percussion (1979); *Cantus II* for String Trio (1980) and *IV: Dedication* for Violin (1987); *Discourse I* and *II* for Oboe and String Quartet (1994). **PIANO:** Pieces (1963–83); *2 Preludes and Fugues* (1965); *For Piano I* (1973) and *II* (1974); *Basso Recitative* for 2 Pianos (1977); *Variable Structures* (1986); *Alliterations* (1993). **VOCAL:** *Songs of Kodr*, oratorio (1966); *Unfinished Lines* for Baritone and Orch. (1970); *October Sun* for Mezzo-soprano, Flute, Violin, Cello, Piano, and Percussion (1974); *Voices* for Voice, Flute, Trombones, Percussion, and Strings (1975); *Day and Night Will Rise to Heaven* for Soprano, Mime, Flute, Trumpet, Trombone, and Percussion (1977); *Memory* for Voice and Orch. (1981); *Life of the World to Come* for Voice and Chamber Orch. (1986); *Letters of Creation* for Voice and Strings (1986); *Circles* for Voice, Clarinet, Cello, and Piano (1987); *Scattered Rhymes* for Chorus and Orch. (1988); *A Poem for the Numbers of the Dead* for Baritone and Chamber Ensemble (1988); *Love Remembered* for Chorus and Orch. (1989).

Korchinska, Maria, Russian-born English harpist; b. Moscow, Feb. 16, 1895; d. London, April 17, 1979. She studied at the Moscow Cons., where she was the first harp student to graduate with the gold medal; then was principal harpist in the orch. of the Moscow Opera (1918–24) and also taught at the Moscow Cons. In 1926 she settled in London, where she pursued a career as a soloist with orchs. and as a recitalist. She was particularly active in promoting the composition of new works for the harp.

Korchmarev, Klimenti (Arkadievich), Russian composer; b. Verkhnedneprovsk, July 3, 1899; d. Moscow, April 7, 1958. He studied at the Odessa Cons. with Maliszewski and Biber (graduated with the gold medal, 1919); then went to Moscow (1923), where he became one of the first Soviet composers to embrace revolutionary themes; he wrote *Leviy marsh* (March on the Left; to words by Mayakovsky) for Chorus and Piano (1923); then composed the operas *Ivan-Soldat* (Ivan the Soldier; 1925–27; Moscow, April 3, 1927) and *Desyat dney, kotoriye potryasili mir* (10 Days That Shook the World; 1929–31) and the ballet *Krepostnaya balerina* (The Serf Ballerina; Leningrad, Dec. 11, 1927). His other works in this vein included the choral syms. *Oktyabr* (October; 1931) and *Narodi sovetskoy strani* (The Peoples of the Soviet Land; 1935). From 1939 to 1947 he was in Turkmenistan, where he collected native songs; also composed the first native ballet, *Vesyoliy obmanschchik* (The Merry Deceiver). In 1950 he wrote a cantata, *Svobodniy Kitay* (Free China), for which he received a Stalin Prize.

Kord, Kazimierz, Polish conductor; b. Pogórze, Nov. 18, 1930. He studied piano at the Leningrad Cons.; then took courses in composition and conducting at the Kraków Academy of Music. He conducted at the Warsaw Opera (1960–62); from 1962 to

1970, was artistic director of the Kraków Opera; from 1968 to 1973, was chief conductor of the Polish Radio and Television Sym. Orch. in Katowice. He was chief conductor with the National Phil. in Warsaw (from 1977); was also principal guest conductor of the Cincinnati Sym. Orch. (1980–82), chief conductor of the South-West Radio Sym. Orch. in Baden-Baden (1980–86), and principal guest conductor and music adviser of the Pacific Sym. Orch. in Santa Ana, California (1989–91).

Koréh, Endre, Hungarian bass; b. Sepsiszentgyörgy, April 13, 1906; d. Vienna, Sept. 20, 1960. He was a student of Arpad Palotay in Budapest. In 1930 he made his operatic debut at the Budapest Opera as Sparafucile, and then sang there regularly. In 1948 he became a member of the Vienna State Opera. He also appeared in Salzburg, Glyndebourne, Florence, Paris, Rome, and other European opera centers. On Jan. 22, 1953, he made his Metropolitan Opera debut in N.Y. as Baron Ochs, remaining on its roster until the close of the season. He was best known for his buffo roles, excelling especially in operas by Mozart, Verdi, and Wagner. He also created the role of Caliban in Frank Martin's opera *Der Sturm,* after Shakespeare's *The Tempest* (Vienna, June 17, 1956).

Kořínek, Miroslav, Slovak composer; b. Brno, Jan. 29, 1925. He studied composition with Alexander Moyzes at the Bratislava Cons.; joined its faculty (1950).

WORKS: ORCH.: Viola Concertino (1951); Accordion Concerto (1956); *Divertimento concertato* for Strings (1962); Flute Concerto (1964); Chamber Concerto for Clarinet and Orch. (1966); Horn Concerto (1968). **CHAMBER:** 2 string quartets (1951, 1963); Trio for 2 Oboes and English Horn (1961); Piano Quintet (1967); Wind Quintet (1970); *2 Capriccios* for Trombone and Piano (1973); *Concertante Fantasy* for Flute and Guitar (1974). **VOCAL:** *Atlantide,* cantata (1972).

Korn, Peter Jona, German composer, conductor, and pedagogue; b. Berlin, March 30, 1922. He studied at the Berlin Hochschule für Musik (1932–33), with Rubbra in London (1934–36), Wolpe at the Jerusalem Cons. (1936–38), Schoenberg at the Univ. of Calif. at Los Angeles (1941–42), and Eisler and Toch at the Univ. of Southern Calif. in Los Angeles (1946–47); also studied film composition with Dahl and Rozsa. He was founder-conductor of the New Orch. of Los Angeles (1948–56); then taught at the Univ. of Calif. at Los Angeles (1964–65). Returning to Germany, he was director of Munich's Richard Strauss Konservatorium from 1967 to 1987. He publ. a book of essays, *Musikalische Unwelt Verschmutzung* (Wiesbaden, 1975). His compositional style is a pragmatic Romanticism marked by polycentric tonality in the framework of strong rhythmic counterpoint.

WORKS: OPERA: *Heidi in Frankfurt (Das fremde Haus),* after Johanna Spyri (1961–63; Saarbrücken, Nov. 28, 1978). **ORCH.:** 4 syms.: No. 1 (1941–46; rev. 1956 and 1977), No. 2 (1950–51), No. 3 (1956; rev. 1969), and No. 4, *Ahasver* (1989–90); *Idyllwild,* overture (1947; rev. 1957); *Tom Paine Overture* (1949–50); *Rhapsody* for Oboe and Strings (1951); Concertino for Horn and Double String Orch. (1952); *In medias res,* overture (1953); *Variations on a Theme from The Beggar's Opera* (1954–55; Louisville, Oct. 1, 1955); Saxophone Concerto (1956; rev. 1982); Violin Concerto (1964–65); *Toccata* (1966); *Exorcism of a Liszt Fragment* (1966–68); *Serenade* for 12 Strings (1968); *4 Pieces* for Strings (1970); *Eine Kleine Popmusik* (1972); *Morgenmusik* for Trumpet and Strings (1973); Overture for Strings (1976); *Beckmesser Variations* (1977); Trumpet Concerto (1979); *Romanza concertante* for Oboe and Small Orch. (1987); *Concerto classico* for Harpsichord and Orch. (1988). **CONCERT BAND:** *Salute to the Lone Wolves,* sym. (1980). **CHAMBER:** Cello Sonata (1948–49); Oboe Sonata (1949); 2 string quartets (1949–50; 1963); *Passacaglia and Fugue* for 8 Horns (1952); Horn Sonata (1952); *Aloysia Serenade* for Flute, Viola, and Cello (1953); *Prelude and Scherzo* for Brass Quintet (1953); *Phantasy* for Horn, Violin, Cello, and Piano (1955); *Serenade* for 4 Horns (1957); *Quintettino* for Flute, Clarinet, Bassoon, Cello, and Piano (1964); Wind Quintet (1966); Trio for Violin, Cello, and Piano (1975); Wind Octet (1976); Duo for Viola and Piano (1978); *Fantasia* for Oboe and Organ (1981); piano pieces; organ works. **VOCAL:** *Eine Kleine Deutsche Stadt,* cantata for Tenor, Harpsichord, and Orch. (1980–81); *Psalm of Courage,* cantata for Baritone, Chorus, and Orch. (1983); songs.

BIBL.: N. Düchtel et al., *P.J. K.* (Tutzing, 1989).

Kornauth, Egon, Austrian pianist and composer; b. Olmütz, May 14, 1891; d. Vienna, Oct. 28, 1959. He began piano training as a child and made his debut at age 15; took a course in theory with Fuchs at the Vienna Academy of Music, winning the Austrian State Prize for his Viola Sonata (1912); then studied musicology with Adler at the Univ. of Vienna (Ph.D., 1915, with the diss. *Die thematische Arbeit in Josef Haydns Streichquartetten seit 1780*). He toured widely with his Vienna Trio (1928–29); then received Vienna's Music Prize (1930). He became a teacher of theory at the Vienna Hochschule für Musik (1940) and a prof. at the Salzburg Mozarteum (1945). His music generally followed along Romantic lines, demonstrating considerable contrapuntal skill.

WORKS: ORCH.: 4 symphonic suites (1913–39); Symphonic Overture (1914; rev. 1925); *Ballade* for Cello and Orch. (Vienna, Feb. 20, 1919); *Romantische Suite* (1932–36; rev. 1940); Suite (1937–38). **CHAMBER:** Viola Sonata (1912); Clarinet Sonata (1912–13); Violin Sonata (1913–14); Piano Sextet (1917); String Sextet (1918–19); 2 string quartets (1920, 1920); Piano Trio (1921); Cello Sonata (1922); 2 string quintets (1923; 1938, rev. 1947); Piano Quintet (1931); Clarinet Quintet (1931); piano pieces. **VOCAL:** Choral works; song cycles.

BIBL.: E. Müller von Asow, *E. K.* (Vienna, 1941); T. Leibnitz, *Österreichische Spätromantiker: Studien zu Emil Nikolaus von Rezniček, Joseph Marx, Franz Schmidt, und E. K.* (Tutzing, 1986).

Korndorf, Nikolai, Russian composer, conductor, and teacher; b. Moscow, Jan. 23, 1947. He studied composition (M.M., 1970; D.M.A., 1973) and conducting (M.M., 1979) at the Moscow Cons., where he served on the faculty from 1972 until emigrating to Canada in 1991.

WORKS: DRAMATIC: *MR (Marina and Rainer),* chamber opera (1989; Munich, May 20, 1994); *. . . si muove!,* music theater (1993). **ORCH.:** 3 syms.: No. 1 (1975; Moscow, Dec. 16, 1977), No. 2 (1980; Moscow, Oct. 25, 1982), and No. 3 for Narrator, Boy's Chorus, Men's Chorus, Piano, and Orch. (1989; Frankfurt am Main, Sept. 8, 1992); *Con sordino* for Harpsichord and 16 Strings (Kraków, Sept. 10, 1984); *Concerto capriccioso* for Cello, Strings, and Percussion (1986); *Hymn I (Sempre tutti)* (1987; Munich, May 27, 1988), *II* (1987; Moscow, March 18, 1989), and *III (In Honor of Gustav Mahler)* (1990; Duisburg, May 8, 1991); *Prologue* (1992); *Epilogue* (1993; Montreal, Dec. 7, 1994). **CHAMBER:** *Confessiones* for 14 Players and Tape (Moscow, Dec. 15, 1979); *Movements* for Percussion Ensemble (Moscow, Nov. 30, 1981); *Primitive Music* for 12 Saxophones (1981; Moscow, April 25, 1984); *Yarilo* for Piano and Tape (Moscow, June 8, 1981); Brass Quintet (1985); *Amoroso* for 11 Players (1986; Witten, April 25, 1987); *In Honor of Alfred Schnittke,* trio for Violin, Viola, and Cello (1986); *The Dance in Metal in Honor of John Cage* for Percussionist (1986); *Mozart-variationen* for String Sextet (1990; Berlin, May 11, 1991); *Continuum* for Organ and Tape (1991); *Let the Earth Bring Forth* for Chamber Ensemble (Amsterdam, Sept. 29, 1992); String Quartet (1992). **PIANO:** *Lullaby* for 2 Pianos (Moscow, Oct. 8, 1984). **VOCAL:** *Yes!!* for 3 Singers, Chamber Ensemble, and Tape (1982; Moscow, Dec. 17, 1984); *Singing* for Mezzo-soprano and Tape (1982; Moscow, March 14, 1983); *Tristful Songs* for Chamber Chorus and Percussionist (1983).

Korngold, Erich Wolfgang, remarkable Austrian-born American composer, son of **Julius Korngold**; b. Brünn, May 29, 1897; d. Los Angeles, Nov. 29, 1957. He received his earliest musical education from his father, then studied with Fuchs, Zemlinsky, and Grädener in Vienna. His progress was astounding; at the age of 12, he composed a Piano Trio, which was soon publ., revealing a competent technique and an ability to write in a style strongly influenced by Richard Strauss. About the same time, he wrote (in piano score) a pantomime, *Der Schneemann*; it was orchestrated by Zemlinsky and performed at the Vienna Court Opera (Oct. 4, 1910), creating a sensation. In 1911 Nikisch conducted Korngold's *Schauspiel-Ouvertüre* with the Leipzig Gewandhaus Orch.; that same year, the youthful composer gave a concert of his works in Berlin, appearing also as a pianist; his *Sinfonietta* was conducted by Weingartner and the Vienna Phil. in 1913. Korngold was not quite 19 when his 2 short operas, *Der Ring des Polykrates* and *Violanta*, were produced in Munich. His first lasting success came with the simultaneous premiere in Hamburg and Cologne of his opera *Die tote Stadt* (Dec. 4, 1920). In 1929 he began a fruitful collaboration with the director Max Reinhardt; in 1934 he went to Hollywood to arrange Mendelssohn's music for Reinhardt's film version of *A Midsummer Night's Dream*. He taught at the Vienna Academy of Music (1930–34) before settling in Hollywood, where he distinguished himself as a composer of film scores. He became a naturalized American citizen in 1943. Korngold's music represents the last breath of the Romantic spirit of Vienna; it is marvelously consistent with the melodic, rhythmic, and harmonic style of the judicious modernity of the nascent 20th century. Korngold never altered his established idiom of composition, and was never tempted to borrow modernistic devices, except for some transitory passages in major seconds or an occasional whole-tone scale.

WORKS: DRAMATIC: OPERAS: *Der Ring des Polykrates* and *Violanta* (Munich, March 28, 1916); *Die tote Stadt* (simultaneous premiere, Hamburg and Cologne, Dec. 4, 1920); *Das Wunder der Heliane* (Hamburg, Oct. 7, 1927); *Die Kathrin* (Stockholm, Oct. 7, 1939). **PANTOMIME:** *Der Schneemann* (Vienna, Oct. 4, 1910). **FILM SCORES:** *A Midsummer Night's Dream* (1934); *Captain Blood* (1935); *Another Dawn* (1936); *Anthony Adverse* (1936); *Give us this Night* (1936); *The Green Pastures* (1936); *Rose of the Ranch* (1936); *The Prince and the Pauper* (1937); *The Adventures of Robin Hood* (1938); *Juarez* (1939); *The Private Lives of Elizabeth and Essex* (1939); *The Sea Hawk* (1940); *King's Row* (1941); *The Sea Wolf* (1941); *The Constant Nymph* (1942); *Devotion* (1943); *Between Two Worlds* (1944); *Of Human Bondage* (1945); *Deception* (1946); *Escape me Never* (1946); *Magic Fire* (1954). **ORCH.:** *Schauspiel-Ouvertüre* (Leipzig, 1911); *Sinfonietta* (Vienna, Nov. 28, 1913); Suite from the music to Shakespeare's *Much Ado about Nothing*, for Chamber Orch. (Vienna, 1919); *Sursum Corda*, symphonic overture (1919); Concerto for Piano, Left-hand and Orch. (1923; written for Paul Wittgenstein); *Babyserenade* for Small Orch. (1928); Cello Concerto (1946); Violin Concerto (1946; St. Louis, Feb. 15, 1947, Heifetz soloist); *Symphonic Serenade* for Strings (1949); Sym. in F-sharp (1950; Munich, Nov. 27, 1972); *Theme and Variations* (1953). **CHAMBER:** Piano Trio (1910); Violin Sonata (1912); String Sextet (1916); Piano Quintet (1921); 3 string quartets (1922, 1935, 1945). **PIANO:** 3 sonatas (1908, 1910, 1932). **VOCAL:** *Psalm* for Soprano, Chorus, and Orch. (1941); *Tomorrow* for Alto, Women's Chorus, and Orch., after the film score *The Constant Nymph* (1942); songs.

BIBL.: R. Hoffmann, *E.W. K.* (Vienna, 1923); L. Korngold, *E.W. K.: Ein Lebensbild* (Vienna, 1967); B. Carroll, "K.'s 'Violanta'," *Musical Times* (Nov. 1980); idem, *E.W. K. 1897–1957: His Life and Works* (Paisley, 1984); J. Korngold, *Die K.s in Wien: Der Musikkritiker und das Wunderkind: Aufzeichnungen* (Zürich, 1991).

Korngold, Julius, noted Austrian music critic, father of **Erich Wolfgang Korngold**; b. Brünn, Dec. 24, 1860; d. Los Angeles, Sept. 25, 1945. He was a law student; at the same time, he studied music with Franz Krenn at the Vienna Cons. In 1902 he became music critic of the influential *Neue Freie Presse*, which position he retained until 1934. He was much in the limelight when his son began his spectacular career at the age of 13 as a child composer, and an unfounded suspicion was voiced that Korngold was using his position to further his son's career. He publ. a book on contemporary German opera, *Deutsches Opernschaffen der Gegenwart* (1922). In 1938 he joined his son in the U.S.

BIBL.: F. Endler, *J. K. und die "Neue Freie Presse"* (diss., Univ. of Vienna, 1981); J. Korngold, *Die K.s in Wien: Der Musikkritiker und das Wunderkind: Aufzeichnungen* (Zürich, 1991).

Kórodi, Andras, Hungarian conductor; b. Budapest, May 24, 1922; d. Treviso, Sept. 17, 1986. He studied with Ferencsik (conducting) and Lajtha (composition) at the Budapest Academy of Music, where he later taught conducting (1957–82). He was a conductor (1946–63) and principal conductor (1963–86) of the Hungarian State Opera in Budapest, where he led the premieres of many contemporary scores; was also conductor of the Budapest Phil. (1967–86).

Korte, Karl (Richard), American composer; b. Ossining, N.Y., Aug. 25, 1928. He studied at Illinois Wesleyan Univ. (1948–49); then took composition courses with Mennin and Bergsma at the Juilliard School of Music in N.Y. (B.S., 1953); in 1953 he went to Italy on a Fulbright grant and studied with Petrassi at the Accademia di Santa Cecilia in Rome. From 1954 to 1956 he was again a student at Juilliard, in the composition class of Persichetti (M.S., 1956); later took private lessons with Luening (1956–59), and also attended seminars given by Copland at the Berkshire Music Center in Tanglewood (1960, 1961). He was awarded Guggenheim fellowships (1960, 1970). He taught at Arizona State Univ. (1963–64), the State Univ. of N.Y. at Binghamton (1964–71), and the Univ. of Texas in Austin (from 1971), where he was co-director of its electronic music studio (from 1984). In 1985 he was a Fulbright lecturer on music in New Zealand. His music is quaquaversal in an attractively scientific manner, with the stylistic spectrum ranging from infrared, so to speak, in his archaically impressed works through the mandatory neo-Baroque essays to the ultra-violet rarefaction of mathematical conceits, abstractions, serialism, and electronics.

WORKS: ORCH.: *Concertato on a Choral Theme* (1955); *For a Young Audience* (1959); Sym. No. 2 (1961); *Southwest*, dance overture (1963); Sym. No. 3 (1968); Concerto for Piano and Wind Instruments (1976). **BAND:** *Ceremonial Prelude and Passacaglia* (1962); *Nocturne and March* (1962); *Prairie Song* for Trumpet and Band (1963); *Gestures* for Wind Ensemble, Amplified Double Bass, Percussion, and Piano (1970); *I Think You Would Have Understood* for Trumpet, Tape, and Band (1971); *Fibers* (1977); *Texarcana*, variations on a Texas Folk Song for Large Wind Ensemble (1992). **CHAMBER:** 2 string quartets (1948, 1965); *Fantasy* for Violin and Piano (1959); Quintet for Oboe and Strings (1960); *Matrix* (1968); *Facets* (1969); *Remembrances* for Flute and Tape (1971); *Symmetrics* (1974); Trio for Piano, Violin, and Cello (1977; rev. 1982); Concertino for Trombone, Winds, and Percussion (1981); Double Concerto for Flute, Double Bass, and Tape (1984); *Vochi*, trio for Clarinet, Violin, and Piano (1984); *Colloquy* for Flute and Tape (1987); *Evocation and Dance* for Trombone and Tape (1988); *Extensions* for Percussion and Tape (1994). **PIANO:** *Epigrams* (2 books, 1993–94). **VOCAL:** *Mass for Youth* for Women's Voices and Orch. (1963); *Aspects of Love* for Chorus (1968); *May the Sun Bless Us* for Men's Voices, Brass, and Percussion (1968); *Psalm XIII* for Chorus and Tape (1970); *Pale Is This Good Prince*, oratorio for Solo Voices, Chorus, 2 Pianos, and 4 Percussion (1973); *Of Time and Season* for Solo Voices, Chorus, Piano, and Marimba (1975); *Sappho Says* for Women's Voices, Solo Voice, Flute, and Piano (1980); *The Whistling Wind* for Mezzo-soprano and Tape (1983); *5 New Zealand Songs* for Voice and Piano (1989); *3 Psalm Settings* for Chorus (1991). **COMPUTER:** *Meeting the Enemy* (1994–95).

Korte, Oldřich František, Czech composer; b. Šala, Slovakia, April 26, 1926. During World War II, he was held in a concentration camp; after his release, he studied with Pícha, and later at the Prague Cons. He toured as a pianist and actor with the modernistic group Laterna Magica; he also worked as a photographer. His music is similarly quaquaversal and quite uninhibited in its methods and resources.

WORKS: MUSICAL: *The Pirates of the Fortune* (Vienna, April 15, 1974). **ORCH.:** *Sinfonietta* (1945–47); *Příběh fléten* (The Story of the Flutes; 1949–51; Prague Radio, Oct. 23, 1953); *Concerto grosso* for Strings, Trumpets, and Piano (1954–62; rev. 1968); *Kouzelný cirkus*, suite (1977); *Canzona a Ritornel* (1979); *Zrcadlení* (1981–82). **CHAMBER:** *Iniuria* for Piano (1942–44); *The Drinker's Transformations*, variations for Piano (1945); *In Praise of Death* for Piccolo and Glockenspiel (1948); *Philosophical Dialogues* for Violin and Piano (1964–68).

Korte, Werner, German musicologist; b. Münster, May 29, 1906; d. there, Nov. 26, 1982. He studied mathematics, natural sciences, and musicology at the univs. of Freiburg im Breisgau and Münster (1924–26); then took courses in musicology, art history, and philosophy at the Univ. of Berlin (1926–28), where his principal mentor was Wolf (Ph.D., 1928, with the diss. *Die Harmonik des fruhen 15. Jahrhunderts in ihrem Zusammenhang mit der Formtechnik*, publ. in Münster, 1929). He completed his Habilitation in 1932 at the Univ. of Münster with his *Studien zur Geschichte der Musik in Italien im ersten Viertel des 15. Jahrhunderts* (publ. in Kassel, 1933). He was an assistant lecturer in musicology at the Univ. of Heidelberg (1928–31), then became director of the musicology dept. at the Univ. of Münster (1932), where he was made reader (1937) and prof. (1946).

WRITINGS: *Deutsche Musikerziehung in Vergangenheit und Gegenwart* (Danzig, 1932); *J.S. Bach* (Berlin, 1935); *Ludwig van Beethoven* (Berlin, 1936); *Robert Schumann* (Potsdam, 1937); *Musik und Weltbild* (Leipzig, 1940); *Händel und der deutsche Geist* (Leipzig, 1942); *Bruckner und Brahms: Die spätromantische Lösung der autonomen Konzeption* (Tutzing, 1963); *De musica: Monolog über die heutige Situation der Musik* (Tutzing, 1966).

Kortekangas, Olli, Finnish composer and teacher; b. Turku, May 16, 1955. He was a student of theory and composition of Rautavaara and Hämeeniemi at the Sibelius Academy in Helsinki (1974–81). In 1977 he was a founding member of the contemporary music society Korvat Auki (Ears Open). Following further training with Schnebel in Berlin (1981–82), he returned to Helsinki and taught at the National Theater Academy (1983–86) and then at the Sibelius Academy. As a composer, Kortekangas has followed an independent course in which he confronts and incorporates various styles and techniques in a stimulating fashion.

WORKS: DRAMATIC: *Short Story*, opera (1979–80; Helsinki, Oct. 15, 1980); *Grand Hotel*, opera (1984–85; Helsinki, Sept. 12, 1987); *Memoria*, radiophonic piece (1989); incidental music. **ORCH.:** *Arr* for Strings (1980); *Fanfares* for 3 Instrumental Groups (1980); *Ökologie 1: Vorspiel* (1983; Helsinki, Jan. 25, 1984) and *2: Konzert* (1986–87; Helsinki, March 11, 1987); *Alba* (1988; Espoo, March 19, 1989); *Fanfare* (Porvoo, June 28, 1991); *Concert Piece* for Clarinet, Cello, and Orch. (1993–94). **CHAMBER:** *Threnody* for Horn and Piano (1977; Helsinki, Dec. 13, 1978); *Konsequenz* for Violin and Piano (1982–83); *Sehr schnell* for Violin (1984); *Koraali "Punavuoren nuottikirjasta"* for Harmonium (1986); *Emotion* for Variable Ensemble and Electronics (Helsinki, Aug. 27, 1988); *Omaggio a M.C. Escher* for Alto Flute and Guitar (Viitasaari, July 22, 1990); *Iscrizione* for Clarinet and Cello (Warsaw, Sept. 12, 1990); *Mi* for Violin and Piano (1991). **KEYBOARD: PIANO:** *Cereal Sweet* for Piano, 4-hands (1978); *Fingerprints* (1980). **ORGAN:** Sonata (Helsinki, Sept. 25, 1979). **VOCAL:** *Vihreä madonna* (The Green Madonna) for Chorus (Espoo, Dec. 7, 1975); *3 Early Songs* for Voice and Piano (1975; rev. 1980); *Tuutulaulu* (Lullaby) for Soprano and Alto Voices (Nilsiä, June 1980); *Memoarer* (Memoirs) for Voice and Piano (1982; Jyväskylä, June 28, 1983); *Paraabeli* (Parable) for 5 Men's Voices (1983; Helsinki, March 1, 1985); *Metamatiikkaa* for Soprano and Alto Voices and Instruments Obbligato (1983); *Madrigaali* for Women's Chorus (Turku, May 12, 1984); *Lumen valo* (The Glow of Snow) for Men's Chorus and Percussion (1984; Helsinki, Dec. 8, 1985); *MAA* (Earth) for Children's Chorus and Instruments (1984–85; Joensuu, June 19, 1985); *3 Texts by Waltari* for Chorus (1985; Helsinki, March 15, 1986); *Istuin meren rannalla* (I Was Sitting by the Sea) for Voice (1987; Helsinki, Jan. 9, 1988); *Verbum* for Double Chorus (1987); *A* for Children's Chorus, Percussion, and Electronics (1987–88; Tampere, Feb. 20, 1988); *Amores*, 3 songs for Mezzo-soprano and Orch. (Oulu, Nov. 30, 1989). **ELECTRONIC:** *Memoria* (1988–89).

Kortschak, Hugo, Austrian-American violinist, conductor, and teacher; b. Graz, Feb. 24, 1884; d. Honolulu, Sept. 20, 1957. He studied violin with Ševčik at the Prague Cons.; went to America and in 1913 organized in Chicago the Kortschak Quartet, later renamed Berkshire String Quartet. He was head of the violin dept. at Yale Univ. (1924–52); then was a member of the Honolulu Sym. Orch. He was awarded the Coolidge Medal (1938).

Kortsen, Bjarne, Norwegian musicologist; b. Haugesund, July 4, 1930. He studied music and electrical engineering; was employed by the Norwegian railways while studying musicology at the Univ. of Oslo (M.A., 1962); later studied at the Univ. of Glasgow (Ph.D., 1964). He publ. *Fartein Valen, Life and Music* (3 vols., Oslo, 1965); *Modern Norwegian Chamber Music* (Haugesund, 1965); *Contemporary Norwegian Orchestral Music* (Berlin, 1969); *Chamber Music Works by Johan Svendsen* (Bergen, 1971).

Kósa, György, Hungarian pianist, teacher, and composer; b. Budapest, April 24, 1897; d. there, Aug. 16, 1984. He exhibited a precocious talent for music, and when he was 10 years old studied piano privately with Bartók and then later with him at the Royal Academy of Music in Budapest (1908–15); also studied composition with Herzfeld and Kodály (1908–12) and piano with Dohnányi (1915–16) there. He was co-répétiteur at the Royal Opera House in Budapest (1916–17); then toured Europe and North Africa as a pianist (1917–20); subsequently was a theater conductor in Tripoli (1920–21). He then returned to Budapest as an accompanist (1921); from 1927 to 1960 he was prof. of piano at the Budapest Academy of Music, with the exception of a period during World War II when he was compelled to work as a manual laborer in a war camp. He was actively engaged in the promotion of modern Hungarian music; played both traditional and contemporary scores. He was awarded the Erkel Prize (1955); was made a Merited Artist (1963) and an Honored Artist (1972) of his homeland. As a composer, he was initially influenced by Bartók, but he later developed an individualistic style of expressionism.

WORKS: DRAMATIC: OPERAS: *A király palástja* (The King's Robe; 1926); *Az két lovagok* (2 Knights), comic opera (1934; Budapest, 1937); *Cenodoxus*, mystery opera (1942); *Anselmus diák* (Student Anselmus; 1945); *A méhek* (The Bees; 1946); *Tartuffe*, comic opera (1951); *Pázmán lovag* (Knight Pázmán), comic opera (1962–63); *Kocsonya Mihály házassága* (The Marriage of Mihály Kocsonya), comic opera (1971); *Kiálts város* (City, Shout!; 1980–81). **BALLETS:** *Fehér Pierrot* (White Pierrot; 1916; Budapest, 1920); *Phaedra* (1918); *Dávid király* (King David; 1936); *Ének az örök bánatról* (Song about the Everlasting Sorrow; 1955). **PANTOMIMES:** *Mese a királykisasszonyról* (A Tale of a Princess; 1919); *Laterna Magica* (1922; Budapest, Feb. 23, 1927); *Árva Józsi három csodája* (The 3 Miracles of Józsi Arva; 1932; Budapest, Feb. 26, 1933). **ORCH.:** Suite (1915); 6 Pieces (1919); 9 syms. (1920, 1927, 1933, 1936, 1937, 1946, 1957, 1959, 1969); Suite, *Ironic Portraits* (1924); *Fantasy on 3 Folksongs* (1948); *Dance Suite* (1951); Concerto for Piano, Violin, Cymbals, Percussion, and Orch. (1973). **CHAMBER:** 8 string quartets (1920, 1929, 1933, 1936, 1956, 1959, 1963, 1965); *Chamber Music* for 17 Instruments (1928); *6 Portraits* for 6 Horns and Harp (1938); *Divertimento* for String Quartet and Cymbals (1938); Quintet for Flute, Clarinet, Bassoon, Horn, and Harp (1938); Trio for Flute, Viola, and Cello (1946); Trio for Soprano, Clarinet, and Violin (1947); Wind Quintet (1960); Piano Trio (1962); *Duo* for Violin and Cello

(1964); Cello Sonata (1965); *6 Intermezzos* for String Trio (1969); *Dialogus* for Bass Tuba and Marimba (1975). **PIANO:** 3 sonatas (1941, 1947, 1956); other works. **CHORAL: ORATORIOS:** *Jonah* (1931); *Easter Oratorio* (1932); *Saulus* (1935); *Joseph*, chamber oratorio (1939); *Elijah*, chamber oratorio (1940); *Christus*, chamber oratorio (1943); *Hajnóczy* (1954); *Villon* (1960). **CANTATAS:** *Laodomeia* (1924); *Job* (1933); *Küldetés* (Mission; 1948); *Szól az úr* (The Lord Is Saying; 1957); *Amor sanctus* (1958); 2 cantatas (1964); *Bárányka* (Lambkin; 1965); *Balázsolás* (St. Blaise Play; 1967); *Cantata humana* (1967); *Orpheus, Eurydike, Hermes* (1967); *Öszikék* (Autumn Songs; 1970); *Johannes* (1972); *Szalkak* (Splints; 1972); *Perlekedő prófécia* (A Quarrelling Prophecy; 1972); 2 cantatas (1973–74); Cantata (1974); *Bikasirato* (Dirge for a Bull; 1975); *Kakasszó* (Crowing of the Cock; 1975). **OTHER WORKS:** *Dies irae* (1937); 2 masses (1946, 1949); 2 requiems (1949, 1966); *Te Deum* (1949); *Biblical Mass* (1951); *De profundis* (1970); some 500 songs.

BIBL.: M. Pándi, *K. G.* (Budapest, 1966).

Kosakoff, Reuven, American pianist and composer; b. New Haven, Conn., Jan. 8, 1898; d. N.Y., May 6, 1987. He studied at Yale Univ. and at the Juilliard School of Music in N.Y.; then went to Berlin as a private piano student of Artur Schnabel. He wrote several biblical cantatas; 2 Sabbath services; Piano Concerto on Hebrew themes (Pittsburgh, March 24, 1941); *Jack and the Beanstalk* for Narrator and Orch. (New Haven, April 22, 1944).

Koshetz, Nina (Pavlovna), Russian-American soprano; b. Kiev, Dec. 30, 1894; d. Santa Ana, Calif., May 14, 1965. Her father, Paul Koshetz, was a tenor; she began piano study when she was 4 and gave her first recital at 9; then enrolled at the Moscow Cons. at 11, studying piano with Igumnov and Safonov and voice with Enzo Masetti; later studied with Félia Litvinne. She toured Russia with Rachmaninoff, of whose songs she was a congenial interpreter; also toured with Koussevitzky and his orch.; made her operatic debut as Donna Anna at the Imperial Opera in St. Petersburg (1913); toured the U.S. with the Ukrainian National Chorus, under the conductorship of her brother (1920); then settled there. She sang the role of Fata Morgana in the first performance of Prokofiev's *The Love for 3 Oranges* (Chicago, Dec. 30, 1921); subsequently devoted herself mainly to concert appearances; later taught voice.

BIBL.: J. Dennis, "N.P. K.," *Record Collector,* XVII (1967–68; with discography).

Košler, Zdeněk, Czech conductor; b. Prague, March 25, 1928; d. there, July 2, 1995. He studied in Prague with Grünfeldová (piano), Jeremiáš and Řídký (theory and composition), and Dědeček (conducting); then took conducting courses with Ančerl, Brock, and Doležil at the Academy of Music (1948–52). He made his conducting debut at the National Theater of Prague with *Il barbiere di Siviglia* (1951), and conducted there until 1958; then conducted the Olomouc (1958–62) and Ostrava (1962–66) operas. In 1956 he won 1st prize in the Besançon competition, and in 1963 1st prize in the Mitropoulos competition. He was chief conductor of the Prague Sym. Orch. (1966–67); also served as Generalmusikdirektor of the Komische Oper in East Berlin (1966–68); then was chief conductor of the Slovak National Theater in Bratislava (1971–79). He was chief conductor of the Prague National Theater from 1980 to 1985, and again from 1989 to 1991. In 1974 he was made an Artist of Merit and in 1984 a National Artist by the Czech government.

Kosma, Joseph, Hungarian-French composer; b. Budapest, Oct. 22, 1905; d. La Roche-Guyon, near Paris, Aug. 7, 1969. He studied at the Budapest Academy of Music; then with Eisler in Berlin (1929). He settled in Paris (1933).

ORCH.: DRAMATIC: COMIC OPERAS: *Les Chansons de Bilitis* (1954); *Un Amour électronique* (Paris, 1962); *La Révolte des canuts* (Lyons, 1964); *Les Hussards* (Lyons, Oct. 21, 1969). **BALLETS:** *Le Rendez-vous* (Paris, June 15, 1945); *Baptiste* (1946); *L'Ecuyère* (1948); *Le Pierrot de Montmartre* (1952). Also film scores to *La Grande Illusion, Les Enfants du paradis,* etc. **OTHER:** *Les Ponts de Paris,* oratorio (1947); piano pieces; songs.

BIBL.: M. Fleuret, ed., *J. K., 1905–1969: Un homme, un musicien* (Paris, 1969).

Kostelanetz, André, highly successful Russian-born American conductor, uncle of **Richard Kostelanetz**; b. St. Petersburg, Dec. 22, 1901; d. Port-au-Prince, Haiti, Jan. 13, 1980. He studied at the St. Petersburg Cons. In 1922 he went to the U.S., becoming a naturalized American citizen (1928). He came to prominence as a conductor on the radio; appeared regularly with the CBS Sym. Orch. (from 1930); later enjoyed tremendous success with his own orch. on radio and recordings, making the lush "Kostelanetz sound" and arrangements his trademark. He married **Lily Pons** in 1938, but they subsequently were divorced. During World War II, he conducted many concerts for the U.S. armed forces. He later appeared as a guest conductor with leading orchs. in North America, Europe, Israel, and Japan. He also conducted popular concerts in America and in Europe; made successful arrangements of light music, his technique of massive concentration of instrumental sonorities and of harmonic saturation by means of filling in harmonies with inner thirds and sixths having influence upon film music. An intelligent musician, he commissioned special works from American composers, of which the most successful was Copland's *Lincoln Portrait.* With G. Hammond, he wrote *Echoes: Memoirs of André Kostelanetz* (N.Y., 1981).

Kostelanetz, Richard, versatile American music critic, writer on contemporary music and the arts, and composer, nephew of **André Kostelanetz**; b. N.Y., May 14, 1940. He studied American civilization and history at Brown Univ. (A.B., 1962) and Columbia Univ. (M.A., 1966); was a Fulbright scholar at King's College, Univ. of London (1964–65), and also attended classes at London's Morley College and the New School in N.Y. He lectured at Harvard Univ., Wellesley College, Carnegie-Mellon Univ., and the Univ. of Calif. at Santa Cruz, among other institutions. His extensive list of publications includes articles, books, poetry, fiction, plays, and experimental prose; among his numerous anthologies on contemporary American arts are several with emphasis on music, including *The Theatre of Mixed Means* (N.Y., 1968), *Master Minds* (N.Y., 1969), *Conversing with Cage* (N.Y., 1988), *On Innovative Musicians* (N.Y., 1989), *On Innovative Art(ist)s* (Jefferson, North Carolina, 1992), *On Innovative Performance(s)* (Jefferson, North Carolina, 1994), and *Cage (Ex)plain(ed)* (N.Y., 1995). Included in his compositional output are audiotapes and videotapes as well as a number of films and holograms, many of which have been exhibited and broadcast around the world. He was a visiting artist at Syracuse Univ. (1975), the Electronic Music Studio of Stockholm (1981–88), and the Experimental Television Center in Oswego, N.Y. (1985–90). He wrote numerous theatrical (*Epiphanies,* 1980) and performance (*Central Park,* 1980) texts; also composed choreographic works (*Invocations,* 1985). He prepared extended features for radio, and his work has appeared in both solo and group exhibitions. Among his awards are a Pulitzer fellowship for critical writing (1965), a Guggenheim fellowship (1967), and annual ASCAP stipends (from 1983). His compositions include audiocassette eds. (*The 8 Nights of Hanukah/Praying to the Lord,* 1983; *Onomatopoeia,* 1988; *Carnival of the Animals/Karneval der Tiere,* 1988) and hörspiels (*Die Evangelien,* 1982; *Invocations,* 1983; *New York City,* 1984; *The Gospels Abridged,* 1986; *Kaddish,* 1990), many of which were commissioned by the West German Radio; also *Lovings* (1990). His videotapes, for which he customarily provides the visuals, include *3 Prose Pieces* (1975), *Epiphanies* (1980), *Seductions/Relationships* (1987), and *Kinetic Writings* (1989). He describes his critical writings and his art as both "avant-garde" and "anarchist libertarian."

Kostić, Dušan, Croatian composer; b. Zagreb, Jan. 23, 1925. He studied at the Belgrade Academy of Music (1947–55); later took a course in conducting with Scherchen in Bayreuth (1955). He was music ed. for Radio Belgrade (1957–59); then taught at his alma mater (from 1964). He incorporated neo-Classical, impressionistic, and serial techniques in his music; also wrote occasional pieces on national folk themes.

WORKS: OPERA BUFFA: *Majstori su prvi ljudi* (Belgrade, April 23, 1962). **ORCH.:** *Contrasts*, symphonic poem (1954); 2 syms. (1957, 1961); *Crnogorska suita* (1957); *Kragujevac*, symphonic poem for Voices and Orch., commemorating the execution of the schoolboys at Kragujevac in 1941 by the Nazi occupation forces (Belgrade, Feb. 5, 1962). **OTHER:** Chamber works, including *Sonata amorosa* for Violin and Piano (1957); piano pieces; choruses; songs.

Kostić, Vojislav, Serbian composer; b. Belgrade, Sept. 21, 1931. He studied in his native city; adopted a sophisticated style of utilitarian music. His *Karakteri* for Clarinet, Piano, and 18 Percussion Instruments (1958) had numerous performances in Yugoslavia. He also wrote a *Divertimento* for Wind Quintet; Suite for Bassoon and Piano; *Ciganska pri-ča* (Gypsy Tale) for Men's Chorus and Chamber Orch., to Gypsy texts (1964).

Kostov, Georgi, Bulgarian composer; b. Sofia, Jan. 21, 1941. He studied composition with Vladigerov and Stoyanov at the Bulgarian State Cons. in Sofia, graduating in 1966; pursued his studies at the Moscow Cons. (1972); then taught at his alma mater.

WORKS: BALLET: *The Broadside of "Avrora"* (1967). **ORCH.:** Clarinet Concerto (1958); Viola Concertino (1965); Concerto for Horn, Strings, and Timpani (1966); *Youth Overture* (1967); *3 Diaphonous Dances* (1972); *Poem* for Trumpet, Percussion, and Strings (1973); *Prelude, Chorale, and Fugue* (1974); *Rhythmic Movements* (1974); *Antiphonous Dialogues* (1974); *September Ballad* (1974). **OTHER:** 2 cantatas: *The Communist Man* (1964) and *We Are Proud of You, Our Party* (1975); 2 oratorios: *Glorious Days* (1969) and *Alive He Is* (1976); chamber music; choral songs; popular music.

Kosugi, Takehisa, inventive Japanese composer and violinist; b. Tokyo, March 24, 1938. He studied at the Tokyo Univ. of Fine Arts and Music, then founded the group Ongaku, which introduced mixed-media improvisational performance in Japan. In 1969 he founded the Taj Mahal Travelers ("TMT"), with which he toured in India, the Near East, and Europe; upon returning to Japan, the group frequently participated in rock and jazz festivals. In 1976 Kosugi was invited to compose for the Merce Cunningham Dance Co., and, after moving to the U.S. in 1977, appeared in performances with John Cage and David Tudor. Kosugi regularly creates installations in which he employs acoustic and self-designed electronic instruments; his aesthetic premise is that a performance must make the invisible aspects of a given situation perceptible, audible, and tangible, revealing what is hidden and enabling sounds to be seen as well as heard. In this original capacity he has performed since 1978 in Paris, Rome, Berlin, Bremen, Cologne, and London. Among his commissioned works for the Merce Cunningham Dance Co. are *S.E. Wave/E.W. Song* (1976), *Interspersion* (1979), *Cycles* (1981), *Spacings* (1984), *Assemblage* (1986), *Rhapsody* (1987), and *Spectra* (1989). His major installations include *Interspersions for 54 Sounds* (1980), *Spacings* (audiovisual version; 1985), and *Loops* (1988). As a violinist, he made a remarkable recording, entitled simply *Violin Improvisations* (1990). In 1995 he succeeded David Tudor as music director of the Cunningham Dance Co.

Köth, Erika, German soprano; b. Darmstadt, Sept. 15, 1925; d. Speyer, Feb. 20, 1989. She was a student in Darmstadt of Elsa Bank. In 1947 she won 1st prize in a Hessian Radio competition, and then made her debut as Adele in a Darmstadt radio broadcast. In 1948 she made her stage debut as Philine in *Mignon* in Kaiserslautern. After singing in Karlsruhe (1950–53), she appeared with the Bavarian State Opera in Munich (from 1953), the Vienna State Opera (from 1953), and in Berlin (from 1961); she also made appearances at the Salzburg (1955–64) and Bayreuth (1965–68) festivals. In 1956 she was named a Bavarian and in 1970 a Berlin Kammersängerin. She taught at the Cologne Hochschule für Musik (from 1973), and then at the Heidelberg-Mannheim Hochschule für Musik (from 1980). Among her esteemed portrayals were Zerbinetta, the Queen of the Night, Susanna, Constanze, Donna Elvira, Lucia, and Sophie.

BIBL.: K. Adam, *Herzlichst! E. K.* (Darmstadt, 1969).

Kotik, Petr, Czech-born American flutist and composer; b. Prague, Jan. 27, 1942. He studied flute with František Cech at the Prague Cons. (B.A., 1962) and at the Prague Academy of Music (M.A., 1969); also had lessons in composition with Rychlik in Prague, and in flute with Hans Resnicek (M.A., 1966) at the Vienna Academy of Music; studied composition at the Vienna Academy of Music with Schiske, Jelinek, and Cerha (B.A., 1966). In 1961 he founded Musica Viva Pragensis, and in 1966 the Prague experimental music ensemble QUAX. He went to the U.S. in 1969; became a naturalized American citizen in 1977. From 1969 to 1974 he was a member of the Center of the Creative and Performing Arts at the State Univ. of N.Y. in Buffalo. In 1970 he founded the S.E.M. Ensemble, with which he toured in the U.S. and abroad; also toured as a solo flutist. He taught flute (1971–77) and composition (1976–77) at the State Univ. of N.Y. in Buffalo; also taught composition at York Univ. in Toronto (1975–76). In 1983 he settled in N.Y.; continued to tour with the S.E.M. Ensemble and as a soloist.

WORKS: *Congo* for Flute, Oboe, Clarinet, Bassoon, Viola, Cello, and Double Bass (1962; Prague, Jan. 18, 1963); *Kontrapunkt II* for Alto Flute, English Horn, Clarinet, Bassoon, Viola, and Cello (1962–63; Vienna, Oct. 8, 1963); *Spontano* for Piano and 10 Wind Instruments (1964; Buffalo, May 22, 1973); *6 Plums* for Orch. (1965–68); *Contraband* for Live Electronics and 2 to 6 Performers (Cologne, April 28, 1967); *Aria*, tape or theater piece (1969; Buffalo, May 27, 1971); *Alley* for Instrumental Ensemble (1969–70; N.Y., March 18, 1971); *There Is Singularly Nothing*, 21 solos for Ensemble (1972; rev. version as *There Is Singularly Nothing II* for Voices and Instruments, N.Y., Dec. 19, 1995); *John Mary* for 2 Voices, 3 Melodic Instruments, and Percussionist (1973–74; Witten, April 27, 1974); *Many Many Women* for 2, 4, or 6 Singers and 2, 4, or 6 Instruments (1975–78); *Drums* for Percussion Ensemble (1977–81); *Explorations in the Geometry of Thinking* for Vocal Ensemble (1978–82); *August/October* for Viola or Cello and Ensemble (1981; rev. as *Apparent Orbit*, 1981–85); *Music* for Winds (1981–82); *Solos and Incidental Harmonies* for Flute, Violin, and 2 Percussion (1983–84); *Integrated Solo* for Flute, Tambourine, Trumpet, and Keyboard (1986–88); *Wilsie Bridge* for Winds, Keyboards, and Percussion (1986–87; N.Y., Jan. 13, 1987); *Letters to Olga* for 5 Voices, Flute, Trumpet, and 3 Guitars (1989–91; N.Y., May 7, 1991); *Quiescent Form* for Orch. (1994–95).

Kotoński, Wlodzimierz, Polish composer; b. Warsaw, Aug. 23, 1925. He studied theory with Rytel at the Warsaw Cons. (1945–51); also privately with Szeligowski in Poznań (1950–51); later took courses in Darmstadt (1957–60). In the meantime, he began experimenting with alteration of sound by electronic means; produced an *Étude concrète* in which a single stroke of cymbals was electronically metamorphosed and expanded into a work of considerable length (1949). He did research in Polish folk music at the State Inst. of Art (1951–59); then studied the problems of musique concrète with Schaeffer in Paris. He subsequently worked at the Electronic Music Studio of the West German Radio in Cologne (1966–67); taught electronic music at the Warsaw Cons. (from 1967) and also lectured at the State Univ. of N.Y. at Buffalo (1978). In 1983 he became president of the Polish Soc. for Contemporary Music. He publ. *Instrumenty perkusyjne we współczesnej orkiestrze* (Percussion Instruments in the Modern Orchestra; Kraków, 1963).

WORKS: ORCH.: *Poème* (1949); *Danses montagnardes* (1950); *Prelude and Passacaglia* (1953); *Musique en relief*, cycle of 5 miniatures for 6 Orch. Groups (Darmstadt, Sept. 5, 1959); *Concerto per quattro* for Harp, Harpsichord, Guitar, Piano, and Chamber Orch. (1960); *Music* for 16 Cymbals and

Strings (Warsaw, Sept. 20, 1969); Oboe Concerto (1972); *Wind Rose* (1976); *Bora* (1979); *Sirocco* (1981); *Terra incognita* (1984). **CHAMBER:** *Étude concrète* for a single stroke of Cymbals electronically metamorphosed (1949; Darmstadt, July 9, 1960); *6 Miniatures* for Clarinet and Piano (1957); *Chamber Music* for 21 Instruments and Percussion (Warsaw, Oct. 2, 1958); Trio for Flute, Guitar, and Percussion (1960); *Canto* for 18 Instruments (1961); *Selection I* for 4 Jazz Players (1962); 2 wind quintets (1964, 1967); *Monochromie* for Oboe (1964); *A battere* for Guitar, Viola, Cello, Harpsichord, and Percussion (1966); *Pour quatre* for Clarinet, Trombone, Cello, and Piano (1968); *Multiplay*, instrumental theater for Brass Quintet (1971); *Promenade* for Clarinet, Trombone, and Cello, all electronically amplified, and 2 Synthesizers (1973); *Spring Music* for Flute, Oboe, Violin, and Synthesizer (1978); *Lyric Scenes* for 9 Performers (1986); *Tialoc*, duo for Harpsichord and Percussion (1987); *Birds*, 8 pieces for Clarinet, Cello, and Piano (1988). **COMPUTER:** *Textures* (1984).

Kounadis, Arghyris, Greek composer; b. Constantinople, Feb. 14, 1924. He was taken to Athens in his infancy; studied piano at home and then with S. Farandatos at the Athens Cons. (graduated, 1952); also studied law at the Univ. of Athens. After studying composition with Papaioannou at Athens's Hellenic Cons. (graduated, 1956), he continued his studies with Fortner in Freiburg im Breisgau (1958–61). In 1963 he joined the faculty of the Freiburg im Breisgau Hochschule für Musik, becoming a prof. there in 1972.

WORKS: DRAMATIC: *Der Gummisarg* (1968); *Die verhexten Notenstander* (1971); *Der Ausbruch* (1975); *Die Bassgeige* (1979; rev. 1987); *Lysistrata*, after Aristophanes (1983); *Der Sandmann* (1986). **ORCH:** *Chorikon I* (1958) and *II* (1960); *Triptychon* (1964); *Heterophonika Idiomela* (1967). **VOCAL:** *Quattro pezzi per trio et soprano* (1968); *Die Nachtigall* for Soprano and 10 or More Double Basses (1975); *9 Gedichte des M. Sochtouris* for Bass, Chorus, and Instrumental Ensemble (1980).

Koussevitzky, Serge (Alexandrovich), celebrated Russian-born American conductor; b. Vishny-Volochok, July 26, 1874; d. Boston, June 4, 1951. His father and his 3 brothers were all amateur musicians. Koussevitzky learned to play the trumpet and took part, with his brothers, in a small wind ensemble, numbering 8 members in all; they earned their living by playing at balls and weddings and occasionally at village fairs. At the age of 14, he went to Moscow; since Jews were not allowed to live there, he became baptized. He then received a fellowship with free tuition at the Musico-Dramatic Inst. of the Moscow Phil. Soc., where he studied double bass with Rambousek; he also studied theory with Blaramberg and Kruglikov. In 1894 he joined the orch. of the Bolshoi Theater, succeeding Rambousek as principal double bass player in 1901, retaining that post until 1905. In the meantime, he became known as a soloist of the first magnitude; made his public debut in Moscow on March 25, 1901. He garnered great attention with a double bass recital in Berlin on March 27, 1903. To supplement the meager repertoire for his instrument, he arranged various works; also wrote several pieces. With some aid from Glière, he wrote a Double Bass Concerto, which he performed for the first time in Moscow on Feb. 25, 1905. On Sept. 8, 1905, he married Natalie Ushkov, daughter of a wealthy tea-merchant family. He soon resigned from the orch. of the Bolshoi Theater; in an open letter to the Russian publication *Musical Gazette,* he explained the reason for his resignation as the economic and artistic difficulties in the orch. He then went to Germany, where he continued to give double-bass recitals; played the 1st Cello Concerto by Saint-Saëns on the double bass. In 1907 he conducted a student orch. at the Berlin Hochschule für Musik; his first public appearance as a conductor took place on Jan. 23, 1908, with the Berlin Phil. In 1909 he established a publishing house, Editions Russes de Musique; in 1915 he purchased the catalog of the Gutheil Co.; among composers with whom he signed contracts were Scriabin, Stravinsky, Prokofiev, Medtner, and Rachmaninoff; the association with Scriabin was particularly fruitful, and in subsequent years Koussevitzky became the greatest champion of Scriabin's music. In 1909 he organized his own sym. orch. in Moscow, featuring works by Russian composers, but also including classical masterpieces; played many Russian works for the first time, among them Scriabin's *Prometheus.* In the summer of 1910 he took his orch. to the towns along the Volga River in a specially chartered steamboat. He repeated the Volga tour in 1912 and 1914. The outbreak of World War I in 1914 made it necessary to curtail his activities; however, he continued to give his concerts in Moscow; in 1915 he presented a memorial Scriabin program. After the Revolution of 1917, he was offered the directorship of the State Sym. Orch. (former Court Orch.) in Petrograd; he conducted it until 1920; also presented concerts in Moscow, despite the hardships of the revolutionary times. In 1920 he left Russia; went first to Berlin, then to Rome, and finally to Paris, where he organized the Concerts Koussevitzky with a specially assembled orch.; presented many new scores by French and Russian composers, among them Ravel's orchestration of Mussorgsky's *Pictures at an Exhibition*, Honegger's *Pacific 231*, and several works by Prokofiev and Stravinsky. In 1924 Koussevitzky was appointed the conductor of the Boston Sym. Orch., a position he held with great eminence until 1949. Just as in Russia he championed Russian composers, in France the French, so in the U.S. he encouraged American composers to write works for him. Symphonic compositions by Copland, Harris, Piston, Barber, Hanson, Schuman, and others were performed by Koussevitzky for the first time. For the 50th anniversary of the Boston Sym. Orch. (1931), he commissioned works from Stravinsky (Symphony of Psalms), Hindemith, Honegger, Prokofiev, Roussel, Ravel (piano concerto), Copland, Gershwin, and others. A highly important development in Koussevitzky's American career was the establishment of the Berkshire Music Center at Tanglewood, Mass. This was an outgrowth of the Berkshire Sym. Festival, organized in 1934 by Henry Hadley; Koussevitzky and the Boston Sym. Orch. presented summer concerts at the Berkshire Festival in 1935 for the first time; since then, the concerts have become an annual institution. The Berkshire Music Center was opened on July 8, 1940, with Koussevitzky as director and Copland as assistant director; among the distinguished guest instructors were Hindemith, Honegger, and Messiaen; Koussevitzky himself taught conducting; he was succeeded after his death by his former student Leonard Bernstein.

Koussevitzky held many honorary degrees: Mus.Doc. from Brown Univ. (1926), Rutgers Univ. (1937), Yale Univ. (1938), Univ. of Rochester (1940), Williams College (1943), and Boston Univ. (1945); LL.D. from Harvard Univ. (1929) and Princeton Univ. (1947). He was a member of the French Legion of Honor and held the Cross of Commander of the Finnish Order of the White Rose. He became a naturalized American citizen on April 16, 1941. His wife died in 1942; he established the Koussevitzky Foundation as a memorial to her, the funds to be used for commissioning works by composers of all nationalities. He married Olga Naoumoff (1901–78), a niece of Natalie Koussevitzky, on Aug. 15, 1947.

As a conductor, Koussevitzky possessed an extraordinary emotional power; in Russian music, and particularly in Tchaikovsky's syms., he was unexcelled; he was capable of achieving the subtlest nuances in the works of the French school; his interpretations of Debussy were notable. As a champion of modern music, he had few equals in his time; his ardor in projecting unfamiliar music before new audiences in different countries served to carry conviction among the listeners and the professional music critics. He was often criticized for the liberties he allowed himself in the treatment of classical masterpieces; undoubtedly his performances of Haydn, Mozart, Beethoven, and other giants of the Austro-German repertoire were untraditional; but they were nonetheless musicianly in the sincere artistry that animated his interpretations.

BIBL.: A. Lourie, *S.A. K. and His Epoch* (N.Y., 1931); H. Leichtentritt, *S. K., The Boston Symphony Orchestra and the New American Music* (Cambridge, Mass., 1946); M. Smith, *K.*

(N.Y., 1947; a controversial biography); K. DeKay, "K.—Review and Commentary," *Le Grand Baton* (Dec. 1983); idem, "K. and His Biographers," *Koussevitzky Recordings Society*, newsletter, II/1 (1988).

Kout, Jiří, Czech conductor; b. Novedvory, Dec. 26, 1937. He received training in organ and conducting at the Cons. and the Academy of Music in Prague. In 1964 he became a conductor at the Plzeň Opera. His protest of the Warsaw Pact invasion of his homeland in 1968 led the Czech authorities to ban him from conducting. However, in 1973, he was allowed to resume his career with an engagement at the Prague National Theater. In 1976 he emigrated to West Germany and became a conductor at the Deutsche Oper am Rhein in Düsseldorf. From 1985 to 1991 he was Generalmusikdirektor of the Saarländisches Staatstheater in Saarbrücken; also appeared as a guest conductor of opera houses in Munich, Berlin, Vienna, Venice, Florence, Paris, Cincinnati, and Los Angeles. From 1991 he was a regular conductor at the Deutsche Oper in Berlin; that same year, he made his Metropolitan Opera debut in N.Y. conducting *Der Rosenkavalier.* In 1993 he conducted *Jenůfa* at London's Covent Garden. In 1993 he became music director of the Leipzig Opera. In addition to his idiomatic interpretations of the operas of Smetana, Dvořák, and Janáček, Kout has acquired a distinguished reputation for his performances of operas by Wagner and Strauss.

Koutzen, Boris, Russian-American violinist, teacher, and composer; b. Uman, near Kiev, April 1, 1901; d. Mount Kisco, N.Y., Dec. 10, 1966. He studied violin with Leo Zetlin and composition with Glière at the Moscow Cons. (1918–22). In 1922 he went to the U.S. and joined the violin section of the Philadelphia Orch. (until 1927); later played in the NBC Sym. Orch. in N.Y. (1937–45). He was head of the violin dept. at the Philadelphia Cons. (1925–62) and a teacher at Vassar College in Poughkeepsie, N.Y. (1944–66). His music possesses an attractive Romantic flavor in an old Russian manner. He composed a number of orch. pieces, among them *Solitude* (Philadelphia, April 1, 1927, composer conducting); *Valley Forge*, symphonic poem (N.Y., Feb. 19, 1940); Concerto for 5 Solo Instruments (Boston, Feb. 23, 1940); Violin Concerto (Philadelphia, Feb. 22, 1952, Nadia Koutzen, composer's daughter, soloist); *Concertante* for 2 Flutes and Orch. (1965); also an opera, *You Never Know* (1962).

Kovačević, Krešimir, significant Croatian musicologist; b. Zagreb, Sept. 16, 1913. He studied at the Univ. of Leipzig (Ph.D., 1943, with a diss. on folk music from the Meotimurje region of Croatia). He taught music in Osijek and Dubrovnik (1940–50) and then at the Zagreb Academy of Music (prof., 1950; vice-dean, 1961–71; dean, from 1971). He was also a repetiteur in Zagreb and Belgrade (1936–39), conductor of the Dubrovnik Orch. (1946–50), and a music critic for several publications. He wrote primarily on Croatian contemporary music; publ. the valuable *Hrvatski kompozitori i njihova djela* (Croatian Composers and Their Works; Zagreb, 1960) and *The History of Croatian Music of the Twentieth Century* (in Eng.; Zagreb, 1967). He also edited the 2nd ed. of the *Muzička enciklopedija* (3 vols., 1971–77) and contributed the Croatian entries to the Slovene reference work *Jugoslovanska glasbena dela* (1980).

Kovacevich, Stephen, distinguished American pianist and conductor; b. Los Angeles, Oct. 17, 1940. He began his piano studies with Lev Schorr in 1948, and in 1951 made his public debut in San Francisco under the name Stephen Bishop. In 1959 he went to London to pursue his piano training with Dame Myra Hess. After making his London recital debut in 1961, he appeared as a soloist with many of the major European and North American orchs., as a recitalist, and as a chamber music artist. In 1975 he began to use the name Stephen Bishop-Kovacevich, and finally assumed his original name Stephen Kovacevich in 1991. In 1984 he made his conducting debut with the Houston Sym. Orch., and thereafter pursued a dual career as a pianist and conductor. In 1986 he was appointed to an international chair at the Royal Academy of Music in London. From 1990 to 1993 he was music director of the Irish Chamber Orch. in Dublin. His wife is **Martha Argerich.** As a pianist, Kovacevich has demonstrated an extraordinary command of an expansive repertoire, ranging from the classics to contemporary scores. As a conductor, he has concentrated on works from the 18th and 19th centuries to good effect.

Koval, Marian (Viktorovich), Russian composer; b. Pristan Voznesenya, Olonets district, Aug. 17, 1907; d. Moscow, Feb. 15, 1971. Following training in Nizhny-Novgorod and Petrograd, he studied composition with Gnessin and Miaskovsky at the Moscow Cons. (1925–30). Inspired by the revolutionary ideas of a new collective society, he organized with others a group named Procoll ("Productive Collective"), dedicated to the propaganda of music in its sociological aspects; was also a member of the Russian Assn. of Proletarian Musicians from 1929 until it was disbanded by the Soviet government in 1931 as being counterproductive. He became known mainly through his choruses and songs on socialist subjects; all of his music is derived from modalities of Russian folk songs and those of the ethnic group of the Urals, to which he belonged. He wrote the operas *Emelian Pugatchev* (Moscow, Nov. 25, 1939) and *Sevastopoltzy* (Perm, Nov. 28, 1946); 3 cantatas: *The People's Sacred War* (1941), *Valery Tchkalov* (1942), and *The Kremlin Stars* (1947); *The Wolf and 7 Little Goats*, children's opera (1939); 2 cycles of songs about Lenin; etc.

BIBL.: G. Polyanovsky, *M. K.* (Moscow, 1968).

Kovaříček, František, Czech composer; b. Liteniny, May 17, 1924. He studied with Hlobil at the Prague Cons. and with Řídký at the Prague Academy of Music, graduating in 1952. He was music director of the Czech Radio in Prague (1953–58). From 1966 to 1985 he taught at the Prague Cons., and from 1990 to 1991 was its director.

WORKS: Cello Sonata (1958); *Serenade* for 9 Instruments (1958); *Divertimento* for Strings (1960); *Larghetto* for Clarinet and Piano (1963); Clarinet Concerto (1964); *Ukradený mesič* (The Stolen Moon), comic opera (1966; Czech Radio, July 1, 1970); *Capriccio* for Chamber Orch. (1970–71); *Music* for Chamber Orch. (1982; Prague, March 23, 1984); 2 piano sonatas; choral pieces; songs.

Kovařovic, Karel, noted Czech conductor and composer; b. Prague, Dec. 9, 1862; d. there, Dec. 6, 1920. He studied clarinet, harp, and piano at the Prague Cons. (1873–79); also studied composition privately with Fibich (1878–80). He was harpist in the orch. of Prague's National Theater (1879–85); also was director of Pivoda's Vocal School (1880–1900). In 1900 he was appointed opera director of the National Theater in Prague, a position he held until his death; he also led sym. concerts in Prague. As a conductor, he demonstrated great craftsmanship and established a high standard of excellence in his operatic productions; his interpretations of Dvořák and Smetana were particularly notable; an ardent believer in the cause of Czech music, he promoted national compositions. In his own music, he also made use of national materials, but his treatment was mostly imitative of the French models; the influences of Gounod and Massenet are particularly noticeable. He publ. some of his lighter works under a series of humorously misspelled names of French composers (C. Biset, J. Héral, etc.).

WORKS: DRAMATIC: OPERAS (all 1st perf. in Prague): *Ženichové* (The Bridegrooms; May 13, 1884); *Cesta oknem* (Through the Window; Feb. 11, 1886); *Noc Šimona a Judy* (The Night of Simon and Jude; original title, *Frasquita*; Nov. 5, 1892); *Psohlavci* (The Dog-Heads; April 24, 1898); *Na starém bělidle* (At the Old Bleaching-House; Nov. 22, 1901). **BALLETS:** *Hashish* (June 19, 1884); *Pohádka o nalezeném štěstí* (A Tale of Found Happiness; Dec. 21, 1886); *Na zaletech* (Flirtation; Oct. 24, 1909). **OTHER:** Symphonic works, including Piano Concerto (1887); chamber pieces, including 3 string quartets (1878, 1887, 1894).

BIBL.: J. Němeček, *Opera Národního divadla za Karla Kovařovice* (Prague, 1968–69).

Kowalski, Július, Slovak composer; b. Ostrava, Feb. 24, 1912. He studied composition with Rudolf Karel and Alois Hába at the Prague Cons. (1929–33); subsequently composition with Suk and conducting with Talich at the Master School there (1933–34); then went to Vienna, where he studied conducting with Clemens Krauss (1939). After World War II, he held administrative and managerial positions in Bratislava. He wrote some microtonal pieces, e.g., Suite for Violin and Viola in the sixth-tone system (1936) and Duo for Violin and Cello in the quarter-tone system (1937), but later composed in a more or less traditional style.

WORKS: CHAMBER OPERA: *Lampionová slávnost* (The Chinese Lantern Celebration; 1961; Ostrava, 1963). **ORCH.:** *Russian Rhapsody* (1933–34); *Serbian Fantasy* (1934); 7 syms. (1954; 1957; 1959; 1970; 1974; 1980; *Peace*, 1981); Concertino for Violin and Chamber Orch. (1955); *Impressions* (1965); Concerto for Cello and Strings (1970); Concerto for String Quartet and Orch. (1973–74; Bratislava, Nov. 14, 1974); *Concertante Symphonietta* for Wind Quintet and Orch. (1976; Bratislava, Feb. 7, 1977). **CHAMBER:** 2 piano trios (1931, 1975); 6 string quartets (1932, 1954, 1965, 1975, 1977, 1979); *Divertimento* for Flute, Oboe, and Bassoon (1966); Violin Sonatina (1966); *Little Fantasy* for Flute and Piano (1969); *Grimaces* for Flute, Clarinet, Trombone, and Tuba (1970).

Kowalski, Max, Polish-born German composer; b. Kowal, Aug. 10, 1882; d. London, June 4, 1956. He was taken to Frankfurt am Main as an infant, and received his primary education there; studied voice with Heinemann in Berlin and composition with Sekles in Frankfurt am Main; also obtained a law degree from the Univ. of Marburg. He wrote a song cycle to Guiraud's *Pierrot Lunaire* (1912), and during the following 20 years composed a number of lieder, which found favor in Germany. After the Nazis came to power (1933), he was sent to the Buchenwald concentration camp; after his release (1939), he settled in London and eked out a living as a teacher, synagogal cantor, and piano tuner.

Kox, Hans, Dutch composer and teacher; b. Arnhem, May 19, 1930. He studied at the Utrecht Cons. and with Badings. After teaching at the Doetinchem Music School (1956–70), he served as a prof. of composition at the Utrecht Cons. In some of his works, he applied a scale of 31 equal intervals, invented by the Dutch physicist Adriaan Fokker. In his series of *Cyclophonies*, he experimented with open-end forms.

WORKS: OPERAS: *Dorian Gray* (1972–73; Scheveningen, March 30, 1974; rev. 1976); *Lord Rochester* (1978); *Das grüne Gesicht* (1991). **ORCH.:** *Little Lethe Symphony* (1956; rev. 1959); *Concertante Music* for Horn, Trumpet, Trombone, and Orch. (1956); Flute Concerto (1957); *Macbeth*, overture (1958); 3 syms.: No. 1 for Strings (1959), No. 2 (1960–66), and No. 3 (1985); *Concerto for Orchestra* (1959); Piano Concerto (1961); 3 violin concertos (1963; 1978, rev. 1981; 1993); Concerto for 2 Violins and Orch. (1964); *Cyclophony I* for Cello and Small Orch. (1964), *II* for 3 Orch. Groups (1964), *V* for Oboe, Clarinet, Bassoon, and 19 Strings (1966), *VI* for Violin, Trumpet, Piano, Vibraphone, and 16 Strings (1967), *IX* for Solo Percussion and Small Orch. (1974), and *XI* for Big Band (1978); *Music for Status Seekers* (1966); Cello Concerto (1969); *Phobos* (1970); *Concerto bandistico* (1973); *Gothic Concerto* for Harp and Chamber Orch. (1975); *Sinfonia Concertante* for Violin, Cello, and Orch. (1976); *Vangoghiana* for Brass Band, Strings, and Percussion (1977); Alto Saxophone Concerto (1978); *Concertino chitarristico* for 3 Guitars and Small Orch. (1981); *Irold's Youth* (1983); *Notturno e danza* for Violin, Viola or Clarinet, Cello, Piano, and Strings (1983); *Le songe du vergier, dispute rêvée* for Cello and Orch. (1986); *Musica reservata* for Symphonic Band and Orch. (1986; rev. 1987); *Sinfonia Concertante* for Saxophone Quartet and Strings (1988); *Ruach* (1990); *Face to face*, concerto for Alto Saxophone and Strings (1992). **CHAMBER:** 4 violin sonatas (1952, 1955, 1961, 1966); 2 trios for 2 Violins and Viola (1952, 1954); String Quartet (1955); 4 sextets (1957, 1957, 1959, 1961); String Quintet (1957); *3 Pieces* for Violin, in the 31-tone system (1958); 2 piano quartets (1959, 1968); Sonata for Solo Cello (1959; rev. 1985); *4 Pieces* for String Quartet, in the 31-tone system (1961); *4 Pieces* for 2 Trumpets and Trombone, in the 31-tone system (1964); *Cyclophony IV* for Treble Recorder and 9 Strings (1965), *VII* for Violin, Piano, and 6 Percussionists (1971), *VIII* for Wind Quintet, Violin, Viola, Cello, and Double Bass (1971; rev. 1982), and *XII* for 8 Cellos (1979); Piano Trio (1976); Suite for Guitar Trio (1977); *Sweerts de Landas*, suite for Violin and Piano (1981); Tenor Saxophone Sonata (1983); 2 saxophone quartets (1985; 1987, rev. 1988); Alto Saxophone Sonata (1985); Cello Sonata (1987); 4 études for Double Bass (1988). **KEYBOARD: PIANO:** 2 sonatas (1954, 1955); 3 études (1961); *Cyclophony III* for Piano and Tape (1964); *Melancholies* (1975); *Looks and Smiles for the Orgellas* for 4 Pianists Playing 2 Pianos (1988). **ORGAN:** *Prelude and Fugue* (1954); *Passacaglia and Chorale*, in the 31-tone system (1960). **VOCAL: CHORUS AND ORCH.:** *Stichtse kantate* (1958); *Zoo*, cantata (1964); *In those days* (1969); *Requiem for Europe* (1971); *Cyclophony X* (1975); *Anne Frank Cantata: A Child of Light* (1984); *Amsterdam cantate* (1985); *Sjoah*, oratorio (1989); *Das Credo Quia Absurdum* (1995).

Koyama, Kiyoshige, Japanese composer; b. Nagano, Jan. 15, 1914. He studied composition with Komei Abe. He wrote a number of works in a Japanese national style, among them *Shina no Bayashi* for Orch. (Tokyo, June 3, 1946); *Kobiki-Uta* for Orch. (Tokyo, Oct. 3, 1957); *Nomen*, symphonic suite, for a Noh play (Tokyo, Dec. 5, 1959); *Ubusuna* for Koto and other Japanese Instruments (1962); *Ainu no Uta* for Strings (Tokyo, May 23, 1964); *Sansho Dayu*, opera (Tokyo, March 29, 1972); several pieces for Japanese instruments.

Kozina, Marjan, Slovenian composer and teacher; b. Novo Mesto, June 4, 1907; d. there, June 19, 1966. He studied mathematics at the Univ. and music at the Cons. (1925–27) in Ljubljana, and then was a student of Marx at the Vienna Academy of Music (1927–30) and of Suk at the Prague Cons. (1930–32); he also studied conducting with Malko. He was conductor and director of the music school Maribor Glasbena Matica (1934–39), and then taught at the Belgrade Academy of Music (1939–43). During the Nazi occupation, he took part in the armed resistance movement. After the liberation, he served as director of the Slovene Phil. (1947–50) before teaching composition at the Ljubljana Academy of Music (1950–60). His finely executed scores made circumspect use of modern harmonies, while deriving their melorhythmic essence from native Slovenian folk song patterns. Among his works were the opera *Ekvinokcij* (Equinox; Ljubljana, May 2, 1946); ballets; orch. music; choral pieces; songs.

Kozlovsky, Ivan (Semyonovich), Russian tenor; b. Maryanovka, near Kiev, March 24, 1900; d. Moscow, Dec. 21, 1993. He studied at the Kiev Cons. with Lysenko and Muravyova. He made his operatic debut as Faust in Poltava in 1918; then sang in Kharkov (1924) and Sverdlovsk (1925); in 1926 he joined the Bolshoi Theater in Moscow, where he was one of the leading singers until 1954. An artist of imaginative power, Kozlovsky expanded his activities into stage direction, striving to synthesize dramatic action with its musical realization. Apart from operatic performances, he gave recitals in programs of the classical repertoire as well as Russian and Ukrainian songs.

BIBL.: G. Polinovsky, *I. K.* (Moscow, 1945); V. Sletov, *I. K.* (Moscow, 1951); A. Kuznetzova, *I. K.* (Moscow, 1964).

Kozma, Matei, Romanian organist and composer; b. Tîrgu-Mureş, July 23, 1929. He acquired the rudiments of music from his father, Géza Kozma, a composer and cellist; then studied at the Cluj Cons. (1947–54), where his teachers were Jodal and Demian. He was organist (1955–57) and director (1959–66) of the Tîrgu-Mureş Phil.; then taught at the Music Inst. there.

WORKS: BALLETS: *Baladă lacului Sf. Ana* (1957); *Baladă celui care cînta in cătuşe* (1963). **ORCH.:** Organ Concerto (1961; rev. 1965); *Omagiu eroilor*, overture (1967). **CHAMBER:** *Rondo* for Piano (1954); *Theme and Variations* for Organ

(1963); Trio for Clarinet (1965); *Toccata, Trio, and Ricercari* for Organ (1968). **VOCAL:** *Trandafirii roşii,* poem for Chorus and Orch. (1962); choruses; songs.

Kozolupov, Semyon Matveievich, Russian cellist and pedagogue; b. Krasnokholmskaya, April 22, 1884; d. Moscow, April 18, 1961. He was a pupil of Wierzbillowicz and Seifert at the St. Petersburg Cons. In 1911 he won the Moscow cello competition. He was principal cellist in the orch. of the Bolshoi Theater in Moscow (1908–12; 1924–31), and also a member of the Moscow Quartet. He taught at the Saratov Cons. (1912–16; 1921–22), the Kiev Cons. (1916–20), and the Moscow Cons. (from 1922), where he was also head of the cello dept. (1936–54). Among his outstanding students were Knushevitzky and Rostropovich.

Krader, Barbara (née **Lattimer**), American ethnomusicologist; b. Columbus, Ohio, Jan. 15, 1922. She studied music with Krenek at Vassar College (A.B., 1942); later took courses in Russian and Slavonic languages, and in literature with Roman Jakobson at Columbia Univ. (A.M., 1948). After a brief period at the Univ. of Prague (1948–49), she completed her education with Jakobson at Radcliffe College (Ph.D., 1955, with the diss. *Serbian Peasant Wedding Ritual Songs: A Formal, Semantic and Functional Analysis*). She worked as a reference librarian in the Slavonic division of the Library of Congress in Washington, D.C. (1959–63) and as a lecturer in Slavonic at Ohio State Univ. (1963–64); in 1965–66 she was executive secretary of the International Folk Music Council in London. On returning to the U.S., she taught at Columbia Univ. (1969) and also served as president of the Soc. for Ethnomusicology (1972–73). She made valuable field recordings in Czechoslovakia, Yugoslavia, Greece, and Romania.

Kraft, Leo (Abraham), American composer and pedagogue; b. N.Y., July 24, 1922. He studied composition with Rathaus at Queens College of the City Univ. of N.Y. (B.A., 1945), Thompson at Princeton Univ. (M.F.A., 1947), and Boulanger in Paris on a Fulbright fellowship (1954–55). He taught at Queens College (1947–89); was Distinguished Composer-in-Residence at N.Y. Univ. (1988–92). From 1976 to 1980 he was president of the American Music Center. He received various ASCAP awards (from 1961); in 1975 and 1978 he held NEA fellowships. Kraft's principal works have developed along atonal lines.

WRITINGS: With S. Berkowitz and G. Frontrier, *A New Approach to Sight Singing* (N.Y., 1960; 3rd ed., 1986); *Gradus: An Integrated Approach to Harmony, Counterpoint, and Analysis* (N.Y., 1976; 2nd ed., 1987); *A New Approach to Ear Training* (Melody) (N.Y., 1967); with others, *A New Approach to Keyboard Harmony* (N.Y., 1978).

WORKS: ORCH.: 6 concertos: No. 1 for Flute, Clarinet, Trumpet, and Strings (1951), No. 2 for 12 Instruments (1966; rev. 1972), No. 3 for Cello, Wind Quintet, and Percussion (1968), No. 4 for Piano and 14 Instruments (1978; rev. 1982), No. 5 for Oboe and Strings (1986), and No. 6 for Clarinet and Orch. (1986); *Larghetto in Memory of Karol Rathaus* for Strings and Timpani (1955); *Variations* (1958); *3 Pieces* (1963); *Music* (1975); Chamber Sym. (1980); *Symphony in 1 Movement* (1985); *A New Ricercar* for Strings (1985); *Pacific Bridges* for Strings and Clarinet obbligato (1989); *Tableaux* for 10 Winds and Piano (1989); *Symphonic Prelude* (1993). **CHAMBER:** Suite for Brass (1947); 4 string quartets (1951, 1959, 1966, 1994); *Short Suite* for Flute, Clarinet, and Bassoon (1951); Sextet for Clarinet, Piano, and String Quartet (1952); Cello Sonata (1954); Violin Sonata (1956); Wind Quintet (1956); *Partita No. 2* for Violin and Viola (1961), *No. 3* for Wind Quintet (1964), *No. 4* for Flute, Clarinet, Violin, Double Bass, and Piano (1975), and *No. 5* for Flute and Guitar (1987); *5 Pieces* for Clarinet and Piano (1962); *Fantasy* No. 1 (1963) and No. 2 (1980) for Flute and Piano; *Trios and Interludes* for Flute, Viola, and Piano (1965); *Dialogues* for Flute and Tape (1968); *Dualities* for 2 Trumpets (1971); *Line Drawings* for Flute and Percussion (1972); *Diaphonies* for Oboe and Piano (1975); *Dialectica* for Flute, Clarinet, Violin, Cello, and Tape (1976); *Conductus Novus* for Trombones (1979); *Strata* for 8 Instruments (1979; rev. 1984); *Interplay* for Trumpet and Percussion (1983); *O Primavera* for Flute, Oboe, and Clarinet (1984); *Inventions and Airs* for Clarinet, Violin, and Piano (1984); *Statements and Commentaries* No. 2 for 2 Cellos (1988); *Tableau* for Double Wind Septet and Piano (1989); *Cloud Studies* for 12 Flutes (1989); *Washington Square* for Flute, Clarinet, Trombone, Cello, Double Bass, Piano, and Percussion (1990); *Green Mountain Notes* for Oboe, Clarinet, Bassoon, Horn, Violin, and Piano (1991); *Omaggio* for Flute, Clarinet, Violin, Viola, and Cello (1992); *No Time Like This Time* for Clarinet and Piano (1993); *7 Bagatelles* for Cello (1994). **PIANO:** *Scherzo* (1949); *Variations* (1951); Sonata (1956); *Partita No. 1* (1958); *Allegro Giocoso* (1958); *Statements and Commentaries No. 1* (1965); *Easy Animal Pieces* (1968); *Antiphonies* for Piano, 4-hands, and Tape (1971); *Sestina* (1971); *10 Short Pieces* (1976); *5 Short Pieces and a Reprise* (1981); *Venetian Reflections* (1989). **VOCAL:** *Festival Song* for Chorus (1948); *Let Me Laugh* for Chorus and Piano (1953); *A Proverb of Solomon* for Chorus and Chamber Orch. (1953); *Thanksgiving* for Chorus (1955); *When Israel Came Forth* for Chorus (1961); *I Waited Patiently* for Men's Voices (1963); *A New Song* for Men's Voices (1964); *Spring in the Harbor* for Soprano, Flute, Cello, and Piano (1969); *3 3-Part Songs* for Women's or Men's Voices (1975); *8 Choral Songs* for Chorus (1975); *4 Songs from the Chinese* for Soprano, Flute, and Percussion (1990).

Kraft, Walter, German organist, pedagogue, and composer; b. Cologne, June 9, 1905; d. in a hotel fire in Antwerp, May 9, 1977. He studied piano with Rebbert and organ with Hannemann in Hamburg, and composition with Hindemith in Berlin. From 1924 to 1927 he was organist of the Markuskirche in Hamburg, and from 1927 to 1929 of the Lutherkirche in Altona-Bahrenfeld. From 1929 he was organist of the Marienkirche in Lübeck; the church was destroyed in 1942, but he resumed his post there after it was restored. He was also a prof. of organ at the Freiburg music college (from 1947); in addition, served as director of the Schleswig-Holstein Academy of Music (1950–55). He composed the oratorios *Christus* (1942–43), *Die Bürger von Calais* (1953–54), *Lübecker Totentanz* (1954), and *Die Gemeinschaft der Heiligen* (1956–57); Mass (1966); *Laudatio 71* for Speaker, Chorus, 5 Wind Groups, Bells, Percussion, and Organ (1971); organ music. As an organist, he gained wide distinction as an interpreter of Baroque music and as an improviser.

Kraft, William, American percussionist, composer, and conductor; b. Chicago, Sept. 6, 1923. His parental name was Kashareftsky, which his parents Americanized to Kraft. The family moved to California and Kraft began to study piano. He took music courses at San Diego State College and at the Univ. of Calif. at Los Angeles, where he also had professional percussion instruction with Murray Spivack. In 1943 he was called to arms, and served in the U.S. forces as pianist, arranger, and drummer in military bands; while in Europe with the army, he attended music courses at the Univ. of Cambridge. Returning to the U.S. after discharge from military duty, he earned a living as percussionist in jazz bands. In the summer of 1948 he enrolled in the Berkshire Music Center in Tanglewood, where he studied composition with Fine and conducting with Bernstein. In 1949 he entered Columbia Univ., where his instructors in composition were Beeson, Luening, Bingham, Ussachevsky, and Cowell; he also attended classes in musicology with Hertzmann and Lang (B.S., 1951; M.A., 1954). He continued to perfect his technique as a percussionist, and took lessons with Morris Goldenberg and Saul Goodman; he attained a high degree of virtuosity as a percussion player, both in the classical tradition and in jazz. In 1955 he became a percussionist with the Los Angeles Phil., retaining this position until 1981. In the meantime he developed his natural gift for conducting; from 1969 to 1972 he served as assistant conductor of the Los Angeles Phil.; in a parallel development, he composed assiduously and successfully. From 1981 to 1985 he was composer-in-residence of the Los Angeles Phil.; also founded the Los Angeles Phil. New Music Group, presenting programs of modern works for chamber orch. combinations. From 1988 to 1990 he was a visiting prof. at the Univ. of Calif. at Los Angeles. He held 2 Guggenheim fellowships (1967, 1972). As a composer, he explores without prejudice a variety of quaquaversal techniques, including serial procedures; naturally, his music coruscates with a rainbow spectrum of asymmetrical rhythms. There is a tendency in the very titles of his works toward textured constructivism, e.g., *Momentum, Configurations, Collage, Encounters, Translucences, Triangles,* and *Mobiles*; but there are also concrete representations of contemporary events, as in *Contextures: Riots-Decade '60.*

WORKS: DRAMATIC: Music for Samuel Beckett's radio drama *Cascando* (1988); film scores. **ORCH.:** *A Simple Introduction to the Orchestra* (1958); *Variations on a Folksong* (Los Angeles, March 26, 1960); Sym. for Strings and Percussion (N.Y., Aug. 21, 1961); *Concerto grosso* for Violin, Flute, Cello, Bassoon, and Orch. (1961; San Diego, March 22, 1963); *American Carnival Overture* (1962); Concerto for 4 Percussionists and Orch. (Los Angeles, March 10, 1966); *Configurations*, concerto for 4 Percussionists and Jazz Orch. (Los Angeles, Nov. 13, 1966); *Contextures: Riots-Decade '60* (1967; Los Angeles, April 4, 1968); Piano Concerto (1972–73; Los Angeles, Nov. 21, 1973); *Tintinnabulations: Collage No. 3* (Anaheim, March 22, 1974); *Dream Tunnel* for Narrator and Orch. (Los Angeles, May 12, 1976); *Andirivieni* for Tuba and Orch. (1977; Los Angeles, Jan. 26, 1978; rev. as Concerto for Tuba, 3 Chamber Groups, and Orch., 1979); *Settlers Suite* (Merced, Calif., March 10, 1981); *Double Play* for Violin, Piano, and Chamber Orch. (1982; St. Paul, Minn., Jan. 7, 1983); Timpani Concerto (1983; Indianapolis, March 9, 1984); *Contextures II: The Final Beast* for Soprano, Tenor, and Chamber Orch. (Los Angeles, April 2, 1984; also for Soprano, Tenor, Boys' Chorus, and Orch., 1986; Los Angeles, April 2, 1987); *Interplay* (Los Angeles, Nov. 1, 1984); *Of Ceremonies, Pageants, and Celebrations* (Costa Mesa, Calif., Sept. 19, 1986; rev. 1987); *A Kennedy Portrait* for Narrator and Orch., in commemoration of the 25th anniversary of the assassination of President John F. Kennedy (Boston, Nov. 19, 1988); *Veils and Variations* for Horn and Orch. (1988; Berkeley, Calif., Jan. 27, 1989); *Vintage Renaissance* (Boston, June 10, 1989); *Vintage 1990–91* (Costa Mesa, Calif., Oct. 9, 1990). **WIND ENSEMBLE:** *Games: Collage I* (Los Angeles, Nov. 21, 1969); *Dialogues and Entertainments* (1980; Ann Arbor, Feb. 13, 1981); *Quintessence*, concerto for 5 Percussionists and Concert Band (1985; Washington, D.C., Nov. 5, 1986). **CHAMBER:** Nonet for 2 Trumpets, Horn, Trombone, Tuba, and 4 Percussion (Los Angeles, Oct. 13, 1958); *Triangles*, concerto for Percussion and 10 Instruments (1965–68; Los Angeles, Dec. 8, 1969); Double Trio for Piano, Prepared Piano, Amplified Guitar, Tuba, and 2 Percussion (Los Angeles, Oct. 31, 1966); *Mobiles* for 3 Instrumental Groups (1970); *Cadenze* for Flute, Oboe, Clarinet, Bassoon, Horn, Violin, and Viola (1971; Los Angeles, March 20, 1972); *In Memoriam Igor Stravinsky* for Violin and Piano (1972–74); *Des Imagistes* for 6 Percussion and Reciter(s) (Los Angeles, March 12, 1974); *Encounters V: In the Morning of the Winter Sea* for Cello and Percussion (1975; N.Y., Jan. 6, 1976); *Encounters IX* for Saxophone and Percussion (Nuremberg, July 9, 1982); *Melange* for Flute, Clarinet, Violin, Cello, Piano, and Percussion (1985; Dallas, March 10, 1986); *Quartet for the Love of Time* for Clarinet, Violin, Cello, and Piano (Portland, Oreg., July 6, 1987); Quartet for Percussion (Sacramento, Calif., Nov. 7, 1988). **PERCUSSION:** *Theme and Variations* for Percussion Quartet (1956); *Suite* for 4 Percussion (1958; Los Angeles, Nov. 6, 1961); *French Suite* (1962); *English Suite* (1973); *Soliloquy: Encounters I* for Percussion and Tape (1975), *VI*, concertino for Roto-toms and Percussion Quartet (Atlantic City, N.J., March 10, 1976), *VII* for 2 Percussion (1977; Boston, Jan. 22, 1978), and *VIII* (1978); *Images* for Timpani (Los Angeles, Nov. 9, 1978); *Variations for King George* for Timpani (1980); *Weavings* for String Quartet and Percussion (San Francisco, Nov. 30, 1984). **VOCAL:** *Silent Boughs* for Soprano and String Orch. (Stockholm, Nov. 15, 1963); *The Sublime and the Beautiful* for Tenor, Flute, Clarinet, Percussion, Piano, Violin, and Cello (1979); *Feerie* for Mezzo-soprano, Flute, Clarinet, Viola, Cello, and Piano (1987; Los Angeles, Feb. 1, 1988); *Mein Bruder* for Soprano, Flute, Clarinet, Violin, Cello, and Piano (1988; Los Angeles, Jan. 25, 1989).

Krainev, Vladimir (Vsevolodovich), Russian pianist; b. Krasnoyarsk, April 1, 1944. He studied with Anaida Sumbatian at Moscow's Central Music School (graduated, 1962), then with Heinrich Neuhaus (1962–64) and Stanislav Neuhaus (1964–67) at the Moscow Cons., where he completed his postgraduate studies (1969). He won 2nd prize in the Leeds Competition (1963); then 1st prize in the Vianna da Motta Competition in Lisbon (1964) and the Tchaikovsky Competition in Moscow (1970). He subsequently made tours of Europe and the U.S.

Kramer, A(rthur) Walter, American music critic, publishing executive, and composer; b. N.Y., Sept. 23, 1890; d. there, April 8, 1969. He studied music with his father; took violin lessons with Carl Hauser and Richard Arnold. After graduating from the College of the City of N.Y. in 1910, he was on the staff of *Musical America* (1910–22) and served as its ed.-in-chief (1929–36); then was managing director of the Galaxy Music Corp. (1936–56). He publ. over 300 compositions, including orch. pieces, choral works, chamber music, piano pieces, and songs.

BIBL.: J. Howard, *A.W. K.* (N.Y., 1926).

Kramer, Jonathan, American composer, music theorist, teacher, and writer on music; b. Hartford, Conn., Dec. 7, 1942. He studied at Harvard Univ. (A.B., 1965) and the Univ. of Calif. at Berkeley (M.A., 1967; Ph.D., 1969); also received training in computer music at Stanford Univ. (1967–68) and was a post-doctoral fellow in criticism and theory at the Univ. of Calif. at Irvine (1976). He taught at the Univ. of Calif. at Berkeley (1969–70), the Oberlin Cons. (1970–71), and Yale Univ. (1971–78); in 1978 he joined the faculty of the Univ. of Cincinnati College-Cons. of Music, where he later was prof. of composition and theory (1983–90); from 1988 he was a prof. of music at Columbia Univ. In 1980 he became program annotator of the Cincinnati Sym. Orch.; also was its composer-in-residence and new music advisor (1984–92). He publ. *The Time of Music* (N.Y., 1988) and *Listen to the Music* (N.Y., 1988).

WORKS: DRAMATIC AND MULTIMEDIA: *For Broken Piano, Truck, Shaving Cream, Fruit Salad, Toilet, Wife, San Francisco, Color TV, Tape, and Slide Projections* (1969–70; Santa Cruz, Calif., April 3, 1970); *Blue Music* for Tape and Actor (1970–72); *An Imaginary Dance* for Tape and Slide Projections (1970–73); *Fanfare* for Actors and Tape (1973–76); *En noir et blanc* for 2 Actor-Pianists and Actor-Dancer (1988). **ORCH.:** *Funeral March* (1957–61); *Rhapsody* (1958); *Prelude and Fugue* (1964); *Sinfonia* (1965); Clarinet Concerto (1965; Sacramento, March 30, 1967); *Requiem for the Innocent* (1970); *Moments in and out of Time* (1981–83; Cincinnati, Feb. 10, 1984); *Musica pro musica* (1986–87; Columbus, Ohio, Nov. 14, 1987); *About Face* (1988–89; Cincinnati, Nov. 10, 1989); *Cincy in C* (1994); also band music. **CHAMBER:** Suite for 10 Instruments (1958); *3 Inventions* for 2 Clarinets and Cello (1960); Trio for Violin, Viola, and Cello (1962–65); *Random Suite* for Clarinet and Piano (1965); *3 Pieces* for Clarinet (1965–66); *Obstacles* for Trumpet, Trombone, and Piano (1967); Septet (1968); *Renaissance Motet* for 2 Flutes and Bassoon (1970); *1 for 5 in 7, Mostly* for Woodwind Quintet (1971); *1 More Piece* for Clarinet (1972); *Moving Music* for Solo Clarinet and 12 Clarinets (1975–76); *Atlanta Licks* for Flute, Clarinet, Violin, Viola, Cello, and Piano (1984); *A Game* for Cello and Piano (1988–92); *Another Anniversary* for Clarinet (1989); *Another Sunrise* for 7 Instrumentalists (1990); *Notta Sonata* for 2 Pianos and 2 or 3 Percussionists (1992–93); keyboard pieces. **VOCAL:** *No Beginning, No End* for Chorus and Orch. (1982–83; Cincinnati, Oct. 30, 1983). **OTHER:** Tape pieces.

Krapf, Gerhard, German-American organist and composer; b. Meissenheim-bei-Lahr, Dec. 12, 1924. He studied piano and organ in Karlsruhe; was church organist in Offenburg (1939–42); was drafted into the German army and taken prisoner of war in Russia; upon his release, he returned to Karlsruhe, where he studied organ, choral conducting, and composition (1950). In 1951 he went to the U.S., where he studied organ at the Univ. of Redlands in California, and took a course in composition with Paul Pisk. He then taught music at Albion, Mich. (1953–54), at the Northwest Missouri State College in Maryville (1954–58), and at the Univs. of Wyoming (1958–61) and Iowa (1961–77). He joined the faculty of the Univ. of Alberta in Edmonton (1977), where he became chairman of the division of keyboard studies. He composed a great number of organ pieces and sacred choral works. He publ. *Liturgical Organ Playing* (Minneapolis, 1964), *Organ Improvisation: A Practical Approach to Chorale Elaborations for the Service* (Minneapolis, 1967), and *Bach: Improvised Ornamentation and Keyboard Cadenzas: An Approach to Creative Performance* (Dayton, Ohio, 1983). He also tr. H. Klotz's *The Organ Handbook* (St. Louis, 1969) and Werckmeister's 1698 *Orgelprobe* (Raleigh, N.C., 1976).

Krapp, Edgar, distinguished German organist and pedagogue; b. Bamberg, June 3, 1947. He studied the organ at the Hochschule für Musik in Munich (1966–71), where he was a pupil of Franz Lehrndorfer; subsequently took organ lessons with Marie-Claire Alain in Paris (1971–72). In 1970 he won 1st prize in the Competition of the German Academies in Munich, and in 1971 the prize of the Mendelssohn Competition in Berlin. In 1974 he was named successor to Helmut Walcha as prof. of organ at the Hochschule für Musik in Frankfurt am Main; from 1982 to 1991 he was a visiting prof. at the Salzburg Mozarteum. In 1993 he became prof. of organ at the Hochschule für Musik in Munich. He is particularly noted for his performances of the organ music of Bach.

Krása, Hans (actually, **Johann**), Czech composer; b. Prague, Nov. 30, 1899; d. probably in the concentration camp in Auschwitz, Oct. 16(?), 1944. He began playing piano and composing as a child. He later studied with Zemlinsky at the Cons. and at the Deutsche Akademie für Musik und darstellende Kunst in Prague. After working at the Kroll Opera in Berlin (1927), he returned to Prague as répétiteur at the New German Theater. He subsequently became involved in avant-garde artistic circles and devoted much time to composition. Following the German occupation of his homeland, Krása was active at the Prague Jewish orphanage until the Nazis deported him to the Jewish ghetto camp in Theresienstadt in 1942. He continued to compose and to have works performed there. On the night of Oct. 16, 1942, Krása was herded into a railway car by the Nazis and never seen again. It is presumed that he was put to death in the concentration camp in Auschwitz. Krása adopted a neo-Classical style of composition enlivened by comedic and grotesque elements.

WORKS: DRAMATIC: *Die Verlobung in Traum*, opera (Prague, May 18, 1933); *Mládí ve hre*, incidental music to A. Hoffmeister's play (1935); *Brundibár* (The Bumble Bee), children's opera (1938; rev. version, Theresienstadt camp, Sept. 23, 1943). **ORCH.:** Sym. for Small Orch. (1923); Overture for Small Orch. (n.d.). **CHAMBER:** 2 string quartets (1923; *Theme and Variations*, 1943–44); *Chamber Music* for Harpsichord and 7 Instruments (1936); *Passacaglia and Fugue* for String Trio (1943); *Dance* for String Trio (1944). **VOCAL:** *Vier Orchesterlieder nach Gedichten von Christian Morgenstern* (1921); *Fünf Lieder* for Voice and Piano (1926); *Die Erde ist des Herrn* for Soli, Chorus, and Orch. (1932); *Tři písně* (3 songs) for High Voice, Clarinet, Viola, and Cello, after Rimbaud (1943).

BIBL.: J. Karas, *Music in Terezín 1941–1945* (N.Y., 1985).

Krasner, Louis, Russian-born American violinist; b. Cherkassy, June 21, 1903; d. Brookline, Mass., May 4, 1995. He was taken to the U.S. as a small child; studied violin with Eugene Gruenberg and composition with Converse at the New England Cons. of Music in Boston, graduating in 1923; then went abroad, where he studied violin with Flesch, Capet, and Ševčik. From 1944 to 1949 he was concertmaster of the Minneapolis Sym. Orch.; then was prof. of violin and chamber music at Syracuse Univ. (1949–71); subsequently taught at the New England Cons. of Music (from 1974). He commissioned and gave the first performance of Berg's Violin Concerto (Barcelona, April 19, 1936); also gave the premiere of Schoenberg's Violin Concerto (Philadelphia, Dec. 6, 1940, Stokowski conducting).

Krásová, Marta, prominent Czech mezzo-soprano; b. Protivín, March 16, 1901; d. Vráž u Berouna, Feb. 20, 1970. She studied with Olga Borová-Valoušková and Růžena Maturová in Prague; then with Ullanovsky in Vienna. She began her career as a soprano at the Slovak National Theater in Bratislava (1922), but soon turned to mezzo-soprano roles. She made her debut at the Prague National Theater as Azucena (1926), then was one of its principal singers (1928–66); also made successful guest appearances in Hamburg, Dresden, Madrid, Paris, Moscow, and Warsaw; toured the U.S. in 1937. In 1935 she married **Karel Boleslav Jirák**; they divorced in 1946. In 1958 she was made a National Artist. She achieved distinction for her roles in Czech operas; was also noted as a Wagnerian singer.

BIBL.: V. Šolín, *M. K.* (Prague, 1960).

Kraus (Trujillo), Alfredo, distinguished Spanish tenor of Austrian descent; b. Las Palmas, Canary Islands, Sept. 24, 1927. He had vocal training with Gali Markoff in Barcelona and Francisco Andrés in Valencia, then completed his studies with Mercedes Llopart in Milan (1955). In 1956 he won 1st prize in the Geneva Competition and made his operatic debut as the Duke of Mantua in Cairo; he also made his European debut in Venice as Alfredo Germont, a role he repeated for his British debut at London's Stoll Theatre in 1957. After he scored a remarkable success in the same role at Lisbon's Teatro São Carlo on March 27, 1958, an international career beckoned. On July 10, 1959, he appeared at London's Covent Garden for the first time as Edgardo in *Lucia di Lammermoor*. His U.S. debut followed at the Chicago Lyric Opera, as Nemorino in *L'elisir d'amore* on Oct. 31, 1962. He made his Metropolitan Opera debut in N.Y. as the Duke of Mantua on Feb. 16, 1966. Thereafter his career took him to most of the major European and North American opera houses. He also toured as a recitalist. In 1996 he celebrated his 40th anniversary on the operatic stage. A consummate artist with a voice of remarkable beauty, he was particularly noted for his portrayals of Rossini's Count Almaviva, Don Ottavio, Ernesto in *Don Pasquale*, Des Grieux, Nadir in *Les Pêcheurs de perles*, and Massenet's Werther.

BIBL.: N. Dentici Bourgoa, *A. K.: Treinta y cinco años de arte en el País Vasco* (Bilbao, 1992).

Kraus, Detlef, distinguished German pianist; b. Hamburg, Nov. 30, 1919. He made a notable debut at the age of 16, performing the complete *Well-tempered Clavier* in 2 successive recitals in Hamburg; then continued his studies with Edwin Fischer and later with Wilhelm Kempff in Berlin and Potsdam. In 1958 he performed a cycle of Beethoven piano sonatas in London; in 1970 he gave Beethoven cycles in Tokyo, Valencia, and Pittsburgh; in 1980 he played all of the solo piano works of Brahms in N.Y. He also taught classes at the Folkwang Hochschule für Musik in Essen. His playing is remarkable for its freedom from pedantry; his interpretations are notable for their spontaneity. He publ. *Johannes Brahms als Klavierkomponist: Wege und Hinweise zu seiner Klaviermusik* (Wilhelmshaven, 1986; Eng. tr., 1988).

Kraus, Ernst, outstanding German tenor, father of **(Wolfgang Ernst) Richard Kraus**: b. Erlangen, June 8, 1863; d. Wörthsee, Sept. 6, 1941. He studied in Munich with Schimon-Regan and then in Milan with Cesare Galliera. He made his concert debut at a Kaim Concert in Munich (Jan. 18, 1893), and then his operatic debut in Mannheim on March 26, 1893, as Tamino; remained on its roster until 1896, and thereafter was a leading member of the Berlin Royal (later State) Opera until 1924. He also was a leading singer with the Damrosch Opera Co. in N.Y. (1896–99) and at the Bayreuth Festivals (1899–1909); appeared at London's Covent Garden (1900, 1907, 1910). He made his Metropolitan Opera debut in N.Y. on Nov. 25, 1903, as Siegmund in *Die Walküre,* remaining on its roster for a season. After retiring from the Berlin State Opera in 1924, he returned to Munich as a singing teacher. He was one of the foremost Wagnerians of his day, excelling in such roles as Siegfried, Siegmund, and Walther von Stolzing.

Kraus, Felix von, noted Austrian bass; b. Vienna, Oct. 3, 1870; d. Munich, Oct. 30, 1937. He studied philology and music history, took a course in harmony with Bruckner in Vienna, and received training in theory from Mandyczewski at the Univ. of Vienna (Ph.D., 1894, with a diss. on Caldara); also received vocal instruction from C. Van Zanten in Amsterdam and from Stockhausen in Frankfurt am Main. He made his debut in a Vienna concert (1896); made his operatic debut as Hagen at the Bayreuth Festival (1899), and continued to appear there until 1909, excelling as Gurnemanz, the Landgrave, and King Marke; sang at London's Covent Garden (1907). In 1908 he became a prof. at the Munich Academy of Music. He married **Adrienne Osborne** (1899).

Kraus, Lili, noted Hungarian-born English pianist; b. Budapest, March 4, 1903; d. Asheville, N.C., Nov. 6, 1986. She entered the Royal Academy of Music in Budapest while still a child, becoming a pupil of Bartók and Kodály; after graduating (1922), she studied with Steuermann at the Vienna Cons. before attending Schnabel's master classes in Berlin (1930–34). From 1935 to 1940 she toured with the violinist Szymon Goldberg. In 1942 she embarked on a major tour, only to be interned by the Japanese when they captured the island of Java during World War II. After the War, she resumed her career and appeared in many of the principal music centers of the world. During the 1966–67 season, she played all the Mozart piano concertos in N.Y. From 1967 to 1983 she served as artist-in-residence at Texas Christian Univ. in Fort Worth. In 1948 she became a naturalized British subject. Kraus was especially esteemed for her interpretations of Mozart and Schubert.

Kraus, Otakar, Czech-born English baritone; b. Prague, Dec. 10, 1909; d. London, July 28, 1980. He was a student of Konrad Wallerstein in Prague and of Fernando Carpi in Milan. He made his operatic debut as Amonasro in Brno (1935); then sang in Bratislava. At the outbreak of World War II, he went to England, where he sang with the Carl Rosa Opera Co. (1940); then joined the English Opera Group (1946), creating Tarquinius in Britten's *The Rape of Lucretia.* He sang with the Netherlands Opera (1950–51); created Nick Shadow in Stravinsky's *The Rake's Progress* (Venice, 1951); subsequently appeared at London's Covent Garden (1951–73), where he created Diomede in Walton's *Troilus and Cressida* (1954) and King Fisher in Tippett's *The Midsummer Marriage* (1955); also appeared as Alberich at the Bayreuth Festivals (1960–62). After his retirement, he devoted himself to teaching. He was made an Officer of the Order of the British Empire (1973).

Kraus, (Wolfgang Ernst) Richard, German conductor, son of **Ernst Kraus**; b. Berlin, Nov. 16, 1902; d. Walchstadt, April 11, 1978. He studied at the Berlin Hochschule für Musik. After working as a répétiteur at the Berlin State Opera (1923–27), he conducted opera in Kassel (1927–28), Hannover (1928–33), and Stuttgart (1933–37). He served as Generalmusikdirektor of the operas in Halle an der Sale (1937–44) and Cologne (1948–53), and then of the Nordwestdeutsche Phil. in Herford (1963–69). He was particularly admired for his performances of Wagner, Mahler, and R. Strauss.

Krause, Tom, Finnish baritone; b. Helsinki, July 5, 1934. He received his training in Helsinki, Vienna, and Berlin. In 1957 he made his debut as a lieder artist in Helsinki, followed by his operatic debut at the Berlin Städtische Oper as Escamillo in 1959. In 1962 he made his first appearance at the Bayreuth Festival as the Herald in *Lohengrin,* and that same year he became a member of the Hamburg State Opera, where he established a reputation as an interpreter of Mozart, Wagner, and Verdi; he also sang in the premieres there of Krenek's *Der goldene Bock* (June 16, 1964) and Searle's *Hamlet* (title role, March 5, 1968). In 1962 he made his British debut as the Count in *Capriccio* at the Glyndebourne Festival. On Oct. 11, 1967, he made his Metropolitan Opera debut in N.Y. as Count Almaviva, remaining on its roster until 1973. He also sang opera in Chicago, San Francisco, and Houston. He also pursued an extensive concert career which took him to most of the leading music centers of the world. Among his prominent roles were Don Alfonso, Guglielmo, Pizarro, Amonasro, Amfortas, Kurwenal, King Philip II, and Golaud.

Krauss, Clemens (Heinrich), eminent Austrian conductor, great-nephew of (Marie) Gabrielle Krauss; b. Vienna, March 31, 1893; d. Mexico City, May 16, 1954. His father was a court figure, and his mother a dancer; of illegitimate birth, he took his mother's maiden name. He was a chorister in the Imperial Choir; then studied piano with Reinhold, composition with Grädener, and theory with Heuberger at the Vienna Cons. (graduated, 1912). He was a chorus master at the Brünn Theater (1912–13), making his conducting debut there with a performance of *Zar und Zimmermann* (Jan. 13, 1913); then was 2nd conductor at Riga's German Theater (1913–14) and in Nuremberg (1915–16); after serving as 1st conductor in Stettin (1916–21), he conducted in Graz (1921–22). In 1922 he became Schalk's assistant at the Vienna State Opera; he also taught conducting at the Vienna Academy of Music (1922–24) and was conductor of the Vienna Tonkünstlerkonzerte (1923–27). He was director of the Frankfurt am Main Opera and its Museumgesellschaft concerts (1924–29), and then of the Vienna State Opera (1929–34); was also conductor of the Vienna Phil. (1930–33). In 1926 he made his first appearance at the Salzburg Festivals, and returned there regularly (1929–34); he also conducted in South America (1927) and was a guest conductor with the N.Y. Phil. and the Philadelphia Orch. (1929); he made his debut at London's Covent Garden in 1934. He was director of the Berlin State Opera (1934–37) and Generalmusikdirektor of the Bavarian State Opera in Munich (1937–44); also conducted at the Salzburg Mozarteum (1939–45) and appeared with the Vienna Phil. (1944–45). Having been a friend of Hitler and Göring, and a prominent figure in the musical life of the Third Reich, Krauss was held accountable for his actions by the Allied authorities after the end of World War II. There was a strain of humanity in Krauss, however, for he had assisted Jews to escape the clutches of the barbarous Führer's fury. In 1947 he was permitted to resume his career with appearances at the Vienna State Opera; he took it to London that same year. He was a conductor with the Vienna Phil. from 1947, and also served as conductor of its famous New Year's Day Concerts. From 1951 to 1953 he conducted at London's Covent Garden, and in 1953–54 at the Bayreuth Festivals. He died during a visit to Mexico. He was married to **Viorica Ursuleac**, who often appeared in operas under his direction; he also accompanied her in recitals. He was a close friend and collaborator of Richard Strauss, who considered him one of the finest interpreters of his works; he conducted the premieres of *Arabella, Friedenstag, Capriccio* (for which he wrote the libretto), and *Die Liebe der Danae.* Krauss was renowned as a conductor of works by Mozart, Wagner, and Verdi, as well as those by the Viennese waltz composers.

BIBL.: A. Berger, *C. K.* (Graz, 1924; 3rd ed., 1929); J. Gregor, *C. K.: Eine musikalische Sendung* (Vienna, 1953); O. van Pander, *C. K. in Munchen* (Munich, 1955); B. Flowers, "C. K. (1893–1954): An Evolution," *Le Grand Baton* (Nov. 1986; with discography); G. Kende and S. Scanzoni, *Der Prinzipal. C. K.: Fakten, Vergleiche, Rückschlüsse* (Tutzing, 1988).

Krauze, Zygmunt, Polish composer and pianist; b. Warsaw, Sept. 19, 1938. He was a student of Sikorski (composition) and Wiłkomirska (piano) at the Warsaw State College of Music (M.A., 1964), and then completed his training with Boulanger in Paris (1966–67). In 1966 he took 1st prize as a pianist in the Gaudeamus Competition for interpreters of contemporary music in Holland, and subsequently specialized in the performance of modern works. In 1967 he founded the Warsaw Music Workshop, a new music group which gave over 100 premieres of contemporary scores. In 1970–71 he taught piano at Cleveland State Univ. In 1973–74 he was active in Berlin on a grant from the Deutscher Akademischer Austauschdienst. He became president of the Polish section of the ISCM in 1980. In 1982–83 he served as artistic advisor to IRCAM in Paris. He also lectured extensively on contemporary music in Europe and the U.S. In 1987 he was elected president of the ISCM. The French government made him a Chevalier dans l'ordre des arts et les Lettres in 1984. In 1989 he received the Polish Composers Union prize and the prize of the Polish Ministry of Culture and Arts.

WORKS: CHAMBER OPERA: *Die Kleider* or *Der Star* (1981; Mannheim, March 26, 1982). **ORCH.:** *Voices* for 15 Instruments (1968–72); *3 Pieces* (1969; 1970; Metz, Oct. 22, 1982); *Folk Music* (Warsaw, Sept. 17, 1972); *Fête galante et pastorale* for Small Orch. and 4 Soloists ad libitum Playing 16 Folk Instruments (1974–75; Warsaw, Sept. 25, 1975; based on the spatial piece, 1974); Piano Concerto (1975–76; Donaueschingen, Oct. 1976); *Suite de danses et de chansons* for Harpsichord and Orch. (Bonn, Dec. 12, 1977); Violin Concerto (1979–80; Lisbon, June 7, 1980); *Tableau vivant* for Chamber Orch. (Vienna, Nov. 20, 1981); *Arabesque* for Piano and Chamber Orch. (1983; Radio France, Paris, Jan. 6, 1984); *Blanc et Rouge, paysage d'un pays* for 4 Brass Orchs., 2 Accordion Orchs., 2 Mandolin Orchs., and 6 Percussion (Strasbourg, Sept. 29, 1985); Double Concerto for Violin, Piano, and Orch. (1985; Radio France, Paris, Oct. 1988); *Symphonie parisienne* for Chamber Orch. (Paris, June 4, 1986). **CHAMBER:** *Prime Numbers* for 2 Violins (1961); 3 string quartets: No. 1 (Warsaw, Sept. 26, 1965), No. 2 (1970; Warsaw, Sept. 15, 1979), and No. 3 (1982; Paris, Jan. 9, 1983); *Entrée* for Clarinet, Trombone, Cello, and Piano (1968); *Polychromy* for Clarinet, Trombone, Piano, and Cello (1968); *Aus aller Welt stammende* for 10 Strings (Innsbruck, April 7, 1973); *Song* for 4 to 6 Melody Instruments (1974; based on the spatial piece); *Idyll* for 4 Hurdy-gurdies, 4 Bagpipes, 4 Folk Violins, 4 Fifes, 16 Bells, and Tape (1974); *Soundscape* for 4 Zithers, 4 Melodicas, 4 Recorders, 8 Little Folk Bells, 4 Glasses, Amplification, and Tape (1975); *Automatophone* for Mandolins, Guitars, and Music Boxes (1974; also as a spatial piece, 1976); *Commencement* for Harpsichord (1981); *Je préfère qu'il chante* for Bassoon (1984); *Quatuor pour la naissance* for Clarinet, Violin, Cello, and Piano (Radio France, Paris, Nov. 10, 1985); *La rivière souterraine* for Clarinet, Trumpet, Guitar, Percussion, Piano, Accordion, Cello, and Tape (1987; based on the spatial piece); *Siegfried und Siegmund* for Cello and Piano (1988); *For Alfred Schlec with Admiration* for String Quartet (1988); Piano Quintet (1993); *Terra incognita* for 10 Strings and Piano (1994). **KEYBOARD: PIANO:** *5 Pieces* (1957–58); *Praeludium, Intermezzo, Postludium* (1958); *2 Inventions* (1958); *7 Interludes* (1958); *Monody and Fugue* (1959); *Ohne Kontraste* (1960); *5 Unitary Piano Pieces* (1964); *Triptychon* (1964); *Esquisse* (1967); *Falling Water* (1971); *Stone Music* (1972); *Gloves Music* (1972); *1 Piano, 8-hands* for 4 Pianists (1973); *Music Box Waltz* (1977); *Ballade* (1978); *From Keyboard to Score* (1987); *Nightmare Tango* (1987–91); *La chanson de mal-aime* (1989); *Blue Jay Way* (1990); *Refrain* (1993). **ORGAN:** *Diptychos* (1981). **VOCAL:** *Malaisische Pantunen* for Woman's Voice and 3 Flutes (1961); *Postcard from the Mountains* for Woman's Voice and 5 Instruments (1990). **SPATIAL:** *Spatial Music Composition No. 1* for 6 Tapes, Architect, and Sculptor (1968) and *No. 2* for 2 Tapes and Architect (1970); *Song* for 4 to 6 Melody Instruments and 6 Music Boxes (1974; also without music boxes); *Automatophone* for 15 Music Boxes, 15 Plucked Instruments, and Amplification (1974; also without amplification, 1976); *Fête galante et pastorale*, spatial music for a Castle for 6 Instrumental Groups and 13 Tapes (1974; also for Orch., 1974–75); *La rivière souterraine: Spatial Music* for 7 Tapes and 2 Architects (1987; also for 7 Instruments and Tape).

Krebs, Helmut, German tenor; b. Dortmund, Oct. 8, 1913. He studied at the Berlin Hochschule für Musik. He made his debut at the Berlin Städtische Oper (1938); then sang with the Düsseldorf Opera (1945–47) and again with the Berlin Städtische Oper. He also sang opera in Hamburg, Munich, Milan, London, Glyndebourne, Edinburgh, and Salzburg; likewise appeared as an oratorio and concert artist. In 1963 he was made a Berlin Kammersanger. He taught at the Frankfurt am Main Hochschule für Musik (1963–75).

Krein, Alexander (Abramovich), Russian composer, brother of **Grigori (Abramovich)** and uncle of **Julian (Grigorievich) Krein**; b. Nizhny-Novgorod, Oct. 20, 1883; d. Staraya Ruza, near Moscow, April 21, 1951. At the age of 13, he entered the Moscow Cons. and studied cello; also studied composition privately with Nikolayev and Yavorsky. He taught at the People's Cons. in Moscow (1912–17); after the Revolution, he worked in the music division of the Commissariat of Education and in the Ethnographic Dept. From 1923 he was associated with the productions of the Jewish Drama Theater in Moscow, and wrote music for many Jewish plays. Together with Gnessin, he was a leader of the National Jewish movement in Russia. In general, his style was influenced by Scriabin and Debussy, but he made considerable use of authentic Hebrew material.

WORKS: DRAMATIC: OPERAS: *Zagmuk*, on a revolutionary subject based on an ancient Babylonian tale (Moscow, May 29, 1930); *Daughter of the People* (1946). **BALLET:** *Laurencie*, after Lope de Vega (1938). Incidental music to plays, including *The Eternal One* (1923), *Sabbati Zewi* (1924), *Ghetto* (1924), *The People* (1925), and *The Doctor* (1925). **ORCH.:** *Elegy* (1914); *The Rose and the Cross* (1917–21); 2 syms. (1922–25; 1946); *Salome* (1923); suites. **CHAMBER:** String Quartet; *Jewish Sketches* for Clarinet and String Quartet; *Elegiac Trio* for Violin, Cello, and Piano; Piano Sonata. **VOCAL:** *Kaddish* for Tenor, Chorus, and Orch. (1921); *U.S.S.R., Shock Brigade of the World Proletariat* for Narrator, Chorus, and Orch. (1925); *Threnody in Memory of Lenin* for Chorus and Orch. (1925); vocalises; songs.

BIBL.: L. Sabaneyev, *A. K.* (Moscow, 1928; in Russian and German); J. Krein and N. Rogozhina, *A. K.* (Moscow, 1964).

Krein, Grigori (Abramovich), Russian composer, brother of **Alexander (Abramovich)** and father of **Julian (Grigorievich) Krein**; b. Nizhny-Novgorod, March 18, 1879; d. Komarovo, near Leningrad, Jan. 6, 1955. He studied with Juon and Glière. His music underwent the influence of Jewish culture, and he wrote many works on Jewish themes; however, he also cultivated strict classical forms, adapting them to his needs. He wrote a descriptive symphonic cycle on Lenin's life (1937); Violin Concerto; *Hebrew Rhapsody* for Clarinet and Orch.; String Quartet; piano pieces.

Krein, Julian (Grigorievich), Russian composer and musicologist, son of **Grigori (Abramovich) Krein**; b. Moscow, March 5, 1913. He studied with his father; wrote his first compositions at the age of 13. In 1927 he went to Paris, where he completed his studies with Dukas at the École Normale de Musique (graduated, 1932). In 1934 he returned to Moscow. He publ. several monographs (all in Moscow), including ones on Falla (1960), Debussy (1962), Ravel (1962), and his uncle **Alexander (Abramovich) Krein** (with N. Rogozhina; 1964). His music was inspired by both Russian and French models, resulting in works of notable lyricism and harmonic inventiveness.

WORKS: ORCH.: *Razrusheniye* (Destruction), symphonic prelude (1929); Cello Concerto (1929); 3 piano concertos (1929, 1942, 1943); *Vesennyaya simfoniya* (Spring Symphony; 1935–59); *Serenade* (1943); *Arkticheskaya poema*, sym. (1943); *Poemasimfoniya* (1954); *Poema* for Violin and Orch. (1956); Violin Concerto (1959); *Rembrandt*, vocal-symphonic picture (1962–69). **CHAMBER:** 4 string quartets (1925, 1927, 1936, 1943); 2 violin sonatas (1948, 1971); Flute Sonata (1957); Piano Trio (1958); Clarinet Sonata (1961); *Sonata-Poema* for Cello and Piano (1972); 2 piano sonatas (1924, 1955); other piano pieces. **VOCAL:** Songs.

BIBL.: Y. Tyulin, *J. K.: Ocherk zhizni i tvorchestva* (J. K.: Sketch of His Life and Work; Moscow, 1971).

Kreisler, Fritz (actually, **Friedrich**), great Austrian-born American violinist; b. Vienna, Feb. 2, 1875; d. N.Y., Jan. 29, 1962. His extraordinary talent manifested itself when he was only 4, and it was carefully fostered by his father, under whose instruction he made such progress that at age 6 he was accepted as a pupil of Jacob Dont; he also studied with Jacques Auber until, at 7, he entered the Vienna Cons., where his principal teachers were Hellmesberger, Jr. (violin), and Bruckner (theory); he gave his first performance there when he was 9 and was awarded its gold medal at 10. He subsequently studied with Massart (violin) and Delibes (composition) at the Paris Cons., sharing the premier prix in violin with 4 other students (1887). He made his U.S. debut in Boston on Nov. 9, 1888; then toured the country during the 1889–90 season with the pianist Moriz Rosenthal, but had only moderate success. Returning to Europe, he abandoned music to study medicine in Vienna and art in Rome and Paris; then served as an officer in the Austrian army (1895–96). Resuming his concert career, he appeared as a soloist with Richter and the Vienna Phil. on Jan. 23, 1898. His subsequent appearance as a soloist with Nikisch and the Berlin Phil. on Dec. 1, 1899, launched his international career. Not only had he regained his virtuosity during his respite, but he had also developed into a master interpreter. On his 2nd tour of the U.S. (1900–1901), both as a soloist and as a recitalist with Hofmann and Gerardy, he carried his audiences by storm. On May 12, 1902, he made his London debut as a soloist with Richter and the Phil. Soc. orch.; was awarded its Gold Medal in 1904. Elgar composed his Violin Concerto for him, and Kreisler gave its premiere under the composer's direction in London on Nov. 10, 1910. At the outbreak of World War I in 1914, Kreisler joined his former regiment, but upon being quickly wounded he was discharged. He then returned to the U.S. to pursue his career; after the U.S. entered the war in 1917, he withdrew from public appearances. With the war over, he reappeared in N.Y. on Oct. 27, 1919, and once again resumed his tours. From 1924 to 1934 he made his home in Berlin, but in 1938 he went to France, and became a naturalized French citizen. In 1939 he settled in the U.S., becoming a naturalized American citizen (1943). In 1941 he suffered a near-fatal accident when he was struck by a truck in N.Y.; however, he recovered and continued to give concerts until 1950.

Kreisler was one of the greatest masters of the violin. His brilliant technique was ably matched by his remarkable tone, both of which he always placed in the service of the composer. He was the owner of the great Guarneri "del Gesù" violin of 1733 and of instruments by other masters. He gathered a rich collection of invaluable MSS; in 1949 he donated the original scores of Brahms's Violin Concerto and Chausson's *Poème* for Violin and Orch. to the Library of Congress in Washington, D.C. He wrote some of the most popular violin pieces in the world, among them *Caprice viennois, Tambourin chinois, Schön Rosmarin,* and *Liebesfreud.* He also publ. a number of pieces in the classical vein, which he ascribed to various composers (Vivaldi, Pugnani, Couperin, Padre Martini, Dittersdorf, Francoeur, Stamitz, and others). In 1935 he reluctantly admitted that these pieces were his own, with the exception of the first 8 bars from the "Couperin" *Chanson Louis XIII,* taken from a traditional melody; he explained his motive in doing so as the necessity of building up well-rounded programs for his concerts that would contain virtuoso pieces by established composers, rather than a series of compositions under his own, as yet unknown name. He also wrote the operettas *Apple Blossoms* (N.Y., Oct. 7, 1919) and *Sissy* (Vienna, Dec. 23, 1932), publ. numerous arrangements of early and modern music (Corelli's *La Folia,* Tartini's *The Devil's Trill,* Dvořák's *Slavonic Dances,* Granados's *Spanish Dance,* Albéniz's *Tango* et al.), and prepared cadenzas for the Beethoven and Brahms violin concertos. He publ. a book of reminiscences of World War I, *Four Weeks in the Trenches: The War Story of a Violinist* (Boston, 1915).

BIBL.: O. Downes, "K.'s Delectable Musical Hoax," *N.Y. Times* (March 3, 1935); L. Lochner, *F. K.* (N.Y., 1950; 3rd ed., rev., 1981); A. Bell, *F. K. Remembered: A Tribute* (Braunton, Devon, 1992).

Kreizberg, Yakov, Russian conductor; b. Leningrad, Oct. 24, 1959. He was the brother of **Semyon Bychkov**. For personal and professional reasons, he assumed the surname of his maternal great-grandfather. Following private training from Musin in Leningrad, he went to the U.S. in 1976 and studied with Bernstein, Ozawa, and Leinsdorf at the Berkshire Music Center in Tanglewood. He was an assistant to Michael Tilson Thomas at the Los Angeles Phil. Inst. From 1985 to 1988 he was music director of the Mannes College of Music Orch. in N.Y. In 1986 he won the Stokowski conducting competition in N.Y. In 1988 he became Generalmusikdirektor of the Niederrheinsichen Sym. Orch. and the Krefeld-Mönchengladbach Opera. He made his debut at the Glyndebourne Festival conducting *Jenůfa* in 1992. In 1994 he conducted *Der Rosenkavalier* at his first appearance at London's Covent Garden. During this period, he also made guest conducting appearances with major European and North American orchs. He was chief conductor of the Komische Oper in Berlin from 1994 and principal conductor of the Bournemouth Sym. Orch. from 1995.

Krejčí, Iša (František), prominent Czech composer and conductor; b. Prague, July 10, 1904; d. there, March 6, 1968. He studied composition with Jirák and Novák and conducting with Talich at the Prague Cons. (graduated, 1929). He conducted at the Bratislava Opera (1928–32), then at the Prague National Theater (1933–34) and at the Prague Radio (1934–45). From 1945 to 1958 he was chief conductor of the Olomouc Opera; then was artistic director of the Prague National Theater (1958–68). His music, in a neo-Classical idiom, is distinguished by vivacious rhythms and freely flowing melody; the national Czech element is not ostentatious, but its presence is well marked.

WORKS: OPERAS: *Antigone* (1934); *Pozdviženi v Efesu* (The Revolt at Ephesus), after Shakespeare's *Comedy of Errors* (1939–43; Prague, Sept. 8, 1946). **ORCH.:** *Maly balet* (Small Ballet) for Chamber Orch. (1927–30); *Sinfonietta* (1929); Concertino for Piano and Wind Instruments (1935); Concertino for Violin and Wind Instruments (1936); Suite (1939); *Sinfonietta-Divertimento* (1939); Cello Concertino (1939–40); *20 Variations on an Original Theme* (1946–47); *Serenade* (1947–50); *14 Variations on the folk song Goodnight, My Beloved* (1951–52); 4 syms. (1954–55; 1956–57; 1961–63; 1961–66); *Vivat Rossini,* overture (1967). **CHAMBER:** *Divertimento-Cassation* for Flute, Clarinet, Bassoon, and Trumpet (1925); 5 string quartets (1928, rev. 1935; 1953; 1960; 1962; 1965); Viola Sonatina (1928–29); Clarinet Sonatina (1929–30); Trio for Oboe, Clarinet, and Bassoon (1935); Trio for Clarinet, Double Bass, and Piano (1936); Nonet (1937); *Sonatina concertante* for Cello and Piano (1939); Wind Quintet (1964); Piano Trio, with Woman's Voice (1967); *4 Pieces* for Violin and Piano (1967). **PIANO:** Sonatina (1934); *3 Scherzinos* (1945). **VOCAL:** *A Little Mourning Music* for Alto, Violin, Cello, Double Bass, and Piano (1936); *Anticke motivy* (Antique Motifs) for Low Man's Voice and Orch. or Piano (1936); *Oblasy* (Night Sounds) for Voice and Wind Quintet (1936); songs.

Krejčí, Miroslav, Czech composer and teacher; b. Rychnov nad Kněžnou, Nov. 4, 1891; d. Prague, Dec. 29, 1964. He studied piano, organ, and theory at home; subsequently took courses in natural history, geography, and music at the Univ. of Prague (1910–14); also studied composition privately with Novák (1911–13). He then taught in Prague and Litoměřice (1915–53); was a prof. at the Prague Cons. (1943–53).

WORKS: OPERAS: *Léto* (Summer; 1937; Prague, Dec. 4, 1940); *Poslední Hejtman* (The Last Captain; 1944; Prague, March 18, 1948). **ORCH.:** *King Lávra,* symphonic poem (1917); *Life and Time* for Horn and Strings (1927); *Vocal Sym.* (1930); 3 numbered syms.: No. 1 (1944–46), No. 2 (1952–54), and No. 3 (1955); Viola Concerto (1947); Clarinet Concerto (1949); *Capriccio* for Viola, Winds, and Percussion (1950); *Dance Suite* (1950); Violin Concerto (1953); *Funeral Music* for Wind Orch.

(1960). **CHAMBER:** 7 string quartets (1913, 1918, 1926, 1941, 1943, 1953, 1955); Clarinet Quintet (1920); 3 string quintets (1926, 1952, 1957); *Divertimento* for Flute, Clarinet, Horn, and Bassoon (1926); 2 violin sonatas (1926, 1952); Viola Sonata (1942); Cello Sonata (1943); Sonatina for Bassoon or Oboe or Horn and Piano (1950); Septet (1950); Nonet (1953); Organ Sonata (1954); Quartet for Oboe, Clarinet, Bassoon, and Piano (1955); Wind Octet (1956); Suite for Horn (1956); *3 Pieces* for 3 Violas and Piano (1957); Flute Sonata (1958); *Divertimento* for 10 Winds (1958); Horn Sonata (1959). **VOCAL:** Cantatas; choruses; songs.

Krek, Uroš, Slovenian composer; b. Ljubljana, May 21, 1922. He studied composition with Škerjanc at the Ljubljana Academy of Music, graduating in 1947. He worked for the Ljubljana Radio (1950–58); then did research for the Ljubljana Ethnomusicological Inst. (1958–67); subsequently taught at his alma mater (1967–86). He was made a member of the Yugoslav Academy of Science and Art (1977) and the Slovene Academy of Science and Art (1979). His style of composition is classical in form, but contains some elements of folk modalities.

WORKS: ORCH.: Violin Concerto (1949); Bassoon Concerto (1954); *Mouvements concertants* for Strings (1956); Horn Concerto (1960); *Inventiones ferales* for Violin and Orch. (1962); Piccolo Concerto (1966); Sinfonia for Strings (1973); Cello Concerto (1984). **CHAMBER:** Violin Sonata (1946); *Capriccio* for Viola and 10 Instruments (1971); Sonata for 2 Violins (1971); *La Journée d'un bouffon* for Brass Quintet (1973); Clarinet Sonata (1976); Trio for Violin, Viola, and Cello (1977); String Quartet (1979); Cello Sonata (1984); *Espressivo* for Flute and Piano (1985); *Jeux pour quatre* (1986). **VOCAL:** *Old Egyptian Stanzas* for Tenor and Orch. (1967); choral pieces. **OTHER:** Film scores.

Kremenliev, Boris, Bulgarian-American musicologist and composer; b. Razlog, May 23, 1911; d. Los Angeles, April 25, 1988. He went to the U.S. in 1929; studied composition with La Violette at De Paul Univ. in Chicago (B.M., 1936; M.M., 1938) and with Hanson at the Eastman School of Music in Rochester, N.Y. (Ph.D., 1942). He was a member of the Psychological Warfare Branch of the U.S. Army in Europe during World War II. In 1947 he was appointed to the faculty of the Univ. of Calif. at Los Angeles. He publ. *Bulgarian-Macedonian Folk Music* (Los Angeles, 1952). Several of his compositions were imbued with Bulgarian melorhythms; of these, the most interesting are *Pravo Horo* for Orch. (Rochester, N.Y., April 18, 1940) and *Bulgarian Rhapsody* for Orch. (1952); he also composed various other orch. works, including *Crucifixion* (1952), *Elegy: June 5, 1968* (1968–69), and *Peasant Dance* (1984); among his chamber works are 2 string quartets (1954, 1965), 2 piano sonatas (1954, 1959), Double Bass Sonata (1966–67), and *Overtones* for Brass (1983–84); his vocal music included choral pieces and songs.

Kremer, Gidon, brilliant Latvian violinist; b. Riga, Feb. 27, 1947. His parents were violinists in the Riga Sym. Orch. He obtained the elements of violin study from his father and grandfather; when he was 16, he won the 1st prize of the Latvian Republic, and then continued professional studies with David Oistrakh at the Moscow Cons. He took part in several competitions, culminating in 1st prizes at the Paganini Competition in Genoa in 1968 and the Tchaikovsky Competition in Moscow in 1970. Subsequently he appeared in Western Europe to notable acclaim. He made an auspicious N.Y. debut at Avery Fisher Hall on Jan. 14, 1977. In subsequent years, he appeared as a soloist with many of the major orchs. of the world, gave recitals, and performed in chamber music settings. He has won special commendation for his efforts to broaden the repertoire for his instrument; his great contribution to modern music has been the consistent presentation of new violin works, particularly those of Soviet composers, among them Alfred Schnittke and Sofia Gubaidulina. He has also given notable performances of the works of the Estonian composer Arvo Pärt.

Kremlev, Yuli (Anatolyevich), Russian musicologist and composer; b. Essentuki, June 19, 1908; d. Leningrad, Feb. 19, 1971. He studied piano at the Leningrad Cons. (1925–28), where he pursued his general musical education (1929–33); later he was granted his Candidate (1944) and Ph.D. (1963) degrees. From 1957 he was head of the music dept. of the Leningrad Inst. of the Theater, Music, and Cinematography. His most significant monographs (all publ. in Moscow) were those on Chopin (1949; 3rd ed., 1971), Grieg (1958), Debussy (1964), Massenet (1969), and Saint-Saëns (1970). He wrote a Sym., 14 piano sonatas, and songs.

Krenek (originally, **Křenek**), **Ernst,** remarkable Austrian-born American composer, whose intellect responded equally to his musical philosophy and his imaginative compositional style; b. Vienna, Aug. 23, 1900; d. Palm Springs, Calif., Dec. 23, 1991. He studied with Schreker at the Vienna Academy of Music (1916–18). Following miltary service (1918), he enrolled at the Univ. of Vienna in 1919 to study philosophy. In 1920 he went to Berlin to continue his studies with Schreker at the Hochschule für Musik. The premiere of Krenek's atonally conceived 2nd Sym. (Kassel, June 14, 1923) brought him considerable notoriety. With his so-called "jazz" opera *Jonny spielt auf* (Leipzig, Feb. 10, 1927), Krenek became internationally known via performances of the score around the world. A commission from the Vienna State Opera led to his composing the 12-tone opera *Karl V* (1932–33). After the Nazis assumed control of Germany in 1933, Krenek was declared a degenerate artist and his works were banned. Pressure was brought to bear on the Austrian authorities and the scheduled premiere of *Karl V* in 1934 at the Vienna State Opera was cancelled. The opera finally received its premiere in Prague on June 22, 1938. Following the Anschluss of 1938, Krenek emigrated to the U.S. In 1945 he became a naturalized American citizen. After teaching at the Malkin Cons. in Boston (1938–39), he taught at Vassar College (1939–42). From 1942 to 1947 he was head of the music dept. at Hamline Univ. in St. Paul, Minn. In 1947 Krenek went to Los Angeles, where he continued to teach. In 1966 he settled in Palm Springs and devoted himself mainly to composing and writing. As a composer, Krenek pursued a modified serial path. After coming into contact with the avant-garde in Darmstadt, he was moved to expand his horizons. In 1957 he embraced total serial writing. In 1970 he adopted the use of rows and serial techniques in a manner which led to a much greater freedom of expression and mastery. Although Krenek was elected to membership in the National Inst. of Arts and Letters (1960) and was awarded honorary titles and degrees from various American institutions, his importance as a composer was most fully realized in Europe. In 1959 he was made an extraordinary member of the Berlin Akademie der Künste. In 1960 he received the Gold Medal of the City of Vienna. He was awarded the Grand Austrian State Prize in 1963. In 1970 he received the Ring of Honor of Vienna, and in 1982 was accorded honorary citizenship of Vienna. In 1986 a composition prize was established in Vienna in his name. His 90th birthday was celebrated by special performances of a number of his scores. Krenek deposited the MS of his autobiography in the Library of Congress in Washington, D.C., in 1950, with the stipulation that it should not be made public until 15 years after his death.

WORKS: DRAMATIC: *Cyrano de Bergerac*, incidental music (1917); *Die Zwingburg*, scenic cantata (1922; Berlin, Oct. 20, 1924); *Napoleon*, incidental music for G. Dietrich's play (1922); *Fiesco*, incidental music for S. Friedrich's play (1922); *Der sprung über den Schatten*, comic opera (1923; Frankfurt am Main, June 9, 1924); *Orpheus und Eurydike*, opera (1923; Kassel, Nov. 27, 1926); *Bluff*, operetta (1924–25; withdrawn); *Mammon*, ballet (1925; Munich, Oct. 1, 1927); *Der vertauschte Cupido*, ballet (Kassel, Oct. 25, 1925); *Das Leben ein Traum*, incidental music for Grillparzer's *La vida es sueño* (Kassel, 1925); *Vom lieben Augustin*, incidental music for Dietzenschmidt's folk play (Kassel, Nov. 28, 1925); *Die Rache des verhöhnten Liebhabers*, incidental music for E. Toller's puppet play (1925; Zürich, 1926); *Das Gotteskind*, incidental music for a radio play (Kassel Radio,

1925); *Der Triumph der Empfindsamkeit*, incidental music for Goethe's play (1925; Kassel, May 9, 1926; suite, 1926–27; Hamburg, Nov. 28, 1927); *Jonny spielt auf*, opera (1926; Leipzig, Feb. 10, 1927); *Ein Sommernachtstraum*, incidental music for Shakespeare's *A Midsummer Night's Dream* (Heidelberg, July 1926); *Der Diktator*, opera (1926; Wiesbaden, May 6, 1928); *Das geheime Königreich*, fairy tale opera (1926–27; Wiesbaden, May 6, 1928); *Marlborough s'en va-t-en guerre*, incidental music for a puppet play after a comedy by M. Archard (Kassel, May 11, 1927); *Schwergewicht, oder Die Ehre der Nation*, operetta (1927; Wiesbaden, May 6, 1928); *Die Kaiserin von Neufundlung*, incidental music for F. Wedekind's play (1927); *Leben des Orest*, opera (1928–29; Leipzig, Jan. 19, 1930); *Kehraus um St. Stephan*, opera (1930); *Herr Reinecke Fuchs*, incidental music for H. Anton's play (1931); *Karl V*, opera (1932–33; Prague, June 22, 1938; rev. 1954; Düsseldorf, May 11, 1958); *Cefalo e Procri*, opera (1933–34; Venice, Sept. 15, 1934); *L'incoronazione di Poppea*, orchestration of Monteverdi's opera (1936; Vienna, Sept. 25, 1937; suite, 1936); *8 Column Line*, ballet (Hartford, Conn., May 19, 1939); *Tarquin*, chamber opera (1940; Poughkeepsie, N.Y., May 13, 1941); *What Price Confidence?*, chamber opera (1945; Saarbrücken, May 22, 1946); *Sargasso*, ballet (1946; N.Y., March 24, 1965; based on the *Symphonic Elegy*); *Dark Waters*, opera (1950–51; Los Angeles, May 2, 1951); *Pallas Athene weint*, opera (1952–53; rev. version, Hamburg, Oct. 17, 1955; also as the *Symphony Pallas Athene*); *The Belltower*, opera (1955–56; Urbana, Ill., March 17, 1957); *Jedermann*, incidental music for Hofmannsthal's play (1960; Salzburg, July 30, 1962; film score, 1961); *Ausgerechnet und verspielt*, television opera (1960–62; Austrian TV, Vienna, July 25, 1962; with entr'acte *Roulette Sestina*, Mannheim, Oct. 15, 1964); *Jest of Cards*, ballet (San Francisco, April 17, 1962; based on *Marginal Sounds* for Chamber Ensemble, 1957); *Alpbach Quintet*, ballet (Alpbach, Austria, Aug. 25, 1962); *Der goldene Bock*, opera (1962–63; Hamburg, June 16, 1964); *Der Zauberspiegel*, television opera (1963; 1965–66; Bavarian TV, Munich, Sept. 6, 1967); *König Oedipus*, incidental music for Sophocles' play (1964; Salzburg, July 27, 1965); *Sardakai, oder Das kommt davon*, opera (1968–69; Hamburg, June 27, 1970); *Flaschenpost vom Paradies, oder Der englische Ausflug*, television play (1972–73; Vienna, March 8, 1974).

ORCH.: Suite for Piano and Orch. (1915–16); *Leonce und Lena*, overture (c.1919); 4 unnumbered syms. (1920; 1924–25, Leipzig, 1926; *Kleine Symphonie* for Chamber Orch., Berlin, Nov. 3, 1928; *Symphony Pallas Athene*, Hamburg, Oct. 11, 1954, based on the opera *Pallas Athene weint*); 5 numbered syms.: No. 1 (1921; Berlin, March 17, 1922), No. 2 (1922; Kassel, June 11, 1923), No. 3 (1922; Berlin, 1923), No. 4 (N.Y., Nov. 27, 1947), and No. 5 (1947–49; Albuquerque, March 16, 1950); 2 concerti grossi: No. 1 (1921–22; Weimar, Aug. 19, 1922; withdrawn) and No. 2 (Zürich, Oct. 14, 1924); *Symphonische Musik* (Donaueschingen, July 30, 1922) and *Symphonische Musik No. 2* for Chamber Orch. (1923; Berlin, Feb. 1, 1924); 4 piano concertos: No. 1 (Winterthur, Dec. 19, 1923), No. 2 (1937; Amsterdam, March 17, 1938), No. 3 (Minneapolis, Nov. 22, 1946), and No. 4 (1950; Cologne, Oct. 22, 1951); Concertino for Flute, Violin, Harpsichord, and Strings (1924; Winterthur, Feb. 18, 1925); 2 violin concertos: No. 1 (1924; Dessau, Jan. 5, 1925) and No. 2 (1953–54; Cologne, Feb. 18, 1955); *Stücke* (1924; Winterthur, Nov. 4, 1926); (3) *Lustige Märsche* for Band (Donaueschingen, 1926); *Potpourri* (Cologne, Nov. 5, 1927; rev. 1954; Stuttgart, Oct. 22, 1957); *Theme and 13 Variations* (N.Y., Oct. 29, 1931); *Campo Marzio*, overture (1937); *Symphonic Piece* for Strings (1939; Basel, June 11, 1940); *Little Concerto* for Piano, Organ, and Chamber Orch. (1939–40; Poughkeepsie, N.Y., May 23, 1940; also for 2 Pianos and Chamber Orch.); *A Contrapuntal Excursion Through the Centuries* for Student String Orch. (1941); *I Wonder as I Wander*, variations on a N.C. folk tune (Minneapolis, Dec. 11, 1942); *Tricks and Trifles* (1945; Minneapolis, March 22, 1946; based on *Hurricane Variations* for Piano, 1944); *Symphonic Elegy* for Strings (Saratoga Springs, N.Y., Sept. 3, 1946; also as the ballet *Sargasso*); *Short Pieces* for Strings (1948; Basel, Jan. 17, 1955; also for String Quartet); Double Concerto for Violin, Piano, and Orch. (1950; Donaueschingen, Oct. 6, 1951); Concerto for Harp and Chamber Orch. (1951; Philadelphia, Dec. 12, 1952); Concerto for 2 Pianos and Orch. (1951; N.Y., Oct. 24, 1953); *Sinfonietta a Brasileira* for Strings (1952; Besançon, Sept. 6, 1953); 2 cello concertos: No. 1 (1952–53; Los Angeles, March 4, 1954) and No. 2 (1982; Salzburg, Aug. 9, 1983); *Scenes from the West* for School Orch. (1952–53); *11 Transparencies* (1954; Louisville, Feb. 12, 1955); Suite for Flute and Strings (1954; also for Flute and Piano); *Capriccio* for Cello and Orch. (Darmstadt, May 31, 1955); *Sieben leichte Stücke* for Strings (Mainz, 1955); Suite for Clarinet and Strings (1955; also for Clarinet and Piano); *Divertimento* (1956; Ossiach, Austria, Aug. 23, 1986); *Kette, Kreis und Spiegel, sinfonische Zeichnung* (1956–57; Basel, Jan. 23, 1958); *Hexahedron* for Chamber Orch. (Darmstadt, Sept. 7, 1958); *Quaestio temporis* (1959; Hamburg, Sept. 30, 1960); *From 3 Make 7* (1960–61; Berlin, March 3, 1965; rev. version, Baden-Baden, Feb. 16, 1968); *6 Profiles* (1965–68; Fargo, N.Dak., March 14, 1970); *Horizon Circled* (Rochester, Mich., Aug. 12, 1967); *Perspektiven* (1967; Chicago, July 6, 1968); *Exercises of a Late Hour* (1967; San Diego, Jan. 19, 1968; rev. 1969); *Fivefold Enfoldment* (1969; Bonn, Jan. 5, 1970); *Kitharaulos* (1971; The Hague, June 20, 1972; also as *Aulokithara* for Oboe, Harp, and Tape); *Statisch und Ekstatisch* (1971–72; Zürich, March 23, 1973); *Von vorn herein* for Chamber Orch. (Salzburg, Aug. 21, 1974); *Auf- und Ablehnung* (1974; Nuremburg, June 13, 1975); *Dream Sequence* for Symphonic Band (1975–76; College Park, Md., March 11, 1977); Concerto for Organ and Strings (1978–79; Ossiach, Austria, July 22, 1979); *Im Tal der Zeit* (1979; Graz, Oct. 26, 1980); *Arc of Life* for Chamber Orch. (1981; Palm Springs, Calif., Feb. 24, 1982); Organ Concerto (1982; Melbourne, May 17, 1983).

CHAMBER: *Variationen über ein lustiges Thema* for Violin, Cello, and Piano (1916); Cello Sonata (1917); *Serenade* for Clarinet, Viola, and Cello (1919; Berlin, Feb. 8, 1921); 2 unnumbered violin sonatas (1919–20, Berlin, June 21, 1921; 1944–45, Minneapolis, Oct. 21, 1945); *Albumblatt* for Violin and Piano (1920); 1 unnumbered string quartet (1920); 8 numbered string quartets: No. 1 (Nuremberg, June 16, 1921), No. 2 (1921; Berlin, April 24, 1922), No. 3 (Salzburg, Aug. 3, 1923), No. 4 (1923–24; Salzburg, Aug. 5, 1924), No. 5 (Copenhagen, Sept. 29, 1930), No. 6 (1936; Darmstadt, Jan. 16, 1953), No. 7 (1943–44; Indianapolis, Nov. 15, 1944), and No. 8 (1980–81; N.Y., June 7, 1981); *Kleine Suite* for Clarinet and Piano (1924; Bamberg, Jan. 7, 1967); 2 sonatas for Solo Violin: No. 1 (1924; Darmstadt, Nov. 28, 1960) and No. 2 (Washington, D.C., Dec. 19, 1948); *Intrada* for Clarinet, Bassoon, Trumpet, 2 Horns, Trombone, and Timpani (Kassel, June 1, 1927); *Triophantasie* for Violin, Cello, and Piano (1929; Berlin, May 15, 1930); *School Music* for Various Instruments (1938–39; Ann Arbor, July 27, 1939); Suite for Cello (Poughkeepsie, N.Y., Nov. 16, 1939); *Deep Sea* for Tuba and Piano (c.1939); Sonatina for Flute and Viola (1942; Buenos Aires, Oct. 22, 1945; also for Flute and Clarinet, Buenos Aires, Oct. 30, 1944); Sonata for Solo Viola (1942; Chicago, April 11, 1947); Trio for Violin, Clarinet, and Piano (Minneapolis, Nov. 27, 1946); *Short Pieces* for String Quartet (1948; also for String Orch.); Viola Sonata (1948; San Francisco, March 1949); String Trio (1948–49; Los Angeles, April 4, 1949); *Parvula corona musicalis* for String Trio (1950; RAI, Rome, Jan. 15, 1951); *Invention* for Flute and Clarinet (1951; Bamberg, Jan. 7, 1967); Quintet for Flute, Clarinet, Oboe, Bassoon, and Horn (1952; rewritten 1957 as *Pentagramm*; Los Angeles, March 31, 1958); *Fantasy* for Cello and Piano (1953; Lucerne, April 6, 1954); Suite for Flute and Piano (1954; Santiago, Chile, July 5, 1956; also for Flute and String Orch.); Suite for Clarinet and Piano (1955; Miami, Nov. 29, 1962; also for Clarinet and String Orch.); Sonata for Solo Harp (1955; N.Y., Jan. 27, 1958); Oboe Sonatina (1956; N.Y., May 9, 1960); *Monologue* for Clarinet (1956; N.Y., May 9, 1960); *Marginal Sounds* for Violin, Piano, Celesta, Vibraphone, Xylophone, and Percussion (1957; N.Y., Feb. 22, 1960; also as the ballet *Jest of Cards*); Suite for Guitar (1957; Los Angeles, Feb. 16, 1959); *Flötenstück neunphasig* for

Flute and Piano (1959; Venice, Sept. 22, 1960); *Hausmusik* for Various Instruments (Berlin, Nov. 22, 1959); *Toccata* for Accordion (1962); *Cello Studien* for 1 to 4 Cellos (1963; Riehen, Switzerland, April 23, 1968); *Fibonacci Mobile* for String Quartet and Piano, 4-hands (1964; Hanover, N.H., July 7, 1965); *Stücke* for Oboe and Piano (1966; Zagreb, May 21, 1967); *Pieces* for Trombone and Piano (Buffalo, Nov. 5, 1967); Duo for Flute, Double Bass, and Tape (1970; Palm Desert, Calif., Jan. 24, 1971); *Aulokithara* for Oboe, Harp, and Tape (1971; Mainz, Oct. 11, 1972; based on *Kitharaulos* for Orch., 1971); *Accomusic* for Accordion (1976); *Opus 231* for Violin and Organ (1979; Vienna, March 10, 1980); *Streichtrio in zwölf Stationen* (1985; Ossiach, Austria, Aug. 23, 1987). **KEYBOARD: PIANO:** 1 unnumbered sonata (1913); 6 numbered sonatas: No. 1 (1919; Salzburg, May 3, 1920), No. 2 (1928; Berlin, March 27, 1929), No. 3 (1942–43; St. Paul, Minn., Dec. 1, 1943), No. 4 (San Francisco, Nov. 5, 1948), No. 5 (1950), and No. 6 (Donaueschingen, Oct. 1951); 1 unnumbered suite (c.1916); 2 numbered suites (Berlin, Dec. 12, 1924); 3 double fugues (1917, Vienna, May 14, 1918; for Piano, 4-hands, 1917; for 2 Pianos, 1918); 5 sonatinas (1–4, 1920; 5, 1928–29); *Tanzstudie* (1920); *Toccata und Chaconne über den Choral Ja ich glaub an Jesum Christum* (Berlin, Oct. 16, 1922); *Eine kleine Suite von Stücken über denselbigen Choral, verschiedenen Charakters* (Berlin, Oct. 16, 1922); *Klavierstücke* (Kassel, Nov. 18, 1925); *Vier Bagatellen* for Piano, 4-hands (1931; Vienna, April 25, 1937); *Zwölf Variationen in drei Sätzen* (Los Angeles, Dec. 16, 1937); *12 Short Piano Pieces Written in the 12-tone Technique* (1938; NBC, Washington, D.C., Jan. 3, 1939); *Hurricane Variations* (1944; also as *Tricks and Trifles* for Orch.); *Piano Pieces* (1946; St. Paul, Minn., Feb. 9, 1947); *George Washington Variations* (Los Angeles, Sept. 24, 1950); *Miniature* (1953); *20 Miniatures* (1953–54; St. Gallen, Sept. 21, 1954); *Sechs Vermessene* (1958; Kassel, Oct. 9, 1960); *Basler Massarbeit* for 2 Pianos (1960; Basel, Jan. 19, 1961); *Piano Piece in 11 Parts* (1967; Chicago, Dec. 4, 1970); *Doppelt beflügeltes Band* for 2 Pianos and Tape (1969–70; Graz, Oct. 26, 1970). **ORGAN:** Sonata (1941; Poughkeepsie, N.Y., May 3, 1942); *Organologia* (1962; Mülheim, Nov. 24, 1968); *10 Choralvorspiele* (1971); *Orga-nastro* for Organ and Tape (Ann Arbor, Oct. 18, 1971); *4 Winds Suite* (1975; Düsseldorf, March 13, 1977).

VOCAL: *Missa in Festo SS. Trinitatis* for Chorus and Organ (1913); *Grosse Ostersonate* for Chorus and Organ (c.1914); *Missa symphonica prima* for Soli, Chorus, Orch., and Organ (c.1915); *Zwischen Erd und Himmel* for Soli, Chorus, Violin, and Orch. (1916); *Um Mitternacht* for Soli, Chorus, and Orch. (1916); *Über einem Grabe* for Soli, Chorus, and Orch. (1916); *Bühnenmusik zu?* for Chorus and Orch. (c.1917); *Gott gib dein Gericht dem König*, motets for Chorus (c.1918); *O meine armen Füsse* for Voice and Small Orch. (c.1921); (7) *Lieder* for Voice and Piano (1921–22); (2) *Lieder* for Voice and Piano (1922); (5) *Lieder* for Voice and Piano (1922); (5) *Lieder* for Voice and Piano (1923; Berlin, March 26, 1926); *Gemischte a cappella Chöre* (1923); (13) *Lieder* for Voice and Piano (1924); (3) *Lieder* for Mezzo-soprano, Clarinet, and String Quartet (1924); *Vier kleine Männerchöre* (1924; Vienna, March 25, 1935); *Die Jahreszeiten* for Chorus (Donaueschingen, July 1925); *Wechsellied zum Tanz* for Soprano and Piano or Orch. (1926); *Vier a cappella Chöre* (1926; Vienna, Dec. 7, 1927); *O Lacrymosa*, 3 songs for High or Medium Voice and Piano or 7 Instruments (1926; Cologne, Jan. 29, 1927); *Gedicht* for Baritone and 5 Instruments (1926); *Kleine Kantate* for Chorus (1927); (4) *Gesänge nach alten Gedichten* for Mezzo-soprano and Piano (1927; Berlin, Nov. 21, 1929; also for Mezzo-soprano and Winds, Munich, Oct. 1927); (3) *Gesänge* for Baritone and Piano (1927; Dresden, Nov. 5, 1928); *Konzert-Arie* for Soprano and Piano (Berlin, June 1928; as *Monolog der Stella* for Soprano and Orch., Hannover, Aug. 1928); (3) *Gemischte Chöre* (1929; Vienna, Nov. 27, 1932); *Reisebuch aus den österreichischen Alpen*, 20 songs for Voice and Piano or Orch. (1929; Leipzig, Jan. 17, 1930); *Kalendar* for 4 Men's Voices (1929–30); (7) *Fiedellieder* for Medium Voice and Piano (Dresden, April 11, 1930); *Wach auf mein Hort* for Chorus (Berlin, June 23, 1930); *Durch die Nacht* for Soprano and Piano (1930–31; Dresden, April 10, 1931; also for Soprano and Orch., Vienna, June 19, 1932); *Die Nachtigall* for Soprano and Piano (Frankfurt am Main, Nov. 26, 1931; also for Soprano and Orch., Bern, Oct. 27, 1931); (11) *Gesänge des späten Jahres* for Voice and Piano (1931; Dresden, March 25, 1932); *Kantate von den Lieden des Menschen* for Chorus and Orch. (1932); *Kantate von der Vergänglichkeit des Irdischen* for Soprano, Chorus, and Piano (1932; Zürich, Oct. 9, 1933); *Fragmente aus dem Bühnenwerk Karl V* for Soprano and Orch. (1932–33; Barcelona, April 19, 1936); *Jagd im Winter* for Men's Chorus, 4 Horns, and Timpani (1933); *Das Schweigen* for Bass and Piano (1933; Winterthur, Jan. 24, 1934); *Währed der Trennung* for Mezzo-soprano, Baritone, and Piano (1933; Winterthur, Jan. 24, 1934); *Vocalise* for Voice and Piano (1934); (4) *Austrian Folk Songs* for Chorus (1934; Vienna, Feb. 25, 1935); *Italian Ballads* for Voice and Piano (1934); *Symeon der Stylit*, oratorio for Soprano, Mezzo-soprano, Tenor, Baritone, Chorus, and Orch. (1935–37; 1987; Salzburg, July 27, 1988); (5) *Lieder nach Worten von Franz Kafka* for Voice and Piano (1937–38; Poughkeepsie, N.Y., March 1, 1942); *The Night is Far Spent* for Voice and Piano (1938); *2 Choruses on Jacobean Poems* (1939; Poughkeepsie, N.Y., Dec. 7, 1940); *Proprium missae in festo SS. Innocentium martyrum (die 28 Decembris)* for Women's Chorus (Poughkeepsie, N.Y., Dec. 15, 1940); *La corona*, cantata for Mezzo-soprano, Baritone, Organ, and Percussion (1941; Copenhagen, 1958); *The Holy Ghost's Ark* for Mezzo-soprano, Oboe, Clarinet, Viola, and Cello (Madison, Wis., July 24, 1941); *Lamentatio Jeremaie prophetae* for Chorus (1941–42; Kassel, Oct. 5, 1958); *Cantata for Wartime* for Women's Chorus and Orch. (1943; Minneapolis, March 24, 1944); *5 Prayers for Women's Voices Over the Pater noster as Cantus Firmus* (1944; St. Paul, Minn., June 3, 1945); *The Ballad of the Railroads* for Medium Voice and Piano (1944; N.Y., April 5, 1950); *Santa Fe Time Table* for Chorus (1945; Los Angeles, Feb. 20, 1961); *Aegrotavit Ezechias*, motet for Women's Chorus and Piano (1945; St. Paul, Minn., March 12, 1947); *Etude* for Coloratura Soprano and Contralto (1945; St. Paul, Minn., 1946); *In paradisum*, motet for Women's Chorus (St. Paul, Minn., May 10, 1946); *O Would I Were*, canon for Chorus (1946); (4) *Songs on Poems by Gerard Manley Hopkins* for Tenor and Piano (1946–47; Waco, Texas, April 25, 1947); *Remember Now*, motet for Women's Voices and Piano (St. Paul, Minn., 1947); *Medea*, monologue for Mezzo-soprano and Orch. (1951; rev. 1952; Philadelphia, March 13, 1953); (2) *Sacred Songs* for Medium Voice and Piano (1952; N.Y., Jan. 4, 1953); (4) *Choruses* with Organ or Piano (1953); *Motette zur Opferung für das ganze Kirchenjahr* for Chorus (1954; Basel, March 27, 1955); *Proprium missae in domenica tertia in quadragesima* for Chorus (1955); *Psalmenverse zur Kommunion für das ganze Kirchenjahr* for Chorus (1955); *Ich singe wieder, wenn es tagt* for Chorus and String Orch. or String Quintet (1955–56; Linz, May 14, 1956); *Spiritus intelligentiae, Sanctus*, oratorio for Pentecost for 2 Singers, Speaker, and Electronics (1955–56; WDR, Cologne, May 30, 1956); *Egregii, carissimi*, 2 voice canon (1956); *Guten Morgen, Amerika* for Chorus (1956); *Psalmverse* for Chorus (1956); *Sestina* for Soprano and 8 Instruments (1957; N.Y., March 9, 1958); *Missa duodecim tonorum* for Women's or Men's Chorus and Organ (1957); *6 Motetten nach Worten von Franz Kafka* for Chorus (Berlin, Sept. 29, 1959); (5) *Holiday Motets* for Chorus (1959–66); *Children's Song: 3 Madrigals* for Women's Chorus (1960); *Children's Songs: 3 Motets* for Women's Chorus (1960); *The Flea* for Tenor or Soprano and Piano (1960; Raleigh, N.C., 1968); *Like Dew* for 3 Voices (1962); *Kanon Igor Strawinsky zum 80. Geburtstag* for 2-voice Chorus (1962); *O Holy Ghost*, motet for Chorus (1964; Berlin, May 3, 1965); *Wechselrahmen* for Soprano and Piano (1964–65; Düsseldorf, Sept. 9, 1965); *Quintina über die fünf Vokale* for Soprano, 6 Instruments, and Tape (Danish Radio, Copenhagen, Oct. 3, 1965); *Glauben und Wissen* for 4 Speakers, Chorus, and Orch. (North German Radio, Hamburg, Dec. 21, 1966); *Proprium für das Dreifaltigkeitsfest* for Soprano, Chorus, 2 Trumpets, Timpani, and Organ (1966–67; Basel, July 2, 1967); *Instant Remembered* for Soprano and Orch. (Hanover, N.H., Aug. 1, 1968); *Proprium Missae per a le festa de la nativitat de la mare de Due (8 de setembre)* for Chorus, Instruments, and Tape (Montserrat, Abadia, Aug. 22, 1968); *Deutsche Messe (Ordinarium)* for Chorus, Clarinet, Trumpet, 2 Trombones, Timpani, and Percussion (1968; Lucerne, Oct. 1969); *Messe Gib uns den Frieden* for Chorus and Orch. (1970; Hamburg, Oct. 17, 1971); *3 Sacred Pieces* for Chorus (Ann Arbor, Oct. 18, 1971); *3 Lessons* for Chorus (Ann Arbor, Oct. 18, 1971); *Zeitlieder* for Mezzo-soprano and String Quartet (1972; Augsburg, May 15, 1974); (3) *Lieder* for Soprano and Piano (1972; Vienna, Sept. 22, 1975); *Spätlese,* 6 songs for Baritone and Piano (1972; Munich, July 22, 1974); *Feiertags-Kantate* for Speaker, Mezzo-soprano, Baritone, Chorus, and Orch. (1974–75; Berlin, Sept. 12, 1975); *2 Silent Watchers* for Voice and Piano (1975; Palm Springs, Calif., 1976); *2 Kanons für Paul Sacher* for Voices (1975–76); (2) *Settings of Poems by William Blake* for Chorus (1976; Honolulu, May 1977); *They Knew What They Wanted* for Narrator, Oboe, Piano, Percussion, and Tape (1976–77; N.Y., Nov. 6, 1978); *Albumblatt* for Voice and Piano (1977); *The Dissembler,* monologue for Baritone and Ensemble (1978; Baltimore, March 11, 1979; *Deutsche Messgesänge zum 29. Sonntag im Jahreskreis* for Narrator, Chorus, and Organ (Graz, Oct. 19, 1980); *Opus sine nomine,* oratorio for Soprano, Mezzo-soprano, 2 Tenors, Baritone, Narrator, Chorus, and Orch. (1980–88); *For Myself, at Eighty-five,* 4-voice canon (1985).

TAPE: *San Fernando Sequence* (San Francisco, March 15, 1963); *Quintona* (1965).

WRITINGS: *Über neue Musik: Sechs Vorlesungen zur Einführung in die theoretischen Grundlagen* (Vienna, 1937; rev. ed., N.Y., 1939, as *Music Here and Now*); *Studies in Counterpoint, Based on the Twelvetone Technique* (N.Y., 1940; Ger. tr., Mainz, 1952, as *Zwölfton-Kontrapunkt Studien*); ed. *Hamline Studies in Musicology* (St. Paul, Minn., 1945, 1947); *Selbstdarstellung* (Zürich, 1948; rev. and enl. as "Self-Analysis," *University of New Mexico Quarterly,* XXIII, 1953); *Musik im goldenen Westen* (Vienna, 1949); autobiography (MS, 1950); *Johannes Okeghem* (N.Y., 1953); *De rebus prius factis* (Frankfurt am Main, 1956); *Zur Sprache gebracht* (Munich, 1958); *Tonal Counterpoint in the Style of the 18th Century* (N.Y., 1958); *Gedanken unterwegs: Dokumente einer Reise* (Munich, 1959); *Modal Counterpoint in the Style of the 16th Century* (N.Y., 1959); *Komponist und Hörer* (Kassel, 1964); *Prosa, Drama, Verse* (Munich, 1965); *Exploring Music* (London, 1966); *Horizons Circled: Reflections on My Music* (Berkeley, 1974); *Das musikdramatische Werk* (Vienna, 1974–82); *Im Zweifelsfalle: Aufsätze über Musik* (Vienna, 1984); *Franz Schubert: Ein Porträt* (Tutzing, 1990); C. Zenck, ed., *Ernst Krenek: Die Amerikanischen Tagebücher, 1937–1942: Dokumente aus dem Exil* (Vienna, 1992).

BIBL.: A. Weissmann, "E. K.," *Modern Music,* IV (1928); R. Erickson, "K.'s Later Music," *Music Review,* IX (1948); W. Grandi, *Il sistema tonale ed il contrappunto dodecafonico di E. K.* (Rome, 1954); F. Saathen, *E. K.* (Munich, 1959); L. Knessl, *E. K.* (Vienna, 1967); E. Marckhl, *Rede für E. K.* (Graz, 1969); W. Rogge, *E. K.s Opern: Spiegel der zwanziger Jahre* (Wolfenbüttel, 1970); C. Maurer-Zenck, *E. K.: Ein Komponist in Exil* (Vienna, 1980); O. Kolleritsch, ed., *E. K.: Studien zur Wertungsforschung* (Vienna, 1982); S. Cook, *Opera During the Weimar Republic: The Zeitopern of E. K., Kurt Weill, and Paul Hindemith* (Ann Arbor, 1987); G. Bowles, *E. K.: A Bio-Bibliography* (London, 1989); J. Stewart, *E. K.: The Man and His Music* (Berkeley, 1991).

Krenn, Fritz, Austrian bass; b. Vienna, Dec. 11, 1897; d. there, July 17, 1964. He studied at the Vienna Academy of Music. He made his operatic debut as the Herald in *Lohengrin* in Trieste in 1917; then sang in Vienna at the Volksoper (1917–18) and in Bratislava (1918–19); subsequently at the Vienna State Opera (1919–25; 1934–42; 1946–59); also sang with the Berlin State Opera (1927–43), and with Covent Garden in London (1935). He made his Metropolitan Opera debut in N.Y. on Jan. 5, 1951, as Baron Ochs; then continued his career in Europe. He was highly successful in buffo roles.

Krenn, Werner, Austrian tenor; b. Vienna, Sept. 21, 1943. He sang in the Vienna Boys' Choir; then studied bassoon, and played in the Vienna Sym. Orch. (1962–66); took voice lessons with Elisabeth Rado in Vienna. In 1966 he made his operatic debut in Purcell's *The Fairy Queen* at the Berlin Deutsche Oper; then sang regularly at the Vienna State Opera. He made his English debut as Jaquino with the Scottish Opera (1970). He also appeared frequently as a concert and oratorio singer. He was married to **Helga Dernesch**.

Krenz, Jan, noted Polish conductor and composer; b. Wloclawek, July 14, 1926. He managed to take music lessons as a boy in Warsaw during the German occupation; after the liberation, he studied composition with Sikorski, conducting with Wilkomirski and Górzyński, and piano with Drzewiecki at the Łódź Academy of Music. In 1948 he became conductor of the Poznań Phil. and Opera; was made 2nd conductor (1950) and conductor (1953) of the Polish Radio National Sym. Orch. in Katowice, which he led on tours of Europe and the Far East; was its regular conductor until 1956, and then again from 1958 to 1967. From 1967 to 1973 he served as artistic director of the Warsaw Opera; then was Generalmusikdirektor in Bonn (1979–82). His music is audaciously modernistic in its orientation, while preserving a classical form.

WORKS: ORCH.: *Toccata* for Piano and Orch. (1943); Sym. No. 1 (1947–49); *Nocturnes* (1950); *Classical Serenade* (1950); *Rustic Serenade* (1951); Piano Concertino (1952); *Rhapsody* for Xylophone, Tam-tam, Timpani, Celesta, and Strings (1952); *Capriccio* for 24 Instruments (1962); *Antisymphony* (1962). **VOCAL:** *Rozmowa dwoch miast* (Conversation of 2 Towns) for 2 Choruses and Orch. (1950).

Kresánek, Jozef, Slovak musicologist and composer; b. Čičmany, Dec. 20, 1913; d. Bratislava, March 14, 1986. He studied composition with Karel at the Prague Cons. (1932–37) and with Novák at the Master School there (1937–39). He taught in Prešov, and in 1944 was appointed a lecturer at the Univ. of Bratislava, becoming a full prof. of musical science in 1963. As a music scholar, he dedicated himself mainly to the stylistic analysis and codification of Slovak folk songs, and publ. numerous treatises on the subject. He also publ. a monograph on Eugen Suchoň (Bratislava, 1961), as well as other musical studies. His compositions include a String Quartet (1935), Piano Trio (1939), 2 suites for Violin and Piano (1947, 1951), 2 suites for Orch. (1951, rev. 1961; 1953), *Prelude and Toccata* for Orch. (1957), and a Piano Quintet (1975).

Kreuder, Peter Paul, German composer; b. Aachen, Aug. 18, 1905; d. Salzburg, June 28, 1981. He studied in Munich and in Hamburg. He was active as music director of the Reinhardt theaters in Berlin (1928–30) and at the drama theater in Munich (1930–33). In 1936 he was appointed state music director in Munich. In 1945 he went to Argentina, where he occupied educational posts under the regime of Juan Perón. He wrote an opera, *Der Zerrissene* (Stockholm, 1940), and several operettas. His song *Schön war die Zeit* became extremely popular in Germany. It also served as the title of his autobiography (Munich, 1955).

Kreutz, Arthur, American composer and teacher; b. La Crosse, Wis., July 25, 1906; d. Oxford, Miss., March 11, 1991. He studied at the Univ. of Wisc. and at Columbia Univ. He taught at the latter (1946–52) and at the Univ. of Mississippi (1952–64).

WORKS: OPERAS: *Acres of Sky* (Fayetteville, Ark., Nov. 16, 1951); *The University Greys* (Clinton, Miss., March 15, 1954); *Shorwood Mountain* (Clinton, Miss., Jan. 8, 1959). **ORCH.:** *Winter of the Blue Snow,* symphonic poem (1942); 2 syms. (1945, 1946); *Mosquito Serenade* (N.Y., Feb. 21, 1948); *Dance Concerto* for Clarinet and Orch. (1958); Violin Concerto (1965). **OTHER:** 2 "jazz" violin sonatas and other "jazz" pieces; choral music.

Křička, Jaroslav, eminent Czech composer and pedagogue; b. Kelc, Moravia, Aug. 27, 1882; d. Prague, Jan. 23, 1969. He studied law in Prague (1900–1902); then studied music at the Prague Cons. (1902–05) and in Berlin (1905–06). He was in Ekaterinoslav (1906–09), where he was active as a teacher and conductor; then returned to Prague as a choirmaster; later was prof. of composition at the Prague Cons. (1918–45), where he also served as rector. His music was influenced by Dvořák and native folk songs.

WORKS: OPERAS: *Hypolita* (1910–16; Prague, Oct. 10, 1917); *Bílý pán* (The White Gentleman), after Oscar Wilde's *The Canterville Ghost* (1927–29; Brno, 1929; rev. 1930; Breslau, Nov. 14, 1931); *Kral Lavra* (King Lawrence; 1936–37; rev. 1938–39; Prague, June 7, 1940); *České jesličky* (The Czech Christmas Manger; 1936–37; rev. 1948; Prague, Jan. 15, 1949); *Jáchym a Juliána* (Joachim and Julia; 1945–48; Opavá, 1951); *Serenáda*, opera buffa (Plzen, 1950); *Kolébka* (The Cradle), musical comedy (1950; Opavá, 1951); *Zahořanský hon* (The Zahorany Hunt; Opavá, 1955). **CHILDREN'S OPERAS:** *Ogaři* (Country Lads; 1918; Nové Město, Sept. 7, 1919); *Dobře to dopadlo* or *Tlustý pradědeček* (It Turned Out Well or The Fat Great-Grandfather; 1932); *Lupici a detekotyvove* (Robbers and Detectives; 1932; both operas, Prague, Dec. 29, 1932); also several small operas for children's theater; television opera, *Kalhoty* (A Pair of Trousers; Czech TV, 1962). **ORCH.:** Sym., *Jarná* (Spring; 1905–06; rev. 1942); *Nostalgie* for Strings and Harp (1905); *Faith*, symphonic poem (1907); *A Children's Suite* (1907); *Scherzo Idyllic* (1908; Prague, Nov. 13, 1910; 3rd movement of an uncompleted Sym. No. 2); *Modrý pták* (A Blue Bird), overture, after a Maeterlinck fairy tale (1911; Prague, March 3, 1912, composer conducting); *Adventus*, symphonic poem (1920–21; Prague, Nov. 6, 1921); *Matěj Kopecký*, overture (1928); *Horácká suita* (Suite montagnarde; Prague, Sept. 8, 1935); *Sinfonietta* for Strings and Timpani (1940–41); *Majales*, overture (1942); Violin Concerto (1944); Concertino for Horn and String Quartet or String Orch. (1951); *Variations on a Theme of Boccherini* for Bassoon and String Quartet or String Orch. (1952); *Sinfonietta semplice* (1962). **CHAMBER:** *Small Suite in Old Style* for 2 Violins and Piano (1907); 3 string quartets (1907; 1938–39; *Wallachian*, 1949); *Doma* (At Home), piano trio (1924–25); Violin Sonata (1925); Sonatina for 2 Violins (1926–27; rev. for Violin and Viola); Concertino (septet) for Violin, Wind Quintet, and Piano (1940); *Partita* for Violin (1941); *Divertimento* for Wind Quintet (1950); Flute Sonatina (1951); *Variations* for Violin (1956); Violin Sonatina (1962); several albums of piano pieces. **VOCAL: CANTATAS:** *Pokušeni na poušti* (Temptation in the Desert; 1921–22); *Jenny, the Thief* (1927–28); *Tyrolese Elegies* (1930–31); *A Eulogy to a Woman* (1933); *Recollections of Student Years* (1934); *Moravian Cantata* (1935–36); *The Golden Spinning Wheel* (1943); *To Prague* (1960); songs; folk song arrangements.

BIBL.: J. Dostál, *J. K.* (Prague, 1944).

Krieger, Armando, Argentine pianist, conductor, and composer; b. Buenos Aires, May 7, 1940. He studied piano with John Montes and Robert Kinsky and composition with Ginastera, later with Copland, Dallapiccola, Maderna, R. Malipiero, and Messiaen at the Di Tella Inst. (1963–64); continued his piano training with Loriod at the Mozarteum Argentino (1964). He became widely known in his native country as a pianist and conductor, often giving performances of avant-garde music; also conducted his own chamber orch. and was active as a teacher. In his works, he adopted a serial technique in which rhythmic, melodic, and harmonic elements follow a predetermined formula of contrasts.

WORKS: Sym. for Strings (1959); Concerto for 2 Pianos and Orch. (1963); *Métamorfosis d'après une lecture de Kafka* for Piano and 15 Instruments (1968); *Angst* for Orch. (1970); several cantatas and various solo vocal works; 2 string quartets (1960, 1961); other chamber music; keyboard pieces.

Krieger, Edino, Brazilian composer; b. Brusque, Santa Catarina, March 17, 1928. He studied music with his father, a conductor, composer, and founder of the local Cons.; later studied violin with Edith Reis (1943) and composition with Koellreutter (1944–48) at the Rio de Janeiro Cons.; subsequently had lessons with Copland at the Berkshire Music Center in Tanglewood (summer, 1948) and with Mennin at the Juilliard School of Music in N.Y. (1948–49); also violin with Nowinsky at N.Y.'s Henry Street Settlement School; completed his studies with Krenek in Brazil (1952) and Berkeley at London's Royal Academy of Music (1955). He was active as a broadcaster, music critic, conductor, and teacher in his homeland; was director of the art and music dept. of the Radio Jornal do Brasil in Rio de Janeiro (1963–73); was also president of the Brazilian Soc. of Contemporary Music (1971–73). His early works were in a late Romantic and Impressionist style; after a brief dodecaphonic period (1947–53), he turned toward neo-Classicism with national allusions; he fused the latter 2 styles from 1966.

WORKS: ORCH.: *Movimento misto* (1947); *Contrastes* (1949); *Música 1952* for Strings (1952); *Chôro* for Flute and Strings (1952); *Suite* for Strings (1954); *Abertura sinfônica* (1955); *Concertante* for Piano and Orch. (1955); *Andante* for Strings (1956); *Divertimento* for Strings (1959); *Brasiliana* for Viola or Alto Saxophone and Strings (1960); *Variações elementares* for Strings (1964); *Ludus symphonicus* (1966); *Toccata* for Piano and Orch. (1967); *Canticum naturale* (1972). **CHAMBER:** Trio for Oboe, Clarinet, and Bassoon (1945); *Peça lenta* for Flute and String Trio (1946); *Música 1947* for String Quartet (1947); *Música de câmara* for Flute, Trumpet, Timpani, and Violin (1948); String Quartet No. 1 (1955); piano pieces. **VOCAL:** *Melopéia* for Soprano, Tenor Saxophone, Trombone, and Viola (1949); choral pieces; songs.

Krips, Henry (Joseph), Austrian-born Australian conductor, brother of **Josef Krips**; b. Vienna, Feb. 10, 1912; d. Adelaide, Jan. 25, 1987. He studied in Vienna at the Cons. and the Univ. He made his conducting debut at Vienna's Burgtheater in 1932; subsequently was conductor in Innsbruck (1933–34), Salzburg (1934–35), and Vienna (1935–38). In 1938 he emigrated to Australia and became a naturalized Australian citizen in 1944. He conducted ballet and opera. He was principal conductor of the West Australia Sym. Orch. in Perth (1948–72) and the South Australia Sym. Orch. in Adelaide (1949–72); also made guest appearances in Europe. He was best known for his performances of light Viennese music.

Krips, Josef, eminent Austrian conductor, brother of **Henry (Joseph) Krips**; b. Vienna, April 8, 1902; d. Geneva, Oct. 13, 1974. He studied at the Vienna Academy of Music; also was a student of Weingartner and Mandyczewski. He was 1st violinist in the Volksoper orch. in Vienna (1918–21); then became répétiteur and chorus master there, making his conducting debut with *Un ballo in maschera* (1921). In 1924–25 he conducted opera in Aussig an der Elbe; in 1925–26, in Dortmund; from 1926 to 1933 he was was Generalmusikdirektor in Karlsruhe. In 1933 he became a conductor at the Vienna State Opera; also was made a prof. at the Vienna Academy of Music. In 1938 he lost these positions, after the annexation of Austria to Germany; he then conducted in Belgrade (1938–39). In 1945 he rejoined the Vienna State Opera as principal conductor; later that year he conducted the first post-war subscription concert of the Vienna Phil., and quickly moved to reestablish the musical life of his native city. In 1947 he appeared with the Vienna State Opera at London's Covent Garden. After leaving the Vienna State Opera in 1950, he served as principal conductor of the London Sym. Orch. until 1954. In 1953 he made his U.S. debut as a guest conductor with the Buffalo Phil., and subsequently was its music director (1954–63); from 1963 to 1970 he was music director of the San Francisco Sym. Orch. He also was a guest conductor of the major opera houses and orchs. of Europe and the U.S.; he conducted at Chicago's Lyric Opera (1960, 1964), at Covent Garden (1963; 1971–74), and at N.Y.'s Metropolitan Opera (1966–67; 1969–70). He excelled in works of the Austro-German repertoire, his interpretations being notable for their authority, insight, warmth, and lyricism. Harrietta Krips ed. and publ. his autobiography (Vienna, 1994).

Kriukov, Nikolai, Russian composer, brother of **Vladimir Kriukov**; b. Moscow, Feb. 2, 1908; d. there (suicide), April 5, 1961. He studied with Vasilenko. He devoted himself chiefly to folk-song arrangements and film music. He wrote orch. suites on folk themes gathered in various republics of the Soviet Union, sometimes including native instruments. He received 2 Stalin prizes for his film scores.

Kriukov, Vladimir, Russian composer, brother of **Nikolai Kriukov**; b. Moscow, July 22, 1902; d. Staraya Rusa, near Moscow, June 14, 1960. He studied composition with Miaskovsky at the Moscow Cons., graduating in 1925. In 1949–50 he was director of the Moscow Phil. Inst.; from 1957 to 1959, taught composition at the Gnessin Inst. in Moscow. His music is harmoniously and melodiously eclectic, while adhering to an effective Russian style.

WORKS: OPERAS: *Railroad Stationmaster*, after Pushkin (Moscow, Oct. 30, 1940); *Dmitri Donskoy* (1947). **ORCH.:** 2 symphonic poems: *January 9*, commemorating the march on the Winter Palace in St. Petersburg in 1905 (1931), and *Dreadnought Potemkin* (1955); *Russian Rhapsody* (1944); Piano Concerto (1959). **CHAMBER:** Various works; piano pieces. **VOCAL:** *October Cantata* (1947); songs.

Krivine, Emmanuel, French conductor; b. Grenoble, May 7, 1947. He studied violin at the Paris Cons., winning a premier prix at age 16; after further studies at Brussel's Chapelle Musicale Reine Elisabeth, he completed his training with Szeryng and Menuhin. While pursuing his career as a violinist, he also launched a 2nd career as a conductor in 1976; received instruction in conducting from Bohm; following an automobile accident in 1981, he was compelled to give up violin playing and devote himself to conducting. Having conducted regularly for the ORTF in Paris, he then was principal conductor of the Orchestre Philharmonique in Lorraine (1981–83). On Jan. 30, 1987, he made his U.S. debut as a guest conductor with the Indianapolis Sym. Orch. He was music director of the Orchestre de Lyon (from 1987). In addition to appearances with leading French orchs., he appeared widely in Europe and North America.

Kroeger, Karl, American musicologist, teacher, and composer; b. Louisville, Ky., April 4, 1932. He studied with Claude Almand and George Perle (composition) at the Univ. of Louisville (B.M., 1954; M.M., 1959) and with Binkerd (composition) and Plamenac (musicology) at the Univ. of Ill. (M.S., 1962); completed his education with Janet Knapp (musicology) at Brown Univ. (Ph.D., 1971). He was curator of the Americana Collection in the Music Division of the N.Y. Public Library (1962–64); was composer-in-residence of the Eugene (Oreg.) public schools (1964–67). He taught at Ohio Univ. (1967–68) and Moorhead (Minn.) State College (1971–72), and then at Wake Forest Univ. in Winston-Salem, N.C., where he was also director of the Moravian Music Foundation (1972–80); subsequently he taught at the Univ. of Keele in England (1980–81) and then became assoc. prof. and music librarian at the Univ. of Colo. at Boulder in 1982. With H. Nathan, he ed. *The Complete Works of William Billings* (4 vols., Charlottesville, Va., 1977–90). He also ed. a *Catalog of the Musical Works of William Billings* (N.Y., 1991) and *American Fuging Tunes, 1770–1820: A Descriptive Catalog* (Westport, Conn., 1994).

WORKS: ORCH.: 2 sinfoniettas (1958, 1965); Chamber Concerto for Oboe and Strings (1961); *Dramatic Overture* (1964); 4 suites (1965, 1966, 1967, 1968); Concerto for Alto Saxophone and Winds (1982); band music. **CHAMBER:** 2 string quartets (1960, 1966); 4 canzonas for Brass Sextet (1961, 1966, 1967, 1988); *Partita* for Brass Quintet (1963); *Toccata* for Clarinet, Trombone, and Percussion (1968); *Fantasy* for Brass Quartet (1969); Sonata for Trombone Quartet (1978); Suite for Oboe and Harp (1979); *Parataxis* for Flute and Percussion (1989); *Banchetto Musicale* for Saxophone Ensemble (1993); piano pieces; organ music. **VOCAL:** Choral works; anthems; songs.

Krohn, Ernst C(hristopher), American musicologist; b. N.Y., Dec. 23, 1888; d. Santa Fe, N.Mex., March 21, 1975. He settled in St. Louis in 1898; studied piano with his father and with Ottmar Moll (1909–13), attaining a modicum of virtuosity. He gave recitals and taught piano in various schools in St. Louis; also taught music history at Washington Univ. there (1938–53) and was director of music at St. Louis Univ. (1953–63).

WRITINGS: *A Century of Missouri Music* (St. Louis, 1924; reprint, with additions, 1965, as *Missouri Music*); *The History of Music: An Index to the Literature Available in a Selected Group of Musicological Publications* (St. Louis, 1952); *Music Publishing in the Middle Western States before the Civil War* (Detroit, 1972).

Krohn, Felix (Julius Theofil), Finnish conductor, teacher, and composer; b. Tampere, May 20, 1898; d. Lahti, Nov. 11, 1963. He studied with his father; later at the Helsinki School of Music and the Hochschule für Musik in Berlin. Returning to Finland in 1922, he was active as a conductor and teacher.

WORKS: *Sotarukous* (War Prayer) for Orch. (1918); *Vuodenajat* (The Seasons), sinfonia brevis (1921); *Kyllikki*, cantata (1923); *Odalisque* for Orch. (1924); 4 suites for Orch.: *Sysmäläinen* (The Man from Sysma; 1938), *Vihreä kulta* (Green Gold; 1939), *Anu and Mikko* (1940), and *Linnaisten kartanon vihreä kamari* (The Green Room at Linnainen Manor; 1944); *Uskollinen sisar* (The Faithful Sister), children's opera (1945); chamber music.

Krohn, Ilmari (Henrik Reinhold), eminent Finnish musicologist; b. Helsinki, Nov. 8, 1867; d. there, April 25, 1960. After studying with Richard Faltin in Helsinki (1885–86), he took courses at the Leipzig Cons. with Papperitz and Reinecke (1886–90); obtained his M.A. in 1894 and his Ph.D. in 1900 from the Univ. of Helsinki with the diss. *Über die Art und Enstehung der geistlichen Volksmelodien in Finnland* (publ. in Helsinki, 1899); later studied with Bausznern in Weimar (1909). He lectured at the Helsinki Music Inst. (1900–1901; 1905; 1907; 1914–16), the Phil. Orch. School (1900–1901; 1904–14), and the Univ. of Helsinki (1900–18); then was its first prof. of musicology (1918–35); also taught at the Church Music Inst. (1923–30; 1933–44). He was active in folk music research from 1886, resulting in his valuable compilation of some 7,000 Finnish folk songs in *Suomen kansan sävelmiä* (1898–1933). He founded the Finnish section of the IMS (1910); was founder (1916) and chairman (1917–39) of the Finnish Musicological Soc. Krohn was also a composer; wrote an opera, *Tuhotulva* (Deluge; 1918; Helsinki, Oct. 25, 1928); 2 oratorios: *Ikiaartehet* (Eternal Treasures; 1912) and *Voittajat* (Victors; 1935); *St. John Passion* (1940); cantatas; Psalms; songs.

WRITINGS: *Musiikin teorian oppijakso* (Principles of Music Theory; 5 vols., Porvoo: I, *Rytmioppi* [Rhythm; 1911–14; rev. ed., 1958]; II, *Säveloppi* [Melody; 1917]; III, *Harmoniaoppi* [Harmony; 1923]; IV, *Polyfoniaoppi* [Polyphony; 1929]; V, *Muoto-oppi* [Form; 1937]); *Puhdasvireisen säveltapailun opas* (Guide to Solfège in Natural Tuning; Helsinki, 1911); *Die Sammlung und Erforschung der Volksmusik in Finnland* (Helsinki, 1933); *Die finnische Volksmusik* (Griefswald, 1935); *Liturgisen sävellystyylin opas* (The Liturgical Style of Composition; Porvoo, 1940); *Der Formenbau in den Symphonien von Jean Sibelius* (Helsinki, 1942); *Der lutherische Choral in Finnland* (Åbo, 1944); *Der Stimmungsgehalt in den Symphonien von Jean Sibelius* (2 vols., Helsinki, 1945–46); *Sävelmuistoja elämäni varrelta* (Porvoo, 1951; memoirs); *Anton Bruckners Symphonien: Untersuchung über Formenbau und Stimmungsgehalt* (3 vols., Helsinki, 1955–57).

Kroll, Erwin, German musicologist; b. Deutsch-Eylau, Feb. 3, 1886; d. Berlin, March 7, 1976. He studied in Königsberg; later took a course in theory with Sandberger in Munich and also in composition with Pfitzner and Braunfels. From 1919 to 1924 he served as répétiteur at the Bavarian State Opera in Munich; was active as a music journalist in Königsberg (1925–33) and then in Berlin (from 1934); later was director of the Berlin studios of the Northwest German Radio (1946–53). He also composed chamber music and songs.

WRITINGS: *E.T.A. Hoffmanns musikalische Anschauungen* (Königsberg, 1909); *E.T.A. Hoffmann* (Leipzig, 1923); *Hans*

Pfitzner (Munich, 1924); *Aus den Werdejahren der neudeutschen Musik* (Königsberg, 1933); *Carl Maria von Weber* (Potsdam, 1934); *Carl Maria von Weber: Sein Leben in Bildern* (Leipzig, 1936); *Musikstadt Königsberg: Geschichte und Erinnerung* (Freiburg im Breisgau, 1966).

Kroll, William, American violinist, teacher, and composer; b. N.Y., Jan. 30, 1901; d. Boston, March 10, 1980. He studied with Marteau (violin) at the Berlin Hochschule für Musik (1911–14); made his debut in N.Y. in 1915, then continued his studies with Kneisel (violin) and Goetschius (theory) at the Inst. of Musical Art there (1917–22). He played in the Elshuco Trio (1922–29), then was 1st violinist of the Coolidge Quartet (1936–44) and subsequently of his own Kroll Quartet (1944–69); toured with these ensembles, and also made solo appearances. He taught at the Inst. of Musical Art (1922–38), the Mannes College of Music in N.Y. (from 1943), the Peabody Cons. of Music in Baltimore (1947–65), and the Cleveland Inst. of Music (1964–67); was made prof. of violin at Queens College of the City Univ. of N.Y. (1969). He composed some chamber orch. works, chamber music, and violin pieces.

Krombholc, Jaroslav, esteemed Czech conductor; b. Prague, Jan. 30, 1918; d. there, July 16, 1983. He studied composition with Novák (1937–40) and conducting with Dědeček, Ostrčil, and Talich (1940–41) at the Prague Cons. and its Master School; also studied quarter tone music with A. Hába and attended V. Nejedlý's classes at the Univ. of Prague. He first gained attention as a composer, winning 1st prize in a Czech Phil. competition with his Suite for Piano and Orch. (1939). He then made his conducting debut at the Prague National Theater (1940); after serving as chief conductor of the Ostrava Opera (1944–45), he rejoined the roster of the Prague National Theater; later was its chief conductor (1968–75), and chief conductor of the Prague Radio Sym. Orch. (1973–78). He also appeared as a guest conductor with leading European opera houses. He was especially renowned for his idiomatic performances of works by Smetana, Dvořák, Janáček, Martinů, and other Czech composers, as well as for his distinguished interpretations of the music of Prokofiev and Shostakovich.

Krombholc, Karlo, Hungarian-Serbian pianist, teacher, and composer; b. Budapest, Dec. 20, 1905. He studied at the Vienna Academy of Music. He was active as a pianist (1927–39); after World War II, settled in Novi Sad as a piano teacher. His works were influenced mainly by Bartók, with ethnic modalities gadrooned by atonal extrapolations. Typical of these was his extensive piano work *Sazvezda* (Constellations; 1969). He also wrote orch. works based on Hungarian and Balkan folk tunes.

Kromolicki, Joseph, Polish-born German choral conductor, musicologist, and composer; b. Posen, Jan. 16, 1882; d. Berlin, Oct. 11, 1961. He studied with Haberl and Haller in Regensburg and with Pfitzner, Kretzschmar, and Wolf in Berlin, where he took his Ph.D. at the Univ. in 1909 with the diss. *Die Practica artis musicae des Amerus.* He was active as a choral conductor in Berlin; ed. *Musica Sacra* from 1908 and vols. 45, 48, and 57 of Denkmäler Deutscher Tonkunst; composed 5 masses, a Te Deum, organ preludes, sacred songs, etc.

Kroó, György, Hungarian musicologist; b. Budapest, Aug. 26, 1926. He studied violin at the National Cons. and at the Academy of Music in Budapest; also attended classes in musicology there with Szabolcsi and Bartha. In 1957 he was named head of music education of the Hungarian Radio; in 1960, became a guest lecturer at the Academy of Music, joining its permanent faculty in 1967; was chairman of its musicology dept. from 1973; was a prof. of musicology (from 1975). His writings include *Robert Schumann* (Budapest, 1958); *Hector Berlioz* (Budapest, 1960); *Bartók Béla szinpadi müvei* (Béla Bartók's Stage Works; Budapest, 1962); *Wenn Schumann ein Tagebuch geführt hätte* (Budapest, 1962); *A "szabadito" opera* (The "Rescue" Opera; Budapest, 1966); *Richard Wagner* (Budapest, 1968); *Bartók kalauz* (A Guide to Bartók; Budapest, 1971; Eng. tr., 1974); *A magyar zeneszerzés harminc éve* (30 Years of Hungarian Composition; Budapest, 1975); *Rácz Aladár* (Budapest, 1979); *Heilawâc. Négy tanulmány Wagner a Nibelung gyürüjéről* (4 Studies on Wagner's *Ring des Nibelungen*; Budapest, 1983); *Az albumtól a szvitig* (From the Album to the Suite; Budapest, 1986).

Kroyer, Theodor, eminent German musicologist; b. Munich, Sept. 9, 1873; d. Wiesbaden, Jan. 12, 1945. He studied piano with Lang, counterpoint with Rheinberger, and musicology with Sandberger; took his Ph.D. from the Univ. of Munich with the diss. *Die Anfänge der Chromatik im italienischen Madrigal des XVI. Jahrhunderts* (publ. in Leipzig, 1902); completed his Habilitation there in 1902 with his *Ludwig Senfl und sein Motettenstil* (publ. in Munich, 1902). He was music critic of the *Münchener Allgemeine Zeitung* (1897–1910). He taught at the Univs. of Munich (1902–20), Heidelberg (1920–23), Leipzig (1923–33), and Cologne (1932–38). In 1925 he purchased for the Univ. of Leipzig the rich collection of instruments, MSS, and portraits from the famous Heyer Museum in Cologne; also in 1925 he began issuing the valuable series Publikationen Älterer Musik. He publ. the studies *Joseph Rheinberger* (Regensburg and Rome, 1916) and *Walter Courvoisier* (Munich and Berlin, 1929). He ed. a vol. (motets and Magnificat) of the complete works of Senfl in Denkmäler der Tonkunst in Bayern, V, Jg. III/2 (1903); also ed. a selection from the works of G. Aichinger for the same series (XVIII, Jg. X/I, 1909).

BIBL.: H. Zenck et al., eds., *T. K.: Festschrift zum 60. Geburtstage am 9. September 1933 überreicht von Freunden und Schülern* (Regensburg, 1933); O. Ursprung, "T. K.," *Zeitschrift für Musikwissenschaft,* XV (1932–33); H. Zenck, "T. K.," *Die Musikforschung,* I (1948).

Krueger, Karl (Adalbert), American conductor; b. Atchison, Kansas, Jan. 19, 1894; d. Elgin, Ill., July 21, 1979. He learned to play the cello and organ in his early youth; then studied at Midland College in his hometown (B.A. 1913), with Chadwick (composition) and Goodrich (organ) at the New England Cons. of Music in Boston (1914–15), and at the Univ. of Kansas (M.A., 1916). He was an organist at St. Ann's Episcopal Church in N.Y. (1916–20). In 1920 he made a concert tour of Brazil as an organist; then went to Vienna, where he studied theory with Robert Fuchs and conducting with Franz Schalk. He also attended classes in economics at the Univs. of Vienna and Heidelberg. He was conductor of the Seattle Sym. Orch. (1926–32), the Kansas City Phil. (1933–43), and the Detroit Sym. Orch. (1943–49). In 1958 he founded the Soc. for the Preservation of the American Musical Heritage and made numerous recordings of American works. He wrote *The Way of the Conductor: His Origins, Purpose and Procedures* (N.Y., 1958).

Krummacher, Friedhelm (Gustav-Adolf Hugo Robert), German musicologist; b. Berlin, Jan. 22, 1936. He studied musicology and philosophy in Berlin, Marburg, and Uppsala before completing his education at the Univs. of Berlin (Ph.D., 1964) and Erlangen-Nuremberg (Habilitation, 1972). In 1975 he became a prof. at the Detmold Hochschule für Musik. He was a prof. at the Christian-Albrechts-Univ. in Kiel from 1976. From 1980 to 1986 he was vice-president of the Gesellschaft für Musikforschung. He served as chairman of the new Brahms Gesamtausgabe from 1983. In addition to his articles in various series and journals, he publ. the studies *Mendelssohn—der Komponist: Studien zur Kammermusik für Streicher* (Munich, 1978) and *Mahlers III. Symphonie* (Kassel, 1991).

Krushelnitskaya, Salomea (Ambrosivna), noted Russian soprano; b. Belavyntsy, near Tarnopol, Sept. 23, 1872; d. Lwów, Nov. 16, 1952. As a child she sang in a village choir; after studying voice with Wysocki in Lemberg, she made her debut there in *La Favorite* in 1892; then went to Milan, where she took lessons with Crespi (1893–96). From 1898 to 1902 she was a member of the Warsaw Opera; then scored a remarkable success as Cio-Cio-San in Brescia (1904). After singing at La Scala in Milan (from 1906) and in Buenos Aires (1906–13), she made her operatic farewell in Naples in 1920; subsequently devoted herself to concert appearances. She taught at the Lwów Cons. (from 1939). Her voice was of particular beauty, spanning fully 3 octaves. Among her most notable roles were Brünnhilde, Isolde, Elisabeth in *Tannhäuser*, Elsa in *Lohengrin*, Aida, Desdemona, and Elektra. In her concert programs she promoted songs by Ukrainian composers. A collection of articles about her career was publ. in Ukrainian (Lwów, 1956).

Kruyf, Ton de, Dutch composer; b. Leerdam, Oct. 3, 1937. He attended the courses in new music in Darmstadt and studied with Fortner in Heidelberg. His works utilize various contemporary procedures, including serialism.

WORKS: DRAMATIC: OPERAS: *Spinoza* (Amsterdam, June 15, 1971); *Quauhquauhtinchan in den vreemde* (Quauhquauhtinchan in Foreign Parts), radio opera (1971; Hilversum, June 3, 1972). **BALLET:** *Chronologie II* (1967). **ORCH.:** *Mouvements symphoniques* (1956); Sinfonietta for Strings (1956; rev. 1965); *5 Impromptus* (1958); *Sinfonia II* (1969); *Quatre pas de deux* for Flute and Orch. (1972); *Echoi* for Oboe and Strings (1973); *Spring-time fantasietta* for Strings (1978); *Canti e capricci* for Cello and Orch. (1984; rev. 1989); *Adagio, in memoriam Wolfgang Fortner* (1987); *Intrada* for Wind Orch. (1989). **CHAMBER:** *Aubade* for Horn, 2 Trumpets, Trombone, and Tuba (1957; rev. 1967); Quartet for Flute, Bassoon, Viola, and Cello (1959); Flute Sonatina (1960); *Music* for String Quartet (1962); *Partita* for String Quartet (1962); Sonata for Solo Cello (1964); *Pas de deux* for Flute and Piano (1968); *Serenata per complesso da camera* for Flute, Clarinet, Harp, and String Quintet (1968); *Mosaico* for Oboe and String Trio (1969); *Séance* for Harp, Piano, 4 Horns, and 5 Percussion (1969); *Musica portuensis* for 4 Saxophones (1983). **PIANO:** *Sgrafitti* (1960); *Arioso* for Piano, 4-hands (1975). **VOCAL:** *Einst dem Grau der Nacht enttaucht . . .* for Mezzo-soprano and Chamber Orch. (1964); *Pour faire le portrait d'un oiseau* for Mezzo-soprano and Chamber Orch. (1965); *Fragment No. IV from Shakespeare Sonnets* for Low Voice, Flute, and Cello (1965); *De blinde zwemmers* for Youth Chorus and Chamber Orch. (1966); *Töne aus der Ferne* for Alto and Chamber Orch. (1967); *Twee uur* for Speaker and Orch. (1973); *Meditations* for Baritone and Chamber Orch. (1976); *Cantate* for Tenor, Chorus, and Chamber Orch. (1978); *Ode to the West Wind* for Chorus and Orch. (1978).

Kubelík, Jan, famous Czech-born Hungarian violinist, father of **(Jeroným) Rafael Kubelík**; b. Michle, near Prague, July 5, 1880; d. Prague, Dec. 5, 1940. He began violin training with his father, then studied with Ševčik (violin) and Foerster (composition) at the Prague Cons. (1892–98). After making his Prague debut in 1898, he continued his studies in Vienna, where he performed for the first time on Nov. 26, 1898. In 1900 he made his London debut, and thereafter made a series of triumphant tours of Europe and the U.S. He was awarded the Gold Medal of the Phil. Soc. of London in 1902. In 1903 he married a Hungarian countess and became a naturalized Hungarian citizen. He continued his active career for over 4 decades, giving a series of farewell concerts in 1939–40. On May 8, 1940, he gave his last concert in Prague, after his beloved homeland had been dismembered by the Nazis. Kubelík was one of the foremost virtuosos of his day. He also composed; wrote 6 violin concertos, as well as a Sym. and some chamber music; likewise prepared cadenzas for the Beethoven, Brahms, and Tchaikovsky violin concertos.

BIBL.: J. Celeda, *J. K.* (Prague, 1930); B. Voldan, *Skladby J.a K.a* (J. K.'s Compositions; Prague, 1933); H. Doležil, *Mistr houslí J. K.* (The Master of the Violin J. K.; Prague, 1941); K. Hoffmiester, *J. K.* (Prague, 1941); J. Dostal, ed., *J. K.* (Prague, 1942).

Kubelík, (Jeroným) Rafael, eminent Czech-born Swiss conductor, son of **Jan Kubelík**; b. Býchory, near Kolín, June 29, 1914; d. Lucerne, Aug. 11, 1996. He studied violin with his father, and then continued his musical training at the Prague Cons. He made his conducting debut with the Czech Phil. in Prague on Jan. 24, 1934, then was conductor at the National Theater in Brno (1939–41). He was chief conductor of the Czech Phil. from 1942 to 1948, one of the most difficult periods in the history of the orch. and the Czech nation. He refused to collaborate with the Nazi occupation authorities; when the Communists took control of the government in 1948, he left the country for the West, vowing not to return until the political situation changed. He appeared as a guest conductor in England and Western Europe, then made his U.S. debut with the Chicago Sym. Orch. on Nov. 17, 1949; his success led to his appointment as the orch.'s music director in 1950; however, his inclusion of many contemporary works in his programs and his insistence on painstaking rehearsals antagonized some of his auditors, including members of the Chicago press, causing him to resign his post in 1953. He subsequently was music director at the Royal Opera House at Covent Garden in London (1955–58); his tenure was notable for important productions of *Les Troyens*, *Boris Godunov* (in the original version), and *Jenůfa*. He then was chief conductor of the Bavarian Radio Sym. Orch. in Munich (1961–79). He made his Metropolitan Opera debut in N.Y. as its first music director on Oct. 22, 1973, conducting *Les Troyens*; however, he again became an epicenter of controversy, and soon submitted his resignation. In spite of the contretemps, his artistic integrity remained intact; he continued to appear widely as a guest conductor in Western Europe and the U.S. In light of his controversial tenure in Chicago, it was ironic that he became an honored guest conductor with that orch. in later years. He retired in 1985. Following the "velvet" revolution which toppled the hard-line Communist regime in Czechoslovakia in 1989, Kubelík was invited to return to his free homeland to conduct Smetana's *Má Vlast* at the Prague Spring Festival in 1990. Kubelík was the foremost Czech conductor of his generation; in addition to his idiomatic and authoritative performances of the music of his native country, he was greatly esteemed for his distinguished interpretations of the standard repertoire, which were marked by a pristine musicianship, unfettered by self-indulgence. Kubelík became a naturalized Swiss citizen in 1966. His 2nd wife was **Elsie Morison**. He also composed several operas, including *Veronika* (Brno, April 19, 1947) and *Cornelia Faroli* (Augsburg, 1972); a Sym. for Chorus and Orch. (1941); Sym. in 1 Movement (WDR, Cologne, 1974); *Sequences* for Orch. (Lucerne Festival, 1976); Sym., *Orphikon* (N.Y., April 2, 1981); *Symphonic Peripeteia* for Organ and Orch. (Chicago Sym. Orch., March 14, 1985); a number of choral works; 6 string quartets and other chamber music works; and songs.

Kubiak, Teresa (originally, **Tersa Wojtaszek**), Polish soprano; b. Ldzan, Dec. 26, 1937. She studied with Olga Olgina at the Łódź Academy of Music. In 1965 she made her debut as Halk in Monziuszko's opera in Łódź, and then appeared with the Warsaw Opera. She made her U.S. debut in a concert performance of Goldmark's *Die Königen von Saba* in N.Y. (1970); then appeared with the San Francisco Opera, with the Chicago Lyric Opera, and at the Glyndebourne Festival (1971). In 1972 she made her first appearance at London's Covent Garden as Cio-Cio-San. She made her Metropolitan Opera debut in N.Y. as Liza in *The Queen of Spades* on Jan. 18, 1973; that same year, she appeared at the Vienna State Opera as Elsa. She continued to make occasional appearances at the Metropolitan Opera until her final appearance there as Elisabeth in *Tannhäuser* on Jan. 31, 1987. In 1990 she joined the faculty of the Indiana Univ. School of Music in Bloomington. Among her other roles were Senta, Aida, Tosca, Jenůfa, and many from the 20th-century repertoire.

Kubik, Gail (Thompson), American composer; b. South Coffeyville, Okla., Sept. 5, 1914; d. Covina, Calif., July 20, 1984. He was a student of Samuel Belov (violin), Rogers (composition), and McHose (theory) at the Eastman School of Music in Rochester, N.Y. (B.M., 1934), Scott Willits (violin) and Sowerby (composition) at the American Cons. of Music in Chicago (M.M., 1936), and Piston (composition) at Harvard Univ. (1937–38); he also worked with Boulanger. After teaching at Monmouth (Ill.) College (1934), Dakota Wesleyan Univ. in

Mitchell, S.Dak. (1936–37), and at Teachers College at Columbia Univ. (1938–40), he was a staff composer and adviser for NBC in N.Y. (1940–42). In 1942–43 he was director of music for the film bureau of the Office of War Information, and then was a composer-conductor for the U.S. Army Air Force Motion Picture Unit (1943–46). He later was composer-in-residence at Kansas State Univ. (1969), Gettysburg College (1970), and Scripps College in Claremont, California (1970–80). In 1944 and 1965 he held Guggenheim fellowships. He held the American Prix de Rome in 1950–51. In 1952 he received the Pulitzer Prize in Music for his *Symphonie concertante.* He composed much music for films, radio, and television which exerted a liberating force on his serious scores. The latter were notable for their neo-Classical bent in which rhythmic patterns were apt to be stimulatingly asymmetric.

WORKS: DRAMATIC: *A Mirror for the Sky,* folk opera (Eugene, Oreg., May 23, 1939); *Boston Baked Beans,* opera piccola (1950; N.Y., March 9, 1952); film scores: *Thunderbolt* (1943–45); *C-Man* (1949); *The Miner's Daughter* (1950); *Gerald McBoing-Boing* (1950; concert version for Narrator, 9 Instruments, and Percussion, 1950); *The Desperate Hours* (1955); radio and television scores. **ORCH.:** *American Caprice* for Piano and Orch. (1933); 2 violin concertos: No. 1 (1934; rev. 1936; Chicago, Jan. 2, 1938) and No. 2 (1940; rev. 1941); Suite (1935); *Scherzo* (1940); *Music for Dancing* (1940–46); *Folk Song Suite* (1941–46); *Bachata* (1947); *Spring Valley Overture* (1947); 3 syms.: No. 1 (1947–49), No. 2 (1955; Louisville, April 7, 1956), and No. 3 (1956; N.Y., Feb. 28, 1957); *Symphonie concertante* for Piano, Viola, Trumpet, and Orch. (1951; N.Y., Jan. 27, 1952; rev. 1953); *Thunderbolt Overture* (1953); *Scenario* (1957); *Scenes* (1964); *Prayer and Toccata* for Organ and Chamber Orch. (1968); Piano Concerto (1982–83). **CHAMBER:** *2 Sketches* for String Quartet (1932); *Trivialities* for Flute, Horn, and String Quartet (1934); Piano Trio (1934); Wind Quintet (1937); Suite for 3 Recorders (1941); Violin Sonatina (1941); *Little Suite* for Flute and 2 Clarinets (1947); *Soliloquy and Dance* for Violin and Piano (1948); *Divertimento No. 1* for 13 Players (1959), *No. 2* for 8 Players (1959), and *No. 3* for Piano Trio (1970–71); *Music for Bells* for Handbells (1975). **PIANO:** *Celebrations and Epilogue* (1938–50); *Song and Scherzo* for 2 Pianos (1940; rev. 1962); Sonatina (1941); Sonata (1947); *Intermezzo: Music for Cleveland* (1967); Sym. for 2 Pianos (1980; based on Sym. No. 1, 1947–49). **VOCAL:** *In Praise of Johnny Appleseed* for Bass-baritone, Chorus, and Orch. (1938; rev. 1961); *Choral Profiles, Folk Song Sketches* for Chorus (1938); *Litany and Prayer* for Men's Chorus, Brass, and Percussion (1943–45); *Memphis Belle* for Speaker and Orch. (1944); *Fables in Song* for Mezzo-soprano or Baritone and Piano (1950–60); *A Christmas Set* for Chamber Chorus and Chamber Orch. (1968); *A Record of Our Time,* cantata for Narrator, Soloist, Chorus, and Orch. (Manhattan, Kansas, Nov. 11, 1970); *Scholastica* for Chorus (1972); *Magic, Magic, Magic!* for Alto, Chamber Chorus, and Chamber Orch. (San Antonio, April 25, 1976).

Kubín, Rudolf, Czech composer and pedagogue; b. Ostrava, Jan. 10, 1909; d. there, Jan. 11, 1973. He was a student at the Prague Cons. (1924–29) of Junek (cello) and A. Hába (composition). In 1929 he became a cellist in the Prague Radio Sym. Orch.; beginning in 1935 he alternated as music director of the Ostrava and Brno sections of the Czech Radio. After World War II, he helped to organize the Ostrava Higher Music Teaching College, of which he served as director in 1953–54; when it became a cons., he was its director also (1958–60). In 1959 the Czech government honored him with the Order of Work. His studies with Hába prompted him to compose several quarter tone pieces early in his career. After pursuing expressionist paths, he took up the cause of socialist realism.

WORKS: DRAMATIC: *Žena, která zdělila muže* (The Woman Who Did Down Men) or *Ženich z prérie* (The Bridegroom from the Prairie), operetta (Prague, March 29, 1930); *Tři mušketýři* (The 3 Musketeers) or *Královnin náhrdelník* (The Queen's Necklace), musical comedy (Prague, April 19, 1931); *Letní noc* (Summer Night), radio opera (Czech Radio, Sept. 26, 1931); *Kavalir* (The Cavalier), operetta (1932); *Cirkus života* (Circus of Life), operetta (Prague, May 15, 1933); *Ta česká muzika, ta srdce pronika* (That Czech Music, It Speaks Straight to the Heart), folk play (1933); *Zasnoubení na paloučku* (A Greenwood Betrothal), folk play (1933); *Zpěv uhlí* (Song of Coal; unfinished; overture, 1936); *Děvčátko z kolonie* (The Girl From the Mining Settlement), operetta (Ostrava, March 22, 1942; rev. version, Ostrava, Sept. 10, 1955); *Naši furianti* (Our Defiant Ones), comic opera (1942–43; rev. version, Ostrava, Sept. 18, 1949); *Selský kníže* (The Village Prince), operetta-burlesque (Prague, April 10, 1947); *Koleje mládí* (The Ways of Youth), play (Brno, Sept. 15, 1949); *Pasekáři* (People of the Glades), operetta (1950–51; rev. version, Ostrava, April 30, 1954); *Jiříkovo vidění* (Jiřík's Vision), folk opera (1952; unfinished); *Heva,* folk operetta (1955–64). **ORCH.:** *Prologue* (1929); *Czech Overture* (1932); *Sinfonietta* (1935–36); Trombone Concerto (1936); *Symphony Concertante* No. 1 for 4 Horns and Strings (1937) and No. 2 for Cello and Orch. (1969); Clarinet Concerto (1939); 2 violin concertos (1940, 1960); *Moravian Rhapsody* (1942); *May,* overture (1945); Accordion Concerto (1950); *Ostrava,* symphonic cycle (1950–51); *Geroj, in memoriam Klement Gottwald* (1953); *Julius Fučík,* overture (1954); Cello Concerto (1960); Tuba Concertino (1962); *Salutation to Frenštát* (1968); *Reminiscence,* sym. (1968); *Ostrava Variations* (1971). **CHAMBER:** String Quartet (1925–26); *Scherzo* for 2 Clarinets and Piano (1933) and for Violin and Piano (1942); *Ballade* for 4 Cellos (1942); Nonet (1944); Suite for Cello (1970). **QUARTER TONE PIANO:** 2 suites (1925, 1927); 2 fantasies (1926, 1927); *Piano Pieces* (1927). **VOCAL:** Cantatas; song cycles; solo songs.

BIBL.: V. Grebor, *R. K.: Obraz života a dila* (Ostrava, 1975).

Kučera, Václav, Czech composer and musicologist; b. Prague, April 29, 1929. He studied musicology and aesthetics at the Charles Univ. in Prague (1948–51), and then composition (with Shebalin) and musicology at the Moscow Cons. (1951–56). Returning to Prague, he worked at the Czech Radio (1956–59). After serving as head of contemporary musical studies for the Union of Czech Composers (1959–62), he was head of studies in music aesthetics for the Inst. of Musicology (1962–69). From 1969 to 1983 he served as general secretary of the Union of Czech Composers and Concert Artists. In 1972 he joined the faculty of the Academy of Music and Dramatic Arts as a teacher of contemporary composition, and later was prof. of composition there from 1988. From 1988 to 1990 he was president of the "Prague Spring" International Music Festival. In 1972 he received the Prix d'Italia for his *Lidice* and in 1983 received the prize of the Union of Czech Composers and Concert Artists for his String Quartet, *Consciousness of Continuities.* In 1986 he was made a Merited Artist by the Czech government. After following the precepts of socialist realism in his scores, he developed an advanced compositional style in which he sometimes utilized electronics. Among his books are a study of Mussorgsky (1959) and a theoretical vol. on creative experiments in music (1973).

WORKS: DRAMATIC: *Zbojnický oheň* (Brigand's Fire), dance drama (1958); *Festivalová pohádka* (Festival Fairy Tale), ballet (1959); *Sdrce a sen* (Heart and Dream), ballet (1973); *Život bez chyby* (Life without Fault), ballet (1979). **ORCH.:** Sym. (1962); *Krysař* (The Pied Piper), stereophonic concertino for Flute and 2 Chamber Orchs. (1964); *Obraz* (Tableau) for Piano and Orch. (1966–70); *Salut,* symphonic mosaic (1975); *Operand* for Chamber Orch. (1979); *Fortunata, Omaggio à Vivaldi* for Chamber Orch. (1979); *Avanti* (1981); *Balada a romance* for Chamber Orch. (1984); *Sapporo,* symphonic poem with chorus (1991). **CHAMBER:** *Dramas* for 9 Instruments (1961); *Protests* for Violin, Piano, and Timpani (1963); *Genesis* for Flute and Harp (1965); *Hic sunt homines* for Piano Quartet (1965); *Spectra* for Dulcimer (1965); *Diptchon* for Flute, Bass Clarinet, Piano, and Percussion (1966); *Duodrama* for Bass Clarinet and Piano (1967); *To be* for Percussion Quartet (1968); *Panta rhei* for Flute, Vibraphone, and Percussion (1969); *Invariant* for Bass Clarinet, Piano, and Tape (1969); *Scenario* for Flute, Violin, and Cello (1970); *Argot* for Brass Quintet (1970); *Diario* for

Guitar (1971); *Taboo a Due Boemi* for Bass Clarinet, Piano, and Percussion (1972); *Spring Manifesto: In Memory of Prague, May 1945* for 4 Players (1974); *Consciousness of Continuities*, string quartet (1976); *Horizons* for 5 Players (1978); *Aphorisms* for Violin and Piano (1978); *Epigrams* for Violin and Cello (1978); *Science Fiction* for Jazz Ensemble (1980); *Rosen für Rosa* for Harpsichord (1980); *Aquarelles* for Flute and Guitar (1981); *Stenograms* for Flute, Cello, and Piano (1981); *Wagnerian Inventions* for Flute (1982); *Capriccios* for Violin and Guitar (1982); *Nouvelles* for Guitar (1984); *Eruptions* for 5 Cellos (1984); *Gogh's Self-Portrait* for Bass Clarinet and Tape (1985); *Prague Ritornelles* for Bass Clarinet and Piano (1986); *Prefigurations, Hommage à Hans Arp* for Guitar (1986); *Ex abrupto* for 2 Percussionists (1987); *Elegy* for Viola (1988); *Duettinos* for Oboe and Bassoon (1988); *Pieter Brueghel Inspirations* for Flute, Bass Clarinet, and Piano (1988); *Pastoralissimo* for Horn (1990); *Consonanza*, trio for 2 Oboes and English Horn (1990); *Celebrations of Phantasy, Hommage à Max Ernst* for 2 Guitars (1991); *Vivaldiana* for 12 Instruments (1991); *Oraculum* for Bass Clarinet and Harp (1992); *Arcades* for Trombone and Piano (1993). **PIANO:** *Cardiograms* (1983); *Tuning* (1990–94). **VOCAL:** *The Time Has Set In*, cantata for Men's Chorus and Orch. (1961); *The Blue Planet* for Men's Chorus (1964); *Orbis pictus* for Chorus and Ancient Instruments (1975); *Amoroso*, song cycle for Mezzo-soprano, Flute, and Harp (1975); *Catharsis* for Soprano and Chamber Ensemble (1979); *Ecce homo* for Bass, Violin, Viola, Cello, Harp, and Percussion (1980); *Listening to Time* for Voice and Percussion (1981); *Bird*, melodrama for Reciter, 2 Violins, Viola, Cello, and Marimba (1983); *The Painter is Painting* for Children's Chorus (1984); *Bitter and Other Songs* for Soprano and Piano (1985); *A Serious Hour*, song cycle for High Voice and Guitar (1986); *The Decisive Time*, cantata for Chorus and Orch. (1988); *Freedom* for Men's Chorus (1991). **ELECTRONIC:** *A Kinetic Ballet* (1968); *Kinechromie* (1969). **OTHER:** *Lidice*, radio musical-dramatic fresco (1972); *Spartacus*, quadrophonic musical score (1976).

Kuckertz, Josef, German ethnomusicologist; b. Würseln, near Aachen, Nov. 24, 1930. After initial schooling at the Rheinische Musikschule in Cologne, he studied musicology with Marius Schneider at the Univ. of Cologne (Ph.D., 1962, with the diss. *Gestaltvariation in den von Bartók gesammelten rumänischen Colinden*). He then taught at the Univ. of Cologne, completing his Habilitation with a study of South Indian music (1967). His research focuses on the music and theory of the more developed Oriental cultures and the relationship between Oriental and European music, with particular emphasis on South India.

Kuerti, Anton (Emil), esteemed Austrian-born pianist; b. Vienna, July 21, 1938. He was taken by his parents to the U.S. as a child and was naturalized in 1944; began his piano studies with Edward Goldman in Boston and made his debut as soloist in the Grieg Piano Concerto with the Boston Pops Orch. at age 9; he also received training in piano from Bodky and Gregory Tucker and in composition from Arthur Shepherd at the Longy School in Cambridge, Mass. (1948–52), in piano from Balogh and in composition from Cowell at the Peabody Inst. in Baltimore (1952–53), in piano from Arthur Loesser and Beryl Rubinstein and in composition from Marcel Dick at the Cleveland Inst. of Music (B.Mus., 1955), and in piano from Rudolf Serkin and Horszowski at the Curtis Inst. of Music in Philadelphia (diploma, 1959). After winning the Levintritt Competition in N.Y. in 1957, he toured widely, settling in 1965 in Toronto, where he later became a naturalized citizen (1984). He was pianist-in-residence (1965–68) and an assoc. prof. (1968–72) at the Univ. of Toronto; in later years, he gave occasional master classes, but he devoted himself mainly to concertizing. In 1988 he exercised his Canadian citizenship by running as a candidate for Parliament. He was awarded honorary doctorates in 1987 by York Univ. in Toronto and Laurentian Univ. in Sudbury. While Kuerti has won accolades for his fine performances of the Viennese classics, he has also played various works by contemporary composers. Among his compositions are 2 string quartets (1954, 1972), *Linden Suite* for Piano (1970), *Magog* for Cello and Piano (1972), *Symphony "Epomeo"* (1973), Violin Sonata (1973), *6 Arrows* for Piano (1973), *Piano Man Suite* (1985), Piano Concerto (1985), and a Trio for Clarinet, Cello, and Piano (1989).

Kuhlmann, Kathleen, American mezzo-soprano; b. San Francisco, Dec. 7, 1950. She studied in San Francisco and at the Chicago Lyric Opera School, making her debut as Maddalena in *Rigoletto* with that company in 1979. She made her European debut in 1980 as Preziosilla in *La forza del destino* at the Cologne Opera; subsequently appeared at Milan's La Scala (as Meg Page in *Falstaff*, Dec. 7, 1980) and at London's Covent Garden (as Ino and Juno in Handel's *Semele*, Nov. 25, 1982). She sang the leading role in *La Cenerentola* at the Glyndebourne Festival in 1983. In 1987 she scored a major success as Falliero in Rossini's *Bianca e Falliero* in its U.S. premiere at the Greater Miami Opera. She made her Metropolitan Opera debut in N.Y. as Charlotte in *Werther* on March 2, 1989. In 1991 she was a soloist in Beethoven's 9th Sym. at the London Promenade Concerts. In 1992 she appeared as Cenerentola at Dresden's Semper Opera. Among her other notable roles are Isabella in *L'Italiana in Algeri*, Dorabella, Rosina, Arsace in *Semiramide*, Bradamante in *Alcina*, and Carmen.

Kuhn, Gustav, Austrian conductor; b. Turrach, Aug. 28, 1947. He studied conducting at the Salzburg Mozarteum and with Swarowsky at the Vienna Hochschule für Musik; later had instruction from Maderna and Karajan, completing his education at the Univ. of Salzburg (Ph.D., 1970). He then served as conductor at the Istanbul Opera (1970–73) and 1st conductor at the Dortmund Stadttheater (1975–77). In 1978 he was named a conductor at the Vienna State Opera; also was chief conductor of the Bern Sym. Orch. and Opera (1979–81); conducted at the Glyndebourne and Salzburg festivals (1980) and made his U.S. debut at the Chicago Lyric Opera (1981). In 1983 he became Generalmusikdirektor of Bonn, a post he held until being dismissed in 1985 after he physically assaulted the director of the Stadttheater during a dispute. He then served as chief conductor of the Rome Opera (from 1987).

Kuhn, Laura (Diane née **Shipcott)**, spirited American musicologist, editor, teacher, and writer on music; b. San Francisco, Jan. 19, 1953. She studied at Dominican College in San Rafael, Calif. (B.A., 1981) and the Univ. of Calif. at Los Angeles (M.A., 1986; Ph.D., 1992, with the diss. *John Cage's Europeras 1 & 2: The Musical Means of Revolution*); also had private instruction in San Francisco (1975–82) with John Hudnall (voice) and Robert Hagopian (piano). She was a member of the San Francisco (1980) and Oakland (1980–82) Sym. Choruses; also appeared as a vocalist in the Daniel Lentz Group (1983–85) in Los Angeles and in Washington, D.C. She was music critic of Marin County's *Independent Journal* from 1980 to 1982; she also wrote book and record reviews for the *Los Angeles* (1982–87) and *N.Y. Times* (1986–89). From 1986 to 1992 she worked extensively with John Cage on various large-scale works, including his *Europeras 1 & 2* for the Frankfurt am Main Opera and his Harvard lectures as holder of the Charles Eliot Norton Chair in Poetry (publ as *I–VI*). Upon Cage's death in 1992, she instituted, with long-time Cage associate Merce Cunningham, the John Cage Trust in N.Y., which she subsequently directed. Kuhn also worked extensively with the seeded Russian-born American lexicographer Nicolas Slonimsky, giving strong editorial assistance to successive editions of his *Baker's Biographical Dictionary of Musicians* (7th and 8th eds., 1984, 1992) and *Music since 1900* (4th and 5th [rev.] eds., 1986, 1994); in 1995 she inherited the editorship of the 9th ed. of *Baker's Biographical Dictionary of Musicians*. In addition to serving as ed. of the present edition of *Baker's*, the first vol. to be devoted exclusively to 20th-century musicians, she also ed. *A Pronouncing Pocket Manual of Musical Terms* (5th ed., 1995); also contributed articles to the *Musical Quarterly*, *Perspectives of New Music*, *Music Today* et al. In 1991 she became an assistant prof. at Arizona State Univ. West in

Phoenix; also lectured widely in the U.S., South America, and Europe. In 1995 she was appointed secretary of the American Music Center. She is also the librettist of Daniel Lentz's collaborative music-theater work, *Apologetica* (1993–96).

Kuhse, Hanne-Lore, German soprano; b. Schwaan, March 28, 1925. She was educated at the Rostock Cons. and the Stern Cons. in Berlin; later studied in Potsdam. She made her debut in Gera in 1951 as Leonore in *Fidelio*; from 1952 to 1959 she was a member of the Schwerin Opera; then sang at the Leipzig Opera (1959–64). In 1964 she joined the East Berlin State Opera. In 1974 she was appointed prof. at the Hochschule für Musik in East Berlin. In 1954 she was named a Kammersängerin. A versatile artist, she was as stylistically faithful to her roles in Mozart's operas as to the heroic and lyric Wagnerian parts.

Kuijken, prominent family of Belgian musicians, all brothers:

(1) Wieland Kuijken, cellist and viola da gambist; b. Dilbeek, near Brussels, Aug. 31, 1938. He studied piano and cello at the Bruges Cons. and the Brussels Cons. (1957), graduating with the prix d'excellence in 1962; was self-taught as a violist. He played in the Baroque group known as the Alarius Ensemble (1959–72) and in the avant-garde Musiques Nouvelles from 1962; later appeared in concerts with his brothers, and also toured extensively as a soloist; likewise taught master classes.

(2) Sigiswald Kuijken, violinist, violist, and conductor; b. Dilbeek, near Brussels, Feb. 16, 1944. He enrolled at the Bruges Cons. at age 8 as a student of violin, then entered the Brussels Cons. in 1960, winning the premier prix in 1964; was autodidact as a Baroque violinist, beginning his career on the instrument in 1970. He played in the Alarius Ensemble and the Musiques Nouvelles before gaining wide recognition with his own Baroque orch., La Petite Bande (founded 1972); subsequently led it on many tours and in numerous recordings; was also active as a teacher.

(3) Barthold Kuijken, flutist and recorder player; b. Dilbeek, near Brussels, March 8, 1949. He studied at the conservatories in Bruges, Brussels, and The Hague, his principal teachers being Franz Vester (flute) and Frans Brüggen (recorder); he was self-taught as a Baroque flutist. He performed in concerts with his brothers and with others; also toured widely and was active as a teacher.

Kuivila, Ron, American composer and instrument designer; b. Boston, Dec. 19, 1955. He studied music and mathematics at Wesleyan Univ. (B.A., 1977) and electronic music and studio recording techniques at Mills College in Oakland, California (M.F.A., 1979); then was artist-in-residence at Media Study in Buffalo (1979–80) and at Wesleyan Univ. (from 1981). His work includes sound installations and electronic instruments of his own design; he pioneered ultrasound (*In Appreciation*, 1979) and sound sampling (*Alphabet*, 1982) in live performance. His installations have appeared throughout the U.S. and Europe. He has also designed commercial music software and exhibited at visual art galleries. His music involves complex, often unpitched, electronic timbres; some of his compositions utilize existing recordings as source material. Among his works are *Minute Differences/Closely Observed* (1984), *Loose Canons* (1986–87), and *Pythagorean Puppet Theatre* (1989).

Kulenkampff, Georg, eminent German violinist and pedagogue; b. Bremen, Jan. 23, 1898; d. Schaffhausen, Oct. 4, 1948. He studied violin with Willy Hess in Berlin. In 1916 he became concertmaster of the Bremen Phil. From 1923 to 1926 he taught at the Berlin Hochschule für Musik; then toured throughout Europe as a soloist; from 1943 he taught at the Lucerne Cons. He was regarded as one of the most brilliant German violinists of his generation; his book *Geigerische Betrachtungen*, partly didactic, partly autobiographical in content, was ed. by G. Meyer-Stichtung (Regensburg, 1952).

Kulenty, Hanna, Polish composer; b. Bialystok, March 18, 1961. She studied with Kotonski at the Warsaw Academy of Music (1981–85) and Louis Andriessen at the Royal Cons. of Music at The Hague (1986–88). Following further training in Berlin (1990–91), she settled in the Netherlands in 1992. Her music makes use of various advanced techniques, including an extensive employment of glissandos, toward a personal style of composition she describes as "polyphony of the arcs."

WORKS: MONODRAMA: *Parable of the Seed* for Alto, Flute, Violin, Double Bass, Percussion, and Tape (1985). **ORCH.:** *Underwater Music* (1983–84); *Ad unum* (Groningen, Sept. 27, 1985); *Quatro* for Chamber Orch. (1986); 2 syms.: No. 1 (1986) and No. 2 for Chorus and Orch. (1989); *Perpetuus* for Chamber Orch. (1989); *Trigon* for Chamber Orch. (1989); 2 piano concertos: No. 1 (1990) and No. 2 for 2 Pianos and Orch. (1991); *Air* for Chamber Orch. (1991); Concerto for Violin and Chamber Orch. (1992; also for Violin with Delay and Orch. 1993); *Passacaglia* (1992); *Sinequan Forte* for Cello and Orch. (1994). **CHAMBER:** 2 string quartets (*Song*, 1984; 1990); *Arci* for Percussionist (1986); *Ride* for 6 Percussionists (1987); *Arcus* for 3 Percussionists (1988); *Cannon* for Violin and Piano (1988); *aaa Tre* for Viola, Cello, and Double Bass (1988); *Cadenza* for Violin and Delay (1992); *Still Life with Cello* for Cello (1993); *Sinequan* for Cello (1993); *4th Circle* for Cello and Piano (1994); *5th Circle* for Flute (1994). **KEYBOARD: PIANO:** *Sesto* (1985); *Quinto* for 2 Pianos (1986). **HARPSICHORD:** *E for E* (1991).

Kulesha, Gary, Canadian composer, conductor, and pianist; b. Toronto, Aug. 22, 1954. He studied composition with Samuel Dolin and piano at the Royal Cons. of Music of Toronto, receiving degrees in piano performance (1973) and composition (1978); continued private studies in England with John McCabe and in N.Y. with John Corigliano. He returned to Canada in 1982, and from 1983 to 1985 was principal conductor of the Stratford Shakespearean Festival Theatre (Ontario), for which he provided incidental music. He was co-principal conductor of the Composer's Orch. of the Canadian Contemporary Music Workshops, where he served as artistic director (from 1987). From 1989 to 1992 he was composer-in-residence of the Kitchener-Waterloo Sym. Orch., and then of the Canadian Opera Co. from 1993 to 1995. His music makes eclectic use of influences as diverse as Prokofiev, Messiaen, musique concrète, jazz, and rock.

WORKS: ORCH.: *Variations* for Winds (1975); *Divertimento* for Strings (1975); *Essay No. 1* (1977), *No. 2* (1984; Kitchener, Jan. 18, 1985), and *No. 3* (1992); Concerto for Tuba and Orch. or Winds (1978–81); *Ensembles* for Winds (1979); *Chamber Concerto No. 1* for Winds and Percussion (Kitchener, Ontario, Nov. 28, 1981), *No. 2* for Trumpet, Piano, and Winds (Toronto, March 28, 1982), *No. 3* for Bass Clarinet and Winds (1982–83; Toronto, Jan. 31, 1984), and *No. 4* for 10 Winds, String Quintet, and Percussion (Kitchener, April 13, 1988); *Celebration Overture* (1985); *Nocturne* for Chamber Orch. (1985); *The Gates of Time* (Kitchener, Oct. 5, 1991); Recorder Concerto (1992); Viola Concerto (1992). **CHAMBER:** String Trio (1971); Sonata for Horn, Tuba, and Piano (1975); Sonata for Tuba and Organ (1976); Duo for Bass Clarinet and Piano (1977); Sonata for Trumpet, Tuba, and Piano (1978); Trio for Flute, Cello, and Piano (1979; rev. 1985); *Concertante Music* for Soprano Saxophone and Wind Quintet (1979); 2 suites for 2 Trumpets (*The Grand Canyon*, 1979; *Pike's Peak*, 1981); Suite for Percussion Quartet (1981); *Passacaglia, Cadenzas, and Finale* for Trumpet, Tuba, and Piano (1981); *Nocturne and Toccata* for Piano and 3 Percussionists (1981); *Mysterium Coniunctionis* for Clarinet, Bass Clarinet, and Piano (1980); *Secrets* for Flute and Piano (1980); *Attitudes* for Clarinet and Piano (1980); *Canticles* for Brass Quintet and Organ (1982); *Pentagram* for 5 Trumpets (1982); *Angels* for Marimba and Tape (1983); *Jazz Music* for Brass Quintet, Marimba, and Piano (1985); *Complex* for Electric Bass Guitar and Tape (1986); Cello Sonata (1986–87); *Demons* for Tuba and Tape (1988); *Political Implications* for Clarinet Quartet (1988). **PIANO:** 3 sonatinas (1969–71); 3 sonatas (1970; 1980, rev. 1984; 1986); Sonata for 2 Pianos (1970–72); *Aphorisms* (1978); *Monument* for Piano, 4-hands (1978); *Mythologies* for 2 Pianos (1987). **OTHER:** Incidental music; *Lifesongs* for Contralto and Strings (Markham, Ontario, Nov. 18, 1985); songs.

Kulka, János, Hungarian conductor; b. Budapest, Dec. 11, 1929. He studied conducting with Ferencsik and Somogyi, and composition with Kodály at the Budapest Academy of Music. He became a répétiteur and choirmaster at the Budapest State Opera (1950); was a conductor there (1953–57). He conducted at the Bavarian State Opera in Munich (1957–59); was 1st conductor at the Württemberg State Theater in Stuttgart (1959–61) and the Hamburg State Opera (1961–64). He subsequently was Generalmusikdirektor in Wuppertal (1964–76) and of the North-West German Phil. in Herford (1975–87).

Kullman, Charles, American tenor; b. New Haven, Conn., Jan. 13, 1903; d. there, Feb. 8, 1983. He entered Yale Univ., and sang at the Yale Glee Club; then took courses at the Juilliard School of Music in N.Y. After singing with the American Opera Co. in Rochester, N.Y., he went to Berlin, where he made his European debut on Feb. 24, 1931, as Pinkerton in *Madama Butterfly* at the Kroll Opera. He sang at the Berlin State Opera (1932–35); also appeared at the Vienna State Opera, at the Salzburg Festivals, and at Covent Garden in London (1934–36). On Dec. 19, 1935, he made his debut at the Metropolitan Opera in N.Y. as Gounod's Faust. He remained on the roster of the Metropolitan until 1960. His repertoire comprised over 30 roles. He scored a signal success in the role of Eisenstein in *Die Fledermaus.* From 1956 to 1971 he taught at the Indiana School of Music in Bloomington.

Kumer, Zmaga, Yugoslav ethnomusicologist; b. Ribnica, April 24, 1924. She studied Slovene literature at the Univ. of Ljubljana (degree, 1948) and musicology at the Ljubljana Academy of Music (degree, 1952); then returned to the Univ., where she received her Ph.D. (1955, with a diss. on Slovene variants of the song *Puer natus in Bethlehem*) and subsequently taught (from 1966). Her studies focus on the texts of Slovene folk songs as well as on the migration and transformation of these songs among other Alpine cultures.

Kunad, Rainer, German composer; b. Chemnitz, Oct. 24, 1936; d. there, July 17, 1995. He studied with Kurzbach and Hübschmann in Chemnitz, at the Dresden Cons. (1955–56), and with Finke, Gerster, and Schenk at the Leipzig Hochschule für Musik. He worked at the Dresden State Opera (1960–75). After serving as a prof. of composition at the Dresden Hochschule für Musik (1978–84), he settled in West Germany. Kunad was principally influenced by Lutosławski, with some indirect inspiration from Penderecki and Henze. He found his métier as a composer for the theater.

WORKS: DRAMATIC: *Bill Brook,* music theater (Dresden, March 14, 1965); *Old Fritz,* music theater (Dresden, March 14, 1965); *Maître Pathelin, oder Die Hammelkomodie,* opera (Dresden, April 30, 1969); *Sabellicus,* opera (Berlin, Dec. 20, 1974); *Der Eiertanz,* mini-opera (DDR-TV, 1975; 1st stage perf., Tübingen, June 7, 1986); *Litauische Claviere,* opera (Dresden, Nov. 4, 1976); *Vincent,* opera (Dresden, Feb. 22, 1979); *Amphytrion,* musical comedy (Berlin, May 26, 1984); *Der Meister und Margarita,* opera (Karlsruhe, March 9, 1986); *Die Menschen von Babel,* scenic mystery play (1986); *Der verborgene Name,* opera (1990); *Kosmischer Advent,* opera (1991). **ORCH.:** *Aphorismen* (1956); *Sinfonia variatione* (1959); 2 syms. (1964, 1967); *Concerto per archi* (1967); *Sinfonietta* (1969); Piano Concerto (1969); *Quadrophonie* for Strings, Winds, and Timpani (1973); *Die sieben Siegel,* choral sym. (1993). **OTHER:** Choral pieces; chamber music; piano works.

Kunc, Božidar, Croatian-American pianist and composer, brother of **Zinka Milanov**; b. Zagreb, July 18, 1903; d. Detroit, April 1, 1964. He was a student of Stančic (piano) and Bersa (composition) at the Zagreb Academy of Music, graduating in 1927; taught there from 1929 to 1951, when he emigrated to the U.S. His music is impressionistic in its harmonic palette.

WORKS: ORCH.: 2 violin concertos (1928, 1955); *Dramatic Prologue* (1929); *Symphonic Intermezzo* (1934); 2 piano concertos: No. 1 (Zagreb, April 27, 1934, composer soloist) and No. 2 (1962); *Marcia funebre* (1936); *Triptihon* for Cello and Orch. (1940); *3 Episodes* for Piano and Strings (1955); syms. **CHAMBER:** Cello Sonata (1927); *Cycle* for Piano and Percussion (1956); *Pieces* for Double Bass (1959). **PIANO:** 4 sonatas (1930–43). **VOCAL:** Songs.

Kunc, Jan, Czech composer; b. Doubravice, Moravia, March 27, 1883; d. Brno, Sept. 11, 1976. He studied at the Brno Teachers' Training College, with Janáček at the Brno Organ School (graduated, 1903), and with Novák in Prague (1905–06). He wrote music criticism in Brno (1909–18); then became an instructor at the Brno Cons. (1919); from 1923 to 1945, was its director; lectured at the Masaryk Univ. in Brno (1947–52). He was best known as a composer of choral music and songs.

WORKS: OPERA: *The Lady from the Seashore* (1919; unfinished). **ORCH.:** *Píseň mládí* (Song of Youth), symphonic poem (1915–16). **CHAMBER:** Piano Trio (1905); String Quartet (1909); Violin Sonata (1931); *Serenade* for Violin and Piano (1952). **PIANO:** Sonata (1903); *4 Compositions* (1917); *Chronicle,* 20 variations on a Slovak folk song (1926); *Miniatures* (1954–57; also for Wind Quintet, 1958). **VOCAL:** *Sedmdesát tisíc* (70,000) for Chorus (1907); *Ostrava* for Men's Chorus (1912); *Stála Kačenka u Dunaja* (Catherine Stood by the Danube), ballad for Alto and Orch. (1918–19); *35 Folk Songs of Moravian Slovakia* for Women's Chorus (1960); many folk-song arrangements.

Kundera, Ludvík, Czech pianist and musicologist; b. Brünn, Aug. 17, 1891; d. there (Brno), May 12, 1971. He studied voice and piano in Vienna and also took courses at the Univ. of Prague. He made his debut in a Prague recital in 1912; later attended Cortot's master classes in piano in Paris (1925) and studied musicology at the Univ. of Brno (Ph.D., 1925). He toured widely in Europe as a soloist and chamber music player, doing much to promote the music of Czech composers. He was prof. of piano and aesthetics at the Brno Cons. from 1922 until his removal by the Nazi occupation authorities in 1941. After the liberation of his homeland, he was director of the Brno Cons. (1945–46), prof. of piano and deputy dean of the Brno branch of the Prague Academy of Music (1946–47), and prof. of piano at the Brno Academy, serving as dean of its music faculty (1948–50) and as rector (1949–62).

WRITINGS: *Omuzike chekhoslovatskovo naroda* (Music of the Czechoslovak Nation; Ekaterinburg, 1919); *Jaroslav Kvapil* (Prague, 1944); *Jak organizovati hudební výchovu v obnoveněm státě* (How to Organize Music Education in the Renewed State; Brno, 1945); *Janáček a Klub přátel umění* (Janáček and the Club of the Friends of Art; Olomouc, 1948); *Janáčkova varhanická škola* (Janáček's Organ School; Olomouc, 1948); *Ludvík van Beethoven* (Prague, 1952); *Beethovenovy klavírní sonáty,* I (Prague, 1964); *Václav Kaprál: Kapitola z historie české meziválečné hudby* (Václav Kaprál: A Chapter in the History of Czech Music between the Wars; Brno, 1968).

BIBL.: J. Vysloužil, *L. K.* (Brno, 1962).

Kunits, Luigi von (actually, **Ludwig Paul Maria**), Austrian violinist, conductor, pedagogue, and composer; b. Vienna, July 20, 1870; d. Toronto, Oct. 8, 1931. He studied composition with Bruuckner, music history with Hanslick, and violin with Grün and Ševčik in Vienna. In 1893 he went to the U.S., where he played at the Chicago World's Columbian Exposition with an Austrian orch.; taught violin in Chicago (1893–96), and then at the Pittsburgh Cons. (1896–1910). He was also concertmaster of the Pittsburgh Sym. Orch. (1897–1910). He toured widely as a soloist in Europe (1910–12) before settling in Toronto; was a teacher at the Canadian Academy of Music, where he was a founder-member of the Academy String Quartet (1912–23); also founded the *Canadian Journal of Music* (1915–19). He was founder-conductor of the New Sym. Orch. (1922), which became the Toronto Sym. Orch. (1927); he remained with the orch. until his death. He wrote an unpubl. book on Beethoven, *The Hero as Musician* (1913). His compositions include 2 violin concertos; *Lullaby* for Violin and Orch. (1916); String Quartet (1890); Viola Sonata (1917); pieces for Violin and Piano; songs.

BIBL.: A. Bridle, *L. v.K.* (Toronto, 1931).

Künneke, Eduard, noted German composer; b. Emmerich-am-Rhein, Jan. 27, 1885; d. Berlin, Oct. 27, 1953. He was a student of Bruch at the Berlin Hochschule für Musik. After composing the operas *Robins Ende* (Mannheim, May 5, 1909) and *Coeur-As* (Dresden, Nov. 1913), he found his métier as a composer of light theater works in Berlin. He attracted favorable notice with his Singspiel *Das Dorf ohne Glocke* (April 5, 1919). The success of his operettas *Der Vielgeliebte* (Oct. 17, 1919) and *Wenn Liebe erwacht* (Sept. 3, 1920) was followed by the outstanding reception accorded his *Der Vetter aus Dingsda* (April 15, 1921). It quickly entered the repertoire as a favorite of the German operetta stage, and was heard all over the globe. After bringing out *Die Ehe im Kreise* (Nov. 2, 1921), *Verliebte Leute* (April 15, 1922), and *Casino-Girl* (Sept. 15, 1923), he failed to find success in N.Y. with the pasticcio *The Love Song* (Jan. 13, 1925) and *Mayflowers* (Nov. 24, 1925). In the interim, he brought out *Die hellblauen Schwestern* (Berlin, Aug. 22, 1925) with considerable success. After the failure in London of *Riki-Tiki* (April 16, 1926), he again found success with *Lady Hamilton* (Breslau, Feb. 25, 1926). His *Die blonde Liselott* (Altenburg, Dec. 25, 1927) became better known in its revised version as *Liselott* (Berlin, Feb. 17, 1932). After bringing out *Die singende Venus* (Breslau, June 9, 1928) and *Der Tenor der Herzogin* (Prague, Feb. 8, 1931), Künneke composed the opera *Nadja* (Kassel, 1931). Returning to the operetta, he then scored the 2nd triumph of his career when he composed *Glückliche Reise* (Berlin, Nov. 23, 1932). It too became a repertoire score of the German operetta stage. Although he never equalled this 2nd success, he went on to compose a number of well-crafted scores, including *Die Fahrt in die Jugend* (Zürich, March 26, 1933), *Die lockende Flamme* (Berlin, Dec. 25, 1933), *Klein Dorrit* (Stettin, Oct. 28, 1933), *Liebe ohne Grenzen* (Vienna, March 29, 1934), *Herz über Bord* (Zürich, March 30, 1935), *Die grosse Sünderin* (Berlin, Dec. 31, 1935), *Zauberin Lola* (Dortmund, April 24, 1937), *Hochzeit in Samarkand* (Berlin, Feb. 14, 1938), *Der grosse Name* (Düsseldorf, May 14, 1938), *Die Wunderbare* (Fürth, Jan. 25, 1941), *Traumland* (Dresden, Nov. 15, 1941), and *Hochzeit mit Erika* (Düsseldorf, Aug. 31, 1949). Künneke also composed film scores, orch. works, and piano pieces.

BIBL.: O. Schneidereit, *E. K. der Komponist aus Dingsda* (Berlin, 1978).

Kunst, Jaap (Jakob), noted Dutch ethnomusicologist; b. Groningen, Aug. 12, 1891; d. Amsterdam, Dec. 7, 1960. He began playing the violin at an early age; soon became interested in Dutch folk songs. He received a degree in law at the Univ. of Groningen (1917), then toured with a string trio in the Dutch East Indies (1919). He remained in Java, where he worked in a government post in Bandung while pursuing his interest in indigenous Javanese music. He subsequently founded an archive there for folk instruments, field recordings, books, and photographs for the Batavia museum. He returned to the Netherlands in 1934; in 1936, became curator of the Royal Tropical Inst. in Amsterdam, which developed into one of the most important organizations of its kind in Europe. He gave lectures at the Univ. of Amsterdam (1953), becoming a member of its faculty (1958). Kunst is credited with having coined the word "ethnomusicology" as a more accurate term than "comparative musicology."

WRITINGS: With C. Kunst Van-Wely, *De toonkunst van Bali* (Weltevreden, 1924; part 2 in *Tijdschrift voor Indische taal-, land- en volkenkunde, LXV, Batavia, 1925); with R. Goris, Hindoe-Javaansche muziekinstrumenten* (Batavia, 1927; 2nd ed., rev., 1968, as *Hindu-Javanese Musical Instruments*); *A Study on Papuan Music* (Weltevreden, 1931); *Musicologisch onderzoek 1930* (Batavia, 1931); *Over zeldzame fluiten en veelstemmige muziek in het Ngada- en Nagehgebied, West-Flores* (Batavia, 1931); *De toonkunst van Java* (The Hague, 1934; Eng. tr., 1949, as *Music in Java*; 3rd ed., aug., 1973); *Verslagen van den ambtenaar voor het systematisch musicologisch onderzoek in den Indischen archipel omtrent de door hem verrichte werkzaamheden* (Bandung, 1934); *Een en ander over den Javaanschen gamelan* (Amsterdam, 1940; 4th ed., 1945); *De waardering van exotische muziek in den loop der eeuwen* (The Hague, 1942); *Music in Flores: A Study of the Vocal and Instrumental Music among the Tribes Living in Flores* (Leiden, 1942); *Music in Nias* (Leiden, 1942); *Een en ander over de muziek en den dans op de Kei-eilanden* (Amsterdam, 1945); *Muziek en dans in de buitengewesten* (Amsterdam, 1946); *De inheemsche muziek en de zending* (Amsterdam, 1947); *Around von Hornbostel's Theory of the Cycle of Blown Fifths* (Amsterdam, 1948); *The Cultural Background of Indonesian Music* (Amsterdam, 1949); *Begdja, het gamelanjongetje* (Amsterdam, 1950); *De inheemsche muziek in Westelijk Nieuw-Guinea* (Amsterdam, 1950); *Metre, Rhythm and Multipart Music* (Leiden, 1950); *Musicologica: A Study of the Nature of Ethno-musicology, Its Problems, Methods and Representative Personalities* (Amsterdam, 1950; 2nd ed., aug., 1955, as *Ethnomusicology*; 3rd ed., 1959; supplement, 1960); *Kulturhistorische Beziehungen zwischen dem Balkan und Indonesien* (Amsterdam, 1953; Eng. tr., 1954); *Sociologische bindingen in der muziek* (The Hague, 1953). **FOLK SONG EDITIONS:** *Terschellinger volksleven* (Uithuizen, 1916; 3rd ed., 1951); *Noord-Nederlandsche volksliederen en -dansern* (Groningen, 1916–18; 2nd ed., 1918–19); *Het levende lied van Nederland* (Amsterdam, 1918–19; 4th ed., 1947); *Songs of North New Guinea* (Weltevreden, 1931); *Oude westersche liederen uit oostersche landen* (Bandung, 1934).

Kunst, Jos, Dutch composer; b. Roermond, Jan. 3, 1936. He studied composition with Joep Straesser (1963–66) and then with Ton de Leeuw at the Amsterdam Cons. (1965–70); also studied electronic music at the Inst. for Sonology at the Univ. of Utrecht. He taught at the Amsterdam Cons. (from 1971). In his music he utilizes a great variety of modernistic techniques, especially metamorphoses of given thematic material.

WORKS: *Marine* for Orch. (1963); *Stenen eten* (The Stone Eaters) for 2 Pianos (1965); *Ijzer* (Iron) for Violin and Piano (1965); *Insecten* for 13 Strings (1966); *Glass Music* for Piano (1966); *Exterieur* for 2-track Tape (1967); *Arboreal* for Orch. (1968; Rotterdam, Sept. 11, 1969); *Expulsion* for 2-track Tape (1969); *Trajectoire* for 16 Voices and 11 Instruments (1970); *XVII One Way* for Small Orch. (Amsterdam, March 13, 1971); *XVIII Outward Bound* for Harp (1971); *Solo Identity I* for Bass Clarinet (1972) and *II* for Piano (1973); *Elements of Logic* for Wind Orch. (1972; in collaboration with J. Vriend); *No Time at All* for Bass Clarinet and Piano (1973; fusion of *Solo Identity I* and *II*); *No Time* for 3 Clarinets, Bass Clarinet, Piano, and 3 Percussionists (1974; amplified version of *No Time at All*); *XXII: Any 2* for Woodwinds (1975).

Kunz, Alfred (Leopold), Canadian organist, conductor, and composer; b. Neudorf, Saskatchewan, May 26, 1929. After training in composition and conducting at the Royal Cons. of Music of Toronto (1949–55), he pursued his composition studies in Europe; he took his diploma in choral conducting at the Mainz Hochschule für Musik in 1965. He settled in Kitchener, Ontario, where he founded the Kitchener-Waterloo Chamber Music Orch. and Choir in 1959. After serving as organist and choirmaster at Mount Zion Evangelical Lutheran Church (1959–64), he was principal of the Canadian Music Teachers' College in Burlington, Ontario (1965–67) and director of musical activities of the Univ. of Waterloo (1965–79). He also conducted various choral groups, including the German-Canadian Choir from 1965. His extensive output included many choral pieces, piano music, and accordion works. Kunz's style ranged from tonal writing to advanced contemporary usages.

WORKS: DRAMATIC: *The Damask Drum*, chamber opera (1961); *The Watchful Gods*, operetta (1962); *Moses*, ballet (1965); *Let's Make a Carol*, play with music (1965); *Ceyx and Alcyone*, opera (1979). **ORCH.:** 2 sinfoniettas (1957, 1961); *Excursion* (1964); *5 Night Scenes* (1971); Percussion Concerto (1973); Piano Concerto (1975); Chamber Sym. (1976); *3 Pieces* for Clarinet and Strings (1977); *Overture for Fun* (1978; rev. 1986); *Classical Arcade* (1984); *Spring into Summer* (1984);

Winterlude (1984; rev. 1986); *Saturday Night Barn Dance: Boy's Night Out* (1988; rev. 1989). Also band music. **CHAMBER:** Violin Sonata (1958); *Emanation No. 1* for Violin, Horn, and Piano (1962) and *No. 2* for Flute, Clarinet, Horn, and Bassoon (1964); *Fun for 2* for 2 Bassoons or 2 Bass Clarinets (1964); Wind Quintet (1964); many pieces for accordion; piano music. **VOCAL:** 2 oratorios: *The Big Land* (1967) and *The Creation* (1972); numerous choral works; many songs.

Kunz, Erich, Austrian bass-baritone; b. Vienna, May 20, 1909; d. there, Sept. 8, 1995. He was a student of Theo Lierhammer and Hans Duhan at the Vienna Academy of Music. In 1933 he made his operatic debut as Osmin in Opava, and than sang in Plauen (1936–37) and Breslau (1937–41). In 1940 he became a member of the Vienna State Opera, and sang with the company during its visit to London's Covent Garden in 1947. He appeared as Beckmesser at the Bayreuth Festivals (1943–44; 1951) and as Guglielmo at the Glyndebourne Festivals (1948, 1950). On Nov. 26, 1952, he made his Metropolitan Opera debut in N.Y. as Leporello, and remained on its roster until 1954. Kunz was greatly esteemed in buffo roles, as an operetta singer, and as an interpreter of popular Viennese songs. His most successful operatic roles were Papageno, Leporello, Figaro, and Beckmesser.

Kunz, Ernst, Swiss conductor and composer; b. Bern, June 2, 1891; d. Olten, Feb. 7, 1980. He went to Munich to study at the Univ. and with Klose and Kellermann at the Academy of Music; after conducting at the Bavarian Court Opera (1916–18), he pursued his career in his homeland. He wrote in a neo-Romantic style principally influenced by Richard Strauss and Pfitzner.

WORKS: DRAMATIC: OPERAS: *Der Fächer* (1924; Zürich, 1929); *Vreneli ab em Guggisberg* (1935); *Die Bremer Stadtmusikanten* (1937); *Der Traum ein Leben* (1968). **SINGSPIEL:** *Die Hochzeitsreise* (1960). **ORCH.:** 5 syms.: (1917, 1921, 1942, 1965, 1966); Viola Concerto (1952); *Drei Lebensalter* (1964); *Serenata strana* (1971); Chamber Concerto for Flute, Piano, and Strings (1971). **CHAMBER:** 3 string quartets; Piano Quartet; piano pieces. **VOCAL: ORATORIOS:** *Vom irdischen Leben* (1931–49); *Weihnachts Oratorium* (1936); *Weisheit des Herzens* (1946); *Einkehr* (1951); *Psalter und Harfe* (1956); over 500 choruses; song cycles.

Kunzel, Erich, American conductor; b. N.Y., March 21, 1935. He was educated at Dartmouth College (B.Mus., 1957); took postgraduate courses at Harvard Univ. and Brown Univ., teaching at the latter (1958–65). He also studied conducting with Monteux, serving as his assistant (1963–64); likewise was assistant conductor of the Rhode Island Phil. (1960–65). He was assistant conductor (1965–67), assoc. conductor (1967–69), and resident conductor (1969–74) of the Cincinnati Sym. Orch.; also taught at the Univ. of Cincinnati College-Cons. of Music (1965–71). He was music director of the New Haven (Conn.) Sym. Orch. (1974–77); subsequently conducted his own Cincinnati Pops Orch. (from 1977). He also toured widely as a guest conductor, leading the pops series of many U.S. orchs.

Kupfer, Harry, German opera director and administrator; b. Berlin, Aug. 12, 1935. He was trained at the Hans Otto Theaterhochschule in Leipzig. In 1958 he launched his career as an opera director with his staging of *Rusalka* at the Halle Landestheater. After holding the position of Oberspielleiter at the Stralsund Theater der Werfstadt (1958–62), he was senior resident producer at the Karl-Marx-Stadt Städtische Theater (1962–66). From 1966 to 1972 he was opera director at the Weimar Nationaltheater, and from 1967 to 1972 he was on the faculty of the Franz Liszt Hochschule für Musik in Weimar. He was opera director and chief producer at the Dresden State Opera from 1972 to 1981, where he esablished himself as one of the leading opera directors of his day through the staging of notable productions of both traditional and contemporary works. In 1978 he garnered acclaim with his thought-provoking staging of *Der Fliegender Holländer* at the Bayreuth Festival. He was the chief producer at the Berlin Komische Oper from 1981 to 1994. In 1994 he became opera director at the Komische Oper and also artistic advisor to the Intendant of the Berlin State Opera. He collaborated with Penderecki in preparing the libretto for *Die schwarze Maske* (Salzburg Festival, Aug. 15, 1986). In 1988 he staged a compelling *Ring* cycle at the Bayreuth Festival. His productions have also been mounted at the Berlin State Opera, the Hamburg State Opera, the Vienna State Opera, and at London's Covent Garden. In his most inspired productions, Kupfer fuses the finest elements of the traditional music theater experience with all that is best in contemporary stage direction.

BIBL.: D. Kranz, *'Ich muss Oper machen': Der Regisseur H. K.* (Berlin, 1988); M. Lewin, *H. K.* (Vienna and Zürich, 1988); R. Lummer, *Regie im Theater: H. K.* (Frankfurt am Main, 1989).

Kupferberg, Herbert, American journalist and music critic; b. N.Y., Jan. 20, 1918. He was educated at Cornell Univ. (B.A., 1939) and Columbia Univ. (M.A., 1940; M.S., 1941). From 1942 to 1966 he was on the staff of the *N.Y. Herald Tribune*; was also music critic of the *Atlantic Monthly* (1962–69) and of the *National Observer* (1967–77). He served as rapporteur for the Twentieth Century Fund's N.Y. task force on cultural exchange with the Soviet Union, which led to the publication of the report *The Raised Curtain* in 1977.

WRITINGS: *Those Fabulous Philadelphians: The Life and Times of a Great Orchestra* (N.Y., 1969); *The Mendelssohns: Three Generations of Genius* (N.Y., 1972); *Opera* (N.Y., 1975); *Tanglewood* (N.Y., 1976); *The Book of Classical Music Lists* (N.Y., 1985); *Basically Bach* (N.Y., 1986); *Amadeus: A Mozart Mosaic* (N.Y., 1986); also 2 books for young readers, *Felix Mendelssohn: His Life, His Family, His Music* (N.Y., 1972) and *A Rainbow of Sound: The Instruments of the Orchestra and Their Music* (N.Y., 1973).

Kupferman, Meyer, American composer, clarinetist, and teacher; b. N.Y., July 3, 1926. He attended N.Y.'s High School of Music and Art and then Queens College of the City Univ. of N.Y. (1943–45). He was active as a clarinetist and taught at Sarah Lawrence College (from 1951); was also composer-in-residence at the Calif. Music Center in Palo Alto (from 1977). With John Yannelli, he founded the recording and publishing company Soundspells Productions in 1986. He publ. the book *Atonal Jazz* (1993). In 1975 he received a Guggenheim fellowship and in 1981 an award from the American Academy and Inst. of Arts and Letters. While he has principally applied serial procedures in his music since 1948, his vast catalog of works is nevertheless highly eclectic, displaying significant examples of neo-Classicism, electronic music, and jazz.

WORKS: DRAMATIC: OPERAS: *In a Garden*, after Gertrude Stein (N.Y., Dec. 29, 1949); *Doctor Faustus Lights the Lights*, after Gertrude Stein (1952; rev. 1963); *The Curious Fern* and *Voices for a Mirror* (both perf. in N.Y., June 5, 1957); *Draagenfut Girl*, children's opera (N.Y., May 8, 1958); *The Judgement (Infinities No. 18a)* (1966–67); *Prometheus* (1975–77); *The Proscenium* (1991); *The Waxing Moon* (1993). **BALLETS:** *Persephone* (1968); *The Possessed* (1974); *O Thou Desire Who Art About to Sing* (1977); *Icarus* (1980). **ORCH.:** 3 piano concertos (1948, 1978, 1993); *Divertimento* (1948); 11 numbered syms.: No. 1 (1950), No. 2, *Chamber Symphony* (1950), No. 3, *Little Symphony* (1952; rev. 1983), No. 4 (1955; Louisville, Jan. 28, 1956), No. 5, *Lyric Symphony* (1956), No. 6, *Symphony of the Yin-Yang* (1972), No. 7 (1974), No. 8, *Steps* (1975), No. 9 (1979), No. 10, *F.D.R.* (1981; for the 100th anniversary of the birth of President Franklin D. Roosevelt), and No. 11 (1983); *Jazz Symphony* for Mezzo-soprano, Jazz Saxophonist, and Orch. (Middletown, N.Y., Oct. 14, 1988); *Ostinato Burlesque* (1954; orchestration of a 1948 piano piece); *Variations* (1958); Concerto for Cello and Jazz Band (*Infinities No. 5*; 1962; rev. 1982); *Infinities No. 14* for Trumpet and Chamber Orch. (1965); *Schemata* (*Infinities No. 20*; 1967); *Infinities No. 24* for Strings (1968); Concerto for Cello, Tape, and Orch. (1974); *Sculptures*

(1974); *Symphonia Breve* (1975); *Passage* for Strings (1976); Violin Concerto (1976); *Atto* (1977); Concerto for 6 Solo Instruments and Orch. (1978); *Sound Objects No. 10* for Small Orch. (1979); *Phantom Rhapsody* for Guitar and Small Orch. (1980); *Sound Phantoms No. 8* (1980); Tuba Concerto (1983); *Challenger* (1983); Clarinet Concerto (1984); *Quasar Infinities* (1984); *Wings of the Highest Tower* (1988); *Overture for Double Orch.* (1988); *Savage Landscape* (1989); *Symphonic Odyssey* (1990); Double Concerto for 2 Clarinets and Orch. (1991); *Ice Cream Concerto*, concerto grosso for 11 Instruments (1992); *Hot Hors D'Oeuvres* for Small Orch. (1993); Concerto for Amplified Guitar and Small Orch. (1993); *Hexagon Skies*, concerto for Amplified Guitar and Small Orch. (1994); *Banners* for Small Orch. (1995). **CHAMBER:** 5 numbered string quartets, including Nos. 4 (1958) and 5 (1959); Concerto for 11 Brass (1948); Wind Quintet (1958); *Infinities*, cycle of 34 pieces on the same tone row, mostly for Chamber Groupings (1961–83); *Moonchild and the Doomsday Trombone* for Oboe, Voice, and Jazz Band (1968); *Fantasy Concerto* for Cello, Piano, and Tape (1974); *Abracadabra Quartet* for Piano and String Trio (1976); *The Red King's Throw* for Clarinet, Cello, Piano, and Percussion (1977); *Masada*, chamber sym. for Flute, Clarinet, Cello, Double Bass, Piano, and Violin (1977); *Sound Objects*, cycle of 10 pieces, mostly for Chamber Groupings (1978–79); *Sound Phantoms*, cycle of 10 pieces, mostly for Chamber Groupings (1979–81); *Jazz Essay* for Saxophone Quartet (1982); *Symphony for 6* for Clarinet, Bassoon, Horn, Violin, Cello, and Bass (1984); Quintet for Piano and Strings (1985); *And 5 Quartets* for 5 String Quartets (1986); Quintet for Clarinet and Strings (1986); *Rock Shadows* for Brass Quintet (1986); *Summer Music* for 2 Guitars, Flute, and Cello (1987); *Top Brass 5* for 5 Trumpets (1989); *Moontrek Fantasy* for Trumpet, Flute, Cello, and Piano (1989); *Triple Suite* for 3 Flutes Doubling Piccolo (1989); *Currents* for Violin and Piano (1992); *Chaconne Sonata* for Flute and Piano (1993); *Going Home* for Guitar Quartet (1994); *Pipe Dream Sonata* for Guitar (1994); piano pieces. **VOCAL:** *Prometheus profundis* for Chorus, Brass, and Percussion (1975); *Ode to Shreveport*, cantata for 4 Soloists, Chorus, and Orch. (1985); *A Crucible for the Moon* for Soprano, Alto Saxophone, and Percussion Orch. (1986); *Wicked Combinations*, song cycle for Mezzo-soprano and Piano (1989); *The Shadows of Jersalem* for Mezzo-soprano, Clarinet, Cello, and Piano (1992).

Kupkovič, Ladislav, Slovak conductor, teacher, and composer; b. Bratislava, March 17, 1936. He studied violin and conducting in Bratislava at the Cons. (1950–55) and at the Academy of Music (1955–61). In 1959–60 he was conductor of the Hungarian Folk Ensemble of Bratislava and then played violin in the Slovak Phil. there (1960–63). In 1963 he organized the chamber ensemble Hudba Dneska (Music of Today). He left Czechoslovakia after the Soviet invasion in 1968 and went to Germany; was a stipendiary at Berlin's Deutscher Akademischer Austauschdienst (1969–71); was made a lecturer (1973) and a prof. (1976) of composition at the Hannover Hochschule für Musik. His music utilizes the cosmopolitan resources of ultramodern music. He initiated "walking concerts," in which a group of musicians walk in the streets playing segments of familiar pieces.

WORKS: SINGSPIEL: *Die Maske* (1986). **ORCH.:** *Dioe* for Orch., with Conductor (1968); *Notausgang* for Orch. and Microphones (1970); *Erinnerungen* for Orch. and Tape (1970); *Monolith* for 48 Strings (1971); *Ein Gespräch mit Gott* (1972); *Das Gebet* for Strings and Percussion (1972–73); *Concours* for the "orchestra of the future" (1973); *Čarovné sláčiky* (Magic Bows) for 30 Violins and Low Strings (1974); *Serenata* (1976); *Postillon-Cornet* for Trumpet and Orch. (1977); *K.-u. K. Musik* (1978); *Cassation* (1979); 3 violin concertos (1980, 1981, 1985); Cello Concerto (1980); Accordion Concerto (1980); Piano Concerto (1980); 2 syms. (1981, 1987); *2 Rococo Symphonies* (1982, 1982); *Little Rococo Symphony* for Strings (1981); Concertante for Violin, Cello, Piano, and Orch. (1982); *B-A-C-H Variations* (1989); *Katinkas Geheimnis*, children's fairy tale for Speaker and Small Orch. (1992). **CHAMBER:** *Maso kríža* (Flesh of the Cross) for Trombone and 10 Percussion Players (1961–62); *Psalm* for 4 Horns (1962); *Výkřiky* (Exclamations) for Flute, Bass Clarinet, Piano, and Percussion (1964); *Rozhovor času s hmotou* (A Conversation between Time and Matter) for Bassoon and 3 Percussion Players (1965); *Ozveny* (Echoes) for 31 Players (1966); *Pred s za* (Before and After) for Chamber Ensemble (1967); *Oktoedr* (Octohedron) for Chamber Ensemble (1968); *Ad libitum*, "happening" for a random group of Performers (1969); *312-SI/723* for 2 Accordions (1975); 3 string quartets (1978, 1978, 1984); String Quintet for 2 Violins, Viola, and 2 Cellos (1978); 2 violin sonatas (1979, 1980); Quartet for Flute, Violin, Viola, and Cello (1980); Wind Serenade (1981); 2 piano sonatas (1981, 1981); Cello Sonata (1984); Trio for Violin, Cello, and Piano (1985); Octet for Clarinet, Bassoon, Horn, 2 Violins, Viola, Cello, and Double Bass (1986); Quintet for 2 Violins, Viola, Cello, and Piano (1984); 2 quartets for Violin, Viola, Cello, and Piano (1986, 1986); Octet for 2 Oboes, 2 Clarinets, 2 Horns, and 2 Bassoons (1988); *24 Caprices* for Violin (1990); piano pieces. **VOCAL:** *Missa Papae Ioannis Pauli Secundi* for Chorus and Orch. (1979). **OTHER:** *Klanginvasion auf Bonn*, spectacle of indeterminate duration, representing the invasion of noise on the population of Bonn (1970).

Kupper, Annelies (Gabriele), German soprano; b. Glatz, July 21, 1906; d. Haar, near Munich, Dec. 8, 1987. She studied at the Univ. of Breslau, and then taught in that city (1929–35). She made her debut at the Breslau Opera (1935), remaining there until 1937. She then sang in Schwerin (1937–38) and Weimar (1938–39). She was a principal member of the Hamburg State Opera (1940–46) and the Bavarian State Opera in Munich (1946–61); also sang at Bayreuth, Salzburg, and London's Covent Garden (Chrysothemis, 1953) and appeared as Danae in the first public performance of Richard Strauss's *Die Liebe der Danae* (Salzburg, 1952). She became a teacher at the Munich Academy of Music (1956). In addition to her Mozart and Strauss roles, she became known for her performances of works by contemporary German composers.

Kurath, Gertrude Prokosch (Tula), American ethnomusicologist; b. Chicago, Aug. 19, 1903. She studied at Bryn Mawr College (B.A., 1922; M.A. in art history, 1928), concurrently studying music and dance in Berlin, Philadelphia, N.Y., and Providence, R.I.; she then attended the Yale School of Drama (1929–30). She conducted field research for the Wenner-Gren Foundation (1949–73), the American Philosophical Soc. (1951–65), and the National Museum of Canada (1962–65; 1969–70); also taught dance, lectured on dance history, and was dance ed. for *Ethnomusicology* (1958–72). She made substantial contributions to the study of American Indian dance and to dance theory and notation.

WRITINGS: *Songs of the Wigwam* (Delaware, Ohio, 1955); *Iroquois Music and Dance: Ceremonial Arts of Two Seneca Longhouses* (Washington, D.C., 1964); *Michigan Indian Festivals* (Ann Arbor, 1966); *Dance and Song Rituals of Six Nations Reserve, Ontario* (Ottawa, 1968); with A. Garcia, *Music and Dance of the Tewa Pueblos, New Mexico* (Santa Fe, 1970: *Radiant Call* (Ann Arbor, 1971); with R. Miller, *With Magnetic Fields Disrupted* (Ann Arbor, 1972); *Tutelo Rituals on Six Nations Reserve, Ontario* (Ann Arbor, 1981); *Dance Memoires* (Cambridge, Mass., 1983).

Kuri-Aldana, Mario, Mexican composer and teacher; b. Tampico, Aug. 15, 1931. He studied piano with Carlos del Castillo at the Academia Juan Sebastián Bach in Mexico City (1948–51) and composition with Tercero, Vazquez, and Michaca at the Escuela Nacional de Música of the Autonomous Univ. of Mexico (1952–60); took conducting courses from Markevitch and Giardino at the National Inst. of Fine Arts (1957–58); then privately studied advanced techniques of composition with Rodolfo Halffter and Luis Herrera de la Fuente (1961–62); took lessons with Ginastera, R. Malipiero, Messiaen, Maderna, Dallapiccola, Copland, and Chase in various venues (1963–64), and with Stockhausen at the Mexico City Cons. (1965). He was active as a teacher from 1955.

WORKS: ORCH.: 3 syms.: No. 1, *Sacrificio* (1959), No. 2 for Strings (1966), and No. 3, *Ce Actal-1521* (1976); *Los cuatro Bacabs*, suite for Double Wind Orch. and optional Narrator (1960); *Máscaras*, concerto for Marimba and Wind Orch. (1962); *Pasos* for Piano and Orch. (1963); *Bacab de las plegarias* for 2 Flutes, 2 Clarinets, Trumpet, Harp, and Strings (1966); *Formas de otros tiempos* for Strings and Harp (1971); *Concierto de Santiago* for Flute, Strings, and 2 Percussion Players (1973); *Concertino mexicano* for Violin and String Orch. (1974). **CHAMBER:** *Canto de 5-Flor* for Cello and Piano (1957); *Sonatina mexicana* for Violin and Piano (1959); *Xilofonías* for Piccolo, Oboe, Bass Clarinet, Double Bassoon, and Percussion (1963); *Puentes* for String Quartet (1965; rev. 1977); *Candelaria*, suite for Wind Quintet (1965); *3-Silvestre*, concerto for 9 Instruments (1966); *Fuga para metales* (1968). **PIANO:** *Suite ingenua* (1953); *Villancico, Canción y Jarabe* (1965); Sonata (1972). **VOCAL:** *Cantares para una niña muerta* for Mezzo-soprano, Flute, and Guitar (1961); *Este, ese y aquel* for Mezzo-soprano, Flute, Violin, Viola, Cello, and Vibraphone (1964); *Amarillo era el color de la Esperanza*, secular cantata for Narrator, Mezzo-soprano, and Jazz Band (1966); *Noche de verano* for Narrator, Soprano, and Small Orch (1975); *A mi hermano* for Baritone, Chorus, and Orch. (1977).

Kurka, Robert (Frank), American composer; b. Cicero, Ill., Dec. 22, 1921; d. N.Y., Dec. 12, 1957. He studied violin with Kathleen Parlow and Hans Letz, and composition with Luening and Milhaud, but considered himself autodidact. He received a Guggenheim fellowship (1951–52), and taught at the City College of N.Y., Queens College, and Dartmouth College. His satirical opera, *The Good Soldier Schweik*, the composition of which was delayed for years due to problems in clearing rights for the libretto and which existed only as an orchestral suite until 1956, was completed shortly before his untimely death from leukemia and was orchestrated by Hershy Kay; it was premiered with extraordinary success at the N.Y. City Center on April 23, 1958. Kurka's music, though quite melodic, makes use of harmonious dissonance, imbuing neo-Classical forms with a rhythmic and harmonic intuition reminiscent of Prokofiev and Shostakovich.

WORKS: OPERA: *The Good Soldier Schweik*, after J. Hašek (1952–57; N.Y., April 23, 1958; as a chamber orch. suite, N.Y., Nov. 24, 1952). **ORCH.:** Chamber Sym. (1946; N.Y., March 7, 1948); Sym. for Brass and Strings (1948; N.Y., March 13, 1950); Violin Concerto (1948); *Music for Orchestra* (1949); *3 Pieces* (1951); 2 numbered syms.: No. 1 (1951) and No. 2 (1953; San Diego, July 8, 1958); *Serenade* for Small Orch. (La Jolla, Calif., June 13, 1954); *John Henry*, portrait (1954); *Julius Caesar*, symphonic epilogue after Shakespeare (San Diego, July 12, 1955); Concertino for 2 Pianos, Strings, and Trumpet (1955); Marimba Concerto (1956; N.Y., Nov. 11, 1959); *Ballad* for Horn and Strings (1956); *Chamber Sinfonietta* (1957). **CHAMBER:** 5 string quartets (1945, 1947, 1949, 1950, 1954); 4 violin sonatas (1946, 1949, 1953, 1955); Sonata for Solo Violin (1947); *Music* for Violin, Trumpet, Clarinet, Horn, and Double Bass (1951); Piano Trio (1951); *7 Moravian Folksongs* for Wind Quintet (1951); Cello Sonatina (1953). **PIANO:** Sonatina (1947); *For the Piano*, suite (1951); Sonata (1952); *Dance Suite* for Piano, 4-hands (1955); *Sonatina for Young Persons* (1957). **VOCAL:** *Who Shall Speak for the People* for Men's Chorus and Orch., after Sandburg (1956); *Song of the Broad-Axe* for Men's Chorus (1956); songs.

Kurt, Melanie, Austrian soprano; b. Vienna, Jan. 8, 1880; d. N.Y., March 11, 1941. She studied piano with Leschetizky at the Vienna Cons. (1887–94), winning the gold medal and Liszt prize; then took vocal lessons from Fannie Mütter in Vienna (1896), but also toured as a pianist (1897–1900). She then made her operatic debut as Elisabeth in *Tannhäuser* (Lübeck, 1902); then sang in Leipzig (1903–04). She then completed her vocal training with Lilli and Marie Lehmann in Berlin. From 1905 to 1908 she sang in Braunschweig; then (1908–12) at the Berlin Royal Opera. She became an outstanding Wagner interpreter and appeared in London (Covent Garden, 1910, 1914), Brussels, Milan, Budapest, etc. When the Deutsches Opernhaus in Charlottenburg was opened in 1912, she was engaged as chief soprano for heroic roles. On Feb. 1, 1915, she made her debut at the Metropolitan Opera in N.Y. as Isolde; remained on its roster until her contract was terminated with the U.S. entry into World War I in 1917. After returning to Germany, she appeared at the Berlin Volksoper (1920–25); also taught there, and later in Vienna. In 1938 she settled in N.Y. Her roles included Pamina, Beethoven's Leonore, Sieglinde, Brünnhilde, Kundry, and the Marschallin.

Kurtág, György, eminent Hungarian composer and teacher; b. Logoj, Romania, Feb. 19, 1926. At 14, he began lessons in piano with Magda Kardos and in composition with Max Eisikovits in Timişoara. In 1946 he went to Budapest and in 1948 became a naturalized Hungarian citizen. He pursued his training at the Academy of Music with Kadosa (piano), Veress and Farkas (composition), and Weiner (chamber music), graduating with diplomas in piano and chamber music in 1951 and in composition in 1955. In 1957–58 he was in Paris to study with Marianne Stein, and also attended the courses at the Cons. of Milhaud and Messiaen. From 1967 to 1986 he was a prof. at the Budapest Academy of Music. In 1971 he was in Berlin under the sponsorship of the Deutscher Akademischer Austauschdienst. From 1993 to 1995 he was a guest at the Wissenschaftskolleg in Berlin. In 1954, 1956, and 1969 he received the Erkel Prize. He was awarded the Kossuth Prize in 1973. In 1980 he was made a Merited Artist and in 1984 an Outstanding Artist by the Hungarian government. In 1987 he became a member of the Bavarian Akademie der Schönen Künste in Munich. He was awarded the Herder Prize in Hamburg in 1992. In 1994 he was honored with the Austrian State Prize. Kurtág has built upon advanced compositional techniques to produce his own distinctive style. His music is notable for its distinguished craftsmanship, integrity, refinement, and lyricism.

WORKS: ORCH.: *Movement* for Viola and Orch. (1954; 1st movement of the Viola Concerto, 1954); Viola Concerto (1954; 1st movement as *Movement* for Viola and Orch., 1954); *Grabstein für Stephan* for Guitar and Spatially Dispersed Instrumental Groups (1978–79; rev. version, Szeged, Oct. 26, 1989); . . . *Quasi una Fantasia* . . . for Piano and Spatially Dispersed Instrumental Groups (1987–88; Berlin, Oct. 16, 1988); Double Concerto for Piano, Cello, and 2 Spatially Dispersed Chamber Ensembles (1989–90; Frankfurt am Main, Dec. 8, 1990); *Stele* (Berlin, Dec. 14, 1994). **CHAMBER:** String Quartet (1959; Budapest, April 24, 1961); Wind Quintet (1959; Budapest, Nov. 17, 1963); 8 Duos for Violin and Cimbalom (1961; Budapest, March 22, 1963); *Signs* for Viola (1961; Budapest, March 22, 1963); *Splinters* for Cimbalom (1973; Budapest, April 12, 1975; also for Piano, 1978); *In Memoriam György Zilcz* for 2 Trumpets, 2 Trombones, and Tuba (1975); *Hommage à András Mihály*, 12 microludes for String Quartet (1977; Witten, April 21, 1978); *The Little Predicament* for Piccolo, Trombone, and Guitar (1978; Budapest, April 27, 1979); *Herdecker Eurythmie* for Flute, Violin, Speaking Voice, and Tenor Lyre (1979); *János Pilinszky: Gérard de Nerval* for Cello (1986); *Officium Breve in Memoriam Andreae Szervánszky* for String Quartet (Witten, April 22, 1988); *Ligatura-Message to Frances-Marie (The Answered Unanswered Question)* for Cello with 2 Bows, 2 Violins, and Celesta (1989; also for 2 Cellos, 2 Violins, and Celesta, and for 2 Organs and Celesta or Upright Piano); *Hommage à R. Sch.* for Clarinet, Viola, and Piano (Budapest, Oct. 8, 1990); *Lebenslauf* for 2 Pianos and 2 Basset Horns (Witten, April 26, 1992). **KEYBOARD: PIANO:** Suite for Piano Duet (1950–51); *8 Piano Pieces* (Darmstadt, July 10, 1960); *Games* (1st series, 4 books, 1973–76; 2nd series, 3 books, 1975–93); *Pre-Games* (1974–75); *3 In Memoriam* (1988–90). **ORGAN:** *Ligature e Versetti* (1990). **VOCAL:** *Beads* for Chorus (1949 or 1950); *The Sayings of Péter Bornemisza*, concerto for Soprano and Piano (1963–68; Darmstadt, Sept. 5, 1968; rev. 1969 and 1975); *3 Old*

Inscriptions for Voice and Piano (1967–86; Berlin, Oct. 16, 1988); *In Memory of Winter Sunset* for Soprano, Violin, and Cimbalom (Debrecen, May 18, 1969); *4 Capriccios* for Soprano and Chamber Orch. (1970; Budapest, Oct. 13, 1971); *4 Songs to Poems by János Pilinszky* for Bass or Bass-baritone and Chamber Ensemble (Budapest, Oct. 1, 1975); *S.K. Remembrance Noise*, 7 songs for Soprano and Violin (1975; Budapest, Dec. 28, 1976); *Omaggio a Luigi Nono* for Chorus (1979; London, Feb. 3, 1981); *Messages of the Late Miss R.V. Troussova* for Soprano and Chamber Ensemble (1976–80; Paris, Jan. 14, 1981); *Songs of Despondency and Grief* for Chorus and Instruments (1980–94; Amsterdam, June 21, 1995); *Attila József Fragments* for Soprano (1981; Budapest, Oct. 26, 1982); *7 Songs* for Soprano and Cimbalom or Piano (1981; Glasgow, Oct. 7, 1985); *Scenes from a Novel* for Soprano, Violin, Double Bass, and Cimbalom (1981–82; Budapest, Oct. 1, 1983); *8 Choruses* (1981–82; rev. version, London, June 1, 1984); *Requiem for the Beloved* for Soprano and Piano (1982–87; London, Oct. 13, 1989); *Kafka-Fragment* for Soprano and Violin (1985–87; Witten, April 25, 1987); *Hölderlin: An . . .* for Tenor and Piano (1988–89; Aachen, June 6, 1989); *Samuel Beckett: What is the Word* for Voice and Piano (1990; Sermoneta, June 5, 1993; also for Alto, Voices, and Spatially Dispersed Chamber Ensembles, Vienna, Oct. 27, 1991); *Friedrich Hölderlin: Im Walde* for Voice (1993). **TAPE:** *Mémoire de Laïka* (1990; Budapest, Jan. 1, 1991; in collaboration with his son, G. Kurtág, Jr.).

BIBL.: F. Spangemacher, ed., *G. K.* (Bonn, 1986).

Kurth, Ernst, eminent Austrian-born Swiss musicologist; b. Vienna, June 1, 1886; d. Bern, Aug. 2, 1946. He studied with Adler at the Univ. of Vienna (Ph.D., 1908, with the diss. *Der Stil der opera seria von Gluck bis zum Orfeo*; publ. in *Studien zur Musikwissenschaft*, I, 1913); completed his Habilitation at the Univ. of Bern in 1912 with his *Die Voraussetzungen der theoretischen Harmonik und der tonalen Darstellungssystems* (publ. in Bern, 1913). He was made a reader (1920) and a prof. of musicology (1927) there. His principal work, *Grundlagen des linearen Kontrapunkts: Bachs melodische Polyphonie* (Bern, 1917; 5th ed., 1956), profoundly influenced musicology and practical composition, and also introduced the term "linear counterpoint." A companion vol., *Romantische Harmonik und ihre Krise in Wagners Tristan* (Bern, 1920; 3rd ed., 1923), is a psychological analysis of Romantic music. His *Musikpsychologie* (Berlin, 1931; 2nd ed., 1947) represents a synthesis of his theoretical ideas on musical perception. He also publ. *Anton Bruckner* (2 vols., Berlin, 1925). Le Rothfarb ed. and tr. *Ernst Kurth: Selected Writings* (Cambridge and N.Y., 1991).

BIBL.: E. Bücken, "K. als Musiktheoretiker," *Melos*, IV (1924–25); K. von Fischer, "In memoriam E. K.," *Der Musikalmanach*, VIII (1948); D. Menstell Hsu, "E. K. and His Concept of Music as Motion," *Journal of Music Theory*, X (1966); L. Rothfarb, *E. K. as Theorist and Analyst* (Philadelphia, 1988).

Kurtz, Efrem, Russian-born American conductor; b. St. Petersburg, Nov. 7, 1900; d. London, June 27, 1995. He studied with N. Tcherepnin, Glazunov, and Wihtol at the St. Petersburg Cons.; then at the Univ. of Riga (1918–20); then took music courses at the Stern Cons. in Berlin, graduating in 1922. He made his conducting debut in Berlin in 1921; then was a guest conductor with the Berlin Phil.; subsequently was conductor of the Stuttgart Phil. (1924–33). He was conductor of the Ballets Russes de Monte Carlo (1933–42), with which he toured throughout Europe and the U.S.; then went to the U.S., becoming a naturalized American citizen in 1944. He was conductor of the Kansas City Phil. (1943–48) and the Houston Sym. Orch. (1948–54); then was joint conductor of the Liverpool Phil. (1955–57). In subsequent years, he appeared as a guest conductor in Europe, the U.S., and Japan. He was married to the flutist Elaine Shaffer from 1955.

Kurz, Selma, noted Austrian soprano; b. Bielitz, Silesia, Nov. 15, 1874; d. Vienna, May 10, 1933. She studied with Johannes Ress in Vienna and Mathilde Marchesi in Paris. She made her first appearance as a mezzo-soprano as Mignon at the Hamburg Opera (May 12, 1895); then sang in Frankfurt am Main (1896–99). She made her first appearance at the Vienna Court Opera as Mignon (Sept. 3, 1899); after singing lyric-dramatic soprano roles, she turned to coloratura roles; continued on its roster when it became the State Opera (1918), singing there until her retirement (1927). She made her London debut at Covent Garden as Gilda (June 7, 1904), creating a profound impression; sang there again in 1905, 1907, and 1924. She appeared as a concert singer in the U.S. She was esteemed for such roles as Elizabeth, Eva, Sieglinde, Lucia, and Mimi; also created Zerbinetta in the rev. version of Richard Strauss's *Ariadne auf Naxos* (1916). She married the Austrian gynecologist Josef Halban in 1910; their daughter was the soprano Desi Halban-Kurz (b. Vienna, April 10, 1912).

BIBL.: H. Goldmann, *S. K.* (Bielitz, 1933); D. Halbin and U. Ebbers, *S. K.: Die Sängerin und ihre Zeit* (Stuttgart and Zürich, 1983).

Kurz, Siegfried, German conductor and composer; b. Dresden, July 18, 1930. He studied conducting with Ernst Hintze, composition with Fidelio Finke, and trumpet with Gerd Seifert at the Staatlichen Akademie für Musik und Theater in Dresden (1945–50). From 1949 to 1960 he was conductor of music for dramatic productions at the Dresden State Theater. In 1960 he became a conductor at the Dresden State Opera; in 1975 he was named its music director; in 1979 he also became a prof. of composition at the Dresden Hochschule für Musik. He toured with the Dresden State Orch. to Austria, Japan, and the U.S. As a conductor, he was honored with the titles of Staatskapellmeister (1965) and Generalmusikdirektor (1971); as a composer, he received the Kunstpreis and the Nationalpreis of the German Democratic Republic. His compositions combine the principles of Classical lucidity with the dissonant counterpoint of the modern era.

WORKS: ORCH.: *Sinfonia piccola* (1953); Trumpet Concerto (1953); 2 syms. (1958, 1959); Chamber Concerto for Wind Quintet and Strings (1962); Piano Concerto (Dresden, Oct. 2, 1964); *Variations* (1968); *Sonatine* (1969); *Music* for Winds, Percussion, and Strings (1969); Horn Concerto (Dresden, Dec. 20, 1973). **CHAMBER:** Wind Quintet (1950); *Sonatine* for 7 Brass Instruments (1952).

Kurz, Vilém, Czech pianist and pedagogue; b. Německý Brod, Dec. 23, 1872; d. Prague, May 25, 1945. He studied piano with Julius Höger (1884–86) and Jakub Holfeld (1886–98); also received training in organ and theory at the Prague Organ School (1886–87) before passing the state music examinations at the Prague Cons. (1892). He was active as a soloist and chamber music player, founding the Czech Trio and playing in the Czech Quartet. He was prof. of piano at the Lwów Cons. (1898–1919) and the Brno Cons. (1919–20). After teaching at the Brno branch of the Prague Cons. (1920–28), he settled in Prague and taught at the Cons. (1928–40), where he also was its rector (1936–37; 1938–39). Kurz was highly regarded as a pedagogue and publ. several piano methods. His most famous pupil was Rudolf Firkušný.

BIBL.: Z. Böhmová-Zahradničkova, *V. K.: Život, práce, methodika* (V. K.: Life, Work, and Methods; Prague, 1954).

Kusche, Benno, German bass-baritone; b. Freiburg im Breisgau, Jan. 30, 1916. He studied in Karlsruhe with his mother and in Freiburg im Breisgau with Fritz Harlan. He made his operatic debut in Koblenz in 1938; then sang in Augsburg (1939–44); subsequently became a leading member of the Bavarian State Opera in Munich (1946). He made his debut at London's Covent Garden as Beckmesser (1952); chose that same role for his Metropolitan Opera debut in N.Y. on Dec. 27, 1971. He was made a Bavarian Kammersanger in 1955. His notable roles included Papageno, Figaro, Leporello, Don Alfonso, and Alberich.

Kussevitsky, Serge (Alexandrovich). See **Koussevitzky, Serge (Alexandrovich).**

Kutavičius, Bronislovas, Lithuanian composer; b. Molainiai, near Panevežys, Sept. 13, 1932. He studied composition with Antanas Račiunas at the Vilnius Cons., graduating in 1964. In 1975 he was appointed to the music faculty at the Arts School in Vilnius. In his music, he evolves a complex system of varied techniques, impressionistic pointillism, intervallic serialism, and aleatory sonorism, all this intertwined with Lithuanian melorhythms.

WORKS: DRAMATIC: *Doddering Old Man on Iron Mountain*, children's opera-ballet (1976); *The Green Bird*, opera-poem (1981). **ORCH.:** *Sinfonietta* (1964); *Divertimento* for Piano and Strings (1967); Sym. for Men's Chorus and Orch. (1973); *Dzukija Variations* for Strings and Tape (1975). **CHAMBER:** Violin Sonata (1962); *Prelude and Fugue* for 4 Violins (1966); *Poem* for Cello, Piano, and Wind Quintet (1967); Viola Sonata (1968); *From Madrigal to Aleatory*, children's suite for Violin and Piano (1972); 2 string quartets: No. 1 (1972) and No. 2, *Anno cum tettigonia* (Year with a Cicada; 1980); *Prutiena* (Buried Village) for Violin, Organ, and Chimes (1977); String Quintet (1978); *Clocks of the Past* for String Quartet and Guitar (1978); *Perpetuum mobile* for Cello and Piano (1978). **PIANO:** *3 Metamorphoses* (1966); *Collages* for 2 Pianos (1970); Sonata (1975); *A Disputation with a Stranger*, concerto for 2 Pianos and Tape (1982). **VOCAL:** *Pantheistic Oratorio* for Soprano, Narrator, 4 Men's Voices, and 12 Instruments (1970); *On the Shore* for High Voice and 4 Violas (1972); *Little Performance* for Actress, 2 Pianos, and 2 Violins (1975); *2 Birds in the Thick of the Woods*, cantata for Soprano, Oboe, Prepared Piano, and Electronic Tape (1978); *The Last Pagan Rites*, oratorio for Soprano, Girls' Chorus, Horns, and Organ (1978).

Kutev, Filip, Bulgarian bandmaster, choral conductor, and composer; b. Aytos, June 26, 1903; d. Sofia, Nov. 27, 1982. He studied at the Sofia Academy of Music (graduated, 1929). He was a bandmaster in Burgas, and then in Sofia; in 1951 he organized an ensemble of largely untutored folksingers, musicians, and dancers; he brought it to a high point of virtuosity and toured in Europe (1958) and the U.S. (1963), eliciting great praise. Virtually all of his compositions are derived from Bulgarian melorhythms; among these are *Bulgarian Rhapsody* for Orch. (1937); *September the 9th*, cantata in honor of the entry of the Soviet army into Bulgaria in 1944; *Stalin Cantata* (1949); Sym. (1950).

BIBL.: S. Stoyanov, *F. K.* (Sofia, 1962).

Kuula, Toivo (Timoteus), Finnish conductor and composer; b. Vasa, July 7, 1883; d. (shot to death during a street fight in the aftermath of the Finnish Civil War) Viipuri, May 18, 1918. He studied at the Helsinki Music Inst. with Sibelius, Wegelius, Nováček, and Järnefelt (1900–1908); then with Bossi in Bologna, in Leipzig, and with Labey in Paris (1908–10); finally in Berlin (1911–12). He taught and conducted in Vasa (1903–05); was conductor of the Oulu Orch. (1910–11), vice-conductor of the Native Orch. (1912–14), and assistant conductor of the Helsinki Municipal Orch. (1914–16); then conducted the orch. of the Viipuri Friends of Music (1916–18). His music, rooted in Finnish folk song, is occasionally touched with Impressionism.

WORKS: *Etelapohjälainen sarja* (South Ostrobothnians Suites) for Orch. (1906–09; 1912–14); *Prelude and Fugue* for Orch. (1909); *Prelude and Intermezzo* for Strings and Organ (1909); *Orjanpoika* (The Son of a Slave), symphonic legend (1910); *Kuolemattomuuden toivo* (Hope of Immortality) for Baritone, Chorus, and Orch. (1910); *Merenkylpijäneidot* (Maids on the Seashore) for Soprano and Orch. (1910); *Impi ja pajarinpoika* (The Maid and the Boyar's Son) for Soprano and Orch. (1911); *Bothnic Poem* for Orch. (Petrograd, Oct. 26, 1918); Violin Sonata; music for plays; piano pieces; songs. He left unfinished a *Jupiter Symphony*; also a *Stabat Mater* for Chorus, Organ, and Orch. (1914–18; completed by Madetoja).

BIBL.: T. Elmgreen-Heinonen and E. Roiha, *T. K.: A Finnish Composer of Genius* (Helsinki, 1952).

Kuusisto, Ilkka Taneli, Finnish composer, conductor, and administrator, son of **Taneli Kuusisto**; b. Helsinki, April 26, 1933. He studied organ at the Sibelius Academy in Helsinki; also composition with Arre Merikanto and Fougstedt. In 1958 he went to N.Y. to study organ with Seth Bingham; later continued his studies in Germany and Vienna. Returning to Helsinki, he was a conductor at the City Theater (1965–68; 1971–75); also was head of the Klemetti Inst. (1969–71); after serving as artistic director of Fazer Music (1981–84), he was general manager of the Finnish National Opera (1984–92).

WORKS: DRAMATIC: OPERAS: *Muumioopperа* (1974); *Miehen kylkiluu* (1977); *Sota valosta* (1980; Helsinki, April 2, 1981); *Jääkäri Stahl* (1981); *Pierrot tai yon salaisuudet* (1991). **MUSICALS:** *Lumikuningatar* (1979); *Robin Hood* (1987). Also music for plays and films. **CHAMBER:** *3 Introductions* for Brass, Percussion, and Organ (1956); Duo for Flute and Cello (1957); *Coelestis aulae nuntius* for Trombone and Organ (1959); *Cassazione* for 2 Clarinets and 2 Horns (1961); *Jazzationes* for Jazz Quartet and String Quartet (1965); *Ritornells* for Viola and Marimba (1970); organ pieces. **VOCAL:** *3 Chinese Songs* for Soprano, Flute, and Piano (1956); *Daybreak*, cantata for Soli, Youth Chorus, and Organ (1957); *Crucifixus* for Baritone and String Quartet (1959); *The Pain* and *Alfbid*, 2 songs for Baritone, 2 Clarinets, and Strings (1972); other songs.

Kuusisto, Taneli, Finnish organist and composer, father of **Ilkka Taneli Kuusisto**; b. Helsinki, June 19, 1905; d. there, March 30, 1988. He studied at the Helsinki Inst. of Church Music (graduated, 1931), in Paris, and in Leipzig with J.N. David. He centered his career on Helsinki; was assistant conductor of the Finnish Radio (1936–42) and chorus director of the Finnish National Opera (1942–46); was organist of Töölö (1942–63). He taught at the Sibelius Academy (1948–57), serving as head of its church music dept. (1955–57); was vice-director (1956–59) and director (1959–71) there. He was a member of the Swedish Royal Academy of Music.

WORKS: ORCH.: *Pastorale* (1934); *Nocturne* for Cello and Orch. (1936); *Laatokka* (Lake Ladoga), symphonic legend (1944); *Toccata* (1953). **CHAMBER:** Sonatina for String Quartet (1927); *Sonatina di Natale* for Flute, Cello, and Piano (1936); Trio for Flute, Viola, and Piano (1945); keyboard pieces. **VOCAL:** *Psalm 40* for Baritone, Chorus, Organ, and Strings (1939); *Jouluyö* (Christmas Night) for Chorus, Organ, and Orch. (1941); *Kangastuksia* (Mirages) for Mezzo-soprano and Orch. (1945); *Saimoon helmi* (The Pearl of Saimaa), cantata (1949); sacred music.

Kuznetsova, Maria (Nikolaievna), prominent Russian soprano; b. Odessa, 1880; d. Paris, April 25, 1966. She studied in St. Petersburg with Tartakov. She made her debut in an operatic production at the Cons. there (1904); then was a member of the Maryinsky Theater (1905–13), where she distinguished herself in Russian roles and as Juliette, Elsa, Carmen, and Madama Butterfly. She made guest appearances in Berlin (1908), at the Opéra (1908, 1910, 1912, 1914) and Opéra-Comique (1910) in Paris, and at Covent Garden in London (debut as Marguerite in *Faust*, 1909; returned in 1910, 1920). In 1915–16 she sang in Petrograd and in 1916 in Chicago. After the Russian Revolution (1918), she fled to Sweden; made appearances in Stockholm and Copenhagen (1920), and then toured with her own opera company; later was artistic adviser of Barcelona's Teatro Liceo.

Kuznetzov, Konstantin (Alexeievich), learned Russian music historian; b. Novocherkassk, Sept. 21, 1883; d. Moscow, May 25, 1953. Following training in law at the Univ. of Moscow (1902–04; 1906–07) and in philosophy at the Univ. of Heidelberg (1906), he returned to the Univ. of Moscow in 1908 to pursue postgraduate studies; he then studied with Wolfram (music history) and Reger (composition) in Germany, and also was awarded a doctorate in civil law from the Univ. of Kharkov in 1916. After teaching at the Univ. of Moscow (1912–14), he was a prof. at the Univ. of Odessa (1914–20). Returning to Moscow, he worked at the State Inst. for Music Research from

1921. He also taught music history at the Cons. (1923–31; 1934–38; 1941–49), where he was made a prof. in 1936 and head of the music history dept. in 1942; he likewise was head of its Russian music dept. (1943–46). In 1946 he became a senior research fellow at the Inst. of Fine Arts.

WRITINGS: *Etyudï o muzïke* (Studies in Music; Odessa, 1919); *Vvedeniye v istoriyu muzïki* (Introduction to the History of Music; Moscow and Petrograd, 1923); *Glinka i evo sovremenniki* (Glinka and His Contemporaries; Moscow, 1926); *Muzïkalno-istoricheskiye portretï: Biografii kompozitorov XVI–XVII vv.* (Musico-Historical Portraits: Biographies of Composers of the XVI–XVII Centuries; Moscow, 1937); with V. Kuznetsova, *Klassiki russkovo romansa* (Classics of Russian Song; Moscow, 1938); with I. Yampolsky, *Arcangelo Corelli* (Moscow, 1953).

Kvam, Oddvar S(chirmer), Norwegian composer; b. Oslo, Sept. 9, 1927. He studied at the Oslo Cons. (1943–52), where he took a degree in harmony and counterpoint (1950) and received training in piano and theory; also obtained a law degree from the Univ. of Oslo (1949); he later studied conducting with Grüner-Hegge (1955–57) and composition with David Monrad Johansen (1964–66) in Oslo, completing his training in composition with Herman Koppel in Copenhagen (1969). He practiced law while devoting much time to composition; was the first composer to hold the influential post of chairman of the Norwegian Arts Council (1985–88). Two of his orch. works, Prologue (1967) and Opening (1974), received awards at the inauguration of the Oslo Concert Hall in 1977. Kvam's compositions tend to be free of tonally based strictures, yet they preserve a feeling of tonality.

WORKS: OPERAS: *The Dream of the 13th Hour* (1986); *The Cabinet*, chamber opera (1989). **ORCH.:** *Prologue* (1967); *Afterwards Everything Is Too Late* (1967; rev. version for Narrator and Orch., 1977); *Concert Overture* (1969); 2 syms.: No. 1, *3 Contrasts* (1972) and No. 2, *Communication* (1981); *Dialogues* for Oboe and Strings (1973; also for Oboe and Clarinet Quintet); *Opening* (1974); *Suffragette* for Piano and Orch. (1975); *Legend* for Strings (1975); *Trim* for School Orch. (1976); *Ostinato festoso* (1976); *Vibrations* (1976–82); *From the Young People's World* for Orch., Percussion, and Electric Guitar (1978); *Phoenix* for Cello and Orch. (1988); *Colors* for Harmonica and Strings (1989); *Towards the End* (1989); *Carpe Diem* (1990–92); *The Cycle of Life* (1991). **SYMPHONIC BAND:** *Concert March* (1977); *Flight 77* (1977); *Blow Out!* (1978); *Vacation* (1982); *Apollonia* (1983); *Homecoming* (1984); *Sightseeing* (1987); *Downwards and Upwards* (1987). **CHAMBER:** *Divertimento* for Flute, Viola, and Cello (1971); 3 string quartets (1973, 1976, 1985); *3 Centrifuges* for Wind Quintet (1975); *Theme with Variations* for Violin (1976); *Trembling Trumpets* for 4 Trumpets (1977); *Drops* for Flute and Harp (1977); *5 Monophonies*, 2 for Each of the Woodwind Quintet Instruments (1977); Trio for Piano, Violin, and Cello (1979); Sonata for Clarinet and Percussion (1979); *Ave Maria* for Violin or Cello and Piano or Guitar (1981); *Duo ostinato* for Violin and Guitar (1981); *Trio ostinato* for Flute, Viola, and Guitar (1982); *Prelude and Rondo* for Violin (1983); *Andando e tornando* for 2 Violins (1984); *Clarimpette* for Clarinet and Trumpet (1985); *Sunset* for Violin and Organ (1988); *Changes* for Violin, Viola, and Cello (1988); *3 Stages* for Flute, Oboe, Violin, and Cello (1992). **PIANO:** *A Rather Ordinary Week* (1960–68); *3 Mini Pieces* for Piano, 4-hands (1970–71); *Encyclopedia* (1976); *12 Proverbs* (1976); *Plastic Arts* (1979); *Hommage à Prokofiev* (1983); *Growing Influence* (1983); *4 Hands across the Sea* for Piano, 4-hands (1984); *Counterplay*, suite (1994). **VOCAL:** *Festival Cantata* for Men's Chorus and Orch. (1966); *Epinikion* for Chorus and Orch. (1971–75); *Clarina the Clarinet*, fairy tale for Narrator and Clarinet (1975); *The Great Language* for Chorus (1977); *Psalmus XVIII* for Chorus and Organ (1979); *Come!* for Chorus and Piano (1982); *Querela pacis* for 2 Choruses and Orch. (1983); *Born Anew* for Chorus (1988); *The Inauguration* for Chorus and 2 Trumpets (1993–94); other choruses and songs.

Kvandal (real name, **Johansen**), **(David) Johan,** distinguished Norwegian composer and organist, son of **David Monrad Johansen;** b. Christiania, Sept. 8, 1919. He graduated as a student of organ (under Sandvold) and of conducting at the Oslo Cons., where he also took courses with Tveitt (composition) and Steenberg (counterpoint and composition); he then pursued his composition studies with Marx in Vienna, Boulanger in Paris (1952–54), and Blacher in Berlin (1970). From 1959 to 1974 he was organist of Oslo's Valerengen Church. Kvandal's works are written in a well-crafted neo-Classical style but with obeisance to Norway's national musical tradition.

WORKS: DRAMATIC: *Skipper Worse*, television score (1967); *Mysteries*, opera (1993; Oslo, Jan. 15, 1994). **ORCH.:** *Divertimento* for Strings (1945); *Norwegian Overture* (1950); *Variations and Fugue* (1954); Sym. (1959); *Symphonic Epos* (1961–62); Concerto for Flute and Strings (1963); *Sinfonia concertante* (1968); *Antagonia*, concerto for 2 String Orchs. and Percussion (1972–73); Concerto for Oboe and Strings (1977); Violin Concerto (1979); *Triptychon* (1979); Concerto for Chamber Orch. (1980); *Poem* for Strings (1985; also for Piano or Organ); *Visions Norvegiennes* (1985); Concerto for 2 Pianos and Orch. (1993–94). **CHAMBER:** String Trio (1951); 3 string quartets (1954, 1966, 1983); Duo for Violin and Cello (1959); *Aria, Cadenza and Finale* for Violin and Piano (1964); *Introduction and Allegro* for Horn and Piano (1969); *Do lontano* for Flute and Piano (1970); Wind Quintet (1971); Sonata for Solo Violin (1973–74); Quartet for Flute, Violin, Viola, and Cello (1975); *Night Music*, nonet (1981); *Overture Fantasy* for 8 Winds and Double Bass (1982); Sonata for Solo Harp (1984); Sonata for Solo Guitar (1984); Sonata for Solo Accordion (1987); Horn Quartet (1988). **KEYBOARD: PIANO:** Sonata (1940); Sonatina (1942); *3 Fantasy Country Dances* (1969); *Duo concertante* for 2 Pianos (1974). **ORGAN:** *Partita* (1971). **VOCAL:** *Song of Stella* for Soprano and Strings (1952); 3 solo cantatas: No. 1 for Soprano or Tenor and Orch. (1953), No. 2, *O Domine Deus*, for Soprano and Organ (1966), and No. 3 for Baritone and Organ (1970); *Nature*, chamber cantata for Baritone, Violin, and Piano (1972); Cantata for the Ibsen celebration (1978); choruses; songs.

BIBL.: *Festskrift til J. K. i anledning 70-årsdagen 8. september 1989* (Oslo, 1989).

Kvapil, Jaroslav, significant Czech composer; b. Fryšták, April 21, 1892; d. Brno, Feb. 18, 1958. He studied with Nešvera in Olmütz (1902–06), Janáček at the Brno Organ School (1906–09), and Reger at the Leipzig Cons. (1911–13). He was in the Austrian army during World War I; then was conductor of the Brno Beseda (1919–47); then taught at the Janáček Academy of Music there (1947–57). His works show the double influence of Janáček's national and rhapsodic style and Reger's strong polyphonic idiom.

WORKS: OPERA: *Pohádka máje* (A Romance in May; 1940–43; Prague, May 12, 1950; rev., Brno, 1955). **ORCH.:** *Thema con variazioni e fuga* (1912); 4 syms.: No. 1 (1913–14), No. 2 (1921), No. 3 (1936–37), and No. 4, *Vitzna* (Victory; 1943); 2 violin concertos (1927–28; 1952); *Z těžkých dob* (From Anxious Times), symphonic variations (1939); *Slavonic* (Jubilee) Overture (1944); *Burlesque* for Flute and Orch. (1945); *Svitani* (Daybreak), symphonic poem (1948–49); Oboe Concerto (1951); Piano Concerto (1954). **CHAMBER:** 3 violin sonatas (1910, 1914, 1931); Piano Trio (1912); Cello Sonata (1913); 6 string quartets (1914, 1926, 1931, 1935, 1949, 1951); Piano Quintet (1914–15); Brass Quintet (1925); *Variations* for Trumpet and Piano (1929); *Suite* for Trombone and Piano (1930); *Intimate Pictures* for Violin and Piano (1934); Wind Quintet (1935); Violin Sonatina (1941); *Fantasy* for Cello and Piano (1942); Nonet (1944); Quartet for Flute, Violin, Viola, and Cello (1948); Duo for Violin and Viola (1949); *Suite* for Viola and Piano (1955). **KEYBOARD: PIANO:** 3 sonatas (1912, 1925, 1946); *Variations* (1914); *Fantasy in the Form of Variations* (1952); *10 Pieces* (1957). **ORGAN:** *Fantasy* (1935). **VOCAL:** 2 cantatas: *A Song on Time That Is Passing* (1924) and *Small Ital-*

ian Cantata (1950); *Lví srdce* (The Lion's Heart), oratorio (1928–31; Brno, Dec. 7, 1931); song cycles.

BIBL.: L. Kundera, *J. K.* (Prague, 1944).

Kvernadze, Bidzina (actually, **Alexander Alexandrovich**), Russian composer; b. Signahi, Georgia, July 29, 1928. He studied with Balanchivadze at the Tbilisi Cons. (graduated, 1953). Among his works were 2 piano concertos (1950, 1965); Violin Concerto (1956); *Dance-Fantasy* for Orch. (1959); Sym. (1961); violin pieces; film music.

Kvitka, Klyment, Ukrainian ethnomusicologist; b. Kiev, Feb. 4, 1880; d. Moscow, Sept. 19, 1953. During his early career, he was a lawyer and a judge; it was not until after 1920 that he devoted himself to music. He was director of the Ethnomusicology Bureau at the Ukrainian Academy of Sciences (1922–33); during the 1920s, he conducted fieldwork on ritual song, the music of minorities (Bulgarians, Albanians, and Greeks in the Ukraine), and that of professional folk musicians. In 1933 he moved to Moscow, where he founded the Folk Music Bureau at the Cons.; he also studied organology and the geographical dispersal of songs and instruments. His song collections (1917–18; 1922), noted for their scholarship and erudition, are landmarks in Ukrainian ethnomusicology.

Kwalwasser, Jacob, American music psychologist and educator; b. N.Y., Feb. 27, 1894; d. Pittsburgh, Aug. 7, 1977. He received his education at the Univs. of Pittsburgh (B.A., B.Ed., 1917) and Iowa (M.A., 1923; Ph.D., 1926). He taught in public schools in Pittsburgh (1918–23); was head of the dept. of public school music at the Univ. of Iowa (1923–26); from 1926 to 1954 he was a prof. at Syracuse Univ., where he served as head of music education (1926–50) and of research in music education (1951–54). He was co-author of the Kwalwasser-Dykema Music Tests; publ. a manual on the subject in 1913; also collaborated in establishing the Kwalwasser-Ruch Musical Accomplishment Test, and various other melodic, harmonic, and instrumental tests; likewise publ. numerous magazine articles on music education. His daughter, Helen Kwalwasser (b. Syracuse, N.Y., Oct. 11, 1927), was a violinist and teacher.

WRITINGS: *Tests and Measurements in Music* (Boston and N.Y., 1927); *Problems in Public School Music* (N.Y., 1932; rev. 1941); *Exploring the Musical Mind* (N.Y., 1955).

Kwast, James, famous German pianist and teacher; b. Nijkerk, the Netherlands, Nov. 23, 1852; d. Berlin, Oct. 31, 1927. He studied with his father and Ferdinand Böhme; later with Reinecke and Richter at the Leipzig Cons., Theodor Kullak and Wüerst in Berlin, and Brassin and Gevaert in Brussels. He taught at the Cologne Cons. (1874–83) and the Frankfurt am Main Hoch Cons. (1883–1903); then went to Berlin as a prof. at the Klindworth-Scharwenka Cons. (1903–06) and the Stern Cons. (from 1906). He was greatly esteemed by his colleagues and students; among the latter were Grainger and Pfitzner. He wrote a Piano Concerto and other piano music. His 1st wife, Antonia Kwast (d. Stuttgart, Feb. 10, 1931), was a daughter of Ferdinand Hiller; his 2nd wife, Frieda Hodapp-Kwast (b. Bargen, Aug. 13, 1880; d. Bad Wiessee, Sept. 14, 1949), was a pianist.

Kwiatkowski, Ryszard, Polish composer; b. Jaranów, June 27, 1931. He was a student of Szeligowski and Rudziński at the Warsaw State College of Music (1958–62) and of Petrassi in Rome. He taught at the Bydgoszcz State College of Music. His music reflects contemporary trends, including some use of dodecaphony.

WORKS: ORCH.: *Serenade* for Trombone and Orch. (1957); 4 syms. (1958, 1964, 1969, 1969); *Baltic Impressions* (1966); *Pictures* for Chamber Orch. (1966); *Baltic Songs* (1966); *Polyphonic Music* (1967); *Pulsation* (1967–69); *Music* for Flutes, Clarinets, Percussion, and Strings (1969); *Music* for Winds, Percussion, and Piano (1969); Concerto for Oboe, 4 Trumpets, Piano, and Strings (1970); *4 Lyrics* (1970–72); Tuba Concerto (1977); *Lyrics of Toruń* for Chamber Orch. (1980); *Sea Stories* for Strings (1984). **CHAMBER:** Wind Quintet (1960); 3 string quartets (1962; 1966–78; 1971); *Musica in memoriam Johannis Ciconia* for 2 Violins, Viola, Cello, and Piano (1967); *Song of the Sea Wind* for Violin and Piano (1967); *Baltic Wave Song* for Clarinet and Piano (1967); Piano Quartet, with metronome (1968); 2 percussion quartets (1968, 1971); *Lyric Music* for Violin and Double Bass (1969); *Baltic Sonnets* for 9 Instruments and Metronome (1971); *Legend* for Viola and Piano (1975); *Pictures from the Seaside* for Violin, Cello, and Piano (1975); Violin Sonata (1976–77); Viola Sonata (1978); Sonata for Viola and 2 Pianos (1978); Sonata for Oboe, Clarinet, and Bassoon (1981); *5 Little Sonatas* for Flute, Oboe, Clarinet, Horn, and Bassoon (1983). **KEYBOARD: PIANO:** *7 Moon Pictures* (1960–69); 2 sonatas (1975, 1983); *Fields Under Water* (1982). **ORGAN:** Sonata (1980). **VOCAL:** *Baltic Pictures* for Mezzo-soprano, 2 Violins, Cello, and Piano (1975).

Kyllönen, Timo-Juhani, Finnish composer; b. Saloinen, Dec. 1, 1955. He was reared in Sweden, where he commenced playing the accordion when he was 9; in 1976 he entered the Gnessin Inst. in Moscow as an accordion student of Friedrich Lips, and also took courses in composition and conducting before graduating in 1982; he then studied composition, orchestration, and counterpoint with Alexei Nikolaiev, Yuri Fortunatov, and Georgi Tchugaiev at the Moscow Cons., graduating in 1986; then taught theory and composition at the Sibelius Academy in Helsinki.

WORKS: DRAMATIC: Stage, film, and television scores. **ORCH.:** 2 syms.: No. 1 (1985–86; Novosibirsk, June 17, 1986) and No. 2 (1991–95). **CHAMBER:** 2 string quartets (1985, 1989); Trio No. 1 for Violin, Cello, and Accordion (1986) and No. 2 for Piano, Violin, and Cello (1988); *Elegia "quasi una sonata"* for Violin and Piano (1987); *Desolazione* for Organ and Oboe (1987); *Contrasts* for 5 Percussionists (1988); several pieces for solo instruments. **VOCAL:** *Passio secularis* for Soprano, Men's Chorus, and Orch. (1988–89; Helsinki, Dec. 8, 1989); choral pieces.

Kyriakou, Rena, Greek pianist; b. Iraklion, Feb. 25, 1918; d. Athens, Aug. 1994. She made her public debut in Athens at 6; later studied in Vienna with Paul Weingarten and Richard Stöhr; then joined the piano class of Isidor Philipp at the Paris Cons.; she also studied composition there with Henri Busser; received its premier prix at the age of 15. She then embarked on a concert career in programs of neglected piano pieces by 18th- and 19th-century composers.

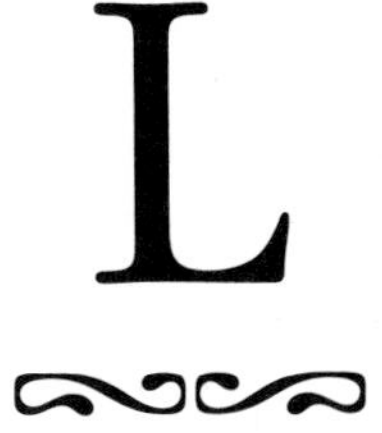

La Barbara, Joan (Linda née **Lotz)**, American composer and experimental vocalist; b. Philadelphia, June 8, 1947. She learned piano from her grandfather; later sang in church and school choirs, and joined a folk music group. She studied voice with Helen Boatwright at the Syracuse Univ. School of Music (1965–68) and music education at N.Y. Univ. (B.S., 1970); also studied voice with Phyllis Curtin at the Berkshire Music Center at Tanglewood (summers, 1967–68) and with Marion Szekely-Freschl at the Juilliard School in N.Y. In 1971 she made her debut as a vocalist at N.Y.'s Town Hall with Steve Reich and Musicians, with whom she continued to perform until 1974; also worked with Philip Glass (1973–76). She toured in the U.S. and Europe; in 1979 she was composer-in-residence in West Berlin under the aegis of the Deutscher Akademischer Austauschdienst; taught voice and composition at the Calif. Inst. of the Arts in Valencia (1981–86). In 1979 she married **Morton Subotnick**. A champion of contemporary music, she developed her performing talents to a high degree; her vocal techniques include multiphonics and circular breathing, with unique throat clicks and a high flutter to match. Her compositions, often incorporating electronics, effectively exploit her vocal abilities. Among her numerous awards and fellowships are NEA grants (1979, 1982, 1986, 1988, 1989, 1991) and ASCAP and ISCM commissions; also numerous radio commissions. La Barbara has collaborated on interdisciplinary projects with visual artists, including Lita Albuquerque, Judy Chicago, Kenneth Goldsmith et al.; she has also given numerous first performances of works written for her by American composers, including Robert Ashley, John Cage, Charles Dodge, Morton Feldman, Daniel Lentz et al. In 1993 she appeared in the N.Y. premiere of Subotnick's opera, *Jacob's Room*, and in 1994 in the N.Y. premiere of Robert Ashley's quartet of operas, *Now Eleanor's Idea.*

WORKS: DRAMATIC: *Twelvesong*, radio work (Radio Bremen, Nov. 1, 1977; also for Voice and Tape, Bremen, May 6, 1978); *Erin*, radio work (1980; also for Voice and Tape, Paris, June 21, 1980); *Prologue* to *The Book of Knowing . . . (and) of Overthrowing*, aria for Voice and Tape with Visual Environment and Costumes, based on female creation myths of 6 cultures (1987–88; N.Y., July 6, 1988); *Anima*, film score for Voice, Percussion, Electronic Keyboard Synthesizers, Gamelan, Hand Drums, Cello, and Indigenous Diablo Canyon Sounds (1991; N.Y., Sept. 25, 1992); *The Misfortune of the Immortals*, interactive media opera (1994–95; in collaboration with M. Coniglio and M. Subotnick). **CHAMBER, WITH VOICE(S):** *Chandra* for Amplified Solo Voice, Men's Voices, and Chamber Orch. (Bremen, May 6, 1978; rev. 1983); *Loisaida* for Voice, Kalimba, Steel Drum, and Hi-hat (N.Y., Feb. 17, 1978); *Silent Scroll* for Voice, Cello or Double Bass, Flute, Zoomoozophone, and Cup Gongs (N.Y., April 25, 1982); *Vlissingen Harbor* for Voice and 7 Instruments (Los Angeles, Dec. 6, 1982); *A Rothko Study* for Voice and Chamber Ensemble (Los Angeles, Nov. 3, 1985); *Helga's Lied* for Voice and Chamber Ensemble (Århus, Oct. 10, 1986); *Urban Tropics*, sound painting for Voice, Percussion, and Indigenous Miami Sounds (Miami, Dec. 12, 1988); *Klangbild Köln*, sound painting for Voice, Percussion, and Indigenous Cologne Sounds (WDR, May 7, 1991); *Awakenings II* for Voice and Chamber Ensemble (Tempe, Ariz., Jan. 28, 1992); *Calligraphy II/Shadows* for Voice and Chinese Instruments (N.Y., June 8, 1995); *In the shadow and act of the haunting place* for Voice and Chamber Ensemble (San Francisco, Jan. 17, 1995). **AMPLIFIED VOICE(S):** *Hear What I Feel* for Voice (1974); *Vocal Extensions* for Voice and Live Electronics (1975); *Space Testing* for Acoustic Voice (1976); *Cathing* for Voice and Tape (1977); *Autumn Signal* for Voice and Synthesizer (Berlin, Oct. 22, 1978); *quatre petites bêtes*, quadraphonic soundance for Voice and Tape (1978–79; Cologne, May 9, 1979); *Twelve for Five in Eight* for 5 Voices (1979); *12 for 5 in 8* for 5 or More Voices (1979); *October Music: Star Showers and Extraterrestrials* for Voice and Tape (Paris, June 21, 1980); *Winds of the Canyon* for Voice and Tape (San Francisco, Nov. 12, 1982; rev. staged version, with visual environment, Los Angeles, March 3, 1986); *After Obervogelsang* for

Voice and Tape (N.Y., June 5, 1984); *Time(d) Trials and Unscheduled Events* for Voice on Tape (1984; rev. for 8 Solo Voices, 1987); *Loose Tongues* for 8 Solo Voices and Tape (1985); *Voice Windows* for Voice and Interactive Video Systems (Los Angeles, March 3, 1986); *Conversations* for Voice (Rome, Aug. 4, 1988); *73 Poems* (1st complete perf., Miami, Dec. 4, 1993; in collaboration with Kenneth Goldsmith). **AMPLIFIED VOICE(S) AND INSTRUMENTS:** *Thunder* for Voice, 6 Timpani, and Electronics (1975); *Ides of March I to VIII* for Voice and Instruments (1975–77); *Chords and Gongs* for Voice, Cimbalom, and Gongs (1976); *Silent Scroll* for Voice, Flute, Cello or Double Bass, Percussion, Gong, and Zoomoozophone (1982); *The Solar Wind I* for Voice and Chamber Ensemble (Los Angeles, Feb. 7, 1983), *II* for 16 Solo Voices, 2 Percussion, Flute/Piccolo, and Electric Keyboard (Copenhagen, Nov. 14, 1983), and *III* for Amplified Voice and Chamber Orch. (San Francisco, May 12, 1984); *Rothko* for Amplified Voice and Tape (Houston, April 5, 1986); *Face to Face* for Voices, Electronics, and Percussion (Houston, Feb. 1, 1992); *"to hear the wind roar"* for Voice, Percussion, and Tape (1991; Santa Fe, Aug. 8, 1992; also for Chamber Vocal Ensemble and Percussion, Pasadena, May 9, 1992, and for Chorus with Handheld Percussion, Adirondack, N.Y., July 18, 1992); *ShamanSong*, suite for Voice, Percussion, and Tape (Athens, March 2, 1992). **OTHER:** *The Executioner's Bracelet*, sound installation after Artemesia Gentileschi's painting *Judith Beheading Holofernes* (1979); *Responsive Resonance with Feathers* for Piano and Tape (1979); *Berliner Träume* for Tape (1983; rev. version for Voice and Tape, Minneapolis, Feb. 18, 1984); *Loose Tongues* for Tape (1985); *l'albero dalle foglie azzurre* for Oboe and Tape (St. Louis, March 20, 1989); *Awakenings* for Chamber Ensemble (1991); *In the Dreamtime*, self-portrait sound collage (WDR, May 7, 1991).

Labèque, Katia (b. Hendaye, March 3, 1950) and **Marielle** (b. Hendaye, March 6, 1952), extraordinarily gifted French sisters, duo-pianists. They began to study piano in early childhood with their mother, a pupil of Marguerite Long, making their formal debut in Bayonne in 1961. After completing their studies with Jean-Bernard Pommier at the Paris Cons., they were awarded 1st prize at their graduation in 1968. They subsequently embarked upon a remarkable career as duo-pianists, touring widely in Europe, North America, the Middle East, and the Far East. In addition to giving numerous recitals, they also appeared with the leading orchs. of the world. Their repertoire is catholic, ranging from the masterworks of the past to contemporary scores by Messiaen, Boulez, Berio, and others; they play popular works as well, from Scott Joplin to Gershwin; they championed the latter's duo-piano versions of *Rhapsody in Blue*, Piano Concerto in F, and *An American in Paris*.

Labey, Marcel, French conductor and composer; b. Le Vésinet, Seine-et-Oise, Aug. 6, 1875; d. Nancy, Nov. 25, 1968. He studied law in Paris, receiving his degree in 1898; then turned his attention to music, studying piano with Delaborde, harmony with Lenormand, and composition with d'Indy at the Paris Schola Cantorum; taught piano there, and at d'Indy's death (1931), became director; was also director of the Cesar Franck School (from 1935). He wrote music in a late Romantic style.

WORKS: OPERA: *Bérengère* (1912; Le Havre, April 12, 1929). **ORCH.:** 3 syms. (1903, 1908, 1934); *Ouverture pour un drame* (Paris, Jan. 22, 1921); *Suite champêtre* (1923). **CHAMBER:** Piano Sonata; Viola Sonata; 2 violin sonatas; String Quartet; Piano Trio; Piano Quartet; Piano Quintet. **VOCAL:** Songs.

Labia, Fausta, Italian soprano, sister of **Maria Labia**; b. Verona, April 3, 1870; d. Rome, Oct. 6, 1935. She studied with her mother and with Aldighieri. After making her operatic debut as Alice in *Robert le Diable* in Verona (1892), she sang in Stockholm (1893–95) and Lisbon (1895–96); then appeared in various Italian opera centers, including Milan's La Scala and Rome's Teatro Costanzi (1901). She sang in Barcelona (1904–05); made her last stage appearance in Buenos Aires (1912); subsequently taught in Rome. In 1907 she married the tenor Emilio Perea. She wrote the method *L'arte del respiro nella recitazione e nel canto* (1936).

Labia, Maria, noted Italian soprano, sister of **Fausta Labia**; b. Verona, Feb. 14, 1880; d. Malcesine del Garda, Feb. 10, 1953. She received her musical education from her mother. Following concert engagements in Milan, Verona, and Padua (1902), and in Russia and Sweden (1903–04), she made her operatic debut as Mimi in Stockholm on May 19, 1905. She scored a remarkable success as Tosca at Berlin's Komische Oper (1907), continuing to sing there until 1911. Among her other notable roles there were Carmen, Thaïs, and Salome. She appeared as Tosca in her debut with the Manhattan Opera on Nov. 9, 1908. After a season there, she continued her career in Europe with engagements in Paris, Vienna, and Milan. She was arrested as a German agent by the Italian authorities in 1916 and spent a year in prison in Ancona. After the close of World War I, she resumed her career in Rome (1919); subsequently became closely associated with the role of Felice in Wolf-Ferrari's *I quatro rusteghi*, which she sang many times from 1922 until 1936. After teaching at the Warsaw Cons. (1930–34), she gave instruction in Rome and Siena. She wrote *Guardare indietro: Che fatica* (1950).

Labinsky, Andrei (Markovich), Russian tenor; b. Kharkov, July 26, 1871; d. Moscow, Aug. 8, 1941. He went to St. Petersburg, where he joined the chorus of the Maryinsky Theater. Following studies with Gabel, he made his operatic debut at the Maryinsky Theater in 1897, where he sang regularly from 1899 to 1912. In 1907 he created the role of Vsevolod in Rimsky-Korsakov's *Kitezh* there. From 1912 to 1924 he was a member of the Bolshoi Theater in Moscow. He taught at the Moscow Cons. from 1920. His finest roles included Don José, Lohengrin, Berendey in *The Snow Maiden*, Sinodal in *The Demon*, and Sobinin in *A Life for the Tsar*.

Labroca, Mario, Italian composer; b. Rome, Nov. 22, 1896; d. there, July 1, 1973. He studied composition with Malipiero and Respighi, and graduated from the Parma Cons. in 1921. He was manager of the Teatro Comunale in Florence (1936–44), artistic director of La Scala in Milan (1947–49), director of the music dept. of the RAI (1949–58), and artistic director of the Teatro La Fenice in Venice (from 1959); also lectured at the Univ. of Perugia (from 1960).

WORKS: DRAMATIC: OPERAS: *La Principessa di Perepepe* (Rome, Dec. 11, 1927); *Le tre figliole di Babbo Pallino* (Rome, Jan. 27, 1928). Also many theater and film scores. **ORCH.:** Sinfonia for Strings (1927); Sym. (1935). **VOCAL:** *Stabat Mater* for Soprano, Chorus, and Orch. (Rome, Dec. 15, 1935); *3 cantate sulla Passione di Cristo* for Baritone, Chorus, and Orch. (1950); *8 madrigali di Tomaso Campanella* for Baritone and Orch. (1958). **CHAMBER:** 3 string quartets (1923, 1932, 1939); Suite for Viola and Piano (1923); Piano Trio (1925).

Labunski, Felix (actually, **Feliks Roderyk**), Polish-born American composer, pedagogue, pianist, and music critic, brother of **Wiktor Labunski;** b. Ksawerynów, Dec. 27, 1892; d. Cincinnati, April 28, 1979. Following piano lessons as a child, he was a pupil of Marczewski and Maliszewski at the Warsaw Cons. (1922–24), and of Dukas and Boulanger (composition) and Migot (musicology) at the École Normale de Musique in Paris (1924–34). In 1927 he was a founder of the Assn. of Young Polish Composers in Paris. After serving as director of classical music for the Polish Radio in Warsaw (1934–36), he emigrated to the U.S. and in 1941 became a naturalized American citizen. In 1940–41 he was a prof. of counterpoint and composition at Marymount College in Tarrytown, N.Y., and thereafter taught at the Cincinnati College of Music (1945–55), and its successor the Univ. of Cincinnati College-Cons. of Music (1955–64). As a pianist, he mainly performed his own works. He composed basically along Romantic lines with some infusions of neo-Classical elements.

WORKS: BALLET: *God's Man* (1937). **ORCH.:** *Danse fantastique* (1926); *Triptyque champêtre* (1931); 2 syms. (1937, 1954); Suite for Strings (1938); *In Memoriam*, symphonic poem in memory of Paderewski (1941); *Variations* (1947); *Elegy* (1955); *Xaveriana*, fantasy for 2 Pianos and Orch. (1956); *Symphonic Dialogues* (1961); *Canto di aspirazione* (1963; based on the slow movement of the Sym. No. 2); *Polish Renaissance Suite* (1967); *Salut à Paris*, ballet suite (1968); *Music* for Piano and Orch. (1968); *Primavera* (1974). **CHAMBER:** 2 string quartets (1935, 1962); *Divertimento* for Flute and Piano (1936); *3 Bagatelles* for Brass Quartet (1955); *Divertimento* for Flute, Oboe, Clarinet, and Bassoon (1956); *Diptych* for Oboe and Piano (1958); *Intrada festiva* for Brass Choir (1968); piano pieces; organ music. **VOCAL:** *Polish Cantata* (1932); *The Birds* for Soprano and Orch. (1934); *Songs without Words* for Soprano and Strings (1946); *There Is No Death*, cantata for Chorus and Orch. (1950); *Images of Youth*, cantata (1956); choruses; songs.

Labunski, Wiktor, Polish-born American pianist, teacher, and composer, brother of **Felix Labunski;** b. St. Petersburg, April 14, 1895; d. Kansas City, Mo., Jan. 26, 1974. He was a student at the St. Petersburg Cons. of Nikolayev (piano) and Kalafati and Wihtol (composition); after further training with F. Blumenfeld and Safonov (piano), he studied conducting in Poland with Mlynarski. He was head of the piano dept. at the Kraków Cons. (1919–28). In 1928 he made his Carnegie Hall debut in N.Y. After teaching at the Nashville (Tenn.) Cons. (1928–31), he was a prof. and director of the Memphis (Tenn.) College of Music (1931–37). He became a teacher at the Kansas City (Mo.) Cons. in 1937, serving as its director from 1941 to 1971. His compositions followed along traditional lines.

WORKS: Piano Concertino (1932); Sym. (1936); Piano Concerto (1937); *Variations* for Piano and Orch. (1945); Concerto for 2 Pianos and Orch. (1951); many piano pieces; songs.

BIBL.: J. Belanger, *W. L.: Polish-American Musician in Kansas City, 1937–1974* (diss., Columbia Univ., 1982).

Laburda, Jiří, Czech composer; b. Soběslav, April 3, 1931. He received private training in composition from Karel Hába and Zdeněk Hůla and in musicology from Eduard Herzog; took courses in music education and philology at the Charles Univ. in Prague (1952–55); after studies at the Prague Teacher Training College (1957–61), he returned to the Charles Univ., where he took his Ph.D. (1970, with a diss. on Shostakovich's syms.) and subsequently served on its faculty. His works follow along traditional paths with infusions of aleatory and dodecaphonic writing; his vocal and chamber pieces are particularly effective.

WORKS: BALLET: *Les Petits Riens* (1967; Liberec, March 15, 1986). **ORCH.:** *Burlesca* for Horn and Orch. (Košice, April 11, 1963); Piano Concerto (1969; Prague, Feb. 5, 1973); Sinfonia (1975); Concerto for Accordion and Strings (Kralupy, April 21, 1980); Concertino for Trumpet and Strings (Mariánské Lazné, July 17, 1981); *Pastorale* for Flute and Strings (1981; Joschkar-Ola, Russia, March 2, 1987); *Overture solenne* (1983; Prague, June 18, 1985); *Divertimento in RE* for Strings (1983; České Budějovice, March 22, 1984); *Concerto da camera* for Violin and Orch. (1986); Double Concerto for Violin, Cello, and Strings (1989); Concerto for Organ and Strings (1991). **CHAMBER:** *Kasace I* for Flute, Clarinet, Horn, Trumpet, and Trombone (1978), *II* for Violin, Clarinet or Oboe d'Amore, Percussion, and Piano (1979), and *III* for Bass Clarinet and Percussion (1979); Partita for Violin (1978); Trumpet Sonatina (1979); Brass Quintet No. 2 (1980); *6 Inventions* for 2 Trumpets and Trombone (1980); Trombone Sonata (1981); Duo for Guitar and Double Bass or Cello (1981); Sonata for Solo Marimba (1983); *Peter with Trumpet* for Trumpet and Piano (1983); *Rondo* for 3 Violins (1984); Bassoon Sonatina (1985); Sonata for 2 Marimbas (1986); Clarinet Sonata (1987); Tuba Sonata (1987); *Signal*, scherzo for Trumpet and Piano (1987); *Aphorismes* for Clarinet (1987); Trio for Oboe, Clarinet, and Bassoon (1989); *Sonata da chiesa* for 2 Trumpets, Horn, Trombone, Tuba, and Organ (1989); Sonata for Solo Accordion (1989); *Sonata da chiesa* for 2 Trumpets, 2 Trombones, and Organ (1990); *Serenata* for 4 Trombones (1991); *Canto pasquale* for Trumpet and Organ (1993); *Partita* for 6 Trumpets (1993); Trumpet Sonatina (1994); *Valse* for Marimba (1994); Suite for Saxophone Quartet (1995); piano pieces. **VOCAL:** *Glagolitica* for Soloists, Chorus, Organ, Brass, and Percussion (1964; Freiburg im Breisgau, Jan. 11, 1990); *Metamorphoses* for Soloists, Chorus, and Orch. (1966; Wolfsburg, May 18, 1969); *Marriage* for Soloists, Women's Chorus, and Piano (1980; Prague, Nov. 12, 1989); *Missa pastoralis* for Soprano, Bass, Chorus, and Organ (1990; Prague, Jan. 12, 1991); *Missa* for Chorus, Trumpet, and Organ (1992); *Missa Sistina* for Chorus (1993; also for Chorus and Organ); *Missa clara* for Voices and Organ (1993).

Laccetti, Guido, Italian singer and composer; b. Naples, Oct. 1, 1879; d. Cava dei Tirreni, Oct. 8, 1943. He studied at the Naples Cons. From 1925 he taught at the Palermo Cons. His works included the operas *La Contessa di San Remo* (1904), *Hoffmann* (Naples, 1912), *Il miracolo* (Naples, 1915), *Carnasciali* (Rome, 1925), and *La favola dei gobbi* (1935).

Lacerda, Francisco (Inácio da Silveira de Sousa Pereira Forjaz) de, Portuguese conductor and composer; b. Ribeira Seca, S. Jorge, Azores, May 11, 1869; d. Lisbon, July 18, 1934. He was a student of Vieira, Gazul, Montinho de Ahmeida, and Soromenho at the Lisbon Cons., where he was made a prof. of theory in 1892. In 1895 he was awarded a government stipend to pursue his training in Paris with Pessard, Bourgault-Ducoudray, Libert, and Widor at the Cons. and with d'Indy and Guilmant at the Schola Cantorum. In 1905 he founded the Concerts Historiques in Nantes. In 1914 he returned to Portugal and in 1923 founded the Orquesta Filarmonica in Lisbon. He ed. the important *Cancioneiro musical português* (Lisbon, 1935–36), a collection of some 500 folk songs. Among his works were ballets; incidental music; the symphonic poems *Adamastor* (1902) and *Almourol* (1926); piano pieces.

BIBL.: F. de Souza, *F.d. L.: Exposição commemorativa do primeiro centenario do nascimento* (Lisbon, 1969).

Lach, Robert, eminent Austrian musicologist and composer; b. Vienna, Jan. 29, 1874; d. Salzburg, Sept. 11, 1958. He studied law at the Univ. of Vienna, but in 1894 he entered the Austrian civil administration without obtaining his degree. He was a composition pupil of R. Fuchs at the Cons. of the Gesellschaft der Musikfreunde in Vienna (1893–99); also studied philosophy and musicology at the Univ. there with Wallaschek and Adler (1896–99); completed his study of musicology with Rietsch at the German Univ. in Prague (Ph.D., 1902, with the diss. *Studien zur Entwicklungsgeschichte der ornamentalen Melopoie;* publ. in Leipzig, 1913). In 1903 he left his government post and in 1911 joined the staff of Vienna's Hofbibliothek; from 1913 to 1918 he was director of its music collection; remained in that post when it became the Staatsbibliothek (1918–20). From 1915 he lectured at the Univ. of Vienna; was prof. of musicology and chairman of its Musicological Inst. (1927–39); was also prof. at the Vienna Academy of Music (from 1924). He recorded for the Phonogram Archives of Vienna the songs of Russian prisoners of World War I (with particular emphasis on Asian and Caucasian nationalities), and publ. numerous papers on these melodies. He was pensioned in 1939, and lived in Vienna in retirement, devoting his time to the compilation of Oriental glossaries (Babylonian, Sumerian, Egyptian, etc.). In 1954 he became general ed. of the new Denkmäler der Tonkunst in Österreich. In addition to his books, he contributed articles to various music journals; also wrote philosophical poems and mystical plays. Among his compositions are 10 syms., 25 string quartets, 14 string quintets, 8 string sextets, other chamber music, 8 masses, cantatas, etc.

WRITINGS (all publ. in Vienna): *Sebastian Sailers "Schöpfung" in der Musik* (1916); *W.A. Mozart als Theoretiker* (1918); *Zur Geschichte des Gesellschaftstanzes im 18. Jahrhundert* (1920); *Eine Tiroler Liederhandschrift aus dem 18. Jahrhundert* (1923); *Zur Geschichte des musikalischen Zunftwesens* (1923); *Die vergleichende Musikwissenschaft: Ihre Methoden und Probleme* (1924); *Das Konstruktionsprinzip der Wiederholung in Musik, Sprache und Literatur* (1925); *Vergleichende Kunst- und*

Musikwissenschaft (1925); *Die Bruckner-Akten des Wiener Universitätsarchivs* (1926); ed. *Gesänge russicher Kriegsgefangener* (1926–52); *Geschichte der Staatsakademie und Hochschule für Musik und darstellende Kunst in Wien* (1927); *Das Ethos in der Musik Franz Schuberts* (1928).

BIBL.: W. Graf, ed., *R. L.: Persönlichkeit und Werk* (Vienna, 1954).

Lachenmann, Helmut Friedrich, German composer and pedagogue; b. Stuttgart, Nov. 27, 1935. He was a student of Jürgen Uhde (piano) and J.N. David (theory and counterpoint) at the Stuttgart Staatliche Hochschule für Musik (1955–58), and of Nono (composition) in Venice (1958–60); he then pursued research at the electronic studio at the Univ. of Ghent (1965). He taught theory at the Stuttgart Hochschule für Musik (1966–70), and then music at the Ludwigsburg Pädagogische Hochschule (1970–76). He also served as coordinator of the composition studio at the Darmstadt Internationale Ferienkurse (1972) and led a master class in composition at the Univ. of Basel (1972–73). In 1976 he became a teacher at the Hannover Hochschule für Musik. He also taught at the Ferienkurse in Darmstadt (1978, 1982). From 1981 he taught at the Stuttgart Hochschule für Musik. Among his honors are the cultural prize for music of Munich (1965), the composition prize of Stuttgart (1968), and the Bach prize of Hamburg (1972). He is also a member of the Akademie der Künste in Berlin, the Akademie der Schönen Künste in Munich, and the Freie Akademie der Künste in Mannheim. While producing works based upon structural techniques, he has made it his central aim as a composer to create scores free of societal expectations.

WORKS: DRAMATIC: *Das Mädchen mit den Schwefelhölzern*, music theater (1990–in progress). **ORCH.:** *Souvenir* for 41 Instruments (1959); *Notturno (Musik für Julia)* for Cello and Small Orch. (1966–68; Brussels, April 25, 1969); *Air* for Percussionist and Orch. (1968–69; Frankfurt am Main, Sept. 1, 1969); *Kontrakadenz* (1970–71; Stuttgart, April 23, 1971); *Klangschatten-mein Saitenspiel* for 3 Grand Pianos and 48 Strings (Hamburg, Dec. 20, 1972); *Fassade* for Orch. and Tape (Bonn, Sept. 22, 1973); *Schwankungen am Rand* for Brass and Strings (1974–75; Donaueschingen, Oct. 17, 1975); *Accanto* for Clarinet and Orch. (1975–76; Saarbrücken, May 30, 1976); *Tanzsuite mit Deutschlandlied* for String Quartet and Orch. (1979–80; Donaueschingen, Oct. 18, 1980); *Harmonica* for Tuba and Orch. (1981–83; Saarbrücken, May 15, 1983); *Mouvement (-vor der Erstarrung)* (1982–84; Paris, Nov. 12, 1984); *Ausklang* for Piano and Orch. (1984–85; Cologne, April 18, 1986); *Staub* (1985–87; Saarbrücken, Dec. 19, 1987); *Tableau* (1988–89; Hamburg, June 4, 1989); *". . . Zwei Gefühle . . .", Musik mit Leonardo* (Stuttgart, Oct. 9, 1992); *Souvenir* (1994). **CHAMBER:** *5 Strophen* for 9 Instruments (1961; Venice, April 13, 1962; *Introversion I* for 6 Instruments (1963; Darmstadt, July 19, 1964) and *II* for 6 Instruments (1964; Munich, Feb. 22, 1965); String Trio (1965; Ghent, March 29, 1966); *Interieur I* for Percussionist (1966; Santa Fe, N.Mex., Aug. 14, 1967); *Trio fluido* for Clarinet, Viola, and Percussion (1966; Munich, March 5, 1968); *temA* for Flute, Mezzo-soprano, and Cello (1968; Stuttgart, Feb. 19, 1969); *Pression* for Cello (1969; Como, Sept. 30, 1970); *Dal niente (Interieur III)* for Clarinet (Nuremberg, June 4, 1970); *Gran Torso* for String Quartet (1971–72; Bremen, May 6, 1972; rev. 1972–76, 1988); *Salut für Caudwell* for 2 Guitars (Baden-Baden, Dec. 3, 1977); *Toccatina*, study for Violin (1986; Stuttgart, May 20, 1988); *Allegro Sostenuto* for Clarinet, Cello, and Piano (1986–88; Cologne, Dec. 3, 1989); String Quartet No. 2, *Reigen seliger Geister* (Geneva, Sept. 28, 1989). **PIANO:** *5 Variationen über ein Thema von Franz Schubert* (1956); *Rondo* for 2 Pianos, 4-hands (1957; Stuttgart, March 12, 1958); *Echo Andante* (Darmstadt, July 18, 1962); *Wiegenmusik* (1963; Darmstadt, April 1, 1964); *Guero* (Hamburg, Dec. 1, 1970; rev. 1988); *Ein Kinderspiel* (1980; Toronto, Feb. 17, 1982). **VOCAL:** *Consolation I* for 12 Voices and 4 Percussion (1967; Bremen, May 3, 1968) and *II* for 16 Voices (1968; Basel, June 15, 1969); *Les Consolations* for 16 Voices and Orch. (1967–68, 1977–78; Darmstadt, Aug. 10, 1978); *Dritte Stimme zu J.S. Bachs zweistimmiger Invention d-moll BWV 775* for 3 Voices (1985). **ELECTRONIC:** *Szenario* (1965).

Lachmann, Robert, noted German musicologist; b. Berlin, Nov. 28, 1892; d. Jerusalem, May 8, 1939. He studied English, French, and Arabic at the Univs. of Berlin and London. He served in the German army during World War I, when he began to collect folk melodies from African and Indian war prisoners; later studied musicology with Stumpf and Johannes Wolf, and Semitic languages with Mittwoch at the Univ. of Berlin; received his Ph.D. there (1922) with the diss. *Die Musik in den tunesischen Städten*, publ. in the *Archiv für Musikwissenschaft*, V (1923). He worked at the Berlin State Library (1924–26); after a period in Kiel, he resumed his work at the Berlin State Library (1927), serving under Wolf; he was ousted by the Nazis as a Jew in 1933. He went to Palestine (1935) and became a member of the faculty of the Univ. of Jerusalem.

WRITINGS: *Musik des Orients* (Breslau, 1929); *Die Musik der aussereuropäischen Natur- und Kulturvölker* (1929); with M. el-Hefni, *Ja'qūb Ikn Ishāq al-Kindī: Risāla fi hubr tā'lif al'alhān-über die Komposition der Melodien* (Leipzig, 1931); E. Gerson-Kiwi, ed., *Robert Lachmann: Posthumous Works*, I (Jerusalem, 1974).

BIBL.: E. Gerson-Kiwi, "R. L.: His Achievement and His Legacy," *Yuval*, III (1974).

La Casinière, Yves de, French composer, music publisher, administrator, and teacher; b. Angers, Feb. 11, 1897; d. Paris, Oct. 28, 1971. He settled in Paris, where he studied with Boulanger (organ), Caussade (counterpoint and fugue), and d'Ollone (composition and harmony) at the École Normale de Musique. In 1935 he became founder-president of the Editions du Musagète. He was also active as an administrator and teacher. Among his works were 2 syms. (1922, 1930), chamber music, piano pieces, and songs.

Laderman, Ezra, notable American composer and teacher; b. N.Y., June 29, 1924. He studied at the High School of Music and Art in N.Y., where he appeared as soloist in the premiere of his 1st Piano Concerto with the school orch. in 1939. He pursued his training in composition with Wolpe in N.Y. (1946–49) and with Gideon at Brooklyn College of the City Univ. of N.Y. (B.A., 1949), and took courses with Leuning and Moore (composition) and Lang (musicology) at Columbia Univ. (M.A., 1952). In 1955, 1958, and 1964 he was awarded Guggenheim fellowships. In 1960–61 he taught at Sarah Lawrence College. After holding the American Prix de Rome (1963–64), he again taught at Sarah Lawrence College (1965–66). From 1971 to 1982 he was composer-in-residence and prof. at the State Univ. of N.Y. in Binghamton. He was also president of the American Music Center (1973–76) and director of the music program of the NEA (1979–82). From 1987 to 1989 he was president of the American Music Council. He was dean of the Yale Univ. School of Music (1989–95), and then was a prof. of music there (from 1995). After composing in a tonal style, Laderman turned to atonal, and later serial writing. Later in his career he came full circle by again exploring the resources of tonality in a synthetic form, utilizing a vast array of techniques and styles.

WORKS: DRAMATIC: OPERAS: *Jacob and the Indians* (1954; Woodstock, N.Y., July 24, 1957); *Goodbye to the Clowns* (1956; N.Y., May 22, 1960); *The Hunting of the Snark*, opera-cantata (1958; concert premiere, N.Y., March 26, 1961; stage premiere, N.Y., April 13, 1978); *Sarah* (CBS-TV, Nov. 30, 1958); *Air Raid* (1965); *Shadows Among Us* (1967); *And David Wept*, opera-cantata (1970; CBS-TV, April 11, 1971); *The Questions of Abraham*, opera-cantata (CBS-TV, Sept. 30, 1973); *Galileo Galilei* (1978; Binghamton, N.Y., Feb. 3, 1979; based on the oratorio *The Trials of Galileo*); *Marilyn* (N.Y., Oct. 6, 1993). **MUSICAL COMEDY:** *Dominique* (1962). **DANCE:** Duet for Flute and Dancer (1956); *Dance Quartet* for Flute, Clarinet, Cello, and Dancer (1957); *Esther* for Narrator, Oboe, and String Orch. (1960); *Song of Songs* for Soprano and Piano (1960); *Solos* *and Chorale* for 4 Mixed Voices (1960). **INCIDENTAL MUSIC:** *Machinal* (N.Y., April 7, 1960); *The Lincoln Mask* (N.Y., Oct. 30, 1972); numerous film and television scores. **ORCH.:** 2 unnumbered piano concertos (N.Y., June 1939; 1957); 2 numbered piano concertos: No. 1 (1978; Washington, D.C., May 12, 1979) and No. 2 (1989; N.Y., Oct. 13, 1991); 1 unnumbered sym. (*Leipzig Symphony*, Wiesbaden, May 1945); 8 numbered syms.: No. 1 (1963; Rome, July 2, 1964), No. 2, *Luther* (1969), No. 3, *Jerusalem* (1973; Jerusalem, Nov. 7, 1976), No. 4 (1980; Los Angeles, Oct. 22, 1981), No. 5, *Isaiah*, for Soprano and Orch. (1982; Washington, D.C., March 15, 1983), No. 6 (1983; rev. version, Houston, March 19, 1988), No. 7 (1984; Dallas, Dec. 7, 1989), and No. 8 (1993); Concerto for Bassoon and Strings (1948); Concerto for Violin and Chamber Orch. (1951; rev. 1960; CBS-TV, Nov. 10, 1963); *Organization No. 1* (1952); Sinfonia (1956); *Identity* (1959); *Stanzas* for 21 Solo Instruments (1959); *Magic Prison* for 2 Narrators and Orch. (N.Y., June 12, 1967); *Concerto for Orchestra* (Minneapolis, Oct. 24, 1968); *Celestial Bodies*, concerto for Flute and Strings (1968); *Priorities* for Jazz Band, Rock Band, and String Quartet (1969); Concerto for Viola and Chamber Orch. (1977; St. Paul, Minn., April 13, 1978); Violin Concerto (1978; Philadelphia, Dec. 12, 1980); *Summer Solstice* (Saratoga, N.Y., Aug. 15, 1980); Concerto for String Quartet and Orch. (1980; Pittsburgh, Feb. 6, 1981); Concerto for Flute, Bassoon, and Orch. (1981; Philadelphia, Jan. 28, 1983); *Sonore* (Denver, Nov. 10, 1983); Cello Concerto (1984; Chicago, Feb. 23, 1990); Flute Concerto (1985; Detroit, Jan. 22, 1987); *Pentimento* (1985; Albany, N.Y., May 16, 1986); *Sanctuary: An Original Theme and Variations* (1986; Louisville, April 2, 1987); Concerto for Violin, Cello, and Orch. (1986; Binghamton, N.Y., Feb. 25, 1988); Sinfonia Concertante (1988; Washington, D.C., June 1, 1989); *A Play Within a Play*, concerto for Double Orch. (1989); Concerto for Chamber Orch. (Martinsville, N.J., May 11, 1989; based on the middle 3 movements of *A Play Within a Play*); *Citadel* (Louisville, May 30, 1990). **CHAMBER:** Cello Sonata (1948); 2 flute sonatas (1951, 1957); Piano Quintet (1951); 1 unnumbered string quartet (1953); 9 numbered string quartets: No. 1 (1959), No. 2 (1962), No. 3 (1966), No. 4 (1974), No. 5 (1976; N.Y., Nov. 24, 1980), No. 6, *The Audubon* (1980; N.Y., April 1981), No. 7 (1983; N.Y., May 2, 1984), No. 8 (1985), and No. 9 (1995); Wind Quintet (1954); *Music* for Winds, Strings, and Harpsichord (1955); Piano Trio (1955; rev. 1959); Violin Sonata (1956); *Theme, Variations, and Finale* for 4 Winds and 4 Strings (1957); Wind Octet (1957); Clarinet Sonata (1958); Sextet for Wind Quintet and Double Bass (1959); Oboe Quartet (1960); *A Single Voice* for Oboe and String Quartet (1967); *Double Helix* for Flute, Oboe, and String Quartet (1968); Nonette for Piano, Strings, Winds, and Brass (1968); *5 Trios and Fantasy* for Wind Quintet (1972); *Partita: Meditations on Isaiah* for Cello (1972); *Elegy* for Viola (1973); *Concerto: Echoes in Anticipation* for Oboe and 7 Instruments (1975); *Cadence* for 2 Flutes and Strings (1978; N.Y., Oct. 23, 1979); *Remembrances* for Violin, Clarinet, Cello, and Piano (1982); Double String Quartet (1983; Washington, D.C., April 1986); Duo for Cello and Piano (N.Y., Dec. 18, 1984); *Fantasy* for Viola (1985); Quintet for Clarinet and Strings (N.Y., Nov. 24, 1987); *Introduction, Barcarolle, and Allegro* for Flute and Harp (1987; N.Y., Dec. 9, 1989); *June 29* for Flute (1987); *MBL Suite* for 2 Flutes and String Quartet (Woods Hole, Mass., Aug. 14, 1988); *A Moment in Time* for Flute (1989; N.Y., Jan. 20, 1990); *Talkin'-Lovin'-Leavin': Recitative, Aria, and Finale* for Alto Recorder and String Quartet (N.Y., March 9, 1990); *Partita* for Violin (N.Y., Feb. 20, 1990). **PIANO:** *Prelude in the Form of a Passacaglia* (n.d.); 2 sonatas (1952, 1955); *3 Pieces* (1956); *Momenti* (1974). **ORGAN:** *25 Preludes for Organ in Different Forms* (1975). **VOCAL:** *The Eagle Stirred*, oratorio for Soloists, Chorus, and Orch. (1961); *Songs for Eve* for Soprano and Piano (1966); *The Trials of Galileo*, oratorio for Soloists, Chorus, and Orch. (1967; reworked into the opera *Galileo Galilei*); *Songs from Michelangelo* for Baritone and Piano (1968); *From the Psalms* for Soprano and Piano (1970); *Thrive Upon the Rock* for Chorus and Piano (1973); *A Handful of Souls*, cantata for Soloists, Chorus, and Organ (1975); *Visions-Columbus*, cantata for Bass-baritone and Orch. (Columbus, Ohio, Oct. 10, 1975); *Worship* for Soprano, Tenor, and Piano (1976); *Song of Songs*, chamber cantata for Soprano, Flute, Viola, and Cello (1977; based on the dance score); *A Mass for Cain*, oratorio for Soloists, Chorus, and Orch. (1983).

Ladmirault, Paul (-Émile), French composer and teacher; b. Nantes, Dec. 8, 1877; d. Kerbili en Kamoel, St. Nazaire, Oct. 30, 1944. As a child, he studied piano, organ, and violin; entered the Nantes Cons. in 1892, winning 1st prize in 1893. He was only 15 when his opera *Gilles de Retz* was staged in Nantes (May 18, 1893); he entered the Paris Cons. in 1895, studying with Tardou (harmony), Fauré (composition), and Gédalge (counterpoint and fugue); subsequently returned to Nantes, where he taught at the Cons. His *Suite bretonne* (1902–03) and symphonic prelude *Brocéliande au matin* (Paris, Nov. 28, 1909) were extracts from a 2nd opera, *Myrdhin* (1902–09), which was never performed; the ballet *La Prêtresse de Koridwen* was premiered at the Paris Opéra (Dec. 17, 1926). Other works included the operetta *Glycère* (Paris, 1928); Sym. (1910); *La Brière* for Orch. (Paris, Nov. 20, 1926); *En forêt*, symphonic poem (1932); incidental music to *Tristan et Iseult* (1929); *Valse triste* for Piano and Orch.; *Airs anciens* for Tenor, String Quartet, and Piano (1897); *Ballet bohémien* for Flute, Oboe, Double String Quartet, and Piano (1898); *Fantaisie* for Violin and Piano (1899); *Chanson grecque* for Flute and Piano (1900); Violin Sonata (1901); *De l'ombre à la clarté* for Violin and Piano (1936); piano pieces; songs; many arrangements of Breton folk songs.

BIBL.: C. Debussy, "P.-E. L.," *Gil Blas* (March 9, 1903).

La Forge, Frank, American pianist, teacher, and composer; b. Rockford, Ill., Oct. 22, 1879; d. while playing at a dinner given by the Musicians Club in N.Y., May 5, 1953. He first had piano lessons with his sister; after studies with Harrison Wild in Chicago (1896–1900), he completed his training in Vienna with Leschetizky, Labor, and Navrátil. He was active in Berlin as a soloist, accompanist, and piano teacher. After touring Europe as accompanist to Sembrich, he appeared in the U.S. with Gadski. Subsequently he was active as accompanist to many of the celebrated artists of the day, gaining distinction for playing his part entirely from memory. In later years, he also was active as a vocal teacher, numbering Marian Anderson, Richard Crooks, and Lawrence Tibbett among his students. He was an accomplished composer of songs, among them *To a Messenger, I Came With a Song, Before the Crucifix, Like a Rosebud, When Your Dear Hands,* and *Song of the Open*. He also wrote piano pieces and publ. practical eds. of selections from the vocal repertoire.

Lagger, Peter, Swiss bass; b. Buchs, Sept. 7, 1930; d. Berlin, Sept. 17, 1979. He studied at the Zürich Cons. and with Hans Duhan in Vienna. In 1953 he made his operatic debut in Graz, and appeared there until 1955; then sang in Zürich (1955–57), Wiesbaden (1957–59), and Frankfurt am Main (1959–63); from 1963 he was a leading member of the Berlin Deutsche Oper. He made appearances in Hamburg, Vienna, Paris, and Geneva, and also at the Salzburg, Aix-en-Provence, and Glyndebourne festivals. His extensive operatic, concert, and lieder repertoire extended from Bach to Henze.

La Grange, Henry-Louis de, eminent French writer on music; b. Paris, May 26, 1924. He was a scion of a distinguished family, his father being French and his mother an American. After studying belles lettres in Aix-en-Provence and at the Sorbonne in Paris, he took courses at the Yale Univ. School of Music (1945–53); then completed his musical training with Y. Lefébure (piano) and Boulanger (harmony, counterpoint, and analysis) in Paris. He wrote music criticism for various American and French periodicals. In 1960 he commenced exhaustive research on the life and works of Gustav Mahler, resulting in his monumental biography *Gustav Mahler: Chronique d'une vie* (3 vols., 1973–84; also in Eng.). He also publ. *Vienne, une histoire musicale* (Arles, 1991). He was a guest lecturer at Columbia Univ., N.Y. Univ., Stanford Univ., and Indiana Univ. (1974–81); in

Geneva (1982), Brussels (1983–84), and Leipzig (1985); and at the Juilliard School, the Univ. of Southern Calif. in Los Angeles, and Johns Hopkins Univ. (1986). In Paris in 1986 he founded the Bibliothèque Musicale Gustav Mahler, a vast repository for researchers. He received many awards and honors, including his being made a Chevalier de la Légion d'honneur.

Laine, Cleo (real name, **Clementina Dinah Campbell**), remarkably gifted and versatile English singer and actress; b. Southall, Middlesex, Oct. 28, 1927. Her father was a Jamaican street entertainer; in spite of the family's poverty, her mother succeeded in finding the means to pay for her singing, dancing, and piano lessons; after performing locally, she quit school when she was 14 to help support her family. In 1951 she became vocalist with **John Dankworth**'s jazz group, making her mark under the name Cleo Laine; they were married in 1958. Her career advanced as she became popular as a singer in cabarets, concerts, and recordings, and on television; she also appeared in stage and film roles as both a singer and an actress. As a concert artist, she made her recitals memorable by encompassing the repertoire from Schumann to Sondheim. She made her U.S. debut at N.Y.'s Alice Tully Hall in 1972, followed by a sensational appearance at Carnegie Hall in 1973. Thereafter she toured throughout the U.S., appearing with her husband and his group and also with the major sym. orchs. In 1985 she appeared on Broadway in Rupert Holmes's musical *The Mystery of Edwin Drood.* With a vocal range of nearly 4 octaves, she failed to be intimidated by any period or genre of the repertoire. She was made an Officer of the Order of the British Empire in 1979.

BIBL.: G. Collier, *C. and John: A Biography of the Dankworths* (London, 1976).

Lajovic, Anton, Slovenian composer and jurist; b. Vače, Dec. 19, 1878; d. Ljubljana, Aug. 28, 1960. He studied at the Ljubljana Gasbena Music School before taking a course in composition with Fuchs at the Vienna Cons. (1897–1902); concurrently studied law at the Univ. of Vienna. In subsequent years, Lajovic served as a judge in Slovenia and Croatia while pursuing a second career as a composer. He was a prominent figure in Slovenian music circles. Among his works were a number of orch. scores, choral pieces, and songs.

BIBL.: L. Skerjanc, *A. L.* (Ljubljana, 1958).

Lajtai, Lajos, Hungarian composer; b. Budapest, April 13, 1900; d. there, Jan. 12, 1966. After training in Budapest and Vienna, he began his career writing various light theater works for the Budapest stage. His first major success came with *A régi nyár* (Once Upon a Time in Summer; June 15, 1928). Among his finest subsequent scores were *Sisters* (March 2, 1929), *Az okos mama* (The Clever Mama; Nov. 26, 1930), *Őfelsége frakkja* (His Majesty's Overcoat; Sept. 19, 1931; rev. version as *Katinka*, Paris, Feb. 22, 1933), *A régi orfeum* (The Old Time Music Hall; March 12, 1932), and *A Rotschildok* (The Rothschilds; Nov. 25, 1932). After a sojourn in Paris, Lajtai made his home in Sweden to escpe the deprivations of World War II.

Lajtha, László, eminent Hungarian ethnomusicologist and composer; b. Budapest, June 30, 1892; d. there, Feb. 16, 1963. He studied piano with Arpád Szendy and theory with Victor von Herzfeld at the Budapest Academy of Music. After travels in Leipzig, Geneva, and Paris, he returned to Budapest in 1913 to take a law degree at the Univ. and to become an assoc. of the Ethnographical Dept. of the Hungarian National Museum. From 1919 to 1949 he was a prof. of composition and chamber music at the National Cons., and from 1952 was a teacher of aesthetics and the theory of Magyar music at the Academy of Music. In 1951 he was awarded the Kossuth Prize for his work on Hungarian folk music. He was a brilliant symphonist; his instrumental music is distinguished by consummate mastery of contrapuntal writing.

WORKS: BALLETS: *Lysistrata* (1933; Budapest, Feb. 25, 1937); *Le Bosquet des quatre dieux* (1943); *Capriccio* (1944). **ORCH.:** *Hortobágy Suite* (1935); 10 syms.: No. 1 (1936), No. 2 (1938), *Les Soli* for Harp, Percussion, and Strings (1941), No. 3 (1947–48), No. 4, *Le Printemps* (1951), No. 5 (1952; Paris, Oct. 23, 1954), No. 6 (1955; Brussels, Dec. 12, 1960), No. 7 (1957; Paris, April 26, 1958), No. 8 (1959; Budapest, May 21, 1960), and No. 9 (1961; Paris, May 2, 1963); 2 *divertissements* (1936, 1939); *In Memoriam* (1941); 2 *sinfoniettas* for Strings (1946, 1956); *11 Variations* (1947). **CHAMBER:** *Dramma per musica*, piano quintet (1922); 10 string quartets (1923; 1926; 1929; 1930; *5 études*, 1934; *4 études*, 1942; 1950; 1951; 1953; *Suite Transylvaine*, 1953); Piano Quartet (1925); 3 string trios (1927, 1932, 1945); Piano Trio (1928); Violin Sonatina (1930); Cello Sonata (1932); 2 trios for Harp, Flute, and Cello (1935, 1949); 2 quintets for Flute, Violin, Viola, Cello, and Harp (*Marionettes*, 1937; 1948); *Sonata en concert* for Cello and Piano (1940); *Sonata en concert* for Flute and Piano (1958); *Sonata en concert* for Violin and Piano (1962). **PIANO:** *Des esquisses d'un musicien* (1913); *Contes I* (1913); Sonata (1914); *Scherzo and Toccata* (1930). **VOCAL:** *3 Nocturnes* for Chorus and Orch. (1941); *Missa in tono phrygio* for Chorus and Orch. (1949–50); *Mass* for Chorus and Organ (1951–52).

BIBL.: *L. L.* (Paris, 1954); *L. L.: Quelques oeuvres* (Paris, 1961); J. Weissmann, "L. L.: The Symphonist," *Music Review*, XXXVI (1975).

Lakes, Gary, American tenor; b. Dallas, Sept. 26, 1950. He studied with Thomas Hayward at Southern Methodist Univ. in Dallas and sang in the Dallas Opera Chorus; also attended the Music Academy of the West in Santa Barbara, California, and pursued extensive vocal training with William Eddy at the Seattle Opera, where he made his professional operatic debut as Froh in 1981. After winning the Heldentenor Foundation competition in N.Y., he appeared as Florestan in Mexico City (1983), Samson in Charlotte, N.C. (1984), and Siegmund in Act I of *Die Walküre* in Paris (1985) before making his Metropolitan Opera debut in N.Y. as the High Priest in *Idomeneo* (Feb. 4, 1986). In return visits to the Metropolitan Opera, he sang Siegmund, Bacchus, Don José, the Emperor in *Die Frau ohne Schatten*, Erik, Parsifal, and Florestan. He also sang in concerts with major orchs. in the U.S. and Europe.

Lakner, Yehoshua, Slovak-born Swiss composer; b. Bratislava, April 24, 1924. He went to Palestine in 1941 and studied with Boscovich, Partos, and Pellig; after further training with Copland at the Berkshire Music Center in Tanglewood (summer, 1952), he went to Cologne and worked under Kagel, Koenig, and Stockhausen at the WDR (1959–60) and also with Zimmermann. In 1963 he went to Switzerland and in 1980 became a naturalized Swiss citizen. From 1965 to 1971 he served as composer-in-residence at the Theater an der Winkelwiese, and then was a teacher at the Zürich Cons. from 1974 to 1987. Lakner has utilized the full panoply of elements available to the contemporary composer. He developed a personalized serial technique, sometimes with Middle Eastern infusions. His later use of computers led him to experiment further with audio-visual time-figures.

WORKS: DRAMATIC: *Dmujoth*, ballet (1962); incidental music; film scores. **ORCH.:** *Toccata* (1953); *Hexachords* for Winds, Brass, and Strings (1959–60). **CHAMBER:** Flute Sonata (1948); Sextet for Winds and Piano (1951); *Improvisation* for Viola (1952); *Dance* for Clarinet, Percussion, and Piano (1955); *Umläufe* for Flute, Bass Clarinet, Piano, and 2 Tapes (1976). **PIANO:** *3 Klavierstücke* (1947); *Notturno* (1949); *Mouvement* (1950); *5 Birthdays* (1965); *Fermaten* (1977); *Kreise und Signale* for 2 Pianos (1985); *Alef-Beth-Gimel* (1991). **VOCAL:** *Ki hineh hastaw awar* for Chorus (1950); *Mohammed's Traum* for Chorus and Tape (1968); *Kaninchen* for Speaker, Percussion, and Tape (1973); songs. **OTHER:** Computer pieces; tape works; audio-visual time-figures.

Laks, Simon (actually, **Szymon**), Polish-born French composer; b. Warsaw, Nov. 1, 1901; d. Paris, Dec. 11, 1983. He studied at the Warsaw Cons. (1921–24) with Melcer (conducting) and Statkowski (composition); went to Paris in 1925, continuing his studies under Rabaud and Vidal at the Cons. He was interned by the Nazis in the Auschwitz and Dachau concentration camps (1941–44), where he was active as a performer and music director; after his liberation, he returned to Paris. He publ. his experiences of his internment as *La Musique d'un autre monde* (Paris, 1948; Eng. tr., 1989).

WORKS: OPERA BUFFA: *L'Hirondelle inattendue* (1965). **ORCH.:** *Farys*, symphonic poem (1924); *Symphonic Blues*, jazz fantasy (1928); *Suite polonaise* (1936); *Sinfonietta* for Strings (1936); *Suite on Silesian Tunes* for Small Orch. (1945); *Songs of the Polish Earth* (1946); *3 Warsaw Polonaises* for Chamber Orch. (1947); Sym. for Strings (1964). **CHAMBER:** 5 string quartets (1928–64); Piano Trio (1950); *Concerto da camera* for Piano, 9 Wind Instruments, and Percussion (1963); Concertino for Wind Trio (1965); Piano Quintet on Polish Themes (1967); piano pieces. **VOCAL:** Songs.

La Laurencie, (Marie Bertrand) Lionel (Jules), Comte de, important French musicologist; b. Nantes, July 24, 1861; d. Paris, Nov. 21, 1933. After studying law and science, he became a pupil of Léon Reynier (violin) and Alphonse Weingartner (harmony) and of Bougault-Ducoudray at the Paris Cons. In 1898 he became a lecturer at the École des Hautes Études Sociales. He contributed regularly to several music journals. In 1916 he became ed. of Lavignac's *Encyclopédie de la musique et dictionnaire du Conservatoire*, to which he contributed articles on French music of the 17th and 18th centuries. The *Catalogue des livres de musiciens de la bibliothèque de l'Arsénal à Paris*, ed. by L. Laurencie and A. Gastoué, was publ. in 1936.

WRITINGS: *La Légende de Parsifal et la drame musical de Richard Wagner* (1888–94); *España* (1890); *Le Goût musical en France* (1905); *L'Académie de musique et le concert de Nantes* (1908); *Rameau* (1908); *Lully* (1911); *Les Créatures de l'opéra français* (1920; 2nd ed., 1930); *L'École française de violon, de Lully à Viotti* (3 vols., 1922–24); *Les Luthistes* (1928); *La Chanson royale en France* (1928); *Inventaire critique du fonds Blancheton à la Bibliothèque du Conservatoire* (2 vols., 1920–31); with Thibault and Mairy, *Chansons du luth et airs du XVIe siècle* (1931); *Orfée de Gluck* (1934).

BIBL.: *Mélanges de musicologie offerts à M. L. d.l.L.* (Paris, 1933); B. Brook, "L. d.l.L.'s *L'École française de violon*," *Notes* (Sept. 1969).

La Liberté, (Joseph-François) Alfred, Canadian pianist, teacher, and composer; b. St.-Jean, Quebec, Feb. 10, 1882; d. Montreal, May 7, 1952. After initial training in Canada, he studied at the Stern Cons. in Berlin (1902–06) with Lutzenko (piano), Baeker (harmony), and Klatte (counterpoint and composition). Following a successful recital debut in Montreal in 1906, he met Scriabin in N.Y. in 1907 who suggested that he pursue his piano training with Carreño in Berlin. Subsequently he became Scriabin's student in Brussels. Upon returning to Montreal in 1911, he became active as a teacher and as a champion of Scriabin's music. He also became an advocate of the music of Madtner and Dupré. Among La Liberté's own works were the opera *Soeur Béatrice* (piano score only); *Passacaille et choeur final* for Piano, Organ, Orch., and Wordless Chorus (unfinished); *La Chanson d'Eve*, song cycle for Orch. or Piano; chamber music; harmonizations of folk songs from several nations.

Lalo, Charles, French aesthetician; b. Périgueux, Feb. 24, 1877; d. Paris, April 1, 1953. He studied aesthetics and philosophy in Bayonne, and then at the Univ. of Paris (Ph.D., 1908, with 2 dissertations: *Esquisse d'une esthétique musicale scientifique*, publ. in Paris, 1908; 2nd ed., aug., 1939 as *Éléments d'une esthétique*, and *L'Esthétique expérimentale contemporaine*, publ. in Paris, 1908). He lectured at the Univ. of Bordeaux, then taught aesthetics and art history at the Sorbonne in Paris (1933–53); was also president of the Société Française d'Esthétique.

WRITINGS (all publ. in Paris): *Les Sentiments esthétiques* (1910); *Introduction à l'esthétique* (1912; 4th ed., rev., 1952 as *Notions de philosophie, notions d'esthétique*); *L'Art et la vie sociale* (1921); *La Beauté et l'instinct sexuel* (1922); *L'Art et la morale* (1922); *L'Expression de la vie dans l'art* (1933); *L'Art loin de la vie* (1939); *L'Économie des passions* (1947); *Les Grandes Évasions esthétiques* (1947).

BIBL.: Special issue of *Revue d'esthétique*, VI/2 (1953).

Lalo, Pierre, French music critic; b. Puteaux, Sept. 6, 1866; d. Paris, June 9, 1943. He was the son of the distinguished French composer of Spanish descent, Édouard (-Victoire-Antoine) Lalo (b. Lille, Jan. 27, 1823; d. Paris, April 22, 1892). He studied literature and philosophy; also took courses in modern languages at the École de Chartes and the École Polytechnique. He began writing music criticism for the *Journal des débats* (1896), then was music critic of *Le Temps* (1898–1914). He became known as a caustic critic of Debussy.

WRITINGS: *La Musique* (Paris, 1898–99; a selection of his articles); *Richard Wagner ou le Nibelung* (Paris, 1933); *De Rameau à Ravel: Portraits et souvenirs* (Paris, 1947).

Laloy, Louis, French musicologist and music critic; b. Grey, Haute-Saône, Feb. 18, 1874; d. Dôle, March 3, 1944. He settled in Paris, where he studied at the École Normale Supérieure (1893; agrégé des lettres, 1896; docteur ès lettres, 1904, with the diss. *Aristoxène de Tarente et la musique de l'antiquité*); also studied with Bordes, Breéille, and d'Indy at the Schola Cantorum (1899–1905). He was co-founder of the *Revue d'Histoire et de Critique Musicale* (1901), the *Mercure musicale* (1905), and the *L'année musicale* (1911); contributed articles to *Revue de Paris, Grande Revue, Mercure de France*, and *Gazette des Beaux-Arts*. He lectured at the Sorbonne; also was prof. of music history at the Paris Cons. (1936–41).

WRITINGS (all publ. in Paris unless otherwise given): *Jean Philippe Rameau* (1908; 3rd ed., 1919); *Claude Debussy* (1909; 2nd ed., 1944); *La Musique chinoise* (1910); *The Future of Music* (London, 1910); *La danse à l'Opéra* (1927); *La Musique retrouvée, 1902–1927* (1928); *Une Heure de musique avec Beethoven* (1930); *Comment écouter la musique* (1942).

Lamb, Joseph F(rancis), remarkable American ragtime pianist and composer; b. Montclair, N.J., Dec. 6, 1887; d. N.Y., Sept. 3, 1960. Although he had no formal musical training and spent most of his life in the textile import business, he was one of the most important composers of piano rags during the heyday of ragtime; also wrote a number of songs for Tin Pan Alley. After almost 30 years, he was rediscovered in 1949 and began composing rags again; also appeared as a ragtime pianist. His most notable piano rags were *Sensation* (1908), *Ethiopia Rag* (1909), *Excelsior Rag* (1909), *Champagne Rag* (1910), *American Beauty Rag* (1913), *Cleopatra Rag* (1915), *Contentment Rag* (1915), *The Ragtime Nightingale* (1915), *Reindeer* (1915), *Patricia Rag* (1916), *Top Liner Rag* (1916), and *Bohemia Rag* (1919). An anthology of his works appeared in N.Y. in 1964.

BIBL.: R. Cassidy, "J. L.: Last of the Ragtime Composers," *Jazz Report*, I (Jan.–Aug. 1961); M. Montgomery, "J.F. L.: A Ragtime Paradox, 1887–1960," *Sound Line*, XII/3–4 (1961); M. Den, *J.F. L., a Ragtime Composer Recalled* (thesis, Brooklyn College, City Univ. of N.Y., 1975); J. Scotti, *J. L.: A Study of Ragtime's Paradox* (diss., Univ. of Cincinnati, 1977; with list of works); idem, "The Musical Legacy of J. L.," in J. Hasse, ed., *Ragtime: Its History, Composers, and Music* (N.Y., 1985).

Lambert, (Leonard) Constant, remarkable English conductor, composer, and writer on music; b. London, Aug. 23, 1905; d. there, Aug. 21, 1951. He won a scholarship to the Royal College of Music in London, where he studied with R.O. Morris and Vaughan Williams (1915–22). His first major score, the ballet *Romeo and Juliet* (Monte Carlo, May 4, 1926), was commissioned by Diaghilev. This early association with the dance proved decisive, for he spent most of his life as a conductor and composer of ballets. His interest in jazz resulted in such fine scores as *Elegiac Blues* for Orch. (1927), *The Rio Grande* for Piano, Chorus, and Orch. (1927; to a text by S. Sitwell), and the Concerto for Piano and 9 Performers (1930–31). Of his many ballets, the most striking in craftsmanship was *Horoscope* (1937). In the meantime, he became conductor of the Camargo

Soc. for the presentation of ballet productions (1930). He was made music director of the Vic-Wells Ballet (1931), and remained in that capacity after it became the Sadler's Wells Ballet and the Royal Ballet, until resigning in 1947; he then was made one of its artistic directors (1948), and subsequently conducted it on its first visit to the U.S. (1949). He also appeared at London's Covent Garden (1937; 1939; 1946–47); was assoc. conductor of the London Promenade Concerts (1945–46), and then frequently conducted broadcast performances over the BBC. He contributed articles on music to the *Nation and Athenaeum* (from 1930) and to the *Sunday Referee* (from 1931). He also penned the provocative book *Music Ho! A Study of Music in Decline* (London, 1934). Lambert was one of the most gifted musicians of his generation. However, his demanding work as a conductor and his excessive consumption of alcohol prevented him from fully asserting himself as a composer in his later years.

WORKS: BALLETS: *Romeo and Juliet* (1924–25; Monte Carlo, May 4, 1926); *Pomona* (1926; Buenos Aires, Sept. 9, 1927); *Horoscope* (1937; London, Jan. 27, 1938, composer conducting); *Tiresias* (1950–51; London, July 9, 1951, composer conducting); also various arrangements. **ORCH.:** *The Bird Actors*, overture (1925; reorchestrated, 1927; London, July 5, 1931, composer conducting; orig. for Piano, 4-hands); *Champêtre* for Chamber Orch. (London, Oct. 27, 1926); *Elegiac Blues* (1927; also for Piano); *Music for Orchestra* (1927; BBC, June 14, 1929); *The Rio Grande* for Piano, Chorus, and Orch., after S. Sitwell (1927; BBC, Feb. 27, 1928, composer conducting); Concerto for Piano, Flute, 2 Clarinets, Bass Clarinet, Trumpet, Trombone, Percussion, Cello, and Double Bass (London, Dec. 18, 1931, composer conducting); *Aubade héroïque* (1942; London, Feb. 21, 1943, composer conducting). **PIANO:** *Pastorale* (1926); *Elegiac Blues* (1927; also for Orch.); Sonata (1928–29; London, Oct. 30, 1929); *Elegy* (1938); *Trois pièces nègres pour les touches blanches* for Piano, 4-Hands (1949). **VOCAL:** *Summer's Last Will and Testament* for Baritone, Chorus, and Orch., after T. Nashe (1932–35; London, Jan. 29, 1936, composer conducting); *Dirge from Cymbeline* for Tenor, Baritone, Men's Chorus, and Strings or Piano, after Shakespeare (with Piano, Cambridge, Nov. 1940; with Strings, BBC, March 23, 1947, composer conducting); numerous songs, including *8 Poems of Li-Po* for Voice and Piano or 8 Instruments (1926–29; with Instruments, London, Oct. 30, 1929).

BIBL.: H. Foss, "C. L.," *Musical Times* (Oct. 1951); D. Webster, "C. L.—an Appreciation," *Opera* (Nov. 1951); R. McGrady, "The Music of C. L.," *Music & Letters* (July 1970); C. Palmer, "C. L.—a Postscript," ibid. (April 1971); R. Shead, *C. L.* (London, 1973; 2nd ed., rev., 1987); K. DeKay, "C. L.: Genius and Tragedy," *Le Grand Baton* (Sept. 1982; with discography by N. Brown).

Lambert, Juan Bautista, Catalan organist, conductor, and composer; b. Barcelona, 1884; d. there, May 4, 1945. He was a pupil of Pedrell and Morera (composition) and of Pellicer and Malats (piano) at the Barcelona municipal music school. He became conductor of its band, as well as of several others; he also served as organist and choirmaster in various churches and colleges, as well as censor of sacred music for the bishopric (from 1940). Lambert particularly distinguished himself as a composer of Catalan sacred music, producing 3 masses, motets, hymns, and organ pieces. Among his other works were 3 operas, 5 zarzuelas, orch. works, chamber music, and piano pieces.

Lambert, Lucien, French composer and pianist; b. Paris, Jan. 5, 1858; d. Oporto, Portugal, Jan. 21, 1945. He studied first with his father; after a tour of America and Europe, returned to Paris to study at the Cons. with Dubois and Massenet, taking the Prix Rossini in 1885 with his cantata *Prométhée enchaîné.* He settled in Portugal in 1914; was a prof. of composition at the Oporto Cons. (1922–37).

WORKS: DRAMATIC: OPERAS: *Brocéliande* (Rouen, Feb. 25, 1893); *Le Spahi* (Paris, Oct. 18, 1897); *La Marseillaise* (Paris, July 14, 1900); *La Flamenca* (Paris, Oct. 31, 1903); *Harald* (1937); *Penticosa; La Sorcière.* **BALLETS:** *La Roussalka* (Paris, Dec. 8, 1911); *Les Cloches de Porto* (1937). **LYRIC COMEDY:** *Florette* (1921). **ORCH.:** *Légende roumaine*, symphonic poem; *Fantaisie monothématique*, on an oriental theme (Paris, March 19, 1933); *Tanger le soir*, Moorish rhapsody; *Esquisses créoles*, suite, on themes by Gottschalk; *Andante et fantaisie tzigane* for Piano and Orch. **CHAMBER:** String Quartet; String Sextet; piano pieces. **VOCAL:** Mass; songs.

Lambro, Phillip, American composer, conductor, and pianist; b. Wellesley Hills, Mass., Sept. 2, 1935. He began his training in Boston, where he made his debut as a pianist in 1952; after further studies in Miami (1953–55), he received a scholarship in 1955 to complete his training at the Music Academy of the West in Santa Barbara with György Sandor (piano) and Donald Pond (composition). Lambro's works have been performed by various major American orchs., and have also been performed abroad. He has also composed and conducted music for several films, including the documentaries *Energy on the Move* and *Mineral King.* As a composer, Lambro is basically autodidact. He learned the art of composition mainly by analyzing the various periods and styles in music, from the Renaissance to the contemporary era. All the same, he developed his own individual means of expression to extend the pathway of valid and divergent statements. Lambro believes in the existence of Elohim Extraterrestrials "who created mankind in a laboratory." To maintain his health, he practices the Japanese Zen Macrobiotic diet and way of life.

WORKS: *Miraflores* for String Orch. (1955); *Dance Barbaro* for Percussion (1958–60); *Toccata* for Piano (1963–65); *2 Pictures* for Solo Percussionist and Orch. (1965–66); *4 Songs* for Soprano and Orch. (1966–67); *Music* for Wind, Brass, and Percussion (1969); *Toccata* for Guitar (1969); *Structures* for String Orch. (1969–70); *Parallelograms* for Flute Quartet and Jazz Ensemble (1969–75); *Obelisk* for Oboist and Percussionist (1970); *Fanfare and Tower Music* for Brass Quintet (1971); *Trumpet Voluntary* (1972); *Biospheres* for 6 Percussionists (1973); *Night Pieces* for Piano (1973); *3 Little Trigrams* for Piano (1979).

Lammers, Gerda, esteemed German soprano; b. Berlin, Sept. 25, 1915. She studied with L. Mysz-Gmeiner and M. Schwedler-Lohmann at the Berlin Hochschule für Musik. After appearances as a concert and lieder artist (1940–55), she made her operatic debut as Ortlinde at the Bayreuth Festival (1955); that same year she made her first appearance at the Kassel State Theater as Marie in Berg's *Wozzeck*, remaining there for some 15 years. She made an acclaimed debut as Elektra at London's Covent Garden (1957), substituting on short notice for an indisposed Christel Goltz; she returned there as Kundry in 1959. She made her Metropolitan Opera debut in N.Y. as Elektra on March 16, 1962. Her other distinguished roles included Alceste, Medea, Senta, Isolde, and Brünnhilde.

Lamond, Frederic(k Archibald), distinguished Scottish pianist; b. Glasgow, Jan. 28, 1868; d. Stirling, Feb. 21, 1948. He played organ as a boy in a local church; also studied oboe and violin; in 1882, entered the Raff Cons. in Frankfurt am Main, studying with Heermann (violin), Max Schwarz (piano), and Urspruch (composition); then piano with Bülow, Clara Schumann, and Liszt. He made his debut in Berlin (Nov. 17, 1885); then appeared in Vienna and Glasgow, and later in London, N.Y., and Russia. He married the German actress Irene Triesch (1904), making Berlin his center of activities until the coming of World War II, when he went to England. While continuing to make tours, he also was engaged as a pedagogue. He became renowned for his performances of Beethoven and Liszt; publ. an ed. of the Beethoven piano sonatas and the book *Beethoven: Notes on the Sonatas* (Glasgow, 1944); his reminiscences appeared as *The Memoirs of Frederic Lamond* (Glasgow, 1949). He was also a composer; wrote a Sym. (Glasgow, Dec. 23, 1889), some chamber music, and numerous piano pieces.

La Montaine, John, American composer and pianist; b. Oak Park, Ill., March 17, 1920. He studied piano with Muriel Parker and Margaret Farr Wilson, then received training in theory in Chicago from Stella Roberts (1935–38); subsequently took courses in piano with Max Landow and in composition with Hanson and Rogers at the Eastman School of Music in Rochester, N.Y. (B.Mus., 1942); after further training from Rudolph Ganz at the Chicago Musical College (1945), he completed his studies in composition with Wagenaar at the Juilliard School of Music in N.Y. and with Boulanger at the American Cons. in Fontainebleau. From 1950 to 1954 he was the pianist and celesta player in the NBC Sym. Orch. in N.Y. As a pianist, he often performed his own works. He received a Guggenheim fellowship (1959–60); in 1961 he was a visiting prof. of composition at the Eastman School of Music; in 1962, served as composer-in-residence at the American Academy in Rome. He received the Pulitzer Prize in Music for his 1st Piano Concerto in 1959. In 1977 he was a Nixon Distinguished Scholar at Nixon's alma mater, Whittier College, in California. While La Montaine's works incorporate various usages ranging from serialism to jazz, his scores reflect his penchant for accessibility and lyricism.

WORKS: OPERAS: Christmas trilogy on medieval miracle plays: *Novellis, Novellis* (Washington, D.C., Dec. 24, 1961), *The Shephardes Playe* (Washington, D.C., Dec. 27, 1967), and *Erode the Greate* (Washington, D.C., Dec. 31, 1969); *Be Glad, Then, America: A Decent Entertainment from the 13 Colonies*, bicentennial opera (Univ. Park, Pa., Feb. 6, 1976). **ORCH.:** *Canons* (n.d.); *6 Sonnets* (n.d.); *Recitative, Aria, and Finale* for Strings (n.d.; Rochester, N.Y., April 28, 1965); *Jubilant Overture* (n.d.); *Colloquy* for Strings (n.d.); *Passacaglia and Fugue* for Strings (n.d.); 4 piano concertos: No. 1 (Washington, D.C., Nov. 25, 1958), No. 2, *Transformations* (1987), No. 3, *Children's Games* (1987), and No. 4 (1989); *From Sea to Shining Sea* (inaugural concert of President John F. Kennedy, Washington, D.C., Jan. 19, 1961); *A Summer's Day* (Washington, D.C., May 25, 1964); *Birds of Paradise* for Piano and Orch. (Rochester, N.Y., April 29, 1964, composer soloist; also as the ballet *Nightwings*, N.Y., Sept. 7, 1966); *Incantations* for Jazz Band (n.d.; 1st concert perf., Rochester, N.Y., April 13, 1976); *Overture: An Early American Sampler* (1976); Flute Concerto (Washington, D.C., April 12, 1981); *2 Scenes from the Song of Solomon* for Flute and Orch. (Carson, Calif., March 8, 1981); Concerto for Strings (Vancouver Radio, March 17, 1981); *Symphonic Variations* for Piano and Orch. (Peninsula Music Festival, Wis., Aug. 20, 1982, composer soloist); *Of Age, after Euripides: An Ode, Epode, and Fanfares* (1990). **CHAMBER:** Cello Sonata; String Quartet; Sonata for Solo Flute; Woodwind Quartet; piano pieces; organ works. **VOCAL:** *Songs of the Nativity* for Chorus (Washington, D.C., Dec. 24, 1954); *Songs of the Rose of Sharon*, biblical cycle for Soprano and Orch. (Washington, D.C., May 31, 1956); *Fragments from the Song of Songs*, biblical cycle for Soprano and Orch. (New Haven, Conn., April 14, 1959); *Wonder Tidings*, Christmas carols for Incidental Solos, Chorus, Harp, Percussion, and Organ (N.Y., Jan. 26, 1964); *Te Deum* for Chorus, Winds, and Percussion (Washington, D.C., May 7, 1964); *Wilderness Journal*, sym. for Bass-baritone, Organ, and Orch., after Thoreau (Washington, D.C., Oct. 10, 1972); *9 Lessons of Christmas* for Incidental Solos, Chorus, Harp, and Percussion (Minneapolis, Nov. 30, 1975); *Mass of Nature (Missa Naturae)* for Chorus and Orch. (Washington, D.C., May 26, 1976); *The Whittier Service*, 9 hymn-anthems for Incidental Solos, Chorus, Guitar, Brass Quintet, Strings, and Optional Organ and Timpani (Washington, D.C., May 20, 1979); *The Lessons of Advent* for Incidental Solos, Chorus, Narrator, Trumpet, Drums, Handbell Choir, Harp, Oboe, Guitar, and Organ (San Francisco, Dec. 4, 1983); *The Marshes of Glynn* for Bass, Chorus, and Orch. (Rochester, N.Y., Nov. 11, 1984); *The Birth of Freedom*, dramatic cantata for 2 Tenors, Bass-baritone, Folk Singer, Chorus, and Orch. (1988); *In Praise of Britain's Queen and Elgar's Enigma* for Chorus (1994).

Lamote de Grignon, Juan, Catalan conductor and composer, father of **Ricardo Lamote de Grignon y Ribas**; b. Barcelona, July 7, 1872; d. there, March 11, 1949. He studied at the Barcelona Cons., and upon graduation, became prof. (1890) and director (1917) there. He made his debut as a conductor in Barcelona (April 26, 1902). In 1910 he founded the Orquesta Sinfónica of Barcelona, which carried on its activity until 1924; also was founder-conductor of the Valencia Municipal Orch. (1943–49). He publ. *Musique et musiciens français à Barcelone: Musique et musiciens catalans à Paris* (Barcelona, 1935). He wrote an opera, *Hesperia* (Barcelona, Jan. 25, 1907); orch. works; an oratorio, *La Nit de Nadal*; numerous songs.

Lamote de Grignon y Ribas, Ricardo, Catalan cellist, conductor, and composer, son of **Juan Lamote de Grignon**; b. Barcelona, Sept. 23, 1899; d. there, Feb. 5, 1962. He studied cello and composition at the Barcelona Cons. He played cello in the Orquesta Sinfónica of Barcelona, conducted by his father; then conducted provincial orchs.; became assistant conductor of the municipal band of Barcelona. He publ. a manual, *Síntesis de técnica musical* (Barcelona, 1948). His *Enigmas* for Orch. won the Barcelona Municipal Prize in 1951.

WORKS: OPERAS: *La caperucita verde*; *La flor*, children's opera. **ORCH.:** *Joan de Os*, symphonic legend (Barcelona, April 19, 1936, composer conducting); *Boires*, symphonic poem; *Triptico de Rabindranath Tagore* for Soprano and Orch.; *Enigmas*. **CHAMBER:** Piano Trio.

Lamy, Fernand, French composer and pedagogue; b. Chauvigny, Vienne, April 8, 1881; d. Paris, Sept. 18, 1966. After training at the Poitiers Cons., he studied with Bleuzet, Caussade, Dukas, and Ropartz in Paris, where he began his career as a conductor at the Théâtre des Champs Elysées. From 1914 to 1943 he was director of the Vallencienne Cons. In 1951 he was made inspector general for the arts and literature. He wrote mainly orch. works and choral music.

Lancen, Serge (Jean Mathieu), French composer and pianist; b. Paris, Nov. 5, 1922. He received training in piano from Marguerite Long and Lazare-Lévy, and later was a composition student of Aubin, Büsser, and N. Gallon at the Paris Cons. (premier prix, 1949). In 1950 he won the Premier Grand Prix de Rome. In later years he was active with the World Assn. for Symphonic Band and Ensembles, serving on the committee of its French section (1985–91).

WORKS: DRAMATIC: *Les Prix*, ballet (Bordeaux, March 13, 1954); *La Mauvaise Conscience*, chamber opera (1962; Paris, Jan. 4, 1964); radio scores. **ORCH.:** Piano Concerto (1947–51); Harmonica Concerto (1954); Concerto for Double Bass and Strings (1960); Concerto for Flute and Strings (1962); *Instants* for Strings, Piano, and Percussion (1963); *Triptyque* (1965); *Fantasie créole* for Piano and Orch. (1967); *Concerto champêtre* for Harp and Small Orch. (1968); *Sinfonietta* (1970); *Concerto-rhapsodie* for Piano and Orch. (1974); Concerto for Harp and Strings (1988). **BAND:** *Manhattan Symphony* (1962); *Ouverture texane* (1971); *Symphonie de Paris* (1973); *Rhapsodie symphonique* (1976); *Symphonie de l'eau* (1985); Concerto for Trombone and Band (1987); *Symphonie ibérique* (1988); Concerto for Horn and Band (1990). **CHAMBER:** String Quartet (1959); *Concert à 6* for 6 Clarinets (1962); *Jeux pour musiciens* for 13 or 14 Instruments (1981); Double Bass Sonata (1982); *Concert* for Violin, Double Bass, and Piano (1985). **VOCAL:** *Narcisse*, secular oratorio (1957); *Poème aecuménique* for 9 Soloists, Chorus, Children's Chorus, Organ, and Orch. (1975); *Missa solemnis* (1986); *Te Deum* (1991).

Lanchbery, John (Arthur), English conductor, composer, and arranger; b. London, May 15, 1923. He held a composition scholarship at the Royal Academy of Music in London (1942–43; 1945–48). He quickly developed a reputation as a ballet conductor in London, where he conducted the Metropolitan Ballet (1948–50), the Sadler's Wells Theatre Ballet (1951–59), and the Royal Ballet at Covent Garden (1960–72). After conducting the Australian Ballet in Melbourne (1972–77), he conducted the American Ballet in N.Y. (1978–80). He also was a guest conductor throughout Europe and the Americas. In addition to his film, radio, and television scores, he also prepared new performing eds. of a number of ballets.

Lancie, John (Sherwood) de. See **de Lancie, John (Sherwood).**

Landau, Siegfried, German-born American conductor and composer; b. Berlin, Sept. 4, 1921. He studied at the Stern Cons. and at the Klindworth-Scharwenka Cons. in Berlin. He continued his studies at the Guildhall School of Music and Drama and at Trinity College of Music in London (1939–40); he pursued conducting studies at the Mannes College of Music in N.Y. (diploma, 1942); also received conducting lessons from Monteux. In 1946 he became a naturalized American citizen. In 1955 he organized the Brooklyn Philharmonia, which he conducted until 1971; concurrently was conductor of the Chattanooga Opera Assn. (1960–73) and of the Music for Westchester (later White Plains) Sym. Orch. (1961–81); likewise served as Generalmusikdirektor of the Westphalian Sym. Orch. (1973–75). He wrote an opera, *The Sons of Aaron* (Scarsdale, N.Y., Feb. 28, 1959), ballet music, orch. pieces, chamber music, and film scores.

Landon, H(oward) C(handler) Robbins, eminent American musicologist; b. Boston, March 6, 1926. He studied music history and theory with Alfred J. Swan at Swarthmore College, and composition there with Harl McDonald; he also took a course in English literature with W.H. Auden (1943–45); then enrolled in the musicology class of Geiringer at Boston Univ. (B.Mus., 1947). In 1948 he traveled to Europe and settled in Vienna; in 1949 he founded the Haydn Soc., with a view to preparing a complete ed. of Haydn's works. He also instituted an energetic campaign to locate music MSS which had disappeared or been removed; thus, he succeeded in finding the MS of Haydn's Mass No. 13; also found the MS of the so-called Jena Sym., erroneously ascribed to Beethoven, and proved that it had actually been composed by Friedrich Witt. In *The Symphonies of Joseph Haydn* (London, 1955; suppl., 1961), he analyzes each sym. and suggests solutions for numerous problems of authenticity; in his new ed. of the syms. (12 vols., Vienna, 1965–68), he carefully establishes the version nearest to the original authentic text. He subsequently publ. his massive study *Haydn: Chronicle and Works* in 5 vols. (Bloomington, Ind., and London): vol. I, *Haydn: The Early Years, 1732–1765* (1980), vol. II, *Haydn at Esterháza, 1766–1790* (1978), vol. III, *Haydn in England, 1791–1795* (1976), vol. IV, *Haydn: The Years of "The Creation," 1796–1800* (1977), and vol. V, *Haydn: The Late Years, 1801–1809* (1977). His other publications include *The Mozart Companion* (ed. with D. Mitchell; London, 1956; 2nd ed., rev., 1965); *The Collected Correspondence and London Notebooks of Joseph Haydn* (London, 1959); a foreword with many emendations to C.S. Terry's *John Christian Bach* (London, 1929; 2nd ed., rev., 1967); *Beethoven: A Documentary Study* (London, 1970; 2nd ed., rev., 1993 as *Beethoven: His Life, Work, and World*); *Essays on the Viennese Classical Style: Gluck, Haydn, Mozart, Beethoven* (London and N.Y., 1970); *Haydn: A Documentary Study* (London, 1981); *Mozart and the Masons* (London, 1983); *1791: Mozart's Last Year* (London, 1988); *Haydn: His Life and Music* (with D. Jones; London, 1988); *Mozart: The Golden Years* (N.Y., 1989); ed. *The Mozart Compendium* (N.Y., 1990); *Mozart and Vienna, including Selections from Johann Pezzl's "Sketch of Vienna" 1786–90* (N.Y., 1991); *Five Centuries of Music in Venice* (London, 1991); *Vivaldi: Voice of the Baroque* (London, 1993); *Mozart Essays* (London, 1995). He was a lecturer of distinction at various American and British colleges and universities. During his early years in Europe, his wife, Christa Landon (b. Berlin, Sept. 23, 1921; d. Funchal, Madeira, Nov. 19, 1977), joined him as a research partner in the search for rare MSS in libraries, churches, and monasteries. She publ. eds. of works by Haydn, Mozart, and Bach; her ed. of Haydn's piano sonatas (3 vols., Vienna, 1963–66) supersedes the one by Hoboken.

Landormy, Paul (Charles-René), French musicologist, music critic, and composer; b. Issy-les-Moulineaux, Jan. 3, 1869; d. Paris, Nov. 17, 1943. He was an agrégé des lettres of the École Normale in Paris; studied voice with Sbriglia and Plancon. With Rolland, he organized a series of lectures on music history at the École des Hautes Études Sociales (1902) and was founder-director of its acoustic laboratory (1904–07); became music critic of *La Victoire* (1918), and contributed articles to other publications. Among his compositions were piano pieces and songs.

WRITINGS (all publ. in Paris): *Histoire de la musique* (1910; 3rd ed., 1923); *Brahms* (1920; rev. ed., 1948); *Bizet* (1924); *La Vie de Schubert* (1928); *Albert Roussel* (1938); *Gluck* (1941); *Gounod* (1942); *La Musique française* (3 vols., 1943–44).

Landowska, Wanda (Alexandra), celebrated Polish-born French harpsichordist, pianist, and pedagogue; b. Warsaw, July 5, 1879; d. Lakeville, Conn., Aug. 16, 1959. She was only 4 when she began to play the piano. Following lessons with Kleczyński, she continued her piano studies at the Warsaw Cons. with Michalowski. In 1896 she went to Berlin and completed her formal training with Moszkowski (piano) and Urban (composition). In 1900 she went to Paris, where she married Henri Lew, an authority on Hebrew folklore. He encouraged her to pursue her interest in the study and performance of 17th- and 18th-century music. While she continued to appear as a pianist, from 1903 she gave increasing attention to playing the harpsichord in public and making it once again an accepted concert instrument. Her tours as a harpsichordist took her all over Europe. In 1913 she went to Berlin to teach harpsichord at the Hochschule für Musik. At the outbreak of World War I in 1914, she and her husband were declared civil prisoners on parole because of their French citizenship. After the Armistice in 1918, Landowska went to Basel to give master classes in harpsichord at the Cons. in 1919. She then returned to Paris to teach at the Sorbonne and at the École Normale de Musique. In 1923 she made her first appearances in the U.S. In 1925 she settled in St.-Leu-la-Forêt, near Paris, where she founded the École de Musique Ancienne for the study, teaching, and performance of early music. She also continued to tour abroad. With the Nazi occupation of Paris in 1940, Landowska fled France and eventually arrived in N.Y. in 1941. In 1947 she settled in Lakeville, Conn. She continued to be active as a performer and teacher during these years. In 1952 she celebrated her 75th birthday in a N.Y. recital. Landowska was the foremost champion of the 20th-century movement to restore the harpsichord to concert settings. Her performance style was an assertive one highlighted by legato playing and variety of articulation. While she was best known for her interpretations of Bach, she also commissioned works from Falla (Harpsichord Concerto, Barcelona, Nov. 5, 1926), Poulenc (*Concert champêtre* for Harpsichord and Small Orch., Paris, May 3, 1929), and other composers. D. Restout and R. Hawkins ed. a collection of her articles as *Landowska on Music* (Briarcliff Manor, N.Y., 1964).

BIBL.: B. Gavoty and R. Hauert, *W. L.* (Geneva, 1957); H. Schott, "W. L.," *Early Music*, VII (1979); D. Alfano, "Remembering W. L. (1879–1959)," *Music and Musicians International* (March 1989); A. Cash, *W. L. and the Revival of the Harpsichord: A Reassessment* (diss., Univ. of Kentucky, 1990).

Landowski, Marcel (François Paul), eminent French composer and administrator; b. Pont-L'Abbé, Finistère, Feb. 18, 1915. He was the great-grandson of Henri Vieuxtemps, and the son of the sculptor Paul Landowski. He received training in piano from Marguerite Long (1922) and in conducting from Monteux (1932), and was a student at the Paris Cons. (1934–37) of Fauchet (harmony), N. Gallon (fugue), Büsser (composition), and Gaubert (conducting). While rising to eminence as a composer, Landowski also became a prominent administrator. From 1960 to 1965 he was director of the Boulogne-Billancourt Cons., and from 1962 to 1966 he was director of music of the Comédie-Française in Paris. In 1964 he was named inspector-general of music for the Ministry of Cultural Affairs, later serving as its chief of the music service (1966–70) and as director of music, lyric art, and dance (1970–74). In 1974 he became inspector-general of music for the Ministry of Education. From

1977 to 1979 he was director of cultural affairs for the City of Paris. He was president of the Théâtre du Châtelet in Paris from 1980 to 1991. He served as president and director-general of the Editions Salabert in Paris from 1991. In 1950 he received the Grand Prix of the City of Paris for composition. The Société des Auteurs, Compositeurs et Editeurs de Musique awarded him its Grand Prix in 1968 and its Prix Maurice Ravel in 1973. In 1975 Landowski was elected a member of the Académie des Beaux-Arts of the Institut de France, serving as its permanent secretary from 1968 to 1994. In 1987 he was made a Commandeur of the Légion d'honneur. In 1994 he was named Chancelier of the Institut de France. He was the author of *L'orchestre* (with L. Aubert; Paris, 1951), *Honegger* (Paris, 1957), *Batailles pour la musique* (Paris, 1979), and *La Musique n'adoucit pas les moeurs* (Paris, 1990). Landowski's compositions reveal his penchant for eclecticism. While his works are always expertly crafted, his generally accessible style is occasionally made more adventuresome by his utilization of atonal, electronic, and electroacoustic diversions. Some of his piano works were written for his wife, Jacqueline Potier, whom he married in 1941.

WORKS: DRAMATIC: *Le Tour d'une aile de pigeon*, operetta (Paris, April 1, 1938; in collaboration with J.-J. Grünewald); *Les Fleurs de la petite Ida*, ballet (Paris, June 19, 1938); *Clairs-obscurs*, ballet (Paris, Nov. 1938); *Après-midi champêtre*, ballet (Versailles, March 30, 1941); *Les Travaux et les jours*, ballet (1943); *Les Djinns*, ballet (Paris, March 11, 1944); *La Rire de Nils Halerius*, lyric legend (1944–48; Mulhouse, Jan. 19, 1951); *Le Fou*, lyric drama (1948–55; Nancy, Feb. 1, 1956); *Rabelais, François de France*, opera-ballet (Tours, July 26, 1953); *Le Ventriloque*, lyric comedy (1954–55; Paris, Feb. 6, 1956); *L'Opéra de Poussière*, lyric drama (1958–62; Avignon, Oct. 25, 1962); *Abîmes*, ballet (Essen, Feb. 12, 1959); *Les Adieux*, lyric drama (Radio Luxembourg, Nov. 1959; 1st stage perf., Paris, Oct. 8, 1960); *Le Leçon d'Anatomie*, ballet (The Hague, 1964; based on the Sym. No. 1); *Le Fantôme de l'Opéra*, ballet (1979; Paris, Feb. 22, 1980); *Les Hauts de Hurlevent*, ballet (Paris, Dec. 28, 1982); *La Sorcière du placard à balais*, children's mini-opera (Sevres, May 2, 1983); *Montségur*, lyric drama (Toulouse, Feb. 1, 1985); *La Vieille Maison*, musical (1987; Nantes, Feb. 25, 1988); *P'tit Pierre et la Sorcière du placard à balais*, children's opera (1991; Colmar, May 7, 1992); *Galina*, opera (1996); incidental music; film scores. **ORCH.:** 2 piano concertos: No. 1, *Poème* (1939–40; Paris, March 1, 1942) and No. 2 (1963; Paris, Feb. 28, 1964); *Brumes*, symphonic poem (1943; Paris, March 5, 1944); Cello Concerto (1944–45; Paris, Nov. 25, 1946); *Edina*, symphonic poem (Paris, Dec. 17, 1946); *Le Petit Poucet*, suite (1946; Cannes, Feb. 1947); *Ballet des Jeux du Monde* (1948); *Le Voyageur et la voyageuse*, suite (1948); 4 syms.: No. 1, *Jean de la Peur* (Paris, April 3, 1949), No. 2 (1964; Paris, Nov. 16, 1965), No. 3, *Les Espaces* (Strasbourg, June 24, 1965), and No. 4 (Paris, Oct. 15, 1988); *Trois histoires de la prairie*, suite (1950); Ondes Martenot Concerto (1954; Vichy, Sept. 16, 1955; also as *Concerto en trio* for Ondes Martenot, Percussion, and Piano, 1975); Bassoon Concerto (1957; Paris, June 1958); *La Passante*, suite (1958); *Mouvement* for Strings (1960); *L'Orage*, symphonic poem (1960); Concerto for Flute and Strings (Bordeaux, May 27, 1968); *Au bout de chagrin, une fenêtre ouverte*, concerto for Trumpet, Orch., and Tape (1976; Paris, June 24, 1977); *L'Horloge*, symphonic poem (Paris, May 6, 1982); *Improvisation* for Trombone and Orch. (Toulon, May 20, 1983; also for Trombone and Piano); *Les Orchestrades* (St. Libéral, Aug. 31, 1985); *Quatre préludes pour l'Opéra des Bastilles* (Paris, Dec. 12, 1989); Concertino for Trombone and Strings (Metz, July 2, 1990); *Adagio Cantabile* for Oboe, English Horn, Percussion, and Strings (1991; Paris, Jan. 7, 1992); Symphonie concertante for Organ and Orch. (1993); *Que ma joie demeure* for Violin and Strings (1994); Flute Concerto (1995); Violin Concerto (1995). **CHAMBER:** Trio for Horn, Trumpet, and Piano (1954); *Quatre préludes* for Percussion and Piano (Paris, June 1963); *Étude de sonorité* for Violin and Piano (1973; Paris, June 10, 1974); *Concerto en trio* for Ondes Martenot, Percussion, and Piano (1975; Paris, Dec. 1, 1976; also as the Ondes Martenot Concerto, 1954); *Souvenir d'un jardin d'enfance* for Oboe and Piano (Paris, June 1, 1977); *Cahier pour quatre jours* for Trumpet and Organ (1977; Munich, Feb. 1978); *Improvisation* for Trombone and Piano (1983; also for Trombone and Orch.); *Sonate brève* for Solo Cello (1985); *Blanc et feu* for Horn, 2 Trumpets, Trombone, and Tuba (1985); *Petite chanson de l'amitié* for 4 Cellos (1987–91). **PIANO:** Sonatine (1940; Paris, May 10, 1941); *Deux nocturnes* (1945); *Le Petit Poucet* (1945); *En trottinant sur le sentier* (1959). **VOCAL:** *Les Sept loups* and *Les Sorcières*, ballades for Women's Chorus and Orch. (Paris, Oct. 24, 1937); *Trois melodies* for Soprano and Orch. (1938; Cannes, Sept. 1942); *Rythmes du Monde*, oratorio (1939–41; Paris, April 26, 1941); *Desbat du cuer et du corps* for Soprano, Tenor, Violin, Cello, and Piano (1943; Paris, Jan. 20, 1944); *La Qûete sans fin*, oratorio (1943–44; Paris, March 1945); *Cantique d'actions de Grâces* for Soloist, Chorus, and Piano or Organ (1945); *Trois révérences à la mort* for Soprano and Piano (1946); *Jésus, là es-tu?*, cantata for Alto, Women's Chorus, and Piano or Strings, and Percussion (Paris, April 1948); *Le Lac d'Undeneur* for Contralto (1948–49); *Quatre chants d'Innocence* for Women's Chorus (1952); *Espoir* for Chorus, Reciter, and Orch. (1959); *Chant de Solitude* for 4 Women's Voices and Orch. (Paris, Aug. 21, 1960); *Les Notes de Nuit* for Reciter and Orch. (1961); *Aux mendiants du Ciel*, cantata for Soprano and Orch. (Fontevrault Abbey, June 11, 1966); *Messe de l'Aurore* for Soprano, Tenor, Baritone, Chorus, and Orch. (Paris, Nov. 14, 1977); *Un enfant appelle* for Soprano, Cello, and Orch. (1978; Washington, D.C., Jan. 9, 1979); *Le Pont de l'espérance*, oratorio for Soprano, Baritone, Chorus, 2 Dancers, and Orch. (Vaison-la-Romaine, Aug. 8, 1980); *La Prison* for Soprano and Orch. (1981; Aix-en-Provence, July 18, 1983; also for Soprano and Chamber Ensemble); *Chant de Paix "Ecoute ma voix . . ."* for Soprano or Child's Voice, Baritone, Children's or Mixed Chorus, and Orch. or Organ (Paris, July 4, 1985); *Help-Help Vatelot* for Soprano, Cello, Chorus, and Small Instrumental Ensemble (Paris, Nov. 1985); *Les Deux soeurs* for Vocal Quartet (Rome, June 24, 1986); *La Symphonie de Montségur* for Soprano, Baritone, and Orch. (Paris, Oct. 18, 1987); *Les Leçons des ténèbres* for Soprano, Bass, Chorus, Organ, and Cello (1991; also for Soprano, Bass, Chorus, Organ, Cello, and Instrumental Ensemble, Paris, Nov. 26, 1991, or Orch.); *Les Rois Mages*, cantata (1994).

BIBL.: C. Baigneres, *M. L.* (Paris, 1959); A. Golea, *M. L.: L'homme et son oeuvre* (Paris, 1969); F. Fabiani, "M. L.: Le musicien de l'Espérance," *La Revue Musicale*, 372–374 (1984).

Landowski, W.-L. (actually, **Alice-Wanda**), French writer on music; b. Paris, Nov. 28, 1899; d. there, April 18, 1959. She studied piano in Paris at the Marguerite Long School; also theory with Gustave Bret. She taught music history at the Clermont Cons.; in 1945, became a prof. at the Rouen Cons.; also was engaged as music critic of *Le Parisien*. She adopted the initials W.-L. (L. for Ladislas, her father's name) to avoid confusion with Wanda Landowska, who was not a relation.

WRITINGS: *L'Année Musicale* (1936–39; annual reports of musical events); *La Musique à travers les âges* (1937); *Maurice Ravel* (1938); *Les Grands Musiciens* (1938); *Histoire universelle de la musique moderne* (1941); *Histoire générale de la musique* (1945); *L'Oeuvre de Claude Delvincourt* (1947); *Chopin et Fauré* (1946); *Le Travail en musique* (1949); *La Musique américaine* (1952); *Paul Paray* (1956).

Landré, Guillaume (Louis Frédéric), important Dutch composer, son of **Willem (Guillaume Louis Frédéric) Landré**; b. The Hague, Feb. 24, 1905; d. Amsterdam, Nov. 6, 1968. He took music lessons from his father and from Zagwijn, and then from Pijper in Utrecht, where he also studied law at the Univ. (M.A., 1929). He subsequently was active as a teacher of commercial law and as a music critic in Amsterdam. He was chairman of the Dutch Music Copyright Soc. (1947–58) and president of the Soc. of Netherlands Composers (1950–62). As a composer, he endeavored to revive the spirit and the polyphonic technique of the national Flemish School of the Renaissance in a 20th-century guise, with euphonious dissonances and impressionistic dynamics creating a modern aura. In his later works, he experimented with serial devices.

WORKS: OPERAS: *De Snoek* (The Pike), comic opera (1934; Amsterdam, March 24, 1938); *Jean Lévecq*, after Maupassant (1962–63; Amsterdam, June 16, 1965); *La Symphonie pastorale*, after André Gide (1965–67; Rouen, March 31, 1968). **ORCH.:** 4 syms.: No. 1 (1932; Amsterdam, June 9, 1933), No. 2 (1942; The Hague, March 6, 1946), No. 3 (Amsterdam, June 16, 1951), and No. 4, *Symphonie concertante* (1954–55; Stockholm, June 5, 1956); *Suite* for Piano and Strings (1936); *4 Pieces* (1937); *Concert Piece* (1938); Cello Concerto (1940); *Sinfonietta* for Violin and Orch. (1941); *Symphonic Music* for Flute and Orch. (1947–48); *Sinfonia sacra in memoriam patris* (1948; Rotterdam, Nov. 7, 1948; uses motifs from his father's *Requiem*); *4 mouvements symphoniques* (1948–49; The Hague, Jan. 17, 1950); Chamber Sym. for 13 Instruments (1952; Amsterdam, Feb. 24, 1953); *Sonata festiva* for Chamber Orch. (1953); *Kaleidoscope*, symphonic variations (1956); *Symphonic Permutations* (1957); Clarinet Concerto (1958; Amsterdam, June 25, 1959); *Concertante* for Contrabass Clarinet and Orch. (1959); *Anagrams* (1960); Sonata for Chamber Orch. (1961); *Variazioni senza tema* (Amsterdam, Dec. 11, 1968). **CHAMBER:** Violin Sonata (1927); 4 string quartets (1927; 1942–43; 1949; 1965); Piano Trio (1929); 2 wind quintets (1930, 1960); *4 Miniatures* for Clarinet and String Quartet or String Orch. (1950); Sextet for Flute, Clarinet, and String Quartet (1959); *Quartetto piccolo* for 2 Trumpets, Horn, and Trombone (1961). **VOCAL:** *Piae memoriae pro patria mortuorum* for Chorus and Orch. (1942); *Groet der martelaren* (Salute to the Martyrs) for Baritone and Orch. (1943–44); *Berceuse voor moede mensen* for Soloists, Chorus, and Orch. (1952).

Landré, Willem (actually, **Guillaume Louis Frédéric**), Dutch writer on music and composer, father of **Guillaume (Louis Frédéric) Landré**; b. Amsterdam, June 12, 1874; d. Eindhoven, Jan. 1, 1948. He was a pupil of Zweers in Amsterdam. In 1901 he became music critic of the *Oprechte Haarlemsche Courant* in Haarlem; was music ed. of the *Nieuwe Courant* in The Hague (1901–05), then of the *Nieuwe Rotterdamsche Courant* in Rotterdam (1905–37). He taught theory, composition, and music history at the Rotterdam Cons.; was ed. of *Caecilia, Het Muziekcollege*.

WORKS: DRAMATIC: OPERAS: *De Roos van Dekama* (Haarlem, 1897); *Beatrijs* (The Hague, 1925). Also incidental music. **ORCH.:** *Nocturne* for Small Orch. (1921); *In memoriam matris* (1923); *Romantisch Pianoconcert* (1935). **OTHER:** Chamber music; piano pieces; vocal works, including *Requiem in memoriam uxoris* for Chorus (1931; rev. by G. Landré, 1954) and songs.

Lane, Eastwood, American composer; b. Brewerton, N.Y., May 22, 1879; d. Central Square, N.Y., Jan. 22, 1951. He attended Syracuse Univ. (1898–1901), but left before graduating; he taught himself piano but did not learn to read music until late in his life. From 1910 to 1933 he was assistant director of N.Y.'s Wanamaker Concerts. He wrote mostly piano pieces in a light, descriptive vein: *In Sleepy Hollow*, 4 tone pictures (1913); *5 American Dances* (1919); *Adirondack Sketches* (1922); *Mongoliana*, suite (1922); *Eastern Seas*, suite (1925; includes *Sea Burial*, orchestrated by F. Grofé); *Persimmon Pucker* (1926; orchestrated by F. Grofé); *Sold Down the River*, ballet suite (1928); *Pantomimes* (c.1933); *4th of July* (1935; orchestrated by F. Grofé); *Here Are Ladies*, 5 pieces (1944).

BIBL.: J. Howard, "E. L.," *Contemporary American Composers* (N.Y., 1925); N. Gentieu, "E. L.," *Journal of Jazz Studies*, III/2 (1976).

Lane, Louis, American conductor; b. Eagle Pass, Texas, Dec. 25, 1923. He studied composition with Kennan at the Univ. of Texas (B.Mus., 1943), Martinů at the Berkshire Music Center in Tanglewood (summer, 1946), and Rogers at the Eastman School of Music in Rochester, N.Y. (M.Mus., 1947); also took a course in opera with Sarah Caldwell (1950). In 1947 he became apprentice conductor to George Szell and the Cleveland Orch.; subsequently was assistant conductor (1956–60), assoc. conductor (1960–70), and resident conductor (1970–73) there; also was co-director of the Blossom Festival School (1969–73). He served as music director of the Akron (Ohio) Sym. Orch. (1959–83) and of the Lake Erie Opera Theatre (1964–72). In 1973 he became principal guest conductor of the Dallas Sym. Orch., and later held various positions with it until 1978. From 1977 to 1983 he was co-conductor of the Atlanta Sym. Orch.; then was its principal guest conductor (1983–88); also was principal guest conductor (1982–83) and principal conductor (1984–85) of the National Sym. Orch. of the South African Broadcasting Corp. in Johannesburg. As a guest conductor, he appeared with major orchs. on both sides of the Atlantic; also was adjunct prof. at the Univ. of Akron (1969–83), visiting prof. at the Univ. of Cincinnati (1973–75), and artistic adviser and conductor at the Cleveland Inst. of Music (from 1982). In 1971 he received the Mahler Medal and in 1972 the Alice M. Ditson Award; in 1979 he was named a Chevalier of the Order of Arts and Letters of France.

Lang, David, American composer; b. Los Angeles, Jan. 8, 1957. He studied with Lou Harrison, Martin Bresnick, and Leland Smith at Stanford Univ. (A.B., 1978), with Richard Hervig, Donald Jenni, and William Hibbard at the Univ. of Iowa (M.M., 1980), and with Bresnick, Druckman, Reynolds, and Subotnick at Yale Univ. (D.M.A., 1989); also trained at the Aspen (Colo.) Music Festival (summers, 1977–81) and the Berkshire Music Center in Tanglewood (summer, 1983). Among his awards were an NEA grant (1986) and the Rome Prize (1990); also BMI awards (1980, 1981). In 1987, with Michael Gordon and Julia Wolfe, he founded the international N.Y. festival BANG ON A CAN. His compositions are starkly dissonant.

WORKS: DRAMATIC: *Judith and Holofernes* (1989; Munich, April 27, 1990). **ORCH.:** *Hammer Amour* for Piano and Chamber Orch. (1979; rev. version, Sept. 25, 1989, Alan Feinberg soloist); *Eating Live Monkeys* (Cleveland, April 19, 1985, Henze conducting); *Spud* for Chamber Orch. (St. Paul, Minn., March 6, 1986); *Are You Experienced?* for Chamber Orch. (Pittsburgh, May 27, 1988); *Dance/Drop* for Chamber Orch. (Toronto, Feb. 10, 1989, composer conducting); *International Business Machine* (Boston, Aug. 25, 1990, Slatkin conducting); *Bonehead* (N.Y., 1990). **CHAMBER:** *Illumination Rounds* for Violin and Piano (N.Y., April 23, 1982); *Frag* for Flute, Oboe, and Cello (Philadelphia, Oct. 1, 1985); *Burn Notice* for Flute, Cello, and Piano (N.Y., Nov. 7, 1988); *Orpheus Over and Under* for 2 Pianos (N.Y., March 27, 1989); *The Anvil Chorus* for Percussion (1990). **VOCAL:** *By Fire* for Chorus (1984; London, June 30, 1986).

Láng, István, Hungarian composer and teacher; b. Budapest, March 1, 1933. He studied with Viski (1951–56) and Szabó (1956–58) at the Budapest Academy of Music. He pursued his career in Budapest, where he first worked at the Academy of Dramatic and Film Arts (1957–60). From 1966 to 1984 he was municipal consultant to the State Puppet Theater. He taught at the Budapest Academy of Music from 1973. From 1978 to 1990 he also was general secretary of the Assn. of Hungarian Musicians. In 1968 and 1975 he received the Erkel Prize. In 1985 he was made a Merited Artist by the Hungarian government. His music is rooted in euphonious dissonance, without venturing into fashionable ugliness.

WORKS: DRAMATIC: OPERAS: *Bernada háza* (Bernarda's House; 1959); *Pathelin mester* (Master Pathelin; Budapest, 1958); *A nagy drámaíró* (The Great Dramatist), television opera (1960; rev. 1974; Budapest, Feb. 14, 1975); *A gyáva* (The Coward; Budapest, 1968); *Álom a színházról* (A Dream about the Theater), television opera (1979–81; Budapest, March 25, 1984). **BALLETS:** *Mario és a varázsló* (Mario and the Magician), after Thomas Mann (1962); *Hiperbola* (1963; suite, 1968); *Lebukott* (Nabbed; 1968); *Csillagra-török* (Starfighters), ballet-cantata (1972; rev. 1977). **ORCH.:** Viola Concerto (1957); Concerto for Strings (1960); Xylophone Concertino (1961; rev. 1967); 4 syms.: No. 1 (1965; withdrawn and reworked as *Vari-*

azioni ed Allegro), No. 2 (1972–74), No. 3 (1981–82; Szombathely, June 7, 1982), and No. 4 (1983; Budapest, Nov. 28, 1984); *Gyászzene* (Funeral Music; 1969); *Impulsioni* for Oboe and Instrumental Groups (1969); *3 Sentences from Romeo and Juliet* for Strings (1969–70); *Concerto bucolico* for Horn and Orch. (1970–71); *Tüzoszlop* (Firepillar; 1972); *Egloga* (1976); Violin Concerto (1976–77; Budapest, May 1, 1980); Double Concerto for Clarinet, Harp, and Orch. (1979–80; Budapest, April 7, 1981); *Pezzo lirico* for Oboe and Orch. (1985); Organ Concerto (1987). **CHAMBER:** Sonata for Solo Cello (1960); 3 string quartets (1961, 1966, 1978); 3 wind quintets (1964; *Transfigurazioni*, 1965; 1975); *Monodia* for Clarinet (1965); *Dramma breve* for Flute (1970); *Cassazione* for Brass Septet (1971); *Rhymes* for Flute, Clarinet, Viola, Cello, and Piano (1972); *Villanások* (Flashes) for Violin (1973); *Improvisazioni* for Cimbalom (1973); *Constellations* for Oboe, Violin, Viola, and Clarinet (1974–75); *Surface Metamorphosis* for Tape (1975); *Constellations* for Oboe and String Trio (1975–76); *Waves II* for Flute, Guitar, and Harpsichord (1976); *2 Preludes for a Postlude* for Bass and String Trio (1977); *Music 2–4-3* for Ensemble (1979); *Prelude, 3 Mobils and Postlude* for Brass Quintet (1980); *Chagall Flies Away over His Sleeping Vitebsk* for Percussion Quartet (1985; Budapest, May 18, 1986); *Interpolations* for Bassoon (1988); *Cimbiosis* for Cimbalom and Chamber Ensemble (1991). **VOCAL:** 2 chamber cantatas: No. 1 for Soprano, Clarinet, Piano, Percussion, and Cello (1962) and No. 2, *Iocaste*, for Soprano, Flute, Clarinet, Harp, and String Trio (1979); *Pezzi* for Soprano, Flute, Clarinet, Percussion, and Viola (1964; rev. 1967); *Laudate hominem*, cantata for Chorus and Orch. (1968); *In Memoriam N. N.*, cantata for Chorus and Orch. (1971); *Fragments* for Alto, Oboe, Bassoon, and Harp (1971–72); *Waves I* for Soprano and Vibraphone (1975); *3 Songs* for Bass and Orch. (1985).

Lang, Margaret Ruthven, American composer; b. Boston, Nov. 27, 1867; d. there, May 29, 1972. She was the daughter of the American pianist, organist, conductor, teacher, and composer Benjamin J(ohnson) Lang (b. Salem, Mass., Dec. 28, 1837; d. Boston, April 3, 1909). She studied piano and composition with her father and violin with Louis Schmidt in Boston; after training in violin with Franz Dreschsler and Ludwig Abel and in counterpoint and fugue with Victor Gluth in Munich (1886–87), she returned to Boston and studied orchestration with Chadwick and MacDowell. She was the first woman composer in the U.S. to have a work performed by a major orch. when Nikisch conducted the premiere of her *Dramatic Overture* with the Boston Sym. Orch. (April 7, 1893). She stopped composing in 1917. She attended the Boston Sym. Orch. concerts from their inception in 1881; was present at a concert 3 days before her 100th birthday, at which Leinsdorf included in the program the psalm tune *Old Hundredth* in her honor.

WORKS: *Witichis*, overture (1893); *Dramatic Overture* (Boston, April 7, 1893); *Sappho's Prayer to Aphrodite* for Mezzo-soprano and Orch. (1895); *Armida* for Soprano and Orch. (1896); *Phoebus' Denunciation of the Furies at the Delphian Shrine* for Bass and Orch.; *Totila*, overture; *Ballade* for Orch. (1901); *Te Deum* for Chorus (1899); *The Lonely Rose*, cantata (1906); *The Night of the Star*, cantata (1913); *The Heavenly Noël* for Chorus (1916); etc.; about 150 songs, including the popular *An Irish Love Song* (1895); piano pieces.

Lang, Paul Henry, eminent Hungarian-born American musicologist, editor, and teacher; b. Budapest, Aug. 28, 1901; d. Lakeville, Conn., Sept. 21, 1991. He studied bassoon with Wieschendorf, chamber music with L. Weiner, composition with Kodály, and counterpoint with Koessler at the Budapest Academy of Music (graduated, 1922); then studied musicology with Kroyer and comparative literature with Ernst Curtius and Friedrich Gundorff at the Univ. of Heidelberg (1924); subsequently studied musicology with Pirro, art history with Henri Focillon, literature with Fernand Baldensperger and Félix Gaiffe, and aesthetics with Victor Basch at the Sorbonne in Paris (degree in literature, 1928). He settled in the U.S. in 1928, becoming a naturalized American citizen in 1934; studied musicology with Kinkeldey and French literature and philosophy with James Frederick Mason at Cornell Univ. (Ph.D., 1934, with the diss. *A Literary History of French Opera*). He was an assistant prof. at Vassar College (1930–31); assoc. prof., Wells College (1931–33); visiting lecturer, Wellesley College (1934–35); assoc. prof. of musicology, Columbia Univ. (1933–39; full prof., 1939; prof. emeritus, 1970). He was vice-president of the American Musicological Soc. (1947–49) and president of the International Musicological Soc. (1955–58). From 1945 to 1973 he was ed. of the *Musical Quarterly*; from 1954 to 1963, music ed. of the *N.Y. Herald Tribune*. He publ. the valuable and very popular book *Music in Western Civilization* (N.Y., 1941; many subsequent reprints) and the important and comprehensive study *George Frideric Handel* (N.Y., 1966); also ed. several vols. of articles reprinted from the *Musical Quarterly*, and the anthologies *The Concerto 1800–1900* (N.Y., 1969) and *The Symphony 1800–1900* (N.Y., 1969).

BIBL.: E. Strainchamps and M. Maniates, eds., *Music and Civilization: Essays in Honor of P. H. L.* (N.Y., 1984).

Lang, Walter, Swiss pianist, conductor, teacher, and composer; b. Basel, Aug. 19, 1896; d. Baden, Aargau canton, March 17, 1966. He was a pupil of Jaques-Dalcroze in Hellerau and Geneva. After teaching at the Jaques-Dalcroze Inst. in Geneva, he completed his studies with Klose in Munich and with Andreae and W. Frey in Zürich. He then was active as a pianist and conductor; he also taught in Basel and Bern, serving as well as prof. of piano at the Zürich Cons. (1922–41) and Academy of Music (1949–64). His wife was the soprano Mimi Lang-Seiber.

WORKS: ORCH.: *Scherzo fugato* for Strings (1929); *Sonata festiva* for Chamber Orch. (1935); Piano Concerto (1940); *Fantasie* for Violin, Cello, and Orch. (1941); Sym. (1946); *Jour de Fête*, overture (1947); Cello Concerto (1951); *Konzertante Suite* for 2 Pianos and Strings (1954); *Divertimento* for Strings (1957). **CHAMBER:** String Quartet (1919); 2 violin sonatas (1920, 1939); Piano Trio (1925); Flute Sonata (1956); many piano pieces.

Langdon, Michael (real name, **Frank Birtles**), English bass; b. Wolverhampton, Nov. 12, 1920; d. Hove, Sussex, March 12, 1991. He studied at the Guildhall School of Music in London; subsequently took voice lessons with Alfred Jerger in Vienna, Maria Carpi in Geneva, and Otakar Kraus in London. In 1948 he joined the chorus at the Royal Opera House, Covent Garden, London; made his operatic debut there in 1950. In subsequent years, he sang with many of the major opera houses of the world. On Nov. 2, 1964, he made his Metropolitan Opera debut in N.Y. as Baron Ochs. He created several bass roles in operas by Benjamin Britten; was also noted for his command of the standard operatic repertoire. After his retirement from the stage in 1977, he was director of the National Opera Studio (1978–86). In 1973 he was made a Commander of the Order of the British Empire. He publ. *Notes from a Low Singer* (with R. Fawkes; London, 1982).

Lange, Francisco Curt (actually, **Franz Curt**), German musicologist; b. Eilenburg, Dec. 12, 1903. He received training in architecture in Munich (diploma, 1927) and pursued his musical studies at the Univs. of Leipzig, Berlin, Munich, and Bonn (Ph.D., 1929, with the diss. *Über die Mehrstimmigket der Niederländischen Motetten*). In 1930 he went to Uruguay, where he founded the Instituto Interamericano de Musicologicá in 1938, which publ. works via its Editorial Cooperativo Interamericano de Compositores (1941–56); he also ed. the *Boletín Latino-Americano de Música* (from 1935) and the *Revista de estudios musicales* (1949–56). In 1943 he was made a corresponding member of the American Musicological Soc.

Langendorff, Frieda, German contralto; b. Breslau, March 24, 1868; d. N.Y., June 11, 1947. She was a student of J. Meyer, M. Mallinger, and A. Iffert. In 1901 she made her operatic debut in Strasbourg. After appearing at Bayreuth (1904), she sang at the German Theatre in Prague (1905–07). On Dec. 7, 1907, she made her Metropolitan Opera debut in N.Y. as Ortrud, remaining on its roster until 1908, and returning in 1910–11. After singing at the Berlin Kroll Opera (1909–11), she gave concerts in the U.S. (1912–13). From 1914 to 1916 she was a member of the Dresden Court Opera. Among her best roles were Dalila, Azucena, Amneris, and Fricka.

Langenus, Gustave, Belgian-American clarinetist and teacher; b. Mechelen, Aug. 6, 1883; d. N.Y., Jan. 30, 1957. He studied at the Brussels Cons. As a youth of 18, he traveled with Sousa's band in Europe; then lived in England. In 1910 he settled in the U.S.; was a clarinetist with the N.Y. Sym. Orch. (1910–20) and the N.Y. Phil. (1920–23). He taught at the Juilliard School of Music and the Dalcroze School of Music. He publ. *Fingered Scale Studies for the Boehm Clarinet* (N.Y., 1911); *Modern Clarinet Playing* (N.Y., 1913); *Virtuoso Studies and Duos for Clarinet* (N.Y., 1915); *Complete Method for the Boehm Clarinet* (8 vols., N.Y., 1916).

Langer, Suzanne K(atherina), important American philosopher of musical aesthetics; b. N.Y., Dec. 20, 1895; d. Old Lyme, Conn., July 17, 1985. She studied philosophy at Radcliffe College (Ph.D., 1926) and at the Univ. of Vienna, her principal teachers being Whitehead and Cassirer. She held teaching positions at Radcliffe and Columbia Univ., then became a prof. at Conn. College in 1954, retiring in 1962. Her publications center on a philosophy of art derived from a theory of musical meaning, which in turn exemplify a general philosophy of mind. According to her theory, modes of understanding are forms of symbolic transformation, i.e., one understands any phenomenon by constructing an object analogous to it or referring to it. She extended this theory to argue that the patterns of musical form are structurally similar to those of human feelings. She later expanded this into a general theory of the fine arts, her final work suggesting that art criticism might form the basis of a new structure for the behavioral sciences. Her lucid, strong-minded writings are widely considered crucial in understanding musical aesthetics.

WRITINGS: *The Practice of Philosophy* (N.Y., 1930); *Philosophy in a New Key* (Cambridge, Mass., 1942); *Feeling and Form* (N.Y., 1953); *Problems of Art* (N.Y., 1957); *Mind: An Essay in Human Feeling* (3 vols., Baltimore, 1967–72).

Langgaard, Rued (Immanuel), distinguished Danish composer and organist; b. Copenhagen, July 28, 1893; d. Ribe, July 10, 1952. His father, Siegfried Langgaard (1852–1914), a student of Liszt, pursued a career as a pianist, composer, and teacher at the Royal Academy of Music in Copenhagen; his mother, Emma Foss, was a pianist. He began his musical training with his parents, then studied organ with G. Helsted, violin with C. Petersen, and theory with V. Rosenberg in Copenhagen. He made his debut as an organist at age 11; subsequently was intermittently active as a church organist until becoming organist of Ribe Cathedral (1940). His early works were influenced by Liszt, Gade, Wagner, and Bruckner; following a period in which he was at times highly experimental (1916–24), he returned to his Romantic heritage; however, even in his last period of production, he produced some works with bizarre and polemical overtones. During his lifetime, he was almost totally neglected in official Danish music circles and failed to obtain an important post. A quarter century after he died, his unperformed works were heard for the first time.

WORKS: DRAMATIC: *Antikrist*, biblical opera (1921–39; Danish Radio, June 28, 1980). **ORCH.:** 16 syms.: No. 1, *Klippepastoraler* (Rock Pastorals; 1908–11; Berlin, April 10, 1913), No. 2, *Vaarbrud* (Awakening of Spring), for Soprano and Orch. (1912–14; Copenhagen, Nov. 17, 1914; rev. 1926–33; Danish Radio, May 21, 1948), No. 3, *Ungdomsbrus* (Youthfulness), for Piano, Chorus ad libitum, and Orch. (1915–16; April 9, 1918; rev. 1925?–29; Danish Radio, May 4, 1934), No. 4, *Løvfald* (Falling Leaves; 1916; Copenhagen, Dec. 7, 1917), No. 5, *Steppenatur* (1917–18, 1920, 1931; 1st version, rev. 1926; Copenhagen, April 11, 1927; 2nd version, Copenhagen, July 8, 1937), No. 6, *Det Himmelrivende* (Tearing the Heavens; 1919–20; Karlsruhe, Jan. 15, 1923; rev. c.1926–30; Danish Radio, May 29, 1935), No. 7, *Ved Tordenskjold i Holmens Kirke* (By Tordenskjold's Tomb in Holmen's Church; 1925–26; Copenhagen, March 8, 1926; rev. 1930–32; Danish Radio, Dec. 10, 1935), No. 8, *Minder om Amalienborg* (Memories at Amalienborg), for Tenor, Chorus, and Orch. (1926–28; rev. 1932–34; not perf.), No. 9, *Fra Dronning Dagmars By* (From the Town of Queen Dagmar; 1942; Copenhagen, May 31, 1943), No. 10, *Hin Tordenbolig* (Yon Dwelling of Thunder; 1944–45; Danish Radio, July 22, 1947), No. 11, *Ixion* (1944–45; Odense, July 29, 1968), No. 12, *Hélsingeborg* (1946; Danish Radio, July 22, 1977), No. 13, *Undertro* (Belief in Miracles; 1947; Danish Radio, Oct. 21, 1970), No. 14, *Morgenen* (The Morning), for Chorus and Orch. (1948; Copenhagen, May 24, 1979), No. 15, *Søstormen* (The Gale at Sea), for Baritone, Men's Chorus, and Orch. (1937–49; Danish Radio, Nov. 23, 1976), and No. 16, *Syndflod af sol* (Flood of Sun; 1950–51; Danish Radio, March 17, 1966); *Heltedøød* (Death of a Hero; 1907); *Drapa* (1907); *Sfinx*, tone picture (1909–10); *Saga blot* (A Thing of the Past; 1917–18); Violin Concerto (1943–44; Danish Radio, July 29, 1968). **CHAMBER:** 8 string quartets (1914–31); 5 violin sonatas (1915–49); Septet for Wind Instruments (1915); *Humoreske* for 5 Wind Instruments and Drum (1923); *Dies irae* for Tuba and Piano (1948); Quartet for Brass Instruments (1949); about 50 works for piano, including 6 sonatas; organ music, including *Messis (Høstens tid)* (Messis [The Time of Harvest]), drama in 3 "evenings" (1932–39), and some 100 preludes. **VOCAL:** *Musae triumphantes*, cantata for Soloists, Men's Chorus, and Orch. (1906); *Drømmen* (The Dream) for Soloists, Chorus, and Orch. (1915–16; rev. 1945); *Angelus* (The Gold Legend) for Soloists, Chorus, and Orch. (1915–37); *Sfaerernes musik* (Music of the Spheres) for Soprano, Chorus, and Orch. (1916–18; Karlsruhe, Nov. 26, 1921); *Endens tid* (The Time of the End; 1921–44); *Fra Højsangen* (From the Song of Solomon), 6 works for Solo Voice and Orch. or Ensemble (1949; Danish Radio, Feb. 24, 1969); *Fra Dybet* (From the Deep) for Chorus and Orch. (1950–52); about 25 motets and 150 songs.

BIBL.: B. Nielsen, "Pettersson and L.," *Nordic Sounds* (March 1988); idem, *R. L.s Kompositioner: Annoteret vaerkfortegnelse* (Odense, 1991); idem, *R. L.: Biografi* (Copenhagen, 1993).

Langlais, Jean (François-Hyacinthe), admired blind French organist, teacher, and composer; b. La Fontenelle, Feb. 15, 1907; d. Paris, May 8, 1991. He was blind from birth. His life was centered on Paris, where he first studied at the Institution des Jeunes Aveugles (1917–30), his principal mentor being Marchal for organ; he then pursued his training at the Cons. with Dupré (organ; premier prix, 1930), N. Gallon (counterpoint), Dukas (composition; 2nd prix, 1935), and Tournemire (improvisation). From 1930 to 1968 he was a prof. at the Institution des Jeunes Aveugles, and from 1961 to 1976 he was prof. of organ and composition at the Schola Cantorum. After serving as organist at Notre-Dame de la Croix and at St.-Pierre de Montrouge (1935–45), he held that position at Ste.-Clotilde (1945–77). He also made tours as a concert artist in Europe, and in 1952 he made his first visit to the U.S. In 1988 he gave his farewell recital at London's Royal Festival Hall. In his compositions, Langlais displayed an adroit use of polymodal harmonies, Gregorian themes, hymn tunes, and Breton folk melodies.

WORKS: ORCH.: *Cloches* (1935); *Essai sur L'évangile de Noël* (1935; Lyons, Feb. 1936); *Hymne d'action des grâces* (1935; Lyons, Feb. 1936); *Piece in Free Form* for Organ and Orch. (1935; Paris, Jan. 28, 1936; also for Organ and String Quartet); *Suite concertante* for Cello and Orch. (1936); *Pièce symphonique* (1937); *Theme, Variations, and Finale* (1937; Paris, June 1938; rev. as *Theme and Variations* for Organ, Brass, and Strings, N.Y., April 21, 1978); *Le Diable qui n'est à personne* for Ondes Martenot and Orch. (1946; Paris, Feb. 14, 1947); *Légende de St. Julien l'hospitalier* (1947; Paris, March 8, 1948); *Premier Concerto* for Organ or Harpsichord and Orch.

(1949); *Le Soleil se leve sur Assise* (Paris, Dec. 30, 1950); *Deuxième Concerto* for Organ and Orch. (1961; Cleveland Heights, Ohio, May 11, 1962); *Troisième Concerto: Reaction* (1971; Potsdam, N.Y., March 2, 1978); *Réminiscences* (Quimper, Aug. 6, 1980). **CHAMBER:** *Ave Maria Stella* for Organ and Horn (1934); *Fantaisie: Pièce en forme libre* for Piano and String Quartet (1935); Trio for Flute, Violin, and Viola (Paris, Feb. 9, 1935); *Ligne* for Cello (1937); *Suite bretonne* for Strings (Paris, Dec. 21, 1938); Duo for Violin and Cello, *Suite concertante* (1943); *Pièces* for Violin and Piano (1951); *Sonnerie* for 4 Trumpets and 4 Trombones (1961); *Elégie* for Flute, Oboe, Clarinet, Horn, Bassoon, and String Quintet (1965; Rennes, March 21, 1966); *Pièce* for Trumpet and Organ (1971; Pittsburgh, April 26, 1972); *Sept Chorals* for Trumpet and Organ (1972); *Diptyque* for Piano and Organ (French Radio, Feb. 11, 1974); Sonatine for Trumpet and Organ (1976; Pittsburgh, April 25, 1978); *Pastorale et rondo* for 2 Trumpets and Organ (1982); *Petite Rapsodie* for Flute and Piano (1983); *Mouvement* for Flute or Oboe or Violin (Pittsburgh, Oct. 6, 1987); *Vitrail* for Clarinet and Piano (1987). **PIANO:** Suite for Piano, 4-hands (1934; rev. 1947); *Prélude et Fugue* (1936); *Suite armoricaine* (Paris, May 3, 1938); *Petite Suite* (1986); *Noël breton* (1987). **ORGAN:** *Prélude et Fugue* (1927); *Trois Poèmes évangéliques* (Paris, May 29, 1932); 3 syms.: No. 1 (1941–42; Paris, June 1943), No. 2 (1959; rev. 1979; Paris, May 31, 1982), and No. 3 (Elsah, Ill., April 3, 1977); *Suite française* (1948; Lorraine Radio, May 8, 1949); *Hommage à Frescobaldi* (1951); *Suite folklorique* (1952); *Organ Book* (1956); *American Suite* (1959–60); *Mosaïque I* (1959, 1976; Pittsburgh, Oct. 21, 1976), *II* (1976; Pittsburgh, Sept. 15, 1977), and *III* (1977; Pittsburgh, April 25, 1978); *Homage to J.Ph. Rameau* (1962–64; N.Y., July 20, 1965); *Poem of Life* (1965); *Poem of Peace* (1965; Washington, D.C., Jan. 16, 1967); *Poem of Happiness* (1966; Paris, May 17, 1969); *Sonate en trio* (1967); *Offrande à Marie* (1971; Washington, D.C., Aug. 20, 1972); *Cinq Méditations sur l'Apocalypse* (1973; Paris, April 11, 1974); *Suite baroque* (Mulhouse, Dec. 2, 1973); *Trois Esquisses gothiques* for 2 Organs (1975; Washington, D.C., Oct. 29, 1976); *Triptych grégorien* (Pittsburgh, Sept. 14, 1978); *Prélude et Allegro* (1982; Cardiff, May 28, 1983); *Huit Préludes* (Pittsburgh, Sept. 9, 1984); *B.A.C.H.*, 6 pieces (Paris, Dec. 21, 1985); *Talitha Koum: Resurrection* (Paris, Nov. 18, 1985); *American Folk Hymn Settings* (St. Louis, June 8, 1986); *Fantasy on 2 Scottish Themes* (1986; Edinburgh, June 10, 1987); many other pieces. **VOCAL:** *Deux Psaumes* for 4 Mixed Voices and Orch. or Piano or Organ (1937; Paris, March 19, 1938); *Psaume solennel I* for Choruses, Organ, Brass, and Timpani (1937; Boys Town, Nebr., Aug. 30, 1963), *II* for Choruses, Organ, and Optional Brass (1963; Providence, R.I., March 7, 1965), and *III* for Choruses, Organ, and Optional Brass (1964; Hartford, Conn., March 7, 1965); *Mystère du vendredi saint* for Chorus, Orch., and Organ (Montrouge, April 23, 1943); *Pie Jésu* for Soprano or Tenor, 2 Violins, Cello, Organ, and Harpsichord (1943; also for Soloists and Orch.); *Trois Motets* for Voice and Orch. or Organ (1943); *La Ville d'Ys* for Soprano, Chorus, and Orch. (1945; Paris, Dec. 19, 1948); *Cantate à St. Vincent de Paul* for Chorus and String Orch. or Organ (1946); *Messe solennelle* for 4 Mixed Voices, Congregation, and 2 Organs or Brass and Organ (1949; Paris, Oct. 15, 1950); *Cantate de Noël* for Soloists, Choruses, and 12 Instruments (Paris, Dec. 25, 1951); *Missa Salve Regina* for Men's Chorus, Congregation, Trumpets, Trombones, and Organs (Paris, Dec. 25, 1954); *La Passion* for 8 Soloists, Narrator, Choruses, and Orch. (1957; Paris, March 27, 1958); *Le Mystère du Christ* for Narrator, Soloists, Chorus, and Orch. (1957); *Psalm 150: Praise Ye the Lord* for Men's Voices and Organ (1958; Boston, Jan. 10, 1959); *Canticle of the Sun* for 3 Treble Voices and Instruments (1965; Philadelphia, March 7, 1967); *Solemn Mass* for 4 Mixed Voices, Congregation, Organ, and Brass (Washington, D.C., Nov. 1, 1969); *Hymn of Praise: Te Deum Laudamus* for 4 Mixed Voices, Congregation, Organ, Trumpets, and Percussion (1973); *Psaume 111: Beatus Via Qui Timet Dominum* for 4 Mixed Voices and Organ (1977; Cambridge, Mass., April 21, 1978); *Hymne de soir* for Men's Voices (Paris, May 14, 1984); *A Morning Hymn* for 4 Mixed Voices and Organ or Piano (1985; San Francisco, Jan. 12, 1986); *Ubi caritas* for 4 Mixed Voices and Organ (Boston, Oct. 12, 1986); *Mort et résurrection: In memoriam Jehan Alain* (1990); numerous other sacred and secular pieces, including songs.

BIBL.: R. Nyquist, *The Use of Gregorian Chant in the Organ Music of J. L.* (diss., Indiana Univ., 1968); K. Thomerson, *J. L.: A Bio-Bibliography* (Westport, Conn., 1988).

Langridge, Philip (Gordon), esteemed English tenor; b. Hawkhurst, Kent, Dec. 16, 1939. He studied violin at the Royal Academy of Music in London; took voice lessons with Bruce Boyce and Celia Bizony. He was active as a violinist but also began to make appearances as a singer from 1962. He first sang at the Glyndebourne Festival in 1964, and made regular appearances there from 1977; also sang at the Edinburgh Festivals from 1970. He appeared at Milan's La Scala in 1979; then sang for the first time at London's Covent Garden as the Fisherman in Stravinsky's *The Nightingale* in 1983. He made his Metropolitan Opera debut in N.Y. as Ferrando in *Così fan tutte* on Jan. 5, 1985. He was chosen to create the role of Orpheus in Birtwistle's opera *The Mask of Orpheus* at London's English National Opera in 1986. In 1992 he appeared as Stravinsky's Oedipus Rex at the inaugural operatic production at the Saito Kinen Festival in Matsumoto. He was made a Commander of the Order of the British Empire in 1994. Admired as both an operatic and a concert singer, Langridge maintains an extensive repertoire ranging from the Baroque masters to contemporary works. He is married to **Ann Murray**.

Lankester, Michael (John), English conductor; b. London, Nov. 12, 1944. He studied at the Royal College of Music in London (1962–67). After making his formal conducting debut with the English Chamber Orch. in London (1967), he was a conductor (1969–80) and head of the opera dept. (1975–80) at the Royal College of Music; also was founder-conductor of Contrapuncti (1967–79) and music director of the National Theatre of Great Britain (1969–74) and of the Surrey Phil. (1974–79). He was assistant conductor (1980–82), assoc. conductor (1982–84), and conductor-in-residence (1984–88) of the Pittsburgh Sym. Orch.; was also music director of the Hartford (Conn.) Sym. Orch. (from 1986).

Lansky, Paul, American composer and teacher; b. N.Y., June 18, 1944. He was a student of Perle and Weisgall at Queens College of the City Univ. of N.Y. (B.A., 1966) and of Babbitt, Cone, and Kim at Princeton Univ. (Ph.D., 1973, with the diss. *Affine Music*). In 1965–66 he played horn in the Dorian Wind Quintet. He taught at Princeton Univ. (from 1969), where he also served as dept. chair (1990–97). He received NEA fellowships (1981, 1988, 1992), an American Academy and Instute of Arts and Letters Award (1977), and commissions from the Koussevitzky Fdn. (1981) and the Fromm Fdn. (1985). He served on the boards of *Perspectives of New Music*, the Fromm Foundation, and the International Music Assn. In 1994, with Joel Chadabe and Neil Rolnick, he founded the Electronic Music Foundation in Albany, N.Y.

WORKS: CHAMBER: *Modal Fantasy* for Piano (1970); *Fanfare* for 2 Horns (1976); *Crossworks* for Piano, Flute, Clarinet, Violin, and Cello (1978); *Dance Suite* for Piano (1977); *Serenade* for Violin, Viola, and Piano (1978); *As If* for String Trio and Tape (1981–82); *Values of Time* for String Quartet, Wind Quartet, and Tape (1987); *Stroll* for Piano, Flute, Cello, Marimba, and Tape (1988); *Hop* for Marimba and Violin (1993); *Dancetracks, for an Improvising Guitarist* for Electric Guitar and Tape (1994). **COMPUTER:** *mild und leise* (1973); *Artifice (on Ferdinand's Reflection)* (1975–76); *Six Fantasies on a Poem by Thomas Campion* (1978–79); *Folk-Images* (1980–91); *As it grew dark* (1983); *Guy's Harp* (1984); *Idle Chatter* (1985); *Wasting* (1985; in collaboration with B. Garton and A. Milburn); *just_more_idle_chatter* (1987); *Notjustmoreidlechatter* (1988); *Smalltalk* (1988); *The Lesson* (1989); *Talkshow* (1989); *Not So Heavy Metal* (1989); *Late August* (1989); *QuakerBridge* (1990);

NightTraffic (1990); *The Sound of Two Hands* (1990); *Table's Clear* (1990); *Now and Then* (1991); *Word Color* (1992); *Memory Pages* (1993); *Still Time* (1994). **VOCAL:** *Three Campion Choruses* for Chorus (1992).

Lanza, Alcides (Emigdio), Argentine-born Canadian pianist, conductor, teacher, and composer; b. Rosario, June 2, 1929. He studied piano with Arminda Canteros in Rosario (1951–52) before going to Buenos Aires to pursue musical training with Ruwin Erlich (1952–59) and Julián Bautista (1960–63); then attended the Instituto Di Tella there (1963–64), where he had advanced training in composition with Copland, Ginastera, Maderna, Malipiero, and Messiaen, and in piano with Loriod. Upon being awarded a Guggenheim fellowship, he went to N.Y. and studied with Ussachevsky and Mimaroglu at the Columbia-Princeton Electronic Music Center (1965–67). After serving as an instructor there (1967–70), he was a prof. of composition at McGill Univ. in Montreal (1971–93) as well as director of its electronic music studio (1974–93). In 1972–73 he was composer-in-residence at the Deutscher Akademischer Austauschdienst in Berlin. In 1976 he became a naturalized Canadian citizen. As a pianist and conductor, he has energetically promoted the cause of contemporary music, especially avant-garde works. As a composer, he has explored the realms of electronics and multimedia in many of his scores.

WORKS: ORCH.: *Transformaciones* for Chamber Orch. (1959); *Eidesis Sinfónica I* (1963), *III* for 1 or 2 Orchs. and Tape (1971), *V* for Chamber Orch. (1981), and *VI* for Strings and Piano (1983); 2 piano concertos: No. 1 for Amplified Piano and Orch. (1964) and No. 2 for Piano and Chamber Orch. (1993); *Bour-drones* for Strings (1985); Concerto for Amplified or Electric Guitar and Orch. (1988). **CHAMBER:** *Concierto de Cámara* for Chamber Ensemble (1960); Trio-Concertante for Any 3 Instruments (1962); *Cuarteto IV* for 4 Horns (1964) and *V* for String Quartet (1967); *Interferences I* for 2 Groups of Winds and Tape (1966), *II* for Percussion Ensemble and Tape (1967), and *III* for Chamber Ensemble and Tape (1983); *Acúfenos I* for Trombone and 4 Instruments (1966), *II* for Chamber Ensemble and Electronics (1971), *III* for Flute, Piano, and Tape (1977), *IV* for Wind Quintet (1978), and *V* for Trumpet, Piano, and Tape (1980); *Eidesis II* for 13 Instruments (1967) and *IV* for Wind Ensemble and Electronics (1977); *Strobo I* for Double Bass, Percussion, and Tape (1967); *Ekphonesis I* for String and/or Keyboard Instrument and Tape (1968) and *III* for Wind, Keyboard, String Instruments, and Tape (1969); *Penetrations II* for Wind, String, Percussion and/or Keyboard Instruments, and Tape (1969); *Hip'nos I* for 1 or More Instruments (1973); *Sensors I* for Percussion Ensemble (1976), *II* for Multiple Trombones (1980), *III* for Organ and Percussion (1982), *V* for Solo Percussion and Percussion Ensemble (1985), and *VI* for Percussion Ensemble (1986); *Módulos III* for Guitar and Chamber Ensemble (1983) and *IV* for Amplified or Electric Guitar and Tape (1986); *Arghanum I* for Accordion, Clarinets, Percussion, and Synthesizer (1986), *II* for Flute, Contrabass, and Chamber Ensemble (1987), and *V* for Accordion or Piano and Tape (1990); *Quodlibet, stylus luxurians* for Organ and Chamber Ensemble (1991). **PIANO:** *Toccata* (1957); *Plectros II* for Piano and Tape (1966), *III* for Piano, Synthesizer, and Tape (1971), and *IV* for 2 Pianists of the Opposite Sex and Tape (1974); *Preludio (Preludio)* (1989). **VOCAL:** *3 Songs* for Soprano and Chamber Ensemble (1963); *Ekphonesis II* for Voice, Piano, and Tape (1968), *V* for Actress-Singer and Tape (1979), and *VI* for Actress-Singer and Tape (1988); *Penetrations VI* for Actress-Singer, Tape, and Chamber Ensemble (1972) and *VII* for Actress-Singer and Tape (1972); *Kron'ikelz 75* for 2 Solo Voices, Chamber Ensemble, and Tape (1975); *Ekphonesis VI* for Actress-Singer and Tape (1988); *Un mondo imaginario* for Chorus and Tape (1989); *The Freedom of Silence* for Voice, Piano, and Tape (1990); *Vôo* for Acting Voice and Tape (1992). **OTHER:** Electronic and tape pieces.

Lanza, Mario (real name, **Alfredo Arnold Cocozza**), popular American tenor and actor; b. Philadelphia, Jan. 31, 1921; d. Rome, Oct. 7, 1959. He studied voice in Philadelphia and then attended the Berkshire Music Center in Tanglewood (summer, 1942) on a scholarship. Subsequently he was drafted and served in the U.S. Army Air Force, during which time he sang in productions of Frank Loesser's *On the Beam* and was a cast member in the *Winged Victory* show. After his discharge in 1945, he went to N.Y. and pursued further vocal training with Rosati. In 1946 he made an impressive appearance as a concert singer at Chicago's Grant Park. In 1947 he scored a major success as a concert artist at the Hollywood Bowl, and that same year he toured the U.S. and Europe as a member of the Bel Canto Trio with Frances Yeend and George London. In 1948 he made his only professional appearances on the operatic stage when he appeared in *Madama Butterfly* at the New Orleans Opera. Lanza then went to Hollywood, where he won a starring role in the film *That Midnight Kiss* (1949). Its success led to his appearance in the film *The Toast of New Orleans* (1950), which included his version of the song *Be My Love.* His recording of the song sold a million copies and made Lanza a rising star. Then followed his starring role in *The Great Caruso* (1951), a film made memorable by his rendition of the song *The Loveliest Night of the Year.* His recording of the song also sold a million copies. Subsequently he starred in the film *Because You're Mine* (1952). His recording of the theme song of the same title likewise sold a million copies. By this time, Lanza's tempermental outbursts, heavy drinking, and overeating had taken a heavy toll. During his filming of *The Student Prince* in 1953, he walked out on the project and only avoided damaging litigation for breach of contract by waiving his rights to the soundtrack. Ironically, the recording of the soundtrack preserved some of his finest singing. After starring in one more Hollywood film, *Serenade* (1956), Lanza settled in Rome. He appeared in the film *The 7 Hills of Rome* (1958), which was made in the Eternal City and made memorable by his performance of the song *Arrivederci, Roma.* In 1958 he appeared at London's Royal Albert Hall and at the Royal Variety Show, and then toured throughout Europe. His last film appearance was in *For the First Time* (1959). While Lanza's death at only 38 in a Rome hospital was initially attributed to a heart attack, rumors later cropped up that he was murdered on orders of the Mafia after refusing to appear at a mobster-organized concert sponsored by Lucky Luciano.

BIBL.: R. Strait and T. Robinson, *L.: His Tragic Life* (N.Y., 1980).

Laparra, Raoul, French composer and music critic; b. Bordeaux, May 13, 1876; d. in an air raid in Suresnes, near Paris, April 4, 1943. He studied at the Paris Cons. (1890–1903) with Diemer, Fauré, Gédalge, and Lavignac; won the Grand Prix de Rome with his cantata *Ulysse* (June 27, 1903). He was music critic of *Le Matin*, resigning in 1937 to dedicate himself entirely to composition. He was at his best in music inspired by Spanish subjects.

WORKS: DRAMATIC: OPERAS: *Peau d'âne* (Bordeaux, Feb. 3, 1899); *La Habanera* (Paris, Feb. 26, 1908); *La Jota* (Paris, April 26, 1911); *Le Joueur de viole* (Paris, Dec. 24, 1925); *Las toreras* (Lille, Jan. 17, 1929); *L'Illustre Fregona* (Paris, Feb. 16, 1931). **INCIDENTAL MUSIC TO:** *El Conquistador.* **ORCH.:** *Un Dimanche basque*, suite for Piano and Orch.

Laplante, (Joseph) André (Roger), Canadian pianist; b. Rimouski, Quebec, Nov. 12, 1949. He commenced piano studies at 7, then continued his training with Nathalie Pépin and Yvonne Hubert at the École Vincent-d'Indy in Montreal (B.Mus., 1968; M.Mus., 1970); then pursued further studies with Gorodnitzki at the Juilliard School in N.Y. (1970–71; 1976–78) and with Lefébure in Paris (1971–74). He won 3rd prizes in the Long-Thibaud (Paris, 1973) and Sydney (1977) competitions, and then shared 2nd prize at the Tchaikovsky Competition in Moscow (1978); made his N.Y. recital debut (Oct. 21, 1978), and subsequently toured throughout North America, Europe, and the Far East. In 1988 he organized his own trio with the violinist Ernö Sebestyén and the cellist Martin Ostertag. He won accolades for his performances of the Romantic repertoire.

Laporte, André, Belgian composer and teacher; b. Oplinter, July 12, 1931. He received training in musicology and philosophy at the Catholic Univ. in Louvain (graduated, 1956), and then was a student of Flor Peeters (organ) and Marinus de Jong (counterpoint) at the Lemmens Inst. in Mechelen (1956–58), where he received the Lemmens-Tinel Prize for organ, piano, and composition (1958); subsequently he attended the courses in new music in Darmstadt (1960–65). In 1963 he joined the staff of the Belgian Radio and Television in Brussels, where he later served as manager of its Phil. Orch. (from 1988). In 1968 he became a teacher of theory and analysis at the Brussels Cons., and then taught composition there from 1988. He also taught composition at the Chapelle Musicale Reine Elisabeth from 1990. In 1971 and 1976 he was awarded the Koopal Prize of the Belgian Ministry of Culture. His oratorio *La vita non è sogno* won the Italia Prize in 1976. In 1991 he was made a member of the Belgian Royal Academy.

WORKS: OPERA: *Das Schloss* (1981–85). **ORCH.:** *Night Music* (1970); *Transit* for 48 Strings (1978–79); *Fantasia-Rondino con tema reale* for Violin and Orch. (1989). **CHAMBER:** *Introduction and Fughetta* for Guitar (1956); *Sequenza I* for Clarinet (1964) and *II* for Bass Clarinet and 3 Clarinets (1965); *Jubilius* for 12 Brasses and 3 Percussion (1966); *Ludus fragilis* for Oboe (1967); *Story* for 3 Viola da Gambas and Harpsichord (1967); *Inclinations* for Flute (1968); *Alliances* for Cello and Piano (1968); *Reflection* for Clarinet (1970); *Péripétie* for Brass Sextet (1973); *Harry's Wonderland* for Bass Clarinet and 2 Tapes (1976); *Incontro notturno* for 13 Winds and Percussion (1976); *Icarus's Flight* for Piano and 13 Strings (1977); *Variaties op een akkoord* for Recorder and Wind Quintet (1979); *A Flemish Round* for Clarinet, Trombone, Cello, and Piano (1980); *C-isme* for Cello (1984). **PIANO:** Sonata (1954); *Ascension* (1967). **VOCAL:** *Psalm* for 6 Voices and Brass (1956); *De profundis* for Chorus (1968); *Le morte chitarre* for Tenor, Flute, and 14 Strings (1969); *La vita non è sogno*, oratorio for Narrator, Tenor, Baritone, Chorus, and Orch. (Ghent, Sept. 13, 1972); *Chamber Music* for Soprano, Flute, Clarinet, Violin, and Piano (1973).

La Prade, Ernest, American violinist and composer; b. Memphis, Tenn., Dec. 20, 1889; d. Sherman, Conn., April 20, 1969. He studied violin at the Cincinnati College of Music, at the Royal Cons. in Brussels with César Thomson, and in London with J. Jongen (composition). He subsequently taught at the Cincinnati College of Music; was a member of the Cincinnati Sym. Orch. (1909–12), the Belgian and Holbrook Quartets in London (1914–17), and the N.Y. Sym. Orch. (1919–28); in 1929, he joined the staff of NBC; in 1950, became supervisor of music research there. He wrote a comic opera, *Xantha* (London, 1917), and songs. He publ. *Alice in Orchestralia* (1925), *Marching Notes* (1929), and *Broadcasting Music* (1947).

La Presle, Jacques de, French composer and teacher; b. Versailles, July 5, 1888; d. Paris, May 6, 1969. He studied at the Paris Cons.; received the Grand Prix de Rome in 1921; in 1937, was appointed prof. of harmony at the Paris Cons. His works included *Apocalypse de St.-Jean* (1928); *Album d'images*, suite for Orch. (1935); Piano Concerto (1949); chamber music; songs.

Laquai, Reinhold, Swiss composer and teacher; b. Zürich, May 1, 1894; d. Oberrieden, Oct. 3, 1957. He studied at the Zürich Cons.; later with Busoni in Berlin. In 1920 he became a teacher at the Zürich Cons. Among his compositions were 2 operas *Der Schleier der Tanit* and *Die Revisionsreise*; many orch. works, including 3 syms., 5 overtures, 2 serenades, a concert piece for Piano and Orch., etc.; chamber music, including trios; sonatas for violin, flute, cello, bassoon, horn, clarinet, etc.; Piano Quintet; piano pieces; and more than 200 songs.

Lara-Bareiro, Carlos, Paraguayan composer; b. Capiatá, March 6, 1914. He played in the boy scout band conducted by his father; then studied violin in Asunción and Rio de Janeiro; during his stay in Brazil, he also took lessons in composition and conducting. Returning to Paraguay in 1951, he organized in Asunción the Sym. Orch. of the Assn. of Musicians of Paraguay. Eventually he moved to Buenos Aires. His works reflected the modes and moods of Paraguayan folk music. He wrote several symphonic suites on Paraguayan themes and a Piano Concerto.

Larchet, John F(rancis), Irish composer and teacher; b. Dublin, July 13, 1884; d. there, Aug. 10, 1967. He studied in Dublin with Esposito at the Royal Irish Academy of Music before completing his training at the Univ. (Mus.B., 1915; Mus.D., 1917). From 1907 to 1934 he was music director of Dublin's Abbey Theatre. He also was prof. of composition at the Royal Irish Academy of Music (1920–55) and prof. of music at Univ. College, Dublin. He composed the orch. works *Lament for Youth* (1939), *Dirge of Oisin* for Strings (1940), and *By the Waters of Moyle* (1957), choral pieces, and songs.

Laredo (y Unzueta), Jaime (Eduardo), Bolivian violinist, conductor, and teacher; b. Cochabamba, June 7, 1941. He was taken to the U.S. as a child; studied violin with Antonio de Grassi and Frank Houser in San Francisco, where he made his debut as a soloist with the San Francisco Sym. at age 11; he continued his training with Gingold in Cleveland and Galamian at the Curtis Inst. of Music in Philadelphia. In 1959, a week before his 18th birthday, he won the Queen Elisabeth of Belgium Competition in Brussels, and subsequently appeared with great success in America and Europe as a soloist with leading orchs. The Bolivian government issued a series of airmail stamps with Laredo's picture and a musical example with the notes A, D, C in the treble clef, spelling his name in solfège notation (La-Re-Do). In 1960 he married **Ruth** (née **Meckler**) **Laredo** (divorced in 1974); his 2nd wife was **Sharon Robinson**. With Robinson and the pianist Joseph Kalichstein, Laredo formed a trio in 1976, which toured extensively. He appeared regularly as a soloist and conductor with the Scottish Chamber Orch. in Glasgow from 1977, and led it on tours of the U.S. He taught at the St. Louis Cons. from 1983; was appointed co-artistic director of the Philadelphia Chamber Orch. in 1985. In 1992–93 he held the title of Distinguished Artist of the St. Paul (Minn.) Chamber Orch. In 1994 he served as president of the jury of the International Violin Competition of Indianapolis.

Laredo, Ruth (née **Meckler**), American pianist; b. Detroit, Nov. 20, 1937. She studied with Rudolf Serkin at the Curtis Inst. of Music in Philadelphia (B.M., 1960). In 1962 she made her debut with Stokowski and the American Sym. Orch. in N.Y. In 1965 she played in Europe with Rudolf and Peter Serkin; in 1977 she toured Japan. In 1960 she married **Jaime Laredo**, with whom she played numerous recitals; they were divorced in 1974. She is particularly fond of Russian music, and plays piano works of Rachmaninoff and Scriabin with passionate devotion.

Larmore, Jennifer, American mezzo-soprano; b. Atlanta, June 21, 1958. She was a student at Westminster Choir College in Princeton, N.J. (1976–80), and later of John Bullock in Washington, D.C. In 1986 she made her European opera debut as Mozart's Sesto in France. From 1990 she pursued a major career, garnering critical accolades for her portrayal of Rossini's Rosina in Paris, London, and Rome. During the 1992–93 season, she sang that role in Berlin, as well as Bellini's Romeo at N.Y.'s Carnegie Hall, Rossini's Angelina in Florence, and Mozart's Dorabella at the Salzburg Festival. In 1993 she made her first appearance at London's Wigmore Hall as a recitalist. She won the Richard Tucker Award in 1994 and gave a recital at Lincoln Center's Walter Reade Theater in N.Y. On Feb. 6, 1995, she made her Metropolitan Opera debut in N.Y. as Rosina. As a soloist with orchs. and as a recitalist, she appeared widely in North America and Europe. Among other operatic roles of note are Monteverdi's Orfeo, Rossini's Arsace and Isabella, and Strauss's Octavian.

La Rosa Parodi, Armando, Italian conductor and composer; b. Genoa, March 14, 1904; d. Rome, Jan. 21, 1977. He studied in Genoa and Milan. He began his career as a conductor in 1929; was active as a guest conductor in Genoa, Milan, Turin, and Rome; in 1963 he was named chief conductor of the RAI

Orch. of Rome, a post he held until his death. He composed the operas *Il Mercante e l'avvocato* (1934) and *Cleopatra* (1938), and several symphonic works.

La Rotella, Pasquale, Italian composer and conductor; b. Bitonto, Feb. 26, 1880; d. Bari, March 20, 1963. He studied in Naples. He was choirmaster at Bari Cathedral (1902–13) and also taught at the Liceo Musicale there (1934–49); toured Italy as an opera conductor. His works included the operas *Ivan* (Bari, Jan. 20, 1900), *Dea* (Bari, April 11, 1903), *Fasma* (Milan, Nov. 28, 1908), *Corsaresca* (Rome, Nov. 13, 1933), and *Manuela* (Nice, March 4, 1948), and much sacred music.

Larrocha (y de la Calle), Alicia de, brilliant Spanish pianist; b. Barcelona, May 23, 1923. She studied piano with Frank Marshall and theory with Ricardo Lamote de Grignon. She made her first public appearance at the age of 5; was soloist with the Orquesta Sinfónica of Madrid at the age of 11. In 1940 she launched her career in earnest; she began making major tours of Europe in 1947; made her first visit to the U.S. in 1955 and thereafter toured throughout the world to great acclaim. She also served as director of the Marshall Academy in Barcelona from 1959. Her interpretations of Spanish music have evoked universal admiration for their authentic quality, but she has also been exuberantly praised by critics for her impeccable taste and exquisitely polished technique in classical works.

Larsen, Jens Peter, distinguished Danish musicologist; b. Copenhagen, June 14, 1902; d. there, Aug. 22, 1988. He studied mathematics and musicology at the Univ. of Copenhagen (M.A., 1928); then joined its staff; later obtained his Ph.D. there in 1939 with the diss. *Die Haydn-Überlieferung* (publ. in Copenhagen, 1939); retired in 1970. A leading authority on the music of Haydn, he served as general ed. of the critical edition sponsored by the Joseph Haydn Inst. of Cologne from 1955 to 1960; his studies on the music of Handel are also of value. He was the son-in-law of **Mogens Wöldike**, with whom he ed. the hymnbook of the Danish Church (1954, 1973).

WRITINGS: *Drei Haydn-Kataloge in Faksimile: Mit Einleitung und erganzenden Themenverzeichnissen* (Copenhagen, 1941; 2nd ed., rev., 1979); *Weyses sange: Deres betydning for sangen i hjem, skole og kirke* (Copenhagen, 1942); *Handel's "Messiah": Origins, Composition, Sources* (Copenhagen, 1957; 2nd ed., rev., 1972); *Essays on Handel, Haydn, and the Viennese Classical Style* (tr. by U. Kramer; Ann Arbor, 1988).

BIBL.: N. Schiørring, H. Glahn, and C. Hatting, eds., *Festskrift J.P. L.: Studier udgivet af Musikvidenskabeligt institut ved Københavns universitet* (Copenhagen, 1972).

Larsen, Libby (actually, **Elizabeth Brown**), American composer; b. Wilmington, Del., Dec. 24, 1950. She was a pupil of Argento, Fetler, and Eric Stokes at the Univ. of Minnesota (B.A., 1971; M.A., 1975; Ph.D., 1978). With Stephen Paulus, she founded the Minnesota Composers Forum in Minneapolis in 1973, serving as its managing composer until 1985; she also was composer-in-residence of the Minnesota Orch. (1983–87). Her works have been widely performed in the U.S. and abroad. One of her most impressive scores, the choral sym. *Coming Forth into Day* (1986), utilizes a text by Jehan Sadat, the widow of the slain leader of Egypt.

WORKS: OPERAS: *The Words upon the Windowpane* (1978); *The Silver Fox*, children's opera (1979); *Tumbledown Dick* (1980); *Clair de lune* (1984); *Frankenstein: The Modern Prometheus* (1989; St. Paul, Minn., May 25, 1990); *Mrs. Dalloway*, chamber opera (1992; Cleveland, July 22, 1993). **ORCH.:** *Tom Twist* for Narrator and Orch. (1975); *Weaver's Song and Jig* for String Band and Chamber Orch. (1978); *Pinions* for Violin and Chamber Orch. (1981); *Ringeltanze* for Men's Chorus, Handbells, and Orch. (1982; Grand Rapids, Mich., Dec. 3, 1983); *Deep Summer Music* (1983); *Parachute Dancing*, overture (1983); 3 syms.: No. 1, *Water Music* (1984), No. 2, *Coming Forth Into Light*, for Soprano, Baritone, Chorus, and Orch. (1985; St. Paul, Minn., April 14, 1986), and No. 3, *Lyric* (1990–91; Albany, N.Y., May 3, 1991); *Coriolis* (1986); *What the Monster Saw* (1987); Trumpet Concerto (1988); *Collage Boogie* (1988); *3 Summer Scenes* (1989); *Cold, Silent Snow*, concerto for Chamber Orch. (1989); Piano Concerto, *Since Armstrong* (1989; Minneapolis, May 8, 1992); *Ghosts of an Old Ceremony* for Orch. and Dancers (Minneapolis, April 17, 1991); Marimba Concerto, *After Hampton* (1992); *Mary Cassatt* for Mezzo-soprano, Trombone, and Orch. (1993); *Ways of Spreading Light* for Orch. and Chorus (1994); *Overture for the End of a Century* (1994). **CHAMBER:** *4 on the Floor* for Violin, Cello, Double Bass, and Piano (1977); *Bronze Veils* for Trombone and Percussion (1979); *Ulloa's Ring* for Flute and Piano (1980); *Scudding* for Cello (1980); *Triage* for Harp (1981); *Aubade* for Flute (1982); *Jazz Variations* for Bassoon (1984); *North Star Fanfare* for Chamber Ensemble (1984); *The Astonishing Flight of Gump* for Chamber Ensemble (1986); *Juba* for Cello and Piano (1986); *Love and Hisses* for Double Wind Quintet (1986); *Black Birds, Red Hills* for Soprano, Clarinet, and Piano (1987); *Vive* for Flute Quartet (1988); *Xibalba* for Bassoon and 2 Percussionists (1989); *Aspects of Glory* for Organ (1990); *Schoenberg, Schenker, Schillinger* for String Quartet (1991); *Celebration of Light* for Chorus and Brass Quintet (1994).

Larsén-Todsen, Nanny, Swedish soprano; b. Hagby, Aug. 2, 1884; d. Stockholm, May 26, 1982. She received her training at the Stockholm Cons., in Berlin, and in Milan. In 1906 she made her operatic debut at the Royal Theater in Stockholm as Agathe, where she then was a member from 1907 to 1922. After appearing at Milan's La Scala (1923–24), she made her Metropolitan Opera debut in N.Y. as Brünnhilde in *Götterdämmerung* on Jan. 31, 1925; she remained on its roster until 1927, singing such roles as Isolde, Rachel in *La Juive*, Fricka, Kundry, Elsa, La Gioconda, and Leonore. Returning to Europe, she sang in various opera centers, including London's Covent Garden (1927, 1930) and the Bayreuth Festivals (1927–28; 1930–31). Shortly before the outbreak of World War II in 1939, she became a voice teacher in Stockholm.

Larsson, Lars-Erik (Vilner), important Swedish composer and pedagogue; b. Åkarp, near Lund, May 15, 1908; d. Hälsingborg, Dec. 27, 1986. After passing the organist's examination in Växjö (1924), he studied with Ernst Ellberg (composition) and Olalla Morales (conducting) at the Stockholm Cons. (1924–29); then completed his training with Berg in Vienna (1929–30) and with Reuter in Leipzig (1930–31). Returning to Stockholm, he was a conductor, composer, and producer with the Swedish Radio (1937–43); he later served as supervisor of its radio orch. (1945–47) and led its chamber orch. (until 1953). He was prof. of composition at the Stockholm Musikshögskolan (1947–59) and director of music at the Univ. of Uppsala (1961–65). His early compositions were in a classical spirit, but with time his idiom became increasingly complex; there are some instances of dodecaphonic procedures in his later compositions. The importance of his works lies in the freedom of application of various techniques without adhering to any current fashion.

WORKS: DRAMATIC: *Prinsessan av Cypern* (The Princess of Cyprus), opera (1930–36; Stockholm, April 29, 1937); *Arresten på Bohus* (The Arrest at Bohus), opera buffa (1938–39); *Linden*, ballet (1958). **ORCH.:** 3 syms. (1927–28; 1936–37; 1945); 3 concert overtures (1929, 1934, 1945); *Symphonic Sketch* (1930); *Sinfonietta* for Strings (1932); *Little Serenade* for Strings (1934); Saxophone Concerto (1934); *Divertimento* for Chamber Orch. (1935); *Little March* (1936); *Ostinato* (Stockholm, Nov. 24, 1937); *En vintersaga* (A Winter Tale), suite (1937); *Pastoral Suite* (1938); *The Earth Sings*, symphonic poem (1940); *The Land of Sweden*, suite (1941); *Gustavian Suite* for Flute, Harpsichord, and Strings (1943); Cello Concerto (1947); *Music for Orchestra* (1948–49); Violin Concerto (1952); 12 concertinos, with Strings, for solo instruments: Flute, Oboe, Clarinet, Bassoon, Horn, Trumpet, Trombone, Violin, Viola, Cello, Double Bass, and Piano (1953–57); *Adagio* for Strings (1960); *3 Pieces* (1960); *Orchestral Variations* (1962); *Lyric Fantasy* for Small Orch. (1967); *2 auguri* (1971); *Barococo*, suite (1973); *Musica permutatio* (1980; Swedish Radio, Feb. 27,

1982). **CHAMBER:** *Intimate Miniatures* for String Quartet (1938); 3 string quartets (1944, 1955, 1975); *4 tempi*, divertimento for Wind Quintet (1968); Cello Sonatina (1969); *Aubade* for Oboe, Violin, and Cello (1972). **PIANO:** 3 sonatinas (1936, 1947, 1950); *Croquiser* (1947); *7 Little Preludes and Fugues* (1969). **VOCAL:** *Förklädd gud* (The Disguised God), lyric suite for Narrator, Soprano, Baritone, Chorus, and Orch. (1940); *Väktarsånger* (Watchman's Songs) for Narrator, Baritone, Men's Chorus, and Orch. (1940); *Missa brevis* for Chorus (1954); *Intrada Solemnis* for 2 Choruses, Boy's Chorus, Winds, and Organ (1964); *Soluret och urnan* (The Sundial and the Urn), cantata (1965–66).

LaRue, (Adrian) Jan (Pieters), eminent American musicologist; b. Kisaran, Sumatra (of American parents), July 31, 1918. During this period in Sumatra, his father invented the budgrafting method now used on all rubber plantations. After attending Harvard Univ. (B.S., 1940), he pursued his studies in composition with Sessions and in musicology with Strunk at Princeton Univ. (M.F.A., 1942). He then saw military service (from 1943), and was active in the Okinawa Campaign. Following his discharge in 1946, he returned to Harvard Univ. to complete his education under Piston and Davison (Ph.D., 1952, with the diss. *The Okinawan Classical Songs: An Analytical and Comparative Study*). Having taught at Wellesley College in 1942–43, he was again on its faculty from 1946 to 1957, and also served as chairman of its music dept. (1950–57). In 1957 he became prof. of music at N.Y. Univ. (dept. chairman, 1970–73; director of graduate studies, 1973–80), retiring in 1988 as prof. emeritus. In addition to a Fulbright Research Followship (Austria, 1954–56), he received grants from the American Council of Learned Societies (1964), the Guggenheim Foundation (1965–66), and the National Endowment for the Humanities (1980–84). From 1966 to 1968 he was president of the American Musicological Soc. LaRue has written pioneering articles on style analysis, authenticity and style in 18th-century music, harmonic rhythm in Beethoven's syms., the music of Okinawa, catalogues and bibliographical methods, watermarks, and computer aids to music. He served as ed. of the *Report of the Eighth Congress of the International Musicological Society* (2 vols., 1961–62), and as co-ed. of the *Festschrift Otto Erich Deutsch* (1963) and of *Aspects of Medieval and Renaissance Music: A Birthday Offering to Gustave Reese* (1966; 2nd. ed., 1978).

WRITINGS: *Guidelines for Style Analysis* (1970; 2nd ed., 1992); *A Catalogue of 18th-Century Symphonies* (1988); with M. Ohmiya, *Methods and Models for Comprehensive Style Analysis* (1988); *Writing on Music Style: Models for a Comprehensive Approach* (1994).

BIBL.: E. Wolf and E. Roesner, eds., *Studies in Musical Sources and Style: Essays in Honor of J. L.* (Madison, Wis., 1990).

Laskine, Lily, noted French harpist and teacher; b. Paris, Aug. 31, 1893; d. there, Jan. 4, 1988. She studied at the Paris Cons. with Alphonse Hasselmans and Georges Marty; won a premier prix there in 1905. She was then a member of the orch. of the Paris Opéra (1909–26); from 1934, made numerous tours as a soloist; was a prof. of harp at the Paris Cons. (1948–58). In 1936 she was awarded the cross of the Légion d'honneur, and in 1958 she was made a chévalier.

László, Alexander, Hungarian-American composer; b. Budapest, Nov. 22, 1895; d. Los Angeles, Nov. 17, 1970. He was a student of A. Szendy (piano) and Herzfeld (composition) at the Royal Academy of Music in Budapest. In 1915 he went to Berlin, where he was active as a pianist and worked in radio and films; he also taught in Munich. He constructed a "color piano" (Farblichtklavier) for the purpose of uniting tones with colors, which he demonstrated at the Kiel music festival (June 14, 1925). To establish a correspondence between the proportional wavelengths in both acoustic elements and light waves, he invented an instrument he called the Sonchromatoscope and a new system of notation he called Sonchromography. His book *Die Farblichtmusik* (1925) discusses his new technique. In 1938 he emigrated to the U.S. and in 1945 settled in Los Angeles, where he composed film and television scores. In addition to his many works for the Sonchromatoscope, he wrote stage music and orch. scores.

Lászlò, Magda, Hungarian soprano; b. Marosvársárhely, 1919. She studied at the Budapest Academy of Music and with Irene Stowasser. In 1943 she made her operatic debut at the Budapest Opera, where she sang until 1946. She then became well known via her appearances on the Italian Radio. On Dec. 4, 1949, she created the role of the Mother in Dallapiccola's *Il Prigionero* in a Turin Radio broadcast, and then sang that role in its first stage performance on May 20, 1950, in Florence. Thereafter she sang in various Italian music centers, and also throughout Europe. In 1953 she appeared as Alceste at the Glyndebourne Festival, returning there in 1954 and again in 1962–63. On Dec. 3, 1954, she created the role of Cressida in Walton's *Troilus and Cressida* at London's Covent Garden. She also sang widely as a concert artist. In addition to roles in operas by such contemporary composers as Dallapiccola, Walton, Casella, Malipiero, and Ghedini, she was admired for her portrayals of Handel's Agrippina, Cherubino, Norma, Senta, Isolde, Busoni's Turandot, and Berg's Marie.

Lateiner, Jacob, American pianist and teacher of Austrian-Polish descent; b. Havana, May 31, 1928. He studied piano with Jascha Fischermann in Havana (1934–40), and with Isabelle Vengerova at the Curtis Inst. of Music in Philadelphia; also attended the chamber music classes given by Piatigorsky and Primrose there; likewise had lessons in compositions with Felix Greissle and Schoenberg. Having won the Philadelphia Youth Competition, he made his debut as soloist in Tchaikovsky's 1st Piano Concerto at a youth concert of the Philadelphia Orch. (Dec. 6, 1944); subsequently performed throughout America and in Europe. He appeared regularly in chamber music recitals with Heifetz and Piatigorsky. From 1963 to 1970 he taught at the Mannes College of Music in N.Y.; in 1966, was appointed to the faculty of the Juilliard School of Music in N.Y. In addition to the standard repertoire, he has played a number of contemporary scores; was soloist in the premiere of Elliott Carter's Piano Concerto (1967).

Latham, William P(eters), American composer and educator; b. Shreveport, La., Jan. 4, 1917. He studied trumpet at the Cincinnati Cons. of Music (1936–38); received his B.S. degree in music education from the Univ. of Cincinnati (1938) and continued his studies at the College of Music in Cincinnati (B.M., 1940; M.M., 1941); subsequently studied composition with Hanson and Elwell at the Eastman School of Music in Rochester, N.Y. (Ph.D., 1951). During World War II, he served in the U.S. Army as a cavalry bandsman and later as an infantry platoon leader in active combat in Germany in 1945. After the war, he taught at Iowa State Teacher's College in Cedars Falls (1946–65); became a prof. at North Texas State Univ. in Denton in 1965, director of graduate studies in music in 1969, and Distinguished Prof. in 1978; he retired in 1984. He excelled as a composer of sacred choruses and band music; in the latter, he boldly experimented with modern techniques, as exemplified by his *Dodecaphonic Set* and, most spectacularly, in *Fusion*, in which he endeavored to translate the process of atomic fusion into musical terms through an ingenious application of asymmetrical rhythms.

WORKS: DRAMATIC: *Orpheus in Pecan Springs*, opera (Denton, Texas, Dec. 4, 1980); *A Modern Trilogy*, ballet (Cincinnati, April 2, 1941). **ORCH.:** *The Lady of Shalott* (1939; Cincinnati, March 7, 1941); *Fantasy Concerto* for Flute, Strings, and Harp (NBC, Cincinnati, May 5, 1941); *Fantasy* for Violin and Orch. (1946; Minneapolis, May 23, 1948); *And Thou America* (1947; Rochester, N.Y., Oct. 18, 1948); 2 syms.: No. 1 (Rochester, N.Y., April 25, 1950) and No. 2, *Sinfonietta* (1953; Fish Creek, Wis., Aug. 20, 1955); Suite for Trumpet and Strings (Rochester, N.Y., May 4, 1951); *Concerto Grosso* for 2 Saxophones and Symphonic Wind Ensemble (Chicago, Dec. 16,

1960; rev. 1962 for 2 Saxophones and Chamber Orch.); Concertino for Saxophone and Symphonic Wind Ensemble (1968; rev. 1969 for Saxophone and Orch.); *American Youth Performs* (Fort Worth, Aug. 1, 1969); *Jubilee 13/50* (Sherman, Texas, Nov. 4, 1978); *Supernovae* (1983); *Excelsior K-2* for Piano and Chamber Orch. (Fort Worth, Texas, Sept. 13, 1994). **BAND:** *Brighton Beach*, march (1954); *Proud Heritage*, march (1955); *3 Chorale Preludes* (1956); *Court Festival* (1957); *Passacaglia and Fugue* (1959); *Plymouth Variations* (1962); *Escapades* (1965); *Dionysian Festival* (1965); *Dodecaphonic Set* (Colorado Springs, Colo., March 11, 1966); *Prayers in Space* (1971); *The Music Makers*, with Chorus, Rock Group, Tape, and Guru (1972); *Dilemmae* (1973); *Prolegomena* (1974); *Revolution!* (1975); *Fusion* (1975; New Orleans, April 12, 1976); *March 6* (Dallas, Feb. 23, 1979); *Drones, Airs, and Games* (1983). **CHAMBER:** 3 string quartets (1938–40); 3 string trios (1938–39); Oboe Sonata (1947); Violin Sonata (1949); *Suite in Baroque Style* for Flute and Piano (1954); Sonata for Recorder and Harpsichord (1959); *Sisyphus 1971* for Alto Saxophone and Piano (1971); *Preludes before Silence*, 9 pieces for Flute and Piccolo (1974); *Eidolons* for Euphonium and Piano (1977); *Ex Tempore* for Alto Saxophone (1978); *Ion, the Rhapsode* for Clarinet and Piano (1984). **VOCAL:** *River to the Sea* for Baritone and Orch. (Cincinnati, Dec. 11, 1942); *Peace* for Chorus and Orch., after Rupert Brook (1943); *Prayer after World War* for Chorus (1945); *Prophecy of Peace* for Chorus, Organ, Piano, and Cymbals (1951; also for Chorus and Orch., 1952, and Chorus and Small Wind Ensemble, 1961); *Music for 7 Poems* for Chorus and Orch., after James Hearst (1958); *Blind with Rainbows*, cantata for Chorus (1962); *Te Deum* for Chorus, Wind Ensemble, and Organ (1964); *A Lenten Letter* for Soprano, Strings, and Percussion, after Alexander Solzhenitsyn (Denton, Texas, Oct. 9, 1974); *St. David's Mass* for Chorus (1977); *Epigrammata* for Chorus (1978); *Gaudeamus Academe* for Chorus, Tenor, Announcer on Tape, Bass Drum, Cymbals, and Slapstick (1981; Denton, Texas, April 27, 1982); *Te Deum Tejas*, 8 songs for Soprano, Flute, and Percussion to texts by the composer (1981); *Bitter Land* for Chorus, Brass Quintet, and Piano (1985); *My Heart Sings*, anthem for Chorus and Organ (1987); *Missa Novella* for Young Choruses (1988); *Metaphors*, 3 songs for Soprano and Piano (1988); *A Green Voice*, cantata for Soprano, Tenor, and Piano (1989); *The Sacred Flame*, cantata for Baritone and Orch. (Denton, Texas, June 9, 1990).

Lattuada, Felice, Italian composer; b. Caselle di Morimondo, near Milan, Feb. 5, 1882; d. Milan, Nov. 2, 1962. He studied at the Milan Cons. with Ferroni, graduating in 1911; then was director of the Milan Civic School of Music (1935–62). He wrote an autobiography, *La passione dominate* (Bologna, 1951).

WORKS: DRAMATIC: OPERAS: *La tempesta* (Milan, Nov. 23, 1922); *Sandha* (Genoa, Feb. 21, 1924); *Le Preziose ridicole* (Milan, Feb. 9, 1929); *Don Giovanni* (Naples, May 18, 1929); *La caverna di Salamanca* (Genoa, March 1, 1938); *Caino* (Milan, Jan. 10, 1957). Also film scores. **ORCH.:** *Sinfonia romantica* (1911); *Cimitero di guerra; Il mistero della Passione di Cristo; Incanti della notte; Divertimento rustico; Prelude and Fugue.* **OTHER:** Chamber works; vocal pieces, including *Canto augurale per la Nazione Eletta* for Tenor, Chorus, and Orch.

Laub, Thomas (Linnemann), significant Danish organist and composer; b. Langaa, Fyn, Dec. 5, 1852; d. Gentofte, near Copenhagen, Feb. 4, 1927. Following training in theology, he studied with Gebauer at the Copenhagen Cons. (1873–76); subsequently was organist at Copenhagen's Hellingåndskirken (1884–91) and Holmens Kirke (1891–1925). He devoted his life to reforming ecclesiastical music in Denmark, restoring the melody, rhythm, and harmony of hymns to their primordial form and composing music reflecting that tradition. The Danish Hymn Soc. was organized in 1922 to propagate his ideas. He publ. the books *Vor musikundervisning og den musikalske dannelse* (Copenhagen, 1884), *Om kirkesangen* (Copenhagen, 1887), and *Musik og kirke* (Copenhagen, 1920; 2nd ed., 1938).

WORKS (all publ. in Copenhagen unless otherwise given): **SACRED:** *80 rytmiske koraler* (1888); *Kirkemelodier, firstemmig udsatte* (1888–90); *Salmemelodier i kirkestil* (1896–1902); *Forspil og melodier: Forsøg i kirkestil* (1890); *Dansk kirkesang: Gamle og nye melodier* (1918; suppl., 1930); *Aandelige sange* (1925); *24 salmer og 12 folkeviser* (ed. by M. Wöldike; 1928); *Liturgisk musik* (ed. by Wöldike; 1937). **SECULAR:** *10 gamle danske folkeviser* (1890); *Danske folkeviser med gamle melodier* (1899–1904; 2nd ed., 1930); with C. Nielsen, *En snes danske viser* (1915–17); *Ti Aarestrupske ritorneller* (1920); *Tolv viser og sange af danske digtere* (Kolding, 1920; 2nd ed., 1938); with Nielsen, O. Ring, and T. Aagaard, *Folkehøjskolens melodibog* (1922; suppl., 1927); *30 danske sange for 3 og 4 lige stemmer* (1922); *Faerøske og danske folkevisemelodier udsatte for mandskor af Henrik Rung og Thomas Laub* (ed. by K. Clausen; 1942); *Danske folkeviser* (ed. by Wöldike and A. Arnholtz; 1948); *Sange med klaver* (ed. by H. Glahn and Wöldike; 1957).

BIBL.: P. Hamburger, *Bibliografisk fortegnelse over T. L.s litteraere og musikalske arbejder* (Copenhagen, 1932); idem, *T. L.: Hans liv og gerning* (Copenhagen, 1942); M. Wöldike, "Erindringer om L. og Carl Nielsen," *Dansk Kirkesangs Årsskrift*, XX (1967–68); J. Jensen, "Musikalisk isolation og gudstjenstligt faellesskab i T. L.s to tidlige skrifter," ibid., XXII (1971–72).

Laubenthal (real name, **Neumann**), **Horst (Rüdiger),** German tenor; b. Duderstadt, March 8, 1939. He began his studies in Munich and continued his training with **Rudolf Laubenthal,** whose surname he took as his own for his professional career. In 1967 he made his operatic debut as Don Ottavio at the Würzburg Festival, and then was a member of the Württemberg State Theater in Stuttgart from 1968 to 1973. In 1970 he appeared as the Steersman in *Der fliegende Holländer* at the Bayreuth Festival, and in 1972 sang Belmonte at the Glyndebourne Festival. In 1973 he became a member of the Deutsche Oper in Berlin. His guest engagements took him to the Vienna State Opera, the Bavarian State Opera in Munich, the Hamburg State Opera, the Paris Opéra, the Aix-en-Provence Festival, and other music centers. He was especially successful for his roles in Mozart's operas, and was particularly noted for his work as a concert artist.

Laubenthal, Rudolf, German tenor; b. Düsseldorf, March 18, 1886; d. Pöcking, Starnberger See, Oct. 2, 1971. At first he studied medicine in Munich and Berlin; simultaneously took vocal lessons with Lilli Lehmann. In 1913 he made his debut in Berlin at the Deutsches Opernhaus, and sang there regularly; from 1919 to 1923 he also was engaged by the Bavarian State Opera in Munich. He made his Metropolitan Opera debut in N.Y. as Walther von Stolzing in *Die Meistersinger von Nürnberg* on Nov. 9, 1923; continued on the company's roster until 1933; he also sang with the Covent Garden Opera in London (1926–30) and made guest appearances in Chicago and San Francisco. In 1937 he retired from the operatic stage. He was primarily noted as a Wagnerian.

Launis (real name, **Lindberg**), **Armas (Emanuel),** Finnish composer; b. Hämeenlinna, April 22, 1884; d. Nice, Aug. 7, 1959. He studied cello and composition at the orch. school of the Helsinki Phil. Soc. (1901–07); after training with Klatte at the Berlin Stern Cons. (1907–08) and with Bauszern in Weimar (1909), he completed his studies with I. Krohn at the Univ. of Helsinki (Ph.D., 1913, with the diss. *Über Art, Entstehung und Verbreitung der Estnisch-Finnischen Runenmelodien*; publ. in Helsinki, 1913). In 1930 he settled in Nice.

WORKS: OPERAS: *Seitsemän veljestäf* (The 7 Brothers; Helsinki, April 11, 1913); *Kullervo* (Helsinki, Feb. 28, 1917); *Aslak Hetta* (Helsinki, 1922); *Noidan laulu* (The Sorcerer's Song; 1932); *Lumottu silkkihuivi* (The Magic Silk Kerchief; 1937); *Jehudith* (1940). **ORCH.:** *Andante religioso* for Violin and Orch. (1932); *Northern Suite* for Violin and Orch. (1950); *Karelian Suite* (1952). **CHAMBER:** Piano Quintet; piano pieces. **VOCAL:** 2 cantatas (1906, 1910); songs.

Laurencie, Lionel de la. See **La Laurencie, (Marie Bertrand) Lionel (Jules), Comte de.**

Lauri-Volpi, Giacomo, famous Italian tenor; b. Lanuvio, near Rome, Dec. 11, 1892; d. Valencia, March 17, 1979. He received training in law before turning to vocal studies with Antonio Cotogni at the Accademia di Santa Cecilia in Rome; he completed his vocal training with Enrico Rosati. In 1919 he made his operatic debut under the name Giacomo Rubini in Viterbo as Arturo in *I Puritani.* He sang for the first time under his real name in Rome in 1920 as Des Grieux in *Manon.* In 1922 he made his debut at Milan's La Scala as the Duke of Mantua, and continued to sing there as a great favorite until the outbreak of World War II in 1939. On Jan. 26, 1923, he made his Metropolitan Opera debut in N.Y. as the Duke of Mantua, and subsequently was one of the principal members on its roster until 1933. While at the Metropolitan, he sang Calaf in the U.S. premiere of *Turandot* on Nov. 16, 1926, and also had notable success in such roles as Cavaradossi, Radamès, Pollione, Alfredo, Canio, Faust, and Rodolfo. In 1925 and in 1936 he was a guest artist at London's Covent Garden. On Feb. 28, 1928, he appeared as Boito's Nerone at the opening of the new Teatro Reale dell'Opera in Rome. He sang Arnold in the centenary staging of Rossini's *Guillaume Tell* at La Scala in 1929, and also appeared at the Paris Opéra and Opéra-Comique that same year. He settled in Burjasot, near Valencia. After World War II ended, he resumed singing in Italy, as well as in Spain. In 1959 he retired from public performances. However, in 1972, when he was in his 80th year, he astounded an audience at a gala performance at Barcelona's Teatro Liceo when he sang *Nessun dorma* from *Turandot.* At the apex of his career, Lauri-Volpi was hailed as one of the foremost lyrico-dramatic tenors of his era. The range and flexibility of his voice, his command of declamation, and his glorious legato, were memorable. He publ. the books *L'equivoco* (Milan, 1938), *Cristalli viventi* (Rome, 1948), *A viso aperto* (Milan, 1953), *Voci parallele* (Milan, 1955), and *Misteri della voce umana* (Milan, 1957).

BIBL.: J. Menéndez, *G. L.-V.* (Madrid, 1990).

Lauro, Antonio, Venezuelan guitarist and composer; b. Ciudad Bolívar, Aug. 3, 1909; d. Caracas, April 17, 1986. He studied in Caracas. He wrote much guitar music, including a Guitar Concerto (Caracas, July 25, 1956, composer soloist); also a choral symphonic poem, *Cantacharo*; several symphonic suites; choruses; songs.

Lautenbacher, Susanne, German violinist; b. Augsburg, April 19, 1932. She studied at the Munich Hochschule für Musik; took private lessons with Szeryng. She then appeared in Europe as a soloist and chamber music player; also taught violin. She was praised for her sensitive performances of the classical violin repertoire.

Laux, Karl, German writer on music; b. Ludwigshafen, Aug. 26, 1896; d. Dresden, June 27, 1978. He studied with Blume while both were prisoners of war in England during World War I; later he pursued his education at the Univ. of Heidelberg (Ph.D., 1926, with the diss. *Der Erziehungsgedanke bei Schleiermacher*). He settled in Dresden and was music ed. of the *Neuen Badischen Landeszeitung* (until 1934), and then of the *Dresdner Neuesten Nachrichten* (until 1945); he also taught at the Akademie für Musik und Theater, and then was music ed. of the *Täglichen Rundschau* (1948–51) before serving as rector of the Hochschule für Musik (1951–63).

WRITINGS: *Joseph Haas* (Mainz, 1931); *Carl Maria von Weber* (Berlin, 1935); *Der Thomaskantor und seine Söhne* (Dresden, 1939); *Anton Bruckner* (Leipzig, 1940; 2nd. ed., 1947); *Joseph Haas* (Hamburg, 1940); *Musik und Musiker der Gegenwart* (Essen, 1949); *Kleine Bach-Biographie* (Berlin, 1950); ed. with H. Draeger, *Bach-Probleme* (Leipzig, 1950); *Joseph Haas* (Berlin and Düsseldorf, 1954); *Die Musik in Russland und in der Sowjetunion* (Berlin, 1958); ed. *10 Jahre Musikleben der DDR* (Leipzig, 1959); *Ottmar Gerster: Leben und Werk* (Leipzig, 1962); *Die Dresdner Staatskapelle* (Leipzig, 1963; Eng. tr., 1967); ed. *Das Musikleben in der Deutschen Demokratischen Republik* (Leipzig, 1963); *Carl Maria von Weber* (Leipzig, 1966); *Kunstansichten, Ausgewählte Schriften Carl Maria von Weber* (Leipzig, 1969); *Robert Schumann* (Leipzig, 1972).

Lavagne, André, French composer; b. Paris, July 12, 1913. He studied at the Paris Cons.; won 1st prize in piano (1933) and Premier 2nd Grand Prix de Rome (1938). In 1941 he was appointed inspector of music in Paris schools.

WORKS: DRAMATIC: OPERAS: *Comme ils s'aiment* (Paris, 1941); *Corinne* (Enghiens-les-Bains, 1956). Also several ballets (*Le Pauvre Jongleur, Kermesse* et al.). **ORCH.:** *Concert dans un parc* for Piano and Orch., inspired by Watteau's painting (1941); *Concerto romantique* for Cello and Orch. (1941). **VOCAL:** *Nox*, symphonic poem for Voice and Orch.; *Spectacle rassurant* for Voice and Orch.

Lavagnino, Angelo Francesco, Italian composer; b. Genoa, Feb. 22, 1909; d. Gavi, Aug. 21, 1987. He studied with Renzo Rossi and Vito Frazzi at the Milan Cons., graduating in 1933. From 1948 to 1962 he was a prof. of film music at the Accademia Musicale in Siena. Among his compositions were an opera, *Malafonte* (Antwerp, 1952); the orch. pieces *Volo d'api* (1932), *Tempo alto* (1938), Violin Concerto (1941), and *Pocket Symphony* (1949); Piano Quintet (1942); Violin Sonata (1943).

Lavalle-García, Armando, Mexican composer; b. Ocotlán, Jalisco, Nov. 23, 1924. He studied violin at the National Cons. of Music in Mexico City and took courses in composition with Bernal Jiménez, Revueltas, and R. Halffter. He subsequently played viola with the National Sym. Orch. of Mexico City and conducted the Xalapa Sym. Orch. His music is permeated with the essence of Mexican folklore, even in pieces of ostensibly abstract connotations.

WORKS: BALLETS: *La canción de los Buenos Principios* (1957); *3 tiempos de amor* (1958); *Corrido* (1959). **ORCH.:** *Mi viaje*, symphonic poem (1950); *Estructuras geométricas* for Strings and Percussion (1960); Concerto for Viola and Strings (1965); Concerto for Violin, Strings, and Percussion (1966). **CHAMBER:** *Divertimento* for Wind Quintet (1953); Violin Sonata (1966); Oboe Sonata (1967); *Potencial* for Guitar, Psaltery, Harp, and Percussion (1967); *Trigonos* for Flute, Clarinet, and Bassoon (1968); Trio for Oboe, Bassoon, Cello, and Percussion (1969).

La Violette, Wesley, American composer and teacher; b. St. James, Minn., Jan. 4, 1894; d. Escondido, Calif., July 29, 1978. He studied at the Northwestern Univ. School of Music (graduated, 1917) and at the Chicago Musical College (D.Mus., 1925), where he was a member of the faculty (1923–33). After teaching at De Paul Univ. in Chicago (1933–40), where he also was director of De Paul Univ. Press, he taught at the Los Angeles Cons. (from 1946). He also was active as a lecturer on philosophy, religion, and the arts. Among his books were *Music and its Makers* (1938) and *The Crown of Wisdom* (1949), the latter devoted to religious mysticism. His compositions followed generally along traditional pathways, although he was not adverse to atonal usages.

WORKS: DRAMATIC: *Shylock*, opera (1927); *Schubertiana*, ballet (1935); *The Enlightened One*, opera (1935). **ORCH.:** *Penetrella* for Strings (Chicago, Nov. 30, 1928); *Osiris* (1929); 2 violin concertos (1929, 1938); 3 syms.: No. 1 (1936; Rochester, N.Y., Oct. 19, 1938), No. 2 (1939; Chicago, May 25, 1942), and No. 3 (1952); *Chorale* (Chicago, July 31, 1936); Piano Concerto (1937); Concerto for String Quartet and Orch. (1939); *Music from the High Sierras* (San Francisco, March 4, 1941); Flute Concertino (1943). **CHAMBER:** 3 string quartets (1926, 1933, 1936); Piano Quintet (1927); Sonata for 2 Violins (1931); Octet (1934); 2 violin sonatas (1934, 1937); Sextet for Piano, Flute, Oboe, Clarinet, Bassoon, and Horn (1940); Flute Quintet (1943). **VOCAL:** Choral pieces; songs.

Lavista, Mario, radical Mexican composer; b. Mexico City, April 3, 1943. He studied harmony with R. Halffter and composition with Quintanar; then attended classes and seminars of

Stockhausen, Pousseur, Xenakis, and Ligeti in Darmstadt and Cologne. Returning to Mexico in 1970, he founded Quanta, an improvisational music group. In his music, he explores all resources of sound, and all idiomatic textures, from deliberate homophony to horrendous explosions of ear-splitting dissonance.

WORKS: *Monologue* for Baritone, Flute, Vibraphone, and Double Bass, after Gogol's *Diary of a Madman* (1966); *5 Pieces* for String Quartet (1967); *Divertimento* for Wind Quintet, 5 Woodblocks, and 3 Shortwave Radios (1968); *Homage to Samuel Beckett* for 3 Amplified Choruses (1968); *Diacronia* for String Quartet (1969); *Kronos* for a minimum of 15 Alarm Clocks, and Loudspeakers and Tapes, with an indeterminate chronometric duration of 5 to 1,440 minutes (1969); *Piece* for 1 Pianist and 1 Piano (1970; also as *Piece* for 2 Pianists and 2 Pianos, in which a 2nd pianist maintains an absolute silence that must be "communicated" to the listeners); *Game* for Flute (1970); *Continuo* for Brass, Percussion, 2 Prepared Pianos, and Strings (1970); Trio for 2 String Instruments and Ring Modulator (1972); *Diafonia* for 1 Performer on 2 Pianos and Percussion (1973); *Cluster* for Piano (1973); *Antinomia* for Tape (1973); *Antifonia* for Flute, 2 Bassoons, and Percussion (1974); *Dialogos* for Violin and Piano (1974); *Espejos* for Piano, 4-hands (1975); *Quotations* for Cello and Piano (1975); *Lyhannh* for Orch. (1976; the title is Swift's word for the "swallow" in Part 4 of *Gulliver's Travels*); Piano Trio (1976); *Jaula* for any number of Prepared Pianos and Pianists (1976); *Ficciones* for Orch. (1980).

Lavrangas, Dionyssios, Greek conductor, composer, and pedagogue; b. Argostólion, Oct. 17, 1860?; d. Razata, Cephalonia, July 18, 1941. After studies with N. Serao (violin) and Olivieri and Metaxas-Tzanis (harmony) in Argostólion, he went to Naples to pursue his training with Scarano (harmony and counterpoint) and Ross (piano); he also was a student at the Cons. of San Pietro a Majella there of Rossi and P. Serao (composition). He then went to Paris and had lessons with Dubois (harmony), Anthiome (piano), and Franck (organ); he also took courses at the Cons. there with Delibes and Massenet. After working as a touring opera conductor, he settled in Athens as conductor of the Phil. Soc. (1894–96); he then was founder-conductor of the Elliniko Melodhrama (Greek Opera; 1900–1935). He also was active as a teacher, and served as director of the opera school of the Hellenic Cons. (1919–24). Lavrangas was an important figure in the development of the Ionian school of composition. His works are reflective of French and Italian models.

WORKS: DRAMATIC: OPERAS: *Elda di Vorn* (c.1886; Naples, c. 1890); *La vita è un sogno* (1887; Act 4 rev. as *Mayissa* [The Sorceress], Athens, Oct. 8, 1901); *Galatea* (c.1887); *Ta dyo adelfia* (The 2 Brothers; Athens, April 24, 1900); *O lytrotis* (The Redeemer; 1900–1903; Corfu, Feb. 24, 1934); *Dido* (1906–09; Athens, April 10, 1909); *Mavri petaloudha* (Black Butterfly; Athens, Jan. 25, 1929); *Aida* (c.1928); *Ikaros* (c.1930); *Ena paramythi,* comic opera (1930); *Fakanapas,* comic opera (1935; Athens, Dec. 2, 1950); *Frosso* (1938). **OPERETTAS:** *I aspri tricha* (The White Hair; Athens, March 22, 1917); *Sporting Club* (Athens, Aug. 4, 1917); *Dhipli Fotia* (Double Flame; Athens, Jan. 10, 1918); *Satore* (n.d.); *O Tragoudistis tou Kazinou* (The Casino Singer; Athens, July 7, 1934; in collaboration with others). **OTHER:** Ballets; orch. works; piano pieces; choral music; songs.

Lavry, Marc, Latvian-born Israeli conductor and composer; b. Riga, Dec. 22, 1903; d. Haifa, March 20, 1967. After attending the Riga Cons., he studied with Teichmüller at the Leipzig Cons.; he also received private instruction from Glazunov. He began his career conducting opera and ballet in Latvia and Germany. In 1935 he went to Palestine; was conductor of the Palestine Folk Opera (1941–47) and then director of the music dept. of the short-wave radio station Kol Zion La Gola (1950–58). In 1952 he visited the U.S. His music is imbued with intense feeling for Jewish folk motifs. Among his works prior to his going to Palestine, the most notable is *Fantastische Suite* for Orch. (1932). He was the composer of the first Palestinian opera in Hebrew to receive a stage performance, *Dan Hashomer* (Dan the Guard; Tel Aviv, Feb. 17, 1945, composer conducting); he also wrote an opera in the form of a series of cantillations with homophonic instrumental accompaniment entitled *Tamar and Judah* (1958; concert perf., N.Y., March 22, 1970); other works include 5 syms., among them the *Tragic* (1945), the *Liberation* (1951), and No. 4 (1957); the symphonic poems *Stalingrad* (c.1943) and *Negev* (c.1954); 2 piano concertos (1945, 1947); Flute Concerto (1965); Harp Concerto; Viola Concerto; the oratorio *Esther ha'malka* (Queen Esther; 1960); many songs.

Lawrence, Dorothea Dix, American soprano and folk-song collector; b. N.Y., Sept. 22, 1899; d. Plainfield, N.J., May 23, 1979. She studied with Cesare Stunai, Henry Russell, and Katherine Opdycke in N.Y. She made her operatic debut as Gounod's Marguerite with the Quebec Opera in Montreal in 1929, then appeared in opera in N.Y., Philadelphia, and elsewhere. She became active as a folk-song collector, presenting recitals in which she sang American Indian songs in their original languages as well as other folk songs and art songs by established composers; toured Europe as a recitalist (1952–54). She publ. the book *Folklore Songs of the United States* (1959).

Lawrence, Gertrude (real name, **Gertrud Alexandra Dagmar Lawrence Klasen**), English actress, singer, and dancer; b. London, July 4, 1898; d. N.Y., Sept. 6, 1952. She began her career with appearances in British revues (from 1910); starred in *André Charlot's Revue* in London, with which she made her N.Y. debut (1924). George and Ira Gershwin wrote for her the musicals *Oh, Kay!* (1926) and *Treasure Girl* (1928). After working mainly as an actress in England and the U.S., she won great critical acclaim as Liza Elliot in the Kurt Weill and Moss Hart musical play *Lady in the Dark* (1941); her last role was as Anna in the Rodgers and Hammerstein musical *The King and I* (1951). She publ. her autobiography as *A Star Danced* (1945).

BIBL.: R. Aldrich, *G. L. as Mrs. A.* (N.Y., 1954); S. Morley, *G. L.* (London, 1981).

Lawrence, Lucile, American harpist and teacher; b. New Orleans, Feb. 7, 1907. She studied with Salzedo and was 1st harpist in his harp ensemble. She organized her own Lawrence Harp Quintet and appeared as a soloist with major orchs., a chamber music artist, and a recitalist. She taught at the Curtis Inst. of Music in Philadelphia (1927–30), then founded the harp dept. at the Philadelphia Musical Academy; also taught at the Mannes College of Music in N.Y. (from 1945), Boston Univ. (from 1966), the Manhattan School of Music in N.Y. (from 1967), and the Berkshire Music Center in Tanglewood (from 1968).

Lawrence, Marjorie (Florence), noted Australian soprano; b. Dean's Marsh, Victoria, Feb. 17, 1907; d. Little Rock, Ark., Jan. 13, 1979. She studied in Melbourne with Ivor Boustead; then in Paris with Cécile Gilly. She made her debut as Elisabeth in *Tannhäuser* in Monte Carlo (1932); then sang at the Paris Opéra (1933–36), gaining success as Donna Anna, Aida, Ortrud, Brangäne, and Brünnhilde. She made her American debut at the Metropolitan Opera in N.Y. on Dec. 18, 1935, as Brünnhilde in *Die Walküre,* where she quickly established herself as a leading Wagnerian on its roster; she also appeared as Alceste, Thaïs, and Salome. She also made guest appearances with the Chicago, San Francisco, St. Louis, and Cincinnati operas. An attack of polio during a performance of *Die Walküre* (1941) interrupted her career. While she never walked again unaided, her determination to return to the operatic stage led to the resumption of her career; her first appearance at the Metropolitan Opera following her illness came on Dec. 27, 1942, when she sang the Venusberg duet in a concert with Melchior, reclining upon a couch. Her last appearance there took place when she sang Venus on April 6, 1944. She continued to make occasional appearances until her retirement in 1952, then devoted herself to teaching. She was a prof. of voice at Tulane Univ. (1956–60) and prof. of voice and director of the opera workshop at Southern Illinois Univ. (from 1960). She publ. an autobiography, *Interrupted Melody, The Story of My Life* (N.Y., 1949), which was made into a film in 1955.

Lawrence (real name, **Cohen**), **Robert,** American conductor; b. N.Y., March 18, 1912; d. there, Aug. 9, 1981. He was educated at Columbia Univ. (M.A., 1934) and the Inst. of Musical Art in N.Y. From 1939 to 1943 he was a music critic for the *N.Y. Herald Tribune.* During World War II, he served in the U.S. Army in Italy. After conducting opera in Rome (1944–45), he was conductor of the Phoenix (Ariz.) Sym. Orch. (1949–52) and the Ankara Sym. Orch. (1957–58). In 1961 he founded the Friends of French Opera in N.Y., with which he conducted performances of many rarely-heard scores. He later conducted opera in Atlanta and served as head of the opera dept. at the Peabody Cons. of Music in Baltimore. He was the author of the books *The World of Opera* (1958) and *A Rage for Opera* (1971).

Lawrence, Vera Brodsky, American pianist and music editor; b. Norfolk, Va., July 1, 1909. She studied piano with Josef and Rosina Lhévinne and theory with Goldmark and Wagenaar at the Juilliard School of Music in N.Y. (1929–32). She gave duo-piano concerts with Harold Triggs, and appeared as a soloist with American orchs. In a radical change of direction, she abandoned her concert career in 1965 to become a historian of American music. In 1967 she was appointed administrator of publications for the Contemporary Music Project, and supervised the publication of numerous works by American composers. She publ. the collected piano works of Gottschalk (5 vols., 1969); the complete works of Joplin (2 vols., 1970); *Music for Patriots, Politicians, and Presidents,* tracing American history as reflected in popular music, profusely illustrated with title pages and musical excerpts from publ. songs and dances celebrating historical events, and campaign ballads written during presidential elections (1975), which received the ASCAP-Deems Taylor Award (1976); *Strong on Music: The New York Music Scene in the Days of George Templeton Strong, 1836–1875: Vol. I: Resonances, 1836–1850* (1988) and *Vol. II: Reverberations, 1850–1856* (1995).

Layton, Billy Jim, American composer and teacher; b. Corsicana, Texas, Nov. 14, 1924. He studied at the New England Cons. of Music in Boston with Francis Judd Cook and Carl McKinley (B.Mus., 1948), at Yale Univ. with Quincy Porter (M.Mus., 1950), and at Harvard Univ. with Piston (composition) and Gombosi and Pirrotta (musicology); obtained his Ph.D. at Harvard with the diss. *Italian Music for the Ordinary of the Mass* (1960); then was on its faculty (1960–66); in 1966 he was appointed a prof. of music at the State Univ. of N.Y. at Stony Brook. His small output is a finely crafted oeuvre which utilizes various contemporary techniques from free atonality to jazz improvisation.

WORKS: *An American Portrait,* symphonic overture (1953); *3 Dylan Thomas Poems* for Chorus and Brass Sextet (1954–56); *Dante Fantasy* for Orch. (1964); chamber music.

Layton, Robert, noted English musicologist; b. London, May 2, 1930. He was educated under Rubbra and Wellesz at Worcester College, Oxford (B.A., 1953); then went to Sweden, learned the language, and took courses at the Univs. of Uppsala and Stockholm (1953–55). In 1959 he joined the staff of the BBC in London, where he prepared music seminars. He became an authority on Scandinavian music. He contributed the majority of the articles on Scandinavian composers to *The New Grove Dictionary of Music and Musicians* (1980), and in a spirit of mischievous fun also inserted a biography of a nonexistent Danish composer, making up his name from the stations of the Copenhagen subway. The editor was not amused, and the phony entry had to be painfully gouged in the galleys for the new printing. Layton also prepared the Eng. tr. of E. Tawaststjerna's *Jean Sibelius* (1976–).

WRITINGS: *Franz Berwald* (in Swedish, Stockholm, 1956; Eng. tr., London, 1959); *Sibelius* (London, 1965; 3rd ed., rev., 1983); *Sibelius and His World* (London, 1970); ed. *A Companion to the Concerto* (London, 1988).

Lažar, Filip, Romanian composer and pianist; b. Craiova, May 18, 1894; d. Paris, Nov. 3, 1936. He was a student of Kiriac (theory), Castaldi (harmony and counterpoint), and Saegiu (piano) at the Bucharest Cons. (1907–12), and of Krehl (harmony and composition) and Teichmüller (piano) at the Leipzig Cons. (1913–14). In subsequent years, he made tours as a pianist in Europe and the U.S. as a champion of modern music. In 1920 he helped to found the Romanian Composers' Soc. In 1928 he founded and served as chairman of the modern music soc. Triton in Paris. He was active as a piano teacher in France and Switzerland from 1928. In 1924 he won the Enesco Prize and in 1931 the prize of the Romanian Radio. His compositions were infused with Romanian folk tunes until he adopted a more adventuresome style in 1928, in which he utilized serial and neo-Classical elements.

WORKS: DRAMATIC: *La bouteille de Panurge,* ballet (1918); *Les images de Béatrice,* opera-cantata (1928). **ORCH.:** *Prelude* (1919); *Suita română* (1921); *Divertisment* (1924; Bucharest, Feb. 9, 1925); *Tziganes,* scherzo (1925); *Suite valaque* for Small Orch. (1925); *Music for an Orchestra* (1927; Boston, March 23, 1928); *Concerto grosso* (1927; Boston, May 1928); *Le Ring,* symphonic suite (1928; Paris, Jan. 10, 1930); *Musique per Radio,* overture for Small Orch. (1930; Paris, Feb. 26, 1931); Concerto for Piano and Small Orch. (1931); Piano Concerto (Paris, Nov. 4, 1934); *Concerto da camera* for Percussion and 12 Instruments (1934; Paris, Dec. 11, 1935). **CHAMBER:** Violin Sonata (1919); *Bagatelle* for Cello and Piano (1925); *3 Dances* for Violin and Piano (1927); Trio for Oboe, Clarinet, and Bassoon (1934); String Trio (1935); *Petite suite* for Oboe, Clarinet, and Bassoon (1936). **PIANO:** 2 sonatas (1913, 1929); 3 suites (1924, 1925, 1926); *Bagatelle* (1927); (6) *Pièces minuscules* for Children (1929); *Dans românesc* (n.d.). **OTHER:** Choral pieces; songs.

BIBL.: V. Tomescu, *F. L.* (Bucharest, 1963).

Lazarev, Alexander, Russian conductor; b. Moscow, July 5, 1945. He was trained in Moscow at the Central Music School and at the Cons., and at the Leningrad Cons. In 1971 he took 1st prize in the Moscow Young Conductors Competition, and then was a prizewinner at the Herbert von Karajan competition in Berlin in 1972. In 1973 he became a conductor at the Bolshoi Theater in Moscow, where he founded the Ensemble of Soloists in 1978 to further the performance of contemporary music. He appeared as both an opera and sym. conductor throughout Europe. From 1987 to 1995 he was chief conductor of the Bolshoi Theater. From 1988 to 1993 he was Generalmusikdirektor of the Duisburg Sym. Orch. From 1992 he was also principal guest conductor of the BBC Sym. Orch. in London.

Lazaro, Hippolito, Spanish tenor; b. Barcelona, Aug. 13, 1887; d. Madrid, May 14, 1974. He studied in Milan; then sang operetta in Barcelona. He went to London in 1912, singing at the Coliseum under the name of Antonio Manuele; in 1913 he returned to Italy, where Mascagni chose him to create the role of Ugo in *Parisina* at La Scala in Milan. He made his Metropolitan Opera debut in N.Y. on Jan. 31, 1918, as the Duke of Mantua in *Rigoletto*; remained on its roster until 1920. In 1921 he created the role of Piccolo Marat in Mascagni's opera in Rome; also the role of Giannetto in *La cena delle beffe* by Giordano at La Scala in 1924. He made guest appearances with the Vienna State Opera, the Budapest Opera, and the Teatro Colón in Buenos Aires. He retired in 1950.

Lazarof, Henri, Bulgarian-born American composer and pedagogue; b. Sofia, April 12, 1932. After initial studies in Sofia, he went to Palestine to pursue his training with Ben-Haim and at the New Cons. of Music in Jerusalem (1949–52); following advanced studies with Petrassi at the Accademia di Santa Cecilia in Rome (1955–57), he completed his training with Berger and Shapiro at Brandeis Univ. (M.F.A., 1959). In 1959 he became a naturalized American citizen, and that same year he became a teacher of French language and literature at the Univ. of Calif. at Los Angeles; subsequently he was prof. of composition there (1962–87). His music is marked by inventive originality in its thematic structure and subtle "sonorism" in instrumentation, with instances of serial procedures.

WORKS: BALLETS: *Events* (1973); *Canti* (1980); *Mirrors, Mirrors* (1981). **ORCH.:** Piano Concerto (1956); *Piccola serenata* (Boston, June 15, 1959); Viola Concerto (1959–60; Monaco, Feb. 20, 1962); Concerto for Piano and 20 Instruments (1960–61; RAI, Milan, May 28, 1963); *Odes* (1962–63); *Tempi concertati*, double concerto for Violin, Viola, and Chamber Orch. (1964); *Structures sonores* (1966); *Mutazione* (1967); Cello Concerto (1968; Oslo, Sept. 12, 1969); *Omaggio*, chamber concerto for 19 Players (1968); *Textures* for Piano and 5 Ensembles (1970); *Konkordia* for Strings (1971); *Spectrum* for Trumpet, Orch., and Tape (1972–73; Salt Lake City, Jan. 17, 1975); Flute Concerto (1973); *Ritratto* (1973); *Chamber Concerto No. 3* (1974); *Volo* for Viola and 2 String Ensembles (1975); Chamber Sym. (1976); *Concerto for Orchestra* No. 1 (1977) and No. 2, *Icarus* (1984; Houston, April 12, 1986); Sym. (1978); Sinfonietta (1981); *Poema* (1985; Seattle, May 10, 1986); Violin Concerto (1985); *Tableaux* for Piano and Orch. (1987); Concertante I for 16 Strings and 2 Horns (1988); Clarinet Concerto (1989; N.Y., May 31, 1992). **CHAMBER:** 3 string quartets (1956; 1961–62; 1980); String Trio (1957); Sonata for Solo Violin (1958); *Concertino da camera* for Wind Quintet (1959); *Inventions* for Viola and Piano (1962); *Asymptotes* for Flute and Vibraphone (1963); *Tempi concertati* for 9 Instruments (1964); *Rhapsody* for Violin and Piano (1966); *Espaces* for 10 Instruments (1966); *Cadence I* for Cello (1969), *II* for Viola and Tape (1969), *III* for Violin and 2 Percussion (1970), *V* for Flute and Tape (1972), and *VI* for Tuba and Tape (1973); *Continuum* for String Trio (1970); *Partita* for Brass Quintet and Tape (1971); *Concertazioni* for 7 Instruments and Tape (1973); Duo for Cello and Piano (1973); *Adieu* for Clarinet and Piano (1974); *Fanfare* for 6 Trumpets (1980); Wind Trio (1981); *Lyric Suite* for Violin (1983); *Serenade* for String Sextet (1985); *La Laurenziana*, string octet (1987); Concertante II, octet for Flute, Oboe, Clarinet, Violin, Cello, Double Bass, Percussion, and Piano (1988); Piano Trio (1989). **PIANO:** *Quantetti* for Piano and 3 Pianos on Tape (1964); *Cadence IV* (1970).

Lazarus, Daniel, French conductor and composer; b. Paris, Dec. 13, 1898; d. there, June 27, 1964. He studied with Diémer, Leroux, and Vidal at the Paris Cons., taking the premier prix in composition (1915). He was conductor of the Théâtre du Vieux Colombier (1921–25), then artistic director of the Paris Opéra-Comique (1936–39); later was chorus master of the Paris Opéra (1946–56), then prof. at the Schola Cantorum in Paris (from 1956). He publ. *Accès à la musique* (Paris, 1960). His compositions include the operas *L'Illustre Magicien* (1924), *La Véritable Histoire de Wilhelm Meister* (1927), *Trumpeldor* (1935), and *La Chambre bleue* (1938); 3 ballets; incidental music; Piano Concerto (1929); 2 syms. (1933, 1934); chamber music; piano pieces; songs.

Lazzari, (Joseph) Sylvio, Austrian-born French conductor and composer; b. Bozen, Dec. 30, 1857; d. Suresnes, near Paris, June 10, 1944. He was born into a wealthy Austro-Italian family. After extensive travels, he settled in Paris and in 1883 he entered the Cons., where he was a student of Gounod, Guiraud, and Franck. In 1896 he became a naturalized French citizen. He became active as a theater conductor, and also wrote operas and incidental music. His most distinguished work was the tragic opera *La lépreuse* or *L'ensorcelé* (Paris, Feb. 7, 1912). His opera *La tour de feu* (Paris, Jan. 28, 1928) was the first to utilize film as an integral part of the score.

WORKS: DRAMATIC: OPERAS: *Armor* (1897; Prague, Nov. 7, 1898); *La lépreuse* or *L'ensorcelé* (1900–1901; Paris, Feb. 7, 1912); *Melaenis* (1913; Mulhouse, March 25, 1927); *Le sauteriot* (1913–15; Chicago, Jan. 19, 1918); *La tour de feu* (1925; Paris, Jan. 28, 1928). Also a pantomime, *Lulu* (Paris, May 1889), and incidental music. **OTHER:** Sym.; symphonic poems; other orch. pieces; chamber music; piano pieces; choral works; songs.

Lazzari, Virgilio, Italian-born American bass; b. Assisi, April 20, 1887; d. Castel Gandolfo, Oct. 4, 1953. He made his stage debut as L'Incognito in Suppe's *Boccaccio* with the Vitale Operetta Co. in 1908, remaining with the company until 1911. After studies with Cotogni in Rome, he made his operatic debut at the Teatro Costanzi there in 1914; then sang in South America. In 1916 he made his U.S. debut as Ramfis in St. Louis. He settled in the U.S. and became a naturalized American citizen. From 1918 to 1933 he was a member of the Chicago Opera. On Dec. 28, 1933, he made his Metropolitan Opera debut in N.Y. as Pedro in *L'Africaine*; remained on the roster until 1940; then returned for the 1943–51 seasons. He also sang at the Salzburg Festivals (1934–39) and appeared as Leporello at London's Covent Garden (1939). He became celebrated for his portrayal of Archibaldo in Montemezzi's *L'amore dei tre re*.

Lear, Evelyn (née **Shulman**), outstanding American soprano; b. N.Y., Jan. 8, 1926. She learned to play the piano and the horn before pursuing vocal training with John Yard in Washington, D.C., and with Sergius Kagen at the Juilliard School of Music in N.Y. She also attended N.Y. Univ. and Hunter College of the City Univ. of N.Y. In 1955 she made her N.Y. recital debut, the same year that she married her 2nd husband, **Thomas Stewart.** For professional reasons, however, she retained her first husband's surname of Lear. After obtaining a Fulbright grant, she pursued her studies with Maria Ivogun at the Berlin Hochschule für Musik. On May 17, 1959, she made her operatic debut as Strauss' Composer at the Berlin Städtische Oper. She attracted wide notice when she essayed the role of Lulu in a concert performance in Vienna in 1960, returning there in 1962 to sing the role on stage. In 1961 she created the title role in Klebe's *Alkmene* in Berlin, and in 1963 the role of Jeanne in Egk's *Die Verlobung in San Domingo* in Munich. At the Salzburg Festivals, she appeared as Cherubino (1962–64) and as Fiordiligi (1965). In 1965 she made her first appearance at London's Covent Garden singing Donna Elvira. On March 17, 1967, she made her Metropolitan Opera debut in N.Y. creating the role of Lavinia in Levy's *Mourning Becomes Electra*. In subsequent seasons, she returned to sing Octavian and Berg's Marie (1969), Strauss' Composer (1970), Tosca and Dido (1973), Donna Elvira (1974), Alice Ford (1975), and Countess Geschwitz (1980). She also created the roles of Irma Arkadina in Pasatieri's *The Seagull* in Houston (1974) and Magda in Ward's *Minutes to Midnight* in Miami (1982). On Oct. 15, 1985, she made her farewell appearance at the Metropolitan Opera as the Marschallin. In 1987 she sang Countess Geschwitz in Chicago. Throughout her operatic career, she also pursued a notably successful concert career. She often appeared in both opera and concerts with her husband.

Leça, Armando Lopes, Portuguese choral conductor, folksong collector, and composer; b. Leça da Palmeira, Aug. 9, 1893; d. Vila Nova de Gaia, Sept. 7, 1977. He studied with Oscar da Silva. He was active as a choral conductor and a collector of native folk songs; publ. an authoritative ed. of popular Portuguese music (1922; expanded ed. in 2 vols., 1947). He wrote several dance suites for Orch., of which the *Dansa de Don Pedro* attained considerable popularity; also 2 operettas: *Maio florido* (1918) and *Bruxa* (1919); many piano pieces of pictorial character; songs.

Le Caine, Hugh, Canadian physicist, acoustician, and innovative creator of prototypical electronic musical instruments; b. Port Arthur, Ontario, May 27, 1914; d. Ottawa, July 3, 1977. Although his childhood training combined music and science, he chose to emphasize science in his formal studies; he received a B.S. degree from Queen's Univ. in Kingston, Ontario, in 1938 and an M.S. in 1939, and obtained his Ph.D. in nuclear physics from the Univ. of Birmingham in England in 1952; he also studied piano briefly at the Royal Cons. of Music of Toronto and privately with Viggo Kihl. His childhood dream was to one day apply scientific techniques to the development and invention of new musical instruments, and he went on to develop ground-breaking electronic musical instruments which ultimately formed the basis of pioneering electronic music studios at the Univ. of Toronto (1959) and McGill Univ. in Montreal (1964). He exhibited electronic music instruments at Expo '67 in Montreal. He contributed numerous articles on his findings in various scholarly journals. While he saw himself as a designer of instruments which assisted others in creative work, he himself realized a number of striking electronic compositions in the course of his development, among them the now-classic *Dripsody* (1959), which used only the sound of a single drop of water falling; other compositions were *Alchemy* (1964) and *Perpetual Motion* for Data Systems Computer (1970). His instruments revolutionized musical composition; his Sackbut synthesizer (1945–48; 1954–60; 1969–73) is today recognized as the first voltage-controlled synthesizer; among his other instruments were the Spectrogram (1959–62; designed to facilitate the use of complex sine tones in composition), the Alleatone (c.1962; "a controlled chance device selecting one of 16 channels with weighted probabilities"), Sonde (1968–70; which can generate 200 sine waves simultaneously), and Polyphone (1970; a polyphonic synthesizer operated by a keyboard with touch-sensitive keys).

BIBL.: G. Young, *The Sackbut Blues: H. L.C.: Pioneer in Electronic Music* (Ottawa, 1989).

Lechthaler, Josef, Austrian composer and pedagogue; b. Rattenberg, Dec. 31, 1891; d. Vienna, Aug. 21, 1948. He studied philology in Innsbruck and then settled in Vienna, where he was a student of Springer and Goller at the Academy of Music and of Adler at the Univ. (Ph.D., 1919, with the diss. *Die kirchenmus: Werke von Uttendal*). In 1924 he became a teacher of theory at the Academy of Music, where he later was director of its church and school music dept. (1933–38; 1945–48). He became best known as a composer of church music, principally of 7 masses (1914–37) and a Stabat mater for Soli, Chorus, Organ, and Orch. (1928). He also wrote choruses, songs, chamber music, and organ pieces.

BIBL.: E. Tittel, *J. L.* (Vienna, 1966).

Lecuna, Juan Vicente, Venezuelan composer; b. Valencia, Nov. 20, 1891; d. Rome, April 15, 1954. He studied at the Escuela Normal, graduating in 1906; then went to Caracas and studied theory with Juan Vicente and piano with Salvador Llamozas at the Cons.; later took a course in composition with Jaime Pahissa in Buenos Airea (1937–41), where he also received instruction from Falla; likewise studied orchestration with Strube in Baltimore (1941). In the meantime, he entered the diplomatic service. In 1936 he was appointed a civil employee at the Venezuelan embassy in Washington, D.C. In 1943 he was sent by the Venezuelan dept. of education to study musical education in Brazil, Uruguay, Argentina, and Chile. In 1947 he was named Secretary of the Legation of Venezuela in Rome, and later was appointed a member of the Venezuelan legation at the Vatican. He composed a Piano Concerto; *Suite venezolana* for 4 Guitars; String Quartet; Harp Sonata; songs; and a suite of 4 Venezuelan dances for Piano.

BIBL.: W. Guido, "Ficha biografica y catálogo de la obra musical de J.V. L.," *Revista Musical de Venezuela* (Jan.-April 1981).

Ledenev, Roman (Semyonovich), Russian composer; b. Moscow, Dec. 4, 1930. He studied composition at the Moscow Cons. with Rakov and Anatoly Alexandrov; later was an instructor there. His music is marked by a typically Russian lyric quality touched with permissible dissonances in harmonic treatment. He composed an oratorio, *The Chronicle of the Campaign of Igor* (1954); *The Song of Freedom* for Chorus, after Asian and African poets (1961); Violin Concerto (1964); Viola Concerto (1964); Sonata in memory of Prokofiev (1956); numerous songs.

Ledger, Philip (Stevens), noted English conductor, organist, harpsichordist, pianist, editor, and arranger; b. Bexhill-on-Sea, Sussex, Dec. 12, 1937. He was educated at King's College, Cambridge, and at the Royal College of Music, London. He served as Master of the Music at Chelmsford Cathedral (1962–65) and as director of music at the Univ. of East Anglia (1965–73), where he served as dean of the School of Fine Arts and Music (1968–71). In 1968 he was named an artistic director of the Aldeburgh Festival; subsequently was engaged as conductor of the Cambridge Univ. Musical Soc. (1973) and director of music and organist at King's College (1974). In 1982 he was appointed principal of the Royal Scottish Academy of Music and Drama in Glasgow. He ed. *The Oxford Book of English Madrigals* (1978) and works of Byrd, Purcell, and Handel. A versatile musician, he is renowned as an elegant performer of early English music. In 1985 he was made a Commander of the Order of the British Empire.

Leduc, Jacques, Belgian composer and teacher; b. Jette, near Brussels, March 1, 1932. He studied music at the Royal Cons. in Brussels and privately with Jean Absil. He was director of the Uccle Academy of Music (1962–83); was made a prof. of harmony (1968), of counterpoint (1972), and of fugue (1979) at the Royal Cons. in Brussels; was also director of the Chapelle Musicale Reine Elisabeth (from 1976). He was made a member of the Royal Academy of Sciences, Letters, and Fine Arts of Belgium in 1983.

WORKS: DRAMATIC: *Nous attendons Sémiramis*, lyric comedy (Belgian TV, Feb. 6, 1973). **ORCH.:** *Antigone*, symphonic poem (1960); Concertino for Oboe and Strings (1962); *Divertissement* for Flute and Strings (1962); *Fantaisie sur le thème de "La Folia"* for Clarinet and Chamber Orch. or Piano (1964); *4 Études* for Chamber Orch. (1966); *Le Printemps*, symphonic sketch (1967); *Ouverture d'été* (1968); Sym. (1969); Piano Concerto (1970); *5 croquis* (1971); *Dialogue* for Clarinet and Chamber Orch. or Piano (1972); *Instantanés*, 5 pieces for String Ensemble (1972); *Suite de danses* (1976); *3 Esquisses concertantes* (1978). **CHAMBER:** Wind Quintet (1960); *3 petites pièces en quatuor* for 4 Flutes or Clarinets (1963); String Trio (1963); *Suite en quatuor* for 4 Saxophones (1964); Flute Sonata (1966); Violin Sonata (1967); *Capriccio* for Wind Quartet (1969); *Serenade* for Wind Quintet (1977); *Rhapsodie* for Saxophone and Piano (1978); *Trois pièces* for 5 Brass Instruments (1980); *Pièces en trio* for 2 Violins and Piano (1984); *Lamento* for Viola (1986). **KEYBOARD: PIANO:** *4 pièces brèves* (1965); *Prelude, Variations, and Fugato* (1965); *Contrastes* (1967); *Apostrophes* (1971); *Pochades* (1977); *4 Miniatures* (1981); *Scherzetto* (1986). Also organ music. **VOCAL:** *L'Aventure*, cantata (1961); *Sortilèges africains*, sequence for Voice, Saxophone, Percussion, and Piano (1966); choruses; songs.

Lee, Dai-Keong, Hawaiian composer of Chinese descent; b. Honolulu, Sept. 2, 1915. Following pre-med training at the Univ. of Hawaii (1933–36), he pursued musical studies with Sessions and Jacobi at the Juilliard Graduate School in N.Y. (1938–41), with Copland at the Berkshire Music Center in Tanglewood (summer, 1941), and with Luening at Columbia Univ. (M.A., 1951). He held 2 Guggenheim fellowships (1945, 1951). Lee's works utilize various native elements for the most part, although he has embraced a neo-Classical approach in some of his more ambitious scores.

WORKS: DRAMATIC: OPERAS: *The Poet's Dilemma* (N.Y., April 12, 1940); *Open the Gates* (1951); *Phineas and the Nightingale* (1952); *Speakeasy* (N.Y., Feb. 8, 1957); *2 Knickerbocker Tales* (1957); *Ballad of Kitty the Barkeep* (1979; based on *Speakeasy*). **MUSICAL PLAYS:** *Noa Noa* (1972); *Jenny Lind* (1981; based on *Phineas and the Nightingale*). **INCIDENTAL MUSIC:** *Teahouse of the August Moon* (1953; orch. suite, 1954). **BALLET:** *Waltzing Matilda* (1951). Also film scores. **ORCH.:** *Prelude and Hula* (1939); *Hawaiian Festival Overture* (1940); *Golden Gate Overture* (1941); *Introduction and Scherzo* for Strings (1941); 2 syms.: No. 1 (1941–42; rev. 1946) and No. 2 (San Francisco, March 14, 1952); *Pacific Prayer* (1943; rev. as *Canticle of the Pacific* for Chorus and Orch., 1968); Violin Concerto (1947; rev. 1955); *Polynesian Suite* (1958); *Mele olili* (Joyful Songs) for Soloists, Chorus, and

Orch. (1960); *Concerto Grosso* for Strings (1985). **OTHER:** Chamber music; songs.

Leech, Richard, American tenor; b. Binghamton, Calif., 1956. During his student years, he made appearances as a baritone and then as a tenor. His professional career began in earnest in 1980. In subsequent years, he sang in Cincinnati, Pittsburgh, Baltimore, Houston, and Chicago. In 1987 he made his European debut as Raoul in *Les Huguenots* at the Berlin Deutsche Oper. He made his first appearance at the N.Y. City Opera as the Duke of Mantua in 1988. In 1990 he made his Metropolitan Opera debut in N.Y. as Gounod's Faust and also sang for the first time at Milan's La Scala as Pinkerton. In the 1991–92 season he made his debut at London's Covent Garden as Raoul. He returned to the Metropolitan Opera in 1994 as Rodolfo.

Leedy, Douglas, American composer, pianist, and conductor; b. Portland, Oreg., March 3, 1938. He studied at Pomona College (B.A., 1959) and at the Univ. of Calif. at Berkeley (M.A., 1962). He played the horn in the Oakland (Calif.) Sym. Orch. and in the San Francisco Opera and Ballet orchs. (1960–65); in 1965–66 he held a joint U.S.-Polish government grant for study in Poland. From 1967 to 1970 he was on the faculty of the Univ. of Calif., Los Angeles; from 1973 to 1978 he taught at Reed College in Portland, Oreg. He was conductor of the Oregon Telemann Ensemble, later known as the Harmonie Universelle. From 1984 to 1985 he was music director of the Portland Baroque Orch. His early works cultivated avant-garde methods of electronic application to mixed media, but later he sought to overcome the restrictions of Western music and its equal temperament; for this purpose, he began in 1979 to work with the Carnatic vocalist K.V. Narayanaswamy in Madras, India. Parallel to that, he evinced an interest in early Western music; ed. *Chansons from Petrucci in Original Notation . . .* in the Musica Sacra et Profana series (1983). He was the author of "A Question of Intonation" in the *Journal of the Conductor's Guild* (Fall 1987).

WORKS: *Exhibition Music* (1965; continued indefinitely); *Decay*, theater piece for Piano, Wagner Tuba, and Tape (1965); *Antifonia* for Brass Quartet (1965); *Usable Music I* for Very Small Instruments with Holes (1966) and *II* for Brass Instruments (1966); *Teddy Bear's Picnic*, audio-tactile electronic theater piece (1968); *Ave Maris Stella* for Soprano, Instrumental Trio, Organ, and Electronic Sound (1968); *88 Is Great*, theater piece for many-handed Piano (1968); *The Electric Zodiac*, electronic music (1969); *Entropical Paradise: 6 Sonic Environments* for Electronic Recordings (1970); *Gloria* for Soprano, Chorus, and Instruments (1970); *The 24th Psalm* for 6 Solo Soprano Voices, Chorus, and Orch. (1972); *Sebastian*, chamber opera for Soprano, Baritone, Chamber Ensemble, and Tape, based on documents of J.S. Bach (1971–74); *Wie schön leuchtet der Morgenstern*, chorale fantasia for Organ and unseen Soprano (1972); String Quartet, in just intonation (1965–75); *Canti: Music* for Contrabass and Chamber Ensemble (1975); *Symphoniae sacrae* for Soprano, Bass, Viola da Gamba, and Harpsichord (1976); *Sur la couche de miettes* for Flute, Oboe, Violin, Viola, Cello, Guitar, Piano, equal-temperament Harpsichord, and just-intonation Harpsichord (1981); *Harpsichord Book, Parts I–II*, in traditional mean-tone temperament (1974, 1982); *Harpsichord Book, Part III*, in just tuning (1982); *4 Hymns from the Rigveda* for Chorus and Javanese or American Gamelan (1982–83); *5 Organ Chorales* (1983); *Music* for Meantone Organ (1983–84); *Canto orphea* for Voice and Harp (1987); *Pastorale* for Solo Voices, Chorus, and Retuned Piano (1987); *Fantasy on "Wondrous Love"* for Organ and Optional Chorus (1990); *3 Symphonies* for Unison Orch. (1993); Piano Sonata (1994); *White Buffalo*, string quartet (1995).

Lees (real name, **Lysniansky**), **Benjamin,** distinguished Russian-born American composer and teacher; b. Harbin, Manchuria, Jan. 8, 1924. He was taken to the U.S. in infancy. At 5, he began piano studies with K. Rodetsky in San Francisco. At 15, he became a piano student of Marguerite Bitter in Los Angeles; he also pursued training in harmony and theory and began to compose. Following studies in theory with Stevens, Dahl, and Kanitz at the Univ. of Southern Calif. in Los Angeles (1945–49), he studied with Antheil (until 1954). In 1954 he held a Guggenheim fellowship and in 1956 a Fulbright fellowship, which enabled him to live in Europe until 1962. In 1966 he held another Guggenheim fellowship. He taught at the Peabody Cons. of Music in Baltimore (1962–64; 1966–68), Queens College of the City Univ. of N.Y. (1964–65), the Manhattan School of Music (1970–72), and the Juilliard School (1973–74). Lees' music possesses an ingratiating quality, modern but not arrogantly so. His harmonies are lucid and are couched in euphonius dissonances. He favors rhythmic asymmetry while the formal design of his works is classical in its clarity.

WORKS: DRAMATIC: OPERAS: *The Oracle* (1956); *Medea in Corinth* (1970; London, Jan. 10, 1971); *The Gilded Cage* (1970–72). **BALLET:** *Scarlatti Portfolio* (1978; San Francisco, March 15, 1979). **ORCH.:** *Profile* (NBC Radio, 1952; 1st concert perf., N.Y., April 18, 1954); 5 syms.: No. 1 (1953), No. 2 (Louisville, Dec. 3, 1958), No. 3 (1968; Detroit, Jan. 16, 1969), No. 4, *Memorial Candles*, for Mezzo-soprano, Violin, and Orch. (Dallas, Oct. 10, 1985), and No. 5, *Kalmar Nyckel* (1986; Wilmington, Del., March 29, 1988); *Declamations* for Piano and Strings (1953; Oklahoma City, Feb. 15, 1956); 2 piano concertos: No. 1 (1955; Vienna, April 26, 1956) and No. 2 (1966; Boston, March 15, 1968); *Divertimento-Burlesca* for Chamber Orch. (Fish Creek, Wis., Aug. 11, 1957); *Interlude* for Strings (Toronto, July 1957); Violin Concerto (1958; Boston, Feb. 8, 1963); *Concertante Breve* for Chamber Orch. (1959; Vancouver, British Columbia, Oct. 1960); *Prologue, Capriccio, and Epilogue* (Portland, Oreg., April 9, 1959); *Concerto for Orchestra* (1959; Rochester, N.Y., Feb. 22, 1962); Oboe Concerto (1963; Philadelphia, Dec. 12, 1964); Concerto for String Quartet and Orch. (1964; Kansas City, Mo., Jan. 19, 1965); *Spectrum* (La Jolla, Calif., June 21, 1964); Concerto for Chamber Orch. (Philadelphia, Oct. 9, 1966); *Fanfare for a Centennial* for Brass and Percussion (Baltimore, Nov. 13, 1966); *Silhouettes* (NET-TV, Oct. 3, 1967); *Etudes* for Piano and Orch. (Houston, Oct. 28, 1974); *Passacaglia* (1975; Washington, D.C., April 13, 1976); *Labyrinths* for Symphonic Band (Bloomington, Ind., Nov. 18, 1975); *Variations* for Piano and Orch. (Dallas, March 31, 1976); Concerto for Woodwind Quintet and Orch. (Detroit, Oct. 7, 1976); *Mobiles* (N.Y., April 13, 1979); Double Concerto for Piano, Cello, and Orch. (N.Y., Nov. 7, 1982); Concerto for Brass Choir and Orch. (Dallas, March 18, 1983); *Portrait of Rodin* (1984; Portland, Oreg., April 5, 1987); Horn Concerto (Pittsburgh, May 14, 1992); *Borealis* (Wichita, Oct. 8, 1993). **CHAMBER:** Horn Sonata (1951); 4 string quartets: No. 1 (N.Y., Nov. 8, 1952), No. 2 (1955; Scranton, Pa., Jan. 31, 1956), No. 3 (1980; N.Y., May 16, 1982), and No. 4 (1989; San Francisco, March 11, 1990); *Evocation* for Flute (1953); 3 violin sonatas: No. 1 (N.Y., Feb. 1953), No. 2 (1972; Washington, D.C., May 4, 1973), and No. 3 (San Francisco, Nov. 21, 1991); *Movemente da camera* for Flute, Clarinet, Piano, and Cello (1954); *3 Variables* for Oboe, Clarinet, Bassoon, Horn, and Piano (Vienna, Oct. 1955); *Invenzione* for Violin (1965; N.Y., Jan. 26, 1966); Duo for Flute and Clarinet (1967); *Study No. 1* for Cello (1969); *Collage* for String Quartet, Wind Quintet, and Percussion (Milwaukee, May 8, 1973); *Dialogue* for Cello and Piano (N.Y., March 2, 1977); Cello Sonata (Washington, D.C., Nov. 13, 1981); Piano Trio (Williamstown, Mass., Sept. 8, 1983). **PIANO:** 4 sonatas: No. 1 (1949), No. 2 (1950), No. 3 (1956), and No. 4 (1963; Oberlin, Ohio, Jan. 7, 1964); Sonata for 2 Pianos (1951); *Toccata* (1953); *Fantasia* (1954); *10 Pieces* (1954); *6 Ornamental Etudes* (1957; N.Y., Feb. 16, 1961); *Kaleidoscopes* (1958); *3 Preludes* (1962; N.Y., Jan. 14, 1963); *Odyssey I* (1970) and *II* (1986; N.Y., May 27, 1992); *Fantasy Variations* (1983; N.Y., Feb. 1, 1984); *Mirrors* (Chicago, May 17, 1992). **VOCAL:** (6) *Songs of the Night* for Soprano and Piano (Los Angeles, June 15, 1952; 4 orchestrated as *4 Songs of the Night* for Soprano and 13 Instruments, Genoa, April 19, 1955); *3 Songs* for Contralto and Piano (1959; N.Y., Feb. 2, 1968); *Cyprian Songs* for Baritone and Piano (1960);

Visions of Poets, cantata for Soprano, Tenor, Chorus, and Orch. (1961; Seattle, May 15, 1962); *The Trumpet of the Swan* for Narrator and Orch. (Philadelphia, May 13, 1972); *Staves* for Soprano and Piano (1977; N.Y., Jan. 29, 1978); *Paumanok* for Mezzo-soprano and Piano (N.Y., Dec. 9, 1980); *Echoes of Normandy* for Tenor, Tape, Organ, and Orch. (Dallas, June 15, 1994).

BIBL.: D. Cooke, "The Music of B. L.," *Tempo* (Summer 1959); idem, "The Recent Music of B. L.," ibid. (Spring 1963); N. Slonimsky, "B. L. in Excelsis," ibid. (Summer 1975).

Leeuw, Reinbert de, Dutch composer and conductor, brother of **Ton de Leeuw**; b. Amsterdam, Sept. 8, 1938. He studied at the Amsterdam Cons. In 1963 he was appointed to the faculty of the Royal Cons. of The Hague. A political activist, he collaborated with Louis Andriessen, Mischa Mengelberg, Peter Schat, and Jan van Vlijmen on the anti-American multimedia spectacle *Reconstructie*, produced during the Holland Festival in Amsterdam on June 29, 1969. He further wrote an opera, *Axel* (with Vlijmen; 1977); *Solo I* for Cello (1961); *3 Positions* for Violin (1963); String Quartet (1963); *Interplay* for Orch. (1965); *Hymns and Chorals* for 15 Winds, 2 Electric Guitars, and Electric Organ (Amsterdam, July 5, 1970); *Duets* for Recorder (1971); *Abschied*, symphonic poem (1971–73; Rotterdam, May 11, 1974). In later years, he was active as a conductor of contemporary music. In 1994 he became director of the Tanglewood Festival of Contemporary Music. He publ. a book about Ives (with J. Bemlef; Amsterdam, 1969) and a collection of 17 articles, *Muzikale anarchie* (Amsterdam, 1973).

Leeuw, Ton (actually, **Antonius Wilhelmus Adrianus) de,** prominent Dutch composer and teacher, brother of **Reinbert de Leeuw;** b. Rotterdam, Nov. 16, 1926. He received training in piano and theory with Toebosch in Breda, and in composition with Badings in Amsterdam (1947–49) and with Messiaen and Hartmann in Paris (1949–50); he studied ethnomusicology with Kunst in Amsterdam (1950–54) and made a study trip to India, Iran, Japan, and the Philippines (1961). After working as director of sound at the Dutch Radio in Hilversum (1954–59), he taught composition at the Amsterdam Cons. (from 1959), where he also was director. From 1962 to 1984 he likewise lectured at the Univ. of Amsterdam. He publ. the book *Muziek van de Twintigste Eeuw* (Music of the Twentieth Century; Utrecht, 1964; 2nd ed., 1977). As a composer, he was honored with the Prix Italia (1956), the Prix des Jeunesses Musicales (1961), the Mathijs Vermeulen Prize (1982), and the Johan Wagenaar Prize (1983). In his varied output, Leeuw has ranged widely, utilizing both contemporary Western and non-Western means of expression. He developed a personal static style in which his modal writing became increasingly diatonic.

WORKS: DRAMATIC: OPERAS: *Alceste*, television opera (Dutch TV, March 13, 1963); *De droom* (The Dream; 1963; Amsterdam, June 16, 1965); *Antigone* (1991). **TELEVISION PLAY:** *Litany of Our Time* (1969–70; Dutch TV, Jan 1, 1971). **BALLETS:** *De Bijen* (The Bees; 1964; Arnhem, Sept. 15, 1965); *Krishna en Radha* (1964). **ORCH.:** Concerto Grosso for Strings (1946); *Treurmuziek, in memoriam Willem Pijper* (1948); 3 syms. (Sym. for Strings and Percussion, 1950; Sym. for Strings, 1951; Sym. of Winds, 1964); *Plutos-Suite* (1952); 2 violin concertos (1953, 1961); Suite for Youth Orch. (1954); *Mouvements rétrogrades* (1957); *Nritta*, orch. dance (1961); *Ombres* (1961); *Syntaxis II* (1966); *Spatial Music I* for 32 to 48 Players (1966), *III* for Chamber Orch. in 4 Groups (1967), and *IV: Homage to Igor Stravinsky* for Chamber Orch. (1968); *Music* for Strings (1970); *Gending, a Western homage to the musicians of the gamelan* for Gamelan Orch. (1975); *Alba*, concerto da camera (1982; rev. 1986); *Résonances* (1985); Concerto for 2 Guitars and Chamber String Orch. (1988); *Danses sacrées* for Piano and Orch. (1990). **CHAMBER:** Trio for Violin, Viola, and Cello (1948); Flute Sonata (1949); Violin Sonata (1951); Trio for Flute, Clarinet, and Piano (1952); *5 Sketches* for Oboe, Clarinet, Bassoon, Violin, Viola, and Cello (1952); *Andante en vivace* for Flute and Piano (1955); Violin Sonatina (1955); 2 string quartets (1958; with tape, 1964); *Antiphonie* for Wind Quintet and Electronics (1960); *Schelp* for Flute, Viola, and Guitar (1964); *The 4 Seasons* for Harp (1964); *Night Music* for Flute (1966); *Music* for Violin (1967); *Music* for Oboe (1969); *Music* for Organ and Chamber Ensemble (1970–71); *Reversed Night* for Flute (1971); *Spatial Music II* for Percussion (1971); *Midare* for Marimba (1972); *Music* for Trombone (1973–74); *Canzone* for 4 Horns, 3 Trumpets, and 3 Trombones (1973–74); *Rime* for Flute and Harp (1974); *Mo-do* for Amplified Clavichord or Harpsichord (1974); *Mountains* for Bass Clarinet and Tape (1977); *Modal Music* for Accordion (1978–79); *Interlude* for Guitar (1984); *Apparances I* for Cello (1987) and *II* for Clarinet Quartet (1987); *Hommage à Henri* for Clarinet and Piano (1989); *Music* for Double Bass (1989–91); Trio for Flute, Bass Clarinet, and Piano (1990); *Fauxbourdon* for Flute, Clarinet, Piano, Synthesizer, Marimba, Mandolin, Violin, and Viola (1991–92; rev. 1993); Saxophone Quartet (1993). **PIANO:** *Scherzo* (1948); Sonatina (1949); Sonata for 2 Pianos (1950); *4 Préludes* (1950); *Variations on a French Popular Song* (1950); *5 études* (1951); *4 Rhythmic Études* (1952); *3 African Études* (1954); *Lydic Suite* (1954); *Zes dansen* (1955); *Men Go Their Ways* (1964); *Linkerhand en rechterhand* (1976); *Les Adieux* (1988). **VOCAL:** *Hiob* (Job) for Soloists, Chorus, Orch., and Tape (1956); *Brabant* for Medium Voice and Orch. (1959); *Psalm 118* for Chorus and 2 Trombones or Organ (1966); *Haiku II* for Soprano and Orch. (1968); *Lamento Pacis* for Chorus and Instruments (1969); *The Magic of Music* for Chorus (1970); *The Birth of Music I* for Chorus (1975) and *II* for Voices, Speaker, and Tape (1978); *And They Shall Reign Forever* for Mezzo-soprano, Clarinet, Piano, and Percussion (1981); *Car nos vignes sont de fleurs (Cantique des Cantigues)* for Chorus (1981); *Invocations* for Chorus and Instruments (1983); *Chimères* for Men's Voices (1984); *Les chants de Kabir* for Men's Voices (1985); *Transparence* for Chorus, 3 Trumpets, and 3 Trombones (1986); *Cinq hymnes* for Chorus, 2 Percussion, and 2 Pianos (1988); *A cette heure du jour* for Chorus (1991–92). **OTHER:** *Electronic Suite* for Tape (1958); *Syntaxis I* for Tape (1966); *Chronos* for 4 Sound Tracks (1980); *Clair-Obscur* for Electronics (1981–82).

BIBL.: W. Markus, "Music and Time: Observations on Arnold Schoenberg and T. d.L.," *Key Notes*, no. 23 (1986); R. de Groot, "Aspects of T. d.L.'s Musical Universe," ibid.; B. Robindoré, "T. d.L.: The Vision of a Composer," ibid. (March 1994).

LeFanu, Nicola (Frances), English composer and teacher; b. Wickham Bishops, Essex, April 28, 1947. She was the daughter of the medical historian William LeFanu and the composer **Elizabeth Maconchy.** Her mother was a major influence on her in her formative years. After initial training in composition with Jeremy Dale Roberts, she pursued her studies at St. Hilda's College, Oxford (B.A., 1968; M.A., 1971) and at the Royal College of Music in London (1968–69). In 1973–74 she held a Harkness fellowship and studied with Earl Kim at Harvard Univ. and Seymour Shifrin at Brandeis Univ. She was active in London as director of music at Francis Holland School (1969–72) and St. Paul's Girls School (1975–77). In 1977 she became a senior lecturer at King's College, Univ. of London. In 1979 she married **David Lumsdaine,** with whom she served as composer-in-residence at the New South Wales State Conservatorium of Music in Sydney that same year. As a composer, she has won several honors, including the Cobbett Prize (1969), the BBC Composers Prize (1972), and the Leverhulme Award (1989). She has developed a well-crafted style in which serial techniques are relieved by a deft handling of dramatic and lyrical writing.

WORKS: DRAMATIC: *Anti-World*, music theater (1972); *The Last Laugh*, ballet (1972; London, April 1973); *Dawnpath*, chamber opera (London, Sept. 29, 1977); *The Story of Mary O'Neill*, radiophonic opera (1986; BBC, Jan. 4, 1989); *The Green Children*, children's opera (1990); *Blood Wedding*, opera (1991–92); *The Wildman*, opera (Aldeburgh, June 9, 1995). **ORCH.:** *Preludio I* for Strings (1967; rev. 1976 as *Preludio II* for Strings); *The Hidden Landscape* (London, Aug. 7, 1973); *Columbia Falls* (Birmingham, Nov. 20, 1975); *Farne* (Bradford, March

28, 1980); *Variations* for Piano and Orch. (London, Dec. 31, 1982); Concerto for Alto Saxophone and Strings (1990). **CHAMBER:** *Soliloquy* for Oboe (1966); *Variations* for Oboe, Violin, Viola, and Cello (1968); *Abstracts and a Frame* for Violin and Piano (1971); *Songs and Sketches* for 6 or More Cellos (1971); Clarinet Quintet (1971); *Collana* for Solo Percussion, Flute, Clarinet, Violin, Cello, and Double Bass (Boston, April 25, 1976); *Deva* for Solo Cello, Alto Flute, Clarinet, Bassoon, Horn, Violin, Viola, and Double Bass (London, March 23, 1979); Trio I for Flute, Cello, and Percussion (1980; London, June 15, 1981); *SPNM Birthday Fanfare* for 2 Trumpets (1983); *Moon Over Western Ridge, Mootwingee* for Saxophone Quartet (Stuttgart, Nov. 6, 1985); *Invisible Places* for Clarinet, 2 Violins, Viola, and Cello (Southampton, June 4, 1986); *Lament 1988* for Oboe, Clarinet, Viola, and Cello (London, March 30, 1988); String Quartet (Bedford, Oct. 13, 1988); *Lullaby* for Clarinet and Piano (1988); *Nocturne* for Cello and Piano (1988). **KEYBOARD: PIANO:** *Chiaroscuro* (1969). **ORGAN:** *Omega* (1971; rev. 1984). **VOCAL:** *Il Cantico dei Cantici II* for Soprano (1968); *But Stars Remaining* for Soprano (1970); *Christ Calls Man Home* for 2 Sopranos and 3 Choruses (Cheltenham, July 4, 1971); *Rondeaux* for Tenor and Horn (1972); *The Valleys Shall Sing* for Chorus, 2 Bassoons, 2 Trumpets, and 3 Trombones (Norwich, Oct. 1973); *Paysage* for Baritone (1973); *The Same Day Dawns* for Soprano, Flute, Clarinet, Violin, Cello, and Percussion (Boston, Nov. 4, 1974); *The Little Valleys* for Women's Chorus (1975); *For We Are the Stars* for 16 Solo Voices (1978; BBC, Sept. 30, 1982); *Verses from Psalm 90* for Soprano and 2 Choruses (London, Dec. 5, 1978); *Like a Wave of the Sea* for Chorus and Early Instruments (Nottingham, March 1, 1981); *The Old Woman of Beare* for Amplified Soprano and Chamber Orch. (London, Nov. 3, 1981); *A Penny for a Song* for Soprano and Piano (1981); *Rory's Rounds* for Young Singers (1983); *Trio 2: Song for Peter* for Soprano, Clarinet, and Cello (London, March 3, 1983); *Stranded on My Heart* for Tenor, Chorus, and Strings (St. Alban's, June 16, 1984); *Wind Among the Pines: 5 Images of Norfolk* for Soprano and Orch. (Aldeburgh, July 31, 1987); *I am Bread* for Soprano and Piano (1987).

Lefébure, Yvonne, French pianist and teacher; b. Ermont, Seine-et-Oise, June 29, 1898; d. Paris, Jan. 23, 1986. She began piano studies at an early age and won the "prix de petits prodigés" of the Paris Cons., where she took courses with Emmanuel, Georges Caussade, and Widor; won 6 premiers prix in all; also studied privately with Cortot. She taught at the École Normale de Musique in Paris (from 1924); was also on the faculty of the Paris Cons. (1952–67). She toured widely as a soloist and recitalist.

Leffler-Burckhard, Martha, German soprano; b. Berlin, June 16, 1865; d. Wiesbaden, May 14, 1954. She was a student in Dresden of Anna von Meichsner and in Paris of Pauline Viardot-Garcia. In 1888 she made her operatic debut in Strasbourg, and then sang in Breslau (1889–90) and Cologne (1891–92). After a tour of North America (1892–93), she appeared in Bremen (1893–97) and Weimar (1898–99). From 1900 to 1912 she sang in Wiesbaden, and also appeared at London's Covent Garden (1903, 1907) and at the Metropolitan Opera in N.Y. (debut as Brünnhilde in *Die Walküre*, March 4, 1908). She was a member of the Berlin Royal Opera from 1913 to 1918. After singing at the Berlin Deutsches Opernhaus (1918–19), she taught voice. Among her best-known roles were Leonore, Isolde, the 3 Brünnhildes, Kundry, Ortrud, and Sieglinde.

Le Flem, Paul, French composer, choral conductor, music critic, and teacher; b. Lézardrieux, Côtes-du-Nord, March 18, 1881; d. Trégastel, Côtes-du-Nord, July 31, 1984. He settled in Paris and studied harmony with Lavignac at the Cons. (1899) before completing his training with d'Indy and Roussel at the Schola Cantorum (1904); he also studied philosophy at the Sorbonne. Le Flem wrote perceptive music criticism for *Comoedia* (1921–36), and also served as prof. of counterpoint at the Schola Cantorum (1923–39). In 1924 he became chorus master at the Opéra-Comique, and from 1925 to 1939 he distinguished himself as director of the St. Gervais Choir. In 1951 he was awarded the Grand Prix Musical of Paris. From his earliest compositional efforts, Le Flem was influenced by his native Brittany. His later works also owe much to Debussy and d'Indy, and are skillfully written.

WORKS: DRAMATIC: *Endrymion et Sélémé*, opera (Paris, 1903); *Aucassin et Nicolette*, chante-fable (1908; private perf., Paris, May 19, 1909); *La folie de Lady Macbeth*, ballet (1934); *Le rossignol de St. Malo*, opera (1938; Paris, May 5, 1942); *Les paralytiques volent*, radio score (1938); *La clairière des fées*, opera (1943); *Magicienne de la mer*, opera (1946; Paris, Oct. 29, 1954); *Macbeth*, radio score (1950); *Côte de granit rose*, film score (1954). **ORCH.:** *En mer* (1901); *Scherzo* (1906); 4 syms. (1907; 1956; 1967; 1977–78); *Les voix de large* (1911); *Fantaisie* for Piano and Orch. (1911); *Pour les morts* (1913); *Le village* (1942); *Le ronde des fées* (1943); *Konzertstück* for Violin and Orch. (1965). **CHAMBER:** *Rèverie grise* for Cello and Piano (1899); Violin Sonata (1905); Piano Quintet (1909); *Claire de lune sous bois* for Flute, Harp, and Strings (1911); *Danse désuète* for Flute, Harp, and Strings (1911); *Pièce* for Horn (1955). **PIANO:** *Par landes* (1907); *Par greves* (1907); *Le vieux calvaire* (1910); *Le chant des genêts* (1910); *Avril* (1912). **VOCAL:** *Invocation* for Voice and Orch. (1920); *Le vin* for Chorus and Wind Orch. (1924); *Le fête de printemps* for Women's Chorus and Orch. (1937); *La maudite* for Voices and Orch. (1967; rev. 1971); choruses; songs.

BIBL.: G. Bernard-Krauss, *Hundert Jahre französischer Musikgeschichte in Leben und Werk P. L.s* (Frankfurt am Main and N.Y., 1993).

Le Fleming, Christopher (Kaye), English composer; b. Wimborne, Feb. 26, 1908; d. Woodbury, Devon, June 19, 1985. He studied at the Brighton School of Music and at the Royal School of Church Music in London; then held many teaching posts. He wrote several orch. works, incidental music to plays, choral music, piano pieces, and songs.

Le Gallienne, Dorian (Leon Marlois), Australian composer and music critic; b. Melbourne, April 19, 1915; d. there, July 27, 1963. He studied at the Univ. of Melbourne Conservatorium (graduated, 1938) and with Benjamin and Howells at the Royal College of Music in London (1938–39); later he took lessons with Jacob in England (1951). He served as music critic for Melbourne's *Argus* (from 1950) and for *The Age* (from 1957). His output reveals English and French traits, along with the bitonal writing of early Stravinsky and late Bartók.

WORKS: DRAMATIC: 2 ballets: *Contes heraldiques* (1947) and *Voyageur* (1954); incidental music; film scores. **ORCH.:** Sinfonietta (1951–56); Overture (1952); Sym. (1952–53); *Symphonic Study* (1962–63; 1st movement of the unfinished 2nd Sym.). **CHAMBER:** Flute Sonata (1943); Violin Sonata (1945); Duo for Violin and Viola (1956); Trio for Oboe, Violin, and Viola (1957); *Piece No. 1* for Violin, Cello, Clarinet, Percussion, and Harp (1959) and *No. 2* for 2 Clarinets and String Quartet (1959); piano pieces. **VOCAL:** Songs; part songs.

Legge, Walter, influential English recording executive, orchestral manager, and writer on music; b. London, June 1, 1906; d. St. Jean, Cap Ferrat, March 22, 1979. He was autodidact in music. In 1927 he joined the staff of the Gramophone Co. (His Master's Voice) of London. He became an ardent champion of first-class recording projects, and in 1931 founded a subscription soc. for the purpose of recording unrecorded works. From 1938 he was active with the British Columbia recording label. He also wrote music criticism for the *Manchester Guardian* (1934–38). In 1938–39 he was assistant artistic director of London's Covent Garden. From 1942 to 1945 he was director of music of the Entertainments National Service Assn. In 1945 he founded the Philharmonia Orch. of London, which he managed with notable results as both a recording and concert ensemble until he unsuccessfully attempted to disband it in 1964. In 1953 he married **Elisabeth Schwarzkopf.**

BIBL.: E. Schwarzkopf, ed., *On and Off the Record: A Memoir of W. L.* (London, 1982; 2nd ed., 1988); A. Sanders, ed., *W. L.: A Discography* (London, 1985).

Leginska (real name, **Liggins**), **Ethel,** English pianist, teacher, and composer; b. Hull, April 13, 1886; d. Los Angeles, Feb. 26, 1970. She showed a natural talent for music at an early age; the pseudonym Leginska was given to her by Lady Maud Warrender, under the illusion that a Polish-looking name might help her artistic career. She studied piano wih Kwast at the Hoch Cons. in Frankfurt am Main, and later in Vienna with Leschetizky. After making her London debut (1907), she toured Europe; on Jan. 20, 1913, she appeared for the first time in America at a recital in N.Y. Her playing was described as having masculine vigor, dashing brilliance, and great variety of tonal color; however, criticism was voiced against an individualistic treatment of classical works. In the midst of her career as a pianist, she developed a great interest in conducting; she organized the Boston Phil. Orch. (100 players), later the Women's Sym. Orch. of Boston; appeared as a guest conductor with various orchs. in America and in Europe. In this field of activity, she also elicited interest, leading to a discussion in the press of a woman's capability of conducting an orch. While in the U.S., she took courses in composition with Rubin Goldmark and Ernest Bloch; wrote music in various genres, distinguished by rhythmic display and a certain measure of modernism. She married **Emerson Whithorne** in 1907 (divorced in 1916). In 1939 she settled in Los Angeles as a piano teacher.

WORKS: OPERAS: *The Rose and the Ring* (1932; Los Angeles, Feb. 23, 1957, composer conducting); *Gale* (Chicago, Nov. 23, 1935, composer conducting). **ORCH.:** *Beyond the Fields We Know,* symphonic poem (N.Y., Feb. 12, 1922); *2 Short Pieces* (Boston, Feb. 29, 1924, Monteux conducting); *Quatre sujets barbares,* suite (Munich, Dec. 13, 1924, composer conducting); *Fantasy* for Piano and Orch. (N.Y., Jan. 3, 1926). **CHAMBER:** String Quartet, inspired by 4 poems by Tagore (Boston, April 25, 1921); *From a Life* for 13 Instruments (N.Y., Jan. 9, 1922); *Triptych* for 11 Instruments (Chicago, April 29, 1928); piano pieces. **VOCAL:** *6 Nursery Rhymes* for Soprano and Chamber Orch.; songs.

Legley, Victor, outstanding Belgian composer; b. Hazebrouck, June 18, 1915; d. Ostend, Nov.28, 1994. He studied viola, chamber music, counterpoint, and fugue at the Brussels Cons. (from 1934); then took private lessons in composition with Absil (1941), subsequently winning the Belgian 2nd Prix de Rome (1943). He was a violist in the Belgian Radio Sym. Orch. (1936–48); then was a music producer for the Flemish dept. of the Belgian Radio, and later was made head of its serious music broadcasts on its 3rd program (1962). He taught at the Brussels Cons. (1949–80). He became a member of the Belgian Royal Academy (1965); was its president (1972); was chairman of the Société Belge des Auteurs, Compositeurs, et Editeurs (from 1981). In his works, Legley adheres to the pragmatic tenets of modern music, structurally diversified and unconstricted by inhibitions against dissonance. His 2nd Violin Concerto was a mandatory work of the 1967 Queen Elisabeth violin competition finals.

WORKS: DRAMATIC: OPERA: *La Farce des deux nus* (Antwerp, Dec. 10, 1966). **BALLET:** *Le Bal des halles* (1954). **ORCH.:** 6 syms. (1942, 1947, 1953, 1964, 1965, 1976); *Concert à 13,* chamber sym. (1944); Suite (1944); *Music for a Greek Tragedy* (1946); *Symphonie miniature* for Chamber Orch. (1946); 2 violin concertos: No. 1 (1947) and No. 2 (1966; Brussels, May 22, 1967); *The Golden River,* symphonic sketch (1948); Piano Concerto (1952); *Serenade* for Strings (1957); *La Cathédrale d'acier,* symphonic sketch after a painting by Fernand Steven (1958); *Overture to a Comedy* by Goldoni (1958); *3 Pieces* for Chamber Orch. (1960); *Dyptiek* (1964); Harp Concerto (1966); *Paradise Regained* (1967); *Prelude for a Ballet* (1969); *3 Movements* for Brass and Percussion (1969); *Espaces* for Strings (1970); Viola Concerto (1971); *Before Endeavors Fade* for Strings (1977); *Festival Overture* for Sym. Orch. and Jazz Band (1978); Concertino for Oboe and Strings (1982); Cello Concerto (1984); *Concert d'automne* for Alto Saxophone and Orch. (1984); *Concerto Grosso* for Violin, Alto Saxophone, and Chamber Orch. (1985). **CHAMBER:** 5 string quartets (1941; 1947; 1956; 1963; *Esquisses,* 1970); Quartet for 4 Flutes (1943); Violin Sonata (1943); Viola Sonata (1943); Sextet for Piano and Wind Quintet (1945); Cello Sonata (1945); *Musique de midi,* nonet (1948); Clarinet Sonata (1952); Trumpet Sonata (1953); *Serenade* for Flute, Violin, and Cello (1957); *5 Miniatures* for 4 Saxophones (1958); Trio for Flute, Viola, and Guitar (1959); Wind Quintet (1961); *4 Pieces* for Guitar (1964); Piano Quartet (1973); Piano Trio (1973); String Trio (1973); *Parades I* for 4 Clarinets (1977), *II* for 6 Saxophones (1978), and *III* for 4 Horns (1981); Duo for Violin and Cello (1983); *Suite en re* for Harpsichord (1986); *2 pieces* for Accordion (1986). **PIANO:** 4 sonatas (1946–85); *4 Portraits* (1954–55); *Music* for 2 Pianos (1966); *3 Marches* (1968); *Brindilles* (1974). **VOCAL:** *Zeng* for Soprano and String Quartet or String Orch. (1965); songs.

BIBL.: R. Wangermée, *V. L.* (Brussels, 1953).

Legrand, Michel (Jean), French composer, arranger, pianist, and conductor; b. Paris, Feb. 24, 1932. He received his training at the Paris Cons. (diploma, 1951). While still a student, he began making jazz arrangements. In 1955 he went to the U.S. and composed for radio, television, and films. He acquired considerable success composing for films, winning Academy awards for his *Windmills of Your Mind* (1968), *Summer of 42* (1970), and *Yentl* (1984). He also made over 100 recordings.

Lehár, Franz (actually, **Ferenc**), celebrated Austrian operetta composer of Hungarian descent; b. Komárom, Hungary, April 30, 1870; d. Bad Ischl, Oct. 24, 1948. He began his music training with his father, Franz Lehár (1838–98), a military bandmaster. He then entered the Prague Cons. at 12 and studied violin with A. Bennewitz and theory with J. Foerster. In 1885 he was brought to the attention of Fibich, who gave him lessons in composition independently from his studies at the Cons. In 1887 Lehár submitted 2 piano sonatas to Dvořák, who encouraged him in his musical career. In 1888 he became a violinist in a theater orch. in Elberfeld; in 1889, entered his father's band (50th Infantry) in Vienna, and assisted him as conductor. From 1890 to 1902 Lehár led military bands in Pola, Trieste, Budapest, and Vienna. Although his early stage works were unsuccessful, he gained some success with his marches and waltzes. With *Der Rastelbinder* (Vienna, Dec. 20, 1902), he established himself as a composer for the theater. His most celebrated operetta, *Die lustige Witwe,* was first performed in Vienna on Dec. 30, 1905; it subsequently received innumerable performances throughout the world. From then on Vienna played host to most of his finest scores, including *Der Graf von Luxemburg* (Nov. 12, 1909), *Zigeunerliebe* (Jan. 8, 1910), and *Paganini* (Oct. 30, 1925). For Berlin, he wrote *Der Zarewitsch* (Feb. 21, 1927), *Friederike* (Oct. 4, 1928), and *Das Land des Lächelns* (Oct. 10, 1929; rev. version of *Die gelbe Jacke*). Lehár's last years were made difficult by his marriage to a Jewish woman, which made him suspect to the Nazis. Ironically, *Die lustige Witwe* was one of Hitler's favorite stage works. After World War II, Lehár went to Zürich (1946); then returned to Bad Ischl shortly before his death. Lehár's music exemplifies the spirit of gaiety and frivolity that was the mark of Vienna early in the 20th century; his superlative gift for facile melody and infectious rhythms is combined with genuine wit and irony; a blend of nostalgia and sophisticated humor, undiminished by the upheavals of wars and revolutions, made a lasting appeal to audiences.

WORKS: DRAMATIC (all 1st perf. in Vienna unless otherwise given): **OPERETTAS:** *Fräulein Leutnant* (1901); *Arabella, die Kubamerin* (1901; unfinished); *Das Club-Baby* (1901; unfinished); *Wiener Frauen (Der Klavierstimmer)* (Nov. 21, 1902; rev. as *Der Schlüssel zum Paradies,* Leipzig, Oct. 1906); *Der Rastelbinder* (Dec. 20, 1902); *Der Göttergatte* (Jan. 20, 1904; rev. as *Die ideale Gattin,* Vienna, Oct. 11, 1913; rev. as *Die Tangokönigin,* Vienna, Sept. 9, 1921); *Die Juxheirat* (Dec. 22,

1904); *Die lustige Witwe* (Dec. 30, 1905); *Peter und Paul reisen im Schlaraffenland (Max und Moritz reisen ins Schlaraffenland)* (Dec. 1, 1906); *Mstislaw der Moderne* (Jan. 5, 1907); *Der Mann mit den drei Frauen* (Jan. 21, 1908); *Das Fürstenkind* (Oct. 7, 1909; rev. as *Der Fürst der Berge*, Berlin, Sept. 23, 1932); *Der Graf von Luxemburg* (Nov. 12, 1909); *Zigeunerliebe* (Jan. 8, 1910; rev. as the opera *Garabonciás diák*, Budapest, Feb. 20, 1943); *Die Spieluhr* (Jan. 7, 1911); *Eva* (Nov. 24, 1911); *Rosenstock und Edelweiss* (Dec. 1, 1912); *Endlich allein* (Jan. 30, 1914; rev. as *Schön ist die Welt*, Berlin, Dec. 3, 1930); *Komm, deutscher Bruder* (Oct. 4, 1914; in collaboration with E. Eysler); *Der Sterngucker* (Jan. 14, 1916; rev. as *La danza delle libellule*, Milan, May 3, 1922; rev. as *Gigolette*, Milan, Oct. 30, 1926); *A Pacsirta (Wo die Lerche singt)* (Budapest, Jan. 1, 1918); *Die blaue Mazur* (May 28, 1920); *Frühling* (Jan. 20, 1922); *Frasquita* (May 12, 1922); *Die gelbe Jacke* (Feb. 9, 1923; rev. as *Das Land des Lächelns*, Berlin, Oct. 10, 1929); *Cloclo* (March 8, 1924); *Paganini* (Oct. 30, 1925); *Der Zarewitsch* (Berlin, Feb. 21, 1927); *Friederike* (Berlin, Oct. 4, 1928); *Das Frühlingsmädel* (Berlin, May 29, 1930); *Giuditta* (Jan. 20, 1934). **OPERAS:** *Der Kurassier* (1891–92; unfinished); *Rodrigo* (1893; unfinished); *Kukuška* (Leipzig, Nov. 27, 1896; rev. as *Tatjana*, Brünn, Feb. 21, 1905). **FILM SCORES:** *Die grosse Attraktion* (1931); *Es war einmal ein Walzer* (1932); *Grossfürstin Alexandra* (1934); *Die ganze Welt dreht sich um Liebe* (1936); *Une Nuit à Vienne* (1937). **OTHER:** Orch. pieces, including several symphonic poems; 2 violin concertos; about 65 waltzes, the most famous being *Gold und Silber* (1899); more than 50 marches; various works for piano, including sonatas; over 90 songs; etc. S. Rourke ed. a thematic index of his works (London, 1985).

BIBL.: E. Decsey, *F. L.* (Munich, 1924; 2nd ed., 1930); S. Czech, *F. L.: Sein Weg und sein Werk* (Berlin, 1940; new ed., 1957, as *Schon ist die Welt: F. L.s Leben und Werk*); M. von Peteani, *F. L.: Seine Musik, sein Leben* (Vienna, 1950); W. Macqueen-Pope and D. Murray, *Fortune's Favourite: The Life and Times of F. L.* (London, 1953); B. Grun, *Gold and Silver: The Life and Times of F. L.* (London, 1970); M. Schönherr, *F. L.: Bibliographie zu Leben und Werk* (Vienna, 1970); O. Schneidereit, *F. L.: Eine Biographie in Zitaten* (Innsbruck, 1984); C. Marten, *Die Operette als Spiegel der Gesellschaft: F. L.s "Die lustige Witwe": Versuch einer sozialen Theorie der Operette* (Frankfurt am Main and N.Y., 1988).

Lehel, György, Hungarian conductor; b. Budapest, Feb. 10, 1926; d. there, Sept. 26, 1989. He was a student in Budapest of Kadosa (composition) and Somogyi (conducting). From 1950 he was a conductor with the Hungarian Radio in Budapest, serving as chief conductor of its radio and television sym. orch. from 1962. As a guest conductor, he made appearances in Europe, the U.S., and Japan. He was honored with the Liszt (1955, 1962) and Kossuth (1973) prizes, and was made an Artist of Merit (1967) by the Hungarian government for his services to the music of his homeland.

Lehmann, Hans Ulrich, Swiss composer and teacher; b. Biel, May 4, 1937. After training in cello and theory at the Biel Cons. (teacher's diplomas), he pursued studies in the composition master classes of Boulez and Stockhausen in Basel (1960–63); he also studied musicology with Fischer at the Univ. of Zürich. From 1961 to 1972 he taught at the Basel Academy of Music, and from 1969 to 1990 he lectured on new music and theory at the Univ. of Zürich. He became a teacher of composition and theory at the Zürich Hochschule für Music in 1972, serving as director of the Hochschule and Cons. from 1976. He also was president of S U I S A, the Swiss copyright soc. for authors of musical works, from 1991. In 1988 he was awarded the composition prize of the Swiss Musician's Assn. In 1993 he received the music prize of the City of Zürich. He has developed an individual style of composition with major serial connotations.

WORKS: ORCH.: *Quanti* for Flute and Chamber Orch. (1962; Geneva, Feb. 14, 1963); *Komposition für 19* (1964–65; Darmstadt, July 25, 1965); *Instants* for Piano and Strings (Geneva, May 2, 1969); Concerto for Flute, Clarinet, and Strings (Lucerne, Sept. 6, 1969); *Positionen* (1971; Zürich, Jan. 7, 1972); *Dis-cantus I* for Oboe and Strings (Zagreb, May 9, 1971); *zu blasen* (1975–76; Graz, Oct. 17, 1976); *Kammermusik I (Hommage à Mozart)* for Small Orch. (1978–79; Lugano Radio, March 29, 1979), *II* for Small Orch. (1979; Zürich, Jan. 4, 1980), and *III* for 12 Solo Strings (1983); *Fragmente* for Small Orch. (1986–87); *Nocturnes* (1990–91). **CHAMBER:** *Régions* for Flute (1963); *Episoden* for Wind Quintet (1963–64); *Mosaik* for Clarinet (1964); *Spiele* for Oboe and Harp (1965); *Regions III* for Clarinet, Trombone, and Cello (1970); *Monodie* for Wind Instrument (1970); *Sonata "da chiesa"* for Violin and Organ (1971); *Tractus* for Flute, Oboe, and Clarinet (1971); *Faces* for Harpsichord or Piano and 5 Instruments (1972); *gegen-(bei-)spiele* for 5 Winds (1973); *". . . zu streichen"* for 2 Cellos, 2 Violins, and 2 Violas (1974); *Air* for Clarinet and Piano (1977); *Contr'aire* for Clarinet and Piano (1979); *flautando* for 3 Recorders (1981); *"stroking"* for Percussionist (1982); *"battuto a tre-tratto"* for 3 Percussion (1983); *Mirlitonnades* for Flute (1983); *Triplum* for 3 Basset Horns or Bass Clarinets (1984); *"sich fragend nach frühster erinnerung"* for Recorder Quartet (1985); *"-ludes"* for Cello and Piano (1985); *"in memoriam S. Nicolai de Flue"* for 2 Flutes, 2 Cellos, and Organ (1986–87); String Quartet (1987–88); *"de profundis"* for Cello, Clarinet, and Percussion (1988–89); *"etwas Klang von meiner Oberfläche"* for Guitar (1991). **PIANO:** *Instants* (1968). **ORGAN:** *Noten* for 1 or 2 Organs (1964–66); *Monolog* (1976); *Fundamentum* (1980). **VOCAL:** *Rondo* for Soprano and Orch. (1967; Donaueschingen, Oct. 20, 1968); *dis-cantus II* for Soprano, Organ, and Chamber Orch. (Bern, Aug. 17, 1971); *a la recherche . . .* for Voices and 2 Organs (1973); *Streuungen* for Chorus and Orch. (1975–76); *Tantris* for Soprano, Flute, and Cello (1976–77); *Motetus Paraburi* for Soprano, Tenor, and Baritone (1977–78); *Duette* for Soprano, Flute, and Cello (1980); *"Lege mich wie ein Stegel auf dein Herz"* for Soprano, Flute, and Clarinet (1980); *Canticum I* and *II* for Soprano and Instrument (1981); *"gottes panarchische nacht"*, cantata for Soprano, Trumpet, Women's Chorus, and Orch. (1981–82); *"Mon amour"* for Mezzo-soprano and Cello (1983); *Alleluja I* for Soprano, Clarinet, Japanese Temple Bell, and Organ (1985); *"Osculetur me"* for Soprano and Basset Horn (1988–89); *"Wandloser Raum"* for Speaker, Flute, Clarinet, and Harp (1989); *"ad missam Prolationum"* for Tenor, Baritone, Bass Clarinet, and Percussion (1989–90).

Lehmann, Lilli, celebrated German soprano, sister of **Marie Lehmann**; b. Würzburg, Nov. 24, 1848; d. Berlin, May 16, 1929. Her father, August Lehmann, was a singer. Her mother, Marie Loew (1807–83), who had sung leading soprano roles and had also appeared as a harpist at the Kassel Opera under Spohr, became harpist at the National Theater in Prague in 1853, and there Lehmann spent her girlhood. At the age of 6 she began to study piano with Cölestin Muller, and at 12 progressed so far that she was able to act as accompanist to her mother, who was her only singing teacher. She made her professional debut in Prague on Oct. 20, 1865, as the 1st Page in *Die Zauberflöte;* then sang in Danzig (1868) and Leipzig (1869–70). In the meantime, she made her first appearance at the Berlin Royal Opera as Marguerite de Valois in *Les Huguenots* (Aug. 31, 1869); then joined its roster (1870) and established herself as a brilliant coloratura. During the summer of 1875 she was in Bayreuth, and was coached by Wagner himself in the parts of Woglinde (*Das Rheingold* and *Götterdämmerung*), Helmwige, and the Forest Bird; these roles she created at the Bayreuth Festival the following summer. She then returned to Berlin under a life contract with the Royal Opera; she was given limited leaves of absence, which enabled her to appear in the principal German cities, in Stockholm (1878), in London (debut as Violetta, June 3, 1880), and in Vienna (1882). She made her American debut at the Metropolitan Opera in N.Y. on Nov. 25, 1885, as Carmen; 5 days later she sang Brünnhilde in *Die Walküre;* then sang virtually all the Wagner roles through subsequent seasons until 1890; her last season there was 1898–99; she also appeared as Norma, Aida, Donna Anna, Fidelio, etc. She sang Isolde at the American premiere of *Tristan und Isolde* (Dec. 1, 1886), and appeared in Italian opera with the De Reszkes and Lassalle during the season of 1891–92. In the meantime, her contract with the Berlin Royal Opera was canceled (1889), owing to her protracted absence, and it required the intervention of Kaiser Wilhelm II to reinstate her (1891). In 1896 she sang the 3 Brünnhildes at the Bayreuth Festival. Her great admiration for Mozart caused her to take an active part in the annual Festivals held at Salzburg (1901–10), where she was artistic director. Her operatic repertoire comprised 170 roles in 114 operas (German, Italian, and French). She possessed in the highest degree all the requisite qualities of a great interpreter; she had a boundless capacity for work, a glorious voice, and impeccable technique; she knew how to subordinate her fiery temperament to artistic taste; on the stage she had plasticity of pose, grace of movement, and regal presence; her ability to project her interpretation with conviction to audiences in different countries was not the least factor in her universal success. Although she was celebrated chiefly as an opera singer, she was equally fine as an interpreter of German lieder; she gave recitals concurrently with her operatic appearances, and continued them until her retirement in 1920; her repertoire of songs exceeded 600. She was also a successful teacher; among her pupils were Geraldine Farrar and Olive Fremstad. On Feb. 24, 1888, in N.Y. she married **Paul Kalisch**, with whom she often sang in opera in subsequent years. They later separated, but never divorced. After her death, Kalisch inherited her manor at Salzkammergut, and remained there until his death in 1946, at the age of 90. Lehmann authored *Meine Gesangskunst* (Berlin, 1902; Eng. tr., 1902, as *How to Sing*; 3rd ed., rev. and supplemented, 1924 by C. Willenbücher); *Studie zu Fidelio* (Leipzig, 1904); *Mein Weg*, autobiography (Leipzig, 1913; 2nd ed., 1920; Eng. tr., 1914, as *My Path through Life*).

BIBL.: J. Wagenmann, *L. L.s Geheimnis der Stimmbänder* (Berlin, 1905; 2nd ed., 1926); L. Andro, *L. L.* (Berlin, 1907).

Lehmann, Liza (actually, **Elizabeth Nina Mary Frederica**), English soprano and composer; b. London, July 11, 1862; d. Pinner, Sept. 19, 1918. She was the daughter of the painter Rudolf Lehmann and the composer and teacher Amelia Lehmann. She received vocal training from Randegger and Lind in London, and studied composition with Raunkilde in Rome, Freudenberg in Wiesbaden, and MacCunn in London. On Nov. 23, 1885, she made her debut in a recital at a Monday Popular Concert in London, and then sang in concerts throughout Europe. On July 14, 1894, she made her farewell concert appearance at St. James' Hall in London, and later that year she married the painter and composer Herbert Bedford. In 1910 she made a tour of the U.S., accompanying herself at the piano in song recitals. In 1911–12 she served as the first president of the Soc. of Women Musicians. In later years, she was a prof. of voice at the Guildhall School of Music in London. Her autobiography appeared as *The Life of Liza Lehmann, by Herself* (London, 1919). As a composer, she became best known for her song cycle *In a Persian Garden* (1896), based on selections from Fitzgerald's tr. of the *Rubaiyāt of Omar Khayyām*. Lehmann was the grandmother of **David** and **Steuart Bedford.**

WORKS: DRAMATIC: *Sergeant Brue*, musical farce (London, June 14, 1904); *The Vicar of Wakefield*, romantic light opera (London, Nov. 12, 1906); *The Happy Prince* (1908); *Everyman*, opera (London, Dec. 28, 1915); incidental music. **CHAMBER:** *Romantic Suite* for Violin and Piano; piano pieces. **VOCAL:** *Young Lochinar* for Baritone, Chorus, and Orch. (1898); *Once Upon a Time*, cantata (1903); *The Golden Threshold* for Soli, Chorus, and Orch. (1907); *Leaves from Ossian*, cantata; song cycles: *The Daisy Chain* (1893); *In a Persian Garden* for Soprano, Alto, Tenor, Bass, and Piano (1896; London, Jan. 10, 1897); *In Memoriam* (1899); (10) *Nonsense Songs* (1908); *4 Cautionary Tales and a Moral* (1909); *More Daisies; Prairie Pictures*; solo songs; part songs.

Lehmann, Lotte, celebrated German-born American soprano; b. Perleberg, Feb. 27, 1888; d. Santa Barbara, Calif., Aug. 26, 1976. She studied in Berlin with Erna Tiedka, Eva Reinhold, and Mathilde Mallinger. She made her operatic debut on Sept. 2, 1910, as the 2nd Boy in *Die Zauberflöte* at the Hamburg Opera; her first major role came before that year was out, and she soon was given important parts in Wagner's operas, establishing herself as one of the finest Wagnerian singers. In 1914 she made her first appearance in London as Sophie at Drury Lane. In 1916 she was engaged at the Vienna Opera. Richard Strauss selected her to sing the Composer in the revised version of his *Ariadne auf Naxos* when it was first performed in Vienna (Oct. 4, 1916); then she appeared as Octavian in *Der Rosenkavalier*, and later as the Marschallin, which became one of her most famous roles. She also created the roles of Fäberin (the Dyer's wife) in his *Die Frau ohne Schatten* (Vienna, Oct. 10, 1919) and Christine in his *Intermezzo* (Dresden, Nov. 4, 1924). In 1922 she toured in South America. In 1924 she made her first appearance at London's Covent Garden as the Marschallin, and continued to sing there regularly with great success until 1935; appeared there again in 1938. On Oct. 28, 1930, she made her U.S. debut as Sieglinde with the Chicago Opera, and on Jan. 11, 1934, sang Sieglinde at her Metropolitan Opera debut in N.Y. She continued to appear at the Metropolitan, with mounting success, in the roles of Elisabeth in *Tannhäuser*, Tosca, and the Marschallin, until her farewell performance as the Marschallin on Feb. 23, 1945. In 1946 she appeared as the Marschallin for the last time in San Francisco. In 1945 she became a naturalized American citizen. She gave her last recital in Santa Barbara, California, on Aug. 7, 1951, and thereafter devoted herself to teaching. Lehmann was universally recognized as one of the greatest singers of the century. The beauty of her voice, combined with her rare musicianship, made her a compelling artist of the highest order. In addition to her unforgettable Strauss roles, she excelled as Mozart's Countess and Donna Elvira, Beethoven's Leonore, and Wagner's Elisabeth, Elsa, and Eva, among others. She publ. a novel, *Orplid mein Land* (1937; Eng. tr., 1938, as *Eternal Flight*); an autobiography, *Anfang und Aufstieg* (Vienna, 1937; in London as *Wings of Song*, 1938; in N.Y. as *Midway in My Song*, 1938); *More Than Singing* (N.Y., 1945); *My Many Lives* (N.Y., 1948); *Five Operas and Richard Strauss* (N.Y., 1964; in London as *Singing with Richard Strauss*, 1964); *Eighteen Song Cycles* (London and N.Y., 1971).

BIBL.: B. Wessling, *L. L. . . . mehr als eine Sängerin* (Salzburg, 1969); B. Glass, *L. L., A Life in Opera & Song* (Santa Barbara, Calif., 1988); A. Jefferson, *L. L.: 1888–1976: A Centenary Biography* (London, 1988); D. Shawe-Taylor, "L. L. and Elisabeth Schumann: A Centenary Tribute," *Musical Times* (Oct. 1988).

Lehmann, (Ludwig) Fritz, esteemed German conductor; b. Mannheim, May 17, 1904; d. Munich, March 30, 1956. He studied at the Mannheim Cons. and the Univs. of Heidelberg and Göttingen. He was a conductor in Göttingen (1923–27), Hildesheim (1927–38), and Hannover (1929–38). In 1934 he became conductor of the Handel Festival in Göttingen; was also Generalmusikdirektor in Bad Pyrmont (1934–38), Wuppertal (1938–47), and Göttingen (1946–50). He subsequently was a teacher at the Hochschule für Musik in Munich (from 1953). A consummate conductor, he led notable performances in both the operatic and symphonic literature, ranging from the Baroque period to the 20th century.

BIBL.: M. Wick, *Bessessen von Musik: Der Dirigent F. L.* (Berlin, 1990).

Lehmann, Marie, esteemed German soprano, sister of **Lilli Lehmann;** b Hamburg, May 15, 1851; d. Berlin, Dec. 9, 1931. She received her training from her mother and her sister. On May 1, 1867, she made her operatic debut as Aennchen in Leipzig, and then appeared in Breslau, Cologne, Hamburg, and Prague. She sang with her sister in the first mounting of Wagner's *Ring* cycle at the Bayreuth Festival in 1876, appearing as Wellgunde and Ortlinde. From 1882 to 1896 she was a leading member of the Vienna Court Opera. In later years, she taught voice in Berlin. Among her notable roles were Mozart's Donna

Elvira and Donna Anna, Bellini's Adalgisa, and Meyerbeer's Marguerite de Valois.

Lehnhoff, Nikolaus, German opera director; b. Hannover, May 20, 1939. He attended the Univs. of Munich and Venice. After gaining experience as an assistant stage director at the Berlin Deutsche Oper, the Bayreuth Festival, and the Metropolitan Opera in N.Y., he staged his first opera, *Die Frau ohne Schatten,* at the Paris Opéra in 1972. In 1975 he produced *Elektra* at the Lyric Opera of Chicago. His mounting of the *Ring* cycle at the San Francisco Opera (1983–85) and at the Bavarian State Opera in Munich (1987) were notably successful. His stagings of *Káť'a Kabanová* (1988) and *Jenůfa* (1989) at the Glyndebourne Festival were outstanding. In 1989 he produced *Salome* at the Metropolitan Opera. He staged *Idomeneo* at the Salzburg Festival in 1990. Lehnhoff places great importance upon his collaborations with the finest designers. He is the author of *Es war einmal* (Munich, 1987).

Lehrman, Leonard J(ordan), American composer, pianist, and conductor; b. Ft. Riley, Kansas, Aug. 20, 1949. He received private composition lessons from Siegmeister (1960–70), and also studied with Kim, Del Tredici, Kirchner, and Foss at Harvard Univ. (B.A., 1971) and attended the American Cons. in Fontainebleau (1969). He continued his training at the École Normale de Musique in Paris (1971–72), the Salzburg Mozarteum (1972), with Husa and Palmer at Cornell Univ. (M.F.A., 1975; D.M.A., 1977), and at the Indiana Univ. School of Music in Bloomington (1975–76). Later he studied library and information science at Long Island Univ. (M.A., 1995). After making his debut as a pianist at N.Y.'s Carnegie Recital Hall in 1979, he conducted at the Bremerhaven City Theater (1981–83) before going to Berlin, where he was founder-president of the Jewish Music Theater (1983–86) and a conductor at the Theater des Westens (1983–85). Returning to N.Y., he became founder-conductor of the Metropolitan Phil. Chorus in 1988. In 1990 he joined the faculty of the Jewish Academy of Fine Arts, which became the Performing Arts Inst. of Long Island in 1993. He served as assoc. ed. of the magazine *Opera Monthly* from 1993.

WORKS: DRAMATIC: OPERAS: *Tales of Malamud,* 2 operas after Malamud: *Idiots First* (completion of Blitzstein's work, 1973; Bloomington, Ind., March 14, 1976) and *Karla* (1974; Bloomington, March 7, 1976); *Sima* (Ithaca, N.Y., Oct. 23, 1976); *Hannah* (Mannheim, May 24, 1980); *The Family Man* (concert perf., Berlin, Jan. 6, 1985; stage perf., N.Y., June 27, 1985); *The Birthday of the Bank* (1988); *New World: An Opera About What Columbus Did to the "Indians"* (1991; Huntington, N.Y., Aug. 11, 1992). **MUSICALS:** *Growing Up Woman,* chamber musical (1980; Berlin, April 30, 1984); *E.G.: A Musical Portrait of Emma Goldman* (1986; N.Y., May 3, 1987); *Superspy! The Secret Musical* (1988; Paris, July 7, 1989). Also incidental music; cabarets, including *A Blitzstein Cabaret, Memories and Music of Leonard Bernstein, An Israel Cabaret, Jewish-American Cabaret,* and *The Jewish Woman in Song.* **ORCH.:** *Bloody Kansas* (1975); Violin Concerto (1975); Flute Concerto (1982). **CHAMBER:** Flute Sonata (1964–65); String Trio (1968); Sonata for Piano and Tape (1968); Piano Trio (1969–70); Sonatina for Solo Tuba (1980). **VOCAL:** *The Universal Declaration of Human Rights* for Chorus and Piano or Winds and Percussion (N.Y., Oct. 26, 1988); *We Are Innocent,* cantata on letters of Julius and Ethel Rosenberg, for Soloists, Optional Chorus, and Piano or Orch. (1988; N.Y., June 11, 1989); *A Requiem for Hiroshima* for Soloists, Chorus, and Orch. or Chamber Ensemble (N.Y., Aug. 5, 1990); song cycles; solo songs.

Leibowitz, René, noted Polish-born French conductor, composer, writer on music, music theorist, and pedagogue; b. Warsaw, Feb. 17, 1913; d. Paris, Aug. 28, 1972. His family settled in Paris in 1926; from 1930 to 1933 he studied in Berlin with Schoenberg and in Vienna with Webern; also studied orchestration with Ravel in Paris (1933). He was active as a conductor from 1937. As a composer, he adopted the 12-tone method of composition, becoming its foremost exponent in France; he had numerous private students, among them Boulez. He publ. the influential books *Schoenberg et son école* (Paris, 1946; Eng. tr., N.Y., 1949) and *Introduction à la musique de douze sons* (Paris, 1949). He also wrote *L'Artiste et sa conscience* (Paris, 1950); *L'Évolution de la musique, de Bach à Schönberg* (Paris, 1952); *Histoire de l'Opéra* (Paris, 1957); with J. Maguire, *Thinking for Orchestra* (N.Y., 1958); with K. Wolff, *Erich Itor Kahn, Un Grand Représentant de la musique contemporaine* (Paris, 1958; Eng. tr., N.Y., 1958); *Schönberg* (Paris, 1969); *Le Compositeur et son double* (Paris, 1971); *Les Fantômes de l'opéra* (Paris, 1973).

WORKS: OPERAS: *La Nuit close* (1949); *La Rumeur de l'espace* (1950); *Ricardo Gonfolano* (1953); *Les Espagnols à Venise,* opera buffa (1963; Grenoble, Jan. 27, 1970); *Labyrinthe,* after Baudelaire (1969); *Todos caerán* (1970–72). **ORCH.:** Sym. (1941); 2 chamber concertos (1942, 1944); Chamber Sym. (1948); Piano Concerto (1954); Viola Concerto (1954); *Fantaisie symphonique* (1956); Violin Concerto (1959); *3 Bagatelles* for Strings (1959); Trombone Concertino (1960); Cello Concerto (1962); *Rapsodie symphonique* (1964–65). **CHAMBER:** 8 string quartets (1940, 1950, 1952, 1958, 1963, 1965, 1966, 1968); *Marijuana* for Violin, Trombone, Vibraphone, and Piano (1960); *Sinfonietta da camera* (1961); *Capriccio* for Flute and Strings (1967); *Suite* for 9 Instruments (1967); Saxophone Quartet (1969); *Petite suite* for Clarinet Sextet (1970). **VOCAL:** *Tourist Death* for Soprano and Chamber Orch. (1943); *L'Explication des métaphores* for Speaker, 2 Pianos, Harp, and Percussion (1947); *Chanson Dada* for Children's Chorus and Instruments (1968); *Laboratoire central* for Speaker and Chorus (1970); numerous songs.

BIBL.: J. Maguire, "R. L.," *Tempo* (Feb. and March 1980).

Leich, Roland (Jacobi), American composer; b. Evansville, Ind., March 6, 1911. He studied composition with Borowski and Sowerby in Chicago, Webern in Vienna (1933–34), Scalero at the Curtis Inst. of Music in Philadelphia (B.M., 1934), and Rogers at the Eastman School of Music in Rochester, N.Y. (M.M., 1942); also studied at Dartmouth College (B.A., 1935), where he served on the faculty (1935–41). In 1946 he became a teacher at the Carnegie Inst. of Technology (later Carnegie-Mellon Univ.) in Pittsburgh, remaining on its faculty until 1976. He was particularly successful as a composer of songs, of which he wrote more than 150.

WORKS: ORCH.: *Rondo* (1942); *Concert Piece* for Oboe and Strings (1952); *Prelude and Fugue* (1954). **CHAMBER:** String Quartet (1936); Flute Sonata (1953); *A Musical Christmas Wreath* for Woodwind Quintet and Harp (1980); piano pieces; organ music. **VOCAL:** *Housman Songs* (1932); 5 songs, after Housman (1939–78); 40 songs, after Milne (1940); 47 songs, after Dickinson (1950–65); 17 songs, after S. Hay (1956–84); also cantatas and other choral works, hymn tunes, and arrangements of folk melodies and hymns.

Leichtentritt, Hugo, eminent German-American music scholar; b. Pleschen, Posen, Jan. 1, 1874; d. Cambridge, Mass., Nov. 13, 1951. He studied with J. K. Paine at Harvard Univ. (B.A., 1894); continued his studies in Paris (1894–95) and at the Berlin Hochschule für Musik (1895–98); obtained his Ph.D. at the Univ. of Berlin in 1901 with the diss. *Reinhard Keiser in seinen Opern: Ein Beitrag zur Geschichte der frühen deutschen Oper* (publ. in Berlin, 1901); he subsequently taught at the Klindworth-Scharwenka Cons. in Berlin (1901–24) and wrote music criticism for German and American publications. In 1933 he left Germany and became a lecturer on music at Harvard Univ. (until 1940); then taught at Radcliffe College and N.Y. Univ. (1940–44). Although known chiefly as a scholar, he also composed a comic opera, *Der Sizilianer* (Freiburg im Breisgau, May 28, 1920); Sym.; Violin Concerto; Cello Concerto; Piano Concerto; much chamber music; several song cycles; numerous piano pieces. His MSS are in the Library of Congress in Washington, D.C.

WRITINGS: *Frédéric Chopin* (Berlin, 1905; 3rd ed., 1949); *Geschichte der Musik* (Berlin, 1905; Eng. tr., N.Y., 1938, as *Everybody's Little History of Music*); *Geschichte der Motette* (Leipzig, 1908); *Musikalische Formenlehre* (Leipzig, 1911; 5th ed., 1952; Eng. tr., Cambridge, Mass., 1951 as *Musical Form*); *Erwin Lendvai* (Berlin, 1912); *Ferruccio Busoni* (Leipzig, 1916); *Analyse der Chopin'schen Klavierwerke* (2 vols., Berlin, 1921–22); *Ignatz Waghalter* (N.Y., 1924); *Händel* (Berlin and Stuttgart, 1924); *Music, History, and Ideas* (Cambridge, Mass., 1938); *Serge Koussevitzky, The Boston Symphony Orchestra and the New American Music* (Cambridge, Mass., 1946); *Music of the Western Nations* (ed. and amplified by N. Slonimsky; Cambridge, Mass., 1956).

Leider, Frida, outstanding German soprano; b. Berlin, April 18, 1888; d. there, June 4, 1975. She was a student of Otto Schwarz in Berlin before completing her training in Milan. She made her operatic debut in Halle in 1915 as Venus in *Tannhäuser*, then sang at Rostock (1916–18), Königsberg (1918–19), and Hamburg (1919–23). She was engaged by the Berlin State Opera in 1923, and remained on its roster until 1940; was also highly successful in Wagnerian roles at London's Covent Garden (1924–38) and at the Bayreuth Festivals (1928–38). In 1928 she made her American debut at the Chicago Civic Opera as Brünnhilde in Die *Walküre*, and continued to appear there until 1932; then made her debut at the Metropolitan Opera in N.Y. on Jan. 16, 1933, as Isolde. In 1934 she returned to Germany; she encountered difficulties because her husband, Rudolf Deman, concertmaster of the Berlin State Opera Orch., was Jewish. She was confronted by the Nazis with the demand to divorce him, but refused; he succeeded in going to Switzerland. After the collapse of the Nazi regime (1945), she maintained a vocal studio at the (East) Berlin State Opera until 1952; also taught at the (West) Berlin Hochschule für Musik from 1948 to 1958. She publ. a memoir, *Das war mein Teil, Erinnerungen einer Opernsängerin* (Berlin, 1959; Eng. tr., N.Y., 1966 as *Playing My Part*). In addition to her celebrated portrayals of Isolde and Brünnhilde, Leider also was acclaimed for her roles of Venus, Senta, Kundry, and the Marschallin. She also was greatly renowned as a concert artist.

Leiferkus, Sergei (Petrovich), Russian baritone; b. Leningrad, April 4, 1946. He was a student of Barsov and Shaposhnikov at the Leningrad Cons. In 1972 he became a member of the Maly Theater in Leningrad, in which city he made his debut at the Kirov Theater in Leningrad as Prince Andrei in *War and Peace* (1977); subsequently sang there with success. In 1982 he appeared as the Marquis in Massenet's *Griselidis* at the Wexford Festival in England. In 1985 he sang for the first time at the Scottish Opera in Glasgow as Don Giovanni. In 1987 he made his debut at the English National Opera in London as Zurga in *Les Pêcheurs de perles*, the same year he appeared as Eugene Onegin and Tomsky with the Kirov Opera at Covent Garden in London. He also made his U.S. debut that year as soloist in Shostakovich's 13th Sym. with the Boston Sym. Orch. In 1989 he returned to London to make his Wigmore Hall recital debut and his first appearance at the Royal Opera at Covent Garden as Luna; also sang for the first time at the Glyndebourne Opera as Mandryka and made his U.S. operatic debut at the San Francisco Opera as Telramund. In 1991 he sang Ruprecht in *The Fiery Angel* at the London Promenade Concerts. He made his Metropolitan Opera debut in N.Y. as Iago in 1994. Among his other notable roles are Germont, Amonasro, Prince Igor, Rangoni, Escamillo, and Scarpia.

Leifs, Jón, eminent Icelandic composer, conductor, and administrator; b. Sólheimar, May 1, 1899; d. Reykjavík, July 30, 1968. He entered the Leipzig Cons. in 1916, where he was a student of Graener and Szendrei (composition), Krehl (theory), Paul (harmony and counterpoint), Teichmüller (piano; diploma, 1921), and Lohse and Scherchen (conducting). With the exception of his tenure as music director of the Icelandic National Broadcasting Service in Reykjavík (1935–37), he worked in Germany as a composer and conductor. In 1926 he appeared as a guest conductor of the Hamburg Phil. on a tour of Norway, the Faeroes, and Iceland. After marrying a woman of Jewish descent, the Nazi regime banned Leifs' music in 1937. He and his family were able to flee to Sweden in 1944. In 1945 they settled in Iceland. He became president of the newly organized Soc. of Icelandic Composers. He also was the founder of STEF, an association of composers and copyright owners (1948), and of Islandia Edition (1949), as well as president of the Nordic Council of Composers (1952–54; 1964–66). Leifs publ. the books *Tónlistarhaettir* (Musical Form; Leipzig, 1922) and *Islands künstlerische Anregung* (Reykjavík, 1951). In his compositions, he utilized various resources, ranging from the medieval Icelandic tvisöngur to folk melos.

WORKS: DRAMATIC: *Galdra-Loftr*, incidental music to the drama (1925; Copenhagen, Sept. 3, 1938; orch. suite, 1925; overture, 1928); *Baldr*, music drama without words for Chorus, Dancers, and Orch. (1948; Reykjavík, March 24, 1991). **ORCH.:** *Trilogia piccoa* (1919–24; Karlsbad, Nov. 28, 1925); *Icelandic Overture*, with optional chorus (1926); *Variazione pastorale*, on a theme of Beethoven (1927; also for String Quartet); Organ Concerto (1927–28; Wiesbaden, April 26, 1935); *Icelandic Dances* (1928; also for Piano); *Sögu-Sinfónia* (Saga Sym.; 1941–42; Helsinki, Sept. 18, 1950); *Reflections from the North* for Strings (1952); *Landsýn* (Landfall), overture with optional chorus (1955; Reykjavík, Feb. 22, 1962); *þrjú óhlutraen málverk* (3 Abstract Pictures; 1955–60; Reykjavík, Dec. 7, 1961); *Geysir* (1961; Reykjavík, Nov. 1, 1984); *Hekla*, overture with optional chorus (1961; Helsinki, Oct. 2, 1964); *Hinzta kveoja* [Last Greeting]: *In memoriam 30. Sept. 1961: Elegie* for Strings (1961); *Víkingasvar* (Viking Answer; 1962); *Fine I* (1963) and *II* for Vibraphone and Strings (1963); *Hughreysting* (Consolation) for Strings (1968). **CHAMBER:** *Étude* for Violin (1924); *Nocturne* for Harp (1931–33); 3 string quartets: No. 1, *Mors et vita* (1939), No. 2, *Vita et mors* (1948–51), and No. 3, *El Greco* (1965); Quintet for Flute, Clarinet, Bassoon, Viola, and Cello (1959); *Scherzso concreto* for 8 Winds, Viola, and Cello (1964). **KEYBOARD: PIANO:** *Intermezzo-Torrek* (1919); 4 Pieces (1922); *Icelandic Dances* (1929); *New Icelandic Dances* (1931); *Juvenile Song* (1960). **ORGAN:** *Praeludia organo* (1951). **VOCAL:** *The Lord's Prayer* for Soprano or Tenor and Organ (1929); *Iceland Cantata* for Chorus, Children's Chorus, and Orch. (1929–30); *Icelandic Dances* for Voice, Chorus, and Orch. (1932); 3 oratorios: *Edda I: The Creation of the World* for Tenor, Bass, Chorus, and Orch. (1936–39), *II: The Life of the Gods* for Mezzo-soprano, Tenor, Bass, Chorus, and Orch. (1951–56), and *III: The Twilight of the Gods* for Chorus and Orch. (1966–68; unfinished); *Lay of Gudrún* for Mezzo-soprano, Tenor, Bass, and Orch. (1940; Oslo, Sept. 29, 1948); *Requiem* for Chorus (1947); *Mountain Songs* for Soli, Men's Chorus, Percussion, and Double Bass (1948); *Vorvísa* (Spring Song) for Chorus and Orch. (1958); *In Memoriam J(ónas) H(allgrímsson)* for Mezzo-soprano or Baritone and Piano (1958; also for Chorus and Orch., 1961); *Hekla* for Chorus and Orch. (1961); *Battle Song* for Chorus and Orch. (1964); *Dettifoss* for Baritone, Chorus, and Orch. (1964); *Night* for Tenor, Bass, and Small Orch. (1964); *Of Helgi the Hunding Killer* for Alto, Bass, and Chamber Orch. (1964); *Hafis* (Drift Ice) for Chorus and Orch. (1965); mixed and men's choruses; solo songs; folk song arrangements.

Leigh, Walter, English composer; b. London, June 22, 1905; d. in battle near Tobruk, Libya, June 12, 1942. He was an organ scholar at Christ's College, Cambridge (1922–26), where he studied with Dent; also took lessons with Darke and later with Hindemith at the Hochschule für Musik in Berlin (1927–29). He was particularly adept in his writing for the theater.

WORKS: 2 light operas: *The Pride of the Regiment, or Cashiered for His Country* (Midhurst, Sept. 19, 1931) and *The Jolly Roger, or The Admiral's Daughter* (Manchester, Feb. 13, 1933); *9 Sharp*, musical revue (London, 1938); incidental music; pieces for amateur orch.; Sonatina for Viola and Piano (Vienna, June 17, 1932); Trio for 3 Pianos (1934); Trio for Flute, Oboe, and Piano (1935); songs; piano pieces.

Leighton, Kenneth, English composer and teacher; b. Wakefield, Yorkshire, Oct. 2, 1929; d. Edinburgh, Aug. 24, 1988. He studied classics (1947–50) and composition with Rose (B.Mus.,

1951) at Queen's College, Oxford, where he later earned his doctorate in music; also won the Mendelssohn Scholarship (1951), which enabled him to study with Petrassi in Rome. He was a lecturer at the Univ. of Edinburgh (1956–68); after serving as a lecturer at Worcester College, Oxford (1968–70), he returned to the Univ. of Edinburgh as Reid Prof. of Music (from 1970). He utilized 12-tone procedures while basically adhering to a diatonic style.

WORKS: OPERA: *Columba* (1980; Glasgow, June 16, 1981). **ORCH.:** *Veris gratia*, suite for Oboe, Cello, and Strings (1950); 3 piano concertos: No. 1 (1951; BBC, Glasgow, March 7, 1958; rev. 1959), No. 2 (1960; BBC, Manchester, Jan. 18, 1962), and No. 3 (1969; Birmingham, March 11, 1970); Violin Concerto (1952; BBC, London, May 5, 1953); Concerto for Viola, Harp, Timpani, and Strings (1952; BBC, London, Sept. 5, 1954); *Burlesque* (1956; London, May 3, 1959); Cello Concerto (Cheltenham, July 20, 1956); *Passacaglia, Chorale, and Fugue* (1957; BBC, London, May 23, 1959); Concerto for Strings (1961; London, June 19, 1962); *Festive Overture* (1962); 3 syms.: No. 1 (1964; Trieste, May 31, 1966), No. 2, *Sinfonia mistica*, for Soprano, Chorus, and Orch. (1974; Edinburgh, March 4, 1977), and No. 3, *Laudes musicae*, for Tenor and Orch. (1983; Glasgow, March 15, 1985); 3 dance suites: No. 1 (Glasgow, July 10, 1968), No. 2 (1970; Farnham, May 12, 1971), and No. 3, *Scottish Dances* (1983; Edinburgh, Feb. 25, 1984); Organ Concerto (1970; Cambridge, Aug. 4, 1971); Concerto for Harpsichord, Recorder, and Strings (1982; Warrington, Feb. 14, 1983). **CHAMBER:** 2 violin sonatas (1951, 1956); 2 string quartets (1956, 1957); Piano Quintet (1959); *Partita* for Cello and Piano (1959); *7 Variations* for String Quartet (1964); Trio for Violin, Cello, and Piano (1965); *Metamorphoses* for Violin and Piano (1966); Sonata for Solo Cello (1967); *Quartet in 1 Movement: Contrasts and Variants* (London, Oct. 13, 1972); *Fantasy on an American Hymn Tune: The Shining River* for Clarinet, Cello, and Piano (1974; Cheltenham, July 8, 1975); *Fantasy on a Chorale* for Violin and Organ (1979; Washington, D.C., May 4, 1980); *Alleluia Pascha Nostrum* for Cello and Piano (1981; Manchester, Feb. 25, 1982); *Fantasy-Octet: Homage to Percy Grainger* for 4 Violins, 2 Violas, and 2 Cellos (Edinburgh, Aug. 29, 1982). **KEYBOARD: PIANO:** *5 Studies* (1953); *Variations* (1955); *Fantasia Contrappuntistica: Homage to Bach* (1956); *9 Variations* (1959); *Conflicts: Fantasy on 2 Themes* (1967); *6 Studies: Study-Variations* (1969); *Household Pets* (1981); Sonata for Piano, 4-hands (1985). **ORGAN:** *Prelude, Scherzo, and Passacaglia* (1963); *Ex Resurrexit: Theme, Fantasy, and Fugue* (1966); *Martyrs: Dialogues on a Scottish Psalm Tune* for Organ Duet (1976); *Missa de Gloria* (1980). **VOCAL:** *The Birds* for Soprano, Tenor, Chorus, and Orch. (1954); *The Light Invisible: Sinfonia Sacra* for Tenor, Chorus, and Orch. (Hereford, Sept. 9, 1958); *Laudes Montium* for Baritone, Semi-chorus, Chorus, and Orch. (1975); *Columbia Mea: The Song of Songs* for Tenor, Chorus, and Orch. (1977; Glasgow, Feb. 5, 1979); *Animal Heaven* for Soprano, Recorder, Cello, and Harpsichord (Manchester, July 24, 1980); many sacred works, including masses, cantatas, anthems, and motets.

Leimer, Kurt, German-born Austrian pianist, teacher, and composer; b. Wiesbaden, Sept. 7, 1920; d. Vaduz, Liechtenstein, Nov. 20, 1974. He studied piano with his great-uncle Karl Leimer (b. Biebrich, June 22, 1858; d. Wiesbaden, July 19, 1944), W. Horbowski, and Edwin Fischer, and composition with Kurt von Wolfurt. In addition to pursuing a career as a pianist, he taught a master class in piano at the Salzburg Mozarteum (from 1953). In 1956 he became a naturalized Austrian citizen. He composed several works for piano, including 4 concertos (No. 2 for left hand) and some sonatas. His works are in an effective late Romantic style.

Leinsdorf (real name, **Landauer**), **Erich,** eminent Austrian-born American conductor; b. Vienna, Feb. 4, 1912; d. Zürich, Sept. 11, 1993. He entered a local music school when he was 5; began piano studies with the wife of Paul Pisk at age 8; then continued his piano studies with Paul Emerich (1923–28), and subsequently studied theory and composition with Pisk. In 1930 he took a master class in conducting at the Mozarteum in Salzburg, and then studied for a short time in the music dept. of the Univ. of Vienna; from 1931 to 1933 he took courses at the Vienna Academy of Music, making his debut as a conductor at the Musikvereinsaal upon his graduation. In 1933 he served as assistant conductor of the Workers' Chorus in Vienna; in 1934 he went to Salzburg, where he had a successful audition with Bruno Walter and Toscanini at the Salzburg Festivals, and was appointed their assistant. In 1937 he was engaged as a conductor of the Metropolitan Opera in N.Y.; he made his American debut there conducting *Die Walküre* on Jan. 21, 1938, with notable success; he then conducted other Wagnerian operas, ultimately succeeding Bodanzky as head of the German repertoire there in 1939. In 1942 he became a naturalized American citizen. In 1943 he was appointed music director of the Cleveland Orch.; however, his induction into the U.S. Army in Dec. 1943 interrupted his tenure there. After his discharge in 1944, he once again conducted at the Metropolitan in 1944–45; also conducted several concerts with the Cleveland Orch. in 1945 and 1946, and made appearances in Europe. From 1947 to 1955 he was music director of the Rochester (N.Y.) Phil. In the fall of 1956 he was briefly music director of the N.Y. City Opera; then returned to the Metropolitan as a conductor and musical consultant in 1957. He also appeared as a guest conductor in the U.S. and Europe. In 1962 he received the prestigious appointment of music director of the Boston Sym. Orch., a post he retained until 1969; then he conducted opera and sym. concerts in many of the major music centers of America and in Europe; from 1978 to 1980 he held the post of principal conductor of the (West) Berlin Radio Sym. Orch. He publ. a semi-autobiographical and rather candid book of sharp comments, *Cadenza: A Musical Career* (Boston, 1976); also *The Composer's Advocate: A Radical Orthodoxy for Musicians* (New Haven, 1981).

Leisner, David, American guitarist, teacher, and composer; b. Los Angeles, Dec. 22, 1953. He was educated at Wesleyan Univ. (B.A., 1976); received instruction in guitar from John Duarte, David Starobin, and Angelo Gilardino, in interpretation from John Kirkpatrick and Karen Tuttle, and in composition from Richard Winslow; won 2nd prize at the Toronto International Guitar Competition (1975) and a silver medal at the Geneva International Guitar Competition (1981). He made his N.Y. debut in 1979, then toured extensively. He taught guitar at Amherst College (1976–78) and at the New England Cons. of Music in Boston (from 1980). From 1993 he taught at the Manhattan School of Music in N.Y. He became well known for his programming of contemporary American music at his concerts. His own compositions include pieces for solo guitar and duos for guitar and viola, cello, or voice.

Leitner, Ferdinand, noted German conductor; b. Berlin, March 4, 1912; d. Forch, Switzerland, June 1996. He studied composition with Schreker and conducting with Pruwer at the Berlin Hochschule für Musik; also studied piano with Schnabel and conducting with Muck. He then was active as a pianist until making his debut as a theater conductor in Berlin in 1943. He became conductor of the Württemberg State Theater in Stuttgart in 1947; was its Generalmusikdirektor (1950–69). He subsequently was chief conductor of the Zürich Opera (1969–84); also of the Residentie Orch. at The Hague (1976–80). From 1986 to 1990 he served as principal conductor of the RAI Orch. in Turin. He was known for his musicianly readings of works by Mozart, Wagner, Bruckner, and Richard Strauss; also conducted a number of modern scores, including premieres of works by Orff and Egk.

Leiviskä, Helvi (Lemmikki), Finnish composer; b. Helsinki, May 25, 1902; d. there, Aug. 12, 1982. She studied under Erkki Melartin at the Helsinki Music Inst. (graduated, 1927) and with Arthur Willner in Vienna; then studied privately with Funtek and Madetoja. She was a librarian at the Helsinki Academy of Music (1933–66).

WORKS: ORCH.: *Folk Dance Suite* (1929; rev. 1971); 2

suites (1934, 1938); Piano Concerto (1935); *Triple Fugue* (1935); 4 syms. (1947; 1954; *Sinfonia brevis*, 1962, rev. 1972; 1971). **CHAMBER:** Piano Quartet (1926); String Quartet (1926); Violin Sonata (1945). **VOCAL:** *Pimeän peikko* (Goblin of Darkness) for Chorus and Orch. (1942); *Mennyt manner* (The Lost Continent) for Soli, Chorus, and Orch. (1957).

Lemacher, Heinrich, German composer, pedagogue, and writer on music; b. Solingen, June 26, 1891; d. Munich, March 15, 1966. He received training in piano, conducting, and composition at the Cologne Cons. (1911–16), and in musicology at the Univ. of Bonn (Ph.D., 1916, with the diss. *Zur Geschichte der Musik am Hofe zu Nassau-Weilburg*). In 1924 he founded the Seminar des Reichsverbandes deutscher Tonkünstler und Musiklehrer, of which he served as director until 1933. He was a teacher of composition, theory, and music history (1925–28) and a prof. (1928–56) at the Cologne Hochschule für Musik. He concurrently taught at the Rheinische Musikschule and the Univ. of Cologne, and then was director of the Cäcilienverband from 1956. He was the author or collaborator of several books, among them *Handbuch der Hausmusik* (Regensburg and Graz, 1948), *Handbuch der Katholischen Kirchenmusik* (Essen, 1949), *Lehrbuch des Kontrapunktes* (Mainz, 1950; 4th ed., 1962), *Generalbassübungen* (Düsseldorf, 1954; 2nd ed., 1965), *Harmonielehre* (Cologne, 1958; 8th ed., 1974), and *Formenlehre der Musik* (Cologne, 1962; 2nd ed., 1968; Eng. tr., 1967, as *Musical Form*). His compositions followed in the paths of Bruckner and Reger. He wrote orch. works, chamber music, and secular vocal pieces but is best remembered for his Catholic church music, including numerous masses, motets, and cantatas.

BIBL.: W. Hammerschlag and A. Schneider, *Musikalisches Brauschtum: Festschrift H. L.* (Cologne, 1956).

Lemare, Edwin (Henry), English-American organist and composer; b. Ventnor, Isle of Wight, Sept. 9, 1865; d. Los Angeles, Sept. 24, 1934. He received his early training from his father, an organist; then studied at the Royal Academy of Music in London. At the age of 17, he played at the Inventions Exhibition in London; in 1892 he began a series of weekly organ recitals at Holy Trinity Church in London, and also became a prof. at the Royal Academy of Music; from 1897 to 1902 he was organist at St. Margaret's, Westminster. In 1900–1901 he made a concert tour through the U.S. and Canada; from 1902 to 1905 he was organist at the Carnegie Inst. in Pittsburgh; continued to tour extensively on both sides of the Atlantic, and also in the Far East; then held the post of municipal organist in San Francisco (1917–21), Portland, Maine (1921–23), and Chattanooga, Tenn. (1924–29). He wrote about 200 organ works, an Easter cantata, anthems, settings of sacred texts, and songs; his *Andantino* acquired wide popularity when it was used for the American ballad *Moonlight and Roses*; he also prepared innumerable transcriptions for the organ. His reminiscences appeared as *Organs I Have Met: The Autobiography of Edwin H. Lemare, 1866–1934, Together With Reminiscences by His Wife and Friends* (Los Angeles, 1956).

Lemeshev, Sergei (Yakovlevich), prominent Russian tenor; b. Knyazevo, near Tver, July 10, 1902; d. Moscow, June 26, 1977. In his youth, he worked at a cobbler's shop in Petrograd; then went to Moscow, where he studied at the Cons. with Raysky, graduating in 1925. He made his operatic debut at Sverdlovsk in 1926; then was a member of the Kharbin Opera in Manchuria (1927–29) and at the Tiflis Opera (1929–31). In 1931 he joined the Bolshoi Theater in Moscow, and gradually created an enthusiastic following; he remained on its roster until 1961 and was particularly admired for his performance of the role of Lensky in *Eugene Onegin*; in 1972, on his 70th birthday, he sang it again at the Bolshoi Theater. Other roles in which he shone, apart from the Russian repertoire, included Faust, Romeo, Werther, Alfredo, and the Duke of Mantua. He also made numerous appearances in solo recitals; he was the first to present an entire cycle of Tchaikovsky's songs in 5 concerts. His autobiography was publ. in Moscow in 1968.

BIBL.: M. Lvov, *S. L.* (Moscow, 1947); E. Grosheva, *S. L.* (Moscow, 1960).

Lemnitz, Tiana (Luise), remarkable German soprano; b. Metz, Oct. 26, 1897; d. Berlin, Feb. 5, 1994. She studied with Hoch in Metz and Kohmann in Frankfurt am Main. She made her operatic debut in Lortzing's *Undine* in Heilbronn (1920), then sang in Aachen (1922–28). Lemnitz subsequently pursued a distinguished career as a member of the Hannover Opera (1928–33), the Dresden State Opera (1933–34), and the Berlin State Opera (1934–57). She also made guest appearances in Vienna, Munich, London's Covent Garden (1936, 1938), and Buenos Aires's Teatro Colón (1936, 1950). Her repertoire included many leading roles in German, Italian, French, and Russian operas. Among her most celebrated portrayals were Pamina, Sieglinde, Desdemona, Micaëla, Octavian, and the Marschallin.

Lenaerts, René Bernard (Maria), distinguished Belgian musicologist; b. Bornem, Oct. 26, 1902; d. Leuven, Feb. 27, 1992. He studied at the Mechelen theological seminary and at the Lemmens Inst., being ordained a priest (1927), then continued his education at the Univ. of Louvain (Ph.D., 1929, with the diss. *Het Nederlands polifonies lied in de zestiende eeuw*; publ. in Mechelen and Amsterdam, 1933); after additional studies with Pirro in Paris (1931–32), he taught in secondary schools in Geel and Antwerp; then was a junior lecturer (1944–46), lecturer (1946–49), and full prof. (1949–73) in musicology at the Catholic Univ. of Louvain; was also a reader in Renaissance music history at the Univ. of Utrecht (1958–71). In 1955 he was made a canon. In 1959 he became ed. of Monumenta Musicae Belgicae. Lenaerts was made a corresponding member of the American Musicological Soc. in 1981. He publ. *Oude Nederlandse muziek* (Brussels, 1937), *Johann Sebastian Bach* (Diest, 1943), *Belangrijke verzamelingen Nederlandse muziek uit de zestiende eeuw in Spanje* (Brussels, 1957), and *De Nederlandse muziek uit de vijftiende eeuw* (Louvain, 1959).

BIBL.: J. Robijns, ed., *Renaissance-Muziek 1400–1600: Donum natalicium R.B. L.* (Louvain, 1969).

Lendvai, Ernő, Hungarian musicologist; b. Kaposvár, Feb. 6, 1925; d. Budapest, Jan. 31, 1993. He studied at the Budapest Academy of Music (1945–49). He was made director of the Szombathely Music School (1949) and the Győr Cons. (1954); was also prof. at the Szeged Cons. (from 1957) and a teacher at the Budapest Academy of Music (1954–56; from 1973). He distinguished himself as a writer on the life and works of Bartók.

WRITINGS: *Bartók stilusa* (Bartók's Style; Budapest, 1955); *Bartók's Dramaturgy: Stage Works and Cantata Profana* (Budapest, 1964); *Toscanini és Beethoven* (Budapest, 1967; Eng. tr., 1966, in *Studia musicologica Academiae scientiarum hungaricae*, VIII); *Bartók költői vilaga* (The Poetic World of Bartók; Budapest, 1971); *Béla Bartók: An Analysis of His Music* (London, 1971); *Bartók és Kodály harmóniavilága* (The Harmonic World of Bartók and Kodály; Budapest, 1975); *The Workshop of Bartók and Kodály* (Budapest, 1983); *Verdi és a 20. század A Falstaff hangzás-dramaturgiája* (Budapest, 1984).

Lendvai, (Peter) Erwin, Hungarian composer; b. Budapest, June 4, 1882; d. Epsom, Surrey, March 31, 1949. He was a student of Koessler in Budapest and of Puccini in Milan. After teaching at the Jaques Dalcroze school in Hellerau (1913–14), the Hoch Cons. in Frankfurt am Main (1914–19), the Klindworth-Scharwenka Cons. in Berlin (1919–22), and the Volksmusikschule in Hamburg (1923–25), he was active as a choral conductor. He eventually settled in England. He publ. the method *Chorschule*. Among his works were the opera *Elga* (Mannheim, Dec. 6, 1916; rev. 1918); Sym. (1909) and other orch. scores; chamber music; vocal pieces.

BIBL.: H. Leichtentritt, *E. L.* (Berlin, 1912).

Lendvay, Kamilló, Hungarian composer, conductor, and teacher; b. Budapest, Dec. 28, 1928. He was a student in composition of Viski at the Budapest Academy of Music (1949–57), and also received lessons in conducting from Somogyi

(1953–55). After conducting at the Szeged Opera (1956–57), he returned to Budapest and was music director of the State Puppet Theater (1960–66) and the Hungarian Army Art Ensemble (1966–68); he then was a conductor (1970–72) and subsequently music director (1972–74) of the Municipal Operetta Theater. From 1962 he was active with the Hungarian Radio. In 1973 he joined the faculty of the Academy of Music, where he was head of its theory dept. from 1978. He also served as president of Artisjus, the Hungarian Copyright Office. In 1962, 1964, and 1978 he was awarded the Erkel Prize. He was made a Merited Artist by the Hungarian government in 1981. In 1989 he received the Bartók-Pásztory Award. In his compositions, serial procedures serve as the foundation of his avant-garde explorations.

WORKS: DRAMATIC: *A bűvös szék* (The Magic Chair), comic opera (1972); *A tisztességtudó utcalány* (The Respectful Prostitute), opera (1976–78); incidental music for plays; film scores. **ORCH.:** *Tragic Overture* (1958); *Mauthausen*, symphonic poem (1958); Concertino for Piano, Winds, Percussion, and Harp (1959; also for Chamber Orch., 1982); *The Indomitable Tin Soldier*, suite (1961); 2 violin concertos (1961–62; 1986); *Quattro invocazioni* (1966); *Expressions* for Strings (1974); *Pezzo concertato* for Cello and Orch. (1975); *The Harmony of Silence* (1980); *Concertino semplice* for Cimbalon and Strings (1986); *Chaconne* (1987–88); Concerto for Trumpet and Wind Orch. (1990); Double Concerto for Violin, Cimbalom, and Strings (1991). **BAND:** *Story-telling Dance* (1952); *Little Suite* (1956); *3 Carnival Masks* (1960); *Scherzo* (1972; arranged by L. Hollós); *Festspiel Overture* (1984). **CHAMBER:** *Trio Serenade* for String Trio (1954); *Rhapsody* for Violin and Piano (1955); String Quartet (1962); *Quattro duetti* for Flute and Piano (1965); *Concerto da camera* for Chamber Ensemble (1969); *Disposizioni* for Cimbalom (1975); *Fifthmusic* for Cello (1978–79); *Metamorphosis of a Cimbalom Piece* for Chamber Ensemble (1979); *5 Arrogant Ideas* for 3 Trumpets, 2 Trombones, and Tuba (1979); *5 Movements in Quotation Marks* for Horn, Trombone, and Tuba (1980); *Senza sordina* for Trumpet and Piano (1983; also for Trumpet and Band, 1985); *As You Like It* for 2 Pianos (1984); 24 Duos for 2 Violins (1985); *8 More Arrogant Ideas* for 2 Trumpets, Horn, Trombone, and Tuba (1986); *Variazioni con tema* for Trumpet and Organ (1986); *Respectfully yours, Mr. Goodman* for Clarinet (1988); *The Cricket, the Ant, and the Others* for 7 Instruments (1993). **VOCAL:** *Orogenesis* for Chorus and Orch. (1969–70); *A Ride at Night* for Contralto and 7 Players (1970); *Pro libertate* for Tenor, Baritone, Men's Chorus, and Orch. (1975); *Scenes* for Soprano, Bass-baritone, and Orch. (1978–81); *Via crucis* for Chorus and 10 Instruments (1988–89); *Stabat Mater* for Soloists, Chorus, Organ, and Chamber Orch. (1991).

Léner, Jenö, Hungarian violinist; b. Szabadka, April 7, 1894; d. N.Y., Nov. 4, 1948. He was a student at the Royal Academy of Music in Budapest. After playing in theater orchs., he founded the Léner Quartet, which made its debut in Budapest in 1919. From 1922 to 1939 it appeared regularly in London. It made its N.Y. debut in 1929, and therefter performed in the U.S. until disbanding in 1942. In was reorganized in 1945 but was dissolved upon Léner's death. The Léner Quartet was one of the most celebrated quartets of its time, being especially renowned for its interpretations of Beethoven's quartets.

BIBL.: A. Molnár, *A L.-vonósnégyes* (The L. Quartet; Budapest, 1968).

Leng, Afonso, Chilean composer; b. Santiago, Feb. 11, 1884; d. there, Nov. 7, 1974. He was a student of Enrique Soro at the Santiago Cons. (1905–06); he also studied dentistry at the Univ. of Chile. While pursuing a career as an odontologist, he also was active as a composer. In 1957 he was awarded the National Arts Prize. His works were in a Romantic vein.

WORKS: ORCH.: *5 dolores* (1920); *La muerte de Alsino*, symphonic poem (1920; Santiago, May 30, 1931); *Canto de Invierno* (1932); *Fantasia* for Piano and Orch. (Santiago, Aug. 28, 1936). **CHAMBER:** *Andante* for Piano and String Quartet (1922). **PIANO:** *Fantasia quasi Sonata* (1909); *10 Preludes* (1919–32); 2 sonatas (1927, 1950); *2 Otoñales* (1932). **VOCAL:** *Psalm 77* for Soloists, Chorus, and Orch. (1941); many songs.

BIBL.: Special issue of *Revista Musical Chilena* (Aug.–Sept. 1957).

Lentz, Daniel (Kirkland), American composer; b. Latrobe, Pa., March 10, 1941. He studied music and philosophy at St. Vincent College (B.A., 1962), music history and composition at Ohio State Univ. (M.A., 1965), and composition with Berger, Lucier, and Shapero at Brandeis Univ. (1965–67) and with Sessions and Rochberg at the Berkshire Music Center at Tanglewood (summer, 1966). He went to Stockholm on a Fulbright grant to study electronic music and musicology (1967–68); then was a visiting lecturer at the Univ. of Calif. at Santa Barbara (1968–70) and at Antioch College in Yellow Springs, Ohio (1973). He formed the performing groups California Time Machine (1969–73) and San Andreas Fault (1974, 1976); later was active with the Los Angeles-based ensemble LENTZ (from 1982), featuring the agile American vocalist Jessica (actually Lynn Mary) Karraker (b. St. Louis, Mo., Sept. 4, 1953), other vocalists, multiple keyboardists, and occasional percussion. He held grants from various organizations, including the NEA (1973, 1975, 1977, 1979, 1993) and the Deutscher Akademischer Austauschdienst in Berlin (1979). Lentz is a proponent of the avant-garde; one of his most interesting early works was *Love and Conception* (1968–69), in which a male pianist and his female page-turner are ultimately directed to crawl under the lid of a grand piano and engage in sexual intercourse. Their performance, which is at first accompanied by 2 tandem AM radio broadcasts of fictional reviews of the piece, is finally replaced by a live, synchronous FM broadcast of the piece itself, which frees them to waltz about the stage, fall into each other's arms, and, overcome with passion, fall into the piano. It was performed at the Univ. of Calif. at Santa Barbara on Feb. 26, 1969; as a result of this and later performances, Lentz was dismissed from his lectureship position there. He then devoted himself to composing, with increasing reliance on computer and synthesizer technologies. In 1991 he became a founding faculty member of a newly-formed interdisciplinary arts and performance degree program at Arizona State Univ. West in Phoenix; in 1992 he was a visiting prof. at the Univ. of Calif., Los Angeles. Since his relocation to the Sonoran desert in 1991, Lentz has collaborated on numerous pieces with Harold Budd, many of which have resulted in recordings, e.g. *Music for Pianos* (1992) and *Walk Into My Voice* (1995). Many of his works, such as the orchestral *An American in L.A.* (1989), are pure sensuality, with less attention given to formal procedures than to rhythmic vibrancy and sonorous effect. His text settings can challenge the ear; frequently phonemes are introduced in the beginning of a piece, which, through a gradual interlocking of parts, form audible words (and occasional truncated sentences) only at the very finish. While retaining its freshness and, at times, almost exquisite beauty, Lentz's music throughout the 1980s was heavily equipment-reliant, demanding much not only from the vocalists and instrumentalists in his ensemble, but from Lentz himself, who has had to function as composer, producer, editor, sound mixer, and recording engineer during live performances. Much of his work dating from 1989 has tended toward acoustic media; his *b.e. cummings* (1991) was his last piece utilizing multi-tracking. In 1993 he commenced work on his first large-scale music theater piece, *Lamentations on the Legacy of Cortez* (1993–95; in collaboration with librettist L. Kuhn and architect/stage designer William Bruder); in its Latin movements, Lentz integrates materials drawn from Requiem masses across time.

WORKS: THEATER AND MIXED MEDIA: *A Piano: Piece* (1965); *Ecumenical Council* (1965); *Gospel Meeting* (1965); *Paul and Judy Meet the Time Tunnel* (1966); *Paul and Judy Meet Startrek* (1966); *Hi-yo Paint* (1968); *Air Meal Spatial Delivery* (1969); *Work of Crow* (1970); *Lamentations on the Legacy of*

Cortez for Chorus, Strings, 2 MIDI-Keyboards, and 2 Percussion (1993–95). **PERFORMERS AND ECHO DELAY:** *Canon and Fugue (Canon and Fugle)* (1971); *King Speech Songs* (1972); *You Can't See the Forest . . . Music* (1972); *Missa umbrarum* (1973); *Song(s) of the Sirens (Les Sirènes)* (1973); *3 Pretty Madrigals* (1976); *Dancing on the Sun* (1980); *Music by Candlelight (Love and Death)* (1980); *Uitoto* (1980); *b.e. cummings* for Soprano, Baritone, and Chamber Ensemble (1991). **PERFORMERS WITH MULTI-TRACKING:** *Is It Love* (1983; Santa Barbara, Calif., Aug. 1984); *On the Leopard Altar* (1983; Santa Barbara, Calif., 1984); *Time Is a Trick* (Rouen, Dec. 1985); *Bacchus with Wineglasses* (Los Angeles, Nov. 1985); *Wild Turkeys* for 3 Keyboard Synthesizers (N.Y., Dec. 1985); *La Tache* with Wineglasses (Boston, June 5, 1987); *Night Breaker* for 4 Pianos (Los Angeles, March 30, 1990). **VOCAL:** *I (Senescence sonorum)*, double concerto for Amplified Body Sounds, Chorus, and Orch. (1970); *Fermentation Notebooks*: 1, *Kissing Song*; 2, *Rising Song*; 3, *Drinking Song* for 28 to 48 Unaccompanied Voices, with Wineglasses in No. 3 (1972); *O-Ke-Wa (North American Eclipse)* for 12 Solo Voices, Bells, Rasps, and Drums (1974); *Sun Tropes* for 7 Solo Voices, Recorders, and Kalimbas (1975); *Composition in Contrary and Parallel Motion* for 16 Solo Voices, Percussion, and 4 Keyboards (1977); *The Elysian Nymph* for 8 Solo Voices and 8 Marimbas (1978); *Wolf Is Dead* for Solo Voices and Percussion (1979; rev. for 6 Solo Voices and 8 Keyboards, 1982); *Wail Song* for Vocal Soloist, 5 Voices, and 8 Keyboards (1983); *wolfMASS* for Vocalist, Keyboards, and Percussion (Rouen, June 1988); *Cathedral of Ecstasy* for Vocalists, Electric Keyboards, and Percussion (1990; Tokyo, Nov. 1991); *Pear Blossom Highway* (aka *Abalone*) for Baritone and Electronic Keyboards (1990); *Talk Radio* for Vocalist and Chamber Ensemble (1990–91; Pittsburgh, Nov. 1991, Joan La Barbara soloist); *White Bee* for Solo Voice (1992; Tempe, Ariz., April 1993). **INSTRUMENTAL:** *Piano Piece for Little Kids with Big Hands* (1962); *3 Episodes from Exodus* for Organ and Percussion (1962); *3 Haiku in 4 Movements* for String Quartet (1963); *8 Dialectics 8* for 18 Instruments (1964); *Funke* for Flute, Vibraphone, Drums, Double Bass, and Piano (1964); *Sermon: Saying Something with Music* for String Quartet and Electronics (1966); *The Last Concert*, in 3: *Love and Conception, Birth and Death*, and *Fate and Death* for Piano and Electronics (1968); *Pastime* for String Instruments and Electronics (1969); *10 Minus 30 Minutes* for Strings (1970); *Point Conception* for 9 Pianos (1981); *Lascaux (Chumash Tombs)* for Vocalists and Wine Glasses (1984); *Topanga Tango* for Chamber Ensemble (Pittsburgh, Oct. 1985); *A Crack in the Bell* for Vocal Soloist, 3 Keyboards, and Optional Chamber Orch. (Los Angeles, Nov. 10, 1986); *An American in L.A.* for Synthesizer and Orch. (Los Angeles, March 30, 1989); *A California Family (Group Portrait)*, trio for Violin, Piano, and Percussion (N.Y., Nov. 1989); *Apache Wine* for Chamber Orch. (1989; Tucson, Feb. 16, 1990). **TAPE:** *Montage Shift* (1963); *No Exit* (1963); *Eleison* (1965); *Medeighnia's* (1965).

BIBL.: G. Elster, "D. L.: Words & Music," *Soundings*, 10 (1976); P. Job, "D. L. pecheur de perles," *Libération*, 19 (Oct. 1980); G. Smith, "D. L.," in *New Voices* (1995).

Lenya, Lotte (real name, **Karoline Wilhelmine Blamauer),** Austrian-American singer and actress; b. Vienna, Oct. 18, 1898; d. N.Y., Nov. 27, 1981. She received training in Classical dance and the Dalcroze method in Zürich (1914–20), where she also worked at the Stadttheater's opera-ballet and at the Schauspielhaus. In 1926 she married **Kurt Weill,** and made her debut as a singer in the premiere of his "songspiel" *Mahagonny* (Baden-Baden, July 17, 1927). She later sang in the first performance of its operatic version as *Aufstieg und Fall der Stadt Mahagonny* (Leipzig, March 9, 1930). She also created the role of Jenny in his *Die Dreigroschenoper* (Berlin, Aug. 31, 1928). In 1933 Lenya and Weill fled Nazi Germany for Paris. During their stay there, she created the role of Anna in his *Die sieben Todsunden der Kleinburger* (June 7, 1933). In 1935 they emigrated to the U.S. She created the roles of Miriam in his *The Eternal Road* (N.Y., Jan 7, 1937) and the Duchess in his *The Firebrand of Florence* (N.Y., March 22, 1945). Following Weill's death in 1950, Lenya devoted herself to reviving many of his works for the American stage. She also was active as an actress on stage and in films. Although she was not a professionally trained singer, she adapted herself to the peculiar type of half-spoken, half-sung roles in Weill's works with total dedication.

BIBL.: H. Marx, ed., *Weill-L.* (N.Y., 1976).

León, Tania (Justina), Cuban-born American composer, conductor, pianist, and teacher; b. Havana, May 14, 1943. She studied in Havana at the Carlos Alfredo Peyrellade Cons. (B.A., 1963; M.A. in music education, 1964). She went in 1967 to the U.S., where she enrolled at N.Y. Univ. (M.S., 1973) and had conducting lessons with Halasz and at the Berkshire Music Center at Tanglewood with Bernstein and Ozawa. In 1968 she joined the Dance Theatre of Harlem as its first music director, a position she held until 1980; also organized the Brooklyn Phil. Community Concert Series (1977). She was a guest conductor with several U.S. and European orchs.; in 1992 she conducted the Johannesburg Sym. during the Dance Theatre of Harlem's historic trip to South Africa, when the company became the first multi-racial arts troupe to perform and teach there in modern times. Among her many awards were the Young Composer's Prize from the National Council of the Arts, Havana (1966), the Alvin John Award from the Council for Emigrés in the Professions (1971), and the Cintas Award (1974–75); she also was an NEA Fellow (1975). In 1978 she was music director for Broadway's smash musical *The Wiz*, and in 1985 served as resident composer for the Lincoln Center Inst. in N.Y.; also joined the composition faculty of Brooklyn College; later was artistic director of the Composers' Forum in N.Y. She has also held composer and/or conducting residencies in the U.S. (Cleveland, Seattle et al.) and in Europe (Italy, Germany et al.). Her compositions are written in an accessible style, rhythmically vibrant, with some novel piano and percussion effects. Her *Kabiosile* for Piano and Orch. (1988) brings together the rich and disparate elements of her own cultural heritage, combining Afro-Cuban, Hispanic, and Latin jazz elements within a classical Western concerto format. Her ballet *Dougla* (with Geoffrey Holder; 1974) was heard in the Soviet Union during the Dance Theatre of Harlem's 1988 tour.

WORKS: DRAMATIC: *Tones*, ballet (1970; in collaboration with A. Mitchell); *The Beloved*, ballet (1972); *Dougla*, ballet (1974; in collaboration with G. Holder); *Maggie Magalita*, theater piece (1980; in collaboration with W. Kesselman); *The Golden Windows*, theater piece (1982; in collaboration with R. Wilson); *Scourge of Hyacinths*, chamber opera, to a libretto by the composer after a play by Wole Soyinka (1992). **ORCH.:** *Concerto criollo* for Piano, 8 Timpani, and Orch. (1980); *Batá* (1985); *Kabiosile* for Piano and Orch. (N.Y., Dec. 4, 1988); *Carabalí* (1991); *Para Viola y Orquesta* for Violin and Orch. (Chicago, July 29, 1994). **CHAMBER:** *Haiku* for Flute, Bassoon, and 5 Percussion (1973); *Pet's Suite* for Flute and Piano (1980); *Ascend* for 4 Horns, 4 Trumpets, 3 Trombones, Tuba, and Percussion (1983); *Permutation Seven* for Flute, Clarinet, Trumpet, Violin, Cello, and Percussion (1985); *A La Par* for Piano and Percussion (1986); *Parajota Delaté* for Flute, Clarinet, Violin, Cello, and Piano (1988; also for Flute, Oboe, Clarinet, Bassoon, and Piano, 1992); *Indigena* for Instrumental Ensemble (1991); *Crossings* for Brass Ensemble (1992); *Aernas d'un Tiempo* for Clarinet, Cello, and Piano (1992); *Son Sonora* for Flute and Guitar (1993); *sin normas, ajenas* for Large Chamber Ensemble (1994); *Hechizos* for Large Chamber Ensemble (1995); various works for solo instruments. **VOCAL:** *De-Orishas* for 2 Sopranos, Countertenor, 2 Tenors, and Bass (1982); *Pueblo Mulato*, 3 songs for Soprano, Oboe, Guitar, Double Bass, Percussion, and Piano, after Nicolás Guillén (1987); *Heart of Ours—A Piece* for Men's Chorus, Flute, 4 Trumpets, and 2 Percussion (1988); *Batéy* for 2 Sopranos, Countertenor, 2 Tenors, and Bass (1989; in collaboration with M. Camilo); *To and Fro* for Medium Voice and Piano (1990); *Journey* for Soprano, Flute, and Harp (1990); *"Or like a . . ."* for Baritone, Cello, and Percussion (1994).

Leoncavallo, Ruggero, noted Italian composer; b. Naples, April 23, 1857; d. Montecatini, Aug. 9, 1919. He attended the Naples Cons. (1866–76), where his teachers were B. Cesi (piano) and M. Ruta and L. Rossi (composition), and then took courses in literature at the Univ. of Bologna (1876–78). His first opera, *Tommaso Chatterton*, was about to be produced in Bologna (1878) when the manager disappeared, and the production was called off. Leoncavallo earned his living playing piano in cafes throughout Europe before going to Paris, where he composed chansonettes and other popular songs. He wrote an opera, *Songe d'une nuit d'été* (after Shakespeare's *Midsummer Night's Dream*), which was privately sung in a salon. He began to study Wagner's scores, and became an ardent Wagnerian; he resolved to emulate the master by producing a trilogy, *Crepusculum*, depicting in epical traits the Italian Renaissance; the separate parts were to be *I Medici, Girolamo Savonarola*, and *Cesare Borgia*. He spent 6 years on the basic historical research; having completed the first part, and with the scenario of the entire trilogy sketched, he returned in 1887 to Italy, where the publisher Ricordi became interested in the project, but kept delaying the publication and production of the work. Annoyed, Leoncavallo turned to Sonzogno, the publisher of Mascagni, whose opera *Cavalleria rusticana* had just obtained a tremendous vogue. Leoncavallo submitted a short opera in a similarly realistic vein; he wrote his own libretto based on a factual story of passion and murder in a Calabrian village, and named it *Pagliacci*. The opera was given with sensational success at the Teatro dal Verme in Milan under the direction of Toscanini (May 21, 1892), and rapidly took possession of operatic stages throughout the world; it is often played on the same evening with Mascagni's opera, both works being of brief duration. Historically, these 2 operas signalized the important development of Italian operatic *verismo*, which influenced composers of other countries as well.

The enormous success of *Pagliacci* did not deter Leoncavallo from carrying on his more ambitious projects. The first part of his unfinished trilogy, *I Medici*, was finally brought out at the Teatro dal Verme in Milan on Nov. 9, 1893, but the reception was so indifferent that he turned to other subjects; the same fate befell his youthful *Tommaso Chatterton* at its production in Rome (March 10, 1896). His next opera, *La Bohème* (Venice, May 6, 1897), won considerable success, but had the ill fortune of coming a year after Puccini's masterpiece on the same story, and was dwarfed by comparison. There followed a light opera, *Zaza* (Milan, Nov. 10, 1900), which was fairly successful, and was produced repeatedly on world stages. In 1894 he was commissioned by the German Emperor Wilhelm II to write an opera for Berlin; this was *Der Roland von Berlin*, on a German historic theme; it was produced in Berlin on Dec. 13, 1904, but despite the high patronage it proved a fiasco. In 1906 Leoncavallo made a tour of the U.S. and Canada, conducting his *Pagliacci* and a new operetta, *La Jeunesse de Figaro*, specially written for his American tour; it was so unsuccessful that he never attempted to stage it in Europe. Back in Italy he resumed his industrious production; the opera *Maia* (Rome, Jan. 15, 1910) and the operetta *Malbrouck* (Rome, Jan. 19, 1910) were produced within the same week; another operetta, *La Reginetta delle rose*, was staged simultaneously in Rome and in Naples (June 24, 1912). In the autumn of that year, Leoncavallo visited London, where he presented the premiere of his *Gli Zingari* (Sept. 16, 1912); a year later, he revisited the U.S., conducting in San Francisco. He wrote several more operettas, but they made no impression; 3 of them were produced during his lifetime: *La Candidata* (Rome, Feb. 6, 1915), *Goffredo Mameli* (Genoa, April 27, 1916), and *Prestami tua moglie* (Montecatini, Sept. 2, 1916); posthumous premieres were accorded the operetta *A chi la giarettiera?* (Rome, Oct. 16, 1919), the opera *Edipo re* (Chicago, Dec. 13, 1920), and the operetta *Il primo bacio* (Montecatini, April 29, 1923). Another score, *Tormenta*, remained unfinished. Salvatore Allegra collected various sketches by Leoncavallo and arranged from them a 3-act operetta, *La maschera nuda*, which was produced in Naples on June 26, 1925.

BIBL.: C. Trevor, "R. L.," *Musical Monthly Record*, XLIX (1919); R. de Rensis, *Per Umberto Giordano e R. L.* (Siena, 1949); J. Klein, "R. L. (1858–1919)," *Opera*, IX (1958); M. Sansone, "The 'Verismo' of R. L.: A Source Study of 'Pagliacci'," *Music & Letters* (Aug. 1989).

Leonhardt, Gustav (Maria), eminent Dutch organist, harpsichordist, conductor, and pedagogue; b. 's Graveland, May 30, 1928. He studied organ and harpsichord with Eduard Müller at the Schola Cantorum in Basel (1947–50), then made his debut as a harpsichordist in Vienna (1950); after studying musicology there, he served as prof. of harpsichord at the Academy of Music (1952–55); was prof. of harpsichord at the Amsterdam Cons. (from 1954); was also active as a church organist there. He made numerous tours of Europe and North America, mainly appearing as a harpsichordist; also led his own Leonhardt Consort on tours from 1955. He ed. Bach's *Die Kunst der Fuge*, pieces by Sweelinck, and other works.

Leoni, Franco, Italian composer; b. Milan, Oct. 24, 1864; d. London, Feb. 8, 1949. He studied at the Milan Cons. with Dominiceti and Ponchielli. In 1892 he went to London, where he remained until 1917; then lived in France and Italy, eventually returning to England.

WORKS: OPERAS: *Raggio di luna* (Milan, June 5, 1890); *Rip van Winkle* (London, Sept. 4, 1897); *Ib and Little Christina*, "picture in 3 panels" (London, Nov. 14, 1901); *L'oracolo* (London, June 28, 1905); *Tzigana* (Genoa, Feb. 3, 1910); *Le baruffe chiozzotte* (Milan, Jan. 2, 1920); *La terra del sogno* (Milan, Jan. 10, 1920); *Falene* (Milan, 1920). **ORATORIOS:** *Sardanapalus* (London, 1891); *The Gate of Life* (London, 1891); *Golgotha* (London, 1909). **OTHER:** Songs.

Leontovich, Mikola (Dmitrovich), prominent Ukrainian composer and teacher; b. Monastïryok, Podolia, Dec. 13, 1877; d. Markovka, near Tulchin, Jan. 25, 1921. He was educated at the seminaries in Stargorod and Kamenets-Podolsky. Although he lacked formal training in music, he was active as a singing teacher in various schools and as a conductor of amateur choirs and orchs. After completing sessions as an external student of the St. Petersburg court chapel choir (1904), he worked with Yavorsky (1909–14); in 1918, became a teacher at the Lissenko Music and Drama Inst. He also was active with various Ukrainian musical organizations. Leontovich possessed a remarkable talent for arranging Ukrainian folk songs for unaccompanied choral groups. Among his own works were several major unaccompanied choral works, instrumental pieces, and an unfinished opera. A number of collections of his works were publ., as well as a vol. of his writings (Kiev, 1947).

BIBL.: V. Diachenko, *M.D. L.* (Kharkov, 1941); M. Gordichuk, *M.D. L.* (Kiev, 1972).

Leoz, Jesús García, Spanish composer; b. Olite, Navarre, Jan. 10, 1904; d. Madrid, Feb. 25, 1953. He was a cantor in Olite before pursuing his studies in Pamplona; later received training from del Campo (composition) and Balsa (piano), and finally from Turina (composition), his most significant influence. Leoz's output included zarzuelas, a ballet, orch. pieces, chamber music, piano pieces, songs, and film scores.

BIBL.: A. Fernández Cid, *J. L.* (Madrid, 1953).

Leplin, Emanuel, American composer; b. San Francisco, Oct. 3, 1917; d. Martinez, Calif., Dec. 1, 1972. He studied violin with Enesco, conducting with Monteux, and composition with Sessions.

WORKS: ORCH.: *Galaxy* for 2 Cellos and Orch. (1942); *Cosmos* for Violin and Orch. (1949); 2 symphonic poems: *Landscapes* and *Skyscrapers* (San Francisco, May 5, 1960); Sym. (San Francisco, Jan. 3, 1962). **CHAMBER:** 3 string quartets; works for various instrumental combinations; piano pieces.

Leppard, Raymond (John), eminent English conductor; b. London, Aug. 11, 1927. He studied harpsichord and viola at Trinity College, Cambridge (M.A., 1952), where he also was active as a choral conductor and served as music director of the

Cambridge Phil. Soc. In 1952 he made his London debut as a conductor, and then conducted his own Leppard Ensemble. He became closely associated with the Goldsbrough Orch., which became the English Chamber Orch. in 1960. He also gave recitals as a harpsichordist, and was a Fellow of Trinity College and a lecturer on music at his alma mater (1958–68). His interest in early music prompted him to prepare several realizations of scores from that period; while his eds. provoked controversy, they had great value in introducing early operatic masterpieces to the general public. His first realization, Monteverdi's *L'incoronazione di Poppea*, was presented at the Glyndebourne Festival under his direction in 1962. He subsequently prepared performing eds. of Monteverdi's *Orfeo* (1965) and *Il ritorno d'Ulisse in patria* (1972), and of Cavalli's *Messa concertata* (1966), *L'Ormindo* (1967), *La Calisto* (1969), *L'Egisto* (1974), and *L'Orione* (1980). During this period, he made appearances as a guest conductor with leading European opera houses, orchs., and festivals. On Nov. 4, 1969, he made his U.S. debut conducting the Westminster Choir and N.Y. Phil., at which occasion he also appeared as soloist in the Haydn D-major Harpsichord Concerto. In 1973 he became principal conductor of the BBC Northern Sym. Orch. in Manchester, a position he retained until 1980. He made his U.S. debut as an opera conductor leading a performance of his ed. of *L'Egisto* at the Santa Fe Opera in 1974. Settling in the U.S. in 1976, he subsequently appeared as a guest conductor with the major U.S. orchs. and opera houses. On Sept. 19, 1978, he made his Metropolitan Opera debut in N.Y. conducting *Billy Budd*. He was principal guest conductor of the St. Louis Sym. Orch. (1984–90). In 1987 he became music director of the Indianapolis Sym. Orch. At the invitation of the Prince of Wales, he conducted his ed. of Purcell's *Dido and Aeneas* at London's Buckingham Palace in 1988. He returned there in 1990 to conduct the 90th-birthday concert of the Queen Mother. On Jan. 27, 1991, he conducted a special concert of Mozart's works with members of the N.Y. Phil. and the Juilliard Orch. at N.Y.'s Avery Fisher Hall in Lincoln Center; telecast live to millions via PBS, it re-created a concert given by Mozart in Vienna on March 23, 1783, and celebrated his 235th birthday and the launching of Lincoln Center's commemoration of the 200th anniversary of his death. In 1993 he conducted the Indianapolis Sym. Orch. on a major tour of Europe, visiting London, Birmingham, Frankfurt am Main, Cologne, Düsseldorf, Vienna, Munich, Geneva, and Zürich. In 1994 he was named artist-in-residence at the Univ. of Indianapolis. Leppard was made a Commander of the Order of the British Empire in 1983. As a composer, he produced film scores for *Lord of the Flies* (1963), *Alfred the Great* (1969), *Laughter in the Dark* (1969), *Perfect Friday* (1970), and *Hotel New Hampshire* (1985). He also orchestrated Schubert's "Grand Duo" Sonata and conducted its first performance with the Indianapolis Sym. Orch. (Nov. 8, 1990). Although long associated with early music, Leppard has acquired mastery of a truly catholic repertoire, ranging from Mozart to Britten. His thoughtful views on performance practice are set forth in his book *The Real Authenticity* (London, 1988). T. Lewis ed. the vol. *Raymond Leppard on Music* (White Plains, N.Y., 1993), an anthology of critical and personal writings, with a biographical chronology and discography.

Lerdahl, (Al)Fred (Whitford), American composer and music theorist; b. Madison, Wis., March 10, 1943. He studied at Lawrence Univ. (B.M., 1965) and Princeton Univ. (M.F.A., 1968), where his teachers included Babbitt, Cone, and Kim; then studied with Fortner at the Freiburg im Breisgau Hochschule für Musik on a Fulbright grant (1968–69); was composer-in-residence at IRCAM (1981–82) and at the American Academy in Rome (1987). He held teaching appointments at the Univ. of Calif. at Berkeley (1969–71), Harvard Univ. (1970–79), Columbia Univ. (1979–85), and the Univ. of Mich. (from 1985). From 1974 he collaborated with linguist Ray Jackendoff on a theory of tonal music based on generative linguistics; several articles along these lines culminated in the innovative *A Generative Theory of Tonal Music* (Cambridge, Mass., 1983). Lerdahl's studies include music cognition and computer-assisted composition. As a composer, he features in his works the dismantling of texts and a technique of "expanding variation" wherein each variation is longer than the preceding by a predetermined ratio.

WORKS: ORCH.: *Chromorhythmos* (1972); *Chords* (1974; rev. 1983); *Crosscurrents* (1987); *Waves* for Chamber Orch. (1988). **CHAMBER:** *Piano Fantasy* (1964); String Trio (1965–66); *6 Études* for Flute, Viola, and Harp (1977); 2 string quartets (1978, 1982); *Episodes and Refrains* for Wind Quintet (1982); *Fantasy Etudes* for Chamber Ensemble (1985); *Marches* for Clarinet, Violin, Cello, and Piano (1992). **VOCAL:** *Wake* for Mezzo-soprano, Violin, Viola, Cello, Harp, and Percussion Ensemble (1968); *Aftermath*, cantata for Soprano, Mezzo-soprano, Baritone, and Chamber Ensemble (1973); *Eros: Variations* for Mezzo-soprano, Alto Flute, Viola, Harp, Piano, Electric Guitar, Electric Bass, and Percussion (1975); *Beyond the Realm of Bird* for Soprano and Chamber Orch. (1981–84).

Lerman, Richard, innovative American composer and sound artist; b. San Francisco, Dec. 5, 1944. He studied composition with Lucier and Shapero at Brandeis Univ. (B.A. in music, 1966), where he also received an M.F.A. in theater and film (1970) and was technical director of its electronic music studio (1965–70). From 1965 to 1970 he was active with numerous film, theater, and media productions; from 1977 he toured throughout North America and Europe; also performed in Australia, New Zealand, Japan, and China. Lerman has made extensive use of self-built transducers and electronics to explore and reveal small sounds inside of materials and objects; his diverse works include real-time performance pieces and sound installations, as well as works on film and video. From 1989 he has produced several collaborations with the installation artist Mona Higuchi, including *Los Desaparecidos* (1989), *Takuhon* (1991), *Kristallnacht* (1992), and *Threading History: The Japanese American Experience* (1995). His *A Matter of Scale* (1986) was premiered in the Houston Astrodome.

WORKS: FILMS: *The Ring Masters* (1966); *3rd Book of Exercises* (1967); *Think Tank* (1971); *Sections for Screen, Performers & Audience* (1974); *Glass Shots with Flower* (1981); *Transducer Series Films (1–54)* (1983–87). **VIDEOS:** *Four Places at South Point* (1988); *A Street Demonstration in Santiago, Chile* (1989); *Windharps at the Tokugawa Women's Grave* (1989); *Hesselt Corn* (1992); *Manzanar and Dachau* (1993); *Tule Lake* (1994). **ELECTROACOUSTIC AND MUSIC THEATER:** *End of the Line: some recent dealings with death* (1973); *Travelon Gamelon* (concert version, 1977; promenade version, 1978); *Accretion Disk, Event Horizon, Singularity* (1978); *Entrance Music* (1979); *Incident at 3 Mile Island, perhaps an elegy for Karen Silkwood* (1980); *Music for Plinky and Straw* (1984); *Transduction System* (1983; in collaboration with T. Plsek); *A Matter of Scale* (1986); *Changing States I–VI* (1985–93); *Kristallnacht Music* (1992); *A Matter of Scale 2* (1993); *Cold Storage* (1994); *Sonic Journeys with Pitch to Midi* (1995). **SOUND INSTALLATIONS:** *Hand-Built Microphones* (1983); *News Filters* (1984); *2 Wind Harps in the Rain & Amplified Dory at Sea* (1986); *Metal Mesh Pieces* (1987); *A Footnote from Chernobyl* (1987); *Pacific Transducer Series* (1988); *20 X 24* (1988); *Sado Island Rice* (1991); *Heselt Corn* (1993); *Metal Mesh Pieces* (1987).

Lerner, Alan Jay, distinguished American lyricist and playwright; b. N.Y., Aug. 31, 1918; d. there, June 14, 1986. He was educated at Harvard Univ. (graduated, 1940); also attended the Juilliard School of Music in N.Y. (summers, 1936, 1937). He met the composer Frederick Loewe in 1942, resulting in their collaboration on the musical *What's Up?* (1943). It proved a failure, but they obtained better luck with their next work, *The Day before Spring* (1945). Their collaborative efforts paid off when they produced the outstanding score of *Brigadoon* (1947). Following the popular *Paint Your Wagon* (1951), they wrote the smashing success *My Fair Lady* (1956), after George Bernard Shaw's *Pygmalion*. There followed their film score *Gigi* (1958; after Colette's story), which garnered 9 Academy Awards. They returned to the Broadway stage with the enormously successful musical *Camelot* (1960). After Loewe's retirement, Lerner continued to write musicals, but he failed to equal his previous successes. His most popular later score was *On a Clear Day You Can See Forever* (1965), written in collaboration with Burton Lane; a film version appeared in 1970. He wrote an autobiography entitled *The Street Where I Live* (1978); also (with D. Shapiro) *We Danced All Night: My Life behind the Scenes* (N.Y., 1990). See A. Sirmay, ed., *The Lerner and Loewe Songbook* (N.Y., 1962) and B. Green, ed., *A Hymn to Him: The Lyrics of Alan Jay Lerner* (N.Y., 1987).

BIBL.: G. Lees, *Inventing Champagne: The Worlds of L. and Loewe* (N.Y., 1990); S. Citron, *The Wordsmiths: Oscar Hammerstein II and A.J. L.* (Oxford, 1995).

Lerner, Bennett, American pianist; b. Cambridge, Mass., March 21, 1944. He was a piano student of Claudio Arrau, Rafael de Silva, German Diez, Sascha Gorodnitski, and Robert Helps; attended Columbia Univ. and the Manhattan School of Music (B.Mus., 1973; M.Mus., 1975); also profited from a close association with Copland, Thomson, and Bowles, whose music he came to champion. He taught at the Manhattan School of Music (1972–82), the Greenwich House Music School (from 1979), Sarah Lawrence College (1983–84), and Brooklyn College's Cons. of Music (from 1987). He appeared as a soloist with the Boston Pops Orch. (1966–68); in 1976 he made his Carnegie Recital Hall debut. On Nov. 14, 1985, he gained national recognition when he appeared as soloist in Copland's Piano Concerto with Mehta and the N.Y. Phil.; the concert, marking Copland's 85th birthday, was telecast live to the nation by PBS. In 1987 Lerner gave a 4-hour marathon recital at N.Y.'s 92nd St. Y in which he performed premieres of works by Thomson, Harris, Barber, Diamond et al. On Feb. 4, 1988, he was the featured performer at Vittorio Rieti's 90th-birthday concert in N.Y., where he was soloist in Rieti's *Enharmonic Variations* for Piano and Orch., a score written especially for him. While Lerner has played much contemporary music, he has also programmed a number of neglected works from the past.

Le Roux, Maurice, French conductor, composer, and writer on music; b. Paris, Feb. 6, 1923; d. Avignon, Oct. 19, 1992. He was a student at the Paris Cons. (1944–52) of Philipp and Nat (piano), Fourestier (conducting), and Messiaen (analysis); he also had private instruction in dodecaphonic techniques with Leibowitz. From 1951 he was active with the French Radio and Television in Paris, where he later was music director of its l'Orchestre National de l'ORTF from 1960 to 1968. After serving as musical councillor of the Paris Opéra (1969–73), he was inspector general of music in the Ministry of Culture (1973–88). He utilized serial procedures in his compositions. Among his works were the ballets *Le Petit Prince* (1949) and *Sables* (1956); incidental music; film scores; the orch. scores *Le Cercle des métamorphoses* (1953) and *Un Koan* (1973); piano pieces, including a Sonata (1946). He publ. in Paris *Introduction à la musique contemporaine* (1947), *Monteverdi* (1947), *La Musique* (1979), and *Boris Godounov* (1980).

Le Roy, René, French flutist and teacher; b. Maisons-Lafitte, near Paris, March 4, 1898; d. Paris, Jan. 3, 1985. He studied at the Paris Cons. with Hennebains, Lafleurance, and Gaubert; in 1918 he won the premier prix for flute. In 1919 he succeeded Gaubert as director of the Société des Instruments à Vent; in 1922 he founded the Quintette Instrumental de Paris, with which he gave numerous concerts in Europe and America. He subsequently occupied various teaching positions; was prof. of chamber music for wind instruments at the Paris Cons. (1955–64). He compiled (with C. Dorgeuille) the manual *Traité de la flûte, historique, technique et pédagogique* (Paris, 1966).

Lert, Ernst (Josef Maria), Austrian operatic Intendant, brother of **Richard (Johanes) Lert**; b. Vienna, May 12, 1883; d. Baltimore, Jan. 30, 1955. He studied at the Univ. of Vienna with G. Adler (Ph.D., 1908). He was a producer and dramaturge in Breslau (1909) and Leipzig (1912–19), then director of the operas in Basel (1919–20) and Frankfurt am Main (1919–23), where he also taught at the Hoch Cons.; from 1923 to 1929 he was producer at La Scala in Milan, and from 1929 to 1931, at the Metropolitan Opera in N.Y. From 1936 to 1938 was head of the opera dept. of the Curtis Inst. of Music in Philadelphia. From 1938 to 1953 he was head of the opera dept. of the Peabody Cons. of Music in Baltimore. He wrote *Mozart auf dem Theater* (Berlin, 1918; 4th ed., 1922) and *Otto Lohse* (Leipzig, 1918).

Lert, Richard (Johanes), Austrian conductor and teacher, brother of **Ernst (Josef Maria) Lert**; b. Vienna, Sept. 19, 1885; d. Los Angeles, April 25, 1980. He studied with Heuberger in Vienna; then served as a conductor in Düsseldorf, Darmstadt, Frankfurt am Main, Hannover, and Mannheim. He later was guest conductor with the Berlin State Opera. He emigrated to the U.S. in 1934 and settled in Pasadena, California, as a conductor and teacher. In 1916 he married the novelist Vicki Baum. He celebrated his 90th birthday in 1975, but continued to be active, conducting summer concerts at Orkney Springs, Va.; also gave courses in conducting.

Lessard, John (Ayres), American composer and teacher; b. San Francisco, July 3, 1920. He commenced piano lessons when he was 5 and trumpet lessons at 9; became a member of the San Francisco Civic Sym. Orch. at age 11. He received instruction in piano and theory from Elsie Belenky; after brief studies with Cowell, he continued his training with Boulanger, Dandelot, Cortot, and Lévy at the École Normale de Musique in Paris (1937–40); completed his studies with Boulanger at the Longy School of Music in Cambridge, Mass. In 1946–47 and 1953–54 he held Guggenheim fellowships; received a National Inst. of Arts and Letters award in 1952 and an NEA grant in 1976. From 1962 to 1990 he taught at the State Univ. of N.Y. at Stony Brook. His works follow along neo-classical lines with occasional adherence to serial procedures.

WORKS: ORCH.: Violin Concerto (1942); *Box Hill Overture* (1946); *Cantilena* for Oboe and Strings (1947); *Little Concert* (1947); Wind Concerto (1949); Concerto for Flute, Clarinet, Bassoon, String Quartet, and String Orch. (1952); *Sinfonietta Concertante* (1961); Harp Concerto (1963–83); *Pastimes and an Alleluia* (1974). **CHAMBER:** *3 Movements* for Violin and Piano (1948); *Partita* for Woodwind Quintet (1952); Wind Octet (1952); Cello Sonata (1956); Trio for Flute, Violin, and Piano (1959); String Trio (1963); *Trio in sei parti* for Violin, Cello, and Piano (1966); *Quodlibets I–III* for 2 Trumpets and Trombone (1967); Woodwind Quintet No. 2 (1970); Brass Quintet (1971); *Trios of Consanguinity* for 8 Combinations of Winds and Strings (1973); *Movements: I* for Trumpet and Vibraphone (1976), *II* for Trumpet and Viola (1976), *III* for Trumpet and Violin (1976), *IV* for Trumpet and Percussion (1976), *V* for Trumpet, Violin, and Cello (1977), *VI* for Trumpet, Viola, Cello, and Percussion (1978), *VII* for Trumpet and Cello (1978), and *VIII* for Trumpet, Marimba, and Vibraphone (1984); *Divertimento* for Guitar (1981–83); *Music* for Guitar and Percussion: *I* for Guitar and Xylophone (1982), *II* for Guitar and Xylophone (1983), and *III* for Guitar, Vibraphone, and Bongos (1983); Duet for Piano and Percussion (1984); *4 Pieces* for Viola and Percussion (1985); *Weatherscenes* for Violin, Guitar, and Cello (1987); *Drift, Follow, Persist* for Horn, Piano, and Percussion (1988); *An Assembled Sequence* for Percussionist (1989); Quintet for Flute, Clarinet, Violin, Cello, and Piano (1993); *Gather and Disperse* for Flute, Clarinet, Trumpet, Trombone, 2 Percussionists, Piano, 2 Violins, and 2 Cellos (1994). **KEYBOARD: PIANO:** Sonata (1940); *Mask* (1946); *New Worlds* (2 vols., 1965); *Threads of Sound Recalled* (1980); *For Aaron* (1981); *4 bagatelles* (1986, 1988, 1990, 1991). **HARPSICHORD:** *Toccata in 4 Movements* (1951); *Perpetual Motion* (1952). **VOCAL:** *Don Quixote and the Sheep* for Bass-baritone and Orch. (1955); *12 Songs from Mother Goose* for Voice and String Trio (1964); *Fragments from the Cantos of Ezra Pound* for Baritone and 9 Instruments (1969); *The Pond in a Bowl* for Soprano, Piano, Marimba, and Vibraphone (1984); *The Seasons* for Soprano, 2 Percussionists, and Piano (1992).

Lesur, Daniel Jean Yves. See **Daniel-Lesur, Jean Yves.**

Lesure, François (-Marie), distinguished French music librarian, musicologist, and writer; b. Paris, May 23, 1923. He studied at the École des Chartres, the École Pratique des Hautes Études, and the Sorbonne, and musicology at the Paris Cons. A member of the music dept. at the Bibliothèque Nationale (from 1950), he was its chief curator (1970–88). From 1953 to 1967 he headed the Paris office (responsible for Series B) of the Répertoire International des Sources Musicales (RISM), for which he himself ed. *Recueils imprimés: XVIe–XVIIe siècles* (Munich, 1960); *Recueils imprimés: XVIIIe siècle* (Munich, 1964; suppl. in *Notes*, March 1972, vol. XXVIII, pp. 397–418), and the 2 vols. of *Écrits imprimés concernant la musique* (Munich, 1971). He also was a prof. at the Free Univ. of Brussels (1965–77), ed. of the early music series known as Le Pupitre (from 1967), president of the Société Française de Musicologie (1971–74; 1988–91), and prof. at the École Pratique des Hautes Études (from 1973). He ed. such non-serial works as *Anthologie de la chanson parisienne au XVIe siècle* (Monaco, 1953); the report of the 1954 Arras Conference, *La Renaissance dans les provinces du Nord* (Paris, 1956); P. Trichet's *Traité des instruments de musique (vers 1640)* (Neuilly, 1957); 6 vols. of *Chansons polyphoniques* (with A.T. Merrit, Monaco, 1967–72; the 1st 5 vols. constitute the collected works of C. Janequin); a collected ed. of Debussy's writings on music, *Monsieur Croche et autres écrits* (Paris, 1971; Eng. tr., 1977); ed. a *Catalogue de l'oeuvre de Claude Debussy* (Geneva, 1977); ed. the letters of Debussy for the period 1884–1918 (Paris, 1980; rev. ed., 1993); was ed.-in-chief of the complete works of Debussy (from 1986). His own publications include a *Bibliographie des éditions d'Adrian Le Roy et Robert Ballard, 1551–1598* (with G. Thibault, Paris, 1955; suppl. in *Revue de Musicologie,* 1957); *Musicians and Poets of the French Renaissance* (N.Y., 1955); *Mozart en France* (Paris, 1956); *Collection musicale A. Meyer* (with N. Bridgman, Abbeville, 1961); *Musica e società* (Milan, 1966; Ger. tr., 1966, as *Musik und Gesellschaft im Bild: Zeugnisse der Malerei aus sechs Jahrhunderten*; Eng. tr., 1968, as *Music and Art in Society*); *Bibliographie des éditions musicales publiées par Estienne Roger et Michel-Charles Le Cene, Amsterdam, 1696–1743* (Paris, 1969); *Musique et musiciens français du XVIe siècle* (Geneva, 1976, a reprinting in book form of 24 articles orig. publ. 1950–69); *Claude Debussy avant 'Pelléas' ou Les Années symbolistes* (Paris, 1992). He contributed *L'Opera classique français: 17e et 18e siècles* (Geneva, 1972) and *Claude Debussy* (Geneva, 1975) to the series Iconographie Musicale. For the Bibliothèque Nationale, he prepared a series of exhibition catalogs, most notably one on Berlioz (Paris, 1969).

BIBL.: J.-M. Fauquet, ed., *Musiques, Signes, Images: Liber amicorum F. L.* (Geneva, 1988).

Letelier (-Llonas), Alfonso, Chilean composer and teacher; b. Santiago, Oct. 4, 1912. He studied with Allende at the Conservatorio Nacional in Santiago (1930–35), where he became a prof. of harmony (1946); was also dean of the faculty of fine arts (1951–62) and vice-rector (1958–62) of the Univ. of Chile. He was made a member of the Chilean Academy of Fine Arts (1967); was awarded the Chilean National Arts Prize (1968). His compositions include *La vida del campo*, symphonic poem for Piano and Orch. (1937); *Los sonetos de la muerte* for Woman's Voice and Orch. (1948); *Aculeo*, suite for Orch. (Louisville, Jan. 30, 1957); Guitar Concerto (1961); Concerto for Strings (1972); choral works; chamber music; piano pieces.

Lettvin, Theodore, American pianist and teacher; b. Chicago, Oct. 29, 1926. He studied with Howard Wells, making his first public appearance at the age of 5 in Chicago; was invited to perform at a young people's concert with the Chicago Sym. Orch. when he was 13; then continued his studies at the Curtis Inst. of Music in Philadelphia with Serkin and Horszowski (Mus.B., 1949); also took courses at the Univ. of Pa. (1947–48). He made his European debut in Paris in 1952, and subsequently appeared as a soloist with American and European orchs. and as a recitalist. He was a visiting lecturer at the Univ. of Colo. (1956–57), then head of the piano dept. at the Cleveland Music School Settlement (1956–68); subsequently was prof. of piano at the New England Cons. of Music in Boston (1968–77), the Univ. of Mich. (1977–87), and Rutgers, the State Univ. of New Jersey (from 1987).

Lev, Ray, Russian-American pianist; b. Rostov na Donau, May 8, 1912; d. N.Y., May 20, 1968. Her father was a synagogue cantor, and her mother a singer. The family went to the U.S. in 1913; she sang in her father's synagogue choirs in N.Y.; studied piano with Walter Ruel Cowles in New Haven and with Gaston Déthier. She also took lessons with Tobias Matthay in London (1930–33); then returned to N.Y. and appeared in recitals.

Levant, Oscar, American pianist and composer; b. Pittsburgh, Dec. 27, 1906; d. Beverly Hills, Aug. 14, 1972. He studied piano with Stojowski; also took a few composition lessons with Schoenberg and Schillinger. As a pianist, he established himself by his authentic performances of Gershwin's music; also emerged as a professional wit on the radio. He publ. a brilliant book, *A Smattering of Ignorance* (1940), and *The Memoirs of an Amnesiac* (1965). He wrote music of considerable complexity, in the modern vein; was soloist in his Piano Concerto (NBC Sym. Orch., Feb. 17, 1942); other works were *Nocturne* for Orch. (Los Angeles, April 14, 1937); String Quartet (1937); piano pieces; film scores.

BIBL.: S. Kashner and N. Schoenberger, *A Talent for Genius: The Life and Times of O. L.* (N.Y., 1994).

Levarie, Siegmund, Austrian-born American musicologist and conductor; b. Lemberg, Galicia, July 24, 1914. He studied conducting with Joseph Mertin at the New Vienna Cons. (diploma, 1935) and musicology with Robert Haas at the Univ. of Vienna (Ph.D., 1938); concurrently took private lessons in composition with Hugo Kauder. He emigrated to the U.S. in 1938; became a naturalized American citizen in 1943. He was director of concerts at the Univ. of Chicago (1938–52); conducted the Collegium Musicum there, mostly in programs of medieval and Renaissance music; he also taught there; was dean of the Chicago Musical College (1952–54). From 1954 to 1962 he served as prof. of music and head of the music dept. at Brooklyn College.

WRITINGS: *Fugue and Form* (Chicago, 1941); *Mozart's "Le Nozze di Figaro": A Critical Analysis* (Chicago, 1952); *Fundamentals of Harmony* (N.Y., 1954); *Guillaume de Machaut* (N.Y., 1954); *Musical Italy Revisited* (N.Y., 1963); with E. Levy, *Tone: A Study in Musical Acoustics* (Kent, Ohio, 1968; 2nd ed., rev., 1980); with E. Levy, *Musical Morphology: A Discourse and a Dictionary* (Kent, Ohio, 1983).

Leventritt, Edgar M(ilton), American music patron; b. San Francisco, Oct. 18, 1873; d. N.Y., May 31, 1939. After training at the Univ. of Calif. (graduated, 1894), he went to N.Y. and studied law. In 1896 he was admitted to the bar. As an amateur pianist, he helped to found the Perolé Quartet in 1925. In his will, he made provision for the establishment of an annual competition for young musicians via the Edgar M. Leventritt Foundation. The first competition was held in 1940.

Levi, Paul Alan, American composer, teacher, and pianist; b. N.Y., June 30, 1941. After training at Oberlin (Ohio) College (B.A. in music, 1963), he was a composition student of Overton and Persichetti at the Juilliard School in N.Y. (M.M., 1972; D.M.A., 1978); also attended the Munich Hochschule für Musik (1973–74), held a Deutscher Akademischer Austauschdienst study grant in Germany (1973–74), and took summer courses in new music in Darmstadt (1974). From 1963 he was active as a piano accompanist. He taught at Baruch (1972–73), Queens (1979), and Lehman (1981–82) colleges of the City Univ. of N.Y. In 1979 he joined the faculty of N.Y. Univ.; also taught at the Manhattan School of Music (from 1992). In 1976 he served as composer-in-residence at the Wolf Trap Farm Park in Vienna, Va. From 1979 to 1982 he was president of the League of Composers. In 1983–84 he held a Guggenheim fellowship. In 1985 he became a founding partner of Mountain Laurel Music, a production company. In his varied output, Levi has revealed an imaginative handling of instrumentation and setting of vocal texts.

WORKS: DRAMATIC: *Thanksgiving*, serio-comic opera (N.Y., Nov. 2, 1977); *In the Beginning . . .* , opera parable (1987–95); incidental music to plays; television and film music. **ORCH.:** *Symphonic Movement* (1972; N.Y., Jan. 30, 1975); *Stringolevio* for Strings and Percussion (1973); *Allegrenino* for Symphonic Band (1973); *Transformations of the Heart* (N.Y., March 7, 1987). **CHAMBER:** String Quartet (1969; Norfolk, Va., Feb. 27, 1971); *5 Progressions for 3 Instruments* for Flute, Clarinet, and Viola (N.Y., Dec. 7, 1971); *Billet Doux/Billiger Duo* for Violin and Viola (Portland, Ore., June 29, 1980); *Elegy and Recreations* for Oboe, Clarinet, Horn, Violin, Viola, Cello, and Piano (N.Y., Nov. 9, 1980); *Bow Jest* for Cello (1983). **PIANO:** *Summer Elegy* (1982; N.Y., April 24, 1987); *Touchings* (1990; N.Y., May 31, 1992); *Suite for the Best of Times* (1991). **VOCAL:** *Jabberwocky* for Voice and Piano (N.Y., April 17, 1968); *The Truth* for Soprano, Cello, Flute, Clarinet, Bassoon, Piano, Harpsichord, and String Quartet (1975; Portland, Oreg., July 31, 1985); *Spring Sestina* for Soprano and 10 Instruments (N.Y., Jan. 13, 1982); *This Much I Know* for Soprano and Piano (N.Y., April 13, 1983); *Mark Twain Suite* for Tenor, Chorus, and Orch. (N.Y., April 30, 1983); *Black Wings* for Soprano and Piano (Columbia, S.C., Oct. 3, 1986); *Songs for the Synagogue* for Cantor, Adult and Children's Choruses, and Quintet or Chamber Orch. (Norwalk, Conn., May 5, 1989; in collaboration with Mark Lipson); *Bow Down Thine Ear, O Lord* for 8 Voices or Double Chorus (N.Y., Dec. 8, 1991); *Holy Willie's Prayer* for Chorus and Chamber Orch. (N.Y., Jan. 27, 1992); *Journeys & Secrets* for Chorus and Chamber Orch. (N.Y., May 25, 1994).

Levi, Yoel, Romanian-born American conductor; b. Sotmar, Aug. 16, 1950. He was taken in infancy to Israel, where he received instruction in violin, percussion, cello, and piano; then pursued training in violin and percussion at the Univ. of Tel Aviv (M.A., 1975); concurrently studied conducting with Rodan at the Jerusalem Academy of Music (graduate degree, 1976); subsequently took instruction in conducting with Ferrara in Siena, at the Accademia di Santa Cecilia in Rome, at the Guildhall School of Music and Drama in London (diploma, 1978), and with Kondrashin in Hilversum. In 1975 he became a percussionist in the Israel Phil.; after winning 1st prize in the Besancon conducting competition in 1978, he was made a conducting assistant with the Cleveland Orch.; was its resident conductor (1980–84). In 1979 he made his European debut as a guest conductor with the (West) Berlin Radio Sym. Orch. In subsequent years, he appeared as a guest conductor with various major North American and European orchs. He became a naturalized American citizen in 1987. In 1988 he assumed the position of music director of the Atlanta Sym. Orch. In 1991 he conducted it on a European tour. During the Olympic Games in Atlanta in 1996, Levi and his orch. gave a series of Cultural Olympiad concerts.

Levidis, Dimitri, Greek-born French composer and teacher; b. Athens, April 8, 1885?; d. Palaeon Phaleron, near Athens, May 29, 1951. He studied at the Lottner Cons. in Athens, then with Boemer, Choisy, Lavrangas, and Mancini at the Athens Cons. (1898–1905). He subsequently studied with Dénéreaz at the Lausanne Cons. (1906–07) and with Klose (fugue), Mottl (orchestration), and Strauss (composition) at the Munich Academy of Music (1907–08). He went to France (1910); served in the French Army during World War I; became a naturalized French citizen in 1929. He returned to Greece about 1932, and was active as a teacher; in 1934 he founded the Phaleron Cons., which became a part of the Hellenic Cons. He was the first to write works for the Martenot Ondes Musicales, including *Poème symphonique pour solo d'Ondes Musicales et Orchestre* (Paris, Dec. 23, 1928) and *De profundis* for Voice and 2 Soli of Ondes Musicales (Paris, Jan. 5, 1930). Other works included a ballet, *Le Pâtre et la nymphe* (Paris, April 24, 1924); *Divertissement* for English Horn, Harps, Strings, Celesta, and Percussion (Paris, April 9, 1927); oratorio, *The Iliad*; *Poem* for Violin and Orch. (1927); *Chant payen* for Oboe and Strings; compositions for the "Dixtuor aeolien d'orchestre"; pieces for chamber ensembles; song cycles; piano pieces.

Levina, Zara, Russian pianist and composer; b. Simferopol, Crimea, Feb. 5, 1906; d. Moscow, June 27, 1976. She studied piano at the Odessa Cons., graduating in 1923; then entered the Moscow Cons., where she was a student of Felix Blumenfeld in piano and of Miaskovsky in composition, graduating in 1931. She subsequently gave piano recitals. She distinguished herself primarily as a composer of children's songs, which achieved great popularity; also set to music some 100 texts by Russian poets; wrote 2 piano concertos (1945, 1975); 2 violin sonatas (1928, 1948); piano pieces.

BIBL.: N. Mikhailovskaya, *Z. L.* (Moscow, 1960).

Levine, Gilbert, American conductor; b. N.Y., Jan. 22, 1948. He attended Reed College (1965–67) and the Juilliard School of Music in N.Y. (1967–68); then studied music history with Mendel and Lockwood, conducting with Monod, and theory with Babbitt and Randall at Princeton Univ. (A.B., 1971), completing his study of theory at Yale Univ. (M.A., 1972); also received instruction in conducting from Ferrara in Siena. In 1973 he made his professional debut as a guest conductor with the Nouvel Orch. Philharmonique de Radio France in Paris; then toured widely as a guest conductor, appearing in Europe and North America. In 1987 he became music director of the Kraków Phil., the first American conductor to hold such a position with a major Eastern European orch. He left his Kraków post in 1991 and was named its conductor laureate-honored guest conductor. In 1993 he conducted it on a tour of the U.S. On April 7, 1994, Levine conducted the Royal Phil. of London and the choir of St. Peter's Basilica in a concert of reconciliation for the victims of the Holocaust in the presence of Pope John Paul II in Rome. On Dec. 19, 1994, Levine became only the 4th Jew in history to receive the papal Equestrian Order of St. Gregory the Great.

Levine, James (Lawrence), brilliant American pianist and conductor; b. Cincinnati, June 23, 1943. His maternal grandfather was a cantor in a synagogue; his father was a violinist who led a dance band; his mother was an actress. He began playing the piano as a small child. At the age of 10, he was soloist in Mendelssohn's 2nd Piano Concerto at a youth concert of the Cincinnati Sym. Orch.; he then studied music with Walter Levin, 1st violinist in the La Salle Quartet; in 1956 he took piano lessons with Serkin at the Marlboro (Vt.) School of Music; in 1957 he began piano studies with Lhévinne at the Aspen (Colo.) Music School. In 1961 he entered the Juilliard School of Music in N.Y., and took courses in conducting with Jean Morel; he also had conducting sessions with Wolfgang Vacano in Aspen. In 1964 he graduated from the Juilliard School and joined the American Conductors Project connected with the Baltimore Sym. Orch., where he had occasion to practice conducting with Wallenstein, Rudolf, and Cleva. In 1964–65 he served as an apprentice to Szell with the Cleveland Orch.; then became a regular assistant conductor with it (1965–70). In 1966 he organized the Univ. Circle Orch. of the Cleveland Inst. of Music; also led the student orch. of the summer music inst. of Oakland Univ. in Meadow Brook, Mich. (1967–69). In 1970 he made a successful appearance as guest conductor with the Philadelphia Orch. at its summer home at Robin Hood Dell; subsequently appeared with other American orchs. In 1970 he also conducted the Welsh National Opera and the San Francisco Opera. He made his Metropolitan Opera debut in N.Y. on June 5, 1971, in a festival performance of *Tosca*; his success led to further appearances and to his appointment as its principal conductor in 1973; he then was its music director from 1975 until becoming its artistic director in 1986. From 1973 to 1993 he was music director of the Ravinia Festival, the summer home of the Chicago Sym. Orch., and served in that capacity with the Cincinnati May Festival (1974–78). In 1975 he began to conduct at the Salzburg Festivals; in 1982 he conducted at the Bayreuth Festival for the first time. He continued to make appearances as a pianist, playing chamber music with impeccable technical precision. But it is as a conductor and an indefatigable planner of the seasons at the Metropolitan Opera that he inspired respect. Unconcerned with egotistical projections of his own personality, he presided over the singers and the orch. with concentrated efficiency.

Levitzki, Mischa, outstanding American pianist; b. Kremenchug (of naturalized Russian-born American parents), May 25, 1898; d. Avon-by-the-Sea, N.J., Jan. 2, 1941. He began his studies with Michalowski in Warsaw at the age of 7; then his parents returned to their adopted country and he continued his training at the Inst. of Musical Art in N.Y. with Stojowski (1906–11). In 1911 he went to Germany, where he studied with Dohnányi at the Hochschule für Musik in Berlin and won the Mendelssohn Prize. Following tours of Germany (1914–15) and Europe (1915–16), he returned to the U.S. and made his N.Y. recital debut on Oct. 17, 1916; subsequently made numerous tours in the U.S. and in the Orient. Levitzki acquired a remarkable reputation as one of the leading keyboard virtuosos of his day. He wrote a number of attractive piano pieces, a Piano Concerto, and a cadenza for Beethoven's 3rd Piano Concerto.

Levy, Burt (Jerome), American composer and teacher; b. N.Y., Aug. 5, 1936. He studied with Keith Robinson in N.Y. (1953–57), Keller at the Univ. of Oregon (1958–60), and Gaburo, Brun, Johnston, and Martirano at the Univ. of Ill. (D.M.A., 1967). He taught at Western Illinois Univ. (1967–68), the Univ. of Wisc. (1968–71), the State Univ. of N.Y. at Albany (1973–77), and at the Wisconsin Cons. in Milwaukee (from 1977). Among his works were *Tryonym* for Orch. (1972), *Orbs* for Flute and Orch. (N.Y., Feb. 5, 1973), *6 Moments* for Piano (1976), and a String Quartet (1978).

Lévy, Ernst, distinguished Swiss pianist, pedagogue, and composer; b. Basel, Nov. 18, 1895; d. Morges, April 19, 1981. He studied in Basel with Huber and Petri, and in Paris with Pugno. He was head of the piano master class at the Basel Cons. (1917–21); then was founder-conductor of the Choeur Philharmonique in Paris (1928). In 1941 he went to the U.S.; taught at the New England Cons. of Music in Boston (1941–45), Bennington (Vt.) College (1946–51), the Univ. of Chicago (1951–54), the Mass. Inst. of Technology (1954–59), and Brooklyn College of the City Univ. of N.Y. (1959–66). In 1966 he returned to Switzerland. He composed 15 syms. (1920–67); many choral works; chamber music; various pieces for solo instruments; etc. Among his publications are *Tone: A Study in Musical Acoustics* (with S. Levarie; Kent, Ohio, 1968; 2nd ed., rev., 1980), *Des rapports entre la musique et l société suivi de réflexions* (Neuchâtel, 1979), *Musical Morphology: A Discourse and a Dictionary* (with S. Levarie; Kent, Ohio, 1983), and *A Theory of Harmony* (Albany, N.Y., 1985).

Lévy, Heniot, Polish-American pianist, teacher, and composer; b. Warsaw, July 19, 1879; d. Chicago, June 16, 1946. He was a pupil at the Hochschule für Musik in Berlin, and of Bruch (composition). He made his debut as a pianist with the Berlin Phil. (1899); in 1900 he emigrated to America, and became a piano teacher at the American Cons. in Chicago. Among his works were *24 Variations on an Original Theme* for Orch. (Chicago, April 9, 1942); Piano Concerto; String Sextet; String Quintet; 2 piano quintets; 4 string quartets; 2 piano trios; Cello Sonata; numerous piano pieces; songs.

Levy, Jules, Bulgarian conductor and composer; b. Salonika, June 19, 1930. He studied in Sofia with Stoyanov at the Bulgarian State Cons., graduating in 1957; then was active as a theater conductor.

WORKS: DRAMATIC: MUSICALS: *The Girl I Was in Love With* (1963); *The World Is Small* (1970); *The Phone Which . . .* (1975). **BALLET:** *Fair in Sofia* (1968). **CHOREOGRAPHIC ORATORIO:** *Onward to the Rising World* (1973). **ORCH.:** *Youth Concerto* for Violin and Orch. (1953); 3 syms.: No. 1, *Life and Death* (1958), No. 2 (1970), and No. 3 (1976); *Divertimento-Concertante No. 1* for Trumpet and Pop Orch. (1961) and *No. 2* for Flute and Orch. (1971); *Overture-Poem* (1962); *The Blacksmith*, symphonic fantasy (1964); *Pirin Mountain Rhapsody* for Jazz and Sym. Orchs. (1972). **OTHER:** *Masks,* string quartet (1974), and other chamber pieces; choral songs; popular music.

Lévy, Lazare, distinguished French pianist and pedagogue; b. Brussels (of French parents), Jan. 18, 1882; d. Paris, Sept. 20, 1964. He studied piano with Diémer at the Paris Cons. (1894–98), where he was awarded 1st prize for piano; also studied harmony with Lavignac and composition with Gédalge there. He gave concerts with the principal orchs. of Europe; in 1920, succeeded Cortot as a prof. at the Paris Cons. He publ. numerous piano pieces.

Levy, Marvin David, American composer; b. Passaic, N.J., Aug. 2, 1932. He studied composition with Philip James at N.Y. Univ., and with Luening at Columbia Univ.; was awarded 2 Guggenheim fellowships (1960, 1964) and 2 American Prix de Rome fellowships (1962–63; 1965). Levy showed a particular disposition toward the musical theater. In his vocal and instrumental writing, he adopted an expressionistic mode along atonal lines, in an ambience of cautiously dissonant harmonies vivified by a nervously asymmetric rhythmic pulse.

WORKS: DRAMATIC: OPERAS: *Sotoba Komachi* (N.Y., April 7, 1957); *The Tower* (Sante Fe, Aug. 2, 1957); *Escorial* (N.Y., May 4, 1958); *Mourning Becomes Electra,* after O'Neill (N.Y., March 17, 1967). **MUSICAL:** *The Balcony* (1981–87). **ORCH.:** *Caramoor Festival Overture* (1959); Sym. (Los Angeles, Dec. 15, 1960); *Kryos,* dance poem for Chamber Orch. (1961); Piano Concerto (Chicago, Dec. 3, 1970); *Trialogues I* and *II* (1972); *In memoriam W.H. Auden* (1974); *Arrows of Time* (Orlando, Fla., Oct. 3, 1988). **CHAMBER:** String Quartet (1955); *Rhapsody* for Violin, Clarinet, and Harp (1956); *Chassidic Suite* for Horn and Piano (1956). **VOCAL:** *Echoes* for Soprano and Ensemble (1956); *For the Time Being,* Christmas oratorio (1959); *One Person,* cantata for Alto and Orch. (1962); *Sacred Service* for the Park Avenue Synagogue in N.Y. (1964); *Masada,* oratorio for Narrator, Tenor, Chorus, and Orch. (1973; rev. version, Chicago, Oct. 15, 1987); *Canto de los Marranos* for Soprano and Orch. (1977).

Lewenthal, Raymond, American pianist; b. San Antonio, Texas, Aug. 29, 1926; d. Hudson, N.Y., Nov. 21, 1988. He was taken to Los Angeles as a child and studied piano with local teachers. He then enrolled at the Juilliard School of Music in N.Y. as a student of Samaroff; continued his studies in Europe with Cortot. Returning to the U.S., he devoted himself to performing the piano music of neglected Romantic composers, among them Thalberg, Hummel, and Henselt. Particularly meritorious was his redemption from undeserved oblivion of the voluminous output of Alkan.

Lewin, David (Benjamin), American music theorist, teacher, and composer; b. N.Y., July 2, 1933. He studied piano, harmony, and composition with Steuermann (1945–50), mathematics at Harvard Univ. (B.A., 1954), and theory and composition with Sessions, Babbitt, Kim, and Cone at Princeton Univ. (M.F.A., 1958); also undertook further graduate work at Yale Univ. (M.A., 1980). He taught at the Univ. of Calif. at Berkeley (1961–67), the State Univ. of N.Y. at Stony Brook (1967–80), and Yale Univ. (1979–85); then was a prof. at Harvard Univ. (from 1985). He held a Guggenheim fellowship (1983–84). He was president of the Soc. for Music Theory (1985–88). Lewin wrote numerous articles for various learned journals.

WORKS: 4 Short Pieces for String Quartet (1956; rev. 1969); Viola Sonata (1957–58); *Essay on a Subject by Webern* for Chamber Orch. (1958); *Classical Variations on a Theme by Schoenberg* for Cello and Piano (1960); 2 Studies for Computer (1961); Fantasia for Organ (1962); *5 Characteristic Pieces* for 2

Pianos (1964); *Fantasy-Adagio* for Violin and Orch. (1963–66); *Quartet Piece* for String Quartet (1969); Woodwind Trio (1969); *Computer Music* for Computer (1970–71); *Just a Minute, Roger* for Piano (1978); *Fanfare* for Bass Clarinet, Cello, and Piano (1980); *For Piano* for Piano (1982); songs.

Lewis, Sir Anthony (Carey), eminent English conductor, musicologist, composer, and teacher; b. Bermuda, March 2, 1915; d. Haslemere, June 5, 1983. He became an organ scholar at Peterhouse, Cambridge (1932); continued his studies with Dent at Cambridge (B.A. and Mus.B., 1935); also took courses with Boulanger in Paris (1934). He joined the music staff of the BBC (1935); then was the creator of its Third Programme (1946). From 1947 to 1968 he was a prof. of music at the Univ. of Birmingham; also was dean of the faculty of fine arts there (1961–64). From 1968 to 1982 he served as principal of the Royal Academy of Music in London. In 1967 he was made a Commander of the Order of the British Empire. He was knighted in 1972. His specialty was the music of the Baroque period; he ed., conducted, and recorded works by Purcell, Rameau, and Handel. He publ. *The Language of Purcell* (Hull, 1968); was a founder and ed. of the prestigious series Musica Britannica (1951). His compositions include *Choral Overture* (1938), *Elegy and Capriccio* for Trumpet and Orch. (1947), Trumpet Concerto (1950), *A Tribute of Praise* for Voices (1951), and Horn Concerto (1959).

Lewis, Daniel, American conductor and pedagogue; b. Flagstaff, Ariz., May 10, 1925. He studied composition with Marcelli in San Diego (1939–41) and received violin lessons in Boston. During World War II, he saw military service in Hawaii, where he was concertmaster of the Honolulu Sym. Orch., 1st violinist in the U.S. Navy String Quartet, and a conductor of navy ensembles. After the War, he pursued his education at San Diego State College (B.M., 1949) and at the Claremont (Calif.) Graduate School (M.A., 1950). He was assistant conductor (1954–56) and assoc. conductor and concertmaster (1956–59) of the San Diego Sym. Orch. In 1959 he held a Fulbright scholarship and studied with Eugen Jochum at the Munich Hochschule für Musik and with Karajan in Salzburg. After conducting the La Jolla (Calif.) Sym. Orch. (1961–69) and the Orange County (Calif.) Sym. Orch. (1966–70), he was music director of the Pasadena (Calif.) Sym. Orch. (1972–84). He also appeared as a guest conductor with major American orchs. He taught at Calif. State Univ. at Fullerton (1963–70) and at the Univ. of Southern Calif. in Los Angeles (from 1970).

Lewis, Henry, black American conductor; b. Los Angeles, Oct. 16, 1932. He learned to play piano and string instruments as a child; at the age of 16, was engaged as a double-bass player in the Los Angeles Phil.; from 1955 to 1959, played double bass in the 7th Army Sym. Orch. overseas, and also conducted it in Germany and the Netherlands. Returning to the U.S., he founded the Los Angeles Chamber Orch.; in 1963, traveled with it in Europe under the auspices of the State Dept. From 1968 to 1976 he was music director of the New Jersey Sym. Orch. in Newark; subsequently conducted opera and orch. guest engagements. From 1989 to 1991 he was chief conductor of the Radio Sym. Orch. in Hilversum. He married **Marilyn Horne** in 1960, but they were separated in 1976.

Lewis, Richard (real name, **Thomas Thomas**), noted English tenor; b. Manchester, May 10, 1914; d. Eastbourne, Nov. 13, 1990. He studied with T.W. Evans, then with Norman Allin at the Royal Manchester College of Music (1939–41) and at the Royal Academy of Music in London (1945). He made his operatic debut with the Carl Rosa Opera Co. in 1939; from 1947 he sang at the Glyndebourne Festivals and at London's Covent Garden. He sang with the San Francisco Opera (1955–60); then appeared there as a guest artist (1962–68). He toured extensively as a concert and oratorio singer. In 1963 he was named a Commander of the Order of the British Empire. His repertoire was extensive, including roles in operas ranging from Monteverdi and Mozart to Schoenberg, Britten, and Tippett.

Lewis, Robert Hall, American composer and teacher; b. Portland, Oreg., April 22, 1926. He studied with Rogers and Hanson at the Eastman School of Music in Rochester, N.Y. (B.M., 1949; M.M., 1951; Ph.D., 1964), Boulanger and Bigot in Paris (1952–53), and Apostel, Krenek, and Schiske in Vienna (1955–57); also received instruction in conducting from Monteux in Hancock, Maine (1954). He taught at Goucher College and the Peabody Cons. of Music in Baltimore (from 1958); also was on the faculty of Johns Hopkins Univ. (1969–80). He held 2 Fulbright scholarships (1955–57) and 2 Guggenheim fellowships (1966, 1980).

WORKS: ORCH.: *Poem* for Strings (1949); *Concert Overture* (1951); *Sinfonia, Expression for Orchestra* (1955); *Prelude and Finale* (1959); *Designs* (1963); 4 syms. (1964; 1971; 1982–85; 1990); *Music* for 12 Players (1965); *3 Pieces* (1965; rev. 1966); Concerto for Chamber Orch. (1967; rev. 1972); *Intermezzi* (1972); *Nuances II* (1975); *Osservazioni II* for Winds, Keyboard, Harpsichord, and Percussion (1978); *Moto* (1980); *Atto* for Strings (1981); Concerto for Strings, 4 Trumpets, Harps, and Piano (1984); *Destini* for Strings and Winds (1985); *Invenzione* (1988); *3 Movements on Scenes of Hieronymous Bosch* (1989); *Images and Dialogues* (1992); *Ariosi* (1995); *Scena* for Strings (1995). **CHAMBER:** 4 string quartets (1956, 1962, 1981, 1993); Trio for Clarinet, Violin, and Piano (1966); *Monophonies I–IX* for Winds (1966–77); *Tangents* for Double Brass Quartet (1968); Violin Sonata (1968); *Inflections I* for Double Bass (1969) and *II* for Piano Trio (1970); *Serenades I* for Piano (1970), *II* for Flute, Piccolo, Cello, and Piano (1976), and *III* for Brass Quintet (1982); *Fantasiemusik I* for Cello and Piano (1973), *II* for Clarinet and Piano (1978), and *III* for Saxophone, Piano, and Percussion (1984); *Combinazioni I* for Clarinet, Violin, Cello, and Piano (1974), *II* for 8 Percussion and Piano (1974), *III* for Narrator, Oboe, English Horn, and Percussion (1977), *IV* for Cello and Piano (1977), and *V* for 4 Violas (1982); *Osservazioni I* for Flutes, Piano, and Percussion (1975); *A due I* for Flute, Piccolo, Alto Flute, and Harp (1981), *II* for Oboe, English Horn, and Percussion (1981), *III* for Bassoon and Harp (1985), *IV* for Soprano and Piano (1986), and *VII* for Bassoon and Trumpet (1991); Wind Quintet (1983); Duo for Cello and Percussion (1987); *Dimensioni* for Clarinet, Violin, Viola, Cello, and Piano (1988); *9 Visions* for Piano Trio (1992); *Monologo* for Timpanist (1992); *Ottetto* (1994). **VOCAL:** *Acquainted with the Night* for Soprano and Chamber Orch. (1951); 5 Songs for Soprano, Clarinet, Horn, Cello, and Piano (1957); 2 madrigals for Chorus (1972); *3 Prayers of Jane Austen* for Small Chorus, Piano, and Percussion (1977); *Kantaten* for Chorus and Piano (1980); *Monophony X* for Soprano (1983).

Lewkowitch, Bernhard, Danish organist and composer; b. Copenhagen (of Polish parents), May 28, 1927. He studied organ, theory, and music history at the Royal Danish Cons. of Music in Copenhagen (graduated in theory, 1948; organ degree, 1949); completed his studies of composition and orchestration there with Jersild and Schierbeck (1950). He was organist and choirmaster at Copenhagen's St. Ansgar Catholic Church (1947–63); also founded the Schola Cantorum choral society (1953), with which he performed medieval and Renaissance music. He served as director of music at Copenhagen's Church of the Holy Sacrament (1973–85). In 1963 he was awarded the Carl Nielsen Prize; in 1966 he was given a lifetime Danish government pension. His music is primarily choral, to Latin texts, and is derived essentially from the Renaissance paradigms of modal counterpoint; it has an affinity with sacred works of Stravinsky, but is otherwise sui generis in its stylized archaisms; several of these works have become repertoire pieces in Denmark, and were also performed at various international festivals.

WORKS: *Mariavise* for Chorus (1947); 2 salmi for Chorus (1952); 3 motets for Chorus (1952); *Mass* for Chorus (1952); *Mass* for Chorus, Harp, and Woodwinds (1954); *Tre madrigali di Torquato Tasso* for Chorus (1954–55); *Tres orationes* for Tenor, Oboe, and Bassoon (1958); *Cantata sacra* for Tenor and Instrumental Ensemble (1959); *Improperia per voci* (1961); *Il* *cantico delle creature* for 8 Voices, after St. Francis of Assisi (1962–63); *Veni creator spiritus* for Chorus and 6 Trombones (1967); *Laudi a nostra Signora* for Chorus (1969); *Stabat Mater* for Chorus (1969); *Sub vesperum* for Chorus (1970); 65 organ chorales (1972); *Folk Mass* for Unison Voices and Organ (1974); 32 motets for Chorus (1975–76); *De Lamentatione Jeremiae Prophetae* for Chorus and Orch. (1977); *Memoria apostolorum* for Chorus (1978); *Mass* for Chorus and 2 Horns (1978); *Vesper in Advent* for Tenor, Chorus, and Organ (1979); 12 organ chorales (1979); *Ad nonam* for Chorus and Orch. (1980); *Requiem* for Baritone, Chorus, and Orch. (1981); *Tenebrae-Responsoria* for Chorus (1983); *Magnificat* for Chorus and Orch. (1983); *Pater noster* for Chorus and 6 Wind Instruments (1983); *Deprecations* for Tenor, Horn, and Trombone (1984); *Songs of Solomon* for Tenor, Clarinet, Horn, and Trombone (1985); *Preacher and Singer* for Tenor and Piano (1986); 6 partitas for Brass (1986–88); *Via Stenonis* for Chorus and Brass Quintet (1987); *6 Partitas* for Organ (1990).

BIBL.: M. Chestnut, "Cantio sacra: The Music of B. L.," *Nordic Sounds* (Dec. 1987).

Ley, Salvador, Guatemalan pianist and composer; b. Guatemala City, Jan. 2, 1907; d. there, March 21, 1985. He studied at the Berlin Hochschule für Musik (1922–30); concurrently studied piano with Georg Bertram (1922–30) and theory and composition with Klatte (1923–25) and Leichtentritt (1928–29). He was director of the National Cons. in Guatemala City (1934–37; 1944–53); then taught at the Westchester (N.Y.) Cons. (1963–70).

WORKS: *Lera*, opera (1959); *Danza exotica* for Piano (1959); Suite for Flute and Piano (1962); *Concertante* for Viola and String Orch. (1962); *Toccatina* for Piano (1965); *Introduction and Movement* for Cello (1965); other piano pieces; songs.

Leyden, Norman, American conductor; b. Springfield, Mass., Oct. 17, 1917. He studied at Yale Univ. (B.A., 1938; Mus.B., 1939) and at Teachers College of Columbia Univ. (M.A., 1965; Ed.D., 1968). He organized the Westchester Youth Sym. Orch. in White Plains, N.Y., in 1957; led it until 1968. In 1974 he became assoc. conductor of the Oregon Sym. Orch. in Portland; also pursued a successful career as a guest conductor with leading U.S. orchs. in concerts of popular fare.

Leygraf, Hans, Swedish pianist, teacher, and composer; b. Stockholm, Sept. 7, 1920. He appeared as a soloist with the Stockholm Orch. at the age of 10; then studied at the Stockholm Cons., in Munich, and in Vienna. He acquired a fine reputation as a concert pianist, becoming particularly noted as a Mozart interpreter. In 1944 he married the Austrian pianist Margarete Stehle (b. Vienna, April 26, 1921). In 1956 he joined the faculty of the Salzburg Mozarteum. He wrote a Piano Concerto, chamber music, and piano pieces.

Lhévinne, Josef, celebrated Russian pianist and pedagogue, husband of **Rosina** (née **Bessie**) **Lhévinne**; b. Orel, Dec. 13, 1874; d. N.Y., Dec. 2, 1944. After some preliminary study in his native town, he was taken to Moscow, and entered Safonov's piano class at the Cons. (1885); at the age of 15, he played the *Emperor Concerto*, with Anton Rubinstein conducting; he graduated in 1891. Lhévinne won the Rubinstein Prize in 1895. He taught piano at the Tiflis Cons. (1900–1902), and then at the Moscow Cons. (1902–06). During this period, he also toured Europe. He made his American debut in N.Y. with the Russian Sym. Orch., conducted by Safonov (Jan. 27, 1906); afterward he made numerous concert tours in America. He lived mostly in Berlin from 1907 to 1919; was interned during World War I, but was able to continue his professional activities. In 1919 he returned to the U.S.; appeared in recitals, and with major American orchs.; also in duo recitals with his wife, whom he married in 1898. They established a music studio, where they taught numerous pupils; also taught at the Juilliard Graduate School in N.Y. (from 1922). He publ. *Basic Principles in Pianoforte Playing* (Philadelphia, 1924). Lhévinne's playing was distinguished not only by its virtuoso quality, but by an intimate understanding of the music, impeccable phrasing, and fine gradations of singing tone. He was at his best in the works of the Romantic school; his performances of the concertos of Chopin and Tchaikovsky were particularly notable.

BIBL.: R. Wallace, *A Century of Music-Making: The Lives of J. and Rosina L.* (Bloomington, Ind., 1976).

Lhévinne, Rosina (née **Bessie**), distinguished Russian pianist and pedagogue, wife of **Josef Lhévinne**; b. Kiev, March 28, 1880; d. Glendale, Calif., Nov. 9, 1976. She graduated from the Moscow Cons. in 1898, winning the gold medal; that same year she married Josef Lhévinne. She appeared as a soloist in Vienna (1910), St. Petersburg (1911), and Berlin (1912); remained in Berlin with her husband through World War I. In 1919 they went to the U.S., where they opened a music studio; also taught at the Juilliard Graduate School in N.Y. (from 1922); later taught privately. Among her famous students were Van Cliburn, Mischa Dichter, John Browning, and Garrick Ohlsson.

BIBL.: R. Wallace, *A Century of Music-Making: The Lives of Josef and R. L.* (Bloomington, Ind., 1976).

Lhotka, Fran, Croatian composer and teacher of Czech descent, father of **Ivo Lhotka-Kalinski**; b. Wožice, Dec. 25, 1883; d. Zagreb, Jan. 26, 1962. He took lessons with Dvořák, Klička, and Stecker in Prague (1899–1905). After teaching in Ekaterinoslav (1908–9), he settled in Zagreb as a member of the Opera orch.; then was conductor of the Lisinski Chorus (1912–20); subsequently was a prof. at the Academy of Music (1920–61), where he also served as rector (1923–40; 1948–52). He publ. a harmony manual (Zagreb, 1948). His music followed in the late Romantic style.

WORKS: DRAMATIC: OPERAS: *Minka* (Zagreb, 1918); *The Sea* (Zagreb, 1920). **BALLETS:** *The Devil of the Village* (Zürich, Feb. 18, 1935); *Ballad of Medieval Love* (Zürich, Feb. 6, 1937); *Luk* (Munich, Nov. 13, 1939). **ORCH.:** Sym.; Violin Concerto (1913); Concerto for String Quartet and Orch. (1924). **OTHER:** Chamber music; choral works; songs.

Lhotka-Kalinski, Ivo, Croatian composer, son of **Fran Lhotka**; b. Zagreb, July 30, 1913; d. there, Jan. 29, 1987. He studied composition with his father and also voice at the Zagreb Academy of Music; after further composition lessons with Pizzetti in Rome (1937–39), he was active as a teacher; then was prof. of singing at the Zagreb Academy of Music (from 1951), becoming its regional director in 1967. He had a natural flair for stage composition in the folk style; he wrote several brilliant musical burlesques, among them *Analfabeta* (The Illiterate; Belgrade, Oct. 19, 1954); *Putovanje* (The Journey), the first television opera in Yugoslavia (Zagreb, June 10, 1957); *Dugme* (The Button; Zagreb, April 21, 1958); *Vlast* (Authority; Zagreb TV, Oct. 18, 1959); *Svjetleći grad* (The Town of Light; Zagreb, Dec. 26, 1967); also a children's opera, *Velika coprarija* (The Great Sorcerer; 1952); Sym. (1937); *Jutro* (Morning), symphonic poem (1941–42); *Misli* (Thoughts) for Clarinet and Strings (1965); chamber music; choral works; songs; piano pieces.

Liapunov, Sergei (Mikhailovich), noted Russian pianist, conductor, teacher, and composer; b. Yaroslavl, Nov. 30, 1859; d. Paris, Nov. 8, 1924. He began piano studies with his mother, a talented pianist, then took courses at the Russian Musical Soc. in Nizhny-Novgorod; later studied piano with Klindworth, Pabst, and Wilborg and composition with Hubert, Tchaikovsky, and Taneyev at the Moscow Cons. (1878–83). He went in 1884 to St. Petersburg, where he entered the Balakirev circle; was assistant director of the Imperial Chapel (1894–1902), inspector of music at St. Helen's Inst. (1902–10), and director of the Free Music School (1905–11); was prof. of piano and theory at the Cons. (1910–17) and a lecturer at the State Inst. of Art (1919). Liapunov toured widely as a pianist in Europe, and also appeared as a conductor; he spent his last years in Paris. He wrote a number of virtuoso pieces for piano, including the *12 études d'exécution transcendante* in sharp keys, written in emulation of Liszt's similarly titled works in flat keys. He also wrote some attractive character pieces for piano and songs. With Balakirev and Liadov, he was commissioned by the Imperial Geographic Soc. in 1893 to collect folk songs from the regions of Vologda, Viatka, and Kostroma; 30 of his arrangements of them for voice and piano were publ. by the society in 1897. He also utilized original folk songs in several of his works.

WORKS: ORCH.: *Ballada*, overture (1883; rev. 1894–96); 2 syms.: No. 1 (1887; St. Petersburg, April 23, 1888) and No. 2 (1910–17; Leningrad, Dec. 28, 1950); 2 piano concertos (1890, 1909); *Solemn Overture on Russian Themes* (St. Petersburg, May 6, 1896); *Polonaise* (1902); *Rhapsody on Ukrainian Themes* for Piano and Orch. (1907; Berlin, March 23, 1908); *Zelazowa Wola*, symphonic poem named after Chopin's birthplace, commemorating his centennial (1909); *Hashish*, symphonic poem (1913); Violin Concerto (1915; rev. 1921). **OTHER:** Numerous piano pieces, including *12 études d'exécution transcendante* (1900–1905) and a Sonata (1906–08); many songs.

BIBL.: A. Liapunova, "S.M. L.," *Sovetskaya Muzyka*, no. 9 (1950); M. Shifman, *S.M. L.: Zhizn i tvorchestvo* (S.M. L.: Life and Works; Moscow, 1960); R. Davis, "S. L. (1859–1924): The Piano Works—A Short Appreciation," *Music Review*, XXI (1960).

Liatoshinsky, Boris (Nikolaievich), significant Ukrainian composer and pedagogue; b. Zhitomir, Jan. 3, 1895; d. Kiev, April 15, 1968. He studied jurisprudence at the Univ. of Kiev, simultaneously taking lessons in composition at the Kiev Cons. with Gliere, graduating in 1919. He was an instructor (1919–35) and then a prof. (1935–68) at the Kiev Cons.; also taught at the Moscow Cons. (1936–37; 1941–43). Liatoshinsky was awarded State Prizes in 1946 and 1952. His style of composition followed the broad outlines of national music, with numerous thematic allusions to folk songs.

WORKS: OPERAS: *The Golden Hoop* (1929; Odessa, March 26, 1930); *Shchors* (1937; Kiev, Sept. 1, 1938; rev. version, Kiev, Feb. 18, 1970). **ORCH.:** 5 syms.: No. 1 (1918–19), No. 2 (1935–36; rev. 1940), No. 3 (1951; rev. 1954), No. 4 (1963), and No. 5 (1965–66); *Poem of Reunification* (1949–50); *Slavonic Concerto* for Piano and Orch. (1953); *Grazina*, ballad (Kiev, Nov. 26, 1955); *On the Banks of the Vistula*, symphonic poem (1958); *Solemn Overture* (1967). **CHAMBER:** 4 string quartets (1915, 1922, 1928, 1943); 2 piano trios (1922, rev. 1925; 1942); Violin Sonata (1926); *Ukrainian Quintet* for Piano (1942; rev. 1945); *Suite on Ukrainian Folk Themes* for String Quartet (1944); other piano pieces. **VOCAL:** Choral works; songs; many folk song arrangements.

BIBL.: I. Boelza, *B.M. L.* (Kiev, 1947); V. Samokhvalov, *B. L.* (Kiev, 1970; 2nd ed., 1974).

Licad, Cecile, Filipino pianist; b. Manila, May 11, 1961. She studied piano with Rosario Picazo. She made her public concert debut at the age of 7; then enrolled at the Curtis Inst. of Music in Philadelphia in the classes of Serkin, Lipkin, and Horszowski. In 1979 she was soloist with the Boston Sym. Orch. at the Berkshire Music Center in Tanglewood; in 1981 she won the Leventritt Gold Medal, which launched her on a fine career; subsequently appeared with major orchs. on both sides of the Atlantic. She married **Antônio Meneses**.

Licette, Miriam, English soprano; b. Chester, Sept. 9, 1892; d. Twyford, Aug. 11, 1969. She was trained in Milan and Paris, her principal mentors being Marchesi, Jean de Reszke, and Sabbatini. In 1911 she made her operatic debut in Rome as Cio-Cio-San. From 1916 to 1920 she sang with the Beecham Opera Co., and from 1919 to 1929 she appeared in the international seasons at London's Covent Garden. She also was a member of the British National Opera Co. from 1922 to 1928. She won particular praise as a Mozartian. Among her other roles were Eurydice, Gutrune, Eva, Desdemona, Juliette, and Louise.

Lichtenwanger, William (John), learned American librarian; b. Asheville, N.C., Feb. 28, 1915. He studied at the Univ. of Mich. at Ann Arbor (B.Mus., 1937; M.Mus., 1940); played double bass, oboe, and other instruments in the band and orch.; wrote pieces with whimsical titles, e.g., *Phrygidair* (in Phrygian mode, naturally). He served as assistant reference librarian of the Music Division at the Library of Congress in Washington, D.C. (1940–53, except for service in the U.S. Army, 1941–45), then assistant head (1953–60) and head (1960–74) of the music reference section there; was assoc. ed. of *Notes* of the Music Library Assn. (1946–60), then its ed. (1960–63); in 1975 he was made a member emeritus of the Music Library Assn. In addition, he was music ed. of *Collier's Encyclopedia* (1947–50) and consultant for the biographical dictionary *Notable American Women* (1971); also was a contributor to supplements II and III of the *Dictionary of American Biography*; was chairman and compiler of *A Survey of Musical Instrument Collections* in the U.S. and Canada (1974). A polyglot and a polymath, Lichtenwanger is fluent in German, French, and Turkish, nearly fluent in Japanese, and fairly fluent in personalized Russian. With his excellent wife, Carolyn, he ed. an analytic index to *Modern Music* (N.Y., 1976). Among his scholarly achievements, perhaps the highest is his incandescent essay "The Music of The Star-Spangled Banner—From Ludgate Hill to Capitol Hill," in the *Quarterly Journal of the Library of Congress* (July 1977), in which he furnishes documentary proof that the tune of the American national anthem was indeed composed by John Stafford Smith, all demurrings by various estimable historians to the contrary notwithstanding. To the 6th ed. of *Baker's Biographical Dictionary of Musicians* he contributed incalculably precious verifications, clarifications, rectifications, and refutations of previous inadvertent and/or ignorant fabrications and unintentional prevarications; he also ed. *Oscar Sonneck and American Music* (Urbana, Ill., 1984) and compiled *The Music of Henry Cowell: A Descriptive Catalog* (Brooklyn, 1986).

Lichtveld, Lou (actually, **Lodewijk Alphonsus Maria**), Dutch composer; b. Paramaribo, Surinam, Nov. 7, 1903. He went to Amsterdam in 1922 and was active as an organist and music critic. In 1936 he joined the International Brigade on the Loyalist side in the Spanish Civil War. During the Nazi occupation of the Netherlands, he served in the resistance movement, and became its representative in the emergency parliament of 1945. He returned to Surinam in 1949, and served as Minister of Education and Public Health and later President of the Exchequer; organized the facilities for musical education. From 1961 to 1969 he was in the diplomatic service of the Netherlands, stationed in Washington, D.C., and at the United Nations. He wrote about 2 dozen novels and essays under the pen name of Albert Helman. His musical works include an oratorio, *Canciones* (1934; MS lost in the Spanish Civil War); Piano Concertino (1932); Flute Sonata (1930); Violin Sonata (1931); *Triptych* for Piano (1925); Piano Sonata (1927); also experimental pieces employing oriental scales. He used a 24-tone scale for 2 Dutch documentary films produced by Joris Ivens: *Regen* (1929; musical score added in 1932) and *Philips-Radio* (1930; also known as *Industrial Symphony*). He also composed several choruses.

Lidholm, Ingvar (Natanael), prominent Swedish composer; b. Jönköping, Feb. 24, 1921. He studied violin with Hermann Gramms and orchestration with Natanael Berg in Södertälje; then received violin training from Alex Ruunqvist and conducting lessons from Tor Mann at the Stockholm Musikhögskolan (1940–45); also studied composition with Hilding Rosenberg (1943–45). He was a violinist in the orch. of the Royal Theater in Stockholm (1943–47); received a Jenny Lind fellowship and pursued his studies in France, Switzerland, and Italy (1947); later studied in Darmstadt (summer, 1949) and with Seiber in England (1954). He served as director of music in Örebro (1947–56); was director of chamber music for the Swedish Radio (1956–65); after holding the position of prof. of composition at the Stockholm Musikhögskolan (1965–75), he returned to the Swedish Radio as director of planning in its music dept. (1975). In 1960 he was elected a member of the Royal Swedish Academy of Music in Stockholm. He became active in Swedish avant-garde circles, contributing greatly to the formulation of methods and aims of contemporary music. In his works, he applies constructivist methods with various serial algorithms.

WORKS: DRAMATIC: *Cyrano de Bergerac*, incidental music (1947); *Riter*, ballet (1959; Stockholm, March 26, 1960); *Holländarn*, television opera (Swedish TV, Dec. 10, 1967); *Ett drömspel*, opera (1990). **ORCH.:** *Toccata e canto* for Chamber Orch. (1944); Concerto for Strings (1945); *Music* for Strings (1952); *Ritornello* (1955; Stockholm, Feb. 17, 1956); *Mutanza* (Örebro, Nov. 15, 1959); *Motus Colores* (Cologne, June 13, 1960); *Poesis* (1963; Stockholm, Jan. 14, 1964); *Greetings (from an Old World)* (N.Y., Nov. 10, 1976); *Kontakion*, hymn (1978; Moscow, Feb. 6, 1979). **CHAMBER:** String Quartet (1945; Stockholm, March 9, 1946); Sonata for Solo Flute (1945); *Little String Trio* (1953); Concertino for Flute, Oboe, English Horn, and Cello (Stockholm, Oct. 16, 1954); *Invention* for Clarinet and Bass Clarinet, or Viola and Cello, or Piano (1954); *4 Pieces* for Cello and Piano (Stockholm, May 16, 1955); *Fanfare* for 2 Trumpets, 2 to 4 Horns, and 2 Percussion (Stockholm, June 1956); *Fantasia sopra Laudi* for Cello (Swedish Radio, June 21, 1977); *Amicizia* for Clarinet (1980); *Tre elegier-Epilog* for String Quartet (1982–86; Stockholm, Oct. 23, 1986). **KEYBOARD: PIANO:** *Rosettas visa* (1942); Sonata (Stockholm, Oct. 25, 1947); 2 sonatinas (1947, 1950); *10 Miniatures* (1948); *Klavierstück 1949* (1949). **ORGAN:** *Variazioni sopra Laudi* (Stockholm, Oct. 27, 1982; in collaboration with K.-E. Welin). **VOCAL:** *Laudi* for Chorus (1947); Cantata for Baritone and Orch. (1949–50); *Canto LXXXI* for Chorus, after Ezra Pound (1956; Stockholm, Feb. 24, 1957); *Skaldens natt* (The Night of the Poet) for Soprano, Chorus, and Orch. (1958; North German Radio, Hamburg, April 6, 1959; rev. version, Swedish Radio, Oct. 23, 1981); *Nausikaa einsam* (Nausikaa Alone) for Soprano, Chorus, and Orch., after a section of Eyvind Johnson's novel *Return to Ithaca* (Ingesund, June 2, 1963); *Stamp Music I* for Soprano and Tam-tam (1971; score printed on a Swedish postage stamp) and *II* for Chorus and Piano (1971; score printed on a Swedish postage stamp); *Och inga träd skall väcka dig* for Soprano, Chorus, String Quartet, and Electronics (1973–74; Swedish TV, March 12, 1974); *Perserna* for Tenor, Baritone, Narrator, and Men's Chorus (Uppsala, April 29, 1978); *2 Madrigals* for Chorus (1981; Minneapolis, Sept. 12, 1982); *De profundis* for Chorus (Stockholm, Oct. 23, 1983); *Inbillningens värld* for Men's Chorus (1990); other choral pieces; songs.

Lídl, Václav, Czech composer; b. Brno, Nov. 5, 1922. He studied with Kvapil at the Brno Cons., graduating in 1948. In addition to writing numerous film scores, he also composed 4 syms. (1965, 1974, 1975, 1979), *Radostná predehra* for Orch. (1981), *Balada o červnovém ránu (Lidice 1942)* for Orch. (1982), *Serenade* for Orch. (1982), chamber music, and choral works.

Lie, Harald, Norwegian composer; b. Christiania, Nov. 21, 1902; d. there (Oslo), May 23, 1942. He studied piano at the Christiania Cons., and later received training in composition from Valen (1930). He was stricken with tuberculosis in 1932. His works were written in a late Romantic style. He withdrew a number of his scores: among those acknowledged are 2 syms. (1934, 1937), a *Symphonic Dance*, the scherzo from his unfinished 3rd Sym. (1942), several fine songs with orch., and choral pieces.

Liebermann, Lowell, American composer, pianist, and conductor; b. N.Y., Feb. 22, 1961. He began piano lessons at the age of 8, becoming a student of Ada Sohn Segal by age 11; at 14, began piano and composition lessons with Ruth Schonthal. In 1977 he made his debut at N.Y.'s Carnegie Recital Hall. In 1978 he commenced private composition lessons with Diamond, who continued as his mentor at the Juilliard School in N.Y. from 1979; also studied there with Lateiner (piano), Halasz (conducting), and Persichetti (composition), taking a B.Mus. (1982), a M.Mus. (1984), and a D.M.A. (1987). In 1986 he won the Victor Herbert/ASCAP Award, and in 1990 the Charles Ives fellowship of the American Academy and Inst. of Arts and Letters and ASCAP's Young Composers Competition. Liebermann's output demonstrates a deft handling of both traditional and modern elements in an accessible style.

WORKS: OPERA: *Dorian Gray* (1993–94; Monte Carlo, May 8, 1995). **ORCH.:** Concertino for Cello and Chamber Orch. (1982); Sym. (1982; N.Y., Feb. 19, 1988); 2 piano concertos: No. 1 (1983; Lake Forest, Ill., Oct. 28, 1988) and No. 2 (Washington, D.C., June 11, 1992); *The Domain of Arnheim* (1990; N.Y., Jan. 12, 1991); Flute Concerto (St. Louis, Nov. 6, 1992); *Revelry* (1995). **CHAMBER:** Cello Sonata (1978); *2 Pieces* for Violin and Viola (1978; N.Y., Oct. 25, 1986); String Quartet (1979); Viola Sonata (1984; N.Y., April 29, 1985); Flute Sonata (1987; Charleston, S.C., May 20, 1988); Contrabass Sonata (1987; Washington, D.C., March 18, 1989); Sonata for Flute and Guitar (1988; N.Y., March 15, 1989); Quintet for Piano, Clarinet, and String Trio (Washington, D.C., Nov. 13, 1988); *Fantasy on a Fugue by J.S. Bach* for Flute, Oboe, Clarinet, Horn, Bassoon, and Piano (N.Y., March 21, 1989); Concerto for Violin, Piano, and String Quartet (Charleston, S.C., May 28, 1989); *Fantasy* for Bass Koto (1989; N.Y., June 1, 1992); Trio for Piano, Violin, and Cello (Cape Cod, Mass., Aug. 8, 1990); Quintet for Piano and Strings (1990; Greenville, S.C., Feb. 2, 1991); *Soliloquy* for Flute (New Orleans, Jan. 30, 1993); Violin Sonata (N.Y., Dec. 1, 1994). **KEYBOARD: PIANO:** 2 sonatas: No. 1 (N.Y., May 15, 1977) and No. 2, *Sonata Notturna* (Wavendon, England, July 7, 1983); *Variations on a Theme by Anton Bruckner* (1986; Charleston, S.C., June 3, 1987); 4 nocturnes: No. 1 (Washington, D.C., Nov. 21, 1986), No. 2 (N.Y., March 28, 1990), No. 3 (San Antonio, Oct. 20, 1991), and No. 4 (London, Nov. 22, 1992); *Variations on a Theme by Mozart* for 2 Pianos (1993); *Album for the Young* (1993). **ORGAN:** *De Profundis* (1985; N.Y., Jan. 16, 1986). **VOCAL:** *2 Choral Elegies* (Stony Brook, N.Y., April 29, 1977); *War Songs* for Bass and Piano (1980; also for Bass and Orch., 1981); *3 Poems of Stephen Crane* for Baritone, String Orch., 2 Horns, and Harp (1983); *Sechs Gesange nach Gedichten von Nelly Sachs* for Soprano and Piano (1985; N.Y., March 19, 1986; also for Soprano and Orch., 1986; N.Y., April 7, 1987); *Missa Brevis* for Tenor, Baritone, Chorus, and Organ (1985; N.Y., March 29, 1986); *Final Songs* for Baritone and Piano (N.Y., Nov. 23, 1987); *Night Songs* for Baritone and Piano (1987); *A Poet to His Beloved* for Tenor, Flute, String Quartet, and Piano (N.Y., Feb. 13, 1993); *Out of the Cradle Endlessly Rocking* for Mezzo-soprano and String Quartet (Lawrence, Kansas, April 2, 1993).

Liebermann, Rolf, esteemed Swiss operatic administrator and composer; b. Zürich, Sept. 14, 1910. He studied law at the Univ. of Zürich and received private instruction in music from José Berr (1929–33); took a conducting course with Scherchen in Budapest (1936), and served as his assistant in Vienna (1937–38); also had composition studies with Vogel (1940). He was a producer at Radio Zürich (1945–50); then was director of the orch. section of the Schweizerische Rundspruchgesellschaft in Zürich (1950–57); subsequently was director of music of the North German Radio in Hamburg (1957–59). He was Intendant of the Hamburg State Opera (1959–73), where he pursued a policy of staging numerous 20th-century operas, including specially commissioned works from leading contemporary composers; then was general administrator of the Paris Opéra (1973–80), bringing enlightened leadership to bear on its artistic policies; subsequently was recalled to his former post at the Hamburg State Opera in 1985, remaining there until 1988. From 1983 to 1988 he also was director of the International Summer Academy of the Salzburg Mozarteum. He was made a Commandeur de la Légion d'honneur in 1975. His autobiography was publ. in English as *Opera Years* (1987). As a composer, he worked mostly in an experimental idiom, sharing the influence of hedonistic eclecticism, French neo-Classicism, and Viennese dodecaphony; he became particularly attracted to theatrical applications of modernistic procedures.

WORKS: OPERAS: *Leonore 40/45* (1951–52; Basel, March 25, 1952); *Penelope* (1953–54; Salzburg, Aug. 17, 1954); *The School for Wives* (1954–55; Louisville, Dec. 3, 1955; rev. as *Die Schüle der Frauen*, Salzburg, Aug. 17, 1957); *La Forêt* or *Der Wald* (1985–86; Geneva, April 11, 1987); *Non lieu pour Medea*

(1992). **ORCH.:** *Furioso* (1947; Dallas, Dec. 9, 1950); *Schweizerische Volksliedersuite* (BBC, Jan. 10, 1947); Sym. No. 1 (1949); Concerto for Jazz Band and Orch. (Donaueschingen Festival, Oct. 17, 1954); *Geigy Festival Concerto* (1958); *Liaison* for Cello, Piano, and Orch. (1983); Violin Concerto (1993). **CHAMBER:** Piano Sonata (1951); *Musique pour clavecin* (1966); *Essai 81* for Cello and Piano (1981). **VOCAL:** *Giraudoux-Cantata: Une des fins du monde* for Medium Voice and Orch. (1944); *Chinesische Liebeslieder* for High Voice, Harp, and String Orch. (1945); *Musik* for Speaker and Orch. (1949); *Streitlied Zwischen Leben und Tod* for Soprano, Mezzo-soprano, Tenor, Bass, Chorus, and Orch. (1950); *Capriccio* for Soprano, Violin, and Orch. (1959); *Ferdinand der Stier* for Speaker and Chamber Ensemble (1984); *Freispruch für Medea* for Soprano, Women's Chorus, and Orch. (1989); *Bundesbrief der Schweizer Eidgenossenschaft 1291* for Chorus and 12 Percussion (1990). **OTHER:** *Concert des echanges* for 52 Industrial Machines recorded on tape (Lausanne, April 24, 1964).

BIBL.: I. Scharberth and H. Paris, eds., *R. L. zum 60. Geburtstag* (Hamburg, 1970); C. Riess, R. L., "Nennen Sie mich einfach Musiker" (Hamburg, 1977).

Lieberson, Goddard, English-American recording executive and composer, father of **Peter Lieberson**; b. Hanley, Staffordshire, April 5, 1911; d. N.Y., May 29, 1977. He was taken to the U.S. as a child; studied composition with George Frederick McKay at the Univ. of Wash. in Seattle and with Bernard Rogers at the Eastman School of Music in Rochester, N.Y. In 1939 he joined the Masterworks division of Columbia Records in N.Y.; was its president (1955–66; 1973–75), during which period he recorded many contemporary works as well as those of the standard repertoire. In 1964 he was named president of the Record Industry Assn. of America; in 1978 the American Academy and Inst. of Arts and Letters set up the Lieberson fellowships to assist young composers. He composed a Sym., a ballet, *Yellow Poodle*, chamber music, choral works, and piano pieces.

Lieberson, Peter, American composer, son of **Goddard Lieberson**; b. N.Y., Oct. 25, 1946. He took a degree in English literature at N.Y. Univ. (1972); after studies with Babbitt, he trained with Wuorinen at Columbia Univ. (M.A. in composition, 1974), then studied Vajrayana Buddhism with Chögyam Trungpa of the Shambhala tradition. After completing his doctoral studies with Martino and Boykan at Brandeis Univ., he taught at Harvard Univ. (1984–88). He then settled in Halifax, Nova Scotia, as international director of Shambhala training, while continuing to pursue his career as a composer. His compositions are written in a well-crafted 12-tone system.

WORKS: ORCH.: Piano Concerto (1980–83; Boston, April 21, 1983); *Drala* (Boston, Oct. 9, 1986); *The Gesar Legend* (Boston, June 12, 1988); *World's Turning* (1990–91; San Francisco, Feb. 6, 1991); Viola Concerto (Toronto, Feb. 18, 1993); *Fire* (1995). **CHAMBER:** *Flute Variations* for Flute (1971); Concerto for 4 Groups of Instruments (1972–73); Concerto for Cello and 4 Trios (1974); *Accordance* for 8 Instruments (1975–76); *Tashi Quartet* for Clarinet, Violin, Cello, and Piano (1978–79); *Lalita-Chamber Variations* for 10 Instrumentalists (1983–84); *Feast Day* for Flute, Oboe, Piano or Harpsichord, and Cello (Washington, D.C., Sept. 21, 1985); *Ziji* for 6 Instruments (1987; N.Y., Jan. 17, 1988); *Raising the Gaze* for 8 Instrumentalists (San Francisco, March 28, 1988); *Elegy* for Violin and Piano (1990); *Wind Messengers* for 13 Instruments (1990); *A Little Fanfare I* for Flute, Trumpet, Violin, and Harp (1991) and *II* for Clarinet, Piano, Violin, Viola, and Cello (1993); *Variations* for Violin and Piano (1993); *Rumble* for Viola, Double Bass, and Percussion (1994); String Quartet No. 1 (Halifax, June 5, 1994). **PIANO:** *Piano Fantasy* (1975); (3) *Bagatelles* (1985); *Scherzo No. 1* (1989); (3) *Fantasy Pieces* (1989); *Garland* (1994). **VOCAL:** *Motetti di Eugenio Montali* for Soprano, Alto, and 4 Instruments (1971–72); *Double Entendre* for Soprano and 3 Instruments (1972); *3 Songs* for Soprano and 13 Instruments (1981); *King Gesar* for Narrator and 8 Instrumentalists (1991–92; Munich, May 20, 1992).

Liebling, Estelle, American soprano and pedagogue, sister of **Leonard** and niece of **Georg Liebling**; b. N.Y., April 21, 1880; d. there, Sept. 25, 1970. She studied with Marchesi in Paris and Nicklass-Kempner in Berlin. She made her operatic debut as Lucia at the Dresden Court Opera; then appeared at the Stuttgart Opera, the Opéra-Comique in Paris, and the Metropolitan Opera in N.Y. (debut Feb. 24, 1902, as Marguerite in *Les Huguenots*); was again on the Metropolitan's roster in 1903–04. She was a soloist with leading orchs. in the U.S., France, and Germany; also with Sousa. From 1936 to 1938 she was a prof. at the Curtis Inst. of Music in Philadelphia; then settled in N.Y. as a vocal teacher. Her most famous pupil was Beverly Sills. She publ. *The Estelle Liebling Coloratura Digest* (N.Y., 1943).

Liebling, Georg, German-American pianist and composer, uncle of **Estelle Liebling**; b. Berlin, Jan. 22, 1865; d. N.Y., Feb. 7, 1946. He studied piano with Theodor and Franz Kullak and Liszt, and composition with Urban and Dorn. He toured Europe (1885–89); was court pianist to the Duke of Coburg (1890). From 1894 to 1897 he directed his own music school in Berlin; from 1898 to 1908, was a prof. at the Guildhall School of Music in London. He settled in the U.S. in 1924, making his N.Y. debut that same year. He used the pseudonym André Myrot.

WORKS: *Concerto eroico* for Piano and Orch. (1925); 2 violin concertos; 2 violin sonatas; 3 Preludes for Violin and Piano; *Aria e Tarantella* for Cello and Piano; *Légende* for Violin and Piano; piano pieces; *Great Mass* for Soli, Chorus, Orch., and Organ (Los Angeles, 1931); songs.

BIBL.: G. Braun, *Hofpianist G. L.* (Berlin, 1896).

Liebling, Leonard, American pianist, music critic, and editor, nephew of **Georg** and brother of **Estelle Liebling**; b. N.Y., Feb. 7, 1874; d. there, Oct. 28, 1945. He studied at City College in N.Y., and privately with Leopold Godowsky (piano); then in Berlin with Kullak and Barth (piano) and Urban (composition). He toured Europe and America as a pianist. In 1902 he joined the staff of the *Musical Courier* in N.Y., and in 1911 became its ed.-in-chief; his weekly columns on topical subjects were both entertaining and instructive. He also served as music critic of the *N.Y. American* (1923–34; 1936–37). He wrote some chamber music, piano pieces, and songs, as well as librettos of several light operas, including Sousa's *The American Maid.*

Lier, Bertus van. See **Van Lier, Bertus.**

Lier, Jacques van. See **Van Lier, Jacques.**

Lierhammer, Theodor, Austrian baritone and teacher; b. Lemberg, Nov. 18, 1866; d. Vienna, Jan. 6, 1937. He was a practicing physician when he began to study singing with Ress in Vienna, Carafa in Milan, and Stockhausen in Frankfurt am Main. He made his debut at Vienna in 1894 in a concert with Fritz Kreisler; toured Austria and Hungary (1896), Germany (1898), Russia (1899), France and England (1900), and the U.S. (1904). From 1904 to 1914 he was a prof. of singing at the Royal Academy of Music in London. He served as an army physician during World War I. From 1922 to 1924 he was in London as a singer and teacher; in 1924 he was named prof. of singing at the Academy of Music in Vienna; from 1932 to 1935, he taught at the Austro-American Summer Cons. in Mondsee (Salzburg). One of his American pupils was Roland Hayes.

Lieurance, Thurlow (Weed), American composer; b. Oskaloosa, Iowa, March 21, 1878; d. Boulder, Colo., Oct. 9, 1963. He learned to play the cornet. After serving as a bandmaster during the Spanish-American War, he took courses in harmony and arranging at the Cincinnati College of Music. His visit to the Crow Indian reservation in 1903 prompted him to develop an intense interest in American Indian music and customs. From 1911 he made field recordings of his travels. He later taught at the Municipal Univ. in Wichita, Kansas, where he served as dean of its music dept. (1940–57). His collection of American Indian music is housed in the Archive of Folk Culture at the Library of Congress in Washington, D.C. In his compositions, Lieurance found inspiration in the music of the American

Indian. His song *By the Waters of Minnetonka* or *Moon Deer* (1917) achieved tremendous popularity.

WORKS: DRAMATIC: *Drama of the Yellowstone.* **ORCH.:** *Minisa* (1930); *Paris, France,* symphonic sketches (1931); *Trails Southwest* (1932); *The Conquistador* (1934); *Colonial Exposition Sketches; Medicine Dance; Water Moon Maiden.* **CHAMBER:** More than 200 salon pieces for various instrumental combinations, including piano pieces (1904–55); numerous arrangements. **VOCAL: CHORAL:** *Queen Esther,* oratorio (1897); (11) *Indian Love Songs* (1925); (10) *Indian Songs* (1934); part songs; numerous arrangements. **SONGS FOR VOICE AND PIANO:** *5 Songs* (1907); *9 Indian Songs* (1913); *By the Waters of Minnetonka* or *Moon Deer* (1917); *Songs of the North American Indian* (1920); *Songs from the Yellowstone* (1920–21); *8 Songs from Green Timber* (1921); *Forgotten Trails* (1923); *3 Songs, Each in His Own Tongue* (1925); *6 Songs from Stray Birds* (1937); *From the Land in the Sky* (1941); *Singing Children of the Sun* (1943).

BIBL.: "T. L. (An Authentic Biography)," *The Etude,* XLI (1923).

Ligabue, Ilva, Italian soprano; b. Reggio Emilia, May 23, 1932. She studied at the Milan Cons. and at the opera school of Milan's La Scala, where she made her operatic debut as Marina in Wolf-Ferrari's *I quattro Rusteghi* in 1953. She subsequently sang in other Italian and German music centers. From 1958 to 1961 she appeared at the Glyndebourne Festivals, where she was heard as Alice Ford, Fiordiligi, Donna Elvira, and Anna Bolena. In 1961 she made her U.S. debut as Boito's Margherita. In 1963 she sang with the American Opera Soc. in N.Y., at the Vienna State Opera, and at London's Covent Garden, returning to the latter in 1974. Her guest engagements took her to many other U.S. and European music centers.

Ligendza, Catarina (real name, **Katarina Beyron**), Swedish soprano; b. Stockholm, Oct. 18, 1937. Her parents sang at Stockholm's Royal Theater; she studied at the Würzburg Cons., in Vienna, and with Greindl in Saarbrücken. She made her debut as Countess Almaviva in Linz (1965); then sang in Braunschweig and Saarbrücken (1966–69); subsequently became a member of the Deutsche Oper in West Berlin and of the Württemberg State Theater in Stuttgart. In 1970 she sang for the first time at Milan's La Scala and at the Salzburg Easter Festival. She made her Metropolitan Opera debut in N.Y. as Leonore in *Fidelio* on Feb. 25, 1971; that summer she appeared at the Bayreuth Festival; her Covent Garden debut in London followed as Senta in 1972. In subsequent years, she sang in principal operatic centers of Europe before retiring from the operatic stage in 1988. Her other roles included Agathe, Isolde, Brünnhilde, Desdemona, Chrysothemis, and Ariadne.

Ligeti, György (Sándor), eminent Hungarian-born Austrian composer and pedagogue; b. Dicsöszentmárton, Transylvania, May 28, 1923. The original surname of the family was Auer; his great-uncle was **Leopold Auer**. He studied composition with Farkas at the Kolozsvar Cons. (1941–43) and privately with Kadosa in Budapest (1942–43); then continued his training with Veress, Járdányi, Farkas, and Bárdos at the Budapest Academy of Music (1945–49), where he subsequently was a prof. of harmony, counterpoint, and analysis (from 1950). After the Hungarian revolution was crushed by the Soviet Union in 1956, he fled his homeland for the West; in 1967 he became a naturalized Austrian citizen. He worked at the electronic music studio of the West German Radio in Cologne (1957–58); from 1959 to 1972 he lectured at the Darmstadt summer courses in new music; from 1961 to 1971 he also was a visiting prof. at the Stockholm Musikhögskolan. In 1972 he served as composer-in-residence at Stanford Univ., and in 1973 he taught at the Berkshire Music Center at Tanglewood. From 1973 to 1989 he was a prof. of composition at the Hamburg Hochschule für Musik. He has received numerous honors and awards. In 1964 he was made a member of the Royal Swedish Academy of Music in Stockholm, in 1968 a member of the Akademie der Künste in Berlin, and in 1984 an honorary member of the American Academy and Inst. of Arts and Letters; in 1986 he received the Grawemeyer Award of the Univ. of Louisville; in 1988 he was made a Commandeur in the Ordre National des Arts et Lettres in Paris; in 1990 he was awarded the Austrian State Prize; in 1991 he received the Praemium Imperiale of Japan; in 1993 he won the Ernst von Siemens Music Prize of Munich. In his bold and imaginative experimentation with musical materials and parameters, Ligeti endeavors to bring together all aural and visual elements in a synthetic entity, making use of all conceivable effects and alternating tremendous sonorous upheavals with static chordal masses and shifting dynamic colors. He describes his orch. style as micropolyphony.

WORKS: OPERA: *Le Grand Macabre* (1974–77; Stockholm, April 12, 1978). **ORCH.:** *Alte ungarische Tänze* for Flute or Clarinet and Strings (1949); *Romanian Concerto* for Small Orch. (1952); *Apparitions* (1958–59; Cologne, June 19, 1960); *Atmosphères* (Donaueschingen, Oct. 22, 1961); *Fragment* for Chamber Orch. (1961; Munich, April 1962); Cello Concerto (1966; Berlin, April 19, 1967); *Lontano* (Donaueschingen, Oct. 22, 1967); *Ramifications* for String Orch. or 12 Solo Strings (1968–69; 1st version, Berlin, April 23, 1969; 2nd version, Saarbrücken, Oct. 10, 1969); Chamber Concerto for 13 Instruments (Ottawa, April 2, 1970); *Melodien* (Nuremberg, Dec. 10, 1971); Double Concerto for Flute, Oboe, and Orch. (Berlin, Sept. 16, 1972); *San Francisco Polyphony* (1973–74; San Francisco, Jan. 8, 1975); Piano Concerto (1985–88; movements 1–3, Graz, Oct. 23, 1986; movements 4–5, Vienna, Feb. 29, 1988); *Macabre Collage* (1991; Florence, May 16, 1992; arranged from the opera *Le Grand Macabre* by E. Howarth); Violin Concerto (1st version, Cologne, Nov. 3, 1990; 2nd version, Cologne, Oct. 8, 1992). **CHAMBER:** Cello Sonata (1948–53); 2 string quartets: No. 1, *Métamorphoses nocturnes* (1953–54; Vienna, May 8, 1958) and No. 2 (1968; Baden-Baden, Dec. 14, 1969); 10 Pieces for Wind Quintet (1968; Malmö, Jan. 20, 1969); Trio for Violin, Horn, and Piano (Hamburg-Bergedorf, Aug. 7, 1982); Sonata for Solo Viola (1991–94; Gütersloh, April 23, 1994). **KEYBOARD: PIANO:** *Musica ricercata* (1951–53); *Trois bagatelles* (1961); *Monument, Selbstportrait, Bewegung* for 2 Pianos (1976); *13 Études* (1985–93). **ORGAN:** *Volumina* (1961–62); 2 studies: No. 1, *Harmonies* (1967) and No. 2, *Coulée* (1969). **HARPSICHORD:** *Continuum* (1968); *Hungarian Rock (Chaconne)* (1978); *Passacaglia ungherese* (1978). **VOCAL:** *Ifúsági kantáta* (Cantata for Youth) for Soprano, Contralto, Tenor, Baritone, Chorus, and Orch. (1949); *Pápainé* for Chorus (1953); *Éjszaka* (Night) and *Reggel* (Morning) for Chorus (1955); *Aventures* for 3 Singers and 7 Instruments (1962; Hamburg, April 4, 1963); *Nouvelles aventures* for Aventures Ensemble (1962–65; Hamburg, May 26, 1966); *Aventures & Nouvelles aventures,* theater piece based on the 2 preceding works (Stuttgart, Oct. 19, 1966); *Requiem* for Soprano, Mezzo-soprano, 2 Choruses, and Orch. (1963–65; Stockholm, March 14, 1965; the Kyrie was used in the film score for *2001: A Space Odyssey*); *Clocks and Clouds* for Women's Chorus and Orch. (1972–73; Graz, Oct. 15, 1973); *Lux aeterna* for 16 Voices (Stuttgart, Nov. 2, 1966); *Drei Phantasien* for 16 Voices (Stockholm, Sept. 26, 1983); *Magyar etüdök* (Hungarian Studies) for 16 Voices (1983); *Nonsense Madrigals* for 6 Men's Voices (1988–93). **ELECTRONIC:** *Glissandi* (1957); *Artikulation* (1958); *Pièce électronique* No. 3 (1957–58). **OTHER:** *Poème symphonique* for 100 Metronomes (1962; Hilversum, Sept. 13, 1963).

BIBL.: E. Salmenhaara, *Das musikalische Material und seine Behandlung in den Werken "Apparitions," "Atmosphères," "Aventures" und "Requiem" von G. L.* (Helsinki and Regensburg, 1969); O. Nordwall, *G. L.: Eine Monographie* (Mainz, 1971); P. Griffiths, *G. L.* (London, 1983); E. Restagno, ed., *L.* (Turin, 1985); H. Sabbe, *G. L.: Studien zur kompositorischen Phänomenologie* (Munich, 1987); R. Richart, *G. L.: A Bio-Bibliography* (N.Y., 1990); P. Peterson, ed., *Für G. L.: Die Referate des L.-Kongresses Hamburg 1988* (Laaber, 1991).

Ligeti, Lukas, Austrian composer and percussionist; b. Vienna, June 13, 1965. He began playing percussion at the age of 18, then studied with Erich Urbanner (composition) and Fritz

Ozmec (jazz drums) at the Vienna Academy of Music (diploma, 1993); also attended summer courses in new music at Darmstadt, taking improvisation workships with John Zorn (1988) and David Moss (1991) and in composition with Crumb (1991). In 1994 he became a visting scholar at the Center for Computer Research in Music and Acoustics at Stanford Univ. Among his awards are composition grants from the city of Vienna (1989, 1993), a Foerderungspreis of the city of Vienna (1990), an Austrian state grant for composition (1991), and a prize of the Austrian Ministry for Science and Research (1993). Ligeti has been strongly influenced by jazz, rock, and traditional musics; he developed a new way of playing drums based on movement patterns derived from central and east African practices, as well as a new tablature. He has also devoted much time to the art of improvisation.

WORKS: *Pattern Transformation* for 4 Percussionists on 2 Marimbas (1988); *Oblique Narratives*, 3 pieces for 2 Pianos (1989–90); *Frozen State of Song* for Saxophone Quartet (1990–93); *Seeking Scapegoat* for Violin, Soprano Saxophone, 2 Electric Guitars, and Drums (1991); *The Chinese Wall* for Orch. (1992); *Groove Magic* for 11 Musicians and Computer-controlled Click Tracks (1992–93); *Tonga Tango* for Chorus (1993).

Lilburn, Douglas (Gordon), notable New Zealand composer and teacher; b. Wanganui, Nov. 2, 1915. He was a student of J.C. Bradshaw at Canterbury Univ. College, Christchurch (1934–36). As winner of the Grainger Competition with his symphonic poem *Forest* (1936), he was able to pursue his studies in London with Vaughan Williams at the Royal College of Music (1937–40). He was composer-in-residence at the Cambridge Summer Music Schools (1946–49; 1951). In 1947 he began teaching at Victoria Univ. in Wellington, where he was a lecturer (1949–55), senior lecturer (1955–63), assoc. prof. (1963–70), and prof. (1970–79). In 1966 he founded New Zealand's first electronic music studio there, serving as its director until 1979. In 1967 he founded the Wai-te-ata Press Music Editions. His Lilburn Trust has done much to encourage the promotion of music in New Zealand. He publ. the lectures *A Search for Tradition* (Wellington, 1984) and *A Search for a Language* (Wellington, 1985). In 1988 Lilburn was made a member of the Order of New Zealand. In his early works, Lilburn found inspiration in traditional forms of expression. About 1953 he embraced an eclectic style, primarily influenced by Stravinsky, Bartók, the 2nd Viennese School, and modern American composers. By 1962 he pursued a more adventuresome path as a proponent of electronic music.

WORKS: DRAMATIC: *Landfall in Unknown Seas*, incidental music (1942). **ORCH.:** *Forest*, symphonic poem (1936); *Drysdale Overture* (1937; rev. 1940 and 1986); *Festival Overture* (1939); *Aotearoa Overture* (London, April 16, 1940); *Introduction and Allegro* for Strings (1942); *4 Canzonas* for Strings (1943–50); *A Song of Islands* or *Song of the Antipodes* (1946; Wellington, Aug. 20, 1947); *Cambridge Overture* (1946); *Diversions* for Strings (1947); 3 syms.: No. 1 (1949; Wellington, May 12, 1951), No. 2 (1951; rev. 1974), and No. 3 (1961); Suite (1955; rev. 1956); *A Birthday Offering* (1956). **CHAMBER:** *Fantasy* for String Quartet (1939); *Allegro concertante* for Violin and Piano (1944; rev. 1945); Trio for Violin, Viola, and Cello (1945); String Quartet (1946; rev. 1981); Clarinet Sonatina (1948); Violin Sonata (1950); *Duos* for 2 Violins (1954); Quartet for 2 Trumpets, Horn, and Trombone (1957); Wind Quintet (1957); *17 Pieces* for Guitar (1962–70). **KEYBOARD: PIANO:** *3 Sea Changes* (1945–72; rev. 1981); *Chaconne* (1946); 2 sonatinas (1946, 1962); Sonata (1949); *9 Short Pieces* (1965–66; rev. 1967). **ORGAN:** *Prelude and Fugue* (1944). **VOCAL:** *Prodigal Country* for Baritone, Chorus, and Orch. (1939); *Elegy: In memoriam Noel Newson* for 2 Voices and Strings (1945); *3 Songs* for Voice and Piano (1947–54); *Elegy* for Baritone and Piano (1951); *Sings Harry* for Baritone and Piano, or Tenor and Guitar (1954); *3 Poems of the Sea* for Narrator and Strings (1958); *3 Songs* for Baritone and Viola (1958). **ELECTRONIC:** *The Return* (1965); *Poem in Time of War* (1967); *Summer Voices* (1969); *Expo '70 Dance Sequence* (1970); *3 Inscapes* (1972); *Carousel* (1976); *Winterset* (1976); *Of Time and Nostalgia* (1977); *Triptych* (1977); *Soundscape with Lake and River* (1979).

BIBL.: V. Harris and P. Norman, eds., *D. L.: A Festschrift for D. L. on His Retirement from the Victoria University of Wellington* (Wellington, 1980); P. Norman, *The Beginnings and Development of a New Zealand Music: The Life and Work of D. L., 1940–65* (diss., Univ. of Canterbury, Christchurch, 1983).

Liljefors, Ingemar (Kristian), Swedish pianist and composer, son of **Ruben (Mattias) Liljefors**; b. Göteborg, Dec. 13, 1906; d. Stockholm, Oct. 14, 1981. He studied at the Royal Academy of Music in Stockholm (1923–27; 1929–31) and in Munich (1927–29). He taught piano (1938–43) and harmony (from 1943) at the Stockholm Musikhögskolan. From 1947 to 1963 he was chairman of the Assn. of Swedish Composers. He publ. a manual on harmony from the functional point of view (1937) and one on harmonic analysis along similar lines (1951). His compositions frequently employed elements of Swedish folk music with a later infusion of some modernistic techniques.

WORKS: OPERA: *Hyrkusken* (The Coachman; 1951). **ORCH.:** *Rhapsody* for Piano and Orch. (1936); Piano Concerto (1940); Sym. (1943); Piano Concertino (1949); Violin Concerto (1956); *Sinfonietta* (1961); *2 Intermezzi* for Strings (1966); *Divertimento* for Strings (1968). **CHAMBER:** 2 piano trios (1940, 1961); Violin Sonatina (1954); 3 piano sonatinas (1954, 1964, 1965); Cello Sonatina (1958); String Quartet (1963); Sonatina for Solo Violin (1968). **VOCAL:** *En Tijdh-Spegel* (A Mirror of the Times) for Soli, Chorus, and Orch. (1959; Swedish Radio, April 16, 1961).

Liljefors, Ruben (Mattias), Swedish composer and conductor, father of **Ingemar (Kristian) Liljefors**; b. Uppsala, Sept. 30, 1871; d. there, March 4, 1936. He studied in Uppsala; then with Jadassohn at the Leipzig Cons.; later in Dresden with Draeseke and with Reger in Leipzig. Returning to Sweden, he was conductor of the Göteborg Phil. (1902–11) and the Gävleborg Orch. Soc. (1912–31). His works, which included a Piano Concerto (1899; rewritten 1922), Sym. (1906), *Sommer-Suite* for Orch. (1920), choral works, chamber music, piano pieces, and songs, followed in the Romantic tradition.

Lill, John (Richard), English pianist; b. London, March 17, 1944. He studied at the Royal College of Music in London (1955–64); also with Kempff in Positano. He made his debut at a concert in the Royal Festival Hall in London in 1963; was joint 1st prizewinner at the Tchaikovsky Competition in Moscow (1970), which was the beginning of his successful international career. In 1978 he received the Order of the British Empire. While Lill's repertoire ranges from the classics to the moderns, he has won particular distinction for his cycles of the music of Beethoven.

Lima, Luis, Argentine tenor; b. Córdoba, Sept. 12, 1948. He was trained in Buenos Aires and at the Madrid Cons. After taking prizes in the Toulouse (1972) and Francisco Viñas (1973) competitions, he took 1st prize in the Lauri-Volpe competition (1973). In 1974 he made his operatic debut as Turiddu in Lisbon, and then appeared throughout Germany. He made his American debut in a concert performance of Donizetti's *Gemma di Vergy* at N.Y.'s Carnegie Hall in 1976. In 1977 he sang for the first time at Milan's La Scala as Donizetti's Edgardo. On March 16, 1978, he made his N.Y. City Opera debut as Alfredo, which role he also chose for his Metropolitan Opera debut in N.Y. on Sept. 20, 1978. He appeared as Cavaradossi at the Teatro Colón in Buenos Aires in 1982. In 1984 he made his debut at London's Covent Garden as Nemorino. He sang Cavaradossi at the Salzburg Easter Festival in 1988; in 1992, appeared as Don Carlos at the San Francisco Opera. Among his other roles were Berlioz's and Boito's Faust, Verdi's Riccardo, Bizet's Don José, Gounod's Faust and Roméo, and Puccini's Rodolfo.

Lin, Cho-Liang, outstanding Chinese-born American violinist; b. Hsin-Chu, Taiwan, Jan. 29, 1960. He began to study the violin as a child and won the Taiwan National Youth Violin Competition at age 10; when he was 12, he became a pupil of Robert Pikler at the New South Wales State Conservatorium of Music in Sydney; at 15, he went to the U.S., where he enrolled at the Juilliard School in N.Y. as a scholarship student of Dorothy DeLay (graduated, 1981). He won wide notice when he was chosen to play at the inaugural concert in Washington, D.C., for President Jimmy Carter in 1977; that same year, he won 1st prize in the Queen Sofia International Competition in Madrid. In subsequent years, he pursued a highly rewarding career as a virtuoso, touring throughout the world; he appeared as a soloist with virtually every major orch., and also was active as a recitalist and chamber music player. In 1988 he became a naturalized U.S. citizen. His extensive repertoire ranges from the standard literature to specially commissioned works. In his performances, he combines effortless technique with a beguiling luminosity of tone.

Lincke, (Carl Emil) Paul, German conductor and composer; b. Berlin, Nov. 7, 1866; d. Klausthal-Zellerfeld, near Göttingen, Sept. 3, 1946. After studies with Rudolf Kleinow in Wittenberge (1880–84), he was active in Berlin as a bassoonist in and later conductor of theater orchs. He also became active as a composer of small operettas and other light theater pieces, scoring his first success with *Venus auf Erden* (June 6, 1897). After a sojourn at the Folies-Bergère in Paris (1897–99), he returned to Berlin and brought out such works as *Frau Luna* (May 1, 1899), *Im Reiche des Indra* (Dec. 18, 1899), *Fräulein Loreley* (Oct. 15, 1900), *Lysistrata* (April 1, 1902; best known for its *Glühwürmchen*-[Glowworm] *Idyll*), *Nakiris Hochzeit* (Nov. 6, 1902), and *Berliner Luft* (Sept. 28, 1904). Among his later works, only *Gri-gri* (Cologne, March 25, 1911) and *Casanova* (Chemnitz, Nov. 5, 1913) attracted much attention. He subsequently devoted himself mainly to conducting and overseeing his own publishing firm, Apollo Verlag. During the Nazi era, Lincke's works were successfully revived and the composer was granted various honors. His new-won fame, however, did not survive the collapse of the Third Reich.

BIBL.: E. Nick, *P. L.* (Hamburg, 1953); O. Schneidereit, *P. L. und die Entstehung der Berliner Operette* (Berlin, 1974).

Lindberg, Christian, extraordinary Swedish trombonist; b. Stockholm, Feb. 12, 1958. He took up the trombone at the age of 17; after playing in the Royal Opera Orch. in Stockholm (1977–78), he studied at the Stockholm Musikhögskolan, in London, and in Los Angeles (1978–82). His remarkable mastery of his instrument led to a career as a trombone virtuoso, and he subsequently appeared as a soloist with the major orchs., a recitalist, and a chamber music player in the principal music centers the worldover; also gave master classes and designed new instruments. Lindberg's repertoire is vast, embracing Baroque works on original instruments, Classical and Romantic scores, and a provocative cornucopia of contemporary pieces, including those by Berio, Cage, Dutilleux, Hindemith, Kagal, and Stockhausen. He also commissioned works, including the trombone concertos of Sandstrom, Xenakis, and Takemitsu.

Lindberg, Magnus (Gustaf Adolf), Finnish pianist and composer; b. Helsinki, June 27, 1958. He began playing the piano at age 11, then at 15 entered the Sibelius Academy in Helsinki, where he studied composition with Rautavaara and Heininen (graduated, 1981); also received instruction in electronic music there with Lindeman and took courses with Grisey and Globokar in Paris, Donatoni in Siena, and Ferneyhough in Darmstadt. His works are cast in a decisive contemporary idiom. He won the Prix Italia for his *Faust* in 1986 and the Nordic Music Prize for his *Kraft* in 1987.

WORKS: ORCH.: *Ritratto* (1979–83; Milan, Feb. 27, 1983); *Drama* (1980–81; Helsinki, Feb. 8, 1981); *Sculpture II* (1981; Helsinki, Oct. 13, 1982); *Tendenza* (1982; Paris, Jan. 27, 1983); *Kraft* (1983–85; Helsinki, Sept. 4, 1985); *Trois sculptures* (1988; Helsinki, March 13, 1989); *Marea* for Chamber Orch. (London, April 26, 1990); *Joy* for Large Chamber Ensemble (Frankfurt am Main, Dec. 9, 1990); Piano Concerto (Helsinki, Sept. 4, 1991); *Corrente I* for Chamber Orch. (1991–92; Helsinki, Feb. 5, 1992) and *II* (1991–92; London, Nov. 27, 1992). **CHAMBER:** *Tre stycken* (3 Pieces) for Horn, Violin, Viola, and Cello (1976; Helsinki, May 25, 1977); *Arabesques* for Wind Quintet (1978; Helsinki, Oct. 5, 1980); *Espressione I* for Cello (1978) and *II* for Violin (1979); *Quintetto dell'estate* for Flute, Clarinet, Violin, Cello, and Piano (1979; Helsinki, May 24, 1980); *Sonatas* for Violin and Piano (1979); *Layers* for Unspecified Ensemble (1979–); *. . . de Tartuffe, je crois* for String Quartet and Piano (Kuhmo, July 27, 1981); *Linea d'ombra* for Flute, Saxophone, Guitar, and Percussion (1981; Milan, March 17, 1983); *Action-situation-signification* for Horn or Clarinets, Piano, Percussion, Cello, and Tape (Jyväskylä, July 6, 1982); *Ablauf* for Clarinet and 2 Percussion ad libitum (Helsinki, April 15, 1983; rev. 1988); *Zona* for Cello, Alto Flute, Bass Clarinet, Percussion, Harp, Piano, Violin, and Double Bass (Hilversum, Dec. 2, 1983); *Metal Work* for Accordion and Percussion (1984; Joensuu, June 18, 1985); *Stroke* for Cello (Helsinki, Dec. 30, 1984); *UR* for 5 Players and Live Electronics (Paris, Oct. 11, 1986); *Moto* for Cello and Piano (1990; Paris, April 13, 1991); *Steamboat Bill JR* for Clarinet and Cello (1990); Duo Concertante for Clarinet, Cello, and 8 Instruments (Witten, April 15, 1992); Clarinet Quintet (Kuhmo, July 16, 1992). **PIANO:** *Music* for 2 Pianos (1976); *Klavierstück* (1977); 3 pieces (1978); *Play I* for 2 Pianos (1979); *Twine* (Bremen, May 19, 1988). **VOCAL:** *Jag vill breda vingar ut* for Mezzo-soprano and Piano (1977–78); *Untitled* for 20 Voices (1978). **TAPE:** *Etwas zarter* (1977); *Ohne Ausdrück* (1978; Helsinki, April 15, 1983); *Faust*, radiophonic score (1985–86; Finnish Radio, Aug. 17, 1986).

Lindberg, Oskar (Fredrik), Swedish organist, pedagogue, and composer; b. Gagnef, Feb. 23, 1887; d. Stockholm, April 10, 1955. He became organist in Gagnef when he was 14. At 16, he entered the Stockholm Cons., where he took diplomas as a church musician (1906) and as a music teacher (1908); he also studied composition with Andreas Hallén and Ernst Ellberg. He served as organist at Stockholm's Trefaldighetskyrka (1906–14) and Engelbrektskyrka (1914–55), and also gave recitals. In 1919 he became a teacher of harmony at the Stockholm Cons., where he was a prof. from 1936. In 1926 he was named a member of the Swedish Royal Academy of Music. In his compositions, he pursued a Romantic path in which folk and national elements predominated.

WORKS: OPERA: *Fredlös* (1936–42; Stockholm, Nov. 25, 1943). **ORCH.:** Sym. (1909); 3 overtures (1909; 1911; *Vår*, 1924); symphonic poems, including *Från de stora skogarna* (1918) and *Gesunda* (1946); *Per spelman, han spelte*, rhapsody (1930); suites. **CHAMBER:** Piano Quartet; Piano Quintet; piano pieces; organ music, including a Sonata (1924) and chorale preludes. **VOCAL:** *Requiem* (1920–22); choral pieces; songs.

Linde, (Anders) Bo (Leif), Swedish composer, pianist, and music critic; b. Gävle, Jan. 1, 1933; d. there, Oct. 2, 1970. Following initial training with Bengtsson and Bökman, he studied at the Stockholm Musikhögskolan (1948–52) with Larsson (composition) and Wibergh (piano) before pursuing studies in conducting in Vienna (1953–54). He taught theory at the Stockholm Citizens' School (1957–60), and then returned to Gävle as a pianist, music critic, and composer. He composed in a well-crafted style notable for its adherence to classical forms in an accessible idiom.

WORKS: DRAMATIC: *Ballet blanc* (1953; Gävle, May 11, 1969); *Slotts-skoj* (Fun in the Castle), children's opera (1959). **ORCH.:** *Sinfonia fantasia* (1951); 2 piano concertos (1954, 1956); *Suite in an Old Style* (1954); *Preludium and Final* for Strings (1955); Violin Concerto (1957); Suite (1959); *Sinfonia* (1960); *Concerto for Orchestra* (1961–62); *Concert Music* for Small Orch. (1963); Cello Concerto (1964); *Suite Boulogne* (1966); *Little Concerto* for Wind Quintet and Strings (1966); *Pensieri sopra un cantico vecchio* (1967; Gävle, Jan. 1, 1968); *Pezzo concertante* for Bass Clarinet and Strings (Gävle, Sept. 9,

1970). **CHAMBER:** 2 piano trios (1953, 1969); String Quartet (1953); Violin Sonata (1953); *Serenata nostalgica* for 11 Strings (1965); *Quartet in Miniature* for Clarinets (1965); String Trio (1968); piano pieces. **VOCAL:** *Varbilder* (Spring Scenes) for Soli, Chorus, and Orch. (1963); songs.

Linde, Hans-Martin, German-born Swiss flutist, recorder player, conductor, pedagogue, and composer; b. Werne, May 24, 1930. He was a student of Gustav Scheck (flute) and Konrad Lechner (composition) at the Freiburg im Breisgau Hochschule für Musik (1947–51). He played solo flute in the Cappella Coloniensis of the West German Radio in Cologne, and from 1955 he toured as a soloist throughout Europe and abroad. In later years, he appeared with his own Linde Consort. From 1957 he was active in Basel, where he served on the faculty of the Academy of Music. He served as director of its Cons. (1976–79), and then director of its choral music department at its Inst. He also was conductor of its Hochschule chorus (to 1991) and chamber chorus (to 1995). From 1980 he pursued an active career as a conductor. In 1993 he was awarded the German Handel Prize. He publ. *Kleine Anleitung zum Verzieren alter Musik* (1958) and *Handbuch des Blockflötenspiels* (1962; Eng. tr., 1967).

WORKS: Trio for Recorder, Transverse Flute, and Harpsichord (1963); *Serenata a tre* for Recorder, Guitar, and Cello (1966); *Consort Music* for 4 Instrumentalists (1972); *Fairy Tale* for Recorder (1981); *Music for 2* for Recorder and Guitar (1983); *5 Studies* for Recorder and Piano (1985); *Browning* for Recorder Quintet (1986); *Una Follia Nuova* for Recorder (1989); Suite for Recorder Quartet (1991); *Carmina pro Lassum* for 5 Recorders and Percussion (1992); *3 Sketches* for Recorder, Violin, and Piano (1993); Concerto for Recorder and String Orch. (1994).

Lindeman, Osmo (Uolevi), Finnish composer; b. Helsinki, May 16, 1929; d. there, Feb. 15, 1987. He studied with Linnala and Fougstedt at the Sibelius Academy in Helsinki (1956–59). In 1959 he was awarded a UNESCO grant to the Hochschule für Musik in Munich, where he studied for a year with Orff; upon returning to Finland, he taught at the Sibelius Academy (1961–84). In his works, he at first adopted a traditional Romantic manner, but after 1968 devoted himself to electronic music.

WORKS: DRAMATIC: *Huutokauppa* (Auction), ballet (1967); film scores. **ORCH.:** 2 syms. (*Sinfonia inornata*, 1959; 1964); 2 piano concertos (1963, 1965); *Music* for Chamber Orch. (1966); Concerto for Chamber Orch. (1966); *Variabile* (1967). **CHAMBER:** String Trio (1958); *Partita* for Percussion (1962); *2 Expressions* for Vibraphone and Marimba (1965); String Quartet (1966). **TAPE:** *Kinetic Forms* (1969); *Mechanical Music* (1969); *Tropicana* (1970); *Midas* (1970); *Ritual* (1972).

Lindholm, Berit (real name, **Berit Maria Jonsson**), Swedish soprano; b. Stockholm, Oct. 18, 1934. She studied with Britta von Vegesack and Käthe Sundström in Stockholm. She made her debut as Mozart's Countess at the Royal Opera there in 1963. She first appeared at London's Covent Garden as Chrysothemis in *Elektra* (1966), and then sang at the Bayreuth Festivals (1967–74). She made her U.S. debut as Brünnhilde with the San Francisco Opera (1972); her Metropolitan Opera debut followed in N.Y. in the same role on Feb. 20, 1975. She became best known for her Wagnerian roles.

Ling, Jahja, Indonesian conductor and pianist of Chinese descent; b. Jakarta, Oct. 25, 1951. He received piano training at the Jakarta School of Music. After winning the Jakarta Piano Competition at 17, he was awarded a Rockefeller grant and pursued his studies at the Juilliard School in N.Y. (M.A.), where he was a pupil of Meczyslaw Munz and Beveridge Webster (piano) and of John Nelson (conducting); also held a Leonard Bernstein Conducting Fellowship at the Berkshire Music Center at Tanglewood (summer, 1980), where he studied with Bernstein, Sir Colin Davis, Ozawa, Previn, Schuller, and Silverstein; completed his conducting studies with Mueller at Yale Univ. (D.M.A., 1985). From 1981 to 1984 he was the Exxon/Arts Endowment Conductor of the San Francisco Sym., and also was founder-music director of its youth orch. and music director of the San Francisco Cons. of Music orch. He then was resident conductor of the Cleveland Orch. (from 1984), where he also was founder-music director of its youth orch.; concurrently served as music director of the Florida Orch. (from 1988). In 1988 he received a Seaver-NEA Conductor's Award. A guest conductor, he appeared with many leading North American orchs. In 1988 he made his European debut with the Gewandhaus Orch. in Leipzig. At his N.Y. Phil. debut on Feb. 26, 1993, he conducted the premiere of Zwilich's 3rd Sym.

Linjama, Jouko (Sakari), Finnish organist and composer; b. Kirvu, Feb. 4, 1934. He studied composition with Merikanto and Kokkonen at the Sibelius Academy in Helsinki (1954–60) and musicology and literature at the Univ. of Helsinki; continued his composition training with Zimmermann and Koenig at the Cologne Staatliche Hochschule für Musik (1962–64) and also worked with Stockhausen in the Cologne course for new music (1963). He was organist at St. Henrik's Catholic Church (1958–60) and then in the Tuusula parish (from 1964); also taught at the Sibelius Academy (1964–68). A prominent composer of sacred music, he was awarded the composition prize of the Finnish church in 1979. In his works, he attempts to fuse Burgundian strict counterpoint with serial techniques.

WORKS: ORCH.: *La Migration d'oiseaux sauvages* (1977). **CHAMBER:** *5 Metamorphosen für 5 Instrumente über 5 Canons Op. 16 von Anton Webern* for Celesta, Vibraphone, Guitar, Harpsichord, and Piano (1963); . . . *lehtiä* . . . (. . . leaves . . .) for Cello and Piano (1974); *Hommage à Dandriaeu* for 2 Cellos or 2 Men's Voices and Organ (1977); 2 string quartets: No. 1, *Cantiones* (1978) and No. 2, *Variazioni* (1979); Concerto for Organ, Marimba, Vibraphone, and 2 Wind Quartets (1981). **ORGAN:** *Sonatina supra b-a-c-h* (1961); *Partita-sonata Veni Creator Spiritus* (1968); *Intrada* (1969); *Magnificat* (1970); Concerto (1971); *Triptychon* for 2 Organs (1971); *Partita* (1973); *Piae cantiones per organo piccolo* (1976); *Missa cum jubilo* (1977); *Consolation pour l'orgue* (1978); *Toccatina, danza e contradanza per organo piccolo* (1981); *Organum supra b-a-c-h* (1982); *Roccata* (1985); *Reflections* for Organ Duet (1991). **VOCAL:** *Millaista on* (How it is), oratorio for Baritone, 6 Men's Voices, Orch., and 3 Tape Recorders (1964–68); *Homage to Aleksis Kivi*, symphonic oratorio for Narrator, Baritone, Women's Chorus, Men's Chorus, Children's Chorus, and Orch. (1970–76); *La sapienza*, chamber oratorio for 2 Choruses (1980); cantatas; song cycles; solo songs.

Linko, Ernst, Finnish composer and pianist; b. Helsinki, July 14, 1889; d. there, Jan. 28, 1960. He studied piano at the Helsinki School of Music (1909–11), and then in Berlin, St. Petersburg, and Paris. He was director of the Sibelius Academy in Helsinki (1939–59); for many years, was active as a concert pianist. He wrote 4 piano concertos (1916, 1920, 1931, 1957); *Symphonie chevaleresque* (1949); *Ariette* for Wind Ensemble; *Rigaudon* for Strings; Piano Trio; String Quartet; numerous piano pieces.

Linn, Robert, American composer; b. San Francisco, Aug. 11, 1925. He studied with Milhaud at Mills College in Oakland, California (1947–49), and with Sessions, Stevens, and Dahl at the Univ. of Southern Calif. in Los Angeles (M.M., 1951); taught there (from 1958) and served as chairman of the theory and composition dept. (from 1973). In his output, Linn makes effective use of traditional forms.

WORKS: ORCH.: *Overture for Symphony Orchestra* (1952); Sym. in 1 Movement (1956; rev. 1961); *Hexameron* for Piano and Orch. (1963; reconstruction of Liszt's orchestration of *Hexaméron*, variations on a theme by Bellini); Sinfonia for Strings (1967; rev. 1972); Concertino for Oboe, Horn, Percussion, and Strings (1972); *Fantasia* for Cello and Strings (1975–76); Concertino for Woodwind Quintet and Strings (1981–82). **WOODWIND ORCH.:** *Elevations* (1964); *Propagula* (1970); Concerto for Flute and Woodwind Orch. (1980); Partita (1980); Concerto for Piano and Woodwind Orch. (1984). **CHAMBER:** Clarinet

Sonata (1949); String Quartet No. 1 (1951); Quartet for 4 Saxophones (1953); 2 piano sonatas (1955, 1964); Quartet for 4 Horns (1957); *Prelude and Dance* for 4 Saxophones (1960); Brass Quintet (1963); Woodwind Quintet (1963); *Dithyramb* for 8 Cellos (1965); Concertino for Violin and Wind Octet (1965); *Vino* for Violin and Piano (1975); *12* for Chamber Ensemble (1976–77); *Saxifrage Blue* for Baritone Saxophone and Piano (1977); *Trompe l'oeil* for Bass Trombone and Piano (1978); *Diversions* for 6 Bassoons (1979); *Trombosis* for 12 Trombones (1979); *Serenade* for Flute, Clarinet, Cello, and Guitar (1982). **VOCAL:** *An Anthem of Wisdom* for Chorus and Orch. (1958); *Pied Piper of Hamlin*, oratorio (1968); choruses; songs.

Linnala, Eino (Mauno Aleksanteri), Finnish composer and teacher; b. Helsinki, Aug. 19, 1896; d. there, June 8, 1973. He studied composition with Melartin (1915–20), at the Univ. of Helsinki, in Berlin (1922), and with Willner in Vienna (1924–27). Linnala taught theory and analysis at the Univ. of Helsinki (1927–66); was also chairman of the Finnish Composers' Copyright Bureau (1960–68). He publ. several textbooks on theory. His compositions, all composed in the Romantic tradition, included 2 syms. (1927, 1935); *Dance Suite* for Orch. (1931); *Suomalainen rapsodia* for Orch. (1932); *Overture* (1933); *Elegia* for Orch. (1945); 4 cantatas (1932–40); more than 100 choral songs; chamber music; about 50 songs.

Linstead, George (Frederick), Scottish organist, choirmaster, music critic, teacher, and composer; b. Melrose, Jan. 24, 1908; d. Sheffield, Dec. 29, 1974. He wrote an oratorio at the age of 13 and an opera, *Agamemnon*, at 16; studied with F. Shera in Sheffield; also with E. Bairstow (composition) and James Ching (piano); was awarded a D.Mus. degree from the Univ. of Durham (1946). He was active as a church organist and choirmaster, as well as a music critic, in Sheffield; was also a part-time lecturer at the Univ. there (1947–74). Among his compositions were an opera, *Eastward in Eden* (1937); a ballet, *Hylas*; Sym.; Sinfonietta; *Moto perpetuo* for Orch.; Overture "In the French Style"; *Anglican Overture*; 2 concertinos for Piano and Orch.; choral music; 2 string quartets and other chamber works; band music; piano pieces; songs.

Lioncourt, Guy de, French composer and teacher; b. Caen, Dec. 1, 1885; d. Paris, Dec. 24, 1961. He studied Gregorian chant with Gastoué, counterpoint with Roussel, and composition with his uncle, d'Indy, at the Paris Schola Cantorum (graduated, 1916); in 1918 he won the Grand Prix Lasserre with his *La Belle au bois dormant* (1912–15). He became prof. of counterpoint (1914) at the Schola Cantorum; at d'Indy's death in 1931, he became subdirector and prof. of composition. He helped to found the École César Franck in Paris (1935), and then was its director. He publ. an autobiography, *Un Témoignage sur la musique et sur la vie au XXe siècle* (Paris, 1956).

WORKS: DRAMA: *Jan de la lune* (1915–21). **LITURGICAL DRAMAS:** *Le Mystère de l'Emmanuel* (1924); *Le Mystère de l'Alléluia* (1925–26); *Le Mystère de l'Esprit* (1939–40). **CHAMBER:** Piano Quintet (1908); Piano Quartet (1925); String Quartet (1933). **KEYBOARD:** Piano pieces; organ music. **VOCAL: SOLOISTS, CHORUS, AND ORCH.:** *Hyalis, le petit faune aux yeux bleus* (1909–11); *La Belle au bois dormant* (1912–15); *Le Réniement de St.-Pierre* (1928); *Le Navrement de Notre Dame* (1943). **OTHER VOCAL:** 3 masses (1914–22; 1942; 1948); *Les Dix Lépreux* for Voice, Women's Chorus, and Orch. (1918–19); *Le Dict de Mme. Saincte Barbe* for Soloists, Chorus, Harp, and Strings (1937); motets.

Lipatti, Dinu (actually, **Constantin**), outstanding Romanian pianist and composer; b. Bucharest, April 1, 1917; d. Chêne-Bourg, near Geneva, Dec. 2, 1950. His father was a violinist who had studied with Sarasate, and his mother, a pianist; his godfather was Enesco. He received his early training from his parents; then studied with Florica Musicescu at the Bucharest Cons. (1928–32). He received a 2nd prize at the International Competition at Vienna in 1934, a judgment which prompted Cortot to quit the jury in protest; Lipatti then studied piano with Cortot, conducting with Munch, and composition with Dukas and Boulanger in Paris (1934–39). He gave concerts in Germany and Italy, returning to Romania at the outbreak of World War II. In 1943 he settled in Geneva as a teacher of piano at the Cons. After the war, he resumed his career; played in England 4 times (1946–48). His remarkable career was tragically cut short by lymphogranulomatosis. He was generally regarded as one of the most sensitive interpreters of Chopin, and was also praised for his deep understanding of the Baroque masters; was also a fine composer. Lipatti was married to the pianist and teacher Madeleine Cantacuzene.

WORKS: ORCH.: *Şătrarii*, symphonic poem (1934; Bucharest, Jan. 23, 19363); *Concertino in the Classic Style* for Piano and Chamber Orch. (1936; Bucharest, Oct. 5, 1939); *Symphonie concertante* for 2 Pianos and Strings (1938; Bucharest, May 4, 1941). **CHAMBER:** Violin Sonatina (1933); *Improvisation* for Piano, Violin and Cello (1939); Concerto for Organ and Piano (1939); *Introduction and Allegro* for Flute (1939); *Aubade* for Wind Quartet (1949). **PIANO:** Sonata (1932); *3 Dances* (1937); nocturnes (1937, 1939); Sonatina for Piano, Left Hand (1941); *Romanian Dances* for 2 Pianos (1943; also for Piano and Orch., Geneva, Oct. 11, 1945). **VOCAL:** Songs.

BIBL.: M. Lipatti, ed., *Hommage à D. L.* (Geneva, 1952); A. Lipatti, *La Vie du pianiste D. L., écrite par sa mère* (Paris, 1954); T. Dragos, *L.* (Bucharest, 1965); C. Păsculescu-Florian, *Vocaţie Şi destin, D. L.* (Bucharest, 1986); D. Tanasescu and G. Bargauanu, *L.* (London, 1988); C. Păsculescu-Florian, *D. L.: Pagini din jurnalul unei regăsiri* (Bucharest, 1989); G. Bargauanu and D. Tanasescu, *D. L.* (Lausanne, 1991).

Lipkin, Malcolm (Leyland), English composer, pianist, and teacher; b. Liverpool, May 2, 1932. He studied piano with Gordon Green in Liverpool; following further piano training from Kendall Taylor at the Royal College of Music in London (1949–53), he studied composition privately with Seiber (1954–57); received his doctorate from the Univ. of London (1972). In 1951 he made his debut as a pianist performing his 3rd Piano Sonata at the Gaudeamus Foundation Music Week in the Netherlands; in 1952 he made his London debut playing the same score. He served as a tutor for the external dept. of the Univ. of Oxford (1965–75) and for the School of Continuing Education at the Univ. of Kent (from 1975).

WORKS: ORCH.: 2 violin concertos: No. 1 (1952) and No. 2 (1960–62; Bournemouth, Oct. 17, 1963); *Movement* for Strings (1956–57; rev. 1960); Piano Concerto (1957; Cheltenham, July 16, 1959); 3 syms.: No. 1, *Sinfonia di Roma* (1958–65; Liverpool, Jan. 18, 1966), No. 2, *The Pursuit* (1975–79; Manchester, Feb. 9, 1983), and No. 3, *Sun* (1979–86); *Pastorale* for Horn and Strings (1963; also for Horn and String Quintet, or Horn and Piano, or Oboe and Piano); *Mosaics* for Chamber Orch. (London, Oct. 23, 1966; rev. 1969); Concerto for Flute and Strings (1974); Oboe Concerto (1988–89; London, June 20, 1989). **CHAMBER:** String Quartet (1951); Violin Sonata (1957); Suite for Flute and Cello (1961); String Trio (1963–64); *Capriccio* for Piano and String Quartet (1966); *Interplay* for Treble Recorder, Viola da Gamba, Harpsichord, and Percussion (London, March 5, 1976; also for Flute, Cello, and Piano); *Recollections* for Percussion (1976); *Clifford's Tower* for 8 Instruments (1977; Cheltenham, July 11, 1980); Trio for Flute, Viola, and Harp (Rye, Sept. 7, 1982); *Naboth's Vineyard* for Recorder, Cello, and Harpsichord (1982); Wind Quintet (1985; London, July 14, 1986); *Prelude and Dance* for Cello and Piano, in memory of Jacqueline DuPré (1987; London, July 5, 1988); *Idyll* for Violin (1988); Piano Trio (1988; London, March 22, 1989); *5 Bagatelles* for Oboe and Piano (1993); Duo for Violin and Cello (1994). **KEYBOARD: PIANO:** 5 sonatas, including No. 3 (Bilthoven, Sept. 6, 1951; rev. 1979), No. 4 (Cheltenham, July 17, 1955; rev. 1987), and No. 5 (1986; Kent, July 21, 1989); *Nocturne* (1987). **HARPSICHORD:** *Metamorphosis* (1974). **VOCAL:** *Psalm 96* for Chorus and Orch. (London, Dec. 17, 1969); *Psalm 117* for Chorus (1969); *4 Departures* for Soprano and Violin (1972); *5 Songs* for Soprano and Piano (1978).

Lipkin, Seymour, American pianist, conductor, and teacher; b. Detroit, May 14, 1927. He studied piano as a child and appeared as soloist in Beethoven's 1st Piano Concerto with the Detroit Civic Orch. (1938); then studied formally at the Curtis Inst. of Music in Philadelphia with Saperton (1938–41) and with Serkin and Horszowski (B.Mus., 1947); also studied conducting with Koussevitzky at the Berkshire Music Center in Tanglewood (summers, 1946; 1948–49) and was apprentice conductor to Szell and the Cleveland Orch. (1947–48). After winning 1st prize in the Rachmaninoff Piano Competition (1948), he played the Tchaikovsky 1st Piano Concerto with Koussevitzky and the Boston Sym. Orch. that same year and subsequently appeared as a soloist with major U.S. orchs. He made his formal conducting debut with the N.Y. City Opera leading Bernstein's *Trouble in Tahiti* (1958); then was an assistant conductor of the N.Y. Phil. (1959–60) and music director of the Long Island Sym. Orch. (1963–79). He was also music director of N.Y.'s Joffrey Ballet (1966–68), then its principal guest conductor (1968–72), and once again its music director (1972–79). He taught at Marymount College in Tarrytown, N.Y. (1963–72; chairman of the music dept., 1968–71), the Curtis Inst. of Music (from 1969), the Manhattan School of Music (1972–87), the New England Cons. of Music in Boston (1984–86), and the Juilliard School in N.Y. (from 1986); also served as artistic director of the Univ. of Maryland International Piano Festival and William Kapell Piano Competition (1988–92).

Lipkovska, Lydia (Yakovlevna), Russian soprano; b. Babino, Khotin district, Bessarabia, May 10, 1882; d. Beirut, Jan. 22, 1955. She studied with Iretzkaya in St. Petersburg and Vanzo in Milan. She made her debut as Gilda at the St. Petersburg Imperial Opera (1907), singing there until 1908 and again from 1911 to 1913. She appeared in Diaghilev's season in Paris (1909), as well as at the Opéra and the Opéra-Comique. Her American debut took place with the Boston Opera on Nov. 12, 1909, when she sang Lakme; on Nov. 18, 1909, she made her Metropolitan Opera debut in N.Y. as Violetta, singing there until 1911 and in Chicago in 1910–11; also appeared at London's Covent Garden as Mimi (July 11, 1911). After the Russian Revolution of 1917, she was active in Paris. In 1920 she toured the U.S. and in 1921–22 appeared at the Chicago Grand Opera. She sang at the Odessa Opera (1941–44) and then returned to Paris. Her last years were spent as a teacher in Beirut.

Lipman, Samuel, American pianist, teacher, and music critic; b. Los Gatos, Calif., June 7, 1934; d. N.Y., Dec. 17, 1994. He commenced piano studies in his youth, making his debut at age 9; attended L'École Monteux in Hancock, Maine (summers, 1951–57), and the Aspen (Colo.) Music School (summers, 1959–61); completed his piano training with Rosina Lhévinne at the Juilliard School of Music in N.Y. (1959–62). He also took courses in government at San Francisco State College (B.A., 1956) and pursued graduate work in political science at the Univ. of Calif. at Berkeley (M.A., 1958). His tours as a pianist took him all over the U.S. and Europe; he also served as music critic of *Commentary* (from 1976) and publ. the *New Criterion* (from 1982); taught at the Aspen Music School (from 1971) and at the Waterloo Music Festival in Stanhope, N.J. (from 1976), where he was artistic director (1985–93). In 1977 he won the ASCAP-Deems Taylor Award for music criticism, and in 1980 for his vol. of essays *Music after Modernism* (1979). He also wrote *The House of Music: Art in an Era of Institutions* (1982), *Arguing for Music, Arguing for Culture: Essays* (1990), and *Music and More: Essays, 1975–1991* (1992). Lipman was a prominent figure in the American neo-conservative movement.

Lipovšek, Marjana, distinguished Yugoslav mezzo-soprano; b. Ljubljana, Dec. 3, 1946. She received her training in Ljubljana, Graz, and Vienna. In 1979 she became a member of the Vienna State Opera, where she developed a notably successful career. In 1981 she made her first appearance at the Salzburg Festival. In 1982 she sang for the first time at the Hamburg State Opera and at Milan's La Scala. In 1983 she joined the Bavarian State Opera in Munich. She made her London debut as a soloist in *Das Lied von der Erde* with the London Sym. Orch. in 1988, returning to London in 1990 to make her Covent Garden debut as Clytemnestra. On Nov. 25, 1993, she made her North American debut as Fricka in *Die Walküre* at the Lyric Opera of Chicago. In addition to her operatic career, Lipovšek has pursued an extensive following as a concert and lieder artist. She has appeared as a soloist with the leading orchs. of Europe and North America, and at many festivals. Among her many roles of note are Gluck's Orfeo, Mistress Quickly, Amneris, Azucena, Brangäne, Orlofsky, Strauss' Composer and Octavian, and Berg's Marie.

Lipp, Wilma, esteemed Austrian soprano; b. Vienna, April 26, 1925. She was a student in Vienna of Sindel, Novikova, Bahr-Mildenburg, and Jerger, and in Milan of Dal Monte. In 1943 she made her operatic debut in Vienna as Rosina, and then was a member of the State Opera there from 1945. She also appeared at the Salzburg Festival from 1948. In 1950 she made her debut at Milan's La Scala as the Queen of the Night, a role she made her own. In 1951 she made her first appearance at London's Covent Garden singing Gilda. In 1953 she sang the Queen of the Night at her debut at the Paris Opéra. She appeared at the Glyndebourne Festival for the first time in 1957 as Constanze. Her U.S. debut followed in 1962 as Nannetta in *Falstaff* at the San Francisco Opera. In 1982 she became a prof. of voice at the Salzburg Mozarteum. She was honored as an Austrian Kammersängerin. Lipp was equally adept in coloratura and lyric roles, ranging from the operas of Mozart to Richard Strauss.

Lipphardt, Walther, German musicologist; b. Wiescherhofen bei Hamm, Oct. 14, 1906; d. Frankfurt am Main, Jan. 17, 1981. He studied musicology with Moser at the Univ. of Heidelberg and with Gurlitt at the Univ. of Freiburg im Breisgau; then took additional courses at the Univ. of Heidelberg with Besseler, graduating with a Ph.D. in 1931 with the diss. *Über die altdeutschen Marienklagen.* He subsequently was on the faculty of the Hochschule für Musik in Frankfurt am Main (1946–70). He publ. numerous valuable papers on liturgical music and ed. works of Renaissance composers.

WRITINGS: *Die Weisen der lateinischen Osterspiele des 12. und 13. Jahrhunderts* (Kassel, 1948); *Die Geschichte des mehrstimmigen Proprium Missae* (Heidelberg, 1950); *Der karolingische Tonar von Metz* (Münster, 1965); *Gesangbuchdrucke in Frankfurt am Main vor 1569* (Frankfurt am Main, 1974).

Lippincott, Joan, American organist and teacher; b. East Orange, N.J., Dec. 25, 1935. She studied piano and organ with William Jancovius, then organ with Alexander McCurdy at Westminster Choir College in Princeton, N.J. (B.M., 1957; M.M., 1961) and at the Curtis Inst. of Music in Philadelphia (diploma, 1960), where she also received instruction in piano from Vladimir Sokoloff; subsequently she pursued graduate studies at the School of Sacred Music at the Union Theological Seminary in N.Y. She made many tours as a recitalist in the U.S. and overseas. She also taught at Westminster Choir College (from 1960), where she served as head of the organ dept. (from 1967). In addition to the standard organ literature, Lippincott has played much contemporary music for her instrument.

Lippman, Edward A(rthur), American musicologist; b. N.Y., May 24, 1920. He was educated at the City College of N.Y. (B.S., 1942), N.Y. Univ. (M.A., 1945), and Columbia Univ. (Ph.D., 1952, with the diss. *Music and Space: A Study in the Philosophy of Music*); held a Guggenheim fellowship (1958–59). He taught at Columbia Univ. (from 1954), where he was a prof. (from 1969).

WRITINGS: *Musical Thought in Ancient Greece* (N.Y., 1964); *A Humanistic Philosophy of Music* (N.Y., 1977); *Musical Aesthetics: A Historical Reader* (3 vols., N.Y., 1986–90); *A History of Western Musical Aesthetics* (Lincoln, Nebr., 1992).

Lipton, Martha, American mezzo-soprano; b. N.Y., April 6, 1913. She was educated at the Juilliard School of Music in N.Y.

On Nov. 27, 1944, she made her debut as Siebel with the Metropolitan Opera in N.Y. and remained on its roster until 1960; also sang with the N.Y. City Opera (1944, 1958, 1961) and at the Chicago Lyric Opera (1956). In Europe she sang in Amsterdam and The Hague, and at the Holland and Edinburgh festivals, the Vienna State Opera, and the Paris Opéra; also made appearances in South America. In 1960 she became a prof. of voice at the Indiana Univ. School of Music in Bloomington. Among her prominent roles were Cherubino, Ulrica, Orlovsky, Herodias, and Octavian. She also appeared extensively as a concert artist.

Lisitsyan, Pavel (Gerasimovich) (actually, **Pogos Karapetovich**), Armenian baritone; b. Vladikavkaz, Nov. 6, 1911. He studied in Leningrad. He sang at the Maly Theater there (1935–37); then was a member of the Armenian Opera Theater in Yerevan (1937–40); in 1940 he joined the Bolshoi Theater in Moscow, remaining on its roster until 1966, but in the interim filled engagements all over Europe, in India, and in Japan; also made his debut at the Metropolitan Opera in N.Y. as Amonasro (March 3, 1960). From 1967 to 1973 he was on the faculty of the Yerevan Cons. He was best known for his roles in Russian operas.

Lissa, Zofia, distinguished Polish musicologist; b. Lemberg, Oct. 19, 1908; d. Warsaw, March 26, 1980. She studied piano and organ at the Lemberg Cons., and then musicology with Chybiński at the Univ. of Lemberg (1925–29), where she also took courses in philosophy, psychology, and art history (Ph.D., 1930, with the diss. *O harmonice Aleksandra Skriabina*; publ. in *Kwartalnik Muzyczny*, II, 1930); subsequently completed her Habilitation at the Univ. of Poznań with her *Oistocie komizmu muzycznege* (The Essence of Musical Humor; publ. in Kraków, 1938) and later took a 2nd Ph.D. there in 1954 with the diss. *Podstawy estetyki muzycznej* (Questions of Music Aesthetics; publ. in Warsaw, 1953). She taught at the Lwów Cons. (1931–41); later was reader (1948–51), prof. (1951–57), and director (from 1957) of the musicological inst. of the Univ. of Warsaw. She was a leading proponent of socialist realism as a critical method of musical evaluation.

WRITINGS: *Zarys nauki o muzyce* (A Short Music Textbook; Lwów, 1934; 4th ed., aug., 1966); *Muzykologia polska na przelomie* (A Turning Point in Polish Musicology; Kraków, 1952); with J. Chomiński, *Muzyka polskiego odrodzenia* (Music of the Polish Renaissance; Warsaw, 1953; 3rd ed., rev., 1958, in *Odrodzenie w Polsce*, V); *Historia muzyki rosyjskiej* (History of Russian Music; Kraków, 1955); *Estetyka muzyki filmowej* (Kraków, 1964); *Skice z estetyki muzycznej* (A Sketch of Musical Aesthetics; Kraków, 1965); *Polonica Beethovenowskie* (Kraków, 1970); *Studia nad twórczością Fryderyka Chopina* (Studies of Frédéric Chopin's Works; Kraków, 1970).

BIBL.: *Studia musicologica aesthetica, theoretica, historica: Z. L. w 70. roku urodzin* (Kraków, 1979).

List (real name, **Fleissig**), **Emanuel,** noted Austrian-born American bass; b. Vienna, March 22, 1886; d. there, June 21, 1967. He was a boy chorister at the Theater-an-der-Wien. Following voice training with Steger in Vienna, he toured Europe as a member of a comic vocal quartet. He went to the U.S. and appeared in vaudeville, burlesque, and minstrel shows. After further vocal studies with Zuro in N.Y., he returned to Vienna in 1920 and in 1922 made his operatic debut as Gounod's Méphistophélès at the Volksoper. He then sang at Berlin's Städtische Oper (1923–25) and State Opera (1925–33), London's Covent Garden (1925; 1934–36), the Salzburg Festivals (1931–35), and the Bayreuth Festival (1933). List made his Metropolitan Opera debut in N.Y. on Dec. 27, 1933, as the Landgrave. While remaining on its roster until 1948, he also appeared in San Francisco and Chicago (1935–37) and gave lieder recitals. He was again on the Metropolitan Opera's roster in 1949–50. In 1952 he returned to Vienna. List was especially admired for the rich vocal resources he brought to such roles as Osmin, the Commendatore, Sarastro, Rocco, King Marke, Hagen, Pogner, Hunding, and Baron Ochs.

List, Eugene, American pianist; b. Philadelphia, July 6, 1918; d. N.Y., March 1, 1985. He was taken to Los Angeles when a year old; studied there at the Sutro-Seyler Studios and made his debut with the Los Angeles Phil. at the age of 12; later studied in Philadelphia with Samaroff, and at the Juilliard Graduate School in N.Y. He played the solo part in the American premiere of Shostakovich's Piano Concerto No. 1 with the Philadelphia Orch. (Dec. 12, 1934). As a sergeant in the U.S. Army, he was called upon to play the piano at the Potsdam Conference in July 1945, in the presence of Truman, Churchill, and Stalin. Subsequently he appeared as a soloist with many American orchs. and as a recitalist. In 1964 he was appointed a prof. of piano at the Eastman School of Music in Rochester, N.Y.; left there in 1975 and then joined the faculty of N.Y. Univ. His repertoire ranged from Mozart to contemporary composers. He championed the cause of Gottschalk, and in later years oversaw a series of "monster concerts" à la Gottschalk in which 10 or more pianos and various pianists were involved. In 1943 he married **Carroll Glenn**.

List, Garrett, American composer; b. Phoenix, Sept. 10, 1943. He studied with Bertram McGarrity at Calif. State Univ. in Long Beach, and in N.Y. with Hall Overton and at the Juilliard School (B.M., 1968; M.M., 1969). He became proficient as a trombonist and was active with various new-music groups, both as performer and as composer; was music director of N.Y.'s Kitchen (1975–77); taught at the Liège Cons. (from 1980).

WORKS: DRAMATIC: *Time and Desire*, dance piece (1984–85). **ORCH.:** *Orchestral Études* (1972–79); *9 Sets of 7* for Chamber Orch. (1975); *Songs* for Chamber Orch. (1975); *I Am Electric* for Jazz Band (1976); *The Girls* for Narrator and Small Orch. (1977); *Escape Story* for Soloists and Orch. (1979); *Fear and Understanding* for Jazz Band (1981). **OTHER INSTRUMENTAL:** *2 Wind Studies* for 9 to 16 Winds (1971); *Songs* for 7 to 12 Instruments (1972); *Your Own Self* for Any Instrument(s) (1972); *Elegy: To the People of Chile* for Any Instrument(s) (1973); *Requiem for Helen Lopez* for Piano and 4 to 6 Instruments (1981); *Flesh and Steel* for Piano, Guitar(s), and Instrument(s) (1982); *Baudelaire* for Instrument(s) (1983); *Hôtel des étrangers* for 5 to 21 Instruments (1983); trombone pieces. **VOCAL:** *American Images*, cantata for Voice and Instrument(s) (1972); *Standard Existence* for Voice and Instrument(s) (1977); many songs.

List, Kurt, Austrian musicologist, music critic, conductor, record producer, and composer; b. Vienna, June 21, 1913; d. Milan, Nov. 16, 1970. He studied at the Vienna Academy of Music (M.A., 1936) and at the Univ. of Vienna (Ph.D., 1938); also took private lessons with Berg (1932–35) and Webern (1935–38). He went to the U.S. in 1938; became active in the field of recording; wrote music criticism. After World War II he returned to Europe and lived mostly in Italy. His String Quartet and a Wind Quintet were performed in N.Y.; he also wrote 2 unperformed operas, *Der Triumph des Todes* and *Mayerling*, stylistically influenced by Richard Strauss.

Listov, Konstantin, Russian composer; b. Odessa, Sept. 19, 1900; d. Moscow, Sept. 6, 1983. He learned music by ear; then studied piano in Tsaritsin and in Saratov. In 1923 he went to Moscow and began to write music for the theater. His Red Army song *Tachanka* became immensely popular. He also wrote a Sym. in commemoration of the centennial of Lenin (1970).

BIBL.: A. Tishchenko, *K. L.* (Moscow, 1962).

Litaize, Gaston, blind French organist, pedagogue, and composer; b. Ménil-sur-Belvitte, Vosges, Aug. 11, 1909; d. Says, Vosges, Aug. 5, 1991. Following initial training at the Institut National des Jeunes Aveugles in Paris (1926–31), he pursued his studies at the Paris Cons. with Dupré (organ), Caussade (fugue), Büsser (composition), and Emmanuel (music history), taking premiers prix for organ and improvisation (1931), fugue

(1933), and composition (1937). In 1938 he won the 2nd Prix de Rome and the Prix Rossini with his musical legende *Fra Diavolo.* From 1946 he served as organist at St.-François-Xavier in Paris, and he also made tours as a recitalist in Europe and abroad. He was a prof. at the Institut National des Jeunes Aveugles. Among his works were various organ pieces and a number of vocal works, including a *Missa solemnior* (1954), a *Missa Virgo gloriosa* (1959), and a *Messe solennelle en français* (1966).

Litinsky, Genrik, distinguished Russian composer; b. Lipovetz, March 17, 1901; d. Moscow, July 26, 1985. He studied composition with Glière at the Moscow Cons., graduating in 1928; subsequently taught there (1928–43); among his students were Khrennikov, Zhiganov, Arutiunian, and other Soviet composers. In 1945 he went to Yakutsk as an ethnomusicologist; in collaboration with native Siberian composers, he produced the first national Yakut operas, based on authentic folk melorhythms and arranged in contemporary harmonies according to the precepts of socialist realism: *Nurgun Botur* (Yakutsk, June 29, 1947); *Sygy Kyrynastyr* (Yakutsk, July 4, 1947); *Red Shaman* (Yakutsk, Dec. 9, 1967). He wrote 3 Yakut ballets: *Altan's Joy* (Yakutsk, June 19, 1963), *Field Flower* (Yakutsk, July 2, 1947), and *Crimson Kerchief* (Yakutsk, Jan. 9, 1968). Other works include: Sym. (1928); *Dagestan Suite* for Orch. (1931); Trumpet Concerto (1934); *Festive Rhapsody* for Orch. (1966); 12 string quartets (1923–61); String Octet (1944); 12 concert studies for Cello (1967); 12 concert studies for Trumpet and Piano (1968); 15 concert studies for Oboe and Piano (1969). He publ. the valuable manuals *Problems of Polyphony* (3 vols., 1965, 1966, 1967), ranging from pentatonic to dodecaphonic patterns and from elementary harmonization to polytonality; also *Formation of Imitation in the Strict Style* (1970). He also collected, transcribed, and organized the basic materials of several Soviet Republics; altogether he compiled musical samples from as many as 23 distinct ethnic divisions of folkloric elements. He was in time duly praised by the Soviet authorities on aesthetics, but not until the policy of the Soviet Union itself had changed. In the meantime, Litinsky became the target of unconscionable attacks by reactionary groups within Soviet musical organizations who denounced him as a formalist contaminated by Western bourgeois culture. In one instance, his personal library was ransacked in search of alleged propaganda. In 1964 he was named a People's Artist of the Yakut S.S.R. and of the Tatar Autonomous S.S.R.

Litton, Andrew, American conductor; b. N.Y., May 16, 1959. He studied piano with Reisenberg and conducting with Ehrling at the Juilliard School in N.Y.; also received lessons in conducting from Weller at the Salzburg Mozarteum, Järvi in Hilversum, and Edoardo Müller in Milan. In 1982 he won the BBC/Rupert Foundation International Conductors' Competition; then was the Exxon-Arts Endowment assistant conductor of the National Sym. Orch. in Washington, D.C. (1982–85), where he subsequently was assoc. conductor (1985–86); also appeared as a guest conductor in North America and Europe. On March 9, 1989, he made his Metropolitan Opera debut in N.Y. conducting *Eugene Onegin.* In 1988 he assumed the position of principal conductor and artistic adviser of the Bournemouth Sym. Orch., with which he established a fine reputation. In 1994 he took it on its first tour of the U.S. before concluding his tenure with it that year to become music director of the Dallas Sym. Orch.

Litvinenko-Wohlgemut, Maria (Ivanova), Russian soprano; b. Kiev, Feb. 6, 1895; d. there, April 4, 1966. She was a student of Alexeyeva-Yunevich and Ivanitsky at the Kiev Music Inst. (graduated, 1912). In 1912 she made her operatic debut as Oxana in Gulak-Artemovsky's *The Cossack Beyond the Danube* in Kiev. She was a member of the Petrograd Music Drama Theater (1914–16), the Kharkov Opera (1923–25), and the Kiev Opera (1935–51). From 1946 she taught at the Kiev Cons. In 1936 she was honored as a People's Artist of the U.S.S.R. In addition to her portrayals of Russian roles, she was admired for her Aida and Tosca.

BIBL.: A. Polyakov, *M.I L.-W.* (Kiev, 1956).

Litvinne, Félia (real name, **Françoise-Jeanne Schütz**), noted Russian soprano; b. St. Petersburg, Aug. 31, 1860?; d. Paris, Oct. 12, 1936. She studied in Paris with Barth-Banderoli, Viardot, and Maurel; made her debut there in 1882 at the Théâtre-Italien as Maria Boccanegra; then sang throughout Europe. In 1885 she made her first appearance in the U.S. with Mapleson's company at N.Y.'s Academy of Music; after singing at the Théâtre Royal de la Monnaie in Brussels (1886–88), at the Paris Opéra (1889), and at Milan's La Scala, in Rome, and in Venice (1890), she appeared at the imperial theaters in St. Petersburg and Moscow (from 1890). She made her Metropolitan Opera debut in N.Y. as Valentine in *Les Huguenots* on Nov. 25, 1896, but remained on the roster for only that season. In 1899 she first appeared at London's Covent Garden as Isolde, and made several further appearances there until 1910. She made her farewell to the operatic stage in Vichy in 1919, but continued to give concerts until 1924. In 1927 she became prof. of voice at the American Cons. in Fontainebleau. Her pupils included Nina Koshetz and Germain Lubin. She publ. her memoirs as *Ma vie et mon art* (Paris, 1933). Her most outstanding roles included Gluck's Alceste, Donna Anna, Aida, Kundry, Brünnhilde, and Selika.

Liuzzi, Fernando, Italian composer and pedagogue; b. Senigallia, Dec. 19, 1884; d. Florence, Oct. 6, 1940. He received training in piano and composition with Fano in Bologna, where he also attended the Univ. (fine arts degree, 1905), and then pursued his studies with Falchi at Rome's Accademia di Santa Cecilia and with Reger and Mottl in Munich. Liuzzi was prof. of theory at the Parma Cons. (1910–17), and also was a teacher of composition at the Naples Cons. (1912–14). After serving as prof. of theory at the Florence Cons. (1917–23), he was prof. of musical aesthetics at the Univs. of Florence (1923–27) and Rome (1927–38). With the promulgation of the Fascist racial laws, he went to Belgium in 1939. After a sojourn in N.Y., he returned to his homeland in 1940. Among his writings were *Estetica della musica* (Florence, 1924) and *Musicista italiani in Francia* (Rome, 1946).

WORKS: *L'augellin bel verde,* puppet opera (Rome, 1917); *Le vergini savie e le vergini folli,* liturgical drama after a 12th-century French MS (Florence, 1930); *La Passione* for Soli, Chorus, and Orch. (1930); orch. music; chamber pieces; songs.

BIBL.: E. Ferand, "In Memoriam: F. L.," *Musical Quarterly* (Oct. 1942).

Liviabella, Lino, Italian composer; b. Macerata, April 7, 1902; d. Bologna, Oct. 21, 1964. He studied with Respighi at the Accademia di Santa Cecilia in Rome. He was director of the Pesaro Cons. from 1953 to 1959; then taught at Parma.

WORKS: DRAMATIC: *Conchiglia,* musical play (1955). **ORCH.:** *L'usignola e la Rosa* for Chamber Orch. (1926); *I canti dell' amore,* triptych for Strings (1929); *Suite per una fiaba* (1933); *Il Vincitore,* for the Berlin Olympiad (1936); *Il Poeta e sua moglia* (1938); *La mia terra* (1942). **CHAMBER:** 3 violin sonatas; String Quartet. **VOCAL:** 3 oratorios: *Sorella Chiara* (1947), *Caterina da Siena* (1949), and *O Crux Ave* (1953); songs.

Ljungberg, Göta (Albertina), Swedish soprano; b. Sundsval, Oct. 4, 1893; d. Lidingö, near Stockholm, June 28, 1955. She studied at the Royal Academy of Music and the Royal Opera School in Stockholm; later was a student of Mme. Cahier, of Fergusson in London, of Vanza in Milan, and of Bachner and Daniel in Berlin. In 1918 she made her operatic debut as Elsa at the Royal Stockholm Opera, remaining there until 1926; was a member of the Berlin State Opera (1926–32); also appeared at London's Covent Garden (1924–29), creating the title role there of Goossens's *Judith* (1929). She made her Metropolitan Opera debut in N.Y. as Sieglinde in *Die Walküre* on Jan. 20, 1932; she remained on the roster until 1935; created the role of Lady Marigold Sandys in Hanson's *Merry Mount* in its first stage production there in 1934. She subsequently taught voice in N.Y., and later in Sweden. Among her notable roles were Isolde, Brünnhilde, Salome, and Elektra.

Llobet, Miguel, famous Catalan guitarist; b. Barcelona, Oct. 18, 1875; d. there, Feb. 22, 1938. He began his career as a painter; then turned to music and studied with Alegre and Tarrega. He lived in Paris (1900–1914); toured in Argentina (1910), Chile (1912), the U.S. (1915–17), and throughout Europe. From 1918 he toured extensively in Latin America. He often appeared in a duo with his former pupil, Maria Luisa Anido. Falla composed his *Homenaje* (for the *Tombeau de Debussy*) for him, and Llobet himself made many outstanding transcriptions and arrangements for the guitar.

Lloyd, A(lbert) L(ancaster), English ethnomusicologist; b. London, Feb. 29, 1908; d. Greenwich, Sept. 29, 1982. He became interested in folk-song research while working on an Australian sheep farm (1926–35). His interest was furthered by his commitment to Socialism. In 1937–38 he collected whaling songs while working as a whaling fisherman in the Antarctic, and then traveled in South America and the Middle East. From 1950 he concentrated his research in southeastern Europe. He gave lectures in England and the U.S., and produced radio programs and documentary films.

EDITIONS: *Come All Ye Bold Miners: Songs and Ballads of the Coalfields* (London, 1952); with R. Vaughan Williams, *The Penguin Book of English Folk Song* (Harmondsworth, 1959).

WRITINGS: *The Singing Englishman: An Introduction to Folk Songs* (London, 1944); *Folk Song in England* (London, 1967).

Lloyd, David, American tenor; b. Minneapolis, Feb. 29, 1920. He was educated at the Minneapolis College of Music (B.A., 1941) and studied voice with Bonelli at the Curtis Inst. of Music in Philadelphia. On Oct. 13, 1950, he made his operatic debut as David in *Die Meistersinger von Nürnberg* at the N.Y. City Opera, where he sang regularly until 1958; he appeared there again in 1965 and 1976. His other operatic engagements took him to Boston, Washington, D.C., New Orleans, and St. Paul. In 1955 he sang at the Athens Festival and in 1957 at the Glyndebourne Festival. He also pursued an active career as a concert and oratorio singer. He taught at the Univ. of Ill. in Urbana (from 1971) and was director of the Lake George Opera Festival in N.Y. (from 1974). Lloyd was particularly admired for his roles in operas by Mozart, Rossini, and Richard Strauss.

Lloyd, David (John) de, Welsh composer and teacher; b. Skewen, April 30, 1883; d. Aberystwyth, Aug. 20, 1948. He studied at the Univ. College of Wales, Aberystwyth (B.A., 1903; B.Mus., 1905), the Leipzig Cons. (1906–07), and the Univ. of Dublin (Mus.D., 1915). He served as a lecturer (1919–26) and a prof. (1926–48) at the Univ. College of Wales. Among his works were the operas *Gwenllian* (1924) and *Tir na n-og* (1930); *Cylch corawl o ganeuon gwerin* (Choral Folksong Cycle) for Chorus and Orch. (1938); *Requiem cymraeg* (Welsh Requiem) for Soloists and Chorus (1947); other choral pieces and songs.

Lloyd, George (Walter Selwyn), English composer and conductor; b. St. Ives, Cornwall, June 28, 1913. He began violin lessons at 5 and commenced composing at 10. He later was a student of Albert Sammons (violin), C.H. Kitson (counterpoint), and Harry Farjeon (composition). In 1933 he attracted notice as a composer with the premiere of his 1st Sym. in Bournemouth, and then had further success with his operas *Iernin* (1933–34) and *The Serf* (1936–38). His career was interrupted when he enlisted in the Royal Marines in 1939. He served on Arctic convoy duty until he was severely shell-shocked in the attack on the HMS Trinidad in 1942. Following a long and arduous recuperation, he resumed composition with great ernestness. He was also active as a conductor and served as principal guest conductor and music advisor of the Albany (N.Y.) Sym. Orch. (1989–91). In his compositions, Lloyd embraced an unabashedly Romantic style of pleasurable accessibility.

WORKS: OPERAS: *Iernin* (1933–34; Penzance, Nov. 6, 1934); *The Serf* (1936–38; London, Oct. 20, 1938); *John Socman* (1949–51; Bristol, May 15, 1951). **ORCH.:** 12 syms. (1932; 1933; 1933; 1945–46; 1947–48; 1956; 1957–59; 1961; 1969; *November Journeys,* 1981; 1985; 1989); 4 piano concertos (*Scapegoat,* 1962–63; 1964; 1967–68; 1970); *Charade,* suite (1969); 2 violin concertos (1970, 1977); *Royal Parks* for Brass Band (1984); *Diversions on a Brass Theme* for Brass Band (1986); *The Forest of Arden* for Wind Band (1987); *English Heritage* for Brass Band (1989). **CHAMBER:** *Lament, Air, and Dance* for Violin and Piano (1975); Violin Sonata (1976); *Intercom Baby* for Violin (1977; also for Piano); *A Miniature Triptych* for Brass Quintet (1981). **PIANO:** *An African Shrine* (1966); *Aubade* for 2 Pianos (1971); *St. Anthony and the Bogside Beggar* (1972); *The Lily Leaf and the Grasshopper* (1972); *The Transformation of the Naked Ape* (1972); *The Aggressive Fishes* (1972); *The Road Through Samarkand* (1972). **VOCAL:** *The Vigil of Venus* for Chorus and Orch. (1979–80; London, Nov. 7, 1989); songs.

Lloyd, Jonathan, English composer; b. London, Sept. 30, 1948. He took composition lessons in London with Emile Spira (1963–65), and with Edwin Roxburgh (1965–66) and John Lambert (1966–69) at the Royal College of Music; also worked with Tristram Cary at the electronic music studio there and then completed his training with György Ligeti at the Berkshire Music Center in Tanglewood (summer, 1973). He was composer-in-residence at the Dartington College Theatre Dept. (1978–79). He has produced a number of compositions of considerable and lasting value, distinguished by a variety of forms and styles. His music theater work *Scattered Ruins* won the Koussevitzky Composition Prize in 1973.

WORKS: DRAMATIC: *Scattered Ruins,* music theater (Tanglewood, Aug. 1973); *Musices genus,* masque (1974); *The Adjudicator,* "community opera" (1985; Blewbury, April 15, 1986); *Blackmail,* music for Hitchcock's silent film (1992–93; Paris, March 13, 1993). **ORCH.:** *Cantique* for Small Orch. (1968; rev. 1970); *Time Caught by the Tail* for Strings and Percussion (1969); Concerto for Viola and Small Orch. (1979–80; London, Nov. 10, 1981); *Fantasy* for Violin and Orch. (1980); *Rhapsody* for Cello and Orch. (1982); 5 syms.: No. 1 (1983; Birmingham, Jan. 19, 1989), No. 2 (1983–84; Baden-Baden, Feb. 12, 1988), No. 3 for Chamber Orch. (Wilde Festival, June 27, 1987), No. 4 (London, July 26, 1988), and No. 5 (1989; Birmingham, Jan. 14, 1990); *Wa Wa Mozart* for Piano and Chamber Orch. (London, Dec. 5, 1991); *There* for Guitar and Strings (1991; Aldeburgh, Jan. 1, 1992); *Tolerance* (1993); *Blessed Days of Blue* for Flute and Strings (1995); Violin Concerto (1995); Piano Concerto (1995). **ENSEMBLE:** *Won't It Ever Be Morning* (1980); *Waiting for Gozo* (1981; London, Jan. 15, 1982); *3 Dances* (Reykjavík, June 18, 1982); *Don't Mention the War* (1982; Montepulciano, Aug. 2, 1983); *The Shorelines of Certainty* (Aldeburgh Festival, June 17, 1984; incorporated in *Songs from the Other Shore,* 1984–86; London, May 11, 1986); *Time between Trains* (Wilde Festival, June 30, 1984); *The New Ear* (Colchester, Sept. 28, 1985); *Almeida Dances* (London, June 25, 1986); *Dancing in the Ruins* (Warwick, July 12, 1990). **CHAMBER:** *John's Journal* for Saxophone and Piano (1980); 2 string quintets: No. 1 for 2 Violins, 2 Violas, and Cello (1982) and No. 2 for Mandolin, Lute, Guitar, Harp, and Double Bass (1982); Brass Quintet for 2 Trumpets, 2 Trombones, and Tuba (1982); Wind Quintet for Flute, Oboe, Clarinet, Bassoon, and Horn (1982; London, Jan. 5, 1984); String Quartet No. 1, "Of Time and Motion" (1984; London, June 25, 1986); Oboe Sonata (1985); *The 5 Senses* for Flute and Guitar (1985); *True Refuge* for Clarinet and Piano (1985); *Feuding Fiddles* for 2 Violins (1986); *1 Step More* for Flute, Oboe, Cello, and Harpsichord (1986); *Airs and Graces* for Violin (1987); *He Will Make It* for Cello (1988); *Restless Night* for Wind Quintet (Bournemouth, June 29, 1991); *There and Then* for Guitar Duo (1991–92; Exeter, June 20, 1992. **VOCAL:** *Coming into Gone* for Chanters and Orch. (1974); *The Other Shore* for Chorus and Orch. (1975); *Everything Returns* for Wordless Soprano and Orch. (1977–78; BBC, Oct. 4, 1979); *3 Songs* for Voice, Viola, and Piano (1980); *Toward the Whitening Dawn* for Chorus and Chamber Orch. (1980; London, March 4, 1981); *If I Could Turn You On* for High Soprano and Chamber Orch.

(1981); *No Man's Land* for Chorus and Orch. (1982); *Mass* for 6 Solo Voices (1983; London, April 10, 1984); *Missa Brevis* for Double Chorus (1984); *Revelation* for Chorus (London, Nov. 4, 1990); *Marching to a Different Song* for Soprano and Chamber Orch. (1990; Bracknell, April 14, 1991); *People Your Dreams* for Voice and Ensemble (1994).

Lloyd, Norman, American music educator and composer; b. Pottsville, Pa., Nov. 8, 1909; d. Greenwich, Conn., July 31, 1980. He was educated at N.Y. Univ. (B.S., 1932; M.S., 1936). After teaching at Sarah Lawrence College (1936–46), he was director of education (1946–49) and a teacher (1949–63) at the Juilliard School of Music in N.Y.; he then was dean of the Oberlin (Ohio) College Cons. of Music (1963–65) before serving as director of arts programming for the Rockefeller Foundation (1965–72). He composed numerous dance and film scores, as well as band music, choruses, and piano pieces. He publ. *The Fireside Book of Favorite American Songs* (1947), *The Fireside Book of Love Songs* (1954), and the *Golden Encyclopedia of Music* (1968).

Lloyd, Robert (Andrew), esteemed English bass-baritone; b. Southend-on-Sea, March 2, 1940. He studied history at Keble College, Oxford, then voice with Otakar Kraus at the London Opera Centre (1968–69), making his debut at London's Collegiate Theatre as Beethoven's Fernando (1969). He was a member of Sadler's Wells (1969–72) and the Royal Opera at Covent Garden (1972–83) in London; also made guest appearances in Berlin, Paris, Hamburg, Milan, Munich, San Francisco, Salzburg, and Vienna. On Oct. 26, 1988, he made his Metropolitan Opera debut in N.Y. as Rossini's Basilio. In 1990 he became the first English singer to appear as Boris Godunov at the Kirov Opera in Leningrad. In 1991 he was made a Commander of the Order of the British Empire. Among his best roles are Sarastro, the Commendatore, Oroveso, Banquo, Boris Godunov, King Philip, and Gurnemanz (he appeared as the latter in the Syberberg film version of *Parsifal* in 1981).

Lloyd-Jones, David (Mathias), English conductor; b. London, Nov. 19, 1934. He studied at Magdalen College, Oxford. He appeared as a guest conductor with the leading British opera houses, including Covent Garden, the English National Opera, the Scottish Opera, and the Welsh National Opera; in 1978 he was named music director of the newly organized English National Opera North in Leeds, which was renamed Opera North in 1981; he retained this post until 1990; in 1989 he became artistic adviser of the Guildhall School of Music and Drama in London. He conducted the English premieres of works from the traditional and modern operatic repertoire; also ed. the full score of Mussorgsky's *Boris Godunov* (1975) and Borodin's *Prince Igor* (1982).

Lloyd Webber, Andrew, Lord Lloyd Webber, tremendously successful English composer, brother of **Julian Lloyd Webber**; b. London, March 22, 1948. His father, William Southcombe Lloyd Webber, was the director of the London College of Music and his mother was a piano teacher; inspired and conditioned by such an environment, Lloyd Webber learned to play piano, violin, and horn, and soon began to improvise music, mostly in the style of American musicals. He attended Westminster School in London, then went to Magdalen College, Oxford, the Guildhall School of Music in London, and the Royal College of Music in London. In college he wrote his first musical, *The Likes of Us*, dealing with a philanthropist. In 1967, at the age of 19, he composed the theatrical show *Joseph and the Amazing Technicolor Dreamcoat*, which was performed at St. Paul's Junior School in London in 1968; it was later expanded to a full-scale production (Edinburgh, Aug. 21, 1972), and achieved considerable success for its amalgam of a biblical subject with rock music, French chansonnettes, and country-western songs. In 1970 it was produced in America and in 1972 was shown on television. He achieved his first commercial success with *Jesus Christ Superstar*, an audacious treatment of the religious theme in terms of jazz and rock. It was premiered in London on Aug. 9, 1972, and ran for 3,357 performances; it was as successful in America. Interestingly enough, the "rock opera," as it was called, was first released as a record album, which eventually sold 3 million copies. *Jesus Christ Superstar* opened on Broadway on Oct. 12, 1971, even before the London production. There were protests by religious groups against the irreverent treatment of a sacred subject; particularly offensive was the suggestion in the play of a carnal relationship between Jesus and Mary Magdalen; Jewish organizations, on the other hand, protested against the implied portrayal of the Jews as guilty of the death of Christ. The musical closed on Broadway on June 30, 1973, after 720 performances; it received 7 Tony awards. In 1981 the recording of *Jesus Christ Superstar* was given the Grammy Award for best cast show album of the year. The great hullabaloo about the musical made a certainty of his further successes. His early musical *Joseph and the Amazing Technicolor Dreamcoat* was revived at the off-Broadway Entermedia Theatre in N.Y.'s East Village on Nov. 18, 1981, and from there moved to the Royale Theater on Broadway. In the meantime, he produced a musical with a totally different chief character, *Evita*, a semi-fictional account of the career of the first wife of Argentine dictator Juan Perón; it was first staged in London on June 21, 1978; a N.Y. performance soon followed, with splendid success. It was followed by the spectacularly successful *Cats*, inspired by T.S. Eliot's *Old Possum's Book of Practical Cats*; it was premiered in London on May 11, 1981, and was brought out in N.Y. in Oct. 1982 with fantastic success; *Evita* and *Joseph and the Amazing Technicolor Dreamcoat* were still playing on Broadway, so that Lloyd Webber had the satisfaction of having 3 of his shows running at the same time. Subsequent successful productions were his *Song and Dance* (London, March 26, 1981) and *Starlight Express* (London, March 19, 1984). His series of commercial successes reached a lucrative apex with the production of *The Phantom of the Opera* (London, Oct. 9, 1986), a gothically oriented melodramatic tale of contrived suspense. On April 17, 1989, his musical *Aspects of Love* opened in London. His musical setting of the 1950 Billy Wilder film *Sunset Boulevard* was first staged in London on July 12, 1993. Apart from popular shows, Lloyd Webber wrote a mini-opera, *Tell Me on a Sunday*, about an English girl living in N.Y., which was produced by BBC Television in 1980. Quite different in style and intent were his *Variations* for Cello and Jazz Ensemble (1978), written for his brother, and his *Requiem Mass* (N.Y., Feb. 24, 1985). He was knighted in 1992 and made a lord in 1996.

BIBL.: G. McKnight, *A. L.W.* (London and N.Y., 1984); J. Mantle, *Fanfare: The Unauthorized Biography of A. L.W.* (London, 1989); M. Walsh, *A. L.W.: His Life and Works* (N.Y., 1989); H. Mühe, *Die Musik von A. L. W.* (Hamburg, 1993).

Lloyd Webber, Julian, talented English cellist, brother of **Andrew Lloyd Webber**; b. London, April 14, 1951. He studied with Douglas Cameron (1964–67) and then at the Royal College of Music in London (1967–71); he subsequently studied with Pierre Fournier in Geneva (1973). He made his London debut as soloist in the Bliss Cello Concerto in 1972; subsequently played many engagements as a soloist with English orchs. He made his American debut in N.Y. in 1980. In 1978 he became prof. of cello at the Guildhall School of Music in London. He publ. an account of his career, *Travels with My Cello* (1984), and also ed. *Song of the Birds: Sayings, Stories and Impressions of Pablo Casals* (London, 1985). His exhaustive repertoire embraces both traditional and contemporary works, ranging from Haydn to Rodrigo.

Lobaczewska (Gérard de Festenburg), Stefania, Polish musicologist; b. Lemberg, July 31, 1888; d. Kraków, Jan. 16, 1963. She studied piano with V. Kurc at the Lemberg Cons., then musicology with Adler at the Univ. of Vienna and with Chybiński at the Univ. of Lemberg (1914–18; Ph.D., 1929, with the diss. *O harmonice Klaudiusza Achillesa Debussy' ego w pierwszym okresie jego twórczosci* [Claude Achille Debussy's Harmony in His First Creative Period]; publ. in Kwartalnik Muzyczny, II/5, 1929–30); completed her Habilitation at the Univ. of Poznań in 1949, with his *Karol Szymanowski: Życie i* *twórczość (1882–1937)* (Karol Szymanowski: Life and Works [1882–1937]; publ. in Kraków, 1950). She taught at the Szymanowski School of Music in Lwów (1931–39) and at the Lwów Cons. (1940–41), then went to Kraków (1945), where she became a prof. at the State College of Music; later served as its rector until 1955; was also head of the musicology dept. at the Univ. of Kraków (1952–63).

WRITINGS: *Zarys estetyki muzycznej* (Outline of Music Aesthetics; Lwów, 1937); *Tablice do historii muzyki* (Kraków, 1949); *Zarys historii form muzycznych: Próba ujecia socjologicznego* (Outline of the History of Musical Form: Attempt at a Sociological Approach; Kraków, 1950); *Ludwik van Beethoven* (Kraków, 1953; 2nd ed., 1955); *W klad Chopina do romantyzmu europejskiego* (Chopin's Contribution to European Romanticism; Warsaw, 1955); *Style muzyczne* (Kraków, 1960–62).

Lockhart, James (Lawrence), Scottish conductor; b. Edinburgh, Oct. 16, 1930. He studied at the Univ. of Edinburgh and at the Royal College of Music in London. He served as apprentice conductor of the Yorkshire Sym. Orch. (1954–55), assistant conductor at Munster (1955–56), the Bavarian State Opera in Munich (1956–57), Glyndebourne (1957–59), and Covent Garden in London (1959–68). Intercalatorily, he was music director of the Opera Workshop of the Univ. of Texas in Austin (1957–59), and conductor of the BBC Scottish Sym. Orch. in Glasgow (1960–61). From 1968 to 1973 he was music director of the Welsh National Opera in Cardiff; from 1972 to 1980 he served as Generalmusikdirektor of the State Theater in Kassel; from 1981 to 1991 he was Generalmusikdirektor of the Rheinische Phil. in Koblenz and at the Koblenz Opera. He was head of the opera school at the Royal College of Music from 1986. In 1992 he became director of opera at the London Royal Schools Vocal Faculty.

Lockhart, Keith, American conductor; b. Poughkeepsie, N.Y., Nov. 7, 1959. He received instruction in piano at the Juilliard School's preparatory division in N.Y., and at the Vienna Hochschule für Musik (1979). Following studies in piano (B.Mus., 1981) and German (B.A., 1981) at Furman Univ. in Greenville, S.C., he took his M.F.A. degree in conducting at Carnegie-Mellon Univ. in Pittsburgh (1983). He also studied conducting at the Aspen (Colo.) Music School (summer, 1980), the American Sym. Orch. League conductor's workshops in Morgantown, W.Va. (summers, 1982–83), and the Dutch Radio's master classes in Hilversum (1988). In 1989 he was a conducting fellow of the Los Angeles Phil. Inst. He was resident conductor (1983–86) and director of orch. activities (1986–89) at Carnegie-Mellon Univ. From 1985 to 1990 he was music director of the Pittsburgh Civic Orch. He was assistant conductor of the Akron (Ohio) Sym. Orch. (1988–90), and concurrently was music director of the Akron Youth Sym. In 1990 he joined the staff of the Cincinnati Sym. Orch. and the Cincinnati Pops Orch., where he was assistant conductor (to 1992), assoc. conductor (1992–95), and artistic director of education and outreach (1995–96). From 1992 he also was music director of the Cincinnati Chamber Orch. In 1995 he became conductor of the Boston Pops Orch. As a guest conductor, he has appeared with various North American orchs.

Locklair, Dan (Steven), American composer, organist, and teacher; b. Charlotte, N.C., Aug. 7, 1949. He was educated at Mars Hill (N.C.) College (B.M., 1971), Union Theological Seminary in N.Y. (S.M.M., 1973), and the Eastman School of Music in Rochester, N.Y. (D.M.A., 1982); among his mentors were Robert Baker (1971–73) and David Craighead (1979–80) in organ and Ezra Laderman (1975–77), Samuel Adler (1979), and Joseph Schwantner (1980) in composition. After serving as a church musician in Binghamton, N.Y. (1973–82), he was composer-in-residence and an assoc. prof. of music at Wake Forest Univ. in Winston-Salem, N.C. (from 1982). He received annual ASCAP awards from 1981; in 1989, won the Barlow International Composition Competition. His works are handsomely wrought within tonal parameters.

WORKS: DRAMATIC: *Good Tidings from the Holy Beast,* opera (Lincoln, Nebr., Dec. 21, 1978); *Scintillations,* ballet (1986; Winston-Salem, N.C., March 13, 1987). **ORCH.:** *Prism of Life* (1980–81; Charlotte, N.C., May 12, 1982); *Dances* (1981; Binghamton, N.Y., May 15, 1982); *Phoenix and Again,* overture (1983; Winston-Salem, N.C., Jan. 29, 1984); *In the Autumn Days,* sym. for Chamber Orch. (1984; Omaha, April 20, 1985); *When Morning Stars Begin to Fall,* tone poem (1986; Knoxville, Tenn., April 23, 1987); *Creation's Seeing Order* (1987; Charlotte, N.C., April 13, 1988); *Dayspring,* fanfare/concertino for Guitar and Orch. (1988; Winston-Salem, N.C., June 13, 1989); Concerto Grosso for Harpsichord, Strings, and Percussion (1990–92); *Hues* (1993; Fayetteville, N.C., Oct. 27, 1994); *Since Dawn,* tone poem for Narrator, Chorus, and Orch. (1995); *"Ere long we shall see . . .",* concerto brevis for Organ and Orch. (1995–96). **CHAMBER:** *Constellations,* concerto for Organ and Percussionists (1980); *Music of Quince* for Flute, Clarinet, Violin, and Piano (1981; New Milford, Conn., Aug. 15, 1984); *Petrus: In Bright Array* for Brass Quintet (1988–89); *Through the Winds* for Wind Quintet and Piano (1989; Winston-Salem, N.C., April 14, 1990); *Dream Steps,* dance suite for Flute, Viola, and Harp (choreographed version, Raleigh, N.C., Oct. 16, 1993; concert version, Washington, D.C., Oct. 24, 1993); *Diminishing Returns* for 7 Percussionists and Piano (1994). **KEYBOARD: PIANO:** *Visions in the Haze* (1982); Sonata (1987); *6 Interval Inventions* (1988); organ pieces; harpsichord music. **VOCAL:** *Lairs of Soundings* for Soprano and Double String Orch. (Binghamton, N.Y., Nov. 13, 1982); *Tapestries* for Chorus, Handbells, and Piano (1982; N.Y., Jan. 31, 1987); *Missa Brevis,* "The Brass Mass" for Chorus and Brass Quintet (1985–87; Oneonta, N.Y., Nov. 14, 1987); *"changing perceptions" and Epitaph* for Chorus and Piano (Portland, Maine, Oct. 25, 1987); *The Columbus Madrigals* for Treble Voices (Stroudsburg, Pa., June 16, 1991); *Windswept (the trees)* for Chorus, Wind Quintet, and Piano (1992; Charlotte, N.C., Feb. 25, 1994); *For Amber Waves* for 5 Choruses (1992); *Brief Mass* for Chorus (1993); *Poems 'n Pairs* for Children's Voices and Piano (1994).

Lockspeiser, Edward, English writer on music; b. London, May 21, 1905; d. Alfriston, Sussex, Feb. 3, 1973. He went to Paris in 1922, where he studied with Tansman. After studies with Boulanger (1925–26), he returned to London and completed his training at the Royal College of Music (1929–30) with Kitson and Sargent. He was on the staff of the BBC (1942–51). Lockspeiser distinguished himself as a writer on French music.

WRITINGS (all publ. in London unless otherwise given): *Debussy* (1936; 5th ed., rev., 1980); *Berlioz* (1939); *Bizet* (1951); ed. *Lettres inédites de Claude Debussy à Andre Caplet (1908–1914)* (Monaco, 1957); *The Literary Clef: An Anthology of Letters and Writings by French Composers* (1958); *Debussy et Edgar Poe: Manuscrits et documents inédits* (Monaco, 1961); *Debussy: His Life and Mind* (2 vols., 1962, 1965; 2nd ed., rev., 1978); *Music and Painting: A Study in Comparative Ideas from Turner to Schoenberg* (1973).

Lockwood, Annea (actually, **Anna Ferguson**), New Zealand composer and instrument builder; b. Christchurch, July 29, 1939. She studied at Canterbury Univ. in New Zealand (B.Mus., 1961); then went to London, where she took courses with Fricker (composition) and E. Kendall Taylor (piano) at the Royal College of Music (diplomas in both, 1963); also attended courses in new music in Darmstadt (1961–62), had lessons with Koenig at the Hochschule für Musik in Cologne (1963–64), and studied at the Bilthoven (Netherlands) Electronic Music Center (1963–64); also worked in computer composition at the Electronic Music Studio in Putney, England (1970), and undertook research at the Univ. of Southampton's Inst. for Sound and Vibration Research (1969–72). In 1968 she gave non-lectures at the Anti-Univ. of London; later taught at Hunter College of the City Univ. of N.Y. (1973–83) and at Vassar College (from 1982), where she subsequently became a prof. and head of the music dept. In 1968, with her then husband, Harvey Matusow, she undertook a series of experiments in total art, including aural, oral, visual, tactile, gustatory, and olfactory demonstrations and sporadic transcendental manifestations; of these, the most remarkable was the summoning (in German) of Beethoven's ghost at a seance held in London on Oct. 3, 1968, with sound recorded on magnetic tape, which in playback revealed some surprisingly dissonant music of apparently metapsychic origin, tending to indicate that Beethoven was a posthumous avant-garde composer. The seance was preceded by the burning of a combustible piano and of an inflammable microphone. Since the mid-1970s, her concerns have been with aural perception and the utilization of sounds found in nature and the environment in participatory or on-site installations and performance pieces. From the mid-1980s she has written largely for acoustic instruments and voices.

WORKS (descriptive materials provided by the composer): Violin Concerto (1962); *À Abélard, Heloïse*, chamber cantata for Mezzo-soprano and 10 Instruments (1963); *Glass Concert* for 2 Performers and Amplified Glass (1966); *River Archives*, recordings of select world rivers and streams (1966–); *Tiger Balm*, tape collage of sensual and erotic sounds including sonic images of a woman and a tiger making love (1972); *Malaman*, solo chant using very old words for sound from many languages, based upon the belief that these words contain and can release specific, useful acoustic energy (1974); *World Rhythms*, 10-channel live mix of the sounds of such natural phenomena as earthquakes, radio waves from a pulsar star, fire, human breathing, tree frogs, geysers, etc., together with a biorhythm produced by a gong player (1975); *Spirit Songs Unfolding* for Tape and Slides (1977); *Delta Run*, mixed-media work for Tape, Slide Projection, and Movement centered around a dying sculptor's reflections on death (1982); *A Sound Map of the Hudson River*, installation work tracing the course of the Hudson, by means of recordings of water and ambient sounds made over the course of a year along its banks, from source to ocean (1982–83); *Night and Fog*, settings of texts by Osip Mandelstam and Carolyn Forché for Baritone, Baritone Saxophone, Percussion, and Tape (1987); *The Secret Life* for Amplified Double Bass, using a form of improvisatory ventriloquism with the player initially talking about his or her relationship with the bass, then the point of view shifting to the bass itself, which talks back to the player, all spoken material being transduced through the bass itself (1989); *Amazonia Dreaming* for Snare Drum (1989); *Red Mesa* for Amplified Piano (1989); *Thousand Year Dreaming* for Conch Shells, 4 Didjeridus, Winds, Trombones, Frame Drums and Other Percussion, and Projections of Images from the Lascaux Caves (1990); *The Angle of Repose* for Baritone, Alto Flute, and Khaen (1991); *I Give You Back* for Mezzo-soprano, after Joy Harjo (1992); *Western Spaces* for Flutes, Zoomoozophone, and Percussion (1995); *Monkey Trips* for Strings, Winds, Percussion, and Non-Western Instruments (1995; in collaboration with the California E.A.R. Unit).

Lockwood, Lewis (Henry), distinguished American musicologist; b. N.Y., Dec. 16, 1930. He was a student of Lowinsky at Queens College in N.Y. (B.A., 1952) and of Strunk and Mendel at Princeton Univ. (M.F.A., 1955; Ph.D., 1960, with the diss. *The Counter-Reformation and the Sacred Music of Vincenzo Ruffo*; publ. in Venice, 1970). In 1958 he joined the faculty of Princeton Univ., where he was an assoc. prof. (1965–68), prof. (1968–80), and chairman of the music dept. (1970–73). In 1980 he became prof. of music at Harvard Univ., where he served as the Fanny Peabody Prof. of Music from 1984. He also was chairman of the music dept. (1988–90). In 1973–74 and 1984–85 he was an NEH Senior Fellow. In 1977–78 he held a Guggenheim fellowship. In 1984 he was elected a member of the American Academy of Arts and Sciences. He served as president of the American Musicological Soc. in 1987–88, and was made an honorary member in 1993. In 1991 he was awarded an honorary doctorate by the Università degli Studi in Ferrara. In addition to his studies of music of the Italian Renaissance, Lockwood has devoted himself to the elucidation of Beethoven's life and works with special emphasis on his creative process as revealed in his sketches and autographs. He publ. the valuable books *Music in Renaissance Ferrara, 1400–1505: The Creation of a Musical Center in the Italian Renaissance* (1984) and *Beethoven: Studies in the Creative Process* (1992), the latter the winner of the ASCAP-Deems Taylor Award in 1993. He also served as general ed. of the series Studies in Musical Genesis and Structure (from 1984) and as co-ed. of the series Studies in Music History (from 1981), *Beethoven Essays: Studies in Honor of Elliot Forbes* (1984), *Essays in Musicology: A Tribute to Alvin Johnson* (1990), and the yearbook *Beethoven Forum* (from 1991).

Lockwood, Normand, American composer and teacher; b. N.Y., March 19, 1906. He studied at the Univ. of Mich. (1921–24), and with Respighi in Rome (1925–26) and Boulanger in Paris (1926–28); he was a Fellow at the American Academy in Rome (1929–31). Upon his return to America, he was an instructor in music at the Oberlin (Ohio) Cons. (1932–43); from 1945 to 1953, was a lecturer at Columbia Univ., then at Trinity Univ. in San Antonio (1953–55); later taught at the Univ. of Hawaii and at the Univ. of Oregon (1955–61). In 1961 he was appointed a member of the faculty of the Univ. of Denver; became prof. emeritus in 1974. Lockwood's compositions are well crafted in an accessible style.

WORKS: OPERAS: *The Scarecrow* (N.Y., May 19, 1945); *Early Dawn* (Denver, Aug. 7, 1961); *The Wizards of Balizar* (Denver, Aug. 1, 1962); *The Hanging Judge* (Denver, March 1964); *Requiem for a Rich Young Man* (Denver, Nov. 24, 1964). **ORCH.:** 2 syms. (1935; 1978–79); *Moby Dick* for Chamber Orch. (1946); 2 concertos for Organ and Brass (1950, 1970); Oboe Concerto (1966); *Symphonic Sequences* (1966); *From an Opening to a Close* for Wind Instruments and Percussion (1967); *Panegyric* for Horn and Strings (1978–79); Concerto for 2 Harps and Strings (1981); *Prayers and Fanfares* for Brass, Strings, and Percussion (1982). **CHAMBER:** 7 string quartets (1933–50); Piano Quintet (1940); *6 Serenades* for String Quartet (1945); Clarinet Quintet (1960); Sonata for 4 Cellos (1968); *Excursions* for 4 String Basses (1976); *Tripartito* for Flute and Guitar (1980); Piano Trio (1985). **VOCAL:** *The Closing Doxology* for Chorus, Symphonic Band, and Percussion (1952); *Prairie* for Chorus and Orch. (1952); *Magnificat* for Soprano, Chorus, and Orch. (1954); oratorios, including *Children of God* (1956; Cincinnati, Feb. 1, 1957), *Light out of Darkness* (1957), *Land of Promise* (1960), and *For the Time Being* (1971); cantatas; choruses; song cycles; solo songs.

BIBL.: K. Norton, *N. L.: His Life and Music* (Metuchen, N.J., 1993).

Loeffler, Charles Martin (Tornow), outstanding Alsatian-born American composer; b. Mulhouse, Jan. 30, 1861; d. Medfield, Mass., May 19, 1935. His father was a writer who sometimes used the nom de plume Tornow, which Loeffler later added to his name. When he was a child, the family moved to Russia, where his father was engaged in government work in the Kiev district; later they lived in Debrecen, and in Switzerland. In 1875 Loeffler began taking violin lessons in Berlin with Rappoldi, who prepared him for study with Joachim; he studied theory with Kiel; also took lessons with Bargiel at the Berlin Hochschule für Musik (1874–77). He then went to Paris, where he continued his musical education with Massart (violin) and Guiraud (counterpoint and composition). He was engaged briefly as a violinist in the Pasdeloup Orch.; then was a member of the private orch. of the Russian Baron Paul von Derwies at his sumptuous residences near Lugano and in Nice (1879–81). When Derwies died in 1881, Loeffler went to the U.S., with letters of recommendation from Joachim; he became a naturalized American citizen in 1887. He played in the orch. of Leopold Damrosch in N.Y. in 1881–82. In 1882 he became 2nd concertmaster of the newly organized Boston Sym. Orch., but was able to accept other engagements during late spring and summer months; the summers of 1883 and 1884 he spent in Paris, where he took violin lessons with Hubert Leonard. He resigned from the Boston Sym. Orch. in 1903, and devoted himself to composition and farming in Medfield. He was married to Elise Burnett Fay (1910). After his death, she donated to the Library of Congress in Washington, D.C., all of his MSS, correspondence, etc.; by his will, he left the material assets of his not inconsiderable estate to the French Academy and the Paris Cons. He was an officer of the French Academy (1906); a Chevalier in the French Legion of Honor (1919); a member of the American Academy of Arts and Letters; Mus. Doc. (*honoris causa*), Yale Univ. (1926).

Loeffler's position in American music is unique, brought up as he was under many different national influences, Alsatian, French, German, Russian, and Ukrainian. One of his most vivid scores, *Memories of My Childhood,* written as late as 1924, reflects the modal feeling of Russian and Ukrainian folk songs. But his aesthetic code was entirely French, with definite leanings toward Impressionism; the archaic constructions that he sometimes affected, and the stylized evocations of "ars antiqua," are also in keeping with the French manner. His most enduring work, *A Pagan Poem,* is cast in such a neo-archaic vein. He was a master of colorful orchestration; his harmonies are opulent without saturation; his rhapsodic forms are peculiarly suited to the evocative moods of his music. His only excursion into the American idiom was the employment of jazz rhythms in a few of his lesser pieces.

WORKS: DRAMATIC: OPERAS: *The Passion of Hilarion* (1912–13); *Les Amants jaloux* (1918); *The Peony Lantern* (c.1919). **INCIDENTAL MUSIC:** *Ouverture pour le T.C. Minstrel Entertainment* (Boston, 1906?); *The Countess Cathleen* (Concord, Mass., May 8, 1924; not extant); *The Reveller* (Boston, Dec. 22, 1925). **ORCH.:** *Les Veillées de l'Ukraine* for Violin and Orch. (1888?–91; Boston, Nov. 20, 1891; rev. version, Boston, Nov. 24, 1899); *Morceau fantastique: Fantastic Concerto* for Cello and Orch. (1893; Boston, Feb. 2, 1894); *Divertissement* for Violin and Orch. (1894; Boston, Jan. 4, 1895); *La Mort de Tintagiles* for 2 Violas d'Amore and Orch. (1897; Boston, Jan. 7, 1898; rev. for Viola d'Amore and Orch., 1900; Boston, Feb. 15, 1901); *Divertissement espagnol* for Saxophone and Orch. (1900; Boston, Jan. 29, 1901); *Poem (La Bonne Chanson; Avant que tu ne t'en ailles*; 1901; Boston, April 11, 1902; rev. 1915; Boston, Nov. 1, 1918); *La Villanelle du diable* (1901; Boston, April 11, 1902; revision of his 3rd song in the set *Rapsodies,* 1898); *A Pagan Poem* (1904–06; Boston, Oct. 29, 1907; revision of *Poème païen* for 13 Instruments, 1901–02); *Memories of My Childhood* (Life in a Russian Village) (Evanston, Ill., May 30, 1924); *Intermezzo (Clowns)* for Jazz Band (Boston, Feb. 19, 1928). **CHAMBER:** *Danse bizarre* for Violin (1881); String Sextet (c.1885–92; Boston, Feb. 27, 1893); Violin Sonata (1886); String Quartet (1889); Quintet for 3 Violins, Viola, and Cello (1894?; Boston, Feb. 18, 1895); Octet for 2 Clarinets, 2 Violins, Viola, Cello, Double Bass, and Harp (1896?; Boston, Feb. 15, 1897); *Le passeur d'eau* for 2 Violins, 2 Violas, and 2 Cellos (1900; Boston, Dec. 10, 1909); *Deux Rapsodies* for Oboe, Viola, and Piano (Boston, Dec. 16, 1901); *Poème païen (d'aprés Virgil)* for 2 Flutes, Oboe, Clarinet, English Horn, 2 Horns, Viola, Double Bass, Piano, and 3 Trumpets (1901–02; also as *Poème antique d'aprés Virgil* for 2 Pianos and 3 Trumpets, 1902–03; Boston, April 13, 1903; rev. 1904–06 as *A Pagan Poem* for Orch.); *Ballade carnavalesque* for Flute, Oboe, Saxophone, Bassoon, and Piano (1902; Boston, Jan. 25, 1904); *Poème (Scène dramatique)* for Cello ad Piano (1916; N.Y., Jan. 27, 1917); *Music for 4 Stringed Instruments* for String Quartet (1917; rev. 1918–19; N.Y., Feb. 15, 1919; rev. 1920); *Historiettes* for String Quartet and Harp (1922); pieces for violin and piano; various unfinished works. **VOCAL:** *L'Archet* for Soprano, Women's Chorus, Viola d'Amore, and Piano (c.1897–99; Boston, Feb. 4, 1902); *The Sermon on the Mount* for Women's Chorus, 2 Violas d'Amore, Viola da Gamba, Harp, and Organ (1901?; unfinished); *Psalm 137 (By the Rivers of Babylon)* for Women's Chorus, Organ, Harp, 2 Flutes, and Cello Obbligato (1901?; Boston, Feb. 28, 1902); *Ave maris stella* for Boy's Voices, Soprano, Strings, Piano, and Organ (c.1906–12); *For One Who Fell in Battle* for Chorus (Boston, Dec. 13, 1906; rev. as *Ode for One Who Fell in Battle* for Chorus, 1911; Boston, March 21, 1912); *Poème mystique* for Boy's Chorus, Chorus, 4 Horns, 2 Contrabasses, Harp, and Organ (1907; also for Baritone, Chorus, 4 Horns, and 2 Contrabasses; unfinished); *Hora mystica* for Men's Chorus and Orch. (1915; Norfolk, Conn., June 6, 1916); *Beat! Beat! Drums!* for Men's Voices and Piano (1917; also 3 other versions, including one for Men's Voices and Band, 1927–32; Cleveland, Dec. 17, 1932); *5 Irish Fantasies* for Voice and Orch. (1920; numbers 2, 3, and 5, Boston, March 10, 1922; numbers 1 and 4, Cleveland, Nov. 7, 1929); *Canticum fratris solis (Canticle of the Sun)* for Voice and Chamber Orch. (Washington, D.C., Oct. 28, 1925); *Evocation* for Women's Voices and Orch. (1930; for the opening of Severance Hall, Cleveland, Feb. 5, 1931); over 45 songs.

BIBL.: C. Engel, "C.M. L.," *Musical Quarterly* (July 1925); idem, "C.M. L.," *Chesterian,* VI (1928); E.B. Hill, "C.M. L," *Modern Music* (Nov.–Dec. 1935); W. Damrosch, *C.M. L.* (N.Y., 1936); E. Waters, "New L.iana," *Library of Congress Quarterly Journal* (April–June 1945); H. Colvin, *C.M. L.: His Life and Works* (diss., Univ. of Rochester, 1959); E. Henry, *Impressionism in the Arts and Its Influence on Selected Works of C.M. L. and Charles Tomlinson Griffes* (diss., Univ. of Cincinnati, 1976); E. Knight, "C.M. L. and George Gershwin: A Forgotten Friendship," *American Music* (Winter 1985); idem, *C.M. L.: A Life Apart in American Music* (Urbana, 1993).

Loesser, Arthur, esteemed American pianist, teacher, and writer on music, half-brother of **Frank (Henry) Loesser**; b. N.Y., Aug. 26, 1894; d. Cleveland, Jan. 4, 1969. He studied with Stojowski and Goetschius at the Inst. of Musical Art in N.Y. He made his debut in Berlin (1913). He first played in N.Y. in 1916; after touring the Orient and Australia (1920–21), he appeared widely in the U.S. In 1926 he was appointed a prof. of piano at the Cleveland Inst. of Music. In 1943 he was commissioned in the U.S. Army as an officer in the Japanese intelligence dept.; mastered the language and, after the war, gave lectures in Japanese in Tokyo; was the first American musician in uniform to play for a Japanese audience (1946). He publ. *Humor in American Song* (N.Y., 1943) and an entertaining vol., *Men, Women and Pianos: A Social History* (N.Y., 1954).

Loesser, Frank (Henry), talented American composer and lyricist, half-brother of **Arthur Loesser**; b. N.Y., June 29, 1910; d. there, July 28, 1969. He was educated at City College in N.Y., where he began writing songs for college activities; he subsequently was active as a reporter, singer, vaudeville performer, and nightclub pianist. In 1936 he settled in Hollywood and devoted himself mainly to writing film scores. During World War II he was in the U.S. Army, and wrote several Army songs, including *Praise the Lord and Pass the Ammunition* (1942) and *Roger Young* (1945). Although he continued to compose successful songs, he found his greatest reward in producing shows for Broadway; these included *Where's Charley?* (Oct. 11, 1948), *Guys and Dolls* (Nov. 24, 1950), *A Most Happy Fella* (May 3, 1956), and *How to Succeed in Business Without Really Trying* (Oct. 14, 1961), which won a Pulitzer Prize and ran for 1,417 performances. His last musical was *Pleasures and Palaces* (Detroit, March 11, 1965).

BIBL.: A. Loesser, "My Brother F.," *Notes* (March 1950); M. Mann, *The Musicals of F. L.* (diss., City Univ. of N.Y., 1974); *F. L. Remembered* (N.Y., 1977); S. Loesser, *A Most Remarkable Fella: F. L. and the Guys and Dolls in his Life* (N.Y., 1993).

Loevendie, Theo, Dutch composer; b. Amsterdam, Sept. 17, 1930. He received training in composition and clarinet at the Amsterdam Cons. (1956–61). He taught at the Haarlem Toonkunst Music School (1960–65) and at the Rotterdam Cons. (from 1968). In 1973 he founded the STAMP concerts for the promotion of contemporary music, ranging from jazz to the avant-garde. His own works reflect his interest in various contemporary styles.

WORKS: OPERAS: *Naima* (1985); *Gassir, the Hero,* chamber opera (1990). **ORCH.:** *Confluxus* for Jazz and Sym. Orchs.

(1966); *Scaramuccia* for Clarinet and Orch. (1969); *Incantations* for Bass Clarinet and Orch. (1975); *Orbits* for Horn and Orch. (1976); *Flexio* (1979; rev. 1981); *Bons* for Improviser on Any Instrument and Chamber Orch. (1991). **CHAMBER:** *3 Pieces* for 3 Clarinets (1968); *10 Easy Sketches* for Clarinet and Piano (1970); *Music* for Bass Clarinet and Piano (1971); *Aulos* for 1 or More Instruments (1972; rev. 1975); *2 Trios* for 3 Percussion (1973); *Timbo* for 6 Percussion (1974); *Prelude* for 6 Percussion (1974; rev. 1980); *Music* for Flute and Piano (1979); Nonet (1980); *Venus and Adonis Suite* for Clarinet, Violin, Mandolin, Guitar, and Percussion (1981); *Dance* for Violin (1986). **PIANO:** *Strides* (1976); *Voor Jan, Piet en Klaas* for 2 Pianos (1979); *Walk* (1985). **VOCAL:** *6 Turkish Folk Poems* for Soprano or Mezzo-soprano and 7 Instruments (1977); *De nachtegaal* for Reciter and 7 Instruments (1979); *Oh oor o hoor: Herfst der muziek, Spreken praten . . . , Visser van Ma Yuan, Nocturne, Het einde* for Bass-baritone and Orch. (1987).

Loewe, Frederick, remarkable Austrian-American composer of popular music; b. Vienna, June 10, 1901; d. Palm Springs, Calif., Feb. 14, 1988. He studied piano in Berlin with Busoni and d'Albert and composition with Rezniček. He emigrated to the U.S. in 1924, and after a period as a concert pianist, devoted himself to composing popular music. Adapting himself adroitly to the American idiom, he became one of the most successful writers of musical comedies. His first musical comedies were *Salute to Spring* (St. Louis, June 12, 1937), *Great Lady* (N.Y., Dec. 1, 1938), and *The Life of the Party* (Detroit, Oct. 8, 1942). He met the lyricist and playwright Alan Jay Lerner in 1942, which led to their collaboration on the unsuccessful musical *What's Up?* (N.Y., Nov. 11, 1943). Their next effort, *The Day before Spring* (N.Y., Nov. 22, 1945), received a respectable hearing, but it was with *Brigadoon* (N.Y., March 13, 1947) that they achieved success. After *Paint Your Wagon* (N.Y., Nov. 12, 1951), they took Broadway by storm with *My Fair Lady* (N.Y., March 15, 1956; with 2,717 subsequent perfs.), based on George Bernard Shaw's *Pygmalion.* They then brought out the film score *Gigi* (1958), after a story by Colette, which won 9 Academy Awards. Their final collaboration was the highly acclaimed musical *Camelot* (N.Y., Dec. 3, 1960). See A. Sirmay, ed., *The Lerner and Loewe Songbook* (N.Y., 1962).

BIBL.: G. Lees, *Inventing Champagne: The Worlds of Lerner and L.* (N.Y., 1990).

Loewenberg, Alfred, German-born English musicologist; b. Berlin, May 14, 1902; d. London, Dec. 29, 1949. He studied at the Univs. of Berlin and Jena (Ph.D., 1925); settled in London in 1934. His unique achievement is the compilation of *Annals of Opera: 1597–1940* (Cambridge, 1943; new ed., Geneva, 1955; rev. and corrected, 1978), tabulating in chronological order the exact dates of first performances and important revivals of some 4,000 operas, with illuminating comments of a bibliographical nature. He also publ. *Early Dutch Librettos and Plays with Music in the British Museum* (London, 1947) and *The Theatre of the British Isles, Excluding London: A Bibliography* (London, 1950).

Logar, Mihovil, Croatian composer; b. Rijieka, Oct. 6, 1902. He went to Prague to study with Jirák and then attended Suk's master classes. In 1927 he settled in Belgrade, where he was a prof. of composition at the Academy of Music (1945–72). In his works, he employed a restrained modern idiom.

WORKS: DRAMATIC: OPERAS: *Sablazan u dolini šentflorijansko* (Blasphemy in the Valley of St. Florian; 1937); *Pokondirena tikva* (Middle Class Noblewoman; Belgrade, Oct. 20, 1956); *Četrdesetprva* (The Year of 1941; Sarajevo, Feb. 10, 1961). **BALLET:** *Zlatna ribica* (The Golden Fish; Belgrade, Nov. 11, 1953). **ORCH.:** *Rondo rustico* (1945); Violin Concerto (1954); Clarinet Concerto (1956); *Kosmonauti* (Cosmonauts), overture (Belgrade, June 8, 1962); *Sinfonia italiana* (Belgrade, Nov. 24, 1964); *Doppio Concerto* for Clarinet, Horn, and Orch. (Belgrade, April 5, 1968). **OTHER:** Vocal music; piano pieces.

Logothetis, Anestis, Bulgarian-born Austrian composer of Greek parentage; b. Burgas, Oct. 27, 1921; d. Lainz, Jan. 6, 1994. He went to Vienna in 1942 and studied at the Technischen Hochschule until 1944; then received training in theory and composition from Ratz and Uhl and in piano and conducting from Swarowsky at the Academy of Music, graduating in 1951. In 1952 he became a naturalized Austrian citizen. He worked with Koenig at the electronic music studio of the West German Radio in Cologne (1957). In 1960 and 1963 he was awarded the Theodor Körner Prize; in 1986 he received the honorary gold medal of the city of Vienna. He exhibited in Vienna galleries a series of polymorphic graphs capable of being performed as music by optional instrumental groups. He employed a highly personalized "integrating" musical notation, making use of symbols, signs, and suggestive images, playing on a performer's psychological associations.

WORKS: DRAMATIC: OPERAS: *Daidalia* (1976–78); *Waraus ist der Stein des Sisyphos?* (1982–84). **MUSIC THEATER:** *Im Gespinst* (1976). **MUSICAL RADIO PLAYS:** *Anastasis* (1969); *Manratellurium* (1970); *Kybernetikon* (1971–72); *Kerbtierparty* (1972–73); *Sommervögel* or *Schmetterlinge* (1973); *Menetekel* (1974); *Vor! stell! Unk!* (1980); *Bienen' Binom* (1980). **BALLETS:** *Himmelsmechanik* (1960); *5 Porträts der Liebe* (1960); *Odyssee* (1963). **ORCH.:** *Agglomeration* for Violin and Orch. (1960); *Koordination* for 5 Orch. Groups (1960); *Kulmination I* and *II* for 2 Orch. Groups (1961); *Mäandros* (1963); *Dynapolis* (1963); *Seismographie I* and *II* (1964); *Enoseis* (1965); *Diffusion* (1965); *Linienmodulationen* (1965); *Integration* (1966); *Enklaven* (1966); *Oasi* (1967); *Desmotropie* (1967); *Polychronon* (1967); *Styx* for Plucked Strings (1968); *Zonen* (1969); *Mensuren* for Chamber Orch. (1969); *Kollisionen 70* (1970); *Komplementäres* (1970); *Klangräume I, II,* and *III* (1972); *Wellen* (1972); *Volant* (1972); *Ghia tin ora* (1975); *Geomusik 76* for Clarinet and Orch. (1976); *Rondo* (1979); *Brunnenburg-Hochzeit-Symphionetten* (1981); *Meridiane I und Breitengrade* (1981). **OTHER:** Many works for variable instrumentation; chamber pieces; piano music; *Wellenformen 1981,* computer piece.

Lokshin, Alexander, Russian composer; b. Biisk, Altai Region, Sept. 19, 1920; d. Moscow, June 11, 1987. He studied with Miaskovsky at the Moscow Cons. (graduated, 1941). The major portion of his output is devoted to his 11 syms., 10 of them vocal, which promote their often poetic and profound expressions through a unique blend of lyricism and contemporary compositional techniques.

WORKS: ORCH.: *Wait for Me,* symphonic poem for Voice and Orch. (1943); *Hungarian Fantasia* for Violin and Orch. (1952); 11 syms.: No. 1, *Requiem,* for Chorus and Orch. (1958), No. 2, *Greek Epigrams,* for Voices and Orch., after ancient Greek poets (1963), No. 3 for Baritone, Men's Chorus, and Orch., after Kipling (1966), No. 4, *Sinfonia stretta* (1967), No. 5, *Sonnets for Shakespeare,* for Baritone, Harp, and Strings (1969), No. 6 for Baritone, Chorus, and Orch., after Alexander Blok (1971), No. 7 for Contralto and Chamber Orch., after Japanese poets of the 7th to the 13th century (1972), No. 8 for Tenor and Orch., after Pushkin (1973), No. 9 for Baritone and Strings, after Martynow (1975), No. 10 for Contralto, Organ, and Orch., after Zabolotsky (1976), and No. 11 for Soprano and Chamber Orch., after Camoëns (1977); *Speaking Out Loud,* symphonic poem for Bass, Organ, and Orch., after Mayakovsky (1968). **CHAMBER:** *Variations* for Piano (1953); Clarinet Quintet (1955); String Quintet (1978). **VOCAL:** *The Giant Cockroach,* comic oratorio (1962); *Songs of Margaret* for Soprano and Chamber Orch., after Goethe's *Faust* (1973); *Mater dolorosa,* cantata (1977).

Lomax, Alan, American ethnomusicologist, son of **John Avery Lomax**; b. Austin, Texas, Jan. 31, 1915. He acquired his métier from his father, the American ethnomusicologist John Avery Lomax (b. Goodman, Miss., Sept. 23, 1867; d. Greenville, Miss., Jan. 26, 1948), founder of the Texas Folklore Soc. and author of the autobiographical *Adventures of a Ballad Hunter* (N.Y., 1947); then studied at Harvard Univ. (1932–33), the Univ. of Texas in Austin (B.A., 1936), and at Columbia Univ. (graduate work in anthropology, 1939). He joined his father as a researcher in 1933; collected folk songs in the Southwestern and Midwestern regions of the U.S.; they supervised field recordings of rural and prison songs, discovering Leadbelly; they also "discovered" Jelly Roll Morton and recorded interviews with him at the Library of Congress in Washington, D.C. (1938). He also collected folk songs in Europe. In 1963 he was made director of the Bureau of Applied Social Research; also of the cantometrics project at Columbia Univ. (1963). Among his eds., compiled with his father, are *American Ballads and Folksongs* (N.Y., 1934); *Negro Folk Songs as Sung by Leadbelly* (N.Y., 1936); *Our Singing Country* (N.Y., 1941); *Folk Song: U.S.A.* (N.Y., 1947; 4th ed., 1954); *Leadbelly: A Collection of World Famous Songs* (N.Y., 1959; 2nd ed., aug., 1965 as *The Leadbelly Legend*); he also prepared *The Folk Songs of North America in the English Language* (N.Y., 1960); *The Penguin Book of American Folk Songs* (Harmondsworth, 1966); *Hard-Hitting Songs for Hard-Hit People* (N.Y., 1967); *Folk Song Style and Culture* (Washington, D.C., 1968).

WRITINGS: With S. Cowell, *American Folk Song and Folk Lore: A Regional Bibliography* (N.Y., 1942); *Mr. Jelly Roll* (N.Y., 1950; 2nd ed., 1973); *Harriett and Her Harmonium* (London, 1955); *The Rainbow Sign* (N.Y., 1959); *Cantometrics: A Handbook and Training Method* (Berkeley, 1976); *Index of World Song* (N.Y., 1977); *The Land Where the Blues Began* (N.Y., 1993).

Lombard, Alain, French conductor; b. Paris, Oct. 4, 1940. He was only 9 when he entered Poulet's conducting class at the Paris Cons., making his debut with the Pasdeloup Orch. when he was 11; later studied with Fricsay. He conducted at the Lyons Opera (1960–64); won the gold medal at the Mitropoulos Competition in N.Y. (1966); then was music director of the Miami Phil. (1966–74). He made his Metropolitan Opera debut in N.Y. conducting *Faust* on Dec. 24, 1966, and continued to appear there until 1973. He was chief conductor of the Strasbourg Phil. (1972–83), artistic director of the Opera du Rhin (1974–80), and music director of the Paris Opéra (1981–83). From 1988 to 1995 he was artistic director of the Orchestre National Bordeaux Aquitaine.

Lombardi, Luca, Italian composer and teacher; b. Rome, Dec. 24, 1945. He was educated at the Univ. of Vienna and the Univ. of Rome (graduated with a thesis on Eisler; publ. in Milan, 1978). He also studied composition with Renzi, Lupi, and Porena at the Pesaro Cons. (graduated, 1970). He also was in Cologne to take courses with Zimmermann and Globokar (1968–72) and to attend the courses in new music with Stockhausen, Pousseur, Kagel, Schnebel, and Rzewski (1968–70). After training in electronic music from Eimert in Cologne and Koenig in Utrecht, he studied with Dessau in Berlin (1973). He taught composition at the Pesaro Cons. (1973–78) and the Milan Cons. (1978–93). From 1983 to 1986 he was one of the artistic directors of the Cantiere Internazionale d'Arte in Montepulciano. With W. Gieseler and R. Weyer, he publ. the orchestration treatise *Instrumentation in der Musik des 20. Jahrhunderts* (Celle, 1985). In his compositions, he pursues an advanced course notable for its eclectic stylistic manifestations.

WORKS: OPERA: *Faust, un travestimento* (1986–90; Basel, Dec. 21, 1991). **ORCH.:** 3 syms.: No. 1 (1974–75), No. 2 (1981), and No. 3 for Soprano, Baritone, Chorus, and Orch. (1992–93); *Variazioni* (1977); *Tre pezzi* for 2 Pianos and Chamber Orch. (1978–87; Cologne, Oct. 25, 1987); *Framework* for 2 Pianos and Orch. (1983); *Due Ritratti* (1987–88; Lugano, June 13, 1989); *Con Faust* (1990); *La Notte di Valpurga* for Orch. and Chorus ad libitum (1990); *Atropos* (Milan, April 20, 1991); Viola Concerto (1995). **CHAMBER:** *Elegia* for Violin and Piano (1965); *Proporzioni* for 4 Trombones (1968–69); *Non Requiescat* for 13 Instruments (1973); *Canzone* for 13 Instruments (1974–75); *Essay I* for Double Bass (1975) and *II* for Bass Clarinet (1979); *Gespräch über Bäume* for 9 Instrumentalists (1976); *Einklang* for Oboe and 7 Instruments (1980); *Winterblumen* for Flute and Harp (1982); *Sie bagatelle di fine estate* for 1 to 11 Instrumentalists (1983); *Schattenspiel* for Bass Flute (1983); *Sisyphos I* for 8 Instruments (1983) and *II* for 14 Instruments (1984); *Thamar y Amnôn* for Guitar (1983); *Schegge* for Flute, Clarinet, and Horn (1984); *Mirium* for 4 Trombones (1984); *Sisifo felice* for 8 Instruments (1985); *Ai piedo del faro* for Double Bass and 8 Instruments (1986); *Für Flori* for Violin and Piano (1990); *Psalmus VI di Josquin Desprez* for 9 Instruments (1991); String Quartet (1991–92); *Jahreswechsel* for 16 Instruments (1994); *Gruss* for Cello (1994); piano pieces. **VOCAL:** *Hasta que caigan las puertas del odio* for 16 Voices (1976–77); *Alle fronde dei salici* for 12 Voices (1977); *Mayakowski*, cantata for Bass, Chorus, and 7 Instruments (1979–80); *Mythenasche* for Soprano, Baritone, Chorus, and Orch. (1980–81); *Ophelia-Fragmente* for Soprano and Piano (1982; Berlin, Feb. 21, 1983); *Nel tuo porto quiete*, requiem for Soprano, Bass, Chorus, and Orch. (1984); *Canto di Eros* for 5 Voices (Cologne, April 29, 1986); *La canzone di Greta* for Soprano and String Quartet (RAI, Rome, May 11, 1987); *Ein Lied* for Soprano and 3 Instruments (1988; Berlin, Feb. 26, 1989); *Sisyphos III* for Reciter and Ensemble (1988–89; Frankfurt am Main, March 3, 1989); *Tum Balalaike* for Soprano and 3 Instruments (1988–89; Witten, April 21, 1989); *Giocate al giuoco mio, grassi giganti* for Chorus (1992); *A chi fa notte il giorno* for Reciter and Double Bass (1993); *Yedid Nefesh* for Mezzo-soprano and Guitar (1994).

Lomon, Ruth, Canadian-born American composer, pianist, and teacher; b. Montreal, Nov. 8, 1930. She studied at McGill Univ. in Montreal; in 1960 she went to the U.S. and continued her training with Frances Judd Cooke and Miklos Schwalb at the New England Cons. of Music in Boston; in 1964 she took a course with Lutosławski at the Dartington Summer School of Music in England; she also attended the Darmstadt summer courses in new music. In 1965 she became a naturalized American citizen. From 1971 to 1983 she was half of the duo-piano team of Lomon and Wenglin, specializing in the performance of works by women composers. Several of her most important works have been inspired by Native American ceremonials.

WORKS: CHAMBER OPERA: *The Fisherman and His Soul* (1963). **ORCH.:** Bassoon Concerto (1979; rev. 1993); *Terra Incognita* (1993)). **CHAMBER:** Trio for Horn, Cello, and Piano (1961); *Dialogue* for Vibraphone and Harpsichord (1964); *Shapes* for Violin, Cello, Guitar, and Piano (1964); *Phase I* for Cello and Piano (1969); *The Furies: Erinnyes* for Oboe, Oboe d'Amore, and English Horn (1977); *Equinox* for Brass (1978); *Solstice* for Brass Quartet (1978); *Celebrations* for 2 Harps (1978); *Vitruvian Scroll* for String Quartet (1981); *Diptych* for Woodwind Quintet (1983); *Iatiku: "bringing to life . . ."* for Bass Clarinet, Marimba, Vibes, Harp, Harpsichord, and Piano (1983); *Janus* for String Quartet (1984); *Desiderata* for Oboe, Marimba, and Optional Bow Chime (1984); *Spells* for Piano, Woodwind Quintet, String Quartet, Trumpet, and Percussion (1985); *Imprints*, concerto for Piano and 4 Percussion (1987; Columbus, Ohio, May 15, 1989); *The Talisman* for B-flat and Bass Clarinets, Violin, Viola, Cello, and Synthesizer (1988; Boston, Feb. 12, 1989); *The Butterfly Effect* for String Quartet (1989); *Shadowing* for Piano Quartet (1993). **KEYBOARD: PIANO:** *Soundings* for Piano, 4-hands (1975); *Triptych* for 2 Pianos (1978); *5 Ceremonial Masks* (1980); *Esquisses* (1986); *Dreams and Drama* (1994). **ORGAN:** *7 Portals of Vision* (1982); *Commentaries* (1988). **VOCAL:** *5 Songs After Poems by William Blake* for Contralto and Viola (1962); *Dartington Quintet* for Soprano, Flute, Clarinet, Violin, and Piano (1964); *Phase II* for Soprano, Cello, and Piano (1974); *Requiem* for Soprano, Chorus, and Instruments (1977); *Songs from a Requiem* for Soprano and Piano (1982); *Winnowing Song* for Chorus, Cello, and Piano (1982); *Symbiosis* for Mezzo-soprano, Percussion, and Piano (1983); *A Fantasy Journey into the Mind of a Machine* for Soprano and Saxophone (1985). **MIXED MEDIA:** *Many Moons* for Chamber Orch., Narrator, Mimes, and Dancers (Lexington, Mass., Oct. 14, 1990).

London, Edwin, American conductor, teacher, and composer; b. Philadelphia, March 16, 1929. After training in horn at the Oberlin (Ohio) College Cons. of Music (B.A., 1952), he studied conducting (M.F.A., 1954) and composition (Ph.D., 1961) at the Univ. of Iowa. He also received private instruction in composition from Dallapiccola, Schuller, Bezanson, Milhaud, and Clapp, and in conducting from Perlea and Solomon. From 1960 to 1969 he taught at Smith College. He was a prof. at the Univ. of Ill. School of Music from 1968 to 1978, where he also was active as a conductor. In 1972–73 he was a visiting prof. of composition at the Univ. of Calif. at San Diego. He was a prof. (from 1978) and chairman of the music dept. (1978–86) at Cleveland State Univ. He was also founder-music director of the Cleveland Chamber Sym. (from 1980). In 1965, 1966, 1970, and 1974 he held MacDowell Colony fellowships. In 1969 he was awarded a Guggenheim fellowship. In 1973, 1974, and 1979 he received NEA grants. His stylistically diverse output includes theater scores, orch. music, chamber pieces, and vocal works.

London (real name, **Burnstein**), **George,** esteemed Canadian-born American bass-baritone; b. Montreal, May 5, 1919; d. Armonk, N.Y., March 23, 1985. The family moved to Los Angeles in 1935; there he took lessons in operatic interpretation with Richard Lert; also studied voice with Hugo Strelitzer and Nathan Stewart. He made his public debut in the opera *Gainsborough's Duchess* by Albert Coates in a concert performance in Los Angeles on April 20, 1941. He appeared as Dr. Grenvil in *La Traviata* on Aug. 5, 1941, at the Hollywood Bowl, and then sang with the San Francisco Opera on Oct. 24, 1943, in the role of Monterone in *Rigoletto.* He took further vocal lessons with Enrico Rosati and Paola Novikova in N.Y.; then, anticipating a serious professional career, he changed his name from the supposedly plebeian and ethnically confining Burnstein to a resounding and patrician London. In 1947 he toured the U.S. and Europe as a member of the Bel Canto Trio with Frances Yeend, soprano, and Mario Lanza, tenor. His European operatic debut took place as Amonasro at the Vienna State Opera on Sept. 3, 1949. He made his Metropolitan Opera debut in N.Y. in the same role on Nov. 13, 1951; this was also the role he sang at his last Metropolitan appearance on March 10, 1966. From 1951 to 1964 he also sang at the Bayreuth Festivals. On Sept. 16, 1960, he became the first American to sing Boris Godunov (in Russian) at the Bolshoi Theater in Moscow. In 1967 he was stricken with a partial paralysis of the larynx, but recovered sufficiently to be able to perform administrative duties. From 1968 to 1971 he was artistic administrator of the John F. Kennedy Center for the Performing Arts in Washington, D.C.; was also executive director of the National Opera Inst. from 1971 to 1977. He was general director of the Opera Soc. of Washington, D.C., from 1975 to 1977, when he suffered a cardiac arrest that precluded any further public activities. For several years before his death, he suffered from a grave neurological disease. Among his best roles were Wotan, Don Giovanni, Scarpia, Escamillo, and Boris Godunov.

BIBL.: N. London, *Aria for G.* (N.Y., 1987).

Long, Kathleen, English pianist and teacher; b. Brentford, July 7, 1896; d. Cambridge, March 20, 1968. She was a pupil of Herbert Sharpe at the Royal College of Music in London (1910–16). Following her debut in 1915, she pursued a fine career as a soloist with orchs., as a recitalist, and as a chamber music artist. Her tours took her throughout Europe and North America. She also taught at the Royal College of Music (1920–64). In 1950 she was awarded the palmes academiques of France and in 1957 was made a Commander of the Order of the British Empire. Long was an admirable interpreter of Bach, Scarlatti, Mozart, Schumann, and the French school, especially of Fauré. She also championed the cause of British music.

Long, Marguerite (Marie-Charlotte), eminent French pianist and pedagogue; b. Nîmes, Nov. 13, 1874; d. Paris, Feb. 13, 1966. She began piano studies as a child with her sister, Claire Long. In 1883 she became a student of her sister at the Nîmes Cons., where she received a Prix d'Honneur in 1886. That same year she made her debut in Nîmes as a soloist in Mozart's D minor Concerto, K.466. In 1889 she entered the Paris Cons. in the class of Mme. Chêné, and then was Henri Fissot's student there (1890–91). After graduating in 1891 with a premier prix, she pursued private studies with Antonin Marmontel. In 1893 she made her formal Paris recital debut, and subsequently acquired a notable reputation as a recitalist and chamber music artist. On Nov. 22, 1903, she made her Paris debut as a soloist when she played Franck's *Variations Symphoniques* with Chevillard and the Orchestre Lamoureux. Her reputation was assured when she appeared for the first time as soloist with the orch. of the Société des Concerts du Conservatoire in Paris performing Fauré's *Ballade* on Jan. 19, 1908. Thereafter she appeared as a soloist with the principal French orchs. until her farewell appearance in the same work with Inghelbrecht and the Orchestre National de la Radiodiffusion Télévision Française in Paris on Feb. 3, 1959. In 1906 Long became a teacher of piano at the Paris Cons. In 1920 she was made a prof. of piano of a Classe Supérieure there, the first woman to hold that position. From 1906 she also was active with her own music school. After retiring from the Cons. in 1940, she joined Jacques Thibaud in founding the École Marguerite Long-Jacques Thibaud in 1941. They also organized the Concours Marguerite Long-Jacques Thibaud, which was first held in 1943. After World War II, it blossomed into one of the principal international competitions. Among Long's many notable students were Samson François, Nicole Henriot, Aldo Ciccolini, Philippe Entremont, and Peter Frankl. Her writings, all publ. in Paris, included *Le piano* (1959), *Au piano avec Claude Debussy* (1960; Eng. tr., 1972), *Au piano avec Gabriel Fauré* (1963; Eng. tr., 1981), and *Au piano avec Maurice Ravel* (1971; Eng. tr., 1973). She was made a Chevalier (1921), an Officier (1930), and a Commandeur (1938) of the Légion d'Honneur. She was the first woman to be accorded the latter honor. In 1965 she was the first woman to be awarded the Grand Croix de l'Ordre du Mérite. In 1906 she married **Joseph de Marliave.** As a pianist, Long won great renown for her interpretations of French music. Her performances of Fauré, Debussy, and Ravel, all of whom she came to know well, were outstanding. She gave the first performance of Ravel's *Le Tombeau de Couperin* (Paris, April 11, 1919). She also was the soloist in the premiere of his Piano Concerto in G major under the composer's direction (Paris, Jan. 14, 1932).

BIBL.: J. Weill, *M. L.: Une vie fascinante* (Paris, 1969); C. Dunoyer, *M. L.: A Life in French Music, 1874–1966* (Bloomington and Indianapolis, 1993).

Longo, Achille, Italian composer and teacher, son of **Alessandro Longo**; b. Naples, March 28, 1900; d. there, May 28, 1954. He studied with his father and with A. Savasta; then at the Naples Cons. (diplomas in piano, 1918, and composition, 1920); he taught harmony there (1926–30); then at the Parma Cons. (1930–34); subsequently taught composition at the Naples Cons. (1934–54).

WORKS: ORCH.: *Scenetta pastorale* (1924); Piano Concerto (Venice, 1932); *La burla del Pievano Arlotto* (1933); Violin Concerto (1937); *Notturno and Corte* (1942); *Serenata in do* (1950). **CHAMBER:** Suite for Flute, Oboe, Clarinet, Bassoon, and Piano (1926; won the Bellini Prize); Piano Quintet (1934). **VOCAL:** *Missa di requiem* (1934).

Longo, Alessandro, Italian pianist, teacher, editor, and composer, father of **Achille Longo**; b. Amantea, Dec. 30, 1864; d. Naples, Nov. 3, 1945. He began his studies with his father, Achille Longo (b. Melicucca, Feb. 27, 1832; d. Naples, May 11, 1919), a pianist and composer; then entered the Naples Cons. (1878), where he studied piano with Cesi, composition with Serrao, and organ (diplomas in all 3, 1885). He was appointed prof. of piano there in 1897, retiring in 1934; later returned as its interim director (1944). Longo also was active as a piano soloist and, from 1909, served as pianist of the Società del Quartetto. In 1892 he founded the Circolo Scarlatti to promote the works of Domenico Scarlatti; ed. the *Opere complete per clavicembalo di Domenico Scarlatti* (11 vols., Milan, 1906–08); also became ed. of the periodical *L'Arte Pianistica* (1914), which became the *Vita Musicale Italiana*; it discontinued publication in 1926. He publ. the study *Domenico Scarlatti e la sua* *figura nella storia della musica* (Naples, 1913). He also was the composer of over 300 works, including numerous pieces for piano solo and piano, 4-hands; chamber music; and songs.

BIBL.: M. Limoncelli, *A. L.* (Naples, 1956).

Longy, (Gustave-) Georges (-Léopold), French oboist, conductor, music educator, and composer; b. Abbeville, Aug. 28, 1868; d. Moreuil, March 29, 1930. He studied oboe with Georges Gillet at the Paris Cons. (premier prix, 1886). He was a member of the Lamoureux Orch. (1886–88) and of the Colonne Orch. (1888–98) in Paris. In 1898 he was engaged as 1st oboe player of the Boston Sym. Orch., and remained there until 1925. From 1899 to 1913 he conducted the Boston Orchestral Club. In 1916 he established his own music school in Boston (later the Longy School of Music in Cambridge, Mass.). In 1925 he returned to France.

Lonque, Georges, Belgian composer and teacher; b. Ghent, Nov. 8, 1900; d. Brussels, March 3, 1967. He studied with Moeremans, Mathieu, and Lunssens at the Ghent Cons.; was awarded the 2nd Prix de Rome for his cantatas *Le Rossignol* (1927) and *Antigone* (1929). He joined the faculty of his alma mater (1926); was a lecturer in harmony there (1932–65); was also director of the Renaix music academy (1938–64). His music was influenced mainly by Franck, Debussy, Fauré, and Ravel.

WORKS: ORCH.: *Impressions d'Hemelrijk* (1925); *Vieux quai* for Violin or Cello and Orch. (1928); *Aura*, symphonic poem and ballet (1930); *Wiener Walzer* for Small Orch. (1933); *Poème de la mer* for Cello and Orch. (1935); *Images d'Orient* for Saxophone or Viola and Orch. (1935); *Porcelaines* de Saxe for Small Orch. (1939); *Prélude et Aria* for Cello and Orch. (1943); *Estrelle* for Violin and Orch. (1944); Violin Concerto (1948); *Afgoden (Idoles)* for Clarinet and Orch. (1950). **CHAMBER:** Violin Sonata (1925); *Caprice* for Violin and Piano (1930); String Quartet (1937); piano pieces, including *Nuit d'automne* (1929), 2 sonatinas (1939, 1944), *Voilier* (1952), *Tableaux d'une chambre bleue* (1952), and *Nocturne* (1955). **VOCAL:** 2 cantatas: *Le Rossignol* (1927) and *Antigone* (1929); *Missa pro pace* for Men's Chorus and Organ (1941); songs.

Loomis, Clarence, American pianist, teacher, and composer; b. Sioux Falls, S.Dak., Dec. 13, 1889; d. Aptos, Calif., July 3, 1965. He studied at the American Cons. of Chicago with Heniot Lévy (piano) and Adolph Weidig (composition); subsequently took lessons with Godowsky in Vienna. Returning to the U.S., he held various positions as a music teacher. As a composer, he was mainly successful in writing light operas in a Romantic vein; among them are *Yolanda of Cyprus* (London, Ontario, Sept. 25, 1929); *A Night in Avignon* (Indianapolis, July 1932); *The White Cloud* (1935); *The Fall of the House of Usher* (Indianapolis, Jan. 11, 1941); *Revival* (1943); *The Captive Woman* (1953); he further wrote a comic ballet, *The Flapper and the Quarterback*, which was first performed in Kyoto, Japan, at the coronation of Emperor Hirohito, Nov. 10, 1928. Among his orch. works were *Gargoyles*, symphonic prelude (1936); *Gaelic Suite* for Strings (1953); *Fantasy* for Piano and Orch. (1954); *Macbeth* (1954); also *The Passion Play* for Chorus and Orch.; 2 string quartets (1953, 1963); cantata, *Song of the White Earth* (1956); numerous sacred choruses; *Susanna Don't You Cry*, stage extravaganza (1939); piano suites; songs; organ pieces.

Loos, Armin, German-born American composer; b. Darmstadt, Feb. 20, 1904; d. New Britain, Conn., March 23, 1971. He studied law at the Univ. of Dresden, then attended the Univs. of Berlin and Geneva and the École Supérieur de Commerce in Neuchâtel, Switzerland; he also had lessons in composition with Paul Buettner. In 1928 he emigrated to the U.S. After living in N.Y., he settled in New Britain, becoming a naturalized American citizen in 1940.

WORKS: ORCH.: 3 syms.: No. 1, "in memoriam Ferruccio Busoni" (1940), No. 2 for Strings (1940), and No. 3, "in canon form" (1941); *Pastoral and Perpetuum mobile* (1941); *Precepts* for Chamber Orch. (1968); *Aquarius 70* for Strings (1970); *Lento: Prelude to Easter* (1970). **CHAMBER:** 4 string quartets (1933–63); Woodwind Quintet (1964); 2 violin sonatas (1968; 1970–71); piano pieces. **VOCAL:** *Te Deum* for Chorus (1934); *Missa spiritorum* for Chorus and Orch. (1948); *Psalm CXX* for Chorus and Orch. (1963); songs.

Loose, Emmy, Austrian soprano; b. Karbitz, Bohemia, Jan. 22, 1914; d. Vienna, Oct. 14, 1987. She was educated at the Prague Cons.; then made her debut as Blondchen in *Die Entführung aus dem Serail* in Hannover (1939). From 1941 she sang with the Vienna State Opera; also appeared at the festivals in Salzburg, Glyndebourne, and Aix-en-Provence, at Milan's La Scala, London's Covent Garden, and in South America. From 1970 she taught at the Vienna Academy of Music. She was admired for her fine soubrette roles in the operas of Mozart and Richard Strauss.

Looser, Rolf, Swiss cellist, teacher, and composer; b. Niederscherli, near Bern, May 3, 1920. He studied at the Cons. and at the Univ. of Bern, his principal teachers being Sturzenegger (cello) and Moeschinger, Zulauf, and Kurth (theory); after taking teaching (1942) and concert (1944) diplomas, he pursued his training with Frank Martin (composition) and Franz Walter (cello) in Geneva, Burkhard (counterpoint) in Zürich, and Fournier (cello) in Paris. He was a cellist in the radio orch. of Studio Monte Ceneri and 1st cellist in the Utrecht Sym. Orch. (1946–49), and then taught at the Bern and Biel Conservatories. He subsequently taught at the Zürich Cons. and Academy of Music (from 1975).

WORKS: ORCH.: Suite (1944–49); *Introduction et Dialogues* for Cello and Chamber Orch. (1950); *Konzertante Musik* (1951); *Musik* for Strings and Organ (1953); *Fantasie* for Violin and Orch. (1958); *Rhapsodia* for Cello and Chamber Orch. (1961); *Pezzo* (1964); *Alyssos*, 5 pieces for Strings and Percussion (1967); *Ponti* (1971); *Arche*, symphonic essay (1986–87); *Es Bilderbuech für d'Ohre* for Small Orch. (1988–89). **CHAMBER:** *6 Stücke* for Flute and Clarinet (1958); *Variationenphantasie über ein eigenes Choralthema* for Trumpet and Piano (1958); *Rezitativ und Hymnus* for Violin (1960); *4 Stücke* for Oboe and Harpsichord (1962); *Fantasia a quattro* for String Quartet (1965); *Dialog* for Violin and Organ (1968); *Monologue, Gestes et Danse* for Cello (1976); *Partita à tre* for 2 Trumpets, Organ, and Percussion (1979–80); *Danza* for Dancer and Cello (1982); *5 kurze Szenen* for Violin and Oboe (1984); *Fantasia à tre* for 3 Flutes (1985); *3 Stücke* for Clarinet and Cello (1987); *Stück* for Flute, Basset Horn, and Organ (1989); *Monochromie* for 5 Clarinets (1991–92). **OTHER:** Organ music; choral pieces; songs.

Lopatnikoff, Nicolai (actually, **Nikolai Lvovich**), outstanding Russian-born American composer; b. Tallinn, Estonia, March 16, 1903; d. Pittsburgh, Oct. 7, 1976. He studied at the St. Petersburg Cons. (1914–17); after the Revolution, continued his musical training at the Helsinki Cons. with Furuhjelm (1918–20); then studied with Grabner in Heidelberg (1920) and Toch and Rehberg in Mannheim (1921); concurrently took civil engineering at the Technological College in Karlsruhe (1921–27). He lived in Berlin (1929–33) and London (1933–39) before settling in the U.S., becoming a naturalized American citizen in 1944. He was head of theory and composition at the Hartt College of Music in Hartford, Conn., and of the Westchester Cons. in White Plains, N.Y. (1939–45); then was a prof. of composition at the Carnegie Inst. of Technology (later Carnegie-Mellon Univ.) in Pittsburgh (1945–69). In 1951 he married the poet Sara Henderson Hay. He was elected to the National Inst. of Arts and Letters in 1963. His music is cast in a neo-Classical manner, distinguished by a vigorous rhythmic pulse, a clear melodic line, and a wholesome harmonic investment. A prolific composer, he wrote music in all genres; being a professional pianist, he often performed his own piano concertos with orchs.

WORKS: DRAMATIC: OPERA: *Danton* (1930–32; *Danton Suite* for Orch., Pittsburgh, March 25, 1967). **BALLET:** *Melting Pot* (1975; Indianapolis, March 26, 1976). **ORCH.:** *Prelude to a Drama* (1920; lost); 2 piano concertos: No. 1 (1921; Cologne,

Nov. 3, 1925) and No. 2 (Düsseldorf, Oct. 16, 1930); *Introduction and Scherzo* (1927–29; 1st complete perf., N.Y., Oct. 23, 1930); 4 syms.: No. 1 (1928; Karlsruhe, Jan. 9, 1929), No. 2 (1938–39; 4-movement version, Boston, Dec. 22, 1939; withdrawn and rev. in 3 movements), No. 3 (1953–54; Pittsburgh, Dec. 10, 1954), and No. 4 (1970–71; Pittsburgh, Jan. 21, 1972); *Short Overture* (1932; lost); *Opus Sinfonicum* (1933; rev. 1942; Cleveland, Dec. 9, 1943); *2 Russian Nocturnes* (1939; orig. the 2 middle movements of the 2nd Sym.); Violin Concerto (1941; Boston, April 17, 1942); Sinfonietta (Berkeley, Calif., Aug. 2, 1942); Concertino (1944; Boston, March 2, 1945); Concerto for 2 Pianos and Orch. (Pittsburgh, Dec. 7, 1951); *Divertimento* (La Jolla, Calif., Aug. 19, 1951); *Variazioni concertanti* (Pittsburgh, Nov. 7, 1958); *Music for Orchestra* (1958; Louisville, Jan. 14, 1959); *Festival Overture* (Detroit, Oct. 12, 1960); *Concerto for Orchestra* (Pittsburgh, April 3, 1964; orch. version of Concerto for Wind Orch.); *Partita concertante* for Chamber Orch. (1966); *Variations and Epilogue* for Cello and Orch. (Pittsburgh, Dec. 14, 1973; orchestration of 1946 chamber piece). **WIND ORCH.:** Concerto for Wind Orch. (Pittsburgh, June 23, 1963); *Music for Band* (1963; transcribed by William Schaefer from *Music for Orchestra*). **CHAMBER:** 2 piano trios (1918, lost; 1935); 3 string quartets (1920; 1924, rev. 1928; 1955); Sonata for Violin, Piano, and Snare Drum (1927; rev. in 1967 as Sonata for Violin, Piano, and Percussion); Cello Sonata (1929); *Arabesque* for Cello or Bassoon and Piano (1931); *Variations and Epilogue* for Cello and Piano (1946; orchestration, 1973); Violin Sonata No. 2 (1948); *Fantasia concertante* for Violin and Piano (1962); *Divertimento da camera* for 10 Instruments (1965). **PIANO:** *4 Small Piano Pieces* (1920); *Prelude and Fugue* (1920); Sonatina (1926; rev. 1967); *2 Pieces* for Mechanical Piano (1927; lost); *2 danses ironiques* (1928; rev. 1967); *5 Contrasts* (1930); *Dialogues* (1932); *Variations* (1933); Sonata (1943); *Intervals*, 7 studies (1957). **VOCAL:** Songs.

BIBL.: W. Critser, compiler, *The Compositions of N. L.: A Catalogue* (Pittsburgh, 1979).

Lopes-Graça, Fernando, eminent Portuguese composer, musicologist, pianist, and pedagogue; b. Tomar, Dec. 17, 1906; d. Lisbon, Nov. 28, 1994. He took piano lessons at home, then studied with Merea and da Motta (piano), Borba (composition), and de Freitas Branco (theory and musicology) at the Lisbon Cons. (1923–31); also studied at the Univ. of Lisbon. He taught at the Coimbra music inst. (1932–36). In 1937 he left his homeland for political reasons; went to Paris, where he studied composition and orchestration with Koechlin, and musicology with Masson at the Sorbonne. After the outbreak of World War II (1939), he returned to Lisbon, where he served as a prof. at the Academia de Amadores de Música (1941–54); from 1950 was director of its chorus, a position he held for 40 years; also made appearances as a pianist. In his music, he pursued an independent path in which he moved from Portuguese folk traditions to atonality in 1962. With M. Giacometti, he publ. the 1st vol. of the *Antologia da Música Regional Portuguesa*, the 1st attempt to collect, in a systematic way, the regional songs of Portugal.

WORKS: DRAMATIC: *La Fièvre du temps*, revue-ballet (1938); *D. Duardos e Flérida*, cantata-melodrama (1964–69; Lisbon, Nov. 28, 1970); *Dançares*, choreographic suite (1984). **ORCH.:** *Poemeto* for Strings (1928); *Prelúdio, Pastoral e Dança* (1929); 2 piano concertos (1940, 1942); 3 Portuguese Dances (1941); Sinfonia (1944); *5 estelas funerárias* (1948); *Scherzo heróico* (1949); *Suite rústica No. 1* (1950–51); *Marcha festiva* (1954); Concertino for Piano, Strings, Brass, and Percussion (1954); *5 Old Portuguese Romances* (1951–55); *Divertimento* for Winds, Kettledrums, Percussion, Cellos, and Double Basses (1957); *Poema de Dezembro* (1961); Viola Concertino (1962); *4 bosquejos* (4 Sketches) for Strings (1965); *Concerto da camera* for Cello and Orch. (Moscow, Oct. 6, 1967, Rostropovich soloist); *Viagens na minha terra* (1969–70); *Fantasia* for Piano and Orch., on a religious song from Beira-Baixa (1974); *Homenagem a Haydn*, sinfonietta (1980); *Em louvor da paz* (1986). **CHAMBER:** *Estudo-Humoresca* for Flute, Oboe, Clarinet, 2 Violins, Viola, and Cello (1930); Piano Quartet (1939; rev. 1963); *Prelúdio, Capricho e Galope* for Violin and Piano (1941; rev. 1951); *Página esquecida* for Cello and Piano (1955); *Canto de Amor e de Morte* for Piano Quintet (1961); String Quartet (1964); *14 anotaçoes* for String Quartet (1966); *7 souvenirs for Vieira da Silva* for Wind Quintet (1966); *The Tomb of Villa-Lobos* for Wind Quintet (1970); *3 capriccetti* for Flute and Guitar (1975); *Quatro peças em suite* for Viola and Piano (1978); *Sete Apotegmas* for Oboe, Viola, Double Bass, and Piano (1981); *Homenagem a Beethoven—Três Equali* for Double-bass Quartet (1986); *Geórgicas* for Oboe, Viola, Double Bass, and Piano (1989). **PIANO:** 6 sonatas (1934; 1939, rev. 1956; 1952; 1961; 1977; 1981); *8 Bagatelles* (1939–48; No. 4, 1950); *Glosas* (Glosses; 1950); *24 Preludes* (1950–55); *Album do jovem pianista* (1953–63); *In Memoriam Béla Bartók*, 8 progressive suites (1960–75); *4 Impromptus* (1961); *Piano Music for Children* (1968–76); *Melodias rústicas portuguesas No. 3* for Piano, 4-hands (1979); *Deploração na morte trágica de Samora Machel* (1986); *Pranto à memória de Francisco Miguel, uma vida heróica* (1988). **GUITAR:** *Prelúdio e Baileto* (1968); *Partita* (1970–71); Sonatina (1974); *Quatro peças* (1979). **VOCAL:** *Pequeno cancioneiro do Menino Jesus* for Women's Chorus, 2 Flutes, String Quartet, Celesta, and Harp (1936–59); *História trágico-marítima* for Baritone, Contralto, Chorus, and Orch. (1942–59); *9 Portuguese Folk Songs* for Voice and Orch. (1948–49); *4 Songs of Federico García Lorca* for Baritone, 2 Clarinets, Violin, Viola, Cello, Harp, and Percussion (1953–54); *Cantos do Nata* for Women's Voices and Instrumental Ensemble (1958); *9 cantigas de amigo* for Voice and Chamber Ensemble (1964); *6 cantos sefardins* for Voice and Orch. (1971); *Requiem pelas vítimas do fascismo em Portugal* for Soloists, Chorus, and Orch. (1979); *Sete Predicações de "Os Lusíadas"* for Tenor, Baritone, Men's Chorus, and 12 Instruments (1980); *. . . meu país de marinheiros . . .* for Narrator, 4 Women's Voices, 4 Men's Voices, Flute, and Guitars (1981); many choruses; songs.

WRITINGS: *Sobre a evolução das formas musicais* (Lisbon, 1940; 2nd ed., rev., 1959, as *Breve ensaio sobre a evolução das formas musicais*); *Reflexões sobre a música* (Lisbon, 1941); *Introdução à música moderna* (Lisbon, 1941; 3rd ed., 1984); *Música e músicos modernos (Aspectos, obras, personalidades)* (Oporto, 1943; 2nd ed., 1985); *A música portuguesa e os seus problemas* (3 vols., 1944, 1959, 1973); *Bases teóricas da músicas* (Lisbon, 1944; 2nd ed., 1984); *Talia, Euterpe e Terpsicore* (Coimbra, 1945); *Pequena história da música de piano* (Lisbon, 1945; 2nd ed., 1984); *Cartas do Abade António da Costa (Introdução e notas)* (Lisbon, 1946; 2nd ed., 1973, as *O Abade António da Costa, músico e epistológrafo setecentista*); *Visita aos músicos franceses* (Lisbon, 1948); *Vianna da Motta (Subsídios para uma biografia, incluindo 22 cartas ao autor)* (Lisbon, 1949; 2nd ed., 1984); *Béla Bartók (Três apontamentos sobre a sua personalidade e a sua obra)* (Lisbon, 1953); *A Canção popular portuguesa* (Lisbon, 1953; 3rd ed., 1981); *Em louvor de Mozart* (Lisbon, 1956; 2nd ed., 1984); with T. Borba, *Dicionário de música* (Lisbon, 1956–58); *Musicália* (Baia, 1960; corrected and aug. ed., 1967); *Lieder der Welt, Portugal (Ausgewält und erlautert von . . .)* (Hamburg, 1961); *Nossa companheira música* (Lisbon, 1964); *Páginas escolhidas de crítica e estética musicale* (Lisbon, 1966); *Disto e daquilo* (Lisbon, 1973); *Um artista intervém/Cartas com alguma moral* (Lisbon, 1974); *A caça aos coelhos e outros escritos polémicos* (Lisbon, 1976); *Escritos musicológicos* (Lisbon, 1977); *A música portuguesa e os seus problemas* (Lisbon, 1989).

BIBL.: M. Henriques, *F. L.G. na música portuguesa contemporanea* (Sacavém, 1956); M. Vieria de Carvalo, *O essencial sobre F. L.-G.* (Lisbon, 1989).

Lopez, Francis(co), French composer; b. Montbéliard, June 15, 1916; d. Paris, Jan. 5, 1995. He studied to be a dentist but after finding success writing songs, he opted for a career as a composer of light works for the French musical theater in Paris. He found an adept librettist and lyricist in Raymond Vincy; they scored an enormous success with their first outing, the operetta

Le Belle de Cadix (Dec. 24, 1945). They subsequently collaborated on a long series of highly successful works, among them *Andlousie* (Oct. 25, 1947), *Quatre Jours à Paris* (Feb. 28, 1948), *Pour Don Carlos* (Dec. 17, 1950), *Le Chanteur de Mexico* (Dec. 15, 1951), *La Route fleurie* (Dec. 19, 1952), *À la Jamïque* (Jan. 24, 1954), *La Toison d'or* (Dec. 18, 1954), and *Méditerranée* (Dec. 17, 1956). Several of these works became classics and were made into films. Lopez and Vincy continued their collaboration until the latter's death in 1968. Among their later scores were *Maria-Flora* (Dec. 18, 1957), *La Secret de Marco Polo* (Dec. 12, 1959), *Visa pour l'amour* (Dec. 1961), *Cristobal le Magnifique* (Dec. 1963), and *Le Prince de Madrid* (March 4, 1967). In subsequent years, Lopez continued to compose prolifically but only infrequently found the inspiration of his earlier years. His autobiography was publ. as *Flamenco: La gloire et les larmes* (Paris, 1987).

Lopez, Vincent (Joseph), American pianist, bandleader, and composer; b. Brooklyn, Dec. 30, 1894; d. North Miami Beach, Fla., Sept. 20, 1975. His father, of Portuguese ancestry, a bandmaster in the U.S. Navy, taught Lopez the rudiments of music. However, he sent him to St. Mary's Passionist Monastery in the hope that he would become a Roman Catholic priest. But Lopez turned to music, and as a teenager played in the beer halls of Brooklyn. Later he led restaurant orchs. in N.Y. In 1927 he inaugurated a regular broadcasting hour of dance band music over radio station WJX in Newark, on which he popularized the song *Nola,* using it as a signature, opening with a greeting, "Hello, everybody . . . Lopez speaking." He had the first sustaining television show, "Dinner Date with Lopez," which featured show-business personalities. Among his song hits were *Rockin' Chair Swing; Knock, Knock, Who's There?;* and *The World Stands Still.* He also gave lectures on numerology and related pseudo-sciences.

López-Buchardo, Carlos, Argentine composer; b. Buenos Aires, Oct. 12, 1881; d. there, April 21, 1948. He studied piano, violin, and harmony in Buenos Aires and composition with Albert Roussel in Paris. He was founder-director of the National Cons. in Buenos Aires (1924–48); also founded the school of fine arts at the Univ. of La Plata, where he was a prof. of harmony. His music is set in a vivid style, rooted in national folk song; particularly successful in this respect is his symphonic suite *Escenas argentinas* (Buenos Aires, Aug. 12, 1922). His other works are the opera *El sueño de alma* (Buenos Aires, Aug. 4, 1914; won the Municipal Prize); 3 lyric comedies: *Madama Lynch* (1932), *La perichona* (1933), and *Amalia* (1935); several piano pieces in an Argentine folk manner; songs.

López-Calo, José, Spanish Jesuit priest and music scholar; b. Nebra, La Coruña, Feb. 4, 1922. After graduating with degrees in philosophy and theology from the Univs. of Comillas and Granada, he studied church music at the Madrid High School of Sacred Music and musicology with Anglès at the Rome Pontifical Inst. for Sacred Music (Ph.D., 1962, with the diss. *La música en la catedral de Granada;* publ. in Granada, 1963). He served as assistant to Anglès (1964–65), then was prof. of musicology at the Pontifical Inst. for Sacred Music (1965–70); also was musical adviser for the Vatican Radio (1962–70) and general secretary of the International Soc. for Church Music (1964–70). In 1970 he returned to Spain to pursue research in Spanish cathedral archives; in 1973 he became prof. of music history at the Univ. of Santiago de Compostela, and was made prof. emeritus upon his retirement in 1988. His valuable research is reflected in his cataloging of musical archives and in the gathering of an immense collection of firsthand documentation on music history.

WRITINGS: *Canti sacri per la Santa Messa* (Rome, 1965; 2nd ed., 1967); *Presente y futuro de la música sagrada* (Madrid, 1967; Italian tr., Rome, 1968); *Catálogo musical del archivo de la santa iglesia catedral de Santiago* (Cuenca, 1972; 2nd ed., rev., 1992–93, as *La música en la catedral de Santiago*); *Hygini Anglès Scripta musicologica* (3 vols., Rome, 1976); *Catálogo del archivo de música de la catedral de Ávila* (Santiago de Compostela, 1978); *Francisco Valls: Missa Scala Aretina* (London, 1978); *Esencia de la música sagrada* (La Coruña, 1980); *La música en la catedral de Palencia* (2 vols., Palencia, 1981); *La música medieval en Galicia* (La Coruña, 1982); *Indices de la revista Tesoro Sacro Musical* (Madrid, 1983); *Historia de la música española en el siglo XVII* (Madrid, 1983); *The Symphony in Spain: 3 Symphonies by José Pons* (N.Y., 1983); *La música en la catedral de Zamora* (Zamora, 1985); *Las sonatas de Beethoven para piano* (Santiago de Compostela, 1985); *Melchor López: Misa de Requiem* (Santiago de Compostela, 1987); *La música en la catedral de Segovia* (Segovia, 1988); *Catálogo del archivo de música de la catedral de Santo Domingo de La Calzada* (Logroño, 1988); *Catálogo del archivo de música de la catedral de Granada* (2 vols., Granada, 1991); *La música en la catedral de Calahorra* (Logroño, 1991); *Catálogo del archivo de música de la capilla réal de Granada* (Granada, 1993).

BIBL.: E. Casares and C. Villanueva, *De música hispana et aliis: Miscelánea en honor al Prof. Dr. J. L.-C., S.J., en su 65º cumpleaños* (2 vols., Santiago de Compostela, 1990).

López-Chavarri y Marco, Eduardo, Spanish musicologist, music critic, and composer; b. Valencia, Jan. 29, 1871; d. there, Oct. 28, 1970. He received a law degree from the Univ. of Valencia (1900) and studied composition with Pedrell. In 1897 he became music critic of *Las provincias* in Valencia, a position he retained until shortly before his death. He also was prof. of aesthetics and music history at the Valencia Cons. (1910–21), where he conducted its orch. and chamber orch. His most important writings were *Historia de la música* (Barcelona, 1914; 3rd ed., 1929) and *Música popular española* (Barcelona, 1927; 3rd ed., 1958). He composed orch. works, choral pieces, chamber music, piano pieces, and songs.

López-Cobos, Jesús, distinguished Spanish conductor; b. Toro, Feb. 25, 1940. He took a doctorate in philosophy at the Univ. of Madrid (1964); studied composition at the Madrid Cons. (diploma, 1966) and conducting with Ferrara in Venice, Swarowsky at the Vienna Academy of Music (diploma, 1969), Maag at the Accademia Musicale Chigiana in Siena, and Morel at the Juilliard School of Music in N.Y. In 1969 he won 1st prize at the Besancon Competition; that same year he conducted at the Prague Spring Festival and at the Teatro La Fenice in Venice; subsequently was a regular conductor at the Deutsche Oper in West Berlin (1970–75). In 1972 he made his American debut with the San Francisco Opera conducting *Lucia di Lammermoor,* and thereafter appeared as a guest conductor throughout the U.S. In 1975 he made his first appearance at London's Covent Garden conducting *Adriana Lecouvreur.* On Feb. 4, 1978, he made his Metropolitan Opera debut in N.Y. conducting the same score. He was Generalmusikdirektor of the Deutsche Oper in West Berlin (1980–90), principal guest conductor of the London Phil. (1982–86), chief conductor of the Orquesta Nacional de Espana in Madrid (1984–89), and music director of the Cincinnati Sym. Orch. (from 1986) and of the Lausanne Chamber Orch. (from 1990). To mark the 100th anniversary of the Cincinnati Sym. Orch. in 1995, he conducted it on a tour to Europe.

Lo Presti, Ronald, American composer; b. Williamstown, Mass., Oct. 28, 1933; d. Tempe, Ariz., Oct. 25, 1985. He studied composition with Mennini and Rogers at the Eastman School of Music in Rochester, N.Y. (M.M., 1956); subsequently was engaged as a clarinet teacher in public schools; in 1964 he was appointed an instructor in theory at Arizona State Univ. in Tempe. He obtained popular success with his score *The Masks* (1955), which was commissioned for the space exhibit at the aerospace building at the Smithsonian Inst. in Washington, D.C.

WORKS: DRAMATIC: *The Birthday,* opera (1962; Winfield, May 1962); *Playback,* children's opera (Tucson, Ariz., Dec. 18, 1970). **ORCH.:** *The Masks* (Rochester, N.Y., May 8, 1955); *Nocturne* for Small Orch. (1955–56); *Nocturne* for Viola and String Orch. (1959); *Kansas Overture* (1960); *Kanza Suite* (1961);

Llano estacado (The Staked Plain; 1961); *Port Triumphant* (1962); 2 syms. (1966, 1968); *From the Southwest* (1967); *Rhapsody* for Marimba, Vibraphone, and Orch. (1975). **SYMPHONIC BAND:** *Pageant* (1956); *Prelude* (1959); *Introduction, Chorale and Jubilee* (1961); *Tundra* (1967); *A Festive Music* (1968). **CHAMBER:** *Suite* for 8 Horns (1952); *Sketch* for Percussion (1956); *Suite* for 4 Horns (1958); *5 Pieces* for Violin and Piano (1960); *Scherzo* for Violin Quartet (1960); *Chorale* for 3 Tubas (1960); *Fanfare* for 38 Brasses (1960); *Requiescat* for Brass Ensemble (1961); *Suite* for 5 Trumpets (1961); *Miniature* for Brass Quartet (1962); *Rondo* for Timpani and Piano (1969); *Trio* for 3 Percussionists (1971); String Quartet (1970); *Suite* for 6 Bassoons (1971); *Fantasy* for 5 Horns (1972); *Cantalena* for Cello Orch. (1972); Wind Quintet (1975). **VOCAL:** *Alleluia* for Chorus, Brass, and Timpani (1960); *Kanza* for 4 Narrators, Chorus, and Orch. (1961); *Tribute* for Chorus and Orch. and/or Band (1962); *Scarecrow* for Children's Ballet Co., Mixed Voices, and Cello Orch. (1973); *Ode to Independence* for Baritone, Chorus, and Band (1974); *Requiem* for Chorus and Orch. (1975); *Memorials* for Chorus and Orch. (1975); choruses; songs.

Lorengar, Pilar (real name, **Pilar Lorenza García**), prominent Spanish soprano; b. Saragossa, Jan. 16, 1928; d. Berlin, June 2, 1996. She studied with Angeles Ottein in Madrid, where she made her debut as a mezzo-soprano in zarzuela (1949); after becoming a soprano in 1951, she made her operatic debut as Cherubino at the Aix-en-Provence Festival in 1955. Her first appearance in the U.S. took place that same year as Rosario in a concert perf. of *Goyescas* in N.Y. She made her debut at London's Covent Garden as Violetta in 1955, making frequent appearances there from 1964; also sang at the Glyndebourne Festivals (1956–60) and the Berlin Deutsche Oper (from 1958). On Feb. 11, 1966, she made her Metropolitan Opera debut in N.Y. as Donna Elvira. She was named a Kammersängerin of the Berlin Deutsche Oper in 1963, and in 1984 Lifetime Member of the company on the occasion of her 25th anniversary with them. Her final appearance there was in 1991. She received the Medallo d'Oro de Zaragoza of Saragossa and the Order of Isabella de Catolica (1965), as well as the San Francisco Opera Medal (1989). Among her finest roles were Donna Anna, Fiordiligi, Countess Almaviva, Alice Ford, Eva, and Mélisande.

BIBL.: W. Elsner and M. Busch, *P. L.: Ein Porträt* (Berlin, 1985).

Lorentzen, Bent, Danish composer; b. Stenvad, Feb. 11, 1935. He studied with Knud Jeppesen at the Univ. of Århus and with Holmboe, Jersild, and Høffding at the Royal Danish Cons. of Music in Copenhagen (graduated, 1960), and worked at the Stockholm electronic music studio (1967–68). After teaching at the Århus Cons. (1962–71), he settled in Copenhagen and devoted himself to composition; in 1982 he was awarded a State Grant for Life. Among his honors are the Prix Italia (1970) and 1st prizes in the "Homage to Kazimierz Serocki" International Competition (1984) and the Spittal International Composition Competition (1987). In his music, he employs a variety of quaquaversal techniques, often utilizing highly sonorous effects.

WORKS: DRAMATIC: OPERAS: *Stalten Mette* (Århus, Nov. 17, 1963; rev. 1980); *Die Schlange* (1964; rev. 1974); *Eurydike* (1965; Danish Radio, Dec. 16, 1969); *Die Musik kommt mir äusserst bekannt vor* (Kiel, May 3, 1974); *Eine wundersame Liebesgeschichte* (Munich, Dec. 2, 1979); *Klovnen Toto* (1982); *Fackeltanz* (1986). **INSTRUMENTAL THEATER:** *Studies for 2* for Cello or Guitar and Percussion (1967); *Studies for 3* for Soprano Cello or Guitar, and Percussion (1968); *The End* for Cello (1969); *Friisholm*, film (1971); *3 Mobiles* for 3 Different Instruments (1979; rev. 1988). **ORCH.:** *Deep* (1967; rev. 1981); *Tide* (Copenhagen, March 31, 1971); *Partita popolare* for Strings (1976); Oboe Concerto (1980; Danish Radio, Feb. 18, 1982); Cello Concerto (Danish Radio, May 11, 1984); Piano Concerto (1984; Odense, Jan. 11, 1985); *Latin Suite I* (1984; also for Symphonic Band) and *II* for Symphonic or Brass Band (1987); Saxophone Concerto (1986; Danish Radio, March 6, 1987); *Regenbogen* for Trumpet and Orch. (1991). **CHAMBER:** *Quadrata* for String Quartet (1963); *Cyclus I* for Viola, Cello, and Double Bass (1966; rev. 1986), *II* for 2 Percussion and Harp (1966; rev. 1987), and *III* for Cello and Tape (1966; rev. 1981); *Syncretism* for Clarinet, Trombone, Cello, and Piano (1970); *Quartetto rustico* for String Quartet (1972); *Contorni* for Violin, Cello, and Piano (1978); *Samba* for Clarinet, Trombone, Cello, and Piano (1980); *Wunderblumen* for 12 Musicians (1982); *Mambo* for Clarinet, Cello, and Piano (1982); *Paesaggio* for Flute, Oboe, Clarinet, Bassoon, Horn, Violin, and Viola (1983); *Paradiesvogel* for Flute, Clarinet, Violin, Cello, Guitar, Percussion, and Piano (1983; Warsaw, July 7, 1984); *Dunkelblau* for Flute, Viola, and Harp (1985); *Quartetto Barbaro* for String Quartet (1990); *Farbentiegel* for Alto Saxophone and Piano (1990); *Cries* for Electric Guitar (1991); *Tears* for Accordion (1992); *Tiefe* for Double Bass (1993); piano pieces; organ music. **VOCAL:** *Genesis V* for Chorus and Orch. (1984; Århus, May 19, 1985); *Comics* for Entertainer, Amateur Tenor Saxophone, Electric Bass, Percussion Group, Children's Chorus, and Chorus (1987; Århus, Aug. 27, 1988); choruses; songs. **TAPE:** *The Bottomless Pit* (1972); *Cloud Drift* (1973); *Visions* (1978).

Lorenz, Alfred (Ottokar), Austrian musicologist, composer, and conductor; b. Vienna, July 11, 1868; d. Munich, Nov. 20, 1939. He studied with Radecke (conducting) and Spitta (musicology) in Berlin. He was a conductor in Königsberg, Elberfeld, and Munich (1894–97), then became a conductor (1898) and later chief conductor (1904) in Coburg; was made director of its Opera (1917); was also director of the Musikverein in Gotha (1901–18) and Coburg (1907–20). He then gave up his conducting career and studied musicology with Moritz Bauer at the Univ. of Frankfurt am Main (graduated, 1922); lectured at the Univ. of Munich from 1923. He made a specialty of Wagnerian research; publ. the comprehensive work *Das Geheimnis der Form bei Richard Wagner* (4 vols., Berlin, 1924–33; 2nd ed., 1966); also publ. *Alessandro Scarlattis Jugendoper* (Augsburg, 1927) and *Abendländische Musikgeschichte im Rhythmus der Generationen* (Berlin, 1928). He composed an opera, *Helges Erwachen* (Schwerin, 1896); incidental music to various plays; symphonic poems: *Bergfahrt* and *Columbus*; chamber music; songs.

BIBL.: F. Herzfeld, "A. L. der Wagner-Forscher," *Archiv für Musikwissenschaft*, LXIII (1936).

Lorenz, Max, greatly admired German tenor; b. Düsseldorf, May 17, 1901; d. Salzburg, Jan. 11, 1975. He studied with Grenzebach in Berlin. He made his debut as Walther von der Vogelweide in *Tannhäuser* at the Dresden State Opera (1927); sang at the Berlin State Opera (1929–44) and the Vienna State Opera (1929–33; 1936–44; 1954). He made his Metropolitan Opera debut in N.Y. as Walther von Stolzing in *Die Meistersinger von Nürnberg* on Nov. 12, 1931; was again on its roster in 1933–34 and from 1947 to 1950. Lorenz also sang at the Bayreuth Festivals (1933–39; 1952), London's Covent Garden (1934; 1937), the Chicago Opera (1939–40), and the Salzburg Festivals (1953–55; 1961). He was particularly esteemed as a Wagnerian; was also a noted Florestan, Othello, and Bacchus.

BIBL.: W. Herrmann, *M. L.* (Vienna, 1976).

Lorenzo Fernândez, Oscar, Brazilian composer and teacher; b. Rio de Janeiro, Nov. 4, 1897; d. there, Aug. 26, 1948. He was a student of João Otaviano (piano and theory) before pursuing his training at the Instituto Nacionale de Música in Rio de Janeiro with Oswald (piano), Nascimento (harmony), and Braga (counterpoint and fugue). In 1924 he joined its faculty as prof. of harmony; later was founder-director of the Brazilian Cons. (1936–48). His works, derived from Brazilian folk songs, followed along national lines.

WORKS: OPERA: *Malazarte* (1931–33; Rio de Janeiro, Sept. 30, 1941; orch. suite, 1941). **ORCH.:** Piano Concerto (1924); *Suite sinfônica sôbre 3 temas populares brasileiros* (1925); *Imbapará, poema amerindio* (1928; Rio de Janeiro, Sept. 2, 1929); *Amayo, bailado incaico* (1930; Rio de Janeiro, July 9, 1939); *Reisado do pastoreio* (Rio de Janeiro, Aug. 22, 1930);

Violin Concerto (1941); 2 syms. (1945, 1947); *Variações sinfônicas* for Piano and Orch. (1948). **CHAMBER:** Piano Trio (1921); *Trio brasileiro* for Piano Trio (1924); Suite for Wind Quintet (1926); 2 string quartets; piano pieces. **VOCAL:** Songs.

Lorenzo, Leonardo de, Italian-American flutist, teacher, and composer; b. Viggiano, Aug. 29, 1875; d. Santa Barbara, Calif., July 27, 1962. He studied at the Naples Cons. From 1897 to 1907 he was a flutist in various traveling orchs. In 1910 he emigrated to the U.S.; was 1st flutist of the N.Y. Phil. (1910–12); later, with the Minneapolis Sym. Orch., the Los Angeles Phil., and the Rochester Phil.; taught flute at the Eastman School of Music in Rochester, N.Y.; in 1935 he settled in California. He publ. several books of flute studies and some solo pieces, and an informative book on flute playing and flute players, *My Complete Story of the Flute* (N.Y., 1951).

Loriod, Yvonne, distinguished French pianist and teacher; b. Houilles, Seine-et-Oise, Jan. 20, 1924. She studied at the Paris Cons., winning no less than 7 premiers prix; among her mentors were Eminger-Sivade, Lévy, Philipp, and Ciampi for piano, Estyle for piano accompaniment, Calvet for chamber music, Plé-Caussade for fugue, and Messiaen and Milhaud for composition. After World War II, she toured extensively; made her U.S. debut in the premiere of Messiaen's *Turangalîla-Symphonie* with the Boston Sym. Orch. (Dec. 2, 1949). She taught at the Paris Cons. from 1967 to 1989. A foremost champion of the music of Messiaen, she married him in 1961. She also excelled in performances of the music of Bartók, Schoenberg, and Boulez.

Lortie, Louis, Canadian pianist; b. Montreal, April 27, 1959. He began piano lessons at age 7 in Montreal at the École de musique Wilfred-Pelletier; later studied at the École normal de musique. In 1975 he won the CBC Talent Festival and International Stepping Stones of the Canadian Music Competition, and subsequently appeared as a recitalist and performed on the CBC. He also completed his training with Deiter Weber in Vienna (1975–76), Menahem Pressler at the Indiana Univ. School of Music in Bloomington, and Marc Durand. In 1978 he won distinction as one of the soloists to accompany Andrew Davis and the Toronto Sym. on their tour of Japan and China. After taking 1st prize in the Busoni Competition in Bolzano and 4th prize in the Leeds Competition in 1984, he made regular tours of Europe and North America. His commanding repertoire ranges from Mozart to the contemporary era.

Los Angeles (real name, **Gómez Cima**), **Victoria de,** famous Spanish soprano; b. Barcelona, Nov. 1, 1923. She studied at the Barcelona Cons. with Dolores Frau. In 1941 she made her operatic debut as Mimi in Barcelona, but then resumed her training. In 1945 she made her formal operatic debut as Mozart's Countess in Barcelona. After winning 1st prize in the Geneva International Competition in 1947, she sang Salud in *La Vida Breve* with the BBC in London in 1948. In 1949 she made her first appearance at the Paris Opéra as Marguerite. In 1950 she sang at the Salzburg Festival for the first time. She made her debut at London's Covent Garden as Mimi in 1950, and continued to appear there regularly with notable success until 1961. She also sang at Milan's La Scala from 1950 to 1956. On Oct. 24, 1950, she made her first appearance in the U.S. in a Carnegie Hall recital in N.Y. She made her Metropolitan Opera debut in N.Y. as Marguerite on March 17, 1951, and remained on its roster until 1956. In 1957 she sang at the Vienna State Opera, and was again on the roster of the Metropolitan Opera from 1957 to 1961. After making her debut at the Bayreuth Festival as Elisabeth in 1961, she devoted herself principally to a concert career. However, she continued to make occasional appearances in one of her favorite operatic roles, Carmen, during the next 2 decades. Her concert career continued as she entered her 7th decade, highlighted by a well-received recital appearance at N.Y.'s Alice Tully Hall on March 7, 1994. Among her other acclaimed operatic roles were Donna Anna, Rosina, Manon, Nedda, Desdemona, Cio-Cio-San, Violetta, and Mélisande. As a concert artist, she excelled particularly in Spanish and French songs.

Lothar, Mark, German composer; b. Berlin, May 23, 1902; d. Munich, April 6, 1985. He studied with Schreker (composition), Juon (harmony), and Krasselt (conducting) at the Berlin Hochschule für Musik (1919–20), and later with Meiszner (piano) and Wolf-Ferrari (composition). He was active as piano accompanist to the Dutch singer Cora Nerry, whom he married in 1934. Lothar served as director of music at Berlin's Deutsche Theater (1933–34) and Prussian State Theater (1934–44), and at the Bavarian State Theater in Munich (1945–55). In addition to his various dramatic scores, he wrote a number of lieder.

WORKS: DRAMATIC: OPERAS: *Tyll* (Weimar, Oct. 14, 1928); *Lord Spleen* (Dresden, Nov. 11, 1930); *Münchhausen* (Dresden, June 6, 1933); *Das kalte Herz*, radio opera (Berlin Radio, March 24, 1935); *Schneider Wibbel* (Berlin, May 12, 1938); *Rappelkopf* (Munich, Aug. 20, 1958); *Der Glücksfischer* (Nuremberg, March 16, 1962); *Liebe im Eckhaus*, Singspiel (n.d.); *Der widerspenstige Heilige* (Munich, Feb. 8, 1968); *Momo und die Zeitdiebe* (Coburg, Nov. 19, 1978); *La bocca della verità: Hommage à Baldassare Galuppi* (1982); incidental music to many plays and radio dramas; film scores. **ORCH.:** *Verwandlung eines Barockthemas* (1958); Concertino for 4 Clarinets, Strings, Harp, and Percussion (1962); Concertino for 2 Pianos, Strings, and Percussion (1972). **OTHER:** Chamber music; piano pieces; choral works; numerous songs.

BIBL.: A. Ott, ed., *M. L.: Ein Musikerporträt* (Munich, 1968); F. Messmer et al., *M. L.* (Tutzing, 1986).

Lott, Felicity (Ann), English soprano; b. Cheltenham, May 8, 1947. She studied in London at Royal Holloway College, Univ. of London, and at the Royal Academy of Music. In 1976 she sang at London's Covent Garden in the premiere of Henze's *We Come to the River*; she also appeared there as Anne Trulove in Stravinsky's *The Rake's Progress*, as Octavian in *Der Rosenkavalier*, and in various other roles. She appeared in Paris for the first time in 1976; made her Vienna debut in 1982 singing the *4 Letze Lieder* of Strauss; in 1984 she was engaged as soloist with the Chicago Sym. Orch. In 1986 she sang at the wedding of the Duke and the Duchess of York at Westminster Abbey. In 1990 she was made a Commander of the Order of the British Empire. On Sept. 4, 1990, she made her Metropolitan Opera debut in N.Y. as the Marschallin. She chose that same role for her San Francisco Opera debut in 1993. Among her finest roles are Pamina, Countess Almaviva, Donna Elvira, Octavian, Arabella, and Anne Trulove.

Loucheur, Raymond, French composer and pedagogue; b. Tourcoing, Jan. 1, 1899; d. Nogent-sur-Marne, Sept. 14, 1979. He was a student of Woollett in Le Havre (1915–18) and of Boulanger, Gédalge, d'Indy, Fauchet, and Vidal at the Paris Cons. (1920–23). In 1928 he won the Premier Grand Prix de Rome with his cantata *Héracles à Delphe*. He was active in Paris, where he taught (1925–40); after serving as inspector of musical education in the city schools (from 1941), he was director of the Cons. (1956–62). His music was chromatically lyrical and displayed rhythmic spontaneity.

WORKS: BALLET: *Hof-Frog* (1935–48; Paris, June 17, 1953). **ORCH.:** 3 syms.: No. 1 (1929–33; Paris, Dec. 15, 1936; rev. 1969), No. 2 (1944; Paris, Feb. 15, 1945), and No. 3 (1971; Paris, Oct. 17, 1972); *Défilé* (1936); *Pastorale* (1939); *Rapsodie malgache* (Paris, Oct. 10, 1945); *Divertissement* (1951); Violin Concerto (1960–63; Paris, Feb. 28, 1965); Percussion Concertino (1963; Paris, Jan. 9, 1966); *Cortège, Interlude, et Danse* for Winds, Harp, and Percussion (1964–66); Cello Concerto (1967–68; Radio Luxembourg, July 11, 1968); *Thrène* for Flute and Strings (1971); *Hommage à Raoul Dufy* (1973; Paris, Oct. 27, 1974); *Évocations* for Wind Orch. (1974; Paris, March 7, 1976). **CHAMBER:** String Quartet (1930); *En famille* for Clarinet Sextet (1932; also for Chamber Orch., 1940); *Portraits* for Clarinet, Oboe, and Bassoon (1947); *4 pièces en quintette* for Harp, Flute, Violin, Viola, and Cello (1953); Concertino for Trumpet and Clarinet Sextet (1954; also for Trumpet and Orch., 1956); Sonata for Solo Violin (1959); *Recontres* for Oboe and Cello (1972); *Reflets* for Brass Quintet (1976). **VOCAL:** *Héracles à Delphe*, cantata (1928; Le Havre, June 12, 1929); *3 Duos* for Soprano, Chorus, and Orch. (1934); *La Ballade des petites filles qui n'ont pas de poupée* for 4 Soli, Chorus, and Piano (1936); *L'Apothéose de la Seine* for Narrator, Mezzo-soprano, Chorus, Ondes Martenot, and Orch. (Paris, July 7, 1937); *5 poèmes de R.-M. Rilke* for Mezzo-soprano and String Quartet (1952–57).

Loudová, Ivana, Czech composer; b. Chlumec nad Cidlinou, March 8, 1941. After training with Kabeláč at the Prague Cons. (1958–61), she was a student of Hlobil at the Prague Academy of Arts (1961–66); she then attended the summer courses in new music in Darmstadt (1967–69), pursued postgraduate studies with Kabeláč at the Prague Academy of Arts (1968–72), and had lessons with Messiaen and Jolivet in Paris (1971). In 1980 she served as composer-in-residence of the American Wind Sym. Orch. in Pittsburgh. In her works, she makes use of both traditional and modern compositional procedures.

WORKS: BALLET: *Rhapsody in Black* (1966). **ORCH.:** *Fantasy* (1961); Concerto for Chamber Orch. (1962); 2 syms.: No. 1 (1964) and No. 2 for Contralto, Chorus, and Orch. (1965); *Spleen (Hommage à Charles Baudelaire)* (1971); *Hymnos* (1972); *Chorale* (1974); Concerto for 6 Percussion, Organ, and Wind Orch. (1974); *Cadenza* for Violin, Flute, and Strings (1975); *Nocturno* for Viola and Strings (1975); *Partita* for Flute, Harpsichord, and Strings (1975); *Magic Concerto* for Xylophone, Marimba, Vibraphone, and Wind Orch. (1976); *Concerto breve* for Flute or Violin and Orch. (1979); *Olympic Overture* for Wind Orch. (1979); *Dramatic Concerto* for Percussion and Wind Orch. (1979); *Luminous Voice* for English Horn and Wind Orch. (1985); Double Concerto for Violin, Percussion, and Strings (1989). **CHAMBER:** Suite for Flute (1959); Violin Sonata (1961); Clarinet Sonata (1964); 2 string quartets (1964, 1978); *Ballata Antica* for Trombone and Piano (1966); *Solo for King David* for Harp (1972); *Air a due boemi* for Bass Clarinet and Piano (1972); *Ritornello* for 2 Trumpets, Horn, Tuba, and Percussion (1973); *Agamemnon* for Solo Percussion (1973); *Romeo and Juliet*, suite for Flute, Violin, Viola, Cello, and Harp or Lute (1974); *Soli e tutti* for Flute, Oboe, Violin, Viola, Cello, and Harps (1976); *Ballata eroica* for Violin and Piano (1976); *Meditations* for Flute, Bass Clarinet, Piano, and Percussion (1977); *Mattinata* for Clarinet, Trombone, and Cello (1978); *Quintetto giubiloso* for 2 Trumpets, Horn, Trombone, and Tuba (1979); *Musica festiva* for 3 Trumpets and 3 Trombones (1981); *Flower for Emmanuel* (in memory of C.P.E. Bach) for Jazz Quintet (1981); *Duo concertante* for Bass Clarinet and Marimba (1982); *2 Eclogues* (in memory of Vergil) for Flute and Harp (1982); *Hukvaldy Suite* (in memory of Janáček) for String Quartet (1984); Trio for Violin, Cello, and Piano (1987); *Trio Italiano* for Clarinet, Bassoon, and Piano (1987); *Don Giovanni's Dream* for Wind Octet (1989); *Variations on a Stamic Theme* for String Quartet (1989); *Mediativo* for Voice and Cello (1994). **OTHER:** Piano pieces and much choral music.

Louël, Jean (Hippolyte Oscar), Belgian composer and conductor; b. Ostend, Jan. 3, 1914. He studied at the Ghent Cons. with Joseph Ryelandt (composition), and at the Brussels Cons. with Joseph Jongen (theory) and Defauw (conducting); then studied conducting with Bigot and Paray at the Paris Cons. (diploma, 1943); won the Belgian Prix de Rome in 1943 for his cantata *La Navigation* d'Ulysse. He became a teacher at the Brussels Cons. (1943); was director of music academies in Alost (1945–49) and Anderlecht (1949–56). He was founder-conductor of the chamber orch. of the Concerts di Midi in Brussels (1949–70). In 1956 he became inspector of music schools in Flemish Belgium; in 1959, became a teacher of composition at the Chapelle Musicale Reine Elisabeth, retiring in 1984.

WORKS: ORCH.: *Fantaisie sur 2 chansons de trouvères* (1942); *Suite* for Chamber Orch. or Piano (1942); *Burlesque* for Bassoon and Orch. (1943); *March funèbre* and *Triomfmarch* (1945); 2 piano concertos (1945, 1949); *Concerto da camera* for Flute and Orch. (1946–47); 2 violin concertos (1950, 1971); 3 syms.: No. 1 (withdrawn), No. 2 for Strings (1968), and No. 3 (1984–85); *Toccata and Fugue* for Winds (1974); *Rhapsody* (1975); Horn Concerto (1981); *Funeral Music* (1984); Cello Concerto (1986). **CHAMBER:** Clarinet Sonata (1935); Brass Trio (1951); Wind Quintet (1958); Violin Sonata (1960); *Suite* for Flute, Cello, Vibraphone, and Harp (1967); *L'Art d'être Grand'père*, 10 pieces for Piano (1978); Saxophone Quartet (1983); Sonata for Solo Violin (1985); Clarinet Quartet (1986).

Loughran, James, Scottish conductor; b. Glasgow, June 30, 1931. He studied with Peter Maag in Bonn, where he was a répétiteur at the City Theater; also studied in Amsterdam and Milan. In 1961 he won 1st prize in a conducting competition sponsored by the Philharmonia Orch. in London. From 1962 to 1965 he was assoc. conductor of the Bournemouth Sym. Orch.; then was principal conductor of the BBC Scottish Sym. Orch in Glasgow (1965–71). He served as principal conductor of the Hallé Orch. in Manchester (1971–83), and chief conductor of the Bamberg Sym. Orch. (1979–83). He was chief guest conductor of the BBC Welsh Sym. Orch. in Cardiff (1987–90) and permanent guest conductor of the Japan Phil. in Tokyo (from 1993).

Lourié, Arthur Vincent (real name, **Artur Sergeievich Lure**), Russian-born American composer; b. St. Petersburg, May 14, 1892; d. Princeton, N.J., Oct. 13, 1966). He studied at the St. Petersburg Cons. but gave up formal training after becoming active in various modernistic groups, including the futurists. With the coming of the Bolshevik Revolution in 1917, he was made chief of the music dept. of the Commisarit for Public Instruction in 1918. In 1921 he went to Berlin, where he met Busoni. In 1924 he proceeded to Paris, where he was befriended by Stravinsky. In 1941 he emigrated to the U.S. and in 1947 became a naturalized American citizen. He was the author of the vol. *Profanation et sanctification du temps* (Paris, 1966). As early as 1915, Lourié experimented with 12-tone techniques in his piano music. He later pursued the practice of stylizing early forms à la Stravinsky.

WORKS: DRAMATIC: *The Feast During the Plague*, opera-ballet (1935; arranged for Soprano, Chorus, and Orch., Boston, Jan. 5, 1945); *The Blackamoor of Peter the Great*, opera (1961). **ORCH.:** *Sonata liturgica* for Piano, Chorus, and Orch. (1928); *Concerto spirituale* for Piano, Chorus, and Double Basses (N.Y., March 26, 1930); 2 syms.: No. 1, *Sinfonia dialectica* (1930; Philadelphia, April 17, 1931) and No. 2, *Kormtschaya* (1939; Boston, Nov. 7, 1941); *Concerto da camera* for Violin and Strings (1957). **CHAMBER:** *Dithyrambes* for Flute (1923); *The Mime* for Clarinet (1956); piano pieces. **VOCAL:** Sacred and secular choral pieces; songs.

BIBL.: D. Gojowy, *A. L. und der Russische Futurismus* (Laaber, 1993).

Love, Shirley, American mezzo-soprano; b. Detroit, Jan. 6, 1940. She studied voice in Detroit with Avery Crew and in N.Y. with Marinka Gurewich and Margaret Harshaw; then sang with the Baltimore Opera (1962). She first appeared in a minor role at the Metropolitan Opera in N.Y. on Nov. 30, 1963; subsequently gained experience as a singer with other American opera companies; returned to the Metropolitan in 1970, remaining on its roster until 1984. She also appeared in opera in Europe, sang in concerts with major American orchs., gave recitals, and appeared in musical comedies. Her operatic repertoire includes more than 100 roles.

Löveberg, Aase (née **Nordmo**), Norwegian soprano; b. Målselv, June 10, 1923. She was born into a peasant family; spent her childhood on a farm near the Arctic Circle. When she was 19 she went to Oslo, where she studied voice with Haldis Ingebjart. She made her operatic debut in Oslo on Dec. 3, 1948; then sang in Stockholm, Vienna, Paris, and London. She made her first American appearance as a soloist with the Philadelphia Orch. (Dec. 6, 1957); then pursued her career mainly in Norway, later serving as manager of the Oslo Opera (1978–81).

Löwe, Ferdinand, noted Austrian conductor; b. Vienna, Feb. 19, 1865; d. there, Jan. 6, 1925. He studied with Dachs, Krenn, and Bruckner at the Vienna Cons.; then taught piano and choral singing there (1883–96) and was conductor of the Vienna Singakademie (1896–98). In 1897 he became conductor of the Kaim Orch. in Munich; then of the Court Opera in Vienna (1898–1900) and of the Vienna Gesellschaftskonzerte (1900–1904). In 1904 he became conductor of the newly organized Vienna Konzertverein Orch., which he made one of the finest instrumental bodies in Europe. He returned to Munich as conductor of the Konzertverein Orch. (1908–14), which comprised members of the former Kaim Orch. From 1918 to 1922 he was head of the Vienna Academy of Music. He was a friend and trusted disciple of Bruckner; ed. (somewhat liberally) several of Bruckner's works, including his 4th Sym., preparing a new Finale (1887–88); he also made a recomposed version of his unfinished 9th Sym., which he conducted in Vienna with Bruckner's *Te Deum* in lieu of the unfinished Finale (Feb. 11, 1903).

Lowens, Irving, eminent American musicologist, music critic, and librarian; b. N.Y., Aug. 19, 1916; d. Baltimore, Nov. 14, 1983. He studied at Teachers College, Columbia Univ. (B.S. in music, 1939). During World War II, he served as an air-traffic controller for the Civil Aeronautics Administration; continued in this capacity at the National Airport in Washington, D.C.; then took special courses in American civilization at the Univ. of Maryland (M.A., 1957; Ph.D., 1965). In 1953 he began to write music criticism for the *Washington Star*, from 1960 to 1978 he was its chief music critic; received the ASCAP-Deems Taylor Award for the best articles on music in 1972 and 1977. From 1960 to 1966 he was a librarian in the Music Division of the Library of Congress in Washington, D.C. From 1978 to 1981 he was dean of the Peabody Inst. of the Johns Hopkins Univ. in Baltimore; also wrote music criticism for the *Baltimore News American*. A linguist, he traveled widely on numerous research grants in Europe. He was a founding member of the Music Critics' Assn., and from 1971 to 1975 served as its president.

WRITINGS: *The Hartford Harmony: A Selection of American Hymns from the Late 18th and Early 19th Centuries* (Hartford, 1953); *Music and Musicians of Early America* (N.Y., 1964); *Source Readings in American Music History* (N.Y., 1966); *Lectures on the History and Art of Music at the Library of Congress, 1946–63* (N.Y., 1968); *A Bibliography of American Songsters Published before 1821* (Worcester, Mass., 1976); *Haydn in America* (Washington, D.C., 1977); with A. Britton and R. Crawford, *American Sacred Music Imprints, 1698–1810: A Bibliography* (Worcester, Mass., 1990).

Lowenthal, Jerome (Nathaniel), American pianist; b. Philadelphia, Feb. 11, 1932. He studied piano at an early age; made his debut with the Philadelphia Orch. at the age of 13; then took lessons with Samaroff at the Philadelphia Cons. (1947–50). While taking courses at the Univ. of Pa. (B.A., 1953), he received private piano instruction from Kapell; continued his studies with Steuermann at the Juilliard School of Music in N.Y. (M.S., 1956) and with Cortot at the École Normale de Musique (licence de concert, 1958). In 1957 he took 1st prize in the Darmstadt competition. He traveled to Israel, where he gave concerts and taught at the Jerusalem Academy of Music; returned to the U.S. in 1961. He made his professional debut as soloist with the N.Y. Phil. in 1963, and subsequently toured throughout North and South America, the Middle East, and the Far East. From 1990 he taught at the Juilliard School in N.Y. His repertoire embraces the standard piano literature as well as contemporary works; among composers who wrote special works for him were George Rochberg and Ned Rorem.

Lowinsky, Edward E(lias), eminent German-born American musicologist; b. Stuttgart, Jan. 12, 1908; d. Chicago, Oct. 11, 1985. He studied at the Hochschule für Musik in Stuttgart (1923–28); took his Ph.D. at the Univ. of Heidelberg in 1933 with the diss. *Das Antwerpener Motettenbuch Orlando di Lassos und seine Beziehungen zum Motettenschaffen der niederländischen Zeitgenössen* (publ. in The Hague, 1937). When the Nazis came to power in Germany in 1933, he fled to the Netherlands; when the dark cloud of anti-Semitism reached the Netherlands, he emigrated to the U.S. (1940), becoming a naturalized American citizen in 1947. He was assistant prof. of music at Black Mountain College (1942–47); assoc. prof. of music at Queens College, N.Y. (1948–56); prof. of music at the Univ. of Calif., Berkeley (1956–61); and prof. of music at the Univ. of Chicago (1961–76), where he also held a post-retirement professorship until 1978. He held Guggenheim fellowships in 1947–48 and 1976–77; was a Fellow at the Inst. for Advanced Study at Princeton Univ. from 1952 to 1954; was made a Fellow of the American Academy of Arts and Sciences in 1973; was named Albert A. Bauman Distinguished Research Fellow of the Newberry Library in Chicago in 1982. He was general ed. of the Monuments of Renaissance Music series; publ. the valuable studies *Secret Chromatic Art in the Netherlands Motet* (N.Y., 1946) and *Tonality and Atonality in Sixteenth-Century Music* (Berkeley and Los Angeles, 1961; rev. printing, 1962; new ed. by B. Blackburn, 1990). He also prepared the vol. *Josquin des Prez. Proceedings of the International Josquin Festival-Conference* (London, 1976) and wrote the study *Cipriano de Rore's Venus Motet: Its Poetic and Pictorial Sources* (Provo, 1986). He was married to **Bonnie Blackburn**. She ed. *Music in the Culture of the Renaissance and Other Essays by Edward E. Lowinsky* (Chicago, 1989). With Lowinsky and C. Miller, she ed. and tr. *A Correspondence of Renaissance Musicians* (Oxford, 1991).

Lualdi, Adriano, Italian composer; b. Larino, March 22, 1885; d. Milan, Jan. 8, 1971. He was a student in Rome of Falchi and in Venice of Wolf-Ferrari. In 1918 he settled in Milan and was active as a music critic and administrator. As a loyal Fascist, he served as director of the Cons. of San Pietro a Majella in Naples (1936–44). After the fall of the Fascist regime, he was forced to withdraw from public life but later resumed his career and was director of the Florence Cons. (1947–56). Lualdi was best known for his dramatic works.

WORKS: DRAMATIC: *Le nozze di Haura*, opera (1908; rev. 1913; Italian Radio, Oct. 19, 1939; stage premiere, Rome, April 18, 1943); *La figlia del re*, opera (1914–17; Turin, March 18, 1922); *Le furie di Arlecchino*, opera (Milan, May 17, 1915; rev. 1925); *Il diavolo nel campanile*, opera (1919–23; Milan, April 21, 1925; rev. 1952; Florence, May 21, 1954); *La grançeola*, opera (Venice, Sept. 10, 1932); *Lumawig e la saetta*, mimodrama (1936; Rome, Jan. 23, 1937; rev. 1956); *Eurydikes diatheke* or *Il testamento di Euridice*, opera (c.1940–62; RAI, Nov. 22, 1962); *La luna dei Caraibi*, opera (1944; Rome, Jan. 29, 1953); *Tre alla radarstratotropojonosferaphonotheca del Luna Park*, satiric radio comedy (c.1953–62). **ORCH.:** 2 symphonic poems: *La leggenda del vecchio marinaio* (1910) and *L'interludio del sogno* (1917); *Suite adriatica* (1932); *Africa*, rhapsody (1936); *Divertimento* (1941). **VOCAL:** *La rosa di Saron* or *Il cantico*, cantata (Milan, May 10, 1915); many choruses.

WRITINGS (all publ. in Milan): *Viaggio musicale in Italia* (1927); *Serate musicali* (1928); *Viaggio musicale in Europa* (1928); *Arte e regime* (1929); *Il rinnovamento musicale italiano* (1931); *Viaggio musicale nel Sud-America* (1934); *L'arte di dirigere l'orchestra* (1940; 3rd ed., 1958); *Viaggio musicale nell'URSS* (1941); *Tutti vivi* (1955); *La bilancia di Euripide: 10 libretti d'opera* (1969).

BIBL.: G. Confalonieri, *L'opera di A. L.* (Milan, 1932).

Lubimov, Alexei, esteemed Russian pianist and fortepianist; b. Moscow, Sept. 16, 1944. Following initial instruction at the Moscow Central Music School, he entered the Moscow Cons. in 1963 and studied with Neuhaus. He first attracted notice with his compelling performances of modern scores. In 1968 he gave the Moscow premieres of works by John Cage and Terry Riley, and subsequently championed the works of such masters as Schoenberg, Ives, Webern, Stockhausen, Boulez, and Ligeti, as well as many contemporary Russian composers. His interests were extensive, leading him to explore not only contemporary works but those from the standard repertoire as well as the early music repertoire for fortepiano. He made regular tours of Europe before making his North American debut as soloist with Andrew Parrott and the Classical Band in N.Y. in 1991.

Lubin, Germaine (Léontine Angélique), noted French soprano; b. Paris, Feb. 1, 1890; d. there, Oct. 27, 1979. She studied at the Paris Cons. (1909–12) and with F. Litvinne and Lilli Lehmann. She made her debut at the Paris Opéra-Comique in 1912 as Antonio in *Les Contes d'Hoffmann.* In 1914 she joined the Paris Opéra, remaining on its roster until 1944; also appeared at London's Covent Garden (1937, 1939); in 1938 she became the first French singer to appear at Bayreuth, gaining considerable acclaim for her Wagnerian roles. She continued her career in Paris during the German occupation and was briefly under arrest after the liberation of Paris in 1944, charged with collaboration with the enemy; she was imprisoned for 3 years. After her release, she taught voice. Her most distinguished roles included Alceste, Ariane, Isolde, Kundry, Donna Anna, Leonore, Brünnhilde, Sieglinde, and the Marschallin.

BIBL.: N. Casanov, *Isolde 39—G. L.* (Paris, 1974).

Lubin, Steven, esteemed American pianist and fortepianist; b. N.Y., Feb. 22, 1942. After initial piano training, he studied philosophy at Harvard Univ. (B.A., 1963); he then continued his piano studies at the Juilliard School of Music in N.Y. (M.A., 1965), where his mentors included Rosina Lhévinne and Beveridge Webster, and studied musicology at N.Y. Univ. (Ph.D., 1974). He made his N.Y. debut in 1977. In 1978 he organized the Mozartean Players, a chamber ensemble devoted to presenting period instrument performances; subsequently he toured with them throughout the U.S. He was equally adept in projecting discriminating interpretations of the Classical and Romantic keyboard repertoire, using the keyboard of the fortepiano modeled after the 1800 type of instrument.

Luboff, Norman, American conductor, composer, and arranger; b. Chicago, May 14, 1917; d. Bynum, N.C., Sept. 22, 1987. He received his training in Chicago, where he attended the Univ., Central College, and American Cons. of Music, in the class of Leo Sowerby. After graduation, he was active as a singer and arranger for radio; then went to Hollywood as an arranger for films and television. He founded the Norman Luboff Choir in 1963, and subsequently conducted it on numerous tours, maintaining a vast repertoire of works ranging from classical to popular genres. As a composer, he devoted himself mainly to choral music.

Luboshutz (real name, **Luboshitz**), **Léa,** Russian-American violinist and teacher, sister of **Pierre Luboshutz**; b. Odessa, Feb. 22, 1885; d. Philadelphia, March 18, 1965. She studied violin with her father; played in public at the age of 7; after study at the Odessa Music School, she went to the Moscow Cons., graduating with a gold medal (1903). She gave concerts in Germany and France, and also took additional lessons from Ysaÿe in Belgium; returned to Russia, and organized a trio with her brother and her sister Anna (cello); left Russia after the Revolution and lived in Berlin and Paris (1921–25). In 1925 she settled in N.Y.; played the American premiere of Prokofiev's 1st Violin Concerto (Nov. 14, 1925); made several appearances in joint recitals with her son, the pianist **Boris Goldovsky**. From 1927 she was on the faculty of the Curtis Inst. of Music in Philadelphia.

Luboshutz (real name, **Luboshitz**), **Pierre,** Russian-American pianist, brother of **Léa Luboshutz**; b. Odessa, June 17, 1891; d. Rockport, Maine, April 17, 1971. He studied violin with his father; then turned to the piano, and entered the Moscow Cons. as a pupil of Igumnov, graduating in 1912; also studied in Paris with Edouard Risler. Returning to Russia, he played in a trio with his 2 sisters, Léa (violin) and Anna (cello); in 1926, went to America as accompanist to Zimbalist, Piatigorsky, and others. In 1931 he married Genia Nemenoff (b. Paris, Oct. 23, 1905; d. N.Y., Sept. 19, 1989); with her he formed a piano duo (N.Y. debut, Jan. 18, 1937); as Luboshutz-Nemenoff, they gave annual concerts with considerable success. From 1962 to 1968 they headed the piano dept. at Michigan State Univ.; then returned to N.Y.

Lubotsky, Mark (Davidovich), Russian violinist and teacher; b. Leningrad, May 18, 1931. He was a pupil of Yampolsky and Oistrakh at the Moscow Cons., where he made his debut as soloist in the Tchaikovsky Violin Concerto (1950). He then performed throughout the Soviet Union and Eastern Europe. After making his British debut as soloist in Britten's Violin Concerto at the London Promenade Concerts (1970), he toured internationally. From 1967 to 1976 he taught at the Gnessin Inst. in Moscow. He became a prof. at the Sweelinck Cons. in Amsterdam in 1976. In 1986 he was made a prof. at the Hamburg Hochschule für Musik. His repertoire encompasses a vast range of works, from the Baroque to the most modern scores.

Luca, Sergiu, noted Romanian-born American violinist and teacher; b. Bucharest, April 4, 1943. He began to study violin as a child; in 1950 his parents took him to Israel, where he made his debut as a soloist with the Haifa Sym. Orch. (1952); later continued his studies with Rostal in London, at the Bern Cons. (1958–61), and with Galamian at the Curtis Inst. of Music in Philadelphia (1961–65). He made his U.S. debut as soloist with the Philadelphia Orch. in 1965; subsequently appeared with many American and European orchs. with considerable success. In 1966 he became a naturalized American citizen. He was founder-director of the Chamber Music Northwest Festival in Portland, Oreg. (1971–80); then was prof. of violin at the Univ. of Ill. (1980–83); subsequently was prof. of violin and violinist-in-residence at the Shepherd School of Music at Rice Univ. in Houston (from 1983) and also served as music director of the Texas Chamber Orch. (1983–88). In 1988 he became founder-general director of the Houston-based arts organization Da Camera. He distinguished himself in a broad repertoire, ranging from the Baroque to the contemporary eras. His performances of early music are notable for their stylistic propriety.

Lucas, Leighton, English conductor and composer; b. London, Jan. 5, 1903; d. there, Nov. 1, 1982. He was trained to be a dancer, and was a member of Diaghilev's Ballets Russes in Paris and in London (1918–21). Then he learned conducting and traveled with various ballet companies. From 1946 he conducted his own orch. He made arrangements of classical pieces for ballet and composed his own ballets, *The Wolf's Ride* (1935), *Death in Adagio*, after Scarlatti (1936), *The Horses* (1945–46), and *Tam O'Shanter* (1972–73). He also wrote *Missa pro defunctis* for Soli, Voices, and Orch. (1934); *Sinfonia brevis* for Horn and 11 Instruments (1935); *Suite française* for Orch. (1940); *Divertissement* for Harp and 8 Instruments (1955); Cello Concerto (1956); Clarinet Concerto (1957); *Concert champêtre* for Violin and Orch. (1959); *Disquisition* for 2 Cellos and Piano, 4-hands (1967); String Trio (1969); etc.

Lucchesini, Andrea, Italian pianist; b. Montecatini, July 8, 1965. He began studies at the age of 7 with Maria Tipo, continuing his training at the Istituto Musicale Giuseppe Verdi. After winning the Dino Ciani Competition in Milan in 1983, he embarked upon a tour of Italy, giving a particularly noteworthy recital at Milan's La Scala; also toured in Germany, France, and Switzerland. He made his U.S. debut at the Newport (R.I.) Music Festival in 1984; also appeared elsewhere in the U.S. and throughout Europe.

Lucier, Alvin (Augustus, Jr.), American composer; b. Nashua, N.H., May 14, 1931. He studied with Boatwright, Donovan, Kraehenbuhl, and Porter at Yale Univ. (1950–54); continued his training with Berger, Fine, and Shapero at Brandeis Univ. (1958–60); also studied with Foss (composition) and Copland (orchestration) at the Berkshire Music Center in Tanglewood (1958, 1959); then went to Rome on a Fulbright scholarship (1960–62). He was on the faculty of Brandeis Univ. (1962–70), where he served as choral director. With Robert Ashley, David Behrman, and Gordon Mumma, he founded the Sonic Arts Union (1966), an electronic music performing group with which he toured the U.S. and Europe. He joined the faculty of Wesleyan Univ. (1970); was music director of the Viola Farber Dance Co. (1972–77). He contributed many articles to music journals and other publications; with D. Simon, he publ. *Chambers* (Middletown, Conn., 1980). In 1990 he was in Berlin on a Deutscher Akademischer Austauschdienst fellowship. His works exploit virtually all known musical and non-musical resources available to the creative artist.

WORKS: *Action Music* for Piano (1962); *Music for Solo Performer* for Amplified Brain Waves and Percussion (1965); *North American Time Capsule* for Voices and Vocoder (1967); *Chambers*, realized by moving large and small resonant environments (1968); *Vespers*, acoustic orientation by means of echolocation (1969); *"I am sitting in a room"* for Voice and Electromagnetic Tape (1970); *The Queen of the South* for Players, Responsive Surfaces, Strewn Material, and Closed-circuit Television System (1972); *Still and Moving Lines of Silence in Families of Hyperbolas* for Singers, Players, Dancers, and Unattended Percussion (1973–74; Paris, Oct. 18, 1974); *Outlines of persons and things* for Microphones, Loudspeakers, and Electronic Sounds (1975); *Bird and Person Dyning* for Performer with Microphones, Amplifiers, Loudspeakers, and Sound-producing Object (1975); *Music on a Long Thin Wire* for Audio Oscillators and Electronic Monochord (1977); *Directions of Sounds from the Bridge* for Stringed Instrument, Audio Oscillator, and Sound-sensitive Lights (N.Y., Feb. 11, 1978); *Clocker* for Amplified Clock, Galvanic Skin Response Sensor, and Digital Delay System (1978–88); *Solar Sounder I*, electronic music system powered and controlled by sunlight (1979; in collaboration with John Fullemann); *Shapes of the Sounds from the Board* for Piano (1979); *Lullaby* for Unamplified or Amplified Voice (1979); *Music* for Pure Waves, Bass Drums, and Acoustic Pendulums (1980); *Reflections of Sounds from the Wall* (1981); *Crossings* for Small Orch. with Pure Wave Oscillator (Chicago, July 6, 1982); *Seesaw*, sound installation (1983); *Still and Moving Lines of Silence in Families of Hyperbolas, Part II, Nos. 1–12* (Oakland, Calif., Feb. 16, 1984); *Spinner*, sound installation (1984); *In Memoriam Jon Higgins* for Clarinet and Slow-sweep, Pure Wave Oscillator (Hartford, Conn., Dec. 8, 1984); *Serenade* for 13 Winds and Pure Wave Oscillator (Aspen, Colo., Aug. 8, 1985); *Sound on Paper*, sound installation (1985); Septet for 3 Strings, 4 Winds, and Pure Wave Oscillator (Middletown, Conn., Sept. 20, 1985); *Music for Men, Women, and Reflecting Walls* for Pure Wave Oscillators (N.Y., June 11, 1986); *Salmon River Valley Songs* for Soprano, English Horn, Xylophone, and Pure Wave Oscillators (Hartford, Conn., Sept. 27, 1986); *Kettles* for 5 Timpani and 2 Pure Wave Oscillators (1987); *Fideliotrio* for Viola, Cello, and Piano (1988); *Silver Streetcar for the Orchestra* for Triangle (1988); *Carbon Copies* for Piano, Saxophone, and Percussion (1988); *Amplifier and Reflector I* for Open Umbrella, Ticking Clock, and Glass Oven Dish (1991); *Navigations* for String Quartet (Frankfurt am Main, Oct. 11, 1991).

Luciuk, Juliusz (Mieczyslaw), Polish composer; b. Brzeźnica, Jan. 1, 1927. He studied in Kraków at the Jagiellonian Univ. (graduated in musicology, 1952) and at the State College of Music (diplomas in theory, 1955, and composition, 1956). After further training in composition with Boulanger and Deutsch in Paris (1958–59), he returned to Poland and devoted himself to composition. In 1974 he won 1st prize in the Monaco competition. He received the Golden Cross of Merit of Poland in 1975. In 1983 he was awarded the prize of the City of Kraków. In his extensive output, Luciuk followed a sui generis compositional path.

WORKS: DRAMATIC: *Niobe*, ballet (1962; Gdańsk, May 20, 1967); *The Frock*, mimodrama (Wroclaw, Oct. 25, 1965); *Brand-Peer Gynt*, mimodrama (Oslo, Sept. 28, 1967); *The Death of Euridice*, ballet (1972; Polish TV, Warsaw, Dec. 27, 1974); *When 5 Years Will Go By: The Legend of Time*, choreodrama (Amsterdam, Oct. 9, 1972); *L'Amour d'Orphée*, opera (1973; Wroclaw, Feb. 22, 1980); *Medea*, ballet (Poznań, Oct. 26, 1975); *Demiurgos*, opera (1976; Kraków, April 26, 1990). **ORCH.:** *4 Symphonic Sketches* (1957); *Symphonic Allegro* (1958; Katowice, June 9, 1959); *Composition* for 4 Orchs. (1960; Wroclaw, Nov. 14, 1965); *Speranza Sinfonica* (1969; Częstochowa, June 17, 1972); *Lamentazioni in memoriam Grażyna Bacewicz* (1970; Częstochowa, March 4, 1971); *Warsaw Legend: Quasi Cradle-Song* (1974; Warsaw, Jan. 10, 1976); Double Bass Concerto (Kraków, June 10, 1986). **CHAMBER:** *Capriccio* for Violin and Piano (Warsaw, June 27, 1956); Clarinet Sonata (1956); Bassoon Sonata (1956; Kraków, Nov. 17, 1958); *Variations* for Cello and Piano (1980; Kraków, April 5, 1982); *3 Miniatures* for Violin and Piano (Kraków, May 25, 1984). **KEYBOARD: PIANO:** *4 Miniatures* (1957; Kraków, March 19, 1962); *Arabesque No. 2* for 2 Pianos (1987). **PREPARED PIANO:** *Marathon* (1963; Warsaw, Sept. 21, 1964); *Lirica di Timbri* (1963; Kraków, Dec. 16, 1964); *Pacem in terris* for 2 Players and Soprano (Poznań, May 29, 1964); *Passacaglia* (Kolonia Radio, April 3, 1968). **ORGAN:** *Image* (1977; Poznań, April 17, 1978); *Marienpräludiem* (1982; Kraków, June 6, 1983); *Tripticum Paschale* (1993; Kraków, May 22, 1994). **VOCAL:** *The Latin Mass* for Men's Chorus and Organ (1958); *Floral Dream* for Voice and Orch. (1960; Wenecja, April 25, 1961); *Pour un Ensemble* for Speaking Voice and 24 Strings (1961; Utrecht, Sept. 13, 1962); *Tool of the Light* for Baritone and Orch. (1966; Wroclaw, Jan. 21, 1968); *Poeme de Loire* for Soprano and Orch. (1968; Wroclaw, Feb. 21, 1970); *Le Souffle du Vent* for Baritone and Orch. (Polish TV, Warsaw, Aug. 21, 1971); *Wings and Hands* for Baritone and Orch. (1972; Poznań, April 3, 1975); *Missa Gratiarum Actione* for Women's Chorus (Warsaw, Sept. 22, 1974); *Portraits lyriques* for Soprano and Orch. (1974; Posnań, April 5, 1976); *St. Francis of Assisi*, oratorio for Soprano, Tenor, Baritone, Chorus, and Orch. (Kraków, Oct. 3, 1976); *Hymnus de Caritate* for Chorus (1976; Poznań, April 7, 1981); *4 Antiphonae* for Men's Chorus (1980–84; Aachen, Dec. 16, 1984); *Manen Suita* for Chorus (1983; Warsaw, Nov. 21, 1984); *Polish Litany*, oratorio for Soloists, Chorus, and String Orch. (1984; Częstochowa, Jan. 27, 1985); *Apocalypsis* for Chorus (1985; Poznań, April 28, 1987); *Partes Variables* for Women's Chorus (1985; Kraków, May 13, 1986); *Assumpta est Maria* for Women's Chorus (1987; Częstochowa, Nov. 17, 1989); *Vesperae in Assumptione Beatae Mariae Virginis* for Women's Chorus (1987–89; Aachen, June 9, 1989); *Magnificat* for Chorus (Częstochowa, May 4, 1991); *Antiphone ex Secundis Vesperis in Assumptione Beatae Mariae Virginis* for Chorus (1992); *The Polish Mass* for Mezzo-soprano, Chorus, and Orch. (Częstochowa, May 1, 1993). **OTHER:** Children's pieces.

Lucký, Štěpán, Czech composer; b. Žilina, Jan. 20, 1919. He was a student at the Prague Cons. (1936–39). During the Nazi occupation, he became active in the resistance and was imprisoned in Budapest before being sent to the concentration camps in Auschwitz and Buchenwald. Following the liberation in 1945, he resumed his training at the master school of the Prague Cons. (graduated, 1947). He also studied musicology and aesthetics at the Charles Univ. in Prague (graduated, 1948; Ph.D., 1990). From 1954 to 1959 he served as artistic director of music broadcasting of Czech-TV. He taught television opera directing at the Prague Academy of Music from 1964 to 1969. In 1972 he was made a Merited Artist by the Czech government. A progressive eye disease hampered his activities from about 1985. His music is couched in a pragmatic contemporary style without circumscription by any particular doctrine or technique.

WORKS (all 1st perf. in Prague unless otherwise given): **DRAMATIC:** *Půlnoční překvapení* (Midnight's Surprise), opera (1958–59; May 15, 1959); 40 feature film scores and over 100 short film scores; incidental music for plays, radio, and television. **ORCH.:** Cello Concerto (1946; Dec. 11, 1947); Piano Concerto (Dec. 16, 1947); Violin Concerto (1965; Mariánské Lázně, Feb. 17, 1967); *Ottetto* for Strings (1970; March 6, 1972); Double Concerto for Violin, Piano, and Orch. (1971; Jan. 24, 1974); *Nenia* for Violin, Cello, and Orch. (1974–75; May 21, 1976); *Concerto for Orchestra* (Suhl, Germany, May 4, 1976); *Fantasia concertante* for Bass Clarinet, Piano, and Orch. (1979–84; March 23, 1984). **CHAMBER:** 2 wind quintets: No. 1 (1946;

April 10, 1947) and No. 2, *Deliciae Suhlenses* (1982; Suhl, June 5, 1983); *Sonata brevis* for Violin and Piano (Nov. 3, 1947); *Elegia* for Horn and Piano (1965; Nov. 30, 1966); Sonata for Solo Violin (1967–69; March 3, 1970); *Tre pezzi di Due Doemi* for Bass Clarinet and Piano (1969–70; Biberach, Germany, June 26, 1970); Double Sonata for 2 Violins (1971; March 29, 1974; Duo concertante for Violin and Guitar (1972; March 12, 1973); Flute Sonata (1973; March 9, 1975); *Divertimento* for Wind Quintet (1974; April 1, 1977); *Pastorale* for Oboe and Piano (1975; March 1, 1976); *Preludio e scherzino* for Clarinet (1975; N.Y., Nov. 29, 1976); *Balada* for Cello (1976; Brno, April 21, 1977); *Invence pro Sonatori* for Flute, Bass Clarinet, Piano, and Percussion (May 25, 1977); *Arietta* for Alto Flute or Bass Clarinet and Piano (1977; Stade an der Elbe, Germany, March 6, 1979); *Introduzione e capriccio* for Bassoon and Piano (1977; March 9, 1978); Concertino for Bass Clarinet, Piano, and Strings (1979; April 15, 1980); *Musica collegialis* for 10 Instruments (1980; March 10, 1982); String Quartet (1984; March 13, 1986); Wind Quartet (1985; Suhl, Sept. 23, 1986); Sonatina for 2 Guitars (1986; Jan. 18, 1988). **KEYBOARD: PIANO:** Sonatina (1945; May 7, 1947). **HARPSICHORD:** *Toccata* (Biberach, April 11, 1973). **ORGAN:** *Rapsodia* (1981; Feb. 24, 1986). **VOCAL:** *Stesk* (Nostalgia), song cycle for Soprano and Piano (1940; Feb. 1, 1946); *Nedopěné písně* (Unsong Songs), song cycle for Soprano and Piano (1944; Jan. 14, 1947); *Jak se hladí kočička* (How to stroke a cat) for Children's Chorus (1983–84; Nov. 23, 1986).

Ludgin, Chester (Hall), American baritone; b. N.Y., May 20, 1925. After service in the U.S. Army (1943–46), he was a student of the American Theatre Wing Professional Training Program (1948–50); studied voice with Armen Boyajian. He began his career by singing in nightclubs; made his operatic debut in 1956 as Scarpia with the New Orleans Experimental Opera Theatre of America. In 1957 he became a member of the N.Y. City Opera; sang leading roles with the San Francisco Opera from 1964; made his European debut with the Netherlands Opera in 1977. He created major roles in Ward's *The Crucible* (N.Y., 1961), Imbrie's *Angle of Repose* (San Francisco, 1967), and Bernstein's *A Quiet Place* (Houston, 1983); also made successful appearances in productions of Broadway musicals.

Ludikar (real name, **Vyskočil**), **Pavel,** Czech bass-baritone; b. Prague, March 3, 1882; d. Vienna, Feb. 19, 1970. He studied law in Prague; then took piano lessons, acquiring sufficient proficiency to accompany singers; then finally devoted himself to his real profession, that of opera singing; studied with Lassalle in Paris. He made his operatic debut as Sarastro at the Prague National Theater (1904); then appeared in Vienna, Dresden, and Milan; was a member of the Boston Civic Opera (1913–14). He made his Metropolitan Opera debut in N.Y. as Timur in *Turandot* on Nov. 16, 1926; remained on its roster until 1932; also sang with Hinshaw's touring opera company. He essayed the role of Figaro in *Il Barbiere di Siviglia* more than 100 times in the U.S. He created the title role in Krenek's opera *Karl V* (Prague, June 22, 1938).

Ludkewycz, Stanislaus, significant Polish composer and pedagogue; b. Jaroslav, Galicia, Jan. 24, 1879; d. Lwów, Sept. 10, 1979. He studied philosophy at the Univ. of Lemberg, graduating in 1901; then went to Vienna, where he studied composition with Gradener and Zemlinsky at the Cons. (Ph.D., 1908). He then settled in Lemberg. From 1910 to 1914 he served as director of the Inst. of Music there; then was recruited in the Austrian army, and was taken prisoner by the Russians (1915). After the Russian Revolution, he was evacuated to Tashkent; liberated in 1918, he returned to Lemberg; from 1939 to 1972 he was a prof. of composition at the Cons. there. When the city was incorporated in the Ukrainian Soviet Republic after World War II, Ludkewycz was awarded the Order of the Red Banner by the Soviet government (1949). On the occasion of his 100th birthday in 1979, he received the Order of Hero of Socialist Labor. His music followed the precepts of European Romanticism, with the representational, geographic, and folkloric aspects in evidence. Stylistically, the influence of Tchaikovsky was paramount in his vocal and instrumental compositions.

WORKS: OPERA: *Dovbush* (1955). **ORCH.:** 2 piano concertos (1920, 1957); 4 symphonic poems: *Valse mélancolique* (1920), *Stone Carvers* (1926), *Dnieper* (1947), and *Moses* (1956); Violin Concerto (1945); *Carpathian Symphony* (1952). **CHAMBER:** Piano Trio (1919); *Variations on a Ukrainian Theme* for Violin and Piano (1949); piano pieces. **VOCAL:** *Eternal Revolutionary* for Chorus and Orch. (1898); *Caucasus,* ode for Chorus and Orch. (1905–13); *The Testament,* cantata (1934; rev. 1955); *Conquistadores* for Chorus and Orch. (1941); *A Testament for the Pioneers* for Chorus and Orch. (1967); songs.

BIBL.: M. Zagaikevycz, *S. L.* (Kiev, 1957); S. Pavlishin, *S. L.* (Kiev, 1974).

Ludwig, Christa, celebrated German mezzo-soprano; b. Berlin, March 16, 1924. She was reared in a musical family. Her father, Anton Ludwig, was a tenor and an operatic administrator, and her mother, Eugenie Besalla, was a mezzo-soprano. She studied with her mother and in Frankfurt am Main with Hüni-Mihacsek. In 1946 she made her debut as Orlovsky there, and continued to sing there until 1952. After appearances in Darmstadt (1952–54), she made her debut at the Salzburg Festival as Cherubino in 1954. In 1954–55 she sang in Hannover. In 1955 she joined the Vienna State Opera, where she became one of its principal artists and was made a Kammersängerin in 1962. In 1959 she made her U.S. debut as Dorabella in Chicago. On Dec. 10, 1959, she made her first appearance at the Metropolitan Opera in N.Y. as Cherubino, and subsequently returned there regularly. Among the many outstanding roles she sang in Vienna and N.Y. were Octavian, the Dyer's Wife, Ortrud, Fricka in *Die Walküre,* the Marschallin, Kundry, Charlotte in *Werther,* Lady Macbeth, Didon in *Les Troyens,* and Strauss' Clytemnestra. In 1966 she sang Brangäne at the Bayreuth Festival and in 1969 made her first appearance at London's Covent Garden as Amneris. In addition to her appearances in other leading operatic centers, she pursued a remarkable career as a soloist with orchs. and as a lieder artist. Her performances of Schubert, Schumann, Brahms, Wolf, Mahler, and Strauss were noteworthy. In 1957 she married **Walter Berry,** but they were divorced in 1970. During their marriage and even afterward, they appeared together in operatic and concert settings. On March 20, 1993, Ludwig gave her last N.Y. recital at Carnegie Hall, and on April 3, 1993, made her farewell appearance at the Metropolitan Opera singing Fricka in *Die Walküre.* Her career closed with concert and operatic farewells in Vienna in 1994. In 1980 she received the Golden Ring of the Vienna State Opera, and in 1981 was made its honorary member. She also was awarded the Silver Rose of the Vienna Phil. in 1980. In 1989 she was honored by the French government as a Chevalier of the Légion d'honneur and as a Commandeur de l'ordre des arts et des lettres. Her autobiography was publ. as *". . . und ich wäre so gern Primadonna geworden"* (Berlin, 1994). Ludwig's fine vocal gifts and compelling musical integrity gained her a distinguished reputation as one of the outstanding operatic and concert artists of her day.

BIBL.: P. Lorenz, *C. L.—Walter Berry: Eine Künstler Biographie* (Vienna, 1968).

Ludwig, Friedrich, eminent German musicologist; b. Potsdam, May 8, 1872; d. Göttingen, Oct. 3, 1930. He studied history at the Univs. of Marburg and Strasbourg (Ph.D., 1896); then musicology with G. Jacobsthal. He was a reader (1905–10) and a prof. (1910–20) at the Univ. of Göttingen. He was an authority on medieval music. His most valuable work was *Repertorium organorum recentioris et motetorum vetustissimi stili,* I: *Catalogue raisonné der Quellen,* part 1: *Handschriften in Quadrat-Notation* (Halle, 1910); part 2: *Handschriften in Mensural-Notation* (ed. by F. Gennrich in Summa Musicae Medii Aevi, VII, 1961); II: *Musikalisches Anfangs Verzeichnis des nach Tenores geordneten Repertorium* (ed. by Gennrich in ibid., VIII, 1962). He also ed. an incomplete collection of the works of Guillaume de Machaut (1926–34).

BIBL.: J. Müller-Blattau, *Dem Andenken F. L.s* (Kassel, 1931).

Ludwig, Leopold, Austrian conductor; b. Witkowitz, Jan. 12, 1908; d. Lüneburg, April 25, 1979. He studied piano at the Vienna Cons.; then conducted in provincial opera houses. He was made Generalmusikdirektor of the Oldenburg State Theater (1936); then was a conductor at the Vienna State Opera (1939–43), the Berlin Städtische Oper (1943–51), and the Berlin State Opera (1945–51). From 1951 to 1970 he was Generalmusikdirektor of the Hamburg State Opera; also conducted at the Edinburgh Festivals (1952, 1956), the San Francisco Opera (1958–68), and the Glyndebourne Festival (1959). On Nov. 14, 1970, he made his Metropolitan Opera debut in N.Y. conducting *Parsifal*, and remained on its roster until 1972. He was known as an unostentatious but thoroughly competent interpreter of the Austro-German operatic and symphonic repertoire.

BIBL.: B. Wessling, *L. L.* (Bremen, 1968).

Ludwig, Walther, German tenor; b. Bad Oeynhausen, March 17, 1902; d. Lahr, May 15, 1981. He studied jurisprudence and medicine before deciding on a singing career; studied voice in Königsberg, where he made his debut in 1928. After singing in Schwerin (1929–32), he was a member of the Berlin Städtische Oper (1932–45). He also made appearances at the Glyndebourne Festival, Milan's La Scala, London's Covent Garden, the Salzburg Festival, and the Vienna State Opera; likewise toured as a concert artist. From 1952 to 1969 he was a prof. at the (West) Berlin Hochschule für Musik. He also completed his medical studies in Berlin (M.D., 1971). He was best known for his Mozart roles.

Luening, Otto (Clarence), noted American composer, music educator, flutist, and conductor; b. Milwaukee, June 15, 1900; d. N.Y., Sept. 2, 1996. His father, Eugene Luening, was a pianist, conductor, and teacher. After the family moved to Munich in 1912, he studied flute, piano, and theory (with Beer-Walbrunn) at the Akademie der Tonkunst. In 1916 he made his debut as a flutist in Munich. In 1917 he went to Zürich and studied with Jarnach and Andreae at the Cons. (until 1920). He also attended the Univ. there (1919–20) and profited from his association with Busoni. His Sextet (1918) and 1st String Quartet (1919–20) won him recognition as a composer in Europe and the U.S. After playing flute in the Tonhalle Orch. and the Opera orch. in Zürich, he went to Chicago in 1920. With Gilbert Wilson, he founded the American Grand Opera Co. in 1922. From 1925 to 1928 he was a faculty member at the Eastman School of Music in Rochester, N.Y. In 1929 he went to N.Y. and conducted on WOR Radio and in the theater. In 1932 he was awarded the David Bispham medal for his opera *Evangeline*. After serving as an assistant prof. at the Univ. of Arizona in Tucson (1932–34), he was head of the music dept. at Bennington (Vt.) College (1934–44). From 1935 to 1937 he was assoc. conductor of the N.Y. Phil. Chamber Orch. He was assoc. prof. and chairman of the music dept. at Barnard College from 1944 to 1948, and then a prof. there from 1948 to 1964. In 1944 he became music director of the Brander Matthews Theater at Columbia Univ., where he conducted the premieres of Menotti's *The Medium* (May 8, 1946), Thomson's *The Mother of Us All* (May 7, 1947), and his own *Evangeline* (May 4, 1948). From 1949 to 1968 he was a prof. of music at Columbia Univ., where he also was a co-director of the Columbia-Princeton Electronic Music Center (1959–80) and music chairman of the School of the Arts (1968–70). From 1971 to 1973 he taught at the Juilliard School in N.Y. He helped to found the American Composers Alliance in 1937 and was its president from 1945 to 1951. In 1940 he co-founded the American Music Center and was it chairman until 1960. In 1954 he was a founder of Composers Recordings, Inc. Luening received various commissions, grants, awards, and honorary doctorates. He held 3 Guggenheim fellowships (1930–31; 1931–32; 1974–75). In 1952 he was elected to membership in the National Inst. of Arts and Letters. He was composer-in-residence at the American Academy in Rome in 1958, 1961, and 1965. His long and distinguished career in American music is recounted in his autobiography, *The Odyssey of an American Composer* (N.Y., 1980). Although a prolific composer in various genres and styles, Luening's most significant contribution to music rests upon his pioneering work as a composer of electronic music. His flute on tape pieces *Fantasy in Space, Invention in 12 Notes*, and *Low Speed*, all premiered at N.Y.'s Museum of Modern Art on Oct. 28, 1952, were the earliest such works ever written. In collaboration with Vladimir Ussachevsky, he also wrote the first work for tape and orch., the *Rhapsodic Variations* (Louisville, March 20, 1954).

WORKS: DRAMATIC: *Sister Beatrice*, incidental music to Maeterlinck's play (Rochester, N.Y., Jan. 15, 1926); *Evangeline*, opera (1930–32; rev. 1947; N.Y., May 5, 1948, composer conducting); *Blood Wedding*, incidental music to García Lorca's play (Bennington, Vt., Dec. 1, 1940); *Of Identity*, ballet for Organ on Tape (1954; N.Y., Feb. 9, 1955; in collaboration with V. Ussachevsky); *Carlsbad Caverns*, electronic television theme for *Wide, Wide World* (1955; in collaboration with Ussachevsky); *King Lear*, incidental music on tape for Shakespeare's play (1955; in collaboration with Ussachevsky); *Theatre Piece No. 2*, ballet for Narrator, Recorded Soprano, and Instrumental Ensemble (N.Y., April 20, 1956, composer conducting); *Back to Methuselah*, electronic incidental music to Shaw's play (1958; in collaboration with Ussachevsky); *Incredible Voyage*, electronic television score for the series *Twenty-First Century* (1968; in collaboration with Ussachevsky). **ORCH.:** Concertino for Flute and Chamber Orch. (1923; Philadelphia, Jan. 30, 1935, composer conducting); *Music* (1923; N.Y., May 26, 1978); *Symphonic Fantasia No. 1* (1924; Rochester, N.Y., Nov. 25, 1925), *No. 2* (1939–49; N.Y., Oct. 13, 1957), *No. 3* (1969–81; N.Y., Jan. 26, 1982), *No. 4* (1969–81; N.Y., May 14, 1984), *No. 5* (1978–85), *No. 6* (1985), *No. 7* (1986), *No. 8* (1986), *No. 9* (1989), *No. 10* (1990), *No. 11* (1991), and *No. 12* (1994); *Serenade* for 3 Horns and Strings (1927; Rochester, N.Y., Jan. 12, 1928); *Short Symphony* (1929–80); *Symphonic Interludes Nos. 1* and *2* (1935; N.Y., April 11, 1936), *3* (1975; Tanglewood, Aug. 13, 1980), *4* (1985), and *5* (1986); *Prelude to a Hymn Tune by William Billings* (N.Y., Feb. 1, 1937, composer conducting); Suite for Strings (Saratoga Springs, N.Y., Sept. 12, 1937); *Serenade* for Flute and Strings (1940; N.Y., Oct. 19, 1956); *Pilgrim's Hymn* (Saratoga Springs, N.Y., Sept. 14, 1946, composer conducting); *Prelude: World Without People* for Chamber Orch. (Saratoga Springs, N.Y., Sept. 14, 1946, composer conducting); *Legend* for Oboe and Strings (WNYC Radio, N.Y., July 1, 1951); *Louisville Concerto*, later renamed *Kentucky Concerto* (Louisville, March 5, 1951, composer conducting); *Wisconsin Suite "Of Childhood Tunes Remembered"* (N.Y., March 28, 1954); *Lyric Scene* for Flute and Strings (1958; Arlington, Va., Oct. 25, 1964); *Fantasia* for String Quartet and Orch. (N.Y., April 18, 1959); *Fantasia* for Strings (1966); *Sonority Forms No. 1* (North Bennington, Vt., Oct. 14, 1973, composer conducting) and *No. 2* (Bennington, Vt., June 4, 1983, composer conducting); *Wisconsin Symphony* (1975; Milwaukee, Jan. 3, 1976); *Potawatomi Legends* for Chamber Orch. (Parkside, Wis., April 13, 1980, composer conducting); *Fanfare for Those We Have Lost* for Wind Orch. (1993). **CHAMBER:** *Minuet und Pollutionen Gavotte* for Cello and Piano (1917); 3 violin sonatas (1917; 1922; 1943–51); Sextet for Flute, Clarinet, Horn, Violin, Viola, and Cello (1918); *Variations on Christus der ist mein Leben* for Horn Quartet (1918); Flute Sonatina (1919); Fugue for String Quartet (1919); 3 string quartets (1919–20; 1924; 1928); Piano Trio (1921); *Variations on the National Air Yankee Doodle* for Piccolo and Piano (c.1922); *Legend* for Violin and Piano (1924); 2 sonatas for Solo Cello (1924, 1992); *Fantasia brevis* for Flute and Piano (1929); *Short Fantasy* for Violin and Horn (1930); *Mañana* for Violin and Piano (1933); *Fantasia brevis* for Clarinet and Piano (1936); *Fantasia brevis* for Violin, Viola, and Cello (1936); *Short Ballad* for 2 Clarinets and Strings (1937); *Short Sonata No. 1* for Flute and Harpsichord or Piano (1937), *No. 2* for Flute and Piano (1971), and *No. 3* for Flute and Piano (1966); *Fuguing Tune* for Woodwind Quintet (1938–39); *Short Fantasy* for Violin and Piano (1938); *The Bass with the Delicate Air* for Flute, Oboe, Clarinet, and Bassoon (1940); *Variations on Bach's Chorale Prelude Liebster Jesu wir sind hier* for Cello and Piano (1942); *Aria* for Cello and Piano (1943); Suite for Violin, Viola, and Cello (1944–66); Suite for Cello or Viola and Piano (1946); 5 suites for Flute (1947, c.1959, 1961, 1963, 1969); *Easy March* for Recorder, Flute, Oboe, and Piano (1950); *3 Nocturnes* for Oboe and Piano (1951); Sonata for Bassoon or Cello and Piano (1952); Trio for Flute, Violin, and Piano (1952); Trombone Sonata (1953); Suite for Double Bass and Piano (1953); *Sonata Composed in 2 Dayturns* for Cello (1958); Sonata for Solo Double Bass (1958); Sonata for Solo Viola (1958); 3 sonatas for Solo Violin (1958, 1968, 1971); *Song, Poem, and Dance* for Flute and String Quartet (1958); *3 Fantasias* for Guitar (1960–81); *Sonority Canon* for 2 to 37 Flutes (1962); *3 Duets* for 2 Flutes (1962); Trio for Flute, Cello, and Piano (1962); Duo for Violin and Viola (1963); *Elegy* for Violin (1963); *March for Diverse High and Low Instruments* (1963); *Suite for Diverse High and Low Instruments* (1963); *Entrance and Exit Music* for 3 Trumpets, 3 Trombones, and Cymbals (1964); *Fanfare for a Festive Occasion* for 3 Trumpets, 3 Horns, 3 Trombones, Timpani, Bells, and Cymbal (1965); *Fantasia* for Cello (1966); *Trio for 3 Flutists* (1966); *14 Easy Duets* for 2 Recorders (1967); *Meditation* for Violin (1968); Trio for Trumpet, Horn, and Trombone (1969); *Introduction and Allegro* for Trumpet and Piano (1971); *Easy Suite* for Strings (1971); *8 Tone Poems* for 2 Violas (1971); *Elegy for the Lonesome Ones* for 2 Clarinets and Strings (1974); *Mexican Serenades* for 11 Instruments (1974); *Prelude and Fugue* for Flute, Clarinet, and Bassoon (1974); *4 Cartoons: Short Suite* for Flute, Clarinet, and Bassoon (1974; also for String Trio); Suite for 2 Flutes, Piano, and Cello ad libitum (1976); *Triadic Canon with Variations* for Flute and 2 Violins (1976); *Potawatomi Legends No. 2: Fantasias on Indian Motives* for Flute (1978); *10 Canons* for 2 Flutes (1980); *2 Fantasias* for Violin, Cello, and Piano (1981, 1993); *Fantasia* for Clarinet (1982); *Fantasia* for Violin (1982); *Serenade* for Violin, Cello, and Piano (1983); *Fantasia and Dance in Memoriam Max Pollikoff* for Violin (1984); *Opera Fantasia* for Violin and Piano (1985); *Serenade and Dialogue* for Flute and Piano (1985); *3 Canons* for 2 Flutes (1985); Duo for Flute and Viola (1985); *3 Fantasias* for Baroque Flute (1986); Suite for Horn (1987); *3 Études* for Cello (1987); *Lament* for Cello(s) (1987); *Divertimento* for Oboe, Violin, Viola, and Cello (1988); *Divertimento* for 2 Trumpets, Horn, Trombone, and Tuba (1988); *Green Mountain Evening, July 25, 1988* for Flute, Oboe, Clarinet, 2 Cellos, and Piano (1988); *Canon with Variations* for Double Bass (1989); Flute Quartet (1989); *Dealer's Choice: Divertimento* for Oboe or Flute, Clarinet, and Bassoon (1990; also for String Trio); Cello Sonata (1992); Sonata for Solo Cello (1992); *Canonical Studies* for 2 Flutes (1993); *Canonical Variations* for String Quartet (1994); *Divertimento* for Clarinet, Violin, and Piano (1994). **PIANO:** *Fuga a tre voce* (1918); *Music for Piano: A Contrapuntal Study* (1921); *Coal-Scuttle Blues* (1922–23; in collaboration with E. Bacon); *2 Bagatelles* (1924); *Hymn to Bacchus* (1926); *Dance Sonata* (1928); *8 Pieces* (1928); *Intermezzo III* (1928); *5 Intermezzi* (1932–36); *Phantasy* (1935); *Andante* (1936); *8 Preludes* (1936); *2 Inventions* (1938); *6 Inventions* (1938–39); *6 Short Sonatas* (1940, 1958, 1958, 1967, 1979, 1979, 1979); *Canonical Study* (1941); *Easy Canons* (1941); *Canon in the Octave* (1945); *10 Pieces for 5 Fingers* (1946); *In Memoriam Ferruccio Busoni*, sonata (1955–66); *Gay Picture* (1957); *The Bells of Bellagio* for Piano, 4 or 6 Hands (1967); *Sonority Forms I* (1983), *II: The Right-hand Path* for Piano, Right Hand (1984), and *III* (1989); *Tango* (1985); *Song Without Words* (1987); *Chords at Night* (1988); *Image* (1989); *2 Études* (1994); *Fantasia Etudes* (1994). **OTHER:** Organ music; harpsichord pieces. **VOCAL:** Trio for Soprano, Flute, and Violin (1923–24); *The Soundless Song* for Soprano, Flute, Clarinet, String Quartet, Piano, and Optional Movement and Light (1924); *When in the Langour of Evening* for Soprano, Chorus, String or Woodwind Quartet, and Piano (1932); Suite for Soprano and Flute (1936–37); *No Jerusalem But This*, cantata for Soloists, Chorus, and Chamber Ensemble (1982); *Lines from the First Book of Urizen and Vala, or a Dream of 9 Nights* for Soloists and Chorus (1983); many choral pieces; numerous songs for voice and piano. **ELECTRONIC:** *Fantasy in Space* for Flute on Tape (N.Y., Oct. 28, 1952); *Invention in 12 Notes* for Flute on Tape (N.Y., Oct. 28, 1952); *Low Speed* for Flute on Tape (N.Y., Oct. 28, 1952); *Gargoyles* for Violin and Synthesized Sound (1961); *A Day in the Country* for Violin and Synthesized Sound (1961); *A Study in Synthesized Sounds* (1961); *Synthesis* for Orch. and Electronic Sound (1962; Erie, Pa., Oct. 22, 1963); *Moonflight* for Flute on Tape (1967); *Variations on Fugue and Chorale Fantasy* for Organ and Electronic Doubles (1973); in collaboration with Ussachevsky: *Incantation* (1953); *Rhapsodic Variations* for Tape and Orch. (1953–54; Louisville, March 20, 1954); *A Poem in Cycles and Bells* for Tape and Orch. (Los Angeles, Nov. 18, 1954); *Concerted Piece* for Tape and Orch. (N.Y., March 31, 1960); in collaboration with H. El-Dabh: *Diffusion of Bells* (1962–65); *Electronic Fanfare* for Recorder, Sound Synthesizer, and Percussion on Tape (1962–65).

BIBL.: R. Hartsock, *O. L.: A Bio-Bibliography* (Westport, Conn., 1991).

Lukács, Miklós, Hungarian conductor; b. Gyula, Feb. 4, 1905; d. Budapest, Nov. 1, 1986. He took courses with A. Schnabel and Hindemith at the Berlin Hochschule für Musik. He conducted in various German theaters (1930–43), then at the Hungarian State Opera in Budapest (1943–78), where he also served as its director (1944; 1966–78).

Lukáš, Zdeněk, Czech composer; b. Prague, Aug, 21, 1928. He studied at the Prague teachers' inst.; also had lessons with Řídký (composition) and Modr (theory). He was active with the Czech Radio in Plzeň (1953–64) and received instruction from Kabeláč in Prague (1961–70). In his works, he explores various compositional forms.

WORKS: OPERAS: *At žije mrtvý* (Long Live the Deceased; Prague, Dec. 11, 1968); *Domácí karneval* (Domestic Carnival; Prague, March 29, 1969); *Planeta a tiše fialovou září* (Planet with Soft Violet Glow; 1978); *Falkenštejn* (1985); *Veta za vetu* (Measure for Measure; 1986). **ORCH.:** Piano Concerto (1955); Violin Concerto (1956); Cello Concerto (1957); 5 syms. (1960, 1961, 1965, 1965, 1972); Concerto for Soprano Saxophone and Orch. (1964); 3 concerti grossi: No. 1 for String Quartet and String Orch. (1964), No. 2 for Flute, Violin, Orch., and Tape (1972), and No. 3 for Chamber Orch. (1977); *Symphonietta solemnis* (1965); *Sonata concertata* for Piano, Winds, and Percussion (1966); *Musica ritmica* for Percussion and Winds (1966); Concerto for Violin, Viola, and Orch. (1968); *Partita* for Chamber Orch. (1969); *Musica da concerto* for 12 Strings and Harpsichord (1974); *Variations* for Piano and Orch. (1970); *Postludium* (1971); Bassoon Concerto (1976); Clarinet Concerto (1976); *Transformations* for Piano and Orch. (1978); *Musica Boema*, 2 symphonic movements for Winds, Percussion, and Harp (1978); Flute Concerto (1981); Viola Concerto (1983); Cello Concerto (1986). **CHAMBER:** 4 string quartets (1960, 1965, 1973, 1987); Trio for Violin, Piano, and Side Drum (1962); *Partita semplice* for 4 Violins and Piano (1964); Wind Quintet (1968); *Duetti* for Chamber Ensemble (1969); *Music for a Private View* for Viola and Piano (1970); *Amoroso* for Clarinet, Bagpipes, and Double Bass (1970); *Divertimento* for Violin and Viola (1973); Trio for Violin, Cello, and Piano (1974); *Meditations* for Viola and Harpsichord (1976); *Cathedrals* for Brass Instruments and Organ (1976); *Intarsia* for Violin, Viola, and Cello (1977); *Sonata di danza* for Violin, Cello, and Piano (1980); *Canzoni da sonar* for Flute, Oboe, Violin, Viola, and Cello (1983); *Duo di basso* for Cello and Double Bass (1987). **VOCAL:** *Adam a Eva*, oratorio (1969); *Nezabiješ* (Thou Shalt Not Kill), oratorio (1971); 2 cantatas (1977; *To Prague*, 1982); many choral works; songs.

Luke, Ray, American composer, conductor, and teacher; b. Forth Worth, Texas, May 30, 1928. He received training in theory at Texas Christian Univ. in Fort Worth (B.M., 1949; M.M., 1950), and in theory and composition at the Eastman School of Music in Rochester, N.Y. (Ph.D., 1960). In 1962 he joined the faculty of Oklahoma City Univ., where he taught for more than 30 years. He also conducted its orch. and opera productions until 1987. From 1963 to 1967 he was music director of the

Lyric Theater of Oklahoma in Oklahoma City. He was assoc. conductor of the Oklahoma City Sym. Orch. from 1968 to 1973, and then was its music director and resident conductor in 1973–74. Thereafter he was a frequent guest conductor with it until 1979. His Piano Concerto won 1st prize in the Queen Elisabeth of Belgium International Composition Competition in 1969. In 1978 he won 1st prize in the Rockefeller Foundation/New England Cons. of Music Competition with his opera *Medea.* As a composer, Luke has utilized various contemporary techniques in his works.

WORKS: DRAMATIC: OPERAS: *Medea* (1978; Boston, May 3, 1979); *Drowne's Wooden Image* (1994); *Mrs. Bullfrog* (1994). **BALLET:** *Tapestry* (Oklahoma City, May 8, 1975). **ORCH.:** *2 Miniatures* (1957); 3 suites (1958, 1967, 1990); *Epilogue* (1958); 4 syms. (1959, 1961, 1963, 1970); Suite for 12 Orch. Woodwinds (1962); *Symphonic Dialogues I* for Violin, Oboe, and Orch. (1965) and *II* for Soprano, Violin, Oboe, Harpsichord, and Strings (1988); Bassoon Concerto (1965); *Fanfare* for Symphonic Winds and Percussion (1967); Piano Concerto (1968); *Incantation* for Cello, Harp, and Strings (1968); *Summer Music*, concert overture (1970); *Compressions I* (1972) and *II* (1973); *Celebration for the Oklahoma Diamond Jubilee* (1982); Sinfonia Concertante for Double Orch. (1989); *Fanfare* for Brass Quintet and Orch. (1990). **CONCERT BAND:** *Prelude and March* (1959); *Antiphonale and Toccata* (1960); *Introduction and Badinage* (1968); *New England Miniatures* (1968); *Intrada and Rondo* (1972); *Sonics and Metrics* (1973); *Design* (1976). **CHAMBER:** *Lament* for Horn and String Quartet (1957); Woodwind Quintet (1958); String Quartet (1966); *4 Dialogues* for Organ and Percussion (1970); Trio for Flute, Clarinet, and Piano (1974); Septet for Winds and Strings (1979); Suite for Trumpet (1986); Suite for Oboe, Bassoon, and Piano (1988); *Compressions III* for Brass Quintet (1988); *4 Scenes* for 8 Flutes (1993); *Contrasts* for Bassoon and Piano (1993); *Splinters From Old Wood* for 2 Trumpets (1994); *Wood From Old Splinters* for 2 Vibraphones (1994). **VOCAL:** *Psalm 51* for Chorus and Concert Band (1960); *2 Odes* for Mezzo-soprano, Flute, and Piano (1965); *Symphonic Songs* for Mezzo-soprano and Orch. (1968); *Epitaphs* for 12 Voices (1979); *4 Foibles* for Voices (1980); *Plaintes and Dirges* for Chorus and Orch. (1982); *Quartz Mountain* for Voices and Orch. (1988); *Cantata Concertante* for Choruses, Instrumental Ensembles, and Orch. (1991).

Lukomska, Halina, Polish soprano; b. Suchedniów, May 29, 1929. She studied at the Warsaw Academy of Music (graduated, 1954), with Giorgio Favaretto at the Accademia Musicale Chigiana in Siena, and with Toti dal Monte in Venice. In 1956 she captured 1st prize in the 's-Hertogenbosch competition. From 1960 she pursued a concert career which took her all over the world. In 1973 she toured North America as a soloist with the Cleveland Orch. She became especially noted for her performances of contemporary music, including the most daunting of avant-garde scores.

Lumsdaine, David (Newton), Australian composer and teacher; b. Sydney, Oct. 31, 1931. He studied in Sydney at the New South Wales State Conservatorium of Music (piano, viola, and theory) and at the Univ. (composition with Raymond Hanson; B.A., 1953) before pursuing his studies in London with Seiber (1954–56) and at the Royal Academy of Music with Berkeley (1956–57). He was a lecturer at the Univ. of Durham (1970–81), where he was founder of an electronic music studio; he was awarded a Mus.Doc. there in 1981. In 1976 he served as a visiting prof. at the Univ. of Adelaide and in 1979 was composer-in-residence at the New South Wales State Conservatorium of Music, sharing the latter position with his wife, **Nicola LeFanu,** whom he married that year. He was a senior lecturer at King's College, Univ. of London, from 1981 to 1993. In his music, Lumsdaine has pursued a highly complex but thoroughly individual mode of expression which ranges from the use of traditional instruments to the application of electronics.

WORKS: ORCH.: *Variations* (1960); *Short Symphony* (1961); *Bach Music* (1965); *Episodes* (1968–69); *Salvation Creek with Eagle* for Chamber Orch. (1974); *Sunflower: To the Memory of Luigi Dallapiccola* (1975); *Evensong* for Brass Band (1975); *Hagoromo* (1977); *Shoalhaven* for Small Orch. (1982); *Mandala V* (1988); *The Arc of Stars* for Strings (1990–91); *Garden of Earthly Delights*, fantasia for Cello and Orch. (1992). **CHAMBER:** *Mandala I* for Wind Quartet (1967), *II* for Flute, Clarinet, Viola, Cello, and Percussion (1969); *III* for Piano, Flute, Clarinet, Viola, Cello, and Chinese Bell (1978), and *IV* for String Quartet (1983); *Looking Glass Music* for Brass Quintet and Tape (1970); *Kangaroo Hunt* for Piano and Percussion (1971); *Caliban Trio* for Piano Trio, Tape, and Live Electronics (1972); *Bagatelles* for Flute, Clarinet, Piano, Violin, Viola, and Cello (1985); *Empty Sky, Mootwingee* for Flute, Trombone or Horn, Cello, Pitched Percussion, and 2 Pianos (1986); *A Dance and a Hymn for Alexander Maconochie* for Flute, Clarinet, Percussion, Mandolin, Guitar, Violin, and Double Bass (1988); *Round Dance* for Sitar, Tabla, Flute, Cello, and Keyboard (1989); *Sine nome* for Alto Saxophone or Clarinet and Pitched Percussion (1990); *Blue Upon Blue* for Cello (1991). **PIANO:** *Ruhe Sanfte, Sanfte Ruh'* (1964); *Kelly Ground* (1966); *Flights* for 2 Pianos (1967); *Cambewarra* (1980); *Garden of Earthly Delights* (1992); *Kali Dances* (1994). **VOCAL:** *The Ballad of Perse O'Reilly* for Tenor, Men's Chorus, and 2 Pianos (1953–81); *Missa brevis* for Chorus and Organ (1964); *Annotations of Auschwitz* for Soprano, Flute or Trumpet, Horn, Violin, Cello, and Piano (1964); *Dum medium silentium* for Chorus (1964–75); *Easter Fresco* for Soprano, Flute, Horn, Harp, and Piano (1966); *Aria for Edward John Eyre* for Soprano, Narrators, Chamber Ensemble, Tape, and Live Electronics (1972); *My Sister's Song* for Soprano (1975); *Tides* for Narrator, 12 Voices, and Percussion (1979); *What Shall I Sing?* for Soprano and 2 Clarinets (1982); *Where the Lilies Grow* for Chamber Chorus (1985); *Just So Stories* for Narrator, Dancers, and Computer-generated Tape (1990); *A Tree Telling of Orpheus* for Soprano, Flute, Clarinet, Violin, Viola, and Cello (1990). **OTHER:** *Big Meeting* for Tape (1978); *Wild Ride to Heaven*, radiophonic piece (1980; in collaboration with N. LeFanu); *4 Soundscapes*, field recordings (1990); *Soundscape 5: Cambewarra* (1991).

Lumsden, Sir David (James), noted English organist, harpsichordist, choirmaster, and music editor; b. Newcastle upon Tyne, March 19, 1928. He studied with Ord and Dart at the Univ. of Cambridge (Mus.B., 1951; Ph.D., 1955) and at the Univ. of Oxford (Ph.D., 1959). He was organist of the Univ. of Nottingham (1954–56); also founder-conductor of the Nottingham Bach Soc.; served as rector chori at Southwell Minster and director of music at the Univ. College of North Staffordshire, Keele (1956–59). He then was organist at New College, Oxford (1959–78); also taught at the Royal Academy of Music in London (1960–62). He was principal of the Royal Scottish Academy of Music in Glasgow (1978–82) and of the Royal Academy of Music in London (1982–92). He was knighted in 1985.

Lundquist, Torbjörn Iwan, Swedish composer and conductor; b. Stockholm, Sept. 30, 1920. He received training in musicology at the Univ. of Uppsala, in composition from Wirén, and in conducting from Suitner in Salzburg and Vienna. He then was active as a conductor in Stockholm, and also appeared as a guest conductor throughout Europe. In 1978 he was awarded a government income to pursue composition. In his works, Lundquist has utilized various styles and techniques, ranging from the traditional to the avant-garde, from jazz to Eastern music.

WORKS: OPERAS: *Sekund av evighet* (Moment of Eternity; 1971–74; Stockholm, May 27, 1974); *Jason and Medea* (1985–89). **ORCH.:** *Divertimento* for Chamber Orch. (1951); 8 syms.: No. 1 (1952–56; rev. 1971), No. 2 (1956–70), No. 3, *Sinfonia dolorosa* (1971–75; Swedish Radio, Malmö, Sept. 14, 1976), No. 4 (1974–85; Göteborg, Nov. 7, 1985), No. 5 (Halmstad, Feb. 13, 1980), No. 6 (1985–86), No. 7 for Soprano, Baritone, Chorus, and Orch. (1986–88; Stockholm, March 22, 1991), and No. 8, *Kroumata* (1989–92); *Concerto da camera* for Accordion and Orch. (1965); *Férvor* for Violino Grande and Orch. (1967); *Hangarmusik*, concerto sinfonico for Piano and

Orch. (1967); *Intarzia* for Accordion and Strings (1967–68); *Confrontation* (Stockholm, Oct. 5, 1968); *Evoluzione* for Strings (1968); *Sogno* for Oboe and Strings (1968); *Galax* (1971); Marimba Concerto (1971–74); Concerto grosso for Violin, Cello, and Strings (1974); *Schatten* (Salzburg, Aug. 25, 1977); Violin Concerto (1978; Örebro, Feb. 11, 1979); *Landscape* for Tuba, Strings, and Piano (1978); *Poetry* for Flute, Strings, and Piano (1978); *Wind Power* for Wind. Orch. (1978); *Serenade* for Strings (1979); *Arktis* for Symphonic Band (1984). **CHAMBER:** *Movements* for Accordion and String Quartet (1966); *Duell* for Accordion and Percussion (1966); *Combinazione* for Violin and Percussion (1966); 2 string quartets (1966, 1969); *Teamwork* for Wind Quintet (1967); *Stereogram III* for Xylorimba, Electric Guitar, and Accordion (1969); *4 rondeaux* for Wind Quartet and Piano (1969); *Tempera* for 6 Brass Instruments (1969); *Trio fiorente* for Piano, Violin, and Cello (1975); Suite for 6 Percussionists (1976); *Integration* for 5 Percussionists (1980–82); *Alla prima* for Saxophone Quartet (1989). **VOCAL:** *Elegies from Bergen* for Tenor, Men's Chorus, and Orch. (1958); *Via the Emptiness* for Soli, Chorus, and Chamber Orch. (1959); *Call* for Soprano and Orch. (1963–64); many songs.

Lundsten, Ralph, Swedish composer, film creator, and artist; b. Ersnäs, Oct. 6, 1936. He was basically autodidact; settled in the wooden fairy-tale mansion of Castle Frankenburg (built 1878) in Saltsjö-Boo, where he founded Andromeda (1959), Sweden's best-known private electronic music studio and film center. A pioneer in electronic music in Sweden, he has gone on to secure an international following via the popularity of the "New Age" movement. In 1982 the Andromeda Fan Soc. was organized to promote his activities as a composer, artist, and "New Age" visionary. In 1984 Radio Sweden International adopted "Out in the Wide World" from his *Nordic Nature Symphony No. 4, A Summer Saga* as its theme signature for its international broadcasts. Much of his output has been recorded and performed throughout the world. In 1991–92 his work as a portrait artist was the subject of a special exhibition at Stockholm's Music Museum.

WORKS: *Aloha Arita* (1966); *Kaleidoscope* (1966); *Mums: EMS No. 1* (1967); *3 Electronic "Pop" Pieces* (1967); *Visions of Flying Saucers* (1967); *Happy Music* (1968); *Winter Music* (1968); *Mizar* (1968); *Tellus* (1969); *Blue Bird* (1969); *Suite for Electronic Accordion* (1969); *Energy for Biological Computer* (1969); *Erik XIV* (1969); *Carvings* (1969); *Ölskog: Through a Landscape of Mirrors* (1970); *Cosmic Love—Trial and Discussion* (1970); *Gustav III* (1971); *Nightmare* (1971); *Ourfather* (1972); *Nordic Nature Sympony No. 1, The Water Sprite* (1972–73); *The Midnight Hour* (1973); *Ode to a Lost Soul* (1973); *On Tottering Toes* (1973); *Feel It* (1973); *Gunnar of Lidarände* (1973); *Shangri-la* (1975); *Winter Music* (1975); *Heaven by Night* (1975); *Raped Planet* (1975); *Icelandic Dancing Pictures* (1975); *Nordic Symphony No. 2, Johannes and the Lady of the Woods* (1975); *Universe* (1977); *Discophrenia* (1978); *Alpha Ralpha Boulevard* (1979); *Paradise Symphony* (1980); *Nordic Nature Symphony No. 3, A Midwinter Saga* (1981); *The New Age* (1982); *Aspects of Nature* (1982); *Nordic Nature Symphony No. 4, A Summer Saga* (1983); *Strangers in Paradise* (1984); *Nordic Nature Symphony No. 5, Bewitched* (1984); *Dreamscape* (1984); *Welcome* (1985); *Fantasia by Starlight* (1986); *The Dream Master* (1986); *Suite amoroso* (1986); *The Gate of Time* (1988); *Nordic Nature Symphony No. 6, Landscape of Dreams* (1990); *The Symphony of Joy* (1994).

Lunelli, Renato, Italian musicologist, organist, and composer; b. Trent, May 14, 1895; d. there, Jan. 14, 1967. He studied at the Händelhochschule in Munich (1913–14) and with Bormioli (organ) and Gianferri (harmony and counterpoint) at the Liceo Musicale in Trent. He then was organist at S. Maria Maggiore in Trent. Lunelli was an authority on the organ. With Tagliavini, he founded the journal *L'organa: Rivista di cultura organaria e organistica* in 1960. Among his compositions were sacred works and vocal pieces.

WRITINGS: *Un ventennio di attività organaria nel Trentino* (Trent, 1931); *Mistica ed estetica delle sonorità organistiche al servizio della liturgia* (Trent, 1950); *Der Oregelbau in Italien in seinen Meisterwerken vom 14. Jahrhundert bis zur Gegenwart* (Mainz, 1956); *L'arte organaria del Rinascimento in Rome e gli organi di S. Pietro in Vaticano, dalle origini a tutto il periodo frescobaldiano* (Florence, 1958); R. Maroni, ed., *Organi trentini: Notizie storiche, iconografia* (Trent, 1964); ed. with R. Maroni, *La musica nel Trentino dal XV al XVIII secolo* (Trent, 1967); ed. with R. Maroni, *Strumenti musicali nel Trentino* (Trent, 1968).

Lunn, Louise Kirkby. See **Kirkby-Lunn, Louise.**

Lunssens, Martin, Belgian conductor and composer; b. Molenbeek-Saint-Jean, April 16, 1871; d. Etterbeek, Feb. 1, 1944. He studied with Gevaert, Jehin, and Kufferath at the Brussels Cons., gaining the 1st Belgian Prix de Rome in 1895 with the cantata *Callirhoé*; then became a prof. there. He subsequently was director of the Music Academy at Courtrai (1905–16); at Charleroi (1916–21); at the Louvain Cons. (1921–24); and finally at the Ghent Cons. (from 1924). He was also known as an excellent conductor; was in charge of the Flemish Opera in Antwerp, where he conducted many Wagner operas.

WORKS: 4 syms., the 1st 3 with the programmatic titles *Symphonie romaine, Symphonie florentine*, and *Symphonie française*; symphonic poems (*Roméo et Juliette; Phèdre; Le Cid; Timon d'Athènes*); 3 violin concertos; Viola Concerto; Cello Concerto; much chamber music; songs.

Lupi, Roberto, Italian conductor, teacher, and composer; b. Milan, Nov. 28, 1908; d. Dornach, Switzerland, April 17, 1971. He graduated in piano (1927), cello (1928), and composition (1934; under Pedrollo) at the Milan Cons. After winning the 1st Rassegna Nazionale in 1937, he was active as a guest conductor. From 1941 to 1971 he also was prof. of harmony and counterpoint at the Cherubini Cons. in Florence. He ed. works by a number of Italian composers and publ. the books *Armonia di gravitazione* (Rome, 1946) and *Il mistero del suono* (Rome, 1955). He composed stage works, orch. pieces, chamber music, choral works, and songs.

Lupu, Radu, outstanding Romanian pianist; b. Galați, Nov. 30, 1945. He began his piano studies at the age of 6, making his recital debut when he was 12; then studied with Florica Muzicescu and on scholarship at the Moscow Cons. (1963), where he studied with Heinrich and Stanislau Neuhaus until 1969. In quick succession he won 1st prize in the Van Cliburn (1966), Enesco (1967), and Leeds (1969) competitions. In 1972 he made his American debut as soloist with the Cleveland Orch., and subsequently played with the Chicago, Los Angeles, N.Y., and Boston orchs. In Europe he made successful appearances in Berlin, Paris, Amsterdam, London, Vienna, and other cities in varied programs ranging from Classical to modern works.

Luria, Juan (real name, **Johannes Lorie**), Polish baritone; b. Warsaw, Dec. 20, 1862; d. in the concentration camp in Auschwitz, 1942. He was a student of Gänsbacher in Vienna. In 1885 he made his operatic debut in Stuttgart. On Dec. 3, 1890, he made his Metropolitan Opera debut in N.Y. as Nevers in *Les Huguenots*, singing there for a season. He subsequently pursued his career in Berlin, Milan, Vienna, Munich, Paris, and other European music centers. In 1893 he sang the role of Wotan at its first performance at Milan's La Scala. From 1914 he taught voice in Berlin. As a Jew, Luria left Germany under the Hitler regime in 1937 and made his way to Holland, where he taught at the conservatories in Amsterdam and The Hague. After the Nazis occupied Holland in 1939, he was unable to flee, and in 1942 was arrested and sent to the Auschwitz concentration camp. Luria was best known as a Wagnerian. He also sang in the premiere of Pfitzner's *Die Rose vom Liebesgarten* (1901).

Lussan, Zélie de, American soprano; b. Brooklyn, Dec. 21, 1862; d. London, Dec. 18, 1949. She was trained in singing by her mother, and made her first public appearance at Chickering

Hall in N.Y. (April 2, 1878). In 1885 she joined the Boston Ideal Opera Co., and then went to London, where she made her debut as Carmen with A. Harris's Italian Opera Co. at Covent Garden (July 7, 1888); subsequently sang with the Carl Rosa Opera Co. and Mapleson's company. She sang Carmen again for her Metropolitan Opera debut in N.Y. on Nov. 26, 1894; after that season, was on its roster again from 1898 to 1900. She was particularly successful at Covent Garden (1890–93; 1895–1900; 1902–03; 1910). She was called upon to sing Carmen more than 1,000 times during her career; she was also a noted Cherubino, Zerlina, Mignon, and Nedda. She was married to the pianist Angelo Fronani.

Lutkin, Peter Christian, American organist, choral conductor, music educator, and composer; b. Thompsonville, Wis., March 27, 1858; d. Evanston, Il., Dec. 27, 1931. He was a chorister at the Episcopal Cathedral in Chicago and a teacher of piano at Northwestern Univ. in Evanston (1879–81) before pursuing studies in Berlin with Raff, Bargiel, and Haupt, and in Paris with Moszkowski (1881–84). Returning to Chicago, he served as organist at St. Clement's (1884–91) and St. James' (1891–97). In 1895 he founded the Northwestern Univ. School of Music and was its first dean until 1928. In 1909 he founded the Chicago North Shore Festival and was its choral conductor until 1930. He publ. *Music in the Church* (1910) and *Hymn-Singing and Hymn-Playing* (1930). He composed mainly sacred works.

Lutosławski, Witold, outstanding Polish composer; b. Warsaw, Jan. 25, 1913; d. there, Feb. 7, 1994. He learned to play the piano as a child; then studied violin with Lidia Kmitowa (1926–32) and theory and composition with Witold Maliszewski (from 1927); also studied mathematics at the Univ. of Warsaw (1931–33). He entered the Warsaw Cons. (1932), where he continued composition studies with Maliszewski and also studied piano with Jerzy Lefeld (graduated as a pianist, 1936, and as a composer, 1937). He served in the Polish Army (1937–38); was mobilized in the summer of 1939 and was taken prisoner of war by the invading Nazi armies at the outbreak of World War II; he managed to escape to Warsaw, where he earned a living by playing piano in cafes (1939–44); also participated in clandestine concerts in private homes. After the war, he worked briefly for the Polish Radio (1945), then devoted himself to composition; when his renommée reached the outside world, he obtained prestigious engagements as a lecturer and instructor on both sides of the Atlantic from 1962; he also appeared as a conductor of his own works from 1963. Lutosl/awski was accorded numerous honors, including the City of Warsaw Prize (1948), the State Music Prize, 1st class (1952, 1955, 1964, 1978), the prize of the Union of Polish Composers (1959, 1973), the Maurice Ravel Prize of Paris (1971), the Sibelius de Wihuri Prize of Helsinki (1973), the "Solidarity" Award of Poland (1984), the 1st Grawemeyer Award of $150,000 from the Univ. of Louisville (1985), the Gold Medal of the Royal Phil. Soc. of London (1985), etc. He was made an honorary member of Hamburg's Freie Akademie der Künste (1966), extraordinary member of West Berlin's Akademie der Künste (1968), honorary member of the ISCM (1969), corresponding member of East Berlin's Deutsche Akademie der Künste (1970), corresponding member of the American Academy of Arts and Letters (1975), honorary member of London's Royal Academy of Music (1976), the Polar Music Prize of Sweden (1993), etc. He also received many honorary doctorates in Europe and the U.S. His early works were marked by a neo-Classical tendency, with an influx of national Polish motifs; gradually he turned to a more structural type of composition in which melodic and rhythmic elements are organized into a strong unifying network, with occasional incursions of dodecaphonic and aleatory practices. He was also extraordinarily open-minded; he was attracted by the music of John Cage, finding useful applications in the operations of chance. The influence of Bartók is felt in the constantly changing colors, angular intervallic progressions, and asymmetrical rhythms. In this respect, Lutosławski's *Funeral Music* for Strings (1958), dedicated to the memory of Bartók, thematically built on a concatenation of upward tritones and downward semitones, is stylistically significant. He freely applied sonorism in building orchestral colors. Although possessing a masterful technique of composition, he allowed himself plenty of time for revisions; willing to make any number of successive changes to attain his goal, it took him fully 10 years to achieve the desired balance of structural contents to complete his 3rd Sym. His list of works is therefore not exceptionally large, but each composition, whatever its length, is an accomplished masterpiece.

WORKS: ORCH.: *Symphonic Variations* (1936–38; Polish Radio, April 1939; 1st concert perf., Kraków, June 17, 1939); 4 syms.: No. 1 (1941–47; Katowice, April 6, 1948), No. 2 (1966–67; Katowice, June 9, 1967), No. 3 (1972–83; Chicago, Sept. 29, 1983), and No. 4 (1992; Los Angeles, Feb. 5, 1993); *Overture* for Strings (Prague, Nov. 9, 1949); *Little Suite* for Chamber Orch. (1950; also for Full Orch., 1951; Warsaw, April 20, 1951); *Concerto for Orchestra* (1950–54; Warsaw, Nov. 26, 1954); *Dance Preludes* for Clarinet, Harp, Piano, Percussion, and Strings (Polish Radio, 1955; 1st concert perf., Aldeburgh, June 1963; also for Clarinet and Piano, 1954, and for Flute, Oboe, Clarinet, Bassoon, Horn, and Solo Strings, 1959); *Funeral Music* for Strings, in memory of Bartók (Katowice, March 26, 1958); *3 Postludes* (1958–60; Kraków, Oct. 8, 1965); *Venetian Games* for Chamber Orch. (Venice, April 24, 1961); *Livre pour orchestre* (Hagen, Nov. 18, 1968); Cello Concerto (1969–70; London, Oct. 14, 1970, Rostropovich soloist); *Preludes and Fugue* for Chamber String Orch. (Graz, Oct. 12, 1972); *Mi-parti* (Rotterdam, Oct. 22, 1976); *Variations on a Theme of Paganini* for Piano and Orch. (1978; Miami, Nov. 18, 1979); *Novelette* (1978–79; Washington, D.C., Jan. 29, 1980); Double Concerto for Oboe, Harp, and Orch. (1979–80; Lucerne, Aug. 24, 1980); *Grave* for Cello and Chamber Strings (1981–82; Paris, Aug. 26, 1982; also for Cello and Piano, 1981); *Chain 1* for Chamber Orch. (London, Oct. 4, 1983), *2* for Violin and Orch. (1985; Zürich, Jan. 31, 1986), and *3* (San Francisco, Dec. 10, 1986); *Fanfare for Louisville* (Louisville, Sept. 19, 1986); Piano Concerto (Salzburg, Aug. 19, 1988); *Partita* for Violin and Orch. (1988; London, Oct. 17, 1990; also for Violin and Piano, 1984); *Interludium* for Chamber Orch. (1989; London, Oct. 17, 1990). **CHAMBER:** Trio for Oboe, Clarinet, and Bassoon (1945); *Recitativo e Arioso* for Violin and Piano (1951); *5 Folk Melodies* for Strings (1952); *Bucoliche*, 5 pieces for Viola and Piano (1952); *Dance Preludes* for Clarinet and Piano (1954; Warsaw, Feb. 15, 1955; also for Clarinet, Harp, Piano, Percussion, and Strings, 1955, and for Flute, Oboe, Clarinet, Bassoon, Horn, and Solo Strings, Louny, Nov. 10, 1959); String Quartet (1964; Stockholm, March 12, 1965); *Sacher Variations* for Cello (1975; Zürich, May 2, 1976); *Epitaph* for Oboe and Piano (1979; London, Jan. 3, 1980); *Grave* for Cello and Piano (1981; Warsaw, April 22, 1981; also for Cello and Chamber Strings, 1982); *Mini Overture* for Horn, 2 Trumpets, Trombone, and Tuba (Lucerne, March 11, 1982); *Partita* for Violin and Piano (1984; also for Violin and Orch., 1988); *Slides* for Flute, Oboe, Clarinet, Bassoon, Horn, Percussion, Piano, Guitar, and String Quartet (N.Y., Dec. 1, 1988); *Subito* for Violin and Piano (1992; WFYI-FM, Indianapolis, Sept. 16, 1994). **PIANO:** Sonata (1934); *Variations on a Theme of Paganini* for 2 Pianos (1941); *Invention* (1983). **VOCAL:** *20 Polish Christmas Carols* for Voice and Piano (1946; rev. 1984); *2 Nightingales* for Women's Chorus and Piano (1947); *About Mr. Tralalinski* for Women's Chorus and Piano (1947); *A Straw Chain and Other Songs* for Women's Chorus, Flute, Oboe, 2 Clarinets, and Bassoon (1951); *3 Children's Songs* for Women's Chorus and Piano (1951); *Silesian Triptych* for Soprano and Orch. (Warsaw, Dec. 2, 1951); *5 Songs* for Woman's Voice and Piano or 30 Solo Instruments (1956–58); *3 Poems of Henri Michaux* for Chorus and Orch. (1962–63; Zagreb, May 9, 1963); *Paroles tissées* for Tenor and Orch. (Aldeburgh, June 20, 1965); *Les Espaces du sommeil* for Baritone and Orch. (1975; Berlin, March 12, 1978); *Chantefleurs et Chantefables* for Soprano and Chamber Orch. (1990; London, Aug. 8, 1991).

BIBL.: S. Jarociński, "W. L.," *Polish Music* (Warsaw, 1965); O.

Nordwall, *L.* (Stockholm, 1968); B. Varga, *L. Profile: W. L. in Conversation with Bálint András Varga* (London, 1976); J.-P. Couchod, *La Musique polonaise et W. L.* (Paris, 1981); S. Stucky, *L. and His Music* (Cambridge, 1981); T. Kaczynski, *Conversations with W. L.* (London, 1984); C. Rae, "L.'s Golden Year," *Musical Times* (Oct. 1986); I. Nikolska, *Conversations with W. L.* (Stockholm, 1994).

Lutyens, (Agnes) Elisabeth, important English composer; b. London, July 9, 1906; d. there, April 14, 1983. She was a daughter of the noted architect Sir Edwin Lutyens, and was brought up in an atmosphere of cultural enlightenment. She studied at the École Normale de Musique in Paris (1922–23) and with H. Darke at the Royal College of Music in London (1926–30). In her vivid autobiography, *A Goldfish Bowl* (London, 1972), she recounted her search for a congenial idiom of musical expression, beginning with the erstwhile fashionable Romantic manner and progressing toward a more individual, psychologically tense writing in an atonal technique using a sui generis dodecaphonic method of composition. In 1969 she was made a Commander of the Order of the British Empire. She was married to **Edward Clark**.

WORKS: DRAMATIC: *the Birthday of the Infanta,* ballet (1932); *The Pit,* dramatic scene for Tenor, Bass, Women's Chorus, and Orch. (Palermo, April 24, 1949); *Penelope,* radio opera (1950); *Infidelio,* chamber opera (1956; London, April 17, 1973); *The Numbered,* opera (1965–67); *Time Off? Not a Ghost of a Chance,* charade (1967–68; London, March 1, 1972); *Isis and Osiris,* lyric drama for 8 Voices and Chamber Orch. (1969); *The Linnet from the Leaf,* musical theater for 5 Singers and 2 Instrumental Groups (1972); *The Waiting Game,* 5 scenes for Mezzo-soprano, Baritone, and Chamber Orch. (1973); *One and the Same,* scena for Soprano, Speaker, and Mimes (1973); *The Goldfish Bowl,* ballad opera (1975); *Like a Window,* extracts from letters of van Gogh (1976). **ORCH.:** *3 Pieces* (1939); 6 chamber concertos, some with Solo Instruments (1939–48); *3 Symphonic Preludes* (1942); Viola Concerto (1947); *Music I* (1954), *II* (1962), *III* (1964), and *IV* (1981); *Quincunx* (1960); *En voyage,* symphonic suite (London, July 2, 1960); *Symphonies* for Piano, Wind Instruments, Harps, and Percussion (London, July 28, 1961); *Music* for Piano and Orch. (1964); Novenaria (1967); *Plenum II* for Oboe and Chamber Orch. (1973; London, June 14, 1974); *The Winter of the World* for Cello and Chamber Ensemble (London, May 5, 1974); *Eos* for Chamber Orch. (1975); *Rondel* (1976); *6 Bagatelles* for Chamber Orch. (1976); *Nox* for Piano and 2 Chamber Orchs. (1977); *Wild Decembers* (1980). **CHAMBER:** Sonata for Solo Viola (1938); 13 string quartets (1938–82); String Trio (1939); *9 Bagatelles* for Cello and Piano (1942); *Aptote* for Violin (1948); *Valediction* for Clarinet and Piano (1954); *Nocturnes* for Violin, Cello, and Guitar (1956); *Capricci* for 2 Harps and Percussion (1956); *6 Tempi* for 10 Instruments (1957); Wind Quintet (1960); String Quintet (1963); Trio for Flute, Clarinet, and Bassoon (1963); *Scena* for Violin, Cello, and Percussion (1964); *Music for Wind* for Double Wind Quintet (1964); *Music for 3* for Flute, Oboe, and Piano (1964); *The Fall of the Leafe* for Oboe and String Quartet (1967); *Horai* for Violin, Horn, and Piano (1968); *The Tides of Time* for Double Bass and Piano (1969); *Driving Out the Death* for Oboe and String Trio (1971); *Rape of the Moone* for Wind Octet (1973); *Plenum III* for String Quartet (1974); *Kareniana* for Viola and Instrumental Group (1974); *Go, Said the Bird* for Electric Guitar and String Quartet (1975); *Mare et Minutiae* for String Quartet (1976); *Fantasia* for Alto Saxophone and 3 Instrumental Groups (1977); *O Absalom* for Oboe and String Trio (1977); *Constants* for Cello and Piano (1977); *Doubles* for String Quartet (1978); *Footfalls* for Flute and Piano (1978); *Prelude* for Violin (1979); Trio for Clarinet, Cello, and Piano (1979); *Morning Sea* for Oboe and Piano (1979); *Rapprochement* for Horn, Harp, Wind Quartet, String Quartet, Piano, and Percussion (1980); *6* for an ensemble of 6 Instruments and Percussion (1980); *Soli* for Clarinet, interchangeable with Bass Clarinet, and Double Bass (1980); *Branches of the Night and of the Day* for Horn and String Quartet (1981); *The Living Night* for Percussion (1981); *Echo of the Wind* for Viola (1981); *Triolet I* for Clarinet, Mandolin, and Cello (1982) and *II* for Cello, Marimba, and Harp (1982). **KEYBOARD: PIANO:** *5 Intermezzi* (1942); *Piano e Forte* (1958); *Plenum I* (1973); *The Ring of Bone* (1975); *5 impromptus* (1977); *3 Books of Bagatelles* (1979); *La natura dell'acqua* (1981). **ORGAN:** *Sinfonia* (1956); *Plenum IV* (1975). **VOCAL:** *O Saisons, O Châteaux,* cantata for Soprano, Mandolin, Guitar, Harp, and Strings (1946); *Requiem for the Living* for Soloists, Chorus, and Orch. (1948); *Bienfaits de la lune* for Soprano, Tenor, Chorus, Strings, and Percussion (1952); *De Amore,* cantata (1957; London, Sept. 7, 1973); *Catena* for Soprano, Tenor, and 21 Instruments (1961–62); *Encomion* for Chorus, Brass, and Percussion (1963); *The Valley of Haisu-Se* for Soprano and Instrumental Ensemble (1965); *Akapotik Rose* for Soprano and Instrumental Ensemble (1966); *And Suddenly It's Evening* for Tenor and 11 Instruments (1967); *Essence of Our Happiness,* cantata (1968; London, Sept. 8, 1970); *Phoenix* for Soprano, Violin, Clarinet, and Piano (1968); *Anerca* for Women's Speaking Chorus, 10 Guitars, and Percussion (1970); *Vision of Youth* for Soprano, 3 Clarinets, Piano, and Percussion (1970); *Islands* for Soprano, Tenor, Narrator, and Instrumental Ensemble (London, June 7, 1971); *The Tears of Night* for Countertenor, 6 Sopranos, and 3 Instrumental Ensembles (1971); *Requiescat,* in memoriam Igor Stravinsky, for Soprano and String Trio (1971); *Dirge* for the Proud World for Soprano, Countertenor, Harpsichord, and Cello (1971); *Counting Your Steps* for Chorus, 4 Flutes, and 4 Percussion Players (1972); *Chimes and Cantos* for Baritone and Instrumental Ensemble (1972); *Voice of Quiet Waters* for Chorus and Orch. (1972; Huddersfield, April 14, 1973); *Laudi* for Soprano, 3 Clarinets, Piano, and Percussion (1973); *Chorale Prelude and Paraphrase* for Tenor, String Quintet, and Percussion, after a letter of Keats (1977); *Cascando* for Contralto, Violin, and Strings (1977); *Elegy of the Flowers* for Tenor and 3 Instrumental Groups (1978); *Echoi* for Mezzo-soprano and Orch. (1979); *Cantata* for Soprano and Instruments (1979); *Cantata* for 3 Soloists and Instrumental Ensemble, after Baudelaire (1979); *The Roots of the World* for Chorus and Cello obbligato, after Yeats (1979); *Echoes* for Contralto, Alto Flute, English Horn, and String Quartet (1979); *Mine Eyes, My Bread, My Spade* for Baritone and String Quartet (1980); *Fleur du silence* for Tenor, Flute, Oboe, Horn, Harp, Violin, Viola, and Percussion, after Rémi de Gourmont (1980); *The Singing Birds* for Actress and Viola (1980).

BIBL.: M. and S. Harries, *A Pilgrim Soul: The Life and Work of E. L.* (London, 1989).

Luvisi, Lee, American pianist and teacher; b. Louisville, Dec. 12, 1937. He studied at the Curtis Inst. of Music in Philadelphia with Serkin and Horszowski; upon graduation in 1957, he joined its faculty. In 1963 he was named artist-in-residence at the Univ. of Louisville School of Music; later became chairman of its piano dept. He appeared as soloist with many of the major American and European orchs., and also gave numerous recitals. In 1983 he became a member of the Chamber Music. Soc. of Lincoln Center in N.Y.

Luxon, Benjamin, esteemed English baritone; b. Redruth, March 24, 1937. He studied with Walter Grünner at the Guildhall School of Music in London, then joined the English Opera Group, with which he sang Sid in *Albert Herring* and Tarquinius in *The Rape of Lucretia* on its tour of the Soviet Union (1963). He was chosen by Britten to create the title role in the opera *Owen Wingrave* (BBC-TV, May 16, 1971); then made his debut at London's Covent Garden as Monteverdi's Ulysses (1972), and subsequently sang there regularly; also appeared at the festivals in Aldeburgh, Edinburgh, and Glyndebourne (from 1972), and with the English National Opera in London (from 1974). On Feb. 2, 1980, he made his Metropolitan Opera debut in N.Y. as Eugene Onegin. In 1986 he made his first appearance at Milan's La Scala. In 1988 he sang Wozzeck in Los Angeles. In 1992 he appeared as Falstaff at the English National

Opera. His last years as a singer were aggravated by increasing deafness. His other roles included Count Almaviva, Don Giovanni, Papageno, Wolfram, and Eisenstein. He also distinguished himself as a concert artist, his repertoire ranging from the standard literature to folk songs. In 1986 he was made a Commander of the Order of the British Empire.

Lybbert, Donald, American composer and teacher; b. Cresco, Iowa, Feb. 19, 1923; d. Norwalk, Conn., July 26, 1981. He studied at the Univ. of Iowa (B.M., 1946), with Ward and Wagenaar at the Juilliard School of Music in N.Y. (1946–48), with Carter and Luening at Columbia Univ. (M.A., 1950), and with Boulanger in Fontainebleau (1961). From 1954 to 1980 he taught at Hunter College of the City Univ. of N.Y. With F. Davis, he wrote *The Essentials of Counterpoint* (1969). His music was freely atonal for the most part, although he utilized serial procedures in some of his scores.

WORKS: DRAMATIC: *Monica*, operetta (Amsterdam, Nov. 2, 1952); *The Scarlet Letter*, opera (1964–67). **ORCH.:** Concert Overture (1952). **CHAMBER:** Wind Octet (1947); *Introduction and Toccata* for Brass and Piano (1955); Trio for Clarinet, Horn, and Bassoon (1956); *Chamber Sonata* for Viola, Horn, and Piano (1957); *Sonorities* for 11 Instruments (1960); *Praeludium* for Brass and Percussion (1962); *Variants* for 5 Winds (1971). **PIANO:** 3 sonatas (1947, 1954, 1962); *Movement* for Piano, 4-hands (1960); Concerto for Piano and Tape (n.d.). **VOCAL:** *Leopardi Canti*, song cycle for Soprano, Flute, Viola, and Bass Clarinet (1959); *Austro terris inflente*, 3 motets (1961); *Lines for the Fallen* for Soprano and 2 Quarter Tone Tuned Pianos (1967); *Zap* for Multiantiphonal Chorus, Instruments, and Rock Group (1970); *Octagon* for Soprano and 7 Instrumentalists (1975).

Lympany, Dame Moura (real name, **Mary Johnstone**), esteemed English pianist; b. Saltash, Aug. 18, 1916. After studies in Liège, she was a scholarship student of Coviello at the Royal College of Music in London. She then continued her training in Vienna with Paul Weingarten and in London with Mathdilde Verne and Tobias Matthay. At age 12, she made her debut as soloist in Mendelssohn's G minor Piano Concerto in Harrogate. In 1938 she took 2nd prize in the Ysaÿe Competition in Brussels. For professional purposes, she took the name Moura Lympany, the surname being a transformation of her mother's maiden name of Limpenny. In 1940 she was soloist in the first London performance of the Khachaturian Piano Concerto, which she later played throughout Europe. After making her first appearances in the U.S. in 1948, she toured throughout the world. In 1979 she was made a Commander of the Order of the British Empire and in 1992 a Dame Commander of the Order of the British Empire. With M. Strickland, she publ. *Moura Lympany, her Autobiography* (London, 1991). Lympany displayed a remarkable capacity for Russian music, particularly of Rachmaninoff. She also championed such English composers as Delius, Ireland, Cyril Scott, and Rawsthorne.

Lynn, George, American choral conductor, organist, teacher, and composer; b. Edwardsville, Pa., Oct. 5, 1915; d. Colorado Springs, Colo., March 16, 1989. He was a student of Weinrich (organ), Williamson (conducting), and Harris (composition) at Westminster Choir College in Princeton, N.J. (B.Mus., 1938) and of Thompson (composition) at Princeton Univ. (M.F.A., 1947). He was active as an organist and music director in various churches in New Jersey, California, Pennsylvania, Colorado, and North Carolina. Lynn served as prof. of choral arts at Westminster Choir College (1946–50) and at the Univ. of Colo. (1950–52). From 1963 to 1969 he was music director of the Westminster Choir. In 1971 he was visiting composer-in-residence at the Univ. of New Mexico. He subsequently was prof. of choral arts at the Colorado School of Mines (1971–80), Loretto Heights College (1971–86), and Rice Univ. (1986–87). Lynn composed in a tonal idiom with a strong modal character. Rhythmic variation was indicative of his style and provided a firm foundation for his long melodic lines.

WORKS: OPERAS: *The Violinden Tree* (1960); *From Time to Time* (1962). **ORCH.:** Piano Concerto (1962); 2 syms. (1964, 1966). **CHAMBER:** 5 string quartets; works for Violin and Piano, Clarinet and Piano, etc.; over 100 piano pieces. **VOCAL:** *Gettysburg Address* for Baritone, Chorus, and Orch. (1941); *Greek Folk Song Rhapsody* for Contralto, Chorus, and Orch. (1958); 3 sacred syms. for Chorus (1959, 1960, 1962); *Second Inaugural* for Chorus and Orch. (1961); *Markings* for Soprano, Men's Chorus, and Orch. (1969); settings of e.e. cummings for Chorus (1984); 2 cantatas: *Under the Shadow* for Chorus, Brass, and Organ (1985) and *The Scandal of Christ* for Soloists, Chorus, and Organ (1986); many other choral pieces; over 100 songs; arrangements.

Lyons, James, American music critic and editor; b. Peabody, Mass., Nov. 24, 1925; d. N.Y., Nov. 13, 1973. He studied musicology with Geiringer at Boston Univ. (graduated, 1947), music history with Warren Storey Smith at the New England Cons. of Music in Boston, and psychology at N.Y. Univ. (M.A., 1964). After serving as assistant ed. of *Musical America* (1953–55), he was ed. and publisher of the *American Record Guide* (1957–73). He also contributed criticism and articles to various other publications. With J. Howard, he publ. *Modern Music* (N.Y., 1957), a rev. version of Howard's *This Modern Music* (1942).

Ma, Yo-Yo, brilliant Chinese cellist; b. Paris, Oct. 7, 1955. He was born into a musical family active in Paris; his father was a violinist, his mother a mezzo-soprano. He began to study violin as a small child, then graduated to the viola and finally the cello; was taken to N.Y. when he was 7, and enrolled at the Juilliard School of Music when he was 9; his principal teachers were Leonard Rose and János Scholz; he subsequently received additional musical training at Harvard Univ. In 1978 he was awarded the Avery Fisher Prize. He quickly established a formidable reputation as a master of the cello in his appearances with the great orchs. of the world, as a recitalist, and as a chamber music player, being deservedly acclaimed for his unostentatious musicianship, his superlative technical resources, and the remarkable tone of his melodious lyricism. In order to extend his repertoire, he made a number of effective transcriptions for his instrument. He also promoted contemporary works and was soloist in the premieres of the cello concertos of Christopher Rouse (Los Angeles, Jan. 23, 1994) and John Williams (Tanglewood, July 7, 1994).

Maag, (Ernst) Peter (Johannes), eminent Swiss conductor; b. St. Gallen, May 10, 1919. His father, Otto Maag, was the Lutheran minister, philosopher, musicologist, and critic; his mother was a violinist and a member of the Capet Quartet. He attended the Univs. of Zürich, Basel, and Geneva, where his principal mentors were Karl Barth and Emil Brunner in theology and Karl Jaspers in philosophy. He also studied piano and theory with Czeslaw Marek in Zürich, and then pursued his training in piano with Cortot in Paris. His conducting mentors were Hoesslin and Ansermet in Geneva. He later profited greatly as an assistant to Furtwängler. He began his career as répétiteur at the Biel-Solothurn theater, where he then served as music director (1943–46). From 1952 to 1955 he held the title of 1st conductor at the Düsseldorf Opera. He was Generalmusikdirektor of the Bonn City Theater from 1955 to 1959. In 1958 he made his first appearance at London's Covent Garden. In 1959 he made his U.S. debut as guest conductor of the Cincinnati Sym. Orch. He was chief conductor of the Vienna Volksoper from 1964 to 1968. On Sept. 23, 1972, he made his Metropolitan Opera debut in N.Y. conducting *Don Giovanni.* He was artistic director of the Teatro Regio in Parma from 1972 to 1974 and of the Teatro Regio in Turin from 1974 to 1976. Thereafter he continued to appear frequently in Italy while continuing to make guest appearances with orchs. and opera houses in Europe, North and South America, and Japan. From 1984 to 1991 he was music director of the Bern Sym. Orch. Maag is particularly esteemed for his remarkable interpretations of the music of Mozart, and also for his efforts to revive forgotten works of the past.

BIBL: D. McIntire, "P. M.: Switzerland's Musical Ambassador," *Northern Light* (Jan. 1979).

Maasalo, Armas (Toivo Valdemar), Finnish composer and teacher; b. Rautavaara, Aug. 28, 1885; d. Helsinki, Sept. 9, 1960. He studied at the Helsinki Music Inst. (1907–10). He taught at the Helsinki Church Music Inst. (1914–51), serving as its director (1923–51); then was director of the church music dept. of the Sibelius Academy in Helsinki (1951–55). He wrote much sacred music.

WORKS: ORCH.: *Ricordanza* for Cello, Piano, and Orch. (1919); Piano Concerto (1919); *Karelian Scenes* (1920); *Partita seria* for Strings (1934); Suite for Organ and Orch. (1945). **VOCAL:** *The Path of Man,* cantata (1926); *2 Stars* for Alto, Chorus, and Orch. (1929); *Christmas Oratorio* (1945); religious songs for chorus and solo voice.

Ma'ayani, Ami, Israeli composer; b. Ramat-Gan, Jan. 13, 1936. He studied at the New Jerusalem Academy of Music (1951–53), with Ben-Haim (1956–60), and with Ussachevsky at Columbia Univ. in N.Y. (1961–62; 1964–65); he also studied architecture at the Israel Inst. of Technology (B.Sc., 1960) and philosophy at the Univ. of Tel Aviv (M.A., 1973).

WORKS: DRAMATIC: *The War of the Sons of Light,* opera-oratorio (1970–72); *A Legend of 3 and 4,* ballet (1978). **ORCH.:** *Divertimento concertante* for Chamber Orch. (1957); 2 harp concertos (1960, 1966); Violin Concerto (1967); Concerto for 8 Wind Instruments and Percussion (1966); Cello Concerto (1967); Concerto for 2 Pianos and Orch. (1969); *Qumran* (1970); *Symphony Concertante* for Wind Quintet and Orch. (1972); Sym. No. 2 (1975) and No. 4, *Sinfonietta on Popular Hebraic Themes*, for Chamber Orch. (1982); Viola Concerto (1975); Guitar Concerto (1976); Concertino for Harp and Strings (1980); Sinfonietta No. 1 for Chamber Orch. (1980); *Ouverture solennelle* (1982); *Scherzo Mediterranean* (1983). **CHAMBER:** *Magamat* for Harp (1960); *Toccata* for Harp (1962); *Poème* for Flute and String Trio (1965); *Improvisation variée* for Flute, Viola or Violin, and Harp (1966); *4 Preludes* for 4 Percussionists and Piano (1968); *2 Madrigals* for Harp and Wind Quintet (1969); Sonatina for Clarinet, Cello, and Piano (1985); piano pieces. **VOCAL:** *Psalms* for Soprano, Flute, Bass Clarinet, Harp, Percussion, and Strings (1965); *Festivals* for Soprano or Tenor and Orch. (1966); Sym. No. 3, *Hebrew Requiem*, for Mezzo-soprano, Chorus, and Orch. (1977).

Maazel, Lorin (Varencove), brilliant American conductor; b. Neuilly, France (of American parents), March 6, 1930. His parents took him to Los Angeles when he was an infant. At a very early age, he showed innate musical ability; he had perfect pitch and could assimilate music osmotically; he began to study violin at age 5 with Karl Moldrem, and then piano at age 7 with Fanchon Armitage. Fascinated by the art of conducting, he went to sym. concerts and soon began to take lessons in conducting with Vladimir Bakaleinikov, who was an assoc. conductor of the Los Angeles Phil.; on July 13, 1938, at the age of 8, he was given a chance to conduct a performance of Schubert's *Unfinished Symphony* with the visiting Univ. of Idaho orch. In 1938 Bakaleinikov was appointed assistant conductor of the Pittsburgh Sym. Orch., and the Maazel family followed him to Pittsburgh. From Bakaleinikov, Maazel quickly learned to speak Russian. On Aug. 18, 1939, he made a sensational appearance in N.Y. conducting the National Music Camp Orch. of Interlochen at the World's Fair, eliciting the inevitable jocular comments (he was compared to a trained seal). Maazel was only 11 when he conducted the NBC Sym. Orch. (1941) and 12 when he led an entire program with the N.Y. Phil. (1942). He survived these traumatic exhibitions, and took academic courses at the Univ. of Pittsburgh. In 1948 he joined the Pittsburgh Sym. Orch. as a violinist, and at the same time was appointed its apprentice conductor. In 1951 he received a Fulbright fellowship for travel in Italy, where he undertook a serious study of Baroque music; he also made his adult debut as a conductor in Catania on Dec. 23, 1953. In 1955 he conducted at the Florence May Festival, in 1957 at the Vienna Festival, and in 1958 at the Edinburgh Festival. In 1960 he became the first American to conduct at the Bayreuth Festival, where he led performances of *Lohengrin*. In 1962 he toured the U.S. with the Orchestre National de France. On Nov. 1, 1962, he made his Metropolitan Opera debut in N.Y. conducting *Don Giovanni*. From 1965 to 1971 he was artistic director of the Deutsche Oper in West Berlin; from 1965 to 1975 he also served as chief conductor of the (West) Berlin Radio Sym. Orch. He was assoc. principal conductor of the New Philharmonia Orch. of London from 1970 to 1972, and its principal guest conductor from 1976 to 1980. In 1972 he became music director of the Cleveland Orch., a position he held with great distinction until 1982; was then made conductor emeritus. He led the Cleveland Orch. on 10 major tours abroad, including Australia and New Zealand (1973), Japan (1974), twice in Latin America, and twice in Europe, and maintained its stature as one of the world's foremost orchs. He was also chief conductor of the Orchestre National de France from 1977 to 1982; then was its principal guest conductor until 1988, and then its music director until 1991. In 1980 he became conductor of the famous Vienna Phil. New Year's Day Concerts, a position he retained until 1986. In 1982 he assumed the positions of artistic director and general manager of the Vienna State Opera, the first American to be so honored; however, he resigned these positions in the middle of his 4-year contract in 1984 after a conflict over artistic policies with the Ministry of Culture. He then served as music consultant to the Pittsburgh Sym. Orch. (1984–86); was its music adviser and principal guest conductor in 1986, becoming its music director that same year. In 1993 he also assumed the post of chief conductor of the Bavarian Radio Sym. Orch. in Munich. In 1994 he again conducted the Vienna Phil. New Year's Day Concert. In 1996 he stepped down as music director of the Pittsburgh Sym. Orch. after a notably distinguished tenure.

Maazel is equally adept as an interpreter of operatic and symphonic scores; he is blessed with a phenomenal memory, and possesses an extraordinary baton technique. He also maintains an avid interest in nonmusical pursuits; a polyglot, he is fluent in French, German, Italian, Spanish, Portuguese, and Russian. Maazel was the recipient of many awards; he received an honorary doctorate from the Univ. of Pittsburgh in 1965, the Sibelius Prize in Finland, the Commander's Cross of the Order of Merit from West Germany, and, for his numerous recordings, the Grand Prix de Disque in Paris and the Edison Prize in the Netherlands.

Macák, Ivan, Slovak ethnomusicologist; b. Gbelce, near Nové Zámky, Aug. 26, 1935. He studied ethnomusicology at the Univ. of Bratislava, where he received his Ph.D. (1969) with the diss. *Štúdie k typológii a histórii slovenskych l'udovych nástrojov* (Studies in the Classification and History of Slovak Folk Instruments). He was ed. of *L'udová tvorivosť* (1959–65), and research fellow in music at the Slovak National Museum in Bratislava (from 1967), where he subsequently built its collection to include over 900 folk instruments and 7,000 pictorial records. He lectured in ethnomusicology at the Bratislava Academy (1962–73) and co-ed. the *Annual Bibliography of European Ethnomusicology* (Bratislava, 1967 et seq.). His chief contribution is in the area of organology, particularly the earliest history of instruments and their methodology.

Macal, Zdenek (originally **Zdeněk Mácal**), prominent Czech-born American conductor; b. Brno, Jan. 8, 1936. He studied with Bakala, Jílek, and Vesélka at the Brno Cons. (1951–56), then at Brno's Janáček Academy of Music. He was conductor of the Moravian Phil. in Olomouc (1963–67). He won the Besançon (1965) and Mitropoulos (1966) competitions. In 1966 he made his first appearance as a guest conductor with the Czech Phil. in Prague, with which he then toured Europe. In 1968 he left his homeland in the wake of the Soviet-led invasion and served as chief conductor of the Cologne Radio Sym. Orch. (1970–74) and the Hannover Radio Orch. (1980–83); also appeared as a guest conductor throughout Europe and the U.S. He was principal guest conductor (1985–86) and music director (1986–95) of the Milwaukee Sym. Orch. He also was chief conductor of the Sydney Sym. Orch. (1986), principal guest conductor (1986–88) and artistic director and principal conductor (1988–92) of the San Antonio Sym. Orch., and artistic advisor (1992–93) and artistic director (from 1993) of the New Jersey Sym. Orch. On Oct. 3, 1992, he became a naturalized American citizen at a special ceremony held during a concert he conducted with the Milwaukee Sym. Orch.

MacArdle, Donald Wales, American musicologist; b. Quincy, Mass., July 3, 1897; d. Littleton, Colo., Dec. 23, 1964. He studied science at the Mass. Inst. of Technology, obtaining an M.S. in chemical engineering; he also took courses at the Juilliard School of Music in N.Y., and studied musicology at N.Y. Univ. Although he earned his living as an engineer, he devoted much time to scholarly research, mainly to the minutiae of Beethoven's biography; he contributed a number of valuable articles on the subject to the *Musical Quarterly* and other journals. He ed., with L. Misch, *New Beethoven Letters* (Norman, Okla., 1957); ed. and tr. Schindler's *Biographie von Ludwig van Beethoven*, 3rd ed., 1860, as *Beethoven as I Knew Him* (London and Chapel Hill, 1966); he also prepared *An Index to Beethoven's Conversation Books* (Detroit, 1962) and, with S. Pogodda, *Beethoven Abstracts* (Detroit, 1973).

Macbeth, Florence, American soprano; b. Mankato, Minn., Jan. 12, 1891; d. Hyattsville, Md., May 5, 1966. She studied in N.Y. and Paris. In 1913 she made her operatic debut as Rosina in *Il Barbiere di Siviglia* in Braunschweig. On Jan. 14, 1914, she made her American debut with the Chicago Opera Co. and remained on its staff as prima coloratura soprano until 1930; for a season she undertook an American tour with the Commonwealth Opera Co., singing in Gilbert and Sullivan operettas. So melodious and mellifluous were her fiorituras that she was dubbed the "Minnesota Nightingale." In 1947 she married the novelist James M. Cain and settled in Maryland.

MacCunn, Hamish (James), Scottish composer, conductor, and teacher; b. Greenock, March 22, 1868; d. London, Aug. 2, 1916. He won a composition scholarship to the Royal College of Music in London when he was 15, and studied there with Parry, Stanford, and Franklin Taylor (until 1886). He remained in London and served as prof. of hamony at the Royal Academy of Music (1888–94). He also taught composition privately and later at the Guildhall School of Music (from 1912). From 1898 he was also active as a theater conductor. After working with the Carl Rosa Opera Co. and the Moody-Manners Co., he served as principal conductor of the Savoy Theatre (1902–05). Thereafter he conducted at various theaters, and in 1910 and 1915 he was a conductor with the Beecham Opera Co. MacCunn's most important work was the opera *Jeanie Deans* (Edinburgh, Nov. 15, 1894), after Scott's *The Heart of Midlothian.* He remains best known, however, for the overture *The Land of the Mountain and the Flood* (London, Nov. 5, 1887).

WORKS: DRAMATIC: *Jeanie Deans,* opera (Edinburgh, Nov. 15, 1894); *Diarmid,* opera (London, Oct. 23, 1897); *Breast of Light* (n.d.; unfinished); *The Masque of War and Peace,* masque (London, Feb. 13, 1900); *The Golden Girl,* light opera (Birmingham, Aug. 5, 1905); *Prue,* light opera (n.d.; unfinished); *The Pageant of Darkness and Light,* stage pageant (1908); *The Sailor and the Nursemaid,* light opera (London, June 27, 1912). **ORCH.:** *Cior Mhor,* overture (London, Oct. 27, 1885); *The Land of the Mountain and the Flood,* overture (London, Nov. 5, 1887); *The Ship o' the Fiend,* ballade (London, Feb. 21, 1888); *The Dowie Dens O'Yarrow,* ballade (London, Oct. 13, 1888); *Highland Memories,* suite (London, March 13, 1897); *5 Dances* (n.d.). **CHAMBER:** String Quintet (n.d.); *3 Romantic Pieces* for Cello and Piano (1894); piano pieces, including *6 Scotch Dances* (1896). **VOCAL:** *The Moss Rose,* cantata (1885); *Lord Ullin's Daughter* for Chorus and Orch. (London, Feb. 18, 1888); *Bonny Kilmeny* for Soloist, Chorus, and Orch. (Edinburgh, Dec. 15, 1888); *The Lay of the Last Minstrel* for Solo Voices, Chorus, and Orch. (Glasgow, Dec. 18, 1888); *The Cameronian's Dream* for Baritone, Chorus, and Orch. (Edinburgh, Jan. 27, 1890); *Queen Hynde of Caledon* for Soloists, Chorus, and Orch. (Glasgow, Jan. 28, 1892); *Psalm VIII* for Chorus and Organ (1901); *The Wreck of the Hesperus* for Chorus and Orch. (London, Aug. 28, 1905); *Livingstone the Pilgrim* for Chorus and Orch. (1913); part songs; over 100 solo songs.

Macdonald, Hugh (John), distinguished English musicologist; b. Newbury, Berkshire, Jan. 31, 1940. He was educated at Pembroke College, Cambridge (B.A., 1961; M.A., 1965; Ph.D., 1969). In 1966 he became a lecturer at the Univ. of Cambridge, then at the Univ. of Oxford in 1971; in 1979 he was a visiting prof. at Indiana Univ. in Bloomington; in 1980 he was named Gardiner Prof. of Music at the Univ. of Glasgow; then was a prof. at Washington Univ. in St. Louis (from 1987). His special field of interest is 19th-century music; he is particularly noted for his studies in French music, and is a leading authority on the life and works of Berlioz; in 1965 he became general ed. of the *New Berlioz Edition.* He publ. *Berlioz: Orchestral Music* (London, 1969), *Skryabin* (London, 1978), and *Berlioz* (London, 1982). He also ed. *Berlioz: Selected Letters* (1995)

MacDonald, Jeanette (Anna), American soprano; b. Philadelphia, June 18, 1903; d. Houston, Jan. 14, 1965. She started a career as a chorus girl and model in N.Y. (1920) and unexpectedly won encomia for her starring role in the musical *The Magic Ring* (1923). She then attained wide recognition as a singing actress via 29 films, especially those in which she paired with Nelson Eddy: *Naughty Marietta* (1935), *Rose Marie* (1936), *Maytime* (1937), *The Girl of the Golden West* (1938), *Sweethearts* (1939), *New Moon* (1940), *Bittersweet* (1940), and *I Married an Angel* (1942). She made a belated operatic debut as Juliette in Montreal (May 1944); she also sang in Chicago, but her voice was too small to fill large opera halls.

BIBL.: S. Rich, *J. M.: A Pictorial Biography* (Los Angeles, 1973); E. Knowles, *Films of J. M. and Nelson Eddy* (South Brunswick, N.J., 1975); J. Parish, *The J. M. Story* (N.Y., 1976); L. Stern, *J. M.* (N.Y., 1977).

MacDowell, Edward (Alexander), greatly significant American composer; b. N.Y., Dec. 18, 1860; d. there, Jan. 23, 1908. His father was a Scotch-Irish tradesman; his mother, an artistically-inclined woman who encouraged his musical studies. He took piano lessons with Juan Buitrago and Paul Desvernine; also had supplementary sessions with Teresa Carreño, who later championed his works. In 1876, after traveling in Europe with his mother, MacDowell enrolled as an auditor in Augustin Savard's elementary class at the Paris Cons.; on Feb. 8, 1877, he was admitted as a regular student; he also studied piano with Antoine-François Marmontel and solfège with Marmontel's son, Antonin. Somewhat disappointed with his progress, he withdrew from the Cons. on Sept. 30, 1878, and went to the Stuttgart Cons. for a brief period of study with Sigmund Lebert; he then proceeded to Wiesbaden to study theory and composition with Louis Ehlert; in 1979 he enrolled at the newly founded but already prestigious Hoch Cons. in Frankfurt am Main as a student of Carl Heymann in piano, Joachim Raff (the Cons. director) in composition, and Franz Böhme in counterpoint and fugue. During MacDowell's stay there, Raff's class had a visit from Liszt, and MacDowell performed the piano part in Schumann's Quintet, op. 44, in Liszt's presence. At another visit, MacDowell played Liszt's *Hungarian Rhapsody* No. 14 for him; 2 years later, he visited Liszt in Weimar, and played his own 1st Piano Concerto for him, accompanied by Eugène d'Albert at the 2nd piano. Encouraged by Liszt's interest, MacDowell sent him the MS of his *Modern Suite,* op. 10, for piano solo; Liszt recommended the piece for performance at the meeting of the Allgemeiner Deutscher Musikverein (Zürich, July 11, 1882); he also recommended MacDowell to the publishers Breitkopf & Härtel, who subsequently brought out the first works of MacDowell to appear in print, the *Modern Suites* for piano, opp. 10 and 14. MacDowell left the Cons. in 1880 and began teaching piano privately. However, he pursued private piano and composition lessons with Heymann and Raff.

Despite his youth, MacDowell was given a teaching position at the Darmstadt Cons. in 1881, but he resigned in 1988; he also accepted private pupils, among them Marian Nevins of Connecticut; they were secretly married on July 9, 1884, in N.Y., followed by a public ceremony in Waterford, Conn., on July 21. During the early years of their marriage, the MacDowells made their 2nd home in Wiesbaden, where MacDowell composed industriously; his works were performed in neighboring communities; Carreño put several of his piano pieces on her concert programs. There were also performances in America. However, the MacDowells were beset by financial difficulties; his mother proposed that he and his wife live on the family property, but MacDowell declined. He also declined an offer to teach at the National Cons. in N.Y. at the munificent fee of $5 an hour. Similarly, he rejected an offer to take a clerical position at the American Consulate in Krefeld, Germany. In 1888 he finally returned to the U.S., making his home in Boston, where he was welcomed in artistic circles as a famous composer and pianist; musical Boston at the time was virtually a German colony, and MacDowell's German training was a certificate of his worth. On Nov. 19, 1888, MacDowell made his American debut as a composer and pianist at a Boston concert of the Kneisel String Quartet, featuring his *Modern Suite,* op.

10. On March 5, 1889, he was the soloist in the premiere performance of his 2nd Piano Concerto with the N.Y. Phil., under the direction of Theodore Thomas. Frank van der Stucken invited MacDowell to play his concerto at the spectacular Paris Exposition on July 12, 1889. MacDowell had no difficulty having his works publ., although for some reason he preferred that his early piano pieces, opp. 1–7, be printed under the pseudonym Edgar Thorn.

In 1896 Columbia Univ. invited MacDowell to becomes its first prof. of music, "to elevate the standard of musical instruction in the U.S., and to afford the most favorable opportunity for acquiring instruction of the highest order." MacDowell interpreted this statement to its fullest; by 1899, 2 assistants had been employed, Leonard McWhood and Gustav Hinrichs, but students received no credit for his courses. At the same time, he continued to compose and to teach piano privately; he also conducted the Mendelssohn Glee Club (1896–98) and served as president of the Soc. of American Musicians and Composers (1899–1900). In the academic year 1902–03, he took a sabbatical; he played concerts throughout the U.S. and in Europe; played his 2nd Piano Concerto in London (May 14, 1903). During his sabbatical, Columbia Univ. replaced its president, Seth Low, with Nicholas Murray Butler, whose ideas about the role of music in the univ. were diametrically opposed to the ideals of MacDowell. MacDowell resigned in 1904 and subsequently became a "cause célèbre," resulting in much acrimony on both sides. It was not until some time later that the Robert Center Chair that MacDowell had held at Columbia Univ. was renamed the Edward MacDowell Chair of Music to honor its first recipient.

Through the combination of the trauma resulting from this episode, an accident with a hansom, and the development of what appears to have been tertiary syphilis, MacDowell rapidly deteriorated mentally into a vegetative state. In 1906 a public appeal was launched to raise funds for his care; among the signers were Horatio Parker, Victor Herbert, Arthur Foote, George Chadwick, Frederick Converse, Andrew Carnegie, J. Pierpont Morgan, and former President Grover Cleveland. MacDowell was only 47 years old when he died. The sum of $50,000 was raised for the organization of the MacDowell Memorial Assn. Mrs. MacDowell, who outlived her husband by nearly half a century (she died at the age of 98, in Los Angeles, on Aug. 23, 1956), deeded to the Assn. her husband's summer residence at Peterborough, N.H. This property became a pastoral retreat, under the name of the MacDowell Colony, for American composers and writers, who could spend summers working undisturbed in separate cottages, paying a minimum rent for lodging and food. During the summer of 1910, Mrs. MacDowell arranged an elaborate pageant with music from MacDowell's works, the sucess of which led to the establishment of a series of MacDowell Festivals at Peterborough.

MacDowell received several awards during his lifetime, including 2 honorary doctorates (Princeton Univ., 1896; Univ. of Pa., 1902) and election into the American Academy of Arts and Letters (1904); in 1940 a 5-cent U.S. postage stamp with his likeness was issued; in 1960 he was the 2nd composer elected to the Hall of Fame at N.Y. Univ., where, in 1964, a bust was revealed.

Among American composers, MacDowell occupies a historically important place as the first American whose works were accepted as comparable in quality and technique with those of the average German composers of his time. His music adhered to the prevalent representative Romantic art. Virtually all of his works bear titles borrowed from mythical history, literature, or painting; even his piano sonatas, cast in Classical forms, carry descriptive titles, indicative of the mood of melodic resources, or as an ethnic reference. Since he lived in Germany during his formative years, German musical culture was decisive in shaping his musical development; even the American rhythms and melodies in his music seem to be European reflections of an exotic art. A parallel with Grieg is plausible, for Grieg was also a regional composer trained in Germany. But Grieg possessed a much more vigorous personality, and he succeeded in communicating the true spirit of Norwegian song modalities in his works. Lack of musical strength and originality accounts for MacDowell's gradual decline in the estimation of succeeding generations; his romanticism was apt to lapse into salon sentimentality. The frequency of performance of his works in concert (he never wrote for the stage) declined in the decades following his death, and his influence on succeeding generations of American composers receded to a faint recognition of an evanescent artistic period.

MacDowell's writings were collected by W. Baltzell and publ. as *Critical and Historical Essays* (1912; reprinted, with new introduction by I. Lowens, N.Y., 1969).

WORKS: ORCH.: *Hamlet and Ophelia*, 2 tone poems, op. 22 (1885; *Ophelia*, N.Y., Nov. 4, 1886; *Hamlet*, N.Y., Nov. 15, 1887; together, Chicago, March 26, 1890); *Lancelot and Elaine*, symphonic poem, op. 28 (1889; Boston, Jan. 10, 1890); *Lamia*, symphonic poem, op. 29 (1889; Boston, Oct. 23, 1908); *The Saracens* and *The Lovely Alda*, 2 fragments after the Song of Roland, op. 30 (Boston, Nov. 5, 1891); 2 suites: No. 1, op. 42 (Worcester Festival, Sept. 24, 1891; 3rd movement, "In October," op. 42a, added in 1894; complete works 1st perf., Boston, 1896), and No. 2, *Indian*, op. 48 (N.Y., Jan. 23, 1896); 2 piano concertos: No. 1, in A minor, op. 15 (movements 2 and 3, N.Y., March 30, 1885, Adele Margulies soloist; complete version, Chicago, July 5, 1888, Teresa Carreño soloist) and No. 2, in D minor, op. 23 (N.Y., March 5, 1889, composer soloist); *Romance* for Cello and Orch., op. 35 (1888).

PIANO: *Amourette*, op. 1 (1896); *In Lilting Rhythm*, op. 2 (1897); *Forgotten Fairy Tales (Sung outside the Prince's Door, Of a Tailor and a Bear, Beauty in the Rose Garden, From Dwarfland)*, op. 4 (1898); *6 Fancies (A Tin Soldier's Love, To a Humming-Bird, Summer Song, Across Fields, Bluette, An Elfin Round)*, op. 7 (1898); *Waltz*, op. 8 (1895); *1st Modern Suite*, op. 10 (1880); *Prelude and Fugue*, op. 13 (1883); *2nd Modern Suite*, op. 14 (1881); *Serenata*, op. 16 (1883); *2 Fantastic Pieces (Legend, Witches' Dance)*, op. 17 (1884); 2 Pieces (*Barcarolle, Humoresque*), op. 18 (1884); *Forest Idyls (Forest Stillness, Play of the Nymphs, Reverie, Dance of the Dryads)*, op. 19 (1884); 4 Pieces (*Humoresque, March, Cradle Song, Czardas*), op. 24 (1887); 6 Idyls after Goethe (*In the Woods, Siesta, To the Moonlight, Silver Clouds, Flute Idyl, The Bluebell*), op. 28 (1887); 6 Poems after Heine (*From a Fisherman's Hut, Scotch Poem, From Long Ago, The Post Wagon, The Shepherd Boy, Monologue*), op. 31 (1887); *4 Little Poems (The Eagle, The Brook, Moonshine, Winter)*, op. 32 (1888); *Étude de concert* in F-sharp, op. 36 (1889); *Les Orientales*, after Victor Hugo (*Clair de lune, Dans le Hamac, Danse Andalouse*), op. 37 (1889); *Marionettes*, 8 Little Pieces (*Prologue, Soubrette, Lover, Witch, Clown, Villain, Sweetheart, Epilogue*), op. 38 (1888; originally only 6 pieces; *Prologue* and *Epilogue* were added in 1901); 12 Studies, Book I (*Hunting Song, Alla Tarantella, Romance, Arabesque, In the Forest, Dance of the Gnomes*) and Book II (*Idyl, Shadow Dance, Intermezzo, Melody, Scherzino, Hungarian*), op. 39 (1890); 4 sonatas: No. 1, *Tragica*, op. 45 (1893), No. 2, *Eroica*, op. 50 (1895), No. 3, *Norse*, op. 57 (1900), and No. 4, *Keltic*, op. 59 (1901); 12 Virtuoso Studies (*Novelette, Moto perpetuo, Wild Chase, Improvisation, Elfin Dance, Valse triste, Burleske, Bluette, Träumerei, March Wind, Impromptu, Polonaise*), op. 46, (1894); *Air* and *Rigaudon*, op. 49 (1894); *Woodland Sketches*, 10 pieces (*To a Wild Rose, Will o' the Wisp, At an Old Trysting Place, In Autumn, From an Indian Lodge, To a Water Lily, From Uncle Remus, A Desert Farm, By a Meadow Brook, Told at Sunset*), op. 51 (1896); *Sea Pieces* (*To the Sea, From a Wandering Iceberg, A.D. 1620, Star-light, Song, From the Depths, Nautilus, In Mid-Ocean*), op. 55 (1898); *Fireside Tales* (*An Old Love Story, Of Br'er Rabbit, From a German Forest, of Salamanders, A Haunted House, By Smouldering Embers*), op. 61 (1902); *New England Idyls*, 10 pieces (*An Old Garden, Midsummer, Midwinter, With Sweet Lavender, In Deep Woods, Indian Idyl, To an Old White Pine, From Puritan Days, From a Log Cabin, The Joy of Autumn*), op. 62 (1902); 6 Little Pieces on Sketches by J.S. Bach (1890); Technical Exercises, 2 Books (1893, 1895).

VOCAL: CHORAL: 2 choruses for Men's Voices, op. 3: *Love and Time* and *The Rose and the Gardener* (1897); *The Witch* for Men's Chorus, op. 5 (1898); *War Song* for Men's Chorus, op. 6 (1898); 3 songs for Men's Chorus, op. 27 (1887); 2 songs for Men's Chorus, op. 41 (1890); *2 Northern Songs* for Mixed Voices, op. 43 (1891); 3 choruses for Men's Voices, op. 52 (1897); *2 Songs from the 13th Century* for Men's Chorus (1897); 2 choruses for Men's Voices, op. 53 (1898); 2 choruses for Men's Voices, op. 54 (1898); *College Songs* for Men's Voices (1901); *Summer Wind* for Women's Chorus (1902). **VOICE AND PIANO:** *2 Old Songs*, op. 9 (1894); 3 songs, op. 11 (1883); 2 songs, op. 12 (1883); *From an Old Garden* (6 songs), op. 26 (1887); 3 songs, op. 33 (1888; rev. 1894); 2 songs, op. 34 (1888); *6 Love Songs*, op. 40 (1890); 8 songs, op. 47 (1893); 4 songs, op. 56 (1898); 3 songs, op. 58 (1899); 3 songs, op. 60 (1902).

BIBL.: L. Gilman, *E. M.: A Study* (N.Y., 1908; corrected reprint, N.Y., 1969); E. Page, *E. M.: His Works and Ideals* (N.Y., 1910); T. Currier, "M. as I Knew Him," *Musical Quarterly* (Jan. 1915); O. Sonneck, *Catalogue of First Editions of E. M.* (Washington, D.C., 1917); W. Humiston, *M.* (N.Y., 1921); J. Matthews, *Commemorative Tributes to M.* (N.Y., 1922); J. Porte, *A Great American Tone Poet: E. M.* (London, 1922); A. Brown, *The Boyhood of E. M.* (N.Y., 1924); J. Cooke, *E. M.: A Short Biography* (Philadelphia, 1928); R. Brown, "A Listener to the Winds, E. M.," in *Lonely Americans* (N.Y., 1929); M. MacDowell, "M.'s Peterborough idea," *Musical Quarterly* (Jan. 1932); idem, *Random Notes on E. M. and His Music* (Boston, 1950); I. Lowens, "E. M.," *Hi-Fi Stereo Review* (Nov. 1967); A. Schwab, "E. M.'s Birthdate: A Correction," *Musical Quarterly* (April 1975); C. Kefferstan, *The Piano Concertos of E. M.* (diss., Univ. of Cincinnati, 1984); D. Pesce, "New Light on the Programmatic Aesthetic of M.'s Symphonic Poems," *American Music* (Winter 1986); F. Brancaleone, "E. M. and Indian Motives," ibid. (Winter 1989).

Maceda, José, notable Filipino ethnomusicologist, composer, and pianist; b. Manila, Jan. 31, 1917. He studied piano with Cortot at the École Normale de Musique in Paris (1937–41) and with Schmitz in San Francisco (1946–49). He pursued an active career as a pianist, principally in his homeland, until 1957. His interest in musicology and ethnomusicology prompted him to pursue his training at Queen's College of the City Univ. of N.Y., Columbia Univ., the Univ. of Chicago, Indiana Univ., and the Univ. of California at Los Angeles (Ph.D., 1963). From 1952 to 1990 he taught at the Univ. of the Philippines College of Music, where he oversaw the enhancement of the Univ.'s Ethnomusicology Archives. His field research took him throughout his native country as well as Southeast Asia, Brazil, and Africa. In addition to his articles in reference books and journals, he publ. *A Manual of Field Music Research with Special Reference to Southeast Asia* (Quezon City, 1981) and *Gongs and Bamboo: A Panorama of Philippine Music Instruments* (Quezon City, 1995). In his compositions, Maceda has pursued an adventuresome course in an attempt to break free of European traditionalism. He has utilized native instruments in repetitive sounds distributed in space (*Pagsamba* and *Ugnayan*); as rhythm, color, and pitch in their simplest forms (*Udlot-Udlot*); and as indefinite and definite pitch levels (*Siasid* and *Srata*), with the participation of several if not hundreds of people. In his recent works, groupings of orchestral instruments according to number and pitch categories operate within the boundaries of equal temperament, which neutralizes the effect of colors and unifies into one consonance the pitches of the whole orch.

WORKS: *Ugma-Ugma* for Native Instruments and Chorus (1963); *Agungan* for Families of Gongs (1965); *Kubing* for Bamboo Instruments and Men's Voices (1966); *Pagsamba*, ritual music for 116 Instrumentalists, 100 Mixed Voices, 25 Men's Voices, and Circular Auditorium (1968); *Cassettes 100* for 100 Cassette-recorder Players (1971); *Ugnayan*, music for 20 Radio Stations (1974); *Udlot-Udlot*, ritual music for Hundreds of Performers of Mixed Instruments and Voices in the Open Air (1975); *Ading* for 100 Instrumentalists, 100 Voices, and the Public (1978); *Aroding* for 40 Mouth Harps, 7 Men's Voices, and 3 Tiny Flutes (1983); *Siasid* for Percussion, 10 Blown Bamboo Tubes, and 5 Violins (1983); *Suling-Suling* for 10 Flutes, 10 Bamboo Percussion, and 10 Flat Gongs (1985); *Strata* for 10 Buzzers, 10 Pairs of Sticks, 5 Tam-tams, 5 Flutes, 5 Cellos, and 5 Guitars (1988); *Dissemination* for Orch. (1990); *Distemperament* for Orch. (1992); *Music* for 5 Pianos (1993).

Mácha, Otmar, Czech composer; b. Ostrava, Oct. 2, 1922. He studied with Hradil (1941–42); then at the Prague Cons. (1943–45), where he subsequently attended Řídký's master class (1945–48). He was active with the Czech Radio (1945–62); then devoted himself to composing; was awarded the State Prize in 1967 and was made a Merited Artist by the Czech government in 1982.

WORKS: DRAMATIC: *Polapená nevěra* (Entrapped Faithlessness), opera (1956–57; Prague, Nov. 21, 1958); *Jezero Ukereve* (Lake Ukereve), opera (1960–63; Prague, May 27, 1966); *Růže pro Johanku (Panichyda za statečné)* (Rose for Jeanne [Homage to the Brave]), dramatic musical fantasy (1971–74); *Svatba na oko* (Feigned Wedding), comic opera (1974–77); *Kolébka pro hříšné panny* (Cradle for Sinful Maidens), musical comedy (1975–76); film scores. **ORCH.:** Sym. (1947–48); *Slovak Rhapsody* (1951); *Symphonic Intermezzo* (1958); *Noc a naděje* (Night and Hope), symphonic poem (1959); *Variace na téma a smrt Jana Rychlíka* (Variations on a Theme by Jan Rychlík; 1964; Prague, March 15, 1966); *Variants*, short studies (1968); 2 sinfoniettas (1970–71; 1978–80); Double Concerto for Violin, Piano, and Orch. (1976). **CHAMBER:** 3 string quartets (1943; 1981–82; 1990); 2 violin sonatas (1948, 1987); Cello Sonata (1949); Bassoon Sonata (1963); *Saxophone Cries* for Saxophone and Piano (1963–68); *Adagio* for Bass Clarinet and Piano (1969); *Variations* for Flute and Piano (1977); *Preludium, Aria, and Toccata* for Accordion (1978); *Elegy* for Violin and Piano (1982); *Sinfonietta da Camera* for Chamber Group (1993); organ music; piano pieces. **VOCAL:** *Odkaz J.A. Komenského* (J.A. Comenius's Legacy), oratorio (1952–55); *4 Monologues* for Soprano, Baritone, and Orch. (1965–66); *Janinka zpívá* (Janinka Sings), suite for Soprano and Orch. (1969); *Small Triptych*, 3 songs for Soprano, Flute, and Tam-tam (1971); *Oči a ruce* (Eyes and Hands), dramatic song for Mezzo-soprano, Clarinet, Viola, and Piano (1975); Concerto grosso for Vocal Soloists and Orch. (1980); choruses; songs.

Machabey, Armand, French musicologist; b. Pont-de-Roide, Doubs, May 7, 1886; d. Paris, Aug. 31, 1966. He studied with d'Indy and Pirro; received his doctorat ès lettres from the Univ. of Paris in 1928 with the diss. *Essai sur les formules usuelles de la musique occidentale (des origines à la fin du XVe siècle)*; publ. in a rev. ed., Paris, 1955, as *Genèse de la tonalité musicale classique*. He was subsequently active as a music historian and essayist; also was one of the eds. of *Larousse de la musique* (Paris, 1957).

WRITINGS (all publ. in Paris unless otherwise given): *Sommaire de la méthode en musicologie* (1930); *Le théâtre musical en France* (1933); *Précis-manuel d'histoire de la musique* (1942; 2nd ed., 1947); *La musique des Hittites* (Liège, 1945); *La Vie et l'oeuvre d'Anton Bruckner* (1945); *Maurice Ravel* (1947); *Traité de la critique musicale* (1947); *Le "bel canto"* (1948); *Portraits de trente compositeurs français* (1950); *Gerolamo Frescobaldi Ferrarensis (1583–1643)* (1952); *La Musique et la médecine* (1952); *La Notation musicale* (1952; 3rd ed., rev., 1971 by M. Huglo); *Guillaume de Machaut: La Vie et l'oeuvre musicale* (1955); *Le cantillation manichéene: Notation hypothétique, métrique, analogies* (1956); *Notations musicales non modales des XIIe et XIIIe siècle* (1957; 3rd ed., Aug., 1959); *Problèmes de notation musicale* (1958); *Mélanges musicologiques d'Aristoxène à Hucbald* (1960); *La Musicologie* (1962; 2nd ed., 1969); *Embryologie de la musique occidentale* (1963); *La Musique de danse* (1966).

Machavariani, Alexei (Davidovich), Russian composer; b. Gory, Sept. 23, 1913. He studied at the Tbilisi Cons., graduating in 1936; then was on its faculty as a teacher of theory (1940–63) and as a prof. of composition (from 1963). He was made a People's Artist of the U.S.S.R. in 1958. His music is profoundly infused with Caucasian melorhythms.

WORKS: DRAMATIC: OPERAS: *Deda da shvili* (Mother and Son; 1944; Tbilisi, May 1, 1945); *Hamlet* (1964). **BALLETS:** *Otello* (1957); *Knight in a Tiger's Skin* (1965). **ORCH.:** 3 symphonic poems: *Mumly Muhasa* (1939), *Satchidao* (1940), and *On the Death of a Hero* (1948); Piano Concerto (1944); 2 syms. (1947, 1973); *The People's Choice*, overture (1950); Violin Concerto (1949). **VOCAL:** *For Peace, for Fatherland*, cantata (1951); *The Day of My Fatherland*, oratorio (1954); many songs.

Mâche, François-Bernard, remarkable French composer, musicologist, and philologist; b. Clermont-Ferrand, April 4, 1935. Following training in piano and harmony (with Emile Passani) at the Clermont-Ferrand Cons., he went to Paris and studied at the Ecole Normale Supérieure (diploma in Greek archaeology, 1957; agrégation in classical literature, 1958) and at the Cons. (composition with Messiaen, 1958–60); he later was awarded his Docteur d'Etat ès Lettres et Sciences Humaines by the Sorbonne for his diss. *L'idée de modèle en musique aujourd'hui* (1980). In 1968 he was made prof. of classical literature at the Lycée Louis-le-Grand in Paris. He became prof. of musicology at the Univ. of Strasbourg in 1983. In addition to many articles and reviews in the periodical literature, he publ. *Musique, mythe, nature ou les dauphins d'Arion* (1983; 2nd. ed., Aug., 1991). In 1977 he received the Prix Italia, in 1984 he was awarded the Prix Chartier de l'Académie des Beaux-Arts, and in 1988 he won the Grand Prix National de la Musique. In 1985 he was made an Officier and in 1990 a Commandeur des Arts et Lettres. While Mâche has been notably influenced as a composer by his study of philology, in particular structural linguistics, he finds the basis of his sound world in nature. His imaginative manipulation of that sound world embraces such procedures as imitation and transliteration.

WORKS: ORCH.: *La Peau du silence I* (1962; Tokyo, Oct. 24, 1986), *II* (1966; Warsaw, Sept. 29, 1968), and *III* (1970; Strasbourg, Jan. 12, 1971); *Synergies* (Paris, March 18, 1963); *Le Son d'une voix* for Chamber Orch. (Warsaw, Sept. 23, 1964); *Rituel d'oubli* for Chamber Orch. and Tape (1968; Strasbourg, June 11, 1970); *Répliques* (Royan, April 3, 1969); *Rambaramb* for Orch. and Tape (1972; Radio-France, Paris, May 8, 1973); *Le Jonc à 3 glumes* (Seillans, July 8, 1974); *Andromède* for Orch. and 2 Choruses (1979; Radio-France, Paris, June 4, 1980); *L'estuaire du temps* (Strasbourg, Sept. 17, 1993); *Planh* for Strings (Warsaw, Sept. 21, 1994). **CHAMBER:** Duo for Violin and Piano (1956); *Canzone I* for 5 Instruments (1957), *II* for 5 Instruments (1963); *III* for 7 Instruments (1967), and *V* for 4 Instruments and Theater Set (1969); *Sporanges* for Harpsichord and Violin (1965); *Kemit* for Darboukka or Zarb (1970); *Korwar* for Modern Harpsichord and Tape (Bourges, June 30, 1972); *Temes Nevinbür* for 2 Pianos, 2 Percussion, and Tape (Royan, April 16, 1973); *Naluan* for 8 Instruments and Tape (Sudwestfunk, Baden-Baden, Feb. 28, 1974); *Maraé* for 6 Amplified Percussion and Tape (1974; Le Roche-Courbon, March 25, 1975); *Solstice* for Modern Harpsichord and Organ or Tape (La Roche-Courbon, March 28, 1975); *Kassandra* for 14 Instruments and Tape (Paris, Oct. 16, 1977); *Octuor* for 8 Instruments (Paris, June 6, 1977); *Aera* for 6 Percussionists (1978; Paris, March 30, 1979); *Amorgos* for 12 Instruments and Tape (Metz, Nov. 16, 1979); *Sopiana* for Flute, Piano, and Tape ad libitum (Pecs, Hungary, July 12, 1980); *Anaphores* for Modern Harpsichord and Percussionist (1981; Radio-France, Paris, March 1, 1982); *Phénix* for Percussionist (Beijing, Sept. 28, 1982); *Aulodie* for Oboe or Soprano Saxophone or Piccolo Clarinet and Tape (Amsterdam, June 25, 1983); *Iter memor* for Cello and Échantillonneur (Radio-France, Paris, Nov. 12, 1985); *Heol an Ankou* for Organ and 3 Trombones (Rennes, Nov. 28, 1985); *Uncas* for 9 Instruments, Voice-tracker, Sequencer, and Tape (Paris, June 9, 1986); *Éridan* for 2 Violins, Viola, and Cello (1986; Radio-France, Paris, Jan. 17, 1987); *Aliunde* for Clarinet or Contrabass Clarinet, Soprano, Percussion, and Échantillonneur (London, July 4, 1988); *Tempora* for 3 Claviers Échantillonneurs and Sequencer (1988; Paris, Feb. 27, 1989); *Figures* for Bass Clarinet and Vibraphone (1989); *Guntur Madu* for Harpsichord (1990); *Khnoum* for Échantillonneur and 5 Percussion (Strasbourg, Sept. 28, 1990); *Athanor* for 10 Instruments (1991; Brussels, March 9, 1992); *Hiérogamie* for Piccolo Flute and Percussion (1993); *Moires* for Quartet and Tape (Radio-France, Paris, Dec. 2, 1994). **KEYBOARD: PIANO:** *Areg* for Piano, 4-hands (1977); *Nocturne* for Piano and Tape (1981); *Autonomie* for Piano, 4-hands (1981; also for other instruments); *Styx* for 2 Pianos, 8-hands (1984); *Léthé* for 2 Pianos, 8-hands (1985); *Mesarthim* for 2 Pianos (1987). **ORGAN:** *Guntur Sari* (1990). **VOCAL:** *Safous Mêlé* for Alto Solo, 4 Sopranos, 4 Altos, and 9 Instruments (1959; Paris, Oct. 5, 1963); *Nuit blanche* for Reciter and Tape (Warsaw, Sept. 18, 1966); *Canzone IV* for 2 Sopranos, Alto, Tenor, and Bass (1968); *Danaé* for 3 Sopranos, 3 Altos, 3 Tenors, 3 Basses, and Percussion (Persepolis, Sept. 3, 1970); *Rituel pour les Mangeurs d'Ombre* for 3 Sopranos, 3 Altos, 3 Tenors, 3 Basses, and Percussion (Bordeaux, May 16, 1979); *Temboctou* for 2 Sopranos, 2 Mezzo-sopranos, 3 Baritones, Tenor, Bass, 8 Instruments, Tape, and Electronics (Colmar, June 16, 1982); *Trois Chants Sacrés*: No. 1, *Muwatalli* for Mezzo-soprano or Baritone and Percussion (1984), No. 2, *Rasna* for Voice (1982), and No. 3, *Maponos* for Voice and Drum (1990); *Cassiopée* for Chorus and 2 Percussionists (1988; Radio-France, Paris, March 20, 1989); *Kengir*, 5 pieces for Mezzo-soprano and Clavier Échantillonneur (1991). **OTHER:** *Da capo* for Organ, 2 Percussion, 3 Medieval Reed Players, 10 Comedians, Sound Environment, and Tape (Avignon, July 15, 1976); many tape pieces.

BIBL.: B. Thomas, *Nature et musique dans l'oeuvre de F.-B. M.* (diss., Univ. of Paris, 1986); special issue of *Cahiers du C.I.R.E.M.*, 22–23 (Rouen, 1992); O. Emery and L. Dixsaut, "F.-B. M.," *Bulletin de la Société des amis de l'Ecole Normale Supérieure* (March 1994).

Machl, Tadeusz, Polish composer, organist, and teacher; b. Lwów, Oct. 22, 1922. After training in piano from Kasparek and in theory from Lachowska, Freiheiter, and Sołtys, he studied at the Kraków State College of Music (1949–52) with Malawski (composition) and Rutkowski (organ). He made tours as an organist in Poland and abroad, and also taught at the Kraków State College of Music, where he was chairman of the composition dept. (1966–72).

WORKS: DRAMATIC: Theater and film scores. **ORCH.:** *3 miniatury symfoniczne* (1946); 5 syms. (1947, 1948, 1949, 1954, 1963); 7 organ concertos (1950, 1952, 1953, 1959, 1969, 1978, 1983); *Lyrical Suite* (1956); Violin Concerto (1961); Harpsichord Concerto (1962); Piano Concerto (1965); Harp Concerto (1967); Double Concerto for Piano, Harpsichord, and Orch. (1967); Horn Concerto (1970); Triple Concerto for 2 Pianos, Organ, and Orch. (1971); *Jubilee Overture* (1971); *Symphonic Scherzo* (1986). **CHAMBER:** 4 string quartets (1952, 1957, 1962, 1972); *Haerbarium*, septet for Organ, English Horn, Horn, Bassoon, Cello, Harp, and Percussion (1980). **ORGAN:** *3 Studies* (1950); *2 Pieces* (1964); *Pièce en cinq mouvements* (1964); *Mini-Suite* (1967); *10 Pieces* (1970); *Triptych* (1972); Sonata for 3 Organs (1973); *Landscapes*, cycle of preludes and fugues (1976, et seq.); *Grand Fantasia* (1979); *Rupicaprae*, 9 studies for Double Organ (1981); *15 Rosary Poems* (1982); *Disonatio* (1989); *Poem* (1992). **VOCAL:** Concerto for Soprano and Orch. (1958); *Icarus's Flight*, cantata for Soprano, Reciter, Organ, and Orch. (1968); *The Blue Cross* for Soprano, 2 Reciters, Organ, Chorus, Orch. and Tape (1974).

Machlis, Joseph, Latvian-born American writer on music and pedagogue; b. Riga, Aug. 11, 1906. He was taken to the U.S. as an infant. He studied at the College of the City Univ. of N.Y. (B.A., 1927), and at the Inst. of Musical Art (teacher's diploma, 1927); also took an M.A. in English literature from Columbia Univ. (1938). He was on the music faculty of Queens College of the City Univ. of N.Y. (1938–74); then on the graduate faculty at the Juilliard School (from 1976). He made English trs. of a number of opera librettos; publ. several well-written texts: the immensely popular *The Enjoyment of Music* (N.Y., 1955; 7th ed., rev., 1995); *Introduction to Contemporary Music* (N.Y., 1961; 2nd ed., 1979); *American Composers of Our Time* (N.Y., 1963); *Getting to Know Music* (N.Y., 1966). He also publ. 5 novels.

Machover, Tod, American cellist, conductor, and composer; b. N.Y., Nov. 24, 1953. He studied composition at the Univ. of Calif. at Santa Cruz (1971–73), Columbia Univ. (1973–74), and the Juilliard School in N.Y. (B.M., 1975; M.M., 1977); among his mentors were Dallapiccola (1973), Sessions (1973–75), and Carter (1975–78); also studied computer music at the Mass. Inst. of Technology and at Stanford Univ. He was 1st cellist in the orch. of the National Opera of Canada in Toronto (1975–76), guest composer (1978–79) and director of musical research (1980–85) at IRCAM in Paris, and a teacher at the Mass. Inst. of Technology (from 1985), where he also was director of its Experimental Media Facility (from 1986). He ed. the books *Le Compositeur et l'Ordinateur* (Paris, 1981) and *Musical Thought at IRCAM* (London, 1984), and was the author of *Quoi, Quand, Comment? La Recherche Musicale* (Paris, 1985; Eng. tr., 1988, as *The Concept of Musical Research*) and *Microcomputers and Music* (N.Y., 1988). Among his honors were the Koussevitzky Prize (1984) and the Friedheim Award (1987).

WORKS: OPERA: *Valis* (Paris, Dec. 2, 1987). **ORCH.:** Concerto for Amplified Guitar and Orch. (1978); *Nature's Breath* for Chamber Orch. (1984–85); *Desires* (1985–89); *Forever and Ever,* concerto for Hyperviolin and Chamber Orch. (St. Paul, Minn., Sept. 24, 1993). **CHAMBER:** *Fresh Spring* for Baritone and 10 Instruments (1977); *Ye Gentle Birds* for Soprano, Mezzo-soprano, and 6 Instruments (1977); *Yoku Mireba* for Flute, Cello, and Piano (1977); *With Dadaji in Paradise* for Cello (1978; rev. 1983); *Light* for 15 Instruments (1979); *Winter Variations* for 9 Instruments (1981); String Quartet No. 1 (1981); *Hidden Sparks* for Violin (1984). **ELECTRONIC:** *Déplacements* for Guitar and Computer Electronics (1979); *Soft Morning, City!* for Soprano, Double Bass, and Tape (1980); *Fusione Fugace* for Live Computer Electronics (1981); *Electric Études* for Cello and Computer Electronics (1983); *Spectres parisiens* for Flute, Horn, Cello, Synthesizer, 18 Instruments, and Computer (1984); *Flora* for Computer Tape (1989); *Bug-Mudra* for 2 Guitars, Percussion, Conductor with Gesture-tracking "Dataglove," and Live Computer (1989–90); *Epithalamion* for Vocal Soloists, 25 Players, and Live and Recorded Computer Electronics (1990); *Begin Again Again . . . ,* concerto for Cello and Computer Electronics (Lenox, Mass., Aug., 15, 1991).

Maciejewski, Roman, Polish-American pianist, organist, choral conductor, and composer; b. Berlin (of Polish parents), Feb. 28, 1910. His mother taught him to play piano at an early age; he then took lessons with Goldenweiser at the Berlin Cons. (1916–19) and with Zeleski at the Poznań Cons. (diploma, 1922); also studied composition with Wiechowicz in Poznań and with Sikorski at the Warsaw Cons. He went to Paris in 1934, and studied with Boulanger; then lived in Sweden (1939–51). In 1952 he emigrated to the U.S., settling in Redondo Beach, California, as a church organist and director of the Roman Choir. He excelled in writing lush, resonant, protracted choruses in self-confident tonal harmonies.

WORKS: ORCH.: *Allegro concertante* for Piano and Orch. (1944; Göteborg, Jan. 11, 1945). **CHAMBER:** Brass Quartet (1937); String Quartet (1938); Violin Sonata (1940); String Trio (1948); *Nocturne* for Flute, Celesta, and Guitar (1951); *Variations* for Wind Quintet (1971). **PIANO:** 2 sonatas (1926, 1932); *25 Mazurkas* (1928–38); *Bajka* (Fairy Tale), children's ballet for 2 Pianos (1931); Concerto for 2 Solo Pianos (1935). **VOCAL:** *Song of Bilitis* for Soprano and Orch. (1932); *Requiem* for Soloists, Chorus, and Orch. (1944–60; Warsaw, Sept. 1960); masses; songs.

Mackerras, Sir (Alan) Charles (MacLaurin), eminent American-born Australian conductor; b. Schenectady, N.Y. (of Australian parents), Nov. 17, 1925. He was taken to Sydney, Australia, as an infant; studied oboe, piano, and composition at the New South Wales State Conservatorium of Music; then was principal oboist in the Sydney Sym. Orch. (1943–46). He subsequently went to London, where he joined the orch. at Sadler's Wells and studied conducting with Michael Mudie; he won a British Council Scholarship in 1947, which enabled him to study conducting with Václav Talich at the Prague Academy of Music. Returning to London in 1948, he was an assistant conductor at Sadler's Wells until 1953; then was engaged as principal conductor of the BBC Concert Orch. (1954–56); subsequently appeared as a guest conductor with British orchs.; also had engagements on the Continent. In 1963 he made his debut at London's Covent Garden conducting Shostakovich's *Katerina Izmailova.* From 1966 to 1970 he held the post of 1st conductor at the Hamburg State Opera. In 1970 he became music director at the Sadler's Wells Opera (renamed the English National Opera in 1974), a position he held until 1978. On Oct. 31, 1972, he made his Metropolitan Opera debut in N.Y. conducting Gluck's *Orfeo et Euridice.* From 1976 to 1979 he was chief guest conductor of the BBC Sym. Orch. in London. After serving as chief conductor of the Sydney (Australia) Sym. Orch. (1982–85), he was artistic director of the Welsh National Opera in Cardiff (1987–92). He was principal guest conductor of the Scottish Chamber Orch. in Glasgow (from 1992), of the Royal Phil. in London (from 1993), and of the San Francisco Opera (from 1993). He was made a Commander of the Order of the British Empire in 1974, and was knighted in 1979. Mackerras has distinguished himself as an opera conductor by championing the works of Janáček. He has also conducted operas by Handel, Gluck, and J.C. Bach. He likewise is a discriminating interpreter of the orch. repertoire.

BIBL.: N. Phelan, *C. M.: A Musicians' Musician* (London, 1987).

Maclean, Alick (actually, **Alexander Morvaren**), English composer and conductor; b. Eton, near Windsor, July 20, 1872; d. London, May 18, 1936. His father was the English organist, editor, and composer Alick (Alexander Morvaren) Maclean (b. Cambridge, March 27, 1843; d. London, June 23, 1916). He studied with Joseph Barnby. In 1899 he became music director to Charles Wyndham and in 1911 to the Spa Co. in Scarborough. From 1915 to 1923 he also was a conductor at Chappell's and led the Ballard Concerts at the Queen's Hall in London.

WORKS: OPERAS: *Quentin Durward* (1892; Newcastle upon Tyne, Jan. 13, 1920); *Petruccio* (London, June 29, 1895); *The King's Price* (London, April 29, 1904); *Die Liebesgeige* (Mainz, April 15, 1906); *Maître Seiler* (London, Aug. 20, 1909); *Waldidyll* (Mainz, March 23, 1913). **OTHER:** *The Annunciation,* oratorio (London, 1909); *Rapsodie monégasque* for Orch. (1935); choral works.

Maclean, Quentin (Stuart Morvaren), English-Canadian organist, composer, and teacher; b. London, May 14, 1896; d. Toronto, July 9, 1962. He began his studies with Harold Osmund, F.G. Shuttleworth, and R.R. Terry (1904–07); after receiving training from H. Grädener in Vienna (1907–09), he completed his studies with Straube (organ) and Reger (composition) in Leipzig (1912–14). At the outbreak of World War I in 1914, he was interned as an enemy alien in the Ruhleben camp near Berlin until 1918. In 1919 he became assistant organist under Terry at Westminster Cathedral in London. He played in various British film theaters (from 1921) and on the BBC (from 1925). In 1939 he emigrated to Canada and played in Toronto film theaters until 1949. He also was organist-choirmaster at Holy Rosary Church in Toronto (1940–62), and was a teacher at the Toronto Cons. of Music and at St. Michael's College, Univ. of Toronto. He frequently appeared on the CBC. As a composer, he followed traditional paths.

WORKS: ORCH.: *Concert Piece* for Organ and Orch. (1932); *Rhapsody on 2 English Folk Tunes* for Harp and Small Orch. (1938); *Algonquin Legend* (1942); *Concerto Grosso in Popular Style* for Solovox, Electric Organ, Electric Guitar, Theremin, and Small Orch. (1942); Concerto for Electric Organ and Dance Orch. (1945); *The Well-tempered Orchestra* (1950); *Concerto Romantico* for Piano and Orch. (1953); *Rustic Rhapsody* (1954);

Theme and Variations for Harpsichord and Orch. (1954); *Concerto Rococo* for Violin and Orch. (1957). **CHAMBER:** String Quartet (1937); Piano Trio (1937); Trio for Flute, Viola, and Guitar (1937); piano pieces; organ music. **VOCAL:** *Stabat Mater* for Tenor, Chorus, Organ, and Strings (1941); 10 masses; cantata; many choruses; songs.

Mac Low, Jackson, American poet, composer, painter, and multimedia performance artist; b. Chicago, Sept. 12, 1922. He studied piano, violin, and harmony at Chicago Musical College (1927–32) and Northwestern Univ. School of Music (1932–36); then took courses in philosophy, poetics, and English at the Univ. of Chicago (A.A., 1941); then studied classical languages at Brooklyn College of the City Univ. of N.Y. (B.A., 1958). He also studied piano with Shirley Rhodes Perle (1943–44), Grete Sultan (1953–55), and Franz Kamin (1976–79), composition with Erich Katz (1948–49), recorder with Tui St. George Tucker (1948–53), experimental music with John Cage at the New School for Social Research in N.Y. (1957–60), Moog synthesizer with Rhys Chatham (1973), and voice with Pandit Pran Nath (1975–76). He taught at N.Y. Univ. (1966–73), the Mannes College of Music in N.Y. (1966), the State Univ. of N.Y. at Albany (1984), Binghamton (1989), and Buffalo (1990), and Temple Univ. (1989); also held guest lectureships at various institutions and in 1990 was Regents Lecturer at the Univ. of Calif. at San Diego. Among his 26 books, many—e.g., *Stanzas for Iris Lezak* (1972), *21 Matched Asymmetries* (1978), *Asymmetries 1–260* (1980), *"Is That Wool Hat My Hat?"* (1982), *Bloomsday* (1984), *Representative Works: 1938–1985* (1986), *Words nd Ends from Ez* (1989), *Twenties: 100 Poems* (1991), *Pieces o' Six: Thirty-three Poems in Prose* (1992), *42 Merzgedichte in Memoriam Kurt Schwitters* (1994), and *Barnesbook* (1995)—comprise or include works realizable as musical-verbal performances. He wrote several quasi-musical plays, some with chance operations, including *The Marrying Maiden* (1958; unpubl.), *Verdurous Sanguinaria* (1961; publ. in anthologies, 1980, 1995), and *The Twin Plays: Port-au-Prince and Adams County Illinois* (1963, 1966). *The Pronouns* (1964, 1971, 1979) comprises works composed by a nonintentional method which are both poems and dance instructions, realized in the U.S., England, and Australia; he also wrote, directed, and performed in several verbal-musical Hörspiele for radio, 5 of which produced and broadcast by the Westdeutscher Rundfunk in Cologne. As both composer and writer, Mac Low adopted nonintentional procedures, including chance operations, indeterminacy, and related methods in 1954; but he has also written and composed extensively by intentional and quasi-intentional means. His many "simultaneities" include musical, verbal, and visual elements; these and other compositions are for live voices, instruments (usually variable), and/or tape multitracking; many are realized by instruction-guided performers' choices. He has performed extensively throughout North America, Europe, and New Zealand, often with his wife, the painter, composer, poet, and performance artist Anne Tardos. Others have performed his work in the U.S., England, Australia, Japan, and South America. A joint concert of his and James Tenney's works and a machine recording sounds as visual traces by Max Neuhaus was presented at N.Y.'s Town Hall in 1966. An 8-hour retrospective concert on the occasion of his 60th birthday was given at Washington Square Church in N.Y. (1982). His awards include fellowships from N.Y. State's Creative Artists Public Service Program (1973–74; 1976–77), the NEA (1979), the Guggenheim Memorial Foundation (1985), and the N.Y. Foundation for the Arts (1988); he also received a Fulbright grant for travel in New Zealand and a composer's grant from New Zealand's Queen Elizabeth II Art Council (both 1986).

WORKS: Overture to Paul Goodman's *Faustina* (1949); Overture, Songs, and Incidental Music for Paul Goodman's *Jonah* (1950); *Hear, O Israel!,* choral canon (1950); *5 biblical poems* (1954–55); Songs and Incidental Music for W.H. Auden's *The Age of Anxiety* (1955); *Rush Hour* (1955); *4 Pianissimo Pieces* (1955); *Peaks & Lamas* (1958–59); *Sade Suit* (1959); *Head-line Glass Material Buildings* (1959); *Stanzas for Iris Lezak* (1960); *A Piece for Sari Dienes* (1960); *Asymmetries 1–501* (1960–61); *Thanks, a simultaneity for people* (1960–61); *Nembutsu Gathas* (1961); *1st Aum Gatha* (1961); *Aum Field* (1961); *1st Mani Gatha* (1961); *An Asymmetry for La Monte Young* (1961); *A Piece for Recorder, Right Hand Moving* (1961); *F# for Simone Forti* (1961); *Pitches* (1961); *A Word Event for George Brecht* (1961); *"The text on the opposite page . . ."* (1961; various realizations, 1965–70); *Gate Gate Gathas* (1961–66); *Jesus Gathas* (1961–66); *Chamber Music for Barney Childs* (1963); *Jail Break* (1963–66); *Hare Krsna Gathas* (1967); *The 10 Bluebird Asymmetries* (1967); *The 6 Asymmetries for Dr. Howard Levy* (1967); *The 5 Young Turtle Asymmetries* (1967); *A Vocabulary for Carl Fernbach-Flarsheim* (1968); *LETT* (1969; quarter tone guitar realization, 1976); *Word Event(s) for Bici Forbes* (1971–72); *A Word Event for Bici Forbes on the Book Title "Lucy Church Amiably"* (1971); *A Word Event for Bici Forbes on the Word "Environmentally"* (1971); *The Black Tarantula Crossword Gathas* (1973; 8-voice multitrack tape realization, 1973); *Guru-Guru Gathas* (1973); *A Vocabulary for Michael Wiater* (1973); *A Vocabulary for Sharon Belle Mattlin* (1973); *The Tennyson Asymmetries* (1973); *Phoneme Dance for/from John Cage* (1974); *Govinda Gathas* (1974); *A Vocabulary for Vera Regina Lachmann* (1974); *A Vocabulary for Charlotte Moorman* (1974); *Counterpoint for Candy Cohen* (multitrack tapes, 1974, 1978); *A Vocabulary for Peter Innisfree Moore* (1974–75); *Heavens* (1974–75); *Mani-Mani Gatha* (1975); *Guru-Guru Gatha* (1975); *Tara Gathas* (1975); *Kaddish Gatha* (1975); *1st Sharon Belle Mattlin Vocabulary Crossword Gatha* (1976); *1st Milarepa Gatha* (1976, 1979); *A Word Event for Bici Forbes on the Word "Bicentennial"* (1976); *Homage to Leona Bleiweiss* (1976); *Stephanie Vevers Vocabulary Gatha* (1977); *Albuquerque Antiphonies* (1977); *Musicwords (for Phill Niblock)* (1977–78); *Free Gatha 1* (1978); *A Notated Vocabulary for Eve Rosenthal* (1978); *A Vocabulary Gatha for Pete Rose* (1978); *A Vocabulary for Custer LaRue* (1978–79); *A Vocabulary for Annie Brigitte Gilles Tardos* (1979; rev. 1980–82); *A Vocabulary Gatha for Anne Tardos* (1980); *"Is That Wool Hat My Hat?"* (1980); *Winds/Instruments* (1980–84); *Dream Meditation* (1980–82); *Words nd Ends from Ez* (text, 1981–83; used in radio work, 1981; arranged as multitrack tape, 1985; music, *"Ezra Pound" and Anagrams for Instrument[s],* 1989–90); *Dialog unter Dichten/Dialog Among Poets,* radio work (1981); *Canon for the Summer Solstice* (1981); *Free Gatha 2* (1981); *Transverse Flute Mime Piece* (1981); *2nd Aum Gatha* (1982); *Milarepa Quartet for 4 Like Instruments* (1982); *Thanks/Danke,* radio work (1983); *Heterophonies from "Hereford Bosons 1 and 2"* (1984); *Phonemicon from "Hereford Bosons 1"* (1984); *A Bean Phonemicon for Alison Knowles* (1984); *Reisen,* radio work (1984); *Locks,* radio work (1984); *Für Stimmen, etc.,* radio work (1985); *Definitive Revised Instructions for Performing Gathas* (1985); *Wörter nd Enden aus Goethe/Words and Ends from Goethe* (arranged as radio work, 1986); *Phoneme Dance for John Cage/Phonemtanz für John Cage,* radio work (1986; in collaboration with A. Tardos); *The Birds of New Zealand* for Multitrack Tape (1986); *Iran-Contra Hearings* (1987–90); *Westron Winde 2* (1987–88); *22nd Merzgedicht in Memoriam Kurt Schwitters* (1988); *Westron Winde 4* (1988–89); *36th–42nd Merzgedichte in Memoriam Kurt Schwitters* (1989; arranged as voice duos, 1989–93); *Definitive Revised Performance Instructions for each of the Vocabularies* (1989–90); *Low Order Travesties,* computer-mediated poems arranged as voice duos (1989–90); *Lucas 1–29* (1990–92); *Motet on a Saying of A.J. Muste* for Chorus (1991); *S.E.M.* for Instrumentalists (1992); *1st, 2nd, and 3rd Four-language Word Events in Memoriam John Cage,* collaborative paintings/scores for Voices (1992–93; in collaboration with A. Tardos); *Phoneme Dance in Memoriam John Cage* for Speaker-Vocalists (1993; in collaboration with A. Tardos); *Trope Market Phonemicons* for Voices and/or Instruments with Optional Tape (1993); *Phoneme Dance in Memoriam John Cage, Bob Watts, and George Maciunas* for Speaker-Vocalists (1994; in collaboration with A. Tardos); A Forties *Opera* for Speaker and Improvising Instrumentalist (1995; in collaboration with P. Oliveros).

BIBL.: J. Cage, "Music and Particularly Silence in the Work of J. M. L.," *Paper Air,* II/3 (1980); H. Smith, "Image, Text, and Performance: Inter-artistic Relationships in Contemporary Poetry," in D. Murray, ed., *Literary Theory and Poetry: Extending the Canon* (London, 1989).

MacMillan, Sir Ernest (Alexander Campbell), eminent Canadian conductor and composer; b. Mimico, Aug. 18, 1893; d. Toronto, May 6, 1973. He began organ studies with Arthur Blakeley in Toronto at age 8, making his public debut at 10; continued organ studies with A. Hollins in Edinburgh (1905–8), where he was also admitted to the classes of F. Niecks and W.B. Ross at the Univ. He was made an assoc. (1907) and a fellow (1911) of London's Royal College of Organists, and received the extramural B.Mus. degree from the Univ. of Oxford (1911). He studied modern history at the Univ. of Toronto (1911–14) before receiving piano instruction from Therese Chaigneau in Paris (1914). In 1914 he attended the Bayreuth Festival, only to be interned as an enemy alien at the outbreak of World War I; while being held at the Ruhleben camp near Berlin, he gained experience as a conductor; was awarded the B.A. degree in absentia by the Univ. of Toronto (1915); his ode, *England,* submitted through the Prisoners of War Education Committee to the Univ. of Oxford, won him his D.Mus. degree (1918). After his release, he returned to Toronto as organist and choirmaster of Timothy Eaton Memorial Church (1919–25). He joined the staff of the Canadian Academy of Music (1920) and remained with it when it became the Toronto Cons. of Music, serving as its principal (1926–42); was also dean of the music faculty at the Univ. of Toronto (1927–52). He was conductor of the Toronto Sym. Orch. (1931–56) and of the Mendelssohn Choir there (1942–57); also appeared as guest conductor in North and South America, Europe, and Australia. He served as president of the Canadian Music Council (1947–66) and of the Canadian Music Centre (1959–70). In 1935 he was the first Canadian musician to be knighted, an honor conferred upon him by King George V; also received honorary doctorates from Canadian and U.S. institutions. He conducted many works new to his homeland, both traditional and contemporary.

WORKS: DRAMATIC: *Snow White,* opera (1907); *Prince Charming,* ballad opera (1931). **ORCH.:** 4 overtures (*Cinderella,* 1915; *Don't Laugh,* 1915; 1924; *Scotch Broth,* 1933); *2 Sketches* for Strings (1927; also for String Quartet); *Fantasy on Scottish Melodies* (1946); *Fanfare for a Festival* for Brass and Percussion (1959); *Fanfare for a Centennial* for Brass and Percussion (1967). **CHAMBER:** String Quartet (1914; rev. 1921); *4 Fugues* for String Quartet (1917); piano pieces; organ music. **VOCAL:** *England,* ode for Soprano, Baritone, Chorus, and Orch., after Swinburne (1917–18; Sheffield, England, March 17, 1921); *2 Carols* for Soprano and String Trio (1927); *Te Deum laudamus* for Chorus and Orch. (1936); many choruses and songs; arrangements.

BIBL.: "Sir E. M., 1893–1973," *Canadian Composer,* 82 (1973); W. Smith, "Reassessing Sir. E. M.," ibid., 181 (1983); E. Schabas, *Sir E. M.: The Importance of Being Canadian* (Toronto, 1994).

MacMillan, James, Scottish composer and teacher; b. Kilwinning, July 16, 1959. He was a student of Rita McAllister at the Univ. of Edinburgh (1977–81) and then pursued postgraduate studies in composition with Casken at the Univ. of Durham (Ph.D., 1987). He was a lecturer in music at the Univ. of Manchester (1986–88). In 1989 he served as composer-in-residence of the St. Magnus Festival in Orkney. In 1990 he became affiliate composer of the Scottish Chamber Orch. in Glasgow and a teacher at the Royal Scottish Academy of Music and Drama there. In 1991 he was a visiting composer of the Philharmonia Orch. in London. He developed an accessible style of composition which found inspiration in his Roman Catholic faith and Scottish nationalism.

WORKS: DRAMATIC: *Búsqueda,* music theater (Edinburgh, Dec. 6, 1988); *Tourist Variations,* chamber opera (1991); *Inés de Castro,* opera (1992–93); *Visitatio Sepulchri,* music theater (1992–93; Glasgow, May 20, 1993). **ORCH.:** *The Keening* (1986); *Festival Fanfares* for Brass Band (Ayr, May 1986); *Into the Ferment* (Irvine, Dec. 19, 1988); *Tryst* (Kirkwall, Orkney, June 17, 1989); *The Exorcism of Rio Sumpul* for Chamber Orch. (1989; Glasgow, Jan. 28, 1990); *The Berserking,* piano concerto (Glasgow, Sept. 22, 1990); *The Confession of Isobel Gowdie* (London, Aug. 22, 1990); *Sowetan Spring* for Wind Band (Glasgow, Sept. 23, 1990); Sinfonietta (1991; London, May 14, 1992); *Veni, Veni, Emmanuel,* percussion concerto (London, Aug. 10, 1992); *Epiclesis,* trumpet concerto (Edinburgh, Aug. 28, 1993); *They saw the stone had been rolled away,* fanfare for Brass and Percussion (Edinburgh, Aug. 27, 1993). **CHAMBER:** *Study on 2 Planes* for Cello and Piano (1981; Edinburgh, March 4, 1984); *The Road to Ardtalla* for Sextet (1983; Manchester, Nov. 6, 1987); *3 Dawn Rituals* for Chamber Ensemble (1983; London, Nov. 2, 1985); *2 Visions of Hoy* for Oboe and Chamber Ensemble (Manchester, June 16, 1986); *Litanies of Iron and Stone* for Clarinet, Soprano Saxophone, Trombone, and Tape (Glasgow, Sept. 14, 1987); *Untold* for Wind Quintet (1987; Ayr, Sept. 13, 1988; rev. 1991); *After the Tryst* for Violin and Piano (1988; Glasgow, Sept. 19, 1990); *Visions of a November Spring* for String Quartet (1988; Glasgow, May 3, 1989; rev. 1991); *The Cumnock Orcadian* for Chamber Ensemble (Kirkwall, Orkney, June 16, 1989); *. . . as others see us . . .* for Chamber Ensemble (London, April 5, 1990); *Tuireadh* for Clarinet and String Quartet (Kirkwall, Orkney, June 25, 1991); *Intercession* for 3 Oboes (Huddersfield, Nov. 26, 1991). **PIANO:** Sonata (1985; Radio Scotland, Sept. 1987); *A Cecilian Variation for J.F.K.* (Washington, D.C., Nov. 22, 1991; 2nd movement of *Kennedy Variations,* in collaboration with G. Victory, W. Mathias, and M. Berkeley); *Barncleupédie* (1992; Edinburgh, Feb. 28, 1993); *Angel* (1993). **VOCAL:** *Beatus Vir* for Chorus and Organ (Norwich, July 2, 1983); *St. Anne's Mass* for Congregation and Organ or Piano (1985); *Variation on Johnny Faa'* for Soprano, Flute, Cello, and Harp (Edinburgh, Aug. 1988); *Cantos Sagrados* for Chorus and Organ (1989; Edinburgh, Feb. 10, 1990); *Catherine's Lullabies* for Chorus, Brass, and Percussion (1990; Glasgow, Feb. 10, 1991); *Scots Song* for Soprano and Chamber Quintet (Brighton, May 10, 1991); *Divo Aloysio Sacrum* for Chorus and Optional Organ (1991); *So Deep* for Chorus, Viola, and Cello (1992); *. . . here in hiding . . .* for 4 Men's Voices (Glasgow, Aug. 10, 1993); *7 Last Words from the Cross* for Chorus and Strings (BBC-TV, April 3, 1994).

MacNeil, Cornell, noted American baritone; b. Minneapolis, Sept. 24, 1922. While working as a machinist, he appeared on the radio as an actor and sang minor parts on Broadway. He then was a scholarship student of Friedrich Schorr at the Hartt College of Music in Hartford, Conn., and also studied with Virgilio Lazzari and Dick Marzollo in N.Y. and with Luigi Ricci in Rome. On March 1, 1950, he made his professional operatic debut as Sorel in the premiere of Menotti's *The Consul* in Philadelphia. On April 4, 1953, he made his N.Y. City Opera debut as Tonio, and subsequently appeared there regularly. He first sang opera in San Francisco as Escamillo in 1955 and in Chicago as Puccini's Lescaut in 1957. On March 5, 1959, he made his debut at Milan's La Scala as Don Carlo in *Ernani.* On March 21, 1959, he made his Metropolitan Opera debut in N.Y. as Rigoletto, and remained on its roster until 1987. He became particularly successful there in Verdi roles, excelling as Amonasro, Germont, Luna, Iago, and Nabucco. In 1964 he made his debut at London's Covent Garden as Macbeth. His other guest engagements took him to Vienna, Rome, Paris, Geneva, Florence, and other European operatic centers. In addition to his Verdi portrayals, he also had success as Barnaba in *La Gioconda,* the Dutchman in Wagner's opera, and as Scarpia. In the later years of his career, he became well known for his verismo roles.

Maconchy, Dame Elizabeth, significant English composer of Irish descent, mother of **Nicola LeFanu;** b. Broxbourne, Hertfordshire, March 19, 1907; d. Norwich, Nov. 11, 1994. She studied composition with Charles Wood and Vaughan Williams, and counterpoint with C.H. Kitson at the Royal College of Music in London (from 1923); she then pursued further training with Jirák in Prague (1929–30). Returning to England, she devoted herself to composition. She also served as chairman of the Composers Guild of Great Britain (1959–60) and as president of the Soc. for Promotion of New Music (from 1977). In 1977 she was made a Commander and in 1987 a Dame Commander of the Order of the British Empire. Maconchy developed a style peculiarly her own: tonally tense, contrapuntally dissonant, and coloristically sharp in instrumentation.

WORKS: DRAMATIC: *Great Agrippa*, ballet (1933); *The Little Red Shoes*, ballet (1935); *Puck Fair*, ballet (1940); *The Sofa*, opera (1956–57; London, Dec. 13, 1959); *The 3 Strangers*, opera (1958–67; Bishop's Stortford College, June 5, 1968); *The Departure*, opera (1960–61; London, Dec. 16, 1962); *Witnesses*, incidental music (1966); *The Birds*, opera (1967–68; Stortford College, June 5, 1968); *Johnny and the Mohawks*, children's opera (1969; London, March 1970); *The Jesse Tree*, church opera (1969–70; Dorchester Abbey, Oct. 7, 1970); *The King of the Golden River*, opera (Oxford, Oct. 29, 1975). **ORCH.:** Concerto for Piano and Chamber Orch. (1928); Concertino for Piano and Strings (1928); *The Land*, suite (1929); Suite for Chamber Orch. (1930); Viola Concerto (1937); *Dialogue* for Piano and Orch. (1940); *Theme and Variations* for Strings (1942); *Variations on a Well-Known Theme* (1942); Concertino for Clarinet and Strings (1945; Copenhagen, June 2, 1947); Sym. (1945–48); Double Concerto for Oboe, Bassoon, and Strings (1950); Concerto for Bassoon and Strings (1950); *Nocturne* (1951); Sym. for Double String Orch. (1952–53); *Proud Thames*, overture (1953); *Serenata concertante* for Violin and Orch. (1962); *Variazioni concertante* for Oboe, Clarinet, Bassoon, Horn, and Strings (1964–65); *An Essex Overture* (1966); *Music* for Winds and Brass (1966); *3 Cloudscapes* (1968); *Epyllion* for Cello and 14 Strings (1975); Sinfonietta (1975–76); *Romanza* for Viola and Chamber Orch. (1978; London, March 12, 1979); *Little Symphony* (1980; Norwich, July 28, 1981); *Music* for Strings (London, July 26, 1983). **CHAMBER:** Quintet for Oboe and String Quartet (1932); 14 string quartets (1933; 1936; 1938; 1943; 1948; 1950; 1955–56; 1966; 1968–69; 1971–72; 1976; 1979; 1983; 1984); Duo for 2 Violins (1934); *Prelude, Interlude, and Fugue* for 2 Violins (Prague, Sept. 4, 1935); 2 violin sonatas (1938, 1944); Sonata for Solo Viola (1938); *Serenade* for Cello and Piano (1944); *Divertimento* for Piano and Cello (1944); *Duo, Theme, and Variations* for Violin and Cello (1951); *3 Pieces* for 2 Clarinets (1956); *Trios* for Strings (1957); *Variations on a Theme from Vaughan Williams's Job* for Cello (1957); *Reflections* for Oboe, Clarinet, Viola, and Harp (1960); Quintet for Clarinet and Strings (1963); Sonatina for String Quartet (1963); *6 Pieces* for Violin (1966); *Conversations* for Clarinet and Viola (1967–68); *Music* for Double Bass and Piano (1970); *3 Bagatelles* for Oboe and Harpsichord or Piano (1972); Oboe Quartet (1972); *3 Preludes* for Violin and Piano (1972); *5 Sketches* for Viola (1972–73); *Morning, Noon, and Night* for Harp (1976); *Contemplation* for Cello and Piano (1978); *Colloquy* for Flute and Piano (1978–79); *Fantasia* for Clarinet and Piano (1979); Trio for Violin, Viola, and Cello (1980); *Trittico* for 2 Oboes, Bassoon, and Harpsichord (1981); *Piccola musica* for String Trio (Cheltenham, July 13, 1981); *Tribute* for Violin and 8 Winds (1983); *Narration* for Cello (1985); *Excursion* for Bassoon (1985). **KEYBOARD: PIANO:** *A Country Town* (1939); *Contrapuntal Pieces* (1941); *The Yaffle* (1962); *Mill Race* (1962); Sonatina (1965); *Preludio, Fugue, and Finale* for Piano, 4-hands (1967). **HARPSICHORD:** Sonatina (1965–66); *Notebook* (1965–66); *3 Pieces* (1977); Sonatina (1977). **VOCAL:** *The Voice of the City* for Women's Voices (1943); *Stalingrad* for Women's Chorus (1946); *Sonnet Sequence* for Soprano and String Orch. (1946); *A Winter's Tale* for Soprano and String Quartet (1949); *6 Yeats Settings* for Soprano, Women's Chorus, Clarinet, 2 Horns, and Harp (1951); *Christmas Morning* for Women's Voices and Piano or Small Ensemble (1962); *The Armado* for Chorus and Piano (1962); *Samson and the Gates of Gaza* for Chorus and Orch. (1963–64); *The Starlight Night* for High Voice and Orch. (1964); *Nocturnal* for Chorus (1965); *Propheta Mendax* for Boy's or Women's Chorus (1965); *I Sing of a Maiden* for Chorus (1966); *Peace* for High Voice and Orch. (1966); *And Death Shall Have No Dominion* for Chorus, 2 Horns, 3 Trumpets, and 3 Trombones (1968–69); *May Magnificat* for High Voice and Orch. (1970); *Ariadne* for Soprano and Orch. (1970); *Fly-by-Nights* for Treble Voices and Harp (1973); *Pied Beauty* for Chorus and Brass (1975); *Heavenhaven* for Chorus and Brass (1975); *The Leaden Echo and the Golden Echo* for Chorus, Alto Flute, Viola, and Harp (1978); *Heloise et Abelard*, cantata for Soprano, Tenor, Bass, Chorus, and Orch. (1978; Croydon, March 1979); *My Dark Heart* for Soprano and Instrumental Ensemble (1982); *L'Horloge* for Soprano, Clarinet, and Piano (1983); *Still Falls the Rain* for Double Chorus (1984); *Butterflies* for Voice and Harp (1986); other choral pieces, song cycles, and solo songs.

Maconie, Robin (John), New Zealand composer and writer on music; b. Auckland, Oct. 22, 1942. He studied at Victoria Univ., Wellington (B.A., 1962; M.A., 1963), and later with Messiaen at the Paris Cons. (1963–64) and with Zimmermann and Eimert at the Cologne Hochschule für Musik (1964–65); also attended Stockhausen's lectures at the Darmstadt summer courses. He returned to New Zealand as a composer for film and theater; also lectured at the Univ. of Auckland (1967–68). In 1969 he settled in England, where he engaged in music criticism and research in musical phenomenology. He publ. *The Works of Karlheinz Stockhausen* (London, 1975; 2nd ed., 1991) and ed. *Stockhausen on Music: Lectures and Interviews* (London, 1989).

WORKS: Clarinet Sonata (1961); *Music for a Masque* for String Orch. (1962); *Basia Memoranda*, song cycle for Low Voice and String Quartet (1962); *Canzona* for Chamber Orch. (1962); *A:B:A:* for Harp (1964); *Ex evangelio Sancti Marci* for Chorus (1964); *A:D:C:* for Piano (1965); Sonata for String Quartet (1964); *Māui*, television ballet for Speaker, Dancers, and Orch. (1967–72); String Quartet (1970); *Limina*, modified sound track (1975).

Macurdy, John, American bass; b. Detroit, March 18, 1929. He studied engineering at Wayne State Univ. in Detroit, and then voice with Avery Crew and Boris Goldovsky. In 1952 he made his operatic debut in New Orleans in *Samson et Dalila.* After singing in Santa Fe, Houston, and Baltimore, he became a member of the N.Y. City Opera in 1959. On Dec. 8, 1962, he made his Metropolitan Opera debut in N.Y. as Tom in *Un ballo in maschera*, and subsequently appeared there regularly. He also sang with other U.S. opera companies, including those of San Francisco and Chicago. In 1973 he appeared as Debussy's Arkel at the Paris Opéra, in 1974 as Beethoven's Pizzaro at Milan's La Scala, and in 1977 as Mozart's Commendatore at the Salzburg Festival. As a concert artist, he was engaged by many orchs. Among his other roles were Sarastro, Hagen, King Marke, Rocco, Pogner, Sparafucile, and Gounod's Méphistophélès.

Maddy, Joe (actually, **Joseph Edgar**), American music educator and conductor; b. Wellington, Kansas, Oct. 14, 1891; d. Traverse City, Mich., April 18, 1966. He received training in violin and clarinet in his youth, and then studied at Bethany College, Wichita College, and the Columbia School of Music in Chicago. He was a member of the Minneapolis Sym. Orch. (1909–14) and St. Paul Sym. Orch. (1914–18). Maddy was supervisor of instrumental music in the public schools of Rochester, N.Y. (1918–20), and Richmond, Ind. (1920–24), and instructor of public school methods at Earlham College (1922–24). In 1924 he was appointed to the faculty of the Univ. of Mich. as a prof. of music education; in 1926 he founded and conducted the National High School Orch., for which he established, with T.P. Giddings, the National Music Camp at Interlochen, Mich., in 1928. In 1962 it became a private high school as the Interlochen Arts Academy.

BIBL.: N. Browning, *J. M. of Interlochen* (Chicago, 1963).

Madeira, Francis, American conductor, pianist, and composer; b. Jenkintown, Pa., Feb. 21, 1917. He received training in piano and conducting at the Juilliard School of Music in N.Y. (1937–43). He was founder-conductor of the Rhode Island Phil. in Providence, R.I. (1945–80), and also appeared as a pianist in the U.S. and Europe. He composed several symphonic works. In 1957 he married **Jean** (née **Browning**) **Madeira.**

Madeira, Jean (née **Browning**), American mezzo-soprano; b. Centralia, Ill., Nov. 14, 1918; d. Providence, R.I., July 10, 1972. She studied piano with her mother; at the age of 12, she was piano soloist with the St. Louis Sym. Orch. She took vocal lessons in St. Louis, then studied both piano and voice at the Juilliard School of Music in N.Y. In 1943 she made her operatic debut as Nancy in *Martha* in Chautauqua, N.Y. In 1948 she joined the Metropolitan Opera in N.Y., where she sang minor roles. She went to Europe, where she first gained notice as Carmen in Vienna, Aix-en-Provence, and Munich in 1955; also sang Erda at her Covent Garden debut in London that same year. She then returned to the Metropolitan, where she appeared as Carmen on March 17, 1956; she remained on the Metropolitan's roster until 1971. Her European tours included appearances at the Vienna State Opera, the Bavarian State Opera in Munich, Milan's La Scala, the Paris Opéra, and Bayreuth. She married **Francis Madeira** in 1957.

Maderna, Bruno, outstanding Italian-born German conductor, composer, and teacher; b. Venice, April 21, 1920; d. Darmstadt, Nov. 13, 1973. He commenced musical studies at 4, and soon took violin lessons; began touring as a violinist and conductor when he was only 7, appearing under the name Brunetto in Italy and abroad. He studied at the Verdi Cons. in Milan, with Bustini at the Rome Cons. (diploma in composition, 1940), and with Malipiero at the Venice Cons.; also took a conducting course with Guarnieri at the Accademia Musicale Chigiana in Siena (1941). He then served in the Italian army during World War II, eventually joining the partisan forces against the Fascists. After the war, he studied conducting with Scherchen in Darmstadt. He taught composition at the Venice Cons. (1947–50); then made his formal conducting debut in Munich (1950). He subsequently became a great champion of the avant-garde; with Berio, he helped to form the Studio di Fonologia in Milan (1954); also with Berio, he was conductor of the RAI's Incontri Musicali (1956–60). He taught conducting and composition in various venues, including Darmstadt (from 1954), the Salzburg Mozarteum (1967–70), the Rotterdam Cons. (from 1967), and the Berkshire Music Center in Tanglewood (1971–72). He was chief conductor of the RAI in Milan from 1971. In 1963 he became a naturalized German citizen. Stricken with cancer, he continued to conduct concerts as long as it was physically possible. He was held in great esteem by composers of the international avant-garde, several of whom wrote special works for him.

WORKS: DRAMATIC: *Don Perlimplin*, radio opera, after García Lorca (1961; RAI, Aug. 12, 1962); *Hyperion*, "lirica in forma di spettacolo" (Venice, Sept. 6, 1964; a composite of *Dimensioni III, Aria de Hyperion*, and tape); *Von A bis Z*, opera (1969; Darmstadt, Feb. 22, 1970); *Oedipe-Roi*, electronic ballet (Monte Carlo, Dec. 31, 1970); *Satyrikon*, opera after Petronius (1972; Scheveningen, the Netherlands, March 16, 1973). **ORCH.:** *Introduzione e Passacaglia* (1947); Concerto for 2 Pianos, Percussion, and 2 Harps (Venice, Sept. 17, 1948); *Composizioni No. 1* (1949) and *No. 2* for Chamber Orch. (1950); *Improvvisazione I* and *II* (1951, 1952); *Composizioni in 3 tempi* (North German Radio, Hamburg, Dec. 8, 1954); Flute Concerto (1954); *Dark Rapture Crawl* (1957); Piano Concerto (Darmstadt, Sept. 2, 1959); 3 oboe concertos: No. 1 (1962; rev. 1965), No. 2 (West German Radio, Cologne, Nov. 10, 1967), and No. 3 (Amsterdam, July 6, 1973); *Dimensioni III* for Flute and Orch. (Paris Radio, Dec. 12, 1963); *Stele per Diotima* for Orch. (1965; West German Radio, Cologne, Jan. 19, 1966); *Dimensioni IV* (combination of *Dimensioni III* and *Stele per Diotima*); *Amanda* for Chamber Orch. (Naples, Nov. 22, 1966); *Quadrivium* for 4 Percussionists and 4 Orch. Groups (1969); Violin Concerto (Venice, Sept. 12, 1969); *Grande aulodia* for Flute, Oboe, and Orch. (1969; Rome, Feb. 7, 1970); *Juilliard Serenade (Free Time I)* for Chamber Orch. and Tape Sounds (1970; N.Y., Jan. 31, 1971); *Music of Gaiety* for Solo Violin, Oboe, and Chamber Orch., based on pieces in the "Fitzwilliam Virginal Book" (1970); *Aura* (1971; Chicago, March 23, 1972); *Biogramma* (1972); *Giardino religioso* for Chamber Ensemble (Tanglewood, Aug. 8, 1972). **CHAMBER:** *Serenata* for 11 Instruments (1946; rev. 1954); *Musica su 2 dimensioni* for Flute and Tape (1952; rev. 1958); String Quartet (1955); *Serenata No. 2* for 11 Instruments (1957) and *No. 4* for 20 Instruments and Tape (1961); *Honey reves* for Flute and Piano (1961); *Aulodia per Lothar* for Oboe d'Amore and Guitar ad libitum (1965); *Widmung* for Violin (1967); *Serenata per un satellite* for 7 Instruments (1969). **PIANO:** *B-A-C-H Variations* for 2 Pianos (1949). **VOCAL:** *3 Greek Lyrics* for Soprano, Chorus, and Instruments (1948); *Studi per "Il Processo" di Kafka* for Narrator, Soprano, and Small Orch. (1949); *4 Briefe* for Soprano, Bass, and Chamber Orch. (1953); *Aria da "Hyperion"* for Soprano, Flute, and Orch. (1964); *Hyperion II* (combination of *Dimensioni III, Cadenza* for Flute, and *Aria da "Hyperion"*); *Hyperion III* (combination of *Hyperion* and *Stele per Diotima*); *Ausstrahlung* for Soprano, Chorus, and Orch. (1971); *Boswell's Journal* for Tenor and Chamber Orch. (N.Y., March 12, 1972). **ELECTRONIC:** *Notturno* (1955); *Syntaxis* for 4 different but unspecified timbres produced electronically (1956); *Continuo* (1958); *Dimensioni II*, "invenzioni sue una voce" (1960); *Serenata No. 3* (1962); *Le Rire* (1964); *Ages* (1972; in collaboration with G. Pressburger).

BIBL.: M. Baroni and R. Dalmonte, eds., *B. M.: Documenti* (Milan, 1985); R. Fearn, *B. M.* (Chur and N.Y., 1990).

Madetoja, Leevi (Antti), outstanding Finnish composer; b. Oulu, Feb. 17, 1887; d. Helsinki, Oct. 6, 1947. He was educated at the Univ. of Helsinki (M.A., 1910) and studied composition with Sibelius at the Helsinki Music Inst. (diploma, 1910); then took courses with d'Indy in Paris (1910–11) and R. Fuchs in Vienna (1911–12) and in Berlin. After serving as deputy conductor of the Helsinki Phil. (1912–14) and as conductor of the Vyborg Music Soc. Orch. (1914–16), he taught at the Helsinki Music Inst. (1916–38); was also music critic of the *Helsingen Sanomat* (1916–32); became a lecturer in music at the Univ. of Helsinki (1928). In 1917 he founded the Finnish Musicians' Assn., with which he remained involved until his death. He was awarded a state composer's pension in 1919. He was one of Finland's leading composers; his music for the stage and his symphonic works are particularly notable.

WORKS (all 1st perf. in Helsinki): **DRAMATIC: OPERAS:** *Pohjalaisia* (The Bothnians; 1923; Oct. 25, 1924); *Juha* (1934; Feb. 17, 1935). **BALLET-PANTOMIME:** *Okon-Fuoko* (Feb. 12, 1930). **ORCH.:** *Symphonic Suite* (Sept. 26, 1910); *Concert Overture* (1911); *Tanssinäky* (Dance Vision; 1911–19); *Kullervo*, symphonic poem (Oct. 14, 1913); 3 syms.: No. 1 (Feb. 10, 1916), No. 2 (Dec. 17, 1918), and No. 3 (April 8, 1926); *Huvinäytelmäalkusoitto* (Comedy Overture; April 12, 1923). **CHAMBER:** Trio for Violin, Cello, and Piano (1910); Violin Sonatina (1913); *Lyric Suite* for Cello and Piano (1922); piano pieces, including the suite *Kuoleman puutarha* (Garden of Death; 1919). **VOCAL:** Much choral music; many songs.

BIBL.: K. Tuukkanen, *L. M.* (Helsinki, 1947); *L. M.: Teokset—Works* (1982); K. Karjalainen, *L. M. oopperat Pohjalaisia ja Juha: Teokset, tekstit ja kontekstit* (Helsinki, 1993).

Madge, Geoffrey Douglas, extraordinary Australian pianist; b. Adelaide, Oct. 3, 1941. He studied with Clemens Leski at the Elder Cons. of the Univ. of Adelaide (graduated, 1959), with Géza Anda in Switzerland (1964), and with Peter Solymos in Hungary (1967). He taught at the Royal Cons. of Music in The Hague from 1971. Madge's outstanding technical resources make him an ideal interpreter of the most formidable avant-garde scores. His repertoire ranges from Barraqué to Wyschnegradsky among the moderns; he performs standard works as well.

Maegaard, Jan (Carl Christian), Danish musicologist and composer; b. Copenhagen, April 14, 1926. He studied at the Royal Danish Cons. of Music in Copenhagen (teacher's diploma in theory and music history, 1953), at the Univ. of Copenhagen (M.A., 1957; Ph.D., 1972, with the diss. *Studien zur Entwicklung des dodekaphonen Satzes bei Arnold Schönberg*; publ. in Copenhagen, 1972), and at the Univ. of Calif. at Los Angeles (1958–59). After teaching at the Royal Danish Cons. of Music (1953–58), he joined the faculty of the Univ. of Copenhagen in 1959, where he was an assoc. prof. (1961–71) and prof. (from 1971). He also was a visiting prof. at the State Univ. of N.Y. at Stony Brook (1974) and prof. of music at the Univ. of Calif. at Los Angeles (1978–81). In 1986 he was made a member of the Royal Danish Academy of Sciences and Letters. As a composer, Maegaard has explored a wide range of styles, from tonal to serial.

WRITINGS: *Musikalsk Modernisme* (Copenhagen, 1964; 2nd. ed., 1971); *Praeludier til Musik af Schönberg* (Copenhagen, 1976); *Indføring i Romantisk Harmonik* (2 vols., Copenhagen, 1980, 1986; vol. I with T. Larsen); ed. *Musikalsk analyse efter Forte-metoden* (Copenhagen, 1988).

WORKS: DRAMATIC: *Don Quixote*, incidental music (1949); *Den hvide souper*, music for a radio play (1954); *Antigone*, incidental music (1966). **ORCH.:** 2 chamber concertos (1949; 1961–62); March for Strings (1956); *Due tempi* (1961); *Marineforeningens jubilaeumsmarch* for Military Orch. (1963); *Danmark trofast* (1971; also for Tenor and Piano); *De profundis* (1976; also for Men's Chorus and Piano); March for Military Orch. (1980); *Triptykon* for Violin and Strings (1984); *Sinfonietta* for Strings (1986); Cello Concerto (1994). **CHAMBER:** Suite for Violin and Piano (1949); Trio for Flute, Clarinet, and Bassoon (1950); Wind Quintet (1951); Suite for 2 Violins (1951); *Quasi una sonata* for Viola and Piano (1952); Bassoon Sonata (1952); *Variations impromptus* for Violin, Viola, Cello, and Piano (1953); *Fem praeludier* for Violin (1956); *O alter Duft aus Märchenzeit*, trio-serenade for Violin, Cello, and Piano (1960); *Octomeri* for Violin and Piano (1962); *ISCM Fanfare* for 4 Trombones (1964); *Movimento* for Clarinet, Horn, String Quartet, Percussion, and Hammond Organ (1967); *Musica riservata No. 1* for String Quartet (1970), *No. 2* for Oboe, Clarinet, Bassoon, and Saxophone (1976), and *No. 3* for Flute, Oboe, Cello, and Harpsichord (1982); *Pastorale* for 2 Clarinets (1976); Canon for 3 Flutes (1980); *Labirinto I* for Viola (1986) and *II* for Guitar (1987); Duo Phantasy for 2 Guitars (1988); *Double* for Cello (1988); *Pierrot in the Ball Room* for 2 Guitars (1988); *Kinderblicke* for Guitar (1989); *Preludio notturno d'estate e contrappunto fugato* for 2 Flutes, String Quartet, and Piano, 4-hands (1991); *Progressive variationer* for Violin and Cello (1993). **KEYBOARD: PIANO:** *Koncertetude/Passacaglia* (1949); Sonata (1955); *5 pezzi* (1959); *Danse til Marina* (1975). **ORGAN:** *Tre orgelkoraler* (1954); *Aus tiefer Not* (1956); *Tre orgelkoraler* (1969); *Passacaglia-fantasia-choral* (1981); *Fantasia: Indsigter—udsigter* (1983). **VOCAL:** *Pigens møde med Pan* for Soprano, Flute, Clarinet, and Piano (1947); *Legend* for Soprano, Violin, and Piano (1949); *Den gyldne harpe* for Mezzo-soprano, Oboe, Cello, and Piano (1952); *Gåudenom sletterne* for Chorus and String Orch. (1953); *Jaevndøgnselegi* (Elegy of Equinox) for Soprano, Cello, and Organ (1955); *Sic enim amavit*, motet for Chorus or Soprano, Trumpet, and Organ (1969); *Liebeslied* for Alto and 2 Guitars (1990); *Te Deum* for 2 Choruses, Children's Chorus, and Organ (1992); many other choral pieces and songs. **OTHER:** Cadenzas; orchestrations; arrangements.

Maes, Jef, Belgian composer; b. Antwerp, April 5, 1905. He studied with N. Distelmans (viola), L. Mortelmans (chamber music), and Karl Candael (harmony, counterpoint, and fugue) at Antwerp's Royal Flemish Cons. of Music. He was a violist in several orchs. in Antwerp; became a teacher of viola (1932) and director (1952) of the Boom Academy of Music; from 1942 to 1970 he was on the faculty of the Royal Flemish Cons. In his compositions, he continues the traditions of the Belgian national school.

WORKS: DRAMATIC: *Marise*, opera buffa (1946); *De antikwaar* (The Antique Dealer), television opera (1959; Antwerp TV, March 1963); *Tu auras nom . . . Tristan*, ballet (1960; Geneva, June 1963; orch. suite, 1963–64). **ORCH.:** *3 rythmen in dansvorm* (1931); *Légende* for Violin and Orch. (1933); Viola Concerto (1937); *Concertstück* (1938); *Ouvertura buffa* (1939); *Concertstück* for Trombone and Orch. (1944); Piano Concerto (1948); Violin Concerto (1951); 3 syms. (1953, 1965, 1975); Concerto for Harpsichord and Strings (1955); *Burlesque* for Bassoon and Orch. (1957); *Kempische Suite* for Orch. or Wind Orch. (1960); *Concertante ouverture* (1961); *Arabesque en scherzo* for Flute and Orch. (1963); *Praeludium, Pantomime, Scherzo*, suite (1966); *Partita* for Strings (1966); *Ouverture op een Belcanto Thema van Verdi* for Orch. or Wind Orch. (1967); *De verloofden* (1969); *Music pour le podium* for Wind Orch. (1971); *Dialogue* for Violin and Orch. (1972); *Intrada* (1980). **CHAMBER:** Sonatina for Flute and Viola (1934); Violin Sonata (1934); *Concertstück* for Trumpet and Piano (1957); *Prelude and Allegro* for 2 Trumpets, Horn, Trombone, and Tuba (1959); *Fantasia* for 2 Pianos (1960); Duo for Violin and Piano (1962); Trio for Violin, Viola, and Percussion (1964); *4 contrastes* for 4 Clarinets (1965); Suite for Percussion and Piano (1968); Piano Quartet (1970); *Studie* for Violin (1978); *Saxo-scope* for Saxophone Quartet (1979); *Adagio en allegretto* for Violin and Piano (1985). **VOCAL:** *Rosa mystica* for Soprano and Orch. or Piano (1959); *Mei 1871* for Narrator and Orch. (1971); choruses; songs.

Magaloff, Nikita, distinguished Russian-born Swiss pianist and teacher; b. St. Petersburg, Feb. 21, 1912; d. Vevey, Dec. 26, 1992. His family left Russia after the Revolution; he enrolled in the Paris Cons. as a student of Isidor Philipp; graduated with a premier prix at the age of 17; also studied composition with Prokofiev in Paris. In 1939 he settled in Switzerland; in 1947 he made his first American tour; also toured Europe, South America, South Africa, etc. From 1949 to 1960 he taught piano at the Geneva Cons.; then gave summer courses at Taormina, Sicily, and at the Accademia Musicale Chigiana in Siena. In 1956 he became a naturalized Swiss citizen. He was renowned for his lyrico-dramatic interpretations of Chopin, with lapidary attention to detail. He was also a composer; wrote a Piano Toccata; Violin Sonatina; songs; cadenzas for Mozart's piano concertos. He was the son-in-law of **Joseph Szigeti**.

Maganini, Quinto, American flutist, conductor, arranger, and composer; b. Fairfield, Calif., Nov. 30, 1897; d. Greenwich, Conn., March 10, 1974. He played flute in the San Francisco Sym. (1917–19) and in the N.Y. Sym. (1919–28). He studied flute with Barrère in N.Y. and composition with Boulanger at the American Cons. in Fontainebleau. In 1928–29 he held a Guggenheim fellowship. In 1930 he became conductor of the N.Y. Sinfonietta. In 1932 he organized his own orch., the Maganini Chamber Sym., with which he toured widely. From 1939 to 1970 he was conductor of the Norwalk (Conn.) Sym. Orch.

WORKS: *Toulumne*, "a Californian Rhapsody," for Orch., with Trumpet obbligato (N.Y., Aug. 9, 1924); *South Wind*, orch. fantasy (N.Y., April 7, 1931); *Sylvan Symphony* (N.Y., Nov. 30, 1932); *Napoleon*, orch. portrait (N.Y., Nov. 10, 1935); *The Royal Ladies*, orch. suite on airs ascribed to Marie-Antoinette (Greenwich, Conn., Feb. 3, 1940); *Tennessee's Partner*, opera (WOR Radio, N.Y., May 28, 1942); numerous arrangements for small orch. of classical and modern works.

Mager, Jörg, German music theorist and pioneer in electronic music; b. Eichstätt, Nov. 6, 1880; d. Aschaffenburg, April 5, 1939. After completing his univ. studies, he became interested in electronic reproduction of sounds; constructed several instruments capable of producing microtonal intervals by electronic means, which he named Sphärophon, Elektrophon, and Partiturophon; he was also active in visual music for film. He publ. *Vierteltonmusik* (Aschaffenburg, 1916) and *Eine neue Epoche der Musik durch Radio* (Berlin, 1924).

Magne, Michel, French composer; b. Lisieux, March 20, 1930; d. (suicide) Cergy-Pontase, Val d'Oise, Dec. 19, 1984. He was mainly self-taught, beginning to compose as a very young man in an ultramodern style; later took lessons with Plé-Caussade.

His film score *Le Pain vivant* (1955) received critical acclaim; he also experimented with electronic music; on May 26, 1955, he conducted in Paris his *Symphonie humaine* for 150 Performers, making use of inaudible "infrasounds" to produce a physiological reaction by powerful low frequencies. He wrote the musical score for Françoise Sagan's ballet *Le Rendez-vous manqué* (1957) and many film scores.

Magomayev, (Abdul) Muslim, Azerbaijani conductor and composer; b. Shusha, Sept. 18, 1885; d. Baku, July 28, 1937. He studied at the Gori teachers' seminary (1899–1904); learned to play violin and clarinet, and taught at Lenkoran College (1905–11). He then settled in Baku as an orch. player, conductor, and teacher at the Azerbaijani Theater; later was associated with the National Commissariat of Enlightenment, becoming artistic director and conductor of the musical theater (1924); was music director of the Azerbaijani Radio (from 1929). The first version of his opera *Shah Ismail* (1916; Baku, 1919) was mainly made up of improvised songs and dialogue; he later revised it with notated improvisatory sections and added recitatives (1920–23; 1930–32). His second opera, *Nergiz* (1934; Baku, Jan. 1, 1936), was fully notated. He also wrote orch. pieces, incidental music, film scores, and numerous arrangements of folk songs and dances.

BIBL.: G. Ismailova, *M. M.* (Baku, 1975).

Mahler, Fritz, Austrian-born American conductor and composer, 2nd cousin of **Gustav Mahler;** b. Vienna, July 16, 1901; d. Winston-Salem, N.C., June 18, 1973. He was a student of Reichwein (conducting) and Adler (musicology) at the Univ. of Vienna (1920–24), concurrently studying composition privately with Schoenberg and Berg. After conducting in Austria and Germany, he was a conductor with the Danish Radio in Copenhagen (1931–35). In 1936 he emigrated to the U.S. and in 1939 became a naturalized American citizen. He conducted the La Scala Opera of Philadelphia (1937–40), the National Youth Administration Orch. (1940–42), the Erie (Pa.) Phil. (1947–53), and the Hartford (Conn.) Sym. Orch. (1953–64). He also taught conducting at the Juilliard Summer School in N.Y. (1938–53), where he served as director of the opera dept. Among his works were a symphonic poem, chamber pieces, and songs.

Mahler, Gustav, great Austrian composer and conductor; b. Kalischt, Bohemia, July 7, 1860; d. Vienna, May 18, 1911. He attended school in Iglau. In 1875 he entered the Vienna Cons., where he studied piano with Julius Epstein, harmony with Robert Fuchs, and composition with Franz Krenn. He also took academic courses in history and philosophy at the Univ. of Vienna (1877–80). In the summer of 1880 he received his first engagement as a conductor, at the operetta theater in the town of Hall in Upper Austria; subsequently he held posts as theater conductor at Ljubljana (1881), Olmutz (1882), Vienna (1883), and Kassel (1883–85). In 1885 he served as 2nd Kapellmeister to Anton Seidl at the Prague Opera, where he gave several performances of Wagner's operas. From 1886 to 1888 he was assistant to Arthur Nikisch in Leipzig. In 1888 he received the important appointment of music director of the Royal Opera in Budapest. In 1891 he was engaged as conductor at the Hamburg Opera; during his tenure there, he developed a consummate technique for conducting. In 1897 he received a tentative offer as music director of the Vienna Court Opera, but there was an obstacle to overcome. Mahler was Jewish, and although there was no overt anti-Semitism in the Austrian government, an imperial appointment could not be given to a Jew. Mahler was never orthodox in his religion, and had no difficulty in converting to Catholicism, which was the prevailing faith in Austria. He held this position at the Vienna Court Opera for 10 years; under his guidance, it reached the highest standards of artistic excellence. In 1898 Mahler was engaged to succeed Hans Richter as conductor of the Vienna Phil. Here, as in his direction of opera, he proved a great interpreter, but he also allowed himself considerable freedom in rearranging the orchestration of classical scores when he felt it would redound to greater effect. He also aroused antagonism among the players by his autocratic behavior toward them. He resigned from the Vienna Phil. in 1901; in 1907 he also resigned from the Vienna Court Opera. It was in the latter year that he was diagnosed as suffering from a lesion of the heart. In the meantime, he became immersed in strenuous work as a composer; he confined himself exclusively to composition of symphonic music, sometimes with vocal parts; because of his busy schedule as conductor, he could compose only in the summer months, in a villa on the Worthersee in Carinthia. In 1902 he married Alma Schindler; they had 2 daughters. The younger daughter, Anna Mahler, was briefly married to Ernst Krenek; the elder daughter died in infancy. Alma Mahler studied music with Zemlinsky, who was the brother-in-law of Arnold Schoenberg.

Having exhausted his opportunities in Vienna, Mahler accepted the post of principal conductor of the Metropolitan Opera in N.Y. in 1907. He made his American debut there on Jan. 1, 1908, conducting *Tristan und Isolde.* In 1909 he was appointed conductor of the N.Y. Phil. His performances both at the Metropolitan and with the N.Y. Phil. were enormously successful with the audiences and the N.Y. music critics, but inevitably he had conflicts with the board of trustees in both organizations, which were mostly commanded by rich women. He resigned from the Metropolitan Opera in 1910. On Feb. 21, 1911, he conducted his last concert with the N.Y. Phil. and then returned to Vienna. The N.Y. newspapers publ. lurid accounts of his struggle for artistic command with the regimen of the women of the governing committee. Alma Mahler was quoted as saying that although in Vienna even the Emperor did not dare to order Mahler about, in N.Y. he had to submit to the whims of 10 ignorant women. The newspaper editorials mourned Mahler's death, but sadly noted that his N.Y. tenure was a failure. As to Mahler's own compositions, the *N.Y. Tribune* said bluntly, "We cannot see how any of his music can long survive him." His syms. were sharply condemned in the press as being too long, too loud, and too discordant. It was not until the second half of the 20th century that Mahler became fully recognized as a composer, the last great Romantic symphonist. Mahler's syms. were drawn on the grandest scale, and the technical means employed for the realization of his ideas were correspondingly elaborate. The sources of his inspiration were twofold: the lofty concepts of universal art, akin to those of Bruckner, and ultimately stemming from Wagner; and the simple folk melos of the Austrian countryside, in pastoral moods recalling the intimate episodes in Beethoven's syms. True to his Romantic nature, Mahler attached descriptive titles to his syms.; the 1st was named the *Titan*; the 2nd, *Resurrection*; the 3rd, *Ein Sommermorgentraum*; and the 5th, *The Giant.* The great 8th became known as "Sym. of a Thousand" because it required about 1,000 instrumentalists, vocalists, and soloists for performance; however, this sobriquet was the inspiration of Mahler's agent, not of Mahler himself. Later in life, Mahler tried to disassociate his works from their programmatic titles; he even claimed that he never used them in the first place, contradicting the evidence of the MSS, in which the titles appear in Mahler's own handwriting. Mahler was not an innovator in his harmonic writing; rather, he brought the Romantic era to a culmination by virtue of the expansiveness of his emotional expression and the grandiose design of his musical structures. Morbid by nature, he brooded upon the inevitability of death; one of his most poignant compositions was the cycle for voice and orch., *Kindertotenlieder;* he wrote it shortly before the death of his little daughter, and somehow he blamed himself for this seeming anticipation of his personal tragedy. In 1910 he consulted Sigmund Freud in Leiden, Holland, but the treatment was brief and apparently did not help Mahler to resolve his psychological problems. Unquestionably, he suffered from an irrational feeling of guilt. In the 3rd movement of his unfinished 10th Sym., significantly titled *Purgatorio,* he wrote on the margin, "Madness seizes me, annihilates me," and appealed to the Devil to take possession of his soul. But he never was clinically insane. His already weakened heart could not withstand the onslaught of a severe bacterial infection of the blood, and he died at the lamentable age of 50.

Mahler's importance to the evolution of modern music is very great; the early works of Schoenberg and Berg show the influence of Mahler's concepts. A society was formed in the U.S. in 1941 "to develop in the public an appreciation of the music of Bruckner, Mahler and other moderns." An International Gustav Mahler Soc. was formed in Vienna in 1955, with Bruno Walter as honorary president. On Mahler's centennial, July 7, 1960, the government of Austria issued a memorial postage stamp of 1 1/2 shillings, with Mahler's portrait.

WORKS: SYMS.: No. 1, in D, *Titan* (1883–88; Budapest, Nov. 20, 1889, composer conducting; a rejected movement, entitled *Blumine*, was reincorporated and perf. at the Aldeburgh Festival, June 18, 1967), No. 2, in C minor, *Resurrection*, for Soprano, Contralto, Chorus, and Orch. (1887–94; Berlin, Dec. 13, 1895, composer conducting), No. 3, in D minor, *Ein Sommermorgentraum* (1893–96; Krefeld, June 9, 1902, composer conducting), No. 4, in G (1899–1901; Munich, Nov. 25, 1901, composer conducting), No. 5, in C-sharp minor, *The Giant* (1901–02; Cologne, Oct. 18, 1904, composer conducting), No. 6, in A minor (1903–05; Essen, May 27, 1906, composer conducting), No. 7, in E minor (1904–06; Prague, Sept. 19, 1908, composer conducting), No. 8, in E-flat, "Symphony of a Thousand," for 8 Solo Voices, Adult and Children's Choruses, and Orch. (1906–07; Munich, Sept. 12, 1910, composer conducting), No. 9, in D (1909–10; Vienna, June 26, 1912, Bruno Walter conducting), and No. 10, in F-sharp minor (sketched 1909–10, unfinished; 2 movements, *Adagio* and *Purgatorio*, perf. in Vienna, Oct. 12, 1924, Franz Schalk conducting; publ. in facsimile, 1924, by Alma Mahler; a performing version, using the sketches then available and leaving the 2 scherzo movements in fragmentary form, was made by D. Cooke; it was broadcast by the BBC, London, Dec. 19, 1960; Alma Mahler approved of Cooke's realization; further sketches were made available, and a full performing version was premiered in London, Aug. 13, 1964; a final revision of the score was made in 1972; there are also other performing versions as well).

VOCAL: *Das klagende Lied* for Soprano, Contralto, Tenor, Chorus, and Orch. (1878–80; rev. 1896–98; Vienna, Feb. 17, 1901, composer conducting); *Lieder und Gesänge aus der Jugendzeit*, 14 songs for Voice and Piano (1880–91); *Lieder eines fahrenden Gesellen*, 4 songs with Orch. (1883–85; Berlin, March 16, 1896, composer conducting); 14 Lieder from *Des Knaben Wunderhorn* for Voice and Orch. (1892–1901); 5 songs, to poems by Rückert (1901–03); *Kindertotenlieder*, 5 songs, with Piano or Orch., to poems by Rückert (1901–04; Vienna, Jan. 29, 1905, composer conducting); *Das Lied von der Erde*, sym. for Contralto or Baritone, Tenor, and Orch. (1907–09; Munich, Nov. 20, 1911, Bruno Walter conducting).

Mahler destroyed the MSS of several of his early works, among them a piano quintet (perf. in Vienna, July 11, 1878, with the composer at the piano) and 3 unfinished operas: *Herzog Ernst von Schwaben*, to a drama by Uhland; *Die Argonauten*, from a trilogy by Grillparzer; and *Rübezahl*, after Grimm's fairy tales. He also made an arrangement of Weber's *Die drei Pintos* (Leipzig, Jan. 20, 1888, composer conducting) and *Oberon* (c.1907); also arranged Bruckner's 3rd Sym. for 2 Pianos (1878). Mahler made controversial reorchestrations of syms. by Beethoven, Schumann, and Bruckner, and a version for String Orch. of Beethoven's String Quartet in C-sharp minor, op. 131.

BIBL.: L. Schiedermair, *G. M.* (Leipzig, 1901); P. Stefan, *G. M.: Eine Studie über Persönlichkeit und Werk* (Munich, 1910; 4th ed., 1921; Eng. tr., N.Y., 1913); R. Specht, *G. M.* (Berlin, 1913); G. Adler, *G. M.* (Vienna, 1916); A. Neisser, "G. M.," *Reclams Universal-Bibliothek* (Berlin, 1918); H. Redlich, *G. M.: Eine Erkenntnis* (Nuremberg, 1919); P. Bekker, *M.s Sinfonien* (Berlin, 1921); A. Roller, *Die Bildnisse G. M.s* (Leipzig, 1922); N. Bauer-Lechner, *Erinnerungen an G. M.* (Vienna, 1923); A. Mahler, *Briefe G. M.s* (Berlin, 1924); W. Hutschenruyter, *G. M.* (The Hague, 1927); H. Holländer, "G. M.," *Musical Quarterly* (Oct. 1931); G. Engel, *G. M.* (Vienna, 1936; Eng. tr., N.Y., 1957); A. Mahler, *G. M.: Erinnerungen und Briefe* (Amsterdam, 1940; Eng. tr., London, 1946); E. Wellesz, "The Symphonies of G. M.," *Music Review* (Jan.–April 1940); B. Walter (with E. Krenek), *G. M.* (N.Y., 1941); D. Newlin, *Bruckner-M.-Schoenberg* (N.Y., 1947; 2nd ed., rev., 1978); N. Loeser, *G. M.* (Haarlem, 1950); H. Tischler, "M.'s Impact on the Crisis of Tonality," *Music Review* (April 1951); D. Mitchell, "Some Notes on M.'s Tenth Symphony," *Musical Times* (Dec. 1955); H. Redlich, *Bruckner and M.* (London, 1955; 2nd ed., rev., 1963); D. Mitchell, *G. M.: I: The Early Years* (London, 1958; rev. 1980), *G. M.: II: The Wunderhorn Years* (Boulder, Colo., 1976), and *G. M.: III: Songs and Symphonies of Life and Death* (London, 1985); W. Reich, ed., *G. M.: Im eigenen Wort, im Wort der Freunde* (Zürich, 1958); T. Adorno, *M.: Eine musikalische Physiognomik* (Frankfurt am Main, 1960); S. Vestdijk, *G. M.* (The Hague, 1960); N. Cardus, *G. M.: His Mind and His Music* (London, 1965); H. Kralik, *G. M.* (Vienna, 1968); K. Blaukopf, *G. M., oder Zeitgenosse der Zukunft* (Vienna, 1969); J. Diether, "Notes on Some M. Juvenilia," *Chord and Discord*, III/I (1969); H.-L. de La Grange, *G. M.: Chronique d'une vie* (3 vols., Paris, 1973–84; also in Eng.); D. Holbrook, *G. M. and the Courage to Be* (N.Y., 1975); K. Blaukopf, ed., *M.: A Documentary Study* (N.Y., 1976; rev. and enl. ed, 1991, as *M.: His Life, Work and World*); A. Shelley, ed., *G. M. in Vienna* (N.Y., 1976); C. Floros, *G. M.* (3 vols., Wiesbaden, 1977–85); P. Ruzicka, *M.: Eine Herausforderung* (Wiesbaden, 1977); E. Gartenberg, *M.: The Man and His Music* (N.Y., 1978); E. Reilly, *G. M. und Guido Adler: Zur Geschichte einer Freundschaft* (Vienna, 1978; Eng. tr., Cambridge, 1982); B. and E. Vondenhoff, *G. M. Dokumentation* (Tutzing, 1978); D. Cooke, *G. M.: An Introduction to His Music* (London, 1980); H. Eggebrecht, *Die Musik G. M.s* (Munich, 1982); E. Seckerson, *M.: His Life and Times* (N.Y., 1982); H. Blaukopf, ed., and E. Jephcott, tr., *G. M.—Richard Strauss: Correspondence 1888–1911* (London, 1984); D. Greene, *M.: Consciousness and Temporality* (N.Y., 1984); C. Lewis, *Tonal Coherence in M.'s Ninth Symphony* (Ann Arbor, 1984); H. Lea, *G. M.: Man on the Margin* (Bonn, 1985); H. Danuser, *G. M.: Das Lied von der Erde* (Munich, 1986); H.-P. Jülg, *G. M.s Sechste Symphonie* (Munich, 1986); H. Blaukopf, ed., *M.'s Unknown Letters* (Boston, 1987); S. Namenwirth, *G. M.: A Critical Bibliography* (3 vols., Wiesbaden, 1987); K.-J. Müller, *M.: Leben, Werke, Dokumente* (Mainz, 1988); M. Oltmanns, *Strophische Strukturen im Werk G. M.s: Untersuchungen zum Liedwerk und zur Symphonik* (Pfaffenweiler, 1988); S. Filler, *G. and Alma M.: A Guide to Research* (N.Y., 1989); E. Nikkels, *"O Mensch! Gib Acht!": Friedrich Nietzsches Bedeutung für G. M.* (Amsterdam and Atlanta, 1989); Z. Roman, *G. M.'s American Years 1907–1911: A Documentary History* (Stuyvesant, N.Y., 1989); T. Bloomfield, "In Search of M.'s Tenth: The Four Performing Versions as Seen by a Conductor," *Musical Quarterly*, no. 2 (1990); R. Hopkins, *Closure and M.'s Music: The Role of Secondary Parameters* (Philadelphia, 1990); H. Danuser, *G. M. und seine Zeit* (Laaber, 1991); P. Franklin, *M.: Symphony No. 3* (Cambridge, 1991); F. Krummacher, *G. M.s III. Symphonie: Welt im Widerbild* (Kassel, 1991); A. Neumayr, *Musik und Medizin: Chopin, Smetana, Tschaikowsky, M.* (Vienna, 1991); P. Russell, *Light in Battle with Darkness: M.'s "Kindertotenlieder"* (Bern, 1991); E. Schmierer, *Die Orchesterlieder G. M.s* (Kassel, 1991); H. Danuser, ed., *G. M.* (Darmstadt, 1992); B. Meier, *Geschichtliche Signaturen der musik bei M., Strauss und Schöberg* (Hamburg, 1992); A. Unger, *Welt, Leben und Kunst als Themen der "Zarathustra-Kompositionen" von Richard Strauss und G. M.* (Frankfurt am Main, 1992); F. Berger, *G. M.: Vision und Mythos: Versuch einer geistigen Biographie* (Stuttgart, 1993); F. Willnauer, *G. M. und die Wiener Oper* (Vienna, 1993); P. Reed, ed., *On M. and Britten: Essays in Honour of Donald Mitchell on his Seventieth Birthday* (Woodbridge, Suffolk, 1995); R. Samuels, *M.'s Sixth Symphony: A Study in Musical Semiotics* (Cambridge, 1995).

Mahrenholz, Christhard (actually, **Christian Reinhard**), prominent German musicologist; b. Adelebsen, near Göttingen, Aug. 11, 1900; d. Hannover, March 15, 1980. He studied piano, organ, and cello, and took courses in theology. He also studied musicology with Schering at the Leipzig Cons., Abert at the Univ. of Leipzig, and Ludwig and Spitta at the Univ. of Göttingen (Ph.D., 1923, with the diss. *Samuel Scheidt: Sein Leben und sein Werk;* publ. in Leipzig, 1924). He served as a pastor in Göttingen; then taught at the Univ. there, being made honorary prof. of church music (1946). He was a member of the Hannover Landes Kirchenant (1930–65), president of the Assn. of Protestant Church Choirs in Germany (1934–73), and chairman of the Neue Bach-Gesellschaft (1949–74). Mahrenholz was co-ed. of *Musik und Kirche* (from 1929), the *Handbuch der deutschen evangelischen Kirchenmusik* (from 1935), the *Jahrbuch für Liturgik und Hymnologie* (from 1955), and the *Handbuch zum Evangelischen Kirchengesangbuch* (from 1956); was the general ed. of the complete works of Samuel Scheidt (from 1932). He was made abbot of the Amelungsborn Cloister in 1960. Mahrenholz retired from active work in 1967. His books include *Die Orgelregister: Ihre Geschichte und ihr Bau* (Kassel, 1930; 2nd ed., 1944); *Luther und die Kirchenmusik* (Kassel, 1937); *Die Berechnung der Orgelpfeifen-Mensuren vom Mittelalter bis zur Mitte des 19. Jahrhunderts* (Kassel, 1938); *Glockenkunde* (Kassel, 1949); with R. Untermöhlen, *Choralbuch zum evangelischen Kirchengesangbuch* (Kassel, 1950); *Das evangelische Kirchengesangbuch: Vorgeschichte, Werden und Grundsätze seiner Gestaltung* (Kassel, 1950); *Das Schicksal der deutschen Kirchenglocken* (Hamburg, 1952); *Kompendium der Liturgik des Hauptgottesdienstes* (Kassel, 1963). K. Müller ed. a collection of his articles as *Musicologica et liturgica: Aufsätze von Christhard Mahrenholz* (Kassel, 1960). His 70th birthday was honored by the Festschrift *Kerygma und Melos* (Kassel and Berlin, 1970).

Maiboroda, Georgi, Ukrainian composer; b. Pelekhovshchina, near Poltava, Dec. 1, 1913. He studied at the Kiev Cons. with Revutsky, graduating in 1941; from 1952 he taught there. His music tends toward heroically patriotic themes according to the precepts of socialist realism.

WORKS: OPERAS: *Milana* (1957); *The Arsenal* (1960); *Taras Shevchenko* (1964); *Yaroslav the Wise* (1975). **ORCH.:** 4 syms. (1940; 1952; 1976; *Autumn,* 1988); Concerto for Voice and Orch. (1969); Violin Concerto (1977); Cello Concerto (1984); *Joyful Overture* (1985). **OTHER:** Numerous vocal pieces, including *Friendship of Peoples,* cantata (1948).

BIBL.: O. Zinkevich, *G. M.* (Kiev, 1973).

Maier, Guy, American pianist and teacher; b. Buffalo, Aug. 15, 1891; d. Santa Monica, Calif., Sept. 24, 1956. He studied at the New England Cons. of Music in Boston (graduated, 1913) and with Schnabel in Berlin (1913–14). He made his U.S. debut in Boston (1914); in addition to solo appearances, he also toured as a duo-pianist with Lee Pattison (1916–31). He taught at the Univ. of Mich. (1924–31), the Juilliard School of Music in N.Y. (1935–42), and the Univ. of Calif. at Los Angeles (1946–56).

Mailman, Martin, American composer, conductor, and teacher; b. N.Y., June 30, 1932. He studied composition with Mennini, Barlow, Rogers, and Hanson at the Eastman School of Music in Rochester, N.Y. (B.M., 1954; M.M., 1955; Ph.D., 1960). He taught at the U.S. Naval School of Music during his naval service (1955–57); after teaching at the Eastman School of Music (1958–59), he was composer-in-residence of Jacksonville, Fla., under a Ford Foundation grant (1959–61). During the summers of 1960–61 and 1983, he taught at the Brevard Music Center; from 1961 to 1966 he was composer-in-residence and prof. of music at East Carolina College; also taught at West Virginia Univ. (summer, 1963). In 1966 he joined the faculty of North Texas State Univ. (later the Univ. of North Texas) in Denton, where he served as Regents Prof. of Music (from 1987) and as composer-in-residence (from 1990). He was active as a guest conductor, composer, and lecturer at more than 80 colleges and univs. In 1982 he won the Queen Marie-Jose Prize for Composition for his Violin Concerto and an NEA grant; in 1983 he received the American Bandmasters Assn./NABIM Award for his *Exaltations*; in 1989 he won the National Band Assn./Band Mans Award and the American Bandmasters Assn./Ostwald Award for his *For Precious Friends Hid in Death's Dateless Night.*

WORKS: DRAMATIC: *The Hunted,* opera (Rochester, N.Y., April 27, 1959); *Mirrors,* multimedia theater piece (1986). **ORCH.:** *Dance in 2 Moods* (1952); *Autumn Landscape* (1954); *Jubilate* (1955); *Elegy* (1955); *Cantiones* (1957); *Prelude and Fugue No. 1* (1959) and *No. 2* (1963); *Partita* for Strings (1960); *Gateway City Overture* (1960); *Suite in 3 Movements* (1961); Sinfonietta (1964); 3 syms. (1969; 1979; *Fantasies,* 1983); *Generations 2* for 3 String Orchs. and Percussion (1969); Violin Concerto (1982); *Elegy* for Strings (1985); *Mirror Music* (1987); Concerto for Wind Orch. (1993). **BAND:** *Partita* (1958); *Commencement March* (1960); *4 Miniatures* (1960); *Geometrics No. 1* (1961), *No. 2* (1962), *No. 3* (1965), *No. 4* (1968), and *No. 5* (1976); *Alarums* (1962); Concertino for Trumpet and Band (1963); *Liturgical Music* (1964); *Associations No. 1* (1968–69); *In Memoriam Frankie Newton* (1970); *Shouts, Hymns and Praises* (1972); *Night Vigil* (1980); *Exaltations* (1981); *Toward the 2nd Century* (1989); Clarinet Concertino (1990); *Bouquets* (1991); *Secular Litanies* (1993). **CHAMBER:** *Promenade* for Brass and Percussion (1953); *Brevard Fanfare* for Brass (1961); String Quartet (1962); *4 Divisions* for Percussion Ensemble (1966); *Partita No. 4* for 9 Players (1967); *2 Fanfares* for Brass (1970); *Clastics: Formations* for Cello (1977); *Clastics 2* for Euphonium and Percussion (1979); *Nocturne* for Trumpet Choir (1985); Trio for Violin, Cello, and Piano (1985); *For Precious Friends Hid in Death's Dateless Night* for Wind Ensemble (1988); *Surfaces* for Wind Quintet (1991). **PIANO:** *Petite Partita* (1961); *Variations on a Short Theme* (1966); *Martha's Vineyard* (1969); *In Memoriam Silvio Scionti* (1974); *Clastics 3* for 2 Pianos (1980); *6 Brief Obituaries* (1988). **VOCAL:** *Alleluia* for Chorus and Band (1960); *Genesis Resurrected* for Narrator, Chorus, and Orch. (1961); *Leaves of Grass* for Narrator, Chorus, and Band (1963); *Shakespearean Serenade* for Chorus and 4 Instruments (1968); *Requiem, Requiem* for Chorus, Soloists, and Orch. (1970); *Let Us Now Praise Famous Men* for Voice, Narrators, and Band (1975); *Wild Across the Nations* for Voice, Piano, Percussion, Flute, and Guitar (1975); *Generations 3: Messengers* for Children's Choruses, Voice, and Stage Band (1977); *Soft Sounds for a Wordless Night* for Chorus (1979); *Secular Hours* for Chorus (1982); Cantata for Soloists, Jazz Chorus, and Large Jazz Ensemble (1984); *Love Letters from Margaret* for Soprano and Orch. (1991); *Agnus Dei* for Chorus (1994).

Mainardi, Enrico, Italian cellist, teacher, and composer; b. Milan, May 19, 1897; d. Munich, April 10, 1976. He studied cello and composition at the Milan Cons. (graduated, 1920), cello with H. Becker in Berlin, and composition with Malipiero in Venice. He made tours of Europe, both as a soloist and a chamber music player.

WORKS: ORCH.: 3 cello concertos: No. 1 (1943; Rome, May 13, 1947; composer soloist), No. 2 (1960), and No. 3, with String Orch. (1966); *Musica per archi*; *Elegie* for Cello and String Orch. (1957); Concerto for 2 Cellos and Orch. (1969; Freiburg im Breisgau, Oct. 12, 1970); *Divertimento* for Cello and String Orch. (1972). **CHAMBER:** 2 unnumbered string trios (1939, 1954); *Suite* for Cello and Piano (1940); Cello Sonatina (1943); *Notturno* for Piano Trio (1947); String Quartet (1951); Cello Sonata (1955); Sonata and *Sonata breve* for Solo Cello; 7 *studi brevi* for Cello (1961); *Sonata quasi fantasia* for Cello and Piano (1962); Violin Sonata; Piano Quartet (1968); Viola Sonata (1968); *Burattini,* suite of 12 pieces for Cello and Piano (1968); Trio for Clarinet, Cello, and Piano (1969); String Quintet (1970); Piano Sonatina (1941); other piano pieces.

BIBL.: *E. M.: Bekenntnisse eines Künstlers* (Wiesbaden, 1977).

Maine, Basil (Stephen), English writer on music and composer; b. Norwich, March 4, 1894; d. Sheringham, Norfolk, Oct. 13, 1972. He studied with Stanford, Rootham, and Dent at Queen's College, Cambridge; was active after graduation as a schoolteacher and occasionally an actor. He was music critic for London's *Daily Telegraph* (1921–26) and *Morning Post* (1926–37); was ordained a priest in the Church of England in

1939. He composed orch. works, choral music, and organ pieces. His writings include *Behold These Daniels* (1928), *Reflected Music and Other Essays* (1930), *Elgar, His Life and Works* (2 vols., 1933), *Chopin* (1933; 2nd ed., 1948), *The Glory of English Music* (1937), *The Best of Me: A Study in Autobiography* (1937), *New Paths in Music* (1940), *Basil Maine on Music* (1945), and *Twang with Our Music, Being a Set of Variants to Mark the Completion of Thirty Years' Practice in the Uncertain Science of Music Criticism* (London, 1957).

Maisenberg, Oleg, Ukrainian pianist; b. Odessa, April 29, 1945. He began piano studies in his youth, and later was a pupil of Alexander Joscheles at the Gnessin Inst. in Moscow (1966–71). From 1971 he was a soloist with the Moscow Phil. After making his Vienna debut in 1981, he performed throughout Europe. In 1983 he made his first appearance in the U.S. In subsequent years, he toured globally. He also made frequent appearances in duo concerts with Gidon Kremer.

Maisky, Mischa, Russian-born Israeli cellist; b. Riga, Jan. 10, 1948. He was a pupil of Rostropovich at the Moscow Cons. In 1965 he won 1st prize in the All Russian Competition and made his formal debut as a soloist with the Leningrad Phil.; in 1966 he was a laureate at the Tchaikovsky Competition in Moscow. Despite his successful career, he got into trouble with the Soviet authorities when he bought a tape recorder without proper permission. In 1969 he was duly arrested and spent a few months in jail. Determined to leave Russia, he approached a liberal-minded psychiatrist, who, like Maisky, was of the Jewish faith, and was committed to an asylum. He was finally permitted to emigrate to Israel in 1971, where he settled and became a naturalized Israeli citizen. In 1973 he captured 1st prize at the Gaspar Cassadó Competition in Florence. He also pursued further studies with Piatigorsky in the U.S. From 1975 he toured throughout the world, appearing as a soloist with orchs., as a recitalist, and as a chamber music artist.

Maison, René, Belgian tenor; b. Frameries, Nov. 24, 1895; d. Mont-Dore, France, July 15, 1962. He was trained at the Brussels Cons. and the Paris Cons. After making his operatic debut as Rodolfo in *La Bohème* in 1920, he sang in Nice and Monte Carlo. From 1925 he sang in Paris at the Opéra and the Opéra-Comique, establishing a reputation as a Wagnerian. He also appeared at the Chicago Opera (1927–32) and the Teatro Colón in Buenos Aires (1934–37). On Feb. 3, 1936, he made his Metropolitan Opera debut in N.Y. as Walther von Stolzing, and remained on its roster until 1943. He later taught voice in N.Y. and Boston. Among his prominent roles were Lohengrin, Loge, Florestan, Samson, Herodes, and Don José.

Maizel, Boris, significant Russian composer; b. St. Petersburg, July 17, 1907; d. Moscow, July 9, 1986. He graduated from the Leningrad Cons. in 1936 in the composition class of Riazanov. During the siege of Leningrad by the Germans in 1942, he was evacuated to Sverdlovsk; in 1944 he settled in Moscow.

WORKS: DRAMATIC: *Snow Queen*, ballet (1940; orch. suite, 1944); *Sombrero*, children's ballet (1959); *The Shadow of the Past*, opera (1964); film music. **ORCH.:** 9 syms.: No. 1 (1940), No. 2, *Ural Symphony* (1944), No. 3, *Victoriously Triumphant*, written in celebration of the victory over Germany (1945), No. 4 (1947), No. 5 (1962), No. 6 (1967), No. 7 (1970), No. 8 (1973), and No. 9 (1976); Double Concerto for Violin, Piano, and Orch. (1949); 3 symphonic poems: *Distant Planet* (1961; also as a ballet, 1962), *Leningrad Novella* (1969), and *Along Old Russian Towns* (1975); Double Concerto for Flute, Horn, Strings, and Percussion (1971); Concerto for 10 Instruments (1977); Concerto for 2 Pianos and Strings (1978). **CHAMBER:** Cello Sonata (1936); 2 string quartets (1937, 1974); Piano Trio (1951); piano pieces. **VOCAL:** Song cycles.

Major, Ervin, Hungarian musicologist and composer; b. Budapest, Jan. 26, 1901; d. there, Oct. 10, 1967. After initial training with his father, the Hungarian pianist, choral conductor, and composer Gyula (Jakab) Major (real name, Mayer) (b. Kassa, Dec. 13, 1858; d. Budapest, Jan. 30, 1925), he studied with Kodály (composition) at the Budapest Academy of Music (1917–21), philosophy at the Budapest Scientific Univ. (1920–24), and musicology at the Univ. of Szeged (Ph.D., 1930, with the diss. *A népies magyar műzene és a népzene kapcsolatai* [The Relation of Hungarian Popular Music to Folk Music]; publ. in Budapest, 1930). He was ed. of the journal *Zenei szemle* (1926–28), and then taught composition, theory, and music history and was librarian at the Budapest Cons. (later known as the Béla Bartók Music School; 1928–44; 1945–63). He also taught Hungarian music history at the Budapest Academy of Music (1935–41; 1945–66). Among his compositions were chamber music, piano pieces, organ music, choral works, and arrangements of Hungarian melodies.

WRITINGS (all publ. in Budapest): *Bihari János* (1928); *Brahms és magyar zene* (Brahms and Hungarian Music; 1933); *Fáy András és a magyar zenetörténet* (András Fáy and the History of Hungarian Music; 1934); *A Rakoczi-indulo koruli kutatasok ujabb eredmenyei* (New Results of Research into the Rakoczi March; 1937); *Lizst Ferenc és a magyar zenetörtenet* (Ferenc Lizst and the History of Hungarian Music; 1940); *Bach és Magyarország* (Bach and Hungary; 1953); *Mozart és Magyarország* (Mozart and Hungary; 1956); *Fejezetek a magyar zene történetéből* (Chapters from the History of Hungarian Music; 1967).

Makarova, Nina, Russian composer; b. Yurino, Aug. 12, 1908; d. Moscow, Jan. 15, 1976. She studied with Miaskovsky at the Moscow Cons., graduating in 1936. Her early works show a Romantic flair, not without some coloristic touches of French Impressionism. She wrote an opera, *Zoya* (1955); a Sym. (1938), which she conducted in Moscow on June 12, 1947; a number of violin pieces; a Sonatina and 6 etudes for piano; several song cycles; *The Saga of Lenin*, cantata (1970). She was married to **Aram Khachaturian**.

BIBL.: I. Martinov, *N. M.* (Moscow, 1973).

Makedonski, Kiril, Macedonian composer; b. Bitol, Jan. 19, 1925; d. Skopje, June 2, 1984. After completing his academic schooling in Skopje, he studied with Krso Odak at the Zagreb Academy of Music; later continued his composition studies with Brkanović in Sarajevo, and in Ljubljana with Škerjanc. He was the composer of the first national Macedonian opera, *Goce* (Skopje, May 24, 1954); his second opera was *Tsar Samuil* (Skopje, Nov. 5, 1968). He also wrote 4 syms., chamber music, and a number of choruses. His idiom follows the fundamental vocal and harmonic usages of the Russian national school.

Maklakiewicz, Jan Adam, Polish composer and teacher; b. Chojnata, Mazuria, Nov. 24, 1899; d. Warsaw, Feb. 7, 1954. He was a student of Biernacki (harmony) and Szopski (counterpoint) at the Chopin Music School in Warsaw. After studies in composition with Statkowski at the Warsaw Cons. (1922–25), he completed his training in composition with Dukas at the École Normale de Musique in Paris. He served as a prof. at the Łódź Cons. (1927–29), and then at the Warsaw Cons. (from 1929). He was director of the Kraków Phil. (1945–47), the Warsaw Phil. (1947–48), and the Kraków Cons. (from 1947). Maklakiewicz composed in an advanced style before developing a highly simplified idiom.

WORKS: DRAMATIC: *Cagliostro w Warszawie* (Cagliostro in Warsaw), ballet (1938; Poznań, Oct. 1, 1946); *Zlota kaczka*, ballet (1950); incidental music; film scores. **ORCH.:** 2 syms.: No. 1, *Wariacje symfoniczne* (1922) and No. 2, *Swięty Boze* (O Holy Lord), for Baritone, Chorus, and Orch. (1928); Cello Concerto (1932); Violin Concerto (1933); *Grundwald*, symphonic poem (1939–44; Kraków, Sept. 1, 1945); *Uwertura praska* (Prague Overture; Prague, May 8, 1947). **OTHER:** Chamber music; *Pieśni japońskie* (Japanese Songs) for Soprano and Orch. (1930; Oxford, July 23, 1931); much sacred music; many arrangements of Polish folk songs.

Maksimović, Rajko, Serbian composer and teacher; b. Belgrade, July 27, 1935. He studied with Predrag Miloševic at the

Belgrade Academy of Music (graduated, 1961; M.A., 1965); continued his training at Princeton Univ. (1965–66), devoting himself mainly to electronic music. He taught at the Belgrade Academy of Music (from 1963). In his works, he utilizes resources ranging from the Ars Nova to the contemporary period.

WORKS: ORCH.: Piano Concerto (1961; Belgrade, Jan. 28, 1964); *Musique de devenir* (1965; Belgrade, Dec. 15, 1967); *Partita concertante* for Violin and Strings (1965); *Not to Be or to Be?* and *Eppur si muove*, diptych (1969–70); *Concerto non grosso* for Student String Orch. (1970); *Nežno* (Tenderly) for Chamber Ensemble (1979); *Prélude à "l'avant midi" d'un faune* for Flute and Strings (Belgrade, May 17, 1994). **CHAMBER:** *Trialogue* for Clarinet, String Trio, and Piano (1968). **PIANO:** Suite (1957); *Ab aqua terraque* (1966); *Jeu à quatre* for 2 Pianos, 8-hands (1977); *Gambit* (1993). **VOCAL:** *Kad su živi zavideli mrtvima* (When the Living Envied the Dead), epic partita for Chorus and Orch. (1963; Belgrade, Feb. 2, 1967); *2 Basho's Haiku* for Voice, Ensemble, and Tape (1966); *3 Haiku* for Women's Chorus and 24 Instruments (Zagreb, May 16, 1967); *Iz tmine pojanje* (Chants out of Darkness), madrigals to ancient Serbian texts for Chorus (1975); *Buna protiv dabija* (Uprising against Dakhias), dramatic oratorio for 4 Actors, Choruses, Orch., and Tape (1978; Belgrade, March 20, 1979); *Palabras en piedra*, madrigal suite to pre-Columbian Mexican Indian texts in Spanish for Chorus and Optional Percussion (1980); *After the Scent of the Blossomed Cherry*, 5 haiku for Voice and Ensemble (1981); *Veče na školju* (An Evening on the Reef) for Chorus (1982); *Les Proverbes de Fenis*, choral suite to ancient French texts (1983; also for 4 Voices and Ancient Instruments, 1984, and for Women's Chorus and Orch., 1986); *Prometheus* for Chorus (1985); *Testament of the Bishop of Montenegro Peter Petrovich Nyegosh* for Chorus (1984; also for Bass, Chorus, Orch., and Tape, 1986); *The St. Prince Lazarus Passion* for Narrator, 4 Soloists, 2 Choruses, and Orch. (Belgrade, June 26, 1989); *She Sleeps Perhaps* for Mezzo-soprano and Chamber Orch. (Novi Sad, May 15, 1993; also for Mezzo-soprano and Piano); *Fate* for Chorus (1993); *This and That* for Chorus (1994); *Temptation, Feat, and Death of St. Peter of Korisha* for Narrator, 3 Soloists, Chorus, Chamber Orch., and Tape (Belgrade, Oct. 19, 1994).

Maksymiuk, Jerzy, Polish conductor and composer; b. Grodno, April 9, 1936. He studied piano with Kirjacka and Lefeld, composition with Perkowski, and conducting with Madey at the Warsaw Cons.; won several composition prizes. He conducted at Warsaw's Wielki Theater (1970–72); then in 1972 he founded the Polish Chamber Orch. in Warsaw, which he led as music director; was also conductor of the Polish Radio National Sym. Orch. in Katowice (1976–77) and principal conductor of the BBC Scottish Sym. Orch. in Glasgow (1983–93). From 1993 he was principal conductor of the Kraków Phil. He appeared as a guest conductor in North and South America. He wrote several ballets, orch. music, and choral pieces.

Malas, Spiro, American bass-baritone; b. Baltimore, Jan. 28, 1933. He studied voice with Nagy at the Peabody Cons. of Music in Baltimore and with Elsa Baklor and Daniel Ferro in N.Y.; was also coached by Ivor Chichagov. In 1959 he made his operatic debut as Marco in *Gianni Schicchi* in Baltimore, and in 1961 won the Metropolitan Opera Auditions. On Oct. 5, 1961, he made his first appearance at the N.Y. City Opera as Spinellocchio in *Gianni Schicchi*, and continued to sing there regularly. In 1965 he toured Australia with the Sutherland-Williamson International Grand Opera Co. In 1966 he made his debut at London's Covent Garden as Sulpice in *La Fille du régiment.* He sang Assur in *Semiramide* for his first appearance at the Chicago Lyric Opera in 1971. On Oct. 8, 1983, he made his Metropolitan Opera debut in N.Y. as Sulpice, and later appeared as Zuniga in *Carmen*, as Mozart's Bartolo, as Frank in *Die Fledermaus*, and as the sacristan in *Tosca.* He also toured widely as a concert artist. In 1992 he scored a fine success on Broadway in the revival of *The Most Happy Fella.*

Malawski, Artur, Polish violinist, conductor, teacher, and composer; b. Przemyśl, July 4, 1904; d. Kraków, Dec. 26, 1957. He was a student of Chmielewski (violin) at the Kraków Cons. (graduated, 1928), where he then taught violin and theory (1928–36). After further training with Sikorski (composition) and Bierdiajew (conducting) at the Warsaw Cons. (1936–39), he taught conducting and composition at the Kraków Cons. (1945–57) and conducting at the Katowice Cons. (1950–54). He pursued a progressive path as a composer from 1945, but in his last years he adopted a more Romantic style.

WORKS: DRAMATIC: *Wierchy* (The Peaks), ballet-pantomime (c.1942; rev. 1950–52; concert perf., Kraków, Jan. 10, 1952); incidental music. **ORCH.:** *Allegro capriccioso* for Small Orch. (1929); *Sinfonietta* (1935); *Fuga w starym stylu* (Fugue in the Old Style; 1936); *Variations* (1937); 2 syms.: No. 1 (1938–43) and No. 2, *Dramatyczna* (1953–56); *Fantazja ukraińska* (1941); (6) *Etiudy symfoniczne* for Piano and Orch. (1947; Sopot, April 30, 1948); *Toccata* for Small Orch. (1947); Overture (1948–49); *Toccata and Fugue in Variation Form* for Piano and Orch. (1949); *Tryptyk góralski* (Mountaineer Triptych) for Small Orch. (1950; also for Piano); *Suite popularna* (1952); *Hungaria 1956* (1957; Warsaw, Feb. 14, 1958). **CHAMBER:** 2 string quartets (1926, destroyed; 1941–43); Sextet for 2 Violins, 2 Violas, and 2 Cellos (1932; destroyed); *Żywioly Tatr* (Elements of the Tatra) for Wind Quintet (1934; partly destroyed); *Burleska* for Violin and Piano (1940); *Sonata na tematy F. Janiewicza* for Violin and Piano (1951); Piano Trio (1951–53); *Siciliana i rondo na tematy F. Janiewicza* for Violin and Piano (1952); piano pieces. **VOCAL:** *Wyspa gorgon* (Gorgon's Island), cantata for Soprano, Baritone, Chorus, and Orch. (1939); *Stara baśń* (Old Tale), cantata (n.d.); songs.

BIBL.: B. Schaffer, ed., *A. M.: Zycie i twórczość* (Kraków, 1969).

Malcolm, George (John), esteemed English harpsichordist, pianist, conductor, and teacher; b. London, Feb. 28, 1917. He enrolled at the Royal College of Music in London at the age of 7 and studied with G. Fryer; after attending Balliol College, Oxford (1934–37), he completed his training at the Royal College of Music in London. Following military service in the Royal Air Force during World War II, he took up a distinguished career as a harpsichord virtuoso, chamber music pianist, and conductor; was also active as a teacher. He was Master of Music at Westminster Cathedral (1947–59), artistic director of the Philomusica of London (1962–66), and assoc. conductor of the BBC Scottish Sym. Orch. in Glasgow (1965–67). He was particularly associated with the Baroque revival. In 1965 he was made a Commander of the Order of the British Empire.

Malcużyński, Witold, outstanding Polish-born Argentine pianist; b. Koziczyn, Aug. 10, 1914; d. Palma, Majorca, July 17, 1977. He was a student of Turczyński at the Warsaw Cons. (graduated, 1936) and took courses in law and philosophy at the Univ. of Warsaw before completing his training with Paderewski in Switzerland (1936). In 1937 he took 3rd prize in the Chopin Competition in Warsaw. In 1938 he married the French pianist Colette Gaveau and went to Paris. With the coming of World War II, he went to South America in 1940 and became a naturalized Argentine citizen. In 1942 he made his U.S. debut at N.Y.'s Carnegie Hall, and in subsequent years made regular tours of the U.S. and South America. After World War II, he toured in Europe and various other regions of the world. He became well known for his performances of the Romantic repertoire, especially of the music of Chopin.

BIBL.: B. Gavoty, *W. M.* (London, 1957).

Malec, Ivo, Yugoslav-born French composer, conductor, and teacher; b. Zagreb, March 30, 1925. He studied at the Univ. and at the Academy of Music in Zagreb (1945–51). He was director of the Rijeka (Fiume) Opera (1952–53); in 1955 he traveled to Paris, where he met Pierre Schaeffer (1957) and participated in his Groupe de Musique Concrète. In 1959 he settled in Paris and joined the Service de la Recherche de l'ORTF in 1960. He also worked with the Groupe de Recherche Musicale and taught at the Paris Cons. (1972–90). In 1992 he won the Grand Prix national de la musique. From 1956 his music has explored the extremes of timbre and complexity.

WORKS: DRAMATIC: *Operabus*, 2 scenes from the collective opera, to a libretto by Schaeffer (1965); *Le Roi Lear*, theater score (1967); *Victor Hugo—Un contre tous*, "musical poster" for 2 Actors, Chorus, Orch., and Tape, after Hugo's political texts (Avignon, Aug. 1, 1971); incidental music. **ORCH.:** Sym. (1951); *Maquettes* for 17 Instruments (1957); *Mouvements en couleur* (1959); *Séquences* for Vibraphone and Strings (1960); *Tutti* for Orch. and Tape (1962); *Sigma* (Zagreb, May 16, 1963); *Vocatif* (1968); *Gam(m)es* (Strasbourg, June 10, 1971); *Tehrana* (1975); *Arco-22* for 22 Strings (1976); *Ottava bassa* for Double Bass and Orch. (1983; Paris, April 10, 1984); *Exemples* (1988). **CHAMBER:** Piano Trio (1950); *Sonata brevis* for Cello and Piano (1956); *Trois stèles* for Instruments (1963); *Miniatures pour Lewis Carroll* for Violin, Flute, Harp, and Percussion (1964); *Échos* for 10 Musicians (1965); *Planètes* for Instruments (1966); *Lumina* for 12 Strings and Tape (Lucerne, Sept. 7, 1968); *Kitica* for Violin, Flute, Clarinet, and Trombone (1972); *Actuor* for 6 Percussionists (Strasbourg, April 1, 1973); *Arco-11* for 11 Strings (Paris, June 12, 1975); *Pieris* for 2 Harps (1985); *Attacca*, concerto for Solo Percussion and Tape (1985–86; Metz, Nov. 20, 1986); *Arco 1* for Violin (1987). **PIANO:** Sonata (1949); *Dialogues* (1961; also for Harpsichord). **VOCAL:** *Poèmes de Radovan* for Voice and Orch. (1956); *Cantate pour elle* for Soprano, Harp, and Tape (Paris, May 25, 1966); *Oral* for Actor and Orch. (Zagreb, May 19, 1967); *Lied* for 18 Voices and 39 Strings (Dubrovnik, July 30, 1969); *Dodecameron* for 12 Solo Voices (1970; Bologna, Feb. 22, 1971); *Vox, vocis, f.* for 3 Women's Voices and 9 Instruments (Metz, Nov. 16, 1979). **TAPE:** *Mavena* (1956); *Reflets* (1960); *Dahovi I* (1961) and *II* (1962); *Luminetudes* (1968); *Bizarra* (1972); *Triola* (Metz, Nov. 18, 1978); *Recitativo* (1980); *Carillon Choral* (1981); *Week-end* for 3 Synthesizers and Tape (Paris, May 3, 1982); *Artemisia* (1991).

Maleingreau (or **Malengreau**), **Paul (Eugène) de,** Belgian organist, pedagogue, and composer; b. Trélon-en-Thiérache, Nov. 23, 1887; d. Brussels, Jan. 9, 1956. He studied with Gilson and Tinel at the Brussels Cons. (1905–12); in 1913, became a prof. of harmony there; in 1919, was appointed instructor of organ, and from 1929 to 1953 was prof. of organ. He was elected president of the Froissart Academy in 1946. His performances of Bach organ works were highly regarded in Belgium.

WORKS: 2 syms.: *Symphonie de Noë* and *Symphonie de la Passion*; *Légende de St. Augustin*, oratorio for Solo Voices, Chorus, and Orch. (1934); masses; motets; chamber music; songs; organ works, including 3 organ syms.; piano pieces.

Maler, Wilhelm, German composer and music educator; b. Heidelberg, June 21, 1902; d. Hamburg, April 29, 1976. He was a student of Kroyer (music history) and Grabner (composition) in Heidelberg, and then of Haas in Munich and Jarnach in Berlin. In 1925 he became a teacher of theory at the Cologne Rheinische Musikschule, and also was made a teacher (1928) and a prof. (1936) of composition at the Cologne Staatliche Hochschule für Musik. In 1945 he was made deputy director of the Hamburg Schule für Musik und Theater. He also helped to reorganize the Detmold Nordwestdeutsche Musik-Akademie in 1946, later serving as its director. From 1959 to 1969 he was director of the Hamburg Hochschule für Musik. From 1967 to 1971 he served as president of the Hamburg Freie Akademie der Künste. He publ. *Beitrag zur Harmonielehre* (3 vols., Leipzig, 1931; 3rd ed., 1950, with G. Bialas and J. Drissler, as *Beitrag zur durmolltonalen Harmonielehre*; 6th ed., 1967). His music was influenced principally by Reger and Busoni, with some infusions of Impressionism and folk melos.

WORKS: ORCH.: Concerto for Harpsichord and Chamber Orch. (1927); Concerto grosso (1928); *Orchesterspiel* (1930); Violin Concerto (1932); *Flämisches Rondo* (1937); *Musik* for Strings (1937); Concerto for Piano Trio and Orch. (1940). **CHAMBER:** 2 string quartets (1935, 1942); String Trio (1938); 6 piano sonatas (1935–46). **VOCAL:** *St.-George-Kantate* for Baritone, Chorus, and Orch. (1930); *Der ewige Strom*, oratorio (1934).

Malfitano, Catherine, admired American soprano; b. N.Y., April 18, 1948. She received her early training at home from her father, a violinist in the Metropolitan Opera orch., then continued her studies at the Manhattan School of Music (B.A., 1971). She made her professional debut as Nannetta in *Falstaff* at Denver's Central City Opera (1972) and then appeared with the Minnesota Opera (1972–73). On Sept. 7, 1974, she made her debut at the N.Y. City Opera as Mimi, remaining on the company's roster until 1979. She made her European debut as Susanna in *Le nozze di Figaro* at the Holland Festival (1974), and then appeared in Salzburg (1976), Vienna (1982), Paris (1984), Munich (1985), London (Covent Garden, 1988), and Geneva (1989). In 1993 she was acclaimed for her Salome in Salzburg. Malfitano made her Metropolitan Opera debut in N.Y. as Gretel on Dec. 24, 1979; she also pursued a career as a concert artist. Her other roles include Rosina, Servilia, Violetta, Julietta, Micaela, and Massenet's Manon; she also created leading roles in Susa's *Transformations* (1973), Floyd's *Bilby's Doll* (1976), Pasatieri's *Washington Square* (1976), and Bolcom's *McTeague* (1992).

Malgoire, Jean-Claude, French oboist, conductor, and musicologist; b. Avignon, Nov. 25, 1940. He studied from 1957 to 1960 at the Paris Cons., where he won 1st prizes in the categories of oboe and chamber music; in 1968 he won the International Prize of Geneva for his performances as an oboist. In 1974 he founded La Grande Écurie et La Chambre du Roy, with the avowed purpose of presenting early French music in historically authentic instrumentation; he toured with this ensemble in Europe, South America, Australia, and the U.S. He also appeared as a guest conductor, leading performances of rarely heard operas in various European music centers.

Malherbe, Edmond Paul Henri, French composer; b. Paris, Aug. 21, 1870; d. Corbeil-Essonnes, Seine-et-Oise, March 7, 1963. He studied at the Paris Cons. with Massenet and Fauré; in 1898, won the Premier Second Prix de Rome, and in 1899, the Deuxième Premier Grand Prix; won the Prix Trémont of the Académie des Beaux-Arts (1907, 1913, 1921); in 1950 he received the Grand Prix Musical of the City of Paris. He publ. *L'Harmonie du système musical actuel à demi-tons* (1920) and *Le Tiers-de-ton: Deux Systèmes: Tempéré et non-tempéré* (1900, 1950).

WORKS: DRAMATIC: OPERAS: *Madame Pierre* (1903; Paris, 1912); *L'Avare* (1907); *L'Emeute* (1911; Paris, 1912); *Cléanthis* (1912); *Anna Karénine* (1914); *Le Mariage forcé* (1924); *Néron* (1945); also *L'Amour et Psyché*, lyric tragedy with ballet (1948); *Monsieur de Pourceaugnac*, pantomime with Chorus (1930). **OTHER:** A series of "tableaux symphoniques" after great paintings; 3 syms. (1948, 1956, 1957); Violin Concerto; Nonet; Sextet; many choruses, songs, and piano pieces.

Malipiero, Gian Francesco, eminent Italian composer and teacher, uncle of **Riccardo Malipiero**; b. Venice, March 18, 1882; d. Treviso, near Venice, Aug. 1, 1973. His grandfather, Francesco Malipiero, was a composer, and his father, Luigi Malipiero, was a pianist and conductor. In 1898 Malipiero enrolled at the Vienna Cons. as a violin student; in 1899 he returned to Venice, where he studied at the Liceo Musicale Benedetto Marcello with Marco Bossi, whom he followed to Bologna in 1904, and took a diploma in composition at the Liceo Musicale G.B. Martini that same year; subsequently worked as amanuensis to Smareglia, gaining valuable experience in orchestration. He studied briefly with Bruch in Berlin (1908); later went to Paris (1913), where he absorbed the techniques of musical Impressionism, cultivating parallel chord formations and amplified tonal harmonies with characteristic added sixths, ninths, and elevenths. However, his own style of composition was determined by the polyphonic practices of the Italian Baroque. Malipiero was prof. of composition at the Parma Cons. (1921–23); afterwards lived mostly in Asolo, near Venice. He was made prof. of composition at the Liceo Musicale Benedetto Marcello in Venice (1932), continuing there when it became the Cons. (1940); was its director (1939–52). He ed. a complete edition of the works of Monteverdi (16 vols., Bologna and Vienna, 1926–42) and many works by Vivaldi, as well as works by other Italian composers. He was made a member of the National Inst. of Arts and Letters in N.Y. in 1949, the Royal Flemish Academy in Brussels in 1952, the Institut de France in 1954, and the Akademie der Künste in West Berlin in 1967.

WORKS: DRAMATIC: OPERAS: *Canossa* (1911–12; Rome, Jan. 24, 1914); *Sogno d'un tramonto d'autunno* (1913–14; concert perf., RAI, Milan, Oct. 4, 1963); *L'Orfeide*, in 3 parts: *La morte della maschere, 7 canzoni*, and *Orfeo* (1918–22; 1st complete perf., Düsseldorf, Nov. 5, 1925; *7 canzoni* [Paris, July 10, 1920] is often perf. separately); *3 commedie goldoniane: La bottega da caffe, Sior Todaro Brontolon*, and *Le baruffe chiozzotte* (1920–22; 1st complete perf., Darmstadt, March 24, 1926); *Filomela e l'Infatuato* (1924–25; Prague, March 31, 1928); *Il mistero di Venezia*, in 3 parts: *Le aquile di aquileia, Il finto Arlecchino*, and *I corvi di San Marco* (1925–28; 1st complete perf., Coburg, Dec. 15, 1932); *Merlino, Maestro d'organi* (1926–27; Rome Radio, Aug. 1, 1934); *Torneo notturno* (1929; Munich, May 15, 1931); *Il festino* (1930; Turin Radio, Nov. 6, 1937); *La favola del figlio cambiato* (1932–33; in German, Braunschweig, Jan. 13, 1934); *Giulio Cesare* (1934–35; Genoa, Feb. 8, 1936); *Antonio e Cleopatra* (1936–37; Florence, May 4, 1938); *Ecuba* (1938; Rome, Jan. 11, 1941); *La vita è sogno* (1940–41; Breslau, June 30, 1943); *I capricci di Callot* (1941–42; Rome, Oct. 24, 1942); *L'allegra brigata* (1943; Milan, May 4, 1950); *Mondi celesti e infernali* (1948–49; RAI, Turin, Jan. 12, 1950; 1st stage perf., Venice, Feb. 2, 1961); *Il Figliuol prodigo* (1952; RAI, Jan. 25, 1953; 1st stage perf., Florence May Festival, May 14, 1957); *Donna Urraca* (1953–54; Bergamo, Oct. 2, 1954); *Il capitan Spavento* (1954–55; Naples, March 16, 1963); *Venere prigioniera* (1955; Florence May Festival, May 14, 1957); *Il marescalco* (1960–68; Treviso, Oct. 22, 1969); *Rappresentazione e festa del Carnasciale e della Quaresima* (1961; concert perf., Venice, April 20, 1962; 1st stage perf., Venice, Jan. 20, 1970); *Don Giovanni* (1962; Naples, Oct. 22, 1963); *Le metamorfosi di Bonaventura* (1963–65; Venice, Sept. 4, 1966); *Don Tartufo bacchettone* (1966; Venice, Jan. 20, 1970); *Gli Eroi di Bonaventura* (1968; Milan, Feb. 7, 1969); *L'Iscariota* (1970; Siena, Aug. 28, 1971); *Uno dei dieci* (1970; Siena, Aug. 28, 1971). **BALLETS:** *Pantea* (1917–19; Venice, Sept. 6, 1932); *La mascherata delle principesse prigioniere* (1919; Brussels, Oct. 19, 1924); *Stradivario* (1947–48; Florence, June 20, 1949); *Il mondo novo* (1950–51; Rome, Dec. 16, 1951; rev. as *La lanterna magica*, 1955). **DIALOGHI:** No. 1, *con M. de Falla*, for Orch., No. 2 for 2 Pianos, No. 3, *con Jacopone da Todi*, for Voice and 2 Pianos, No. 4 for Wind Quintet, No. 5 for Viola and Orch., No. 6 for Harpsichord and Orch., No. 7 for 2 Pianos and Orch., and No. 8, *La morte di Socrate*, for Baritone and Small Orch. (all 1956–57). **OTHER WORKS FOR ORCH.:** *Sinfonia degli eroi* (1905); *Sinfonia del mare* (1906); *Sinfonie del silenzio e della morte* (1909–11); *Impressioni dal vero* in 3 parts (1910–11; 1st part, Milan, May 15, 1913; 2nd part, Rome, March 11, 1917; 3rd part, Amsterdam, Oct. 25, 1923); *Armenia*, on Armenian folk songs (1917); *Ditirambo tragico* (1917; London, Oct. 11, 1919); *Pause del silenzio* in 2 parts (1st part, 1917; Rome, Jan. 27, 1918; 2nd part, 1925–26; Philadelphia, April 1, 1927); *Per una favola cavalleresca* (1920; Rome, Feb. 13, 1921); *Oriente immaginario* for Chamber Orch. (Paris, Dec. 23, 1920); *Variazioni senza tema* for Piano and Orch. (1923; Prague, May 19, 1925); *L'esilo dell'eroe*, symphonic suite (1930); *Concerti per orchestra* (1931; Philadelphia, Jan. 29, 1932); *Inni* (1932; Rome, April 6, 1933; rev. 1934); 2 violin concertos: No. 1 (1932; Amsterdam, March 5, 1933) and No. 2 (1963; Venice, Sept. 14, 1965); *7 invenzioni* (1932; Rome, Dec. 24, 1933); *4 invenzioni* (1932; Dresden, Nov. 11, 1936); 11 numbered syms.: No. 1 (1933–34; Florence, April 2, 1934), No. 2, *Elegiaca* (1936; Seattle, Jan. 25, 1937), No. 3, *Delle campane* (1944–45; Florence, Nov. 4, 1945), No. 4, *In Memoriam* (1946; Boston, Feb. 27, 1948; in memory of Natalie Koussevitzky), No. 5, *Concertante, in eco*, for 2 Pianos and Orch. (London, Nov. 3, 1947), No. 6, *Degli archi*, for Strings (1947; Basel, Feb. 11, 1949), No. 7, *Delle canzoni* (1948; Milan, Nov. 3, 1949), No. 8, *Symphonia brevis* (1964), No. 9, *Dell'ahimè* (Warsaw, Sept. 21, 1966), No. 10, *Atropo* (1967), and No. 11, *Delle cornamuse* (1969); 6 piano concertos: No. 1 (1934; Rome, April 3, 1935), No. 2 (1937; Duisburg, March 6, 1939), No. 3 (1948; Louisville, March 8, 1949), No. 4 (1950; RAI, Turin, Jan. 28, 1951), No. 5 (1957–58), and No. 6, *Delle macchine* (1964; Rome, Feb. 5, 1966); Cello Concerto (1937; Belgrade, Jan. 31, 1939); *Concerto a 3* for Violin, Cello, Piano, and Orch. (1938; Florence, April 9, 1939); *Sinfonia in un tempo* (1950; Rome, March 21, 1951); *Sinfonia dello zodiaco* (1951; Lausanne, Jan. 23, 1952); *Passacaglie* (1952); *Fantasie di ogni giorni* (1953; Louisville, Nov. 17, 1954); *Elegy-Capriccio* (1953); *4 Fantasie concertanti* (all 1954): No. 1 for Strings, No. 2 for Violin and Orch., No. 3 for Cello and Orch., and No. 4 for Piano and Orch.; *Notturno di canti e balli* (1956–57); Concerto for 2 Pianos and Orch. (Besançon, Sept. 11, 1957); *Serenissima* for Saxophone and Orch. (1961); *Sinfonia per Antigenida* (1962); Flute Concerto (1967–68); *San Zanipolo* (1969); *Undicesima Sinfonia, delle cornamuse* (1969); *Omaggio a Belmonte* (1971). **OTHER CHAMBER:** 8 string quartets: No. 1, *Rispetti e Strombotti* (1920), No. 2, *Stornelli e Ballate* (1923), No. 3, *Cantari alla madrigalesca* (1930; also for String Orch.), No. 4 (1934), No. 5, *Dei capricci* (1940), No. 6, *L'arca di Noè* (1947), No. 7 (1949–50), and No. 8, *Per Elisabetta* (1964); *Ricercari* for 11 Instruments (Washington, D.C., Oct. 7, 1926); *Ritrovari* for 11 Instruments (1926; Gardone, Oct. 26, 1929); *Sonata a 3* for Piano Trio (1926–27); *Epodi e giambi* for Violin, Viola, Oboe, and Bassoon (1932); *Sonata a 5* for Flute, Violin, Viola, Cello, and Harp (1934); Cello Sonatina (1942); *Sonata a 4* for 4 Winds (1954); *Serenata mattutini* for 10 Instruments (1959); *Serenata* for Bassoon and 10 Instruments (1961); *Macchine* for 14 Instruments (1963); *Endecatode*, chamber sym. for 14 Instruments and Percussion (1966; Hanover, N.H., July 2, 1967). **OTHER WORKS FOR PIANO:** *6 morceaux* (1905); *Bizzarrie luminose dell' alba, del meriggio e della notte* (1908); *Poemetti lunari* (1909–10); *Preludi autunnali* (1914); *Poemi asolani* (1916); *Barlumi* (1917); *Risonanze* (1918); *Maschere che passano* (1918); *3 omaggi* (1920); *Omaggio a Claude Debussy* (1920); *Cavalcate* (1921); *La siesta* (1921); *Il tarlo* (1921–22); *Pasqua di Resurrezione* (1924); *Preludi a una fuga* (1926); *Epitaffio* (1931); *Omaggio a Bach* (1932); *Preludi, ritmi e canti gregoriani* (1937); *Preludio e fuga* (1940); *Hortus conclusus* (1946); *5 studi per domani* (1959); *Variazione sulla "Pantomima" dell'Amor brujo di Manuel de Falla* (1960); *Bianchi e neri* (1964). **OTHER VOCAL:** *San Francesco d'Assisi*, mystery for Soli, Chorus, and Orch. (1920–21; N.Y., March 29, 1922); *La Principessa Ulalia*, cantata (1924; N.Y., Feb. 19, 1927); *La cena* for Soli, Chorus, and Orch. (1927; Rochester, N.Y., April 25, 1929); *Il commiato* for Baritone and Orch. (1934); *La Passione* for Soli, Chorus, and Orch. (Rome, Dec. 15, 1935); *De Profundis* for Voice, Viola, Bass Drum, and Piano (1937); *Missa pro mortuis* for Baritone, Chorus, and Orch. (Rome, Dec. 18, 1938); *4 vecchie canzoni* for Voice and 7 Instruments (1940; Washington, D.C., April 12, 1941); *Santa Eufrosina*, mystery for Soli, Chorus, and Orch. (Rome, Dec. 6, 1942); *Universa Universis* for Men's Chorus and Chamber Orch. (1942; Liviano, April 11, 1943); *Vergilii Aeneis*, heroic sym. for 7 Soli, Chorus, and Orch. (1943–44; Turin, June 21, 1946; scenic version, Venice, Jan. 6, 1958); *Le 7 allegrezze d'amore* for Voice and 14 Instruments (1944–45; Milan, Dec. 4, 1945); *La Terra* for Chorus and Orch. (1946; Cambridge, Mass., May 2, 1947, with Organ); *I 7 peccati mortali* for Chorus and Orch. (1946; Monteceneri, Nov. 20, 1949); *Mondi celesti* for Voice and 10 Instruments (1948; Capri, Feb. 3, 1949); *La festa de la Sensa* for Baritone, Chorus, and Orch. (1949–50; Brussels Radio, July 2, 1954); *5 favole* for Voice and Small Orch. (Washington, D.C., Oct. 30, 1950); *Passer mortuus est* for Chorus (Pittsburgh, Nov. 24, 1952); *Magister Josephus* for 4 Voices and Small Orch. (1957); *Preludio e Morte di Macbeth* for Baritone and Orch. (1958); *L'asino d'oro* for

Baritone and Orch., after Apuleius (1959); *Concerto di concerti ovvero Dell'uom malcontento* for Baritone, Concertante Violin, and Orch. (1960); *Abracadabra* for Baritone and Orch. (1962); *Ave Phoebe, dum queror* for Chorus and 20 Instruments (1964); *L'Aredodese* for Reciter, Chorus, and Orch. (1967).

WRITINGS: *L'orchestra* (Bologna, 1920; Eng. tr., 1920); *Teatro* (Bologna, 1920; 2nd ed., 1927); *Oreste e Pilade, ovvero "Le sorprese dell'amicizia"* (Parma, 1922); *I profeti di Babilonia* (Milan, 1924); *Claudio Monteverdi* (Milan, 1929); *Strawinsky* (Venice, 1945; new ed., 1982); *La pietra del bando* (Venice, 1945; new ed., 1990); *Anton Francesco Doni, musico* (Venice, 1946); *Cossí va lo mondo* (Milan, 1946); *L'armonioso labirinto (da Zarlino a Padre Martini, 1558–1774)* (Milan, 1946); *Antonio Vivaldi, il prete rosso* (Milan, 1958); *Il filo d'Arianna (saggi e fantasie)* (Turin, 1966); *Ti co mi e mi co ti (soliloqui di un veneziano)* (Milan, 1966); *Così parlò Claudio Monteverdi* (Milan, 1967); *Di palo in frasca* (Milan, 1967); *Da Venezia lontan* (Milan, 1968); *Maschere della commedia dell'arte* (Bologna, 1969).

BIBL.: F. Alfano, *A. Casella, M. Castelnuovo-Tedesco et al., M. e le sue "Sette canzoni"* (Rome, 1929); special issue of *La Rassegna Musicale*, XV (1942); F. Ballo, *"I 'Capricci' di Callot" di G.F. M.* (Milan, 1942); M. Bontempelli and R. Cumar, *G.F. M.* (Milan, 1942); F. D'Amico, "G.F. M.," *Melos*, XVII (1950); G. Scarpa, ed., *L'opera di G.F. M.* (Treviso, 1952); M. Labroca, *M., musicista veneziano* (Venice, 1957; 2nd ed., 1967); special issue of *L'Approdo Musicale*, 9 (Rome and Turin, 1960); special issue of *Musica d'Oggi*, new series, IV (Milan, 1961); F. Degrada, "G.F. M. e la tradizione musicale italiana," *Quadrivium*, XIV (1973); A. Gianuario, *G.F. M. e l'arte monteverdiana* (Florence, 1973); M. Messinis, ed., *Omaggio a M.* (Florence, 1977); J. Waterhouse, *La musica G.F. M.* (Turin, 1990).

Malipiero, Riccardo, prominent Italian composer, pedagogue, administrator, and writer on music, nephew of **Gian Francesco Malipiero;** b. Milan, July 24, 1914. He received training in piano at the Milan Cons. (diploma, 1932) and in composition at the Turin Cons. (diploma, 1937) before completing his studies in composition in his uncle's master classes in Venice (1937–39). Between 1945 and 1976 he was active as a music critic for various newspapers and magazines. In 1949 he organized the first congress on dodecaphonic music in Milan. From 1969 to 1984 he served as director of the Civico Liceo Musicale in Varese. He also lectured and gave master classes abroad. He was awarded the gold medals of Milan (1977) and Varese (1984) for his services to Italian music. As a composer, Malipiero adopted 12-tone procedures in 1945 but without doctrinaire proclivities. Among his books were *G.S. Bach* (Brescia, 1948), *C. Debussy* (Brescia, 1948; 2nd ed., 1958), *Guida alla dodecafonia* (Milan, 1961), and, with G. Severi, *Musica ieri oggi* (6 vols., Rome, 1970).

WORKS: DRAMATIC: *Minnie la Candida*, opera (Parma, Nov. 19, 1942); *La Donna è mobile*, opera buffa (1954; Milan, Feb. 22, 1957); *Battono alla Porta*, television opera (Italian TV, Feb. 12, 1962; 1st stage perf., Genoa, May 24, 1963); *L'ultima Eva*, opera (1992–95). **ORCH.:** 2 piano concertos: No. 1 (1937) and No. 2 for Piano and Chamber Orch. (Fulda, Oct. 11, 1955); *3 Dances* (1937); 2 cello concertos: No. 1 (1938) and No. 2 (1957; Milan, Oct. 30, 1958); *Balleto* (1939); *Piccolo concerto* for Piano and Orch. (1945); 3 syms.: No. 1 (1949), No. 2, *Sinfonia cantata*, for Baritone and Orch. (1956; N.Y., Feb. 19, 1957), and No. 3 (1959; Miami, April 10, 1960); Violin Concerto (1952; Milan, Jan. 31, 1953); *Studi* (Venice, Sept. 11, 1953); *Ouverture-Divertimento "del Ritorno"* (Milan, Oct. 30, 1953); *Concerto breve* for Ballerina and Chamber Orch. (Venice, Sept. 11, 1956); Sonata for Oboe and Strings (1961; Naples, Jan. 4, 1962; also for Oboe and Piano, 1960); *Concerto per Dimitri* for Piano and Orch. (Venice, April 27, 1961); *Nykteghersia* (Besançon, Sept. 8, 1962); *Cadencias* (1964; Geneva Radio, Jan. 13, 1965); *Muttermusik* (1965–66; Milan, Feb. 28, 1966); *Mirages* (1966; RAI, Milan, Feb. 6, 1970); *Carnet de notes* for Chamber Orch. (1967; Milan, Feb. 4, 1968); *Cassazione II* for Strings (London, Nov. 10, 1967; also for String Sextet); *Rapsodia* for Violin and Orch. (1967; Indianapolis, Nov. 16, 1972); *Serenata per Alice Tully* for Chamber Orch. (1969; N.Y., March 10, 1970); Concerto for Violin, Cello, Piano, and Orch. (1971; RAI, Milan, Jan. 16, 1976); *Capriccio* for Chamber Orch. (1972; Milan, Feb. 12, 1975); Concerto for 2 Pianos and Orch. (1974); *Requiem 1975* (1975; Florence, Nov. 6, 1976); *Due pezzi sacri* (1976–77); *Canti* for Viola and Orch. (1978; Milan, May 17, 1982); *Divertimento* for Oboe, Bassoon, and Strings (1978; Milan, Jan. 14, 1979); *Preludio e rondo* (1979); *Composizione concertata* for English Horn, Oboe, Oboe d'Amore, and Strings (Turin, Oct. 9, 1982); *Notturno* for Cello and Chamber Orch. (1983; Milan, Jan. 29, 1984); *Racconto* (1985); *Ombre* for Chamber Orch. (1986; Milan, May 14, 1988). **CHAMBER:** *Musik I* for Cello and 9 Instruments (1938); 3 string quartets: No. 1 (1941), No. 2 (Milan, Jan. 27, 1954), and No. 3 (Florence, May 14, 1960); Violin Sonata (1956; London, May 21, 1957); Piano Quintet (1957; London, March 1, 1960); *Musica da camera* for Wind Quintet (1959; N.Y., Feb. 18, 1960); Oboe Sonata (1960; Milan, May 4, 1961; also for Oboe and String Orch., 1961); *Mosaico* for Wind and String Quintets (1961; Munich, April 21, 1964); *Nuclei* for 2 Pianos and Percussion (Venice, Sept. 7, 1966); *Cassazione* for String Sextet (1967; Siena, Sept. 2, 1968; also as *Cassazione II* for Strings); Trio for Piano, Violin, and Cello (1968; Rome, Jan. 13, 1970); *Ciaccona di Davide* for Viola and Piano (Washington, D.C., Nov. 20, 1970); *Fantasia* for Cello (1970–71); *Giber Folia* for Clarinet and Piano (1973; Milan, April 30, 1974); *Memoria* for Flute and Harpsichord (1974); *Winter Quintet* for Clarinet and String Quartet (Venice, Oct. 17, 1976); *Musica* for 4 Cellos (1979; Turin, March 24, 1980); *Diario* for Oboe and String Trio (1981); *Aprèsmirò* for 11 Instruments (1981–82; Venice, May 5, 1984); *Liebesspeil* for Flute and Guitar (1982; Milan, Feb. 16, 1983); *Diario d'Agosto* for Piano, Clarinet, and Cello (1985; Venice, March 26, 1986); *Rinelcàrlido* for Oboe and Piano (1986); *Mosaico secondo* for Violin (1987). **PIANO:** *14 Invenzioni* (1938); *Musik* for 2 Pianos (1939); *Piccola musica* (1941); *Invenzioni* (1949); *Costellazioni* (1965); *Le Rondini de Alessandro* (1971); *Diario secondo* (1985). **VOCAL:** *Antico sole* for Soprano and Orch. (1947); *Cantata sacra* for Soprano, Chorus, and Orch. (1947); *Sette variazione su "Les Roses"* for Soprano and Piano (1951); *Cantata de natale* for Soprano, Chorus, and Orch. (Milan, Dec. 21, 1959); *6 poesie di Dylan Thomas* for Soprano and 10 Instruments (Rome, June 13, 1959); *Motivi* for Voice and Piano (1959); *Preludio, Adagio e Finale* for Voice and Percussion (Buenos Aires, Aug. 1, 1963); *In Time of Daffodils* for Soprano, Baritone, and 7 Instrumentalists (Washington, D.C., Oct. 30, 1964); *Due ballate* for Voice and Guitar (1965; Milan, June 20, 1966); *Monologo* for Voice and Strings (1969; Milan, April 22, 1971); *Go Placidly . . .*, cantata for Baritone and Chamber Orch. (1974–75; N.Y., Nov. 10, 1976); *Tre frammenti* for Voice and Piano (1979; Turin, Feb. 11, 1980); *Loneliness* for Voice and Orch. (1986–87; Rome, April 8, 1989); Vocal Quintet for Soprano and String Quartet (1988; Milan, Feb. 22, 1994); *Tre sonetti* for Soprano and 10 Instruments (1989); *Meridiana* for Soprano and Chamber Orch. (1989–90; N.Y., Oct. 24, 1990); *Lieder etudes* for Soprano and Piano (1989–90; Mendrisio, Jan. 31, 1991; also for Soprano and Instrumental Ensemble, 1992); *Dalla prigione un suono* for Soprano, Baritone, Violin, Piano, Chorus, and Orch. (1992).

BIBL.: C. Sartori, *R. M.* (Milan, 1957); P. Franci et al., *Piccolo omaggio a R. M.* (Milan, 1964); C. Sartori and P. Santi, *Due tempi di R. M.* (Milan, 1964).

Maliponte (real name, **Macciaïoli), Adriana,** Italian soprano; b. Brescia, Dec. 26, 1938. She was a student of Suzanne Steppen at the Mulhouse Cons. and of Carmen Melis in Como. In 1958 she made her operatic debut as Mimi at Milan's Teatro Nuovo. In 1960 she won the Geneva Competition. After singing Micaëla at the Paris Opéra in 1962, she was chosen to create the role of Sardulla in Menotti's *Le dernier sauvage* at the Paris Opéra-Comique in 1963. In 1963 she made her U.S. debut as Leila in *Les Pêcheurs de Perles* with the Philadelphia Lyric Opera, and thereafter sang with various U.S. opera companies. In 1970 she made her first appearance at Milan's La Scala as Massenet's Manon. On March 19, 1971, she made her Metropolitan Opera debut in N.Y. as Mimi, and continued to sing there regularly in subsequent years. In 1976 she made her debut at London's Covent Garden as Nedda. Among her other roles were Gluck's Eurydice, Pamina, Luisa Miller, and Gounod's Juliet.

Maliszewski, Witold, Polish composer and pedagogue; b. Mohylev-Podolsk, July 20, 1873; d. Zalesie, July 18, 1939. He received training in piano in Warsaw and in violin in Tiflis. After obtaining a degree in medicine at the Univ. of St. Petersburg (1897), he studied composition with Rimsky-Korsakov at the St. Petersburg Cons. (1898–1902). From 1908 to 1921 he taught composition, harmony, and counterpoint and was director of the Odessa Cons. He also was conductor of the Odessa orch. Settling in Warsaw, he was director of the Chopin Music School (1925–27), head of the music dept. of the Ministry of Culture (1927–34), and a prof. at the Cons. (1931–39). In 1933 he helped to organize the Chopin Inst. His works followed in the Russian Romantic tradition until 1921 when he began to make use of Polish folk music.

WORKS: BALLETS: *Syrena* (The Mermaid; 1927); *Boruta* (1929). **ORCH.:** 5 syms., including No. 1 (1902), No. 2 (1903), No. 3 (1907), and No. 4, *Odrodzonej i odnalezionej ojczyźnie* (To the Newborn and Recovered Homeland; 1925); Suite for Cello and Orch. (1923); *Fantazja kujawska* for Piano and Orch. (1928); Piano Concerto (1931); *Bajka* (Fairytale), scherzo (1932); *Legenda o Borucie*, symphonic poem (n.d.). **CHAMBER:** Violin Sonata (1902); 3 string quartets (1903, 1905, 1914); String Quintet (1904); many piano pieces. **VOCAL:** *Great Bible Cantata* for Soloists, Chorus, and Orch. (1902); *Requiem* for Soloists, Chorus, and Orch. (1930); *Missa pontificalis Papae Pii XI* for Soloists, Chorus, Organ, and Orch. (1930); songs.

BIBL.: E. Wrocki, "W. M.: Rys życia i dzialalności artystycznej," *Śpiewak*, XI (1931).

Malkin, Jacques, Russian-American violinist and teacher, brother of **Joseph** and **Manfred Malkin**; b. Slobodka, near Odessa, Dec. 16, 1875; d. N.Y., Dec. 8, 1964. He studied in Odessa, and later enrolled at the Paris Cons. From 1893 he played the viola d'amore in the Société des Instruments Anciens in Paris. In 1918 he settled in N.Y. as a violin teacher. He also played in a trio with his brothers.

Malkin, Joseph, Russian-American cellist and pedagogue, brother of **Jacques** and **Manfred Malkin;** b. Propoisk, near Odessa, Sept. 24, 1879; d. N.Y., Sept. 1, 1969. He was trained in Odessa and at the Paris Cons. (premier prix, 1898). After touring France and Germany, he was 1st cellist in the Berlin Phil. (1902–08). On Nov. 28, 1909, he made his U.S. debut in N.Y., and then toured the country as a member of the Brussels Quartet. After playing 1st cello in the Boston Sym. Orch. (1914–19) and the Chicago Sym. Orch. (1919–22), he played with his brothers in the Malkin Trio. He was founder-director of the Malkin Cons. of Music in Boston (1933–43). From 1944 to 1949 he was a cellist in the N.Y. Phil. He publ. studies and arrangements for cello.

Malkin, Manfred, Russian-American pianist and teacher, brother of **Jacques** and **Joseph Malkin**; b. Odessa, Aug. 11, 1884; d. N.Y., Jan. 8, 1966. He studied at the Paris Cons. In 1905 he went to the U.S.; established his own music school in N.Y. (1914–31); also played in a trio with his brothers.

Malko, Nicolai (actually, **Nikolai Andreievich),** eminent Russian-born American conductor and teacher; b. Brailov, May 4, 1883; d. Sydney, Australia, June 23, 1961. He went to St. Petersburg to study philology at the Univ. (graduated, 1906), composition and orchestration with Rimsky-Korsakov, Liadov, and Glazunov, and conducting with N. Tcherepnin at the Cons. After completing his training in conducting with Mottl in Munich, he returned to St. Petersburg in 1908 to commence his conducting career. He subsequently appeared as a conductor in the major Russian music centers, and also was a prof. at the Moscow Cons. (1918–25) and the Leningrad Cons. (1925–28). From 1926 to 1928 he was chief conductor of the Leningrad Phil., with which he programmed many new works by Soviet composers. He then left Russia and was active as a guest conductor in Vienna, Prague, Buenos Aires, and Copenhagen. From 1928 to 1932 he was permanent guest conductor of the Danish State Radio Sym. Orch. in Copenhagen. He also was active as a teacher there, the King of Denmark being one of his students. In 1933 he made his London debut conducting the orch. of the Royal Phil. Soc. From 1938 he appeared as a guest conductor in the U.S. In 1946 he became a naturalized American citizen. In 1954–55 he was conductor of the Yorkshire Sym. Orch. In 1956 he became conductor of the Sydney Sym. Orch. He publ. the manual *The Conductor and His Baton* (1950; new ed., 1975, by E. Green as *The Conductor and His Score*; 2nd ed., 1985, as *The Conductor's Score*), and the memoir *A Certain Art* (1966). The Danish Radio sponsors a triennial international conducting competition in his memory. While Malko was particularly admired for his idiomatic readings of the Russian repertoire, he also acquitted himself well in the Viennese classics.

Malm, William P(aul), distinguished American ethnomusicologist; b. La Grange, Ill., March 6, 1928. He studied composition at Northwestern Univ. (B.M., 1949; M.M., 1950) and ethnomusicology at the Univ. of Calif. at Los Angeles (Ph.D., 1959, with the diss. *Japanese Nagauta Music*). He taught at the Univ. of Ill. (1950), the U.S. Naval School of Music in Washington, D.C. (1951–53), and at the Univ. of Calif. at Los Angeles (1958–60); was assistant prof. (1960–63), assoc. prof. (1963–66), and prof. (from 1966) at the Univ. of Mich. He was president of the Soc. for Ethnomusicology (1978–80). He received many honors and awards for his research on Asian studies; lectured widely in the U.S. and abroad; was a Distinguished Visiting Prof. at Baylor Univ. (1977), the Ernst Bloch Prof. of Music at the Univ. of Calif. at Berkeley (1981), a Distinguished Visiting Prof. at the Univ. of Iowa (1982), and a research fellow at the National Univ. of Australia (1987). He contributed many articles to learned journals and reference books.

WRITINGS: *Japanese Music and Musical Instruments* (Tokyo, 1959); *Nagauta: The Heart of Kabuki Music* (Tokyo, 1963); *Music Cultures of the Pacific, the Near East and Asia* (Englewood Cliffs, N.J., 1967; 2nd ed., 1977); ed., with J. Crump, *Chinese and Japanese Music Drama* (Ann Arbor, 1975); with J. Brandon and D. Shively, *Studies in Kabuki* (Honolulu, 1977); *Six Hidden Views of Japanese Music* (Berkeley, 1985); *Music as Theater* (1991).

Malotte, Albert Hay, American organist and composer; b. Philadelphia, May 19, 1895; d. Los Angeles, Nov. 16, 1964. He was a chorister at St. James Episcopal Church; studied with W.S. Stansfield, and later in Paris with Georges Jacob. He settled in Hollywood, where he became a member of the music staff of the Walt Disney Studios; composed the scores for some of Disney's "Silly Symphonies" and "Ferdinand, the Bull." He was the composer of the enormously popular setting *The Lord's Prayer* (1935); he also set to music the 23rd Psalm and other religious texts.

Malovec, Jozef, Slovak composer; b. Hurbanovo, March 24, 1933. After initial musical studies with Ján Zimmer, he studied with Alexander Moyzes at the Bratislava Academy of Music (1952–54) and with Řídký and Sommer at the Prague Academy of Music (1954–57); later he attended the summer courses in new music in Darmstadt (1965). He worked at the Czech Radio in Bratislava (1957–81), where he was active with its electroacoustic studio (1977–81). While dodecaphonic and electroacoustic explorations permeate his output, he has infused a number of his works with Slovakian folkloristic elements.

WORKS: DRAMATIC: Incidental music; film scores; music for radio plays. **ORCH.:** *Scherzo* (1956); Overture (1957); *Bagatelles* (1961); *2 Movements* for Chamber Orch. (1963); *Concertante Music* (1967); *Preludio alla valse* (1975); *Ode* for Piano and Orch. (1979); Chamber Symphony (1980); *Divertimento per* *archi* (1980); 2 syms. (1988, 1989). **CHAMBER:** Cassation for Wind Quartet (1953); *3 Bagatelles* for String Quartet (1962); *Little Chamber Music,* octet (1964; rev. 1970); *Cryptogram 1* for Bass Clarinet, Piano, and Percussion (1965); 4 suites for Harpsichord and Strings (1975–80); *Divertimento* for Wind Quintet (1976); *Canzona* for Flute and Guitar (1976); 5 string quartets (*Meditazioni notturne e coda,* 1976; 1979–80; 1985; 1986; *Symetric Music,* 1987); *Poem* for Violin, in memory of Dmitri Shostakovich (1977); *Avvenimento ricercato* for Chamber Ensemble (1978); *Melancholic Romance* for Violin and Piano (1979); *Canto di speranza* for Violin and Piano (1979); *Amoroso* for Violin and Piano (1981); *3 Inventions* for Wind Quintet (1983); *Pastorale* for Wind Trio (1984); *Epigrams* for Violin and Guitar (1984); *Little Poetical Suite* for 3 Clarinets (1985); *Balladic Impression* for Viola and Piano (1987); *Capriccio* for Violin and Viola (1987); *Yeoman Dances* for String and Other Instruments (1987–90); *Lyrical Suite* for Wind Quintet (1988); *Epitaph* for Viola and Piano (1988); *Folk Dances* for 2 Cimbaloms and Strings (1989). **KEYBOARD: PIANO:** 3 sonatinas (1954, 1956, 1977); *5 Quiet Pieces* (1980); *Poetical Meditations* (1981); *2 Lyrical Compositions,* in memory of Casella (1983); *Partita* (1986); *4 Preludes* (1987–88). **ORGAN:** *Postludio serale* (1980); *Quasi una sonata* (1983); *Prelude and Enigmatic Fantasia* (1985); *Concerto da chiesa* (1988); *Prelude and Toccata* (1988); *Introduzione e corrente* (1988); *Summer Preludes* (1990). **VOCAL:** *Songs from Kysuce* for Chorus (1977); *Prasnica,* madrigal for Women's Chorus, Percussion, and Tape (1979); *A Year with a Song,* cycle for Children's Chorus and Percussion (1982); *In These Places* for Reciter and String Quartet (1990). **ELECTROACOUSTIC:** *Orthogenesis* (1966); *Punctum alfa* (1967); *Putty* (1968); *Taboo* (1969); *Theorema* (1970); *B-A-C-H* (1975); *The Garden of Joy* (1981); *Elegiac Concerto* for Clarinet, Tape, and Digital Sound Processor (1988).

Mamangakis, Nikos, Greek composer; b. Rethymnon, Crete, March 3, 1929. He studied at the Hellikon Cons. in Athens (1947–53); then composition with Orff and Genzmer at the Hochschule für Musik in Munich (1957–61) and electronic music at the Siemens Studio in Munich (1961–64). His works reflect modern quasi-mathematical procedures, with numerical transformations determining pitch, rhythm, and form.

WORKS: *Music for 4 Protagonists* for 4 Voices and 10 Instrumentalists, after Kazantzakis (1959–60); *Constructions* for Flute and Percussion (1959–60); *Combinations* for Solo Percussionist and Orch. (1961); *Speech Symbols* for Soprano, Bass, and Orch. (1961–62); "Cycle of Numbers": No. 1, *Monologue,* for Cello (1962), No. 2, *Antagonisms,* for Cello and 1 Percussionist moving in an arc along the stage (1963), No. 3, *Trittys* (Triad), for Guitar, 2 Double Basses, Santouri, and Percussion (1966), and No. 4, *Tetraktys,* for String Quartet (1963–66); *Kassandra* for Soprano and 6 Performers (1963); *Erotokritos,* ballad for 3 Voices and 5 Instruments (1964); *Ploutos,* popular opera after Aristophanes (1966); *Theama-Akroama,* visual-auditive event (happening) for Actor, Dancer, Painter, Singer, and 8 Instruments (Athens, April 3, 1967); *Scenario* for 2 Improvised Art Critics for Voice, Instruments, and Tape (1968); *Antinomies* for Voice, Flute, Electric Double Bass, 2 Harps, 4 Cellos, 2 Percussionists, Hammond Organ, 4 Basses, and 4 Sopranos (Athens, Dec. 18, 1968); *Bolivar,* folk cantata in pop-art style (1968); *The Bacchants,* electronic ballet (1969); *Parastasis* for various Flutes, Voice, and Tape (1969); *Askesis* for Cello (1969–70); *Perilepsis* for Flute (1970); *Erophili,* popular opera (1970); *Anarchia* for Solo Percussion and Orch. (Donaueschingen, Oct. 16, 1971); *Penthima,* in memory of Jani Christou, for Guitar (1970–71); *Monologue II* for Violin and Tape (1971); *Kykeon* for several Solo Instruments (1972); *Olophyrmos* for Tape (1973); *Folk Liturgy* for Women's Voices and Chamber Ensemble (1976).

Mamiya, Michio, Japanese composer; b. Asahikawa, Hokkaido, June 29, 1929. He was a student of Ikenouchi at the Tokyo National Univ. of Fine Arts and Music. In his works, Mamiya cultivates national Japanese music in modern forms, with inventive uses of dissonant counterpoint and coloristic instrumentation.

WORKS: DRAMATIC: *Mukashi banashi hitokai Tarobê* (A Fable from Olden Times about Tarobê, the Slave Dealer), opera (1959); *Elmer's Adventure,* musical (Tokyo Radio, Aug. 28, 1967); *Narukami,* opera (1974); *Yonagahime and Mimio,* chamber opera (1990). **ORCH.:** 3 piano concertos: No. 1 (1954), No. 2 (1970), and No. 3 (1989–90; Savonlinna, July 22, 1990); Sym. (1955); 2 violin concertos: No. 1 (Tokyo, June 24, 1959) and No. 2 (1975); *2 Tableaux* (1965); *Serenade* (1974); Cello Concerto (1975); *Tableau '85* for Orch. and 8 Tenors (1985); *Antler* (1989); *Singing Birds in the Mountains* for Strings (1991). **CHAMBER:** Cello Sonata (1950); Violin Sonata (1953); Sonata for 2 Violins (1958); *Uta* for Cello and Piano (1960); *3 Movements* for Wind Quintet (1962); Quartet for Japanese Instruments (1962); 2 string quartets (1963, 1980); Sonata for Violin, Piano, Percussion, and Double Bass (1966); Sonata for Solo Cello (1966; rev. 1969); Sonata for Solo Violin (1971); Concerto for 9 Strings (1972); *4 Visions: Tomb of the Fireflies* for Chamber Ensemble (1987). **PIANO:** *3 Inventions* (1955); 3 sonatas (1955; 1973; *Spring,* 1987); *Diferencias* (1983); *3 Préludes* (1983); *Friends of the Earth* for Piano, 4-hands (1985); *Piano Trail* (1986). **VOCAL:** *Composition for Chorus* Nos. 1–13 (1958–93; many with varying instrumental accompaniment); *King of Crow,* oratorio (1959); *June 15, 1960,* oratorio (1961); *Serenade I* for Soprano, String Quartet, and Piano (1971) and *II* for Soprano, Viola, and Piano (1986); *Brahma-nada* for Narrator, Soli, 2 Pianos, Synthesizer, and Percussion (1987); *Nilch'i Ligai* for 5 Singers and 3 Percussionists (1992); cantatas; choruses; songs.

Mamlok, Ursula, German-born American composer and teacher; b. Berlin, Feb. 1, 1928. She studied piano and composition in childhood in Berlin; after her family went to Ecuador, she continued her training there and then emigrated to the U.S., settling in N.Y. in 1941. In 1945 she became a naturalized American citizen. She studied with Szell at the Mannes College of Music (1942–46) and with Giannini at the Manhattan School of Music (M.M., 1958); also took instruction from Wolpe, Sessions, Steuermann, and Shapey. She taught at N.Y. Univ. (1967–76), the Manhattan School of Music (from 1968), and Kingsborough Community College (1972–75). In 1989 she received the Walter Hinrichsen Award of the American Academy and Inst. of Arts and Letters. Her works reveal a fine craftsmanship, lyricism, and wit; in a number of her works she utilizes serial techniques.

WORKS: ORCH.: Concerto for Strings (1950); *Grasshoppers: 6 Humoresques* (1957); Oboe Concerto (1974; also for Oboe, 2 Pianos, and Percussion); Concertino for Wind Quintet, 2 Percussion, and Strings (1987); *Constellations* (1993; San Francisco, Feb. 9, 1994). **CHAMBER:** Wind Quintet (1956); Sonatina for 2 Clarinets (1957); *Variations* for Flute (1961); *Designs* for Violin and Piano (1962); String Quartet (1962); *Composition* for Cello or Viola (1962); *Concert Piece for 4* for Flute, Oboe, Percussion, and Viola (1964); *Music* for Viola and Harp (1965); *Capriccios* for Oboe and Piano (1968); *Polyphony* for Clarinet (1968); *Variations and Interludes* for Percussion Quartet (1971); Sextet for Flute, Clarinet, Bass Clarinet, Piano, Cello, and Double Bass (1978); *Festive Sounds* for Wind Quintet (1978); *When Summer Sang* for Flute, Clarinet, Piano, Violin, and Cello (1980); *Panta Rhei* for Piano, Violin, and Cello (1981); String Quintet (1981); *From My Garden* for Violin or Viola (1983); *Fantasie Variations* for Cello (1983); *Alarina* for Recorder or Flute, Clarinet, Bassoon, Violin, and Cello (1985); *3 Bagatelles* for Harpsichord (1987); *Bagatelles* for Clarinet, Violin, and Cello (1988); *Rhapsody,* trio for Clarinet, Viola, and Piano (1989); Violin Sonata (1989); *Girasol,* sextet for Flute, Clarinet, Violin, Viola, Cello, and Piano (1990); *Music for Stony Brook* for Flute, Violin, and Cello (1990); *5 Intermezzi* for Guitar (1991). **PIANO:** Various didactic pieces, including *6 Recital Pieces for Children* (1983) and *4 Recital Pieces for Young Pianists* (1983). **VOCAL:** *Daybreak* for Soprano or Mezzo-soprano and Piano (1948); *4 German Songs* for Soprano or Mezzo-soprano and Piano (1957);

Stray Birds for Soprano, Flute, and Cello (1963); *Haiku Settings* for Soprano and Flute (1967); *Der Andreas Garten* for Mezzo-soprano, Flute, Alto Flute, and Harp (N.Y., Oct. 5, 1987). **TAPE:** *Sonar Trajectory* (1966).

Mamoulian, Rouben, Russian-born director of operas, musicals, and films; b. Tiflis, Oct. 8, 1897; d. Los Angeles, Dec. 4, 1987. He showed an early interest in theater, founding a drama studio in his native city in 1918; in 1920 he toured England with the Russian Repertory Theater. Later he directed several hit plays in London during a 3-year span. In 1923 he emigrated to the U.S. to become director of operas and operettas at the George Eastman Theater in Rochester, N.Y. He was an innovator of both stage and screen, using an imaginative and bold blend of all the components of film with the new dimension of sound. He directed the noted early "talkie" *Applause* in 1929, as well as the film version of Gershwin's *Porgy and Bess* in 1935. He was the first director to use a mobile camera in a sound movie, and among the first to use a multiple-channel sound track. He directed the film of the Rodgers and Hammerstein musical *Oklahoma!* (1955), which was the first musical to utilize songs and dance as an integral part of the dramatic flow of the plot.

Mana-Zucca (real name, **Gizella Augusta Zuckermann**), American composer, pianist, and singer; b. N.Y., Dec. 25, 1887; d. Miami Beach, March 8, 1981. She began playing piano as a child and took the name Mana-Zucca as a teenager. In 1902 she played in one of Frank Damrosch's young people's concerts at N.Y.'s Carnegie Hall. After training from Alexander Lambert, she toured as a pianist in Europe from about 1907. She also made some appearances as a singer, attracting notice in Lehár's *Der Graf von Luxemburg* in London in 1919. From 1921 she was active mainly in Florida, where she devoted herself fully to composition. She became best known as a composer of lyrically soaring songs, the most famous being *I Love Life* (1923).

WORKS: *Hypatia,* opera (c.1920); *The Queue of Ki-Lu,* opera (c.1920); *The Wedding of the Butterflies,* ballet; Piano Concerto (N.Y., Aug. 20, 1919); Violin Concerto (N.Y., Dec. 9, 1955); chamber music; choral pieces; over 170 songs; didactic pieces.

Mandac, Evelyn (Lorenzana), Filipino soprano; b. Malaybalay, Mindanao, Aug. 16, 1945. After training at the Univ. of the Philippines (B.A., 1963), she pursued her studies at the Oberlin (Ohio) College Cons. of Music and then at the Juilliard School of Music in N.Y. (M.A., 1967). In 1968 she made her formal debut in Orff's *Carmina burana* in Mobile, Ala. Her operatic debut followed as Mimi in Washington, D.C., in 1969. On Dec. 19, 1975, she made her Metropolitan Opera debut in N.Y. as Lauretta in *Gianni Schicchi,* and remained with the company until 1978. She also sang opera in San Francisco, Glyndebourne, Rome, Houston, Geneva, and other cities, and she also toured as a concert artist. Among her roles were Despina, Zerlina, Susanna, Pamina, Juliet, and Mélisande. She also created roles in Pasatieri's *Black Widow* (1972) and *Inez de Castro* (1976).

Mandel, Alan (Roger), gifted American pianist and teacher; b. N.Y., July 17, 1935. He began taking piano lessons with Hedy Spielter at the incredible underage of 3 1/2 , and continued under her pianistic care until he was 17. In 1953 he entered the class of Rosina Lhévinne at the Juilliard School of Music in N.Y. (B.S., 1956; M.S., 1957); later took private lessons with Leonard Shure (1957–60). In 1961 he obtained a Fulbright fellowship; went to Salzburg, where he studied advanced composition with Henze (diplomas in composition and piano, 1962); completed his training at the Accademia Monteverdi in Bolzano (diploma, 1963). He made his debut at N.Y.'s Town Hall in 1948. In later years, he acquired distinction as a pianist willing to explore the lesser-known areas of the repertoire, from early American music to contemporary scores. He taught piano at Pa. State Univ. (1963–66); then was head of the piano dept. at the American Univ. in Washington, D.C. (from 1966); also founded the Washington (D.C.) Music Ensemble (1980) with the aim of presenting modern music of different nations. As a pianist, he made numerous tours all over the globe. One of Mandel's chief accomplishments was the recording of the complete piano works of Charles Ives. He composed a Piano Concerto (1950); Sym. (1961); piano pieces; songs.

Mandelbaum, (Mayer) Joel, American composer; b. N.Y., Oct. 12, 1932. He studied with Piston at Harvard Univ. (B.A., 1953), with Fine and Shapero at Brandeis Univ. (M.F.A., 1955), and at Indiana Univ. (Ph.D., 1961, with the diss. *Multiple Division of the Octave and the Tonal Resources of 19-tone Temperament*); also studied with Dallapiccola at the Berkshire Music Center at Tanglewood and with Blacher at the Berlin Hochschule für Musik. He held a Fulbright fellowship (1957) and was a fellow at the MacDowell Colony (1968). He taught at Queens College of the City Univ. of N.Y. (from 1961), where he served as director of its Aaron Copland School of Music. Many of his compositions reflect his study of microtonal music and the utilization of the Scalatron, an instrument with a color-coordinated keyboard that can be rearranged into divisions of the octave up to and including 31 tones.

WORKS: DRAMATIC: OPERAS: *The Man in the Man-made Moon* (1955); *The 4 Chaplains* (1956); *The Dybbuk* (1971; rev. 1978); light operas; musicals; incidental music; film scores. **ORCH.:** *Convocation Overture* (1951); Piano Concerto (1953); *Sursum corda* (1960); *Sinfonia Concertante* for Oboe, Horn, Violin, Cello, and Small Orch. (1962); *Memorial* for Strings (1965); Trumpet Concerto (1970). **CHAMBER:** *Moderato* for Cello and Piano (1949); Flute Sonata (1950); Wind Quintet (1957); 2 string quartets (1959, 1979); *Xenophony No. 1* for 3 Horns and Trombone (1966) and *No. 2* for Violin, Cello, Double Bass, Wind Quintet, and Organ (1979); *Romance* for String Trio (1973); *Fanfare* for Brass (1974); 3 Tonal Studies for Large Chamber Ensemble (1979); Oboe Sonata (1981); Clarinet Sonata (1983). **KEYBOARD:** Piano Sonata (1958); 9 Preludes in 19-tone temperament for 2 Specially Tuned Pianos (1961); 10 Studies for Fokker Organ based on the Conora Suler (1964); *Moderato* for 2 Pianos (1965); *Allegro agitato* for 2 Pianos (1979); 4 Miniatures in 31-tone temperament for Architone or Scalatron (1979). **VOCAL:** Mass for Men's Voices and Organ (1954); choruses; songs.

Manén, Juan, Catalan violinist and composer; b. Barcelona, March 14, 1883; d. there, June 26, 1971. He received training in solfège and piano at a very early age from his father. At 5, he began to study violin and, at 7, made his public debut as a violinist. At 9, he made his first appearances in America. Following studies with Ibarguren, he made tours of Europe from 1898. He spent some years in Germany, where his orch. compositions were influenced by Wagner and Strauss. After returning to his homeland, he devoted himself principally to composition. Much of his music was redolent of Catalan melorhythms. His writings, all publ. in Barcelona, included *Mis experiencias* (1944), *Variaciones sin tema* (1955), *El violin* (1958), *El jóven artista* (1964), and *Diccionario de celebridades musicales* (1974).

WORKS: DRAMATIC: *Juana de Nápoles,* opera (Barcelona, Jan. 1903); *Acté,* opera (Barcelona, Dec. 3, 1903; rewritten as *Neró i Akté,* Karlsruhe, Jan. 28, 1928); *Der Fackeltanz,* opera (Frankfurt am Main, 1909); *Heros,* opera (n.d.); *Camino del sol,* theater sym. (Leipzig, 1913); *Don Juan,* tragic comedy (n.d.); *Soledad,* opera (n.d.); *Triana,* ballet (1952). **OTHER:** Many orch. works, including pieces for violin and strings; chamber music; violin pieces; guitar music.

Mann, Alfred, German-born American musicologist and choral conductor; b. Hamburg, April 28, 1917. He was a pupil of Kurt Thomas, Hans Mahlke, and Max Seiffert at the Berlin Hochschule für Musik (certificate, 1937); after teaching at the Berlin Hochschule für Kirchen- und Schulmusik (1937–38), he continued his training at the Milan Cons. (1938); taught at the Scuola Musicale di Milano (1938–39). In 1939 he emigrated to the U.S., and became a naturalized citizen in 1943; studied at the Curtis Inst. of Music in Philadelphia (diploma, 1942), where he also taught (1939–42); completed his education with Paul

Henry Lang, William J. Mitchell, and Erich Hertzmann at Columbia Univ. (M.A., 1950; Ph.D., 1955, with the diss. *The Theory of Fugue*). He was on the faculty of Rutgers Univ. from 1947 to 1980; in 1978 he was a visiting prof. at Columbia Univ.; was on the faculty of the Eastman School of Music in Rochester, N.Y. (1980–87). From 1952 to 1959 he was conductor of the Cantata Singers in N.Y. and later of the Bach Choir in Bethlehem, Pa. (1970–80). He ed. works for the critical editions of Mozart, Fux, Handel, and Schubert; was ed. of the Rutgers Documents of Music series (1951–88) and the *American Choral Review* (from 1962); contributed many articles to scholarly journals.

WRITINGS: Ed. J. Fux's *Gradus ad Parnassum (Die Lehre vom Kontrapunkt*, Celle, 1938; 2nd ed., 1951; partial Eng. tr., N.Y., 1943, as *Steps to Parnassus*; 2nd ed., N.Y. and Toronto, 1965, as *The Study of Counterpoint*); *The Study of Fugue* (New Brunswick, N.J., 1958; 3rd ed., 1987); *Bethlehem Bach Studies* (N.Y., 1985); *Theory and Practice: The Great Composer as Student and Teacher* (N.Y. and London, 1987); ed. *Modern Music Librarianship* (Stuyvesant, N.Y., and Kassel, 1988); *Handel: The Orchestral Music* (N.Y., 1995).

BIBL.: M. Parker, ed., *Eighteenth-Century Music in Theory and Practice: Essays in Honor of A. M.* (Stuyvesant, N.Y., 1993).

Mann, Leslie (Douglas), Canadian composer and clarinetist; b. Edmonton, Alberta, Aug. 13, 1923; d. Balmoral, Manitoba, Dec. 7, 1977. He began to study clarinet at 13 and composition at 15. He was 1st clarinetist of the CBC Winnipeg Orch. (1958) and of the Winnipeg Sym. Orch. (1960–71). His music followed along traditional lines in an accessible manner.

WORKS: CHAMBER OPERA: *The Donkey's Tale* (1971). **ORCH.:** *Concertino in the Old Style* for Strings (1955); Flute Concerto (1964); Clarinet Concerto (1970); *Sinfonia concertante* for Bassoon and Chamber Orch. (1971); *Concerto grosso No. 1* for Chamber Orch. (1972); *Meditations on a Chorale* for Strings (1972); 3 syms. (1973; 1974; *Typhoon*, 1976). **CHAMBER:** *5 Bagatelles* for Clarinet or Viola and Piano (1951); Trio for Flute, Clarinet, and Cello (1952); Cello Sonata (1953); *5 Improvisations* for Flute and Piano (1954); *Toccata alla Barocco* for Flute, Clarinet, and Cello (1956); Wind Quintet (1961); Clarinet Sonata (1962); Suite for Clarinet (1963); *Suite* for Flute (1963); Trio for Clarinet, Cello, and Piano (1967); *4 Studies in the Blues Idiom* for Wind Quintet (1969); *Music* for Clarinet, Viola, and Piano (1971); *Partita* for Violin and Bassoon (1972); Sonata for Solo Violin (1974); *Vocalise* for Oboe or Clarinet and Piano (1974); String Quartet (1975); Suite for Saxophone (1976); Flute Sonata (1977). **VOCAL:** *My Master Have a Garden*, cantata for Soprano and Orch. (1963); *Weep You No More Sad Fountains* for Voice and Chamber Orch., after Elizabethan poems (1974).

Mann, Robert (Nathaniel), American violinist, conductor, teacher, and composer; b. Portland, Oreg., July 19, 1920. He studied violin with Déthier at the Juilliard Graduate School in N.Y., and had instruction in chamber music with Betti, Salmond, and Letz; also took courses with Schenkman in conducting, and Wagenaar and Wolpe in composition. In 1941 he won the Naumburg Competition, and made his N.Y. debut as a violinist. From 1943 to 1946 he was in the U.S. Army; then joined the faculty of the Juilliard School and in 1948 founded the Juilliard String Quartet, in which he played 1st violin, and which was to become one of the most highly regarded chamber music groups; in 1962 it was established as the quartet-in-residence under the Whittall Foundation at the Library of Congress in Washington, D.C., without suspending its concert tours in America and abroad. As a conductor, Mann specialized in contemporary music; was associated as a performer and lecturer with the Music Festival and Inst. at Aspen, Colo., and also served with the NEA; in 1971 he was appointed president of the Walter W. Naumburg Foundation. He has composed a String Quartet (1952); Suite for String Orch. (1965); several "lyric trios" for Violin, Piano, and Narrator.

Mann, William (Somervell), English music critic, writer on music, and translator; b. Madras, Feb. 14, 1924; d. Bath, Sept. 5, 1989. He studied piano with Kabos and composition with Seiber; also studied at Magdalene College, Cambridge (1946–48), with Patrick Hadley, Hubert Middleton, and Robin Orr. He was on the music staff of the *Times* of London (1948–60); was its chief music critic (1960–82). He made many serviceable Eng. trs. of opera librettos and lieder texts. He publ. *Introduction to the Music of Johann Sebastian Bach* (London, 1950), *Richard Strauss: A Critical Study of the Operas* (London, 1964), and *The Operas of Mozart* (London, 1977).

Manneke, Daan, Dutch composer; b. Kruiningen, Nov. 7, 1939. He was a student of Houet and Toebosch (organ) and of Van Dijk (composition) at the Brabant Cons. (1960–66), and then of D'Hooghe (organ) and de Leeuw (composition) in Amsterdam (1967–73). From 1958 to 1969 he was organist at St. Gertrudes in Bergen op Zoom, and then taught at the Amsterdan Cons. (from 1972).

WORKS: OPERAS: *De passie van Johannes Mattheus Lanckohr* (1977); *Jules*, chamber opera (1988). **ORCH.:** *4 Sonatas* (1972); *Sine nome* for 3 Instrumental Groups (1972); *Motet* for Orch. of Renaissance Instruments (1975); 2 sinfonias (1975, 1982); *En passant* for Small Orch. (1977); *Ruimten* for Strings (1978); *Babel* for 6 Orchs. (1985); *Organum II* (1986; also for Organ as *Organum*); *Archipel V: Les ponts* for Wind Orch. (1990–92). **CHAMBER:** *Chiasma* for Piano Quartet (1970); *Walking in Fog Patches* for Wind Quintet (1971); *Jeux* for Flute (1971); *Plein jeu* for Brass Quintet (1972); *Stages III* for Variable Ensemble (1972); *Diaphony for Geoffrey* for Horn, Trumpet, Trombone, and Piano (1973); *Ordre* for 4 Recorders (1976); *Clair obscur* for Recorder and Organ (1978; also for Piano and Harpsichord); *Vice versa* for 5 Instruments (1979); *Ramificazioni* for Piano Trio (1979); *Wie ein Hauch . . . (eine kleine Nachtmusik)* for Flute (1979); *Gesti* for Clarinet (1979; also for Bass Tuba or Bass Trombone); *Rondeau* for Percussion (1979); *Gestures* for Bass Clarinet and Marimba (1981); *Archipel II* for Viola, Cello, and Double Bass (1985) and *III* for Guitar (1987); *Arc* for String Quartet (1994). **ORGAN:** *Diaspora* (1969); *Pneoo* (1979); *Organum* (1986; also for Orch. as *Organum II*). **VOCAL:** *Qui iustus est, iustificetur adhuc*, cantata for Chorus, Clarinet, Trombone, Electric Guitar, and Percussion (1970); *3 Times* for Chorus and Orch. (1975); *Job* for Baritone/Reciter, Men's Chorus, 4 Brasses, and 3 Percussionists (1976); *Chants and Madrigals* for Chorus (1980); *Trans* for Chorus and 8 Instruments (1982); *Messe de Notre Dame* for Chorus (1986); *Plenum* for Chorus and Orch. (1989); songs.

Mannes, Leopold (Damrosch), American pianist, teacher, composer, and inventor; b. N.Y., Dec. 26, 1899; d. Martha's Vineyard, Mass., Aug. 11, 1964. He was the son of David and Clara (née Damrosch) Mannes. He studied at Harvard Univ. (B.A., 1920) and took courses at the Mannes School of Music and the Inst. of Musical Arts in N.Y.; among his teachers were Quaile, Maier, Berthe Bert, and Cortot in piano, and Johannes Schreyer, Goetschius, and Scalero in composition. He won a Pulitzer scholarship (1925) and a Guggenheim fellowship (1927). In 1922 he made his debut in N.Y. as a pianist; taught theory and composition at the Mannes School (1927–31), then worked for the Eastman Kodak Co. in Rochester, N.Y., where he invented the Kodachrome process of color photography with Loepold Godowsky, son of the pianist, in 1935. He subsequently was director (1940–48) and a teacher of theory and composition (1946–48) at the Mannes School; was its co-director (1948–52) and president (1950–64); was also active with his own Mannes Trio (1948–55). He wrote *3 Short Pieces* for Orch. (1926); incidental music to Shakespeare's *Tempest* (1930); String Quartet (1928); Suite for 2 Pianos (1924); songs.

Manning, Jane (Marian), English soprano; b. Norwich, Sept. 20, 1938. She was a student of Greene at the Royal Academy of Music in London (1956–60), of Husler at the Scuola di Canto in Cureglia, Switzerland, and of Frederick Jackson and Yvonne Rodd- Marling in London. In 1964 she made her debut in London singing songs of Webern, Messiaen, and Dallapiccola, and subsequently established herself as a leading proponent of modern music. From 1965 she sang regularly on the BBC, and also toured extensively around the globe. In all, she sang in more than 300 premieres of contemporary scores. In 1988 she founded her own Jane's Minstrels in London, an ensemble devoted to the furtherance of contemporary music. She was active as a lecturer, serving as a visiting prof. at Mills College in Oakland, California (1982–86) and as a lecturer at the Univ. of York (1987). She publ. the book *New Vocal Repertory: An Introduction* (Oxford, 1994). In 1990 she was made a member of the Order of the British Empire. In 1966 she married **Anthony Payne.**

Manning, Kathleen Lockhart, American composer and singer; b. Hollywood, Oct. 24, 1890; d. Los Angeles, March 20, 1951. She was a student of Moszkowski in Paris (1908). She sang in France and England, including an engagement with the Hammerstein Opera Co. in London (1911–12), and later in the U.S. (1926), but she devoted herself principally to composition. Her output reflected her interest in oriental subjects à la the French impressionists.

WORKS: DRAMATIC: *Operetta in Mozartian Style* (n.d.); *Mr. Wu,* opera (1925–26); *For the Soul of Rafael,* opera (n.d.). **ORCH.:** 4 symphonic poems; Piano Concerto. **CHAMBER:** String Quartet; many piano pieces. **SONGS:** *Water Lily* (1923); *Japanese Ghost Songs* (1924); *Sketches of Paris* (1925); *Sketches of London* (1929); *Chinese Impressions* (1931); *5 Fragments* (1931); *Vignettes* (1933); *Sketches of N.Y.* (1936).

Mannino, Franco, Italian conductor, pianist, composer, novelist, and playwright; b. Palermo, April 25, 1924. He was a student of Silvestri (piano) and Mortari (composition) at the Accademia di Santa Cecilia in Rome. At 16, he made his debut as a pianist. After the end of World War II, he toured as a pianist in Europe and the U.S. He also took up conducting and appeared as a guest conductor throughout Europe, North and South America, and the Far East. In 1968 he founded the Incontri Musicale Romani. From 1969 to 1971 he served as artistic director of the Teatro San Carlo in Naples, where he subsequently was its artistic advisor. He was principal conductor and artistic advisor of the National Arts Centre Orch. in Ottawa from 1982 to 1986, and then was its principal guest conductor from 1986 to 1989. In 1990–91 he was president of the Accademia Filarmonica of Bologna. The Italian Republic gave him its gold medal in 1968 and honored him as Commendatore ordine al merito in 1993. In his compositions, Mannino has generally followed traditional modes of expression with occasional excursions into modernistic practices. In addition to his prolific compositions, he has also written novels, plays, essays, and articles.

WORKS: DRAMATIC: *Mario e il Mago,* azione coreografia (1952; Milan, Feb. 25, 1956); *Vivi,* lyric drama (1955; Naples, March 28, 1957); *La speranza,* melodrama (1956; Trieste, Feb. 14, 1970); *La stirpe di Davide,* tragedy (1958; Rome, April 19, 1962); *La notti della paura,* melodrama (1960; RAI, Rome, May 24, 1963); *Il diavolo in giardino,* comedy (1962; Palermo, Feb. 28, 1963); *Luisella,* drama (1963; Palermo, Feb. 28, 1969); *Il quadro delle meraviglie,* intermezzo-ballet (Rome, April 24, 1963); *Il ritratto di Dorian Gray,* drama (1973; Catania, Jan. 12, 1982); *Roma Pagana,* ballet (1978); *Il Principe Felice,* theater piece (1981; Milan, July 7, 1987); *Soltanto il rogo,* drama (1986; Agrigento, Oct. 21, 1987); *Le notte Bianche,* Liederopera (1987; Rome, April 14, 1989); *Le teste Scambiate,* legend (1988); *Anno domini 3000,* opera buffa (1993); film scores. **ORCH.:** *Concertino lirico* for Cello, Strings, and Piano (1938); *Tre tempi* (1951); 2 piano concertos (1954, 1974); 12 syms.: No. 1, *Sinfonia Americana* (1954; Florence, Nov. 11, 1956), No. 2 (1972), No. 3 (1978), No. 4, *Leningrad* (1981), No. 5, *Rideau Lake* (1984; Ottawa, Feb. 12, 1986), No. 6 (1986), No. 7 (1989), No. 8, *Degli Oceani* (1990), No. 9 (Rome, June 27, 1991), No. 10, *Da Colomba a Broadway,* for Baritone, Trombone, Chorus, and Orch. (1991), No. 11 for Baritone and Orch. (1993; Sanremo, Oct. 1994), and No. 12, *Panormus* (1994); *Demoniaca Ouverture* (1963); *Mottetti strumentali* (1964; Rome, June 1, 1965); *Music for Angels* for Piano and Strings (1964; RAI, Naples, Feb. 14, 1966); Concerto for 3 Violins and Orch. (1965); *Suite galante* for Flute, Trombone Obbligato, and Small Orch. (1966); *Otto commenti* (1966); *Laocoonte* (1966; RAI, Turin, April 4, 1969); *Capriccio di capricci* (1967); Concerto for Piano, 3 Violins, and Orch. (1969); *Notturno Napoletano* (1969); Concerto grosso (1970); 2 violin concertos (1970, 1993); 4 cello concertos (1974–90); *Enigma* for Strings (1975; Ottawa, April 1993); *Cinque romanze* for Viola and Orch. (1975); *Sons enchantes* for Flute, Alpine Horn, and Strings (1976); *Molto vibrato* for Violin and Orch. (1978); *Settecento* (1979); *Olympic Concert* for 6 Violins, 2 Pianos, and Orch. (1979); *Nirvana* (1980); Concerto for 6 Violins, 2 Pianos, and Orch. (1980); *Tropical Dances* for Cello Ensemble (1984; RAI, Rome, Nov. 3, 1986; also for Orch., Rome, April 10, 1987); *Piccolo concerto grosso* for Flute, Oboe, and Strings (Rome, Nov. 6, 1985); *Introduzione e aba* for Organ and Orch. (1987); *Atmosfere delle notti Bianche di Pietroburgo* for Trombone and Orch. (1987); *Inquietudini* for Clarinet and Orch. (1987); *6 Romanze senza parole* for Piano, Violin, Viola, Cello, and Orch. (1988); Concerto for Horn and Strings (1990); Concerto for Trombone and Strings (1990); *Suite Italiana* for Clarinet and Strings (1991); *Evanescenze* for Harp and Orch. (1992; Palermo, Dec. 1994; also for Harp and Piano); *La grotta della maga Circe,* overture (1995). **CHAMBER:** *Melodica e contrappunti* for Flute and Bamboo Pipes (1959); *Variazione capricciose* for 3 Violins (1966); *Piccolo sonata* for Viola and Piano (1966); *Melange capriccioso* for 3 Violins (1966); *Sonata breve* for Guitar (1967); *Cinque duetti* for 2 Violins (1967); *Improvvisazione* for Violin, Horn, and Piano (1969); 3 cello sonatas (1970, 1971, 1986); Sonata for Solo Viola (1970); *Ballata dramatica* for Violin, Viola, Cello, and Piano (1970); String Trio (1974); *Quattro cantabili, un intermezzo e un rondo* for Violin and Piano (1976); 3 Pieces for Viola (1983); *Suoni astrali* for 8 Violas (1985); 7 Pieces for Violin (1985); Suite for Wind Quintet (1986); 2 string quartets (1989, 1994); *Love* for Clarinet and Piano (1990); *Quindici pezzi per l'Adelchi* for Cello (1992); Trio for Violin, Cello, and Piano (1992); Violin Sonata (1994); Quintet for Clarinet and Strings (1995). **PIANO:** 5 sonatas (1950, 1971, 1975, 1979, 1980); many other pieces. **OTHER:** Choral works; song cycles; solo songs; transcriptions; cadenzas for concertos by Haydn and Mozart.

Manojlović, Kosta, Serbian composer; b. Krnjevo, Dec. 3, 1890; d. Belgrade, Oct. 2, 1949. He studied in Munich and at the Univ. of Oxford (B.A., 1919). He wrote a Serbian liturgy, and a cantata, *By the Waters of Babylon*; characteristic piano pieces; and songs. He publ. several studies on Serbian folk music; his collection of 337 songs of east Serbia was publ. posthumously (Belgrade, 1953).

Manowarda, Josef von, esteemed Austrian bass; b. Kraków, July 3, 1890; d. Berlin, Dec. 24, 1942. He studied in Graz, making his debut there (1911); sang at the Vienna Volksoper (1915–18) and in Wiesbaden (1918–19); then was a principal member of the Vienna State Opera (1919–42); also appeared at the Salzburg Festivals (from 1922), the Bayreuth Festivals (1931, 1934, 1939, 1942), and the Berlin State Opera (1934–42); in addition, he taught at the Vienna Academy of Music (1932–35). Among his notable roles were Osmin, King Marke, Gurnemanz, and King Philip; created the role of the Messenger in Strauss's *Die Frau ohne Schatten* (1919). He also pursued a fine concert career.

Manschinger, Kurt, Austrian conductor and composer; b. Zeil-Wieselburg, July 25, 1902; d. N.Y., Feb. 23, 1968. He studied musicology at the Univ. of Vienna, and at the same time took private lessons with Webern (1919–26). After graduation, he was mainly active as a theatrical conductor in Austria and Germany. His practical acquaintance with operatic production led to his decision to write operas, for which his wife, the singer Greta Hartwig, wrote librettos. Of these his first opera, *Madame Dorette,* was to be performed by the Vienna State Opera, but the Anschluss in 1938 made this impossible. He and his wife fled to London, where they organized an émigré theater, The Lantern. In 1940 they emigrated to America; Manschinger changed his name to Ashley Vernon and continued to compose; earned his living as a musical autographer by producing calligraphic copies of music scores for publishers.

WORKS: OPERAS: *The Barber of New York* (N.Y., May 26, 1953); *Grand Slam* (Stamford, Conn., June 25, 1955); *Cupid and Psyche* (Woodstock, N.Y., July 27, 1956); *The Triumph of Punch* (N.Y., Jan. 25, 1969). **OTHER:** *Der Talisman* for Voices, Violin, Viola, Cello, and Piano (London, Feb. 24, 1940); Sinfonietta (1964); Sym. (1967); chamber music.

Manski, Dorothée, German-American soprano and teacher; b. Berlin, March 11, 1891; d. Atlanta, Feb. 24, 1967. She studied in Berlin, where she made her debut at the Komische Oper (1911); then sang in Mannheim (1914–20) and Stuttgart (1920–24). She was a member of the Berlin State Opera (1924–27); also sang in Max Reinhardt's productions; then appeared as Isolde at the Salzburg Festival (1933) and the Vienna State Opera (1934). She made her Metropolitan Opera debut in N.Y. as the Witch in *Hänsel und Gretel* on Nov. 5, 1927, and remained on the company's roster until 1941; also sang opera in Philadelphia, Chicago, and San Francisco, and appeared as a concert singer with leading European and U.S. orchs. She was prof. of voice at the Indiana Univ. School of Music in Bloomington (1941–65). Among her other roles were Sieglinde, Venus, Gutrune, Brünnhilde, Freia, and Elsa.

Mansurian, Tigran, prominent Armenian composer and teacher; b. Beirut, Lebanon, Jan. 27, 1939. His family moved to Soviet Armenia in 1947, where he studied with Baghdasaryan at the Yerevan Music School (1956–60) and with Sarian at the Yerevan Cons. (1960–65). After completing his postgraduate studies at the Cons. (1965–67), he taught modern theory there until being made a teacher of composition in 1986. Mansurian's music owes much to his Armenian heritage. While his early works reflect the influence of the serialists, he pursued an independent road in which Armenian and contemporary elements were effectively synthesized. In his later works, Armenian elements flourished as he infused his creative efforts with modal harmonies and folk-like melodies.

WORKS: DRAMATIC: *The Ice Queen*, ballet (1988); incidental music; film scores. **ORCH.:** Concerto for Organ and Chamber Orch. (1964); *Partita* (1965); *Preludes* (1975); 3 cello concertos: No. 1 (1976), No. 2 (1978), and No. 3 for Cello and 13 Winds (1983); *Canonical Ode* for 2 String Orchs., 4 Harps, and Organ (1977); Double Concerto for Violin, Cello, and Strings (1977); *Nachtmusik* (1980); Concerto for Violin and Strings (1981). **CHAMBER:** 2 unnumbered string quartets (1960, 1964); 2 numbered string quartets (1984, 1984); Viola Sonata (1962); Flute Sonata (1963); 2 violin sonatas (1964, 1965); *Allegro barbaro* for Cello (1964); Piano Trio (1965); *Psalm* for 2 Flutes and Violin (1966); *Music* for 12 Strings (1966); *Arabesques I* for 6 Winds and Harp (1969) and *II* for 10 Instruments (1970); *Elegy* for Cello and Piano (1971); *Interior* for String Quartet (1972); *Bird's Silhouette*, suite for Harpsichord and Percussion (1973); 2 cello sonatas (1973, 1974); Quintet for Flute, Oboe, Clarinet, Bassoon, and Horn (1974); *The Rhetorician* for Harpsichord, Flute, Violin, and Double Bass (1978); *Tovem* for 15 Instrumentalists (1979); *Commemorating Stravinsky* for 15 Instruments (1981); *4 Duets* for Violin Ensemble (1983); *Capriccio* for Cello (1984); *5 Bagatelles* for Violin, Cello, and Piano (1985); *Le Tombeau* for Cello and Percussion (1989); *Postlude* for Clarinet and Cello (1991–92). **PIANO:** Sonatina (1963); Sonata (1967); *3 Pieces* (1971); *Nostalgia* (1976). **VOCAL:** *3 Nairain Songs* for Baritone and Orch. (1975); *3 Madrigals* for Voice, Flute, Cello, and Piano (1981); *Miserere* for Voice and String Orch. (1989); choruses; other songs.

Manuel, Roland. See **Roland-Manuel.**

Manziarly, Marcelle de, Russian-born French conductor, pianist, and composer; b. Kharkov, Sept. 13, 1899; d. Ojai, Calif., May 12, 1989. She studied in Paris with Boulanger, in Basel with Weingartner (1930–31), and in N.Y. with Vengerova (1943). She appeared as a pianist and conductor in the U.S. and taught privately in Paris and N.Y. Her works extend the boundaries of tonality through such resources and procedures as polytonality, serialism, and atonality.

WORKS: OPERA: *La Femme en flèche* (1954). **ORCH.:** Piano Concerto (1932); *Sonate pour Notre-Dame de Paris* (1944–45); *Musique pour orchestre* for Small Orch. (1950); *Incidences* for Piano and Orch. (1964). **CHAMBER:** String Quartet (1943); Trio for Flute, Cello, and Piano (1952); *Trilogue* for Flute, Viola da Gamba, and Harpsichord (1957); *Dialogue* for Cello and Piano (1970); *Périple* for Oboe and Piano (1972). **PIANO:** *Mouvement* (1935); *Arabesque* (1937); *Toccata* (1939); *Bagatelle* (1940); Sonata for 2 Pianos (1946); *6 études* (1949); *Stances* (1967). **VOCAL:** *3 fables de La Fontaine* (1935); *Choeurs pour enfants* (1938); *Poèmes en trio* for 3 Women's Voices and Piano (1940); Duos for 2 Sopranos or 2 Tenors and Piano (1952); Duos for Soprano and Clarinet (1953); 3 chants for Soprano and Piano (1954); *2 odes de Grégoire de Marek* for Alto and Piano (1955); *3 sonnets de Petrarque* for Baritone and Piano (1958); *Le Cygne et le cuisinier* for 4 Solo Voices and Piano (1959).

Manzoni, Giacomo, Italian composer, teacher, and writer on music; b. Milan, Sept. 26, 1932. He studied composition with Contilli at the Messina Liceo Musicale (1948–50); then pursued training at the Milan Cons., where he received diplomas in piano (1954) and composition (1956); also obtained a degree in foreign languages and literature at the Bocconi Univ. in Milan (1955). He was ed. of *Il Diapason* (1956), music critic of the newspaper *L'Unità* (1958–66), and music ed. of the review *Prisma* (1968); later was on the editorial staff of the review *Musica/Realtà.* He taught harmony and counterpoint at the Milan Cons. (1962–64; 1968–69; 1974–91) and composition at the Bologna Cons. (1965–68; 1969–74); also taught at the Scuola di musica in Fiesole (from 1988). In 1982 he was a guest of the Deutscher Akademischer Austauschdienst in Berlin. He contributed articles to Italian and other journals and publications; tr. works of Schoenberg and Adorno into Italian; publ. the books *Guida all'ascolto della musica sinfonica* (Milan, 1967) and *Arnold Schonberg: L'uomo, l'opera, i testi musicati* (Milan, 1975). Collections of his writings were ed. by C. Tempo (Florence, 1991) and A. De Lisa (Milan, 1994). As a composer, Manzoni has embraced advanced forms of expression. While pursuing a highly individual serial path, he has explored microstructures, macrostructures, and multiphonics with interesting results.

WORKS: OPERAS: *La sentenza* (1959–60; Bergamo, Oct. 13, 1960); *Atomtod* (1963–64; Milan, March 27, 1965); *Per Massimiliano Robespierre* (1974; Bologna, April 17, 1975); *Doktor Faustus*, after Thomas Mann (1985–88; Milan, May 16, 1989). **ORCH.:** *Fantasia-Recitativo-Finale* for Chamber Orch. (1956; Milan, Jan. 21, 1957); *Studio per 24* for Chamber Orch. (Venice, April 13, 1962); *Studio No. 2* for Chamber Orch. (1962–63; Milan, April 20, 1963); *Insiemi* (1966–67; Milan, Sept. 30, 1969); *Multipli* for Chamber Orch. (1972; Washington, D.C., Feb. 23, 1973); *Variabili* for Chamber Orch. (1972–73; Bolzano, March 8, 1973); *Masse: Omaggio a Edgar Varèse* for Piano and Orch. (1976–77; Berlin, Oct. 6, 1977); *Lessico* for Strings (Piacenza, March 23, 1978); *Modulor* (1978–79; Venice, Oct. 7, 1979); *Ode* (1982; Milan, March 11, 1983); *Nuovo incontro* for Violin and Strings (Florence, June 5, 1984); *Adagio e solenne* (1990; San Marino, May 12, 1991); *Malinamusik* (1990; Rome, Sept. 14, 1991). **CHAMBER:** *2 Piccola suites* for Violin and Piano (1952–55; 1956); *Improvvisazione* for Viola and Piano (1958); *Musica notturna* for 7 Instrumentalists (1966; Venice, Sept. 12, 1967); *Quadruplum* for 2 Trumpets and 2 Trombones (1968); *Spiel* for 11 Strings (1968–69; London, April 26, 1969); *Parafrasi con finale* for 10 Instrumentalists (Bavarian Radio, Munich, June 6, 1969); Quartet for Violin, Viola, and Cello (1971); 6 pieces utilizing the title *Percorso*: *C* for Bassoon and Tape (1974), *a otto* for Double Wind Quartet (1975), *C2* for Bassoon and 11 Strings (1976; Graz, Oct. 15, 1977), *F* for Double Bass (1976), *GG* for Clarinet and Tape (1979), and *H* for

Flute (1987); *Epodo* for Flute, Oboe, Clarinet, Horn, and Bassoon (1976); *Sigla* for 2 Trumpets and 2 Trombones (1976); *Echi* for Guitar (1977–81); *Hölderlin: Epilogo* for 10 Instrumentalists (1980); *D'improvviso* for Percussionists (1981); *Incontro* for Violin and String Quartet (Naples, Nov. 22, 1983); *Opus 50 (Daunium)* for 11 Instrumentalists (Foggia, Nov. 14, 1984); *Die Strahlen der Sonne . . .* for 9 Instrumentalists (Milan, April 21, 1985); *Frase* for Clarinet and Piano (1988); *To Planets and to Flowers* for Saxophone Quartet (1989); *Essai* for Flute, Bass Clarinet, and Piano (1991); *Frase 2B* for 3 Violins and Percussion (1993). **VOCAL:** *Preludio: Grave: di Waring Cuney—Finale* for Woman's Voice, Clarinet, Violin, Viola, and Cello (1956; Rome, June 30, 1958); *Cinque Vicariote* for Chorus and Orch. (1958; Turin, Nov. 29, 1968); *Tre liriche di Paul Éluard* for Woman's Voice, Flute, Clarinet, Trumpet, Violin, and Cello (Rome, May 14, 1958); *Don Chisciotte* for Soprano, Small Chorus, and Chamber Orch. (1961; Venice, Sept. 14, 1964); *Due sonetti italiani* for Chorus (1961; Siena, Aug. 5, 1987); *Quattro poesie spagnole* for Baritone, Clarinet, Viola, and Guitar (Florence, March 21, 1962); *Ombre (alla memoria di Che Guevara)* for Chorus and Orch. (1967–68; Bologna, May 10, 1968); Parole da Beckett for 2 Choruses, 3 Instrumental Groups, and Tape (1970–71; Rome, May 21, 1971); *Hölderlin (frammento)* for Chorus and Orch. (Venice, Sept. 17, 1972); *Omaggio a Josquin* for Soprano, Chorus, 2 Violas, and Cello (1985; Rome, Feb. 24, 1987); *Uei prea al biele stele* for Men's Chorus and Timpani (Udine, Nov. 25, 1987); *Dedica* for Bass, Flute, and Orch. (1985; Parma, May 9, 1986); *Dieci versi di Emily Dickinson* for Soprano, String Quartet, 10 Strings, and 2 Harps (1988); *Poesie dell'assenza* for Narrator and Orch. (1990; Parma, Sept. 1992); *Finale e aria* for Soprano, String Quartet, and Orch. (1991; RAI, Milan, April 23, 1992); *Il deserto cresce* for Chorus and Orch. (1992; Ravenna, July 4, 1993).

BIBL.: M. Romito, *Le composizioni sinfonico-corali di G. M.* (Bologna, 1982); J. Noller, *Engagement und Form: G. M.s Werk in kulturtheoretischen und musikhistorischen Zusammenhangen* (Frankfurt am Main, 1987); F. Dorsi, *G. M.* (Milan, 1989); *Omaggio a G. M.: 1992 sesant'annil il 26 settembre* (Milan, 1992).

Marais, Josef, South African-born American folksinger and composer; b. Sir Lowry Pass, Nov. 17, 1905; d. Los Angeles, April 27, 1978. He studied at the South African College of Music and at the Royal Academy of Music in London; then took violin lessons with Sevčik in Prague. He emigrated to the U.S. in 1939; worked at the Office of War Information in N.Y. and broadcast songs from the South African *veld*; in 1947 married Roosje Baruch de la Bardo, a Dutch immigrant *chanteuse*, who took on the professional name Miranda. Together they publ. a number of song collections; Marais wrote the music for several stage productions, including Alan Paton's *Too Late the Phalarope*; he composed the orch. work *Paul Gauguin Suite* and other descriptive pieces.

Mařák, Otakar, Czech tenor; b. Esztergom, Hungary, Jan. 5, 1872; d. Prague, July 2, 1939. He was a student at the Prague Cons. of Paršova-Zikešová. After making his operatic debut as Faust in Brünn in 1899, he sang in Prague at the Deutsches Theater (1900–1901) and the National Theater (1901–07). Following guest engagements in Vienna (1903), Berlin (1906), London (Covent Garden, 1908), and Chicago (1914), he was a principal member of the National Theater in Prague (1914–34). He lost his financial security in a business venture, and went to the U.S. to seek his fortune. However, he ended up selling newspapers on Chicago streets. After funds were raised for his assistance, he was able to return to Prague to eke out his last days in straitened circumstances. At the zenith of his career, he was dubbed the Czech Caruso. Among his best roles were Turiddu, Canio, and Don José.

Marbe, Myriam (Lucia), Romanian composer and teacher; b. Bucharest, April 9, 1931. After initial studies with her mother, the piano pedagogue Angela Marbe, she pursued her training at the Bucharest Cons. (1944–54), where her mentors included Florica Musicescu and Silvia Căpăţînă (piano), Ioan Chirescu (theory), Marţian Negrea and Ion Dumitrescu (harmony), Mihail Jora and Leon Klepper (counterpoint and composition), and Theodor Rogalski (orchestration); later she attended the summer courses in new music in Darmstadt (1968–69; 1972). From 1954 to 1988 she taught at the Bucharest Cons. She received prizes from the Romanian Composers Union (1970–71; 1973–74; 1980; 1982). In 1972 she was awarded the Bernier Prize of the Académie des Beaux-Arts in Paris. She was honored with the prize of the Romanian Academy in 1977. In her music, she has pursued an advanced path in which she has experimented with serialism, sonorism, and spatial music.

WORKS: ORCH.: *In memoriam* (1959); *Musica festiva* (1961); *Le temps inévitable* for Piano and Orch. (1971); *Serenata-Eine kleine Sonnenmusik* for Chamber Orch. (Braşov, June 29, 1974); *Evocări* for Strings and Percussion (Tîrgu Mureş, June 22, 1976); Viola Concerto (Braşov, Feb. 1977); *La parabole du grenier II* for Harpsichord and Chamber Orch. (Zagreb, May 13, 1977); *Trium* (1978); Concerto for Viola da Gamba or Cello and Orch. (1982; Ploieşti, May 31, 1983); Sonata for Strings (1986; also as String Quartet No. 2, 1985); Saxophone(s) Concerto (1986); Sym. No. 1, *Ur-Ariadne*, for Mezzo-soprano and Orch. (1988). **CHAMBER:** Viola Sonata (1955); Clarinet Sonata (1961); *Incantatio*, sonata for Solo Clarinet (1964); Sonata for 2 Violas (1965); *Cyclus* for Flute, Guitar, and Percussion (1974); *Vocabulaire II-Rythme* for 3 Percussion (1975); *La parabole du grenier I* for Piano, Harpsichord, and Celesta, with Glockenspiel and Bells ad libitum (1975–76); Concerto for Harpsichord and 8 Instruments (1978); *Narratio* for Flute, Violin, Viola, and Percussion (1979); 4 string quartets: No. 1, *Les musiques compatibles* (1981), No. 2 (1985; also as the Sonata for Strings, 1986), No. 3, *Lui Nau* (1988), and No. 4 (1990; also as *Preţuitorul* for String Quartet, Trombone, Percussion, Speaker, and Tenor); *Sonate per due* for Flute and Viola (1985); *Trommelbass* for String Trio and Drum Bass (1985); *Des-Cântec* for Wind Quintet (1985); *After Nau*, sonata for Cello and Organ (1987); *The World is a stage . . .* for Violin, Double Bass, Clarinet, Trombone, and Percussion (1987); *Diapente* for 5 Cellos (1990); *E-Y-Thé* for Clarinet and 4 Cellos (1990); *Et in Arcadia . . .* for Flute, Bass Clarinet, Percussion, and Piano (1993); *Yorick* for Clarinet or Recorder, Violin, Piano, and Percussion (1993); *Haikus* for Flute and Piano (1993–94). **PIANO:** Sonata (1956); *Le temps inévitable I* and *II* (1968); *Clusterstudie I* and *II* (1970); *Accents* (1971). **VOCAL:** *Noapte ţărănească*, cantata for Chorus and Orch. (1958); *Madrigals After Japanese Haikus* for Women's Chorus (1964); *Clime* for Mezzo-soprano, Women's Chorus, Children's Chorus, and Chamber Orch. (1966); *. . . de aducere aminte* for Chorus and Small Orch. (1967); *Ritual pentru setea pământului* for 7 Voices and Instruments (1968); *Jocus secundus* for Small Vocal Group, Instruments, and Tape ad libitum (1969); *Vocabulaire I-Chanson* for Soprano, Clarinet, Piano, and Bells (1974); *Chiuituri* for Children's Chorus and Small Orch. (1978); *Les oiseaux artificiels* for Narrator and 6 Instruments (1979); *Timpul regăsit* for Soprano or Tenor and 7 Instruments (1982); *An die Musik* for Alto, Flute, and Organ (1983); *An die Sonne* for Mezzo-soprano and Wind Quintet (1986); *Fra Angelico-Marc Chagall-Voroneţ-Requiem* for Mezzo-soprano, Chorus, and Instrumental Ensemble (1990); *Stabat Mater* for 12 Voices and Instrumental Ensemble (1991); *Na Castelloza* for Mezzo-soprano, Oboe, Viola, and Percussion (1993); *Mirail-Jeu sur des fragments de poemes de femmes troubadours* for Soprano, 2 Mezzo-sopranos, Flute, Oboe, Violin, and Viola (1993); *Überzeitliches Gold* for Soprano, Percussion, and Saxophone(s) (1994); *Passages in the wind* for Tenor, Recorder, Cello, and Harpsichord (1994).

BIBL.: G. Gronemeyer, ed., *Klangportrait: M. L. M.* (Berlin, 1991); T. Beimel, *Vom Ritual zur Abstraktion: Über die rumänische Komponistin M. M.* (Wuppertal, 1994).

Marc, Alessandra, accomplished American soprano; b. Berlin, July 29, 1957. She received her training at the Univ. of Maryland. In 1987 she made her operatic debut in Giordano's *La Cene delle Beffe* at the Wexford Festival in England. In 1988 she sang Maria in Strauss's *Friedenstag* at the Santa Fe Opera. During the 1988–89 season, she appeared as Leonora in *La Forza del Destino* at the Greater Miami Opera, as Madame Lidoine in *Les Dialogues des Carmelites* at the Houston Grand Opera, as Strauss's Ariadne at the Washington (D.C.) Concert Opera, and as Aida at the Lyric Opera in Chicago. On Oct. 14, 1989, she made her Metropolitan Opera debut in N.Y. as Aida. In 1992 she sang for the first time at the Philadelphia Opera as Turandot. During the 1992–93 season, she made her debut at the Berlin State Opera as Strauss's Ariadne. In 1993 she made her Italian operatic debut at the Rome Opera as Aida. During the 1994–95 season, she appeared for the first time at London's Covent Garden as Turandot. Her other opera engagements included the Vienna State Opera, the San Francisco Opera, the Cologne Opera, the Bavarian State Opera in Munich, and the Hamburg State Opera. Among her other prominent roles are Norma, Sieglinde in *Die Walküre*, and Chrysothemis in *Elektra*. As a concert artist, she has appeared with many of the finest orchs. and festivals in a repertoire ranging from classical standards to Samuel Barber.

Marcel (real name, **Wasself**), **Lucille,** American soprano; b. N.Y., 1885; d. Vienna, June 22, 1921. She studied in N.Y., Berlin, and with J. de Reszke in Paris, where she made her debut as Mallika in *Lakmé* at the Opéra-Comique (1903). After marrying the conductor **Felix Weingartner** (1907), she sang the title role in Elektra at its first Viennese staging under his direction (March 24, 1908); continued to sing at the Court Opera until 1911, then was a member of the Hamburg Opera (1912–14). She made her U.S. debut as Tosca with the Boston Opera Co. (Feb. 14, 1912), and remained on its roster until 1914. After a period in Darmstadt, she settled in Vienna. Her other roles included Eva, Marguerite, Desdemona, and Aida.

Marchal, André (-Louis), distinguished blind French organist and pedagogue; b. Paris, Feb. 6, 1894; d. St. Jean-de-Luz, Aug. 27, 1980. He was blind from birth; studied at the Institution Nationale des Jeunes Aveugles; later entered the Paris Cons. in the class of Gigout. In 1915 he became organist at St. Germain-des-Prés in Paris; then served at St. Eustache from 1945 to 1963. He began a concert career in 1923; was greatly admired for his exhaustive repertoire and brilliance as an improviser. He was also esteemed as a teacher.

Marchant, Sir Stanley (Robert), English organist, teacher, and composer; b. London, May 15, 1883; d. there, Feb. 28, 1949. He studied organ at the Royal Academy of Music in London; completed his studies at Oxford (D.Mus., 1914). He occupied various posts as organist in London churches from 1899; was made prof. (1913) and principal (1936) at the Royal Academy of Music; was named King Edward VII Prof. of Music at London Univ. (1937); was knighted (1943). He wrote sacred music, secular choral works, songs, and organ pieces.

Marchesi (de Castrone), Blanche, French soprano and teacher of Italian-German descent; b. Paris, April 4, 1863; d. London, Dec. 15, 1940. She was the daughter of the distinguished Italian bartione and teacher Salvatore Marchesi de Castrone (b. Palermo, Jan. 15, 1822; d. Paris, Feb. 20, 1908) and the famous German mezzo-soprano and pedagogue Mathilde (née Graumann) Marchesi de Castrone (b. Frankfurt am Main, March 24, 1821; d. London, Nov. 17, 1913). After studying violin, she turned to vocal training with her mother. She began her career singing in private and charity concerts in Paris, and then appeared in Berlin and Brussels in 1895. On June 19, 1896, she made her London debut in a concert and made England her home. In 1900 she made her operatic debut as Brünnhilde in *Die Walküre* in Prague, and then returned to England to sing with the Moody-Manners Co. In 1902 she appeared at London's Covent Garden as Elisabeth, Elsa, and Isolde. For the most part, however, she pursued a career on the concert stage. Later she was also active as a teacher. She made her farewell concert appearance in 1938. She publ. the memoir *A Singer's Pilgrimage* (London, 1923), and the didactic vol. *The Singer's Catechism* (London, 1932).

Marco, Tomás, Spanish composer; b. Madrid, Sept. 12, 1942. He studied violin and composition at the Univ. of Madrid (1959–64); also attended the Darmstadt summer course in new music (1967). An ardent modernist, he founded in 1967 the magazine *Sonda*, dedicated to new music. His compositions are of an experimental, almost exhibitionistic, theatrical nature.

WORKS: BALLET: *Llanto por Ignacio Sanchez Mejias* (1984–85). **ORCH.:** *Los caprichos* (1959–67); *Glasperlenspiel* for Chamber Orch. (1963–64); *Vitral (Música celestial No. 1)* for Organ and Strings (1968); *Anábasis* (1968–70); *Mysteria* for Chamber Orch. (1970–71); *Angelus novus (Hommage à Mahler)* (1971); Violin Concerto, *Les Mécanismes de la mémoire* (1971–72; Royan Festival, April 19, 1973); Cello Concerto (1974–75); 5 syms.: No. 1, *Sinfonía Aralar* (1976), No. 2, *Espacio cerrado* (1985), No. 3 (1985), No. 4, *Espacio guebrado* (1987), and No. 5, *Modelos de Universo* (1988–89); *Concierto del Alma* for Violin and String Orch. (1982); *Concerto austral* for Oboe and Orch. (1982); *Pulsar* (1986); Triple Concerto for Violin, Cello, Piano, and Orch. (1987); *Settecento* for Piano and Chamber Orch. (1988); *Campo de Estrellas* (1989); *Espejo de viento* for 12 Saxophones (1989). **CHAMBER:** *Roulis-Tangage* for Trumpet, Cello, Guitar, Piano, Vibraphone, and 2 Percussionists (1962–63); *Trivium* for Piano, Tuba, and Percussion (1963); *Car en effet* for 3 Clarinets and 3 Saxophones (1965); *Schwan* for Trumpet, Trombone, Viola, Cello, and 2 Percussionists (1966); *Maya* for Cello and Piano (1968–69); *Rosa-Rosae*, quartet for Flute, Clarinet, Violin, and Cello (1969); *Floreal* for a Percussionist (1969); *Kukulcan* for Wind Quintet (1969–72); *Albor* for Flute, Clarinet, Violin, Cello, and Piano (1970); *Necronomicon*, choreography for 6 Percussionists (1971); *Jetztzeit* for Clarinet and Piano (1971); *Nuba* for Flute, Oboe, Clarinet, Violin, Cello, and Percussion (1973). **PIANO:** *Piraña* (1965); *Evos* (1970); *Espejo Desierto* for String Quartet (1987). **VOCAL:** *Jabberwocky* for Actors, Tenor, Saxophone, Piano, 4 Percussionists, Tape, 6 Radios, Lights, and Slides (1966); *Cantos del pozo artesiano* for Actress, 3 Chamber Ensembles, and Lights (1967); *Tea Party* for 4 Vocal Soloists, Clarinet, Trombone, Cello, and Vibraphone (1969); *L'Invitation au voyage* for Soprano, optional Narrator, 3 Clarinets, Piano, and Percussion (1971); *Ultramarina* for Soprano, Clarinet, Piano, and Percussion (1975); *Concierto Coral 1* for Violin and 2 Choral Groups (1980) and *2: Espacio Sagrado* for Piano, Chorus, and Orch. (1983).

Marcoux, Vanni (actually, **Jean Émile Diogène**), remarkable French bass-baritone who was also known as **Vanni-Marcoux;** b. Turin (of French parents), June 12, 1877; d. Paris, Oct. 22, 1962. He received training in law at the Univ. of Turin, and in voice from Taverna and Collino in Turin and from Boyer in Paris. He was only 17 when he made his operatic debut at Turin as Sparafucile. His formal operatic debut followed in 1899 when he sang Frère Laurent in *Roméo et Juliette* in Bayonne. After singing in Nice, Brussels, and The Hague, he distinguished himself at London's Covent Garden (1905–12). In 1908 he made his debut at the Paris Opéra as Méphistophélès. On Jan. 13, 1909, he created the role of Guido Colonna in Février's *Monna Vanna* there. Massenet composed the title role of his opera *Don Quichotte* for Marcoux, who sang in its first Paris staging on Dec. 29, 1910. He appeared as a guest artist at Milan's La Scala (1910), the Boston Opera Co. (1911–12), and the Chicago Grand Opera Co. (1913–14). From 1918 to 1936 he was a principal member of the Paris Opéra-Comique. He also sang again in Chicago (1926–32) and at Covent Garden (1937). From 1938 to 1943 he taught at the Paris Cons. In 1940 he retired from the operatic stage, although he made a final appearance as Don Quichotte at the Opéra-Comique in 1947. From 1948 to 1951 he served as director of the Grand Théâtre in Bordeaux. Marcoux's outstanding repertoire consisted of over 240 roles, of which the most famous were Don Giovanni,

Rossini's Don Basilio, Iago, Boris Godunov, Baron Ochs, Golaud, Scarpia, and Don Quichotte.

Marcovici, Silvia, Romanian violinist; b. Bacau, Jan. 30, 1952. She studied in Bacau and at the Bucharest Cons.; her principal teacher was S. Gheorghiu. She made her professional debut in The Hague in 1967; in 1969 she won the Long-Thibaud Competition in Paris and in 1970 the Enesco Competition in Bucharest. She appeared for the first time in London in 1970; in 1977, performed in N.Y.; subsequently appeared with many of the world's major orchs.

Marcuse, Sibyl, German-born American musicologist; b. Frankfurt am Main (of Swiss-English parents), Feb. 13, 1911. After studies in Europe, she lived in China (1932–35); emigrated to the U.S. with the coming of World War II, becoming a naturalized citizen in 1945; studied at a N.Y. school for piano technicians and then worked as a keyboard technician. She was curator of the Yale Univ. Collection of Musical Instruments (1953–60); publ. *Musical Instruments, A Comprehensive Dictionary* (1964; 2nd ed., rev., 1975) and *A Survey of Musical Instruments* (1975).

Maréchal, Adolphe, Belgian tenor; b. Liège, Sept. 26, 1867; d. Brussels, Feb. 1, 1935. He studied at the Liège Cons. He made his operatic debut in Tournai in 1891; then sang in Rheims, Bordeaux, and Nice; in 1895 he became a member of the Opéra-Comique in Paris, where he remained until 1907; during that time, he created the roles of Julien in *Louise* (1901), Alain in *Grisélidis* (1901), and Danielo in *La Reine fiammette* (1903); also Jean in *Le Jongleur de Notre-Dame* at Monte Carlo (1902). In 1902 he appeared at London's Covent Garden as Don José, Des Grieux, and Faust. He retired in 1907 after the loss of his singing voice.

Marek, Czeslaw (Josef), Polish-born Swiss pianist, teacher, and composer; b. Przemysl, Sept. 16, 1891; d. Zürich, July 17, 1985. He studied with Loewenhoff (piano) and Niewiadomski (harmony) at the Lemberg Music Inst., Leschetizky (piano) and Weigl (composition) in Vienna, and Pfitzner (composition) in Strasbourg. He made his debut in Lemberg (1909), where he taught at the Music Inst. until 1915; then settled in Zürich as a pianist, teacher, and composer, becoming a naturalized Swiss citizen (1932); was also prof. of composition at the Poznań Cons. (1929–30). He publ. the manual *Lehre des Klavierspiels* (Zürich, 1972).

WORKS: ORCH.: *Méditations* (1911–13); *Scherzo symfoniczne* (1914); *Sinfonietta* (1914–16); *Serenade* for Violin and Orch. (1916–18); Suite (1925); Sinfonia (1927). **OTHER:** Violin Sonata (1914); piano pieces; songs.

Marescotti, André-François, Swiss composer, organist, choirmaster, and teacher; b. Geneva, April 30, 1902. Following training at the Geneva Technicum, he studied at the Geneva Cons. with Mottu (piano), Montillet (organ), Chaix (harmony, counterpoint, and composition), and Lauber (instrumentation), and in Paris with Roger-Ducasse (composition). In 1921 he became organist in Compesières. In 1924 he became choirmaster at the Sacré-Coeur, and in 1940 at the St.-Joseph Church in Geneva. He also was on the faculty of the Geneva Cons. (1931–73). He publ. the valuable folio vol. *Les Instruments d'orchestre, leurs caractères, leurs possibilités et leur utilisation dans l'orchestre moderne* (with 900 musical examples; Paris, 1950). Marescotti's early works followed along French Impressionist lines, but he later embraced serialism.

WORKS: BALLET: *Les Anges du Grèco* (Zürich, June 1, 1947). **ORCH.:** *Ouverture pour celui qui épousa une femme muette* (1930); *Prélude au Grand Meaulnes* (1934); *Aubade* (1936); *Concert Carougeois I* (1942), *II* (1959), *III* (1964–65), and *IV* (1985); *Giboulées* for Bassoon and Orch. (1949; also for Solo Bassoon); Piano Concerto (1954–57); *Festa* (1961); *Hymnes* (1961–64); *Rondeau capriccioso* (1972); *Ballade* for Violin and Orch. (1975; also for Solo Violin); Cello Concerto (1977); *Nuage sur la vigne*, suite (1984). **CHAMBER:** *Mouvement* for Harp (1941); *Giboulées* for Bassoon (1949; also for Bassoon and Orch.); *Ballade* for Violin (1975; also for Violin and Orch.); *Méditation alternée* for Winds, Timpani, and Percussion (1979). **PIANO:** *Esquisses et Croquis* (3 series, 1923–40); 3 suites (1928–44); *Fantasque* (1939); *Variations sur un thème de J.-J. Rousseau* (1978); *Ittocséram* (1980–82). **VOCAL:** *Messe St.-André* for Chorus and Organ (1925); *Réveillez-vous Pastoureaux*, 10 carols for Voices and Piano or Orch. (1944); *Vergers* for Medium Voice and Piano (1945–46); *La Lampe d'argile* for Soloists and Chorus (1947); *Insomnies* for Voice and Orch. (1950–64); *Trois Incantations* for Chorus and 4 Percussionists (1969); *Salve Regina, Regina Coeli*, 2 motets for Women's Chorus and Organ (1990).

BIBL.: A. Golea, *A.-F. M., Biographie. Études analytiques. Liste des Oeuvres. Discographie* (Paris, 1963); C. Tappolet, *A.-F. M.* (Geneva, 1986).

Marez Oyens, Tera de, Dutch composer, pianist, conductor, and teacher; b. Velzen, Aug. 5, 1932. She was a piano student of Jan Ode at the Amsterdam Cons., graduating when she was 20. She also took courses there in harpsichord, violin, and conducting. After further training with Henkemens (composition and orchestration), she studied electronic music with Koenig at the Inst. of Sonology at the Univ. of Utrecht. She was active as a pianist and conductor. She also was a prof. at the Zwolle Cons. (until 1988). In her music, she has utilized both traditional and contemporary modes of expression.

WORKS: ORCH.: *Introduzione* (1969); *Transformation* (1972); *Human* for Orch. and Tape (1975); *Shoshadre* for Strings (1976); *Episodes* for Orch. and Adaptable Ensemble (1976); *In Exile*, concertino for Piano and Strings (1977); *Litany of the Victims of War* (1985); *Structures and Dance*, violin concerto (1986; Hilversum, Jan. 22, 1987); 3 syms.: No. 1, *Sinfonia Testimonial*, for Chorus, Orch., and Tape (The Hague, Nov. 1987), No. 2, *Squaw Sachem* (1993), and No. 3, *Ceremonies* (1993); *Symmetrical Memories*, cello concerto (1988; Scheveningen, March 19, 1989); *Confrontations*, piano concerto (1990; Utrecht, Dec. 1991); *Interface* for Strings (1991); *Linzer Concert*, accordion concerto (Linz, Nov. 1991); Alto Saxophone Concerto (1992). **CHAMBER:** *Deducties* for Oboe and Harpsichord (1964); Wind Octet (1972); *Mahpoochah* for 7 or More Instruments (1978); *Mosaic* for Oboe, Clarinet, Horn, Bassoon, and Piano (1979); Concerto for Horn and Tape (1980); *Polskie Miasta* for Flute, Oboe, Violin, Viola, Cello, and Piano (1981); 3 string quartets, including *Contrafactus* (1981) and No. 3 (1988); *Lenaia* for Flute (1982; also as *Lenaia Quintet* for Flute, 2 Violins, Viola, and Cello); *Octopus* for Bass Clarinet and Percussion (1982); *Möbius by Ear* for Viola and Piano (1983); *Ambiversion* for Bass Clarinet and Tape (1983); *Trajectory* for Saxophone Quartet (1985); *Powerset* for Saxophone Quartet and Percussion (1986); *Free for All* for 5 Instruments (1986); *Gilgamesh Quartet* for 4 Trombones (1988); *Dublin Quartet* for Violin, Viola, Cello, and Piano (1989); *NamSan* for Marimba (1993); *A Wrinkle in Time* for Flute, Violin, Viola, and Piano (1994). **KEYBOARD: PIANO:** Sonatine (1961); Sonatine for 2 Pianos (1963); *Ballerina on a Cliff* (1980); *Charon's Gift* for Piano and Tape (1982); *Sentenced to Dream* (1990); *The Uncarved Block* for Piano and Tape (1994). **ORGAN:** *Partita* (1958). **VOCAL:** *Zuid Afrikaanse Liederen* for Soprano or Tenor and Piano (1951); *Tragödie* for Men's Chorus (1957); *Der Chinesische Spiegel* for Tenor and Orch. (1962); *Deposuit Potentos de Sede* for Chorus (1970); *Pente Sjawoe Kost* for 7 Narrators and Chorus (1970); *Canto di Parole* for Chorus (1971); *Bist du Bist II* for Chorus (1973); *From Death to Birth* for Chorus (1974); *Ode to Kelesh* for Chorus and Instruments (1975); *The Lover* for Chorus (1975); *The Odyssey of Mr. Goodevil*, oratorio for 4 Soloists, 2 Narrators, 2 Choruses, and Orch. (1976–81); *The Fire and the Mountains*, cantata for Chorus and Orch. (1978; rev. 1984); *Takadon* for Voices and Chamber Ensemble (1978); *And Blind She Remained* for Voice, Keyboard, and Percussion (1978); *3 Hymns* for Mezzo-soprano and Piano (1979); *Black* for Chorus (1981); *Het Lied van de Duizend Angsten* for 2 Soloists, 2 Choruses, and Orch. (1984); *Vignettes* for Soprano, Flute, Percussion, and Piano (1986); *Music for a Small Planet* for Voice, 8 Melody Instruments, and Percussion (1988); *Shadow of a Prayer* for Soprano, Flute, and Piano (1989); *From a Distant Planet* for Baritone or Alto or Mezzo-soprano and Piano (1990); *Recurrent Thoughts of a Haunted Traveller* for Soprano and Saxophone Quartet (1991); *If Only* for Soprano, Flute, Percussion, and Piano (1991); *Carichi pendenti* for Soprano, Accordion, and Cello (1993); *Strange Logic* for Contralto and Orch. (1994). **ELECTRONIC:** *Etude II* (1964); *Safed* (1968); *Photophonie* for 4 Tracks and 8 Light Sources (1971); *Mixed Feelings* for 4 Tracks and Percussion (1973); *Dances of Illusion*, verbosonic-electronic ballet (1985); *Lier* for Voices and Electronics (1991). **OTHER:** Pieces for school orch. and amateur groups.

Margola, Franco, Italian composer and teacher; b. Orzinuovi, near Brescia, Oct. 30, 1908; d. Brescia, March 10, 1992. He studied violin with Romanini and composition with Guerrini, Jachino, Longo, and Casella at the Parma Cons. (diplomas in piano, 1926, and in composition, 1934); then took a course in advanced theory with Casella at the Accademia di Santa Cecilia in Rome. After serving as director of the Messina Cons. (1938–40), he taught at the conservatories in Cagliari, Bologna, Milan, Rome, and Parma. He publ. a manual, *Guida pratica per lo studio della composizione* (Milan, 1954).

WORKS: OPERA: *Il mito di Caino* (Bergamo, 1940). **ORCH.:** Piano Concerto (1943; Florence, Feb. 12, 1944); Cello Concerto (1949); 2 syms. (1950, 1961); Children's Concerto for Piano and Small Orch. (1954); Children's Concerto for Violin and Small Orch. (1955); Concerto for Strings (1958); Concerto for Violin, Piano, and Strings (1960); Horn Concerto (1960); Double Concerto for Violin, Piano, and Strings (1960); Concerto for Oboe and Strings (1962); Passacaglia for Strings, Piano, and Percussion (1970). **CHAMBER:** 3 cello sonatas (1931–45); 4 violin sonatas (1932–44); 2 piano quintets (1933, 1946); 8 string quartets (1936–50); *4 Episodi* for Flute and Guitar (1970); piano pieces.

Margulies, Adele, Austrian-born American pianist and teacher; b. Vienna, March 7, 1863; d. N.Y., June 6, 1949. She was a student of Door and Grädner at the Vienna Cons., where she took 1st prize for 3 consecutive years. On Nov. 3, 1881, she made her N.Y. recital debut. On March 30, 1885, she played the premiere of the last 2 movements of MacDowell's 2nd Piano Concerto there. In 1887 she became the first prof. of piano at the National Cons. of Music of America in N.Y., continuing in that capacity until 1936. She also was active with the Margulies Trio (1890–92; 1904–25).

Marguste, Anti, Estonian composer and teacher; b. Are, Aug. 5, 1931. He studied with M. Saar and A. Garshnek at the Tallinn Cons. (graduated, 1960), then taught at the Tallinn Music School from 1962. His output is marked by the use of folk elements.

WORKS: ORCH.: 6 syms. (1960, 1963, 1966, 1967, 1970, 1981); *Pieces* for Reed-pipe, Flutes, and Strings (1967); *Symphonic Runes* (1974); *Organ Tunes* for Organ and Orch. (1974). **CHAMBER:** *Concertino piccolo* No. 1 for Woodwind Quintet (1967) and No. 2 for 12 Flutes and Percussion (1979); piano pieces. **VOCAL:** *Old Proverb—Old Silver*, cycle for Children's Chorus, Women's Chorus, and Mixed Chorus (1974); *Red Data Book* for Soprano, Mezzo-soprano, Tenor, Bass, Chorus, Trumpet, Trombone, Horn, Tuba, and Piano (1980); songs.

Marić, Ljubica, remarkable Serbian composer; b. Kragujevac, March 18, 1909. She studied with Josip Slavenski in Belgrade; then went to Prague, where she took composition courses with Suk and Alois Hába at the Cons.; also studied conducting with Malko in Prague (1929–32) and with Scherchen in Strasbourg (1933); she returned to Prague for more study with Hába in his special quarter tone classes (1936–37). She subsequently taught at the Stanković School of Music in Belgrade. During the period of Nazi occupation of Serbia, she was an active participant in the resistance. After the liberation, she was a member of the teaching staff of the Belgrade Academy of Music (1945–67). In her music, she adopted a global type of modern technique, utilizing variable tonal configurations, atonal melodic progressions, and microtonal structures while adhering to traditional forms of composition.

WORKS: ORCH.: *Passacaglia* (Belgrade, April 21, 1958). **CHAMBER:** String Quartet (1931); Wind Quintet (1932); Trio for Clarinet, Trombone, and Double Bass (1937); Violin Sonata (1948); numerous piano pieces. **VOCAL:** 2 cantatas: *Pesme prostora* (Songs of Space), based on inscriptions on the graves of Bogomils, a heretical religious sect of the Middle Ages (Belgrade, Dec. 8, 1956) and *Prag sna* (Threshold of Dream), chamber cantata for Narrator, Soprano, Alto, and Instrumental Ensemble (1961; Opatija, Oct. 30, 1965); *Slovo svetlosti* (Sound of Light), oratorio, after medieval Serbian poetry (1966); songs. **OTHER:** 4 modern realizations of the Serbian Octoichos: *Muzika oktoiha No. 1* for Orch. (Belgrade, Feb. 28, 1959), *Vizantijski koncert* (Byzantine Concerto) for Piano and Orch. (Belgrade, June 4, 1963), *Ostinato super thema octoicha* for String Quintet, Harp, and Piano (Warsaw, Sept. 27, 1963), and *Simfonija oktoiha* (1964).

Marinov, Ivan, Bulgarian composer and conductor; b. Sofia, Oct. 17, 1928. He studied conducting with Goleminov and composition with Stoyanov and Khadziev at the Bulgarian State Cons. in Sofia, graduating in 1955.

WORKS: ORCH.: *Suite on 4 Folk Songs* (1955); *Ilinden*, symphonic poem (1956); *Paraphrases* (1957); *Fantastic Scenes* (1959); *Divertimento* (1961); *Festive Suite* (1968); *Ode on Liberty* (1969). **CHAMBER:** Various works. **VOCAL:** *Dvuboj* (Duel), poem for Tenor and Orch. (1953); *Pentagram* for Bass, Strings, Piano, and Timpani (1965–66); Sym. No. 1 for Bass and Orch. (1967); songs.

Marinuzzi, Gino, noted Italian conductor and composer, father of **Gino Marinuzzi;** b. Palermo, March 24, 1882; d. Milan, Aug. 17, 1945. He was a student of Zuelli at the Palermo Cons. He commenced his career conducting at the Teatro Massimo in Palermo, where he conducted the first local performance of *Tristan und Isolde* in 1909. After conducting in various Italian operatic centers, he toured in South America. In 1913 he conducted the first local performance of *Parsifal* at the Teatro Colón in Buenos Aires. From 1915 to 1918 he was director of the Bologna Liceo Musicale. On March 27, 1917, he conducted the premiere of Puccini's *La Rondine* in Monte Carlo. He was artistic director of the Chicago Grand Opera Co. from 1919 to 1921. From 1928 to 1934 he was chief conductor of the Teatro Reale dell'Opera in Rome. In 1934 he conducted at London's Covent Garden. From 1934 to 1944 he conducted at Milan's La Scala, where he served as its superintendent in 1944. Marinuzzi was especially admired as a conductor of the Italian operatic repertoire, but he also won distinction for his performances of Wagner and Strauss. Among his compositions were the operas *Barberina* (Palermo, 1903), *Jacquerie* (Buenos Aires, Aug. 11, 1918), and *Palla de' Mozzi* (Milan, April 5, 1932), a Sym. (1943), and chamber music.

BIBL.: A. Garbelotto, *G. M.* (Ancona, 1965).

Marinuzzi, Gino, Italian conductor and composer, son of **Gino Marinuzzi**; b. N.Y., April 7, 1920. He studied at the Milan Cons. with Calace (piano) and Paribeni and Bossi (composition), graduating in 1941. From 1946 to 1951 he was assistant conductor at the Teatro dell'Opera in Rome, and then conducted in other Italian opera houses. He was one of the first Italian composers to explore the potentialities of electronic music; in collaboration with Ketoff, he developed an electronic synthesizer, the "Fonosynth," and was a founder of an electronic studio in Rome. His compositions include a radio opera, *La Signora Paulatim* (Naples, 1966); Violin Concerto; Piano Concerto; chamber music; piano pieces; film scores; pieces for electronic tape.

Mario (real name, **Tillotson**), **Queena,** American soprano and teacher; b. Akron, Ohio, Aug. 21, 1896; d. N.Y., May 28, 1951. She went to N.Y. to work as a journalist in order to raise funds to pursue her vocal training with Saenger and Sembrich. On Sept.

4, 1918, she made her operatic debut as Olympia in *Les Contes d'Hoffmann* with the San Carlo Opera Co. in N.Y. She remained with the company until 1920, and then was a member of the Scotti Grand Opera Co. (1920–22). On Nov. 30, 1922, she made her Metropolitan Opera debut in N.Y. as Micaëla. She remained on its roster until 1938, winning favor for her portrayals of Gilda, Juliette, Marguerite, Nedda, Sophie, and Antonia. She was particularly associated with the role of Gretel, which she sang in the first complete opera to be broadcast on radio by the Metropolitan (Dec. 25, 1931), and also at her farewell appearance with the company (Dec. 26, 1938). Mario also sang with the San Francisco Opera (1923–24; 1929–30; 1932). In 1931 she became a teacher at the Curtis Inst. of Music in Philadelphia. In 1934 she opened her own vocal studio in N.Y., and in 1942 became a teacher at the Juilliard School of Music there. She wrote 3 mystery novels, including *Murder in the Opera House*. In 1925 she married **Wilfred Pelletier**, but they divorced in 1936.

Mariotte, Antoine, French composer; b. Avignon, Dec. 22, 1875; d. Izieux, Loire, Nov. 30, 1944. He was trained at the Naval Academy. In 1897 he became a pupil of d'Indy at the Schola Cantorum in Paris. In 1899 he was appointed conductor of the sym. concerts at St.-Etienne, Loire; from 1902 to 1919 he taught at the Orléans Cons.; in 1920, was appointed its director; from 1936 to 1938 he was director of the Paris Opéra-Comique.

WORKS: OPERAS: *Salomé* (Lyons, Oct. 30, 1908); *Le Vieux Roi* (Lyons, 1911); *Léontine Soeurs* (Paris, May 21, 1924); *Esther, Princesse d'Israël* (Paris, May 5, 1925); *Gargantua* (1924; Paris, Feb. 13, 1935); *Nele Dooryn* (1940). **OTHER:** *Impressions urbaines*, symphonic suite (1921); numerous teaching pieces for piano; songs.

Mariz, Vasco, Brazilian musicologist and diplomat; b. Rio de Janeiro, Jan. 22, 1921. He was a student of Lorenzo Fernández, Vera Janacópulos, Francisco Mignone, and Ernest Tempele at the Conservatório Brasileiro de Música in Rio de Janeiro. He also studied law at the Univ. of Rio de Janeiro (D.J., 1943). In 1945 he sang bass roles in Mozart's operas in Porto Alegre, and in 1947 made his recital debut in Rio de Janeiro. However, after entering the Brazilian diplomatic service in 1945, he devoted himself mainly to a dual career as a diplomat and musicologist. Following diplomatic posts in Oporto, Portugal (1948–49) and Belgrade (1950–51), he was consul in Rosario, Argentina (1951–54) and Naples (1956–58). From 1959 to 1962 he was cultural affairs officer at the Brazilian Embassy in Washington, D.C. In 1969–70 he was the Brazilian assistant secretary of state for cultural affairs. He subsequently served as Brazil's ambassador to Israel (1977–82), Peru (1983–84), and Germany (1985–87).

WRITINGS: *A Canção da câmara no Brasil* (Oporto, 1948; rev. and enl. ed., 1959, as *A canção brasileira: Eruita folclórica e popular*, 5th ed., 1985); *Figuras da música brasileira contemporânea* (Oporto, 1948; 2nd ed., 1970); *Dicionário bio-bibliográfico musical (brasileiro e internacional)* (Rio de Janeiro, 1948; new ed., 1985, as *Dicionário bio-bibliográfico musical: Compositores intérpretes e musicólogos*, 3rd ed., 1991); *Heitor Villa-Lobos* (Rio de Janeiro, 1949; 11th ed., 1990); *Vida musical I* (Oporto, 1950); *Alberto Ginastera, en adhesión a la fecha nacional argentina* (Rosario, 1954); *Vida musical II* (Rio de Janeiro, 1970); *História de musica no Brasil* (Rio de Janeiro, 1981; 4th ed., 1994); *Tres musicólogos brasileiros: Mário de Andrade, Renato Almeida, Luiz Heitor Correa de Azevedo* (Rio de Janeiro, 1983); *Cláudio Santoro* (Rio de Janeiro, 1994).

BIBL.: R. Stevenson, "Tribute V. M.," *Inter-American Music Review*, II (1993).

Markevitch, Igor, greatly talented Russian-born Italian, later French composer and conductor; b. Kiev, July 27, 1912; d. Antibes, France, March 7, 1983. He was taken to Paris in his infancy; in 1916 the family settled in Vevey, Switzerland, which remained Markevitch's home for the next decade. He began to study piano with his father, and subsequently took piano lessons with Paul Loyonnet; he also took academic courses at the Collège de Vevey. In 1925 he joined the piano class of Cortot in Paris at the École Normale de Musique, and studied harmony, counterpoint, and composition with Boulanger and orchestration with Rieti. He attracted the attention of Diaghilev, who commissioned him to write a piano concerto and also to collaborate with Boris Kochno on a ballet. Markevitch was soloist in his Piano Concerto at Covent Garden in London on July 15, 1929. Diaghilev died on Aug. 19, 1929, and Markevitch interrupted his work on the ballet for him; he used the musical materials from it in his *Cantate*, which achieved an extraordinary success at its Paris premiere on June 4, 1930. On Dec. 8, 1930, his Concerto Grosso was performed for the first time in Paris with even greater acclaim. Finally, his ballet *Rébus* was produced in Paris on Dec. 15, 1931, to enthusiastic press reviews. Markevitch was hailed, only half-facetiously, as "Igor II" (the first Igor being, of course, Stravinsky). His ballet *L'Envol d'Icare* was premiered in Paris on June 26, 1933, prompting Milhaud to opine that the occasion would probably "mark a date in the evolution of music." But swift as was Markevitch's Icarus-like ascent as a composer, even more precipitous was his decline. He began to be sharply criticized for his penchant toward unrelieved dissonance. When he conducted the premiere of his oratorio *Le Paradis perdu* (London, Dec. 20, 1935), it was roundly condemned for sins of dissonance. Although he continued to compose, Markevitch turned his attention more and more to conducting. He made his professional conducting debut with the Concertgebouw Orch. of Amsterdam in 1930. In 1934–35 he took conducting lessons in Switzerland with Scherchen. During World War II, he was in Italy; after the war, he devoted himself to conducting. He conducted in Stockholm (1952–55). He made his U.S. debut as a guest conductor with the Boston Sym. Orch. (1955). Markevitch was then conductor of the Montreal Sym. Orch. (1957–61), the Havana Phil. (1957–58), and the Lamoureux Orch. in Paris (1957–62). He was founder-conductor of the Spanish Radio and Television Sym. Orch. (1965); then conducted the U.S.S.R. State Sym. Orch. in Moscow (1965), the Monte Carlo Orch. (1967–72), and the orch. of the Accademia di Santa Cecilia in Rome (1973–75). He also gave master classes in conducting in various European music centers. In 1947 he became a naturalized Italian citizen. He became a naturalized French citizen in 1982. Markevitch wrote *Introduction à la musique* (Paris, 1940), *Made in Italy* (London, 1949), and *Point d'orgue* (Paris, 1959). In addition to the Russian repertoire, he exhibited special affinity for the works of Stravinsky, Bartók, and other 20th-century composers.

WORKS: BALLETS: *Rébus* (Paris, Dec. 15, 1931); *L'Envol d'Icare* (Paris, June 16, 1933; also for Piano as *La Mort d'Icare*). **ORCH.:** Sinfonietta (Brussels, Nov. 30, 1929); Piano Concerto (London, July 15, 1929, composer soloist); Concerto Grosso (Paris, Dec. 8, 1930); *Ouverture symphonique* (1931); *Hymnes* (Paris, June 26, 1933, composer conducting); *Petite suite d'après Schumann* (1933); *Hymne à la mort* for Chamber Orch. (1936); *Cantique d'amour* for Chamber Orch. (Rome, May 14, 1937); *Le Nouvel Age*, sinfonia concertante (1937; Warsaw, Jan. 21, 1938, composer conducting); *Le Bleu Danube* for Chamber Orch. (Florence, May 24, 1946, composer conducting). **CHAMBER:** *Serenade* for Violin, Clarinet, and Bassoon (Wiesbaden, Aug. 5, 1931); *Partita* (Paris, May 13, 1932); *Galop* for 8 Players (1932); Duo for Flute and Bassoon (1939). **PIANO:** *Noces*, suite (1925); *La Mort d'Icare* (1933; also as the ballet *L'Envol d'Icare*); *Stefan le poète* (1939–40); *Variations, Fugue and Envoi on a Theme of Handel* (Rome, Dec. 14, 1941). **VOCAL:** Cantate, after Jean Cocteau (Paris, June 4, 1930); *Psaume* for Soprano and Chamber Orch. (Amsterdam, Dec. 3, 1933, composer conducting); *Le Paradis perdu*, oratorio, after Milton (London, Dec. 20, 1935, composer conducting); *3 poèmes* for Voice and Piano (1935); *La Taille de l'homme* for Soprano and 12 Instruments (1939; unfinished; 1st perf. as *Oraison musicale*, Maastricht, Feb. 7, 1982); *Lorenzo il magnifico*, sinfonia concertante for Soprano and Orch. (1940; Florence, Jan. 12, 1941); *Inno della liberazione nazionale*, songs for the Italian underground resistance (1943–44).

BIBL.: B. Gavoty, *I. M.* (Geneva, 1954); special issue of *Tempo* (Sept. 1980); J. Heinzelmann, *I. M.* (Bonn, 1982).

Markova, Juliana, gifted Bulgarian pianist; b. Sofia, July 8, 1945. She studied at the Bulgarian State Cons. in Sofia (1963–65) and then with Ilonka Deckers at the Milan Cons., graduating with the highest honors in 1969. She won prizes in the Enesco Competition in Bucharest (1964) and the Long-Thibaud Competition in Paris (1965). In 1973 she made her recital debut at the Berlin Festival, and that same year her U.S. recital debut in Chicago. After appearing as soloist in the Tchaikovsky 1st Piano Concerto with the Los Angeles Phil. in 1974, she appeared as soloist with the leading orchs. of Europe and the U.S., including the London Sym., Philharmonia Orch., Royal Phil., Chicago Sym., Cleveland Orch., and Philadelphia Orch.; also toured in solo recitals. During the 1991–92 season, she toured Japan as soloist with the San Francisco Sym. She settled in London and married **Michael Roll**. A technically brilliant pianist, she excels in the Romantic and the early modern repertoire.

Markowski, Andrzej, Polish conductor and composer; b. Lublin, Aug. 22, 1924; d. Warsaw, Oct. 30, 1986. He studied theory and composition with Malawski in Lublin (1939–41); after studies in composition with Rowley at Trinity College of Music in London (1946–47), he completed his training as a composer with Rytel and Szeligowski and studied conducting with Rowicki at the Warsaw State High School of Music (1947–55). He conducted the Szczecin Theater (1949–50), the Poznań Phil. (1954–55), the Silesian Phil. in Katowice (1955–59), and the Kraków Phil. (1959–64), with which he toured the U.S. (1961). After conducting the Wroclaw Phil. (1965–69), he was one of the conductors of the National Phil. in Warsaw (1971–78); toured with it in Europe and Japan; then was conductor of the Artur Rubinstein Phil. in Łódź (1982–86), touring Italy with this orch. in 1984. He was best known as an interpreter of contemporary music. He wrote instrumental works, chamber music, film and theater scores, and electronic pieces.

Marks, Alan, talented American pianist; b. Chicago, May 14, 1949; d. Berlin, July 12, 1995. His family moved to St. Louis when he was a child; he studied piano with Shirley Parnas Adams. In 1965 he won a prize in Interlochen; gave his first piano recital in St. Louis in 1966. In 1967 he went to N.Y., where he studied at the Juilliard School of Music with Irwin Freundlich (B.M., 1971); then with Leon Fleisher at the Peabody Cons. of Music in Baltimore (1971–72). He took 2nd prize in the Univ. of Maryland (1973) and Geza Anda (1979) competitions. In 1981 he settled in Berlin. He gave successful recitals in Boston, Washington, Philadelphia, Los Angeles, San Francisco, and other cities. In 1976 he played the first performance of *Caprichos* for Piano by Carlos Chávez; also participated in numerous concerts of chamber music. He possessed an innate virtuoso technique, and was able to interpret with perfect stylistic fidelity piano works by classical as well as modern composers.

Marlowe (real name, **Sapira**), **Sylvia,** American harpsichordist and teacher; b. N.Y., Sept. 26, 1908; d. there, Dec. 11, 1981. She studied piano; went to Paris to take courses with Boulanger at the École Normale de Musique; later became a student of Landowska in harpsichord. In 1953 she joined the faculty of the Mannes School of Music in N.Y. In 1957 she founded the Harpsichord Music Soc., which commissioned works by Elliott Carter, Ned Rorem, Vittorio Rieti, Henri Sauguet, and others. Although her primary devotion was to the Baroque style of composition, she adventurously espoused the cause of popular American music; she was a member of the pop group called Chamber Music Soc. of Lower Basin Street and even performed in nightclubs, ostentatiously proclaiming her belief in music as an art in flux.

Maros, Miklós, Hungarian-born Swedish composer and teacher, son of **Rudolf Maros**; b. Pécs, Nov. 14, 1943. He studied composition in Budapest with Sugár at the Béla Bartók Cons. (1958–63) and with Szabó at the Franz Liszt Academy of Music (1963–67); settled in Stockholm, where he continued his training with Lidholm and Ligeti at the Musikhögskolan (1968–72); in 1975 he became a naturalized Swedish citizen. He taught electronic music at the Stockholm Electronic Music Studio (1971–78) and at the Musikhögskolan (1976–80); also taught privately. In 1972, with his wife, the singer Ilona Maros, he founded the Maros Ensemble, which championed contemporary music. In 1980–81 he held a Deutscher Akademischer Austauschdienst fellowship in West Berlin; in 1982–83 he was composer-in-residence of the Swedish Inst. for National Concerts. In his music, Maros utilizes both traditional and experimental techniques, including electronics.

WORKS: DRAMATIC: *Jag önkar jag vore* (I Wish I Could Be), opera (1971); *Stora grusharpan* (The Huge Gravel-sifter), radio opera (1982); *Att i denna natt . . .* (In This Night . . .), church opera (1986). **ORCH.:** *Pezzo* for Chamber Orch. (1967); *Mutazioni* for Wind Orch. (1971); Concertino for Double Bass or Tuba, and 6 to 24 Instruments (1971); *Confluentia* for Strings (1972); *Proportio* for Wind Orch. (1973); 2 syms.: No. 1 (1974; Stockholm, Feb. 14, 1976) and No. 2 for Wind and Percussion Orch. (Stockholm, Sept. 22, 1979); Concerto for Harpsichord and Chamber Orch. (1978; Reykjavík, Jan. 20, 1980); *Circulation* for Strings (1980); Concerto for Wind Quintet and Orch. (1980); *Coalottino II* for Bass Clarinet and Strings (1981); *Konzertsatz* for Accordion and Strings (1982); *Fantasi* (1983); Trombone Concerto (1983; Gävle, Oct. 6, 1984); *Sinfonietta* for Chamber Orch. (1985); *Sinfonia Concertante* for Strings (1986); *Introduzione e Marcia* for Wind Orch. (1986); *Concerto grosso* for Saxophone Quartet and Orch. (1988; Wuppertal, March 2, 1990); Clarinet Concerto (1989; Stockholm, March 6, 1991); Alto Saxophone Concerto (1990; Stockholm, Jan. 19, 1991); *Vice-Concertino* for Harpsichord, Violin, and Strings (1993); *Saxazione* for 18 Saxophones (1994); *Aurora* for Double Wind Quintet and Wind Band (1995). **CHAMBER:** 2 wind quintets (1962, 1980); *Spel* (Game) for Clarinet, Trombone, Cello, and Percussion (1969); *Festeggiamento* for Recorder, Violin, and Harp (1971); *Oolit* for 10 Instruments (1974); *Divertimento* for Wind Quintet, Violin, and Piano (1976); String Quartet No. 1 (1977); *Åtbörder* (Gestures) for Flute, Clarinet, Violin, Viola, Cello, Piano, and Percussion (1979); *Speglingar* (Reflections) for Winds, Guitars, Pianos, and Strings (1983); Saxophone Quartet (1984); *Picchiettato* for 5 Percussionists (1986); *Aulos*, trio for Oboe, Cello, and Harpsichord (1987); *Goboj* for Oboe and Guitar (1987); *Res mobilis* for Brass Quintet (1990); *Partita* for Viola and Piano (1991); *Burattinata* for Alto Saxophone and Piano (1992); *Konzertmusik* for Chamber Ensemble (1992); *Feinschnitten* for Flute and Percussion (1993); *Lyria* for Trumpet and Harp (1993). **VOCAL:** *Prelude* for Mezzo-soprano and Orch. (1967); *Inversioni* for Soprano and Chamber Ensemble (1968); *Erotikon* for Mezzo-soprano and Orch. (1968); *Anenaika* for Soprano, Chamber Ensemble, and Tape (1970); *Denique* for Soprano and Orch. (1970); *Diversion* for Soprano, Contralto, Alto Flute, Viola, Guitar, and 3 Percussionists (1971); *Laus Pannoniae* for Soprano, Chorus, and Chamber Ensemble (1972); *Xylographia* for Soprano, Violin, Bassoon, Harp, Harpsichord, and Vibraphone (1972); *Lunovis* for Soprano, Violin, Bassoon, Harp, and Celesta (1973); *Fabula* for Alto, Cello, 2 Pianos, and Percussion (1974); *Elementen* for Soprano, Reciter, Women's Trio, and Youth Orch. (1975); *Psalm 98* for Soprano, Flute, Clarinet, Bassoon, Violin, Viola, Cello, and Percussion (1978); *4 sanger ur Gitanjali* (4 Songs from Gitanjali) for Soprano, Flute, Clarinet, and 2 Percussionists (1979); *Clusters for Clusters* for Flute, Soprano Saxophone, Guitar, and Percussion (1981); *Drehlieder* for Tenor, Hurdy-gurdy, Cello, and Harpsichord (1984); choruses; songs. **OTHER:** Live electronic pieces; electroacoustic works.

Maros, Rudolf, Hungarian composer, father of **Miklós Maros**; b. Stachy, Jan. 19, 1917; d. Budapest, Aug. 3, 1982. He studied at the Györ teachers' training college (graduated, 1937), and then took courses in composition with Kodály and Siklós and viola with Temesváry at the Budapest Academy of Music (1938–42); later attended A. Hába's master class there (1949).

He played viola in the Budapest Concert Orch. (1942–49); from 1949 to 1978 he was on the faculty of the Budapest Academy of Music. In 1971–72 he held a Deutscher Akademischer Austauschdienst scholarship in West Berlin. In 1954, 1955, and 1957 he received Erkel prizes. In 1973 he was made a Merited Artist and in 1980 an Outstanding Artist by the Hungarian government. The early period of his music is marked by nationalistic tendencies; later he adopted serial techniques and began to explore the field of "sonorism," or sound for sound's sake, making use of all available sonorous resources, such as tone clusters and microtones.

WORKS: BALLETS: *The Wedding at Ecser* (1950); *Bányászballada* (Miner's Ballad; 1961); *Cinque studi* (1967; after the orch. set of the same title); *Quadros soltos (Musica da ballo)* (1968); *Reflexionen* (1970); *Dance Pictures* (1971); *Metropolis* (1972); *The Poltroon* (1972). **ORCH.:** *Puppet Show Overture* (1944); 2 sinfoniettas (1944, 1948); Bassoon Concertino (1954); *Symphony for Strings* (1956); *Ricercare* (1959); *Musica da ballo,* suite (1962; based on the ballet *Bányászballada*); *Cinque studi* (1960; as a ballet, 1967); *3 Eufonias: I* for Strings, 2 Harps, and Percussion (1963), *II* for 24 Winds, 2 Harps, and Percussion (1964), and *III* for Orch. (1965); *Gemma (In Memoriam Kodály)* (1968); *Monumentum* (1969); *Notices* for Strings (1972); *Landscapes* for Strings (1974); *Fragment* (1977). **CHAMBER:** String Quartet (1948); *Serenade* for Oboe, Clarinet, and Bassoon (1952); *Musica leggiera* for Wind Quintet (1956); String Trio (1957); *Musica da camera per 11* (1966; Hanover, N.H., July 12, 1967); Trio for Violin, Viola, and Harp (1967); *Consort* for Wind Quintet (1970); *Albumblätter* for Double Bass (1973); *Kaleidoscope* for 15 Instruments (1976); *4 Studies* for 4 Percussionists (1977); *Contrasts* for Chamber Ensemble (1979). **VOCAL:** *2 Laments* for Soprano, Alto Flute, Harp, Piano, and Percussion (1962); *Lament* for Soprano and Chamber Ensemble (1967); *Messzésegek* (Remoteness) for Chorus (1975); *Strophen* for Soprano, Harp, and Percussion (1975); *Nyúlfarkkantáta* (Tiny Cantata) for Voices, Strings, and Piano (1976); *Cheremiss Folksongs* for Chorus (1977).

BIBL.: P. Várnai, *M. R.* (Budapest, 1967).

Marriner, Sir Neville, outstanding English conductor; b. Lincoln, April 15, 1924. He studied violin with his father, and then with Frederick Mountney; subsequently entered the Royal College of Music in London when he was 13, but his studies were interrupted by military service during World War II; after resuming his training at the Royal College of Music, he completed his violin studies in Paris with René Benedetti and took courses at the Cons. He was active as a violinist in chamber music ensembles; was a prof. of violin at the Royal College of Music (1949–59); joined the Philharmonia Orch. of London as a violinist (1952), and then was principal 2nd violinist of the London Sym. Orch. (1956–58). His interest in conducting was encouraged by Pierre Monteux, who gave him lessons at his summer school in Hancock, Maine (1959). In 1958 he founded the Academy of St.-Martin-in-the-Fields; served as its director until 1978, establishing an international reputation through recordings and tours. From 1968 to 1978 he also served as music director of the Los Angeles Chamber Orch.; then was music director of the Minnesota Orch. in Minneapolis (1978–86). In 1981 he became principal guest conductor of the Stuttgart Radio Sym. Orch.; was its chief conductor from 1983 to 1989. He appeared as a guest conductor with many of the world's leading orchs. On Sept. 29, 1994, he opened the 1994–95 season of N.Y.'s Carnegie Hall conducting the Academy of St. Martin-in-the-Fields in a program featuring Cecilia Bartoli as the soloist of the evening. The concert was subsequently telecast throughout the U.S. by PBS. In 1979 he was made a Commander of the Order of the British Empire. He was knighted in 1985. Marriner has proved himself one of the most remarkable conductors of his day. His extensive activities as a chamber music player, orch. musician, and chamber orch. violinist-conductor served as an invaluable foundation for his career as a sym. conductor of the first rank. His enormous repertoire encompasses works from the Baroque era to the great masterworks of the 20th century. In all of his performances, he demonstrates authority, mastery of detail, and impeccable taste.

Marrocco, W(illiam) Thomas, American violinist and musicologist; b. West New York, N.J., Dec. 5, 1909. After initial music studies in the U.S., he went to Italy and entered the Cons. di Musica S. Pietro a Majella in Naples, receiving his diploma di Magistero in 1930; then studied violin and musicology at the Eastman School of Music in Rochester, N.Y. (B.M., 1934; M.A., 1940); earned his Ph.D. at the Univ. of Calif. at Los Angeles with the diss. *Jacopo da Bologna and His Works* (1952; publ. as *The Music of Jacopo da Bologna,* Berkeley, 1954). After teaching at Elmira (N.Y.) College (1936–39) and serving as a visiting lecturer at the Univ. of Iowa (1945–46), he was on the music faculty of the Univ. of Kansas in Lawrence (1946–49); was prof. of music at the Univ. of Calif. at Los Angeles (1950–77); also played in the Roth String Quartet. He publ. numerous informative essays dealing with early Italian and American music; ed. Vols. VI–IX of Polyphonic Music of the Fourteenth Century: Italian Secular Music (Monaco, 1967–78); also publ. *Fourteenth Century Italian Cacce* (Cambridge, Mass., 1942; 2nd ed., rev. and aug., 1961); *Music in America: An Anthology* (with H. Gleason; N.Y., 1964); *Medieval Music* (with N. Sandon; London, 1977); *Inventory of Fifteenth Century Bassedanze, Balli and Balletti in Italian Dance Manuals* (N.Y., 1981); *Memoirs of a Stradivarius* (N.Y., 1988).

Marsalis, Wynton, outstanding black American trumpeter; b. New Orleans, Oct. 18, 1961. He was born into a cultured musical family; his father, Ellis Marsalis, was a trained pianist and active as a jazz musician; he insisted that his sons receive professional training. In 1974 the elder Marsalis founded the jazz program for the nascent New Orleans Center for the Creative Arts, which nurtured important new talent. Wynton took up the trumpet at age 6; later studied with John Longo, and also received instruction at his father's school. He appeared as soloist in the Haydn Trumpet Concerto with the New Orleans Phil. when he was 14; also performed with local groups in classical, jazz, and rock settings. He won the Harvey Shapiro Award as the most gifted brass player at the Berkshire Music Center at Tanglewood at age 17; then attended the Juilliard School in N.Y. (1979–81). He was a member of Art Blakey's Jazz Messengers (1980–81); played with them at the jazz festival at Montreux, Switzerland (1980); then toured with his own quintet, which included his brother Branford, a fine saxophonist; he also worked with Miles Davis. In 1984 he achieved unprecedented success when he won Grammy awards in both the jazz and classical categories for his recordings. In all, he won a grand total of 8 Grammy awards. He is credited with leading a jazz revival which has brought forward many young musicians of great talent. On Oct. 30, 1990, Marsalis hosted a benefit concert for Graham-Windham (a private child-care agency), the Autism Soc. of America, and the Immunohematology Research Foundation at Alice Tully Hall in N.Y.; featured were the musical members of his family: patriarch Ellis on piano, youngest brother Jason, making his debut on drums, Branford on saxophone, and Wynton on trumpet; absent was Delfeayo, a trombonist. The Marsalis clan was joined by the members of Wynton's jazz septet in an evening of critically acclaimed hard-bop. In 1993 he was invited to perform at the White House in Washington, D.C., for President Clinton. He publ. the book *Sweet Swing Blues on the Road* (N.Y., 1994) and the companion vol. to the PBS series, *Marsalis on Music* (N.Y., 1995).

Marsh, Robert C(harles), noted American music critic; b. Columbus, Ohio, Aug. 5, 1924. He took courses in journalism (B.S., 1945) and philosophy (A.M., 1946) at Northwestern Univ. In 1946–47 he was a Sage fellow at Cornell Univ., where he received training in theory from Robert Palmer. He pursued postgraduate studies at the Univ. of Chicago (1948), and then studied at Harvard Univ. (Ed.D., 1951), where he also attended Hindemith's lectures (1949–50). After attending the Univ. of

Oxford (1952–53), he studied musicology with Thurston Dart and theory of criticism with H.S. Middleton at the Univ. of Cambridge (1953–56). He taught social sciences at the Univ. of Ill. (1947–49), was a lecturer in the humanities at Chicago City Junior College (1950–51), and assistant prof. of education at the Univ. of Kansas (1951–52). After serving as visiting prof. of education at the State Univ. of N.Y. (1953–54), he taught the humanities at the Univ. of Chicago (1956–58). He was contributing ed. of *High Fidelity* magazine (1955–66; 1971–77). He served as music critic of the *Chicago Sun-Times* from 1956 to 1991. In addition to his music reviews and books, he contributed articles on music to various literary and philosophical publications. His books on music comprise *Toscanini and the Art of Orchestral Performance* (1956; 2nd ed., rev., 1962 as *Toscanini and the Art of Conducting*), *The Cleveland Orchestra* (1967), *Ravinia* (1987), and *James Levine at Ravinia* (1993).

Marsh, Roger (Michael), English composer and teacher; b. Bournemouth, Dec. 10, 1949. He studied with Ian Kellam at the London College of Music and privately (1966–68); continued his training at the Univ. of York (B.A., 1971), where he became a composition student of Bernard Rands (Ph.D., 1975); received a Harkness fellowship to study at the Univ. of Calif. at San Diego (1976–78). Returning to England, he was a lecturer at the Univ. of Keele (1978–88), where he was founder-director of the Keele New Music Ensemble (1979–88) and head of the music dept. (1985–88); then accepted a position as lecturer at the Univ. of York (from 1988).

WORKS: MUSIC THEATER: *Cass* (1970); *PS* (1971); *Calypso* (1973); *Scènes de ballet* (London, Feb. 17, 1974); *Dum* (1973; rev. version, San Diego, April 29, 1977; also for Orch. as *Dum's Dream*, 1973); *Time Before* (1977; London, Jan. 19, 1979); *Bits and Scraps* (London, May 6, 1979); *Spit and Blow* (1981; Birmingham, Feb. 27, 1983); *Samson* (1983; London, Oct. 20, 1984); *Love on the Rocks* (1989); *The Big Bang* (part 1, 1989). **ORCH.:** *Dum's Dream* (1973; also a music theater version as *Dum*); *Still* (1980; Birmingham, Nov. 13, 1981; rev. version, Liverpool, May 12, 1987); *Stepping Out* (1990). **CHAMBER:** *Jesters (for sicks)* for 2 Oboes, 2 Clarinets, and 2 Bassoons (1972); *Serenade* for Amplified Double Bass and 15 Strings (London, July 16, 1974); *Sweet and Short* for Clarinet, Piano, and Double Bass (1974); *Variations* for [4] Trombones (1977; Los Angeles, Feb. 5, 1979); *Point to Point* for 2 Oboes, 2 Clarinets, 2 Horns, and 2 Bassoons (1979); *2 Movements* for 2 Flutes, 2 Clarinets, Harp, and String Quartet (London, Oct. 9, 1979); *Heaven Haven* for Harp (1982); *Music* for Piano and Wind Instruments (York, March 17, 1986); *Dying for it* for 9 Instruments (1988); Trio for Piano, Clarinet, and Cello (1988). **PIANO:** *Easy Steps* (1987). **VOCAL:** *Streim* for Soprano, Flute, Clarinet, Trumpet, and Double Bass (1972); *The Lover's Ghost*, folk song for Soprano, 2 Flutes, 2 Clarinets, and Cello (1972; also for High Voice and Harp, 1976); *On and On*, folk song for Soprano, 2 Clarinets, and Bass Clarinet (1975); *3 Hale Mairies* for 3 Sopranos, Flute, Clarinet, Trumpet, Harp, Piano, 2 Percussion, Viola, and Cello (1976; San Diego, March 17, 1977); *Another Silly Love Song* for Soprano, Clarinet, and Piano (1976); *Not a Soul but Ourselves . . .* for 2 Women's and 2 Men's Voices with independent amplification (San Diego, Nov. 29, 1977); *A Psalm and a Silly Love Song* for Soprano, Mezzo-soprano, Flute, Clarinet, Trumpet, Harp, Viola, and Cello (London, April 25, 1979); *The Wormwood and the Gall* for Mezzo-soprano, Flute, Clarinet, Percussion, Harp, Viola, and Cello (London, July 6, 1981); *Words of Love* for Baritone, 2 Oboes, Bassoon, and Harpsichord (1982); *Songs of Devotion* for Soprano, Clarinet, and Guitar (1983; York, March 10, 1984); *3 Biblical Songs* for Soprano, Baritone, Small Women's Chorus, and Orch. (1985); *The Song of Abigail* for Soprano and Orch. (London, March 7, 1986).

Marshall, Ingram D(ouglass), American composer; b. Mount Vernon, N.Y., May 10, 1942. He studied at Lake Forest (Ill.) College (B.A., 1964); after studies in musicology with Lang and in electronic music with Ussachevsky at Columbia Univ. (1964–66), he pursued training with Subotnick at N.Y.'s School of the Arts (1969–70); continued his studies with Subotnick and with K.R.T. Wasitodipura (traditional Indonesian music) at the Calif. Inst. of the Arts in Valencia (M.F.A., 1971), where he subsequently taught (until 1974). He was active as both a composer and a music critic; was awarded various grants and commissions. His compositions reflect his extensive travels, as well as an artful incorporation of non-traditional instruments, live electronics, and improvisation. His highly successful *Fog Tropes* (1982) makes use of electronically manipulated taped sounds gathered around the San Francisco Bay that include not only foghorns but the falsetto keenings of seagulls and the lowing of a gambuh (a Balinese flute).

WORKS: *Transmogrification* for Tape (1966); *3 Buchla Studies* for Synthesizer (1968–69); *Cortez*, text-sound piece (1973); *Vibrosuperball* for 4 Amplified Percussion (1975); *Non confundar* for String Sextet, Alto Flute, Clarinet, and Electronics (1977); *Adendum: In aeternum* for Clarinet, Flute, and String Sextet (1979); *Spiritus* for 6 Strings, 4 Flutes, Harpsichord, and Vibraphone (1981; rev. for String Orch., 1983); *Fog Tropes* for Brass Sextet and Tape (1982); *Voces resonae*, string quartet (1984).

Marshall, Lois (Catherine), prominent Canadian soprano, later mezzo-soprano; b. Toronto, Jan. 29, 1924. She began her vocal training at age 12 with Weldon Kilburn, whom she married in 1968; also studied lieder interpretation with Emmy Heim (1947–50). She first gained notice as a soloist in Bach's *St. Matthew Passion* with Sir Ernest MacMillan and the Toronto Sym. Orch. (1947). In 1952 she made her operatic stage debut as the Queen of the Night in Toronto, won the Naumburg Award, and made her N.Y. recital debut. She appeared as a soloist in Beethoven's *Missa solemnis* with Toscanini and the NBC Sym. Orch. in 1953, and subsequently sang with many other important American orchs. She made her London debut in 1956 with Beecham and the Royal Phil., and began a series of world concert tours in 1960; began singing as a mezzo-soprano in the mid-1970s. Although she gave her official farewell performance at a Toronto concert on Dec. 10, 1982, she made occasional appearances in subsequent years. She was made a Companion of the Order of Canada (1968).

Marshall, Margaret (Anne), Scottish soprano; b. Stirling, Jan. 4, 1949. She studied at the Royal Scottish Academy of Music in Glasgow; also took voice lessons with Edna Mitchell and Peter Pears in England and with Hans Hotter in Munich. In 1974 she won 1st prize at the International Competition in Munich. She made her London concert debut in 1975; in 1978 she made her operatic debut in Florence as Euridice in *Orfeo*; she then sang the role of the Countess in the 1979 Florence production of *Le nozze di Figaro*, and made her Covent Garden debut in London in the same role in 1980. In 1982 she appeared as Fiordiligi at La Scala in Milan and at the Salzburg Festival. She made her first appearances in the U.S. in 1980 as a soloist with the Boston Sym. Orch. and N.Y. Phil.; subsequently made several American tours as a concert artist. In 1988 she made her first appearance at the Vienna State Opera as Mozart's Countess.

Marshall, Mike, American mandolinist and guitarist; b. Newcastle, Pa., July 17, 1957. He studied with James Hilligoos in Lakeland, Fla. He performed in various ensembles, including the Sunshine Bluegrass Boys (1972–76), the David Grisman Quintet (1979–84), and Montreux (1984–89). In 1986 he formed, with mandolinist Dana (William) Rath (b. West Bend, Wis., May 21, 1956), the Modern Mandolin Quartet, the first mandolin quartet, comprising mandolins, mandola, and mandocello, corresponding to the string quartet; other members are Paul Binkley (b. Minneapolis, May 9, 1954) and John Eric Imholz (b. San Francisco, June 9, 1953). Marshall helped to spearhead the New Acoustic movement with the David Grisman Quintet and New Age music as a recording artist for Windham Hill; an accomplished international performer, he performs in bluegrass, jazz, classical, and New Acoustic Music styles. His goal as a composer and performer is to "fuse musical styles such as jazz, bluegrass, world music, and classical to form new styles reflective of a less-structured, freer world." Among his compositions are *Gator Strut, Dolphins,* and *Free D;* also songs.

Marshall, Robert L(ewis), distinguished American musicologist; b. N.Y., Oct. 12, 1939. After training at Columbia Univ. (A.B., 1960), he studied at Princeton Univ. with Babbitt, Lockwood, Mendel, and Strunk (M.F.A., 1962; Ph.D., 1968, with the diss. *The Compositional Process of J.S. Bach: A Study of the Autograph Scores of the Vocal Works;* publ. in Princeton, 1972). In 1966 he joined the faculty of the Univ. of Chicago, where he served as chairman of the music dept. (1972–77) and then as a prof. (1977–83). He was a prof. at Brandeis Univ. from 1983. From 1977 to 1987 he was general ed. of the series Recent Researches in the Music of the Baroque Era. Marshall has particularly distinguished himself in Bach and Mozart studies, and has contributed scholarly articles to various journals. His book *The Music of Johann Sebastian Bach: The Sources, the Style, the Significance* (N.Y., 1989) won the ASCAP-Deems Taylor Award in 1990. His other books include *Mozart Speaks: Views on Music, Musicians, and the World* (N.Y., 1991) and *Eighteenth-Century Keyboard Music* (N.Y., 1994).

Marsick, Armand (Louis Joseph), Belgian conductor, teacher, and composer; b. Liège, Sept. 20, 1877; d. Haine-St.-Paul, April 30, 1959. He was the nephew of the distinguished Belgian violinist Martin (-Pierre-Joseph) Marsick (b. Jupille-sur-Neuse, near Liège, March 9, 1848; d. Paris, Oct. 21, 1924). Armand Marsick studied with his father, Louis Marsick; then took a course in composition with Dupuis at the Liège Cons., with Ropartz at the Nancy Cons., and d'Indy in Paris. After playing 1st violin in the Municipal Théâtre in Nancy, he became concertmaster at the Concerts Colonne in Paris (1898); in 1908 he obtained the position of instructor at the Athens Cons., where he remained until 1921; was appointed director at the Bilbao Cons. in 1922. He was a prof. at the Liège Cons. (1927–42) and conductor of the Société des Concerts Symphoniques (1927–39).

WORKS: DRAMATIC: OPERAS: *La Jane* (1903; 1st perf. as *Vendetta corsa,* Rome, 1913; Liège, March 29, 1921); *Lara* (1913; Antwerp, Dec. 3, 1929); *L'Anneau nuptial* (1920; Brussels, March 3, 1928). **RADIO PLAY:** *Le Visage de la Wallonie* (1937). **ORCH.:** 2 symphonic poems: *Stèle funéraire* (1902) and *La Source* (1908); *Improvisation et Final* for Cello and Orch. (1904); 2 suites: *Scènes de montagnes* (1910) and *Tableaux grecs* (1912); *Tableaux de voyage* for Small Orch. (1939); *Loustics en fête* for Small Orch. (1939); *3 morceaux symphoniques* (1950). **CHAMBER:** Violin Sonata (1900); Quartet for 4 Horns (1950); *4 pièces* for Piano (1912). **VOCAL:** Choruses; songs.

Marteau, Henri, greatly esteemed French-born Swedish violinist and pedagogue; b. Rheims, March 31, 1874; d. Lichtenberg, Bavaria, Oct. 3, 1934. He studied violin with Léonard and Garcin at the Paris Cons. (premier prix, 1892) and began his concert career as a youth; played in Vienna when he was 10 and in London when he was 14. In 1892, 1893, 1894, 1898, and 1906 he also toured the U.S.; gave concerts in Scandinavia, Russia, France, and Germany. In 1900 he was appointed prof. of violin at the Geneva Cons., and in 1908 succeeded Joachim as violin teacher at the Hochschule für Musik in Berlin. He conducted the Göteborg orch. (1915–20) and became a naturalized Swedish citizen (1920); then taught at the German Academy of Music in Prague (1921–24), the Leipzig Cons. (1926–27), and the Dresden Cons. (from 1928). He was greatly appreciated by musicians of Europe; Reger, who was a personal friend, wrote a violin concerto for him, as did Massenet; his teacher Léonard bequeathed to him his magnificent Maggini violin, once owned by the Empress Maria Theresa. He championed the music of Bach and Mozart. Marteau was also a competent composer; he wrote an opera, *Meister Schwable* (Plauen, 1921); *Sinfonia gloria naturae* for Orch. (Stockholm, 1918); 2 violin concertos; Cello Concerto; much chamber music; many choral works; numerous violin pieces and arrangements of classical works.

BIBL.: B. Marteau, *H. M., Siegeszug einer Geige* (Tutzing, 1971); G. Weiss, ed., *Der Lehrer und Wegbereiter von H. M., Hubert Léonard* (Tutzing, 1987); K. Bangerter, *H. M. als Komponist im Spiegel der Kritik: Eine Studie zum Begriff der "Einheit" in der Musikkritik um 1900* (Tutzing, 1991).

Martelli, Henri, French composer; b. Santa Fe, Argentina, Feb. 25, 1895; d. Paris, July 15, 1980. He studied law at the Univ. of Paris; simultaneously took courses in fugue and composition with Widor at the Paris Cons. (1912–24). From 1940 to 1944 he was head of orch. and chamber music programs of the French Radio; he was secretary of the Société Nationale de Musique (1945–67) and director of programs there from 1968; from 1953 to 1973, he also was president of the French section of the ISCM. In his compositions, he attempted to re-create the spirit of early French music using modern techniques.

WORKS: DRAMATIC: OPERAS: *La Chanson de Roland* (1921–23; rev. 1962–64; Paris, April 13, 1967); *Le Major Cravachon* (1958; French Radio, June 14, 1959). **BALLETS:** *La Bouteille de Panurge* (1930; Paris, Feb. 24, 1937); *Les Hommes de sable* (1951). **ORCH.:** *Rondo* (1921); *Sarabande, Scherzo et Final* (1922); *Divertissement sarrasin* (1922); *Sur la vie de Jeanne d'Arc* (1923); *Scherzo* for Violin and Orch. (1925); *Mors et Juventas* (1927); *Bas-reliefs assyriens* (1928; Boston, March 14, 1930); *Passacaille sur un thème russe* (1928); *Concerto for Orchestra* (1931; Boston, April 22, 1932); 3 suites: No. 1, *Suite sur un thème corse* (1936), No. 2 (1950), and No. 3 (1971); 2 concertos for Violin and Chamber Orch. (1938, 1954); *Ouverture pour un conte de Boccace* (1942); *Suite concertante* for Wind Quintet and Orch. (1943); *Divertimento* for Wind Orch. (1945); *Fantaisie* for Piano and Orch. (1945); *Sinfonietta* (1948); 3 syms.: No. 1 for Strings (1953; French Radio, March 13, 1955), No. 2 for Strings (1956; Paris, July 17, 1958), and No. 3 (1957; Paris, March 8, 1960); Concertino for Oboe, Clarinet, Horn, Bassoon, and Strings (1955); Double Concerto for Clarinet, Bassoon, and Orch. (1956); *Le Radeau de la Meduse,* symphonic poem (1957); *Variations* for Strings (1959); *Scènes a danser* (1963); *Rapsodie* for Cello and Orch. (1966); Oboe Concerto (1971). **CHAMBER:** *Invention* for Cello and Piano (1925); Duo for Oboe and English Horn (1925); 2 string quartets (1932–33; 1944); Piano Trio (1935); Violin Sonata (1936); *Suite* for 4 Clarinets (1936); *Introduction et Final* for Violin and Piano (1937); Wind Octet (1941); *Scherzetto, Berceuse et Final* for Cello and Piano (1941); Bassoon Sonata (1941); Cello Sonatina (1941); Flute Sonata (1942); *3 esquisses* for Saxophone and Piano (1943); *Preambule et Scherzo* for Clarinet and Piano (1944); 7 Duos for Violin and Harp (1946); *Fantaisiestück* for Flute and Piano (1947); Wind Quintet (1947); Cornet Sonatina (1948); *Adagio, Cadence et Final* for Oboe and Piano (1949); 2 quintets for Flute, Harp, and String Trio (1950, 1952); Trio for Flute, Cello, and Piano (1951); *Cadence, Interlude et Rondo* for Saxophone and Piano (1952); *15 études* for Bassoon (1953); Bass Trombone Sonata (1956); Viola Sonata (1959); Suite for Guitar (1960); *Concertstück* for Viola and Piano (1962); Concertino for Cornet and Piano (1964); *Dialogue* for Trombone, Tuba or Bass Saxophone, and Piano (1966); Oboe Sonata (1972); String Trio (1973–74); Trio for Flute, Cello, and Harp (1976). **PIANO:** *Suite galante* (1924); *Guitare* (1931); *3 Petites suites* (1935, 1943, 1950); Suite (1939); Sonata for 2 Pianos (1946); *Sonorités* for Piano, left-hand (1974). **VOCAL:** *Le Temps,* cantata for Voice and 8 Instruments (1945); *Chrestomathie* for Chorus (1949); songs. **OTHER:** 17 radiophonic works (1940–62).

Martenot, Maurice (Louis Eugène), French inventor of the electronic instrument "Ondes musicales," a.k.a. "Ondes Martenot"; b. Paris, Oct. 14, 1898; d. there, Oct. 10, 1980. He studied composition at the Paris Cons. with Gédalge. He constructed an electronic musical instrument with a keyboard, which he called Ondes musicales. He gave its first demonstration in Paris on April 20, 1928, and, on Dec. 23, 1928, the first musical work for the instrument, *Poème symphonique pour solo d'Ondes musicales et orchestre,* by Dimitri Levidis, was presented in Paris. Martenot publ. *Méthode pour l'enseignement des Ondes musicales* (Paris, 1931). The instrument became popular, especially among French composers: it is included in the score of Honegger's *Jeanne d'Arc au bûcher* (1935); Koechlin's *Le Buisson ardent*, part 1 (1938); Martinon's 2nd Sym., *Hymne à la vie* (1944); and Messiaen's *Turangalila-Symphonie* (1946–48). It was used as a solo instrument in Koechlin's *Hymne* (1929), Jolivet's *Concerto* (1947), Landowski's *Concerto* (1954), Bondon's *Kaleidoscope* (1957), and Charpentier's *Concertino "alla francese"* (1961). Many other composers were attracted to it as well. Of all the early electronic instruments—Ondes Martenot, Trautonium, and Theremin—only Martenot's has proved a viable musical instrument. When Varèse's *Ecuatorial*, written in 1934 for a brass ensemble and including a Theremin, was publ. in 1961, the score substituted an Ondes Martenot for the obsolescent Theremin. Martenot's sister, Ginette Martenot (b. Paris, Jan. 27, 1902), became the chief exponent of the Ondes Martenot in concert performances in Europe and the U.S.

Martienssen, Carl Adolf, German musicologist; b. Güstrow, Dec. 6, 1881; d. Berlin, March 1, 1955. He received training in piano from Klindworth and Berger in Berlin, and from Reisenauer in Leipzig. After teaching at the Bromber Cons., he studied with Kretzchmar, Stumpf, Wolf, and Wundt at the Univ. of Berlin. In 1914 he became a piano teacher at the Leipzig Cons. He also served as director of the piano classes at the Leipzig Inst. of Church Music, where he was made a prof. in 1932. From 1932 he was a prof. at the Berlin Musical Inst. for Foreigners. He taught at the Hochschules für Musik in Berlin (1934–45), Rostock (1945–50), and East Berlin (1950–52). Martienssen prepared Urtexts of the Haydn, Mozart, and Beethoven piano sonatas.

WRITINGS (all publ. in Leipzig): *Die individuelle Klaviertechnik auf der Grundlage des schöpferischen Klangwillens* (1930); *Die Methodik des individuellen Klavierunterrichts* (1934); *Grundlage einer deutschen Klavierlehre* (1942); *Das Klavierkunstwerk* (1950).

Martín, Edgardo, Cuban composer and music educator; b. Cienfuegos, Oct. 6, 1915. He began his initial musical training with his maternal grandmother, the pianist Aurea Suárez, in Cienfuegos (1925–35). Settling in Havana, he studied piano with Jascha Fischermann (1936–37), attended the Univ. (1937–41), and received training in composition from José Ardévol at the Cons. (1939–46). From 1943 to 1967 he was active as a music critic. He also taught music history and aesthetics at the Cons. (1945–68) and music analysis at the Escuela nacional de Arte (1969–73). From 1962 to 1971 he was executive secretary of the National Committee of Music for UNESCO. As a Castro partisan, he was a principal figure in the reform of music teaching under the Communist regime. He composed in an accessible style.

WORKS: BALLET: *El Caballo de coral* (1960). **ORCH.:** 2 syms. (1947, 1948). **CHAMBER:** Concerto for 9 Winds (1944); Trio for Oboe, Clarinet, and Bassoon (1963); 2 string quartets (1967, 1968); *Recitativo y aria* for Viola and Piano (1979); guitar pieces. **PIANO:** Sonata (1943); 2 preludes (1950); 3 *Soneras* (1950, 1971, 1975). **VOCAL:** *Los 2 abuelos* for Chorus and Instruments (1949); *Canto de héroes* for Voices and Orch. (1967); *La carta del soldado* for Narrator, Tenor, Chorus, Speaking Chorus, and Orch. (1970); *Granma* for Chorus and Instruments (1976); cantatas; songs.

Martin, Frank (Théodore), greatly renowned Swiss composer and pedagogue; b. Geneva, Sept. 15, 1890; d. Naarden, the Netherlands, Nov. 21, 1974. He was the last of 10 children of a Calvinist minister, a descendant of the Huguenots. He studied privately with Joseph Lauber in Geneva (1906–14), who instructed him in the basics of the conservative idiom of Swiss music of the fin de siècle; then had lessons with Hans Huber and Frederic Klose, who continued to emphasize the conservative foundations of the religious and cultural traditions of the Swiss establishment. However, Martin soon removed himself from the strict confines of Swiss scholasticism, encouraged in this development by Ernest Ansermet. In 1918 Martin went to Zürich and, in 1921, to Rome; finally settled in Paris in 1923, then the center of modern music. He returned to Geneva in 1926 as a pianist and harpsichordist; taught at the Inst. Jaques-Dalcroze (1927–38), was founder and director of the Technicum Moderne de Musique (1933–39), and served as president of the Assn. of Swiss Musicians (1942–46). He moved to the Netherlands in 1946; also taught composition at the Cologne Hochschule für Musik (1950–57). His early music showed the influence of Franck and French impressionists, but soon he succeeded in creating a distinctive style supported by a consummate mastery of contrapuntal and harmonic writing, and a profound feeling for emotional consistency and continuity. Still later he became fascinated by the logic and self-consistency of Schoenberg's method of composition with 12 tones, and adopted it in a modified form in several of his works. He also demonstrated an ability to stylize folk-song materials in modern techniques. In his music, Martin followed the religious and moral precepts of his faith in selecting several subjects of his compositions. In 1944 the director of Radio Geneva asked him to compose an oratorio to be broadcast immediately upon the conclusion of World War II. He responded with *In terra pax* for 5 Soli, Double Chorus, and Orch., which was given its broadcast premiere from Geneva at the end of the war in Europe, May 7, 1945; a public performance followed in Geneva 24 days later. He publ. *Responsabilité du compositeur* (Geneva, 1966); M. Martin ed. his *Un compositeur médite sur son art* (Neuchâtel, 1977).

WORKS: DRAMATIC: *Oedipe-Roi*, incidental music (Geneva, Nov. 21, 1922); *Oedipe à Colone*, incidental music (1923); *Le Divorce*, incidental music (Geneva, April 1928); *Roméo et Juliette*, incidental music (Mézières, June 1, 1929); *Die blaue Blume*, ballet music (1935); *Das Märchen vom Aschenbrodel*, ballet, after *Cinderella* (1941; Basel, March 12, 1942); *La Voix des siècles*, incidental music (Geneva, July 4, 1942); *Ein Totentanz zu Basel im Jahre 1943*, outdoor dance spectacle (Basel, May 27, 1943); *Athalie*, incidental music (1946; Geneva, May 7, 1947); *Der Sturm*, opera, after Shakespeare (1952–55; Vienna, June 17, 1956); *Monsieur de Pourceaugnac*, opera, after Molière (1960; Geneva, April 23, 1963).

ORCH.: Suite (St. Gallen, June 14, 1913); *Symphonie pour orchestre burlesque* (1915; Geneva, Feb. 1916); *Esquisse* (Geneva, Oct. 30, 1920); *Entr'acte pour grand orchestre* (1924; also as a Concerto for Winds and Piano, and as the *Chamber Fox Trot*, Boston, Dec. 20, 1927; all based on the *Ouverture et foxtrot* for 2 Pianos); *Rhythmes*, 3 symphonic movements (1926; Geneva, March 12, 1927); 2 piano concertos: No. 1 (1933–34; Geneva, Jan. 22, 1936) and No. 2 (1968; ORTF, Paris, June 24, 1970); *Quatre pièces brèves* (Geneva, Nov. 21, 1934; also for Guitar or for Piano, 1933); *Danse de la peur* for 2 Pianos and Chamber Orch. (1935; Geneva, June 28, 1944; based on the ballet music *Die blaue Blume*); Sym. (1936–37; Lausanne, March 7, 1938); *Ballade* for Alto Saxophone and Strings (1936–37); *Du Rhône au Rhin*, march for Band (Zürich, May 6, 1939); *Ballade* for Flute and Orch. (orchestrated by E. Ansermet; Lausanne, Nov. 27, 1939; based on the *Ballade* for Flute and Piano; also for Flute, Strings, and Piano, Basel, Nov. 28, 1941); *Ballade* for Piano and Orch. (1939; Zürich, Feb. 1, 1944); *Ballade* for Trombone and Chamber Orch. (1941; Geneva, Jan. 26, 1942; based on the *Ballade* for Trombone and Piano, 1940); *Petite symphonie concertante* for Harp, Harpsichord, Piano, and Double String Orch. (1944–45; Zürich, May 17, 1946; also for Full Orch. as *Symphonie concertante*, 1946; Lucerne, Aug. 16, 1947); *Ballade* for Cello and Chamber Orch. (1949; Zürich, Nov. 17, 1950; based on the *Ballade* for Cello and Piano); Concerto for 7 Winds, Percussion, and Strings (Bern, Oct. 25, 1949); Violin Concerto (1950–51; Basel, Jan. 24, 1952); Concerto for Harpsichord and Small Orch. (1951–52; Venice, Sept. 14, 1952); *Sonata da chiesa* for Viola d'Amore and Strings (1952; Turin, April 29, 1953; based on the *Sonata da chiesa* for Viola d'Amore and Organ, 1938; also for Flute and Strings, 1958; Lausanne, Oct. 15, 1959); *Passacaille* for Strings (1952; Frankfurt am Main, Oct. 16, 1953; based on the *Passacaille* for Organ, 1944; also for Full Orch., 1963; Berlin, May 30, 1963); *Pavane couleur du temps* for Chamber Orch. (1954; based on the piece for String Quintet, 1920; also for Piano, 4-hands); *Études* for Strings (1955–56; Basel, Nov. 23, 1956; also for 2 Pianos, 1957); *Ouverture en hommage à Mozart* (Geneva, Dec. 10, 1956); *Ouverture en rondeau* (Lucerne, Aug. 13, 1958); *Inter arma caritas* (Geneva, Sept. 1, 1963); *Les Quatre éléments*, symphonic études (1963–64; Lausanne, Oct. 5, 1964); Cello Concerto (1965–66; Basel, Jan. 26, 1967); *Erasmi monumentum* for Organ and Orch. (Rotterdam, Oct. 27, 1969); *Trois danses* for Oboe, Harp, String Quintet, and String Orch. (Zürich, Oct. 9, 1970); *Ballade* for Viola and Wind Orch. (1972; Salzburg, Jan. 20, 1973); *Polyptyque: Six images de la passion du Christ* for Violin and Double String Orch. (Lausanne, Sept. 9, 1973).

CHAMBER: 2 violin sonatas: No. 1 (1913; Thoune, July 10, 1915) and No. 2 (1931–32; Geneva, Oct. 7, 1932); Piano Quintet (1919); *Pavane couleur de temps* for String Quintet (1920; also for Piano, or for Chamber Orch., 1954); *Trio sur des mélodies populaires irlandais* for Violin, Cello, and Piano (1925; Paris, April 1926); *Quatre pièces brèves* for Guitar (1933; also for Piano, and for Orch., 1934); *Rhapsodie*, quintet for 2 Violins, 2 Violas, and Double Bass (1935; Geneva, March 10, 1936); String Trio (Brusses, May 2, 1936); *Sonata da chiesa* for Viola d'Amore and Organ (1938; Basel, Dec. 8, 1939; also for Flute and Organ, 1941, Lausanne, June 11, 1942, for Viola d'Amore and String Orch., 1952, and for Flute and String Orch., 1958); *Ballade* for Flute and Piano (1939; also for Flute and Orch., 1939, and for Flute, String Orch., and Piano, 1941); *Ballade* for Trombone and Piano (Geneva, Sept. 1940; also for Trombone and Chamber Orch., 1941); *Petite fanfare* for 2 Trumpets, 2 Horns, and 2 Trombones (1945); *Ballade* for Cello and Piano (1949; also for Cello and Chamber Orch.); String Quartet (1966–67; Zürich, June 20, 1968). **KEYBOARD: PIANO:** *Overture et foxtrot* for 2 Pianos (1924; also as *Entr'acte pour grand orchestre*, as a Concerto for Winds and Piano, and as the *Chamber Fox Trot*); *Quatre pièces brèves* (1933; also for Guitar or for Orch.); *Petite marche blanche et trio noir les grenouilles, le rossignol* for 2 Pianos (1937); *Huit préludes* (1947–48; Lausanne, March 22, 1950); *Clair de lune* (1952); *Au clair de lune* for Piano, 4-hands (1955); *Études* for 2 Pianos (Cologne, Oct. 28, 1957; based on the *Études* for String Orch., 1955–56); *Étude rythmique* (Geneva, Feb. 22, 1965); *Esquisse* (Munich, Sept. 1965); *Fantaisie sur des rhythmes flamenco* for Piano and Dancer ad libitum (1973; Lucerne, Aug. 18, 1974). **ORGAN:** *Passacaille* (Bern, Sept. 26, 1944; also for String Orch., 1952, and for Full Orch., 1962).

VOCAL: *Trois poèmes païens* for Baritone and Orch. (1910; Vevey, May 20, 1911); *Ode et sonnet* for 3 Treble Voices and Cello ad libitum (1912); *Les Dithyrambes* for 4 Soloists, Chorus, Children's Chorus, and Orch. (1915–18; Lausanne, June 16, 1918); *Le Roy a fait battre tambour* for Alto and Chamber Orch. (1916); *Chantons, je vous en prie* for Chorus (1920); *Quatre sonnets à Cassandre* for Mezzo-soprano, Flute, Viola, and Cello (1921; Geneva, April 7, 1923); Mass for Double Chorus (1922, 1926; Hamburg, Nov. 2, 1963); *Chanson du Mezzetin* for Soprano and Mandolin or Oboe, Violin, and Cello (1923); *La Nique à Satan* for Soprano, Baritone, Choruses, Winds, Percussion, and Piano (1928–31; Geneva, Feb. 25, 1933); *Le Vin herbé*, secular oratorio in 3 parts (part 1, 1938; Zürich, April 16, 1940; parts 2 and 3, 1940–41; 1st complete perf., Zürich, March 28, 1942); *Cantata pour le ler août*, secular cantata for Chorus and Piano or Organ (Geneva, Aug. 1, 1941); *Der Cornet*, song cycle for Alto and Chamber Orch., after Rilke (1942–43; Basel, Feb. 9, 1954); *Sechs Monologe aus "Jedermann,"* song cycle for Baritone and Piano, after Hofmannsthal (1943–44; Gastaad, Aug. 6, 1944; also for Baritone or Alto and Orch., 1949); *In terra pax*, oratorio brève for 5 Soloists, 2 Mixed Choruses, and Orch. (1944; radio broadcast, Geneva, May 7, 1945; 1st public perf., Geneva, May 31, 1945); *Dédicace* for Tenor and Piano (Geneva, July 6, 1945); *Golgotha*, passion oratorio for 5 Soloists, Chorus, Organ, and Orch. (1945–48; Geneva, April 29, 1949); *Quant n'ont assez fait, do-do*, song for Tenor, Guitar, and Piano, 4-hands (Lauren, Oct. 9, 1947); *Trois Chants de Noël* for Soprano, Flute and Piano (private family perf., Amsterdam, Dec. 25, 1947); *5 Ariel Songs* for Chorus (1950; Amsterdam, March 7, 1953); *Le Mystère de la Nativité*, Christmas oratorio for 9 Soloists, Mixed Chamber Chorus, Men's Chorus, Mixed Chorus, and Orch. (1957, 1959; Geneva, Dec. 23, 1959); *Pseaumes de Genève*, cantata for Chorus, Boy's Chorus, Organ, and Orch. (1958; Geneva, May 1959); *Drey Minnelieder*, song cycle for Soprano and Piano (1960); *Ode à la musique* for Chorus, Brass, Double Bass, and Piano (1961; Bienne, June 23, 1962); *Verse à boire* for Chorus (1961; Amsterdam, June 26, 1963); *Pilate*, oratorio breve for Baritone, Mezzo-soprano, Tenor, Bass, Chorus, and Orch. (RAI, Rome, Nov. 14, 1964); *Magnificat* for Soprano, Violin, and Orch. (1967; Lucerne, Aug. 14, 1968; incorporated into the *Maria-Triptychon*); *Maria-Triptychon* for Soprano, Violin, and Orch. (1968; Rotterdam, Nov. 13, 1969); *Ballade des pendus* for 3 Men's Voices and 3 Electric Guitars (1969; incorporated into the *Poèmes de la mort*); *Poèmes de la mort* for 3 Men's Voices and 3 Electric Guitars (1969, 1971; N.Y., Dec. 12, 1971); *Requiem* for 4 Soloists, Chorus, Organ, and Orch. (1971–72; Lausanne, May 4, 1973); *Et la vie l'emporta*, chamber cantata for Alto, Baritone, Small Chorus, and Instrumental Ensemble (1974; completed by B. Reichel; private premiere, Montreux, June 12, 1975; public premiere, Lucerne, Aug. 24, 1975); a few other short choruses and songs, as well as arrangements and harmonizations.

BIBL.: R. Klein, *F. M.: Sein Leben und Werk* (Vienna, 1960); A. Koelliker, *F. M.: Biographie, les oeuvres* (Lausanne, 1963); B. Billeter, *F. M.: Ein Aussenseiter der neuen Musik* (Frauenfeld, 1970); B. Martin, *F. M. ou la réalité du rêve* (Neuchâtel, 1973); special issue of *Schweizerische Musikzeitung*, CXVI (1976); W. Misteli, ed., *F. M.: Né le 15 septembre 1890, décédé le 21 novembre 1974: Liste des oeuvres: Werkverzeichnis* (Zürich, 1981); M. Martin, ed., *Apropos de . . . commentaires de F. M. sur ses oeuvres* (Neuchâtel, 1984); C. King, *F. M.: A Bio-Bibliography* (Westport, Conn., 1990).

Martin, Janis, American mezzo-soprano, later soprano; b. Sacramento, Aug. 16, 1939. She studied in San Francisco and N.Y., making her operatic debut as Teresa in *La Sonnambula* at the San Francisco Opera in 1960; subsequently sang Marina, Venus, and Meg Page there. On March 25, 1962, she made her first appearance at the N.Y. City Opera as Mrs. Grose in Britten's *The Turn of the Screw*. She won the Metropolitan Opera Auditions, making her debut as Flora in *La Traviata* on Dec. 19, 1962, in N.Y. After singing for 3 seasons as a mezzo-soprano, she returned to the Metropolitan Opera in 1973 as a soprano and sang such roles as Kundry, Sieglinde, and Berg's Marie in *Wozzeck*. In 1968 she appeared as Magdalene and as Fricka at the Bayreuth Festival. She sang Tosca at the Chicago Lyric Opera in 1971. From 1971 to 1988 she appeared at the Berlin Deutsche Oper. She made her Covent Garden debut in London as Marie in *Wozzeck* in 1973. In 1980 she sang the Woman in *Erwartung* at Milan's La Scala. She appeared as Isolde at the Geneva Opera in 1985. In 1990 she sang Beethoven's Leonore at the Deutsche Opera am Rhein in Düsseldorf. Among her other roles are Ortrud, Brangäne, Senta, Elisabeth in *Tännhauser*, Ariadne, and Judith in *Duke Bluebeard's Castle*.

Martin, Mary (Virginia), American singer, dancer, and actress; b. Weatherford, Texas, Dec. 1, 1913; d. Rancho Mirage, Calif., Nov. 3, 1990. The daughter of a lawyer and a violinist, she first established a dance school in Weatherford. She studied at the Ward-Belmont School in Nashville, Tenn.; then went to N.Y., where, although totally unknown to the general public, she stopped the show with her rendition of the song *My Heart Belongs to Daddy* in Cole Porter's musical comedy *Leave It to Me* (1938). Her N.Y. success brought her a film contract with Paramount studios in Hollywood, which was short-lived, as she preferred the theater. On the stage she scored a series of hits, beginning with a starring role in the Rodgers and Hammerstein musical *South Pacific* (1949) and later in *The Sound of Music* (1959), two of the longest-running musicals in Broadway history. She became best known for her 1954 creation of the lead character in the musical *Peter Pan*, in which she seemed to fly through the air; her career was once interrupted when she suffered an accident during levitation. In 1969 she retired to Brazil with her husband; after his death, she resumed her career (1979). In 1989 Martin received a Kennedy Center Honor in Washington, D.C., for her achievements in the theater. Her autobiography, *My Heart Belongs*, was publ. in 1976. Her son, Larry Hagman, was a veteran television actor whose fame was assured when he was cast as the villainous J.R. Ewing in the nighttime soap series *Dallas*.

BIBL.: B. Rivadue, *M. M.: A Bio-Bibliography* (N.Y., 1991).

Martin, Riccardo (actually, **Hugh Whitfield**), American tenor, teacher, and composer; b. Hopkinsville, Ky., Nov. 18, 1874; d. N.Y., Aug. 11, 1952. He received training in composition from MacDowell at Columbia Univ. and in voice from Sbriglia in Paris (1901), Franklin Cannone in Milan, and Vincenzo Lombardi in Florence (1908). In Oct. 1904 he made his operatic debut as Gounod's Faust in Nantes under the name Richard Martin. In 1905 he appeared as Andrea Chénier in Verona under the name Riccardo Martin. After making his U.S. debut as Canio in New Orleans in 1906, he toured with the San Carlo Opera Co. (1906–07). On Nov. 20, 1907, he made his Metropolitan Opera debut in N.Y. as Boito's Faust, remaining on its roster until 1915. During his years with the Metropolitan Opera, he appeared in such roles as Pinkerton, Cavaradossi, Canio, Manrico, Rodolfo, and Turiddu; he also created the roles of Quintus in Horatio Parker's *Mona* (March 14, 1912) and Christian in Walter Damrosch's *Cyrano de Bergerac* (Feb. 27, 1913) while there. In 1910 he appeared as Pinkerton at London's Covent Garden. In 1910–11 and 1912–13 he made appearances with the Boston Grand Opera Co. In 1917–18 he was again on the roster of the Metropolitan Opera, and then sang with the Chicago Grand Opera Co. (1920–22). He also made appearances as a concert artist before settling in N.Y. as a voice teacher. Among his compositions were a ballet, orch. music, and songs. Martin possessed a beautiful spinto voice and dramatic stage gifts, but his career was overshadowed by his celebrated colleague Enrico Caruso.

Martinelli, Giovanni, famous Italian tenor; b. Montagnana, Oct. 22, 1885; d. N.Y., Feb. 2, 1969. He sang and played the clarinet in his youth. His potential as a singer was discovered by a bandmaster during Martinelli's military service. In 1908 he first appeared on the operatic stage in Montagnana as the Messenger in *Aida*. He then studied voice with Mandolini in Milan, where he made his concert debut as a soloist in Rossini's *Stabat Mater* on Dec. 3, 1910. His formal operatic debut followed there at the Teatro del Varme as Ernani on Dec. 29, 1910. Puccini was impressed with his vocal gifts and invited Martinelli to sing Dick Johnson in the European premiere of the composer's *La Fanciulla del West* in Rome on June 12, 1911. He subsequently sang that role in various Italian music centers, including Milan's La Scala in 1912. On April 22, 1912, he made his first appearance at London's Covent Garden as Cavaradossi, and sang there again in 1913–14, 1919, and 1937. Martinelli made his 1st appearance with the Metropolitan Opera in that same role during the company's visit to Albany, N.Y., on Nov. 18, 1913. His formal debut at the Metropolitan Opera in N.Y. followed as Rodolfo on Nov. 20, 1913, with remarkable success. He rapidly acquired distinction there and, after Caruso's death in 1921, became one of the principal tenors on the Metropolitan Opera roster. He sang there every season until 1943, winning acclaim for his portrayals of such roles as Otello, Radames, Manrico, Eléazar in *La Juive*, Don José, Canio, Faust, Samson, and Andrea Chénier. He also appeared in Boston (1914), San Francisco (1923–39), Chicago (1924–31; 1933–44), St. Louis (1934–41), and Cincinnati (1940–45). In 1944 he returned to the Metropolitan Opera, where he made his farewell appearance as Pollione on March 8, 1945. During the 1945–46 season, he returned to the Metropolitan Opera as a concert artist. After singing in Philadelphia (1945–50), he taught voice in N.Y. while making occasional appearances as a singer. The Metropolitan Opera honored him on the 50th anniversary of his debut with the company with a gala on Nov. 20, 1963. He made his last public appearance as a singer in his 82nd year when he sang the Emperor in *Turandot* in Seattle. Martinelli's brilliant vocal and dramatic gifts made him one of the foremost singers of heroic roles of his era.

Martinet, Jean-Louis, French composer; b. Ste.-Bazeille, Nov. 8, 1912. He received his training in Paris with Koechlin (fugue) at the Schola Cantorum and with Roger-Ducasse (composition), Messiaen (analysis), and Munch and Desormière (conducting) at the Cons., where he took the premier prix in composition (1943). He later pursued studies in 12-tone music with Leibowitz (1945). He was a prof. at the Montreal Cons. from 1971. The early influence of Impressionism and neo-Classicism in his works gave way to dodecaphony à la française before he returned to tonal writing in his later output.

WORKS: *Orphée*, symphonic poem (1945–46); *2 images* for Orch. (1953–54); pieces entitled *Mouvement symphonique* (1953–63); Sym., *In memoriam* (1962–63); *Divertissement pastoral* for Piano and Orch. (1966); *La triomphe de la mort*, dramatic sym. (1967–73); *Variations* for String Quartet (1946); vocal pieces.

Martinez, José Daniel, Puerto Rican composer and pianist; b. San Juan, Sept. 8, 1956. He studied with Luis Antonio Ramírez and Luz N. Hutchinson at the Cons. of Music in Puerto Rico (certificate of diploma, 1975) and at the Eastman School of Music in Rochester, N.Y. (B.A. in composition, 1977; M.A. in piano, 1980). He taught piano and theory at the Hochstein School of Music in Rochester (1977–80) and at the Cons. of Music in Puerto Rico (1981–82); in 1982–83 he worked as an accompanist in N.Y. In 1985 he made a recording of Puerto Rican "Danzas" for the Círculo de Recreo de San Germán, where he subsequently taught at the Interamerican Univ. of Puerto Rico.

WORKS: *Dos preludios* for Piano (1971); *Fantasía* for Violin and Piano (1973); *Tema y variaciones* for Piano (1974); *Tiempo sinfónico* for Chamber Orch. (1976); *Impromptu* for Chamber Ensemble (1983); *Música para la Interamericana* for Organ and Baroque Orch. (1984); *Concierto para aulos . . . Reflexiones sobre el retorno de un cometa* for Flute, Piccolo, Oboe, Horn, and Piano (1986); Cello Sonata (1987).

Martínez, Miguel Angel Gomez. See **Gomez Martínez, Miguel Angel.**

Martinez, Odaline de la, Cuban-born American conductor, pianist, and composer; b. Matanzas, Oct. 31, 1949. She emigrated to the U.S. in 1961 and in 1971 became a naturalized American citizen. Following training at Tulane Univ. (B.F.A., 1972), she settled in London and studied composition with Paul Patterson at the Royal Academy of Music (1972–76) and with Reginald Smith Brindle at the Univ. of Surrey (M.M., 1977); subsequently she pursued postgraduate studies in computer music (1977–80). In 1976 she helped organize and was conductor of the chamber ensemble Lontano, with which she toured extensively. In 1981 she also organized the Contemporary Chamber Orch., for which she served as principal conductor. Among her various awards were a Guggenheim followship (1980–81) and the Villa-Lobos Medal (1987). Martinez has embraced an inclusive course as a composer in which she utilizes various styles and techniques.

WORKS: OPERA: *Sister Aimee*, on the life of the American evangelist Aimee Semple McPherson (1978–83). **ORCH.:** *Phasing* for Chamber Orch. (1975). **CHAMBER:** *Little Piece* for Flute (1975); *A Moment's Madness* for Flute and Piano (1977); *Improvisations* for Violin (1977); *Litanies* for Flutes, Harp, and String Trio (1981); *Asonancias* for Violin (1982); Suite for English Horn and Cello (1982); String Quartet (1984–85). **KEYBOARD: PIANO:** *Colour Studies* (1978). **ORGAN:** *Eos* (1976). **VOCAL:** *5 Imagist Songs* for Soprano, Clarinet, and Piano (1974); *After Sylvia* for Soprano and Piano (1976); *Absalom* for Countertenor, 2 Tenors, Baritone, and Bass (1977); *Psalmos* for Chorus, Brass Quintet, Timpani, and Organ (1977); *2 American Madrigals* for

Chorus (1979); *Canciones* for Soprano, Percussion, and Piano (1983); *Cantos de amor* for Soprano, Piano, and String Trio (1985). **OTHER:** *Hallucination* for Tape (1975); *Visions and Dreams* for Tape (1977–78); *Lamento* for Amplified Soprano, Alto, Tenor, and Bass , and Tape (1978); *3 Studies* for Percussion and Electronics (1980).

Martino, Donald (James), American composer, clarinetist, and teacher; b. Plainfield, N.J., May 16, 1931. He learned to play the clarinet, oboe, and saxophone in his youth; then studied composition with Bacon at Syracuse Univ. (B.M., 1952), Babbitt and Sessions at Princeton Univ. (M.F.A., 1954), and Dallapiccola in Florence on a Fulbright scholarship (1954–56). In 1958–59 he was an instructor at Princeton Univ.; from 1959 to 1969, taught theory and composition at Yale Univ.; then was a prof. of composition at the New England Cons. of Music in Boston (1970–80), where he served as chairman of the composition dept. He was Irving Fine Prof. of Music at Brandeis Univ. (1980–83); in 1983, became a prof. of music at Harvard Univ., serving as Walter Bigelow Rosen Prof. of Music from 1989 until his retirement in 1993. He held 3 Guggenheim fellowships (1967, 1973, 1982); was awarded the Pulitzer Prize in Music in 1974 for his chamber piece *Notturno*; in 1981, was made a member of the American Academy and Inst. of Arts and Letters, and in 1987 a fellow of the American Academy of Arts and Sciences.

WORKS: ORCH.: *Contemplations* (1956; Lenox, Mass., Aug. 13, 1964; originally entitled *Composition*); Piano Concerto (1965; New Haven, March 1, 1966); *Mosaic for Grand Orchestra* (Chicago, May 26, 1967); Cello Concerto (1972; Cincinnati, Oct. 16, 1973); *Ritorno* (1975; Plainfield, N.J., Dec. 12, 1976); Triple Concerto for Clarinet, Bass Clarinet, Contrabass Clarinet, and Chamber Orch. (1977; N.Y., Dec. 18, 1978); *Divertissements* for Youth Orch. (1981); Concerto for Alto Saxophone and Chamber Orch. (1987); Violin Concerto (1995). **CHAMBER:** 4 string quartets (n.d., withdrawn; 1952, withdrawn; 1954, withdrawn; 1983); Clarinet Sonata (1950–51); *A Suite of Variations on Medieval Melodies* for Cello (1952; rev. 1954); *A Set* for Clarinet (1954; rev. 1974); *Quodlibets* for Flute (1954); *Sette canoni enigmatici,* puzzle canons with various solutions for 2 Violas and 2 Cellos or 2 Bassoons, or for String Quartet, or for 4 Clarinets (1955–56); Quartet for Clarinet and String Trio (1957); Trio for Clarinet, Violin, and Piano (1959); *Cinque frammenti* for Oboe and Double Bass (1961); *Fantasy-Variations* for Violin (1962); Concerto for Wind Quintet (1964); *Parisonatina al'dodecafonia* for Cello (1964); *B,A,B,B,I,T,T* for Clarinet with Extensions (1966); *Strata* for Bass Clarinet (1966); *Notturno* for Piccolo, Flute, Alto Flute, Clarinet, Bass Clarinet, Violin, Viola, Cello, Piano, and Percussion (1973); *Quodlibets II* for Flute (1980); *Canzone e Tarantella sul nome Petrassi* for Clarinet and Cello (1984); *From the Other Side,* divertimento for Flute, Cello, Percussion, and Piano (1988); *15, 5, 92, A. B.: A Musical Birthday Card for Arthur Berger* for Clarinet (1992); *3 Sad Songs* for Viola and Piano (1993). **PIANO:** *Fantasy* (1958); *Pianississimo,* sonata (1970); *Impromptu for Roger* (1977; for Sessions's 80th birthday); *Fantasies and Impromptus* (1978); *Suite in Old Form: Parody Suite* (1982); *12 Préludes* (1991). **VOCAL:** *Portraits: A Secular Cantata* for Mezzo-soprano, Bass, Chorus, and Orch., after Walt Whitman, Edna St. Vincent Millay, and e.e. cummings (1954); *7 Pious Pieces* for Chorus and Optional Piano or Organ, after Robert Herrick (1972); *Augenmusik: A Mixed Mediacritique* for "actress, danseuse or uninhibited female percussionist and electronic tape" (1972); *Paradiso Choruses,* oratorio for 12 Soloists, Chorus, Children's Chorus ad libitum, Tape, and Orch., after Dante's *Divine Comedy* (1974; Boston, May 7, 1975); *The White Island* for Chorus and Chamber Orch., after Robert Herrick (1985; Boston, April 8, 1987); songs.

Martinon, Jean, significant French conductor and composer; b. Lyons, Jan. 10, 1910; d. Paris, March 1, 1976. He studied violin at the Lyons Cons. (1924–25) and at the Paris Cons. (1926–29), winning the premier prix; then took lessons in composition with Roussel and d'Indy and in conducting with Munch and Desormière; obtained his M.A. degree in arts from the Sorbonne (1932). He was in the French army during World War II; was taken prisoner in 1940 and spent 2 years in a German prison camp (Stalag IX); during imprisonment, he wrote several works of a religious nature, among them *Psalm 136, Musique d'exil ou Stalag IX,* and *Absolve Domine,* in memory of French musicians killed in the war. After his release, he appeared as a conductor with the Pasdeloup Orch. in Paris (1943); then was conductor of the Bordeaux Sym. Orch. (1943–45), assistant conductor of the Paris Cons. Orch. (1944–46), and assoc. conductor of the London Phil. (1947–49). After conducting the Radio Eireann Orch. in Dublin (1948–50), he was artistic director of the Lamoureux Orch. in Paris (1950–57). He made his American debut with the Boston Sym. Orch. on March 29, 1957, conducting the U.S. premiere of his 2nd Sym. Martinon was artistic director of the Israel Phil. (1958–60) and Generalmusikdirektor of the Düsseldorf Sym. Orch. (1960–66). In 1963 he was appointed music director of the Chicago Sym. Orch.; during the 5 years of his tenure, he conducted about 60 works by American and European composers of the modern school; this progressive policy met opposition from some influential people in Chicago society and in the press, and he resigned in 1968. He subsequently was chief conductor of the Orchestre National de la Radio Télévision Française in Paris (from 1968) and the Residente Orch. in The Hague (from 1974). As a conductor, he became best known for his idiomatic performances of the French repertoire. His own compositions follow the spirit of French neo-Classicism, euphonious in their modernity and expansive in their Romantic élan.

WORKS: DRAMATIC: OPERA: *Hécube,* after Euripides (1949–54; 1st scenic perf., Strasbourg, Nov. 10, 1956). **BALLET:** *Ambohimanga ou La Cité bleue* (1946; Paris, 1947). **ORCH.:** 4 syms.: No. 1 (1934–36; Paris, March 1940), No. 2, *Hymne à la vie* (1942–44; Paris, Feb. 13, 1944), No. 3, *Irlandaise* (Radio Eirean, Dublin, 1949), and No. 4, *Altitudes* (Chicago, Dec. 30, 1965); *Symphoniette* for Strings, Piano, Harp, and Percussion (1935; Paris, May 30, 1938); 2 violin concertos: No. 1, *Concerto giocoso* (1937–42) and No. 2 (1958; Selle, Bavaria, May 28, 1961); *Musique d'exil ou Stalag IX,* musical reminiscence of imprisonment (1941; Paris, Jan. 11, 1942); *Divertissement* (1941); *Obsession* for Chamber Orch. (1942); *Romance bleue,* rhapsody for Violin and Orch. (1942); *Concerto lyrique* for String Quartet and Chamber Orch. (1944; transcribed as Concerto for 4 Saxophones and Chamber Orch. in 1974); *Overture for a Greek Tragedy* (1949; prelude to the 2nd act of *Hécube*); *Symphonies de voyages* (1957); *Introduction and Toccata* (1959; orchestration of the piano piece *Prelude and Toccata*); Cello Concerto (1963; Hamburg, Jan. 25, 1965); *Le Cène* (1962–63); *Hymne, Variations et Rondo* (1967; Paris, Feb. 15, 1969); Flute Concerto (1970–71); *Sonata movimento perpetuo* (1973). **CHAMBER:** 7 sonatinas: No. 1 for Violin and Piano (1935), No. 2 for Violin and Piano (1936), No. 3 for Piano (1940), No. 4 for Wind Trio (1940), No. 5 for Solo Violin (1942), No. 6 for Solo Violin (1958), and No. 7 for Flute and Piano (1958); *Domenon* for Wind Quintet (1939); String Trio (1943) *Suite nocturne* for Violin and Piano (1944); Piano Trio (1945); *Scherzo* for Violin and Piano (1945); 2 string quartets (1946; 1963–66); *Prelude and Toccata* for Piano (1947); *Duo* for Violin and Piano (1953); *Introduzione, Adagio et Passacaille* for 13 Instruments (1967); *Vigentuor* for 20 Instruments (1969); Octet (1969). **VOCAL:** *Absolve Domine* for Men's Chorus and Orch. (1940; perf. at Stalag IX prison camp, Nov. 2, 1940); *Appel de parfums* for Narrator, Men's or Mixed Chorus, and Orch. (1940); *Psalm 136 (Chant de captifs)* for Narrator, Soloists, Chorus, and Orch. (1942); *Ode au Soleil né de la Mort* for Narrator, Chorus, and Orch. (1945); *Le Lis de Sharon,* oratorio (1951; Tel Aviv, 1952); songs.

Martins, João Carlos, Brazilian pianist; b. São Paulo, June 25, 1940. He studied piano with José Kliass. He made his professional debut at Teresopolis in 1954; other concerts followed in Brazilian cities; in 1960 he made his American debut at Carnegie Hall in N.Y., evoking superlatives for his "passionate subjectivity" from the critics; later he made a specialty of performing all of Bach's 48 preludes and fugues in 2 consecutive concerts; he also appeared as a soloist with orchs. in N.Y., Philadelphia, and Boston. But at the height of his successes, in 1969, he was knocked down during a soccer match, and hurt his arm to the point of a painful neuralgia, so that he had to stop playing piano. But in a surprising change of direction, he went into banking, managed a champion prizefighter, started a construction company, and became a multimillionaire in devalued Brazilian currency. An even more surprising development followed when, in 1981, he was appointed to the post of the Brazilian state secretary of culture; in this capacity, he exhibited an extraordinary knack for urban recovery in the direction of futuristic Americanization. In the meantime, his neurological ailment subsided, and he returned to his career as a virtuoso pianist. Following a recording session in Sofia in 1995, he was beaten senseless by two Bulgarian thugs. The tragic incident left him with a disabled right hand, which eventually was relieved by biofeedback. In 1996 he returned to the concert stage with an appearance at N.Y.'s Carnegie Hall.

Martinů, Bohuslav (Jan), remarkable Czech-born American composer; b. Polička, Dec. 8, 1890; d. Liestal, near Basel, Aug. 28, 1959. He was born in the bell tower of a church in the village where his father was a watchman. He studied violin with the local tailor when he was 7; from 1906 to 1909 he was enrolled at the Prague Cons.; then entered the Prague Organ School (1909), where he studied organ and theory, but was expelled in 1910 for lack of application. He played in the 2nd violin section in the Czech Phil. in Prague (1913–14), returning to Polička (1914–18) to avoid service in the Austrian army; after World War I, he reentered the Prague Cons. as a pupil of Suk, but again failed to graduate; also played again in the Czech Phil. (1918–23). In 1923 he went to Paris and participated in progressive musical circles; took private lessons with Roussel. In a relatively short time his name became known in Europe through increasingly frequent performances of his chamber works, ballets, and symphonic pieces; several of his works were performed at the festivals of the ISCM. In 1932 his String Sextet won the Elizabeth Sprague Coolidge Award. He remained in Paris until June 1940, when he fled the German invasion and went to Portugal; finally reached the U.S. in 1941 and settled in N.Y.; personal difficulties prevented him from accepting an offer to teach at the Prague Cons. after the liberation of Czechoslovakia in 1945; later was a visiting prof. of music at Princeton Univ. (1948–51). In 1952 he became a naturalized American citizen. Although Martinů spent most of his life away from his homeland, he remained spiritually and musically faithful to his native country. He composed a poignant tribute to the martyred village of Lidice where, in 1943, the Nazi authorities ordered the execution of all men and boys over the age of 16 to avenge the assassination of the local Gauleiter. Martinů immortalized the victims in a heartfelt lyric work entitled *Memorial to Lidice.* In 1953 he returned to Europe, spending the last 2 years of his life in Switzerland. On Aug. 27, 1979, his remains were taken from Schonenberg, Switzerland, to Polička, Czechoslovakia, where they were placed in the family mausoleum. Martinů's centennial was celebrated in 1990 all over Czechoslovakia. As a musician and stylist, he belonged to the European tradition of musical nationalism. He avoided literal exploitation of Czech or Slovak musical materials, but his music is nonetheless characterized by a strong feeling for Bohemian melorhythms; his stylizations of Czech dances are set in a modern idiom without losing their authenticity or simplicity. In his large works, he followed the neo-Classical trend, with some impressionistic undertones; his mastery of modern counterpoint was extraordinary.

WORKS: DRAMATIC: OPERAS: *Voják a tanečnice* (The Soldier and the Dancer; 1926–27; Brno, May 5, 1928); *Les Larmes du couteau* (The Knife's Tears; 1928); *Trois souhaits, ou Les Vicissitudes de la vie,* "opera-film in 3 acts" (1929; Brno, June 16, 1971); *La Semaine de bonté* (1929; unfinished); *Hry o Marii* (The Miracle of Our Lady; 1933–34; Brno, Feb. 23, 1935); *Hlas lesa* (The Voice of the Forest), radio opera (Czech Radio, Oct. 6, 1935); *Divadlo za bránou* (The Suburban Theater), opera buffa (1935–36; Brno, Sept. 20, 1936); *Veselohra na mostě* (Comedy on a Bridge), radio opera (1935; Czech Radio, March 18, 1937; rev. 1950); *Julietta, or The Key to Dreams,* lyric opera (1936–37; Prague, March 16, 1938); *Alexandre bis,* opera buffa (1937; Mannheim, Feb. 18, 1964); *What Men Live By* (Čím člověk žije), pastoral opera after Tolstoy (1951–52; N.Y., May 20, 1955); *The Marriage* (Ženitba), television opera after Gogol (1952; NBC-TV, N.Y., Feb. 7, 1953); *La Plainte contre inconnu* (1953; unfinished); *Mirandolina,* comic opera (1954; Prague, May 17, 1959); *Ariadne,* lyric opera (1958; Gelsenkirchen, March 2, 1961); *Řecké pašije* (Greek Passion), musical drama after Kazantzakis (1955–59; Zürich, June 9, 1961). **BALLETS:** *Noc* (Night), "meloplastic scene" (1913–14); *Stín* (The Shadow; 1916); *Istar* (1918–22; Prague, Sept. 11, 1924); *Who Is the Most Powerful in the World?* (Kdo je na světě nejmocnější), ballet comedy, after an English fairy tale (1922; Brno, Jan. 31, 1925); *The Revolt* (Vzpoura), ballet sketch (1922–23; Brno, Feb. 11, 1928); *The Butterfly That Stamped* (Motýl, ktery dupal), after Kipling (1926); *La Revue de cuisine* (Prague, 1927); *On tourne* (Natáčí se), for a cartoon and puppet film (1927); *Le Raid merveilleux* (Báječný let), "ballet mécanique" for 2 Clarinets, Trumpet, and Strings (1927); *Echec au roi,* jazz ballet (1930); *Špalíček* (The Chapbook), with Vocal Soloists and Chorus (1931; Prague, Sept. 19, 1933; rev. 1940; Prague, April 2, 1949); *Le Jugement de Paris* (1935); *The Strangler* (Uškreovač), for 3 Dancers (New London, Conn., Aug. 15, 1948).

ORCH.: *Anděl smrti* (Angel of Death), symphonic poem (1910; also for Piano); *Komposition* (1913–14); *Nocturno No. 1* for Viola and Orch. (1914); *Ballada* (1915); *Míjející půlnoc* (Vanishing Midnight; 1921–22); *Half Time,* rondo (Prague, Dec. 7, 1924); Concertino for Cello, Winds, Piano, and Percussion (1924; Prague, March 24, 1949); 5 piano concertos: No. 1 (1925; Prague, Nov. 21, 1926), No. 2 (1934; Prague, 1935; rescored 1944), No. 3 (1947–48; Dallas, Nov. 20, 1949), No. 4, *Incantation* (N.Y., Oct. 4, 1956), and No. 5, *Fantasia concertante* (1957; Berlin, Jan. 31, 1959); *La Bagarre,* rondo (1926; Boston, Nov. 18, 1927); *Divertimento* for Piano, Left-hand, and Orch. (1926; Prague, Feb. 26, 1947; rev. 1928 as the Concertino for Piano, Left-hand, and Orch.); *Jazz Suite* for Chamber Orch. (Baden-Baden, June 7, 1928); *Allegro symphonique,* rhapsody (Boston, Dec. 14, 1928); *Praeludium* (1930); *Serenade* for Chamber Orch. (1930); 2 cello concertos: No. 1 for Cello and Chamber Orch. (1930; rev. for Full Orch., 1939; rescored 1955) and No. 2 (1944–45); Concerto for String Quartet and Orch. (1931); 2 violin concertos: No. 1 for Cello and Chamber Orch. (1931–32; Chicago, Oct. 25, 1973) and No. 2 (Boston, Dec. 31, 1943); *Sinfonia concertante* for 2 Orchs. (1932); *Partita:* Suite No. 1 (1932); *Divertimento: Serenade No. 4* for Violin, Viola, Oboe, Piano, and Strings (1932); Concertino for Piano Trio and Strings (1933; Basel, Oct. 16, 1936); *Invence* (Inventions; Venice, Sept. 1934); Concerto for Harpsichord and Chamber Orch. (1935); Concerto for Flute, Violin, and Orch. (Paris, Dec. 27, 1936); *Duo concertante* for 2 Violins and Orch. (1937); *Suite concertante* for Violin and Orch. (1937; rev. 1945); Piano Concertino (1938; London, Aug. 5, 1948); Concerto Grosso for Small Orch. (1938; Boston, Nov. 14, 1941); *3 ricercari* for Chamber Orch. (1938); Double Concerto for 2 String Orchs., Piano, and Timpani (1938; Basel, Feb. 9, 1940); *Sonata da camera* for Cello and Chamber Orch. (1940; Geneva, Nov. 25, 1943); *Sinfonietta giocosa* for Piano and Chamber Orch. (1940; rev. 1941; N.Y., March 16, 1942); *Concerto da camera* for Violin, String Orch., Piano, and Timpani (1941; Basel, Jan. 23, 1942); 6 syms.: No. 1 (Boston, Nov. 13, 1942), No. 2 (Cleveland, Oct. 28, 1943), No. 3 (1944; Boston, Oct. 12, 1945), No. 4 (Philadelphia, Nov. 30, 1945), No. 5 (1946; Prague, May 27, 1947), and No. 6, *Fantaisies symphoniques* (1951–53; Boston, Jan. 7, 1955); *Memorial to Lidice* (N.Y., Oct. 28, 1943); Concerto for 2 Pianos and Orch. (Philadelphia, Nov. 5, 1943); *Thunderbolt P-47,* scherzo (Washington, D.C., Dec. 19, 1945); *Toccata e due canzone* for Small Orch. (1946; Basel, Jan. 21, 1947); *Sinfo-*

nia concertante for Oboe, Bassoon, Violin, Cello, and Small Orch. (1949; Basel, Dec. 8, 1950); Concerto for 2 Violins and Orch. (1950; Dallas, Jan. 8, 1951); *Sinfonietta La Jolla* for Piano and Chamber Orch. (1950); *Intermezzo* (N.Y., Dec. 29, 1950); *Rhapsody-Concerto* for Viola and Orch. (1952; Cleveland, Feb. 19, 1953); Concerto for Violin, Piano, and Orch. (1955); *Les Fresques de Piero della Francesca* (1955; Salzburg Festival, Aug. 28, 1956); Oboe Concerto (1955); *The Rock*, symphonic prelude (1957; Cleveland, April 17, 1958); *The Parables* (1957–58; Boston, Feb. 13, 1959); *Estampes*, symphonic suite (1958; Louisville, Feb. 4, 1959).

CHAMBER: 1 unnumbered string quartet (1917; Zürich, May 7, 1994); 7 numbered string quartets: No. 1 (1918; reconstructed, with the addition of a newly discovered 4th movement, by Jan Hanuš, 1972), No. 2 (1925), No. 3 (1929), No. 4 (1937; Donaueschingen, Oct. 15, 1960), No. 5 (1938; Prague, May 25, 1958), No. 6 (1946; Cambridge, Mass., May 1, 1947), and No. 7, *Concerto da camera* (1947); 2 unnumbered violin sonatas (1919; 1926, Prague, March 30, 1963); 3 numbered violin sonatas (1929, 1931, 1944); 2 string trios (1923, 1934); Quartet for Clarinet, Horn, Cello, and Drum (1924); 2 unnumbered nonets: for Violin, Viola, Cello, Flute, Clarinet, Oboe, Horn, Bassoon, and Piano (1924–25), and for Violin, Viola, Cello, Double Bass, Flute, Clarinet, Oboe, Horn, and Bassoon (1959); 2 duos for Violin and Cello (1927, 1957); *Impromptu* for Violin and Piano (1927); String Quintet (1927); Sextet for Winds and Piano (1929); *5 Short Pieces* for Violin and Piano (1929); Wind Quintet (1930); *Les Rondes*, 6 pieces for 7 Instruments (1930; Paris, March 18, 1932); 3 piano trios (*5 Brief Pieces*, 1930; 1950; 1951); Sonatina for 2 Violins and Piano (1930); *Études rythmiques* for Violin and Piano (1931); *Pastorales and Nocturnes* for Cello and Piano (both 1931); *Arabesques* for Violin or Cello and Piano (1931); String Sextet (1932); Sonata for 2 Violins and Piano (London, Feb. 1932); *Serenade* No. 1 for 6 Instruments, No. 2 for 2 Violins and Viola, and No. 3 for 7 Instruments (all 1932 and 1st perf. in Prague, Oct. 16, 1947; No. 4 is the *Divertimento* for Violin, Viola, Oboe, Piano, and String Orch.); 2 piano quintets (1933, 1944); Sonata for Flute, Violin, and Piano (1936; Paris, July 1, 1937); *4 Madrigals* for Oboe, Clarinet, and Bassoon (1937); Violin Sonatina (1937); *Intermezzo*, 4 pieces for Violin and Piano (1937); Trio for Flute, Violin, and Bassoon (1937); 3 cello sonatas (1939, 1944, 1952); *Bergerettes* for Piano Trio (1940); *Promenades* for Flute, Violin, and Harpsichord (1940); Piano Quartet (1942); *Madrigal Sonata* for Flute, Violin, and Piano (1942); *Variations on a Theme of Rossini* for Cello and Piano (1942); *Madrigal Stanzas*, 5 pieces for Violin and Piano (1943); Trio for Flute, Cello, and Piano (1944); Flute Sonata (1945); *Czech Rhapsody* for Violin and Piano (1945); *Fantasia* for Theremin, Oboe, String Quartet, and Piano (1945); 2 duos for Violin and Viola (3 Madrigals, 1947; 1950); Quartet for Oboe, Violin, Cello, and Piano (1947); *Mazurka-Nocturne* for Oboe, 2 Violins, and Cello (1949); *Serenade* for Violin, Viola, Cello, and 2 Clarinets (1951); Viola Sonata (1955); Clarinet Sonatina (1956); Trumpet Sonatina (1956); *Divertimento* for 2 Flutes-à-bec (1957); *Les Fêtes nocturnes* for Violin, Viola, Cello, Clarinet, Harp, and Piano (1959); *Variations on a Slovak Theme* for Cello and Piano (Prague, Oct. 17, 1959). **KEYBOARD: PIANO:** *Puppets*, small pieces for children (3 sets, 1914–24); *Scherzo* (1924); *Fables* (1924); *Film en miniature* (1925); *3 Czech Dances* (1926); *Le Noël* (1927); *4 Movements* (1928); *Borová*, 7 Czech dances (1929; also for Orch.); *Préludes (en forme de . . .)* (1929); *Fantaisie* for 2 Pianos (1929); *À trois mains* (1930); *Esquisses de danse*, 5 pieces (1932); *Les Ritournelles* (1932); *Dumka* (1936); *Fenêtre sur le jardin*, 4 pieces (1938); *Fantasia and Toccata* (1940); *Mazurka* (1941); *Études and Polkas* (3 books, 1945); *The 5th Day of the 5th Moon* (1948); *3 Czech Dances* for 2 Pianos (1949); Sonata (1954); *Reminiscences* (1957). **HARPSICHORD:** *2 Pieces* (1935); Sonata (1958); *Impromptus* (1959). **ORGAN:** *Vigilie* (1959).

VOCAL: *Nipponari*, 7 songs for Woman's Voice and Chamber Ensemble (1912); *Ceska rapsódie*, cantata (1918; Prague, Jan. 12, 1919); *Kouzelné noci* (Magic Nights), 3 songs for Soprano and Orch. (1918); *Le Jazz* for Voice and Orch. (1928); *Kytice* (Bouquet of Flowers), cantata on Czech folk poetry (1937; Czech Radio, May 1938); *Polní mše* (Field Mass) for Men's Chorus, Baritone, and Orch. (1939; Prague, Feb. 28, 1946); *Hora tří světel* (The Hill of 3 Lights), small oratorio for Soloists, Chorus, and Organ (1954; Bern, Oct. 3, 1955); *Hymnus k sv. Jakubu* (Hymn to St. James) for Narrator, Soloists, Chorus, Organ, and Orch. (1954; Polička, July 31, 1955); *Gilgameš* (The Epic of Gilgamesh) for Narrator, Soloists, Chorus, and Orch. (1954–55; Basel, Jan. 24, 1958); *Otvírání studánek* (The Opening of the Wells) for Narrator, Soloists, Women's Chorus, 2 Violins, Viola, and Piano (1955); *Legend from the Smoke of Potato Fires* for Soloists, Chorus, and Chamber Ensemble (1957); *Mikeš z hor* (Mikesh from the Mountains) for Soloists, Chorus, 2 Violins, Viola, and Piano (1959); *The Prophecy of Isaiah* (Proroctví Izaiášovo) for Men's Chorus, Soloists, Viola, Trumpet, Piano, and Timpani (1959; Jerusalem, April 2, 1963); numerous partsongs and choruses.

BIBL.: M. Šafránek, "B. M.," Musical Quarterly (July 1943); idem, *B. M.: The Man and His Music* (N.Y., 1944); J. Löwenbach, *M. pozdravuje domov* (Prague, 1947); M. Šafránek, *B. M.: His Life and Works* (London, 1962); H. Halbreich, *B. M.* (Zürich, 1968); C. Martinů, *Můj život s B. M.* (My Life with B. M.; Prague, 1971); B. Large, *M.* (N.Y., 1975); J. Brabcová, ed., *B. M. anno 1981: Papers From an International Musicological Conference, 26–28 May, 1981* (Prague, 1990); G. Erismann, *M., un musicien à l'éveil des sources* (Arles, 1990).

Martirano, Salvatore, American composer and teacher; b. Yonkers, N.Y., Jan. 12, 1927; d. Urbana, Ill., Nov. 17, 1995. He studied piano and composition at the Oberlin (Ohio) Cons. of Music (B.M., 1951); then composition at the Eastman School of Music in Rochester, N.Y., with Rogers (M.M., 1952); later took courses with Dallapiccola at the Cherubini Cons. in Florence (1952–54). He served in the U.S. Marine Corps; played clarinet and cornet with the Parris Island Marine Band; from 1956 to 1959 he held a fellowship to the American Academy in Rome, and in 1960 received a Guggenheim fellowship and the American Academy of Arts and Letters Award. In 1963 he joined the faculty of the Univ. of Ill. at Urbana. Martirano wrote in a progressive avant-garde idiom, applying the quaquaversal techniques of unmitigated radical modernism, free from any inhibitions.

WORKS: Sextet for Wind Instruments (1949); Prelude for Orch. (1950); Variations for Flute and Piano (1950); String Quartet No. 1 (1951); *The Magic Stones*, chamber opera after the *Decameron* (Oberlin Cons., April 24, 1952); *Piece for Orchestra* (1952); Violin Sonata (1952); *Contrasto* for Orch. (1954); *Chansons innocentes* for Soprano and Piano (1957); *O, O, O, O, That Shakespeherian Rag* for Chorus and Instrumental Ensemble (1958); *Cocktail Music* for Piano (1962); Octet (1963); *Underworld* for 4 Actors, 4 Percussion Instruments, 2 Double Basses, Tenor Saxophone, and Tape (1965; video version, 1982); *Ballad* for Amplified Nightclub Singer and Instrumental Ensemble (1966); *L's.G.A.* for a gas-masked Politico, Helium Bomb, 3 16mm Movie Projectors, and Tape (1968); *The Proposal* for Tapes and Slides (1968); *Action Analysis* for 12 People, Bunny, and Controller (1968); *Selections* for Alto Flute, Bass Clarinet, Viola, and Cello (1970); *Sal-Mar Construction I–VII* for Tape (1971–75); *Fast Forward* for Tape (1977); *Fifty One* for Tape (1978); *In Memoriam Luigi Dallapiccola* for Tape (1978); *Omaggio a Sally Rand*, video piece (1982); *Thrown*, sextet for Wind and Percussion (1984); *Look at the Back of My Head for Awhile*, video piece (1984); *Sampler: Everything Goes When the Whistle Blows* for Violin and Synthetic Orch. (1985; rev. 1988); *Dance/Players I* and *II*, video pieces (1986); *3 not 2*, variable-forms piece (1987); *Phleu* for Amplified Flute and Synthetic Orch. (1988); *LON/dons* for Chamber Orch. (1989).

Martland, Steve, English composer; b. Liverpool, Oct. 10, 1958. After graduating from the Univ. of Liverpool (1981), he studied composition with Louis Andriessen at the Royal Cons. of Music at The Hague (1982–85) and with Schuller at the Berkshire Music Center at Tanglewood (summer, 1984). He was active with his own Steve Martland Band, finding inspiration in the world of pop and rock music in pursuit of his own fiercely independent course as a serious composer.

WORKS: DRAMATIC: *Ghost Story,* incidental music to a television play (1989); *The Task,* incidental music (1989); *Home, Away from Home,* incidental music to a television play (1989); *Cult,* soundtrack to a dance-theater piece for television (1990). **ORCH.:** *Lotta continua* for Jazz Band and Orch. (1981; rev. 1984); *Babi Yar* (1983; Liverpool, Nov. 22, 1985); *Orc* for Horn and Small Orch. (1984; Amsterdam, Jan. 14, 1985); *Dividing the Lines* for Brass Band (1986); *Crossing the Broder* for Strings (1990–91; also for String Quartet and Tape). **CHAMBER:** *Remembering Lennon* for 7 Players (1981; rev. 1985); Duo for Trumpet and Piano (1982); *American Invention* for 13 Players (Aldeburgh, June 10, 1985); *Shoulder to Shoulder* for 13 Players (Amsterdam, Dec. 9, 1986); *Remix* for Jazz Ensemble (Amsterdam, Nov. 6, 1986); *Big Mac I* for 4 Players (The Hague, May 27, 1987) and *II* for 8 Players (1987); *Principia* for Jazz Ensemble (1989; Leeds, March 7, 1990); *Wolf-gang,* arrangements of 6 Mozart arias for Wind Octet (1991); *Crossing the Border* for String Quartet and Tape (1991; also for String Orch.); *Patrol* for String Quartet (1992); *Bach Toccata and Fugue BWV565,* arrangement for String Quartet (1992). **PIANO:** *Kgakala* (1982); *Drill* for 2 Pianos (1987; Rotterdam, Jan. 14, 1988); *Birthday Hocket* for 2 Pianos (Amsterdam, June 6, 1989). **VOCAL:** *Canto a la Esperanza* for Soprano, Electric Guitar, and Chamber Orch. (1982); *El Pueblo unido James Sera Vencido* for Voices and 13 Players (1987); *Glad Day* for Voices and 12 Players (1988); *Skywalk* for 5 Voices or Chorus (1989); *Terra Firma* for 5 Voices, Amplification, and Video (1989); *The Perfect Act* for Voice and Amplified Ensemble (1991). **OTHER:** *Divisions* for Tape (1986–87); *Albion,* audio-visual piece (BBC-TV, Dec. 18, 1988).

Marton, Eva, outstanding Hungarian soprano; b. Budapest, June 18, 1943. She studied with Endre Rősler and Jenő Sipos at the Franz Liszt Academy of Music in Budapest. She made her formal operatic debut as the Queen of Shemakha in *Le Coq d'or* at the Hungarian State Opera there in 1968, remaining on its roster until joining the Frankfurt am Main Opera in 1971; then became a member of the Hamburg State Opera in 1977. On Feb. 23, 1975, she made her U.S. debut in N.Y. as a soloist in the world premiere of Hovhaness's folk oratorio *The Way of Jesus*; then made her first appearance at the Metropolitan Opera there as Eva in *Die Meistersinger von Nürnberg* on Nov. 3, 1976. After singing at the Bayreuth Festivals (1977–78) and at Milan's La Scala (1978), she scored a notable success as the Empress in *Die Frau ohne Schatten* at the Metropolitan Opera in 1981; thereafter she was one of its most important artists, appearing as Elisabeth in *Tännhauser* (1982), Leonore in *Fidelio* (1983), Ortrud in *Lohengrin* (1984), Tosca (1986), and Lady Macbeth (1988). She first sang Turandot at the Vienna State Opera in 1983; appeared as Elektra there in 1989. In 1987 she made her debut at London's Covent Garden as Turandot, and in 1990 she returned there as Elektra. In 1992 she appeared as Turandot in Chicago and as the Dyer's Wife at the Salzburg Festival. Her appearances as an oratorio and lieder artist were also well received.

BIBL.: C. Wilkens, *E. M.* (Hamburg, 1982); H. Waleson, "E. M.," *Ovation* (Oct. 1987).

Martopangrawit, R.L., significant Indonesian composer, teacher, performer, and music theorist; b. Surakarta, Central Java, April 4, 1914; d. there, April 17, 1986. He was a descendant of many generations of royal musicians and became a member of the royal gamelan at the Kraton (palace) Surakarta at 13. In 1948 he joined the offices of the Central Javanese Ministry of Education and Culture; also taught in Surakarta at the Konservatori Karawitan (K.O.K.A.R., 1951–64) and Akademi Seni Karawiten Indonesia (A.S.K.I., from 1964; later Sekolah Tinggi Seni Indonesia [S.T.S.I.]). Considered among the finest of traditional musicians, Martopangrawit garnered fame for his inventive and stylistically diverse compositions, which numbered over 100; his earliest dated work was *Ladrang Biwadhapraja* (1939), and his last was *Ra Ngandel* (1986); others included *Ladrang Cikar Bobrok* (1943), *Ketawang ASKI, Ladrang Asri* (1946), *Ladrang Gandasuli* (1946), *Ladrang Lo Kowe Nang* (1954), *Lancaran Kebat* (1961), *Lancaran Uyal-uyel* (1962), *Ketawang Pamegatsih* (1966), *Nglara Ati* (1970), *Mijil Anglir Medung* (1981), and *Gending Parisuka* (1982). He was also active in the preservation and development of many classical music and dance forms, particularly those associated with the Kraton Surakarta, where he was promoted to "Bupati Anon-anon" and given the honorary title Raden Tumenggung Martodipura (1984). He also publ. many books on the Central Javanese gamelan; some of these comprise collections of music notation, including those of his own pieces—*Gending-gending Martopangrawit* (1968) and *Lagu Dolanan Anggitan Martopangrawit* (children's songs). Among his theoretical works is his landmark treatise *Pengetahuan Karawitan* (The Theory of Classical Javanese Music; Surakarta, 1972; Eng. tr. by M. Hatch, in J. Becker and A. Feinstein, eds., *Karawitan: Source Readings in Javanese Gamelan and Vocal Music,* vol. I, Ann Arbor, 1984). Other publications include a book of drumming notation, *Titilaras Kendangan*; a compendium of melodic patterns used by the gender (an important instrument in the Javanese gamelan), *Titilaras Cengkok-cengkok Genderan Dengan Wiledannya* (2 vols.); and a collection of children's songs, *Lagu Dolanan Lare-lare.*

Marttinen, Tauno (Olavi), Finnish composer, pedagogue, and conductor; b. Helsinki, Sept. 27, 1912. He received training in conducting and composition at the Viipuri Inst. of Music (1920–35), and then was a student of Peter Akimov, Ilmari Hannikainen, and Selim Palmgren at the Sibelius Academy in Helsinki (1935–37); later he studied with Vogel in Switzerland (1958). From 1949 to 1958 he was conductor of the Hämeenlinna City Orch. In 1950 he founded the Hämeenlinna Inst. of Music, serving as its director until 1975. In 1982 he was awarded an honorary prize by the Soc. of Finnish Composers and the Kalevala Soc. He received the 1st Sibelius Award in 1990. After composing in a late Romantic style, Marttinen developed a free serial mode of expression. Later he embraced free tonality before finding renewed creative resources in neo-Baroque and neo-Classical styles.

WORKS: DRAMATIC: OPERAS: *Neiti Gamardin talo* (The House of Lady Gamard; 1960–71); *Päällysviitta* (The Cloak; 1962–63); *Kihlaus* (The Engagement; 1964; Helsinki, June 12, 1966); *Apotti ja ikäneito* (The Abbot and the Old Maid; 1965); *Tulitikkuja lainaamassa* (Borrowing Matches; Helsinki, Aug. 20, 1966); *Lea* (1967; Turku, Sept. 19, 1968); *Poltettu oranssi* (Burnt Orange), television opera (1968; Finnish TV, Oct. 6, 1971; 1st stage perf., Helsinki, Nov. 3, 1975); *Mestari Patelin* (Master Patelin; 1969–72; Hämeenlinna, July 31, 1983); *Noitarumpu* (Shaman's Drum; 1974–76); *Psykiatri* (The Psychiatrist; 1974); *Laestadiuksen saarna* (Laestadius's Sermon; 1974–76; Oulu, April 29, 1976); *Meedio* (The Medium), chamber opera (1975–76); *Jaarlin sisar* (The Jarl's Sister; 1977; Hämeenlinna, April 3, 1979); *Faaraon kirje* (Pharaoh's Letter; 1978–80; Tampere, Oct. 18, 1982); *Suuren joen laulu eli Najaadi* (The Song of a Great River; 1980; Kemi, May 2, 1982); *Häät* (The Wedding), chamber opera (1984–85; Helsinki, Jan. 31, 1986); *Noidan kirous* (1987); *Seitsemän veljestä* (7 Brothers; 1989); *Mooses* (1990); *Minna Graucher* (1992). **MUSICAL:** *Kullanmuru* (The Golden Treasure; 1980). **BALLETS:** *Tikkaat* (The Ladder; 1955); *Dorian Grayn muotokuva* (The Picture of Dorian Gray; 1969); *Lumikuningatar* (The Snow Queen; 1970); *Beatrice* (1970); *Päivänpäästö* (The Sun Out of the Moon; 1975–77); *Ruma ankanpoikanen* (The Ugly Duckling; 1976, 1982–83). **ORCH.:** 9 syms.: (1958; 1959; 1960–62; 1964; *The Shaman,* 1967–72; 1974–75; 1977; 1983; 1986); *The Milky Way* (1960–61); *Rembrandt* for Cello and Orch. (1962); Violin Concerto (1962); 4 piano concertos (1964, 1972, 1981, 1984); *Birds of the Underworld* (1964); *Fauni* (1965); *Panu, God of Fire* (1966); *Dalai Lama,* cello concerto (1966; rev. 1979); *Creation of the Earth* (1966); *Mont Saint Michel* (1968); *Pentalia* (1969); *The North* for Wind Orch. (1970–71); Bassoon Concerto (1971; rev. 1983–84);

Flute Concerto (1972); *On the Tracks of the Winter Moose*, clarinet concerto (1974); *Concerto espagnole* for Flute and Orch. (1978); *Night on the Fortress* for Wind Orch. (1978); *Elegia* for Harp and Strings (1979); *Voces polaris* (1979); *Sirius* for Wind Orch. (1980); Concerto for 2 Pianos and Orch. (1981); *Väinämöisen's Birth* (1981); *Adagio* (1982); *Väinämöisen's Departure for Pohjola* (1982); *The Maid of Pohjola* (1982); Concerto grosso for Violin, Viola, Cello, and Orch. (1983); *Profeetta* (1984); *A Trip to the Land of Dawn*, homage to Hermann Hesse, for Strings (1984); *Tiibetilainen fantasia* (1985); *Faustus*, violin concerto (1987); Zither Concerto (1988); *Uuden aamun soitto* for Violin and Orch. (1990); *Andante religioso* for Strings (1990). **CHAMBER:** *Delta* for Clarinet and Piano (1962); *Silhouettes* for Piano and Percussion (1962); *The Conjuration* for 3 Percussionists (1963); *Alfa* for Flute and 7 Cymbals (1963); 4 nonets for Flute, Oboe, Clarinet, Bassoon, Horn, Violin, Viola, Cello, and Double Bass (1963, 1968, 1973, 1985); *Visit to the Giant Sage Vipunen* for 7 Double Basses (1969); 3 string quartets (1969, 1971, 1983); Duo for Clarinet and Percussion (1971); *Ilman, Virgin of the Air* for Piccolo (1974); *Septemalia* for 7 Double Basses (1975); *3 Preludes* for Guitar (1975); *Homage to Johann Sebastian Bach* for Guitar (1977); *Divertimento* for Oboe or English Horn and Percussion (1977); *Intermezzo* for Flute and Guitar (1977–78); *Impression* for Cello (1978); Trio for Piano, Violin, and Cello (1978); *The Old Mill Tells Its Tale* for Clarinet (1978); *Le Commencement* for Flute, Oboe, and Piano (1978); *Quo vadis* for Flute, Oboe, Bassoon, and Harpsichord (1979); *The Gnome* for Bass Clarinet (1981); Duo for Viola and Piano (1981); *Illusio* for Clarinet (1982); Trio for Violin, Viola, and Cello (1982); *Idyll* for Oboe or Clarinet (1984); Suite for Wind Quintet (1984); *Elegy* for Violin and Cello (1985); *Isis* for Violin and Guitar (1986); *Fantasia concertante* for Flute and Piano (1986); *Vedenhaltija*, trio for Violin, Cello, and Piano (1990); *Lasi* for 5 Instruments (1991). **KEYBOARD: PIANO:** *4 Preludes* (1965); *Titisee* (1965); *Taara* (1967); Sonatina (1970); *Easter* (1971); Sonata (1975); *Giant Stride* for 2 Pianos (1973); *Water Drops* (1976); *Vibrations* (1976); *Glittering* (1977); *Japanese Garden* (1983); *Faustus* (1987). **ORGAN:** *Intrada* (1967); *Adagio* (1967); *Notre Dame* (1970); *The Cupola* (1971); *Larghetto* (1972); *Orgelstück* (1972); *In the Beginning Was the Word . . .* (1975); *Prelude* (1978); *Largo religioso* (1980); *Fantasia on the Theme B-A-C-H* (1982); *Prophet* (1984). **VOCAL:** *Eagle, Bird of the Air* for Mezzo-soprano and Orch. (1965); *The Bow of Fire* for Bass and Piano Trio (1969); *Jesus and Peter* for Baritone and Organ (1969–70); *Sounds from Noah's Ark* for Men's Chorus (1971); *Love Songs from Ancient Times* for Voice and Orch. (1972); *Thus Was the Beginning* for Soloists, Children's Chorus, and Instruments (1977–80); *The Bosom Friend* for Bass and Wind Quintet (1977); *Cantate Jehovae canticum novum* for Mixed or Boy's Chorus, Organ, and String Orch. (1978); *Canticum canticorum* for Mezzo-soprano and Piano or Harp (1978); *Rohkea ratsastaja* for Reciter and Men's Chorus (1980); *Kaupunkini* for Voice and Orch. (1980); *The Kiss of Judas* for Bass, 2 Baritones, Tenor, Mixed Chorus, Men's Chorus, and Organ (1981); *Offenbarung Johannes* for Bass, Men's Chorus, and Organ (1981); *The Maid of Pohjola* for Reciter and Orch. (1982); *Faunit* for Voice and Orch. (1985); *Seunalan Anna* for Soprano, Speaker, Chorus, and Orch. (1989); *Lemminkäinen's Departure to the North* for Chorus and Orch. (1990–91).

Martucci, Paolo, Italian-American pianist and teacher; b. Naples, Oct. 8, 1881; d. N.Y., Oct. 18, 1980. He was the won of the esteemed Italian pianist, conductor, teacher, and composer Giuseppe Martucci (b. Capua, Jan. 6, 1856; d. Naples, June 1, 1909), with whom he studied. On June 27, 1902, he made his debut as soloist in Tchaikovsky's 1st Piano Concerto. After teaching at the Cincinnati Cons. (1911–13), he taught in N.Y.

Martzy, Johanna, Hungarian violinist; b. Timişoara, Oct. 26, 1924; d. Glarus, Switzerland, Aug. 13, 1979. She received instruction from Hubay before entering the Budapest Academy of Music at age 10. She made her debut in Budapest when she was 13, and graduated from the Academy (1942). After winning 1st prize in the Geneva Competition (1947), she toured widely; first played in England in 1953 and in the U.S. in 1957. She acquired a fine reputation as a soloist and chamber music artist.

Marvin, Frederick, American pianist and musicologist; b. Los Angeles, June 11, 1923. He studied with Maurice Zam (1935–39) and Milan Blanchet (1940–41; 1945–48) in Los Angeles, with Serkin at the Curtis Inst. of Music in Philadelphia (1939–40), and with Arrau (1950–54). He made his professional debut when he was 15; then made his N.Y. debut in 1948; subsequently toured widely in North America, Europe, and India; was a prof. and artist-in-residence at Syracuse Univ. (1968–90). As a pianist, he made it a practice to include rarely heard works on his programs; he particularly championed the music of Antonio Soler; ed. a number of Soler's works, and developed a numbering system (Marvin Verzeichnis) that was widely adopted.

Marx, Josef, German-American oboist, English horn player, musicologist, and music publisher; b. Berlin, Sept. 9, 1913; d. N.Y., Dec. 21, 1978. He emigrated to America in his early youth; studied oboe with Dandois at the Cincinnati Cons. and with Goossens in London; then took lessons in theory with Wolpe. He was an oboist in the Palestine Orch. (1936–37) and the Pittsburgh Sym. Orch. (1942–43); then played English horn in the orch. of the Metropolitan Opera in N.Y. (1943–51); in addition, he appeared as an oboe soloist; several contemporary composers wrote special works for him. In 1945 he founded the McGinnis-Marx Edition in N.Y., which publ. works by Wolpe, Wuorinen, Sydeman, Schuller, and other contemporary composers. From 1956 to 1960 he taught oboe at the Hartt College of Music in Hartford.

Marx, Joseph (Rupert Rudolf), Austrian composer, pedagogue, and music critic; b. Graz, May 11, 1882; d. there, Sept. 3, 1964. He was a student of Degner and took courses in musicology at the Univ. of Graz (Ph.D., 1909, with the diss. *Über die Funktion von Intervallen, Harmonie und Melodie beim Erfassen von Tonkomplexen*). In 1914 he became a prof. of theory and composition at the Vienna Academy of Music, where he was made director in 1922. After it was made the Hochschule für Musik in 1924, he served as its first director until 1927. He continued to teach there until 1952. From 1931 to 1938 he was music critic of the *Neues Wiener Journal*. Following World War II, he was music critic of the *Wiener Zeitung*. From 1947 to 1957 he was an honorary prof. at the Univ. of Graz. Marx established his reputation as a composer early in his career with his songs, of which he wrote about 120. They are in a late Romantic vein à la Hugo Wolf.

WRITINGS (all publ. in Vienna): *Harmonielehre* (1934; 3rd ed., 1948); *Kontrapunkt-Lehre* (1935); *Betrachtungen eines romantischen Realisten* (1947); *Weltsprache Musik* (1964).

WORKS: ORCH.: *Romantische Klavierkonzert* (1919–20); *Eine Herbstsymphonie* (1920–21; Vienna, Feb. 5, 1922); *Naturtrilogie: Eine symphonische Nachtmusik, Idylle*, and *Eine Frühlingsmusik* (1922–25); *Nordlands-Rhapsodie* (1928–29); *Castelli Romani* for Piano and Orch. (1930); *Alt-Wiener Serenaden* (1941–42; Vienna, April 14, 1942); *Sinfonietta in modo classico* for Strings (1944; also as the 3rd string quartet); *Feste im Herbst* (1945); *Sinfonia in modo antico* for Strings (1947; also as the 2nd string quartet). **CHAMBER:** *Ballade* for Piano Quartet (1911); *Scherzo* for Piano Quartet (1911); *Quartett in Form einer Rhapsodie* for Piano Quartet (1911); *Frühlingssonate* for Violin and Piano (1913); *Trio Phantasie* for Piano Trio (1913); 3 string quartets: No. 1, *Quartetto in modo chromatico* (1937), No. 2, *in modo antico* (1938; also as the *Sinfonia in modo antico* for Strings), and No. 3, *in modo classico* (1941; also as the *Sinfonietta in modo classico* for Strings). **VOCAL:** *Morgengesang* for Men's Chorus, Winds, and Organ (1910; also for Men's Chorus and Orch., 1934); *Lieder und Gesänge* (3 vols., 1910–17); *Herbstchor an Pan* for Chorus, Children's Chorus, Orch., and Organ (1911); *Italienisches Liederbuch* (3 vols., 1912); *5 Lieder* for Voice and Orch. (1921); *Verklärtes Jahr*, 5 Songs for Medium Voice and Orch. (1930–32).

BIBL.: J. Bistron, *J. M.* (Vienna, 1923); A. Liess, *J. M.: Leben und Werk* (Graz, 1943); E. Werba, *J. M.* (Vienna, 1964); J. Meyers, *The Songs of J. M.* (diss., Univ. of Missouri, 1972); T. Leibnitz, *Österreichische Spätromantiker: Studien zu Emil Nikolaus von Reznicek, J. M., Franz Schmidt und Egon Kornauth* (Tutzing, 1986).

Marx, Karl, German composer and pedagogue; b. Munich, Nov. 12, 1897; d. Stuttgart, May 8, 1985. He served in the German army during World War I and was a prisoner of war in England; after the Armistice, he returned to Munich to study with Orff; then took courses with Beer-Walbrunn, Hausegger, and Schwickerath at the Akademie der Tonkunst (1920–24). In 1924 he joined its faculty and in 1928 he became the conductor of the Bach Soc. Chorus in Munich; from 1939 to 1946 he was instructor at the Hochschule für Musikerziehung in Graz; subsequently taught at the Hochschule für Musik in Stuttgart (1946–66). A master of German polyphony, Marx distinguished himself as a composer of both sacred and secular choral music.

WORKS: ORCH.: Concerto for 2 Violins and Orch. (1926); Piano Concerto (1929; rev. 1959); Viola Concerto (1929); *Passacaglia* (1932); Violin Concerto (1935); Concerto for Flute and Strings (1937); *15 Variations on a German Folk Song* (1938); *Musik nach alpenländischen Volksliedern* for Strings (1940); *Festival Prelude* (1956); Concerto for Strings (1964; a reworking of his 1932 *Passacaglia*); *Fantasia sinfonica* (1967; rev. 1969); *Fantasia concertante* for Violin, Cello, and Orch. (1972). **CHAMBER:** *Fantasy and Fugue* for String Quartet (1927); *Variations* for Organ (1933); *Divertimento* for 16 Winds (1934); *Turmmusik* for 3 Trumpets and 3 Trombones (1938); *Divertimento* for Flute, Violin, Viola, Cello, and Piano (1942); 6 sonatinas for various instrumental combinations (1948–51); *Kammermusik* for 7 Instruments (1955); Trio for Piano, Flute, and Cello (1962); Cello Sonata (1964); *Fantasy* for Violin (1966); *Partita über "Ein' feste Burg"* for String Quartet or String Orch. (1967); Wind Quintet (1973). **VOCAL:** Several large cantatas, including *Die heiligen drei Könige* (1936); *Rilke-Kantate* (1942); *Und endet doch alles mit Frieden* (1952); *Raube das Licht aus dem Rachen der Schlange* (1957); *Auftrag und Besinnung* (1961); chamber cantatas, including *Die unendliche Woge* (1930); also cantatas for special seasons, children's cantatas, and the like; a cappella pieces; songs, many with Orch., including *Rilke-Kreis* for Voice and Piano (1927; also for Mezzo-soprano and Chamber Orch., 1952) and *3 Songs*, to texts by Stefan George, for Baritone and Chamber Orch. (1934).

BIBL.: R. von Saalfeld, "K. M.," *Zeitschrift für Musik*, XXI (1931); F. Oberborbeck, "K. M.," *Hausmusik*, XXI (1957); E. Karkoschka, "Über späte Instrumentalwerke von K. M.," *Musica*, XXVI (1972).

Marx, Walter Burle, Brazilian-American conductor, teacher, and composer; b. São Paulo, July 23, 1902; d. Akron, Ohio, Dec. 29, 1990. He first studied piano with his mother, then pursued training in Rio de Janeiro with Enrique Oswald; in 1921, went to Berlin and studied piano with Kwast and composition with Reznicek. After touring as a pianist, he returned to Rio de Janeiro and was founder-conductor of its Phil. (1931–33); later appeared as a guest conductor in Europe and the U.S., conducting the N.Y. Phil. at the World's Fair in 1939; in 1947 he was conductor of the Rio de Janeiro Opera. In 1952 he settled in Philadelphia, where he taught piano and composition at the Settlement Music School until 1977. Among his works were 4 syms., concertos, chamber music, and vocal pieces.

Maryon (-d'Aulby), (John) Edward, English composer; b. London, April 3, 1867; d. there, Jan. 31, 1954. He began to compose early in life; went to Paris, where his first opera, *L'Odalisque*, won the Gold Medal at the Exposition of 1889; however, he regarded the work as immature and destroyed the score. In 1891 he studied with Max Pauer in Dresden; later took lessons with Wullner in Cologne. From 1914 to 1919 he was in Montclair, N.J., where he established a cons. with a fund for exchange of music students between England and America; in 1933 he returned to London. He wrote the operas *Paolo and Francesca; La Robe de plume; The Smelting Pot; The Prodigal Son; Werewolf; Rembrandt; Greater Love*; and *Abelard and Heloise*. In his *Werewolf* he applied a curious system of musical symbolism, in which the human part was characterized by the diatonic scale and the lupine self by the whole-tone scale; Maryon made a claim of priority in using the whole-tone scale consistently as a leading motive in an opera. His magnum opus was a grandiose operatic heptalogy under the title *The Cycle of Life*, comprising 7 mystical dramas: *Lucifer, Cain, Krishna, Magdalen, Sangraal, Psyche*, and *Nirvana*. He also wrote a symphonic poem, *The Feather Robe*, subtitled *A Legend of Fujiyama* (1905), which he dedicated to the Emperor of Japan; and *Armageddon Requiem* (1916), dedicated to the dead of World War I. After Maryon's death, his complete MSS were donated to the Boston Public Library. Maryon developed a theory of universal art, in which colors were associated with sounds; an outline of this theory was publ. in his *Marcotone* (N.Y., 1915).

Märzendorfer, Ernst, Austrian conductor; b. Oberndorf, May 26, 1921. He was a student in Graz and of Krauss at the Salzburg Mozarteum. In 1940 he began his conducting career in Salzburg. He conducted at the Graz (1945–51) and then Salzburg (from 1951) Landestheaters. From 1951 he taught conducting at the Mozarteum. In 1952–53 he conducted at the Teatro Colón in Buenos Aires. From 1953 to 1958 he was conductor of the Mozarteum Orch., which he led on a U.S. tour in 1956. He subsequently conducted throughout Europe. He also recorded all the Haydn syms. with the Vienna Chamber Orch. (1969–71) and prepared a completion of Bruckner's 9th Sym. (1969).

Mascagni, Pietro, famous Italian opera composer; b. Livorno, Dec. 7, 1863; d. Rome, Aug. 2, 1945. His father was a baker who wished him to continue in that trade, but yielded to his son's determination to study music. Thanks to aid from an uncle, he was able to take some music lessons with Soffredini in Livorno and then to attend the Milan Cons., where he studied with Ponchielli and Saladino (1882). However, he became impatient with school discipline, and was dismissed from the Cons. in 1884. He then was active as a double bass player in the orch. of the Teatro dal Verme in Milan. After touring as a conductor with operetta troupes, he taught music in Cerignola, Puglia. He composed industriously; in 1888 he sent the MS of his 1-act opera *Cavalleria rusticana* to the music publisher Sonzogno for a competition, and won 1st prize. The opera was performed at the Teatro Costanzi in Rome on May 17, 1890, with sensational success; the dramatic story of village passion, and Mascagni's emotional score, laden with luscious music, combined to produce an extraordinary appeal to opera lovers. The short opera made the tour of the world stages with amazing rapidity, productions being staged all over Europe and America with never-failing success; the opera was usually presented in 2 parts, separated by an "intermezzo sinfonico" (which became a popular orch. number performed separately). *Cavalleria rusticana* marked the advent of the operatic style known as verismo, in which stark realism was the chief aim and the dramatic development was condensed to enhance the impressions. When, 2 years later, another "veristic" opera, Leoncavallo's *Pagliacci*, was taken by Sonzogno, the 2 operas became twin attractions on a single bill. Ironically, Mascagni could never duplicate or even remotely approach the success of his first production, although he continued to compose industriously and opera houses all over the world were only too eager to stage his successive operas. Thus, his opera *Le Maschere* was produced on Jan. 17, 1901, at 6 of the most important Italian opera houses simultaneously (Rome, Milan, Turin, Genoa, Venice, Verona); it was produced 2 days later in Naples. Mascagni himself conducted the premiere in Rome. But the opera failed to fire the imagination of the public; it was produced in a revised form in Turin 15 years later (June 7, 1916), but was not established in the repertoire even in Italy. In 1902 he made a tour of the U.S. conducting his *Cavalleria rus-*

ticana and other operas, but, owing to mismanagement, the visit proved a fiasco; a South American tour in 1911 was more successful. He also appeared frequently as a conductor of sym. concerts. In 1890 he was made a Knight of the Crown of Italy; in 1929 he was elected a member of the Academy. At various times he also was engaged in teaching; from 1895 to 1902 he was director of the Rossini Cons. in Pesaro. His last years were darkened by the inglorious role that he had played as an ardent supporter of the Fascist regime, so that he was rejected by many of his old friends. It was only after his death that his errors of moral judgment were forgiven; his centennial was widely celebrated in Italy in 1963. D. Stivender ed. and tr. his autobiography into Eng. (N.Y., 1975).

WORKS: DRAMATIC: OPERAS: *Pinotta* (c.1880; San Remo, March 23, 1932); *Guglielmo Ratcliff* (c.1885; Milan, Feb. 16, 1895); *Cavalleria rusticana* (Rome, May 17, 1890); *L'Amico Fritz* (Rome, Oct. 31, 1891); *I Rantzau* (Florence, Nov. 10, 1892); *Silvano* (Milan, March 25, 1895); *Zanetto* (Pesaro, March 2, 1896); *Iris* (Rome, Nov. 22, 1898; rev. version, Milan, Jan. 19, 1899); *Le Maschere* (simultaneous premiere in Rome, Milan, Turin, Genoa, Venice, and Verona, Jan. 17, 1901); *Amica* (Monte Carlo, March 16, 1905); *Isabeau* (Buenos Aires, June 2, 1911); *Parisina* (Milan, Dec. 15, 1913); *Lodoletta* (Rome, April 30, 1917); *Scampolo* (1921); *Il piccolo Marat* (Rome, May 2, 1921); *Nerone* (Milan, Jan. 16, 1935); *I Bianchi ed i Neri* (1940). **OPERETTAS:** *Il re a Napoli* (n.d.); *Sí* (Rome, Dec. 13, 1919). **OTHER:** 2 syms. (1879, 1881); *Poema leopardiano* (for the centenary of G. Leopardi, 1898); Hymn in honor of Admiral Dewey (July 1899); *Rapsodia satanica* for Orch. (music for a film, Rome, July 2, 1917); *Davanti Santa Teresa* (Rome, Aug. 1923); chamber music; choral works; songs; piano pieces.

BIBL.: G. Monaldi, *P. M.: L'Uomo e l'artista* (Rome, 1899); G. Marvin, *P. M.: Biografia aneddotica* (Palermo, 1904); G. Bastianelli, *P. M., con nota delle opere* (Naples, 1910); G. Orsini, *L'arte di P. M.* (Milan, 1912); E. Pompei, *P. M., nella vita e nell'arte* (Rome, 1912); "Bibliografia delle opere di P. M.," *Bolletino Bibliografico Musicale*, VII (1932); A. Donno, *M. nel 900 musicale* (Rome, 1935); A. Jeri, *M., 15 Opere, 1000 Episodi* (Milan, 1940); D. Cellamare, *M. e la "Cavalleria" visti da Cerignola* (Rome, 1941); *M. parla* (Rome, 1945); *Comitato nazionale delle onoranze a P. M. nel primo centenario della nascità* (Livorno, 1963); M. Morini, ed., *P. M.* (2 vols., Milan, 1964); G. Gavazzeni, *Discorso per M. nel centenario della nascità* (Rome, 1964); D. Cellamare, *P. M.* (Rome, 1965); H. Goetz, "Die Beziehungen zwischen P. M. und Benito Mussolini," *Analecta Musicologica*, 17 (1976); R. Iovino, *M: L'avventuroso dell'opera* (Milan, 1987); C. and L. Pini, *M. aquattro mani* (Viareggio, 1992).

Mascheroni, Edoardo, distinguished Italian conductor; b. Milan, Sept. 4, 1852; d. Ghirla, near Varese, March 4, 1941. As a boy, he showed special interest in mathematics and literature; wrote literary essays for the journal *La Vita Nuova* before he decided to study music seriously; took lessons with Boucheron in Milan, and composed various pieces. In 1880 he began a career in Brescia as a conductor, and it was in that capacity that he distinguished himself. He was first a theater conductor in Livorno; then went to Rome, where he established his reputation as an opera conductor at the Teatro Apollo (1884). From 1891 to 1894 he was chief conductor of Milan's La Scala, where Verdi chose him to conduct the premiere of his *Falstaff* (Feb. 9, 1893). After conducting in Germany, Spain, and South America, he continued his career in Italy until retiring about 1925. He wrote 2 operas, *Lorenza* (Rome, April 13, 1901) and *La Perugina* (Naples, April 24, 1909), 2 Requiems, and chamber music. His brother, Angelo Mascheroni (1855–95), was also a conductor.

BIBL.: G. Roncaglia, "M.ana," *La Scala*, VI (1950).

Masetti, Enzo, Italian composer; b. Bologna, Aug. 19, 1893; d. Rome, Feb. 11, 1961. He studied with Franco Alfano at the Liceo Musicale in Bologna. He devoted his life mainly to film music; from 1942 until his death he was connected with the Centro Sperimentale di Cinematografia in Rome. He publ. *La musica nel film* (Rome, 1950) and composed about 60 film scores. He also wrote several dramatic fables, among them *La fola delle tre ochette* (Bologna, 1928), *La mosca mora* (Bologna, 1930), and *La bella non puo dormire* (Bologna, 1957); also *Contrasti* for Orch. (1921); *Il gioco del cucu* for Piano and Orch. (1928); piano pieces; songs.

Masini, Galliano, Italian tenor; b. Livorno, 1896; d. there, Feb. 15, 1986. He received his training in Milan. In 1923 he made his operatic debut as Cavaradossi in Livorno, and then sang in various Italian music centers. In 1930 he made his first appearance in Rome as Pinkerton, and continued to sing there until 1950. He also sang at Milan's La Scala, in Rio de Janeiro, Buenos Aires, Vienna, and Paris. In 1937–38 he appeared at the Chicago Opera. On Dec. 14, 1938, he made his Metropolitan Opera debut in N.Y. as Edgardo, where he remained on the roster for the season. In subsequent years, he pursued his career in Europe, making his farewell appearance in 1957. Among his other roles were Radames, Rodolfo, Turiddu, and Enzo.

Masley, Michael, American instrumentalist, composer, and instrument maker; b. Trenton, Mich., Sept. 22, 1952. He studied creative writing at Northwestern Michigan College (1970–72); in 1973 he began working with hammer dulcimer player Bob Spinner, who became a mentor. He played using traditional 2-hammer technique until 1979; during months at a fishing lodge in northern Michigan, he developed a 10-fingered "finger-hammer" technique. In 1982 he engaged the dulcimer maker William Webster of Detroit to make him a cymbalom; he added sections of violin bow to the finger hammers in 1983, creating his unique "bowhammers." In 1982 he moved to Palo Alto, California, where he met guitarist Barry Cleveland (1983); they performed as the duo Thin Ice, releasing the recordings *Thin Ice Live* (1984) and *1st Frost* (1985); he also played on Cleveland's later albums, *Mythos* (1986) and *Voluntary Dreaming* (1990). In 1985 he settled in Berkeley, California. His own recordings include *Cymbalom Songs* (1985), *The Moment's River* (1987), *Bells & Shadows* (1989), *Mystery Loves Company* (1990), *Sky Blues* (1992), and *Life in the Vast Lane* (1993); also the compilation *Mystery Repeats Itself* (1994). His innovative cymbalom technique enables the player to strike, bow, or pluck notes with all 10 fingers in any combination. The resulting timbral distinctions are used to create unusually complex contrapuntal textures for a solo instrument, to which he often adds pitched and tunable percussion instruments.

Mason, Daniel Gregory, eminent American composer and educator; b. Brookline, Mass., Nov. 20, 1873; d. Greenwich, Conn., Dec. 4, 1953. He was a scion of a famous family of American musicians; his grandfather was the distinguished American organist, conductor, music educator, and composer Lowell Mason (b. Medfield, Mass., Jan. 8, 1792; d. Orange, N.J., Aug. 11, 1872) and his uncle was the esteemed American pianist, pedagogue, and composer William Mason (b. Boston, Jan. 24, 1829; d. N.Y., July 14, 1908); his father, Henry Mason, was a co-founder of the piano manufacturing firm Mason & Hamlin. He entered Harvard Univ., where he studied with J.K. Paine (B.A., 1895); after graduation, he continued his studies with Arthur Whiting (piano), Goetschius (theory), and Chadwick (orchestration). Still feeling the necessity for improvement of his technique as a composer, he went to Paris, where he took courses with d'Indy (1913). In 1905 he became a member of the faculty of Columbia Univ. in N.Y.; in 1929, was appointed MacDowell Professor of Music; he was chairman of the music dept. until 1940, and continued to teach there until 1942, when he retired. As a teacher, Mason developed a high degree of technical ability in his students; as a composer, he represented a conservative trend in American music; while an adherent to the idea of an American national style, his conception was racially and regionally narrow, accepting only the music of Anglo-Saxon New England and the "old South"; he was an outspoken opponent of the "corrupting" and "foreign" influences of 20th-century Afro-American and Jewish-American music. His ideals were the German masters of the Romantic school; but there is an admixture of impressionistic colors in his orchestration; his harmonies are full and opulent, his melodic writing expressive and songful. The lack of strong individuality, however, has resulted in the virtual disappearance of his music from the active repertoire.

WORKS: ORCH.: 3 syms.: No. 1 (1913–14; Philadelphia, Feb. 18, 1916; radically rev. version, N.Y., Dec. 1, 1922), No. 2 (Cincinnati, Nov. 23, 1928), and No. 3, *Lincoln* (1935–36; N.Y., Nov. 17, 1937); *Prelude and Fugue* for Piano and Orch. (1914; Chicago, March 4, 1921); *Scherzo-Caprice* for Chamber Orch. (N.Y., Jan. 2, 1917); *Chanticleer*, festival overture (1926; Cincinnati, Nov. 23, 1928); *Suite* (1933–34); *Prelude and Fugue* for Strings (1939). **CHAMBER:** Violin Sonata (1907–08); Quartet for Piano and Strings (1909–11); *Pastorale* for Violin, Clarinet or Viola, and Piano (1909–12); 3 pieces for Flute, Harp, and String Quartet (1911–12); Sonata for Clarinet or Violin and Piano (1912–15); *Intermezzo* for String Quartet (1916); *String Quartet on Negro Themes* (1918–19); *Variations on a Theme of John Powell* for String Quartet (1924–25); *Divertimento* for Flute, Oboe, Clarinet, Horn, and Bassoon (1926); *Fanny Blair*, folksong fantasy for String Quartet (1929); *Serenade* for String Quartet (1931); *Sentimental Sketches*, 4 short pieces for Violin, Cello, and Piano (1935); *Variations on a Quiet Theme* (1939). **VOCAL:** *Russians* for Voice and Piano (1915–17; also for Baritone and Orch.); *Songs of the Countryside* for Chorus and Orch. (1923); *Soldiers* for Baritone and Piano (1948–49).

WRITINGS (all publ. in N.Y.): *From Grieg to Brahms* (1902; rev. 1930); *Beethoven and His Forerunners* (1904; 2nd ed., 1930); *The Romantic Composers* (1906); with T. Surette, *The Appreciation of Music* (1907) *The Orchestral Instruments and What They Do* (1909); *A Guide to Music* (1909); *A Neglected Sense in Piano Playing* (1912); with M. Mason, *Great Modern Composers* (1916; 2nd ed., 1968); *Short Studies of Great Masterpieces* (1917); *Contemporary Composers* (1918); *Music as a Humanity: And Other Essays* (1921); *From Song to Symphony* (1924); *Artistic Ideals* (1925); *The Dilemma of American Music* (1928); *Tune In, America!* (1931); *The Chamber Music of Brahms* (1933); *Music in My Time and Other Reminiscences* (1938); *The Quartets of Beethoven* (1947).

BIBL.: B. Tuthill, "D.G. M.," *Musical Quarterly* (Jan. 1948); M. Klein, *The Contribution of D.G. M. to American Music* (diss., Catholic Univ. of America, 1957); R. Lewis, *The Life and Music of D.G. M.* (diss., Univ. of Rochester, 1959); D. Kapec, *The Three Symphonies of D.G. M.: Style-Critical and Theoretical Analyses* (diss., Univ. of Florida, 1982).

Mason, Edith (Barnes), American soprano; b. St. Louis, March 22, 1893; d. San Diego, Nov. 26, 1973. She studied in Cincinnati, and then with Enrico Bertran and Edmond Clément in Paris. Following her operatic debut in Marseilles (1911), she sang in Boston (1912), Montreal (1912), Nice (1914), and N.Y. (Century Co., 1914–15). On Nov. 20, 1915, she made her Metropolitan Opera debut in N.Y. as Sophie in *Der Rosenkavalier*, remaining on its roster until 1917. After singing in Paris (1919–21), she was a principal member of the Chicago Opera (1921–29). She also sang at Milan's La Scala (1923), was again on the roster of the Metropolitan Opera (1934–36), and appeared at the Salzburg Festival (1935). In 1941 she made her farewell appearance in Chicago as Mimi. She was married twice to **Giorgio Polacco**. Among her other roles were Gilda, Gounod's Marguerite, Thaïs, Elsa, and Cio-Cio-San.

Mason, Marilyn (May), American organist and pedagogue; b. Alva, Okla., June 29, 1925. She studied at Oklahoma State Univ. and the Univ. of Mich.; also took lessons with Boulanger, Duruflé, and Schoenberg, completing her studies at the Union Theological Seminary in N.Y. (D.S.M., 1954). She became a teacher at the Univ. of Mich. in Ann Arbor (1946); was made chairman of its organ dept. in 1962 and a prof. in 1965. She made many tours as a recitalist in North America, Europe, South America, and the Far East, performing commissioned works from such composers as Cowell, Finney, Kay, Krenek, and Sowerby.

Massa, Juan Bautista, Argentine composer; b. Buenos Aires, Oct. 29, 1885; d. Rosario, March 7, 1938. He studied violin and composition. He became a choral conductor; moved to Rosario, where he was active as a teacher.

WORKS: DRAMATIC: OPERAS: *Zoraide* (Buenos Aires, May 15, 1909); *L'Evaso* (Rosario, June 23, 1922); *La Magdalena* (Buenos Aires, Nov. 9, 1929). **OPERETTAS:** *Esmeralda* (1903); *Triunfo del corazon* (1910); *La eterna historia* (1911). **BALLET:** *El cometa* (Buenos Aires, Nov. 8, 1932). **ORCH.:** *La muerte del Inca*, symphonic poem (Buenos Aires, Oct. 15, 1932); 2 Argentine suites; other pieces on native themes.

BIBL.: F. Lange, "J.B. M.," *Boletín Latino-Americano de Música* (Dec. 1938).

Massarani, Renzo, Italian-born Brazilian composer; b. Mantua, March 26, 1898; d. Rio de Janeiro, March 28, 1975. He studied with Respighi at Rome's Accademia di Santa Cecilia (diploma, 1921), then was active as music director of Vittorio Podrecca's puppet theater Il Teatro dei Piccoli and as a music critic. He left Fascist Italy and settled in Rio de Janeiro in 1935, becoming a naturalized Brazilian citizen in 1945; was active as a music critic. Through the banning of his works during the Mussolini dictatorship, the havoc of World War II, and his own destruction of many scores, much of his output is not extant. His surviving music reveals a composer of considerable talent.

WORKS: DRAMATIC: OPERAS: *Noi due* (c.1921); *La Donna nel pozzo* (1930); *Eliduc* (1938; unfinished). **OPERINAS:** *Bianco e nero* (Rome, 1921); *Le nozze di Takiu* (Rome, 1927); *Gilbetto e Gherminella* (Rome, 1929); *I dolori della principessa Susina* (Rome, 1929). **BALLETS:** *Guerin detto il meschino* (1928); *Boe* (Bergamo, 1937). **ORCH.:** Sinfonietta (1924); *Introduzione, tema e 7 variazioni* for Small Orch. (1934); *Il molinaro* for Violin and Orch. (1935); *Squilli e danze per il 18BL* (1937). **OTHER:** Chamber music; piano pieces; songs.

BIBL.: G. Rossi-Doria, "Laborca—M.—Rieti," *Il Pianoforte*, V (1924); A. Casella, "Jeunes et independants: R. M.," *La Revue Musicale*, VIII/3 (1927).

Masselos, William, American pianist and teacher; b. Niagara Falls, N.Y., Aug. 11, 1920; d. N.Y., Oct. 23, 1992. He studied at N.Y.'s Inst. of Musical Art and the Juilliard Graduate School, his principal mentors being Friedberg (piano), Salmond and Persinger (ensemble playing), and Wagenaar (theory); later he studied with Saperton and Dounis. In 1939 he made his debut in N.Y., and subsequently appeared as a soloist with orchs. and as a recitalist in the U.S. In later years he also toured in Europe. He taught at Indiana Univ. in Bloomington (1955–57), the Catholic Univ. of America in Washington, D.C. (1965–71; 1976–86), Georgia State Univ. in Atlanta (1972–75), and the Juilliard School (from 1976). Masselos acquired a fine reputation as an exponent of modern music. He gave the belated premiere of Ives's 1st Piano Sonata (1949), as well as the premieres of Copland's *Piano Fantasy* (1957) and Ben Weber's Piano Concerto (1961).

Massenet, Jules (-Émile-Frédéric), famous French composer and pedagogue; b. Montaud, near St.-Etienne, Loire, May 12, 1842; d. Paris, Aug. 13, 1912. He was 6 when he began to study piano with his mother. At 9, he was admitted to the Paris Cons. to study piano and theory. He had to leave the Cons. in 1854 when his father's ill health compelled the family to move to Chambéry. In 1855 he was able to resume his studies at the Cons., where he received instruction in piano from Laurent. In 1858 he made his public debut as a pianist in a Paris recital. In 1859 he won the premier prix for piano at the Cons., where he also pursued training with Reber (harmony), Benoist (organ), and Thomas (composition). In 1863 he won the Grand Prix de Rome with his cantata *David Rizzio.* His first major success as a composer came with the premiere of his oratorio *Marie-Magdeleine* (Paris, April 11, 1873). His next oratorio, *Ève* (Paris, March 18, 1875), won him the Légion d'honneur. His first operatic success came with the premiere of *Le roi de Lahore* at the Paris Opéra on April 27, 1877. The success of his opera *Hérodi-*

ade (Brussels, Dec. 19, 1881) resulted in his being made a Knight of the Order of Leopold of Belgium. He scored a triumph with the first performance of his opera *Manon* at the Paris Opéra on Jan. 19, 1884. This score is generally acknowledged as his finest opera. *Werther*, another distinguished opera, added to his renown when it was premiered at the Vienna Court Opera on Feb. 16, 1892. Equally noteworthy was his opera *Thaïs* (Paris Opéra, March 16, 1894). Among his later operatic efforts, the most important were *Le jongleur de Notre-Dame* (Monte Carlo, Feb. 18, 1902) and *Don Quichotte* (Monto Carlo, Feb. 24, 1910). Of his incidental scores, that for Leconte de Lisle's drama *Les Érinnyes* (Paris, Jan. 6, 1873) was particularly notable. In 1878 Massenet was appointed prof. of composition at the Paris Cons., a position he held with distinction until 1896. He was a highly influential teacher, numbering among his students Bruneau, Charpentier, Pierné, Koechlin, and Schmitt. In 1878 he was elected a member of the Institut of the Académie des Beaux-Arts, ascending to the rank of Grand-Officier in 1900. Massenet wrote an autobiography, *Mes souvenirs* (completed by X. Leroux; Paris, 1912; Eng. tr., 1919, as *My Recollections*). He was one of the leading French opera composers of his era. His operas are the work of a fine craftsman, marked by a distinctive style, sensuous melodiousness, and lyricism which proved immediately appealing to audiences of his day. However, even before his death, developments in the lyric theater had passed him by. In succeeding years, his operas were heard infrequently, and almost disappeared from the active repertoire. Even the celebrated *Meditation* for Violin and Orch. from *Thaïs*, long a favorite concert piece with violinists and audiences, was seldom performed. Today, revivals of *Manon, Werther*, and *Thaïs* have won Massenet new audiences around the world.

WORKS: DRAMATIC: OPERAS: *Esmeralda* (1865; not extant); *La coup du roi de Thulé* (1866?); *La grand'tante* (Paris, April 3, 1867); *Manfred* (1869?; unfinished); *Méduse* (1870; unfinished); *Don César de Bazan* (Paris, Nov. 30, 1872); *L'adorable bel'-boul'* (Paris, April 17, 1874; not extant); *Les templiers* (1875?; not extant); *Bérangère et Anatole* (Paris, Feb. 1876); *Le roi de Lahore* (Paris, April 27, 1877); *Robert de France* (1880?; not extant); *Les Girondins* (1881; not extant); *Hérodiade* (Brussels, Dec. 19, 1881); *Manon* (Paris, Jan. 19, 1884); *Le Cid* (Paris, Nov. 30, 1885); *Esclarmonde* (Paris, May 14, 1889); *Le mage* (Paris, March 16, 1891); *Werther* (Vienna, Feb. 16, 1892); *Thaïs* (Paris, March 16, 1894); *Le portrait de Manon* (Paris, May 8, 1894); *La navarraise* (London, June 20, 1894); *Amadis* (1895?; Monte Carlo, April 1, 1922); *Sapho* (Paris, Nov. 27, 1897; rev. 1909); *Cendrillon* (Paris, May 24, 1899); *Grisélidis* (Paris, Nov. 20, 1901); *Le jongleur de Notre-Dame* (Monte Carlo, Feb. 18, 1902); *Chérubin* (Monte Carlo, Feb. 14, 1903); *Ariane* (Paris, Oct. 31, 1906); *Thérèse* (Monte Carlo, Feb. 7, 1907); *Bacchus* (Paris, May 5, 1909); *Don Quichotte* (Monte Carlo, Feb. 24, 1910); *Roma* (Monte Carlo, Feb. 17, 1912); *Panurge* (Paris, April 25, 1913); *Cléopâtre* (Monte Carlo, Feb. 23, 1914). **BALLETS:** *Le carillon* (Vienna , Feb. 21, 1892); *Cigale* (Paris, Feb. 4, 1904); *Espada* (Monte Carlo, Feb. 13, 1908). **INCIDENTAL MUSIC** (all 1st perf. in Paris unless otherwise given): *Les Érinnyes* (Jan. 6, 1873); *Un drame sous Philippe II* (April 14, 1875); *La vie de Bohème* (1876); *L'Hetman* (Feb. 2, 1877); *Notre-Dame de Paris* (June 4, 1879); *Michel Strogoff* (Nov. 17, 1880); *Nana-Sahib* (Dec. 20, 1883); *Théodora* (Dec. 26, 1884); *Le crocodile* (Dec. 21, 1886); *Phèdre* (Dec. 8, 1900); *Le grillon du foyer* (Oct. 1, 1904); *Le manteau du roi* (Oct. 22, 1907); *Perce-Neige et les sept gnomes* (Feb. 2, 1909); *Jérusalem* (Monte Carlo, Jan. 17, 1914). **ORCH.:** *Ouverture de concert* (1863); 7 suites: No. 1, *Première suite d'orchestre* (1865), No. 2, *Scènes hongroises* (1871), No. 3, *Scènes dramatiques* (1873), No. 4, *Scènes pittoresques* (1874), No. 5, *Scènes napolitaines* (1876?), No. 6, *Scènes de féerie* (1879), and No. 7, *Scènes alsaciennes* (1881); *Ouverture de Phèdre* (1873); *Sarabande du XVIe siècle* (1875); *Marche héroïque de Szabady* (1879); *Parade militaire* (1887); *Visions, poème symphonique* (1890); *Devant la Madone* (1897); *Fantaisie* for Cello and Orch. (1897); *Marche solennelle* (1897); *Brumaire*, overture (1899); *Les grand violons du roi* (1900?); *Les Rosati* (1902); Piano Concerto (1903). **OTHER:** 4 oratorios: *Marie-Magdeleine* (Paris, April 11, 1873); *Ève* (Paris, March 18, 1875); *La Vierge* (Paris, May 22, 1880); *La terre promise* (Paris, March 15, 1900); the choral pieces *Narcisse* (1877) and *Biblis* (1886); secular cantatas, including *David Rizzio* (1863); part songs; about 200 songs; piano pieces; completion and orchestration of Delibes's opera *Kassya* (Paris, March 24, 1893).

BIBL.: E. de Solenière, *M.: Étude critique et documentaire* (Paris, 1897); C. Fournier, *Étude sur le style de M.* (Amiens, 1905); L. Schneider, *M.: L'homme, le musicien* (Paris, 1908; 2nd ed., 1926); H. Finck, *M. and His Operas* (London and N.Y., 1910); O. Séré, *M.* (Paris, 1911); special issue of *Musica* (Sept. 1912); A. Soubies, *M. historien* (Paris, 1913); A. Pougin, *M.* (Paris, 1914); C. Widor, *Notice sur la vie et les travaux de M.* (Paris, 1915); H. Twitchell, "M. as a Teacher," *Musician*, XXV (1920); J. Loisel, *Manon de M.: Étude historique et critique* (Paris, 1922); C. Bouvet, *M.* (Paris, 1929); J. d'Udine, *L'art du lied et le mélos de M.* (Paris, 1931); M. Delmas, *M., sa vie, ses oeuvres* (Paris, 1932); A. Bruneau, *M.* (Paris, 1935); A. Morin, *J. M. et ses opéras* (Montreal, 1944); N. Boyer, *Trois musiciens français: Gounod, M., Debussy* (Paris, 1946); P. Colson, *M.: Manon* (London, 1947); J. Bruyr, *M.* (Geneva, 1948); idem, *M., musicien de la belle époque* (Lyons, 1964); A. Coquis, *J. M.: L'homme et son oeuvre* (Paris, 1965); E. Bouilhol, *M.: Son rôle dans l'évolution du théâtre musicale* (St.-Etienne, 1969); L. Stocker, *The Treatment of the Romantic Literary Hero in Verdi's "Ernani" and in M.'s "Werther"* (diss., Florida State Univ., 1969); J. Harding, *M.* (London, 1970); O. Salzer, *The M. Compendium* (Fort Lee, N.J., 1984); G. Marschall, *M. et la fixation de la forme mélodique française* (Saarbrücken, 1988); D. Irvine, *M.: A Chronicle of His Life and Times* (Portland, Oreg., 1993).

Masséus, Jan, Dutch composer; b. Rotterdam, Jan. 28, 1913. He received training in piano from Callenbach and Aribo and in composition from Badings, the latter continuing as his mentor at the Rotterdam Cons.; later he worked in the electronic music studio of the Delft Technical High School. He was a music critic in Rotterdam (1956–60), and then director of the Leeuwarden Music School (1961–72).

WORKS: ORCH.: Sinfonietta for Chamber Orch. (1952); Concerto for Violin and Chamber Orch. (1953); Concerto for 2 Flutes and Orch. (1956); *Cassazione*, 4 dances for Small Orch. (1960); Piano Concerto (1966); *Iowa Serenade* (1981); *Skriabinade*, symphonic suite (1983); *Homo Ludens* (1986); *Nada Brahma* (1988); *Pandora* (1991; rev. 1992). **CHAMBER:** 2 violin sonatas (1946, 1950); Trio for Flute, Violin, and Piano (1948); *Quintetto* for Piano and String Quartet (1952); *Introduction and Allegro* for Oboe, Clarinet, and Piano (1952); *Partita* for Violin and Piano (1956); Flute Sonata (1957); *Serenade* for Oboe, Bassoon, Violin, and Viola (1958); *7 Minutes of Organized Sound* for 3 Winds, Guitar, and Percussion (1968); *Contemplations* for Brass Ensemble (1972); Concertino for 5 Accordions and Flute (1977); *Sept pièces breves* for Oboe, Clarinet, and Piano (1980). **PIANO:** *Symphonic Fantasy* for 2 Pianos (1947); *Helicon Suite* for Piano, 4-hands (1952); *Zoological Impressions* for Piano, 4-hands (1954); *Balletto piccola* for 2 Pianos (1955); *Confetti* for Piano, 4-hands (1969); *Pentatude*, 5 studies (1974). **VOCAL:** *Gezelle liederen* for Soprano, Alto, Piano, 4-hands, and Percussion (1955); *Camphuysen-liederen* for Chorus, 3 Trumpets, 3 Trombones, and Tuba (1967); *4 Songs* for Chorus, 9 Brasses, Double Bass, and Percussion (1970); *The 7 Tile Tableaux* for Baritone, Brass Instruments, Double Bass, and Percussion (1973); *Schermutselingen* for Chorus and Orch. (Leeuwarden, Dec. 17, 1975); *Het meezennestje* for Chorus and Piano (1979); *Triptyque maconnique* for Bass, Flute, and Organ (1981); *Drentse metamorfosen* for Chorus and Orch. (1985).

Massey, Andrew (John), English conductor; b. Nottingham, May 1, 1946. He studied cello, flute, and trumpet while in high school, and also began to compose; then pursued musical training at the Univ. of Oxford (B.A., 1968; M.A., 1981) and at the Univ. of Nottingham (M.A., 1969); he also studied composition with Berio, Lutosławski, and Keller at the Dartington Summer School and conducting with Hurst at the Canford Summer School. He was principal conductor of the Derby Concert Orch. (1969–76), the Apollo Sym. Orch. (1969–78), and the Reading Sym. Orch. (1972–78); from 1972 to 1978, also was senior lecturer in music at the Middlesex Polytechnic, where he was principal conductor of the Middlesex Phil. (1972–75). After serving as assistant conductor of the Cleveland Orch. (1978–80), he was assoc. conductor of the New Orleans Sym. Orch. (1980–86) and the San Francisco Sym. (1986–88). From 1985 to 1991 he was music director of the Rhode Island Phil. in Providence. In 1986–87 he was music advisor of the Fresno (Calif.) Phil., and then was its music director from 1987 to 1993. He was music director designate (1990–91) and then music director (from 1991) of the Toledo (Ohio) Sym. Orch. In addition to his admirable interpretations of the standard repertory, Massey has displayed remarkable facility with works by contemporary composers, among them Ligeti, Boulez, Messiaen, Carter, Bolcom, Knussen, and Drew.

Másson, Áskell, Icelandic composer; b. Reykjavík, Nov. 21, 1953. He began clarinet lessons at the age of 8. After taining at the Reykjavík College of Music, he went to London and studied with Patrick Savill (harmony and counterpoint) and James Blades (percussion). In 1972 he became a composer and instrumentalist with the ballet of the National Theater in Reykjavík. From 1978 to 1983 he worked as a producer for the Icelandic State Radio. He was secretary-general of the Iceland League of Composers (1983–85), then president of STEF, the association of composers and copyright owners (from 1989). Másson's output is generally marked by an intensity and brilliance of expression, complemented by a judicious infusion of lyricism.

WORKS: DRAMATIC: *Eldtröllid* (The Fire Troll), ballet (1974); *Höfudskepnurnar* (The Elements), ballet (1974); *Svart-Hvítt* (Black and White), ballet (1975); *Klakahöllin* (The Ice Palace), opera (1993); incidental music to players; music for radio and television. **ORCH.:** *Galda-Loftur* (The Wish; Icelandic State Radio, June 19, 1980); Clarinet Concerto (1980; Reykjavík, Jan. 31, 1981); *Konzertstück* for Snare Drum and Orch. (Reykjavík, Sept. 25, 1982); *Októ Nóvember* (Octo November for Strings (Reykjavík, Dec. 19, 1982); Viola Concerto (1983; Reykjavík, May 3, 1984); *Myndhvörf* (Metamorphoses) for Brass Orch. (Reykjavík, Nov. 29, 1983); Piano Concerto (1985; Reykjavík, Oct. 5, 1987); *Impromptu* (1986; Reykjavík, Jan. 1989); Marimba Concerto (1987; Göteborg, Oct. 1991); Trombone Concerto (1987); *Hvörf* for Strings (1992; Reykjavík, June 2, 1993); *Sinfonia Trilogia* (1992). **CHAMBER:** *Silja* for 3 Percussionists (1970–72); *Lafasafn* (Melodies) for 2 Flutes and Vibraphone (1974); *Vatnsdropinn* (The Drop of Water) for 2 Percussionists and Tape or 3 Percussionists (1977); *Bláa Ljósid* (The Blue Light) for 2 Flutes and 2 Percussionists (1978); *Helfró* (Transcendental Visions) for 2 Percussionists and Tape or 4 Percussionists (1978); Sonata for Marimba and Tuned Percussion (1981; also as Sonata for Solo Marimba, 1985); Trio for Clarinet, Violin, and Viola (1983; also as *Triology* for Clarinet, Violin, and Viola, 1985); *Partita* for Guitar and Percussion (1984); *Divertimento* for Clarinet, Guitar, Percussion, and Hand Drums (1986); *Fantasy on a Chinese Poem* for Clarinet and Hand Drum (1987); *Sindur* (Sparks) for Percussion Quartet (1989); *Fantasia* for Oboe or Clarinet and Harpsichord (1991); Wind Quintet (1991); *Snow* for Violin, Cello, Vibraphone or Crotales, and Piano (1992); also numerous works for solo instrument, including a Violin Sonata (1993). **ORGAN:** *Elegie* (1981); *Brúdarmars* (Wedding March; 1984; also with optional trumpet); Sonata (1986); *Meditation* (1992). **VOCAL:** *Sýn* (Vision) for Women's Voices and Percussionist (1974–75); *Snjór* (Snow) for High Voice and Piano (1982; rev. 1992); *Introitus* for Chorus, 14 Brass Players, Timpani, and Organ (1985); *Fjörg* (The Gods) for Chorus and Percussionists (1989); *Baen* (Prayer) for High or Low Voice and Bells (1994).

Masson, Diego, French conductor; b. Tossa, Spain, June 21, 1935. He studied percussion, harmony, and chamber music at the Paris Cons. (1953–59); also received training in fugue, counterpoint, and composition from Leibowitz (1955–59), in composition from Maderna (1964), and in conducting from Boulez (1965). In 1966 he founded the Musique Vivante, with which he gave numerous performances of contemporary music. He also was music director of the Marseilles Opéra until 1982, and of the Ballet-Théâtre Contemporain in Amiens (from 1968), which removed to Angers in 1972 under his direction as part of the Théâtre-Musical d'Angers.

Masson, Gérard, French composer; b. Paris, Aug. 12, 1936. He took courses in advanced techniques with Stockhausen, Pousseur, and Earle Brown in Cologne (1965–66), working along the lines of serial methods and acoustical coordination of sonorous blocs; experienced profound influence of the theory and practice of Varèse's "organized sound." His music is marked by strict constructivism, enlivened by lyric exoticism. Stravinsky, who had opportunity to examine some of Masson's scores, commended him in one of his last publ. interviews.

WORKS: *Pièce* for 14 Instruments and Percussion (1964); *Dans le deuil des vagues I* for 14 Instruments (Royan Festival, April 1, 1967) and *II* for Orch. (London, Nov. 20, 1968); *Ouest I* for 10 Instruments (Vienna, April 25, 1968) and *II* for Voice and Instruments (Paris, April 26, 1971); *Bleu loin* for 12 Strings (1970); *Ici c'est la tyrannie* for Orch. (1973); String Quartet (1973); *Hymnopsie* for Orch. (1974); 2 piano concertos (1977, 1990); *Pas seulement des moments, des moyens d'amour* for 2 Pianos and Orch. (1980); *Gymnastique de l'éponge* for Piano and 10 Instrumentalists (1985); *Offs* for Orch. (1988); *La Mort de Germanicus* for Piano and Cello (1991); *Bud* for Orch. (1992).

Masson, Paul-Marie, eminent French musicologist; b. Sète, Hérault, Sept. 19, 1882; d. Paris, Jan. 27, 1954. He studied at the lycée, the arts faculty, and the Lycée Henri IV in Montpellier before going to Paris, where he pursued his education at the École Normale Superieure and concurrently was a student of Rolland and Lefranc at the École des Haute Études (agregation, 1907, with the diss. *La Musique mesurée à l'Antique au XVIe siècle*); after further training with d'Indy and Koechlin (fugue, counterpoint, and composition) at the Schola Cantorum, he completed his education at the Univ. of Paris (docteur ès lettres, 1930, with the diss. *L'opéra de Rameau*; publ. in Paris, 1930). In 1910 he served as chargé de conférences at the Univ. of Grenoble, and also taught the history of French literature and music at the Institut Français in Florence (1910–14). In 1918 he was again at the Institut Français, and then went to Naples, where he founded its Institut Français in 1919. He taught music history at the Sorbonne in Paris from 1931 to 1952. In 1951 he founded the Institut de Musicologie of the Univ. of Paris. In 1937 he was elected vice-president of the Société Française de Musicologie, and in 1949 was elected its president. He contributed numerous articles to journals and publ. the book *Berlioz* (Paris, 1923). He also composed the *Chant des peuples unis*, a cantata; *Suite pastorale* for Wind Quintet; piano pieces; songs.

BIBL.: *Mélanges d'histoire et d'esthétique musicale offertes à P.-M. M.* (Paris, 1955).

Masterson, Valerie, English soprano; b. Birkenhead, June 3, 1937. She studied at the Matthay School of Music in Liverpool and the Royal College of Music in London; also in Milan. She made her debut as Frasquita in *Carmen* at the Salzburg Landestheater in 1963; then sang with the D'Oyly Carte Opera Co. in London (1966–70); became a member of the Sadler's Wells Opera in London in 1970; from 1974, sang at Covent Garden in London. She made her debut at the Paris Opéra as Marguerite (1978); made her U.S. debut as Violetta with the San Francisco Opera (1980). As a guest artist, she appeared in opera and concert around the world. In 1988 she was made a Commander of the Order of the British Empire.

Mastilović, Danica, Yugoslav soprano; b. Negotin, Nov. 7, 1933. She was a pupil of Nikola Cvejić in Belgrade; while still a student, she sang with the Belgrade Operetta Theater (1955–59);

in 1959 she made her formal operatic debut as Tosca at the Frankfurt am Main Opera, where she sang until 1969. Her guest appearances took her to Hamburg, Vienna, Munich, Bayreuth, Paris, and London. In 1963 she made her first U.S. appearance at the Chicago Lyric Opera as Abigaille, and on Nov. 25, 1975, her Metropolitan Opera debut in N.Y. as Elektra. In 1973 she made her first appearance at London's Covent Garden as Elektra. In 1978–79 she was again on the roster of the Metropolitan Opera. She became principally known for her roles in operas by Verdi, Wagner, and Strauss.

Masur, Kurt, eminent German conductor; b. Brieg, Silesia, July 18, 1927. He received training in piano and cello at the Breslau Music School (1942–44); then studied conducting with H. Bongartz and took courses in piano and composition at the Leipzig Hochschule für Musik (1946–48). In 1948 he commenced his career with appointments as répétiteur and conductor at the Halle Landestheater; held the title of 1st conductor at the Erfurt City Theater (1951–53) and at the Leipzig City Theater (1953–55). He was conductor of the Dresden Phil. (1955–58), Generalmusikdirektor of the Mecklenburg State Theater in Schwerin (1958–60), and senior director of music at the Komische Oper in East Berlin (1960–64). In 1967 he returned to the Dresden Phil. as its music director, a position he retained until 1972. In 1970 he assumed the time-honored position of Gewandhauskapellmeister of Leipzig, where he served as music director of the Gewandhaus Orch. with notable distinction until 1998. He also made extensive tours with his orch. in Europe and abroad. In 1973 he made his British debut as a guest conductor with the New Philharmonia Orch. of London; his U.S. debut followed in 1974 as a guest conductor with the Cleveland Orch. On Oct. 9, 1981, he conducted the Beethoven 9th Sym. at the gala opening of the new Gewandhaus in Leipzig. In 1988 he was named principal guest conductor of the London Phil. In the autumn of 1989, during the period of political upheaval in East Germany, Masur played a major role as peacemaker in Leipzig. In 1990 he was appointed music director of the N.Y. Phil., which position he assumed in 1991 while retaining his title in Leipzig until 1997. On Dec. 7, 1992, he conducted the N.Y. Phil. in a performance of Dvořák's *New World Symphony* as part of the orch.'s 150th anniversary concert, which was televized live throughout the U.S. by PBS. While he has earned a reputation as a faithful guardian of the hallowed Austro-German repertoire, he frequently programs contemporary scores as well.

BIBL.: D. Härtwig, *K. M.* (Leipzig, 1975); A. Fritzsch and M. Simon, *Der Gewandhauskapellmeister K. M.* (Leipzig, 1987).

Masurok, Yuri (Antonovich), Polish-born Russian baritone; b. Krasnik, July 18, 1931. He studied at the Lwów Inst. and the Moscow Cons.; won prizes in singing competitions in Prague (1960), Bucharest (1961), and Montreal (1967); in 1964 he made his debut as Eugene Onegin at the Bolshoi Theater in Moscow, where he later sang Prince Andrei in Prokofiev's *War and Peace.* He made his London debut at Covent Garden in 1975 as Anckarström, the same role he chose for his U.S. debut with the San Francisco Opera in 1977. In 1979 he sang Escamillo in Zeffirelli's production of *Carmen* at the Vienna State Opera, and also appeared there as Scarpia and Luna. In 1991 he became a member of the Mannheim National Theater. His other roles include Rossini's Figaro, Giorgio Germont, and Rodrigo in *Don Carlos.*

Mata, Eduardo, Mexican conductor and composer; b. Mexico City, Sept. 5, 1942; d. in an airplane crash in Cuernavaca, Jan. 4, 1995. He studied composition with Halffter at the National Cons. of Mexico City (1954–60); then took lessons in composition and conducting with Chávez (1960–65) and Orbón (1960–63) there; in 1964 he went to the Berkshire Music Center at Tanglewood, where he attended conducting seminars led by Rudolf, Schuller, and Leinsdorf. He was conductor of the Mexican Ballet Co. (1963–64), the Guadalajara Sym. Orch. (1964–66), and the Phil. Orch. of the National Univ. of Mexico (1966–76). From 1970 to 1978 he was principal conductor of the Phoenix (Ariz.) Sym. Orch. Mata served as music director of the Dallas Sym. Orch. from 1977 to 1993. He also appeared as a guest conductor with leading orchs. throughout North America and Europe. In 1990 he became principal guest conductor of the Pittsburgh Sym. Orch. At the beginning of his career, he was active as a composer; however, he virtually abandoned composition after 1970. Among his works were 3 syms. (1962; 1963; 1966–67), the ballet music *Débora* (1963), and chamber music.

Matačić, Lovro von, noted Slovenian conductor; b. Sušak, Feb. 14, 1899; d. Zagreb, Jan. 4, 1985. He studied with Herbst and Nedbal at the Vienna Cons.; later worked under Brechner at the Cologne Opera, where he made his debut in 1919; then conducted in Ljubljana (1924–26), Belgrade (1926–32), and Zagreb (1932–38). He was chief conductor of the Belgrade Opera (1938–42); then conducted at the Vienna Volksoper (1942–45); subsequently was Generalmusikdirektor of the Dresden State Opera (1956–58); also conducted at the (East) Berlin State Opera. He was chief conductor of the Frankfurt am Main Opera (1961–65), the Zagreb Phil. (1970–80), and the Monte Carlo Opera (1974–78). His guest conducting engagements included appearances in Europe, the U.S., and South America.

Matěj, Josef, Czech composer; b. Brušperk, Feb. 19, 1922; d. there, March 28, 1992. He learned to play the trombone from his father; studied composition with Hlobil at the Prague Cons. (1942–47) and Řídký and Janeček at the Prague Academy of Musical Arts (1947–51). His early works are characterized by folk-song inflections of the Lachian region of his birth; after 1960 he introduced into his works some coloristic oriental elements; also made discreet use of dodecaphonic techniques.

WORKS: OPERA: *Čtyřicet dní hory Musa Dagh* (40 Days of Musa Dagh Mountain; 1979–82). **ORCH.:** 2 trombone concertos (1947–51; 1952); *3 Symphonic Dances* (1952); 5 syms.: No. 1 for Soloists, Chorus, and Orch. (1953–55), No. 2 (1959–60), No. 3, *Sinfonia dramatica* (1969–70), No. 4 (1974), and No. 5 (1977); *Sonata da camera* for Oboe and Chamber Orch. (1955); Violin Concerto (1961); *Rhapsody* for Viola and Orch. (1962); Trumpet Concerto (1963; Prague, April 15, 1965); Concerto for Flute, Strings, and Harpsichord (1967); Concerto for Clarinet, Strings, and Piano (1970); Cello Concerto (1972; Prague, March 7, 1973); Triple Concerto for Trumpet, Horn, Trombone, and Chamber Orch. (1974). **CHAMBER:** 2 string quartets (1947–48; 1966); *Invocation* for 4 Trombones (1950); Wind Quintet (1955–56); Sonata for Trombone and Strings (1965); Violin Sonata (1971); Music for 5 Brass Instruments, *Omaggio à Leos Janáček* (1978); *Canzona* for Trumpet and Piano (1980); *Fantasia* for Organ (1981); *Inventions* for Flute and Piano (1982–83). **VOCAL:** Choral works; songs.

Mather, (James) Bruce, Canadian composer, pianist, and teacher; b. Toronto, May 9, 1939. He studied at the Royal Cons. of Music of Toronto (1952–57) and at the Univ. of Toronto (B.Mus., 1959), his principal mentors being Alberto Guerrero, Earle Moss, and Uninsky in piano and Ridout, Morawetz, and Weinzweig in theory and composition. During the summers of 1957–58, he also attended the Aspen (Colo.) Music School. He then studied at the Paris Cons. (1959–61) with Milhaud (composition), Plé-Caussade (counterpoint and fugue), Messiaen (analysis), and Lévy (piano). Following further training in composition with Leland Smith and Roy Harris at Stanford Univ. (M.A., 1964), he returned to the Univ. of Toronto to take his D.Mus. in 1967. In 1969 he studied conducting with Boulez in Basel. After teaching at the Brodie School of Music and Dance and at the Univ. of Toronto (1964–66), he taught at McGill Univ. in Montreal from 1966. As a pianist, he won approbation as an interpreter of contemporary scores. He appeared in duo piano concerts with his wife, Pierrett LePage. In 1979 he won the Jules Léger Prize for his *Musique pour Champigny.* In 1987 he was one of the winners of the Micheline Coulombe Saint-Marcoux prize for his *Barbaresco.* In his music, Mather has utilized various contemporary modes of expression, ranging from serialism to microtonality. He has displayed a special affinity in composing chamber and vocal pieces.

WORKS: OPERA: *La Princesse Blanche* (1993; Montreal, Feb. 2, 1994). **ORCH.:** Concerto for Piano and Chamber Orch. (Aspen, Colo., Aug. 20, 1958); *Elegy* for Saxophone and Strings (1959); *Symphonic Ode* (1964; Toronto, March 28, 1965); *Orchestra Piece 1967* (1966; Toronto, Jan. 11, 1967); *Ombres* (1967; Montreal, May 1, 1968); *Music for Vancouver* for Chamber Orch. (Vancouver, Sept. 17, 1969); *Musique pour Rouen* for Strings (1970; Rouen, June 9, 1971); *Musigny* (1980; Metz, Nov. 20, 1981); *Scherzo* (Toronto, Dec. 4, 1987; also for 18 Instruments, 1988; Montreal, March 16, 1989); *Dialogue* for Viola, Cello, Double Bass, and Orch. (Montreal, Nov. 4, 1988). **CHAMBER:** *Étude* for Clarinet (1962); *Mandola* for Mandolin and Piano (1971); *Music* for Organ, Horn, and Gongs (Toronto, Oct. 20, 1973); *Eine kleine Bläsermusik* for Wind Quintet (1975; Ottawa, April 11, 1976); *Clos du Vougeot* for Percussion Quartet (1977; Toronto, April 3, 1978); *Barolo* for Cello and Tape (1978–85); *Ausone* for Flute, or for Flute and 2 Harps, or for Flute, 2 Harps, 2 Guitars, 2 Violins, 2 Violas, and 2 Cellos (1979); *Coulée de Serrant* for Harp and Piano (1980); *Sassicaia* for Clarinet and Piano (1981); *Gattinara* for Viola and Marimba (1982; Montreal, April 28, 1983); *Elegy* for Flute, Cello, Piano, and Percussion (Burnaby, Dec. 1, 1983); *Barbaresco* for Viola, Cello, and Double Bass (Metz, Oct. 7, 1984); *Clos d'Audignac* for Marimba and 3 Percussion (1984; Toronto, May 11, 1985); *Vourray* for Oboe and Harp (1986); Viola Duet (1987); *Vega Sicilia* for Guitar, Viola, Cello, Harp, and Marimba (1989); *Aux victimes de la guerre de Vendée* for Horn, 2 Pianos, and Tape (Metz, Nov. 17, 1990); *Yquem* for 4 Ondes Martenot and 4 Pianos (1991; Montreal, Jan. 15, 1993); *Romance* for Bassoon and Synthesizer (N.Y., Nov. 6, 1992); *Standing Ware* for Clarinet, Cello, Piano, and Percussion (1994; Vancouver, Feb. 10, 1995). **KEYBOARD: PIANO:** *Smaragdin* (1960); *Like Snow* (1960); *Mystras* (1962); *Fantasy 1964* (CBC, Toronto, Nov. 22, 1964); Sonata for 2 Pianos (Manitoba, Oct. 14, 1970); *In Memoriam Alexandre Uninsky* (1974; Paris, Nov. 24, 1975); *Régime Onze, Type A* for 2 Pianos (Metz, Nov. 16, 1978); *Poème du Delire* for 3 Pianos (1982; Metz, April 21, 1983). **ORGAN:** *6 Études* (1982; Sinzig, Germany, March 7, 1983). **VOCAL:** 2 Songs for Bass-baritone and Orch. (1956; Toronto, April 20, 1958); *Venice* for Soprano, Clarinet, Cello, and Piano (Aspen, Colo., Aug. 23, 1957); *3 Poems of Robert Graves* for Soprano and String Orch. (1957–58); *Cycle Rilke* for Tenor and Guitar (1959; Paris, April 20, 1960); *Sick Love* for Soprano and Orch. (1960); *The Song of Blodeuwedd* for Baritone, Percussion, Harp, Piano, and Strings (1961); *Lament for Pasiphae* for Chorus and Chamber Orch. (1962; Stanford, Calif., April 28, 1963); *Orphée* for Soprano, Piano, and Percussion (San Francisco, Dec. 14, 1963); *La Lune Mince* for Chorus (1965; Montreal, April 2, 1970); *Madrigal I* for Soprano, Contralto, and 5 Instruments (Toronto, April 16, 1967), *II* for Soprano, Contralto, and 5 Instruments (Stratford, Ontario, July 27, 1968), *III* for Contralto and 3 Instruments (Toronto, July 21, 1971), *IV* for Soprano, Flute, Piano, and Tape (1972; Montreal, April 13, 1973), and *V* for Soprano, Contralto, and Chamber Orch. (Montreal, April 12, 1973); *Au Château de Pompairain* for Mezzo-soprano and Orch. (1975; Ottawa, May 4, 1977); *Musique pour Champigny* for Soprano, Mezzo-soprano, Contralto, and 5 Instruments (1976; Montreuil, France, March 3, 1977); *Les Grandes Fontaines* for Soprano and Piano (1981); *Un cri qui durerait la mer* for Mezzo-soprano or Contralto and Piano (1985; Montreal, April 25, 1986); *Travaux de Nuit* for Baritone and Chamber Orch. (1989; N.Y., June 24, 1990).

Mathews, Max (Vernon), American computer scientist and composer; b. Columbus, Nebr., Nov. 13, 1926. He studied electrical engineering at the Calif. Inst. of Technology (B.S., 1950) and at the Mass. Inst. of Technology (M.S., 1952; D.Sc., 1954). He joined the Bell Telephone Laboratories in Murray Hill, N.J. (1955), and developed its MUSIC programs, the first computer sound-synthesis languages; with other scientists, he developed its GROOVE (Generated Real-time Operations on Voltage-controlled Equipment) system; he also developed electronic violins. He wrote the book *The Technology of Computer Music* (1969). His compositions for computer include *May Carol II* (1960); *Numerology* (1960); *The 2nd Law* (1961); *Masquerades* (1963); *Slider* (1965); *International Lullaby* (1966; in collaboration with O. Fujimura); *Swansong* (1966).

Mathias, William (James), prominent Welsh composer and teacher; b. Whitland, Nov. 1, 1934; d. Menai Bridge, July 29, 1992. He was a student of Ian Parrott at Univ. College of Wales, Aberystwyth (B.Mus., 1956); in 1957 he went to London to continue his training with Lennox Berkeley (composition) and Peter Katin (piano) at the Royal Academy of Music, where he was made a Fellow in 1965. Upon returning to his homeland, he received his D.Mus. from the Univ. of Wales (1966). From 1959 to 1968 he lectured at Univ. College of North Wales, Bangor. In 1968–69 he taught at the Univ. of Edinburgh. In 1969 he rejoined the faculty of Univ. College of North Wales, where he then was a prof. and head of the music dept. from 1970 to 1988. From 1972 he also served as artistic director of the North Wales Music Festival in St. Asaph. In 1968 he received the Bax Soc. Prize and in 1981 the John Edwards Memorial Award. In 1985 he was made a Commander of the Order of the British Empire. In his music, Mathias followed a basically tonal path notable for its craftsmanship, adept handling of instrumental and vocal forces, and euphonious appeal.

WORKS: DRAMATIC: *Culhwch and Olwen*, entertainment (1966); *As You Like It*, incidental music to Shakespeare's play (1967); *The Servants*, opera (Cardiff, Sept. 15, 1980); *Jonah: A Musical Morality* (Guildford, July 6, 1988).

ORCH.: 3 piano concertos: No. 1 (1955), No. 2 (1960), and No. 3 (Swansea, Oct. 15, 1968); *Berceuse* (1956); *Divertimento* for Strings (London, March 1958); *Music* for Strings (1960; London, Dec. 3, 1961); *Dance Overture* (Wales, Aug. 10, 1962); *Invocation and Dance* (Cardiff, March 1, 1962); *Serenade* for Chamber Orch. (Carmarthen, June 5, 1962); *Prelude, Aria, and Finale* for Strings (Caerphilly, May 23, 1964); *Concerto for Orchestra* (1965–66; Liverpool, March 29, 1966); 3 syms.: No. 1 (Llandaff, June 23, 1966), No. 2, *Summer Music* (Liverpool, May 14, 1983), and No. 3 (1991); Sinfonietta (Leicester, May 1, 1967); *Litanies: Concertante Music* (BBC, Feb. 28, 1968); *Festival Overture* (Caernarvon, June 1970); Harp Concerto (Bournemouth, June 1, 1970); *Intrada* for Small Orch. (1970–71; Aberystwyth, April 8, 1971); Concerto for Harpsichord, Strings, and Percussion (Fishguard, Aug. 26, 1971); *Holiday Overture* (Llandudno, Sept. 30, 1971); *Celtic Dances* (1972); *Laudi* (Llandaff, June 11, 1973); Clarinet Concerto (Bangor, Sept. 22, 1975); *Vistas* (Swansea, Oct. 25, 1975); *Dance Variations* (London, July 1, 1977); *Melos* for Flute, Harp, Percussion, and Strings (Abbotsham, April 24, 1977); *Vivat regina* for Brass Band (London, June 11, 1977); *Helios* (Llandaff, June 16, 1977); *Requiescat* (1977; Portmadoc, Feb. 9, 1978); *Reflections on a Theme of Tomkins* for Flute, Oboe, Organ, Harpsichord, and Strings (1980); Organ Concerto (London, Sept. 12, 1984); Horn Concerto (Llandaff, June 9, 1984; also for Horn and Piano); *Anniversary Dances* (1984; Bangor, Feb. 16, 1985); *Carnival of Wales* (Cardiff, July 24, 1987); Violin Concerto (1989–91); Oboe Concerto (Llantilio Crossenny, May 6, 1990).

CHAMBER: *Divertimento* for Violin and Piano (n.d.); Clarinet Sonatina (1956; Cheltenham, July 13, 1957); Sextet for Clarinet, String Quartet, and Piano (1958); *Improvisations* for Harp (1958); 2 violin sonatas: No. 1 (1961; Cheltenham, July 12, 1962) and No. 2 (Swansea, Oct. 1984); Quintet for Flute, Oboe, Clarinet, Horn, and Bassoon (Cheltenham, July 4, 1963); *Divertimento* for Flute, Oboe, and Piano (1963); Piano Trio (Cheltenham, July 9, 1965); 3 string quartets: No. 1 (1967; Cardiff, April 25, 1968), No. 2 (1980; St. David's, March 6, 1981), and No. 3 (Harrogate, Aug. 7, 1986); Concertino for Flute or Recorder, Oboe, Bassoon, and Harpsichord or Piano (London, March 6, 1974); *Zodiac Trio* for Flute, Viola, and Harp (Glamorgan, Aug. 19, 1976); *Ceremonial Fanfare* for 2 Trumpets (Whitland, Oct. 20, 1979); Flute Sonatina (Beaumaris, June 12, 1986); *Soundings* for Brass Quintet (1988); *Santa Fe Suite* for Harp (London, Sept. 1988). **KEYBOARD: PIANO:** *Toccata alla danza* (1961); 2 sonatas: No. 1 (1963; Bangor, March 11, 1964) and No. 2 (1979). **ORGAN:** Postlude (1962); *Partita* (London, Oct. 26, 1962); *Variations on a Hymn Tune (Braint)* (Llandaff, Dec. 7, 1962); Processional (1964); *Invocations* (1966; Liverpool, April 4, 1967); *Toccata Giocosa* (1967); *Fantasy* (Manchester, Sept. 7, 1978); *Canzonetta* (1978); *Antiphonies* (Cardiff, May 13, 1982); *Berceuse* (Newbury, May 9, 1985); *Fenestra* (1989–90; Keele, Jan. 22, 1990); Carillon (1990–91).

VOCAL: *7 Poems of R.S. Thomas* for Tenor, Harp, and Chamber Orch. (1957); *Festival Te Deum* for Chorus and Organ (1964); *3 Medieval Lyrics* for Chorus, 2 Trumpets, Percussion, and Organ (1966); *Psalm 150* for Mixed Voices, Orch., and/or Organ (Worcester, Aug. 24, 1969); *Ave Rex* for Mixed Voices and Organ or Orch. (Llandaff, Dec. 6, 1969); *Gloria* for Men's Voices and Organ (Swansea, Dec. 5, 1970); *Elegy for a Prince* for Baritone and Orch. (Llandaff, June 10, 1972); *A Vision of Time and Eternity* for Contralto and Piano (Bangor, Sept. 27, 1972); *Ceremony After a Fire Raid* for Chorus, Piano, and Percussion (London, Sept. 19, 1973); *This Worldes Joie* for Soprano, Tenor, Bass, Chorus, Boy's or Girl's Chorus, and Orch. (Fishguard, Aug. 17, 1974); *The Fields of Praise* for Tenor and Piano (1976; Bangor, March 3, 1977); *A Royal Garland* for Chorus (Paris, Sept. 1977); *A May Magnificat* for Double Chorus and Chime Bars (Cork, May 5, 1978); *Shakespeare Songs* for Chorus and Piano (Cardiff, Feb. 8, 1979); *Songs of William Blake* for Mezzo-soprano, Harp, Piano, Celesta, and Strings (Fishguard, July 29, 1979); *Rex Gloriae* for Mixed Voices (Stuttgart, May 1981); *Te Deum* for Soprano, Mezzo-soprano, Tenor, Chorus, and Orch. (Aberdeenshire, Oct. 10, 1981); *Let the People Praise Thee O Lord* for Chorus and Organ or Orch. (London, July 29, 1981); *Lux Aeterna* for Soprano, Mezzo-soprano, Contralto, Boy's Chorus, Chorus, Organ, and Orch. (Hereford, Aug. 26, 1982); *Salvator Mundi* for Women's Chorus, Piano Duet, Percussion, and String Orch. (Cheltenham, Dec. 10, 1982); *Let Us Now Praise Famous Men* for Chorus and Organ or Orch. (Worcester, Aug. 18, 1984); *Missa aedis Christi (in memoriam William Walton)* for Chorus and Organ (Oxford, June 10, 1984); *Veni Sancte Spiritus* for Chorus, Organ, 2 Trumpets, and Percussion (Hereford, Aug. 20, 1985); *Let All the World in Every Corner Sing* for Chorus, Organ, and Optional Brass (1985; London, June 25, 1987); *O Lord, Our Lord* for Chorus, Organ, and Optional Brass (Princeton, N.J., May 16, 1987); *Cantate Domino* for Chorus and Organ (Ludlow, June 1987); *Riddles* for 6 Soloists, Chorus, Piano, and Bells (1987; Vancouver, Feb. 6, 1988); *Learsongs* for Women's Chorus and Piano Duet or Clarinet, Trumpet, Piano Duet, Percussion, and Double Bass (1989); *World's Fire* for Soloists, Chorus, and Orch. (St. Asaph, Sept. 30, 1989); *Doctrine of Wisdom* for Chorus and Organ (London, May 17, 1990); various other sacred and secular pieces.

Mathieson, Muir, Scottish conductor and composer; b. Stirling, Jan. 24, 1911; d. Oxford, Aug. 2, 1975. He studied conducting at the Royal College of Music in London with Sargent. While he made appearances as a conductor at the Sadler's Wells Opera in London, it was as a music director for films that he became best known. After working for the film producer Sir Alexander Korda (1931–39), he was music director of government film enterprises (1940–45) and then for J. Arthur Rank films. Through his efforts, such composers as Vaughan Williams, Bliss, Walton, and Britten were persuaded to write for films. In 1957 he was made an Officer of the Order of the British Empire.

Mathieu, (René) André (Rodolphe), remarkable Canadian pianist and composer, son of **(Joseph) Rodolphe Mathieu**; b. Montreal, Feb. 18, 1929; d. there, June 2, 1968. A child prodigy, he received lessons in piano and compositions at a very early age with his father; his *3 Études* for piano date from his 4th year. On Feb. 25, 1935, he created a stir in Montreal with his recital debut as a pianist at the Ritz-Carlton Hotel. In 1936 he received a Quebec government grant to pursue his studies in Paris, where he had lessons in piano with Yves Nat and in harmony and composition with Jacques de la Presle. While in Paris, he gave recitals with notable success. On Feb. 3, 1940, he made a highly successful Town Hall recital debut in N.Y.; then continued his studies in composition in N.Y. with Harold Morris while touring as a pianist in North America. In 1946–47 he was again in Paris to complete his studies with Arthur Honegger (composition) and Jules Gentil (piano). Returning to Canada, he devoted himself principally to teaching and composing. Among his works, all composed in a late Romantic vein, were 4 piano concertos; Piano Trio; Piano Quintet; pieces for Violin and Piano; numerous solo piano pieces; several vocal scores.

BIBL.: J. Rudel-Tessier, *A. M., un génie* (Montreal, 1976).

Mathieu, (Joseph) Rodolphe, Canadian composer, teacher, and pianist, father of **(René) André (Rodolphe) Mathieu;** b. Grondines, near Quebec City, July 10, 1890; d. Montreal, June 29, 1962. He went to Montreal and studied piano with Alphonse Martin and voice with Céline Marier (1906–08). After training in composition with Alexis Contant (c.1910), he went to Paris in 1920 and studied composition with d'Indy and orchestration with Aubert at the Schola Cantorum, and conducting with Golschmann at the Collège de France. Settling in Montreal in 1927, he became a teacher at the Institut pédagogique of the Sisters of the Congregation of Notre Dame and at the convent of the Sisters of Ste. Anne in Lachine. He organized the Canadian Institute of Music in 1929. He was also active as director of the International Soc. of Music, which became the Édition exclusive de musique canadienne in 1934 and which publ. various Canadian scores, including some by Mathieu. In addition to teaching privately, he was on the faculty of the Montreal Cons. (1955–59). He was the author of *Parlons . . . musique* (Montreal, 1932). His *Tests d'aptitudes musicales* (1930–56) remains in MS. In his early works, he was influenced by Debussy and more especially Wagner, but he later embraced post-Romantic elements in his output.

WORKS: CHAMBER: *Lied* for Violin and Piano (1915); String Quartet (1920); Trio for Piano, Violin, and Cello (1921); *12 Études modernes* or *Monologues* for Violin (1924); *22 Dialogues* for Violin and Cello (c.1924); Violin Sonata (1928; also as a Cello Sonata); Quintet for Piano and String Quartet (1942). **KEYBOARD: PIANO:** *Chevauchée* (1911); *3 Préludes* (1912–15; also orchestrated); Sonata (1927). **ORGAN:** Variations on *Venez, divin Messie!* (1910). **VOCAL:** *Un peu d'ombre* for Soprano and Orch. (1913); *Harmonie du soir* for Soprano or Tenor, Violin, and Orch. (1924); *Saisons canadiennes* for Bass and Piano (c.1925); *Symphonie-ballet avec choeurs* for Chorus and Orch. (1927; unfinished); *Deux Poèmes* for Tenor or Soprano and String Quartet (1928); *Sanctus et Benedictus* for Chorus (1931); *Prière: "O Jésus vivant en Marie"* for Men's Voices and Organ (1933); *Lève-toi, Canadien* for Chorus and Orch. or Band (1934); *Symphonie pour voix humaines* for 12 Voices and Piano or Brass ad libitum (1960; unfinished).

BIBL.: J. Bourassa-Trépanier, *R. M., musicien canadien (1890–1962)* (diss., Laval Univ., 1972).

Mathis, Edith, admired Swiss soprano; b. Lucerne, Feb. 11, 1938. She received her training at the Lucerne Cons. and from Elisabeth Bosshart in Zürich. In 1956 she made her operatic debut as the 2nd boy in *Die Zauberflöte* in Lucerne. From 1959 to 1962 she sang at the Cologne Opera. In 1960 she appeared at the Salzburg Festival, which led to engagements in Vienna and Munich. From 1960 to 1975 she appeared with the Hamburg State Opera, and in 1962 made her debut at Glyndebourne as Cherubino. From 1963 she also sang at the Berlin Deutsche Oper. On Jan. 19, 1970, she made her Metropolitan Opera debut in N.Y. as Pamina, remaining on its roster until 1974. She sang for the first time at London's Covent Garden in 1970 as Mozart's Susanna, returning there until 1972. Her frequent Munich engagements led to her being made a Kammersängerin in 1980. In addition to her operatic appearances, she won notable distinction as a concert and lieder artist. She married **Bernhard Klee**, with whom she often appeared. Among her most memorable operatic roles, in addition to those already noted, were Zerlina, Zdenka, Nannetta, Mélisande, the Marschallin, Sophie, and Arabella.

Matsudaira, Yoriaki, Japanese composer, son of **Yoritsune Matsudaira;** b. Tokyo, March 27, 1931. He studied biology at the Tokyo Metropolitan Univ. (1948–57); as a composer, he was autodidact. In 1958 he became a teacher of physics and biology at Rikkyo Univ. in Tokyo. He was also active with the composing collective Group 20.5, which he founded to promote contemporary music. In his output, Matsudaira has followed an avant-garde path in which he has utilized serialism, aleatory, tape, and electronics. He publ. the book *Conpyuta to ongaku* (Computers in Music; Tokyo, 1972).

WORKS: DRAMATIC: *Sara*, opera (Tokyo, Nov. 12, 1960); *Ishikawa no iratsume*, dance drama (Tokyo, July 1964). **ORCH.:** *Configuration* for Chamber Orch. (1961–63; Tokyo, March 29, 1967); *The Symphony* for Chamber Orch. (1971); *Messages* for Wind Orch. and Tape (1972); *Revolution* for Piano and Orch. (1991). **CHAMBER:** *Variations* for Piano Trio (Tokyo, Nov. 15, 1957); *Speed Co-Efficient* for Flute, Piano, and Keyboard Percussion (1958); *Orbits I–III* for Flute, Clarinet, and Piano (1960); *Variations on a Noh Theme* for Flute, Clarinet, 3 Percussion, Piano, Violin, Viola, and Cello (1960; in collaboration with others); *Co-Action I & II* for Cello and Piano (1962); *Parallax* for Flute, Oboe, Clarinet, Bassoon, and Saxophone (1963); *Rhymes for Severino Gazzelloni* for Flute (1965–66; Venice, Sept. 10, 1966); *Distributions* for String Quartet and Ring Modulator (1966–67; Tokyo, March 16, 1968); *Alternations* for Trumpet, Piano, Double Bass, Drums, and Ring Modulator (1967); *Gradations* for Violin, Viola, and Oscillator (1971); *Trichromatic Form* for Harp (1973); *Transient '74* for Guitar, Organ, Harp, and Percussion (1974); *Simulation* for Tuba (1974); *Coherency for Ark* for Flute, Clarinet, Percussion, Harp, and Keyboard (1976); *Brilliancy* for Flute and Piano (1978); *Metathesis* for Accordion (1990); *Domain* for String Quartet (1991); *Response* for Double Bass and Oboe (1992). **PIANO:** *Instruction* (1961); *Allotropy* (1970); *Erixatone* for Electric Piano (1979); *Perspective* (1988); *Gala* (1990); *Recollection* (1990); *Multistrata* (1990); *Morphogenesis I–II* (1991–92); *Acrostics* (1992). **VOCAL:** *What's Next?* for Soprano and 2 Noisemakers (1967–71; Graz, Oct. 12, 1972); *Wand Waves* for Narrator and Tape (1970); *Substitution* for Soprano and Piano (1972). **OTHER:** *Transient '64* for Tape (1964); *Assemblages* for Tape (1968); *Why Not?* for 4 to 5 Operators and Live Electronics (1970); *Where Now?* for 3 Dancers and Ensemble (1973); *Shift* for Dance and Tape (1976).

Matsudaira, Yoritsune, Japanese composer, father of **Yoriaki Matsudaira;** b. Tokyo, May 5, 1907. He took courses in French literature at Keio Univ. and pursued private instruction in composition with Komatsu, and with Tansman and Tcherepnin (1935–37). In 1937 he helped organize and was co-director of the Nihon Gendai Sakkyokuka Renmei, which later became the Japanese Soc. for Contemporary Music. He served the Soc. as its secretary (1953–55) and chairman (1956–60). He was the author of *Kindai waseigaku* (Harmony Today; Tokyo, 1955; rev. 1969–70). Among his honors were the Weingartner Prize (1937), the ISCM Prize (1952), the Zerboni Prize (1954), and the International Composition Competition Prize of Rome (1962). In his early works, he followed neo-Classical trends. His use of gagaku with modern methods became a hallmark of his style. He first utilized 12-tone procedures in his *Theme and Variations on Etenraku* for Piano and Orch. in 1951. Still later he explored the use of gagaku with various other avant-garde procedures.

WORKS: ORCH.: *Pastorale* (1935); *Theme and Variations on a Folk Song from the Nanbu District* for Piano and Orch. (Tokyo, Dec. 17, 1939); *Theme and Variations on Etenraku* for Piano and Orch. (1951); *Ancient Japanese Dance* (1952; Berlin, Oct. 9, 1953); *Negative and Positive Figures* (Tokyo, May 28, 1954); *Figures sonores* (1956; Zürich, June 1, 1957); *U-Mai* (Ancient Dance; 1957; Darmstadt, Sept. 11, 1958); *Samai* for Chamber Orch. (1958; Rome, June 15, 1959); *Danse sacre* (1959); *Danse finale* (1959); *Dance Suite* for 3 Orchs. (Donaueschingen, Oct. 18, 1959); *Bugaku* for Chamber Orch. (1961; Palermo, Oct. 6, 1962); *3 Movements* for Piano and Orch. (1962; Stockholm, March 20, 1964); *Ritual Dance and Finale* (1963); 2 piano concertos: No. 1 (1964; Madrid, March 20, 1965) and No. 2 (1980); *Music* for 17 Performers (1967); *Rotating Movements* for 2 Chamber Orchs. (1971; Graz, Oct. 10, 1972); *Prelude, Interlude, and Aprèslude* (1973); *2 Synthese* for Chamber Orch. (1983). **CHAMBER:** Flute Sonatina (1936); Sonatina for Flute and Clarinet (1940); Cello Sonata (1942; rev. 1947); Piano Trio (1948); 2 violin sonatas (1948, 1952); 2 string quartets (1949, 1951); Suite for Flute, Horn, and Piano (1950); *Somakusha* for Flute (1961; rev. 1970; also for Flute, Oboe, Harp, Percussion, Piano, and Strings); *Serenade* for Flute, Oboe, Percussion, and Strings (1962); Suite for 10 Instruments (1963); *Concerto da camera* for Harpsichord, Harp, and Instrumental Ensemble (1964); *Dialogue choréographique* for Wind Quintet, Harp, 2 Pianos, and Percussion (1966; Royan, April 3, 1967); *Portrait* for 2 Pianos and 2 Percussion (1967–68); *Rhapsody on a Theme of Gagaku* for Chamber Ensemble (1982); *Netori et Rôëi* for Cello and Ensemble (1985); Concertino for Piano and Chamber Ensemble (1988); *Petite Piece* for Clarinet, Piano, Marimba, and Percussion (1988); *Bonguen* for Shō, Flute, Clarinet, and Percussion (1992). **PIANO:** *Lullaby and Music Box* (1928–31); 2 preludes (1934, 1940); *6 Pastoral Dances* (1939–40); Concertante for 2 Pianos (1946); Sonatina (1948); Sonata (1949); *Portrait* for 2 Pianos (1967); *Pieces for Children* (1968); *Lullabies* (1969); *Pieces for Children from Nursery Rhymes and Folk Songs* (1969–70); *Études on Japanese Melodies* (1970). **VOCAL:** *Folk Songs from the Nanbu District* for Voice and Piano (2 sets, 1928–36; 1938); *Kokin-shu* for Soprano and Piano (1939–45; also for Soprano and Orch., 1950); *Metamorphoses on an Old Japanese Melody* (*Saibara*) for Soprano and Chamber Orch. (1953; Haifa, June 3, 1954); *Koromogae* (Love Song) for Soprano and Chamber Orch. (1954; Venice, Dec. 11, 1968); *Katsura* for Soprano, Guitar, Harp, Harpsichord, and Percussion (1957; rev. 1967); *Jesei, a rôëi* (2 Stars in Vega) for Soprano, Flute, Oboe, Harp, Piano, Vibraphone, and Percussion (1967); *Kashin, a rôëi* for Women's Voices and Orch. (1969); *3 Airs du Genji Monogatari* for Soprano and Japanese Instruments (1990); *Requiem* for Soprano and Chamber Ensemble (1992).

Matsumura, Teizo, Japanese composer and pedagogue; b. Kyoto, Jan. 15, 1929. He was orphaned at an early age. After lessons from Tsuneharu Takahashi (piano) and Toshio Nagahiro (harmony), he settled in Tokyo in 1949 to pursue his training with Ikenouchi (harmony, counterpoint, and composition) and Ifukube (composition). Between 1950 and 1955 his life was seriously threatened by tuberculosis. During his convalescence, he began to compose and in 1955 won 1st prize in the NHK-Mainichi Music Competition with his *Introduction and Allegro Concertante* for Orch. From 1970 to 1987 he was prof. of composition at the National Univ. of Fine Arts and Music. In 1994 he won the Mainichi Art Prize and the Grand Prize of the Kyoto Music Awards. Matsumura rebelled early on against dodecaphonism, the then-prevailing musical ideology in Japan. Instead, he pursued an independent course in which he combined the use of Western instruments and forms with the rich inheritance of Asian culture. Among his notable works were his Sym. (1965) and his *Prélude pour orchestre* (1968), the latter winning the Otaka Prize.

WORKS: DRAMATIC: *Flute of Devil's Passion*, mono-opera (1965); *Silence*, opera (1980–93; Tokyo, Nov. 3, 1993); incidental music; film scores. **ORCH.:** *Introduction and Allegro Concertante* (Tokyo, Oct. 22, 1955); *Cryptogame* for Chamber Orch. (1958); Sym. (Tokyo, June 15, 1965); *Prélude pour Orchestre* (NHK Radio, Nov. 7, 1968); 2 piano concertos: No. 1 (NHK Radio, Nov. 4, 1973) and No. 2 (Tokyo, May 13, 1978); Cello Concerto (Tokyo, Feb. 27, 1984); *Pneuma* for Strings (Tokyo, Sept. 19, 1987); *Hommage à Akira Ifukube* (1988); *Offrande Orchesrale* (Tokyo, Sept. 21, 1989). **CHAMBER:** *Music* for

String Quartet and Piano (1962); *Poem I* for Shakuhachi and 13-String Koto (1969) and *II* for Shakuhachi (1972); *Courtyard of Apsaras*, trio for Flute, Violin, and Piano (1971); *Poem* for Shinobue and Biwa (NHK Radio, Nov. 1979); *Fantasy* for 13-String Koto (1980); *Poem* for Alto Saxophone and Biwa (1980); *Air of Prayer* for 17-String Koto (1984; also for Cello, 1985); *Spelmatica* for Cello (1985); Trio for Violin, Cello, and Piano (1987; NHK Radio, April 1, 1988); *Nocturne* for Harp (1994). **PIANO:** *Deux Berceuses à la Grèce* (1969). **VOCAL:** *Achime* for Piano and Chamber Ensemble (1957); *Totem Ritual* for Soprano, Chorus, and Orch. (1969); *Apsaras* for Women's Voices and Small Orch. (1969); *2 Poems by the Prince of Karu* for Soprano and Piano (1973; NHK Radio, March 12, 1974); *Hymn to Aurora* for Chorus and Chamber Ensemble (Tokyo, Nov. 15, 1978); *The Drifting Reed* for Voice and Orch. (NHK-TV, July 1979); *The Patient Waters* for Chorus and Orch. (1985).

Matsushita, Shinichi, Japanese composer; b. Osaka, Oct. 1, 1922; d. there, Dec. 25, 1990. He graduated in mathematics from the Kyushu Univ. in Fukuoka in 1947; concurrently studied music. In 1958 he went to work in an electronic music studio in Osaka; taught both mathematics and music at the Univ. of Osaka City. In his music, he followed cosmopolitan modernistic techniques, mostly of a functional, pragmatic nature.

WORKS: RADIO OPERAS: *Comparing Notes on a Rainy Night* (1960); *Amayo* (1960). **ORCH.:** *Ouvrage symphonique* for Piano and Orch. (1957); *Isomorfismi* (1958); *Sinfonia "Le Dimensioni"* (1961); *Successioni* for Chamber Orch. (Radio Palermo, Oct. 1, 1962); *Serenade* for Flute and Orch. (1967); *Sinfonie Pol* for Orch., Harp, and Piano (1968); *Astrate Atem* for Orch., Harp, and Piano (1969–70); *Idylle*, violin concerto (1983); *Ein Neues Lied* (1984); *Ethno* (1984); *Nippon Capriccio* (1987); Sym. No. 7 (1988). **CHAMBER:** *Correlazioni per 3 gruppi* for 12 Players (1958); *Composizione da camera per 8* (1958); *5 tempi per undici* for 11 Instruments (1958–59); *Faisceaux* for Flute, Cello, and Piano (1959); *Cube for 3 Players* for Flute, Celesta, and Viola (1961); *Meta-Musique No. 1* for Piano, Horn, and Percussion (1962); *Uro* for Chamber Ensemble (1962); *Sinfonia "Vita"* (1963); *Fresque sonore* for 7 Instruments (1964); *Hexahedra A, B* and *C* for Piano and Percussion (1964–65); *Kristalle* for Piano Quartet (1966); *Alleluja in der Einsamkeit* for Guitar, Piccolo, and 2 Percussionists (1967); *Subject 17* for Piano, Percussion, Horn, Trumpet, and Trombone (San Francisco, Oct. 31, 1967); *Haleines astrales* for Chamber Ensemble (1968); *Musik von der Liebe* for Flute, Vibraphone, Harp, Piano, Electone, and Tape (1970); *Musik der Steinzeit* for Violin, Ondes Martenot, Tape, and the sound of Cracking Stone (1970); String Quartet (1988). **KEYBOARD: PIANO:** *Spectra 1–4* (1964; 1967; for 2 Players, 1971; 1971); *Ostinato obbligato* (1972); *Spectra No. 6, 12 Bagatelles* (1984). **ORGAN:** *Mini-Max* for Organ, 4-hands (1984); *Konzentrazion* (1988). **VOCAL:** *Le Croitre noir* for Chorus, Electronic and Musique Concrète Sounds, Piano, Harp, and Percussion (Osaka, Nov. 14, 1959); *Jet Pilot* for Narrator, Orch., String Quartet, and Women's Chorus (1960); *Musique* for Soprano and Chamber Ensemble (Osaka, Sept. 14, 1964); *Requiem on the Place of Execution* for 4 Soloists, Chorus, Orch., and Tape (1970).

Mattfeld, Julius, American librarian, organist, and musicographer; b. N.Y., Aug. 8, 1893; d. there, July 31, 1968. He studied at the N.Y. German Cons. In 1910 he joined the staff of the N.Y. Public Library; resigned in 1926 to become music librarian of NBC (until 1929); then was librarian of CBS; was also organist of the Fordham Lutheran Church in N.Y. (1915–32). He publ. *The Folk Music of the Western Hemisphere* (1925); *A Hundred Years of Grand Opera in New York, 1825–1925* (1927); *Variety Music Cavalcade, 1620–1950* (N.Y., 1952; rev. 1962); *A Handbook of American Operatic Premieres, 1731–1962* (Detroit, 1963).

Mattfeld, Victor Henry, American organist, conductor, music editor, and teacher; b. Bunceton, Mo., Sept. 1, 1917. He studied at the Univ. of Chicago (B.A. in psychology, 1942), the American Cons. of Music, Chicago (B.Mus., 1944; M.Mus., 1946, both in organ), and Yale Univ. (Ph.D. in music history, 1960); also studied orch. conducting privately with Malko (1945–47) and choral conducting at the Berkshire Music Center at Tanglewood (summer, 1946). He was active as a church organist and music director in Chicago, N.Y., New Haven, and Boston (1938–63); was ed. in chief of E.C. Schirmer Music Co. (1956–58) and the Ione Press (1963–68); taught at the American Cons. of Music (1945–47), Yale Univ. (1952–55), and the Mass. Inst. of Technology (1957–66) before becoming associated with N.Y.'s Richmond College (1967–76) and College of Staten Island (1976–82). He publ. *Georg Rhaw's Publications for Vespers* (1966). He married the musicologist Jacquelyn Mattfeld (b. Baltimore, Oct. 5, 1925); she studied at Goucher College (B.A., 1948) and Yale Univ. (Ph.D., 1959); taught at the Mass. Inst. of Technology (1963–65), Sarah Lawrence College (1965–71), and Brown Univ. (from 1971).

Matthaei, Karl, Swiss organist and musicologist; b. Olten, April 23, 1897; d. Winterthur, Feb. 8, 1960. He studied piano and organ at the Basel Cons.; also took courses in musicology there with Karl Nef; then went to Leipzig, where he pursued his organ studies with Straube (1920–23). He subsequently was organist in Wadenswil; from 1925, was organist and director of the Winterthur music school; from 1938 served also as organist of the city church. He ed. *J. Pachelbel: Ausgewählte Orgelwerke* (4 vols., Kassel, 1928–36), *M. Praetorius: Sämtliche Orgelwerke* (Wolfenbüttel, 1930), and *J.J. Froberger: Ausgewählte Orgelwerke* (Kassel, 1932). He also ed. a *Bach-Gedenkschrift* (Zürich, 1950); publ. the books *Vom Orgelspiel* (Leipzig, 1936) and *Die Baugeschichte der Stadtkirchenorgel in Winterthur* (Winterthur, 1941).

BIBL.: *K. M.: Gedenkschrift* (Winterthur, 1960).

Matthay, Tobias (Augustus), eminent English pianist and pedagogue; b. London, Feb. 19, 1858; d. High Marley, near Haslemere, Surrey, Dec. 14, 1945. He began to play the piano at the age of 6; was taught by private teachers; in 1871 he entered the Royal Academy of Music in London as a pupil of Dorrell (piano); won the Sterndale Bennett scholarship, and continued to study piano (with Macfarren); took courses with Sterndale Bennett, and after the latter's death (1875) completed his studies with Ebenezer Prout and Arthur Sullivan. He subsequently was on the faculty of the Royal Academy of Music as a sub-prof. (1876–80) and full prof. (1880–1925); in 1900 he established his own piano school in London. The Matthay System, as his teaching method was known, stressed mastery of both the psychological and physiological aspects of piano performance; it became famous not only in England but on the Continent and in America. Students flocked to him and carried his method abroad. Matthay also composed *In May*, an overture; Piano Quartet; numerous piano pieces; songs.

WRITINGS (all publ. in London unless otherwise given): *The Art of Touch in All Its Diversity* (1903); *The First Principles of Pianoforte Playing* (1905; 2nd ed., rev., 1906); *Relaxation Studies . . . in Pianoforte Playing* (Leipzig, 1908); *Some Commentaries on the Teaching of Pianoforte Technique* (1911); *The Child's First Steps in Pianoforte Playing* (1912); *The Fore-arm Rotation Principle in Pianoforte Playing* (1912); *Musical Interpretation* (1913); *On Method in Teaching* (1921); *An Epitome of the Laws of Pianoforte Technique* (1931); *The Visible and Invisible in Pianoforte Technique* (1932; 2nd ed., rev., 1947); etc.

BIBL.: J. Henderson Matthay, *The Life and Work of T. M.* (London, 1945); A. Coviello, *What M. Meant* (London, 1948); R. Hoare, "What Did M. Mean?," *Piano Teacher*, IV (1962).

Matthews, Colin, English composer, writer on music, and broadcaster, brother of **David (John) Matthews;** b. London, Feb. 13, 1946. He studied classics (B.A., 1967) and received instruction in composition from Arnold Whittal (M.Phil., 1969) at the Univ. of Nottingham. He also studied composition with Nicholas Maw before completing his education at the Univ. of Sussex (Ph.D., 1977, with the diss. *Mahler at Work: A Study of the Creative Process*). With his brother, he collaborated with Deryck Cooke on a performing ed. of Mahler's 10th Sym.

(1964–74). From 1971 to 1976 he was associated with Benjamin Britten, and later edited many of his early and unpubl. scores. He also worked with Imogen Holst on eds. of her father's scores (1972–84). He contributed articles to various journals and was active as a broadcaster.

WORKS: ORCH.: 6 sonatas, including No. 4 (1974–75) and No. 5, *Landscape* (1977–81); *Night Music* for Small Orch. (1977); Cello Concerto (1984); *Night's Mask* for Chamber Orch. (1984); *Cortège* (1988); *Chiaroscuro* (1990); *Machines and Dreams: Toy Symphony* (1991); *Broken Symmetry* (1991–92); *Hidden Variations* (1992; also for 15 Players, 1988–89); *Memorial* (1993). **CHAMBER:** *Ceres* for 3 Flutes, Guitar, Percussion, 2 Cellos, and Double Bass (1972); *Specula* for Flute, Keyed Percussion, Harp, and Viola (1976–77); *Rainbow Studies* for Flute, Oboe, Clarinet, Bassoon, and Piano (1977–78); 3 string quartets (1979; 1985; 1993–94); 2 oboe quartets (1981; 1988–89); *Divertimento* for Double String Quartet (1982); *Triptych* for Piano Quintet (1984); *Sun's Dance* for Piccolo, Oboe, Bass Clarinet, Double Bass, Horn, and String Quintet (1984–85); 5 Duos for Cello and Piano (1987); *Hidden Variables* for 15 Players (1988–89; also for Orch., 1992); *3-Part Chaconne* for String Trio and Piano, Left-hand (1989); *Quatrain* for Wind, Brass, and Percussion (1989); *Duologue* for Oboe and Piano (1991); *To Compose without the least Knowledge of Music . . .*, wind sextet (1991); *Contraflow* for 14 Players (1992). **PIANO:** *5 Studies* (1974–76); Suite (1977–79); *11 Studies in Velocity* (1987). **VOCAL:** *Cantata on the Death of Antony* for Soprano and Chamber Ensemble (1988–89); *Strugnells Haiku* for Voice and Piano or Chamber Ensemble (1989); choruses; solo songs.

Matthews, David (John), English composer and writer on music, brother of **Colin Matthews;** b. London, March 9, 1943. He studied classics at the Univ. of Nottingham (1962–65) and composition with Anthony Milner. He was associated with Benjamin Britten and the Aldeburgh Festival (1966–69). With his brother, he collaborated with Deryck Cooke on a performing ed. of Mahler's 10th Sym. He wrote articles on music and publ. *Michael Tippett: An Introductory Study* (1980) and *Landscape into Sound* (1992).

WORKS: ORCH.: 4 syms.: No. 1 (Stroud Festival, Oct. 8, 1975; rev. 1978), No. 2 (1976–79; London, May 13, 1982), No. 3 (1983–85; Sheffield, Sept. 27, 1985), and No. 4 for Chamber Orch. (1989–90); *September Music* (1979; BBC, Glasgow, April 28, 1980; rev. 1982); *White Nights* for Violin and Small Orch. (1980; rev. 1988); *Introit* for 2 Trumpets and Strings (Windsor, Nov. 13, 1981); Violin Concerto (1980–82; BBC, Manchester, Nov. 2, 1983); *In the Dark Time* (1984–85; London, Dec. 11, 1985); *Variations* for Strings (1986; Uppingham, March 23, 1987); *Chaconne* (1986–87; Manchester, Oct. 7, 1988); *The Music of Dawn* (1989–90); *Romanza* for Cello and Chamber Orch. (1990); *Scherzo capriccioso* (1990); *Capriccio* for 2 Horns and Strings (1991); Oboe Concerto (1991–92); *From Sea to Sky*, overture (1992); *A Vision and a Journey* (1993). **CHAMBER:** 6 string quartets (1970, rev. 1980; 1976, rev. 1979; 1978, rev. 1981; 1981; 1984, rev. 1985; 1991); *Toccatas and Pastorals* for Oboe d'Amore, English Horn, Bassoon, and Harpsichord (1976; rev. 1979); *Duet Variations* for Flute and Piano (1982); Piano Trio (1983); Clarinet Quintet (1984); *Aria* for Violin and Piano (1986); Concertino for Oboe and String Quartet (1986–87); String Trio (1989); *3 to Tango*, piano trio (1991); piano pieces, including a sonata (1989). **VOCAL:** *3 Songs* for Soprano and Orch. (1968–71); *Stars* for Chorus and Orch. (1970); *Eclogue* for Soprano and 7 Instrumentalists (1975–79); *Cantiga* for Soprano and Chamber Orch. (1987–88); *Marina* for Baritone, Basset Horn, Cello, and Piano (1988); *The Sleeping Lord* for Soprano, Flute, Clarinet, Harp, and String Quartet (1992); *Spell of Sleep* for Soprano, 2 Clarinets, Viola, Cello, and Double Bass (1992); choral pieces; other songs.

Matthews, Denis (James), English pianist, teacher, and writer on music; b. Coventry, Feb. 27, 1919; d. (suicide) Birmingham, Dec. 24, 1988. He studied with Harold Craxton (piano) and Alwyn (composition) at the Royal Academy of Music in London (1935–40). He made his London debut in 1939. During World War II, he served in the Royal Air Force while continuing to make appearances as a pianist; after the war, he toured throughout the world. Matthews was the first prof. of music at the Univ. of Newcastle upon Tyne (1971–84). In 1975 he was made a Commander of the Order of the British Empire.

WRITINGS: *In Pursuit of Music* (autobiography; London, 1966); *Beethoven's Piano Sonatas* (London, 1967); *Arturo Toscanini* (Tunbridge Wells and N.Y., 1982); *Beethoven* (London, 1985).

Matthews, Michael Gough, English pianist and music educator; b. Wanstead, Essex, July 12, 1931. He studied at the Royal College of Music in London, where he received the Hopkinson Gold Medal (1953); then took a course at the Accademia di Santa Cecilia in Rome, and subsequently toured as pianist in Europe and the Far East. From 1964 to 1971 he was on the staff of the Royal Scottish Academy of Music and Drama in Glasgow; then was prof. of piano at the Royal College of Music (1972–75), where he was vice-director (1978–84) and director (1985–93).

Matthus, Siegfried, German composer; b. Mallenuppen, East Prussia, April 13, 1934. He studied composition with Wagner-Régeny at the Deutsche Hochschule für Musik (1952–58) and with Eisler at the Deutsche Akademie der Künste (1958–60) in East Berlin. In 1964 he was appointed a composer and dramatist at the (East) Berlin Komische Oper; in 1972 he became a member of the presidium of the Deutsche Akademie der Künste.

WORKS: OPERAS: *Lazarillo vom Tormes* (1960–63; Karl-Marx-Stadt, May 26, 1964); *Der letzte Schuss* (1966–67; Berlin, Nov. 5, 1967); *Noch ein Löffel Gift, Liebling?* (1971–72; Berlin, April 16, 1972); *Omphale* (1972–73; Weimar, Aug. 29, 1976); *Die Weisse von Liebe und Tod des Cornet Christoph Rilke*, opera vision (1983–84; Dresden, May 12, 1985); *Judith* (Berlin, Sept. 28, 1985); *Eine Opernvision* (1985); *Mirabeau* (1989); *Desdemona und ihre Schwestern*, opera monologues (1991; Schwetzingen, May 12, 1992). **ORCH.:** *Concerto for Orchestra* for 2 Flutes, 3 Trombones, Harp, Piano, Percussion, and Strings (1963); *Inventions* (1964); *Tua res agitur* for 15 Instruments and Percussion (1965); Violin Concerto (1968; Berlin, Feb. 24, 1969); 2 syms.: No. 1, *Dresdener Sinfonie* (1969), and No. 2 (1976); Piano Concerto (1970; Berlin, Feb. 18, 1971); *Orchesterserenade* (1974); Cello Concerto (1975); *Werther*, "musical metaphor" (1976); *Responso*, concerto for Orch. (1977); *Visions* for Strings (1978); Flute Concerto (1978); *Kammerkonzert* for Flute, Harpsichord, and Strings (1980–81); *Der Wald*, concerto for Kettledrum and Orch. (Dresden, June 6, 1985); Oboe Concerto (1985); *Die Windsbraut*, concerto (1985); *Das Triangelkonzert*, divertimento (1985); *Nächtliche Szenen im Park* (1987); *O namenlose Freude*, concerto for 3 Trumpets and Strings (1989); *Tiefist der Brunnen der Vergangenheit* (1991; Berlin, Jan. 23, 1992); *Manhattan Concerto* (N.Y., May 16, 1994); Piano Concerto, after the Brahms Piano Quartet, op. 25 (Berlin, June 1, 1994). **CHAMBER:** Percussion Sonatina (1960); Sonata for Brasses, Piano, and Kettledrums (1968); *Music* for 4 Oboes and Piano (1968); Octet (1970); String Quartet (1971); Harp Trio for Flute, Viola, and Harp (1971). **PIANO:** *Variations* (1958); *Konzertstück* (1958). **VOCAL:** *Es wird ein grosser Stern in meinen Schoss fallen*, 5 love songs for Soprano and Orch. (1961–62; East Berlin, Oct. 5, 1962); *Das Manifest*, cantata (1965); *Kammermusik* for Alto, 3 Women's Voices, and 10 Instruments (1965); *Galileo* for Voice, 5 Instruments, and Tape (1966); *Vokalsinfonie* for Soprano, Baritone, 2 Choruses, and Orch. (1967; from the opera *Der letzte Schuss*); *Kantate von den Beiden* for Narrator, Soprano, Baritone, and Orch. (1968); *Vokalisen* for Soprano, Flute, Double Bass, and Percussion (1969); *Laudate pacem*, oratorio (1974); *Unter dem Holunderstrauch*, scene after Kleist for Soprano, Tenor, and Orch. (1976); *Holofernes-Portrait* for Baritone and Orch. (1981); *Nachtlieder* for Baritone, String Quartet, and Harp (1987); *Die Sonne sinkt* for Speaker and String Quartet (1994); choruses; songs.

Mattila, Karita (Marjatta), Finnish soprano; b. Somero, Sept. 5, 1960. She was a pupil of Liisa Linko-Malmio and Kim Borg at the Sibelius Academy in Helsinki and of Vera Rozsa in London. In 1982 she made her operatic debut as Mozart's Countess at the Finnish National Opera in Helsinki; after winning the Singer of the World Competition in Cardiff in 1983, she appeared as a soloist with many of the world's major orchs. In 1983 she sang Fiordiligi at the Munich Festival and also made her U.S. debut as Donna Elvira in Washington, D.C.; in 1986 she made her first appearance at London's Covent Garden as Fiordiligi. Her other operatic engagements include the Hamburg State Opera, the Chicago Lyric Opera, the Vienna State Opera, and N.Y.'s Metropolitan Opera (from 1990). In addition to her Mozart roles, she also became well known as a Wagnerian.

Matton, Roger, Canadian composer and ethnomusicologist; b. Granby, Quebec, May 18, 1929. He studied with Sister Yvette Dufault (piano and theory) before pursuing his training at the Conservatoire de musique du Québec à Montréal with Champagne (composition), Delorme (solfege and harmony), and Letondal (piano). He went to Paris to study with Messiaen (analysis) at the Cons. (1950; 1953–54), and also was a student of Vaurabourg-Honegger (piano privately, 1950, and at the École Normale de Musique, 1952–53). He also studied with Boulanger (analysis, counterpoint, and composition privately, 1952–55). From 1956 to 1976 he was a researcher and ethnomusicologist at the Archives de Folklore at Laval Univ. in Quebec City. He also taught there, later serving as a teacher of composition and then of the history of contemporary music at its school of music (1960–63) and finally of ethnomusicology at its Dept. of Canadian Studies and Dept. of History (1963–89). While his compositions partake of various contemporary trends, his works remain generally tonally anchored. In a number of his works, folk melos may be discerned.

WORKS: ORCH.: *Danse lente (Gymnopédie)* for Chamber Orch. (1947); Concerto for Saxophone and Strings (1948); *Pax* (1950); *L'Horoscope*, suite choregraphique (1957; CBC Radio, Oct. 12, 1958; as a ballet, CBC-TV, Nov. 6, 1958); *Mouvement symphonique I* (Quebec City, Nov. 14, 1960), *II: Musique pour un drame* (Montreal, April 17, 1962), *III* (Quebec City, May 7, 1974), and *IV* (1978); Concerto for 2 Pianos and Orch. (Quebec City, Nov. 30, 1964). **CHAMBER:** *Étude* for Clarinet and Piano (1946); *Esquisse* for String Quartet (1949); Concerto for 2 Pianos and Percussion (1955). **KEYBOARD: PIANO:** *Berceuse* (1945); *Danse brésilienne* (1946; orchestrated 1971); *Trois Préludes* (1949). **ORGAN:** *Suite de Paques* (1952); *Tu es Petrus* (1984). **VOCAL:** *L'Escaouette* for Soprano, Mezzo-soprano, Tenor, Baritone, Chorus, and Orch. (1957); *Te Deum* for Baritone, Chorus, Orch., and Tape (1967).

Mattox, Janis, American composer; b. St. Paul, Minn., March 18, 1949. She studied at the Univ. of Minnesota (B.A., 1972) and Northwestern Univ. in Evanston, Ill. (M.A., 1974). In 1978 she began composing and producing works involving computer music technologies and live performers at Stanford Univ.'s Center for Computer Research in Music and Acoustics (CCRMA); among the virtuoso performers she has collaborated with are jazz bassist Mel Graves (*Voice of the Ancestors*, 1983), actor Bob Ernst (*Spirits Rising*, 1984), flutist (Moroccan ney) Richard Horowitz (*Night Flyer*, 1985), and drummer George Marsh (*Adowa*, 1987); works for dance include *Song from the Center of the Earth* for belly dancer Rachel Dutton (1982) and *Beehive Suite* (1985) for Jim Self and Beehive. Mattox taught and gave lecture demonstrations on computer music at CCRMA; also lectured in Los Angeles and Venice. She is project consultant for Good Sound Foundation and a performing member (piano) of the Good Sound Band. Her other works include *Dragon's View* for Computer-generated Quadraphonic Tape (1980); *Shaman*, music theater piece for Percussionist, Belly Dancer, Bassist, Actor/Vocalist, Live Digital Processing, and Computer-generated Tape (1984); *Adowa* for Percussionist and Dancer (1987); *Book of Shadows, Part I*, for Film, 2 Pianos in just intonation, Soprano, Violin, Garden Hose, Ney, Didjeridu, Contrabass, Saxophone, Accordion in just intonation, and Live Digital Processing (1989); and Pulse for 2 Drummers (1990). She is married to **Loren Rush**.

Matys, Jiří, Czech composer and teacher; b. Bakov, Oct. 27, 1927. He studied with František Michálek (organ) at the Cons. (graduated, 1947) and with Kvapil (composition) at the Janáček Academy of Music (graduated, 1951) in Brno. He taught at the latter, served as head of Brno's public art school Královo Pole, and was a prof. of composition at the Brno Cons.

WORKS: ORCH.: *Morning Music* for Strings, 2 Trumpets, and Percussion (1961–62); *Music* for String Quartet and Orch. (1971); Symphonic Overture (1973–74); *Music* for Strings (1982); *The Urgency of Time* for Viola and Orch. (1986–87). **CHAMBER:** Viola Sonata (1954); 5 string quartets (1957; 1961; 1963–64; 1973; 1989–90); Sonata for Solo Viola (1963); Violin Sonata (1964–65); Concert Piece for 2 Accordions (1968); *Inventions* for Flute and Cello (1969); *Music* for Winds (1970–71); *Allusions* for 4 Flutes (1971); Suite for Viola and Bass Clarinet (1972–73); *Suita Giocosa* for Flute and Bassoon (1974); Suite for Clarinet and Piano (1974–75); 4 sonatas for Solo Violin (1977, 1991, 1993, 1994); Suite for Flute and Guitar (1977); *Divertimento* for 4 Horns (1981); Suite for Wind Quintet (1984); *Music for 2*, suite for Violin and Marimba (1986); *The Soul of My District I* for Viola and Guitar or Cello (1987) and *II* for Viola (1988); *Scenes* for Clarinet and Piano (1989); *Visions* for Bass Clarinet and Guitar (1991); piano pieces. **VOCAL:** *Lyrical Melodramas* for Reciter and Piano (1957); *Variations on Death* for Reciter, String Quartet, and Horn (1959); *The Red Toadstool* for Soloist, Children's Chorus, Piano, and Flute (1968); *Written by Grief into Silence . . .*, song cycle for Medium Voice and Orch. or Piano (1972); *4-Leaf Clover* for Reciter and Flute (1979–80); *To the Czech-Moravian Uplands* for Girl's or Women's Chorus (1991).

Matz, Rudolf, Croatian cellist and composer; b. Zagreb, Sept. 19, 1901. He studied cello and composition at the Zagreb Academy of Music. In 1950 he was appointed instructor in cello there; then taught chamber music at the Ljubljana Academy of Music. He publ. a manual for cello playing (Zagreb, 1951).

WORKS: ORCH.: *Classical Concert* for Cello and Orch. (1949); *Lyric Sketches* for Cello and Strings (1959); Flute Concerto (1963). **CHAMBER:** 4 string quartets (1924, 1932, 1935, 1944); Violin Sonata (1941); 2 cello sonatas (1941, 1942); *Baroque Concerto* for 3 Cellos and Piano (1952); *12 Pieces* for 3 Cellos and Piano (1960); *11 Caprices* for Cello (1964). **VOCAL:** *24 Songs on Croatian Folk Poems* and other pieces based on native themes.

Matzenauer, Margarete, celebrated Hungarian soprano and contralto; b. Temesvár, June 1, 1881; d. Van Nuys, Calif., May 19, 1963. Her father was a conductor and her mother a soprano; she grew up in favorable musical surroundings, and began to study singing at an early age, first in Graz, then in Berlin, and finally in Munich. In 1901 she joined the staff of the Strasbourg Opera; then sang contralto roles at the Munich Court Opera (1904–11); also sang at Bayreuth in 1911. She made her American debut as Amneris in *Aida* at the Metropolitan Opera in N.Y. (Nov. 13, 1911) and remained one of its leading members until 1930; in the interim, she sang in opera in Germany and South America. She gave her farewell concert recital in Carnegie Hall, N.Y., in 1938, and settled in California. She had one of the most remarkable singing careers of her day; she sang both soprano and contralto roles until 1914, and thereafter concentrated on contralto roles. Among her many outstanding roles were Brünnhilde, Venus, Isolde, Fricka, Ortrud, Eboli, Azucena, Leonora, and Laura in *La Gioconda*.

Mauceri, John (Francis), American conductor; b. N.Y., Sept. 12, 1945. He studied with Gustav Meier at Yale Univ. (B.A., 1967; M.Phil., 1972) and with Maderna, Colin Davis, Ozawa, and Bernstein at the Berkshire Music Center at Tanglewood (summer, 1971). He conducted the Yale Univ. Sym. Orch. (1968–74); subsequently appeared widely as a guest conductor of opera, musical theater, and sym. orchs. He was music director of the Washington (D.C.) Opera (1980–82), the American Sym. Orch. in N.Y. (1984–87), the Scottish Opera in Glasgow (1987–93), and the Hollywood Bowl Orch. (from 1990).

Mauersberger, Rudolf, German organist, choral conductor, teacher, and composer; b. Mauersberg, Erzgebirge, Jan. 29, 1889; d. Dresden, Feb. 22, 1971. He studied piano, organ, and composition at the Leipzig Cons. (1912–14; 1918–19); won the Nikisch Prize for composition in 1914. He served as organist and choirmaster in Aachen (1919–25); then was in charge of church music in Thuringia (1925–30), directing the choir at Eisenach's Georgenkirche. In 1930 he became choirmaster of the Kreuzkirche in Dresden, and directed its famous boy's choir, taking it on numerous tours in Europe and abroad. He composed a number of choral works, including the *Dresdner Requiem* (1948), written in memory of those who lost their lives during the barbarous bombing of the beautiful porcelaneous city just a few weeks before the end of World War II.

BIBL.: M. Grun, *R. M.: Studien zu Leben und Werk* (Regensburg, 1986); M. Herrmann, *R. M. (1889–1971): Werkverzeichnis (RMWV)* (Dresden, 1991).

Maurice, Pierre, Baron de, Swiss composer; b. Allaman, Nov. 13, 1868; d. Geneva, Dec. 25, 1936. He attended the Geneva Cons., then for a short time studied at Stuttgart, finishing his musical education with Lavignac and Massenet at the Paris Cons. He composed the operas *Die weisse Flagge* (Kassel, 1903), *Misé brun* (Stuttgart, 1908), *Lanval* (Weimar, 1912), *Kalif Storch* (not perf.), *Andromède* (1923), *Le Mystère de la Nativité* (1933) et al.; a biblical drama, *La Fille de Jephthé* (Geneva, 1899); a symphonic suite, *Die Islandfischer* (after Loti); *Chanson des quatre saisons* for Piano, and other piano pieces; songs.

BIBL.: M. Maurice, *P. M.* (Geneva, 1938).

Mauro, Ermanno, Italian-born Canadian tenor; b. Trieste, Jan. 20, 1939. He emigrated to Canada in 1958 and became a naturalized Canadian citizen in 1963; after vocal training with Jean Létourneau in Edmonton, he entered the Royal Cons. Opera School in Toronto in 1964 and studied with George Lambert, Herman Geiger-Torel, and Ernesto Barbini. In 1962 he made his operatic debut as Manrico in Edmonton; after appearances in opera productions at the Royal Cons. in Toronto and with the Canadian Opera Co., he sang at London's Covent Garden (1967–72). On Feb. 3, 1975, Mauro made his debut at the N.Y. City Opera, remaining with the company until 1979; on Jan. 6, 1978, he made his Metropolitan Opera debut in N.Y. as Canio, and continued to sing there in subsequent seasons. Among his other roles are Ernani, Des Grieux, Alfredo, Faust, Pinkerton, and Rodolfo.

Maury, Lowndes, American composer; b. Butte, Mont., July 7, 1911; d. Encino, Calif., Dec. 11, 1975. He earned his B.A. degree in music at the Univ. of Montana in 1931; went to Los Angeles, where he studied composition with Wesley La Violette and Schoenberg. He became active in Hollywood as a pianist, arranger, and teacher. He publ. *Magic Lines and Spaces,* a series of piano instruction books in correlated notation, a system employing a 3-line staff (1974).

WORKS: *In Memory of the Korean War Dead* for Violin and Piano (1952); *Proud Music of the Storm,* cantata after Walt Whitman (1953); *Passacaglia* for String Orch. (1959); *Springtime Digressions* for Piano, Flute, and String Quintet (1961); *Speculations* for Piano and 3 String Instruments (1964); *Summer of Green,* rhapsody for Alto Flute and String Orch. (1964); *Scène de ballet* for Piccolo and String Quartet (1965); 11 *Sketches* for Piano Trio (1968); *The Imprisoned Cellist,* suite for Cello (1973).

Maw, (John) Nicholas, distinguished English composer and teacher; b. Grantham, Lincolnshire, Nov. 5, 1935. After studies with Berkeley (composition) and Steinitz (theory) at the Royal Academy of Music in London (1955–58), he held a French government scholarship for further training in Paris with Deutsch and Boulanger (1958–59). In 1959 he was awarded the Lili Boulanger Prize. He taught at the Royal Academy of Music (1964–66), and then was fellow commoner (composer-in-residence) at Trinity College, Cambridge (1966–70). He was a lecturer in music at the Univ. of Exeter, Devon (1972–74), and also served as composer-in-residence of the South Bank Summer Music series in London (1973). In 1984–85 and 1989 he was a visiting prof. of music at the Yale School of Music. From 1989 he was a prof. of music at the Milton Avery Graduate School of the Arts at Bard College in Annandale-on-Hudson, N.Y. In his music, Maw pursued a personal compositional path that utilizied neo-Classical and late Romantic elements before finding fulfillment in a style notable for its expansive lyrical qualities.

WORKS: DRAMATIC: *One-Man Show,* opera (London, Nov. 12, 1964; rev. 1966 and 1970); *The Rising of the Moon,* opera (1967–70; Glyndebourne, July 19, 1970); incidental music; film scores. **ORCH.:** *Sinfonia* for Small Orch. (Newcastle upon Tyne, May 30, 1966); *Severn Bridge Variations* (1967; in collaboration with M. Arnold, M. Tippett, A. Hoddinott, G. Williams, and D. Jones); Sonata for 2 Horn and Strings (Bath, June 7, 1967); *Concert Music* (London, Oct. 19, 1972; based on the opera *The Rising of the Moon,* 1967–70); *Odyssey* (1972–87; 1st complete perf., London, April 8, 1989); *Life Studies I–VIII* for 15 Solo Strings (Cheltenham, July 9, 1973; also nos. *II, III,* and *VI–VIII* for String Orch.); *Serenade* (Singapore, March 31, 1973; rev. 1977); *Summer Dances* for Youth Orch. (1980; Aldeburgh, July 27, 1981); *Toccata* (1982); *Morning Music* (1982); *Spring Music* (1982–83); *Sonata notturna* for Cello and Strings (1985; King's Lynn, May 30, 1986); *Little Concert* for Oboe, 2 Horns, and Strings (Wymondham, May 28, 1988); *The World in the Evening* (London, Oct. 21, 1988); *American Games* for Wind Band (1990–91; London, July 23, 1991); *Shahnama* (1992); Violin Concerto (N.Y., Sept. 29, 1993). **CHAMBER:** Flute Sonatina (1957); *Chamber Music* for Oboe, Clarinet, Horn, Bassoon, and Piano (1962); 2 string quartets: No. 1 (Harlow, July 12, 1965) and No. 2 (1982; London, Jan. 13, 1983); *Epitaph-Canon in Memory of Igor Stravinsky* for Flute, Clarinet, and Harp (1971); Flute Quartet (London, May 7, 1981); *Night Thoughts* for Flute (London, June 10, 1982); *Ghost Dances* for 5 Players (N.Y., May 16, 1988); *Music of Memory* for Guitar (1989). **PIANO:** *Personae I* (1973) and *IV–VI* (1985–86). **VOCAL:** *Nocturne* for Mezzo-soprano and Chamber Orch. (1957–58); *5 Epigrams* for Chorus (1960); *Our Lady's Song* for Chorus (1961); *Scenes and Arias* for Soprano, Mezzo-soprano, Contralto, and Orch. (1961–62; London, Aug. 31, 1962; rev. 1966); *The Angel Gabriel* for Chorus (1963); *Round* for Children's Chorus, Mixed Chorus, and Piano (1963); *Corpus Christi Carol* for Chorus (1964); *Balulalow* for Chorus (1964); *6 Interiors* for High Voice and Guitar (1966; London, May 5, 1970); *The Voice of Love* for Mezzo-soprano and Piano (London, Oct. 6, 1966); *5 Irish Songs* for Chorus (1972; Cork, May 4, 1973); *Te Deum* for Treble or Soprano, Tenor, Chorus, Congregation, and Orch. (Bruton, May 29, 1975); *Reverdie* for Men's Chorus (Glasgow, Oct. 29, 1975); *20 Nonsense Rhymes* for Children's Voices and Piano (Darsham, Sept. 4, 1976); *La Vita Nuova* for Soprano and Chamber Ensemble (London, Sept. 2, 1979); *The Ruin* for Double Chorus and Horn Obbligato (Edinburgh, Aug. 27, 1980); *5 American Folksongs* for High Voice and Piano (1988); *3 Hymns* for Chorus and Organ (1989); *Roman Canticle* for Mezzo-soprano, Flute, Viola, and Harp (1989); *One Foot in Eden, Here I Stand* for Soprano, Alto, Tenor, Bass, and Chorus (1990); *The Head of Orpheus* for Soprano and 2 Clarinets (1992).

Maxakova, Mariya (Petrovna), Russian mezzo-soprano; b. Astrakhan, April 8, 1902; d. Moscow, Aug. 11, 1974. She was a student of Maximilian Maxakov, whom she married. After singing in Astrakhan, she appeared at Moscow's Bolshoi Theater in 1923. From 1925 to 1927 she sang at the Leningrad Academy Opera. In 1927 she became a member of the Bolshoi Theater, where she sang until 1953. She also appeared as a concert artist. In addition to her distinguished Russian roles, she won particular notice for her Ortrud, Dalila, and Carmen.

BIBL.: M. Lvov, *M.P. M.* (Moscow and Leningrad, 1947).

Maxfield, Richard (Vance), American composer; b. Seattle, Wash., Feb. 2, 1927; d. (suicide) Los Angeles, June 27, 1969. He studied at the Univ. of Calif., Berkeley, with Sessions, and at Princeton Univ. with Babbitt (M.F.A., 1955); also took courses with Krenek; held a Fulbright fellowship (1955–57), which enabled him to continue his training with Dallapiccola in Florence and Maderna in Milan. He became deeply engaged in acoustical electronics; taught experimental music at the New School for Social Research in N.Y. (1959–62) and then at San Francisco State College. He contributed essays to avant-garde publications; 2 of them, in free verse, were publ. in *Contemporary Composers on Contemporary Music,* ed. by E. Schwartz and B. Childs (N.Y., 1967). He acquired an excellent technique of composition in the traditional idiom before adopting an extreme avant-garde style. He took his own life by self-defenestration from a hotel room.

WORKS: *Classical Overture* (1942); Trio for Clarinet, Cello, and Piano (1943); Septet for 2 Flutes, 3 Clarinets, Horn, and Bassoon (1947); Sonata for Solo Violin (1949); Violin Sonata (1950); String Trio (1951); Sonata for Solo Flute (1951); *Structures* for 10 Wind Instruments (1951); *11 Variations* for String Quartet (1952); *5 Movements* for Orch. (1956); Chamber Concerto for 7 Instruments (1957); *Structures* for Orch. (1958); *Sine Music* (1959); *Stacked Deck,* opera for Tape, Actors, and Lighting (1959); *Perspectives* for Violin and Tape (1960); *Peripeteia* for Violin, Saxophone, Piano, and Tape (1960); *Clarinet Music* for 5 Clarinets and Tape (1961); *Cough Music,* with sonic materials obtained from coughs and other bronchial sound effects recorded during a modern dance recital and electronically arranged in a piece of tussive polyphony (N.Y., Jan. 13, 1961); *Toy Symphony* for Flute, Violin, Wooden Boxes, Ceramic Vase, and Tape (1962); *African Symphony* (1964); *Venus Impulses* for Electronic Sound (1967).

Maxwell Davies, Sir Peter. See **Davies, Sir Peter Maxwell.**

Mayer, Sir Robert, industrious German-born English music patron; b. Mannheim, June 5, 1879; d. London, Jan. 9, 1985. His love for music was established early when he entered the Mannheim Cons. as a piano student; there he also met Brahms. His father sent him at age 17 to relatives in England to establish himself, since business opportunities were limited for Jews in Germany. So totally immersed did he become in English life that his family asserted he even spoke his native German with a British accent. He was an entrepreneur in the grand manner of the Victorian age. He never wrote music, but he promoted the art with youthful enthusiasm. In 1923, inspired by Walter Damrosch's concerts for children in N.Y., Mayer and his wife, the singer Dorothy Moulton-Mayer, began a series of children's concerts, whose first regular conductor was Adrian Boult. The tremendous success of making serious classical music available to young children everywhere in England, from slums to suburbs, encouraged a new enterprise in 1954, Youth and Music, which was specifically offered to adolescents, with the view to creating lifetime participants in musical culture. Mayer's business acumen launched this program successfully as well. In 1939 he was knighted, and in 1973 made a Companion of Honour. His centennial was gloriously celebrated, with himself as the center of festivities, at the Royal Festival Hall in London, and he was elevated to Knight Commander of the Royal Victorian Order. His autobiography was publ. as *My First Hundred Years* (London, 1979). He had the wit to proclaim that music exercised a curative power over the human body and mind, and he adjusted his entire life accordingly.

Mayer-Serra, Otto, eminent Spanish musicologist; b. Barcelona (of German-Catalan parents), July 12, 1904; d. Mexico City, March 19, 1968. He studied in Germany with H. Abert, Curt Sachs, J. Wolf, and E. von Hornbostel; received his Ph.D. in 1929 with the diss. *Die romantische Klaviersonaten* from the Univ. of Greifswald. He returned to Spain in 1933, and was music critic of the Catalan weekly *Mirador.* In 1936, at the outbreak of the Spanish Civil War, he was appointed head of the music division of the propaganda ministry of the Catalan government; served in the Loyalist army in 1938–39; after its defeat, he fled to France. In 1940 he reached Mexico, where he became active as a writer, editor, lecturer, and manager.

WRITINGS (all publ. in Mexico City): *El romanticismo musical* (1940); *Panorama de la musica mexicana desde la independencia hasta la actualidad* (1941); *Música y músicios de Latino-América* (2 vols., 1947); *Breve diccionaria de la música* (1948); *La música contemporánea* (1954).

Mayer, William (Robert), American composer; b. N.Y., Nov. 18, 1925. He was a student of Richard Donovan and Herbert Baumgartner at Yale Univ. (B.A., 1949), of Sessions at the Juilliard School of Music in N.Y. (summer, 1949), of Salzer at the Mannes College of Music in N.Y. (1949–52), and of Izler Solomon (conducting) at the Aspen (Colo.) Music School (summer, 1960). In 1966 he held a Guggenheim fellowship. In 1980 he was secretary of the National Music Council. He received the National Inst. for Musical Theater Award in 1983.

WORKS: DRAMATIC: *The Greatest Sound Around,* children's opera (1954); *Hello World!,* children's opera (N.Y., Nov. 10, 1956); *The Snow Queen,* ballet (1963); *One Christmas Long Ago,* opera (Philadelphia, Dec. 12, 1964); *Brief Candle,* "micro-opera" (1964); *A Death in the Family,* opera (Minneapolis, March 11, 1983); *A Sobbing Pillow of Man* (N.Y., Dec. 7, 1995). **ORCH.:** *Andante* for Strings (1955); *Hebraic Portrait* (1957); *Overture for an American* (1958); *2 Pastels* (1960); *Octago* for Piano and Orch. (N.Y., March 21, 1971); *Inner and Outer Strings* for String Quartet and Orch. (1982); *Of Rivers and Trains* (Albany, N.Y., Nov. 4, 1988). **OTHER:** Chamber music; children's piano pieces; choruses; songs.

Maynor, Dorothy (Leigh), noted black American soprano and music educator; b. Norfolk, Va., Sept. 3, 1910. She was educated at the Hampton Inst. (B.S., 1933). She began her career singing in various choirs, and later toured with the inst.'s famous chorus in Europe; subsequently studied at Westminster Choir College and with William Kamroth and John Alan Haughton in N.Y. After a successful appearance at the Berkshire Music Festival at Tanglewood in 1939, she made her Town Hall debut in N.Y. on Nov. 19, 1939. In subsequent years, she toured widely in the U.S. and Europe as a concert singer, appearing with leading orchs. She founded the Harlem School of the Arts in 1963 to provide music education for underprivileged children, and served as its executive director until her retirement in 1979.

BIBL.: W. Rogers, *D. M. and the Harlem School of the Arts: The Diva and the Dream* (Lewiston, N.Y., 1993).

Mayuzumi, Toshirō, eminent Japanese composer; b. Yokohama, Feb. 20, 1929. He was a student of Ikenouchi and Ifukube at the Tokyo National Univ. of Fine Arts and Music (1945–51) and of Aubin at the Paris Cons. (1951–52). With Akutagawa and Dan, he organized the contemporary music group Ars Nova Japnica, Sannin no Kai (Group of 3). In 1959 and 1962 he won the Otaka Prize, and in 1964 the Mainichi Music Prize. His style of composition embodies sonorous elements from Japanese and other Asian traditions, modified serial techniques, and electronic sounds, all amalgamated in a remarkably effective manner.

WORKS: DRAMATIC: *Bugaku,* ballet (1962; N.Y., March 20, 1963); *The Bible,* film score (1965); *Kinkakuji* (The Temple of the Golden Pavilion), opera (Berlin, June 23, 1976); *The Kabuki,* ballet (1985); incidental music; dance dramas. **ORCH.:** *Serenade Fantastic* (1946); *Rumba Rhapsody* (1948); *Symphonic Mood* (1950); *Bacchanale* (1953); *Ectoplasme* for Electronic Instruments, Percussion, and Strings (1954; Stockholm, June 5, 1956); *Phonologie symphonique* (Tokyo, May 28, 1957); *Nirvana Symphony* (Tokyo, April 2, 1958); *Manadala Symphony* (Tokyo, March 27, 1960); *Music with Sculpture* for Wind Orch. (Pittsburgh, June 29, 1961); *Samsara,* symphonic poem (Tokyo, June 12, 1962); *Textures* for Band (Pittsburgh, June 10, 1962); *Essay in Sonorities: Mozartiana* (1962; Osaka, Jan 21, 1963);

Essay for Strings (1963); *Fireworks* for Band (Pittsburgh, June 13, 1963); *Ritual Overture* for Band (Pittsburgh, July 2, 1964); *The Birth of Music*, symphonic poem (Tokyo, Oct. 10, 1964); Xylophone Concertino (1965); Concerto for Percussion and Winds (1966); *Incantation* (1967); *Ancient and Modern Music*, symphonic poem (1969–70; Tokyo, Oct. 31, 1970); *Tateyama*, symphonic poem (1974); *Aria in G* for Violin and Orch. (1978); *Capriccio* for Violin and Strings (1988); *Perpetuum mobile* (1989); *Rhapsody for the 21st Century* for Orch., Electric Piano, and Synthesizer (1991). **CHAMBER:** Violin Sonata (1946); *Divertimento* for 10 Instruments (1948); *Poem* for Violin and Piano (1950); String Quartet (1952); Sextet for Flute, Clarinet, Bass Clarinet, Horn, Trumpet, and Piano (1955); *Tone Pleromas 55* for 5 Saxophones, Musical Saw, and Pianos (1955); *Mikrokosmos* for Claviolin, Guitar, Vibraphone, Xylophone, Piano, Percussion, and Musical Saw (Karuizawa, Aug. 12, 1957); *Pieces* for Prepared Piano and String Quartet (1957); *A hun* for Japanese Flute, Kotsuzumi, and Otsuzumi (1958); *Bunraku* for Cello (1960); *Metamusic* for Violin, Saxophone, Piano, and Conductor (1961); *Prelude* for String Quartet (1961); *Showa Tenpyo-raku* for Gagaku Ensemble (1970). **PIANO:** *12 Preludes* (1946); *Poesie* (1946); *Hors d'oeuvre* (1947). **VOCAL:** *Elegy* for Soprano and Piano (1948); *Sphenogramme* for Voice, Flute, Saxophone, Marimba, Piano 4-hands, Violin, and Cello (1950; Frankfurt am Main, June 25, 1951); *Wedding Song* for Chorus and Orch. (1959); *U-So-Ri*, oratorio for Soloists, Chorus, and Orch. (Tokyo, June 12, 1959); *Sange* for Men's Voices (1959); *Pratidesana*, Buddhist cantata for Voices (Kyoto, Sept. 5, 1963); *Mori*, cantata for Voices (1963); *Mandala* for Voice and Tape (1969); *Hymn to Japan* for Narrator, Chorus, and Orch. (1972); *Hymn to Buddha* for Chorus and Orch. (1983); *The World Prayers* for Chorus, Orch., and Tape (1991).

Mazura, Franz, Austrian bass-baritone; b. Salzburg, April 21, 1924. He studied in Detmold. He made his operatic debut in Kassel (1949); later appeared at the opera houses of Mainz, Braunschweig, and Mannheim. In 1963 he made his first appearance at the Berlin Städtische Oper and in 1967 at the Hamburg State Opera; also sang at the Bayreuth Festivals (from 1971). In 1979 he sang Dr. Schön in the premiere of the 3-act version of *Lulu* in Paris, which role he also sang at his Metropolitan Opera debut in N.Y. (Dec. 12, 1980). In addition to the Wagnerian repertoire, he sang Pizzaro in *Fidelio*, Jochanaan in *Salome*, and Moses in Schoenberg's *Moses und Aron*.

Mazurek, Ronald, American composer and teacher; b. Perth Amboy, N.J., Dec. 2, 1943. He received training in clarinet and piano at Montclair (N.J.) College (B.A., 1966) and N.Y. Univ. (M.A., 1967); completed his studies there in composition with Ghezzo (Ph.D., 1986). He taught composition at N.Y. Univ. (from 1982) and electronic music at William Paterson College of N.J. in Wayne (from 1990); served as vice president of the Composers Guild of N.J. (1983–91) and as founder-director of the Fairleigh Dickinson Univ. Concerts of Contemporary Music (1984–90). In his music, he frequently integrates acoustic and electronic elements.

WORKS: *Meditation* for Clarinet and Percussion (1978); *Voices* for Wind Quintet (1979); *Meditation* for Oboe and Percussion (1980); *Anima* for Flute, Clarinet, and Piano (1980); *Encounters* for Percussion Quartet (1981); *Dialogues* for Trumpets (1981); *Fusion/Defusion* for Clarinet (1982); *Focusing* for Alto Saxophone (1984); *Cantos* for Brass Quintet (1984); *The Voice Within* for Piano and Tape (1986); *The Mirror of Wisdom* for Wind Quintet (1987); *In Search of . . .* for Percussion and Tape (1987); *Yu-Chou* for Tape (1988); *Trigrams* for Clarinet, Piano, and Tape (1988); *3 Songs in Memoriam* for Soprano and Tape (1989); *3 Etudes* for Piano and Tape (1990); *Alleluia* for Chamber Orch. and Tape (1990); *Satori* for Clarinet and Tape (1991); *3 Preludes* for Piano and Tape (1992); *Visions* for Ensemble and Tape (1992).

Mazzoleni, Ettore, Canadian conductor, teacher, and composer of Italian-Swiss descent; b. Brusio, Switzerland, June 19, 1905; d. in an automobile accident in Oak Ridges, near Toronto, June 1, 1968. He studied mathematics and music at Oxford Univ. (B.A., 1927; B.Mus., 1927) and piano at the Royal College of Music in London, where he later taught (1927–29). He then settled in Toronto, where he was music master and later an English instructor at Upper Canada College (1929–45); also taught music history at the Toronto Cons. (from 1932) and conducted its sym. orch. (from 1934); was made its principal in 1945, continuing in that capacity when it became the Royal Cons. of Music of Toronto in 1952; retired in 1966. He was assoc. conductor of the Toronto Sym. Orch. (1942–48); also appeared as a conductor in other Canadian cities. In 1949 he became a naturalized Canadian citizen. He made several transcriptions of folk songs for various instrumental and vocal groups.

McAllester, David (Park), American ethnomusicologist; b. Everett, Mass., Aug. 6, 1916. He studied anthropology at Harvard Univ. (B.A., 1934) and Columbia Univ. (Ph.D., 1939). He taught anthropology at Wesleyan Univ. from 1947; from 1972 he served as prof. of anthropology and music there. He devoted much time to the study of American Indian culture.

WRITINGS: *Peyote Music* (N.Y., 1949); *Enemy Way Music* (Cambridge, Mass., 1954); *The Myth and Prayers of the Great Star Chant* (Santa Fe, N.Mex., 1956); ed. *Readings in Ethnomusicology* (N.Y., 1971); with S. McAllester, *Hogans: Navajo Houses and House Songs* (Middletown, Conn., 1980).

McArthur, Edwin, American conductor, pianist, and pedagogue; b. Denver, Sept. 24, 1907; d. N.Y., Feb. 24, 1987. He studied piano in Denver and with Rosina Lhévinne in N.Y. He toured widely as a piano accompanist to various celebrated artists of the day, becoming well known as accompanist to Kirsten Flagstad. In 1938 he made his debut as an opera conductor in Chicago, and then appeared with the San Francisco Opera in 1939. On April 1, 1940, he made his Metropolitan Opera debut in N.Y. conducting *Tristan und Isolde*, remaining on its roster until 1941. From 1945 to 1950 he was director of the St. Louis Municipal Opera. He was conductor of the Harrisburg (Pa.) Sym. Orch. from 1950 to 1974. He also served as director of the opera dept. at the Eastman School of Music in Rochester, N.Y. (1967–72) before devoting himself to private teaching. McArthur was the author of the book *Flagstad: A Personal Memoir* (N.Y., 1965).

McBride, Robert (Guyn), American composer; b. Tucson, Ariz., Feb. 20, 1911. He learned to play clarinet, saxophone, organ, and piano, and played in dance bands as a youth. He studied theory at the Univ. of Arizona (1928–35) and was a member of the Tucson Sym. Orch. (1928–35). From 1935 to 1946 he taught wind instruments at Bennington (Vt.) College; was then an arranger for Triumph Films, N.Y. (1946–57); from 1957 to 1978 he was on the music faculty of the Univ. of Arizona. An exceptionally prolific composer, he wrote over 1,000 pieces in various genres, many of them on American or Mexican themes with an infusion of jazz elements.

WORKS: ORCH.: *Mexican Rhapsody* (1934); *Side Show* (1944); Violin Concerto (1954); *Hill Country Symphony* (1964); *Symphonic Melody* (1968); *Folk-Song Fantasy* (1973); *Light Fantastic* (1976–77). **CHAMBER:** *Workout* for Oboe and Piano (1936); *Swing Stuff* for Clarinet and Piano (1938); *Jam Session* for Woodwind Quintet (1941); *Swing Foursome* for String Quartet (1957); *5 Winds Blowing* for Wind Quintet (1957); *Lament for the Parking Problem* for Trumpet, Horn, and Trombone (1968).

McCabe, John, esteemed English pianist, music educator, and composer; b. Huyton, April 21, 1939. He learned to play piano, violin, and cello as a child; studied with Proctor Gregg (composition) at the Univ. of Manchester and with Pitfield (composition) and Green (piano) at the Royal Manchester College of Music; later took courses at the Munich Academy of Music (1964–65) and also studied privately there with Genzmer. He was pianist-in-residence at Univ. College, Cardiff (1965–67); then settled in London as a pianist, excelling in the music of

Haydn and contemporary composers. He was director of the London College of Music from 1983 to 1990. In 1985 he was made a Commander of the Order of the British Empire.

WORKS: THEATER: *The Lion, the Witch, and the Wardrobe,* children's opera (1968; Manchester, April 29, 1969); *This Town's a Corporation Full of Crooked Streets,* entertainment for Speaker, Tenor, Children's Chorus, Mixed Chorus, and Instrumental Ensemble (1969); *Notturni ed Alba,* ballet (1970); *The Teachings of Don Juan,* ballet (Manchester, May 30, 1973); *The Play of Mother Courage,* chamber opera (Middlesbrough, Oct. 3, 1974); *Mary Queen of Scots,* ballet (1975; Glasgow, March 3, 1976); *Edward II,* ballet (1995). **ORCH.:** 2 violin concertos: No. 1, *Sinfonia concertante* (1959) and No. 2 (Birmingham, March 20, 1980); Concerto for Chamber Orch. (1962; rev. 1968); *Concerto funèbre* for Viola and Chamber Orch. (1962); *Variations on a Theme of Hartmann* (1964; Manchester, Nov. 24, 1965); Chamber Concerto for Viola, Cello, and Orch. (1965); *Concertante* for Harpsichord and Chamber Ensemble (1965); 3 syms.: No. 1, *Elegy* (1965; Cheltenham, July 4, 1966), No. 2 (Birmingham, Sept. 26, 1971), and No. 3, *Hommages* (London, July 11, 1978); 3 piano concertos: No. 1 (1966), No. 2, *Sinfonia concertante* (1970; Middlesbrough, Nov. 23, 1971), and No. 3, *Dialogues* (1976; rev. 1977; Liverpool, Aug. 5, 1977); Concertino for Piano Duet and Orch. (1968); *Concertante Music* (Bath, June 24, 1968); *Metamorphosen* for Harpsichord and Orch. (1968; Liverpool, Feb. 19, 1972); *Concertante Variations on a Theme of Nicholas Maw* for Strings (1970; Bristol, March 3, 1971); Oboe d'Amore Concerto (Portsmouth, April 26, 1972); *The Chagall Windows* (1974; Manchester, Jan. 9, 1975); *Sonata on a Motet* for Strings (Manchester, March 20, 1976); *Jubilee Suite* (London, April 17, 1977); Clarinet Concerto (1977; London, July 11, 1978); *The Shadow of Light* (London, Dec. 6, 1979); *Concerto for Orchestra* (1982; London, Feb. 10, 1983); *Tuning* ('s Hertogenbosch, July 27, 1985); *Fire at Durilgai* (London, Aug. 7, 1989); Flute Concerto (1990); *Red Leaves* (1991); *Canyons* for Wind Band (1991); *Northern Lights,* overture for Brass Band (1992). **CHAMBER:** 5 string quartets (1960, 1972, 1979, 1982, 1989); *Partita* for String Quartet (1960); Sym. for 10 Wind Instruments (1964); String Trio (1965); *Nocturnal* for Piano Quintet (1966); *Fantasy* for Brass Quartet (1967); *Rounds* for Brass Quintet (1967); Oboe Quartet (1968); Concerto for Piano and Wind Quintet (1969); *Canzona* for Wind and Percussion (1970); *The Goddess Trilogy* for Horn and Piano: Part 1, *The Castle of Arianrhod* (1973)m Part 2, *Floraison* (1975), and Part 3, *Shape-Shifter* (1975); *Desert I: Lizard* for Flute, Oboe, Clarinet, Bassoon, and Percussion (1981), *II: Horizon* for 10 Brass Instruments (1981), *III: Landscape* for Violin, Cello, and Piano (1982), and *IV: Vista* for Recorder (1983); *Rainforest* for 10 Players (N.Y., Nov. 30, 1984); *January Sonatina* for Clarinet (1990); *Harbour with Ships: 5 Impressions* for Brass Quintet (1991); *Postcards* for Wind Quintet (1991); piano pieces; organ works. **VOCAL:** *Voyage,* cantata for Vocal Soloists, Boy's Chorus, Mixed Chorus, and Organ (Worcester, Aug. 30, 1972); *Stabat Mater* for Soprano, Chorus, and Orch. (Northampton, Oct. 28, 1976); *Reflections of a Summer Night,* cantata for Chorus and Orch. (1977; Fishguard, July 26, 1978); *Scenes from America Deserta* for 6 Voices (1986); works for solo voices, including *Time Remembered* for Soprano and Instrumental Ensemble (Malvern, Oct. 4, 1973).

BIBL.: S. Craggs, *J. M.: A Bio-Bibliography* (N.Y., 1991).

McCalla, James, American musicologist; b. Lawrence, Kansas, Aug. 25, 1946. He received a B.Mus. in piano and a B.A. in French from the Univ. of Kansas in Lawrence (1968), and an M.M. in music literature from the New England Cons. of Music in Boston (1973); then took a Ph.D. in musicology, specializing in 20th-century music, with Kerman at the Univ. of Calif. at Berkeley (1976, with the diss. *"Between Its Human Accessories": The Art of Stéphane Mallarmé and Pierre Boulez*). He taught at the Univ. of Virginia (1976–78), the State Univ. of N.Y. at Stony Brook (1978–85), and Bowdoin College in Maine (from 1985). His textbooks include *Jazz: A Listener's Guide* (Englewood Cliffs, N.J., 1982) and *Chamber Music of Our Time* (1991). His research employs literary critique to analyze the interface between complex musical and textual works, with subjects including indeterminacy and jazz.

McCauley, William (Alexander), Canadian conductor and composer; b. Tofield, Alberta, Feb. 14, 1917. He studied at the Univ. of Toronto (M.B., 1947), with Parsons (piano, 1947) and Willan (composition) at the Toronto Cons., and with Hanson and Rogers at the Eastman School of Music in Rochester, N.Y. (M.M., 1959; D.M.A., 1960); also was a conducting pupil of Monteux in Hancock, Maine (summer, 1959). He was 1st trombone for the Ottawa Phil. and the National Film Board (1947–49); then was music director of Crawley Films (1949–60), where he composed and conducted music for over 100 television films and documentaries; then was music director of York Univ. (1960–69), the O'Keefe Centre (1960–87), Christopher Chapman Films (1969–70), Seneca College (1970–78), and the North York Sym. Orch. (1972–88). His music is pleasing, lyrical, and inoffensive, with some officious modernities.

WORKS: ORCH.: *Newfoundland Scene* (1952); *Saskatchewan Suite* (1956); *5 Miniatures* for Flute and Strings (1958); *Contrasts* (1958); Horn Concerto (1959); *5 Miniatures* for Bass Trombone, Harp, and Strings (1959); *Theme and Deviations* (1960); *Wilderness,* music from the film (1963); *Canadian Folk Song Fantasy* for Symphonic Band (1966); *Metropolis,* concert suite for Symphonic Band (1967); *2 Nocturnes* for Strings (1968); *Sunday Morning at Wabanowin* for Strings (1968); *Concerto grosso* for Brass Quintet and Orch. (1973); *Christmas Carol Fantasies* (1975). **CHAMBER:** *5 Miniatures* for 6 Percussionists (1962), for 10 Winds (1968), for 4 Saxophones (1972), and for Brass Quintet (1974); *Miniature Overture* for Brass Quintet (1973); *Kaleidoscope québécois* for Flute, Clarinet, Violin, Cello, and 2 Pianos (1974). **PIANO:** *Space Trip* (1968). **VOCAL:** Choruses; songs.

McClain, Ernest Glenn, American music scholar; b. Canton, Ohio, Aug. 6, 1918. He studied at Oberlin (Ohio) College (B.Mus., 1940), Northwestern Univ. (M.Mus., 1946), and Columbia Univ. (Ed.D., 1959). He was band director at Denison Univ. (1946–47) and the Univ. of Hawaii (1947–50); then taught at Brooklyn College, City Univ. of N.Y., from 1950 until his retirement in 1981. He developed an effective way of teaching tuning systems using the monochord. His articles and books are sophisticated explorations of the interface between acoustics, mathematics, philosophy, and religion in ancient and medieval cultures.

WRITINGS: *The Myth of Invariance: The Origin of the Gods, Mathematics, and Music from the Rig-Veda to Plato* (Boulder, Colo., 1976); *The Pythagorean Plato: Prelude to the Song Itself* (York Beach, Maine, 1978); *Meditations through the Quran: Tonal Images in an Oral Culture* (1981).

McClary, Susan, progressive American musicologist; b. St. Louis, Oct. 2, 1946. She studied piano at Southern Illinois Univ. (B.Mus., 1968) and musicology at Harvard Univ. (A.M., 1971; Ph.D., 1976, with the diss. *The Transition from Modal to Tonal Organization in the Works of Monteverdi*). She taught at Harvard Univ. (1969–73) and Trinity College in Hartford, Conn. (1977); joined the faculty of the Univ. of Minnesota in 1977, becoming a prof. in 1990; was acting director of its Center for Humanistic Studies (1984–85) and director of its Collegium Musicum. Her early research disputed the view of 17th-century music that treats it as primitive tonality, arguing instead for its theoretical integrity. From 1982 she publ. articles on the political, economic, and feminist critique of music, on subjects including Mozart, Madonna, Bach, and Laurie Anderson; these studies won her attention and infamy and led to her being called "the first radical feminist musicologist." Her books include *Feminine Endings: Music, Gender, and Sexuality* (Minneapolis, 1990) and *Power and Desire in Seventeenth-Century Music* (Princeton, 1991); also co-ed., with R. Leppert, *Music* *and Society: The Politics of Composition, Performance and Reception* (Cambridge, 1987).

McCorkle, Donald M(acomber), American musicologist; b. Cleveland, Feb. 20, 1929; d. Vancouver, Feb. 6, 1978. He studied at Brown Univ., at Bradley Univ. (B.Mus., 1951), and with W. Apel and P. Nettl at Indiana Univ. (M.A., 1953; Ph.D., 1958, with the diss. *Moravian Music in Salem: A German-American Heritage*). He was assistant prof. of musicology at Salem College, Winston-Salem, N.C. (1954–64); was also director of the Moravian Music Foundation (1956–64); then was prof. of musicology at the Univ. of Maryland (1964–72); subsequently was a prof. and head of the music dept. at the Univ. of British Columbia (1972–75).

McCormack, John, famous Irish-born American tenor; b. Athlone, June 14, 1884; d. "Glena," Booterstown, County Dublin, Sept. 16, 1945. In 1902 he became a member of the Palestrina Choir of Dublin's Cathedral, where he received lessons from the choirmaster, Vincent O'Brien. In 1903 he won the gold medal in the tenor section of the Feis Ceoil (National Music Festival) in Dublin, and began making concert appearances there. He first sang in the U.S. at the St. Louis Exposition in 1904; that same year he commenced making recordings. After vocal studies with Vincenzo Sabatini in Milan (1905), he made his operatic debut under the name Giovanni Foli in the role of Fritz in *L'Amico Fritz* in Savona (Jan. 13, 1906); then went to London, where he began appearing in concerts in 1907; made his Covent Garden debut as Turiddu (Oct. 15, 1907), and subsequently sang there during the 1908–14 summer seasons in such roles as Edgardo, the Duke in *Rigoletto*, Rodolfo, Count Almaviva in *Il Barbiere di Siviglia*, Pinkerton, Gounod's Romeo, Cavaradossi, and Elvino. He made his U.S. operatic debut as Alfredo in *La Traviata* at the Manhattan Opera House (Nov. 10, 1909), a role he also chose for his Metropolitan Opera debut in N.Y. (Nov. 29, 1910), remaining on the company's roster until 1911 and returning from 1912 to 1914 and from 1917 to 1919; also sang with the Chicago Opera (1910–11). After making his formal concert debut at the Manhattan Opera House (Nov. 18, 1909), McCormack devoted much of his time to a concert career, which he furthered through his many recordings. After World War I, he made few appearances in opera, giving his last performance as Gritzko in Mussorgsky's *The Fair at Sorochinsk* in Monte Carlo on March 25, 1923. He applied for American citizenship in 1914; this action, coupled with his strong support of the Irish cause, cost him the support of the British public during World War I. He became a naturalized U.S. citizen in 1919. After an absence of 10 years, he made a triumphant return to England at a Queen's Hall Concert in London in 1924. In subsequent years he pursued a far-flung concert career with enormous success, although his vocal powers began to wane about 1930. He bade his farewell to the U.S. in Buffalo on March 17, 1937. He gave his last concert in London at the Royal Albert Hall on Nov. 27, 1938. At the outbreak of World War II (1939), he came out of retirement to aid the Red Cross; sang on the radio; continued to make recordings until 1942. He received a number of honors, including being made a Papal Count by Pope Pius XI in 1928. McCormack was an incomparable recitalist, his repertoire ranging from the works of the great masters to popular Irish songs and ballads.

BIBL.: P. Key, *J. M.: His Own Life Story* (Boston, 1918); L. Strong, *J. M.* (London, 1941); L. McCormack (his widow), *I Hear You Calling Me* (Milwaukee, 1949); L. MacDermott Roe, *J. M.: The Complete Discography* (London, 1956; 2nd ed., 1972); R. Foxall, *J. M.* (London, 1963); G. Ledbetter, *The Great Irish Tenor* (London, 1977).

McCoy, Seth, black American tenor and teacher; b. Sanford, N.C., Dec. 17, 1928. He studied at the North Carolina Agricultural and Technical College (graduated, 1950), then pursued vocal training with Pauline Thesmacher at the Cleveland Music School Settlement and with Antonia Lavanne in N.Y. He first gained notice as a soloist with the Robert Shaw Chorale (1963–65), with which he toured throughout the U.S. and South America; later appeared with the Bach Aria Group (1973–80); also was a soloist with such leading U.S. orchs. as the N.Y. Phil., Boston Sym. Orch., Chicago Sym. Orch., and Los Angeles Phil. In 1978 he made his European debut at the Aldeburgh Festival. On Feb. 17, 1979, he made his Metropolitan Opera debut in N.Y. as Tamino. His London debut was as soloist in Bach's Christmas Oratorio in 1986. He taught at the Eastman School of Music in Rochester, N.Y. (from 1982).

McCracken, James (Eugene), remarkable American tenor; b. Gary, Ind., Dec. 16, 1926; d. N.Y., April 29, 1988. After working at the Roxy Theatre in N.Y., he sang at Radio City Music Hall and appeared in minor roles on Broadway; following formal vocal studies with Wellington Ezekiel, he made his operatic debut as Rodolfo with the Central City Opera in Colorado (1952). On Nov. 21, 1953, he made his first appearance at the Metropolitan Opera in N.Y. as Parpignol; continued to sing minor roles there until he decided to try his fortune in Europe in 1957. After further vocal training with Marcello Conati in Milan, he joined the Zürich Opera in 1959 and proved himself in major roles there. He soon gained wide recognition for his portrayal of Verdi's Otello, a role he sang to great acclaim at the Metropolitan Opera on March 10, 1963; remained on its roster until quitting the company in a dispute with the management in 1978. In 1983 he returned to the Metropolitan Opera as a participant in its Centennial Gala; he rejoined its roster in 1984, singing there with distinction until his death. He also appeared as a guest artist with major U.S. and European opera houses, and as a soloist with leading orchs. He often made joint appearances with his wife, **Sandra Warfield**. In addition to Otello, he won renown as Canio, Florestan, Don José, Radames, Samson in Saint-Saëns's opera, and Bacchus in Strauss's *Ariadne auf Naxos*. With his wife, he publ. the memoir *A Star in the Family* (ed. by R. Daley; N.Y., 1971).

McCreesh, Paul, remarkable English conductor and music scholar; b. London, May 24, 1960. He received his education at the Univ. of Manchester, where he specialized in music, performance, and musicology (Mus.B., 1981). While still a student there, he formed his own chamber choir and period-instrument ensemble. In 1982 he founded the Gabrieli Consort and Players in London, which he molded into an outstanding choral and period-instrument ensemble, known for its extraordinary technical expertise and refinement. He conducted his ensemble throughout England, on British radio and television, and on tours of Europe. As both an interpreter and music scholar, McCreesh has brought insight and erudition to his handling of works from the Venetian High Renaissance and Baroque eras. While he sometimes provokes controversy, he always elicits respect and often accolades for his imaginative performances.

McCurdy, Alexander, American organist, choirmaster, and pedagogue; b. Eureka, Calif., Aug. 18, 1905; d. Philadelphia, June 1, 1983. He was a student of Farnum (1924–27) and at the Curtis Inst. of Music in Philadelphia (graduated, 1934). In 1926 he made his debut at N.Y.'s Town Hall, and thereafter toured extensively as a recitalist, often appearing in duo recitals with his wife, harpist Flora Greenwood. From 1927 to 1972 he was organist and choirmaster at Philadelphia's Second Presbyterian Church. He was head of the organ dept. at the Curtis Inst. of Music (1935–72) and Westminster Choir College in Princeton, N.J. (1940–65).

McDaniel, Barry, American baritone; b. Lyndon, Kansas, Oct. 18, 1930. He was a student at the Juilliard School of Music in N.Y. and of Alfred Paulus and Hermann Reutter at the Stuttgart Hochschule für Musik. In 1953 he made his recital debut in Stuttgart. After appearing in opera in Mainz (1954–55), Stuttgart (1957–59), and Karlsruhe (1960–62), he was a principal member of the Deutsche Opera in Berlin (from 1962). On Jan. 19, 1972, he made his Metropolitan Opera debut in N.Y. as Pelléas, remaining on the roster for that season. His guest engagements took him to most of the leading opera houses and festivals. He also appeared widely as a concert artist and recitalist. His expansive repertoire ranged from early music to contemporary scores.

McDermott, Vincent, American composer and teacher; b. Atlantic City, N.J., Sept. 5, 1933. He studied with Rochberg at the Univ. of Pa. (B.F.A. in composition, 1959; Ph.D. in music history and theory, 1966) and took a course in music history at the Univ. of Calif. at Berkeley (M.A., 1961); also received instruction in composition from Milhaud and Stockhausen. He studied the tabla at the Ali Akbar Khan College in Oakland, California (1973), and the Javanese gamelan at the Akademi Seni Karawitan Indonesia in Surakarta (1971, 1978). He taught at the Hampton Inst. in Virginia (1966–67), at the Wisconsin Cons. of Music in Milwaukee (1967–77), and at Lewis and Clark College in Portland, Oreg. (from 1971); in 1980 he held the directorship of the Venerable Showers of Beauty gamelan. His music draws freely upon both Western and Eastern elements.

WORKS: DRAMATIC: *A Perpetual Dream*, chamber opera (1978); *Spirits among the Spires*, chamber opera (1987); *The King of Bali*, opera (Portland, Oreg., April 20, 1990); *Mata Hari*, chamber opera (1994; Dallas, April 21, 1995). **ORCH.:** *Siftings upon Siftings* (1976); *Solonese Concerto* for Piano, Voice, and Orch. (1979); *Prelude, Waltz, and Chorale* for String Quartet and Chamber Orch. (1985); *Titus Magnificus*, fanfare (Cincinnati, Sept. 23, 1994); *Titus Magnificat* (1994). **CHAMBER:** *3 for 5* for Flute, Alto Saxophone, Vibraphone, Piano, Tabla or Bongos, and Cymbal (1970); *Komal Usha-Rudra Nisha* for Sitar, Flute, Guitar, and Double Bass (1972); *Time Let Me Plan and Be Golden in the Mercy of His Means* for Guitar and Harpsichord (1973); *Dreams, Listen* for Viola and Piano (1974); *Kagoklaras* for Prepared Piano and Gamelan (1981); *The Bells of Tajilor* for Gamelan (1984); String Quartet No. 1, *Fugitive Moons* (1991); *Price's Fancy and Gavotte* for Viola and Piano (1992). **VOCAL:** 4 numbered cantatas: *Mixes* No. 1 for Voices, Violin, and Percussion (1971), No. 2, *Thou Restless Ungathered* for Soprano or Tenor, Clarinet, and Tape (1973), No. 3, *Swift Wind* for High Voice and Double Bass (1974), and No. 4, *Slayer of Time, Ancient of Days* for Soloists, Chorus, English Horn, Guitar, and Percussion (1977); *Laudamus* (1980); *The Book of the Lover, the Beloved, and the Alone* for Voice and Instruments (1980); *Tagore Songs* for Soprano and Guitar (1981); *Sweet-breathed Minstrel* for 2 Voices, Viola, and Gamelan (1982); *The Dark Laments of Ariadne and of Attis*, 2 songs for Soprano, Narrator, Viola, and Tape, after Catullus (1983); *Sir Christemas* for Men's Chorus and Percussion (1990). **TAPE AND MIXED MEDIA:** *He Who Ascends by Ecstasy into Contemplation of Sublime Things Sleeps and Sees a Dream* for Piano and Tape (1972); *Pictures at an Exhibition*, multimedia piece (1975); *Orpheus* for Tape and Video (1975); *Rain of Hollow Reeds* for Tape (1977); *A Perpetual Dream* for Voice, Tape, and 1 or 2 Dancers (1978); *Execution—what! what? what*, multimedia piece (1980).

McDonald, Harl, American pianist, music administrator, and composer; b. near Boulder, Colo., July 27, 1899; d. Princeton, N.J., March 30, 1955. He studied at the Univ. of Southern Calif. in Los Angeles (Mus.B., 1921); continued his studies in Leipzig at the Cons. and the Univ. (diploma, 1922). He made tours of the U.S. as a pianist from 1923; taught at the Philadelphia Musical Academy (1924–26) and the Univ. of Pa. (1926–46), where he later was a prof. and director of its music dept.; was also general manager of the Philadelphia Orch. (1939–55).

WORKS: ORCH. (all 1st perf. in Philadelphia unless otherwise given): 4 syms.: No. 1, *The Santa Fe Trail* (1932; Nov. 16, 1934), No. 2, *The Rhumba* (1934; Oct. 4, 1935), No. 3, *Lamentations of Fu Hsuan*, for Soprano, Chorus, and Orch. (1935; Jan. 3, 1936), and No. 4, *Festival of the Workers* (1937; April 8, 1938); *3 Poems on Aramaic Themes* (1935; Dec. 18, 1936); Concerto for 2 Pianos and Orch. (1936; April 2, 1937); *San Juan Capristrano*, 2 nocturnes (1938; Boston, Oct. 30, 1939); *The Legend of the Arkansas Traveler* (1939; Detroit, March 3, 1940); *Chameleon Variations* (1940); *From Childhood* for Harp and Orch. (1940; Jan. 17, 1941); *Bataan* (Washington, D.C., July 3, 1942); *Saga of the Mississippi* (1943; April, 9, 1948); *My Country at War*, symphonic suite (1943); Violin Concerto (1943; March 16, 1945); *Song of the Nations* for Soprano and Orch. (1945); *Overture for Children* (1950). **CHAMBER:** 2 piano trios (1931, 1932); *Fantasy* for String Quartet (1932); *String Quartet on Negro Themes* (1933); numerous piano pieces. **VOCAL:** *The Breadth and Extent of Man's Empire* for Chorus (1938); *Songs of Conquest* for Chorus (1938); *Lament for the Stolen* for Women's Voices and Orch. (1939); *Dirge for 2 Veterans* for Women's Voices and Orch. (1940); *Wind in the Palm Trees* for Women's Voices and Strings (1940); *God Give us Men* for Voices and Orch. (1950); numerous other vocal pieces.

McDonald, Susann, noted American harpist and pedagogue; b. Rock Island, Ill., May 26, 1935. She began harp study when she was 6, then took lessons with Marcel Grandjany in N.Y. (1948) and Marie Ludwig in Chicago (1948–52); continued her training in Paris at the École Normale de Musique and privately with Henriette Renie (1952; 1953–55); was also a scholarship student of Lily Laskine at the Paris Cons. (1954–55), graduating with the premier prix in 1955, the first American to attain that distinction for harp. She subsequently pursued an outstanding concert career, playing with most of the leading orchs. of the world and appearing as a recitalist in the major music centers. She was artist-in-residence (1963–70) and assoc. prof. (1970–81) at the Univ. of Arizona; was also a lecturer at the Univ. of Southern Calif. in Los Angeles (1966–81) and head of the harp dept. at the Juilliard School in N.Y. (1975–85); was chairman of the harp dept. at the Indiana Univ. School of Music in Bloomington (from 1981); served as artistic director of the World Harp Congress (from 1981). She ed. a number of works for her instrument. A remarkable virtuoso, she maintains an extensive repertoire, which ranges from early works to contemporary scores.

McDonnell, Donald (Raymond), American composer and teacher; b. Helena, Mont., Feb. 14, 1952. He studied saxophone and gained practical experience as a jazz player and arranger. He pursued his education at the Berklee College of Music (B.Mus., 1975), Boston Univ. (M.Mus., 1982), and Brandeis Univ. (Ph.D., 1987), his principal composition mentors being Imbrie, Del Tredici, Berger, and Boykan. In 1975 he joined the faculty of the Berklee College of Music.

WORKS: Sonata for Alto Flute and Guitar (1982); *The Road Not Taken* for Soprano and Piano (1982); *Introduction and Fanfare* for 7 Brass and 2 Percussion Instruments (1982); Concertino for Alto Saxophone and Orch. (1982); *A Warm Tension From the Curved Line* for Piano (1983); Saxophone Quartet (1984); *Parvis Mundi* for Piano (1985); *Nexus/Dreamscape* for Flute, Clarinet, Bassoon, Violin, Viola, Cello, and Piano (1986); *Wall Music*, computer-realized music synthesis (1987); *Flow Gently Sweet Afton* for Chorus (1987); *Psalm XL* for Chorus, Brass Quintet, and Organ (1988); *Midwinter Sauna* for Soprano and Piano (1989).

McDowell, John Herbert, American composer; b. Washington, D.C., Dec. 21, 1926; d. Scarsdale, N.Y., Sept. 3, 1985. He studied at Colgate Univ. (B.A., 1948) and at Columbia Univ. with Luening, Beeson, and Goeb (M.A., 1957); held a Guggenheim fellowship in 1962. He devoted his energies chiefly to music for the theater and dance.

WORKS: *Good News from Heaven*, cantata (1957); *Four Sixes and a Nine* for Orch. (1959); *Accumulation* for 35 Flutes, Strings, and Percussion (1964); 100-odd pieces for dance, among them *Insects and Heroes* (1961); *From Sea to Shining Sea*, an homage to Ives (1965); *Dark Psalters* (1968).

McEwen, Sir John (Blackwood), Scottish composer and pedagogue; b. Hawick, April 13, 1868; d. London, June 14, 1948. He studied at Glasgow Univ. (M.A., 1888) and at the Royal Academy of Music in London with Corder, Matthay, and Prout. He taught piano in Glasgow (1895–98) and composition at the Royal Academy of Music in London (1898–1936); in 1924 he succeeded Alexander Mackenzie as principal, retiring in 1936. He was knighted in 1931.

WORKS: ORCH.: 2 syms.: No. 1 (1892–98) and No. 2, *Solway* (1911); 4 suites (1893, 1935, 1935, 1941); Viola Concerto (1901). **CHAMBER:** 17 string quartets (1893–1947); 7 violin sonatas (1913–39); 7 Bagatelles "Nugae" for Strings (1912); *Scottish Rhapsody* for Violin and Piano (1915); Viola Sonata (1930); piano pieces. **VOCAL:** Songs.

McFerrin, Bobby (actually, **Robert**), gifted black American vocalist and conductor, son of **Robert McFerrin**; b. N.Y., March 11, 1950. He studied theory from the age of 6 and played piano in high school, forming a quartet that copied the styles of Henry Mancini and Sergio Mendes. In 1970 he heard Miles Davis's fusion album *Bitches Brew* and completely changed his musical direction. He studied music at Sacramento State Univ. and at Cerritos College; then played piano professionally until 1977, when he began to develop his voice; toured in 1980 with jazz vocalist Jon Hendricks, and debuted a solo act in 1982. His recordings include *Bobby McFerrin* (1982), *The Voice* (1984), *Spontaneous Improvisation* (1986), *Simple Pleasures* (1988; includes the song *Don't Worry, Be Happy*, which made him a household name), and *Medicine Music* (1991); he also made several music videos and sang with Herbie Hancock, Yo-Yo Ma, Manhattan Transfer, and others. In 1989 he created the sound track for *Common Threads*, a 1989 documentary on the AIDS quilt. McFerrin began studying conducting in 1989, making his debut with a performance of Beethoven's Sym. No. 7 with the San Francisco Sym. on March 11, 1990. From 1994 to 1996 he held the Creative Chair of the St. Paul (Minn.) Chamber Orch. Technically, McFerrin is a virtuoso, using a remarkable range of voices with sophisticated control and accompanying them with body percussion, breath, and other self-generated sounds. Aesthetically, he fuses a number of musical styles, including jazz, rock, and New Age, in a brilliant palette; his solo and ensemble shows are based on various improvisatory structures through which he produces highly polished, expertly burnished works.

McFerrin, Robert, black American baritone, father of **Bobby** (actually, **Robert**) **McFerrin**; b. Marianna, Ariz., March 19, 1921. He studied at Fisk Univ. in Nashville, Chicago Musical College (B.M., 1948), and Kathryn Turney Long School in N.Y. In 1949 he appeared in Kurt Weill's *Lost in the Stars*, in William Grant Still's *Troubled Island* (with the N.Y. City Opera), and as Amonasro in *Aida* (with Mary Cardwell Dawson's National Negro Opera Co.); joined the New England Opera Co. in 1950, creating roles in Marc Connelly's play *The Green Pastures* (N.Y., 1951; music by Hall Johnson) and *My Darlin' Aida* (1952), a version of Verdi's opera set in the time of the Confederacy. He won the Metropolitan Auditions of the Air in 1953; became the first black male to join the company, making his debut on Jan. 27, 1955, as Amonasro. After singing in Naples at the Teatro San Carlo, he sang the role of Porgy (played by Sidney Poitier) in the film version of Gershwin's *Porgy and Bess* (1959); also sang on the recording. He toured internationally, giving recitals of arias, art songs, and spirituals.

McGegan, Nicholas, English keyboard player, flutist, and conductor; b. Sawbridgeworth, Hertfordshire, Jan. 14, 1950. He studied piano at London's Trinity College of Music (1968) and also learned to play the flute, specializing in the Baroque flute; pursued his education at Corpus Christi College, Cambridge (B.A., 1972), and at Magdalen College, Oxford (M.A., 1976). He was active as a flutist, harpsichordist, fortepianist, and pianist in London, where he was also a prof. of Baroque flute (1973–79) and music history (1975–79) and director of early music (1976–80) at the Royal College of Music. From 1979 to 1984 he was artist-in-residence at Washington Univ. in St. Louis; then became music director of the Philharmonia Baroque Orch. in San Francisco (1985), the Ojai (Calif.) Festival (1988), and the Göttingen Handel Festival (1991). From 1993 to 1995 he was principal conductor of the Drottningholm Court Theater in Stockholm. He also appeared widely in Europe and North America as a guest conductor.

McGlaughlin, William, American conductor; b. Philadelphia, Oct. 3, 1943. He studied at Temple Univ. (B.M., 1967; M.M., 1969). He played trombone in the Pittsburgh Sym. Orch. and the Philadelphia Orch., and was founder-conductor of the Pittsburgh Sym. Players and the Pittsburgh Camerata (1973). He became assistant conductor of the Pittsburgh Chamber Orch. in 1975; was also a conductor with the St. Paul (Minn.) Chamber Orch. (1975–78). He was music director of the Eugene (Oreg.) Sym. Orch. (1981–85) and the Tucson Sym. Orch. (1983–87). From 1986 to 1998 he was music director of the Kansas City (Mo.) Sym. Orch. He also was the congenial host of the successful public radio program "St. Paul Sunday."

McGlinn, John, American conductor; b. Philadelphia, Sept. 18, 1953. His academic and musical studies led him to pursue an intensive investigation of the scores of the American musical theater. As a result, he dedicated himself to restoring the classic American musicals to their pristine state via original orchestrations and texts. In 1985 he won critical accolades when he conducted the Jerome Kern Centennial Festival at N.Y.'s Carnegie Hall. In subsequent years, he returned there with major success and also appeared as a guest conductor with various major North American orchs. His recordings were especially valuable in documenting America's golden era on Broadway. He occasionally appeared as an opera conductor as well. In 1988 he made his first appearance in London leading the London Sym. Orch.'s 70th birthday concert in honor of Leonard Bernstein. His championship of Jerome Kern, George Gershwin, Cole Porter, Vincent Youmans, and Richard Rodgers has been particularly notable.

McGurty, Mark, remarkably gifted American composer whose music possesses an aura of new classicism; b. Newark, N.J., April 28, 1955. He studied at the Juilliard School in N.Y., where his major teachers were Diamond and Carter. He also took lessons in violin with Frank Scocozza, piano with Frances Goldstein, and conducting with Abraham Kaplan. However, he did not at once pursue the occupation of a professional composer or performer, but had to earn a living elsewhere. He was manager of the Orquesta Filarmónica de Caracas in Venezuela (1979–83); concurrently was active as an instructor at the Simon Bolivar Univ. in Caracas, and occasional director for the Opera Nacional of Caracas. His next engagement was with the Opera of the Dominican Republic. In 1985 he moved to California, where he worked on the production of recordings for the Pacific Sym. Orch. During all these years, he was intensely working on a number of compositions for theater, orch., and chamber ensembles. In all cases, he favors complex ensembles of variegated instruments marked by a resilient rhythmic beat while the flow of governing melody is never muted.

WORKS: BALLETS: *The Castle*, after Kafka (1974); *Journey to the Land of the Tarahumaras* (1975). **ORCH.:** Symphonic Poem (1975); *Variations on a Gregorian Chant* (1976); Concerto for Viola and 24 Players (1982); Violin Concerto (1982); Sym. for Strings (1983); *Concerto grosso* for Piano and Strings (1983); *Dirige Domine* for Strings (1985); 2 piano concertos (1985, 1987); *Concerto for Orchestra* (1985); *Sinfonie pour un tombeau d'Anatole* (1987–88); *Oisin and the Gwragedd Annwn* (1988); *Denizens of the Realm Faerie* (1990). **CHAMBER:** Violin Sonata (N.Y., 1974); Quintet (N.Y., 1974); 2 piano sonatas (1975, 1985); *Partita for Violin Alone* (1976); 8 string quartets, including No. 1 (1976), No. 3 (1978), No. 4 (1981), No. 5 (1983), No. 7 (1987), and No. 8, *Armadillo Quartet* (1987); Flute Sonata (1977); *Concert Etudes* for Piano (1983); Chamber Sym. (1983); Woodwind Quintet (1985); Piano Sonata (1985); *Fantasies and Cadenzas* for Oboe Quartet (1987); *Clarinet Alone* (1987); *Sonata and Its Double* for 2 Pianos (1 pianist with midi equipment) (1987); *Whitening* for Soprano and Ensemble (1987); *Songs of the Gwrageth Anoon* for 21 Instruments (Los

Angeles, 1987); *Sonata for Violin Alone* (1988); *Scene Concertante* for Flute, Harp, and Strings (Los Angeles, 1988).

McHose, Allen Irvine, American music theorist and educator; b. Lancaster, Pa., May 14, 1902; d. Canandaigua, N.Y., Sept. 14, 1986. He studied at Franklin and Marshall College (B.S., 1923; D.F.A., 1948), the Eastman School of Music in Rochester, N.Y. (B.M., 1928; M.M., 1929), and Oklahoma City Univ. (D.Mus., 1945). From 1930 to 1967 he was on the faculty at the Eastman School; from 1931 to 1962, he was chairman of the theory dept. there. He developed a theory of musical analysis based upon a statistical survey of works of J.S. Bach, and propounded it persuasively in his books *Contrapuntal Harmonic Technique of the 18th Century* (1947) and *Basic Principles of the Technique of 18th and 19th Century Composition* (1951). He also publ. *Sight Singing Manual* (1944; with R. Tibbs); *Keyboard and Dictation Manual* (1949; with D. White); *Teachers' Dictation Manual* (1948); and *Musical Style 1850–1920* (1950).

McIntire, Dennis K(eith), diligent American music historian and lexicographer; b. Indianapolis, June 25, 1944. His innate love of music was manifested at a very early age when he discovered his maternal grandmother's Edison Amberola and a cornucopia of playable cylinders. His rejection of the rudiments of formal music schooling did not preclude his being able to give authentic performances of such works as John Cage's famous silent masterpieces, *4'33"* and *0'00"*. By 1985 his mastery of musical reproductive technique reached its summit, so that he could play difficult scores on the compact disc player. As a lexicographer, he was autodidact, being mainly inspired by the example of the great Samuel Johnson. His precocious self-assurance was such that at the age of 13 he undertook a systematic attack on imperfections in reference books, beginning with misinformative vols. such as *The Lincoln Library of Essential Information.* After 10 years of badgering its eds., he was made an assistant and research ed. of the aforesaid encyclopedia in 1967. His fascination for reference books spurred him on to consume virtually the entire contents of several voluminous standard sources, among them *Baker's Biographical Dictionary of Musicians, Grove's Dictionary of Music and Musicians,* and even the monumental *Encyclopaedia Britannica.* Appalled by the surprising percentage of errors in such dignified reference publications, he undertook a systematic correspondence with their eds., suggesting corrections and additions. In the meantime, he undertook a thorough study of 20th-century European history at Indiana Univ., but managed to depart the halls of academe without a devastating critique of any deficiencies in instruction; continued to fulfill editorial duties all the while. His capacity of total recall and indefatigability in corresponding with far corners of the musical world enabled him to make valuable additions to the 7th and 8th eds. of *Baker's Biographical Dictionary of Musicians* (1984, 1992); he also contributed material to Slonimsky's *Supplement to Music since 1900* (1986) and the 5th ed. of *Music since 1900* (1994). It is no wonder that he became known to intimates as "Dennisimo," the superlative of his first name, in appreciation of his quaquaversal and, indeed, immarcescible super-duper contribution to the art of musical lectionary. He also lent assistance to *The Concise Oxford Dictionary of Opera* (1979), *The Oxford Dictionary of Music* (1985; 2nd ed., 1994), and *The New Everyman Dictionary of Music* (1988); served as an adviser and contributor to *The New Grove Dictionary of American Music* (1986) and was co-consultant ed. (with D. Cummings) of the 12th ed. of *The International Who's Who in Music* (1990), and subsequently was a contributing ed. to the 13th to 15th eds. (1992–96). In 1995 he served as assoc. ed of the present edition of *Baker's.* From 1991 he was an adviser to the *Encyclopaedia Britannica.* He also was a contributor to *The New Grove Dictionary of Opera* (1992).

McIntyre, Sir Donald (Conroy), esteemed New Zealand bass-baritone; b. Auckland, Oct. 22, 1934. He studied at the Guildhall School of Music in London. He made his operatic debut as Zachariah in *Nabucco* with the Welsh National Opera in Cardiff (1959); then was a member of the Sadler's Wells Opera in London (1960–67). In 1967 he made his debut as Pizzaro at Covent Garden in London; that same year he made his first appearance at the Bayreuth Festival as Telramund, returning there annually until 1981; sang Wotan there during the centenary *Ring* production in 1976. On Feb. 15, 1975, he made his Metropolitan Opera debut in N.Y. as Wotan. He made guest appearances with many of the leading opera houses of the world. In 1977 he was made an Officer of the Order of the British Empire, and in 1985 a Commander of the Order of the British Empire. In 1992 he was knighted. His other roles include Kaspar in *Der Freischütz,* Attila, Klingsor, Amfortas, the Dutchman, Golaud, and Escamillo.

McKay, George Frederick, American composer and teacher; b. Harrington, Wash., June 11, 1899; d. Stateline, Nev., Oct. 4, 1970. He was a student of Palmgren and Sinding at the Eastman School of Music in Rochester, N.Y., where he was the first student in composition to graduate there (B.M., 1923). In 1927 he joined the faculty of the Univ. of Wash. in Seattle, where he later was a prof. (1943–68). He publ. the book *Creative Orchestration* (1963). In his music, McKay often made use of folk melodies.

WORKS: ORCH.: 4 sinfoniettas (1925–42); *Fantasy on a Western Folk Song* (Rochester, N.Y., May 3, 1933); *From a Mountain Town* (1934); *Port Royal, 1861,* suite for Strings (1939); *Bravura Prelude* for Brass Ensemble (Rochester, N.Y., April 30, 1939); *To a Liberator: A Lincoln Tribute* (1939–40; Indianapolis, March 15, 1940); *Introspective Poem* for Strings (Philadelphia, April 3, 1941); *A Prairie Portrait* (San Francisco, Sept. 4, 1941); *Pioneer Epic* (Oakland, Calif., Feb. 17, 1942); Cello Concerto (1942); *Music of the Americas,* suites (1947–50); *Evocation Symphony* (1951); *Song Over the Great Plains* (1954); *6 Pieces on Winter Moods and Patterns* (1961). **CHAMBER:** Wind Quintet (1930); Piano Trio (1931); *American Street Scenes* for Clarinet, Bassoon, Trombone, Saxophone, and Piano (1935); *Trombone Sonata* (1951); Suite for Chamber Ensemble (1958); Suite for Harp and Flute (1960); *Sonatina expressiva* for Brass Quintet (1966); *Andante mistico* for 8 Cellos and Piano (1968); 4 string quartets; piano pieces; organ music. **VOCAL:** Choral works; part songs; various other pieces, including works for students.

McKellar, Kenneth, Scottish tenor; b. Paisley, June 23, 1927. He took a course in philology at the Univ. of Aberdeen and received a B.S. degree; then studied voice at the Royal College of Music in London. He subsequently sang with the Carl Rosa Opera Co. in London; later toured the U.S. as a concert singer. He was also a fine interpreter of traditional Scottish ballads, which he included in his concert programs.

McKinley, William Thomas, American composer, pianist, and teacher; b. New Kensington, Pa., Dec. 9, 1938. He began piano lessons at 5, and began playing in local bands around age 10. At 13, he began piano studies with the jazz pianist Johnny Costa. He pursued his academic training with Lopatnikoff, Haieff, and Dorian at the Carnegie Inst. of Technology (B.F.A., 1960). After attending sessions given by Copland, Schuller, and Foss at the Berkshire Music Center at Tanglewood (summer, 1963), he completed his studies with Powell and Moss at Yale Univ. (M.M., 1968; M.F.A., 1969). He taught at the State Univ. of N.Y. at Albany (1968–69), Yale Univ. (1969), the Univ. of Chicago (1969–73), and the New England Cons. of Music in Boston (1973–92). Throughout the years, he was active as a pianist with frequent appearances in jazz settings. In 1991 he founded Master Musicians Collective recordings. Among his various honors were a BMI prize (1963), 8 NEA awards (1976–86), a Koussevitzky Music Foundation commission (1983), and a Guggenheim fellowship (1985–86). As a composer, McKinley has developed a style which he describes as "neo-tonal," one made imaginative by his use of jazz improvisation.

WORKS: ORCH.: Triple Concerto for Piano, Double Bass,

Drums, and Orch. (1970); 3 piano concertos (1974; *O'Leary*, 1987; 1994); *October Night* (1976); 6 syms.: No. 1 (1977; Minneapolis, Jan. 3, 1979), No. 2, *Of Time and Future Monuments* (1978), No. 3, *Romantic* (N.Y., May 18, 1984), No. 4 (1985; N.Y., March 25, 1986), No. 5, *Irish* (Pasadena, Calif., March 18, 1989), and No. 6 (St. Lucia, Australia, Sept. 8, 1990); Cello Concerto (1977); 3 clarinet concertos: No. 1 (1977), No. 2 (Norwalk, Conn., June 2, 1990), and No. 3, *The Alchemical* (1994); *The Mountain* (Pittsburgh, Oct. 17, 1982); *Boston Overture* (Boston, May 6, 1986); Concerto for Flute and Strings (1986); *Tenor Rhapsody* for Tenor Saxophone and Orch. (1988); *Huntington Horn Concerto* (1989); *N.Y. Overture* (1989; N.Y., May 12, 1990); *Jubilee Concerto* for Brass Quintet and Orch. (1990); *Concerto for the New World* for Wind Quintet, Strings, and Percussion (1991; N.Y., Jan. 9, 1992); Chamber Concerto No. 3 (Pittsburgh, April 29, 1991); *Concerto Domestica* for Trumpet, Bassoon, and Orch. (1991; Richmond, Va., March 6, 1992); Concerto No. 3 for Viola and Orch. (1992; N.Y., Feb. 22, 1993); *Silent Whispers* for Piano and Orch. (1992); *Andante and Scherzo* for Piano and Orch. (1993); *Fantasia Variazioni* for Harpsichord and Orch. (1993); *Concerto for Orchestra No. 2* (Seattle, Sept. 27, 1993); *Concert Variations* for Violin, Viola, and Orch. (1993; N.Y., Jan. 31, 1994); *Patriotic Variations: Reading Festival Overture* (1993; Reading, Pa., May 7, 1994); *Lightning*, overture (1993; N.Y., March 30, 1994). **CHAMBER:** 9 string quartets (1959–92); *Attitudes* for Flute, Clarinet, and Cello (1967); *Studies* for String Trio (1968); *Paintings I–VIII* for Various Instrumental Combinations (1972–86); *Tashi*, quartet for Piano, Clarinet, Violin, and Cello (1977); *August Symphony* for Flute, Clarinet, Violin, Cello, and Piano (1983); *Quintet Romantico* (1987); *Ancient Memories* for Viola and Chamber Ensemble (1989); *Glass Canyons* for Clarinet, Percussion, and Piano (1990); *Der Baum des Lebens* for 2 Violins, Viola, and Cello (1993); *Elegy* for Flute (1993); many pieces for solo instrument. **VOCAL:** *Deliverance, Amen*, oratorio for Chorus, Chamber Ensemble, and Organ (Boston, Dec. 12, 1983); *N.Y. Memories* for Soprano and Piano (1987); *When the Moon is Full* for Mezzo-soprano, Baritone, and 7 Instruments (1989); *Emsdettener Totentanz* for Soprano, Alto, Baritone, and Chamber Ensemble (1991); *Westfälischer Pan* for Mezzo-soprano, Clarinet, and Piano (1991; also for Mezzo-soprano and 6 Instruments, 1992); *Jenseits der Mauer* for Baritone, Trumpet, and Organ (1992); *3 Poems of Pablo Neruda* for Soprano and Orch. (1992).

BIBL.: J. Sposato, *W. T. M.: A Bio-Bibliography* (Westport, Conn., 1995).

McKinney, Baylus Benjamin, American composer and editor of gospel hymns; b. Heflink, La., July 22, 1886; d. Bryson City, N.C., Sept. 7, 1952. He was educated at Mt. Lebanon Academy in Louisiana, Louisiana College, and the Southwestern Baptist Theological Seminary, where he subsequently taught (1919–32). He was music ed. for the Robert H. Coleman publishing firm in Dallas (1918–35) and for the Baptist Sunday School Board's widely used Broadman Hymnal (1941). He wrote both words and music to some 150 gospel hymns and set more than 100 texts to music.

BIBL.: W. Reynolds and A. Faircloth, *The Songs of B.B. M.* (Nashville, Tenn., 1974); T. Terry, *B.B. M.: A Shaping Force in Southern Protestant Music* (diss., North Texas State Univ., 1981); R. Hastings, *Glorious Is Thy Name!: B.B. M., the Man and His Music* (Nashville, Tenn., 1986).

McLean, Barton (Keith), American composer; b. Poughkeepsie, N.Y., April 8, 1938. He studied music education at the State Univ. of N.Y. at Potsdam (B.S., 1960), with Cowell at the Eastman School of Music in Rochester, N.Y. (M.M., 1965), and composition at Indiana Univ. in Bloomington (Mus.D., 1972). He taught at the State Univ. of N.Y. at Potsdam (1960–66). He then was head of theory and composition and director of the electronic music center at Indiana Univ. in South Bend (1969–76); after teaching and serving as director of the electronic music center at the Univ. of Texas in Austin (1976–83), he taught and was co-director at the I-Ear Studios at the Rensselaer Polytechnic Inst. (1987–89). In 1974 he married **Priscilla McLean**; together they toured in the U.S. and abroad as the McLean Mix electro-acoustic music duo. In 1976 and 1982 he received NEA fellowships; also held MacDowell Colony fellowships (1979, 1981, 1984, 1985). Most of his compositional efforts have been devoted to electronic and computer music.

WORKS: ORCH.: *Metamorphosis* (1972); *Rainforest Reflections* for McLean Mix Duo and Orch. (Chico, Calif., March 6, 1993). **CHAMBER:** *Ritual of the Dawn* for 6 Players (1982); *Pathways* for Symphonic Winds (1983); *From the Good Earth*, "foot-stompin' homage to Bartók" for String Quartet (1985). **VOCAL:** *3 Songs on Sandburg Poems* for Voice and Piano (1970). **TAPE AND ELECTRONICS:** *The Sorcerer Revisited* for Tape (1975); *Mysteries from the Ancient Nahuatl* for Soloists, Chorus, Narrator, Instrumentalists, and Tape (1978); *Etunytude* for Computer (1982); *In Wilderness Is the Preservation of the World: Voices of the Wild, Passages of the Night*, electronic piece (1985); *Voices of the Wild: Primal Spirits* for McLean Mix Synthesizer, Soloists, and Orch. (1987; Troy, N.Y., Feb. 26, 1988); *Earth Music*, improvisation installation-performance computer piece (1988); *Visions of a Summer Night* for Computer (1988); *Rainforest*, environmental audience-interactive quasi-installation computer piece (1989). **OTHER:** *Rainforest Images*, audio piece (Cincinnati, Feb. 24, 1993; in collaboration with P. McLean); *Forgotten Shadows*, musical-historical installation (1994).

BIBL.: J. Aikin, "B. and Priscilla M.: Composing for Piano, Synthesizer and Electronic Tape," *Keyboard* (Sept. 1983).

McLean, Priscilla (Anne née **Taylor)**, American composer; b. Fitchburg, Mass., May 27, 1942. She studied at Fitchburg State College (B.E.E., 1963) and the Univ. of Lowell (B.M.E., 1965) in Massachusetts, and with Heiden and Beversdorf at Indiana Univ. (M.M., 1969). She was an assoc. lecturer at Indiana Univ.'s Kokomo campus (1971–73) and at St. Mary's College in Notre Dame, Ind. (1973–76); in 1975–76 she was composer-in-residence at the electronic music center at Indiana Univ.'s South Bend campus, and in 1985 served as visiting prof. of music at the Univ. of Hawaii in Manoa. In 1974 she married **Barton McLean**; together they toured in Europe and the U.S. as the McLean Mix electro-acoustic music duo. She appeared as a singer, pianist, and percussionist, and also played synthesizer and native wooden flutes. She received numerous NEA grants (1979–87) and MacDowell Colony fellowships (1979, 1981, 1984, 1986). Her compositions make innovative use of man-made or animal sounds with synthesized music.

WORKS: ORCH.: *Holiday for Youth* for Concert Band (1965); *Variations and Mosaics on a Theme of Stravinsky* (Indianapolis, April 24, 1975); *A Magic Dwells* for Orch. and Tape (1984); *Voices of the Wild: 1 (Printemps) Rites* (Albany, N.Y., Feb. 26, 1988). **CHAMBER:** *Spectra I* for Percussion and Synthesizer (1971) and *II* for Percussion and Prepared Piano (1972); *Ah-Syn!* for Autoharp and Synthesizer (1976); *Fire and Ice* for Trombone and Piano (1977); *Beneath the Horizon I* for Tuba Quartet and Taped Whales (1978) and *III* for Tuba and Taped Whale Ensemble (1979); *The Inner Universe*, 8 tone poems for Piano and Tape (1981); *Elan! A Dance to All Rising Things from the Earth* for Instrumental Ensemble (1984). **VOCAL:** *3 Songs in Season* for Chorus (1963; rev. 1967); *Rainer Maria Poems*, 3 songs for Voice and Violin (1967; rev. 1974); *Messages* for 4 Soloists, Chorus, and Chamber Ensemble (1974); *Fantasies for Adults and Other Children*, 8 songs for Voice and Amplified Piano (1980); *In Celebration* for Chorus (1987); *Wilderness* for Soprano, Percussionist, and Tape (1989; Baltimore, April 8, 1990); *Everything Awakening Alert and Joyful!* for Narrator and Orch. (1991–92; Berkeley, Feb. 1, 1992). **OTHER:** *The Dance of Shiva* for Tape and Multiple Slide Projections (1989–90); *Rainforest Images*, audio piece (Cincinnati, Feb. 24, 1993; in collaboration with B. McLean).

McNair, Sylvia, talented American soprano; b. Mansfield, Ohio, June 23, 1956. She studied with Margarita Evans at Wheaton (Ill.) College (B.M., 1978) and with Virginia MacWatters (1978–80), John Wustman (1978–82), and Virginia Zeani (1980–82) at the Indiana Univ. School of Music in Bloomington

(M.M., 1982). She made her formal concert debut as a soloist in *Messiah* with the Indianapolis Sym. Orch. (1980). Her operatic debut followed as Sandrina in Haydn's *L'Infedeltà delusa* at N.Y.'s Mostly Mozart Festival (1982). In 1984 she created the title role in Kelterborn's opera *Ophelia* at her European debut at the Schwetzingen Festival, and immediately thereafter sang the role at Berlin's Deutsche Oper. In 1990 she was honored with the Marian Anderson Award. In 1993 she sang Poppea at the Salzburg Festival. On Nov. 27, 1994, she made her Alice Tully Hall recital debut in N.Y. Her extensive repertoire ranges from Monteverdi to contemporary composers.

McNeill, Lloyd, black American artist, musician, painter, photographer, and poet; b. Washington, D.C., April 12, 1935. He studied art and zoology at Morehouse College (B.A., 1961), painting and printmaking at Howard Univ. (M.F.A., 1963), lithography at the École des Beaux Arts in Paris (1964–65), and sound recording and animation at N.Y. Univ. (1974); also studied composition with Hale Smith and flute with Frank Albright, Eric Dolphy, Harold Jones, and others. A true Renaissance man, McNeill excels in a variety of art forms; his drawings were praised by Picasso, whom he befriended in the 1960s, and have been exhibited widely with his paintings; he also appears in readings of his own poetry. He appeared as a congo drummer with Nina Simone and in a variety of ensembles as a flutist; in 1968 he formed the Lloyd McNeill Band. He taught at Dartmouth College, Spelman College, and Howard Univ.; in 1969 he joined the visual arts faculty at Rutgers Univ. (Mason Gross School of the Arts); subsequently was a prof. there. He produced 6 record albums: *Asha, Tanner Suite, Washington Suite, Treasures, Tori,* and *Elegia*; among his other compositions is *Sketches* for Flute (1986); certain movements are often performed separately (e.g., *Tori Suite,* 3 pieces), while others have been arranged for different instrumental combinations, including *The Falling Snow* for Flute and Violin (1987) and *Calypso Facto* for Flute and Violin (1987; also arranged for Harpsichord); he also wrote and performed dance pieces and film scores.

McPhee, Colin (Carhart), outstanding American composer and ethnomusicologist; b. Montreal, Canada, March 15, 1900; d. Los Angeles, Jan. 7, 1964. He studied piano and composition with Harold Randolph and Gustav Strube at the Peabody Cons. in Baltimore (graduated, 1921), then took piano lessons with Arthur Friedheim in Toronto (1921–24); continued his studies with Le Flem (composition) and Philipp (piano) in Paris (1924–26). Returning to the U.S. (1926), he joined the modern movement in N.Y. and was briefly a student of Varèse; wrote scores for the experimental films *H20* and *Mechanical Principles* in 1931. He became infatuated with the gamelan music of Java and Bali; moved to Indonesia in 1931 and, except for brief interruptions, remained there until 1939. He then returned to the U.S. and was a consultant to the Office of War Information during World War II; later was active with the Inst. of Ethnomusicology at the Univ. of Calif. at Los Angeles (1958–64). His *Tabuh-Tabuhan* for 2 Pianos, Orch., and Exotic Percussion, composed and premiered during an interlude in Mexico City (1936), is the quintessential work in his Bali-influenced style. He wrote the books *A House in Bali* (N.Y., 1946), *A Club of Small Men* (N.Y., 1948), and *Music in Bali* (New Haven, 1966).

WORKS: ORCH.: 2 piano concertos: No. 1, *La Mort d'Arthur* (Baltimore, May 26, 1920; not extant) and No. 2 (1923; Toronto, Jan. 15, 1924; not extant); *Sarabande* (1927); 3 syms.: No. 1 in 1 movement (1930; not extant), No. 2, *Pastorale* (1957; Louisville, Jan. 15, 1958), and No. 3 (1960–62; incomplete); *Tabuh-Tabuhan* for 2 Pianos, Orch., and Exotic Percussion (Mexico City, Sept. 4, 1936); *4 Iroquois Dances* (1944); *Transitions* (1954; Vancouver, March 20, 1955); *Nocturne* for Chamber Orch. (N.Y., Dec. 3, 1958); Concerto for Wind Orch. (1959; Pittsburgh, July 1960). **CHAMBER:** *Pastorale and Rondino* for 2 Flutes, Clarinet, Trumpet, and Piano (1925; not extant); Concerto for Piano and Wind Octet (1928; Boston, March 11, 1929). **PIANO:** *4 Piano Sketches* (1916); *Invention* (1926); *Kinesis* (1930); *Balinese Ceremonial Music* for 2 Pianos (1934–38). **VOCAL:** *Sea Shanty Suite* for Baritone, Men's Chorus, 2 Pianos, and Timpani (N.Y., March 13, 1929); *From the Revelation of St. John the Divine* for Men's Chorus, 3 Trumpets, 2 Pianos, and Timpani (1935; N.Y., March 27, 1936; not extant).

BIBL.: W. Riegger, "Adolph Weiss and C. M.," in H. Cowell, ed., *American Composers on American Music* (Stanford, Calif., 1933); C. Sigmon, "C. M.," *American Composers Alliance Bulletin,* XII/1 (1964); R. Mead, *Henry Cowell's New Music 1925–1936* (Ann Arbor, 1981); R. Mueller, *Imitation and Stylization in the Balinese Music of C. M.* (diss., Univ. of Chicago, 1982); C. Oja, *C. M.: Composer in Two Worlds* (Washington, D.C., 1990).

Meader, George, American tenor; b. Minneapolis, July 6, 1888; d. Los Angeles, Dec. 19, 1963. He studied law at the Univ. of Minnesota (graduated, 1908) and concurrently took vocal lessons with Anna Schoen-René; then studied with Pauline Viardot-Garcia in Paris. He made his operatic debut as the Steersman in *Der fliegende Hollander* in Leipzig (1911); then was a member of the Stuttgart Opera until 1919. Returning to America in 1919, he gave recitals before making his operatic debut with the Metropolitan Opera in N.Y. as Victorin in Korngold's *Die tote Stadt* (Nov. 19, 1921); he left the Metropolitan in 1931 and sang in operetta; was particularly successful in Jerome Kern's *Cat and the Fiddle.*

Meale, Richard (Graham), notable Australian composer and teacher; b. Sydney, Aug. 24, 1932. He received training in piano, clarinet, harp, and theory at the New South Wales State Conservatorium of Music in Sydney (1946–55). As a composer, he was autodidact. In 1960 he received a Ford Foundation grant and studied non-Western music at the Inst. of Ethnomusicology at the Univ. of Calif. at Los Angeles. From 1961 to 1969 he was on the music staff of the Australian Broadcasting Corp. He was also active as a pianist and conductor of contemporary music. From 1969 to 1988 he taught at the Elder Conservatorium of Music at the Univ. of Adelaide. In 1974 he received a senior fellowship in composition from the state government of South Australia. He was awarded an Australian Creative Fellowship in 1989. In 1971 he was made a Member of the Order of the British Empire, and in 1985 a Member of the Order of Australia. By the 1960s, Meale was recognized as one of Australia's principal avant-garde composers. His visit to France and Spain, as well as his study of Japanese ritual and theater music, was influential in his development as a composer. By the close of the 1970s, Meale made a profound change of course and became one of Australia's leading composers of the neo-Romantic persuasion.

WORKS: DRAMATIC: *Voss,* opera (1979–86; Adelaide, March 1, 1986); *Mer de Glace,* opera (1986–91; Sydney, Oct. 3, 1991); ballets. **ORCH.:** Flute Concerto (1959); *Sinfonia* for Piano, 4-hands, and Strings (1959); *Homage to García Lorca* for Double String Orch. (Sydney, Oct. 15, 1964); *Images (Nagauta)* (Adelaide, March 1966); *Nocturnes* for Vibraphone, Harp, Celesta, and Orch. (Sydney, April 1, 1967); *Very High Kings* (Sydney, Aug. 13, 1968); *Clouds Now and Then* (Perth, Feb. 1969); *Soon It Will Die* (Sydney, March 29, 1969); *Variations* (Brisbane, March 5, 1970); *Evocations* for Oboe, Chamber Orch., and Violin Obbligato (1973; Zürich, March 8, 1974); *Viridian* (Adelaide, May 18, 1979); Sym. (1994). **CHAMBER:** *Rhapsody* for Violin and Piano (1952); Quintet for Oboe and Strings (1952); *Rhapsody* for Cello and Piano (1953); Horn Sonata (1954), Sonata for Solo Flute (1957); *Divertimento* for Piano Trio (1959); Flute Sonata (1960); *Las Alborados* for Flute, Violin, Horn, and Piano (1963); *Intersections* for Flute, Viola, Vibraphone, and Piano (1965); *Cyphers* for Flute, Viola, Vibraphone, and Piano (1965); *Interiors/Exteriors* for 2 Pianos and 3 Percussion (Adelaide, March 11, 1970); Wind Quintet (1970); *Incredible Floridas (Homage to Arthur Rimbaud)* for Flute, Clarinet, Violin, Cello, Piano, and Percussion (London, June 5, 1971); *Plateau* for Wind Quintet (1971); 2 string quartets: No. 1 (London, Feb. 1975) and No. 2 (Adelaide, March 12, 1980).

PIANO: *Sonatina patetica* (1957); *Orenda* (1959); *Coruscations* (London, April 1971).

Mechem, Kirke (Lewis), American composer, conductor, and lecturer on music; b. Wichita, Kansas, Aug. 16, 1925. He was a pupil of Harold Schmidt, Leonard Ratner, and Sandor Salgo at Stanford Univ. (B.A., 1951) and of Walter Piston, Randall Thompson, and A. Tillman Merritt at Harvard Univ. (M.A., 1953). After serving as director of music at Menlo College in California (1953–56) and as a teacher and conductor at Stanford Univ. (1953–56), he was active in Vienna (1956–57; 1961–63). He was composer-in-residence at the Univ. of San Francisco's Lone Mountain College (1964–65; 1966–72) and a teacher and conductor at San Francisco State College (1965–66). In his works he adopts a candidly euphonious method of composition, not shirking resolvable dissonances and circumtonal patterns, but faithfully observing basic tonality. He became well known as a composer of choral works and instrumental pieces. His opera *Tartuffe* (1977–80) proved an immediate success at its premiere and was subsequently performed more than 100 times.

WORKS: OPERAS: *Tartuffe*, after Molière (1977–80; San Francisco, May 27, 1980); *John Brown* (1988–89). **ORCH.:** 2 syms.: No. 1 (1958–59; San Francisco, Jan. 6, 1965) and No. 2 (1966; San Francisco, March 29, 1967; rev. 1968; San Francisco, Jan. 15, 1969); *Haydn's Return*, fugue and variations on Haydn's *Farewell Symphony* (1960; Santa Rosa, Calif., Feb. 12, 1961); *The Jayhawk*, overture to a mythical comedy (1974; Topeka, Kansas, March 19, 1975). **CHAMBER:** Suite for 2 Violins (1952–53); Suite for Piano (1954); Trio for Oboe, Clarinet, and Bassoon (1955); Trio for Piano, Violin, and Cello (1956–57); Divertimento for Flute, Violin, Viola, and Cello (1958); String Quartet No. 1 (1962–63). **PIANO:** Sonata (1964–65); *Whims*, 15 easy vignettes (1967; also as *Brass Buttons* for Brass Quintet, 1969). **VOCAL:** *Songs of Wisdom*, sacred cantata for 4 Soloists and Chorus (1958–59; San Francisco, March 10, 1960); *The King's Contest*, cantata for 4 Soloists, Chorus, and Orch. or Chamber Ensemble (1960–61; San Rafael, Calif., May 1, 1965; rev. 1972); *The Winged Joy: A Woman's Love by Women Poets* for Mezzo-soprano, Treble Chorus, and Piano (1963–64; Boston, Feb. 21, 1965); *7 Joys of Christmas*, sequence of carols for Soprano, Chorus, and Harp or Keyboard Instrument (San Francisco, Dec. 9, 1964; also for Soprano, Chorus, and Chamber Orch., 1974); *The Shepherd and His Love* for Chorus, Piano, Piccolo, and Viola (Cambridge, Mass., Aug. 17, 1967); *Singing is So Good a Thing: An Elizabethan Recreation*, cantata for Soprano or Tenor, Chorus, and Chamber Orch. or Instrumental Ensemble (1970–71; Elgin, Ill., Jan. 23, 1972); *Speech to a Crowd* for Baritone, Chorus, and Orch. or 2 Pianos (Anaheim, Calif., March 26, 1974); *American Madrigals* for Chorus and Instrumental Ensemble or Piano (1975; Palo Alto, Calif., Feb. 13, 1976); *Songs of the Slave* for Bass-baritone, Chorus, and Orch. (1993; Los Angeles, June 12, 1994); *Barter* for Women's Chorus, Trumpet, and Piano, 4-hands (1994; Florence, July 1995).

Medek, Tilo, German composer; b. Jena, Jan. 22, 1940. He went to Berlin and studied musicology at Humboldt Univ., attended the Deutsche Hochschule für Musik, and received training in composition from Wagner-Régeny at the Deutsche Akademie der Künste. Thereafter he devoted himself to composition.

WORKS: DRAMATIC: OPERAS: *Einzug* (1969); *Katharina Blum* (1984–91; Bielefeld, April 20, 1991). **SINGSPIELS:** *Icke und die Hexe Yu* (1971); *Appetit auf Frühkirschen* (1971). **BALLET:** *David und Goliath* (1972). **ORCH.:** *Triade* (1964); *Porträt eines Tangos* (1968); *Das zögernde Lied* (1970); Flute Concerto (1973); *Grosser Marsch* (1974); 3 cello concertos (1978, 1984, 1992); 2 organ concertos (1979, 1994); *König Johann oder Der Ausstieg* (1980); Violin Concerto (1980); *Konzertstuck* for Timpani and Orch. (1982); *Eisenblätter* (1983); *Rheinische Sinfonie* (1986); Trumpet Concerto (1989); *Zur Lage der Nation* (1990); *Schattenbrenner* for Symphonic Wind Orch. (1991); Percussion Concerto (1993); *Sorbische Wehrstücke* (1994); *Air* for Vibraphone and Orch. (1994); Children's Piano Concerto (1994). **CHAMBER:** 4 wind quintets (1965; 1974–76; 1979; 1989); *Stadtpfeifer, ein Schwanengesang* for Clarinet, Trombone, Cello, and Piano (1973); *Tagtraum* for Flute, Oboe, Trumpet, Violin, Cello, Double Bass, and Piano (1976); *Giebichenstein* for Chamber Ensemble (1976); *Reliquienschrein* for Organ and Percussion (1980); *Spiegelszenen* for Oboe, Clarinet, Horn, Bassoon, and Piano (1986–89); *Bündelungen* for 3 Guitars (1990); *Biedermaier-Variationen* for Flute, Violin, and Cello (1991–92); *Dezett* for Double Wind Quintet (1993); piano pieces; organ music. **VOCAL:** *Altägyptische Liebslieder* for 2 Voices and Orch. (1963); *Johann Wallbergens natürliche Zauberkünste 1768* for Narrator, Soprano, and Salon Orch. (1965); *Todesfuge nach Paul Celan* for Soprano and 16 Voices (1966); *De mirabili effectu amoris/Von der wunderbaren Wirkung der Liebe* for 2 Choruses (1967); *Deutschland 1952* for Children's Chorus (1971); *Kindermesse* for Children's Chorus (1974); *Sinnsprüche des Angelus Silesius*, 12 pieces for 6 Solo Voices or Chamber Chorus (1978); *Gethsemane*, cantata for Soprano, Tenor, Chorus, and Orch. (1980); *Der Greis* for Voice, Violin, Guitar, and Percussion (1992).

Mediņš, family of prominent Latvian musicians, all brothers:

(1) Jāzeps Mediņš, conductor and composer; b. Kaunas, Feb. 13, 1877; d. Riga, June 12, 1947. He studied at the Riga Music Inst. (graduated, 1896), where he later was a teacher and director. He was a conductor at the Riga Theater (1906–11), the Baku Opera (1916–22), and the Latvian National Opera in Riga (1922–25); later taught piano at the Riga Cons. (1945–47).

WORKS: OPERAS: *Vaidelote* (The Priestess; 1922–24; Riga, 1927); *Zemdegi* (The Zemdegs Family; 1947; completed by M. Zarinš). **ORCH.:** Sym. No. 2, *Ziedonī* (In Springtime; 1937); Sym. No. 3 (1941); Violin Concerto (1911). **CHAMBER:** String Quartet (1941); other works. **VOCAL:** Choral works; songs.

BIBL.: M. Zālīte, *J. M.* (Riga, 1951).

(2) Jēkabs Mediņš, conductor, teacher, and composer; b. Riga, March 22, 1885; d. there, Nov. 27, 1971. He studied at the Riga Music Inst. (graduated, 1905) and at the Berlin Hochschule für Musik (1910–14). He taught at the Jelgava Teachers' Inst. (1921–44), and was director of the People's Cons. there (1921–41); later taught choral conducting at the Riga Cons. (1944–71), serving as its rector (1949–51). He wrote an autobiography, *Silueti* (Silhouettes; Riga, 1968).

WORKS: ORCH.: Clarinet Concerto (1948); 2 horn concertos (1949, 1962); Kokle Concerto (1952); Organ Concerto (1954). **OTHER:** Chamber music; cantatas; songs.

(3) Jānis Mediņš, conductor and composer; b. Riga, Oct. 9, 1890; d. Stockholm, March 4, 1966. He studied at the Riga Music Inst. (graduated, 1909). He was a violist and conductor at the Latvian Opera in Riga (1913–15), then a military bandmaster in St. Petersburg (1916–20). He conducted at the Latvian National Opera (1920–28); subsequently was chief conductor of the Latvian Sym. Orch. (1928–44); was also a prof. at the Riga Cons. (1929–44). As the Soviet army approached his homeland (1944), he went to Germany; then settled in Stockholm (1948). He wrote an autobiography, *Toni un pustoni* (Tones and Semitones; Stockholm, 1964). He distinguished himself as a composer of both vocal and instrumental works. His *Mīlas uzvara* (Love's Victory; 1935) was the first Latvian ballet.

WORKS: DRAMATIC: OPERAS: *Uguns un nakts* (Fire and Night; 1st written as 2 operas, 1913–19; Riga, May 26, 1921; rev. as a single opera, 1924); *Dievi un cilvēki* (Gods and Men; Riga, May 23, 1922); *Sprīdītis* (Tom Thumb; Riga, 1927); *Luteklīte* (The Little Darling), children's opera (Riga, 1939). **BALLET:** *Mīlas uzvara* (Love's Victory; 1935). **ORCH.:** Cello Concerto (1928); Piano Concerto (1934); several suites for Orch., including No. 3, *Dzimtene* (The Fatherland; 1933); other orch. pieces and music for band. **CHAMBER:** 2 piano trios (1930, 1958); Cello Sonata (1945); String Quartet (1946); 2 sonatas for Violin and Piano (1946, 1954); various piano pieces. **VOCAL:** 8 cantatas; some 130 songs.

Medtner, Nicolai (actually, **Nikolai Karlovich**), notable Russian pianist and composer of German descent; b. Moscow, Jan.

5, 1880; d. London, Nov. 13, 1951. He first studied piano with his mother, and then with his uncle, Theodore Goedicke; in 1892, entered the Moscow Cons., where he took courses with Sapelnikov and Safonov (piano) and Arensky and Taneyev (composition); graduated in 1900, winning the gold medal; that same year he won the Rubinstein prize in Vienna. For the next 2 years he appeared with much success as a pianist in the European capitals; returning to Russia, he taught at the Moscow Cons. (1902–03; 1909–10; 1914–21); then lived in Berlin and Paris; eventually settled in London (1935). He made tours of the U.S. (1924–25; 1929–30) and the Soviet Union (1927). He publ. a collection of essays as *Muza i moda* (The Muse and Fashion; Paris, 1935; Eng. tr., 1951). In Russian music he was a solitary figure; he never followed the nationalist trend, but endeavored to create a new type of composition, rooted in both the Classical and the Romantic traditions; his sets of fairy tales in sonata form are unique examples of his favorite genre. He wrote his best compositions before he left Russia; although he continued to compose during his residence abroad, his late music lacks the verve and Romantic sincerity that distinguish his earlier works. He wrote almost exclusively for the piano and for the voice. A revival of his music was begun in Russia after his death, and a complete ed. of his works appeared in Moscow (12 vols., 1959–63).

WORKS: 3 piano concertos: No. 1 (1914–18), No. 2 (1920–27; Moscow, March 13, 1927), and No. 3 (1940–43; London, Feb. 19, 1944, composer soloist); Piano Quintet (1904–49); 3 violin sonatas (1909–10; 1926; 1938); numerous piano pieces, including *34 Fairy Tales* (1905–29), 6 sonatas (1896–1915), *Sonaten-Triade* (1904–08), *Sonata romantica* (1931–32), *Sonata minacciosa* (1931–32), and *Sonata idillica* (1935); also sets of piano pieces, including *4 Lyric Fragments* (1910–11), 3 sets of *Forgotten Melodies* (1918–20), and 4 sets of *Romantic Sketches for the Young* (1932); also 107 songs.

BIBL.: V. Yakovlev, *N. M.* (Moscow, 1927); R. Holt, *M. and His Music* (London, 1948); idem, ed., *N. M. (1879–1951): A Tribute to His Art and Personality* (London, 1955); E. Dolinskaya, *N. M.* (Moscow, 1966); H. Milne, "N. M.: A Centenary Appraisal," *Music and Musicians*, XXVIII/5 (1980); B. Martyn, *N. M.: His Life and Music* (Brookfield, Vt., 1995).

Meester, Louis de, Belgian composer; b. Roeselare, Oct. 28, 1904; d. Ghent, Dec. 12, 1987. He was mainly autodidact as a composer. After serving as director of the Meknes Cons. in French Morocco (1933–37), he returned to Belgium and studied with Absil. From 1945 to 1961 he worked for the Belgian Radio. He was director of the Inst. for Psychoacoustics and Electronic Music at the Univ. of Ghent from 1961 to 1969.

WORKS: DRAMATIC: *Van een trotse vogel*, musical comedy (1948); *La Grande Tentation de Saint Antoine*, opera buffa (1957; Antwerp, Nov. 11, 1961); *2 is te weining, 3 is te veel* (2 is too little, 3 is too much), opera (1966; Palermo, June 13, 1969); *Paradijsgeuzen* (Beggars in Heaven), opera (1966; Ghent, March 26, 1967); incidental music. **ORCH.:** *Magreb* for Viola and Orch. (1946); *Capriccio* (1948); *Sprookjesmuziek* (1949); *Sinfonietta Buffa* (1950); 2 piano concertos (1952, 1956); *Musica per archi* (1955); *Amalgames* (1956); *Marine* (1957); Concertino for 2 String Orchs. (1965); *Serenade* for Flute, Oboe, and Strings (1967); *Tombeau voor P.-P. Rubens* (1977). **CHAMBER:** Cello Sonatina (1945); *Divertimento* for Wind Quintet (1946); 3 string quartets (1947, 1949, 1954); String Trio (1951); *Tafelmuziek* for Flute, Oboe, Violin, Viola, and Cello (1953); Sonata for Solo Guitar (1954); Violin Sonata (1957); *Serenade* for Harpsichord and 11 Strings (1958–59); *Postludium* for Organ and Brass (1959); *Divertimento* for Piano Quartet (1970); *3 Interludes* for Flute and Organ (1975); piano pieces. **VOCAL:** *La Voix du silence*, cantata for Baritone, Narrator, Women's Chorus, and Chamber Orch. (1951–54); *Ballade van de gebarste trommel* for Narrator and Orch. (1973); choruses. **OTHER:** Electronic pieces.

Meeuwisse, Willy, Dutch pianist and composer; b. Arnhem, Dec. 18, 1914; d. Amsterdam, Aug. 6, 1952. He was a student of Sem Dresden in Amsterdam. His *Suite of Old Dutch Dances* for Piano Solo enjoyed a certain popularity; also was active as a concert pianist.

Méfano, Paul, French composer; b. Basra, Iraq, March 6, 1937. He studied at the Paris Cons. with Dandelot, Messiaen, Martenot, and Milhaud; attended seminars of Boulez, Stockhausen, and Pousseur in Basel. He received a grant from the Harkness Foundation for residence in the U.S. (1966–68) and in Berlin (1968–69). In his music, he pursues a constructivist style, with an emphasis on rhythmic percussion and electronic sound; the influences of Stravinsky and Varèse are particularly in evidence.

WORKS: OPERA: *Micromegas* for 4 Singers, Narrator, 3 Actors, 10 Instruments, and Tape, after Voltaire (1979). **ORCH.:** *Incidences* for Orch. and Piano (1960); *Interférences* for Chamber Group (1966). **CHAMBER:** *Ondes, Espaces mouvants* for 12 Players (Metz, Nov. 20, 1975); *Mouvement calme* for String Quartet (1976); *Traits suspendus* for Double Bass and Flute (1980). **VOCAL:** *Paraboles* for Soprano and Chamber Ensemble (Paris, Jan. 20, 1965); *Aurelia* for 3 Choruses, 3 Orchs., and 3 Conductors (1968); *Lignes* for Bass, Brass, Percussion, Bassoon, and Amplified Double Bass (1968); *La Cérémonie* for 3 Solo Voices, Instrumental Groups, and 12-voice Speaking Chorus (1970); *La Messe des voleurs* for 4 Solo Voices, Chamber Ensemble, and Electronic Equipment (Royan Festival, March 28, 1972). **ELECTRONIC:** *Intersection* for 2 Generators and Ring Modulator (1971).

Mehta, Mehli, Indian violinist and conductor, father of **Zubin Mehta**; b. Bombay, Sept. 25, 1908. He studied at the Univ. of Bombay and at Trinity College of Music in London (licentiate, 1929). He founded the Bombay Sym. Orch. in 1935; was its concertmaster (until 1945) and then its conductor (until 1955); subsequently was assistant concertmaster of the Hallé Orch. in Manchester (1955–59). He settled in the U.S., where he played in the Curtis String Quartet in Philadelphia (1959–64); then went to Los Angeles, where he founded the American Youth Sym. Orch. (1964); also taught at the Univ. of Calif. there (1964–76), serving as conductor of its sym. and chamber orchs.

Mehta, Zubin, notable Indian conductor, son of **Mehli Mehta;** b. Bombay, April 29, 1936. His first mentor was his father. He received training in violin and piano in childhood, and at 16 had his first taste of conducting when he led a rehearsal of the Bombay Sym. Orch. He studied medicine in Bombay but the lure of music compelled him to abandon his medical training to pursue musical studies at the Vienna Academy of Music. While playing double bass in its orch., he found a conducting mentor in Swarowsky. During the summers of 1956 and 1957, he also studied conducting with Carlo Zecchi and Alceo Galliera at the Accademia Musicale Chigiana in Siena. In 1957 he made his professional conducting debut with the Niederösterreichisches Tonkünstler-Orch. in Vienna. He won the 1st Royal Liverpool Phil. conducting competition in 1958, and then served for a season as its assistant conductor. In the summer of 1959 he attended the Berkshire Music Center in Tanglewood, where he took 2nd prize in conducting. He made his North American debut conducting the Philadelphia Orch. in 1960. Later that year his successful appearances with the Montreal Sym. Orch. led to his appointment as its music director in 1961. That same year he also became assoc. conductor of the Los Angeles Phil. His London debut came later in 1961 when he appeared as a guest conductor with the Royal Phil. In 1962 he became music director of the Los Angeles Phil. while retaining his Montreal post until 1967. He made his first appearance at the Salzburg Festival in 1962. He first conducted opera in Montreal in 1964 when he led a performance of *Tosca*. On Dec. 29, 1965, he made his Metropolitan Opera debut in N.Y. conducting *Aida*. In 1966 he conducted for the first time at Milan's La Scala. He was named music advisor of the Israel Phil. in 1968. His success with that ensemble led to his appointment as its music director in 1977 and as its music director for life in 1981. He led it on major tours of Europe, North and South America, and the Far East. In 1977 he made his debut at London's Covent Garden conducting *Otello*. During his tenure in Los Angeles, Mehta was glamorized in the colorful Hollywood manner. This glamorization process was abetted by his genuine personableness and his reputation as a bon vivant. As a conductor, he secured the international profile of the Los Angeles Phil. through recordings and major tours. He became particularly known for his effulgent and expansive readings of the Romantic repertoire, which he invariably conducted from memory. His success in Los Angeles led the management of the N.Y. Phil. to appoint him as music director in 1978 with the hope that he could transform that ensemble in the wake of the austere Boulez tenure. Although Mehta served as music director of the N.Y. Phil. until 1991, he was unable to duplicate the success he attained in Los Angeles. Critics acknowledged his abilities but found his interpretations often indulgent and wayward. On July 7, 1990, Mehta served as conductor of the 3 tenors extravaganza in Rome with Carreras, Domingo, and Pavarotti in a concert telecast live to the world. He returned to the N.Y. Phil. for its 150th anniversary concert on Dec. 7, 1992, when he conducted a performance of *Till Eulenspiegels lustige Streich*. On July 16, 1994, he was conductor of the Carreras, Domingo, and Pavarotti reunion when he led the Los Angeles Phil. in a concert again telecast live around the globe. In 1995 he was appointed Generalmusikdirektor of the Bavarian State Opera in Munich, which post he was to assume in 1998.

BIBL.: M. Bookspan and R. Yockey, *Z.: The Z. M. Story* (N.Y., 1978).

Meier, Johanna, American soprano; b. Chicago, Feb. 13, 1938. She was a scholarship student at the Manhattan School of Music in N.Y. She made her debut with the N.Y. City Opera in 1969 as the Countess in Strauss's *Capriccio*; continued to appear there regularly until 1979; made her Metropolitan Opera debut in N.Y. as Strauss's Ariadne on April 9, 1976, and subsequently appeared there regularly; also sang opera in Chicago, Cincinnati, Pittsburgh, Seattle, and Baltimore. In Europe, she had guest engagements in opera in Zürich, Vienna, Hamburg, Berlin, and Bayreuth; also appeared in concerts.

Meier, Waltraud, distinguished German mezzo-soprano; b. Würzburg, Jan. 9, 1956. She was a pupil of Dietger Jacob in Cologne. In 1976 she made her operatic debut as Cherubino at the Würzburg Opera, singing there until joining the Mannheim National Theater in 1978; then was a member of the Dortmund Opera (1980–83). In 1980 she appeared as Fricka at the Teatro Colón in Buenos Aires, and in 1984 sang Brangäne at the Paris Opéra and Eboli at London's Covent Garden. From 1984 to 1987 she appeared at the Bayreuth Festivals, where she won notable success as Kundry. From 1986 she sang at the Württemberg State Theater in Stuttgart. In 1987 she made her Metropolitan Opera debut in N.Y. as Fricka, and then sang Venus at the Vienna State Opera. In 1993 she sang the role of Isolde at Bayreuth. In addition to her roles in operas by Wagner, Verdi, and Strauss, she is a notable concert artist.

Meitus, Yuli (Sergievich), eminent Ukrainian composer; b. Elizavetgrad, Jan. 28, 1903. He studied piano at a local music school, where he soon began to compose. Later he moved to Kharkov, where he composed music to theatrical productions on contemporary revolutionary subjects. In 1924 he wrote a melodeclamation commemorating the death of Lenin, and in 1930 he composed a symphonic suite, *Dneprostroy*, on the subject of the building of the hydroelectric station on the Dnieper River; in the score he included a number of percussion instruments representing various mechanical aspects of the project. During the Russian Civil War (1918–20), he wrote the opera *Perekop*, on the subject of the protracted struggle between the red and white armies on the Crimean Peninsula (Kiev, Jan. 20, 1939). When Russia was invaded by the Nazi armies (1941), Meitus was forced to move to Turkestan in Central Asia. There he produced the operas *Gaidamaki* (Ashkhabad, Oct. 15, 1943) and *Leili and Medzhiun* (Ashkhabad, Nov. 2, 1946). Returning to the Ukraine, he produced the operas *The Young Guard* (Kiev, Nov. 7, 1947), *Dawn over the River Dvina* (Kiev, July 5, 1955), *Stolen Happiness* (Lvov, Galicia, Sept. 10, 1960), and *The Daughter of the Wind* (Odessa, Oct. 24, 1965). There followed *The Brothers Ulyanov* (Ufa, Nov. 25, 1967), on the subject of the family of Lenin, whose real name was Ulyanov (Lenin's brother was executed by hanging for participation in a conspiracy to kill the Czar). Other operas include *Makhtunkuli*, on Turkmenian themes (Ashkhabad, Dec. 29, 1962); *Yaroslav the Wise*, on the rule of an early Russian chieftain (Donetsk, March 3, 1973); *Richard Sorge*, on the life of a German Soviet agent working in Nazi circles in Tokyo (Lvov, 1976); *Ivan the Terrible* (1980–82); and *Maria Volkonskaya*, on the wife of one of the Decembrist rebels against Czar Nicholas I; she followed her husband to his Siberian exile (1986–89). Apart from operas, which constitute his main contribution to Soviet music, Meitus composed a number of instrumental works, which were invariably connected with themes of socialist structures; in this connection, he joined the Assn. of Revolutionary Ukrainian Composers. It was only when such proletarian groups were disbanded by the Soviet government in 1932 that Meitus devoted himself mainly to opera. He also composed a considerable number of choruses and solo songs to Russian and Ukrainian words. Stylistically, most of his music follows the tenets of socialist realism, observing clear tonality but freely using dissonant harmonies when necessary for dramatic effect; he also applied considerable variety in asymmetrical meters and rhythms, especially in his works based on Turkmenian themes.

BIBL.: Y. Malishev, *Y. M., Essays on His Work* (Moscow, 1962); L. Arkhimovich and I. Mamchur, *Y. M.* (Moscow, 1983).

Mekeel, Joyce, American harpsichordist and composer; b. New Haven, Conn., July 6, 1931. She studied at the Longy School of Music in Cambridge, Mass. (1952–55); received instruction in keyboard playing from Boulanger at the Paris Cons. (1955–57), from Leonhardt (1957), and from Kirkpatrick (1957–59); took courses in theory and composition at Yale Univ. (B.M., 1959; M.M., 1960) and studied privately with Earl Kim (1960–62); completed her education at Boston Univ. (Ph.D., 1983, with the diss. *Social Influences on Changing Audience Behavior in the Mid-Victorian London Theatre*). She made appearances as a harpsichordist, and was a composer for several dance and theater companies (1961–75); taught at the New England Cons. of Music in Boston (1964–70) and at Boston Univ. (1970–92).

WORKS: DRAMATIC: *Jaywalk* for Viola and Dancer (1969); *Moveable Feast* (1973–75; in collaboration with P. Earls and L. Davidson); *Kisses and Kazoos* (1977); *Alarums and Excursions* for Violin, Viola, Cello, Piano, Flute, Clarinet, Percussion, and Actress/Mezzo-soprano (1978); *Museum* (1980); *Sigil* for String Quintet, Clarinet, English Horn, 2 Horns, 2 Tubas, Harp, Actor, and Actress/Mezzo-soprano (1981); *Journeys of Remembrance* (1986). **ORCH.:** *String Figures Disentangled by a Flute* for Flute and Strings (Boston, April 2, 1969); *Vigil* (Boston, Oct. 19, 1978). **CHAMBER:** *Spindrift* for String Quartet (1970); *Hommages* for Brass Quintet (1973); *Rune* for Flute and Percussion (1976); *Tessera* for String Quintet, Saxophone, English Horn, Contrabassoon, Trumpet, Horn, and Harps (1981); *Fertile Vicissitudes* for Harp and Oboe (1981); *Voices* for Violin, Clarinet, and Piano (1983); *An Insomnia of Owls* for Woodwind Quintet (1985); numerous solo works. **VOCAL:** *White Silence* for Chorus (1965); *Waterwalk* for Speaking Chorus (1970); *Corridors of Dream* for Mezzo-soprano, Flute, Clarinet, Harp, Viola, and Cello (1972); *Toward the Source* for Chorus and Orch. (1974); *Serena* for Mezzo-soprano, Speaker, and Prepared Piano (1975); songs.

Melartin, Erkki (Gustaf), Finnish composer; b. Käkisälmi, Feb. 7, 1875; d. Pukinmäki, Feb. 14, 1937. He was a pupil of Wegelius at the Helsinki Music Inst. and of Robert Fuchs in Vienna. He taught theory at the Helsinki Music Inst. (1898; 1901–07); succeeded Wegelius as director in 1911, and remained at this post until 1936. His compositions are marked by a lyrical strain, with thematic materials often drawn from Finnish folk songs.

WORKS: DRAMATIC: *Aino*, opera (1907; Helsinki, Dec. 10, 1909); *Sininen helmi* (The Blue Pearl), ballet (1930); incidental music. **ORCH.:** 8 syms. (1902; 1904; 1906–7; 1912; *Sinfonia brevis*, 1916; 1924–25; 2 unfinished); 3 symphonic poems; 3 lyric suites; Violin Concerto; Serenade for Strings; *Karjalaisia kuvia* (Karelian Pictures). **CHAMBER:** 4 string quartets; Quartet for 2 Trumpets, Trombone, and Horn; Quartet for 4 Horns; Trio for Flute, Clarinet, and Bassoon; 2 violin sonatas; Sonata for Flute and Harp; piano pieces; violin works. **VOCAL:** Choruses; about 300 songs.

Melba, Dame Nellie (actually, **Helen Porter Mitchell**), famous Australian soprano; b. Burnley, near Richmond, May 19, 1861; d. Sydney, Feb. 23, 1931. Her father, who had decided objections to anything connected with the stage, was nevertheless fond of music and proud of his daughter's talent. When she was only 6 years old he allowed her to sing at a concert in the Melbourne Town Hall, but would not consent to her having singing lessons; instead, she was taught piano, violin, and harp, and even had instruction in harmony and composition. As she grew older she frequently played the organ in a local church, and was known among her friends as an excellent pianist, while all the time her chief desire was to study singing. Not until after her marriage in 1882 to Captain Charles Armstrong was she able to gratify her ambition, when she began to study with a local teacher, Cecchi; her first public appearance as a singer was on May 17, 1884, in a benefit concert in Melbourne. The next year her father received a government appointment in London, and she accompanied him, determined to begin an operatic career. She studied with Mathilde Marchesi in Paris. Melba gave her first concert in London (June 1, 1886). Her debut as Gilda at the Théâtre Royal de la Monnaie in Brussels (Oct. 13, 1887) created a veritable sensation; the famous impresario Augustus Harris immediately engaged her for the spring season at London's Covent Garden, where she appeared on May 24, 1888, as Lucia, to only a half-full house. However, she scored a major success at the Paris Opéra as Ophelia in Thomas's *Hamlet* (May 8, 1889); then sang with great success in St. Petersburg (1891), Milan (La Scala, 1893; immense triumph over a carefully planned opposition), Stockholm and Copenhagen (Oct. 1893), N.Y. (Metropolitan Opera, as Lucia, Dec. 4, 1893), and Melbourne (Sept. 27, 1902). From her first appearance at Covent Garden she sang there off and on until 1914; besides being one of the most brilliant stars of several seasons at the Metropolitan Opera in N.Y., she also sang with Damrosch's Opera Co. (1898) and at Hammerstein's Manhattan Opera (1906–07 and 1908–09), and made several transcontinental concert tours of the U.S. Bemberg wrote for her *Elaine* (1892), and Saint-Saëns, *Hélène* (1904), in both of which she created the title roles. In 1915 she began teaching at the Albert Street Conservatorium in Melbourne; returned to Covent Garden for appearances in 1919, 1923, and a farewell performance on June 8, 1926. Then she returned to Australia and retired from the stage. Melba was by nature gifted with a voice of extraordinary beauty and bell-like purity; through her art she made this fine instrument perfectly even throughout its entire extensive compass and wonderfully flexible, so that she executed the most difficult fioriture without the least effort. As an actress she did not rise above the conventional, and for this reason she was at her best in parts demanding brilliant coloratura (Gilda, Lucia, Violetta, Rosina, Lakmé et al.). On a single occasion she attempted the dramatic role of Brünnhilde in *Siegfried* (Metropolitan Opera, N.Y., Dec. 30, 1896), and met with disaster. In 1918 she was created a Dame Commander of the Order of the British Empire. She was a typical representative of the golden era of opera; a prima donna assoluta, she exercised her powers over the public with perfect self-assurance and a fine command of her singing voice. Among her other distinguished roles were Mimi, Else, Nedda, Aida, Desdemona, and Marguerita. As a measure of Melba's universal popularity, it may be mentioned that her name was attached to a delicious dessert (Peach Melba) and also to Melba toast, patented in 1929 by Bert Weil. A film based on her life was produced in 1953 with Patrice Munsel as Melba. She wrote an autobiography, *Melodies and Memories* (London, 1925).

BIBL.: A. Murphy, *M., A Biography* (London, 1909; contains a chapter on singing written by Melba); P. Colson, *M., An Unconventional Biography* (London, 1931); J. Wechsberg, *Red Plush and Black Velvet: The Story of M. and Her Times* (Boston, 1961); G. Hutton, *M.* (Melbourne, 1962); J. Hetherington, *M.* (London, 1967); W. Moran, *N. M.: A Contemporary Review* (Westport, Conn., 1985); T. Radic, *M.: The Voice of Australia* (Melbourne and London, 1986).

Melcer (-Szczawiński), Henryk, esteemed Polish pianist, conductor, teacher, and composer; b. Kalisch, Sept. 21, 1869; d. Warsaw, April 18, 1928. He was a pupil of Noszkowski (composition) and Strobl (piano) at the Warsaw Music Inst. (graduated, 1890); after touring Russia as an accompanist, he received further piano training from Leschetizky in Vienna. After successful concert tours of Russia, Germany, and France, he taught at the Helsinki Cons. (1895–96) and was a prof. at the Lemberg Cons. (1896–99); was director of the Łódź music society (1899–1902) and director-conductor of the Łódź Phil. (from 1902); was conductor of the Warsaw Phil. (1910–12) and Opera (1915–16). He subsequently taught at the Warsaw Cons. (from 1919), serving as head of piano studies (until 1928), orchestration (1925–26), and composition (1925–28).

WORKS: 2 operas: *Protasilas i Laodamia* (1902; Paris, 1925) and *Marja* (Warsaw, Nov. 16, 1904); 2 piano concertos (1895, 1898); *Pani Twardowska*, ballad for Tenor, Chorus, and Orch. (1898); Piano Trio (1895); Violin Sonata (c.1896); piano pieces; songs.

BIBL.: J. Reiss, *H. M.* (Warsaw, 1949).

Melchers, H(enrik) Melcher, Swedish composer and teacher; b. Stockholm, May 30, 1882; d. there, April 9, 1961. He studied at the Stockholm Cons., taking his diploma as a music teacher in 1903. After further studies with Lindegren (composition, 1903–05), he attended the Paris Cons. (1908–12). In 1913 he took his diploma as an organist and precentor in Visby. He later took conducting courses in Brussels and Sonderhausen in 1921. In 1926 he joined the faculty of the Stockholm Cons., where he was a prof. from 1939 to 1947. In 1932 he was made a member of the Royal Academy of Music in Stockholm. In his music, Melchers was greatly influenced by his Parisian sojourn. On the whole, his output followed along Romantic lines.

WORKS: *Swedish Rhapsody* for Orch. (1914); Sym. in D minor (Stockholm, April 1926); symphonic poems; 2 piano concertos; Violin Concerto; String Quartet; Violin Sonata; Cello Sonata; songs.

Melchior, Lauritz (real name, **Lebrecht Hommel**), celebrated Danish-born American tenor; b. Copenhagen, March 20, 1890; d. Santa Monica, Calif., March 18, 1973. He studied with Paul Bang at the Royal Opera School in Copenhagen, making his operatic debut in the baritone role of Silvio in *Pagliacci* at the Royal Theater there (April 2, 1913); continued on its roster while studying further with Vilhelm Herold, and then made his tenor debut as Tannhäuser (Oct. 8, 1918). In 1921 he went to London to continue his training with Beigel, and then studied with Grenzebach in Berlin and Bahr-Mildenburg in Munich. On May 24, 1924, he made his Covent Garden debut in London as Siegmund, returning there regularly from 1926 to 1939. He was in Bayreuth in 1924 to study with Kittel; made his first appearance at the Festspielhaus there as Siegfried on July 23, 1924, and continued to make appearances there until 1931. On Feb. 17, 1926, he made his Metropolitan Opera debut in N.Y. as Tannhäuser, and quickly established himself as one of its principal artists; with the exception of the 1927–28 season, he sang there regularly until his farewell performance as Lohengrin on Feb. 2, 1950. In 1947 he became a naturalized American citizen. After the close of his operatic career, Melchior appeared on

Broadway and in films; also continued to give concerts. He was accorded a preeminent place among the Wagnerian Heldentenors of his era.

BIBL.: H. Hanse, *L. M.: A Discography* (Copenhagen, 1965; 2nd ed., 1972); S. Emmons, *Tristanissimo: The Authorized Biography of Heroic Tenor L. M.* (N.Y., 1990).

Melichar, Alois, Austrian music critic and composer; b. Vienna, April 18, 1896; d. Munich, April 9, 1976. He studied theory at the Vienna Academy of Music with Joseph Marx (1917–20) and at the Hochschule für Musik in Berlin with Schreker (1920–23). From 1923 to 1926 he was in the Caucasus, where he collected materials on Caucasian folk songs; then lived in Berlin and Vienna. As a composer, he followed the safe footpath of Reger, Pfitzner, and Graener; he wrote a symphonic poem, *Der Dom* (1934); *Rhapsodie über ein schwedisches Volkslied* (1939); *Lustspiel-Ouvertüre* (1942); lieder; film music. As a music critic, he acquired notoriety by his intemperate attacks on better composers than himself. His publications, written in his virulent, polemical manner, include *Die unteilbare Musik* (Vienna, 1952), *Musik in der Zwangsjacke* (Vienna, 1958), and (particularly vicious) *Schönberg und die Folgen* (Vienna, 1960).

Melik-Pashayev, Alexander (Shamilievich), noted Russian conductor; b. Tiflis, Oct. 23, 1905; d. Moscow, June 18, 1964. He studied with N. Tcherepnin at the Tiflis Cons. He was pianist and concertmaster of the Tiflis Opera orch. (1921–24), and then its conductor; after conducting studies with Gauk at the Leningrad Cons. (graduated, 1930), he returned to the Tiflis Opera as chief conductor (1930–31); then conducted at Moscow's Bolshoi Theater, later serving as its chief conductor (1953–62). He was highly esteemed for his interpretations of Russian operas; was awarded 2 Stalin prizes (1942, 1943) and was made a People's Artist of the U.S.S.R. (1951).

Melikov, Arif (Djangirovich), Russian composer; b. Baku, Sept. 13, 1933. He studied the tar (an oriental lute) at the Baku Zeinalla Music College (1948–53) and composition with Kara Karayev at the Gadjibekov Azerbaijan State Cons. (1953–58); in 1965 he joined its faculty. His early music hewed to the tenets of socialist realism, representational and stylistically inoffensive to untutored ears. In his later works, he made use of various modern techniques.

WORKS: DRAMATIC: BALLETS: *The Legend of Love* (Leningrad, March 23, 1961); *The 2* (1969); *Poem of 2 Hearts* (1983). **MUSICAL:** *Waves* (1967). Also incidental music to plays; film scores. **ORCH.: SYMPHONIC POEMS:** *Fairy Tale* (1957); *In Memory of Fizuli* (1959); *Metamorphoses* (1963); *Motherland* for Voice and Orch. (1964); *The Last Pass* (1976); *Remember* (1978). **OTHER ORCH.:** Flute Concertino (1956); 6 syms. (1958; 1969; 1975; 1977; 1979–82; 1985); *2 Suites* (1965); *Suite* for Folk Orch. (1967); *Pictures* for Folk Orch. (1967); *8 Pieces* (1968); *2 Suites* (1970); *12 Pieces* (1971); *Symphonic Dances* (1976). **CHAMBER:** *Suite* for Violin and Piano (1954); *Scherzo* for Violin and Piano (1954); Sonata for Solo Violin (1980); *Scherzo* for 2 Pianos (1983). **VOCAL:** *Voice of the Earth*, cantata (1972); choruses; songs.

Melikyan, Romanos Hovakimi, Armenian composer; b. Kiziyar, northern Caucasus, Dec. 1, 1883; d. Yerevan, March 30, 1935. He studied at the Rostov College of Music (graduated, 1905), then with Ippolitov-Ivanov, Taneyev, and Yavorsky in Moscow (1905–07); subsequently with Kalafati and Steinberg at the St. Petersburg Cons. (1910–14). He founded the Tiflis Music League (1908); became director of music at the Armenian House of Culture in Moscow (1918), then founded the Yerevan Cons. (1923); was also founder-director of the Yerevan Theater of Opera and Ballet (1933). He was a major figure in Armenian music circles; as a composer, he was highly regarded for his songs and folk song arrangements.

BIBL.: G. Geodakyan, *R. M.* (Yerevan, 1960); K. Tordjyan, *R. M.* (Yerevan, 1960).

Melis, Carmen, Italian soprano; b. Cagliari, Aug. 14, 1885; d. Longone al Segrino, Dec. 19, 1967. She was a student of Teresina Singer and Carlo Carignani in Milan, of Cotogni in Rome, and of Jean de Reszke in Paris. In 1905 she made her operatic debut in Novara, and then sang in Naples (1906) and Russia (1907). On Nov. 26, 1909, she made her U.S. debut as Tosca at the Manhattan Opera in N.Y., and then appeared in Boston, Chicago, and other U.S. cities. In 1913 she made her first appearance at London's Covent Garden. She later sang at Milan's La Scala, and sang regularly at the Rome Opera. Following her retirement in 1935, she taught voice. Among her most impressive roles were Musetta, Thaïs, Nedda, Zazà, Mistress Ford, Fedora, and the Marschallin.

Melkus, Eduard, Austrian violinist, conductor, and teacher; b. Baden-bei-Wien, Sept. 1, 1928. He studied violin with Ernst Moravec at the Vienna Academy of Music (1943–53) and musicology with Schenk at the Univ. of Vienna (1951–53); continued his violin training with Firmin Touche in Paris (1953), Alexander Schaichet in Zürich (1956), and Peter Rybar in Winterthur (1958). After playing in several Swiss orchs., he became prof. of violin and viola at the Vienna Hochschule für Musik (1958); also toured as a soloist in Europe and the U.S.; founded the Capella Academica of Vienna (1965), which he conducted in performances of works ranging from the Renaissance to the early Classical era, utilizing modern instruments as well as original instruments or reproductions.

Mell, Gertrud Maria, Swedish composer, organist, and sea captain; b. Ed, Aug. 15, 1947. She studied at the Lund Cons. (diploma in organ, 1967) and in Stockholm (music teacher's diploma, 1968); later pursued training at the Univ. of Marine Officers in Göteborg (1978–81), passing examinations as a mate (1979), ship mechanic (1979), sea captain (master mariner, 1981), radio telephone operator (1982), and ship engineer (1985). She began her career as a church organist in Ed at age 17 and became adept at improvisation; was organist in Töftedal (1967–76) and also taught music in Ed (1969–71) and Bengtsfors (1972–76). After working as a seaperson on transatlantic ships (1976–78), she pursued both music and navigation; served as organist of the Pater Noster Church in Göteborg (from 1982); also appeared as a recitalist in concert, radio, and television settings, and even made an appearance as a pop singer in her recording *Mermaid* (1977).

WORKS: ORCH.: 4 syms. (1964, 1965, 1966, 1967); *Melodie aus dem Meer*, symphonic poem (1980; also for Violin and Piano, 1976); *Solvind* (1984; also for Flute and Piano, 1975); *Celeste cordialis* for Strings (1985); *Andante*, symphonic poem (1988); *Pacem* for Strings (1990). **OTHER:** String Quartet No. 1 (1969); piano pieces, including *Fantasie* (1961) and *Impromptu* (1971); organ music; improvisations for both piano and organ; choral works, including *Pater noster* for Soloists, Chorus, and Instruments (1983); songs; various pop pieces.

Mellers, Wilfrid (Howard), English musicologist and composer; b. Leamington, Warwickshire, April 26, 1914. He studied at the Univ. of Cambridge (B.A., 1936; M.A., 1939); was a pupil in composition of Wellesz and Rubbra; received his D.Mus. from the Univ. of Birmingham (1960). He was a lecturer in music at Downing College, Cambridge (1945–48); after serving as a staff tutor in the extramural dept. at the Univ. of Birmingham (1948–59), he served as Andrew W. Mellon Prof. of Music at the Univ. of Pittsburgh (1960–63); then was prof. of music at the Univ. of York (1964–81). In 1982 he was made an Officer of the Order of the British Empire.

WRITINGS: *Music and Society: England and the European Tradition* (London, 1946); *Studies in Contemporary Music* (London, 1947); *François Couperin and the French Classical Tradition* (London, 1950; 2nd ed., rev., 1987); *Music in the Making* (London, 1952); *Romanticism and the 20th Century* (London, 1957; 2nd ed., rev., 1988); *The Sonata Principle* (London, 1957; 2nd ed., rev., 1988); *Music in a New Found Land: Themes and Developments in the History of American Music* (London, 1964;

2nd ed., rev., 1987); *Harmonious Meeting: A Study of the Relationship between English Music, Poetry and Theatre, c.1600–1900* (London, 1965); *Caliban Reborn: Renewal in Twentieth-Century Music* (N.Y., 1967); *Twilight of the Gods: The Music of the Beatles* (N.Y., 1973); *Bach and the Dance of God* (N.Y., 1980); *Beethoven and the Voice of God* (London, 1983); *A Darker Shade of Pale: A Backdrop to Bob Dylan* (London, 1984); *Angels of the Night: Popular Female Singers of Our Time* (London, 1986); *The Masks of Orpheus: Seven Stages in the Story of European Music* (Manchester, England, and Wolfeboro, N.H., 1987); *Le Jardin Parfume: Homage to Frederic Mompou* (1989); *Vaughan Williams and the Vision of Albion* (London, 1989); *Percy Grainger* (Oxford, 1992); *Francis Poulenc* (Oxford, 1994).

WORKS: DRAMATIC: OPERAS: *The Tragicall History of Christopher Marlowe* (1952); *The Shepherd's Daughter*, chamber opera (1953–54); *Mary Easter*, ballad opera (1957). **MONODRAMA:** *The Ancient Wound* (Victoria, British Columbia, July 27, 1970). **ORCH.:** *Sinfonia ricercata* (1947); *Alba, in 9 Metamorphoses* for Flute and Orch. (1961); *Noctambule and Sun Dance* for Wind Sym. (1966); *Shaman Songs* for Jazz Paraphernalia (1980); *The Wellspring of Loves*, concerto for Violin and String Orch. (1981); *The Spring of the Year* for Double String Orch. (1985); *Hortus Rosarium* for 11 Solo Strings (1986). **CHAMBER:** String Trio (1945); Viola Sonata (1946); *Eclogue* for Treble Recorder, Violin, Cello, and Harpsichord (1961); Trio for Flute, Cello, and Piano (1963); *Ghost Dance* for Flute, Viola, and Harpsichord (1972); *Aubade for Indra* for Clarinet and String Quartet (1981); *The Happy Meadow*, eclogue for Flute and Guitar (1986); piano pieces. **VOCAL:** *Voice of the Earth*, cantata (1972); choruses; songs.

Melles, Carl, Hungarian conductor; b. Budapest, July 15, 1926. He received his musical training in Budapest. In 1951 he was appointed conductor of the Hungarian State Orch. and the Sym. Orch. of Hungarian Radio and Television; was also a prof. at the Budapest Academy of Music (1954–56). After the abortive rebellion in 1956, he led the Radio Orch. of Luxembourg (1958–60); also conducted at Bayreuth and Salzburg. He eventually made his home in Vienna and became a regular conductor of the Vienna Sym. Orch. and on the Austrian Radio.

Mellnäs, Arne, Swedish composer and teacher; b. Stockholm, Aug. 30, 1933. He entered the Stockholm Musikhögskolan in 1953, where he studied composition with Koch, Larsson, Blomdahl, and Wallner (1958–61). He also was a student of Blacher at the Berlin Hochschule für Musik (1959) and of Deutsch in Paris (1961). After further training with Ligeti in Vienna (1962), he worked at the San Francisco Tape Music Center (1964). He made Stockholm the center of his activities, where he taught at the Citizen's School (1961–63) and at the Musikhögskolan (from 1963). From 1983 he also served as chairman of the Swedish section of the ISCM. In 1984 he was elected a member of the Royal Swedish Academy of Music. He was awarded the Atterberg Prize in 1994. Mellnäs is one of Sweden's most innovative composers, and has done much to advance the cause of contemporary music in his homeland.

WORKS: DRAMATIC: *Minibuff*, opera (1966); *Kaleidovision*, television ballet (1969); *Erik den helige*, church opera (1975; Stockholm, May 18, 1976); *Spöket på Canterville*, opera (Umeå, April 25, 1981); *Dans på rosor*, opera buffa (1984); *Doktor Glas*, opera (1987–90). **ORCH.:** Concerto for Clarinet and Strings (1957); *Music* (1959); *Chiasmos* (1961); *Collage* (1962); *Aura* (Malmö, June 5, 1964); *Transparence* (1972); *Blow* for Wind Orch. (1974); *Moments musicaux* (1977; Lillehammer, March 12, 1978); *Besvärjelser* (1978); *Capriccio* (Stockholm, May 6, 1978); *Ikaros*, sym. (1986; Stockholm, March 18, 1987); *Passages* (1989; Sydney, April 21, 1990). **CHAMBER:** Oboe Sonata (1957); *Per caso* for Saxophone, Trombone, Violin, Double Bass, and 2 Percussionists (1963); *Tombola* for Horn, Trombone, Electric Guitar, and Piano (1963); *Sic transit* for Instruments and Tape (1964); *Siamfoni* for Trumpet, Horn, and Trombone (1964); *Quasi niente* for 1 to 4 String Trios (1968); *Capricorn Flakes* for Piano, Harpsichord, and Vibraphone (1970); *Cabrillo* for Clarinet, Trombone, Cello, and Percussion (1970); *Ceremus* for Flute, Clarinet, Trumpet, Trombone, Double Bass, and Percussion (1973); *The Mummy and the Hummingbird* for Flute and Harpsichord ad libitum (1974); *Riflessioni* for Clarinet or Bass Clarinet and Tape (1981); *31 Variations on C A G E* for 2 Pianos and Percussion (1982); *Rendez-vous* for 2 Flutes and Percussion (1983); *Stampede* for Saxophone Quartet (1985); *Gardens* for Flute, Clarinet, Percussion, Violin, Cello, and Piano (Stockholm, April 13, 1987); *No roses for Madame F* for Saxophone Quartet (1991); *Rolando furioso* for Violin and Harpsichord (1991); String Quartet No. 1, *Hommages* (1993); piano pieces. **OTHER:** Choral works; songs; electronic music.

Melton, James, American tenor; b. Moultrie, Ga., Jan. 2, 1904; d. N.Y., April 21, 1961. He studied with Gaetano de Luca in Nashville and Enrico Rosati in N.Y. and then with Michael Raucheisen in Berlin. He began his career on the radio; made his concert debut in N.Y. on April 22, 1932, and his operatic debut as Pinkerton in *Madama Butterfly* in Cincinnati on June 28, 1938. On Dec. 7, 1942, he appeared for the first time with the Metropolitan Opera in N.Y. as Tamino in *Die Zauberflöte*; remained on its roster until 1950; also toured the U.S. as a concert singer and later appeared in films.

Menasce, Jacques de, Austrian-born American pianist and composer; b. Bad Ischl (of a French-Egyptian father and a German mother), Aug. 19, 1905; d. Gstaad, Switzerland, Jan. 28, 1960. He studied in Vienna with Sauer (piano) and with J. Marx, Paul Pisk, and Berg (composition). From 1932 to 1940 he gave concerts in Europe as a pianist; in 1941 he went to America, living mostly in N.Y., but continued his concert career in Europe. He became a naturalized American citizen.

WORKS: BALLETS: *The Fate of My People* (1945); *Status Quo* (1947). **ORCH.:** 2 piano concertos (1935, 1939); *Divertimento* for Piano and Strings (1940). **CHAMBER:** Violin Sonata (1940); Viola Sonata (1950); piano pieces. **VOCAL:** Choruses; songs.

Mendel, Arthur, eminent American music scholar; b. Boston, June 6, 1905; d. Newark, N.J., Oct. 14, 1979. He studied at Harvard Univ. (A.B., 1925); then took courses in theory with Boulanger in Paris (1925–27). Returning to America, he was literary ed. of G. Schirmer, Inc. (1930–38); also wrote music criticism in the *Nation* (1930–33). From 1936 to 1953 he conducted in N.Y. a chorus, the Cantata Singers, specializing in Baroque music; taught at the Dalcroze School of Music from 1938; was its president (1947–50); also lectured at Columbia Univ. (1949) and the Univ. of Calif., Berkeley (1951). He was prof. of music and chairman of the music dept. at Princeton Univ. (1952–67); held the Henry Putnam Univ. Professorship there from 1969 to 1973. He ed. (with H. David) the valuable "documentary biography" *The Bach Reader* (N.Y., 1945; 2nd ed., rev., 1966); ed. Bach's *St. John Passion* (1951), Schütz's *Christmas Story* (1949) and *Musicalische Exequien* (1957), and other works of the Baroque period. He publ. numerous important articles on the history of pitch, reprinted in *Studies in the History of Musical Pitch* (Amsterdam, 1969), and also promoted the possibility of music analysis with the aid of a computer, publ. in *Computers and the Humanities* (1969–70).

BIBL.: R. Marshall, ed., *Studies in Renaissance and Baroque Music in Honor of A. M.* (Kassel, 1974).

Mendelsohn, Alfred, Romanian composer, conductor, and teacher; b. Bucharest, Feb. 17, 1910; d. there, May 9, 1966. He was a student of Schmidt and Marx (composition) and of Lach and Wellesz (music history) in Vienna (1927–31). Returning to Bucharest, he completed his training with Jora (composition) at the Cons. (1931–32). He taught harmony (1932–36) and was director (1936–40) at the E. Massini Cons. From 1946 to 1954 he was assistant music director of the Romanian Opera. From 1949 until his death he also was a prof. at the Cons. In 1945 he received the Enesco Prize and in 1949 was awarded the Romanian Academy Prize. While his music primarily reflects the influence of the Romantic Viennese School, he also probed the potentialities of motivic structures, suggesting the serial concepts of modern constructivists while remaining faithful to basic tonalitarianism.

WORKS: DRAMATIC: *Imnul iubirii* (The Love Hymn), dramatic sym. (1946); *Harap-Alb* (The White Moor), ballet (1948; Bucharest, March 30, 1949); *Meşterul Manole*, lyric drama (1949); *Călin*, choreographic poem (1956; Bucharest, May 2, 1957); *Anton Pann*, operetta (1961); *Michelangelo*, opera (1964; Timişoara, Sept. 29, 1968); *Spinoza*, lyric scene (1966). **ORCH.:** *Suită concertantă în stil clasic* for Violin and Strings (1938; rev. 1961); *Divertisment* for Flute and Strings (1938); *Rapsodie* (1940); Suite for Chamber Orch. (1940); 9 syms.: No. 1, *Înainte* (1944), No. 2, *Veritas* (1947), No. 3, *Reconstrucţia* (1949), No. 4, *Apelul păcii* (1951), No. 5 (1953), No. 6 (1955), No. 7 (1960), No. 8 (1963; Bucharest, Feb. 11, 1965), and No. 9, concertante for Organ and Orch. (1964; Bucharest, July 1, 1965); 2 piano concertos (1945, 1949); *Sinfonietă* (1946); 2 cello concertos (1950, 1962); *Praăbuşirea Doftanei* (Doftana's Assault), poem (1950; Bucharest, May 7, 1955); 3 violin concertos (1950–54; 1957; 1963); *Eliberare* (Liberation), poem (1954); *Va înflori acel arminden* (The May Tree Will Blossom), festive poem (1956); Concerto grosso for String Quartet and String Orch. (1956); Concertino for Harp and Strings (1956); Concertino for Violin and Strings (1957); *Divertisment* for Horn and Strings (1957); Concerto for Organ and Strings (1958–59); Piano Concertino (1959); *Schiţe dobrogene* (Dobrudjan Sketches; 1960–61); *Concertino în stil clasic* for 2 Violins and Strings (1961); Concerto for 2 Violins and Orch. (1962); *6 Schite* (Sketches; 1963); Tuba Concerto (1963); *Concerto for Orchestra* (1965); Viola Concerto (1965); *Epitaf* (1965). **CHAMBER:** 10 string quartets (1930; 1930; 1953; 1954; 1955; 1955; 1955–56; 1958; 1959–61; 1964); 4 Pieces for Clarinet and Piano (1952); Piano Quintet (1953); String Sextet (1956); 4 Pieces for Cello and Piano (1959); 2 piano trios (1957, 1960); 3 violin sonatas (all 1957); *Sonata brevis* for Violin and Organ (1960); *12 Preludii în stil clasic* for Violin (1962); *Variatiumi rapsodice* for Cello and Piano (1963); Sonata for Solo Cello (1965); piano pieces, including a Sonata (1947). **VOCAL:** *Cantata Bucureştiului* for Reciter, Chorus, and Orch. (1953; Bucharest, Oct. 31, 1954); *Horia*, heroic oratorio for Soloists and Orch. (1954–56); *1907*, oratorio for Soloists, Chorus, and Orch. (1956; Bucharest, March 21, 1957); *Glasul lui Lenin*, cantata for Chorus and Orch. (Bucharest, Nov. 2, 1957); *Sub cerul de vară*, sym.-cantata for Soloists, 2 Reciters, Chorus, and Orch. (Bucharest, Oct. 8, 1959); *Pentru Marele Octombrie*, oratorio for Soloists, Chorus, and Orch. (Bucharest, Nov. 3, 1960).

Meneely-Kyder, Sarah, American composer, pianist, and sitar player; b. Albany, N.Y., Feb. 18, 1945. She studied theory and piano at Goucher College (B.A., 1967); also had composition studies with Robert Hall Lewis (from 1966), Earle Brown at the Peabody Cons. of Music in Baltimore (M.M., 1969), and Robert Morris at the Yale School of Music (M.M.A., 1973); also studied the sitar and vina for 10 years. Her early works were serial or atonal in design; later she experimented with controlled improvisation, and spatial and proportional systems; still later she concentrated upon fusing disparate musical styles, making use of North Indian notational systems and instrumentations. She hails from a family of bell manufacturers who established the Meneely Foundry in Troy, N.Y.

WORKS: Piano Concerto (1967); *Homegrown* for Piano (1973); *Lament* for Sitar and Renaissance Instruments (1978); *Filarmonico* for Chorus, Piano, Vibraphone, and Gamelan Chimes (1980; rev. 1986, 1988); *Now I Sing Only 1 Song* for 2 Pianos (1980); *Weep, the Mighty Typhoons* for Mezzo-soprano and Piano (1982); *Narcissus* for Clarinet (1983); *Season Phases* for Piano (1987–88); *The 3 Gunas* for Piano, 4-hands, Violin, Cello, Flute, Clarinet, and Bassoon (1989).

Meneses, António, talented Brazilian cellist; b. Recife, Aug. 23, 1957. His father was 1st hornist in the opera orch. in Rio de Janeiro. António began his musical training when he was 8, then became a pupil of Janigro in Düsseldorf and Stuttgart at 16. He won 2nd prize in the Barcelona International Maria Casals Competition (1976) and in the Rio de Janeiro International Competition (1976); after winning 1st prize in the International ARD Competition in Munich (1977), he captured the prestigious gold medal at the Tchaikovsky Competition in Moscow (1982). He subsequently appeared as soloist with many major European orchs. He made his first tour of North America in 1985. His wife is **Cecile Licad**.

Mengelberg, Karel (Willem Joseph), Dutch composer and conductor, father of **Misha** and nephew of **(Josef) Willem Mengelberg**; b. Utrecht, July 18, 1902; d. Amsterdam, July 11, 1984. He studied with Pijper and later took a course at the Hochschule für Musik in Berlin. He conducted theater orchs. in provincial German towns and was a musician with Berlin Radio (1930–33); subsequently was conductor of the municipal band in Barcelona (1933); then went to Kiev, where he was in charge of the music dept. in the Ukrainian film studio. He returned to Amsterdam in 1938. In addition to his own compositions, in 1961 he completed the revision, with a simplified orchestration, of Willem Pijper's 2nd Sym. (Pijper's own rev. score was destroyed during a Nazi air raid on Rotterdam in May 1940).

WORKS: BALLETS: *Bataille* (1922); *Parfait amour* (1945). **ORCH.:** *Requiem* (1946); *Divertimento* for Small Orch. (1948); Horn Concerto (1950); *Anion*, symphonic sketch (1950); *Serenade* for Strings (1952); *Suite* for Small Orch. (1954); *De bergen* (1982). **CHAMBER:** String Quartet (1938); Sonata for Solo Oboe (1939); Trio for Flute, Oboe, and Bassoon (1940); *Toccata* for Piano (1950); *Soliloquio* for Flute (1951); *Ballade* for Flute, Clarinet, Harp, and String Quartet (1952); *Soneria, Romanza e Mazurca* for Harp (1958). **VOCAL:** *3 songs from Tagore's "The Gardener"* for Soprano and Orch. (1925); *Jan Hinnerik* for Chorus (1950); *Recitatief* for Baritone, Viola da Gamba, and Harpsichord (1953); *Roland Holst*, cantata for Chorus and Small Orch. (1955).

Mengelberg, Kurt Rudolf, German-born musicologist and composer of Dutch descent, nephew of **(Josef) Willem Mengelberg**; b. Krefeld, Feb. 1, 1892; d. Beausoleil, near Monte Carlo, Oct. 13, 1959. He studied piano with Neitzel in Cologne and musicology with Hugo Riemann at the Univ. of Leipzig, receiving his doctorate in 1915. He then went to Amsterdam, where he studied theory with his uncle; in 1917, through his uncle's intervention, he became artistic assistant of the Concertgebouw Orch. in Amsterdam; then was artistic manager there (1925–35), and finally director (1935–54). Among his publications were the valuable program book *Das Mahler-Fest, Amsterdam Mai 1920* (Vienna, 1920); a biography of Mahler (Leipzig, 1923); *Nederland, spiegeleener beschaving* (The Netherlands, Mirror of a Culture; Amsterdam, 1929); a commemorative publication on the semicentennial of the Concertgebouw (Amsterdam, 1938); *Muziek, spiegel des tijds* (Music, Mirror of Time; Amsterdam, 1948); and a biography of Willem Mengelberg. His compositions were mainly liturgical; among them are *Missa pro pace* (1932), *Stabat Mater* (1940), and *Victimae Paschali laudes* (1946); he also wrote *Symphonic Variations* for Cello and Orch. (1927); Violin Concerto (1930); *Capriccio* for Piano and Orch. (1936); Concertino for Flute and Chamber Orch. (1943); piano pieces; songs.

Mengelberg, Misha, Dutch composer, son of **Karel (Willem Joseph) Mengelberg**; b. Kiev, June 5, 1935. He was born in Kiev while his father was working in the U.S.S.R.; went in 1938 to the Netherlands, where he studied with Kees van Baaren at the Royal Cons. in The Hague, graduating in 1964.

WORKS: *Musica* for 17 Instruments (1959); *Medusa* for String Quartet (1962); *Commentary* for Orch. (1965); *Exercise* for Flute (1966); *Omtrent een componistenactie* (Concerning a Composer's Action) for Wind Quintet (1966); *3 Piano Pieces + Piano Piece 4* (1966); *Amaga* for 3 Different Guitars and Electronic Equipment (1968); *Anatoloose* for Orch. and Tape (1968; Holland Festival, July 8, 1971); *Hello Windy Boys* for Double

Wind Quintet (1968); *Reconstructie*, opera (1968–69; Holland Festival, June 29, 1969; in collaboration with L. Andriessen, R. de Leeuw, P. Schat, and J. van Vlijmen); *Met welbeleefde groet van de kameel* (With the Very Polite Greetings of the Camel) for Orch. with Electronic Sawing and Excavating Drills (1971–73); *Onderweg* (On the Way) for Orch. (1973; Bergen, Jan. 13, 1974); *Dressoir* for Wind Instruments and Piano (1977).

Mengelberg, (Josef) Willem, celebrated Dutch conductor, uncle of **Karel (Willem Joseph)** and **Kurt Rudolf Mengelberg**; b. Utrecht, March 28, 1871; d. Chur, Switzerland, March 21, 1951. He studied at the Utrecht Cons., and later at the Cologne Cons. with Seiss, Jensen, and Wüllner. He was appointed municipal music director in Lucerne in 1891, and his work there attracted so much attention that in 1895 he was placed at the head of the Concertgebouw Orch. in Amsterdam, holding this post for 50 years (resigning in 1945); during his directorship, he elevated that orch. to a lofty position in the world of music. In 1898 he also became conductor of the Tonkoonst choral society in Amsterdam, and from 1908 to 1921 he was director of the Museumgesellschaft concerts in Frankfurt am Main. He appeared frequently as guest conductor in all the European countries; in England he was an annual visitor from 1913 until World War II. He first appeared with the N.Y. Phil. in 1905; then conducted it regularly from 1922 to 1930, with Toscanini serving as assoc. conductor in 1929–30. In 1928 he received the degree of Mus.Doc. at Columbia Univ. (honoris causa); in 1933 he was appointed prof. of music at the Univ. of Utrecht. During the occupation of the Netherlands by the Germans, Mengelberg openly expressed his sympathies with the Nazi cause, and lost the high respect and admiration that his compatriots had felt for him; after the country's liberation (1945), he was barred from professional activities there, the ban to be continued until 1951, but he died in that year in exile in Switzerland. Mengelberg was an outstanding representative of the Romantic tradition in symphonic conducting. His performances of the Beethoven syms. were notable for their dramatic sweep and power, if not for their adherence to stylistic proprieties. He was a great champion of many of the major composers of his era, including Mahler and Strauss; both men appeared as guest conductors of the Concertgebouw Orch., and became Mengelberg's friends. Mahler dedicated his 5th and 8th syms. to Mengelberg and the Concertgebouw Orch., and Strauss dedicated *Ein Heldenleben* to the same forces. Mengelberg was the first to lead a major cycle of Mahler's works, in Amsterdam in 1920.

BIBL.: H. Nolthenius, *W. M.* (Amsterdam, 1920); A. Van den Boer, *De psychologische beteekenis van W. M. als dirigent* (Amsterdam, 1925); E. Sollitt, *M. and the Symphonic Epoch* (N.Y., 1930); idem, *M. spreckt* (speeches by M.; The Hague, 1935); W. Paap, *W. M.* (Amsterdam, 1960).

Menges, (Siegfried Frederick) Herbert, English conductor, brother of **Isolde (Marie) Menges**; b. Hove (of German parents), Aug. 27, 1902; d. London, Feb. 20, 1972. He played violin as a child; then took piano lessons with Mathilda Verne and Arthur de Greef; later attended courses in composition with Vaughan Williams and Holst at the Royal College of Music in London. He began his conducting career in Brighton, and conducted the Brighton Phil. Soc. (which was founded by his mother) from 1925 until his death. He was also a music director of the Old Vic Theatre in London (1931–50) and of the Southern Phil. Orch. at Southsea (from 1945). In 1963 he was made an Officer of the Order of the British Empire.

Menges, Isolde (Marie), English violinist and teacher, sister of **(Siegfried Frederick) Herbert Menges**; b. Hove (of German parents), May 16, 1893; d. Richmond, Surrey, Jan. 13, 1976. Both her parents were violinists, and she studied at home; then went to St. Petersburg for lessons with Auer. She made her London debut on Feb. 4, 1913, and her N.Y. debut on Oct. 21, 1916. In 1931 she was appointed to the faculty of the Royal College of Music in London; also organized the Menges Quartet there.

Mennin (real name, **Mennini**), **Peter,** eminent American composer and music educator, brother of **Louis (Alfred) Mennini**; b. Erie, Pa., May 17, 1923; d. N.Y., June 17, 1983. His family stemmed from Italy; his brother did not cut off the last letter of his name as Peter did. His early environment was infused with music, mostly from phonograph recordings. He studied piano with Tito Spampani. In 1940 he enrolled in the Oberlin (Ohio) Cons., where he took courses in harmony with Normand Lockwood. He quickly learned the basics of composition, and at the age of 18 wrote a sym. and a string quartet. In 1942 he enlisted in the U.S. Army Air Force; was discharged in 1943, and resumed his musical studies at the Eastman School of Music in Rochester, N.Y., where his teachers were Hanson and Rogers. He worked productively; wrote another sym. in 1944; a movement from it, *Symphonic Allegro*, was performed by the N.Y. Phil., Leonard Bernstein conducting, on March 27, 1945. His 3rd Sym. was performed by Walter Hendl with the N.Y. Phil. on Feb. 27, 1947. Mennin progressed academically as well; he obtained his Ph.D. from the Eastman School of Music in 1947. He received a Guggenheim fellowship grant in 1948; a 2nd Guggenheim grant followed in 1956. From 1947 to 1958 he taught composition at the Juilliard School of Music in N.Y.; in 1958 he assumed the post of director of the Peabody Cons. of Music in Baltimore. In 1962 he received his most prestigious appointment, that of president of the Juilliard School of Music, serving in that capacity until his death. Despite his academic preoccupations, he never slackened the tempo of his activities as a composer; he diversified his syms. by adding descriptive titles; thus his 4th Sym. was subtitled *The Cycle* and was scored for chorus and orch.; his 7th Sym. was called *Variation Symphony*; the 4 movements of his 8th Sym. bore biblical titles. Increasingly also, he began attaching descriptive titles to his other works; his Concertato for Orch. was named *Moby Dick*; there followed a *Canto for Orchestra*, a *Cantata de Virtute, Voices*, and *Reflections of Emily*, after Emily Dickinson. Mennin's musical mind was directed toward pure structural forms; his music is characterized by an integrity of purpose and teleological development of thematic materials, all this despite the bold infusion of dissonant sonorities in contrapuntal passages.

WORKS: ORCH.: 9 syms.: No. 1 (1941; withdrawn), No. 2 (1944; Rochester, N.Y., March 27, 1945), No. 3 (1946; N.Y., Feb. 27, 1947), No. 4, *The Cycle*, for Chorus and Orch. (1948; N.Y., March 18, 1949), No. 5 (Dallas, April 2, 1950), No. 6 (Louisville, Nov. 18, 1953), No. 7, *Variation Symphony* (1963; Cleveland, Jan. 23, 1964), No. 8 (1973; N.Y., Nov. 21, 1974), and No. 9, *Sinfonia capricciosa* (Washington, D.C., March 10, 1981); Concertino for Flute, Strings, and Percussion (1944); *Folk Overture* (Washington, D.C., Dec. 19, 1945); *Sinfonia* for Chamber Orch. (1946; Rochester, N.Y., May 24, 1947); *Fantasia* for Strings (1947; N.Y., Jan. 11, 1948); *Canzona* for Band (1951); Concertato, *Moby Dick* (Erie, Pa., Oct. 20, 1952); Cello Concerto (N.Y., Feb. 19, 1956); Piano Concerto (Cleveland, Feb. 27, 1958); *Canto for Orchestra* (San Antonio, March 4, 1963); *Symphonic Movements*, renamed *Sinfonia* (1970; Minneapolis, Jan. 21, 1971; withdrawn); Flute Concerto (1983; N.Y., May 25, 1988). **CHAMBER:** Organ Sonata (1941; withdrawn); 2 string quartets (1941, withdrawn; 1951); *5 Pieces* for Piano (1949); *Sonata concertante* for Violin and Piano (Washington, D.C., Oct. 19, 1956); Piano Sonata (1963). **VOCAL:** *4 Songs* for Soprano and Piano (1941; withdrawn); *Alleluia* for Chorus (1941); *4 Chinese Poems* for Chorus (1948); 2 choruses for Women's Voices and Piano (1949); *The Christmas Story* for Soprano, Tenor, Chorus, Brass Quintet, Timpani, and Strings (1949); *Cantata de Virtute: Pied Piper of Hamelin* for Narrator, Tenor, Bass, Mixed Chorus, Children's Chorus, and Orch. (Cincinnati, May 2, 1969); *Voices* for Voice, Piano, Harp, Harpsichord, and Percussion, after Thoreau, Melville, Whitman, and Emily Dickinson (1975; N.Y., March 28, 1976); *Reflections of Emily* [Dickinson] for Boy's Chorus, Harp, Piano, and Percussion (1978; N.Y., Jan. 18, 1979).

Mennini, Louis (Alfred), American composer and music educator, brother of **Peter Mennin**; b. Erie, Pa., Nov. 18, 1920. He studied at the Oberlin (Ohio) Cons. (1939–42); then served in the U.S. Army Air Force (1942–45); subsequently studied composition with Rogers and Hanson at the Eastman School of Music, Rochester, N.Y. (B.M., 1947; M.M., 1948). He was a prof. at the Univ. of Texas (1948–49); then was a prof. of composition at the Eastman School of Music, receiving his doctorate in composition from the Univ. of Rochester in 1961. After serving as dean of the School of Music at the North Carolina School of the Arts in Winston-Salem (1965–71), he became chairman of the music dept. at Mercyhurst College in Erie, Pa., in 1973, where he founded the D'Angelo School of Music and D'Angelo Young Artist Competition. In 1983 he founded the Virginia School of the Arts in Lynchburg, serving as its head until his retirement in 1988. His music is pragmatic and functional, with occasional modernistic touches.

WORKS: OPERAS: *The Well* (Rochester, N.Y., May 8, 1951); *The Rape*, chamber opera, after Eugene O'Neill (Tanglewood, Aug. 8, 1955). **ORCH.:** *Overtura breve* (1949); *Cantilena* (1950); *Canzona* for Chamber Orch. (1950); 2 syms. (*Da Chiesa*, 1960; *Da Festa*, 1963); *Tenebrae* (1963); Concerto Grosso (1975). **CHAMBER:** Violin Sonata (1947); Cello Sonatina (1952); String Quartet (1961); many piano works.

Menotti, Gian Carlo, remarkable Italian composer; b. Cadegliano, July 7, 1911. He was the 6th of 10 children. He learned the rudiments of music from his mother, and began to compose as a child, making his first attempt at an opera, entitled *The Death of Pierrot*, at the age of 10. After training at the Milan Cons. (1924–27), he studied with Scalero at the Curtis Inst. of Music in Philadelphia (1927–33). Although Menotti associated himself with the cause of American music, and spent much of his time in the U.S., he retained his Italian citizenship. As a composer, he is unique on the American scene, being the first to create American opera possessing such an appeal to audiences as to become established in the permanent repertoire. Inheriting the natural Italian gift for operatic drama and an expressive singing line, he adapted these qualities to the peculiar requirements of the American stage and to the changing fashions of the period; his serious operas have a strong dramatic content in the realistic style stemming from the Italian verismo. He wrote his own librettos, marked by an extraordinary flair for drama and for the communicative power of the English language; with this is combined a fine, though subdued, sense of musical humor. Menotti made no pretensions at extreme modernism, and did not fear to approximate the successful formulas developed by Verdi and Puccini; the influence of Mussorgsky's realistic prosody is also in evidence, particularly in recitative. When dramatic tension required a greater impact, Menotti resorted to atonal and polytonal writing, leading to climaxes accompanied by massive dissonances. His first successful stage work was *Amelia Goes to the Ball*, an opera buffa in 1 act (originally to an Italian libretto by the composer, as *Amelia al ballo*), staged at the Academy of Music, Philadelphia, on April 1, 1937. This was followed by another comic opera, *The Old Maid and the Thief*, commissioned by NBC, first performed on the radio, April 22, 1939, and on the stage, by the Philadelphia Opera Co., on Feb. 11, 1941. Menotti's next operatic work was *The Island God*, produced by the Metropolitan Opera, N.Y., on Feb. 20, 1942, with indifferent success; but with the production of *The Medium* (N.Y., May 8, 1946), Menotti established himself as one of the most successful composer-librettists of modern opera. The imaginative libretto, dealing with a fraudulent spiritualist who falls victim to her own practices when she imagines that ghostly voices are real, suited Menotti's musical talent to perfection; the opera had a long and successful run in N.Y., an unprecedented occurrence in the history of the American lyric theater. A short humorous opera, *The Telephone*, was first produced by the N.Y. Ballet Soc., Feb. 18, 1947, on the same bill with *The Medium*; these 2 contrasting works were subsequently staged all over the U.S. and in Europe, often on the same evening. Menotti then produced *The Consul* (Philadelphia, March 1, 1950), his finest tragic work, describing the plight of political fugitives vainly trying to escape from an unnamed country but failing to obtain the necessary visa from the consul of an anonymous power; very ingeniously, the author does not include the title character in the cast, since the consul never appears on the stage but remains a shadowy presence. *The Consul* exceeded Menotti's previous operas in popular success; it had a long run in N.Y., and received the Pulitzer Prize in Music. On Christmas Eve, 1951, NBC presented Menotti's television opera *Amahl and the Night Visitors*, a Christmas story of undeniable poetry and appeal; it became an annual television production every Christmas in subsequent years. His next opera was *The Saint of Bleecker Street*, set in a N.Y. locale (N.Y., Dec. 27, 1954); it won the Drama Critics' Circle Award for the best musical play of 1954, and the Pulitzer Prize in Music for 1955. A madrigal ballet, *The Unicorn, the Gorgon and the Manticore*, commissioned by the Elizabeth Sprague Coolidge Foundation, was first presented at the Library of Congress, Washington, D.C., Oct. 21, 1956. His opera *Maria Golovin*, written expressly for the International Exposition in Brussels, was staged there on Aug. 20, 1958. In 1958 he organized the Festival of 2 Worlds in Spoleto, Italy, staging old and new works; in 1977 he inaugurated an American counterpart of the festival in Charleston, S.C. In many of the festival productions Menotti acted also as stage director. In the meantime, he continued to compose; he produced in quick succession *Labyrinth*, a television opera to his own libretto (N.Y., March 3, 1963); *Death of the Bishop of Brindisi*, dramatic cantata with the text by the composer (Cincinnati, May 18, 1963); *Le Dernier Sauvage*, opera buffa, originally with an Italian libretto by Menotti, produced at the Opéra-Comique in Paris in a French tr. (Oct. 21, 1963; produced in Eng. at the Metropolitan Opera, N.Y., Jan. 23, 1964); *Martin's Lie*, chamber opera to Menotti's text (Bath, England, June 3, 1964); *Help, Help, the Globolinks!*, "an opera in 1 act for children and those who like children" to words by Menotti, with electronic effects (Hamburg, Dec. 19, 1968); *The Most Important Man*, opera to his own libretto (N.Y., March 12, 1971); *The Hero*, comic opera (Philadelphia, June 1, 1976); *The Egg*, a church opera to Menotti's own libretto (Washington Cathedral, June 17, 1976); *The Trial of the Gypsy* for Treble Voices and Piano (N.Y., May 24, 1978); *Miracles* for Boy's Chorus (Fort Worth, April 22, 1979); *La loca*, opera to Menotti's own libretto dealing with a mad daughter of Ferdinand and Isabella (San Diego, June 3, 1979); *A Bride from Pluto*, children's opera (Washington, D.C., April 14, 1982); *The Boy Who Grew Too Fast*, opera for young people (Wilmington, Del., Sept. 24, 1982); *The Wedding*, opera (Seoul, Sept. 16, 1988); *Singing Child*, children's opera (Charleston, S.C., May 31, 1993). Among Menotti's non-operatic works are the ballets *Sebastian* (1944) and *Errand into the Maze* (N.Y., Feb. 2, 1947); 2 piano concertos: No. 1 (Boston, Nov. 2, 1945) and No. 2 (Miami, June 23, 1982); *Apocalypse*, symphonic poem (Pittsburgh, Oct. 19, 1951); Violin Concerto (Philadelphia, Dec. 5, 1952, Zimbalist soloist); *Triplo Concerto a Tre*, triple concerto (N.Y., Oct. 6, 1970); *Landscapes and Remembrances*, cantata to his own autobiographical words (Milwaukee, May 14, 1976); *First Symphony*, subtitled *The Halcyon* (Philadelphia, Aug. 4, 1976); *Nocturne* for Soprano, String Quartet, and Harp (N.Y., Oct. 24, 1982); Double Bass Concerto (N.Y. Phil., Oct. 20, 1983, James VanDemark, soloist, Zubin Mehta conducting); *For the Death of Orpheus* for Tenor, Chorus, and Orch. (Atlanta, Nov. 8, 1990). He also wrote a number of *pièces d'occasion* such as *Trio for a House-Warming Party* for Piano, Cello, and Flute (1936); *Variations on a Theme by Schumann*; *Pastorale* for Piano and Strings; *Poemetti per Maria Rosa* (piano pieces for children); etc. He is also the author of the librettos for Samuel Barber's operas *Vanessa* (Metropolitan Opera, N.Y., Jan. 15, 1958) and *A Hand of Bridge* (1959); also wrote a play without music, *The Leper* (Tallahassee, April 22, 1970).

Menotti's last years were plagued with disputes over his role as an artistic director. In 1991 a major dispute arose between the composer and the director of the Spoleto Festival USA in Charleston, but ultimately Menotti retained control. However, in

1993 he announced that he was taking the festival away from Charleston, but the city's mayor intervened and Menotti lost control of his festival. That same year he was named artistic director of the Rome Opera, but again conflicts over artistic policy between the composer and the superintendent led to Menotti's dismissal in 1994.

BIBL.: J. Gruen, *M.: A Biography* (N.Y., 1978); J. Ardoin, *The Stages of M.* (Garden City, N.Y., 1985).

Menuhin, Hephzibah, American pianist, sister of **Sir Yehudi Menuhin, Lord Menuhin of Stoke d'Abernon**; b. San Francisco, May 20, 1920; d. London, Jan. 1, 1981. Like her brother, she appeared in public at a very early age in San Francisco (1928); studied there and later with Ciampi in Paris. She toured widely as a recitalist with her brother in the U.S. and Europe.

Menuhin, Sir Yehudi, Lord Menuhin of Stoke d'Abernon, celebrated American violinist, brother of **Hephzibah Menuhin**; b. N.Y., April 22, 1916. He was born of Russian-Jewish parents (the family surname was originally Mnuhin). As a child, he was taken to San Francisco, where he began to study violin with Sigmund Anker; in 1923 he began taking lessons with Louis Persinger, who was then concertmaster of the San Francisco Sym. Orch. On Feb. 29, 1924, he made his public debut in Oakland playing Bériot's *Scène de ballet* with Persinger as accompanist; Menuhin was only 7 at the time. On Jan. 17, 1926, when he was 9 years old, he played a recital in N.Y. He made his European debut in Paris on Feb. 6, 1927, with Paul Paray and the Lamoureux Orch. In Paris he began to study with Enesco, who became his most influential teacher, and who guided his future career. Returning to America, Menuhin played the Beethoven Concerto with Fritz Busch and the N.Y. Sym. Orch. on Nov. 25, 1927, winning unanimous acclaim from the public and the press. He subsequently made tours throughout America and Europe; on April 12, 1929, he appeared with Bruno Walter and the Berlin Phil., playing concertos by Bach, Beethoven, and Brahms on the same program; on Nov. 10, 1929, he made his London debut. He continued to pursue his studies with Enesco, and also received additional instruction from Adolf Busch. On the sesquicentennial of the first concert given at the Gewandhaus in Leipzig, he appeared as soloist with the Gewandhaus Orch. in the Mendelssohn Concerto (Nov. 12, 1931). In 1935 he completed his first world tour. In subsequent years, he toured regularly throughout the world. After giving numerous concerts for the Allies during World War II, he resumed his international career. He also became active in organizing music festivals; in 1956 he established the Gstaad Festival in Switzerland. In 1959 he made his home in London, and founded the Bath Festival, which he directed until 1968; he also founded the Windsor Festival and directed it from 1969 to 1972. In 1963 he founded his own boarding school for musically gifted children at Stoke d'Abernon, Surrey. In 1965 he received an honorary knighthood from Queen Elizabeth II. In 1970 he received honorary citizenship from the community of Saanen, Switzerland, and assumed Swiss national allegiance while preserving his American citizenship. In 1971 he succeeded Barbirolli as president of Trinity College of Music in London. In 1976 he was awarded an honorary doctorate by the Sorbonne of Paris, the first musician to be so honored during its entire history. On Sept. 10, 1981, he celebrated the 50th anniversary of his first appearance in Leipzig by performing the Brahms Concerto with Kurt Masur and the Gewandhaus Orch. In 1985 he was granted honorary British citizenship, and thereby formally became Sir Yehudi. In 1986 President Mitterand made him a Grand Officer of the Légion d'honneur of France. In 1987 he was made a member of the Order of Merit. He was created a life peer as Lord Menuhin of Stoke d'Abernon in 1993.

Apart from his musical activities, Menuhin became deeply interested in art, politics, and above all, psychology and philosophy. He embraced the cause of Oriental religions, practiced yoga exercises, and even lectured on these abstruse subjects. In 1963 he appeared on the BBC in London in a discussion entitled "Yehudi Menuhin and His Guru." He also adopted a health diet, eschewing carbohydrates and some other foods. In his political utterances, he antagonized many factions in many lands. He was enthusiastically received in Israel during his tours in 1950, 1951, 1952, and 1953, but aroused Israeli animosity when he gave benefit concerts for Palestinian refugees. He embarrassed the Russians at a music congress in Moscow in 1971 when in his speech, which he read in understandable Russian, he appealed to them on behalf of human rights. In the meantime, his artistry suffered somewhat; critics began to notice a certain unsteadiness in his intonation and technique. In later years, he devoted himself to conducting, a career which failed to equal his former renown as a violin virtuoso. Still, he never slackened his energetic activities, musical or non-musical. He publ. a collection of essays under the title *Theme and Variations* (London, 1972); an autobiography, *Unfinished Journey* (N.Y., 1977); with Curtis W. Davis, *The Music of Man* (London, 1980), based on the television series of the same title, and *Life Class* (London, 1986).

BIBL.: B. Gavoty, *Y. M. et Georges Enesco* (Geneva, 1955); R. Magidoff, *Y. M.: The Story of the Man and the Musician* (Garden City, N.Y., 1955; 2nd ed., 1973); N. Wymer, *Y. M.* (London, 1961); E. Fenby, *M.'s House of Music* (London, 1969); R. Daniels, *Conversations with M.* (London, 1979); M. Menuhin, *The M. Saga* (London, 1984); D. Menuhin, *Fiddler's Moll* (London, 1985); B. Land, "The Indefatigable Y. M. at Seventy," *Ovation* (June 1986); K. Pohl and A. Zipf-Pohl, eds., *Hommage à Y. M.: Festschrift zum 70. Geburtstag am 22. April 1986* (Baden-Baden, 1986); T. Palmer, *M.: A Family Portrait* (London and Boston, 1991).

Mercure, Pierre, Canadian composer; b. Montreal, Feb. 21, 1927; d. in an ambulance between Avallon and Auxerre, France, Jan. 29, 1966, after an automobile crash while driving from Paris to Lyons. He studied harmony and counterpoint with Marvin Duchow and Claude Champagne and bassoon with Roland Gagnier and Louis Letellier at the Montreal Cons. (1944–49); then studied composition with Boulanger and conducting with Barzin in Paris (1949–50); later studied orchestration with Hoérée and Milhaud and conducting with Fournet there (1962); also took courses with Dallapiccola at the Berkshire Music Center in Tanglewood (summer, 1951), and at Darmstadt and Dartington with Pousseur, Nono, and Berio (1962). He played bassoon with the Montreal Sym. Orch. (1947–52); then joined the CBC (1952), where he served as its first producer of television music programming (1954–59). In his music, he explored electronic sonorities in combinations with traditional instrumentation.

WORKS: ORCH.: *Kaléidoscope* (1947–48); *Pantomime* for Winds and Percussion (1948); *Divertissement* for Solo String Quartet and String Orch. (1957); *Triptyque* (1959); *Lignes et points* (1964; Montreal, Feb. 16, 1965). **CHAMBER:** *Emprise* for Clarinet, Bassoon, Cello, and Piano (1950); *Tetrachromie*, ballet for 3 Winds, 4 Percussionists, and Tape (1963); *H2O per Severino* for 4–10 Flutes and/or Clarinets (1965). **VOCAL:** *Cantate pour une joie* for Soprano, Chorus, and Orch. (1955); *Psaume pour abri*, radiophonic cantata for Narrator, 2 Choruses, Chamber Ensemble, and Tape (Montreal, May 15, 1963). **TAPE:** 6 pieces with optional choreography: *Improvisation, Incandescense, Structures métalliques I* and *II* (all 1961), *Manipulations* (1963), and *Surimpressions* (1964); *Répercussions*, for Japanese Wind Chimes on Tape (1961); *Jeu de Hockey* (1961); *Structures metalliques III* (1962). **OTHER:** 3 short choreographed pieces: *Dualité*, with Trumpet and Piano, *La Femme archaïque*, with Viola, Piano, and Timpani, and *Lucrèce Borgia*, with Trumpet, Piano, and Percussion (all 1949); film scores.

Merian, Wilhelm, Swiss musicologist; b. Basel, Sept. 18, 1889; d. there, Nov. 15, 1952. He studied with Nef at the Univ. of Basel (Ph.D., 1915, with the diss. *Die Tabulaturen des Organisten Hans Kotter: Ein Beitrag zur Musikgeschichte des beginnenden 16. Jahrhunderts*; publ. in Leipzig, 1916); subsequently completed his Habilitation there in 1921 with his *Die Klavier-*

musik der deutschen Koloristen, and joined its faculty that same year. From 1920 to 1951 he was music critic and music ed. of the *Basler Nachrichten.* With Paul Sacher, he helped to found the Schola Cantorum Basiliensis (1933).

WRITINGS: Ed. *Gedenkschrift zum 50 jährigen Bestehen der Allgemeinen Musikschule in Basel* (1917); *Basels Musikleben im XIX. Jahrhundert* (1920); *Der Tanz in den deutschen Tabulaturbuchern . . .* (1927); *Hermann Suter: Ein Lebensbild als Beitrag zur schweizerischen Musikgeschichte* (1936).

Merikanto, Aarre, Finnish composer and teacher, son of **(Frans) Oskar Merikanto**; b. Helsinki, June 29, 1893; d. there, Sept. 29, 1958. He studied composition with Melartin at the Helsinki Music Inst.; then in Leipzig with Reger (1912–14) and with Vasilenko in Moscow (1915–16). In 1936 he joined the faculty at the Sibelius Academy in Helsinki, and in 1951 succeeded Palmgren as head of the dept. of composition there; held this post until his death. Like his father, he wrote on themes of Finnish folklore, but some of his early works reveal Russian and French traits.

WORKS: OPERA: *Juha* (1920–22; Finnish Radio, Helsinki, Dec. 3, 1958; 1st stage perf., Lahti, Oct. 28, 1963). **ORCH.:** 3 piano concertos (1913, 1937, 1955); 3 syms. (1916, 1918, 1953); 4 violin concertos (1916, 1925, 1931, 1954); *Lemminkainen,* symphonic suite (1916); 2 cello concertos (1919; 1941–44); *Pan,* symphonic poem (1924); Concerto for Violin, Clarinet, Horn, and String Sextet (1925); *Concert Piece* for Cello and Chamber Orch. (1926); *Symphonic Study* (1928; mutilated; reconstructed by P. Heininen, 1981; Helsinki, Aug. 26, 1982); *Notturno,* symphonic poem (1929); *Kyllikin ryöstö* (The Abduction of Kyllikki), symphonic poem (1935); *Scherzo* (1937); *3 Impressions* (1940); *Soitelma kesäyölle* (Music to the Summer Night; 1942). **CHAMBER:** 2 string quartets (1913, 1939); String Trio (1912); Piano Trio (1917); Nonet (1926); String Sextet (1932); *Partita* for Harp and Woodwinds (1936). **VOCAL:** *Genesis* for Soprano, Chorus, and Orch. (1956); *Tuhma* (Simpleton) for Men's Chorus and Orch. (1956); songs.

Merikanto, (Frans) Oskar, Finnish composer, conductor, and organist, father of **Aarre Merikanto**; b. Helsinki, Aug. 5, 1868; d. Hausjärvi-Oiti, Feb. 17, 1924. After preliminary study in his native city, he studied at the Leipzig Cons. (1887–88) and in Berlin (1890–91). Returning to Finland, he became organist of St. John's Church, and from 1911 to 1922 was conductor of the National Opera in Helsinki. He wrote manuals for organ playing. He wrote the first opera in Finnish, *Pohjan Neiti* (The Maid of the North; 1899; Vyborg, June 18, 1908); also the operas *Elinan surma* (Elina's Death; Helsinki, Nov. 17, 1910) and *Regina von Emmeritz* (Helsinki, Jan. 30, 1920); various instrumental pieces; organ works; numerous songs, many of which became popular in his homeland.

BIBL.: Y. Suomalainen, *O. M.* (Helsinki, 1950).

Meriläinen, Usko, Finnish composer and teacher; b. Tampere, Jan. 27, 1930. He studied with Aarre Merikanto and Funtek at the Sibelius Academy in Helsinki (1951–55); then took private lessons with Krenek in Darmstadt and with Vogel in Switzerland. In 1956–57 he was a conductor and teacher in Kuopio; subsequently was theater conductor in Tampere (1957–60); then taught at the music inst. there (1961–66) and from 1965 at the Univ. In his music, he adopted a pragmatic modern idiom, with structural foundations of tonal and/or dodecaphonic procedures, depending on the basic concept.

WORKS: DRAMATIC: BALLETS: *Arius* (1958–60; also 2 suites, 1960, 1962); *Psyche* (1973). **DANCE PANTOMIME:** *Alasin* (The Anvil; 1975; also listed as his 4th Sym.). **ORCH.:** 5 syms.: No. 1 (1953–55), No. 2 (1964), No. 3 (1971), No. 4, *Alasin* (The Anvil; 1975; also listed as the dance pantomime under the same name), and No. 5 (1976); 2 piano concertos (1955, 1969); Concerto (1956); Chamber Concerto for Violin, 2 Percussionists, and Double String Orch. (1962); *Epyllion* (1963); *Musique du printemps* (1969); Cello Concerto (1975); *Dialogues* for Piano and Orch. (1977); *Mobile—ein Spiel für Orchester* (1977); *A Kinetic Poem* for Piano and Orch. (1981); *Kivenmurskaajat* (The Stone Crushers; 1982); *Visions and Whispers* for Flute and Orch. (1985); *". . . but this is a landscape, monsieur Dali!"* (1986); Flute Concerto (1986); *Aikaviia,* concerto (1989); *Timeline,* concerto No. 2 for Orch. (1989); Guitar Concerto (1991); *Summer Concert* for Chamber Orch. (1993–94). **CHAMBER:** *Partita* for Brass (1954); *4 Bagatelles* for String Quartet (1962); 3 string quartets (1965, n.d., 1992); *Divertimento* for Wind Quintet, Harp, Viola, and Cello (1968); *Metamorfora for 7* for Clarinet, Bassoon, Trumpet, Trombone, Percussion, Violin, and Double Bass (1969); *Concerto for 13* for 7 Violins, 3 Violas, 2 Cellos, and Double Bass (1971); Concerto for Double Bass and Percussion (1973); *Aspects of the Ballet "Psyche"* for Tape and Instrumental Ensemble (1973); *Simultus for 4* for Flute, Alto Saxophone, Guitar, and Percussion (1979); *Kyma* for String Quartet (1979); *Suvisoitto: Summer Sounds for Flute and Grasshoppers* for Flute and Tape (1979); *Paripeli (For 2)* for Cello and Piano (1980); Alto Saxophone Sonata (1982); *Mouvements circulaires en douceur* for 4 Flutes (1985); *Fêtes d'Henriette* for Flute, Cello, and Piano (1995). **PIANO:** Suite (1955); Sonatina (1958); 5 sonatas (1960, 1966, 1972, 1974, 1992); *Tre Notturni* (1967); *Papillons* for 2 Pianos (1969). **OTHER:** *Yö, vene ja punaiset purjeet* (Night, a Boat and Red Sails) for Chorus (1987); 2 electroacoustic works: *The Concert Where I Dozed Off—Consciousness Streaming Free,* radiophonic poem (1982), and *Oratorio Picassolle* (1984).

Merli, Francesco, Italian tenor; b. Milan, Jan. 27, 1887; d. there, Dec. 12, 1976. He studied with Borghi and Negrini in Milan. He made his first appearance at Milan's La Scala as Alvaro in Spontini's *Fernando Cortez* (1916), and subsequently sang there regularly until 1942; also appeared at the Teatro Colón in Buenos Aires; between 1926 and 1930 he sang at Covent Garden in London. He made his debut at the Metropolitan Opera in N.Y. as Radames in *Aida* on March 2, 1932; then returned to Italy. He retired from the stage in 1948 and was active mainly as a voice teacher. His other roles included Don José, Otello, Canio, Samson, Calaf, and Dick Johnson.

Merola, Gaetano, Italian-American conductor and opera manager; b. Naples, Jan. 4, 1881; d. while conducting a performance of the San Francisco Sym. Orch. at Sigmund Stern Grove in San Francisco, Aug. 30, 1953. He studied at the Naples Cons. He went to the U.S. in 1899, and was appointed assistant conductor at the Metropolitan Opera in N.Y.; also conducted the Henry Savage English Opera in N.Y. (1903) and at the Manhattan Opera; subsequently became music director and manager of the San Francisco Opera in 1923, where he remained until his death; also conducted opera in Los Angeles (1924–32).

Merrem-Nikisch, Grete, German soprano; b. Düren, July 7, 1887; d. Kiel, March 12, 1970. She studied with Schulz-Dornburg in Cologne and Marie Hedmondt at the Leipzig Cons. In 1910 she made her operatic debut at the Leipzig Opera, where she sang until 1913. In 1911 she made her first appearance at the Berlin Royal Opera, where she was a member (1913–18), and then of its successor, the State Opera (1918–30). She was known for her lyric roles, and for her Eva and Sophie. She also sang in Dresden, where she appeared in the premieres of *Die toten Augen* (1916), *Intermezzo* (1924), and *Cardillac* (1926). From 1918 she likewise pursued a fine career as a lieder artist. In later years, she taught at the Univ. of Kiel. In 1914 she married the eldest son of Arthur Nikisch.

Merriam, Alan P(arkhurst), American anthropologist and ethnomusicologist; b. Missoula, Mont., Nov. 1, 1923; d. in an airplane crash near Warsaw, March 14, 1980. He studied at the Univ. of Montana (B.A., 1947) and took courses in anthropology from Melville Herskovits and Richard Waterman at Northwestern Univ. (M.M., 1948; Ph.D., 1951). He taught anthropology there (1953–54; 1956–62) and at the Univ. of Wisc. (1954–56); in 1962 he became a prof. of anthropology at Indiana Univ. in Bloomington; was chairman of the dept. there from 1966 to 1969. In 1976 he was engaged as a senior scholar in anthropology at the

Univ. of Sydney. He was involved in field research among the Flathead Indians and the tribes in Zaire.

WRITINGS: *The Anthropology of Music* (Evanston, Ill., 1964); with F. Gillis, *Ethnomusicology and Folk Music: An International Bibliography of Dissertations and Theses* (Middletown, Conn., 1966); *Ethnomusicology of the Flathead Indians* (Chicago, 1967); *African Music on LP: An Annotated Discography* (Evanston, 1970); *The Arts and Humanities in African Studies* (Bloomington, Ind., 1972).

Merrick, Frank, English pianist, pedagogue, and composer; b. Clifton, Bristol, April 30, 1886; d. London, Feb. 19, 1981. He studied piano and composition with his father; made his debut in 1895, then studied piano with Leschetizky in Vienna (1898–1901; 1905). Returning to England, he taught at the Royal Manchester College of Music (1911–29); then became a prof. at the Royal College of Music in London; in 1956 he joined the piano faculty of Trinity College of Music in London. In 1928 he entered a rather ill-conceived contest launched by the Columbia Phonograph Co. to nail down the centenary of Schubert's death by finishing his "Unfinished" Sym. Merrick did finish it, and won a prize. He was married to the pianist Hope Squire and gave duo-piano concerts with her. He championed the music of British composers in his concerts. In 1978 he was made a Commander of the Order of the British Empire. Somewhat off-center in his propensities, proclivities, and predilections, he learned Esperanto and wrote songs to his own texts in that artificial language. He also composed 2 piano concertos and some instrumental pieces. He publ. a didactic vol., *Practising the Piano* (London, 1958), and ed. John Field's piano concertos.

Merrill, Robert, noted American baritone; b. N.Y., June 4, 1917. He first studied voice with his mother, Lillian Miller Merrill, a concert singer; then took lessons with Samuel Margolis. He began his career as a popular singer on the radio; then made his operatic debut as Amonasro in Trenton, N.J., in 1944. After winning the Metropolitan Opera Auditions of the Air in N.Y., he made his debut there with the Metropolitan Opera on Dec. 15, 1945, as Germont. He remained on the roster of the Metropolitan Opera until 1976, and was again on its roster in 1983–84; he also gave solo recitals. In 1961 he made his European operatic debut as Germont in Venice; sang that same role at his Covent Garden debut in London in 1967. He became highly successful through many radio, television, and film appearances; gave recitals and sang with the major American orchs.; also starred in *Fiddler on the Roof* and other popular musicals. Among his numerous roles were Don José, Iago, Figaro, Rigoletto, Ford, and Scarpia. He was briefly married to **Roberta Peters**. He publ. 2 autobiographical books, *Once More from the Beginning* (N.Y., 1965) and *Between Acts* (N.Y., 1977).

Merriman, Nan (actually, **Katherine-Ann**), American mezzo-soprano; b. Pittsburgh, April 28, 1920. She studied with Alexia Bassian in Los Angeles. She made her operatic debut as La Cieca in *La Gioconda* with the Cincinnati Summer Opera in 1942; from 1943 she sang with Toscanini and the NBC Sym. Orch.; also appeared in opera at Aix-en-Provence, Edinburgh, and Glyndebourne. She retired in 1965. Her best operatic roles were Gluck's Orfeo, Maddalena in *Rigoletto*, Dorabella in *Così fan tutte*, Emilia in *Otello*, Baba the Turk in *The Rake's Progress*, and Meg in *Falstaff*.

Merritt, A(rthur) Tillman, American musicologist and pedagogue; b. Calhoun, Mo., Feb. 15, 1902. He studied at the Univ. of Missouri (B.A., 1924; B.F.A., 1926) and Harvard Univ. (M.A., 1927); then went to Europe on a J.K. Paine traveling scholarship from Harvard, and studied in Paris with Boulanger and Dukas; upon his return to America, he taught at Trinity College in Hartford, Conn. (1930–32). In 1932 he joined the faculty of the music dept. of Harvard Univ.; was its chairman from 1942 to 1952 and from 1968 to 1972, when he retired. He publ. the valuable treatise *Sixteenth-century Polyphony: A Basis for the Study of Counterpoint* (Cambridge, Mass., 1939); also ed. works by Janequin. On his retirement, he was honored with a Festschrift, *Words and Music: The Scholar's View* (Cambridge, Mass., 1972).

Mersmann, Hans, distinguished German musicologist; b. Potsdam, Oct. 6, 1891; d. Cologne, June 24, 1971. He studied in Munich with Sandberger and Kroyer, in Leipzig with Riemann and Schering, and with Wolf and Kretzschmar at the Univ. of Berlin, where he received his Ph.D. in 1914 with the diss. *Christian Ludwig Boxberg und seine Oper "Sardanapalus" (Ansbach 1698), mit Beiträgen zur Ansbacher Musikgeschichte*; completed his Habilitation at the Berlin Technische Hochschule in 1921 with his *Grundlagen einer musikalischen Volksliedforschung* (publ. in Leipzig, 1930); was a reader there from 1927. He subsequently taught at the Stern Cons. in Berlin, and at the Technische Hochschule there, until 1933; was in charge of the folk song archives of the Prussian Volksliederkommission (1917–33); also organized numerous seminars on musicology and modern music; from 1924, ed. the periodical *Melos*; wrote music criticism. He was removed from all of his positions by the Nazi regime in 1933; then devoted himself to private musicological research. After the collapse of the 3rd Reich, he taught at the Staatliche Hochschule für Musik in Munich (1946–47); from 1947 to 1958 he was director of the Hochschule für Musik in Cologne. As a historian and analyst of modern music, Mersmann occupied an important position in 20th-century research.

WRITINGS: *Kulturgeschichte der Musik in Einzeldarstellungen* (4 vols., Berlin, 1921–25); *Angewandte Musikästhetik* (Berlin, 1926); *Das Musikseminar* (Leipzig, 1931); *Kammermusik* (vols. 2–4, Leipzig, 1930; vol. 1, Leipzig, 1933); *Eine deutsche Musikgeschichte* (Potsdam, 1934; 2nd ed., rev. and aug., 1955, as *Musikgeschichte in der abendländischen Kultur*, 3rd ed., 1973); *Volkslied und Gegenwart* (Potsdam, 1936); *Musikhören* (Berlin, 1938; aug. ed., 1952); *Neue Musik in den Strömungen unserer Zeit* (Bayreuth, 1949); *Die Kirchenmusik im XX. Jahrhundert* (Nuremberg, 1958); *Stilprobleme der Werkanalyse* (Mainz, 1963).

BIBL.: W. Wiora, ed., *Musikerkenntnis und Musikziehung. Dankesgaben für H. M. zu seinem 65. Geburtstag* (Kassel, 1957).

Messager, André (Charles Prosper), celebrated French composer and conductor; b. Montiuçon, Allier, Dec. 30, 1853; d. Paris, Feb. 24, 1929. He studied at the École Niedermeyer in Paris with Gigout, Fauré, and Saint-Saëns (composition), A. Lassel (piano), and C. Loret (organ). In 1874 he became organist at St.-Sulpice. He was active as a conductor at the Folies-Bergère, where he produced several ballets. After conducting Brussels's Eden-Théâtre (1880), he returned to Paris as organist of St. Paul-St. Louis (1881) and as maître de chapelle at Ste. Marie-des-Baugnolles (1882–84). He subsequently was music director at the Opéra-Comique (1898–1903); also managed the Grand Opera Syndicate at London's Covent Garden (1901–07). He was conductor of the Concerts Lamoureux (1905) and music director of the Paris Opéra (1907–14); was also conductor of the Société des Concerts da Conservatoire from 1908 until 1919; under the auspices of the French government, he visited the U.S. with that orch., giving concerts in 50 American cities (1918); also toured Argentina (1916). Returning to Paris, he again conducted at the Opéra-Comique; led a season of Diaghilev's Ballets Russes in 1924. As a conductor, Messager played an important role in Paris musical life; he conducted the premiere of *Pelléas et Mélisande* (1902), the score of which Debussy dedicated to him. His initial steps as a composer were auspicious; his Sym. (1875) was awarded the gold medal of the Société des Compositeurs and performed at the Concerts Colonne (Jan. 20, 1878); his dramatic scene *Don Juan et Haydée* (1876) was awarded a gold medal by the Academy of St. Quentin. He wrote several other works for orch. (*Impressions orientals, Suite funambulesque*, etc.) and some chamber music, but he was primarily a man of the theater. His style may be described as enlightened eclecticism; his music was characteristically French, and more specifically Parisian, in its elegance and gaiety. He was honored in France; in 1926 he was elected to the Académie des Beaux Arts. He was married to Hope Temple (real name, Dotie Davis; 1858–1938), who was the author of numerous songs. His stage works (1st perf. in Paris unless otherwise given) included *François les-Bas-Bleus* (Nov. 8, 1883; score begun by F. Bernicat and completed after his death by Messager); *La Fauvette du temple* (Nov. 17, 1885); *La Béarnaise* (Dec. 12, 1885); *Le Bourgeois de Calais* (April 6, 1887); *Isoine* (Dec. 26, 1888); *La Basoche* (May 30, 1890; greatly acclaimed); *Madame Chrysanthème* (Jan. 26, 1893; to a story similar to Puccini's *Madame Butterfly*, produced 11 years later; but Puccini's dramatic treatment eclipsed Messager's lyric setting); *Le Chevalier d'Harmental* (May 5, 1896); *Véronique* (Dec. 10, 1898); *Les Dragons de l'impératrice* (Feb. 13, 1905); *Fortunio* (June 5, 1907); *Béatrice* (Monte Carlo, March 21, 1914); *Monsieur Beaucaire* (Birmingham, April 7, 1919). Other stage works were *Le Mart de la Reine* (Dec. 18, 1889); *Mies Dollar* (Jan. 22, 1893); *La Fiancée* en loterie (Feb. 15, 1896); *Les Pittes Michu* (Nov. 18, 1897); *La Petite Fonctionnaire* (May 14, 1921); *Passionnément* (Jan. 15, 1926). His ballets included *Fleur d'oranger* (1878); *Les Vins de France* (1879); *Mignons et villains* (1879); *Les Deux Pigeons* (1886); *Scaramouche* (1891); *Amants éternels* (1893); *Le Chevalier aux fleurs* (1897); *Le Procès des roses* (1897); *Une Aventure de la guimard* (1900). He also wrote incidental music.

BIBL.: Special issue of *Musica*, LXXII (1908); O. Séré, *Musiciens français d'aujourd'hui* (Paris, 1911; 2nd ed., 1921); H. Février, *A. M.: Mon maître, mon ami* (Paris, 1948); M. Augé-Laribé, *A. M.: Musicien de théâtre* (Paris, 1951); J. Wagstaff, *A. M.: A Bio-Bibliography* (N.Y., 1991).

Messiaen, Olivier (Eugène Prosper Charles), outstanding French composer and pedagogue; b. Avignon, Dec. 10, 1908; d. Clichy, Hauts-de-Seine, April 27, 1992. A scion of an intellectual family (his father was a translator of English literature; his mother, Cécile Sauvage, a poet), he absorbed the atmosphere of culture and art as a child. A mystical quality was imparted by his mother's book of verses *L'Âme en bourgeon*, dedicated to her as yet unborn child. He learned to play piano; at the age of 8, he composed a song, *La Dame de Shalott*, to a poem by Tennyson. At the age of 11, he entered the Paris Cons., where he attended the classes of Jean and Noël Gallon, Dupré, Emmanuel, and Dukas, specializing in organ, improvisation, and composition; he carried 1st prizes in all these depts. After graduation in 1930, he became organist at the Trinity Church in Paris. He taught at the École Normale de Musique and at the Schola Cantorum (1936–39). He also organized, with Jolivet, Baudrier, and Daniel-Lesur, the group La Jeune France, with the aim of promoting modern French music. He was in the French army at the outbreak of World War II in 1939; was taken prisoner; spent 2 years in a German prison camp in Görlitz, Silesia; he composed there his *Quatuor pour la fin du temps*; was repatriated in 1941 and resumed his post as organist at the Trinity Church in Paris. He was prof. of harmony and analysis at the Paris Cons. (from 1948). He also taught at the Berkshire Music Center in Tanglewood (summer, 1948) and in Darmstadt (1950–53). Young composers seeking instruction in new music became his eager pupils; among them were Boulez, Stockhausen, Xenakis, and others who were to become important composers in their own right. He received numerous honors; was made a Grand Officier de la Légion d'honneur; was elected a member of the Institut de France, the Bavarian Academy of the Fine Arts, the Accademia di Santa Cecilia in Rome, the American Academy of Arts and Letters, and other organizations. He married **Yvonne Loriod** in 1961.

Messiaen was one of the most original of modern composers; in his music, he made use of a wide range of resources, from Gregorian chant to Oriental rhythms. A mystic by nature and Catholic by religion, he strove to find a relationship between progressions of musical sounds and religious concepts; in his theoretical writing, he postulated an interdependence of modes, rhythms, and harmonic structures. Ever in quest of new musical resources, he employed in his scores the Ondes Martenot and exotic percussion instruments; a synthesis of these disparate tonal elements found its culmination in his grandiose orch. work *Turangalîla-Symphonie*. One of the most fascinating aspects of Messiaen's innovative musical vocabulary was the phonetic emulation of bird song in several of his works; in order to attain ornithological fidelity, he made a detailed study notating the rhythms and pitches of singing birds in many regions of several countries. The municipal council of Parowan, Utah, where Messiaen wrote his work *Des canyons aux étoiles*, glorifying the natural beauties of the state of Utah, resolved to name a local mountain Mt. Messiaen on Aug. 5, 1978. On Nov. 28, 1983, his opera, *St. François d'Assise*, was premiered, to international acclaim, at the Paris Opéra.

WORKS: OPERA: *St. François d'Assise* (Paris Opéra, Nov. 28, 1983). **ORCH.:** Fugue (1928); *Le Banquet eucharistique* (1928); *Simple chant d'une âme* (1930); *Les Offrandes oubliées* (1930; Paris, Feb. 19, 1931); *Le Tombeau resplendissant* (1931; Paris, Feb. 12, 1933); *Hymne au Saint Sacrement* (1932; Paris, March 23, 1933); *L'Ascension* (1933; Paris, Feb. 1935); *3 Talas* for Piano and Orch. (Paris, Feb. 14, 1948); *Turangalîla-Symphonie* (1946–48; Boston, Dec. 2, 1949); *Réveil des oiseaux* for Piano and Orch. (Donaueschingen, Oct. 11, 1953); *Oiseaux exotiques* for Piano, 2 Wind Instruments, Xylophone, Glockenspiel, and Percussion (Paris, March 10, 1956); *Chronochromie* (Donaueschingen, Oct. 16, 1960); *7 Haï-kaï* for Piano, 13 Wind Instruments, Xylophone, Marimba, 4 Percussion Instruments, and 8 Violins (1962; Paris, Oct. 30, 1963); *Couleurs de la cité céleste* for Large Orch., with imitations of 2 New Zealand birds and 1 from Brazil (Donaueschingen, Oct. 17, 1964); *Et expecto resurrectionem mortuorum* for 18 Woodwinds, 16 Brass Instruments, and 3 Percussion Instruments (1964; Paris, May 7, 1965); *Des canyons aux étoiles* (1970–74; N.Y., Nov. 20, 1974); *Éclairs sur l'Au-Delà* (1987–91; N.Y., Nov. 5, 1992). **CHAMBER:** *Thème et variations* for Violin and Piano (1932); *Quatuor pour la fin du temps* for Violin, Clarinet, Cello, and Piano (Stalag 8A, Görlitz, Jan. 15, 1941, composer pianist); *Le Merle noir* for Flute and Piano (1951); *Le Tombeau de Jean-Pierre Guézec* for Horn (1971). **KEYBOARD: PIANO:** *8 Préludes* (1929); *Pièce pour le tombeau de Paul Dukas* (1935); *Visions de l'Amen* for 2 Pianos (1942); *20 regards sur l'enfant Jésus* (1944); *Cantéyodjayâ* (1948); *4 études de rythme* (1949); *Catalogue d'oiseaux* (1956–58). **ORGAN:** *Variations écossaises* (1928); *Le Banquet céleste* (1928); *Diptyque* (1929); *Apparition de l'église éternelle* (1932); *L'Ascension* (1934; based on the orch. piece, 1933); *La Nativité du Seigneur* (1935); *Les Corps glorieux* (1939); *Messe de la Pentecôte* (1950); *Livre d'orgue* (1951); *Verset pour la fête de la dédicace* (1960); *Méditations sur le mystère de la Sainte Trinité* (1969). **VOCAL:** *2 ballades de Villon* (1921); *3 mélodies* (1930); *La Mort du nombre* for Soprano, Tenor, Violin, and Piano (1930; Paris, March 25, 1931); Mass for 8 Sopranos and 4 Violins (1933); *Poèmes pour Mi* for Soprano and Piano (1936; Paris, April 28, 1937; orch. version, 1937; Paris, 1946); *O sacrum convivium!* for Chorus and Organ (1937); *Chants de terre et de ciel*, song cycle for Soprano and Piano, after texts by the composer (1938); *Choeurs pour une Jeanne d'Arc* for Chorus (1941); *3 petites liturgies de la Présence Divine* for 18 Sopranos, Piano, Ondes Martenot, and Orch. (1944; Paris, April 21, 1945); *Harawi*, "chant d'amour et de mort," for Soprano and Piano (1945); *5 rechants* for Chamber Chorus (1949); *La Transfiguration de Notre Seigneur Jésus-Christ* for Chorus and Orch. (Lisbon, June 7, 1969).

WRITINGS: *20 leçons de solfèges modernes* (Paris, 1933); *20 leçons d'harmonie* (Paris, 1939); *Technique de mon langage musical* (2 vols., Paris, 1944; Eng. tr., 1957, as *The Technique of My Musical Language*).

BIBL.: B. Gavoty, *Musique et mystique: Le "Cas" M.* (Paris, 1945); V. Zinke-Bianchini, *O. M. Notice biographique; catalogue détaillé des oeuvres éditées* (Paris, 1946); C. Rostand, *O. M.* (Paris, 1958); A. Goléa, *Rencontres avec O. M.* (Paris, 1961); C. Samuel, *Entretiens avec O. M.* (Paris, 1967); S. Waumsley, *The Organ Music of O. M.* (Paris, 1969; rev. 1975); R. Johnson, *M.* (Berkeley, Calif., 1975); R. Nichols, *M.* (London, 1975; 2nd ed.,

1985); C. Bell, *O. M.* (Boston, 1984); P. Griffiths, *O. M. and the Music of Time* (London, 1985); J. Gallatin, *An Overview of the Compositional Methods in Representative Works of O. M.* (diss., Univ. of Cincinnati, 1986); A. Michaely, *Die Musik O. M.s: Untersuchungen zum Gesamtschaffen* (Hamburg, 1987); T. Hirsbrunner, *O. M., Leben und Werk* (Laaber, 1988); B. Carl, *O. M.s Orchesterwerk des Canyons aux Etoiles* (Kassel, 2 vols., 1994); P. Hill, ed., *The M. Companion* (Portland, Oreg., 1995).

Messner, Joseph, Austrian organist, conductor, and composer; b. Schwaz, Tirol, Feb. 27, 1893; d. St. Jakob Thurn, near Salzburg, Feb. 23, 1969. He studied at the Univ. of Innsbruck; after his ordination (1918), he took courses in organ and composition with Friedrich Klose at the Munich Akademie der Tonkunst. In 1922 he was appointed Cathedral organist in Salzburg; from 1926 to 1967 he led the concerts at the Salzburg Cathedral; at the same time, he gave a seminar in church music at the Mozarteum there. He wrote 4 operas: *Hadassa* (Aachen, March 27, 1925), *Das letzte Recht* (1932), *Ines* (1933), and *Agnes Bernauer* (1935); 3 syms.; Violin Concerto; Cello Concerto; String Quartet; several sacred works, including 11 masses.

Mester, Jorge, talented Mexican-born American conductor; b. Mexico City (of Hungarian parents), April 10, 1935. He settled in the U.S. and became a naturalized citizen in 1968. He studied with Morel at the Juilliard School of Music in N.Y. (M.A., 1958); also with Bernstein at the Berkshire Music Center in Tanglewood (summer, 1955) and with A. Wolff in the Netherlands. From 1956 to 1967 he taught conducting at the Juilliard School of Music. In 1967 he was appointed music director of the Louisville Orch., holding this post until 1979. Following the Louisville Orch.'s unique policy of commissioning new works and then giving their premieres, Mester conducted, during his tenure, something like 200 first performances, and made about 70 recordings of some of them. Concurrently, he served as musical adviser and principal conductor of the Kansas City Phil. (1971–74). In 1970 he became music director of the Aspen (Colo.) Music Festival. From 1980 he again taught at the Juilliard School, where he was chairman of the conducting dept. (1984–87). In 1984 he became music director of the Pasadena (Calif.) Sym. Orch. He also was concurrently music director of the West Australian Sym. Orch. in Perth (1990–93). Equally at home in the classical and modern repertoires, in symphonic music and in opera, Mester knows how to impart a sense of color with a precision of technical detail.

Mestres-Quadreny, Josep (Maria), Spanish composer; b. Manresa, March 4, 1929. He studied composition with Taltabull at the Univ. of Barcelona (1950–56). In 1960 he collaborated in the founding of Música Abierta, an organization of avant-garde musical activity; later he joined composers Xavier Benguerel, Joaquim Homs, and Josep Soler in founding the Conjunt Català de Másica Contemporània, for the propagation of Catalan music. In his music, he consciously attempts to find a counterpart to Abstract Expressionism in art, as exemplified by the paintings of Miró; for this purpose he applies serial techniques and aleatory procedures.

WORKS: DRAMATIC: OPERA: *El Ganxo* (1959). **BALLETS:** *Roba i ossos* (1961); *Petit diumenge* (1962); *Vegetació submergida* (1962). **MUSIC THEATER:** *Concert per a representar* for 6 Voices, 6 Instrumentalists, and Tape (1964); *Suite bufa* for Ballerina, Mezzo-soprano, Piano, and Electronic Sound (1966). **ORCH.:** *Triade per a Joan Miró* (1961; a superimposition of *Música da cámara I* for Flute, Piano, Percussion, Violin, and Double Bass, *Música da cámara II* for 3 Clarinets, English Horn, Trumpet, Trombone, Percussion, and String Trio, and *3 Moviments per a orquesta de cámara* for 15 Instruments); *Digodal* for Strings (1963); *Conversa* for Chamber Orch. (1965); *Quadre* for Chamber Orch. (1969); Double Concerto for Ondes Martenot, Percussion, and Orch. (1970). **CHAMBER:** Piano Sonata (1957); *3 invenció mòvils: I* for Flute, Clarinet, and Piano, *II* for Voice, Trumpet, and Electric Guitar, and *III* for String Quartet (all 1961); *Tramesa a Tàpies* for Violin, Viola, and Percussion (1961); *Quartet de Catroc* for String Quartet (1962); *3 cànons en homenatge a Galile*, in 3 versions: for Piano (1965), for Percussion (1968), and for Ondes Martenot (1969), each with Tape; String Trio (1968); *Ibemia* for 13 Instrumentalists (1969); *Micos i Papellones* for Guitar and Metal Percussion (1970); *Variacions essencials* for String Trio and Percussion (1970); *Homenatge a Joan Prats* for 6 Actors, Electroacoustical Installation, String Quartet, 4 Percussionists, Flute, Clarinet, Trumpet, 2 Trombones, and Tuba (1972); *Frigoli-Frigola* for Any Instruments (1969); *Aronada* for Any Instruments (1972). **VOCAL:** *Epitafios*, cantata for Soprano, Strings, Harp, and Celesta (1958); *Tríptic carnavalesc*, cantata for Soprano, Flute, Clarinet, Trumpet, Trombone, 2 Percussionists, and Piano (1966); *Música per a Anna* for Soprano and String Quartet (1967).

Metcalf, Frank J(ohnson), American hymnologist; b. Ashland, Mass., April 4, 1865; d. Washington, D.C., Feb. 25, 1945. He studied at Boston Univ. (B.A., 1886). He owned a private collection of more than 2,000 hymn books; also a MS bibliography containing about 10,000 entries. He publ. *American Psalmondy, or Titles of Books Containing Tunes Printed in America from 1721 to 1820* (N.Y., 1917); *American Writers and Compilers of Sacred Music* (N.Y., 1925); *Stories of Hymn Tunes* (N.Y., 1928); also numerous articles.

Metianu, Lucian, Romanian composer; b. Cluj, June 3, 1937. He studied with Olah, Vancea, Constantinescu, and Chirescu at the Bucharest Cons. (1957–63).

WORKS: ORCH.: Concerto for Strings (1959); *2 Choreographic Tableaux* (1964); *Echo* (1966); *Ergodica* (1967); *Conexe* for Speaking Chorus and Orch. (1969); *Elogiu* (1969); *Evocare* (1972); *Evolutio II* (1976). **CHAMBER:** Piano Quintet (1960); 2 string quartets (1961, 1968); Piano Sonata (1962); *Pithagoreis* for Tape (1970–71); *Evolutio '73*, sonata for Solo Double Bass (1973); Duo for Double Bass and Cello (1974); *Evolutio '74* for Cello (1974). **VOCAL:** *Cantata de camera* for Chorus and Chamber Orch. (1953).

Metner, Nikolai. See **Medtner, Nicolai.**

Metternich, Josef, German baritone; b. Hermuhlheim, near Cologne, June 2, 1915. He studied in Berlin and Cologne. After singing in the opera choruses in Bonn and Cologne, he made his operatic debut as Tonio at the Berlin Städtische Opera in 1945. In 1951 he sang the Dutchman at his first appearance at London's Covent Garden. On Nov. 21, 1953, he made his Metropolitan Opera debut in N.Y. as Carlo in *La forza del destino*, and remained on its roster until 1956. In 1954 he became a member of the Bavarian State Opera in Munich, where he created the role of Johannes Kepler in Hindemith's *Die Harmonie der Welt* in 1957. His guest engagements took him to Cologne, Hamburg, Vienna, Milan, Edinburgh, and other European music centers. In 1963 he sang Kothner in *Die Meistersinger von Nürnberg* at the reopening of the National Theater in Munich. He retired from the operatic stage in 1971. From 1965 he was a prof. at the Cologne Hochschule für Musik. Among his other roles were Kurwenal, Wolfram, Amfortas, Amonasro, Jochanaan, and Scarpia.

Metzger, Heinz-Klaus, German writer on music; b. Konstanz, Feb. 6, 1932. He studied at the Staatliche Musikhochschule in Freiburg im Breisgau (1949–52), then studied composition with Deutsch in Paris and musicology in Tübingen (1952–54). He qualified in 1956 at the Akademie für Tonkunst in Darmstadt, where he later was active in the Darmstadt summer courses. His theoretical, philosophical, and cultural writings on modern and avant-garde music were influenced by Adorno, who recognized his talent. Metzger co-founded the journal *Musik-Konzepte* with Rainer Riehn in 1977. His relationship with Sylvano Bussotti led to his remarkable studies of music considered unanalyzable by other writers, by composers including Bussotti, Schnebel, and Kagel.

Metzger-Lattermann, Ottilie, German contralto; b. Frankfurt am Main, July 15, 1878; d. in the concentration camp in

Auschwitz, Feb. 1943. She was a pupil of Selma Nicklass-Kempner and Emanuel Reicher in Berlin. In 1898 she made her operatic debut in Halle, and then appeared in Cologne (1900–1903), at the Bayreuth Festivals (1901–12), the Hamburg Opera (1903–15), and the Dresden Court Opera (1915–18), and its successor, the State Opera (1918–21). In 1910 she was the first to sing Herodias in *Salome* in London under Beecham's direction. She made guest appearances in Berlin, Vienna, Munich, and other European cities, and in 1923 she toured the U.S. with the German Opera Co. As a Jew, she was forced to leave Germany in 1935 and went to Brussels, where she taught voice. In 1942 she was arrested by the Nazi henchmen and was sent to Auschwitz.

Meulemans, Arthur, eminent Belgian composer; b. Aarschot, May 19, 1884; d. Brussels, June 29, 1966. He was a student of Tinel at the Lemmens Inst. in Mechelen (1900–1906), and then was a prof. there until 1914. In 1916 he founded the Limburg School for organ and song in Hasselt, serving as its director until 1930. He subsequently settled in Brussels, where he was a conductor with the Belgian Radio (1930–42). In 1954 he became president of the Royal Flemish Academy of Fine Arts. Meulemans composed a prodigious body of music, excelling especially as a composer of orch. works.

WORKS: OPERAS: *Vikings* (1919); *Adriaen Brouwer* (1926); *Egmont* (1944). **ORCH.:** 2 cello concertos (1920, 1944); 15 syms.: No. 1 (1931), No. 2 (1933), No. 3, *Dennensymphonie* (1933), No. 4 for Winds and Percussion (1934), No. 5, *Danssymphonie*, for Women's Chorus and Orch. (1939), No. 6, *Zeesymphonie*, for Contralto, Chorus, and Orch. (1940), No. 7, *Zwaneven* (1942), No. 8, *Herfstsymphonie*, for Soloists, Chorus, and Orch. (1942), No. 9 (1943), No. 10, *Psalmen-Symphonie*, for 2 Narrators, Soloists, Chorus, and Orch. (1943), No. 11 (1946), No. 12 (1948), No. 13, *Rembrandt-Symphonie* (1950), No. 14 (1954), and No. 15 (1960); 2 horn concertos (1940, 1961); 3 piano concertos (1941, 1956, 1960); 3 violin concertos (1942, 1946, 1950); Viola Concerto (1942); Flute Concerto (1942); Oboe Concerto (1942); 2 organ concertos (both 1942); Trumpet Concerto (1943); 3 sinfoniettas (1952; 1959–60; 1960); 2 concertos for orch. (1953, 1956); Harp Concerto (1953); Timpani Concerto (1954); Harpsichord Concerto (1958); Concerto for 2 Pianos and Orch. (1959); Concerto grosso for Winds, Strings, Harp, and Percussion (1962); symphonic poems, suites, etc. **CHAMBER:** 5 string quartets (1915, 1932, 1933, 1944, 1952); Piano Quartet (1915); 2 violin sonatas (1915, 1953); 3 wind quintets (1931, 1932, 1958); 2 woodwind trios (1933, 1960); 2 brass trios (1933, 1960); Piano Trio (1941); String Trio (1941); Saxophone Quartet (1953); Viola Sonata (1953); Cello Sonata (1953); Trumpet Sonata (1959); Woodwind Quartet (1962). **KEYBOARD: PIANO:** 3 sonatas (1916, 1917, 1951); *Refleksen* (1923); 3 sonatinas (1927, 1928, 1941); *Préludes* (1951); *Atmosferiliën* (1962). **ORGAN:** Sonata (1915); 2 syms. (both 1949); *7 Pieces* (1959); *Pièce heroïque* (1959). **VOCAL:** Oratorios; choral pieces; songs.

BIBL.: M. Boereboom, *A. M.* (Kortrijk, 1951); *Aan Meester A. M. bij zijn tachtigs verjaardag* (Antwerp, 1964).

Mewton-Wood, Noel, remarkable Australian pianist; b. Melbourne, Nov. 20, 1922; d. (suicide) London, Dec. 5, 1953. After training with Seidel at the Melbourne Cons., he went to London and at age 14 was admitted to the Royal Academy of Music. Later he completed his studies with Schnabel. In 1940 he made an auspicious London debut as soloist in Beethoven's 1st Piano Concerto under Beecham's baton. Subsequently he was active as a soloist with orchs., as a recitalist, as a chamber music player, and as an accompanist. In 1947 he appeared at the London Promenade Concerts. His extensive repertoire ranged widely, from the classics to contemporary scores.

Meyer, Ernst Hermann, German musicologist and composer; b. Berlin, Dec. 8, 1905; d. there, Oct. 8, 1988. His father was a medical doctor of artistic interests who encouraged him to study music; he took piano lessons with Walter Hirschberg and played in chamber music groups. During the economic disarray in Germany in the 1920s, Meyer was obliged to do manual labor in order to earn a living. In 1926 he was able to enroll in the Univ. of Berlin, where he studied musicology with Wolf, Schering, Blume, Hornbostel, and Sachs; in 1928 he had additional studies with Besseler at the Univ. of Heidelberg, obtaining his Ph.D. in 1930 with the diss. *Die mehrstimmige Spielmusik des 17. Jahrhunderts in Nord- und Mitteleuropa* (publ. in Kassel, 1934). In 1929 he met Eisler, who influenced him in the political aspect of music. In 1930 he joined the German Communist party. He conducted workers' choruses in Berlin and composed music for the proletarian revue *Der rote Stern.* He also attended classes on film music given by Hindemith. In 1931 he took a course in Marxism-Leninism with Hermann Duncker at the Marxist Workers' School in Berlin. He also began a detailed study of works by modern composers; in his own works, mostly for voices, he developed a style characteristic of the proletarian music of the time, full of affirmative action in march time adorned by corrosive discords, and yet eminently singable. When the Nazis bore down on his world with a different march, he fled to London, where, with the help of Alan Bush, he conducted the Labour Choral Union. During World War II, he participated in the Chorus of the Free German Cultural Union in London and wrote propaganda songs; of these, *Radio Moskau ruft Frau Kramer* was widely broadcast to Germany. In 1948 he went to East Berlin, where he was a prof. and director of the musicological inst. of the Humboldt Univ. until 1970. He was acknowledged as one of the most persuasive theoreticians of socialist realism in music; he founded the periodical *Musik und Gesellschaft*, which pursued the orthodox Marxist line. He publ. *English Chamber Music: The History of a Great Art from the Middle Ages to Purcell* (London, 1946; in Ger. as *Die Kammermusik Alt-Englands*, East Berlin, 1958; new ed., rev., 1982, with D. Poulton as *Early English Chamber Music*); *Das Werk Beethovens und seine Bedeutung für das sozialistisch-realistische Gegenwartsschaffen* (East Berlin, 1970); and the autobiographical *Kontraste-Konflikte* (East Berlin, 1979). A Festschrift was publ. in his honor in Leipzig in 1973.

WORKS: DRAMATIC: OPERA: *Reiter der Nacht* (1969–72; Berlin, Nov. 17, 1973); film music. **ORCH.:** Sym. for Strings (1946–47; rev. 1958); *Symphonischer Prolog* (1949); Sym. for Piano and Orch. (1961); *Poem* for Viola and Orch. (1962); Violin Concerto (1964); *Serenata pensierosa* (1965); Concerto Grosso (1966); Sym. (1967); Harp Concerto (1969); Toccata (1971); *Divertimento* (1973); Concerto for Orch. with Piano obbligato (1975); *Kontraste, Konflikte* (1977); Viola Concerto (1978); *Sinfonietta* (1980); *Berliner Divertimento* (1981); *Kammersinfonie* (1983; transcription of the 5th String Quartet); *Sinfonische widmung* for Orch. and Concertante Organ (1983). **CHAMBER:** Trio for Flute, Oboe, and Harp (1935); Clarinet Quintet (1944); Piano Trio, *Reflections and Resolution* (1948); 6 string quartets (1956, 1959, 1967, 1974, 1978, 1982); *Sonatina Fantasia* for Solo Violin (1966); Viola Sonata (1979); Piano Trio (1980); Violin Sonata (1984); piano pieces. **CHORAL:** *Mansfelder Oratorium* (1950); *Nun, Steuermann*, cantata, after Walt Whitman's *Now Voyager* (1946; rev. 1955); *Gesang von der Jugend* for Soloists, Chorus, Children's Chorus, and Orch. (1957); *Das Tor von Buchenwald* (1959); *Der Staat* for Chorus and Orch. (1967); *Lenin hat gesprochen* (1970); more than 200 mass songs.

BIBL.: K. Niemann, *E.H. M.: Für Sie porträtiert* (Leipzig, 1975); M. Hansen, ed., *E.H. M.: Das kompositorische und theoretische Werk* (Leipzig, 1976); A. Cross, "The Music of E.H. M.," *Musical Times* (Dec. 1980).

Meyer, Kerstin (Margareta), Swedish mezzo-soprano; b. Stockholm, April 3, 1928. She studied at the Royal Academy of Music (1948–50) and at the Opera School (1950–52) in Stockholm; also at the Accademia Musicale Chigiana in Siena and at the Salzburg Mozarteum. In 1952 she made her operatic debut as Azucena at the Royal Theater in Stockholm, where she subsequently sang regularly; also made guest appearances in numerous European opera centers and toured widely as a concert artist. In 1960 she made her first appearance at London's Covent Garden as Dido in the English-language production of Les Troyens. On Oct. 29, 1960, she made her Metropolitan Opera debut in N.Y. as Carmen, remaining on its roster until 1963; also appeared at the Bayreuth Festivals (1962–65). In 1963 she was made a Royal Swedish Court Singer. Following her retirement, she served as director of the Opera School in Stockholm (from 1984). In 1985 she was made an honorary Commander of the Order of the British Empire. She excelled particularly in contemporary operas, most notably in the works of Schuller, Searle, Henze, Maw, and Ligeti; among her standard portrayals were Orfeo, Dorabella, Fricka, Octavian, and Clytemnestra.

Meyer, Krzysztof, remarkable Polish composer and teacher; b. Kraków, Aug. 11, 1943. He commenced piano lessons when he was 5. At 11, he began to take lessons in theory and composition with Wiechowicz. He pursued his training at the Kraków College of Music with Penderecki (composition diploma, 1965) and Frączkiewicz (theory diploma, 1966). He also studied in Fontainebleau and Paris with Boulanger in 1964, 1966, and 1968. From 1965 to 1967 he was a pianist with the contemporary music group MW-2. He was prof. of theoretical subjects at the Kraków College of Music from 1966 to 1987, and was also head of its theory dept. from 1972 to 1975. From 1985 to 1989 he was president of the Union of Polish Composers. He was prof. of composition at the Cologne Hochschule für Musik from 1987. In addition to his various articles on contemporary music, he publ. the first monograph on the life and works of Shostakovich in Poland (Kraków, 1973; 2nd ed., 1986; Ger. tr., 1980; new ed., enl., Paris, 1994, and Bergish Gladbach, 1995). He prepared his own version of Shostakovich's unfinished opera *The Gamblers* (1980–81; Wuppertal, Sept. 9, 1984). His 3rd Sym. won 1st prize in the Young Polish Composers' Competition in 1968. In 1970 he won the Grand Prix of the Prince Pierre of Monaco composers' competition for his opera *Cyberiada.* He received awards from the Polish Ministry of Culture and Art in 1973 and 1975. In 1974 his 4th Sym. won 1st prize in the Szymanowski Competition in Warsaw. In 1984 he received the Gottfried von Herder Prize of Vienna. In 1987 he was made a member of the Freien Akademie der Künste in Mannheim. He received the annual award of the Union of Polish Composers in 1992. As a composer, he abandoned the early influence of Penderecki and Boulanger and pursued his own advanced course without ever transcending the practical limits of instrumental and vocal techniques or of aural perception. His scores are the product of a rare musical intelligence and acoustical acuity.

WORKS: DRAMATIC: *Cyberiada*, fantastic comic opera (1967–70; Act. 1, Polish-TV, May 12, 1971; 1st complete perf., Wuppertal, May 11, 1986); *Hrabina* (The Countess), ballet (1980; Poznań, Nov. 14, 1981); *Igroki* (The Gamblers), completion of Shostakovich's opera (1980–81; Wuppertal, Sept. 9, 1984); *Klonowi bracia* (The Maple Brothers), children's opera (1988–89; Poznań, March 3, 1990). **ORCH.:** *Concerto da camera* for Flute, Percussion, and Strings (1964; Kraków, June 25, 1965), for Oboe, Percussion, and Strings (1972; Zielona Góra, May 24, 1984), and for Harp, Cello, and Strings (1984; Cologne, Oct. 7, 1987); 6 numbered syms.: No. 1 (Kraków, June 12, 1964), No. 2, *Epitaphium Stanisław Wiechowicz in memoriam,* for Chorus and Orch. (1967; Wrocław, Feb. 15, 1969), No. 3, *Symphonie d'Orphée,* for Chorus and Orch. (1968; Warsaw, Sept. 16, 1972), No. 4 (1973; Zagreb, May 14, 1975), No. 5 for Chamber String Orch. (1978–79; Białystok, Sept. 17, 1979), and No. 6, *Polish* (Hamburg, Nov. 15, 1982); *Symphony in D major in Mozartean Style* (1976; Poznań, April 1, 1977); Violin Concerto (1965; Poznań, March 22, 1969); Cello Concerto (1971–72; Poznań, April 3, 1975); Trumpet Concerto (1973; Poznań, April 2, 1976); *Fireballs* (1976; Warsaw, April 20, 1978); Piano Concerto (1979–89; Cologne, June 14, 1992); *Hommage à Johannes Brahms* (1982; Hamburg, May 15, 1983); Flute Concerto (1983; Berlin, Dec. 1, 1984); *Canti Amadei* for Cello and Orch. (Kraków, Dec. 19, 1984); *Concerto retro* for Flute, Violin, Harpsichord, and Strings (1986; Kraków, April 10, 1988); *Musica incrostata* (Cologne, June 6, 1988); *Caro Luigi* for 4 Cellos and Strings (Stuttgart, Sept. 29, 1989); *Carillon* (1992–93; Flensburg, Aug. 5, 1993). **CHAMBER:** Sonata for Solo Cello (1959–61; Kamien Pomorski, Aug. 15, 1969); *Introspection* for 5 Cellos (1960; Kraków, May 28, 1961); *Music* for 3 Cellos, Kettledrums, and Piano (1962; Kraków, May 9, 1963); 10 string quartets: No. 1 (1963; Warsaw, Sept. 26, 1965), No. 2 (Warsaw, Sept. 28, 1969), No. 3 (1971; Warsaw, Sept. 29, 1973), No. 4 (1974; Curitiba, Jan. 29, 1975), No. 5 (1977; Białystok, March 10, 1978), No. 6 (1981; Plock, June 11, 1982), No. 7 (Wrocław, April 16, 1985), No. 8 (1985; Munich, March 16, 1986), No. 9 (1989–90; Cologne, Dec. 28, 1991), and No. 10 (1993–94; Poznań, Oct. 3, 1994); *Interludio statico* for Clarinet and 4 Cellos (1963–64; Poznań, April 19, 1967); *Hommage à Nadia Boulanger* for Flute, Viola, and Harp (1967–71; Zagreb, May 14, 1971); *Quattro colori* for Clarinet, Trombone, Cello, and Piano (1970); Sonata for Solo Violin (1975; Poznań, April 22, 1977); *Concerto retro* for Flute, Violin, Cello, and Harpsichord (1976; Curitiba, Feb. 4, 1977); *Moment musical* for Cello (1976); *3 Pieces* for Percussionist (Copenhagen, June 8, 1977); *Interludio drammatico* for Oboe and Chamber Ensemble (1980; Leipzig, Jan. 19, 1981); Piano Trio (1980; Wrocław, April 16, 1985); Sonata for Solo Flute (1980; Darmstadt, March 30, 1985); *Canzona* for Cello and Piano (1981; Hamburg, Nov. 1, 1982); *6 Préludes* for Violin (1981); *Pezzo capriccioso* for Oboe and Piano (1982; Princeton, N.J., April 18, 1983); Cello Sonata (1983; Klagenfurt, Nov. 22, 1984); Clarinet Quintet (Ulm, Nov. 2, 1986); *Capriccio per sei instrumenti* (1987–88; Lanaudière, Canada, July 10, 1989); *Wittener Kammermusik* for Flute, Oboe, and Clarinet (1988; Witten, Germany, April 22, 1989); *Monologue* for Cello (Hamburg, Oct. 5, 1990); Piano Quartet (1990–91; Cologne, May 25, 1992); String Trio (1993; Munich, March 6, 1994); *Misterioso* for Violin and Piano (Hannover, Nov. 2, 1994). **KEYBOARD: PIANO:** *Aphorisms* (1961; Kraków, June 20, 1962); 5 sonatas: No. 1 (Katowice, April 26, 1962), No. 2 (Kraków, June 3, 1963), No. 3 (Kraków, May 18, 1966), No. 4 (1968; Kraków, June 5, 1969), and No. 5 (1975; Katowice, Jan. 19, 1977); *24 Préludes* (1978; Stalowa Wola, May 17, 1979). **HARPSICHORD:** Sonata (1972–73; Paris, Oct. 28, 1974). **ORGAN:** *Fantasia* (1990; Berlin, June 15, 1991). **VOCAL:** *Songs of Resignation and Denial* for Soprano, Violin, and Piano (1963; Prague, April 28, 1966); *Quartettino* for Soprano, Flute, and Cello (Szczecin, Sept. 11, 1966); *5 Chamber Pieces* for Soprano, Clarinet, and Viola (1967; Kraków, April 17, 1969); *Polish Chants* for Soprano and Orch. (1974; Bydgoszcz, Sept. 9, 1977); *Lyric Triptych* for Tenor and Chamber Orch. (1976; Aldeburgh, June 22, 1978); *9 Limericks of Stanisław Jerzy Lec* for Soprano and Piano (Baranow Sandomierski, Sept. 7, 1979); *Sunday Colloquy* for Baritone and Piano (1981; Kraków, March 26, 1987); *Mass* for Chorus and Organ (1987–92; Cologne, Jan. 24, 1993); *Wjelitchalnaja* for Chorus (1988; L'Hermitage, May 15, 1989).

Meyer, Leonard B., eminent American musicologist; b. N.Y., Jan. 12, 1918. He was educated at Bard College (1936–37), Columbia Univ. (B.A., 1940; M.A., 1948), and the Univ. of Chicago (Ph.D., 1954). In 1946 he joined the faculty of the Univ. of Chicago, where he served as head of the humanities section (1958–60), chairman of the music dept. (1961–70), prof. of music (1961–75), and the Phyllis Fay Horton Distinguished Service Prof. (1972–75). In 1971–72 he held a Guggenheim fellowship. From 1975 to 1988 he was the Benjamin Franklin prof. of music at the Univ. of Pa., and subsequently held its emeritus title. In 1971 he was the Ernest Bloch Prof. of Music at the Univ. of Calif. at Berkeley, and later was a senior fellow at the School of Criticism and Theory (1975–88). He was a resident scholar at the Bellagio Study and Conference Center in Italy in 1982. In 1984 he was the Tanner lecturer at Stanford Univ. and in 1985 the Patten lecturer at Indiana Univ. In 1987 he was made an honorary member of the American Musicological Soc. Many of his erudite books and articles have been tr. into various foreign languages, among them French, Italian, Spanish, Polish, Serbo-Croatian, Japanese, and Chinese.

WRITINGS: *Emotion and Meaning in Music* (Chicago, 1956); with G. Cooper, *The Rhythmic Structure of Music* (Chicago, 1960); *Music, the Arts, and Ideas: Patterns and Predictions in Twentieth Century Culture* (Chicago, 1967; with new postlude, 1994); *Explaining Music: Essays and Explorations* (Berkeley and Los Angeles, 1973); *Style and Music: Theory, History, and Ideology* (Philadelphia, 1989).

BIBL.: E. Narmour and R. Solie, eds., *Explorations in Music, the Arts, and Ideas: Essays in Honor of L. B. M.* (Stuyvesant, N.Y., 1989).

Meyers, Anne Akiko, American violinist; b. San Diego, May 15, 1970. She began her musical training at age 4, making her public debut as a soloist with orch. at age 7. Following studies with Alice Schoenfeld at the R.D. Colburn School of Performing Arts in Los Angeles, she had advanced training with Josef Gingold at the Indiana Univ. School of Music in Bloomington and with Dorothy DeLay, Masao Kawasaki, and Felix Galimir at the Juilliard School in N.Y. In 1993 she was awarded the Avery Fisher Career Grant. She has appeared as a soloist with most of the leading orchs. of North America, and has appeared with major orchs. abroad. As a recitalist, she has performed throughout North America, Europe, and the Far East.

Meyer-Siat, Pie, French musicologist; b. Ribeauvillé, Haut-Rhin, Oct. 15, 1913; d. Strasbourg, April 4, 1989. He was educated at the Univ. of Strasbourg; received a degree in philosophy in 1937; took the agrégation in German in 1948; was awarded his Ph.D. in musicology in 1962 with the diss. *Les Callinet, facteurs d'orgues à Rouffach, et leur oeuvre en Alsace*, publ. in Strasbourg, 1965. He was an authority on organs in Alsace; contributed important articles for *Les Cahiers de la Société d'Histoire de Saverne.*

WRITINGS: *L'Orgue Callinet de Masevaux* (Mulhouse, 1962); *L'Orgue Joseph Callinet de Mollau (Haut-Rhin)* (Strasbourg, 1963); *Les Orgues de Niedernai et d'Obernai* (Colmar, 1972); *Stiehr-Mockers, facteurs d'orgues* (Hagenau, 1972); *Historische Orgeln im Elsass, 1489–1869* (Munich, 1983).

Meyerowitz, Jan (actually, **Hans-Hermann**), German-born American composer and teacher; b. Breslau, April 23, 1913. In 1927 he went to Berlin, where he studied with Gmeindl and Zemlinsky at the Hochschule für Musik. Compelled to leave Germany in 1933, he went to Rome, where he took lessons in advanced composition with Respighi and Casella, and in conducting with Molinari. In 1938 he moved to Belgium and later to southern France, where he remained until 1946; he then emigrated to the U.S., becoming a naturalized American citizen in 1951. He married the French singer Marguerite Fricker in 1946. He held a Guggenheim fellowship twice (1956, 1958). He taught at the Berkshire Music Center in Tanglewood (summers, 1948–51) and at Brooklyn (1954–61) and City (1962–80) Colleges of the City Univ. of N.Y. He publ. a monograph on Schoenberg (Berlin, 1967) and *Der echte judische Witz* (Berlin, 1971). His music is imbued with expansive emotionalism akin to that of Mahler; in his works for the theater, there is a marked influence of the tradition of 19th-century grand opera. His technical idiom is modern, enlivened by a liberal infusion of euphonious dissonance, and he often applies the rigorous and vigorous devices of linear counterpoint.

WORKS: DRAMATIC: OPERAS: *Simoon* (1948; Tanglewood, Aug. 2, 1950); *The Barrier*, after Langston Hughes (1949; N.Y., Jan. 18, 1950); *Eastward in Eden*, later renamed *Emily Dickinson* (Detroit, Nov. 16, 1951); *Bad Boys in School* (Tanglewood, Aug. 17, 1953); *Esther*, after Langston Hughes (Urbana, Ill., May 17, 1957); *Port Town*, after Langston Hughes (Tanglewood, Aug. 4, 1960); *Godfather Death* (N.Y., June 2, 1961); *Die Doppelgängerin*, after Gerhart Hauptmann, later renamed *Winterballade* (1966; Hannover, Jan. 29, 1967). **ORCH.:** *3 Comments on War* for Band (1957); 3 syms.: *Silesian Symphony* (1957), *Esther Midrash* (N.Y., Jan. 31, 1957), and *Sinfonia brevissima* (1968); *Flemish Overture* (1959); Oboe Concerto (1962); Flute Concerto (1962); *6 Pieces* (Pittsburgh, May 27, 1967); *7 Pieces* (1974); *4 Romantic Pieces* for Band (1978). **CHAMBER:** Cello Sonata (1946); Trio for Flute, Cello, and Piano (1946); Woodwind Quintet (1954); String Quartet (1955); Violin Sonata (1960); Flute Sonata (1961). **PIANO:** *Homage to Hieronymus Bosch* for 2 Pianos (1945); Sonata (1958). **VOCAL:** *The Glory Around His Head* for Bass, Chorus, and Orch. (N.Y., April 14, 1955); *the 5 Foolish Virgins* for Chorus and Orch. (1956); *Stabat Mater* for Chorus and Orch. (1957); *Hebrew Service* for Tenor, Mezzo-soprano, Chorus, and Organ (1962); *I rabbini* for Soli, Chorus, and Orch. (1962); *Missa Rachel plorans* for Soprano, Tenor, Chorus, and Organ ad libitum (1962); 6 Songs for Soprano and Orch., after August von Platen (1976; Cologne, Feb. 12, 1977); other choral works and songs.

Meyrowitz, Selmar, German conductor; b. Bartenstein, East Prussia, April 18, 1875; d. Toulouse, March 24, 1941. He studied at the Leipzig Cons., and later with Max Bruch in Berlin. In 1897 he became assistant conductor at the Karlsruhe Opera under Mottl, with whom he went to America as conductor at the Metropolitan Opera in N.Y. (1903); subsequently conducted at the Prague National Theater (1905–06), the Berlin Komische Oper (1907–10), the Munich Opera (1912–13), and the Hamburg Opera (1913–17). After appearing as a guest conductor with the Berlin Phil., he conducted at the Berlin Radio and the State Opera (1924–33); also toured with the German Grand Opera Co. in the U.S. (1929–31); settled in France (1933).

Miaskovsky, Nikolai (Yakovlevich), eminent Russian composer and teacher; b. Novogeorgievsk, near Warsaw, April 20, 1881; d. Moscow, Aug. 8, 1950. His father was an officer of the dept. of military fortification; the family lived in Orenburg (1888–89) and in Kazan (1889–93). In 1893 he was sent to a military school in Nizhny-Novgorod; in 1895 he went to a military school in St. Petersburg, graduating in 1899. At that time he developed an interest in music, and tried to compose; took lessons with Kazanli; his first influences were Chopin and Tchaikovsky. In 1902–03 he was in Moscow, where he studied harmony with Glière. Returning to St. Petersburg in 1903, he took lessons with Kryzhanovsky, from whom he acquired a taste for modernistic composition in the impressionist style. In 1906, at the age of 25, he entered the St. Petersburg Cons. as a pupil of Liadov and Rimsky-Korsakov, graduating in 1911. At the outbreak of World War I in 1914, Miaskovsky was called into active service in the Russian army; in 1916 he was removed to Reval to work on military fortifications; he remained in the army after the Bolshevik Revolution of 1917; in 1918 he became a functionary in the Maritime Headquarters in Moscow; was finally demobilized in 1921. In that year he became prof. of composition at the Moscow Cons., remaining at that post to the end of his life. A composer of extraordinary ability, a master of his craft, Miaskovsky wrote 27 syms., much chamber music, piano pieces, and songs; his music is marked by structural strength and emotional élan; he never embraced extreme forms of modernism, but adopted workable devices of tonal expansion short of polytonality, and freely modulating melody short of atonality. His style was cosmopolitan; only in a few works did he inject folkloric elements. His autobiographical notes were publ. in *Sovetskaya Muzyka* (June 1936); S. Shlifstein ed. a vol. of articles, letters, and reminiscences (Moscow, 1959) and a vol. of articles, notes, and reviews (Moscow, 1960).

WORKS: ORCH. (all 1st perf. in Moscow unless otherwise given): **SYMS.:** No. 1 in C minor, op. 3 (1908; Pavlovsk, June 2, 1914), No. 2 in C-sharp minor, op. 11 (1910–11; July 24, 1912), No. 3 in A minor, op. 15 (1913–14; Feb. 27, 1915), No. 4 in E minor, op. 17 (1917–18; Feb. 8, 1925), No. 5 in D major, op. 18 (1918; July 18, 1920), No. 6 in E-flat minor, op. 23 (1922–23; May 4, 1924), No. 7 in B minor, op. 24 (1922; Feb. 8, 1925), No. 8 in A major, op. 26 (1924–25; May 23, 1926), No. 9 in E minor, op. 28 (1926–27; April 29, 1928), No. 10 in F minor, op. 30 (1927; April 7, 1928), No. 11 in B-flat minor, op. 34 (1931–32; Jan. 16, 1933), No. 12 in G minor, op. 35 (June 1, 1932), No. 13

in B-flat minor, op. 36 (1933; Winterthur, Oct. 16, 1934), No. 14 in C major, op. 37 (1933; Feb. 24, 1935), No. 15 in D minor, op. 38 (1933–34; Oct. 28, 1935), No. 16 in F major, op. 39 (Oct. 24, 1936), No. 17 in G-sharp minor, op. 41 (Dec. 17, 1937), No. 18 in C major, op. 42 (Oct. 1, 1937), No. 19 in E-flat major for Band (Feb. 15, 1939), No. 20 in E major, op. 50 (Nov. 28, 1940), No. 21 in F-sharp minor, op. 51 (Nov. 16, 1940; perf. as a commissioned work as *Symphonie fantaisie* by the Chicago Sym. Orch., Dec. 26, 1940), No. 22 in B minor, op. 54, *Symphonie ballade* (1941; Tbilisi, Jan. 12, 1942), No. 23 in A minor, op. 56, *Symphony-Suite* (1941; July 20, 1942), No. 24 in F minor, op. 63 (Dec. 8, 1943), No. 25 in D-flat major, op. 69 (1946; March 6, 1947), No. 26 in C major, op. 79 (Dec. 28, 1948), No. 27 in C minor, op. 85 (Dec. 9, 1950). **OTHER ORCH.:** Overture in G major for Small Orch. (1909; rev. 1949); *Molchaniye* (Silence), op. 9, symphonic poem after Poe (1909; June 13, 1914); Sinfonietta in A major, op. 10, for Small Orch. (1910; rev. 1943); *Alastor*, op. 14, symphonic poem after Shelley (1912–13; Nov. 18, 1914); Serenade in E-flat major, op. 32/1, for Small Orch. (Oct. 7, 1929); Sinfonietta in C minor, op. 32/2, for Strings (May 1930); *Lyric Concertino* in G major, op. 32/2, for Small Orch. (Oct. 7, 1929); Violin Concerto in D minor, op. 44 (Leningrad, Nov. 14, 1938); 2 Pieces, op. 46/1, for Strings (1945); 2 Pieces, op. 46/2, for Violin, Cello, and Strings (1947); *Privetstvennaya uvertyura* (Salutatory Overture) in D major, op. 48, for Stalin's birthday (Dec. 21, 1939); *Zvenya*, op. 65, suite (1908; rev. 1945); Cello Concerto in C minor, op. 66 (March 17, 1945); *Slavonic Rhapsody*, op. 71 (1946); *Divertissement*, op. 80 (1948). **BAND:** 2 marches (1930); 3 marches (1941); *Dramatic Overture* (1942). **CHAMBER:** 2 cello sonatas (1911, rev. 1945; 1948–49); 13 string quartets (1929–49); Violin Sonata (1946–47). **PIANO:** 9 sonatas (1907–49); sets of piano pieces. **VOCAL:** 2 cantatas: *Kirov s nami* (Kirov is With Us) for 2 Soloists, Chorus, and Orch. (1942) and *Kreml nochyu* (Kremlin at Night) for Voice, Chorus, and Orch. (1947); choruses; song cycles. A collected edition of his works was publ. in Moscow (12 vols., 1953–56).

BIBL.: A. Ikonnikov, *M.: His Life and Work* (N.Y., 1946); T. Livanova, *N.Y. M.* (Moscow, 1953); V. Vinogradov, *Spravochnik-putevoditel* (a guide to the syms.; Moscow, 1954); S. Shlifstein, ed., *Notograficheskii spravochnik* (list of works; Moscow, 1962).

Michaelides, Solon, Greek conductor, musicologist, and composer; b. Nicosia, Nov. 25, 1905; d. Athens, Sept. 9, 1979. He studied at London's Trinity College of Music (1927–30) before pursuing his training in Paris with Boulanger (harmony, counterpoint, and fugue) and Maize and Cortot (piano) at the École Normale de Musique (1930–34), and with Labey (conducting) and Lioncourt (composition) at the Schola Cantorum. In 1934 he founded the Limassol Cons. in Cyprus, for which he served as director until 1956. He also taught music at its Lanitis Communal High School (1941–56). From 1957 to 1970 he was director of the Salonica State Cons. He also was director-general and principal conductor of the Salonica State Orch. from 1959 to 1970. As a guest conductor, he appeared in Europe and the U.S.

WRITINGS: *Synchroni angliki moussiki* (Modern English Music; Nicosia, 1939); *I kypriaki laiki moussiki* (Cypriot Folk Music; Nicosia, 1944; 2nd ed., 1956); *Harmonia tis synchronis moussikis* (Harmony of Contemporary Music; Limassol, 1945); *The Neo-Hellenic Folk-Music* (Limassol, 1948); *I neo-elleniki moussiki* (Neo-Hellenic Music; Nicosia, 1952); *The Music of Ancient Greece: An Encyclopedia* (London, 1978).

WORKS: DRAMATIC: *Nausicaa*, ballet (1950); *Ulysses*, opera (1951; rev. 1972–73); incidental music for Greek tragedies. **ORCH.:** *De profundis* (1933; rev. 1949); *2 Byzantine Sketches* for Strings (1934); *Cypriot Wedding* for Flute and Strings (1935); *2 Greek Symphonic Pictures* (1936); *Byzantine Offering* for Strings (1944); *Archaic Suite* for Flute, Oboe, Harp, and Strings (1954); *Kypriaka eleftheria* (To Cypriot Freedom; 1959); Piano Concerto (1966); *In memoriam* for Strings (1974; based on the Piano Sonata, 1934). **CHAMBER:** String Quartet (1934); Piano Sonata (1934); Piano Trio (1946); many piano pieces. **VOCAL:** *O táfos* (The Tomb) for Mezzo-soprano, Baritone, Chorus, and Orch. (1936); *I eleftheroi poliorkimenoi* (The Free Besieged) for Soprano, Baritone, Chorus, and Orch. (1955); *Hymnos stin eleftheria* (Hymn to Freedom), the Cypriot national anthem; songs.

Michalsky, Donal, American composer and teacher; b. Pasadena, Calif., July 13, 1928; d. in a fire at his home in Newport Beach, Calif., Dec. 31, 1975. After clarinet training in his youth, he studied with Stevens (theory) and Dahl (orchestration) at the Univ. of Southern Calif. at Los Angeles (Ph.D., 1965) and on a Fulbright scholarship with Fortner in Freiburg im Breisgau (1958). From 1960 until his tragic death he was a prof. of composition at Calif. State College in Fullerton. His music was marked by robust dissonant counterpoint, often in dodecaphonic technique, and yet permeated with a lyric and almost Romantic sentiment.

WORKS: OPERA: *Der arme Heinrich* (unfinished MS destroyed in the fire that took his life). **ORCH.:** Concertino for Trombone and Band (1953); *6 Pieces* for Chamber Orch. (1956); Little Sym. for Band (1959); 3 syms.: No. 1, *Wheel of Time*, for Chorus and Orch. (1967), No. 2, Sinfonia concertante, for Clarinet, Piano, and Orch. (1969), and No. 3 (1975). **CHAMBER:** Quintet for 2 Trumpets, 2 Clarinets, and Piano (1951); *Divertimento* for 2 Clarinets and Bass Clarinet (1952); *Partita* for Oboe d'Amore, String Trio, and Strings (1958); Cello Sonata (1958); *Morning Music* for Chamber Ensemble (1959); *Trio Concertino* for Flute, Oboe, and Horn (1961); *Variations* for Clarinet and Piano (1962); *Fantasia alla marcia* for Brass Quartet (1963); *Partita piccola* for Flute and Piano (1964); *Allegretto* for Clarinet and Strings (1964); *3 × 4* for Saxophone Quartet (1972). **PIANO:** Sonata for 2 Pianos (1957); *Sonata concertante* (1961); *Song Suite* (1970). **VOCAL:** *Cantata memoriam* for High Voice and 12 Instruments (1971); songs.

Micheau, Janine, French soprano; b. Toulouse, April 17, 1914; d. Paris, Oct. 18, 1976. She studied in Toulouse and at the Paris Cons. In 1933 she made her operatic debut in *Louise* at the Paris Opéra-Comique, where she was a distinguished member until 1956. In 1937 she made her debut at London's Covent Garden as Micaëla. She made her U.S. debut as Mélisande in San Francisco in 1938, a role she subsequently sang with remarkable success on both sides of the Atlantic. In 1939 she appeared for the first time at the Teatro Colón in Buenos Aires. From 1940 to 1956 she was a member of the Paris Opéra. Among her other esteemed roles were Pamina, Juliet, Violetta, Gilda, Zerbinetta, Sophie, and Anne Trulove.

Micheelsen, Hans Friedrich, German organist, teacher, and composer; b. Hennstedt, Dithmarschen, June 9, 1902; d. Glüsing, Holstein, Nov. 23, 1973. He studied in Hamburg and Berlin. He was active as a church organist until 1938, when he was drafted into the German army; after demobilization, he settled in Hamburg, where he taught at the Hochschule für Musik until 1962. He wrote primarily choral music and pieces for organ; among his works were a *Luther Mass* (1933); a German Requiem, *Tod und Leben* (1938); an oratorio, *Wachstum und Reife* (1953); *Passion according to St. Mark* (1954); *Land der Vater*, cantata (1955); *Unser Wandel ist im Himmel*, evangelical mass (1957); *St. John's Passion* for Chorus (1961); also a Singspiel, *Munchhausen*; Organ Concerto (1952); Suite for Flute and Piano (1970); some songs in the Hamburg dialect.

Michel, Paul-Baudouin, Belgian composer; b. Haine-St.-Pierre, Sept. 7, 1930. He studied humanities at the Mons Cons.; then took courses in composition with Absil at the Queen Elisabeth Music Chapel in Brussels (1959–62) and in conducting at the Royal Cons. in Brussels; attended summer courses in Darmstadt with Ligeti, Boulez, Maderna, and Messiaen. He was later appointed director of the Academy of Music in Woluwe-St.-Lambert. His music adheres to the doctrine of precisely planned structural formations in a highly modern idiom.

WORKS: DRAMATIC: *Pandora*, ballet (1961); *Jeanne la Folle*, opera (1983–87). **ORCH.:** *Variations symphoniques* (1960); *5 inframorphoses* for Strings (1963); *Symphonium*

(1966); *Concaténation* for Chamber Orch. (1967); *Hors-Temps* (1970); *Confluences* for 2 Chamber Groups (1974); *Lamobyl-rinthe ou Dovetailed Forms*, concerto for Piano and 21 Instruments (1979); *Humoresque-Nocturne-Rondo* for Chamber Orch. (1979–80); *Trois nocturnes* (1981); Piano Concerto (1986); Harpsichord Concerto (1986); Concertinetto for Piano and Orch. (1987); *Symphonium "Jeanne la Folle"* (1988). **CHAMBER:** String Trio (1956); Violin Sonata (1960); *Hommage à François Rabelais*, wind quintet (1960); Clarinet Sonatina (1960); String Quartet (1961); *Sérénade concertante* for Violin and Piano (1962); *Quadrance* for String Quartet (1965); *Conduit et Danse hiératique* for Harp (1964); *Monologue double* for Flute and Tape (1965); *Ultramorphoses* for Flute, Clarinet, Saxophone, Percussion, Piano, Violin, Viola, and Cello (1965); *Clarbassonance* for Bass Clarinet and Tape (1966); *Bassonance* for Bassoon and Tape (1966); *Oscillonance* for 2 Violins and Piano (1967); *Colloque* for Piano, Trumpet, and Percussion (1967); *Gravures* for 2 Trumpets and Horn (1972); *Intonations* for Brass (1972); *Parelléloide* for Clavichord and Tape (1974); *Trois sur quatre* for Flute, Cello, and Piano (1979); *Décentrement* for Wind Quintet (1980); *Expansion I* for String Quartet (1981); *Versets* for 2 Ondes Martenot (1982); *Ellipse* for 4 Saxophones and 2 Harps (1983); *Poème* for Cello and Piano (1985); *Hommage à Paul Delvaux* for Saxophone and Harpsichord (1986); *Polyèdre* for 2 Percussionists (1988). **KEYBOARD: PIANO:** *Partita* No. 1 (1955); *Transsonance* (1965); *Libration I* (1971; rev. 1973); *Lithophanie* for Prepared Piano (1971); *Variations concentriques* (1971); *Musicoïde* for 2 Prepared Pianos (1971); *Orbe* (1972). **ORGAN:** *Transphonies pour plusieurs nefs* (1969); *Puzzlephonie* (1972). **VOCAL:** *Equateur*, cantata (1962); *Motet aléatoire sur le "Veni creator"* for Chorus, 19 Instruments, and Percussion (1962); *Rex pacificus*, radiophonic motet for Bass, Chorus, Orch., and Tape (1968); *Le Feu et le monde* for Narrator, Soli, Chorus, Organ, 12 Trumpets, and Percussion (1970); *Systoles—Diastoles* for Soprano and Instruments (1973); *Le Graal gras, ode au pétrole* for Speaker, Soprano, 10 Instruments, and Tape (1980); *Ecce Homo* for Bass and Chorus (1983); *Itinerrance* for Soprano, Clarinet, and Piano (1988).

Michelangeli, Arturo Benedetti, celebrated Italian pianist and pedagogue; b. Brescia, Jan. 5, 1920; d. Lugano, June 12, 1995. He began his training with his father and studied violin with Paolo Chiuieri at the Venturi Inst. in Brescia. When he was 10, he entered the Milan Cons. to pursue piano studies with Giuseppe Anfossi. He was awarded his diploma at age 13. In 1939 he captured 1st prize in the Geneva competition and that same year was made a prof. at the Bologna Cons. From 1941 to 1943 he served in the Italian Air Force, and then joined the anti-Fascist partisan movement. Although taken prisoner by the German occupation forces, he soon managed to escape and awaited the complete liberation of Italy to resume his career. With World War II over in 1945, he played in his homeland. In 1946 he made his first tour of Europe, and played for the first time in the U.S. in 1948. In subsequent years, he appeared in selected major music centers of the world while acquiring a legendary reputation as a virtuoso. Unfortunately, he also developed a reputation for cancelling engagements at the last minute; when he did perform, however, his concerts were invariably sold out and accorded ovations by public and critics alike. From 1964 to 1969 he was director of his own piano academy in Brescia. In his later years, he devoted most of his time to teaching. While his technical mastery made him one of the great keyboard exponents of the Romantic repertoire, his sympathies ranged widely, from early music to the 20th century.

Michelet (real name, **Levin**), **Michel,** Russian-American composer; b. Kiev, June 26, 1894. He studied cello in Kiev. After further training with J. Klengel (cello) and Reger (composition) at the Leipzig Cons., he returned to Kiev and completed his studies with Glière (composition). In 1921 he went to Paris, where he was active as a film composer. In 1941 he settled in the U.S. His music evinced a Russian lyric quality with some infusions of early French Impressionism.

WORKS: *Hannele*, opera (1972); some 200 film scores; Violin Concerto; 2 cello sonatas (1937, 1977); *Lisztiana*, trio for Violin, Cello, and Piano (1943); Balalaika Sonata (1972); 3 violin sonatas; piano pieces; songs.

Micheletti, Gaston, French tenor; b. Tavaco, Corsica, Jan. 5, 1892; d. Ajaccio, May 21, 1959. He was a student at the Paris Cons. In 1922 he made his operatic debut as Gounod's Faust in Rheims. In 1925 he became a member of the Paris Opéra-Comique, where he remained a principal artist for 2 decades. He also made guest appearances in Brussels, Nice, and Monte Carlo. In later years, he was active as a voice teacher in Paris and then in Ajaccio. Among his admired roles were Don José, Des Grieux, and Werther.

Middelschulte, Wilhelm, eminent German organist and teacher; b. Werne, near Dortmund, April 3, 1863; d. there, May 4, 1943. He studied at the Inst. für Kirchenmusik in Berlin with Löschhorn (piano), Haupt (organ), and Commer and Schroder (composition). After serving as organist at the Church of St. Luke in Berlin (1888–91), he settled in Chicago; was organist at the Cathedral of the Holy Name (1891–95); subsequently was organist at Milwaukee's St. James's Church (1899–1919) and also a prof. of organ at the Wisconsin Cons. of Music there. He was greatly distinguished for his interpretations of Bach. In 1935 he became instructor of theory and organ at the Detroit Foundation Music School; in 1939 he returned to Germany.

BIBL.: J. Becker, "W. M.," *Musical Quarterly* (April 1928).

Middleton, Hubert Stanley, English organist, teacher, and composer; b. Windsor, May 11, 1890; d. London, Aug. 13, 1959. He studied at the Royal Academy of Music in London and at the Univ. of Cambridge (M.A., 1920). He was appointed organist and director of music at Trinity College, Cambridge, in 1931; also taught at the Royal Academy of Music in London. His specialty was cathedral music. He composed a number of anthems and organ pieces. He was greatly esteemed as an educator, and his teaching methods exercised profound influence on his students, many of whom became educators in their own right.

Middleton, Robert (Earl), American composer and teacher; b. Diamond, Ohio, Nov. 18, 1920. He was educated at Harvard Univ. (B.A., 1948; M.A., 1954); also studied composition with Boulanger at the Longy School of Music (1941–42) and piano with Beveridge Webster at the New England Cons. of Music in Boston (1941–42) and with K.U. Schnabel (1946–49). While holding the John Knowles Paine Traveling Fellowship from Harvard Univ. (1948–50), he pursued his composition studies with Boulanger in Paris. In 1965–66 he held a Guggenheim fellowship. After teaching at Harvard Univ. (1950–53), he joined the faculty of Vassar College in 1953, where he was a prof. from 1966 to 1985 and chairman of the music dept. from 1973 to 1976. He publ. *Harmony in Modern Counterpoint* (Boston, 1967). He displayed a deft handling of genres and forms throughout his basically conservative course as a composer.

WORKS: DRAMATIC: *Life Goes to a Party*, opera (1947; Tanglewood, Aug. 12, 1948); *The Nightingale is Guilty*, opera (1953; Boston, March 1954); *Command Performance*, opera-concerto (1958–60; rev. 1987–88). **ORCH.:** *Andante* (1948); Violin Concerto (1949; rev. 1984); *Concerto di Quattro Duetti* for Solo Winds and String Orch. (1962; rev. 1986); *Variations* for Piano and Orch. (1965; rev. 1984–85); *Sinfonia Filofonica* (Poughkeepsie, N.Y., May 4, 1969); *Gardens 1 2 3 4 5* (1972); *Overture to The Charterhouse of Parma* (1981). **CHAMBER:** 3 violin sonatas (n.d., 1941, 1948); 3 string quartes (1950, 1989, 1990); *Ritratti della Notte* (*Portraits of the Night*) for Flute and Piano (1966); *Approximations* for Viola and Piano (1967); *Vier Trio-Sätze in romantischer Manier* for Violin, Cello, and Piano (1970); *2 Duologues* for Violin and Piano (1973); *4 Nocturnes* for Clarinet and Piano (1979). **KEYBOARD: PIANO:** *Passacaglia and Fugue* for Piano, 4-hands (1940); Sonata (1957); *12 Inventions* (1960–61); *Notebooks of Designs* (book 1, 1968; book 2, 1968, rev. 1978); *vARIAzioni—variAZIONI* (1970). **ORGAN:** *4 Preludes* (1956). **VOCAL:** Choral pieces; songs.

Midori (real name, **Goto Mi Dori**), outstanding Japanese violinist; b. Osaka, Oct. 25, 1971. She studied with her mother, Setsu Goto; in 1981, went to the U.S., where she took violin lessons with Dorothy DeLay at the Aspen (Colo.) Music School and continued her training with that mentor at N.Y.'s Juilliard School. She attracted the attention of Zubin Mehta when she was 10 years old; he subsequently engaged her as a soloist with the N.Y. Phil., with which she traveled on an extensive Asian tour that included Hong Kong, Singapore, Korea, Thailand, and her native Japan. There followed concerts with the Berlin Phil., the Boston Sym. Orch., the Chicago Sym. Orch., the Cleveland and Philadelphia Orchs., the Los Angeles Phil., the London Sym. Orch., and other European and American orchs., in programs that included not only classical concertos but also modern works, under the direction of such renowned conductors, besides Mehta, as Bernstein, Previn, Maazel, Dohnányi, Leppard, and Barenboim. She also attracted the attention of popular television programs, and appeared as a guest of President and Mrs. Reagan at the White House during the NBC-TV special Christmas in Washington (1983). Most importantly, she won the admiration of orch. members for her remarkable artistic dependability. On one occasion, when a string broke on the concertmaster's violin during an orch. introduction, she demonstrated her sangfroid; since she had a few minutes to spare before her entrance as a soloist, she handed her own violin to the player and coolly changed the broken string in time to continue the performance without pause. On Oct. 21, 1990, she made her N.Y. recital debut at Carnegie Hall. In 1992 she created the Midori Foundation to promote the cause of classical music.

Miedél, Rainer, German conductor; b. Regensburg, June 1, 1937; d. Seattle, March 25, 1983. He studied cello with Navarra in Paris, and conducting with Ferrara in Siena and Kertész in Salzburg. In 1965 he became a cellist in the Stockholm Phil. That same year, he won 1st prize in the Swedish Radio conducting competition. In 1967 he made his formal conducting debut with the Stockholm Phil., and then was its assistant conductor (1969–76). He also was music director of the Gävleborgs Sym. Orch. (1969–76), and assistant conductor (1969–72) and assoc. conductor (1972–73) of the Baltimore Sym. Orch. From 1976 until his death he was music director of the Seattle Sym. Orch. He also was interim music director of the Florida Phil. (1980–82).

Mieg, Peter, Swiss composer and painter; b. Lenzburg, Sept. 5, 1906; d. there, Dec. 7, 1990. He studied composition, piano, and theory with C.A. Richter in Lenzburg, and then continued his musical training with H. Münch in Basel, E. Frey in Zürich, and Landowska in Basel. He also was drawn to painting, taking his Ph.D. in 1933 at the Univ. of Zürich with a diss. on modern Swiss art. While he devoted much of his time to composition, he also was active as a painter. In 1961 he held his first major exhibition of paintings in Zürich, Paris, Vienna, and other cities. As a composer, his output took on a pronounced individual style after 1950. His autobiography was publ. as *Laterna magica* (Lenzburg, 1986).

WORKS: BALLETS: *La fête de la ligne* (1935); *Daphne* (1943). **ORCH.:** Concerto for 2 Pianos and Orch. (1939–42); 2 piano concertos (1947, 1961); Violin Concerto (1948–49); *Concerto da camera* (1952); Concerto for Harpsichord and Chamber Orch. (1953); *Concerto veneziano* for Strings (1955); Oboe Concerto (1957); Sym. (1958); Concerto for Flute and Strings (1962); *Rondeau symphonique* (1964); Cello Concerto (1966–67); Concerto for Harp and Strings (1970); Concerto for 2 Flutes and Strings (1973–74); *Combray* for Strings (1977); *Triple concerto le goût italien* for Violin, Viola, Cello, and String Orch. (1978); *Schlossbildermusik* (1980); Double Concerto for Piano, Cello, and Orch. (1983–84); *Ouverture pour Monsieur Lully* for Strings (1986). **CHAMBER:** Violin Sonata (1936); 3 string quartets (1936–37; 1944–45; 1987); *Divertimento* for Oboe, Violin, Viola, and Cello (1950); *Musik* for Harpsichord, Flute, Oboe, Violin, Viola, Cello, and Double Bass (1954); Flute Sonata (1963); Quintet for Flute, 2 Violins, Cello, and Harpsichord (1969); Wind Quintet (1977); Piano Trio (1984–85); Cello Sonata (1986); keyboard pieces, including 5 piano sonatas (1944; 1944; 1959; 1975; 1987–88), harpsichord pieces, and organ music. **VOCAL:** Choral works; songs.

BIBL.: U. Däster, W. Kläy, and W. Labhart, *P. M.: Eine Monographie* (Aarau and Frankfurt am Main, 1976).

Miereanu, Costin, Romanian-born French composer and teacher; b. Bucharest, Feb. 27, 1943. He studied in Bucharest at the School of Music (B.M., 1960) and the Cons. (M.F.A., 1966), and then attended the summer courses in new music given by Stockhausen, Ligeti, and Karkoschka in Darmstadt (1967–68). In 1968 he settled in France and in 1977 became a naturalized French citizen. He pursued training in musical semiotics at the École des Hautes Études en Sciences Sociales in Paris (D.M.A., 1978) and in the liberal arts at the Univ. of Paris (Ph.D., 1979). In 1978 he joined the faculty of the Univ. of Paris. He also was associated with Editions Salabert (from 1981), and taught at the Sorbonne in Paris (from 1982) and at the summer courses in new music in Darmstadt (from 1982). His music represents a totality of the cosmopolitan avant-garde: semiotics, structuralism, serialism, electronic sound, aleatory, musical-verbal theater, etc.

WORKS: DRAMATIC: *L'Avenir est dans les oeufs*, opera (1980); *La Porte du paradis*, lyric fantasy (1989–91); film scores. **ORCH.:** *Monostructures I* (1966) and *II* (1967); *Finis coronat opus* (1966); *Couleur du temps* for Strings (1966–68); *Espace dernier* (1966–69; also for Chorus, 6 Instrumental Groups, and Tape); *Rosario* (1973–76); *Rosenzeit* (1980); *Miroirs celestes* (1981–83); *Voyage d'hiver II* (1982–85); *Doppel(kammer)konzert* for Saxophonist, Percussion, and Chamber Orch. (1985); *Un temps sans mémoire* (1991). **CHAMBER:** *Variants* for Clarinet (1966); *Sursum corda triplum* for 7 Instruments (1967–82); *Espace au delà du dernier* for Chamber Ensemble (1968); *Dans La Nuit des temps* for Variable Ensemble and Tape (1968–69); *Polymorphies 5 × 7 (A)* for Variable Ensemble and Tape (1968–69) and *(B)* for 8 Instruments (1969–70); *Altar* for 6 Players or Singers, Tape, and Visuals ad libitum (1973); *Aquarius* for 2 Pianos and 2 Percussion (1974–80); *Musique élémentaire de concert* for Chamber Ensemble (1977); *Piano-Miroir* for Piano, Polyphonic Synthesizer or Electric Organ, Tape, and Visuals ad libitum (1978); *Do-Mi-Si-La-Do-Re* for Saxophonist and Tape (1980–81); *Variants-invariants* for Alto or Soprano Saxophone or Bass Clarinet and Korg SE 500 Echo Chamber (1982); *Bucharest-Grenade* for Guitar (1983); *Aksax* for Bass Saxophone (1983); *Bolero des Balkans (C)* for Saxophone(s) and Percussion (1984); *Gyrasol I* for Recorder Quartet, Percussion, and Tape (1984); *Ombres lumineuses* for Chamber Group and Synthesizers (1986); *Miroir liquide* for 6 Players (1986); *Tension en cycle* for 6 Percussion and Tape (1987); *Limping Rock* for Amplified Harpsichord (1988). **OTHER:** Various vocal, tape, and electronic scores.

Mies, Paul, noted German musicologist and pedagogue; b. Cologne, Oct. 22, 1889; d. there, May 15, 1976. He studied musicology, mathematics, and physics at the Univ. of Bonn, receiving his Ph.D. there in 1912 with the diss. *Über die Tonmalerei.* He then was active as a teacher of mathematics in Cologne (1919–39) while continuing his musicological work; in 1946 he became director of the Institut für Schulmusik at the Cologne Staatliche Hochschule für Musik, retaining this post until 1954.

WRITINGS: *Stilmomente und Ausdrucksstilformen im Brahmsschen Lied* (Leipzig, 1923); *Die Bedeutung der Skizzen Beethovens zur Erkenntnis seines Stiles* (Leipzig, 1925; Eng. tr., London, 1929); *Musik im Unterricht der höheren Lehranstalten* (2 vols., Cologne, 1925–26); *Skizzen aus Geschichte und Ästhetik der Musik* (Cologne, 1926); *Das romantische Lied und Gesänge aus Wilhelm Meister; Musik und Musiker in Poesie und Prosa* (2 vols., Berlin, 1926); *Schubert, der Meister des Liedes: Die Entwicklung von Form und Inhalt im Schubertschen Lied* (Berlin, 1928); *Johannes Brahms: Werke, Zeit, Mensch* (Leipzig,

1930); *Der Charakter der Tonarten: Eine Untersuchung* (Cologne, 1948); *Von Sinn und Praxis der musikalischen Kritik* (Krefeld, 1950); with N. Schneider, *Musik im Umkreis der Kulturgeschichte: Ein Taballenwerk aus der Geschichte der Musik, Literatur, bildenden Künst, Philosophie und Politik Europas* (Rodenkirchen, 1953); *Franz Schubert* (Leipzig, 1954); *Textkritische Untersuchungen bei Beethoven* (Munich and Duisburg, 1957); *Die geistlichen Kantaten Johann Sebastian Bachs und der Hörer von heute* (3 vols., Wiesbaden, 1959–60; 2nd ed., 1964); *Bilder und Buchstaben werden Musik* (Rodenkirchen, 1964); with H. Grundmann, *Studien zum Klavierspiel Beethovens und seiner Zeitgenossen* (Bonn, 1966; 2nd ed., 1970); *Die weltlichen Kantaten Johann Sebastian Bachs und der Horer von heute* (Wiesbaden, 1967); *Das instrumentale Rezitativ: Von seiner Geschichte und seinen Formen* (Bonn, 1968); *Die Krise der Konzertkadenz bei Beethoven* (Bonn, 1970); *Das Konzert im 19. Jahrhundert: Studien zu Kadenzen und Formen* (Bonn, 1972); ed. *Reihenfolge*, a collection for school orchs.

Migenes-Johnson, Julia, American soprano; b. N.Y., March 13, 1945. She studied at the High School of Music and Art in N.Y., and while still a student sang in a televised concert performance of Copland's *The 2nd Hurricane* under Bernstein's direction; then appeared in *West Side Story* and *Fiddler on the Roof* on Broadway. On Sept. 29, 1965, she made her operatic debut at the N.Y. City Opera as Annina in *The Saint of Bleecker Street*; then pursued training in Vienna, where she sang at the Volksoper; also studied with Gisela Ultmann in Cologne. In 1978 she made her first appearance at the San Francisco Opera as Musetta. Her Metropolitan Opera debut in N.Y. took place on Dec. 10, 1979, as Jenny in *The Rise and Fall of the City of Mahagonny*. In 1983 she sang with the Vienna State Opera. She gained international acclaim for her sultry portrayal of Carmen in Francesco Rosi's film version of Bizet's opera in 1984. In 1985 she returned to the Metropolitan Opera as Berg's Lulu. She won accolades for her compelling performances as Strauss's Salome.

Mignone, Francisco (Paulo), eminent Brazilian composer and pedagogue; b. São Paulo, Sept. 3, 1897; d. Rio de Janeiro, Feb. 20, 1986. He studied with his father; then took courses in piano, flute, and composition at the São Paulo Cons. (graduated, 1917); then studied with Ferroni at the Milan Cons. (1920). Returning to Brazil, he taught at the São Paulo Cons. (1929–33); was appointed to the faculty of the Escola Nacional de Música in Rio de Janeiro (1933), and taught there until 1967. His music shows the influence of the modern Italian school of composition; his piano pieces are of virtuoso character; his orchestration shows consummate skill. In many of his works he employs indigenous Brazilian motifs, investing them in sonorous modernistic harmonies not without a liberal application of euphonious dissonances.

WORKS: DRAMATIC: OPERAS: *O Contractador dos diamantes* (Rio de Janeiro, Sept. 20, 1924); *O inocente* (Rio de Janeiro, Sept. 5, 1928); *O Chalaca* (1972). **OPERETTA:** *Mizú* (1937). **BALLETS:** *Maracatú de Chico-Rei* (Rio de Janeiro, Oct. 29, 1934); *Quadros amazónicos* (Rio de Janeiro, July 15, 1949); *O guarda chuva* (São Paulo, 1954). **ORCH.:** *Suite campestre* (Rio de Janeiro, Dec. 16, 1918); *Congada*, from the opera *O Contractador dos diamantes* (São Paulo, Sept. 10, 1922); *Scenas da Roda*, symphonic dance (São Paulo, Aug. 15, 1923); *Festa dionisiaca* (Rome, Oct. 24, 1923); *Intermezzo lirico* (São Paulo, May 13, 1925); *4 fantasias brasilieras* for Piano and Orch. (1931–37); *Momus*, symphonic poem (Rio de Janeiro, April 24, 1933); *Suite brasileira* (Rio de Janeiro, Dec. 9, 1933); *Sonho de um Menino Travesso* (São Paulo, Oct. 30, 1937); *Seresta* for Cello and Orch. (Rio de Janeiro, March 31, 1939); *Miudinho*, symphonic dance (São Paulo, June 28, 1941); *Festa das Igrejas* (N.Y., April 22, 1942); *Sinfonia tropical* (1958); Piano Concerto (1958); Violin Concerto (1961); Concerto for Violin, Piano, and Orch. (1966); Concertino for Clarinet and Small Orch. (1957); Bassoon Concertino (1957); Concerto for Violin and Chamber Orch. (1975). **CHAMBER:** 2 sextets (1935, 1968); String Octet (1956); 2 string quartets (1956, 1957); 2 wind quintets (1960, 1962); 2 sonatas for 2 Bassoons (1960, 1965); *Trifonia* for Oboe, Flute, and Bassoon (1963); *Tetrafonia* for Flute, Oboe, Clarinet, and Trumpet (1963); 3 violin sonatas (1964, 1965, 1966); Sonata for 4 Bassoons (1966); Cello Sonata (1967); 2 wind trios (1967, 1968); 2 sonatas for Flute and Oboe (1969, 1970); *Sonata à tre* for Flute, Oboe, and Clarinet (1970); Sonata for Solo Trumpet (1970); Clarinet Sonata (1971). **PIANO:** 4 sonatas (1941, 1962, 1964, 1967); *Samba rítmico* for 2 Pianos (1953); *Sonata humorística* for 2 Pianos (1968); *Rondo* (1969); waltzes. **VOCAL:** 2 oratorios: *Alegrias de Nossa Senhora* (Rio de Janeiro, July 15, 1949) and *Santa Claus* (1962); many songs.

BIBL.: B. Kiefer, *F. M.* (Porto Alegre, 1984).

Migot, Georges, significant French composer; b. Paris, Feb. 27, 1891; d. Levallois, near Paris, Jan. 5, 1976. He began taking piano lessons at the age of 6; entered the Paris Cons. in 1909; after preliminary courses in harmony, he studied composition with Widor, counterpoint with Gédalge, and music history with Emmanuel; then orchestration with d'Indy and organ with Gigout and Guilmant. Before completing his studies at the Paris Cons., he was mobilized into the French army, was wounded at Longuyon in 1914, and was released from military service. In 1917 he presented in Paris a concert of his own works; received the Lily Boulanger Prize in 1918. He competed twice for the Prix de Rome in 1919 and 1920, but failed to win and abandoned further attempts to capture it. In the meantime, he engaged in a serious study of painting; in fact, he was more successful as a painter than as a composer in the early years of his career; he exhibited his paintings in Paris art galleries in 1917, 1919, 1923, and subsequent years. He also wrote poetry; virtually all of his vocal works are written to his own words. In his musical compositions, he endeavored to recapture the spirit of early French polyphony, thus emphasizing the continuity of national art in history. His melodic writing is modal, often with archaic inflections, while his harmonic idiom is diatonically translucid; he obtains subtle coloristic effects through unusual instrumental registration. Profoundly interested in the preservation and classification of early musical instruments, he served as curator of the Instrumental Museum of the Paris Cons. (1949–61). He wrote *Essais pour une esthétique générale* (Paris, 1920; 2nd ed., 1937); *Appoggiatures résolues et non résolues* (Paris, 1922–31); *Jean-Philippe Rameau et le génie de la musique française* (Paris, 1930); *Lexique de quelques termes utilisés en musique* (Paris, 1947); 2 vols. of poems (Paris, 1950, 1951); *Matériaux et inscriptions* (Toulouse, 1970); *Kaléidoscope et miroirs ou les images multipliées et contraires* (autobiography; Toulouse, 1970).

WORKS: DRAMATIC: *Hagoromo*, symphonie lyrique et chorégraphique (Monte Carlo, May 9, 1922); *Le Rossignol en amour*, chamber opera (1926–28; Geneva, March 2, 1937); *Cantate d'amour*, concert opera (1949–50); *La Sulamite*, concert opera (1969–70); *L'Arche*, polyphonie spatiale (1971; Marseilles, May 3, 1974). **ORCH.:** 13 numbered syms.: No. 1, *Les Agrestides* (1919–20; Paris, April 29, 1922), No. 2 (1927; Besançon, Sept. 7, 1961), No. 3 (1943–49), No. 4 (1946–47), No. 5, *Sinfonia da chiesa*, for Wind Orch. (Roubaix, Dec. 4, 1955), No. 6 for Strings (1944–51; Strasbourg, June 22, 1960), No. 7 for Chamber Orch. (1948–52), No. 8 for 15 Winds and 2 Double Basses (1953), No. 9 for Strings (n.d.; unfinished), No. 10 (1962), No. 11 for Wind Orch. (1963), No. 12 (1954–64; Lille, May 29, 1972), and No. 13 (1967); 1 unnumbered sym.: *Petite symphonie en trois mouvements enchaînés* for Strings (1970; Beziers, July 23, 1971); *La Paravent de laque aux cinq images* (1920; Paris, Jan. 21, 1923); *La Fête de la bergère* (1921; Paris, Nov. 21, 1925); *Trois ciné-ambiances* (1922); *Dialogue* for Piano and Orch. (1922–25; Paris, March 25, 1926); *Dialogue* for Cello and Orch. (1922–26; Paris, Feb. 7, 1927); Suite for Violin and Orch. (1924; Paris, Nov. 14, 1925); Suite for Piano and Orch. (Paris, March 12, 1927); *Suite en concert* for Harp and Orch. (Paris, Jan. 15, 1928); *La Jungle* for Organ and Orch. (1928; Paris, Jan. 9, 1932); *Prélude pour un poète* (Paris, June 7,

1929); *Le Livre des danceries*, suite (Paris, Dec. 12, 1931); *Le Zodiaque* (1931–39); Piano Concerto (1962; Paris, June 26, 1964); *Phonie sous-marine* (1962); Concerto for Harpsichord and Chamber Orch. (Paris, Dec. 12, 1967). **CHAMBER:** Trio for Oboe, Violin, and Piano (1906); *Les Parques* for 2 Violins, Viola, and Piano (1909); Violin Sonata (1911); Trio for Violin, Viola, and Piano (1918); 3 string quartets (1921, 1957, 1966); *Dialogue No. 1* (1922) and *No. 2* (1929) for Cello and Piano; *Dialogue No. 1* (1923) and *No. 2* (1925) for Violin and Piano; Quartet for 2 Clarinets, Corno di Bassetto, and Bass Clarinet (1925); Suite for Flute (1931); Piano Trio (1935); Trio for Oboe, Clarinet, and Bassoon (1944); String Trio (1944–45); Flute Sonata (1945); *Sonate luthée* for Solo Harp (1949); *Pastorale* for 2 Flutes (1950); 2 sonatas for Solo Violin (1951, 1959); Sonata for Solo Clarinet (1953); Sonata for Solo Bassoon (1953); Quintet for Flute, Oboe, Clarinet, Horn, and Bassoon (1954); Sonata for Solo Cello (1954); Quartet for 2 Violins and 2 Cellos (1955); Saxophone Quartet (1955); Cello Sonata (1958); Sonata for Solo Cello (1958); Quartet for Flute, Violin, Cello, and Piano (1960); Guitar Sonata (1960); Quartet for Violin, Viola, Cello, and Piano (1961); Suite for 2 Cellos (1962); Suite for English Horn and Piano (1963); *Introduction pour un concert de chambre* for 5 Strings and 5 Winds (1964); Trio for Flute, Cello, and Harp (1965); piano pieces; organ music. **VOCAL:** 4 oratorios: *La Passion* (1939–46; Paris, July 25, 1957), *L'Annonciation* (1943–46), *La Mise au tombeau* (1948–49), and *La Résurrection* (1953; Strasbourg, March 28, 1969); *Mystère orphique* for Voice and Orch. (1951; Strasbourg, March 18, 1964); *La Nativité de Notre Seigneur* for Soloists, Chorus, and Instruments (1954); sacred and secular choruses; trios; quartets; etc.

BIBL.: L. Vallas, *G. M.* (Paris, 1923); P. Wolff, *La Route d'un musicien: G. M.* (Paris, 1933); M. Pinchard, *Connaissance de G. M., musicien français* (Paris, 1959); M. Honegger, ed., *Catalogue des oeuvres musicales de G. M.* (Strasbourg, 1977); C. Latham, ed. and tr., *G. M.: The Man and His Work* (Strasbourg, 1982).

Mihalovici, Marcel, significant Romanian-born French composer; b. Bucharest, Oct. 22, 1898; d. Paris, Aug. 12, 1985. After studies with Bernfeld (violin), Cuclin (harmony), and Cremer (counterpoint) in Bucharest (1908–19), he settled in Paris and completed his training with d'Indy (composition), Saint Requier (harmony), Gastoué (Gregorian chant), and Lejeune (violin) at the Schola Cantorum (1919–25). With Martinů, Conrad Beck, and Harsányi, he founded the "École de Paris" of emigrants. In 1932 he helped to organize the contemporary music society Triton. He became a naturalized French citizen in 1955. In 1964 he was elected a member of the Institut de France. His wife was **Monique Haas**. Mihalovici's music presents a felicitous synthesis of French and Eastern European elements, tinted with a roseate impressionistic patina and couched in euphoniously dissonant harmonies.

WORKS: DRAMATIC: OPERAS: *L'Intransigeant Pluton* (1928; Paris, April 3, 1939); *Phèdre* (1949; Stuttgart, June 9, 1951); *Die Heimkehr* (Frankfurt am Main, June 17, 1954); *Krapp ou La Dernière Bande*, after Samuel Beckett (1959–60; Bielefeld, Feb. 25, 1961); *Les Jumeaux*, opera buffa (1962; Braunschweig, Jan. 23, 1963). **BALLETS:** *Une Vie de Polichinelle* (1923); *Le Postillon du Roy* (1924); *Divertimento* (1925); *Karagueuz*, marionette ballet (1926); *Thésée au labyrinthe* (1956; Braunschweig, April 4, 1957; rev. version as *Scènes de Thésée*, Cologne, Oct. 15, 1958); *Alternamenti* (1957; Braunschweig, Feb. 28, 1958); *Variations* (Bielefeld, March 28, 1960). Also incidental music for plays. **ORCH.:** *Notturno* (1923); *Introduction au mouvement symphonique* (1923; Bucharest, Oct. 17, 1926); *Fantaisie* (1927; Liège, Sept. 6, 1930); *Cortège des divinités infernales* (1928; Bucharest, Dec. 7, 1930); *Chindia* for 13 Wind Instruments and Piano (1929); *Concerto quasi una Fantasia* for Violin and Orch. (1930; Barcelona, April 22, 1936); *Divertissement* (1934); *Capriccio roumain* (1936); *Prélude et Invention* for Strings (1937; Warsaw, April 21, 1939); *Toccata* for Piano and Orch. (1938; rev. 1940); *Symphonies pour le temps présent* (1944); *Variations* for Brass and Strings (1946); *Séquences* (1947); *Ritournelles* (1951); 5 syms.: *Sinfonia giocosa* (Basel, Dec. 14, 1951), *Sinfonia partita* for Strings (1952), *Sinfonia cantata* for Baritone, Chorus, and Orch. (1953–63), *Sinfonia variata* (1960), and No. 5 for Soprano and Orch., in memory of Hans Rosbaud (1966–69; Paris, Dec. 14, 1971); *Étude en 2 parties* for Piano Concertante, 7 Wind Instruments, Celesta, and Percussion (Donaueschingen, Oct. 6, 1951); *Elegie* (1955); *Ouverture tragique* (1957); *Esercizio* for Strings (1959); *Musique nocturne* for Clarinet, Strings, Harpsichord, and Celesta (1963); *Aubade* for Strings (1964); *Périples* for Piano and Orch. (1967; Paris, March 22, 1970); *Prétextes* for Oboe, Bass Clarinet, and Chamber Orch. (1968); *Variantes* for Horn and Orch. or Piano (1969); *Borne* (1970); *Rondo* (1970); *Chant premier* for Saxophone and Orch. (1973–74); *Follia* (1976–77). **CHAMBER:** 2 violin sonatas (1920, 1941); Piano Quartet (1922); 3 string quartets (1923; 1931; 1943–46); Oboe Sonatina (1924); *Serenade* for String Trio (1929); Sonata for 3 Clarinets (1933); Viola Sonata (1942); Sonata for Violin and Cello (1944); *Egloge* for Flute, Oboe, Clarinet, Bassoon, and Piano (1945); Sonata for Solo Violin (1949); Sonata for Solo Cello (1949); Wind Trio (1955); *Pastorale triste* for Flute and Piano (1958); Bassoon Sonata (1958); Clarinet Sonata (1958); *Improvisation* for Percussion (1961); *Dialogues* for Clarinet and Piano (1965); *Serioso* for Bass Saxophone and Piano (1971); *Récit* for Clarinet (1973); *Melopeia* for Oboe (1973). **PIANO:** *3 Nocturnes* (1928); *4 Caprices* (1929); *Ricercari* (1941); *3 pièces nocturnes* (1948); Sonata (1964); *Cantus Firmus* for 2 Pianos (1970); *Passacaglia* for Piano, Left-hand (1975). **VOCAL:** *La Genèse*, cantata (1935–40); *Cascando* for Voice and Instruments (1962); *Cantilène* for Mezzo-soprano and Chamber Orch. (1972); motets; songs.

BIBL.: G. Beck, *M. M.: Esquisse biographique* (Paris, 1954).

Mihály, András, Hungarian composer, conductor, administrator, and teacher; b. Budapest, Nov. 6, 1917; d. there, Sept. 19, 1993. He was a student of Adolf Schiffer (cello) and of Leó Weiner and Imre Waldbauer (chamber music) at the Budapest Academy of Music. He also received private instruction in composition from Pál Kadosa and István Strasser. After playing 1st cello in the orch. of the Budapest Opera (1946–48), he was general secretary of the Opera (1948–50). From 1950 to 1978 he taught chamber music at the Budapest Academy of Music. He also was a music reader with the Hungarian Radio (1962–78). From 1978 to 1986 he was director of the Hungarian State Opera in Budapest, and then of the student orch. at the Budapest Academy of Music (from 1986). In 1952, 1954, and 1964 he received the Erkel Prize, and in 1955 was awarded the Kossuth Prize. He was made a Merited Artist (1969) and an Outstanding Artist (1974) by the Hungarian government.

WORKS: DRAMATIC: *Együtt és egyedül* (Together and Alone), opera (1964–65; Budapest, Nov. 5, 1966); incidental music for plays and films. **ORCH.:** 3 syms. (1946, 1950, 1962); Cello Concerto (1953); Piano Concerto (1954); *Fantasy* for Wind Quintet and Orch. (1955); Violin Concerto (1959); *Festive Overture* (1959); *Monodia* (1971). **CHAMBER:** Piano Trio (1940); 3 string quartets (1942, 1960, 1977); *Rhapsody* for Viola and Piano (1947); *Serenade* for Wind Trio (1956); Suite for Cello and Piano (1957); *Movement* for Cello and Piano (1962); *3 Movements* for Chamber Ensemble (1969); *Musica per 15* for Chamber Ensemble (1975); *Musica* for Viola and Piano (1977). **PIANO:** Sonata (1958); *Rondo* (1958); *4 Little Piano Pieces* (1958); *Ciaccona* (1961). **VOCAL:** *Liberty and Peace* for Chorus and Orch. (1942; not extant; 2nd version, 1949); *Youth! Defend Peace!* for Chorus and Orch. (1950); *My Beloved Hungarian Fatherland* for Chorus and Orch. (1952); *The Red Cart* for Chorus and Orch. (1957); *1871* for Chorus and Orch. (1960); *Apocrypha* for 3 Women's Voices, Clarinet, and Percussion (1962); *Fly, Poem!* for Chorus and Orch. (1967); choruses; songs.

BIBL.: J. Kárpáti, *M. A.* (Budapest, 1965).

Mikhailova, Maria (Alexandrovna), Russian soprano; b. Kharkov, June 3, 1866; d. Moscow, Jan. 18, 1943. She studied in St. Petersburg, and then in Paris and Milan. In 1892 she made her debut at the Imperial Opera in St. Petersburg as Marguerite de Valois in *Les Huguenots*; she remained a member there until 1912. On Oct. 29, 1895, she created the role of Electra in Taneyev's *Oresteia*. She visited Tokyo in 1907. She made over 300 recordings, achieving a considerable reputation through the gramophone alone.

Mikhailovich, Maxim (Dormidontovich), Russian bass; b. Koltsovka, near Kazan, Aug. 25, 1893; d. Moscow, March 30, 1971. He studied in Kazan with Oshustovich and in Moscow with Osipov. After appearing as a soloist with Moscow's All-Union Radio (1930–32), he sang with Moscow's Bolshoi Theater (from 1932). He was admired for his many portrayals in Russian operas. In 1940 he was made a People's Artist of the U.S.S.R.

BIBL.: V. Endrzheyevsky and E. Osipov, *M. M.* (Moscow, 1957).

Mikhashoff, Yvar (real name, **Ronald Mackay**), American pianist and composer; b. Troy, N.Y., March 8, 1941; d. Buffalo, Oct. 11, 1993. He studied at the Eastman School of Music in Rochester, N.Y.; then enrolled at the Juilliard School of Music in N.Y. as a piano student of Beveridge Webster and Adele Marcus; subsequently studied composition on a Fulbright scholarship with Boulanger in Paris (1968–69); also studied at the Univ. of Houston (B.M., 1967; M.M., 1968) and the Univ. of Texas in Austin (D.M.A. in composition, 1973). He taught at the State Univ. of N.Y. in Buffalo (from 1973); toured extensively in the U.S. and Europe, being particularly noted for his championship of American music of the 19th and 20th centuries. He also appeared as a multimedia performer. In 1980 he played the principal acting role in the La Scala premiere of Bussotti's opera *La Racine* in Milan. In 1982 he organized the Holland Festival's 2-week-long celebration of 200 years of Dutch-American friendship through a series of 9 thematic concerts covering 250 years of American music.

WORKS: *Dances for Davia I–II* for Flute and Piano (1958, 1979); Concerto No. 1 for Piano, Winds, and Percussion (1965); Viola Concerto (1969); *Nocturne* for Cello and Piano (1977); *Light from a Distant Garden* for String Quartet (1983); *Grand Bowery Tango* for Flute and Ensemble (1985); *Night Dances* for String Trio (1985); *Twilight Dances* for Violin, Contrabass, Piano, and Percussion (1986); *Evening Dances* for Violin and Piano (1987); piano pieces; several vocal works, including *In Memoriam Igor Stravinsky* for Voice, Flute, Clarinet, and Cello (1971) and *Improvisations on the Last Words of Chief Seattle* for Speaker, Percussion, Mime Dancer, and Syllabist (1976).

Miki, Minoru, Japanese composer; b. Tokushima, March 16, 1930. He studied with Ifukube and Ikenouchi at the National Univ. of Fine Arts and Music in Tokyo (1951–55). He was a founder of the Nihon Ongaku Shūdan (Pro Musica Nipponia; 1964), an ensemble dedicated to performing new music for traditional Japanese instruments; later served as its artistic director. He lectured at the Tokyo College of Music; was founder-director of UTAYOMI-ZA (1986), a musical-opera theater.

WORKS: DRAMATIC: OPERAS: *Mendori Teishu* (A Henpecked Husband), chamber opera (1963); *Shunkin-shō* (Tokyo, 1975); *An Actor's Revenge* (London, 1979); *Toge no muko ni naniga aruka*, choral opera (1983); *Utayomizaru*, musical-opera (1983); *Joruri* (St. Louis, 1985); *At the Flower Garden*, mini-opera (1985); *Wakahime* (1991); *Orochi-den* (1992); *Shizuka and Yoshitsume* (1993). **CHAMBER MUSICAL:** *Yomigaeru* (1992). **BALLET:** *From the Land of Light* (1987). **ORCH.:** *Trinita sinfonica* (1953); *Sinfonia Gamula* (1957); *Symphony: Joya* (1960); Marimba Concerto (1969); *Jo-no-Kyoku*, prelude for Shakuhachi, Koro, Shamisen, and Strings (1969); *Convexity*, concerto for 3 Groups of Sankyoku and a Japanese Drum (1970); *Ha-no-Kyoku*, koto concerto (1974); *Hote* for Japanese Orch. (1976); *Symphony from Life* (1980); *Concerto Requiem* for Koto and Japanese Instruments (1980); *Kyu-no-Kyoku* (Sym. for 2 Worlds; Leipzig, Nov. 12, 1981); *3 Pieces*: 1, *March 1930*; 2, *August 1945*; 3, *September 1950* (1983); *Japan*, overture (1990); *Z Concerto* for Marimba, Percussion, and Orch. (1992); *Mai* (1992). **CHAMBER:** *Osabai* for 12 Wind Instruments and Percussion (1955); Sextet for Wind Instruments and Piano (1965); *Figures for 4 Groups* for Various Instruments (1967–69); *Ballades* for Koto (3 vols., 1969, 1976, 1983); *Tennyo* for Koto (1969); *Hakuyo* for Violin and Koto (1973); *Danses concertantes No. 1, 4 Seasons*, for Ensemble of Japanese Instruments (1973–74), *No. 2, Naruto-Hicho*, for Ensemble of Japanese Instruments (1977), *No. 3, A Tale of Hachirō*, for Ensemble of Japanese Instruments (1981), and *No. 4, Kita-no-Uta* (1984); *Yui I* for Shō and Piano (1982), *II* for Cello and Koto (1980–83), and *III, Flowers and Water*, for Shakuhachi, Koto, Shamisen, Harp, and String Quartet (1985); *Marimba Spiritual* for Marimba and 3 Percussionists (1984); Trio for Violin, Cello, and Piano (1986); *Organ Nirvana* for Organ (1988–89); String Quartet (1989). **VOCAL:** *Paraphrase after Ancient Japanese Music* for Soprano and Ensemble of 10 Japanese Instruments (1966); *Matsu-no-Kyoko* for Women's Chorus and Ensemble of Japanese Instruments (1974); *Sinfonia concertante per Wasan* for Bass, Women's Chorus, Nohkan, Koto, and Orch. (1976); *Taro*, cantata for 5 Soloists, Children's Chorus, and 17 Japanese Instruments (1977); *Awa Kitobun, I, II, III* (1981); *Beijing Requiem* (1990).

Mila, Massimo, Italian writer on music; b. Turin, Aug. 14, 1910; d. there, Dec. 26, 1988. He studied literature at the Univ. of Turin; after graduation, he became a regular contributor to many Italian musical publications; was music critic of *L'Espresso* (1955–68) and of *La Stampa* (1968–74). He taught music history at the Turin Cons. (1953–73) and at the Univ. of Turin (from 1960).

WRITINGS: *Il melodramma di Verdi* (Bari, 1933); *Cent' anni di musica moderna* (Milan, 1944); *W.A. Mozart* (Turin, 1945); *Breve storia della musica* (Milan, 1946; 2nd ed., 1963); *L'esperienza musicale e l'estetica* (Turin, 1950; 3rd ed., 1965); *"La carriera d'un libertino" di Strawinsky* (Milan, 1952); *Cronache musicale, 1955–1959* (Turin, 1959); *La musica pianistica di Mozart* (Turin, 1963); *Le sinfonie di Mozart* (Turin, 1967); *"I vespri siciliani" di Verdi* (Turin, 1973); *Lettura del Don Giovanni di Mozart* (Turin, 1988); R. Garavaglia and A. Sinigaglia, eds., *Massimo Mila alla Scala: Scritti, 1955–1988* (Milan, 1989).

BIBL.: G. Pestelli, ed., *Il melodramma italiano dell'ottocento: Studi e ricerche per M. M.* (Turin, 1977).

Milanov, Zinka (née **Kunc**), famous Croatian-American soprano; b. Zagreb, May 17, 1906; d. N.Y., May 30, 1989. She studied at the Zagreb Academy of Music, then with Milka Ternina, Maria Kostrenćić, and Fernando Carpi. She made her debut as Leonora in *Il Trovatore* in Ljubljana (1927); subsequently was principal soprano of the Zagreb Opera (1928–35), where she sang in over 300 performances in Croatian. After appearing at Prague's German Theater (1936), she was invited by Toscanini to sing in his performance of the Verdi *Requiem* at the Salzburg Festival (1937). She then made her Metropolitan Opera debut in N.Y. as Verdi's Leonora on Dec. 17, 1937; was one of the outstanding members on its roster (1937–41; 1942–47; 1950–66); gave her farewell performance there as Maddalena in *Andrea Chénier* on April 13, 1966. In addition to appearing in San Francisco and Chicago, she also sang at Buenos Aires's Teatro Colón (1940–42), Milan's La Scala (1950), and London's Covent Garden (1966–67). Her brother was **Božidar Kunc**. She married Predrag Milanov in 1937, but they were divorced in 1946; she then married Ljubomir Ilic in 1947. Blessed with a voice of translucent beauty, she became celebrated for her outstanding performances of roles in operas by Verdi and Puccini.

Mildmay, (Grace) Audrey (Louise St. John), English soprano; b. Herstmonceux, Dec. 19, 1900; d. London, May 31, 1953. She studied in London with Johnstone Douglas and in Vienna with Jani Strasser. In 1927–28 she toured North America as Polly Peachum in *The Beggar's Opera*, and then returned to England as a member of the Carlo Rosa Opera Co. (1928–31). In 1931 she married John Christie, with whom she helped to found the Glyndebourne Festival in 1934. She sang there from 1934 to 1936 and again in 1938–39. In 1939 she appeared at the Sadler's Wells Theatre in London. She retired from the operatic stage in 1943. Mildmay was co-founder of the Edinburgh Festival with Rudolf Bing in 1947. Her finest roles were Susanna, Zerlina, and Norina.

Miles, Maurice, English conductor; b. Epsom, Feb. 25, 1908; d. Hereford, June 26, 1985. He studied with Curzon (piano) and with Wood and Reed (conducting) at the Royal Academy of Music in London; later with Krauss at the Salzburg Mozarteum. He was on the staff of the BBC (1930–36); then conducted in Buxton and Bath (1936–39); after service in the British army, he rejoined the BBC (1943). He then was conductor of the Yorkshire Sym. Orch. (1947–54); later conducted the City of Belfast Orch. (1955–66) and the Ulster Orch. (1966–67); also taught at the Royal Academy of Music (from 1953).

Miles, Philip Napier, English composer and conductor; b. Shirehampton, Jan. 21, 1865; d. King's Weston, near Bristol, July 19, 1935. He studied in London with Parry and Dannreuther. He organized the Shirehampton Choral Soc. on his own estate and conducted festivals in various localities in England. He wrote the operas: *Westward Ho!* (London, Dec. 4, 1914), *Fire Flies* (Clifton, Oct. 13, 1924; on the same program with his opera *Markheim*), *Good Friday, Demeter*, and *Queen Rosamond*; also some chamber music and many songs.

Miletić, Miroslav, Croatian violinist and composer; b. Sisak, Aug. 22, 1925. He studied in Zagreb, where he organized the renowned Pro Arte String Quartet, specializing in performances of modern music.

WORKS: DRAMATIC: OPERAS: *Hasanaginica* and *Der Fall Ružena*; *Auvergnanski Senatori*, radio opera (1957). **TELEVISION BALLET:** *Vision* (1958). **ORCH.:** Suite for Strings (1955); Violin Concerto (1958); Viola Concerto (1959); Sym. (1959). **CHAMBER:** *Rhapsodic Variations* for Violin and Piano (1962); 4 string quartets; Violin Sonata; *Proportions* for 6 Instruments; *Lamentation* for Viola and Magnetic Tape; piano pieces; Croatian songs arranged for recorder.

Milford, Robin (Humphrey), English composer and teacher; b. Oxford, Jan. 22, 1903; d. Lyme Regis, Dec. 29, 1959. He was a student of Holst, Vaughan Williams, and R.O. Morris at the Royal College of Music in London. Thereafter he was active as a composer and teacher. He was best known for his chamber music, choral pieces, and songs.

WORKS: DRAMATIC: OPERA: *The Scarlet Letter* (1959). **BALLET:** *The Snow Queen* (1946). **ORCH.:** Suite for Chamber Orch. (1924); *Miniature Concerto* for Harpsichord and Chamber Orch. (1927); *Miniature Concerto* for Strings (1933); Violin Concerto (1937); *Ariel* for Small Orch. (1940); *Elegiac Meditation* for Viola and Strings (1947); *A Festival* for Strings (1951); *Fishing by Moonlight* for Piano and Strings (1952). **CHAMBER:** Flute Sonata (1944); *Fantasia* for String Quartet (1945); Violin Sonata (1945); Trio for Clarinet, Cello, and Piano (1948); Trio for 2 Violins and Piano (1949); piano pieces. **VOCAL:** *The Pilgrim's Progress*, oratorio (1932); *The Forsaken Merman* for Tenor, Women's Chorus, Strings, and Piano (1938–50); *A Liturgy to the Holy Spirit* (1947); songs.

BIBL.: I. Copley, *R. M.* (London, 1985).

Milhaud, Darius, eminent French composer; b. Marseilles, Sept. 4, 1892; d. Geneva, June 22, 1974. He was the descendant of an old Jewish family, settled in Provence for many centuries. His father was a merchant of almonds; there was a piano in the house, and Milhaud improvised melodies as a child; then began to take violin lessons. He entered the Paris Cons. in 1909, almost at the age limit for enrollment; studied with Berthelier (violin), Lefèvre (ensemble), Leroux (harmony), Gédalge (counterpoint), Widor (composition and fugue), and d'Indy (conducting); played violin in the student orch. under Dukas. He received 1st "accessit" in violin and counterpoint, and 2nd in fugue; won the Prix Lepaulle for composition. While still a student, he wrote music in a bold modernistic manner; became associated with Satie, Cocteau, and Claudel. When Claudel was appointed French minister to Brazil, he engaged Milhaud as his secretary; they sailed for Rio de Janeiro early in 1917; returned to Paris (via the West Indies and N.Y.) shortly after the armistice of Nov. 1918. Milhaud's name became known to a larger public as a result of a newspaper article by Henri Collet in *Comoedia* (Jan. 16, 1920), grouping him with 5 other French composers of modern tendencies (Auric, Durey, Honegger, Poulenc, and Tailleferre) under the sobriquet Les Six, even though the association was stylistically fortuitous. In 1922 he visited the U.S.; lectured at Harvard Univ., Princeton Univ., and Columbia Univ.; appeared as pianist and composer in his own works; in 1925 he traveled in Italy, Germany, Austria, and Russia; returning to France, he devoted himself mainly to composition and teaching. At the outbreak of World War II in 1939, he was in Aix-en-Provence; in July 1940 he went to the U.S.; taught at Mills College in Oakland, Calif. In 1947 he returned to France; was appointed prof. at the Paris Cons., but continued to visit the U.S. as conductor and teacher almost annually, despite arthritis, which compelled him to conduct while seated; he retained his post at Mills College until 1971; then settled in Geneva. Exceptionally prolific from his student days, he wrote a great number of works in every genre; introduced a modernistic type of music drama, "opéra à la minute," and also the "miniature symphony." He experimented with new stage techniques, incorporating cinematic interludes; also successfully revived the Greek type of tragedy with vocal accompaniment. He composed works for electronic instruments, and demonstrated his contrapuntal skill in such compositions as his 2 String Quartets (No. 14 and No. 15), which can be played together as a string octet. He was the first to exploit polytonality in a consistent and deliberate manner; applied the exotic rhythms of Latin America and the West Indies in many of his lighter works; of these, his *Saudades do Brasil* are particularly popular; Brazilian movements are also found in his *Scaramouche* and *Le Boeuf sur le toit*; in some of his works he drew upon the resources of jazz. His ballet *La Création du monde* (1923), portraying the Creation in terms of Negro cosmology, constitutes the earliest example of the use of the blues and jazz in a symphonic score, anticipating Gershwin in this respect. Despite this variety of means and versatility of forms, Milhaud succeeded in establishing a style that was distinctly and identifiably his own; his melodies are nostalgically lyrical or vivaciously rhythmical, according to mood; his instrumental writing is of great complexity and difficulty, and yet entirely within the capacities of modern virtuoso technique; he arranged many of his works in several versions.

WORKS: DRAMATIC: OPERAS: *La Brebis égarée*, "roman musical" (1910–15; Paris, Dec. 10, 1923); *Le Pauvre Matelot*, "complainte en trois actes" (1926; Paris, Dec. 12, 1927); *Les Malheurs d'Orphée* (Brussels, May 7, 1926); *Esther de Carpentras*, opéra-bouffe (1925; Paris, Feb. 1, 1938); 3 "minute operas": *L'Enlèvement d'Europe* (Baden-Baden, July 17, 1927), *L'Abandon d'Ariane*, and *La Délivrance de Thésée* (Wiesbaden, April 20, 1928); *Christophe Colomb* (Berlin, May 5, 1930); *Maximilien* (Paris, Jan. 4, 1932); *Médée* (Antwerp, Oct. 7, 1939); *Bolivar* (1943; Paris, May 12, 1950); *Le Jeu de Robin et Marion*, mystery play after Adam de la Halle (Wiesbaden, Oct. 28, 1951); *David* (Jerusalem, June 1, 1954); *La Mère coupable*, to a libretto by Madeleine Milhaud, after Beaumarchais (Geneva, June 13, 1966); *Saint Louis, Roi de France*, opera-oratorio (1970–71; Rio de Janeiro, April 14, 1972). **INCIDENTAL MUSIC:** *Agamemnon* (1913; Paris, April 16, 1927); *Les Choéphores* (concert version, Paris, June 15, 1919; stage version, Brussels, March 27, 1935); *Les Euménides* (1922; Antwerp, Nov. 27, 1927); *Jeux d'enfants*, 3 children's plays: *A propos de bottes* (1932), *Un Petit Peu de musique* (1933), and *Un Petit Peu d'exercise* (1937). **BALLETS:** *L'Homme et son désir* (Paris, June 6, 1921); *Le Boeuf sur le toit* (Paris, Feb. 21, 1920); *Les Mariés de la Tour Eiffel* (Paris, June 19, 1921; in collaboration with Honegger, Auric, Poulenc, and Tailleferre); *La Création du monde* (Paris, Oct. 25, 1923); *Salade*, "ballet chanté" (Paris, May 17, 1924); *Le Train bleu*, "danced operetta" (Paris, June 20, 1924); *Polka* for the ballet *L'Éventail de Jeanne*, in homage to the music patroness Jeanne

Dubost (Paris, June 16, 1927; in collaboration with Ravel, Ibert, Roussel et al.); *Jeux de printemps* (Washington, D.C., Oct. 30, 1944); *The Bells*, after Poe (Chicago, April 26, 1946); *'adame Miroir* (Paris, May 31, 1948); *Vendange* (1952; Nice, April 17, 1972); *La Rose des vents* (1958); *La Branche des oiseaux* (1965).

ORCH.: *Suite symphonique No. 1* (Paris, May 26, 1914) and *No. 2* (from incidental music to Claudel's *Protée*; Paris, Oct. 24, 1920); 5 syms. for Small Orch.: No. 1, *Le Printemps* (1917), No. 2, *Pastorale* (1918), No. 3, *Sérénade* (1921), No. 4, *Dixtuor à cordes* (1921), and No. 5, *Dixtuor d'instruments à vent* (1922); 12 syms. for Large Orch.: No. 1 (Chicago, Oct. 17, 1940, composer conducting), No. 2 (Boston, Dec. 20, 1946, composer conducting), No. 3, *Hymnus ambrosianus*, for Chorus and Orch. (Paris, Oct. 30, 1947), No. 4 (Paris, May 20, 1948, composer conducting), No. 5 (Turin, Oct. 16, 1953), No. 6 (Boston, Oct. 7, 1955, composer conducting), No. 7 (Chicago, March 3, 1956), No. 8, *Rhodanienne* (Berkeley, Calif., April 22, 1958), No. 9 (Fort Lauderdale, Fla., March 29, 1960), No. 10 (Portland, Oreg., April 4, 1961), No. 11, *Romantique* (Dallas, Dec. 12, 1960), and No. 12, *Rural* (Davis, Calif., Feb. 16, 1962); *Cinéma-Fantaisie sur Le Boeuf sur le toit* for Violin and Orch. (Paris, Dec. 4, 1920); *Caramel mou, a shimmy*, for Jazz Band (1920); *5 études* for Piano and Orch. (Paris, Jan. 20, 1921); *Saudades do Brasil*, suite of dances (1920–21; also for Piano); *Ballade* for Piano and Orch. (1921); *3 Rag Caprices* (Paris, Nov. 23, 1923); *Le Carnaval d'Aix* for Piano and Orch. (N.Y., Dec. 9, 1926, composer soloist); *2 hymnes* (1927); 3 violin concertos: No. 1 (1927), No. 2 (Paris, Nov. 7, 1948), and No. 3, *Concerto royal* (1958); Viola Concerto (Amsterdam, Dec. 15, 1929); Concerto for Percussion and Small Orch. (Paris, Dec. 5, 1930); 5 piano concertos: No. 1 (Paris, Nov. 23, 1934), No. 2 (Chicago, Dec. 18, 1941, composer soloist), No. 3 (Prague, May 26, 1946), No. 4 (Boston, March 3, 1950), and No. 5 (1955; N.Y., June 25, 1956); *Concertino de printemps* for Violin and Orch. (Paris, March 21, 1935); 2 cello concertos: No. 1 (Paris, June 28, 1935) and No. 2 (N.Y., Nov. 28, 1946); *Suite provençale* (Venice, Sept. 12, 1937); *L'Oiseau* (Paris, Jan. 30, 1938); *Cortège funèbre* (N.Y., Aug. 4, 1940); Clarinet Concerto (1941; Washington, D.C., Jan. 30, 1946); *Suite* for Harmonica and Orch. (1942; Paris, May 28, 1947, Larry Adler soloist; also for Violin and Orch., Philadelphia, Nov. 16, 1945, Zino Francescatti soloist); Concerto for 2 Pianos and Orch. (Pittsburgh, Nov. 13, 1942); *Opus americanum* (San Francisco, Dec. 6, 1943); *Suite française* (for Band, N.Y., June 13, 1945; for Orch., N.Y., July 29, 1945); *Cain and Abel* for Narrator and Orch. (Los Angeles, Oct. 21, 1945); *Le Bal martiniquais* (N.Y., Dec. 6, 1945, composer conducting); *2 Marches* (CBS, N.Y., Dec. 12, 1945); *Fête de la Victoire* (1945); *L'Apothéose de Molière* for Harpsichord and Strings (Capri, Sept. 15, 1948); *Kentuckiana* (Louisville, Jan. 4, 1949); Concerto for Marimba, Vibraphone, and Orch. (St. Louis, Feb. 12, 1949); *West Point Suite* for Band (West Point, May 30, 1952); *Concertino d'hiver* for Trombone and Strings (1953); *Ouverture méditerranéenne* (Louisville, May 22, 1954); Harp Concerto (Venice, Sept. 17, 1954); Oboe Concerto (1957); *Aubade* (Oakland, Calif., March 14, 1961); *Ouverture philharmonique* (N.Y., Nov. 30, 1962); *A Frenchman in New York* (Boston, June 25, 1963); *Odes pour les morts des guerres* (1963); *Murder of a Great Chief of State*, in memory of President John F. Kennedy (Oakland, Calif., Dec. 3, 1963); *Pacem in terris*, choral sym. (Paris, Dec. 20, 1963); *Music for Boston* for Violin and Orch. (1965); *Musique pour Prague* (Prague, May 20, 1966); *Musique pour l'Indiana* (Indianapolis, Oct. 29, 1966); *Musique pour Lisbonne* (1966); *Musique pour Nouvelle Orléans* (commissioned by the New Orleans Sym. Orch., but unaccountably canceled, and perf. for the 1st time in Aspen, Colo., Aug. 11, 1968, composer conducting); *Musique pour l'Univers Claudelien* (Aix-en-Provence, July 30, 1968); *Musique pour Graz* (Graz, Nov. 24, 1970); *Musique pour San Francisco*, "with the participation of the audience" (1971); *Suite in G* (San Rafael, Calif., Sept. 25, 1971); *Ode pour Jerusalem* (1972).

CHAMBER: 2 violin sonatas (1911, 1917); 18 string quartets (1912–51), of which No. 14 and No. 15 are playable together, forming an octet (1st perf. in this form in Oakland, Calif., Aug. 10, 1949); Sonata for Piano and 2 Violins (1914); *Le Printemps* for Piano and Violin (1914); Sonata for Piano, Flute, Clarinet, and Oboe (1918); Flute Sonatina (1922); *Impromptu* for Violin and Piano (1926); *3 caprices de Paganini* for Violin and Piano (1927); Clarinet Sonatina (1927); *Pastorale* for Oboe, Clarinet, and Bassoon (1935); Suite for Oboe, Clarinet, and Bassoon (1937); *La Cheminée du Roi René*, suite for Flute, Oboe, Clarinet, Horn, and Bassoon (1939); Sonatina for 2 Violins (1940); *Sonatine à trois* for Violin, Viola, and Cello (1940); Sonatina for Violin and Viola (1941); *Quatre visages* for Viola and Piano (1943); 2 viola sonatas (1944); *Elegie* for Cello and Piano (1945); *Danses de Jacarémirim* for Violin and Piano (1945); Sonata for Violin and Harpsichord (1945); Duo for 2 Violins (1945); String Trio (1947); *Aspen Serenade* for 9 Instruments (1957); String Sextet (1958); Chamber Concerto for Piano, Wind Instruments, and String Quintet (1961); String Septet (1964); Piano Quartet (1966); Piano Trio (1968); *Stanford Serenade* for Oboe and 11 Instruments (1969; Stanford, Calif., May 24, 1970); *Musique pour Ars nova* for 13 Instruments (1969); Wind Quintet (1973). **PIANO:** *Le Printemps*, suite (1915–19); 2 sonatas (1916, 1949); *Saudades do Brasil*, 12 numbers in 2 books (1921); *3 Rag Caprices* (1922; also for Small Orch.); *L'Automne*, suite of 3 pieces (1932); *4 romances sans paroles* (1933); 2 sets of children's pieces: *Touches noires* and *Touches blanches* (1941); *La Muse ménagère*, suite of 15 pieces (1944; also for Orch.); *Une Journée*, suite of 5 pieces (1946); *L'Enfant aimé*, suite of 5 pieces (1948; also for Orch.); *Le Candélabre à sept branches*, suite (Ein Gev Festival, Israel, April 10, 1952); *Scaramouche*, version for 2 Pianos (1939); Le Bal martiniquais, version for 2 Pianos (1944); *Paris*, suite of 6 pieces for 4 Pianos (1948); *6 danses en 3 mouvements* for 2 Pianos (Paris, Dec. 17, 1970).

VOCAL: 3 albums of songs after Francis Jammes (1910–12); *7 poèmes de la Connaissance de l'Est*, after Claudel (1913); *3 poèmes romantiques* for Voice and Piano (1914); *Le Château*, song cycle (1914); *4 poèmes* for Baritone, after Claudel (1915–17); *8 poèmes juifs* (1916); *Child poems* (1916); *3 poèmes*, after Christina Rossetti (1916); *Le Retour de l'enfant prodigue*, cantata for 5 Voices and Orch. (1917; Paris, Nov. 23, 1922, composer conducting); *Chansons bas* for Voice and Piano, after Mallarmé (1917); *2 poèmes de Rimbaud* for Voice and Piano (1917); *Psalm 136* for Baritone, Chorus, and Orch. (1918); *Psalm 129* for Baritone and Orch. (1919); *Les Soirées de Pétrograd*, in 2 albums: *L'Ancien Régime* and *La Révolution* (1919); *Machines agricoles* for Voice and 7 Instruments, to words from a commercial catalog (1919); *3 poèmes de Jean Cocteau* for Voice and Piano (1920); *Catalogue de fleurs* for Voice and Piano or 7 Instruments (1920); *Feuilles de température* for Voice and Piano (1920); *Cocktail* for Voice and 3 Clarinets (1921); *Psalm 126* for Chorus (1921); *4 poèmes de Catulle* for Voice and Violin (1923); *6 chants populaires hébraïques* for Voice and Piano (1925); *Hymne de Sion* for Voice and Piano (1925); *Pièce de circonstance* for Voice and Piano, after Cocteau (1926); *Cantate pour louer le Seigneur* for Soli, Choruses, and Orch. (1928); *Pan et Syrinx*, cantata (1934); *Les Amours de Ronsard* for Chorus and Small Orch. (1934); *Le Cygne* for Voice and Piano, after Claudel (1935); *La Sagesse* for Voices and Small Orch., after Claudel (1935; Paris Radio, Nov. 8, 1945); *Cantate de la paix*, after Claudel (1937); *Cantate nuptiale*, after *Song of Songs* (Marseilles, Aug. 31, 1937); *Les Deux Cités*, cantata (1937); *Chanson du capitaine* for Voice and Piano (1937); *Les Quatre Éléments* for Soprano, Tenor, and Orch. (1938); *Récréation*, children's songs (1938); *3 élégies* for Soprano, Tenor, and Strings (1939); *Incantations* for Men's Chorus (1939); *Quatrains valaisans* for Chorus, after Rilke (1939); *Cantate de la guerre* for Chorus, after Claudel (1940); *Le Voyage d'été*, suite for Voice and Piano (1940); *4 chansons de Ronsard* for Voice and Orch. (1941); *Reves*, song cycle (1942); *La Libération des Antilles* for Voice and Piano (1944); *Kaddisch* for Voice, Chorus, and Organ (1945); *Sabbath Morning Service* for Baritone, Chorus, and Organ (1947); *Naissance de Vénus*, cantata for Chorus (Paris Radio, Nov. 30, 1949); *Ballade-Nocturne* for Voice and Piano

(1949); *Barba Garibo*, 10 French folk songs, for Chorus and Orch. (for the celebration of the wine harvest in Menton, 1953); *Cantate de l'initiation* for Chorus and Orch. (1960); *Cantate de la croix de charité* (1960); *Invocation à l'ange Raphael* for 2 Women's Choruses and Orch. (1962); *Adam* for Vocal Quintet (1964); *Cantate de Psaumes* (Paris, May 2, 1968); *Les Momies d'Égypte*, choral comedy (1972).

WRITINGS: *Études* (essays; Paris, 1926); *Notes sans musique* (autobiography; Paris, 1949; Eng. tr., London, 1952, as *Notes without Music*); *Entretiens avec Claude Rostand* (Paris, 1952); *Ma vie heureuse* (Paris, 1973).

BIBL.: P. Landormy, "D. M.," *Le Ménestrel* (Aug. 14, 21, 28, 1925); G. Augsbourg, *La Vie de D. M. en images* (Paris, 1935); M. Bauer, "D. M.," *Musical Quarterly* (April 1942); G. Beck, *D. M.: Étude suivie du catalogue chronologique complet* (Paris, 1949; supplement, 1957); C. Mason, "The Chamber Music of M.," *Musical Quarterly* (July 1957); J. Roy, *D. M.* (Paris, 1968); A. Braga, *D. M.* (Naples, 1969); C. Palmer, *M.* (London, 1976); P. Collaer, *D. M.* (Geneva and Paris, 1982; with complete catalog of works, eds., writings, trs., and recordings; Eng. tr., 1988); H. Ehrler, *Untersuchungen zur Klaviermusik von Francis Poulenc, Arthur Honegger und D. M.* (Tutzing, 1990); F. Bloch, *D. M., 1892–1974* (Paris, 1992); A. Lunel, *Mon ami D. M.: Inédits* (Aix-en-Provence, 1992); H. Malcomess, *Die opéras minute von D. M.* (Bonn, 1993); J. Roy, *Le groupe des six: Poulenc, M., Honegger, Auric, Tailleferre, Durey* (Paris, 1994).

Miller, Dayton C(larence), American physicist and flutist; b. Strongsville, Ohio, March 13, 1866; d. Cleveland, Feb. 22, 1941. After graduation from Baldwin College and Princeton Univ. (D.Sc., 1890), he was prof. of physics at the Case School of Applied Science in Cleveland (from 1893). An early interest in the flute led to his experimentation with various versions of the instrument (including a double-bass flute); he accumulated an extensive collection of flutes and various materials relating to the flute, which he left to the Library of Congress in Washington, D.C. A leading authority in the field of acoustics and light, he was president of the American Physical Soc. (1925–26) and of the Acoustical Soc. of America (1931–32), and vice-president of the American Musicological Soc. (1939). His books included *The Science of Musical Sounds* (1916; 2nd ed., rev., 1926), *Catalogue of Books and Literary Material Relating to the Flute and Other Musical Instruments* (1935), *Anecdotal History of the Science of Sound to the Beginning of the 20th Century* (1935), and *Sound Waves, Their Shape and Speed* (1937).

BIBL.: H. Fletcher, *Biographical Memoir of D.C. M.* (Washington, D.C., 1944); L. Gilliam and W. Lichtenwanger, *The D.C. M. Flute Collection: A Checklist of the Instruments* (Washington, D.C., 1961).

Miller, (Alton) Glenn, famous American trombonist and bandleader; b. Clarinda, Iowa, March 1, 1904; d. during an airplane flight from London to Paris, Dec. 15, 1944. He spent his formative years in Fort Morgan, Colo., where he began his musical training; played with the local Boyd Senter Orch. (1921) and took courses at the Univ. of Colo. After performing with Ben Pollack's band on the West Coast (1924–28), he followed Pollack to N.Y. and then became active as a free-lance musician; helped to found an orch. for Ray Noble (1934), and subsequently studied orchestration with Joseph Schillinger; began experimenting with special effects, combining clarinets with saxophone in the same register. He organized his first band in 1937, but it failed to find an audience and dissolved in 1938; that same year he organized another band, which caught on only in 1939 through its radio broadcasts and recordings. It subsequently became one of the most successful aggregations of the day, producing such popular recordings as *Moonlight Serenade* (1939), *In the Mood* (1939), *Tuxedo Junction* (1940), *Chattanooga Choo Choo* (1941), and *A String of Pearls* (1941); it also appeared in the films *Sun Valley Serenade* (1941) and *Orchestra Wives* (1942). Miller joined the U.S. Army Air Force as a captain in 1942 and put together a band for entertaining the troops; it was based in England from 1944. A film, *The Glenn Miller Story*, was produced in 1953.

BIBL.: S. Bedwell, *A G. M. Discography and Biography* (London, 1955; 2nd ed., 1956); J. Flower, *Moonlight Serenade: A Bio-Discography of the G. M. Civilian Band* (New Rochelle, N.Y., 1972); G. Simon, *G. M. and His Orchestra* (N.Y., 1974); J. Green, *G. M. and the Age of Swing* (London, 1976); G. Butcher, *Next to a Letter from Home: Major G. M.'s Wartime Band* (Edinburgh, 1986).

Miller, Jonathan (Wolfe), English opera director; b. London, July 21, 1934. He studied the natural sciences at St. John's College, Cambridge, taking his M.D. degree in 1959. However, his abiding interest in the arts led him to pursue work in television and the theater. Turning to opera direction, he attracted notice with his staging of Alexander Goehr's *Arden Must Die* with the New Opera Co. in 1974. From 1974 to 1981 he was an opera director with the Kent Opera, where his stagings of *Così fan tutte, Orfeo, Falstaff,* and *Evgeny Onegin* were highly praised; also worked regularly with the English National Opera in London, winning special acclaim for his stagings of *Rigoletto* (1982) and *The Mikado* (1986). In 1991 he staged *Le Nozze di Figaro* at the Vienna Festival and *Kát'a Kabanová* at the Metropolitan Opera in N.Y.

BIBL.: M. Romain, *A Profile of J. M.* (Cambridge, 1992).

Miller, Mildred, American soprano; b. Cleveland, Dec. 16, 1924. Her parents came from Germany; the original family name was Müller. She studied at the Cleveland Inst. of Music (B.M., 1946), then with Sundelius at the New England Cons. of Music in Boston (diploma, 1948). In 1949 she went to Germany; sang with the Stuttgart Opera and with the Bavarian State Opera in Munich. In 1950 she married the American pilot Wesley W. Posvar. Returning to the U.S., she made her debut with the Metropolitan Opera in N.Y. as Cherubino (Nov. 17, 1951); remained there until 1975; also appeared widely as a concert singer. She was founder-artistic director of the Pittsburgh Opera Theater (from 1978).

Miller, Mitch(ell William), American oboist, recording executive, and conductor; b. Rochester, N.Y., July 4, 1911. He studied at the Eastman School of Music (B.Mus., 1932). He played oboe in the Rochester Phil. (1930–33) and the CBS Sym. Orch. (1935–47); was director of artists and repertoire for the classical division of Mercury Records (1947–50); was in charge of the popular division of Columbia Records (1950–61); starred in his own television program, "Sing-Along with Mitch" (1960–65), which became extremely popular. He appeared as a guest conductor of pop concerts with many U.S. orchs. From 1994 to 1996 he was principal pops conductor of the New Jersey Sym. Orch.

Miller, Philip Lieson, American music librarian and writer on music; b. Woodland, N.Y., April 23, 1906. He received training in piano and theory at the Manhattan School (1923–27) and in singing at the Inst. of Musical Art (1927–29) in N.Y. In 1927 he joined the staff of the N.Y. Public Library, where he was assistant chief (1946–59) and then chief (1959–66). In 1963–64 he was president of the Music Library Assn. He was president of the Assn. for Recorded Sound Collections (1966–68). His articles and reviews were publ. in many journals. He also publ. the books *Vocal Music* (N.Y., 1955) and *The Ring of Words: An Anthology of Song Texts* (N.Y., 1963).

Miller, Robert, American pianist and lawyer; b. N.Y., Dec. 5, 1930; d. Bronxville, N.Y., Nov. 30, 1981. He studied piano with Mathilde McKinney and Abbey Simon; then enrolled at Princeton Univ., where he took classes in composition with Babbitt and Cone, graduating in 1952; also studied jurisprudence at Columbia Univ. Law School, graduating in 1957. He was admitted to the bar in 1958 and became a practicing Wall Street lawyer; among his clients were several composers. As a pianist, he made his debut in Carnegie Hall in N.Y. in 1957; he had a fairly active, though unhappily brief, career as a recitalist, excelling particularly in ultramodern music. He gave the first performance in N.Y. in 1980 of a piano concerto by John Harbison; George Crumb wrote his *Makrokosmos* (vol. II) for him.

Millet, Luis, Catalan composer and conductor; b. Masnou, near Barcelona, April 18, 1867; d. Barcelona, Dec. 7, 1941. He studied with Vidiella and Pedrell. He became a choral conductor. In 1891 he founded the famous choral society Orfeo Català, which he led until the last years of his life; was also director of the municipal music school in Barcelona. He composed several orch. fantasies on Catalan folk songs and many choral works; also publ. 2 books on folk music: *De la cancion popular catalana* and *Pel nostre ideal* (1917).

BIBL.: B. Sampler, *L. M.* (Barcelona, 1926).

Milligan, Harold Vincent, American organist, writer on music, and composer; b. Astoria, Oreg., Oct. 31, 1888; d. N.Y., April 12, 1951. He studied with Carl and Noble. He was a church organist in Portland, Oreg., before going to N.Y. in 1907; then taught organ at various schools and colleges; was church organist in New Jersey and N.Y.; also lectured on American music. He ed. 4 vols. of 18th-century American songs and, with G. Souvaine, *The Opera Quiz Book* (N.Y., 1948); also wrote a biography of Stephen Foster (N.Y., 1920) and *Stories of Famous Operas* (N.Y., 1950; 2nd ed., rev., 1955). He composed 2 children's operettas, *The Outlaws of Etiquette* (1914) and *The Laughabet* (1918); incidental music; choral works; many songs; organ works.

Millo, Aprile (Elizabeth), talented American soprano; b. N.Y., April 14, 1958. Her father was a tenor and her mother a soprano; after living in Europe, Millo's family moved to Los Angeles when she was 11; during her high school years, she studied voice with her parents and augmented her training by listening to recordings of the great divas. In 1977 she won 1st place in the San Diego Opera competition, received the Geraldine Farrar Award, and sang in the opening concert of the new opera center there. In 1978 she won 1st prize in the Concorso Internazionale di Voci Verdiane in Busseto and received the Montserrat Caballe Award at the Francisco Vinas competition in Barcelona. In 1981 she sang with the N.Y. City Opera and also joined the Metropolitan Opera's Young Artists Development Program; later studied with Rita Patane. On Jan. 4, 1983, she made her first appearance at La Scala in Milan as Elvira in *Ernani*, a role she repeated with the Welsh National Opera in 1984. She made her Metropolitan Opera debut in N.Y. as Amelia in *Simon Boccanegra* on Dec. 3, 1984, substituting for the ailing Anna Tomowa-Sintow. In 1985 she received the Richard Tucker Award. Subsequently she appeared at the Metropolitan Opera in such roles as Elisabetta in *Don Carlos*, Li in *Turandot*, Luisa Miller, Leonora in *Il Trovatore*, Desdemona in *Otello*, and Aida. She also sang in concert performances with the Opera Orch. of N.Y., appearing as Giselda in *I Lombardi alla prima crociata* (1986) and as Lida in *La battaglia di Legnano* (1987). In 1992 she made her San Francisco Opera debut as Maddalena.

Mills, Charles (Borromeo), American composer; b. Asheville, N.C., Jan. 8, 1914; d. N.Y., March 7, 1982. In his youth, he played in dance bands. In 1933 he went to N.Y. and engaged in serious study of composition, first with Max Garfield and then with Copland (1935–37), Sessions (1937–39), and Harris (1939–41). He wrote mostly in a severe but eloquent contrapuntal style; in virtually his entire career as a composer, he pursued the ideal of formal cohesion; his style of composition may be described as Baroque à l'américaine. His quest for artistic self-discipline led him to the decision to become a Roman Catholic. He was baptized according to the Roman Catholic rite on May 14, 1944. In 1952 he was awarded a Guggenheim fellowship. In his last works, Mills gradually adopted serial methods, which seemed to respond to his need of strong discipline.

WORKS: ORCH.: 6 syms.: No. 1 (1940), No. 2 (1942), No. 3 (1946), No. 4, *Crazy Horse* (Cincinnati, Nov. 28, 1958), No. 5 for Strings (1980), and No. 6 (1981); Piano Concerto (1948); *Theme and Variations* (N.Y., Nov. 8, 1951); Concertino for Oboe and Strings (1957); *Serenade* for Winds and Strings (1960); *In a Mule-Drawn Wagon* for Strings (1968); *Symphonic Ode* for Strings (1976). **CHAMBER:** 5 string quartets (1939–58); 6 violin sonatas (1940–77); 2 cello sonatas (1940, 1942); Piano Trio (1941); Chamber Concerto for 10 Instruments (1942); 2 suites for Solo Violin (1942, 1944); English Horn Sonata (1946); *Concerto sereno* for Woodwind Octet (1948); *Prologue and Dithyramb* for String Quartet (1951); Brass Quintet (1962); Brass Sextet (1964); *Sonata da chiesa* for Recorder and Harpsichord (1972); *The 5 Moons of Uranus* for Recorder and Piano (1972); *Duo eclogue* for Recorder and Organ (1974). **PIANO:** 2 sonatas (1941–42); 11 sonatinas (1942–45); *30 Penitential Preludes* (1945). **VOCAL:** *Canticles of the Sun* for Voice and Piano (1945); *The Ascension Cantata* for Tenor and Chorus (1954); *The 1st Thanksgiving*, cantata for Chorus and Organ (1956). **JAZZ ENSEMBLE:** *The Centaur and the Phoenix* (1960); *Summer Song* (1960); *Paul Bunyan Jump* (1964).

Mills, Erie, American soprano; b. Granite City, Ill., June 22, 1953. She attended the National Music Camp in Interlochen, Mich., then studied voice with Karl Trump at the College of Wooster, Ohio, with Grace Wilson at the Univ. of Ill., and with Elena Nikolaidi. In 1979 she made her professional operatic debut as Ninette in *The Love for 3 Oranges* at the Chicago Lyric Opera; on Oct. 13, 1982, she made her first appearance with the N.Y. City Opera as Cunegonde in *Candide*, and subsequently sang there regularly; she made her Metropolitan Opera debut in N.Y. as Blondchen in *Die Entführung aus dem Serail* on Nov. 26, 1987. She also made guest appearances with the Cincinnati Opera, Cleveland Opera, San Francisco Opera, Minnesota Opera, Opera Soc. of Washington, D.C., Santa Fe Opera, Houston Grand Opera, Hamburg State Opera, La Scala in Milan, and Vienna State Opera. On March 17, 1989, she made her N.Y. recital debut. On Oct. 5, 1992, she sang Orazio in the U.S. premiere of Handel's *Muzio* in N.Y. Among her other prominent roles are Rossini's Rosina, Donizetti's Lucia, Offenbach's Olympia, Johann Strauss's Adele, and Richard Strauss's Zerbinetta.

Mills, Kerry (real name, **Frederick Allen**), American composer and music publisher; b. Philadelphia, Feb. 1, 1869; d. Hawthorne, Calif., Dec. 5, 1948. He was active as a violinist; taught violin at a private cons. in Ann Arbor, Mich., known as the Univ. School of Music (1892–93); adopting the name Kerry Mills, he publ. his own cakewalk march *Rufus on Parade* (1895); encouraged by its favorable sales, he moved to N.Y., where he became one of the most important publishers of minstrel songs, cakewalks, early ragtime, and other popular music. His own compositions were particularly successful; *At a Georgia Campmeeting* (1897) became the standard against which all other cakewalks were measured; performed in Europe by John Philip Sousa, it became popular there as well; it was roundly denounced in the *Leipzig Illustrierte Zeitung* (Feb. 5, 1903), and may well have been the inspiration for Debussy's *Golliwog's Cakewalk*. Some of his other hits also reached Europe; his *Whistling Rufus* (1899) was publ. in Berlin as *Rufus das Pfeifergigerl*. He also wrote the popular song *Meet Me in St. Louis, Louis* (1904) for the Louisiana Purchase Exposition held in St. Louis that year; it was revived for the film of that title starring Judy Garland (1944). He also wrote sacred songs as Frederick Allen Mills.

Mills, Richard (John), Australian conductor and composer; b. Toowoomba, Queensland, Nov. 14, 1949. After initial training at the Queensland Conservatorium of Music in North Quay (1964–69), he pursued his education at the Univ. of Queensland in St. Lucia (B.A., 1969) before completing his studies at the Guildhall School of Music in London (1969–71) with Rubbra (composition) and Gilbert Webster (percussion). He was principal percussionist in the Tasmanian Sym. Orch. in Hobart (1976–79) and the Queensland Sym. Orch. in Brisbane (1980–81). He lectured in composition at the Univ. of Northern

Rivers in Lismore, New South Wales (1982–84), and in composition and conducting at the Queensland Conservatorium of Music (1985–86). In 1989–90 he served as artist-in-residence of the Australian Broadcasting Corp. He was artistic director of the Adelaide Chamber Orch. (1991–92) and artistic consultant of the Queensland Sym. Orch. (1991–92). His early diatonic style evolved into one in which more complex uses of harmony and counterpoint appeared.

WORKS: DRAMATIC: *Snugglepot and Cuddlepie*, ballet (1988). **ORCH.:** *Toccata* (1976); *Music* for Strings (1977); *Fantasia on a Rondel* (1981); *Overture with Fanfares* (1981); Trumpet Concerto (1982); *Soundscapes* for Percussion and Orch. (1983); *Castlemaine Antiphons* for Brass Band and Orch. (1984); *Bamaga Diptych* (1986); *Sequenzas/Concertante* (1986); *Fantastic Pantomimes* for Flute, Oboe, Clarinet, Horn, Trumpet, and Orch. (1987–88); *Aeolian Caprices* (1988); *Seaside Dances* for 18 Solo Strings (1989); Flute Concerto (1990); Cello Concerto (1990); Violin Concerto (1992). **CHAMBER:** Brass Quintet (1986); Sonatina for String Quartet (1986); *Miniatures and Refrains* for String Quartet (1986); String Quartet No. 1 (1989). **VOCAL:** *Festival Folksongs* for Tenor, Mezzo-soprano, Chorus, Children's Chorus, 2 Optional Brass Choirs, and Orch. (1985); *Voyages and Visions* for 4 Soloists, Chorus, 3 Brass Bands, 4 Percussion, Orch., and Tape (1987); *Visionary Fanfare* for Chorus, 2 Brass Bands, 6 Trumpets, 6 Trombones, and Orch. (1988); *5 Meditations on the Poetry of David Campbell* for Soprano, Baritone, Chorus, and Orch. (1988).

Mills-Cockell, John, Canadian composer; b. Toronto, May 19, 1943. He studied composition and electronic music at the Univ. of Toronto and at the Royal Cons. of Music there. In 1966 he developed, in collaboration with the writer Blake Parker, artist Michael Hayden, and designer Dick Zander, a method of composition and performance called Intersystems; he joined the rock bands Kensington Market in Toronto (1969), Hydro-Electric Streetcar in Vancouver (1969–70), and Syrinx in Toronto (1970–72), which he founded; then devoted himself to composing and recording. He wrote numerous pieces for mixed media, works utilizing tape, electronic music for films, etc.

Milner, Anthony (Francis Dominic), English composer and teacher; b. Bristol, May 13, 1925. He studied composition privately with Matyas Seiber (1944–48); also took courses with R.O. Morris (composition) and Herbert Fryer (piano) at the Royal College of Music in London (1945–47). From 1948 to 1964 he taught at Morley College in London; served as director and harpsichordist of the London Cantata Ensemble (1954–65); was a part-time teacher (1961–80) and principal lecturer (1980–89) at the Royal College of Music; was also a lecturer at King's College, London (1965–71), and senior lecturer (1971–74) and principal lecturer (1974–80) at Goldsmiths' College, London.

WORKS: ORCH.: *Variations* (1958; Cheltenham, July 6, 1959); *Divertimento* for Strings (London, Aug. 17, 1961); *Overture: April Prologue* (London, Dec. 5, 1961); *Sinfonia pasquale* for Strings (1963; Dorchester, May 5, 1964); Chamber Sym. (1967; London, March 31, 1968); 3 syms.: No. 1 (1972; London, Jan. 17, 1973), No. 2 for Soprano, Tenor, Boy's Chorus, Chorus, and Orch. (Liverpool, July 13, 1978), and No. 3 (1986; London, Nov. 26, 1987); Concerto for Symphonic Wind Band (Ithaca, N.Y., Oct. 10, 1979); Concerto for Strings (1982; Wells, June 19, 1984). **CHAMBER:** Quartet for Oboe and Strings (1953); Quintet for Wind Instruments (1964); String Quartet No. 1 (1975); piano music; organ pieces. **VOCAL:** Cantatas: *Salutatio Angelica* for Contralto or Mezzo-soprano, Chorus, and Chamber Orch. (1948; London, Nov. 11, 1951); *The City of Desolation: A Cantata of Hope* for Soprano, Chorus, and Orch. (Totnes, Devon, Aug. 12, 1955); *The Harrowing of Hell* for Tenor, Bass, and Chorus (BBC, Nov. 14, 1956); *Roman Spring* for Soprano, Tenor, Chorus, and Orch. (London, Oct. 13, 1969); *Midway* for Mezzo-soprano and Chamber Orch. (London, July 10, 1974); *Emmanuel*, Christmas cantata for Countertenor, Soprano, Contralto, Tenor, Bass, Chorus, Audience, and Orch. (1974; Kingston upon Thames, Dec. 13, 1975); other vocal works, including *The Gates of Spring*, ode for Soprano, Tenor, Chorus, and String Orch. (1988), many sacred works, and songs.

BIBL.: S. Dodgson, "Retrospect and Prospect: M. at 60," *Musical Times* (May 1985); J. Siddons, *A. M.: A Bio-Bibliography* (Westport, Conn., 1989).

Milnes, Sherrill (Eustace), distinguished American baritone; b. Downers Grove, Ill., Jan. 10, 1935. He learned to play piano and violin at home, then played tuba in a school band; after a period as a medical student at North Central College in Naperville, Ill., he turned to music; subsequently studied voice with Andrew White at Drake Univ. in Des Moines and with Hermanus Baer at Northwestern Univ. He sang in choral performances under Margaret Hillis in Chicago; then was a member of the chorus at the Santa Fe Opera, where he received his first opportunity to sing minor operatic roles. In 1960 he joined Boris Goldovsky's Boston opera company and toured widely with it. He met Rosa Ponselle in Baltimore in 1961, and she coached him in several roles; he first appeared with the Baltimore Civic Opera as Gérard in *Andrea Chénier* in 1961. He made his European debut as Figaro in *Il Barbiere di Siviglia* at the Teatro Nuovo in Milan on Sept. 23, 1964; then made his first appearance at the N.Y. City Opera on Oct. 18, 1964, singing the role of Valentin in *Faust.* His Metropolitan Opera debut in N.Y. followed in the same role on Dec. 22, 1965. He rose to a stellar position at the Metropolitan, being acclaimed for both vocal and dramatic abilities; also sang with other opera houses in the U.S. and Europe. His notable roles included Don Giovanni, Escamillo, the Count di Luna, Tonio, Iago, Barnaba, Rigoletto, and Scarpia.

Milojević, Miloje, Serbian conductor, musicologist, and composer; b. Belgrade, Oct. 27, 1884; d. there, June 16, 1946. He was taught piano by his mother; then entered the Serbian School of Music at Novi Sad; then studied with Mayer G'schray (piano), Mottl (conducting), and Klose (composition) at the Munich Academy of Music and took courses in musicology with Sandberger and Kroyer at the Univ. of Munich; subsequently studied musicology with Nejedlý at the Univ. of Prague (D.Mus., 1925). He was active as a choirmaster in Belgrade; was conductor of the Collegium Musicum at the Univ. there (1925–41); also wrote music criticism and taught composition at the Academy of Music there (1939–46). He publ. *Osnovi muzičke umetnosti* (Elements of Music; Belgrade, 1922), *Smetana* (Belgrade, 1924), *Smetanin harmonski stil* (Smetana's Harmonic Style; Belgrade, 1926), and *Muzičke studije i članci* (Music Studies and Articles; Belgrade, 1926, 1933, 1953). As a composer, he wrote mostly in small forms; was influenced successively by Grieg, Strauss, Debussy, and Russian modernists; his music contains an original treatment of Balkan folk songs. His piano suite, *Grimaces rythmiques* (in a modern vein), was performed at the Paris Festival on June 26, 1937. His list of works contains choral pieces, chamber music, songs, and piano pieces.

BIBL.: P. Konjović, *M. M.: Kompozitor i muzički pisac* (Belgrade, 1954).

Milstein, Nathan (Mironovich), celebrated Russian-born American violinist; b. Odessa, Dec. 31, 1903; d. London, Dec. 21, 1992. His father was a well-to-do merchant in woolen goods; his mother was an amateur violinist who gave him his first lessons. He then began to study with Stoliarsky in Odessa, remaining under his tutelage until 1914; then went to St. Petersburg, where he entered Auer's class at the St. Petersburg Cons. (1915–17). He began his concert career in 1919, with his sister as piano accompanist. In Kiev he met Horowitz, and they began giving duo recitals in 1921; later they were joined by Piatigorsky, and organized a trio. In 1925 Milstein went to Berlin and then to Brussels, where he met Ysaÿe, who encouraged him in his career. He gave several recitals in Paris, then proceeded to South America. On Oct. 28, 1929, he made his American debut with the Philadelphia Orch. conducted by Stokowski. In 1942 he became a naturalized American citizen.

After the end of the World War II in 1945, Milstein appeared regularly in all of the principal music centers of the world. He performed with most of the great orchs. and gave numerous recitals. He celebrated the 50th anniversary of his American debut in 1979 by giving a number of solo recitals and appearing as soloist with American orchs. As an avocation, he began painting and drawing, arts in which he achieved a certain degree of self-satisfaction. He also engaged in teaching; held master classes at the Juilliard School of Music in N.Y., and also in Zürich. Milstein was renowned for his technical virtuosity and musical integrity. He composed a number of violin pieces, including *Paganiniana* (1954); also prepared cadenzas for the violin concertos of Beethoven and Brahms. His autobiography was publ. as *From Russia to the West* (N.Y., 1990).

BIBL.: B. Gavoty, *N. M.* (Geneva, 1956).

Milstein, Yakov (Isaakovich), Russian pianist, pedagogue, and writer on music; b. Voronezh, Feb. 4, 1911; d. Moscow, Dec. 4, 1981. He studied piano with Igumnov at the Moscow Cons. (Ph.D., 1942); was a member of its faculty (from 1935). His main interest was an analysis of works of masters of Romantic music; particularly important is his biography of Liszt (Moscow, 1956; Hungarian ed., Budapest, 1965; 2nd ed., rev., 1971). He contributed an essay on the piano technique of Chopin and Liszt to *The Book of the First International Musicological Congress Devoted to the Works of Chopin* (Warsaw, 1963). He also publ. a monograph on Igumnov (Moscow, 1975).

Milveden, (Jan) Ingmar (Georg), Swedish composer, organist, and musicologist; b. Göteborg, Feb. 15, 1920. He studied cello and organ; then took a course in composition with Sven Svensson and in musicology with C.A. Moberg at the Univ. of Uppsala (graduated, 1945; Fil.lic., 1951; Ph.D., 1972, with the diss. *Zu den liturgischen "Hystorie" in Schweden. Liturgie- und choralgeschichtliche Untersuchungen*). He was organist at Uppsala's St. Per's Church (1967–78); lectured at the Univ. of Stockholm (1970–73) and at the Univ. of Uppsala (1972–86). He distinguished himself as a composer of church music.

WORKS: CHURCH OPERA: *Vid en Korsväg* (1971; Lund, Nov. 30, 1974). **ORCH.:** *Serenade* for Strings (1942); *Pezzo concertante* (1969; Uppsala, Feb. 5, 1970); *Concerto al fresco* for Clarinet and Orch. (1970; Uppsala, Nov. 25, 1971). **CHAMBER:** Piano Sonatina (1943); Duo for Flute and Piano (1953; rev. 1975); Trio for Flute, Clarinet, and Viola (1955; rev. 1973); *Threnodia* for 3 Cellos (1970); *Toccata* for Organ (1973); *3 assaggi* for Cello (1975). **VOCAL:** *Canticula linnaeana* for Chorus (1965); *Mässa i skördetid* (Mass of the Harvest Time) for Congregation, Liturgist, 2 Choruses, 2 Organs, 2 Orch. Groups, and Tape (1969); *Nu . . .*, 4 Linne quotations for Solo Voices, Chorus, and Instrumental Groups (1972; Ingesund, March 17, 1974); *Magnificat* for 2 Choral Groups, Organ, Winds, and Percussion (1973); *Musica in honorem Sanctae Eugeniae* for Voices (1982); *Alleluia "Terribilis est"* for Voices (1987); choruses; songs.

Mimaroglu, Ilhan Kemaleddin, Turkish composer and writer on music; b. Constantinople, March 11, 1926. He studied law at the Univ. of Ankara; in 1955 he traveled to the U.S. on a Rockefeller fellowship, and settled in N.Y., where he studied theory with Jack Beeson and Chou Wen-Chung, musicology with Lang, and electronic music with Ussachevsky at Columbia Univ.; he took lessons in modern composition with Wolpe, and also received inspiring advice from Varèse. He was subsequently a recipient of a Guggenheim fellowship (1971–72). He publ. several books in Turkish. In 1963 he began his association with the Columbia-Princeton Electronic Music Center, where he composed most of his electronic works, among them *Le Tombeau d'Edgar Poe* (1964), *Anacolutha* (1965), *Preludes* for Magnetic Tape (1966–76), *Wings of the Delirious Demon* (1969), and music for Jean Dubuffet's *Coucou Bazar* (1973). He developed compositional methods viewing electronic music in a parallel to cinema, resulting in works for tape in which recorded performance dominates individual rendition. Concurrently, he displayed a growing political awareness in his choice of texts, conveying messages of New Left persuasion in such works as *Sing Me a Song of Songmy*, a protest chant against the war in Vietnam (1971), *Tract* (1972–74), *To Kill a Sunrise* (1974), and String Quartet No. 4 with Voice obbligato on poems by Nâzim Hikmet (1978). Other works include *Pieces sentimentales* for Piano (1957); *Music Plus 1* for Violin and Tape (1970); *Still Life 1980* for Cello and Tape (1983); *Immolation Scene* for Voice and Tape (1983); *Valses ignobles et sentencieuses* for Piano (1984). He destroyed all of his non-performed compositions, as well as those not recorded for posterity within a year of completion. Since the late 1980s, he has been working on a documentary film in which various composers respond to his question dealing with the condition of the contemporary composer in a cultural environment dominated by commercial determinants.

Minami, Satoshi, Japanese composer; b. Tokyo, July 17, 1955. He was a student of Teruyuki Noda and Toshirō Mayazumi at the Tokyo National Univ. of Fine Arts and Music (degree, 1983). He won 2nd prize in the Japan Music Competition (1983) and at the World Buddhist Music Festival (1986). His concept of "music on the pluralistic structure" is exemplified in his *UTA no KAGE yori* (1990).

WORKS: *Reliquiae* for Cello and Piano (1976–79); *Plants II* for 2 Violins and 3 Harps (1977–79); *Fresco* for Orch. (1980; rev. 1985); *Francesco Parmigiamino's Hand* for Piano, Glockenspiel, Tubular Bells, and Tape (1984); *Tatoereba . . .* for Viola and Piano (1986); *Coloration Project I* for Piano (1989), *II* for Electric Organ (1989), *III* for Niju-gen (1989), *IV* for Organ (1989), *V* for Orch. (1990), *VI* for Mandolin Orch. (1991), *VII* for Percussion (1992), and *VIII* for Viola, Cello, and Double Bass (1992); *The Window by the Metaphor* for Piano (1989); *UTA no KAGE yori* for Voice, Harp, Violin, Cello, and Piano (1990); *The Autobiography for Moon* for Cello and Piano (1990); *Latticed Eye* for Violin and Piano (1991); *The Garden of Joyful Intellection* for Flute, Violin, Piano, and Chamber Orch. (1991); *The Night of the Milky Way Railroad* for Narrator, Clarinet, Cello, and Piano (1991); *Window, the Coming Florescence*, Prelude I for Orch. (1992).

Minchev, Georgi, Bulgarian composer; b. Sofia, Jan. 29, 1939. He studied composition with Goleminov at the Bulgarian State Cons. in Sofia, graduating in 1963; went to Moscow and studied with Shchedrin (1968–70); in 1972 he traveled to France, Great Britain, and the U.S. on a UNESCO scholarship. Returning to Bulgaria, he became chief of productions at the Committee for Television and Radio in Sofia.

WORKS: Sym. (1967); *Music* for 3 Orch. Groups (1968); *Starobulgarski hroniky* (Old Bulgarian Chronicles), oratorio for Narrator, Soloists, Mixed Chorus, Folk Music Chorus, and Orch. (Sofia, Dec. 22, 1971); *Intermezzo and Aquarelle* for Strings, 2 Flutes, and Harpsichord (1972); *3 Poems* for Mezzo-soprano and Orch. (1973); *Concert Music* for Orch. (1975); Piano Concerto (1976); *Symphonic Prologue* (1980); choruses; solo songs; folk song arrangements.

Minghetti, Angelo, Italian tenor; b. Bologna, Dec. 6, 1889; d. Milan, Feb. 10, 1957. He began his career in 1911, and then sang in various Italian music centers. After appearing in Rio de Janeiro (1921), he was a member of the Chicago Opera (1922–24). In 1923 he made his debut at Milan's La Scala as Rodolfo, and sang there until 1932. He also was a guest artist at Buenos Aires's Teatro Colón (1924) and London's Covent Garden (1926; 1930; 1933–34).

Minter, Drew, American countertenor; b. Washington, D.C., Jan. 11, 1955. He studied at Indiana Univ. and with Marcy Lindheimer, Myron McPherson, Rita Streich, and Erik Werba. After singing with many early music ensembles, he made his stage debut as Handel's Orlando at the St. Louis Baroque Festival in 1983; in subsequent years, appeared in performances of early operas in Boston, Brussels, Los Angeles, Omaha, and Milwaukee; also sang in the U.S. premiere of Judith Weir's *A Night* *at the Chinese Opera* at the Santa Fe (N.M.) Opera in 1989. He is best known for his roles in operas by Monteverdi, Handel, and Landi.

Minton, Yvonne (Fay), noted Australian mezzo-soprano; b. Sydney, Dec. 4, 1938. She studied with Marjorie Walker in Sydney and with Henry Cummings and Joan Cross in London; won the Kathleen Ferrier Prize and the 's Hertogenbosch Competition (both 1961). She sang the role of Maggie Dempster in the premiere of Maw's *One Man Show* (London, 1964); made her Covent Garden debut in London as Lola in *Cavalleria rusticana* (1965), and subsequently sang there regularly; also sang at the Cologne Opera (from 1969) and at the Bayreuth Festivals (from 1974). She made her first appearance in the U.S. in Chicago (1970); made her Metropolitan Opera debut in N.Y. as Octavian in *Der Rosenkavalier* on March 16, 1973; also appeared in concerts with the Chicago Sym. Orch. In 1983 she retired from the operatic stage, but continued her concert career. She resumed an active career in 1990 with an engagement in Florence. In 1994 she made her debut at the Glyndebourne Festival as Madame Larina in *Eugene Onegin*. In 1980 she was made a Commander of the Order of the British Empire. Among her finest roles were Gluck's Orfeo, Cherubino, Sextus in *La clemenza di Tito*, Dorabella, Waltraube, Fricka, Dido, and Brangäne; she also created the role of Thea in Tippett's *The Knot Garden* (1970) and sang the role of the Countess in the first perf. of the complete version of Berg's *Lulu* (1979).

Mintz, Shlomo, Russian-born Israeli violinist and conductor; b. Moscow, Oct. 30, 1957. His family emigrated to Israel when he was 2; he became a pupil of Ilona Feher there at age 6; gave his first recital (1966) and appeared as soloist in the Mendelssohn Concerto with Mehta and the Israel Phil. (1968). He completed his training with Dorothy DeLay at N.Y.'s Juilliard School (1973), the same year in which he made his U.S. debut in the Bruch Concerto No. 1 with Steinberg and the Pittsburgh Sym. Orch. at Carnegie Hall in N.Y. After making his European debut at the Brighton Festival in England (1976), he made a major tour of Europe (1977). In subsequent years, he appeared in all the leading music centers of the world, performing as a soloist with orchs., as a recitalist, and as a chamber music artist. In 1989 he was appointed music adviser of the Israel Chamber Orch. In 1994 he became music advisor and principal guest conductor of the Limburg Sym. Orch. in Maastricht.

Mirouze, Marcel, French composer and conductor; b. Toulouse, Sept. 24, 1906; d. in an automobile accident in Aude, Aug. 1, 1957. He studied with Büsser at the Paris Cons. He conducted the Paris Radio Orch. (1935–40) and in Monte Carlo (1940–43). He wrote an opera, *Geneviève de Paris*, for the 2,000th anniversary of the founding of the city of Paris; it was produced first as a radio play with music in 1952, and then on stage in Toulouse in the same year; he also composed 2 ballets, *Paul et Virginie* (1942) and *Les Bains de mer* (1946); 2 symphonic tableaux, *Afrique* (1936) and *Asie* (1938); Piano Concerto (1948); film music; piano pieces; songs.

Mirovitch, Alfred, Russian-American pianist; b. St. Petersburg, May 4, 1884; d. Whitefield, N.Mex., Aug. 3, 1959. He graduated from the St. Petersburg Cons. with the 1st prize in piano as a student of Anna Essipova in 1909. He began his concert career in 1911; made 9 world tours; made his American debut in 1921. He conducted master classes in piano at the Juilliard School of Music in N.Y. (1944–52); then joined the faculty of Boston Univ.; was also an ed. of piano music for G. Schirmer, Inc.; likewise wrote some piano pieces.

Mirzoyan, Edvard (Mikaeli), Armenian composer and pedagogue; b. Gori, Georgia, May 12, 1921. He studied in Yerevan at the Music School (1928–36) and with Talyan at the Cons. (1936–41) before completing his training with Litinsky and Peyko at the House of Armenian Culture in Moscow (1946–48). Returning to Yerevan, he was a teacher (1948–65) and a prof. (from 1965) at the Cons., where he served as head of the composition dept. (1972–87). In 1981 he was made a People's Artist of the U.S.S.R. His music followed in a lucid neo-Classical style, while his thematic materials were of Armenian provenance.

WORKS: DRAMATIC: Film scores. **ORCH.:** *Sako from Lhore*, symphonic poem (1941); *Symphonic Dances*, suite (1946); Overture (1947); *Introduction and Perpetuum Mobile* for Violin and Orch. (1957); Sym. for Strings (1962); *Epitaph*, symphonic poem (1988). **CHAMBER:** String Quartet (1947); Cello Sonata (1967); piano pieces. **VOCAL:** 3 cantatas (1948, 1949, 1950) and other pieces.

BIBL.: T. Arazyan, *E. M.* (Yerevan, 1963); M. Ter-Simonyan, *E. M.* (Moscow, 1969).

Misch, Ludwig, German-American organist, conductor, music critic, and musicologist; b. Berlin, June 13, 1887; d. N.Y., April 22, 1967. He studied theory with Max Friedlaender at the Univ. of Berlin; simultaneously took courses in law, obtaining his D.Jur. degree at the Univ. of Heidelberg in 1911. He was music critic for the *Allgemeine Musikzeitung* (1909–13); conducted theater orchs. in Berlin, Essen, and Bremen. From 1921 to 1933 he was music critic of the *Berliner Lokalanzeiger*. Under the Nazi regime, he conducted a Jewish madrigal choir in Berlin until he was sent to a concentration camp. In 1947 he emigrated to N.Y., where he became active as an organist and musicologist. He publ. the valuable books *Johannes Brahms* (Bielefeld, 1913; 2nd ed., Berlin, 1922); *Beethoven-Studien* (Berlin, 1950; Eng. tr., Norman, Okla., 1953); tr. and annotated (with D. MacArdle) *New Beethoven Letters* (Norman, 1957); *Die Faktoren der Einheit in der Mehrsatzigkeit der Werke Beethovens: Versuch einer Theorie der Einheit des Werkstils* (Bonn, 1958); *Neue Beethoven-Studien und andere Themen* (Bonn, 1967).

Mischakoff (real name, **Fischberg**), **Mischa**, Russian-born American violinist; b. Proskurov, April 3, 1895; d. Petoskey, Mich., Feb. 1, 1981. Owing to a plethora of Russian-Jewish violinists named Fischberg, he decided to change his name to Mischakoff, formed by adding the Russian ending -koff to his first name, the Russian diminutive for Michael. He studied with Korguyev at the St. Petersburg Cons., graduating in 1912; made his debut that year in Berlin and then was active as an orch. player and teacher. He emigrated to the U.S. in 1921 and became a naturalized citizen in 1927. He was concertmaster of the N.Y. Sym. Orch. (1924–27), the Philadelphia Orch. (1927–29), the Chicago Sym. Orch. (1930–36), the NBC Sym. Orch. in N.Y. (1937–52), and the Detroit Sym. Orch. (1952–68); then guest concertmaster of the Baltimore Sym. Orch. (1968–69); was also concertmaster and soloist with the Chautauqua Sym. Orch. (summers, 1925–65); likewise led his own Mischakoff String Quartet. He taught at the Juilliard School of Music in N.Y. (1940–52), at Wayne State Univ. in Detroit (from 1952), and at various other schools.

Mitchell, Donald (Charles Peter), eminent English writer on music and publishing executive; b. London, Feb. 6, 1925. He studied at Dulwich College in London (1939–42) and with A. Hutchings and A.E.F. Dickinson at the Univ. of Durham (1949–50). After noncombatant wartime service (1942–45), he founded (1947) and then became co-ed. (with Hans Keller) of *Music Survey* (1949–52). From 1953 to 1957 he was London music critic of the *Musical Times*. In 1958 he was appointed music ed. and adviser of Faber & Faber, Ltd.; in 1965 he became managing director, and in 1976 vice chairman; became chairman in 1977 of its subsidiary, Faber Music. He also ed. *Tempo* (1958–62); was on the music staff of the *Daily Telegraph* (1959–64); in 1963–64 he served as music adviser to Boosey & Hawkes, Ltd. From 1971 to 1976 he was prof. of music, and from 1976 visiting prof. of music, at the Univ. of Sussex; in 1973 he was awarded by it an honorary M.A. degree; received his doctorate in 1977 from the Univ. of Southampton with a diss. on Mahler. He lectured widely in the United Kingdom, U.S., and Australia; contributed articles to the *Encyclopaedia Britannica* and other reference publications. As a music scholar, Mitchell made a profound study, in Vienna and elsewhere, of the life and works of Gustav Mahler; was awarded in 1961 the Mahler Medal of Honor by the Bruckner Soc. of America and in 1987 the Mahler Medal of the International Gustav Mahler Soc. His major work is a Mahler biography: vol. 1, *Gustav Mahler: The Early Years* (London, 1958; rev. ed., 1980); vol. 2, *The Wunderhorn Years* (London, 1976); vol. 3, *Songs and Symphonies of Life and Death* (London, 1985). His other publications include: ed. with H. Keller, *Benjamin Britten: A Commentary on All His Works from a Group of Specialists* (London, 1952); *W.A. Mozart: A Short Biography* (London, 1956); with H.C. Robbins Landon, *The Mozart Companion* (N.Y., 1956; 2nd ed., 1965); *The Language of Modern Music* (London, 1963; 3rd ed., 1970); ed. and annotated Alma Mahler's *Gustav Mahler: Memories and Letters* (London, 1968; 3rd ed., rev., 1973); ed. with J. Evans, *Benjamin Britten, 1913–1976: Pictures from a Life* (London, 1978); *Britten and Auden in the Thirties* (London, 1981); *Benjamin Britten: Death in Venice* (Cambridge, 1987); *Cradles of the New: Writings on Music, 1951–1991* (1995).

BIBL.: P. Reed, ed., *On Mahler and Britten: Essays in Honour of D. M. on his Seventieth Birthday* (Woodbridge, Suffolk, 1995).

Mitchell, Howard, American cellist and conductor; b. Lyons, Nebr., March 11, 1911; d. Ormond Beach, Fla., June 22, 1988. He studied piano and trumpet in Sioux City, Iowa; after studying cello at the Peabody Cons. of Music in Baltimore, he completed his training with Felix Salmond at the Curtis Inst. of Music in Philadelphia (1930–35). He was 1st cellist of the National Sym. Orch. in Washington, D.C. (1933–44); then was its assistant (1944–48), assoc. (1948–49), and principal (1949–69) conductor. He then became conductor of the SODRE Sym. Orch. in Montevideo.

Mitchell, Leona, talented black American soprano; b. Enid, Okla., Oct. 13, 1948. She was one of 15 children; her father, a Pentecostal minister, played several instruments by ear; her mother was a good amateur pianist. She sang in local church choirs; then received a scholarship to Oklahoma City Univ., where she obtained her B.Mus. degree in 1971. She made her operatic debut in 1972 as Micaëla in *Carmen* with the San Francisco Spring Opera Theater. She then received the $10,000 Opera America grant (1973), which enabled her to study with Ernest St. John Metz in Los Angeles. On Dec. 15, 1975, she made her Metropolitan Opera debut in N.Y. as Micaëla; subsequently sang there as Pamina in *Die Zauberflöte* and Musetta in *La Bohème*; she won critical acclaim for her portrayal of Leonora in *La forza del destino* in 1982. In 1987 she appeared as Massenet's Salome in Nice. She sang the 3 leading soprano roles in Puccini's *Trittico* at the Paris Opéra-Comique in 1988. She sang Verdi's Elvira in Parma in 1990. In 1992 she appeared as Aida with the New Israeli Opera.

Mitchell, William J(ohn), American musicologist; b. N.Y., Nov. 21, 1906; d. Binghamton, N.Y., Aug. 17, 1971. He studied at the Inst. of Musical Art in N.Y. (1925–29); then at Columbia Univ. (B.A., 1930); went to Vienna for further studies (1930–32). Upon his return to N.Y., he was on the staff at Columbia Univ.; received his M.A. there in 1938; became a full prof. in 1952, then served as chairman of the music dept. from 1962 to 1967; concurrently he taught at the Mannes College of Music in N.Y. (1957–68); he subsequently joined the faculty of the State Univ. of N.Y. in Binghamton. He was president of the American Musicological Soc. (1965–66). He publ. *Elementary Harmony* (N.Y., 1939; 3rd ed., rev., 1965); ed. and tr. Herriot's *La Vie de Beethoven* (1935) and *C.P.E. Bach's Versuch über die wahre Art das Clavier zu spielen* (1949); was co-ed. of the first 3 vols. of *Music Forum* (1967–73).

Mitrea-Celarianu, Mihai, Romanian composer; b. Bucharest, Jan. 20, 1935. He studied with Rogalski, Mendelsohn, Vancea, and Negrea at the Bucharest Cons. (1948–53); also took private lessons with Jora (1949–51). He was a prof. of harmony and music history in Bucharest (1954–60; 1962–68); then attended summer courses in new music given by Aloys Kontarsky, Caskel, and Karkoschka in Darmstadt (1968), and further studied with the Groupe de Recherches Musicales in Paris (1968–69) and with Schaeffer and Pousseur at the Paris Cons. (1968–69). His trademarks in composition are aleatory, electronic, and variable scoring.

WORKS: ORCH.: *Variations* (1958); *Petite histoire d'avant-monde* for Small Chamber Ensemble (1967); *Trei pentru cinci* for Aleatorily Structured Orch. (1969; in collaboration with Miereanu and Bosseur); *Milchstrassenmusik* (1983); *Jokari* for String Trio and String Orch. (1990); *Plateaux* for Strings (1990). **CHAMBER:** Violin Sonata (1957); Piano Sonata (1958); Piano Sonatina (1960); *Glosa* (Comment) for Viola (1965); *Convergences II (Colinda)* for Electronic Instruments and Percussion (1967) and *IV* for 1 Performer on Optional Instrument or Variable Ensemble (1968); *Seth* for 7 Instruments (1969); *ZN*, "idéogramme photographique" for 3, 4, or 5 Performers (1971); *Signaux (Sur l'Océan U)* for 13 Players (1971); *Inaugural 71*, "action" for a Flutist, with Electroacoustical Devices and a Projector (1971); *Piano de matin (Écoute pour Anne Frank)*, "action" for 5 Instruments, 5 Persons manipulating Divergent Sound Sources, Electroacoustical Devices, and Projectors (1972); *Natalienlied* for 10 Instrumentalists (1986); *Evian, Evian* for Instrumental Ensemble (1987). **VOCAL:** *Le Chant des étoiles*, cantata for Mezzo-soprano and 33 Instruments (1964); *Convergences III (Ideophonie M)*, aleatory music for Narrator, Children's Chorus, and 19 Instruments (1968) and *V (Jeux dans le blanc)* for Chorus, Percussion, and Tape (1969); *Prérêve* for Voice, Harpsichord, Flute, and Percussion (1975); *Weil Paul Celan* for Vocal Ensemble, Chorus, and Orch. (1988); *La Reine manquante* for Soprano and 14 Performers (1991); *Par ce fil d'or* for Tenor, Baritone, and 15 Performers or Orch. (1993).

Mitropoulos, Dimitri, celebrated Greek-born American conductor and composer; b. Athens, March 1, 1896; d. after suffering a heart attack while rehearsing Mahler's 3rd Sym. with the orch. of the Teatro alla Scala, Milan, Nov. 2, 1960. He studied piano with Wassenhoven and harmony with A. Marsick at the Odeon Cons. in Athens; wrote an opera after Maeterlinck, *Soeur Béatrice* (1918), performed at the Odeon Cons. (May 20, 1919); in 1920, after graduation from the Cons., he went to Brussels, where he studied composition with Gilson; in 1921 he went to Berlin, where he took piano lessons with Busoni at the Hochschule für Musik (until 1924); concurrently was répétiteur at the Berlin State Opera. He became a conductor of the Odeon Cons. orch. in Athens (1924); was its co-conductor (1927–29) and principal conductor (from 1929); was also prof. of composition there (from 1930). In 1930 he was invited to conduct a concert of the Berlin Phil.; when the soloist Egon Petri became suddenly indisposed, Mitropoulos substituted for him as soloist in Prokofiev's Piano Concerto No. 3, conducting from the keyboard (Feb. 27, 1930). He played the same concerto in Paris in 1932 as a pianist-conductor, and later in the U.S. His Paris debut as a conductor (1932) obtained a spontaneous success; he conducted the most difficult works from memory, which was a novelty at the time; also led rehearsals without a score. He made his American debut with the Boston Sym. Orch. on Jan. 24, 1936, with immediate acclaim; that same year he was engaged as music director of the Minneapolis Sym. Orch.; there he frequently performed modern music, including works by Schoenberg, Berg, and other representatives of the atonal school; the opposition that naturally arose was not sufficient to offset his hold on the public as a conductor of great emotional power. He resigned from the Minneapolis Sym. Orch. in 1949 to accept the post of conductor of the N.Y. Phil.; shared the podium with Stokowski for a few weeks, and in 1950 became music director. In 1956 Leonard Bernstein was engaged as assoc. conductor with Mitropoulos, and in 1958 succeeded him as music director. With the N.Y. Phil., Mitropoulos continued his policy of bringing out important works by European and American modernists; he also programmed modern operas (*Elektra, Wozzeck*) in concert form. A musician of astounding technical ability, Mitropoulos became very successful with the general public as well as with the musical vanguard whose cause he so boldly espoused. While his time was engaged mainly in the U.S., Mitropoulos continued to appear as guest conductor in Europe; he also appeared on numerous occasions as conductor at the Metropolitan Opera in N.Y. (debut conducting *Salome*, Dec. 15, 1954) and at various European opera theaters. He became a naturalized American citizen in 1946. As a composer, Mitropoulos was one of the earliest among Greek composers to write in a distinctly modern idiom.

WORKS: DRAMATIC: *Soeur Béatrice*, opera (1918; Odeon Cons., Athens, May 20, 1919); incidental music to *Electra* (1936) and *Hippolytus* (1937). **ORCH.:** *Burial* (1925); Concerto Grosso (1928). **CHAMBER:** *Concert Piece* for Violin and Piano (1913); *Fauns* for String Quartet (1915); Violin Sonata, *Ostinata* (1925–26). **PIANO:** Sonata (1915); *Piano Piece* (1925); *Passacaglia, Preludio e Fuga* (c.1925); *4 Dances from Cythera* (1926). **VOCAL:** *10 Inventions* for Soprano and Piano (1926).

BIBL.: S. Arfanis, *The Complete Discography of D. M.* (Athens, 1990); W. Trotter, *Priest of Music: The Life of D. M.* (Portland, Oreg., 1995).

Mitsukuri, Shukichi, Japanese composer; b. Tokyo, Oct. 21, 1895; d. Chigasaki, Kanagawa Prefecture, May 10, 1971. He graduated in applied chemistry from the engineering dept. of the Imperial Univ. in Tokyo in 1921; then went to Berlin and studied composition with Georg Schumann. Returning to Japan in 1925, he became an Imperial Navy engineering officer. In 1930 he founded a contemporary Japanese composers' society, Shinko Sakkyokuka; in 1954, was appointed a prof. at the Music Academy in Tokyo.

WORKS: ORCH.: *Sinfonietta classica* (Paris, March 6, 1936); *10 Haikai de Basho* (Paris, Dec. 10, 1937); *Elegy* for Chorus and Orch. (1949); 2 syms.: No. 1 (Tokyo, Aug. 22, 1951) and No. 2 (1963); Piano Concertino (Tokyo, Aug. 22, 1953); Piano Concerto (Tokyo, April 23, 1955). **CHAMBER:** Violin Sonata (1935); Piano Quintet (1955); piano pieces, including *Night Rhapsody* (1935). **VOCAL:** 3 albums of Japanese folk songs (1950, 1954, 1955).

Mittler, Franz, Austrian composer and pianist; b. Vienna, April 14, 1893; d. Munich, Dec. 28, 1970. He studied in Vienna with Heuberger and Prohaska and later in Cologne with Steinbach and Friedberg. From 1921 to 1938 he lived in Vienna as a pianist and accompanist; in 1939 he settled in N.Y. He wrote an opera, *Rafaella* (Duisburg, 1930); Piano Trio; a number of piano pieces. In America he wrote numerous popular songs (*In Flaming Beauty, From Dreams of Thee, Soft through My Heart, Over the Mountains* et al.); also light piano suites (*Manhattan Suite, Suite in 3/4 Time, Newsreel Suite, Boogie-Woogie, Waltz in Blue*, and *One-Finger Polka*).

BIBL.: D. Mittler Battipaglia, *F. M.: Composer, Pedagogue and Practical Musician* (diss., Univ. of Rochester, 1974).

Miyagi (real name, **Wakabe**), **Michio,** Japanese koto player, teacher, and composer; b. Kobe, April 7, 1894; d. in a railroad accident in Kariya, near Tokyo, June 25, 1956. He was given the surname of Suga in infancy; became blind at age 7; studied the koto with Nakajima Kengyō II and made his debut when he was 9. He went to Inchon (1908) to teach the koto and shakuhachi; then taught in Seoul. After receiving his certificate as a koto player with highest honors, he was given the professional name of Nakasuga; was known as Michio Miyagi from 1913. He settled in Tokyo (1917); with Seiju Yoshida, he founded the New Japanese Music Movement (1920); became a lecturer (1930) and a prof. (1937) at the Tokyo Music School; taught at the National Univ. of Fine Arts and Music (from 1950). He wrote more than 1,000 works for koto and other Japanese instruments; also an opera, *Kariteibo* (1924); choral works; solo vocal music.

BIBL.: E. Kikkawa, *Miyagi Michio den* (The Life of M. M.; Tokyo, 1962).

Miyoshi, Akira, Japanese composer and teacher; b. Tokyo, Jan. 10, 1933. He joined the Jiyû-Gakuen children's piano group at the age of 3, graduating at the age of 6. He studied French literature; in 1951 he began to study music with Hirai, Ikenouchi, and Gallois-Montbrun, who was in Tokyo at the time. He obtained a stipend to travel to France and took lessons in composition with Challan and again with Gallois-Montbrun (1955–57); upon his return to Japan, he resumed his studies in French literature at the Univ. of Tokyo, obtaining a degree in 1961. In 1965 he was appointed instructor at the Toho Gakuen School of Music in Tokyo.

WORKS: POETICAL DRAMAS: *Happy Prince* (1959); *Ondine* (1959). **ORCH.:** *Symphonie concertante* for Piano and Orch. (1954); *Mutation symphonique* (1958); *3 mouvements symphoniques* (1960); Piano Concerto (1962); Concerto (Tokyo, Oct. 22, 1964); Violin Concerto (1965); *Odes metamorphosées* (1969); Concerto for Marimba and Strings (1969); *Ouverture de fête* (1973); *Leos* (1976); *Noesis* (1978); *Distant As I Am* (1982); *En Passant* for Violin and Orch. (1986); *Fuji Litany*, symphonic poem (1988); *Etoiles à cordes* for Violin and Strings (1991); *Creation Sonore* (1991). **CHAMBER:** Sonata for Clarinet, Bassoon, and Piano (1953); Violin Sonata (1954–55); Sonata for Flute, Cello, and Piano (1955); *Torse I* for Chamber Orch. (1959), *III* for Marimba (1968), *IV* for String Quartet and 4 Japanese Instruments (1972), and *V* for 3 Marimbas (1973); 2 string quartets (1962, 1967); *Conversation*, suite for Marimba (1962); *8 poèmes* for Flute Ensemble (1969); *Transit* for Electronic and Concrete Sounds, Percussion, and Keyboard Instruments (1969); *Hommage à musique de chambre, I, II, III*, and *IV* for Flute, Violin and Piano (1970, 1971, 1972, 1974); *Nocturne* for Marimba, Percussion, Flute, Clarinet, and Double Bass (1973); *Protase de loin à rien* for 2 Guitars (1974); *Concert Étude* for 2 Marimbas (1977); *Message Sonore* for Flute, Clarinet, Marimba, Percussion, and Double Bass (1985); *Constellation noir* for String Quartet (1992). **PIANO:** Sonata (1958); *In Such Time*, suite (1960); *Études en forme de Sonate* (1967); *Kyōshō* for 2 Pianos (1983). **VOCAL:** *Torse II* for Chorus, Piano, Electone, and Percussion (1962); *Duel* for Soprano and Orch. (1964); 2 works of musical poesy: *The Red Mask of Death I* for Narrator, Orch., and Electronic Sound (1969) and *II* for Voice, Chorus, Orch., and Electronic Sound (1970); *Shihenshôei* for Flute, Chorus, and Orch. (1980); *Kyōmon* for Children's Chorus and Orch. (1984); choruses; songs.

Mizelle, (Dary) John, American composer and teacher; b. Stillwater, Okla., June 14, 1940. He studied trombone at Calif. State Univ. in Sacramento (B.A., 1965) and composition at the Univ. of Calif. at Davis (M.A., 1967) and at the Univ. of Calif. at San Diego (Ph.D., 1977); also studied computer music at Columbia Univ. (1979–83). He taught at the Univ. of South Florida in Tampa (1973–75) and at the Oberlin (Ohio) College Cons. of Music (1975–79); in 1990, joined the faculty of the State Univ. of N.Y. at Purchase. He served as assoc. ed. of *Source* magazine (1966–69). Interest in Mizelle's music increased greatly when a 25-year retrospective concert was given in N.Y. in 1988. His compositions, which number over 200, have been lauded for their stylistic assimilation of such disparate Western composers as Bartók, Messiaen, and Xenakis, their admixtures of ancient, traditional acoustic, and electronic instruments, the mathematical exactitude of their construction, their generous reliance upon the improvisational skills of performers, and their varied use of extended vocal techniques.

WORKS: 3 string quartets (1964, 1975, 1983); *Green and Red*, quartet for 9 Instruments (1965); *Straight Ahead* for Violin, Flute, Trumpet, Trombone, Percussion, and Tape (1965); *Radial Energy I* for Unspecified Instruments (1967) and *II* for Orch. (1968); *Mass* for Chorus and Live Electronics (1968); *Quanta I & Hymn to Matter* for 8 Multiphonic Volcalists, Chorus, and Orch. (1972–76); Contrabass Concerto (1974–85); *Parameters* for Solo Percussion and Orch. (1974–87); *Polyphonies I* for Quadraphonic Tape, Shakuhachi, and Electronics (1975), *II* for Tape and Dance (1976), and *III* for Quadraphonic Tape and Theater (1978); *Transforms I–XIII* for Piano (1975–94); *Soundscape* for Percussion Ensemble (1976); *Polytempus I* for Trumpet and

Tape (1976) and *II* for Marimba and Tape (1979); *Primavera-Heterophony* for 24 Cellos (1977); *Samadhi* for Quadraphonic Tape (1978); *Quanta II & Hymn of the Word* for Wind Ensemble, Percussion, Organ, and 2 Choruses (1979); *Lake Mountain Thunder* for English Horn and Percussion Ensemble (1981); *The Thunderclap of Time I* (1981) and *II* (1982), music for a planetarium; *Requiem* Mass for Chorus and Orch. (1982); *Sonic Adventures*, 15 process pieces for Various Multiple Instrumental Ensembles (1982); Quintet for Woodwinds (1983); Contrabass Quartet (1983); *Indian Summer* for String Quartet and Oboe (1983); *Sounds* for Orch. (1984); *Genesis* for Orch. (1985); *Blue* for Orch. (1985–86); Percussion Concerto (1985–87); *Earth Mountain Fire*, 80 minutes of music for Compact Disc (1987); *Fossy: A Passion Play*, music theater (1987); *Chance Gives Me What I Want*, dance piece (1988); *I Was Standing Quite Close to Process* for Piano (1991–92); *Sun/The Gentle (The Penetrating Wind)* for Violin and Dance (1992); *SPAMDA*, "macrocomposition" of 198 pieces (1995 et seq.).

Mlynarski, Emil (Simon), Polish violinist, conductor, and composer; b. Kibarty, July 18, 1870; d. Warsaw, April 5, 1935. He studied at the St. Petersburg Cons. (1880–89), taking up both the violin, with Leopold Auer, and piano, with Anton Rubinstein; also took a course in composition with Liadov. He embarked on a career as a conductor; in 1897 he was appointed principal conductor of the Warsaw Opera, and concurrently conducted the concerts of the Warsaw Phil. (1901–05); from 1904 to 1907 he was director of the Warsaw Cons. He achieved considerable success as a conductor in Scotland, where he was principal conductor of the Scottish Orch. in Glasgow (1910–16). Returning to Warsaw, he was director of the Opera (1918–29) and Cons. (1919–22). After teaching conducting at the Curtis Inst. of Music in Philadelphia (1929–31), he returned to Warsaw. He composed an opera, *Noc letnia* (Summer Night; 1914; Warsaw, March 29, 1924); Sym., *Polonia* (1910); 2 violin concertos (1897, Paderewski prize; 1914–17); violin pieces.

BIBL.: A. Wach, *Zycie i twórczość Emila M.ego* (Life and Works of E. M.; diss., Univ. of Kraków, 1953); J. Mechanisz, *E. M.: W setną rocznicę urodzin (1870–1970)* (Warsaw, 1970).

Moberg, Carl Allan, eminent Swedish musicologist; b. Östersund, June 5, 1896; d. Uppsala, June 19, 1978. He studied with Norlind at the Univ. of Uppsala (1917–24); then took some lessons with Berg in Vienna, and took a course in musicology with Wagner in Fribourg (1924–27); received his Ph.D. in 1927 from the Univ. of Uppsala; later studied with Handschin in Basel (1934–35). He was a reader (1928–47) and a prof. (1947–61) at the Univ. of Uppsala; was ed. of *Svensk tidskrift för musikforskning* (1945–61) and of *Studia musicologica upsaliensia* (1952–61). Among his achievements was a journey to Lapland in the north to collect native songs. He was honored with a Festschrift on his 65th birthday in 1961. Moberg distinguished himself particularly in the study of music history and ethnomusicology.

WRITINGS: *Kyrkomusikens historia* (Stockholm, 1932); *Tonkonstens historia i Västerlandet* (2 vols., Stockholm, 1935); *Dietrich Buxtehude* (Hälsingborg, 1946); *Die liturgischen Hymnen in Schweden* (2 vols., Uppsala, 1947, and with A.-M. Nilsson, 1991); *Musikens historia i Västerlandet intill 1600* (Oslo, 1973).

Mödl, Martha, esteemed German mezzo-soprano, later soprano; b. Nuremberg, March 22, 1912. She studied at the Nuremberg Cons. and in Milan. She made her operatic debut as Hansel in Nuremberg (1942), then sang in Düsseldorf (1945–49) and at the Hamburg State Opera (1947–55), appearing in soprano roles from 1950 with notable success. She sang at London's Covent Garden (1949–50; 1953; 1959; 1966); appeared as Kundry at the resumption of the Bayreuth Festival productions in 1951, and continued to sing there regularly until 1967; sang Leonore in the first performance at the rebuilt Vienna State Opera in 1955. On March 2, 1957, she made her Metropolitan Opera debut in N.Y. as Brünnhilde in *Götterdämmerung*, remaining on the roster there until 1960; was again a member of the Hamburg State Opera (1956–75). In 1981 she sang in the premiere of Cerha's *Baal* in Salzburg. She was made both a German and an Austrian Kammersängerin. Among her finest mezzo-soprano roles were Dorabella, Carmen, Eboli, Octavian, the Composer, and Marie in *Wozzeck*; as a soprano, she excelled as Brünnhilde, Isolde, Gutrune, Venus, and Sieglinde.

BIBL.: W. Schafer, *M. M.* (Hannover, 1967).

Moeck, Hermann, German music publisher and instrument maker; b. Elbing, July 9, 1896; d. Celle, Oct. 9, 1982. He established his publ. business in Celle in 1930; in 1960 he handed it over to his son Hermann Moeck, Jr. (b. Lüneburg, Sept. 16, 1922). The firm was influential in the revival of the manufacture of the vertical flute (recorder) and other Renaissance and early Baroque instruments; Moeck also publ. arrangements and authentic pieces for recorders and the theretofore obsolete fidels. Hermann Moeck, Jr., wrote a valuable monograph, *Ursprung und Tradition der Kernspaltflöten* (2 vols., 1951; abridged ed., 1967, as *Typen europäischer Blockflöten*).

Moeran, E(rnest) J(ohn), English composer of Anglo-Irish descent; b. Heston, Middlesex, Dec. 31, 1894; d. Kenmare, County Kerry, Ireland, Dec. 1, 1950. His father was a clergyman, and he learned music from hymnbooks; then studied at the Royal College of Music in London; was an officer in the British army in World War I, and was wounded. Returning to London, he took lessons in composition with John Ireland (1920–23); also became interested in folk music; he collected numerous folk songs in Norfolk, some of which were publ. by the Folksong Soc. (1922). In his early music, he was influenced by Ireland and Delius, but later found inspiration in the works of Vaughan Williams, Holst, and Warlock.

WORKS: ORCH.: *In the Mountain Country*, symphonic impression (1921); 2 rhapsodies (1922; 1924, rev. 1941); *Whythorne's Shadow* (1931); *Lonely Waters* (1932); Sym. (1934–37; London, Jan. 13, 1938); Violin Concerto (London, July 8, 1942); *Rhapsody* for Piano and Orch. (London, Aug. 19, 1943); *Overture to a Masque* (1944); *Sinfonietta* (1944); Cello Concerto (Dublin, Nov. 25, 1945, with Moeran's wife, Peers Coetmore, as soloist); *Serenade* (London, Sept. 2, 1948). **CHAMBER:** Piano Trio (1920); String Quartet (1921); Violin Sonata (1930); String Trio (1931); *Fantasy Quartet* for Oboe, Violin, Viola, and Cello (1946); Cello Sonata (1947); piano pieces; organ music. **VOCAL:** Choral pieces; songs.

BIBL.: H. Foss, *Compositions of E.J. M.* (London, 1948); S. Wild, *E.J. M.* (London, 1973); G. Self, *The Music of E.J. M.* (London, 1986).

Moeschinger, Albert, Swiss composer; b. Basel, Jan. 10, 1897; d. Thun, Sept. 25, 1985. He received training in piano and theory in Bern, Leipzig, and Munich (1917–23). In 1927 he returned to Bern to teach piano and theory, and later was on the faculty of the Cons. there (1937–43). After experimenting with various styles, he embraced dodecaphony in 1954.

WORKS: BALLET: *Amor und Psyche* (1955). **ORCH.:** 5 syms.; 5 piano concertos; *Erratique* (1969); *Tres Caprichos* (1972); *Homo et fatum* (1975); *Blocs sonores* (1976); *Étude* (1978). **CHAMBER:** 6 string quartets; 2 piano trios; quintets; Piano Sextet; piano pieces; organ music. **VOCAL:** *Die kleine Meerjungfrau*, dramatic cantata for Soli, Chorus, and Orch. (1947); choral pieces; songs.

Moevs, Robert W(alter), American composer and teacher; b. La Crosse, Wis., Dec. 2, 1920. He studied with Piston at Harvard College (A.B., 1942), with Boulanger at the Paris Cons. (1947–51), and at Harvard Univ. (A.M., 1952). From 1952 to 1955 he was a Rome Prize Fellow in music at the American Academy in Rome; he held a Guggenheim fellowship (1963–64). He taught at Harvard Univ. (1955–63); was composer-in-residence at the American Academy in Rome (1960–61); in 1964 he joined the faculty of Rutgers Univ. in New Jersey, where he was a prof. (1968–91) and chairman of the music dept. at its New Brunswick campus (1974–81). In addition to his activities as a composer and teacher, he made appearances as a pianist, often in performances of his own works. In 1978 he was awarded the Stockhausen International Prize for his Concerto Grosso for Piano, Percussion, and Orch. As a composer, he developed a compositional method based on intervallic control as opposed to specific pitch sequence that he described as systematic chromaticism.

WORKS: ORCH.: *Passacaglia* (1941); *Introduction and Fugue* (1949); Overture (1950); *14 Variations* (1952); *3 Symphonic Pieces* (1954–55; Cleveland, April 10, 1958); Concerto Grosso for Piano, Percussion, and Orch. (1960; 2nd version with Amplified Instruments, 1968); *In Festivitate* for Wind Instruments and Percussion (Dartmouth, N.H., Nov. 8, 1962); *Main-Travelled Roads, Symphonic Piece No. 4* (1973); *Prometheus: Music for Small Orchestra, I* (1980); *Pandora: Music for Small Orchestra, II* (1986). **CHAMBER:** *Spring* for 4 Violins and Trumpets (1950); 3 string quartets: No. 1 (1957; Cambridge, Mass., Feb. 17, 1960), No. 2 (1989), and No. 3 (1994–95); *Variazioni sopra una Melodia* for Viola and Cello (1961); *Musica da camera I* (1965), *II* (1972), and *III* (1992) for Chamber Ensemble; *Fanfare canonica* for 6 Trumpets (1966); *Paths and Ways* for Saxophone and Dancer (1970); Trio for Violin, Cello, and Piano (1980); *Dark Litany* for Wind Ensemble (1987); Woodwind Quintet (1988); *Echo* for Guitar (1992); *Conundrum* for 5 Percussionists (1993); solo pieces; various keyboard works. **VOCAL:** *Cantata sacra* for Baritone, Men's Chorus, Flute, 4 Trombones, and Timpani (1952); *Attis* for Tenor, Chorus, Percussion, and Orch. (1958–59; 1963); *Et Nunc, reges* for Women's Chorus, Flute, Clarinet, and Bass Clarinet (1963); *Ode to an Olympic Hero* for Voice and Orch. (1963); *Et Occidentem Illustra* for Chorus and Orch. (1964); *A Brief Mass* for Chorus, Organ, Vibraphone, Guitar, and Double Bass (1968); *The Aulos Player* for Soprano, 2 Choruses, and 2 Organs (1975); choruses; songs.

Moffo, Anna, noted American soprano; b. Wayne, Pa., June 27, 1932. She was of Italian descent. She studied voice at the Curtis Inst. of Music in Philadelphia; later went to Italy on a Fulbright fellowship and studied at the Accademia di Santa Cecilia in Rome. She made her debut as Norina in Spoleto in 1955, and, progressing rapidly in her career, was engaged at La Scala in Milan, at the Vienna State Opera, and in Paris. She made her U.S. debut as Mimi with the Chicago Lyric Opera in 1957; on Nov. 14, 1959, she made her debut at the Metropolitan Opera in N.Y. as Violetta, obtaining a gratifying success; sang regularly at the Metropolitan and other major opera houses in the U.S. and Europe until she suffered a vocal breakdown in 1974; then resumed her career in 1976. In her prime, she became known for her fine portrayals of such roles as Pamina, the 4 heroines in *Les Contes d'Hoffmann*, Gilda, Massenet's Manon, Mélisande, Juliet, Luisa Miller, and Gounod's Marguerite.

Mohaupt, Richard, German composer; b. Breslau, Sept. 14, 1904; d. Reichenau, Austria, July 3, 1957. He studied with J. Prüwer and R. Bilke. He began his musical career as an opera conductor; also gave concerts as a pianist. After the advent of the Nazi regime in 1933, he was compelled to leave Germany because his wife was Jewish; he settled in N.Y. in 1939, and continued to compose; was also active as a teacher. In 1955 he returned to Europe.

WORKS: DRAMATIC: OPERAS: *Die Wirtin von Pinsk* (Dresden, Feb. 10, 1938); *Die Bremer Stadtmusikanten* (Bremen, June 15, 1949); *Double Trouble* (Louisville, Dec. 4, 1954); *Der grüne Kakadu* (Hamburg, Sept. 16, 1958). **BALLETS:** *Die Gaunerstreiche der Courasche* (Berlin, Aug. 5, 1936); *Max und Moritz*, dance-burlesque (1945; Karlsruhe, Dec. 18, 1950); *Lysistrata* (1946; rev. for Orch. as *Der Weiberstreik von Athen*, 1955); *The Legend of the Charlatan*, mimodrama (1949). Also incidental music. **ORCH.:** *Stadtpfeifermusik* (1939; London, July 7, 1946; rev. for Winds, 1953); Sym., *Rhythmus und Variationen* (1940; N.Y., March 5, 1942); Concerto (1942); Violin Concerto (1945; N.Y., April 29, 1954); Banchetto musicale for 12 Instruments and Orch. (1955); *Offenbachiana* (1955). **CHAMBER:** Piano pieces and other works. **VOCAL:** *Trilogy* for Alto and Orch. (1951); *Bucolica* for 4 Soloists, Chorus, and Orch. (1955); lieder; children's songs.

Moiseiwitsch, Benno, outstanding Russian-born English pianist; b. Odessa, Feb. 22, 1890; d. London, April 9, 1963. He studied in Odessa, and won the Anton Rubinstein prize at the age of 9; then went to Vienna at 14 and studied with Leschetizky. He made his British debut in Reading on Oct. 1, 1908, and subsequently made London his home; made his American debut in N.Y. on Nov. 29, 1919, and toured many times in Australia, India, Japan, etc. He became a naturalized British subject in 1937. He represented the traditional school of piano playing, excelling mostly in Romantic music.

BIBL.: M. Moiseiwitsch, *B. M.* (London, 1965).

Mojsisovics (-Mojsvár), Roderich, Edler von, Austrian composer; b. Graz, May 10, 1877; d. there, March 30, 1953. He studied with Degner in Graz, with Wüllner and Klauwell at the Cologne Cons., and with Thuille in Munich. He conducted a choral group in Brünn (1903–07); then taught in various Austrian towns. He became director of the Graz Steiermarkische Musikverein (1912); it became the Graz Cons. in 1920, and he remained as director until 1931; from 1932 to 1935 he taught music history at the Univ. of Graz; then lectured at the Trapp Cons. in Munich (1935–41) and at the Mannheim Hochschule für Musik (1941–44); he returned to teach at the Graz Cons. from 1945 to 1948. He publ. *Bach-Probleme* (Würzburg, 1931). As a composer, he followed Regerian precepts. Among his stage works were 5 operas, a melodrama, a musical comedy, etc.; also wrote 5 syms.; a symphonic poem, *Stella*; 2 overtures; Violin Concerto; 3 string quartets and other chamber music; choral works; songs; piano pieces; organ works.

BIBL.: K. Haidmayer, *R. v.M.: Leben und Werk* (diss., Univ. of Graz, 1951).

Mokranjac, Vasilije, Serbian composer; b. Belgrade, Sept. 11, 1923; d. there, May 27, 1984. He was brought up in a musical enviroment (his father was a cellist, a nephew of Stevan Mokranjac). He studied piano and composition at the Belgrade Academy of Music. His early works are Romantic in style, but he gradually began experimenting with serial techniques, while safeguarding the basic tonal connotations.

WORKS: Incidental music; *Dramatic Overture* (1950); Concertino for Piano, 2 Harps, and Strings (Belgrade, March 15, 1960); 3 syms.: No. 1 (Belgrade, Feb. 2, 1962), No. 2 (Belgrade, April 1, 1966), and No. 3 (Belgrade, Oct. 25, 1968); chamber music; piano pieces.

Molchanov, Kirill (Vladimirovich), Russian composer; b. Moscow, Sept. 7, 1922; d. there, March 14, 1982. He was attached to the Red Army Ensemble of Song and Dance during World War II; after demobilization, he studied composition with Anatoly Alexandrov at the Moscow Cons., graduating in 1949. From 1973 to 1975 he served as director of the Bolshoi Theater in Moscow and accompanied it on its American tour in 1975. He was primarily an opera composer; his musical style faithfully followed the precepts of socialist realism. His most successful work, the opera *The Dawns Are Quiet Here*, to his own libretto depicting the Russian struggle against the Nazis, was first performed at the Bolshoi Theater on April 11, 1975. It became the melodramatic event of the year, accompanied by an unabashed display of tearful emotion; however, its American performance during the visit of the Bolshoi Theater to N.Y. in June 1975 met with a disdainful dismissal on the part of the critics.

WORKS: OPERAS: *The Stone Flower* (Moscow, Dec. 2, 1950); *Dawn* (1956); *Romeo, Juliet, and Darkness* (1963); *The Unknown Soldier* (1967); *A Woman of Russia* (1969); *The Dawns Are Quiet Here* (Moscow, April 11, 1975). **ORCH.:** 3 piano concertos (1945, 1947, 1953). **VOCAL:** *Song of Friendship*, cantata (1955); *Black Box*, suite for Voice, Recitation, and Piano (1968).

BIBL.: Y. Korev, *K. M.* (Moscow, 1971).

Moldenhauer, Hans, German-American musicologist; b. Mainz, Dec. 13, 1906; d. Spokane, Wash., Oct. 19, 1987. He studied music with Dressel, Zuckmayer, and Rosbaud in Mainz; was active as a pianist and choral conductor there. In 1938 he went to the U.S., and settled in Spokane, Wash.; as an expert alpinist, he served in the U.S. Mountain Troops during World War II. He founded the Spokane Cons. (1942), incorporating it as an educational institution in 1946; also continued his own studies at Whitworth College there (B.A., 1945) and at the Chicago Musical College of Roosevelt Univ. (D.F.A., 1951). With his wife, the pianist Rosaleen Moldenhauer (1926–82), he inaugurated a series of radio broadcasts of 2-piano music; the outgrowth of this was the publication of his valuable book *Duo-Pianism* (Chicago, 1950). As a music reseacher, he became profoundly interested in the life and works of Webern; he organized 6 international Webern festivals, in Seattle (1962), Salzburg (1965), Buffalo (1966), at Dartmouth College, Hanover, N.H. (1968), in Vienna (1972), and at Louisiana State Univ., Baton Rouge (1976). His major achievement in research was the formation of the Moldenhauer Archives ("Music History from Primary Sources"), embodying a collection of some 10,000 musical autographs, original MSS, correspondence, etc., of unique importance to musical biography. Particularly rich is the MS collection of works of Webern, including some newly discovered works; for this accomplishment, Moldenhauer was awarded in 1970 the Austrian Cross of Honor for Science and Art. In 1988 the archives became a part of the Library of Congress in Washington, D.C. Moldenhauer's publications concerning Webern include *The Death of Anton Webern: A Drama in Documents* (N.Y., 1961); ed. with D. Irvine, *Anton von Webern: Perspectives: 1st Webern Festival, Seattle 1962* (Seattle, 1966; catalog of the Webern Archive); *Anton von Webern: Sketches 1926–1945* (N.Y., 1968); with R. Moldenhauer, *Anton von Webern: Chronicle of His Life and Work* (N.Y., 1978). Moldenhauer suffered from Retinitis pigmentosa, and became totally blind in 1980. He remarried in 1982, a few months after his first wife's death.

Moldovan, Mihai, Romanian composer; b. Dej, Nov. 5, 1937; d. Medgidia, Sept. 11, 1981. He studied with Toduţa and Comes at the Cluj Cons. (1956–59) and with Vancea, Vieru, and Jora at the Bucharest Cons. (1959–62). He was active in various branches of Romanian radio and television. His music fuses a Romanian ethos with modern harmonic textures.

WORKS: OPERAS: *Trepte ale istoriei* (1972); *Micul prinţ* (1977–78). **ORCH.:** Oboe Concerto (1964); *Texturi* (1967); *Poem* for Ondes Martenot and Chamber Orch. (1967); *Vitralii* (Stained Glass Windows; 1968); *Scoarţe* (Tapestry; 1969); *Tulnice* for 4 Flutes, 8 Horns, Harp, 4 Cellos, 4 Double Basses, and Percussion (1971); *Sinfonia* for Strings (1972); Concerto for Double Bass and Orch. (1973); *Cantemirian* (1976); *Omagiu lui Anton Pann* (1976); *Rezonante* (1976); *Memoria Putnei* for Strings (1978). **CHAMBER:** Violin Sonatina (1967); 2 string quartets (1968, 1978); *Incantations* for Clarinet and Piano (1968); *Cadenza I* for Trombone and Percussion, *II* for Double Bass, *III* for Flute and Percussion (all 1971), and *V* for Cello and Trumpet (1980); *Imaginati-vă un spectacol Kabuki* for Chamber Ensemble (1978). **VOCAL: CANTATAS:** *Soare al păcii* (Sun of Peace; 1962); *Prefigurarea primăverii,* chamber cantata (1962); *Bocet* (1963); *6 stări de nuanţă* (1966); *Cintare omului* (1967); *Luceafăru de ziua* (1977). **OTHER VOCAL:** *Rituale,* suite for Soprano and Orch. (1963); *Cîntece străbune* (Ancient Songs) for Soprano, Flute, Clarinet, Horn, Trumpet, Trombone, Piano, Vibraphone, Xylophone, and String Quintet (1972).

Moldoveanu, Vasile, Romanian tenor; b. Konstanza, Oct. 6, 1935. He was a student of Badescu in Bucharest, where he made his operatic debut in 1966 as Rinuccio. In 1972 he made his first appearance in Stuttgart as Edgardo, and then sang Alfredo at the Vienna State Opera and Rodolfo at the Bavarian State Opera in Munich in 1976. In 1977 he sang at the Deutsche Oper in Berlin and at the Chicago Lyric Opera, and on May 19 of that year he made his Metropolitan Opera debut in N.Y. as Rodolfo. He appeared as Don Carlos at the Hamburg State Opera in 1978, and sang that role at his debut at London's Covent Garden in 1979. His later engagements took him to Zürich (1980), Monte Carlo (1982), Nice (1988), Rome (1990), and other European music centers.

Molina, Antonio (Jesus), Filipino conductor, music administrator, and composer; b. Manila, Dec. 26, 1894; d. there, Jan. 29, 1980. He studied at the S. Juan de Letran College and at the Univ. of the Philippines Cons.; became a teacher at the latter (1925); was also active as a conductor; was director of the Centro Escolar Univ. Cons. (1948–71) and founder-director of a string group, Rondalla Ideal.

WORKS: *Ritorna Vincitor,* lyric drama (Manila, March 10, 1918); 2 zarzuelas: *Panibuglo* (Manila, April 16, 1918) and *Ang Ilaw* (Manila, Nov. 23, 1918); *The Living Word,* Christmas cantata for Chorus and Orch. (Manila, Dec. 18, 1936); *Ang batingaw* (The Bells), choral sym. (1972); Piano Quintet, based on native folk songs (1929; Manila, Jan. 21, 1950); Trio (1931); many songs; numerous piano pieces.

Molinari, Bernardino, eminent Italian conductor; b. Rome, April 11, 1880; d. there, Dec. 25, 1952. He studied with Falchi and Renzi at Rome's Liceo di Santa Cecilia (graduated, 1902). He was artistic director of Rome's Augusteo Orch. (1912–43); also conducted throughout Europe and South America. In 1928 he made his American debut with the N.Y. Phil., which he conducted again during the 1929–30 and 1930–31 seasons; he also appeared with other American orchs. He was head of the advanced conducting class at Rome's Accademia di Santa Cecilia (from 1936), serving as a prof. there (from 1939). Molinari championed the modern Italian school, and brought out many works by Respighi, Malipiero, and other outstanding Italian composers; publ. a new ed. of Monteverdi's *Sonata sopra Sonata Maria* (1919) and concert transcriptions of Carissimi's oratorio *Giona,* Vivaldi's *Le quattro stagioni* et al.; also orchestrated Debussy's *L'Isle joyeuse.*

BIBL.: E. Mucci, *B. M.* (Lanciano, 1941).

Molinari-Pradelli, Francesco, Italian conductor; b. Bologna, July 4, 1911; d. Marano di Castenaso, Aug. 7, 1996. He studied with d'Ivaldi and Nordio in Bologna, and with Molinari at the Accademia di Santa Cecilia in Rome. In 1938 he launched his career as a conductor; in 1939 he appeared for the first time as an opera conductor, leading *L'elisir d'amore* in Bologna. He conducted at Milan's La Scala from 1946; made his first appearance at London's Covent Garden in 1955, at the San Francisco Opera in 1957, and at the Vienna State Opera in 1959. On Feb. 7, 1966, he made his Metropolitan Opera debut in N.Y. conducting *Un ballo in maschera,* and remained on the company's roster until 1973. He was also active as a pianist. He was best known as an interpreter of the Italian operatic repertoire.

Molitor, Raphael, German musicologist; b. Sigmaringen, Feb. 2, 1873; d. Beuron, Oct. 14, 1948. He was the son of Johann Baptist Molitor, a cathedral organist; he studied philosophy and theology in the Benedictine Monastery of Beuron; was ordained a priest in 1897; lectured there on canon law (1898–1904); in 1904, was appointed a member of the advisory board of the Editio Vaticana. He was one of the foremost authorities on Gregorian chant.

Moll, Kurt, outstanding German bass; b. Buir, near Cologne, April 11, 1938. He learned to play the guitar and cello and sang in a school choir in his youth; then studied voice at the Cologne Hochschule für Musik and with Emmy Müller. After singing minor roles at the Cologne Opera (1958–61), he sang in Aachen (1961–63), Mainz (1963–66), and Wuppertal (1966–69); subsequently pursued a career of great distinction, appearing regularly in Hamburg, Bayreuth, Salzburg, Vienna, Paris, Milan, and London. He made his U.S. debut as Gurnemanz at the San Francisco Opera in 1974; on Sept. 18, 1978, came his Metropolitan Opera debut in N.Y., in which he essayed the role of the Landgrave; he subsequently appeared there regularly. He made his first appearance at the Chicago Lyric Opera as Daland in 1983.

He also sang widely as a concert artist and recitalist; made his North American recital debut at N.Y.'s Carnegie Hall in 1984. Among his other notable roles are the Commendatore, Sarastro, King Marke, Pogner, Nicolai's Falstaff, and Baron Ochs.

Molnár, Antal, distinguished Hungarian musicologist and composer; b. Budapest, Jan. 7, 1890; d. there, Dec. 7, 1983. He was a pupil in composition of Herzfeld at the Budapest Academy of Music (1907–10). He was a violist in the Waldbauer String Quartet (1910–13) and the Dohnányi-Hubay Piano Quartet (1915–17). After teaching music history and solfège at the Budapest Music School (1912–18), he was a prof. at the Budapest Academy of Music (1919–59), where he taught courses in music history, theory, solfège, and chamber music. In 1914 he received the Franz Joseph Prize, in 1957 the Kossuth Prize, and in 1970 was made an Eminent Artist by the Hungarian government.

WRITINGS (all publ. in Budapest): *A zenetörténet szelleme* (The Spirit of the History of Music; 1914); *Bartók Béla—táncjátéka alkalmából* (Béla Bartók—On the Occasion of His Ballet; 1917); *Az európai zene története 1750-ig* (History of European Music Until 1750; 1920); *Bach és Händel zenéjének lelki alapjai* (Spiritual Basis of Bach's and Handel's Music; 1920); *Bartók Két elégiájának elemzése* (Two Eagles: An Analysis; 1921); *A zenetörténet: Szociológiája* (The Sociology of Music History; 1923); *Az uj zene* (New Music; 1925); *Az uj magyar zene* (The New Hungarian Music; 1926); *Bevezetés a zenekulturába* (Introduction to Musical Culture; 1928); *Bevezetés a mai muzsikába* (Introduction to Contemporary Music; 1929); *Fizika és muzsika* (Physics and Music; 1930); *A gyermek és a zene* (The Child and Music; 1931); *A zenetörténet megvilágitása* (Light on Musical History; 1933); *Zeneesztétika és szellemtudomány* (Musical Aesthetics and "Geisteswissenschaft"; 1935); *A ma zenéje* (Music Today; 1936); *Az óvodáskoru gyermek zenei nevelése* (Musical Education in the Nursery School; 1936); *Kodály Zoltán* (1936); *Zeneesztétika* (Musical Aesthetics; 1938); *Népszerü zeneesztétika* (Popular Musical Aesthetics; 1940); *Az uj muzsika szelleme* (The Spirit of the New Music; 1948); *Bartók müvészete, emlékezésekkel a müvész életére* (The Art of Bartók with Reminiscences of his Life; 1948); *Repertórium a barokk zene történetébez* (Repertory of the History of Baroque Music; 1959); *Irások a zenéről* (Writings on Music; 1961); *A Léner-vonósnégyes* (The Léner Quartet; 1968); *A zeneszerző világa* (The World of the Composer; 1969); *Gyakorlati zeneesztétika* (Practical Musical Aesthetics; 1971); *Magamról— másokról* (On Myself—On Others; autobiography; 1974).

WORKS: DRAMATIC: *Savitri* (1912). **ORCH.:** *Grotesque March* (1914); Cello Concerto (1916); *Hungarian Dances* (1917); *Operetta Music* (1920); *Budapest,* overture (1921); *Past and Present* for Violin and Orch. (1923); Suite (1925); *Variations on a Hungarian Theme* (1928); *Hungarian Comedy Overture* (1928); *Kuruc Music* for 4 Tárogatós and Chamber Orch. (1936); *Overture to a Comedy* (1948); Harp Concerto (1952). **CHAMBER:** Various works, including piano pieces and organ music. **VOCAL:** Sacred and secular pieces; folk song arrangements.

Mompou (Semblança), Federico, significant Spanish composer; b. Barcelona, April 16, 1893; d. there, June 30, 1987. After preliminary studies at the Barcelona Cons., he went to Paris, where he studied piano with Philipp and composition with Rousseau. He returned to Barcelona in 1914; then was again in Paris from 1921 to 1941, when he once more went back to Spain. His music is inspired by Spanish and Catalan melos, but its harmonic and instrumental treatment is entirely modern. He wrote mostly for piano: *6 impressions intimes* (1911–14); *Scènes d'enfants* (1915); *Suburbis* (1916–17); *3 pessebres* (1918); *Cants magics* (1919); *Festes Llunyanes* (1920); *6 charmes* (1921); *3 variations* (1921); *Dialogues* (1923); *Canción y Danza* (1918–53); *10 preludes* (1927–51); *3 paisajes* (1942, 1947, 1960); *Música callada* (4 albums, 1959–67); *Suite compostelana* for Guitar (1963); choral works and songs.

BIBL.: S. Kastner, *F. M.* (Madrid, 1946); A. Iglesias, *F. M.* (Madrid, 1977); C. Janés, *F. M.: Vida, textos, documentos* (Madrid, 1987); W. Mellers, *Le Jardin Parfume: Homage to F. M.* (1989); R. Paine, *Hispanic Traditions in Twentieth-Century Catalan Music with Particular Reference to Gerhard, M., and Montsalvatge* (N.Y. and London, 1989); *F.M. S. (1893–1987): Palau de la Música Catalana, 13 d'abril–13 de maig de 1993* (Marid, 1993).

Monaco, Mario del. See **Del Monaco, Mario.**

Moncada, Eduardo Hernández. See **Hernández Moncada, Eduardo.**

Moncayo García, José Pablo, Mexican composer and conductor; b. Guadalajara, June 29, 1912; d. Mexico City, June 16, 1958. He studied with Chávez at the Mexico City Cons. From 1932 he was a member of the Mexico Sym. Orch.; was conductor of the National Sym. Orch. (1949–52). In company with Ayala, Contreras, and Galindo (also pupils of Chávez), he formed the so-called Grupo de Los Cuatro for the purpose of furthering the cause of Mexican music.

WORKS: OPERA: *La mulata de Córdoba* (Mexico City, Oct. 23, 1948). **ORCH.:** *Huapango* (1941); Sym. (1944); Sinfonietta (1945); *Homenaje a Cervantes* for 2 Oboes and Strings (Mexico City, Oct. 27, 1947); *Cumbres* (Louisville, June 12, 1954). **OTHER:** Choruses; piano pieces.

Monckton, (John) Lionel (Alexander), English composer; b. London, Dec. 18, 1861; d. there, Feb. 15, 1924. He was educated at Oriel College, Oxford, where he first composed for productions of the univ. dramatic society. He was active as a drama and music critic before launching his career as a composer of musical comedies in London in 1891. With John Crook, he collaborated on his first musical, *Claude Du-Val* (Sept. 25, 1894). After contributing to successful scores by Ivan Caryll and Sidney Jones, he worked with Howard Talbot on *Kitty Grey* (Sept. 7, 1901). He then won success in his own right with the musicals *A Country Girl* (Jan. 18, 1902) and *The Cingalee* (May 14, 1904). Collaborating again with Talbot, he created his most outstanding work in *The Arcadians* (April 28, 1909), which was performed throughout the world to great acclaim. Further success followed with his *The Quaker Girl* (Nov. 5, 1910). Collaborating once more with Talbot, he produced *The Mousme* (Sept. 9, 1911). His final collaboration with Talbot brought forth the enormously successful *The Boy* (Sept. 14, 1917).

Monestel, Alejandro, Costa Rican organist and composer; b. San José, April 26, 1865; d. there, Nov. 3, 1950. He studied at the Brussels Cons. Returning to Costa Rica in 1884, he was organist at the San José Cathedral (until 1902); then lived in N.Y. (1902–37), where he was active as a church organist and composer. He wrote 14 masses; 4 Requiems; 5 cantatas; *Rapsodia costarricense* for Orch. (San Jose, Aug. 28, 1935); arrangements of Costa Rican songs.

Monfred, Avenir de, Russian composer of French descent; b. St. Petersburg, Sept. 17, 1903; d. Paris, April 11, 1974. He studied piano, organ, and composition at the Petrograd Cons., graduating in 1922. In 1924 he went to Paris and studied with d'Indy at the Schola Cantorum (1925–27). He promulgated an interesting theory of composition, "diatonic polymodality," expounded in detail in his book *The New Diatonic Modal Principle of Relative Music* (N.Y., 1970).

WORKS: DRAMATIC: *Suite New-yorkaise,* ballet (Monte Carlo, Nov. 19, 1956); film scores. **ORCH.:** *Rapsodie juive* (1926); *Vienna, 1850,* symphonic poem (1941); 2 syms. (1955, 1957); *Manhattan Sketches,* symphonic suite (1958). **CHAMBER:** 3 violin sonatas (1922, 1926, 1947); Cello Sonata (1938); String Quartet (1939); piano pieces; organ works. **VOCAL:** Choruses.

Monk, Meredith (Jane), American composer, singer, and filmmaker; b. Lima, Peru (of American parents), Nov. 20, 1942. She studied eurythmics from an early age; was educated at Sarah Lawrence College (B.A., 1964), then was a pupil in voice of

Vicki Starr, John Devers, and Jeanette Lovetri, in composition of Ruth Lloyd, Richard Averee, and Glenn Mack, and in piano of Gershon Konikow. She pursued an active career as a singer, filmmaker, director, choreographer, recording artist, and composer. In 1968 she organized The House in N.Y., a company devoted to interdisciplinary approaches to the arts; in 1978 she founded there her own vocal chamber ensemble, with which she toured widely in the U.S. and abroad. In 1972 and 1982 she held Guggenheim fellowships; received various ASCAP awards and many commissions; in 1995 she was awarded a MacArthur fellowship. Her unique soprano vocalizations employ a wide range of ethnic and avant-garde influences. As one of the first and most natural of performance artists, she developed a flexible, imaginative theatrical style influenced by dream narrative and physical movement.

WORKS: *16 Millimeter Earrings* for Voice and Guitar (1966); *Candy Bullets and Moon* for Voice, Electric Organ, Electric Bass, and Drums (1967; in collaboration with D. Preston); *Blueprint: Overload/Blueprint 2* for Voice, Echoplex, and Tape (1967); *Juice*, theater cantata for 85 Voices, Jew's Harp, and 2 Violins (1969); *A Raw Recital* for Voice and Electric Organ (1970); *Needle-Brain Lloyd and the Systems Kid* for 150 Voices, Electric Organ, Guitar, and Flute (1970); *Key*, album of invisible theater for Voice, Electric Organ, Vocal Quartet, Percussion, and Jew's Harp (1970–71); *Plainsong for Bill's Bojo* for Electric Organ (1971); *Vessel*, opera epic for 75 Voices, Electric Organ, Dulcimer, and Accordion (1971); *Paris* for Piano and Vocal Duet (1972); *Education of the Girlchild*, opera for 6 Voices, Electric Organ, and Piano (1972–73); *Our Lady of Late* for Voice and Wine Glass (1972–73); *Chacon* for 25 Voices, Piano, and Percussion (1974); *Anthology and Small Scroll* for Voice and Piano (1975); *Quarry*, opera for 38 Voices, 2 Pump Organs, 2 Soprano Recorders, and Tape (1976); *Venice/Milan* for 15 Voices and Piano, 4-hands (1976); *Songs from the Hill* for Voice (1976–77); *Tablet* for 4 Voices, Piano, 4-hands, and 2 Soprano Recorders (1977); *The Plateau Series* for 5 Voices and Tape (1977); *Dolmen Music* for 6 Voices, Cello, and Percussion (1979); *Recent Ruins* for 14 Voices, Tape, and Cello (1979); *Turtle Dreams (Waltz)* for 4 Voices and 2 Electric Organs (1980–81); *Specimen Days* for 14 Voices, Piano, and 2 Electric Organs (1981); *View No. 1* for Piano, Synthesizer, and Voice (1981) and *No. 2* for Voice and Synthesizer (1982); *Ellis Island* for 2 Pianos (1982); *Tokyo Cha-Cha* for 6 Voices and 2 Electric Organs (1983); *Engine Steps* for Tape Collage (1983); *2 Men Walking* for 3 Voices and Electric Organs (1983); *The Games* for 16 Voices, Synthesizer, Keyboards, Flemish Bagpipes, Bagpipes, Chinese Horn, and Rauschpfeife (1983); *Panda Chant I* for 4 Voices and *II* for 8 Voices (both 1984); *Graduation Song* for 16 Voices (1984); *Book of Days* for 25 Voices, Synthesizer, and Piano (1985); *Scared Song* for Voice, Synthesizer, and Piano (1986); *I Don't Know* for Voice and Piano (1986); *Double Fiesta* for Voice and 2 Pianos (1986); *String* for Voice (1986); *Window in 7's (for Nurit)* for Piano (1986); *Duet Behavior* for 2 Voices (1987); *The Ringing Place* for 9 Voices (1987); *Do You Be* for 10 Voices, 2 Pianos, Synthesizer, Violin, and Bagpipes (1987); *Book of Days*, film score for 10 Voices, Cello, Shawm, Synthesizer, Hammered Dulcimer, Bagpipe, and Hurdy Gurdy (1988); *Fayum Music* for Voice, Hammered Dulcimer, and Double Ocarina (1988); *Light Songs* for Voice (1988); *Raven* for Piano (1988); *Cat Song* for Voice (1988); *Parlour Games* for 2 Pianos (1988); *Waltz* for 2 Pianos (1988); *Processional* for Piano and Voice (1988); *Phantom Waltz* for 2 Pianos (1990); *Facing North* for 2 Voices and Tape (1990; in collaboration with R. Een); *Atlas*, opera (Houston, Feb. 22, 1991); *3 Heavens and Hells* for 4 Voices (1992); *Custom Made* for Piano and 1 or 2 Voices (1993); *American Archeology No. 1: Roosevelt Island* for 9 Voices, Organ, Bass, Medieval Drum, and Shawm (1994); *Volcano Songs* for Voice, Tape, and Piano (1994); *Nightfall* for 16 Voices (1995); *Denkai Krikiki Chants* for 4 Voices (1995).

Monk, Thelonious "Sphere," noted black American jazz pianist and composer; b. Rocky Mount, N.C., Oct. 10, 1917; d. Englewood, N.J., Feb. 17, 1982. He spent most of his life in Harlem, where he played in nightclubs; gradually surfaced as a practitioner of bebop, set in angular rhythms within asymmetrical bar sequences. His eccentric behavior was signalized by his external appearance; he wore skullcaps and dark sunglasses; time and again he would rise from the keyboard and perform a tap dance. Although not educated in the formal sense, he experimented with discordant harmonies, searching for new combinations of sounds. Paradoxically, he elevated his ostentatious ineptitude to a weirdly cogent modern idiom, so that even deep-thinking jazz critics could not decide whether he was simply inept or prophetically innovative. Monk's own tunes, on the other hand, seemed surprisingly sophisticated, and he gave them impressionistic titles, such as *Crepuscule with Nellie* (Nellie was the name of his wife) and *Epistrophy*, or else ethnically suggestive ones, as in *Rhythm-a-ning*. A profoundly introspective neurotic, he would drop out of the music scene for years, withdrawing into his inner self. From 1973 to 1976, he stayed with an admirer, the Baroness Pannonica de Koenigswarter, in her mansion in Weehawken, N.J., but was visited daily by his wife, Nellie. He made his last public appearance at the Newport Jazz Festival in 1976, but seemed a faint shadow, a weak echo of his former exuberant personality. His song *Criss-Cross* (1951) was used by Gunther Schuller for his *Variations on a Theme of Thelonious Monk*.

BIBL.: N. Hentoff, *T. M.* (N.Y., 1961); L. Bijl and F. Conté, *M. on Record: A Discography of T. M.* (Amsterdam, 1982); T. Fitterling, *T. M.: Sein Leben, seine Musik, seine Schallplatten* (Waakirchen, 1987).

Monleone, Domenico, Italian opera composer; b. Genoa, Jan. 4, 1875; d. there, Jan. 15, 1942. He studied at the Milan Cons. From 1895 to 1901 he was active as a theater conductor in Amsterdam and in Vienna. He attracted attention by producing in Amsterdam (Feb. 5, 1907) an opera, *Cavalleria rusticana*, to a libretto by his brother Giovanni, on the same subject as Mascagni's celebrated work; after its first Italian performance (Turin, July 10, 1907), Mascagni's publisher, Sonzogno, brought a lawsuit against Monleone for infringement of copyright. Monleone was forced to change the title; his brother rewrote the libretto, and the opera was produced as *La Giostra dei falchi* (Florence, Feb. 18, 1914). Other operas were: *Una novella di Boccaccio* (Genoa, May 26, 1909); *Alba eroica* (Genoa, May 5, 1910); *Arabesca* (Rome, March 11, 1913; won 1st prize at the competition of the City of Rome); *Suona la ritrata* (Milan, May 23, 1916); *Il mistero* (Venice, May 7, 1921); *Fauvette* (Genoa, March 2, 1926); *La ronda di notte* (Genoa, March 6, 1933); also an opera in Genovese dialect, *Scheuggio Campann-a* (Genoa, March 12, 1928). For some of his works he used the pseudonym W. di Stolzing.

Monnikendam, Marius, Dutch music critic, teacher, and composer; b. Haarlem, May 28, 1896; d. Heerlen, May 22, 1977. He studied composition with Dresden, and organ and piano with de Pauw at the Amsterdam Cons.; in 1925 he went to Paris, where he took courses with Aubert and d'Indy at the Schola Cantorum. Returning to the Netherlands, he taught composition at the Rotterdam Cons. and in Amsterdam; also served as music critic of the newspaper combine *De Tijd* and *De Maasbode*. He wrote a number of church works, in which he revived the most ancient form of plainchant, but injected asymmetric rhythms in a modern style; in his larger works, he employed the resources of advanced harmony, including polytonality. He publ. monographs on Franck (Amsterdam, 1949) and Stravinsky (Haarlem, 1951); also *50 Masterpieces of Music* (The Hague, 1953) and *Nederlandse Componisten van heden en verleden* (Amsterdam, 1968).

WORKS: ORCH.: *Arbeid* (Labor), symphonic movement (1931); *Sinfonia super "Merck toch hoe sterck"* for Chamber Orch. (1944); *Mouvement symphonique* (1950); Concerto for Trumpet, Horn, and Orch. (1952); *Variations symphoniques super "Merck toch hoe sterck"* (1954); Concerto for Organ and Strings (1958); *Ouverture* for Organ and Orch. (1960); *Vision* for Chamber Orch. (1963); Concerto for Organ, Wind Instruments, Harp, Double Bass, and Percussion (1968); Piano Concertino

(1974). **CHAMBER:** Cello Sonata (1925); *2 toccatas* for Organ (1931, 1970); Concerto for Organ, 2 Trumpets, and 2 Trombones (1956); *10 Inventions* for Organ (1959); *Suite* for Flute, Oboe, Clarinet, Bassoon, and Harp (1960); Piano Sonatina (1967); *Suite biblique* for Piano, 4-hands (1967); *The Bells*, prelude for Organ (1971); *Toccata batalla* for Organ, 2 Trumpets, and 2 Trombones (1972); numerous small organ pieces. **VOCAL:** 2 Te Deums for Chorus and Orch. (1919, 1946); *Missa Nova* for 3 Voices and Organ (1928); *7 Boetpsalmen* (7 Penitential Psalms) for Chorus and Orch. (1934); *Noah*, oratorio (1937); *Samson*, oratorio (1938); *Solomon*, oratorio (1939); *Missa antiphonale* (1939); *Sinfonia sacra I* for Men's Chorus and Orch. (1947) and *II (Domine salvum fac)* for Chorus and Orch. (1952); *Passion* for Speaker, Chorus, and Orch. (1948); *Van Riebeeck-Taferelen* for 2 Speakers, Chorus, and Orch. (1952); *Noe ou La Destruction du Premier Monde*, oratorio (1955); *Magnificat* for Soprano, Men's Chorus, and Orch. without Strings (1956; transcribed for Mixed Chorus and Full Orch., 1965); *Missa festiva* for Chorus and Orch. (1956); *Lamentations of Jeremiah* for Chorus and Orch. (1956); *Hymne* for Alto, Men's Chorus, and Orch. (1957); *Missa solenissima* for Chorus, Organ, and 7 Wind Instruments (1959); *Missa pro defunctis* for 3 Soloists, Organ, and Percussion (1961); *Apocalypse* for Chorus and Organ (1966); *Madrigalesca* for Chorus, 9 Winds, and Percussion (1966); *De Kinderkruistocht* (The Children's Crusade) for Mixed or Women's Chorus, 7 Woodwinds, and Percussion (1967); *Via sacra* (Way of the Cross) for Speaker, Chorus, Organ, Percussion, and Projection Slides (1969); *3 psaumes pour le temps present* for Soloists, Chorus, and Chamber Orch. (1971); *Missa concertanta* for Soloists, Chorus, and Orch. (1971); *Elckerlyc* (Everyman), mystery play for Chorus, Organ, and Orch. (1975; The Hague, May 28, 1976); *Heart Rhythm* for Speaker, Men's Chorus, Organ, Double Bass, and Percussion (1975); *Gloria* for Chorus, Organ, and Orch. (1976).

Monod, Jacques-Louis, French pianist, conductor, music editor, and composer; b. Asnières, near Paris, Feb. 25, 1927. He was admitted to the Paris Cons. before he had reached the official entrance age of 9, later studying with Messiaen (1944) and receiving instruction in theory, composition, and analysis from Leibowitz (1944–50); subsequently studied composition with Wagenaar at N.Y.'s Juilliard School of Music and conducting with Rudolf Thomas at Columbia Univ., and then took courses with Blacher and Rufer in Berlin. As a pianist and conductor, he became a proponent of modern music. He was married for a time to **Bethany Beardslee**, with whom he gave many song recitals. He was chief music ed. of the Boelke-Bomart firm (1952–82); was also active as a teacher at various U.S. academic institutions. He wrote orch. works, chamber music, and songs.

Mononen, Sakari (Tuomo), Finnish organist, teacher, and composer; b. Korpiselkä, July 27, 1928. He studied composition with Fougstedt and Englund at the Sibelius Academy in Helsinki, graduating in 1962. He then was an organist and theory teacher at the Kuopio Music Inst., where he was made head of the church music dept. (1970) and prorector (1976).

WORKS: ORCH.: Sym. (1961); Concerto Grosso for Winds and Strings (1968); *Divertimento* (1971); *Legenda con espressione* (1971); *Perspectives* (1972). **CHAMBER:** 2 suites for Piano (1959, 1970); String Trio (1960); String Quartet (1961); 3 organ sonatas (1963, 1964, 1965); Clarinet Sonata (1973). **VOCAL:** *Vuorela Suite* for Chorus (1972).

Monrad Johansen, David. See **Johansen, David Monrad.**

Montagu-Nathan, M(ontagu) (real name, **Montagu Nathan**), English writer on music; b. Banbury, Sept. 17, 1877; d. London, Nov. 15, 1958. He legally changed his name to Montagu Montagu-Nathan on March 17, 1909. He studied in Birmingham; then took violin lessons with Ysaÿe in Brussels, with Heermann in Frankfurt am Main, and with Wilhelmj in London. He appeared as a violinist in Belfast and Leeds, but soon abandoned concerts in favor of music journalism. He learned the Russian language and wrote several books on Russian music: *A History of Russian Music* (London and N.Y., 1914; 2nd ed., 1918); *An Introduction to Russian Music* (London and Boston, 1916); *Contemporary Russian Composers* (London, 1917); *Handbook to the Piano Works of A. Scriabin* (London, 1917); also monographs on Glinka (London, 1916; 2nd ed., 1921), Mussorgsky (London, 1916), and Rimsky-Korsakov (London, 1916).

Montague, Stephen (Rowley), American composer and pianist; b. Syracuse, N.Y., March 10, 1943. Following studies in piano, conducting, and composition at Florida State Univ. (B.M., 1965; M.M., 1967), he pursued his education at Ohio State Univ. (D.M.A., 1972) and worked at the Studio for Experimental Music at the Polish Radio in Warsaw on a Fulbright scholarship (1972–74). In 1974 he made London the center of his activities, but also toured widely as a pianist championing contemporary music. From 1985 he also toured with the pianist Philip Mead in the duo known as Montague/Mead Piano Plus. In 1980 he helped organize the Electro-Acoustic Music Assn. of Great Britain. In 1992 and 1995 he was a guest prof. at the Univ. of Texas at Austin. From 1993 he was a visiting guest prof. at the Royal College of Music in London, and chairman of the SPNM (Soc. for the Promotion of New Music) of Great Britain. In 1995–96 he also was composer-in-residence with the Orch. of St. John's Smith Square in London. Montague's extensive output includes various electroacoustic pieces and acoustic scores.

WORKS: DRAMATIC: *Largo con moto*, graphic/text piece for Dancer and Tape (London, March 15, 1975); *Criseyde*, theater piece for Soprano Playing Ocarina, Slide, and Tape (Mexico City, Oct. 19, 1976); *Into the Sun*, ballet for 4-Channel Tape, Percussion, and Prepared Piano (Manchester, Oct. 31, 1977); *The West of the Imagination*, music for a television drama/documentary series (1986); many other pieces. **ORCH.:** *Voussoirs* for Orch. and Tapes (1970–72); *Sound Round* for Orch. and Digital Delay (1973; Manchester, July 11, 1988); *At the White Edge of Phrygia* for Chamber Orch. (London, June 20, 1983; for Full Orch. as *From the White Edge of Phrygia*, 1984; also as part of the ballet, *Median*, 1984); *Prologue* (1984; London, Jan. 3, 1985; also as part of the ballet, *Median*, 1984); Piano Concerto (London, June 11, 1988). **CHAMBER:** *The Eyes of Ambush* for 1 to 5 Instruments or Voices and Digital Delay (1973); *Caccia* for Trombone, Piano, Tape, and Amplification (1974); *Quiet Washes* for 3 Trombones and 3 Pianos or Harps or Pre-recorded Versions (1974); *Strummin'* for Piano, Strings, Lighting, and Tape (1974–81); *Inundations I: Trio* for 3 Amplified Pianos, 12 Pianists, and Tape (1975) and *II: Willow* for Soprano, Piano, and Tape (1976); *E Pluribus Unum*, graphic/text piece for Any Chamber Group (1976); *Introduction* for Voice, Acoustic Feedback, and Tape (1976); *Paramell I* for Muted Trombone and Muted Piano (1977), *II: Entity* for 6 Percussionists (1977), *III* for Piano, Chorus of Humming Audience, and Pre-recorded Cassette (1981), *IV* for Tuba or Bass Trombone and Tape (1979), *V* for 2 Pianos (1981), and *VI* for Piano, Flute, Clarinet, and Cello or Percussion (1981); Quintet, graphic/text piece for Any Instrument and Pre-recorded 4-Channel Tape (1978); Trio, graphic/text piece for Any Instrument and Pre-recorded Stereo Tape (1978); *Gravity's Rainbow* for Flute, Live Electronics, and Tape (1980); Duo, graphic/text piece for Any Instrument and Pre-recorded Tape (1982); *Tongues of Fire* for Piano, Live Electronics, and Tape (1983–90); *Haiku* for Piano, Flanger, and Electronic Tape (1987); 2 string quartets: No. 1, *in memoriam Barry Anderson and Tomasz Sikorski*, with Live Electronics and Tape (1989–93) and No. 2, *Shaman*, with Live Electronics and Tape (1993); *Behold a Pale Horse* for Organ (1990); *After Ives . . .* for Piano, Tape, Live Electronics, and Optional Flute and String Quartet (1991–93); *Vlug* for Flute, Tape, and Live Electronics (1992); *Aeolian Furies* for Accordion (1993); *Silence: John, Yvar, and Tim* for Prepared String Quartet, Prepared Piano, 2 Tapes, and Live Electronics (1994); *Phrygian Tucket* for Harpsichord and Tape (1994). **VOCAL:** *Varshavian Spring* for Chorus and Orch. (1973–80); *Sotto Voce*, graphic/text piece for Multiphonic Chorus, Tape Recorder, and Playback System (1976); *Tigida Pipa* for Amplified Voices, Woodblocks, Claves, and Electronic Tape (1983–89); *3 Temper-*

ance Songs for Woman's Voice and 6 Instruments or Synthesizer, Piano, and Optional Tape (1988); *Boombox Virelai* for 4 Men's Voices (1992); *Wild Nights* for Soprano, Clarinet, Viola, and Piano (1993). **ELECTROACOUSTIC:** *A Presto Patch* (1973); *Scythia* (1981); *Quartet* (1982); *Slow Dance on a Burial Ground* (1982–84); *Bright Interiors* (1992).

Monte, Toti dal. See **Dal Monte, Toti.**

Montemezzi, Italo, eminent Italian opera composer; b. Vigasio, near Verona, Aug. 4, 1875; d. there, May 15, 1952. He was a pupil of Saladino and Ferroni at the Milan Cons., and graduated in 1900; his graduation piece, conducted by Toscanini, was *Cantico dei Cantici,* for Chorus and Orch. He then devoted himself almost exclusively to opera. In 1939 he went to the U.S.; lived mostly in California; in 1949 he returned to Italy. Montemezzi's chief accomplishment was the maintenance of the best traditions of Italian dramatic music, without striving for realism or overelaboration of technical means. His masterpiece in this genre was the opera *L'amore dei tre re* (Milan, April 10, 1913), which became a standard work in the repertoire of opera houses all over the world. Other operas are *Giovanni Gallurese* (Turin, Jan. 28, 1905); *Hellera* (Turin, March 17, 1909); *La nave* (libretto by Gabriele d'Annunzio; Milan, Nov. 1, 1918); *La notte di Zoraima* (Milan, Jan. 31, 1931); and *L'incantesimo* (NBC, Oct. 9, 1943, composer conducting). He also wrote *Paolo e Virginia* for Orch. (1929) and *Italia mia, nulla fermera il tuo canto* for Orch. (1944).

BIBL.: L. Tretti and L. Fiumi, eds., *Omaggio a I. M.* (Verona, 1952).

Monteux, Pierre, celebrated French-born American conductor; b. Paris, April 4, 1875; d. Hancock, Maine, July 1, 1964. He studied at the Paris Cons. with Berthelier (violin), Lavignac (harmony), and Lenepveu (composition); received 1st prize for violin (1896). He began his career as a violist in the Colonne Orch. in Paris, where he later was chorus master; also was a violist in the orch. of the Opéra-Comique in Paris. He then organized his own series, the Concerts Berlioz, at the Casino de Paris (1911); that same year, he also became conductor for Diaghilev's Ballets Russes; his performances of modern ballet scores established him as one of the finest technicians of the baton. He led the premieres of Stravinsky's *Petrouchka, Le Sacre du printemps,* and *Le Rossignol*; Ravel's *Daphnis et Chloé;* and Debussy's *Jeux.* Monteux conducted at the Paris Opéra (1913–14); founded the Société des Concerts Populaires in Paris (1914); appeared as guest conductor in London, Berlin, Vienna, Budapest, and other music centers. In 1916–17 he toured the U.S. with the Ballets Russes; in 1917, conducted the Civic Orch. Soc., N.Y.; from 1917 to 1919, at the Metropolitan Opera there. In 1919 he was engaged as conductor of the Boston Sym. Orch., and held this post until 1924; from 1924 to 1934 he was assoc. conductor of the Concertgebouw Orch. in Amsterdam; from 1929 to 1938 he was principal conductor of the newly founded Orch. Symphonique de Paris. From 1936 until 1952 he was conductor of the reorganized San Francisco Sym. Orch. He became a naturalized American citizen in 1942. He appeared as a guest conductor with the Boston Sym. Orch. from 1951, and also accompanied it on its first European tour in 1952, and then again in 1956; likewise was again on the roster of the Metropolitan Opera (1953–56). In 1961 (at the age of 86) he became principal conductor of the London Sym. Orch., retaining this post until his death. He was married in 1927 to Doris Hodgkins (b. Salisbury, Maine, 1895; d. Hancock, Maine, March 13, 1984), an American singer who co-founded in 1941 the Domaine School for Conductors and Orchestral Players in Hancock, Maine, of which Monteux was director. She publ. 2 books of memoirs, *Everyone Is Someone* and *It's All in the Music* (N.Y., 1965). After Monteux's death, she established the Pierre Monteux Memorial Foundation. As an interpreter, Monteux endeavored to bring out the inherent essence of the music, without imposing his own artistic personality; unemotional and restrained in his podium manner, he nonetheless succeeded in producing brilliant performances in an extensive repertoire ranging from the classics to the 20th century.

BIBL.: D. Schneider, *The San Francisco Symphony Orchestra: Music, Maestros, and Musicians* (Novato, Calif., 1983); J. Canarina, "P. M.: A Conductor for All Repertoire," *Opus* (April 1986).

Montgomery, Kenneth (Mervyn), Irish conductor; b. Belfast, Oct. 28, 1943. He received his formal musical education at the Royal College of Music in London; studied conducting in Siena with Celibidache, and in London with Boult; also had instruction with Pritchard and Schmidt-Isserstedt. In 1964 he joined the conducting staff of the Glyndebourne Festival; in 1966 he conducted at the Sadler's Wells Opera in London. In 1970 he became assistant conductor of the Western Orch. Soc. at Bournemouth; in 1972, its assoc. conductor; in 1973 was appointed music director of the Bournemouth Sinfonietta. He was music director of the Glyndebourne Touring Opera (1975–76). From 1976 to 1980 he was principal conductor of the Netherlands Radio; in 1981 he became chief conductor of its Groot Omroep Koor. He was music director of Opera Northern Ireland in Belfast from 1985.

Montgomery, Merle, American music educator, editor, and composer; b. Davidson, Okla., May 15, 1904; d. Arlington, Va., Aug. 25, 1986. She studied at the Univ. of Okla. (B.F.A., 1924), with Philipp (piano) and Boulanger (composition) at the American Cons. in Fontainebleau (diploma, 1933), and at the Eastman School of Music in Rochester, N.Y. (M.M., 1938; Ph.D. in theory, 1948). She was head of the music dept. at Southwestern Inst. in Weatherford, Okla. (1938–41); after teaching at the Eastman School of Music (1943–45), she went to N.Y. as national educational representative and later vice-president of the Carl Fischer firm; ed. music and books on music; taught at the Westchester Cons.; was president of the National Music Council (1975–79). She composed mainly songs and piano pieces, often using the name Aline Campbell.

Montoya, Carlos, popular Spanish flamenco guitarist; b. Madrid, Dec. 13, 1903; d. Wainscott, N.Y., March 3, 1993. He began to play the guitar when he was 8; within a few years he performed professionally with various dance groups, and later gave solo recitals which attracted faithful aficionados; he traveled in the U.S., South America, and Japan. He also improvised a number of attractive pieces, among them a *Suite flamenca* for Guitar and Orch. (1966); they were notated by helpers, since Montoya himself never learned to read music.

Montsalvatge, (Bassols) Xavier, Spanish composer, music critic, and teacher; b. Gerona, March 11, 1911. He settled in Madrid and studied at the Cons. His mentors in composition were Morera and Pahissa. He was active as a teacher and as a music critic, writing for the newspaper *La Vanguardia* (1960–72) and serving as ed. of the newspaper *Destino* (1962–70). His autobiography was publ. in Barcelona in 1987. Montsalvatge composed in a well-crafted tonal style in which he occasionally made use of bracing dissonance.

WORKS: DRAMATIC: *El gato con botas,* magic opera (1948); *Una voce in off,* opera (1961); incidental music; film scores. **ORCH.:** 2. syms. (*Sinfonia mediterranea,* 1949; *Sinfonia da requiem,* 1986); *Concierto breve* for Piano and Orch. (1952); *Partita 1958* (1958); *Desintegración morfología de la chacona de Bach* (1962); *Laberinto* (1970); *Cinco invocaciones al Crucificado* (1970); *Reflexus obertura* (1974); *Serenata a Lydia de Cadaques* for Flute and Orch. (1974; also for Flute and Piano, 1969); *Concerto capriccio* for Harp and Orch. (1975); *Concertino 1+13* for Violin and Chamber String Orch. (1975); *Concierto del Albayzin* for Harpsichord and Orch. (1977); *Metamorfosis de concierto* for Guitar and Orch. (1982); *Música per a un diumenge* for Band (1984); *Fanfarría para la Alegría de la Paz* (1985). **CHAMBER:** *Cuarteto Indiano* for String Quartet (1952); *Sef-paragrasis* for Clarinet and Piano (1968); *Serenata a Lydia de Cadaques* for Flute and Piano (1969; also for Flute and Orch., 1974); *Sonata concertante* for Cello and Piano (1972);

Parafrasis concertante for Violin and Piano (1975); *Questions and Answers* for Brass Quintet (1979); *Cuadrivio para tres Stradivarius* for String Trio (1984); *Fantasis* for Guitar and Harp (1984); Trio for Violin, Cello, and Piano (1987); piano pieces; organ music. **VOCAL:** *Cinco canciones negras* for Soprano and Piano or Orch. (1945); *Cant espiritual* for Chorus and Orch. (1959); *Homenaje a Manolo Hugue* for Soprano and Orch. (1973); *Sum vermis* for Voice, 2 Pianos, and 2 Percussion (1974); solo songs.

BIBL.: M. Valls, *X. M.* (Barcelona, 1969); E. Franco, *X. M.* (Madrid, 1975); R. Paine, *Hispanic Traditions in Twentieth-Century Catalan Music with Particular Reference to Gerhard, Mompou, and M.* (N.Y. and London, 1989).

Moodie, Alma, Australian violinist; b. Brisbane, Sept. 12, 1900; d. Frankfurt am Main, March 7, 1943. She studied with Thomson in Brussels (1907–10). She played at a concert as a child prodigy (with Reger); gave concerts in Germany, where she lived most of her life; taught at the Frankfurt am Main Academy of Music. Her prestige as a musician was high in Germany; she performed many new works; Pfitzner wrote his Violin Concerto for her.

Moody, Fanny, English soprano; b. Redruth, Cornwall, Nov. 23, 1866; d. Dundrum, County Dublin, July 21, 1945. She studied with Charlotte Sainton-Dolby, making her debut in a memorial concert for her teacher at Prince's Hall in London (1885). She made her operatic debut as Arline in *The Bohemian Girl* with the Carl Rosa Opera Co. in Liverpool (1887), and subsequently was the company's principal soprano until 1898; she married the Irish bass and impresario Charles Manners (1890), with whom she founded the Moody-Manners Opera Co. (1898), and thereafter toured widely with it until it was disbanded (1916). Among her best roles were Gounod's Marguerite and Juliet, Verdi's Leonora, and Santuzza.

BIBL.: P. Graves, "The M.-Manners Partnership," *Opera*, IX (1958).

Moog, Robert (Arthur), American designer of electronic instruments; b. Flushing, N.Y., May 23, 1934. He studied at Queens College (B.S. in physics, 1957), Columbia Univ. (B.S. in electrical engineering, 1957), and Cornell Univ. (Ph.D. in engineering physics, 1965). He founded the R.A. Moog Co. in 1954 for the purpose of designing electronic musical instruments; in 1964 he introduced the first synthesizer modules; his company was incorporated in 1968, with its headquarters at Trumansburg, N.Y. In 1970 he brought out the Minimoog, a portable monophonic instrument; in 1971 the company became Moog Music and went to Buffalo, N.Y.; in 1973 it became a division of Norlin Industries, with which Moog was associated until 1977. He founded another firm, Big Briar, in Leicester, N.C., which manufactured devices for precision control of analog and digital synthesizers. He was associated with Kurzweil Music Systems of Boston (1984–89). His synthesizers and other electronic devices were used by both classical and rock musicians.

BIBL.: D. Crombie, "The M. Story," *Sound International*, 6 (1978); T. Rhea, "The M. Synthesizer," *Contemporary Keyboard*, VII/3 (1981).

Moór, Emanuel, Hungarian pianist, inventor, and composer; b. Kecskemet, Feb. 19, 1863; d. Mont Pelerin, near Montreux, Switzerland, Oct. 20, 1931. He studied in Budapest and Vienna. He toured the U.S. from 1885 to 1887 as director of the Concerts Artistiques, for which he engaged Lilli Lehmann, Ovide Musin, and other celebrated artists, and also acted as their accompanist. He then lived in London, Lausanne, and Munich. He invented the Moór-Duplex piano, consisting of a double keyboard with a coupler between the two manuals (an octave apart). With the introduction of this piano, a new technique was made possible, facilitating the playing of octaves, tenths, and even chromatic glissandos. Some piano manufacturers (Steinway, Bechstein, Bösendorfer) put the Moór mechanism into their instruments. His 2nd wife, Winifred Christie (b. Stirling, Feb. 26, 1882; d. London, Feb. 8, 1965), an English pianist, aided him in promoting the Moór keyboard, and gave many performances on it in Europe and the U.S. She publ. (in collaboration with her husband) a manual of technical exercises for the instrument.

WORKS: OPERAS: *La Pompadour* (Cologne, Feb. 22, 1902); *Andreas Hofer* (Cologne, Nov. 9, 1902); *Hochzeitsglocken* (Kassel, Aug. 2, 1908; in London as *Wedding Bells*, Jan. 26, 1911); *Der Goldschmied von Paris* (n.d.); *Hertha* (unfinished). **ORCH.:** 3 piano concertos (1886, 1888, 1906); 8 syms. (1893–1910); 4 violin concertos (1905–07); 2 cello concertos (1905–06); Triple Concerto for Violin, Cello, Piano, and Orch. (1907); Harp Concerto (1913). **OTHER:** *Requiem* (1916); much chamber music; numerous songs.

BIBL.: L. Deutsch, *Die Technik der Doppelklaviatur M.* (Leipzig, 1932); M. Pirani, *E. M.* (London, 1959); H. Shead, *The History of the E. M. Double Keyboard Piano* (1978).

Moor (real name, **Mohr**), **Karel**, Czech conductor, composer, and writer; b. Bělohrad, Dec. 26, 1873; d. Prague, March 30, 1945. He studied at the Prague Cons. and in Vienna. From 1900 to 1923 he was active as a theatrical director and conductor in Bohemia and Serbia; then lived mainly in Prague. He achieved his first success as a composer with the operetta *Pan profesor v pekle* (Mr. Professor in Hell), produced in Brunn in 1908; his other operas, *Hjördis* (1899; rev. 1901; Prague, Oct. 22, 1905) and *Viy*, after Gogol's fantastic tale (1901; Prague, July 14, 1903), were also successful. A facile writer, he publ. an autobiography in the form of a novel as *Karl Martens* (Prague, 1906); a vol. of reminiscences, *Vzpomínsky* (Pilsen, 1917); and a semifictional book, *V dlani osudu* (In the Hands of Fate; Nový Bydżov, 1947).

Moore, Carman (Leroy), versatile black American composer, conductor, teacher, and writer on music; b. Lorain, Ohio, Oct. 8, 1936. He studied with Martin Morris (horn), Peter Brown (cello), and Cecil Isaacs (conducting) at the Oberlin (Ohio) College Cons. of Music; after further studies at Ohio State Univ. (B.M., 1958), he went to N.Y., where he studied at the Juilliard School of Music with Persichetti and Berio (B.M., 1966); completed his studies with Wolpe (1967). He helped to launch the Soc. of Black Composers in 1968; taught at Manhattanville College (1969–71), Yale Univ. (1969–71), and Queens (1970–71) and Brooklyn (1972–74) Colleges of the City Univ. of N.Y. He presented concerts with his own group, Carman Moore and Ensemble, which he transformed into the Skymusic Ensemble in 1985. In addition to writing music criticism, he publ. a biography of Bessie Smith as *Somebody's Angel Child* (1970) and a textbook on teaching popular music (1980). In his compositions, he makes imaginative use of various genres, ranging from jazz to the avant-garde.

WORKS: DRAMATIC: OPERA: *The Masque of Saxophone's Voice* (1981). **MUSIC THEATER:** *Wild Gardens of the Loup Garou* (1983); *Distraughter, or The Great Panda Scanda* (1983); *Paradise Re-Lost* (1987). **MUSICAL:** *Franklin and Eleanor* (1989). **BALLETS:** *A Musical Offering* (1962); *Catwalk* (1966); *Tryst* (1966); *They Tried to Touch* (1986); *La Dea delle Acque* (Milan, March 29, 1988). **DANCE PIECE:** *Shipwreck* (1989). **INTERMEDIA:** *Broken Suite* for Instrumental Ensemble (1969); *The Illuminated Workingman* for 11 Instruments and Tape (1971); *American Themes and Variations* for Narrator and Instrumental Ensemble (1980); *Sky Dance/Sky Time* for Instrumental Ensemble, Dance Ensemble, and Sculpture (1984); *The Persistence of Green* for Dance, Dance Projections, and Instrumental Ensemble (N.Y., April 16, 1988); *The Magical Turn About Town* for Instrumental Ensemble (N.Y., July 18, 1989); *Tales of Exile* for Dancers and Instrumental Ensemble (N.Y., July 15, 1989); *Magic Circle* for Dancer, Projections, and Instrumental Ensemble (N.Y., Dec. 28, 1989). **ORCH.:** *Sinfonia* (1964); *Saratoga Festival Overture* (1966); *Gospel Fuse* for 4 Women's Voices and Orch. (San Francisco, Jan. 22, 1975); *Wildfires and Field Songs* (N.Y., Jan. 23, 1975); *Hit*, percussion concerto (1978); Concerto for Blues Piano and Orch. (1982); *Concertos (The Theme Is Freedom)* (N.Y., Nov. 11, 1985); Concerto for Jazz Violin and Orch. (1987). **CHAMBER:** Piano Sonata

(1963); Mandolin Sonata (1966); Cello Sonata (1966); *Drum Major* for Chamber Ensemble and Tape (1969); Quartet for Saxophones and Echo Device (1978); *Dawn of the Solar Age* for Brass, Percussion, and Synthesizer (1978); *Music for the Flute Alone* for Flute, Piano, Double Bass, and Tape (1981); *Deep Night with Tree* for Flute and Taped Flute (1986); *Journey to: Journey through* for 9 Instruments (1987); Concerto for Tap and Chamber Ensemble (1989). **VOCAL:** *Wedding Cantata* for Voices and Instruments (1963); *Variations on a Theme of Abraham Lincoln* for Soprano and Instrumental Ensemble (1973); *The Great American Nebula*, cantata for Narrator, Chorus, Orch., and Synthesizer (1976); *Follow Light* for Chorus, Percussion, and Double Bass (1981); *Celestial Intervals or Triptych* for Soprano, Tenor, and Instrumental Ensemble (N.Y., April 14, 1989); *Mass for the 21st Century* for Soloists, Chorus, and Orch. (N.Y., Aug. 10, 1994).

Moore, Dorothy Rudd, black American composer; b. New Castle, Del., June 4, 1940. She studied with Mark Fax at Howard Univ. (B.Mus., 1963), with Boulanger at the American Cons. at Fontainebleau (1963), and with Chou Wen-chung in N.Y. (1965). She then taught at the Harlem School of the Arts (1965–66), N.Y. Univ. (1969), and Bronx Community College (1971); also appeared as a singer in N.Y. and wrote poetry. In 1968 she helped to found the Soc. of Black Composers. She is married to the cellist Kermit Moore, who has given premiere performances of her works.

WORKS: OPERA: *Frederick Douglass* (1979–85). **ORCH.:** *Reflections* for Symphonic Winds (1962); Sym. (1963). **CHAMBER:** *Baroque Suite* for Cello (1965); *Adagio* for Viola and Cello (1965); *3 Pieces* for Violin and Piano (1967); *Modes* for String Quartet (1968); *Moods* for Viola and Cello (1969); Piano Trio (1970); *Dirge and Deliverance* for Cello and Piano (1971); *Night Fantasy* for Clarinet and Piano (1978); also piano pieces, including *Dream and Variations* (1974) and *A Little Whimsy* (1982). **VOCAL:** Numerous works, including song cycles (*12 Quatrains from the Rubaiyat* for Soprano and Oboe [1962], etc.) and solo songs.

Moore, Douglas (Stuart), distinguished American composer and pedagogue; b. Cutchogue, N.Y., Aug. 10, 1893; d. Greenport, Long Island, July 25, 1969. After initial musical training in N.Y., he studied with D.S. Smith and Horatio Parker at Yale Univ. (B.A., 1915; B.M., 1917). He composed several univ. and popular songs, including the football song *Good Night, Harvard*, which became a favorite among the Yale student body. After serving in the U.S. Navy, he studied organ with Tournemire and composition with d'Indy and Boulanger in Paris. He was organist at the Cleveland Museum of Art (1921–23) and at Adelbert College, Western Reserve Univ. (1923–25). During this period, he pursued training with Ernest Bloch. In 1925 he received a Pulitzer traveling scholarship, which enabled him to study in Europe. From 1926 to 1962 he taught at Barnard College and at Columbia Univ., serving as chairman of the latter's music dept. from 1940 to 1962. In 1934 he held a Guggenheim fellowship. In 1951 he won the Pulitzer Prize in Music for his opera *Giants in the Earth*. His opera *The Ballad of Baby Doe* won the N.Y. Music Critics' Circle Award in 1958. In 1941 he was elected to the National Inst. of Arts and Letters, and in 1951 to the American Academy of Arts and Letters. He was the author of the books *Listening to Music* (1932; 2nd ed., aug., 1937) and *From Madrigal to Modern Music: A Guide to Musical Style* (1942). Moore was a fine musical craftsman who applied his technical mastery to American subjects in his operas and symphonic scores. He achieved popular success with his operas *The Devil and Daniel Webster* (N.Y., May 18, 1939) and *The Ballad of Baby Doe* (Central City, Colo., July 7, 1956).

WORKS: DRAMATIC: OPERAS: *Jesse James* (1928; unfinished); *White Wings*, chamber opera (1935; Hartford, Conn., Feb. 9, 1949); *The Headless Horseman*, high school opera (1936; Bronxville, N.Y., March 4, 1937); *The Devil and Daniel Webster*, folk opera (1938; N.Y., May 18, 1939); *The Emperor's New Clothes*, children's opera (1948; N.Y., Feb. 19, 1949; rev. 1956); *Giants in the Earth* (1949; N.Y., March 28, 1951; rev. 1963); *The Ballad of Baby Doe*, folk opera (Central City, Colo., July 7, 1956); *Gallantry*, soap opera (1957; N.Y., March 19, 1958); *The Wings of the Dove* (N.Y., Oct. 12, 1961); *The Greenfield Christmas Tree*, Christmas entertainment (Baltimore, Dec. 8, 1962); *Carrie Nation* (Lawrence, Kansas, April 28, 1966). **MUSICAL COMEDY:** *Oh, Oh, Tennessee* (1925). **CHILDREN'S OPERETTA:** *Puss in Boots* (1949; N.Y., Nov. 18, 1950). **BALLET:** *Greek Games* (1930). **INCIDENTAL MUSIC TO:** plays and for the films *Power in the Land* (1940), *Youth Gets a Break*, and *Bip Goes to Town* (1941). **ORCH.:** *4 Museum Pieces* (1923; based on the organ piece); *The Pageant of P.T. Barnum*, suite (1924; Cleveland, April 15, 1926); *Moby Dick*, symphonic poem (1927); 2 syms.: No. 1, *A Symphony of Autumn* (1930) and No. 2 (1945; Paris, May 5, 1946); *Overture on an American Tune* (N.Y., Dec. 11, 1932); *Village Music*, suite (N.Y., Dec. 18, 1941); *In Memoriam*, symphonic poem (1943; Rochester, N.Y., April 27, 1944); *Farm Journal*, suite for Chamber Orch. (1947; N.Y., Jan. 19, 1948); *Cotillion*, suite for Strings (1952). **CHAMBER:** Violin Sonata (1929); String Quartet (1933); Wind Quintet (1942; rev. 1948); *Down East Suite* for Violin and Piano (1944; also for Violin and Orch.); Clarinet Quintet (1946); Piano Trio (1953). **KEYBOARD: PIANO:** *3 Contemporaries: Careful Etta, Grievin' Annie*, and *Fiddlin' Joe* (c.1935–40); *Museum Piece* (1939); Suite (1948); *4 Pieces* (1955); *Dance for a Holiday* (1957); *Prélude* (1957); *Summer Holiday* (1961). **ORGAN:** *Prélude and Fugue* (1919–22); *4 Museum Pieces* (1922; also for Orch.); *March* (1922); *Scherzo* (1923); *Passacaglia* (1939; arranged by K. Wilson as *Dirge* for Band). **VOCAL:** *Perhaps to Dream* for Women's Voices (1937); *Simon Legree* for Men's Voices and Piano (1937); *Dedication* for Chorus (1938); *Prayer for England* for Men's Voices (1940); *Prayer for the United Nations* for Alto or Baritone, Chorus, and Piano or Orch. (1943); *Western Winde*, canon for Chorus (c.1946); *Vayechulu* for Cantor, Chorus, and Organ (1947–48); *Bird's Courting Song* for Tenor, Chorus, and Piano (c.1953); *The Mysterious Cat* for Chorus (1960); *Mary's Prayer* for Soprano and Women's Voices (1962); many songs for Voice and Piano; arrangements of hymns and carols.

Moore, Earl Vincent, American music educator and composer; b. Lansing, Mich., Sept. 27, 1890; d. La Jolla, Calif., Dec. 29, 1987. He studied at the Univ. of Mich. (B.A., 1912; M.A., 1915) and later in Europe with Widor, Holst, Boult, Heger, and others. He was an organist and teacher of theory at the Univ. of Mich. (1914–23), and then director of its School of Music, while continuing to teach (was a prof. there, 1923–46); from 1946 to 1960 he was dean of the School of Music. In 1939–40 he was national director of the WPA Music Project. From 1960 to 1970 he was chairman of the music dept. at the Univ. of Houston. He was a founder-member of the National Assn. of Schools of Music and its president from 1936 to 1938. He composed parts of the Michigan Union Operas and other pieces, but is famous at the Univ. of Mich. as composer of the football song Varsity.

Moore, Gerald, renowned English piano accompanist; b. Watford, July 30, 1899; d. Penn, Buckinghamshire, March 13, 1987. He first studied with Wallis Bandey at the local music school; after the family went to Canada in 1913, he continued his studies with Michael Hambourg; then made appearances as a solo recitalist and accompanist; following his return to England (1919), he completed his training with Mark Hambourg. He began recording in 1921 and first gained distinction as accompanist to John Coates in 1925; he subsequently achieved well-nigh legendary fame as the preeminent accompanist of the day, appearing with such celebrated singers as Kathleen Ferrier, Dietrich Fischer-Dieskau, Elisabeth Schwarzkopf, Janet Baker, and others. He retired from the concert platform in 1967 but continued to make recordings. He was made a Commander of the Order of the British Empire (1954); was made an honorary D.Litt. by the Univ. of Sussex (1968) and Mus.D. by the Univ. of Cambridge (1973). As a witty account of his experiences at the piano, he publ. a sort of autobiography, *The Unashamed Accompanist* (London, 1943; rev. 1957), followed by an even more unzipped opus, *Am I Too Loud? Memoirs of an Accompanist* (London, 1962), and concluding with a somewhat nostalgic vol., *Farewell Recital: Further Memoirs* (London, 1978), and a rip-roaring sequel, *Furthermoore [sic]: Interludes in an Accompanist's Life* (London, 1983). Of a purely didactic nature are his books *Singer and Accompanist: The Performance of 50 Songs* (London, 1953), *The Schubert Song Cycles* (London, 1975), and *"Poet's Lore" and Other Schumann Cycles and Songs* (London, 1984).

Moore, Grace, popular American soprano; b. Nough, near Del Rio, Tenn., Dec. 5, 1898; d. in an airplane crash near Copenhagen, Jan. 26, 1947. She studied at the Wilson Greene School of Music in Chevy Chase, Md., and with Marafioti in N.Y.; she first appeared in musical comedy in N.Y. (1921–26); then continued her studies in Antibes with Richard Berthelemy. Upon returning to America, she made her operatic debut as Mimi at the Metropolitan Opera in N.Y. (Feb. 7, 1928), and sang there off and on until 1946; made successful appearances also at the Paris Opéra-Comique (1928), Covent Garden, London (1935), and other European centers; also sang with the Chicago City Opera (1937) and appeared in several films, including *One Night of Love* (1934). She publ. an autobiography, *You're Only Human Once* (1944). Her finest roles were Mimi, Tosca, Louise, Fiora, and Manon.

Moore, Jerrold Northrop, American editor and writer on music; b. Paterson, N.J., March 1, 1934. He studied at Swarthmore College (B.A., 1955) and Yale Univ. (M.A., 1956; Ph.D., 1959). He taught English at the Univ. of Rochester (1958–61), then was curator of historical sound recordings at Yale Univ. (1961–70). He wrote the authoritative biography *Edward Elgar: A Creative Life* (1984); was also an editor of the complete critical ed. of Elgar's works (from 1981). His other publications include *Elgar: A Life in Photographs* (1972), *Elgar on Record: The Composer and the Gramophone* (1974), *A Voice in Time: The Gramophone of Fred Gaisberg* (1976; U.S. ed. as *A Matter of Records*), *Music and Friends: Letters to Adrian Boult* (1979), *Spirit of England: Edward Elgar in His World* (1984), *Elgar and His Publishers: Letters of a Creative Life* (2 vols., 1987), *Edward Elgar: Letters of a Lifetime* (1990), and *Vaughan Williams: A Life in Photographs* (1992).

Moore, Mary (Louise) Carr, American composer and teacher; b. Memphis, Tenn., Aug. 6, 1873; d. Inglewood, Calif., Jan. 9, 1957. Her father was a cavalry officer in the U.S. Army who sang; her mother authored several theater dramas; her uncle, John Harraden Pratt, was an organist; after the family went to California (1885), she studied composition with her uncle and singing with H.B. Pasmore in San Francisco. She began her career as a teacher, composer, and singer; sang the lead role in her first operetta, *The Oracle* (San Francisco, March 19, 1894), but soon devoted herself fully to teaching and composition. She taught in Lemoore, California (1895–1901), and in Seattle (1901–15), where she founded the American Music Center (1909); after teaching in San Francisco (1915–26), she went to Los Angeles as an instructor at the Olga Steeb Piano School (1926–43) and was prof. of theory and composition at Chapman College (1928–47); was a founder of the Calif. Soc. of Composers (1936–38) and the Soc. of Native Composers (1938–44). As a composer, she devoted herself mainly to writing vocal works, particularly operas on American themes; her most important score was *Narcissa, or The Cost of Empire* (Seattle, April 22, 1912), which was awarded the David Bispham Memorial Medal.

WORKS: OPERAS: *The Oracle* (San Francisco, March 19, 1894); *Narcissa, or The Cost of Empire* (1909–11; Seattle, April 22, 1912); *The Leper* (1912); *Memories* (Seattle, Oct. 31, 1914); *Harmony* (San Francisco, May 25, 1917); *The Flaming Arrow, or The Shaft of Ku'pish-ta-ya* (1919–20; San Francisco, March 27, 1922); *David Rizzio* (1927–28; Los Angeles, May 26, 1932); *Los rubios* (Los Angeles, Sept. 10, 1931); *Legende provençale* (1929–35); *Flutes of Jade Happiness* (1932–33; Los Angeles, March 2, 1934). **ORCH.:** *Ka-mi-a-kin* (1930); Piano Concerto (1933–34); *Kidnap* (1937–38). **CHAMBER:** 3 piano trios (1895, 1906, 1941); Violin Sonata (1918–19); 2 string quartets (1926, 1930); String Trio (1936); *Brief Furlough* for Quintet (1942); some 20 pieces for Various Instruments and Piano; 57 piano pieces. **VOCAL:** 57 choral works; some 250 songs (1889–1952).

BIBL.: C. Smith and C. Richardson, *M.C. M., American Composer* (Ann Arbor, 1989).

Moorman, (Madeline) Charlotte, avant-garde American cellist; b. Little Rock, Ark., Nov. 18, 1933; d. N.Y., Nov. 8, 1991. She took a B.A. degree in music at Centenary College in Shreveport, La., before studying cello with Horace Britt at the Univ. of Texas in Austin (1956–57); then completed her training at N.Y.'s Juilliard School of Music. She was a cellist in the Boccherini Players (1958–63) and in the American Sym. Orch. in N.Y. A fascination with the avant-garde led her to found the N.Y. Avant-Garde Art Festival in 1963, with which she remained active until 1982. She first attracted attention in 1965 when she performed the *Cello Sonata No. 2 for Adults Only*. In 1967 she became something of a sensation when she performed Nam June Paik's *Opéra Sextronique* in accordance with the composer's instructions, i.e. nude from the waist up. Her performance was halted by her arrest; although she was tried and convicted for unseemly exposure, her sentence was eventually suspended and she resumed her championship of the avant-garde unhindered. Among her other notable performances were *TV Bra for Living Sculpture* (1969), which called for a bra made of 2 small televisions, and Paik's *The TV Cello* (1971), in which she played a cello made out of 3 television sets. Varèse was so taken with Moorman that he dubbed her the "Jeanne d'Arc of New Music."

Moos, Paul, German writer on music and aesthetics; b. Bad Buchau, near Ulm, March 22, 1863; d. Raeren, Belgium, Feb. 27, 1952. He studied with Thuille, Rheinberger, and others at Munich's Akademie der Tonkunst.

WRITINGS: *Moderne Musikästhetik in Deutschland: Historisch-kritische Übersicht* (Berlin and Leipzig, 1902; rev. and aug., 1922, as *Die Philosophie der Musik von Kant bis Eduard von Hartmann*); *Richard Wagner als Ästhetiker* (Berlin and Leipzig, 1906); *Die deutsche Ästhetik der Gegenwart: Mit besonderer Berucksichtigung der Musikästhetik*, I: *Die psychologische Ästhetik* (Berlin and Leipzig, 1920) and II: *Die deutsche Ästhetik der Gegenwart: Versuch einer kritischen Darstellung* (Berlin, 1931).

Mooser, R(obert) Aloys, Swiss writer on music; b. Geneva, Sept. 20, 1876; d. there, Aug. 24, 1969. He was the great-grandson of the noted Swiss organist and organ builder (Jean Pierre Joseph) Aloys Mooser (b.Niederhelfenschwyl, June 27, 1770; d. Fribourg, Dec. 19, 1839). His mother was a Russian, and he acquired the knowledge of the Russian language in childhood. He studied with his father and Otto Barblan in Geneva. In 1896 he went to St. Petersburg, where he served as organist at the French church, wrote music criticism for the *Journal de St. Petersbourg*, and made an extensive study of Russian music in the archives. He took courses with Balakirev and Rimsky-Korsakov. In 1909 he returned to Geneva and wrote music criticism for the periodical *La Suisse* (1909–62); was also founder, ed., and publisher of the periodical *Dissonances* (1923–46). His reviews were collected in the vols. *Regards sur la musique contemporaine: 1921–1946* (Lausanne, 1946); *Panorama de la musique contemporaine: 1947–1953* (Geneva, 1953); *Aspects de la musique contemporaine: 1953–1957* (Geneva, 1957); and *Visage de la musique contemporaine, 1957–1961* (Paris, 1962). He wrote the following books on Russian music: *Contribution à l'histoire de la musique russe: L'Opéra comique française en Russie au XVIIIe siècle* (Geneva, 1932; 2nd ed., 1954); *Violonistes-compositeurs italiens en Russie au XVIIIe siècle* (Milan, 1938–50); *Opéras, intermezzos, ballets, cantates, oratorios joués en Russie durant le XVIIIe siècle* (Geneva, 1945; 3rd ed., 1964); *Annales de la musique et des musiciens en Russie au XVIIIe siè-*

cle (of prime importance; 3 vols., Geneva, 1948–51); also wrote *Deux violonistes genevois: Gaspard Fritz* (1716–1783) and *Christian Haensel (1766–1850)* (Geneva, 1968).

Morales, Carlos O., Puerto Rican composer; b. San Juan, June 17, 1953. He studied at the Cons. of Music in Puerto Rico, graduating with degrees in guitar performance (1976) and music education (1977); subsequently taught there; also studied at the Accademia Musicale Chigiana in Siena. In 1979 he went to California, where he continued his composition studies. He is known primarily for his transcriptions to guitar of music originally written for the Renaissance laud. He was a prof. of music history at the Interamerican Univ. of Puerto Rico in Germán. Among his original compositions are *Thanks after Communion* for Men's Chorus (1980); *Etapas* for Flute (1981); 2 symphonic poems, *Guanina* (1981) and *La Campana del Ingenio* (1984); and numerous works for solo guitar, including *Nocturno* (1984) and *Canción de Cuna* (1985).

Morales, Olallo (Juan Magnus), Spanish-born Swedish conductor, music critic, and composer; b. Almería (of a Spanish father and Swedish mother), Oct. 15, 1874; d. Tällberg, April 29, 1957. Taken to Sweden as a child, he received his education there, first at Göteborg, then at the Stockholm Cons., with W. Stenhammar and others (1891–99), and in Berlin with H. Urban (composition) and Carreño (piano). In 1901 he returned to Sweden; was conductor of the Göteborg Orch. (1905–09); was a teacher (1917–21) and a prof. (1921–39) at the Stockholm Cons.; was also secretary of the Royal Academy of Music (1918–40). With T. Norlind, he publ. *Kungliga muskaliska akademien* (Royal Academy of Music; Stockholm; vol. I, 1771–1921 [1921]; vol. II, 1921–31 [1932]; vol. III, 1931–41 [1942]); also publ. a handbook on conducting (Stockholm, 1946). His works include a Sym. (1901); several overtures; Violin Concerto (1943); String Quartet; Piano Sonata; *Balada andaluza* for Piano (1946); *Nostalgia* (1920) and other character pieces for piano; choral works; songs.

Moralt, Rudolf, esteemed German composer, nephew of **Richard (Georg) Strauss**; b. Munich, Feb. 26, 1902; d. Vienna, Dec. 16, 1958. He studied in Munich at the Univ. and the Academy of Music, his principal teachers being Courvoisier and Schmid-Lindner. After serving as répétiteur at the Bavarian State Opera in Munich (1919–23), he was conductor at the Kaiserslautern Stadtische Oper (1923–28; 1932–34) and music director of the German Theater in Brno (1932–34); then conducted opera in Braunschweig (1934–36) and Graz (1937–40); subsequently was a principal conductor at the Vienna State Opera (1940–58); also appeared as a guest conductor in Europe. In addition to his natural affinity for the music of his uncle, he also conducted fine performances of Mozart, Wagner, Johann Strauss, and Pfitzner.

Moran, Robert (Leonard), American composer; b. Denver, Jan. 8, 1937. He studied piano; went to Vienna in 1957 and took lessons in 12-tone composition with Apostel. Returning to America, he enrolled at Mills College in Oakland, California, where he attended seminars of Berio and Milhaud (M.A., 1963); completed his training with Haubenstock-Ramati in Vienna (1963); also painted in the manner of Abstract Expressionism. He was active in avant-garde music circles; with Howard Hersh, he was founder and co-director of the San Francisco Cons.'s New Music Ensemble; was composer-in-residence at Portland (Oreg.) State Univ. (1972–74) and at Northwestern Univ. (1977–78), where he led its New Music Ensemble; also appeared extensively as a pianist in the U.S. and Europe in programs of contemporary music. In his compositions, he combines the "found art" style with aleatory techniques; some of his works are in graphic notation animated by a surrealistic imagination.

WORKS: DRAMATIC: OPERAS: *Let's Build a Nut House,* chamber opera in memory of Paul Hindemith (San Jose, April 19, 1969); *Divertissement No. 3: A Lunchbag Opera* for Paper Bags and Instruments (BBC-TV, 1971); *Metamenagerie,* department store window opera (1974); *Hitler: Geschichten aus der Zukunft* (1981); *Erlösung dem Erlöser,* music drama for Tape Loops and Performers (1982); *The Juniper Tree,* children's opera (1985; in collaboration with P. Glass); *Desert of Roses* (Houston, Feb. 1992). **BALLETS:** *Spin Again* for Amplified Harpsichord(s) and Electric Keyboards (1980); *Chorale Variations: 10 Miles High over Albania* for 8 Harps (1983). **OTHER DRAMATIC:** *Durch Wüsten und Wolken* for Shadow Puppets and Instruments (1975); *Marketmenagerie* for Children and Musique Concrète (1975); *Es war einmal,* children's show for Film, Slides, and Musique Concrete (1976); *Music for Gamelan,* incidental music (1978); *Am 29. 11. 1780* for Tape and Dancers (1979). **ORCH.:** *Interiors* for Orch., Chamber Orch., or Percussion Ensemble (1964; San Francisco, April 12, 1965); *Bombardments No. 2* for 1 to 5 Percussion (1964); *L'Après-midi du Dracoula* for Any Group of Instruments capable of producing Any Kind of Sound (1966); *Elegant Journey with Stopping Points of Interest* for Any Ensemble (1967); *Jewel-encrusted Butterfly Wing Explosions* (1968); *Silver and the Circle of Messages* for Chamber Orch. (San Francisco, April 24, 1970); *Emblems of Passage* for 2 Orchs. (1974); *Angels of Silence* for Viola and Chamber Orch. (1975); *Enantiodromia* for 8 Orchs. and Dancers (1977). **CHAMBER:** *4 Visions* for Flute, Harp, and String Quartet (1964); *Eclectic Boogies* for 13 Percussionists (N.Y., Jan. 14, 1965); *Within the Momentary Illumination* for 2 Harps, Electric Guitar, Timpani, and Brass (Tokyo, Dec. 1, 1965); *Scream Kiss No. 1* for Harpsichord and Stereophonic Tape (1968); *Evening Psalm of Dr. Dracula* for Prepared Piano and Tape (1973); *The Last Station of the Albatross* for 1 to 8 Instruments (1978); *BASHA* for 4 Amplified Clavichords (1983); *Survivor from Darmstadt* for Bass Oboes (1984). **OTHER:** *Smell Piece for Mills College* for Frying Pans and Foods (Mills College, Nov. 20, 1967; originally intended to produce a conflagration sufficiently thermal to burn down the college); *39 Minutes* for 39 Autos for 30 Skyscrapers, 39 Auto Horns, Moog Synthesizer, and Players, employing 100,000 Persons, directed from atop Twin Peaks in San Francisco, and making use of Autos, Airplanes, Searchlights, and local Radio and Television Stations (San Francisco, Aug. 20, 1969); *Titus* for Amplified Automobile and Players (1969); *Hallelujah,* "a joyous phenomenon with fanfares" for Marching Bands, Drum and Bugle Corps, Church Choruses, Organs, Carillons, Rock-'n'-Roll Bands, Television Stations, Automobile Horns, and Any Other Sounding Implements, commissioned by Lehigh Univ. for the city of Bethlehem, Pa., with the participation of its entire population of 72,320 inhabitants (Bethlehem, April 23, 1971); *Pachelbel Promenade* for Guitar Ensemble, Folk Instruments, String Ensemble, and Jazz Ensemble (1975); *From the Market to Asylum* for Performers (1982); *Music for a Fair* (1984).

Moravec, Ivan, distinguished Czech pianist and pedagogue; b. Prague, Nov. 9, 1930. He studied with Grünfeld at the Prague Cons. (graduated, 1948); after further training with Štěpánova-Kurzova in Prague (1952–53), he attended Michelangeli's master classes in Arezzo (1957, 1958). He made his debut with the Prague Radio (1946); later toured in Europe, making his London debut in 1959; first appeared in the U.S. as soloist with the Cleveland Orch. in N.Y. (Jan. 30, 1964). He taught at the Prague Academy of Music (from 1967), where he headed its master class in piano (from 1969). Moravec is particularly noted for his performances of the standard 19th- and 20th-century repertoires.

Morawetz, Oskar, significant Czech-born Canadian composer; b. Světlá nad Sázavou, Jan. 17, 1917. He studied with Jaroslav Křička at the Univ. of Prague (1933–36); after the invasion of Czechoslovakia by the Nazis in 1938, he went to Vienna, where he studied with Julius Isserlis, and then to Paris, where he had lessons with Lévy; emigrated to Canada in 1940, becoming a naturalized citizen in 1946; completed his training at the Univ. of Toronto (B.M., 1944; D.Mus., 1953). He taught at the Royal Cons. of Music of Toronto (1946–51) and at the Univ. of Toronto (1951–82). In 1989 he received the Order of Canada. His music is Classical in format, Romantic in spirit, impressionistic in coloring, and modernistic in harmonic usage.

WORKS: ORCH.: *Carnival Overture* (1945; Montreal, July 1, 1947); *Divertimento* for Strings (1948; rev. 1954); 2 syms.: No. 1 (1950–53; 1st complete perf., Toronto, March 5, 1956; each movement is titled for separate perf.: *Fantasy, Dirge,* and *Scherzo*) and No. 2 (1959; Toronto, Feb. 2, 1960); *Overture to a Fairy Tale* (Halifax, Feb. 8, 1957); *Capriccio* (1960); Piano Concerto (1962; Montreal, April 23, 1963); *Sinfonietta* for Strings (1963; rev. 1983, 1989); *Passacaglia on a Bach Chorale* (Toronto, Nov. 24, 1964); *Sinfonietta* for Winds and Percussion (1965; Montreal, Feb. 22, 1966); Concerto for Brass Quintet and Chamber Orch. (Toronto, March 28, 1968); *Memorial to Martin Luther King,* elegy for Cello and Orch. (1968; the last movement employs the popular spiritual *Free at Last*; rev. 1973); *Reflections after a Tragedy* (1968); Harp Concerto (1976); Concerto for Clarinet and Chamber Orch. (1989). **CHAMBER:** 5 string quartets (1944; 1952–55; 1959; 1978; 1990); Duo for Violin and Piano (1947; rev. 1959); 3 violin sonatas (1956; 1965, rev. 1976; 1985); Trio for Flute, Oboe, and Harpsichord or Piano (1960); *2 Fantasies* for Cello and Piano (1962; rev. 1970); *2 Preludes* for Violin and Piano (1965); Flute Sonata (1980); Horn Sonata (1980); Oboe Sonata (1980–81); Clarinet Sonata (1981); Bassoon Sonata (1981); Sonata for Viola and Harp (1985–86); Trumpet Sonata (1986). **PIANO:** *Sonata tragica* (1945); *Ballade* (1946; rev. 1982); *Scherzo* (1947); *Fantasy in D Minor* (1948); *Fantasy on a Hebrew Theme* (1951); *Scherzino* (1953); *Fantasy, Elegy and Toccata* (1956); *10 Preludes* (1961); *Suite* (1968); *Fantasy* (1973); *4 Contrasting Moods* (1985–86). **VOCAL:** *Keep Us Free* for Chorus and Orch. (1951); *From the Diary of Anne Frank* for Soprano or Mezzo-soprano, and Orch. (CBC, May 20, 1970); *A Child's Garden of Verses* for Mezzo-soprano or Alto or Baritone and Orch., after R.L. Stevenson (Toronto, Feb. 10, 1973); *Psalm 22: God, Why Have You Forsaken Me?* for Baritone or Mezzo-soprano or Contralto, and Piano or Orch. (1980; orch. version, Toronto, Jan. 4, 1984); *5 Biblical Songs* for Chorus (1981; Vancouver, Sept. 12, 1982); solo songs.

Morawski-Dąbrowa, Eugeniusz, Polish composer and pedagogue; b. Warsaw, Nov. 2, 1876; d. there, Oct. 23, 1948. He was a student of Noskowski at the Warsaw Music Inst., and then of Gédalge (counterpoint) and Chevillard (orchestration) in Paris. In 1930 he became director of the Poznań Cons. From 1932 to 1939 he was director and prof. of composition at the Warsaw Cons. His music followed the precepts of late Romanticism, He wrote the operas *Aspazja, Lilla Weneda,* and *Salammbô*; ballets; 6 syms.; 2 piano concertos; Violin Concerto; symphonic poems; 7 string quartets; 2 violin sonatas; 8 piano sonatas.

Mordden, Ethan, American writer on music; b. Heavensville, Pa., Jan. 27, 1949. He studied piano at an early age; was educated in Quaker schools, including Friends Academy in Locust Valley, N.Y.; then studied at the Univ. of Pa. (B.A. in history, 1969). He worked as a musical director and coach in N.Y. (1971–74), then was assistant ed. of *Opera News* (1974–76); also was a visiting fellow at Yale Univ. (1980). He is a regular contributor to the *New Yorker*, won a National Magazine Award in 1989; also wrote for the *N.Y. Times* and *Christopher Street,* among other publications. In addition to his numerous books on music, film, and theater, he publ. fiction on gay life, especially the *Buddies Trilogy* (*I've a Feeling We're Not in Kansas Anymore* [1985], *Buddies* [1986], and *Everybody Loves You* [1988]). He also composed *Reminiscences de Mahagonny* for Piano (1986).

WRITINGS: *Better Foot Forward: The Story of America's Musical Theatre* (1976); *Opera in the Twentieth Century* (1978); *That Jazz!: An Idiosyncratic Social History of the American Twenties* (1978); *A Guide to Orchestral Music* (1979); *The Splendid Art of Opera: A Concise History* (1980); *The Hollywood Musical* (1983); *Demented: The World of the Opera Diva* (1985); *Opera Anecdotes* (1986); *A Guide to Opera Recordings* (1987).

Moreau, Léon, French composer; b. Brest, July 13, 1870; d. Paris, April 11, 1946. He studied at the Paris Cons.; won the Grand Prix de Rome in 1899. Among his works were the operas *Myriade* and *Pierrot décoré*; the symphonic poems *Sur la mer lointaine* and *Dionysos*; Piano Concerto; many songs.

Morel, (Joseph Raoul) François (d'Assise), Canadian composer, teacher, pianist, and conductor; b. Montreal, March 14, 1926. After private instruction in piano (1935–43), he pursued his training at the Cons. de Musique de Québec à Montréal (1944–53) with Champagne (composition), Papineau-Couture (acoustics), Delorme (harmony, counterpoint, and fugue), and Letondal, Malépart, and Trudel (piano). He also received some training in conducting from Gagnier. From 1954 he was active in contemporary music circles. In 1956 he helped found the new music group Musique de notre temps. Between 1956 and 1979 he was active with the CBC Radio. After teaching at the Inst. Nazareth in Montreal (1959–61), he was director of the Académie de musique de Québec (1972–78). In 1979–80 he taught at the Univ. of Montreal. He was on the faculty of Laval Univ. in Montreal from 1979. Morel's music parallels the aesthetic fashions of modern times, from Debussyan coloristic imagism to motoric neo-Classicism to the organized sound world of Varèse with a circumspect handling of serial procedures.

WORKS: ORCH.: *Esquisse* (Montreal, Oct. 7, 1947); *Suite pour petite orchestre,* renamed *Dyptique* (1948; rev. 1956); *Antiphonie* (1953); *Boréal* (1959); *Rituel de l'espace* (1959; Montreal, April 6, 1960); *L'Étoile noire (Tombeau de Borduas)* (Montreal, March 13, 1962); *Trajectoire* (Montreal, April 20, 1967); *Neumes d'espace et Reliefs* (Edmonton, Oct. 29, 1967); *Prismes-Anamorphoses* (1967); *Radiance* for Small Orch. (1972); *Melisma* for Piano and Orch. (1980). **BAND:** *Aux marges du silence* (1982); *Aux couleurs du ciel* (1985–87); *De subitement lointain* (1989). **CHAMBER:** 2 string quartets (1952, 1963); *Cassation* for Woodwind Septet (1954); *Symphonies* for Brass and Percussion (1956); *Rythmologue* for 6 or 8 Percussion (1957; rev. 1970); Brass Quintet (1962); *Étude en forme de toccate* for 2 Percussion (1965); *Nuvattuq* for Flute (1967); *Départs* for 2 Percussion, Guitar, Harp, and 14 Strings (1969); *IIKKII (Froidure)* for 18 Instruments (1971); *Me Duele España* for Guitar (1975; rev. 1977); *Duolet I* (1982) and *II* (1988) for 2 Flutes; *L'Oiseau-Demain* for 12 Flutes, 2 Clarinets, and 3 Percussion (1982); *Divergences* for Violin and Guitar (1983); *Talea (Couleur)* for Flute, Oboe, and Clarinet (1984); *Area* for Brass Ensemble (1986); *Fulgurane I* for Flute, Horn, Cello, Piano, Harp, and 2 Percussion (1986) and *II* for Alto Flute, Oboe d'amore, Clarinet, Horn, Violin, Viola, Cello, Piano, Harp, and 2 Percussion (1990); *Lyre de crystal* for 6 Percussion (1986); *Les Voix de l'ombre* for Brass Ensemble (1987); *Figures-Segments-Ellipses* for 2 Clarinets and String Quartet (1990); *Paysage dépaysé* for 2 Violins, Viola, and 2 Cellos (1990); *Distance intime* for Flute and Piano (1991); piano pieces; organ music.

Morel, Jean (Paul), French-American conductor and pedagogue; b. Abbeville, Jan. 10, 1903; d. N.Y., April 14, 1975. He was a student of Philipp (piano), N. Gallon (theory), Emmanuel (music history), Pierné (composition), and Hahn (lyric repertoire) in Paris. From 1921 to 1936 he taught at the American Cons. in Fontainebleau. He conducted the Orchestre National (1936–39) and the Orchestre Symphonique de Paris (1938). In 1939 he emigrated to the U.S. He taught at Brooklyn College of the City Univ. of N.Y. (1940–43). From 1949 to 1971 he was a teacher and conductor at the Juilliard School of Music in N.Y., where he proved influential in producing a generation of musicians. On Nov. 12, 1944, he made his debut at the N.Y. City Opera conducting *La Traviata.* He made his Metropolitan Opera debut in N.Y. on Dec. 21, 1956, conducting *La Périchole.* He remained on the roster there until 1962, and then returned for the 1967–68 and 1969–71 seasons.

Morell, Barry, American tenor; b. N.Y., March 30, 1927. He received his training in N.Y. On March 26, 1955, he made his first appearance at the N.Y. City Opera as Pinkerton. He chose that same role for his Metropolitan Opera debut in N.Y. on Nov. 1, 1958, and continued to make occasional appearances there until 1979. As a guest artist, he also sang in Europe and South America. He was best known for his roles in Italian opera.

Morelli (real name, **Zanelli**), **Carlo,** Chilean baritone; b. Valparaiso (of an Italian father and a Chilean mother), Dec. 25, 1897; d. Mexico City, May 12, 1970. He studied voice in Bologna with Angelo Queize and in Florence with Leopoldo Mugnone. He sang at La Scala, Milan (1922); toured South America (1925–31). He made his first U.S. appearence with the Chicago Opera in 1932; made his debut at the Metropolitan Opera in N.Y. on Dec. 21, 1935, as Marcello; remained there until 1940; then sang with the San Carlo Opera at the City Center, N.Y. (1940–49). In 1949 he settled in Mexico.

Morena (real name, **Meyer**), **Berta,** noted German soprano; b. Mannheim, Jan. 27, 1878; d. Rottach-Egern, Oct. 7, 1952. Her buxom beauty attracted the attention of the famous painter von Lenbach, who persuaded her to study voice with Sophie Röhr-Brajnin and Aglaja von Orgeni in Munich; after additional training with Regina de Sales, she made her operatic debut as Agathe in *Der Freischütz* at the Munich Court Opera (1898); remained on its roster until 1927. She made her American debut with the Metropolitan Opera in N.Y. as Sieglinde (March 4, 1908), remaining on its roster until 1909; then returned from 1910 to 1912 and in 1924–25. She was regarded in Germany as an intelligent and musicianly singer, excelling particularly in Wagnerian roles, including Elisabeth, Elsa, Eva, Isolde, and the 3 Brünnhildes.

BIBL.: A. Vogl, *B. M. und ihre Kunst* (Munich,1919).

Moreno (Andrade), Segundo Luis, Ecuadorian musicologist and composer; b. Cotacachi, Aug. 3, 1882; d. Quito, Nov. 18, 1972. He played the clarinet in a civil band in Quito. He studied at the Quito Cons.; then was active as a military band leader in various localities in Ecuador; in 1937, took over the newly established Cons. Nacional de Música in Cuenca; later was director of the Guayaquil Cons. (1940–45). He composed mostly for military band; many of his pieces celebrate various patriotic events in Ecuador, as the cantata *La emancipación* (1920), the overture *9 de Julio* (1925), and various pieces on native motifs, among them *3 suites ecuatorianas* for Orch. (1921, 1944, 1945). He publ. *Música y danzas autoctonas del Ecuador* (Quito, 1949) and *La música de los Incas* (Quito, 1957).

Morera, Enrique (Enric), Spanish composer; b. Barcelona, May 22, 1865; d. there, March 11, 1942. As a child, he was taken to Argentina, and studied in Buenos Aires; then took courses at the Brussels Cons. Returning to Barcelona, he studied piano with Albéniz and harmony with Felipe Pedrell. In 1895 he founded the choral society Catalunya Nova, which he conducted until 1909; then taught at the Escuela Municipal de Música in Barcelona (1910–28). He was an ardent propagandist of Catalan music, and wrote a number of songs to Catalan words; also collected 193 melodies of popular origin. His opera *Emporium*, originally to a Catalan text, was performed first in Italian (Barcelona, Jan. 20, 1906); he wrote more than 50 other stage works (lyric comedies, zarzuelas, operettas, intermezzos, etc.); several symphonic poems, including *Introducció a l'Atlántida* (1893); Cello Concerto (1917); *Poema de la nit i del dia* for Orch. (1919); chamber music; much choral music; many sardanas.

BIBL.: I. Iglesias, *Enric M.* (Barcelona, 1921); J. Pena, *Enric M.* (Barcelona, 1937).

Mörike, Eduard, German conductor; b. Stuttgart, Aug. 16, 1877; d. Berlin, March 14, 1929. He was a great-nephew of the poet Eduard Friedrich Mörike. He studied at the Leipzig Cons. with Ruthard and Sitt, and received private piano instruction from Siloti. In 1899 he went to the U.S. and made appearances as a pianist. After working as a coach at the Metropolitan Opera in N.Y., he returned to Germany and conducted in various theaters. From 1906 to 1909 he was an assistant conductor at the Bayreuth Festivals. He held the post of 1st conductor at the Deutsches Opernhaus in Berlin from 1912 to 1922, and also made appearances as a guest conductor with the Berlin Phil. He subsequently was active as a conductor in Europe and the U.S. From 1924 until his death he was chief conductor of the Dresden Phil.

Morillo, Roberto García, Argentine composer and music critic; b. Buenos Aires, Jan. 22, 1911. He studied composition with Aguirre and Juan José Castro; later took courses with Gaito and Ugarte. From 1926 to 1930 he was in Paris. Returning to Argentina, he taught at the National Cons. in Buenos Aires and wrote music criticism for *La Nación*. He publ. monographs on Mussorgsky (1943), Rimsky-Korsakov (1945), and Carlos Chávez (1960); also *Julian Bautista en la música española contemporánea* (1949). His music is marked by propulsive rhythms and a strong sense of dissonant counterpoint.

WORKS: ORCH.: *Berseker*, symphonic poem (Buenos Aires, Dec. 29, 1932); Piano Concerto (Buenos Aires, Nov. 7, 1940); *The Fall of the House of Usher*, after Poe (Buenos Aires, May 12, 1943); 3 syms. (1948, 1955, 1961); *Variaciones olímpicas* (1958); *3 pinturas de Piet Mondrian* (1960); *Ciclo de Dante Alighieri* for Chamber Orch. (1970); *Dionysos* (1971); *Concerto a 9* for 3 Clarinets and Strings (1943). **CHAMBER:** Quartet for Violin, Cello, Clarinet, and Piano (1937); *Las pinturas negras de Goya* for Piano, Violin, Cello, Flute, Clarinet, and Bassoon (Montevideo, May 27, 1940); String Quartet (1951). **PIANO:** 5 sonatas (1935–62); *Divertimento sobre temas de Paul Klee* for Wind Quintet (1967; orchestrated 1971). **VOCAL:** *Cantata de los caballeros* for Soprano and Orch., after García Lorca (1965); *Cantata fèstiva* for Chorus (1971). **OTHER:** Film music.

Morini (real name, **Siracusano), Erica,** Austrian-born American violinist; b. Vienna, Jan. 5, 1904; d. N.Y., Oct. 30, 1995. Her father was Italian and her mother Austrian. She first studied at her father's music school in Vienna. At 7, she became a student of Ševčik at the Vienna Cons. She was 12 when she made her professional debut in Vienna, and then was invited to appear as a soloist with the Leipzig Gewandhaus Orch. and the Berlin Phil. On Jan. 26, 1921, she made her U.S. debut as soloist in 3 concertos with Bodanzky and the Metropolitan Opera orch. in N.Y. She subsequently appeared as a soloist with various U.S. orchs. until returning to Europe in 1924 to pursue her career. After the Anschluss in 1938, she emigrated to the U.S. and in 1943 became a naturalized American citizen. After World War II ended in 1945, she toured extensively at home and abroad.

Morison, Elsie (Jean), Australian soprano; b. Ballarat, Aug. 15, 1924. She studied with Clive Carey at the Melbourne Cons. She made her London debut at the Royal Albert Hall in London in 1948; then sang with the Sadler's Wells Opera (1948–54) and at Covent Garden (1953–62). She married **Rafael Kubelik** in 1963. Her roles included Pamina, Susanna, Marzelline, Micaëla, and Anne Trulove.

Moroi, Makoto, Japanese composer and teacher, son of **Saburo Moroi;** b. Tokyo, March 12, 1930. He was a student of his father and of Ikenouchi at the Tokyo National Univ. of Fine Arts and Music (1948–52), and subsequently devoted himself to composition and teaching. He has utilized ancient Japanese elements, serial procedures, and sonorism in developing his compositional style.

WORKS: ORCH.: *Composition 1* (1951–53), *2* (1958), and *5, Ode to Arnold Schoenberg*, for Chamber Orch. (1961); *Suite classique* (1953); *Suite concertante* for Violin and Orch. (1963); Piano Concerto (1966); *Vision of Cain* (1966); Sym. (Tokyo, Nov. 7, 1968); Concerto for Shakuhachi, Strings, and Percussion (1970–71); Sym. for Voice, Percussion, Japanese Instruments, and Tape (1972); Sinfonia concertante No. 3, *Demise of Mythologies*, for Marimba, Sanjū-gen, Organ, and Orch. (1992). **CHAMBER:** *Musica da camera 3* for Viola and Wind Quintet (1951) and *4* for String Quartet (1954); *Ordre* for Cello and Piano (1958); *5 epigrammes* for 7 Instruments (1964); *Toccata, Sarabande, and Tarantella* for Strings and Piano (1964); *Les Farces* for Violin (1970); piano music; pieces for Solo Japanese

Instruments. **VOCAL:** *Développements rarefiants* for Soprano and Chamber Group (1957); *Composition 3* for Narrator, Men's Chorus, and Orch. (1958) and *4* for Narrator, 3 Speaking Sopranos, Chorus, and Orch. (1960); *Stars of Pythagoras* for Narrator, Chorus, Chamber Orch., and Tape (1959); *Cantata da camera 1* for Narrator, Men's Chorus, Ondes Martenot, Harpsichord, and 3 Percussionists (1959) and *2, Blue Cylinder*, for Narrator, Soprano, Chorus, and Chamber Orch. (1959); *The Red Cocoon* for Narrator, Pantomime, 2 Choruses, Orch., and Tape (1960); *Phaeton, the Coachman* for Narrator, Voice, Chorus, and Tape (1965); *Izumo, My Home!* for Baritone, Soprano, Chorus, Orch., and Tape (1970).

Moroi, Saburo, Japanese composer, teacher, and writer on music, father of **Makoto Moroi**; b. Tokyo, Aug. 7, 1903; d. there, March 24, 1977. He studied literature at the Univ. of Tokyo (1926–28), and later took lessons in composition with Max Trapp, orchestration with Gmeindl, and piano with Robert Schmidt at the Hochschule für Musik in Berlin (1932–34). Upon returning to Japan, he was active as a music teacher; was inspector of music and adult education for the Ministry of Culture (1946–64) and director of Tokyo's Gakuen Academy of Music (1967–77); among his students, in addition to his son, were Dan and Irino. Among his numerous publications are *Junsui tai i ho* (Strict Counterpoint; Tokyo, 1949) and *Gakushiki no kenkyū* (Historical Research on Musical Forms; 5 vols., Tokyo, 1957–67).

WORKS: ORCH.: 2 piano concertos (1933, 1977); 5 syms.: No. 1 (Berlin, Oct. 2, 1934), No. 2 (Tokyo, Oct. 12, 1938), No. 3 for Organ and Orch. (Tokyo, May 26, 1950), No. 4 (Tokyo, March 26, 1951), and No. 5 (Tokyo, 1971); Cello Concerto (1936); Bassoon Concerto (1937); Violin Concerto (1939); 2 Symphonic Movements (1942); *Sinfonietta* (1943); *Allegro* for Piano and Orch. (1947). **CHAMBER:** Violin Sonata (1930); String Quartet (1933); Piano Quartet (1935); Viola Sonata (1935); Flute Sonata (1937); String Sextet (1939); String Trio (1940). **PIANO:** 2 sonatas (1933, 1940); *Preludio ed Allegro giocoso* (1971). **VOCAL:** *2 Songs* for Soprano and Orch. (1935); *A Visit of the Sun*, fantasy-oratorio (Tokyo, June 30, 1969).

Moross, Jerome, American composer; b. N.Y., Aug. 1, 1913; d. Miami, July 25, 1983. He studied at the Juilliard School of Music in N.Y. (1931–32) and at N.Y. Univ. (graduated, 1932). He became associated with various ballet groups and wrote a number of scores for the dance, most of them on American subjects, all of them in a vivid folklike manner. In 1940 he went to Hollywood as an arranger; collaborated with Copland on the score for *Our Town*. He held 2 Guggenheim fellowships (1947, 1948). His first film score was *Close Up* (1948); his other film scores included *The Cardinal, The Proud Rebel*, and *The Big Country*. For Broadway he wrote music for *Parade* (1935). His works for the dance included *Paul Bunyan* (1934); *American Patterns* (1937); *Frankie and Johnny* (1938); *Guns and Castanets* (1939); *The Eccentricities of Davy Crockett* (1946); *Robin Hood* (1946). He also wrote operas: *Susanna and the Elders* (1940); *Willie the Weeper* (1945); *The Golden Apple* (1948–50); *Gentleman, Be Seated!* (1955–56; N.Y., Oct. 10, 1963); *Sorry, Wrong Number* (1977); a ballet suite, *The Last Judgment* (1953); several orch. works, including *Beguine* (N.Y., Nov. 21, 1934); *A Tall Story* (N.Y., Sept. 25, 1938); and a Sym. (1941–42; Seattle, Oct. 18, 1943); chamber music, including Sonatina for Clarinet Choir (1966); Sonatina for Strings, Double Bass, and Piano (1967); Sonatina for Brass Quintet (1968); Sonatina for Woodwind Quintet (1970); Sonatina for Divers Instruments (1972); Sonata for Piano Duet and String Quartet (1975); and Concerto for Flute and String Quartet (1978).

Morris, Harold, American composer, teacher, and pianist; b. San Antonio, March 17, 1890; d. N.Y., May 6, 1964. He studied at the Univ. of Texas (B.A.) and the Cincinnati Cons. (M.M., 1922). He was on the faculty of the Juilliard School of Music (1922–39) and Teachers College, Columbia Univ. (1935–46). He was one of the principal founders of the American Music Guild in N.Y. (1921). In his music, he revealed himself as a Romanticist; in the main direction of his creative development, he was influenced by Scriabin. Many of his works were of programmatic content; some of them included American thematic material.

WORKS: ORCH.: *Poem*, after Tagore's *Gitanjali* (1915; Cincinnati, Nov. 29, 1918); *Dum-A-lum*, variations on a Negro spiritual for Chamber Orch. (1925); 3 syms.: No. 1, after Browning's *Prospice* (1925), No. 2, *Victory* (1943; Chicago, Dec. 23, 1952), and No. 3, *Amaranth*, after E.A. Robinson (1946; Houston, March 13, 1948); Piano Concerto on 2 Negro Themes (1927; Boston, Oct. 23, 1931); Suite for Chamber Orch. (1927; N.Y., Nov. 1, 1941); Violin Concerto (1938; N.Y., May 25, 1939); *Passacaglia and Fugue* (1939); *American Epic* (1942); *Heroic Overture* (1943); *Passacaglia, Adagio, and Finale* (1955). **CHAMBER:** 2 piano trios (1917, 1933); Violin Sonata (1919); 2 string quartets (1928, 1937); 2 piano quintets (1929, 1937); Suite for Piano and Strings (1943); also many works for solo piano, including 4 sonatas (1915, 1915, 1920, 1939) and *Ballade* (1938).

Morris, James (Peppler), outstanding American bass-baritone; b. Baltimore, Jan. 10, 1947. After studies with a local teacher, he won a scholarship to the Univ. of Maryland; concurrently received invaluable instruction from Rosa Ponselle; continued his studies with Frank Valentino at the Peabody Cons. of Music in Baltimore (1966–68). He made his debut as Crespel in *Les Contes d'Hoffmann* with the Baltimore Civic Opera (1967). After further training with Nicola Moscona at the Philadelphia Academy of Vocal Arts (1968–70), he made his Metropolitan Opera debut in N.Y. as the King in *Aida* on Jan. 7, 1971; appeared with the Opera Orch. of N.Y. and sang widely in Europe. In 1975 he scored a notable success as Don Giovanni at the Metropolitan. Although closely associated with the Italian and French repertoires, he appeared as Wotan in *Die Walküre* at the Baltimore Civic Opera in 1984; subsequently sang that role in the San Francisco Opera's *Ring* cycle in 1985, eliciting extraordinary critical acclaim. In 1986 he appeared at the Salzburg Festival as Mozart's Guglielmo and Figaro. In 1990 he sang Méphistophélès in Cincinnati and at the Metropolitan Opera, where he also appeared as Wotan, and as the Wanderer in *Siegfried* at London's Covent Garden. His other roles include Count Almaviva, Philip II, the Dutchman, the 4 villains in *Les Contes d'Hoffmann*, Timur in *Le Roi de Lahore*, Scarpia, and Claggart in *Billy Budd*. In 1995 he appeared as Iago at the Metropolitan Opera.

Morris, Joan (Clair), American mezzo-soprano; b. Portland, Oreg., Feb. 10, 1943. She studied voice with Lyle Moore at Gonzaga Univ. (1963–65), and received training in speech and voice from Clifford Jackson, first at the American Academy of Dramatic Arts (diploma, 1968), and then privately (1968–73); also had private instruction from Frederica Schmitz-Svevo in N.Y. (1968–74). In 1975 she married **William Bolcom**, with whom she subsequently appeared regularly in concerts. Morris became notably successful as an interpreter of both serious scores and popular music, ranging from the early American period to works by Bolcom. In 1983 she was featured in the PBS-TV special, *Fascinating Rhythms*. In 1987 she appeared at Weill Recital Hall at N.Y.'s Carnegie Hall. From 1981 she taught at the Univ. of Mich.

Morris, R(eginald) O(wen), English composer and pedagogue; b. York, March 3, 1886; d. London, Dec. 14, 1948. He studied with Charles Wood at the Royal College of Music in London, where he later taught (1920–26). After teaching at the Curtis Inst. of Music in Philadelphia (1926–28), he again taught at the Royal College of Music (1928–48). He became best known as a teacher, serving as a discerning mentor to many notable students. He was the brother-in-law of **Ralph Vaughan Williams**.

WORKS: ORCH.: Violin Concerto (1930); *Concerto piccolo* for 2 Violins and String Orch. (1930); Sym. (1935). **CHAMBER:** *Fantasy* for String Quartet (1922); other chamber works. **VOCAL:** Songs; folk-song arrangements.

WRITINGS (all publ. in London unless otherwise given):

Contrapuntal Technique in the 16th Century (Oxford, 1922); *Foundations of Practical Harmony and Counterpoint* (1925); with H. Ferguson, *Preparatory Exercises in Score Reading* (1931); *Figured Harmony at the Keyboard* (1931); *The Structure of Music* (1935); *Introduction to Counterpoint* (1944); *Oxford Harmony* (1946).

BIBL.: W. Mellers, "The Music of R.O. M.," *Musical Opinion*, LXIV (1940–41); E. Rubbra, "R.O. M.: An Appreciation," *Music & Letters* (Jan. 1949).

Morris, Robert (Daniel), English-born American composer, teacher, and music theorist; b. Cheltenham, Oct. 19, 1943. He studied composition at the Eastman School of Music in Rochester, N.Y. (B.Mus., 1965), and at the Univ. of Mich. (M.Mus., 1966; D.M.A., 1969). He taught at the Univ. of Hawaii (1968–69); then was on the faculty of Yale Univ. (1969–77), where he was director of the electronic music studio (1972–77) and chairman of the composition dept. (1973–77). From 1976 to 1980 he served on the staff of the music dept. of the Univ. of Pittsburgh. In 1980 he joined the faculty at the Eastman School of Music, where he was prof. of theory and composition from 1985. In 1992 he became chairman of the editorial board of *Perspectives of New Music*. He publ. *Composition with Pitch-Classes: A Theory of Compositional Design* (New Haven, 1987) and *Class-Notes for Atonal Theory* (1990).

WORKS: DRAMATIC: *Hagoromo* for Soprano, Bass, Men's Chorus, 2 Flutes, 3 Violins, String Bass, and Bells (1977); also incidental music. **ORCH.:** *Syzygy* (Ann Arbor, April 13, 1966); *Continua* (New Haven, Dec. 14, 1972); *Streams and Willows*, flute concerto (Pittsburgh, Nov. 12, 1974); *In Different Voices* for Symphonic Band (New Haven, Feb. 28, 1976); *Tapestries* for Chamber Orch. (1976); *Interiors* (Pittsburgh, March 7, 1978); *Cuts* for Large Wind Ensemble (1984; Rochester, N.Y., April 4, 1986); *Just Now and Again* (1987); *Clash* (Rochester, N.Y., May 25, 1988); *Piano in the Winds*, concerto for Piano and Wind Ensemble (1988); *Bad Lands*, concerto for Flute and Wind Ensemble (1991); Concerto for Piano and Strings (1994). **CHAMBER:** *Sangita 67* for Flutes, Strings, and Percussion (1967); *Varnam* for 5 Melody Instruments and Percussion (1972); *Motet on Doo-Dah* for Alto Flute, Double Bass, and Piano (1973); *Not Lilacs* for Alto Saxophone, Trumpet, Piano, and Drums (1974); *Throughout (Anyway)* for 4 Flutes (1975); *The Dreamer Once Removed* for Carillon and 4 Trumpets (1976); String Quartet (1976); *3/4/5* for 3, 4, or 5 Players (1977); *Plexus* for Woodwind Quartet (1978); *Tigers and Lilies* for 12 Saxophones (1979); *Vira* for Tuba, Flute, Crotales, and Gongs (1980); *Tournament* for 12 or 24 Trombones (1981); *2's Company* for 8 Instruments (1982); *Saraswati's Children* for Melody Instruments, Percussion, and Drone (1985); *Arci* for String Quartet (1988); *Pari Passu* for Violin and Percussion (1988); *Out and Out* for Clarinet and Piano (1989); *3 Musicians* for English Horn, Horn, and Bass (1989); *Traces* for Flute and Piano (1990); *A Fabric of Seams* for 8 Instruments (1990); *Along a Rocky Path* for Clarinet, Violin, and Piano (1993); *Broken Consort in 3 Parts* for 6 Players (1994). **PIANO:** *Trip, Tusk, Night Vapors* (1967); *Cairn* (1969); *Phrases* (1970); *Bhayanaka* for Piano, 4-hands (1977); *Either Ether* (1978); *Allies* for Piano, 4-hands (1979); *Variations on a Theme of Steve Reich* (1980); *Diamond* (1982); *4 Voices in 3 Voices* (1983); *Alter Egos* (1985); *Twice* (1987); *Clear Sounds Above Hills and Water* (1989); *Little Harmonic Labyrinth* (1989); *Terrane* (1990); *Doing Time*, suite (1991); *Canonic Variations* for 2 Pianos (1992); *Where a Cord Ends* (1994); *Bits and Pieces* (1994). **VOCAL:** *Forgotten Vibrations* for Soprano and Chamber Ensemble (1967); *. . . Versus . . .* for 5 Altos, Chamber Ensemble, Jazz Ensemble, and Double Bass obbligato (1968); *Lorelei* for Soprano, Bass, Flutes, Cellos, and Piano, 4-hands (1970–71); *Q* for Chorus and Orch. (1976); *Haiku Cycle* for Soprano and Piano (1978); *Hamiltonian Cycle: Chorus* (1979); *4-fold Heart Sutra* for Baritone, Men's Chorus, Piano, and Vibraphone (1984); *Wang River Cycle* for Mezzo-soprano and 8 Instruments (1985); *A Time* for Soprano and 8 Instruments (1987–88); (19) *Cold Mountain Songs* for Soprano and Piano (1993). **ELECTRONIC:** *Entelechy* for Voice, Cello, Piano, and Electronics (1969); *Phases* for 2 Pianos and Electronics (1970); *. . . Delay . . .* for String Trio and Tape (1971; rev. 1972); *Thunders of Spring over Distant Mountains* (1973); *Bob's Plain Bobs* for 4 Percussionists and Tape (1975); *Curtains* for Pipe Organ and Tape (1976); *Entelechy '77* for Piano and Electronics (1977); *Flux Mandala* for Tape (1977–78); *Shanti* for Clarinet and Tape (1979); *Ghost Dances* for Flutes and Tape (1980); *Aubade* for Tape (1981); *Exchanges* for Piano and Tape (1982); *Night Sky Scroll* for Tape (1984–85); *Amid Flock and Flume* for Flute and Tape (1986); *To the 9* for Guitar and Tape (1991); *Ma* for Electronics (1992).

Morris, Wyn, Welsh conductor; b. Trlech, Feb. 14, 1929. He studied at the Royal Academy of Music in London and the Salzburg Mozarteum. He was apprentice conductor with the Yorkshire Sym. Orch. (1950–51) and conductor of an army band (1951–53). In 1954 he founded the Welsh Sym. Orch.; in 1957 he went to the U.S., where he led the Cleveland Chamber Orch. and other groups. In 1960 he returned to Great Britain; served as conductor of the choir of the Royal National Eisteddfod of Wales (1960–62), of the Royal Choral Soc. of London (1968–70), and of the Huddersfield Choral Soc. (1969–74); then organized the Symphonica of London, with which he gave regular concerts in ambitious programs, particularly of Mahler's music.

Morse, Theodore, American music publisher and composer; b. Washington, D.C., April 13, 1873; d. N.Y., May 25, 1924. He settled in N.Y. when he was 14 and worked as a clerk in various publishing firms; after operating his own publishing concern (1898–1900), he worked for the firm of Howley, Haviland, & Dresser; after the firm dissolved (1905), he and Haviland ran their own company until 1910; Morse then operated independently until selling out to Leo Feist in 1915. He became best known as a composer of sentimental ballads, love songs, and novelty pieces; his most successful song was *M-O-T-H-E-R* (1915). His wife, Alfreda Theodora Strandberg Morse (b. Brooklyn, July 11, 1890; d. White Plains, N.Y., Nov. 10, 1953), wrote the texts to several of his songs.

Mortari, Virgilio, Italian composer and pedagogue; b. Passirana di Lainate, near Milan, Dec. 6, 1902; d. Rome, Sept. 6, 1993. He began his training at the Milan Cons. with Bossi and Pizzetti, and then completed his studies at the Parma Cons. (composition diploma, 1928). After appearances as a pianist, he taught composition at the Venice Cons. (1933–40). From 1940 to 1973 he was a prof. of composition at the Rome Cons. He also served as superintendent of the Teatro La Fenice in Venice from 1955 to 1959. With A. Casella, he wrote the book *Le tecnica dell'orchestra contemporanea* (Milan, 1947; 2nd ed., 1950). Mortari completed Mozart's unfinished score *L'Oca del Cairo* (Salzburg, Aug. 22, 1936).

WORKS: DRAMATIC: OPERAS: *Secchi e Sberlecchi* (1927); *La scuola delle moglie* (1930; rev. 1959); *La Figlia del diavolo* (Milan, March 24, 1954); *Il contratto* (1964). **BALLETS:** *L'allegro piazetta* (1945); *Specchio a tre luci* (1973). **ORCH.:** *Fantasia* for Piano and Orch. (1933); Concerto for String Quartet and Orch. (1937); *Notturno incantato* (1940); 2 piano concertos (1952, 1960); Viola Concerto (1966); Double Bass Concerto (1966); Violin Concerto (1967); *Eleonora d'Arborea*, overture (1968); Double Concerto for Violin, Piano, and Orch. (1968); Cello Concerto (1969); Tripartita (1972); Harp Concerto (1972). **CHAMBER:** Harp Sonatina (1938); *Piccola serenata* for Cello (1946) and for Violin (1947); *Duettini concertati* for Violin and Double Bass (1966); *Capriccio* for Violin (1967); *Les Adieux* for Flute, Violin, Viola, and Cello (1978); *Offerta musicale* for Violin, Cello, and Double Bass (1980); *Divertimento* for Bassoon and Cello (1986). **VOCAL:** *2 Funeral Psalms* in memory of A. Casella for Voice and Instruments (1947); *Stabat Mater* (1947); *Requiem* (1959); *Alfabeto a sorpresa* for 3 Voices and 2 Pianos (1959); *Gloria* for Chorus, 2 Pianos, and Orch. (1980); *Domande e risposte* for Soprano, Baritone, and String Quartet (1983); *Missa pro pace* for Chorus and Organ (1984); songs.

Mortelmans, Ivo (Oscar), Belgian conductor, teacher, and composer, son of **Lodewijk Mortelmans**; b. Antwerp, May 19, 1901; d. Ostend, Aug. 20, 1984. He studied at the Antwerp Cons.; upon graduation, taught academic subjects and theory in Berchem (1925–66), Deurne (1939–70), and Mortsel (1946–67). He was also active as an opera conductor. He wrote an oratorio, *Eeuwig vlecht de bruid haar kroon* (1964), and numerous other choral works, both sacred and secular.

Mortelmans, Lodewijk, Belgian conductor, teacher, and composer, father of **Ivo (Oscar) Mortelmans**; b. Antwerp, Feb. 5, 1868; d. there, June 24, 1952. He was a chorister in the Dominican Church; then studied with Benoit in Antwerp. In 1889 he won the 2nd Belgian Prix de Rome; gained 1st prize with his cantata Lady Macbeth in 1893; then taught at the Antwerp Cons. from 1902. In 1921 he made a tour in the U.S. He was director of the Antwerp Cons. from 1924 to 1933. His finest creations were his songs to Flemish texts, which prompted Gilson to call him the "Prince of the Flemish song."

WORKS: OPERA: *De kinderen der Zee* (Antwerp, 1920). **ORCH.:** 5 symphonic poems: *Helios* (1894), *Mythe du printemps* (1895), *Avonlied* (1928), *Weemoedig aandenken* (1942), and *Eenvoud* (1950); *Symphonie homérique* (1898); 4 elegies: *In memoriam* (1917), *Elevation du coeur* (1917), *Solitude* (1919), and *Treurdicht* (1925). **PIANO:** 3 sets of *Miniatures*; *27 Old Flemish Folksongs.* **VOCAL:** *Jong Vlaanderen*, church cantata (1907); songs.

BIBL.: J. Broeckx, *L. M.* (Antwerp, 1945).

Mortensen, Finn (Einar), Norwegian teacher and composer; b. Christiania, Jan. 6, 1922; d. there (Oslo), May 21, 1983. He studied harmony with Thorlief Eken (1942) and counterpoint with Klaus Egge (1943) in Oslo; received instruction in composition with Bentzon in Copenhagen (1956). He taught theory at the Norwegian Correspondence School (1948–66); then composition at the Oslo Cons. (1970–73); subsequently was prof. of composition at the Oslo Musikkho/gskolan (from 1973); also served as chairman of the Norwegian Soc. of Composers (1972–74). In some of his compositions, he adopted a modified 12-tone idiom, supplemented by the devices of permutation and thematic rotation.

WORKS: ORCH.: Sym. (1953; Bergen, Jan. 21, 1963); *Pezzo orchestrale* (1957); *Evolution* (1961); *Tone Colors* (1961); Piano Concerto (Oslo, Sept. 11, 1963); *Fantasia* for Piano and Orch. (Oslo, May 6, 1966); *Per orchestra* (Oslo, Nov. 27, 1967); *Hedda* (1974–75); *Fantasia* for Violin and Orch. (1977). **CHAMBER:** String Trio (1950); Wind Quintet (1951); Sonata for Solo Flute (1953); Duo for Soprano and Violin (1956); Sonatina for Solo Clarinet (1957); Balalaika Sonatina (1957); *5 Studies* for Flute (1957); Sonatina for Solo Viola (1959); Oboe Sonatina (1959); *Fantasia* for Bassoon (1959); Violin Sonata (1959); Viola Sonatina (1959); Piano Quartet (1960); *3 Pieces* for Violin and Piano (1961–63); *Constellations* for Accordion, Guitar, and Percussion (1971); *Neoserialism I* for Flute and Clarinet (1971), *II* for Flute, Clarinet, and Bassoon (1972), and *III* for Violin, Viola, and Cello (1973); Suite for Wind Quintet (1972); *Serenade* for Cello and Piano (1972); *3 Pieces* for Accordion (1973); *Construction* for Horn (1974–75); *Adagio and Fugue* for 16 Horns (1976); Sonata for Oboe and Harpsichord (1976); *Fantasia* for Trombone (1977); Suite for 5 Recorders and String Quintet (1978–79); String Quartet (1981). **PIANO:** 2 sonatinas (1943, 1949); 2 sonatas (1956, 1977); *Fantasia and Fugue* (1957–58); Sonata for 2 Pianos (1964); *Drawing* (1966); *Impressions* for 2 Pianos (1971).

Mortensen, Otto (Jacob Hubertz), Danish pianist, teacher, and composer; b. Copenhagen, Aug. 18, 1907; d. Århus, Aug. 30, 1986. He studied with Christiansen (piano), Rung-Keller (organ), and Jeppeson (theory) at the Copenhagen Cons. (1925–29). He made his debut as a pianist in Copenhagen (1930), and continued his studies in Berlin (1930), with Milhaud and Desormière in Paris (1939), and at the Univ. of Copenhagen (M.A., 1956). He taught at the Copenhagen Cons. (1942–66) and at the Univ. of Århus (1966–74). He wrote mostly vocal music, including many songs; also a Piano Concerto (1945); Sym. (1956); 2 string quartets (1937, 1955); Quartet for Flute, Violin, Cello, and Piano (1938); Wind Quintet (1944); Oboe Sonata (1947); piano pieces.

Morthenson, Jan W(ilhelm), Swedish composer; b. Örnsköldsvik, April 7, 1940. He studied composition with Mangs, Lidholm, and Metzger in Stockholm and aesthetics at the Univ. of Uppsala; received instruction in electronic techniques from Koenig in Cologne and attended the new music courses in Darmstadt. He devised a "non-figurative" method in which "individual changes in sound are imperceptible"; publ. a treatise on the subject (Copenhagen, 1966).

WORKS: *Coloratura I* for Strings and Tape (1960), *II* for Orch. (1962), *III* for Chamber Orch. (1962–63), and *IV* for Orch. (1963); *3 Wechselspiel: I* for Cello (1960), *II* for Flute and 3 Loudspeakers (1961), and *III* for Piano and Percussion (1961); *Canzona* for 6 Choral Groups, Percussion, and Loudspeakers (1961); *Chains-Mirrors*, electroacoustic work for Soprano (1961); *Some of these . . .* , graphic music for Organ (1961); *Courante I, II,* and *III,* graphic music for Piano (1962); *Pour Madame Bovary* for Organ (1962); *3 Antiphonia: I* for Orch. (1963), *II* for Chamber Orch. (1963), and *III* for Chamber Orch. (1970); *Eternes* for Organ (1964); *Decadenza I* for Organ and Tape (1968) and *II* for Orch. with Tape and Film (1970; Uppsala, Jan. 18, 1972); *Colossus* for Orch. (1970; Berlin, Nov. 26, 1972); *Farewell* for Organ (1970); *Senza* for Strings (1970); *Labor* for Chamber Orch. (1971); *Life* for Tenor, Orch., and Instrumental Group (1972); *Video I* for 8 Solo Strings (1972); *Alla marcia* for Women's Chorus, Orch., Tape, and 8 Stroboscopes (1972–73; Stockholm, March 31, 1974); *5 Pieces* for Orch. (1973); *Soli* for Wind Quintet (1974); *Morendo* for Chorus, Orch., and Tape (Swedish Radio, Oct. 21, 1977); *Musica nera* for 9 Instruments, Tape, and Projection (1979); Organ Concerto (1981; Stockholm, Feb. 9, 1982); *Trauma,* radio opera (Swedish Radio, Aug. 30, 1981); *Energia I* for Symphonic Band (1984); *1984* for Orch. and Electronics (Swedish Radio, Sept. 21, 1984); *Materia* for Soprano, Chorus, Synthesizer, and Organ (1985); *Paraphonia* for Orch. (Stockholm, March 29, 1987); *Once* for Clarinet, Cello, and Piano (1988); *Silence XX* for Laser and Tape (1988); *Contra* for Chamber Orch. (1990); computer and electronic pieces.

Morton, Lawrence, American music critic, impresario, and musicologist; b. Duluth, Minn., July 13, 1904; d. Santa Monica, Calif., May 8, 1987. He earned a living as a film theater organist in Chicago and N.Y. In 1937 he moved to Los Angeles, where he devoted himself mainly to music criticism. In 1954 he joined Peter Yates to organize the famous West Coast concert series Evenings on the Roof (later Monday Evening Concerts), which was devoted to the performance of modern music and lesser-known works from earlier repertoires. He championed Boulez, and, among lesser lights, Dahl, in his programs, as well as Stravinsky, Copland, Schoenberg, and other celebrated masters. The Lawrence Morton Fund was established in 1987 to facilitate the completion of his historical documentation of the above-named concert series; his rich and extensive archives were donated to the Special Collections aspect of the Research Library at the Univ. of Calif. at Los Angeles.

Moscona, Nicola, Greek bass; b. Athens, Sept. 23, 1907; d. Philadelphia, Sept. 17, 1975. He studied at the Athens Cons. with Elena Teodorini. He sang opera in Greece and Eygpt; then was engaged to sing at the Metropolitan Opera in N.Y., and made a successful American debut there as Ramfis in *Aida* (Dec. 13, 1937); remained on its roster until 1962. He then went to Philadelphia, where he taught at the Academy of Vocal Arts.

Moser, Edda (Elisabeth), prominent German soprano, daughter of **Hans Joachim Moser**; b. Berlin, Oct. 27, 1938. She studied with Hermann Weissenborn and Gerty König at the Berlin Cons. She made her debut as Kate Pinkerton at the Berlin

Städtische Oper (1962); after singing in the Würzburg Opera chorus (1962–63), she sang opera in Hagen and Bielefeld; subsequently appeared with the Frankfurt am Main Opera (1968–71) before joining the Vienna State Opera; also sang in Berlin, Salzburg, Hamburg, and other major music centers. She made her U.S. debut as Wellgunde in *Das Rheingold* at the Metropolitan Opera in N.Y. on Nov. 22, 1968, and later appeared there as Donna Anna, the Queen of the Night, and Li. Her last appearance there was in 1984. She maintained an extensive repertoire, singing both coloratura and lyrico-dramatic roles, being equally successful in standard and contemporary works; also sang widely as a concert artist.

Moser, Hans Joachim, eminent German musicologist, father of **Edda (Elisabeth) Moser**; b. Berlin, May 25, 1889; d. there, Aug. 14, 1967. He studied violin with his father, the noted German violin pedagogue and music scholar Andreas Moser (b. Semlin an der Donau, Nov. 29, 1859; d. Berlin, Oct. 7, 1925); then took courses in musicology with Kretzschmar and Wolf at the Univ. of Berlin, with Schiedermair at the Univ. of Marburg, and with Riemann and Schering at the Univ. of Leipzig; also studied voice with Oskar Noë and Felix Schmidt, and took courses in composition with H. van Eyken, Robert Kahn, and G. Jenner; he received his Ph.D. from the Univ. of Rostock in 1910 with the diss. *Die Musikergenossenschaften im deutschen Mittelalter*. Returning to Berlin, he was active as a concert singer (bass-baritone); then served in the German army during World War I. He subsequently completed his Habilitation at the Univ. of Halle in 1919 with his *Das Streichinstrumentenspiel im Mittelalter* (publ. in A. Moser's *Geschichte des Violinspiels*, Berlin, 1923; 2nd ed., rev. and enl., 1966–67). In 1919 he joined the faculty of the Univ. of Halle as a Privatdozent of musicology, and then became a reader there in 1922; he then was a reader at the Univ. of Heidelberg from 1925 to 1927; he was honorary prof. at the Univ. of Berlin from 1927 to 1934, and also served as director of the State Academy for Church and School Music in Berlin from 1927 to 1933; he received the degree of doctor of theology at Königsberg in 1931. He retired from his public positions in 1934 but continued his musicological pursuits in Berlin; he later served as head of the Reichsstelle für Musik-Bearbeitungen from 1940 to 1945. After World War II, he resumed teaching by accepting appointments as a prof. at the Univ. of Jena and the Hochschule für Musik in Weimar in 1947; he then served as director of the Berlin Cons. from 1950 until 1960. Moser was an outstanding music historian and lexicographer; his numerous writings are notable for their erudition. However, his unquestionable scholarship was marred by his ardent espousal of the Nazi racial philosophy; so ferocious was his anti-Semitism that he excluded Mendelssohn from his books publ. during the 3rd Reich. He served as ed. of a projected complete edition of Weber's works (Augsburg and Leipzig, 1926–33), but it remains unfinished. Other works he ed. include *Luthers Lieder, Werke*, XXXV (Weimar, 1923; with O. Albrecht and H. Lucke); *Minnesang und Volkslied* (Leipzig, 1925; 2nd ed., enl., 1933); *Das Liederbuch des Arnt von Aich* (Kassel, 1930; with E. Bernoulli); *Das deutsche Sololied und die Ballade, Das Musikwerk*, XIV (1957; Eng. tr., 1958); *Heinrich Schütz: Italienische Madrigale, Neue Ausgabe sämtlicher Werke*, XXII (Kassel, 1962). He also contributed countless articles to various German music journals; likewise wrote novels, short stories, and a comedy. He also tried his hand at composing, producing the school opera *Der Reisekamerad*, choruses, and songs. He arranged operas by Handel and Weber; wrote an entirely new libretto for Weber's Euryanthe and produced it under the title *Die sieben Raben* (Berlin, March 5, 1915).

WRITINGS: *Technik der deutschen Gesangskunst* (Berlin, 1911; 3rd ed., 1955, with Oskar Noë); *Geschichte der deutschen Musik* (3 vols., Stuttgart and Berlin, 1920, 1922, and 1924; 2nd ed., enl., 1968); *Musikalisches Wörterbuch* (Leipzig and Berlin, 1923); *Paul Hofhaimer: Ein Lied- und Orgelmeister des deutschen Humanismus* (Stuttgart and Berlin, 1929; 2nd ed., enl., 1966); *Die Ballade* (Berlin, 1930); *Die Epochen der Musikgeschichte im Überblick* (Stuttgart and Berlin, 1930; 2nd ed., 1956); *Die mehrstimmige Vertonung des Evangeliums* (2 vols., Leipzig, 1931 and 1934); *Musiklexikon* (Berlin, 1932–35; 2nd ed., 1943, withdrawn; 3rd ed., 1951; 4th ed., 1955; supplement, 1963); *Corydon: das ist: Geschichte des mehrstimmigen Generalbass-Liedes und des Quodlibets im deutschen Barock* (2 vols., Braunschweig, 1933); *Die Melodien der Luther-Lieder* (Leipzig and Hamburg, 1935); *Johann Sebastian Bach* (Berlin, 1935; 2nd ed., 1943); *Tönende Volksaltertümer* (Berlin, 1935); *Heinrich Schütz: Sein Leben und Werk* (Kassel, 1936; 2nd ed., rev., 1954; Eng. tr., 1959); *Lehrbuch der Musikgeschichte* (Berlin, 1936; 13th ed., 1959); *Das deutsche Lied seit Mozart* (Berlin and Zürich, 1937; 2nd ed., rev., 1968); *Die Musikfibel* (Leipzig, 1937); *Kleine deutsche Musikgeschichte* (Stuttgart, 1938; 4th ed., 1955); *Allgemeine Musiklehr* (Berlin, 1940); *Christoph Willibald Gluck* (Stuttgart, 1940); *Kleines Heinrich-Schütz-Buch* (Kassel, 1940; Eng. tr., 1967); *Carl Maria von Weber* (Leipzig, 1941; 2nd ed., 1955); *George Friedrich Händel* (Kassel, 1941; 2nd ed., 1952); *Goethe und die Musik* (Leipzig, 1949); *Lebensvolle Musikerziehung* (Vienna, 1952); *Musikgeschichte in hundert Lebensbildern* (Stuttgart, 1952); *Die evangelische Kirchenmusik in Deutschland* (Berlin, 1953); *Musikästhetik* (Berlin, 1953); *Die Musikleistung der deutschen Stämme* (Vienna, 1954); *Die Tonsprachen des Abendlandes* (Berlin and Darmstadt, 1954); *Dietrich Buxtehude* (Berlin, 1957); *Musik in Zeit und Raum* (Berlin, 1960; collected essays); *Bachs Werke: Ein Führer für Musikfreunde* (Kassel, 1964); etc.

BIBL.: *Festgabe für H.J. M.* (Kassel, 1954; with complete list of writings).

Moser, Rudolf, Swiss composer, conductor, violist, and teacher; b. Niederuzwyl, Jan. 7, 1892; d. in a mountain-climbing accident in Silvaplana, Aug. 20, 1960. He studied musicology with Nef and received training in theology at the Univ. of Basel. After further studies with Reger, Sitt, and Klengel at the Leipzig Cons. (1912–14), he completed his training with Huber in Basel and Lauber in Geneva. He settled in Basel, where he conducted the Cathedral Choir, played viola in a string quartet, and taught at the Cons.

WORKS: DRAMATIC: *Die Fischerin*, Singspiel (1935); *Der Rattenfänger*, dance play (1950). **ORCH.:** Concerto Grosso for Strings (Basel, June 26, 1927); 3 violin concertos; Piano Concerto; Viola Concerto; Organ Concerto; Concerto for Violin, Viola, Cello, and Orch.; suites. **CHAMBER:** 4 string quartets: String Sextet; Piano Trio; organ music. **VOCAL:** *Das Lied von der Sonne* for Soli, Chorus, Organ, and Orch.; *Odes of Horace* for Baritone, Chorus, and Orch.

BIBL.: H. Buchli, *R. M.* (Zürich, 1964).

Moser, Thomas, American tenor; b. Richmond, Va., May 27, 1945. After training at the Richmond (Va.) Professional Inst., he studied at the Curtis Inst. of Music in Philadelphia; later pursued vocal training with Martial Singher, Gérard Souzay, and Lotte Lehmann. In 1974 he was a winner in the Metropolitan Opera Auditions; then joined the Graz Landestheater in 1975. In 1976 he appeared as Mozart's Belmonte with the Bavarian State Opera in Munich. From 1977 he sang with the Vienna State Opera, where he appeared as Mozart's Tamino, Ottavio, Titus, and Idomeneo, Strauss's Flamand and Henry, and Gluck's Achilles. He made his first appearance with the N.Y. City Opera in 1979 as Titus. In 1983 he sang at the Salzburg Festival, returning there in 1984 to create the role of the tenor in Berio's *Un re in ascolto*. In 1985 he made his debut at Milan's La Scala as Tamino. In 1986 he sang for the first time at the Rome Opera as Achilles. In 1988 he appeared in the title role of Schubert's *Fierrabras* at the Theater an der Wien. In 1992 he sang the Emperor in *Die Frau ohne Schatten* in Geneva. As a concert artist, he appeared with leading North American and European orchs. His expansive operatic and concert repertoire ranges from early music to the cosmopolitan avant-garde.

Mosko, Lucky (actually, **Stephen L.**), American composer and conductor; b. Denver, Dec. 7, 1947. He studied conducting and piano with Antonia Brico (1959–65), then entered Yale Univ. as a composition student of Donald Martino and a conducting student of Gustav Meier (B.A., 1969); also studied composition at the Calif. Inst. of the Arts with Powell, Subotnick, and Stein (M.F.A., 1972). He traveled on a Fulbright grant to Iceland to research folk and contemporary music (1974, 1978). He taught at the Calif. Inst. of the Arts (1970–90); was director of its conducting program (1976–82), conductor of its orch. (1980–82), and founder-director of its Twentieth Century Players (1974–87). He was composer-in-residence at the Aspen (Colo.) Music Festival (1986, 1987). He joined the faculty at Harvard Univ. in 1990. Mosko was principal conductor of the San Francisco Contemporary Music Players (from 1987) and the Griffen Ensemble of Boston (from 1990); also was a guest conductor with the San Francisco Sym. (from 1983) and the Los Angeles Phil. (from 1985); was director of the Ojai Music Festival in 1990. Mosko is an important conductor of new music, giving first performances of works by Cage, Scelsi, Stockhausen, Xenakis, and others. His own compositions are peculiar, somewhat abstruse, and characterized by wide-ranging fragments of sound in delicately controlled timbral contexts. He is married to the flutist Dorothy Stone, a long-time member of the California E.A.R. Unit.

WORKS: *Lovely Mansions* for Chamber Ensemble (1971); *Night of the Long Knives* for Soprano and Chamber Ensemble (1974); *3 Clerks in Niches* for Chamber Ensemble (1975); *Darling* for Contrabass (1976); *Rais Murad* for Cello and Piano (1978); *Cosmology of Easy Listening* for Percussion Trio (1979); *Indigenous Music I* for Chorus (1981) and *II* for Solo Instruments and Chamber Ensemble (1984); *Superluminal Connections I* for Chamber Orch. (1985) and *II: The Atu of Tahiti* for Voices and Orch. (1986); *The Road to Tiphareth* for Chamber Ensemble (1986); *for Morton Feldman* for Flute, Cello, and Piano (1987); *Schweres Loos* for Alto, Piccolo, Bass Clarinet, and Violin (1988); *A Garden of Time* for Orch. (1989).

Mosolov, Alexander (Vasilievich), Russian composer; b. Kiev, Aug. 11, 1900; d. Moscow, July 12, 1973. He fought in the Civil War in Russia (1918–20); was wounded and decorated twice with the Order of the Red Banner for heroism. After the war, he studied composition with Glière in Kiev; then studied harmony and counterpoint with Glière, composition with Miaskovsky, and piano with Prokofiev and Igumnov at the Moscow Cons. (1922–25). He played his 1st Piano Concerto in Leningrad on Feb. 12, 1928. In his earliest works, he adopted modernistic devices; wrote songs to texts of newspaper advertisements. His ballet *Zavod* (Iron Foundry; Moscow, Dec. 4, 1927) attracted attention because of the attempt to imitate the sound of a factory at work by shaking a large sheet of metal. However, Mosolov's attempt to produce "proletarian" music by such means elicited a sharp rebuke from the official arbiters of Soviet music. On Feb. 4, 1936, he was expelled from the Union of Soviet Composers for staging drunken brawls and behaving rudely to waiters in restaurants. He was sent to Turkestan to collect folk songs as a move toward his rehabilitation. After settling in Moscow in 1939, he continued to make excursions to collect folk songs in various regions of Russia.

WORKS: DRAMATIC: OPERAS: *Geroy* (The Hero; 1927; Baden-Baden, July 15, 1928); *Plotina* (The Dam; 1929); *The Signal* (1941); *Maskarad* (Masquerade; 1940). **MUSICAL COMEDY:** *Friedrich Barbarossa.* **ORCH.:** 2 piano concertos (1927, 1932); 6 syms. (1928, 1932, 1937, 1942, 1947, 1950); 5 suites: No. 1, *Turkmenian* (1933), No. 2, *Uzbekian Dance* (1935), No. 3, *Native Lands*, with Folk Instruments (1951), No. 4 (1955), and No. 5, *Festive* (1955); Harp Concerto (Moscow, Nov. 18, 1939); *Concerto for Orchestra* (1943); Cello Concerto (1946); *Elegiac Poem* (1961). **CHAMBER:** 2 string quartets (1926, 1942); Trio for Clarinet, Cello, and Piano (1926); Piano Trio (1927); Cello Sonata (1927); Viola Sonata (1928); *Dance Suite* for Piano Trio (1928). **PIANO:** 4 sonatas (1923, 1924, 1925, 1926). **VOCAL:** 4 oratorios, including *M.I. Kalinin* (1940) and *Moscow* (1948); cantatas, including *Minin and Pozharsky*; *Kirghiz Rhapsody* for Mezzo-soprano, Chorus, and Orch. (1933); *Ukraine* for Soloist, Chorus, and Orch. (1942); choruses; songs.

Moss, David (Michael), avant-garde American percussionist and vocalist; b. N.Y., Jan. 21, 1949. He studied South Indian drumming with Tanjore Ranganathan (1970) and composition with Bill Dixon (1971–73). From 1972 he toured Europe, Japan, Australia, and the U.S. as a soloist and leader of his own ensembles in more than 950 concerts; worked with David Van Tieghem, John King, John Zorn, and others. Moss has collaborated with numerous dance, visual, theater, and video artists; his recordings include *Terrain: Solo Percussion and Voice* (1980), *David Moss Dense Band 'Live' in Europe* (1988), and *The Day We Forgot* (1990); he also created and produced new music programs for radio (from 1981). Moss's solo performances combine a wide range of pitched and unpitched percussion, "found" objects, sound sculpture, and electronics with extended vocalizations.

WORKS: *Light no. 18* (1983); *Full House*, duets (1983); *King Lear*, incidental music (1983); *N.Y. Objects & Noise nos. 1 and 2* (1984); *Vox Box* (1984); *Mossmen* (1984); *Intimate Solos* (1985); *Light no. 20* (1985); *Operadio* (1986); *Slow Talking* (1987); *Slant Lines* (1987); *Operadio no. 2* (1987); *Conjuring Calvino* (1988); *Language Linkage nos. 1–3* (1988); *That Tempest* (1989); *After That Tempest* (1989); *Stolen Voice* (1990).

Moss, Lawrence (Kenneth), American composer and teacher; b. Los Angeles, Nov. 18, 1927. He studied at the Univ. of Calif. at Los Angeles (B.A., 1949), at the Eastman School of Music in Rochester, N.Y. (M.A., 1950), and with Kirchner at the Univ. of Southern Calif. in Los Angeles (Ph.D., 1957); held a Fulbright scholarship (1953–54), 2 Guggenheim fellowships (1959–60; 1968–69), and 3 NEA grants (1975, 1977, 1980). He taught at Mills College (1956–59) and Yale Univ. (1960–68); then was a prof. and director of the composition dept. at the Univ. of Maryland at College Park (from 1969); in 1986 he was composer-in-residence at the Rockefeller Center in Bellagio, Italy. His style of composition tends toward polycentric tonality, with sporadic application of serial techniques and electronic sounds.

WORKS: DRAMATIC: OPERAS: *The Brute*, comic opera (1960; Norfolk, Conn., July 15, 1961); *The Queen and the Rebels* (1989). **THEATER:** *Unseen Leaves* for Soprano, Oboe, Tapes, Slides, and Lights (Washington, D.C., Oct. 20, 1975); *Nightscape* for Soprano, Flute, Clarinet, Violin, Percussion, Dancer, Tape, and Slides (1978); *Dreamscape* for Dancer, Tape, and Lights (1980); *Images* for Clarinet, Tape, and Dancer (1981); *Rites* for Tape, Slides, Lights, and Dancers (1983); *Song to the Floor* for Dancer and Tape (1984); *That Gong-Tormented Sea* for Tape and Dance (1985); *Lesbia's Sparrow* for Singer, Tape, and Dancer (1985); *Incidental Music* for Percussion and Mime/Dancer (1986); *Blackbird* for Clarinet, Mime/Dancer, and Tape (1987); *Summer Night on the Yogahenney River* for Soprano, Dancer, and Tape (1989). **ORCH.:** *Suite* (1950); *Scenes* for Small Orch. (1961); *Paths* (1970); *Symphonies* for Brass Quintets and Chamber Orch. (1977); *Clouds* for Chamber Ensemble (1989); *Chinese Lullaby* for Band (1994). **CHAMBER:** 3 string quartets (1958, 1975, 1980); Violin Sonata (1959); *Music for 5* for Brass Quintet (1963); *Patterns* for Flute, Clarinet, Viola, and Piano (1967); *Auditions* for Woodwind Quintet and Tape (1971); *B.P.: A Melodrama* for Trombone, Piano, and Tape (1976); *Chanson* for Flute Choir (1979); *Apresludes* for Flute and Percussion (1983); *Music of Changes* for 7 Performers and Conductor (1986); *Various Birds* for Woodwind Quintet (1987); *Violaria, una dramma per musica* for Viola and Tape (1988); *Clouds* for Chamber Ensemble (1990); *Through a Window . . .* for Flute, Clarinet, and Contrabassoon (1991); Quartet for Flute, Cello, Percussion, and Piano (1992); *Saxpressivo* for Alto Saxophone and Tape (1992); *6 Little Pieces* for Saxophone and Piano (1993); piano pieces. **VOCAL:** *A Song of Solomon* for Chorus and Piano (1956); *Song of Myself* for Baritone and Chamber Ensemble (1957); *Ariel* for Soprano and Orch. (1969); *Loves* for Soprano, Flute, Clarinet, Viola, Harp, and Piano

(1982); *Voyages* for Tenor, Flute, Clarinet, Percussion, Violin, Viola, and Cello (1985); *Grand is the Seen* for 6 Soloists and Chorus (1989); *Love Songs* for Baritone and Harp (1990); *Songs of the Earth and Sky* for Mezzo-soprano, Clarinet, Violin, and Piano, 4-hands (1990); *10 Miracles*, song cycle for Tenor, Oboe, and Harp (1993); *From Dawn to Dawn* for Baritone, Oboe, and Orch. (1994).

Moss, Piotr, Polish composer; b. Bydgoszcz, May 13, 1949. He received training at the Warsaw Academy of Music.

WORKS: Violin Concerto (1971); Wind Quintet (1971); *Per esempio*, music for 13 Performers (1972); String Quartet (1973); *Charon*, sym. (1973); Piano Concertino (1973); *Vowels* for 12 Voices and Instrumental Ensemble (1974); Piano Trio (1974); *Giorno* for 10 Performers (1975); Cello Concerto (1975); *Poem* for Cello and Orch. (1978); Concerto for Harpsichord and 2 String Orchs. (1980); Sonata for String Quartet (1982); *Incontri* for Orch. (1982; Paris, May 7, 1984); *Musique en trois mouvements* for Cello and Chamber Ensemble (Versailles, Nov. 17, 1983); *Abendmusik*, quartet for Oboe, Violin, Viola, and Cello (1985); *Mesto* for Wind Quartet, Organ, and Percussion (1986; Salzburg, May 27, 1987); *Elegy: Alexander Tansman in memoriam* for 2 Cellos (1986; also for Cello and String Orch., 1987).

Moszumańska-Nazar, Krystyna, Polish composer and pedagogue; b. Lwów, Sept. 5, 1924. She was a student of Wiechowicz at the Kraków State College of Music (1948–55). In 1964 she joined its faculty, becoming a prof. in 1981 and rector in 1987. In 1988 she received the Polish Composers Union award for her life's work and in 1989 the Polish government Award of Merit. While her music is classical in its formal design, she often makes use of densely dissonant harmonic writing.

WORKS: ORCH.: Piano Concertino (1954); 2 overtures (1954, 1956); *Allegro symphonique* (1957); *4 Symphonic Essays* (1957); *Hexaèdre* (1960; Kraków, June 22, 1962); *Music* for Strings (1961; Warsaw, Sept. 9, 1963); *Exodus* for Orch. and Tape (1964; Wrocłow, Nov. 10, 1967); *Variazioni concertanti* for Flute and Chamber Orch. (1965–66); *Pour orchestre* (1969; Poznań, March 29, 1973); *Rhapsody No. 1* (1975) and *No. 2* (Kraków, Sept. 12, 1980); Sinfoniette for Chamber String Orch. (1983; Baranów, Sept. 10, 1986); *Concerto for Orchestra* (1985–86); *Fresco No. 1* (Kraków, Nov. 25, 1988), *No. 2* (1992), and *No. 3* (1993–94; Kraków, Nov. 24, 1994); *2 Dialogues* (1994; Szczecin, March 16, 1995; 2nd version, Odense, Nov. 23, 1994). **CHAMBER:** *3 Miniatures* for Clarinet and Piano (1957); 5 Duets for Flute and Clarinet (1959); *Interpretations* for Flute, Percussion, and Tape (1967; Kraków, Feb. 7, 1968); *3 Concert Studies* for Percussionist (1969); 2 string quartets: No. 1 (1973–74) and No. 2 (Lusławice, Aug. 28, 1980); *From End to End Percussion* for Percussionist (1976; Berkeley, Calif., May 24, 1978); *Variants* for Piano and Percussion (1979; London, Feb. 5, 1980); *Canzona* for Violin (1985); *Fantasy* for Marimbaphone (Wrocław, Feb. 19, 1988); *Music for 5* for Percussion (1989–90; Munich, Feb. 24, 1990); *3 Moments musicaux* for Double Bass (1990; Wrocław, April 28, 1991; also for Cello, Kraków, Nov. 9, 1994); *Recitativo* for Cello (1991; Kraków, Nov. 9, 1994); *Un petit cadeau*, trio for Flute, Cello, and Percussion (1993; Kraków, Jan. 17, 1994). **PIANO:** *Variations* (1949); *Suite of Polish Dances* (1954); Sonatina (1957); *Bagatelle* (1971); *Constellations* (1972). **VOCAL:** *Intonations* for 2 Choruses and Orch. (1968); *Bel canto* for Soprano, Celesta, and Percussion (1972; Avignon, July 1973; also for Soprano, Cello, and Percussion); *Polish Madonnas* for Chorus and Orch. (1974; Kraków, April 23, 1976); *Challenge* for Baritone and Chamber Ensemble (Poznań, April 28, 1977); *The Song of Songs* for Soprano, Reciting Voice, Reciting Chorus, and Chamber Ensemble (Poznań, March 24, 1984).

Motta, José Vianna da. See **Vianna da Motta, José.**

Mottu, Alexandre, Swiss pianist, organist, teacher, and composer; b. Geneva, June 11, 1883; d. there, Nov. 24, 1943. He studied organ with Otto Barblan in Geneva and piano with Teresa Carreño in Berlin. He was appointed prof. of piano and organ at the Geneva Cons. in 1907. His works include various pieces for piano, violin, and organ, and much choral music.

Moulaert, Pierre, Belgian composer and teacher, son of **Raymond (Auguste Marie) Moulaert**; b. Brussels, Sept. 24, 1907; d. there, Nov. 13, 1967. He studied at the Royal Cons. in Brussels with his father and Joseph Jongen, and taught there from 1937 until his death. He was not a prolific composer, and wrote mostly in small forms, but his music had a distinctive quality of fine craftsmanship.

WORKS: ORCH.: Concertino for Flute, Oboe, and Strings (1954); *Sérénade* (1956); *Petite musique concertante* (1961); *Introduction et Fugue* for Flute, Oboe, Clarinet, Bassoon, and Strings (Uccle, March 7, 1963); *Séquences* (1964). **CHAMBER:** *Passepied en Rondo* for Wind Quintet (1940); String Quartet (1956).

Moulaert, Raymond (Auguste Marie), Belgian pianist, teacher, and composer, father of **Pierre Moulaert**; b. Brussels, Feb. 4, 1875; d. there, Jan. 18, 1962. He studied at the Brussels Cons. with Arthur de Greef (piano) and Edgar Tinel (theory); then was appointed to its staff and taught composition (from 1927); concurrently was director of his own music school in St.-Gilles (1913–38); also lectured at the Queen Elizabeth Chapel of Music in Brussels.

WORKS: ORCH.: *Theme and Variations* for Trumpet and Orch. (1910); *Appels pour un tournoi de chevalerie* for Wind Orch. (1923); *Passacaglia* (1931); *Symphonie de valses* (1936); Trumpet Concertino (1937); Piano Concerto (1938); *Rhapsodie écossaise* for Clarinet and Orch. (1940); *Tango-caprice* for Saxophone and Orch. (1942); *Symphonie de fugues* (1942–44); *Études symphoniques* (1943); *Eroica* for Horn and Chamber Orch. (1946); *Légende* for Flute and Orch. (1951); *Variations symphoniques* (1952); *Sinfonietta* for Strings (1955; not extant). **CHAMBER:** *Andante* for 4 Horns (1903); *Andante, Fugue et Final* for 4 Saxophones (1907); Sextet for Wind Quintet and Piano (1925); *Passacaglia* for Double Bass (1928); *Études rythmiques* for Percussion (1929); *Divertimento* for String Trio (1936); *Choral varie* for 4 Cellos (1937); *Suite* for 3 Trombones (1939); *Sonata en forme de passacaille* for Cello and Piano (1942); *Concert* for Wind Quintet and Harp (1950); *Bagatelles* for 2 Violins (1960). **KEYBOARD: PIANO:** Sonata (1917); *Toccata* (1938); *Ciels* (1938); *Études-paraphrases*, after Paganini (1948). **ORGAN:** Sonata (1907); *2 Pieces* (1910); *3 poèmes bibliques* (1916–20); *2 Fugues* (1929); *Prélude et Choral* (1948). **VOCAL:** 5 sets of *Poemes de la Vieille France* for Variable Vocal Groups (1917–43); *L'Eau passe*, song cycle for Solo Voice.

Moyse, Louis, French-American flutist, pianist, and composer, son of **Marcel (Joseph) Moyse**; b. Scheveningen, the Netherlands, July 14, 1912. He was taken to Paris as an infant; learned to play the piano and flute at home; later took private piano lessons with Philipp (1925–27); in 1930 he entered the Paris Cons., where he studied flute with Gaubert and composition with Bigot; he graduated in 1932 with the premier prix in flute; then was his father's teaching assistant at the Paris Cons., and filled in with various jobs playing at movie theaters and restaurants. He served in the French army during World War II; after the war, he organized the Moyse Trio, with his father as flutist, his wife, Blanche Honegger-Moyse, as violinist, and himself as pianist. In 1948 he went with his wife to the U.S.; became a naturalized American citizen in 1959; was active at the Marlboro (Vt.) Music Festival (from 1950); was prof. of flute and chamber music at the Univ. of Toronto (from 1975).

WORKS: Suite for 2 Flutes and Viola (1957); *4 Dances* for Flute and Violin (1958); Woodwind Quintet (1961); *Divertimento* for Double Woodwind Quintet, 2 Cellos, Double Bass, and Timpani (1961); *4 Pieces* for 3 Flutes and Piano (1965); *3 Pieces* for Flute and Guitar (1968); *Marlborian Concerto* for Flute, English Horn, and Orch. (1969); *A Ballad for Vermont* for Narrator, Soloists, Chorus, and Orch. (1971–72); Flute Sonata (1975); *Serenade* for Piccolo, 4 Flutes, Alto Flute, Bass Flute, and Piano

(1977); several collections of didactic flute pieces; various arrangements for flute and instrumental groups of works by Bach, Handel, Telemann, Mozart, Beethoven, and Weber.

Moyse, Marcel (Joseph), celebrated French flutist and pedagogue, father of **Louis Moyse;** b. St. Amour, Jura, May 17, 1889; d. Brattleboro, Vt., Nov. 1, 1984. He studied flute (premier prix, 1906) with Taffanel, Hennebains, and Gaubert, and chamber music with Capet at the Paris Cons. In 1908 he made his debut as soloist with the Pasdeloup Orch. in Paris. From 1913 to 1938 he played flute in the orch. of the Opéra-Comique in Paris. He also played in the Concerts Staram in Paris (1922–33). From 1932 to 1949 he was prof. of flute at the Paris Cons. In 1933 he formed the Moyse Trio with his son as pianist and his daughter-in-law Blanche Honegger Moyse as violinist. In 1949 he settled in the U.S. In 1950 he helped found the Marlboro (Vt.) Music Festival, where he was active as both a performer and teacher. He also gave master classes abroad. In 1934 Moyse was made a member of the Légion d'honneur. As a performer, he played various modern works. Ibert composed his Flute Concerto for Moyse, who gave the first performance in 1933. Moyse wrote many didactic works for the flute as well as the manual *Tone Development through Interpretation.*

BIBL.: T. Wye, *M. M.: An Extraordinary Man: A Musical Biography* (Cedar Falls, 1993); A. McCutchan, *M. M.: Voice of the Future* (Portland, Oreg., 1995).

Moyzes, Alexander, Slovak composer and teacher, son of **Mikuláš Moyzes**; b. Kláštor pod Znievom, Sept. 4, 1906; d. Bratislava, Nov. 20, 1984. He studied conducting with Ostrčil, composition with Karel and Šin, and organ with Wiedermann at the Prague Cons. (1925–28); then studied in Novák's master class there (1929–30). He taught at the Bratislava Academy of Music and Drama (from 1929); was chief music adviser to the Bratislava Radio and a prof. at the Bratislava Cons. (from 1941); became a prof. of composition at the Bratislava College of Musical Arts (1949), serving as its rector (1965–71). He won the State Prize (1956) and was made an Artist of Merit (1961) and a National Artist (1966). His music uses the melodic resources of Slovak folk songs; his Sym. No. 1 is the first national Slovak sym.

WORKS: OPERA: *Udatný král'* (The Brave King; 1966; Bratislava, 1967). **ORCH.:** 12 syms.: No. 1 (Bratislava, Feb. 11, 1929), No. 2 (1932; rev. 1941), No. 3 (1942; orch. version of the Wind Quintet), No. 4 (1939–47), No. 5 (1948), No. 6 (1951), No. 7 (Bratislava, Oct. 23, 1955), No. 8 (1968), No. 9 (1971), No. 10 (1978), No. 11 (1978), and No. 12 (1983); *Symphonic Overture* (1929); Concertino (1933); *Jánošik's Rebels* (1933); *Nikola Šuhaj*, overture (1933); *Down the River Vah*, symphonic suite (1936; rev. 1945); *Dances from the Hron Region* (1950); *February Overture* (1952); *Dances from Gemer*, suite (1955); Violin Concerto (1958); *Sonatina giocosa* for Violin, Chamber String Orch., and Harpsichord (1962); Flute Concerto (1966); *Keeper of the House*, overture (1972); *Bonfires on the Mountains*, symphonic suite (1973); *Musica istropolitana* for Chamber String Orch. (1974); *Music to Woman*, symphonic study (1975; Bratislava, May 13, 1976); *The Tale about Jánošik*, rhapsodic suite (1976). **CHAMBER:** 4 string quartets (1928, 1969, 1981, 1983); Wind Quintet (1933); *Poetic Suite* for Violin and Piano (1948); *Duetta* for Violin and Piano (1960); *Small Suite* for Violin and Piano (1968); Sonatina for Flute and Guitar (1975). **PIANO:** *Divertimento* (1929); *Jazz Sonata* for 2 Pianos (1932); Sonata (1942). **VOCAL:** 2 cantatas: *Svätopluk* (1935) and *Znejú piesne na chotari* (Songs Resound in the Meadows; 1948); 2 song cycles: *Jeseň* (In Autumn) for Mezzo-soprano and Orch. or Piano (1960) and *Morning Dew* for Mezzo-soprano and Orch. or Piano (1963).

BIBL.: L. Burlas, *A. M.* (Bratislava, 1956).

Moyzes, Mikuláš, Slovak composer and teacher, father of **Alexander Moyzes**; b. Zvolenská, Slatina, Dec. 6, 1872; d. Prešov, April 2, 1944. He was a non-resident student at the Budapest Academy of Music; then was a music teacher and organist in various Slovak towns; settled in Prešov as a teacher (1908). He was a leading figure in the development of Slovak national music.

WORKS: MELODRAMAS: *Siroty* (Orphans; 1921); *Lesná panna* (Maid of the Woods; 1922); *Čertova rieka* (The Devil's River; 1940). **ORCH.:** 2 suites (1931, 1935); *Malá vrchovská symfónia* (Little Highland Sym.; 1937); *Naše Slovensko* (Our Slovakia), festival overture (1938). **CHAMBER:** 4 string quartets (1926, 1929, 1932, 1943); Wind Sextet (1934); organ pieces. **VOCAL:** *Missa solemnis* for Chorus (1906); *Mass* for Chorus (1929); songs; folk song arrangements.

BIBL.: Z. Bokesová, *Sedemdesiatročný M. M.* (M. M. at 70; Bratislava, 1942).

Mraczek (actually, **Mraček**), **Joseph Gustav**, Czech composer, violinist, conductor, and teacher; b. Brünn, March 12, 1878; d. Dresden, Dec. 24, 1944. He received his first instruction from his father, the cellist Franz (František) Mraček (1842–98); was a chorister in various churches in Brünn before going to Vienna, where he studied with Hellmesberger, Stocker, and Löwe at the Cons. From 1897 to 1902 he was concertmaster at the Stadttheater in Brünn; then taught violin at the Cons. there (1898–1919). He settled in Dresden and conducted the Phil. (1919–24) and taught composition at the Cons. (from 1919).

WORKS: OPERAS: *Der glaserne Pantoffel* (Brünn, 1902); *Der Traum* (Brünn, Feb. 26, 1909); *Aebelö* (Breslau, 1915); *Ikdar* (Dresden, 1921); *Herrn Dürers Bild oder Madonna am Wiesenzaun* (Hannover, Jan. 29, 1927); *Der Liebesrat* (not perf.); *Der arme Tobias* (1936). **ORCH.:** *Rustans Traum*, symphonic poem (1911); *Max und Moritz*, symphonic burlesque (1911); *Orientalische Skizzen* for Chamber Orch. (1918); *Eva*, symphonic poem (1922); *Variété*, scenes (1928). **CHAMBER:** Piano Quintet; String Quartet; piano pieces. **VOCAL:** Choral pieces; songs.

BIBL.: E. Müller, *J.G. M.* (Dresden, 1917).

Mravinsky, Evgeni (Alexandrovich), eminent Russian conductor; b. St. Petersburg, June 4, 1903; d. there (Leningrad), Jan. 19, 1988. He studied biology at the Univ. of St. Petersburg; then joined the Imperial Ballet as a pantomimist and rehearsal pianist; in 1924 he enrolled in the Leningrad Cons., where he studied conducting with Gauk and Malko, graduating in 1931; also had courses in composition with Shcherbachev. He then was conductor of the Leningrad Theater of Opera and Ballet (1932–38). In 1938 he was appointed principal conductor of the Leningrad Phil., which position he held with imperious authority for 50 years. Mravinsky represented the best of the Soviet school of conducting, in which technical precision and fidelity to the music were combined with individual and even Romantic interpretations. He was especially noted for his fine performances of Tchaikovsky's operas, ballets, and syms.; he gave first performances of several syms. of Prokofiev and Shostakovich; also conducted works by Bartók and Stravinsky. In 1973 he was awarded the order of Hero of Socialist Labor.

BIBL.: V. Bogdanov-Berezovsky, *The Soviet Conductor M.* (Leningrad, 1956); V. Fomin, *M. Conducts* (Leningrad, 1976).

Mshvelidze, Shalva (Mikhailovich), Russian ethnomusicologist, teacher, and composer; b. Tiflis, May 28, 1904; d. there (Tbilisi), March 4, 1984. He studied with Bagrinovsky at the Tiflis Cons., graduating in 1930, and with Shcherbachev, Tyulin, Steinberg, and Ryazanov at the Leningrad Cons. He was made a teacher (1929) and a prof. (1942) at the Tbilisi Cons. He was a leading figure in Georgian music.

WORKS: DRAMATIC: OPERAS: *Legend of Tariel* (Tbilisi, Feb. 25, 1946; rev. 1966); *The Grandmaster's Right Hand* (Tbilisi, June 3, 1961); *Widow of a Soldier* (1967); *Aluda Ketelauri* (1972). Also incidental music; film scores. **ORCH.:** 4 symphonic poems: *Azar* (1933), *Zviadauri* (1940), *Mindia* (1949), and *Youngling and Tiger* (1962); 5 syms. (1943, 1944, 1952, 1968, 1974). **OTHER:** Chamber music; vocal works, including 2 oratorios: *Caucasiana* (1949) and *The Legacy of Posterity*, for the centennial of Lenin's birth (1970), and songs.

BIBL.: V. Donadze, *S. M.* (Tbilisi, 1946); A. Shaverzashvili, *Fugi S. M.* (Tbilisi, 1964); A. Tsulukidze, *S. M.* (Tbilisi, 1964).

Muck, Karl, great German conductor; b. Darmstadt, Oct. 22, 1859; d. Stuttgart, March 3, 1940. He received his first musical instruction from his father; then studied piano with Kissner in Würzburg; later pursued academic studies (classical philology) at the Univs. of Heidelberg and Leipzig (Ph.D., 1880). He also attended the Leipzig Cons., and shortly before graduation made a successful debut as pianist with the Gewandhaus Orch. However, he did not choose to continue a pianistic career, but obtained a position as chorus master at the municipal opera in Zürich; his ability soon secured him the post of conductor there. In subsequent years, he was a theater conductor in Salzburg, Brünn, and Graz; there Angelo Neumann, impresario of a traveling opera company, heard him, and engaged him as conductor for the Landestheater in Prague (1886), and then as Seidl's successor for his traveling Wagner Co. It was during those years that Muck developed his extraordinary qualities as a masterful disciplinarian and faithful interpreter possessing impeccable taste. In 1889 he conducted the Wagner tetralogy in St. Petersburg, and in 1891, in Moscow. In 1892 he was engaged as first conductor at the Berlin Royal Opera, and also frequently conducted sym. concerts of the Royal Chapel there. From 1894 to 1911 he led the Silesian Music Festivals; in 1899 he conducted the Wagner repertoire at London's Covent Garden. He also appeared, with outstanding success, in Paris, Rome, Brussels, Madrid, Copenhagen, and other European centers. In 1901 he was selected to conduct the performances of Parsifal at Bayreuth; appeared there regularly until 1930. Muck was one of the conductors of the Vienna Phil. (1904–06); then was conductor of the Boston Sym. Orch. (1906–08) before returning to Berlin as Generalmusikdirektor. He returned to America in 1912 and again assumed the post of conductor of the Boston Sym. Orch.; held that post with the greatest distinction until the U.S. entered World War I in 1917. Muck's position then became controversial; a friend of Kaiser Wilhelm II, he saw no reason to temper his ardent German nationalism, nor was he inclined to alter certain aspects of his private life. Protests were made against his retention as conductor, but despite the efforts to defend him by Major Higginson, the founder of the Boston Sym. Orch., Muck's case proved hopeless. In order to avoid prosecution under the Mann Act, he subsequently submitted to being arrested at his home on March 25, 1918, as an enemy alien and was interned until the end of the war. In 1919 he returned to Germany; conducted the Hamburg Phil. from 1922 until his retirement in 1933. Muck was one of the foremost conductors of his era. A consummate musician, endowed with a masterful technique, he was renowned for his authoritative performances of the revered Austro-German repertoire. His sympathies were wide, however, and he programmed such contemporary musicians as Mahler, Debussy, Sibelius, and even Schoenberg and Webern at his concerts. His penchant for stern disciplinarianism and biting sarcasm made him a feared podium figure for the musicians who played under him, but the results he obtained were exemplary.

BIBL.: N. Stücker, *K. M.* (Graz, 1939); J. Baker-Carr, *Evening at Symphony: A Portrait of the Boston Symphony Orchestra* (Boston, 1977).

Muczynski, Robert, American composer, pianist, and teacher; b. Chicago, March 19, 1929. He received training from Walter Knupfer (piano) and A. Tcherepnin (composition) at De Paul Univ. (B.M., 1950; M.M., 1952), playing his own *Divertimento* for Piano and Orch. at his graduation; pursued further training with Tcherepnin in Nice (summer, 1961). In 1958 he made his N.Y. recital debut, and in subsequent years continued to be active as a pianist. He taught at De Paul Univ. (1955–58) and served as chairman of the piano dept. at Loras College in Dubuque, Iowa (1956–59); in 1964–65 he was a visiting lecturer at Roosevelt Univ. in Chicago; then was a prof. and head of the composition dept. at the Univ. of Arizona in Tucson from 1965 until 1988, when he became prof. emeritus. Muczynski is a particularly fine composer of chamber music and piano pieces, whose output reflects the influence of Bartók and Piston, among others.

WORKS: ORCH.: *Divertimento* for Piano and Orch. (1951–52); Sym. No. 1 (1953); Piano Concerto (1954; Louisville, Jan. 12, 1955); *Galena: A Town*, suite (1957–58); *Dovetail Overture* (Oakland, Calif., March 13, 1960); *Dance Movements* for Chamber Orch. (1962–63); *Symphonic Dialogues* (Washington, D.C., Oct. 31, 1965); *Charade* (1970–74); *A Serenade for Summer* for Chamber Orch. (1976; Tucson, Sept. 15, 1978); *Symphonic Memoir* (1978; Tucson, Jan. 11, 1979); Concerto for Alto Saxophone and Chamber Orch. (Kalamazoo, Mich., Oct. 31, 1981). **CHAMBER:** *Allegro deciso* for Brass Sextet and Timpani (1952); *Fragments* for Woodwind Trio (1958); Trumpet Trio (1959); *3 Designs* for 3 Timpani (1960); Flute Sonata (1960–61); *Movements* for Wind Quintet (1962); 3 piano trios (1966–67; 1975; 1986–87); *Gallery*, suite for Cello (1966); Cello Sonata (1968); *Fantasy Trio* for Clarinet, Cello, and Piano (1969); *Voyage*, 7 pieces for Trumpet, Horn, and Trombone (1969); Alto Saxophone Sonata (1970); Trio for Violin, Viola, and Cello (1971–72); *Time Pieces* for Clarinet and Piano (1983); Wind Quintet (1985); also numerous piano pieces. **VOCAL:** *Alleluia* for Chorus (1961); *I Never Saw a Moor* for Chorus (1967); *Synonyms for Life* for Chorus and Piano (1973).

Mueller, Otto-Werner, German-American conductor and pedagogue; b. Bensheim, June 23, 1926. He studied at the Frankfurt am Main Musisches Gymnasium. He was made music director of the Stuttgart Radio's chamber music dept. (1945), where he founded and conducted its chamber choir; then became conductor at the Heidelberg Theater (1947). After moving to Canada in 1951, he conducted with the CBC and joined the faculty of the Montreal Cons. (1958). He was founder-director of the Victoria School of Music in British Columbia (1963–65) and music director of the Victoria Sym. Orch. (1963–67). He then went to the U.S., where he was prof. of music at the Univ. of Wisc. (1967–77) and of conducting at the Yale Univ. School of Music (1977–86); then taught at N.Y.'s Juilliard School and at Philadelphia's Curtis Inst. of Music (from 1986).

Mueller (actually, **Müller**) **von Asow, Erich H(ermann),** noted German musicologist; b. Dresden, Aug. 31, 1892; d. Berlin, June 4, 1964. He studied with Riemann and Schering at the Univ. of Leipzig (Ph.D., 1915, with the diss. *Die Mingottischen Opernunternehmungen, 1732–1756*; publ. in Dresden, 1917, as *Angelo und Pietro Mingotti: Ein Beitrag zur Geschichte der Oper im XVIII. Jahrhundert*). During World War I, he was active as a military bandmaster. After serving as assistant director of Leipzig's Neue Theater, he was artistic director of Dresden's international festival for modern music (1917–18); was director of the Wernow Theater (1918–19) and then was active as a music critic in Berlin and Dresden; joined the staff of Dresden's Pädagogium der Tonkunst (1926), serving as its director (1927–33). He went to Austria (1936); was briefly under arrest by the Gestapo (1943); returned to Germany in 1945, where he founded the Internationales Musiker-Brief-Archiv in Berlin.

WRITINGS: *Joseph Gustav Mraczek* (Dresden, 1917); *Die Musiksammlung der Bibliothek zu Kronstadt* (Kronstadt, 1930); *Dresdner Musikstätten* (Dresden, 1931); *Egon Kornauth: Ein Bild von Leben und Schaffen des mährischen Komponisten* (Vienna, 1941); *Max Reger und seine Welt* (Berlin, 1944); *Richard Strauss: Thematisches Verzeichnis* (3 vols., Vienna and Wiesbaden, 1959–74; completed by A. Ott and F. Trenner); also ed. numerous vols.

Muench, Gerhart, German-born Mexican pianist, teacher, and composer; b. Dresden, March 23, 1907; d. Tacambaro, Nov. 9, 1988. He studied piano with his father, a prof. at the Dresden Cons.; gave a public piano recital in Dresden at the age of 9. His auspicious career was halted by the Nazi takeover in Germany; Muench was drafted into the German army, but was discharged in 1944 as physically unfit. He went to the U.S. in 1947. In 1953 he settled in Mexico City and taught at the Univ. Nacional. In his piano recitals he introduced the new music of Stockhausen, Boulez, Pousseur, and others to Mexican audiences.

WORKS: CHAMBER OPERA: *Tumulus Veneris* (1950). **ORCH.:** *Concerto da camera* for Piano and Chamber Orch. (1926); *Capriccio variato* for Piano and Orch. (1941); *Vocationes* for Piano and Chamber Orch. (1951); Bassoon Concerto (1956); *Muerte sin fin* (1957); Concerto for Piano and Strings (1957); Violin Concerto (1959); *Labyrinthus Orphei* (1965); *Itinera duo* for Piano and Orch. (1965); *Oxymora* (1967); *Auditur* (1968); *Epitomae tacambarensiae* (1974). **CHAMBER:** Cello Sonata (1938); *Tesauras Orphei* for Oboe, Clarinet, Viola, Double Bass, and Harp (1951); *Tessellata tacambarensia*, cycle of 9 chamber pieces for various instrumental groups or soloists (1964–76); *Out of Chaos* for Cello and Piano (1975); *Signa Flexanima* for Piano Trio (1975); *Tetrálogo* for String Quartet (1977); *Mini-Dialogos* for Violin and Cello (1977); *Proenza* for Piano Trio (1977); *Yuriko* for Violin and Piano (1977); *Pentalgo* for Flute, Oboe, Clarinet, Violin, and Cello (1985). **PIANO:** *Evoluta* for 2 Pianos (1961); *Pièce de résistance* (1962). **VOCAL:** *Asociaciones* for Soprano and Instruments (1969); 5 masses; choruses; songs.

Mugnone, Leopoldo, noted Italian conductor; b. Naples, Sept. 29, 1858; d. there, Dec. 22, 1941. He studied with Cesi and Serrao at the Naples Cons.; began to compose as a young student; when he was 16, he produced a comic opera, *Don Bizarro e le sue figlie* (Naples, April 20, 1875); other operas were *Il Biricchino* (Venice, Aug. 11, 1892; fairly successful) and *Vita Brettone* (Naples, March 14, 1905). He also composed an attractive Neapolitan song, *La Rosella*, and other light music. But it was as a fine opera conductor that Mugnone achieved fame; his performances of Italian stage works possessed the highest degree of authority and an intense musicianly ardor. He also brought out Wagner's music dramas in Italy; conducted the first performances of Mascagni's *Cavalleria rusticana* (Rome, May 17, 1890) and Puccini's *Tosca* (Rome, Jan. 14, 1900).

Mul, Jan, Dutch organist, choral conductor, and composer; b. Haarlem, Sept. 20, 1911; d. Overveen, near Haarlem, Dec. 30, 1971. He was a student of H. Andriessen and Dresden in Amsterdam, and of the Roman Catholic School of Church Music in Utrecht. From 1931 to 1960 he was an organist and choral conductor in Overveen. He also was music ed. of the Amsterdam daily *De Volkskrant*. He orchestrated Dresden's opera *François Villon* from the vocal score (Amsterdam, June 12, 1958) and Sweelinck's *Keyboard Variations on an Old Song* (Amserdam, June 12, 1963). Mul composed some fine sacred choral music.

WORKS: OPERAS: *De Varkenshoeder* (The Swineherd; Amsterdam, June 25, 1953); *Bill Clifford* (Hengelo, Oct. 5, 1964). **ORCH.:** Piano Concerto (1938); *Felicitatie* (1952); *Concerto for Orchestra* (1956); Sinfonietta (1957; based on the Piano Sonata, 1940); *Mein junges Leben* (1961); Concerto for Piano, 4-hands, and Small Orch. (1962); *Confetti musicali* (1965); *Ik, Jan Mul* (I, Jan Mul; 1965); *Divertimento* for Piano and Orch. (1967); *Balladino* for Cello and Orch. or Piano (1968); *Variazioni "I due orsini"* (1968). **CHAMBER:** Quintet for Clarinet, Bassoon, Violin, Viola, and Cello (1957); Trio for 2 Violins and Double Bass (1969). **KEYBOARD: PIANO:** 2 sonatinas (1928, 1942); Sonata (1940; orchestrated as the Sinfonietta, 1957); *Intervallen*, 6 inventions (1942; orchestrated 1954); Sonata for 2 Pianos (1953); *Les Donemoiselles*, 6 pieces (1968). **ORGAN:** Sonata (1942). **VOCAL:** *Stabat Mater* for Chorus and Small Orch. (1934); *4 Coplas* for Voice and Orch. (1936); *Egmont onthalsd* (Egmont Beheaded) for Chorus and Orch. (1938); Sonata for Mezzo-soprano, Baritone, and Small Orch. (1940–53); *Galant Quartet* for Soprano and Small Orch. or Flute, Cello, and Piano (1952); *Te Deum laudamus* for Chorus and Orch. (1955); *Lettre de M. l'Abbé d'Olivet à M. le President Bouhier* for Baritone and Orch. (1962); *De kwink*, ballad for Men's Chorus, Bassoon, and Percussion (1965); *L'Homme désarmé*, cantata for Chorus and Orch. (1970–71; Leiden, Sept. 25, 1973); masses.

Mulder, Ernest Willem, Dutch composer, conductor, and teacher; b. Amsterdam, July 21, 1898; d. there, April 12, 1959. He was a pupil of Schulz (piano) and Zweers (composition) at the Amsterdam Toonkunst cons., where he later was a prof. of theory and composition. From 1938 to 1947 he lectured at the Univ. of Utrecht. He also was director of the Bussum Music School and conductor of the Toonkunst Musical Soc.

WORKS: OPERA: *Dafne* (1932–34). **ORCH.:** Piano Concerto (1935); *Sinfonia sacra III: Super psalmos* (1948) and *IV: Super passionem* (1949–50). **CHAMBER:** 2 violin sonatas (both 1920); *Ars contrapunctica*, 7 pieces for Various Instrumental Combinations (1938–40); *Sonata (in modo classico)* for Solo Violin (1941); Trio for 3 Bassoons (1942); String Quartet (1942); Sextet for Winds and Piano (1946); Quartet for Oboe, Bassoon, Cello, and Harp (1946). **VOCAL:** *3 chansons* for Soprano and Orch. (1921–28); *Sinfonia sacra I* for 6 Soloists, Chorus, and Orch. (1922–32) and *II: Dialogue mystique* for Baritone, Chorus, and Orch. (1936–40); *Requiem (Missa pro defunctis)* for Soloists, Chorus, and Orch. (1927–32); *Holland* for Chorus and Orch. (1942); *Maria-motetten*, 5 pieces for Soprano and Various Instrumental Ensembles (1945); *Stabat Mater dolorosa* for Soloists, Chorus, and Orch. (1948); *Te Deum laudamus* for Chorus and Orch. (1951); *Symphonietta* for Medium Voice and Orch. (1958); songs.

Mulder, Herman, Dutch composer; b. Amsterdam, Dec. 12, 1894; d. there, April 28, 1989. He received training in harmony and voice. After a brief career as a singer, he became a prolific composer.

WORKS: ORCH.: 14 syms. (1940; 1952; 1954; 1959–60; 1961; 1962; 1964; 1967; 1968; 1971; 1972–73; 1974–75; 1976; 1981); Suite (1941); Piano Concerto (1943); *Concerto for Orchestra* (1956); Violin Concerto (1964); *Music* for Violin and Chamber Orch. (1967); *Ouverture* (1967–70); Concerto for 2 Pianos and Orch. (1968); *Funerailles* (1971); *Introduction, Chaconne, and Finale* (1978). **CHAMBER:** 13 string quartets (n.d.–1970); Piano Quintet (1947); 2 string sextets (1957, 1973); 6 violin sonatas (1958–82); Viola Sonata (1960); Trio for Flute, Oboe, and Bassoon (1960); 2 wind quintets (1961, 1966); 2 piano trios (1965, 1978); Piano Quartet (1965); 2 string trios (both 1972); *2 Divertimenti* for Violin (1978); other sonatas, including 6 for piano. **VOCAL:** *De snaren hebben getrild*, cantata for Soprano and Orch. (1977); songs.

Muldowney, Dominic (John), English composer; b. Southampton, July 19, 1952. He received his training from Harvey at the Univ. of Southampton, Birtwistle in London, and Rands and Blake at the Univ. of York (1971–74). In 1976 he became music director of the National Theatre in London. He composes within tonal parameters with a penchant for adventuresome harmonic explorations.

WORKS: DRAMATIC: *An Heavyweight Dirge*, music theater (1971); *Klavier-Hammer*, music theater (1973); *Da Capo al Fine*, ballet (1975); *The Earl of Essex's Galliard*, music theater (1975–76); *Macbeth*, ballet (1979); *Carmen*, ballet (1984–85); incidental music; film scores. **ORCH.:** *Driftwood to the Flow* for Strings (1972); *Music at Chartres* for Chamber Orch. (1974); *Perspectives* (1975); Concerto for 4 Violins and Strings (1980); Piano Concerto (1983); Saxophone Concerto (1984); *Sinfonietta* for Small Orch. (1986); Violin Concerto (1989–90); *3 Pieces* (1990–91); Percussion Concerto (1991); Oboe Concerto (1991–92); Trumpet Concerto (1992–93). **CHAMBER:** 2 string quartets (1973, 1980); *Love Music for Bathsheba Everdene and Gabriel Oak* for Chamber Ensemble (1974); *Solo/Ensemble* (1974); *3-part Motet* for 11 Instruments (1976); *Variations after Sweelinck* for Chamber Ensemble (1977); *Double Helix* for Octet (1977); *In a Hall of Mirrors* for Alto Saxophone and Piano (1979); Piano Trio (1980); *6 Chorale Preludes* for Chamber Ensemble (1986); *Ars subtilor* for Chamber Ensemble and Tape (1987); *Un carnaval Cubiste* for 10 Brass and Metronome (1989). **PIANO:** *A Little Piano Book*, 24 pieces (1979); *Paraphrase on Machaut's Hoquetus David* (1987); *The Ginger Tree*

(1989). **VOCAL:** *Cantata* for Soloists, Speakers, 2 Cellos, and Percussion (1975); *Procurans Odium* for Soprano and 8 Instruments (1977); *5 Psalms* for Soprano, Tenor, Chorus, Wind, and Tape (1979); *5 Theatre Poems* for Mezzo-soprano and Ensemble (1980–81); *In Dark Times* for Soprano, Alto, Tenor, Bass, and Ensemble (1981); *The Duration of Exile* for Mezzo-soprano and Ensemble (1983); *A Second Show* for Contralto, Harp, Violin, Alto Saxophone, and Tape (1983); *Maxims* for Baritone and Ensemble (1986); *Lonely Hearts* for Woman's Voice and Ensemble (1988); *On Suicide* for Voice and Ensemble (1989); *Out of the East* for 2 Voices and Ensemble or Piano (1990).

Mulè, Giuseppe, Italian composer and pedagogue; b. Termini, Imerese, Sicily, June 28, 1885; d. Rome, Sept. 10, 1951. He studied at the Palermo Cons.; graduated as a cellist as well as in composition. In 1922 he was engaged as director of the Palermo Cons. (until 1925); in 1925 he succeeded Respighi as director of the Accademia di Santa Cecilia in Rome; remained there until 1943. He wrote mostly for the stage, and was particularly successful in providing suitable music for revivals of Greek plays. He composed numerous operas in the tradition of the Italian verismo: *La Baronessa di Carini* (Palermo, April 16, 1912); *La Monacella della fontana* (Trieste, Feb. 17, 1923); *Dafni* (Rome, March 14, 1928); *Liola* (Naples, Feb. 2, 1935); *Taormina* (San Remo, 1938); *La zolfara* (Rome, 1939); also the oratorio *Il Cieco di Gerico* (1910); 2 symphonic poems, *Sicilia canora* (1924) and *La Vendemmia* (1936); *3 canti siciliani* for Voice and Orch. (1930); a String Quartet and other chamber music; songs.

Mulet, Henri, French organist, teacher, and composer; b. Paris, Oct. 17, 1878; d. Draguignan, Sept. 20, 1967. He studied with Delsart (premier prix in cello, 1893), Leroux and Pugno (premier prix in harmony, 1896), and Guilmant and Widor (2nd prix in organ, 1897) at the Paris Cons. He taught at the École Niedermeyer (1899–1917) and the Schola Cantorum (1924–31) in Paris, and also held various positions as an organist. In 1937 he settled in Draguignan, where he played organ at the Cathedral until entering a convent in 1958. Mulet composed various orch. and organ works but destroyed most of his MSS in 1937. His best known works are the organ pieces *Esquisses byzantines* and *Carillon sortie.*

Müller, Maria, Austrian soprano; b. Leitmeritz, Jan. 29, 1898; d. Bayreuth, March 13, 1958. She studied with Erik Schmedes in Vienna and Max Altglass in N.Y. She made her operatic debut as Elsa in Linz in 1919; then sang at the German Theater in Prague (1921–23) and at the Bavarian State Opera in Munich (1923–24). On Jan. 21, 1925, she made her Metropolitan Opera debut in N.Y. as Sieglinde, remaining on its roster until 1935. In 1926 she joined the Berlin Städtische Oper. From 1927 to 1943 she sang at the Berlin State Opera. She also sang at the Wagner festivals in Bayreuth (1930–44) and in Salzburg.

Müller, Sigfrid Walther, German composer; b. Plauen, Jan. 11, 1905; d. in a Russian prison camp in Baku, Nov. 2, 1946. He studied at the Leipzig Cons. with Karg-Elert and Martienssen; also church music and organ with Straube. He taught at the Leipzig Cons. (1929–32) and at the Hochschule für Musik in Weimar (1940–41); then was in the German army on the eastern front. His output comprised 62 opus numbers, mostly chamber music and organ works; also an opera, *Schlaraffenhochzeit* (Leipzig, 1937); *Böhmische Musik* for Orch.; *Gohliser Schlossmusik* for Small Orch.; Concerto for Flute and Chamber Orch. (1941).

Müller-Blattau, Joseph (Maria), noted German musicologist; b. Colmar, Alsace, May 21, 1895; d. Saarbrücken, Oct. 21, 1976. He studied musicology with Friedrich Ludwig at the Univ. of Strasbourg, and composition and conducting with Pfitzner and organ with Ernst Münch at the Strasbourg Cons. He served in the German army during World War I; after the Armistice of 1918, he resumed his studies in musicology with Wilibald Gurlitt at the Univ. of Freiburg im Breisgau (Ph.D., 1920, with the diss. *Grundzüge einer Geschichte der Fuge*, publ. in Königsberg, 1923; 3rd ed., rev., 1963). He then completed his Habilitation at the Univ. of Königsberg in 1922 with his *Die Kompositionslehre Heinrich Schützens in der Fassung seines Schulers Christoph Bernhard* (publ. in Leipzig, 1926; 2nd ed., 1963). He taught at the Univ. of Königsberg; was promoted to reader there in 1928; then taught at the Univs. of Frankfurt am Main (1935–37) and Freiburg im Breisgau (1937–39); subsequently served in military administration (1939–42); then lectured at the Univ. of Strasbourg during the last years of World War II. From 1952 to 1958 he was director of the Staatliche Hochschule für Musik in Saarbrücken; he also taught at the Univ. of Strasbourg from 1952 to 1964. He was the editor of the abortive 12th ed. of Riemann's *Musiklexikon* (1937–39), of which only a few issues appeared before the outbreak of World War II made further publication impossible.

WRITINGS: *Das Elsass, ein Grenzland deutscher Musik* (Freiburg im Breisgau, 1922); *Geschichte der Musik in Ost- und Westpreussen von der Ordenszeit bis zur Gegenwart* (Königsberg, 1931; 2nd ed., enl., 1968); *Hamann und Herder in ihren Beziehungen zur Musik* (Königsberg, 1931); *Das deutsche Volkslied* (Berlin, 1932; 2nd ed., 1958); *Einführung in die Musikgeschichte* (Berlin, 1932; 2nd ed., 1941); *Johannes Brahms* (Potsdam, 1933); *Georg Friedrich Händel* (Potsdam, 1933; 2nd ed., 1959); *Zur Erforschung des ostpreussischen Volksliedes* (Halle, 1934); *Johann Sebastian Bach* (Leipzig, 1935; 2nd ed., Stuttgart, 1950); *Geschichte der deutschen Musik* (Berlin, 1938; 3rd ed., 1942); *Hans Pfitzner* (Potsdam, 1940; 2nd ed., rev., 1969); *Gestaltung—Umgestaltung: Studien zur Geschichte der musikalischen Variation* (Stuttgart, 1950); *Das Verhältnis von Wort und Ton in der Geschichte der Musik: Grundzüge und Probleme* (Stuttgart, 1952); *Die Volksliedsammlung des jungen Goethe* (Kassel, 1955); *Von der Vielfalt der Musik: Musikgeschichte—Musikerziehung—Musikpflege* (Freiburg im Breisgau, 1966); *Goethe und die Meister der Musik* (Stuttgart, 1969).

BIBL.: W. Salmen, ed., *Festgabe für J. M.-B. zum 65. Geburtstag* (Saarbrücken, 1960; 2nd ed., 1962); C.-H. Mahling, ed., *Zum 70. Geburtstag von J. M.-B.* (Kassel, 1966).

Müller-Hartmann, Robert, German composer; b. Hamburg, Oct. 11, 1884; d. Dorking, Surrey, Dec. 15, 1950. He studied at the Stern Cons. in Berlin. He was a lecturer on music at the Univ. of Hamburg (1923–33); in 1937 he settled in England, where he worked mainly as an arranger and translator. He wrote a number of symphonic works, some of which were first performed by Richard Strauss and Karl Muck: a Sym. (1926), a Symphonic Ballad, several sets of variations, etc.; a Trio for Flute, Violin, and Viola; 2 violin sonatas; many organ works; piano pieces.

Müller-Hermann, Johanna, Austrian composer and pedagogue; b. Vienna, Jan. 15, 1878; d. there, April 19, 1941. She studied with Nawrátil, Josef Labor, Guido Adler, Zemlinsky, and J.B. Foerster. She began to compose at an early age, in a Romantic vein, influenced chiefly by Mahler and Reger; was regarded as one of the foremost European women composers of orch. and chamber music of her time. She wrote an oratorio, *In Memoriam*, to Walt Whitman's words; a Sym. for Voices with Orch.; a Symphonic Fantasy on Ibsen's play *Brand*; String Quartet; String Quintet; Piano Quintet; Violin Sonata; Cello Sonata; Piano Sonata; several song cycles.

Müller-Kray, Hans, German conductor and composer; b. Essen, Oct. 13, 1908; d. Stuttgart, May 30, 1969. He studied piano, cello, and theory in Essen; then was a conductor at the theater there. He conducted in Münster (1934–41), Frankfurt am Main (1942–45), and Wiesbaden (1945–48). In 1948 he became chief conductor of the Stuttgart Radio Sym. Orch., a post he held until his death. He wrote several ballet scores and other works.

Müller von Kulm, Walter, Swiss composer; b. Kulm, Aug. 31, 1899; d. Arlesheim, near Basel, Oct. 3, 1967. He studied in

Aarau and at the conservatories and in Basel and Zürich, and took courses in musicology, philosophy, and psychology at the Univ. of Basel. He was director of the Basel Cons. (1947–64). He publ. the manual *Grundriss der Harmonielehre* (Basel, 1948). Among his works were the opera *Der Erfinder* (1944); a ballet, *Die blaue Blume* (1936); the oratorios *Vater unser* (1945) and *Petrus* (1960); Sym. (1928); chamber music; keyboard pieces; etc.

Müller-Zürich (real name, **Müller**), **Paul,** esteemed Swiss conductor and composer; b. Zürich, June 19, 1898; d. Lucerne, July 21, 1993. He studied with Andreae and Jarnach at the Zürich Cons. (1917–19) and in Paris and Berlin; then taught in Zürich at the Cons. (1927–69) and at the Univ. (1959–70). He was active as a choral and sym. conductor, serving as director of the Elisabeth Schmid Choir (1931–39), the Lucerne Chamber Orch. (1948–55), and other ensembles. His music evolved from early Romantic influences to reflect neo-Baroque practices in a contemporary, tonal style.

WORKS: ORCH.: 4 syms.: *Little Symphony* (1920), Sym. for Strings (1944), Sym. (1947), and Sym. for Flute and Strings (1952); *Little Serenade* for Chamber Orch. (1921); *Hymnus* (1927); Concerto for Viola and Small Orch. (1934); 2 violin concertos: No. 1 for Violin and Small Orch. (1935) and No. 2 (1957); Concerto for Organ and Strings (1938); Cello Concerto (1954); *Sinfonischer Prolog* (1955); *Sinfonische Suite* (1956–57); Concerto for 2 Violins, Harpsichord, and Strings (1958); *Sinfonietta* (1964); *Sonata* for Strings (1967–68); *Consenso*, suite (1974). **CHAMBER:** String Quintet (1919); 2 string quartets (1921, 1960); 3 violin sonatas (1922, 1941, 1952); *Marienleben* for 10 Instruments (1928); *Praludium, Arie und Fuge* for Oboe, Bassoon, Horn, Trumpet, and String Quintet (1933); *Petite sonate* for Clarinet and Piano (1942); *Fantasie und Fugue* for Violin and Organ (1949); String Trio (1950); *Canzone* for String Quartet (1961); Trio for Flute, Clarinet, and Piano (1965–66); Sonata for Solo Viola (1979); *Fantasie* for Oboe and Organ (1980); *Serenata turicensis* for Basset Horn, Viola, and Cello (1981); organ music. **OTHER:** Dramatic works; choral music; songs.

BIBL.: F. Jakob, *P. M.: Biographie und Werkverzeichnis* (Zürich, 1963).

Mullings, Frank (Coningsby), distinguished English tenor; b. Walsall, March 10, 1881; d. Manchester, May 19, 1953. He studied voice in Birmingham. He made his operatic debut in Coventry in 1907 as Faust; then sang Tristan in London in 1913, and performed the role of Otello in Manchester in 1916. In 1919 he was the first to sing Parsifal in English, at Covent Garden in London. From 1922 to 1926 he was the principal dramatic tenor of the British National Opera Co., and appeared with it as Apollo in the first performance, in 1924, of Rutland Boughton's *Alkestis.* He taught at the Birmingham School of Music (1927–46) and at the Royal Manchester College of Music (1944–49). His other roles included Siegfried, Tannhäuser, Canio, and Radames.

Mullova, Viktoria, Russian violinist; b. Moscow, Nov. 27, 1959. She began violin lessons in childhood and made her public debut as soloist in Vieutemps's 5th Concerto when she was 12; studied in Moscow with Bronin at the Central Music School (1969–78) and with Kogan at the Moscow Cons. She won 1st prize in the Sibelius Competition in Helsinki in 1981 and took the Gold Medal in the Tchaikovsky Competition in Moscow in 1982. She then left Russia to pursue an international career, touring as a concert recitalist and appearing as soloist with major orchs.

Mumma, Gordon, innovative American composer, performer, electronic-music engineer, teacher, and writer on music; b. Framingham, Mass., March 30, 1935. He received private instruction in piano, horn, and composition; attended the Univ. of Mich. in Ann Arbor (1952–53). In 1958 he became cofounder of Ann Arbor's Cooperative Studio for Electronic Music, remaining active with it until 1966; also was co-director of the ONCE Festival and ONCE Group there (1960–66). He helped to develop a revolutionary theatrical art based on projected images, resulting in an aesthetic medium called "Manifestations: Light and Sound" and, later, "Space Theatre"; in 1964 he participated in a memorable presentation of "Space Theatre" at Venice's Biennial Exhibition, a pioneering demonstration of the electronic light show. Having attended the Inst. of Science and Technology at the Univ. of Mich. (1959–62), he returned there as a research assoc. in acoustics and seismics (1962–63). From 1966 to 1974 he was active as a composer and performer with the Merce Cunningham Dance Co. in N.Y.; also was active with the Sonic Arts Union in N.Y. (from 1966). He taught at the Univ. of Ill. at Urbana (1969–70) and at the Univ. of Calif. at Santa Cruz (1973–75), where he subsequently was a prof. of music (from 1975). He also was a visiting lecturer at Brandeis Univ. (1966–67), the State Univ. of N.Y. at Buffalo (1968), and the Ferienkurse für Neue Musik in Darmstadt (1974); in 1981 he held the Darius Milhaud Professorship at Mills College in Oakland, California; after serving as a visiting prof. at the Univ. of Calif. at San Diego (1985, 1987), he returned to Mills College as Distinguished Visiting Composer in 1989. Mumma has contributed various articles on contemporary music to journals and other publications. He pioneered the process of "cybersonic music," the control of acoustical and electronic media by means of feedback; also applied computer techniques to composition.

WORKS: *Sinfonia* for 12 Instruments and Tape (1958–60; Ann Arbor, March 4, 1961); *Mographs*, pieces for Various Combinations of Pianos and Pianists (1962–64); *Retrospect*, stereophonic electro-acoustic music (1962–82; Santa Cruz, Calif., Oct. 6, 1982); *Megaton for William Burroughs*, live electronic piece for 10 Electronic, Acoustic, and Communication Channels (1963; Ann Arbor, Feb. 28, 1964); *Music for the Venezia Space Theatre* for 4-channel Magnetic Tape with Live Electronic Music (Venice, Sept. 1, 1964); *The Dresden Interleaf 13 February 1945*, quadraphonic electronic music on magnetic tape (Ann Arbor, Feb. 13, 1965); *Horn* for Cybersonic Horn and Voices (1965); *Mesa*, live electronic music for Cybersonic Bandoneon (St. Paul de Vence, France, Aug. 6, 1966); *Hornpipe* for Cybernetic Horn and Waldhorn (1967); *Schoolwork* for Bowed Psaltery, Piano Melodica, and Bowed Crosscut Saw (1970); *Telepos* for Dancers, Telemetry Belts, and Accelerometers (1971; N.Y., Feb. 2, 1972); *Cybersonic Cantilevers*, cybersonic electronic system with public participation (Syracuse, N.Y., May 19, 1973); *Some Voltage Drop*, variable-duration theater piece with electroacoustical implementation (Paris, Oct. 13, 1974); *Earheart: Flights, Formations, and Starry Nights* for Dancers and Electronics (Portland, Oreg., Sept. 9, 1977); *Echo-BCD* for Dancers and Electronics (Portland, Oreg., Oct. 15, 1978); *11 Note Pieces and Decimal Passacaglia* for Harpsichord (1979); *Pontpoint* for Dancers and Electronics (1979; Portland, Oreg., March 14, 1980); *Faisandage et galimafrée*, divertimento for Trios of Diverse Instruments (Santa Cruz, Calif., June 10, 1984); *Epifont (Spectral Portrait in memoriam George Cacioppo)*, stereophonic electroacoustic music on magnetic tape (1984; Ann Arbor, April 14, 1985); *Than Particle* for Percussion and Digital Computer (Los Angeles, Nov. 7, 1985); *Aleutian Displacement* for Chamber Orch. (1987); *Orait* for Dancers and Vocal Ensemble (Santa Cruz, Calif., June 17, 1988); *Ménages à deux* for Violin, Piano, Vibraphone, and Marimba (1989; Berkeley, Calif., Feb. 10, 1990).

Munch (originally, **Münch**), **Charles,** eminent Alsatian-born French conductor; b. Strasbourg, Sept. 26, 1891; d. Richmond, Va., Nov. 6, 1968. He was the son of the Alsatian organist and choral conductor Ernst Münch (b. Niederbronn, Dec. 31, 1859; d. Strasbourg, April 1, 1928). He studied violin at the Strasbourg Cons. and with Lucien Capet in Paris. At the outbreak of World War I (1914), he enlisted in the German army; made a sergeant of artillery, he was gassed at Peronne and wounded at Verdun; after the end of the war (1918) and his return to Alsace-Lorraine (1919), he became a naturalized French citizen. Having received further violin training from Flesch in Berlin, he pursued a career as a soloist; was also prof. of violin at the Leipzig Cons. and concertmaster of the Gewandhaus Orch. there. On Nov. 1, 1932, he made his professional conducting debut in Paris with the Straram Orch. He studied conducting with Szendrei in Paris (1933–40). He quickly rose to prominence; was conductor of Paris's Orch. de la Société Philharmonique (1935–38) and became a prof. at the École Normale de Musique (1936). In 1938 he became music director of the Société des Concerts du Conservatoire de Paris, remaining in that post during the years of the German occupation during World War II; refusing to collaborate with the Nazis, he gave his support to the Resistance, being awarded the Légion d'honneur in 1945. He made his U.S. debut as a guest conductor of the Boston Sym. Orch. on Dec. 27, 1946; a transcontinental tour of the U.S. with the French National Radio Orch. followed in 1948. In 1949 he was appointed music director of the Boston Sym. Orch., which he and Monteux took on its first European tour in 1952; they took it again to Europe in 1956, also touring in the Soviet Union, making it the first U.S. orch. to do so. After retiring from his Boston post in 1962, Munch made appearances as a guest conductor; also helped to launch the Orchestre de Paris in 1967. Munch acquired an outstanding reputation as an interpreter of the French repertoire, his performances being marked by spontaneity, color, and elegance. French music of the 20th century also occupied a prominent place on his programs; he brought out new works by Roussel, Milhaud, Honegger, and others. He wrote *Je suis chef d'orchestre* (Paris, 1954; Eng. tr., N.Y., 1955).

BIBL.: P. Olivier, *C. M.: Une Biographie par le disque* (Paris, 1987); G Honegger, *C. M.* (Strasbourg, 1992).

Münch, Hans, Alsatian-born Swiss conductor and composer; b. Mulhouse, March 9, 1893; d. Basel, Sept. 7, 1983. His father, Eugen Munch, was a conductor. His uncle was the Alsatian organist and choral conductor Ernst Münch (b. Niederbronn, Dec. 31, 1859; d. Strasbourg, April 1, 1928). After studying with Albert Schweitzer, he settled in Basel (1912) and became a naturalized Swiss citizen; took courses with Hans Huber (composition), Adolf Hamm (organ), and Emil Braun (cello) at the Cons. He played cello in the city orch. (1914–16); then taught piano at the Cons. (1918–32) and conducted the Bach Choir (1921–26); subsequently led the Gesangverein and the Liedertafel, was conductor of the Allgemeine Musikgesellschaft (1935–66), and served as director of the Music School and Cons. (1935–47). He composed a Sym. (1951), *Symphonische Improvisationen* (1971), and several cantatas.

Münchinger, Karl, German conductor; b. Stuttgart, May 29, 1915; d. there, March 13, 1990. He studied at the Hochschule für Musik in Stuttgart; then with Abendroth at the Leipzig Cons. From 1941 to 1943 he was 1st conductor of the orch. in Hannover, and in 1945 founded the Stuttgart Chamber Orch. He toured America, Japan, and Russia; made his U.S. debut in San Francisco in 1953, and during the following season made a U.S. tour with his Stuttgart Chamber Orch.; he visited the U.S. again in 1977. In 1966 he organized the "Klassische Philharmonie" in Stuttgart, with which he gave regular performances. He retired in 1988.

Munclinger, Milan, Czech flutist and conductor; b. Košice, July 3, 1923; d. Prague, March 30, 1986. He began to study the flute in his youth; then enrolled at the Prague Cons.; also studied at the Prague Academy of Musical Arts and the Univ. of Prague. He gained distinction as founder-conductor of the Ars Ridiviva ensemble (1951), with which he gave performances of the Baroque and Classical repertoires with much success; also toured widely with his ensemble.

Münnich, Richard, German music educator and theorist; b. Berlin, June 7, 1877; d. Weimar, June 4, 1970. After training in piano with his father and in cello with Otto Hutschenreuter, he studied musicology with Bellermann, Friedlaender, and Stumpf at the Univ. of Berlin (Ph.D., 1902, with the diss. *Johann Kuhnau: Sein Leben und seine Werke*; publ. in the *Sammelbände der Internationalen Musik-Gesellschaft*, III, 1901–02), and composition with Grabert. He taught in Berlin at the Klindworth-Scharwenka Cons. (1910–35) and the Charlottenburg Akademie für Kirchen- und Schulmusik (1928–34). From 1935 to 1964 he was a prof. at the Weimar Hochschule für Musik, where he also served as director from 1935 to 1949. He was co-ed. (1928–34) and ed. (from 1934) of the *Zeitschrift für Schulmusik*. He was honored with Festschriften in 1947 and 1957. In his numerous writings on harmony, he followed Riemann's analytical theories. He publ. *Zilchers Dehmel-Zyklus* (Charlottenburg, 1911), *Jale, Ein Beitrag sur Tonsilbenfrage und zer Schulmusik-Propädeutik* (Lahr, 1930; 2nd ed., Wolfenbüttel, 1959), and *Die Suite* (Berlin, 1931; 2nd ed., 1957, by H. Schmidt).

Munrow, David (John), gifted English recorder player; b. Birmingham, Aug. 12, 1942; d. (suicide) Chesham Bois, Buckinghamshire, May 15, 1976. He studied English at Pembroke College, Cambridge; during this period (1961–64), he founded an ensemble for the furtherance of early English music and organized a recorder consort. In 1967 he formed the Early Music Consort of London, with which he gave many successful concerts of medieval and Renaissance music; also was active with his own BBC radio program. He lectured on the history of early music at the Univ. of Leicester (from 1967) and was prof. of recorder at London's Royal Academy of Music (from 1969). He publ. the vol. *Instruments of the Middle Ages and Renaissance* (London, 1976). He killed himself for obscure reasons in his early maturity.

Munsel, Patrice (Beverly), American soprano; b. Spokane, Wash., May 14, 1925. She studied in N.Y. with William Herman and Renato Bellini. She won an audition at the Metropolitan Opera and made a successful debut there on Dec. 4, 1943, in the role of Philine in Thomas's *Mignon*, being the youngest singer to appear there to that time; she remained on the staff until 1958, excepting the 1945–46 season. She subsequently made several European tours. Her best roles were Gilda, Lucia, Rosina, Violetta, and Lakme. She portrayed Melba in a film of Melba's life (1953); also made successful appearances in operetta and in Broadway musicals.

Munz, Mieczyslaw, esteemed Polish-American pianist and pedagogue; b. Kraków, Oct. 31, 1900; d. N.Y., Aug. 25, 1976. He studied piano and composition at the Vienna Academy of Music, and later at the Hochschule für Musik in Berlin; his principal teacher there was Busoni. He made a brilliant debut in Berlin in 1920 as soloist in 3 works on the same program: the Brahms Piano Concerto in D minor, Liszt's Piano Concerto in A, and *Variations symphoniques* by Franck. His American debut took place in a solo recital in N.Y. on Oct. 20, 1922; he subsequently was soloist with a number of orchs. in the U.S.; also toured Europe, South America, Australia, and Japan. He taught at the Cincinnati Cons. of Music (1925–30); then was on the faculty of the Curtis Inst. of Music in Philadelphia (1930–32; 1941–63); from 1946 to 1965 he taught at the Peabody Inst. in Baltimore; also was a prof. of piano at the Juilliard School of Music in N.Y. (1963–75). In 1975 he was given a tenured appointment at the Toho Gakuen School of Music in Tokyo, but he was forced to return to the U.S. due to illness. He was highly esteemed as a teacher; his students included Emanuel Ax and Ilana Vered. His piano playing was distinguished by a fine Romantic flair supported by an unobtrusive virtuoso technique.

Muradeli, Vano (Ilyich), Russian composer; b. Gori, Georgia, April 6, 1908; d. Tomsk, Siberia, Aug. 14, 1970. As a child he improvised songs, accompanying himself on the mandolin; he studied with Barchudarian and Bagrinsky at the Tiflis Cons. (graduated, 1931) and with Shekhter and Miaskovsky at the Moscow Cons. (graduated, 1934). His early compositions were influenced by his native folk music; he wrote a *Georgian Suite* for Piano (1935) and incidental music to plays on Caucasian subjects. His first important work was a sym. in memory of the assassinated Soviet dignitary Kirov (Moscow, Nov. 28, 1938);

his 2nd Sym. (1946) received a Stalin prize. The performance of his opera *Great Friendship* (Moscow, Nov. 7, 1947) gave rise to an official condemnation of modernistic trends in Soviet music, culminating in the resolution of the Central Committee of the Communist Party of Feb. 10, 1948, which described the opera as "chaotic, inharmonious, and alien to the normal human ear." His reputation was rehabilitated by his subsequent works: *The Path of Victory*, symphonic poem for Chorus and Orch. (1950); a series of choruses (*Stalin's Will Has Led Us; Song of the Fighters for Peace*; and *Hymn to Moscow*, which received a Stalin prize in 1951); and an opera, *October* (Moscow, April 22, 1964).

Murail, Tristan, remarkable French composer; b. Le Havre, March 11, 1947. He received training in Arabic and economics (1963–70), taking courses at the École Nationale des Langues Orientales and at the Institut d'Études Politiques in Paris. He also studied composition with Messiaen at the Paris Cons. (1967–71), taking the premier prix (1971). After winning the Prix de Rome, he pursued training at the French Academy in Rome (1971–73). Upon his return to Paris, he helped to found the contemporary instrumental music ensemble L'Intinéraire. In 1982–83 he was active at IRCAM in Paris. From 1989 to 1991 he was prof. of composition at the American Cons. in Fontainebleau. He also was a consultant at IRCAM from 1990 to 1992. Murail has explored innovative approaches to all aspects of composition, often through imaginative uses of the computer.

WORKS: ORCH.: *Couleur de mer* for 15 Instruments (Le Havre, May 13, 1969); *Altitude 8000* for Small Orch. (1970; Paris, Jan. 18, 1971); *Au delà du mur du son* (Rome, June 10, 1972); *Sables* (1974–75; Royan, March 22, 1975); *Les courants de l'espace* for Ondes Martenot, Synthesizer, and Small Orch. (1979; Paris, Dec. 20, 1980); *Gondwana* (Darmstadt, July 21, 1980); *Désintégrations* for 17 Instruments and Tape (1982; Paris, Feb. 15, 1983); *Sillages* (Kyoto, Sept. 9, 1985; rev. 1990); *Time and again* (1985; Birmingham, Jan. 21, 1986); *Les Sept Paroles du Christ en Croix: I, De Ciel et de Terre* (1986–87); *La dynamique des fluides* (1990–91; Parma, June 17, 1991); *Serendib* for 22 Instruments (1991–92; Paris, June 18, 1992). **CHAMBER:** *Mach 2, 5* for 2 Ondes Martenot (1971; Paris, Feb. 2, 1972; also for 6 Ondes Martenot, 1975); *L'Attente* for 7 Instruments (Paris, Nov. 18, 1972; rev. 1992); *Les Nuages de Magellan* for 2 Ondes Martenot, Electric Guitar, and Percussion (Orleans, March 23, 1973); *Mémoire/Erosion* for Horn and 9 Instruments (1975–76; Orleans, March 5, 1976); *Ethers* for 6 Instruments (Lisbon, June 6, 1978); *Treize couleurs du soleil* for 5 Instruments (1978; Madrid, Dec. 4, 1979); *Random Access Memory* for 6 Instrumentalists (1984–85; Metz, Oct. 4, 1985; rev. 1987); *Atlantys* for 2 Synthesizers (King's Lynn, July 26, 1986); *Vision de la cité interdite* for 2 Synthesizers (King's Lynn, July 26, 1986); *Vues aériennes* for Horn, Violin, Cello, and Piano (London, Dec. 1, 1988); *Allégories* for 7 Instruments (1989–90; Brussels, March 13, 1990); *Le four à pattes bleues* for Flute and Piano (1990; Radio France, Nov. 21, 1991); *La Barque Mystique* for 5 Instruments (Bern, Oct. 16, 1993); *L'Esprit des Dunes* for 11 Instruments (1993–94; Paris, May 28, 1994); also pieces for Solo Instruments. **PIANO:** *Estuaire* (1971–72); *Territoires de l'oubil* (1976–77; Rome, May 22, 1978); *Cloches d'adieu, et un sourire . . . in memoriam Olivier Messiaen* (1992); *La Mandragore* (Tokyo, Nov. 27, 1993). **VOCAL:** *O tremblant des contours* for 2 Altos (Paris, Nov. 20, 1970); *La dérive des continents* for Alto and 12 Strings (1973; Royan, March 23, 1974); *Les Sept Paroles du Christ en Croix II: Les Sept Paroles* for Chorus and Orch. (1987–88; London, Oct. 28, 1989); *. . . amaris et dulcibus aquis . . .* for Chorus and 2 Synthesizers (1994).

Murakumo, Ayako, Japanese composer; b. Gifu Prefecture, Feb. 25, 1949. She graduated from the Graduate School of Aichi Prefecture Univ. of the Arts (degree, 1982). She received the Nagoya City Cultural Promotion Prize (1985), the Incentive Prize for Original Theatrical Art from the Agency of Cultural Affairs (1986), and an award from the Kyūshū competition (1988).

WORKS: ORCH.: *Hishō* (1980); *Chronos* (1982); *Wave* (1982). **CHAMBER:** *Reflection* for Flute, Clarinet, Cello, and Percussion (1982); *Fuha* for Flute, Cello, and Piano (1984); *Chiku-in Sō-Sho* for Shakuhachi and Koto (1985); *Interspersion* for Viola, Cello, and Contrabass (1988); *Polymorph II* for Recorder and Guitar (1989). **VOCAL:** *Projection* for Mezzo-soprano, Cello, and Piano (1984); *Ondine* for Chorus (1985).

Muratore, Lucien, prominent French tenor and teacher; b. Marseilles, Aug. 29, 1876; d. Paris, July 16, 1954. He studied at the Marseilles Cons., graduating with honors in 1897, but began his career as an actor. Later he studied opera at the Paris Cons. He made his operatic debut at the Paris Opéra-Comique on Dec. 16, 1902, as the King in Hahn's *La Carmélite*, with extraordinary success. Muratore also sang in the premieres of several operas by Massenet: *Ariane* (1906), *Bacchus* (1909), and *Roma* (1912); Février's *Monna Vanna* (1909), and Giordano's *Siberia* (1911) et al. In 1913 he made his American debut with the Boston Opera Co.; on Dec. 15, 1913, he sang Faust with the Chicago Opera Co. In 1914 he joined the French army; then returned to the Chicago Grand Opera (1915–19; 1920–22). In 1922 he went back to France; for 7 years he served as mayor of the town of Biot. He was married 3 times; his first 2 marriages (to Marguerite Beriza, a soprano, and to **Lina Cavalieri**) ended in divorce; his 3rd wife was Marie Louise Brivaud. Among his finest roles were Faust, Don José, and Des Grieux.

Muro, Bernardo de, Italian tenor; b. Tempio Pausanio, Sardinia, Nov. 3, 1881; d. Rome, Oct. 27, 1955. He studied at the Accademia di Santa Cecilia in Rome and with Alfredo Martinio. He made his operatic debut as Turiddu at Rome's Teatro Costanzi in 1910; in 1911 he appeared at Milan's La Scala as Folco in Mascagni's *Isabeau* and returned there in the title role of *Don Carlos* in 1912; then sang in various Italian music centers, winning admiration for his portrayal of Otello; also appeared in Europe and South America. After marrying the American soprano Barbara Wait, he toured in the U.S. with minor opera companies; following his retirement from the stage (1943), he devoted himself to teaching. He never became a star in the operatic firmament, yet knowledgeable critics regarded him as worthy of comparison with Caruso, both in the carrying force of his natural voice and in emotional appeal. He wrote an autobiographical vol., *Quandro ero Folco* (Milan, 1956).

Murray, Ann, Irish mezzo-soprano; b. Dublin, Aug. 27, 1949. She studied at the Royal Manchester College of Music and in London. In 1974 she made her operatic debut as Alceste at Glasgow's Scottish Opera, and then appeared regularly at London's English National Opera; in 1976 she made her Covent Garden debut in London as Cherubino, and subsequently sang there frequently. On Oct. 18, 1985, she made her Metropolitan Opera debut in N.Y. as Sextus in *La clemenza di Tito*. In 1990 she scored a notable success as Berlioz's Beatrice with the English National Opera. In 1994 she appeared as Giulio Cesare in Munich. She also sang as a guest artist with various opera houses and festivals at home and abroad, and likewise pursued a notably successful career as a concert artist. Among her finest roles are Handel's Xerxes, Mozart's Dorabella and Zerlina, and Strauss's Composer. Her husband is **Philip Langridge**.

Murray, Bain, American composer and teacher; b. Evanston, Ill., Dec. 26, 1926; d. Cleveland, Jan. 16, 1993. He was a student of Elwell at Oberlin (Ohio) College (A.B., 1951), of Thompson and Piston at Harvard Univ. (A.M., 1952), and of Boulanger in Paris. He taught at Harvard Univ. (1954–55), Oberlin College (1955–60), and Cleveland State Univ. (from 1960), wherehe was head of its theory and composition dept. (from 1966).

WORKS: *The Legend*, opera-oratorio (1986; Cleveland, May 8, 1987); *Mary Stuart: A Queen Betrayed*, opera (Cleveland, March 1, 1991); *Peter Pan*, ballet; *Epitaph* for Strings; 2 string quartets; Trio for Flute, Cello, and Piano; Woodwind Quintet; piano pieces; many choral works; song cycles.

Murray, Michael, American organist; b. Kokomo, Ind., March 19, 1943. He studied with Dorothy Cleveland Hopkins in

Kokomo (1958–59), Mallory Bransford in Indianapolis (1959–61), Haskell Thomson at Oberlin (Ohio) College (1961; 1965), and Marcel Dupré in Paris (1961–64). He served as organist (1967–80) and music director (1970–80) at Cleveland Heights Christian Church. He formally launched his career as a concert artist with a series of the complete organ works of J.S. Bach in Cleveland (1968–69). He made his European debut in Leiden, the Netherlands, in 1972; thereafter he regularly toured the U.S. and Europe, making his N.Y. debut at St. James Episcopal Church in 1986. He was a contributor of articles to the journals *Diapason* and *American Organist*; publ. *Marcel Dupré: The Work of a Master* (Boston, 1985) and *Albert Schweitzer, Musician* (Aldershot, 1994).

Murray, Thomas (Mantle), American organist and choral conductor; b. Los Angeles, Oct. 6, 1943. He studied with Clarence Mader (organ) and Howard Swan (choral conducting) at Occidental College (B.A., 1965), then was organist at Los Angeles's Immanuel Presbyterian Church (1965–73) and organist and choirmaster at Boston's St. Paul's Episcopal Church (1973–80). He taught at the Yale Univ. School of Music from 1981 and toured widely as a recitalist, acquiring a fine reputation as an interpreter of the Romantic organ repertoire.

Murray, William, American baritone; b. Schenectady, N.Y., March 13, 1935. He studied at Adelphi Univ. In 1956 he received a Fulbright scholarship and continued his training in Rome. After making his operatic debut as Count Gil in *Il segreto di Susanna* in Spoleto in 1956, he sang in Detmold, Braunschweig, Munich, Frankfurt am Main, Amsterdam, and Salzburg. In 1969 he became a member of the Deutsche Oper in Berlin, where he was made a Kammersanger. In 1970 he created the title role in Dallapiccola's *Ulisse* at Milan's La Scala. In 1973 he sang in the premiere of Nabokov's *Love's Labours Lost* in Brussels. Among his other roles were Don Giovanni, Rigoletto, Don Carlo, Wolfram, Macbeth, and Scarpia.

Murrill, Herbert (Henry John), English organist, choral conductor, broadcasting executive, and composer; b. London, May 11, 1909; d. there, July 24, 1952. He studied at the Royal Academy of Music in London with York Bowen, Stanley Marchant, and Alan Bush (1925–28); then was an organ scholar at Worcester College, Oxford (1928–31), where he took courses with Ernest Walker and Sir Hugh Allen. He occupied various posts as organist and choral director; was prof. of composition at the Royal Academy of Music (1933–52); joined the staff of the BBC (1936), where he was program organizer (1942); after working in the British intelligence service (1942–46), he returned to the BBC as assistant head (1948) and head (1950) of music. His relatively small output was in a modern vein, exemplified by a "jazz opera," *Man in Cage* (London, 1930). He also wrote 2 cello concertos (1935; *El cant dels ocells*, 1950), choral works, chamber music, piano pieces, and songs.

Mursell, James L(ockhart), English-born American music educator; b. Derby, June 1, 1893; d. Jackson, N.H., Feb. 1, 1963. Following training in England and at the Univ. of Queensland in Brisbane, Australia (B.A., 1915), he studied philosophy with Josiah Royce at Harvard Univ. (Ph.D., 1918); then pursued training for the ministry at N.Y.'s Union Theological Seminary (1918–20). He taught psychology and education at Lake Erie College in Painesville, Ohio (1921–23), and then philosophy, psychology, and education at Lawrence College in Appleton, Wis. (1923–25), where he also studied at the Cons. with Gladys Brainard. In 1935 he became prof. of education at Teachers College, Columbia Univ., where he later was chairman of the music education dept. (1939–57). Mursell was a proponent of a humanistic approach to music education.

WRITINGS (all publ. in N.Y. unless otherwise given): *Principles of Musical Education* (1927); with M. Glenn, *The Psychology of School Music Teaching* (1931; 2nd ed., 1938); *Human Values in Music Education* (1934); *The Psychology of Music* (1937); *Music in American Schools* (1943); *Education for Musical Growth* (Boston, 1948); *Music and the Classroom Teacher* (1951); *Music Education: Principles and Programs* (Morristown, N.J., 1956).

BIBL.: L. Simutis, *J.L. M. as Music Educator* (diss., Univ. of Ottawa, 1961); D. Metz, *A Critical Analysis of the Thought of J.L. M. in Music Education* (diss., Case Western Reserve Univ., 1968); V. O'Keefe, *J.L. M.: His Life and Contributions to Music Education* (diss., Teachers College, Columbia Univ., 1970).

Musgrave, Thea, remarkable Scottish composer; b. Barnton, Midlothian, May 27, 1928. She pursued preliminary medical studies at the Univ. of Edinburgh, and concurrently studied with Mary Grierson (musical analysis) and Hans Gál (composition and counterpoint), receiving her B.Mus. (1950) and winning the Donald Tovey Prize; then studied privately and at the Paris Cons. with Boulanger (1952–54); later was a scholarship student of Copland at the Berkshire Music Center in Tanglewood (summer, 1959). She taught at the Univ. of London (1958–65), then was a visiting prof. of composition at the Univ. of Calif. at Santa Barbara (1970); also lectured at various other U.S. and English univs.; likewise made appearances as a conductor on both sides of the Atlantic. She held 2 Guggenheim fellowships (1974–75; 1982). In 1971 she married the American violinist Peter Mark, who later served as conductor of the Virginia Opera Assn. in Norfolk. She was named Distinguished Prof. of Music at Queens College in N.Y. in 1987. At the outset of her career, she followed the acceptable modern style of composition, but soon the diatonic lyricism of the initial period of her creative evolution gave way to increasingly chromatic constructions, eventually systematized into serial organization. She described her theatrical works as "dramatic abstracts" in form, because even in the absence of a programmatic design, they revealed some individual dramatic traits. Appreciated by critics and audiences alike, her compositions enjoy numerous performances in Europe and America.

WORKS: DRAMATIC: OPERAS: *The Abbott of Drimock*, chamber opera (London, 1955); *The Decision* (1964–65; London, Nov. 30, 1967); *The Voice of Ariadne* (1972–73; Aldeburgh, June 11, 1974); *Mary, Queen of Scots* (1976; Edinburgh, Sept. 6, 1977); *A Christmas Carol* (Norfolk, Va., Dec. 7, 1979); *An Occurrence at Owl Creek Bridge*, radio opera (1981; London, Sept. 14, 1982); *Harriet, the Woman Called Moses* (Norfolk, Va., March 1, 1985); *Simon Bolivar* (1994; Norfolk, Va., Jan. 20, 1995). **BALLETS:** *A Tale for Thieves* (1953); *Beauty and the Beast* (London, Nov. 19, 1969); *Orfeo* (1975; BBC-TV, March 17, 1977; as *Orfeo II* for Flute and Strings, Los Angeles, March 28, 1976; as *Orfeo I* for Flute and Tape, Chichester, July 5, 1976). **ORCH.:** *Divertimento* for Strings (1957); *Obliques* (1958); *Scottish Dance Suite* (1959); *Perspectives* (1961); *Theme and Interludes* (1962); *Sinfonia* (1963); *Festival Overture* (1965); *Nocturnes and Arias* (1966); *Variations* for Brass Band (1966); *Concerto for Orchestra* (1967); Clarinet Concerto (London, Feb. 5, 1969); *Night Music* for Chamber Orch. (1969); *Memento vitae* (1969–70); Horn Concerto (1971); Viola Concerto (London, Aug. 13, 1973); *Peripeteia* (1981); *Moving into Aquarius* (1984; London, Jan. 23, 1985; in collaboration with R.R. Bennett); *The Seasons* (London, Dec. 4, 1988); *Rainbow* (Glasgow, Oct. 8, 1990); *Autumn Sonata,* bass clarinet concerto (1993); *Journey Through a Japanese Landscape,* concerto for Marimba and Wind Orch. (1993–94); *Helios,* oboe concerto (1995). **CHAMBER:** String Quartet (1958); *Colloquy* for Violin and Piano (1960); Trio for Flute, Oboe, and Piano (1960); *Serenade* for Flute, Clarinet, Harp, Viola, and Cello (1961); Chamber Concerto No. 1 for 9 Instruments (1962), No. 2 for 5 Instruments (1966), and No. 3 for 8 Instruments (1966); *Sonata for 3* for Flute, Violin, and Guitar (1966); *Impromptu No. 1* for Flute and Oboe (1967) and *No. 2* for Flute, Oboe, and Clarinet (1970); *Music* for Horn and Piano (1967); *Soliloquy No. 1* for Guitar and Tape (1969); *Elegy* for Viola and Cello (1970); *From 1 to Another I* for Viola and Tape (1970; arranged as *From 1 to Another II* for Viola and 15 Strings, 1980); *Space Play,* concerto for 9 Instruments (London, Oct. 11, 1974); *Fanfare* for Brass Quintet (1982); *Pierrot* for Clarinet, Violin, and Piano (1985); *The Golden Echo I* for Horn and Tape (1986; as *The Golden Echo II* for Solo Horn and 16

Accompanying Horns, 1986); *Narcissus* for Flute with Digital Delay (1987); *Wild Winter* for Chamber Ensemble (1993). **VOCAL:** *4 Madrigals* for Chorus (1953); *A Suite o' Bairnsangs* for Voice and Piano (1953); *Cantata for a Summer's Day* for Vocal Quartet, Speaker, Flute, Clarinet, String Quartet, and Double Bass (1954); *Song of the Burn* for Chorus (1954); *5 Love Songs* for Tenor and Guitar (1955); *A Song for Christmas* for Voice and Piano (1958); *Triptych* for Tenor and Orch. (1959); *The Phoenix and the Turtle* for Chorus and Orch. (1962); *The 5 Ages of Man* for Chorus and Orch. (1964); *Memento creatoris* for Chorus (1967); *Rorate coeli* for Chorus (1974); *The Last Twilight* for Chorus, Brass, and Percussion (Santa Fe, July 20, 1980); *The Lord's Prayer* for Chorus and Organ (1983); *Black Tambourine* for Women's Voices, Piano, and Percussion (1985); *For the Time Being: Advent* for Narrator and Chorus (1986; London, April 27, 1987).

BIBL.: D. Hixon, *T. M.: A Bio-Bibliography* (Westport, Conn., 1984).

Mustonen, Olli, Finnish pianist and composer; b. Helsinki, June 7, 1967. He was only 5 when he began studying piano, harpsichord, and composition; after piano lessons with Ralf Gothoni, he pursued his studies with Eero Heinonen (piano) and Einojuhani Rautavaara (composition). After making his debut in 1984, he appeared with the principal Finnish orchs. and soon performed with orchs. on the Continent. In 1986 he made his U.S. debut at the Newport (R.I.) Festival. In 1987 he appeared for the first time in London. He toured the Far East with the Stockholm Phil. in 1989; in 1991, played at the London Promenade Concerts. In addition to his engagements with the world's leading orchs., Mustonen also pursued an active recital and chamber music career. His extraordinary technique is matched by a challenging spontaneous approach to interpretation. Among his compositions are 2 piano concertos.

Muti, Riccardo, greatly talented Italian conductor; b. Naples, July 28, 1941. His father was a physician who possessed a natural Neapolitan tenor voice; after receiving instruction in violin and piano from his father, Riccardo studied composition with Napoli and Rota at the Conservatorio di Musica San Pietro a Majella in Naples, taking a diploma in piano; then studied conducting with Votto and composition with Bettinelli at the Verdi Cons. in Milan; also attended a seminar in conducting with Ferrara in Venice (1965). After winning the Guido Cantelli Competition in 1967, he made his formal debut with the RAI in 1968; then conducted in several of the major Italian music centers. His success led to his appointment as principal conductor of the Teatro Comunale in Florence in 1970; also conducted at the Maggio Musicale Fiorentino, becoming its artistic director in 1977. In the meantime, he began his advancement to international fame with guest conducting appearances at the Salzburg Festival in 1971 and with the Berlin Phil. in 1972. He made his U.S. debut with the Philadelphia Orch. on Oct. 27, 1972. In 1973 he conducted at the Vienna State Opera, and that same year became principal conductor of the New Philharmonia Orch. in London (it resumed its original name of Philharmonia Orch. in 1977). In 1974 he conducted the Vienna Phil. and in 1977 appeared at London's Covent Garden. His successful appearances with the Philadelphia Orch. led to his appointment as its principal guest conductor in 1977. In 1979 he was also named music director of the Philharmonia Orch. In 1980 he succeeded Eugene Ormandy as music director of the Philadelphia Orch., and subsequently relinquished his posts in London and Florence in 1982. In 1986 he became music director of Milan's La Scala, but retained his Philadelphia position. Muti announced his resignation as music director of the Philadelphia Orch. in 1990, but agreed to serve as its laureate conductor from 1992. His brilliance as a symphonic conductor enabled him to maintain, and even enhance, the illustrious reputation of the Philadelphia Orch. established by Stokowski and carried forward by Ormandy. Unlike his famous predecessors, he excels in both the concert hall and the opera pit.

BIBL.: J. Kurnick, ed., *R. M.: Twenty Years in Philadelphia* (Philadelphia, 1992).

Mutter, Anne-Sophie, talented German violinist; b. Rheinfeldin, June 29, 1963. At the age of 6 she won "1st Prize with Special Distinction" at the "Jungen Musiziert" National Competition, the youngest winner in its annals. In 1976 she came to the notice of Karajan during her appearance at the Lucerne Festival; in 1977 he invited her to be a soloist with him and the Berlin Phil. at the Salzburg Easter Festival; this was the beginning of an auspicious career. She subsequently appeared regularly with Karajan and the Berlin Phil., and also recorded standard violin concertos with him; likewise appeared as soloist with many other leading conductors and orchs. on both sides of the Atlantic. She held the 1st International Chair of Violin Studies at London's Royal Academy of Music (from 1986). On Dec. 14, 1988, she made her N.Y. recital debut.

Muzio, Claudia (real name, **Claudina Muzzio**), oustanding Italian soprano; b. Pavia, Feb. 7, 1889; d. Rome, May 24, 1936. She studied with Casaloni in Turin and Viviani in Milan. She made her operatic debut as Manon in Arezzo (Jan. 15, 1910); then sang in Turin (1911; 1914–15), at Milan's La Scala (1913–14), and at London's Covent Garden (1914). She made her Metropolitan Opera debut in N.Y. as Tosca (Dec. 4, 1916), remaining on its roster until 1922; created the role of Giorgetta in Puccini's *Il tabarro* there (Dec. 14, 1918). In 1922 she made her first appearance with the Chicago Opera as Aida, and continued to sing there regularly until 1932; also sang in South America and again at La Scala (1926–27); after returning to the Metropolitan (1933–34), she pursued her career mainly in Rome. She was one of the most gifted dramatic sopranos of her time, excelling in such roles as Desdemona, Mimi, Santuzza, Margherita in *Mefistofele*, Violetta, and Madeleine de Coigny.

BIBL.: H. Barnes, *C. M.: A Biographical Sketch and Discography* (Austin, Texas, 1947); J. Richards, "C. M.," *Record Collector*, XVII (1968); J. Steane, "C. M.: A Centenary Tribute," *Musical Times* (Feb. 1989).

Mycielski, Zygmunt, Polish music critic and composer; b. Przeworsk, Aug. 17, 1907; d. Warsaw, Aug. 5, 1987. He studied with Rizzi in Kraków and with Dukas and Boulanger at the Paris École Normale de Musique, where he was a member of the Soc. of Young Polish Musicians (1928–36). After World War II, he became active as a journalist; ed. the principal Polish music magazine, *Ruch Muzyczny* (1945–48; 1960–68); publ. 2 collections of essays: *Uzieczki z pieciolinii* (Flight of the Staff Lines; Warsaw, 1956) and *Notatki o muzyce i muzykach* (Notes on Music and Musicians; Kraków, 1961). His music, couched in a modern idiom, contains elements of Polish folk inflections, but dodecaphonic usages are also encountered.

WORKS: BALLET: *Zabawa w Lipinach* (Merrymaking at Lipiny; 1953). **ORCH.:** *Lamento di Tristano* for Small Orch., in memory of Szymanowski (1937); *5 Symphonic Essays* (1945); 6 syms.: No. 1 (1947), *Polish Sym.* (1951), No. 2 (1960), No. 3, *Sinfonia breve* (1967; Warsaw, Sept. 23, 1972), No. 4 (1972–73; Poznań, April 2, 1976), and No. 5 (1977); *Silesian Overture* (1948); Piano Concerto (1954); *Variations* for Strings (1980). **CHAMBER:** Piano Trio (1934); *5 Preludes* for Piano Quintet (1967). **VOCAL:** *Portrait of a Muse* for Narrator, Chorus, and 15 Instruments (1947); *Nowy lirnik mazowiecki* (New Mazovian Bard), 9 songs and finale for Soprano, Baritone, Chorus, and Orch. (1955); *Psalms* for Baritone, Chorus, and Orch. (1982); *Liturgia sacra* for Chorus and Orch. (1983–84); *Fragments* for Chorus and Small Orch. (1987); songs.

Myers, Rollo (Hugh), English music critic and writer on music; b. Chislehurst, Kent, Jan. 23, 1892; d. Chichester, Jan. 1, 1985. He was educated at Balliol College, Oxford, and at the Royal College of Music in London. From 1919 to 1934 he was the Paris music correspondent of *The Times* and the *Daily Telegraph* of London. He was on the staff of the BBC in London from 1935 to 1944. After serving as music officer of the British

Council in Paris (1944–45), he returned to London as ed. of *The Chesterian* (from 1947) and of *Music Today* (from 1949).

WRITINGS (all publ. in London unless otherwise given): *Modern Music: Its Aims and Tendencies* (1923); *Music in the Modern World* (1939; 2nd ed., rev., 1948); *Debussy* (1948); *Erik Satie* (1948); *Introduction to the Music of Stravinsky* (1950); *Ravel: Life and Works* (1960); ed. *Twentieth Century Music* (1960; 2nd ed., aug., 1968); ed. and tr., *Richard Strauss and Romain Rolland: Correspondence* (1968); *Emmanuel Chabrier and his Circle* (1969); *Modern French Music* (Oxford, 1971).

Mysz-Gmeiner, Lula (née **Gmeiner**), noted Hungarian contralto; b. Kronstadt, Transylvania, Aug. 16, 1876; d. Schwerin, Aug. 7, 1948. She studied violin in her native town, and singing in Berlin with Etelka Gerster and Lilli Lehmann. She made her concert debut in Berlin in 1899; then traveled in Europe as a concert singer; was greatly praised for her interpretations of German lieder. She was a prof. at the Berlin Hochschule für Musik (1920–45), numbering among her students Peter Anders and Elisabeth Schwarzkopf.

Nabokov, Nicolas (actually, **Nikolai**), distinguished Russian-born American composer; b. near Lubcha, Novogrudok district, Minsk region, April 17, 1903; d. N.Y., April 6, 1978. He was a scion of a distinguished Russian family; his uncle was a liberal member of the short-lived Duma (Russian parliament); the famous writer Vladimir Nabokov was his 1st cousin. Nabokov received his early education with Rebikov in St. Petersburg and in Yalta; after taking courses at the Stuttgart Cons. (1920–22), he continued his studies with Juon and Busoni at the Berlin Hochschule für Musik (1922–23); finally moved to Paris, where he was introduced to Diaghilev, who commissioned him to write his first major score, the ballet-oratorio *Ode: Méditation sur la majesté de Dieu* (1927), for the Ballets Russes. In 1933 he went to the U.S., and in 1939 became a naturalized American citizen; taught at Wells College in Aurora, N.Y. (1936–41) and at St. John's College in Annapolis (1941–44); after working for the U.S. government in Berlin (1944–47), he taught at the Peabody Cons. of Music in Baltimore (1947–52). From 1951 to 1963 he was secretary-general of the Congress for Cultural Freedom; then served as artistic director of the Berlin Music Festivals (1963–68); lectured on aesthetics at the State Univ. of N.Y. at Buffalo (1970–71) and at N.Y. Univ. (1972–73). He was elected to membership in the National Inst. of Arts and Letters in 1970. In addition to writing articles for various periodicals, he wrote a book of essays, *Old Friends and New Music* (Boston, 1951), and the vols. *Igor Stravinsky* (Berlin, 1964) and *Bagazh: Memoirs of a Russian Cosmopolitan* (N.Y., 1975). In his music, he adopted a cosmopolitan style, with an astute infusion of fashionable bitonality; in works of Russian inspiration, he reverted to melorhythms of Russian folk songs.

WORKS: DRAMATIC: OPERAS: *The Holy Devil* (1954–58; Louisville, April 16, 1958; rev. version as *Der Tod des Grigorij Rasputin*, Cologne, Nov. 27, 1959); *Love's Labour's Lost* (1970–73; Brussels, Feb. 7, 1973). **BALLETS:** *Ode: Méditation sur la majesté de Dieu*, ballet-oratorio (1927; Paris, June 6, 1928); *La vie de Polichinelle* (Paris, 1934); *Union Pacific* (Philadelphia, April 6, 1934); *The Last Flower* (1941); *Don Quixote* (1966); *The Wanderer* (1966). **ORCH.:** 3 syms.: No. 1, *Symphonie lyrique* (Paris, Feb. 16, 1930), No. 2, *Sinfonia biblica* (N.Y., Jan. 2, 1941), and No. 3, *A Prayer* (N.Y., Jan. 4, 1968); Piano Concerto (1932); *Le Fiancé*, overture (1934); Flute Concerto (1948); Cello Concerto, *Les Hommages* (Philadelphia, Nov. 6, 1953); *Symphonic Variations* (1967); *Variations on a Theme by Tchaikovsky* for Cello and Orch. (1968). **CHAMBER:** *Serenata estiva* for String Quartet (1937); Bassoon Sonata (1941); *Canzone, Introduzione, e Allegro* for Violin and Piano (1950); 2 piano sonatas (1926, 1940), and other piano pieces. **VOCAL:** *Job*, oratorio for Men's Voices and Orch. (1933); *Collectionneur d'échos* for Soprano, Bass, and 9 Percussion Instruments (1933); *The Return of Pushkin*, elegy for Soprano or Tenor and Orch. (Boston, Jan. 2, 1948); *America Was Promises*, cantata for Alto, Baritone, and Men's Voices (N.Y., April 25, 1950); *Vita nuova* for Soprano, Tenor, and Orch. (Boston, March 2, 1951); *Symboli chrestiani* for Baritone and Orch. (1953); *Quatre poèmes de Boris Pasternak* for Voice and Piano (1961; arr. for Voice and Strings, 1969); *5 Poems by Anna Akhmatova* for Voice and Orch. (1964).

Nadel, Arno, German composer; b. Vilnius, Oct. 3, 1878; d. in the Auschwitz concentration camp, March 1943. He studied in Königsberg with Birnbaum and Schwalm; then at the Jewish Seminary in Berlin with Loewengard and L. Mendelssohn. In 1916 he became conductor of the Jewish Community Choir in Berlin. He compiled several anthologies of Jewish songs, among them *Jontefflieder* (10 vols., 1919) and *Jüdische Volkslieder* (2 vols., Leipzig, 1921; new ed., 1926).

Nagano, Kent (George), American conductor; b. Morro Bay, Calif. (of Japanese-American parents), Nov. 22, 1951. He studied at the Univ. of Oxford (1969), with Grosvenor Cooper at the Univ. of Calif. at Santa Cruz (B.A., 1974), at San Francisco State Univ. (M.M., 1976), and at the Univ. of Toronto; also had instruction in conducting from Laszlo Varga in San Francisco. He was associated with Sarah Caldwell's Opera Co. of Boston (1977–79); was made music director of the Berkeley (Calif.)

Sym. Orch. (1978) and of the Ojai (Calif.) Music Festival (1984). While working as an assistant conductor with the Boston Sym. Orch., he was called upon to substitute for Ozawa at the last moment and led a notably successful performance of Mahler's 9th Sym. without benefit of rehearsal (Nov. 30, 1984). In 1985 he was the first co-recipient (with Hugh Wolff) of the Affiliate Artist's Seaver Conducting Award. He subsequently appeared as a guest conductor with various orchs. on both sides of the Atlantic. From 1989 to 1998 he was chief conductor of the Opéra de Lyon. In 1991 he also was named principal conductor designate of the Hallé Orch. in Manchester, serving as its principal conductor from 1994 to 1998. In 1992 he made his San Francisco Opera debut conducting Milhaud's *Christoph Colomb*. He was made an Officier in the Order of Arts and Letters of France in 1993.

Naginski, Charles, American composer; b. Cairo, Egypt, May 29, 1909; d. (drowned) Lenox, Mass., Aug. 4, 1940. He was taken to America at an early age; studied piano with his father and other teachers; from 1928 to 1933, held a fellowship at the Juilliard Graduate School in N.Y. as a pupil in composition of Rubin Goldmark.

WORKS: BALLET: *The Minotaur* (1938). **ORCH.:** *Suite* (1931); 2 syms. (1935, 1937); *1936*, symphonic poem (1936); Sinfonietta (1937); *3 Movements* for Chamber Orch. (1937); *Nocturne and Pantomime* (1938); *5 Pieces from a Children's Suite* 1940); *Movement for Strings*. **OTHER:** 2 string quartets (1933); songs.

Nancarrow, Conlon, remarkable American-born Mexican composer, innovator in the technique of recording notes on a player-piano roll; b. Texarkana, Ark., Oct. 27, 1912. He played the trumpet in jazz orchs.; then took courses at the Cincinnati Cons. of Music (1929–32); subsequently traveled to Boston, where he became a private student of Slonimsky, Piston, and Sessions (1933–36). In 1937 he joined the Abraham Lincoln Brigade and went to Spain to fight in the ranks of the Republican Loyalists against the brutal assault of General Franco's armies. Classified as a premature anti-Fascist after the Republican defeat in Spain, he was refused a U.S. passport and moved to Mexico City, where he remained for 40 years, eventually obtaining Mexican citizenship (1956). In 1981, with political pressures defused in the U.S., Nancarrow was able to revisit his native land and to participate in the New American Music Festival in San Francisco. In 1982 he was a composer-in-residence at the Cabrillo Music Festival in Aptos, California; also traveled to Europe, where he participated at festivals in Austria, Germany, and France. An extraordinary event occurred in his life in 1982, when he was awarded the "genius grant" from the MacArthur Foundation of Chicago, enabling him to continue his work. The unique quality of Nancarrow's compositions is that they can be notated only by perforating player-piano rolls to mark the notes and rhythms, and can be performed only by activating such piano rolls. This method of composition gives him total freedom in conjuring up the most complex contrapuntal, harmonic, and rhythmic combinations that no human pianist or number of human pianists could possibly perform. The method itself is extremely laborious; a bar containing a few dozen notes might require an hour to stamp out on the piano roll. Some of his studies were publ. in normal notation in Cowell's *New Music Quarterly*. Copland, Ligeti, and other contemporary composers expressed their appreciation of Nancarrow's originality in high terms of praise. On Jan. 30, 1984, Nancarrow gave a concert of his works in Los Angeles, in a program including his *Prelude and Blues for Acoustic Piano* and several of his studies. An audiovisual documentary on Nancarrow was presented on slides by Eva Soltes. A number of Nancarrow's *Studies for Player Piano* that could be adequately notated were publ. in *Soundings 4* (1977), accompanied with critical commentaries by Gordon Mumma, Charles Amirkhanian, John Cage, Roger Reynolds, and James Tenney. On Oct. 15, 1988, his 3rd String Quartet was given its premiere performance in Cologne by the London-based Arditti Quartet, perhaps the only ensemble in the world capable of realizing Nancarrow's exceedingly complex score.

BIBL.: P. Carlsen, *The Player-Piano Music of C. N.: An Analysis of Selected Studies* (Brooklyn, 1988); K. Gann, *The Music of C. N.* (Cambridge, 1995).

Naoumoff, Émile, Bulgarian-born French pianist and composer; b. Sofia, Feb. 20, 1962. He began piano training at the age of 5; at 9, became a student of Boulanger, working with her first at the American Cons. in Fontainebleau and later at the École Normale de Musique in Paris (until 1979); also studied at the Paris Cons. (from 1975), taking premiers prix in piano and chamber music (1978). He subsequently studied conducting with Dervaux (1979–81). In 1973 and 1977 he won the Prix de Composition of Paris; in 1974, took the medal in the Robert Casadesus piano competition. In subsequent years, he toured extensively as a pianist in Europe and North America in a repertoire extending from the masters to the contemporary scene; also was a prof. at the École Normale de Musique (from 1981) and at the Paris Cons. (from 1984). In 1987 the French Académie des Beaux Arts awarded him its Grand Prix de Composition. His compositions include orch. works, chamber music, and piano pieces, all written in a free, tonal style.

Napoli, Gennaro, Italian composer and teacher, father of **Jacopo Napoli**; b. Naples, May 19, 1881; d. there, June 28, 1943. He was a student of d'Arienzo and de Nardis at the Royal Cons. in Naples. In 1906 he won the Pensionato Nazionale per la Musica. He taught composition in Naples at the Liceo Musicale (1912–15) and at the Royal Cons. (from 1915), where he served as assistant director (from 1926). He ed. *L'Arte Pianistica* and publ. *Bassi imitati e fugati* (1915).

WORKS: *Jacopo Ortis*, opera; *Armida abbandonata*, dramatic scene (1906); Sym.; *In montagna*, symphonic suite (1906); *Il sole risorto* for Soli, Chorus, and Orch. (1909); songs; piano pieces.

Napoli, Jacopo, Italian composer, son of **Gennaro Napoli**; b. Naples, Aug. 26, 1911; d. Ascea Marina, Oct. 20, 1994. He studied at the Cons. San Pietro a Majella in Naples, with his father and S. Cesi; was subsequently appointed to the faculty, and eventually was its director (1954–62); subsequently was director of the Milan Cons. (1962–72) and then of the Rome Cons. (1972–76). He specialized in opera, often with a Neapolitan background, which gave him the opportunity to use Neapolitan songs in his scores. His operas include *Il Malato immaginario* (Naples, 1939); *Miseria e nobilità* (Naples, 1945); *Un curioso accidente* (Bergamo, 1950); *Masaniello* (1951; won a prize of La Scala, Milan); *I Peccatori* (1954); *Il tesoro* (Rome, 1958); *Il rosario* (Brescia, 1962); *Il povero diavolo* (Trieste, 1963); *Il Barone avaro* (Naples, 1970).

Narmour, Eugene, American musicologist; b. Deming, N.J., Oct. 27, 1939. He studied at the Eastman School of Music in Rochester, N.Y. (B.M., 1961; M.A., 1962), and with Leonard Meyer, Grosvenor Cooper, and Howard M. Brown at the Univ. of Chicago (Ph.D., 1974). He taught at East Carolina Univ. (1963–67), the Univ. of Chicago (1968–71), and the Univ. of Pa. (from 1971), where he became a prof. (1987) and also served as dept. chairman and conductor of the univ. orch.; was a Fellow at Oxford (1984, 1989–90); lectured widely in North America, Europe, and Asia. His first book, *Beyond Schenkerism: The Need for Alternatives in Music Analysis* (Chicago, 1977), was an important turning point in contemporary analysis, focusing on the interface between music theory and cognition and addressing problems of composition and perception. His other publications include *The Analysis and Cognition of Basic Melodic Structures* (Chicago, 1990) and *The Analysis and Cognition of Melodic Complexity* (Chicago, 1991).

Nash, Heddle, admired English tenor; b. London, June 14, 1896; d. there, Aug. 14, 1961. He was a chorister at Westminster Abbey in London. After training in London, he studied with Borgatti in Milan, where he made his operatic debut at the Teatro Carcano as Rossini's Count Almaviva in 1924. Returning to London, he sang the Duke of Mantua at his first appearance at the Old Vic Theatre in 1925. From 1926 to 1929 he appeared with the British National Opera Co. In 1929 he made his debut at Covent Garden as Don Ottavio, singing there until 1939. During World War II, he appeared with the Carl Rosa Opera Co. In 1947–48 he again sang at Covent Garden. In 1957–58 he appeared with the New Opera Co. He was greatly esteemed for his roles in operas by Mozart and Rossini. Among his other distinguished roles were David in *Die Meistersinger von Nürnberg*, Gounod's Faust, and Rodolfo. He also was a notable concert singer, winning particular renown for his interpretation of Elgar's Gerontius. His son, John Heddle Nash (b. London, March 30, 1928; d. there, Sept. 29, 1994), was a baritone who sang at the Sadler's Wells Theatre and with the Carl Rosa Opera Co.

Nasidze, Sulkhan, Russian composer; b. Tiflis, March 17, 1927. He studied piano and composition at the Tbilisi Cons.; in 1963 he joined its staff; in 1974 he became artistic director of the State Phil. of Georgia in Tbilisi. His music is imbued with Georgian melorhythms, and is set in a fairly advanced idiom. He wrote 2 piano concertos (1954, 1961); 5 syms. (1958, 1964, 1970, 1972, 1975); *Rhapsody on themes of old Tiflis* for Orch. (1964); Cello Concerto (1974); Piano Trio (1958); 2 string quartets (1968, 1971); *Polyphonic Sonata* for Piano; many vocal works.

Nastasijević, Svetomir, Serbian composer; b. Gornje Milanovec, April 1, 1902; d. Belgrade, Aug. 17, 1979. He studied engineering and architecture; at the same time, he learned to play the violin; wrote music criticism and publ. 2 manuals on theory. His works include the music drama *Medjulu*ško *blago* (The Treasure of the Medjuluzje; Belgrade, March 4, 1937); *Durad Branković*, national opera from medieval Serbian history (Belgrade, June 12, 1940); several symphonic poems and choruses. In his operas, he adopted the Wagnerian system of leitmotifs.

Nat, Yves, French pianist, pedagogue, and composer; b. Béziers, Dec. 28, 1890; d. Paris, Aug. 31, 1956. A gifted child, he conducted his own orchestral *Fantaisie* when he was 10. After studying with Diémer at the Paris Cons. (premier prix in piano, 1907), he toured in Europe and the Americas (1909–34). He was also active as accompanist to Ysaÿe, Enesco, and Thibaud. From 1934 he was a prof. of piano at the Paris Cons. He was especially esteemed as an interpreter of Beethoven and Schumann. Among his compositions were *L'enfer* for Chorus and Orch. (1942), a Piano Concerto (1953), piano pieces, and songs.

Nataletti, Giorgio, Italian ethnomusicologist; b. Rome, June 12, 1907; d. there, July 16, 1972. He studied at the Pesaro Cons., then pursued ethnomusicological research in Italy, the Maritime Alps, and Tunisia (from 1926). He was technical director of Le Arti di le Tradizioni Popolari dell'OND (ENAL) (1926–36; 1946–61) and secretary of the Comitato Nazionale delle Arti Popolari (1947–52). In 1948, with Pizzetti and others, he founded the Centro Nazionale Studi di Musica Popolare. In addition, he was active as broadcaster and music director of the RAI; also was artistic director of RCA Italiana and taught folk music (from 1940) and music history (from 1961) at the Rome Cons. With A. Lomax and D. Carpitella, he prepared the Italian section of *The Columbia World Library of Folk and Primitive Music* (vols. XV and XVI).

WRITINGS (all publ. in Rome unless otherwise given): With G. Petrassi, *Canti della campagna romana* (Milan, 1930); *Musica e canti della patria* (Tunis, 1933); *Trenta ninna nanne popolari italiene* (1934); *Catalogo del Museo strumentale di Tunisi* (1935); *I poeti a braccio della campagna romana* (1936); *La raccolta dei canti popolari della CIATP* (1936); *Verdi e le sue medaglie* (1941); *Il folklore musicale Italia* (1948); *La musica folklorica italiana nel cinema* (1959).

BIBL.: *1922–1962: Quaranti anni di attività di G. N.* (Rome, 1962).

Natanson, Tadeusz, Polish composer and pedagogue; b. Warsaw, Jan. 26, 1927; d. Wroclaw, Nov. 10, 1990. He studied composition with K. Wilkomirski, P. Perkowski, and S. Poradowski at the Wroclaw Academy of Music (1952–56); was on its faculty (from 1957), and also taught at the Warsaw Academy of Music (from 1977), where he received his Ph.D. (1977; with a diss. on music therapy as a function of music). He also taught at the Univ. of Silesia in Cieszyn (from 1983), where he served as head of the Inst. for Music Therapy (from 1984).

WORKS: DRAMATIC: *Quo Vadis*, ballet-pantomime (1970); *Tamango*, opera (1972). **ORCH.:** *Toccata* (1956); 2 piano concertos (1956, 1980); *Polifonie* for 2 String Orchs. (1958); *Rondo concertante* for Violin and Orch. (1958); Double Concerto for 2 Saxophones and Orch. (1959); 7 syms.: No. 1, *Wroclaw*, for Piano and Orch. (1961), No. 2 (1964), No. 3, *"John Kennedy in Memoriam"* (1965), No. 4 (1969), No. 5 for Baritone, Chorus, and Orch. (1974), No. 6 (1980), and No. 7 (1982); *Concerto breve* for Trombone and Orch. (1963); Viola Concerto (1971); *Triptyque* (1976); *Symphoniette classique* (1979). **CHAMBER:** 2 wind quartets (1960, 1987); *Toccata* for 2 Clarinets, 2 Horns, and Piano (1964); 2 trios for Violin, Cello, and Piano (1965, 1966); Oboe Sonata (1977); *Sonata antiqua* for Wind Quintet (1978); Sextet for 3 Trumpets and 3 Trombones (1981). **VOCAL:** *Satires* for Chorus and Instrumental Ensemble (1960); *I Prayed to Jehovah* for Reciter and Orch. (1964); *Cain's Question* for Reciter and Orch. (1967; also for Reciter and Men's Voices); *A Salt Shaker Full of Pepper* for Men's Chorus (1968); *Familiale* for Reciter and Chamber Ensemble (1979).

Nathan, Hans, German-born American musicologist; b. Berlin, Aug. 5, 1910; d. Boston, Aug. 4, 1989. He took courses in musicology at the Univ. of Berlin (Ph.D., 1934, with the diss. *Das Rezitativ der Frühopern Richard Wagners: Ein Beitrag zur Stilistik des Opernrezitativs in der ersten Hälfte des 19 Jahrhunderts*); studied piano with Rudolph Schmidt and Claudio Arrau, theory with Grete von Zieritz, and conducting with Michael Taube. He was active as a music critic in Berlin (1932–36). In 1936 he went to the U.S. and became a naturalized American citizen in 1944. From 1936 to 1938 he did postgraduate study at Harvard Univ. After a year of teaching at Tufts Univ., he joined the faculty of Michigan State Univ. in East Lansing in 1946; held a Guggenheim fellowship in 1957; was a visiting prof. at the Inst. for Advanced Study in Princeton, N.J., in 1957–58 and again in the summer of 1979; he retired in 1981. In the U.S. he devoted himself chiefly to subjects of American music; publ. the valuable books *Dan Emmett and the Rise of Early Negro Minstrelsy* (Norman, Okla., 1962) and *William Billings: Data and Documents* (Detroit, 1976). He was the ed. of vol. 2 (1977) of the complete, critical ed. of works by William Billings, in 4 vols.; contributed articles on folk music, history, and modern biography to various publications.

Nathan, Montagu. See **Montague-Nathan, M(ontagu).**

Natra, Sergiu, Romanian-born Israeli composer and teacher; b. Bucharest, April 12, 1924. He studied composition with Leon Klepper at the Bucharest Cons. (1945–52). He emigrated to Israel in 1961, where he became active mainly as a teacher; became a teacher at the Rubin Academy of Music in Tel Aviv (1975); was prof. at the Univ. of Tel Aviv (from 1976).

WORKS: BALLET: *Diary of a Choreographer* (1982). **ORCH.:** *Divertimento in a Classical Style* for Strings (1943); *March and Chorale* (1944); *Suite* (1948); Sym. No. 1 (1952); *Sinfonia* for Strings (1960); *Toccata* (1963); *Music* for Oboe and Strings (1965); *Variations* for Piano and Orch. (1966); *Pages from a Composer's Diary* for Chamber Orch. (1978); *Development* for Viola and Chamber Orch. (1988); *Concerto a quattro* for Clarinet, Cello, Trombone, Organ, and Strings (1993). **CHAMBER:** 2 string quartets (1947, 1991); *Music* for Violin and Harp (1959); *Music* for Harpsichord and 6 Instruments (1964); Sonatina for Solo Harp (1965; rev. 1978); 3 solo sonatinas: for Trombone, for Trumpet, and for Oboe (all 1969); Piano Trio (1971); *Music for Nicanor* (Zabaleta) for Harp, Flute, Clarinet, and String Quartet (1988); *Ancient Walls* for Oboe and Trombone (1990); Sonata for 4 Harps (1993). **VOCAL:** *4 Poems* for Baritone and Orch. (1958); *Song of Deborah* for Mezzo-soprano and Chamber Orch. (1967); *Commentary on Nehemia* for Baritone, Chorus, and Orch. (1967); *Miracle of the Peoples*, cantata (1984). **OTHER:** *Environment for an Exhibition*, sound collage on tape (1970).

Nattiez, Jean-Jacques, learned French-born Canadian musicologist; b. Amiens, Dec. 30, 1945. He studied piano privately while pursuing musical training at the Amiens Cons. Following further studies in Aix-en-Provence (L.Litt. in modern languages, 1967; Licentiate in linguistics, 1968; M.Litt. in modern languages, 1968), he studied in Paris (Certificat d'aptitude pédagogique à l'enseignement secondaire, 1970; Ph.D., 1973, with a diss. on musical semiology). He also received instruction in conducting from Jacques Clément in Montreal, Fernand Quattrochi and Pierre Dervaux in Nice, and Charles Bruck in Hancock, Maine. He settled in Canada, becoming a naturalized Canadian citizen in 1975. In 1970 he became a prof. at the Univ. of Montreal, where he taught musicology (from 1972) and also was director of the Groupe de recherches en sémiologie musicale (1974–80). From 1980 to 1985 he was co-ed. of the *Canadian University Music Review/Revue de musique des universités canadiennes.* With Pierre Boulez, he became co-ed. of the series Musique/Passé/Présent of Paris in 1981. From 1984 to 1987 he was music director of the Joliette-Lanaudière Sym. Orch. In 1988 he was elected to membership in the Royal Soc. of Canada and was awarded the Dent Medal of the Royal Musical Assn. of England. In 1990 he was made a Member of the Order of Canada. Nattiez is a foremost authority on musical semiotics. His study, *Fondements d'une sémiologie de la musique* (Paris, 1975; rev. and expanded, 1987, as *Musicologie générale et sémiologie*), is notable for its erudite investigation of structural linguistics as applied to musical analysis.

WRITINGS: *Fondements d'une sémiologie de la musique* (Paris, 1975; rev. and expanded, 1987, as *Musicologie générale et sémiologie*); *Tétralogies "Wagner, Boulez, Chéreau," essai sur l'infidélité* (Paris, 1983); *Proust musicien* (Paris, 1989); *Il discorso musicale, Per una semiologia della musica* (Turin, 1987); *De la sémiologie à la musique* (Montreal, 1988); ed. *Pierre Boulez, John Cage: Correspondance et documents* (vol. I, Basel, 1990); *Wagner adrogyne: Essai sur l'interprétation* (Paris, 1990); *Le combat de Chronos et d'Orphée Essais* (Paris, 1993).

Naumann, Siegfried, Swedish conductor, teacher, and composer; b. Malmö, Nov. 27, 1919. He received instruction in violin, theory, and composition from his father, then studied with Wolf (violin) and Myrtelius (instrumentation), and also took courses with Melchers, Mann, and Broström at the Stockholm Musikhögskolan (1942–45); after conducting the Örnsköldsvik Music Soc. (1945–49), he studied composition with Pizzetti at Rome's Accademia di Santa Cecilia (1949–53); also with Malipiero and Orff. He later received instruction in conducting at the Salzburg Mozarteum and with Furtwängler and Scherchen. He was conductor of the Gävleborgs Sym. Orch. (1954–55); in 1962 he founded the Musica Nova ensemble, which he conducted on tours of Scandinavia, Germany, and England; was its conductor until 1977. He taught conducting at the Stockholm Musikhögskolan (1963–83), becoming a prof. there in 1976; then taught at the Malmö Musikhögskolan and Teaterhögskolan (from 1983). He wrote 3 syms. and some other works in a traditionally acceptable infra-modern idiom, but at the age of 40 decided to adopt an austere structural style governed by serial procedures and diversified by aleatory passages. To mark this decisive avatar, he designated his first serial work, *Ruoli* (Roles) for 4 Clarinets, as op. 1 (1959). Among his subsequent works were: *7 Sonetti di Petrarca* for Tenor, Harp, Vibraphone, and 4 Cellos (1959); *Phaedri: 4 Fabulae* for Soli, Chorus, and 8 Instruments (1961); *Improvviso sopra 28 strutture* for Keyboard and Percussion Instruments (1961); *Transformations* for Orch. (1962; Gävleborg, April 29, 1962); *Risposte I* for Flute and Percussion (1963), *II* for Piano, Hammond Organ, Electric Guitar, Trombone, and Percussion (1963), and *III* for Flute, Percussion, Harp, and Strings (1994); *Il cantico del sole* for Soli, Chorus, 10 Solo Instruments, and Orch. (1963; Stockholm, Sept. 14, 1966); *Cadenza* for 9 Players (1964); *Missa in onore della Madonna de Loreto* for Chorus, Organ, and Percussion (1964); *Spettacolo I* for Soprano and Orch. (1967) and *II* for 3 Soli, Chorus, and Orch. (1969); *Estate* for Chamber Orch. (1968); *Ljudposter* (Soundposts) for Wind Orch. (1970); *Due cori su testi latini* for Chorus, Double Bass, Hammond Organ, and Percussion (1970); *Teatro strumentale* for Chamber Ensemble (1971); *Il cielo del ponte a Moriano*, dialogue for Tenor, Chorus, and Chamber Orch. (1972); *Materialstudier i improvisation* for Orch. (1974); *Fanfarer* for Wind Ensemble (1974–76); *Strutture per Giovanni*, Version B for Wind Orch. (1980); *Ljudspel/Giuoco di suono* for 3 Instrumental Groups (1984); *Och lärka slår och Skånes somrar ila* for Chorus and Orch. (Malmö, Sept. 8, 1985); *Strutture* for Orch. (1986); *Tripla* for Flute, Cello, and Piano (1987); *Arie di battaglia* for Soprano, Tenor, and Orch. (Stockholm, Nov. 26, 1989); *Il pianot della Madonna: Lauda drammatica* for Soprano, Tenor, Baritone, Chorus, and Orch. (1990); *Skåne* for Contralto and Orch. (1992); *Versi da Francesco d'Assisi* for Soprano, Flute, and Percussion (1992); *Cadenze* for Voices and Instruments (1993).

Naumburg, Walter W(ehle), American music patron; b. N.Y., Dec. 25, 1867; d. there, Oct. 17, 1959. He received cello lessons in his youth. After graduating from Harvard Univ. in 1889, he returned to N.Y. and entered the mercantile business of his father, Elkan Naumburg, who founded a series of free concerts in N.Y.'s Central Park in 1905. Walter and his brother George continued the series after their father's death in 1924. In 1925 Walter founded a series of auditions to find young talent for Town Hall debuts, an effort continued under the auspices of the Walter W. Naumburg Foundation (from 1926).

Navarra, André (-Nicolas), noted French cellist and pedagogue; b. Biarritz, Oct. 13, 1911; d. Siena, July 31, 1988. He studied at the Paris Cons. with J. Loeb (cello) and Tournemire (chamber music), winning a premier prix at 16. He was a member of the Krettly String Quartet (1929–35); made his debut as a soloist with the Paris Colonne Orch. (1931); in subsequent years, he appeared as a soloist with various European orchs. He was prof. of cello at the Paris Cons. (from 1949) and at the North West German Music Academy (from 1958); also taught in Siena (1954–88). He gave premiere performances of cello concertos by Jolivet (1962) and Tomasi (1970).

BIBL.: S. Milliot, *Entretiens avec A. N.* (Béziers, 1993).

Navarro, (Luis Antonio) García, Spanish conductor; b. Chiva, April 30, 1941. He was educated at the Valencia Cons., where he studied oboe; also took courses at the Madrid Cons. He then went to Vienna to study conducting with Hans Swarowsky, Karl Oesterreicher, and Reinhold Schmid; also took composition lessons with Alfred Uhl. In 1967 he won 1st prize at the conducting competition in Besançon. He was music director of the Valencia Sym. Orch. (1970–74); then was assoc. conductor of the Noordhollands Phil. in Haarlem (1974–78), and music director of Lisbon's Portuguese Radio Sym. Orch. (1976–78) and National Opera at the São Carlos Theater (1980–82). In 1979 he made his debut as an opera conductor at London's Covent Garden, and then appeared for the first time in the U.S. in 1980. He was Generalmusikdirektor of the Württemberg State Theater in Stuttgart from 1987 to 1991.

Naylor, Bernard (James), English-born Canadian organist, conductor, and composer; b. Cambridge, Nov. 22, 1907; d. Keswick, Cumbria, England, May 20, 1986. He was the son of the organist and composer Edward (Woodall) Naylor (b. Scarborough, Feb. 9, 1867; d. Cambridge, May 7, 1934). He studied composition with Vaughan Williams, Holst, and Ireland at the Royal College of Music in London (1924–27) and was an organ scholar at Exeter College, Oxford (1927–31); also served as conductor of the Oxford Univ. Opera Club (1927–31). In 1932 he went to Canada, where he was active in Winnipeg as conductor of its Male Voice Choir, Phil. Choir, and Sym. Orch.; returned to England in 1936 and was organist and director of music at Queen's College, Oxford, until 1939; once more in Canada, he conducted the Little Sym. Orch. in Montreal (1942–47); returned again to England and taught at Oxford (1950–52) and at Reading Univ. (1952–59). He moved permanently to Canada in 1959. As a composer, he specialized in sacred choral music.

WORKS: ORCH.: *Variations* for Small Orch. (1960). **CHAMBER:** String Trio (1960). **VOCAL:** *The Living Fountain*, cycle of 4 songs for Tenor and String Orch. (1947); *Missa da camera* for 4 Vocal Soloists, Chorus, and Chamber Orch. (1954–66); *The Resurrection According to Saint Matthew*, Easter cantata (1965); *The Nymph Complaining for the Death of Her Faun* for Mezzo-soprano, Flute, Oboe, Clarinet, Bassoon, and String Quartet (1965); *Festal Te Deum* for Chorus and Orch. (1968); *Scenes and Prophecies* for Soprano, Chorus, Brass, and Percussion (1968–69); several a cappella choruses, including 9 Motets (1952), *Magnificat & Nunc Dimittis* (1964), and *Missa sine Credo* (1969); songs.

Nazareth, Daniel, Indian conductor; b. Bombay, June 8, 1948. He received training in piano and theory in Bombay and London, and then studied composition and conducting in Vienna and with Bernstein at the Berkshire Music Center in Tanglewood. He appeared as a guest conductor with various orchs. in Europe, and made his debut as an opera conductor with *Così fan tutte* in Spoleto in 1977. From 1982 to 1985 he was chief conductor of the Berlin Sym. Orch. In 1988 he became music director of the Teatro San Carlo in Naples. He was chief conductor of the sym. orch. of the Mitteldeutschen Radio in Leipzig from 1992.

Neary, Martin (Gerard James), English organist and conductor; b. London, March 28, 1940. He was an organ scholar at Gonville and Caius College, Cambridge, and also held a conducting scholarship to the Berkshire Music Center in Tanglewood (summer, 1963). He was assistant organist (1963–65) and organist and master of music (1965–71) at St. Margaret's, Westminster. From 1963 to 1972 he was prof. of organ at Trinity College of Music in London. He was conductor of the Twickenham Musical Soc. (1966–72) and founder-conductor of St. Margaret's Westminster Singers (1967–71). In 1972 he became founder-conductor of his own Martin Neary Singers. He also was organist and master of music at Winchester Cathedral (1972–87) and conductor of the Waynflete Singers (1972–88). In 1988 he became organist and master of the choristers at Westminster Abbey. As both an organist and conductor, Neary has made numerous appearances in England and has toured extensively abroad. As a conductor, he has led performances of a vast repertoire, conducting premieres of many scores by English composers.

Neblett, Carol, American soprano; b. Modesto, Calif., Feb. 1, 1946. She studied voice privately with William Vennard, then with Lotte Lehmann and Pierre Bernac at the Univ. of Southern Calif. in Los Angeles; quitting school before graduating (1965), she toured as a soloist with the Roger Wagner Chorale; then made her operatic debut as Musetta with the N.Y. City Opera (March 8, 1969). She garnered wide public exposure when she appeared as Thaïs with the New Orleans Opera (1973), choosing to disrobe at the close of Act 1; subsequently made debuts with the Chicago Lyric Opera (Chrysothemis in *Elektra*, 1975), the Dallas Civic Opera (Antonia in *Les Contes d'Hoffmann*, 1975), the Vienna State Opera (1976), and London's Covent Garden (1977); also sang widely as a soloist with U.S. orchs. On March 8, 1979, she made her Metropolitan Opera debut in N.Y. as Senta. She made occasional appearances there in subsequent years, and also sang with various opera houses in North America and Europe. In 1975 she married **Kenneth Schermerhorn**.

Nechayev, Vasily, Russian pianist and composer; b. Moscow, Sept. 28, 1895; d. there, June 5, 1956. He studied at the Moscow Cons. with Goldenweiser (piano), graduating in 1917; then took composition lessons with Vasilenko. In 1925 he joined the staff of the Moscow Cons. He made a systematic study of the folk songs of the Ural region and made arrangements of folk songs of other lands. He composed the operas *7 Princesses*, after Maeterlinck (1923), and *Ivan Bolotnikov* (1930); Septet; Quartet; Violin Sonata; Cello Sonata; songs; and a number of piano pieces.

Nedbal, Oskar, distinguished Czech violist, conductor, and composer; b. Tábor, Bohemia, March 26, 1874; d. (suicide) Zagreb, Dec. 24, 1930. He was a pupil of Bennewitz (violin), Knittl and Stecker (theory), and Dvořák (composition) at the Prague Cons., where he graduated in 1892. From 1891 to 1906 he played viola in the famous Bohemian String Quartet; from 1896 to 1906 he conducted the Czech Phil.; from 1906 to 1918 he was conductor of the Tonkünstler-Orch. in Vienna; later was director of the Slovak National Theater in Bratislava (1923–30) and a conductor with the Radio there (1926–30). He was a notable interpreter of Czech music, and also was admired for his fine performances of the standard repertory.

WORKS: DRAMATIC: OPERA: *Sedlák Jakub* (Peasant Jacob; 1919–20; Brno, Oct. 13, 1922; rev. version, Bratislava, Dec. 15, 1928). **OPERETTAS:** *Die keusche Barbora* (Vienna, Oct. 7, 1911); *Polenblut* (Vienna, Oct. 25, 1913); *Die Winzerbraut* (Vienna, Feb. 11, 1916); *Die schöne Saskia* (Vienna, Nov. 16, 1917); *Eriwan* (Vienna, Nov. 29, 1918). **BALLETS:** *Pohádka o Honzovi* (Legend of Honza; Prague, Jan. 24, 1902); *Z pohádky do pohádky* (From Fairy Tale to Fairy Tale; Prague, Jan. 25, 1908); *Princezna Hyacinta* (Prague, Sept. 1, 1911); *Des Teufels Grossmutter* (Vienna, April 20, 1912); *Andersen* (Vienna, March 1, 1914). **OTHER:** *Scherzo caprice* for Orch. (1892); piano pieces.

BIBL.: J. Květ, *In memoriam O.a N.a* (Bratislava, 1931); idem, *O. N.* (Prague, 1947); M. Šulc, *O. N.* (Prague, 1959); A. Buchner, *O. N.: Život a dílo* (O N.: Life and Works; Prague, 1976).

Neel, (Louis) Boyd, English-born Canadian conductor; b. Blackheath, Kent, July 19, 1905; d. Toronto, Sept. 30, 1981. He studied at the Royal Naval College in Dartmouth; after taking medical courses at Caius College, Cambridge (B.A., 1926; M.A., 1930), he studied theory and orchestration at the Guildhall School of Music in London (1931). In 1932 he organized the Boyd Neel Orch., which gave its first performance in London on June 22, 1933; it quickly gained a fine reputation, excelling in performances of contemporary British music; also played Baroque works. He commissioned Britten's *Variations on a Theme of Frank Bridge* and conducted its premiere at the Salzburg Festival in 1937. He remained active with his ensemble until 1952; also appeared as a conductor with various English orchs. and theaters. He conducted at the Sadler's Wells Theatre (1945–47) and with the D'Oyly Carte Opera (1948–49); was also conductor of the Robert Mayer Children's Concerts (1946–52). After serving as founder-conductor of the Hart House Orch. in Toronto (1954–71), with which he made many tours, he conducted the Mississauga Sym. Orch. (1971–78); was also dean of the Royal Cons. of Music of Toronto (1953–71). He became a naturalized Canadian citizen in 1961. He was made a Commander of the Order of the British Empire (1953) and an Officer of the Order of Canada (1973). His book, *The Story of an Orchestra* (London, 1950), recounted his years with the Boyd Neel Orch.

Nees, Staf (Gustaaf Frans), Belgian carillonneur, teacher, and composer; b. Mechelen, Dec. 2, 1901; d. there, Jan. 2, 1965. He was a pupil of Van Nuffel, Mortelmans, and Depuydt at the Lemmens Inst. (1916–22) and of Denijn at the Carillonneurs's school (1922–24) in Mechelen. He taught at the Lemmens Inst. (1924–44), and then was director of the Carillonneurs's school (from 1944). From 1932 he also served as town carillonneur in Mecheln. Nees toured extensively throughout Europe and North America, and also gave master classes. In addition to music for the carillon, he composed choral works.

Nef, Albert, Swiss conductor and composer, brother of **Karl Nef**; b. St. Gallen, Oct. 30, 1882; d. Bern, Dec. 6, 1966. He studied at the Leipzig Cons. and with Kretzschmar at the Univ. of Berlin (Ph.D., 1906). From 1907 he was an opera conductor in Lübeck, Neustrelitz, and Rostock; from 1912, was in Bern, and was conductor of the Orch. Society there from 1922; from 1920, was president of the Swiss Stage Artists' Alliance. He was the author of *Das Lied in der deutschen Schweiz Ende des 18. und am Anfang des 19. Jahrhunderts* (1909); also of *50 Jahre Berner Theater* (Bern, 1956). He composed a Singspiel, *Graf Strapinski* (Bern, 1928); *Appenzeller Tänze* for Orch. (1926); *Wanderschaft*, song cycle for Tenor, Chorus, and Orch. (Bern, 1924); choruses; piano pieces; songs.

Nef, Isabelle (Lander), Swiss harpsichordist, pianist, and teacher; b. Geneva, Sept. 27, 1898; d. Bossy, near Geneva, Jan. 2, 1976. She studied with Marie Panthès (piano) at the Geneva Cons., and with Philipp (piano), d'Indy (composition), and Landowska (harpsichord) in Paris. She made extensive concert tours of Europe, North and South America, South Africa, and Australia. In 1936 she was appointed the first prof. of harpsichord at the Geneva Cons.

Nef, Karl, Swiss musicologist, brother of **Albert Nef**; b. St. Gallen, Aug. 22, 1873; d. Basel, Feb. 9, 1935. He entered the Leipzig Cons. in 1891, studying with Reckendorf (piano), Julius Klengel (cello), and Jadassohn (theory); attended Kretzschmar's lectures on musicology at the Univ. of Leipzig, and in 1896 received a Ph.D. with his diss. *Die Collegia musica in der deutschen reformierten Schweiz* (publ. in St. Gallen, 1897); subsequently completed his Habilitation in 1900 at the Univ. of Basel. He settled in Basel in 1897; from 1897 to 1925 he was music critic of the *Basler Nachrichten* and from 1898 to 1909, ed. the *Schweizerische Musikzeitung*; in 1900, became Privatdozent for musicology at the Univ.; in 1909, assoc. prof.; in 1923, prof.

WRITINGS: *Schriften über Musik und Volksgesang* (Bern, 1908); *Einführung in die Musikgeschichte* (Basel, 1920; 3rd ed., 1945; Eng. tr., 1935, as *Outline of the History of Music*); *Geschichte der Sinfonie und Suite* (Leipzig, 1921); *Geschichte unserer Musikinstrumente* (Leipzig, 1926; new ed., 1949); *Die neun Sinfonien Beethovens* (Leipzig, 1928); *Aufsätze* (Basel, 1936).

BIBL.: *Festschrift K. N. zum 60. Geburtstag* (Zürich, 1933).

Negrea, Marţian, Romanian composer and teacher; b. Vorumloc, Feb. 10, 1893; d. Bucharest, July 13, 1973. He studied with Timotei Popovici (theory and harmony) at the Andréien Seminary in Sibiu (1910–14) and of Mandyczewski (harmony, counterpoint, and music history) and Franz Schmidt (composition) at the Vienna Academy of Music (1918–21). He was a prof. of harmony at the Cluj Cons. (1921–41) and the Bucharest Cons. (1941–63). In his music, Negrea sought a balance between post-Romantic and Impressionist elements, to which he brought an infusion of folk melos.

WORKS: OPERA: *Marin Pescarul* (Marin the Fisherman; 1933; Cluj, Oct. 3, 1934). **ORCH.:** *Fantezie simfonică* (1921); *Rapsodia română I* (1938) and *II* (1950; Bucharest, April 8, 1951); *Poveşti din Grui* (Fairytale from Grui; 1940; Bucharest, March 21, 1943); *Baia-Mare* (1949); *Divertisement* (1951); *Prin Munţii Apuseni* (Through the Western Mountains; 1952); *Recrutul* (The Recruit), symphonic poem (1953); *Simfonia primăverii* (Spring Sym.; 1956); *Sărbătoarea muncii* (Celebration of Work), symphonic poem (1958; Bucharest, May 6, 1961); *Concerto for Orchestra* (1963; Bucharest, Jan. 1965). **CHAMBER:** *Prélude and Fugue* for String Quartet (1920); *4 Pieces* for Harp (1945); String Quartet (1949); Suite for Clarinet and Piano (1960). **PIANO:** Rondo (1920); Sonata (1921); *Impresii de la tară*, suite (1921); Sonatina (1922). **VOCAL:** *Povestea rozei* for Voice and Orch. (Bucharest, Dec. 12, 1943); *Requiem* for Soloists, Chorus, and Orch. (1957); songs.

Negri, Gino, Italian composer; b. Milan, May 25, 1919; d. Cernusco Montevecchia, July 19, 1991. He studied at the Milan Cons. with Renzo Bossi and Paribeni, graduating in 1942. In 1959 he was appointed artistic director of the Teatro del Popolo in Milan. He wrote a number of light operas, all to his own librettos, among them *Vieni qui, Carla* (Milan, Feb. 28, 1956); *Massimo* (Milan, April 12, 1958); *Il tè delle tre* (Como, Sept. 12, 1958); *Il Circo Max* (Venice, Sept. 23, 1959); *Publicità, ninfa gentile* (Milan, 1970).

Negri, Vittorio, Italian conductor, record producer, and musicologist; b. Milan, Oct. 16, 1923. He was educated at the Milan Cons., graduating with a degree in composition and conducting in 1946. He began his professional career at the Salzburg Mozarteum, working with Bernhard Paumgartner; then served as a guest conductor of the Orch. del Teatro alla Scala in Milan, the Orchestre National de France in Paris, the Dresden Staatskapelle, and the Boston Sym. Orch.; also made festival appearances in Salzburg, Montreux, Monte Carlo, and Versailles.

Neidlinger, Gustav, noted German bass-baritone; b. Mainz, March 21, 1910; d. Bad Ems, Dec. 26, 1991. He studied at the Frankfurt am Main Cons. In 1929 he made his operatic debut in Mainz, where he was a member of the Opera (1931–34). After singing with the Plauen Opera (1934–35), he was a member of the Hamburg Opera (1936–50). In 1950 he became a member of the Stuttgart Opera. In 1952 he made his first appearance at the Bayreuth Festival, where he won renown as Alberich; among his other distinguished roles there were Kurwenal, Telramund, Klingsor, and Hans Sachs. He was made a German Kammersänger in 1952. In 1953 he sang at Milan's La Scala, and from 1956 he appered with the Vienna State Opera. In 1963 he made his debut at London's Covent Garden as Telramund. On Nov. 17, 1972, he made his Metropolitan Opera debut in N.Y. as Alberich, but remained on the roster for only one season. He continued to sing in Europe until his retirement in 1977.

Neighbour, O(liver) W(ray), English music bibliographer and musicologist; b. Merstham, Surrey, April 1, 1923. He pursued the study of modern languages at Birbeck College (B.A., 1950). He joined the dept. of printed books at the British Museum (1946); then was on the music room staff (1951–76), subsequently serving as its superintendent (1976–85). He publ. *English Music Publishers: Plate Numbers in the First Half of the Nineteenth Century* (with A. Tyson; London, 1965) and *Consort and Keyboard Music*, vol. III of *The Music of William Byrd* (London, 1978); also ed. *Music and Bibliography: Essays in Honour of Alec Hyatt King* (London, 1980).

BIBL.: C. Banks, A. Searle, and M. Turner, eds., *Sundry Sorts of Music Books: Essays on the British Library Collections; Presented to O. W. M. on his 70th Birthday* (London, 1993).

Neikrug, Marc (Edward), American pianist and composer; b. N.Y., Sept. 24, 1946. He was a student of Klebe at the Northwest Music Academy in Detmold (1964–68), of Schuller at the Berkshire Music Center in Tanglewood, and at the State Univ. of N.Y. at Stony Brook (M.M., 1971). In 1972 he was composer-in-residence at the Marlboro (Vt.) Music Festival. From 1975 he toured extensively in duo concert appearances with Pinchas Zukerman. From 1978 to 1986 he was a consultant on contemporary music to the St. Paul (Minn.) Chamber Orch. As a composer, Neikrug has produced both tonal and atonal scores.

WORKS: OPERAS: *Through Roses* (1979–80); *Los Alamos* (Berlin, Oct. 1, 1988). **ORCH.:** Piano Concerto (1966); Clarinet Concerto (1967); Viola Concerto (1974; Boston, Oct. 14, 1979); *Eternity's Sunrise* (1979–80); *Mobile* (1982); Violin Concerto (1984); Concerto for 2 Violins, Viola, Cello, and Chamber Orch. (1987); *Chetro Ketl* (1988); Flute Concerto (Pittsburgh, Sept. 8, 1989); Sym. No. 1 (1991); *Flamenco Fanfare* (1994). **CHAMBER:** 2 string quartets (1966, 1972); Suite for Cello and Piano (1974); Concertino for Flute, Oboe, Clarinet, Violin, Viola, Cello, and Piano (1978); *Rituals* for Flute and Harp (1978); *Kaleidoscope* for Clarinet and Piano (1978); *Continuum* for Cello and Piano (1978); Duo for Violin and Piano (1983); *Voci* for Piano, Clarinet, Violin, and Cello (1988); *Stars the Mirror* for String Quartet (1989); *Take Me T'Susan's Gift* for Percussion (1989); Sonata Concertante for Violin and Piano (1994); String Quintet (1995). **VOCAL:** *Nachtlieder* for Soprano and Orch. (1988).

Nejedlý, Vít, Czech composer, conductor, and musicologist, son of **Zdeněk Nejedlý**; b. Prague, June 22, 1912; d. Dukla,

Slovakia, Jan. 1, 1945. He was a student of Svěceny and Jeremiáš (composition) and Talich (conducting) at the Charles Univ. in Prague, obtaining his Ph.D. in musicology in 1936. From 1936 to 1938 he was a répétiteur and conductor at the Olomouc Theater. After the Nazi occupation of his homeland in 1939, he fled to the Soviet Union and served as an ed. of Czech programs for Radio Moscow's foreign broadcasts. In 1943 he joined the Czech contingent of the Red Army.

WORKS: DRAMATIC: *The Dying*, melodrama (1933); *Tkalci* (The Weavers), opera (1938; unfinished; completed by J. Hanus((SQ)); Plzen((SQ)), May 7, 1961). **ORCH.:** 3 syms.: No. 1 (1931), No. 2, *Bídy a smrti* (Poverty and Death, 1934), and No. 3, *Španělská* (Spanish, 1937–38); *Dawn*, overture (1932); *Commemoration* (1933); *Sinfonietta* (1937); *Dramatic Overture* (1940); *Popular Suite* (1940); military marches. **CHAMBER:** *2 Compositions* for Wind Quintet (1934); *2 Compositions* for Nonet (1934); *Small Suite* for Violin and Piano (1935); String Quartet (1937); *Fantasy* for Piano (1937); Concertino for Nonet (1940). **VOCAL:** 2 cantatas: *Den* (The Day; 1935) and *To You-the Red Army* (1943); choruses; songs.

BIBL.: J. Plavec, *Vzpominky na Víta Nejedlého* (Memories of V. N.; Prague, 1948); J. Jiránek, *V. N.* (Prague, 1959).

Nejedlý, Zdeněk, Czech musicologist and politician, father of **Vít Nejedlý**; b. Litomyšl, Feb. 10, 1878; d. Prague, March 9, 1962. He studied in Prague with Fibich, and took courses with Jaroslav Goll (history) and Hostinský (aesthetics) at the Charles Univ., where he qualified in 1900. He was an archivist at the National Museum (1899–1909); joined the staff of the Charles Univ. (1905), serving as a reader (1908–19) and prof. (1919–39) in musicology. He joined the Czech Communist Party in 1929; after the Nazi occupation of his country (1939), he went to the Soviet Union and was a prof. of history at the Univ. of Moscow. After the liberation of Czechoslovakia (1945), he returned to Prague; was minister of education (1948–53) and deputy premier (1953).

WRITINGS (all publ. in Prague): *Zdenko Fibich, zakladatel scénického melodramu* (Zdenko Fibich, Founder of the Scenic Melodrama; 1901); *Katechismus estetiky* (A Manual of Aesthetics; 1902); *Dějinv české hudby* (A History of Czech Music; 1903); *Dějiny předhusitského v Čechách* (A History of Pre-Hussite Song in Bohemia; 1904; 2nd ed., 1954, as *Dějiny husitského zěpvu*); *Počátky husitského zěpvu* (The Beginnings of Hussite Song; 1907; 2nd ed., 1954–55, as *Dějiny husitského zpěvu*); *Zpěvohry Smetanovy* (Smetana's Operas; 1908; 3rd ed., 1954); *Josef Bohuslav Foerster* (1910); *Dějiny husitského spěvu za válek husitských* (A History of Hussite Song during the Hussite Wars; 1913; 2nd ed., 1955–56, as *Dějiny husitského zpěvu*); *Gustav Mahler* (1913; 2nd ed., 1958); *Richard Wagner* (1916; 2nd ed., 1961); *Všeobecné dějiny hudby, I: O původy hudby, Antika* (A General History of Music, I: Origin and Antiquity; 1916–30); *Vitězslav Novák* (1921; articles and reviews); *Otakara Hostinského estetika* (Otakar Hostinský's Aesthetics; 1921); *Smetaniana* (1922); *Bedřich Smetana* (4 vols., 1924–33; 2nd ed., 1950–54); *Zdeňka a Fibicha milostný denik* (Zdeňka Fibich's Erotic Diary; 1925; 2nd ed., 1949); *Otakar Ostrčil, Vzrůst a uzráni* (Otakar Ostrčil: Growth and Maturity; 1935; 2nd ed., 1949); *Sovětská hudba* (Soviet Music; 1936–37); *Otakar Hostinský* (1937; 2nd ed., 1955); *Kritiky* (2 vols., 1954, 1965).

BIBL.: J. Teichmann, *Z. N.* (Prague, 1938); V. Pekárek, *Z. N.* (Prague, 1948); J. Jiránek, *Z. N.* (Prague, 1952); A. Sychra, *Estetika Z.a Nejedlého* (Z. N.'s Aesthetics; Prague, 1956); F. Cervinka, *Z. N.* (Prague, 1959); V. Pekárek and J. Kubát, eds., *Na pamět' Z.a Nejedlébo* (In Memory of Z. N.; Prague, 1966); *Z. N.: Doba—život—dilo* (Z. N.: Times—Life—Work; Prague, 1975); M. Ransdorf, *Z. N.* (Prague, 1988).

Nelhybel, Vaclav, Czech-born American composer and conductor; b. Polanka nad Odrou, Sept. 24, 1919. He studied composition and conducting with Ridký at the Prague Cons. (1938–42) and musicology at the Univ. of Prague (1938–42); in 1942, went to Switzerland and took courses in medieval and Renaissance music at the Univ. of Fribourg. He was affiliated with the Swiss Radio (1946–50); then was music director of Radio Free Europe in Munich (1950–57). In 1957 he settled in the U.S., becoming a naturalized American citizen in 1962; subsequently evolved energetic activities as a lecturer and guest conductor at American colleges and high schools. As a composer, he is especially notable for his fine pieces for symphonic band. His harmonic idiom is of a freely dissonant texture, with melorhythmic components gravitating toward tonal centers.

WORKS: DRAMATIC: OPERAS: *A Legend* (1953–54); *Everyman*, medieval morality play (Memphis, Oct. 30, 1974); *The Station* (1978). **BALLETS:** *In the Shadow of a Lime Tree* (1946); *The Cock and the Hangman* (Prague, Jan. 17, 1947). **ORCH.:** Sym. No. 1 (1942); *Ballade* (1946); *Etude symphonique* (1949); Concertino for Piano and Chamber Orch. (1949); *Sinfonietta Concertante* (1960); Viola Concerto (1962); *Houston Concerto* (1967); *Concertino da camera* for Cello, 15 Winds, and Piano (1971); *Polyphonies* (1972); *Toccata* for Harpsichord, 13 Winds, and Percussion (1972); *Cantus and Ludus* for Piano, 17 Winds, and Percussion (1973); *Polyphonic Variations* for Strings and Trumpet (1975); *Slavonic Triptych* (1976). **SYMPHONIC BAND:** *Caucasian Passacaglia* (1963); *Concerto Antiphonale* for 14 Brasses (1964); *Symphonic Requiem*, with Baritone (1965); *Estampie* (1965); *Yamaha Concerto* (1971); *Introit* (1972); *Dialogues* for Piano and Symphonic Band (1976); *Ritual* (1978); *Toccata* (1993). **CHAMBER:** *3 Organa* for 4 Bassoons (1948); 2 string quartets (1948, 1962); 3 wind quintets (1948, 1958, 1960); Quartet for 4 Horns (1957); Quartet for Piano and 3 Brass Instruments (1959); *4 Miniatures* for String Trio (1959); *Numismata* for Brass Septet (1961); Brass Trio (1961); 2 brass quintets (1961, 1965); *Impromptus* for Wind Sextet (1963); 9 clarinet trios (1963); *Scherzo concertante* for Horn and Piano (1963); *3 Pieces* for Saxophone Quartet (1965); *Quintetto concertante* for Violin, Trombone, Trumpet, Xylophone, and Piano (1965); Concerto for Percussion (1972); *Concerto spirituoso No. 1* for 12 Flutes, Electric Harpsichord, and Voice (1974), *No. 2* for 12 Saxophones, Electric Harpsichord, and Voice (1974), *No. 3* for Electric Violin, English Horn, Horn, Tuba, Vibraphone, Winds, Percussion, and Voice (1975), and *No. 4* for Voice, String Quartet, and Chamber Orch. (1977); *Oratio No. 1* for Piccolo, Trumpet, Chimes, and String Quartet or String Orch. (1974) and *No. 2* for Oboe and String Trio (1976); *Music* for 6 Trumpets (1975); *Ludus* for 3 Tubas (1975); Bassoon Quartet (1976); *Variations* for Harp (1977). **KEYBOARD: PIANO:** *103 Short Pieces* (1965). **ORGAN:** *Trois danses liturgiques* (1964); *26 Short Preludes* (1972); *Preambulum*, with Timpani (1977). **VOCAL:** *Caroli antiqui varii*, 7 choruses for 7 Voices (1962); *Epitaph for a Soldier* for Soloists and Chorus (1964); *Peter Piper* for Chorus and Clarinet Choir or Piano (1965); *Cantata pacis* for 6 Soloists, Chorus, Winds, Percussion, and Organ (1965); *Dies ultima* for 3 Soloists, Chorus, Speaking Chorus, Orch., and Jazz Band (1967); *Sine nomine* for 4 Soloists, Chorus, Orch., and Tape (1968); *America Sings* for Baritone, Chorus, and Band (1974); *Estampie natalis* for Double Chorus, Piccolo, Viola, Cello, and Percussion (1976); *6 Fables for All Time* for Narrator, Chorus, and Orch. (Ridgefield, Conn., Oct. 25, 1980).

Nelson, John (Wilton), American conductor; b. San José, Costa Rica (of American parents), Dec. 6, 1941. He studied at Wheaton (Ill.) College and with Morel at the Juilliard School of Music in N.Y. He was music director of the Indianapolis Sym. Orch. (1976–87), the Caramoor Festival in Katonah, N.Y. (1983–90), and the Opera Theatre of St. Louis (1985–91).

Nelson, Judith (Anne née **Manes**), American soprano; b. Chicago, Sept. 10, 1939. She studied at St. Olaf College in Northfield, Minn. She sang with music groups of the Univ. of Chicago and the Univ. of Calif. at Berkeley; made her operatic debut as Drusilla in Monteverdi's *L'incoronazione di Poppea* in Brussels in 1979. She appeared widely as a soloist and recitalist. Although she is particularly noted for her performances of Baroque music, she also introduced compositions by American and English composers.

Nelson, Oliver (Edward), black American saxophonist, composer, and arranger; b. St. Louis, June 4, 1932; d. Los Angeles, Oct. 27, 1975. He studied piano, saxophone, taxidermy, dermatology, and embalming. After serving in the U.S. Marines, he studied composition with Robert Wykes at Washington Univ. in St. Louis (1954–58); had private lessons with Elliott Carter in N.Y. and George Tremblay in Los Angeles. In the 1950s and early 1960s, he played saxophone in several jazz orchs., among them those led by Wild Bill Davis, Louis Bellison, Duke Ellington, and Count Basie; then moved to Hollywood. He publ. a valuable saxophone improvisation book, *Patterns for Jazz* (Los Angeles, 1966; originally titled *Patterns for Saxophone*).

WORKS: Saxophone Sonata (1957); *Songs* for Contralto and Piano (1957); *Divertimento* for 10 Woodwinds and Double Bass (1957); *Afro-American Sketches* for Jazz Ensemble (1960); *Blues and the Abstract Truth* for Jazz Ensemble (1960); Woodwind Quintet (1960); *Dirge* for Chamber Orch. (1961); *Soundpiece* for Contralto, String Quartet, and Piano (1963); *Soundpiece* for Jazz Orch. (1964); *Patterns* for Jazz Ensemble (1965); *A Study in 5/4* for Wind Ensemble (1966); Concerto for Xylophone, Marimba, Vibes, and Wind Orch. (1967); *The Kennedy Dream Suite* for Jazz Ensemble (1967); *Jazzhattan Suite* for Jazz Orch. (N.Y., Oct. 7, 1967); Septet for Wind Orch. (1968); *Piece* for Orch. and Jazz Soloists (1969); *A Black Suite* for Narrator, String Quartet, and Jazz Orch. (1970); *Berlin Dialogue* for Jazz Orch. (Berlin, 1970); *Concert Piece* for Alto Saxophone and Studio Orch. (1972); *Fugue and Bossa* for Wind Orch. (1973); also a sterling jazz arrangement of Prokofiev's *Peter and the Wolf* (1966) and music for films and television.

BIBL.: D. Baker et al., eds., *The Black Composer Speaks* (Metuchen, N.J., 1978).

Nelson, Robert U(riel), American musicologist; b. Brush, Colo., Sept. 16, 1902. He studied at the Univ. of Calif. at Berkeley (A.B., 1923); later worked with Déthier and Goetschius at the Inst. of Musical Art, N.Y. (diplomas in piano and organ, 1925), and with Piston and Apel at Harvard Univ. (M.A., 1937; Ph.D., 1944). He also studied composition with Holst and Zador. From 1925 to 1937 he was a faculty member at Washington State Univ.; in 1938, became an instructor at the Univ. of Calif. at Los Angeles; was a prof. from 1955; retired in 1970. He publ. a valuable study, *The Technique of Variation* (Berkeley, 1948); contributed numerous articles to music magazines.

Nelson, Ron(ald Jack), American composer and teacher; b. Joliet, Ill., Dec. 14, 1929. He studied composition with Hanson, Rogers, Mennini, and Barlow at the Eastman School of Music in Rochester, N.Y. (B.Mus., 1952; M.Mus., 1953; D.M.A., 1956) and with Aubin at the École Normale de Musique in Paris on a Fulbright grant (1955). In 1956 he joined the faculty of Brown Univ. in Providence, R.I., where he was chairman of the music dept. (1963–73) and a prof. (1968–93). In addition to numerous commissions, he received a Ford Foundation fellowship (1963), a Howard Foundation grant (1965–66), NEA grants, and the John Philip Sousa Medal of Honor (1994). His widely-known scores are stylistically diverse and generally accessible.

WORKS: DRAMATIC: *Dance in Ruins*, ballet (1954). *The Birthday of the Infanta*, opera (1955–56); *Hamaguchi*, opera (1981); many documentary and educational film scores. **ORCH.:** *Sarabande: For Katharine in April* (1954); *Savannah River Holiday* (1955; also for Band, 1973); *This Is the Orchestra*, with narrator (1960); *Jubilee* (1960); *Overture for Latecomers* (1961); *Toccata* (1961); *Rocky Point Holiday* (1969; also for Band); *Trilogy: JFK-MLK-RFK* for Orch. and Tape (1969); *5 Pieces for Orchestra after Paintings by Andrew Wyeth* (1976); *Meditation and Dance* (1977); *Fanfare for a Celebration* (1983; also for Band, 1982); *Morning Alleluias* for Wind Orch. (1989); *Epiphanies: Fanfares and Chorales* (1993; also for Band, 1994). **BAND:** Concerto for Piano and Symphonic Band (1948); *Mayflower Overture* (1958); *Medieval Suite* (1982); *Aspen Jubilee* (1984); *Lauds: Praise High Day* (1991); *To the Airborne* (1992); *Passacaglia: Homage on B-A-C-H* (1992); *Chaconne: In Memoriam* (1994); *Sonoran Desert Holiday* (1994). **OTHER INSTRUMENTAL:** 6 Pieces for Chamber Ensemble (1977); *Kristen's Song* for Violin, Flute, and Organ (1982); *Pebble Beach Sojourn* for Organ, Brass, and Percussion (1983); *Danza Capriccio* for Alto Saxophone and Wind Ensemble (1988); *Elegy II* for Strings (1988); *Fanfare for the Hour of Sunrise* for Winds and Percussion (1989); *Resonances I* for Winds and Percussion (1990). **VOCAL:** *The Christmas Story*, cantata for Chorus, Organ, Brass, and Timpani (1958; also for Chorus and Orch.); *Glory to God* for Chorus, Organ, and Brass (1958); *All Praise to Music* for Chorus, Brass, and Timpani (1960); *3 Ancient Prayers* for Chorus and Organ (1962); *Triumphal Te Deum* for Chorus, Brass, Organ, and Percussion (1963); *What Is Man?*, oratorio for Soprano, Baritone, Narrator, Chorus, and Orch. (1964); *Meditation of the Syllable OM* for Narrator and Men's Chorus (1970); *Psalm 95* for Chorus and Ensemble (1971); *Prayer of the Emperor of China on the Altar of Heaven, Dec. 21, 1539* for Chorus and Ensemble (1972); *Prayer of St. Francis of Assisi* for Chorus and Organ (1975); *4 Pieces after the Seasons* for Chorus and Small Ensemble (1977); *3 Autumnal Sketches* for Chorus and Small Ensemble (1980); *For Freedom of Conscience* for Chorus, Organ, and Trumpets (1980); *Mass of St. LaSalle* for Chorus and Ensemble (1981); *3 Nocturnal Pieces* for Chorus, Viola, and Small Ensemble (1982); *Make Music in the Lord's Honor* for Chorus, Organ, and Brass (1982); *Te Deum Laudamus* for Chorus and Wind Ensemble (1985); *Festive Anthem* for Chorus, Brass, and Organ (1985); *Prime: The Hour of Sunrise* for Chorus and Band (1986); *Another Spring* for Chorus and String Quintet (1987); *Invoking the Powers* for Chorus, Piano, and Percussion (1990); *And This Shall be for Music* for Chorus and Brass Instruments or Band (1990); *Songs of Praise and Reconciliation* for Chorus, Piano, and Percussion (1991); many other vocal pieces.

Nelsova (real name, **Katznelson**), **Zara,** brilliant Canadian-born American cellist of Russian descent; b. Winnipeg, Dec. 23, 1918. Her father, a flutist, gave her music lessons; she later studied with Dezso Mahalek (1924–28). In 1929 she went to London, where she continued her studies with Herbert Walenn (until 1935). In 1931, at the age of 13, she appeared as soloist with the London Sym. Orch. With her 2 sisters, a pianist and a violinist, she organized a group billed as the Canadian Trio, and toured in England, Australia, and South Africa. Returning to Canada, she served as principal cellist of the Toronto Sym. Orch. (1940–43); she was also a member of another Canadian Trio, this time with Kathleen Parlow and Sir Ernest MacMillan (1941–44). In 1942 she made her U.S. debut at Town Hall in N.Y.; also continued her studies, receiving valuable instruction from Feuermann, Casals, and Piatigorsky. In 1962 she joined the faculty of the Juilliard School of Music in N.Y. In 1953 she became a naturalized American citizen. From 1963 to 1973 she was the wife of **Grant Johannesen**. She received rather rapturous press reviews for her lyrical interpretations of classical and modern cello music in a purportedly "Russian" (i.e., wonderful) style.

Nelsson, Woldemar, Russian-born German conductor; b. Kiev, April 4, 1938. His father, a conductor, gave him violin lessons in Kiev; after conducting studies at the Novosibirsk Cons., he attended master classes at the Moscow Cons. and the Leningrad Cons. He won 1st prize in the All-Union Conducting Competition in Moscow (1971); then became assistant to Kondrashin and the Moscow Phil.; also appeared as a guest conductor throughout the Soviet Union. In 1977 he emigrated to West Germany, where he served as Generalmusikdirektor of the Kassel State Theater (1980–87). From 1980 he was a regular conductor at the Bayreuth Festivals. In 1990 he became chief conductor of the Royal Opera and Orch. in Copenhagen.

Nemescu, Octavian, Romanian composer; b. Pascani, March 29, 1940. He studied with Jora, Mendelsohn, Vieru, Ciortea, Vancea, and Paul Constantinescu at the Bucharest Cons. (1956–63); attended the summer courses of new music held in Darmstadt (1972). He devoted himself to composing and teaching. In his output, he pursued an advanced course.

WORKS: Clarinet Sonata (1961–62); *Poliritmii* for Clarinet, Piano, and Prepared Piano (1962–63); *Triunghi* (Triangle) for Orch. (1964; Bucharest, Dec. 3, 1967); *Patru dimensiuni în timp* (4 Dimensions in Time): *I* for Orch. (1965), *II* for Chorus and Orch. (1966), *III* for Orch. (1967), and *IV* for Orch. (1968); *Combinații în cercuri* (Combinations of Circles) for Cello, Tape, and Multimedia Action (1965); *Plurisens*, cycle for Variable Group and Multimedia Action (1965–68); *Concentric and Efemeride*, both for Variable Ensemble, Tape, and Multimedia Action (1968–69); *Memorial I–V* for various combinations of Instruments, Tape, and Multimedia Action (1968–70); *Ego*, multimedia spectacle (1970); *Le Roi va mourir* for an Instrumentalist, Clock, Tape, and Multimedia Action (1971–72); *Ulysse* for Variable Group, Tape, and Multimedia Action (1972–73); *Jeu des sens*, music for a pair of ears, eyes, hands, a nose, and a mouth (1973–74); *Pourras-tu seul?* and *Cromoson*, both "imaginary music" (1973–74); *Natural!*, space music (1973–74); *Kalendrier*, permanent music for the atmosphere of a room (1974); *Natural-Cultural* for Chamber Ensemble and Tape (1973–83); *Sugestii II* for Chamber Ensemble (1974), *III: "Cumpăna porții"* for Viola and Tape (1977–78), *IV* for Piano (1979), and *V* for Clarinet, Piano, and Tape (1981); *Combinații în cercuri* for Chamber Ensemble and Tape (1979–80); *Metabizantinirikon* for Clarinet and Tape (1983–84); *Sonatu(h)r*, electronic piece (1986); *Trisson*, electronic piece (1987); *Finalpha*, electronic piece (1990).

Németh, Mária, Hungarian soprano; b. Körmend, March 13, 1897; d. Vienna, Dec. 28, 1967. She studied with Georg Anthes and Géza Laszló in Budapest, Giannina Russ in Milan, Fernando De Lucia in Naples, and Felicie Kaschowska in Vienna. She made her operatic debut as Sulamith in *Königin von Saba* in Budapest in 1923. In 1924 she became a member of the Vienna State Opera, where she remained until 1946; also made appearances at Covent Garden in London, La Scala in Milan, Munich, Rome, Paris, and Salzburg. She sang both lyric and coloratura roles during her career, excelling as the Queen of the Night, Aida, Donna Anna, and Tosca, among others.

Némethy, Ella, Hungarian mezzo-soprano; b. Sátoraljaujhely, April 5, 1895; d. Budapest, June 14, 1961. She studied at the Budapest Academy of Music and with Panizza in Milan. In 1919 she made her operatic debut as Dalila at the Budapest Opera, where she remained as one of its principal artists until 1948. She was especially known as a Wagnerian, garnering particular success as Brünnhilde, Isolde, and Kundry.

Nemiroff, Isaac, American composer and teacher; b. Cincinnati, Feb. 16, 1912; d. N.Y., March 5, 1977. He studied at the Cincinnati Cons., and with Stefan Wolpe at the N.Y. College of Music; taught at various music schools in N.Y. and Brooklyn.

WORKS: Duo for Violin and Cello (1939); Concerto for Oboe and String Orch. (1955); Concertino for Flute, Violin, and String Orch. (1958); *Lorca*, solo cantata for Voice, Flute, and Strings (1963); Woodwind Quintet (1968); Quintet for Flute, Clarinet, Cello, Voice, and Piano (1969); *Atomyriades* for Oboe (1972); Duo for Oboe and Bass Clarinet (1973); 2 string quartets; 2 violin sonatas; Saxophone Sonata.

Nemtin, Alexander, Russian composer; b. Perm, July 13, 1936. He studied at the Moscow Cons., graduating in 1960. He writes music in different genres, but his most notable creation is an intimately plausible reification of Scriabin's *Acte préalable*, the "preliminary act" of the planned *Mysterium*. Nemtin put together the score from sketches left by Scriabin, supplemented by materials from his late opus numbers, endeavoring to recreate Scriabin's symphonic textures. The first part of this work was performed in Moscow on March 16, 1973.

Nenov, Dimiter, Bulgarian composer, pianist, and teacher; b. Razgrad, Jan. 1, 1902; d. Sofia, Aug. 30, 1953. He went to Dresden to study architecture at the Technische Hochschule and piano with Feling and composition with Blumer and Bitner at the Cons.; after working as an architect, he continued his studies with Petri in Zakopane (1931) and attended the Bologna Cons. (1932). He taught piano in Sofia (1930–33), then at the State Academy of Music there (1933–35), where he later was made a reader (1937) and a prof. (1943).

WORKS: ORCH.: 2 syms. (1922; 1923, unfinished); *Ballad* (1926); Piano Concerto (1932–36); *2 ballads* for Piano and Orch. (1942, 1943); *Rhapsodic Fantasy* (1942–52). **CHAMBER:** Violin Sonata (1921); Piano Sonata (1922).

BIBL.: L. Nikolov, ed., *D. N.: Spomeni i materijali* (Sofia, 1969).

Neri, Giulio, Italian bass; b. Turilla di Siena, May 21, 1909; d. Rome, April 21, 1958. He studied with Ferraresi in Florence. He made his operatic debut at the Teatro delle Quattro Fontane in Rome in 1935; then sang at the Teatro Reale dell'Opera in Rome, where he soon established himself as a principal bass; also made guest appearances at La Scala in Milan, Florence, Venice, London, and Munich. An outstanding Verdi interpreter, he was equally distinguished as a Wagnerian.

Nerini, Emile, French composer; b. Colombes, near Paris, Feb. 2, 1882; d. Paris, March 22, 1967. Son of a piano manufacturer, he studied with Decombes, Diémer, Lenepveu, and Caussade at the Paris Cons.

WORKS: 4 lyric dramas: *Manoel* (Paris, May 11, 1905), *Le Soir de Waterloo* (Paris, April 17, 1910), *L'Epreuve dernière* (Monte Carlo, March 16, 1912), and *Mazeppa* (Bordeaux, 1925); *Mademoiselle Sans-Gêne*, operetta (1944; Bordeaux, 1966); orch. pieces; chamber music; choral works; songs.

Nero, Peter (Bernard), popular American pianist and conductor; b. N.Y., May 22, 1934. He studied at the Juilliard School of Music in N.Y.; then toured as a pianist with Paul Whiteman; subsequently launched a highly successful career as a pianist in the popular music genres. He also appeared as a conductor in his own arrangements of popular music and in his original compositions. He wrote the score for the film *A Sunday in New York*, in which he also played a cameo part.

Nessi, Giuseppe, Italian tenor; b. Bergamo, Sept. 25, 1887; d. Milan, Dec. 16, 1961. He studied at the Bergamo Cons. with Vezzani and Melli. In 1910 he made his operatic debut as Alfredo in Saluzzo. From 1921 to 1959 he was a valued member of Milan's La Scala, where he excelled in comprimario roles. He also sang in other Italian opera centers and at London's Covent Garden (1927–37). Among his most notable roles were Bardolfo, Spoletta, Missail, and Goro. He also created the roles of Gobrias in *Nerone* (1924) and Pong in *Turandot* (1926).

Nesterenko, Evgeni (Evgenievich), distinguished Russian bass; b. Moscow, Jan. 8, 1938. He went to Leningrad to pursue training in architectural engineering at the Structural Inst. (graduated, 1961) and in voice with Lukanin at the Cons. In 1963 he made his operatic debut as Prince Gremin at the Maly Theater in Leningrad, where he sang until 1967. From 1967 to 1971 he was a member of the Kirov Opera and Ballet Theater in Leningrad. In 1970 he captured 1st prize in the Tchaikovsky Competition in Moscow. In 1971 he became a member of the Bolshoi Theater in Moscow, with which he toured as Boris Godunov to Milan's La Scala (1973), the Vienna State Opera (1974), and N.Y.'s Metropolitan Opera (1975). In 1978 he made his debut at London's Covent Garden as Don Basilio. In subsequent years, he appeared as a guest artist with many European opera houses. His festival appearances took him to Verona (1978, 1985, 1989, 1991), Bregenz (1986), and Orange (1990). He also toured widely as a concert artist. Among his various honors are the People's Artist of the U.S.S.R. (1976), the Vercelli Prize (1981), the Lenin Prize (1982), and the Verona Prize (1986). Among his other outstanding roles are Ruslan, Kutuzov, King Philip, Zaccaria, and Méphistophélès.

Nestyev, Izrail (Vladimirovich), Russian musicologist; b. Kerch, April 17, 1911. He received training in theory and composition at the Moscow Cons. (graduated, 1937), and then pursued postgraduate studies there with Ferman (1940; degree,

1946). From 1945 to 1948 he was ed. of music broadcasting in the U.S.S.R. He was on the staff of *Sovetskaya muzika* from 1949 to 1959. He also taught at the Moscow Cons. (from 1956) and was a senior research fellow at the Inst. of the History of the Arts in Moscow (from 1960), which awarded him his Ph.D. in 1971 for his study on Bartók (publ. in Moscow, 1969). His major work was a biography of Prokofiev (Moscow, 1946; Eng. tr., N.Y., 1946; rev. ed., Moscow, 1957; Eng. tr., Stanford, Calif., 1960, with a foreword by N. Slonimsky; new ed. rev. and aug., Moscow, 1973).

Nettl, Bruno, distinguished Czech-born American ethnomusicologist, son of **Paul Nettl**; b. Prague, March 14, 1930. He was taken to the U.S. in 1939; studied at Indiana Univ. (A.B., 1950; M.A., 1951; Ph.D., 1953, with the diss. *American Indian Music North of Mexico: Its Styles and Areas*; publ. as *North American Indian Musical Styles,* Philadelphia, 1954); he also received an M.A. degree in library science from the Univ. of Mich. in 1960. He taught at Wayne State Univ. (1953–64); in 1964 he joined the faculty of the Univ. of Ill. at Urbana, becoming a prof. of music and anthropology in 1967; in 1992 he was made prof. emeritus but continued to teach there part time. He ed. the periodical *Ethnomusicology* (1961–65), serving as president of the Soc. for Ethnomusicology (1969–71); was also ed. of the yearbook of the *International Folk Music Council* (1974–77), and contributed articles to scholarly journals.

WRITINGS: *Music in Primitive Culture* (Cambridge, Mass., 1956); *An Introduction to Folk Music in the United States* (Detroit, 1960; 3rd ed., rev. and aug. by H. Myers, 1976, as *Folk Music in the United States, an Introduction*); *Cheremis Musical Styles* (Bloomington, Ind., 1960); *Reference Materials in Ethnomusicology* (Detroit, 1961; 2nd ed., rev., 1968); *Theory and Method in Ethnomusicology* (N.Y., 1964); *Folk and Traditional Music of the Western Continents* (Englewood Cliffs, N.J., 1965; 3rd ed., rev. by V. Goertzen, 1990); with B. Foltin, Jr., *Daramad of Chahargah: A Study in the Performance Practice of Persian Music* (Detroit, 1972); with C. Hamm and R. Byrnside, *Contemporary Music and Music Cultures* (Englewood Cliffs, N.J., 1975); ed. *Eight Urban Musical Cultures, Tradition and Change* (Urbana, Ill., 1978); *The Study of Ethnomusicology: 29 Issues and Concepts* (Urbana, Ill., 1983); *The Western Impact on World Music: Change, Adaptation, and Survival* (N.Y., 1985); *The Radif of Persian Music: Studies of Structure and Cultural Context* (Champaign, Ill., 1987; 2nd ed., rev., 1991); *Blackfoot Musical Thought: Comparative Perspectives* (Kent, Ohio, 1989); ed. with P. Bohlman, *Comparative Musicology and Anthropology in Music: Essays on the History of Ethnomusicology* (Chicago, 1991); with others, *Excursions in World Music* (Englewood Cliffs, N.J., 1992); ed. with others, *Community of Music: An Ethnographical Seminar in Champaign-Urbana* (Champaign, Ill., 1993); *Heartland Excursions: Ethnomusicological Reflections on Schools of Music* (Urbana, Ill., 1995).

Nettl, Paul, eminent Czech-born American musicologist, father of **Bruno Nettl**; b. Hohenelbe, Bohemia, Jan. 10, 1889; d. Bloomington, Ind., Jan. 8, 1972. He studied jurisprudence (Jur.D., 1913) and musicology (Ph.D., 1915) at the German Univ. of Prague; from 1920 to 1937 he was on its faculty. In 1939 he emigrated to the U.S.; became a naturalized U.S. citizen (1945). After teaching at Westminster Choir College and in N.Y. and Philadelphia, he was a prof. of musicology at Indiana Univ. in Bloomington (1946–59); remained a part-time teacher there until 1963.

WRITINGS: *Vom Ursprung der Musik* (Prague, 1918); *Alte jüdische Spielleute und Musiker* (Prague, 1923); *Musik und Tanz bei Casanova* (Prague, 1924); *Musik-Barock in Böhmen und Mähren* (Brünn, 1927); *Der Prager Kaufruf* (Prague, 1930); *Das Wiener Lied im Zeitalter des Barock* (Vienna, 1934); *Mozart in Böhmen,* after Prochazka's *Mozart in Prag* (Prague, 1938); *The Story of Dance Music* (N.Y., 1947); *The Book of Musical Documents* (N.Y., 1948); *Luther and Music* (N.Y., 1948); *Casanova und seine Zeit* (Esslingen, 1949); *Goethe und Mozart: Eine Betrachtung* (Esslingen, 1949); *The Other Casanova* (N.Y., 1950); *Forgotten Musicians* (N.Y., 1951); *National Anthems* (N.Y., 1952; 2nd ed., enl., 1967); *Beethoven Encyclopedia* (N.Y., 1956; 2nd ed., rev., 1967, as *Beethoven Handbook*); *Mozart and Masonry* (N.Y., 1957); *Beethoven und seine Zeit* (Frankfurt am Main, 1958); *Georg Friedrich Handel* (Berlin, 1958); *Mozart und der Tanz* (1960); *The Dance in Classical Music* (N.Y., 1963); R. Daniel, ed., *P.N.: Selected Essays* (Bloomington, 1975).

BIBL.: T. Atcherson, *Ein Musikwissenschaftler in zwei Welten: Die musikwissenschaftlen und literarischen Arbeiten von P. N.* (Vienna, 1962).

Neuhaus, Heinrich (Gustavovich), eminent Russian pianist and pedagogue; b. Elizavetgrad, April 12, 1888; d. Moscow, Oct. 10, 1964. He studied piano with his father, Gustav Neuhaus (1847–1938); other musical members of his family were his uncle, Felix Blumenfeld, and his 1st cousin, **Karol Szymanowski**. Neuhaus began giving concerts at the age of 9; he made a concert tour in Germany in 1904, then studied composition with Paul Juon in Berlin; from 1912 to 1914 he took piano lessons with Leopold Godowsky in Vienna. Returning to Russia, he taught piano at the Kiev Cons. (1918–22); then was a prof. from 1922 to his death at the Moscow Cons. Among his outstanding students were Emil Gilels, Sviatoslav Richter, Yakov Zak, and Radu Lupu. He excelled as an interpreter of the Romantic and 20th-century Russian repertory; publ. *Ob iskusstve fortepiannoy igrï* (The Art of Piano Playing; Moscow, 1958; 3rd ed., 1967; Eng. tr., London, 1973).

BIBL.: V. Delson, *H. N.* (Moscow, 1966).

Neuhaus, Rudolf, German conductor and pedagogue; b. Cologne, Jan. 3, 1914; d. Dresden, March 7, 1990. He first studied violin; then took conducting lessons with Hermann Abendroth, and also studied theory with Philipp Jarnach at the Cologne Hochschule für Musik (1932–34). He was music director of the Landestheater in Neustrelitz (1934–44); then was conductor of the Landestheater in Schwerin (1945–50), serving as its Generalmusikdirektor from 1950 to 1953. In 1953 he joined the Dresden State Opera, where he was deputy Generalmusikdirektor until 1975. From 1953 he was a member of the faculty of the Dresden Hochschule für Musik; in 1959, was named prof. there.

Neumann, Frederick (actually, **Fritz**), distinguished Austrian-born American violinist and musicologist; b. Bielitz, Dec. 15, 1907; d. Richmond, Va., March 21, 1994. He studied violin with Ondříček, Ševčik, and Marteau in Prague, and also took courses at the Univ. of Berlin (Ph.D., 1934, in political science and economics); subsequently studied violin with H. Kaplan in Berlin and A. Busch in Basel. He emigrated to the U.S. in 1939, and served as head of the string dept. of the Cornish School of Music and Arts in Seattle (1939–42); during World War II (1942–45), he was in the intelligence service of the U.S. Army, becoming a naturalized American citizen (1943). After the war, he studied at Teachers College, Columbia Univ. (M.A., 1947), and at Columbia Univ. (Ph.D., 1952). He was prof. of music and concertmaster of the orch. at the Univ. of Miami (1948–51) and prof. of music at the Univ. of Richmond (Va.) (1955–78); also was concertmaster of the Richmond Sym. Orch. (1957–64), and a visiting prof. at Princeton (1970–71), Yale (1975–76), and Indiana (1978–79) Univs. He made valuable contributions to the field of 17th- and 18th-century performance practices. He publ. the books *Contemporary Violin Technique* (with F. Galamian; 2 vols., N.Y., 1966, 1977), *Violin Left Hand Technique: A Critical Survey of the Literature* (Urbana, Ill., 1969), *Ornamentation in Baroque and Post-Baroque Music* (Princeton, N.J., 1978), *Essays in Performance Practice* (Ann Arbor, 1982), *Ornamentation and Improvisation in Mozart* (Princeton, N.J., 1986), *New Essays on Performance Practice* (Ann Arbor, 1989), and *Performance Practices of the Seventeenth and Eighteenth Centuries* (N.Y., 1992).

Neumann, Václav, prominent Czech conductor; b. Prague, Sept. 29, 1920; d. Vienna, Sept. 2, 1995. He studied violin with J. Micka and conducting with Pavel Dědeček and Metod Doležil at the Prague Cons. (1940–45). While still a student, he was active as a chamber-music player; became a founding member of the Smetana Quartet (1945); that same year he was made 1st violist of the Czech Phil., making his conducting debut in 1948. He was chief conductor of the Karlovy Vary Sym. Orch. (1951–54) and of the Brno Sym. Orch. (1954–56); then conducted at East Berlin's Komische Oper (1956–64), and concurrently was conductor of Prague's FOK Sym. Orch. From 1964 to 1968 he held the post of 2nd conductor of the Czech Phil. in Prague; during that same period, he was the conductor of the Gewandhaus Orch. and Generalmusikdirektor of the Opera in Leipzig; then held the latter post at the Württemberg State Theater in Stuttgart (1969–72). He was chief conductor of the Czech Phil. (1968–90), touring widely with it in Europe and abroad.

Neumann, Věroslav, Czech composer and music educator; b. Citoliby, near Louny, May 27, 1931. He studied with Řídký at the Prague Academy of Music (1950–54). Thereafter he was active as a composer and teacher, working in both professional and amateur circles, and with young people. In 1991 he was appointed director of the Prague Cons. and made it his goal to restore that once venerable institution to its pre-Communist days of educational distinction. In his works, Neumann has developed an accessible style with touches of leavening wit.

WORKS: DRAMATIC: *Opera o komínku* (Chimney Opera; 1965–66); *Glorie*, radio opera (1970); *Příběh se starou lenoskou* (Story of an Old Armchair), comic opera (1987). **ORCH.:** *Ode* (1965–66); *Invitation to a Cocktail Party* (1967); *Dedication* for Chamber Orch. (1977); Concerto for Trumpet, Strings, and Tape (1980); *Symphonic Dances* (1984); *Soothing* (1989). **CHAMBER:** *Music* for Viola and Piano (1968); *5 Pieces* for 2 Violins (1968); String Quartet (1969); *5 Dramatic Sequences* for Cello and Piano (1978); *Proclamation* for Tuba and Piano (1981); *Portraits of a Man* for Violin and Piano (1987); *An Aging Elegant Gentleman's Afternoon in a Spa* for Clarinet and Piano (1987). **VOCAL:** *Panorama of Prague* for Baritone and Orch. (1962); Chamber Sym. for 16 Singers and 13 Instrumentalists (1972); *Christmas for Young Singers* for Children's Chorus and Chamber Orch. (1976); *In Bohemia*, cantata for Girl's Chorus and Orch. (1983); *Elements* for Medium Voice, Cello, and Organ (1989); various choruses; other songs. **OTHER:** Didactic pieces.

Neumann, Werner, respected German musicologist; b. Königstein, Jan. 21, 1905; d. Leipzig, April 24, 1991. He studied piano and theory at the Leipzig Cons., and musicology with Kroyer and Zenck at the Univ. of Leipzig (Ph.D., 1938, with the diss. *J.S. Bachs Chorfuge: Ein Beitrag zur Kompositions-Technik Bachs*; publ. in Leipzig, 1938; 2nd ed., 1950), where he also took courses in psychology and philosophy. He taught at the Leipzig Hochschule für Musik; in 1950 he founded the Leipzig Bach Archive, and in 1953 became co-ed. of the *Bach-Jahrbuch* and the *Neue Bach-Ausgabe*, retiring in 1973. The vol. *Bach-Studien, V* (Leipzig, 1975), was publ. as a Festschrift in his honor.

WRITINGS: *Handbuch der Kantaten Johann Sebastian Bachs* (Leipzig, 1947; 4th ed., 1971); *Auf den Lebenswegen Johann Sebastian Bachs* (Berlin, 1953; 4th ed., 1962); *Johann Sebastian Bach: Sämtliche Kantatatexte* (Leipzig, 1956; 2nd ed., 1967); *Bach: Eine Bildbiographie* (Munich, 1960; 2nd ed., 1961; Eng. tr., 1961, as *Bach and His World*; 2nd ed., 1969); ed. with H.-J. Schulze, *Schriftstücke von der Hand Johann Sebastian Bachs, Bach-Dokumente, I* (Leipzig, 1963); ed. with H.-J. Schulze, *Fremdschriftliche und gedruckte Dokument zur Lebensgeschichte Johann Sebastian Bachs 1685–1750*, Bach-Dokumente, II (Leipzig, 1969); ed. *Bilddokumente zur Lebensgeschichte Johann Sebastian Bachs*, Bach-Dokumente, IV (Leipzig, 1978).

Nevada (real name, **Wixom**), **Emma,** noted American soprano, mother of **Mignon (Mathilde Marie) Nevada**; b. Alpha, near Nevada City, Calif., Feb. 7, 1859; d. Liverpool, June 20, 1940. She studied from 1877 with Marchesi in Vienna. She made her operatic debut as Amina at London's Her Majesty's Theatre (May 17, 1880); then sang in the leading Italian music centers, including Milan's La Scala (1881). Her first appearance in Paris was at the Opéra-Comique, May 17, 1883, as Zora in F. David's *Perle du Bresil.* During the 1884–85 season, she was a member of Col. Mapleson's company at the Academy of Music in N.Y., singing on alternate nights with Patti. She sang in Chicago at the Opera Festival in 1885, and again in 1889. She then sang mostly in Europe; retired in 1910.

BIBL.: W. Armstrong, ed., "Reminiscences of E. N.," *N.Y. Tribune Sunday Magazine* (Oct. 28, 1906).

Nevada, Mignon (Mathilde Marie), American soprano, daughter of **Emma Nevada**; b. Paris (of American parents), Aug. 14, 1886; d. Long Melford, England, June 25, 1971. She studied with her mother. She made her operatic debut at Rome's Teatro Costanzi as Rosina in *Il Barbiere di Siviglia* in 1907; then sang a season at the Teatro San Carlos in Lisbon; after a season at the Pergola Theater in Florence, she made her London debut at Covent Garden as Ophelia (Oct. 3, 1910), and sang there in subsequent seasons; also appeared at the Théâtre Royal de la Monnaie in Brussels, and at La Scala in Milan (1923). During World War II, she engaged in war work at Liverpool, England; from 1954 she lived in London.

Neveu, Ginette, brilliant French violinist; b. Paris, Aug. 11, 1919; d. in an airplane crash in San Miguel, Azores Islands, Oct. 28, 1949. She was a grandniece of **Charles-Marie Widor**. She studied with her mother, making her debut when she was 7 as soloist with the Colonne Orch. in Paris; after further studies at the Cons. there, she won the premier prix at age 11; then completed her training with Enesco and Flesch. She won the Wieniawski Competition (1935), and then embarked on an acclaimed career as a virtuoso, touring Poland and Germany that same year, the Soviet Union (1936), and the U.S. and Canada (1937). After the close of World War II, she made her London debut (1945); then appeared in South America, Boston, and N.Y. (1947). Her tragic death occurred on a flight to the U.S. for a concert tour; her brother, Jean-Paul, a talented pianist and her accompanist, also lost his life. Her performances were notable for their controlled and yet impassioned intensity, ably supported by a phenomenal technique.

BIBL.: M.-J. Ronze-Neveu, *G. N.: La Fulgurante Carrière d'une grande artiste* (Paris, 1952; Eng. tr., London, 1957).

Nevin, Arthur (Finley), American composer and pedagogue; b. Edgeworth, Pa., April 27, 1871; d. Sewickley, Pa., July 10, 1943. He received musical training at home, mainly from his father, then at the New England Cons. of Music in Boston (1889–93); in 1893 he went to Berlin, where he studied piano with Klindworth and composition with Boise and Humperdinck. Returning to the U.S., he devoted himself to teaching, research, composition, and conducting; lived with the Blackfoot Indians in Montana (summers, 1903 and 1904), and later wrote and lectured on his experiences. He was a prof. of music at the Univ. of Kansas (1915–20) and director of the municipal music dept. of Memphis, Tenn. (1920–22); he settled in Sewickley as a private teacher (1926). His brother, Ethelbert (Woodbridge) Nevin (b. Edgeworth, Pa., Nov. 25, 1892; d. New Haven, Conn., Feb. 17, 1901) was also a composer who excelled in popular piano pieces and songs.

WORKS: DRAMATIC: *A Night in Yaddo Land*, masque (1900); *Poia*, opera (Berlin, April 23, 1910); *A Daughter of the Forest*, opera (Chicago, Jan. 5, 1918). **OTHER:** 2 cantatas: *The Djinns* (N.Y., 1913) and *Roland*; *Bakawali Dances* for Orch.; 3 orch. suites, including *Lorna Doone* and *Love Dreams*; chamber music; piano pieces; songs.

Neway, Patricia, American soprano; b. N.Y., Sept. 30, 1919. She was educated at Notre Dame College for women; received vocal instruction from Morris Gesell, who later became her husband. She made her stage debut as Fiordiligi at the Chautauqua Festival in 1946. After several appearances in minor roles, she achieved her first significant success as Magda Sorel in Menotti's opera *The Consul* (Philadelphia, March 1, 1950); created the role of the Mother in another Menotti opera, *Maria Golovin*, at the Brussels World's Fair (Aug. 20, 1958). Her repertoire also included parts in operas by Berg and Britten.

Newbould, Brian (Raby), English musicologist; b. Kettering, Feb. 26, 1936. He studied at the Univ. of Bristol (B.Mus., 1958; M.A., 1961). He was a lecturer at the Royal Scottish Academy of Music in Glasgow (1960–65) and at the Univ. of Leeds (1965–79). He became prof. of music and head of the music dept. at the Univ. of Hull in 1979. He prepared effective realizations of Schubert's Sym. No. 7, D.729, and Sym. No. "10," D.936a; also completed the scherzo and trio of Schubert's Sym. No. 8, D.759, "Unfinished." Newbould is also the author of the study *Schubert and the Symphony: A New Perspective* (Surbiton, Surrey, 1992).

Newcomb, Ethel, American pianist; b. Whitney Point, N.Y., Oct. 30, 1875; d. there, July 3, 1959. She went to Vienna in 1895, and studied with Leschetizky until 1903; served as his assistant from 1904 to 1908. She made her debut on Feb. 28, 1903, with the Vienna Sym. Orch.; returning to America, she appeared in recitals; then settled at her home in Whitney Point. She publ. *Leschetizky as I Knew Him* (London, 1921).

Newlin, Dika, American writer on music and composer; b. Portland, Oreg., Nov. 22, 1923. She studied piano and theory at Michigan State Univ. (B.A., 1939) and at the Univ. of Calif. at Los Angeles (M.A., 1941); later took courses at Columbia Univ. in N.Y. (Ph.D., 1945, with the diss. *Bruckner-Mahler-Schoenberg*; publ. in N.Y., 1947; 2nd ed., rev., 1978); concurrently received instruction in composition from Farwell, Schoenberg, and Sessions, and in piano from Serkin and A. Schnabel. She taught at Western Maryland College (1945–49), Syracuse Univ. (1949–51), Drew Univ. (1952–65), North Texas State Univ. (1965–73), and Virginia Commonwealth Univ. (from 1978). She ed. and tr. several books by and about Schoenberg; also publ. *Schoenberg Remembered: Diaries and Recollections, 1938–1976* (N.Y., 1980). Her compositions follow the Schoenbergian idiom and include 3 operas, a Sym. for Chorus and Orch., a Piano Concerto, chamber music, piano pieces, and songs.

BIBL.: T. Albrecht, ed., *D. Caecilia: Essays for D. N., November 22, 1988* (Kansas City, Mo., 1988).

Newman, Alfred, American film composer and conductor; b. New Haven, Conn., March 17, 1900; d. Los Angeles, Feb. 17, 1970. He was the uncle of the well-known popular singer, pianist, and songwriter Randy Newman (b. Los Angeles, Nov. 28, 1943). He studied piano with Sigismund Stojowski and composition with Rubin Goldmark; also had private lessons with Schoenberg in Los Angeles. He began his career in vaudeville shows billed as "The Marvelous Boy Pianist"; later, when he led theater orchs. on Broadway, he was hailed as "The Boy Conductor" and "The Youngest Conductor in the U.S." In 1930 he went to Hollywood and devoted himself entirely to writing film music; he wrote scores for about 230 films, 45 of which were nominated for Academy Awards and 9 were winners. Among his most successful scores were *The Prisoner of Zenda* (1937), *The Hunchback of Notre Dame* (1939), *Wuthering Heights* (1939), *Captain from Castille* (1947), *The Robe* (1953), and *The Egyptian* (1954; partly written by the original assignee, Bernard Herrmann). Stylistically, Newman followed an eclectic type of theatrical Romanticism, often mimicking, almost literally, the most popular works of Tchaikovsky, Rachmaninoff, Wagner, and Liszt, and amalgamating these elements in colorful free fantasia.

BIBL.: F. Steiner, *The Making of an American Film Composer: A Study of A. N.'s Music in the First Decade of the Sound Era* (diss., Univ. of Southern Calif., 1981).

Newman, Anthony, American organist, harpsichordist, fortepianist, conductor, and composer; b. Los Angeles, May 12, 1941. He received keyboard training before pursuing studies in Paris with Cortot, Boulanger, and Cochereau, receiving a diplome superieur from the École Normale de Musique. Following further studies at the Mannes College of Music in N.Y. (B.S., 1962) and composition with Kirchner and Berio at Harvard Univ. (M.A., 1963), he completed his education at Boston Univ. (D.M.A., 1966). In 1967 he made his professional debut in a pedal harpsichord recital at N.Y.'s Carnegie Hall, and subsequently toured extensively in the U.S. and abroad as both a keyboard player and conductor. He also was active as conductor of his own period-instrument orch., the Brandenburg Collegium. After teaching at the Juilliard School in N.Y. (1968–73), he was on the faculty of the State Univ. of N.Y. at Purchase (from 1975), where he later was head of its graduate program in music. He also taught at the Indiana Univ. School of Music in Bloomington (1978–81) and gave master classes. He publ. the vol. *Bach and the Baroque: A Performing Guide with Special Emphasis on the Music of J.S. Bach* (N.Y., 1985). Among his works are a Violin Concerto (Indianapolis, Oct. 26, 1979); Sym. for Strings and Percussion (1987); *Sinfonia: On Fallen Heroes* (1988); Organ Concerto (1994; Englewood, N.J., Feb. 23, 1995); chamber music; piano pieces; organ music, including 2 solo organ syms.; vocal pieces.

Newman, Ernest (real name, **William Roberts**), renowned English music critic and writer on music; b. Everton, Lancashire, Nov. 30, 1868; d. Tadworth, Surrey, July 7, 1959. He was educated at Liverpool College and the Univ. of Liverpool; while employed as a bank clerk (1889–1904), he pursued various studies on his own and began to publ. books on music; assumed his *nom de plume* to symbolize an "earnest new man." In 1904 he accepted an instructorship in Birmingham's Midland Inst., and took up music as a profession; in 1905–06 he was in Manchester as critic of the *Guardian*; from 1906 to 1918 he was in Birmingham as critic for the *Daily Post*; in 1919–20 he was in London as critic for the *Observer*; from 1920 to 1958 he was on the staff of the *London Sunday Times*; from 1923 he was also a contributor to the *Glasgow Herald*; in 1924–25, was guest critic of the *N.Y. Evening Post*. One of the best equipped and most influential of English music critics, Newman continued to write his regular column in the *Sunday Times* in his 90th year.

WRITINGS (all publ. in London unless otherwise given): *Gluck and the Opera* (1895); *A Study of Wagner* (1899); *Wagner* (1904); *Musical Studies* (1905; 3rd ed., 1914); *Elgar* (1906); *Hugo Wolf* (1907); *Richard Strauss* (1908); *Wagner as Man and Artist* (1914; 2nd ed., 1924); *A Musical Motley* (1919); *The Piano-Player and Its Music* (1920); *Confessions of a Musical Critic* (1923); *Solo Singing* (1923); *A Musical Critic's Holiday* (1925); *The Unconscious Beethoven* (1927); *What to Read on the Evolution of Music* (1928); *Stories of the Great Operas* (3 vols., 1929–31); *Fact and Fiction about Wagner* (1931); *The Man Liszt* (1934); *The Life of Richard Wagner* (4 vols., 1933, 1937, 1941, 1946); *Opera Nights* (1943; U.S. ed. as *More Stories of Famous Operas*); *Wagner Nights* (1949; U.S. ed. as *The Wagner Operas*); *More Opera Nights* (1954; U.S. ed. as *17 Famous Operas*); *From the World of Music: Essays from "The Sunday Times"* (selected by F. Aprahamian; London, 1956); *More Musical Essays* (2nd selection from the *Sunday Times*, London, 1958); *Testament of Music* (selected essays; 1962); *Berlioz, Romantic Classic* (ed. by P. Heyworth; 1972).

BIBL.: H. van Thal, ed., *Fanfare for E. N.* (London, 1955); V. Newman, *E. N.: A Memoir by His Wife* (London, 1963).

Newman, William S(tein), distinguished American music scholar; b. Cleveland, April 6, 1912. He studied piano with Riemenschneider and Arthur Loesser; composition with Elwell and Shepherd in Cleveland; received his Ph.D. at Western Reserve Univ. in 1939 with the diss. *The Present Trend of the Sonata Idea*; then pursued postdoctoral studies with Lang and Hertzmann at Columbia Univ. in 1940. During World War II, he served in the U.S. Army Air Force Intelligence. From 1945 to 1970 he taught at the Univ. of North Carolina at Chapel Hill; became prof. emeritus in 1976. He focused most of his research on the evolution of the instrumental sonata. His chief project was *A History of the Sonata Idea* (Chapel Hill; Vol. I, *The Sonata in the Baroque Era*, 1959; 4th ed., rev., 1983; Vol. II, *The*

Sonata in the Classic Era, 1963; 3rd ed., rev., 1983; Vol. III, *The Sonata since Beethoven*, 1969; 3rd ed., rev., 1983). He also publ. *The Pianist's Problems* (N.Y., 1950; 4th ed., 1984), *Understanding Music* (N.Y., 1953; 3rd ed., rev., 1967), *Performance Practices in Beethoven's Piano Sonatas* (N.Y., 1971), and *Beethoven on Beethoven: Playing His Piano Music His Way* (N.Y. and London, 1989). He contributed articles to various reference works and music journals.

Newmarch, Rosa (Harriet née **Jeaffreson)**, English writer on music; b. Leamington, Dec. 18, 1857; d. Worthing, April 9, 1940. Growing up in an artistic atmosphere, she entered the Hetherley School of Art to study painting, but after a time abandoned that career for literary pursuits; settled in London in 1880 as a contributor to various journals. There she married Henry Charles Newmarch in 1883. She visited Russia in 1897 and many times afterward; established contact with the foremost musicians there; her enthusiasm for Russian music, particularily that of the Russian national school of composition, was unlimited, and she publ. several books on the subject which were of importance to the appreciation of Russian music in England, though her high-pitched literary manner was sometimes maintained to the detriment of factual material.

WRITINGS (all publ. in London unless otherwise given): *Tchaikovsky: His Life and Works* (1900; 2nd ed., 1908, ed. by E. Evans); *Henry J. Wood* (1904); *The Russian Opera* (1914); *A Quarter of a Century of Promenade Concerts at Queen's Hall* (1928); *The Concert-goer's Library of Descriptive Notes* (6 vols., 1928–48); *The Music of Czechoslovakia* (Oxford, 1942); *Jean Sibelius* (1944).

Newmark, John (real name, **Hans Joseph Neumark**), German-born Canadian pianist; b. Bremen, June 12, 1904; d. Montreal, Oct. 17, 1991. He studied piano with Karl Boerner in Bremen (1912–19) and Annie Eisele in Leipzig (1920–21). He began his career as an accompanist to Szymon Goldberg (1925); with August Wenzinger, he founded the Neue Kammermusik society in Bremen for the performance of modern music (1929); was director of music programs for the Bremen Radio (1930–33). After going to London (1939), he was interned as an alien (1940), and sent to Canada; after his release, he studied harmony and conducting with Mazzoleni in Toronto (1942). Following World War II, he pursued a far-flung career as an accompanist, traveling all over the world with the most celebrated artists of the day. He became a naturalized Canadian citizen in 1946, and in 1974 was made an Officer of the Order of Canada.

Newsom, Hugh Raymond, American concert manager and composer; b. Cawnpore, India (of American parents), Dec. 20, 1891; d. Baltimore, May 19, 1978. He was taken to America as an infant; studied at the Oberlin (Ohio) Cons. and with Chadwick at the New England Cons. of Music in Boston. He became a successful concert manager; in 1937, married the harpist Marjorie Brunton. In the meantime, he composed industriously, producing works which were disarmingly euphonious in an attractive lyric vein. He wrote an oratorio-drama, *The Divine Tragedy*; several other oratorios; a Harp Concerto (N.Y., Nov. 6, 1968, Brunton soloist); song cycles; character pieces for Piano.

Newton, Ivor, English pianist; b. London, Dec. 15, 1892; d. there, April 21, 1981. He studied piano with Arthur Barclay; then went to Berlin, where he studied lieder with Zur Muhlen and the art of accompaniment with Conraad van Bos. An earnest student of the history of song and the proper role of accompaniment, Newton became one of the most appreciated piano accompanists of his time, playing at recitals with celebrated singers and instrumentalists, among them Dame Nellie Melba, John McCormack, Fyodor Chaliapin, Kirsten Flagstad, Pablo Casals, Yehudi Menuhin, and Maria Callas. His career, which spanned more than 60 years, is chronicled in his interesting autobiography, *At the Piano—Ivor Newton* (London, 1966). In 1973 he was made a Commander of the Order of the British Empire.

Ney, Elly, German pianist and pedagogue; b. Düsseldorf, Sept. 27, 1882; d. Tutzing, March 31, 1968. She was a piano student of Leschetizky and Sauer in Vienna. She made her debut in Vienna in 1905; gave successful recitals in Europe and America; then devoted herself mainly to teaching; lived mostly in Munich. From 1911 to 1927 she was married to **Willem van Hoogstraten**; in 1928 she married P.F. Allais of Chicago. She publ. an autobiography, *Ein Leben für die Musik* (Darmstadt, 1952; 2nd ed., 1957, as *Erinnerungen und Betrachtungen; Mein Leben aus der Musik*).

BIBL.: C. von Pidoll, *E. N.* (Leipzig, 1942); Z. Maurina, *Begegnung mit E. N.* (Memmingen, 1956); E. Valentin, *E. N., Symbol einer Generation* (Munich, 1962).

Nezhdanova, Antonina (Vasilievna), distinguished Russian soprano; b. Krivaya Balka, near Odessa, June 16, 1873; d. Moscow, June 26, 1950. She studied at the Moscow Cons. (graduated, 1902). She made her operatic debut as Antonida in *A Life for the Tsar* in Moscow (1902); shortly thereafter, became a principal member of the Bolshoi Theater there, remaining on its roster for almost 40 years; also appeared in other Russian music centers, as both an opera singer and a concert singer; sang Gilda in Paris (1912). She taught at the Stanislavsky Opera Studio and the Bolshoi Theater Opera Studio (from 1936); was prof. of voice at the Moscow Cons. (from 1943). Her husband was **Nikolai Golovanov**. She was made a People's Artist of the U.S.S.R. (1936). She was notably successful in lyric, coloratura, and dramatic roles, her range extending to high G; in addition to Antonida, she excelled as Tatiana, Marguerite, Marfa, Lakme, and Juliette. Her memoirs were publ. posthumously in Moscow (1967).

BIBL.: M. Lvov, *A.V. N.* (Moscow, 1952); G. Polyanovsky, *A. N.* (Moscow, 1970).

Niblock, Phill, American composer and teacher; b. Anderson, Ind., Oct. 2, 1933. He studied economics at Indiana Univ. in Bloomington (B.A., 1956), and then settled in N.Y., where he was active as both a composer and filmmaker. From 1971 he taught at the College of Staten Island of the City Univ. of N.Y. In 1978 he received a Guggenheim fellowsip; also received awards and grants from the N.Y. State Council on the Arts (1981–89), the NEA (1982–88), the City Univ. of N.Y. Research Foundation (1985–89), Meet the Composer, N.Y. (1991), and N.Y.'s Foundation for Contemporary Performance Arts (1994). Niblock's works have been heard in a variety of venues, including galleries and museums around the world, including London (1982), Holland (1989), Brussels (1989), and N.Y. (1990). He has long been associated with the important N.Y.-based organization Experimental Intermedia. In 1994 a double CD collection was released as *The Young Persons Guide to Phill Niblock*.

WORKS: *3 to 7–196* for Cello (1974); *Cello & Bassoon* (1975); *First Performance* for English Horn (1976); *261.63 + and -* for Chamber Ensemble (1976); *Tymps in E* for Percussion (1978); *Earpiece* for Bassoon (1978); *A Trombone Piece* (1978); *Twelve Tones* for Bass (1979); *Voice and Violin* (1979); *A Third Trombone* (1979); *Second 2 Octaves & a Fifth* for Oboe (1980); *Every Tune* for Clarinet (1980); *PK AND SLS* for 2 Flutes (1981); *S L S* for Flute (1981); *P K* for Flute (1981); *E for Gibson* for Cello (1982); *Held Tones* for Flute (1982); *B Poore* for Tuba (1982); *Not Untitled, Knot Untied—Old* for Chamber Ensemble (1984); *Unmentionable Piece for Trombone and Sousaphone* (1984); *New Newband Work* for (the Newband) Ensemble (1984); *Summing I, II, III,* and *IV* for Cello (1985); *Fall and Winterbloom* for Bass Flute (1987); *According to Guy,* versions *I, II,* and *III* (a.k.a. *Aversion I, II,* and *III*) for Accordion (1987–88); *Weld Tuned* for Computer-controlled Synthesizers (1990); *Wintergreen* for Computer-controlled Synthesizers (1990); *MTPNC* for Computer-controlled Synthesizers (1992); *Didjeridoos and Don'ts* (1992); *Early Winter* for Flute, Bass Flute (prerecorded), 38 sampled and synthesized voices (computer-controlled), and String Quartet (1991–93); *Five More String Quartets* (1991–93); *Ten Auras* and *Ten Auras Live* for Tenor Saxophone (1992).

Nicholls, Agnes, English soprano; b. Cheltenham, July 14, 1877; d. London, Sept. 21, 1959. She studied singing with Visetti at the Royal College of Music in London. She made her operatic debut in Manchester on Nov. 20, 1895, as Dido in a revival of Purcell's opera. From 1901 to 1924 she sang with the Denhof, Beecham, and British National Opera companies. On July 15, 1904, she married **Hamilton Harty**. She was quite successful in Wagnerian roles; in 1908 she sang Sieglinde in *Die Walküre* at Covent Garden in London under the direction of Hans Richter.

Nicholson, George (Thomas Frederick), English pianist, teacher, and composer; b. Great Lumley, Sept. 24, 1949. He was educated at the Univ. of York (B.A. in English and music, 1971; Ph.D. in composition, 1979), his mentors in music being Bernard Rands and David Blake. He then was active as a teacher and performer; from 1988 he served as lecturer in music and director of composition at the Univ. of Keele.

WORKS: ORCH.: *1132* (1976); *The Convergence of the Twain* for Chamber Orch. (1978); Chamber Concerto for 13 Instruments (1979–80); *Sea-Change* for 14 Strings (1988); Cello Concerto (1990); Flute Concerto (1993). **CHAMBER:** *Recycle* for 11 Instruments (1975–76); 2 string quartets (1976–77; 1984–85); Brass Quintet (1977); *Winter Music* for Clarinet, Harp, and Percussion (1978); *Ancient Lights* for 7 Instruments (1982); *Sound Progressions Newly Minted* for Brass Quintet (1983); *Stilleven* for 5 Instruments (1985); *Romanza* for Violin and Piano (1987); *Spring Songs* for Recorder (1991); *Muybridge Frames* for Trombone and Piano (1992). **PIANO:** Sonata (1983); *Cascate* (1985); *Impromptu* (1988); *All Systems Go* (1989); *For Miles* (1991–92). **VOCAL:** *Alla Luna* for Soprano, Clarinet, and Piano (1981); *Aubade* for Soprano and 5 Instruments (1981); *The Arrival of the Poet in the City* for Narrator and 7 Instruments (1982–83); *A World of Imagination* for Chorus (1984); *Blisworth Tunnel Blues* for Soprano and Chamber Orch. (1986–87); songs.

Nicholson, Sir Sydney (Hugo), English organist, music educator, and composer; b. London, Feb. 9, 1875; d. Ashford, Kent, May 30, 1947. He was educated at Oxford, the Royal College of Music in London, and in Frankfurt am Main. He served as organist of the Lower Chapel, Eton (1900–1904), acting organist of Carlisle Cathedral (1904–08), and organist of Manchester Cathedral (1908–19) and of Westminster Abbey, London (1919–28). Nicholson then founded the School of English Church Music, which became the Royal School of Church Music in 1945. In 1938 he was knighted. He composed a comic opera, *The Mermaid* (1928), an opera for boy's voices, *The Children of the Chapel* (1934), church music, and organ pieces. He publ. *Church Music: A Practical Handbook* (London, 1920), *A Manual of English Church Music* (with G. Gardner; London, 1923; 2nd ed., 1936), and *Quires and Places where they sing* (London, 1932; 2nd ed., 1942).

Nicolet, Aurèle, prominent Swiss flutist and pedagogue; b. Neuchâtel, Jan. 22, 1926. He studied flute and theory with André Jamet and Willy Burkhard in Zürich, then pursued training with Marcel Moyse and Yvonne Drappier at the Paris Cons., where he won the premier prix for flute in 1947. In 1948 he captured 1st prize for flute at the Geneva Competition. After playing flute in the Zürich Tonhalle Orch. (1945–47), the Winterthur orch. (1948–50), and the Berlin Phil. (1950–59), he pursued an international career as a soloist, recitalist, and chamber music player. He also was a prof. at the Berlin Hochschule für Musik (1953–65) and later taught in Fribourg and Basel. In addition to traditional scores, he also played much modern music for his instrument, including works by Denisov, C. Halffter, Holliger, Kelterborn, Ligeti et al. He publ. a flute method (1967).

Niculescu, Ştefan, Romanian composer and teacher; b. Moreni, July 31, 1927. He was a student of Jora (harmony and counterpoint), Rogalski (orchestration), and Andricu (composition) at the Bucharest Cons. (1951–59), of Kagel at the Siemens Studio in Munich (1966), and of Ligeti, Stockhausen, and Karkoschka at the summer courses in new music in Darmstadt (1966–68). After serving as head of research at the Bucharest Inst. of the Arts (1960–63), he taught at the Bucharest Cons. (1963–87). He was director of the International Festival of New Music in Bucharest from 1990. In addition to his various articles on music, he publ. a vol. of reflections on music (Bucharest, 1980). He first composed in a stringent adherence to serial dictates before adopting a more freely inspired personal mode of expression in which he utilized aleatory and diatonic harmony while remaining true to nontonal precepts. He later enhanced his works with enriched melodic and harmonic elements.

WORKS: DRAMATIC: *Cartea cu "Apolodor,"* opera (Cluj-Napoca, April 13, 1975); *Le Prince né des larmes*, ballet (1982). **ORCH.:** 3 syms.: No. 1 (1955–56; Bucharest, April 12, 1960), No. 2, *Opus dacicum* (1979–80; Timişoara, Nov. 19, 1984), and No. 3, *Cantos* (Timişoara, Nov. 19, 1984); *Scenes* (1962; Cluj-Napoca, March 13, 1965); Sym. for Small Orch. (1963; Bucharest, June 16, 1964); *Hétéromorphie* (1967; Bucharest, April 12, 1968); *Formants* for Chamber Orch. (Bucharest, Aug. 15, 1968); *Unisonos I* (Mainz, Sept. 26, 1970) and *II* (1971; Ljubljana, Oct. 17, 1972); *Ison I* (1973; also for 14 Instruments) and *II*, concerto for Winds and Percussion (Romanian TV, Bucharest, Nov. 13, 1975); *Sincronie II, Omaggio a Enescu e Bartók* (Cluj-Napoca, May 22, 1981). **CHAMBER:** Clarinet Sonata (1953–55); Trio for Violin, Viola, and Cello (1957; Bucharest, Feb. 18, 1976); *Inventions* for Clarinet and Piano (1963–64; Bucharest, Jan. 29, 1965); *Invenţiuni* for Viola and Piano (1965); Sextet for Flute, 2 Clarinets, 2 Oboes, and Trumpet (1969; based on the 3rd cantata, 1960); *Triplum I* for Flute, Cello, and Piano (Royan, April 8, 1971) and *II* for Clarinet, Cello, and Piano (1972; Bucharest, April 18, 1973); *Echoes I* for Violin (1977; Bucharest, Feb. 21, 1978) and *II* for Violin and Synthesizer (1984; Turin, Oct. 1, 1985); *Sincronie I* for 2 to 12 Instruments (Bucharest, Nov. 5, 1979), *V* for Wind Quintet (1982), *III* for Flute, Oboe, and Bassoon (1985; Lugar, Spain, Feb. 22, 1986), and *IV* for Clarinet, Piano, and Percussion (1987; Bucharest, March 21, 1989); *Duplum I* for Cello and Piano or Synthesizer (Bucharest, Nov. 7, 1984) and *III* for Clarinet and Piano (1986); *Ricercare in uno* for Clarinet, Violin, and Synthesizer (Bucharest, March 27, 1984); *Sincronie per quattro* for Flute, Oboe, Violin, and Cello (1985); *Octuplum* for Chamber Ensemble (Den Bosch, the Netherlands, March 31, 1985); *Hétérofonies pour Montreux* for Flute, English Horn, Clarinet, Bassoon, and Horn (Vevey, Aug. 29, 1986); *A Due* for Clarinet and Bassoon (1986); *Monophonie* for Bassoon (1988; Bucharest, Feb. 4, 1989); *Chant-son* for Soprano or Alto Saxophone (1989). **VOCAL:** *Cantata I* for Women's and/or Children's Chorus and Orch. (1959; Cluj-Napoca, June 16, 1961), *II* for Tenor, Chorus, and Orch. (1960; Warsaw, Feb. 15, 1963), and *III, Răscruce*, for Mezzo-soprano and Wind Quintet (Cluj-Napoca, Dec. 11, 1965); *Aphorismes d'Heraclite* for Chorus (Zagreb, May 1969); *Fragments I* for 12 Voices and Instruments (1977; Bucharest, March 23, 1978), *II* for Voice and Instruments (1977), and *III* for Voice and Instruments (1977); *Invocatio* for Voices (Paris, April 18, 1989).

Nielsen, Alice, American soprano; b. Nashville, Tenn., June 7, 1868?; d. N.Y., March 8, 1943. She sang in a church choir in Kansas City; then joined the Burton Stanley Opera Co., where she sang in operettas; she made her debut as a grand-opera singer in Naples as Marguerite in *Faust* (Dec. 6, 1903); made her first American appearance in N.Y. (Nov. 10, 1905). In 1908 she toured with the San Carlo Co. in the U.S.; then achieved the status of a prima donna with the Boston Opera Co. (1909–13) and also sang concurrently with the Metropolitan Opera in N.Y. She eventually settled in N.Y. as a singing teacher.

Nielsen, Carl (August), greatly significant Danish composer; b. Sortelung, near Nørre-Lyndelse, June 9, 1865; d. Copenhagen, Oct. 3, 1931. He received violin lessons in childhood from his father and the local schoolteacher; played 2nd violin in the village band, and later in its amateur orch. After studying cornet with his father, he played in the Odense military orch. (1879–83), serving as its signal horn and alto trombone player; also taught himself to play piano. While in Odense, he began to compose, producing several chamber pieces; then received financial assistance to continue his training at the Royal Cons. in Copenhagen, where he studied violin with Tofte, theory with J.P.E. Hartmann and Orla Rosenhoff, and music history with Gade and P. Matthison-Hansen (1884–86). He was a violinist in Copenhagen's Royal Chapel Orch. (1889–1905); in the interim, he achieved his first success as a composer with his *Little Suite* for Strings (1888); then continued private studies with Rosenhoff. In 1901 he was granted an annual pension. He was conductor of the Royal Theater (1908–14) and the Musikföreningen (1915–27) in Copenhagen; also appeared as a guest conductor in Germany, the Netherlands, Sweden, and Finland; taught theory and composition at the Royal Cons. (1916–19), being appointed its director a few months before his death. The early style of Nielsen's music, Romantic in essence, was determined by the combined influences of Gade, Grieg, Brahms, and Liszt, but later on he experienced the powerful impact of modern music, particularly in harmony, which in his works grew more and more chromatic and dissonant; yet he reserved the simple diatonic progressions, often in a folk-song manner, for his major climaxes; in his orchestration, he applied opulent sonorities and colorful instrumental counterpoint; there are instances of bold experimentation in some of his works, as, for example, the insertion of a snare-drum solo in his 5th Sym., playing independently of the rest of the orch.; he attached somewhat mysterious titles to his 3rd and 4th syms. (*Expansive* and *Inextinguishable*). Nielsen is sometimes described as the Sibelius of Denmark, despite obvious dissimilarities in idiom and sources of inspiration; while the music of Sibelius is deeply rooted in national folklore, both in subject matter and melodic derivation, Nielsen seldom drew on Danish popular modalities; Sibelius remained true to the traditional style of composition, while Nielsen sought new ways of modern expression. It was only after his death that Nielsen's major works entered the world repertoire; festivals of his music were organized on his centennial in 1965, and his syms. in particular were played and recorded in England and America, bringing him belated recognition as one of the most important composers of his time. In 1988 Queen Margrethe II dedicated the Carl Nielsen Museum in Odense. His writings include *Levende musik* (Copenhagen, 1925; Eng. tr., London, 1953, as *Living Music*) and *Min fynske barndom* (Copenhagen, 1927; Eng. tr., London, 1953, as *My Childhood*). A new ed. of his works commenced publication in Copenhagen in 1994 as *The New Carl Nielsen Edition*.

WORKS (all 1st perf. in Copenhagen unless otherwise given): **DRAMATIC:** *Saul og David*, opera (1898–1901; Nov. 28, 1902); *Maskarade*, opera (1904–06; Nov. 11, 1906); *Snefrid*, melodrama (1893; April 10, 1894; rev. 1899); incidental music to A. Munch's *En aften paa Giske* (1889; Jan. 15, 1890), G. Wied's *Atalanta* (Dec. 19, 1901), Drachmann's *Hr. Oluf han rider—* (Master Oluf Rides—; Oct. 9, 1906), L. Holstein's *Tove* (1906–08; March 20, 1908), L. Nielsen's *Willemoes* (1907–08; Feb. 7, 1908), O. Benzon's *Foraeldre* (Feb. 9, 1908), J. Aakjaer's *Ulvens søn* (Århus, Nov. 14, 1909), A. Oehlenschlaeger's *Hagbarth og Signe* (June 4, 1910) and *Sankt Hansaftenspil* (June 3, 1913), Christiansen's *Faedreland* (1915; Feb. 5, 1916), H. Rode's prologue to the Shakespeare Memorial Celebrations (Elsinore, June 24, 1916), J. Sigurjónsson's *Løgneren* (Feb. 15, 1918), Oehlenschlaeger's *Aladdin*, op. 34 (1918–19; Feb. 15 and 22, 1919), Rode's *Moderen*, op. 41 (1920; Jan. 30, 1921), Christiansen's *Cosmus* (1921–22; Feb. 25, 1922), H. Bergstedt's *Ebbe Skammelsen* (June 25, 1925), S. Michaelis's *Amor og Digteren*, op. 54 (Odense, Aug. 12, 1930), and N. Grundtvig's *Paaske-aften* (April 4, 1931).

ORCH.: *Little Suite* for Strings, op. 1 (Sept. 8, 1888; rev. 1889); *Symphonic Rhapsody* (1888; Feb. 24, 1893; not extant); 6 syms.: No. 1, op. 7 (1890–92; March 14, 1894), No. 2, op. 16, *Die fire temperamenter* (The 4 Temperaments; Dec. 1, 1902), No. 3, op. 27, *Sinfonia espansiva* (1910–11; Feb. 28, 1912), No. 4, op. 29, *Det uudslukkelige* (The Inextinguishable; 1914–16; Feb. 1, 1916), No. 5, op. 50 (Jan. 24, 1922), and No. 6, *Sinfonia semplice* (Dec. 11, 1925); *Helios*, overture, op. 17 (Oct. 8, 1903); *Saga-drøm* (Dream of Saga), op. 39 (April 6, 1908); Violin Concerto, op. 33 (1911; Feb. 28, 1912); paraphrase on "Naermere Gud til dig" ("Near My God to Thee") for Wind Orch. (1912; Aug. 22, 1915); *Pan og Syrinx*, op. 49, pastorale (Feb. 11, 1918); Flute Concerto (Paris, Oct. 21, 1926); *En fantasirejse til Faerøerne* (A Fantasy-Journey to the Faroe Islands), rhapsodic overture (Nov. 27, 1927); Clarinet Concerto, op. 57 (Humlebaek, Sept. 14, 1928); *Bohmisk-Dansk folketone* (Bohemian and Danish Folk Tunes), paraphrase for Strings (Nov. 1, 1928).

CHAMBER: 2 numbered violin sonatas: No. 1 (1881–82) and No. 2, op. 35 (1912); 1 unnumbered violin sonata, op. 9 (1895); 5 string quartets: No. 1 (1882–83), No. 2, op. 13 (1887–88; rev. 1897–98), No. 3, op. 5 (1890), No. 4, op. 14 (1897–98), and No. 5, *Piacevolezza*, op. 19 (1906; rev. as the Quartet in F major, op. 44, 1919); Duet for 2 Violins (1882–83); Piano Trio (1883); String Quintet for 2 Violins, 2 Violas, and Cello (1888); *Fantasistykke* for Clarinet and Piano (c.1885); *Ved en ung kunstners baare* (At the Bier of a Young Artist) for String Quartet and Double Bass (1910); *2 Fantasistykker* for Oboe and Piano, op. 2 (1889); *Canto serioso* for Horn and Piano (1913); *Serenata in vano* for Clarinet, Bassoon, Horn, Cello, and Double Bass (1914); Wind Quintet, op. 43 (1922); *Prelude and Theme with Variations* for Violin, op. 48 (1923); *Preludio e presto* for Violin, op. 52 (1927–28); *Allegretto* for 2 Recorders (1931).

KEYBOARD: PIANO: 2 character pieces (1882–83); 5 pieces, op. 3 (1890); *Symphonic Suite*, op. 8 (1894); *Humoreske-bagateller*, op. 11 (1894–97); *Fest-praeludium: "Ved Aarhundredskiften"* (1900); *Drømmen om "Glade Jul"* (1905); *Chaconne*, op. 32 (1916); *Theme and Variations*, op. 40 (1917); Suite "Den Luciferiske," op. 45 (1919–20); 3 pieces, op. 59 (1928); *Klaviermusik for smaa og store*, op. 53 (2 vols., 1930). **ORGAN:** 29 Little Preludes, op. 51 (1929); 2 Preludes (1930); *Commotio*, op. 58 (1931).

VOCAL: CANTATAS: For the Lorens Frølich Festival (1900), the Students' Assn. (1901), the anniversary of the Univ. of Copenhagen, op. 24 (1908), the commemoration of Feb. 11, 1659 (1909), the national exhibition in Århus (1909; in collaboration with E. Bangert), the commemoration of P. Krøyer (1909), the centenary of the Merchants' Committee (1917), the centenary of the Polytechnic High School (1929), the 50th anniversary of the Danish Cremation Union (1930), the 50th anniversary of the Young Merchants' Education Assn. (1930), and *Digtning i sang og toner*, for the opening of the swimming baths (1930); also *Hymnus amoris* for Soprano, Tenor, Baritone, Chorus, and Orch., op. 12 (April 27, 1897); *Søvnen* (Sleep) for Chorus and Orch., op. 18 (1903–4; March 21, 1905); *Fynsk foraar* (Springtime in Funen), lyrical humoresque for Soprano, Tenor, Bass, Chorus, and Orch., op. 42 (1921; Odense, July 8, 1922); *Hyldest til Holberg* for Solo Voices, Chorus, and Orch. (1922); *Hymne til kunsten* for Soprano, Tenor, Chorus, and Wind Orch. (1929). **UNACCOMPANIED CHORAL:** *Sidskensang* (1906); *Kom Guds engel* (1907); *Aftenstemning* (1908); *Paaskeliljen* (1910); *Der er et yndigt land* (1924); 2 school songs (1929); 3 Motets, op. 55 (1929; April 30, 1930); *Til min fødeø* (1929); *6 Rounds* (1930); etc. **SOLO VOCAL:** 2 melodramas: *Franz Neruda in memoriam* for Speaker and Orch. (1915) and *Island* for Speaker and Piano (1929). **SONGS:** 5 Songs, op. 4 (1891); *Viser og vers*, op. 6 (1891); 6 Songs, op. 10 (1894); *Du danske mand* (1906); *Strophic Songs*, op. 21 (1902–07); *De unges sang* (1909); *Hymns and Sacred Songs* (1913–14); 20 Danish Songs (vol. I, 1914; in collaboration with T. Laub); 20 Danish Songs (vol. II, 1914–17; in collaboration with T. Laub); *Studie efter naturen* (1916); *Blomstervise* (1917); 20 Popular Melodies (1917–21); 4 Popular Melodies (1922); *Balladen om bjørnen*, op. 47 (1923); 10 Little Danish Songs (1923–24); 4 Jutish Songs (1924–25); *Vocalise-étude* (1927); etc.

BIBL.: H. Seligmann, *C. N.* (Copenhagen, 1931); K. Jeppesen, "C. N.: A Danish Composer," *Music Review* (1946); T. Meyer and F. Schandorf Petersen, *C. N.: Kunstneren og mennes-*

ket (2 vols., Copenhagen, 1947–48); H. Riis-Vestergaard, *C. N.s symfoniske stil, dens forudsaetninger og saerpraeg* (diss., Univ. of Copenhagen, 1952); I. Møller and T. Meyer, eds., *C. N.s breve i udvalg og med kommentarer* (Copenhagen, 1954); K. Jeppesen, "C. N. paa hundredaarsdagen: Nogle erindringer," *Dansk aarbog for musikforskning,* IV (1964–65); J. Balzer, ed., *C. N. i hundredåret for hans fødsel* (Copenhagen, 1965; Eng. tr., 1965); J. Fabricius, *C. N. 1865–1931: A Pictorial Biography* (Copenhagen, 1965); D. Fog and T. Schousboe, *C. N.: kompositioner: En bibliografi* (Copenhagen, 1965); R. Simpson, "C. N. and Tonality," *Dansk musiktidsskrift,* XL (1965); idem, *Sibelius and N.: A Centenary Essay* (London, 1965); A. Telmányi, *Mit barndomschjem* (Copenhagen, 1965); J. Waterhouse, "N. Reconsidered," *Musical Times,* CVI (1965); T. Schousboe, ed., *C. N.: Dagboger og brevvesling med Anna Marie Carl Nielsen* (2 vols., Copenhagen, 1983); M. Miller, *C. N.: A Guide to Research* (N.Y., 1987); J. Jensen, *C. N.: Danskeren: Musikbiografi* (Copenhagen, 1991); B. Bjørnum and K. Møllerhøj, eds., *Kongelige Bibliotek (Denmark): C. N.s samling: Katalog over komponistens musikhåndskrifter i Det kongelige Bibliotek: The C. N. Collection: A Catalogue of the Composer's Musical Manuscripts in the Royal Library* (Copenhagen, 1992); M. Miller, ed., *The N. Companion* (Portland, Oreg., 1995).

Nielsen, (Carl Henrik) Ludolf, Danish violist, conductor, and composer; b. Nørre-Tvede, Jan. 29, 1876; d. Copenhagen, Oct. 16, 1939. He was a pupil of V. Tofte (violin), A. Orth (piano), Bondesen (harmony), and O. Malling and J.P.E. Hartmann (composition) at the Copenhagen Cons. (1896–98); then was a violist at the Tivoli and violist and deputy conductor at the Palekoncerter. He won the Ancker stipend and traveled in Germany, Austria, and Italy (1907); later played in the Bjørvig Quartet; subsequently was conductor of the musical society Euphrosyne (1914–20). His music represents an expansive late Romantic style.

WORKS: DRAMATIC: OPERAS: *Isbella* (Copenhagen, Oct. 8, 1915); *Uhret* (The Clock; 1911–13); *Lola* (1917–20). **BALLETS:** *Lackschmi* (1921; Copenhagen, March 4, 1922); *Rejsekammeraten* (1928). Also incidental music to plays; music for radio. **ORCH.:** 3 syms.: No. 1 (1903), No. 2 (1909; Copenhagen, April 25, 1910), and No. 3 (1913; Copenhagen, May 4, 1914); other orch. works. **CHAMBER:** 3 string quartets (1900, 1904, 1920); piano pieces; organ music. **VOCAL:** Choral works; songs.

Nielsen, Ludvig, Norwegian organist, conductor, and composer; b. Borge in Østfold, Feb. 3, 1906. He studied with Sandvold and Lange at the Oslo Cons., then with Straube, Raphael, and Hochkofler at the Leipzig Cons. (1931–32) and with Steenberg and Walle-Hansen in Oslo. He was organist at the Høvik Church, Baerum, Akershus (1924–32), and organist and choirmaster at Trondheim Cathedral (1935–76); also taught at the Oslo Cons. (1934–35) and the Trondheim Music School (from 1942). He distinguished himself primarily as a composer of sacred music. Among his organ works are a Concerto for Organ and Strings (1965), chorales, fugues, fantasies, and other pieces; his choral works include a *Te Deum* (1944–45), the oratorio *Draumkvedet* (1962), and motets.

BIBL.: B. Moe, *L. N.* (diss., Univ. of Trondheim, 1974).

Nielsen, Riccardo, Italian composer and administrator; b. Bologna, March 3, 1908; d. Ferrara, Jan. 30, 1982. He studied with Casella and Gatti. He served as director of the Teatro Comunale in Bologna (1946–50). In 1952 he became director of the Liceo Musicale (later Cons.) in Ferrara. In his early works, he was influenced by Casella. He later wrote in a 12-tone idiom, which eventually evolved into a post-Webern style.

WORKS: DRAMATIC: *L'incuba,* monodrama (1948); *La via di Colombo,* radio opera (1953). **ORCH.:** Sinfonia concertante for Piano and Orch. (1931); Violin Concerto (1932); 2 syms. (1933, 1935); *Concerto for Orchestra* (1935); *Musica per archi* (1946); *Variations* (1956); *Varianti* (1965); *6 + 5 fascie sonore* for Strings (1968). **CHAMBER:** *Divertimento* for Clarinet, Bassoon, Trumpet, Violin, Viola, and Cello (1934); *7 aforismi* for Clarinet and Piano (1958); Cello Sonata (1958); Piano Quartet (1961); *Cadenza a due* for Cello and Piano (1967). **VOCAL:** *Musik für Chor und Orchester* (1944); *Requiem nella miniera* for Soloists, Chorus, and Orch. (1957); *4 Goethelieder* for Soprano and Orch. (1958); *Invenzioni e sinfonie* for Soprano and Orch. (1959); songs.

Nielsen, Svend, Danish composer and teacher; b. Copenhagen, April 20, 1937. He studied theory with Holmboe at the Royal Danish Cons. of Music in Copenhagen (graduated, 1967). After advanced composition studies with Nørgård, he taught at the Jutland Cons. of Music in Århus.

WORKS: CHAMBER OPERA: *Bulen* (1968). **ORCH.:** *Metamorfoser* for 23 Solo Strings (1968); *Nuages* (1972); Sym. (1978–79); Violin Concerto (1985); Concertino for Viola and Strings (1988; also for Viola and Orch., 1990); *Nightfall* for Chamber Orch. (1989); *Aria* (1991); *Aubade* (1994); Sinfonia concertante for Cello and Orch. (1994). **CHAMBER:** Rondo for Flute, Violin, Viola, Cello, and Piano (1985); String Quartet (1987); *Black Velvet* for Clarinet and String Quartet (1988); *Variations* for Chamber Ensemble (1990); *Vindbilleder* for 5 Instruments (1990); *Akvareller* for Oboe and Piano (1992); *Luftkasteller* for Woodwind Quintet (1992); *Reflekser* for Flute and Organ (1994). **PIANO:** *Fall* (1987). **VOCAL:** *Duetter* for Soprano, Contralto, Flute, Cello, Vibraphone, and Percussion (1964); *Prisma-suite* for Contralto, Flute, Viola, and Strings (1965); *Paraphrase on "Auf dem Wasser zu singen"* for Soprano and Ensemble (1985); *Det dybe smil I–III* for Chorus (1986); *Så stille* for Alto and 4 Instruments (1986); *Dreamsongs* for Soprano, Flute, Electric Guitar, and Cello (1988); *På bunden af min drom . . .* for Mezzo-soprano, Clarinet, Piano, and Cello (1993).

Nielsen, Tage, Danish composer, pedagogue, and administrator; b. Copenhagen, Jan. 16, 1929. He received training in music and French at the Univ. of Copenhagen (M.A., 1955). In 1951 he joined the music dept. of Radio Denmark, where he was program secretary (from 1954) and later program ed. and deputy head of the dept. (from 1957). In 1963 he became director of the Jutland Academy of Music in Århus, where he was prof. of theory and music history from 1964. From 1983 to 1989 he was director of the Accademia di Danimarca in Rome. He served as managing director of the Soc. for the Publication of Danish Music from 1989 to 1993. In 1992 he received the Schierbeck Prize. His stylistic development proceeded through neo-Classicism, expressionism, the Danish New Simplicity mode, to neo-Romanticism.

WORKS: OPERA: *Laughter in the Dark* (1986–91). **ORCH.:** *Intermezzo gaio* (1952; rev. 1963); *Bariolage* (1965; Århus, Feb. 7, 1966); *Il giardino magico* (1967–68; Århus, Feb. 24, 1969); *Passacaglia* (1981; Copenhagen, Nov. 24, 1983). **CHAMBER:** *Variants* for Alto Flute (1963); *2 Impromptus* for Viola and Organ (1967); *Recitative and Elegy* for Guitar (1975); *Arrangement and Landscape* for Flute (1981); *Ballade* for Percussion (1984); *Salon,* trio for Flute, Viola, and Harp (1984); *3 Opera Fragments* for 13 Instruments (1986); *Tramonto* for Cello and Percussion (1989); *The Frosty Silence in the Gardens* for Guitar (1990); *Uccelli* for Clarinet (1992); *A Winter's Tale,* clarinet sonatina (1994). **KEYBOARD: PIANO:** Sonata (1949–50); *2 Nocturnes* (1960–61); *3 Character Pieces and an Epilogue* (1972–74); *Paesaggi* for 2 Pianos (1985). **ORGAN:** Toccata (1951); *Divertimento: Fields and Meadows* (1971); *Lamento* (1993); *Chorale Fantasy* (1994–95). **VOCAL:** *5 Songs* for Mezzo-soprano and Piano (1946–70); *Attic Summer* for Soprano, Guitar, and Percussion (1974); *8 Choral Songs* (1974); *3 Shakespeare Fragments* for Soprano, Oboe, Cello, and Piano (1977–78); *3 Black Madrigals* for Chorus (1978); *5 Poems by William Blake* for Soprano and Vibraphone (1979); *3 Mexican Poems* for Soprano, Alto, Tenor, Bass, and Piano (1982); *2 Choral Songs* (1984); *In tribulatione mea,* motet for Chorus (1985); *Ritual* for Mezzo-soprano, Flute, Piano, and Percussion (1989); *3 Choral Songs* (1990); *5 Romantic Songs* for Mezzo-soprano and Guitar (1994).

Niemann, Walter, German writer on music and composer; b. Hamburg, Oct. 10, 1876; d. Leipzig, June 17, 1953. He was a pupil of his father, Rudolph (Friedrich) Niemann, and of Humperdinck (1897); from 1898 to 1901, studied at the Leipzig Cons. with Reinecke and von Bose, and at the Univ. of Leipzig with Riemann and Kretzschmar (musicology); received a Ph.D. in 1901 with the diss. *Über die abweichende Bedeutung der Ligaturen in der Mensuraltheorie der Zeit vor Johannes de Garlandia* (publ. in Leipzig, 1902). From 1904 to 1906 he was ed. of the *Neue Zeitschrift für Musik* in Leipzig; from 1907 to 1917 he was a teacher at the Hamburg Cons.; in 1907–17 he was again in Leipzig as a writer and critic of the *Neueste Nachrichten*, then gave up this position to devote himself to composition. Besides a Violin Sonata and a few works for orch. and string orch., he wrote numerous piano pieces (over 150 opus numbers).

WRITINGS (all publ. in Leipzig unless otherwise given): *Musik und Musiker des 19. Jahrhunderts* (1905); *Die Musik Skandinaviens* (1906); *Das Klavierbuch* (1907; 5th ed., 1920); with G. Schjelderup, *Edvard Grieg: Biographie und Wurdigung seiner Werke* (1908); *Das Norlandbuch* (Weimar, 1909); *Die musikalische Renaissance des 19. Jahrhunderts* (1911); *Taschenlexikon für Klavierspieler* (1912; 4th ed., 1918, as *Klavierlexikon*); *Die Musik seit Richard Wagner* (1913; 5th and later eds. as *Die Musik der Gegenwart seit Wagner*); *Jean Sibelius* (1917); *Die nordische Klaviermusik* (1918); with O. Klauwell, *Die Formen der Instrumentalmusik* (2nd ed., 1918); *Die Virginalmusik* (1919); *Meister des Klaviers* (1919); *Brahms* (1920; 14th ed., 1933; Eng. tr., N.Y., 1929).

Niemöller, Klaus Wolfgang, esteemed German musicologist; b. Gelsenkirchen, July 21, 1929. He was a student of Fellerer at the Univ. of Cologne (Ph.D., 1955, with the diss. *Nikolaus Wollick [1480–1541] und sein Musiktraktat*; publ. in Cologne, 1956); in 1955–56, continued his studies in Paris, Rome, and Freiburg im Breisgau. In 1958 he became an assistant lecturer in the musicology dept. at the Univ. of Cologne, where he completed his Habilitation in 1964 with his *Untersuchungen zu Musikpflege und Musikunterricht an den deutschen Lateinschulen vom ausgehenden Mittelalter bis um 1600* (publ. in Regensburg, 1969); subsequently held appointments on its faculty as a lecturer, ausserplanmässiger Professor (1969–70), and research fellow and prof. (from 1970), and, from 1983 to 1994, as director of its Musikwissenschaftlichen Inst. In 1977 he became chairman of the Joseph Haydn Inst. in Cologne. From 1989 to 1993 he was president of the Gesellschaft für Musikforschung. In 1971 he received the Dent Medal of England, and, in 1975, was made a member of the Nordheim-westfälischen Akademie der Wissenschaften. Niemöller's learned articles have appeared in various Festschriften, series, and journals. He is an authority on sources for the study of the history of early music theory and other aspects of early music, as well as of the music of the 19th century.

Nigg, Serge, prominent French composer and teacher; b. Paris, June 6, 1924. He entered the Paris Cons. at age 17, where he studied harmony with Messiaen and then counterpoint and fugue with Plé-Caussade (until 1945). He subsequently studied dodecaphonic composition with Liebowitz. His *Variations* for Piano and 10 Instruments (1946) was the first strictly dodecaphonic score to be composed in France. In 1956 he was made a member of the music committee of Radiodiffusion Française. From 1967 to 1982 he was inspector of the French lyrical theaters for the Ministry of Culture. He served as prof. of composition (1978–82) and of instrumentation and orchestration (1982–89) at the Paris Cons. From 1982 to 1989 he was president of the Société National de Musique. Among his honors are the Italia Prize (1958), the Musical Grand Prix of the City of Paris (1974), the Grand Prix of the SACEM (1978), and prizes of the Académie des Beaux-Arts (1976, 1983, 1987, 1991). In 1989 he was elected a member of the Institut de France (Académie des Beaux-Arts), becoming president in 1995. After composing orthodox serial pieces, Nigg opted for a synthesis of nondoctrinal serial writing and accessible French refinement.

WORKS: BALLET: *Billard* (1950). **ORCH.:** *Timour*, symphonic poem (Paris, Feb. 1944); *Pour un poète captif*, symphonic poem (1950; Prague, May 1951); 2 piano concertos: No. 1 (1954) and No. 2 (Strasbourg, June 10, 1971); Violin Concerto (1957; Paris, May 27, 1960); *Musique funèbre* for Strings (1959); *Jérôme Bosch Symphonie* (1959; Strasbourg, June 21, 1960); Concerto for Flute and Strings (Vichy, July 26, 1961); *Visages d'Axël* (1965–67; Besançon, Sept. 4, 1967); *Fulgur* (Paris, Oct. 7, 1969); *Fantes de l'Imaginaire* (Paris, June 1974); *Scènes concertantes* for Piano and Strings (1975; French Radio, Paris, March 26, 1976); *Mirrors for William Blake*, sym. for Orch. and Piano (1978; French Radio, Paris, Oct. 25, 1979); *Millions d'oiseaux d'or* (1980–81; Boston, March 20, 1981); Viola Concerto (1988); *Poème* (1989; Quebec, Feb. 12, 1990). **CHAMBER:** *Variations* for Piano and 10 Instruments (1946; Paris, Jan. 29, 1947); Suite for Violin, Viola, Cello, and Harp (1952); Sonata for Solo Violin (N.Y., Nov. 10, 1965); *Pièce* for Trumpet and Piano (1972); *Pièce* for Flute and Piano (1976); String Quartet (1982; Radio France, Paris, April 11, 1983); *Duo élégiaque* for Cello and Piano (1985); *Arioso* for Violin and Piano (1987); Violin Sonata (1994). **PIANO:** 3 sonatas (1943, 1964, 1984); *Deux pièces* (1947). **VOCAL:** *Quatre mélodies sur des poèmes de Paul Eluard* for Soprano and Piano (1948); *Prière pour le Premier Jour de l'Eté* for Baritone, Reciter, Chorus, Children's Chorus, and Orch. (1956); *L'Etrange Aventure de Gulliver à Lilliput* for Reciter, Children's Chorus, and Instrumental Ensemble (1958); *La Croisade des Enfants* for Chorus, Children's Chorus, and Instrumental Ensemble (1959); *Histoire d'Oeuf* for 2 Reciters, 6 Percussion, Piano, and Celesta (1961; Strasbourg, Jan. 17, 1962; choreographed version, 1977); *Le Chant du dépossédé* for Baritone, Reciter, and Orch. (Strasbourg, June 25, 1964); *Du clair au sombre* for Soprano and Chamber Orch. (1986; French Radio, Paris, March 7, 1987).

Niimi, Tokuhide, Japanese composer; b. Nagoya, Aug. 5, 1947. After graduating from the Univ. of Tokyo (1970), he studied composition with Miyoshi, Noda, Yashiro, and Mamiya at the Tokyo National Univ. of Fine Arts and Music (1971–78). He taught at the Toho Gakuen School of Music in Tokyo and served on the board of directors of the Japanese Composers Society.

WORKS: ORCH.: Percussion Concerto (1973); 2 syms. (1981; with chorus, 1986); *Waving* for Japanese Drums and Orch. (1982); 2 piano concertos (1984; *Eyes of the Creator*, 1993); *Ohju* (1986); *Heteorhythmix* (1991); *Chain of Life* for Small Orch. (1993). **CHAMBER:** *Enlaçage II* for 3 Percussionists (1978) and *III* for 2 Marimbas and 2 Percussionists (1980); *Fuin I* for Saxophone and Cello (1987) and *II* for 3 Shakuhachis (1988); *Ohju* for Cello (1987); *Kazane* for Clarinet, Violin, and Cello (1989); *Far Away from the Far Past*, concerto for 17-String Koto and Koto Ensemble (1987); *Planets Dance* for 6 Percussionists (1993); String Quartet (1994). **KEYBOARD: PIANO:** *In the Twilight*, preludes for 2 Pianos (1983); *Various Divines* (1983); *3 Valses* for Piano Duet (1986); *Preludes of the Wind* (1992). **ORGAN:** *Wind Spiral* (1991). **VOCAL:** *Enlaçage I* for Chorus and Orch. (1977); *Under Blue Skies* for Children's Chorus, Mixed Chorus, and Orch. (1986); *Au-Mi* for Soprano, Violin, Cello, and Piano (1989); also choruses; songs.

Nikolais, Alwin (Theodore), American choreographer, stage director, and composer; b. Southington, Conn., Nov. 25, 1912; d. N.Y., May 8, 1993. He studied piano and played in movie houses for the silent films. In 1929 he began to study dance with a pupil of Mary Wigman; became director of the Hartford (Conn.) Parks Marionette Theater and later chairman of the dance dept. of the Hartt School of Music there. From 1942 to 1946 he served in military counterintelligence in Europe; then studied with Hanya Holm in N.Y. He became director of the Henry Street Settlement Playhouse in N.Y. (1948), where he organized the Alwin Nikolais Dance Theatre. He wrote music for many of his dance productions, including works in the electronic medium. His principal choreographic innovation is the technique of body extension by tubular projections and disks attached to the head and upper and nether limbs, so that a biped dancer becomes a stereogeometrical figure; often in his productions clusters of dancers form primitivistic ziggurats.

Nikolayev, Leonid (Vladimirovich), Russian pianist, pedagogue, and composer; b. Kiev, Aug. 13, 1878; d. Tashkent, Oct. 11, 1942. He was a pupil of Taneyev and Ippolitov-Ivanov at the Moscow Cons.; then settled in St. Petersburg, where he became prof. of piano at the Cons. in 1906, achieving a fine reputation as a teacher; among his piano pupils was Shostakovitch. Nikolayev went to Tashkent in Central Asia after the German invasion of Russia in 1941, and died there shortly afterward. He composed several symphonic works; *Hymn to Beauty* for Soloists, Chorus, and Orch.; 3 string quartets; Cello Sonata; Violin Sonata; a number of piano works; etc.

BIBL.: S. Savshinsky, *L.V. N.* (Moscow, 1960).

Nikolayeva, Tatiana (Petrovna), esteemed Russian pianist, pedagogue, and composer; b. Bezhitz, May 4, 1924; d. San Francisco, Nov. 22, 1993. She began her piano training with Goldenweiser at Moscow's Central Music School, continuing as his pupil at the Moscow Cons. (graduated, 1947); also studied composition there with Golubev (graduated, 1950). After a highly successful series of concerts in Russia, she won 1st prize at Leipzig's Bach festival for her performance of Bach's clavier works (1950); subsequently toured in Eastern Europe and later made visits to Western Europe; gave several highly acclaimed recitals in London (1986). She was a teacher (1959–65) and a prof. (from 1965) at the Moscow Cons. She was stricken with a cerebral hemorrhage while giving a recital in San Francisco on Nov. 13, 1993; she died 9 days later. Nikolayeva was a remarkably gifted virtuoso; Shostakovich wrote his 24 Preludes and Fugues expressly for her. She was made an Honored Artist of the R.S.F.S.R. in 1955. Among her works are several syms.; 2 piano concertos; Piano Quintet; Piano Sonata; many piano pieces.

Nikolov, Lazar, Bulgarian composer; b. Burgas, Aug. 26, 1922. He studied composition with Vladigerov at the Bulgarian State Cons. in Sofia (1942–47); in 1961, joined its faculty. An experimenter by nature, Nikolov was one of the few composers in Bulgaria who adopted modern procedures of composition, melodically verging on atonality and harmonically on polytonality.

WORKS: OPERAS: *Prometheus Bound*, chamber opera (1963–69; Ruse, March 24, 1974); *Uncles* (1975). **ORCH.:** 2 piano concertos: No. 1 (1947–48; Ruse, Nov. 21, 1949) and No. 2 (1954–55; Sofia, Feb. 28, 1963); Concerto for Strings (1949; Ruse, Nov. 30, 1951); Violin Concerto (1951–52; Varna, March 25, 1955); 2 syms.: No. 1 (1953; Varna, Feb. 16, 1956) and No. 2 for 2 Pianos and Orch. (1960–61); Piano Concertino (1964); *Symphonies* for 13 Strings (1965); *Divertimento concertante* for Chamber Orch. (1968); Cello Concertino (1973). **CHAMBER:** Violin Sonata (1953–54); Viola Sonata (1955); Piano Quintet (1958–59); Flute Sonata (1962); Cello Sonata (1962); Clarinet Sonata (1962); 2 string quartets (1965, 1970); Sonata for 2 Harps (1971); Double Bass Sonata (1972); Bassoon Sonata (1976); Oboe Sonata (1976). **PIANO:** 4 sonatas (1950, 1952, 1955, 1964); Sonata for 2 Pianos (1952). **VOCAL:** *Chants* for Soloists, Chorus, and Chamber Instrumental Group (1969).

Nikolovski, Vlastimir, Macedonian composer; b. Prilep, Dec. 20, 1925. Both his parents were professional musicians from whom he received elementary musical education. In 1944 he obtained a baccalaureate in Prilep; subsequently studied theory with Evlahov at the Leningrad Cons. In 1955 he returned to Yugoslavia, where he took courses at the Belgrade Academy of Music. Upon graduation, he settled in Skopje and became active as a teacher and as director of musical programming for the state radio. In 1976 he was appointed a corresponding member of the Academy of Arts of Macedonia. In his music he makes use of a number of native instruments, particularly percussion. Among his works are 3 syms., a Piano Concerto, 2 oratorios, a Violin Sonata, a Cello Sonata, a Piano Sonata, a String Quartet, and a number of choruses on Macedonian themes.

Niles, John Jacob, American folksinger, folk-music collector, and composer; b. Louisville, Ky., April 28, 1892; d. at his Boot Hill farm, near Lexington, Ky., March 1, 1980. He began collecting and transcribing Appalachian songs when he was 15, and subsequently traveled throughout the Southern Appalachians; studied at the Cincinnati Cons. (1919), and later took courses at the Univ. of Lyons and at the Paris Schola Cantorum. After making his operatic debut in Massenet's *Manon* with the Cincinnati Opera (1920), he devoted himself to teaching, performing folk music, collecting, and composing. His own works include such favorites as *I Wonder as I Wander, Go 'way from my Window,* and *Black Is the Color of My True Love's Hair.* With Douglas Moore, he also brought out *Songs My Mother Never Taught Me* (1929). Many of his works were included in the collection *The Songs of John Jacob Niles* (1975). The greater part of his MSS, field notebooks, instruments, etc., are housed in the John Jacob Niles Collection at the Univ. of Kentucky. Among his publications are *7 Kentucky Mountain Songs* (1929); *7 Negro Exultations* (1929); *Songs of the Hill Folk* (1934); *10 Christmas Carols* (1935); *More Songs of the Hill Folk* (1936); *Ballads and Tragic Legends* (1937); *The Anglo-American Ballad Study Book* (1945); *The Anglo-American Carol Study Book* (1948); *The Shape-Note Study Book* (1950).

Nilsson, (Märta) Birgit, greatly renowned Swedish soprano; b. Vastra Karups, May 17, 1918. She studied with Joseph Hislop at the Royal Academy of Music in Stockholm. She made her debut as Agathe in *Der Freischütz* at the Royal Theater in Stockholm (1946), gaining her first success as Verdi's Lady Macbeth (1947); then sang major roles in operas by Wagner, Puccini, and Strauss with increasing success. She first appeared as Brünnhilde in *Götterdämmerung* in Stockholm during the 1954–55 season, and sang this role in the *Ring* cycle for the first time in Munich during the same season; likewise appeared at the Vienna State Opera (1954) and at the Bayreuth Festival (1954), to which she returned regularly from 1959 to 1970. On Aug. 9, 1956, she made her U.S. debut at the Hollywood Bowl; then sang Brünnhilde in *Die Walküre* at the San Francisco Opera (Oct. 5, 1956); subsequently made her first appearance at London's Covent Garden (1957). She made her long-awaited Metropolitan Opera debut in N.Y. as Isolde on Dec. 19, 1959. Nilsson was universally acclaimed as one of the greatest Wagnerian dramatic sopranos of all time. After an absence of 5 years, she returned to the Metropolitan Opera for a gala concert on Nov. 4, 1979. She then rejoined the co., appearing as Elektra in 1980. She retired from the operatic stage in 1982. In addition to her brilliant Wagnerian roles, she excelled as Beethoven's Leonore, Puccini's Turandot, and Strauss's Salome and Elektra. She publ. *Mina minnesbilder* (Stockholm, 1977; Eng. tr., 1981, as *My Memoirs in Pictures*).

Nilsson, Bo, radical Swedish composer; b. Skellefteå, May 1, 1937. Largely autodidact, he experimented with techniques of serial composition, the phonetic possibilities of vocal music, and electronic sonorities; attended seminars on modern techniques in Cologne and Darmstadt. His works are constructed on precise quasi-mathematical, serial principles, often given abstract titles in German. He publ. his memoirs as *Livet i en mössa* (Life in a Cap; 1984).

WORKS: ORCH.: *Buch der Veränderungen* (1957); *Plexus* (1959); *Szene III* for Chamber Orch. (1961); *Versuchungen* for 3 Orch. Groups (1961); *Entrée* for Tape and Orch. (1963); *Litanei über das verlorene Schlagzeug* for Orch. without Percussion, to conform to the title (1965); *Revue* (1967); *Quartets* for 36 Winds, Percussion, and Tape (1969); *Caprice* (1970); *Exit* for Tape and Orch. (1970); *Eurythmical Voyage* for Piano, Tape, and Orch. (1970). **CHAMBER:** *Frequenzen* for Piccolo, Flute, Percussion, Guitar, Xylophone, Vibraphone, and Double Bass (1955–56); *Zeiten im Umlauf* for 8 Woodwinds (1957); *Kreuzungen* for Flute, Vibraphone, Guitar, and Xylophone (1957); *20 Gruppen* for Piccolo, Oboe, and Clarinet, or any 3 Instruments (1958); *Stenogramm* for Percussion or Organ (1959); *Reaktionen* for 1–4 Percussionists (1960); *Szene I* for 2

Flutes, 2 Trumpets, Piano, Harp, and 2 Percussionists (1960) and *II* for 6 Trumpets, 6 Violins, 4 Percussionists, Piano, Harp, Celesta, and Vibraphone (1961); *Déjà-vu* for Wind Quartet (1967); *Attraktionen* for String Quartet (1968); *Design* for Violin, Clarinet, and Piano (1968); *Déjà-connu* for Wind Quintet (1973); *Déjà connu, déjà entendu* for Wind Quintet (1976); Piano Quintet (1979); *Wendepunkt* for Brass and Live Electronics (1981); *Carte postale a Sten Frykberg* for Brass Quintet (1985). **PIANO:** *Bewegungen* (1956); *Schlagfiguren* (1956); *Quantitäten* (1958); *Rendezvous* (1968). **VOCAL:** *Ett blocks timme*, chamber cantata for Soprano and 6 Instrumentalists (1957–58); *Szene IV* for Saxophone, Orch., and Chorus (1974–75); *La Bran* for Chorus and Orch. (1961); *La Bran* for Saxophone, Chorus, and Orch. (1963–76; Stockholm, March 19, 1976); *Nazm* for Speakers, Vocal Soloists, Chorus, Orch., and Tape (1972–73). **TAPE:** *Audiogramme* (1957–58).

Nilsson, Leo, Swedish composer; b. Malmö, Feb. 20, 1939. He studied organ and music pedagogy at the Stockholm Musikhögskolan (1958–62). After working at the electronic-music studio of the ORTF in Paris, he returned to Sweden and was active in electronic-music circles; collaborated with Ralph Lundsten for a time, and also organized his own electronic-music studio in Skäne; taught at the Stockholm Musikshögskolan (from 1982). He composed various experimental works utilizing electronics.

WORKS: *Vilda livet fortsätter*, electronic score (1974); *Star-75*, multimedia piece (1975); *Zoo*, intermedia piece (1975); *String Play Video*, video piece (1976); *Vad speglar ögat själens spegel*, electronic score (1976); *Identitet* for Trombone, Violin, Double Bass, Synthesizer, and Electronics (1978); *Incostante* for Instrument and Electronics (1978); *Musica mobile*, electronic score (1978); *Signs of Presence*, sonographic piece (1978); *Sonata grafica Y* for Brass Quintet and Live Electronics (1978); *Va-et-vient monsieur Satie* for Piano and Live Electronics (1979); *Lek*, electronic score (1979); *Stenens hjärta*, electronic score (1979); *Animagica* (1980); *Sonata infernale*, electronic score (1981); *Early Ear*, electronic score (1982); *An der Quelle* for Piano (1983); *Musique d'ameublement* for 16 Winds, Cello, and Tape (Stockholm, Oct. 5, 1983); *Niente subito* for Cello and Tape (1983); *Svart vår-vår tiger* for Narrator, Piano, Cello, Live Electronics, and Tape (1983); *Voice of Glass*, electroacoustic piece (1985); *Passage* for Amplified Viola and Percussion (1986).

Nilsson, Sven, Swedish bass; b. Gävle, May 11, 1898; Stockholm, March 1, 1970. He studied with Gillis Bratt and Hjaldis Ingebjarth in Stockholm, and then with Ivar Andresen in Dresden (1928–30). From 1930 to 1944 he was a member of the Dresden State Opera, where he became well known for his Mozart and Wagner portrayals, and also sang in the premieres of Strauss's *Arabella* (1933) and *Daphne* (1938). He likewise sang Wagner in Zoppot from 1934 to 1942. In 1946 he became a member of the Royal Theater in Stockholm, where he appeared until his death. On Nov. 9, 1950, he made his Metropolitan Opera debut in N.Y. as Daland, remaining there on the roster for a season. His guest engagements also took him to London, Milan, Amsterdam, Brussels, Barcelona, and other Eoropean music centers. Among his other roles were Osmin, Sarastro, Pogner, and Baron Ochs.

Nilsson, Torsten, Swedish organist, choirmaster, teacher, and composer; b. Höör, Jan. 21, 1920. He studied church music and pedagogy at the Stockholm Musikhögskolan (1938–42); also had instruction in organ from Alf Lindner and in organ and composition from Anton Heiller in Vienna (1961, 1965). He was organist in Köping (1943–53), Hälsingborg (1953–62), and at the Oscar Church in Stockholm (1962–79); also was conductor of the Oscar Motet Choir. He taught theory at the Stockholm Citizen's School (1962–73) and liturgical singing at the Stockholm Theological Inst. (1964–70) and the Univ. of Uppsala (1966–70). He excels in liturgical works; in his organ music he introduces many innovations, such as static tone-clusters and specified periods of thematic improvisation.

WORKS: CHURCH OPERA-ORATORIOS: *Ur jordens natt* (Out of the Night of the Earth) for Improvising Soli and Vocal Groups, with Organ (Stockholm, April 12, 1968); *Dantesvit* (Dante Suite) for Soli, Vocal Group, Percussion, Organ, Harpsichord, and Tape (Stockholm, April 23, 1969); *Skapelse* (The Creation) for Narrator, Chorus, Organ, and Instruments (Stockholm, May 11, 1970); *Ur jordens natt. Del 2* (Out of the Night of the Earth, Part 2; Stockholm, April 12, 1974); *Den sista natten* (The Last Night) for 2 Actors, Mixed and Children's Chorus, Flute, Harp, Organ, and Percussion (Stockholm, Nov. 25, 1973). **OPERA:** *Malin: Pictures of History* for Chorus and Archaeological Instruments (1987; Nashville, Tenn., April 8, 1988). **ORCH.:** 2 concertos: No. 1 for Piano and Strings (1974–77) and No. 2, *On the Threshold*, for Piano, Wind Instruments, and Percussion (1975); Concerto for Trombone and Strings (1978); *Om ett brev*, lyric suite for Strings (1983); *A Lyric Suite* for Strings (1986–87). **CHAMBER:** Concertino for Trombone and Organ (1978); *Verwerfungen* for Organ and Percussion (1980); *Rondo* for Trombone (1981); Concertino for Trombone and Organ (1981–85); Concertino for Horn and Brass Quartet or Organ (1983); *Signals with 7 Structures* for Organ and 5 Percussionists (1985); *Rondo Sueziae* for Trombone and Piano (1987); *Revelations*, concerto for Organ and Piano (1988); *Barrage: Marche de dressage (marche surréaliste)* for 4 Trombones (1990); *Musica* for Winds (1992); organ music; piano pieces.

Nimas, Lithuanian composer and conductor; b. Viduklé, April 17, 1907. He studied with his father, an organist, then went to Prague, where he took advanced composition lessons with Jaroslav Křička and Alois Hába; subsequently occupied various conducting posts in Lithuania. After numerous misadventures during World War II, he finally emigrated to the U.S. His music reflects the influences of Scriabin and the French Impressionists. He wrote a Trumpet Concerto, 2 string quartets, and piano pieces.

Nimsgern, Siegmund, German bass-baritone; b. Stiring-Wendel, Jan. 14, 1940. He was a student in Saarbrücken of Sibylle Fuchs, Jakob Stämpfli, and Paul Lohmann. In 1965 he made his debut as a concert artist; his operatic debut followed in 1967 when he appeared as Lionel in Tchaikovsky's *The Maid of Orleans* in Saarbrücken, where he sang until 1971. In 1970 he made his Salzburg Festival debut. From 1971 to 1974 he was a member of the Deutsche Oper am Rhein in Düsseldorf. He made his British debut in 1972 as a soloist in *La Damnation de Faust.* In 1973 he made his first appearance at London's Covent Garden as Amfortas, and he also made debuts as Milan's La Scala and the Paris Opéra. In 1974 he made his U.S. debut as Jokanaan at the San Francisco Opera. He made his Metropolitan Opera debut in N.Y. as Pizarro on Oct. 2, 1978, and returned there as Jokanaan in 1981. From 1983 to 1985 he appeared as Wotan at the Bayreuth Festivals. Among his other roles were Telramund, Alberich, Günther, the Dutchman, Macbeth, Iago, and Luna.

Nin (y Castellanos), Joaquín, Spanish-born Cuban pianist and composer, father of **Joaquín (María) Nin-Culmell**; b. Havana, Sept. 29, 1879; d. there, Oct. 24, 1949. He studied with Carlos Vidiella (piano) in Barcelona and with Moszkowski (piano) and d'Indy (composition) at the Paris Schola Cantorum, teaching piano at the latter (1905–08). After living in Berlin, Havana, and Brussels, he settled in Paris. He was a member of the French Légion d'honneur and a corresponding member of the Spanish Academy. He was especially noted as an interpreter of early piano music. He championed the music of the Bach family and works by early Spanish composers, advocating their performance on the piano as opposed to the harpsichord. He wrote articles on aesthetics; ed. 2 valuable collections of keyboard music: *16 sonates anciennes d'auteurs espagnols* (Paris, 1925) and *17 sonates et pièces anciennes d'auteurs espagnols* (Paris, 1929); these 2 collections contained the first contemporary eds. of Padre Antonio Soler, and led to the rediscovery of Spain's outstanding 18th-century master; also ed. *Sept* *chants lyriques espagnols anciens* (1926) and *Sept chansons picaresques espagnoles anciennes* (1926), both for Voice and Piano, 10 pieces by Herrando for Violin and Piano (1937), and *Vocalise (Chant elégiaque)* for Voice and Piano.

WORKS: *20 cantos populares españoles* for Voice and Piano (1923); *10 noëls espagnols* for Voice and Piano (1932); *Aus jardín de Lindaraja* for Violin and Piano (1927); *5 commentarios* for Violin and Piano (1929); many solo piano pieces, including *Danza ibérica* (1926), *Mensaje a Claude Debussy* (1929), *Cadena de valses* (1929), *"1830" variaciones* (1930), and *Canto de cuna para los huérfanos de España* (1939).

Nin-Culmell, Joaquín (María), Cuban-American composer, pianist, and teacher, son of **Joaquín Nin (y Castellanos)**; b. Berlin, Sept. 5, 1908. He went to Paris and studied piano at the Schola Cantorum and composition with Dukas at the Cons. From 1930 to 1935 he pursued training in composition with Falla in Granada. He also continued piano studies with Cortot and Viñes. In 1938 he emigrated to the U.S., where he taught at Williams College in Williamstown, Mass. (1940–50) and the Univ. of Calif. at Berkeley (1950–74). He ed. and annotated the Spanish Choral Tradition (1975 et seq.), a series devoted to secular music of the Renaissance. His own music exhibits Spanish influence in its basic lyricism and vital rhythmic energy, but it combines these elements with 20th century harmonies in transparent textures that are essentially homophonic and tonal.

WORKS: DRAMATIC: *Yerma*, incidental music to García Lorca's play (1956); *El burlador de Sevilla*, ballet (1957–65); *La Celestina*, opera (1965–85); *Le rêve de Cyrano*, ballet (1978); *Cymbeline*, incidental music to Shakespeare's play (1980). **ORCH.:** *Homenaje a Falla* (1933–90); Piano Concerto (1946); *3 Piezas antiguas españolas* (1959–61); *Diferencias* (1962); Cello Concerto (1962; also as a Guitar Concerto, 1992). **CHAMBER:** Piano Quintet (1934–36); *Celebration for Julia* for String Quartet and Glockenspiel (1981). **GUITAR:** *6 Variations on a Theme by Luis de Milán* (1945); *La Matilda y El Emilio* (1990). **KEYBOARD: PIANO:** *Tres impresiones* (1929); *Sonata brève* (1932); *3 Homages* (1941–90); *Tonadas* (4 vols., 1956–61); *Alejandro y Luis* (1983); *12 Danzas Cubanas* (1985). **ORGAN:** *Variations on a Theme by Bach* (1987); *Sinfonia de los Misterios* (1993–94). **VOCAL:** Cantata for Voice, Harpsichord, and Strings (1965–66); *Dedication Mass* for Chorus and Organ (1970); *6 Popular Sephardic Songs* for Voice and Orch. or Piano (1982); *10 de Octubre!* for Chorus and Brass (1985–90); *Ragpicker's Song* for Chorus and Piano (1995); art songs; 49 Spanish and Cuban folk songs.

Nishimura, Akira, Japanese composer; b. Osaka, Sept. 8, 1953. He studied with Ikenouchi, Yashiro, and Mamiya at the Tokyo National Univ. of Fine Arts and Music (1973–80). He taught at the Tokyo College of Music and served on the board of the Japanese Composers Society. In 1993–94 he was composer-in-residence of the Kanazawa Orch. Ensemble. He won the Queen Elisabeth of Belgium International Music Competition (1977), the Dallapiccola Composition Award (1977), and the Otaka Prize (1988, 1992, 1993). His energetic and colorfully chromatic music explores the universe of sound and its transfigurations, with a special affinity for percussion.

WORKS: DRAMATIC: *Hot Rain in August*, television opera (1986). **ORCH.:** *Prelude* (1974); 2 syms. (1976, 1979); *Mutazioni* (1977); 2 piano concertos (*Guren*, 1979; 1982); *Nostalgia* (1983); *Heterophony* for 2 Pianos and Orch. (1987); *Navel of the Sun* for Hichiriki and Orch. (1989); Cello Concerto (1990); *Into the Light of the Eternal Chaos* (1990); *Tapas*, concerto for Bassoon, Percussion, and Strings (1990); *A Ring of Lights*, double concerto for Violin, Piano, and Orch. (1991); *Music of Dawn* for Japanese Instruments and Orch. (1991); *Hoshi-Mandala* (1992); *Astral Concerto: A Mirror of Lights* for Ondes Martenot and Orch. (1992); *Birds Heterophony* (1993); *Birds in Light* (1993–94). **CHAMBER:** 2 string quartets (*Heterophony*, 1975, rev. 1987; *Pulse of the Lights*, 1992); *Kecak* for 6 Percussionists (1979); *Tāla* for 6 Percussionists (1982); *Khyāl* for Flute and Piano (1985); *Mātra* for Marimba, Timpani, and 5 Percussionists (1985); *Gaka I: Concrete of Heterophony* for Shakuhachi, Flute, Koto, and Cello (1987), *III: Generalize of Heterophony* for Violin and 2 Pianos (1987), and *IV: Heterophony on Drone* for Violin and Cello (1988); *Padma in Meditation* for 6 Percussionists (1988); Timpani Concerto for Timpani and 5 Percussionists (1988); *Kāla* for Marimba and 6 Percussionists (1989); *Organums* for Flute, Clarinet, Violin, Piano, and Vibraphone (1989); *Pipa* for 3 Guitars (1989); *Honey of Lights* for Nonet (1990); *Voice of the Sun* for Marimba, Oboe, Soprano Saxophone, and 2 Percussionists (1991); *Ektāl* for 3 Marimba Players and 2 Percussionists (1992); *Silver Cord* for Ondes Martenot and Cello (1993). **PIANO:** Sonata (1972); *Tritrope* (1978); *Penguin Suite* (1983; rev. 1989); *Vibrancy Mirrors* for 2 Pianos (1985); *Because* (1991); *Mirror of the Stars* (1992). **VOCAL:** *Ceremony* for 2 Sopranos and Orch. (1973); *Gaka II: Abstraction of Heterophony* for Soprano, Clarinet, Violin, and 2 Pianos (1987); *Mana II* for Mezzo-soprano and 5 Percussionists (1989); *Mantra of the Light* for Women's Chorus and Orch. (1993).

Nishizaki, Takako, Japanese violinist; b. Aichi Prefecture, April 14, 1944. She was born to musical parents and received early instruction from her father; then was the first student of Suzuki, and subsequently pursued training with Broadus Erle (violin) and Saito (cello) at the Toho Gakuen School of Music in Tokyo (1960–63). In 1962 she was accepted as a violin student of Joseph Fuchs at the Juilliard School of Music in N.Y., where she took 1st prize in its concerto competition in 1967. After winning 2nd prize in the Leventritt competition in 1964, she toured extensively in the Far East, North America, and Europe. In addition to the standard repertoire, she has won particular notice for her championship of rarely-performed concertos by Spohr, Bériot, Joachim, Cui, Anton Rubinstein, and Respighi. She has also acquired a notable reputation as a performer of scores by Chinese composers.

Nissen, Hans Hermann, distinguished German bass-baritone; b. Zippnow, near Marienwerder, West Prussia, May 20, 1893; d. Munich, March 28, 1980. He studied with Julius von Raatz-Brickmann in Berlin, where he made his concert debut (1920); then made his operatic debut as the Caliph in *Der Barbier von Bagdad* at the Berlin Volksoper (1924); subsequently joined the Bavarian State Opera in Munich (1925). In 1930 he went to the U.S., where he was a member of the Chicago Civic Opera (until 1932); on Nov. 23, 1938, he made his debut with the Metropolitan Opera in N.Y. as Wotan and remained with it for a season. He then rejoined the Bavarian State Opera in Munich, retiring in 1967. He remained in Munich as a voice teacher.

Nissman, Barbara, American pianist; b. Philadelphia, Dec. 31, 1944. She was educated at the Univ. of Mich. (B.M., 1966; M.M., 1966; D.M.A., 1969); her principal mentor was György Sandor. In 1971 she made her U.S. orch. debut as soloist with Ormandy and the Philadelphia Orch.; she subsequently appeared as soloist with leading orchs. throughout the U.S. and Europe, and also gave concerts in Latin America and the Far East. She has become particularly known for her performances of contemporary music, most especially the works of Ginastera, who dedicated his 3rd piano sonata to her.

Nixon, Marni (née **Margaret Nixon McEathron**), American soprano; b. Altadena, Calif., Feb. 22, 1930. She studied with Carl Ebert at the Univ. of Southern Calif. in Los Angeles, Jan Popper at Stanford Univ., and Boris Goldovsky and Sarah Caldwell at the Berkshire Music Center at Tanglewood. She pursued a multifaceted career; sang on the soundtrack of the films *The King and I*, *West Side Story*, and *My Fair Lady*, and also starred in her own children's program on television; appeared in musical comedy and opera; was a soloist with major orchs. in the U.S. and abroad. She taught at the Calif. Inst. of the Arts (1969–71) and the Music Academy of the West in Santa Barbara (from 1980).

Nixon, Roger, American composer and teacher; b. Tulare, Calif., Aug. 8, 1921. He studied clarinet with a local teacher; in

1940, attended a seminar in composition with Bliss at the Univ. of Calif. at Berkeley, and in 1941, with Bloch. From 1942 to 1946 he was in the U.S. Army; he returned in 1947 to Berkeley, where he studied with Sessions (M.A., 1949; Ph.D., 1952); in the summer of 1948 he took private lessons with Schoenberg. In 1960 he joined the faculty of San Francisco State College (later Univ.), where he retired as prof. emeritus in 1991. A prolific composer, Nixon writes in a consistent modern idiom anchored in fluctuating tonality and diversified by atonal protuberances. His music is marked by distinctly American melorhythms; his miniature opera, *The Bride Comes to Yellow Sky*, is an exemplar of adroit modernistic Westernism fashioned in a non-ethnomusicological manner.

WORKS: OPERA: *The Bride Comes to Yellow Sky* (Charleston, Ill., Feb. 20, 1968; rev. version, San Francisco, March 22, 1969). **ORCH.:** *Air* for Strings (1953); Violin Concerto (1956); *Elegiac Rhapsody* for Viola and Orch. (1962); *3 Dances* (1963); Viola Concerto (1969; San Francisco, April 29, 1970); *San Joaquin Sketches* for Orch. or Band (1982); various works for Band, including *Chamarita!* (1980), *California Jubilee* (1982), *Golden Jubilee* (1985), *Flower of Youth* (1989–90), and *A Centennial Overture* (1993). **CHAMBER:** String Quartet No. 1 (1949); *Conversations* for Violin and Clarinet (1981); *Music* for Clarinet and Piano (1986); *Variations* for Clarinet and Cello (1991). **VOCAL:** *Christmas Perspectives* for Chorus (1980); *Festival Mass* for Chorus (1980); *Chaunticleer* for Men's Voices (1984); *The Canterbury Tales* for Chorus (1986); *The Daisy* for Chorus (1987); *Wonders of Christmas* for Chorus (1988); other choral works; song cycles and songs; etc.

Niyazi (real name, **Taghi-zade-Khadzhibekov**), Russian conductor and composer; b. Tiflis, Aug. 20, 1912; d. Baku, Aug. 2, 1984. His father was the composer Zulfugar Khadzhibekov. He studied music in Moscow, Yerevan, and Baku. From 1937 to 1965 he served, off and on, as conductor of the Azerbaijani Ballet. In 1961 he was named principal conductor of the Leningrad Theater of Opera and Ballet. He conducted a number of first performances of works by Azerbaijani composers. Among his works are *Hosrov and Shirin*, opera (1942); *Chitra*, ballet, after Rabindranath Tagore (1961); *In Combat*, symphonic poem (1944); popular concert pieces; songs.

BIBL.: E. Abasova, *N.* (Baku, 1965).

Nketia, J(oseph) H(ansen) Kwabena, Ghanaian ethnomusicologist; b. Mampong Ashanti, near Kumasi, June 22, 1921. He attended the Teacher Training College in Akropong-Akwapim (1937–40); then taught music and languages at Presbyterian Training College there (1942–44; 1949–52), where he made his first collection of Akan songs (publ. 1949), and composed original works and arrangements of Ghanaian music. He also studied at the School of Oriental and African Studies, Univ. of London (1944–46; B.A., 1949), where he developed an interdisciplinary approach to ethnomusicology. He taught at the Univ. of Ghana (1951–81) and at the Univ. of Calif. at Los Angeles (1969–83); became Andrew Mellon Prof. of Music at the Univ. of Pittsburgh in 1983; also was director of the Inst. of African Studies at the Univ. of Ghana (1965–80). His numerous publications include collections and studies of African music and performance (publ. in Ghana), as well as the important *Music of Africa* (N.Y., 1974; won the ASCAP-Deems Taylor Award).

Nobel, Felix de, Dutch choral conductor, pianist, and teacher; b. Haarlem, May 27, 1907; d. Amsterdam, March 25, 1981. He studied with Martha Autengruber (piano) and Dresden (composition) at the Amsterdam Cons. He was a piano accompanist with the Dutch Radio and was a pianist in the Concergebouw Quintet. From 1939 to 1973 he conducted the Netherlands Chamber Choir, which he led on numerous tours abroad. He also taught at the Amsterdam Cons. and the Royal Cons. of Music at The Hague. As a choral conductor, his expansive repertoire extended from Obrecht to contemporary Dutch composers.

Noble, Dennis (William), English baritone; b. Bristol, Sept. 25, 1899; d. Jávea, Spain, March 14, 1966. He was trained as a chorister at Bristol Cathedral. In 1924 he made his operatic debut at London's Covent Garden as Marullo in *Rigoletto*, and then sang there until 1938 and again in 1947. He also appeared with the British National Opera Co. and the Carl Rosa Opera Co. In 1931 he was soloist in the premiere of Walton's *Belshazzar's Feast* in Leeds. In 1936–37 he appeared in Cleveland. In addition to his various French and Italian roles, he also sang in many contemporary British operas.

Nobre, Marlos, notable Brazilian composer, pianist, and conductor; b. Recife, Feb. 18, 1939. He studied piano and theory at the Pernambuco Cons. of Music (1948–59). Following studies in composition with Koellreutter and Guarnieri (1960–62), he held a Rockefeller Foundation scholarship to pursue training with Ginastera, Messiaen, Copland, and Dallapiccola at the Latin American Center in Buenos Aires (1963–64). In 1969 he worked with Goehr and Schuller at the Berkshire Music Center in Tanglewood and studied at the Columbia-Princeton Electronic Music Center in N.Y. From 1971 to 1976 he was music director of Radio MEC and the National Sym. Orch. in Rio de Janeiro, and then was the first director of the National Inst. of Music (1976–79). In 1982–83 he was in Berlin under the sponsorship of the Deutscher Akademischer Austauschdienst. He held a Guggenheim fellowship in 1985–86. In 1986–87 he was president of the international Music Council of UNESCO. In 1992 he was a visiting prof. at Yale Univ. As a pianist and conductor, he appeared in South America and Europe. In 1988 he was made an Officer of the Order of Merit of Brasilia. Nobre has developed a strong, individual style in which various contemporary techniques are effectively complemented by his inventive handling of native musical elements.

WORKS: BALLET: *Football* (1980). **ORCH.:** Concertino for Piano and Strings (Rio de Janeiro, Nov. 23, 1959); *Divertimento* for Piano and Orch. (1963; Rio de Janeiro, Nov. 10, 1965); *Convergências* (Rio de Janeiro, June 11, 1968; rev. version, Maracaibo, Nov. 20, 1977); *Desafio I* for Viola and Strings (1968; Rio de Janeiro, Oct. 30, 1974; also for Viola and Piano), *II* for Cello and Strings (1968; Porto Alegre, Nov. 17, 1978; also for Cello and Piano), *III* for Violin and Strings (1968; Recife, May 11, 1978; also for Violin and Piano), *IV* for Double Bass and Strings (1968; also for Double Bass and Piano), *VI* for Strings (1968–79), and *VII* for Piano and Strings (1968–80; Fribourg, May 26, 1980); *Concerto breve* for Piano and Orch. (Rio de Janeiro, May 27, 1969); *Ludus instrumentalis* for Chamber Orch. (Tanglewood, Aug. 18, 1969); *Biosfera* for Strings (1970; Lisbon, Jan. 27, 1971); *Mosaico* (Rio de Janeiro, May 12, 1970); *In memoriam* (1973–76; Rio de Janeiro, Sept. 18, 1976); Concerto I (1976) and II (Bloomington, Ind., Aug. 6, 1981) for Strings; Guitar Concerto (1980); *Elegia* for Strings (Recife, Dec. 21, 1981); *Abertura festiva* (Rio de Janeiro, Oct. 10, 1982); Concerto for Piano and Strings (Nice, July 24, 1984); *4 Latin American Dances* for Chamber or Full Orch. (1989); Concerto for Trumpet and Strings (1989); *Concertante do imaginário* for Piano and Strings (Rio de Janeiro, Dec. 15, 1989); *Xingú* (1989); Concerto for 2 Guitars, Strings, Timpani, and Percussion (1994–95). **CHAMBER:** Trio for Violin, Cello, and Piano (Rio de Janeiro, Nov. 28, 1960); *Musicamera* for Chamber Ensemble (1962; N.Y., April 29, 1981); Sonata for Solo Viola (1963; Rio de Janeiro, Dec. 16, 1968); *Variações ritmicas* for Piano and Percussion (Buenos Aires, Nov. 25, 1963); 2 string quartets: No. 1 (Madrid, Oct. 23, 1967) and No. 2 (1985); *Canticum instrumentale* for Flute, Harp, Piano, and Timpani (1967); Wind Quintet (1968); *Tropicale* for Piccolo, Clarinet, Piano, and Percussion (Rio de Janeiro, March 15, 1968); *Sonâncias I* for Piano and Percussion (Munich, Aug. 4, 1972), *II* for Flute, Guitar, Piano, and Percussion (1980), and *III* for 2 Pianos and Percussion (1980); *Solo I* for Flute (Rio de Janeiro, May 23, 1984), *II* for Bass Clarinet (1994), and *III* for Vibraphone (1994); *Circulos magicos* for Bass Clarinet and Percussion (1989); Duo for Guitar and Percussion (1989); *Sonante I* for Marimba (Oviedo,

April 19, 1994), *II* for Mallet Percussion (1995), and *III* for Flute, Clarinet, Bass Clarinet, Violin, Cello, Piano, and Guitar (1995); also numerous guitar pieces, including *Momentos I–VII* (1974–84), *Homenagem a Villa-Lobos* (1977; N.Y., April 17, 1978), *Fandango* for Guitar Ensemble (1985), *Reminiscencias* (1990; London, Sept. 8, 1991), *Relembrando* (1990), and *Rememórias* (1993). **PIANO:** *Nazarethiana* (1960); *16 Variations on a Theme by Frutuoso Vianna* (1962; Brasilia, Aug. 7, 1970); 2 sonatas: No. 1, *Sonata breve* (1966), and No. 2 (on a theme by Bartók; 1977); *Tango* (Toronto, Sept. 25, 1984). **VOCAL:** *Ukrinmakrinkrin* for Soprano, Piccolo, Oboe, Horn, and Piano (Buenos Aires, Nov. 20, 1964); *O canto multiplicado* for Voice and String Orch. (Rio de Janeiro, Aug. 5, 1972; also for Voice and Piano); *Yanomâni* for Tenor, Chorus, and Guitar (1980; Fribourg, Feb. 6, 1981); *Cantata do Chimborazo* for Soloists, Chorus, and Orch. (1982; Maracaibo, Oct. 24, 1983); *Columbus*, cantata for Soloists, Chorus, and Orch. (1990); *Amazonia (Desafio XVIII)* for Voice and Guitar (1993; N.Y., April 4, 1994); other choral pieces; songs.

Nobutoki, Kiyoshi, Japanese composer and pedagogue; b. Kyoto, Dec. 29, 1887; d. Tokyo, Aug. 1, 1965. He studied music in Japan and in Germany, and then was active mainly as a teacher in Tokyo. He composed a militant cantata, *Kaido Tosei* (Along the Coast, Conquer the East; Tokyo, Nov. 26, 1940), and other choral works.

Noda, Ken, American pianist and composer; b. N.Y., Oct. 5, 1962. He studied piano with Adele Marcus at the Juilliard School in N.Y., and also had lessons in composition with Sylvia Rabinof and Thomas Pasatieri. In 1977 he made his professional debut as a soloist with the Minnesota Orch. in Minneapolis, followed by his London debut as soloist with the English Chamber Orch. in 1979. After further studies with Barenboim in Paris (1979–83), he made appearances on both sides of the Atlantic until giving up his career in 1990. In 1991 he became musical assistant to the artistic director, artistic administration, at the Metropolitan Opera in N.Y. Among his works were several operas, song cycles, and piano pieces.

Noda, Teruyuki, Japanese composer; b. Mie Prefecture, June 15, 1940. He was a pupil of Ikenouchi and Yashiro at the Tokyo Univ. of Fine Arts and Music.

WORKS: ORCH.: 4 syms.: *Symphony in One Movement* (1963), Choral Sym. (Tokyo, July 10, 1968), Sym. No. 2 (1983), and *Mie Ode* (1990); *A Mirror or a Journey* (1968); *Dislocation* (Tokyo, Feb. 10, 1971); *Mutation* for 4 Japanese Instruments and Orch. (1971); Piano Concerto (1977); Guitar Concerto (1984); *Fresque Symphonique* (1987); *Rapsodie Adriatique* for Guitar and Strings (1988); *Carnaval* (1989); *Liturgical Overture* for Winds (1991); *Forest Echoes* for Marimba, 2 Percussionists, and Strings (1992). **CHAMBER:** Trio for Violin, Horn, and Piano (1963); Quartet for Horn, Cello, Timpani, and Piano (1965); *Morning Song* for Marimba, 3 Flutes, and Contrabass (1968); 2 quartets for Japanese Instruments (1969, 1973); *Poems I* and *II* for 7 Instruments (1980); *Novelette* for String Quartet (1983); String Quartet (1985); *In the Garden* for Violin and Piano (1986); *Ode Capricious* for Piano (1986). **VOCAL:** Choral music.

Noehren, Robert, American organist, organ builder, and composer; b. Buffalo, Dec. 16, 1910. He studied at the Inst. of Musical Art in N.Y. and at the Curtis Inst. of Music in Philadelphia. He served in the U.S. Army in World War II. After demobilization, he studied at the Univ. of Mich. (B.Mus., 1948). He taught at Davidson College in N.C. (1946–49) and at the Univ. of Mich. (1949–76); also toured extensively as a recitalist in North America and overseas. He built organs for churches in Milwaukee, Buffalo, San Francisco, and other cities. Among his works are a number of solo organ pieces, including 2 sonatas.

Noelte, A. Albert, German-American music pedagogue and composer; b. Starnberg, March 10, 1885; d. Chicago, March 2, 1946. He went to the U.S. in 1901 and studied music and literature in Boston; in 1908 he returned to Germany, but frequently visited the U.S.; in 1931, settled there and was appointed a prof. at Northwestern Univ. in Evanston, Ill. He earned a fine reputation as a teacher; many American scholars and composers were his pupils. Among his works were the opera *François Villon* (1920) and the orch. piece *Prologue to a Romantic Drama* (Chicago, Jan. 16, 1941).

Noetel, Konrad Friedrich, German composer; b. Posen, Oct. 30, 1903; d. Berlin, April 9, 1947. Following training in engineering and law, he studied music in Hannover and Königsberg. He completed his studies with Hindemith at the Berlin Hochschule für Musik, where he subsequently was on the faculty (1936–47). Noetel's works were in a late Romantic idiom. He composed a Sym.; Suite for Chamber Orch. (1934); Concertino for Flute, Violin, and Strings (1942); *Konzertmusik* for Strings (1944); Concerto for Flute, Oboe, and Strings (1947); chamber music; choral pieces; songs.

Nolte, Ewald V(alentin), American organist, choirmaster, teacher, and composer; b. Utica, Nebr., Sept. 21, 1909; d. Winston-Salem, N.C., March 31, 1991. He studied at Concordia Teachers College in Seward, Nebr. (certificate, 1929) and later was a student of Albert Noelte at Northwestern Univ. in Evanston, Ill. (M.Mus., 1945; Ph.D., 1954, with the diss. *The Instrumental Works of Johann Pachelbel*). He also studied with Hindemith and Schrade at Yale Univ. (1950–51). From 1929 to 1944 he was a Lutheran church organist and choirmaster in Ill. and Ohio. He was an assistant prof. of music at Northwestern Univ. from 1944 to 1964, and then was a prof. of music at Salem College in Winston-Salem from 1964 to 1980. From 1964 to 1972 he also was executive director of the Moravian Music Foundation and ed. numerous works in its archive. He composed sacred choral music, supplied accompaniments to hymns, and arranged American folk songs.

Noni, Alda, Italian soprano; b. Trieste, April 30, 1916. After studies in piano and voice in Trieste, she pursued vocal training in Vienna. In 1937 she made her operatic debut as Rossini's Rosina in Ljubljana, and then sang in Zagreb, Belgrade, and Trieste. She was a member of the Vienna State Opera (1942–44), where she sang the role of Zerbinetta at Strauss's 80th birthday celebration in 1944. In 1946 she appeared as Norina in London. In 1949 she sang with the Glyndebourne Opera at the Edinburgh Festival, and then appeared at Glyndebourne (1950; 1952–54). From 1949 to 1953 she also sang at Milan's La Scala. Among her notable roles were Despina, Papagena, Zerlina, Nannetta, Clorinda in *La Cenerentola*, and Oscar.

Nono, Luigi, remarkable Italian composer who earned a unique place in the history of modern music through his consistent devotion to social problems; b. Venice, Jan. 29, 1924; d. there, May 8, 1990. He became a student at the Venice Cons. (1941), where he received instruction in composition with Malipiero (1943–45); also studied law at the Univ. of Padua (graduated, 1946); later had advanced harmony and counterpoint lessons with Maderna and Scherchen. A man of extraordinary courage, he joined the Italian Communist Party while the country was still under the dictatorship of Mussolini, and was an active participant in the Italian Resistance Movement against the Nazis. In 1975 he was elected to the Central Committee of the Communist Party, and remained a member until his death. Although his works were extremely difficult to perform and practically all of them were devoted to Leftist propaganda, he found support among a number of liberal composers and performers. At the end of his life, he acquired an enormous reputation as a highly original composer in the novel technical idiom as well as a fearless political agitator. In his technique of composition, he followed the precepts of Schoenberg without adhering to the literal scheme of dodecaphonic composition. As a resolutely "engaged" artist, Nono mitigated the antinomy between the modern idiom of his music and the conservative Soviet ideology of Socialist Realism by his militant political attitude and his emphasis on revolutionary subjects in his works, so that even extreme dissonances may be dialectically justified as representing the horrors of Fascism. He made several visits to Russia, the last in 1988, but his works were rarely performed there because of the intransigence of his idiom. He made use of a variety of techniques: serialism, "sonorism" (employment of sonorities for their own sake), aleatory and concrete music, and electronics. Perhaps his most militant composition, both politically and musically, is his opera *Intolleranza 1960*, utilizing texts by Brecht, Eluard, Sartre, and Mayakovsky; the work is a powerful protest against imperialist policies and social inequities. At its premiere in Venice on April 13, 1961, a group of neo-Fascists showered the audience with leaflets denouncing Nono for his alleged contamination of Italian music by alien doctrines, and even making a facetious allusion to his name as representing a double negative. Nono was married to Schoenberg's daughter, Nuria, in 1955; they separated on friendly terms after several years; they had 2 daughters. Nuria settled in her father's last residence in Los Angeles, while Nono traveled widely in Europe. He died of a liver ailment at the age of 66.

WORKS: *Variazioni canoniche* for Orch., based on the 12-tone row of Schoenberg's *Ode to Napoleon Buonaparte* (Darmstadt, Aug. 27, 1950); *Polifonica, monodia, ritmica* for Flute, Clarinet, Bass Clarinet, Saxophone, Horn, Piano, and Percussion (Darmstadt, July 10, 1951); *España en el corazón* for Voices and Instruments, to words by García Lorca (Darmstadt, July 21, 1952); *Der rote Mantel*, ballet (Berlin, Sept. 20, 1954); *La Victoire de Guernica* for Voices and Orch. (1954); *Canti* for 13 Instruments (Paris, March 26, 1955); *Incontri* for 24 Instruments (Darmstadt, May 30, 1955); *Varianti* for Violin, Strings, and Woodwinds (Donaueschingen, Oct. 20, 1957); *La terra e la compagna* for Soli, Chorus, and Instruments (Hamburg, Jan. 13, 1958); *Il canto sospeso* for Solo Voices, Chorus, and Orch., to texts from letters by young men and women condemned to death by the Fascists (Cologne, Oct. 24, 1956); *Intolleranza 1960*, opera (1960–61; Venice, April 13, 1961); *Sarà dolce tacere* for 8 Solo Voices, to texts from "La terra e la morte" by Cesare Pavese (Washington, D.C., Feb. 17, 1961); *La fabbrica illuminata* for Voice and Magnetic Tape (1964); music for the documentary play *Die Ermittlung* by Peter Weiss, dealing with the trial of Nazi guards (Frankfurt am Main, Oct. 19, 1965); *Sul ponte di Hiroscima* for 2 Soloists and Orch., commemorating the victims of the atomic bomb attack on Hiroshima (1962); *A Floresta é jovem e cheja de vida*, oratorio to texts from declarations by the Vietnam guerrilla fighters (1966); *Per Bastiana* for Electronic Tape and 3 Orch. Groups (1967); *Non consumiano Marx* for Electronic Sound (1968); *Voci destroying Muros* for Women's Voices and Instruments in Mixed Media, featuring a machine gun pointed toward the audience (1970); *Y entonces comprendió* for Voices and Magnetic Tape, dedicated to Ché Guevara (1970); *Ein Gespenst geht um in der Welt* for Voice and Orch., to words from the Communist Manifesto (Cologne, Feb. 11, 1971); *Como una ola de fuerza y luz* for Singer, Piano, Magnetic Tape, and Orch. (1972); 2 piano concertos (1972, 1975); *Al gran sole carico d'amore*, opera (1974); *. . . sofferte onde serene . . .* for Piano and Tape (1976); *Con Luigi Dallapiccola* for 6 Percussionists and Live Electronics (1979); *Fragmente-Stille, an Diotima* for String Quartet (1979–80); *Das atmende Klarsein* for Bass Flute, Chorus, and Live Electronics (1980–81); *Quando stanno morendo . . .* for 4 Women's Voices, Bass Flute, Cello, and Live Electronics (1982); *Omaggio a György Kurtág* for Trombone and Live Electronics (1983); *A C. Scarpa architetto, ai suo infiniti possibili* for Orch. (1984); *Guai ai gelidi mostri* for 2 Altos, Flute, Clarinet, Tuba, Viola, Cello, Double Bass, and Live Electronics (1984); *Prometeo, Tragedia dell'ascolto* (1984; rev. 1985); *A Pierre: Dell'azzurro silenzio, inquietum* for Chorus, Flute, Clarinet, and Live Electronics (1985); *Risonanze erranti a M. Cacciari* for Alto, Flute, Tuba, Percussion, and Live Electronics (1986); *Découvrir la subversion: Omaggio a E. Jabés* for Mezzo-soprano, Narrator, Tuba, Horn, and Live Electronics (1987); *No hay caminos, hay que caminar . . . A. Tarkovsky* for Orch. (1987).

BIBL.: J. Stenzl, ed., *L. N.: Texte: Studien zu seiner Musik* (Zürich, 1975); F. Spangemacher, *L. N., die elektronische Musik* (Regensburg, 1983); C. Henius, *Schnebel, N., Schönberg, oder, Die wirkliche und die erdachte Musik: Essays und autobiographisches* (Hamburg, 1993); M. Taibon, *L. N. und sein Musiktheater* (Vienna, 1993).

Norby, Erik, Danish composer; b. Copenhagen, Jan. 9, 1936. He studied with Kayser at the Royal Danish Cons. of Music in Copenhagen (diploma in composition and theory, 1966) and with Nørgård at the Jutland Cons. He taught at the Alborg Cons. until 1975. His music reveals deft handling of styles ranging from the late Romantic to Darmstadt schools.

WORKS: ORCH.: *Folkesang-suite* (1962); *Variations* (1963); *Music for 8 Sextets* (1966); *Nocturne* (1969); *Corps celeste*, symphonic poem (1970); *Regnbueslangen* (Rainbow Snake), symphonic poem (Copenhagen, Nov. 20, 1975); *Illuminations*, capriccio for Flute and Strings (1978); *3 Dances* for Wind Orch. (1983); Concerto for 2 Sopranos and Orch. (1987); *Cortège II* (1992). **CHAMBER:** *Illustrations* for 6 Percussion (1965); *Schubert Variations* for 4 Flutes (1974); *Kuhlau Metamorphoses* for 4 Flutes (1978); *Partita* for Flute and Organ (1981); *Tivoli Collage* for 5 Percussion (1983); organ pieces. **VOCAL:** *Edvard Munch Triptych* for Chorus and Orch. (Danish Radio, Oct. 11, 1979); Cantata for the 150th anniversary of the Copenhagen Cathedral (1979); *Abendstern* for Soprano, English Horn, Harp, and Cello (1984); *Södergran-Lieder* for Alto and Orch. (1992).

Nordal, Jón, Icelandic composer; b. Reykjavík, March 6, 1926. He studied with Kristjánsson and Thórarinsson at the Reykjavík College of Music; then in Zürich with Burkhard (1949–51); finally in Paris and Rome (1956–57) and in Darmstadt (1957). He taught at the Reykjavík College of Music before becoming its director in 1959. In 1968 he became a member of the Royal Swedish Academy. His early works are in the neo-Classical mold, but in the course of time he adopted colorism in the French impressionist vein.

WORKS: ORCH.: *Concerto Grosso* (1950); Concerto (1954); *Sinfonietta seriosa* (1954); Piano Concerto (1957); *Brotaspil* (A Play of Fragments; 1963); *Adagio* for Flute, Harp, Piano, and Strings (1965); *Stiklur* (1969); *Canto elegiaco* for Cello and Orch. (1971); *Leidsla* (Rapture; 1973); *Epitafion* (1974); *Langnaetti* (The Winter Night; 1976); *Tvisong* (Twinsong), double concerto for Violin, Viola, and Orch. (1979); *Tileinkun* (Dedication; 1981); *Choralis* (Washington, D.C., Nov. 23, 1982); Cello Concerto (1983). **CHAMBER:** Violin Sonata (1952); *Rórill* for Flute, Oboe, Clarinet, and Bass Clarinet; Duo for Violin and Cello (1983); *Carvings* for Clarinet and Piano (1985); organ music. **VOCAL:** Choral pieces; songs.

Nordgren, Pehr Henrik, Finnish composer; b. Saltvik, Jan. 19, 1944. He studied composition with Kokkonen and musicology at the Univ. of Helsinki, and composition and traditional Japanese music at the Tokyo Univ. of Arts and Music (1970–73). In his works, he utilizes traditional and advanced harmonies and both Western and traditional Japanese instruments.

WORKS: DRAMATIC: *Den svarte munken* (The Black Monk), chamber opera (1981; Stockholm, March 20, 1984); *Alex*, television opera (1983; Helsinki, Sept. 6, 1986). **ORCH.:** *Epiphrase* (1966); *Koko maailma valittanee* (The Whole World Will Lament) for Strings (1966–74); *Euphonie I* (Helsinki, Feb. 25, 1967), *II* (1967; Helsinki, Jan. 30, 1969), *III* (Lahti, April 12, 1975), and *IV* (1981); *Minore* (1968); 3 violin concertos: No. 1 (1969; Helsinki, Feb. 12, 1970), No. 2 for Violin and Strings (Helsinki, Nov. 15, 1977), and No. 3 for Violin and Strings (1981; Kaustinen, Jan. 31, 1982); 3 viola concertos: No. 1 (1970), No. 2 (Helsinki, Dec. 7, 1979), and No. 3 for Viola and Chamber Orch. (Vaasa, July 2, 1986); Concerto for Clarinet, Folk Instruments, and Small Orch. (1970; Helsinki, April 22, 1971); *The Turning Point* (1972; Helsinki, March 12, 1974); *Autumnal Concerto* for Traditional Japanese Instruments and Orch. (Helsinki, Aug. 28, 1974); 2 syms.: No. 1 (Turku, Oct. 10, 1974) and No. 2 (1990); Piano Concerto (Helsinki, April 22, 1975); *Pelimannimuotokuvia* (Portraits of Country Fiddlers) for Strings (Seinäjoki, April 5, 1976); *Summer Music* (Kaustinen,

July 18, 1977); Sym. for Strings (1978; Kokkola, Jan. 14, 1979); 3 cello concertos: No. 1 for Cello and Strings (Kuhmo, July 28, 1980), No. 2 (Helsinki, March 21, 1984), and No. 3 (1992); Concerto for Strings (1982; Kokkola, Nov. 27, 1983); *Elegy to Vilho Lampi* (1984; Oulu, Feb. 21, 1985); Concerto for Kantele and Small Orch. (Joensuu, June 19, 1985); *Tanse-Choral* for 15 Strings (Kokkola, Jan. 6, 1986); *HATE-LOVE* for Cello and Strings (1987); *Cronaca* (1991). **CHAMBER:** 7 string quartets (1967–92); *Nachtwache*, suite from the music to the radio play by Nelly Sachs, for Chamber Ensemble (1967); *Neljä kuolemankuvaa* (4 Pictures of Death) for Chamber Ensemble (1968); *Kolme maanitusta* (3 Enticements): 2 wind quintets: No. 1 (1970) and No. 2 (1975); 2 quartets for Traditional Japanese Instruments (1974; *Seita*, 1978); Piano Quintet (1978); Piano Trio (1980); *Equivocations* for Kantele and String Trio (1981). **VOCAL:** *Agnus Dei* for Soprano, Baritone, Chorus, and Orch. (1970; Helsinki, May 11, 1971); *Kuninkaan kämmenella* (In the Palm of the King's Hand), cantata for Soprano, Baritone, Chorus, and Orch. (1979; Kokkola, Feb. 24, 1980); *Taivaanvalot* (The Lights of Heaven) for Soprano, Tenor, Chorus, Children's Chorus, and Orch. (Kaustinen, Feb. 3, 1985).

Nordheim, Arne, significant Norwegian composer; b. Larvik, June 20, 1931. He studied at the Oslo Cons. (1948–52). His principal mentors in composition were Andersen, Baden, and Brustad. Following further studies with Holmboe in Copenhagen, he returned to Oslo and wrote music criticism for the *Morgenpost* (1959–63) and *Dagbladet* (1963–69). In 1960 he was awarded the Bergen Festival prize. His *Eco* for Soprano, Choruses, and Orch. took the Nordic Council Music Prize in 1972. He was made a member of the Royal Swedish Academy of Music in Stockholm in 1975 and in 1982 he was named a knight 1st class in the Royal Norwegian Order of St. Olav. In 1990 he received the Norwegian Cultural Council's prize. Nordheim is one of Norway's most important composers, one long in the forefront of avant-garde developments in his country. His works are marked by extraordinary craftsmanship and imagination, and are notable for their experimental use of pointillistic tone colors and for their motivic method of seemingly spontaneous melorhythmic structures.

WORKS: DRAMATIC: BALLETS: *Katharsis* (1962); *Stages* (1971); *Strender* (1974); *Stoolgame* (1974); *Greening* (1975); *Ariadne* (1977); *The Tempest* (1979; also as a suite for Soprano, Baritone, and Orch.); incidental music; film scores. **ORCH.:** *Nachruf* for Strings (1956); *Canzona* (1961); *Epitaffio* for Chamber Orch. and Tape (1964); *Floating* (Graz, Oct. 20, 1970); *Greening* (Los Angeles, April 12, 1973); *Spur* for Accordion and Orch. (1975); *Tenebrae*, cello concerto (Washington, D.C., Nov. 23, 1982); *Boomerang* for Oboe and Chamber Orch. (1985); *Rendezvous* for Strings (1986; orchestration of the String Quartet, 1956); *Tractatus* for Flute and Chamber Ensemble (1986); *Magma* (1988); *Monolith* (1990); *Acantus Firmus Olympiadis* for Hardanger Fiddle, Trumpets, Strings, and Electro-Acoustic Sounds (1992; Lillehammer, Jan. 1993); *Ad fontes* for Orch. and Electro-Acoustic Sounds (1993); *Adieu* for Strings and Bells (Warsaw, Sept. 9, 1994). **CHAMBER:** String Quartet (1956; orch. as *Rendezvous* for Strings, 1986); *Response* for 2 Percussionists and Tape (1966; also for Organ, 4 Percussionists, and Tape, 1967–75, Percussionist and Tape, 1968, and 4 Percussionists and Tape, 1977); *Signals* for Accordion, Percussion, and Electric Guitar (1968); *Partita II* for Electric Guitar (1969); *Dinosauros* for Accordion and Tape (1971); *Listen* for Piano (1971); *The Hunting of the Snark* for Trombone (1976); *Clamavi* for Cello (1980); *Partita für Paul* for Violin and Electronic Delay (1985); *Flashing* for Accordion (1986); *Duplex* for Violin and Viola (1990). **VOCAL:** *Aftonland* (Evening Land) for Soprano and Chamber Ensemble (1959); *Eco* for Soprano, Chorus, Children's Chorus, and Orch. (1968); *Doria* for Tenor and Orch. (1975); *Tempora Noctis* for 2 Sopranos and Orch. (1979); *Aurora* for 4 Singers, Chotales, and Tape (1983; also for 4 Singers, Chorus, Percussion, and Tape); *Wirklicher Wald* for Soprano, Cello, Chorus, and Orch. (1983); *Music to 2 Fragments to Music by Shelley* for Women's Chorus (1985); *Tres Lamentationes* for Chorus (1985); *Tre Voci* for Soprano and Chamber Ensemble (1988); *Be Not Afeard* for Soprano, Baritone, and Orch. (1989); *Draumkvedet* for 9 Voices, Chorus, and Electro-Acoustic Sounds (Oslo, Feb. 1, 1994); *Lacrimosa*, a movement for the international *Requiem of Reconciliation*, for Soprano, Chorus, and Orch. (Stuttgart, Aug. 16, 1995). **ELECTRONIC:** *Evolution* (1966); *Warszawa* (1968); *Solitaire* (1968); *Pace* (1970); *Lux et tenebrae* (1971).

Nordoff, Paul, American composer and music therapist; b. Philadelphia, June 4, 1909; d. Herdecke, Germany, Jan. 18, 1977. He studied piano with Olga Samaroff at the Philadelphia Cons. (B.M., 1927; M.M., 1932) and composition with Rubin Goldmark at the Juilliard School of Music in N.Y. (1928–33); later received the degree of Bachelor of Music Therapy at Combs College (1960). In 1993–94 and 1935–36 he held Guggenheim fellowships. He taught composition at the Philadelphia Cons. (1937–42), Michigan State College (1945–49), and Bard College (1949–59). From 1959 he devoted himself mainly to music therapy for handicapped children. With C. Robbins, he publ. *Music Therapy for Handicapped Children: Investigations and Experience* (N.Y., 1965), *Music Therapy in Special Education* (N.Y., 1971), *Therapy in Music for Handicapped Children* (N.Y., 1971), and *Creative Music Therapy: Individualized Treatment for the Handicapped Child* (N.Y., 1977).

WORKS: DRAMATIC: OPERAS: *Mr. Fortune* (1936–37; rev. 1956–57); *The Sea Change* (1951). **OPERETTA:** *The Masterpiece* (1940; Philadelphia, Jan. 24, 1941). **BALLETS:** *Every Soul Is a Circus* (1937); *Salem Shore* (1943); *Tally Ho* (1943). **ORCH.:** *Prelude and 3 Fugues* for Chamber Orch. (1932–36); Piano Concerto (1935); Suite (1938); Concerto for Violin, Piano, and Orch. (1948); Violin Concerto (1949); *The Frog Prince* for Narrator and Orch. (1954); *Winter Symphony* (1954); *Spring Symphony* (1956); *Gothic Concerto* for Piano and Orch. (1959). **CHAMBER:** Piano Quintet (1936); Quintet for Winds and Piano (1948); Violin Sonata (1950); Flute Sonata (1953); piano pieces. **VOCAL:** Choral pieces; songs. **OTHER:** Many pieces for handicapped children.

Nordqvist, Gustaf (Lazarus), Swedish organist, teacher, and composer; b. Stockholm, Feb. 12, 1886; d. there, Jan. 28, 1949. He studied organ (diploma, 1903), piano (with Lundberg), and composition (with Ellberg) at the Stockholm Cons. (1901–10) before completing his training with Willner in Berlin (1913–14). Returning to Stockholm, he served as organist of the Adolf Fredrik Church (1914–49), as a teacher (1925–44) and a prof. (1944–49) of harmony at the Cons., and as a teacher of organ at Wohlfart's music school (1926–49). In 1932 he was made a member of the Royal Swedish Academy of Music in Stockholm. He composed some chamber music, piano pieces, organ music, and choral works, but it was as a composer of art songs that he established his reputation in Sweden.

Norena, Eidé (real name, **Kaja Andrea Karoline Hansen-Eidé**), Norwegian soprano; b. Horten, April 26, 1884; d. Lausanne, Nov. 19, 1968. She studied voice with Ellen Gulbranson in Christiania; later in Weimar, London, and Paris; was a pupil of Raimund von Zur Mühlen. She began her career as a concert singer in Scandinavia. She made her operatic debut as Amor in Gluck's *Orfeo* in Christiania (1907), subsequently singing at the National Theater there (1908–18). After appearances at Stockholm's Royal Theater, she sang at La Scala in Milan (1924), Covent Garden in London (1924–25; 1930–31; 1934; 1937), and at the Paris Opéra (1925–37). She was a member of the Chicago Opera (1926–28); from 1933 to 1938, of the Metropolitan Opera in N.Y. (made her debut as Mimi, on Feb. 9, 1933); toured the U.S. in concert. Among her finest roles were Mathilde in *Guillaume Tell*, Violetta, Marguerite in *Les Huguenots*, the 3 heroines in *Les contes d'Hoffmann*, and Desdemona.

Nørgård, Per, prominent Danish composer and pedagogue; b. Gentofte, near Copenhagen, July 13, 1932. He began piano lessons when he was 8; in 1949 he became a private composition pupil of Holmboe; after entering the Royal Danish Cons. of Music in Copenhagen (1952), he continued his training with Holmboe there and also took courses with Høffding (theory), Koppel (piano), and Jersild (solfège), passing his examinations in theory, composition, and pedagogy (1955); following further studies with Boulanger in Paris (1956–57), he was awarded the Lily Boulanger Prize in 1957. He was a music critic for Copenhagen's *Politiken* (1958–62); also taught at the Odense Cons. (1958–60); after teaching at the Royal Danish Cons. of Music in Copenhagen (1960–65), he joined the faculty of the Århus Cons. in 1965, where he was made prof. of composition in 1987. In 1988 he was awarded the Henrik-Steffens-Preis of Germany. In 1995 he was made an honorary member of the ISCM, the first Dane ever to be accorded that distinction. In 1996 he received the Léonie Sonning Music Prize of Denmark. After a period of adolescent emulation of Sibelius, Nørgård plunged into the mainstream of cosmopolitan music-making, exploring the quasi-mathematical serial techniques based on short tonal motifs, rhythmic displacement, metrical modulation, pointillism, graphic notation, and a "horizontal" invariant fixing certain notes to specific registers; then shifted to a pointillistically impressionistic colorism evolving in a tonal bradykinesis.

WORKS: DRAMATIC: OPERAS: *The Labyrinth* (1963; Copenhagen, Sept. 2, 1967); *Gilgamesh* (1971–72; Århus, May 4, 1973); *Siddharta* (1977–79; Stockholm, March 18, 1983); *The Divine Tivoli*, chamber opera (1982). **BALLETS:** *Le Jeune Homme à marier* (1964; Danish TV, April 2, 1965; 1st stage perf., Copenhagen, Oct. 15, 1967); *Tango Chicane* (Copenhagen, Oct. 15, 1967); Trio for 3 Dancers and Percussion (Paris, Dec., 1972). **ORCH.:** *Metamorphose* for Strings (1952); 5 syms.: No. 1, *Sinfonia austera* (1954; Danish Radio, Aug. 19, 1958), No. 2 (Århus, April 13, 1970), No. 3 (1972–75; Copenhagen, Sept. 2, 1976), No. 4, *Indian Rose Garden and Chinese Witch Lake* (Hamburg, Oct. 30, 1981), and No. 5 (1990); *Constellations*, concerto for 12 Solo Strings or 12 String Groups (Copenhagen, Nov. 3, 1958); *Lyse Danse* for Chamber Orch. (1959); *Fragment VI* for 6 Orch. Groups: Winds, Brass, Percussion, Harp, Pianos, and Timpani (1959–61; Århus, Feb. 12, 1962); *Iris* (Copenhagen, May 19, 1967); *Luna, 4 Phases* (Danish Radio, Sept. 5, 1968); *Recall* for Accordion and Orch. (1968); *Voyage into the Golden Screen* for Chamber Orch. (Copenhagen, March 24, 1969); *Mosaic* for 16 Winds (1969); *Doing* for Wind Orch. (1969); *Dream Play* for Chamber Orch. (1975); *Twilight* for Orch. and Conga Player Obbligato with Dancer ad libitum (1976–77); *For a Change*, percussion concerto (1982); *Burn* (Glasgow, Sept. 17, 1984); *Between* for Cello and Orch. (Copenhagen, Aug. 30, 1985); *Prelude to Breaking* (Göteborg, Sept. 26, 1986); *Remembering Child* for Viola and Chamber Orch. (St. Paul, Minn., Sept. 12, 1986); *Helle Nacht*, violin concerto (1987); *Pastorale* for Strings (1988); *King, Queen, and Ace* for Harp and Chamber Ensemble (1989); *Night Symphonies, Day Breaks* (1991); *Spaces of Time* (1991); Piano Concerto (1995). **CHAMBER:** Quintet for Flute, Violin, Viola, Cello, and Piano (1951–52); *Suite* for Flute and Piano (1952); 7 string quartets: No. 1, *Quartetto Breve* (1952), No. 2, *Quartetto Brioso* (1952–58), No. 3, *3 Miniatures* (1959), No. 4, *Dreamscape* (1969), No. 5, *Inscape* (1969), No. 6, *Tintinnabulary* (1986), and No. 7 (1993); *Solo intimo* for Cello (1953); *Diptychon* for Violin and Piano (1953); 2 trios for Clarinet, Cello, and Piano (1955, 1974); *Songs from Aftonland* for Contralto, Flute, Harp, Violin, Viola, and Cello (1956); *Waves* for Percussion (1969); *Returns* for Guitar (1976); *I Ching* for Percussion (1982); *9 Friends* for Harmonica or Piano (1985); *Lin* for Clarinet, Cello, and Piano (1986); *Hut ab* for 2 Clarinets (1988); *Syn* for Brass Quintet (1988); *Swan Descending* for Harp (1989); *Nemo Dynamo* for Percussion and Computer (1991); *Tjampuan* for Violin and Cello (1992). **KEYBOARD: PIANO:** 2 sonatas (1952, 1957); *Sketches* (1959); *9 Studies* (1959); *4 Fragments* (1959–60); *Grooving* (1967–68); *Turn* (1973); *Achilles and the Tortoise* (1983). **ORGAN:** *Canon* (1971); *Triapartita* (1988). **VOCAL:** *Triptychon* for Mixed Voices and Wind Instruments or Organ (1957); *Nocturnes*, suite for Soprano and Piano or 19 Instruments (1961–62); *3 Love Songs* for Contralto and Orch. (1963); *Prism* for 3 Vocalists and Instrumental Ensemble (1964); *The Fourth Day* for Chorus and Orch. (1984–85; 4th movement of a collaborative work, *Hexaemeron*, depicting the 7 days of creation); *Entwicklungen* for Alto and Instrumental Ensemble (1986); *L'Enfant et l'aube* for Soprano, Tenor, and Chamber Ensemble (Radio France, Paris, June 7, 1988).

Nørholm, Ib, Danish composer, organist, and teacher; b. Copenhagen, Jan. 24, 1931. He studied theory with Holmboe, music history with Hjelmborg, and form and analysis with Bentzon and Høffding at the Royal Danish Cons. of Music in Copenhagen (1950–54), passing his examinations in theory and music history (1954), organ and teaching (1955), and sacred music (1956). He was active as a music critic (1956–64); was a church organist in Elsinore (1957–63) and then at Copenhagen's Bethlemskirken (from 1964); also taught part-time at the Royal Danish Cons. of Music in Copenhagen (from 1961) and at the Odense Cons.; subsequently taught theory at the Royal Danish Cons. of Music in Copenhagen (from 1973). His musical idiom is permeated with Scandinavian lyricism, even when he introduces modernistic devices.

WORKS: DRAMATIC: *Invitation to a Beheading*, opera after Nabokov (1965, Danish TV, Oct. 10, 1967); *The Young Park*, chamber opera (Århus, Oct. 14, 1970); *The Garden Wall*, choral opera (1976); *The Revenge of the Truth*, chamber opera (1985). **ORCH.:** 9 syms.: No. 1 (Danish Radio, Aug. 13, 1959), No. 2, *Isola Bella* (Copenhagen, April 27, 1972), No. 3, *Day's Nightmare* (Copenhagen, Oct. 9, 1973), No. 4, *Modskabelse*, for Soloists, Chorus, and Orch. (1979), No. 5 (1981), No. 6 (1982), No. 7, *Ecliptical Instincts* (Copenhagen, May 20, 1983), No. 8, *Faith and Longing* (1989–90), and No. 9, *The Sun Garden in 3 Shades of Light* (1990); *Fluctuations* for 34 Solo Strings, 2 Harps, Harpsichord, Mandolin, and Guitar (1962); *Relief I* and *II* for Chamber Ensemble (both 1963) and *III* for Orch. (1964); *Serenade of Cincinnatus* for Chamber Orch. (1964); *Exile* (Copenhagen, Sept. 8, 1966); *Efter Ikaros* (After Icarus), suite (1967); *Heretic Hymn*, fresco (1974); Violin Concerto (1974); *Idylles d'Apocalypse* for Organ and 20 Instruments (1980); *Spirales* for Accordion and Orch. (1986–87); Cello Concerto (1989). **CHAMBER:** *Rhapsody* for Viola and Piano (1955); 8 string quartets: No. 1, *In Vere* (1955), No. 2, *5 Impromptus* (1965), No. 3, *From My Green Herbarium* (1966), No. 4, *September—October—November* (1966), No. 5 (1976), No. 6, *Skygerne Frosner* (1978), No. 7, *En passant* (1985), and No. 8, *Memories* (1988); *Tombeau* for Cello and Piano (1956); Violin Sonata (1956–57); Trio for Clarinet, Cello, and Piano (1957); *Mosaic Fragments* for Flute and String Trio (1958); Piano Trio (1959); *Signature from a Province* for Piano (1970); *Dialogue in 3 Courses* for Guitar, Accordion, and Percussion (1975); Guitar Sonata (1976); *Essai prismatique* for Piano Trio (1979); *The Garden with Paths That Part* for 7 Instruments (1982); 6 Short Motets (1986); Saxophone Quartet (1992). **VOCAL:** *Jongleurs—69* for Soloists, Chorus, Ensembles, Loudspeaker Voice, and Orch. (Odense, Nov. 25, 1969); *Tys og lovsang* (Light and Hymn of Thanksgiving) for Soloists, Chorus, Organ, and Instrumental Ensemble (Copenhagen, Dec. 5, 1972); *Day's Nightmare II* for Soloists, Chorus, and Orch. (Copenhagen, Nov. 29, 1973); *Proprium Missae Dominicae Pentacostis* for 2 Choruses, Winds, and Organ (1977); *Lux Secunda* for Soprano, Baritone, Chorus, and Small Orch. (1984); songs.

Norlind, (Johan Henrik) Tobias, distinguished Swedish musicologist; b. Vellinge, May 6, 1879; d. Stockholm, Aug. 13, 1947. He studied piano and music in Lund; then took courses in composition with Jadassohn at the Leipzig Cons. (1897–98) and with Thuille in Munich (1898–99); he also studied musicology with Sandberger at the Univ. of Munich, and subsequently with Friedlaender at the Univ. of Berlin. Returning to Sweden in 1900, he attended the Univs. of Uppsala and Lund, obtaining the degree of Ph.D. in 1909. He then held several positions as an instructor in colleges and univs.; taught music history at the Stockholm Cons. (1918–45).

WRITINGS (all publ. in Stockholm unless otherwise given): *Svensk musikhistoria* (Hälsingborg, 1901; 2nd ed., 1918; abr. Ger. tr., 1904); *Allmänt musiklexikon* (1912–16; 2nd ed., 1927–28); *Jenny Lind: en minnesbok till hundraårsdagen* (1919); *Allmän musikhistoria* (1922); *Kristina Nilsson, sångerskan och konstärinnan* (1923); *Beethoven och hans tid* (1924–25); with E. Trobäck, *Kunglia hovkapellets historia 1526–1926* (1926); *Systematik der Saiteninstrumente*: Vol. I, *Geschichte der Zither* (1936), and Vol. II, *Geschichte des Klaviers* (1939; 2nd ed., 1941); *Bilder ur svenska musikens historia från äldsta tid till medeltidens slut* (1947).

Norman, Jessye, exceptionally gifted black American soprano; b. Augusta, Ga., Sept. 15, 1945. She received a scholarship to study at Howard Univ. in Washington, D.C. (1961), where she had vocal lessons from Carolyn Grant; continued her training at the Peabody Cons. of Music in Baltimore and at the Univ. of Mich., where her principal teachers were Pierre Bernac and Elizabeth Mannion. She won the Munich Competition (1968), and then made her operatic debut as Elisabeth in *Tannhäuser* at the Berlin Deutsche Oper (1969); appeared in the title role of *L'Africaine* at Florence's Maggio Musicale (1971), and the following year sang Aida at Milan's La Scala and Cassandra in *Les Troyens* at London's Covent Garden; subsequently made major recital debuts in London and N.Y. (1973). After an extensive concert tour of North America (1976–77), she made her U.S. stage debut as Jocasta in *Oedipus rex* and as Purcell's Dido on a double bill with the Opera Co. of Philadelphia on Nov. 22, 1982. She made her Metropolitan Opera debut in N.Y. as Cassandra on Sept. 26, 1983. In 1986 she appeared as soloist in Strauss's *Vier letzte Lieder* with the Berlin Phil. during its tour of the U.S. On Sept. 20, 1989, she was the featured soloist with Zubin Mehta and the N.Y. Phil. in its opening concert of its 148th season, which was telecast live to the nation by PBS. In 1992 she sang Jocasta at the opening operatic production at the new Saito Kinen Festival in Matsumoto. On Sept. 20, 1995, Norman was again the featured soloist with the N.Y. Phil., this time under Kurt Masur's direction, in a gala concert telecast live to the nation by PBS making the opening of the orch.'s 53rd season. Her extraordinary repertory ranges from Purcell to Richard Rodgers; she commended herself in Mussorgsky's songs, which she performed in Moscow in the original Russian; in her recitals she gave performances of the classical German repertory as well as contemporary masterpieces, such as Schoenberg's *Gürrelieder* and the French moderns, which she invariably performed in the original tongue. This combination of scholarship and artistry contributed to her consistently successful career as one of the most versatile concert and operatic singers of her time.

Norrington, Roger (Arthur Carver), scholarly English conductor; b. Oxford, March 16, 1934. He was educated at Clare College, Cambridge, and the Royal College of Music in London; was active as a tenor. In 1962 he founded the Schütz Choir in London, with which he first gained notice as a conductor. From 1966 to 1984 he was principal conductor of the Kent Opera, where he produced scores by Monteverdi utilizing his own performing eds. He served as music director of the London Baroque Players (from 1975) and the London Classical Players (from 1978); also was principal conductor of the Bournemouth Sinfonietta (1985–89). On April 2, 1989, he made an auspicious N.Y. debut at Carnegie Hall conducting Beethoven's 8th and 9th syms. In 1990 he became music director of the Orch. of St. Luke's in N.Y., which post he held until 1994. In 1980 he was made an Officer of the Order of the British Empire; in 1990, a Commander of the Order of the British Empire. Norrington entered controversy by insisting that the classical tempo is basic for all interpretation. He also insisted that Beethoven's metronome markings, not usually accepted by performers, are in fact accurate reflections of Beethoven's inner thoughts about his own music. He obtained numerous defenders of his ideas (as one critic put it, "inspired literalism") for the interpretation of classical music, which aroused sharp interest as well as caustic rejection. However that might be, his performances, especially in the U.S., received a great deal of attention, and he was particularly praised for the accuracy and precision of his interpretations. In 1985 he began an annual series of musical "experiences": weekends devoted to in-depth exploration of some major classical work, comprising lectures, open rehearsals, research exhibits, and performances of other works by the same composer (which have included Haydn and Berlioz as well as the inevitable Beethoven) and his contemporaries, selected to explicate the musical centerpiece.

Norris, David Owen, English pianist and teacher; b. Northampton, June 16, 1953. He studied at Keble College, Oxford (1972–75) and was an organ scholar at the Royal Academy of Music in London (1975–77). Following the completion of his training in Paris (1977–78), he returned to London as a prof. at the Royal Academy of Music (from 1978). In 1982 he won 3rd prize in the Geneva competition. He secured his reputation as both a pianist and broadcaster via frequent appearances with the BBC; also made extensive tours of Europe and North America. In 1991 he was honored as the first recipient of the Gilmore Artist Award of Kalamazoo, Mich. In 1992 he became chairman of the faculty of the Steans Inst. for Singers in Chicago and artistic director of the Cardiff Festival in Wales. In 1993 he was honored with the Gresham professorship in music in London. Norris has eschewed the usual path of the virtuoso, opting instead for a steady enhancement of his interpretive powers in a varied repertoire ranging from the classics to the contemporary era.

North, Alex, gloriously gifted American composer and conductor with a predilection for uniquely colored film music; b. Chester, Pa., Dec. 4, 1910; d. Pacific Palisades, Calif., Sept. 8, 1991. His father, a blacksmith, was an early immigrant from Russia. North studied piano and theory at the Curtis Inst. of Music in Philadelphia; later received a scholarship to study at the Juilliard School of Music in N.Y., where he took courses in composition (1929–32). A decisive change in his life came with his decision to go to Russia as a technology specialist at a time when Russia was eager to engage American technicians. He became fascinated with new Russian music and received a scholarship to attend the Moscow Cons., where he studied composition with Anton Weprik and Victor Bielyi (1933–35). He also was music director of the propaganda group of German Socialists called "Kolonne Links" (Column to the Left!). He mastered the Russian language and acquired a fine reputation in Russia as a true friend of Soviet music. Returning to the U.S., he took additional courses in composition with Copland (1936–38) and Toch (1938–39). In 1939 he conducted 26 concerts in Mexico as music director of the Anna Sokolow Dance Troupe; during his stay in Mexico City, he had some instruction from Silvestre Revueltas. In 1942 North entered the U.S. Army; promoted to captain, he became responsible for entertainment programs in mental hospitals. He worked closely with the psychiatrist Karl Menninger in developing a theatrical genre called "psychodrama," which later became an accepted mode of psychological therapy. During his Army years, North also worked with the Office of War Information, composing scores for over 25 documentary films. During all these peregrinations he developed a distinct flair for theater music, while continuing to produce estimable works in absolute forms. His concerto, *Revue* for Clarinet and Orch., was performed by Benny Goodman in N.Y. under the baton of Leonard Bernstein on Nov. 18, 1946. He further expanded his creative talents to write a number of modern ballets. The result of these multifarious excursions into musical forms was the formation of a style peculiarly recognizable as the specific art of North. His concentrated efforts, however, became directed mainly toward the art of film music, a field in which he triumphed. John Huston stated in 1986 that "it is the genius of Alex North to convey an emotion to the audience"; other directors praised North's cinemusical abilities in similar terms. Among the writers with whom he worked were Tennessee Williams, John Steinbeck, and Arthur Miller. But no success is without disheartening frustration. North was commissioned to write the score for *2001: A Space Odyssey*, on which he worked enthusiastically. But much to his dismay, the director, Stanley Kubrick, decided to replace it by a pasticcio that included such commonplaces as Strauss's *The Blue Danube Waltz*. North refused to be downhearted by this discomfiture and used the discarded material for his 3rd Sym. He was nominated 15 times for an Academy Award for best film music, but it was not until 1986 that the Academy of Motion Picture Arts and Sciences finally awarded him an Oscar for lifetime achievement. Among his outstanding scores are *A Streetcar Named Desire* (1951), *Death of a Salesman* (1951), *Viva Zapata!* (1952), *The Rose Tattoo* (1955), *The Bad Seed* (1956), *The Rainmaker* (1956), *The Sound and the Fury* (1959), *Spartacus* (1960), *The Children's Hour* (1961), *The Misfits* (1961), *Cleopatra* (1963), *The Agony and the Ecstasy* (1965), *Who's Afraid of Virginia Woolf?* (1966), *The Shoes of the Fisherman* (1968), *Shanks* (1973), *Bite the Bullet* (1975), *Dragonslayer* (1981), *Under the Volcano* (1984), *Prizzi's Honor* (1985), *The Penitent* (1986), *The Dead* (1987), and *Good Morning, Vietnam* (1988). His song *Unchained Melody* (1955) became a popular hit in its rendition by The Righteous Brothers.

WORKS: DRAMATIC: BALLETS: *Ballad in a Popular Style*, for Anna Sokolow (1933); *Case History* (1933); *War Is Beautiful* (1936); *Slaughter of the Innocents* (N.Y., Nov. 14, 1937); *American Lyric*, for Martha Graham (N.Y., Dec. 26, 1937); *Inquisition* (1938); *Lupe* (1940); *Design for 5* (1941); *Exile* (Mansfield, March 3, 1941); *Golden Fleece*, for Hanya Holm (Mansfield, March 17, 1941); *Clay Ritual* (Hartford, Conn., May 20, 1942); *Intersection* (1947); *A Streetcar Named Desire* (Montreal, Oct. 9, 1952); *Daddy Long Legs Dream Ballet* (1955; for Fred Astaire and Leslie Caron in the film *Daddy Long Legs*); *Mal de siècle* (Brussels, July 3, 1958). **CHILDREN'S OPERA AND THEATER:** *The Hither and Thither of Danny Dither* (1941); *Little Indian Drum* for Narrator and Orch. (N.Y., Oct. 19, 1947). **ORCH.:** *Rhapsody* for Piano and Orch. (N.Y., Nov. 11, 1941); *Revue* for Clarinet and Orch. (N.Y., Nov. 18, 1946); 3 syms.: No. 1 (1947), No. 2 (1968), and No. 3 (1971; based upon the unused original score for *2001: A Space Odyssey*); *Holiday Set* (Saratoga, N.Y., July 10, 1948). **OTHER:** *Morning Star Cantata* for Chorus and Orch. (N.Y., May 18, 1947); *Negro Mother Cantata* for Chorus and Orch. (N.Y., May 17, 1948); chamber music.

Noske, Frits (Rudolf), Dutch musicologist; b. The Hague, Dec. 13, 1920; d. Ariolo, Switzerland, Sept. 15, 1993. He studied cello and theory at the Amsterdam Cons. and at the Royal Cons. in The Hague (1940–45), then pursued musicological training with Bernet Kempers and Smits van Waesberghe at the Univ. of Amsterdam (Ph.D., 1954, with the diss. *La Mélodie française de Berlioz à Duparc*; publ. in Amsterdam, 1954; Eng. tr., rev., 1970); also had lessons with Masson at the Sorbonne in Paris (1949–50). He taught music history at the Amsterdam Cons. and at the Bussum Toonkunst Music School; was librarian at the Amsterdam Music Library (1951–54), and subsequently was its director (1954–68); also was a reader in musicology at the Univ. of Leiden (1965–68) and prof. of musicology at the Univ. of Amsterdam (from 1968).

WRITINGS: *Forma formans: Een strutuuranalytische methode, toegepast op de instrumentale muziek van Jan Pieterszoon Sweelinck* (Amsterdam, 1969; Eng. tr., rev., 1976, in the *International Review of the Aesthetics and Sociology of Music*, VII); *The Signifier and the Signified: Studies in the Operas of Mozart and Verdi* (The Hague, 1977); *Sweelinck* (Oxford, 1988); *Saints and Sinners: The Latin Musical Dialogue in the Seventeenth Century* (Oxford, 1992).

Nottara, Constantin, Romanian violinist, conductor, teacher, and composer; b. Bucharest, Oct. 13, 1890; d. there, Jan. 19, 1951. He studied with Klenck (violin), Kiriac (theory), and Castaldi (composition) at the Bucharest Cons. (1900–1907), with Enesco and Bethelier (violin) in Paris (1907–09), and with Klinger (violin) and Schatzenhalz (composition) at the Berlin Royal Academy (1909–13). His career was centered in Bucharest, where he was a violinist in the Phil. (1905–07; 1918–20) and 1st violinist in a string quartet (1914–33). From 1916 to 1947 he taught at the Cons. He also was a conductor with the Municipal Orch. (1929–32) and the Radio Sym. Orch. (1933–38).

WORKS: DRAMATIC: *Iris*, drama (1926; Moravska Ostrava, Nov. 13, 1931); *La drumul mare* (In the Highway), opera (1931; Cluj-Napoca, Oct. 3, 1934); *Cu dragostea nu se glumeşte* (Love is Not a Joke), comic opera (1940; Bucharest, Feb. 8, 1941); *Ovidiu* (Ovid), opera (1941–43; unfinished; completed by W. Berger); *Se face ziuă* (At Dawn), opera (1943); ballets. **ORCH.:** 3 suites: No. 1 (1917; Iaşi, Feb. 28, 1918), No. 2 (1930), and No. 3 (1930; Bucharest, Dec. 9, 1932); *Poem elegiac* for Cello and Orch. (1919); *Poem* for Violin and Orch. (1920; Bucharest, April 10, 1932); *Schiţă simfonică olteneasca* (1943); *Variaţiuni pe un cîntec popular bihorean* (1943); *Poemul păcii* (1947); *Poemul pentru pace* (1948); Violin Concerto (1950; Bucharest, Oct. 10, 1951). **CHAMBER:** 2 violin sonatas (1914, 1949); *Suită românească* for Viola and Piano (1945); Suite for Piano, Violin, and Cello (1949); *Suită în stil românesc* for Cello and Piano (1949); Nonet (1950); piano pieces, including *Rapsodie olteana* (1943) and a Sonata (1947). **VOCAL:** *Mircea şi Baiazil* for Baritone and Orch. (1931); many solo songs.

Nouguès, Jean, French composer; b. Bordeaux, April 25, 1875; d. Auteuil, Aug. 28, 1932. He showed remarkable precocity as a composer, having completed an opera, *Le Roi du Papagey*, before he was 16. After regular study in Paris, he premiered his opera *Yannha* at Bordeaux in 1897. The next 2 operas, *Thamyris* (Bordeaux, 1904) and *La Mort de Tintagiles* (Paris, 1905), were brought out without much success; but after the production of his spectacular *Quo Vadis?* (libretto by H. Cain, after Sienkiewicz's famous novel; Nice, Feb. 9, 1909), he suddenly found himself famous. The work was given in Paris on Nov. 26, 1909, and in N.Y. on April 4, 1911; had numerous revivals in subsequent years. His later operas, not nearly so successful, included *L'Auberge rouge* (Nice, Feb. 21, 1910), *La Vendetta* (Marseilles, 1911), *L'Aiglon* (Rouen, Feb. 2, 1912), and *Le Scarabée bleu* (1931).

Novães, Guiomar, extraordinary Brazilian pianist; b. São João da Bõa Vista, Feb. 28, 1895; d. São Paulo, March 7, 1979. She was the 17th of 19 offspring in a highly fecund family; studied piano with Luigi Chiafarelli; soon began performing in public recitals. The Brazilian government sent her to France to take part in a competition for entering the Paris Cons.; she won 1st place among 389 contestants from a jury that included Debussy and Fauré; Debussy praised her for "the power of total inner concentration, rare among artists." She enrolled in the class of Philipp, who later described her as a true "force of nature." She graduated from the Paris Cons. in 1911, and made a successful concert tour in France, England, and Italy. She made her U.S. debut at a N.Y. recital on Nov. 11, 1915, and subsequently made numerous tours of the U.S. Reviewing one of her concerts, James Huneker described her as "the Paderewska of the Pampas." In 1922 she married **Octavio Pinto**. She made her home in São Paulo, with frequent sojourns in N.Y. In 1956 the Brazilian government awarded her the Order of Merit as a goodwill ambassador to the U.S. She made her last U.S. appearance in 1972. She was especially praised for her interpretations of the music of Chopin, Schumann, and other composers of the Romantic era; she also played pieces by South American composers, including some works written for her by her husband. Her playing was notable for its dynamic colors; she exuded a personal charm, while often disregarding the more pedantic aspects of the music.

Novák, Jan, Czech composer; b. Nová Říše na Morave, April 8, 1921; d. Ulm, Germany, Nov. 17, 1984. He studied composition with Petrželka at the Brno Cons. (1940–46; interrupted by the Nazi occupation) and Bořkovec at the Prague Academy of Musical Arts (1946–47), then with Copland at the Berkshire Music Center at Tanglewood (summer, 1947) and Martinů in N.Y. (1947–48). He subsequently made his home in Brno; being outside his homeland at the time of the Soviet invasion (1968), he chose not to return, and went to Denmark before settling in Rovereto, Italy (1970), where he taught piano at the municipal music school. Predictably, his works ceased to be performed in his native land until the Communist regime collapsed in 1989. His early music is influenced by Martinů; with the Concertino for Wind Quintet (1957) and the *Capriccio* for Cello and Orch. (1958), he adopted jazz elements; beginning in 1958 he applied dodecaphonic techniques, and after 1960 his interest in all things Latin and vocal almost completely dominates his output.

WORKS: DRAMATIC: *Svatební Košile* (The Specter's Bride), ballet-ballad (1954; Plzen((SQ)), 1955); *Komedie o umučenie a slavném vzkříšení Pána a spasitele našeho Ježíše Krista* (Play of the Passion and Glorious Resurrection of the Lord Our Savior Jesus Christ; Brno, 1965); *Dulcitius*, lyric drama (1977); *Aesopia*, fable-cantata with introit and exit (1981; version for 2 Pianos and Orch. as *Aesopia minora*). **ORCH.:** Oboe Concerto (1953); Concerto for 2 Pianos and Orch. (1954); *Capriccio* for Cello and Orch. (1958); *Variations on a Theme of Martinů* (1959; orchestration of a 1949 piece for 2 Pianos); *Musica Caesariana* for Wind Orch. (1960); *Concentus Eurydicae* for Guitar and Strings (1971); *Odarum contentus*, 5 Meditations for Strings (1973); *Concentus biiugis* for Piano, 4-hands, and Small Orch. (1976); *Ludi symphoniaci I* (1978); *Choreae vernales* for Flute, Harp, Celesta or Piano, and Small Orch. (1980); *Ludi concentantes* for 18 Instruments (1981); *Symphonia bipartita* (1983). **CHAMBER:** *Ioci pastorales* for Oboe, Clarinet, Horn, and Bassoon (1974); *Rosarium*, 9 divertimenti for 2 Guitars (1975); *Quadricinium fidium I* for String Quartet (1978); *Sonata solis fidibus* for Solo Violin (1980); *Sonata da chiesa I* for Violin and Organ and *II* for Flute and Organ (both 1981); *Sonata rustica* for Accordion and Piano (1982); *Aeolia* for 2 Flutes and Piano (1983); piano pieces, including *Variations on a Theme of Martinů* for 2 Pianos (1949; orchestrated 1959); harpsichord and organ works. **VOCAL:** *Píseň Závišova* (Songs of Zavis) for Tenor and Orch. (1957); *Passer Catulli* for Bass and 9 Instruments (1961); *Ioci vernales* for Bass, 8 Instruments, and Bird Songs on Tape (1964); *Testamentum* for Chorus and 4 Horns (1966); *Dido*, oratorio (1967); *Ignis pro Ioanne Palach*, cantata (1968; Prague, April 15, 1969); *Planctus Troadum*, chamber cantata for Contralto, Women's Chorus, 8 Cellos, 2 Double Basses, and 2 Percussionists (1969); *Vernalis temporis symphonia* for Soli, Chorus, and Orch. (1982); songs and choruses.

Novák, Vitězslav (Augustín Rudolf), eminent Czech composer and pedagogue; b. Kamenitz, Dec. 5, 1870; d. Skutec((SQ)), July 18, 1949. He studied in Jindřichův Hradec with Vilím Pojman; subsequently won a scholarship to study law at the Univ. of Prague, but concentrated his studies on music at the Prague Cons., where he received instruction in piano from Jiránek, harmony from Knittl, and counterpoint from Strecker; later attended Dvořák's master class there. After graduating in 1892, he continued to study piano until 1896 and also remained a student of philosophy at the Univ. until 1895. He then taught privately and was active as a folk-song collector; through such orch. works as *V tatrách* (In the Tatra Mountains; 1902), *Slovácká svita* (Slovak Suite; 1903), and *O věčne touzé* (Eternal Longing; 1903–05), the cantata *Bouře* (The Storm; 1910), and the piano tone poem *Pan* (1910), he acquired a notable reputation as a composer; he devoted himself to teaching, serving as a prof. at the Prague Cons. (1909–39). His importance as a composer was enhanced in later years by such works as the *Podzimni symfonie* (Autumn Sym.; 1931–34) and *Jihočeská svita* (South Bohemian Suite) for Orch. (1936–37). He was honored with the title of National Artist of the Czech Republic in 1945. The first vol. of his unfinished autobiography, *O sobě a jiných*, was publ. in Prague in 1946. Novák's earliest works followed the general line of German Romanticism; Brahms was so impressed with them that he recommended Novák to his own publisher, Simrock. Novák's interest in folk music made a substantial impact on his music, although he rarely incorporated original folk material in his compositions. His late works espoused patriotic themes.

WORKS (all 1st perf. in Prague unless otherwise given): **DRAMATIC:** *Zvikovský rarášek* (The Imp of Zvikov), comic opera (1913–14; Oct. 10, 1915); *Karlštejn*, opera (1914–15; Nov. 18, 1916); *Lucerna* (The Lantern), musical fairy tale (1919–22; May 13, 1923); *Dědův odkaz* (Old Man's Bequest; 1922–25; Brno, Jan. 16, 1926); 2 ballet-pantomimes: *Signorina Gioventu* (1926–28; Feb. 10, 1929) and *Nikotina* (Feb. 10, 1929); incidental music to F. Rachlik's *Žižka* (1948). **ORCH.:** *Korzár* (The Corsair), overture (1892; Nov. 20, 1927; rev. 1943); *Serenade* in F major for Small Orch. (Sept. 27, 1895); Piano Concerto (1895; Nov. 21, 1915); *Maryša*, dramatic overture (1898; Jan. 28, 1899); *V. Tatrách* (In the Tatra Mountains), symphonic poem (1902; Dec. 7, 1907); *Slovácká svita* (Slovak Suite) for Small Orch. (1903; Feb. 4, 1906); *O věčné touze* (Eternal Longing; 1903–05; Feb. 8, 1905); Serenade for Small Orch. (1905; March 6, 1906); *Toman a lesni panna* (Toman and the Wood Nymph), symphonic poem (1906–07; April 5, 1908); *Lady Godiva*, overture (Nov. 24, 1907); *Podzimni symfonie* (Autumn Sym.) for Men's Chorus, Women's Chorus, and Orch. (1931–34; Dec. 18, 1934); *Jihočeská svita* (South Bohemian Suite; Dec. 22, 1937); *De profundis*, symphonic poem (Brno, Oct. 9, 1941); *Svatováclavský triptych* (St. Wenceslas Triptych) for Organ and Orch. (1941; March 6, 1942); *Májová symfonie* (May Sym.) for Solo Voices, Chorus, and Orch. (1943; Dec. 5, 1945). **CHAMBER:** Violin Sonata (1891); Piano Trio (1892); Piano Quartet (1894; rev. 1899); Piano Quintet (1896; rev. 1897); 3 string quartets (1899, 1905, 1938); *Piano Trio quasi una ballata* (1902); Cello Sonata (1941); various piano pieces. **VOCAL:** Choral works; songs; folk song arrangements.

BIBL.: Z. Nejedlý, *V. N.: Studie a kritiky* (Prague, 1921); B. Vomáčka and S. Hanus((SQ)), eds., *Sborník na počest 60. narozenin V.a N.a* (Prague, 1930); A. Srba, ed., *V. N.: Studie a vzpominky* (Prague, 1932; supplements, 1935, 1940); A. Hába, *V. N.: K 70. narozeninám* (Prague, 1940); V. Štěpán, *N. a Suk* (Prague, 1945); K. Hoffmeister, *Tvorba V.a N.a z let 1941–1948* (Prague, 1949); V. Lébl, *V. N.: Zivot a dilo* (Prague, 1964); idem, *V. N.* (Prague, 1968; in Eng.); special issue of *Hudební Věda*, VIII (1971); K. Padrta and B. Štědron((SQ)), eds., *Národni umelec V. N., Studie a vzpominsky k 100. vyroci narozeni* (Studies and Reminiscences on the 100th Anniversary of V. N.'s Birth; České Budějovice, 1972).

Novello-Davies (real name, **Davies**), **Clara,** Welsh singer, choral conductor, and composer; b. Cardiff, April 7, 1861; d. London, March 1, 1943. Her father (who was also her first teacher) called her "Clara Novello" after the celebrated singer of that name, and she adopted the combined name professionally. She sang at concerts; in 1881 she turned to choral conducting; organized a Royal Welsh Ladies' Choir, with which she traveled with fine success in Great Britain, France, America, and South Africa; at the World's Fair in Chicago (1893) and at the Paris Exposition (1900) the chorus was awarded 1st prize. She was commended by Queen Victoria (1894) and by King George V and Queen Mary (1928). She publ. a number of successful songs (*A Voice from the Spirit Land*, *The Vigil*, and *Comfort*); authored *You Can Sing* and an autobiography, *The Life I Have Loved* (London, 1940). Her son, Ivor Novello (real name, David Ivor Davies) (b. Cardiff, Jan. 15, 1893; d. London, March 6, 1951), was a composer, playwright, and actor; at his mother's request, he wrote the popular World War I song *Till the Boys Come Home (Keep the Home Fires Burning*; 1914); wrote musical comedies and revues, and was also active as an actor; after working as a playwright, he resumed composing for the stage; his most successful musical was *The Dancing Years* (London, March 23, 1939).

BIBL.: S. Wilson, *I.* (London, 1975).

Novotná, Jarmila, Czech soprano; b. Prague, Sept. 23, 1907; d. N.Y., Feb. 9, 1994. She studied with Destinn in Prague; made her operatic debut as Mařenka in *The Bartered Bride* there (1925), then continued her studies in Milan. She sang in Berlin (from 1928); was a member of the Vienna State Opera (1933–38), where she gained distinction as Octavian; also created the title role in Lehár's *Giuditta* (1934). She made her American debut at San Francisco as Madama Butterfly (Oct. 18, 1939); first sang at the Metropolitan Opera in N.Y. as Mimi in *La Bohème* on Jan. 5, 1940; remained on its roster until 1951; was there again from 1952 to 1956; also appeared in films and on Broadway. Her other fine roles included Pamina, Donna Elvira, Violetta, Mélisande, and various roles in Czech operas. She was the author of *Byla jsem stastná* (Prague, 1991).

Nowak, Leopold, eminent Austrian musicologist; b. Vienna, Aug. 17, 1904; d. there, May 27, 1991. He studied piano and organ with Louis Dité and counterpoint with Franz Schmidt at the Vienna Academy of Music; then took courses in musicology with Guido Adler and Robert Lach at the Univ. of Vienna; received his Ph.D. there in 1927 with the diss. *Das deutsche Gesellschaftslied bei Heinrich Finck, Paul Hofhaymer und Heinrich Isaac*; publ. in an augmented version as "Das deutsche Gesellschaftslied in Österreich von 1480 bis 1550," *Studien zur Musikwissenschaft*, XVII, 1930; completed his Habilitation in 1932 with his *Grundzüge einer Geschichte des Basso ostinato* (publ. in Vienna, 1932). He lectured at the Univ. of Vienna from 1932 until 1973; in 1945 he became ed. of the critical edition of Bruckner's works, a position he held until 1990; from 1946 to 1969 he was director of the music division of the Nationalbibliothek in Vienna, where he compiled valuable catalogues for special exhibitions on Bruckner, Bach, Mozart, Haydn, and others. His exhaustive studies on the life and music of Bruckner are of prime value.

WRITINGS: *Franz Liszt* (Innsbruck, 1936); *Te Deum laudamus: Gedanken zur Musik Anton Bruckners* (Vienna, 1947); *Joseph Haydn* (Vienna, 1951; 3rd ed., 1965); with F. von Rezniček, the composer's daughter, *Gegen den Strom: Leben und Werk von Emil Nikolaus von Rezniček* (Vienna, 1960); *Anton Bruckner: Musik und Leben* (a brief study; Vienna, 1964); *Reden und Ansprachen* (Vienna, 1964); *Anton Bruckner: Musik und Leben* (a voluminous pictorial biography; Linz, 1973); *Das Geburtshaus Anton Bruckners [Ansfelden]: Führer* (Linz, 1975).

BIBL.: F. Grasberger, ed., *Bruckner-Studien: L. N. zum 60. Geburtstag* (Vienna, 1964).

Nowak, Lionel (Henry), American pianist, teacher, and composer; b. Cleveland, Sept. 25, 1911. He studied piano with Beryl Rubinstein and Edwin Fischer, and took courses in composition with Elwell, Sessions, and Porter at the Cleveland Inst. of Music (B.Mus., 1933; M.Mus., 1936). In 1924 he made his formal debut as a soloist with the Cleveland Orch.; was director of music at Fenn College in Cleveland (1932–38) and of the Doris Humphrey-Charles Weidman Modern Dance Co. (1938–42). He was prof. of music at Converse College in Spartanburg, S.C. (1942–46); also conducted the Spartanburg Sym. Orch. (1942–45); was prof. of music at Syracuse Univ. (1946–48) and at Bennington (Vt.) College (from 1948). Following a stroke in 1980, he composed works for piano, right-hand, and also commissioned such scores from other composers. He wrote some effective dance pieces.

WORKS: DANCE: *Square Dances* (1938); *Danzas mexicanas* (1939); *On My Mother's Side* (1939); *The Green Land* (1941); *Flickers* (1942); *House Divided* (1944); *Story of Mankind* (1946). **ORCH.:** Piano Concerto (1944); *Concert Piece* for Timpani and Strings (1961). **CHAMBER:** Oboe Sonata (1949); *Orrea Pernel*, sonata for Violin (1950); 3 cello sonatas (1950, 1951, 1960); *Diptych* for String Quartet (1951); Quartet for Oboe and Strings (1952); Piano Trio (1954); *Soundscapes*: for Piano (1964), String Quartet (1970), Bassoon and Piano (1971), Violin, Piano, and Percussion (1971), and Woodwind Trio (1973); Suite for 2 Cellos (1981); Suite for Flute and Harpsichord (1989). **VOCAL:** Vocal pieces.

Nowowiejski, Felix, Polish organist, conductor, and composer; b. Wartenburg, Feb. 7, 1877; d. Poznań, Jan. 18, 1946. He studied in Berlin with Bussler at the Stern Cons., with Bruch at the Königliche Musikakademie, and with Friedlaender, Bellermann, and Dessoir at the Univ.; also received some instruction from Dvořák in Prague; won the Paderewski Prize in 1903. He was director of the Kraków Music Soc. (1909–14) and a prof. at the Poznań Cons. (1920–27). A competent composer, he followed the line of German Romanticism.

WORKS: 2 operas: *Emigranci* (The Emigrants; 1917) and *Legenda Baltyku* (Baltic Legend; Poznań, 1924); several ballets; 5 syms. (1903–41; 1st not extant); Cello Concerto (1938); Piano Concerto (1941); much choral music, including oratorios, masses, cantatas, patriotic works, etc.; songs; piano pieces; organ music.

BIBL.: J. Boehm, *F. N.* (Olsztyn, 1968).

Nucci, Leo, prominent Italian baritone; b. Castiglione dei Pepuli, near Bologna, April 16, 1942. He studied with Giuseppe Marchesi and Ottaviano Bizzarri. He made his operatic debut as Rossini's Figaro in Spoleto (1967). After singing in the chorus of Milan's La Scala (1969–75), he attracted attention with his portrayal of Schaunard in *La Bohème* at Venice's Teatro La Fenice (1975); then was engaged as a member of La Scala, where he appeared as Rossini's Figaro, Rodrigo in *Don Carlos*, Miller in *Luisa Miller*, Marcello, and Sharpless. In 1978 he made his first appearance at the Vienna State Opera and at London's Covent Garden; he made his Metropolitan Opera debut in N.Y. as Renato in *Un ballo in Maschera* on Feb. 22, 1980. He first sang at the Paris Opera and the Chicago Lyric Opera in 1981. He also sang in San Francisco, Berlin, Rome, Hamburg, and Geneva.

Nummi, Seppo (Antero Yrjönpoika), Finnish composer, music critic, and festival administrator; b. Oulu, May 30, 1932; d. Tampere, Aug. 1, 1981. He studied at the Univ. of Helsinki and at the Sibelius Academy; his private composition teacher was Yrjö Kilpinen. He began writing music criticism for the newspaper *Uusi Suomi* in 1953; in 1967 he founded the Savonlinna Opera Festival; then was executive director of the Helsinki Festival (1969–77). As a composer, he is best known for his many songs in a fine lyrical mode, in the tradition of Hugo Wolf and Kilpinen; he also wrote some chamber music. He publ. *Musica fennica* (with T. Makinen; Helsinki, 1965) and *Modern Musik* (Stockholm, 1966).

Nunes, Emmanuel, Portuguese-born French composer and teacher; b. Lisbon, Aug. 31, 1941. He studied at the Lisbon Academy of Music (until 1964), at the summer courses in new music at Darmstadt (1963–65), with Pousseur and Stockhausen at the Cologne Staatliche Hochschule für Musik (1965–67), and with Marcel Beaufils at the Paris Cons. (premier prix in aesthetics, 1970). In 1978–79 he was in Berlin under the auspices of the Deutscher Akademischer Austauschdienst. He taught at the Freiburg im Breisgau Hochschule für Musik and lectured at the Paris Cons. His works are technically assured and inventive. They have become increasingly compact, tense, and extreme in character.

WORKS: ORCH.: *Seuils I* and *II* (1966–67; rev. 1977–78); *Un calendrier révolu* for Chamber Orch. (1968); *Purieu* for 21 Strings (1971); *Down Wo* for 13 Winds (1971–72); *Omens I* (1972) and *II* (1975); *Fermata* (1973); *Es webt* (1974–75; rev. 1977); *Ruf* (1975–77); *Chessed I* for 4 Orch. Groups (1979), *II* for 16 Solo Instruments (1979), and *IV* for String Quartet and Orch. (1992); *Tif'ereth* for 6 Solo Instruments, 6 Orch. Groups, and 2 Conductors (1978–85); *Musik der Frühe* for 18 Instruments (1980; rev. 1984–86); *Nachtmusik II* (1981); *Stretti* for 2 Orchs. (1982–83); *Wandlungen* for 25 Instruments and Electronics (1986); *Lichtung* for Orch. and Electronics (1988–92); *Quodlibet* for 3 Instrumental Ensembles (1990–91). **CHAMBER:** *Degrés* for String Trio (1965); *Esquisses* for String Quartet (1967; rev. 1980); *Impromptu pour un voyage I* for Trombone, Flute, Viola, and Harp (1973) and *II* for Alto Flute, Viola, and Harp (1974–75; rev. 1992); *The Blending Season* for Flute, Alto, Clarinet, Electric Organ, and Amplification (1973; rev. 1976–77 and 1992); *Nachtmusik I* for Viola, Cello, English Horn, Bass Clarinet, Trombone, and Modulation (1977–78); *Einspielung I* for Violin (1979), *II* for Cello (1980), and *III* for Viola (1981);

Grund for Flute and Tape (1982–83); *Aura* for Flute (1983–89); *Sonate a tre* for String Trio (1986); *Clivages I* (1987); and *II* (1988) for 6 Percussionists; *Chessed III* for String Quartet (1990–91). **VOCAL:** *Minnesang* for 12 Voices (1975–76); *Vislumbre* for Chorus (1981–86); *Machina Mundi* for Chorus and Orch. (1991–92).

Nurimov, Chari, Russian composer; b. Buiramali, Turkmenia, Jan. 1, 1941. He studied with Litinsky at the Gnessin Inst. in Moscow (graduated, 1964); returning to Turkmenia, he worked for the Ashkhabad radio and taught at the music inst. He received awards as a national Turkmenian composer; his Trumpet Concerto became popular.

WORKS: DRAMATIC: BALLETS: *The End of Sukhovei* (1967); *Immortality* (1972); *A Kughitang Tragedy* (1976); film scores. **ORCH.:** 3 overtures (1959, 1961, 1974); Sym. No. 1 (1963); Trumpet Concerto (1968); *Concerto-Poem* for Voice and Orch. (1971); Piano Concerto (1973); *Ghazels* for Oboe, Percussion, Piano, and Strings (1976); *The Flame of October*, poem (1979); *Sinfonietta* (1981); *Destan Concerto* for Flute, Oboe, Percussion, Piano, and Strings (1983). **CHAMBER:** Suite for String Quartet (1960); Violin Sonata (1961); *Partita* for String Quartet (1963); Oboe Sonatina (1964); *The Tekin Frescoes* for 11 Instruments (1969); *Concert Piece* for Trombone and Piano (1971); *Pastoral* for Flute and Piano (1973); Woodwind Quintet (1979); String Quartet (1980). **PIANO:** 2 sonatinas (1960, 1965); 3 Fugues (1962); *Impromptu-Fantasia* (1964); 12 Polyphonic Pieces (1968). **VOCAL:** Over 70 songs.

Nurock, Kirk, innovative American composer and originator of "natural sound"; b. Camden, N.J., Feb. 28, 1948. He held scholarships for study at the Juilliard School in N.Y. and at the Eastman School of Music in Rochester, N.Y. His teachers in composition were Persichetti, Sessions, and Berio. He was awarded the Elizabeth Sprague Coolidge Prize in chamber music in 1970. From his earliest essays in composition, he adhered to extraordinary and unusual sound production; became active as a conductor of idiosyncratic theater productions, among them the temporarily objectionable musical *Hair*, which aroused indignant protests on the part of tender-minded listeners. He further developed a natural ability to perform advanced keyboard jazz music. In 1971 he developed an experimental vocal technique which he called "natural sound," founded on the assumption that every person's vocal cords, as well as other parts of their bodies, are capable of producing variegated sound. In several works he annexed animal noises; the most challenging of them being *Sonata for Piano and Dog* (1982) and *Gorilla, Gorilla* for Piano (1988). Audience participation is welcomed as an integral part of "natural sound" productions. Several of Nurock's works are specifically scored for untrained, improvisatory participants. Interestingly enough, many newspaper reviews of his presentations seem to revive the alarmed outcries of shocked innocence that greeted first performances of the now-recognized works of Prokofiev, Stravinsky, Schoenberg, and Varèse.

WORKS: MUSIC THEATER: *Mowgli*, after Kipling, with 12 Singing Actors and 6 Musicians (1978–84). **ORCH.:** *Accumulations* (1968); *Assemblage* (1969). **CHAMBER:** Clarinet Chant for 6 Clarinets and Bass Clarinet (1970); *Creature Memory* (1979). **"NATURAL SOUND," INCLUDING ANIMALS:** *Elemental Chant* (1972); *Audience Oratorio*, with Audience Participation (1975); *Howl* for 20 Voices and 4 Canines (N.Y., Jan. 15, 1980); *Bronx Zoo Events* (Bronx Zoo, N.Y., Oct. 24, 1980); Sonata for Piano and Dog (1982; N.Y., March 16, 1983); *Expedition* for Jazz Trio and Siberian Husky (N.Y., Jan. 14, 1984); *Sendings* for 5 Winds and 4 Creatures (N.Y., March 17, 1984); *Haunted Messages* for Piano and Barking Audience (1984; N.Y., March 20, 1990); *Listening Bach* for Orch., Chorus, Narrator, and Animals (1986–88); *Gorilla, Gorilla* for Piano (N.Y., March 19, 1988). **OTHER:** *The Incurable Dorothy Parker*, song cycle for Soprano and Piano (Philadelphia, Nov. 10, 1986); *3 Screams* for 2 Amplified Pianos (N.Y., March 20, 1990); numerous ensemble numbers for plays.

Nussio, Otmar, Italian composer; b. Grosseto, Oct. 23, 1902; d. Lugano, July 22, 1990. He studied flute, piano, and composition at the Milan Cons. and with Respighi in Rome. He conducted concerts of light music and wrote a number of overtures and orch. suites, among them *Escapades musicales* (1949); *Rubensiana* (Rubens House, Antwerp, May 21, 1950); *Tzigana* (1954); *Portraits musicaux* (1955); *Episodio* (1958); *Monologhi di vita e di morte* (1958); *Alborada* (1971); also a Flute Concerto (1936); Piano Concerto (1960); *Cantata ticinese* for Voices and Orch. (1962); *Passatempo donchisciottesco* for Clarinet and Orch. (1971).

Nyiregyházi, Erwin, remarkable and eccentric Hungarian-American pianist; b. Budapest, Jan. 19, 1903; d. Los Angeles, April 13, 1987. He absorbed music by a kind of domestic osmosis, from his father, a professional tenor, and his mother, an amateur pianist. An exceptionally gifted *Wunderkind*, he had perfect pitch and a well-nigh phonographic memory as a very small child; played a Haydn sonata and pieces by Grieg, Chopin, and himself at a concert in Fiume at the age of 6. In 1910 he entered the Budapest Academy of Music, studying theory with Siklós and Weiner, and piano with Thomán. In 1914 the family moved to Berlin, where he became a piano student of Dohnányi. He made his debut in Germany playing Beethoven's 3rd Piano Concerto with the Berlin Phil. (Oct. 14, 1915). In 1916 he began studying with Frederic Lamond, a pupil of Liszt, who was instrumental in encouraging Nyiregyházi to study Liszt's music, which was to become the most important part of his concert repertoire. In 1920 he went to the U.S.; his American debut (Carnegie Hall, N.Y., Oct. 18, 1920) was sensationally successful; the word "genius" was freely applied to him by critics usually restrained in their verbal effusions. Inexplicably, his American career suffered a series of setbacks; he became involved in a lawsuit with his manager; he married his next manager, a Mrs. Mary Kelen, in 1926, but divorced her a year later. He then went to California, where he became gainfully employed as a studio pianist in Hollywood; in 1930 he made a European tour; then lived in N.Y. and in Los Angeles. Beset by personal problems, he fell into a state of abject poverty, but resolutely refused to resume his concert career; he did not even own a piano. He married frequently, and as frequently divorced his successive wives. In 1972 he married his 9th wife, a lady 10 years his senior; she died shortly afterward. Attempts were made in vain by friends and admirers in California to induce him to play in public; a semi-private recital was arranged for him in San Francisco in 1974; a recording of his playing of Liszt was issued in 1977; it was greeted with enthusiastic reviews, all expressing regret for his disappearance from the concert stage. Nyiregyházi composed several hundred works, mostly for piano; they remain in MS. As a child, Nyiregyházi was the object of a "scientific" study by Géza Révész, director of the Psychological Laboratory in Amsterdam, who made tests of his memory, sense of pitch, ability to transpose into different keys at sight, etc.; these findings were publ. in German as *Psychologische Analyse eines musikalisch hervorragenden Kindes* (Leipzig, 1916; Eng. tr., 1925), but the examples given and the tests detailed in the book proved to be no more unusual than the capacities of thousands of similarly gifted young musicians.

Nystedt, Knut, esteemed Norwegian choral conductor, organist, pedagogue, and composer; b. Christiania, Sept. 3, 1915. He studied organ with Sandvold, conducting with Fjeldstad, and composition with Per Steenberg and Brustad at the Oslo Cons. (1931–43); then pursued training with Ernest White (organ) and Copland (composition) in N.Y. (1947). From 1946 to 1982 he was organist at Oslo's Torshov Church; also was a prof. of choral conducting at the Oslo Cons. (1964–85). In 1950 he founded Det Norske Solistokor (the Norwegian Soloist Choir), which he conducted for the first time in Oslo on May 23, 1951; in subsequent years, he developed it into one of the finest choral groups in the world, conducting it in a comprehensive literature with a special regard for contemporary scores. In

1960 he conducted it for the first time in the U.S.; later led it on tours of Japan, Korea, Hong Kong, and Thailand (1978), China (1982), and Israel (1984, 1988). On March 18, 1990, he conducted his farewell concert as its conductor in Oslo. In 1966 he was made a Knight of the Order of St. Olav; in 1978 he was awarded the Spellemannsprisen; in 1980 he received the music prize of the Norwegian Council for Cultural Affairs. He is an outstanding composer of choral music; his orch. works have also won approbation both at home and abroad.

WORKS: OPERAS: *Med krone og stjerne* (With Crown and Star), Christmas opera (1971); *Salomos hoysang* (The Song of Songs), church opera (1989). **ORCH.:** *Høgfjell* (The Mountains), suite (1940–41); Concerto grosso for 3 Trumpets and Strings (1946); *Spenningens land* (Land of Suspense), symphonic fantasy (1947; Oslo, Sept. 29, 1948); *Festival Overture* (1950); Sym. for Strings (1950); Concertino for English Horn, Clarinet, and Strings (1952); *De syv segl* (The 7 Seals), visions (1958–60); *Collocations* (1963); Mirage (1974); *Fisken* (Fish; 1976); *Exsultate* (1980; Oslo, Sept. 5, 1985; also for Organ); *Sinfonia del mare* (1983); Horn Concerto (Helsinki, Oct. 13, 1986); *Concerto Arctandriae* for Strings (1991); also works for Band. **CHAMBER:** 5 string quartets (1938; 1948; 1956; 1966, Norwegian Radio, Feb. 6, 1989; 1988); *The Moment* for Soprano, Celesta, and Percussion (1962); *Pia memoria*, Requiem for 9 Brass Instruments (1971); *Rhapsody in Green* for Brass Quintet (1978); *Music* for 6 Trombones (1980); organ pieces. **CHORAL:** *Nådevegen*, oratorio for Soli, Chorus, and Orch. (1943–46); *Norge mitt land* (Norway, My County) for Baritone, Chorus, and Orch. (1944); *De profundis* (1964); *Spes Mundi* (The Hope of the World), Mass for Chorus, Drama Group, Trumpet, Organ, Percussion, Narrator, and Congregation (1970); *Dies Irae* for 4 Choruses, Wind, and Percussion (1976); *A Hymn of Human Rights* for Chorus, Organ, and Percussion (1982; Des Moines, Iowa, March 6, 1983); *For a Small Planet* for Chorus, String Quartet, Harp, and Narrator (1983; Eugene, Oreg., July 13, 1984); *Missa Brevis* (1984; Bergen, June 17, 1985); *The Lamentations of Jeremiah* (1985); *Stabat Mater* for Chorus and Cello (1986); *Salomo* (Song of Songs) for Soli, Chorus, Dancers, Instruments, and Organ (1990); *One Mighty Flowering Tree* for Chorus and Brass Orch. (1994); *Kristnikvede* for Chorus and Orch. to celebrate the 1,000th anniversary of Christianity in Norway (1994; Moster, June 4, 1995); *Libertas Vincit* for Reciter, Chorus, and Chamber Orch. to celebrate the 50th anniversary of the liberation of Norway from Nazi occupation (1994; Oslo, May 10, 1995).

Nystroem, Gösta, Swedish composer; b. Silvberg, Oct. 13, 1890; d. Särö, near Göteborg, Aug. 9, 1966. He studied piano, harmony, and composition with his father; then piano and harmony with Lundberg and Bergenson in Stockholm; took courses at the Cons. there (1913–14), and also studied composition with Hallén; after further training in Copenhagen and Germany, he went to Paris (1920) and studied composition and instrumentation with d'Indy and Sabaneyev and conducting with Chevillard; subsequently wrote music criticism in Göteborg (1932–47). After following neo-Baroque practices, he developed an independent mode of composition.

WORKS: DRAMATIC: *De Blinda* (The Blind), radio drama (1949); *Ungersvennen och de sex prinsessorna* (The Young Lad and the 6 Princesses), ballet (1951); *Herr Arnes penningar* (Sir Arne's Hoard), opera (Swedish Radio, Nov. 26, 1959); incidental music. **ORCH.:** *Rondo capriccioso* for Violin and Orch. (1917; rev. 1920); 2 symphonic poems: *Is havet* (The Arctic Ocean; 1924) and *Babels torn* (The Tower of Babel; 1928); 2 concertos for Strings (1930, 1955); 6 syms.: No. 1, *Sinfonia breve* (1931; Göteborg, Oct. 19, 1932), No. 2, *Sinfonia espressiva* (1932–35; Göteborg, Feb. 18, 1937), No. 3, *Sinfonia del mare*, for Soprano and Orch. (1947–48; Stockholm, March 24, 1949), No. 4, *Sinfonia Shakespeareana* (Göteborg, Nov. 5, 1952), No. 5, *Sinfonia seria* (Stockholm, Oct. 9, 1963), and No. 6, *Sinfonia Tramontana* (1965; Stockholm, Oct. 30, 1966); Suite for Small Orch. (1950); *Partita* for Flute, Strings, and Harp (1953); Violin Concerto (1954); *Concerto ricercante* for Piano and Orch. (1959; Stockholm, May 15, 1960). **CHAMBER:** 2 string quartets (1956, 1961); piano pieces. **VOCAL:** *3 Havsvisioner* (Visions of the Sea) for Chorus (1956); *Summer Music* for Soprano and Orch. (1964); solo songs.

BIBL.: P. Christensen, *The Orchestral Works of G. N.: A Critical Study* (diss., Univ. of Wash., 1961; publ. in London, 1965).

Oberhoffer, Emil (Johann), German-born American conductor; b. near Munich, Aug. 10, 1867; d. San Diego, May 22, 1933. He received his initial musical training from his father, an organist; learned to play violin and organ; later studied piano in Paris with Isidor Philipp. He went to N.Y. (1885) and became a naturalized American citizen (1893); in 1897 he settled in St. Paul, Minn. He became conductor of the Schubert Club chorus and orch. and the Apollo Club; was also prof. of music at the Univ. of Minnesota (1902–05). He became conductor of the Phil. Choral Soc. in Minneapolis (1901), and having succeeded in securing an endowment for the establishment of a permanent orch., gave his first concert with the newly-organized Minneapolis Sym. Orch. on Nov. 5, 1903; he remained its conductor until 1923; then settled in Los Angeles. Upon the death of Walter Henry Rothwell (1927), the conductor of the Los Angeles Phil., he led the remaining concerts of the 1926–27 season with that orch.

Oberlin, Russell (Keys), American countertenor; b. Akron, Ohio, Oct. 11, 1928. He studied at the Juilliard School of Music in N.Y., graduating in 1951. In 1952 he joined the N.Y. Pro Musica Antiqua, appearing as a soloist in works from the medieval and Renaissance periods; in 1960 he sang the role of Oberon in Britten's *A Midsummer Night's Dream* at Covent Garden, London. In 1966 he joined the faculty at Hunter College in N.Y.

Oborin, Lev (Nikolaievich), Russian pianist, pedagogue, and composer; b. Moscow, Sept. 11, 1907; d. there, Jan. 5, 1974. He studied with Elena Gnessina at the Gnessin Music School in Moscow and with Igumnov at the Moscow Cons. (graduated, 1926). He made his debut in 1924; won the Chopin Competition in Warsaw (1927), then toured widely; was also on the faculty of the Moscow Cons. (1928–74). He was made a People's Artist of the U.S.S.R. in 1964. He was known for his wide sympathies as an interpreter, ranging from the classics to the Soviet school; was soloist in the premiere of Khachaturian's Piano Concerto. He wrote piano sonatas and other works for piano, as well as several orch. pieces.

BIBL.: S. Khentova, *L. O.* (Moscow, 1964).

Obouhov, Nicolas (actually, **Nikolai**), remarkable Russian composer; b. Kursk, April 22, 1892; d. Paris, June 13, 1954. He studied at the St. Petersburg Cons. with Nikolai Tcherepnin and Maximilian Steinberg; after the Revolution in 1917, he emigrated to Paris, where he received instruction from Ravel. As early as 1914 he began experimenting with harmonic combinations containing 12 different notes without duplication (he called his system "absolute harmony"). In 1915 he devised a special notation for this type of harmony, entirely enharmonic, with crosses indicating sharps or flats; several composers, among them Honegger, wrote pieces in Obouhov's notation. He gave a demonstration of his works written and notated in this system in Petrograd at a concert organized by the eds. of the review *Muzykalnyi Sovremennik* on Feb. 3, 1916. He devoted his entire life to the composition of his magnum opus, *Le Livre de vie*, for Solo Voices, Chorus, 2 Pianos, and Orch. The MS score, some 2,000 pages in length, was deposited after his death at the Bibliothèque Nationale in Paris. A mystic, Obouhov signed his name "Nicolas l'illuminé" and used his own blood to mark sections in the score; the finale represented the spiritual and religious apotheosis in which both the old and the new Russian societies and political factions are reunited. In this and some other scores, Obouhov introduced shouting, screaming, sighing, and groaning sounds for the voice parts. A section of *Le Livre de vie* was performed by Koussevitzky in Paris on June 3, 1926. In quest of new sonorities, Obouhov devised an electronic instrument, the "croix sonore," in the form of a cross, and composed works for it, which were performed by Mme. Aussenac de Broglie. He publ. *Traité d'harmonie tonale, atonale et totale* (Paris, 1946), which presents an exposition of his system.

BIBL.: C. Laronde, *Le Livre de vie de N. O.* (Paris, 1932).

Oboussier, Robert, Swiss composer; b. Antwerp (of Swiss parents), July 9, 1900; d. (stabbed to death by his roommate) Zürich, June 9, 1957. He studied at the Zürich Cons. with Andreae and Jarnach (composition); then with Ochs (conducting) at the Berlin Hochschule für Musik. He then lived in Florence (1922–28); was music ed. of the *Deutsche Allgemeine Zeitung*; but in 1939 political conditions in Germany impelled him to leave for Switzerland; in 1942 he became director of the Central Archive of Swiss Music, and in 1948 of Suisa (the Swiss assn. of writers, composers, and publishers). Of cosmopolitan background, Oboussier combined in his music the elements of both Germanic and Latin cultures. He publ. *Der Sänger* (with others; Berlin, 1934; 2nd ed., rev., 1959) and *Die Sinfonien Beethovens* (Berlin, 1937); also a collection of critical reviews, *Berliner Musik-Chronik 1930–38* (1969).

WORKS: OPERA: *Amphitryon* (1948–50; Berlin, March 13, 1951). **ORCH.:** Piano Concerto (1932–33; rev. 1944); Sym. (1935–36); *Chant de deuil* (1942–43); *Introitus* for Strings (1946); Violin Concerto (1952–53). **CHAMBER:** Several pieces, including piano music. **VOCAL:** *Trilogia sacra* for Solo Voices, Chorus, and Orch. (1925–29); *Antigone* for Voice and Orch. (1938–39); *3 Psaumes* for Solo Voices, Chorus, and Orch. (1946–47); solo songs.

BIBL.: K. Wörner, "R. O.," *Musica* (Oct. 1954); F. Wohlfahrt, "Das Werk R. O.s," *Schweizerische Musikzeitung/Revue musicale suisse*, XCIX (1959).

Obradović, Aleksandar, Yugoslav composer and teacher; b. Bled, Aug. 22, 1927. He studied with Logar at the Belgrade Academy of Music (graduated, 1952), with Berkeley in London (1959–60), and at the Columbia-Princeton Electronic Music Center in N.Y. (1966–67). From 1955 to 1991 he taught at the Belgrade Academy of Music, where he also served as rector (1977–83). He was secretary general of the Union of Yugoslav Composers (1962–66). In 1959 he received the Award of the City of Belgrade for his *Symphonic Epitaph* and in 1980 the award of the Republic of Serbia for his creative oeuvre. Formally, his music adheres to the architectonic Classical design with strongly discernible tonal centers, but he also experiments with atonal thematics, polytonal harmonies, and dodecaphonic formulas.

WORKS (all 1st perf. in Belgrade unless otherwise given): **DRAMATIC:** *Prolećni uranak* (Spring Outing), ballet (1948); music for radio plays; film scores. **ORCH.:** 8 syms.: No. 1 (1952; March 11, 1953), No. 2 (1959–61; Jan. 22, 1965), No. 3, *Microsymphony* (1967; Opatija, Oct. 27, 1968), No. 4 (May 24, 1972), No. 5, *Intima* (Opatija, Nov. 17, 1974), No. 6, *Explicatio duplex, expressio triplex* (1977; May 12, 1978), No. 7 (1985; Oct. 6, 1987), and No. 8, *Na davnom proplanku detinjstva* (In childhood's bygone meadow), for 2 Voices, Chorus, and Orch. (1989; Nov. 26, 1991); *Prelude and Fugue* for Strings (1954); Concertino for Piano and Strings (1956); Concerto for Clarinet and Strings (1958; March 26, 1959); *Scherzo Overture* (1959); *Kroz svemir* (Through Outer Space), suite (1961); *Epitaph H* for Orch. and Tape (Berlin, Oct. 6, 1965); *Dramatična fuga* for Wind Orch. (Nov. 17, 1972); Cello Concerto (1979; April 23, 1980); *Askeza* (Ascetism) for Strings and Celesta (1991); Concerto for Violin and Strings (1991; Sept. 28, 1992; also as a Concerto for Cello and Strings); *Music* for Piano and Strings (1992; Sept. 24, 1993). **CHAMBER:** Quintet for Flute, Clarinet, and String Trio (1951); *Microsonata I* for Clarinet (1969) and *II* for Bassoon (1970); *Divertimento* for Wind Quintet (1983); piano pieces. **VOCAL:** *Mala horska svita* (Little choral suite; 1947); *Plameni vjetar* (Wing of Flame), song cycle for Baritone and Orch. (1955); *Symphonic Epitaph* for Reciter, Chorus, and Orch. (May 21, 1959); *Sutjeska* for 2 Reciters, Chorus, and Orch. (1968; Dec. 19, 1971); *Dačko doba Šumarica* (School Days in Šumarice) for Reciters, Chorus, Children's Chorus, and Wind Orch. (Kragujevac, Oct. 21, 1972); *Mezomed Muzi* (Mesomedes to the Muse), song cycle for Mezzo-soprano and Chamber Trio (1972); *Zeleni vitez* (The Green Knight), song cycle for Voice and Strings (1990); *Stradum*, song cycle for Voice and Piano (1990). **ELECTRONIC:** *Electronic Toccata and Fugue* (1967).

Obraztsova, Elena (Vasilievna), outstanding Russian mezzo-soprano; b. Leningrad, July 7, 1937. Her father was an engineer who played the violin. She studied at the Leningrad Cons., graduating in 1964. She made her operatic debut as Marina in *Boris Godunov* at Moscow's Bolshoi Theater (1963). In 1970 she won 1st prize at the Tchaikovsky Competition in Moscow. She made her first tour of the U.S. with the Bolshoi troupe in June-July 1975; on Oct. 12, 1976, she made her Metropolitan Opera debut in N.Y. as Amneris in Verdi's *Aida*. She appeared in recital in N.Y. in 1987, and was also invited to sing again at the Metropolitan Opera after an absence of some 10 years. In 1973 she was named a National Artist of the R.S.F.S.R. and in 1976 she was awarded the Lenin prize. She possessed a remarkably even tessitura, brilliant in all registers; her roles included virtually the entire Russian operatic repertoire, and such standard roles as Norma, Carmen, Eboli, and Dalila.

Obretenov, Svetoslav, Bulgarian choral conductor and composer; b. Provadia, Nov. 25, 1909; d. Sofia, May 16, 1955. He studied at the Sofia Cons., then was active as a choral conductor. He wrote mostly for chorus; his oratorio *The Partisans* was performed for the first time in Sofia on June 25, 1949.

BIBL.: V. Krstev, *S. O.* (Sofia, 1959).

O'Brien, Eugene, American composer and teacher; b. Paterson, N.J., April 24, 1945. He studied with Robert Beadell at the Univ. of Nebraska (B.M., 1967; M.M., 1969) and on a Fulbright fellowship with Zimmermann at the Cologne Staatliche Hochschule für Musik (1969–70); after further training with Eaton and Xenakis at Indiana Univ. (1970–71), he completed his studies with Erb at the Cleveland Inst. of Music (D.M.A., 1983). In the meantime, he taught composition at the Cleveland Inst. of Music (1973–81), subsequently serving as its composer-in-residence and as chairman of its composition and theory dept. (1981–85); he was assoc. prof. of music and chairman of the composition dept. at the school of music at the Catholic Univ. of America in Washington, D.C. (1985–87); then assoc. prof. of music at the Indiana Univ. School of Music in Bloomington (from 1987), where he was chairman of the composition dept. (from 1994). He held the Rome Prize Fellowship at the American Academy in Rome (1971–73); also received NEA (1977, 1979) and Guggenheim (1984–85) fellowships.

WORKS: BALLET: *Taking Measures* (Cleveland, Oct. 10, 1984). **ORCH.:** Sym. (Lincoln, Nebr., May 16, 1969); Cello Concerto (1971; Rome, Dec. 5, 1972); *Rites of Passage* (1978); *Mysteries of the Horizon* (1987; also for Chamber Orch., 1988); Alto Saxophone Concerto (1989; Bloomington, Ind., Dec. 1, 1993); *The Clouds of Magellan* for the 175th anniversary of Indiana Univ. (1995). **CHAMBER:** *Intessitura* for Cello and Piano (1975); *Embarking for Cythera* for 8 Instruments (1978); *Tristan's Lament* for Cello (1979); *Allures* for Percussion Trio (1979); *Black Fugatos* for 5 Instruments (1983); *Psalms and Nocturnes* for Flute, Viola da Gamba, and Harpsichord (1985); *Close Harmony* for 2 Pianos (1986); *Mysteries of the Horizon* for 11 Instruments (1987); *Rhyme and Reason* for Marimba (1993); *Fancies and Goodnights* for Flute, Clarinet, and Double Bass (1994). **PIANO:** *Ambages* for Piano, 4-hands (1972). **VOCAL:** *Ceremony after a Fire Raid* for Baritone and String Quartet (1965); *Requiem Mass* for Soprano, Chorus, and Wind Ensemble (1966); Nocturne for Soprano and 10 Instruments (1968); *Elegy for Bernd Alois Zimmermann* for Soprano, Trumpet, 2 Percussion, and Cello (1970); *Lingual* for Soprano, Flute, and Cello (1972); *Dédales* for Soprano and Orch. (1973; Rome, Dec. 18, 1976); *Dreams and Secrets of Origin* for Soprano and Orch. (Cleveland, Oct. 19, 1983); *Mareas* for Soprano and Orch. (1991).

Obukhova, Nadezhda (Andreievna), Russian mezzo-soprano; b. Moscow, March 6, 1886; d. Feodosiya, Aug. 14, 1961. She studied with Masetti at the Moscow Cons., graduating in 1912. She made her operatic debut at the Bolshoi Theater there in 1916 as Pauline in *The Queen of Spades;* remained on its roster until 1948. In addition to the Russian repertoire, she was noted for her portrayals of Carmen, Dalila, Amneris, and Fricka. She was greatly esteemed in Russia; in 1943 she was awarded the State Prize of the U.S.S.R.

BIBL.: E. Grosheva, *N. O.* (Moscow, 1953); G. Polyanovsky, *My Meetings with N. O.* (Moscow, 1971).

Očenáš, Andrej, Slovak composer; b. Selce, near Banská Bystrica, Jan. 8, 1911. He studied composition with Alexander Moyzes at the Bratislava Academy of Music, graduating in 1937; then took a course with Novák at the Prague Cons., graduating in 1939. He worked at the Czech Radio in Bratislava (1939–50) and was music deputy to the regional director of broadcasting there (1956–62); taught at the Bratislava Cons. (1943–73), serving as director from 1950 to 1954. His music is imbued with a Slovak ethos.

WORKS: DRAMATIC: *At the Brigand's Ball* (1941); *Year in a Village*, musical play (Bratislava, Dec. 11, 1948); *Highlander's Songs*, ballet (1954–56); *The Romance of the Rose*, stage sym. for Narrator, Soloists, Chorus, and Orch. (1969–71). **ORCH.:** *Tales of My Native Land* (1943); *Resurrection*, symphonic trilogy (1945–53); *To My Nation*, symphonic cycle (1947); Cello Concerto (1952); *Ruralia Slovaca* for Strings, 2 Flutes, 2 Clarinets, 2 Trumpets, Horns, and Piano (1957); Piano Concerto (1959); *Concertino rustico* for Cimbalom, Strings, and Piano (1963); Sinfonietta (1966); *The Flames of May*, prelude (1972); Violin Concerto (1974); *The Depiction of Life*, symphonic cycle (1980); *Gilding of Traditions* (1984). **CHAMBER:** 2 string quartets (*Pictures of the Soul*, 1942; *Étude*, 1970); Concertino for Flute and Piano (1961–62); Piano Trio (1967); *Frescoes* for Violin and Piano (1967); *Poem of the Heart* for Violin (1968); *Don Quixote*, duo for Violin and Cello (1969). **PIANO:** *Zvony* (The Bells), sonata (1972); other piano pieces. **VOCAL:** *Prophecies*, cantata tetralogy (1949–52); *About Earth and Man*, sym. for Chorus and Small Orch. (1970); choral pieces; songs.

Ochman, Wieslaw, Polish tenor; b. Warsaw, Feb. 6, 1937. He studied in Kraków, Bytom, and Warsaw. He made his operatic debut as Edgardo in *Lucia di Lammermoor* in Bytom (1959), appearing there regularly until 1963; then sang in Kraków and Warsaw. He subsequently made debuts at Berlin's Deutsche Oper (1966), the Hamburg State Opera (1967), the Chicago Lyric Opera (1972), the San Francisco Opera (1972), the Paris Opéra (1974), and the Vienna State Opera (1975); made his Metropolitan Opera debut in N.Y. as Arrigo in *Les Vêpres siciliennes* (March 12, 1975). Among his best known roles were those in Mozart's operas as well as Rossini's Count Almaviva, Ernesto, the Duke of Mantua, and Cavaradossi.

O'Connell, Charles, American conductor and recording executive; b. Chicopee, Mass., April 22, 1900; d. N.Y., Sept. 1, 1962. He studied at the Catholic School and College of the Holy Cross (B.A., 1922); also had instruction in organ from Widor in Paris. From 1930 to 1944 he was head of the artist and repertoire dept. of the RCA Victor Red Seal label, then music director of Columbia Masterworks (1944–47). He publ. *The Victor Book of the Symphony* (1934; new ed., 1948); *The Victor Book of the Opera* (1937); *The Other Side of the Record* (1947); *The Victor Book of Overtures, Tone Poems and Other Orchestral Works* (1950).

O'Conor, John, Irish pianist; b. Dublin, Jan. 18, 1947. He was only 3 when he began lessons with his sister; after studies with Sheila Rumbold (1953–57), he attended the Dublin College of Music (1957–68); also pursued his general education at Belvedere College, Dublin (graduated, 1965) and studied music at Univ. College, Dublin (B.Mus., 1969). His postgraduate studies followed with Dieter Weber at the Vienna Hochschule für Musik (1971–75); also attended master classes given by C. Zecchi at the Salzburg Mozarteum (1967–68), Agosti at the Accademia Musicale Chigiana in Siena (1972), and Kempff in Positano, Italy (1974, 1980). He took 1st prize in both the Beethoven (1973) and Bösendorfer (1975) competitions in Vienna. On Nov. 12, 1968, he made his formal debut in Dublin. He first played in London at the Wigmore Hall in Feb. 1974. In May 1976 he made his Tokyo debut at the Bunka Kaikan Hall. On Jan. 10, 1983, he made his first appearance in N.Y. at Alice Tully Hall. In 1985 he was awarded an honorary D.Mus. degree from the National Univ. of Ireland and in 1994 he was made a fellow of the Royal Irish Academy of Music. O'Conor is a particularly sensitive and refined interpreter of the Austro-German masters. He has also championed the music of his neglected countryman, John Field.

Odak, Krsto, Croatian composer and teacher; b. Siverić, Dalmatia, March 20, 1888; d. Zagreb, Nov. 4, 1965. He studied composition with P. Hartmann in Munich (1912–13) and with Novák in his master class at the Prague Cons. (1919–22). Upon his return to Yugoslavia, he was prof. of composition at the Zagreb Academy of Music, retiring in 1961.

WORKS: DRAMATIC: OPERAS: *Dorica pleše* (Dorica Dances; Zagreb, April 16, 1934); *Majka Margarita* (Mother Margaret), radio opera (Zagreb, March 25, 1955); incidental music; film scores. **ORCH.:** 2 passacaglias (1938, 1955); 4 syms. (1940, 1951, 1961, 1965); Concertino for Bassoon and Strings (1958). **CHAMBER:** 4 string quartets (1923, 1927, 1934, 1956); Violin Sonata (1922); Flute Sonata (1946). **VOCAL:** *Radost* (Gaiety), cantata (1959); masses; motets; songs.

Odaka, Hisatada. See **Otaka, Hisatada.**

Oddone Sulli-Rao, Elisabetta, Italian composer; b. Milan, Aug. 13, 1878; d. there, March 3, 1972. She studied at the Milan Cons. She composed a one-act opera, *A gara colle rondini* (Milan, 1920), and a children's opera, *Petruccio e il cavallo cappuccio* (Milan, 1916); also several oratorios; chamber music; and a number of songs. She did some valuable work on dissemination of Italian folk songs; publ. *Canzoniere popolare italiano, Canzoncine per bimbi, Cantilene popolari dei bimbi d'Italia*, etc.

Odnoposoff, Adolfo, Argentine cellist and teacher, brother of **Ricardo Odnoposoff**; b. Buenos Aires, Feb. 22, 1917; d. Denton, Texas, March 13, 1992. He studied with Alberto Schiuma; then went to Berlin, where he took lessons with Feuermann, and to Paris, where he became a student of Diran Alexanian. He was subsequently active as a concert cellist in Palestine (1936–38), Peru (1938–40), Chile (1940–44), Havana (1944–58), and Mexico City, where he also taught at the Cons. Nacional de Música (1958–64); then was a prof. of cello and chamber music at the Cons. of Music in San Juan, Puerto Rico. In 1975 he became a prof. of cello at North Texas State Univ. in Denton. Several Latin American composers (Roque Cordero, Rodolfo Halffter, Eduardo Mata, Floro Ugarte, Antonio Tauriello, and others) wrote special works for him.

Odnoposoff, Ricardo, Argentine violinist and teacher, brother of **Adolfo Odnoposoff**; b. Buenos Aires, Feb. 24, 1914. He studied with Aaron Klasse in Buenos Aires (1919–26), Rudolph Deman in Berlin (1927–28), and Carl Flesch at the Berlin Hochschule für Musik (1928–32). A precocious musician, he played in public as an infant; was a soloist with the Berlin Phil. at 17; won 1st prize at the Vienna (1932) and Ysaÿe (1937) competitions. He evolved a brilliant career as a concert violinist, appearing in all parts of the world. He taught at the Vienna (1956), Stuttgart (from 1964), and Zürich (1975–84) Hochschules für Musik.

O'Dwyer, Robert, English-Irish composer and conductor; b. Bristol, Jan. 27, 1862; d. Dublin, Jan. 6, 1949. He was a conductor of the Carl Rosa Opera Co. in London and on tour (1891); then with the Arthur Rousbey Opera Co. in England and Ireland (1892–99); in 1899, became music director at the Univ. of Ireland in Dublin; from 1914 to 1939, was prof. of music there. He was music director (from 1901) of the Gaelic League choir, for which he arranged many Irish songs. He wrote one of the earliest operas with a Gaelic text, *Eithne* (Dublin, May 16, 1910); also composed songs and organ pieces. He left a book in MS, *Irish Music and Its Traditions.*

Oehl, Kurt (Helmut), eminent German musicologist; b. Mainz, Feb. 24, 1923. He was educated at the Mainz Cons. and at the Johannes Gutenberg Univ. in Mainz; obtained his Ph.D. (1952)

with the diss. *Beitrage zur Geschichte der deutschen Mozart-Übersetzungen.* After working as a dramaturg (1952–60), he became a member of the editorial staff of the *Riemann Musiklexikon* in 1960. In this capacity, he helped to prepare the vol. on musical terms and historical subjects (*Sachteil*) for the 12th ed. (Mainz, 1967); also served as a biographical ed. for the *Supplement* (2 vols., Mainz, 1972, 1975). He then became an ed. for the *Brockhaus-Riemann Musiklexikon* (2 vols., Mainz, 1978–79; supplements, 1989 and 1995). From 1973 to 1987 he also was on the faculty of the Johannes Gutenberg Univ. With K. Pfarr, he publ. *Musikliteratur im Überblick: Eine Anleitung zum Nachschlagen* (Mainz, 1988).

Oestvig, Karl (Aagaard), Norwegian tenor; b. Christiania, May 17, 1889; d. there (Oslo), July 21, 1968. He studied in Cologne. He made his operatic debut at the Stuttgart Opera in 1914; remained on its roster until 1919; was then a member of the Vienna State Opera (1919–27), where he created the role of the Emperor in Strauss's *Die Frau ohne Schatten* in 1919; also sang at the Berlin State Opera (until 1926) and the Städtische Oper (1927–30), and made concert tours of Europe and North America. He retired from the stage in 1932 and devoted himself to teaching; accepted the post of director of the Oslo Opera (1941) during the Nazi occupation of Norway, an action which brought him disgrace after the liberation. He was married to the soprano Maria Rajdl. Among his finest roles were Walther von Stolzing, Lohengrin, and Parsifal.

Ogden, Will (actually, **Wilbur Lee**), American composer and teacher; b. Redlands, Calif., April 19, 1921. He studied at the Univ. of Wisc. in Madison (B.M., 1942) and at Hamline Univ. in St. Paul, Minn. (M.A., 1947); after graduate studies at the Univ. of Calif. at Berkeley (1949–50) and at Indiana Univ. in Bloomington (1950–52), he went to Paris on a Fulbright grant and attended the École Normale de Musique (1952–53); returning to the U.S., he obtained his Ph.D. in 1955 from Indiana Univ. with the diss. *Series and Structure: An Investigation into the Purpose of the Twelve-Note Row in Selected Works of Schoenberg, Webern, Krenek, and Leibowitz;* his teachers in the U.S. included Krenek, Sessions, Bukofzer, Apel, and P. Nettl, and in Paris, Leibowitz. He taught at the Univ. of Texas in Austin (1947–50), at St. Catherine College in St. Paul, Minn. (1954–55), and at Illinois Wesleyan Univ. in Bloomington (1956–65); then became a prof. at the Univ. of Calif. at San Diego (1966), where he served as founder-chairman of its music dept. (1966–71). He retired in 1991. His compositions display an effective utilization of serial procedures.

WORKS: CHAMBER OPERA: *The Awakening of Sappho* (1976–80). **ORCH.:** *Movements for Dance* for Chamber Orch. (1948); *Diversions* for Wind Band (1964); *5 Comments and Capriccio* (1979); *5 Preludes* for Violin and Chamber Orch. (1985). **CHAMBER:** String Quartet (1947); *Palindrome and Variations* for String Quartet (1961–62); *Suite* for Flute and Double Bass (1978); *6 Small Trios* for Marimba, Trumpet, and Piano (1982); 2 serenades for Wind Quintet (1986–87; 1991–94); *7 Pieces and a Capriccio* for Violin and Piano (1988–89); *13 Expressions* for Solo Violin, Flute, Oboe, Clarinet, Viola, Cello, and Piano (1993); *15 Variants* for Clarinet and Strings (1994); piano pieces. **VOCAL:** *3 Statements* for Chorus (1955); *Intrada* for Women's Voices and Instruments (1957); *3 Sea Choruses* (1959; 1960–76); *Orpheus Song* for Chorus (1963); *Un Tombeau de Jean Cocteau II* for Soprano, Clarinet or Mime, Pianist or Conductor, and 13 Instruments (1972) and *III* for Narrator, Soprano, Oboe or Mime, Piano, Slides, and Tape (1976–77); *Summer Images and Reflections,* song cycle for Soprano, Flute, Clarinet, Trumpet, and Piano (1984–85); *Hurricane* for Soprano, Baritone, and Percussion (1985; rev. 1986); *2 Sea Chanteys* for Soprano, Baritone, and 2 Percussionists (1987–88); *4 Chamber Songs* for Soprano, Flute, Oboe, Clarinet, Harp, Viola, and Cello (1989); songs.

Ogdon, John (Andrew Howard), remarkable English pianist; b. Manchester, Jan. 27, 1937; d. London, Aug. 1, 1989. He studied with Iso Elinson at the Royal Manchester College of Music (1945), and then pursued training with Denis Matthews, Egon Petri, and Ilona Kabos. He began his career while still a student, premiering works by Goehr and Maxwell Davies; made his London debut as soloist in the Busoni Piano Concerto (1958). After winning joint 1st prize (with Ashkenazy) at the Tchaikovsky Competition in Moscow (1962), he pursued a far-flung international career. He also taught at the Indiana Univ. School of Music in Bloomington (1976–80). His extraordinary talent and success were marred by the tragedy of his life, acute schizophrenia. His father, Howard Ogdon, who also had the disease, described his misfortunes in *Kingdom of the Lost.* His wife also wrote a book, *Virtuoso: The Story of John Ogdon* (London, 1981), in which she described in detail Ogdon's suffering. Physically he presented a picture of astute well-being, being large of body, powerful of manual dexterity, and sporting a spectacular triangular beard. Despite numerous stays in sanatoriums, electric shock and drug treatment, and suicide attempts, he continued to appear as a concert artist. He maintained a vast repertory. His death at the age of 52 was mourned by a multitude of friends and admirers.

Ogihara, Toshitsugu, Japanese composer; b. Osaka, June 6, 1910; d. Odawara, June 14, 1992. He studied composition with Matsudaira at Nihon Univ.; took private lessons with A. Tcherepnin during the latter's stay in Japan. His music follows the classical models.

WORKS: BALLET: *Springtime* (1973). **ORCH.:** *2 Movements* for Percussion and Orch. (1942); *Sôshun no Hiroba,* symphonic poem (1955); Sym. No. 1 (1958); *Rhapsody* (1960); 2 violin concertos (1962, 1963); Violin Concertino (1962); *Capriccio* for Strings (1964); *4 Pieces* for Horn and Strings (1972); *Fancy Parade* (1983). **CHAMBER:** 4 string quartets (1940, 1949, 1953, 1969); 2 string trios (1947, 1961); Violin Sonata (1959); Concerto for Clarinet and String Quartet (1955); *Capriccio* for Woodwinds and Strings (1958); Trio for Clarinet, Cello, and Piano (1962); English Horn Sonata (1962); Quartet for 4 Flutes (1963); Trio for Flute, Violin, and Piano (1965); Piano Quintet (1970); *Serenade* for Cello, Violin, and Clarinet (1972); *4 Pieces* for Tuba, 3 Tenor Trombones, and Bass Trombone (1972); *2 Suites* for Flute and Piano (1974); *Duet No. 1* for Violin and Piano (1983); *Suite* for Flute and Piano (1984); piano pieces, including a *Fantasia* (1984). **VOCAL:** *7 Poems* for Soprano, Violin, Cello, and Piano (1971); other songs.

Ogura, Roh, Japanese composer and teacher; b. Kitakyūshu, Jan. 19, 1916; d. Kamakura, Aug. 26, 1990. He studied with Fukai, Sugawara, and Ikenouchi, and then engaged in teaching.

WORKS: OPERA: *Neta* (1957). **ORCH.:** 3 syms. (1941; Tokyo, April 25, 1951; 1968); Piano Concerto (Tokyo, March 24, 1946); *5 Movements on Japanese Folk Songs* (1957); Violin Concerto (1971); Cello Concerto (1980). **CHAMBER:** 3 string quartets (1941, 1946, 1954); Violin Sonata (1950); Violin Sonatina (1960); *Divertimento* for 7 (1964) and 8 (1972) Winds; piano music. **VOCAL:** *Orly—A Bugbear at Sea* for Narrator and Orch. (1963); choruses; songs.

Ohana, Maurice, French composer and pianist; b. Casablanca (of Spanish parents), June 12, 1914; d. Paris, Nov. 13, 1992. He studied piano with Frank Marshall in Barcelona and with Lazare Lévy at the Paris Cons.; also had lessons in counterpoint with Daniel-Lesur at the Schola Cantorum in Paris (1937–40). Following service in the British Army during World War II, he completed his training with Casella at Rome's Accademia di Santa Cecilia (1944–46), then settled in Paris. In 1981 he was made a Commandeur des Arts et Lettres. He won the Prix National de Musique (1975) and the Honegger (1982) and Ravel (1985) prizes.

WORKS: DRAMATIC: OPERAS: *Syllabaire pour Phèdre* (1967; Paris, Feb. 5, 1968); *Autodafé* (Lyons, May 23, 1972); *Trois contes de l'Honorable Fleur* (Avignon, July 16, 1978); *La Célestine* (1982–86; Paris, June 13, 1988). **RADIOPHONIC SCORES:** *Les Hommes et les autres* (1955); *Histoire véridique de Jacotin* (1961); *Hélène* (1963); *Les Héraclides* (1964); *Iphigénie* *en Tauride* (1965); *Hippolyte* (1965–66); film music. **ORCH.:** *Trois graphiques*, concerto for Guitar and Orch. (1950–57; BBC, London, Feb. 1961); *Synaxis* for 2 Pianos, 4 Percussionists, and Orch. (1965–66); *Chiffres de clavecin* for Harpsichord and Chamber Orch. (1967–68); *Silenciaire* for 6 Percussion and Strings (1969); *T'harân-Ngô* (Paris, Oct. 1974); *Anneau du Tamarit* for Cello and Orch. (1976); *Livre des Prodiges* (Lyons, Oct. 4, 1979); *Crypt* for Strings (1980); Piano Concerto (1980–81); Cello Concerto No. 2 (1988–89; Tokyo, May 13, 1991). **CHAMBER:** *Tiento* for Guitar (1955); *Quatre improvisations* for Flute (1961); *Cinq séquences* for String Quartet (1963); *Signes* for Flute, 2 Guitars, Piano, and 4 Percussion (1965); *Syrtes* for Cello and Piano (1970); *Sacral d'Ilx* for Harpsichord, Oboe, and Horn (1975); *Satyre* for 2 Flutes (1976); String Quartet No. 2 (1980) and No. 3 (1990); *Kypris* for 4 Instruments (1985); piano pieces; harpsichord music. **VOCAL:** *Llanto por Ignacio Sanchez Mejias* for Baritone, Reciter, Women's Voices, and Instrumental Ensemble (Paris, May 22, 1950); *Cantigas* for Soprano, Mezzo-soprano, Chorus, and Instrumental Ensemble (1953); *Récit de l'ano zéro*, scenic oratorio (1958–59); *Tombeau de Claude Debussy* for Soprano, Guitar, Piano, and Chamber Orch. (1962; Paris, Jan. 8, 1964); *Cris* for 12 Voices (1968); *Stream* for Bass and String Trio (1970); *Office des oracles* for 3 Vocal Groups and Instruments (Ste. Baume, Aug. 9, 1974); *Lys de Madrigaux* for Women's Chorus and Instrumental Ensemble (Paris, June 1, 1976); *Messe* for Soprano, Mezzo-soprano, Chorus, and Instrumental Ensemble (Avignon, July 30, 1977); *Lux Noctis—Die Solis* for 4 Choral Groups and 2 Organs (1981–88; Paris, Dec. 9, 1988); *Swan Songs* for 12 Voices (1988); *Tombeau de Louise Labbé* for 12 Voices (1988–90); *Nuit de Pouchine* for 12 Voices, Solo Man's Voice, and Viola da Gamba or Cello (Leningrad, Nov. 16, 1990); *Avoaha* for Chorus, Percussion, and 2 Pianos (1991; Aix-les-Bains, Feb. 14, 1992).

BIBL.: N. Quist, *M. O.* (diss., Univ. of Heidelberg, 1973).

O'Hara, Geoffrey, Canadian-born American composer; b. Chatham, Ontario, Feb. 2, 1882; d. St. Petersburg, Fla., Jan. 31, 1967. He settled in the U.S. in 1904 and became a naturalized American citizen in 1919. He studied with Homer Norris and J. Vogler; then acted in vaudeville as a pianist, singer, and composer; wrote the song *Your eyes have told me* for Caruso. In 1913 he was appointed an instructor in American Indian music as part of a program of the Dept. of the Interior; in 1917, became an army song leader; was instructor in community singing at Teachers College, Columbia Univ. (1936–37). He wrote the operettas *Peggy and the Pirate* (1927), *Riding Down the Sky* (1928), *The Count and the Co-ed* (1929), and *The Smiling Six-pence* (1930); also about 300 songs, of which the following were extremely popular: *K-K-K-Katy, I Love a Little Cottage, The Living God, I Walked Today Where Jesus Walked*, and *Give a Man a Horse He Can Ride.*

Ohlsson, Garrick (Olof), talented American pianist; b. Bronxville, N.Y., April 3, 1948. At the age of 8, he became a pupil of Thomas Lishman at the Westchester (N.Y.) Cons. He entered the preparatory division of the Juilliard School of Music in N.Y. in 1961 as a student of Sascha Gorodnitzki and later of Rosina Lhévinne (B.Mus., 1971); also studied privately with Olga Barabini and Irma Wolpe. He won the Busoni (1966) and Montreal (1968) competitions; then made his N.Y. recital debut on Jan. 5, 1970; later that year he gained international recognition when he became the first American pianist to win the prestigious quinquennial Chopin Competition in Warsaw. A Polish writer described Ohlsson as a "bear-butterfly" for his ability to traverse the entire spectrum of 18 dynamic degrees discernible on the modern piano, from the thundering fortississimo to the finest pianississimo, with reference also to his height (6 foot, 4 inches), weight (225 lbs.), and stretch of hands (an octave and a 5th in the left hand and an octave and a 4th in the right hand). Thereafter, Ohlsson pursued a distinguished global career. In 1994 he was awarded the Avery Fisher Prize. His interpretations are marked by a distinctive Americanism, technically flawless and free of Romantic mannerisms.

Ohms, Elisabeth, Dutch soprano; b. Arnhem, May 17, 1888; d. Marquardstein, Oct. 16, 1974. She studied in Amsterdam, Frankfurt am Main, and Berlin. She made her operatic debut in Mainz in 1921; in 1922 she joined the Bavarian State Opera in Munich, of which she was a principal member until 1936; also sang at La Scala in Milan (1927–29), Covent Garden in London (1928–29, 1935), and the Bayreuth Festival (1931). On Jan. 17, 1930, she made her debut with the Metropolitan Opera in N.Y. as Brünnhilde; remained on its roster until 1932. She excelled in Wagner's operas; among her finest roles were Brünnhilde, Kundry, Venus, and Isolde.

Oistrakh, David (Fyodorovich), great Russian violinist, outstanding pedagogue, and esteemed conductor; b. Odessa, Sept. 30, 1908; d. Amsterdam, Oct. 24, 1974. He studied violin as a child with Stoliarsky in Odessa; made his debut there at the age of 6; then continued his studies with Stoliarsky at the Odessa Cons. (1923–26); then appeared as soloist in Glazunov's Violin Concerto under the composer's direction in Kiev in 1927. In 1928 he went to Moscow and in 1934 he was appointed to the faculty of the Cons. His name attracted universal attention in 1937 when he won 1st prize at the Ysaÿe Competition in Brussels, in which 68 violinists from 21 countries took part. This launched a career of great renown as a violin virtuoso. He played in Paris and London in 1953 with extraordinary success; made his first American appearances in 1955, as soloist with major American orchs. and in recitals, winning enthusiastic acclaim; also made appearances as a conductor from 1962. He died while on a visit to Amsterdam as a guest conductor with the Concertgebouw Orch. Oistrakh's playing was marked, apart from a phenomenal technique, by stylistic fidelity to works by different composers of different historical periods. Soviet composers profited by his advice as to technical problems of violin playing; he collaborated with Prokofiev in making an arrangement for violin and piano of his Flute Sonata. A whole generation of Soviet violinists numbered among his pupils, first and foremost his son Igor (Davidovich) Oistrakh (b. Odessa, April 27, 1931), who has had a spectacular career in his own right; he won 1st prize at the International Festival of Democratic Youth in Budapest (1949) and the Wieniawski Competition in Poznań (1952); some critics regarded him as equal to his father in virtuosity; from 1958 he taught at the Moscow Cons.

BIBL.: V. Bronin, *D. O.* (Moscow, 1954); I. Yampolsky, *D. O.* (Moscow, 1964); D. Naberin, *D. und Igor O.* (Berlin, 1968); V. Josefowitsch, *D. O.* (Stuttgart, 1977); Y. Soroker, *D. O.* (Jerusalem, 1982).

Oki, Masao, Japanese composer; b. Iwata, Shizuoka, Oct. 3, 1901; d. Kamakura, April 18, 1971. He studied engineering and music; then devoted himself mainly to teaching and composition. He wrote 6 syms., including No. 5, *Atomic Bomb* (Tokyo, Nov. 6, 1953) and No. 6, *Vietnam* (1970). His other works included a cantata, *Take Back the Human* (1961–63); String Quartet; choral works.

Olah, Tiberiu, Romanian composer; b. Arpăşel, Jan. 2, 1928. He studied at the Cluj Cons. (1946–49) and the Moscow Cons. (1949–54); in each of the years from 1966 to 1971, he attended the summer courses in new music at Darmstadt. From 1954 to 1988 he taught at the Bucharest Cons. In his music he adopts a strong contrapuntal style, with some excursions into the atonal domain and dodecaphonic organization.

WORKS: ORCH.: *Little Suite* (1954); 4 syms. (1952–55; 1985–87; 1989; 1991); *Coloana fără sfîşit* (Endless Column), symphonic poem inspired by the works of the Romanian sculptor Constantin Brâncuşi (1962); *Poarta sărutului* (Archway of the Kiss), symphonic poem (1966); *Masa tăcerii* (The Table of Silence), symphonic poem (1967–68); *5 Pieces* (1966); *Crescendo* (1972); *Evenimente 1907* (1972); *Harmonies: No. 1* (1975), *No. 3* (1977–78), and *No. 4*, concerto for 23 Instruments (1981). **CHAMBER:** String Quartet (1952); Trio for Violin, Clarinet, and Piano (1954); Violin Sonatina (1955); 2 sonatas for Solo Clarinet (1963, 1982); *Spaţiu şi ritm* (Space and Rhythm), étude for 3 Percussion Groups (1964); *Translations* for 16 Strings (1968); *Perspectives* for 13 Instruments (1969); Sonata for Solo Cello (1971); *Invocations* for Various Instruments (1971); *Time of Memory* for Chamber Ensemble (1973; N.Y., Dec. 6, 1974); *Harmonies: No. 2* for Winds and Percussion (1976); Sonata for Solo Flute (1978); Sonata for Violin and Percussion (1985); Sonata for Saxophone and Tape (1986). **PIANO:** Sonatina (1950). **VOCAL:** 4 cantatas: *Cantata* for Women's Chorus, 2 Flutes, Strings, and Percussion (1956), *Prind visele aripi* (Dreams Become Reality, 1959), *Lumina lui Lenin* (The Light of Lenin, 1959), and *Constelaţia omului* (The Galaxy of Man, 1960); *Echinocţii* (Equinoxes) for Voice, Clarinet, and Piano (1967).

Olczewska, Maria (real name, **Marie Berchtenbreitner**), prominent German mezzo-soprano; b. Ludwigsschwaige bei Donauwörth, near Augsburg, Aug. 12, 1892; d. Klagenfurt, Austria, May 17, 1969. She studied with Karl Erler in Munich. She began her career singing in operetta; made her operatic debut in Krefeld (1915), then appeared in Leipzig (1916–20) and Hamburg (1920–23); also in Vienna (1921–23). She was a favorite at London's Covent Garden in Wagnerian roles (1924–32); also sang in Munich (1923–25) and again in Vienna (1925–30); likewise appeared in Chicago (1928–32). She made her Metropolitan Opera debut in N.Y. as Brängane on Jan. 16, 1933, remaining on its roster until 1935. From 1947 to 1969 she taught at the Vienna Academy of Music. She had a powerful voice, which made it possible for her to master the Wagner roles; but she was also excellent in dramatic parts, such as Carmen. Furthermore, she had a genuine talent as a stage actress. She was married for a time to **Emil Schipper**.

Oldberg, Arne, American composer; b. Youngstown, Ohio, July 12, 1874; d. Evanston, Ill., Feb. 17, 1962. He studied composition with Middelschulte; then went to Vienna, where he was a piano pupil of Leschetizky (1893–95); also took courses with Rheinberger in Munich. Returning to America in 1899, he became head of the piano dept. at Northwestern Univ.; retired in 1941. Most of his orch. works were performed by the Chicago Sym. Orch., among them *Paolo and Francesca* (Jan. 17, 1908), *At Night* (April 13, 1917), Sym. No. 4 (Dec. 31, 1942), Sym. No. 5 (Jan. 19, 1950), and *St. Francis of Assisi* for Baritone and Orch. (Ravinia Festival, July 16, 1954). Other works are: *Academic Overture* (1909); *The Sea*, symphonic poem (1934); 2 piano concertos, of which the 2nd won the Hollywood Bowl prize and was performed there (Aug. 16, 1932); Violin Concerto (1933; Chicago, Nov. 7, 1946); 2 rhapsodies for Orch.; chamber music; piano pieces.

Oldham, Arthur (William), English pianist, chorus master, and composer; b. London, Sept. 6, 1926. He studied at the Royal College of Music in London with Howells, and privately with Britten. He was music director of the Ballet Rambert; served as chorus master of Scottish Opera in Glasgow (1966–74) and was director of the London Sym. Orch. Chorus (1969–76). In 1990 he was made an Officer of the Order of the British Empire. He wrote the ballets *Mr. Punch* (1946), *The Sailor's Return* (1947), *Circus Canteen* (1951), and *Bonne-Bouche* (1952); also *The Apotheosis of Lucius*, symphonic poem (1952); *The Land of Green Ginger*, musical for children (1964); *Hymns for the Amusement of Children* for Voices and Organ (1962); various sacred and secular choral works.

Oldman, C(ecil) B(ernard), English librarian and bibliographer; b. London, April 2, 1894; d. there, Oct. 7, 1969. He studied at Exeter College, Oxford. In 1920 he received an appointment in the Dept. of Printed Books in the British Museum in London; from 1948 to 1959, was Principal Keeper. In 1952 he was made a Companion of the Order of the Bath and in 1958 a Commander of the Royal Victorian Order. He was an authority on Haydn, Mozart, and Beethoven bibliographical matters; annotated the letters of Constanze Mozart to J.A. André in E. Anderson's *The Letters of Mozart and His Family* (3 vols., London, 1938; 2nd ed., rev., 1966 by A. Hyatt King and M. Carolan; 3rd ed., rev., 1985 by S. Sadie and F. Smart); his essay "Musical First Editions" in J. Carter, ed., *New Paths in Book-collecting* (London 1934) was publ. separately (1938).

Oldroyd, George, English organist and composer; b. Healey, Yorkshire, Dec. 1, 1886; d. London, Feb. 26, 1951. He studied organ and theory with Eaglefield Hull and violin with Frank Arnold. After a year in Paris as organist of the English Church (1915), he played at various London churches; taught at Trinity College of Music; from 1949 he was prof. at the Univ. of London. He wrote a number of sacred works, of which a *Stabat Mater* is notable. He publ. *The Technique and Spirit of Fugue: An Historical Study* (London, 1948), *Polyphonic Writing for Voices, in 6 and 8 Parts* (London, 1953), and some essays on Gregorian chant.

Olenin, Alexander, Russian composer, brother of **Marie (Alexeievna) Olénine d'Alheim**; b. Istomino, Riazan district, June 13, 1865; d. Moscow, Feb. 15, 1944. He studied with P. Pabst and with Erdmannsdörfer. He lived most of his life in Moscow. He wrote an opera in a folk style, *Kudeyar* (Moscow, Nov. 26, 1915); a symphonic poem, *After the Battle*; *Préludes prairiales* for 2 Oboes, Violin, and Piano (1927); Piano Sonata; Violin Sonata; several song cycles (*The Street, The Peasant's Son, The Autumn, Home*, etc.); 52 songs to texts by Heine.

Olénine d'Alheim, Marie (Alexeievna), Russian soprano, sister of **Alexander Olenin**; b. Istomino, Riazan district, Oct. 2, 1869; d. Moscow, Aug. 27, 1970. She studied in Russia and later in Paris, where she made her debut in 1896. Through her brother she met Stasov, Balakirev, and Cui, and became interested in Russian vocal music. In 1893 she married the French writer Pierre d'Alheim (1862–1922), tr. of the text of *Boris Godunov;* together they organized, in Moscow and in Paris, numerous concerts and lectures on Russian music, particularly on Mussorgsky. She was an outstanding interpreter of Russian songs; publ. a book, *Le Legs de Mussorgsky* (Paris, 1908). In 1935 she settled in Paris as a voice teacher; in 1949 she joined the French Communist Party and in 1959 she returned to Russia.

Olevsky, Julian, German-born American violinist; b. Berlin, May 7, 1926; d. Amherst, Mass., May 25, 1985. After studies in Germany, he went with his family to Buenos Aires (1935), where he made his debut at age 10; then settled in the U.S. (1947), becoming a naturalized American citizen (1951). He made his N.Y. debut at Town Hall (1949), and then toured as a soloist, recitalist, and chamber music player. He taught at the Univ. of Mass. in Boston (1967–74), and then in Amherst.

Olitzka, Rosa, German-American contralto and teacher, aunt of **Walter Olitzki**; b. Berlin, Sept. 6, 1873; d. Chicago, Sept. 29, 1949. She studied with Julius Hey in Berlin and with Désirée Artôt in Paris. She sang at Berlin (1891); then was engaged at the Hannover Opera (1892–93), at Covent Garden in London (1894), and in N.Y. with the German Opera Co. (1895–97); was also with the Metropolitan Opera (1895–97; 1899–1901). After a season with the Chicago Grand Opera (1910–11), she made guest appearances in opera and concert in Europe and North America; later taught voice in Chicago.

Olitzki, Walter, German-American baritone, nephew of **Rosa Olitzka**; b. Hamburg, March 17, 1903; d. Los Angeles, Aug. 2, 1949. He received his training in Germany, where he developed his career. On Dec. 2, 1939, he appeared as Beckmesser at the Metropolitan Opera in N.Y., where he remained until 1947. He specialized in Wagnerian roles.

Oliveira, Elmar, talented American violinist; b. Waterbury, Conn., June 28, 1950. He studied violin with Raphael Bronstein on a scholarship at the Hartt College of Music in Hartford, Conn. and later at the Manhattan School of Music in N.Y. He made his formal debut as a soloist with the Hartford (Conn.) Sym. Orch. (1964); appeared with Bernstein at a N.Y. Phil. Young People's Concert (1966), which was telecast to the nation; made his N.Y. recital debut at Town Hall (1973). After winning the Naumburg Award in 1975, he became the first American violinist to capture the Gold Medal at the Tchaikovsky Competition in Moscow (1978); thereafter he pursued a rewarding international career. In 1990 he joined the faculty of the Manhattan School of Music in N.Y. His enormous repertoire ranges from the standard literature to contemporary works.

Oliveira, Jocy de, Brazilian pianist and composer of French and Portuguese descent; b. Curitiba-Parana, April 11, 1936. She studied piano in São Paulo with J. Kliass, in Paris with Marguerite Long, and at Washington Univ. in St. Louis (M.A., 1968). She appeared as a piano soloist with major orchs. in Europe and America, specializing in the modern repertoire; in 1966 she played the piano part in Stravinsky's *Capriccio* in St. Louis, under Stravinsky's direction. As a composer, she occupies the aphelion of ultra-modernism, experimenting in electronic, environmental, theatrical, cinematic, and television media, as exemplified by her *Probabilistic Theater I, II,* and *III* for Musicians, Actors, Dancers, Television and Traffic Conductor, and other environmental manifestations. Her *Polinteracões I, II, III* present the culmination of "total music," involving the visual, aural, tactile, gustatory, and olfactory senses, with an anatomic chart serving as a score for guidance of the participants, supplemented by a phonemic table indicating the proper verbalization of vocal parts. (Complete score and illustrations were reproduced in *Source,* no. 7, Sacramento, Calif., 1970.) A performance of *Polinteracoes* was attempted on the occasion of the Catalytic Celebration of the 10th Anniversary Festival of the New Music Circle in St. Louis on April 7, 1970, but was stopped by the management as a noisy, noisome nuisance. She also composed a number of advanced sambas, precipitating the vogue of the Brazilian bossa nova. Active in belles-lettres, she penned a sociological fantasy, *O 3° Mundo* (The Third World), a controversial play, *Apague meu* (Spotlight), poetical works, etc. She married **Eleazar de Carvalho**.

Oliver, John, American conductor and teacher; b. Teaneck, N.J., June 4, 1939. He was educated at the Univ. of Notre Dame (B.M., 1961) and the New England Cons. of Music (M.M. in choral conducting, 1967). From 1964 he was on the staff of the Mass. Inst. of Technology, where he was a technical instructor (1969–77), lecturer (1977–81), and senior lecturer (from 1981). He also was conductor of its glee club (1971–74), choral society (1972–88), schola cantorum (1973–75), and chamber chorus and concert choir (from 1988). From 1970 to 1991 he was head of vocal and choral activities at the Berkshire Music Center in Tanglewood. He also was founder-conductor of the Tanglewood Festival Chorus (from 1970) and of the John Oliver Chorale (from 1977). Oliver's repertoire ranges from the 18th century to the present era.

Oliver, Stephen (Michael Harding), English composer; b. Liverpool, March 10, 1950; d. London, April 29, 1992. He was a student at Worcester College, Oxford (1968–72), receiving training from Leighton (composition) and Sherlaw Johnson (electronic music). Oliver revealed a special talent for composing dramatic scores.

WORKS: DRAMATIC: *Slippery Soules,* Christmas drama (Oxford, Dec. 1969; rev. 1976; orchestrated version, London, Dec. 12, 1988); *The Duchess of Malfi* (1971; rev. version, Santa Fe, N.Mex., Aug. 5, 1978); *3 Instant Operas: Paid Off, Time Flies,* and *Old Haunts* (1973); *Sufficient Beauty* (1973); *Past Tense* (1973); *Cadenus Observ'd* (1974; London, Jan. 26, 1975); *Perseverance* (1974); *Tom Jones* (1974–75; Snape, April 6, 1976); *Bad Times* (London, June 24, 1975); *The Great McPorridge Disaster* (1976); *The Waiter's Revenge,* short opera (Nottingham, June 15, 1976); *Il Giardino,* short opera (Batignano, July 27, 1977; Eng. version as *The Garden,* London, April 17, 1980); *A Stable Home,* short opera (1977); *The Girl and the Unicorn* (London, Dec. 9, 1978); *The Dreaming of the Bones* (1979); *Jacko's Play,* short opera (1979); *A Man of Feeling,* short opera (London, Nov. 17, 1980); *Nicholas Nickelby,* incidental music (London, June 1980); *The Lord of the Rings,* incidental music (1981); *Euridice,* after Peri's score of 1600 (London, March 4, 1981); *Sasha* (1982; Banff, April 7, 1983); *Peter Pan,* incidental music (London, Dec. 16, 1982); *Blondel,* musical (Bath, Sept. 5, 1983); *Britannia Preserv'd,* masque (Hampton Court, May 30, 1984); *The Ring* (Manchester, May 31, 1984); *La Bella e la bestia* (Batignano, July 26, 1984; Eng. version as *Beauty and the Beast,* London, June 21, 1985); *Exposition of a Picture* (London, June 24, 1986); *Mario ed il mago* (Batignano, Aug. 5, 1988; Eng. version as *Mario and the Magician*); *Tables Meet* (London, May 1990); *Timon of Athens* (London, May 17, 1991); *L'Oca del Cairo* (Batignano, July 30, 1991). **ORCH.:** *The Boy and the Dolphin* (1974); *Luv* (1975); Sym. (Liverpool, May 23, 1976; rev. version, Kuopio, Oct. 13, 1983); *O No* for Brass Band (London, Oct. 10, 1976; rev. 1985); Concerto for Recorder and Strings (Aldeburgh, June 19, 1988). **CHAMBER:** *Music for the Wreck of the Deutschland* for Piano Quintet (1972); *Ricercare I* for Clarinet, Violin, Cello, and Piano (1973; London, Jan. 11, 1974), *II* for 2 Oboes, 2 Clarinets, 3 Bassoons, and 2 Horns (Canterbury, June 7, 1981), *III* for Guitar, Viola, and Cello (1983; London, Jan. 7, 1984), and *V* for 2 Trumpets, Horn, Trombone, and Tuba (Sevenoaks, June 15, 1986); Guitar Sonata (1979; Ludwigsburg, May 16, 1981); *Character Pieces* for 2 Oboes, 2 Clarinets, 2 Horns, and 2 Bassoons (Glyndebourne, July 12, 1991); piano pieces; organ music. **VOCAL:** *The Elixir* for 4 Soloists, Chorus, and Melody Instrument (1976); *Magnificat and Nunc Dimittis* for Chorus (1976); *The Dong with a Luminous Nose* for Narrator and 5 String Quartets (Woodfords, July 31, 1976; rev. version, London, Oct. 17, 1989); *A Dialogue Between Mary and Her Child* for Soprano, Baritone, and Chorus (1979); *The Child from the Sea,* cantata for Treble Voice, Chorus, and Orch. (Newcastle upon Tyne, Oct. 30, 1980); *The Key to the Zoo* for Narrator, 2 Oboes, Bassoon, and Harpsichord (Anglia TV, Feb. 5, 1980); *A String of Beads,* cantata for Chorus, 2 Oboes, Bassoon, and Strings (1980; Milton Keynes, Feb. 15, 1981); *Namings,* cantata for Chorus, Brass Quintet, and Timpani (Edinburgh, Sept. 3, 1981); *Trinity Mass* for Chorus (Norwich, July 5, 1981); *7 Words,* cantata for Chorus and String Orch. (Norwich, Oct. 15, 1985); *Forth in Thy Name* for Soprano, Bass, and Chorus (St. Albans, Oct. 5, 1985); *Festal Magnificat and Nunc Dimittis* for Chorus and Organ (Norwich, July 6, 1986); *2 Songs and a Scene from Cymbeline* for Baritone and Piano (Bromsgrove, Sept. 26, 1986); *Ricercare IV* for Countertenor, 2 Tenors, and Baritone (1986); *Prometheus,* cantata for Chorus and Orch. (Guildford, Nov. 26, 1988); *The Vessel,* cantata for Soprano, Tenor, Bass, Chorus, and Orch. (Nottingham, Oct. 19, 1990).

Olivero, Magda (actually, **Maria Maddalena**), remarkable Italian soprano; b. Saluzzo, near Turin, March 25, 1912. She studied at the Turin Cons. She made her operatic debut as Lauretta in *Gianni Schicchi* in Turin in 1933; then sang in the Italian provinces. She temporarily retired from the stage when she married in 1941, but resumed her career in 1951; made successful appearances at La Scala in Milan, and in Paris and London. On Nov. 4, 1967, she made her U.S. debut in Dallas in the title role of Cherubini's *Medea*; she was 63 years old when she made her first appearance with the Metropolitan Opera in N.Y., on April 3, 1975, as Tosca; on Dec. 5, 1977, she gave a highly successful recital in a program of Italian art songs at Carnegie Hall, N.Y. Among her other notable operatic roles were Violetta, Fedora, Li, Suor Angelica, and Minnie; she was praised mainly for her dramatic penetration of each character and her fine command of dynamic nuances.

Oliveros, Pauline, American composer, performer, teacher, author, and philosopher; b. Houston, May 30, 1932. She received rudimentary instruction in music from her mother and grandmother, and then had lessons with William Sydler (violin), Marjorie Harrigan (accordion), and J.M. Brandsetter (horn). Following studies in composition with Paul Koepke and in accordion with William Palmer at the Univ. of Houston (1949–52), she studied with Robert Erickson (1954–60) and at San Francisco State College (B.A. in composition, 1957). In 1966–67 she was director of the Mills College Tape Music Center in Oakland, California. From 1967 to 1981 she was a prof. of music at the Univ.

of Calif. at San Diego, where she also was director of its Center for Music Experiment (1976–79). In 1985 she was a prof. at the Theater School for New Dance in Amsterdam. In 1985 she founded and became president and co-artistic director of the Pauline Oliveros Foundation, Inc. Among her writings are *Pauline's Proverbs* (1976), *Initiation Dream* (1982), and *Software for Peoples* (1984). In 1973 she held a Guggenheim fellowship. She received annual ASCAP awards from 1982 to 1994. In 1984, 1988, and 1990 she held NEA composer's fellowships. In 1994 she was awarded the Foundation for Contemporary Performance Arts grant. In her life and work, Oliveros has been absorbed by the potentialities of meditation, ritual, and myth. In her music, she has extended the boundaries of her art by an innovative approach to the sound and non-sound worlds, from the use of improvisation to electronics and beyond.

WORKS: 3 Songs for Soprano and Piano (1957); *Variations for Sextet* for Flute, Clarinet, Trumpet, Horn, Cello, and Piano (1959); *Sound Patterns* for Chorus (1961); Trio for Flute, Piano, and Page Turner (1961); *Outline* for Flute, Percussion, and String Bass (1963); Trio for Accordion, Trumpet, and String Bass (1963); *Pieces of 8*, theater piece for Flute, Oboe, Clarinet, Bass Clarinet, Trumpet, Horn, and Trombone (1965); *Aeolian Partitions*, theater piece for Flute, Clarinet, Violin, Cello, and Piano (1968); *Double Basses at 20 Paces*, theater piece for 2 Basses, Their Seconds, and a Referee with Slide and Tape (1968); *Meditation on the Points of the Compass* for Chorus (1970); *To Valerie Solanas and Marilyn Monroe in Recognition of Their Desperation* for Ensemble or Orch. (1970); *Deep Listening Pieces* for Voices and Instruments (1970–90); *Bonn Feier*, environmental theater piece with knowing and unknowing performers (1971); *Sonic Meditations* for Voices and Instruments (1971); *Rose Moon*, ritual theater piece for Chorus (1977); *Spiral Mandala* for Clarinets, Tuned Crystal Glasses, and Bass Drum with 4 Players and Chant (1978); *Music for Stacked Deck* for 4 Players (1979); *El Relicario de los Animales* for Singer and 20 Players (1979); *The Witness* for Solo or Duo or Any Ensemble (1979); *Traveling Companions* for Percussion and Dancers (1980); *Tashi Gomang* for Orch. (1981); *The Wanderer* for Accordion Ensemble and Percussion (1982); *Earth Ears* for Any Ensemble (1983); *Gathering Together* for Piano, 8-hands (1983); *Tree/Peace* for Violin, Cello, and Piano (1983); *The Well and the Gentle* for Ensemble (1983); *The Wheel of Time* for String Quartet (1983); *Wings of Dove* for Double Wind Quintet and 2 Pianos (1984); *Lion's Eye* for Javanese Gamelan and Sampler (1985); *Portraits* for Solo or Any Ensemble (1987); *Dream Horse Spiel* for Voices and Sound Effects (1988); *Dream Gates* for Solo or Ensemble (1989); *Wind Horse* for Chorus (1989); *All Fours for the Drum Bum* for Solo Drum Set (1990); *Contenders*, dance piece (1991); *Njinga the Queen King*, theater piece (1993); *Hommage a Serafina*, dance piece (1996); *Ghost Dance*, dance piece (1996).

BIBL.: H. von Gunden, *The Music of P. O.* (Metuchen, N.J., 1983).

d'Ollone, Max(imilien-Paul-Marie-Félix), French conductor, writer on music, and composer; b. Besançon, June 13, 1875; d. Paris, May 15, 1959. He studied with Lavignac, Massenet, and Lenepveu at the Paris Cons.; received the Grand Prix de Rome in 1897 with his cantata *Frédégonde.* He was active as an opera conductor in Paris and the French provinces. He wrote the books *Le langage musical* (Paris and Geneva, 1952) and *Le Théâtre lyrique et le public* (Paris, 1955). He wrote 5 operas: *Le Retour* (Angers, Feb. 13, 1913), *Les Uns et les autres* (Paris, Nov. 6, 1922), *L'Arlequin* (Paris, Dec. 24, 1924), *George Dandin* (Paris, March 19, 1930), and *La Samaritaine* (Paris, June 25, 1937); *Fantaisie* for Piano and Orch. (1899); *Dans la cathédrale* for Orch. (1906); chamber music; many songs.

Olsen, Poul Rovsing, Danish composer and ethnomusicologist; b. Copenhagen, Nov. 4, 1922; d. there, July 2, 1982. He studied law at the Univ. of Århus (1940–42) and at the Univ. of Copenhagen (1942–48); concurrently, studied harmony and counterpoint with Jeppesen and piano with Christiansen at the Copenhagen Cons. (1943–46); later studied composition with Boulanger and analysis with Messiaen in Paris (1948–49). Between 1958 and 1963 he took part in ethnomusicological expeditions to Arabia, India, Greece, and eastern Greenland and wrote numerous valuable papers on the folklore and musical cultures of the areas he visited. He worked until 1960 for the Danish Ministry of Education as a legal expert on music copyright; served as chairman of the Danish Soc. of Composers (1962–67); taught ethnomusicology at the Univ. of Lund, Sweden (1967–69), and subsequently at the Univ. of Copenhagen. He was president of the International Council of Traditional Music (formerly the International Folk Music Council) from 1977 until his death. He was a music critic for the newspapers *Morgenbladet* (1945–46), *Information* (1949–54), and *Berlingske Tidende* (1954–74). Much of his music embodies materials of non-European cultures, reflecting the influence of his travels. His *Elegy* for Organ (1953) is the first serial work written by a Danish composer.

WRITINGS: *Musiketnologi* (Copenhagen, 1974); with J. Jenkins, *Music and Musical Instruments in the World of Islam* (London, 1976).

WORKS: DRAMATIC: OPERAS: *Belisa*, after García Lorca (1964; Copenhagen, Sept. 3, 1969); *Usher*, after Poe (1980). **BALLETS:** *Ragnarök* (Twilight of the Gods; 1948; Copenhagen, Sept. 12, 1960); *La Création* (1952; Copenhagen, March 10, 1961); *Brylluppet* (The Wedding; 1966; Copenhagen, Sept. 15, 1969); *Den Fremmede* (The Stranger; 1969; Copenhagen, July 17, 1972). **ORCH.:** *Symphonic Variations* (1953); Piano Concerto (1953–54); *Sinfonia I* (1957–58; Copenhagen, April 13, 1959) and *II: Susudil* (Copenhagen, Oct. 31, 1966); *Capriccio* (1961–62); *Et russisk bal* (The Russian Ball), 3 dances (1965); *Au Fond de la nuit* for Chamber Orch. (1968); *Randrussermarchen* (1977); *Lux Coelestis* (1978). **CHAMBER:** *2 Pieces* for Clarinet and Piano (1943); *Romance* for Cello and Piano (1943); Violin Sonata (1946); 2 string quartets (1948, 1969); *Serenade* for Violin and Piano (1949); 2 piano trios (1950, 1976); *Prolana* for Clarinet, Violin, and Piano (1955); Cello Sonata (1956); *The Dream of Pan* for Flute (1959); *Nouba*, 6 movements for Harp (1960); *Passacaglia* for Flute, Violin, Cello, and Piano (1960); *Patet* for 9 Musicians (1966); *How to Play in D major without Caring about It*, fantasy for 2 Accordions (1967); *Arabesk* for 7 Musicians (1968); *Shangri-La* for Flute, Viola d'Amore, and Piano (1969); *Pour une Viola d'Amour* (1969); *Rencontres* for Cello and Percussion (1970); *Poème* for Accordian, Guitar, and Percussion (1973); Concertino for Clarinet, Violin, Cello, and Piano (1973); *Partita* for Cello (1974); *Nostalgie* for Guitar (1976); *Danse élégiaque* for Flute and Guitar (1978); *A Dream of Violet* for String Trio (1982). **PIANO:** 3 sonatinas (1941, 1951, 1967); *Theme with Variations* (1947); 2 sonatas for Piano, 4-hands (1948, 1967); *12 Préludes* (1948); 2 sonatas (1950, 1952); *3 Nocturnes* (1951); *Medardus*, suite (1956); *5 Inventions* (1957); *Bagatelles* (1962); *Images* (1965); *4 Innocent Sonatas* (1969); *Many Happy Returns* (1971). **VOCAL:** *Schicksalslieder*, after 4 Hölderlin poems, for Soprano or Tenor and 7 Instruments (1953); *Evening Songs* for Mezzo-soprano and Flute (1954); *Alapa-Tarana*, vocalise for Mezzo-soprano and Percussion (1959); *A l'inconnu* for Soprano or Tenor and 13 Instruments (1962); *Kejseren* (The Emperor) for Tenor, Men's Chorus, and Orch. (1963; Copenhagen, Sept. 5, 1964); *A Song of Mira Bai* for Chorus, 3 Trumpets, and Percussion (1971); *Air* for Mezzo-soprano, Saxophone, and Piano (1976); *The Planets* for Mezzo-soprano, Flute, Viola, and Guitar (1978).

Olsen, (Carl Gustav) Sparre, Norwegian composer; b. Stavanger, April 25, 1903; d. Oslo, Nov. 8, 1984. He studied composition with Valen and Brustad in Christiania (1925–30), Butting in Berlin, in Vienna, and with Grainger in London. He was violinist in the Christiania Phil. (1923–33); was active as a music teacher, music critic, and choral conductor in Bergen (1934–40). In 1936 he received a government life pension; in 1968, was awarded the Order of St. Olav. He publ. the books *Percy Grainger* (Oslo, 1963), *Tor Jonsson-Minne* (Oslo, 1968), and *Sparretonar* (Oslo, 1973). His music followed in the national tradition.

WORKS: ORCH.: *Symphonic Fantasia I* (Oslo, Sept. 21, 1939), *II* (Oslo, Oct. 6, 1957), and *III* (1973; Bergen, Nov. 28, 1974); *Serenade* for Flute and Strings (1954); *Intrada* (1956); *Canticum* (1972). **CHAMBER:** Wind Quintet (1946); String Quartet (1972); *Metamorfose* for Cello (1982). **VOCAL:** *2 Edda Songs* for Voice and Orch. or Piano (1931); *Draumkvedet* (The Dream Ballad) for Narrator, Soloists, Chorus, and Orch. (Bergen, April 19, 1937); sacred choruses; other songs.

Olson, Lynn (Freeman), American composer and piano pedagogue; b. Minneapolis, June 5, 1938; d. N.Y., Nov. 18, 1987. He studied at the Univ. of Minnesota. After graduation, he devoted himself mainly to musical education; he also ran a successful radio series under the inviting title "It's Time for Music." He publ. hundreds of semi-classical piano pieces suitable for teaching, songs, and choruses.

Olsson, Otto (Emanuel), eminent Swedish organist, pedagogue, and composer; b. Stockholm, Dec. 19, 1879; d. there, Sept. 1, 1964. He studied with Lagergren and Dente at the Stockholm Cons. (1897–1901), where he subsequently taught (1908–45); also was organist of the Gustav Vasa Church in Stockholm (1908–56). He became a member of the Royal Academy of Music in 1915.

WORKS: *Requiem* for Soli, Chorus, and Orch. (1903; Stockholm, Nov. 14, 1976); 3 string quartets (1903, 1906, 1947); 2 organ syms. (1903, 1918); *Te Deum* for Chorus, Strings, Harp, and Organ (1906); 3 sets of *Preludes and Fugues* for Organ (1910–11; 1918; 1935); piano pieces; choral works; songs.

O'Mara, Joseph, Irish tenor; b. Limerick, July 16, 1861; d. Dublin, Aug. 5, 1927. He studied with Moretti in Milan. On Feb. 4, 1891, he made his debut as Sullivan's Ivanhoe at the Royal English Opera House in London. After further training from Perini and Edwin Holland, he toured under the auspices of Augustus Harris. From 1902 to 1908 he was the principal tenor of the Moody-Manners Opera Co. In 1910 he became a member of Beecham's Co. at London's Covent Garden. From 1912 to 1924 he was director of his own O'Mara Grand Opera Co., with which he often appeared in leading roles.

Oncina, Juan, Spanish tenor; b. Barcelona, April 15, 1925. He was a student in Oran, Algeria, and of Mercedes Caspir in Barcelona. In 1946 he made his Italian operatic debut as Count Almaviva in Bologna, and subsequently appeared with leading Italian opera houses. From 1952 to 1961 he also sang at the Glyndebourne Festivals. While he was best known for his roles in operas by Mozart, Rossini, and Donizetti, he also appeared in operas by Verdi and Puccini.

Ondříček, Emanuel, Czech violinist and pedagogue; b. Pilsen, Dec. 6, 1882; d. Boston, Dec. 30, 1958. He studied with his father, then with Ševčik at the Prague Cons. (1894–99). After touring Europe, he emigrated to the U.S. (1912); then taught in Boston and N.Y. He publ. *The Mastery of Tone Production and Expression on the Violin* (1931).

Onégin, (Elisabeth Elfriede Emilie) Sigrid (née **Hoffmann**), noted German contralto; b. Stockholm (of a German father and a French mother), June 1, 1889; d. Magliaso, Switzerland, June 16, 1943. She studied in Frankfurt am Main with Resz, in Munich with E.R. Weiss, and with di Ranieri in Milan. She made her first public appearance, under the name Lilly Hoffmann, in Wiesbaden, Sept. 16, 1911, in a recital, accompanied by the Russian pianist and composer Eugene Onégin (real name, Lvov; b. St. Petersburg, Oct. 10, 1883; d. Stuttgart, Nov. 12, 1919; he was a grandnephew of Alexis Lvov, composer of the Russian Czarist hymn). She married him on May 25, 1913; after his death, she married a German doctor, Fritz Penzoldt (Nov. 20, 1920). She made her first operatic appearance as Carmen in Stuttgart on Oct. 10, 1912; made her first appearance in London in 1913; was a member of the Bavarian State Opera in Munich (1919–22). On Nov. 22, 1922, she made her Metropolitan Opera debut in N.Y. as Amneris, continuing on its roster until 1924. She subsequently sang in Berlin (1926–31), at London's Covent Garden (1927), the Salzburg Festivals (1931–32), in Zürich (1931–35), and at the Bayreuth Festivals (1933–34). She made her last appearances in the U.S. as a recitalist in 1938. Among her most distinguished roles were Gluck's Orfeo, Eboli, Fidès, Erda, Lady Macbeth, Fricka, Waltraute, and Brangäne.

BIBL.: F. Penzoldt, *Alt-Rhapsodie; S. O., Leben und Werk* (Magdeburg, 1939; 3rd ed., 1953).

O'Neill, Norman (Houstoun), English conductor and composer; b. London, March 14, 1875; d. there, March 3, 1934. He was a direct descendant of John Wall Callcott; his father was a painter. He studied in London with Arthur Somervell (1890–93), and later with Knorr in Frankfurt am Main (1893–97). Returning to London in 1899, he married the pianist Adine Rückert (1875–1947). He wrote incidental music for the Haymarket Theatre, of which he was music director from 1908 to 1919 and again 1920 to 1934; from 1924 to 1934 he taught at the Royal Academy of Music in London. He also composed 3 ballets, orch. works, chamber music, choral works, piano pieces, and songs.

BIBL.: D. Hudson, *N. O.: A Life of Music* (London, 1945).

Ono, Yoko, Japanese-born American vocalist, songwriter, and performance artist; b. Tokyo, Feb. 18, 1933. She was born to a wealthy banking family. In 1947 she moved to N.Y., where she entered Sarah Lawrence College (1953). She became active in Manhattan conceptual-art circles, and in 1966 met John Lennon of the Beatles; they became companions and collaborators, marrying in 1969. Under her influence, Lennon became interested in avant-garde ideas that drew him away from rock, contributing to the breakup of the Beatles in 1970. After Lennon's death in 1980, Ono produced several posthumous collaborations. Her solo recordings include *Yoko Ono/Plastic Ono Band* (1970), *Fly* (1971), *Approximately Infinite Universe* (1973), *Feeling the Space* (1973), *Seasons of Glass* (1981), *It's Alright* (1982), and *Every Man Has a Woman* (1984). Her recordings with Lennon include *Unfinished Music no. 1: 2 Virgins* (1968) and *no. 2: Life with the Lions* (1969), *Wedding Album* (1969), *Live Peace in Toronto* 1969 (1970), *Double Fantasy* (1980), *Milk and Honey* (1982), and *Heart Play: Unfinished Dialogue* (1983). Ono's work is often bizarre, her shrill tremolo voice moving over a fluid, arrhythmic background reflecting Asian influences; some of her recordings, notably those between 1980 and 1984, are popular in style. In 1992 she released *Onobox*, a collection of 6 compact discs featuring a wide range of music, from pop to serious scores. Her musical *N.Y. Rock* was premiered in N.Y. on March 30, 1994.

BIBL.: J. Cott and C. Doudna, eds., *The Ballad of John and Yoko* (N.Y., 1982).

Opieński, Henryk, Polish conductor, music scholar, teacher, and composer; b. Kraków, Jan. 13, 1870; d. Morges, Switzerland, Jan. 21, 1942. He studied with Zeleński in Kraków, with d'Indy in Paris, and with H. Urban in Berlin; then went to Leipzig, where he studied musicology with Riemann and conducting with Nikisch. In 1907 he was appointed an instructor at the Warsaw Musical Soc.; from 1908 to 1912 he conducted the Warsaw Opera; in 1912 he went again to Germany, where he took his degree of Ph.D. (Univ. of Leipzig, 1914). He spent the years of World War I in Morges, Switzerland; returning to Poland, he was director of the Poznań Cons. (1919–26); then settled again in Morges. He publ. several books and essays on Chopin (Lemberg, 1910; 2nd ed., 1922); also the collected letters of Chopin in Polish, German, French, and Eng. (1931); other writings include a history of Polish music (Warsaw, 1912; 2nd ed., 1922); *La Musique polonaise* (Paris, 1918; 2nd ed., 1929); a monograph on Paderewski (Lemberg, 1910; 2nd ed., 1928; Fr. tr., Lausanne, 1928; 2nd ed., 1948); a valuable monograph on Moniuszko (Warsaw, 1924).

WORKS: 2 operas: *Maria* (1904; Poznań, April 27, 1923) and *Jakub lutnista* (Jacob the Lutenist; 1916–18; Poznań, Dec. 21, 1927); 2 symphonic poems: *Lilla Weneda* (1908) and *Love and*

Destiny (1912); *Scènes lyriques en forme de quatuor* for String Quartet; violin pieces; *The Prodigal Son*, oratorio (1930); many songs.

BIBL.: A. Forenerod, *H. O.* (Lausanne, 1942).

Oppens, Ursula, talented American pianist; b. N.Y., Feb. 2, 1944. She studied economics and English literature at Radcliffe College (B.A., 1965); then studied with Rosina Lhévinne and Leonard Shure at the Juilliard School of Music in N.Y. She won 1st prize at the Busoni Competition in Italy in 1969. Returning to the U.S., she co-founded Speculum Musicae in N.Y., a chamber music ensemble devoted to performing contemporary music; also appeared with other chamber music groups, as a recitalist, and as a soloist with major U.S. orchs. In 1976 she was awarded the Avery Fisher Prize. Her expansive repertory ranges from the classics to the cosmopolitan avant-garde.

Oppitz, Gerhard, German pianist and teacher; b. Frauenau, Feb. 5, 1953. He began piano lessons as a child and made his first public appearance when he was 12. In 1973 he pursued further training in the master class of Wilhelm Kempff. After winning 1st prize in the Rubinstein Competition in Tel Aviv in 1977, he appeared as a soloist with the world's major orchs. and gave recitals in the leading music centers. From 1981 he was also a prof. at the Munich Hochschule für Musik. His catholic repertoire ranges from the standard literature to the contemporary era.

Orbán, György, Hungarian composer; b. Tîrgu-Mureş, Romania, July 12, 1947. He was a student of Toduţa and Jagamas at the Cluj Cons. (1968–73). After serving on its faculty (1973–79), he went to Budapest and was an ed. at Editio Musica Budapest and a teacher at the Academy of Music.

WORKS: ORCH.: 2 serenades (1984, 1985). **CHAMBER:** Sonata for Solo Violin (1970); Triple Sextet (1980); Wind Quintet (1985); Brass Quintet (1987); Sonata Concertante for Clarinet and Piano (1987); Bassoon Sonata (1987); 2 violin sonatas (1989, 1991); piano pieces. **VOCAL:** *5 Canons to Poems by Attila József* for Soprano and Chamber Ensemble (1977); Duo No. 1 for Soprano and Clarinet (1979), No. 2 for Soprano and Double Bass (1987), No. 3 for Soprano and Cello (1989), and No. 4 for Soprano and Violin (1992); *Stabat Mater* for Chorus (1987); 7 masses (1990–93); *Rotate Coeli*, oratorio for Chorus and Orch. (1992); *Regina Martyrum*, oratorio for Chorus and Orch. (1993); several choral cycles.

Orbón (de Soto), Julián, Spanish-American composer; b. Aviles, Aug. 7, 1925; d. Miami Beach, May 20, 1991. He entered the Oviedo Cons. when he was 10. In 1938 he went with his family to Havana, where he continued his training under his father (piano) and Ardévol (composition). After completing his training in composition with Copland at the Berkshire Music Center in Tanglewood (summer, 1945), he returned to Havana and became director of his father's Orbón Cons. in 1946. In the wake of the Cuban Revolution, he went to Mexico City in 1960 and worked with Chávez at the National Cons. until 1963. In 1964 he settled in the U.S. In 1964–65 he taught at the State Univ. of N.Y at Purchase and at Washington Univ. in St. Louis. He subsequently concentrated his efforts on composition. In 1959 and 1969 he held Guggenheim fellowships. In 1967 he received an award from the American Academy of Arts and Letters. After composing works revealing Spanish and Cuban stylistic traits, he turned to a more expressive Romantic style in his later scores.

WORKS: ORCH.: Sym. (1945); *Homenaje a la tonadilla* (1947); *Tres versiones sinfónicas* (1953; Caracas, Dec. 11, 1954); *Danzas sinfónicas* (1955; Miami, Nov. 17, 1957); Concerto Grosso (1958; N.Y., Nov. 8, 1961); *Partita* No. 3 (1965) and No. 4 for Piano and Orch. (1982–85; Dallas, April 11, 1985). **CHAMBER:** *Concerto da camera* for Horn, English Horn, Trumpet, Cello, and Piano (1944); String Quartet (1951); *Preludio y danza* for Guitar (1951); *Partita* No. 1 for Harpsichord (1963) and No. 2 for Harpsichord, Vibraphone, Celesta, Harmonium, and String Quartet (1964); numerous piano pieces; organ music. **VOCAL:** *Crucifixus*, motet for Chorus (1953); *Hymnus ad galli cantum* for Soprano, Flute, Oboe, Clarinet, Harp, and String Quartet (1956); *Tres cantigas del rey* for Soprano, String Quartet, Harpsichord, and Percussion (1960); *Monte Gelboe* for Tenor and Orch. (1962); *Introito* for Chorus (1967–68); *Oficios: Liturgia de tres días* for Chorus and Orch. (1970–75); *Dos canciones folklóricas* for Chorus (1972); *Libro de cantares* for Mezzo-soprano and Piano (1987).

BIBL.: V. Yedra, *J. O.: A Biographical and Critical Essay* (Miami, 1990).

Orchard, William (Arundel), English-born Australian pianist, conductor, and composer; b. London, April 13, 1867; d. during a voyage in the South Atlantic off the coast of South Africa (23°49′S; 9°33′E), April 17, 1961. He studied in London and Durham. In 1903 he went to Australia and lived in Sydney, where he was active as a conductor and music educator; served as director of the New South Wales State Cons. (1923–34); later taught at the Univ. of Tasmania. He wrote an opera, *The Picture of Dorian Gray*; Violin Concerto; String Quartet; String Quintet; choruses; songs. He publ. 2 books on Australian music: *The Distant View* (Sydney, 1943) and *Music in Australia* (Melbourne, 1952).

Ord, Boris, English organist, harpsichordist, and conductor; b. Bristol, July 9, 1987; d. Cambridge, Dec. 30, 1961. He was educated at the Royal College of Music in London and was an organ scholar at Corpus Christi College, Cambridge. From 1929 to 1957 he was organist and choirmaster at King's College, Cambridge, where he made the Christmas Eve Festival of 9 Lessons and Carols celebrated via the radio. He also was a lecturer on music at the Univ. of Cambridge (1936–58) and was conductor of its Musical Soc. (1938–54). He composed the carol *Adam lay y-bounden* (1957). In 1958 he was made a Commander of the Order of the British Empire. As both a solo artist and conductor, Ord distinguished himself in an extensive repertoire.

BIBL.: P. Radcliffe, *B. O.: A Memoir* (Cambridge, 1962).

Ore, Cecilie, Norwegian composer; b. Oslo, July 19, 1954. She studied piano at the Norwegian State Academy of Music in Oslo and in Paris; then pursued training in composition at the Sweelinck Cons. in Amsterdam with Ton de Leeuw and attended the Inst. of Sonology at the Univ. of Utrecht. In 1988 her *Prophyre* for Orch. was named the Norwegian composition of the year, and she was awarded the Norwegian state guaranteed income for artists. In her output, Ore creates multi-layered constructs in which sonority and rhythm play essential roles. Her use of the computer has become highly significant in her approach to composition.

WORKS: DRAMATIC: THEATER: *Prologos*, electro-acoustic music (1990). **FILM:** *Kald Verden*, electro-acoustic music (1986). **TELEVISION:** *Im-Mobile*, electro-acoustic music (1984); *Contracanthus* for Double Bass (1987). **ORCH.:** *Prophyre* (1986); *Nunc et Nunc* (1994). **CHAMBER:** *Helices* for Wind Quintet (1984); *Janus* for Cello (1985); *Praesens Subitus* for Amplified String Quartet (1989); *Erat Erit Est* for Amplified Chamber Ensemble (1991); *Futurum Exactum* for Amplified String Ensemble (1992); *Lex Temporis* for Amplified String Quartet (1992). **VOCAL:** *Carnatus* for Soprano and Chorus (1982); *Calliope* for Soprano (1984); *Ex Oculus* for 2 Tenors, Baritone, and Bass (1985); *Cantus Aquatoris* for Soprano, Alto, Tenor, and Bass (1987). **TAPE:** *Vacuus* (1986); *Etapper* (1988). **MULTIMEDIA:** *Im-Moible (I+II+III)*, electro-acoustic music sculptures (1984).

Orel, Alfred, distinguished Austrian musicologist; b. Vienna, July 3, 1889; d. there, April 11, 1967. He studied law at the Univ. of Vienna, graduating in 1912; then was employed in the Ministry of Finance until 1918; subsequently studied musicology with Guido Adler at the Univ. of Vienna, where he received his Ph.D. in 1919 with the diss. *Die Hauptstimme in den "Salve regina" der Trienter Codices*; he completed his Habilitation there in 1922 with his *Über rhythmische Qualität in mehrstimmigen Tonsätzen des 15. Jahrhunderts*. He was director of the music division of the Vienna Stadtbibliothek (1918–40); was also librarian of the Inst. of Musicology (1918–22) and a reader in music history (1929–45) at the Univ. of Vienna. He was particularly noted for his work on the life and music of Anton Bruckner.

WRITINGS: *Unbekannte Frühwerke Anton Bruckners* (Vienna, 1921); *Ein Wiener Beethoven-Buch* (Vienna, 1921); *Anton Bruckner: Das Werk—Der Künstler—Die Zeit* (Vienna and Leipzig, 1925); *Wiener Musikerbriefe aus zwei Jahrhunderten* (Vienna, 1925); *Beethoven* (Vienna, 1927); with R. Stöhr and H. Gál, *Formenlehre der Musik* (Leipzig, 1933; 2nd ed., 1954); *Anton Bruckner, 1824–1896: Sein Leben in Bildern* (Leipzig, 1936); *Kirchenmusikalische Liturgik* (Augsburg, 1936); *Franz Schubert, 1797–1828: Sein Leben in Bildern* (Leipzig, 1939); *Aufsätze und Vorträge* (Vienna and Berlin, 1939); *Ein Harmonielehrekolleg bei Anton Bruckner* (Vienna and Berlin, 1940); *Der junge Schubert* (Vienna, 1940); *Mozarts deutscher Weg: Eine Deutung aus Briefen* (Vienna, 1940; 2nd ed., 1943); *Grillparzer und Beethoven* (Vienna, 1941); *Mozart in Wien* (Vienna, 1944); *Hugo Wolf: Ein Künstlerbildnis* (Vienna, 1947); *Johannes Brahms: Ein Meister und sein Weg* (Olten, 1948); *Goethe als Operndirektor* (Bregenz, 1949); *Bruckner-Brevier: Briefe, Dokumente, Berichte* (Vienna, 1953); *Musikstadt Wien* (Vienna, 1953); *Mozart, Gloria Mundi* (Salzburg, 1956); ed. *Johannes Brahms und Julius Allgeyer: Eine Künstlerfreundschaft in Briefen* (Tutzing, 1964).

BIBL.: H. Federhofer, ed., *Festschrift A. O. zum 70. Geburtstag überreicht von Kollegen, Freunden und Schülern* (Vienna and Wiesbaden, 1960).

Orel, Dobroslav, Czech ecclesiastical music scholar and choral conductor; b. Ronov, near Prague, Dec. 15, 1870; d. Prague, Feb. 18, 1942. He studied music with Novák and Hostinský in Prague; later musicology with Adler at the Univ. of Vienna. In 1914 he received a Ph.D. there with the diss. *Der Mensuralkodex Speciálník: Ein Beiträg zur Geschichte der Mensuralmusik und der Notenschrift in Böhmen bis 1540.* He was ordained a priest; was a prof. at the Prague Cons. (1907–19); from 1909 to 1918 he was ed. of the Prague church music periodical *Cyrill*; from 1921 to 1938 he was a prof. of musicology at the Komensky Univ., Bratislava; was active as a conductor of various choral societies. He greatly distinguished himself as an authority on Czech liturgical music.

WRITINGS (all in Czech and publ. in Bratislava unless otherwise given): *A Theoretical and Practical Manual of Roman Plainsong* (Hradec Králové, 1899); *A Czech Hymnbook* (Prague, 1921; 5th ed., 1936); *The Franus Hymnbook* (Prague, 1922); *The Beginnings of Polyphony in Bohemia* (1925); *Ján Levoslav Bella* (1924); *František Liszt a Bratislava* (1925); *Musical Sources in the Franciscan Library in Bratislava* (1930); *St. Wenceslas Elements in Music* (Prague, 1937); J. Potúček, ed., *Contributions to the History of Slovak Music* (1968).

Orff, Carl, outstanding German composer and music educator; b. Munich, July 10, 1895; d. there, March 29, 1982. He took courses with Beer-Walbrunn and Zilcher at the Munich Academy of Music (graduated, 1914); later had additional instruction from Heinrich Kaminski in Munich. He was a conductor at the Munich Kammerspiele (1915–17); after military service during World War I (1917–18), he conducted at the Mannheim National Theater and the Darmstadt Landestheater (1918–19); later was conductor of Munich's Bach Soc. (1930–33). Orff initiated a highly important method of musical education, which was adopted not only in Germany but in England, America, and Russia. It stemmed from the Günther School for gymnastics, dance, and music, founded in Munich in 1924 by Orff with Dorothee Günther with the aim of promoting instrumental playing and understanding of rhythm among children. He commissioned the piano manufacturer Karl Maendler to construct special percussion instruments that would be extremely easy to play; these "Orff instruments" became widely adopted in American schools. Orff's ideas of rhythmic training owe much to the eurhythmics of Jaques-Dalcroze, but he simplified them to reach the elementary level; as a manual, he compiled a set of musical exercises, *Schulwerk* (1930–35; rev. 1950–54). He also taught composition at the Munich Staatliche Hochschule für Musik (1950–55). As a composer, Orff sought to revive the early monodic forms and to adapt them to modern tastes by means of dissonant counterpoint, with lively rhythm in asymmetrical patterns, producing a form of "total theater." His most famous score is the scenic oratorio *Carmina Burana* (Frankfurt am Main, June 8, 1937), with words (in Latin and German) drawn from 13th-century student poems found in the Benediktbeuren monastery in Bavaria ("Burana" is the Latin adjective of the locality). His other works include: *Der Mond*, opera, after a fairy tale by Grimm (1937–38; Munich, Feb. 5, 1939; rev. 1945; Munich, Nov. 26, 1950); *Die Kluge*, opera, after a fairy tale by Grimm (1941–42; Frankfurt am Main, Feb. 20, 1943); *Catulli Carmina*, scenic cantata after Catullus (Leipzig, Nov. 6, 1943); *Die Bernauerin*, musical play (1944–45; Stuttgart, June 15, 1947); *Antigonae*, musical play after Sophocles (1947–48; Salzburg, Aug. 9, 1949); *Trionfo di Afrodite* (1950–51; 3rd part of a triology under the general title *Trionfi*, the 1st and 2nd parts being *Carmina Burana* and *Catulli Carmina*; Milan, Feb. 13, 1953); *Astutuli*, opera-ballet (1945–46; Munich, Oct. 20, 1953); *Comoedia de Christi Resurrectione*, Easter cantata (1955; Munich, March 31, 1956); *Oedipus der Tyrann*, musical play after Sophocles (1957–58; Stuttgart, Dec. 11, 1959); *Ludus de nato infante mirificus*, Nativity play (Stuttgart, Dec. 11, 1960); *Prometheus*, opera (1963–67; Stuttgart, March 24, 1968); *Rota* for Voices and Instruments, after the canon *Sumer is icumen in*, composed as a "salute to youth" for the opening ceremony of the Munich Olympics (1972); *De temporum fine comoedia*, stage play (1969–71; Salzburg, 1973). He further wrote a dance play, *Der Feuerfarbene* (1925); *Präludium* for Orch. (1925); Concertino for Wind Instruments and Harpsichord (1927); *Entrata* for Orch., based on melodies of William Byrd (1928; rev. 1940); *Festival Music* for Chamber Orch. (1928); *Bayerische Musik* for Small Ensemble (1934); *Olympischer Reigen* for Various Instruments (1936); 3 stage works after Monteverdi: *Klage der Ariadne* (Karlsruhe, 1925; rev. version, Gera, 1940), *Orpheus* (Mannheim, April 17, 1925; 2nd version, Munich, Oct. 13, 1929; 3rd version, Dresden, Oct. 4, 1940), and *Tanz der Spröden* (Karlsruhe, 1925; rev. version, Gera, 1940). In 1984 the Carl Orff Foundation was organized.

BIBL.: W. Trittenhoff, *O.-Schulwerk: Einführung* (Mainz, 1930); A. Liess, *C. O.: Idee und Werk* (Zürich, 1955; 2nd ed., rev., 1977; Eng. tr., 1966); K. Ruppel, G. Sellner, and W. Thomas, *C. O., ein Bericht in Wort und Bild* (Mainz, 1955; 2nd ed., rev., 1960; Eng. tr., 1960); I. Kiekert, *Die musikalische Form in den Werken C. O.s* (Regensburg, 1957); M. Devreese-Papgnies, *Sur les traces du Schulwerk de C. O., Méthodologie pour l'usage des instruments d'orchestre scolaire* (Brussels, 1968); F. Willnauer, ed., *Prometheus: Mythos, Drama, Musik: Beiträge zu C. O.s Musikdrama nach Aischylos* (Tübingen, 1968); U. Klement, *Das Musiktheater C. O.s: Untersuchungen zu einem bürgerlichen Kunstwerk* (diss., Univ. of Leipzig, 1969); G. Keetman, *Elementaria: Erster Umgang mit dem O.Schulwerk* (Stuttgart, 1970; Eng. tr., 1974); R. Münster, ed., *C. O.: das Bühnenwerk* (Munich, 1970); H. Wolfgart, ed., *Das O.- Schulwerk im Dienste der Erziehung und Therapie behinderter Kinder* (Berlin, 1971); W. Thomas, *C. O.: De temporum fine comoedia . . . eine Interpretation* (Tutzing, 1973); G. Orff, *The O. Music Therapy* (London, 1980); U. Klement, *Das Musiktheater C. O.s* (Leipzig, 1982); H. Leuchtmann, *C. O.: ein Gedenkbuch* (Tutzing, 1985); G. Orff-Büchtemann, *Mein Vater und ich: Erinnerungen an C. O.* (Munich, 1992); A. Fassone, *C. O.* (Lucca, 1994).

Orgad, Ben-Zion, German-born Israeli composer; b. Gelsenkirchen, Aug. 21, 1926. He went to Palestine in 1933 and studied with Ben-Haim (1942–47), and also took courses at the Rubin Academy of Music (graduated, 1947). He later studied with Copland at the Berkshire Music Center in Tanglewood (summers, 1949, 1951, 1961) and with Fine and Shapero at Brandeis Univ. (M.F.A. in musicology, 1962). From 1950 to 1988 he worked for the Israeli Ministry of Education and Culture.

WORKS: ORCH.: *Building the King's Stage* (1957); *Music* for Horn and Orch. (1960; rev. 1988); *Kaleidoscope* (1961); *Movement on A* (1965); *First Watch* for Strings (1969); *Melodic Dialogues on 3 Scrolls* (1969); *Ballad* (1971); *Second Watch* for Chamber Orch. (1973; rev. for Orch., 1982); *Dialogues on the First Scroll* for Chamber Orch. (1975); *A Vigil in Jerusalem: Third Watch* (1978); *Song of Praise* (1979); *Individuations I*, concertante for Clarinet and Chamber Orch. (1981; rev. 1984) and *II*, concertante for Violin, Cello, and Chamber Orch. (1990); *She'arim* for Brass Orch. (1986); *Filigrees V*, concertante for Chamber Orch. (1993) and *VI* for Strings (1993); *Toccata in Galilean Maqam: Choregraphic Tonescapes* (Tel Aviv, Nov. 24, 1994). **CHAMBER:** *Ballad* for Violin (1947); *Monolog* for Viola (1957); Septet for Clarinet, Bassoon, Horn, Violin, Viola, Cello, and Double Bass (1959); Duo for Violin and Cello (1960); String Trio (1961); *Tak'sim* for Harp (1962); *Landscapes* for Wind Quintet (1969); *Songs without Words* for Flute, Piano, Clarinet, Violin, Cello, Piano, and Percussion (1970); *Filigrees I* for Clarinet and String Quartet (1989–90), *II* for Oboe or English Horn and String Quartet (1990), *III* for Bassoon and String Quartet (1992), and *IV*, septet for Clarinet, Bassoon, Horn, Violin, Viola, Cello, and Double Bass (1993); *Melosalgia* for 2 Trumpets (1993). **PIANO:** *Toccata* (1946); *2 Preludes in Impressionistic Mood* (1960); *7 Variations on C* (1961); *Reshuyoth* (1978). **VOCAL:** *Leave Out My Name*, song cycle for Mezzo-soprano and Flute (1947); *The Beauty of Israel*, sym. for Baritone and Orch. (1949); *Isaiah's Vision*, biblical cantata for Chorus and Orch. (1952); *The Story of the Spies*, biblical cantata for Chorus, Narrator ad libitum, and Orch. (1952); *Out of the Desert*, quintet for Mezzo-soprano or Contralto, Flute, Bassoon, Viola, and Cello (1956); *Mizmorim*, cantata for Soloists and Chamber Orch. (1966–68); (4) *Songs of an Early Morning* for Mezzo-soprano, Baritone, and Chamber Orch. (1968); *Death Came to the Wooden Horse Michael*, ballad for 2 Mezzo-sopranos and Chamber Ensemble (1968; rev. 1977); *The Old Decrees*, Passion in 5 Testimonies for Soloists, Chorus, and Chamber Orch. (1970; rev. 1987; Cologne, Nov. 3, 1990); *Story of a Pipe* for Soloists, Chorus, and Orch. (1971); *Sufferings for Redemption*, cantata for Mezzo-soprano, Women's Chorus, and Chamber Orch. (1974); *Songs Out of Hoshen Valley* for Chorus (1981); *Sh'ar Larashut* for Chorus (1988).

O'Riley, Christopher, talented American pianist; b. Chicago, April 17, 1956. He began piano lessons with Lilli Simon when he was only 4; later studied with Russell Sherman at the New England Cons. of Music in Boston. After winning 2nd prize in the Montreal Competition (1980), 5th prize in both the Van Cliburn and Leeds competitions (1981), and 6th prize in the Busoni Competition (1981), he made his formal recital debut in N.Y. in 1981; that same year he made his European debut in a recital in Amsterdam. He subsequently appeared as soloist with leading orchs. of the U.S. and Europe, gave recitals, and played in chamber music concerts. His programs often include rarely heard works both in the standard and the contemporary piano literature.

Orlov, Nikolai (Andreievich), talented Russian pianist; b. Elets, Orlov district, Feb. 26, 1892; d. Grantown-on-Spey, Scotland, May 31, 1964. He studied in Moscow at the Gnessin Music School and then with Igumnov at the Cons. (graduated, 1910); also studied privately with Taneyev. He launched his career in 1912; was also a teacher at the Phil. School (1913–15) and a prof. at the Cons. (1916–21) in Moscow; then toured extensively in Europe, the U.S., and Latin America, settling in England in 1948. He was one of the finest Russian pianists of his day.

Ormandy, Eugene (real name, **Jenö Blau**), outstanding Hungarian-born American conductor; b. Budapest, Nov. 18, 1899; d. Philadelphia, March 12, 1985. He first studied violin at a very early age with his father, and at age 5 he was admitted to the Royal Academy of Music in Budapest. At 9, he became a student of Hubay there, receiving his artist's diploma at 13. When he was 17 he joined its faculty. He also pursued training in philosophy at the Univ. of Budapest. In 1917 he became concertmaster of the Blüthner Orch. in Germany, and also made tours as a soloist and recitalist. In 1921 he emigrated to the U.S. and in 1927 became a naturalized American citizen. He became a violinist in the pit orch. at the Capitol Theater in N.Y. in 1921, and soon thereafter became its concertmaster. In Sept. 1924 he made his debut as a conductor with the orch., and in 1926 he was named its assoc. music director. He appeared as a guest conductor with the N.Y. Phil. at the Lewisohn Stadium in 1929 and with the Philadelphia Orch. at Robin Hood Dell in 1930. Ormandy first attracted national attention when he substituted for an indisposed Toscanini at a Philadelphia Orch. concert on Oct. 30, 1931. His unqualified success led to his appointment as conductor of the Minneapolis Sym. Orch. in 1931. In 1936 he was invited to serve as assoc. conductor with Stokowski of the Philadelphia Orch. On Sept. 28, 1938, Ormany was formally named music director of the Philadelphia Orch., a position he retained with great distinction until his retirement in 1980. Thereafter he held its title of Conductor Laureate. Ormandy's 42-year tenure as music director of the Philadelphia Orch. was the longest of any conductor of a major American orch. Under his guidance, the Philadelphia Orch. not only retained its renown from the Stokowski era but actually enhanced its reputation through many tours in North America and abroad, innumerable recordings, and radio and television broadcasts. Between 1937 and 1977 Ormandy led it on 9 transcontinental tours of the U.S. In 1949 he took it to England, in 1955 and 1958 to the Continent. In 1973 he took it to the People's Republic of China, the first U.S. orch. to visit that nation. Ormandy received numerous honors. In 1952 he was made an Officier and in 1958 a Commandeur of the French Légion d'honneur. In 1970 he was awarded the U.S. Medal of Freedom by President Richard M. Nixon. In 1976 Queen Elizabeth II made him an honorary Knight Commander of the Order of the British Empire. He also received various doctorates. Ormandy excelled as an interpreter of the Romantic repertoire, in which his mastery of orch. resources was most evident. It was his custom to conduct most of his concerts from memory.

Ornstein, Leo, remarkable Russian-born American pianist, teacher, and composer; b. Kremenchug, Dec. 11, 1892. The son of a synagogal cantor, he studied music at home; then with Vladimir Puchalsky in Kiev and, at the age of 10, with Essipova at the St. Petersburg Cons. As a consequence of anti-Semitic disturbances in Russia, the family emigrated to the U.S. in 1907. Ornstein studied piano with Bertha Feiring Tapper and Goetschius at the Inst. of Musical Art in N.Y. He gave his first concert in N.Y., as a pianist, on March 5, 1911; then played in Philadelphia and other cities. About 1910 he began to compose; he experimented with percussive sonorities, in dissonant harmonies; made a European tour in 1913–14; played in Norway, Denmark, and in Paris; appeared in London on March 27, 1914, in a piano recital announced as "futuristic music" and featuring his Sonata and other works. Returning to the U.S. early in 1915, he gave a series of recitals at the Bandbox Theater in N.Y., comprising works by Debussy, Ravel, Schoenberg, Scriabin, and other modern composers as well as his own; his *Danse sauvage* excited his audiences by its declared wildness and placed him in the center of controversy; he was hailed as the prophet of a new musical era. After several years as an active virtuoso, he turned mainly to teaching; was made head of the piano dept. of the Philadelphia Musical Academy (1920); also founded the Ornstein School of Music in Philadelphia (1940), and continued to teach until 1955. His 90th birthday was celebrated by a special concert of his works in N.Y. in 1982.

WORKS: ORCH.: *3 Moods: Anger, Peace, Joy* (1914); *The Fog*, symphonic poem (1915); *Evening Song of the Cossack* for Chamber Orch. (1923); Piano Concerto (1923; Philadelphia, Feb. 13, 1925); *Lysistrata Suite* (1930); *Nocturne and Dance of the Fates* (St. Louis, Feb. 12, 1937). **CHAMBER:** 2 violin sonatas (c.1915, c.1918); *3 Russian Impressions* for Violin and Piano (1916); 2 cello sonatas (c.1918, c.1920); Piano Quintet (1927); 3

string quartets (?, c.1929, 1976); 6 Préludes for Cello and Piano (1931); *Allegro (Intermezzo)* for Flute and Piano (1959); *Fantasy Pieces* for Viola and Piano (1972); *Hebraic Fantasy* for Violin and Piano (1975); *Poem* for Flute and Piano (1979); numerous piano works, including 6 sonatas and many solo pieces. **VOCAL:** *3 Russian Dances* (1918); songs.

BIBL.: F. Martens, *L. O.: The Man, His Ideas, His Work* (N.Y., 1918); V. Perlis, "The Futurist Music of L. O.," *Notes* (June 1975); T. Darter, Jr., *The Futurist Piano Music of L. O.* (diss., Cornell Univ., 1979).

Orozco, Rafael, Spanish pianist; b. Córdoba, Jan. 24, 1946; d. April 25, 1996. He studied at the Córdoba Cons., then at the Madrid Cons., where he graduated in 1964; also took piano lessons with Alexis Weissenberg at the Accademia Musicale Chigiana in Siena. In 1966 he won the Leeds Competition; subsequently toured extensively, receiving praise as a fine interpreter of the Romantic repertoire.

Orr, C(harles) W(ilfred), English composer; b. Cheltenham, July 31, 1893; d. Painswick, Gloucestershire, Feb. 24, 1976. He studied at the Guildhall School of Music in London. He wrote songs in the manner of German lieder, to words by English poets; his set of 7 songs to texts from Housman's *A Shropshire Lad* is notable.

BIBL.: S. Northcote, "The Songs of C.W. O.," *Music & Letters*, XVIII (1937).

Orr, Robin (actually, **Robert Kemsley**), Scottish composer, organist, and teacher; b. Brechin, June 2, 1909. He studied at the Royal College of Music in London (1926–29), and then was an organ scholar at Pembroke College, Cambridge (Mus.B., 1932); subsequently took his Mus.B. (1938) and Mus.D. (1950) at the Univ. of Cambridge; he also studied composition with Casella at the Accademia Musicale Chigiana in Siena (1934) and with Boulanger in Paris (1938). He was director of music at Sidcot School in Somerset (1933–36), and then was an assistant lecturer at the Univ. of Leeds (1936–38). From 1938 to 1941, and again from 1945 to 1951, he was organist and director of music at St. John's College, Cambridge. From 1947 to 1956 he was a lecturer at the Univ. of Cambridge, and from 1950 to 1956 he was a prof. at the Royal College of Music in London. After serving as the Gardiner prof. of music at the Univ. of Glasgow from 1956 to 1965, he was prof. of composition at the Univ. of Cambridge from 1965 to 1976. From 1962 to 1976 he served as the first chairman of the Scottish Opera in Glasgow. He was director of the Welsh National Opera in Cardiff from 1977 to 1983. In 1972 he was made a Commander of the Order of the British Empire. As a composer, Orr has been particularly adept at investing traditional forms with an individual voice of distinction.

WORKS: DRAMATIC: *A Winter's Tale*, incidental music to Shakepeare's play (1947); *Oedipus et Colonus*, incidental music to Sophocles's play (1950); *Deirdre of the Sorrows*, incidental music (1951); *Full Circle*, opera (Perth, April 10, 1968); *Hermiston*, opera (Edinburgh, Aug. 27, 1975); *On the Razzle*, comic opera (1986; Glasgow, June 27, 1988). **ORCH.:** *The Prospect of Whitby*, overture (1948); *Italian Overture* (1952); *Rhapsody* for Strings (1956); 3 syms.: No. 1, *Symphony in 1 Movement* (Glasgow, Dec. 12, 1963), No. 2 (1970; Glasgow, March 28, 1971), and No. 3 (Llandaff, June 14, 1978); *Sinfonietta Helvetica* (1990; Glasgow, Dec. 6, 1991). **CHAMBER:** Cello Sonatina (1938); Violin Sonatina (1941); Viola Sonata (1947); *Serenade* for String Trio (1948); *Sicilienne and Chaconne* for Viola and Piano (1949); 2 serenades for Horn and Piano (1951, 1960); Duo for Violin and Cello (1953; rev. 1965); Sonata for Violin and Harpsichord or Piano (1956); *Rondeau des Oiseaux* for Recorder or Flute (1994). **KEYBOARD: PIANO:** 2 Pieces (1940); *3 Lyric Pieces* (1994). **ORGAN:** *Toccata alla marcia* (1937); *3 Preludes on Scottish Psalm Tunes* (1958); *Elegy* (1968). **VOCAL:** *3 Songs of Innocence* for Voice and String Quartet (1932); *4 Romantic Songs* for Tenor, Oboe, and String Quartet (1950); *Festival Te Deum* for Chorus and Organ or Orch. (1950–51); *3 Pastorals* for Soprano, Flute, Viola, and Piano (1951); *Te Deum* and *Jubilate* for Chorus and Organ (1952); *Spring Cantata* for Mezzo-soprano, Chorus, Piano, Timpani, Percussion, and Strings (1955); *Come and Let Yourselves Be Built* for Chorus and Organ (1961); *Magnificat and Nunc Dimittis (Short Service)* for Voices (1967); *From the Book of Philip Sparrow* for Mezzo-soprano and Strings (1969); *Journeys and Places* for Mezzo-soprano and String Quintet or String Orch. (1970); *Liebeslied* for Mezzo-soprano and Piano or Organ (1978); *Versus from Ogden Nash* for Medium Voice and Strings (1978); *O God, Ruler of the World*, anthem for Chorus and Organ (1982); *Jesu, Sweet Son Dear* for Chorus (1989); other choral pieces and songs.

Orrego-Salas, Juan (Antonio), distinguished Chilean composer and musicologist; b. Santiago, Jan. 18, 1919. He studied composition at the National Cons. (1936–43) and architecture at the Catholic Univ. (graduated, 1943) in Santiago. In the meantime, he became a teacher of music history at the Univ. of Chile and in 1938 founder-conductor of the Catholic Univ. Chorus. After receiving a Rockefeller Foundation grant and a Guggenheim fellowship, he studied musicology with Lang and Herzog at Columbia Univ. (1944–45), and composition with Thompson at Princeton Univ. (1945–46) and Copland at the Berkshire Music Center in Tanglewood (summer, 1946). Upon returning to Santiago in 1947, he became prof. of composition at the Univ. of Chile; he also resumed his post as conductor of the Catholic Univ. Chorus. In 1949 he became ed. of the *Revista Musical Chilena* and in 1950 music critic of the newspaper *El Mercurio*. In 1953 he was made Distinguished Prof. of composition at the Univ. of Chile. In 1954 he received a 2nd Guggenheim fellowship and revisited the U.S. Upon returning to Santiago, he was director of the Instituto de Extension Musical until 1956. He then became the first director of the music dept. at the Catholic Univ. while continuing to teach at the Univ. of Chile. In 1961 he became a prof. at the Indiana Univ. School of Music in Bloomington, where he was founder-director of its Latin American Music Center. From 1975 to 1980 he also was chairman of its composition dept. He retired as prof. emeritus in 1987. In addition to monographs on composers, Orrego-Salas publ. numerous articles in journals in the U.S., England, and Latin America. In 1956 and 1958 he won the Olga Cohen prize for composition. He was made a corresponding member of the Chilean Academy of Fine Arts in 1971. In 1988 the OAS awarded him the Inter-American Gabriela Mistral Cultural Prize. In 1992 the Chilean government honored him with the Premio Nacional de Arte. As a composer, Orrego-Salas has revealed himself as a refined craftsman and an assured master of neo-Classical techniques.

WORKS: DRAMATIC: *Juventud*, ballet (Santiago, Nov. 19, 1948; based on Handel's *Solomon*); *El Retablo del rey pobre*, opera-oratorio (1950–52; 1st stage perf., Bloomington, Ind., Nov. 10, 1990); *Umbral del sueño*, ballet (Santiago, Aug. 8, 1951); *La Veta del diablo*, film score (1953); *Caleta olvidada*, film score (1959); *The Tumbler's Prayer*, ballet (concert perf., Santiago, Nov. 1960; stage perf., Santiago, Oct. 1961); *Versos del ciego*, incidental music (Santiago, June 1961); *Widows*, opera (1987–90); *The Goat That Couldn't Sneeze*, musical comedy (Bloomington, Ind., Oct. 25, 1992).

ORCH.: *Escenas de cortes y pastores*, 7 symphonic scenes (1946; Santiago, May 16, 1947); *Obertura festiva* (Santiago, April 1948); 4 syms.: No. 1 (1949; Santiago, July 14, 1950), No. 2, *to the memory of a wanderer* (1954; Minneapolis, Feb. 17, 1956), No. 3 (Washington, D.C., April 22, 1961), and No. 4, *of the distant answer* (1966; Bloomington, Ind., April 7, 1967); 2 piano concertos: No. 1 (Santiago, Nov. 24, 1950) and No. 2 (1985; Bloomington, Ind., Oct. 28, 1988); *Concierto de cámara* (Santiago, Nov. 28, 1952); *Serenata concertante* (1954; Louisville, May 14, 1955); *Jubileaus musicus* (Valparaíso, Chile, Dec. 15, 1956); *Psalms* for Wind Orch. (Pittsburgh, July 1962); *Concerto a tre* for Violin, Cello, Piano, and Orch. (1962; Washington, D.C., May 7, 1965); Concerto for Wind Orch. (1963–64; Pittsburgh, June 1964); *Quattro liriche brevi* for Saxophone and Chamber Orch. (1967; Washington, D.C., May 1, 1974; also for Alto Saxophone and Piano); *Volte* for Chamber Orch. (Rochester, N.Y., Dec. 11, 1971); *Variaciones serenas* for Strings (Santiago, Nov. 23, 1971); Concerto for Oboe and Strings (1980; Santiago, June 16, 1981); Violin Concerto (1983; Bloomington, Ind., Oct. 3, 1984); *Riley's Merriment*, scherzo (Indianapolis, Oct. 7, 1986); *Fantasia* for Piano and Wind Orch. (1986; San Antonio, April 29, 1987); Fanfare for the 10th Pan American Games (1986–87; Indianapolis, June 27, 1987); Cello Concerto (1991–92; Bloomington, Ind., Feb. 5, 1995).

CHAMBER: Violin Sonata (N.Y., April 1945); *Sonata a duo* for Violin and Viola (1945; Santiago, Aug. 1947); Bandoneon Suite (1952; Paris, June 2, 1953); Sextet for Clarinet, String Quartet, and Piano (1953; Tanglewood, Aug. 15, 1954); *Duos concertantes* "in memoriam Hans Kindler" for Cello and Piano (1955; Washington, D.C., Jan. 9, 1956); *Pastorale y scherzo* for Violin and Piano (1956; N.Y., April 1957); 2 divertimentos for Flute, Oboe, and Bassoon (Santiago, Aug. 23, 1956); String Quartet No. 1 (1957; Washington, D.C., April 19, 1958); Concertino for Brass Quartet (Bloomington, Ind., Nov. 19, 1963); *Sonata a quattro (Edgewood Sonata)* for Flute, Oboe, Harpsichord, and Contrabass (Washington, D.C., Oct. 31, 1964); 2 trios for Violin, Cello, and Piano: No. 1 (Caracas, May 12, 1966) and No. 2 (1977; N.Y., May 13, 1981); *Quattro liriche brevi* for Alto Saxophone and Piano (1967; London, Jan. 19, 1969; also for Saxophone and Chamber Orch.); *Mobili* for Viola and Piano (1967; Santiago, Nov. 1969); *A Greeting Cadenza* for Viola (1970; Bloomington, Ind., Nov. 1, 1971); *Esquinas* for Guitar (1971; Winona Lake, Ind., March 10, 1973); *Serenata* for Flute and Cello (Columbus, Ohio, Feb. 22, 1972); *Sonata de estío* for Flute and Piano (1972; Bloomington, Ind., Oct. 27, 1974); *Presencias* for Flute, Oboe, Clarinet, Harpsichord, Violin, Viola, and Cello (1972; Washington, D.C., May 5, 1977); *De Profundis* for Tuba and Cello Quartet (1979; N.Y., Jan. 5, 1981); *Variations for a Quiet Man* for Clarinet and Piano for Copland's 80th birthday (1980; Miami, Oct. 3, 1982); *Tangos* for 11 Players (Miami, Oct. 2, 1982); *Balada* for Cello and Piano (1982–83; Bloomington, Ind., Sept. 26, 1983); *Glosas* for Violin and Guitar (1984; Buenos Aires, April 9, 1985); *Variations on a Chant* for Harp (1984; Jerusalem, July 24, 1985); *Gyrocantus* for Flute, Clarinet, Percussion, Harpsichord or Celesta, Violin, and Cello (Santiago, Sept. 1987); *Midsummer Diversions* for Cello and Tuba (Bloomington, Ind., Sept. 27, 1987); *Partita* for Alto Saxophone and Piano Trio (1988); 3 Fanfares for Brass Quintet (Santiago, Nov. 1994). **PIANO:** 2 suites: No. 1 (N.Y., July 31, 1946) and No. 2 (Santiago, Aug. 1951); *Variaciones y fuga sobre el tema de un pregón* (Santiago, July 15, 1946); *Diez piezas simples* (1951; Santiago, Dec. 1, 1952); *Canción y danza* (1951); *Rústica* (1952; Santiago, Jan. 15, 1954); Sonata (Minneapolis, Nov. 18, 1967); *Dialogues in Waltz* for Piano, 4-hands (1984); *Rondo-Fantasia* (Boulder, Colo., Oct. 16, 1984).

VOCAL: *Villancico* for Chorus (1942; Santiago, June 9, 1947); *Romance a lo divino* for Chorus (1942; Washington, D.C., April 14, 1947); *Let Down the Bars, O Death!* for Chorus (1945); *Romances pastorales* for Chorus (1945; Santiago, Sept. 28, 1950); *Canciones en tres movimientos* for Soprano and String Quartet (1945); *Cantata de Navidad* for Soprano and Orch. (Rochester, N.Y., Oct. 23, 1946); *Romance a la muerte del Señor Don Gato* for Men's Voices (1946); *Cânones y rondas* for Children's Chorus (1946); *Canciones castellanas* for Soprano and 8 Instrumentalists (Santiago, Dec. 12, 1948); *Cànticos de Navidad* for Women's or Children's Chorus (N.Y., Dec. 12, 1948); *Cantos de Advenimiento* for Woman's Voice, Cello, and Piano (Santiago, June 26, 1948); *El Alba del Alhelí*, song cycle for Soprano and Piano (1950; Santiago, July 10, 1951); *Garden Songs* for Soprano, Flute, Viola, and Harp (1959; Santiago, Nov. 28, 1960); *Alabanzas a la Virgen* for Voice and Piano (1959; Valparaíso, Chile, Feb. 1960); *Alboradas* for Women's Chorus, Harp, Piano, Timpani, and Percussion (Bloomington, Ind., March 17, 1965); *América, no en vano invocamos tu nombre*, cantata for Soprano, Baritone, Men's Chorus, and Orch. (Ithaca, N.Y., May 10, 1966); *Tres madrigales* for Chorus (Bloomington, Ind., Nov. 9, 1967); *Missa "in tempore discordiae"* for Tenor, Chorus, and Orch. (1968–69; Louisville, April 20, 1979); *Palabras de Don Quijote* for Baritone and Chamber Ensemble (Washington, D.C., Oct. 31, 1970); *The Days of God*, oratorio for Soprano, Alto, Tenor, Baritone, Chorus, and Orch. (1974–76; Washington, D.C., Nov. 2, 1976); *Psalms* for Baritone and Piano (Bloomington, Ind., Aug. 3, 1977); *Un Canto a Bolivar*, cantata for Men's Voices and Folk Instruments (1980–81; Athens, Nov. 1981); *Canciones en el estilo popular* for Voice and Guitar (1981; Bloomington, Ind., Jan. 23, 1983); *Bolívar* for Narrator, Chorus, and Orch. (1981–82); *Yo digo lo que no digo* for Voices and Popular Instruments (1983); *Biografía Mínima de Salvador Allende* for Voice, Guitar, Trumpet, and Percussion (San Diego, Aug. 16, 1983); *Cinco canciones a seis* for Mezzo-soprano, 2 Violins, Clarinet, Cello, and Piano (Bloomington, Ind., Dec. 6, 1984); *Ash Wednesday*, 3 songs for Mezzo-soprano and String Orch. (1984); *Saludo* for Unison Voices (1988); *Cancion de Cuna* for Voice and Piano (1991); *La Ciudad Celeste*, cantata for Baritone, Chorus, and Orch. (1992); *3 Sacred Songs* "in memoriam Alfonso Letelier" (1994–95).

Orthel, Léon, Dutch pianist, pedagogue, and composer; b. Roosendaal, North Brabant, Oct. 4, 1905; d. The Hague, Sept. 6, 1985. He studied composition with Wagenaar at the Royal Cons. of Music in The Hague (1921–26) and with Juon at the Hochschule für Musik in Berlin (1928–29). From 1941 to 1971 he taught piano and theory at the Royal Cons. of Music in The Hague; concurrently taught composition at the Amsterdam Cons. (1949–71); was chairman of the Composers' Section of the Royal Dutch Society of Musicians (1947–70) while continuing to appear as a pianist.

WORKS: ORCH.: *Concertstuk* for Violin and Orch. (1924); *Scherzo* for Piano and Orch. (1927); 2 cello concertos (1929, 1984); *Concertino alla burla* for Piano and Orch. (1930); 6 syms.: No. 1 (1931–33), No. 2, *Piccola sinfonia* (1940; Rotterdam, Oct. 31, 1941), No. 3 (1943), No. 4, *Sinfonia concertante* for Piano and Orch. (1949), No. 5, *Musica iniziale* (1959–60), and No. 6 (1960–61); *2 Scherzos* (1954–55; 1956–57); *3 movimenti ostinati* (1971–72; Amsterdam, Sept. 1, 1973); *Album di disegni* (1976–77); *Evocazione* (1977); Suite No. 2 (1980); *Music* for Double Bass and Orch. (1981). **CHAMBER:** 2 violin sonatas (1924, 1933); 2 cello sonatas (1925, 1958); *5 pezzettini* for Clarinet and Piano (1963); String Quartet (1964); Viola Sonata (1964–65); *Ballade* for Flute and Piano (1970); *8 abbozzi* for Flute, Cello, and Piano (1971); *5 Schizzetti* for Harp (1977). **PIANO:** Sonata (1923); *4 Pieces* (1923–24); 9 sonatinas (1924; *Minatuure sonatine*, 1942; 1945; 1953; for the left hand, 1959; 1974; *Uit 1920 en 1922*, 1975; *Sonatina capricciosa*, 1975; 1977); pieces for children. **VOCAL:** 13 separate song cycles to texts by Rilke (1934–72).

Ortiz, Cristina, Brazilian-born English pianist; b. Bahia, April 17, 1950. She studied in Rio de Janeiro; after training with Magda Tagliaferro in Paris, she won 1st prize in the Van Cliburn Competition (1969). She made her N.Y. recital debut in 1971. Following further studies with R. Serkin at the Curtis Inst. of Music in Philadelphia, she pursued an international career (from 1973). In 1977 she became a naturalized British subject. She maintains an extensive repertoire, which includes both standard and rarely-heard works.

Ortmann, Otto Rudolph, American music educator; b. Baltimore, Jan. 25, 1889; d. there, Oct. 22, 1979. After studying at the Peabody Cons. of Music in Baltimore, he joined its faculty (1917–41), serving as its director (1928–41); also taught the psychology of music at Johns Hopkins Univ. (1921–24) and was on the music faculty at Goucher College (1942–57), serving as its music dept. chairman (1948–57); subsequently gave private instruction in piano, voice, and corrective speech despite advanced age and almost total blindness. Among his publications are *The Physical Basis of Piano Touch and Tone* (1925) and *The Psychological Mechanics of Piano Technique* (1929; 2nd ed., 1962).

Osborne (real name, **Eisbein**), **Adrienne,** American contralto; b. Buffalo, Dec. 2, 1873; d. Zell am Ziller, Austria, June 15, 1951.

She studied with August Gotze and Max Stagemann in Leipzig; later with Felix von Kraus, whom she married in 1899. She sang at the Leipzig City Theater; in 1908 she settled in Munich, where she received the rank of Royal Chamber Singer. After the death of her husband in 1937, she went to Zell am Ziller.

Osborne, Nigel, English composer and teacher; b. Manchester, June 23, 1948. He received training in composition from Leighton and in 12-tone procedures from Wellesz at the Univ. of Oxford (B.Mus., 1970), and then worked in Warsaw with Rudziński and at the Polish Radio Experimental Studio (1970–71). In 1976 he became a lecturer in music at the Univ. of Nottingham. In 1990 he became prof. of music at the Univ. of Edinburgh. His *7 Words* won the International Opera Prize of the Radio Suisse Romande in 1971, his *Heaventree* received the Gaudeamus Prize in 1973, and his *I Am Goya* was honored with the Radcliffe Award in 1977. Osborne's works are in a thoroughly contemporary style pointing the way to postmodernism.

WORKS: OPERAS: *Hell's Angels* (1985; London, Jan. 4, 1986); *The Electrification of the Soviet Union* (1986–87; Glyndebourne, Oct. 5, 1987); *Terrible Mouth* (1992); *Sarajevo* (1993–94). **ORCH.:** Cello Concerto (1977); Concerto for Flute and Chamber Orch. (1980); *Sinfonia I* (1982) and *II* (1983); *Esquisse I* (Bath, June 5, 1987) and *II* (Frankfurt am Main, April 17, 1988) for Small String Orch.; *Stone Garden* (London, Feb. 18, 1988); *Eulogy (for Michael Vyner)* for Small Orch. (London, May 6, 1990); Violin Concerto (London, Sept. 21, 1990); *The Sun of Venice* (1991); *Hommage à Panufnik* (1992). **CHAMBER:** *Kinderkreuzzug* for Chamber Ensemble and Tape (1974); *Remembering Esenin* for Cello and Piano (1974); *Musica da camera* for Violin, Tape Delay, and Audience (1975); *Prélude and Fugue* for Chamber Ensemble (1975); *After Night* for Guitar (1977); *Kerenza at the Zawn* for Oboe and Tape (1978); *Quasi una fantasia* for Cello (1979); *In Camera* for Chamber Ensemble (1979); *Mythologies* for Flute, Clarinet, Trumpet, Harp, Violin, and Cello (1980); *Fantasia* for Chamber Ensemble (1983); *Wildlife* for Chamber Ensemble and Optional Live Electronics (1984); *Zansa* for Chamber Ensemble (1985); *Mbira* for Violin and Piano (1985); *Lumière* for String Quartet and 4 Children's Groups (Devon, Sept. 24, 1986); *The Black Leg Miner* for Oboe, English Horn, Bassoon, and Harpsichord (Southfields, March 6, 1987); *Zone* for Oboe, Clarinet, and String Trio (1989); *Canzona* for 4 Trumpets, Horn, 4 Trombones, and Tuba (London, July 13, 1990); *Adagio for Vedran Smailovic* for Cello (1993). **PIANO:** *Figure/Ground* (1978; rev. 1979); Sonata (1981). **VOCAL:** *7 Words* for 2 Tenors, Bass, Chorus, Orch., and Optional Ondes Martenot (1971); *Heaventree* for Chorus (1973); *The Sickle* for Soprano and Orch. (1975); *Chansonnier* for Soprano, Alto, Tenor, Bass, Chorus, and Chamber Ensemble (1975); *Passers By* for Bass Recorder, Cello, 3 Voices, and Slides (1976); *Vienna. Zürich. Constance.* for Soprano, Violin, Cello, 2 Clarinets, and Percussion (1977); *I Am Goya* for Bass-baritone, Flute, Oboe, Violin, and Cello (1977); *Orlando furioso* for Chorus and Chamber Ensemble (1978); *Under the Eyes* for Voice, Percussion, Piano, Oboe, and Flute (1979); *Songs from a Bare Mountain* for Women's Chorus (1979); *Poem without a Hero* for Soprano, Mezzo-soprano, Tenor, Bass, and Live Electronics (1980); *Gnostic Passion* for Chorus (1980); *The Cage* for Tenor, Chamber Ensemble, and Optional Live Electronics (1981); *For a Moment* for Women's Chorus, Cello, and Optional Kandyan Drum (1981); *Choralis I* (1981), *II* (1981; rev. 1982), and *III* (1982) for Soprano, 2 Mezzo-sopranos, Tenor, Baritone, and Bass; *Cantata Piccola* for Soprano and String Quartet (1982); *Alba* for Mezzo-soprano, Chamber Ensemble, and Tape (1984); *The 4-Loom Weaver* for Mezzo-soprano and Tape (1985); *Pornography* for Mezzo-soprano and Chamber Ensemble (1985); *Tracks* for 2 Choruses, Orch., and Wind Band (Rochester, Kent, April 21, 1990).

Osborn-Hannah, Jane, American soprano; b. Wilmington, Ohio, July 8, 1873; d. N.Y., Aug. 13, 1943. After vocal instruction from her mother, she studied with Marchesi and Sbriglia in Paris and with Sucher in Berlin. In 1904 she made her operatic debut as Elisabeth in *Tannhäuser* in Leipzig, and sang there until 1907. After appearances in Dresden, Munich, and Berlin, she sang at London's Covent Garden in 1908. On Jan. 5, 1910, she made her Metropolitan Opera debut in N.Y. as Elisabeth, and continued on its roster for the 1910–11 season. She also was a member of the Chicago Grand Opera (1910–14). While she was best known as a Wagnerian, she also sang such roles as Desdemona, Cio-Cio-San, and Nedda with conviction.

Osghian, Petar, Serbian composer; b. Dubrovnik, April 27, 1932. He studied at the Belgrade Academy of Music; was on its faculty (from 1964). He adopted a free neo-Romantic style of composition.

WORKS: ORCH.: *Poema eroico* (Belgrade, Dec. 8, 1959); *Symphoniette* for Strings (Belgrade, Dec. 20, 1960); *Concerto for Orchestra* (Belgrade, Feb. 25, 1964); *Sigogis* for Chamber Orch. (Zagreb, May 12, 1967); *Differencias* for Violin and Orch. (1970). **CHAMBER:** String Quartet (1958); *Divertimento* for Double String Quartet (1973); numerous piano pieces.

Osten, Eva von der, German soprano; b. Insel, Aug. 19, 1881; d. Dresden, May 5, 1936. She studied with August Iffert and Marie Söhle in Dresden. She made her operatic debut as Urbain in *Les Huguenots* in Dresden in 1902; was a principal member of the Dresden Court (later State) Opera until 1927, where she created the role of Octavian in *Der Rosenkavalier* in 1911; she also appeared at London's Covent Garden (1912–14) and in the U.S. with the German Opera Co. (1923–24). After her retirement from the stage, she became a producer of opera in Dresden. She was married to **Friedrich Plaschke**. Among her other outstanding roles were Kundry, Isolde, Senta, Ariadne, and Tosca.

Osterc, Slavko, Slovenian composer and teacher; b. Veržej, June 17, 1895; d. Ljubljana, May 23, 1941. He began his training with Beran in Maribor; then studied at the Prague Cons. (1925–27); subsequently taught at Ljubljana's Cons. and Academy of Music. He experimented with various techniques, including quarter tone writing.

WORKS: DRAMATIC: OPERAS: *Salome* (1919–30); *Krst pri Savici* (Baptism at the Savica; 1921); *Iz komične opere* (1928); *Krog s kredo* (The Chalk Circle; 1928–29); *Medea* (1930); *Dandin v vicah* (Dandin in Purgatory; 1930). **BALLETS:** *Iz Satanovega dnevnika* (From Satan's Diary; 1924); *Maska rdeče smrti* (The Masque of the Red Death; 1930); *Illusions* (1938–40); *Illegitimate Mother* (1940). **ORCH.:** Sym. (1922); Concerto (1932); Concerto for Piano and Winds (1933; Prague, Sept. 1, 1935); *Passacaglia and Chorale* (Warsaw, April 14, 1934); *Mouvements symphonique* (1936; London, June 24, 1938); *Nocturne* for Strings (1940). **CHAMBER:** 2 string quartets (1927, 1934); Sonata for 2 Clarinets (1929); Wind Quintet (1932); Saxophone Sonata (1935); piano pieces; organ music.

Osthoff, Helmuth, distinguished German musicologist, father of **Wolfgang Osthoff**; b. Bielefeld, Aug. 13, 1896; d. Würzburg, Feb. 9, 1983. He studied music in Bielefeld and in Münster. He served in the German army during World War I; after the Armistice, he resumed his studies at the Univ. of Münster (1919), and later (1920–22) took courses with Wolf, Kretzschmar, and Schünemann at the Univ. of Berlin, where he received his Ph.D. in 1922 with the diss. *Der Lautenist Santino Garsi da Parma: Ein Beitrag zur Geschichte der oberitaliensischen Lautenmusik der Spätrenaissance* (publ. in Leipzig, 1926). He subsequently studied conducting with Brecher, composition with Klatte, and piano with Kwast at Berlin's Stern Cons. (1922–23). From 1923 to 1926 he served as répétiteur at the Leipzig Opera; in 1926 he became assistant lecturer to Arnold Schering in the dept. of musicology at the Univ. of Halle; in 1928 he was appointed chief assistant to Schering in the dept. of music history at the Univ. of Berlin; completed his Habilitation there in 1932 with his treatise *Die Niederländer und das deutsche Lied 1400–1640* (publ. in Berlin, 1938). In 1938 he became a prof. and director of the inst. of musicology at the

Univ. of Frankfurt am Main, positions he held until his retirement in 1964. He was especially noted for his astute studies of Renaissance music. His other publications include *Adam Krieger; Neue Beiträge zur Geschichte des deutschen Liedes in 17. Jahrhundert* (Leipzig, 1929; 2nd ed., 1970); *Johannes Brahms und seine Sendung* (Bonn, 1942); *Josquin Desprez* (2 vols., Tutzing, 1962–65). A Festschrift was publ. in Tutzing in 1961 to honor his 65th birthday, a 2nd in 1969 for his 70th birthday (contains a bibliography of his writings), and a 3rd in 1977 for his 80th birthday.

Osthoff, Wolfgang, German musicologist, son of **Helmuth Osthoff**; b. Halle, March 17, 1927. He studied piano and theory at the Frankfurt am Main Staatliche Hochschule für Musik (1939–43); then took lessons in conducting with Kurt Thomas (1946–47). He subsequently studied musicology with his father at the Univ. of Frankfurt am Main (1947–49) and with Georgiades at the Univ. of Heidelberg (1949–54); received his Ph.D. there in 1954 with the diss. *Das dramatische Spätwerk Claudio Monteverdis* (publ. in Tutzing, 1960). He taught at the Univ. of Munich (1957–64); completed his Habilitation there in 1965 with his *Theatergesang und darstellende Musik in der italienischen Renaissance* (publ. in Tutzing, 1969). He became a lecturer at the Univ. of Munich in 1966. In 1968 he was named a prof. of musicology at the Univ. of Würzburg. In addition to many scholarly articles dealing with music history from the 15th to the 19th century, he also contributed to many music reference works. With R. Wiesend, he ed. *Bach und die italienische Musik (Bach e la musica italiana)* (Venice, 1987). He publ. the vol. *St. George und "Les deux Musiques"—Tönende und vertonte Dichtung im Einklang und Widerstreit* (Stuttgart, 1989).

BIBL.: M. Just and R. Wiesend, eds., *Liedstudien: W. O. zum 60. Geburtstag* (Tutzing, 1989).

Östman, Arnold, Swedish conductor; b. Malmö, Dec. 24, 1939. He received training in art history at the Univ. of Lund and in music history at the univs. of Paris and Stockholm. From 1969 to 1979 he was artistic director of the Vadstena Academy, where he attracted notice with his productions of operas of the 17th and 18th centuries. He then was artistic director of the Drottningholm Court Theater in Stockholm from 1980 to 1992, where he mounted performances of early operas utilizing period instruments, costumes, and stagings. He also appeared frequently with the Cologne Opera, taking its productions of *Il matrimonio segreto* on tour to London (1983) and Washington, D.C. (1986). In 1984 he conducted *Don Giovanni* at London's Covent Garden. In 1985 he conducted *Le Siège de Corinthe* at the Paris Opéra. He conducted *Lucio Silla* at the Vienna State Opera in 1990. Östman also appeared as a guest conductor with various European orchs. While he has become best known for his performances of early operas, he has also commissioned and conducted the premieres of many contemporary works.

Ostrčil, Otakar, eminent Czech conductor and composer; b. Smichov, near Prague, Feb. 25, 1879; d. Prague, Aug. 20, 1935. He studied languages at the Univ. of Prague, and then taught at a school in Prague (until 1919); at the same time, he took courses in piano with Adolf Mikeš (1893–95) and studied composition privately with Fibich (1895–1900). From 1908 to 1922 he conducted the amateur orch. assn. in Prague; also conducted opera there (from 1909); in 1920 he succeeded Karel Kovařovic as principal conductor at the Prague National Theater; also taught conducting at the Prague Cons. (1926–29). In his compositions, Ostrčil continued the Romantic tradition of Czech music, with some modern elaborations revealing the influence of Mahler.

WORKS: OPERAS: *Vlasty skon* (The Death of Vlasta; 1900–03; Prague, Dec. 14, 1904); *Kunálovy oči* (Kunala's Eyes; Prague, Nov. 25, 1908); *Poupě* (The Bud; 1909–10; Prague, Jan. 25, 1911); *Legenda z Erinu* (The Legend of Erin; 1913–19; Brno, June 16, 1921); *Honzovo království* (Honza's Kingdom; 1928–33; Brno, May 26, 1934). **ORCH.:** Sym. (1905); *Sinfonietta* (1921); *Léto* (Summer), symphonic poem (1925–26); *Křížová cesta* (Way of the Cross), symphonic variations (1928). **CHAMBER:** String Quartet; Trio for Violin, Viola, and Piano. **VOCAL:** Choral pieces; song cycles.

BIBL.: Z. Nejedlý, *O. O.: Vzrůst a uzrání* (O. O.: Development and Maturity; Prague, 1935); J. Bartoš, *O. O.* (Prague, 1936).

Oswald, John, provocative Canadian composer and sound engineer; b. Kitchener-Waterloo, May 30, 1953. In 1989 he produced and distributed, free of charge, *Plunderphonic,* a CD anthology of original pieces made up of "plunderphones" ("electroquotes or macrosamples of familiar sound") derived from revised performances of recordings by well-known artists, including James Brown, Lorin Maazel with the Cleveland Orch., George Harrison, Dolly Parton, Glenn Gould, Bing Crosby, Michael Jackson, and Count Basie. Oswald's "plunderphones" are the substance of each of his 24 tracks, themselves sequenced into typical genre groupings, with the exception of "compilation tracks of a particular performer, juxtapositions of complimentary performances by unrelated performers, unusual rearrangements of existing compositions, and the James Brown tracks, which are vehicles for various types and sources of appropriation." Virtually no extraneous music is added, all of the sounds heard being accurate, unprocessed reproductions of the originals. The overall effect is both less and more complicated than Oswald's explanation—repelling and compelling, with referential musical modules flitting around like bytes of information in the bowels of a computer. Oswald is actively involved in the issue of copyright morality; he has lectured widely on the subject and also wrote extensively for a variety of publications (*Keyboard, The Whole Earth Review, Grammy Pulse,* etc.). *Plunderphonic* itself carries no copyright warning; in its place is a "shareright" insignia, which encourages reproduction but prohibits sale. Since 1980 Oswald has been director of Mystery Laboratory of Toronto, the "aural research, production, and dissemination facility" where Plunderphonic was produced; he is also music director of the North American Experience Dance Co. (from 1987) and co-founder of *Musicworks,* an informative Canadian journal that emphasizes the experimental and avant-garde. Among his other compositions are *Burroughs,* vocal concrète (1974), *Warm Wind Pressure and Aura* for Ensemble without Instruments (1979), and *Fossils,* vocal concrète (1985); he also wrote 3 full-length dance scores: *Skindling Shades* for Tape (1987), *Wounded* for Miming Musicians (1988), and *Zorro* for a cappella Duet (1989); numerous tape pieces, including *Jazz Edit* (1982) and *Bell Speeds* (1983).

Otaka, Hisatada, Japanese conductor and composer; b. Tokyo, Sept. 26, 1911; d. there, Feb. 16, 1951. While still a teenager, he studied in Vienna. Following composition lessons with Pringsheim in Tokyo (1932–34), he returned to Vienna and studied with J. Marx (composition) and Weingartner (conducting) at the Academy of Music (1934–38); he also studied privately with Franz Moser. In 1940 he returned to Japan. From 1942 until his death he was conductor of the Nippon Sym. Orch. in Tokyo.

WORKS: ORCH.: *Sinfonietta* for Strings (1937); *Japanese Suite* No. 1 (Budapest, Nov. 8, 1938) and No. 2 (Vienna, Nov. 3, 1939); *Midare* (Berlin, Dec. 10, 1939); Cello Concerto (Tokyo, May 23, 1943); *Rhapsody* for Piano and Orch. (Tokyo, Dec. 10, 1943); *Fatherland* (Tokyo, Oct. 22, 1945); Sym. (1948); Flute Concerto (Tokyo, March 5, 1951). **CHAMBER:** Violin Sonata (1932); 2 string quartets (1938, 1943); Piano Trio (1941); many piano pieces. **VOCAL:** Songs.

Otaka, Tadaaki, Japanese conductor; b. Kamakura, Nov. 8, 1947. He received training at the Toho Gakuen School of Music in Tokyo and at the Hochschule für Musik in Vienna. In 1970 he joined the faculty of the Toho Gakuen School of Music. From 1974 to 1981 he was principal conductor of the Tokyo Phil., and then of the Sapporo Sym. Orch. from 1981 to 1986. In 1987 he became principal conductor of the BBC Welsh Sym. Orch. in Cardiff, which position he retained when it was renamed the BBC National Orch. of Wales in 1993. In 1991 he became principal conductor of the Yomiuri Sym. Orch. in Tokyo, leaving his Cardiff post in 1995. As a guest conductor, he appeared with various orchs. in Japan and abroad.

Otaño (y Eugenio), (José María) Nemesio, Spanish musicologist and composer; b. Azcoitia, Dec. 19, 1880; d. San Sebastián, April 29, 1956. He became a member of the Soc. of Jesus and organist of the Basilica of Loyola in 1896. In 1903 he went to Valladolid and studied counterpoint and composition with Vincent Goicoechea. In 1907 he founded the journal *Música Sacro-Hispana*, which he ed. until 1922. He also founded the Schola Cantorum at the Comillas seminary in 1911, which he led on tours of Europe. In 1937 he was made music director of the Spanish Radio. From 1939 to 1951 he was director of the Madrid Cons. He pursued the study of Spanish folk music and the villancico, and ed. collections of Spanish organ music and military music of the 18th century. He publ. an essay on folklore, *El canto popular montañes* (Santander, 1915) and publ. the books *La música religiosa y la legislación eclesiastica* (Barcelona, 1912) and *Antonio Eximeno* (Madrid, 1943). Among his compositions were numerous choral works, songs, and organ pieces.

Otescu, Ion (Nonna), Romanian conductor, teacher, and composer; b. Bucharest, Dec. 15, 1888; d. there, March 25, 1940. He was a student of Kiriac (theory) and Castaldi (composition) at the Bucharest Cons. (1903–07), and then completed his training in composition in Paris with d'Indy at the Schola Cantorum and with Widor at the Cons. (1908–11). Returning to Budapest, he was a teacher of harmony and composition (1913–40) and director (1918–40) of the Cons. He also was a conductor of the National Theater (1921–39) and the Bucharest Phil. (from 1927). In 1920 he helped to organize the Soc. of Romanian Composers, serving as its vice-chairman until his death. In 1913 he won the Enesco Prize and in 1928 the National Prize for composition. Otescu's music followed along traditional lines with infusions of folk and French elements.

WORKS: DRAMATIC: *Buby*, musical comedy (1903); *Ileana Cosinzeana*, ballet (1918; to a libretto by Queen Marie of Romania); *Rubinul miraculos*, ballet (1919); *Iderim*, opera (1920); *De la Matei cetire*, opera buffa (1926–38; completed by A. Stroe; Cluj, Dec. 27, 1966). **ORCH.:** *Le temple de Gnid*, symphonic poem (1908; Bucharest, March 2, 1914); Overture (1908); *Narcisse*, symphonic poem (Bucharest, Dec. 9, 1912); *Cuvente din betrani*, symphonic sketch (1912; Bucharest, April 5, 1913); *Impresiuni de iarnă*, symphonic tableau (1913; Bucharest, March 2, 1914); *Vrăjile Armidei*, symphonic poem for Violin and Orch. (1915; Bucharest, Nov. 20, 1922); *Scherzo* (1923; Bucharest, Nov. 19, 1939). **OTHER:** Chamber music; songs.

Ott, David, American composer; b. Crystal Falls, Mich., July 5, 1947. He studied at the Univ. of Wisc., Platteville (B.S. in music education, 1969); after training in piano with Alfonso Montecino at the Indiana Univ. School of Music (M.M., 1971), he took courses in theory and composition at the Univ. of Kentucky (D.M.A., 1982). He taught at Houghton (N.Y.) College (1972–75), the Univ. of Kentucky, Lexington (1976–77), Catawba College, Salisbury, N.C. (1977–78), Pfeiffer College, Misenheimer, N.C. (1978–82), and DePauw Univ., Greencastle, Ind. (from 1982); also was active as an organist and conductor. In 1991 he became composer-in-residence of the Indianapolis Sym. Orch.

WORKS: DRAMATIC: *Lucinda Hero*, opera (1985); *Visions: The Isle of Patmos*, ballet (1988). **ORCH.:** *Genesis II* (1980); Piano Concerto (1983); 4 numbered syms.: No. 1, *Short Symphony*, for Chamber Orch. (1984), No. 2 (1990; Grand Rapids, Mich., Jan. 18, 1991), No. 3 (1991; Grand Rapids, Mich., Oct. 9, 1992), and No. 4 (Fort Wayne, Ind., Oct. 15, 1994); Percussion Concerto (1984); Cello Concerto (1985); *Water Garden* (1986); *Celebration at Vanderburgh* (1987); Saxophone Concerto (1987); Viola Concerto (1988); Concerto for 2 Cellos and Orch. (1988); *Vertical Shrines* (1989); *Music of the Canvas* (Indianapolis, Oct. 11, 1990); *String Symphony* (1990); Triple Brass Concerto for Trumpet, Trombone, Horn, and Orch. (1990); Violin Concerto (Reading, Pa., Oct. 17, 1992); Trombone Concerto (1992; San Diego, April 22, 1993); *Overture on an American Hymn* for Chamber Orch. (1992); *Indianapolis Concerto for Orchestra* (1992–93; Indianapolis, Sept. 30, 1993); *The 4 Winds* (1993); *Improvisation on "Freudvoll und Leidvoll" (Egmont)* (1993); Triple Concerto for Clarinet, Violin, Piano, and Orch. (Grand Rapids, Mich., Nov. 4, 1993). **CHAMBER:** Viola Sonata (1982); *Sabado* for Woodwind Quintet (1985); Trombone Sonata (1986); *DodecaCelli* for 12 Cellos (1988); String Quartet No. 1 (1989); *5 Interludes* for Cello and Piano (1990); organ pieces. **VOCAL:** Choral works; songs.

Otte, Hans (Günther Franz), German composer and pianist; b. Plauen, Dec. 3, 1926. He was a student of Hindemith and J. N. David (composition), Pozniak and Gieseking (piano), Germani (organ), and Abendroth, conducting). In 1959 he won the Prix de Rome. From 1959 to 1984 he served as head of music for Radio Bremen, where he was a proponent of contemporary music. As a composer, he pursued an experimental course which ranged from serial and aleatoric techniques to electronic pieces and sound installations.

WORKS: DRAMATIC: *voicing*, radiophonic piece (1988); *jetzt*, theater piece (1992); *im garten den klänge*, vocal theater (1993). **ORCH.:** *realisationen* for Piano and Orch. (1956); *momente* (1958; Paris, May 1960); *ensemble* for Strings (Palermo, Sept. 1961); *passages* for Piano and Orch. (1965–66); *Buch* (1968); *zero* for Orch. and Chorus (North German Radio, Hamburg, Jan. 1971); *terrain* (Bavarian Radio, Munich, Dec. 1974). **CHAMBER:** *montaru* for 2 Pianos, Brass, and Percussion (South German Radio, Stuttgart, Dec. 1955); *folie et sens* for Piano Trio (1955–56; South German Radio, Stuttgart, May 1956); *daidalos* for Piano, Guitar, Harp, and 2 Percussionists (1960); *valeurs* for Winds (1969); *rendezvous* for Chamber Ensemble (Rome, Oct. 1969); *text* for Percussionist (Stuttgart, May 1972); *orient: occident* for 2 Winds and Tape (1978); *einklang* for Acoustic and Electronic Strings (South West Radio, Baden-Baden, April 1979; also for 2 Wind Groups and Tape, South West Radio, Baden-Baden, April 1979); *wassermann-musik* for Harp (1984); *text* for Vibraphone (1986); *eins* for Alto Flute (1987); *septuor* for Flute, Clarinet, Percussion, Piano, Violin, Cello, and Harp (1988); *phoenix-piece* for Clarinet (1989); *alltagsmusik* for Violin (1992). **KEYBOARD: PIANO:** *dromenon* for 3 Pianos (1957; North German Radio, Hamburg, Jan. 1960); *tropismen* (1959; South German Radio, Stuttgart, April 1960); *interplay* for 2 Pianists (1962); *face à face* for Piano and Tape (1965); *intervall* (Buenos Aires, June 1974); *biographie* for Piano and Tape (South West Radio, Baden-Baden, Jan. 1976); *das buch der klänge* (1979–82). **ORGAN:** *touches* (1965); *minimum: maximum*, simultaneous piece for 2 Organists on 2 Organs (Swedish Radio, Stockholm, and Radio Bremen, Oct. 1973); *sounds* (1992). **VOCAL:** *tasso concetti* for Soprano, Flute, Piano, and Percussion (1961); *schrift* for Chorus, Lights, Loudspeaker, and Organ (1976); *siebengesang* for 3 Singers, Piano, and 3 Winds (1985); *philharmonie* for Chorus and Orch. (1986); *das lied der welt* for 10 Choruses in 10 Countries (European Broadcasting Union, Dec. 1, 1986).

Otter, Anne Sofie von, Swedish mezzo-soprano; b. Stockholm, May 9, 1955. She began her training at the Stockholm Musikhögskolan; then studied with Erik Werba in Vienna and Geoffrey Parsons in London, and later with Vera Rozsa. In 1982 she joined the Basel Opera; in 1984 she sang at the Aix-en-Provence Festival. She made her first appearance at London's Covent Garden in 1985 as Cherubino; that same year, she made her U.S. debut as soloist in Mozart's C-minor Mass with the Chicago Sym. Orch. In 1987 she sang at La Scala in Milan and at the Bavarian State Opera in Munich. In 1988 she appeared as Cherubino at the Metropolitan Opera in N.Y. In 1989 she made her first appearance at the Salzburg Festival as Marguerite in *La Damnation de Faust* with Solti and the Chicago Sym. Orch. In 1992 she returned to Salzburg to sing Ramiro. She sang widely as a soloist with major orchs. and as a recitalist. Her other operatic roles include Gluck's Orfeo, Mozart's Idamantes and Dorabella, Tchaikovsky's Olga, and R. Strauss's Octavian.

Otterloo, (Jan) Willem van, prominent Dutch conductor; b. Winterswijk, Dec. 27, 1907; d. in a automobile accident in Melbourne, Australia, July 27, 1978. He studied with Orobio de Castro (cello) and Sem Dresden (composition) at the Amsterdam Cons. In 1932 he became a cellist in the Utrecht Sym. Orch.; from 1933 to 1937, served as its assistant conductor, and from 1937 to 1949, as its chief conductor. He was chief conductor of the Residente Orch. in The Hague (1949–73); took it on a tour of the U.S. in 1963. He was also chief conductor (1967–68) and principal guest conductor (1969–71) of the Melbourne Sym. Orch.; then was chief conductor of the Sydney Sym. Orch. from 1973 until his tragic death; was also Generalmusikdirektor of the Düsseldorf Sym. Orch. (1974–77). His unmannered readings of the classics were esteemed. He also composed, producing a Sym., suites for Orch., chamber music, etc.

Ottman, Robert W(illiam), American music theorist and pedagogue; b. Fulton, N.Y., May 3, 1914. He studied theory with Rogers at the Eastman School of Music in Rochester, N.Y. (M.Mus., 1943). He served in U.S. Army infantry (1943–46); then took lessons in composition with Alec Rowley at Trinity College of Music in London; in 1946, was engaged as a lecturer in music at North Texas State Univ., from which he also received his Ph.D. (1956); became prof. emeritus in 1980.

WRITINGS (all publ. in Englewood Cliffs, N.J., unless otherwise given): *Music for Sight Singing* (1956; 3rd ed., 1986); with P. Kreuger, *Basic Repertoire for Singers* (San Antonio, 1959); *Elementary Harmony, Theory and Practice* (1961; 3rd ed., 1983); *Advanced Harmony, Theory and Practice* (N.Y., 1961; 4th ed., 1992); with F. Mainous, *The 371 Chorales of J.S. Bach* (N.Y., 1966; with Eng. texts); with F. Mainous, *Rudiments of Music* (1970; 2nd ed., 1987); *Workbook for Elementary Harmony* (1974; 2nd ed., 1983); with F. Mainous, *Programmed Rudiments of Music* (N.Y., 1979); *More Music for Sight Singing* (1981); with P. Dworak, *Basic Ear Training Skills* (1991).

Otto, Lisa, German soprano; b. Dresden, Nov. 14, 1919. She was educated at the Hochschule für Musik in Dresden. She made her operatic debut as Sophie in 1941 at the Landestheater in Beuthen. In 1945–46 she sang at the Nuremberg Opera. She was a member of the Dresden State Opera (1946–51); then joined the Berlin Stadtische Oper (1952); also sang in Salzburg (from 1953), and made tours of the U.S., South America, and Japan. She was made a Kammersängerin in 1963. She became best known for her roles in Mozart's operas.

Ötvos, Gabor, Hungarian-born German conductor; b. Budapest, Sept. 21, 1935. He began his training at the Franz Liszt Academy of Music in Budapest. Following the abortive Hungarian Revolution in 1956, he pursued studies in Venice and Rome. In 1958 he became a conductor at the Teatro Verdi in Trieste, and served as its music director in 1960–61. From 1961 to 1967 he was chief conductor of the Hamburg Sym. Orch. He held the title of 1st conductor and deputy Generalmusikdirektor of the Frankfurt am Main Opera from 1967 to 1972. In 1969 he made his debut with the N.Y. City Opera. On Oct. 27, 1971, he made his first appearance with the Metropolitan Opera in N.Y. conducting *Carmen*, returning there in 1973 and 1974. From 1972 to 1981 he was Generalmusikdirektor of Augsburg. He served as chief conductor of the Royal Danish Theater in Copenhagen from 1981 to 1990.

Oue, Eiji, Japanese conductor; b. Hiroshima, Oct. 3, 1956. He was a student of Saito at the Toho School of Music in Tokyo (B.M., 1978) and of Larry Livingston at the New England Cons. of Music in Boston (Artist Diploma, 1981); also worked with Ozawa (1978–84), Bernstein (1980–90), and Calibidache (1982–83). In 1980 he received the Koussevitzky Prize at Tanglewood, in 1981 he took 1st prize at the Salzburg conducting competition, and in 1982 he was a fellow at the Los Angeles Phil. Inst. He was music director of the New Bedford (Mass.) Sym. Orch. (1982–84) and the Boston Mozarteum Orch. (1982–89); was also music director of the Greater Boston Youth Sym. Orch. (1982–88), the Brown Univ. Orch. (1985–86), and the Empire State Youth Sym. Orch. (1986–88). From 1986 to 1990 he was assoc. conductor of the Buffalo Phil. In 1990 he took the London Sym. Orch. on a tour of Japan, and in 1990 and 1991 he served as resident conductor of the new Pacific Music Festival in Sapporo. From 1990 he was music director of the Erie (Pa.) Phil. In 1995 he became music director of the Minnesota Orch. in Minneapolis. As a guest conductor, he appeared with leading orchs. throughout North America, Europe, and the Far East.

Ousset, Cécile, French pianist; b. Tarbes, Jan. 23, 1936. A child prodigy, she made her public debut when she was only 5. She studied with Marcel Ciampi at the Paris Cons., where she graduated with the premier prix at age 14. In 1953 she won the Claire Pagès Prize. She subsequently won prizes in several competitions, including the Geneva (2nd prize co-winner, 1954), Queen Elisabeth of Belgium (4th prize winner, 1956), Busoni (2nd prize co-winner, 1959), and Van Cliburn (4th prize winner, 1962) competitions. She appeared regularly as a soloist with French orchs. and as a recitalist. In 1980 she made her British debut at the Edinburgh Festival. In 1984 she made her U.S. debut as a soloist with the Los Angeles Phil., and that same year she made her first tour of Japan. In subsequent years, she pursued an international career. In addition to her idiomatic interpretations of the French repertoire, she has also won distinction in the Austro-German repertoire.

Ovchinnikov, Viacheslav, Russian conductor and composer; b. Voronezh, May 29, 1936. He studied composition with Khrennikov at the Moscow Cons., graduating in 1962; also studied conducting with Lev Ginzburg; upon graduation, he conducted various orchs. in Moscow and on Soviet radio and television.

WORKS: DRAMATIC: *Sulamith*, ballet (1962); *On the Dawn of Misty Youth*, opera (1974–78); also scores for films, including *War and Peace* (1961–67). **ORCH.:** 6 symphonic suites (1955–72); 3 syms. (1956, 1973, 1978); *Yuri Gagarin* (1974); *Elegy in Memory of Rachmaninoff* (1973); also orch. arrangements of Rachmaninoff's piano works. **OTHER:** *Hymn to the Fatherland*, oratorio (1974); choral works; songs; piano pieces.

Overton, Hall (Franklin), American pianist, teacher, and composer; b. Bangor, Mich., Feb. 23, 1920; d. N.Y., Nov. 24, 1972. He studied piano at the Chicago Musical College and counterpoint at the Juilliard School of Music in N.Y. (1940–42). He served in the U.S. Army overseas (1942–45). After World War II, he studied composition with Persichetti at the Juilliard School of Music, graduating in 1951; also took private lessons with Riegger and Milhaud. At the same time, he filled professional engagements as a jazz pianist and contributed articles to the magazine *Jazz Today*. He was awarded 2 Guggenheim fellowships (1955, 1957). He taught at Juilliard (1960–71), the New School for Social Research in N.Y. (1962–66), and at the Yale Univ. School of Music (1970–71).

WORKS: OPERAS: *The Enchanted Pear Tree*, after Boccaccio's *Decameron* (N.Y., Feb. 7, 1950); *Pietro's Petard* (N.Y., June 1963); *Huckleberry Finn*, after Mark Twain (N.Y., May 20, 1971). **ORCH.:** 2 syms.: No. 1 for Strings (1955) and No. 2 (1962); *Interplay* (1964); *Sonorities* (1964); *Rhythms* for Violin and Orch. (1965); *Pulsations* for Chamber Orch. (1972). **CHAMBER:** 3 string quartets (1950, 1954, 1967); String Trio (1957); Viola Sonata (1960); Cello Sonata (1960); various piano works, including *Polarities Nos. 1* (1959) and *2* (1971), and a Sonata (1963). **VOCAL:** Songs.

Owen, Morfydd Llywn, Welsh composer, pianist, and singer; b. Treforest, Oct. 1, 1891; d. Gowerton, near Swansea, Sept. 7, 1918. She studied with David Evans at the Univ. of South Wales in Cardiff (B.M., 1912), then with F. Corder at the Royal Academy of Music in London (1912–17), where she later taught. On Feb. 4, 1917, she married Ernest Jones, the Welsh disciple and biographer of Sigmund Freud. Her early death from complications following an operation for appendicitis was greatly lamented, for she had already established herself as a promising composer of vocal works. Her *Nocturne* for Orch. received the Lucas Prize in Composition from the Royal Academy of Music. She appeared frequently at the semi-annual Eisteddfods, both as a vocalist and as a composer. A 4-vol. ed. of her works, containing a biographical memoir by Jones, was publ. in London (1924).

WORKS: ORCH.: *Nocturne* (1913; Dallas, June 23, 1987); *Morfa Rhuddlan*, tone poem (1914); *The Passing of Branwen* (1917). **CHAMBER:** *Romance* for Violin and Piano (1911); Piano Trio (1912). **PIANO:** Sonata (1910); *Étude* (1911); *Rhapsody* (1911); *Prélude after the Style of Bach* (1912); *Fantasie appassionata* (1912); *Rhapsodie* (1913); *Prélude* (1913); 3 préludes: *Waiting for Eirlys, Beti Bwt*, and *Nant-y-ffrith* (1914–15); *Preludio e Fuga grotesca* (1914); *Little Eric*, humoresque (1915); *Talyllyn* (1916); *3 Welsh Impressions: Llanbynmair, Glantaf*, and *Beti Bwt* (1917). **VOCAL:** *Ave Maria* for Soprano, Chorus, and Orch. (1912); *Choric Songs* for Chorus and Orch. (1913); *Towards the Unknown Region*, vocal scena after Walt Whitman for Tenor and Orch. (1915); *Pro Patria*, cantata (1915); choral pieces, including *The Refugee*, after Schiller (1910), *Fierce Raged the Tempest*, after Thring (1911), *Sweet and Low*, after Tennyson (1911), *Sweet and Low* (1911), and *Jubilate* (1913); songs; hymns.

Owen, Richard, American lawyer, judge, and composer; b. N.Y., Dec. 11, 1922. He graduated from Dartmouth College in 1947 and from Harvard Law School in 1950; subsequently he served as a senior trial attorney, and then was appointed to the bench by President Nixon to the U.S. District Court in N.Y. (1974). In between he attended night school at the Mannes School of Music, took courses in harmony and counterpoint with Vittorio Giannini and Robert Starer, and attended the Berkshire Music Center at Tanglewood. He wrote several operas deeply influenced by Puccini and Menotti, including *Dismissed with Prejudice* (1956), *A Moment of War* (1958), *A Fisherman Called Peter* (1965), *Mary Dyer* (dealing with a woman Quaker who was hanged in Boston on June 1, 1660; N.Y., June 12, 1976, with Owen's wife singing the title role), *The Death of the Virgin* (N.Y., March 31, 1983), *Abigail Adams* (N.Y., March 18, 1987), and the children's opera *Tom Sawyer* (N.Y., April 2, 1989).

Ozawa, Seiji, brilliant Japanese conductor; b. Fenytien, China (of Japanese parents), Sept. 1, 1935. His father was a Buddhist, his mother a Christian. The family returned to Japan in 1944, at the end of the Japanese occupation of Manchuria. Ozawa began to study piano; at 16, he enrolled at the Toho School of Music in Tokyo, where he studied composition and conducting; one of his teachers, Hideo Saito, profoundly influenced his development as a musician; he graduated in 1959 with 1st prizes in composition and conducting. By that time he had already conducted concerts with the NHK (Japan Broadcasting Corp.) Sym. Orch. and the Japan Phil.; upon Saito's advice, he went to Europe; to defray his expenses, he became a motorscooter salesman for a Japanese firm, and promoted the product in Italy and France. In 1959 he won 1st prize at the international competition for conductors in Besançon, and was befriended by Charles Munch and Eugène Bigot; he then studied conducting with Bigot in Paris. Munch arranged for Ozawa to go to the U.S. and to study conducting at the Berkshire Music Center in Tanglewood; in 1960 he won its Koussevitzky Prize, and was awarded a scholarship to work with Karajan and the Berlin Phil. Bernstein heard him in Berlin and engaged him as an assistant conductor of the N.Y. Phil. On April 14, 1961, he made his first appearance with the orch. at Carnegie Hall; later that year, he accompanied Bernstein and the orch. on its tour of Japan. In 1962 he was invited to return as a guest conductor of the NHK Sym. Orch., but difficulties arose between him and the players, who objected to being commanded in an imperious manner by one of their own countrymen; still, he succeeded in obtaining engagements with other Japanese orchs., which he conducted on his periodic visits to his homeland.

After serving as sole assistant conductor of the N.Y. Phil. (1964–65), Ozawa's career advanced significantly; from 1964 to 1968 he was music director of the Ravinia Festival, the summer home of the Chicago Sym. Orch.; in 1969 he served as its principal guest conductor; from 1965 to 1969 he also was music director of the Toronto Sym. Orch., which he took to England in 1965. From 1970 to 1976 he was music director of the San Francisco Sym. Orch., and then its music adviser (1976–77); took it on an extensive tour of Europe in 1977, garnering exceptional critical acclaim. Even before completing his tenure in San Francisco, he had begun a close association with the Boston Sym. Orch.; with Schuller, he became co-artistic director of its Berkshire Music Center in 1970; in 1972 he assumed the post of music adviser of the Boston Sym. Orch., and in 1973 he became its music director, and sole artistic director of the Berkshire Music Center, an astonishing event in American music annals, marking the first time an oriental musician was chosen solely by his merit to head the Boston Sym. Orch., which was for years since its foundation the exclusive preserve of German, and later French and Russian, conductors. In 1976 Ozawa took the Boston Sym. Orch. on a tour of Europe; in 1978 he escorted it to Japan, where those among Japanese musicians who had been skeptical about his abilities greeted his spectacular ascendance with national pride. Another unprecedented event took place in the spring of 1979, when Ozawa traveled with the Boston Sym. Orch. to the People's Republic of China on an official cultural visit; in Aug. 1979 Ozawa and the orch. went on a tour of European music festivals. The centennial of the Boston Sym. Orch. in 1981 was marked by a series of concerts, under Ozawa's direction, which included appearances in 14 American cities and a tour of Japan, France, Germany, Austria, and England. On Sept. 24, 1991, he conducted the Saito Kinen Orch. of Japan at its first appearance in the U.S. at N.Y.'s Carnegie Hall. One Sept. 5, 1992, he inaugurated the Saito Kinen Festival in Matsumoto. He made his Metropolitan Opera debut in N.Y. on Dec. 4, 1992, conducting *Eugene Onegin*. In 1994 the Boston Sym. Orch.'s new concert hall at Tanglewood was named the Seiji Ozawa Hall in his honor.

After Ozawa consolidated his music directorship in Boston, his reputation rose to universal recognition of his remarkable talent. He proved himself a consummate master of orchestral playing, equally penetrating in the classical repertoire as in the works of modern times; his performances of such demanding scores as Mahler's 8th Sym. and Schoenberg's *Gürrelieder* constituted proofs of his commanding technical skill, affirmed *a fortiori* by his assured presentation of the rhythmically and contrapuntally intricate 4th Sym. of Charles Ives. All these challenging scores Ozawa consuetudinarily conducted from memory, an astonishing feat in itself. He was married twice: first to the Japanese pianist Kyoko Edo, and 2nd, to a Eurasian, Vera Ilyan. He received an honorary doctorate in music from the Univ. of San Francisco in 1971, and one from the New England Cons. of Music in 1982. His remarkable career was the subject of the documentary film "Ozawa," which was telecast by PBS in 1987.

Ozim, Igor, Slovenian violinist and teacher; b. Ljubljana, May 9, 1931. He studied with Leon Pfeifer at the Ljubljana Academy of Music and with Rostal in London (1949–51), then won the Flesch (1951) and Munich (1953) competitions. He toured widely in Europe and the U.S.; also taught at the Ljubljana Academy of Music (1960–63) and then at the Cologne Hochschule für Musik. In 1990 he served on the jury of the International Violin Competition of Indianapolis. He was a notable advocate of contemporary music.

P

Paap, Wouter, eminent Dutch musicologist and composer; b. Utrecht, May 7, 1908; d. Lage Vuursche (Baarn), Oct. 7, 1981. He studied piano and theory at the Utrecht School of Music (1928–32). He taught at the Netherland's Inst. for Catholic Church Music (1934–47); was founder-ed. of the journal *Mens en Melodie* (1946–75).

WRITINGS: *Anton Bruckner* (Bilthoven, 1936); *Toscanini* (Amsterdam, 1938); *Mens en melodie: Inleiding tot de muziek* (Utrecht, 1940); *Ludwig van Beethoven* (Amsterdam, 1941); with E. Reeser, *Moderne kerkmuziek in Nederland* (Bilthoven, 1942); *De symfonieën van Beethoven* (Utrecht, 1946); *Die kunst van het moduleren* (Utrecht, 1948); *Eduard van Beinum* (Baarn, 1956); *De symfonie* (Bilthoven, 1957); ed. with A. Corbet, *Algemene muziekencyclopedie* (6 vols., Amsterdam, 1957–63; suppl. ed. by J. Robijns, Ghent, 1972); *Willem Mengelberg* (Amsterdam and Brussels, 1960); *Muziek, moderne en klassiek* (Utrecht, 1961); *Mozart: Portret van een muziekgenie* (Utrecht, 1962); *Honderd jaar muziekonderwijs te Utrecht* (Utrecht, 1974); *Een eeuu koninklijke Nederlandse toonkunstenaars vereniging* (Amsterdam, 1975).

WORKS: ORCH.: *Sinfonietta* for Chamber Orch. (1938); *Wals* for Chamber Orch. (1940); *Passacaglia* (1943); *Studentenmuziek* for Strings (1948); *Guirlanden van Muziek* for Strings (1951); *Ballet Suite* for Chamber Orch. (1953); *Overture Electora* (1956); *Trompetten en klaretten*, 3 pieces for Wind Orch. (1960). **CHAMBER:** *Luchtige suite* for Carillon (1955); Carillon Sonatina (1963); various pieces for Wind Instruments. **VOCAL:** *Sterre der zee* for Soprano, Chorus, and Orch. (1937); *Declamatorium* for Reciter and Orch. (1940); *Muziek ter Bruiloft*, cantata for Tenor and Orch. (1945); *5 Liederen* for Voice and Orch. (1956).

Pablo (Costales), Luís (Alfonso) de, eminent Spanish composer and teacher; b. Bilbao, Jan. 28, 1930. He commenced his musical training in Fuenterrabía when he was 8. After settling in Madrid, he pursued the study of law at the Universidad Complutense (graduated, 1952) while continuing his musical training on his own. In 1958 he joined the Nueva Música group. In 1959 he organized the Tiempo y Música group, with which he presented concerts of contemporary chamber music until 1963. He founded the Forum Musical in 1963 for the purpose of giving concerts of contemporary music. In 1964 he served as the artistic organizer of the first gathering of the Música Contemporánea of Madrid. He founded the new music group Alea and the first electroacoustic music laboratory in Spain in 1965. In 1967 he was in Berlin as a guest of the Deutscher Akademischer Austauschdienst. In 1968 he founded Alea, Música electronica libre, a group which presented performances of live electroacoustic music. He became a prof. of contemporary music analysis at the Madrid Cons. in 1971. With José Luis Alexanco, he served as co-director of the Encuentros de Arts in Pamplona in 1972. In 1973 he was the Visiting Slee Prof. at the State Univ. of N.Y. at Buffalo, and in 1974 he was a prof. of contemporary music analysis at the Univs. of Ottawa and Montreal. In subsequent years, he lectured widely on contemporary music in Spain and abroad. He became president of the Spanish section of the ISCM in 1981. In 1983 he was made director of the Centro para la Difusión de la Música Contemporánea of the Ministry of Culture. In 1994 he was composer-in-residence at the Spanish Academy in Rome. In 1973 the French government honored him with the title of Chevalier des Arts et des Lettres, and in 1986 it bestowed upon him the Médaille d'Officier de l'Ordre des Arts et des Lettres. In 1986 King Juan Carlos of Spain presented him with the Medalla de Oro al Mérito en las Bellas Artes españolas. He was made a full member of the Real Academia de Bellas Artes de San Fernando of Madrid and a corresponding member of the Academy of Granada in 1988. In 1991 he was awarded the Premio Nacional de Música by the Ministry of Culture, and in 1993 he was awarded its diploma of the Consejo Internacional de la Música. In his compositions, he has demonstrated a remarkable versatility in handling various techniques. All the while, he has remained true to himself by finding his own compositional path in which each score becomes a thoroughly new adventure in sound. This is so whether he utilizes traditional instruments or ranges into other sound worlds, such as electronic manifestations.

WORKS: DRAMATIC: *Per diversos motivos* for 2 Actors, Soprano, 12 Voices, and Piano (1969); *Berceuse* for Actor, Soprano, 3 Flutes, 2 Percussionists, and Hammond Organ (1973–74; Buffalo, Jan. 26, 1975); *Sólo un paso* for Actor and Flute (Bremen Radio, May 1974); *Very Gentle* for Soprano, Countertenor, and 2 Instrumentalists (Royan, April 3, 1974); *Kiu*, opera (1979–82; Madrid, April 16, 1983); *El viajero indiscreto*, opera (1984–88; Madrid, March 12, 1990); *Llanto*, ballet (1987); *La madre invita a comer*, opera (1992; Venice, June 19, 1993); incidental music; film scores. **ORCH.:** *Sinfonías* for Chamber Orch. (1954–66; Madrid, Dec. 17, 1966); *Invenciones* (1955; rev. 1959–60; Madrid, June 15, 1960); *Radial* for 24 Instruments (1960); *Tombeau* (1962–63); *Iniciativas* (1965–66); *Módolus II* for 2 Orchs. (1966; Madrid, Oct. 24, 1967); *Imaginario II* (1967); *Quasi una fantasía* for String Sextet and Orch. (1969); *Oroitaldi* (1971; Monte Carlo, Dec. 3, 1972); *Éléphants ivres I* (1972; Madrid, April 27, 1973), *III* (1973), and *IV* (1973); *Je mange, tu manges* for Chamber Orch. (1972); *Latidos* (1974–80; Radio France, Paris, Jan. 23, 1981); *Tinieblas del agua* (Metz, Nov. 18, 1978); 2 piano concertos: No. 1 (1978–79; Madrid, March 1, 1980; also as *Concierto de cámara* for Piano and Chamber Orch., 1979; Quebec, Dec. 11, 1980) and No. 2 (1979–80; Santander, Aug. 5, 1982; also as Concerto for Harpsichord, 2 Percussion, and Strings, Naples, Dec. 16, 1983); *Adagio* (1983; Hilversum, March 2, 1984); *Adagio-Cadenza-Allegro spiritoso* for Oboe and Orch. (Murcia, April 18, 1987); *Fiesta* for 6 Percussionists and Orch. (1987; Rennes, Feb. 1988; also for 6 Percussionists, 1989); *Senderos del aire* (1987; Tokyo, Nov. 4, 1988); *Une couleur* for Saxophone and Orch. (1988; Fontenai, Jan. 20, 1989); *Figura en el mar* for Flute and Orch. (1989; Metz, Nov. 17, 1990); *Cinco impromptus* (1990; San Sebastian, Jan. 28, 1991); *Las orillas* (1990; Tenerife, Jan. 7, 1991); *Sueños* for Piano and Orch. (1991; Parma, June 5, 1992). **CHAMBER:** *Coral* for 7 Instruments (1954; rev. 1958); *Polar* for 11 Instruments (1961); *Prosodía* for 6 Instruments (1962); *Condicionado* for Flute (1962); *Recíproco* for Flutes, Piano, and Percussion (Venice, April 13, 1963); *Cesuras* for 6 Instruments (Madrid, Dec. 11, 1963); *Módulos I* for 11 Instruments (1964–65; Darmstadt, July 31, 1965), *IV* for String Quartet (1965–67), *III* for 17 Instruments (1967; North German Radio, Hamburg, Jan. 9, 1968), and *V* for Organ (1967); *Imaginario I* for Harpsichord and 3 Percussion (1967); *Paráfrasis* for 12 Instruments (1968); *La libertad sonríe* for 15 Instruments (Salamanca, May 7, 1971); *Promenade sur un corps* for Flute and Percussion (1971); *Éléphants ivres II* for Chamber Ensemble (1972); *Historia natural* for 2 Organs, Percussion, and Tape (1972); *Pardon* for Clarinet and Trombone (Warsaw, Sept. 1972); *Soirée* for Clarinet and Violin (1972); *Le prie-dieu sur la terrasse* for Percussionist (1973; Barcelona, Feb. 22, 1974); *Vielleicht* for 6 Percussionists (1973; Royan, March 27, 1975); *Déjame hablar* for Strings (1974; Royan, March 27, 1975); *Visto de cerca* for 3 Instrumentalists and Tape (1974); *A modo concierto* for Percussion and Instruments (1975–76); *Credo* for 2 Flutes, 2 Oboes, 2 Clarinets, 2 Bassoons, and 2 Horns (1976; Madrid, April 30, 1977); *Invitación a la memoria* for Chamber Ensemble (1976–77; Saintes, July 18, 1978); *Lerro* for Flute (1977); *Oculto* for Bass Clarinet or Saxophone (1977); Trio for Violin, Viola, and Cello (1978; Madrid, Nov. 3, 1980); *Dibujos* for Flute, Clarinet, Violin, and Cello (1979–80; Madrid, April 29, 1980); *Tornasol* for 2 Flutes, 2 Clarinets, Violin, Viola, Cello, Double Bass, and Tape (1980–81; Marseilles, Feb. 23, 1982); *Ofrenda (Seis piezas a la memoria de Manuel Azaña)* for Cello (1980–82; N.Y., April 1983); *Saturno* for 2 Percussionists (1983); *Cinco meditaciones* for Chamber Ensemble (1983–84; San Sebastián, Aug. 26, 1984); *J. H.* for Clarinet and Cello (1983–84); *Cuatro fragmentos de Kiu* for Violin and Piano (1984–86; also for Flute and Piano, 1985–86; Madrid, June 18, 1986); *Caligrafías (Federico Mompou in memoriam)* for Piano, Violin, and Cello (1987; Santander, Aug. 9, 1988); *Notturnino* for Chamber Ensemble (1987); *Il violino spagnolo* for Violin (1988); *Compostela* for Violin and Cello (1989); *Fiesta* for 6 Percussionists (1989; also for 6 Percussionists and Orch., 1987); *Metáforas* for Piano, 2 Violins, Viola, and Cello (1989–90; Madrid, Nov. 7, 1990); *Melisma furioso* for Flute (Tokyo, Sept. 1, 1990); Sextet, *Paráfrasis e interludio*, for 2 Violins, 2 Violas, Cello, and Double Bass (1990; Reykjavík, Feb. 1991); *Monólogo* for Viola (1990–92); *Libro de imágenes* for 9 Instruments (Amsterdam, June 1992); *Fábula* for Guitar (1991–92; Madrid, March 12, 1992); *Paraíso y Tres danzas macabras* for Chamber Ensemble (1992); *Parodia* for 2 Violins, Viola, and Cello (Madrid, Dec. 6, 1992); *Ritornello* for 8 Cellos (1992–93; Santander, Aug. 22, 1993); *Segunda lectura* for 10 Instruments (1992–93); *Umori* for Flute, Oboe, Clarinet, Trumpet, and Bassoon (1992–93; Bologna, April 28, 1993); *Caligrafía serena* for 2 Violins, Viola, and Cello (1993); Trio for Violin, Cello, and Piano (1993). **PIANO:** *Móvil* for 2 Pianos (1957) and *II* for Piano, 4-hands (1959–67); Sonata (1958; Madrid, March 6, 1960); *Libro para el pianista* (1961–62); *Comme d'habitude* for 1 Pianist on 2 Pianos (1970); *Affettuoso* (1973); *Cuaderno* (1982); *Retratos y transcripciones* (1984–92); *Amable sombra* for 2 Pianos (1989). **VOCAL:** *Comentarios a dos textos de Gerardo Diego* for Soprano or Tenor, Piccolo, Vibraphone, and Double Bass (1956; Barcelona, May 11, 1960); *Escena* for Chorus, 2 Percussion, and 15 Strings (1964); *Ein Wort* for Soprano, Piano, Violin, and Clarinet (1965); *Heterogéneo* for 2 Reciters, Hammond Organ, and Orch. (1967); *Yo lo vi* for Chorus (1970); *Visto de cerca* for 3 Men's Voices and Electronics (1974); *Al son que tocan* for Soprano, 4 Basses, 8 Instruments, and Tape (1974–75; Madrid, Nov. 18, 1975); *Portrait imaginé* for Chorus, Chamber Orch., and Tape (1974–75; Ottawa, Oct. 1, 1975); *Zurezko olerkia* for Chorus, 2 Txalapartas, and 4 Percussionists (1975; Bonn, May 24, 1976); *Bajo el sol* for Chorus (1977; Cuenca, March 25, 1978); *Ederki* for Soprano, Viola, and Percussion (1977–78; Naples, June 17, 1978); *Canción* for Soprano, Oboe, Trumpet, Celesta, and Harp (1979); *Pocket zarzuela* for Mezzo-soprano, 2 Flutes, Clarinet, Violin, Cello, and Piano (Bonn, Oct. 9, 1979); *Retratos de la conquista* for Chorus (Lille, Nov. 15, 1980); *Sonido de la guerra* for Soprano, Tenor, Reciter, Small Women's Chorus, Flute, Harp, Celesta, 2 Percussionists, and Cello (1980; Madrid, Dec. 17, 1981); *Una cantata perdida* for Soprano, Double Bass, and Percussion (N.Y., Nov. 1981); *Viatges i flors* for Soprano, Reciter, Chorus, and Orch. (1981–84; Brussels, Oct. 10, 1985); *El manantial* for Soprano, Flute, Celesta, Harp, Piano, and 2 Violins (Valladolid, Nov. 12, 1982); *Malinche* for Soprano, Percussion, and Tape (1983; Naples, Sept. 1984; also for Soprano and Piano, Rome, April 25, 1985); *Serenata* for Chorus and Band (1984–85; Lille, Dec. 1990); *Zu Strassburg auf der Schanz* for Baritone and Orch. (Radio France, Paris, Feb. 28, 1985); *Tarde de poetas* for Soprano, Baritone, Chorus, and Chamber Orch. (1985–86); *Com um epilog* for Men's Chorus and Orch. (1988; Paris, May 1989); *Antigua fe* for Soprano, Men's Chorus, and Orch. (1990; Madrid, Jan. 28, 1992); *Ricercare recordare* for Reciter, Chorus, and Chamber Ensemble (1990); *De la América pretérita* for Soprano and Orch. (1991); *Variaciones de Léon* for 2 Sopranos, Contralto, Tenor, Baritone, and Bass (1992–93; Royaumont, Sept. 11, 1993). **ELECTROACOUSTIC:** *We* (1969–70; Paris, Oct. 1970; 2nd version, 1984; Madrid, Jan. 28, 1985); *Tamaño natural* (Paris, Oct. 1970); *Soledad interrumpida* (Buenos Aires, July 20, 1971); *Chamán* (1975–76; Ottawa, Feb. 1, 1976).

BIBL.: T. Marco, *L.d. P.* (Madrid, 1976); J. García del Busto, *L.d. P.* (Madrid, 1979); idem, *Escritos sobre L.d. P.* (Madrid, 1987).

Pachmann, Vladimir de, eccentric Russian-born Italian pianist; b. Odessa, July 27, 1848; d. Rome, Jan. 6, 1933. He received his primary music education at home from his father, an Austrian lawyer and amateur musician; his mother was Turkish. He then was a pupil of J. Dachs at the Vienna Cons. (1866–68), graduating with the Gold Medal. He began his concert career with a tour of Russia in 1869; he was 40 years old before he made a decisive impact on the international scene; his first American tour, in 1891, was sensationally successful, and it was in America that he began exhibiting his curious eccentricities, some of them undoubtedly calculated to produce shock effect: he made grimaces when he did not like his own playing, and shouted "Bravo!" when he played to his satisfaction; even more bizarre was his crawling under the grand piano after the concert, claiming that he was looking for the wrong notes he had accidentally hit; all this could be explained as idiosyncratic behavior; but he also allowed himself to mutilate the music itself, by inserting arpeggios between phrases and extra chords at the end of a piece. Most American critics were outraged by his shenanigans, but some, notably Philip Hale, found mitigation in the poetic quality of his interpretations. Pachmann was particularly emotional in playing Chopin, when his facial contortions became quite obnoxious; James Huneker dubbed him "Chopinzee." Pachmann did not lack official honors; in 1855, on his tour of Denmark, he was made a Knight of the Order of Danebrog; in 1916 the Royal Phil. Soc. of London awarded him its Gold Medal. He made his last tour of the U.S. in 1925; spent his last years in Italy, becoming a naturalized Italian citizen in 1928. His personal life was turbulent; he married frequently (the exact number of his wives is in dispute). His first wife was his pupil, the Austrian Maggie Oakey (1864–1952), who toured as Marguerite de Pachmann from the time of their marriage (1884) until their divorce (1895); she later married a French lawyer, becoming known as Marguerite de Pachmann-Labori. Pachmann and his first wife had a son, Adrian de Pachmann (c.1893–1937), who also became a pianist.

BIBL.: K. Sorabji, "P. and Chopin," *Around Music* (London, 1932).

Paciorkiewicz, Tadeusz, Polish composer and organist; b. Sierpc, Oct. 17, 1916. He studied organ with Rutkowski at the Warsaw Cons. (graduated, 1942) and composition with Sikorski at the Łódź State College of Music (graduated, 1951). He taught in music schools in Plock (1945–49) and Łódź (1949–59); also taught at the Warsaw State College of Music (from 1954), becoming a permanent faculty member (1959); was dean of its composition, theory, and conducting dept. (1963–69), and then its rector (1969–71).

WORKS: DRAMATIC: OPERAS: *Ushico*, radio opera (1962); *The Maiden from the Dormer Window* (1964); *Ligea*, radio opera (1967). **BALLET:** *Warsaw Legend* (1959). **ORCH.:** 2 piano concertos (1952, 1954); 4 syms. (1953, 1957, 1989, 1992); Violin Concerto (1955); *Duet koncertujacy* for Organ and Orch. (1962); 2 organ concertos (1967, 1988); *Divertimento* for Clarinet and Strings (1968); Trombone Concerto (1971); Viola Concerto (1975–76); *Concerto alla Barocco* (1979); Concerto for Harp, Flute, and Strings (1980); Oboe Concerto (1982); Concerto for 2 Violins and Orch. (1983); Horn Concerto (1986); Concerto for Viola, Organ, and Orch. (1990); Concerto for Cello and Chamber Orch. (1991). **CHAMBER:** Wind Quintet (1951); Violin Sonata (1954); 2 string quartets (1960, 1982); 4 caprices: *Quasi una sonata* for Clarinet and Piano (1960); Trio for Flute, Viola, and Harp (1966); *6 Miniatures* for 4 Trombones (1972); Piano Quintet (1972); *Concertante Duet* for Clarinet and Piano (1973); Cello Sonata (1974–75); *3 Musical Moments* for 5 Clarinets (1985); *Duo Serenade* for Flute and Piano (1987); *Decet* for Wind Quintet and String Quintet (1988); Viola Sonata (1988); Flute Quintet (1988); *Klangdialog* for Mandolin and Guitar (1989); *Klanspiele* for 6 to 7 Percussionists; organ pieces, including a Sonata (1946–47); piano works. **VOCAL:** *De Revolutionibus*, oratorio for 4 Solo Voices, Reciter, Boy's Chorus, Chorus, Organ, and Orch. (1972); *2 Psalms* for Soprano and Organ (1985); *Psalm 150* for 5 Solo Voices and Organ (1990).

Paderewski, Ignacy (Jan), celebrated Polish pianist and composer; b. Kurylowka, Podolia (Russian Poland), Nov. 18, 1860; d. N.Y., June 29, 1941. His father was an administrator of country estates; his mother died soon after his birth. From early childhood, Paderewski was attracted to piano music; he received some musical instruction from Peter Sowinski, who taught him 4-hand arrangements of operas. His first public appearance was in a charity concert at the age of 11, when he played piano with his sister. His playing aroused interest among wealthy patrons, who took him to Kiev. He was then sent to Warsaw, where he entered the Cons., learned to play trombone, and joined the school band. He also continued serious piano study; his teachers at the Warsaw Cons. were Schlözer, Strobl, and Janotha. In 1875 and 1877 he toured in provincial Russian towns with the Polish violinist Cielewicz; in the interim periods, he took courses in composition at the Warsaw Cons., and upon graduation in 1878 was engaged as a member of the piano faculty there. In 1880 he married a young music student named Antonina Korsak, but she died 9 days after giving birth to a child, on Oct. 10, 1880. In 1882 he went to Berlin to study composition with Kiel; there he met Anton Rubinstein, who gave him encouraging advice and urged him to compose piano music. He resigned from his teaching job at the Warsaw Cons. and began to study orchestration in Berlin with Heinrich Urban. While on a vacation in the Tatra Mountains (which inspired his *Tatra Album* for piano), he met the celebrated Polish actress Modjeska, who proposed to finance his further piano studies with Leschetizky in Vienna. Paderewski followed this advice and spent several years as a Leschetizky student. He continued his career as a concert pianist. On March 3, 1888, he gave his first Paris recital, and on Nov. 10, 1888, played a concert in Vienna, both with excellent success. He also began receiving recognition as a composer. Anna Essipova (who was married to Leschetizky) played his piano concerto in Vienna under the direction of Hans Richter. Paderewski made his London debut on May 9, 1890. On Nov. 17, 1891, he played for the first time in N.Y., and was acclaimed with an adulation rare for pianists; by some counts he gave 107 concerts in 117 days in N.Y. and other American cities and attended 86 dinner parties; his wit, already fully developed, made him a social lion in wealthy American salons. At one party, it was reported, the hostess confused him with a famous polo player who was also expected to be a guest, and greeted him effusively. "No," Paderewski is supposed to have replied, "he is a rich soul who plays polo, and I am a poor Pole who plays solo." American spinsters beseeched him for a lock of his luxurious mane of hair; he invariably obliged, and when his valet observed that at this rate he would soon be bald, he said, "Not I, my dog." There is even a story related by a gullible biographer that Paderewski could charm beasts by his art and that a spider used to come down from the ceiling in Paderewski's lodgings in Vienna and sit at the piano every time Paderewski played a certain Chopin etude. Paderewski eclipsed even Caruso as an idol of the masses. In 1890 he made a concert tour in Germany; also toured South America, South Africa, and Australia. In 1898 he purchased a beautiful home, the Villa Riond-Bosson on Lake Geneva, Switzerland; in 1899 he married Helena Gorska, Baroness von Rosen. In 1900, by a deed of trust, Paderewski established a fund of $10,000 (the original trustees were William Steinway, Henry Lee Higginson, and William Mason), the interest from which was to be used for triennial prizes given "to composers of American birth without distinction as to age or religion" for works in the categories of syms., concertos, and chamber music. In 1910, on the occasion of the centennial of Chopin's birth, Paderewski donated $60,000 for the construction of the Chopin Memorial Hall in Warsaw; in the same year, he contributed $100,000 for the erection of the statue of King Jagiello in Warsaw, on the quinquecentennial of his victory over the Teutonic Knights in 1410. In 1913 he purchased a ranch in Paso Robles in California.

Although cosmopolitan in his culture, Paderewski remained a great Polish patriot. During the First World War he donated the entire proceeds from his concerts to a fund for the Polish people caught in the war between Russia and Germany. After the establishment of the independent Polish state, Paderewski served as its representative in Washington; in 1919 he was named prime minister of the Polish Republic, the first musician to occupy such a post in any country at any period. He took part in the Versailles Treaty conference; it was then that Prime Minister Clemenceau of France welcomed Paderewski with the famous, if possibly apocryphal, remark: "You, a famous pianist, a prime minister! What a comedown!" Paderewski resigned his post on Dec. 10, 1919. He reentered politics in 1920 in the wake of the Russian invasion of Poland that year, when he became a delegate to the League of Nations; he resigned on May 7, 1921, and resumed his musical career. On Nov. 22, 1922, he gave his first concert after a hiatus of many years at Carnegie Hall in N.Y. In 1939 he made his last American tour. Once more during his lifetime Poland was invaded, this time by both Germany and Russia. Once more Paderewski was driven to political action. He joined the Polish government-in-exile in France and was named president of its parliament on Jan. 23, 1940. He returned to the U.S. on Nov. 6, 1940, a few months before his death. At the order of President Roosevelt, his body was given state burial in Arlington National Cemetery, pending the return of his remains to Free Poland. While his body was buried at Arlington National Cemetery, his heart was buried in Brooklyn and finally entombed at the Shrine of Our Lady of Czestochowa in Doylestown, Pa., in 1986. His body was finally removed from Arlington National Cemetery and returned to Free Poland, where a Mass and state burial was accorded him at the St. John the Baptist Cathedral in Warsaw on July 5, 1992, with President Bush of the U.S. and President Walesa of Poland in attendance. Paderewski received many honors. He held the following degrees: Ph.D. from the Univ. of Lemberg (1912); D.Mus. from Yale Univ. (1917); Ph.D. from the Univ. of Kraków (1919); D.C.L. from the Univ. of Oxford (1920); LL.D. from Columbia Univ. (1922); Ph.D. from the Univ. of Southern Calif. (1923); Ph.D. from the Univ. of Poznań (1924); and Ph.D. from the Univ. of Glasgow (1925). He also held the Grand Cross of the French Legion of Honor (1922). A postage stamp with his picture was issued in Poland in 1919, and 2 postage stamps honoring him in the series "Men of Liberty" were issued in the U.S. in 1960.

As an artist, Paderewski was a faithful follower of the Romantic school, which allowed free, well-nigh improvisatory declensions from the written notes, tempi, and dynamics; judged by 20th-century standards of precise rendering of the text, Paderewski's interpretations appear surprisingly free, but this very personal freedom of performance moved contemporary audiences to ecstasies of admiration. Also, Paderewski's virtuoso technique, which astonished his listeners, has been easily matched by any number of pianists of succeeding generations. Yet his position in the world of the performing arts remains undiminished by the later achievements of younger men and women pianists. As a composer, Paderewski also belongs to the Romantic school. At least one of his piano pieces, the *Menuet in G* (a movement of his set of *6 Humoresques de concert*), achieved enormous popularity. His other compositions, however, never sustained a power of renewal and were eventually relegated to the archives of unperformed music. His opera *Manru* (1897–1900), dealing with folk life in the Tatra Mountains, was produced in Dresden on May 29, 1901, and was also performed by the Metropolitan Opera in N.Y. on Feb. 14, 1902. Another major work, a Sym. in B minor, was first performed by the Boston Sym. Orch. on Feb. 12, 1909. His other works included a Piano Concerto in A minor (1888); *Fantaisie polonaise* for Piano and Orch. (1893); Violin Sonata (1880); songs; and the following compositions for piano solo: *Prelude and Capriccio; 3 Pieces (Gavotte, Mélodie, Valse mélancholique); Krakówiak; Élégie; 3 Polish Dances; Introduction and Toccata; Chants du voyageur* (5 pieces); *6 Polish Dances; Album de mai* (5 pieces), *Variations and Fugue; Tatra Album* (also arr. for Piano, 4-hands); *6 Humoresques de concert* (which includes the famous *Menuet in G*); *Dans le désert; Miscellanea* (7 pieces); *Légende*; Sonata in E-flat minor (1903). A complete list of Paderewski's works was publ. in the *Bolletino bibliografico musicale* (Milan, 1932).

BIBL.: F. Buffen, *I. P.* (N.Y., 1891); C. Tretbar, *P.: A Biographical Sketch* (N.Y., 1892); H. Finck, *P. and His Art* (N.Y., 1895); A. Nossig, *P.* (Leipzig, 1901); E. Baughan, *I. P.* (London, 1908); A. Chybiński, *P.* (Warsaw, 1910); S. Popielowna, *I. P.* (Tarnow, 1919); F. Martens, *P.* (N.Y., 1923); B. Sidorowicz, *I. P.* (Poznań, 1924); J. Cooke, *P.* (Philadelphia, 1928); H. Opieński, *I.J. P.* (Warsaw, 1928; 3rd ed., rev. and aug., 1960); C. Philips, *P.* (N.Y., 1933); R. Landau, *I. P.: Musician and Statesman* (N.Y., 1934); *P.'s Diamond Anniversary* (N.Y., 1936); M. Lawton, *The P. Memoirs* (to 1914 only; N.Y., 1938); E. Ligocki, *Homage to P.* (Edinburgh, 1941); A. Gronowicz, *P.: Pianist and Patriot* (Edinburgh, 1943); B. Sarrazin, *Imageries de P.* (Annonay, 1945); A. Baumgartner, *La Vérité sur le prétendu drame P.* (Geneva, 1948); S. Giron, *Le Drame P.* (Geneva, 1948); A. Strakacz, *P. as I Knew Him* (New Brunswick, N.J., 1949); C. Kellogg, *P.* (N.Y., 1956); J. Cieplinski, *I. P.* (N.Y., 1960); R. and P. Hume, *The Lion of Poland: The Story of P.* (N.Y., 1962); R. Halski, *P.* (London, 1964); W. Dulaba, *I. P.* (Kraków, 1966); A. Zamoyski, *P.* (N.Y., 1982); J. Hoskins, *I.J. P., 1860–1941: A Biographical Sketch and a Selective List of Reading Materials* (Washington, D.C., 1984); E. Lipmann, *P., l'idole des années folles* (Paris, 1984); M. Perkowska, *Diariusz koncertowy I.ego J.a. P.ego* (Kraków, 1990).

Padlewski, Roman, Polish violinist, choral conductor, music critic, and composer; b. Moscow, Oct. 7, 1915; d. in the Warsaw uprising, Aug. 16, 1944. He went to Poznań and studied with Jahnke (violin) and Wiechowicz (composition) at the Cons. (1927–29) and with Kamienski (musicology) at the Univ. (1932–35). He was active as an orch. musician, choral conductor, and music critic until being taken prisoner by the Nazis at the outbreak of World War II in 1939. However, he managed to escape to Warsaw, where he resumed his studies in 1943 with Rutkowski (organ), Bierdiajew (conducting), and Sikorski (composition). Many of his MSS were destroyed during the Warsaw uprising, but a Suite for Violin and Orch., 2 string quartets, a Violin Sonata, and several vocal pieces are extant. These reveal Padlewski as a composer of marked talent.

Page, Robert, esteemed American conductor and pedagogue; b. Abilene, Texas, April 27, 1927. Following studies at Abilene Christian College (B.A., 1948) and Indiana Univ. (M.M., 1951), he pursued graduate training at N.Y. Univ. (1955–59). He was director of choral activities at Eastern New Mexico Univ. in Portales (1951–55) and at Temple Univ. in Philadelphia (1956–75). From 1964 to 1976 he was music director of the Mendelssohn Club of Philadelphia. He served as director of choruses for the Cleveland Orch. from 1971 to 1989. He also was director of the Blossom Festival Chorus (1973–89) and assistant conductor of the Cleveland Orch. (1979–89). From 1975 to 1980 he was head of the music dept. at Carnegie-Mellon Univ. in Pittsburgh. In 1979 he became music director of the Mendelssohn Choir of Pittsburgh. He also was a conductor and chorus master of the Cleveland Opera (1980–86), founder-music director of the Robert Page Singers (from 1982), director of choral studies of Carnegie-Mellon Univ. (from 1988), and director of special projects and choral activities of the Pittsburgh Sym. Orch. (from 1989). He likewise served as president of Chorus America (1990–93). Page has won notable distinction as a choral conductor and teacher.

Pagliughi, Lina, American-born Italian soprano; b. N.Y., May 27, 1907; d. Rubicone, Oct. 2, 1980. She was encouraged to pursue a career as a singer by Tetrazzini; studied voice in Milan with Manlio Bavagnoli. She made her operatic debut at the Teatro Nazionale in Milan as Gilda in 1927; then made appearances throughout Italy; sang at La Scala in Milan in 1930, and continued to make appearances there until 1947; then sang with the RAI until her retirement in 1956. She was married to the tenor Primo Montanari. She was best known for her roles in operas by Rossini, Bellini, and Donizetti.

Pahissa, Jaime, Catalan-born Argentine writer on music, teacher, and composer; b. Barcelona, Oct. 7, 1880; d. Buenos Aires, Oct. 27, 1969. He was a practicing architect for 4 years before turning to music as a profession; studied composition with Morera in Barcelona. He associated himself with the Catalan nationalist movement in art, obtaining his first important success in 1906 with the Romantic opera *La presó de Lledida* (The Prison of Lérida), which had 100 consecutive performances in Barcelona; it was later revised and produced in

Barcelona on Feb. 8, 1928, as *La Princesa Margarita*, again obtaining a notable success. Other operas produced in Barcelona were *Gala Placidía* (Jan. 15, 1913) and *Marianela* (March 31, 1923). Among his orch. works, the most remarkable is *Monodía* (Barcelona, Oct. 12, 1925), written in unisons, octaves, double octaves, etc., without using any other intervals, and depending for its effect only on instrumental variety; in a different vein is his *Suite Intertonal* (Barcelona, Oct. 24, 1926), based on his own method of free tonal and polytonal composition. In 1935 Pahissa emigrated to Argentina, settling in Buenos Aires, where he continued to compose; he also established himself as a teacher and writer. He publ. in Buenos Aires the books: *Espíritu y cuerpo de la música* (1945); *Los grandes problemas de la música* (1945; 2nd ed., 1954); *Vida y obra de Manuel de Falla* (1947; Eng. tr., London, 1954); *Sendas y cumbres de la música española* (1955).

Paik, Byung-Dong, Korean composer and pedagogue; b. Seoul, Jan. 26, 1936. He studied at Seoul National Univ. (B.A., 1959), and later with Fritz von Block and Alfred Koerppen (theory) and Isang Yun (composition) at the Hannover Staatliche Hochschule für Musik (1969–71). In 1976 he became a prof. at the College of Music at Seoul National Univ., where he also was head of its composition dept. (1981–87). Among his awards are the Annual Korean New Composer's Prize (1962, for his *Symphony in 3 Movements*), the 5th Wolgan Musicians Prize (1975), the 1st Korean National Composer's Prize (1977, for his *Zweite Streichquartett*), and the Cultural Prize of Seoul (1983). Several of his works combine Korean musical traditions and instruments with contemporary Western instruments and practices. His style of composition tends toward strict formal procedures utilizing academic musical vocabularies.

WORKS (all 1st perf. in Seoul unless otherwise given): **ORCH.:** *Symphony in 3 Movements* (1962; July 9, 1963); Cello Concerto (Oct. 30, 1969); *Stimmung* (1971; March 28, 1974); Viola Concerto (Oct. 11, 1972); Piano Concerto (March 26, 1974); *Metamorphosen für 83 Spieler* (Oct. 23, 1974); *Requiescat* for 3 Oboes and Orch. (1974; Feb. 11, 1976); *Youlmok* for Strings (June 23, 1982); *Sansudo* (Sept. 22, 1983); *Pogu* (Pusan, May 2, 1986); *In September* (1987). **CHAMBER:** *Zeite Streichquartett* (Nov. 29, 1977); *Sori* for Flute, Guitar, and Cello (Tokyo, Feb. 26, 1981); Piano Trio (June 30, 1985); *Zweite Kammerkonzert* (March 11, 1988); *Contra* for Marimbaphone and 2 Percussion (Tokyo, June 21, 1988); *5 Pieces* for Cello and Contrabass (March 9, 1989). **TRADITIONAL KOREAN INSTRUMENTS:** *Shin Byul Gock* (April 18, 1972); *Un-Rack* (April 14, 1976); *3 Essays of GAYO* (Dec. 13, 1985); *Hwan Myung* (May 17, 1988). **OTHER:** Numerous works for Solo Instruments; dance music. **VOCAL:** Numerous works, including songs.

Paik, Kun-Woo, Korean pianist; b. Seoul, March 10, 1946. He studied music with his father, making his public debut when he was 8. He went to the U.S. in 1960 to continue his studies at the Juilliard School of Music in N.Y. with Rosina Lhévinne; won the Naumburg Award, and also studied with Ilona Kabos in London and Wilhelm Kempff in Italy. He subsequently developed a fine concert career, appearing as soloist with leading orchs. of North America as well as in Europe.

Paik, Nam June, innovative avant-garde Korean-American composer and visual arts; b. Seoul, July 20, 1932. He studied first at the Univ. of Tokyo; then took courses in theory with Georgiades in Munich and with Fortner in Freiburg im Breisgau; then attended the summer courses in new music in Darmstadt (1957–61) and worked at the Cologne Electronic Music Studio (1958–60). In his showings, he pursues the objective of total art as the sum of integrated synesthetic experiences, involving all sorts of actions: walking, talking, dressing, undressing, drinking, smoking, moving furniture, engaging in quaquaversal commotion intended to demonstrate that any human or inhuman action becomes an artistic event through the power of volitional concentration of an ontological imperative. Paik attracted attention at his duo recitals with the topless cellist Charlotte Moorman, at which he acted as a surrogate cello, with his denuded spinal column serving as the fingerboard for Moorman's cello bow, while his bare skin provided an area for intermittent pizzicati. About 1963 Paik began experimenting with videotape as a medium for sounds and images; his initial experiment in this field was *Global Groove*, a high-velocity collage of intermingled television bits, which included instantaneous commercials, fragments from news telecasts, and subliminal extracts from regular programs, subjected to topological alterations. His list of works (some of them consisting solely of categorical imperatives) includes *Ommaggio a Cage* for piano demolition, breakage of raw eggs, spray painting of hands in jet black, etc. (Düsseldorf, Nov. 13, 1959); *Symphony for 20 Rooms* (1961); *Variations on a Theme of Saint-Saëns* for Cello and Piano, with the pianist playing *Le Cygne* while the cellist dives into an oil drum filled with water (N.Y., Aug. 25, 1965, composer at the keyboard, cellist Moorman in the oil drum); *Performable Music*, wherein the performer is ordered to make with a razor an incision of no less than 10 centimeters on his left forearm (Los Angeles, Dec. 2, 1965); *Opéra sextronique* (1967); *Opéra électronique* (1968); *Creep into the Vagina of a Whale* (c.1969); and *Young Penis Symphony*, a protrusion of 10 erectile phalluses through a paper curtain (c.1970; first perf. at "La Mamelle," San Francisco, Sept. 21, 1975, under the direction of Ken Friedman, who also acted as one of the 10 performers). Of uncertain attribution is a sym. designated as No. 3, which Paik delegated to Friedman, who worked on it in Saugus, California, the epicenter of the earthquake of Feb. 9, 1971, and of which the earthquake itself constituted the finale. Among his subsequent works were *Video Buddha* (1974); *VIDEA* (1980); *The More the Better* (1988); *My Faust/The Stations* (1988–91); *Video Opera* (1993).

BIBL.: C. Tomkins, "Video Visionary," *New Yorker* (May 5, 1975).

Pailliard, Jean-François, noted French conductor; b. Vitry-le-François, April 12, 1928. He received his musical training at the Paris Cons.; later took courses in conducting with Markevitch at the Salzburg Mozarteum. In 1953 he founded the Jean-Marie Leclair Instrumental Ensemble, which became the Jean-François Pailliard Chamber Orch. in 1959, with which he toured widely; also appeared extensively as a guest conductor. He ed. the series Archives de la Musique Instrumentale; publ. the study *La musique française classique* (Paris, 1960).

Paita, Carlos, Argentine conductor; b. Buenos Aires, March 10, 1932. He studied piano with Juan Neuchoff, composition with Jacobo Fischer, and conducting with Rodzinski; greatly impressed by Fürtwangler's concerts in Argentina, he became determined to pursue a conducting career. After appearances in Buenos Aires, he conducted in Europe; made his U.S. debut as a guest conductor with the Houston Sym. Orch. (1979). He was active mainly in South America and Europe; recorded with an orch. in London created especially for him. A conductor of passionate Latin tempermant, he won both fervent admirers and intrepid detractors with his supercharged performances of the Romantic repertory.

Pakhmutova, Alexandra (Nikolaievna), Russian composer; b. Beketovka, near Stalingrad, Nov. 9, 1929. She studied at the Moscow Cons. with Shebalin, graduating in 1953. She was particularly successful in the genre of urban ballads, close to contemporary reality; of these, especially popular were her *Songs of Turbulent Youth* (1961); *Cuba, My Love* (1962); *Keep Your Heart Young* (1963); *Young Eagles Learn to Fly* (1965); *A Coward Will Not Play Hockey* (1968); *Let Us Embrace the Sky* (1966); *Gagarin's Constellation* (1971); *Sport Heroes* (1972); and *Hope* (1974). Her Trumpet Concerto acquired great popularity in Russia.

WORKS: BALLET: *Lucid Vision* (1973). **ORCH.:** *Russian Suite* (1952); Trumpet Concerto (Moscow, June 11, 1955); Concerto (1971). **CHAMBER:** *4 Miniatures on Russian Folk Themes* for String Quartet (1950); *Nocturne* for Horn and Piano (1956). **VOCAL:** *Lenin Is in Our Hearts*, suite for Narrator, Children's

Chorus, and Orch. (1957); *Young Pioneer Songs*, cantata (1972); choruses; songs.

BIBL.: E. Dobrynina, *A. P.* (Moscow, 1973).

Palange, Louis S(alvador), American conductor, composer, and arranger; b. Oakland, Calif., Dec. 17, 1917; d. Burbank, Calif., June 8, 1979. He played the clarinet and bassoon in school bands; also studied composition with his father and at Mills College in Oakland, California with Domenico Brecia before going to Los Angeles (1936), where he continued his studies with Wesley La Violette. He subsequently pursued a varied career as a conductor, composer, and arranger, working mainly in Los Angeles from 1946.

WORKS: ORCH.: 2 tone poems: *Evangeline* (1943) and *The Plagues of Egypt* (1945); 2 syms.: No. 1, *Invasion* (1946) and No. 2 (1950; Los Angeles, March 22, 1968); *Pictures* for Flute and Orch. (1948); *Poker Deck Ballet Suite* (1949; Redondo Beach, Calif., Dec. 9, 1960); *A Romantic Concerto* for Piano and Orch. (1949); 2 violin concertos (1950, n.d.). **SYMPHONIC BAND:** *Symphony in Steel* (1940; Los Angeles, March 8, 1941); *Hollywood Panorama*, tone poem (1950; Burbank, Sept. 21, 1952); various other pieces. **CHAMBER:** *Classical Trio* for Flute, Violin, and Viola (1942); *4 Generations* for String Quartet (1950). **OTHER:** Film scores; arrangements for Band or Orch.

Palau Boix, Manuel, Spanish conductor, teacher, and composer; b. Alfara de Patriarca, Jan. 4, 1893; d. Valencia, Feb. 18, 1967. He studied first at the Valencia Cons.; later in Paris, where he took lessons from Koechlin and Ravel. Returning to Valencia, he established himself as a teacher, conductor, and composer. Most of his thematic material is inspired by Catalan folk songs; his instrumental music usually bears programmatic content; his technique of composition follows the French impressionist procedures.

WORKS: ORCH.: *Poemas de juventud* (1926); *Gongoriana* (1927); *Siluetas* (1928); *Homenaje a Debussy* (1929); *Valencia* for Piano and Orch. (1936); *Marcha burlesca* (1936); *Divertimento* (1938); *Poemes de Ilum* (1939); 3 syms. (1945, 1946, 1950); *Concierto dramático* for Piano and Orch. (1948); *Mascarada sarcastica* (1949). **OTHER:** Zarzuelas; chamber works; piano pieces; choral music; songs.

BIBL.: A. Mingote, *M. P.* (Valencia, 1946); F. León Tello, *La obra pianistica de M. P.* (Valencia, 1956).

Páleníček, Josef, Czech pianist, pedagogue, and composer; b. Travnik, July 19, 1914; d. Prague, March 7, 1991. He made his debut as a pianist at 11. After training with Hoffmeister (piano) and Šín and Novák (composition) at the Prague Cons., he studied in Paris with Alexanian and Fournier (chamber music), Roussel, and Cortot. Returning to Prague, he co-founded the Smetana Trio in 1934, which later became the Czech Trio. He toured widely from 1935. In 1963 he became a teacher at the Prague Academy of Music. In 1967 he was made an Artist of Merit and in 1977 was awarded the State Prize by the Czech government. As a solo pianist, he distinguished himself as an interpreter of Janáček.

WORKS: BALLET: *Kytice* (Bouquet; 1980–82). **ORCH.:** Concertino (1937–45); 3 piano concertos (1939, 1953, 1961); Saxophone Concerto (1944); Flute Concerto (1955); *Concertino da camera* for Clarinet and Orch. (1957); *Symphonic Variations on an Imaginary Portrait of Ilya Ehrenburg* (1971); Cello Concerto (1973); *Sinfonietta* for Strings (1977). **CHAMBER:** Piano Quintet (1933); *Preludium a capriccio* for Violin and Piano (1935); Clarinet Sonatina (1936); *Choral Variations* for Cello and Piano (1942); *Little Suite* for Clarinet and Piano (1943); String Quartet (1954); *Masks* for Saxophone and Piano (1957); *Little Suite* for Violin and Piano (1958); *Variations* for Cello and Piano (1972); *Rondo concertante* for Cello and Piano (1972); *Suita in modo antico* for Cello and Piano (1973); *Concertant Etudes* for Double Bass and Piano (1975); *Pictures* for Flute, Bass, Clarinet, Piano, and Percussion (1976); *Tre concertini* for Clarinet and Piano (1977); piano pieces. **VOCAL:** *Song of Man*, oratorio (1952–58); Trio Sonata for Mezzo-soprano, Oboe, and Piano (1965).

Palester, Roman, Polish composer; b. Śniatyñ, Dec. 28, 1907; d. Paris, Aug. 25, 1989. After training in piano from Soltysowa at the Lwów Cons., he entered the Warsaw Cons. in 1925 and studied composition with Sikorski. He subsequently pursued the study of art history at the Univ. of Warsaw. In 1931 he obtained diplomas in composition and theory. After dividing his time between Poland and France, he taught at the Warsaw Cons. from the end of World War II until 1948, when he settled in Paris. In 1981 he was reinstated as a member of the Polish Composers Union. In his music, he was particularly influenced by French music but sought to preserve elements of Polish folk melos in the thematic structure of his scores. Harmonically he did not choose to transcend the limit of enhanced tonality.

WORKS: DRAMATIC: OPERAS: *Zywe kamienie* (The Living Stones; 1944; unfinished); *La Mort de Don Juan* (1959–60). **BALLET:** *Piesn o ziemi* (Song of the Earth; 1937). **ORCH.:** *Muzyka symfoniczna* (1930; London, July 27, 1931; not extant); Piano Concerto (1935; not extant); *Danse polonaise* (1935; Barcelona, April 22, 1936); 5 syms.: No. 1 (1935; not extant), No. 2 (1942), No. 3 for Chamber Orch. (1949), No. 4 (1940–51; rev. 1972), and No. 5 (1977–81; Warsaw, Sept. 23, 1988); Saxophone Concertino (1937); *Suita symfoniczna* (1938); Violin Concerto (1941; London, July 14, 1946); Piano Concertino (1942); *Notturno* for Strings (1947); *Serenade* for 2 Flutes and Strings (Kraków, Nov. 9, 1947); *Passacaglia* (1950); *Variations* (1955); Concertino for Harpsichord and Instrumental Ensemble (1955); *Adagio* for Strings (1956); *Music* for 2 Pianos and Orch. (1957); *Study 58* for Chamber Orch. (1958); Sonata for Strings (1959); Piccolo Concerto for Chamber Orch. (1959); *Metamorphosen* (1965–66); Viola Concerto (1977–78). **CHAMBER:** Sonatina for Violin and Cello (1930; not extant); 3 string quartets (1932, not extant; 1935; 1943); Sonata for 2 Violins and Piano (1939); 2 string trios (1945, 1958); *Divertimento* for 9 Instruments (1949); Trio for Flute, Viola, and Harp (1969); Duo for 2 Violins (1972); *Suite à quatre* for Oboe and String Trio (1973); Trio for Flute, Viola, and Harp (1985). **PIANO:** 2 sonatas (1970, 1980); *Passacaille et Variations* (1974). **VOCAL:** *Psalm V* for Baritone, Chorus, and Orch. (1931); *Requiem* for Soloists, Chorus, and Orch. (1945); *Wisla*, cantata for Chorus (1945–48); *Missa brevis* for Chorus (1948); *Sonnets for Orpheus* for Voice and Chamber Ensemble (1952); *Songs* for Soprano and Chamber Orch. (1976); *Te Deum* for 3 Choruses and Instruments (1978–79).

Palisca, Claude V(ictor), esteemed American musicologist; b. Fiume, Yugoslavia, Nov. 24, 1921. He was taken to the U.S. as a child and in 1929 he became a naturalized American citizen. He was a student of Rathaus (composition) at Queens College of the City Univ. of N.Y. (B.A., 1943), and of Piston and Thompson (composition) and Kinkeldey, Gombosi, and Davison (musicology) at Harvard Univ. (M.A., 1948; Ph.D., 1954, with the diss. *The Beginnings of Baroque Music: Its Roots in Sixteenth-century Theory and Polemics*). In 1949–50 he held a John Knowles Paine Traveling fellowship, and then studied in Italy on a Fulbright grant (1950–52). From 1953 to 1959 he taught at the Univ. of Ill. in Urbana. He was assoc. prof. (1959–64) and prof. (1964–80) of the history of music at Yale Univ., where he then was the Henry L. and Lucy G. Moses Prof. of Music from 1980 until being made a prof. emeritus in 1992. He also served as chairman of the music dept. (1969–75), and later as director of its graduate studies (1987–92). From 1966 he was ed. of the Yale Music Theory Translation Series. In 1971–72 he was president of the American Musicological Soc. In 1960–61 and 1981–82 he held Guggenheim fellowships. In 1972–73 he was a senior fellow of the NEH. He became a member of the American Academy of Arts and Sciences in 1986 and of the Accademia filarmonica of Bologna in 1987. In 1991 he was made an honorary member of the American Musicological Soc.

WRITINGS: *Girolamo Mei: Letters on Ancient and Modern Music to Vincenzo Galilei and Giovanni Bardi* (Rome, 1960; 2nd ed., 1977); with others, *Seventeenth Century Science and the Arts* (Princeton, N.J., 1961); with others, *Musicology* (Englewood Cliffs, N.J., 1963); *Baroque Music* (Englewood Cliffs, N.J.,

1968; 3rd ed., 1991); *Music in Our Schools: A Search for Improvement* (Washington, D.C., 1964); with D. Grout, *A History of Western Music* (3rd ed., N.Y., 1980; 5th ed., 1995); ed. *Norton Anthology of Western Music* (2 vols., N.Y., 1980; 3rd. ed., 1995); *Humanism in Italian Renaissance Musical Thought* (New Haven, 1985); *The Florentine Camerata: Documentary Studies and Translations* (New Haven, 1989); *Studies in the History of Italian Music and Music Theory* (Oxford, 1994).

BIBL.: N. Baker and B. Hanning, *Musical Humanism and Its Legacy: Essays in Honor of C. V. P.* (Stuyvesant, N.Y., 1992).

Palkovský, Oldřich, Czech composer, father of **Pavel Palkovský**; b. Brušperk, Feb. 24, 1907; d. Gottwaldov, March 15, 1983. He studied with Petrželka at the Brno Cons. (1925–31) and Suk at the Prague Cons. (1931–33). He was director of the State Testing Commission for Music (1939–54), and taught at the Kroměříž branch of the Brno Cons. (1950–67).

WORKS: ORCH.: 6 syms. (1933–34; 1939; 1944; 1947; 1956–57; 1962); Concerto for Cimbalom and Small Orch. (1952–53); *Scherzo capriccio* (1953); *Morvarian Dances* (1956); *Variations and Fugue* for Cimbalom, Strings, and Timpani (1959); Flute Concerto (1959); Oboe Concerto (1961); Accordion Concerto (1961); *3 Symphonic Movements* (1971); *Sinfonietta* (1978); Small Suite (1981). **CHAMBER:** 10 string quartets (1931–81); 2 piano trios (1940, 1968); Violin Sonata (1942); 2 viola sonatas (1944, 1966); Concertino for Winds (1945); Cello Sonata (1946); Clarinet Sonata (1947); 4 wind quintets (1949–79); Quartet for Flute, Violin, Viola, and Cello (1950); Horn Sonata (1963); *Chamber Music* for 8 Instruments (1964); *Balladic Sonata* for Bassoon and Piano (1969); *Sonnets* for Flute, Bass Clarinet, and Piano (1969); Tuba Sonata (1978); Trumpet Sonata (1980); Sextet for Wind Instruments (1981); Wind Quartet (1982); piano pieces. **VOCAL:** Songs.

Palkovský, Pavel, Czech composer, son of **Oldřich Palkovský**; b. Zlín, Dec. 18, 1939. He studied composition with Schaefer at the Brno Cons. (graduated, 1960), and with Kapr at the Janáček Academy of Music in Brno (graduated, 1964).

WORKS: ORCH.: 2 syms.: No. 1 (1964) and No. 2 for Piano and Orch. (1968–69); *Chamber Music I* for Strings, Piano, and Percussion (1964). **CHAMBER:** Cello Sonata (1963); *Chamber Music II* for Piano, Organ, Celesta, and Percussion (1968); Horn Sonata (1967); *3 Studies* for Accordion and 9 Winds (1969); Trio for 3 Accordions (1969); Suite for Tuba and Piano (1979); *Musica polyphonica* for Clarinet and Piano (1983).

Pallandios, Menelaos, Greek composer and pedagogue; b. Piraeus, Feb. 11, 1914. He studied with Mitropoulos in Athens and with Casella in Rome. In 1936 he became an instructor at the Athens Cons., and in 1962 was appointed its director. In 1969 he was elected to the Athens Academy. He wrote music to several ancient Greek tragedies, endeavoring to re-create the classical modes in modern investiture.

WORKS: DRAMATIC: OPERA: *Antigone* (1942). **BALLETS:** *Pombi ston Aheronta* (Procession Towards Acheron; 1942); *Prosefhi se archaeo nao* (Prayer in the Ancient Temple; 1942); *Electra* (1944); *Penthesilea* (1944); *3 Archaic Suites* (1949); *Greek Triptych* (1960). Also incidental music to Greek dramas; film scores. **ORCH.:** *Suite in Ancient Style* for Strings (1941); *Prosefhi stin Akropoli* (Prayer on the Akropolis; 1942); *Narcissus* (1942); *Greek Classical Overture* (1944); Sym. (1948); *Divertimento* (1952); Piano Concerto (1958). **CHAMBER:** *5 Character Pieces* for Oboe, Clarinet, and Bassoon (1962); piano music.

BIBL.: M. Pallandios, ed., *M.G. P., moussourgos* (Athens, 1968).

Pallo, Imre, Hungarian-American conductor; b. Budapest, May 15, 1941. He was a student of Kodály at the Budapest Academy of Music and of Swarowsky at the Vienna Academy of Music. After conducting in Europe, he made his U.S. debut as a guest conductor with the National Sym. Orch. in Washington, D.C., in 1973. He subsequently conducted at the N.Y. City Opera. From 1976 to 1991 he was music director of the Hudson Valley Phil. in Poughkeepsie, N.Y. He also held the post of 1st conductor of the Frankfurt am Main Opera from 1987. In 1994 he joined the faculty of the Indiana Univ. School of Music in Bloomington.

Palm, Siegfried, noted German cellist, pedagogue, and operatic administrator; b. Barmen, April 25, 1927. He studied cello with his father, a member of the City Orch. in Wuppertal. After playing in the City Orch. in Lübeck (1945–47), he joined the North German Radio Sym. Orch. in Hamburg (1947). He served as a member of the Cologne Radio Sym. Orch. (1962–67); in 1962, joined the faculty of the Cologne Hochschule für Musik; was appointed its director in 1972. From 1977 to 1981 he was Intendant of the Deutsche Oper in West Berlin, while continuing his career as a cellist. From 1981 to 1988 he was president of the ISCM. He traveled widely in Africa and Asia with the purpose of studying native music. He commissioned several modern composers, among them Blacher, Kagel, Keleman, Ligeti, Penderecki, Xenakis, and Zimmermann, to write special works which he premiered. He also contributed scholarly treatises on the new techniques of string instruments.

Palma, Athos, Argentine composer and teacher; b. Buenos Aires, June 7, 1891; d. Miramar, Jan. 10, 1951. He studied with C. Troiani (piano) and other teachers in Buenos Aires; in 1904, went to Europe, returning to Buenos Aires in 1914. There he was busily engaged as a teacher. He publ. *Teoría razonada de la música* (5 vols., n.d.) and *Tratado completo de armonía* (1941). His music follows the Italian tradition, although the subject matter is derived from South American history and literature.

WORKS: OPERAS: *Nazdah* (Buenos Aires, June 19, 1924); *Los Hijos del Sol* (Buenos Aires, Nov. 10, 1928). **ORCH.:** *Cantares de mi tierra* for Strings (1914); 2 symphonic poems: *Jardines* (1926) and *Los Hijos del Sol* (1929). **CHAMBER:** Cello Sonata (1912); Violin Sonata (1924); Piano Sonata. **VOCAL:** Many songs.

BIBL.: N. Lamuraglia, *A. P.: Vida, arte, educación* (Buenos Aires, 1954).

Palmer, Felicity (Joan), admired English soprano; b. Cheltenham, April 6, 1944. She received her training at the Guildhall School of Music in London (1962–67) and from Marianne Schech at the Munich Hochschule für Musik. She first sang in the John Alldis Choir and the Purcell Consort in London. In 1970 she won the Kathleen Ferrier Memorial Scholarship and made her formal debut in Purcell's *Dioclesian* at London's Queen Elizabeth Hall. She made her operatic debut as Dido with the Kent Opera in 1971. In 1973 she made her U.S. operatic debut as Mozart's Countess with the Houston Grand Opera. In 1975 she made her first appearance with the English National Opera in London as Pamina. She continued to make regular appearances in opera in London in subsequent years. She also pursued a highly successful career as a soloist with orchs. and as a recitalist. In 1973, 1977, and 1984 she toured Europe as soloist with the BBC Sym. Orch. After singing opera in Bern (1977), Frankfurt am Main (1978), and Zürich (1980), she made her Glyndebourne debut as Florence in *Albert Herring* in 1985. In 1986 she appeared as Kabanicha in *Kát'a Kabanová* at the Chicago Lyric Opera. In 1987 she sang in the first perf. of Testi's *Riccardo III* at Milan's La Scala. She made her debut at the Salzburg Festival in 1988 as a soloist in *Messiah*. In 1992 she sang the title role in the stage premiere of Roberto Gerhard's *The Duenna* in Madrid. Palmer's operatic and concert repertoire is notable for its range, from early music to the avant-garde.

Palmer, Larry, American harpsichordist, organist, and teacher; b. Warren, Ohio, Nov. 13, 1938. He studied at the Oberlin (Ohio) College Cons. of Music and with David Craighead (organ) at the Eastman School of Music in Rochester, N.Y. (D.M.A., 1963). He also received training in harpsichord from Ahlgrimm at the Salzburg Mozarteum and from Leonhardt in Haarlem. In 1969 he became the harpsichord ed. of *The Diapason*. From 1970 he served as prof. of harpsichord and organ at Southern Methodist Univ. in Dallas. He also toured widely as a harpsichordist and organist in the U.S. and Europe. He publ.

the vols. *Hugo Distler and his Church Music* (1967) and *Harpsichord in America: A 20th Century Revival* (1989; 2nd ed., 1992). Palmer has championed the organ music of Distler and has performed an extensive repertoire of harpsichord music, ranging from the 17th century to the present era.

Palmer, Robert (Moffat), American composer and teacher; b. Syracuse, N.Y., June 2, 1915. He studied at the Eastman School of Music in Rochester, N.Y., with Hanson and Rogers (B.M., 1938; M.M., 1940); also studied with Harris (1939), Copland (1940), and Porter. He held 2 Guggenheim fellowships (1952–53; 1960–61) and a Fulbright Senior fellowship for study in Italy (1960–61). From 1940 to 1943 he was on the faculty at the Univ. of Kansas; from 1943 to 1980, taught at Cornell Univ. In his music, he generally adhered to neo-Classical principles while producing works of a distinctive originality.

WORKS: ORCH.: *Poem* for Violin and Chamber Orch. (1938); Concerto for Small Orch. (1940); *K 19*, symphonic elegy for Thomas Wolfe (1945); Chamber Concerto for Violin, Oboe, and Strings (1949); *Variations, Chorale and Fugue* (1947; rev. 54); 2 syms. (1953, 1966); *Memorial Music* (1960); *Centennial Overture* (1965); *Choric Songs and Toccata* for Band (1968); Piano Concerto (1971); *Overture on a Southern Hymn* for Symphonic Band (1979); Concerto for 2 Pianos, 2 Percussion, Strings, and Brass (1984). **CHAMBER:** 4 string quartets (1939; 1943, rev. 1947; 1954; 1959); 2 piano quartets (1947, 1973); Piano Quintet (1950); Viola Sonata (1951); Quintet for Clarinet, Strings, and Piano (1952; rev. 1953); Violin Sonata (1956); Piano Trio (1958); *Organon I* for Flute and Clarinet (1962) and *II* for Violin and Viola (1975); Trumpet Sonata (1972); *Sinfonia Concertante* for 9 Instruments (1972); 2 cello sonatas (1978, 1983). **PIANO:** 3 sonatas (1938, rev. 1946; 1942, rev. 1948; 1979); Sonata for 2 Pianos (1944); Sonata for Piano, 4-hands (1952); *Evening Music* (1956); *7 Epigrams* (1957–59); *Morning Music* (1973). **VOCAL:** *Abraham Lincoln Walks at Midnight* for Chorus and Orch. (1948); *Carmina amoris* for Soprano, Clarinet, Violin, and Piano (1951; also for Soprano and Chamber Orch.); *Of Night and the Sea*, chamber cantata (1956); *Nabuchodonosor*, dramatic oratorio (1964); *Portents of Aquarius (Visions and Prophecies)* for Narrator, Chorus, and Organ (1975).

BIBL.: W. Austin, "The Music of R. P.," *Musical Quarterly* (Jan. 1956).

Palmgren, Selim, eminent Finnish composer and teacher; b. Björneborg, Feb. 16, 1878; d. Helsinki, Dec. 13, 1951. He studied piano and composition at the Helsinki Cons. (1895–99); then went to Berlin, where he continued his piano studies with Ansorge, Berger, and Busoni. Returning to Finland, he became active as a choral conductor in Helsinki (1902–04); from 1909 to 1912 he was director of the Music Soc. in Turku. In 1921 he made a tour of the U.S. as a pianist; from 1923 to 1926 he taught piano and composition at the Eastman School of Music in Rochester, N.Y.; then returned to Helsinki; became a prof. of harmony and composition at the Sibelius Academy in 1936, remaining there until his death. He was married to the Finnish soprano Maikki Pakarinen in 1910, after her divorce from Armas Järnefelt. He publ. *Minusta tuli muusikko* (Helsinki, 1948). He excelled in piano compositions, often tinged with authentic Finnish colors; some of his pieces are marked by effective impressionistic devices, such as whole-tone scales and consecutive mild dissonances. Among his piano miniatures, *May Night* enjoyed considerable popularity with music students and their teachers.

WORKS: OPERAS: *Daniel Hjort* (Turku, April 15, 1910; rev. version, Helsinki, 1938); *Peter Schlemihl*. **ORCH.:** 5 piano concertos: No. 1 (1903), No. 2, *Virta* (The Stream; 1913), No. 3, *Metamorphoses* (1915), No. 4, *Huhtikuu* (April; 1924–26), and No. 5 (1939–41); *Pastorale* (1920); *Ballet Music* (1944); *Concert Fantasy* for Violin and Orch. (1945). **PIANO:** 2 sonatas; *Fantasia; 24 Preludes; Ballade; Finnische Lyrik* (12 pieces); *Finnische Suite (The Seasons); Maskenball*, suite; *24 Etudes* (1921–22); etc. **VOCAL:** *Turun lilja* (The Lily of Turku), cantata (1929); songs and men's choruses.

Palombo, Paul (Martin), American composer; b. Pittsburgh, Sept. 10, 1937. He was trained in electronics; studied composition at the Peabody Cons. of Music in Baltimore and at the Eastman School of Music in Rochester, N.Y. (Ph.D., 1969), with Barlow and Rogers. In 1969 he was appointed to the faculty of the Univ. of Cincinnati (Ohio) College-Cons. of Music; in 1973, assumed the direction of the electronic music studio there; then was director of the music school of the Univ. of Wash. in Seattle (1978–81); in 1981 he became dean of the College of Fine Arts at the Univ. of Wisc. in Stevens Point.

WORKS: BALLET: *Proteus* (1969). **ORCH.:** *Serenade* for Strings (1964); *Sinfonietta* for Chamber Orch. (1965); *Movement* (1967); *Variations* (1967–68). **CHAMBER:** Cello Sonata (1966); String Quartet No. 1 (1966–67); *Metatheses* for Flute, Oboe, Double Bass, and Harpsichord (1970); *Montage* for Violin and Piano (1971); *Ritratti anticamente* for Viola and Piano (1972; rev. 1974); *4 Sonos: I* for Harpsichord and Tape (1972), *II* for Harp and Tape (1972), *III* for Double Bass and Tape (1973), and *IV* for String Trio and Tape (1974); *Variatione da camera* for Flute, Clarinet, Viola, Cello, Piano, and 2 Percussion (1980). **KEYBOARD:** Piano Sonata (1965); *Variants* for Harpsichord (1975). **VOCAL:** *Moody Blues* for Voices and Dance Band (1981); *Morning Memories* for Voice and Piano (1981); *It's Over* for Voice and Piano (1981). **ELECTRONIC:** *Morphosis*, ballet (1970); *Crystals*, multimedia score (1971); *Etcetera*, ballet (1973); *Stegowagenvolkssaurus*, music for a sculpture (1973–74); *Music for Triceratops Americus* (1977). **OTHER:** *Laser Music* for Tape (1975); *The Dance* for Dance Band (1980).

Pálsson, Páll (Pampichler), Icelandic composer and conductor; b. Graz (of Icelandic parents), May 9, 1928. He studied with Michl, Mixa, and Brugger in Graz and conducting at the Hamburg Hochschule für Musik (1959–60). He settled in Iceland in 1949 and was 1st trumpeter in the Iceland Sym. Orch. in Reykjavík. He was director of the Reykjavík Male Choir (from 1964) and artistic director of the Reykjavík Chamber Ensemble (from 1974).

WORKS: *Divertimento* for 18 Winds (1963); *Hringspil I* for Violin, Viola, Clarinet, and Bassoon (1964) and *II* for 2 Trumpets, Horn, and Trombone; *Crystals* for String Quartet and Wind Quintet (1970); *Requiem* for Chorus (1970); *Dialog* for Orch. (1973); *Mixed Things* for Flute and Piano (1977); *Hugledhing um L* (Meditation über L) for Orch. (1977; the "L" is for Ludwig van Beethoven); Clarinet Concerto (Reykjavík, Jan. 6, 1983).

Pampanini, Rosetta, Italian soprano; b. Milan, Sept. 2, 1896; d. Corbola, Aug. 2, 1973. She studied with Emma Molajoli in Milan. She made her operatic debut as Micaëla in Rome in 1920; then continued her vocal studies; in 1925 she joined La Scala in Milan, remaining on its roster until 1937, with the exception of the 1931–33 seasons; also sang at Covent Garden in London (1928, 1929, 1933) and in Chicago (1931–32). After retiring in 1942, she taught voice. She was particularly admired for her Puccini roles, most notably Manon, Cio-Cio-San, and Mimi.

Pandolfini, Angelica, Italian soprano; b. Spoleto, Aug. 21, 1871; d. Lenno, July 15, 1959. She was the daughter of the Italian baritone Francesco Pandolfini (b. Termini Imerese, Palermo, Nov. 22, 1836; d. Milan, Feb. 15, 1916). She studied with Jules Massart in Paris. She made her debut as Marguerite in 1894 in Modena; after singing in the Italian provinces, she appeared at La Scala in Milan (1897–99; 1906). She created the title role in *Adriana Lecouvreur* at the Teatro Lirico in Milan in 1902; retired from the stage in 1908. She was best known for her convincing portrayals of verismo roles.

Panenka, Jan, Czech pianist and teacher; b. Prague, July 8, 1922. He was a student of Maxián in Prague and of Serebryakov in Leningrad. In 1944 he made his debut in Prague. After winning the Prague Piano Competition in 1951, he toured widely as a soloist. He devoted much time to chamber music, serving as a member of the Suk Trio of Prague from 1957. He also taught at the Prague Academy of Music. In 1972 he was made an Artist of Merit by the Czech government.

Panerai, Rolando, Italian baritone; b. Campi Bisenzio, near Florence, Oct. 17, 1924. He studied at the Florence Cons. with Frazzi; also with di Armani and Tess in Milan. After winning 1st prize in the voice competition in Spoleto, he made his debut as Faraone in *Mosé* in Naples (1947); in 1951 he joined La Scala in Milan; also sang at Covent Garden in London, the Vienna State Opera, and the Salzburg Festivals. He specialized in the Italian repertoire.

Panizza, Ettore, Argentine conductor and composer of Italian descent; b. Buenos Aires, Aug. 12, 1875; d. Milan, Nov. 27, 1967. He studied at the Milan Cons., graduating in 1898 with prizes for piano and composition. From 1907 to 1914 and again in 1924 he conducted at London's Covent Garden. He made his first appearance at the Teatro Colón in Buenos Aires (1908), conducting there regularly from 1921. He joined the roster of Milan's La Scala (1916), serving as assistant to Toscanini (1921–29); was a regular conductor there (1930–32; 1946–48); also conducted at the Chicago Civic Opera (1922–24) and N.Y.'s Metropolitan Opera (1934–42). He publ. an autobiography, *Medio siglo de vida musical* (Buenos Aires, 1952).

WORKS: OPERAS: *Il Fidanzato del mare* (Buenos Aires, Aug. 15, 1897); *Medio evo latino* (Genoa, Nov. 17, 1900); *Aurora* (Buenos Aires, Sept. 5, 1908); *Bisanzio* (Buenos Aires, July 25, 1939). **OTHER:** *Il Re della foresta* for Soli, Chorus, and Orch.; *Tema con variaciones* for Orch.; Violin Sonata; Cello Sonata; String Quartet; piano pieces; songs.

Pannain, Guido, distinguished Italian musicologist and composer; b. Naples, Nov. 17, 1891; d. there, Sept. 6, 1977. He studied composition with C. de Nardis at the Naples Cons. (graduated, 1914). He was prof. of music history at the Naples Cons. (1915–61); also wrote music criticism. As a musicologist, he devoted much of his time to the study of Neapolitan music.

WRITINGS: *La teoria musicale di Giovanni Tinctoris* (Naples, 1913); *Le origini della scuola musicale napoletana* (Naples, 1914); *Le origini e lo sviluppo dell'arte pianistica in Italia dal 1500 fino al 1730 circa* (Naples, 1917); *Lineamenti di storia della musica* (Naples, 1922; 9th ed., rev., 1970); *Musica e musicisti in Napoli nel secolo XIX* (Naples, 1922); *Musicisti dei tempi nuovi* (Milan, 1932; Eng. tr., 1932, as *Modern Composers*; 2nd Italian ed., 1954); with A. della Corte, *Storia della musica* (Turin, 1936; 4th ed., 1964); *Il Conservatorio di musica di S. Pietro in Maiella* (Florence, 1942); *La vita del linguaggio musicale* (Milan, 1947; 2nd ed., 1956); *Ottocento musicale italiano: Saggi e note* (Milan, 1952); *L'opera e le opere ed altri scritti di letteratura musicale* (Milan, 1958); *Giuseppe Verdi* (Turin, 1964); *Richard Wagner: Vita di un artista* (Milan, 1964).

WORKS: OPERAS: *L'Intrusa* (1926; Genoa, 1940); *Beatrice Cenci* (Naples, Feb. 21, 1942); *Madame Bovary* (Naples, April 16, 1955). **ORCH.:** 2 violin concertos (1930, 1960); Viola Concerto (1955); Harp Concerto (1959); Piano Concerto (1969). **VOCAL:** *Requiem* (1912); *Stabat Mater* (1969).

Panufnik, Sir Andrzej, eminent Polish-born English conductor and composer; b. Warsaw, Sept. 24, 1914; d. London, Oct. 27, 1991. His father was a Polish manufacturer of string instruments, his mother an Englishwoman who studied violin in Warsaw. He began his musical training with his mother; after studying composition with Sikorski at the Warsaw Cons. (diploma, 1936), he took conducting lessons with Weingartner at the Vienna Academy of Music (1937–38); subsequently completed his training with Gaubert in Paris, and also studied in London (1938–39). He returned to Warsaw in 1939, remaining there during the Nazi occupation, playing piano in the underground. After the liberation, he conducted the Kraków Phil. (1945–46) and the Warsaw Phil. (1946–47); he then left his homeland in protest of the Communist regime (1954), settling in England, where he became a naturalized British subject (1961). After serving as music director of the City of Birmingham Sym. Orch. (1957–59), he devoted himself to composition. His wife, Scarlett Panufnik, publ. *Out of the City of Fear* (London, 1956), recounting his flight from Poland; his autobiography was publ. as *Composing Myself* (London, 1986). In 1988 he appeared as a guest conductor of his own works with the N.Y. Chamber Sym. and in 1990 with the Chicago Sym. Orch. In 1991 he was knighted. In his early years, he belonged to the vanguard group of Polish composers. He made use of advanced techniques, including quarter tones, and made certain innovations in notation; in several of his orch. works, he left blank spaces in the place of rests to indicate inactive instrumental parts. In his later music, he adopted a more circumspect idiom — expressive, direct, and communicative. His compositions to 1944 were destroyed during the Warsaw uprising.

WORKS: ORCH.: *Tragic Overture* (1942; Warsaw, 1943; reconstructed 1945; rev. 1955); *Nocturne* (1947; Paris, 1948; rev. 1955); *Lullaby* for 29 Strings and 2 Harps (1947; Kraków, 1948; rev. 1955); *Divertimento* for Strings, after trios by Felix Janiewicz (1947; Kraków, 1948; rev. 1955); 10 syms.: No. 1, *Sinfonica Rustica* (1948; Kraków, 1949; rev. 1955), No. 2, *Sinfonica Elegiaca* (Houston, Nov. 21, 1957; rev. 1966), No. 3, *Sinfonia Sacra* (1963; Monte Carlo, Aug. 12, 1964), No. 4, *Sinfonia Concertante*, for Flute, Harp, and Strings (1973; London, May 20, 1974), No. 5, *Sinfonia di Sfere* (1974–75; London, April 13, 1976), No. 6, *Sinfonia Mistica* (1977; Middlesborough, England, Jan. 17, 1978), No. 7, *Metasinfonia*, for Organ, Timpani, and Strings (Manchester, England, Sept. 9, 1978), No. 8, *Sinfonia Votiva* (1981; Boston, Jan. 28, 1982; rev. 1984), No. 9, *Sinfonia di Speranza* (1986; London, Feb. 25, 1987), and No. 10 (1989; Chicago, Feb. 1, 1990); *Old Polish Suite* for Strings (1950; Warsaw, 1951; rev. 1955); *Concerto in modo antico* for Trumpet and Orch. (Kraków, 1951; rev. 1955); *Heroic Overture* (Helsinki, July 27, 1952; rev. 1969); *Rhapsody* (1956; BBC, London, Jan. 11, 1957); *Polonia* (London, Aug. 21, 1959); Piano Concerto (Birmingham, England, Jan. 25, 1962; rev. 1970, 1972, and 1982); *Landscape* for Strings (1962; rev. version, Twickenham, Nov. 13, 1965); *Autumn Music* (1962; rev. 1965; Paris, Jan. 16, 1968); *Jagiellonian Triptych* for Strings (London, Sept. 24, 1966); *Katyn Epitaph* (1967; N.Y., Nov. 17, 1968; rev. 1969); Concerto for Violin and String Orch. (1971; London, July 18, 1972); *Concerto Festivo* (London, June 17, 1979); Concertino for Timpani, Percussion, and Strings (1979–80; London, Jan. 24, 1981); *A Procession for Peace* (1982–83; London, July 16, 1983); *Arbor Cosmica*, 12 evocations for 12 Strings or String Orch. (1983; N.Y., Nov. 14, 1984); Concerto for Bassoon and Small Orch. (1985; Milwaukee, May 18, 1986); *Harmony* (N.Y., Dec. 16, 1989); Cello Concerto (1991; London, June 24, 1992). **CHAMBER:** Piano Trio (1934; Warsaw, 1935; reconstructed 1945; rev. 1977); *Quintetto Accademico* for Flute, Oboe, 2 Clarinets, and Bassoon (1953; rev. 1956); *Triangles* for 3 Flutes and 3 Cellos (BBC-TV, April 14, 1972); 3 string quartets: No. 1 (London, Oct. 19, 1976), No. 2, *Messages* (St. Asaph's Cathedral, North Wales, Sept. 25, 1980), and No. 3, *Wycinanki* (1990; London, April 15, 1991); String Sextet, *Trains of Thought* (1987; London, Feb. 21, 1988). **PIANO:** *12 Miniature Studies* (1947; rev. 1955–64); *Reflections* (1968; London, April 21, 1972); *Pentasonata* (1984; Aldeburgh, June 23, 1989). **VOCAL:** *5 Polish Peasant Songs* for Soprano or Treble Voices, 2 Flutes, 2 Clarinets, and Bass Clarinet (1940; reconstructed 1945; Kraków, 1945; rev. 1959); *Song to the Virgin Mary* for Chorus or 6 Solo Voices (London, April 26, 1964; rev. 1969); *Universal Prayer* for Soloists, Chorus, 3 Harps, and Organ (1968–69; N.Y., May 24, 1970); *Thames Pageant*, cantata for Young Players and Singers (1969; Twickenham, Feb. 7, 1970); *Winter Solstice* for Soprano, Baritone, Chorus, 3 Trumpets, 3 Trombones, Timpani, and Glockenspiel (Kingston-upon-Thames, Dec. 16, 1972); *Invocation for Peace* for Treble Voices, 2 Trumpets, and 2 Trombones (Southampton, England, Nov. 28, 1972); *Love Song* for Mezzo-soprano and Harp or Piano (1976; also for Mezzo-soprano, Harp or Piano, and Strings, London, Nov. 28, 1991); *Dreamscape* for Mezzo-soprano and Piano (London, Dec. 12, 1977); *Prayer to the Virgin of Skempe* for Voice or Chorus, Organ, and Piano or Instruments (1990; 1st perf. at the composer's funeral, St. Mary's Church, Twickenham, Nov. 5, 1991).

Panula, Jorma, Finnish conductor, pedagogue, and composer; b. Kauhajoki, Aug. 10, 1930. He studied in Helsinki at the School of Church Music and with Leo Funtek at the Sibelius Academy (1948–53); then pursued conducting studies with Dean Dixon in Lund (1953), and with Albert Wolff (1957) and Franco Ferrara (1958) in Hilversum. He conducted theater orchs. in Lahti (1953–55), Tampere (1955–58), and Helsinki (1958–62); after conducting the Finnish National Opera (1962–63), he conducted the Turku Phil. (1963–65), the Helsinki Phil. (1965–72), the Århus Sym. Orch. in Denmark (1972–75), and the Espoo City Orch. (1986–88); also appeared as a guest conductor throughout Europe and in North America. He served as a prof. of conducting at the Sibelius Academy (from 1972), the Stockholm Musikhögskolan (1980–86), and the Copenhagen Royal Danish Cons. of Music (1986–91).

WORKS: DRAMATIC: 2 folk operas: *Jaakko Ilkka* (1978) and *Jokiooppera* (The River Opera; 1982); *Vallan Miehet* (Men of Power), television opera (1987); musicals; scores for films, radio, and television. **ORCH.:** Violin Concerto (1954); *Adagio and Allegro* (1957); *Orkesteriesittely* (Orchestral Introduction; 1965); *Jazz Capriccio* for Piano and Orch. (1965); Concertino (1972). **OTHER:** Choral music; numerous arrangements of folk music.

Panzéra, Charles (Auguste Louis), noted Swiss-born French baritone and teacher; b. Geneva, Feb. 16, 1896; d. Paris, June 6, 1976. He studied at the Paris Cons. He made his operatic debut as Albert in *Werther* at the Paris Opéra-Comique in 1919; then gave concerts in Europe and America; also taught at the Juilliard School of Music in N.Y. In 1949 he was appointed a prof. at the Paris Cons. He excelled in the interpretation of French songs. He publ. *L'Art de chanter* (Paris, 1945), *L'Amour de chanter* (Paris, 1957), *L'Art vocal: 30 leçons de chant* (Paris, 1959), and *Votre voix: Directives générales* (Paris, 1967).

Papaioannou, Yannis (Andreou), Greek composer and teacher; b. Kavala, Jan. 6, 1911; d. Athens, May 11, 1989. He studied piano and theory at the Hellenic Cons. in Athens (1922–34); then had some composition lessons with Honegger in Paris (1949). In 1953 he was appointed to the staff of his alma mater. His music traversed from a fairly conservative neo-Classical idiom to dodecaphony and eventually integral serialism.

WORKS: DRAMATIC: Theater music, including the ballet *Winter Fantasy* (1950). **ORCH.:** *Idyll* (1938); *Choreographic Prelude* (1939); 7 symphonic poems: *The Corsair* (1940), *Poem of the Forest* (1942), *Vassilis the Albanian* (1945), *Matins of Souls* (1947), *Pygmalion* (1951), *Hellas* (1956), and *Symphonic Tableau* (1968); 5 syms. (1946, 1951, 1953, 1963, 1964); *Triptych* for Strings (1947); Piano Concerto (1950); *Concerto for Orchestra* (1954); 3 suites (Nos. 1 and 2, *Pictures from Asia*; No. 3, *Egypt*, 1961); Concertino for Piano and Strings (1962); *India*, suite (1969); Concerto for Violin and Chamber Orch. (1971); Concerto for Violin, Piano, and Orch. (1972–73). **CHAMBER:** Violin Sonata (1947); String Quartet (1959); Suite for Guitar (1960); Sonatina for Flute and Guitar (1962); Quartet for Flute, Clarinet, Guitar, and Cello (1962); Trio for Oboe, Clarinet, and Bassoon (1962); *Archaic* for 2 Guitars (1962); String Trio (1963); Trio for Flute, Viola, and Guitar (1967); Quartet for Oboe, Clarinet, Viola, and Piano (1968); *5 Characters*, brass quintet (1970); *Aphigissis* (Narration) for Violin (1970); *The Harlequin's Prattling* for Tuba (1971); *Portrait* for Tuba (1972); *Syneirmoi* (Associations) for 9 Instruments (1973); *Echomorphes* (Sound-figures) for Violin (1975); *Rhythms and Colors* for Cello (1976); *Puck* for Cello (1976); Piano Trio (1977). **PIANO:** Several pieces, including a sonata (1958). **VOCAL:** *Daphnis and Chloe* for Chorus and Orch. (1934); *Sarpidon's Funeral*, cantata (1965); *3 Byzantine Odes* for Soprano and Chamber Ensemble (1966); *Electra Monologues* for Soprano and Instrumental Ensemble (1968); *Footsteps* for Mezzo-soprano, Narrator, Chorus, and Instrumental Ensemble (1969); *4 Orphic Hymns* for Narrator and Instrumental Ensemble (1971); choruses; songs.

Papandopulo, Boris, Croatian conductor and composer; b. Bad Honnef am Rhein, Feb. 25, 1906; d. Zagreb, Oct. 17, 1991. He studied in Zagreb and Vienna. Returning to his homeland, he was active as a conductor and composer; in 1959 he was appointed conductor of the National Theater in Zagreb; from 1964 to 1968 he conducted in Split and Rijeka; later filled engagements as a guest conductor in Yugoslavia. His operas and most of his instrumental works were written in a national Croatian idiom; but he also experimented with the 12-tone techniques, as exemplified by his pointedly titled *Dodekafonski concert* for 2 Pianos (1961).

WORKS: DRAMATIC: OPERAS: *Amiftrion* (Zagreb, Feb. 17, 1940); *Sunčanica* (The Sun Girl; Zagreb, June 13, 1942); *Rona* (Rijeka, May 25, 1955); *Marulova Pisan* (Marul's Song; Split, Aug. 14, 1970); *Madame Buffault* (1972). **BALLETS:** *Zlato* (Gold; Zagreb, May 31, 1930); *Žetva* (The Harvest; Sarajevo, March 25, 1950); *Intermezzo* (Sarajevo, May 25, 1953); *Beatrice Cenci* (Gelsenkirchen, 1959); *Gitanella* (1965); *Doktor Atom: $Qu + H^3 + H^2 = He^4 + n + 9$* (Rijeka, Oct. 29, 1966); *Ljudi u hotelu* (People in a Hotel; Vienna, May 27, 1967); *Teuta* (1973). **ORCH.:** 2 syms.: No. 1 (1930) and No. 2 (Zagreb, May 8, 1946); Sinfonietta (1938); 4 piano concertos (1938, 1942, 1947, 1958); Concerto for Harpsichord and Strings (1962); Double Bass Concerto (1968); Concerto for 4 Timpani and Orch. (1969). **CHAMBER:** 5 string quartets (1927, 1933, 1945, 1950, 1970); Piano Quartet (1938); Clarinet Quintet (1940); Viola Sonata (1956); *Mozaik* for Strings and Jazz Quartet (1963); piano pieces. **VOCAL:** Many cantatas; choruses; songs;

Papi, Gennaro, Italian-American conductor; b. Naples, Dec. 21, 1886; d. N.Y., Nov. 29, 1941. He received training in piano, organ, violin, and theory at the Naples Cons. (graduated, 1904). He was a chorus master at S. Severo (1906), Warsaw (1909–10), Turin (1911), and London's Covent Garden (1911–12). After serving as Toscanini's assistant on a tour of Argentina (1912), Toscanini made him his assistant at the Metropolitan Opera in N.Y. On April 29, 1915, he made his debut there conducting *Rigoletto*. He was on the conducting roster there from 1916 to 1926, and again from 1935 until his death. He also conducted at Chicago's Ravinia Festival (1916–31) and Civic Opera (1925–32).

Papineau-Couture, Jean, prominent Canadian composer, teacher, and administrator; b. Montreal, Nov. 12, 1916. He was the grandson of the Canadian musician Guillaume Couture. At 6, he commenced piano lessons with his mother. From 1926 to 1939 he was a student of Françoise D'Amour, receiving instruction in piano, harmony, sight reading, and music history. He also studied counterpoint with Gabriel Cusson (1937–40). His training continued with Léo-Pol Morin (piano; 1939–40), and then at the New England Cons. of Music in Boston (B.Mus., 1941), where he was a student of Quincy Porter (composition), Francis Findlay (conducting), and Beveridge Webster (piano). He completed his studies with Boulanger at the Longy School in Cambridge, Mass. (1941–43) and in Madison, Wis., and Lake Arrowhead, California (1944–45). He taught at the Jean-de-Brébeuf College in Montreal (1943–44; 1945–46), and then was on the faculty of the Cons. de Musique de Québec à Montréal (1946–63). From 1951 to 1982 he also taught at the Univ. of Montreal, where he was dean of the music faculty from 1968 to 1973. He served as president of the Canadian League of Composers (1957–59; 1963–66), the Académie de musique de Québec (1962–63), the Sociétè de Musique Contemporaine du Québec (1966–72), the Canadian Music Council (1967–68), the Canadian Music Centre (1973–74), and the Humanities Research Council of Canada (1977–78). In 1962 he received the Prix de musique Calixa-Lavallée. He was made an Officer of the Order of Canada in 1968. In 1973 he was awarded the Canadian Music Council Medal. In 1986 the Canadian Conference of the Arts honored him with its Diplôme d'honneur. He was made a Grand Officier of the Ordre national du Québec in 1988. After composing works in an impressionist and neo-Classical manner, he adopted a personal style in which structuralist, chromatic, and symmetrical writing predominated.

WORKS: DRAMATIC: *Papotages*, ballet (1949; Montreal, Nov. 20, 1950); puppet shows. **ORCH.:** Concerto Grosso for

Chamber Orch. (1943; rev. 1955; Montreal, April 10, 1957); Sym. No. 1 (1948; Montreal, Feb. 20, 1949; rev. 1956); *Aria* (1949; Vancouver, Jan. 22, 1960; from the Suite for Piano, 1942–43); Concerto for Violin and Chamber Orch. (1951–52; Montreal, Feb. 3, 1954); *Marche de Guillaumet* (Montreal, Dec. 1952); *Ostinato* for Harp, Piano, and Strings (1952); *Poème* (1952; Montreal, Jan. 27, 1953); *Prélude* (Montreal, May 25, 1953); *Pièce concertante No. 1: Repliement* for Piano and Strings (Montreal, April 6, 1957), *No. 2: Eventails* for Cello and Chamber Orch. (1959), *No. 3: Variations* for Flute, Clarinet, Violin, Cello, Harp, and Strings (Montreal, March 24, 1959), *No. 4: Additions* for Oboe and Strings (1959), and *No. 5: Miroirs* (Montreal, Sept. 21, 1963); *Trois Pièces* (1961; Saskatoon, Nov. 25, 1962); Piano Concerto (1965; Toronto, Feb. 6, 1966); *Suite Lapitsky* (1965; Montreal, Feb. 2, 1966); *Oscillations* for Chamber Orch. (Vancouver, Sept. 27, 1969); *Obsession* for Small Orch. (Montreal, Oct. 18, 1973); *Clair-obscur* for Contrabassoon, Double Bass, and Orch. (Montreal, Dec. 10, 1986); *Célébrations* (Toronto, Feb. 24, 1991). **CHAMBER:** Violin Sonata (1944; Montreal, April 1946; rev. 1953); Suite for Flute and Piano (1944–45); *Aria* for Violin (1946); Suite for Flute, Clarinet, Bassoon, Horn, and Piano (1947; Montreal, Jan. 31, 1955); 2 string quartets: No. 1 (Forest Hill, Ontario, Dec. 8, 1953) and No. 2 (1967; Orford Arts Centre, June 24, 1970); Rondo for 4 Recorders (1953); Suite for Violin (1956); *Éclosion* for Piano, Violin, and Tape (Montreal, April 1961); *Trois Caprices* for Violin and Piano (Orford Arts Centre, July 5, 1962); *Fantaisie* for Wind Quintet (Winnipeg, June 1963); Canons for Brass Quintet (1964); *Dialogues* for Violin and Piano (Montreal, Aug. 19, 1967); Sextet for Horn, Clarinet, Bassoon, Violin, Viola, and Cello (Montreal, Aug. 15, 1967); *Nocturnes* for Flute, Clarinet, Violin, Cello, Guitar, Harpsichord, and Percussion (Montreal, Nov. 28, 1969); *Trio in 4 Movements* for Viola, Clarinet, and Piano (Montreal, March 15, 1974); *Départ* for Alto Flute (1974; Montreal, April 17, 1980); *Verségères* for Bass Flute (Vancouver, May 29, 1975); *J'aime les tierces mineures* for Flute (1975; Orford Arts Centre, July 6, 1976); *Slano* for String Trio (1975; Paris, Dec. 2, 1976); *Exploration* for Guitar (London, Sept. 1983); *Prouesse* for Viola (1985; Montreal, Nov. 21, 1986); *Arcadie* for 4 Flutes (1986); *Thrène* for Violin and Piano (1988; Montreal, Feb. 7, 1991); *Les Arabesques d'Isabelle* for Flute, English Horn, Clarinet, Bassoon, and Piano (1989; Winnipeg, Feb. 13, 1990); *Automne* for 10 Instruments (1992); *Vents capricieux sur le clavier* for Flute, Oboe, Clarinet, Bassoon, and Piano (1993; Montreal, April 11, 1994); *Chocs sonores* for Marimba (1994); *Fantasque* for Cello (1995). **KEYBOARD: PIANO:** Suite (1942–43; Montreal, June 1957); *Mouvement perpétuel* (1943; WNYC Radio, N.Y., Feb. 22, 1947); *Deux valses* (1943–44; Montreal, Feb. 17, 1950); *Étude* (1944–45); Rondo for Piano, 4-hands (1945); *Aria* (1960); *Complémentarité* (1971; Toronto, Jan. 24, 1972); *Nuit* (1978; Toronto, Jan. 20, 1981); *Idée* (1982; Ottawa, Sept. 1984). **HARPSICHORD:** *Dyarchie* (Boston, March 30, 1971). **ORGAN:** *Vers l'extinction* (1987; Montreal, Nov. 1, 1989); *Courbes* (1988; Montreal, Nov. 1, 1989); *Quasapassacaille* (1988; Paris, April 26, 1990); *Autour du Dies Irae* (1991); *C'est bref* (1991); *Tournants* (1992). **VOCAL:** *Églogues* for Alto, Flute, and Piano (1942; Cambridge, Mass., Feb. 23, 1943); *Pater noster* for Mezzo-soprano or Baritone and Organ (Montreal, June 15, 1944); *Ave Maria* for Mezzo-soprano or Baritone or Organ (Montreal, June 23, 1945); *Complainte populaire* for Soprano, Bass, and Piano (1946; Montreal, March 21, 1953); *Quatrains* for Soprano and Piano (1947; Montreal, May 14, 1948); *Offertoire "Père, daignez recevoir"* for Tenor and Organ or Harmonium (1949); *Psaume CL* for Soprano, Tenor, Chorus, Winds, and Organ (1954; Montreal, April 11, 1955); *Mort* for Alto and Piano (Montreal, Nov. 15, 1956); *Te mater* for 3 Voices (1958); *À Jésus, mon roi, mon grand ami, mon frère* for 2 Soloists and Chorus (Montreal, May 1960); *Viole d'amour* for Chorus (1966); *Paysage* for 8 Voices, 8 Speakers, and Chamber Orch. (1968; Zagreb, May 9, 1969); *Contraste* for Voice and Orch. (1970); *Chanson de Rabit* for Voice, Clarinet, and Piano (1972; Montreal, March 3, 1973); *Le Débat du coeur ed du corps de Villon* for Speaker, Cello, and Percussion (1977; Montreal, Feb. 22, 1979); *Nuit polaire* for Contralto and 10 Instruments (1986; Montreal, Jan. 29, 1987); *Glanures* for Soprano and Chamber Orch. (Ottawa, Nov. 5, 1994).

BIBL.: L. Bail-Milot, *J. P.-C.: La vie, la carrière et l'oeuvre* (Montreal, 1986).

Paranov, Moshe (Morris Perlmutter), American pianist, conductor, and music educator; b. Hartford, Conn., Oct. 28, 1895; d. West Hartford, Conn., Oct. 7, 1994. He began his musical studies as a child and sang in synagogues. At 14, he commenced piano playing in theaters and hotels. He was 17 when he made his formal debut as a pianist in Hartford. He pursued training in piano with Julius Hartt and Harold Bauer, and in composition with Ernest Bloch and Rubin Goldmark. After making his N.Y. recital debut as a pianist at Aeolian Hall in 1920, he made appearances as a soloist with orchs. and as a recitalist. With Hartt and others, he founded a music school in Hartford in 1920 as Julius Hartt, Moshe Paranov, and Associated Teachers, which soon became the Hartt School of Music. In 1934 Paranov became its director and proceeded to develop it into one of the finest schools of its kind. After it became a part of the Univ. of Hartford in 1957, he continued to preside over the school until 1971. He also served as music director of WTIC Radio in Hartford (1938–49), and as conductor of the Hartt Opera Theater, the Hartford Sym. Orch. (1947–53), and the Brockton (Mass.) Sym. Orch. (1954–64). His 95th birthday was marked by a special celebration at the Univ. of Hartford on May 16, 1991, at which occasion he conducted a sprightly rendition of Offenbach's overture to *Orpheus in the Underworld.* An endowed chair was also created in his honor to further his efforts in promoting music education.

Paratore, Anthony (b. Boston, June 17, 1944) and his brother, **Joseph Paratore** (b. Boston, March 19, 1948), outstanding American duo-pianists. They followed separate courses of study as pianists, graduating from the Boston Univ. School of Fine and Applied Arts; both entered the Juilliard School of Music in N.Y., in the class of Rosina Lhévinne, who suggested that they try a career as duo-pianists; they subsequently appeared as duo-pianists with Arthur Fiedler and the Boston Pops Orch., and then made their N.Y. recital debut in 1973. In 1974 they won 1st prize at the Munich International Competition, and thereafter scored international successes as duo-pianists. In addition to the standard repertory, they also perf. contemporary works; commissioned and gave the premiere of Michael Schelle's Concerto for 2 Pianos and Orch. (Indianapolis, Jan. 14, 1988). They also gave the premiere of William Bolcom's Sonata for 2 Pianos (Lafayette, Ind., April 6, 1994).

Paray, Paul, distinguished French conductor and composer; b. Le Tréport, May 24, 1886; d. Monte Carlo, Oct. 10, 1979. He began his musical education with his father, a church organist; in 1904 he entered the Paris Cons. as a composition student; studied there with Leroux, Caussade, Lenepveu, and Vidal; received the Premier Grand Prix de Rome with his cantata *Yanitza* (1911). He was drafted into the French army during World War I and was taken prisoner by the Germans; composed a String Quartet while interned at Darmstadt; after the Armistice (1918), he became conductor of the orch. of the Casino de Cauterets. Substituting for an ailing Caplet, Paray made his Paris debut on Feb. 20, 1920, and soon became assistant conductor of the Lamoureux Orch., succeeding Chevillard as 1st conductor in 1923; was appointed conductor of sym. concerts in Monte Carlo in 1928, and in 1932 succeeded Pierné as conductor of the Concerts Colonne, remaining until the orch. was disbanded by the Nazi occupiers of Paris in 1940. He conducted briefly in Marseilles and, following the liberation of Paris, resumed his duties with the Concerts Colonne (1944–52). Paray made his American debut in N.Y. on July 24, 1939, in a program of French music. In 1952 he became music director of the reorganized Detroit Sym. Orch., and on Oct. 18, 1956, inaugurated the new Ford Auditorium in Detroit in a program that included his own *Mass for the 500th Anniversary of the Death of Joan of Arc,* a work first heard in the Rouen Cathedral in France in 1931; he resigned in 1963 and returned to France, although he continued to guest-conduct internationally. In July 1977, at the age of 91, he conducted an orch. concert in honor of Marc Chagall's 90th birthday celebration in Nice, and, at age 92, made his last conducting appearance in the U.S., leading the orch. of the Curtis Inst. of Music in Philadelphia. As a conductor, he concentrated on the Classics and Romantics, and French music. He was the composer of several highly competent works, including, besides *Yanitza* and his *Mass,* a ballet entitled *Artémis troublée* (Paris, April 28, 1922, perf. as a symphonic poem, *Adonis troublé*); *Fantaisie* for Piano and Orch. (Paris, March 25, 1923); 2 syms. (1935, 1940); Sym. for Strings; String Quartet (1918); Violin Sonata (1908); Cello Sonata (1919); piano pieces.

BIBL.: W. Landowski, *P. P.* (Lyons, 1956).

Parelli (real name, **Paparella**), **Attilio,** Italian conductor and composer; b. Monteleone d'Orvieto, near Perugia, May 31, 1874; d. there, Dec. 26, 1944. He studied at the Accademia di Santa Cecilia in Rome, graduating in 1899. He held various posts as a conductor in Italy and France; went to the U.S. as assistant conductor to Campanini at the Manhattan Opera in N.Y. (1906); also conducted for the Chicago Grand Opera Co. In 1925 he returned to Europe. He wrote the operas *Hermes* (Genoa, Nov. 8, 1906), *I dispettosi amanti* (Philadelphia, March 6, 1912), and *Fanfulla* (Trieste, Feb. 11, 1921); also a Sym.; *Rapsodia umbra,* orch. suite; *La Chimera,* symphonic poem; songs.

Pareto, Graziella (actually, **Graciela**), Spanish soprano; b. Barcelona, March 6, 1888; d. Rome, Sept. 1, 1973. She studied with Vidal in Milan. She made her operatic debut as Micaëla in Barcelona in 1906; then sang at the Teatro Colón in Buenos Aires, in Turin, and in St. Petersburg. In 1914 she appeared at La Scala in Milan; subsequently sang at Covent Garden in London (1920), in Chicago (1923–25), and in Salzburg (1931). Among her prominent roles were Rosina, Ophelia, Marguerite de Valois, Violetta, and Norina.

Paribeni, Giulio Cesare, Italian music critic, teacher, and composer; b. Rome, May 27, 1881; d. Milan, June 13, 1960. He studied at the Univ. of Rome and at the Liceo di S. Cecilia of Rome. He was first a conductor, then, from 1911 to 1915, head of the publishing firm of Sonzogno; from 1914, was a teacher of composition and harmony at the Royal Cons. in Milan; from 1922, an opera critic of *L'Ambrosiano* in Milan. He was the author of *Storia e teoria della antica musica greca* (Milan, 1912) and *Muzio Clementi* (Milan, 1921). Among his compositions were orch. works, chamber pieces, and church music.

Parík, Ivan, Slovak composer and pedagogue; b. Bratislava, Aug. 17, 1936. Following private instruction from Alexander Albrecht (1951–53), he studied with Očenáš (composition) and Schimpl (conducting) at the Bratislava Cons. (until 1958); he completed his composition studies with Moyzes at the Bratislava Academy of Music and Drama (1958–62). From 1959 to 1968 he worked as a program director for the Czechoslovak TV in Bratislava. He was a part-time teacher at the Bratislava Academy of Music and Drama from 1962 to 1968, and then taught there full time. In 1984 he became head of its theory dept. In 1990 he was made a prof. and vice-rector of the Academy. In his output, Parík has made use of both tonal and serial resources with excursions into the realm of electroacoustic music.

WORKS: DRAMATIC: *Fragment,* ballet (1969); film music. **ORCH.:** Overture (1962); *Tower Music* for 12 Winds and Tape (1968); *Music to Ballet* (1968); *Introduction to Haydn's Sym. No. 102 in B major* (1971); *Music* for Winds, Double Basses, and Percussion (1981); *Musica pastoralis* (1984); *Music* for Flute, Viola, and Orch. (1987). **CHAMBER:** *Meditation* for Viola and Piano (1956); *Music* for 4 Strings (1958); *Epitaph in the Style of Improvisations,* trio for Flute, Viola, and Cello (1961); Flute Sonata (1962); *Song About a High, Old Tree* for Cello and Piano (1962); *Microstudies* for Flute, Viola, and Harpsichord (1963); *Music for 3* for Flute, Oboe, and Clarinet (1964); Trumpet Sonata (1965); Cello Sonata (1967); Oboe Sonata (1973); Clarinet Sonata (1974); Bassoon Sonata (1975); *Epitaph II* for Flute and Guitar (1976); Violin Sonata (1976); *Nocturne* for Violin and Piano (1979); *Music for Miloš Urbásek* for String Quartet (1981); Duet for 2 Violas (1981); Viola Sonata (1983); *Quadrophony* for 4 Cellos (1987); *Chant* for Flute (1991); piano pieces. **VOCAL:** *Seen Closely above the Lake* for Speaker, Wind Quintet, Piano, and String Quartet or Orch. (1979); *2 Arias* on fragments of the *Stabat mater* for High Voice and Orch. (1989; also for High Voice and Piano or Organ); *How One Drinks from a Well* for Speaker and Chamber Orch. (1990); choruses; solo songs. **ELECTROACOUSTIC:** *Hommage to William Croft* (1969); *Variations on Pictures by Miloš Urbásek* (1970); *Sonata-Canon* for Cello and 4 Electronic Voices (1971); *Tower Music* (1971); *In memoriam Ockeghem* (1971); *Outside the Door* (1974); *Sonata pastoralis 44* (1974); *Cantica feralia* (1975); *Hommage to Hummel* (1980); Concerto grosso (1990).

Parikian, Manoug, Turkish-born English violinist and teacher of Armenian descent; b. Mersin, Sept. 15, 1920; d. Oxford, Dec. 24, 1987. He was a student of Louis Pecsaki at London's Trinity College of Music (1936–39). In 1947 he made his debut as a soloist in Liverpool, and then was concertmaster of the Liverpool Phil. (1947–48) and the Philharmonia Orch. in London (1949–57). From 1957 he made tours of Europe as a soloist. He also was active as a performer in chamber music groups and as a duo recitalist. From 1980 to 1984 he was music director of the Manchester Camerata. He taught in London at the Royal College of Music (1954–56) and the Royal Academy of Music (1959–87). Parikian became well known as an advocate of contemporary British music.

Pâris, Alain, French conductor and writer on music; b. Paris, Nov. 22, 1947. He had a conducting course with Dervaux at the École Normal de Musique in Paris (Licence de concert, 1967), where he also was a student of Dandelot (1965–68); then studied conducting with Fourestier. In 1968 he won 1st prize in the Besançon conducting competition; subsequently appeared as a guest conductor with various French orchs. In 1976–77 he was assistant conductor of the Orchestre de Capitole de Toulouse. In 1980 he organized the Ensemble à Vent in Paris, which he led in programs of rarely-heard works as well as premiere performances of many contemporary scores. From 1983 to 1987 he was permanent conductor of the Opéra du Rhin in Strasbourg. From 1986 to 1989 he was a prof. of conducting at the Strasbourg Cons. As a guest conductor, he appeared throughout Europe. He publ. the *Dictionnaire des interprètes et de l'interprétation musicale au XXe siècle* (Paris, 1982; 4th ed., rev., 1995) and *Les Livrets d'opéra* (Paris, 1991); also made French translations of the *New Oxford Companion to Music* (Paris, 1988) and *Baker's Biographical Dictionary of Musicians* (Paris, 1995).

Parkening, Christopher (William), outstanding American guitarist; b. Los Angeles, Dec. 14, 1947. He began guitar lessons when he was 11 with Celedonio and Pepe Romero in Los Angeles, making his public recital debut in 1959; when he was 15, he entered Andrés Segovia's master class at the Univ. of Calif., Berkeley; also received instruction from cellist Gregor Piatigorsky and harpsichordist Malcolm Hamilton. He attended the Univ. of Calif., Los Angeles (1964–65); then entered the Univ. of Southern Calif. as a cello student of Gabor Retjo (there were no guitar teachers on its faculty); by the close of his sophomore year, he was asked by the Univ. to teach guitar, thus initiating its guitar studies; was head of its guitar dept. (1971–75). In the meantime, he launched a brilliant career as a guitar virtuoso; after his first major tour of North America (1969), he regularly performed throughout the U.S. and Canada; also made extensive tours throughout the world, garnering acclaim as one of the foremost masters of his instrument. He publ. a valuable guitar method (1973) and made effective transcriptions of works by Bach, Dowland, Debussy, Ravel, and others.

Parker, Jamie (real name, **James Edward Kimura**), Canadian pianist, brother of **Jon Kimura Parker**; b. Burnaby, British Columbia, May 31, 1963. He began his studies with his uncle, Edward J. Parker; later was a pupil of Marek Jablonski at the Banff School of Fine Arts (1978–87) and of Kum-Sing Lee at the Vancouver Academy of Music (performance certificate, 1981); after obtaining his B.Mus. at the Univ. of British Columbia (1985), he completed his training with Adele Marcus at the Juilliard School in N.Y. (M.Mus., 1987). In 1981 he made his debut as a soloist in Prokofiev's 1st Piano Concerto with the Calgary Phil., and thereafter performed with principal Canadian orchs. and was active as a recitalist and chamber music artist. In addition to the standard repertoire, Parker also programs the works of contemporary Canadian composers.

Parker, Jon Kimura (real name, **John David Kimura**), Canadian pianist, brother of **Jamie Parker**; b. Vancouver, Dec. 25, 1959. He studied with Jessie Morrison and was only 5 when he appeared as soloist with the Vancouver Youth Orch. After further training with his uncle, Edward J. Parker, with Kum-Sing Lee at the Vancouver Academy of Music (performance certificate, 1977), and with Marek Jablonski at the Banff School of Fine Arts, he completed his studies with Adele Marcus at the Juilliard School in N.Y. (B.Mus. and M.Mus., 1981; D.M.A., 1989). In 1982 he won the Viña del Mar Competition in Chile, and in 1983 toured Europe as a soloist with the Juilliard Orch. After capturing 1st prize in the Leeds Competition in 1984, he appeared as a soloist with principal orchs. the world over and as a recitalist. His commanding technical resources are notably refined by a gift for poetic lyricism, which serves him well as an interpreter of the Romantic repertoire. He has also played much out-of-the-ordinary music, ranging from rags to contemporary Canadian works.

Parker, William, American baritone; b. Butler, Pa., Aug. 5, 1943; d. N.Y., March 29, 1993. He took German language and literature courses at Princeton Univ. (B.A., 1965); after singing in the U.S. Army Chorus in Washington, D.C., he pursued serious vocal training with Bernac and Ponselle. He won 1st prize in the Toulouse Competition and the special Poulenc Prize in the Paris Competition; then gained wide recognition in 1979 when he took 1st prize in the Kennedy Center-Rockefeller Foundation International Competition for Excellence in the Performance of American Music. In subsequent years, Parker acquired a fine reputation as a concert singer; also sang with various opera companies in the U.S. and abroad. He was especially admired for his cultured approach to art song interpretation and for his advocacy of contemporary American music. After contracting AIDS, he commissioned a number of composers to contribute selections to *The AIDS Quilt Songbook.* With the baritones Kurt Ollman, William Sharp, and Sanford Sylvan, he gave the premiere of the cycle at N.Y.'s Alice Tully Hall in 1992. Parker continued to make appearances until his last public concert in Minneapolis on Jan. 1, 1993.

Parlow, Kathleen, Canadian violinist and teacher; b. Calgary, Alberta, Sept. 20, 1890; d. Oakville, Ontario, Aug. 19, 1963. Her family moved to San Francisco when she was a child, where she had early instruction in violin; in 1906 she was sent to St. Petersburg, where she was accepted by Leopold Auer in his violin class at the Cons. She subsequently developed an extensive concert career; played in England, Scandinavia, the U.S., and the Orient. From 1929 to 1936 she was a violin instructor at Mills College in Oakland, California; in 1941, joined the faculty of the Royal Cons. of Music of Toronto; there she organized in 1941 the Parlow String Quartet. She was head of the string dept. at the London (Ontario) College of Music (from 1959). The Kathleen Parlow Scholarship was established at the Univ. of Toronto from proceeds from her estate.

BIBL.: M. French, *K. P.: A Portrait* (Toronto, 1967).

Parmeggiani, Ettore, Italian tenor; b. Rimini, Aug. 15, 1895; d. Milan, Jan. 28, 1960. He was a pupil of Mandolini in Milan, making his operatic debut there in 1922 at the Teatro dal Verme as Cavaradossi. In 1927 he made his first appearance at Milan's La Scala as Max in *Der Freischütz,* and continued to sing there for a decade. In addition to his Wagnerian roles, he appeared in the premieres of Mascagni's *Nerone* (1935) and Respighi's *Lucrezia* (1937) there. In 1936 he also sang in the premiere of Malipiero's *Giulio Cesare* in Genoa. In later years, he taught voice in Milan and led the claque at La Scala.

Parnas, Leslie, American cellist and teacher; b. St. Louis, Nov. 11, 1931. He studied with Piatigorsky at the Curtis Inst. of Music in Philadelphia (1948–53). He won a number of prizes, including 2nd prize in the Geneva Competition (1957), the Prix Pablo Casals in the International Cello Competition in Paris (1957), and the joint 2nd prize (no 1st prize was given) in the Tchaikovsky Competition in Moscow (1962). He was 1st cellist in the St. Louis Sym. Orch. (1954–62); then appeared worldwide as a soloist with orchs., recitalist, and chamber music player. He taught at Boston Univ. (from 1962) and the St. Louis Cons. of Music (from 1982).

Parris, Herman, Russian-American physician and composer; b. Ekaterinoslav, Oct. 30, 1903; d. Philadelphia, Jan. 14, 1973. He was taken to America in his infancy. He studied at the Jefferson Medical College in Philadelphia, obtaining his M.D. in 1926. Concurrently he studied music at the Univ. of Pa., and graduated in 1921. He was a diligent and competent composer; wrote 4 syms. (1946, 1947, 1949, 1952), 8 piano concertos (1946–53), 4 string quartets (1946, 1948, 1960, 1964), 22 piano sonatas (1946–65), 115 piano preludes (1946–65), *Hebrew Rhapsody* for Orch. (1949), *Lament* for Strings (in memory of O. Downes; 1956), and various pieces of chamber music. He gained a flickering moment of notoriety with his orch. piece entitled *Hospital Suite,* realistically portraying bloody events in the sickroom; it was brought to light in a collegiate spirit by the Doctors' Orch. Society in N.Y. on May 13, 1948. Unfortunately, no further performances were given (all the patients in the suite died).

Parris, Robert, American composer, pianist, and teacher; b. Philadelphia, May 21, 1924. He studied piano in his youth and later pursued his education at the Univ. of Pa. (B.S., 1945; M.S., 1946). He then studied composition with Mennin at the Juilliard School of Music in N.Y. (B.S., 1948), Ibert and Copland at the Berkshire Music Center in Tanglewood (summers, 1950–51), and Honegger at the École Normale de Musique in Paris on a Fulbright fellowship (1951–52). After teaching at Washington State College in Pullman (1948–49) and the Univ. of Maryland (1961–62), he joined the faculty of George Washington Univ. in Washington, D.C., in 1963, where he was a prof. from 1976. Between 1961 and 1975 he also acted as an occasional music critic for the *Washington Post* and the *Washington Evening Star.* While some of his music veered toward tonal writing, he was particularly successful in utilizing serial procedures in works marked by effective handling of expressionistic and chromatic elements.

WORKS: ORCH.: *Symphonic Movement No. 1* (N.Y., June 1948) and *No. 2* (1951); *Harlequin's Carnival* (1949; Tanglewood, Aug. 11, 1951); Sym. (1952); Piano Concerto (1954); Concerto for 5 Kettle Drums and Orch. (1955; Washington, D.C., March 25, 1958); Viola Concerto (1956; Washington, D.C., May 20, 1971); Violin Concerto (1958); *Lamentations and Praises* for Brass and Percussion (1962; Philadelphia, May 24, 1966); Sinfonia for Brass (1963); Flute Concerto (1964); Concerto for Trombone and Chamber Orch. (Washington, D.C., Sept. 19, 1964); *The Golden Net* for Chamber Orch. (1968); *The Phoenix,* timpani concerto (1969; Detroit, Jan. 2, 1970); *The Messengers,* later renamed *Angels* (1974; Albany, N.Y., March 14, 1975); *Rite of Passage* for Clarinet, Electric Guitar, and Chamber Orch. (1978); *The Unquiet Heart* for Violin and Orch. (1981); *Chamber Music for Orchestra* (1984; Glasgow, Feb. 12, 1985); *Symphonic Variations* (1987; Washington, D.C., Jan. 28,

1988). **CHAMBER:** Cello Sonata (c.1946); 2 string trios (1947, 1951); Sonatina for Brass Quintet (1948; Pullman, Wash., May 1, 1949); 2 string quartets: No. 1 (1951; Washington, D.C., May 11, 1958) and No. 2 (1952); Sonatina for Winds (1954); *Fantasy and Fugue* for Cello (1955); Violin Sonata (1956); Viola Sonata (1957); Quintet for Violin, Cello, Flute, Oboe, and Bassoon (1957); Trio for Clarinet, Piano, and Cello (1959); *Cadenza, Caprice, and Ricercar* for Piano and Cello (1961); Sonatina for Recorder Quartet (1964); Duo for Flute and Violin (1965); Sonata for Solo Violin (1965); *4 Pieces* for Brass or Wind Trio (1965); *St. Winefred's Well* for 6 Players (1967); Concerto for Percussion, Violin, Cello, and Piano (1967); *The Book of Imaginary Beings I* for Flute, Violin, Cello, Piano, and Percussion (1972) and *II* for Clarinet, Violin, Viola, Cello, and Percussion (1983); 3 Duets for Electric Guitar and Amplified Harpsichord (1985); *Metamorphic Variations* for Flute, Clarinet, Violin, Cello, and Percussion (1986); *13 Pieces* for Trumpet, Violin, Viola, Cello, and Percussion (1989); *2 Small Duets and a Solo* for Violin and Piano (1989); *Nocturnes I* for Flute, Violin, Viola, Cello, and Percussion (Washington, D.C., Nov. 2, 1992) and *II* for Clarinet, Viola, Cello, Bass, and Percussion (1994). **PIANO:** *Toccata* for 2 Pianos (1950); *Variations* (1952); *6 Little Studies* (1960). **VOCAL:** 3 Songs for Baritone, Piano, and Celesta (1947); *The Hollow Men* for Tenor, Men's Chorus, and Chamber Ensemble (1949; N.Y., Feb. 16, 1951); *Night* for Baritone, String Quartet, and Clarinet (1951; Washington, D.C., Oct. 31, 1958); *Alas, for the Day,* cantata for Chorus (1954); *3 Passacaglias* for Soprano, Violin, Harpsichord, and Cello (1957); *Mad Scene* for 2 Baritones, Soprano, and Chamber Orch. (1960); *The Raids* for Soprano, Piano, and Violin (1960); *The Leaden Echo and the Golden Echo* for Baritone and Orch. (1960; Washington, D.C., Jan. 10, 1962); *Hymn for the Nativity* for Chorus and Brass Ensemble (1962); *Reflections on Immortality* for Chorus and Brass (1966); *Jesu duclis memoria* for Voices (1966); *Dirge for the New Sunrise* for Chorus (1970); *Walking Around* for Chorus, Clarinet, Violin, Piano, and 2 Percussionists (1973); *Dreams* for Soprano and Chamber Orch. (1976); *Cynthia's Revells* for Baritone and Guitar or Piano (1979); *3 Lyrics by Ben Jonson* for Baritone and Piano (1979).

Parrish, Carl, American musicologist and composer; b. Plymouth, Pa., Oct. 9, 1904; d. (as a result of injuries incurred in an automobile accident) Valhalla, N.Y., Nov. 27, 1965. He studied at the American Cons. in Fontainebleau (1932), the MacPhail School of Music (B.M., 1933), Cornell Univ. (M.A., 1936), and Harvard Univ. (Ph.D, 1939, with the diss. *The Early Piano and Its Influences on Keyboard Technique and Composition in the Eighteenth Century*). He taught at Wells College (1929–43), Fisk Univ. (1943–46), Westminster Choir College (1946–49), and Pomona College (1949–53); from 1953 to 1965 he was a prof. at Vassar College. He publ. *The Notation of Medieval Music* (N.Y., 1957; 2nd ed., 1959) and *A Treasury of Early Music* (N.Y., 1958). With J. Ohl, he publ. *Masterpieces of Music before 1750* (N.Y., 1951). He wrote orch. pieces, choral music, a String Quartet, a song cycle, piano pieces, and folk song arrangements for chorus.

Parrott, Andrew, English conductor; b. Walsall, March 10, 1947. He studied at the Univ. of Oxford, where he pursued research into the performing practices of 16th- and 17th-century music. In 1973 he founded the Taverner Choir, and subsequently the Taverner Consort and Players. He conducted Monteverdi's *Vespers* at London's Promenade Concerts in 1977; gave the first performance in London of Bach's *B-minor Mass* with period instruments; also presented in authentic style the *St. Matthew Passion* and the *Brandenburg Concertos.* He appeared as a guest conductor with the English Chamber Orch., the London Bach Orch., and the Concerto Amsterdam. In 1987 he made his first appearance at the Salzburg Festival conducting Monteverdi's *Vespers.* In 1989 he became artistic director of Kent Opera. In 1993 he made his debut at London's Covent Garden conducting *Die Zauberflöte.* With H. Keyte, he ed. *The New Oxford Book of Carols* (Oxford, 1992).

Parrott, (Horace) Ian, English composer, teacher, and writer on music; b. London, March 5, 1916. At 12, he began lessons in harmony with Benjamin Dale. Following studies at the Royal College of Music in London (1932–34), he completed his education at New College, Oxford (D.Mus., 1940; M.A., 1941). From 1940 to 1945 he saw service in the Royal Signals. He was a lecturer at the Univ. of Birmingham from 1947 to 1950. From 1950 to 1983 he was the Gregynog Prof. of Music at the Univ. College of Wales in Aberystwyth. In his music, Parrott remained faithful to the tonal tradition. In a number of his works, he was inspired by the culture of Wales.

WRITINGS: *Pathways to Modern Music* (1947); *A Guide to Musical Thought* (1955); *Method in Orchestration* (1957); *The Music of "An Adventure"* (1966); *The Spiritual Pilgrims* (1969); *Elgar* (1971); *Rosemary Brown: Music from Beyond* (1977); *Cyril Scott and His Piano Music* (1992); *The Crying Curlew: Peter Warlock: Family & Influences: Centenary 1994* (1994).

WORKS: OPERAS: *The Sergeant-Major's Daughter,* burlesque opera (1942–43); *The Black Ram* (1951–53; Aberystwyth, March 9, 1966); *Once Upon a Time,* comic opera (1959; Christchurch, New Zealand, Dec. 3, 1960); *The Lady of Flowers,* chamber opera (1981; Colchester, Sept. 17, 1982). **ORCH.:** *Malvern Music* (1937); *Malvern March* (1938); *De l'Estuaire à la source* (1939); *Russian Dance* for Small Orch. (1941); *A Dream* for Small Orch. (1941); *Scherzo No. 2* (1941–43); 5 syms.: No. 1 (1943–46), No. 2, *Round the World* (1960–61), No. 3 (1966), No. 4, *Sinfonietta* (1978), and No. 5 (1979; Coventry, May 23, 1981); *El Alamein* (1944; Guildford, Oct. 1945); *Miniature Concerto* for Violin and Small Orch. (1945); *Luxor* (1947; London, Oct. 17, 1950); Piano Concerto (1948–49); *Maid in Birmingham* (1949); *Pensieri,* concerto grosso for Strings (1950); *Solemn Overture: Romeo and Juliet* (1951–53; Bournemouth, Oct. 24, 1957); *Flourish for a Royal Visit* for Small Orch. (1955); *Orchestral Variations on Dufay's Se la face ay pale* (1955); *4 Shakespeare Dances* (1956); English Horn Concerto (1956; Cheltenham, July 18, 1958); *Cwyn Mam Y'ghyfraith* (1958); *Hen Ferchetan* (1958); *Mae 'Nghariad i'n Fenws* for Strings (1958); *Seithenin,* overture (1959); Cello Concerto (1961; Newtown, May 2, 1963); *Ian Parrott's Attempt* for Strings (1962); *Broncastell* (1964); Suite for Violin and Orch. (1965); Concerto for Trombone and Winds (1967; based on the Sonatina for Trombone and Piano, 1958); *Fantasia on Welsh Tunes* for Brass Band (1968); *Homage to 2 Masters* (1970; also for Organ); *Harrow March* for Brass (1970); *Reaching for the Light* (Attingham Park, Aug. 21, 1971); Concertino for 2 Guitars and Small Orch. (1973); *Rumbustuoso VERNONcello Am GRIFFbrett* for Strings (Christchurch, New Zealand, Feb. 1, 1974); Fanfare-Overture (Montacute, July 3, 1993). **CHAMBER:** Oboe Sonata (1935); Trio for Flute, Violin, and Piano (1937); 5 string quartets: No. 1 (1946; London, May 2, 1950), No. 2 (1954–55), No. 3 (1957; Bangor, May 1961), No. 4 (1963; Aberystwyth, Sept. 1964), and No. 5 (1994; BBC, May 5, 1995); Duet for 2 Flutes (1946); Oboe Quartet (1946; Oxford, Oct. 19, 1947); 2 wind quintets: No. 1 (1947–48; Birmingham, May 6, 1949) and No. 2 (1970; Cardiff, May 14, 1971); *Fantasy* for Cello and Piano (Birmingham, Oct. 8, 1948); *Fantasy Trio* for Violin, Cello, and Piano (1950; Birmingham, May 24, 1951); *Hobos Riding* for Oboe, Oboe d'Amore, English Horn, and Heckelphone (1951); *Dafydd y Garreg Wen* for Viola and Piano (1951); *Capriccio* for Trumpet and Piano (1956); *Ceredigion* for Harp (1957); *Rhapsody* for Violin and Piano (1957); Trombone Sonatina (1958; reworked as the Concerto for Trombone and Winds, 1967); *Fantasy for James Blades* for Percussion (1959); *Blackbird Piece* for Flute, Oboe, Clarinet, Horn, Bassoon, and Piano (Bournemouth, Feb. 22, 1960); *Septet 1962* (1961–62; Cheltenham, July 10, 1962); *Abergenny* for Crwth and Optional Clarinet (1965); *Big Hat Guy* for Violin and Piano (1965); *Partita on 2 Welsh Tunes* for Harp (1967); *Pant Glas* for Violin, Glockenspiel, and Piano (1967); *4 Silhouettes* for Flute (1969); *2 Dances* for Flute and Harp (1969); *Arabesque and Dance* for Treble Recorder and Harpsichord or Piano (1972); *Fanfare and March* for 2 Trumpets, Trombone, and Bass Tuba (1973); *Devil's Bridge Jaunt* for Cello and Piano (1974); *Polished Brass* or *Gleaming Brass* for

Brass Quintet (1976); *Duo fantastico I* (1976) and *II* (1990) for Violin and Piano; *Rhapsody* for Trumpet and Organ (1977); *Arfon* for Harp (1978); *Fantasy Sonata* for Clarinet and Piano (1979; New Haven, Conn., Oct. 1986); *Reflections* for Violin and Piano (1982); *Suite for Stefan Popov* for Cello and Piano (1982; London, Feb. 5, 1985); Duo for Clarinet and Trumpet (1983; London, May 17, 1984); *Autumn Landscape* for Oboe and Piano (1983; BBC, March 6, 1986); Duo for 2 Guitars (1988); *3 North Wales Tunes* for 2 Guitars (1993); *Fantasising* (on a Welsh Tune) for Flute, Oboe, and Piano (1993). **KEYBOARD: PIANO:** *Siberian March* (1928); *Scherzo No. 1* (1933); *Foursome* for Piano, 4-hands (1935–39); *Caprice* (1937); *Nocturne* (1937); *Malvern Hills* (1938); *Betinka* (1939); *Westerham* (1940); *Fuga giocosa* (1942); *Impromptu* (1942); *Theme and 6 Variants* (London, Oct. 17, 1946); *Fantasy and Allegro* for 2 Pianos (1946; London, May 1, 1947); *The Birds of Glanyrafon* (1953); *By the Ystwyth* (1954); *Little Fugato* (1954); *Fantasy* (1964; Bangor, March 8, 1965); *Aspects* (1975; Copenhagen, March 12, 1976); *Humoresque* (1993). **ORGAN:** Sonata (1933); *Agincourt* (1948); *Elegy* (1957); *Toccata* (Cambridge, May 13, 1962); *Mosaics* (1968); *Fantasia* (1974); 2 suites: No. 1 (1977; London, June 1, 1978) and No. 2 (BBC, April 13, 1991); *Hands Across the Years: In Memoriam Gerald Finzi* (1980; Harrogate, Aug. 8, 1983). **VOCAL:** *2 Nature Pieces* for Chorus and Orch. (1936–37); *Jolly Good Ale & Old* for Basses (1939); *Earth Rejoices* for Chorus (1939); *Psalm 91* for Bass, Chorus, and Orch. (1946–47; Belfast, March 16, 1951); *All the Woods Answer* for Voices (1949); *Voices in a Giant City* for Men's Voices and Piano (1949); *3 Kings Have Come* for Women's Voices or Soprano or Baritone or Chorus, Piano, and Strings (1951; Cambridge, Nov. 22, 1952); *Magnificat and Nunc Dimittis* for Voices and Organ (1961); *Cantata jubilate Deo* for Soloists, Chorus, and Orch. (1963; London, Oct. 20, 1967); *The 3 Moorish Princesses* for Narrator and Orch. (1963–64); *The Song of the Stones of St. David's* for Chorus and Organ (1968); *Offertory Motet: Diffusa est gratia in labiis tuis* for Voices (1968; London, March 20, 1969); *Cymun bendigaid* for Voice(s) and Organ or Piano or Guitar and Percussion Band (1972; also as the *Folksong Mass*); *Song for Dyfed* for 2 Narrators, Chorus, and Piano (1973–74); *Master Hugues of Saxe-Gotha* for Men's Voices and Piano (1975); *My Cousin Alice* for Mezzo-soprano, Tenor, Chorus, Piano, and Tape of Birds (1982; Aberystwyth, May 16, 1983); *Eastern Wisdom* for Voice and Chamber Orch. (1987; Machynlleth, May 6, 1990); *Arglwydd ein Ior ni* for Voices (Lower Machen, June 30, 1991); various solo songs.

Parry, Sir C(harles) Hubert H(astings), eminent English composer, pedagogue, and writer on music; b. Bournemouth, Feb. 27, 1848; d. Rustington, Oct. 7, 1918. While attending a preparatory school in Twyford, near Winchester, he began piano lessons with a local organist. He then had training in piano, harmony, and counterpoint with Edward Brind, the organist at Highnam Church. In 1861 he entered Eton, where he became active in its musical society. During this time, he also had composition lessons with George Elvey, organist at St. George's Chapel, Windsor. In 1866 he took his B.Mus. exercise at New College, Oxford, with his cantata *O Lord, Thou hast cast us out.* In 1867 he entered Exeter College, Oxford, to study law and history. During the summer of that year, he pursued training in instrumentation and composition with Pierson in Stuttgart. After graduating from Exeter College in 1870, he had a few lessons with Sterndale Bennett. Between 1873 and 1877 he was engaged in business in London, but he also pursued training in piano with Dannreuther (from 1873) and in composition with Macfarren (1875–77). In 1875 Grove made him subeditor of his *Dictionary of Music and Musicians,* to which Parry contributed a number of the major articles. In 1883 he was named prof. of music history at the newly organized Royal College of Music in London and was awarded an honorary Doc.Mus. from Trinity College, Cambridge. In 1884 he was elected Choragus at the Univ. of Oxford, where he received an honorary doctorate. In 1894 Parry was elevated to the directorship of the Royal College of Music, a position he retained with distinction for the rest of his life. He also served as the Heather Prof. of Music at the Univ. of Oxford from 1900 to 1908. In 1898 he was knighted and in 1905 he was made a Commander of the Royal Victorian Order. Parry secured his reputation as a composer with his distinguished choral ode *At a Solemn Music: Blest Pair of Sirens* (1887). There followed a series of ethical choral works in which he attempted to build upon the British choral tradition. His coronation anthem *I was glad* (1902) is a masterwork in the genre. Also notable is his *Ode on the Nativity* (1910). His unison song *Jerusalem* (1916) quickly established itself as a national song. Among his other fine works are his *Songs of Farewell* and his collections of *English Lyrics.* In his orchestral music, Parry played a significant role in the fostering of the British symphonic tradition. While his orchestral works owe much to the German Romanticists, particularly Mendelssohn, Schumann, and Brahms, he nevertheless developed a personal style notable for its fine craftsmanship and mastery of diatonic writing. His 5 syms. reveal a growing assurance in handling large forms. He also wrote some effective incidental music and fine chamber pieces.

WRITINGS (all publ. in London unless otherwise given): *Studies of the Great Composers* (1887); *The Art of Music* (1893; enl. ed., 1896, as *The Evolution of the Art of Music*); *Summary of the History and Development of Medieval and Modern European Music* (1893; 2nd ed., 1904); *The Music of the Seventeenth Century,* vol. III of *The Oxford History of Music* (1902); *Johann Sebastian Bach* (1910); *Style in Musical Art* (1911); *Instinct and Character* (c.1915–18; MS); H. Colles, ed., *College Addresses* (1920).

WORKS: DRAMATIC: OPERA: *Guenever* (1886). **BALLET:** *Proserpine* (London, June 25, 1912). **INCIDENTAL MUSIC TO:** Aristophanes' *The Birds* (Cambridge, Nov. 27, 1883; rev. 1903); Aristophanes' *The Frogs* (Oxford, Feb. 24, 1892; rev. version, Oxford, Feb. 19, 1909); S. Ogilvie's *Hypatia* (London, Jan. 2, 1893; orch. suite, London, March 9, 1893); P. Craigie's *A Repentance* (London, Feb. 28, 1899); Aeschylus' *Agamemnon* (London, Nov. 16, 1900); Aristophanes' *The Clouds* (Oxford, March 1, 1905); Aristophanes' *The Acharnians* (Oxford, Feb. 21, 1914). **ORCH.:** *Allegretto Scherzando* (1867); *Intermezzo Religioso* (Gloucester, Sept. 3, 1868); *Vivien,* overture (1873); Concertstück (1877); Piano Concerto (1878–80; London, April 3, 1880; rev. 1895); *Guillem de Cabestanh,* overture (London, March 15, 1879); 5 syms.: No. 1, in G major (1880–82; Birmingham, Aug. 31, 1882), No. 2, in F major, *Cambridge* (Cambridge, June 12, 1883; rev. version, London, June 6, 1887; 2nd rev. version, London, May 30, 1895), No. 3, in C major, *English* (London, May 23, 1889; rev. version, Leeds, Jan. 30, 1895; 3rd rev. version, Bournemouth, Dec. 18, 1902), No. 4, in E minor (London, July 1, 1889; rev. version, London, Feb. 10, 1910), and No. 5, *Symphonic Fantasia 1912* (London, Dec. 5, 1912); *Suite Moderne* or *Suite Symphonique* (Gloucester, Sept. 9, 1886; rev. 1892); *An English Suite* for Strings (1890–1918; London, Oct. 20, 1922); *Overture to an Unwritten Tragedy* (Worcester, Sept. 13, 1893; rev. 1897 and 1905); *Lady Radnor Suite* for Strings (London, June 29, 1894; also for Piano, 1905, and for Violin and Piano, 1915); *Elegy for Brahms* (1897; London, Nov. 9, 1918); *Symphonic Variations* (London, June 3, 1897); *From Death to Life,* symphonic poem (Brighton, Nov. 12, 1914). **WIND BAND:** *Foolish Fantasia* (n.d.). **CHAMBER:** 3 movements for Violin and Piano (1863); 2 string quartets (1867, c.1879); *2 Duettinos* for Cello and Piano (1868); *Short Trios* for Violin, Viola, and Piano (1868); *Freundschaftslieder,* 6 pieces for Violin and Piano (1872); 3 violin sonatas (1875; *Fantasie Sonate,* 1878; 1889, rev. 1894); Nonet for Winds (1877); 3 piano trios (1878, 1884, 1890); Piano Quartet (1879); Cello Sonata (1880); String Quintet (1884; rev. 1896 and 1902); *Partita* for Violin and Piano (1886); *12 Short Pieces* for Violin and Piano (1895); Piece for Violin and Piano (1896); *Romance* for Violin and Piano (1896); 2 suites for Violin and Piano (1907, 1907). **KEYBOARD: PIANO:** 4 fugues (1865); *Andante non troppo* (1865); Overture for Piano Duet (1865); Sonata for Piano Duet (1865); *Andante* (1867); *Sonnets and Songs Without Words,* 3 sets (1868; 1867–75; 1870–77); 7

Charakterbilder (1872); *Variations on an air by Bach* (1873–75); *Grosses Duo* for 2 Pianos (1875–77); 2 sonatas (1877; 1876–77); *Theme and 19 Variations* (1878); *Shulbrede Tunes* (1914); *Hands across the Centuries*, suite (1918). **ORGAN:** Fugue (1865); Fantasia and Fugue (1877; new Fantasia, 1882; new Fugue, 1912); Chorale Preludes, 2 sets (1912, 1916); Toccata and Fugue, *Wanderer* (1912–18); *Elegy* (1913); 3 Chorale Fantasias (1915). **VOCAL: CHORAL** (all with orch. unless otherwise given): *O Lord, Thou hast cast us out*, cantata (Eton College, Dec. 8, 1867); *Scenes from Shelley's "Prometheus Unbound"*, dramatic cantata (Gloucester, Sept. 7, 1880; rev. 1881 and 1885); *The Contention of Ajax and Ulysses: The Glories of Our Blood and State*, ode (Gloucester, Sept. 4, 1883; rev. 1908 and 1914); *At a Solemn Music: Blest Pair of Sirens*, ode (London, May 17, 1887); *Judith* or *The Regeneration of Manasseh*, oratorio (Birmingham, Aug. 29, 1888); *Ode on St. Cecilia's Day*, ode (Leeds, Oct. 11, 1889); *L'Allegro ed Il Penseroso*, cantata (Norwich, Oct. 15, 1890; rev. 1909); *Eton*, ode (Eton College, June 28, 1891); *De Profundis* (Hereford, Sept. 10, 1891); *The Lotos-Eaters*, choric song (Cambridge, June 13, 1892); *Job*, oratorio (Gloucester, Sept. 8, 1892); *Hear my words ye people*, anthem for Chorus, Organ, Brass, and Timpani (Salisbury Cathedral, May 10, 1894); *King Saul*, oratorio (Birmingham, Oct. 3, 1894); *Invocation to Music*, ode (Leeds, Oct. 2, 1895); *Magnificat* (Hereford, Sept. 15, 1897); *A Song of Darkness and Light* (Gloucester, Sept. 15, 1898); *Thanksgiving Te Deum* (Latin version, Hereford, Sept. 1900; Eng. version, rev., Gloucester, Sept. 11, 1913); *Ode to Music* (London, June 13, 1901); *I was glad*, coronation anthem (London, Aug. 9, 1902; rev. version, London, June 23, 1911); *War and Peace*, symphonic ode (London, April 30, 1903); *Voces Clamantium*, motet (Hereford, Sept. 10, 1903); *The love that casteth out fear*, sinfonia sacra (Gloucester, Sept. 7, 1904); *The Pied Piper of Hamelin*, cantata (Norwich, Oct. 26, 1905; rev. 1910); *The Soul's Ransom: A Psalm of the Poor*, sinfonia sacra (Hereford, Sept. 12, 1906); *The Vision of Life*, symphonic poem (Cardiff, Sept. 26, 1907; rev. 1914); *Beyond these voices there is peace*, motet (Worcester, Sept. 9, 1908); *Eton Memorial Ode* (Eton College, Nov. 18, 1908); *Coronation Te Deum* (London, June 23, 1911); *Ode on the Nativity* (Hereford, Sept. 12, 1912); *God is our hope* (London, April 24, 1913); *The Chivalry of the Sea*, naval ode (London, Dec. 12, 1916). **LITURGICAL:** *Te Deum* (c.1864); *Magnificat and Nunc Dimittis* (1864); *Te Deum and Benedictus* (1868); Communion, Morning, and Evening Services (1869); *Te Deum* (1873); Evening Service (1881); 10 anthems; 28 hymns, etc. **OTHER:** Part songs; unison songs, including the famous *Jerusalem* (1916); numerous solo songs, including 12 sets of *English Lyrics* (publ. 1885–1920); *Songs of Farewell*, 6 motets (1916–17).

BIBL.: C. Graves, *H. P.: His Life and Works* (2 vols., London, 1926); J. Dibble, *C. H. H. P.: His Life and Music* (Oxford, 1992).

Parsch, Arnošt, Czech composer and teacher; b. Bučovice, Moravia, Feb. 12, 1936. He was a pupil of J. Podešva and M. Ištvan; later took courses at the Janáček Academy of Music in Brno; subsequently served on its faculty.

WORKS: ORCH.: *Suite* for Strings (1963); Concerto for Winds, Percussion, and Piano (1964); Sonata for Chamber Orch. (1967); 2 syms. (1967, 1973); *Musica concertante con ommagio* (1970); *The Flight* (1973); *The Bird Flew above the Clouds* for Oboe and Orch. (1975); Double Concerto for Flute, Trumpet, and Orch. (1977); *The Message* for 2 String Orchs. (1978); *Divisi. Non divisi!* (1979); Sym.-Concerto for Horn and Orch. (1982); *Rondo* for Orch. with Concertante Violin (1983); *2 Rondos* for Strings (1984); *Poema*, concerto for Cimbalom and Orch. (1986); Concerto for Bass Clarinet, Piano, and Orch. (1989); *Rapsodietta* for 11 Strings (1991); *Wells* for Chamber Orch. (1992). **CHAMBER:** *Music* for String Quartet and Percussion (1964); *Trasposizioni I* for Flute, Oboe, Clarinet, Bassoon, and Horn (1967); Organ Sonata (1968); 3 string quartets (1970, 1973, 1994); *Esercizii per uno, due, tre e quatro* for 2 Flutes, Guitar, and Cello (1971); *Quatro pezzi per quatro stromenti* for Violin, Clarinet, Double Bass, and Piano (1972); *Early Spring* for Reciter, Flute, Bass Clarinet, and Piano (1972); *Hold Fast!* for 2 Trumpets, Horn, 2 Trombones, and Tuba (1979); *Drawings* for Violin, Clarinet, and Piano (1989); *Distant Skylines* for Flute, Bass Clarinet, and Piano (1990); *Musica per i montanari* for 2 Horns (1991); *Meditation* for Guitar (1993); *The Voice of the River* for 9 Players (1994); *Hillside* for Violin and Percussion (1995). **VOCAL:** *Simple Truths* for Soprano, 2 Flutes, Guitar, and Cello (1973); *The Sun Rose Once*, cantata for Chorus, Clarinet, Saxophone, and Jazz Orch., after a text by Sitting Bull (1974); *Kings' Ride* for Tenor, Bass, Chorus, and Chamber Ensemble (1984); *Invocation of Love*, 5 songs for Tenor and Piano (1987); *Spring Rites* for Mezzo-soprano, Tenor, Bass-baritone, Chorus, Children's Chorus, and Orch. (1990); *Lullabies* for Woman's Voice, 2 Cymbals, Double Bass, and Chimes (1991); *Etudes Amoureuses* for Mezzo-soprano, Violin, Marimba, and Percussion (1995). **ELECTROACOUSTIC:** *Poetica No. 3* (1967); *Trasposizioni II* (1969) and *III* (1970); *Rotae rotarum* (1971); *Prologos* (1971); *Labyrinthos* (1972); *In High Mountains* (1973); *Daybreak* (1983); *Metamorphoses of Time* (1989).

Parsons, Geoffrey (Penwill), notable Australian piano accompanist and teacher; b. Sydney, June 15, 1929; d. London, Jan. 26, 1995. He received his training from Winifried Burston at the New South Wales State Conservatorium of Music in Sydney (1941–48) and from Wührer in Munich (1956). In 1948 he made his first tour of Australia. In 1950 he first appeared in London, where he settled. In subsequent years, he pursued an international career as a piano accompanist to many of the leading artists of the day. He toured Australia some 30 times and performed in more than 40 nations. He also gave master classes in the art of piano accompaniment. In 1977 he was made an Officer of the Order of the British Empire.

Pärt, Arvo, outstanding Estonian-born Austrian composer; b. Paide, Sept. 11, 1935. He was a student of Heino Eller at the Tallinn Cons., graduating in 1963. From 1958 to 1967 he worked for the Estonian Radio in Tallinn. In 1980 he emigrated to the West, becoming a naturalized Austrian citizen. In his early works, Pärt followed a modern path in which he utilized serial, aleatoric, and collage techniques. This course, along with his deeply felt spiritual convictions, caused him difficulties with Soviet officialdom. Pärt's intense interest in medieval and Renaissance music led to a remarkable change of course in the mid-1970s as he developed a tintinnabular technique which resulted in scores notable for their beauty, strong character, and spirituality. In 1978 he was awarded the Estonian Music Prize for his *Tabula rasa*, a score which established his international reputation.

WORKS: ORCH.: *Nekrolog* (1960); 3 syms. (1963, 1966, 1971); *Perpetuum mobile* (1963); *Pro et contra*, cello concerto (1966); *Wenn Bach Bienen gezüchtet hätte* for Piano, Wind Quintet, and Strings (1976–84); *Cantus in Memory of Benjamin Britten* for Strings and Bell (1977); *Tabula rasa*, double concerto for 2 Violins or Violin and Viola, Strings, and Prepared Piano (1977); *Fratres* for Strings and Percussion (1977; rev. 1991; also for Violin, String Orch., and Percussion, 1992); *Spiegel im Spiegel* for Violin, Piano, and Strings (1980; also for Violin and Piano, 1978); *Summa* for Strings (1980–91); *Dreiklang*, concerto for Violin, Cello, and Chamber Orch. (1981); *Festina lente* for Strings and Harp ad libitum (1988; rev. 1990); *Silouan's Song: My Soul Yearns After the Lord . . .* for Strings (1991); *The Introductory Prayers* for Strings (1992; rev. 1995). **CHAMBER:** String Quartet (1959); Wind Quintet (1964); *Musica syllabica* for 12 Instruments (1964); *Collage über B-A-C-H* for Strings, Oboe, Harpsichord, and Piano (1964); *Fratres* for Chamber Ensemble (1977; also for Violin and Piano, 1977–80, for 4, 8, or 12 Cellos, 1977–83, for String Quartet, 1977–85, etc.); *Arbos* for 7 Flutes and 3 Triangles ad libitum (1977; also for 8 Brass and Percussion, 1977–86); *Spiegel im Spiegel* for Violin and Piano (1978; also for Violin, Piano, and String Orch., 1980); *Pari intervallo* for 4 Flutes (1980; also for Organ); *Summa* for Violin, 2 Violas, and Cello (1980–90; also for String

Quartet, 1980–91); *Psalom* for String Quartet (1986–91); *Adagio* for Violin, Cello, and Piano (1992); *Darf ich . . .* for Violin, Tubular Bells ad libitum, and Strings (1995). **KEYBOARD: PIANO:** 2 sonatinas (1958, 1959); *Partita* (1959); *Diagrams* (1964); *Für Alina* (1976); *Variationen zur gesundung von Arinuschka* (1977). **ORGAN:** *Trivium* (1976); *Pari intervallo* (1980; also for 4 Flutes); *Annum per annum* (1980); *Mein Weg hat Gipfel und Wellentäler* (1985). **VOCAL:** *Meie aed* (Our Garden) for Children's Chorus and Orch. (1958); *Maailma samm* (The World's Stride), oratorio for Chorus and Orch. (1961); *Solfeggio* for Chorus and String Quartet (1964); *Credo* for Chorus, Piano, and Orch. (1968); *Laul armastatule* (Song for the Beloved) for 2 Solo Voices, Chorus, and Orch. (1973); *Calix* for Chorus and Instruments (1976); *By the Waters of Babylon*, Psalm 137 for Voices and Instruments (1976–84; rev. 1994); *Modus* for Soprano and Instruments (1976); *In spe* for 4 Voices and Instruments (1976); *Sarah was 90 Years Old* for 3 Voices, Percussion, and Organ (1977–90); *Cantate Domino Canticum Novum*, Psalm 95 for Voices and Instruments (1977–91); *Missa Syllabica* for Voices and Instruments (1977–91); *Summa* for Chorus or 4 Soloists (1980–90); *De profundis* for Men's Chorus, Organ, and Optional Percussion (1980); *Passio Domini nostri Jesu Christi secundum Joannem* for Tenor, Bass, Vocal Quartet, Chorus, Instrumental Quartet, and Organ (1982); *2 Slavic Psalms* (117 and 131) for Soprano, Alto, Countertenor, Tenor, and Bass (1984); *Ein Wallfahrtslied*, Psalm 121 for Tenor or Baritone and String Quartet (1984); *Es sang vor Langen Jahren* for Alto or Countertenor, Violin, and Viola (1984); *Te Deum* for 3 Choruses, Piano, Strings, and Tape (1984–85; rev. 1986); *Stabat Mater* for Soprano, Alto, Tenor, Violin, Viola, and Cello (1985); *7 Magnificat-Antiphonen* for Chorus (1988; rev. 1991); *Magnificat* for Chorus (1989); *Nun eile ich zu euch* for Chorus or Soloists (1989); *Miserere* for Soloists, Chorus, Ensemble, and Organ (1989; rev. 1990); *Mother of God and Virgin* for Chorus (1990); *Beatus Petronius* for 2 Choruses and 2 Organs (1990); *Statuit ei Dominus* for 2 Choruses and 2 Organs (1990); *The Beatitudes* for Chorus or Soloists and Organ (1990; rev. 1991); *Berliner Messe* for Chorus or Soloists and Organ or String Orch. (1990; rev. 1991); *And One of the Pharisees . . .* for 3 Voices (1992); *Litany: Prayers of St. John Chrysostom for Each Hour of the Day and Night* for Soloists, Chorus, and Orch. (1994).

Partch, Harry, innovative American composer, performer, and instrument maker; b. Oakland, Calif., June 24, 1901; d. San Diego, Sept. 3, 1974. Largely autodidact, he began experimenting with instruments capable of producing fractional intervals, which led him to the formulation of a 43-tone scale; he expounded his findings in his book, *Genesis of a Music* (1949; 2nd ed., rev. and aug., 1974). Among new instruments constructed by him were elongated violas, a chromelodeon, kitharas with 72 strings, harmonic canons with 44 strings, boos (made of giant Philippine bamboo reeds), cloud-chamber bowls, blow-boys (a pair of bellows with an attached automobile horn), etc. Seeking intimate contact with American life, he wandered across the country, collecting indigenous expressions of folkways, inscriptions on public walls, etc., for texts in his productions. T. McGeary ed. a vol. devoted to Partch as *Bitter Music: Collected Journals, Essays, Introductions, and Librettos* (Urbana, Ill., 1991).

WORKS: *17 Lyrics by Li Po* for Voice and Adapted Viola (1930–33; San Francisco, Feb. 9, 1932); *2 Psalms* for Voice and Adapted Viola (1931; San Francisco, Feb. 9, 1932; rev. 1941); *The Potion Scene from Romeo and Juliet* for Voice and Adapted Viola (1931; San Francisco, Feb. 9, 1932; rev. 1955); *The Wayward Barstow: 8 Hitchhiker Inscriptions from a Highway Railing at Barstow, California* for Voice and Adapted Guitar (1941; N.Y., April 22, 1944; rev. 1954); *U.S. Highball: A Musical Account of a Transcontinental Hobo Trip* for Voices, Guitar I, Kithara, and Chromelodeon (1943; N.Y., April 22, 1944; rev. 1955); *San Francisco: A Setting of the Cries of 2 Newsboys on a Foggy Night in the 20s* for 2 Baritones, Adapted Viola, Kithara, and Chromelodeon (1943; N.Y., April 22, 1944); *The Letter: A Depression Message from a Hobo Friend* for Intoning Voices and Original Instruments (1943; N.Y., April 22, 1944); *Dark Brother* for Voice, Chromelodeon, Adapted Viola, Kithara, and Bass Marimba (1942–43); *2 Settings from Joyce's Finnegans Wake* for Soprano, Kithara, and 2 Flutes (1944); *Yankee Doodle Fantasy* for Soprano, Tin Flutes, Tin Oboes, Flex-a-tones, and Chromelodeon (N.Y., April 22, 1944); *11 Intrusions* for Large Ensemble of Original Instruments (1946–50); *Plectra and Percussion Dances* for Voices and Original Instruments (1949–52; Berkeley, Calif., Nov. 19, 1953); *Oedipus*, dance music for 10 Solo Voices and Original Instruments, after Sophocles (1951; Oakland, Calif., March 14, 1952; rev. 1952–54); *2 Settings from Lewis Carroll* for Voice and Original Instruments (Mill Valley, Calif., Feb. 13, 1954); *Ulysses at the Edge* for Alto Saxophone or Trumpet, Baritone Saxophone, and Original Instruments (1955; adapted to *The Wayward*); *The Bewitched*, dance satire for Soprano and Ensemble of Traditional and Original Instruments (1955; Urbana, Ill., March 26, 1957); *Windsong*, film score (1958; rev. as the ballet *Daphne of the Dunes*, 1967); *Revelation in the Courthouse Park* for 16 Solo Voices, 4 Speakers, Dancers, and Large Instrumental Ensemble (1960; Urbana, Ill., April 11, 1962); *Rotate the Body in All Its Planes*, film score (Urbana, Ill., April 8, 1961); *Bless This Home* for Voice, Oboe, and Original Instruments (1961); *Water! Water!*, farcical "intermission" (1961; Urbana, Ill., March 9, 1962); *And on the 7th Day Petals Fell in Petaluma* for Large Ensemble of Original Instruments (1963–66; Los Angeles, May 8, 1966); *Delusion of the Fury: A Ritual of Dream and Delusion*, dramatic piece for Large Ensemble (1965–66; Los Angeles, Jan. 9, 1969); *The Dreamer That Remains: A Study in Loving*, film score (1972).

BIBL.: G. Hackbarth, *An Analysis of H. P.'s "Daphne of the Dunes"* (Ann Arbor, 1979); T. McGeary, *The Music of H. P.: A Descriptive Catalog* (Brooklyn, 1991).

Partos, Oedoen (actually, **Ödön**), Hungarian-born Israeli violinist, violist, pedagogue, and composer; b. Budapest, Oct. 1, 1907; d. Tel Aviv, July 6, 1977. He was a student of Hubay (violin) and Kodály (composition) at the Budapest Academy of Music (1918–24). He served as concertmaster of the Lucerne City Orch. (1924–26) and the Budapest Concert Orch. (1926–27; 1937–38), and also toured throughout Europe as a soloist. In 1938 he emigrated to Israel, where he was 1st violinist in the Palestine Orch. (later the Israel Phil.) until 1956. He also was the violist in the Israel Quartet (1939–54). In 1951 he became director of the Tel Aviv Academy of Music (later the Rubin Academy of Music of the Univ. of Tel Aviv), where he was a prof. from 1961. In 1954 he was awarded the 1st Israel State Prize for composition for his symphonic fantasy *Ein Gev*. In many of his works, he utilized eastern Jewish folk modalities. In 1960 he embraced 12-tone composition. Late in his life he experimented with the 31-tone scale.

WORKS: ORCH.: *Rondo on a Sephardic Theme* for Strings (1939); *Yizkor* (In memoriam) for Viola or Violin or Cello and Strings (1947; also for Viola or Violin or Cello and Piano); 2 viola concertos: No. 1, *Shir Tehillah* (Song of Praise; 1948; Tel Aviv, Jan. 22, 1949) and No. 2 (1957); *Ein Gev*, symphonic fantasy (1951–52; Ein Gev, Oct. 1, 1953); *Mourning Music (Oriental Ballad)* for Viola or Cello and Chamber Orch. (1956; also for Cello or Viola and Piano); Violin Concerto (1958); *Iltur* (Improvisation) for 12 Harps (1960); *Dmuyoth* (Images; 1960); *Tehilim* (Psalms) for Strings (1960; also as String Quartet No. 2); *Sinfonia concertante* for Viola and Orch. (1962); *Symphonic Movements* (1966); *Netivim* (Paths), symphonic elegy (1969); *Shiluvim* (Fusions) for Viola and Chamber Orch. (Tel Aviv, June 21, 1970); *Music* for Chamber Orch. (1971); *Arabesque* for Oboe and Chamber Orch. (1975). **CHAMBER:** 2 string quartets: No. 1, *Concertino* (1932; rev. 1939; N.Y., May 24, 1941) and No. 2, *Tehilim* (Psalms; 1960; also for String Orch.); *Rondo* for Violin and Piano (1947); *4 Israeli Tunes* for Violin or Viola or Cello and Piano (1948); *Maqamat* for Flute and String Quartet (1959); *Agada* (A Legend) for Viola, Piano, and Percussion (1960; London, June 6, 1962); *Arpiliyot* (Nebulae) for Wind Quintet

(1966); Concertino for Flute and Piano (1969); *3 Fantasies* for 2 Violins (1972; composed in the 31-tone system); *Elegy* for Violin and Piano (1973); *Ballad* for Piano Quartet (1977); *Fantasia* for Violin, Cello, and Piano (1977); *Invenzione a 3 (Homage à Debussy)* for Flute, Harp, and Viola (1977). **PIANO:** *Prelude* (1960); *Metamorphoses* (1971). **VOCAL:** *4 Folk Songs* for Alto and String Quartet (1939); *Daughter of Israel*, cantata for Soprano or Tenor, Chorus, and Orch. (1961); *5 Israeli Songs* for Tenor, Oboe, Piano, and Cello (1962); choruses; other songs.

BIBL.: W. Elias, *O. P.* (Tel Aviv, 1978).

Partridge, Ian (Harold), English tenor; b. Wimbledon, June 12, 1938. He was a chorister at New College, Oxford, and a music scholar at Clifton College before pursuing his training in London at the Royal College of Music and the Guildhall School of Music. He commenced his career as a piano accompanist while singing in the Westminster Cathedral Choir (1958–62). In 1958 he made his formal debut as a singer in Bexhill, and from 1962 he pursued a solo career. In 1969 he made his debut at London's Covent Garden as Iopas in *Les Troyens*. He appeared as a soloist with many major orchs. in England and abroad, gave many recitals, and sang on radio and television. In 1989 he made his debut at the Salzburg Festival in Bach's *St. John Passion*. In 1991 he was made a Commander of the Order of the British Empire. His sister, Jennifer Partridge (b. New Malden, June 17, 1942), is a pianist who has often served as his accompanist.

Pasatieri, Thomas, talented American opera composer; b. N.Y., Oct. 20, 1945. He began to play the piano by spontaneous generation, and picked up elements of composition, particularly vocal, by a similar subliminal process; between the ages of 14 and 18 he wrote some 400 songs. He persuaded Boulanger to take him as a student by correspondence between Paris and N.Y. when he was 15; at 16, he entered the Juilliard School of Music in N.Y., where he became a student of Giannini and Persichetti; he also took a course with Milhaud in Aspen, Colo., where his first opera, *The Women*, to his own libretto, was performed when he was only 19. It became clear to him that opera was his natural medium, and that the way to achieve the best results was by following the evolutionary line of Italian operatic productions characterized by the felicity of *bel canto*, facility of harmonic writing, and euphonious fidelity to the lyric and dramatic content of the subject. In striving to attain these objectives, Pasatieri ran the tide of mandatory inharmoniousness; while his productions were applauded by hoi polloi, they shocked music critics and other composers; one of them described Pasatieri's music as "a stream of perfumed urine." This attitude is akin to that taken by some toward Giannini and Menotti (interestingly, all 3 are of Italian genetic stock). From 1967 to 1969 Pasatieri taught at the Juilliard School; then was engaged at the Manhattan School of Music (1969–71); from 1980 to 1983 he was Distinguished Visiting Prof. at the Univ. of Cincinnati (Ohio) College-Cons. of Music.

WORKS: OPERAS: *The Women* (Aspen, Aug. 20, 1965); *La Divina* (N.Y., March 16, 1966); *Padrevia* (N.Y., Nov. 18, 1967); *Calvary* (Seattle, April 7, 1971); *The Trial of Mary Lincoln*, television opera (Boston, Feb. 14, 1972); *Black Widow* (Seattle, March 2, 1972); *The Seagull*, after Chekhov (Houston, March 5, 1974); *Signor Deluso*, after Molière's *Sganarelle* (Vienna, Va., July 27, 1974); *The Penitentes* (Aspen, Aug. 3, 1974); *Inez de Castro* (Baltimore, April 1, 1976); *Washington Square*, after Henry James (Detroit, Oct. 1, 1976); *Three Sisters*, after Chekov (1979; Columbus, Ohio, March 13, 1986); *Before Breakfast* (N.Y., Oct. 9, 1980); *The Goose Girl*, children's opera (Fort Worth, Texas, Feb. 15, 1981); *Maria Elena* (Tucson, April 8, 1983). **PIANO:** 2 sonatas (1976); other works. **VOCAL:** *Heloise and Abelard* for Soprano, Baritone, and Piano (1971); *Rites de passage* for Voice and Chamber Orch. or String Quartet (1974); *3 Poems of James Agee* for Voice and Piano (1974); *Far from Love* for Soprano, Clarinet, and Piano (1976); *Permit Me Voyage*, cantata for Soprano, Chorus, and Orch. (1976); *Mass* for 4 Solo Voices, Chorus, and Orch. (1983).

Pasero, Tancredi, noted Italian bass; b. Turin, Jan. 11, 1893; d. Milan, Feb. 17, 1983. He studied in Turin. He made his operatic debut in 1917 as Rodolfo in *La Sonnambula* in Vicenza; from 1924 to 1930 he sang at the Teatro Colón in Buenos Aires; in 1926 he joined La Scala in Milan, remaining on its roster until 1952. He made his Metropolitan Opera debut in N.Y. on Nov. 1, 1929, as Alvise in *La Gioconda*; continued on its roster until 1933. He also had guest engagements at London's Covent Garden (1931) and the Paris Opéra (1935). His repertoire was extensive and included Italian, German, French, and Russian operas; he excelled in Verdi's operas, and made a distinctive appearance as Mussorgsky's Boris Godunov.

BIBL.: C. Clerico, *T. P.: Voce verdiana* (Scomegna, 1985).

Pashchenko, Andrei (Filippovich), prolific Russian composer; b. Rostov, Aug. 15, 1883; d. Moscow, Nov. 16, 1972. He studied with Wihtol and Steinberg at the St. Petersburg Cons., graduating in 1917. He occupied various clerical positions; was librarian of the St. Petersburg Court Orch. (from 1911), remaining with it when it became the State Orch. (1917) and the Leningrad Phil. (1924); left his post in 1931; in 1961 he went to live in Moscow. An exceptionally fertile composer, he wrote some 14 operas and 15 syms.; the style of his music is a natural continuation of the traditions of the Russian national school; in his later works he allowed a certain influx of impressionistic harmonies and unresolved dissonant combinations.

WORKS: OPERAS: *Eagles in Revolt* (Leningrad, Nov. 7, 1925); *King Maximilian* (1927); *The Black Cliff* (Leningrad, June 12, 1931); *The Pompadours* (1939); *Jester Balakirev* (1949); *The Capricious Bride* (1956); *Radda and Loyko* (1957); *Nila Snishko* (1961); *The Great Seducer* (1966); *Woman, This Is the Devil* (1966); *African Love* (1966); *The Horse in the Senate* (1967); *Portrait* (1968); *Master and Margarita* (1971). **ORCH.:** 15 syms. (1915, 1929, 1933, 1938, 1952, 1954, 1956, 1957, 1958, 1963, 1964, 1966, 1969, 1969, 1970); 4 sinfoniettas (1943, 1945, 1953, 1964); *Volga Fantasy* (1961); *Ukrainiada*, symphonic poem (1963); *Icarus*, symphonic poem (1964); *Dance Triptych* (1965); *The Voice of Peace*, symphonic poem (1971); *Poem of Stars*, symphonic poem (1971); Cello Concerto (1964). **CHAMBER:** 9 string quartets. **VOCAL:** Numerous works for chorus.

BIBL.: Y. Meylikh, *A.F. P.* (Leningrad, 1960).

Pasini, Laura, Italian soprano; b. Gallarate, Jan. 28, 1894; d. Rome, Sept. 30, 1942. She studied piano with Appiano at the Milan Cons., and made her debut as a pianist in Rome in 1912. After vocal training from Pietro at the Accademia di Santa Cecilia in Rome, she made her operatic debut as Zerlina in Auber's *Fra Diavolo* at Milan's Teatro Eden in 1921. She sang in Rome (1922–23), at Milan's La Scala (1923–26; 1930–31) and Buenos Aires's Teatro Colón (1925), and in Turin (1925–27), Salzburg (1931), and Florence (1933) before settling in Cagliari as a voice teacher.

Pasini (-Vitale), Lina, Italian soprano; b. Rome, Nov. 8, 1872; d. there, Nov. 23, 1959. She studied in Rome. She made her operatic debut in 1893 as Cecilia in Cilea's *Tilda* at the Teatro dal Verme in Milan; then sang at La Scala in Milan, Turin, the Teatro Colón in Buenos Aires, Rome, and Naples; retired from the stage in 1928. She married the conductor Edoardo Vitale in 1897. At the height of her career, she was widely regarded as one of the finest Wagnerian sopranos on the Italian stage. Her sister, Camilla Pasini (b. Rome, Nov. 6, 1875; d. there, Oct. 29, 1935), was also a soprano; she studied in Rome; created the role of Musetta in *La Bohème* (Turin, Feb. 1, 1896); retired from the stage in 1905.

Paskalis, Kostas, Greek baritone; b. Levadia, Sept. 1, 1929. He received training in voice in Athens, where he concurrently took courses in piano and composition at the Cons. In 1951 he made his operatic debut as Rigoletto at the National Opera in Athens, where he sang until 1958. In 1958 he made his debut at the Vienna State Opera as Renato, and continued to appear there regularly until 1979. He made his British debut as Macbeth at the Glyndebourne Festival in 1964. On Feb. 17, 1965, he made his Metropolitan Opera debut in N.Y. as Carlo in *La forza del destino*. He made occasional appearances there until 1975. In 1965–66 he sang in Rome. In 1966 he appeared as Pentheus in the premiere of Henze's *The Bassarids* at the Salzburg Festival. In 1967 he made his first appearance at Milan's La Scala as Valentin. He first sang at London's Covent Garden in 1969 as Macbeth, returning there in 1971–72. From 1988 he was director of the National Opera in Athens. Among his other roles were Don Giovanni, Donizetti's Alfonso, Posa, Nabucco, Iago, and Escamillo.

Pasquotti, Corrado, Italian composer; b. Vittorio Veneto, March 11, 1954. He studied in Padua, Venice, and Milan. In 1977 he received the diploma of merit of the Teatro Angelicum in Milan. He subsequently taught at the Rossini Cons. of Pesaro. In his works, he strives to achieve intimate synergy of visual images and auditory projections; his written scores literally follow the parameters of a given painting, with notes corresponding to the lines of the design and rests occupying the spaces of the object; depending on a chart for such correspondences, different musical versions are achieved in actual performances. A typical product of this method is *Forma Magistra Ludi* for Chamber Orch., to images by Yasmin Brandolini d'Adda (1980). He also composed a string quartet, *Quartet "i reflessi"* (1983).

Pásztory, Ditta, Hungarian pianist; b. Rimaszombat, Oct. 31, 1903; d. Budapest, Nov. 21, 1982. She studied piano with Bartók at the Budapest Academy of Music (1922–23); on Aug. 28, 1923, she became his second wife. Although she subsequently abandoned her solo career, she was encouraged by her husband to appear with him in duo performances. She joined him in the premiere of his Sonata for 2 Pianos and Percussion in Basel on Jan. 16, 1938, after which they made tours of Europe and the U.S.; they settled in the U.S. in 1940. After her husband's death in 1945, Pásztory returned to Hungary (1946), where she championed a number of her husband's piano works on recordings. Her will provided for the establishment of the Bartók-Pásztory Award, the most important annual Hugarian prize for composers and performers.

Patachich, Iván, Hungarian composer; b. Budapest, June 3, 1922. He studied with Albert Siklós, János Viski, and Ferenc Szabó at the Budapest Academy of Music. After working as a theater conductor, he became music director of the Budapest Film Studio in 1952; established the electronic music studio EXASTUD (Experimentum Auditorii Studii) in Budapest in 1971.

WORKS: DRAMATIC: OPERAS: *Theomachia* (1962); *Fuente ovajuna* (1969); *Brave New World* (1988–89). **BALLETS:** *Feketefehér* (Black and White; 1958); *Bakaruhában* (Sunday Romance; 1963); *Mngongo and Mlaba* (1965); *Studio sintetico* (1973). **PANTOMIME:** *Möbius tér* (Mobius Space; 1980). **ORCH.:** 2 harp concertos (1956, 1968); *Poema sinfonico* (1958); Flute Concerto (1958); Viola Concerto (1959); Oboe Concerto (1959); *Serenata* for Strings (1960); Guitar Concerto (1961); *Concerto breve* for Cello and Orch. (1962); 2 divertimentos (1962, 1969); 2 piano concertos (1963, 1968); *Sinfonietta Savariensis* (1964); Violin Concerto (1964); 2 syms. (1965, 1966); *Quadri di Picasso* (1965); Bassoon Concerto (1965); Concerto for 3 Percussionists and Orch. (1966); Concerto for Violin, Piano, and Strings (1969); Organ Concerto (1972); *Presentazioni*, concertino for Cimbalom or Marimba, and Orch. (1975); *Coordinate* (1979); Trumpet Concerto (1985); *Naconxypan szigetén* (On the Island of Naconxypan), 5 symphonic poems (1986); *DX7 Reports No. 2* for Synthesizer and Orch. (1987); Trombone Concerto (1988). **CHAMBER:** 2 violin sonatas (1948, 1964); Sextet for Harp and Winds (1957); Quintet for Harp, Flute, and Strings (1958); Trio for Violin, Viola, and Harp (1958); Wind Quintet (1960); Quartet for 2 Harps, Viola, and Double Bass (1962); 2 piano trios (1962, 1967); Viola Sonata (1962); Cello Sonata (1963); Sonata for Harp and Horn (1964); Wind Trio (1965); String Trio (1965); *Elementi* for Percussion (1966); *Quattro studii* for 6 Percussionists (1968); *Costruzioni* for 4 Percussionists (1969); Sonata for Oboe and Harp (1971); *Bagatelli* for Organ, Flute, and Horn (1971); *Proporzioni* for 4 Percussionists (1972); *Ja amidohele*, quintet for 5 Cellos (1976); *Quintetto* for Trombone and Tuba (1981); Trio for Bassoons (1982); *Terzettino* for Saxophones (1987); *Quartettino* for Trombones (1988); *Anpro-Sifi* for Percussion Quartet (1988); *Play 88* for Saxophone Quartet (1988); also piano pieces, including a Sonata (1965) and Sonatina (1966). **VOCAL: CANTATAS:** *Szirtország* (Country of Cliffs) for Chorus and Orch. (1953); *Music of the Bible* for Tenor, Chorus, and Orch. (1968); *Cantus Profani Silvae* for Chorus and Tape (1978); *Canti stravaganti* for Chorus and Tape (1981); *Az éjszaka csodái* (Miracles of the Night) for Chorus, Orch., and Tape (1985); *Cantus discipulus* for Chorus and Tape (1986); *Miracle of the Hermit Thrush* for Chorus, Orch., and Tape (1987). **OTHER VOCAL:** *Missa simplex* for Chorus and Organ (1949); *Messe di Santa Marguerita* for Chorus and Orch. (1967); *Canticum Canticorum* for Chorus and Instruments (1985). **OTHER:** Live electronic scores; tape pieces.

Pataky, Kálmán, Hungarian tenor; b. Alsolenda, Nov. 14, 1896; d. Los Angeles, March 3, 1964. He studied in Budapest. In 1922 he made his operatic debut as the Duke of Mantua at the Budapest Opera, where he subsequently appeared regularly. From 1926 he also sang at the Vienna State Opera. He made guest appearances at the Paris Opéra (1928), the Glyndebourne Festival (1936), the Salzburg Festival (1936), and at Milan's La Scala. He also appeared frequently at the Teatro Colón in Buenos Aires. After the Anschluss in Austria in 1938, he sang mainly in Hungary. After World War II, he settled in the U.S. Pataky was admired for his Mozart roles, particularly his Belmonte, Ottavio, and Tamino. He was a fine concert artist. Strauss dedicated several of his lieder to him.

BIBL.: V. Somogyi and I Molnár, *P. K.* (Budapest, 1968).

Patanè, Giuseppe, Italian conductor; b. Naples, Jan. 1, 1932; d. (fatally stricken while conducting *Il Barbiere di Siviglia* at the Bavarian State Opera) Munich, May 30, 1989. He was a son of Franco Patane (1908–68), a conductor. He studied at the Cons. S. Pietro a Majella in Naples and made his debut as a conductor at the age of 19, when he led a performance of *La Traviata* at the Teatro Mercadante in Naples. He was subsequently 2nd conductor at the Teatro San Carlo in Naples (1951–56); became principal conductor of the Linz Landestheater in 1961, and in 1962 to 1968 was a conductor of the Deutsche Oper in Berlin; he further filled engagements at La Scala in Milan, at the Vienna State Opera, and in Copenhagen. On Oct. 18, 1975, he made his Metropolitan Opera debut in N.Y. conducting *La Gioconda*. In 1982 he was appointed co-principal conductor of the American Sym. Orch. in N.Y., remaining at this post until 1984; then was chief conductor of the Mannheim National Theater (from 1987) and of the Munich Radio Orch. (from 1988).

Patorzhinsky, Ivan (Sergeievich), noted Ukrainian bass; b. Petrovo-Svistunovo, March 3, 1896; d. Kiev, Feb. 22, 1960. He studied at the Ekaterinoslav Cons., graduating in 1922. From 1925 to 1935 he was a member of the Kharkov Opera, and from 1935 to 1960 of the Kiev Opera. He also pursued a concert career. From 1946 he taught at the Kiev Cons. In 1944 he was made a People's Artist of the U.S.S.R. Patorzhinsky was the leading Ukrainian bass of his day, excelling particularly in roles in Ukrainian operas. He also was a fine Don Basilio, Boris Godunov, and Méphistophélès.

BIBL.: M. Stefanovich, *I.S. P.* (Moscow, 1960).

Patterson, Annie Wilson, Irish organist, folk song collector, writer on music, and composer; b. Lurgan, Oct. 27, 1868; d. Cork, Jan. 16, 1934. She studied organ with Robert Stewart at the Royal Irish Academy of Music; also studied at the Royal Univ. of Ireland (Mus.B., B.A., 1887; Mus.D., 1889). She held several posts as an organist before being made organist at Cork's Shandon Church (1904); was named to the chair of Irish music at the Univ. College, Cork (1924). She organized the Feis Ceoil (Irish Music Festival), held annually from 1897. Among her compositions were 2 operas, *The High-King's Daughter* and

Oisin, as well as symphonic poems; cantatas; choruses; songs; and arrangements of Irish airs.

WRITINGS (all publ. in London): *The Story of Oratorio* (1902); *Schumann* (1903; 2nd ed., rev., 1934); *The Profession of Music* (1926); *Great Minds in Music* (1926); *The Music of Ireland* (1926).

Patterson, Paul (Leslie), English composer and teacher; b. Chesterfield, June 15, 1947. He studied with Richard Stoker at the Royal Academy of Music in London (1964–68), and also received instruction from Elizabeth Lutyens, Hans Keller, and Harrison Birtwistle. He pursued private training with Richard Rodney Bennett (1968–70). In 1971 he became the Manson Fellow at the Royal Academy of Music, where he served as head of composition and 20th-century music from 1985. From 1974 to 1980 he also was director of contemporary music at the Univ. of Warwick. In 1989 he became composer-in-residence of the Southwark Festival. In 1990–91 he was composer-in-residence of the Exeter Festival, and in 1991 its artistic director. Patterson has developed a compositional style which combines such contemporary usages as aleatory and electronics with more accessible means of expression.

WORKS: DRAMATIC: Film scores; television music. **ORCH.:** Trumpet Concerto (1968; Bristol, Nov. 19, 1969); *Symphonic Study II* (1968); Chamber Concerto (1969); *Partita* for Chamber Orch. (Nottingham, March 5, 1970); *Piccola sinfonia* for Strings (1970; Oakham, March 11, 1971); Concerto for Horn and Strings (Nottingham, July 21, 1971); *Fiesta sinfonica* (1971; Nottingham, July 22, 1972); *Sonors* (1972; Southend, Jan. 10, 1973); *Fusions* for Orch. and Tape (Croydon, March 9, 1974); *Chromascope* for Brass Band (Harrogate, Aug. 9, 1974); *Count Down* for Brass Band (1974; London, Oct. 11, 1975); *Strange Meeting* for Orch. and Tape (Croydon, May 5, 1975); *Cataclysm* for Brass Band (Hull, Aug. 9, 1975); *The Circular Ruins* (Exeter, Dec. 10, 1975); *Wildfire* for Orch. and Tape (London, March 27, 1976); Concerto for Clarinet and Strings (London, May 19, 1976); *Concerto for Orchestra* (Birmingham, Nov. 13, 1981); *Sinfonia* for Strings (1982; Warsaw, Sept. 22, 1983); *Europhony* for Chamber Orch. (Cardiff, June 11, 1985); *Upside-Down-Under-Variations* (London, March 3, 1985); *Propositions* for Harmonica and Strings (London, April 25, 1987); *White Shadows on the Dark Horizon* (1988); *Fanfare for the Future* for Brass and Percussion (London, Oct. 29, 1989); Sym. (1989–90); *Little Red Riding Hood* for Narrators and Orch. (1992); Concerto for Violin and Strings (1992); *Festivo* (1993). **CHAMBER:** Wind Quintet (San Remo, Aug. 4, 1967); Wind Trio (London, Oct. 16, 1968); *Monologue* for Oboe (1969; London, May 5, 1970); *Fanfares for Great Occasions* for 3 Trumpets, 2 Trombones, Bass Trombone, and Tuba (1969–75; 1, *Chichester Fanfare*, Chichester, June 6, 1975; 2, *Warwick Fanfare*, Warwick, Sept. 11, 1974); 3, *St. Bartholomew's Fanfare*, London, June 21, 1973; 4, *Exeter Fanfare*, Exeter, July 19, 1969); *Comedy* for 5 Winds (Mayfield, May 15, 1972); *Intersections* for Chamber Ensemble (N.Y., July 8, 1973); *Conversations* for Clarinet and Piano (London, Nov. 18, 1974); *Floating Music* for Flute, Clarinet, Violin, Cello, Piano or Celesta, and Percussion (London, Oct. 21, 1974); *Shadows* for Clarinet and Tape (Cincinnati, April 6, 1975); *Diversions* for Saxophone Quartet (1975); *Cracowian Counterpoint* for Chamber Ensemble (London, June 3, 1977); *At the Still Point of the Turning World* for 8 Instruments (1979; Stockholm, Jan. 5, 1980); *Deception Pass* for Brass Ensemble (Cheltenham, July 5, 1980); *Spiders* for Harp (St. Asaph, Wales, Sept. 27, 1983); *Duologue* for Oboe and Piano (Christchurch, July 20, 1984); *Luslawice Variations* for Violin (Luslawice, Sept. 10, 1984); *Mean Time* for Brass Quintet (London, June 16, 1985); String Quartet (Chester, July 24, 1986); *Memories of Quiberville* for Trombone Quartet (1986; Manchester, Feb. 7, 1987); Suite for Cello (Bristol, Nov. 19, 1987); *Tides of Mananan* for Viola (1987). **KEYBOARD: PIANO:** *Country Search* (1974); *3 Portraits* (1984); *A Tunnel of Time* (1988). **ORGAN:** *Jubilate* (1969); *Intrada* (1969); *Visions* (1972); *Interludium* (1972); *Fluorescence* (1973); *Games* (1977). **VOCAL:** *Rebecca* for Speaker and Chamber Ensemble (1965; Dartington, Aug. 21, 1966); *Kyrie* for Chorus and Piano, 4-hands (1971; N.Y., March 21, 1972); *Time Piece* for Men's Voices (1972; London, March 10, 1973); *Gloria* for Chorus and Piano, 4-hands (1972); *The Abode of the Dead/You'll Never be Alone* for Voices and Chamber Orch. (BBC, Oct. 10, 1973); *Requiem* for Chorus, Boy's Chorus, and Orch. (1974; Coventry, June 21, 1975); *Spare Parts* for Chorus (1976; London, Jan. 18, 1978); *Brain Storm* for Soprano, Alto, Tenor, Bass, and Live Electronics (London, Feb. 9, 1978); *Voices of Sleep* for Soprano, Chorus, and Orch. (Washington, D.C., April 19, 1979); *The Canterbury Psalms* for Chorus and Orch. or Organ (Canterbury, April 15, 1981); *Vampireen* for 6 Men's Voices (St. Albans, June 5, 1983); *Mass of the Sea* for Soprano, Bass, Chorus, and Orch. (Gloucester, Aug. 22, 1983); *Christ is the King* for Chorus (Chichester, July 19, 1984); *Missa brevis* for Chorus (1985); *Stabat mater* for Mezzo-soprano, Chorus, and Orch. (1985–86; Huddersfield, March 27, 1986); *Magnificat and Nunc Dimittis* for Chorus and Organ (Norwich, July 4, 1986); *Te Deum* for Soprano, Chorus, Boy's Chorus, and Orch. (Hereford, Aug. 25, 1988); *The End* for Chorus (1989); *O be Joyful* for Chorus and Organ (1991); *Revolting Rhymes* for Narrator and Ensemble (1992).

Pattiera, Tino, Croatian tenor; b. Čavtat, near Ragusa, June 27, 1890; d. there, April 24, 1966. He studied at the Vienna Academy of Music with Ranieri. In 1915 he joined the Dresden Court (later State) Opera, where he was a principal member of the company until 1941; also sang with the Berlin State Opera (1924–29); was a guest artist in Chicago, Vienna, Budapest, Paris, Prague, and other music centers. He gave his farewell concert in Dresden in 1948; from 1950 he taught voice at the Vienna Academy of Music. He was most renowned for the lyric roles in Verdi's operas.

Pattison, Lee, American pianist, teacher, and composer; b. Centralia, Wis., July 22, 1890; d. Claremont, Calif., Dec. 22, 1966. He first studied at the New England Cons. of Music in Boston; later in Berlin with Schnabel. In 1916 he formed a duo-piano team with Guy Maier; they gave a number of successful concerts until 1931, when the partnership was dissolved. From 1932 to 1937 he was head of the piano dept. at Sarah Lawrence College; also taught at the Juilliard Summer School; lived mostly in N.Y. His compositions include *Florentine Sketches* for Piano and a piano suite of 7 pieces, *Told in the Hills.*

Patzak, Julius, distinguished Austrian tenor; b. Vienna, April 9, 1898; d. Rottach-Egern, Bavaria, Jan. 26, 1974. He studied musicology and conducting with Adler, Schmidt, and Mandyczewski at the Univ. of Vienna; was autodidact as a singer. He made his operatic debut as Radames in Reichenberg (1923). After singing in Brno (1927–28), he was a principal member of the Bavarian State Opera in Munich (1928–45) and the Vienna State Opera (1945–59); first appeared at London's Covent Garden as Tamino (1938), returning there with the visiting Vienna State Opera (1947), and then singing there regularly (1951–54). He was a teacher at the Vienna Academy of Music and the Salzburg Mozarteum; retired from the stage in 1966. Patzak was noted for his roles in Mozart's operas, but he became best known for his compelling portrayals of Beethoven's Florestan and Pfitzner's Palestrina.

Pauer, Jiří, Czech composer and arts administrator; b. Libušín, near Kladno, Feb. 22, 1919. He studied composition with Otakar Šin; then with Alois Hába at the Prague Cons. (1943–46) and with Bořkovec at the Prague Academy of Musical Arts (1946–50). He occupied various administrative posts with the Ministry of Education and Culture and with the Czech Radio; was artistic director of the Opera of the National Theater in Prague (1953–55; 1965–67; 1979–89); also taught at the Prague Academy. He was director of the Czech Phil. from 1958 to 1980. His music followed the pragmatic precepts of socialist realism in its modern application, broadly lyrical and tensely dramatic by turns.

WORKS: DRAMATIC: OPERAS: *Žvanivý Slimejš* (Prattling Snail; 1949–50; Prague, April 5, 1958); *Zuzana Vojířová*

(1954–57; Prague, May 11, 1958); *Červená Karkulka* (Little Red Riding Hood; 1959; Olomouc, 1960); *Manželské kontrapunkty* (Marital Counterpoints; 1961; 3 operatic satirical sketches, Ostrava, 1962; 2nd version as 5 satires, Liberec, 1967); *Zdravý nemocný* (The Imaginary Invalid), after Molière (1966–69; Prague, May 22, 1970). **MONODRAMA:** *Labutí píseň* (The Swan Song; 1973). **BALLET:** *Ferda Mravenec* (Ferdy the Ant; 1975). **ORCH.:** *Comedy Suite* (1949); Bassoon Concerto (1949); *Youth Suite* (1951); *Scherzo* (1951); *Children's Suite* for Chamber Orch. (1953); *Rhapsody* (1953); Oboe Concerto (1954); Horn Concerto (1958); Sym. (1963); *Commemoration*, symphonic picture (1969); *Canto festivo* (1970–71); Trumpet Concerto (1972); *Initials* (1974); *Aurora*, overture for Large Wind Orch. (1976; also for Orch., 1978); Sym. for Strings (1978); Concerto for Marimba and Strings (1984); Suite (1987). **CHAMBER:** *Partita* for Harp (1947); *Divertimento* for 3 Clarinets (1949); *Capriccio* for Flute or Oboe or Clarinet or Bassoon and Piano (1952); Violin Sonatina (1953); Cello Sonata (1954); 4 string quartets (1960, 1969, 1970, 1976); *Divertimento* for Nonet (1961); Wind Quintet (1961); Piano Trio (1963); *Concertant Music* for 13 Winds (1971); *Intrada* for 3 Pianos, 3 Trumpets, and 3 Trombones (1975); *Characters* for Brass Quintet (1977–78); Episodes for String Quartet (1980); Trio for 3 Horns (1986); Violin Sonata (1987); Nonet No. 2 (1988–89); piano pieces. **VOCAL:** Cantatas; choruses; songs.

Pauer, Max von, eminent Austrian pianist and teacher; b. London, Oct. 31, 1866; d. Jugenheim, May 12, 1945. He studied with his father, the Austrian pianist, teacher, editor, and composer Ernst Pauer (b. Vienna, Dec. 21, 1826; d. Jugenheim, near Darmstadt, May 9, 1905), and with V. Lachner. He embarked on several successful concert tours in Germany; in 1887, was appointed prof. of piano at the Cologne Cons.; in 1897, became a prof. at the Stuttgart Cons.; was its director from 1908 to 1920; in 1920 it became the Hochschule für Musik, which he directed until 1924; then he was director of the Leipzig Cons. (1924–32) and of the Mannheim Hochschule für Musik (1933–34). He made an American tour in 1913–14. Following his father's excellent example in arranging Classical syms. for piano, he made transcriptions of syms. by Mozart and Haydn for piano solo and piano, 4-hands. He publ. an ironic autobiography, *Unser seltsames Ich: Lebensschau eines Künstlers* (Stuttgart, 1942).

Pauk, György, Hungarian-born English violinist and teacher; b. Budapest, Oct. 26, 1936. He commenced violin lessons when he was only 5, and later pursued his musical training at the Franz Liszt Academy of Music in Budapest with Zathureczky, Weiner, and Kodály. At 14, he made his debut as a soloist with orch. and then toured Eastern Europe. Following the unsuccessful Hungarian revolution in 1956, he left his homeland and won the Paganini (Genoa, 1956), Munich (1957), and Long-Thibaud (Paris, 1959) competitions. In 1961 he settled in England and in 1967 became a naturalized British subject. He made his British debut as a soloist with orch. and as a recitalist in London in 1961, and thereafter he toured internationally. He also played in a trio with the pianist Peter Frankl and the cellist Ralph Kirshbaum from 1972. In 1964 he became a prof. of violin at the Royal Manchester College of Music, and then at the Royal Academy of Music in London in 1987. He also gave master classes in violin interpretation.

Paul, Les (real name, **Lester Polfus**), American guitarist and inventor; b. Waukesha, Wis., June 9, 1915. He was mainly autodidact as a guitarist; after performing as a country music artist, he formed his own jazz group, the Les Paul Trio, which appeared with Fred Waring, Bing Crosby, and the Andrews Sisters. His interest in guitar amplification led to his development of the solid-body electric guitar (1941); later he experimented with recording techniques, being the initiator of so-called "sound-on-sound" or overdubbing technique. He made a number of recordings with his wife, the singer Mary Ford (nee Colleen Summers; b. Pasadena, Calif., July 7, 1924; d. Los Angeles, Sept. 30, 1977).

BIBL.: M. Shaughnessy, *L. P.: An American Original* (N.Y., 1993).

Paul, Thomas (Warburton), distinguished American bass; b. Chicago, Feb. 22, 1934. He studied with Howard Swan and Robert Gross at Occidental College in Los Angeles (B.A., 1956); then took courses in conducting with Jean Morel and Frederic Waldman at the Juilliard School of Music in N.Y.; also studied voice privately in N.Y. He made his vocal debut in Handel's *Belshazzar* at Carnegie Hall in N.Y. on April 10, 1961. He sang with the N.Y. City Opera (1962–71; debut Oct. 4, 1962), and with other U.S. opera companies. He made his European debut in Zürich on April 3, 1976, in a performance of Bach's *St. Matthew Passion*. In 1980 he made his recital debut in N.Y. He made many appearances as a soloist with the major North American orchs. He was a visiting prof. (1971–74) and prof. (from 1974) at the Eastman School of Music in Rochester, N.Y., and also taught at the Aspen (Colo.) Music School. His finest roles include Boris Godunov, Figaro, and Méphistophélès.

Paull, Barberi, avant-garde American composer; b. N.Y., July 25, 1946. She began to play piano as an infra-adolescent, in private and in public; with the awakening of consciousness, she opted for jazz and multimedia forms of self-expression, but went through the motions of academic training at the Juilliard School of Music in N.Y., where she studied composition with Overton and Druckman (1970–71); later she took courses with Wuorinen at the Manhattan School of Music (1972) and attended the Musical Theatre Workshop conducted by Lehman Engel (1973). She founded the Barberi Paull Musical Theatre, Inc., with which she presented a series of mixed-media events. In her compositions, she elevates eclecticism to an article of democratic faith, embracing jazz, pop tunes, and electronic sound in a context of ostentatious and unapologetic cosmic sentimentality.

WORKS: *Time*, electronic ballet (1971); *Earth Pulse*, choreographic cantata, making use of musique concrète (1971); *The Mass* for Tape, Percussion, and Visual Projections (1974); *A Land Called The Infinity of Love* for Multimedia (1975); *Sheer Silver Sheen Flower Sky* for Chorus (1971–74); *O Wind* for Mezzo-soprano and String Quartet (1975); *Song for Orchestra* (1977); *A Christmas Carol* for Chorus and Instrumental Trio, after Dickens (1977; also in a jazz version); many unabashed pop tunes.

Paulson, Gustaf, Swedish composer and organist; b. Hälsingborg, Jan. 22, 1898; d. there, Dec. 17, 1966. He studied composition in Copenhagen with Peder Gram. From 1929 until his death, served as church organist in Hälsingborg. He was an extraordinarily prolific composer. His music reflected the type of Scandinavian Romanticism associated with Sibelius and Nielsen, pervaded by streaks of coherent polyphony.

WORKS: ORCH.: 13 syms.: No. 1 (1928), No. 2 (1933), No. 3, *Sinfonia da chiesa* (1945), No. 4, *Uppstandelse* (The Resurrection; 1947), No. 5, *Aron Bergenson in memoriam* (1948), No. 6 (1952), No. 7 (1953), No. 8 (1954), No. 9 (1956), No. 10 (1957), No. 11, *Stabat Mater* (1959; Hälsingborg, March 26, 1961), No. 12 (1963; Hälsingborg, Nov. 28, 1963), and No. 13 (1966); 2 sinfonias for Strings (1953, 1954); 19 concertos: 2 for Piano (1940, 1961), 2 for Cello (1944, 1957), 2 for Oboe (1950, 1957), 2 for English Horn and Strings (1958, 1959), 2 for Clarinet (1958, 1959), and one each for Bassoon (1959), Saxophone (1959), Violin (1960), Flute and Women's Chorus, *Arets tider* (1962), Horn (1964), Trombone (1965), Trumpet (1965), Viola (1965), and Double Bass (1965–66); *Symphonic Variations* (1934); *Metamorphoses on a Theme by Clementi* (1951); *Passion* for Cello and Orch. (1961). **CHAMBER:** 5 string quartets; Violin Sonata (1958); Cello Sonata (1960); piano pieces; organ pieces. **VOCAL:** *Stabat Mater* for Soli, Women's Chorus, Strings, and Percussion (1956; Hälsingborg, March 17, 1957); *Vid korset*, oratorio (1957); songs.

Paulus, Stephen (Harrison), American composer; b. Summit, N.J., Aug. 24, 1949. He studied with Paul Fetler and Dominick Argento at the Univ. of Minnesota (B.M., 1971; M.M., 1974;

Ph.D., 1978). In 1973 he founded the Minnesota Composers Forum in Minneapolis with Libby Larsen, and was managing composer until 1984. He served as composer-in-residence of the Minnesota Orch. (1983–87), the Santa Fe Chamber Music Festival (1986), the Atlanta Sym. Orch. (1988–92), the Dale Warland Singers (1991–92), and the Aspen (Colo.) Music Festival (1992). In 1987 his Violin Concerto No. 1 won the Kennedy Center Friedheim 3rd Prize. In 1983 he held a Guggenheim fellowship. Paulus has demonstrated fine craftsmanship in both vocal and instrumental writing.

WORKS: OPERAS: *The Village Singer* (1977; St. Louis, June 9, 1979); *The Postman Always Rings Twice* (1981; St. Louis, June 19, 1982; also an orch. suite, Minneapolis, July 26, 1986); *The Woodlanders* (1984; St. Louis, June 13, 1985); *Harmoonia*, children's opera (1991). **ORCH.:** *Spectra* for Small Orch. (Houston, April 12, 1980); *Translucent Landscapes* (Peninsula Music Festival, Aug. 6, 1982); *7 Short Pieces* (1983; Minneapolis, Feb. 9, 1984); *Divertimento* for Harp and Chamber Orch. (1983); *Concerto for Orchestra* (Minneapolis, April 6, 1983); *Ordway* Overture (1984); *Reflections: 4 Movements on a Theme of Wallace Stevens* (1984; St. Paul, Minn., March 22, 1985); *Symphony in 3 Movements (Soliloquy)* (1985; Minneapolis, Jan. 15, 1986); *Ground Breaker*, overture (Minneapolis, Oct. 7, 1987); 2 violin concertos: No.1 (Atlanta, Nov. 5, 1987) and No. 2 (1992); *Night Speech* (Spokane, Wash., April 21, 1989); *Concertante* (Atlanta, April 27, 1989); *Symphony for Strings* (Oregon Bach Festival, July 5, 1989); *Street Music* (1990); *Ice Fields* for Guitar and Orch. (1990; in collaboration with L. Kottke); Sinfonietta (1991); Trumpet Concerto (1991); Organ Concerto (1992); *The Veil of Illusion*, concerto for Violin, Cello, and Orch. (1994); *3 Places of Enlightenment*, concerto for String Quartet and Orch. (1995); *Manhattan Sinfonietta* (1995). **CHAMBER ENSEMBLE:** *Exploration* (1974); *Village Tales: A Tree of Life* (1975); *Graphics* (1977); *Lunar Maria* (1977). **OTHER CHAMBER:** *Colors* for Brass Quintet (1974); *Wind Suite* for Woodwind Quartet (1975); 2 string quartets: No. 1, *Music for Contrasts* (1980) and No. 2 (1987); *Courtship Songs for a Summer's Eve* for Flute, Oboe, Cello, and Piano (1981); *Partita* for Violin and Piano (1986); *American Vignettes* for Cello and Piano (1988); *Fantasy in 3 Parts* for Flute and Guitar (1989); *Bagatelles* for Violin and Piano (1990); *Quartessence* for String Quartet (1990); Concerto for Brass Quintet (1991); *Air on Seurat: The Grand Canal* for Cello and Piano (1992); *Music of the Night* for Violin, Cello, and Piano (1992). **KEYBOARD: PIANO:** *Translucent Landscapes* (1979); *Dance* (1986); *Preludes* (1992). **ORGAN:** *The Triumph of the Saint* for Organ Duet (1994); *Meditations of the Spirit* (1995). **VOCAL:** *Personals* for Chorus, Flute, and Percussion (1975); *Canticles: Songs and Rituals for Easter and the May* for Soloists, Chorus, and Orch. (1977); *North Shore* for Soloists, Chorus, and Orch. (1977); *Letters for the Times* for Chorus and Chamber Ensemble (1980); *Echoes between the Silent Peaks* for Chorus and Chamber Ensemble (1984); *Letters from Colette* for Soprano and Chamber Ensemble (1986); *Madrigali di Michelangelo* for Chorus (1987); *Voices* for Chorus and Orch. (1988); *Canticum Novum* for Chorus, Flute, Oboe, Percussion, and Harp (1990); *Sacred Songs* for Chorus, Flute, Oboe, Percussion, and Organ (1990); *Visions of Hildegard* for Chorus and Instruments (1992–95); *Whitman's Dream* for Double Chorus and Instruments (1994); *The Earth Sings* for Women's Voices, Percussion, and Piano (1995).

Pauly, Rosa (actually, **Rose** née **Pollak**), noted Hungarian soprano; b. Eperjes, March 15, 1894; d. Kfar Shmaryahn, near Tel Aviv, Dec. 14, 1975. She studied voice with Rosa Papier in Vienna, and made her operatic debut at the Vienna State Opera as Desdemona in Verdi's *Otello* in 1918. She subsequently sang in Hamburg, Cologne, and Mannheim. From 1927 to 1931 she was a member of the Kroll Opera in Berlin; also of the Vienna State Opera (1929–35); in 1934 she sang the challenging role of Elektra in Strauss's opera in Salzburg, gathering encomiums; in 1935 she appeared at La Scala in Milan. She made her American debut as Elektra in a concert performance with the N.Y. Phil. on March 21, 1937; sang it again at her first appearance with the Metropolitan Opera in N.Y. on Jan. 7, 1938; appeared there until 1940; also sang at the Teatro Colón in Buenos Aires in 1939. In 1946 she went to Palestine, and devoted herself to teaching in Tel Aviv. She was esteemed for her roles in the operas of Mozart, Verdi, and Wagner, but most particularly for her compelling portrayals of such Strauss roles as Elektra, the Dyer's Wife, and Helena.

Paumgartner, Bernhard, eminent Austrian musicologist and conductor; b. Vienna, Nov. 14, 1887; d. Salzburg, July 27, 1971. He was a son of the pianist Hans Paumgartner (1843–96) and the mezzo-soprano Rosa Papier. He learned to play the horn, violin, and piano in his youth; began to conduct while still in school. After receiving a doctorate in law from the Univ. of Vienna (1911), he studied musicology privately with Adler. He was répétiteur at the Vienna Court Opera (1911–12); then was director of the Salzburg Mozarteum (from 1917), which he headed until 1938, and again from 1945 to 1959; was also closely associated with the Salzburg Festival from its founding (1920), serving as its president (1960–71). He also composed; wrote the operas *Die Hohle von Salamanca* (Dresden, 1923) and *Rossini in Neapel* (Zürich, March 27, 1936), various other stage pieces, including several ballets, orch. music, and songs.

WRITINGS: *Mozart* (Berlin, 1927; 6th ed., aug., 1967); *Franz Schubert: Eine Biographie* (Zürich, 1943; 3rd ed., 1960); *Johann Sebastian Bach: Leben und Werk, I: Bis zur Berufung nach Leipzig* (Zürich, 1950); *Erinnerungen* (Salzburg, 1969); G. Croll, ed., *Bernhard Paumgartner: Vorträge und Essays* (Salzburg, 1972).

BIBL.: E. Preussner, ed., *Wissenschaft und Praxis: Eine Festschrift zum 70. Geburtstag von B. P.* (Zürich, 1957); G. Croll, ed., *B. P.* (Salzburg and Munich, 1971).

Paunović, Milenko, Serbian composer; b. Šajkaš, Nov. 28, 1889; d. Belgrade, Oct. 1, 1924. He studied in Leipzig with Reger and Riemann; became a choral conductor in Novi Sad. In his music he followed Wagnerian concepts, and wrote several music dramas to his own texts; also a *Yugoslav Symphony* (Ljubljana, March 17, 1924).

Pavarotti, Luciano, greatly renowned Italian tenor; b. Modena, Oct. 12, 1935. His father, a baker by trade, sang in the local church choir; Luciano learned to read music and began singing with the boy altos; later joined his father in the choir, and also sang in the chorus of the local Teatro Comunale and the amateur Chorale Gioacchino Rossini. To prepare himself for a career as a schoolteacher, he attended the local Scuola Magistrale; then taught in an elementary school, augmenting his income by selling insurance. In the meantime, he began vocal studies with Arrigo Polo in Modena (1955), then went to Mantua, where he continued his training with Ettore Campogalliani (1960). He made his operatic debut as Rodolfo in *La Bohème* at the Teatro Municipale in Reggio Emilia on April 29, 1961. He obtained his first major engagement when he appeared as the Duke of Mantua at the Teatro Massimo in Palermo (March 15, 1962). His first important appearance outside his homeland was as Edgardo with the Netherlands Opera in Amsterdam (Jan. 18, 1963). On Feb. 24, 1963, he made his Vienna State Opera debut as Rodolfo, a role he also sang for his first appearance at London's Covent Garden (Sept. 21, 1963). On Feb. 15, 1965, he made his U.S. debut as Edgardo opposite Joan Sutherland's Lucia with the Greater Miami Opera. After his first appearance at Milan's La Scala as Alfredo (April 28, 1965), he made a summer tour of Australia with the Sutherland Williamson International Grand Opera Co., a venture featuring the celebrated diva. He subsequently scored his first triumph on the operatic stage when he essayed the role of Tonio in *La Fille du regiment* at Covent Garden (June 1, 1966); with insouciant aplomb, he tossed off the aria *Pour mon âme*, replete with 9 successive high C's, winning an ovation. He was dubbed the "King of the High C's," and a brilliant international career beckoned. He made his debut at the San Francisco Opera as Rodolfo (Nov.

11, 1967), a role he chose for his first appearance at the Metropolitan Opera in N.Y. (Nov. 23, 1968). In subsequent seasons, he became a mainstay at both houses, and also appeared regularly with other opera houses on both sides of the Atlantic. He also made frequent appearances in solo recitals and concerts with orchs. In 1977 he starred as Rodolfo in the first "Live from the Met" telecast by PBS. In 1978 he made an acclaimed solo recital debut at the Metropolitan Opera, which was also telecast by PBS. In 1980 he founded the Opera Co. of Philadelphia/Luciano Pavarotti International Voice Competition. On Oct. 22, 1983, he was one of the featured artists at the Metropolitan Opera Centennial Gala. In 1984 he gave a concert before 20,000 admirers at N.Y.'s Madison Square Garden, which was also seen by millions on PBS. He celebrated the 25th anniversary of his operatic debut by singing his beloved Rodolfo at the Teatro Comunale in Modena on April 29, 1986. In 1988 he sang Nemorino at the Berlin Deutsche Oper, eliciting thunderous applause and no less than 15 curtain calls. On Jan. 9, 1989, he appeared in concert with the N.Y. City Opera orch. in a special program at Avery Fischer Hall at N.Y.'s Lincoln Center for the Performing Arts, which was televised live by PBS. In 1990 he appeared at the Bolshoi Theater in Moscow. On July 7, 1990, he made an unprecedented concert appearance with fellow tenors José Carreras and Plácido Domingo in Rome in an extravaganza telecast to the world. Pavarotti celebrated the 30th anniversary of his career with a special concert at London's Hyde Park on July 30, 1991, which event was telecast throughout Europe and overseas. On July 26, 1993, he gave a concert before some 500,000 people in N.Y.'s Central Park, which was seen by countless others via a live telecast by PBS. He celebrated the 25th anniversary of his debut at the Metropolitan Opera on Sept. 27, 1993, singing Otello in the first act of Verdi's opera in a live radio broadcast heard around the world. On July 6, 1994, he again appeared with Carreras and Domingo in concert in Los Angeles, an event telecast live around the globe.

The most idolized tenor since Caruso, Pavarotti made such roles as Nemorino in *L'elisir d'amore*, Riccardo in *Un ballo in maschera*, Fernando in *La Favorite*, Manrico in *Il Trovatore*, Cavaradossi in *Tosca*, and Radames in *Aida*, as well as the ubiquitous Rodolfo, virtually his own. Indeed, through recordings and television appearances, he won an adoring global following. Always of a jocular rotundity, he announced in 1988 that he had succeeded in dropping 85 pounds from his original body weight. His autobiography was publ. as *Pavarotti: My Own Story* (with W. Wright; Garden City, N.Y., 1981).

BIBL.: M. Mayer, *Grandissimo P.* (Garden City, N.Y., 1986; with career chronology and discography by G. Fitzgerald); A. Pavarotti and W. Dallas, *P.: Vivere con L.* (Trento, 1992; Eng. tr., 1992, as *P.: Life with L.*); C. Bonvicini, *The Tenor's Son: My Days with P.* (N.Y., 1993); L. Magiera, *P.: Mythos, Methode und Magie* (Zürich, 1993); E. Ruggieri, *P.* (Paris, 1993).

Payne, Anthony (Edward), English composer and music critic; b. London, Aug. 2, 1936. He studied at Dulwich College and the Univ. of Durham (1958–61). He was a music critic for the London *Daily Telegraph* (1965–87) and the *Independent* (from 1987). In 1966 he married **Jane Manning**. His style of composition is structurally disciplined, but inwardly Romantic and inspired by northern moods and modes.

WORKS: ORCH.: *Suite from a Forgotten Ballet* (1955; rev. 1986); *Contrapuncti* for String Quartet and String Orch. (1958; rev. 1979); *Concerto for Orchestra* (1974; London, Jan. 8, 1975); *Songs of the Clouds* (1979–80; Cheltenham, June 29, 1980); *Spring's Shining Wake* (1980–81; BBC, Dec. 21, 1983); *Songs and Seascapes* for Strings (London, June 6, 1984); *The Spirit's Harvest* (London, July 31, 1985); *Half-heard in the Stillness* (Derby, Sept. 17, 1987); *Time's Arrow* (1990). **CHAMBER:** *Sonatas and Ricercars* for Flute, Oboe, Clarinet, Bassoon, and Horn (1970; BBC, May 28, 1974); String Quartet (London, Dec. 4, 1978); *The Stones and Lonely Places Sing* for Flute, Clarinet, Horn, and Piano (London, Sept. 2, 1979); *A Day in the Life of a Mayfly* for Flute, Clarinet, Percussion, Piano, Violin, and Cello (London, Sept. 25, 1981); *The Song Streams in the Firmament* for Clarinet, String Quartet, and Double Bass (N.Y., April 19, 1986); *Fanfares and Processional* for Horn, 4 Trumpets, 4 Trombones, and Tuba (London, Sept. 19, 1986); *Echoes of Courtly Love* for Horn, Trumpet, Flugelhorn, Trombone, and Tuba (1987; London, May 13, 1988); *Consort Music* for 2 Violins, 2 Violas, and Cello (Cambridge, July 27, 1987); *Sea Change* for Flute, Clarinet, Harp, and String Quartet (London, June 12, 1988); *The Enchantress Plays* for Bassoon and Piano (1990); *Symphonies of Wind and Rain* for Chamber Ensemble (1993). **VOCAL:** *Phoenix Mass* for Chorus, 3 Trumpets, and 3 Trombones (1965–72; BBC, Oct. 2, 1973); *2 Songs without Words* for Men's Vocal Quintet (1970; London, Feb. 4, 1971); *First Sight of Her and After* for 16 Solo Voices (London, Dec. 11, 1975); *The World's Winter* for Soprano, Flute, Oboe, Clarinet, Horn, Harp, and String Trio (Cheltenham, July 4, 1976); *A Little Whitsuntide Cantata* (1977; rev. 1984); *Alleluias and Hockets* for Chorus and 10 Instruments (1987); choruses; songs.

WRITINGS (all publ. in London): *Schoenberg* (1968); with L. Foreman, *Frank Bridge* (1976); *Frank Bridge: Radical and Conservative* (1984).

Paz, Juan Carlos, significant Argentine composer; b. Buenos Aires, Aug. 5, 1901; d. there, Aug. 25, 1972. He studied composition with Constantino Gaito in Argentina and later with d'Indy in Paris. In 1929, with several young composers of radical tendencies, he organized in Buenos Aires the "Grupo Renovación," and in 1937 inaugurated a series of concerts of new music. He became a music critic and author of several books. His early works, after 1921, are marked by strong polyphony, in a neo-Classical style; about 1927 he adopted atonal and polytonal procedures; in 1934 he began to compose almost exclusively in the 12-tone idiom; after 1950 he modified his musical language, adopting a less rigid and more personal style of composition.

WORKS: ORCH.: *Canto de Navidad* (1927; orchestrated 1930); *Movimiento sinfonico* (1930); Suite for Ibsen's *Juliano Emperador* (1931); *3 Pieces* (1931); *Passacaglia* (1936; Paris, June 25, 1937; rev. 1952–53); *Música (Preludio y fuga)* (1940); *Passacaglia* for Strings (1944; rev. 1949); *Ritmica constante* (1952); *6 superposiciones* (1954); *Transformaciones canónicas* (1955–56); *Música* for Bassoon, Strings, and Percussion (1955–56); *Continuidad 1960* (1960–61; Caracas, May 11, 1966); *Estructuras 1962* for Chamber Orch. (1962); *Música* for Piano and Orch. (1964; Washington, D.C., May 12, 1965). **CHAMBER:** *Tema y transformaciones* for 11 Winds (1929); Wind Octet (1930); 3 sonatinas: No. 1 for Clarinet and Piano (1930), No. 2 for Flute and Clarinet (1932), and No. 3 for Oboe and Bassoon (1933; later transcribed for Piano); *Concierto No. 1* for Flute, Oboe, Clarinet, Bassoon, Trumpet, and Piano (1932) and *No. 2* for Oboe, Trumpet, 2 Trombones, Bassoon, and Piano (1935); *4 Composiciónes dodecafónica*: No. 1 for Flute, English Horn, and Cello (1934; lost), No. 2 for Flute and Piano (1935), No. 3 for Clarinet and Piano (1937), and No. 4 for Violin (1938); Overture for 12 Instruments (1936); 4 pieces for Clarinet (1936); *3 Composiciónes en trio*: No. 1 for Flute, Clarinet, and Bassoon (1937), No. 2 for Clarinet, Trumpet, and Alto Saxophone (1938), and No. 3 for Flute, Oboe, and Bass Clarinet or Bassoon (1940; rev. 1945); 2 string quartets (1938, 1940–43); *Música* for Flute, Saxophone, and Piano (1943); *Dedalus 1950* for Flute, Clarinet, Violin, Cello, and Piano (1950–51); *Continuidad 1953* for Piano and Percussion (1953–54); *3 contrapuntos* for Clarinet, Electric Guitar, Celesta, Trumpet, Trombone, and Cello (1955); *Invención* for String Quartet (1961); *Concreción* for Flute, Clarinet, Bassoon, Horn, Trumpet, Trombone, and Tuba (1964). **KEYBOARD: PIANO:** 3 sonatas (1923, 1925, 1935); *Tema con transformaciones* (1928); *3 movimientos de jazz* (1932); Sonatina No. 3 (1933; originally for Oboe and Bassoon); *10 piezas sobre una serie dodecafónica* (1936); *Música 1946; Núcleos*, 1st series (1962–64). **ORGAN:** *Galaxia 64* (1964).

BIBL.: J. Beschinsky, *J.C. P.* (Buenos Aires, 1964); J. Romano, "J.C. P.," *Boletín Latino-Americano de Música*, no. 54 (1966); idem, *J.C. P.: Tribulaciones de un músico* (Buenos Aires, 1970).

Pazovsky, Ariy (Moiseievich), Russian conductor; b. Perm, Feb. 2, 1887; d. Moscow, Jan. 6, 1953. He received violin training as a child, and then was a student of Krasnokutsky and Auer at the St. Petersburg Cons. (1897–1904). After conducting provincial opera companies (1905–08), he was conductor of Zimin's opera company in Moscow (1908–10), and then conducted in Kharkov, Odessa, and Kiev. He was music director of the Petrograd People's Opera (1916–18). After conducting at Moscow's Bolshoi Theater (1923–24; 1925–28), he conducted in Baku, Sverdlovsk, Kharkov, and Kiev (1926–36). He was artistic director of Leningrad's Kirov Theater (1936–43), and then of the Bolshoi Theater (1943–48). In 1940 he was made a People's Artist of the U.S.S.R. He publ. *Zapiski dirizhora* (The Writings of a Conductor; Moscow, 1966).

Pearlman, Martin, American conductor, harpsichordist, and composer; b. Chicago, May 21, 1945. He received training in composition, violin, piano, and theory in his youth. Following studies in composition with Husa at Cornell Univ. (B.A., 1967), he pursued training in harpsichord with Leonhardt on a Fulbright scholarship in the Netherlands (1967–68). He subsequently took his M.M. in composition under Wyner at Yale Univ. (1971), and also studied with Ralph Kirkpatrick (harpsichord) and Arel (electronic music). In 1972 he won the Erwin Bodky Award and in 1974 he was a prize winner in the Bruges Competition. In 1973 he founded and became music director of Banchetto Musicale, the first permanent Baroque orch. established in North America. In 1992 he was renamed Boston Baroque. From 1976 to 1981 he taught at the Univ. of Mass. in Boston, and also at Brandeis Univ. in 1980–81. As a harpsichordist, Pearlman has become well known for his performances of the Couperin family and of D. Scarlatti. As a conductor, he has led numerous period instrument performances and has given the American premieres of many Baroque and Classical scores, including those of Bach, Handel, Rameau, Mozart, and Beethoven. He has also appeared as a guest conductor of modern instrument groups and sym. orchs., as well as of Baroque ensembles. In 1995 he made his Kennedy Center debut in Washington, D.C., conducting Handel's *Semele*. Pearlman has prepared performing eds. of Monteverdi's *L'Incoronazione di Poppea*, Purcell's *Comical History of Don Quixote*, and Mozart's *Lo sposo deluso*. He has also prepared a complete ed. of the keyboard music of Armand-Louis Couperin. Among his own compositions are pieces for horn, violin, and piano and for solo horn.

Pears, Sir Peter (Neville Luard), renowned English tenor; b. Farnham, June 22, 1910; d. Aldeburgh, April 3, 1986. He began his career as temporary organist at Hertford College, Oxford (1928–29), then was director of music at the Grange School, Crowborough (1930–34). He was a scholarship student at the Royal College of Music in London (1933–34); concurrently sang in the BBC Chorus, and then was a member of the BBC Singers (1934–38) and the New English Singers (1936–38). During this period, he received vocal instruction from Elena Gerhardt and Dawson Freer. In 1936 he also met Benjamin Britten; they gave their first joint recital in 1937, and thereafter remained lifelong personal and professional companions. After singing in the Glyndebourne Chorus (1938), he accompanied Britten to the U.S. (1939); continued his vocal training with Thérèse Behr and Clytie Hine-Mundy. In 1942 he returned to England with Britten, making his stage debut that same year in the title role of *Les Contes d'Hoffmann* at London's Strand Theatre. In 1943 he joined the Sadler's Wells Opera Co., gaining fame when he created the title role in Britten's *Peter Grimes* (June 7, 1945). In 1946 he became a member of the English Opera Group, and thereafter greatly distinguished himself in operas by Britten; among the roles he created were Albert Herring, the Male Chorus in *The Rape of Lucretia*, Captain Vere in *Billy Budd*, Essex in *Gloriana*, Quint in *The Turn of the Screw*, Flute in *A Midsummer Night's Dream* (was co-librettist with the composer), the Madwoman in *Curlew River*, Sir Philip Wingrave in *Owen Wingrave*, and Aschenbach in *Death in Venice*. It was in the latter role that he made his Metropolitan Opera debut in N.Y. on Oct. 18, 1974. He was one of the founders of the Aldeburgh Festival (1948), serving as a director and as a teacher of master classes until his death. Pears also sang in several first performances of Britten's non-operatic works, including the *Serenade* for Tenor, Horn, and Strings, the *Michelangelo Sonnets*, and the *War Requiem*. He also excelled in the works of other English composers, among them Elgar, Holst, Vaughan Williams, and Walton, as well as those by Schütz, Bach, Mozart, Schubert, and Schumann. He was made a Commander of the Order of the British Empire in 1957, and was knighted in 1978. P. Reed ed. and annotated the *Diaries of Peter Pears, 1939–1979* (Rochester, 1994).

BIBL.: M. Thorpe, ed., *P. P.: A Tribute on His 75th Birthday* (London, 1985); C. Headington, *P. P.: A Biography* (London and Boston, 1993).

Pease, James, American bass-baritone; b. Indianapolis, Jan. 9, 1916; d. N.Y., April 26, 1967. He studied at the Curtis Inst. of Music in Philadelphia. In 1941 he made his operatic debut as Gounod's Méphistophélès at the Philadelphia Opera. On May 9, 1946, he made his first appearance at the N.Y. City Opera as Sparafucile, where he sang until 1953 and again in 1959–60 and 1967. From 1952 to 1959 he also was a member of the Hamburg State Opera. As a guest artist, Pease appeared at London's Covent Garden, the Zürich Opera, the San Francisco Opera, the Chicago Lyric Opera, and other opera centers. Among his best roles were Don Giovanni, Figaro, King Marke, Hans Sachs, and Baron Ochs.

Pechner, Gerhard, German-American baritone; b. Berlin, April 15, 1903; d. N.Y., Oct. 21, 1969. He studied in Berlin, making his debut there in 1927. After singing at the German Theater in Prague (1933–39), he emigrated to the U.S. In 1940 he made his U.S. debut as Mozart's Bartolo at the San Francisco Opera. On Nov. 27, 1941, he made his Metropolitan Opera debut in N.Y. as the Notary in *Der Rosenkavalier*, and remained on its roster until 1965. In 1966–67 he was again on its roster. Pechner was especially admired for such roles as Alberich, Beckmesser, Melitone in *La Forza del destino*, and the Sacristan in *Tosca*.

Pederzini, Gianna, noted Italian mezzo-soprano; b. Vo di Avio, Feb. 10, 1903; d. Rome, March 12, 1988. She studied with De Lucia in Naples. She made her operatic debut as Preziosilla in 1923 in Messina; in 1930 she joined La Scala in Milan, where she sang until 1943; also appeared in Rome (1939–52), at Covent Garden, London (1931), and at the Teatro Colón in Buenos Aires (1937–39; 1946–47). She returned to La Scala in 1956–57, creating the role of the Prioress in Poulenc's *Dialogues des Carmelites*. She was an outstanding interpreter of roles in Rossini's operas; was also greatly admired for her interpretation of Carmen.

Pedrell, Carlos, Uruguayan composer, nephew of **Felipe Pedrell**; b. Minas, Oct. 16, 1878; d. Montrouge, near Paris, March 3, 1941. He studied in Madrid with his uncle; later went to Paris, where he took lessons with d'Indy and Breville at the Schola Cantorum. Returning to South America, he was inspector of music in the Buenos Aires schools; lectured at the Univ. of Tucumán; in 1921 he went to Paris, where he remained for the rest of his life. His works are cast in the French style, but the rhythmic elements are related to Spanish and South American sources; his songs, with richly developed accompaniments, are the best among his works.

WORKS: DRAMATIC: OPERAS: *Ardid de Amor* (Buenos Aires, June 7, 1917); *Cuento de Abril*; *La Guitare* (Madrid, 1924). **BALLETS:** *La Rose et le gitan* (Antwerp, 1930); *Alleluia* (Buenos Aires, 1936). **ORCH.:** *Une Nuit de Schéhérazade*

(1908); *Danza y canción de Aixa* (1910); *En el estrado de Beatriz* (1910); *Fantasia Argentina* (1910); *Ouverture catalane* (1912); *Pastorales* for Voice and Orch. (Paris, 1928); choruses; songs.

BIBL.: A. Suarès, "C. P.," *Revue Musicale* (June 1931).

Pedrell, Felipe, eminent Spanish musicologist and composer, uncle of **Carlos Pedrell**; b. Tortosa, Feb. 19, 1841; d. Barcelona, Aug. 19, 1922. He became a chorister at Tortosa Cathedral when he was about 7, receiving instruction from Juan Antonio Nin y Serra. In 1873 he went to Barcelona as deputy director of the Light Opera Co., where he produced his first opera, *L'ultimo Abenzeraggio* (April 14, 1874). After a visit to Italy (1876–77) and a sojourn in Paris, he settled in Barcelona (1881), where he devoted himself mainly to musicological pursuits. In 1882 he founded the journals *Salterio Sacro-Hispano* and *Notas Musicales y Literarias*, both of which ceased publication in 1883. He then was founder-ed. of the important journal *La Illustración Musical Hispano-Americana* (1888–96). During this period, he worked on his operatic masterpiece, the trilogy *Los Pirieneos/Els Pirineus* (1890–91), and also publ. the book *Por nuestra música* (1891), which served as its introduction and as a plea for the creation of a national lyric drama based on Spanish folk song. In 1894 he went to Madrid, where he was named prof. of choral singing at the Cons. and prof. of advanced studies at the Ateneo; was also elected a member of the Royal Academy of Fine Arts. Upon his return to Barcelona (1904), he devoted himself to writing, teaching, and composing. Among his outstanding pupils were Albéniz, Falla, Granados, and Gerhard. Although Pedrell was admired as a composer by his contemporaries, his music has not obtained recognition outside his homeland. His lasting achievement rests upon his distinguished as a musicologist, in which he did much to restore interest in both historical and contemporary Spanish sacred music.

WRITINGS: *Gramática musical or manual expositivo de la teoria del solfeo, en forma de diálogo* (Barcelona, 1872; 3rd ed., 1883); *Las sonatas de Beethoven* (Barcelona, 1873); *Los músicos españoles en sus libros* (Barcelona, 1888); *Por nuestra música* (Barcelona, 1891); *Diccionario técnico de la música bibliográfico de músicos y escritores de música españoles, portugueses y hispano-amerianos antiguos y modernos* (Barcelona, 1895–97); *Emporio cientifico e histórico de organografia musical española antigua* (Barcelona, 1901); *Prácticas preparatorias de instrumentación* (Barcelona, 1902); *La cançó popular catalana* (Barcelona, 1906); *Documents pour servir à l'histoire de théâtre musical: La Festa d'Elche ou le drame lyrique liturgique espagnol* (Paris, 1906); *Musicalerias* (Valencia, 1906); *Catàlech de la Biblioteca musical de la Diputació de Barcelona* (Barcelona, 1909); *Músicos contemporáneos y de otros tiempos* (Paris, 1910); *Jornadas de arte* (Paris, 1911; memoirs and articles, 1841–1902); *La lirica nacionalizada* (Paris, 1913); *Tomás Luis de Victoria Abulense* (Valencia, 1918); *P. Antonio Eximeno* (Madrid, 1920); *Jornados postreras* (Valls, 1922; autobiography); *Musiquerias* (Paris, n.d.; autobiography).

EDITIONS: *Hispaniae schola musical sacra* (Barcelona, 1894–98); *Teatro lirico español anterior al siglo XIX* (La Coruña, 1897–98); *T.L. de Victoria: Opera omnia* (Leipzig, 1902–13); *El organista litúrgico español* (Barcelona, 1905); *Antologia de organistas clásicos españoles* (Madrid, 1908); *Cancionero musical popular español* (Valls, 1918–22; 2nd ed., 1936); with H. Anglès, *Els madrigals i la missa de difunts d'en Brudieu* (Barcelona, 1921).

BIBL.: G. Tebaldini, *F. P. ed il dramma lirico spagnuolo* (Turin, 1897); R. Mitjana, *La música contemporanea en España y F. P.* (Málaga, 1901); H. de Curzon, *F. P. et "Les Pyrénées"* (Paris, 1902); "F. P.," *La Nouvelle Revue* (Jan. 1912); A. Reiff, "F. P.," *Zeitschrift für Musikwissenschaft* (Feb. 1912); L. Vilalba Muñoz, *F. P.: Semblanza y biografia* (Madrid, 1922); M. Falla, "F. P.," *Revue Musicale* (Feb. 1923); E. Istel, "F. P.," *Musical Quarterly* (April 1925); F. Bonastre, *F. P.: Acotaciones a una idea* (Tarragona, 1977).

Pedrollo, Arrigo, Italian composer and pedagogue; b. Montebello Vicentino, Dec. 5, 1878; d. Vicenza, Dec. 23, 1964. He studied at the Milan Cons. (1891–1900); at his graduation, he wrote a Sym., which was performed by Toscanini. He was the director of the Istituto Musicale in Vicenza (1920–30); then a prof. of composition at the Milan Cons. (1930–41); from 1942 to 1959 he was director of the Vicenza Cons. In 1914 he won the Sonzogno competition with his opera *Juana*. His other operas include *Terra promessa* (Cremona, 1908); *La Veglia* (Milan, Jan. 2, 1920); *L'Uomo che ride* (Rome, March 6, 1920); *Maria di Magdala* (Milan, 1924); *Delitto e castigo*, after Dostoyevsky (Milan, Nov. 16, 1926); *L'Amante in trappola* (Verona, Sept. 22, 1936); and *Il Giglio di Ali* (1948). He also wrote orch. pieces, chamber music, choral works, and songs.

Peerce, Jan (real name, **Jacob Pincus Perelmuth**), noted American tenor; b. N.Y., June 3, 1904; d. there, Dec. 15, 1984. He played the violin in dance bands, and sang at various entertainment places in N.Y. In 1932 he was engaged as a singer at Radio City Music Hall in N.Y. He made his operatic debut in Philadelphia as the Duke of Mantua in *Rigoletto* (May 14, 1938), and gave his first solo recital in N.Y. on Nov. 7, 1939. His lyrical voice attracted attention, and he was engaged by the Metropolitan Opera in N.Y.; made his debut there as Alfredo in *La Traviata* on Nov. 29, 1941; sang also the parts of Cavaradossi in *Tosca*, Rodolfo in *La Bohème*, and Gounod's Faust; remained on the staff of the Metropolitan until 1966, appearing again in 1967–68. He continued to make occasional appearances until his retirement in 1982. He was the brother-in-law of **Richard Tucker**.

BIBL.: A. Levy, *The Bluebird of Happiness: The Memoirs of J. P.* (N.Y., 1976).

Peeters, Flor, outstanding Belgian organist, pedagogue, and composer; b. Tielen, July 4, 1903; d. Antwerp, July 4, 1986. He studied organ with Depuydt and Gregorian chant with van Nuffel at the Lemmens Inst. in Mechelen; he succeeded Depuydt as prof. of organ there in 1925, holding this position until 1952. From 1931 to 1938 he was a prof. at the Ghent Cons., and then at the Tilbourg Cons. from 1935 to 1948. He became a prof. of organ at the Antwerp Cons. in 1948, and was its director from 1952 to 1968. He was elevated to the peerage as Baron Peeters by King Baudoin in 1971. He composed nearly 500 works for organ alone, and also wrote much sacred choral music. His works for organ include *Passacaglia and Fugue* (1938); *Sinfonia* (1940); Organ Concerto (1944); *Lied Symphony* (1948); *30 Short Chorale Preludes* (1959); *213 Hymn Preludes for the Liturgical Year* (24 installments, 1959–67); and *6 Lyrical Pieces* (1966). He also publ. several vols., including *Anthologia pro organo* (4 vols., Brussels, 1949–59), *Ars organi* (3 vols., Brussels, 1952–54), and *Little Organ Book* (Boston, 1957).

BIBL.: P. Visser, *F. P., Organist* (Turnhout, 1950); J. Hofmann, *F. P.: His Life and His Organ Works* (Fredonia, 1978).

Peiko, Nikolai, Russian composer; b. Moscow, March 25, 1916. He studied with Litinsky, Rakov, and Miaskovsky at the Moscow Cons. (1933–40). After graduation, he was commissioned to collect folk-song materials in the remote Yakutsk district of Siberia, and produced *Suite on a Yakutsk Theme* for Orch. (1941); then investigated Bashkir folk music and composed a Bashkir opera, *Aikhylu* (1943). Returning to Moscow, he taught at the Cons. (1942–59); also taught at the Gnessin Musical Inst. His music faithfully follows the precepts of socialist realism, national in thematic derivation and realistic in social content. His 1st and 5th syms. are inspired by the heroism and suffering of the war of 1941–45; his 4th Sym. depicts the glory of the 1917 Soviet Revolution.

WORKS: DRAMATIC: OPERA: *Aikhylu*, on a Bashkir subject (1943; rev. 1953). **BALLETS:** *Spring Winds*, on a Tatar subject (1950); *Jeanne d'Arc* (1957). **ORCH.:** *Suite on Yakutsk Themes* (1941); Piano Concerto (1943; rev. 1954); 7 syms.: No. 1 (1945), No. 2 (1946), No. 3 (1957), No. 4 (1965), No. 5 (1968), No. 6 (1972), and No. 7, for Russian Folk Instruments (1977);

From Russia's Remote Past, suite (1949); *Moldavian Suite* (Moscow, Dec. 14, 1950); *Festive Overture* on Kabardin themes (1951); *2 Concert Fantasies* for Violin and Orch., on Finnish themes (1953, 1965); *Symphonic Ballad* (1959); *Concerto-Symphony* (1974); *In the Throes of War,* 5 symphonic tableaux (1975); *Concerto-Poem* for Clarinet, Balalaika, and Orch. (1979). **CHAMBER:** Piano Quintet (1961); 3 string quartets (1964, 1965, 1966); *Decimet* for 10 Instruments (1971); Violin Sonata (1976). **PIANO:** 2 sonatinas (1942, 1957); *Sonatina Fairy Tale* (1943); 2 sonatas (1951, 1975).

BIBL.: G. Grigorieva, *N. P.* (Moscow, 1965).

Peinemann, Edith, German violinist and teacher; b. Mainz, March 3, 1937. She learned the rudiments of music from her father, concertmaster of the Mainz orch.; continued her studies with Heinz Stanske in Heidelberg (1951–53) and Max Rostal in London (1953–56), where she also took courses at the Guildhall School of Music. At the age of 19, she won the Munich International Competition, and then played with many major German orchs.; also gave duo recitals with the Austrian pianist Jorg Demus. In 1962 she made her first tour of America. She was a prof. at the Frankfurt am Main Hochschule für Musik (from 1976).

Peixinho, Jorge (Manuel Rosada Marques), Portuguese composer and teacher; b. Montijo, Jan. 20, 1940; d. Lisbon, June 30, 1995. He received training in piano and composition (with Santos and Vasconcelos) at the Lisbon Cons. (1951–58). After attending the Univ. of Lisbon (1959), he studied composition with Nono in Venice (1960) and Petrassi and Porena at the Accademia di Santa Cecilia in Rome (1960–61). Between 1960 and 1970, he attended the summer courses in new music in Darmstadt, and in 1962–63 he studied at the Basel Academy of Music. In 1965–66 he taught at the Oporto Cons. In 1970 he became director of the Grupo de Música Contemporanea in Lisbon. He was prof. of composition at the National Cons. in Lisbon from 1985. In 1974 he received the Gulbenkian Prize. In 1988 he was awarded Portugal's Medal of Cultural Merit. Peixinho is one of the leading avant-garde composers of Portugal. In developing his own advanced compositional course, he experimented with almost every resource available to the contemporary composer.

WORKS: DRAMATIC: *O gebo a sombra,* theater music (1966); *Recitativo II,* music theater (1966–70); *As quatro estações,* theater music (1968); *Shakespeare's Sonnets,* ballet (1970); *Mariana Pineda,* theater music (1975); film music. **ORCH.:** *Políptico* for Chamber Orch. (1960); *Sobreposições* (1960); Saxophone Concerto (1961); *Diafonia* for Harp, Harpsichord, Piano, Celesta, Percussion, and Strings (1962–65); *Kinetofonias* for 25 Strings and 3 Tapes (1965–69); *Nomos* (1967); *Sucessões simétricas II* (1971) and *III* for Chamber Orch. (1974); *Voix-en-jeux* (1972–76); *Retrato de Helena* (1982); *Concerto de outono* for Oboe and Orch. (1983); *Viagem da natural invenção* (1991). **CHAMBER:** *Do espressioni* for Trumpet and Harpsichord (1959); *Evocação* for Flute, Oboe, Clarinet, Harp, Vibraphone, and Xylophone (1960); *Episodios* for String Quartet (1960); *Imagens sonoras* for 2 Harps (1962); *Domino* for Flute and Percussion (1963–64); *Sequência* for Flute, Celesta, and Percussion (1963–64); *Morfocromia* for 12 Instruments (1963–68); *Situações 66* for Flute, Clarinet, Trumpet, Harp, and Viola (1966); *Recitativo III* for Flute, Harp, and Percussion (1966–69), *V* for Octet (1966–74), *I* for Harp (1971), and *IV* for 8 Instruments (1974); *As quatro estações* for Trumpet, Harp, Piano, and Cello (1968–72); *C D E* for Clarinet, Violin, Cello, and Piano (1970); *A idade do ouro* for 2 Clarinets, 2 Violins, Organ, Piano, Harp, and Harpsichord (1970–73); *Quatro pecas para setembro vermelho* for Chamber Ensemble (1972); *Ma Fin est mon commencement: Homage to Machaut* for Trombone, Viol, Viola, Harp, Recorders, Piano, and Celesta (1972); *Welkom* for Violin and Viola (1972); *Morrer em Santiago* for 6 Percussion (1973); *. . . e isto é só o início, hein?* for Chamber Ensemble (1975); *A aurora do socialismo: Madrigale capriccioso* for Flute, Horn, Violin, Piano, Percussion, and Short Wave Receiver (1975); *Canto da sibila* for Clarinet, Piano, Percussion, Lights, and Smells (1976); *Solo* for Double Bass (1976); *Elegia* for Trombone, Viola, Piano, and Percussion (1976); *Madrigal II* for Clarinet Quintet (1977); *Música en água e mármore* for 7 Instruments (1977); *Lov II* for Cello, Flute, Piano, and Percussion (1978); *Faites vox jeux* for Flute, Cello, Harp, and Piano (1979–81); *Mémoires . . . miroirs . . .* for Amplified Clavichord and 12 Strings (1980); *Warsaw Workshop Waltz* for Clarinet, Trombone, Cello, and Piano (1980); *Ciclo-Valsa* for Variable Instrumental Ensemble, Percussion, Velophonem, Music Boxes, and Voices ad libitum (1980–85); *Novo canto da sibila* for Clarinet, Piano, and Percussion (1981); *Sax-Blue* for Alto Saxophone or Sopranino Saxophone and Electro-acoustics (1982–85); *Serenata per A* for Flutes, Guitar, Piano, and Percussion (1983); *O jardim de Belisa* for 7 Instruments (1984); *Metaformoses* for Bass Clarinet and 7 Instruments (1984); *Remake* for Flute, Cello, Harp, and Piano (1985); *Ougam a soma dos sons que soam* for 9 Instruments (1986); *O quadrado azul* for Oboe, Viola, Double Bass, and Piano (1987); *Passage intérieur* for Saxophone and Electric Instruments (1989); *Alis* for 15 Instruments (1990); *Glosa I* for Piano, *II* for Flute, *III* for Violin, and *IV* for Cello (all 1990); *Fantasia-impromptu* for Alto Saxophone and Piano (1990); *Mediterrânea* for 7 or 8 Instruments (1991). **VOCAL:** *Fascinação* for Soprano, Flute, and Clarinet (1959); *Alba* for Soprano, Mezzo-soprano, Women's Chorus, and 11 Instruments (1959); *Triptico* for Solo Voices and Instrumental Ensemble (1959–60); *A cabeça do grifo* for Soprano, Mandolin, and Piano (1960; also for Soprano, Viola, Harp, and Piano, 1980); *Coração habitado* for Mezzo-soprano, Flute, Cello, and Piano (1965); *Euridice reamada* for Solo Voices, Chorus, and Orch. (1968); *Voix* for Mezzo-soprano and Chamber Orch. (1972); *A lira destemperada* for Soprano, Trombone, and Percussion (1973); *Madrigal* for Chorus (1975); *Leves veus celam* for Soprano, Flute, Viola, Harp, and Marimba (1980); *Canto para Anna Livia* for 3 Women's Voices and 11 Instruments (1981); *A flor das águas verdes* for 15 Voices (1982); *Ulivi aspri e forti* for Mezzo-soprano and Piano (1982; also for Mezzo-soprano, Flute, Clarinet, Trumpet, Harp, Guitar, Viola, and Cello, 1984); *Greetings* for Mezzo-soprano, Flute, Bassoon, Cello, and Percussion (1985); *Llanto por Mariana* for Soprano, Flute, Clarinet, Piano, and String Quartet (1986); *Credo* for Tenor, Alto Saxophone, Piano, Double Bass, and Percussion (1988); *A capela de Janas* for Soprano and Instrumental Ensemble (1989); *Memoria de Marília* for Soprano, Baritone, Oboe, Clarinet, 2 Guitars, Violin, and Cello (1990); *Cantos de Sophia* for Chorus (1990). **ELECTRONIC:** *Elegia a Amilcar Cabral* (1973); *Luis Vaz 73* (1973–74); *Electronicolirica* (1979); *Canto germinal* (1989).

Pekinel, Güher and **Süher,** remarkable Turkish-Spanish duo pianist; b. identical twins, Istanbul, March 29, 1951. They were only 5 when they began piano lessons with their mother. At 6, they played for the first time in public. When they were 9 they attracted wide notice when they appeared with the Ankara Phil. in a broadcast throughout Turkey. At 12, they went to Paris to pursue training with Loriod at the Cons. They continued their studies with August Leopolder at the Frankfurt am Main Hochschule für Musik, and Güher took a degree in psychology and Süher a degree in philosophy at the Johann Wolfgang Goethe Univ. in Frankfurt am Main. Following additional studies at the Curtis Inst. of Music in Philadelphia, where they received training as soloists under Serkin and as duo artists under Horszowski, they completed their studies at the Juilliard School in N.Y. under Adele Marcus. In 1978 they captured 1st prize at the UNESCO World Music Week in Bratislava. Thereafter they pursued a highly rewarding career in appearances with major orchs. and festival throughout the world.

Pelemans, Willem, Belgian composer; b. Antwerp, April 8, 1901; d. Brussels, Oct. 28, 1991. He studied music history at the Malines Cons. A highly prolific composer, he adopted an attractive idiom of writing music in a Romantic manner.

WORKS: DRAMATIC: *La Rose de Bakawali,* chamber opera (1938); *Het tinnen soldaatje,* musical play, after Andersen

(1945); *Floris en Blancefloer*, lyric drama (1947); *Le Combat de la vierge et du diable*, chamber opera (1949); *De mannen van Smeerop* (1952); *De nozem en de nimf*, chamber opera (1960). **BALLETS:** *Miles gloriosus* (1945); *Herfstgoud* (1959); *Pas de quatre* (1969). **ORCH.:** Concertos: one each for Harpsichord (1931), Violin (1954), Viola (1963), 2 Trumpets and Strings (1963), Organ (1965), 2 Pianos (1973), Saxophone (1973), and Clarinet Quartet (1983), 3 for Piano (1945, 1950, 1967), and 7 for Orch. (1948–83); 8 ballades (1933–35); 6 syms. (1936, 1937, 1937, 1938, 1938, 1939); 5 concertinos (1948–66); *Schetsen voor een buffa-opera* for Chamber Orch. (1952); *Ouvertura buffa* (1959); *Petite suite* (1962). **CHAMBER:** 3 piano trios (1932, 1942, 1972); 3 trios for Oboe, Clarinet, and Bassoon (1940, 1941, 1960); 8 string quartets (1942, 1943, 1943, 1943, 1944, 1955, 1961, 1970); 3 violin sonatas (all 1942); String Trio (1945); Viola Sonata (1945); Sonata for Cello and Bassoon (1946); Sonata for Solo Cello (1947); 2 wind quintets (1948, 1968); Quintet for Flute, Clarinet, Violin, Viola, and Cello (1950); 2 sonatas for Flute, Oboe, and Piano (1955, 1956); Sonata for Trumpet, Horn, and Trombone (1955); Sonata for Solo Violin (1955); Cello Sonata (1959); Sonata for Flute and Harpsichord or Piano (1959); 2 clarinet quartets (1961, 1976); Clarinet Sonata (1961); Quintet for Harp, Flute, Violin, Viola, and Cello (1962); Saxophone Quartet (1965); Wind Quartet (1965); Piano Quartet (1967); Sonata for Flute and Harp (1967); Sonata for 2 Guitars (1967); Brass Sextet (1968); Trio for 2 Oboes and English Horn (1971). **PIANO:** 4 suites (1932–33); 19 sonatas (1935–69); *10 Banalities* (1944); 2 sonatas for 2 Pianos (1947, 1954); 3 toccatas (1948, 1951, 1951); Sonata for 4 Hands (1961). **VOCAL:** *De wandelende jood*, oratorio (1929); *Van Ostaijen*, suite for Soprano, Tenor, Women's Chorus, Men's Chorus, and Orch. (1980–81); cantatas; songs.

Pelletier, (Louis) Wilfred, noted Canadian conductor and music educator; b. Montreal, June 20, 1896; d. N.Y., April 9, 1982. His father, a baker by trade, was an amateur musician who gave Pelletier his primary instruction; at the age of 14, he played piano in the orch. of the National Theatre in Montreal; in 1915 he won the Prix d'Europe and went to Paris, where he studied piano with Philipp, composition with Widor, and opera repertoire with Bellaigue. In 1917 he returned to America and was engaged as rehearsal pianist at the Metropolitan Opera in N.Y.; in 1921 he was appointed an assistant conductor there; from 1928 to 1950 he was a principal conductor there, specializing in the French repertoire; in 1936 he founded the popular Metropolitan Opera Auditions of the Air. He also was active as a conductor in Canada; from 1935 to 1951 he was conductor of the Société des Concerts Symphoniques de Montréal, and from 1951 to 1966, of the Orchestre Symphonique de Québec. From 1943 to 1961 he served as director of the Cons. de Musique in Montreal. In 1968 he was made a Companion of the Order of Canada. He was married consecutively to **Queena Mario** (1925–36) and **Rose Bampton** (from 1937). He publ. an autobiographical sketch, *Une Symphonie inachevée* (Quebec, 1972).

Pembaur, Joseph, Jr., Austrian pianist, brother of **Karl Maria Pembaur**; b. Innsbruck, April 20, 1875; d. Munich, Oct. 12, 1950. He was a pupil of his father, the Austrian composer and teacher Joseph Pembrauer, Sr. (b. Innsbruck, May 23, 1848; d. there, Feb. 19, 1923), then studied with Rheinberger and Thuille at the Munich Academy of Music. He was a prof. of piano at the Munich Musikschule (1897–1900); subsequently was on the faculty of the Leipzig Cons. (1902–21); in 1921, was appointed a prof. at the Munich Academy of Music. He wrote a Violin Sonata and a number of songs. He publ. *Von der Poesie des Klavierspiels* (1910; 2nd ed., 1911).

BIBL.: C. Werner, *J. P. zum 60. Geburtstag* (Berlin, 1935).

Pembaur, Karl Maria, Austrian organist and conductor, brother of **Joseph Pembauer, Jr.**; b. Innsbruck, Aug. 24, 1876; d. Dresden, March 6, 1939. He studied with his father, the Austrian composer and teacher Joseph Pembrauer, Sr. (b. Innsbruck, May 23, 1848; d. there, Feb. 19, 1923), then with Rheinberger at the Munich Academy of Music. In 1901 he went to Dresden, where he became court organist and choral conductor; also conducted at the Dresden Opera. He wrote the singspiel *Seien Sie vorsichtig*; *Geistliche Sonette* for 5 Solo Voices and Piano; *Bergbilder* for Woodwind Quintet and Piano; marches; songs. He publ. *Drei Jahrhunderte Kirchenmusik am sächsischen Hofe* (Dresden, 1920).

Penderecki, Krzysztof, celebrated Polish composer, pedagogue, and conductor; b. Debica, Nov. 23, 1933. He went to Kraków, where he attended the Jagellonian Univ. Following private composition lessons with Skolyszewski, he studied theory with Malawski and Wiechowicz at the State Higher School of Music (1955–58). In 1958 he joined its faculty as a lecturer in composition, later serving as a prof. (from 1972) and as rector (1972–87). He also lectured at the Essen Folkwang-Hochschule (1966–68) and was a prof. at Yale Univ. (1973–78). In later years, he also was active as a conductor. In 1988 he became principal guest conductor of the North German Radio Sym. Orch. in Hamburg. In 1995 he conducted the Sinfonia Varsovia on a tour of the U.S. Penderecki's rapid ascent as one of the most original composers of his time prompted many honors to come his way. In 1959 he won the 1st, 2nd, and 3rd prizes in the Competition of Young Polish Composers. His *Threnos* received the UNESCO Prize in 1961. In 1967 his *St. Luke Passion* won the Prix Italia, and in 1968 his *Dies Irae* won another Prix Italia. He received the award of the Union of Polish Composers in 1970. In 1977 he was honored with the Gottfried von Herder Prize of the F.v.S. Foundation in Hamburg. In 1983 he won the Sibelius Prize of the Wihouri Foundation and the Polish State Prize. He was honored with the Premio Lorenzo Magnifico in 1985. In 1992 he received the Grawemeyer Award of the Univ. of Louisville.

After a few works of an academic nature, he developed a hyper-modern technique of composition in a highly individual style, in which no demarcation line is drawn between consonances and dissonances, tonal or atonal melody, traditional or innovative instrumentation; an egalitarian attitude prevails toward all available resources of sound. While his idiom is naturally complex, he does not disdain tonality, even in its overt triadic forms. In his creative evolution, he has bypassed orthodox serial procedures; his music follows an athematic course, in constantly varying metrical and rhythmic patterns. He utilizes an entire spectrum of modern sonorities, expanding the domain of tone to unpitched elements, making use of such effects as shouting, hissing, and verbal ejaculations in vocal parts, at times reaching a climax of aleatory glossolalia; tapping, rubbing, or snapping the fingers against the body of an instrument; striking the piano strings with mallets, etc. For this he designed an optical notation, with symbolic ideograms indicating the desired sound; thus, a black isosceles triangle denotes the highest possible pitch; an inverted isosceles triangle, the lowest possible pitch; a black rectangle for a sonic complex of white noise within a given interval; vertical lines tied over by an arc for arpeggios below the bridge of a string instrument; wavy lines of varying amplitudes for extensive vibrato; curvilinear figures for aleatory passages; dots and dashes for repetitions of a pattern; sinusoidal oscillations for quaquaversal glissandos; etc. He applies these modern devices to religious music, including masses in the orthodox Roman Catholic ritual. Penderecki's most impressive and most frequently performed works is his *Tren pamieci ofiarom Hiroszimy* (Threnody for the Victims of Hiroshima) for 52 Strings (1959–60), rich in dynamic constrasts and ending on a tone cluster of 2 octavefuls of icositetraphonic harmony.

WORKS: OPERAS: *The Devils of Loudun* (1968–69; Hamburg, June 20, 1969); *Paradise Lost* (1976–78; Chicago, Nov. 29, 1978); *Die schwarze Maske* (1984–86; Salzburg, Aug. 15, 1986); *Ubu rex*, opera buffa (1990–91; Munich, July 6, 1991).

ORCH.: *Emanacje* (Emanations) for 2 String Orchs. (1958–59); *Anaklasis* for 42 Strings and Percussion (1959–60; Baden-Baden, Oct. 16, 1960); *Tren pamieci ofiarom Hiroszimy*

(Threnody for the Victims of Hiroshima) for 52 Strings (1959–60; Warsaw Radio, May 31, 1960); *Fonogrammi* for 3 Flutes, Strings, and Percussion (1961); *Polymorphia* for 48 Strings (1961; Hamburg, April 16, 1962); *Fluorescences* (1961–62; Baden-Baden, Oct. 21, 1962); *Kanon* for Strings and 2 Tapes (Warsaw, Sept. 21, 1962); *3 Pieces in Olden Style* for Strings (1963; Kraków, June 11, 1988); Sonata for Cello and Orch. (1964); *Capriccio No. 1* for Oboe and Strings (1965) and *No. 2* for Violin and Orch. (Donaueschingen, Oct. 22, 1967); *De natura sonoris No. 1* (Royan, April 7, 1966) and *No. 2* (N.Y., Dec. 3, 1971); 2 cello concertos: No. 1 (1966–67; rev. 1971–72) and No. 2 (1982; Berlin, Jan. 11, 1983); Violino Grande Concerto (Östersund, Sweden, July 1, 1967; rev. version, Hanover, N.H., Aug. 4, 1968); *Pittsburgh Overture* for Winds (1967); *Partita* for Harpsichord, Electric Guitar, Bass Guitar, Harp, Double Bass, and Orch. (1971; Rochester, N.Y., Feb. 11, 1972; rev. 1991; Munich, Jan. 5, 1992); *Actions* for Jazz Ensemble (Donaueschingen, Oct. 17, 1971); *Prélude* for Winds, Percussion, and Double Basses (Amsterdam, July 4, 1971); 5 syms.: No. 1 (1972–73; London, July 19, 1973), No. 2, *Christmas* (1979–80; N.Y., May 1, 1980), No. 3 (1988–95; Munich, Dec. 8, 1995), No. 4, *Adagio* (Paris, Nov. 26, 1989), and No. 5 (1991–92; Seoul, Aug. 14, 1992); *Intermezzo* for 24 Strings (Zürich, Nov. 30, 1973); *Als Jakob erwachte* (Monte Carlo, Aug. 14, 1974); 2 violin concertos: No. 1 (1976–77; Basel, April 27, 1977; rev. 1988) and No. 2 (1992–95; Leipzig, June 24, 1995); *Adagietto*, from *Paradise Lost* (Osaka, April 8, 1979); Viola Concerto (Caracas, July 21, 1983; also for Viola and Chamber Orch., Moscow, Oct. 20, 1985, and as a Cello Concerto, Wuppertal, Dec. 15, 1989); *Passacaglia* (Lucerne, Aug. 20, 1988); 2 sinfoniettas: No. 1 for Strings (Warsaw, Feb. 17, 1992) and No. 2 for Clarinet and Strings (Bad Kissingen, July 13, 1994); Concerto for Flute and Chamber Orch. (1992; Lausanne, Jan. 11, 1993); *Entrata* for 4 Horns, 3 Trumpets, 3 Trombones, Tuba, and Timpani (Cincinnati, Nov. 4, 1994).

CHAMBER: Violin Sonata (1953; Houston, Jan. 7, 1990); *3 Miniatures* for Violin and Piano (1959); 2 string quartets: No. 1 (1960) and No. 2 (1968; Berlin, Sept. 30, 1970); *Capriccio per Siegfried Palm* for Cello (Bremen, May 4, 1968); *Capriccio* for Tuba (Kraków, June 20, 1980); *Cadenza* for Viola (Luslawice, Sept. 10, 1984; also for Violin, Warsaw, Oct. 28, 1986); *Per Slava* for Cello (1985–86); *Prélude* for Clarinet (1987); *Der unterbrochene Gedanke* for String Quartet (Frankfurt am Main, Feb. 4, 1988); String Trio (1990–91; Metz, Nov. 15, 1991); Quartet for Clarinet and String Trio (Lübeck, Aug. 13, 1993).

VOCAL: *Psalmy Dawida* (Psalms of David) for Chorus and Chamber Ensemble (1958; Kraków, June 26, 1962); *Strophy* (Strophes) for Soprano, Narrator, and 10 Instruments (Warsaw, Sept. 17, 1959); *Wymiary czasu i ciszy* (Dimensions of Time and Silence) for Chorus, Strings, and Percussion (1959–60; Warsaw, Sept. 18, 1960); *Stabat Mater* for 3 Choruses (1962); *Passio et mors Domini Nostri Jesu Christi secundum Lucam* for Narrator, Soprano, Baritone, Bass, Boy's Chorus, 3 Mixed Choruses, and Orch. (1962–65; Münster, March 30, 1966); *Cantata in honorem almae matris Universitatis Jagellonicae* for Chorus and Orch. (1964); *Dies irae*, oratorio for Soprano, Tenor, Bass, Chorus, and Orch. (1966–67; Kraków, April 14, 1967); *Utrenja* (Morning Prayer) *I: The Entombment of Christ* for Soprano, Alto, Tenor, Bass, Basso Profundo, 2 Choruses, and Orch. (1969–70; Altenberg, April 8, 1970) and *II: Resurrection* for Soprano, Alto, Tenor, Bass, Basso Profundo, 2 Choruses, and Orch. (1970–71; Münster, May 28, 1971); *Kosmogonia* for Soprano, Tenor, Bass, Chorus, and Orch. (N.Y., Oct. 24, 1970); *Canticum Canticorum Salomonis* for Chorus, Chamber Orch., and 2 Dancers ad libitum (1970–73; Lisbon, June 5, 1973); *Ecloga VIII* for 6 Men's Voices (Edinburgh, Aug. 22, 1972); *Magnificat* for Bass, 7 Men's Voices, 2 Mixed Choruses, Children's Chorus, and Orch. (1973–74; Salzburg, Aug. 17, 1974); *De Profundis* for Chorus and Orch. (Graz, Oct. 16, 1977); *Prélude, Visions, and Finale*, from *Paradise Lost*, for 6 Soloists, Chorus, and Orch. (Salzburg, Aug. 10, 1979); *Te Deum* for Soprano, Mezzo-soprano, Tenor, Bass, 2 Choruses, and Orch. (1979–80; Assisi, Sept. 27, 1980); *Lacrimosa*, from the *Polish Requiem*, for Soprano, Chorus, and Orch. (Gdańsk, Dec. 16, 1980); *Polish Requiem* for 4 Soloists, Chorus, and Orch. (1980–84; Stuttgart, Sept. 28, 1984; rev. 1984–93; Stockholm, Nov. 11, 1993); *Agnus Dei*, from the *Polish Requiem*, for Chorus (1981; Nuremberg, June 21, 1982); *Song of Cherubim* for Chorus (1986; Washington, D.C., March 27, 1987); *Veni creator* for Chorus (Madrid, April 28, 1987); *2 Scenes and Finale from the Opera Die schwarze Maske* for Soprano, Mezzo-soprano, Chorus, and Orch. (Poznań, Nov. 6, 1988); *Benedicamus Domino* for Men's Chorus (Lucerne, April 18, 1992); *Benedictus* for Chorus (1993). **TAPE:** *Psalmus* (1961); *Brigade of Death* (1963).

BIBL.: K. Lisicki, *Szkice o K. P.m* (Warsaw, 1973); W. Schwinger, *P.: Begegnungen, Lebensdaten, Werkkommentare* (Stuttgart, 1979); R. Robinson, *K. P.: A Guide to His Works* (1983); R. Robinson and A. Winold, *A Study of the P. St. Luke Passion* (Celle, 1983); W. Schwinger, *K. P.: His Life and Work* (London, 1989).

Penherski, Zbigniew, Polish composer; b. Warsaw, Jan. 26, 1935. He studied composition with Stefan Poradowski at the Poznań Cons. (1955–56) and with Tadeusz Szeligowski at the Warsaw Cons. (1956–59).

WORKS: OPERAS: *Girls Through Will* (1961); *The Little Prince* (1962); *Samson Put on Trial* (1967; Warsaw, Sept. 23, 1969); *Mice* (1971–72); *The Fall of Peryn* (1972; Poznań, Oct. 6, 1974); *Edgar, Son of Walpor* (1982); *The Island of the Roses* (1989). **ORCH.:** *Mazurian Chronicles II* for Orch. and Tape (1973; new version, Glasgow, Sept. 27, 1985); *Anamnesis* (1975; Kraków, May 19, 1978); *String Play* for Strings (Ludzmierz, March 2, 1980); *Scottish Chronicles* (Glasgow, March 29, 1987); *Signals* (1992). **CHAMBER:** *Street Music* for Chamber Ensemble (1966); String Quartet (1966); Quartet for Keyboard and 3 Optional Instruments (1970); *Incantation I* for 6 Percussionists (1972) and *II* for 7 Performers (1976); *Jeux partis* for Saxophone and Percussion (1984); piano pieces, including *4 Preludes* (1956) and *Studies in Color* (1961). **VOCAL:** *Ostinata* for Chorus and Orch. (1960); *Choral Pictures* (1960); *3 Gipsy Songs* for Women's Chorus (1961); *Contrasts* for Vocal Ensemble, Selected Instruments, and String Orch. (1962; Lublin, March 5, 1965); *Musica humana* for Baritone, Chorus, and Orch. (1963; Warsaw, Jan. 20, 1967); *Missa abstracta* for Tenor, Narrator, Chorus, and Orch. (Kragujevac, Yugoslavia, Oct. 21, 1966); *Hymnus laudans* for Chorus and Chamber Orch. (1970; Wroclaw, Feb. 24, 1972); *3 Impressions* for Soprano, Piano, and 4 Percussionists (1985); *Cantus* for Chorus (1992). **OTHER:** Tape and didactic pieces.

Pennario, Leonard, brilliant American pianist; b. Buffalo, July 9, 1924. He received instruction from Guy Maier, Isabelle Vengerova, and Olga Steeb (piano) and Ernst Toch (composition). He played in public at 7; made his formal debut as soloist in the Grieg Concerto with the Dallas Sym. Orch. when he was 12. He made his Carnegie Hall debut as soloist in Liszt's 1st Concerto with the N.Y. Phil (Nov. 17, 1943), toured Europe for the first time (1952), and subsequently appeared throughout the world. He played chamber music with Heifetz and Piatigorsky; was active as a teacher.

Pentland, Barbara (Lally), Canadian composer and teacher; b. Winnipeg, Jan. 2, 1912. After taking piano lessons at a Montreal boarding school, she went to N.Y. and studied with Jacobi and Wagenaar at the Juilliard School of Music (1936–39); also took summer courses with Copland at the Berkshire Music Center in Tanglewood (summers, 1941–42). She was an instructor at the Toronto Cons. (1943–49) and the Univ. of British Columbia in Vancouver (1949–63). In her compositions, she adopts a pragmatic method of cosmopolitan modernism, employing dissonant linear counterpoint and dodecaphonic melodic structures within the framework of Classical forms.

WORKS: DRAMATIC: *Beauty and the Beast*, ballet-pantomine (1940); *The Lake*, chamber opera (1952; Vancouver, March 3, 1954). **ORCH.:** *Concert Overture* (1935); *2 Pieces* for Strings (1938); *Lament* (1939); *Holiday Suite* for Chamber Orch.

(1941); *Arioso and Rondo* (1941); Concerto for Violin and Small Orch. (1942); 4 syms.: No. 1 (1945–48), No. 2 (1950; Toronto, Feb. 9, 1953), No. 3, *Symphony in 10 Parts* for Chamber Ensemble (1957; Vancouver, Sept. 18, 1959), and No. 4 (1959); *Colony Music* for Piano and Strings (1947); *Variations on a Boccherini Theme* (1948); Concerto for Organ and Strings (1949); *Ave atque vale* (1951); *Ricercar* for Strings (1955); Concerto for Piano and Strings (1956); *Strata* for Strings (1964); *Ciné scene* for Chamber Orch. (1968); *Variations concertante* for Piano and Small Orch. (1970); *Res musica* for Strings (1975). **CHAMBER:** Piano Quartet (1939); Cello Sonata (1943); 5 string quartets (1945, 1953, 1969, 1980, 1985); *Vista* for Violin and Piano (1945); Violin Sonata (1946); Wind Octet (1948); *Weekend Overture* for Resort Combo of Clarinet, Trumpet, Piano, and Percussion (1949); Sonata for Solo Violin (1950); Sonatina for Solo Flute (1954); Piano Trio (1963); *Variations* for Viola (1965); *Trio con Alea* for String Trio (1966); Septet for Horn, Trumpet, Trombone, Violin, Viola, Cello, and Organ (1967); *Reflections* for Free Bass Accordion (1971); *Interplay* for Accordion and String Quartet (1972); *Occasions* for Brass Quintet (1974); *Trance* for Flute, Piano, and Harp (1978); *Eventa* for Flute, Clarinet, Trombone, 2 Percussion, Harp, Violin, and Cello (1978); *Elegy* for Horn and Piano (1980); *Tellus* for Flute, Cello, Piano, Percussion, and Celesta (1982); Piano Quintet (1983); *Tides* for Violin, Marimba, and Harp (1984); *Elegy* for Cello and Piano (1985). **PIANO:** *Studies in Line* (1941); *Variations* (1942); Sonata (1945); *Sonata Fantasy* (1947); 2 sonatinas (1951); *Mirror Study* (1952); Sonata for 2 Pianos (1953); *Toccata* (1958); *3 Duets after Pictures by Paul Klee* (1959); *Fantasy* (1962); *Puppet Show* (1964); *Shadows* (1964); *Signs* (1964); *Suite borealis* (1966); *Space Studies* (1967); *Arctica* for Young Pianists (1971–73); *Vita brevis* (1973); *Ephemera* (1974–78); *Tenebrae* (1976); *Vincula* (1983); *Horizons* (1985). **VOCAL:** *News* for Virtuoso Voice and Orch., after texts from the news media (1970); *Disasters of the Sun* for Mezzo-soprano, 9 Instruments, and Tape (1976); choruses; other songs.

BIBL.: S. Eastman and T. McGee, *B. P.* (Toronto, 1983).

Pépin, (Jean-Josephat) Clermont, Canadian composer; b. St.-Georges-de-Beauce, May 15, 1926. He studied piano and harmony as a child with Georgette Dionne; then studied piano with Arthur Letondal and harmony and counterpoint with Claude Champagne in Montreal (1937–41). He was a student of Jeanne Behrend (piano) and Rosario Scalero (composition) at the Curtis Inst. of Music in Philadelphia (diploma, 1945); after further training from Lubka Kolessa (piano) and Arnold Walter (composition) at the Toronto Cons., he won the Prix d'Europe (1949) and went to Paris to complete his composition studies with Jolivet, Honegger, and Messiaen. He taught composition at the Montreal Cons. from 1955 to 1964, and later was its director from 1967 to 1973. He taught there again from 1978 to 1987. In 1981 he was made an Officer of the Order of Canada and in 1990 an Officier of the Ordre national du Québec. In his music, he has explored various aspects of serialism while adhering to classical forms.

WORKS: BALLETS: *Les Portes de l'enfer* (1953); *L'Oiseaux-Phénix* (1956); *Le Porte-rêve* (1957–58). **ORCH.:** 2 piano concertos (1946, 1949); *Variations symphoniques* (1947); 5 syms.: No. 1 (1948), No. 2 (Montreal, Dec. 22, 1957), No. 3, *Quasars* (Montreal, Feb. 7, 1967), No. 4, *La Messe sur le monde*, for Narrator, Chorus, and Orch. (1975), and No. 5, *Implosion* (Montreal, Sept. 13, 1983); *Guernica*, symphonic poem after Picasso's painting (Quebec, Dec. 8, 1952); *Le Rite de soleil noir*, symphonic poem (Luxembourg, Sept. 1955); *Monologue* for Chamber Orch. (1961); *Nombres* for 2 Pianos and Orch. (Montreal, Feb. 6, 1963); *Monade* for Strings (1964); *Prismes et cristaux* for Strings (Montreal, April 9, 1974); *Monade* for Violin and Orch. (1972); *Chroma* (Guelph, Ontario, May 5, 1973); Marimba Concerto (1988). **CHAMBER:** Piano Sonata (1947); 5 string quartets (1948, 1955, 1956, 1960, 1976); *Musique pour Athalie* for Woodwinds and Brass (1956); Suite for Piano Trio (1958); *Sequences* for Flute, English Horn, Violin, Viola, and Cello (1972); *Monade IV-Réseaux* for Violin and Piano (1974); *Monade VI-Réseaux* for Violin (1974–76); *Interactions* for 7 Groups of Percussion and 2 Pianos (1977); Trio No. 2 for Violin, Cello, and Piano (1982); *Monade VII* for Violin and Piano (1986). **VOCAL:** *Cycle-Eluard* for Soprano and Piano (1948–49); *Hymne au vent du nord*, cantata (1960); *Paysage* for Soprano, Clarinet, Cello, and Piano (1987); *Trois incantations* for Voice and Piano (1987).

Pepöck, August, Austrian composer; b. Gmunden, May 10, 1887; d. there, Sept. 5, 1967. He studied in Vienna with Heuberger and R. Fuchs. He was active as a conductor of theater music in various provincial towns in Germany; subsequently lived mostly in Vienna. He scored great success with his operettas *Mädel ade!* (Vienna, Oct. 5, 1930) and *Der Reiter de Kaiserin* (Vienna, April 30, 1941). He also wrote some chamber music and songs.

Pepping, Ernst, distinguished German composer and pedagogue; b. Duisburg, Sept. 12, 1901; d. Berlin, Feb. 1, 1981. He studied with Gmeindl at the Berlin Hochschule für Musik. He taught at the Berlin-Spandau Church Music School (from 1934); was also a prof. at the Berlin Hochschule für Musik (1953–68). He publ. *Stilwende der Musik* (Mainz, 1934) and *Der polyphone Satz*: vol. I, *Der cantus-firmus-Satz* (Berlin, 1943; 2nd ed., 1950), and vol. II, *Übungen im doppelten Kontrapunkt und im Kanon* (Berlin, 1957). In 1989 the Ernst-Pepping-Gesellschaft was organized. By virtue of his lifelong association with Lutheran Church culture, Pepping acquired a profound understanding of German polyphonic music, both sacred and secular. He was a significant composer of German chorales; also produced 3 notable syms. A neo-Baroque penchant is discernible in all of his works.

WORKS: ORCH.: *Prelude* (1929); *Invention* (1930); *Partita* (1934); *Lust hab ich g'habt zur Musika: Variationen zu einem Liedsatz von Senfl* (1937); 3 syms.: No. 1 (1939), No. 2 (1942), and No. 3, *Die Tageszeiten* (1944); *Serenade* (1944–45); *Variations* (1949); Piano Concerto (1950); *2 Orchesterstücke über eine Chanson des Binchois* (1958). **CHAMBER:** String Quartet (1943); Flute Sonata (1958). **KEYBOARD: PIANO:** Various pieces, including 4 sonatas (1937–45). **ORGAN:** *Grosses Orgelbuch* (3 vols., 1939); 2 concertos (both 1941); 3 Fugues on BACH (1943); 3 partitas: No. 1, *Ach wie flüchtig* (1953), No. 2, *Wer weiss, wie nahe mir mein Ende* (1953), and No. 3, *Mit Fried und Freud* (1953); *12 Chorale Preludes* (1958); Sonata (1958). **VOCAL** (all for a cappella chorus unless otherwise given): **SACRED:** *Deutsche Choralmesse* (1928); *Choralbuch* (30 works; 1931); *Spandauer Chorbuch* (20 vols., 1935–38; rev. by G. Grote, 4 vols., 1962); *Missa "Dona nobis pacem"* (1948); *Te Deum* for Solo Voices, Chorus, and Orch. (1956); *Die Weihnachtsgeschichte des Lukas* (1959); *Aus hartem Weh die Menschheit klagt* (1964); *Psalm CXXXIX* for Alto, Chorus, and Orch. (1964); *Deines Lichtes Glanz* (1967). **SECULAR:** *Sprüche und Lieder* (1930); *Lob der Träne* (1940); *33 Volkslieder* for Women's or Children's Chorus (1943); *Die wandelnde Glocke* (1952); also song cycles.

BIBL.: H. Poos, ed., *Festschrift E. P.* (Berlin, 1972); K. Hüschen, *Studien zum Motettenschaffen E. P.s* (Regensburg, 1987).

Peragallo, Mario, Italian composer; b. Rome, March 25, 1910. He was a student of Casella. In his early works, he followed the line of Italian traditionalism, characterized by modern but euphonious polyphony; later he adopted a radical quasi-dodecaphonic idiom, with frequent reversions to diatonic structures.

WORKS: OPERAS: *Ginevra degli Almieri* (Rome, Feb. 13, 1937); *Lo stendardo di S. Giorgio* (Genoa, 1941); *La collina* (Venice, 1947); *La Gita in campagna* (Milan, March 24, 1954); *La parrucca dell'imperatore* (Spoleto, 1959). **ORCH.:** *Concerto for Orchestra* (1939); 2 piano concertos (1949, 1951); *Fantasia* (1950); Violin Concerto (1954); *Forme sovrapposte* (1959); *Emircal* for Orch. and Tape (1980). **CHAMBER:** 3 string quartets (1933, 1934, 1937); *Vibrazioni* for Flute, "Tiptofono," and Piano

(1960); *Perclopus*, chamber concerto for Clarinet, Wind Quintet, String Quintet, and Tape (1982); piano pieces; organ works. **VOCAL:** Choral pieces; songs.

Perahia, Murray, outstanding American pianist of Spanish-Jewish descent; b. N.Y., April 19, 1947. He studied piano with J. Haien (1953–64); then entered the Mannes College of Music, where he studied conducting and composition (B.S., 1969); he also continued his piano studies with Balsam and Horszowski. In 1968 he made his Carnegie Hall debut in N.Y.; in 1972 he became the first American to win (by unanimous vote of the jury) the Leeds International Pianoforte Competition; in 1975 he was awarded the 1st Avery Fisher Prize, sharing it with the cellist Lynn Harrell. He appeared as soloist with the leading orchs. of the U.S. and Europe; also gave many recitals in the U.S. and abroad. In 1982 he was appointed co-artistic director of the Aldeburgh Festival, which post he retained until 1989. In 1992 he sustained a crippling hand injury which compelled him to withdraw from public performances. In 1994 he returned to the concert stage as soloist in Beethoven's 4th Piano Concerto in London. He excels in Classical music; mastered all of Mozart's concertos, often conducting from the keyboard; he is praised also for his congenial interpretation of the standard concert repertoire.

Pereira-Salas, Eugenio, Chilean musicologist; b. Santiago, May 19, 1904; d. there, Nov. 17, 1979. He studied at the Univ. of Chile in Santiago; in 1926 he went to Europe and took courses at the Sorbonne in Paris and at the Univ. of Berlin; later enrolled at the Univ. of Calif., Berkeley, on a Guggenheim fellowship (1933–34). Returning to Santiago, he was a lecturer in geography and history at the Univ. of Chile; in 1938 he organized there a dept. of Chilean folklore. He publ. a number of informative books on Chilean music, among them *Los origines del arte musical en Chile* (Santiago, 1941); *La canción nacional de Chile* (Santiago, 1941); *Juegos y alegrías coloniales de Chile* (Santiago, 1947); *Historia de la música en Chile (1850–1900)* (Santiago, 1957); *Art and Music in Contemporary Latin America* (London, 1968).

Perera, Ronald (Christopher), American composer and teacher; b. Boston, Dec. 25, 1941. He studied composition with Kirchner at Harvard Univ. (B.A., 1963; M.A., 1967) and then traveled on its John Knowles Paine Traveling Fellowship to study electronic music and computer composition with Koening at the Univ. of Utrecht (1967–68); also studied privately in the U.S. with Thompson in choral music and electronic music with Davidovsky. After teaching at Syracuse Univ. (1968–70), he served as director of the Dartmouth College Electronic Music Studio (1970–71); then taught theory, composition, and electronic music at Smith College in Northampton, Mass. (from 1971); was also active as a visiting scholar at the Columbia-Princeton Electronic Music Center (1975–76). With Appleton, he ed. *The Development and Practice of Electronic Music* (1975). He received annual ASCAP awards from 1972, and in 1978 and 1988 grants from the NEA.

WORKS: OPERAS: *The Yellow Wallpaper*, chamber opera (Northampton, Mass., May 17, 1989); *S.* (1995). **ORCH.:** *Chanteys* (1976; Concord, Mass., Feb. 4, 1977; rev. 1979); Chamber Concerto for Brass Quintet, 9 Winds, Piano, and Percussion (1983; Cambridge, Mass., April 19, 1984); *The Saints* (N.Y., Dec. 1990); *Music* for Flute and Orch. (1990). **CHAMBER:** *Reverberations* for Organ and Tape (1970); *Reflex* for Viola and Tape (1973); *Fantasy Variations* for Piano and Live Electronics (1976); *Bright Angels* for Organ, Percussion, and Tape (Hartford, Conn., June 6, 1977); *Tolling* for 2 Pianos and Tape (1979; Northampton, Mass., Feb. 3, 1980); *Fanfare* for Viola and Piano (1987); *Augmented Forces* for Piano and Synthesizer (1987; Northampton, Mass., May 19, 1988). **VOCAL:** *Mass* for Soloists, Chorus, and Orch. (1967); *Did You Hear the Angels Sing?* for Soprano, Chorus, and Organ (1968); *3 Night Pieces* for Soprano, Alto, Women's Chorus, Cello, Piano, and Percussion (1974); *The White Whale* for Baritone and Orch. (1981; Northampton, Mass., Feb. 14, 1982); *Crossing the Meridian* for Tenor, Flute, Clarinet, Violin, Viola, Cello, Piano, and Percussion (Cambridge, Mass., Dec. 8, 1982); *Earthsongs* for Women's Chorus and Orch. (1983; Northampton, Mass., May 19, 1984); *As Freedom Is a Breakfastfood* for Women's Chorus and Piano (Rye, N.Y., May 10, 1984); *The Canticle of the Sun* for Narrator, Chorus, and Digitally Synthesized Instruments (1984; Groton, Mass., April 21, 1985); *The Outermost House* for Soprano, Narrator, Chorus, and Chamber Orch. (West Yarmouth, Mass., Nov. 16, 1991); *Visions* for 2 Sopranos and Chamber Ensemble (1993); *A Fondness for Music* for Women's Chorus and Piano (1993; Northampton, Mass., April 17, 1994); songs. **ELECTRONIC:** *Improvisation* for Loudspeakers (1969); *Time Machine* (1970); *Alternate Routes* (1971).

Peress, Maurice, American conductor; b. N.Y., March 18, 1930. He studied at N.Y. Univ. (B.A., 1951) and with H. Freistadt and J. Cnudde (trumpet) and P. James and C. Bamberger (conducting) at N.Y.'s Mannes College of Music (1955–57). After serving as assistant conductor of the N.Y. Phil. (1961–62), he was music director of the Corpus Christi (Texas) Sym. Orch. (1962–75), the Austin (Texas) Sym. Orch. (1970–73), and the Kansas City Phil. (1974–80).

Pérez Casas, Bartolomeo, Spanish conductor and composer; b. Lorca, near Murcia, Jan. 24, 1873; d. Madrid, Jan. 15, 1956. He studied at the Madrid Cons. He played the clarinet in various military bands; also was a bandmaster. He then established himself in Madrid as a teacher at the Cons.; from 1915 to 1936, conducted the Orquesta Filarmonica de Madrid. He wrote a lyric drama, *Lorenzo*; *A mi tierra*, orch. suite; String Quartet; pieces for band.

Pergament, Moses, Finnish-born Swedish music critic and composer; b. Helsinki, Sept. 21, 1893; d. Gustavsberg, near Stockholm, March 5, 1977. He studied violin at the St. Petersburg Cons. and conducting at Berlin's Stern Cons. In 1915 he settled in Sweden and became a naturalized Swedish citizen (1918); from 1923 to 1966 he was active as a music critic in Swedish newspapers; he publ. 4 books on music. His musical style was initially circumscribed by Russian paradigms; later he was influenced by Sibelius; still later he adopted some modernistic procedures. Several of his compositions reflect an ancestral strain of Jewish melos.

WORKS: DRAMATIC: OPERAS: *Himlens hemlighet* (The Secret of Heaven), chamber opera (1952); *Eli*, radio opera (1958; Swedish Radio, March 19, 1959); *Abrams Erwachen*, opera-oratorio (1970–73). **BALLETS:** *Krelantems and Eldeling* (1920–28); *Vision* (1923). Also incidental music and film scores. **ORCH.:** *Romance* for Violin and Orch. (1914); *Adagio* for Clarinet and Strings (1915); *Rapsodia ebraica* (1935); *Concerto romantico* for Strings (1935); *Dibbuk*, fantasy for Violin and Orch. (1935); *Almquistiana*, 2 suites (1936, 1938); *Swedish Rhapsody* (1941); Violin Concerto (1948); *Kol Nidre* for Cello and Orch. (1949); Piano Concerto (1951); Concerto for 2 Violins and Orch. (1954); Cello Concerto (1955); *Canto lirico* for Violin and Orch. (1956); *Pezzo intimo* for 16 Solo Cellos (1957); Viola Concerto (1964–65); *Fantasia differente* for Cello and Strings (1970); *Sonatina* for Flute and Strings (1973). **CHAMBER:** Piano Trio (1912–13; rev. 1940); Violin Sonata (1918–20); 3 string quartets (1922, 1952, 1956); Sonata for Solo Violin (1961); Flute Sonata (1968); *Little Suite* for Woodwinds (1970). **VOCAL:** *Nedanförmänskliga visor* (Subhuman Songs) for Narrator, Soli, Chorus, and Orch. (1936); *Den judiska sången* (The Jewish Song), choral sym. (1944); *De sju dödssynderna* (The 7 Deadly Sins), oratorio (1963); *4 Poems by Edith Södergran* for Soprano and Orch. (1965–66); *Årstider*, 4 songs for Baritone and Orch. (1968); *Drömmen om mullen och vindarna* (The Dream of the Earth and the Winds) for Baritone and Orch. (1969); *Biblical Cantata* for Chorus and Orch. (1974); over 100 solo songs.

Peričić, Vlastimir, Serbian composer and musicologist; b. Vršac, Dec. 7, 1927. He studied in Vienna with Uhl. He became active as a pedagogue in Belgrade; publ. manuals on harmony and form; compiled a valuable reference work on Serbian composers, *Muzički Stvaraoci u Srbiji* (Belgrade, 1969). Among his compositions were String Quartet (1950); *Symphonic Movement* (Belgrade, Oct. 14, 1952); *Fantasia quasi una sonata* for Violin and Piano (1954); Sinfonietta for Strings (Zagreb, Nov. 13, 1957); piano pieces.

Perick (real name, **Prick**), **Christof,** German conductor; b. Hamburg, Oct. 23, 1946. He was a student in Hamburg of Brückner-Rüggeberg. After serving as an assistant conductor at the Hamburg State Opera, he conducted at the operas in Trier (1970–72) and Darmstadt (1972–74). He was Generalmusikdirektor in Saarbrücken (1974–77) and Karlsruhe (1977–84), and also held the title of 1st conductor at the Deutsche Oper in Berlin (1977–84). He was music director (1991–94) and music advisor (from 1994) of the Los Angeles Chamber Orch. In 1993 he became Generalmusikdirektor of the Niedersächsische State Theater and Orch. in Hannover. Perick appeared as a guest conductor of opera and sym. throughout Europe and North America.

Périer, Jean (Alexis), French baritone; b. Paris, Feb. 2, 1869; d. there, Nov. 3, 1954. He studied at the Paris Cons., obtaining the premier prix for singing (1892). He made his debut at the Paris Opéra-Comique as Monostatos in *Die Zauberflöte* on Dec. 16, 1892; was engaged there until 1894, and again from 1900 to 1920. He created the role of Pélleas at the premiere of Debussy's opera (1902), and sang the leading tenor parts in several other premieres of French operas; sang at N.Y.'s Manhattan Opera House (1908). A talented comedian, Périer also appeared in variety shows in Paris. He publ. an instructive album, *Mes exercises, tirés des chansons populaires de France* (Paris, 1917).

Perkins, John MacIvor, American composer and teacher; b. St. Louis, Aug. 2, 1935. He studied at Harvard Univ. (B.A., 1958), at the New England Cons. of Music in Boston (B.Mus., 1958), with Boulanger in Paris and Gerhard and Rubbra in London (1958–59), and at Brandeis Univ. (M.F.A., 1962). After teaching at the Univ. of Chicago (1962–65) and at Harvard Univ. (1965–70), he was assoc. prof. of music (from 1970) and chairman of the music dept. (1970–75) at Washington Univ. in St. Louis. In 1966 he received an American Academy and National Inst. of Arts and Letters award.

WORKS: DRAMATIC: *Divertimento*, chamber opera (1958); *Andrea del Sarto*, operatic monologue (1981). **ORCH.:** *Fantasy and Variations* (1961; orchestration of the piano pieces *Fantasy*, 1959, and *Variations*, 1960); *Music* (1965). **CHAMBER:** *Canons* for 9 Instruments (1957); *Variations* for Flute, Clarinet, Trumpet, Piano, and Percussion (1962); *Music* for Carillon (1963); *Music* for 13 Players (1964); *Music for Brass* for 3 Trumpets and 3 Trombones (1965); *After a Silence-Alpha* for 12 Instruments (1976); *Canzona* for Harpsichord and Piano (1982); *Divisions* for Bass Gamba and Harpsichord (1982); Quartet for Strings and Tape (1984); *Sequence* for 5 Brass Instruments (1986); *Lyric Variations* for Violin and Piano (1989); *Reflections on a Bach Fugue* for Flute and Piano (1995). **KEYBOARD: PIANO:** *Fantasy* (1959), *Intermezzo* (1962), and *Variations* (1960); *Caprice* (1963); *Cadenza* (1978). **ORGAN:** *Fugue in C, The Relief* (1977). **VOCAL:** 7 Songs for Voice and Piano (1955–62); *3 Studies* for Chamber Chorus (1958); *Alleluia* for Chorus (1966; also for Chorus and Percussionist, 1971); *4 Songs on Transience* for Voice and Piano (1988).

Perkowski, Piotr, Polish composer and pedagogue; b. Oweczacze, Ukraine, March 17, 1901; d. Otwock, near Warsaw, Aug. 12, 1990. He studied composition with Statkowski at the Warsaw Cons. (1923–25); then took private lessons with Szymanowski in Warsaw and with Roussel in Paris. He was director of the Toruń Cons. (1936–39); taught composition at the Warsaw Cons. (1946–51; 1954–73); was artistic director of the Kraków Phil. (1949–51) and dean of the Music Academy in Wroclaw (1951–55); served as councilor for cultural development for the city of Warsaw (1965–74). In his earlier years, he followed the fashionable cosmopolitan trend of absolute music without reference to national or general programmatic subjects, but under the influence of social changes he began introducing concrete, historic, and pictorial representations.

WORKS: DRAMATIC: OPERA: *Garlands* (Warsaw, 1962). **BALLETS:** *Swantewit* (1930; rev. 1945–47; Poznań, June 19, 1948); *Rhapsody* (1949); *Fantasia* (1950); *Clementine* (1960–63); *Balladyna* (1960–64; Warsaw, 1965). **ORCH.:** 2 syms.: No. 1 for Chorus and Orch. (1925; lost; reconstructed 1955) and No. 2 (1949); *Geometric Suite* (1930); 2 violin concertos (1933, 1960); *Warsaw Overture* (1954); *Sinfonia drammatica* (1963); *Scottish Impressions* (1968); *Amphiction* (1970); Cello Concerto (1973). **CHAMBER:** 2 string quartets (1930, 1977); *Elegia* for Cello and Organ (1945); Trumpet Sonatina (1954); Flute Sonata (1954); piano pieces. **VOCAL:** 5 cantatas: *Wisla* (1951), *Epitaphe pour Nicos Belojannis* (1952), *Suita weselna* (Merry Suite) for Soprano, Tenor, Chorus, and Orch. (1952), *Suita epicka* (1953), and *Alexiares*, with Narrator and Tape (1966–69); *Niebo w plomieniach* (The Sky in Flames), song cycle, for Voice and Orch. (1969).

Perle, George, eminent American composer, music theorist, and pedagogue; b. Bayonne, N.J., May 6, 1915. Following training in composition and theory with La Violette at DePaul Univ. in Chicago (graduated, 1938), he pursued private lessons in composition with Krenek (1939–41) and obtained his M.M. degree at the American Cons. of Music in Chicago (1942). Later he studied musicology with Sachs, Reese, and Bernstein at N.Y. Univ. (Ph.D., 1956). In 1941 Perle founded the New Music Group of Chicago with Robert Erickson and Ben Weber. After teaching music history and composition at the Univ. of Louisville (1949–57), he was prof. of theory and composition at the Univ. of Calif. at Davis (1957–61) and at Queens College of the City Univ. of N.Y. (1961–85). With Hans Redlich and Igor Stravinsky, he organized the International Alban Berg Soc. in 1968. He was composer-in-residence at the Berkshire Music Center in Tanglewood (summers, 1967, 1980, and 1987), of the San Francisco Sym. (1989–91), and at the Marlboro (Vt.) Music Festival (summer, 1993). Among his positions as a visiting prof. were the Birge-Cary Prof. of Music at the State Univ. of N.Y. at Buffalo (1971–72), the Visiting Ernest Bloch Prof. of Music at the Univ. of Calif. at Berkeley (1989), and the Visiting Distinguished Prof. of Music at N.Y. Univ. (1994). In 1966–67 and 1974–75 he held Guggenheim fellowships. In 1977 he received an award from the American Academy and Inst. of Arts and Letters, and was elected to its membership in 1978. The 1st vol. of his study *The Operas of Alban Berg* (Berkeley, 1980) was honored with the ASCAP-Deems Taylor Award in 1981. He was elected a member of the National Academy of Arts and Sciences in 1985. His 4th wind quintet was awarded the Pulitzer Prize in Music in 1986, the same year he was named a MacArthur fellow. Perle was one of the earliest American serialists, and one of the most innovative. He developed a highly personal and distinctive "12-tone tonality," one made notable by expert craftsmanship.

WRITINGS: *Serial Composition and Atonality: An Introduction to the Music of Schoenberg and Webern* (Berkeley, 1962; 6th ed., 1991); *Twelve-Tone Tonality* (Berkeley, 1977; 2nd ed., 1995); *The Operas of Alban Berg* (2 vols., Berkeley, 1980, 1985); *The Listening Composer* (Berkeley, 1990); *The Right Notes: 23 Selected Essays on 20th-Century Music* (Stuyvesant, N.Y., 1994); *Style and Idea in the Lyric Suite of Alban Berg* (Stuyvesant, N.Y., 1995).

WORKS: DRAMATIC: *The Birds*, incidental music to Aristophanes' play (Berkeley, Sept. 28, 1961). **ORCH.:** *3 Movements* (1960; Amsterdam, June 14, 1963); *Serenade No. 1* for Viola and Chamber Orch. (N.Y., May 10, 1962), *No. 2* for 11 Players (1968; Washington, D.C., Feb. 28, 1969), and *No. 3* for Piano and Chamber Ensemble (N.Y., Dec. 14, 1983); *6 Bagatelles* (1965; Riverhead, N.Y., Nov. 18, 1977); Cello Concerto (1966; N.Y., Nov. 14, 1987); Concertino for Piano, Winds, and Timpani (Chicago, April 20, 1979); *A Short Symphony* (Tanglewood, Aug. 16, 1980); *Dance Overture*, renamed *Dance Fantasy* (1986; Houston, May 16, 1987); *New Fanfares* for Brass Ensemble (Tanglewood, Aug. 1, 1987); *Lyric Intermezzo* for 15 Players (Seattle, Nov. 8, 1987); *Sinfonietta I* (1987; St. Paul, Minn., Jan. 29, 1988) and *II* (San Francisco, Feb. 19, 1990); 2 piano concertos: No. 1 (1990; San Francisco, Jan. 24, 1991) and No. 2 (1991; Columbus, Ohio, Jan. 28, 1992); *Adagio* (1992; N.Y., April 13, 1993); *Transcendental Modulations* (1993). **CONCERT BAND:** *Solemn Procession* (1947). **CHAMBER:** Sonata for Solo Viola (1942); *3 Sonatas* for Solo Clarinet (1943; Chicago, Aug. 7, 1955); *Hebrew Melodies* for Cello (1945; N.Y., Jan. 24, 1947); *Lyric Piece* for Cello and Piano (1946); Sonata for Solo Cello (1947; N.Y., Feb. 22, 1949); String Quintet (1958; San Francisco, Feb. 19, 1960); 4 wind quintets: No. 1 (Berkeley, April 8, 1959), No. 2 (1960; N.Y., May 6, 1962), No. 3 (1967; Chicago, April 5, 1968), and No. 4 (1984; N.Y., Oct. 2, 1985); 2 sonatas for Solo Violin: No. 1 (1959; Davis, Calif., March 13, 1960) and No. 2 (1963; Boston, Feb. 20, 1966); String Quartet No. 5 (1960; rev. version, Tanglewood, Aug. 13, 1967), No. 7 (1973; Buffalo, March 19, 1974), and No. 8, *Windows of Order* (1988; Washington, D.C., April 6, 1989); *Monody I* for Flute (1960; N.Y., May 10, 1962) and *II* for Bass (N.Y., Nov. 2, 1962); *3 Inventions* for Bassoon (1962; N.Y., March 26, 1963); *Solo Partita* for Violin and Viola (Chicago, April 23, 1965); *Sonata quasi una fantasia* for Clarinet and Piano (Buffalo, March 19, 1972); *Sonata a quattro* for Flute, Clarinet, Violin, and Cello (N.Y., May 17, 1982); Cello Sonata (N.Y., April 13, 1985); *Sonata a cinque* for Bass Trombone, Clarinet, Violin, Cello, and Piano (1986; N.Y., Feb. 28, 1987); *For Piano and Winds* (1988; N.Y., March 19, 1989); *Nightsong* for Flute, Clarinet, Violin, Cello, and Piano (1988; N.Y., March 7, 1991). **PIANO:** *Pantomime, Interlude, and Fugue* (1937; N.Y., Feb. 27, 1982); *Little Suite* (Chicago, Oct. 23, 1939); *6 Préludes* (1946); Sonata (1950; N.Y., Feb. 11, 1951); *Short Sonata* (1964; N.Y., May 5, 1965); *Toccata* (1969; N.Y., Nov. 20, 1972); Suite in C (1970; Washington, D.C., April 29, 1987); *Fantasy-Variations* (1971; Sacramento, Calif., Nov. 6, 1986); *6 Études* (Boston, Oct. 29, 1976); *Ballade* (1981; N.Y., Feb. 17, 1982); *6 New Études* (1984; Beijing, May 7, 1985); Sonatina (Sacramento, Calif., Nov. 6, 1986); *Lyric Intermezzo* (Seattle, Nov. 7, 1987); *Improvisation* (N.Y., Oct. 22, 1989); *Phantasieplay* (1994). **VOCAL:** *2 Rilke Songs* for Voice and Piano (1941; N.Y., May 6, 1949); *Sonnets to Orpheus* for Chorus (1974; N.Y., Feb. 18, 1975); *Songs of Praise and Lamentation* for Soli, Chorus, and Orch. (1974; N.Y., Feb. 18, 1975); *13 Dickinson Songs* for Voice and Piano (Princeton, N.J., June 19, 1978).

Perlea, Jonel, Romanian-born American conductor, teacher, and composer; b. Ograda, Dec. 13, 1900; d. N.Y., July 29, 1970. He studied piano and composition in Munich (1918–20) and conducting in Leipzig (1920–23). He made his conducting debut in Bucharest in 1919; held posts as a conductor in Leipzig (1922–23) and Rostock (1923–25); then conducted the Bucharest Opera (1929–32; 1934–36) and the Bucharest Radio Orch. (1936–44), of which he was a founder. He led conducting classes at the Bucharest Cons. (1941–44); during the last year of World War II, he was interned in a German concentration camp. After the war, he conducted opera in Rome (1945–47); in 1950, conducted at La Scala in Milan. He made his American debut at the Metropolitan Opera in N.Y. on Dec. 1, 1949, conducting *Tristan und Isolde;* appeared at the San Francisco Opera and the Lyric Opera of Chicago; from 1955 to 1970, was conductor of the Conn. Sym. Orch. He taught conducting at the Manhattan School of Music from 1952 until shortly before his death. Perlea became a naturalized American citizen in 1960. He suffered a heart attack in 1957 and a stroke in 1958, as a result of which he lost the use of his right arm, but he continued to conduct with his left hand.

WORKS: ORCH.: *2 Sketches* (1919); *Variations on an Original Theme* (Bucharest, Dec. 5, 1935); *Don Quichotte*, symphonic scherzo (1946); Sym. (1951); *Adagio* (1952); Sinfonia Concertante for Violin and Orch. (1968); *3 Studies* (1969). **CHAMBER:** Violin Sonata (1921); Cello Sonata (1921); String Quartet (1922); piano pieces, including a Sonata (1930). **VOCAL:** Songs.

Perlemuter, Vlado, esteemed French pianist and pedagogue of Polish descent; b. Kaunas, Lithuania, May 26, 1904. He was taken to Paris at age 3; entered the Paris Cons. when he was 13, taking the premier prix at 15; his principal mentors were Moszkowski and Cortot. He devoted much time to teaching while making occasional appearances principally as a recitalist; was a prof. at the Paris Cons. (1950–77); also gave master classes. He acquired a remarkable reputation for his insightful interpretations of Chopin and Ravel. In 1968 he was made a member of the Légion d'honneur. With H. Jourdan-Morhange, he publ. *Ravel d'après Ravel* (Lausanne, 1953; Eng. tr., 1988, as *Ravel According to Ravel*).

Perlman, Itzhak, brilliant Israeli-born American violinist; b. Tel Aviv, Aug. 31, 1945. He was stricken with polio when he was 4, which left his legs paralyzed; thereafter he had to walk on crutches. Despite this handicap, he began to play the violin and gave regular recitals at Tel Aviv. In 1958 he was discovered in Israel by Ed Sullivan, the TV producer, and appeared on his show in N.Y. on Feb. 15, 1959. Perlman's courage and good humor endeared him to the public at once. He remained in N.Y., where his parents soon joined him, and was accepted as a scholarship student in the classes of Galamian and DeLay at the Juilliard School of Music. He made his professional American debut on March 5, 1963, playing with the National Orch. Assn. in N.Y. In 1964 he won 1st prize in the Leventritt Competition, which carried, besides the modest purse ($1,000), a significant bonus—an appearance with the N.Y. Phil. It also brought about a lasting friendship with Isaac Stern, who promoted him with all the enthusiasm of a sincere admirer. Perlman's career was assured: he toured the U.S. from coast to coast in 1965–66 and toured Europe in 1966–67. He also began to teach, and in 1975 was appointed to the faculty of Brooklyn College. He seemed to be overflowing with a genuine love of life; he played not only so-called serious works but also rag music and jazz; with Stern and Pinchas Zukerman, he indulged in public charivari on television to which he furnished enjoyable commentaries. And he became quite a habitué of the White House, being particularly popular with President Reagan, who savored Perlman's show-biz savvy and who, in 1986, awarded him the U.S. Medal of Freedom. As a virtuoso, Perlman has demonstrated an extraordinary mastery of technical resources. His playing is equally infused with a genuine humanity and joie de vivre.

BIBL.: C. Behrman, *Fiddler to the World: The Inspiring Life of I. P.* (White Hall, Va., 1992).

Perlongo, Daniel, American composer and teacher; b. Gaastra, Mich., Sept. 23, 1942. He was a student of Bassett and Finney at the Univ. of Mich. (M.M., 1966), and of Petrassi at the Accademia di Santa Cecilia in Rome (1966–68). He won the American Prix de Rome and was in residence at the American Academy in Rome (1970–72). Upon returning to the U.S., he became an assoc. prof. of composition and theory at Indiana Univ. of Pa. In 1980 and 1995 he held NEA fellowships.

WORKS: ORCH.: *7 Pieces* (1965); *Myriad* (1968); *Changes* for Wind Ensemble (1970); *Ephemeron* (1972); *Variations* for Chamber Orch. (1973); *Voyage* for Chamber Orch. (1975); Concertino for Chamber Orch. (1980); *Montalvo Overture* for Wind Ensemble (1984); *Lake Breezes* for Chamber Orch. (1990); *Preludes and Variations* for Wind Ensemble (1991); Piano Concerto (1992); *Shortcut from Bratislava* (1994); *2 Movements* (1995); *Sunburst* for Clarinet and Orch. (1995). **CHAMBER:** *Episodes* for Double Bass (1966); *Movement* for 8 Players (1967); *Intervals* for String Trio (1967); *For Bichi* for Percussion Quartet (1968); *Movement in Brass* for 12 Brass Instruments (1969); *Process 7, 5, 3 for 6 in 12* for Flute, Oboe, Clarinet, and 3 Percussion (1969); 2 string quartets (*Semblance*, 1973; 1983); *Tre Tempi* for Flute, Clarinet, Horn, Violin, and Cello (1971); *Solo* for Violin (1971); *Fragments* for Flute and Cello (1972); *Ricercar* for Oboe, Clarinet, and Bassoon (1976); *Summer Music* for Brass Quintet (1978); *Aureole* for Saxophone Quartet (1979); *Soliloquy* for Bass Clarinet (1980); *A Day at Xochimilco* for Wind Quintet and Piano (1987); *Novella* for Trombone and Organ (1988); *Arcadian Suite* for Horn and Harp (1993). **KEYBOARD: PIANO:** Sonata (1965); *Serenade* (1977); Suite (1988); *First Set* (1990). **ORGAN:** *Tapestry* (1981). **VOCAL:** *Missa Brevis* for Chorus (1967); *6 Songs* for Soprano and Piano (1980); *By Verse Distills* for Mezzo-soprano, Clarinet, Violin, and Piano (1989); *3 Songs* for Chorus (1994).

Pernet, André, French bass; b. Rambervillers, Jan. 6, 1894; d. Paris, June 23, 1966. He studied at the Paris Cons. with Gresse. He made his operatic debut in 1921 in Nice; was a principal member of the Paris Opéra (1928–45); appeared there again in 1948; also sang at the Paris Opéra-Comique (1931–48). His most notable roles included Don Giovanni, Boris Godunov, and Méphistophélès; he also sang in many contemporary operas.

Pernerstorfer, Alois, Austrian bass-baritone; b. Vienna, June 3, 1912; d. there, May 12, 1978. He took courses with Lierhammer and Josef Krips at the Vienna Academy of Music. In 1936 he made his operatic debut as Biterolf in Graz, where he sang until 1939. He was a member of the Volksoper (1939–45) and State Opera (from 1945) in Vienna. He also sang in Zürich (1947–51), and at the Salzburg Festivals (from 1948), the Glyndebourne Festival (1951), and the Metropolitan Opera in N.Y. (debut as Sparafucile, Nov. 15, 1951). He was known for such roles as Figaro, Leporello, King Marke, Alberich, Pogner, and Baron Ochs.

Perosi, Don Lorenzo, distinguished Italian composer of church music; b. Tortona, Dec. 21, 1872; d. Rome, Oct. 12, 1956. He studied at the Milan Cons. (1892–93); also took courses at Haberl's School for Church Music at Regensburg (1893). He became maestro di cappella at Imola, and then at San Marco in Venice (1894–98). He was ordained a priest in 1895; in 1898 he became music director of the Sistine Chapel and leader of the papal choir; he resigned this post in 1915 owing to a severe mental disturbance; spent some time in a sanatorium (1922–23), after which he nominally held these duties again until his death, although with many relapses. Shortly after his 80th birthday, he led a performance of his oratorio *Il natale del Redentore* at the Vatican before Pope Pius XII (Dec. 28, 1952). He was a self-denying and scholarly worker for the cause of the cultivation of a pure church style, both in composition and in performance, and was esteemed above all others as a church musician at the Vatican.

WORKS: ORATORIOS: *La passione di Cristo secondo San Marco* (I, *La cena del Signore*; II, *L'orazione al monte*; III, *La morte del Redentore*; Milan, Dec. 2, 1897); *La trasfigurazione del nostro Signore Ges Cristo* (Venice, March 20, 1898); *La risurrezione di Lazaro* (Venice, July 27, 1898); *La risurrezione di Cristo* (Rome, Dec. 13, 1898); *Il natale del Redentore* (Como, Sept. 12, 1899); *L'entrata di Cristo in Gerusalemme* (Milan, April 25, 1900); *La strage degli innocenti* (Milan, May 18, 1900); *Mosè* (Milan, Nov. 16, 1901); *Dies iste* (Rome, Dec. 9, 1904); *Transitus animae* (Rome, Dec. 18, 1907); *In patris memoriam* (1909; Naples, May 15, 1919); *Giorni di tribulazione* (Milan, Oct. 1916). **OTHER:** Some 40 masses, with Organ; *Requiem*, with Instrumental Accompaniment; *Stabat Mater* for Solo Voices, Chorus, and Orch.; *Vespertina oratio* for Solo Voices, Chorus, and Orch.; about 150 motets, *Psalms*, etc.; 2 symphonic poems: *Dovrei non piangere* and *La festa del villaggio*; a series of 8 orch. pieces, each named after an Italian city: *Roma, Firenze, Milano, Venezia, Messina, Tortona, Genoa*, and *Torino*; Piano Concerto; 2 violin concertos; chamber music; many organ works.

BIBL.: L. Seytre, *L'Abbé P.: Sa biographie, son oeuvre* (Nice, 1901); A. Damerini, *L. P.* (Rome, 1924); A. Della Corte, *L. P.* (Turin, 1936); A. Paglialunga, *L. P.* (Rome, 1952); M. Glinsky, *L. P.* (Milan, 1953); M. Rinaldi, *L. P.* (Rome, 1967); M. Bruni, *L. P., el cantore evangelico* (Turin, 1972).

Perrault, Michel (Brunet), Canadian composer, percussionist, and conductor; b. Montreal, July 20, 1925. He studied theory and timpani with Louis Decair at the McGill Cons. in Montreal (1941–43), oboe with Réal Gagnier at the Montreal Cons. (1943–44), and harmony with Gabriel Cusson (1943–46). After further training with Boulanger, Honegger, and Dandelot at the École Normale de Musique in Paris (1946–47), he returned to Montreal and completed his studies with Conrad Letendre. He was a timpanist in the Montreal Sym. Orch. (1944–46) and the Little Sym. of Montreal (1945–46). He was a percussionist with the Montreal Sym. Orch. (1949–65), and also served as its assistant conductor (1957–60). From 1949 to 1968 he was active as a composer and conductor with the CBC. He also was music director of Les Grands Ballets Canadiens (1958–62). In his music, Perrault is a convinced traditionalist who finds inspiration in Quebec folk music.

WORKS: BALLETS: *Commedia del arte* (1958); *Sea Gallows* (1958); *Suite canadienne* (1965). **ORCH.:** *Les Trois Cones* for Cello and Orch. (1949); *La Belle Rose* for Cello and Orch. (1952); *Fête et parade* for Trumpet and Orch. (1952); *Monologues* for Strings (1954); *Margoton* for Harp and Orch. (1954); *Le Saucisson canadien* for 4 Saxophones and Strings (1955); *Pastiche espagnol* for Trumpet and Orch. (1956); *Pastiche tzigane* for 2 Trumpets and Orch. (1957); *Berubée* for Piano and Orch. (1959); *Jeux de quartes* for Harp and Orch. (1961); *Serenata per tre fratelli* for 3 Horns and Orch. (1962); Double Bass Concerto (1962); *Homage*, overture (1966); Horn Concerto (1967). **CHAMBER:** Violin Sonata (1946); Saxophone Quartet (1953); Piano Trio (1954); Sextet for Clarinet, Harp, and String Quartet (1955); *Georgian Rhapsody* for Alto Saxophone and Piano (1987). **VOCAL:** *Esquisses en plein air* for Soprano and String Orch. (1954); songs. **OTHER:** Pieces for jazz ensemble.

Perry, Janet, American soprano; b. Minneapolis, Dec. 27, 1944. She received piano and violin lessons at home, and appeared in local young people's theater productions; then studied voice with Eufemia Giannini Gregory at the Curtis Inst. of Music in Philadelphia (B.M., 1967). In 1969 she made her operatic debut as Zerlina at the Linz Landestheater, remaining on its roster until 1971; following guest appearances at the Gärtnerplatztheater in Munich and at the Cologne Opera, she became a member of the Bavarian State Opera in Munich. She further made guest appearances in opera and concert in Hamburg, Düsseldorf, Paris, Zürich, Vienna, Berlin, Glyndebourne, and Salzburg. In 1983 she made her formal U.S. debut as Despina in Washington, D.C. Among her most successful roles were Susanna, Pamina, Constanze, Gilda, and Sophie.

Perry, Julia (Amanda), black American composer; b. Lexington, Ky., March 25, 1924; d. Akron, Ohio, April 29, 1979. After studying at the Westminster Choir College in Princeton, N.J. (M.Mus., 1948), she took a course in composition with Dallapiccola at the Berkshire Music Center in Tanglewood (summer, 1951); then took composition lessons, intermittently, with Boulanger in Paris and again with Dallapiccola in Italy (1952–56); she also attended classes in conducting in Siena (1956–58). She received 2 Guggenheim fellowships and an award from the National Inst. of Arts and Letters.

WORKS: OPERAS: *The Bottle* (n.d.); *The Cask of Amontillado* (N.Y., Nov. 20, 1954); *The Selfish Giant*, opera-ballet (1964); *3 Warnings* (n.d.). **ORCH.:** *Short Piece* (1952); 12 syms. (1959–72), including No. 11, *Soul Symphony* (1972); *Pastoral* for Flute and Strings (1959); 2 piano concertos (1964); Violin Concerto (1964); *Module* (1975). **CHAMBER:** *Homunculus C.F.* for Harp and 10 Percussion (1960); Woodwind Trio; String Quartet; etc. **VOCAL:** *Chicago*, cantata for Baritone, Narrator, Chorus, and Orch. (1948); *Ruth*, cantata for Chorus and Organ (1950); *Stabat Mater* for Alto and Strings (1951); numerous songs.

Persen, John, Norwegian composer; b. Porsanger, Norwegian Lapland, Nov. 9, 1941. He studied composition with Finn Mortensen at the Oslo Cons. (1968–73). From 1974 to 1976 he was president of Ny Musikk, the Norwegian section of the ISCM. His music follows the lines of the cosmopolitan avant-garde, with a mixture of jazz, rock, sonorism, and special effects (*ČSV* requires 2 pistol shots to be heard at the end of the work). Persen is a nationalistic Lapp from the extreme Polar North; some titles of his compositions are political in their allusions.

WORKS: *Øre-Verk* for Orch. (1972; the title suggests both "earache" and "aural work"); *Orkesterwerk II* (Oslo, May 4, 1974); *Sámesiidat—ČSV* for Chorus (1976; based on a "joik," a Lapp folk song); *ČSV* for Orch. (1976; Oslo, March 22, 1977; the ambiguous acronym of the title means either "Dare to show that you are a Lapp" or "the secret Lapp host"); *Stykket har ingen tittel* (i.e., This Piece Has No Name), subtitled *Dreietoner for Orchestra* (1976; Trondheim, Jan. 20, 1977); *Music for Resting Marching Band* for Brass Band (1977); *Under Kors og Krone* (Under Cross and Crown), opera (1978–85; based on a revolt of the Lapp population against the authorities in the late 19th century); *TTT-Things Take Time*, electronic piece (1985); *Enn!* for Chorus, 2 Narrators, and Tape (1986); *NotaBene*, electronic piece (1988); *Fuglan Veit*, electronic pieces (1988–89); *The John Persen's Guide to the Orchestra* (1990); *til a'Lisa* for Mezzo-soprano, Piano, and Percussion (1995).

Persichetti, Vincent (Ludwig), remarkable American composer and pedagogue whose finely amalgamated instrumental and symphonic music created an image of classical modernity; b. Philadelphia, June 6, 1915; d. there, Aug. 13, 1987. His father was a native of Abruzzi, Italy, who emigrated to the U.S. in 1894. His mother was of German descent, hailing from Bonn. Persichetti's middle name was given to him not to honor Beethoven but to commemorate his maternal grandfather who owned a saloon in Camden, N.J. He studied piano, organ, double bass, tuba, theory, and composition as a youth; began his career as a professional musician when he was only 11 years old; became a church organist at 15. He took courses in composition with Russell King Miller at the Combs Cons. (Mus.B., 1936); then served as head of the theory and composition dept. there; concurrently studied conducting with Reiner at the Curtis Inst. of Music (diploma, 1938) and piano with Samaroff and composition with Nordoff at the Philadelphia Cons. (M.Mus., 1941; D.Mus., 1945); also studied composition with Harris at Colorado College. From 1941 to 1947 he was head of the theory and composition dept. of the Philadelphia Cons.; in 1947, joined the faculty of the Juilliard School of Music in N.Y.; in 1963, was named chairman of the composition dept. there. In 1952 he became director of music publishing of Elkan-Vogel, Inc. With F. Schreiber, he wrote a biography of William Schuman (N.Y., 1954). He publ. a valuable manual, *Twentieth Century Harmony: Creative Aspects and Practice* (N.Y., 1961). His music is remarkable for its polyphonic skill in fusing the ostensibly incompatible idioms of Classicism, Romanticism, and stark modernism, while the melodic lines maintain an almost Italianate diatonicism in a lyrical manner. The skillful concatenation of ostensibly mutually exclusive elements created a style that was characteristically Persichetti's. He was not interested in program music or in any kind of descriptive tonal works (exceptionally, he wrote a piece of background music for the Radio City Music Hall organs which was performed in 1969). His significance for American music, therefore, is comprised in his 9 syms., and, most particularly, in his 12 piano sonatas and 6 piano sonatinas. Although he stood far from the turmoil of musical politics, he unexpectedly found himself in the center of a controversy when he was commissioned by the 1973 Presidential Inauguration Committee to write a work for narrator and orch. for a perf. at President Richard Nixon's 2nd inauguration. Persichetti selected the text of a speech by President Abraham Lincoln, his 2nd inaugural address, but, surprisingly, objections were raised by certain groups to the passionate denunciation of war in the narrative, at a time when the Vietnam War was very much in the news. The scheduled performance by the Philadelphia Orch. was hurriedly canceled, and the work's premiere was deferred to a performance by the St. Louis Sym. Orch. on Jan. 25, 1973. In 1987 Persichetti contracted a cancer of the lungs, but even when racked by disease he continued to work on his last opus, *Hymns and Responses for the Church Year, Vol. II.* He requested that his body be donated to medical science. His devoted wife suffered a stroke and died on Thanksgiving Day in the same year. Her monograph on her husband (1960) remains unpublished.

WORKS: OPERA: *Parable XX: The Sibyl* (1976; Philadelphia, April 13, 1985). **ORCH.:** Piano Concertino (1941; Rochester, N.Y., Oct. 23, 1945); 9 syms.: No. 1 (1942; Rochester, N.Y., Oct. 21, 1947), No. 2 (1942), No. 3 (1946; Philadelphia, Nov. 21, 1947), No. 4 (1951; Philadelphia, Dec. 17, 1954), No. 5, for Strings (1953; Louisville, Aug. 28, 1954), No. 6, for Band (St. Louis, April 16, 1956), No. 7, *Liturgical* (1958; St. Louis, Oct. 24, 1959), No. 8 (Berea, Ohio, Oct. 29, 1967), and No. 9, *Sinfonia Janiculum* (1970; Philadelphia, March 5, 1971); *Dance Overture* (1942; Tokyo, Feb. 7, 1948); *Fables* for Narrator and Orch. (1943; Philadelphia, April 20, 1945); *The Hollow Men* for Trumpet and Strings (1944; Germantown, Pa., Dec. 12, 1946); *Serenade No. 5* (Louisville, Nov. 15, 1950); *Divertimento* for Band (N.Y., June 16, 1950); *Fairy Tale* (1950; Philadelphia, March 31, 1951); *Psalm* for Band (Louisville, May 2, 1952); *Pageant* for Band (Miami, May 7, 1953); *Serenade No. 11* for Band (1960; Ithaca, N.Y., April 19, 1961); *Bagatelles* for Band (Hanover, N.H., May 21, 1961); Piano Concerto (1962; Hanover, N.H., Aug. 2, 1964); *So Pure the Star*, chorale prelude for Band (Durham, N.C., Dec. 11, 1962); *Introit* for Strings (1964; Kansas City, Mo., May 1, 1965); *Masquerade* for Band (1965; Berea, Ohio, Jan. 23, 1966); *Turn Not Thy Face*, chorale prelude for Band (1966; Ithaca, N.Y., May 17, 1967); *Night Dances* (Kiamesha Lake, N.Y., Dec. 9, 1970); *O Cool is the Valley*, poem for Band (1971; Columbus, Ohio, Feb. 5, 1972); *Parable IX* for Band (1972; Des Moines, April 6, 1973); *A Lincoln Address* for Narrator and Orch. (1972; St. Louis, Jan. 25, 1973; also for Narrator and Band, Russelville, Arks., Feb. 1, 1974); Concerto for English Horn and Strings (N.Y., Nov. 17, 1977); *O God Unseen*, chorale prelude for Band (Winston-Salem, N.C., Nov. 4, 1984). **CHAMBER:** *Serenade No. 1* for 10 Winds (1929), *No. 3* for Violin, Cello, and Piano (1941), *No. 4* for Violin and Piano (1945), *No. 6* for Trombone, Viola, and Cello (1950), *No. 9* for 2 Recorders (1956), *No. 10* for Flute and Harp (1957), *No. 12* for Tuba (1961), *No. 13* for 2 Clarinets (1963), and *No. 14* for Oboe (1984); 4 string quartets (1939; 1944; 1959; *Parable X*, 1972); Suite for Violin and Cello (1940); Violin Sonata (1940); *Concertato* for Piano Quintet (1940); *Fantasy* for Violin and Piano (1941); *Pastoral* for Woodwind Quintet (1943; Philadelphia, April 20, 1945); *Vocalise* for Cello and Piano (1945); *King Lear* for Woodwind Quintet, Timpani, and Piano (1948; 1st perf. as *The Eye of Anguish*, Martha Graham Dance Co., Montclair, N.J., Jan. 31, 1949); Sonata for Solo Cello (1952); Piano Quintet (1954; Washington, D.C., Feb. 4, 1955); *Little Recorder Book* (1956); *Infanta Marina* for Viola and Piano (1960); *Masques* for Violin and Piano (1965); *Parable I* for Flute (1965), *II* for Brass Quintet (1968), *III* for Oboe (1968), *IV* for Bassoon (1969), *VII* for Harp (1971), *VIII* for Horn (1972), *XI* for Alto Saxophone (1972), *XII* for Piccolo (1973), *XIII* for Clarinet (1973), *XIV* for Trumpet (1973), *XV* for English Horn (1973), *XVI* for Viola (1974), *XVII* for Double Bass (1974), *XVIII* for Trombone (1975), *XXI* for Guitar (1978), *XXII* for Tuba (1981), and *XXIII* for Violin, Cello, and Piano (1981). **KEYBOARD: PIANO:** *Serenade No. 2* (1929), *No. 7* (1952), and *No. 8* for Piano, 4-hands (1954); 12 sonatas (1939, 1939, 1943, 1949, 1949, 1950, 1950, 1950, 1952, 1955, 1965, 1980); *Poems* (3 vols., 1939, 1939, 1941); Sonata for 2 Pianos (1940); *Variations for an Album* (1947); 6 sonatinas (1950, 1950, 1950, 1954, 1954, 1954); Concerto for Piano, 4-hands (1952); *Parades* (1952); *Little Piano Book* (1953); *Parables XIX* (1975); *Reflective Studies* (1978); *Little Mirror Book* (1978); *4 Arabesques* (1978); *3 Toccatinas* (1979); *Mirror Etudes* (1979). **ORGAN:** Sonatine (1940); Sonata (1960); *Shimah b'koli* (1962); *Drop, Drop Slow Tears*, chorale prelude (1966); *Parable VI* (1971); *Do Not Go Gentle* (1974); *Auden Variations* (1977); *Dryden Liturgical Suite* (1980); *Song of David* (1981). **HARPSICHORD:** 8 sonatas (1951, 1981, 1981, 1982, 1982, 1982, 1983, 1984); *Parable XXIV* (1982); *Little Harpsichord Book* (1983); *Serenade No. 15* (1984). **VOCAL:** *Magnifi-*

cat and Nunc dimittis for Chorus and Piano (1940); *Canons* for Chorus (1947); *2 Cummings Choruses* for 2 Voices and Piano (1948); *Proverb* for Chorus (1948); *2 Cummings Choruses* for Women's Chorus (1950); *Hymns and Responses for the Church Year* for Chorus (1955; Philadelphia, Oct. 7, 1956); *Seek the Highest* for Voices and Piano (1957); *Song of Peace* for Men's Chorus and Piano (1959); Mass for Chorus (1960; N.Y., April 20, 1961); *Stabat Mater* for Chorus and Orch. (1963; N.Y., May 1, 1964); *Te Deum* for Chorus and Orch. (1963; Philadelphia, March 15, 1964); *Spring Cantata* for Women's Chorus and Piano (1963; Boston, April 1, 1964); *Winter Cantata* for Women's Chorus, Flute, and Marimba (1964; Troy, N.Y., April 9, 1965); *4 Cummings Choruses* for 2 Voices and Piano (1964); *Celebrations* for Chorus and Wind Ensemble (River Falls, Wis., Nov. 18, 1966); *The Pleiades* for Chorus, Trumpet, and Strings (1967; Potsdam, N.Y., May 10, 1968); *The Creation* for Soprano, Alto, Tenor, Baritone, Chorus, and Orch. (1969; N.Y., April 17, 1970); *Love* for Women's Chorus (1971); *Glad and Very* for 2 Voices (1974); *Flower Songs* (Cantata No. 6) for Chorus and Strings (1983; Philadelphia, April 20, 1984); several songs, including the major cycle *Harmonium* for Soprano and Piano, after poems of Wallace Stevens (1951; N.Y., Jan. 20, 1952).

BIBL.: D. and J. Patterson, *V. P.: A Bio-Bibliography* (Westport, Conn., 1988).

Persinger, Louis, eminent American violinist and teacher; b. Rochester, Ill., Feb. 11, 1887; d. N.Y., Dec. 31, 1966. He began his violin studies at an early age in Colorado, making his public debut when he was 12; then studied with Hans Becker at the Leipzig Cons. (1900–04), with Ysaÿe in Brussels, and with Thibaud in Paris. He toured Belgium and Germany; served as concertmaster of the Berlin Phil. (1914–15) and the San Francisco Sym. Orch. (1915–16). He then led his own string quartet and served as director of San Francisco's Chamber Music Society (1916–28); subsequently devoted himself mainly to teaching; in 1930 he joined the staff of the Juilliard School of Music in N.Y. He achieved a great reputation as a teacher who subordinated technical demands to the paramount considerations of formal balance and expressiveness of the melodic line. Among his pupils were Yehudi Menuhin, Ruggiero Ricci, and Isaac Stern.

BIBL.: Y. Menuhin, "L. P.," *Juilliard Review Annual* (N.Y., 1966–67).

Pertile, Aureliano, noted Italian tenor; b. Montagnana, Nov. 9, 1885; d. Milan, Jan. 11, 1952. He studied with Orefice and Fugazzola. He made his operatic debut in *Martha* in Vicenza in 1911; then sang in Naples (1914), at Milan's La Scala (1916), and the Teatro Colón in Buenos Aires (1918); made his Metropolitan Opera debut in N.Y. as Cavaradossi in *Tosca* (Dec. 1, 1921). He then returned to La Scala, where he gained renown for his portrayal of Faust in *Mefistofele* (1922); was a leading tenor there until 1937; also appeared at London's Covent Garden (1927–31); retired from the stage (1946); taught at the Milan Cons. (from 1945). He was esteemed for such roles as Andrea Chénier, Manrico, Radames, Canio, and Don Alvaro; he created Boito's Nerone and Mascagni's Nerone.

Pešek, Libor, admirable Czech conductor; b. Prague, June 22, 1933. He received his training at the Prague Academy of Music, graduating in 1956. He was founder-conductor of the Prague Chamber Harmony (1959) and the Prague Sebastian Orch. (1965). From 1969 to 1975 he was music director of the Frysk Orch. in the Netherlands, and also of the Czech State Chamber Orch. in Prague from 1969 to 1977. He was music director of the Overijssels Phil. in the Netherlands as well from 1975 to 1979. In 1981–82 he was conductor of the Slovak Phil. in Bratislava. In 1982 he was made conductor-in-residence of the Czech. Phil. in Prague. He also was principal conductor and artistic adviser of the Royal Liverpool Phil. from 1987 to 1995, which he led on its first tour of the U.S. in 1992. As a guest conductor, he appeared with many of the leading European and North American orchs. He is an especially distinguished interpreter of the 19th- and 20th-century Czech repertoire.

Peskanov, Mark, Russian-born American violinist; b. Odessa, Aug. 30, 1956. At age 7, he entered the Stoliarsky School of Music in Odessa, where he was a pupil of Boris Brant. In 1973 he emigrated to the U.S., where he pursued studies with Dorothy DeLay at the Juilliard School in N.Y. (B.A., 1979). On Nov. 1, 1977, he made his debut as soloist in Wieniawski's 1st Violin Concerto with Rostropovich and the National Sym. Orch. in Washington, D.C. During the 1978–79 season, he made his London debut with Rostropovich and the London Phil. In 1985 he won the Avery Fisher Career Grant and the 1st Isaac Stern Award of N.Y.'s Carnegie Hall. After appearing as soloist with the Philadelphia Orch. at the Mann Music Center in 1987, he received the 1st Frederick R. Mann Young Artist Award. Subsequently, he was engaged as soloist by many principal American orchs.; he also appeared as a chamber music artist in the U.S. and abroad. He made frequent appearances with the Chamber Music Soc. of Lincoln Center in N.Y.

Peskó, Zoltán, Hungarian-born Italian conductor and composer; b. Budapest, Feb. 15, 1937. He studied at the Budapest Academy of Music (graduated, 1962); also took courses in composition with Petrassi and in conducting with Ferrara in Italy, and in conducting with Boulez in Switzerland (1963–66). He was assistant conductor to Maazel and the Deutsche Oper and Berlin Radio Sym. Orch. in the Western sector (1966–69); then conducted at the Berlin State Opera in East Berlin (1969–73); also served on the faculty at the Berlin Hochschule für Musik (1969–72). From 1974 to 1976 he was chief conductor of the Teatro Comunale in Bologna; subsequently was chief conductor of Venice's Teatro La Fenice (1976–77) and Milan's Orchestra Sinfonica della RAI (1978–82). He wrote some orch. music, chamber works, and keyboard pieces.

Pesonen, Olavi, Finnish composer and teacher; b. Helsinki, April 8, 1909. He studied with Ilmari Krohn and Leevi Madetoja at the Univ. of Helsinki (M.A., 1932); also took courses with Arthur Willner in Vienna and Seiber in London, and studied organ with Ramin in Leipzig. He then devoted himself to teaching and composing in Helsinki. His works follow along traditional lines.

WORKS: DRAMATIC: *Havahtuminen* (Awakening), melodrama for Narrator and Orch. (1936); *Huutokauppa* (Auction), music to A. Leinonen's play (1949). **ORCH.:** *Pieni sarja* (Little Suite; 1936); *Juhla-alkusoitto* (Festive Overture; 1938; rev. 1946); *Fuga fantastica* (1948; based on the organ piece, 1939); *Tanhusoitto* (Folk Dances; 1949); 2 syms. (1949, 1953); *Suite ancienne* (1978); *Pieces* for Strings, after Finnish folk songs (1980); *In dulci jubilo* for Strings (1981). **OTHER:** Various works for Chorus and Orch., including the cantatas *Ah autuus suuri* (O Great Bliss; 1939; rev. 1978), *Koulukantaatti* (School Cantata; 1941), and *Silenivät pitkospuut* (The Causeway Became Smoother; 1966); a cappella choruses; songs; organ music, including *Fuga fantastica* (1939; also for Orch., 1948) and *Jesu dulcis memoria* (1981).

Peters (real name, **Petermann**), **Roberta,** outstanding American soprano; b. N.Y., May 4, 1930. She studied voice with William Pierce Hermann. At the age of 20, she made her operatic debut with the Metropolitan Opera in N.Y. as Zerlina in *Don Giovanni* on Nov. 17, 1950, as a substitute on short notice; she subsequently remained on its roster for more than 40 years. She also sang with the opera companies of San Francisco and Chicago, at Covent Garden in London, at the Salzburg Festivals, and at the Vienna State Opera. She was one of the leading coloratura sopranos of her generation; also appeared with success on television, films, and in musical comedies. She was briefly married to **Robert Merrill**. With Louis Biancolli, she wrote *A Debut at the Met* (1967).

Petersen, Wilhelm, German composer and teacher; b. Athens, March 15, 1890; d. Darmstadt, Dec. 18, 1957. He studied in Germany and worked as a theater conductor; served in the German army during World War I; in 1922, settled in Darmstadt as a teacher. He wrote the opera *Der goldne Topf* (Darmstadt,

March 29, 1941); 5 syms. (1921, 1923, 1934, 1941, 1957); 3 violin sonatas; 3 string quartets; several sacred choruses and songs. He was highly regarded in Darmstadt as a musician and pedagogue. In 1972 a Wilhelm Petersen Society was founded to memorialize his work.

BIBL.: A. Petersen, *W. P., Skizze seines Wesens und Lebens* (Darmstadt, 1962).

Peterson, Wayne, American composer and teacher; b. Albert Lea, Minn., Sept. 3, 1927. He studied with Early Rymer (piano) and with Paul Fetler, Earl George, and James Aliferis (composition) at the Univ. of Minnesota (B.A., 1951; M.A., 1953; Ph.D., 1960); also with Lennox Berkeley and Howard Ferguson at the Royal Academy of Music in London. He served on the music faculty of the Univ. of Minnesota (1953–54), Chico (Calif.) State College (1959–60), and San Francisco State College (later Univ.; from 1960). He held numerous NEA awards. In 1989–90 he held a Guggenheim fellowship (1989–90). In 1992 he won the Pulitzer Prize in Music for his orch. works *The Face of the Night, the Heart of the Dark.*

WORKS: ORCH.: *Introduction and Allegro* (1953); *Free Variations* (1954–58); *Exaltation, Dithyramb and Caprice* (1959–60); *Cataclysms* (1968); *Clusters and Fragments* for Strings (1969); *Transformations II* for Chamber Orch. (1985; San Francisco, April 11, 1986); *Trilogy* (1987; Saratoga, Calif., June 18, 1988); *The Widening Gyre* (1990; N.Y., Feb. 10, 1991); *The Face of the Night, the Heart of the Dark* (1990–91). **CHAMBER:** *Metamorphosis* for Wind Quintet (1967); *Phantasmagoria* for Flute, Clarinet, and Double Bass (1968); *Capriccio* for Flute and Piano (1973); *Transformations* for String Quartet (1974); *Encounters* for 9 Players (1976); *An Interrupted Serenade* for Flute, Harp, and Cello (1978); Sextet (1982); String Quartet (1983–84); *Ariadne's Thread* for Harp, Flute, Clarinet, Horn, Percussion, and Violin (1985); *Duodecaphony* for Viola and Cello (1986–87).

Peterson-Berger, (Olof) Wilhelm, esteemed Swedish music critic, teacher, and composer; b. Ullånger, Feb. 27, 1867; d. Östersund, Dec. 3, 1942. He studied with J. Dente and O. Bolander at the Stockholm Cons. (1886–89); then in Dresden with Scholtz (piano) and Kretzschmar (composition). He eventually settled in Stockholm, where he became active as a pedagogue and music critic of *Dagens Nyheter* (1896–1908; 1910–20; 1921–30). His opera *Arnljot* was one of the finest Swedish operas in the national tradition; his other notable works included his 3rd Sym., Violin Concerto, songs, and piano pieces.

WORKS: DRAMATIC: *Sveagaldrar,* festival play for the silver jubilee of the accession of Oscar II (1897); 4 music dramas (all 1st perf. in Stockholm): *Ran* (1899–1900; May 20, 1903), *Arnljot* (1907–09; April 13, 1910), *Domedagsprofeterna* (The Prophets of Doom; 1912–17; Feb. 21, 1919), and *Adils och Elisiv* (1921–24; Feb. 27, 1927); *Lyckan* (Luck), fairy opera (Stockholm, March 27, 1903). **ORCH.:** 5 syms.: No. 1, *Baneret* (The Banner; 1889–90; 1903; Stockholm, Feb. 23, 1904; rev. 1932–33), No. 2, *Sunnanfärd* (The Journey to the South; 1910; Göteborg, March 22, 1911), No. 3, *Same Ätnam* (Lappland; 1913–15; Stockholm, Dec. 11, 1917), No. 4, *Holmia* (1929; Stockholm, April 9, 1930), and No. 5, *Solitudo* (1932–33; Stockholm, April 11, 1934); 3 orch. suites: *I somras* (Last Summer; 1903), *Earina* (Spring; 1917), and *Italiana* (1922); *Romans* for Violin and Orch. (1915); Violin Concerto (1928; Stockholm, Feb. 6, 1929). **CHAMBER:** 2 violin sonatas (1887, 1910); Suite for Violin and Piano (1896); over 100 piano pieces. **VOCAL: CANTATAS:** *Norrbotten* (1921); *Operakantaten* (1922; rev. 1935–36); *Soluppgång* (1929). Also 40 songs for choruses; nearly 100 solo songs.

WRITINGS: *Svensk Musikkultur* (1911); *Richard Wagner som kulturföreteelse* (Richard Wagner as a Phenomenon of Civilization; 1913; Ger. tr., 1917, as *Richard Wagner als Kulturerscheinung*). A selection of his essays was publ. in Stockholm in 2 vols. (1923); another, in one vol., in Östersund (1951). His reminiscences were publ. posthumously (Uppsala, 1943).

BIBL.: B. Carlberg, *W. P.-B.* (Stockholm, 1950); S. Beite, *W. P.-B.: En känd och okänd tondiktare* (Östersund, 1965); G. Norell, *W. P.-B. och dikten* (vol. 1, Arboga, 1991).

Petit, Raymond, French music critic and composer; b. Neuilly-sur-Seine, July 6, 1893; d. Annemasse, Haute-Savoie, Sept. 25, 1976. He studied with Tournemire in Paris; then devoted himself mainly to music criticism.

WORKS: OPERA: *La Sulamithe.* **ORCH.:** *Suite grave* (1920). **CHAMBER:** 2 *méditations* for String Quartet (1921); *Dialogue* for 2 Violins. **VOCAL:** *Hymnus* for Voice and Flute (1924); *Il cantico del sole* for Voice and Wind Instruments (Frankfurt am Main, July 3, 1927); songs.

Petkov, Dimiter, Bulgarian composer and conductor; b. Smolyan, May 4, 1919. He studied composition with Veselin Stoyanov at the State Academy of Music in Sofia, graduating in 1950; then went to Moscow for postgraduate studies in theory at the Cons. (1952–54). He taught theory at the State Academy of Music in Sofia (1949–52; 1954–58) and was director of the National Opera Theater; later served as president of the Union of Bulgarian Composers (1972–80).

WORKS: DRAMATIC: *The Winding Path,* children's operetta (1956; Michailovgrad, Oct. 29, 1975); *Restless Hearts,* musical comedy (1960). **CHAMBER:** *3 Polyphonic Pieces* for Flute, Clarinet, and Bassoon (1953). **VOCAL:** *The Sparks of October* for Soloists, Children's Chorus, and Orch. (1967); *Rozhan Comes Down from Rhodopa,* oratorio (1965); 5 cantatas: *September Legend* (1953), *Communists* (1956), *Requiem for a Sailor* (1967), *Cantata about Paissy* (1973), and *Festive Cantata* (1974); choruses; folk song arrangements.

BIBL.: E. Pavlov, *D. P.* (Sofia, 1987).

Petra-Basacopol, Carmen, Romanian composer and teacher; b. Sibiu, Sept. 5, 1926. She studied philosophy at the Univ. of Bucharest (1945–49); then took courses with Jora (composition and counterpoint), Rogalski (orchestration), and Constantinescu (harmony) at the Bucharest Cons. (1949–56); attended courses in new music in Darmstadt (1968); later completed her training at the Sorbonne in Paris (Ph.D., 1976, with the diss. *L'Originalité de la musique roumaine à travers les oeuvres d'Enesco, Jora et Constantinesco;* publ. in Bucharest, 1979). She taught at the Bucharest Cons. (from 1962). She received the Order of Cultural Merit (1969) and the Georges Enesco composition prize of the Romanian Academy (1980). Her music is lyrical, with colorful and effective instrumentation.

WORKS: BALLETS: *Fata şi masca* (The Girl and the Mask; 1970); *Ciuleandra* (1985–86). **ORCH.:** Sym. No. 1 (1956); *Tara de piatra* (Stone Country; 1959); Piano Concerto (1961); *Symphonic Triptych* (1962); 2 violin concertos (1963, 1965); Concertino for Harp, Kettledrums, and Strings (1975); Concerto for Strings (1981); Cello Concerto (1982). **CHAMBER:** Suite for Flute and Piano (1950); Cello Sonata (1952); Trio for Violin, Cello, and Piano (1959); Sonata for Flute and Harp (1961); *Divertissement* for Harp, Wind Quintet, Double Bass, and Xylophone (1969); Trio for Flute, Clarinet, and Bassoon (1974); Quartet for Flute, Violin, Cello, and Piano (1978); Suite for Cello (1981); Trio for Flute, Clarinet, and Harp (1987); piano pieces. **VOCAL:** Choral music; songs.

Petrassi, Goffredo, outstanding Italian composer and teacher; b. Zagarolo, near Rome, July 16, 1904. He went to Rome and had private piano lessons with Bastini; then commenced the study of harmony with Donato (1925); subsequently entered the Conservatorio di Santa Cecilia (1928), where he studied composition with Bustini (diploma, 1932) and organ with Germani (diploma, 1933). He taught at the Accademia di Santa Cecilia (1934–36), where he also received instruction from Molinari; was general director of Venice's Teatro La Fenice (1937–40). After teaching composition at the Conservatorio di Santa Cecilia (1939–59), he taught again at the Accademia di Santa Cecilia (1959–74); also taught at Siena's Accademia Musicale Chigiana (1966–67). He publ. the vol. *Autoritratto* (Rome, 1991). Despite the late beginning, Petrassi acquired a solid technique of composition; the chief influence in his music was that of Casella; later he became interested in 12-tone procedures.

WORKS: DRAMATIC: OPERAS: *Il Cordovano* (1944–48; Milan, May 12, 1949; rev. 1958; Milan, Feb. 18, 1959); *La morte dell'aria* (1949–50; Rome, Oct. 24, 1950). **BALLETS:** *La follia di Orlando* (1942–43; Milan, April 12, 1947); *Il ritratto di Don Chisciotte* (1945; Paris, Nov. 21, 1947). **ORCH.:** *Divertimento* (1930); *Ouverture da concerto* (1931); *Passacaglia* (1931); *Partita* (1932; Rome, April 2, 1933); 8 concertos: No. 1 (1933–34; Rome, March 31, 1935), No. 2 (1951; Basel, Jan. 24, 1952), No. 3, *Récréation concertante* (1952–53; Aix-en-Provence Festival, July 23, 1953), No. 4 for Strings (1954; Rome, April 28, 1956), No. 5 (Boston, Dec. 2, 1955), No. 6, *Invenzione concertata*, for Brass, Strings, and Percussion (1956–57; London, Sept. 9, 1957), No. 7 (1961–64; Bologna, March 18, 1965), and No. 8 (1970–72; Chicago, Sept. 28, 1972); Piano Concerto (1936–39; Rome, Dec. 10, 1939); Flute Concerto (1960; Hamburg, March 7, 1961); *Estri*, chamber sym. for 15 Performers (Hanover, N.H., Aug. 2, 1967; as a ballet, Spoleto, July 11, 1968); *Frammento* (1983). **CHAMBER:** *Sinfonia, Siciliana e Fuga* for String Quartet (1929); *Introduzione e allegro* for Violin and Piano (1933; also with 11 Instruments); *Preludio, Aria e Finale* for Cello and Piano (1933); *Sonata da camera* for Harpsichord and 10 Instruments (1948); *Dialogo angelico* for 2 Flutes (1948); *Musica a 2* for 2 Cellos (1952); String Quartet (1958); *Serenata* for Flute, Viola, Double Bass, Harpsichord, and Percussion (1958); String Trio (1959); *Serenata II*, trio for Harp, Guitar, and Mandolin (1962); *Musica di Ottoni* for Brass and Timpani (1963); *3 per 7* for 3 Performers on 7 Wind Instruments (1966); *Ottetto di Ottoni* for 4 Trumpets and 4 Trombones (1968); *Souffle* for 1 Performer on 3 Flutes (1969); *Elogio per un'Ombra* for Violin (1971); *Nunc* for Guitar (1971); *Ala* for Flute and Harpsichord (1972); *4 odi* for String Quartet (1973–75); *Fanfare* for 3 Trumpets (1974–76); *Alias* for Guitar and Harpsichord (1977); *Sestina d'autunno* for 6 Instruments (1981–82); *Inno* for 4 Trumpets, 4 Cornets, and Trombone (1984); *Duetto* for Violin and Viola (1985). **PIANO:** *Siciliana e marcetta* for 2 Pianos (1930); *Toccata* (1933); *Invenzioni* for 2 Pianos (1944); *Oh les beaux jours!* (1976); *Petite pièce* (1976). **VOCAL:** *3 Choruses* for Chorus and Small Orch. (1932); *Psalm IX* for Chorus, Strings, Brass, 2 Pianos, and Percussion (1934–36); *Magnificat* for Soprano, Chorus, and Orch. (1939–40); *Coro di morti*, dramatic madrigal for Men's Chorus, Brass, Double Basses, 3 Pianos, and Percussion (Venice, Sept. 28, 1941); *2 liriche di Saffo* for Voice, and Piano or 11 Instruments (1941); *Quattro inni sacri* for Tenor, Baritone, and Organ (1942; also for Tenor, Baritone, and Orch., Rome, Feb. 22, 1950); *Noche oscura*, cantata (Strasbourg, June 17, 1951); *Nonsense* for Chorus, after Edward Lear (1952); *Propos d'Alain* for Baritone and 12 Performers (1960); *Sesto nonsenso* for Chorus, after Edward Lear (1964); *Mottetti per la Passione* for Chorus (1966); *Beatitudines*, chamber oratorio for Baritone and 5 Instruments, in memory of Martin Luther King, Jr. (Fiuggi, July 17, 1969); *Orationes Christi* for Chorus, Brass, 8 Violins, and 8 Cellos (1974–75; Rome, Dec. 6, 1975); *Laudes creaturarum* for Reciter and 6 Instruments (1982); *Tre cori sacri* for Chorus (1980–83); *Kyrie* for Chorus and Strings (1990).

BIBL.: J. Weissmann, *G. P.* (Milan, 1957; 2nd ed., 1980); C. Annibaldi, *G. P.: Catalogo delle opere e bibliografia* (Milan, 1971); G. Zosi, *Ricerca e sintesi nell'opera di G. P.* (Rome, 1978); E. Restagno, ed., *P.* (Turin, 1986); S. Sablich et al., *A G. P., per i suoi 90 anni* (Milan, 1994; in Italian and Eng.).

Petrauskas, Kipras, Lithuanian tenor, brother of **Mikas Petrauskas**; b. Vilnius, Nov. 23, 1885; d. there, Jan. 17, 1968. He studied with his brother. He appeared in his brother's opera *Birute* (Vilnius, Nov. 6, 1906); then was a singer at the Imperial Opera in St. Petersburg (1911–20); also appeared in Berlin, Paris, and Milan, and made a tour of the U.S. He returned to Lithuania before World War II. In 1950 he received the Stalin Prize.

Petrauskas, Mikas, Lithuanian composer, brother of **Kipras Petrauskas;** b. Kaunas, Oct. 19, 1873; d. there, March 23, 1937. He studied organ with his father and was a student at the St. Petersburg Cons. of Rimsky-Korsakov. During the abortive revolution in 1905, he was implicated in political activities and imprisoned. After his release, he brought out the opera *Birute* (Vilnius, Nov. 6, 1906). In 1907 he went to the U.S. He settled in Boston in 1914, where he founded the Lithuanian Cons. and brought out the operas *The Devil Inventor* (May 20, 1923) and *Egle, Queen of the Snakes* (May 30, 1924; he sang the role of the King of the Snakes). In 1930 he returned to Lithuania.

Petrella, Clara, Italian soprano; b. Greco Milanese, March 28, 1918; d. Milan, Nov. 19, 1987. She studied with her sister, Micaela Oliva, and with Giannina Russ in Milan. She made her operatic debut in 1939 as Li at the Teatro Puccini in Milan; then sang in several provincial Italian theaters. She made her first appearance at La Scala in Milan in 1941, becoming a principal member of the company in 1947; also sang in Rome and Naples; in addition, she appeared in concerts. She was particularly noted for her performances of contemporary operas by Italian composers.

Petri, Egon, eminent German pianist and pedagogue of Dutch descent; b. Hannover, March 23, 1881; d. Berkeley, Calif., May 27, 1962. His father, Henri Wilhelm Petri (1856–1914), was a Dutch violinist who served as concertmaster in Hannover and of the Leipzig Gewandhaus Orch.; his mother was a singer. He studied violin and organ, as well as piano, from an early age; began piano lessons with Carreño, later studying with Buchmayer, Draeseke, and Busoni; also received composition lessons from Kretzchmar. Having pursued a career as an orch. violinist and as a member of his father's string quartet, he launched his career as a piano virtuoso in 1902; subsequently toured extensively in Europe; was also active as a teacher, serving on the faculties of the Royal Manchester College of Music (1905–11) and the Berlin Hochschule für Musik (1921–26); then taught in Zakopane. On Jan. 11, 1932, he made his U.S. debut in N.Y., then performed on both sides of the Atlantic until the outbreak of World War II; also taught at Boston's Malkin Cons. (1934–35). After World War II, he resumed his extensive tours. Having taught at Cornell Univ. (1940–46), he then settled in California to teach at Mills College in Oakland (1947–57) and at the San Francisco Cons. of Music (1952–62). He made his farewell concert appearance in a recital in 1960. As Busoni's foremost student, he followed in his mentor's grand manner of piano virtuosity. His performances of Bach and Liszt were formidable; he also championed the works of Alkan and Medtner as well as Busoni.

Petri, Michala, gifted Danish recorder player; b. Copenhagen, July 7, 1958. She began to play at the incredible age of 3 and appeared on Danish radio when she was 5; made her concert debut as a soloist in Copenhagen in 1969. She formed a trio with her mother, a harpsichordist, and her cellist brother, and toured widely with it. She studied with Ferdinand Conrad at the Hannover Staatliche Hochschule für Musik (1970–76). In addition to chamber music performances, she toured extensively as a soloist; made her U.S. debut with N.Y.'s 92nd St. Y Chamber Orch. in 1982, and first played in Japan in 1984. Her repertoire ranges from the early Baroque era to contemporary music; she has commissioned a number of composers to write works for her.

Petrić, Ivo, Slovenian composer; b. Ljubljana, June 16, 1931. He studied composition with Škerjanc and conducting with Švara at the Ljubljana Academy of Music (1950–58). In 1962 he founded a group dedicated to the promotion of new music; was ed.-in-chief of the publ. division of the Union of Slovenian Composers (from 1970), serving as secretary of the latter (1969–80). His compositions are Romantic in their inspiration, and agreeably modernistic in technical presentation.

WORKS: ORCH.: 3 syms. (1954, 1957, 1960); *Concerto Grosso* for Strings (1955); Concerto for Flute and Chamber Orch. (1955–57); Divertimento (1956); Concerto for Clarinet and Chamber Orch. (1958); *Concertante Suite* for Bassoon and Strings (1959); *Concertante Overture* (1960); *Concertante Music* for Wind Quintet, Timpani, and Strings (1962); *Croquis sonores* for Harp and Chamber Ensemble (1963); *Mosaics* for Clarinet and Chamber Ensemble (1964); *Symphonic Mutations* (1964); *Epitaph* for Harp, Clarinet, Violin, Cello, Strings, and Percussion (1965); *Integrali v barvah* (Integrals in Colors; 1968); *Burlesque pour les temps passés* for Trombone and Orch. (1969); *Music Concertante* for Piano and Orch. (1970); *Dialogues concertants* for Cello and Orch. (1972); *3 Images* for Violin and Orch. (1973); *Nocturnes and Games* (1973); *Fresque symphonique* (1973); *Episodes lyriques* for Oboe and Chamber Orch. (1974); *Gemini Concerto* for Violin, Cello, and Orch. (1975); *Thus Played Kurent*, symphonic poem for Viola and Orch. (1976); *Jeux concertants* for Flute and Orch. (1978); *Hommage à Johannes* (1978); *Toccata concertante* for 4 Percussionists and Orch. (1979); *Concerto for Orchestra* (1982); *The Picture of Dorian Gray* (1984); Trumpet Concerto (1986); *Dresden Concerto* for 15 Strings (1987); *Moods and Temperaments* (1987); *After So Many Years*, symphonic reminiscences (1989); *Toccata* (1989); *Gallus Metamorphoses* (1992); *Spring Concertino* for Percussionist and Orch. (1993); *Jubilee Concerto for Celea* for Strings (1994); *Scottish Impressions* (1995). **CHAMBER:** 3 wind quintets (1953, 1959, 1974); Bassoon Sonata (1954); Oboe Sonata (1955); Flute Sonata (1955); Clarinet Sonata (1956–57); *7 Movements* for 7 Instruments (1963); *Jeux à 3* for Cello, Percussion, and Harp (1965); *Jeux à 4* for Flute, Piano, Harp, and Cello (1966); *Little Chamber Concerto* for Oboe, English Horn, Bass Clarinet, Horn, Harp, Piano, and String Quartet (1966); *5 Movements* for Oboe, and Harp or String Quartet (1967); *Intarzije* (Inlaid Work) for Wind Trio, Horn, Trumpet, Trombone, Percussion, and String Quintet (1968); *Quatuor 69* for String Quartet (1969); *Capriccio* for Cello and 8 Instruments (1974); Violin Sonata (1976); Concerto for 5 Percussionists (1978); *Episodes poétiques* for Oboe and 9 Instruments (1979); *Leipzig Chamber Music* for 5 Players (1983); *Quatuor 1985* for String Quartet (1985); *Fantasies and Nocturnes* for Violin, Clarinet, and Piano (1986); *Rondeau* for Piano Quartet (1987); Chamber Sonata No. 1, . . . *meditations and nocturnes* . . . , for Oboe, Viola, Bass Clarinet, and Harp (1991) and No. 2, . . . *capriccio* . . . , for Flute, English Horn, Violin, Cello, and Harpsichord (1991); *Portrait d'automne* for String Quartet (1992); *Quatres pièces d'été* for Violin and Harp (1992); Alto Saxophone Sonata (1992); *Deux portraits* for 2 Violins and Piano (1993); Trio Sonata for Flute, Viola, and Double Bass (1993); *Burlesque* for 4 Saxophones (1994); *Elégie* for English Horn and String Quartet (1994); *Hommage à Serge Prokofiev*, variations for Oboe, Clarinet, Violin, Viola, and Double Bass (1994). **VOCAL:** *Pierre de la mort*, cantata (1962); *The Song of Life* for Mezzo-soprano and Orch. (1981).

Petridis, Petros (John), eminent Turkish-born Greek composer; b. Nigdé, July 23, 1892; d. Athens, Aug. 17, 1977. He studied in Constantinople at the American Robert College; received instruction in piano from Hegey and in harmony from Selvelli; then went to Paris and read law at the Sorbonne and political science at the École Libre des Sciences Politiques (1911–14); later studied with Wolff (1914) and Roussel (1919). He became a naturalized Greek citizen (1913); subsequently was a music critic for English, American, and Greek publications, dividing his time between Paris and Athens. His use of Byzantine modalities, adorned with contemporary harmonies, reveals the influence of Greek culture.

WORKS: DRAMATIC: *Zefyra*, opera (1923–25; rev. 1958–64); *Iphigenia in Tauris*, incidental music to Euripides' play (Athens, Oct. 15, 1941); *O pramateftis* (The Pedlar), ballet (1941–43; Athens, May 6, 1944). **ORCH.:** *Kleftikoi horoi* (Cleftic Dances; 1922); 5 syms.: No. 1, *Greek* (1928–29; Athens, Jan. 16, 1933), No. 2, *Lyric* (1941; Athens, Dec. 11, 1949), No. 3, *Parisian* (1944–46; Geneva, 1949), No. 4, *Doric* (1941–43; Athens, May 20, 1945), and No. 5, *Pastoral* (1949–51; rev. 1972–73); *Concerto Grosso* for Winds and Timpani (c.1929); *Greek Suite* (1929–30; Athens, Nov. 27, 1932); *Dighenis Akritas* (1933–39; Athens, May 17, 1940); *Studies* for Small Orch. (Athens, Jan. 29, 1934); 2 piano concertos (1934, rev. c.1948; 1937); *Vyzantini thyssia* (Byzantine Offering; 1934–35); *Ionian Suite* (c.1935); Cello Concerto (1936); *Chorale and Variations on Kyrie ton dynameon* for Strings (1940; Athens, June 28, 1941); *Chorale and Variations on Christos anesti for* Strings (1941–43; Athens, May 20, 1945); *Largo* for Strings (Athens, Feb. 6, 1944); *Issagoghi pentihimi ke heroiki* (Funeral and Heroic Overture; 1944; Athens, May 20, 1945); Violin Concerto (1972); Concerto for 2 Pianos (1972). **CHAMBER:** Piano Trio (c.1933); String Quartet (1951; unfinished); piano pieces. **VOCAL:** *Hayos Pavlos*, oratorio for Narrator, Soloists, Chorus, and Orch. (1950; Athens, June 29, 1951); *Requiem ya ton aftorkratora* (Requiem for the Emperor) for Soloists, Chorus, and Orch. (1952–64); songs.

Petrobelli, Pierluigi, prominent Italian musicologist; b. Padua, Oct. 18, 1932. He studied composition with Pedrollo at Padua's Liceo Musicale and musicology with Ronga at the Univ. of Rome (arts degree, 1957). Upon receiving a Fulbright grant, he continued his studies with Lockwood, Mendel, and Strunk at Princeton Univ. (M.A., 1961), and also took courses at Harvard Univ. and the Univ. of Calif., Berkeley. He was librarian-archivist at Parma's Istituto di Studi Verdiani (1964–69); became a lecturer (1968) and later a reader in music history at the Univ. of Parma; was named librarian of the Pesaro Cons. (1970). He received his libera docenza in 1972, and then served as a lecturer in music (1973–77) and reader in musicology (1977–80) at King's College, London. In 1980 he was made director of the Istituto di Studi Verdiani in Parma; from 1981 to 1983 he served as prof. of music history at the Univ. of Perugia; then was a prof. at the Univ. "La Sapienza" of Rome (from 1983). With W. Rhem, he ed. the critical edition of Mozart's *Il Re pastore* for the *Neue Mozart Ausgabe*.

WRITINGS: *Giuseppe Tartini: Le fonti biografiche* (Vienna, London, and Milan, 1968); with S. Durante, *Storia della musica al Santo di Padova* (Vicenza, 1990); *Tartini, le sue idee e il suo tempo* (Lucca, 1992); *Music in the Theater: Essays on Verdi and Other Composers* (Princeton, N.J., 1994).

Petrov, Andrei (Pavlovich), Russian composer; b. Leningrad, Sept. 2, 1930. He studied composition at the Leningrad Cons. with Evlakhov, graduating in 1954. In 1957 he joined the Communist party. In his music he follows the general precepts of socialist realism, ethnic in thematic material, euphonious in harmony, energetic in rhythm, stimulating in modalities, optimistic in contemporary philosophy, and realistic in treatment.

WORKS: DRAMATIC: OPERA: *Peter the First* (Leningrad, 1975). **BALLETS:** *The Magic Apple Tree* (Leningrad, Nov. 8, 1953); *The Station Master*, after Pushkin (Leningrad, May 9, 1955); *The Shore of Hope* (1959); *The Creation of the World* (1971); *Pushkin* (1979). **MUSICAL:** *We Want to Dance* (1967). **ORCH.:** *Pioneer Suite* (1951); *Sport Suite* (1953); *Radda and Lioko*, symphonic poem (1954); *Festive Overture* (1955); *Songs of Today*, symphonic cycle (1965); *Poem*, in memory of those fallen in the siege of Leningrad, for Strings, Organ, 4 Trumpets, 2 Pianos, and Percussion (1965). **VOCAL:** *The Poem of a Young Pioneer* for Soprano, Mezzo-soprano, and Orch. (1959); *Poème pathétique* for Baritone, 2 Pianos, and Percussion, commemorating the centennial of Lenin's birth, after Soviet poets (1970); *Pushkin*, vocal-poetic sym. for Narrator, Mezzo-soprano, Chorus, 2 Harps, and Orch. (1978).

BIBL.: A. Kenigsberg, *A. P.* (Moscow, 1959); L. Markhasev, *A. P., Familiar and Unfamiliar* (Leningrad, 1974).

Petrov, Ivan (Ivanovich), prominent Russian bass; b. Irkutsk, Feb. 29, 1920. He studied with A. Mineyev at the Glazunov Music College in Moscow (1938–39). He then joined the Kozlovsky opera group; became a soloist with the Moscow Phil. in 1941. In 1943 he joined the staff of the Bolshoi Theater in Moscow; his most celebrated interpretation was in the title role of *Boris Godunov*, inviting comparisons with Chaliapin. He made several tours as a member of the Opera of the Bolshoi Theater in Europe, Japan, and the U.S.

BIBL.: I. Nazarenko, *I. P.* (Moscow, 1957).

Petrov, Nikolai (Arnoldovich), outstanding Russian pianist; b. Moscow, April 14, 1943. He studied with Tatiana Kestner at the Moscow Central Music School (1951–61), then continued his training with Yakov Zak at the Moscow Cons. (graduated, 1967). He won 2nd prize in both the Van Cliburn (1962) and Queen Elisabeth of Belgium (1964) competitions; then pursued a remarkable career as a virtuoso, touring widely in the Soviet Union and Eastern Europe; also performed in Western Europe and North America. As a result of the renewed U.S.-Soviet cultural exchange program, he appeared as soloist with Yuri Termirkanov and the N.Y. Phil. at N.Y.'s Avery Fisher Hall in 1986. His repertoire ranges from Classical to contemporary Soviet music; he has given first performances of works by Khachaturian, Khrennikov, Shchedrin, and other Soviet composers, and also tackled the original version of the Liszt transcriptions of the Paganini études.

Petrovics, Emil, Hungarian composer; b. Zrenjanin, Yugoslavia, Feb. 9, 1930. He went to Budapest (1941) and studied at the Academy of Music with Sugár (1949–51), Viski (1951–52), and Farkas (1952–57). He was director of the Petőfi Theater (1960–64); taught at the Academy of Music (from 1969); served as director of the Hungarian State Opera (1986–90). His opera *C'est la guerre* (1961) was awarded the Kossuth Prize in 1966.

WORKS: DRAMATIC: OPERAS: *C'est la guerre* (Budapest Radio, Aug. 17, 1961; 1st stage perf., Budapest, March 11, 1962); *Lysistrate*, after Aristophanes (1962; rev. 1971); *Bün és bűnhődés* (Crime and Punishment), after Dostoyevsky (Budapest, Oct. 26, 1969). **BALLET:** *Salome* (1978). **ORCH.:** Flute Concerto (1957); Sym. for Strings (1962). **CHAMBER:** *Cassazione* for Brass (1953); String Quartet (1958); *4 Self-Portraits in Masks* for Harpsichord (1958); Wind Quintet (1964); *Passacaglia in Blues* for Bassoon and Piano (1964; as a ballet, Budapest, 1965); *Deux mouvements* for 1 or 2 Cimbaloms (1977); *Rhapsody No. 1* for Violin (1982) and *No. 2* for Viola (1983). **VOCAL:** 2 oratorios: *Jónás könyve* (The Book of Jonah; 1966) and *Ott essem el én* (Let Me Die There) for Men's Chorus and Orch. (1972); cantatas; choruses.

Petrushka, Shabtai (Arieh), German-born Israeli composer; b. Leipzig, March 15, 1903. He studied at the Inst. of Technology in Berlin-Charlottenburg, and received an engineering diploma; studied music at the Leipzig Cons. He was a violinist in various Berlin theater orchs. (1928–33); after the advent of the Nazis in 1933, he was a member of the orch. of the Jewish Kulturbund, for which he wrote incidental music. He emigrated to Palestine in 1938; served as an arranger and conductor of the Palestine Broadcasting Service (1938–48); then was assistant director of music of the Israel Broadcasting Service (1948–58) and head of the music division of the Israel Broadcasting Authority (1958–68); from 1969 to 1981 he taught at the Rubin Academy of Music in Jerusalem.

WORKS: String Trio (1939); *4 Movements* for Symphonic Band (1953); *5 Oriental Dances* for Orch. (1954); *The Broken Blackboard*, children's musical (1969); *Piccolo Divertimento* for Symphonic Band (1970); *3 Jewish Melodies* for 2 Flutes and 3 Clarinets (1972); *Hebrew Melodies* for Wind Quintet (1974); Wind Quartet (1975); *Jewish Melodies* for Brass Quintet (1974); *3 Sephardic Songs* for Women's Chorus (1976); Sonatina for Horn and String Quartet (1982); *Little Suite* for Band (1986).

Petrželka, Vilém, noted Czech composer and pedagogue; b. Královo Pole, near Brünn, Sept. 10, 1889; d. Brno, Jan. 10, 1967. He studied with Janáček at the Brno Organ School (1905–08) and in 1910 became his assistant at the school; subsequently took private lessons in Prague with Vítězslav Novák. He taught at the Phil. Society School in Brno (1914–19), and in 1919 became a prof. at the newly formed Brno Cons. In his compositions, he continued the national tradition of modern Moravian music; he was mainly influenced by Janáček, but expanded his resources and on occasion made use of jazz rhythms, quarter-tones, and other modernistic procedures.

WORKS: DRAMATIC: *Námořník Mikuláš* (Mariner Nicholas), symphonic drama for Narrator, Soli, Chorus, Organ, Jazz Band, and Orch. (1928; Brno, Dec. 9, 1930); *Horník Pavel* (The Miner Paul), opera (1935–38). **ORCH.:** *Věčný návrat* (Eternal Return), symphonic poem (1922–23; Brno, Feb. 10, 1924); *Suite* for Strings (1924–25); *Dramatic Overture* (1932; Brno, March 26, 1933); *Partita* for Strings (1934); *Sinfonietta* (1941; Brno, Jan. 22, 1942); Violin Concerto (1943–44; rev. 1946); *Pastoral Sinfonietta* (1951–52); Sym. (1956). **CHAMBER:** 5 string quartets (1909; 1914–15; *Fantasy*, 1927; Suite, 1932; 1947); *Z intimních chvil* (From Intimate Moments) for Violin and Piano (1918); Sonata for Solo Cello (1930); Violin Sonata (1932); Piano Trio (1936–37); *4 Impromptus* for Violin and Piano (1939–40); *Divertimento* for Wind Quintet (1941); *Serenade* for Nonet or Chamber Orch. (1945); *2 Pieces* for Cello and Piano (1947); Violin Sonatina (1953); *Miniatures* for Wind Quintet (1953); *2 Pieces* for Viola and Piano (1959); *Fantasy* for String Quartet (1959); *Suite* for String Trio (1961). **PIANO:** Sonata (1908); *Songs of Poetry and Prose* (1917); *Suite* (1930); *5 nálad* (5 Moods; 1954). **VOCAL:** *Modlitba k slunci* (A Prayer to the Sun), cantata (1921; Brno, Feb. 13, 1922); *Štafeta* (The Courier), 4 songs for Voice and String Quartet (1926–27); choruses, including the popular patriotic part song for Men's Chorus *To je má zem* (This Is My Land; 1940); song cycles; folk song arrangements.

BIBL.: L. Firkušný, *V. P.* (Prague, 1946).

Pettersson, Gustaf Allan, remarkable sui generis Swedish composer; b. Västra Ryd, Sept. 19, 1911; d. Stockholm, June 20, 1980. His father was a blacksmith; his mother was a devout woman who also sang; the family moved to Stockholm, and lived in dire poverty. Pettersson sold Christmas cards and bought a violin from his meager returns. He also practiced keyboard playing on a church organ. In 1930 he entered the Stockholm Cons., studying violin and viola with J. Ruthström and theory with H. M. Melchers. From 1940 to 1951 he played viola in the Stockholm Concert Society Orch., and also studied composition with Otto Olsson, Tor Mann, and Blomdahl. In his leisure hours he wrote poetry; he set 24 of his poems to music. In 1951 he went to Paris to study with Honegger and Leibowitz. Returning to Sweden, he devoted himself to composition in large forms. His music is permeated with dark moods, and he supplied deeply pessimistic annotations to his syms. and other works. In 1963 he began suffering from painful rheumatoid arthritis; he stubbornly continued to compose while compulsively proclaiming his misfortunes in private and in public print. He described himself as "a voice crying out, drowned in the noise of the times." The Stockholm Phil. played several of his syms., but when his 7th Sym., originally scheduled for its American tour in 1968, was taken off the program, Pettersson, wrathful at this callous defection, forbade performance of any of his music in Sweden. Stylistically, Pettersson's music is related to Mahler's symphonic manner, in the grandiosity of design and in the passionate, exclamatory dynamism of utterance. Most of his syms. are cast in single movements, with diversity achieved by frequent changes of mood, tempo, meter, and rhythm. Characteristically, all, except No. 10, are set in minor keys.

WORKS (all 1st perf. in Stockholm unless otherwise given): **ORCH.:** 2 violin concertos: No. 1 for Violin, String Quartet, and Orch. (1949; March 10, 1951) and No. 2 (1977–78; Jan. 25, 1980); 3 concertos for Strings: No. 1 (1949–50; April 6, 1952), No. 2 (1956; Dec. 1, 1968), and No. 3 (1956–57; March 14, 1958); 16 syms.: No. 1 (1950–51; withdrawn with instructions to perform it only posthumously), No. 2 (1952–53; Swedish Radio, May 9, 1954), No. 3 (1954–55; Goteborg, Nov. 21, 1956), No. 4 (1958–59; Jan. 27, 1961), No. 5 (1960–62; Nov. 8, 1963), No. 6 (1963–66; Jan. 21, 1968), No. 7 (1966–67; Oct. 13, 1968), No. 8 (1968–69; Feb. 23, 1972), No. 9 (1970; Göteborg, Feb. 18, 1971), No. 10 (1971–72; Swedish TV, filmed Dec. 16, 1973, for delayed broadcast of Jan. 14, 1974), No. 11 (1971–73; Bergen, Oct. 24, 1974), No. 12, *De döda på torget* (The Dead on the Square) for Chorus and Orch., after Pablo Neruda (1973–74; Sept. 29, 1977),

No. 13 (1976; Bergen, June 7, 1978), No. 14 (1978; Nov. 26, 1981), No. 15 (1978; Nov. 19, 1982), and No. 16, originally Concerto for Alto Saxophone and Orch. (Feb. 24, 1983); *Symphonic Movement* (1st perf. as *Poem*, Swedish TV, Dec. 24, 1976). **CHAMBER:** *2 Elegies* for Violin and Piano (1934); *Fantasy Piece* for Viola (1936); *4 Improvisations* for Violin, Viola, and Cello (1936); *Andante espressivo* for Violin and Piano (1938); *Romanza* for Violin and Piano (1942); *Fugue in E* for Oboe, Clarinet, and Bassoon (1948); 7 sonatas for 2 Violins (1951–52). **VOCAL:** *6 songs* for Voice and Piano (1935); *24 Barfotasånger* (24 Barefoot Songs) for Voice and Piano (1943–45); *Vox humana*, 18 songs for Soprano, Alto, Tenor, Baritone, Chorus, and String Orch., after American Indians (1974; March 19, 1976).

BIBL.: L. Aare, *A. P.* (Stockholm, 1978); P. Rapoport, *Opus Est: 6 Composers from Northern Europe* (London, 1978); idem, *A. P.* (Stockholm, 1981); M. Kube, ed., *A. P. (1911–1980): Texte-Materialien-Analysen* (Hamburg, 1994).

Petyrek, Felix, Czech composer and teacher; b. Brünn, May 14, 1892; d. Vienna, Dec. 1, 1951. After training with Godowsky and Sauer (piano), he studied with Schrecker (composition) and Adler (musicology) at the Univ. of Vienna (graduated, 1919). He taught at the Salzburg Mozarteum (1919–21), the Berlin Hochschule für Musik (1921–23), the Athens Odeon Athenon (1926–30), the Stuttgart Cons. (1930–39), the Cons. and Univ. in Leipzig (1939–49), and the Vienna Academy of Music (1949–51). In his melodic writing, he adopted the scale of alternating whole tones and semitones as a compromise between tonality and atonality.

WORKS: DRAMATIC: *Die arme Mutter und der Tod*, musical fairy play (1923); *Der Garden des Paradieses*, opera (1923–41; Leipzig, Nov. 1, 1942); pantomimes. **ORCH.:** Sym. (1919); *Sinfonietta* (1921); 2 concertos for 2 Pianos and Orch. (1931, 1949). **CHAMBER:** String Quartet (1913); Violin Sonata (1913); String Quartet (1914); Piano Trio (1921); *Divertimento* for 8 Winds (1923); Sextet for Clarinet, String Quartet, and Piano (Donaueschingen, July 30, 1922); piano pieces. **VOCAL:** Choral music; songs.

Petzold, Rudolf, German composer and teacher; b. Liverpool (of a German father and English mother), July 17, 1908; d. Michaelshoven, Nov. 17, 1991. He was a pupil of Jarnach at the Cologne Hochschule für Musik (1930–33), where he taught (1937–38). After teaching at the Frankfurt am Main Hochschule für Musik (1941–42), he again taught at the Cologne Hochschule für Musik (1946–70), where he also was its deputy director (1960–69).

WORKS: ORCH.: 3 syms.: (1942, 1953, 1956); Concerto for Violin and Strings (1960). **CHAMBER:** 4 string quartets (1932, 1948, 1955, 1972); Piano Trio (1961); Cello Sonata (1964); Sonata for Solo Violin (1965); Piano Sonata (1967); Violin Sonata (1969). **VOCAL:** Sacred cantatas; choruses.

Petzoldt, Richard (Johannes), German musicologist; b. Plauen, Nov. 12, 1907; d. Leipzig, Jan. 14, 1974. He studied at the Univ. of Berlin, where his teachers were Abert, Schering, Moser, Sachs, Hornbostel, Schünemann, and Blume; received his Ph.D. in 1933 with the diss. *Die Kirchenkompositionen und weltlichen Kantaten Reinhard Keisers* (publ. in Düsseldorf, 1935). He ed. the *Allgemeine Musikalische Zeitung* (1935–39) and the periodical *Musik in der Schule* (1949–59). He was a prof. of music history at the Univ. of Leipzig (1952–67). His publs. include *Beethoven* (Leipzig, 1938; 2nd ed., 1947); *Schubert* (Leipzig, 1940; 2nd ed., 1947); *Schumann* (Leipzig, 1941; 2nd ed., 1947); *Mozart* (Wiesbaden, 1948; 2nd ed., 1965); *Johann Sebastian Bach und Leipzig* (Leipzig, 1950); *Die Oper in ihrer Zeit* (Leipzig, 1956); iconographies of Bach (Leipzig, 1950; 2nd ed., 1970), Verdi (Leipzig, 1951), Beethoven (Leipzig, 1952; 7th ed., rev., 1968), Schubert (Leipzig, 1953), Tchaikovsky (Leipzig, 1953), Handel (Leipzig, 1954; 2nd ed., 1960), Glinka (Leipzig, 1955), Schumann (Leipzig, 1956), Mozart (Leipzig, 1956; 3rd ed., 1961), *Beethoven* (Leipzig, 1970; 2nd ed., 1973), and Schütz (Kassel, 1972).

Peyser, Joan (née **Gilbert**), American musicologist, editor, author, and journalist; b. N.Y., June 12, 1931. She played piano in public at 13; majored in music at Barnard College (B.A., 1951); studied musicology with Lang at Columbia Univ. (M.A., 1956). She then devoted herself mainly to musical journalism; enlivened the music pages of the Sunday *N.Y. Times* with book reviews and breezy colloquies with composers; wrote scripts for the television series "The World of Music"; acted as musical adviser to the N.Y. City Board of Education. She publ. the popular book *The New Music: The Sense Behind the Sound* (N.Y., 1971; 2nd ed., rev., 1981 as *Twentieth Century Music: The Sense Behind the Sound*); created considerable excitement in the music world with her biography *Boulez: Composer, Conductor, Enigma* (N.Y., 1976); trying to penetrate the eponymous enigma, she undertook a journey to the interior of France, where she interviewed family and friends of her subject, with a fervor suggesting that Boulez was indeed the 4th B of music. From 1977 to 1984 she was ed. of the *Musical Quarterly*, the first woman to occupy this position; during her tenure, she attempted to veer away from the prevalent musicological sesquipedalianism toward plain diction. Among her other publs. are *The Orchestra: Origins and Transformations* (N.Y., 1986), *Leonard Bernstein: A Biography* (N.Y., 1987), and *The Memory of All That: The Life of George Gershwin* (N.Y., 1993).

Pfatteicher, Carl F(riedrichs), American organist and teacher; b. Easton, Pa., Sept. 22, 1882; d. Philadelphia, Sept. 29, 1957. He studied theology in Germany and at Harvard Univ. (Th.D., 1912). He taught Latin and German at various schools; then was a prof. of music at Phillips Academy in Andover, Mass. (1912–47); from 1949 he was a lecturer in musicology at the Univ. of Pa. He publ. a number of useful school manuals and collections of sacred music, among them *The Christian Church Year in Part Songs* (1915); *The Christian Church Year in Chorals* (1917); and *Thesaurus musicae sacrae* (1920); *The Oxford American Hymnal* (1930). He was co-ed. of *The Office Hymns of the Church in Their Plainsong Settings and The Church Organist's Golden Treasury.*

Pfitzner, Hans (Erich), eminent German composer and conductor; b. Moscow (of German parents), May 5, 1869; d. Salzburg, May 22, 1949. He studied piano with James Kwast and composition with Iwan Knorr at the Hoch Cons. in Frankfurt am Main; in 1899 he eloped with Kwast's daughter and took her to England, where they were married. In 1892–93 he taught piano and theory at the Cons. of Koblenz; then served as assistant conductor of the Municipal Theater in Mainz (1894–96); from 1897 to 1907 he was on the faculty of the Stern Cons. in Berlin; concurrently he conducted at the Theater Westens (1903–06). During the 1907–08 season he led the renowned Kaim Concerts in Munich. From 1908 to 1918 he was in Strasbourg as municipal music director and also served as dean at the Strasbourg Cons.; from 1910 to 1916 he conducted at the Strasbourg Opera. During the 1919–20 season he was music director of the Munich Konzertverein; from 1920 to 1929 he led a master class at the Berlin Academy of Arts; from 1929 to 1934 he taught composition at the Akademie der Tonkunst in Munich. Being of certified German stock, though born in Russia, Pfitzner was favored by the Nazi authorities, and became an ardent supporter of the Third Reich; he reached the nadir of his moral degradation in dedicating an overture, *Krakauer Begrüssung*, to Hans Frank, the murderous Gauleiter of occupied Poland in 1944. After the collapse of Hitler's brief millennium, Pfitzner had to face the Denazification Court in Munich in 1948; owing to his miserable condition in both body and soul, he was exonerated. He was taken to a home for the aged in Munich, and later was transferred to Salzburg, where he died in misery. Eventually, his body was honorably laid to rest in a Vienna cemetery.

In his better days, Pfitzner was hailed in Germany as a great national composer. He presented a concert of his works in Berlin on May 12, 1893, with excellent auguries. After the premiere of his opera *Der arme Heinrich* in Mainz on April 2,

1895, the critics, among them the prestigious Humperdinck, praised the work in extravagant terms. Even more successful was his opera *Palestrina*, making use of Palestrina's themes, written to his own libretto, which was conducted by Bruno Walter at its first performance on June 12, 1917, in Munich. The Pfitzner Soc. was formed in Munich as early as 1904, and a Hans Pfitzner Assn. was established in Berlin in 1938, with Furtwängler as president. Although Pfitzner's music is traditional in style and conservative in harmony, he was regarded as a follower of the modern school, a comrade-in-arms of his close contemporary Richard Strauss. Very soon, however, his fame began to dwindle; there were fewer performances of his operas and still fewer hearings of his instrumental works; he himself bitterly complained of this lack of appreciation of his art. It was a miserable end for a once important and capable musician.

WORKS: DRAMATIC: OPERAS: *Der arme Heinrich* (1891–93; Mainz, April 2, 1895); *Die Rose vom Liebesgarten* (1897–1900; Elberfeld, Nov. 9, 1901); *Das Christ-Elflein* (Munich, Dec. 11, 1906); *Palestrina* (1911–15; Munich, June 12, 1917). **INCIDENTAL MUSIC:** *Das Fest auf Solhaug*, after Ibsen (Mainz, Nov. 28, 1890); *Das Käthchen von Heilbronn*, after Kleist (Berlin, Oct. 19, 1905); *Gesang der Barden* for *Die Hermannsschlacht*, after Kleist (1906). **ORCH.:** Scherzo in C minor (1887; Frankfurt am Main, Nov. 8, 1888); *3 Preludes*, symphonic excerpts from the opera *Palestrina* (1917); Piano Concerto (Dresden, March 16, 1921; Walter Gieseking soloist); Violin Concerto (1923; Nuremberg, June 4, 1924); Sym. in C-sharp minor, after the 2nd String Quartet (1932; Munich, March 23, 1933, composer conducting); 2 cello concertos: No. 1 (Frankfurt am Main, 1935) and No. 2 (Solingen, April 23, 1944, composer conducting); *Duo* for Violin, Cello, and Chamber Orch. (Frankfurt am Main, Dec. 3, 1937, composer conducting); *Kleine Symphonie* (Berlin, Nov. 19, 1939, Furtwängler conducting); Sym. in C (Frankfurt am Main, Oct. 11, 1940); *Elegie und Reigen* (1940; Salzburg, April 4, 1941); *Krakauer Begrüssung* (1944); *Elegie* (1947). **CHAMBER:** 4 string quartets (1886, 1903, 1925, 1942); Cello Sonata (1890); Piano Trio (1896); Piano Quintet (1908); Violin Sonata (1918); *5 Klavierstücke* (1941); *6 Studien* for Piano (1943); *Sextet* for Clarinet, Violin, Viola, Cello, Double Bass, and Piano (1945). **VOCAL:** *Von deutscher Seele*, romantic cantata, after J. von Eichendorff (1921; Berlin, Jan. 27, 1922); *Das dunkle Reich* for Solo Voices and Orch. (1929; Cologne, Oct. 21, 1930); *Fons salutatis* for Chorus and Orch. (1941); *Kantate*, after Goethe (1948–49; left unfinished; completed by R. Rehan); 106 lieder (1884–1931).

WRITINGS: *Gesammelte Schriften* (2 vols., Augsburg, 1926, 1929; containing Pfitzner's vicious pamphlets against modern ideas about music, including *Futuristengefahr*, dedicated against Busoni [1917], and *Neue Aestetik der musikalischen Impotenz*, denouncing the critic Paul Bekker); *Über musikalische Inspiration* (Berlin, 1940); *Philosophie und Dichtung in meinem Leben* (Berlin, 1944); *Eindrücke und Bilder meines Lebens* (Hamburg, 1947); W. Abendroth, ed., *Reden, Schriften, Briefe* (Berlin, 1955).

BIBL.: P. Cossmann, *H. P.* (Munich, 1904); R. Louis, *H. P.s "Rose vom Liebesgarten"* (Munich, 1904); C. Wandrey, *H. P.* (Leipzig, 1922); E. Kroll, *H. P.* (Munich, 1924); W. Lütge, *H. P.* (Leipzig, 1924); E. Valentin, *H. P.: Werk und Gestalt eines Deutschen* (Regensburg, 1939); H. Lindlar, *H. P.s Klavier-Lied* (Würzburg, 1940); J. Müller-Blattau, *H. P.: Ein Bild in Widmungen anlässlich seines 75. Geburtstages* (Leipzig, 1944); H. Rutz, *H. P.: Musik zwischen den Zeiten* (Vienna, 1949); K. Müller, *In memoriam H. P.* (Vienna, 1950); D. Henderson, *H. P.: The Composer and His Instrumental Music* (diss., Univ. of Mich., 1963); H. Rectanus, *Leitmotivik und Form in den musikdramatischen Werken H. P.s* (Würzburg, 1967); W. Dietz, *H. P.s Lieder: Versuch einer Stilbetrachtung* (Regensburg, 1968); W. Abendroth and K.-R. Danler, eds., *Festschrift aus Anlass des 100. Geburtstags und des 20. Todestags H. P.s* (Munich, 1969); E. Busse, *Die Eichendorff-Rezeption im Kunstlied: Versuch einer Typologie anhand von Kompositionen Schumanns, Wolfs, und P.s* (Würzburg, 1975); W. Osthoff, ed., *Symposium H. P. (1981: Berlin, Germany)* (Tutzing, 1984); R. Ermen, *Musik als Einfall: H. P.s Position im ästhetischen Diskurs nach Wagner* (Aachen, 1986); E. Wamlek-Junk, *H. P. und Wien: Sein Briefwechsel mit Victor Junk und andere Dokumente* (Tutzing, 1986); J. Williamson, "P. and Ibsen," *Music & Letters* (April 1986); J. Vogel, *H. P.: Mit Zelbstzeugnissen und Bilddokumenten* (Reinbek bei Hamburg, 1989); G. Busch-Salmen and G. Weiss, *H. P.: Münchner Dokumente, Bilder und Bildnesse* (Regensburg, 1990); J. Williamson, *The Music of H. P.* (Oxford, 1992).

Philip, Achille, French composer and teacher; b. Arles, Oct. 12, 1878; d. Béziers, Hérault, Oct. 12, 1959. He studied at the Paris Cons. with Guilmant (organ) and d'Indy (composition). From 1905 to 1950 he taught organ at the Schola Cantorum in Paris. He wrote an opera, *L'Or du Menhir* (Rouen, 1934); 3 symphonic poems: *Les Djinns* (1913), *Dans un parc enchanté* (1917), and *Nymphes et Naiades* (1920); sacred works; chamber music; songs.

Philipp, Isidor, eminent French pianist and pedagogue of Hungarian descent; b. Pest, Sept. 2, 1863; d. Paris, Feb. 20, 1958. He was taken to Paris as an infant; studied piano with Georges Mathias at the Paris Cons., winning 1st prize in 1883; then took lessons with Saint-Saëns, Stephen Heller, and Ritter. His concert career was brief, but he found his true vocation in teaching; was a prof. at the Paris Cons. (1893–1934), where he was mentor to many notable pupils, including Albert Schweitzer. In Paris he continued to perform, mostly in chamber music groups; formed a concert trio with Loeb and Berthelier, with which he gave a number of successful concerts. After the outbreak of World War II, he went to the U.S.; arrived in N.Y. in 1941; despite his advanced age he accepted private students, not only in N.Y., but also in Montreal. At the age of 91, he played the piano part in Franck's Violin Sonata (N.Y., March 20, 1955); then returned to France. He publ. some technical studies for piano, among them *Exercises journaliers; École d'octaves; Problèmes techniques; Études techniques basées sur une nouvelle manière de travailler*, and *La Gamme chromatique*; made arrangements for 2 pianos of works by Bach, Mendelssohn, Saint-Saëns, and others; also brought out *La Technique de Liszt* (2 vols., Paris, 1932).

BIBL.: H. Bellamann, "I. P.," *Musical Quarterly* (Oct. 1943).

Philippot, Michel, French composer and teacher; b. Verzy, Marne, Feb. 2, 1925; d. Paris, July 28, 1996. He was a student at the Paris Cons. (1945–47) and of Leibowitz (1945–49). After working with the Radiodiffusion française (1949–59), he was associated with Schaeffer's Groupe de recherches musicales de la RTF (1959–61). From 1963 to 1975 he was active with the ORTF. He taught at the Univ. of Paris (1969–76) and was a prof. of composition at the Paris Cons. (1970–90). He also was active in Brazil, where he founded and directed the music dept. at the Univ. of São Paulo (1976–79) and was a prof. at the Univ. of Rio de Janeiro (1979–81). In 1987 he was awarded France's Grand Prix national for music. He publ. the vols. *Électronique et techniques compositionnelles* (Paris, 1956), *Pierre Boulez aujourd'hui, entre hier et demain* (Paris, 1964), *Stravinski* (Paris, 1965), *Diabolus in musica: Analyse des variations "Diabelli" de Beethoven* (São Paulo, 1978), and *Traité de l'écriture musicale* (São Paulo, 1984).

WORKS: ORCH.: *Ouverture* for Chamber Orch. (1949); *Composition No. 1* for Strings (1959) and *No. 2* for Strings, Piano, and Harp (1974), and *No. 4* (1980); *Composition* for Double Orch. (1960); *Carrés magiques* (1983); Concerto for Violin, Viola, and Orch. (1984). **CHAMBER:** Piano Trio (1953); *Variations* for 10 Instruments (1957); *Pièces* for 10 Instruments (1961); *Transformations triangulaires* for 12 Instruments (1963); *Composition No. 1* (1965) and *No. 3* (1976) for Violin; *Scherzo* for Accordion (1972); *Passacaille* for 12 Instruments (1973); Octet for Clarinet, Bassoon, Horn, String Quartet, and Double Bass (1975); 4 string quartets (1976, 1982, 1985, 1988); Septet (1977); Piano Quintet (1986); *Concerto de chambre* for

Piano and 6 Instruments (1986); Wind Quintet (1988); *Composition* for Violin and Piano (1990). **KEYBOARD: PIANO:** 2 sonatas (1947, 1973); *3 Compositions* (1958); *Composition No. 4* (1975), *No. 5* (1976), and *No. 6* (1977). **ORGAN:** Sonata (1971). **OTHER:** *Contrapunctus X* (1994).

Phillips, Burrill, American composer and teacher; b. Omaha, Nov. 9, 1907; d. Berkeley, Calif., June 22, 1988. He studied music with Edwin Stringham in Denver; then with Hanson and Rogers at the Eastman School of Music in Rochester, N.Y. (B.M., 1932; M.M., 1933). He taught at the Eastman School of Music (1933–49; 1965–66), the Univ. of Ill. in Urbana (1949–64), the Juilliard School in N.Y. (1968–69), and Cornell Univ. (1972–73). His early music was cast in a neo-Classical style; later he incorporated free serial techniques.

WORKS: DRAMATIC: OPERAS: *Don't We All* (1947; Rochester, N.Y., May 9, 1949); *The Unforgiven* (1981). **BALLETS:** *Katmanusha* (1932–33); *Play Ball* (Rochester, N.Y., April 29, 1938); *Step into My Parlor* (1942); *La piñata* (1969). Also incidental music. **ORCH.:** *Selections from McGuffey's Reader* (1933; Rochester, N.Y., May 3, 1934); *Sinfonia concertante* (Rochester, N.Y., April 3, 1935); *American Dance* for Bassoon and Strings (Rochester, N.Y., April 25, 1940); *3 Satiric Fragments* (Rochester, N.Y., May 2, 1941); Piano Concerto (1942); *Scherzo* (1944); *Tom Paine Overture* (1946; N.Y., May 15, 1947); Concerto grosso for String Quartet and Chamber Orch (1949); Triple Concerto for Clarinet, Viola, Piano, and Orch. (1952); *Perspectives in a Labyrinth* for 3 String Orchs. (1962); *Soleriana concertante* (1965); *Yellowstone, Yates, and Yosemite* for Tenor Saxophone and Symphonic Band (1972). **CHAMBER:** Trio for 3 Trumpets (1937); 2 string quartets (1939–40; 1958); Violin Sonata (1941); *Partita* for Piano Quartet (1947); Cello Sonata (1948); *4 Figures in Time* for Flute and Piano (1952); Oboe Quintet (1967); *Intrada* for Wind Ensemble, Percussion, Piano, Violin, and Cello (1975); *Scena da camera* for Violin and Cello (1978); *Canzona VI* for Wind Quintet (1985). **PIANO:** 4 sonatas (1942–60); *9 by 9*, a set of 9 variations, each in a meter of 9 beats (1942); *Toccata* (1944); *Commentaries* (1983). **VOCAL:** *Declaratives* for Women's Chorus and Chamber Orch. (1943); *The Return of Odysseus* for Baritone, Narrator, Chorus, and Orch. (1956); *Letters from Italy Hill* for Soprano, Flute, Clarinet, String Quartet, and Piano (1984).

Phillips, Harvey (Gene), outstanding American tuba player and teacher; b. Aurora, Mo., Dec. 2, 1929. He played the sousaphone in high school; after attending the Univ. of Missouri (1947–48), he joined the Ringling Brothers and Barnum & Bailey Circus Band; then took general music courses at the Juilliard School of Music (1950–54) and at the Manhattan School of Music (1956–58) in N.Y. He played in various ensembles there, including the N.Y. City Ballet Orch., the N.Y. City Opera Orch., the Goldman Band, and the Sym. of the Air; he also was a founding member of the N.Y. Brass Quintet. From 1967 to 1971 he held an administrative position at the New England Cons. of Music in Boston. In 1971 he became a prof. of music at the Indiana Univ. School of Music; was named a distinguished prof. of music there in 1979. He commissioned works for tuba from Gunther Schuller, Robert Russell Bennett, Alec Wilder, and Morton Gould. With W. Winkle, he publ. *The Art of Tuba and Euphonium* (Secaucus, N.J., 1992).

Phillips, Karen, American pianist, violist, and composer; b. Dallas, Oct. 29, 1942. She studied piano at the Eastman School of Music, and theory at the Juilliard School in N.Y.; she also took lessons in viola, and gave recitals both as a violist and a pianist. She wrote 4 syms., a Cello Concerto, some chamber music, and piano pieces.

Phillips, Montague (Fawcett), English composer and pedagogue; b. London, Nov. 13, 1885; d. Esher, Jan. 4, 1969. He studied with F. Corder at the Royal Academy of Music in London; subsequently taught there. He wrote a light opera, *The Rebel Maid* (London, March 12, 1921), which enjoyed some success; also a Sym. (1911), 2 piano concertos (1907, 1919), overtures, including *In Praise of My Country* (1944), *Empire March* for Orch. (1941), and many choral works.

Phillips, Peter, notable English choral conductor; b. Southampton, Oct. 15, 1953. He was educated at Winchester College and at St. John's College, Oxford. In 1978 he founded the Tallis Scholars, a choral group, which he conducted in admired performances of the Renaissance masters throughout Great Britain, including its debut at the London Promenade Concerts in 1988; the group also toured extensively abroad, appearing in Australia, the U.S., and the Far East. Phillips publ. the vol. *English Sacred Music, 1549–1649* (1991).

Piastro, Josef, Russian-American violinist, brother of **Mishel Piastro**; b. Kerch, Crimea, March 1, 1889; d. Monrovia, Calif., May 14, 1964. He studied with Auer at the St. Petersburg Cons. He went to the U.S. in 1920; was concertmaster of the Los Angeles Phil., and conducted children's concerts in Hollywood. In America he assumed the pseudonym Borissoff, to avoid confusion with his brother. He composed *Crimean Rhapsody* for Violin and Piano (1920).

Piastro, Mishel, Russian-American violinist and conductor, brother of **Josef Piastro**; b. Kerch, Crimea, July 1, 1891; d. N.Y., April 10, 1970. He studied with Auer at the St. Petersburg Cons. In 1920 he settled in the U.S.; was concertmaster of the San Francisco Sym. Orch. (1925–31) and of the N.Y. Phil. (1931–43). He was conductor of WOR radio's "Longines Symphonette," sponsored by the Longines-Wittnauer Watch Co. (1941–66).

Piatigorsky, Gregor, great Russian-born American cellist and pedagogue, brother of **Alexander Stogorsky**; b. Ekaterinoslav, April 17, 1903; d. Los Angeles, Aug. 6, 1976. He received his first music lessons from his father, a violinist; then took cello lessons with Alfred von Glehn at the Moscow Cons. He played in various orchs. in Moscow. In 1921 he left Russia and took cello lessons with Julius Klengel in Leipzig. After serving as 1st cellist of the Berlin Phil. (1924–28), he devoted himself to a solo career. He played the solo part in Richard Strauss's *Don Quixote* under the composer's direction many times in Europe, and was probably unexcelled in this part; Strauss himself called him "mein Don Quixote." He went to America in 1929, and made his American debut in Oberlin, Ohio, on Nov. 5, 1929; played the Dvořák Concerto with the N.Y. Phil., eliciting great praise (Dec. 29, 1929). He was regarded as the world's finest cellist after Casals; continued giving solo recitals and appearing with major European and American orchs. for many years; gave first performances of several cello works commissioned by him from Hindemith, Dukelsky, Castelnuovo-Tedesco, and others. He became a naturalized American citizen in 1942. He taught at the Curtis Inst. of Music in Philadelphia (1942–51) and at the Berkshire Music Center in Tanglewood; was a prof. at the Univ. of Southern Calif. in Los Angeles (1962–76); presented a series of trio concerts with Heifetz and Pennario. He was the recipient of honorary D.Mus. degrees from Temple Univ., Columbia Univ., the Univ. of Calif., Los Angeles, etc. He publ. an autobiographical vol., *Cellist* (N.Y., 1965).

Piazzolla, Astor, fiery Argentine bandoneón player, bandleader, composer, and arranger; b. Mar del Plata, March 11, 1921; d. Buenos Aires, July 5, 1992. He was taken to N.Y. in 1924, where he took up the bandoneón when he was 12. Upon settling in Buenos Aires in 1937, he began a career as a bandoneón player and arranger; also pursued training with Ginastera, and later was a scholarship student in Paris of Boulanger (1954–55). Upon his return to Buenos Aires, he organized his own band, and in 1960 founded the innovative Quinteto Nuevo Tango. From 1974 to 1985 he made his home in Paris; then returned to his homeland. Piazzolla was a master of the modern tango, embracing an avant-garde style incorporating classical and jazz elements with a piquant touch of modern dissonances. His other works included operas, theater music, film scores, concertos (including one for Bandoneón [1979]), and chamber music.

BIBL.: C. Kuri, *P., la música límite* (Buenos Aires, 1992).

Piccaver (real name, **Peckover**), **Alfred,** English tenor; b. Long Sutton, Lincolnshire, Feb. 15, 1884; d. Vienna, Sept. 23, 1958. He studied at the Metropolitan School in N.Y. He made his operatic debut as Romeo in Prague in 1907; then continued his studies there and in Milan. In 1910 he deputized at the Vienna Court (later State) Opera in the Italian season; remained in Vienna as a leading lyric tenor until 1937. His repertoire included Don José, Florestan, Walther von Stolzing, Lensky, and Andrea Chénier; he also took part in the first Austrian performance of *La Fanciulla del West* in 1913. He appeared in Chicago (1923–25); in 1924 he sang Cavaradossi and the Duke of Mantua at Covent Garden in London. From 1937 to 1955 he taught voice in London; then returned to Vienna to attend the opening of the new building of the Staatsoper; he remained in Vienna as a voice teacher until his death.

Picchi, Mirto, Italian tenor; b. Florence, March 15, 1915; d. there, Sept. 25, 1980. He was a pupil of Florence of Giuseppe Armani and Giulia Tess. After making his operatic debut as Radames in Milan in 1946, he sang in various Italian music centers. In 1947–48 he sang at London's Cambridge Theatre, appearing as Rodolfo, Cavaradossi, and the Duke of Mantua. In 1949 he appeared with the Glyndebourne company as Verdi's Riccardo during its visit to Edinburgh. In 1952 he sang at London's Covent Garden. In 1957 he appeared at Milan's La Scala, where he gave his farewell appearance as Don Basilio in 1974. Picchi was especially known for his roles in contemporary operas.

Picchi, Silvano, Argentine composer; b. Pisa, Italy, Jan. 15, 1922. His family emigrated to Argentina while he was a child; he studied composition with Constantino Gaito, Alberto Ginastera, Arturo Luzzatti, Gilardo Gilardi, and Floro Ugarte in Buenos Aires. He was the music critic of *La Prensa* in Buenos Aires.

WORKS: ORCH.: *Suite irreverente* (1949); *Música para caballos* (1952); Piano Concerto (Buenos Aires, July 23, 1967); Violin Concerto (Buenos Aires, Aug. 12, 1968); *Euè*, funeral chant for Strings, on an African theme (Buenos Aires, March 18, 1969); *Sinfonia breve* (1970); *Mozartiana* for Strings (1971). **CHAMBER:** *Discantus* for Guitar and Bassoon (1968); 2 trios for Oboe, Violin, and Piano; guitar pieces. **VOCAL:** Songs.

Pícha, František, Czech composer and teacher; b. Řipec, Oct. 3, 1893; d. Prague, Oct. 10, 1964. He studied with Foerster, Křička, and Jirák at the Prague Cons., and later attended Suk's master class there. He subsequently served on its faculty and at the Academy of Fine Arts. Pícha publ. a textbook on harmony (Prague, 1949). Among his compositions were *Night Song of a Pilgrim*, symphonic poem (1924); *Štepančikovo*, overture (1931); *Vyzva* (The Challenge) for Orch. (1933); Violin Concerto (1960); chamber music; choral works; song cycles; and folk song arrangements.

Pick-Mangiagalli, Riccardo, Italian pianist and composer; b. Strakonice, Bohemia, July 10, 1882; d. Milan, July 8, 1949. He was of mixed Italian and Bohemian parentage; studied at the Cons. Giuseppe Verdi in Milan with Appiani (piano) and Ferroni (composition). He began his career as a successful concert pianist, but later turned exclusively to composition. In 1936 he succeeded Pizzetti as director of the Cons. Giuseppe Verdi, and held this post until his death.

WORKS: DRAMATIC: OPERAS: *Basi e Bote* (1919–20; Rome, March 3, 1927); *Casanova a Venezia* (Milan, Jan. 19, 1929; orch. suite as *Scene carnevalesche*, Milan, Feb. 6, 1931); *L'Ospite inatteso* (Milan-Turin-Genoa Radio, Oct. 25, 1931); *Il notturno romantico* (Rome, April 25, 1936). **DANCE:** *Il salice d'oro*, ballet (1911–12; Milan, 1914); *Sumitra* (1917; Frankfurt am Main, 1922); *Mahit*, ballet-fable (Milan, March 20, 1923); *La Berceuse* (San Remo, Feb. 21, 1933); *Variazioni coreografiche* (San Remo, April 13, 1935). **ORCH.:** *Notturno e rondo fantastico* (1914; Milan, May 6, 1919); *Humoresque* for Piano and Orch. (1916); *Sortilegi*, symphonic poem for Piano and Orch. (Milan, Dec. 13, 1917); *2 preludi* (Rome, March 1, 1921); *4 poemi* (Milan, April 24, 1925); *Piccola suite* (Milan, June 12, 1927); *Preludio e fuga* (Rome, March 11, 1928); *Preludio e scherzo sinfonico* (Milan, Oct. 22, 1938); Piano Concerto (1944). **CHAMBER:** Violin Sonata; String Quartet (1909); piano pieces. **VOCAL:** Songs.

BIBL.: F. Abbiati, "Musicisti contemporanei: R. P.-M.," *Emporium*, LXXIII (Bergamo, 1931).

Picken, Laurence (Ernest Rowland), English zoologist, biologist, musicologist, and ethnomusicologist; b. Nottingham, July 16, 1909. He studied the natural sciences at Trinity College, Cambridge (B.A., 1931; M.A., 1935; Ph.D., 1935; D.Sc., 1952). In 1944 he became a Fellow at Jesus College, Cambridge; from 1946 to 1966 he was assistant director of research in zoology at Univ. of Cambridge; from 1966 to 1976 he was engaged at the Faculty of Oriental Studies there. In 1944 he went to China as a member of the British Council Scientific Mission; studied the *ch'in* there with Hsu Yuan-Pai and Cha Fu-Hsi; in 1951 he took lessons in Turkish music from Nejdet Senvarol in Istanbul. In 1962 he became ed. of the *Journal of the International Folk Music* Council. He was ed. of *Musica Asiatica* (1977–84); ed. the series Music from the Tang Court (from 1981); contributed articles to many learned journals. He publ. the comprehensive study *Folk Musical Instruments of Turkey* (London, 1975); also ed., with E. Dal, E. Stockmann, and K. Vetterl, *A Select Bibliography of European Folk Music* (Prague, 1966), and, with K. Pont, *Ancient Chinese Tunes* (London, 1973).

Picker, Tobias, American composer; b. N.Y., July 18, 1954. He was a student of Wuorinen at the Manhattan School of Music (B.M., 1976) and of Carter at the Juilliard School (M.M., 1978) in N.Y. From 1985 to 1987 he served as composer-in-residence of the Houston Sym. Orch. In addition to various awards and commissions, he held a Guggenheim followship in 1981. In his music, Picker has generally used serial techniques without abandoning tonality.

WORKS: ORCH.: 3 piano concertos: No. 1 (1980; Manchester, N.H., Jan. 16, 1981), No. 2, *Keys to the City*, for the 100th anniversary of the Brooklyn Bridge (1982–83; Fulton Ferry Landing, Brooklyn, N.Y., May 24, 1983), and No. 3 (1986; Honolulu, Jan. 10, 1988); Violin Concerto (1981; N.Y., Feb. 1, 1982); 3 syms.: No. 1 (1982; San Francisco, April 23, 1983), No. 2, *Aussöhnung*, for Soprano and Orch. (Houston, Oct. 25, 1986), and No. 3 for Strings (1989); *Encantadas* for Narrator and Orch. (1983); *Dedication Anthem* for Band (1984); *Old and Lost Rivers* (1986; also for Piano); *Romances and Interludes*, after Schumann, for Oboe and Orch. (1990); *2 Fantasies* (1991); *Séance* (1991); *Bang!* for Piano and Orch. for the opening of the 150th anniversary season of the N.Y. Phil. (N.Y., Sept. 24, 1992); Viola Concerto (1992–94). **CHAMBER:** 4 sextets for Various Instruments (1973; 1973; 1977; *The Blue Hula*, 1981); *Rhapsody* for Violin and Piano (1979); *Nova* for Piano, Violin, Viola, Cello, and Double Bass (1979); *Serenade* for Piano and Wind Quintet (1983); String Quartet No. 1, *New Memories* (1986–87); Piano Quintet (N.Y., May 6, 1988); Violin Sonata, *Invisible Lilacs* (1992; N.Y., Jan. 8, 1993). **PIANO:** *Piano-o-rama* for 2 Pianos (1984); *Old and Lost Rivers* (1986; also for Orch.).

Pickett, Philip, esteemed English recorder player, conductor, and teacher; b. London, Nov. 17, 1950. He was initiated into the world of early wind instruments by Anthony Baines and David Munrow, and subsequently made that field his specialty. He mastered the recorder and learned to play other early instruments, including the shawm, crumbhorn, and rackett. He appeared as recorder soloist wih the leading British ensembles. He also founded and directed the New London Consort, which he conducted throughout Europe. From 1972 he served as prof. of recorder at the Guildhall School of Music in London. As both performer and conductor, Pickett brings erudition and mastery to his vast early music repertoire.

Pierné, (Henri-Constant-) Gabriel, noted French composer, conductor, and organist; b. Metz, Aug. 16, 1863; d. Ploujean, near Morlaix, July 17, 1937. He studied at the Paris Cons. (1871–82), where his teachers were Marmontel (piano), Franck (organ), and Massenet (composition); he won 1st prizes for piano (1879), counterpoint and fugue (1881), and organ (1882); was awarded the Grand Prix de Rome (1882) with the cantata *Edith*; succeeded Franck as organist at Ste.-Clotilde (1890), where he remained until 1898. He was assistant conductor (1903–10) and conductor (1910–34) of the Concerts Colonne. Pierné was elected a member of the Académie des Beaux-Arts in 1925. His music reveals the hand of an expert craftsman.

WORKS: DRAMATIC: OPERAS: *La Coupe enchantée* (Royan, Aug. 24, 1895; rev. version, Paris, Dec. 26, 1905); *Vendée* (Lyons, March 11, 1897); *La Fille de Tabarin* (Paris, Feb. 20, 1901); *On ne badine pas avec l'amour* (Paris, May 30, 1910); *Sophie Arnould*, lyric comedy, based on episodes from the life of the famous singer (Paris, Feb. 21, 1927). **BALLETS AND PANTOMIMES:** *Le Collier de saphirs* (1891); *Les Joyeuses Commères de Paris* (1892); *Bouton d'or* (1893); *Le Docteur Blanc* (1893); *Salomé* (1895); *Cydalise et le chèvre-pied* (1919; Paris, Jan. 15, 1923; as an orch. suite, 1926); *Impressions de Music-Hall*, "ballet à l'Américaine" (Paris, April 6, 1927); *Giration* (1934); *Fragonard* (1934); *Images, "divertissement sur un thème pastoral"* (Paris, June 19, 1935). **ORCH.:** *Suite de concert* (1883); *Première suite d'orchestre* (1883); *Ouverture symphonique* (1885); Piano Concerto (1887); *Marche solonnelle* (1889); *Pantomime* (1889); *Scherzo-Caprice* for Piano and Orch. (1890); *Poème symphonique* for Piano and Orch. (1901); *Ballet de cour* (1901); *Paysages franciscains* (1920); *Gulliver au pays de Lilliput* (Paris, June 23, 1937). **CHAMBER:** *Pastorale variée dans le style ancien* for Wind Instruments (also for Piano); *Berceuse* for Violin and Piano; *Caprice* for Cello and Piano; *Canzonetta* for Clarinet and Piano; *Solo de concert* for Bassoon and Piano; *Variations libres et Finale* for Flute, Violin, Viola, Cello, and Harp. **PIANO:** *15 pièces* (1883); *Étude de concert; Album pour mes petits amis* (containing the famous *Marche des petits soldats de plomb*); *Humoresque; Rêverie; Ariette dans le style ancien; Pastorale variée; Sérénade à Colombine; Sérénade vénitienne; Barcarolle* for 2 Pianos; folk song arrangements. **VOCAL: ORATORIOS:** *La Croisade des enfants* for Chorus of Children and Adults (Paris, Jan. 18, 1905); *Les Enfants à Bethléem* for Soloists, Children's Chorus, and Orch. (Amsterdam, April 13, 1907); *Les Fioretti de St. François d'Assise* (1912). **SONG CYCLES:** *Contes* (1897); *3 Adaptations musicales* (1902); *3 mélodies* (1904); 38 other songs; folk song arrangements.

BIBL.: G. Masson, *G. P., musicien lorrain* (Nancy and Metz, 1987).

Pijper, Willem, renowned Dutch composer and pedagogue; b. Zeist, Sept. 8, 1894; d. Leidschendam, March 18, 1947. He received a rudimentary education from his father, an amateur violinist; then went to the Toonkunst School of Music in Utrecht, where he studied composition with Johan Wagenaar and piano with Mme. H.J. van Lunteren-Hansen (1911–16). From 1918 to 1923 he was music critic of *Utrecht Dagblad*, and from 1926 to 1929, co-ed. of the monthly *De Muziek*. He taught theory at the Amsterdam Cons. (from 1918), and was a prof. of composition there from 1925 to 1930; served as director of the Rotterdam Cons. from 1930 until his death. In his music, Pijper continued the Romantic tradition of Mahler, and also adopted the harmonic procedures of the modern French School. He postulated a "germ-cell theory," in which an opening chord or motif is the source of all succeeding harmonic and melodic development; he also cultivated the scale of alternating whole tones and semitones, regarding it as his own, not realizing that it was used abundantly by Rimsky-Korsakov (in Russian reference works it is termed the Rimsky-Korsakov scale); the "Pijper scale," as it became known in the Netherlands, was also used by Anton von der Horst and others. During the German bombardment of Rotterdam in May 1940, nearly all of Pijper's MSS were destroyed by fire, including the unpubl. reduced scoring of his large 2nd Sym. (restored in 1961 by Pijper's student Karel Mengelberg); also destroyed was the unpubl. *Divertimento* for Piano and Strings.

WORKS: DRAMATIC: OPERAS: *Halewijn* (1932–33; Amsterdam, June 13, 1933; rev. 1934); *Merlijn* (1939–45; incomplete; Rotterdam, June 7, 1952). **INCIDENTAL MUSIC TO:** Sophocles' *Antigone* (1920; rev. 1922 and 1926); Euripides' *Bacchantes* (1924) and *The Cyclops* (1925); Shakespeare's *The Tempest* (1930); Vondel's *Phaëton* (1937). **ORCH.:** *Orchestral Piece* for Piano and Orch. (Utrecht, Dec. 11, 1915; originally titled "Piano Concerto No. 1," causing confusion with his later and only Piano Concerto [Amsterdam, Dec. 22, 1927], in turn sometimes incorrectly referred to as "Piano Concerto No. 2"); 3 syms.: No. 1, *Pan* (1917; Amsterdam, April 23, 1918), No. 2 for Large Orch. (1921; Amsterdam, Nov. 2, 1922; reduced scoring by K. Mengelberg, 1961), and No. 3 (Amsterdam, Oct. 28, 1926); *6 Symphonic Epigrams* (Amsterdam, April 12, 1928); Cello Concerto (Amsterdam, Nov. 22, 1936; rev. 1947); Violin Concerto (1938–39; Amsterdam, Jan. 7, 1940); *6 Adagios* (1940; Utrecht, Nov. 14, 1951). **CHAMBER:** 2 piano trios (1913–14, 1921); 5 string quartets (1914; 1920; 1923; 1928; 1946, unfinished); *Passepied* for Carillon (1916); 2 violin sonatas (1919, 1922); 2 cello sonatas (1919, 1924); Septet for Wind Quintet, Double Bass, and Piano (1920); Sextet for Wind Quintet and Piano (1922–23); Flute Sonata (1925); Trio for Flute, Clarinet, and Bassoon (1926–27); Wind Quintet (1928–29); Sonata for Solo Violin (1931). **PIANO:** *Theme with 5 Variations* (1913); *3 Aphorisms* (1915); 3 sonatinas (1917, 1925, 1925); *3 Old Dutch Dances* (1926); Sonata (1930); Sonata for 2 Pianos (1935). **VOCAL:** *Fêtes galantes* for Mezzo-soprano and Orch., after Verlaine (1916; Schweningen, Aug. 2, 1917); *8 vieilles chansons de France* for Voice and Piano (1918); *8 Noëls de France* for Voice and Piano (1919); *Romance sans paroles* for Mezzo-soprano and Orch., after Verlaine (1919; Amsterdam, April 15, 1920); *8 Old Dutch Love Songs* for Voice and Piano (1920; rev. 1943); *Heer Halewijn* for Chorus (1920); *8 Old Dutch Songs* for Voice and Piano (2 sets: 1924, 1935); *Heer Danielken* for Chorus (1925); *Hymne* for Bass-baritone and Orch., after Boutens (1941–43; Amsterdam, Nov. 1945).

BIBL.: W. Kloppenburg, *Thematisch-bibliografische Catalogus van de Werken van W. P.* (Assen, 1960); H. Ryker, *The Symphonic Music of W. P.* (diss., Univ. of Wash., 1971).

Piket, Frederick, Austrian-American composer; b. Constantinople (of Austrian parents), Jan. 6, 1903; d. Long Island, N.Y., Feb. 28, 1974. He studied at the Vienna Academy of Music and with Schreker in Berlin; settled in N.Y. in 1940.

WORKS: *Curtain Raiser for an American Play*, overture (Minneapolis, Dec. 30, 1948); Piano Concerto; Violin Concerto; Saxophone Concerto; Concerto for Strings: *The Funnies*, suite (after "Superman" and "Little Orphan Annie"); *Sea Charm* for Chorus; *Legend and Jollity* for 3 Clarinets; *Reflection and Caprice* for 4 Clarinets; Woodwind Trio; numerous choral works for the Jewish service.

Pilarczyk, Helga (Käthe), German soprano; b. Schöningen, March 12, 1925. She studied piano and aspired to a concert career; then took voice lessons and sang in operetta. She found her true vocation in opera; made her debut at Braunschweig in 1951; was a member of the Hamburg State Opera from 1953 until 1968. She made a specialty of modern music; sang Schoenberg's dramatic monologue *Erwartung*, and the leading parts in Berg's *Wozzeck* and *Lulu* as well as in works by Stravinsky, Prokofiev, Dallapiccola, Honegger, Krenek, and others. She appeared as a guest artist at the Bavarian State Opera in Munich, the Vienna State Opera, La Scala in Milan, the Paris Opéra, Covent Garden in London, and the Metropolitan Opera in N.Y. (debut, Feb. 19, 1965, as Marie in *Wozzeck*). She publ. an interesting essay, *Kann man die moderne Oper singen?* (Hamburg, 1964).

Pilati, Mario, Italian composer; b. Naples, Oct. 16, 1903; d. there, Dec. 10, 1938. He studied at the Naples Cons.; was an instructor there (1930–38).

WORKS: ORCH.: *Notturno* (1923). **CHAMBER:** Flute Sonata (1926); Piano Quintet (1928); Violin Sonata (1929); Cello Sonata (1929); String Quartet (1930); piano pieces. **VOCAL:** *La sera* for Women's Voices and Orch. (1926); *Il battesimo di Cristo* for Soli, Chorus, and Orch. (1927).

Pimsleur, Solomon, Austrian-American pianist and composer; b. Paris (of Austrian-Jewish parents), Sept. 19, 1900; d. N.Y., April 22, 1962. He was taken to the U.S. in 1903. He studied piano privately and majored in Eng. literature at Columbia Univ. in N.Y. (M.A., 1923), where he also received instruction in composition from Daniel Gregory Mason. He was a fellowship student of Rubin Goldmark at the Juilliard School of Music in N.Y. (1926), and then studied at the Salzburg Mozarteum. Returning to the U.S., he was active as a pianist and lecturer. He also ran his own artists agency and production company. His compositions followed along Romantic lines, and included an unfinished opera *The Diary of Anne Frank; Ode to Intensity,* symphonic ballad (N.Y., Aug. 14, 1933); *Shakespearean Sonnet Symphony* for Chorus and Orch.; chamber music; many piano pieces.

Pincherle, Marc, noted French musicologist; b. Constantine, Algeria, June 13, 1888; d. Paris, June 20, 1974. He studied musicology in Paris with Pirro, Laloy, and Rolland. He served in both world wars; was taken prisoner of war in June 1940 and was interned in Germany until March 1941. He taught at the Paris École Normale de Musique; was artistic director of the Société Pleyel (1927–55) and president of the Société Française de Musicologie (1948–56). As a musicologist, he devoted himself mainly to the study of 17th- and 18th-century French and Italian music.

WRITINGS (all publ. in Paris unless otherwise given): *Les Violonistes compositeurs et virtuoses* (1922); *Feuillets d'histoire du violon* (1927; 2nd ed., 1935); *Corelli* (1933); *Les Musiciens peints par eux-mêmes* (160 letters of famous composers from his own autograph collection; 1939); *Antonio Vivaldi et la musique instrumentale* (2 vols., 1948); *Les Instruments du quatuor* (1948; 3rd ed., 1970); *L'Orchestre de chambre* (1948); *Jean-Marie Leclair l'âiné* (1952); *Petit lexique des termes musicaux d'usage courant* (1953; 2nd ed., 1973); *Corelli et son temps* (1954; Eng. tr., 1956, as *Corelli, His Life, His Work*); *Vivaldi* (1955; Eng. tr., 1957, as *Vivaldi: Genius of the Baroque*); *Fritz Kreisler* (Geneva, 1956); *Albert Roussel* (Geneva, 1957); *Histoire illustrée de la musique* (1959; 2nd ed., 1962; Eng. tr., 1959); *Le Monde des virtuoses* (1961; Eng. tr., 1963); *Musical Creation* (Washington, D.C., 1961); *L'orchestra da camera* (Milan, 1963); *Le Violon* (1966; 2nd ed., 1974).

Pingoud, Ernest, Russian-born Finnish composer; b. St. Petersburg, Oct. 14, 1888; d. Helsinki, June 1, 1942. He studied piano in St. Petersburg with Siloti; then went to Leipzig, where he took courses in music history with Riemann and in composition with Reger. In 1918 he settled in Finland, where he served as managing director of the Helsinki Phil. (1924–42). In his music, he was influenced by the Russian modern school, particularly by Scriabin, from whom he acquired his predilection for mystical titles, often in French.

WORKS: BALLETS: *Suurkaupungin kasvot* (The Face of the Big City; 1936); *Epäjumala* (The Idol; n.d.). **ORCH.:** *Prologue* (1916); *Confessions* (1916); *La Dernière Aventure de Pierrot* (1916); *Diableries galantes "Le fétiche"* (1917); 3 piano concertos (1917, 1921, 1922); *Hymneja yolle* (Hymns to the Night; 1917); *5 Sonnets* for Chamber Orch. (1918); *Ritari peloton ja moitteeton* (The Knight without Fear or Reproach), an "adventure" (1918); *Mysterium* (1919); *Flambeaux éteints* (1919); *Chantecler* (1919); *Le Sacrifice* (1919); 3 syms. (1920; 1920; 1923–27); *Profeetta* (The Prophet; 1921); *Cor ardens* (1927); *Narcissos* (1930); *Le Chant d'espace* (1931; rev. 1938); *La Flamme éternelle* (1938–39). **OTHER:** Chamber music; piano works; *Kuolemantanssi* (Danse macabre) for Chorus and Orch. (1918); songs.

Pinkham, Daniel (Rogers, Jr.), esteemed American composer, organist, choral conductor, and teacher; b. Lynn, Mass., June 5, 1923. He received training in organ and harmony from Carl Pfatteicher at the Phillips Academy in Andover, Mass., before pursuing his studies with Merritt, Piston, Davison, and Copland at Harvard Univ. (A.B., 1943; M.A., 1944). He also received instruction in harpsichord from Aldrich and Landowska, and in organ from Biggs. He likewise attended the composition courses given by Honegger and Barber at the Berkshire Music Center in Tanglewood, and then studied with Boulanger. Pinkham taught at Simmons College in Boston, Boston Univ., and Dartington Hall in Devon, England. In 1957–58 he was a visiting lecturer at Harvard Univ. In 1958 he became music director of the King's Chapel in Boston. He also taught at the New England Cons. of Music in Boston from 1959. In 1950 he held a Fulbright fellowship and in 1962 received a Ford Foundation fellowship. He was awarded honorary Mus.D. degrees from Westminster Choir College in Princeton, N.J. (1979), the New England Cons. of Music (1993), and Ithaca College (1994). In 1990 he was named composer of the year by the American Guild of Organists. In his prolific output as a composer, Pinkham has demonstrated a fine capacity for producing versatile scores. The formal design of his music is compact and contrapuntally cohesive. The rhythmic element is often propulsive while he occasionally introduces modernistic devices without disrupting the tonal fabric of his scores.

WORKS: DRAMATIC: Theater works; chamber operas; some 20 documentary film scores. **ORCH.:** 3 sonatas for Organ and Strings (1943, 1954, 1986; also for Organ and Chamber Ensemble); 2 violin concertos: No. 1 (Falmouth, Mass., Sept. 8, 1956) and No. 2 (1968); 4 syms.: No. 1 (Washington, D.C., April 29, 1961), No. 2 (1962; Lansing, Mich., Nov. 23, 1963), No. 3 (1985), and No. 4 (Washington, D.C., Nov. 4, 1990); *Catacoustical Measures* (N.Y., May 28, 1962); *Signs of the Zodiac* for Orch. and Optional Narrator (Portland, Maine, Nov. 10, 1964); 2 organ concertos: No. 1 (1970) and No. 2 (Rheinland-Pfalz, Sept. 1, 1995); *Serenades* for Trumpet and Wind Orch. (1979; Cambridge, Mass., March 7, 1980); *Concerto piccolo* for Piccolo, String Orch. or Quintet, and Percussion (New Orleans, Aug. 20, 1989); *Overture Concertante* (Boston, Oct. 29, 1992). **CHAMBER:** Piano Concertino (Cambridge, Mass., May 3, 1950); Concerto for Celesta and Harpsichord (1954; N.Y., Nov. 19, 1955); Concertante for Organ, Celesta, and Percussion (1963); *Toccatas for the Vault of Heaven* for Organ and Tape (1972); *Masks* for Harpsichord and Chamber Ensemble (1978); *Diversions* for Organ and Harp (1980); Brass Quintet (1983); *Sonata da chiesa* for Viola and Organ (1988); String Quartet (Boston, April 8, 1990); Reed Trio (Boston, Sept. 29, 1994); numerous organ pieces. **VOCAL:** *Wedding Cantata* for Optional Soprano and Tenor, Chorus, and Orch. (Cambridge, Mass., Sept. 22, 1956); *Christmas Cantata* for Chorus and Orch. (1957); *Easter Cantata* for Chorus and Orch. (1961); *Requiem* for Alto, Tenor, Chorus, and Orch. (1962; N.Y., Jan. 24, 1963); *Stabat Mater* for Soprano, Chorus, and Orch. (Lenox, Mass., Aug. 10, 1964); *St. Mark Passion* for Chorus and Orch. (Southboro, Mass., May 22, 1965); *Magnificat* for Soprano, Women's Chorus, and Orch. (1968); *Ascension Cantata* for Chorus and Orch. (Columbus, Ohio, March 20, 1970); *Daniel in the Lion's Den* for Narrator, Tenor, Baritone, Bass, Chorus, 5 Instrumentalists, and Tape (1972); *The Passion of Judas* for Soloists, Chorus, and 5 Instrumentalists (1975; Washington, D.C., June 6, 1976); *The Descent into Hell* for Soprano, Tenor, Bass, Chorus, Orch., and Tape (1979; Buckhannon, W.Va., Oct. 17, 1980); *Hezekiah* for Chorus and Orch. (1979; Shaker Heights, Ohio, April 8, 1981; rev. 1987); *When God Arose* for Chorus and Orch. (1979; Norman, Okla., Feb. 15, 1980); *Before the Dust Returns* for Chorus and Orch. (Lewisburg, Pa., Nov. 21, 1981); *In Heaven Soaring Up* for Alto, Tenor, Chorus, Oboe, and Harp (1985); *Getting to Heaven* for Soprano, Chorus, Brass Quintet, and Harp (1987); *Stabat Mater* (1990); *Advent Cantata* (Albany, N.Y., Dec. 4, 1991); numerous other vocal works, both sacred and secular.

BIBL.: M. Johnson, *The Choral Works of D. P.* (diss., Univ. of Iowa, 1966); M. Corzine, *The Organ Works of D. P.* (diss., Eastman School of Music, 1979); M. Stallings, *Representative Works* *for Mixed Chorus by D. P.: 1968–1983* (diss., Univ. of Miami, 1984); K. Deboer and J. Ahouse, *D. P.: A Bio-Bibliography* (Westport, Conn., 1988).

Pinnock, Trevor (David), outstanding English harpsichordist and conductor; b. Canterbury, Dec. 16, 1946. He became a chorister at Canterbury Cathedral when he was 7; after receiving instruction in piano and organ, he served as a church organist; at 19, he entered the Royal College of Music in London, where he took courses in organ and later harpsichord. While still a student, he organized the Gailliard Harpsichord Trio (1966); also toured Europe with the Academy of St. Martin-in-the Fields. In 1973 he founded the English Concert, an ensemble devoted to the performance of early music on original instruments; through numerous tours and recordings, his ensemble acquired an international reputation; toured North America with it for the first time in 1983. He also pursued a distinguished career as a harpsichord virtuoso. On Sept. 27, 1988, he made his Metropolitan Opera debut in N.Y. conducting *Giulio Cesare.* In 1989 he founded the Classical Band of N.Y., which he led in performances of the Classical repertoire from Haydn to Mendelssohn on period instruments until resigning unexpectedly in 1990. In 1991 he was named artistic director and principal conductor of the National Arts Centre Orch. in Ottawa. In 1995 he conducted it on a critically acclaimed tour of Europe. In 1996 he stepped down from his post but served as its artistic advisor during the 1996–97 season. In 1992 he was made a Commander of the Order of the British Empire.

Piňos, Alois Simandl, Czech composer and teacher; b. Vyškov, Oct. 2, 1925. He studied forestry at the Univ. of Brno (graduating in 1953), music with Petrželka at the Brno Cons. (1948–49) and at the Janáček Academy of Music in Brno with Kvapil and Schaeffer (1949–53); attended the summer courses of new music at Darmstadt (1965) and an electronic music seminar in Munich (1966). In 1953 he joined the faculty of the Janáček Academy of Music in Brno. In 1967 he founded in Brno a modern music group, with which he produced a number of works by the local avant-garde, some composed collectively.

WORKS: DRAMATIC: CHAMBER OPERA: *The Criers* (1970). **AUDIO-VISUAL:** *The Lattice* for Piano and Film (1970); *The Genesis* for Chamber Orch. and Film (1970); *Static Music* for Tape and Slides (1970). **ORCH.:** *Czech Dances* (1951); *Wedding Suite* (1952); Horn Concerto (1953); *Concertino* (1963); *Abbreviations* (1963); Concerto for Orch. and Tape (1964); Double Concerto for Cello, Piano, Winds, and Percussion (1965–66; Prague, March 7, 1967); Chamber Concerto for Strings (1967); *Concerto on the Name B-A-C-H* for Bass Clarinet, Cello, Piano, Strings, and Percussion (1968); *Apollo XI,* sym. (1970); *Symphonic Diptych* (1973–74); Concerto for Harp and Strings (1978); *Ballad* for Chamber Orch. and Synthesizer (1981); Organ Concerto (1985). **CHAMBER:** Cello Sonata (1950); 2 wind quintets (1951, 1959); Sonata for Viola and Cello (1960); Piano Trio (1960); Suite for String Trio (1961); *Monologues* for Bass Clarinet (1962); *Caricatures* for Flute, Bass Clarinet, and Piano (1962); 3 string quartets (1962–93); *Conflicts* for Violin, Bass Clarinet, Piano, and Percussion (1964); *3 Pieces* for Bass Clarinet and Piano (1965); *Pulsus intermissi* for Percussionist (1965); *Hyperboles,* 7 pieces for Harp (1966); *16 January 1969* for Piano Quintet and Kettledrums (1969); *Dialogues* for Bass Clarinet (1969); *2 campanari* for Bass Clarinet, Piano, and Ringing Instruments (1971); *Be Beaten* for Percussionist (1972); *Sonata Concertante* for Cello and Piano (1974); *Composition for 3* for Flute, Clarinet, and Marimbaphone (1975); Nonet (1982–83). **PIANO:** *Paradoxes* (1965); *2-3-1,* 3 pieces (1969); *Esca* for Prepared Piano (1971). **VOCAL:** *Hunting Music* for Baritone and 4 Horns (1963); *2 Lyrical Sketches* for Narrator, Flute, and Violin (1964); *4 Lyrical Sketches* for Narrator, Flute, Bass Clarinet, and Piano (1965); *Ludus floralis,* 5 songs for Baritone, Women's Chorus, Percussion, and Tape (1966); *Gesta Machabaeorum* for Chorus, Flute, Trumpet, Harp, and Percussion (1967–68); *Power of Love* for Baritone and String Quartet (1974); *Acquaintance* for Soprano, Bass-baritone, and Guitar or Harpsichord, to texts from advertisements (1975); choruses; other songs. **TAPE:** *Home* (1972–73); *Speleophony* (1976).

Pinto, Alfredo, Italian-Argentine pianist, conductor, and composer; b. Mantua, Oct. 22, 1891; d. Buenos Aires, May 26, 1968. He studied piano with Longo and composition with De Nardis in Naples. He then went to Buenos Aires, where he became active as a pianist and conductor. He wrote the operas *La última esposa, o Sheherazade* and *Gualicho* (Buenos Aires, 1940); 3 symphonic poems: *Nostalgias* (1929), *Eros* (1930), and *Rebelión* (1939); numerous piano pieces, choruses, and songs.

Pinto, Octavio, Brazilian composer; b. São Paulo, Nov. 3, 1890; d. there, Oct. 31, 1950. He was trained as an architect and built apartment houses in Brazil; also studied piano with Isidor Philipp. In 1922 he married **Guiomar Novães**. Villa-Lobos wrote his suite *Prole do bébé* for their children. Pinto publ. a number of effective piano miniatures, of which *Scenas infantis* (1932) and *Children's Festival* (1939) are best known.

Pinza, Ezio (baptized **Fortunio**), celebrated Italian bass; b. Rome, May 18, 1892; d. Stamford, Conn., May 9, 1957. The family moved to Ravenna when he was an infant; he studied engineering. He began to study voice at the age of 18 with Ruzza and Vizzani at the Bologna Cons. He made his operatic debut as Oroveso in *Norma* in Soncino (1914); after military service in World War I, he resumed his career, making his first important appearance as Comte Des Grieux in Rome (1920); then sang at La Scala in Milan (1922–24); was selected by Toscanini for the leading part in the premiere of Boito's *Nerone* (May 1, 1924). He made his American debut at the Metropolitan Opera in N.Y. as Pontifex Maximus in Spontini's *La Vestale* (Nov. 1, 1926), and remained on its staff until 1947; appeared also in San Francisco, Chicago, and other cities in the U.S.; also sang in Europe and in South America. His most celebrated roles were Méphistophélès in Gounod's *Faust,* Don Giovanni, and Boris Godunov. In 1949 he appeared as a musical comedy star in *South Pacific,* and immediately became successful in this new career; also appeared in films.

BIBL.: R. Magidoff, ed., *E.P.: An Autobiography* (N.Y., 1958).

Pipkov, Lubomir, noted Bulgarian composer, son of **Panayot Pipkov**; b. Lovec, Sept. 19, 1904; d. Sofia, May 9, 1974. He studied piano and composition with his father; entered the Sofia Music School (1919); completed his training with Boulanger and Dukas (composition) and Lefébure (piano) at the Paris École Normale de Musique (1926–32). Returning to Bulgaria, he occupied several administrative posts, including the directorship of the National Theater in Sofia (1944–47). His style of composition is determined by the inherent asymmetry of Bulgarian folk songs; there is a similarity in his compositions with those of Bartók, resulting from common sources in Balkan and Macedonian music; his harmonic investiture is often polytonal or polymodal.

WORKS: DRAMATIC: OPERAS: *Yaninite devet bratya* (The 9 Brothers of Yanina; 1929–37; Sofia, Sept. 19, 1937); *Momchil* (1939–44; Sofia, April 24, 1948); *Antigone 43* (1961–62; Ruse, Dec. 23, 1963). **ORCH.:** Concerto for Winds, Percussion, and Piano (1930); 4 syms.: No. 1 (1939–40), No. 2 (1954), No. 3 for Strings, Trumpet, 2 Pianos, and Percussion (1965), and No. 4 for Strings (1970); *Heroic Overture* (1950); *Journey through Albania,* variations for Strings (1950); Violin Concerto (1951); Piano Concerto (1954); *Symphony-Concerto* for Cello and Orch. (1963; Moscow, April 20, 1964); Concerto for Clarinet and Chamber Orch. (1966); *The Partisan's Grave* for Trombone and Strings (1970). **CHAMBER:** 3 string quartets (1928, 1948, 1966); 2 violin sonatas (1929, 1969); Piano Trio (1930); Piano Quartet (1939); Sonata for Solo Violin (1969). **PIANO:** *Tableaux et études métrorythmiques* (1972); *Suggestions printanières* (1972). **VOCAL:** 2 cantatas: *The Wedding* (1934) and *Cantata of Friendship* (1958); *Oratorio for Our Time* (Plovdiv, Dec. 18, 1959); choruses; songs.

BIBL.: K. Iliev, *L. P.* (Sofia, 1958); L. Koen, *L. P.* (Sofia, 1968).

Pipkov, Panayot, Bulgarian composer, father of **Lubomir Pipkov**; b. Plovdiv, Dec. 2, 1871; d. Sofia, Aug. 25, 1942. He studied violin before attending the Milan Cons. (1893–95). After conducting in Rusa, he settled in Sofia in 1905. In addition to his musical career, he also pursued acting and literary activities. He composed 2 children's operettas, many choral works, and piano pieces.

Pires, (Luis) Filipe, Portuguese composer; b. Lisbon, June 26, 1934. He studied piano with Mendes and composition with Croner de Vasconcelos at the Lisbon Cons. (1946–54), and then took courses at the Hannover Hochschule für Musik (1957–60); taught composition at the Oporto Cons. (1960–70) and at the Lisbon Cons. (1972–75); subsequently worked in an electronic studio in Paris with Pierre Schaeffer. His music hewed resolutely to the tenets of the cosmopolitan avant-garde.

WORKS: String Quartet (1958); Piano Trio (1960); *Eternal Return* for Baritone and Orch. (1961); *Perspectivas* for 3 Groups of Instruments (1965); *Metromonie* for Flute, Viola, and Harp (1966); *Portugaliae Genesis* for Baritone, Chorus, and Orch. (1968; Lisbon, May 21, 1969); *Homo sapiens* for Magnetic Tape (1972); *Dialogues* for 8 Instrumentalists and Tape (1975).

Pires, Maria-João, Portuguese pianist; b. Lisbon, July 23, 1944. She began piano lessons at a very early age, making her recital debut at 5 and appearing as soloist in a Mozart Concerto when she was 7; studied piano with Campos Coelho at the Lisbon Academy of Music (1953–60), and concurrently received instruction in composition, theory, and music history from Francine Benoit; then pursued piano training with R. Schmid at the Munich Staatliche Hochschule für Musik and with Karl Engel. She appeared throughout her homeland and in Spain and Germany; after winning 1st prize in the Beethoven Competition in Brussels (1970), she gave concert tours in Europe, Africa, and Japan. In 1986 she made her North American debut as a soloist with the Montreal Sym. Orch., and in 1988 she made her first U.S. tour. In 1993 she was a soloist with Raymond Leppard and the Indianapolis Sym. Orch. on a major tour of Europe. Her readings of Mozart, Beethoven, Schubert, Schumann, and Chopin are finely etched and poetically outlined.

Pirogov, Alexander (Stepanovich), noted Russian bass; b. Novoselki, Riazan district, July 4, 1899; d. Bear's Head Island, June 26, 1964. He studied voice at the Moscow Phil. Inst., and simultaneously attended classes in history and philology at the Univ. of Moscow. In 1924 he joined the Bolshoi Theater in Moscow, remaining on its roster until 1954. He specialized in the Russian operatic repertoire; his performance of the role of Boris Godunov received a prize in 1949; also notable were his interpretations of Méphistophélès in *Faust* and Don Basilio in *Il Barbiere di Siviglia.* His 2 brothers, Grigori (1885–1931) and Mikhail (1887–1933), were also notable basses.

Pironkoff, Simeon, Bulgarian composer; b. Lom, June 18, 1927. He took courses in violin, conducting (with A. Dimitrov), and composition (with P. Khadzhiev) at the Bulgarian State Cons. in Sofia (graduated, 1952). He was active as a composer and conductor at Sofia's Youth Theater (1951–61) and served as secretary of the Bulgarian Composer's Union (1966–69). He received the Gottfried von Herder Prize of the Univ. of Vienna (1985). His music is rhythmically animated, harmonically tense, melodically modal, and instrumentally coloristic.

WORKS: DRAMATIC: OPERAS: *A Good Woman from Szechwan* (1965); *The Motley Bird* (1979); *Ah, You, My Dream . . .* (1985). Also film and theater music. **ORCH.:** Sym. for Strings (1960); *Movements* for Strings (1967); *Night Music* (1968); *Requiem for an Unknown Young Man* for Strings (1968); *A Big Game* for Small Orch. (1970); *Ballet Music in Memory of Igor Stravinsky* for Small Orch. (1972); *Concerto rustico* for Cello and Orch. (1982); *Entrata and Bulgarian Folk Dance* (1983); *Lyric Suite* for Strings (1983); *Symphonic Sketch on a Popular Melody: Rum and Coca-Cola* (1986); Flute Concerto (1987); Violin Concerto (1989); Chamber Sym. (1990); *Passacaglia* (1991); *Bosnian Lullaby* (1993). **CHAMBER:** 3 trios (1949, 1950, 1987); 3 string quartets (1951, 1966, 1985); Sonata for Solo Violin (1955); *Berceuse* for Clarinet and Piano (1983); *Thema con variationi* for Violin and Piano (1985); *Ecological Trio* for Clarinet, Violin, and Double Bass (1987); *3 Movements* for Harp (1992); piano pieces. **VOCAL:** *The True Apology of Socrates* for Bass, Strings, and Percussion (1967); *The Life and the Sufferings of the Sinful Sofronii,* oratorio for Narrator, Tenor, Chorus, and Orch. (1976); *In the Eye of the Storm* for Tenor and Orch. (1986); choruses; songs.

Pirro, André (Gabriel Edme), distinguished French musicologist and organist; b. St.-Dizier, Haute-Marne, Feb. 12, 1869; d. Paris, Nov. 11, 1943. He first studied with his father, the local organist, then went to Paris, where he served as organist and maître de chapelle at the Collège Stanislas; also audited the organ classes given by Franck and Widor at the Paris Cons. (1889–91). He studied law at the Sorbonne and continued private studies in music; also studied in the faculty of arts in Nancy (1898–99); received his doctorat ès lettres from the Sorbonne in 1907 with the diss. *L'Esthétique de Jean-Sébastien Bach* (publ. in Paris, 1907), which was followed that same year by the supplementary diss. *Descartes et la musique* (publ. in Paris, 1907). When the Schola Cantorum was founded in 1896, he was made a member of its board of directors and prof. of music history and organ; was organist at St. Jean-Baptiste de Belleville (1900–1904); lectured on music history at the École des Hautes Études Sociales (1904–14); was prof. of music history at the Sorbonne (1912–37). His outstanding students included Plamenac, Machabey, Rokseth, and Pincherle. In addition to his valuable books, he wrote many important articles on various aspects of music.

WRITINGS: *L'Orgue de Jean-Sébastien Bach* (Paris, 1895; Eng. tr., 1902); *J.-S. Bach* (Paris, 1906; 2nd ed., 1949; Eng. tr., 1957); *Dietrich Buxtehude* (Paris, 1913); *Schütz* (Paris, 1913); *Jean Sébastien Bach auteur comique* (Madrid, 1915); *Les Clavecinistes: Étude critique* (Paris, 1924); *La Musique à Paris sous le règne de Charles VI, 1380–1422* (Strasbourg, 1930); ed. with A. Gastoué et al., *Bibliothèque nationale: La Musique française du moyen-âge à la Révolution* (Paris, 1934); *Histoire de la musique de la fin du XIVe siècle à la fin du XVIe* (Paris, 1940); *Mélanges: Recueil d'articles publié sous le patronage de la Société française de musicologie* (Geneva, 1971).

BIBL.: R. Rolland et al., "Hommage à A. P.," *Information musicale,* IV (Paris, 1943).

Pirrotta, Nino (actually, **Antonino**), eminent Italian musicologist; b. Palermo, June 13, 1908. He studied at the Conservatorio Vincenzo Bellini in Palermo; then received a diploma in organ and organ composition at the Florence Cons. (1930) and a liberal arts degree at the Univ. of Florence (1931). He was a lecturer in music history and a librarian at the Palermo Cons. (1936–48); was chief librarian at the Santa Cecilia Cons. in Rome (1948–56); was also a visiting prof. at Princeton Univ. (1954–55), the Univ. of Calif., Los Angeles (summer, 1955), and Columbia Univ. (1955). He then was a prof. at Harvard Univ. (1956–72), where he also was chairman of the music dept. (1965–68); subsequently was prof. of music history at the Univ. of Rome (1972–83). He was made a member of the American Academy of Arts and Sciences (1967) and an honorary member of the American Musicological Soc. (1980). An erudite scholar of wide interests, Pirrotta greatly distinguished himself in the study of Renaissance polyphony and Baroque opera. In addition to his important books, he ed. *The Music of Fourteenth-century Italy* in the Corpus Mensurabilis Musicae series (1954–64), and contributed valuable articles to music journals and other publications.

WRITINGS: With E. Li Gotti, *Il Sacchetti e la tecnica musicale del trecento italiano* (Florence, 1935); *Il codice estense lat.568 e la musica francese in Italia al principio del '400* (Palermo, 1946); *Li due Orfei: Da Poliziano a Monteverdi* (Turin, 1969; 2nd ed., 1975; Eng. tr., 1981); *Music and Culture in Italy from the Middle Ages to the Baroque: A Collection of Essays* (Cambridge, Mass., and London, 1984); *Musica tra*

Medioevo e Rinascimento (Turin, 1984); *Scelte poetiche di musicisti: Teatro, poesia e musica da Willaert a Malipiero* (Venice, 1987); *Don Giovanni's Progress: A Rake Goes to the Opera* (N.Y., 1994).

BIBL.: F. Della Seta and F. Piperno, eds., *In Cantu et in sermone: For N. P. on His 80th Birthday* (Florence, 1989).

Pirumov, Alexander, Russian composer; b. Tiflis, Feb. 6, 1930. He studied composition with Kabalevsky at the Moscow Cons. (graduated, 1956). He taught piano first at the music school attached to the Cons. (1956–62), then at the Cons. itself (1962–71; lecturer, from 1971). His *Prelude and Toccata* (1962) and *Scherzo* (1974) were required pieces for the Tchaikovsky Piano Competition.

WORKS: ORCH.: 4 syms. (1956; for Strings and Percussion, 1963; 1965; 1973); *Concert Variations* for Piano and Orch. (1972). **CHAMBER:** 4 string quartets (1954, 1955, 1959, 1967). **KEYBOARD: PIANO:** 2 sonatinas (1961, 1966); *Children's Album* (24 pieces; 1968); *Variations on a Theme of Bartók* (1968); Sonata (1973). **ORGAN:** *5 Preludes* (1967). **VOCAL:** *October Days*, oratorio (1967); *Requiem in Memory of My Brother* (1975; in memory of his brother, who was killed in World War II).

Pisk, Paul A(madeus), Austrian-born American composer, pedagogue, and musicologist; b. Vienna, May 16, 1893; d. Los Angeles, Jan. 12, 1990. He studied piano with J. Epstein, composition with Schreker and Schoenberg, and orchestration with Hellmesberger in Vienna; studied musicology with Adler at the Univ. of Vienna (Ph.D., 1916, with the diss. *Das Parodieverfahren in den Messen des Jacobus Gallus*); later studied at the Vienna Cons. (graduated, 1919). From 1922 to 1934 he taught at the Volkshochschule Volksheim in Vienna; in 1925–26, was instructor in theory at the New Vienna Cons.; from 1931 to 1933, lectured at the Austro-American Cons. in Mondsee, near Salzburg. He also wrote music criticism for the Socialist newspaper *Wiener Arbeiterzeitung*; with Paul Stefan, he founded the progressive music journal *Musikblätter des Anbruch*. He was closely associated with Schoenberg, Berg, and Webern, and espoused the tenets of the New Vienna School, adopting in many of his own works the methods of 12-tone composition. As the dark cloud of ignorance and barbarity fell on Germany and approached Austria, Pisk left Vienna and emigrated to the U.S. (1936); became a naturalized American citizen (1941). He occupied with great honor teaching posts at the Univ. of Redlands, Calif. (1937–51), the Univ. of Texas in Austin (1951–63), and Washington Univ. in St. Louis (1963–72); he also gave courses at summer sessions at the Univ. of Calif., Los Angeles (1966), the Univ. of Cincinnati (1969), and Dartmouth College (1972). In 1973 he settled in Los Angeles. His 90th birthday was celebrated by his many disciples and admirers in 1983. He continued to compose prolifically, accumulating an impressive catalogue of works, mostly chamber music. He wrote (with H. Ulrich) *History of Music and Musical Style* (N.Y., 1963); ed. masses by Jacobus Gallus for Denkmäler der Tonkunst in Österreich. A Festschrift, *Paul A. Pisk, Essays in His Honor*, ed. by J. Glowacki, was publ. in 1966.

WORKS: DRAMATIC: *Schattenseite*, monodrama (1931); *American Suite*, ballet (Redlands, Calif., Feb. 19, 1948). **ORCH.:** *Partita* (Prague, May 17, 1925); *Suite on American Folksongs* for 24 Instruments (1944); *Bucolic Suite* for Strings (Saratoga Springs, Sept. 10, 1946); *Rococo Suite* for Viola and Orch. (1953); *Baroque Chamber Concerto* for Violin and Orch. (1953); *Canzona* for Chamber Orch. (1954); *3 Ceremonial Rites* (1957–58); *Elegy* for Strings (1958); *Sonnet* for Chamber Orch. (1960). **CHAMBER:** 4 violin sonatas (1921, 1927, 1939, 1977); String Quartet (1924); *Fantasy* for Clarinet and Piano (1925); *Rondo* for Violin and Piano (1932); *Variations on a Waltz by Beethoven* for Violin, Viola, and Guitar (1933); Piano Trio (1933–35); *Moresca Figures* for Violin, Clarinet, and Piano (1934); *Berceuse slave* for Oboe and Piano (1939); *Bohemian Dance Rondo* for Bassoon and Piano (1939); Suite for 4 Clarinets (1939); *Shanty-Boy Fantasy* for Oboe and Piano (1940); *Variations on an Old Trumpet Tune* for Brass Sextet (1942); *Little Woodwind Music* (1945); *Cortege* for Brass Choir (1945); *Variations and Fugue on an American Theme* for Violin and Cello (1946); Clarinet Sonata (1947); Suite for Oboe and Piano (1947); *Introduction and Rondo* for Flute and Piano (1948); 2 flute suites (1950, 1969); *Intermezzo* for Clarinet and Piano (1950); *Elegy and Scherzino* for Oboe, 2 Clarinets, and Bassoon (1951); Quartet for 2 Trumpets, Horn, and Trombone (1951); Horn Sonata (1953); Suite for 2 Flutes (1953); Flute Sonata (1954); Suite for Oboe, Clarinet, and Piano (1955); *Eclogue* for Violin and Piano (1955); *Idyll* for Oboe and Piano (1957); String Trio (1958); Woodwind Quintet (1958); Woodwind Trio (1960); *Music* for Violin, Clarinet, Cello, and Bassoon (1962); *Envoi* for 6 Instruments (1964); *Duo* for Clarinet and Bassoon (1966); *Perpetuum mobile* for Organ and Brass Quartet (1968); Suite for Woodwind and Piano (1970); *Variables* for Clarinet and Piano (1973); *Discussions* for Oboe, Clarinet, Bassoon, Viola, and Cello (1974); Brass Quintet (1976); Violin Sonata (1977); *Three Vignettes* for Clarinet and Bassoon (1977); *3 Movements* for Violin and Piano (1978); Trio for Oboe, Clarinet, and Bassoon (1979); *Music* for Oboe and Piano (1982); Suite for Cello (1983); piano pieces. **VOCAL:** *3 Songs* for Voice and String Quartet (Salzburg, Aug. 10, 1922); *Die neue Stadt*, "cantata for the people" (Vienna, Nov. 1926); *Der grosse Regenmacher*, scenic ballad for Narrator and Orch. (1931); *Requiem* for Baritone and Orch. (1942); *A Toccata of Galuppi* for Soprano and Orch. (1947); songs.

BIBL.: T. Collins, *The Instrumental Music of P.A. P.* (diss., Univ. of Missouri, 1972).

Piston, Walter (Hamor, Jr.), outstanding American composer and pedagogue; b. Rockland, Maine, Jan. 20, 1894; d. Belmont, Mass., Nov. 12, 1976. The family name was originally Pistone; his paternal grandfather was Italian. He received his primary education in Boston; took courses in architectural drawing at the Massachusetts Normal Art School, graduating in 1916; then took piano lessons with Harris Shaw, and studied violin with Fiumara, Theodorowicz, and Winternitz. He played in restaurants and places of public entertainment as a youth. During World War I, he was in the U.S. Navy; after the Armistice, he entered Harvard Univ., graduating in musical subjects summa cum laude in 1924; while at Harvard, he conducted concerts of the univ. orch., the Pierian Sodality. For a time he was employed as a draftsman for Boston Elevated Railway. In 1924 he went to Paris on a John Knowles Paine Traveling Fellowship, and became a student of Boulanger; also took courses with Dukas at the École Normale de Musique (1925). Returning to the U.S. in 1926, he was appointed to the faculty of Harvard Univ.; in 1944, became a prof. of music; was named prof. emeritus in 1960. As a teacher, he was greatly esteemed, not only because of his consummate knowledge of music and pedagogical ability, but also because of his immanent humanity in instructing students whose aesthetics differed from his own; among his grateful disciples was Leonard Bernstein. As a composer, Piston followed a cosmopolitan course, adhering to classical forms while extending his harmonic structures toward a maximum of tonal saturation; he was particularly expert in contrapuntal writing. Beginning about 1965, Piston adopted a modified system of 12-tone composition, particularly in initial thematic statements; his Sym. No. 8 (1964–65) and *Variations* for Cello and Orch. (1966) are explicitly dodecaphonic. Piston rejected the narrow notion of ethnic Americanism in his music, and stated once that an artist could be as American working in the Library of the Boston Atheneum as roaming the Western prairie; yet he employed upon occasion the syncopated rhythms of jazz. He received Pulitzer Prizes in Music for his Sym. No. 3 and Sym. No. 7, and N.Y. Music Critics' Circle Awards for his Sym. No. 2, Viola Concerto, and String Quartet No. 5. He held the degree of D.Mus. *honoris causa* from Harvard Univ.; was elected a member of the National Inst. of Arts and Letters (1938), the American Academy of Arts and Sciences (1940), and the American Academy of Arts and Letters (1955). He traveled little and declined invitations to go to South America and to Russia under the auspices of the State Dept., preferring to live in his house in suburban Belmont, near Boston. His working habits were remarkably methodical; he rarely altered or revised his music once it was put on paper, and his handwriting was calligraphic. With 2 exceptions, he never wrote for voices.

WORKS: BALLET: *The Incredible Flutist* (Boston, May 30, 1938; suite, 1938; Pittsburgh, Nov. 22, 1940). **ORCH.:** *Symphonic Piece* (1927; Boston, March 23, 1928); 2 suites: No. 1 (1929; Boston, March 28, 1930) and No. 2 (1947–48; Dallas, Feb. 29, 1948); *Concerto for Orchestra* (1933; Boston, March 6, 1934); *Prelude and Fugue* (1934; Cleveland, March 12, 1936); 8 syms.: No. 1 (1937; Boston, April 8, 1938), No. 2 (1943; Washington, D.C., March 5, 1944), No. 3 (1947; Boston, Jan. 9, 1948), No. 4 (1950; Minneapolis, March 30, 1951), No. 5 (1954; for the 50th anniversary of the Juilliard School of Music, N.Y., Feb. 24, 1956), No. 6 (for the 75th anniversary of the Boston Sym. Orch., Nov. 25, 1955), No. 7 (1960; Philadelphia, Feb. 10, 1961), and No. 8 (1964–65; Boston, March 5, 1965); Concertino for Piano and Chamber Orch. (CBS Radio, N.Y., June 20, 1937); 2 violin concertos: No. 1 (1939; N.Y., March 18, 1940) and No. 2 (Pittsburgh, Oct. 28, 1960); Sinfonietta (Boston, March 10, 1941); *Prelude and Allegro* for Organ and Strings (CBS, Cambridge, Mass., Aug. 8, 1943); *Fugue on a Victory Tune* (N.Y., Oct. 21, 1944); *Variation on a Theme by Eugene Goossens* (1944; Cincinnati, March 23, 1945); *Toccata* (Bridgeport, Conn., Oct. 14, 1948); *Fantasy* for English Horn, Harp, and Strings (1952; Boston, Jan. 1, 1954); *Serenata* (Louisville, Oct. 24, 1956); Viola Concerto (1957; Boston, March 7, 1958); Concerto for 2 Pianos and Orch. (1959; Hanover, N.H., July 4, 1964); *3 New England Sketches* (Worcester, Mass., Oct. 23, 1959); *Symphonic Prelude* (Cleveland, April 20, 1961); *Lincoln Center Festival Overture* (N.Y., Sept. 25, 1962); *Capriccio* for Harp and String Orch. (1963; Madrid, Oct. 19, 1964); *Variations on a Theme by Edward Burlingame Hill* (Boston, April 30, 1963); *Pine Tree Fantasy* (Portland, Maine, Nov. 16, 1965); *Variations* for Cello and Orch. (1966; N.Y., March 2, 1967); Clarinet Concerto (Hanover, N.H., Aug. 6, 1967); *Ricercare* (1967; N.Y., March 7, 1968); *Fantasia* for Violin and Orch. (1970; Hanover, N.H., March 11, 1973); Flute Concerto (1971; Boston, Sept. 22, 1972); *Bicentennial Fanfare* (Cincinnati, Nov. 14, 1975); Concerto for String Quartet, Wind Ensemble, and Percussion (Portland, Maine, Oct. 26, 1976). **BAND:** *Tunbridge Fair: Intermezzo* (1950). **CHAMBER:** *3 Pieces* for Flute, Clarinet, and Bassoon (1926); Flute Sonata (1930); Suite for Oboe and Piano (1931); 5 string quartets (1933, 1935, 1947, 1951, 1962); 2 piano trios (1935, 1966); Violin Sonata (1939); *Fanfare for the Fighting French* for Brass and Percussion (Cincinnati, Oct. 23, 1942); *Interlude* for Viola and Piano (1942); Quintet for Flute and Strings (1942); *Partita* for Violin, Viola, and Organ (1944); Sonatina for Violin and Harpsichord or Piano (1945); *Divertimento* for 9 Instruments (1946); *Duo* for Viola and Cello (1949); Piano Quintet (1949); Wind Quintet (1956); Sextet for Strings (1964); Piano Quartet (1964); *Souvenirs* for Flute, Viola, and Harp (1967); *Ceremonial Fanfare* for Brass and Percussion (1969; N.Y., Feb. 10, 1970); *Duo* for Cello and Piano (1972); *3 Counterpoints* for Violin, Viola, and Cello (1973). **KEYBOARD: PIANO:** Sonata (1926); *Passacaglia* (1943); *Improvisation* (1945). **ORGAN:** *Chromatic Study on B.A.C.H.* (1940). **VOCAL:** *Carnival Song* for Men's Chorus and 11 Brasses (1938; Cambridge, Mass., March 7, 1940); *Psalm and Prayer of David* for Chorus, Flute, Clarinet, Bassoon, Violin, Viola, Cello, and Double Bass (1958).

WRITINGS: *Principles of Harmonic Analysis* (Boston, 1933); *Harmony* (N.Y., 1944; 5th ed., rev. and enl. by M. DeVoto, 1987); *Counterpoint* (N.Y., 1947); *Orchestration* (N.Y., 1955).

BIBL.: N. Slonimsky, "W. P.," in H. Cowell, *American Composers on American Music* (Stanford, Calif., 1933); I. Citkowitz, "W. P.—Classicist," *Modern Music* (Jan.–Feb. 1936); E. Carter, "W. P.," *Musical Quarterly* (July 1946); W. Austin, "P.'s Fourth Symphony," *Music Review* (May 1955); O. Daniel et al., *W. P.* (N.Y., 1964); H. Lindenfeld, *Three Symphonies of W. P.: An Analysis* (diss., Cornell Univ., 1975); H. Gleason and W. Becker, "W. P.," *20th-century American Composers* (Bloomington, Ind., 2nd ed., rev., 1981); H. Pollack, *W. P.* (Ann Arbor, Mich., 1981).

Pistor, Gotthelf, German tenor; b. Berlin, Oct. 17, 1887; d. Cologne, April 4, 1947. He began his career as an actor in Berlin. Following vocal training from Luria, he made his operatic debut in Nuremberg in 1923. He had engagements in Würzburg (1924–25), Darmstadt (1925–27), and Magdeburg (1928–29) before serving as a principal member of the Cologne Opera (from 1929). He also made guest appearances at the Bayreuth Festivals (1925; 1927–31), at the Zoppot Festivals (1930–38), and in San Francisco (1931). In his last years, he taught voice in Cologne. Pistor was esteemed for such Wagnerian roles as Tristan, Parsifal, Siegfried, and Siegmund.

Pitfield, Thomas B(aron), English composer, teacher, artist, and writer; b. Bolton, April 5, 1903. He was educated at the Royal Manchester College of Music and the Bolton School of Arts. He taught at Tettenhall College (1935–45) and the Royal Manchester College of Music (1947–72), and finally at the latter's successor, the Royal Northern College of Music (1972–73). In addition to his musical interests, he also was active as an artist and writer. He publ. 2 autobiographical vols., *No Song, No Supper* (1986) and *A Song After Supper* (1991). His compositions were in a simple style, and included dramatic scores, orch. works, brass band pieces, chamber music, piano pieces, and choral works.

Pitt, Percy, English conductor and composer; b. London, Jan. 4, 1870; d. there, Nov. 23, 1932. He studied with Jadassohn and Reinecke at the Leipzig Cons. and with Rheinberger at the Akademie der Tonkunst in Munich. Returning to England in 1893, he pursued his career in London; was musical advisor (1902–07) and musical director (1907–24) of the Grand Opera Syndicate at Covent Garden; was the first English conductor to appear at Covent Garden (1907), returning there in 1909–10 and 1919–20; was artistic director of the British National Opera Co. (1922–24) and musical advisor to the BBC (1922–24), serving as the latter's musical director (1924–30). He wrote stage music, a *Ballade* for Violin and Orch. (1900) for Ysaÿe, a Clarinet Concerto, and a *Sérénade du passant* for Tetrazzini.

BIBL.: J. Chamier, *P. P. of Covent Garden and the BBC* (London, 1938).

Pittaluga, Gustavo, Spanish composer; b. Madrid, Feb. 8, 1906. He studied law at the Univ. of Madrid and composition with Oscar Esplá. He was a member of the Grupo de los 8 in Madrid and of the Paris group of modern musicians, Triton (1935); from 1936 to 1939, was a member of the staff of the Spanish Embassy in Washington, D.C. (for the Loyalist government); then settled in the U.S., where he was active with the film library at the Museum of Modern Art in N.Y. (1941–43).

WORKS: *Vocalise-Étude* for Voice and Piano (1932); *La Romería de los Cornudos*, ballet (1933); *El Loro*, zarzuela (1933); *Concerto militaire* for Violin and Orch. (1933); *Ricercare* for Violin, Clarinet, Bassoon, and Trumpet (1934); *Petite suite* for 10 Instruments (1935; also as *3 pièces pour une espagnolade* for Piano); *Berceuse* for Violin and Piano (1935); *6 danses espagnoles en suite* for Piano (1935); *Capriccio alla romantica* for Piano and Orch. (1936); *5 canciones populares* for Chorus and 10 Instruments (1939); *Habañera* for Violin and Piano (1942); *Lament for Federico García Lorca* for Narrator and Orch. (1942).

Pittel, Harvey, American saxophonist; b. Great Falls, Mont., June 22, 1943. He studied with Kalman Bloch and Franklyn Stokes; then took courses at the Univ. of Southern Calif. in Los Angeles (1961–65), where he received his doctorate in music education. After studies with Frederick Hemke at Northwestern Univ. (1965–66), he played in the U.S. Military Academy Band (1966–69), during which time he continued his studies, with Joseph Allard. He won the silver medal at the Geneva International Competition (1970). He made his formal debut as a soloist in Ingolf Dahl's Saxophone Concerto with the Boston Sym. Orch. (1971), and his recital debut at N.Y.'s Carnegie Recital Hall (1973); subsequently toured throughout North America and Europe, appearing as a soloist with the leading orchs., as a recitalist, and as a chamber music player.

Pitzinger, Gertrude, Bohemian contralto; b. Mährisch-Schönberg, Aug. 15, 1904. She studied music with Joseph Marx at the Vienna Academy of Music, and voice with various teachers. After several concert tours in central Europe, she went to the U.S. and gave a N.Y. recital on Jan. 17, 1938, with excellent success. She specialized in German lieder; her repertoire included some 400 songs. She taught singing at the Hochschule für Musik in Frankfurt am Main (1960–73).

Pizzetti, Ildebrando, eminent Italian composer and teacher; b. Parma, Sept. 20, 1880; d. Rome, Feb. 13, 1968. He studied piano with his father, Odvardo Pizzetti, in Parma and composition with Tebaldini at the Parma Cons., graduating in 1901. He was on the faculty of the Parma Cons. (1907–08); then of the Florence Cons. (1908–24), where he became director in 1917; from 1924 to 1936, was director of the Milan Cons.; then taught at the Accademia di Santa Cecilia in Rome (1936–58); from 1947 to 1952 he was also its president. In 1914 he founded (with G. Bastianelli) in Florence a modernistic periodical, pointedly named *Dissonanza,* to promote the cause of new music. In 1930 he made a trip to the U.S. to attend the performance of his *Rondo veneziano,* conducted by Toscanini with the N.Y. Phil.; in 1931 Pizzetti conducted his opera *Fra Gherardo* at the Teatro Colón in Buenos Aires. Pizzetti's music represents the Romantic trend in 20th century Italy; in his many works for the theater, he created the modern counterpart of medieval mystery plays; the mystical element is very strong in his own texts for his operas. He employed astringent chromatic harmony, but the mainstream of his melody flows along pure diatonic lines.

WORKS: DRAMATIC: OPERAS: *Fedra* (1909–12; Milan, March 20, 1915); *Debora e Jaele* (1915–21; Milan, Dec. 16, 1922); *Lo straniero* (1922–25; Rome, April 29, 1930); *Fra Gherardo* (1925–27; Milan, May 16, 1928); *Orséolo* (1931–35; Florence, May 4, 1935); *L'Oro* (1938–42; Milan, Jan. 2, 1947); *Vanna Lupa* (1947–49; Florence, May 4, 1949); *Ifigenia* (RAI, Oct. 3, 1950; 1st stage perf., Florence, May 9, 1951); *Cagliostro* (RAI, Nov. 5, 1952; 1st stage perf., Milan, Jan. 24, 1953); *La figlia di Iorio* (Naples, Dec. 4, 1954); *Assassinio nella cattedrale,* after T.S. Eliot (1957; Milan, March 1, 1958); *Il calzare d'argento* (Milan, March 23, 1961); *Clitennestra* (1961–64; Milan, March 1, 1965). **INCIDENTAL MUSIC TO:** G. d'Annunzio's *La nave* (1905–07; Rome, March 1908) and *La Pisanella* (Paris, June 11, 1913); F. Belcare's *La sacra rappresentazione di Abram e d'Isaac* (1915–17; Florence, June 1917; expanded into an opera, 1925; Turin, March 11, 1926); Aeschylus' *Agamemnon* (Syracuse, April 28, 1930); Sophocles' *Le trachiniae* (1932; Syracuse, April 26, 1933); Sophocles' *Edipo a Colono* (Syracuse, April 24, 1936); *La festa delle Panatenee* (1935; Paestum, June 1936); Shakespeare's *As You Like It* (Florence, May 1938). **ORCH.:** *Ouverture per una farsa tragica* (1911); *Concerto dell'estate* (1928; N.Y., Feb. 28, 1929); *Rondo veneziano* (1929; N.Y., Feb. 27, 1930; as a ballet, Milan, Jan. 8, 1931); Cello Concerto (Venice, Sept. 11, 1934); Sym. (1940); Violin Concerto (1944; Rome, Dec. 9, 1945); *Canzone di beni perduti* (1948; Venice, Sept. 4, 1950); Harp Concerto (1958–60). **CHAMBER:** 2 string quartets (1906; 1932–33); Violin Sonata (1918–19); Cello Sonata (1921); Piano Trio (1925). **PIANO:** *Da un autunno già lontano,* 3 pieces (1911); *Sonata 1942* (1942). **VOCAL:** *Messa di requiem* (1922); *De profundis* (1937); *Epithalamium,* cantata for Soloists, Chorus, and Orch. (1939); *Oritur sol et occidit,* cantata for Brass and Orch. (1943); *Cantico di gloria "Attollite portas"* for 3 Choruses, 22 Wind Instruments, 2 Pianos, and Percussion (1948); *Vanitas vanitatum,* cantata for Soloists, Men's Chorus, and Orch. (1958); *Filiae Jerusalem, adjuro vos,* cantata for Soprano, Women's Chorus, and Orch. (1966); songs.

WRITINGS: *La musica dei Greci* (Rome, 1914); *Musicisti contemporanei* (Milan, 1914); *Intermezzi critici* (Florence, 1921); *Paganini* (Turin, 1940); *Musica e dramma* (Rome, 1945); *La musica italiana dell' 800* (Turin, 1947).

BIBL.: R. Fondi, *I. P. e il dramma musicale italiano d'oggi* (Rome, 1919); special issue of *Il pianoforte,* II (Turin, 1921); G. Gatti, "I. P.," *Musical Quarterly* (Jan., April 1923); G. Tebaldini, *I. P. nelle memorie* (Parma, 1931); G. Gatti, *I. P.* (Turin, 1934; 2nd ed., 1955; Eng. tr., 1951); G. Gavazzeni, *Tre studi su P.* (Como, 1937); special issue of *La Rassegna Musicale,* XIII (1940); V. Bucchi, L. Dallapiccola et al., *Firenze a I. P.* (Florence, 1947); G. Gavazzeni, *Altri studi pizzettiani* (Bergamo, 1956); M. la Morgia, ed., *La citta d'annunziana a I. P.: Saggi e note* (Pescara, 1958); B. Pizzetti, ed., *I. P.: Cronologia e bibliografia* (Parma, 1980).

Pizzini, Carlo Alberto, Italian composer; b. Rome, March 22, 1905; d. there, Sept. 9, 1981. He studied with Respighi at the Accademia di Santa Cecilia in Rome, graduating in 1929; later was an administrator there and with the RAI.

WORKS: DRAMATIC: *Dardanio,* opera (Rome, 1928); theater, film, and radio music. **ORCH.:** *Sinfonia in stile classico* (1930); *Il poema delle Dolomiti* (1931); *Strapaese* (1932); *Al Piemonte* (1941); *Grotte di Postumia* (1941); *Concierto para tres hermanas* for Guitar and Orch. (1969). **OTHER:** Chamber music; piano pieces.

Plaichinger, Thila, Austrian soprano; b. Vienna, March 13, 1868; d. there, March 17, 1939. She studied with Gänsbacher at the Vienna Cons. and with Dustmann and Mampe-Babbnigg. In 1893 she made her operatic debut in Hamburg. She was a principal member of the Strasbourg Opera (1894–1901) and of the Berlin Royal Opera (1901–14). In 1904 and 1910 she was a guest artist at London's Covent Garden, and also appeared in Munich, Dresden, and Vienna. Among her finest roles were Isolde, Brünnhilde, Ortrud, Venus, and Elektra.

Plakidis, Peteris, Latvian composer; b. Riga, March 4, 1947. He graduated from the Latvian Cons. in Riga (1970), where he studied composition with V. Utkins and Gederts Ramans; taught there from 1973, and also was secretary of the Latvian Composer's Union (1978–84; from 1989). In 1990 he made a tour of the U.S. as harpsichordist of the Latvian Chamber Orch.

WORKS: ORCH.: *Music* for Piano, Timpani, and Strings (1969); Piano Concerto (1975); *Legend* (1976); *Interchanges* for a Group of Soloists (1977); Concerto for 2 Oboes and Chamber Orch. (1982); *Concerto-Ballad* for 2 Violins, Piano, and Strings (1984); *Canto* (1989). **CHAMBER:** *Improvisation and Burlesque* for Piano Trio (1966); *Prelude and Pulsation* for Wind Quintet (1975); *2 Sketches* for Oboe (1975); *Fifths,* invention for 2 Pianos (1976); *2 Retrospections* (1977); *A Short Canon and Animated Cartoon Film* for Flute, Oboe, and Piano (1979); *Romantic Music* for Piano Trio (1980); *Homage to Haydn* for Piano, Flute, and Cello (1982). **VOCAL:** *The Rifleman* for Voice and Orch. (1972); choruses; songs.

Plamenac, Dragan, eminent Croatian-born American musicologist; b. Zagreb, Feb. 8, 1895; d. Ede, the Netherlands, March 15, 1983. He studied jurisprudence at the Univ. of Zagreb; then took courses in composition with Schreker at the Vienna Academy of Music and with Novák in Prague. In 1919 he went to Paris and attended lectures at the Sorbonne given by Pirro; then had a seminar with Adler at the Univ. of Vienna, receiving his Ph.D. there in 1925 with the diss. *Johannes Ockeghem als Motetten- und Chansonkomponist.* From 1928 to 1939 he taught at the Univ. of Zagreb; after the outbreak of World War II, he went to the U.S., becoming a naturalized citizen in 1946. In 1947 he received a Guggenheim fellowship. He taught at the Univ. of Ill., Urbana (1954–63). Plamenac's chief accomplishment was his painstaking and fruitful research into the sources of the music of the Renaissance. He prepared a major ed. of the works of Ockeghem in the Publikationen älterer Musik, Jg. I/2 (Leipzig, 1927); a 2nd ed., rev. in 1959, was publ. in N.Y. as *Masses I–VIII in the Collected Works,* I; *Masses and Mass Sections IX–XVI* appeared as vol. II (N.Y., 1947; 2nd ed., 1966).

BIBL.: G. Reese and R. Snow, eds., *Essays in Musicology in Honor of D. P. on his 70th Birthday* (Pittsburgh, 1969).

Plantinga, Leon (Brooks), American musicologist; b. Ann Arbor, Mich., March 25, 1935. He studied at Calvin College (B.A., 1957), Michigan State Univ. (M.Mus., 1959), and Yale Univ. (Ph.D., 1964, with the diss. *The Musical Criticism of Robert Schumann in the "Neue Zeitschrift für Musik"*). He taught there from 1963, he became a prof. (1974), acting chairman (1978–79), and chairman (1979–86) of its music dept. In 1985 he received the ASCAP-Deems Taylor Award for his study *Romantic Music: A History of Musical Style in Nineteenth-Century Europe.*

WRITINGS: *Schumann as Critic* (New Haven, Conn., and London, 1967); *Muzio Clementi: His Life and Music* (London, 1977); *Romantic Music: A History of Musical Style in Nineteenth-Century Europe* (N.Y. and London, 1984); *Anthology of Romantic Music* (N.Y. and London, 1984).

Plaschke, Friedrich (real name, **Bedřich Plaške**), Czech bass-baritone; b. Jaroměr, Jan. 7, 1875; d. Prague, Nov. 20, 1951. He studied with Leontine von Döttcher and Ottilie Sklenář-Mala in Prague, and then with Karl Scheidemantel in Dresden. He made his operatic debut with the Dresden Court (later State) Opera as the Herald in *Lohengrin* in 1900; was on its roster until 1939; during his tenure there, he created the following roles in operas by Richard Strauss: Pöschel in *Feuersnot*, the 1st Nazarene in *Salome*, Da-Ud in *Die ägyptische Helena*, Count Waldner in *Arabella*, and Sir Morosus in *Die schweigsame Frau.* He made many guest appearances at Vienna and Munich; also sang at Bayreuth, at Covent Garden in London, and in the U.S. with the German Opera Co. in 1923–24.

Plasson, Michel, French conductor; b. Paris, Oct. 2, 1933. He received training in piano from Lazare-Lévy, and then studied percussion at the Paris Cons., where he took the premier prix. In 1962 he won 1st prize in the Besançon conducting competiton, and then studied conducting in the U.S. with Leinsdorf, Monteux, and Stokowski. From 1966 to 1968 he was music director of the Théâtre de Metz. In 1968 he became conductor of the Théâtre du Capitole in Toulouse, where he served as its music and general director from 1973 to 1982. In 1974 he became music director of the Orchestre du Capitole in Toulouse, which became the Orchestre National du Capitole in 1980. He took the orch. on various tours of Europe and North America. As a guest conductor, he appeared with many of the major orchs. and opera houses of the world. In 1987 he became principal guest conductor of the Tonhalle Orch. in Zürich. In 1994 he became music director of the Dresden Phil.

Plath, Wolfgang, German musicologist; b. Riga, Latvia, Dec. 27, 1930; d. Augsburg, March 19, 1995. He studied musicology at the Free Univ. of Berlin with Gerstenberg, and later at the Univ. of Tübingen (Ph.D., 1958, with the diss. *Das Klavierbüchlein für Wilhelm Friedemann Bach*). In 1960 he was named co-ed. (with Wolfgang Rehm) of the *Neue Mozart-Ausgabe.* His studies of Mozart autographs and texts are valuable; he contributed important articles to the *Mozart-Jahrbuch.*

Plaza (-Alfonzo), Juan Bautista, Venezuelan composer and organist; b. Caracas, July 19, 1898; d. there, Jan. 1, 1964. He went to Rome in 1920 to study at the Pontifical Inst. of Sacred Music; upon returning to Venezuela, became organist of the Cathedral of Caracas. He wrote a number of sacred choral works; also symphonic poems: *El picacho abrupto, Vigilia, Campanas de Pascua, Las horas,* etc.; *Fuga criolla* for Orch.; *Sonatina venezolana* for Piano; songs.

Plé-Caussade, Simone, French pianist, pedagogue, and composer; b. Paris, Aug. 14, 1897; d. Bagnères-de-Bigorre, Aug. 6, 1985. She studied piano at the Paris Cons. with Cortot and composition with **Georges Caussade**, whom she later married. In 1928 she was appointed prof. of harmony and counterpoint at the Paris Cons.; among her students were Gilbert Amy and Betsy Jolas. She wrote a number of orch. and chamber music works in a fine impressionistic manner.

Pleasants, Henry, American music critic and writer on music; b. Wayne, Pa., May 12, 1910. He was educated at the Philadelphia Musical Academy and the Curtis Inst. of Music in Philadelphia. From 1930 to 1942 he was music critic of the *Philadelphia Evening Bulletin*, and then central European music correspondent of the *N.Y. Times* from 1945 to 1955. From 1950 to 1964 he was also active with the U.S. Foreign Service. In 1967 he became the London music critic of the *International Herald Tribune* and the London ed. of *Stereo Review.* He was active as a guest lecturer throughout the U.S. and England, and also appeared on radio and television programs of the BBC, as well as those in North America and Europe. His writings appeared in many leading American and English music magazines, and he also was a contributor to the *Encyclopaedia Britannica* and *The New Grove Dictionary of Music and Musicians.* As a tr. and ed., he publ. *Vienna's Golden Years of Music 1850–1900* (writings of Hanslick: 1950); *The Musical Journeys of Louis Spohr* (1961), *The Musical World of Robert Schumann* (1965), *The Music Criticism of Hugo Wolf* (1979), and *Piano and Song* (by Friedrich Wieck; 1988).

WRITINGS (all publ. in N.Y.): *The Agony of Modern Music* (1955); *Death of a Music? The Decline of the European Tradition and the Rise of Jazz* (1961); *The Great Singers from the Dawn of Opera to Our Own Time* (1966; 3rd ed., rev. and enl., 1985); *Serious Music, and All That Jazz* (1969); *The Great American Popular Singers* (1974); *Opera in Crisis: Tradition, Present, Future* (1989).

Pleeth, William, English cellist and teacher; b. London, Jan. 12, 1916. He studied at the London Violoncello School and with Klengel at the Leipzig Cons. In 1932 he made his debut in Leipzig, and then returned to London, where he first appeared in 1933. In subsequent years, he appeared as a soloist with various British orchs. He also was a member of the Blech (1936–41) and Allegri (1953–67) string quartets. From 1948 to 1978 he was prof. of cello at the Guildhall School of Music in London. In 1989 he received the Order of the British Empire. Pleeth's most famous student was Jacqueline Du Pré.

Pleshakov, Vladimir, Russian-American pianist; b. Shanghai (of Russian parents), Oct. 4, 1934. He studied piano with Russian teachers in Shanghai; in 1949 he went to Sydney, where he took piano lessons with Alexander Sverjensky. In 1955 he emigrated to the U.S. and studied medicine at the Univ. of Calif., Berkeley (A.B., 1958). Turning back to music, he entered Stanford Univ. in the graduate school of music (Ph.D., 1973). He made a special study of piano manufacture in Beethoven's era, and performed on reconstructed pianos at his concerts of classical music.

Pleskow, Raoul, Austrian-born American composer and teacher; b. Vienna, Oct. 12, 1931. He went to the U.S. in 1939, and became a naturalized citizen in 1945; took courses at N.Y.'s Juilliard School of Music (1950–52), with Rathaus at Queens College (B.M., 1956), and with Luening at Columbia Univ. (M.M., 1958). He taught at C.W. Post College, Long Island Univ. (from 1959). His works combine both tonal and atonal means of expression.

WORKS: ORCH.: *2 Movements* (1968); *Music* (1980); *4 Bagatelles* (1981); *6 Epigrams* (1985); *Consort* for Strings (1988). **CHAMBER:** *Movement* for Flute, Cello, and Piano (1964); *Music* for 7 Players (1966); *Movement* for 9 Players (1967); *3 Bagatelles* for Flute, Viola, and Piano (1969); Trio for Flute, Cello, and Piano (1978); String Quartet (1979); *4 Pieces* for Flute, Cello, and Piano (1979); *Variations on a Lyric Fragment* for Cello and Piano (1980); *4 Short Pieces* for 7 Players (1981); *Divertimento: Sua sei canzoni* for 5 Players (1984); *Intrada* for Flute, Clarinet, Violin, and Cello (1984); *Composition* for 4 Instruments (1987); solo pieces for Violin, Viola, Cello, Brass, and Piano. **VOCAL:** 2 cantatas for Soloists, Chorus, and Orch. 1975, 1979); *6 Brief Verses* for 2 Sopranos and/or Women's

Voices, Strings, and Piano (1983); *Paumanok* for Soprano, Chorus, and Chamber Ensemble (1985); *Serenade* for Chorus and Orch. (1988); also many settings for Solo Voice with a variety of accompaniments.

Plessis, Hubert (Lawrence) du, distinguished South African composer, pedagogue, pianist, harpsichordist, and writer on music; b. Malmesbury District, June 7, 1922. He was a student of W. H. Bell. After training in piano at the Univ. of Stellenbosch (B.A., 1943), he studied with Friedrich Hartmann at Rhodes Univ. College in Grahamstown (B.Mus., 1945) and with Alan Bush and Howard Ferguson (composition and orchestration) at the Royal Academy of Music in London (1951–54). He was on the faculty of Rhodes Univ. College (1944–51), the Univ. of Cape Town (1955–57), and the Univ. of Stellenbosch (1956–82). In 1963 he was awarded the Gold Medal of the South African Academy for Arts and Sciences. He received an honorary D.Mus. degree from the Univ. of Stellenbosch in 1989. In 1994 State President F. W. de Klerk presented him with the Order for Meritorious Service, 1st class. Among his writings were *Johann Sebastian Bach* (1960), *Dagboek van "Die Dans von die Reën"* (1970), and *Letters from William Henry Bell* (1973). In his music, he followed a tonal course with some excursions into serial byways.

WORKS: DRAMATIC: Incidental music. **ORCH.:** Sym. (1953–54); *Music After 3 Paintings by Henri Rousseau* for Large Chamber Orch. (1962); *Feestelike Suite* for Chamber Orch. (1977–78). **CHAMBER:** String Quartet (1953); Trio for Piano, Violin, and Cello (1957–60); *3 Pieces* for Flute and Piano (1962–63); *Variasies Op 'n volkswysie* for Harp (1968); *4 Antique Dances* for Flute and Harpsichord or Piano (1972–74); Sonata for Solo Viola (1977); Suite for 2 Clarinets (1982); *'n Kleine hulde aan Bach* for 2 Oboes and Bassoon (1984); Sonata for Solo Cello (1991; rev. 1994). **PIANO:** 4 pieces (1943–45; rev. 1962); *6 Miniatures* (1945–49); 2 sonatas (1952; 1974–75); Sonata for Piano Duet (1953); *Prelude, Fugue, and Postlude* for Piano Duet (1954–55); *Inspiré par mes chats* (1963–64); 4 pieces (1964–65); *Toe ek 'n kind was* (When I was a child), suite (1970–71). **VOCAL:** *2 Christmas Carols* for Chorus (1953); *Malay Scenes* for Chorus, Clarinet, Harp, and String Orch. (1959); *The Dance of the Rain* for Chorus and Orch. (1959–60); *Kersliedjie* for Soprano, Mezzo-soprano, Alto, and Piano (1962); *Night and Dawn* for Soprano, Chorus, and Orch. (1965–66); *Requiem aeternam* for Chorus (1974–75); *Krokos* for Chorus (1982–83); *Hugenote-Kantata* for Soloists, Chorus, and Orch. (1986–87); other choral pieces and solo songs.

Pletnev, Mikhail, Russian pianist and conductor; b. Arkhangel'sk, April 14, 1957. He began piano lessons at age 7 with Julia Shashkina in Kazan; at 13, entered the Moscow Central Music School as a student of Yevgeni Timakin, and later attended master classes of Yakov Flier and Lev Vlasenko at the Cons. In 1977 he won the All-Union Competition; captured 1st prize in the Tchaikovsky Competition in Moscow in 1978. Following appearances in England and the U.S. in 1979, he made tours of Europe and Japan. He also took up conducting; in 1990 he founded the Russian National Orch. in Moscow, which he led on its debut tour of the U.S. (1992–93). As a pianist, Pletnev's repertoire extends from Bach to contemporary scores; he has won particular distinction for his interpretations of the Classical and Romantic masterworks. Among his compositions are orch. works and chamber pieces.

Plishka, Paul (Peter), American bass; b. Old Forge, Pa., Aug. 28, 1941. He studied at Montclair, N.J., State College. From 1961 to 1965 he was a member of the Paterson (N.J.) Lyric Opera; in 1965 he joined the Metropolitan Opera National Co., and sang with it on tour. On June 27, 1967, he made his Metropolitan Opera debut in a concert performance at the Botanical Gardens in the Bronx as the Uncle-Priest in *Madama Butterfly*; he first sang on the Metropolitan's stage as the Monk in *La Gioconda* on Sept. 21, 1967; remained on its roster for many years, most notably in such roles as King Marke, Leporello, Varlaam, Oroveso, Pimen, Gounod's Méphistophélès, and Henry VIII in *Anna Bolena*. In 1992 he celebrated his 25th anniversary at the Metropolitan Opera in an acclaimed appearance as Falstaff. In 1993 he won critical accolades as Philip II at the Seattle Opera. He also appeared as a concert singer with many of the major U.S. orchs.

Plotnikov, Eugene, Russian conductor; b. Odessa, Aug. 29, 1877; d. N.Y., Sept. 28, 1951. He studied at the Moscow Cons. He was a coach and assistant conductor at the Moscow Opera; also conducted at the Paris Opéra (1921). In 1922 he settled in the U.S.; conducted Russian operas in N.Y. and other American cities.

Plowright, Rosalind (Anne), English mezzo-soprano, later soprano; b. Worksop, May 21, 1949. She was a student of F. R. Cox at the Royal Manchester College of Music, where she made her operatic debut in the college's first British production of J. C. Bach's *Temistocle* in 1968. In 1975 she made her first appearance with the English National Opera in London as Page in *Salome*, and as Agathe with the Glyndebourne Touring Opera. In 1979 she won the Sofia International Competition and sang Miss Jessel in *The Turn of the Screw* at the English National Opera. She made her debut at London's Covent Garden as Ortlinde in 1980. In 1981 she sang at the Frankfurt am Main Opera and at the Bavarian State Opera in Munich. In 1982 she made her U.S. debut as a soloist with Muti and the Philadelphia Orch., and then her U.S. operatic debut in *Il Corsaro* in San Diego. In 1983 she appeared at Milan's La Scala, the Edinburgh Festival, and in San Francisco. She sang Aida at Covent Garden in 1984, and appeared at the Deutsche Oper in Berlin. In 1986 she sang Senta at Covent Garden. In 1987 she appeared as Gluck's Alceste at La Scala. In 1990 she made her debut at the Vienna State Opera as Amelia. She also toured widely as a soloist with orchs. and as a recitalist. Among her other operatic roles were Médée, Rossini's Desdemona, Norma, Ariadne, and Maddalena in *Andrea Chénier*.

Plush, Vincent, remarkable Australian composer; b. Adelaide, April 18, 1950. He studied piano, organ, and voice before embarking on regular courses at the Univ. of Adelaide (B.M., 1971), where his principal instructors in composition were Andrew McCredie and Richard Meale. From 1973 to 1980 he taught at the New South Wales State Conservatorium of Music in Sydney. In 1976 he founded the Seymour Group, an ensemble devoted to the performance of contemporary music. In 1981 he joined the staff of the Australian Broadcasting Commission (A.B.C.) in Sydney. From his earliest independent activities as a lecturer, radio commentator, and conductor, Plush dedicated his efforts to the promotion of Australian music. Thanks to a generous Harkness fellowship, he was able to spend a couple of years at Yale Univ., conducting interviews with a number of American composers for its Oral History Project; also worked at the Univ. of Minnesota (1981), and participated in an Australian Arts Festival in Minneapolis (1982). He then spent a year at the Center for Music Experiment and the Computer Music Facility at the Univ. of Calif. at San Diego. Returning to Australia in 1983, he became composer-in-residence for the A.B.C., where he inaugurated a series of radio broadcasts pointedly entitled "Mainstreet U.S.A.," dedicated to new American music. A firm believer in the authentic quality of Australian folk music, he organized in Sydney the whimsically named ensemble Magpipe Musicians, which gave performances of native music in schools and art galleries, on the radio, in the concert hall, at country festivals, citizenship ceremonies, railway openings, and suchlike events, public and private. Their programs were deliberately explorative, aggressive, and exhortatory, propagandistic of new ideas, often with a decided revolutionary trend. The titles of Plush's own works often pay tribute to revolutionary or heroic events, e.g., *On Shooting Stars—Homage to Victor Jara* (a Chilean folksinger murdered by the fascistic Chilean police), *Bakery Hill Rising* (memorializing the suppression of the rebellion of Australian gold miners in 1854), *Gallipoli Sunrise* (commemorating the sacrificial attempt at capturing the Gallipoli Straits in World War I, during which thousands of Australians perished), and *The Ludlow Lullabies* (recalling the brutal attack on striking coal miners in the region of Ludlow, Colo., in 1914). The musical setting of each of these works varies from astutely homophonic to acutely polyphonic, according to the requirements of the subject.

WORKS: DRAMATIC: *Australian Folksongs*, musical theater piece for Baritone and Ensemble (Sydney, July 19, 1977); *The Maitland and Morpeth String Quartet* for Narrator and String Quartet (Sydney, April 1, 1979; rev. 1985); *Facing the Danger* for Narrator and Instruments, after the poem *Say No* by Barbara Berman (1982; Las Vegas, Jan. 18, 1983); *Grody to the Max* for "Val"- (i.e. San Fernando "Valley Girl") speaker and Trumpeter (1983); *The Wakefield Chronicles*, pageant for Narrator, Solo Trumpet and Trombone, and Ensemble, after Edward Gibbon Wakefield (Adelaide, March 5, 1986); *The Muse of Fire* for Narrator, Baritone, Trumpet, Flute, Piano, Chorus, 2 Brass Bands, Children's Chorus, and Organ, after Andrew Torning (1986–87). **ORCH.:** *Pacifica* (1986; rev. 1987; Aspen, July 10, 1988); *Concord/Eendracht* (Utrecht, May 18, 1990); *Pilbara* for Strings (1991). **BRASS BAND:** *The Wakefield Chorales* (1986); *March of the Dalmatians* (1987). **CHAMBER:** *Aurores* for Horn, Piano, and Ensemble (from *O Paraguay!*; Kensington, New South Wales, July 31, 1979); *Bakery Hill Rising* for Solo Horn and 8 Other Horns (1980; Ballarat, Victoria, Feb. 14, 1981); *On Shooting Stars—Homage to Victor Jara* for Ensemble (Sydney, Sept. 11, 1981); *FireRaisers*, "Concertino in the Style of a Vaudeville Entertainment" for Trumpet and Ensemble (Brisbane, Queensland, Sept. 30, 1984); *Gallipoli Sunrise* for Tenor Trombone and 7 Other Trombones (1984); *Helices* for Percussion Quartet (from *The Wakefield Chronicles*; 1985); *The Wakefield Convocation* for Brass Quintet (1985); *The Wakefield Invocation* for Trumpet and Organ (1986); *The Ludlow Lullabies* for Violin and Piano (Colorado Springs, Oct. 19, 1989); *SkyFire* for 10 Pianos and Tape (Colorado Springs, Nov. 19, 1989); *Aunt Kelly's Book of Tangos* for Violin, Cello, and Piano (1990); *Florilegium I, II, and III* (Sydney, Sept. 28, 1990); *Los Dios de Los Muertos* for Percussion Quartet (1990); *The Love-Songs of Herbert Hoover* for Horn Trio (1991); also pieces for Solo Instruments, including *Franz Liszt Sleeps Alone*, piano nocturne (1985; Budapest, March 12, 1986) and *Encompassings* for Organ (Canberra, March 16, 1975). **TAPE:** *Estuary* (1978); *Stevie Wonder's Music* for Flute and Tape (Sydney, Nov. 4, 1979); *All Ears* (1985); *Metropolis: Sydney* (WDR, Cologne, Nov. 14, 1988). **VOCAL:** *Magnificat* for Soprano, Flute, and 3 Vocal Quartets (1970; Sydney, Sept. 8, 1976); *3 Carols* for Soprano, Contralto, and Children's Chorus (1978, 1979, 1982); *The Hymn of the Winstanly Levellers* for Speaking/Singing Chorus (Sydney, May 23, 1981); *Ode to Knocks* for Mixed Voices and Instruments (Knox, Victoria, Sept. 6, 1981); *Letters from the Antipodes: 6 English Reflections on Colonial Australia* for Small Chorus (1984; Sydney, July 9, 1989); *Letters from the Antipodes: 6 English Reflections on Colonial Australia* for Small Chorus (1984; Sydney, July 9, 1989); *All Ears*, radiophonic composition for Voices (Radio 2MBS-FM, Sydney, March 16, 1985); *The Muse of Fire*, pageant for Voices and Instruments (Penrith, New South Wales, Oct. 17, 1987); *Cornell Ceremonial Music* for Brass Instruments and Chorus (Winter Park, Fla., Nov. 10, 1988); *Andrew Torning's March to Victory* for Small Chorus and Piano (1989); *The Arraignment of Henry Lawson* for Voices and Instruments (1991); songs.

Pochon, Alfred, Swiss violinist; b. Yverdon, July 30, 1878; d. Lutry, Feb. 26, 1959. He made his first public appearance at the age of 11; then went to Liège to study with César Thomson, who engaged him as 2nd violin in his string quartet. In 1902 the philanthropist E. de Coppet asked Pochon to organize a string quartet, later to become famous as the Flonzaley Quartet, so named after Coppet's summer residence near Lausanne; Pochon remained a member until it was disbanded in 1929. In 1938 Pochon returned to Switzerland; was director of the Lausanne Cons. until 1957. He publ. *A Progressive Method of String-Quartet Playing* (N.Y., 1924).

Podéšt, Ludvík, Czech composer; b. Dubňany, Dec. 19, 1921; d. Prague, Feb. 27, 1968. He was a student of Kvapil (composition) at the Brno Cons. (1945–48) and of Racek and B. Štědroň (musicology) at the Univ. of Brno (Ph.D., 1949). After working at the Brno Radio (1947–51), he was music director of the Vit Nejedlý Army Artistic Ensemble (1953–56) and head of the music dept. of the Czech TV (1958–60).

WORKS: OPERAS: *Tři apokryfy* (3 Apocryphas; 1957–58); *Hrátky s čertem* (Frolics with the Devil; 1957–60; Liberec, Oct. 12, 1963). **ORCH.:** Sym. (1947–48; rev. 1964); *Raymonda Dienová*, symphonic poem (1950–51); 4 suites (1951, 1954, 1956, 1960); 2 piano concertos (1951–53; 1958–59); Violin Concerto, *Jarní Serenáda* (1953); *Advent Rhapsody* (1956–57); Cimbalom Concertino (1963); *The Seconds of a Day*, symphonic variations (1965); Concertino for 2 Cellos and Chamber Orch. (1965); *Partita* for Strings, Guitar, and Percussion (1967). **CHAMBER:** 2 string quartets (1942, 1942); *Litanie* for String Quartet (1944); Wind Quintet (1946); Violin Sonata (1947); Cello Sonata (1947); *Hojačky* for 2 Clarinets and Piano (1947); Suite for Viola and Piano (1955–56). **PIANO:** Sonatina (1945); Sonata (1946). **VOCAL:** *Smrt* (Death), cantata (1942); *Písně z koncentráku* (Songs from the Concentration Camp) for Baritone and Orch. (1946); *Měsíce* (Months) for Soprano and Orch. (1948; rev. 1957–58).

Podešva, Jaromír, Czech composer and teacher; b. Brno, March 8, 1927. He learned to play the piano, violin, and viola and to compose in childhood. After attending the Brno Cons. (1946–47), he pursued training in composition with Kvapil at the Janáček Academy of Music in Brno (1947–51; postgraduate studies, 1951–53). In 1960–61 he traveled abroad, studying with Copland at the Berkshire Music Center in Tanglewood and with Dutilleux in Paris. His travels are recounted in the book *Současná hudba na Západě* (Current Music in the West; Prague, 1963). From 1969 to 1987 he taught at the Ostrava Cons. He publ. the treatise *Možnosti kadence v dvanáctitónovém poli* (The Possibilities of Cadences in the Twelve-tone System; Prague, 1974). As a composer, Podešva reacted positively to his travels abroad and composed works in a style embracing both tonality and dodecaphony.

WORKS: DRAMATIC: *Bambini di Praga*, buffa-ballet-pantomime (1968). **ORCH.:** 10 syms.: No. 1 (1950–51), No. 2 for Flute and Strings (1961), No. 3, *Culmination—The Pearl Deep Down* (1966), No. 4, *Soláň Music*, for Flute, Harpsichord, and Small String Orch. (1967), No. 5, *3 Fragments of the Quinguennium*, for Baritone and Orch. (1967), No. 6 (1970), No. 7, *In memoriam J.P. jun. (1951–1972)* (1982–83), No. 8, *Ostrava* (1986), No. 9 (1989), and No. 10, *Initium ultimum* (1993); *Kounic Halls* (1952); Flute Concerto (1965); Concerto for String Quartet and Orch. (1971); Piano Concerto (1973); *Beskydy Suite* (1974); Violin Concerto (1974–75); Trumpet Concerto (1975); *Homage to Léos Janáček* (1977); *Sinfonietta festiva* for Chamber String Orch. (1983); Viola Concerto (1986); *5 Pieces* for Chamber String Orch. (1994). **CHAMBER:** 6 string quartets (1950, 1951, 1955, 1960, 1964, 1976); 2 nonets (1954–55; 1972); Violin Sonata (1958); Cello Sonatina (1960); Wind Quintet (1961); *5 Pieces* for Violin and Piano (1967); Suite for Viola and Piano, *In Search of a Smile* (1969); Concertino for 2 Violins and Piano (1972); Quartet for Violin, Clarinet, Cello, and Piano (1977); Sonata for Solo Viola, *Circle* (1982); Clarinet Quintet (1984); Clarinet Sonatina (1984); *Fantasia quasi una sonata* for Violin and Piano (1987); Trio for Violin, Cello, and Piano (1990); *Movement* for Viola and Piano (1992); piano pieces. **VOCAL:** Choral works; songs.

Pogorelich, Ivo, provocative Yugoslav pianist; b. Belgrade, Oct. 20, 1958. He commenced piano lessons in Belgrade when he was 7; when he was 11 he became a pupil of A. Timakin in Moscow; after studies at its Central Music School, he continued his training at the Moscow Cons., where he became a student of Aliza Kezeradze in 1976; they married in 1980. After winning 5 competitions in his homeland and the Casagrande Competition in Terni, Italy (1978), he captured 1st prize in the Montreal Competition in 1980; later that year he entered the Chopin Competition in Warsaw, where he became the center of a major controversy after he was eliminated from its final round; one of the jurors, Martha Argerich, resigned in protest and declared that Pogorelich was a "genius"; a group of Polish music critics were moved to give him a special prize. In 1981 he made his Carnegie Hall debut in N.Y. in a recital, and that same year he made his London debut. He subsequently toured all over the world, appearing both as a soloist with orchs. and as a recitalist. His phenomenal technical mastery is well suited in showcasing his brilliant but idiosyncratic interpretations of works ranging from Bach to Bartók. He and his wife founded the Ivo Pogorelich International Solo Piano Competition, a triennial event first held in Pasadena in 1993.

Poister, Arthur (William), American organist and pedagogue; b. Galion, Ohio, June 13, 1898; d. Durham, N.C., Feb. 25, 1980. He studied at the American Cons. in Chicago (B.M., 1925; M.M., 1931), with Dupré in Paris (1925–26; 1927–28), and with Straube in Leipzig (1933–34). He was a teacher of organ and theory at the Univ. of Redlands, Calif. (1928–37), and then prof. of organ at the Univ. of Minnesota (1937–38), the Oberlin (Ohio) Cons. (1938–48), and Syracuse Univ. (1948–67), where he served as univ. organist and director of music at Hendricks Chapel. While Poister also made recital tours, it was as a teacher that he proved most influential. Even after his formal retirement, he continued to teach. He also was a consultant to Walter Holtkamp, Sr., the Cleveland organ builder.

Pokrass, Dimitri, Russian composer; b. Kiev, Nov. 7, 1899; d. Moscow, Dec. 20, 1978. He studied piano at the St. Petersburg Cons. (1913–17). In 1919 he joined the Soviet cavalry during the Civil War, and wrote the song *The Red Cavalry.* This was the first of a series of many songs which acquired great popularity, among them *If War Comes Tomorrow* (1938), *March of the Tank Brigade, Farewell,* etc. He also wrote music for films.

Polacco, Giorgio, Italian conductor; b. Venice, April 12, 1873; d. N.Y., April 30, 1960. He studied in St. Petersburg, at Venice's Liceo Benedetto Marcello, and at the Milan Cons. He became assistant conductor at London's Covent Garden (1890), then conducted in Europe and South America; appeared in the U.S. for the first time for Tetrazzini's debut in San Francisco (1905); toured the U.S. with the Savage Opera Co. (1911). He made his Metropolitan Opera debut in N.Y. with *Manon Lescaut* (Nov. 11, 1912), remaining on its roster until 1917; conducted the Chicago Grand Opera (1918–19; 1921) and in Boston (1927); was principal conductor of the Chicago Civic Opera (1922–30). He was married twice to the soprano Edith (Barnes) Mason.

Polansky, Larry, American composer, music theorist, writer, and teacher; b. N.Y., Oct. 16, 1954. He studied anthropology and music at New College in Sarasota, Fla. (1974); subsequently studied mathematics and music at the Univ. of Calif., Santa Cruz (B.A., 1976), and undertook graduate work at York Univ. in Toronto (1977); finally majored in composition at the Univ. of Ill. in Champaign-Urbana (M.A., 1978); also studied composition privately with James Tenney, Ben Johnston, and Ron Riddle, jazz guitar with Chuck Wayne, George Barnes, and Michael Goodwick, bluegrass mandolin with Frank Wakefield and Paul Kramer, and jazz theory and improvisation with Lee Konitz. He performed and arranged pieces in various styles, particularly jazz and folk, on guitar and other plectra, piano, and electronics (from 1966); he was a dance accompanist (1977–81), and composed works for the choreographers Ann Rodiger and Anita Feldman. He worked as a computer programmer, systems analyst, and studio engineer (from 1975); taught at Mills College in Oakland, California (1981–90), where he also was involved with its Center for Contemporary Music (1981–87; interim director, 1988) and directed its Contemporary Performance Ensemble (1981–86); in 1990 he became an assistant prof. at Dartmouth College, where he also co-directed its Bregman Electro-Acoustic Music Studio. He is married to Jody Diamond, with whom he founded and directed the American Gamelan Inst. and also ed. its journal, *Balungan.* Together they also founded the publishing firm Frog Peak Music, A Composers' Collective. His own compositions reflect sophisticated technical concerns in acoustics, intonation, and morphological processes; they are generally in variation or canonic forms, based on single ideas worked out in textures that sometimes resemble those of minimalism. His *51 Harmonies* for Percussion Trio, Live Computer Electronics, and Electric Guitar (1994) was commissioned by Cologne's Westdeutscher Rundfunk. In 1995–96 he held a Fulbright Senior Scholar/Teacher Fellowship in Melbourne, Australia. Polansky's extensive articles and reviews have appeared in the *Journal of New Music Research, Perspectives of New Music, Computer Music Journal* et al.; he served as music advisor ed. to the journal *Leonardo* (from 1985) and assoc. ed. of *Perspectives of New Music* (from 1988); he also authored HMSL (Hierarchical Music Specification Language), a widely used computer music language, as well as the books *Early Works of James Tenney* (1983) and *New Instrumentation and Orchestration* (1986).

WORKS: *Dance of the Tombstone/Gauss Music* for Dancer and Live Electronics (1976); *Silence Study #4* for 4 Actors and Violist (1976); *Four Voice Canon #3,* computer-generated work (1978); *Quartet in F for Paula Ravitz* for Piano, Viola, Clarinet, and Trombone (1979); *Unhappy Set of Coincidences* for Guitar and Bass, Flute and Bass, or any 2 Melody Instruments (1979); *Another You,* 17 variations for Harp in just intonation (1981); *Three Monk Tunes* for Tap Dancer and Percussionist (1982); *Sascha's Song (for the peoples of Chile)* for Tape (1983); *Four Bass Studies* for Double Bass (1985); *Hensley Variations* for Flute, Viola, and Harp (1985); *The Time is Now* for Soprano and Chamber Ensemble (1985); *V'leem'shol* (. . . And to rule) *(Cantillation Study #2)* for 5 Flutes (1985); *Will You Miss Me* for Flute, Double Bass, Harp, and Untrained Man's Voice (1985); *Buy Some for Spare Parts,* live (HMSL) computer music installation with audience (1986); *Conversation,* live electronic installation for large numbers of microphones, speakers, computer-controlled matrix switcher, and specially designed software and hardware (1986; in collaboration with J. Levin and R. Povall); *Hitting the Open Man,* graphic score (1986); *Sweet Sue* for Guitar and Baritone Saxophone (1986); *Al Het (for the people of Nicaragua)* for Voice and Slendro Gender/Pelog Gambang (1 player) (1987); *B'rey'sheet* (In the beginning) *(Cantillation Study #1)* for Voice and Live Interactive Computer (1987); *Milwaukee Blues* for 2 Tap Dancers and 5 Saxophones (1987); *Simple Actions* for Solo Live Interactive Computer (1987); *Study for Milwaukee Blues* for 3 Tap Dancers (1987); *17 Simple Melodies of the Same Length* for Melody Instrument and Live Interactive Computer (1988); *The Birth of Peace,* live computer work (HMSL and 3DIS System) with Video-computer Interactive Goldfish (1989; in collaboration with C. Mann, A. Riddle, S. Veitch et al.); *Horn* for Horn and Live Computer (1990); *Movement in E Major for John Cage* for Violin and Piano (1990); *Three Studies* for Performers and Live Computer (1990); *. . . Slippers of Steel . . .* for 2 Electric Guitars and Real-time Interactive Computer Electronics (1991); *Bedhaya Sadra/Bedhaya Guthrie* for Clarinet (1992); *51 Melodies* for 2 Electric Guitars and Rock Band (1992); *Two Children's Songs* for Tuba and Trombone or Any 2 Bass Wind Instruments (1992); *Field Holler* for Double Bass and Sustaining Instruments (1994); *51 Harmonies* for Percussion Trio, Live Computer Electronics, and Electric Guitar (1994); *The Casten Variation* for Piano (1994); *Always Cut Off the Baseline* for Trumpet and Live Interative Computer Electronics (1995); *for jim, ben and lou,* 3 pieces for Guitar, Harp, and Percussion: *I. Preamable, II. Rue Plats (Resting Place),* and *III. The World's Longest Melody (Trio): "The Ever-Widening Halfstep"* (1995); *Four Voice Canon #5* for 4 Percussion (1995); *Four Voice Canon #9 (Anna canon)* for Tape (1995); *Lonesome Road (The Crawford Variations),* 51 variations for Piano (1995); *Roads to Cimacum* for String or Mandolin

Quartet (1995); *Study: Anna, the long and the short of it*, computer-synthesized work (1995).

BIBL.: K. Gann, "Downtown Beats for the 1990s: Rhys Chatham, Mikel Rouse, Michael Gordon, L. P., Ben Neil," *Contemporary Music Review*, 10/1 (1994); M. Perlman, "American Gamelan in the Garden of Eden: Intonation in a Cross-Cultural Encounter," *Musical Quarterly* (1994); N. Hossfield, "Music to our Eyes: Envisioning Music Theoretic Principles," *Interface: Computing News of Dartmouth College* (Spring 1995).

Poleri, David (Samuel), American tenor; b. Philadelphia, Jan. 10, 1921; d. in a helicopter accident in Hanalei, Hawaii, Dec. 13, 1967. He studied at the Philadelphia Academy of Vocal Arts, the Berkshire Music Center in Tanglewood, and with Alberto Sciarretti. In 1945 he sang with the Philadelphia Orch. In 1949 he made his operatic debut as Gounod's Faust with Gallo's San Carlo Opera on a tour in Chicago. He subsequently was a guest artist with various opera companies and a soloist with various orchs. in the U.S. He also sang at the Edinburgh Festivals (1951, 1955) and at London's Covent Garden (1956). In 1954 he created the role of Michele in Menotti's *The Saint of Bleecker Street.* In 1955 he appeared as Cavaradossi on NBC-TV.

Polgar, Tibor, Hungarian-born Canadian composer, conductor, pianist, and teacher; b. Budapest, March 11, 1907. He was a pupil of Kodály at the Budapest Academy of Music (composition diploma, 1925), and earned a degree in philosophy (1931). He was active as a performer and composer with the Hungarian Radio, later serving as its artistic director (1948–50). From 1962 to 1964 he was assoc. conductor of the Philharmonia Hungarica in Marl kreis Recklinghausen; then emigrated to Canada and became a naturalized citizen (1969). He conducted the Univ. of Toronto Sym. Orch. (1965–66), and later was on the staff of the Univ.'s opera dept. (1970–75); also taught at the Royal Cons. of Music of Toronto (1966–68); then taught orchestration at York Univ. in Toronto (1976–77).

WORKS: DRAMATIC: OPERAS: *Kérök* (The Suitors; 1954); *The Troublemaker* (1968); *The Glove* (1973); *A Strange Night* (1978–88). **MUSICAL SATIRE:** *A European Lover* (1965). **ORCH.:** *Variations on a Hungarian Folk Song* for Harp and Orch. (1969; also for Solo Harp); *Ilona's 4 Faces* for Clarinet or Saxophone and Orch. (1970; also for Clarinet or Saxophone and Piano); *Notes on Hungary* for Concert Band (1971); *Pentatonia* for Concert Band (1976; Toronto, Feb. 15, 1977); *3 Poems in Music* (1977; also for Piano); *2 Symphonic Dances in Latin Rhythm* for Trumpet and Symphonic Band (1979); *Fanfare of Pride and Joy* for Symphonic Band (1982); *Concerto romantico* for Harp and Orch. (1986); *The Voice of the Soul* for Concert Band (1989). **CHAMBER:** *Improvisazione* for 4 Horns (1962); *In Private* for Violin and Viola (1964); *Rhapsody of Kallo* for Violin and Harp (1970); Sonatine for 2 Flutes (1971); *Romantic Minutes* for Harp (1980); *Frère Jacques* for 4 Harps (1984); *Hide and Seek* for Horn and Piano (1988). **VOCAL:** *The Last Words of Louis Riel*, cantata for Contralto, Baritone, Chorus, and Orch. (1966–67); *Lest We Forget the Last Chapter of Genesis*, cantata for Low Voice and Piano or Orch. (1970); *How Long Shall the Ungodly Triumph?* for 6 Voices and Organ (1974); *Annabel Lee* for Voice, Flute, and Harp (1974); songs; arrangements.

Poliakin, Miron, Russian violinist and pedagogue; b. Cherkassy, Feb. 12, 1895; d. Moscow, May 21, 1941. He received his early training from his father, a noted violinist, then studied with Elena Vonsovskaya in Kiev and with Auer at the St. Petersburg Cons. (1908–18). He developed a notable international career, making his N.Y. debut on Feb. 27, 1922. Returning to Russia in 1928, he became prof. of violin at the Leningrad Cons., and in 1936 joined the faculty of the Moscow Cons. With Yampolsky and Yankelevich, he produced a pleiad of fine violinists who dominated the concert annals and competition circuits in Russia and elsewhere.

BIBL.: L. Raaben, *M. P.* (Moscow, 1963).

Poliakov, Valeri(an), Russian composer and conductor; b. Orel, Oct. 24, 1913; d. Kishinev, Jan. 17, 1970. He studied clarinet and composition in Kharkov (1928–34). In 1935 he joined the staff of the Kiev Opera; in 1937 was appointed head of the music dept. of the Moldavian Music Theater in Kishinev, and taught at a music school there until 1940; then taught in Armenia (1941–45) and Riga (1945–51). He was music ed. and conductor of the Moldavian Radio (1951–54); conducted the dance ensemble Zhok (1955–57) and the jazz band Bukuria (1965–66); also taught at the Kishinev Cons. (1961–70). In 1960 he was made an Honored Artist of the Moldavian S.S.R.

WORKS: DRAMATIC: OPERA: *Where?* (1969). **BALLETS:** *Iliana, An Ancient Tale* (1936); *Legend of the Architect* (1959); *Eternity* (1961). **ORCH.:** *Suite on Moldavian Themes* (1938); *Moldavia*, poem (1938); *Pictures of Drinking* (1939); *Fantasia Capriccio on European Themes* (1939); 7 syms. (1944; 1946; 1947; *Chkalov*, 1950; 1958; *Heroic Fantasy*, 1961; 1966); *Triumphant Overture* (1947); 2 piano concertos (1948, 1955); *Rhapsody-Poem* (1951); *Through the Flames*, poem (1952); Violin Concerto (1953); Cello Concerto (1960); *Burleska* for Trombone and Orch. (1960); *Concerto rustico* (1963); *Vernal Garden*, sinfonietta (1969). **CHAMBER:** *3 Pieces in Memory of Prokofiev* for Violin and Piano (1962); *Ballade* for Cello and Piano (1963); String Quartet (1965); *Concert études* for Clarinet and Piano (1966) *Concert études* for Bassoon and Piano (1966). **VOCAL:** *Ballad to the Soldier* for Voices and Orch. (1948); songs.

Polignac, Armande de, French composer; b. Paris, Jan. 8, 1876; d. Neauphle-le-Vieux, Seine-et-Oise, April 29, 1962. She studied with Fauré and d'Indy. She composed the operas *Morgane* and *L'Hypocrite sanctifie*; *Judith de Béthulie*, dramatic scene (Paris, March 23, 1916); *La Source lointaine*, Persian ballet (Paris, 1913); *Les 1,001 Nuits*, Arabian ballet (Paris, 1914); *Chimères*, Greek ballet (Paris, June 10, 1923); *Urashima*, Japanese ballet; *La Recherche de la vérité*, Chinese ballet for Small Orch.; *Petite suite pour le clavecin* (1939).

Polin, Claire, American flutist, teacher, and composer; b. Philadelphia, Jan. 1, 1926. She studied flute with Kincaid and composition with Persichetti in Philadelphia, Mennin at the Juilliard School of Music in N.Y., and Sessions and Foss at the Berkshire Music Center in Tanglewood; held the degrees of B.Mus. (1948), M.Mus. (1950), and D.Mus. (1955). She taught at the Philadelphia Musical Academy (1949–64) and at Rutgers Univ. (1958–91). A versatile scholar, she wrote and lectured on music, and traveled and played flute in distant lands, including Israel, Russia, and Japan; advanced bold theories, suggesting, for example, a link between Hebrew and Welsh legends, and composed industriously in a cogently modernistic manner, often with recursive ancient modalities.

WORKS: ORCH.: 2 syms. (1961; *Korean*, 1976); *Scenes from Gilgamesh* for Flute and Strings (1972); *Amphion* (1978); *Mythos* for Harp and String Orch. (1982). **CHAMBER:** 3 string quartets (1953, 1959, 1969); Flute Sonata (1954); *Structures* for Flute (1964); *Consecutivo* for Flute, Clarinet, Violin, Cello, and Piano (1964); *Cader Idris* for Brass Quintet (1970); *The Journey of Owain Madoc* for Brass Quintet and Percussion (1971); *Makimono I* for Flute, Clarinet, Violin, Cello, and Piano (1972) and *II* for Brass Quintet (1972); Sonata for Flute and Harp (1972); *Aderyn Pur* for Flute, Alto Saxophone, and Bird Tape (1973); *Tower Sonata* for Flute, Clarinet, and Bassoon (1974); *Death of Procris* for Flute and Tuba (1974); *Serpentine* for Viola (1974); *Telemannicon* for Oboe and Self-Tape (1975); *Klockwork* for Alto Saxophone, Horn, and Bassoon (1977); *Synaulia* for Flute, Clarinet, and Piano (1977); *Vigniatures* for Harp and Violin (1980); *Felina* for Harp and Violin (1981); *Res naturae* for Woodwind Quintet (1982); *Kuequenaku-Cambriola* for Piano and Percussion (1982); *Freltic Sonata* for Violin and Piano (1986); *Garden of Earthly Delights* for Woodwind Quintet (1987); *Regensburg* for Flute, Guitar, and Dancer (1989); *Taliesin* for Flute, Oboe, and Cello (1993); piano pieces. **VOCAL:** *Welsh Bardic Odes* for Soprano, Flute, and Piano (1956); *Canticles* for Men's Voices (1959); *Lorca Songs* for Voices and Piano (1965); *Infinito* for Alto Saxophone, Soprano, Chorus, and Narrator (1973); *Biblical Madrigals* for Chorus (1974); *Windsongs* for Soprano and Guitar (1977); *Isaiah Syndrome* for Chorus (1980); *Mystic Rondo* for Man's or Woman's Voice, Violin, and Piano (1987–88).

Polisi, Joseph W(illiam), American bassoonist and music educator; b. N.Y., Dec. 30, 1947. He had primary lessons in bassoon with his father, William Polisi, principal bassoonist of the N.Y. Phil.; then turned to legal studies, and took a course in political science at the Univ. of Conn. (B.A., 1969) and international relations at the Fletcher School of Law and Diplomacy at Tufts Univ. (M.A., 1970). He then resumed his musical training at Yale Univ. (M.M., 1973; M.M.A., 1975; D.M.A., 1980); also studied bassoon with Maurice Allard at the Paris Cons. (1973–74). He performed widely as a soloist and chamber music player; taught at the Univ. of Nevada (1975–76); then was executive officer of the Yale Univ. School of Music (1976–80); subsequently was dean of faculty at the Manhattan School of Music (1980–83). After serving as dean of the Univ. of Cincinnati (Ohio) College-Cons. of Music (1983–84), he became president of the Juilliard School in N.Y. (1984).

Polívka, Vladimír, Czech pianist and composer; b. Prague, July 6, 1896; d. there, May 11, 1948. He studied piano at the Prague Cons., and took lessons in composition from Vítězslav Novák at the Master School there (1912–18). He traveled in Europe, America, and Japan with the violinist Jaroslav Kocián; from 1923 to 1930, taught piano in Chicago. In 1938 he returned to Prague and taught at the Cons.; was chairman of Pritomnost, an association for contemporary music. He publ. several collections of children's pieces, collaborated on a book about Smetana (Prague, 1941), and wrote a book of travels, describing his world tour (Prague, 1945).

WORKS: DRAMATIC: *Polobůh* (The Demigod), opera (1930); *A Ballad of a Deaf-Mute,* melodrama (1936); incidental music. **ORCH.:** *Jaro* (Spring), symphonic poem (1918); *Little Symphony* (1921); Suite for Viola and Small Orch. (1934); Concerto for Piano and Small Orch. (1934); Overture (1942). **CHAMBER:** 2 violin sonatas (1918, 1919); Suite for Viola and Wind Quintet (1934); String Quartet (1937); *Divertimento* for Wind Quintet (1939); *Giacona* for Viola and Piano (1944); Viola Sonata (1945). **PIANO:** *Dni v Chicagu* (Days in Chicago; 1926); *3 Impromptus* (1930); *Merry Music* (1932–33); *Krajiny z let okupace* (Landscapes in the Years of Occupation), suite (1941). **VOCAL:** Choruses; songs.

Pollak, Anna, English mezzo-soprano of Austrian descent; b. Manchester, May 1, 1912. She studied in the Netherlands and in Manchester. Following appearances as an actress and singer in musical comedy and operetta, she studied voice with Joan Cross. In 1945 she made her operatic debut as Dorabella at the Sadler's Wells Opera in London, where she was one of its leading artists until 1962. In 1952 she made her first appearance at the Glyndebourne Festival as Dorabella and at London's Covent Garden as Cherubino. Between 1962 and her retirement in 1968 she was a guest artist at the Sadler's Wells Opera. In 1962 she was made an Officer of the Order of the British Empire. She created the role of Bianca in Britten's *The Rape of Lucretia* (1946) and the title role in Berkeley's *Ruth* (1956).

Pollak, Egon, esteemed Czech-born Austrian conductor; b. Prague, May 3, 1879; d. there (of a heart attack while conducting a performance of *Fidelio*), June 14, 1933. He studied with Knittl at the Prague Cons. He was chorus master at the Prague Deutsches Theater (1901–05); conducted opera in Bremen (1905–10), Leipzig (1910–12), and Frankfurt am Main (1912–17); also conducted in Paris and at London's Covent Garden (1914). He led Wagner's *Ring* cycle at the Chicago Grand Opera (1915–17); was able to leave the U.S. with the Austrian diplomatic legation as the U.S. entered World War I (1917). He was Generalmusikdirektor of the Hamburg Opera (1917–31); also conducted in Rio de Janeiro and at Buenos Aires's Teatro Colón (1928); appeared at the Chicago Civic Opera (1929–32) and in Russia (1932); led performances of the ensemble of the Vienna State Opera in Cairo and Alexandria (1933). He was a distinguished interpreter of the operas of Wagner and Richard Strauss.

Pollikoff, Max, American violinist and concert director; b. Newark, N.J., March 30, 1904; d. N.Y., May 13, 1984. He studied with Auer. He made his N.Y. debut in a recital (1923); subsequently devoted himself to contemporary music; he organized the series "Music of Our Time" in 1954, giving periodic concerts at the 92nd Street Y in N.Y.; the series continued until 1974 with programs including works by Ives, Bernstein, Sessions, Dello Joio, and Cage.

Pollini, Maurizio, famous Italian pianist and conductor; b. Milan, Jan. 5, 1942. A precocious child, he began piano studies at an early age with Lonati. He made his debut at age 9, then studied with Vidusso at the Milan Cons. After sharing 2nd prize in the Geneva Competition in 1958, he took his diploma in piano at the Milan Cons. (1959); also studied with Michelangeli. After capturing 1st prize in the Chopin Competition in Warsaw (1960), he launched an acclaimed career as a virtuoso; appeared throughout Europe as a soloist with the leading orchs. and as a recitalist; made his U.S. debut at N.Y.'s Carnegie Hall (Nov. 1, 1968). In later years, he made appearances as a conductor, leading concerts from the keyboard and also mounting the podium and taking charge in the opera pit. Pollini is a foremost master of the keyboard; he has won deserved renown for making his phenomenal technical resources a means of exploring a vast repertoire, ranging from Bach to the cosmopolitan avant-garde. In 1987 he was awarded the Ehrenring of the Vienna Phil.

Pololáník, Zdeněk, Czech composer; b. Brno, Oct. 25, 1935. Following training with Vladimír Malacka and František Suchý, he was a student of Josef Černocký (organ) at the Cons. (graduated,1957) and of Vilém Petrželka and Theodor Schafer (composition) at the Janáček Academy of Music (graduated, 1961) in Brno. Thereafter, he devoted himself fully to composing. In his music, Pololáník reveals an assured handling of form, structure, color, and unusual instrumental combinations.

WORKS: DRAMATIC: MELODRAMA: *Malá mytologická cvičení* (Small Mythological Exercises; 1991). **BALLETS:** *Mechanismus* (Mechanism; 1964); *Popelka* (Cinderella; 1966); *Pierot* (About; 1976; orch. suite, 1977); *Sněhová královna* (Snow Queen; 1978); *Paní mezi stíny* (Lady Among Shadows; 1984). Also much incidental music and numerous radio, television, and film scores. **ORCH.:** *Sinfonietta* (1958); *Toccata* for Double Bass and Ensemble (1959); *Divertimento* for 4 Horns and Strings (1960); 5 syms.: No. 1 (1961), No. 2 for 11 Winds (1962), No. 3 for Percussion and Organ (1962), No. 4 for Strings (1963), and No. 5 (1969); *Concentus resonabilis* for 19 Soloists and Tape (1963); Piano Concerto (1966); Concerto grosso I for Clarinet or Flute, Guitar, Harpsichord, and Strings (1966) and II for Clarinet, Bassoon, and Strings (1988); Suite from the oratorio *Sheer hash sheereem* (1975); *Musica giocosa* for Violin and Chamber Ensemble (1980); Concertino for Piano and Strings (1985). **CHAMBER:** *Variations* for Organ and Piano (1956); Suite for Violin and Piano (1957); String Quartet (1958); *Scherzo contrario* for Xylophone or Guitar, Bass Clarinet or Clarinet, and Violin (1961); *Musica spingenta I* for Double Bass and Wind Quintet (1961), *II* for String Quartet and Harpsichord (1962), and *III* for Bass Clarinet and 13 Percussion (1962); *Dodici preludii* for 2 Pianos and Organ (1963); *Tre scherzi* for Wind Quintet (1969); *Musica concisa* for Flute, Bass Clarinet, Harpsichord, Piano, and Percussion (1963); Horn Sonata (1965); *Oratio,* nonet for Key, Plucked, and Percussion Instruments (1968); *Musica trascurata* for Bass Clarinet and Piano (1970); *Ballad* for Cello and Piano (1992); *Christmas Triptych* for Bugle and 4 Trombones (1993). **KEYBOARD: PIANO:** *Piano Preludes* (1957); *7 Preludes* (1960); *Seguidilla* (1983). **ORGAN:** *Sonata bravura* (1959); *Sonata laetitiae* (1962); *Allegro affanato* (1963); *Esultatio e pianto* (1972); *Burlesca* (1982); *Pastorale* (1986); *Preludio festivo* (1992). **VOCAL:** *Nabuchodonosor* for Chorus, 3 Trumpets, and 4 Kettledrums (1960); *Zpěv mrtvých dětí* (Cantus mortuorum liberorum) for Chorus, 3 Trumpets, and Percussion (1963); *Liturgical Mass* for Chorus, Brass, Harp, and Organ (1965); *Tiché světlo* (Silent Light) for Baritone and Organ (1965); *Cantus psalmorum* for Bass-baritone, Organ, Harp, and Percussion (1966); *Missa brevis* for Children's Chorus and Organ (1969); *Sheer hash sheereem* (Song of Songs), oratorio for Soli, Chorus, and Orch. (1970; orch. suite, 1975); *Proglas* for Soprano, Horn, Harpsichord, Percussion, and Orch. (1980); *Slavnosti léta* (Summer Festivities) for Chorus and 2 Pianos (1985); *Vánoční poselství* (Christmas Message) for Men's Chorus, Electric Guitar, Synthesizer, and Percussion (1987); *Gloria! Co to nového . . .* (Gloria! What's New . . .), carols for Soprano, Tenor, Flute, Oboe, Cello, and Piano (1988–89; also for Men's Chorus, Piano, and Synthesizer); *Velikonočni cesta* (Easter Way), 14 songs for Soprano, Flute, Oboe, Cello, and Piano (1990; also for High Voice and Organ, 1991); *Cinderella of Nazareth*, chamber oratorio for Medium Voice and Synthesizer (1991); *Andělské poselství světu* (The Angel's Message to the World), Christmas pastoral for Soprano, Alto, Chorus, and Strings (1991); *Te Deum* for Chorus and Organ (1991); *First One Must Carry the Cross*, chamber oratorio for Medium Voice and Synthesizer (1992); *Time of Joy and Merrymaking*, cycle of 19 carols for Children's or Women's Chorus and Piano (1992); *God is Love*, chamber oratorio for Medium Voice and Synthesizer (1993); *Eulogies*, Psalms for Chorus (1993); *Cantus laetitiae*, Psalms for Children's or Women's Chorus (1993).

Polovinkin, Leonid (Alexeievich), Russian composer; b. Kurgan, Aug. 13, 1894; d. Moscow, Feb. 8, 1949. He studied at the Moscow Cons. with Glière and Vassilenko. He began his career as a composer by writing theater music in Moscow after the Revolution of 1917; adopted a modernistic idiom; emphasized the element of humor. Later he devoted more time to abstract instrumental music. He wrote 9 syms., 4 string quartets, 2 piano trios, several overtures on folk themes, 5 piano sonatas, 24 postludes for Piano, and songs.

Pommier, Jean-Bernard, French pianist and conductor; b. Béziers, Aug. 17, 1944. He began piano lessons at 4 with Mina Kosloff. In 1958 he entered the Paris Cons., where he continued his studies with Yves Nat and Pierre Sancan. After taking the premier prix there in 1961, he completed his training with Eugene Istomin. In 1960 he won 1st prize in the Jeunesses Musicales competition in Berlin, and then began to make regular appearances in Europe. In 1971 he made his first appearance at the Salzburg Festival. During the 1973–74 season, he made his first appearances in the U.S. In subsequent years, his career took him to most of the principal music centers of the world. From 1980 he also pursued a career as a conductor.

Ponc, Miroslav, Czech violinist, conductor, and composer; b. Vysoké Mýto, Dec. 2, 1902; d. Prague, April 1, 1976. He studied organ with Wiedermann at the Prague Cons. (1920–22) and composition with Alois Hába there (1922–23; 1925–27).; went to Berlin and took lessons with Schoenberg. Upon returning to Prague, he studied violin with Suk at the Cons., graduating in 1930, and attended the quarter tone composition class of Hába, graduating in 1935; also took lessons in conducting with Scherchen in Strasbourg (1933). After World War II, he was active mainly as a theater conductor in Prague; wrote a number of scores of incidental music for plays.

WORKS: *5 Polydynamic Compositions* for Piano, Xylophone, and String Quartet (1923); 2 song cycles: *A Bad Dream* (1925) and *A Black Swan* (1926); *3 Merry Pieces* for Wind Quintet (1929); *Little Pieces* for Flute or Cello and Piano (1930); Piano Concertino (1930); *Overture to an Ancient Tragedy*, with the application of quarter tones in the Greek enharmonic mode (Prague, Feb. 18, 1931); Nonet (1932); *Osudy* (The Fates), 2 antique ballet pictures (1935); Suite for Piano with 2 manuals tuned in quarter tones (1935); String Trio (1937); over 100 scores of incidental music and much music for films and radio.

Ponce, Manuel (Maria), distinguished Mexican composer; b. Fresnillo, Dec. 8, 1882; d. Mexico City, April 24, 1948. He studied piano with his older sister; in 1904 he went to Europe, where he took lessons in composition with Enrico Bossi at Bologna and in piano with Martin Krause in Berlin. Upon his return to Mexico, he taught piano at the Mexico City Cons. (1909–15). He gave a concert of his compositions in Mexico City on July 7, 1912, which included a Piano Concerto. In 1917 he again became a teacher at the Mexico City Cons., and also was conductor of the National Sym. Orch. (1917–19); then went to Paris for additional study, and took lessons with Dukas (1925). In 1933 he rejoined the faculty of the Mexico City Cons., serving as its director in 1934–35. His contact with French music wrought a radical change in his style of composition; his later works are more polyphonic in structure and more economical in form. He possessed a great gift of melody; one of his songs, *Estrellita* (1914), became a universal favorite, and was often mistaken for a folk song. In 1941 he made a tour in South America, conducting his own works. He was the first Mexican composer of the 20th century to employ an identifiably modern musical language, and his place in the history of Mexican music is thus very important. His works are often performed in Mexico; a concert hall was named after him in the Instituto de Bellas Artes.

WORKS: ORCH.: Piano Concerto (1912); *Balada mexicana* for Piano and Orch. (1914); *Estampas nocturnas* (1923); *Chapultepec, 3 bocetos sinfonicos* (Mexico City, Aug. 25, 1929; rev. version, Mexico City, Aug. 24, 1934); *Canto y danza de los antiguos Mexicanos* (1933); *Suite en estilo antiguo* (1935); *Poema elegiaco* for Chamber Orch. (Mexico City, June 28, 1935); *Instantáneas mexicanas* (1938); *Ferial, divertimento sinfónico* (Mexico City, Aug. 9, 1940); *Concierto del Sur* for Guitar and Orch. (Montevideo, Oct. 4, 1941); Violin Concerto (Mexico City, Aug. 20, 1943). **CHAMBER:** Piano Trio (1911); Cello Sonata (1922); *4 miniaturas* for String Quartet (1929); *Pequeña suite en estilo antiguo* for Violin, Viola, and Cello (1933); Sonata for Violin and Viola (1935); numerous piano pieces, some based on Mexican rhythms; 6 guitar sonatas. **VOCAL:** About 30 songs; 34 arrangements of Mexican folk songs.

BIBL.: D. López Alonso, *M.M. P.: Ensayo biográfico* (Mexico City, 1950); J. Romero, "Efemérides de M. P.," *Nuestra Música*, V/2 (1950).

Poné, Gundaris, Latvian-born American conductor and composer; b. Riga, Oct. 17, 1932; d. Kingston, N.Y., March 15, 1994. In 1944 his family went to Germany, where he studied violin. In 1950 he emigrated to the U.S., becoming a naturalized American citizen in 1956. He studied violin and composition at the Univ. of Minnesota (B.A., 1954; M.A., 1956; Ph.D., 1962). In 1966 he made his conducting debut in N.Y., and subsequently appeared as a guest conductor in the U.S. and in Europe; served as music director of the Music in the Mountains Festivals (from 1981). His compositions captured 1st prizes in the Concorso Internazionale "Citta di Trieste" (1981), the Kennedy Center Friedheim Awards Competition (1982), the International Louisville Orch. Competition (1984), the International Hambach Prize Competition (1985), and the International Georges Enesco Competition (1988). His concern as a composer was to develop a musical language capable of communicating with the general audience while maintaining the high intellectual standards of contemporary composition.

WORKS: OPERA: *Rosa Luxemburg* (1968). **ORCH.:** Violin Concerto (1959); *Composizione per quattro orchestre* (1967–69); *Vivos voco, Mortuos plango* (1972); *Avanti!* (1975); Horn Concerto (1976); *La Serenissima*, 7 Venetian portraits (1979–81; Trieste, Sept. 25, 1982); *American Portraits* (1982–84); *Titzarin* (1984–86); *La bella veneziana*, overture (1987). **CHAMBER:** *Hetaera Esmeraldo*, string quartet (1963); *Serie-Alea* for Flute, Oboe, Clarinet, Bassoon, and Piano (1965); Sonata for Solo Cello (1966); *San Michele della Laguna* for Clarinet, Violin, and Piano (1969); *De Mundo Magistri Ioanni* for Chamber Ensemble (1972); *Diletti dialettici*, concerto for 9 Virtuosos (1973); *Eisleriana*, concerto for 11 Players (1978); *Woodland Elegies*, 5 pieces for 5 Instruments (1980); *Propositions for Opus 32*, 6 pieces for Woodwind Quartet and Piano (1982); *Cyprian Sketches*, 4 pieces for Clarinet, Cello, and Piano (1983); *Gran duo funebre* for Viola and Cello (1987); *Pezzi del tramonto* for Violin and Piano (1989); piano pieces, including Oltre questa porta geme la terra for 3 Pianos (1969) and 3 Farewell Pieces (1984); works for solo instruments. **VOCAL:** *Quattro temperamenti d'amore* for Baritone and Orch. or Piano (1960); *Daniel Propheta* for 3 Soloists, Chorus, and Orch. (1962); *Junius Broschure* for 4 Speakers, 18 Women's Voices, and Instrumental Ensemble (1970); *5 American Songs* for Medium Voice and Small Orch. (1975).

Pongrácz, Zoltán, Hungarian composer and teacher; b. Diószeg, Feb. 5, 1912. He studied with Kodály at the Budapest Academy of Music (1930–35); then took lessons in conducting from Nilius in Vienna (1935–38) and Krauss in Salzburg (1941). He served as director of the music dept. of Hungarian Radio in Budapest (1943–44) and then conducted the Debrecen Phil. (1946–49). He taught composition at the Debrecen Cons. (1947–58) and electronic composition at the Budapest Academy of Music (from 1975).

WORKS: DRAMATIC: OPERAS: *Odysseus and Nausikaa* (1949–50; Debrecen, 1960); *The Last Station* (1983). **BALLET:** *The Devil's Present* (1936). **ORCH.:** Sym. (1943); *Ballo ongaro* for Youth Orch. (1955); *3 Orchestral Etudes* (1963); *Hangok és zörejek* (Tones and Noises; 1966); *Színek és vonalak* (Colors and Lines) for Youth Orch. (1971). **CHAMBER:** *Pastorale* for Clarinet, Organ, 6 Winds, and Percussion (1941); *Javanese Music*, on a South Asiatic motif, for Chamber Ensemble (1942); *Music* for 5 Cellos (1954); Wind Quintet (1956); *Toccata* for Piano (1957); *3 Small Pieces* for Orff Ensemble (1966); *Phonothèse* for Tape (1966); *Sets and Pairs*, electronic variations for Piano and Celesta (1968); *3 Improvisations* for Piano, Percussion, and 3 Tape Recorders (1971); *3 Bagatelles* for Percussion (1972); *Zoophonia*, concrete music synthesized from animal sounds (1973); Concertino for Soprano Saxophone and Tape (1982); Concertino for Cimbalon and Electronics (1988). **VOCAL:** *Christmas Cantata* (1935); *St. Stephen Oratorio* (1938); *Apollo musagètes*, cantata (1958); *Negritude* for Speaking Chorus, Chorus, and Percussion (1962); *Ispirazioni* for Chorus, Orch., and Tape (1965); *Music from Nyírség* for Soloists, Chorus, and Folk Orch. (1965). **ELECTRONIC:** *Polar and Successive Contrasts* (1986).

Poniridis, Georges, distinguished Greek composer; b. Constantinople (of Greek parents), Oct. 8, 1892; d. Athens, March 29, 1982. He studied violin with Ysaÿe at the Brussels Cons. and composition with d'Indy and Roussel at the Schola Cantorum in Paris, where he remained until the outbreak of World War II; then returned to Athens and served in the Music Division of the Greek Ministry of Education (1954–58). In his music, he made use of authentic Greek motifs, at times endeavoring to emulate the simple monody of ancient Greek chants and the rhythms of classical prosody.

WORKS: DRAMATIC: Incidental music to ancient Greek plays. **ORCH.:** 2 syms. (1935, 1942); *Triptyque symphonique* (Athens, Nov. 22, 1937); *3 Symphonic Preludes* (1938); Chamber Sym. for Strings and Percussion (n.d.); *Petite symphonie* (1956); Piano Concerto (1968); Violin Concerto (1969). **CHAMBER:** Flute Sonata (1956); String Quartet (1959); Clarinet Sonata (1962); Quartet for Oboe, Clarinet, Bassoon, and Xylophone (1962); Trio for Xylophone, Clarinet, and Bassoon (1962); Trio for Flute, Oboe, and Clarinet (1962); 2 violin sonatas; Viola Sonata (1967); Cello Sonata (1967); 3 piano sonatas. **VOCAL:** Arrangements of Greek folk songs.

Ponnelle, Jean-Pierre, French opera designer and producer; b. Paris, Feb. 19, 1932; d. Munich, Aug. 11, 1988. He received his training in Paris. He gained early recognition for his staging of Henze's *Boulevard Solitude* at its premiere in Hannover in 1952; worked mostly in German opera houses. In 1962 he began to produce opera. He also distinguished himself in film productions.

Pons, Charles, French composer; b. Nice, Dec. 7, 1870; d. Paris, March 16, 1957. He studied organ, and earned his living as a church organist in his youth; then turned to theater music, and produced a long series of operas: *L'Epreuve* (Nice, 1904); *Laura* (Paris, 1906); *Mourette* (Marseilles, 1909); *Le Voile du bonheur* (Paris, April 26, 1911); *Françoise* (Lyons, 1913); *Loin du bal* (Paris, 1913); *Les Fauves* (Paris, 1917); *Le Drapeau* (Paris, 1918); *Le Passant de Noël* (Nice, 1935); *L'Envol de la Marseillaise* (Marseilles, 1947); also wrote *Pyrrhusm*, overture; *Heures vendéennes*, symphonic poem; *Symphonie tragique*; several orch. suites; *La Samaritaine*, oratorio (Nice, 1900); other vocal works, with Orch., including *La Mort de Démosthène* (Paris, 1928) and *Dans la forêt normande* (1934); chamber music; songs.

Pons, Lily (actually, **Alice Josephine**), glamorous French soprano; b. Draguignan, April 12, 1898; d. Dallas, Feb. 13, 1976. She studied piano as a child; took voice lessons with Alberti di Gorostiaga. She made her debut as an opera singer in Mulhouse in 1927 in the title role in *Lakmé*; sang in provincial theaters in France; then was engaged at the Metropolitan Opera in N.Y., and sang Lucia at her debut there on Jan. 3, 1931, with excellent success; she remained on its roster until 1944 (again from 1945 to 1958; on Dec. 14, 1960, made a concert appearance there). While in N.Y., she continued vocal studies with Maria Gay and Giovanni Zenatello. Her fame as an extraordinary dramatic singer spread rapidly; she was engaged to sing at the Grand Opéra and the Opéra-Comique in Paris, at Covent Garden in London, the Teatro Colón in Buenos Aires, in Mexico, and in Cuba. She went to Hollywood and appeared in films, among them *That Girl from Paris* (1936) and *Hitting a New High* (1938). During World War II, she toured the battlefronts of North Africa, India, China, and Burma; received numerous honors. So celebrated did she become that a town in Maryland was named Lillypons in her honor. She was married twice (divorced both times) to the publisher August Mesritz, and once to **André Kostelanetz**. She possessed an expressive coloratura voice, which she used with extraordinary skill. In addition to Lakmé, she won great renown for her portrayals of Philine in *Mignon*, Gilda, Marie in *La fille du régiment*, Rosina, Olympia in *Les contes d'Hoffmann*, and Amina in *La sonnambula*.

Ponse, Luctor, Swiss-born Dutch composer; b. Geneva, Oct. 11, 1914. He studied at the Valenciennes Cons. in France, winning the Prix d'Excellence for theory in 1930 and for piano in 1932; after further study at the Geneva Cons. (1933–35), he went to the Netherlands, and in 1964 became a member of the staff of the Inst. of Sonology at Univ. of Utrecht; he also taught at the Groningen Cons.

WORKS: BALLET: *Feestgericht* (1957). **ORCH.:** *Divertissement* for Strings (1946); Piano Concerto (1951–55); 3 sinfoniettas (1952, 1959, 1961); 3 syms. (1953; 1957; 1981–85); Concerto for 2 Pianos and Orch. (1961–62); *Concerto da camera* for Oboe and Strings (1962); 2 violin concertos (1963, 1965); Concerto for Piano, Orch., and Tape (1967; rev. 1980); Harp Concerto (1986); Suite for Piano and Orch. (1987); *5 études* for Piano and Orch. (1991). **CHAMBER:** Trio for Flute, Clarinet, and Piano (1940–41); 2 string quartets (1941, 1947); 2 cello sonatas (1943, 1950); *2 Pieces* for Wind Quintet (1943); *Duo* for Violin and Cello (1946); Violin Sonata (1948); Quintet for Flute, Oboe, Violin, Viola, and Cello (1956); *2 Caprices* for Flute and Piano (1956); Sextet for Flute, Oboe, Violin, Viola, Cello, and Harpsichord (1958); *Variations* for Flute and Harpsichord (1962); *Euterpe Suite* for 11 Instruments (1964); *Musique concertante* for Viola, Double Bass, Piano, Percussion, and Electronics (1977); Sonata for Clarinet and Tape (1981); Suite for Piano and Percussion (1982); *Toccata* for Harpsichord (1985); piano pieces.

Ponselle (real name, **Ponzillo**), **Carmela,** American mezzo-soprano and teacher, sister of **Rosa (Melba) Ponselle**; b. Schenectady, N.Y., June 7, 1892; d. N.Y., June 13, 1977. She began to study singing rather late in life. She made her professional debut as Amneris in N.Y. in 1923, which role she also sang at her Metropolitan Opera debut there on Dec. 5, 1925; she remained on its roster until 1928; was reengaged for the seasons 1930–35; then devoted most of her time to teaching.

Ponselle (real name, **Ponzillo**), **Rosa (Melba),** brilliant American soprano, sister of **Carmela Ponselle**; b. Meriden, Conn., Jan. 22, 1897; d. Green Spring Valley, Md., May 25, 1981. Her parents, who emigrated to the U.S. from southern Italy, gave her, with a prescient hope, the middle name Melba. Her father owned a grocery store in Meriden; she studied music with her mother, an amateur singer, and sang in a local church choir. Her older sister, Carmela, also learned to sing, and the 2 sisters, billed under their real name, Ponzillo, as "Italian Girls," sang in vaudeville shows in Pittsburgh and in N.Y. Later she took voice lessons in N.Y. with William Thorner, who became her manager; he introduced her to Caruso, who in turn arranged for her audition at the Metropolitan Opera. She made a fine impression, and was engaged for a debut on Nov. 15, 1918, in the role of Leonora in *La forza del destino*, opposite Caruso, who sang the male lead of Don Alvaro. She was immediately successful, and the critics, including the usually skeptical James Huneker, praised her. She subsequently sang at the Metropolitan Opera a rich assortment of Italian roles. She was equally successful in London when she appeared at Covent Garden as Norma (May 28, 1929). In 1936 she was married to Carl Jackson, son of the former mayor of Baltimore, who built for her a magnificent villa at Green Spring Valley, near Baltimore; she divorced him in 1950. She made her last appearance at the Metropolitan Opera in N.Y. as Carmen on Feb. 15, 1937. After her retirement, she became active in social affairs. Her 80th birthday was celebrated in 1977 at her estate, with a multitude of friends and itinerant celebrities in attendance.

BIBL.: T. Villella and B. Park, "R. P. Discography," *Le Grand Baton* (Sept. 1975); J. Hines, "R. P.," *Great Singers on Great Singing* (Garden City, N.Y., 1982); E. Aloi, *My Remembrances of R. P.* (N.Y., 1994).

Ponti, Michael, American pianist; b. Freiburg im Breisgau (of American parents), Oct. 29, 1937. He was taken to the U.S. as a child. He studied piano with Gilmour MacDonald; in 1955 he returned to Germany to continue his studies at the Frankfurt am Main Hochschule für Musik. In 1964 he won 1st prize in the Busoni Competition in Bolzano, which launched him on a successful career. In his programs, he specialized in bringing out neglected or forgotten piano masterpieces of the sonorous Romantic past.

Poot, Marcel, remarkable Belgian composer; b. Vilvoorde, near Brussels, May 7, 1901; d. Brussels, June 12, 1988. He received his first musical training from his father; continued his studies with Gilson (1916); then studied at the Brussels Cons. with Sevenants, Lunssens, and de Greef (1916–20), and at the Royal Flemish Cons. of Antwerp with Lodewijk Mortelmans (1921–23). In 1925, with 7 other Gilson pupils, he founded the Groupe des Synthétistes, dedicated to propaganda of new musical ideas (the group disbanded in 1930). Also in 1925, Poot was co-founder, with Gilson, of *La Revue Musicale Belge*, to which he contributed until its dissolution in 1938. He was on the staff of the Brussels Cons. from 1938 to 1966, and was its director from 1949 until his retirement. The most striking element of his music is its rhythmic vivacity; his harmony is well within the tonal sphere. His Piano Concerto (1959) was a compulsory work for finalists of 1960 Queen Elisabeth piano competition, won by Malcolm Frager.

WORKS: DRAMATIC: CHAMBER OPERA: *Moretus* (1943; Brussels, 1944). **BALLETS:** *Paris et les 3 divines* (1933); *Camera* (1937); *Pygmalion* (1952). Also incidental music. **ORCH.:** *Variations en forme de danses* (1923); *Charlot*, 3 sketches inspired by Charlie Chaplin films (1926); *Rondo* for Piano and Small Orch. (1928); *Capriccio* for Oboe and Orch. (1928); 7 syms. (1929; *Triptyque symphonique*, 1938; 1952; 1970; 1974; 1978; 1982); *Poème de l'espace*, symphonic poem inspired by Lindbergh's flight (1929; Liège, Sept. 4, 1930); *Jazz Music* (1930; Brussels, Feb. 21, 1932); *Allegro symphonique* (1935); *Fantaisie rythmique* (1936); *Ballade* for String Quartet and Orch. (1937); *Légende épique* for Piano and Orch. (1938); *Suite* for Small Orch. (1940); *Ballade* for Clarinet and Orch. (1941); *Concertstück* for Cello and Orch. (1942); *Fantasia* (1944); Sinfonietta (Chicago, Oct. 22, 1946); *Mouvement symphonique* for Wind Orch. (1946); *Divertimento* for Small Orch. (1952); *Mouvement perpétuel* (1953); *Ballade* for Violin and Orch. (1955); Piano Concerto (1959; Brussels, May 25, 1960); *2 mouvements symphoniques* (1960); *Concertstück* for Violin and Orch. (1962); *Concerto Grosso* for 11 Strings (1962); *Music* for Strings (1963); *Concerto Grosso* for Piano Quartet and Orch. (1969); Trumpet Concerto (1973); Alto Saxophone Concerto (1980). **CHAMBER:** Piano Quartet (1932); *3 Pièces en trio* for Piano Trio (1935); *Scherzo* for 4 Saxophones (1941); *Divertimento* for Oboe, Clarinet, and Bassoon (1942); Octet for Winds and Strings (1948); String Quartet (1952); *Ballade* for Oboe, Clarinet, and Bassoon (1954); *Fantaisie* for 6 Clarinets (1955); *Concertino* for Wind Quintet (1958); *Musique* for Wind Quintet (1964); *Légende* for 4 Clarinets or Saxophones (1967); Quartet for 4 Horns (1969); *Mosaïque* for 8 Winds (1969); *Musique de chambre* for Piano Trio (1971); several Ballades and other pieces for Solo Instruments with Piano; solo piano pieces. **VOCAL:** 2 oratorios: *Le Dit du routier* (1943) and *Icare* (1945); choral works; songs.

Popov, Alexander, Bulgarian composer; b. Kolarovgrad, July 14, 1927. He studied composition with Veselin Stoyanov at the Bulgarian State Cons., graduating in 1954. He played viola in the orch. of the National Opera in Sofia; was a member of the Sofia Soloists chamber ensemble.

WORKS: ORCH.: *Suite* (1956); *Native Land*, variations (1958); *The Artist*, suite for String Quartet and String Orch. (1961); *Sinfonietta* (1964); *Concerto Grosso* for Strings (1966); *Prelude and Dance* (1972); *Adagio* (1973); *Variants* for 13 Strings (1973). **CHAMBER:** 2 string quartets. **VOCAL:** 2 cantatas: *Cantata about the April Uprising* (1952) and *Land of Songs* (1969); choruses; songs.

Popov, Gavriil, outstanding and original Russian composer; b. Novocherkassk, Sept. 12, 1904; d. Repino, near Leningrad, Feb. 17, 1972. He studied at the St. Petersburg Cons. with Nikolayev (piano) and Shcherbachev (composition). From his student days, he adopted the procedures of modern music; his Septet (Moscow, Dec. 13, 1927) was written in a system of dissonant counterpoint then fashionable in Western Europe; his 1st Sym. (1927–34) was in a similar vein. When modern music became the target of attack in Russia, Popov modified his style toward a more popular conception, following the tenets of socialist realism. Among his other works were 6 syms., including No. 2, *Fatherland* (Moscow, Feb. 15, 1944), No. 3 for Strings, on Spanish themes (Moscow, Jan. 31, 1947), No. 4, *Glory Be to the Fatherland* (1949), No. 5 (1965), and No. 6 (Moscow, Jan. 23, 1970); an Organ Concerto (1970); film scores, among them *Communist Youth Union* and *Leader of Electrification* (1932).

Popovici, Doru, Romanian composer; b. Reşiţa, Feb. 17, 1932. He studied at the Bucharest Cons. with Constantinescu, Negrea, Andricu, Rogalski, Jora, and Vancea (1950–55) and attended the summer courses in new music in Darmstadt.

WORKS: OPERAS: *Prometeu* (1958; Bucharest, Dec. 16, 1964); *Mariana Pineda*, after García Lorca (Bucharest, Dec. 22, 1966); *Interogateriul din zori* (Bucharest, Feb. 6, 1975); *Noaptea cea mai lungă* (Bucharest, March 30, 1978). **ORCH.:** *Triptyque* (1955); *2 Symphonic Sketches* (1955); *Concertino* for Strings (1956); Concerto (1960); 4 syms.: No. 1 (1962), No. 2, *Spielberg* (1966), No. 3, *Bizantina*, for Chorus and Orch. (1968), and No. 4 for Chorus and Orch. (1973); *Poem bizantin* (1968); *Codex Cajoni* for Strings (1968); *Pastorale transilvane* for Strings (1979); *Pastorale din Oltenia*, suite (1982). **CHAMBER:** Cello Sonata (1952); Violin Sonata (1953); String Quartet No. 1 (1954; rev. 1964); *Fantasy "Orphée"* for String Trio (1955); Sonata for 2 Cellos (1960); Sonata for 2 Violas (1965); *Omagiu lui Tuculescu*, quintet for Piano, Violin, Viola, Cello, and Clarinet (1967); *Musique solennelle* for Violin and Piano (1969); Trio for Violin, Cello, and Piano (1969–70); *Madrigal* for Flute, Clarinet, Violin, Viola, Cello, and Trombone (1979); piano pieces. **VOCAL:** 5 cantatas: *Porumbeii morții* (1957), *Noapte de August* for Baritone and Orch. (1959), *In memoriam poetae Mariana Dumitrescu* (1967), *1877* (1976–77), and *Cîntec de speranță* (1977); choruses; many songs.

Popp, Lucia, esteemed Czech-born Austrian soprano; b. Uhorška Veš, Nov. 12, 1939; d. Munich, Nov. 16, 1993. She studied at the Bratislava Academy of Music (1959–63) and in Prague, her principal mentor being Anna Prosenč-Hřusková. After singing at the Bratislava Opera, she went to Vienna and appeared as Barbarina at the Theater an der Wien (1963); that same year, she joined the Vienna State Opera, where she established herself as a principal member; also became a favorite at the Salzburg Festivals. In 1966 she made her first appearance at London's Covent Garden as Oscar; then made her Metropolitan Opera debut in N.Y. in one of her finest roles, the Queen of the Night, on Feb. 19, 1967. She sang with many of the world's leading opera houses, and also won distinction as a gifted concert and lieder artist. In 1979 she was made an Austrian Kammersängerin, and was awarded the Silver Rose of the Vienna Phil. She won accolades for her roles in operas by Mozart and Strauss, especially Pamina, Despina, Zerlina, Susanna, Zdenka, Sophie, and the Countess, as well as the Queen of the Night. For some years she was married to **György Fischer**.

Poradowski, Stefan (Boleslaw), Polish composer and pedagogue; b. Wloclawek, Aug. 16, 1902; d. Poznań, July 9, 1967. He studied composition with Opieński at the Poznań Cons. (1922–26); then took private lessons with Rezniček in Berlin (1929). Returning to Poland, he taught composition and theory at the Poznań Cons. (1930–39; 1945–67); also gave courses (from 1956) at the Wroclaw Cons. He publ. *Nauka harmonii* (Science of Harmony; Poznań, 1931; 5th ed., rev., 1964), *Ogólne wiadomości z akustyki* (General Knowledge on Acoustics; Poznań, 1947), and *Sztuka pisania kanonów* (Art of Writing Canons; Poznań, 1965).

WORKS: DRAMATIC: *Odkupienie* (Redemption), passion play for Mezzo-soprano, Chorus, and Orch. (1939–41); *Plomienie* (Flames), opera (1961–66). **ORCH.:** *Sinfonietta* (1925); *Concerto antico* for Viola d'Amore and Orch. (1925); *Triptych* for Strings (1926); 8 syms. (1928; 1930; 1932; 1934; 1937–38; 1951–52; 1961; 1967); Double Bass Concerto (1929); *Capriccio on a Theme by Kreutzer* for Strings (1930); *Serenada klasyczna* for Strings (1940); *Rapsodia polska* for Violin and Orch. (1944); Concert Overture (1947); *Ratusz poznański* (The Town Hall of Poznań), symphonic poem (1950); Concerto for Flute, Harp, and String Orch. (1954); Violin Concerto (1965). **CHAMBER:** 4 string quartets (1923, 1923, 1936, 1947); Violin Sonata (1925); 5 trios: I and II for Violin, Viola, and Double Bass (1929, 1930), III for String Trio (1935), IV for 3 Double Basses (1952), and V for String Trio (1955); piano pieces; organ music. **VOCAL:** *Pieśń wiosenna* (Spring Song) for Soprano, Chorus, and Orch. (1926); *Koń Światowida* (The Horse of Sviatovid), fantastic poem for Tenor, Baritone, Chorus, and Orch. (1931); 3 cantatas (1950, 1954, 1954); 3 masses; 4 hymns; songs; folk song arrangements.

Porcelijn, David, Dutch composer; b. Achtkarspelen, Friesland, Jan. 7, 1947. He studied flute with Frans Vester (1964–68) and composition with Baaren and Vlijmen (1966–70) at the Royal Cons. of Music at The Hague; then studied conducting with Stotijn; later took lessons in conducting and composition with Tabachnik in Geneva. A modernist par excellence, Porcelijn makes explorations in every direction; his music ranges from the infraclassical to ultramathematical.

WORKS: *4 Interpretations* for Various Instruments (1967–69); *Continuations* for 11 Wind Instruments (1968); *Combinations* for 26 Solo Instruments (1969–70); *Requiem*, in memory of Varèse, for Percussion Ensemble (1969–70); *Zen* for Flute (1970); *1,000 Frames* for 1 + Wind Instruments and/or 1 + Pianos (1970); *Confrontation and Indoctrinations* for Jazz Band and 19 Instruments (Scheveningen, June 23, 1972); *Cybernetic Object* for Orch. (The Hague, June 18, 1971); *Amoeba* for x Flutes (1971); *Pole*, ballet for 26 Instruments (1971–72); *10-5-6-5(a)* for 2 String Quartets, Wind Quintet, and 2 Vibraphones (1972); *Pulverizations I* for 52 Strings (1972) and *II* for Alto Saxophone, 22 Winds, 5 Percussion Groups, and 52 Strings (1973); *Pulverizations* for Wind Quintet (1972); Concerto for Flute, Harp, and Orch. (1973); Flute Concerto (1975); *Shades* for Flute, Violin, and Viola (1975); *Rhythm Song* for Men's Chorus and Percussion (1976); *Into the Earth* for 14 Brass and 2 Percussionists (1976); *12 November 1819* for Wind Quintet (1976); *Terrible Power* for Orch. (1977); *Explosions* for 10 Instruments (1977); *Groupings* for 5 Groups of Instruments (1979); *Sinfonia Concertante* for Orch. (1985–86); *Unfinished Songs for an Elusive Sphinx* for Oboe, Clarinet, and Bassoon (1986); *97 Endeavors to Propitiate Ra* for Flute (1986).

Porfetye, Andreas, Romanian composer; b. Zădăreni, July 6, 1927. He studied with Drăgoi, Constantinescu, Rogalski, and Vancea at the Bucharest Cons. (1948–54). He was ed. of the journal *Muzica* (1954–69); taught at the Bucharest Cons. (from 1969).

WORKS: ORCH.: 3 syms. (1955; 1965; *La Dramatique*, 1970); *Partita* for Strings (1958); Organ Concerto (1962; rev. 1967); *Sinfonia-Serenata* (1964); Violin Concerto (1966); *Sonata* (1971). **CHAMBER:** Horn Sonata (1956); Wind Quintet (1957); *Piccola sonata* for Violin and Organ (1962); Sonata for Cello and Organ (1963); *6 Pieces* for Clarinet and Harp (1965); Violin Sonata (1967); String Quartet No. 2 (1969). **KEYBOARD: PIANO:** Sonata (1963); Sonatina (1965). **ORGAN:** *Passacaglia and Fugue* (1955); *Toccata, Chorale, and Fugue* (1957); 3 sonatas (1960–68); *Toccata* (1966); *Fantasy* (1968). **VOCAL:** *Cantata de camera* for Mezzo-soprano, Cello, and Chamber Orch. (1959); Cantata No. 2, *Comunistul*, for Mezzo-soprano, Chorus, and Orch. (1962); *In memorian Mihail Sadoveanu*, Requiem for Soprano, Tenor, and Orch. (1962).

Porrino, Ennio, Italian composer and teacher; b. Cagliari, Sardinia, Jan. 20, 1910; d. Rome, Sept. 25, 1959. He studied at the Accademia di Santa Cecilia in Rome with Mule, and later took a course with Respighi (1932–35). He subsequently taught in Rome, Venice, and Naples; from 1956 he was director of the Cagliari Cons.

WORKS: DRAMATIC: OPERAS: *Gli orazi* (Milan, 1941); *L'organo di bambu* (Venice, 1955); *I shardana* (Naples, 1959). **BALLETS:** *Proserpina* (Florence, 1938); *Altair* (Naples, 1942); *Mondo tondo* (Rome, 1949); *La bambola malata* (Venice, 1959). **ORCH.:** *Tartatin de Tarascon*, overture (Rome, 1933); *Sardegna*, symphonic poem, based on Sardinian folk themes (Rome, 1933); Trumpet Concertino (1934); *La visione di Ezechiele* (1935); *Sinfonia per una fiaba* (1936); *Notturna e Danza* (1936); *3 canzoni italiane* for Chamber Orch. (1937); *Preludio in modo religioso e ostinato* (1942; also for Piano); *Sinfonietta dei fanciulli* (1947); *Sonata drammatica* for Piano and Orch. (1947); *Ostinato* for Piano and Strings (1951; Milan, Feb. 3, 1952); *Nuraghi*, 3 primitive dances (1952); *Concerto dell'Argentarola* for Guitar and Orch. (1953); *Sonar per musici* for Harpsichord and Strings (1959). **OTHER:** *I canti dell'esilio*, 15 songs for Voice and Chamber Orch. (1947); *Il processo di Cristo*, oratorio (1949); other songs; chamber pieces, including *Preludio, Aria e Scherzo* for Trumpet and Piano (1942).

Porter, Andrew (Brian), brilliant English writer on music; b. Cape Town, South Africa, Aug. 26, 1928. He studied music at Diocesan College in Cape Town; then went to England and continued his education at Univ. College, Oxford; became a proficient organist. In 1949 he joined the staff of the Manchester Guardian; then wrote music criticism for the *Financial Times* of London (1953–74); also served as ed. of the *Musical Times* of London (1960–67). In 1972 he became the music critic of the *New Yorker*. In 1992 he became the chief music critic of *The Observer* in London. He was made a corresponding member of the American Musicological Soc. in 1993. A polyglot, a polymath, and an uncommonly diversified intellectual, Porter expanded his interests far beyond the limited surface of purely musical studies; he mastered German, Italian, and French; made an exemplary tr. into Eng. of the entire text of *Der Ring des Nibelungen*, taking perspicuous care for the congenial rendition of Wagner's words and melodic inflections; his tr. was used to excellent advantage in the performance and recording of the cycle by the conductor Reginald Goodall with the English National Opera. Porter also tr. texts of Verdi's operas, Mozart's *Die Zauberflöte*, and some French operas. His mastery of English prose and his unostentatious display of arcane erudition make him one of the most remarkable music critics writing in the English language. Selections from his reviews have been publ. in *A Musical Season* (N.Y., 1974), *Music of Three Seasons, 1974–1977* (N.Y., 1978), *Music of Three More Seasons, 1977–1980* (N.Y., 1981), *Musical Events: A Chronicle, 1980–1983* (N.Y., 1987), and *Musical Events: A Chronicle, 1983–1986* (N.Y., 1989); also was co-ed. of *Verdi's Macbeth: A Sourcebook* (N.Y., 1983).

Porter, Hugh, American organist and pedagogue; b. Heron Lake, Minn., Sept. 18, 1897; d. N.Y., Sept. 22, 1960. He studied at the American Cons. in Chicago (B.M., 1920), Northwestern Univ. (B.A., 1924), with Middelschulte, Farnam, Noble, and Boulanger, and at the Union Theological Seminary in N.Y. (M.S.M., 1930; D.S.M., 1944). He taught at Northwestern Univ., the Juilliard School of Music in N.Y., N.Y. Univ., and the Mannes College of Music in N.Y. In 1931 he joined the faculty of the Union Theological Seminary, where he was director (from 1945) and a prof. (from 1947). Porter also held many positions as a church organist, toured as a recitalist, and was organist at the Chatauqua Institution. With his wife Ethel Porter, he ed. the United Church of Christ *Pilgrim Hymnal* (1958).

Porter, (William) Quincy, significant American composer and teacher; b. New Haven, Conn., Feb. 7, 1897; d. Bethany, Conn., Nov. 12, 1966. He was brought up in an intellectual atmosphere; his father and his grandfather were profs. at Yale Univ. He studied with David Stanley Smith and Horatio Parker at the Yale Univ. School of Music (B.A., 1919; B.Mus., 1921); submitted a violin concerto for the American Prix de Rome and received an honorable mention; also won the Steinert and Osborne prizes. After graduation he went to Paris, where he took courses with Capet (violin) and d'Indy (composition). Returning to America in 1922, he earned a living as a violinist in theater orchs. in N.Y. while taking a course in composition with Bloch. He taught at the Cleveland Inst. of Music (1922–28; 1931–32); played the viola in the Ribaupierre String Quartet there; also spent 3 years in Paris on a Guggenheim fellowship (1928–31). He was a prof. at Vassar College and conductor of the Vassar Orch. (1932–38); in 1938 he succeeded Converse as dean of the New England Cons. of Music in Boston; from 1942 to 1946, was its director; from 1946 to 1965, was a prof. at Yale Univ. In 1954 he won the Pulitzer Prize in Music for his Concerto for 2 Pianos and Orch., later renamed the *Concerto Concertante.* His music is built on strong contrapuntal lines, with incisive rhythms; his harmonic procedures often reach stridently polytonal sonorities, while the general idiom of his works combines elements of both the modern German and the modern French styles of composition.

WORKS: ORCH.: *Ukrainian Suite* for Strings (Rochester, N.Y., May 1, 1925); Suite in C minor (1926); *Poem and Dance* (Cleveland, June 24, 1932, composer conducting); 2 syms.: No. 1 (1934; N.Y., April 2, 1938, composer conducting) and No. 2 (1961–62; Louisville, Jan. 14, 1964); *Dance in Three-Time* for Chamber Orch. (St. Louis, July 2, 1937); *Music for Strings* (1941); *Fantasy on a Pastoral Theme* for Organ and Strings (1942); *The Moving Tide* (1944); Viola Concerto (N.Y., May 16, 1948); *Fantasy* for Cello and Small Orch. (1950); Concerto for 2 Pianos and Orch., renamed *Concerto Concertante* (1952–53; Louisville, March 17, 1954); *New England Episodes*, symphonic suite (Washington, D.C., April 18, 1958); Concerto for Wind Orch. (1959); Harpsichord Concerto (1959; New Haven, Jan. 19, 1960); Concerto for Wind Orch. (1960); *Ohio*, overture (1963). **CHAMBER:** 10 string quartets (1923, 1925, 1930, 1931, 1935, 1937, 1943, 1950, 1958, 1965); 2 violin sonatas (1926, 1929); *In Monasterio* for String Quartet (1927); Piano Quintet (1927); *Little Trio* for Flute, Violin, and Viola (1928); Clarinet Quintet (1929); Suite for Viola (1930); *Quintet on a Childhood Theme* for Flute and Strings (1937); Horn Sonata (1946); *String Sextet on Slavic Folk Tunes* (1947); 4 pieces for Violin and Piano (1947); Duo for Violin and Viola (1954); Duo for Flute and Harp (1957); *Divertimento* for Wind Quintet (1960); Oboe Quintet (1966). **PIANO:** Sonata (1930); *8 Pieces for Bill* (1941–42; nos. 2 and 8 not extant); *6 Miniatures* (1943); *Day Dreams* (1957; based on *8 Pieces for Bill*). **VOCAL:** *The Desolate City* for Baritone and Orch. (1950); choruses.

BIBL.: H. Ewell, "Q. P.," *Modern Music*, XXIII (1946); H. Boatwright, "Q. P.," *American Composers Alliance Bulletin*, VI/3 (1957); idem, "Q. P. (1897–1966)," *Perspectives of New Music*, V/2 (1967).

Pospíšil, Juraj, Slovak composer and teacher; b. Olomouc, Jan. 14, 1931. He received training in piano, organ, and theory at the Olomouc School of Music (1949–50). After studying composition with Petrželka at the Janáček Academy of Music and Drama in Brno (1950–52), he completed his studies in composition with Moyzes and Cikker at the Bratislava Academy of Music and Drama (1952–55). From 1955 to 1991 he lectured on theory and composition at the Bratislava Cons. In 1988 he received an award from the Union of Slovak Composers. Pospíšil developed a compositional style which owed much to the Second Viennese School while paying homage to Slovak tradition.

WORKS: DRAMATIC: *Inter arma*, cycle of 3 operas (1969–70); *Manon Lescaut*, scenic drama (1993). **ORCH.:** *The Mountains and the People*, symphonic poem (1954; Bratislava, Dec. 20, 1955); 5 syms.: No. 1 (1958; Bratislava, June 4, 1961), No. 2, *Nebula in Andromeda* (1963; Bratislava, June 3, 1964), No. 3 for Chamber Ensemble and Kettledrums (1967; Bratislava, Feb. 27, 1968), No. 4, *Warsaw*, for Narrator, Soprano, Chorus, and Orch. (1978), and No. 5 (1986; Bratislava, Feb. 27, 1988); *Reflections* (1958); *Song About a Man*, symphonic variations (1961); Trombone Concerto (1962; Bratislava, Jan. 20, 1964); Violin Concerto (1968); Clarinet Concerto (1972; also for Clarinet and Organ, 1977); 3 symphonic frescoes: No. 1 (1972; Kosice, Oct. 6, 1976), No. 2 (1976; Bratislava, Feb. 24, 1985), and No. 3 (1981; Bratislava, Feb. 10, 1985); *Concerto eroico* for Horn and Orch. (1973); *Through the Land of Childhood* (1983); Concerto for Soprano and Orch. (1984; Bratislava, Feb. 14, 1986); *Dramatic Overture* (1984); Dulcimer Concerto (1989); Sonata for Alto Trombone and Strings (1991); Bass Tuba Concerto (1994). **CHAMBER:** *In Reveries* for Strings (1953); Sonata for Strings (1961; Berlin, Dec. 14, 1963); *3 Inventions* for Wind Trio (1961); *Music* for Brass (1962); *Glosses* for Wind Quintet (1964); Double Bass Sonata (1964); *Contradictions* for Clarinet and String Quartet (1964); *Music* for 12 Strings (1965; Bratislava, Feb. 27, 1968); 2 sonatas for Solo Violin (1965, 1976); 4 string quartets (1970, 1979, 1985, 1990); Flute Quartet (1971); *Chamber Sinfonietta* for Strings and Brass (1974); 2 trios for Violin, Cello, and Piano (1977, 1987); Sonata for English Horn and String Quartet (1983); Trio for Violin, Cello, and Accordion (1985); *Melancholic Suite* for Oboe, English Horn, and Bassoon (1986); Trio for Flute, Guitar, and Cello (1986); Wind Sextet (1988); *Grand duo (quasi una sonata)* for Bass Clarinet and Piano (1989); Trio for Trombones (Bratislava, Oct. 12, 1990); Brass Quintet (1991; Bratislava, Nov. 26, 1992); piano pieces; organ music. **VOCAL:** *Margita and Besná* for Soli, Chorus, and Orch. (1955; Bratislava, June 4, 1961); *To Bratislava* for Baritone and Orch. or Piano (1973); *Dazzlement* for Narrator and Chamber Ensemble (1973); *November Triptych* for Chamber Chorus, Wind Quintet, and Piano (1977); *The Lord's Prayer of the Hussites*, sacred cantata for Mezzo-soprano, Bass, Chorus, and Orch. (1990); *Autumn Bottling* for Bass and String Quartet (1994).

Posselt, Ruth, American violinist; b. Medford, Mass., Sept. 6, 1914. She studied with E. Ondříček. She gave numerous recitals in America and Europe; gave the premieres of violin concertos by Walter Piston, Vladimir Dukelsky, Edward Burlingame Hill, and others. On July 3, 1940, she married **Richard Burgin**.

Postnikova, Viktoria (Valentinovna), Russian pianist; b. Moscow, Jan. 12, 1944. She studied at the Moscow Central Music School and later at the Moscow Cons., graduating in 1967. In 1966 she received 2nd prize at the Leeds Competition; then embarked upon a major career, appearing widely as a soloist with leading orchs. and as a recitalist. She married **Gennadi Rozhdestvensky** in 1969.

Poštolka, Milan, Czech musicologist; b. Prague, Sept. 29, 1932; d. there, Dec. 14, 1993. He studied with Očadlik and Sychra at the Univ. of Prague (1951–56), passing the state examination in musicology (1956), taking the C.Sc. (1966), and obtaining his Ph.D (1967; with the diss. *Leopold Koželuh: Život a dílo* [Leopold Kozeluh: Life and Works]; publ. in Prague, 1964). He worked in the music division of Prague's National Museum (from 1958), and also taught at the Univ. of Prague (1966–79); was director of a research team studying 17th- and 18th-century Czech music at the Czech Academy of Sciences (1972–86). He publ. books on Czech music of the 18th century (Prague, 1961) and on the young Haydn (Prague, 1988).

Poston, Elizabeth, English pianist and composer; b. Highfield, Hertfordshire, Oct. 24, 1905; d. there, March 18, 1987. She studied piano with Harold Samuel; also took courses at the Royal Academy of Music in London. During World War II, she was in charge of music in the European Service of the BBC in London. Her works follow along neo-Classicial lines.

WORKS: *The Holy Child* for Soloists, Chorus, and Strings (1950); *Concertino da Camera on a Theme of Martin Peerson* for Ancient Instruments (1950); *The Nativity* for Soloists, Chorus, and Strings or Organ (1951); Trio for Flute, Clarinet or Viola, and Piano (1958); *Peter Halfpenny's Tunes* for Recorder and Piano (1959); *Lullaby and Fiesta,* 2 pieces for Piano (1960); *Magnificat* for 4 Voices and Organ (1961); *3 Scottish Carols* for Chorus and Strings or Organ (1969); *Harlow Concertante* for String Quartet and String Orch. (1969); *An English Day Book* for Mixed Voices and Harp (1971); Sonatina for Cello and Piano (1972); hymn tunes; Christmas carols; music for films and radio.

Potter, A(rchibald) J(ames), Irish composer and teacher; b. Belfast, Sept. 22, 1918; d. Greystones, July 5, 1980. He received training under W. Vale at the choir school of All Saints, Margaret Street, in London (1929–33), D.G.A. Fox at Clifton College in Bristol (1933–36), and Vaughan Williams at the Royal College of Music in London (1936–38); later he took his D.Mus. at the Univ. of Dublin (1953). From 1955 to 1973 he was a prof. of composition at the Royal Irish Academy of Music in Dublin. His output followed in the path of tradition and opted for Romantic qualities.

WORKS: DRAMATIC: OPERAS: *Patrick,* television opera (1962; RTE, March 17, 1965); *The Wedding* (1979; Dublin, June 8, 1981). **BALLETS:** *Careless Love* (1959; Dublin, April 12, 1960); *Caitlín Bhocht* (1963; Radio Ireland, June 27, 1964). **ORCH.:** *Overture to a Kitchen Comedy* (1950); *Rhapsody Under a High Sky* (1950); *Concerto da chiesa* for Piano and Orch. (1952); *Variations on a Popular Tune* (1955); *Phantasmoraggio* (1956); *Elegy* for Clarinet, Harp, and Strings (1956); *Caonie* (Dirge; 1956); *Finnegans Wake* (1957; also for Concert Band); *Fantasia Gaelach* (1957); *Fantasie Concertante* for Violin, Cello, and Orch. (1959); *Irish Rhapsody* (1963); *Caprice* for Cello and Orch. (1964); *Hunter's Holiday* for Horn and Orch. (1964); *Sound the Sackbuts* for 3 Trombones and Orch. (1965); *Fantasie* for Clarinet and Orch. (1965); *Spanish Point* for Guitar and Orch. (1965); *Rapsóid Deireadh lae* (Rhapsody for the End of the Day) for Violin and Orch. (1966); *Concerto for Orchestra* (Dublin, March 13, 1967); *Concertino Bennio* for Trumpet and Orch. (1967); *Dance Fantasy* (1967); *Binneadán Bél* for Horn and Orch. (1967); 2 syms.: No. 1, *Sinfonia de Profundis* (1968; Dublin, March 23, 1969) and No. 2 (1976; Springfield, Mass., Dec. 11, 1981); *Madra Líath na Mara* (Grey Dog of the Sea) for English Horn and Chamber Orch. (1977); *Salala's Castle* for Winds and Percussion (1980). **CHAMBER:** String Quartet (1938); *A House Full of Harpers* for Irish Harp Ensemble and Concert Harp (1963); *Arklow Quartet* for Brass or Winds (1976–77). **VOCAL:** *Hail Mary* for Mezzo-soprano, Tenor, Chorus, and Orch. (1966); *The Cornet of Horse* for Baritone, Men's Chorus, and Orch. (1975); choruses; songs.

Poueigh, Jean (Marie-Octave-Géraud), French composer and writer on music; b. Toulouse, Feb. 24, 1876; d. Olivet, Loiret, Oct. 14, 1958. After music study in his native city, he entered the Paris Cons. as a student of Caussade, Lenepveu, and Fauré; also received advice from d'Indy; settled in Paris. He harmonized and ed. a number of folk songs of Languedoc and Gascogne in *Les Chansons de France* (1907–09), *3 chansons des Pays d'Oc,* and *14 chansons anciennes*; also ed. the collection *Chansons populaires des Pyrénées françaises* (vol. 1, 1926). Under the pen name of Octave Séré, he publ. *Musiciens français d'aujourd'hui* (Paris, 1911; 7th ed., 1921); contributed numerous articles to various French periodicals. His original compositions include the operas *Les Lointains* (1903); *Le Meneur de louves* (1921); *Perkin,* a Basque legend (Bordeaux, Jan. 16, 1931); *Le Roi de Camargue* (Marseilles, May 12, 1948); *Bois-brûlé* (1956); 3 ballets: *Fünn* (1906), *Frivolant* (Paris, May 1, 1922), and *Chergui,* Moroccan ballet; *La Basilique aux vainqueurs,* symphonic tableau; piano pieces and songs.

Pouishnov, Lev, Russian-born English pianist; b. Odessa, Oct. 11, 1891; d. London, May 28, 1959. He made his public debut at age 5; after studies in Kiev, he received instruction in piano from Essipova and in composition from Liadov, Rimsky-Korsakov, and Glazunov at the St. Petersburg Cons. (graduated with the Gold Medal and the Rubinstein Prize, 1910); then toured while also being active as a teacher in Tiflis (1913–17). He left Russia as a result of the Bolshevik Revolution, and pursued a career in the West; toured widely in Europe and also made appearances in the U.S. (from 1923); made his home in England, becoming a naturalized subject in 1935. He became best known for his performances of works from the Romantic repertoire.

Poulenc, Francis (Jean Marcel), brilliant French composer; b. Paris, Jan. 7, 1899; d. there, Jan. 30, 1963. He was born into a wealthy family of pharmaceutical manufacturers; his mother taught him music in his childhood; at 16, he began taking formal piano lessons with Ricardo Viñes. A decisive turn in his development as a composer occurred when he attracted the attention of Erik Satie, the arbiter elegantiarum of the arts and social amenities in Paris. Deeply impressed by Satie's fruitful eccentricities in the then-shocking manner of Dadaism, Poulenc joined an ostentatiously self-descriptive musical group called the Nouveaux Jeunes. In a gratuitous parallel with the Russian Five, the French critic Henri Collet dubbed the "New Youths" Le Groupe de Six, and the label stuck under the designation Les Six. The 6 musicians included, besides Poulenc: Auric, Durey, Honegger, Milhaud, and Tailleferre. Although quite different in their styles of composition and artistic inclinations, they continued collective participation in various musical events. Poulenc served in the French army (1918–21), and then began taking lessons in composition with Koechlin (1921–24). An excellent pianist, Poulenc became in 1935 an accompanist to the French baritone Pierre Bernac, for whom he wrote numerous songs. Compared with his fortuitous comrades-in-six, Poulenc appears a classicist. He never experimented with the popular devices of "machine music," asymmetrical rhythms, and polyharmonies as cultivated by Honegger and Milhaud. Futuristic projections had little interest for him; he was content to follow the gentle neo-Classical formation of Ravel's piano music and songs. Among his other important artistic contacts was the ballet impresario Diaghilev, who commissioned him to write music for his Ballets Russes. Apart from his fine songs and piano pieces, Poulenc revealed himself as an inspired composer of religious music, of which his choral works *Stabat Mater* and *Gloria* are notable. He also wrote remarkable music for the organ, including a concerto that became a minor masterpiece. A master of artificial simplicity, he pleases even sophisticated listeners by his bland triadic tonalities, spiced with quickly passing diaphonous discords.

WORKS: DRAMATIC: OPERAS: *Les Mamelles de Tirésias*, opéra-bouffe (1944; Paris, June 3, 1947); *Dialogues des Carmélites*, religious opera (1953–56; Milan, Jan. 26, 1957); *La Voix humaine*, monodrama for Soprano (1958; Paris, Feb. 6, 1959). **BALLETS:** *La Baigneuse de Trouville and Discours de Général*, 2 movements for *Les Mariés de la Tour Eiffel*, ballet-farce (Paris, June 18, 1921; other movements by members of Les Six, except for Durey); *Les Biches*, with Chorus (1923; Monte Carlo, Jan. 6, 1924); *Pastourelle*, 9th movement of an 11-movement collective ballet, *L'Eventail de Jeanne* (1927; 1st perf. of orch. version, Paris, March 4, 1929; movements by Roussel, Ravel, Ibert, Milhaud et al.); *Aubade*, choreographic concerto for Piano and 18 Instruments (private perf., Paris, June 18, 1929; public perf., London, Dec. 19, 1929); *Les Animaux modèles* (1940–41; Paris, Aug. 8, 1942).

ORCH.: *Concert champêtre* for Harpsichord or Piano and Orch. (1927–28; Paris, May 3, 1929); Concerto for 2 Pianos and Orch. (Venice, Sept. 5, 1932); *2 marches et un intermède* for Chamber Orch. (Paris, 1937); Concerto for Organ, Strings, and Timpani (1938; private perf., Paris, June 21, 1939; public perf., Paris, June 10, 1941); *Sinfonietta* (1947; London, Oct. 24, 1948); Piano Concerto (1949; Boston, Jan. 6, 1950); *Matelote provençale*, movement from a collective work of 7 composers, *La Guirlande de Campra* (1952); *Bucolique: Variations sur la nom de Marguerite Long* (1954; movement from a collective work of 8 composers).

CHAMBER: Sonata for 2 Clarinets (1918; rev. 1945); Sonata for Clarinet and Bassoon (1922); Sonata for Horn, Trumpet, and Trombone (1922; rev. 1945); Trio for Oboe, Bassoon, and Piano (1926); Sextet for Piano and Wind Quintet (1930–32; rev. 1939); *Suite française* for 9 Winds, Percussion, and Harpsichord (1935); Violin Sonata (1942–43; rev. 1949); Cello Sonata (1948); Flute Sonata (1956); *Élégie*, to the memory of Dennis Brain, for Horn and Piano (1957); *Sarabande* for Guitar (1960); Clarinet Sonata (1962); Oboe Sonata (1962). **PIANO:** Sonata for Piano, 4-hands (1918); *3 mouvements perpétuels* (1918); *Valse* (1919); *Suite in C* (1920); *6 impromptus* (1920); *Promenades* (1921); *Napoli*, suite of 3 pieces (1921–25); *2 novelettes* (1928); *3 pièces* (1928); *Pièce brève sur la nom d'Albert Roussel* (1929); *8 nocturnes* (1929–38); *15 improvisations* (1932–59); *Villageoises* (1933); *Feuillets d'album* (1933); *Les Soirées de Nazelles* (1930–36); *Mélancolie* (1940); *Intermezzo* (1943); *L'Embarquement pour Cythère* for 2 Pianos (1951); *Thème varié* (1951); Sonata for 2 Pianos (1952–53); *Élégie* for 2 Pianos (1959); *Novelette sur un thème de Manuel de Falla* (1959).

VOCAL: CHORAL: *Chanson à boire* for Men's Chorus (1922); *7 chansons* for Chorus (1936); *Litanies à la vièrge noire* for Women's Chorus and Organ (1936); Mass in G for Chorus (1937; Paris, May 1938); *Secheresses* (Dryness), cantata for Chorus and Orch., after Edward James (1937; Paris, 1938); *4 motets pour un temps de penitence* for Chorus (1938–39); *Exultate Deo* for Chorus (1941); *Salve regina* for Chorus (1941); *Figure humaine*, cantata for Double Chorus (1943); *Un Soir de neige*, chamber cantata for 6 Voices (1944); 2 books of traditional French songs, arr. for Chorus (1945); *4 petites prières de Saint François d'Assise* for Men's Chorus (1948); *Stabat Mater* for Soprano, Chorus, and Orch. (1950; Strasbourg, June 13, 1951); *4 motets pour le temps de Noël* for Chorus (1951–52); *Ave verum corpus* for Women's Chorus (1952); *Laudes de Saint Antoine de Padoue* for Men's Chorus (1957–59); *Gloria* for Soprano, Chorus, and Orch. (1959; Boston, Jan. 20, 1961); *7 répons des ténèbres* for Boy Soprano, Boy's and Men's Chorus, and Orch. (1961; N.Y., April 11, 1963). **VOICE AND INSTRUMENTS:** *Rapsodie nègre* for Baritone, String Quartet, Flute, Clarinet, and Piano (Paris, Dec. 11, 1917; rev. 1933); *Le Bestiaire* for Mezzo-soprano, String Quartet, Flute, Clarinet, and Bassoon, after Apollinaire (1918–19); *Cocardes* for Voice, Violin, Cornet, Trombone, Bass Drum, and Triangle, after Cocteau (1919); *Le Bal masque* for Voice, Oboe, Clarinet, Bassoon, Violin, Cello, Percussion, and Piano, after Max Jacob (1932); *La Dame de Monte Carlo*, monologue for Soprano and Orch. (Paris, Dec. 5, 1961). **VOICE AND PIANO:** *Histoire de Babar le petit éléphant* for Narrator and Piano (1940–45; orchestrated by Jean Françaix, 1962). **SONG CYCLES:** *Le Bestiaire* (1919; arrangement); *Cocardes* (1919; arrangement); *Poèmes de Ronsard* (1924–25; later orchestrated); *Chansons gaillardes* (1925–26); *Airs chantés* (1927–28); *8 chansons polonaises* (1934); *4 chansons pour enfants* (1934); *5 poèmes*, after Éluard (1935); *Tel jour, telle nuit* (1936–37); *3 poèmes*, after de Vilmorin (1937); *2 poèmes*, after Apollinaire (1938); *Miroirs brûlants* (1938–39); *Fiançailles pour rire* (1939); *Banalités* (1940); *Chansons villageoises* (1942; orchestrated 1943); *Métamorphoses* (1943); *3 chansons*, after García Lorca (1947); *Calligrammes* (1948); *La Fraîcheur et le feu* (1950); *Parisiana* (1954); *Le Travail du peintre* (1956); *2 mélodies* (1956); *La Courte Paille* (1960). **SONGS:** *Toréador* (1918; rev. 1932); *Vocalise* (1927); *Épitaphe* (1930); *À sa guitare*, after Ronsard (1935); *Montparnasse* (1941–45); *Hyde Park* (1945); *Paul et Virginie* (1946); *Le Disparu* (1947); *Mazurka* (1949); *Rosemonde* (1954); *Dernier poème* (1956); *Une Chanson de porcelaine* (1958); others.

WRITINGS: *Emmanuel Chabrier* (Paris, 1961); *Moi et mes amis* (Paris, 1963; Eng. tr., London, 1978 as *My Friends and Myself*); *Journal de mes mélodies* (Paris, 1964); S. Buckland, tr. and ed., *Francis Poulenc: Selected Correspondence, 1915–1963: Echo and Source* (1991).

BIBL.: A. Schaeffner, "F. P., musicien français," *Contrepoints*, 1 (1946); C. Rostand, *F. P.: Entretiens avec Claude Rostand* (Paris, 1954); H. Hell, *P., musicien français* (Paris, 1958); J. Roy, *F. P.* (Paris, 1964); P. Bernac, *F. P.: The Man and His Songs* (London, 1977); K. Daniel, *F. P.: His Artistic Development and Musical Style* (N.Y., 1982); F. Bloch, *F. P.* (Paris, 1984); M. Rosenthal, *Satie, Ravel, P.: An Intimate Memoir* (Madras and N.Y., 1987); G. Keck, *F. P.: A Bio-Bibliography* (Westport, Conn., 1990); H. Ehrler, *Untersuchungen zur Klaviermusik von F. P., Arthur Honegger und Darius Milhaud* (Tutzing, 1990); W. Mellers, *F. P.* (Oxford, 1994); J. Roy, *Le groupe des six: P., Milhaud, Honegger, Auric, Tailleferre, Durey* (Paris, 1994); C. Schmidt, *The Music of F. P. (1899–1963): A Catalogue* (Oxford, 1995).

Poulet, Gaston, French violinist and conductor, father of **Gérard Poulet**; b. Paris, April 10, 1892; d. Draveil, Essonne, April 14, 1974. He studied violin at the Paris Cons., winning the premier prix (1910). He made his debut as soloist in the Beethoven Concerto in Brussels (1911); organized a string quartet in 1912 and gave concerts in Europe; from 1927 to 1936 he conducted the Concerts Poulet at the Théâtre Sarah-Bernhardt in Paris; from 1932 to 1944 he served as director of the Cons. of Bordeaux and conducted the Phil. Orch. there; from 1940 to 1945 he conducted the Concerts Colonne in Paris; was a guest conductor with the London Sym. Orch. (1947) and in Germany (1948); also in South America. He played the violin in the first performance of Debussy's Violin Sonata, with Debussy himself at the piano (1917). He was a prof. of chamber music at the Paris Cons. from 1944 to 1962. In 1948 he founded the famous Besançon Festival.

Poulet, Gérard, French violinist, son of **Gaston Poulet**; b. Bayonne, Aug. 12, 1938. He entered the Paris Cons. at the age of 11 in the class of André Asselin, and won 1st prize at 12; in the same year (1950), he played 3 violin concertos with the Colonne Orch. in Paris, under his father's direction; then appeared with other Paris orchs.; subsequently gave concerts and played with orchs. in England, Germany, Italy, Austria, and the Netherlands. In 1956 he won 1st Grand Prix at the Paganini competition of Genoa, and was given the honor of performing on Paganini's own violin, the famous Guarneri del Gesù.

Pound, Ezra (Loomis), greatly significant American man of letters and amateur composer; b. Hailey, Idaho, Oct. 30, 1885; d. Venice, Nov. 1, 1972. He was educated at Hamilton College (Ph.B., 1905) and the Univ. of Pa. (M.A., 1906). He went to England, where he established himself as a leading experimental poet and influential critic. He also pursued a great interest in early music, especially that of the troubadours, which led him to try his hand at composing. With the assistance of George Antheil, he composed the opera *Le Testament*, after poems by François Villon (1923; Paris, June 19, 1926); it was followed by a 2nd opera, *Calvacanti* (1932), and a 3rd, left unfinished, based on the poetry of Catullus. In 1924 he settled in Rapallo. Although married to Dorothy Shakespear, daughter of one of Yeats's friends, he became intimate with the American violinist Olga Rudge; Rudge bore him a daughter in 1925 and his wife bore him a son in 1926. Through the influence of Rudge, his interest in music continued, and he became a fervent champion of Vivaldi; he also worked as a music reviewer and ran a concert series with Rudge, Inverno Musicale. A growing interest in economic history and an inordinate admiration for the Fascist dictator Benito Mussolini led Pound down the road of political obscurantism. During World War II, he made many broadcasts over Rome Radio on topics ranging from literature to politics. His condemnation of Jewish banking circles in America and the American effort to defeat Fascism led to his arrest by the Allies after the collapse of Il Duce's regime. In 1945 he was sent to a prison camp in Pisa. In 1946 he was sent to the U.S. to stand trial for treason, but was declared insane and confined to St. Elizabeth's Hospital in Washington, D.C. Finally, in 1958, he was released and allowed to return to Italy, where he died. Among his writings on music is *Antheil and the Treatise on Harmony* (1924). He also composed several works for solo violin for Rudge, including *Fiddle Music* (1924) and *Al poco giorno* (Berkeley, March 23, 1983); he also arranged Gaucelm Faidit's *Plainte pour la mort du roi Richart Coeur de Lion*. The uncatalogued collection of Pound's musical MSS at Yale Univ. includes various musical experiments, including rhythmic and melodic realizations of his poem *Sestina: Altaforte*. Among the composers who have set his poems to music are Copland, Luytens, and Berio.

BIBL.: S. Adams, *E. P. and Music* (diss., Univ. of Toronto, 1974); R. Schafer, ed., *E. P. and Music* (N.Y., 1977; a complete collection of his writings on music).

Pountney, David (Willoughby), English opera director; b. Oxford, Sept. 10, 1947. He received his education at Radley College and at the Univ. of Cambridge. In 1967 he staged his first opera, A. Scarlatti's *Il trionfo dell'onore*, with the Cambridge Opera Soc. In 1971 he produced *The Rake's Progress* at Glasgow's Scottish Opera, and in 1972 at the Netherlands Opera in Amsterdam. He first directed opera in the U.S. in 1973 when he mounted *Macbeth* at the Houston Grand Opera. From 1975 to 1980 he served as director of productions at the Scottish Opera; in collaboration with the Welsh National Opera in Cardiff, he produced a celebrated cycle of Janáček's operas. In 1977 he oversaw the production of the premiere of Blake's *Toussaint* at the English National Opera in London, and in 1980 he was responsible for the staging of the premiere of Glass's *Satyagraha* at the Netherlands Opera. Pountney garnered critical accolades during his tenure as director of productions at the English National Opera from 1982 to 1993. His productions have also been staged in Berlin, Rome, Paris, Chicago, and N.Y. Pountney's imaginative approach to opera production aims to create a total theater experience, running the gamut from the purely visual to the psychological.

Pourtalès, Guy (Guido James) de, French writer on music; b. Berlin, Aug. 4, 1881; d. Lausanne, June 12, 1941. He studied in Bonn, Berlin, and Paris; was in the French army during World War I; then settled in Paris as a music critic. He publ. *La Vie de Franz Liszt* (1925); *Chopin, ou Le Poète* (1927; 2nd ed., 1946; Eng. tr., London, 1930 as *Chopin: A Man of Solitude*); *Wagner, Histoire d'un artiste* (1932; 2nd ed., rev. and aug. 1942); *Berlioz et l'Europe romantique* (1939).

Pousseur, Henri (Léon Marie Thérèse), radical Belgian composer and pedagogue; b. Malmédy, June 23, 1929. He studied at the Liège Cons. (1947–52) and the Brussels Cons. (1952–53); had private lessons in composition from Souris and Boulez. Until 1959, he worked in the Cologne and Milan electronic music studios, where he came in contact with Stockhausen and Berio; was a member of the avant-garde group of composers "Variation" in Liège. He taught music in various Belgian schools (1950–59); was founder (1958) and director of the Studio de Musique Électronique APELAC in Brussels, from 1970 a part of the Centre de Recherches Musicales in Liège; gave lectures at the summer courses of new music in Darmstadt (1957–67), Cologne (1966–68), Basel (1963–64), the State Univ. of N.Y. in Buffalo (1966–69), and the Liège Cons. (from 1970), where he became director in 1975. In his music he tries to synthesize all the expressive powers of which man, as a biological species, Homo sapiens (or even Homo insipiens), is capable in the domain of art (or non-art); the technological resources of the subspecies Homo habilis (magnetic tape, electronics/synthesizers, aleatory extensions, the principle of indeterminacy, glossolalia, self-induced schizophasia) all form part of his rich musical (or non-musical) vocabulary for multimedia (or nullimedia) representations. The influence of his methods (or non-methods) of composition (or non-composition) is pervasive. He publ. *Fragments théoriques I. Sur la musique experimentale* (Brussels, 1970).

WORKS: *3 chants sacrés* for Soprano and String Trio (1951); *Seismogrammes* for Tape (1953); *Symphonies* for 15 Solo Instruments (1954–55); *Quintet to the Memory of Webern* for Violin, Cello, Clarinet, Bass Clarinet, and Piano (1955); *Mobile* for 2 Pianos (1956–58); *Scambi* for Tape (1957); *Madrigal I* for Clarinet (1958) *II* for Flute, Violin, Viola da Gamba, and Harpsichord (1961), and *III* for Clarinet, Violin, Cello, 2 Percussionists, and Piano (1962); *Rimes pour différentes sources sonores* for 3 Orch. Groups and Tape (1958–59; Donaueschingen, Oct. 17, 1959); *Électre*, "musical action" (1960); *Répons* for 7 Musicians (1960; rev. with Actor added, 1965); *Ode* for String Quartet (1960–61); *3 visages de Liège and Prospective* for Tape (1961); *Votre Faust*, an aleatory "fantasy in the manner of an opera" for 5 Actors, Vocal Quartet, 12 Musicians, and Tapes, for which the audience decides the ending (1961–67; Milan, 1969; concert version as *Portail de Votre Faust* for 4 Voices, Tape, and 12 Instruments; in collaboration with Michel Butor); *Trait* for 15 Strings (1962); *Miroir de Votre Faust* for Piano and Soprano ad libitum (Caracteres II, 1964–65); *Caractères madrigalesques* for Oboe (*Madrigal IV* and *Caractère III*, 1965); *Phonèmes pour Cathy* for Voice (*Madrigal V*, 1966); *Echoes I* for Cello (1967) and *II, de Votre Faust* for Mezzo-soprano, Flute, Cello, and Piano (1969); *Couleurs croisées* for Orch., a series of cryptic musical variations on the civil rights song *We Shall Overcome* (1967; Brussels Radio, Dec. 20, 1968); *Mnemosyne I*, monody, after Hölderlin, for Solo Voice, or Unison Chorus, or one Instrument (1968), and *II*, an instrumental re-creation of *Mnemosyne I*, with ad libitum scoring (1969); *Croisées des couleurs croisées* (an intensified sequel to *Couleurs croisées*) for Woman's Voice, 2–5 Pianos, Tape Recorders, and 2 Radio Receivers dialed aleatorily, to texts from Indian and Negro materials and political speeches (N.Y., Nov. 29, 1970); *Icare apprenti* for an undetermined number of instruments (1970); *Les Éphémerides d'Icare 2* for Piano and Instruments (Madrid, April 20, 1970); *Invitation à l'Utopie* for Narrator, 2 Women's Voices, Chorus, and Instruments (Brussels Radio, Jan. 25, 1971); *L'Effacement du Prince Igor*, scene for Orch. (Brussels, Jan. 18, 1972); *Le Temps des paraboles* (1972); *Die Erprobung des Petrus Herbraicus*, chamber opera (Berlin, Sept. 12, 1974); *Vue sur les jardins interdits* for Organ or Saxophone Quartet (1974); *19$\sqrt{}$8/4* for Cello (1975); *Les ruines de Jeruzona* for Chorus, Piano, Double Bass, and Percussion (1978); *Humeurs du futur quotidien* for Reciter and Orch. (Paris, March 12, 1978); *Tales and Songs from the*

Bible of Hell for 4 Voices, Narrator, and Electronics (1979); *Les Îles déchainées* for Jazz Group, Electroacoustic Ensemble, and Orch. (Brussels, Nov. 27, 1980); *Le Seconde Apothéose de Rameau* for Chamber Orch. (Paris, Nov. 9, 1981); *La Rose des voix* for Voice, Chorus, Reciter, and Instruments (Namur, Aug. 6, 1982); *La Passion selon quignol* for Vocal Quartet and Orch. (1982; Liège, Feb. 24, 1983; in collaboration with C. Paulo); *Cinquième vue sur les jardins interdits* for Vocal Quartet (1982); *Trajets dans les arpents du ciel* for Soloists and Orch. (Metz, Nov. 18, 1983); *Cortèjes des belles ténébreuses au jardin boréal* for English Horn, Viola, Horn, Tuba, and Percussion (1984); *L'Étoile des langues* for Chamber Chorus and Speaker (1984); *Patchwork des tribus américaines* for Wind Orch. (1984); *Nuits des Nuits* for Orch. (1985); *Sur le Qui-Vive* for Woman's Voice, Clarinet, Cello, Tuba, Keyboards, and Percussion (1985); *Arc-en-ciel de remparts* for Student Orch. and Chorus ad libitum (1986); *Un Jardin de panacailles* for Original Orchestration Globally Organized from the works of Lully, Bach, Beethoven, Brahms, and Webern with an *Original Prologue, Interlude, and Grand Finale* for 12 Musicians (1987); *Traverser la forêt*, cantata for Speaker, 2 Vocal Soloists, Chorus, and 12 Instruments (1987); *Ode No. 2, Mnemosyne (doublement) obstinée* for String Quartet and Soprano ad libitum (London, June 1989); *Leçons d'enfer*, musical theater (Metz, Nov. 14, 1991); *Dichterliebesreigentraum*, grand paraphrase after Schumann's cycle for 2 Pianos, Soprano, Baritone, Chamber Chorus, and Chamber Orch. (1992–93; Amsterdam, June 1993).

Powell, John, American pianist, composer, and ethnomusicologist; b. Richmond, Va., Sept. 6, 1882; d. Charlottesville, Va., Aug. 15, 1963. His father was a schoolteacher, his mother an amateur musician; he received his primary musical education at home; then studied piano with F.C. Hahr, a pupil of Liszt; subsequently entered the Univ. of Virginia (B.A., 1901) and then went to Vienna, where he studied piano with Leschetizky (1902–07) and composition with Navrátil (1904–07). He gave successful piano recitals in Paris and London; returning to the U.S., he toured the country as a pianist, playing some of his own works. His most successful piece was *Rapsodie nègre* for Piano and Orch., inspired by Joseph Conrad's *Heart of Darkness*; Powell was the soloist in its first performance with the Russian Sym. Orch. (N.Y., March 23, 1918). The titles of some of his works disclose a whimsical propensity. Perhaps his most important achievement lies in ethnomusicology; he methodically collected rural songs of the South; was the organizer of the Virginia State Choral Festivals and of the White Top Mountain Folk Music Festivals. A man of versatile interests, he was also an amateur astronomer, and discovered a comet.

WORKS: ORCH.: Piano Concerto (n.d.); Violin Concerto (1910); *Rapsodie nègre* for Piano and Orch. (1917; N.Y., March 23, 1918); *In Old Virginia*, overture (1921); *Natchez on the Hill*, 3 Virginian country dances (1932); *A Set of 3* (1935); Sym. in A (1945; Detroit, April 23, 1947; substantially rev. version as *Virginia Symphony*, Richmond, Va., Nov. 5, 1951). **CHAMBER:** *Sonate Virginianesque* for Violin and Piano (1906); 2 string quartets (1907, 1922); Violin Sonata (1918); *From a Loved Past* for Violin and Piano (1930). **PIANO:** 3 sonatas: *Sonate psychologique*, "on the text of St. Paul's 'The wages of sin is death'" (1905), *Sonate noble* (1908), and *Sonata Teutonica* (1905–13); *In the South*, suite (1906); *At the Fair*, suite (1907); *In the Hammock* for 2 Pianos, 8-hands (1915); *Dirge*, sextet for 2 Pianos, 12-hands (1928). **VOCAL:** Choral pieces, including the folk carol *The Babe of Bethlehem* (1934); songs, including *5 Virginian Folk Songs* for Voice and Piano (1938).

Powell, Laurence, English-born American organist, conductor, teacher, and composer; b. Birmingham, Jan. 13, 1899; d. Victoria, Texas, Jan 29, 1990. He studied at Ratcliffe College, Leicester (1909–15), Ushaw College, Durham (1915–17), with Bantock at the Birmingham Midland Inst. School of Music (1919–22), and at the Univ. of Birmingham (Mus.Bac.). In 1923 he emigrated to the U.S. and in 1936 became a naturalized American citizen. He completed his education at the Univ. of Wisc. (M.A., 1926), where he also taught (1924–26). Subsequently he taught at the Univ. of Ark. (1926–34) and Little Rock Junior College (1934–39). He was founder-conductor of the Little Rock Sym. Orch. (1934–39), and then conducted the Grand Rapids (Mich.) Federal Sym. Orch. (1939–41). After serving as organist at St. Mary's Church in Victoria, Texas (1947–52), he was organist and choirmaster at St. Francis Cathedral in Sante Fe (1952–68), where he also was founder-conductor of the Sante Fe Orch., later known as the Rio Grande Sym. Orch. (1953–55). He was organist and choirmaster at Assumption Church in Albuquerque (1968–70) and at Our Lady of Victory Church in Victoria, Texas (1970–75).

WORKS: ORCH.: *The Ogre of the Northern Fastness* (1921); *Keltic Legend* (Bournemouth, Aug. 27, 1924; rev. version, Madison, Wis., May 20, 1931); *Charivari*, suite (1925); 2 syms. (1929, 1943); Suite for Strings (1931; Grand Rapids, May 9, 1940); *Deirdre of the Sorrows* (1933; Little Rock, March 18, 1937); *The Country Fair*, suite (1936); *Picnic* for Strings (Oklahoma City, March 21, 1936); *Variations* (Rochester, N.Y., Oct. 28, 1941); *Duo concertante* for Recorders and Orch. (1941); *Penny Overture* (1960); *Overture on French Folk Tunes* (1970); *Oracle* (1975). **CHAMBER:** Piano Quartet (1933); Quartet for Clarinets (1936); 3 recorder sonatinas (1977). **VOCAL:** *Halcyone* for Chorus and Orch. (1923); *Alleluya*, cantata for Chorus and Orch. (1926); *The Seasons* for Chorus (1928); *The Santa Fe Trail* for Baritone, Narrator, and Orch. (Santa Fe, April 22, 1958); masses; songs.

Powell, Mel (real name, **Melvin Epstein**), remarkable American composer and teacher; b. N.Y., Feb. 12, 1933. He acquired an early fascination for American jazz, and was barely 14 when he was chosen as pianist for Benny Goodman's band. It was then that he changed his name to the more mellifluous Mel Powell, restructured from that of his paternal uncle, Poljanowsky. He was drafted into the Army, where he was selected for the Air Force Band led by Glenn Miller. While playing jazz, Powell also began to compose. Tragedy struck at the height of his powers as a jazz musician and composer when he suddenly contracted muscular dystrophy; the disease affected his quadriceps, and he was ultimately confined to a wheelchair. He could still play the piano, but he could no longer travel with a band. He turned to serious composition and became an excellent teacher. While he was working with the Goodman band, he took lessons with Wagenaar and Schillinger in N.Y. (1937–39); later studied composition privately with Toch in Los Angeles (1946–48). A turning point in his career occurred in 1948 when he entered the Yale Univ. School of Music in the class of Hindemith, from whom he acquired the matchless skill of Teutonic contrapuntal writing; he received his B.Mus. degree in 1952. From then on, Powell dedicated himself mainly to teaching; served on the faculty of Yale Univ. (1957–69), and was dean of music at the Calif. Inst. of the Arts in Valencia (from 1969), serving as provost (1972–76) and as a prof. and fellow (from 1976). As a composer of growing strength, he revealed versatile talents, being technically at home in an incisive jazz idiom, in a neo-Classical manner, tangentially shadowing Stravinsky, and in an expressionist mode of Schoenberg, occasionally paralleling the canonic processes of Webern. He also evolved a sui generis sonorism of electronic music. In all these asymptotic formations, he nevertheless succeeded in projecting his own personality in a curious and, indeed, quaquaversal way; while absorbed in atonal composition, he was also able to turn out an occasional march tune or waltz figure. In all these mutually enhanced formulas, he succeeds in cultivating the unmistakable modality of his personal style without venturing into the outer space of musical entropy. In 1990 he received the meritorious Pulitzer Prize in Music for his *Duplicates*, a concerto for 2 Pianos and Orch. Powell describes this work as a "perpetual cadenza," an expression he attributes to Debussy.

WORKS: ORCH.: *Cantilena concertante* for English Horn and Orch. (1948); *Symphonic Suite* (1949); *Capriccio* for Concert Band (1950); *Intrada and Variants* (1956); *Stanzas* (1957); *Setting* for Cello and Orch. (1961); *Immobiles I–IV* (1967); *Set-*

tings for Jazz Band (1982); *Modules*, intermezzo for Chamber Orch. (1985); *Duplicates*, concerto for 2 Pianos and Orch. (Los Angeles, Jan. 26, 1990); *Settings* for Small Orch. (Los Angeles, Sept. 23, 1992). **CHAMBER:** 2 string quartets: No. 1, *Beethoven Analogs* (1949) and No. 2, *String Quartet 1982* (1982); Harpsichord Sonata (1952); Trio for Piano, Violin, and Cello (1954); *Divertimento* for Violin and Harp (1954); *Divertimento* for 5 Winds (1955); Quintet for Piano and String Quartet (1956); *Miniatures for Baroque Ensemble* for Flute, Oboe, Violin, Viola, Cello, and Harpsichord (1958); *Filigree Setting* for String Quartet (1959); *Improvisation* for Clarinet, Viola, and Piano (1962); *Nocturne* for Violin (1965; rev. 1985); *Cantilena* for Trombone and Tape (1981); Woodwind Quintet (1984–85); *Setting* for Guitar (1986); *Invocation* for Cello (1987); *Amy-abilities* for Percussion (1987); *3 Madrigals* for Flute (1988). **PIANO:** 2 sonatinas (1951); *Etude* (1957); *Intermezzo* (1984); *Piano Preludes* (1987). **VOCAL:** *6 Choral Songs* (1950); *Sweet Lovers Love the Spring* for Women's Voices and Piano (1953); *Haiku Settings* for Soprano and Piano (1961); *2 Prayer Settings* for Tenor, Oboe, and String Trio (1963); *Cantilena* for Voice, Violin, and Tape (1969); *Settings* for Soprano and Chamber Group (1979); *Little Companion Pieces* for Soprano and String Quartet (1979); *Strand Settings: Darker* for Soprano and Electronics (1983); *Letter to a Young Composer* for Soprano (1987); *Die Violine* for Soprano, Violin, and Piano (1987). **ELECTRONIC:** *Electronic Setting* (1958); *2nd Electronic Setting* (1961); *Events* (1963); *Analogs I–IV* (1963); *3 Synthesizer Settings* (1970–80); *Inscape*, ballet (1976); *Variations* (1976); *Computer Prelude* (1988).

Powers, Harold S(tone), American musicologist and teacher; b. N.Y., Aug. 5, 1928. He received his early education at Stanford Univ. and Syracuse Univ. (B.Mus., 1950); then studied with Babbitt and Cone (theory) and Strunk and Mendel (musicology) at Princeton Univ. (M.F.A., 1952; Ph.D., 1959, with a diss. on the Indian rāga system). He also studied in India under Rangaramanuja Ayyangar, Balwant Ray Bhatt, and Prem Lata Sharma on Fulbright and Rockefeller grants (1952–54; 1960–61; 1967–68). He taught at Princeton Univ. (1955–58), Harvard Univ. (1958–60), and the Univ. of Pa. (1960–73), where he became prof. of music and South Asian studies (1971); in 1973 he rejoined the faculty at Princeton Univ. as a full prof. He has written extensively on Indian music, Italian opera, and music theory.

Pozdro, John (Walter), significant American composer and pedagogue; b. Chicago, Aug. 14, 1923. He began training in piano and theory at an early age with Nina Shafran, and later studied piano with Edward Collins at the American Cons. of Music in Chicago (1941–42). After serving in military intelligence in the U.S. Army, he pursued his training with Robert Delaney at Northwestern Univ., taking B.M. and M.M. (1949) degrees. He completed his studies with Hanson, Rogers, and Barlow at the Eastman School of Music in Rochester, N.Y. (Ph.D. in composition, 1958). In 1950 he joined the faculty of the Univ. of Kansas in Lawrence, becoming chairman of theory and composition in 1961; from 1958 to 1968 he also chaired its Annual Symposium of Contemporary Music. He retired from teaching in 1992. In 1993 he served as guest composer for the International Carillon Congress in Berkeley, where he was awarded the Univ. of Calif. at Berkeley Medal for distinguished service in music. His music is inherently pragmatic, with tertian torsion resulting in the formation of tastefully enriched triadic harmony, and with asymmetric rhythms enhancing the throbbing pulse of musical continuity.

WORKS: DRAMATIC: *Hello, Kansas!*, musical play (Lawrence, Kansas, June 12, 1961); *Malooley and the Fear Monster*, "family opera" (1976; Lawrence, Kansas, Feb. 6, 1977). **ORCH.:** Overture (1948; Evanston, Ill., Nov. 30, 1949); 3 syms.: No. 1 (1949), No. 2 (1957; Rochester, N.Y., May 4, 1958), and No. 3 (Oklahoma City, Dec. 12, 1960); *A Cynical Overture* (1952; Austin, Texas, March 24, 1953); *Lament of Judas* (1954; Austin, Texas, March 30, 1955); *Lament in Memory of a Friend* (1956; Rochester, N.Y., April 1957); *Rondo giocoso* for Strings (1964; Pittsburg, Kansas, March 9, 1965); *Music for a Youth Symphony* (Lawrence, Kansas, March 4, 1969); *Waterlow Park: 1970* (Lawrence, Kansas, May 8, 1972); *Processional* for Band (1973). **CHAMBER:** Wind Quintet (Evanston, Ill., Dec. 11, 1947); 2 string quartets (1947, 1952); Sextet for Flute and Strings (Evanston, Ill., Nov. 23, 1948); *Elegy* for Trumpet and Piano (1953; Lawrence, Kansas, Jan. 6, 1954); *Interlude* for Winds (Lawrence, Kansas, April 26, 1954); *Trilogy* for Clarinet, Bassoon, Trumpet, and Piano (Manhattan, Kansas, Nov. 22, 1960); Sonata for Brass and Percussion (1966; Lawrence, Kansas, Jan. 18, 1967); Violin Sonatine (1971); *Impressions* for Flute, Oboe, Clarinet, Bassoon, and Piano (1984); *2 Movements* for Cello and Piano (1987). **KEYBOARD: PIANO:** 6 sonatas (1947, 1963, 1964, 1976, 1979, 1982); March (1950); 8 preludes (1950–74); *3 Short Pieces* (1951); Rondo (1953); *Ballade-Fantasy* (1981); *For Nancy* (1987). **CARILLON:** *Landscape I* (1954) and *II: Ostinato* (1969); *Rustic Landscape* (1981); *Variations on a Slavonic Theme* (1982); *Tryptich* (1980); *Richard's Träume* (1993). **VOCAL:** *John Anderson* for Women's Voices (1950; Lawrence, Kansas, April 18, 1951); *All Pleasant Things* for Chorus (Lawrence, Kansas, May 3, 1960); *The Creation* for Children's Voices (1967); *They That Go Down to the Sea* for Chorus (Oklahoma City, Sept. 1967); *After the Dazzle* for Chorus (1970); *This is the Hour, O Soul* for Chorus (1970); *Alleluia* for Chorus (1979); *King of Glory* for Chorus, Organ, and Piano (1983); *Spirit of Oread* for Soloists, Chorus, and Organ (1989–90); *The Lord's Prayer* for Chorus and Organ (1994).

Pratella, Francesco Balilla, Italian music critic, musicologist, and composer; b. Lugo di Romagna, Feb. 1, 1880; d. Ravenna, May 17, 1955. He studied with Ricci-Signorini, then at the Liceo Rossini in Pesaro with Cicognani and Mascagni. He taught in Cesana (1908–09); was director of the Istituto Musicale in Lugo (1910–29), and of the Liceo Musicale Giuseppe Verdi in Ravenna (1927–45). He joined the Italian futurist movement in 1910 (Russolo's manifesto of 1913 was addressed to "Balilla Pratella, grande musicista futurista"), and in 1913 wrote his first composition in a "futurist" idiom, the choral work *Inno alla vita*. After World War I, he broke with futurism.

WORKS: DRAMATIC: OPERAS: *Lilia* (1903; Lugo, Nov. 13, 1905); *La Sina d'Vargöun* (1906–08; Bologna, Dec. 4, 1909); *L'Aviatore Dro* (1911–14; Lugo, Nov. 4, 1920); *La ninnananna della bambola*, children's opera (1920–22; Milan, May 21, 1923); *La leggenda di San Fabiano* (1928–32; Bologna, Dec. 9, 1939); *L'uomo* (1934–49; not perf.); *Dono primaverile*, comedy with music (Bologna, Oct. 17, 1923). Also incidental music. **ORCH.:** *Romagna*, 5 symphonic poems (1903–04); *Musica futurista*, renamed *Inno alla vita* (1912; rev. 1933). **OTHER:** Chamber music; piano pieces; choral works; songs.

WRITINGS: *Cronache e critiche dal 1905 al 1917* (Bologna, 1918); *L'evoluzione della musica: Dal 1910 al 1917* (Milan, 1918–19); *Saggio di gridi, canzoni, cori e danze del popolo italiano* (Bologna, 1919); *Luci ed ombre: per un musicista italiano ignorato in Italia* (Rome, 1933); *Scritti vari di pensiero, di arte, di storia musicale* (Bologna, 1933); Autobiografia (Milan, 1971).

BIBL.: A. Ghigi, *F.B. P.* (Ravenna, 1930); *F.B. P., Appunti biografici e bibliografici* (Ravenna, 1931); R. Payton, *The Futurist Musicians: F.B. P. and Luigi Russola* (diss., Univ. of Chicago, 1974).

Pratt, Awadagin, black American pianist; b. Philadelphia, March 6, 1966. He began to study the piano at the age of 6 and the violin at age 9. At 16, he became a student at the Univ. of Ill., where he received training in piano, violin, and conducting. In 1986 he entered the Peabody Cons. of Music in Baltimore, where he was its first student ever to obtain diplomas in piano, violin, and conducting. In 1992 he won the Naumburg Competition in N.Y., and in 1994 he was awarded an Avery Fisher Career Grant. As a soloist, Pratt appeared with major American orchs., including the N.Y. Phil., the National Sym. Orch. in Washington, D.C., the St. Louis Sym. Orch., the Cincinnati Sym. Orch., the Minnesota Orch. in Minneapolis, and the Los Angeles Phil. He also toured widely as a recitalist at home and abroad.

Pratt, Waldo Selden, distinguished American music historian and pedagogue; b. Philadelphia, Nov. 10, 1857; d. Hartford, Conn., July 29, 1939. He studied at Williams College and at Johns Hopkins Univ., specializing in classical languages; was practically self-taught in music. He was assistant director of the Metropolitan Museum of Art in N.Y. (1880–82); in 1882 he was appointed to the faculty of the Hartford Theological Seminary, where he taught hymnology; remained there until his retirement in 1925; he also taught music history at Smith College (1895–1908), and later at the Inst. of Musical Art in N.Y. He ed. the American supplement to *Grove's Dictionary of Music and Musicians* (N.Y., 1920; rev. 1928) and *The New Encyclopedia of Music and Musicians* (N.Y., 1924; 2nd ed., rev., 1929). He also publ. *The History of English Hymnody* (Hartford, Conn., 1895); *Musical Ministries in the Church* (N.Y., 1901; 4th ed., rev., 1915); *The History of Music* (N.Y., 1907; 3rd ed., aug., 1935); *The Music of the Pilgrims* (Boston, 1921); *The Music of the French Psalter of 1562* (N.Y., 1939).

BIBL.: O. Kinkeldey, "W.S. P.," *Musical Quarterly* (April 1940).

Prausnitz, Frederik (actually, **Frederick William**), German-born American conductor and teacher; b. Cologne, Aug. 26, 1920. He went to the U.S. in his youth and studied at the Juilliard School of Music in N.Y.; later served on its faculty (1947–61); then was conductor of the New England Cons. of Music sym. orch. in Boston (1961–69). He was music director of the Syracuse (N.Y.) Sym. Orch. from 1971 to 1974. In 1976 he joined the Peabody Cons. of Music in Baltimore as conductor of its sym. orch. and opera; from 1980 he acted as director of its conducting program and conductor of its Contemporary Music Ensemble. He appeared widely as a guest conductor in the U.S. and Europe, garnering a reputation as a leading advocate of contemporary music; was awarded the Gustav Mahler Medal of Honor of the Bruckner Society of America (1974). He publ. *Score and Podium: A Complete Guide to Conducting* (1983) and *Roger Sessions: A Critical Biography* (1983).

Prégardien, Christoph, German tenor; b. Limburg an der Lahn, Jan. 18, 1956. He gained experience as a member of the Cathedral boy's choir and later the Cathedral choir in his native city. He studied voice with Martin Gründler at the Frankfurt am Main Hochschule für Musik (graduated, 1983) and with Carla Castellani in Milan. In 1978 he won the Federal Republic of Germany vocal competition in Berlin. He sang opera in Frankfurt am Main, Stuttgart, Hamburg, Antwerp, Karlsruhe, Ghent, and other European cities, becoming well known for his roles in Baroque and Classical operas. As a concert and lieder artist, he appeared in major European music centers with notable success. In 1989 he gave a series of early music concerts in London, returning there in 1993 to make his Wigmore Hall recital debut. Prégardien has won particular praise for his interpretations of works by Schütz, Bach, Handel, Buxtehude, Haydn, and Mozart.

Premru, Raymond (Eugene), American trombonist, conductor, and composer; b. Elmira, N.Y., June 6, 1934. He studied at the Oberlin (Ohio) College Cons. of Music, at the Eastman School of Music in Rochester, N.Y. (B.Mus., 1956), and with Peter Racine Fricker in London. From 1958 to 1988 he played in the Philharmonia Orch. in London; also was a member of the Philip Jones Brass Ensemble (1960–86) and co-director of the Bobby Lamb-Ray Premru Big Band. He gave master classes in trombone virtuosity throughout the world; taught at various institutions, including the Oberlin College Cons. of Music (from 1988). Among his works are a *Concerto for Orchestra* (1976), 2 syms. (1981; Cleveland, Nov. 23, 1988), Concerto for Trumpet and Strings (1983), *Celebrations* for Timpani and Orch. (1984), *Music* for 3 Trombones, Tuba, and Orch. (1985), other instrumental pieces, and choral works.

Pressler, Menahem, German-born American pianist and teacher; b. Magdeburg, Dec. 16, 1923. He was taken to Palestine by his family after the Hitlerization of Germany; he studied piano with Eliah Rudiakow and Leo Kestenberg; then played with the Palestine Sym. Orch. In 1946 he won the Debussy Prize at the piano competition in San Francisco. In 1955 he became a member of the School of Music at Indiana Univ. in Bloomington; that year he became pianist in the Beaux Arts Trio, with which he made numerous tours; he also continued his career as a soloist.

BIBL.: N. Delbanco, *The Beaux Arts Trio: A Portrait* (London, 1985).

Preston, Simon (John), distinguished English organist, harpsichordist, conductor, and pedagogue; b. Bournemouth, Aug. 4, 1938. He was a chorister at King's College, Cambridge (1949–51), where he received instruction in organ from Hugh McLean; after further keyboard training from Anthony Brown at Canford School, he continued his studies with C.H. Trevor at the Royal Academy of Music in London (1956–58); subsequently was an organ scholar at King's College, Cambridge (1958–62). He made his formal debut as an organist at the Royal Festival Hall in London in 1962; was sub-organist at Westminster Abbey (1962–67); after conducting the Oxford Bach Choir (1967–68), he was organist and lecturer at Christ Church, Oxford (1970–81); then was organist and master of the choristers at Westminster Abbey (1981–87). He toured widely as an organ virtuoso and gave master classes on both sides of the Atlantic; also conducted much choral music. His repertoire ranges from Handel to Messiaen.

Prêtre, Georges, prominent French conductor; b. Waziers, Aug. 14, 1924. He studied at the Douai Cons.; then at the Paris Cons.; also received instruction in conducting from Cluytens. He made his debut as a conductor at the Marseilles Opera in 1946; subsequently had guest engagements in Lille, Casablanca, and Toulouse; then was music director of the Paris Opéra-Comique (1955–59); subsequently conducted at the Paris Opéra (from 1959), where he served as music director (1970–71). In 1959 he made his U.S. debut at the Chicago Lyric Opera; in 1961 he appeared for the first time in London. On Oct. 17, 1964, he made his first appearance at the Metropolitan Opera in N.Y., conducting *Samson et Dalila.* He appeared as a guest conductor with many of the major opera houses and orchs. of the world in succeeding years; also served as principal guest conductor of the Vienna Sym. Orch. (1986–91).

Previn, André (George) (real name, **Andreas Ludwig Priwin**), brilliant German-born American pianist, conductor, and composer; b. Berlin, April 6, 1929. He was of Russian-Jewish descent. He showed an unmistakable musical gift as a child; his father, a lawyer, was an amateur musician who gave him his early training; they played piano, 4-hands, together at home. At the age of 6, he was accepted as a pupil at the Berlin Hochschule für Musik, where he studied piano with Breithaupt; as a Jew, however, he was compelled to leave school in 1938. The family then went to Paris; he continued his studies at the Cons., Dupré being one of his teachers. In 1939 the family emigrated to America, settling in Los Angeles, where his father's cousin, Charles Previn, was music director at Universal Studios in Hollywood. He took lessons in composition with Joseph Achron, Toch, and Castelnuovo-Tedesco. He became a naturalized American citizen in 1943. Even before graduating from high school, he obtained employment at MGM; he became an orchestrator there and later one of its music directors; he also became a fine jazz pianist. He served in the U.S. Army (1950–52); stationed in San Francisco, he took lessons in conducting with Monteux, then music director of the San Francisco Sym. During these years, he wrote much music for films; he received Academy Awards for his arrangements of *Gigi* (1958), *Porgy and Bess* (1959), *Irma la Douce* (1963), and *My Fair Lady* (1964). Throughout this period he continued to appear as a concert pianist. In 1962 he made his formal conducting debut with the St. Louis Sym. Orch., and conducting soon became his principal vocation. From 1967 to 1969 he was conductor-in-chief of the Houston Sym. Orch. In 1968 he assumed the post of principal conductor of the London

Sym. Orch., retaining it with distinction until 1979; then was made its conductor emeritus. In 1976 he became music director of the Pittsburgh Sym. Orch., a position he held with similar distinction until a dispute with the management led to his resignation in 1984. He had already been engaged as music director of the Royal Phil. of London in 1982, a position he held from 1985 to 1987; then served as its principal conductor from 1987 to 1992, and thereafter was its Conductor Laureate. Previn also accepted appointment as music director of the Los Angeles Phil., after resigning his Pittsburgh position; he formally assumed his duties in Los Angeles in 1985, but gave up this position in 1990 after disagreements with the management over administrative procedures. During his years as a conductor of the London Sym. Orch., he took it on a number of tours to the U.S., as well as to Russia, Japan, South Korea, and Hong Kong. He also took the Pittsburgh Sym. Orch. on acclaimed tours of Europe in 1978 and 1982. He continued to compose popular music, including the scores for the musicals *Coco* (1969) and *The Good Companions* (1974); with words by Tom Stoppard, he composed *Every Good Boy Deserves Favour* (1977), a work for Actors and Orch. His other compositions include Sym. for Strings (1962); *Overture to a Comedy* (1963); Violin Sonata (1964); Flute Quartet (1964); *Elegy* for Oboe and Strings (1967); Cello Concerto (1967); Horn Concerto (1968); Guitar Concerto (1972); *Principals* for Orch. (1980); *Reflections* for Orch. (1981); *Divertimento* for Orch. (1982); Piano Concerto (1985); piano pieces; songs. He ed. the book *Orchestra* (Garden City, N.Y., 1979); also publ. *André Previn's Guide to Music* (London, 1983) and the autobiographical *No Minor Chords: My Days in Hollywood* (N.Y., 1991). He was married four times (and divorced thrice): to the jazz singer Betty Bennett, to the jazz poet Dory Langdon (who made a career of her own as composer and singer of pop songs), to the actress Mia Farrow, and in 1982 to Heather Hales.

BIBL.: E. Greenfield, *A. P.* (N.Y., 1973); M. Bookspan and R. Yockey, *A. P.: A Biography* (Garden City, N.Y., 1981); a "profile" in the *New Yorker* (Jan. 10 and 17, 1983); H. Ruttencutter, *P.* (London, 1985).

Previtali, Fernando, prominent Italian conductor; b. Adria, Feb. 16, 1907; d. Rome, Aug. 1, 1985. He studied cello, piano, and composition at the Turin Cons.; then was Gui's assistant at the Maggio Musicale Fiorentino (1928–36). He was chief conductor of the Rome Radio orch. (1936–43; 1945–53); also conducted at Milan's La Scala and at other major Italian opera houses. From 1953 to 1973 he was chief conductor of the Orchestra Sinfonica dell'Accademia Nazionale di Santa Cecilia in Rome, which he led on tours abroad. On Dec. 15, 1955, he made his U.S. debut as a guest conductor with the Cleveland Orch. Previtali became well known for his advocacy of contemporary Italian composers, and conducted the premieres of numerous operas and orch. works. He was also a composer; wrote the ballet, *Allucinazioni* (Rome, 1945), choral works, chamber music, etc. He publ. *Guida allo studio della direzione d'orchestra* (Rome, 1951).

Prévost, (Joseph Gaston Charles) André, Canadian composer; b. Hawkesbury, Ontario, July 30, 1934. He studied harmony and counterpoint with Isabelle Delorme and Papineau-Couture and composition with Pépin (premier prix, 1960) at the Montreal Cons.; after studying analysis with Messiaen at the Paris Cons., and receiving further instruction from Dutilleux at the Paris École Normale de Musique (1961), he returned to Canada (1962) and was active as a teacher; following studies in electronic music with Michel Phillipot at the Paris ORTF (1964), he worked with Schuller, Martino, Copland, and Kodály at the Berkshire Music Center in Tanglewood (summer, 1964); then taught at the Univ. of Montreal (from 1964). In 1986 he was made an Officer of the Order of Canada.

WORKS: ORCH.: *Poème de l'infini*, symphonic poem (1960); *Scherzo* for Strings (1960); *Fantasmes* (Montreal, Nov. 22, 1963; posthumously dedicated to President John F. Kennedy); *Pyknon*, pièce concertante for Violin and Orch. (1966); *Célébration* (1966); *Diallèle* (Toronto, May 30, 1968); *Evanescence* (Ottawa, April 7, 1970); *Hommage (à Beethoven)* for 14 Strings (1970–71); *Chorégraphie I (. . . Munich, September 1972 . . .)* (1972–73; Toronto, April 22, 1975; inspired by the Munich Olympics tragedy), *II (E = MC²)* (1976), *III* (1976), and *IV* (1978; London, Ontario, Jan. 10, 1979); *Ouverture* (1975); Cello Concerto (1976; Winnipeg, Dec. 6, 1979); *Paraphrase* for String Quartet and Orch. (Toronto, April 29, 1980); *Cosmophonie* (1985); *Cantate pour cordes* for Chamber Orch. (1987). **CHAMBER:** *Pastorale* for 2 Harps (1955); *Fantasie* for Cello and Piano (1956); 2 string quartets (1958; *Ad pacem*, 1971–72); *Mobiles* for Flute, Violin, Viola, and Cello (1959–60); Violin Sonata (1960–61; arr. as a ballet as *Primordial*, 1968); 2 cello sonatas (1962, arr. for Violin and Piano or Ondes Martenot, 1967; 1985); *Triptyque* for Flute, Oboe, and Piano (1962); *Mouvement* for Brass Quintet (1963); *Ode au St. Laurent* for Optional Narrator and String Quartet (1965); Suite for String Quintet (1968); *Improvisation II* for Cello (1976) and *III* for Viola (1976); Violin Sonata (1979); Clarinet Quintet (London, England, Oct. 26, 1988). **KEYBOARD: PIANO:** *4 Préludes* for 2 Pianos (1961). **ORGAN:** *5 Variations sur un thème grégorien* (1956); *Variations en Passacaille* (1984). **VOCAL:** *Terre des hommes* for 2 Narrators, 3 Choruses, and Orch. (Montreal, April 29, 1967); *Psaume 148* for Chorus, Brass, and Organ (Guelph, May 1, 1971); *Hiver dans l'âme* for Baritone and Orch. (1978); *Missa de profundis* for Chorus and Organ (1973); other choruses; songs.

Prey, Claude, French composer; b. Fleury-sur-Andelle, Eure, May 30, 1925. After studies at the Sorbonne in Paris and with Milhaud and Messiaen at the Paris Cons., he pursued his training with Mignone in Rio de Janeiro (1953–54) and with Frazzi in Siena before completing his studies at Laval Univ. in Quebec. In 1963 he won the Prix Italia. He devoted himself principally to composing dramatic scores.

WORKS: DRAMATIC: *Le Phénix*, opera (1957); *Lettres perdues*, radiophonic opera (1960); *La Dictée*, lyric monodrama (1961); *Le Coeur révélateur*, chamber opera (1962); *L'Homme occis*, opera (1963); *Jonas*, opera-oratorio (1964; 1st stage perf., Lyons, Dec. 2, 1969); *Donna mobile I*, opera (1965; Avignon, July 15, 1972); *La Noirceur du lait*, "opéra-test" (1967); *On veut la lumière? Allons-y!*, opera parody (1969); *Fêtes de la faim*, opera (1969); *Jeu de l'oie*, opera (1970); *Théâtrophonie*, opera (1971); *Donna mobile II*, "opéra-kit" (1972); *Les liaisons dangereuses*, "opéra épistolaire" (1973); *Young libertad*, "opéra-study" (1975); *Les Trois Langages*, children's opera (1978); *Utopopolis*, "opéra-chanson(s)" (1980); *L'Escalier de Chambord*, opera (1981); *Scenarios VII*, opera (1982); *Lunedi blu*, "opéra-flash" (1982); *Paulina*, chamber opera (1983); *O comme eau*, madrigal opera (1984); *Paysages pacifiques*, "mélo-cycle" (1986); *Le Rouge et le Noir*, opera (1989); *Sommaire soleil*, "mélo(d)rama" (1991); *Parlons fric!* (1992); *Sitôt le septuor*, opera (1994).

Prey, Hermann, outstanding German baritone; b. Berlin, July 11, 1929. He studied with Günther Baum and Harry Gottschalk at the Berlin Hochschule für Musik; won 1st prize in a vocal competition organized by the U.S. Army (1952), and that same year made his operatic debut as the 2nd prisoner in *Fidelio* in Wiesbaden. After appearing in the U.S., he joined the Hamburg State Opera (1953); also sang in Vienna (from 1956), Berlin (from 1956), and in Salzburg (from 1959). In 1959 he became a principal member of the Bavarian State Opera in Munich; made his Metropolitan Opera debut in N.Y. as Wolfram (Dec. 16, 1960); appeared for the first time in England at the Edinburgh Festival (1965), and later sang regularly at London's Covent Garden (from 1973). He also appeared as a soloist with the major orchs. and as a recitalist; likewise starred in his own Munich television show. In 1982 he became a prof. at the Hamburg Hochschule für Musik. His autobiography was publ. as *Premierenfieber* (1981; Eng. tr., 1986, as *First Night Fever: The Memoirs of Hermann Prey*). Among his finest operatic roles were Count Almaviva, Papageno, Guglielmo, and Rossini's

Figaro; he also sang a number of contemporary roles. As a lieder artist, he distinguished himself in Schubert, Schumann, and Brahms.

Preyer, Carl Adolph, German-American pianist, composer, and teacher; b. Pforzheim, Baden, July 28, 1863; d. Lawrence, Kansas, Nov. 16, 1947. He studied at the Stuttgart Cons.; then with Navrátil in Vienna, and with H. Urban and H. Barth in Berlin. In 1893 he settled in the U.S.; became a piano teacher at the School of Fine Arts of the Univ. of Kansas, and remained with that institution throughout his life. He publ. several instructive collections for piano; also character pieces.

BIBL.: H. Gloyne, *C.A. P.: The Life of a Kansas Musician* (Lawrence, 1949).

Přibyl, Vilém, Czech tenor; b. Náchod, April 10, 1925; d. Brno, July 13, 1990. After making his debut with an amateur opera company in Hradec Králové (1952), he pursued vocal instruction there with Jakoubková (1952–62); sang at the opera in Ústí nad Labem (1960) and at the Janáček Opera in Brno (1960); also received further training from Vavrdová at the Brno Academy of Music. He gained notable success with his portrayal of Dalibor with the Prague National Theater Opera during its visit to the Edinburgh Festival (1964); then appeared in various European music centers; also taught at the Janáček Academy of Arts in Brno (from 1969). In 1969 he was made an Artist of Merit and in 1977 a National Artist by the Czech government. His repertoire included Lohengrin, Radames, and Otello, as well as roles in operas by Prokofiev, Martinů, and Shostakovich; he was especially esteemed for his roles in operas by Janáček.

Price, Florence B(eatrice née **Smith)**, black American teacher and composer; b. Little Rock, Ark., April 9, 1888; d. Chicago, June 3, 1953. She studied with Chadwick and Converse at the New England Cons. of Music in Boston, graduating in 1906. She had been publishing her compositions since she was 11 (1899); in 1928 she won a prize from G. Schirmer for her *At the Cotton Gin* for Piano; around this time she was also writing musical jingles for radio commercials. Her first notable success came in 1932 with her 1st Sym. (winner of the Wanamaker Award; perf. by the Chicago Sym. Orch. at the Century of Progress Exhibition in 1933); she became known as the first black woman to write syms.

WORKS: ORCH.: 6 syms.: No. 1 (1931–32), *Mississippi River Symphony* (1934), D minor (n.d.), No. 3 (1940), G minor (n.d.), and *Colonial Dance Symphony* (n.d.); *Ethiopia's Shadow in America* (1932); Piano Concerto (1934); 2 violin concertos: No. 1 (n.d.) and No. 2 (1952); 2 concert overtures on Negro spirituals; Piano Concerto in 1 Movement; *Rhapsody* for Piano and Orch.; *Songs of the Oak*, tone poem. **CHAMBER:** *Negro Folksongs in Counterpoint* for String Quartet; 2 piano quintets; pieces for Violin and Piano; piano works; organ music. **VOCAL:** Choral music; songs; arrangements of spirituals.

BIBL.: B. Jackson, "F. P., Composer," *Black Perspective in Music* (Spring 1977); M. Green, "F. P.," *Black Women Composers: A Genesis* (Boston, 1983).

Price, (Mary Violet) Leontyne, remarkably endowed black American soprano; b. Laurel, Miss., Feb. 10, 1927. She was taught piano by a local woman, and also learned to sing. On Dec. 17, 1943, she played piano and sang at a concert in Laurel. She went to Oak Park High School, graduating in music in 1944; then enrolled in the College of Education and Industrial Arts in Wilberforce, Ohio, where she studied voice with Catherine Van Buren; received her B.A. degree in 1948, and then was awarded a scholarship at the Juilliard School of Music in N.Y.; there she received vocal training from Florence Page Kimball, and also joined the Opera Workshop under the direction of Frederic Cohen. Virgil Thomson heard her perform the role of Mistress Ford in Verdi's opera *Falstaff* and invited her to sing in the revival of his opera *4 Saints in 3 Acts* in 1952. She subsequently performed the role of Bess in Gershwin's *Porgy and Bess* on a tour of the U.S. (1952–54) and in Europe (1955). On Nov. 14, 1954, she made a highly acclaimed debut as a concert singer in N.Y. On Dec. 3, 1954, she sang at the first performance of Samuel Barber's *Prayers of Kierkegaard* with the Boston Sym. Orch., conducted by Charles Munch. On Jan. 23, 1955, she performed Tosca on television, creating a sensation both as an artist and as a member of her race taking up the role of an Italian diva. Her career was soon assured without any reservations. In 1957 she appeared with the San Francisco Opera; on Oct. 18, 1957, she sang Aida, a role congenial to her passionate artistry. In 1958 she sang Aida with the Vienna State Opera under the direction of Herbert von Karajan; on July 2, 1958, she sang this role at Covent Garden in London and again at La Scala in Milan in 1959, becoming the first black woman to sing with that most prestigious and most fastidious opera company. On Jan. 27, 1961, she made her first appearance with the Metropolitan Opera in N.Y. in the role of Leonora in *Il Trovatore*. A series of highly successful performances at the Metropolitan followed: Aida on Feb. 20, 1961; Madama Butterfly on March 3, 1961; Donna Anna on March 25, 1961; Tosca on April 1, 1962; Pamina on Jan. 3, 1964; Cleopatra in the premiere of Samuel Barber's opera *Antony and Cleopatra* at the opening of the new Metropolitan Opera House at Lincoln Center in N.Y. on Sept. 16, 1966. On Sept. 24, 1973, she sang Madama Butterfly at the Metropolitan once more. On Feb. 7, 1975, she appeared there in the title role of *Manon Lescaut*; and on Feb. 3, 1976, she sang Aida, a role she repeated for her farewell performance in opera in a televised production broadcast live from the Metropolitan Opera in N.Y. by PBS on Jan. 3, 1985. She then continued her concert career, appearing with notable success in the major music centers. She was married in 1952 to **William Warfield** (who sang Porgy at her performances of *Porgy and Bess*), but separated from him in 1959; they were divorced in 1973. She received many honors during her remarkable career; in 1964 President Johnson bestowed upon her the Medal of Freedom, and in 1985 President Reagan presented her with the National Medal of Arts.

BIBL.: H. Lyon, *L. P.: Highlights of a Prima Donna* (N.Y., 1973); R. Steins, *L. P., Opera Superstar* (Woodbridge, Conn., 1993).

Price, Dame Margaret (Berenice), outstanding Welsh soprano; b. Blackwood, near Tredegar, South Wales, April 13, 1941. She commenced singing lessons when she was 9; then won the Charles Kennedy Scott scholarship of London's Trinity College of Music at 15, and studied voice with Scott for 4 years. After singing in the Ambrosian Singers for 2 seasons, she made her operatic debut as Cherubino with the Welsh National Opera (1962); then sang that same role at her Covent Garden debut in London (1963). She made her first appearance at the Glyndebourne Festival as Constanze in *Die Entführung aus dem Serail* (1968); then made her U.S. debut as Pamina at the San Francisco Opera (1969); subsequently sang Fiordiligi at the Chicago Lyric Opera (1972). In 1973 she sang at the Paris Opéra, later joining its cast during its U.S. tour in 1976, eliciting extraordinary praise from the public and critics for her portrayal of Desdemona; made an auspicious Metropolitan Opera debut in N.Y. in that same role on Jan. 21, 1985. She also toured widely as a concert singer. Her other notable roles include Donna Anna, Aida, Adriana Lecouvreur, and Strauss's Ariadne. Her voice is essentially a lyric soprano, but is capable of technically brilliant coloratura. She was made a Commander of the Order of the British Empire in 1982. In 1992 she was made a Dame Commander of the Order of the British Empire.

Priestman, Brian, English conductor and music educator; b. Birmingham, Feb. 10, 1927. He received his training at the Univ. of Birmingham (B.Mus., 1950; M.A., 1952) and the Brussels Cons. (diploma, 1952). After serving as founder-conductor of the Opera da Camera and the Orch. da Camera in Birmingham, he was music director of the Royal Shakespeare Theatre at Stratford-upon-Avon (1960–63). He conducted the Edmonton (Alberta) Sym. Orch. (1964–68) and the Baltimore Sym. Orch. (1968–69), and then was music director of the Denver Sym. Orch. (1970–78). He also was principal conductor of the New

Zealand National Orch. in Wellington (1973–76) and music director of the Florida Phil. (1977–80). From 1980 to 1986 he was principal conductor of the Cape Town Sym. Orch., prof. and chairman of the music dept. at the Univ. of Cape Town, and director of the South African College of Music. He was principal guest conductor of the Malmö Sym. Orch. (1988–90). In 1992 he became artist-in-residence, prof., and director of orch. studies at the Univ. of Kansas at Lawrence.

Prigozhin, Lucian (Abramovich), Russian composer; b. Tashkent, Aug. 15, 1926. He received training in piano and theory in Tashkent, and then completed his studies with Shcherbachev, Evlakhov, and Kochurov at the Leningrad Cons. He became a convinced modernist in his music, introducing the concept of "supplementary tones" in the 12-tone method of composition by allowing members of the tone-row to permutate freely. However, he preserved the basic tonality even when he no longer used the key signatures.

WORKS: DRAMATIC: *Doctor Aybolit* (Ay! It Hurts!), children's radio opera (1956); *Circle of Hades,* ballet (1964; orch. suite, 1965); *Malchish-Kibalchish,* children's radio opera (1969); *Robin Hood,* opera (1972); film music. **ORCH.:** *Sinfonietta* (1953); 3 syms. (1955, rev. 1975; 1960, rev. 1963; 1970); *Music* for Flute and Strings (1961). **CHAMBER:** 2 violin sonatas (*Sonata-burlesque,* 1967; 1969); 2 string quartets (1970, 1979); *Musica rustica* for Wind Quintet (1973); Horn Sonata (1974). **PIANO:** Sonatina (1973); Sonata (1973); *Calendar of Nature,* 12 pieces (1974). **VOCAL:** *Stenka Razin* for 2 Soloists and Orch. (1949); *Prometheus Unbound* for Chorus and Orch. (1959–60); *The Chronicle of Igor's Campaign* for Mezzo-soprano, Bass, Chorus, and Chamber Ensemble (1966); *Snowstorm,* chamber oratorio (1968); *In Memory of the Great Battle* for Bass, Chorus, and Orch. (1975); cantatas.

BIBL.: E. Ruchyevskaya, *L. P.* (Moscow, 1977).

Přihoda, Váša, noted Czech violinist and teacher; b. Vodnany, Aug. 22, 1900; d. Vienna, July 26, 1960. He received his first instruction from his father, a professional violinist. He made his public debut at the age of 12 in Prague; in 1920, went on an Italian tour; in 1921, appeared in the U.S., and in 1927 played in England; then gave recitals throughout Europe. He continued to concertize after the absorption of Austria and Czechoslovakia into the Nazi Reich, and was briefly charged with collaboration with the occupying powers. He eventually resumed his career, and later became a prof. at the Vienna Academy of Music.

BIBL.: J. Vratislavský, *V. P.* (Prague, 1970).

Primrose, William, eminent Scottish-born American violist and pedagogue; b. Glasgow, Aug. 23, 1903; d. Provo, Utah, May 1, 1982. He studied violin in Glasgow with Camillo Ritter, at London's Guildhall School of Music, and in Belgium (1925–27) with Ysaÿe, who advised him to take up viola so as to avoid the congested violin field. He was the violist in the London String Quartet (1930–35), with which he made several tours. In 1937 he settled in the U.S., and was engaged as the principal violist in the NBC Sym. Orch. in N.Y. under Toscanini, holding this post until 1942. In 1939 he established his own string quartet. In 1953 he was named a Commander of the Order of the British Empire. He became a naturalized American citizen in 1955. From 1954 to 1962 he was the violist in the Festival Quartet. He also became active as a teacher; was on the faculty of the Univ. of Southern Calif. in Los Angeles (1962) and at the School of Music of Indiana Univ. in Bloomington (1965–72). In 1972 he inaugurated a master class at the Tokyo Univ. of Fine Arts and Music. Returning to the U.S., he taught at Brigham Young Univ. in Provo, Utah (1979–82). Primrose was greatly esteemed as a viola virtuoso; he gave first performances of viola concertos by several modern composers. He commissioned a viola concerto from Bartók, but the work was left unfinished at the time of Bartók's death, and the task of reconstructing the score from Bartók's sketches remained to be accomplished by Bartók's friend and associate Tibor Serly; Primrose gave its first performance with the Minneapolis Sym. Orch. on Dec. 2, 1949. He publ. *A Method for Violin and Viola Players* (London, 1960), *Technique in Memory* (1963), and an autobiography, *Walk on the North Side* (1978); also ed. various works for viola, and made transcriptions for the instrument.

BIBL.: D. Dalton, *Playing the Viola: Conversations with W. P.* (Oxford, 1988).

Pringsheim, Klaus, German conductor and composer; b. Feldafing, near Munich, July 24, 1883; d. Tokyo, Dec. 7, 1972. A scion of a highly cultured family, he studied mathematics with his father, a prof. at the Univ. of Munich, and physics with Röntgen, the discoverer of X-rays. His twin sister, Katherine, was married to Thomas Mann. In Munich, Pringsheim took piano lessons with Stavenhagen and composition with Thuille. In 1906 he went to Vienna and was engaged as assistant conductor of the Court Opera, under the tutelage of Mahler, who took him as a pupil in conducting and composition, a relationship that developed into profound friendship. Mahler recommended him to the management of the German Opera in Prague; Pringsheim conducted there from 1909 to 1914; then was engaged as conductor and stage director at the Bremen Opera (1915–18) and music director of the Max Reinhardt theaters in Berlin (1918–25). In 1923–24 he conducted in Berlin a Mahler cycle of 8 concerts, featuring all of Mahler's syms. and songs with orch. In 1927 he became the music critic of the socialist newspaper *Vorwärts.* A turning point in Pringsheim's life came in 1931 with an invitation to teach music at the Imperial Academy of Music in Tokyo, where he taught until 1937; several of his Japanese students became prominent composers. From 1937 to 1939 Pringsheim served as music adviser to the Royal Dept. of Fine Arts in Bangkok, Thailand. In 1939 he returned to Japan; was briefly interned in 1944 as an opponent of the Axis policies. In 1946 he went to California; after some intermittent activities, he returned to Japan in 1951; was appointed director of the Musashino Academy of Music in Tokyo; continued to conduct; also wrote music reviews for English-language Tokyo newspapers. As a composer, Pringsheim followed the neo-Romantic trends, deeply influenced by Mahler. His compositions include a *Concerto for Orchestra* (Tokyo, Oct. 13, 1935); *Yamada Nagasama,* Japanese radio opera (1953); Concertino for Xylophone and Orch. (1962); *Theme, Variations, and Fugue* for Wind Orch. (his last composition, 1971–72); and a curious album of 36 2-part canons for Piano (1959). A chapter from his theoretical work *Pythagoras, die Atonalität und wir* was publ. in *Schweizerische Musikzeitung* (1957). His reminiscences, "Mahler, My Friend," were publ. posthumously in the periodical *Composer* (1973–74). Pringsheim was a signatory of a letter of protest by surviving friends of Mahler against the film *Death in Venice,* after a novel of Thomas Mann, in which the central character, a famous writer who suffers a homosexual crisis, was made to resemble Mahler.

Pritchard, Sir John (Michael), distinguished English conductor; b. London, Feb. 5, 1921; d. Daly City, Calif., Dec. 5, 1989. He studied violin with his father, and then continued his musical training in Italy, returning to England to serve in the British army during World War II. In 1947 he joined the staff of the Glyndebourne Festival Opera as a répétiteur; became chorus master and assistant to Fritz Busch in 1948; conducted there regularly from 1951, serving as its music director (1969–77). He made his first appearance at London's Covent Garden in 1952. He was principal conductor of the Royal Liverpool Phil. (1957–63) and the London Phil. (1962–66), touring widely abroad with the latter. In 1963 he made his U.S. debut as a guest conductor with the Pittsburgh Sym. Orch.; also conducted at the Chicago Lyric Opera (1969) and the San Francisco Opera (1970). On Oct. 25, 1971, he made his Metropolitan Opera debut in N.Y. conducting *Così fan tutte.* As a guest conductor, he appeared with many of the world's leading opera houses and orchs. He was chief conductor of the Cologne Opera (1978–89). In 1979 he became chief guest conductor of the BBC Sym. Orch. in London, and subsequently was made its chief conductor in 1982. He was also joint music director of the Opera National in Brussels (1981–89), and served as the 1st music director of the San Francisco Opera (1986–89). In 1962 he was made a Commander of the Order of the British Empire, and was knighted in 1983. Pritchard was esteemed for his unpretentious but assured command of a vast operatic and symphonic repertory, extending from the Baroque masters to the leading composers of the present era.

BIBL.: H. Conway, *Sir J. P.: His Life in Music* (London, 1993).

Procter, Alice McElroy, American pianist, teacher, and composer; b. Albany, N.Y., April 18, 1915; d. Newton, Mass., Dec. 20, 1987. She studied composition at Smith College and at the Eastman School of Music in Rochester, N.Y., where she received her Ph.D. Subsequently, she taught piano in Boston and its environs. She publ. some ingratiating teaching pieces for piano, among them *Jumping Cat* and *Footsteps in the Night.* She was the wife of **Leland Procter**.

Procter, Leland, American composer and teacher; b. Newton, Mass., March 24, 1914; d. Hampden, Mass., Feb. 20, 1994. He studied composition at the Eastman School of Music in Rochester, N.Y., with Hanson and Rogers, and later at the Univ. of Okla. Returning to Boston, he taught at the New England Cons. of Music. He publ. some teaching pieces for piano, and wrote symphonic works. He was the husband of **Alice McElroy Procter**.

Procter, (Mary) Norma, English contralto; b. Cleethorpes, Feb. 15, 1928. She studied voice with Roy Henderson and Alec Redshaw. She made her debut in Handel's *Messiah* at Southwark Cathedral in 1948; soon established herself as an outstanding concert singer; in 1961 she made her operatic debut at London's Covent Garden as Gluck's Orpheus.

Prod'homme, J(acques)-G(abriel), industrious French librarian and music critic; b. Paris, Nov. 28, 1871; d. Neuilly-sur-Seine, near Paris, June 18, 1956. He studied philology and music history at the Paris École des Hautes Études Sociales (1890–94); then became a writer on musical and other subjects in the socialist publications, among them *La Revue Socialiste, Droits de l'Homme*, and *Messidor.* An ardent believer in the cause of peace, he ed. in Munich the *Deutsche-französische Rundschau,* dedicated to the friendship between the French and German peoples (1899–1902). His hopes for peace were shattered by 2 devastating world wars within his lifetime. Back in Paris, he founded, with Dauriac and Écorcheville, the French section of the IMS (1902), serving as its secretary (1903–13); with La Laurencie, he founded the French Musicological Society (1917), serving as its secretary (1917–20) and vice-president (1929–36). He was curator of the library and archivist of the museum at the Paris Opéra (1931–40); was also librarian at the Paris Cons. (1934–40). He was made a Chevalier of the Légion d'honneur (1928). With others, he tr. Wagner's prose works (13 vols., 1907–25); also Wagner's music dramas (1922–27) and Beethoven's conversation books (1946).

WRITINGS (all publ. in Paris): *Le Cycle Berlioz*, in 2 vols.: *La Damnation de Faust* (1896) and *L'Enfance du Christ* (1899); with C. Bertrand, *Guides analytiques de l'Anneau du Nibelung. Crépuscule des dieux* (1902); *Hector Berlioz 1803–1869: Sa vie et ses oeuvres* (1905; 2nd ed., rev., 1913); *Les Symphonies de Beethoven (1800–1827)* (1906; 15th ed., 1938); *Paganini* (1907; 2nd ed., 1927; Eng. tr., 1911); *Franz Liszt* (1910); with A. Dandelot, *Gounod 1818–93: Sa vie et ses oeuvres d'après des documents inédits* (2 vols., 1911); *Écrits de musiciens (XVe–XVIIIe siècles)* (1912); *Richard Wagner et la France* (1921); *La jeunesse de Beethoven, 1770–1800* (1921; 2nd ed., 1927); *L'Opéra, 1669–1925* (1925); *Pensées sur la musique et les musiciens* (1926); *Beethoven raconté par ceux qui l'ont vu* (1927); *Mozart raconté par ceux qui l'ont vu 1756–1791* (1928); *Schubert raconté par ceux qui l'ont vu* (1928); with E. Crauzat, *Paris qui disparaît: Les Menus plaisirs du roi; L'École royale et le Conservatoire de Paris* (1929); *Wagner raconté par ceux qui l'ont vu* (1929); *Les Sonates pour piano de Beethoven, 1782–1823* (1937; 2nd ed., rev., 1950); *L'Immortelle bien-aimée de Beethoven* (1946); *Gluck* (1948); *François-Joseph Gossec, 1734–1829* (1949).

Profeta, Laurențiu, Romanian composer; b. Bucharest, Jan. 12, 1925. He studied with Constantinescu and Mendelsohn (harmony, counterpoint, and composition) at the Bucharest Cons. (1945–49) and with Messner (composition) at the Moscow Cons. (1954–56). He pursued his career in Bucharest, where he was assistant director of the Romanian Radio (1948–52). From 1952 to 1960 he was director of the music dept. of the Ministry of Culture. He was secretary of the Romanian National Committee of the International Music Council from 1960 to 1970. From 1968 he was also secretary of the Union of Composers and Musicologists, serving as a member of its directory council from 1990. It awarded him its prize 8 times (1968, 1969, 1976, 1979, 1980, 1986, 1990, 1993). In his music, Profeta has followed in the path of neo-Classicism while utilizing various contemporary elements in his scores.

WORKS: DRAMATIC: *The Captain's Wife*, ballet (1946); *The Prince and the Pauper*, ballet (Bucharest, Sept. 15, 1967); *The Wistful Mariner*, ballet (1976); *The Hours of the Sea*, dance piece (1979); *The Triumph of Love*, ballet (1983); *Peter Pan's Story*, children's comic opera (Bucharest, Dec. 20, 1984); *Rica*, ballet (1986); *Hershale*, musical (1989); *The Loosers*, musical (Bucharest, Oct. 22, 1990); *Of the Carnival*, ballet (1991); *Maria Tănase*, musical (1992); *Turandot*, musical (1992); *Eva Now*, musical (1993); film scores. **ORCH.:** *A Suite for Marionettes: Images from the World of Childhood* for Chamber Orch. (1945); *Poem of the Motherland* (1952); *Days of Vac*, suite (1956). **VOCAL:** *The Happening in the Garden*, oratorio for Soloists, Reciter, Children's Chorus, and Orch. (1958); *Cantata of the Motherland* for Mezzo-soprano, Reciter, Chorus, and Orch. (1959); *6 Humorous Pieces* for Soloists, Children's Chorus, Small Orch., and Tape (1966); *Echoes* for Chorus and Electric Organ (1967); *The Poem of the Forest* for Children's Chorus, Electric Organ, and Tape (1968); *Madrigal '75*, pop cantata (1975); *Romanian Christmas Carols* for Children's Chorus and Orch. (1994). **OTHER:** *Symphonic Pop Music* for Synthesizer (1994).

Prohaska, Carl, Austrian composer, father of **Felix Prohaska**; b. Mödling, near Vienna, April 25, 1869; d. Vienna, March 28, 1927. He studied piano with Anna Assmayr in Vienna and with Eugen d'Albert in Berlin and composition with Franz Krenn and musicology with Mandyczewski in Vienna. In 1908 he joined the faculty of the Vienna Academy of Music, where he taught piano and theory. He wrote an opera, *Madeleine Guinard*; an oratorio, *Frühlingsfeier* (1913); String Quartet; Piano Trio; Quintet for 2 Violins, Viola, Cello, and Double Bass; a group of piano pieces.

Prohaska, Felix, Austrian conductor, son of **Carl Prohaska**; b. Vienna, May 16, 1912; d. there, March 29, 1987. He received his primary music education at home with his father; then studied piano with Steuermann, and theory with Kornauth, Gál et al. He served as répétiteur at the Graz Opera (1936–39); conducted opera in Duisburg (1939–41) and in Strasbourg (1941–43); then was 1st conductor of the Vienna State Opera (1945–55) and the Frankfurt am Main Opera (1955–61). He again conducted at the Vienna State Opera (1964–67); conducted at the opera in Hannover (1965–74), and also served as director of the Hochschule für Musik there (1961–75).

Prohaska, Jaro(slav), Austrian bass-baritone; b. Vienna, Jan. 24, 1891; d. Munich, Sept. 28, 1965. He sang in the Wiener Sangerknaben; studied voice with Otto Müller in Vienna. He made his operatic debut in Lübeck in 1922; then sang in Nuremberg (1925–31). In 1932 he joined the Berlin State Opera, remaining on its roster until 1953; also made many appearances at the Bayreuth Festivals (1933–44), where he excelled in such roles as Hans Sachs, Wotan, and the Dutchman. He was director of the West Berlin Hochschule für Musik (1947–59), where he also directed its opera school (1952–59).

Prokofiev, Sergei (Sergeievich), great Russian composer of modern times, creator of new and original formulas of rhythmic, melodic, and harmonic combinations that became the recognized style of his music; b. Sontsovka, near Ekaterinoslav, April 27, 1891; d. Moscow, March 5, 1953. His mother was born a serf in 1859, 2 years before the emanicipation of Russian serfdom, and she assumed (as was the custom) the name of the estate where she was born, Sontsov. Prokofiev was born on that estate on April 27, 1891, although he himself erroneously believed that the date was April 23; the correct date was established with the discovery of his birth certificate. He received his first piano lessons from his mother, who was an amateur pianist; he improvised several pieces, and then composed a children's opera, *The Giant* (1900), which was performed in a domestic version. Following his bent for the theater, he put together 2 other operas, *On Desert Islands* (1902) and *Ondine* (1904–07); fantastic subjects obviously possessed his childish imagination. He was 11 years old when he met the great Russian master, Taneyev, who arranged for him to take systematic private lessons with Glière, who became his tutor at Sontsovka during the summers of 1903 and 1904 and by correspondence during the intervening winter. Under Glière's knowledgeable guidance in theory and harmony, Prokofiev composed a sym. in piano version and still another opera, *Plague*, based upon a poem by Pushkin. Finally, in 1904, at the age of 13, he enrolled in the St. Petersburg Cons., where he studied composition with Liadov and piano with Alexander Winkler; later he was accepted by no less a master than Rimsky-Korsakov, who instructed him in orchestration. He also studied conducting with Nikolai Tcherepnin, and form with Wihtol. Further, he entered the piano class of Anna Essipova. During the summers, he returned to Sontsovka or traveled in the Caucasus and continued to compose, already in quite an advanced style; the Moscow publisher Jurgenson accepted his first work, a piano sonata, for publication; it was premiered in Moscow on March 6, 1910. It was then that Prokofiev made his first visit to Paris, London, and Switzerland (1913); in 1914 he graduated from the St. Petersburg Cons., receiving the Anton Rubinstein Prize (a grand piano) as a pianist-composer with his Piano Concerto No. 1, which he performed publicly at the graduation concert. Because of audacious innovations in his piano music (he wrote one piece in which the right and left hands played in different keys), he was described in the press as a "futurist," and because of his addiction to dissonant and powerful harmonic combinations, some critics dismissed his works as "football music." This idiom was explicitly demonstrated in his *Sarcasms and Visions fugitives*, percussive and sharp, yet not lacking in lyric charm. Grotesquerie and irony animated his early works; he also developed a strong attraction toward subjects of primitive character. His important orch. work, the *Scythian Suite* (arr. from music written for a ballet, *Ala and Lolly*, 1915), draws upon a legend of ancient Russian sun-worship rituals. While a parallel with Stravinsky's *Le Sacre du printemps* may be drawn, there is no similarity between the styles of the 2 works. The original performance of the *Scythian Suite*, scheduled at a Koussevitzky concert in Moscow, was canceled on account of the disruption caused by war, which did not prevent the otherwise intelligent Russian music critic Sabaneyev, blissfully unaware that the announced premiere had been canceled, from delivering a blast of the work as a farrago of atrocious noises. (Sabaneyev was forced to resign his position after this episode.) Another Prokofiev score, primitivistic in its inspiration, was the cantata *Seven, They Are Seven*, based upon incantations from an old Sumerian religious ritual. During the same period, Prokofiev wrote his famous *Classical Symphony* (1916–17), in which he adopted with remarkable acuity the formal style of Haydn's music. While the structure of the work was indeed classical, the sudden modulatory shifts and subtle elements of grotesquerie revealed decisively a new modern art.

After conducting the premiere of his *Classical Symphony* in Petrograd on April 21, 1918, Prokofiev left Russia by way of Siberia and Japan for the U.S. (the continuing war in Europe prevented him from traveling westward). He gave concerts of his music in Japan and later in the U.S., playing his first solo concert in N.Y. on Oct. 29, 1918. Some American critics greeted his appearance as the reflection of the chaotic events of Russia in revolution, and Prokofiev himself was described as a "ribald and Bolshevist innovator and musical agitator." "Every rule in the realm of traditional music writing was broken by Prokofiev," one N.Y. writer complained. "Dissonance followed dissonance in a fashion inconceivable to ears accustomed to melody and harmonic laws." Prokofiev's genteel *Classical Symphony* struck some critics as "an orgy of dissonant sound, an exposition of the unhappy state of chaos from which Russia suffers." One N.Y. critic indulged in the following: "Crashing Siberians, volcano hell, Krakatoa, sea-bottom crawlers. Incomprehensible? So is Prokofiev." But another critic issued a word of caution, suggesting that "Prokofiev might be the legitimate successor of Borodin, Mussorgsky, and Rimsky-Korsakov." The critic was unintentionally right; Prokofiev is firmly enthroned in the pantheon of Russian music.

In 1920 Prokofiev settled in Paris, where he established an association with Diaghilev's Ballets Russes, which produced his ballets *Chout* (a French transliteration of the Russian word for buffoon), *Le Pas d'acier* (descriptive of the industrial development in Soviet Russia), and *L'Enfant prodigue*. In 1921 Prokofiev again visited the U.S. for the production of the opera commissioned by the Chicago Opera Co., *The Love for 3 Oranges*. In 1927 he was invited to be the pianist for a series of his own works in Russia. He gave a number of concerts in Russia again in 1929, and eventually decided to remain there. In Russia he wrote some of his most popular works, including the symphonic fairy tale *Peter and the Wolf*, staged by a children's theater in Moscow, the historical cantata *Alexander Nevsky*, the ballet *Romeo and Juliet*, and the opera *War and Peace*.

Unexpectedly, Prokofiev became the target of the so-called proletarian group of Soviet musicians who accused him of decadence, a major sin in Soviet Russia at the time. His name was included in the official denunciation of modern Soviet composers issued by reactionary Soviet politicians in 1948. He meekly confessed that he had been occasionally interested in atonal and polytonal devices during his stay in Paris, but insisted that he had never abandoned the ideals of classical Russian music. Indeed, when he composed his 7th Sym., he described it specifically as a youth sym., reflecting the energy and ideals of new Russia. There were also significant changes in his personal life. He separated from his Spanish-born wife, the singer Lina Llubera, the mother of his 2 sons, and established a companionship with Myra Mendelson, a member of the Young Communist League. She was a writer and assisted him on the libretto of his *War and Peace*. He made one final attempt to gain favor with the Soviet establishment by writing an opera based on a heroic exploit of a Soviet pilot during the war against the Nazis. But this, too, was damned by the servile Communist press as lacking in true patriotic spirit, and the opera was quickly removed from the repertory. Prokofiev died suddenly of heart failure on March 5, 1953, a few hours before the death of Stalin. Curiously enough, the anniversary of Prokofiev's death is duly commemorated, while that of his once powerful nemesis is officially allowed to be forgotten. O. Prokofiev tr. and ed. his *Soviet Diary, 1927, and Other Writings* (London, 1991).

WORKS: DRAMATIC: OPERAS: *Maddalena* (1912–13, piano score only; orchestrated by Edward Downes, 1978; BBC Radio, March 25, 1979; 1st stage perf., Graz, Nov. 28, 1981; U.S. premiere, St. Louis, June 9, 1982); *The Gambler*, after Dostoyevsky (1915–16; rev. 1927; Brussels, April 29, 1929); *The Love for 3 Oranges*, after Gozzi (1919; Chicago, Dec. 30, 1921); *The Fiery Angel* (1919; 2 fragments perf., Paris, June 14, 1928; 1st complete concert perf., Paris, Nov. 25, 1954; 1st stage perf., Venice, Sept. 14, 1955); *Semyon Kotko* (1939; Moscow, June 23, 1940); *Betrothal in a Convent*, after Sheridan's *Duenna* (1940; Leningrad, Nov. 3, 1946); *War and Peace*, after Tolstoy (1941–52; concert perf. of 8 of the original 11 scenes, Ensemble of Soviet Opera of the All-Union Theatrical Society, Oct. 16, 1944; concert perf. of 9 of the original 11 scenes with scenes 6 and 8 omitted, Moscow Phil., June 7, 1945; stage perf. of Part I [*Peace*] with new Scene 2, Maly Theater, Leningrad, June 12, 1946; "final" version of 11 scenes, Prague, June 25, 1948; another "complete" version, Leningrad, March 31, 1955; rev. version in 13 scenes with cuts, Moscow, Nov. 8, 1957; 13 scenes with a choral epigraph, Moscow, Dec. 15, 1959); *A Tale about a Real Man* (1947–48; private perf., Leningrad, Dec. 3, 1948; severely censured by Soviet critics and not produced in public until given at the Bolshoi Theater, Moscow, Oct. 8, 1960). **BALLETS:** *Buffoon* (1920; Paris, May 17, 1921); *Trapeze* (1924; music used in his Quintet); *Le Pas d'acier* (1924; Paris, June 7, 1927); *L'Enfant prodigue* (1928; Paris, May 21, 1929); *Sur le Borysthène* (1930; Paris, Dec. 16, 1932); *Romeo and Juliet* (1935–36; Brno, Dec. 30, 1938); *Cinderella* (1940–44; Moscow, Nov. 21, 1945); *A Tale of the Stone Flower* (1948–50; Moscow, Feb. 12, 1954). **INCIDENTAL MUSIC TO:** *Egyptian Nights* (1933); *Boris Godunov* (1936); *Eugene Onegin* (1936); *Hamlet* (1937–38; Leningrad, May 15, 1938). **FILM MUSIC:** *Lt. Kijé* (1933); *The Queen of Spades* (1936); *Alexander Nevsky* (1938); *Lermontov* (1941); *Tonya* (1942); *Kotovsky* (1942); *Partisans in the Ukrainian Steppes* (1942); *Ivan the Terrible* (1942–45).

ORCH.: *Rêves*, symphonic tableau (St. Petersburg, Dec. 5, 1910); *Autumn*, symphonic tableau (Moscow, Aug. 1, 1911); 5 piano concertos: No. 1 (Moscow, Aug. 7, 1912, composer soloist), No. 2 (Pavlovsk, Sept. 5, 1913, composer soloist), No. 3 (1917–21; Chicago, Dec. 16, 1921, composer soloist), No. 4, for the Left Hand (1931; Berlin, Sept. 5, 1956), and No. 5 (Berlin, Oct. 31, 1932, composer soloist); Sinfonietta (1914; Petrograd, Nov. 6, 1915; rev. 1929; Moscow, Nov. 18, 1930); *Scythian Suite* (1914; Petrograd, Jan. 29, 1916); 2 violin concertos: No. 1 (1916–17; Paris, Oct. 18, 1923) and No. 2 (Madrid, Dec. 1, 1935); 7 syms.: No. 1, *Classical* (1916–17; Petrograd, April 21, 1918, composer conducting), No. 2 (1924; Paris, June 6, 1925; 2nd version not completed), No. 3 (1928; Paris, May 17, 1929), No. 4 (Boston, Nov. 11, 1930; radically rev. version, 1947), No. 5 (1944; Moscow, Jan. 13, 1945), No. 6 (1945–47; Leningrad, Oct. 11, 1947), and No. 7 (1951–52; Moscow, Oct. 11, 1952); *Buffoon*, suite from the ballet (1923; Brussels, Jan. 15, 1924); *The Love for 3 Oranges*, suite from the opera (Paris, Nov. 29, 1925); *Divertissement* (1925–29; Paris, Dec. 22, 1929); *Le Pas d'acier*, suite from the ballet (1926; Moscow, May 27, 1928); *American Overture* for Chamber Orch. (Moscow, Feb. 7, 1927; also for Orch., 1928; Paris, Dec. 18, 1930); *L'Enfant prodigue*, suite from the ballet (1929; Paris, March 7, 1931); *4 Portraits*, suite from the opera *The Gambler* (1931; Paris, March 12, 1932); *On the Dnieper*, suite from the ballet (1933); 2 cello concertos: No. 1 (1933–38; Moscow, Nov. 26, 1938, Lev Berezovsky soloist) and No. 2 (rev. version of No. 1; Moscow, Feb. 18, 1952, M. Rostropovich soloist; further rev. as *Sinfonia Concertante*, Copenhagen, Dec. 9, 1954, Rostropovich soloist); *Symphonic Song* (Moscow, April 14, 1934); *Lt. Kijé*, suite from the film music (1934; Paris, Feb. 20, 1937); *Egyptian Nights*, suite from the incidental music (Radio Moscow, Dec. 21, 1934); *Romeo and Juliet*, 3 suites from the ballet (No. 1, Moscow, Nov. 24, 1936, No. 2, Leningrad, April 15, 1937, and No. 3, Moscow, March 8, 1946); *Peter and the Wolf*, symphonic fairy tale (Moscow, May 2, 1936); *Semyon Kotko*, suite from the opera (1940); *A Summer Day*, children's suite for Chamber Orch. (1941); *Symphonic March* (1941); *The Year 1941* (1941; Sverdlovsk, Jan. 21, 1943); *Ivan the Terrible*, suite from the film music (1942–45); March for Military Orch. (Moscow, April 30, 1944); *Ode on the End of the War* for 8 Harps, 4 Pianos, Military Band, Percussion Ensemble, and Double Basses (Moscow, Nov. 12, 1945); *Cinderella*, 3 suites from the ballet (No. 1, Moscow, Nov. 12, 1946, No. 2, 1946, and No. 3, Radio Moscow, Sept. 3, 1947); *Waltzes*, suite (1946; Moscow, May 13, 1947); *Festive Poem* (Moscow, Oct. 3, 1947); *Pushkin Waltzes* (1949); *Summer Night*, suite from the opera *Betrothal in a Convent* (1950); *Wedding Scene*, suite from the ballet *A Tale of the Stone Flower* (Moscow, Dec. 12, 1951); *Gypsy Fantasy* from the ballet *A Tale of the Stone Flower* (Moscow, Nov. 18, 1951); *Ural Rhapsody* from the ballet *A Tale of the Stone Flower* (1951); *The Mistress of the Copper Mountain*, suite from the ballet *A Tale of the Stone Flower* (1951; unfinished); *The Meeting of the Volga with the Don River*, for the completion of the Volga-Don Canal (1951; Moscow, Feb. 22, 1952); Cello Concertino (1952; unfinished; completed by M. Rostropovich and D. Kabalevsky); Concerto for 2 Pianos and Strings (1952; unfinished).

CHAMBER: *Humorous Scherzo* for 4 Bassoons (1912; London, Sept. 2, 1916); *Ballade* for Cello and Piano (1912; Moscow, Feb. 5, 1914); *Overture on Hebrew Themes* for Clarinet, 2 Violins, Viola, Cello, and Piano (N.Y., Jan. 26, 1920); Quintet for Oboe, Clarinet, Violin, Viola, and Double Bass (1924; Moscow, March 6, 1927); 2 string quartets: No. 1 (Washington, D.C., April 25, 1931) and No. 2 (1941; Moscow, Sept. 5, 1942); Sonata for 2 Violins (Moscow, Nov. 27, 1932); 2 violin sonatas: No. 1 (1938–46; BBC, London, Aug. 25, 1946) and No. 2 (Moscow, June 17, 1944; transcribed from the Flute Sonata); Flute Sonata (Moscow, Dec. 7, 1943); Sonata for Solo Violin (1947; Moscow, March 10, 1960); Cello Sonata (1949; Moscow, March 1, 1950). **PIANO:** 10 sonatas (1909; 1912; 1917; 1917; 1923; 1940; 1942; 1944; 1947; 1953, unfinished); 4 Etudes (1909); 4 Pieces (1911); 4 Pieces (1912); Toccata (1912); *Sarcasms*, suite of 5 pieces (1912–14); 10 Pieces (1913); *Visions fugitives*, suite of 20 pieces (1915–17); *Tales of an Old Grandmother*, 4 pieces (1918); *March and Scherzo* from the opera *The Love for 3 Oranges* (1922); *Things in Themselves* (1928); 6 Pieces (1930–31); 2 sonatinas (1931–32); 3 Pieces (1934); *Pensées* (1933–34); *Children's Music*, 12 easy pieces (1935); *Romeo and Juliet*, 10 pieces from the ballet (1937); 3 pieces from the ballet *Cinderella* (1942); 3 Pieces (1941–42); 10 pieces from the ballet *Cinderella* (1943); 6 pieces from the ballet *Cinderella* (1944).

VOCAL: CHORAL: 2 poems for Women's Chorus and Orch: *The White Swan* and *The Wave* (1909); *Seven, They Are Seven*, cantata for Tenor, Chorus, and Orch. (1917–18; Paris, May 29, 1924); Cantata for the 20th anniversary of the October Revolution, for 2 Choruses, Military Band, Accordions, and Percussion, to texts by Marx, Lenin, and Stalin (1937; perf. in Moscow, April 5, 1966, but not in its entirety; the section which used a text from Stalin was eliminated); *Songs of Our Days*, suite for Solo Voices, Chorus, and Orch. (Moscow, Jan. 5, 1938); *Alexander Nevsky*, cantata for Mezzo-soprano, Chorus, and Orch. (Moscow, May 17, 1939); *Zdravitsa: Hail to Stalin*, cantata for Chorus and Orch., for Stalin's 60th birthday (Moscow, Dec. 21, 1939); *Ballad of an Unknown Boy*, cantata for Soprano, Tenor, Chorus, and Orch. (Moscow, Feb. 21, 1944); *Hymn to the Soviet Union* (1943; submitted to the competition for a new Soviet anthem but failed to win; a song by Alexander Alexandrov was selected); *Flourish, Powerful Land*, cantata for the 30th anniversary of the October Revolution (Moscow, Nov. 12, 1947); *Winter Bonfire*, suite for Narrators, Boys' Chorus, and Orch. (Moscow, Dec. 19, 1950); *On Guard for Peace*, oratorio for Mezzo-soprano, Narrators, Chorus, Boys' Chorus, and Orch. (Moscow, Dec. 19, 1950). **SONGS:** *2 Poems* (1911); *The Ugly Duckling*, after Hans Christian Andersen (1914); *5 Poems* (1915); *5 Poems* (1916); *5 Songs without Words* (1920; also for Violin and Piano); *5 Poems* (1921); *6 Songs* (1935); *3 Children's Songs* (1936); *3 Poems* (1936); *3 songs* from the film *Alexander Nevsky* (1939); *7 Songs* (1939); *7 Mass Songs* (1941–42); 12 transcriptions of folk songs (1944); 2 duets (1945); *Soldiers' March Song* (1950).

BIBL.: I. Nestyev, *S. P.* (Moscow, 1946; Eng. tr., N.Y., 1946; enl. Russian ed., Moscow, 1957; Eng. tr. with a foreword by N. Slonimsky, Stanford, Calif., 1961); S. Schlifstein, ed., *S. P., Materials, Documents, Reminiscences* (Moscow, 1956); M. Sabinina, *S. P.* (Moscow, 1958); L. Gakkel, *Piano Works of S. P.* (Moscow, 1960); C. Samuel, *P.* (Paris, 1960; Eng. tr., 1971); F. Streller, *P.* (Leipzig, 1960); L. Berger, ed., *Traits of P.'s Style* (Moscow, 1962); I. Nestyev and G. Edelman, eds., *S. P., Articles and Materials* (Moscow, 1962); M. Hofmann, *P.* (Paris, 1963); H. Brockhaus, *S. P.* (Leipzig, 1964); L. and E. Hanson, *P., The Prodigal Son* (London, 1964); M. Rayment, *P.* (London, 1965); S. Schlifstein, ed., *P.* (album of pictures annotated in Russian and Eng.; Moscow, 1965); L. Danko, *S.S. P.* (Moscow, 1966); M. Brown, *The Symphonies of P.* (diss., Florida State Univ., 1967); S. Morozov, *P.* (Moscow, 1967); V. Serov, *S. P., A Soviet Tragedy* (N.Y., 1968); R. McAllister, *The Operas of S. P.* (diss., Cambridge Univ., 1970); I. Martynov, *P.* (Moscow, 1974); D. Appel, ed., and G. Daniels, tr., *P. by P.: A Composer's Memoir* (Garden City, N.Y., 1979); V. Blok, ed., *S. P.: Materials, Articles, Interviews* (London, 1980); H. Robinson, *The Operas of S. P. and Their Russian Literary Sources* (diss., Univ. of Calif., Berkeley, 1980); M. Nesteyeva, *S.S. P.* (Moscow, 1981); N. Savkina, *S.S. P.* (Moscow, 1982; Eng. tr., Neptune City, N.J., 1984); D. Gutman, *P.* (London, 1988); S. Fiess, *The Piano Works of S. P.* (Metuchen, N.J., 1994).

Prošev, Toma, Yugoslav conductor, teacher, and composer; b. Skopje, Nov. 10, 1931. He studied with Škerjanc at the Ljubljana Academy of Music, graduating in composition in 1960; then made a musical pilgrimage to Boulanger in Paris (1964). Upon returning to his homeland, he was active as a conductor, teacher, and composer. His music is moderately modern.

WORKS: DRAMATIC: OPERAS: *Paučina* (The Cobweb; 1957); *Mali princ* (The Little Prince; 1966). **BALLETS:** *Okviri i odjeci* (Frames and Echoes; 1961); *Pesma nad pesmama* (Song of Songs; 1967); *Relacije* (Relaxations; 1969). **ORCH.:** Piano Concertino (1958); *Makete* (Dummies; 1960); *Concertante Music* for Cello and String Orch. (1960); *Improvisations concertante* for Violin and String Orch. (1962); 4 syms. (1962–79); 2 violin concertos (1963, 1969); *Tempera I–IV* for Strings (1963–70); *Metastasis* (1963); Ondes Martenot Concerto (1964); *Relations* (1964); *Morphographie* for Chamber Orch. (1965); *3 Movements* for Clarinet and Strings (1966); *Tempera X* for Chamber Orch. (1974). **CHAMBER:** Violin Sonata (1953); String Quartet (1959); *Intergrali* for Piano and Chamber Ensemble (1971); *Musandra 3* for Brass Quintet (1974). **VOCAL:** 4 oratorios: *Jama* (The Pit; 1961), *Skopje* (1965), *Sunce prastare zemlje* (Sun of the Ancient Country; 1967), and *Prouka* (The Message; 1968); *Diametry* for Voice and Chamber Orch. (1966); *Colors* for 6 Solo Voices and Ensemble (1967).

Prota-Giurleo, Ulisse, distinguished Italian musicologist; b. Naples, March 13, 1886; d. Perugia, Feb. 9, 1966. He studied with Salvatore di Giacomo in Naples; then devoted himself to the study of Neapolitan music and theater. In addition to his valuable books, he contributed important articles to various journals, including "Breve storia del teatro di corte e della musica a Napoli nei secoli XVII e XVIII," in *Il teatro di corte del Palazzo reale di Napoli* (Naples, 1952).

WRITINGS (all publ. in Naples unless otherwise given): *Musicisti napoletani in Russia* (1923); *La prima calcofragia musicale a Napoli* (1923); *Musicisti napoletani alla corte di Portogallo* (1924); *Alessandro Scarlatti "il Palermitano"* (1926); *La grande orchestra del Teatro San Carlo nel '700* (1927); *Nicola Logroscino "il dio dell'opera buffa"* (1927); *Francesco Cirillo e l'introduzione del melodramma a Napoli* (Grumo Nevano, 1952); *Francesco Durante nel 27 centenario della sua morte* (Frattamaggiore, 1955); *La famiglia napoletana dei Prota nella storia della musica* (Milan, 1957); *Miserere, tradotto in dialetto napoletano da Nicola Valletta* (1960); *I teatri di Napoli nel '600: La commedia e le maschere* (1962); *Gian Leonardo dell'Arpa nella storia della musica* (1964); with A. Giovine, *Giacomo Insanguine detto Monopoli, musicista monopolitano: Cenno biografici, elenco di rappresentazioni, bibliografia, indice vari e iconografia* (Bari, 1969).

BIBL.: A. Giovine, *U. P.-G.: Ricordo di un mio maestro* (Bari, 1968).

Protopopov, Sergei, Russian choral conductor, teacher, and composer; b. Moscow, April 2, 1893; d. there, Dec. 14, 1954. He studied medicine at the Univ. of Moscow (1913–17) and composition with Yavorsky at the Kiev Cons. (1918–21). He was active as a choral conductor and later taught at the Moscow Cons. (1938–43). His piano sonatas reflect the influence of Yavrosky's theory of model rhythms and are dissonant in the vein of the Lourié, Roslavetz, and Mossolov piano pieces of the period. His compositions included an opera; *Suite of 6 Folk Pieces* for Orch. (1945); *Poem* for Cello and Piano (1935); *3 Poems* for Cello and Piano (1938); piano pieces, including 3 sonatas (1920–22; 1924; *Sonata Terza,* 1924–28) and *3 Preludes* (1938); and numerous songs.

Pruett, James W(orrell), prominent American music librarian and musicologist; b. Mount Airy, N.C., Dec. 23, 1932. He studied music and comparative literature at the Univ. of North Carolina in Chapel Hill (B.A., 1955; M.A., 1957; Ph.D., 1962); was a member of its library staff (1955–61), serving as music librarian (1961–76); in 1963 he joined its music dept., serving as prof. of music (1974–87) and chairman of the dept. (1976–86); also was president of the Music Library Assn. (1973–75) and ed. of its journal *Notes* (1974–77). He was chief of the music division of the Library of Congress in Washington, D.C. (from 1987). He ed. *Studies in Musicology: Essays in the History, Style, and Bibliography of Music in Memory of Glen Haydon* (Chapel Hill, 1969); with T. Stevens, he publ. *Research Guide to Musicology* (Chicago, 1985).

Prüfer, (Hermann Bernhard) Arthur, German musicologist; b. Leipzig, July 7, 1860; d. Würzburg, June 3, 1944. He was a law student; then turned to music and studied at the Leipzig Cons. (1887–88), also attending the lectures on musicology of Paul and Kretzschmar at the Univ.; studied further in Berlin (1888–89) with Spitta and Bargiel; took the degree of Ph.D. (Univ. of Leipzig, 1890) with the diss. *Über den ausserkirchlichen Kunstgesang in den evangelischen Schulen des 16. Jahrhunderts*; completed his Habilitation there in 1895 with his *Johann Hermann Schein* (publ. in Leipzig, 1895). He joined its faculty as a lecturer (1895) and as an assoc. prof. (1902). He ed. the first collected edition of Schein's works (7 vols., 1901–23); publ. *Die Bühnenfestspiele in Bayreuth* (1899; 2nd ed., 1909, as *Das Werk von Bayreuth*; new ed., 1930, as *Tannhäuser und der Sängerkrieg auf der Wartburg*); *Johann Hermann Schein und das weltliche deutsche Lied des 17. Jahrhunderts* (1908); *Die Musik als tönende Faust-Idee* (1920); *Deutsches Leben im Volkslied und Wagners Tannhäuser* (1929).

Prunières, Henry, eminent French musicologist; b. Paris, May 24, 1886; d. Nanterre, April 11, 1942. He studied music history with Rolland at the Sorbonne (1906–13), receiving his doctorat ès lettres from the Univ. of Paris in 1913 with the diss. *L'Opéra italien en France avant Lulli* (publ. in Paris, 1913); also wrote a supplementary diss. in 1913, *La Ballet de cour en France avant Benserade et Lully,* publ. in Paris in 1914. From 1909 to 1914, was an instructor at the École des Hautes Études Sociales in Paris; in 1920, founded the important journal *La Revue Musicale,* of which he was ed.-in-chief until 1939; was head of the French section of the ISCM. He was general editor of a complete ed. of Lully's works (10 vols., Paris, 1930–39).

WRITINGS (all publ. in Paris): *Lully* (1910; 2nd ed., 1927); *La Musique de la chambre et de l'écurie* (1912); *La Vie et l'oeuvre de Claudio Monteverdi* (1924; Eng. tr., 1926; 2nd French ed., 1931); *La Vie illustre et libertine de Jean-Baptiste Lully* (1929); *Cavalli et l'opéra vénitien au XVII*[e] *siècle* (1931); *Nouvelle histoire de la musique* (2 vols., 1934, 1936; Eng. tr., 1943).

Pruslin, Stephen (Lawrence), American pianist, writer on music, and composer; b. N.Y., April 16, 1940. He studied at Brandeis Univ. (B.A., 1961) and Princeton Univ. (M.F.A., 1963); also studied piano with Luise Vosgerchian and Steuermann; received a Hertz Memorial Scholarship from the Univ. of Calif. (1964), which enabled him to go to Europe. He settled in London, where he made his recital debut (1970); that same year he became a founding member of the Fires of London with Peter Maxwell Davies, and subsequently appeared with it frequently; also toured widely as a soloist. He became especially known as an interpreter of and a writer on contemporary music; ed. *Peter Maxwell Davies: Studies from Two Decades* (1979); composed scores for the theater, films, and television.

Prüwer, Julius, Austrian conductor; b. Vienna, Feb. 20, 1874; d. N.Y., July 8, 1943. He studied piano with Friedheim and Moriz Rosenthal, and theory with R. Fuchs and Krenn; also profited greatly by his friendly association with Brahms. He studied conducting with Hans Richter. Prüwer began his career as a conductor in Bielitz; then conducted at the Cologne Opera (1894–96) and at the Breslau Opera (1896–1923), where he distinguished himself by conducting numerous new works. From 1924 to 1933 he conducted popular concerts of the Berlin Phil. In 1933 he was compelled to leave Germany owing to the barbarous racial laws of the Nazi regime; he conducted in Russia and in Austria; eventually reached N.Y., where he remained until his death.

Pryor, Arthur (Willard), American trombonist, conductor, and composer; b. St. Joseph, Mo., Sept. 22, 1870; d. Long Branch, N.J., June 18, 1942. He began his professional career in 1889 as a performer on the slide trombone. When Sousa formed his own band in 1892, he hired Pryor as his trombone soloist; from 1895 until he left to form his own band in 1903, Pryor was assistant conductor for Sousa. Pryor's Band gave its first major concert at the Majestic Theatre in N.Y. on Nov. 15, 1903, but beginning in 1904 it initiated series of summer outdoor concerts at Asbury Park, Coney Island, and other amusement parks. From 1903 to 1909 it made 6 coast-to-coast tours. Unlike Sousa, who had little to do with "canned music," Pryor was quick to take advantage of the developing recording industry; he made some 1,000 acoustic recordings before 1930. He also entered upon a series of commercial radio broadcasts. He composed about 300 works, including operettas, ragtime and cakewalk tunes, and novelties such as *The Whistler and His Dog*, Pryor's best-known work. He was a charter member of ASCAP in 1914 and of the American Bandmasters Assn. in 1929. In 1933 he retired to Long Branch.

BIBL.: D. Frizane, *A. P. (1870–1942) American Trombonist, Bandmaster, Composer* (diss., Univ. of Kansas, 1984).

Przybylski, Bronisław Kazimierz, Polish composer and teacher; b. Łódź, Dec. 11, 1941. He was a student of Franciszek Wesolowski (theory diploma, 1964) and Tomasz Kiesewetter (composition diploma, 1969) at the Łódź State College of Music, of Szabelski in Katowice, and of Haubenstock-Ramati at the Vienna Hochschule für Musik (1975–76). From 1964 he taught at the Łódź State College of Music.

WORKS: DRAMATIC: *Miriam*, ballet (1985); *The Strange Adventures of Mr. Hare*, musical fairy tale (1985); *Wawelski Smok*, ballet (1987); *3 Cheers for the Elephant*, musical fairy tale (1989). **ORCH.:** *Quattro studi* (1970); *Suite of Polish Dances* (1971); *In honorem Nicolai Copernici* (1972); *Scherzi musicali* for Strings (1973); *Memento* (1973); *4 Kurpian Nocturnes* for Harp or Guitar and Strings (1973, 1975); *Concerto Polacco* for Accordion and Orch. (1973); *Guernica: Pablo Picasso in memoriam* (1974); 5 syms.: *Sinfonia Polacca* (1974–78), *Sinfonia da Requiem* (1976), *Sinfonia-Corale* (1981), *Sinfonia-Affresco* (1982), and *Jubiläums-Sinfonie* (1983, 1995); *Radogoszca*, funeral music for Chamber Orch. (1975); *Drammatico* (1976); *Animato e Festivo* (1978); *Cottbuser Ouvertüre* (1980); *A Varsovie* (1981); *Program S*, hommage à Karol Szymanowski for Piano and Strings (1982); Concerto for Harpsichord and Strings (1983); *Folklore*, suite for Strings (1983); *Return*, quasi symphonic poem (1984); *Midnight Echoes Music* for Strings (1985); *Concerto Classico* for Accordion and Orch. or Strings (1986); *Scherzi* for Violin and Chamber Orch. (1990; also for Cello and Symphonic Band); *Lacrimosa 2000* for Strings (1991). **CHAMBER:** Wind Quintet (1967); String Quartet, *Quartetto di Tritone* (1969); *La Follia* for Accordion (1974); *The 4 Seasons* for Accordion (1976); *Arnold Schönberg in memoriam* for String Quartet (1977); *The Royal Tournament* for Wind Quintet (1977); *Asteroedides I–V* for Accordion Quintet (1978); *Quasi un sonata* for Violin and Piano (1980); 3 accordion sonatinas (1983); *Metamorphosen* for Accordion and String Quartet (1985); Trio for Violin, Cello, and Accordion (1986); *Modal Piece I–II* for Accordion Quintet (1986); *Bimodal Piece* for 2 Accordion Quintets (1986); *Musica concertante* for Organ and Percussion (1986); *Folklore II* for Guitar and Harpsichord (1986); *Double Play* for 2 Accordions (1987); *A.B. Sonata* for Accordion (1988); *Night Music* for Flute, Guitar, and Accordion (1988); *Spring Sonata* for Accordion (1989); *Concerto della morte e della vita* for Chamber Group (1991); *Scherzo-Trio* for Violin, Cello, and Piano (1992); *Autumn Multiplay* for 6 Instruments (1994); *A Sleeping Bear* for Accordion (1995); *A Porcelain Dancer* for Accordion (1995). **VOCAL:** *A Tale of the Life and Death of Karol Walter-Swierczewskiego*, cantata for Tenor, Bass, Reciter, and Men's Chorus or Mixed Chorus and Orch. (1969); *Midnight*, monodrama for Actor and Chamber Ensemble (1973); *Voices* for 3 Actors and Chamber Ensemble (1974); *Requiem* for Soprano, 2 Reciters, Boy's Chorus, and Orch. (1976); *Jagsagen* for Speaker and Brass Quintet (1978); *Mazowsze* for Reciter, 4 Optional Melodic Instruments, and Percussion (1979); *The City of Hope*, cantata for Bass, Chorus, and 2 Orchs. (1979); *In Memoriam*, 4 songs for Voice and Chamber Ensemble (1982); *Portrait of a Lady* for Voices and Chamber Ensemble (1982); *Basnie*, fairy tales for Voices and Chamber Ensemble (1982); choruses; solo songs.

Ptaszyńska, Marta, Polish composer and percussionist; b. Warsaw, July 29, 1943. She studied piano and timpani at the Music Lyceum in Warsaw (1957–62); then took courses in composition with Dobrowolski and Rudziński at the Warsaw Cons. (1962–68), and worked out problems of electronic music with Kotoński in his studio; had supplementary practice in percussion at the Poznań Cons. (1963–67); in 1969 she traveled to Paris, where she had lessons with Boulanger. In 1972 she received a grant from the Kosciuszko Foundation to travel to the U.S., and studied percussion at the Cleveland Inst. of Music (until 1974). From 1974 to 1977 she taught percussion at Bennington (Vt.) College; in 1977, became an instructor in composition at the Univ. of Calif., Berkeley. She played with the "Percussions de Strasbourg"; was a composer and percussionist at the Claremont Music Festival in California. Her music is entirely free of any strictures, whether academically traditional or fashionably modern. Being a virtuoso drummer, she naturally gives a prominent place to percussion in her scores; she also makes use of stereophony by spatial separation of players or groups of instruments.

WORKS: DRAMATIC: *Oscar from Alva*, television opera (1972); *Helio, centricum, musicum*, multimedia spectacle for Voices, Dancers, and Instrumentalists (1973). **ORCH.:** *Improvisations* (1968; Kraków, March 26, 1971); *Spectri sonori* (1973; Cleveland, Jan. 22, 1974); *Crystallites* (1973; Bydgoszcz, Jan. 24, 1975); Concerto for Percussion Quartet and Orch. (Bennington, Vt., Oct. 20, 1974); *Chimes, Bells, Wood, Stones* for Wind and String Instruments and Percussion (Bennington, Vt., June 9, 1977); *Conductus*, ceremonial for Symphonic Wind Ensemble (1982); *La Novella d'inverno* for Strings (1984); Marimba Concerto (1985). **CHAMBER:** *Preludes* for Vibraphone and Piano (1965); *Scherzo* for Xylophone and Piano (1967); *Recitative, Arioso, Toccata* for Violin (1969–75); *Projections sonores* for Chamber Ensemble (1970); *Madrigals*, in memory of Stravinsky, for Wind Instruments, String Quartet, Trumpet, Trombone, and Gong (1971); *Sonospheres No. 1* for Clarinet, Trombone, Cello, and Piano (1971), *No. 2* for 8 Instruments (1971), and *No. 3* for Flute, Clarinet, Trombone, Cello, Piano, and Percussion (1972); *Siderals* for 2 Percussion Quintets and Light Projections (Urbana, Nov. 21, 1974); *Ornaments in Wood* for Flute, Clarinet, Bass Clarinet, and Bassoon (1975); *Classical Variations* for 4 Timpani and String Quartet (1976); *Linear Constructions in Space* for Percussion Quartet (1977); *Soirée snobe chez la Princesse*, instrumental theater (1979); *Dream Lands, Magic Spaces* for Violin, Piano, and Percussion (1979); *Moon Flowers* for Cello and Piano (1986); piano pieces; percussion music for children. **VOCAL:** *A Tale of Nightingales* for Baritone and 6 Instruments (1968); *Chant for All the People on Earth*, oratorio (1969); *Epigrams* for 20 Women's Voices, Flute, Harp, Piano, and Percussion (1976–77); *Un Grand Sommeil noir* for Soprano,

Flute, and Harp, after Verlaine (1977); *Ave Maria* for 4 Men's Voices, Brass, Percussion, and Organ (1982; also for Men's Chorus and Orch., 1987).

Puccini, Giacomo (Antonio Domenico Michele Secondo Maria), celebrated Italian composer; b. Lucca, Dec. 22, 1858; d. Brussels, Nov. 29, 1924. He was the 5th of 7 children of Michele Puccini, the Italian teacher and composer (b. Lucca, Nov. 27, 1813; d. there, Jan. 23, 1864), who died when Giacomo was only 5; his musical training was thus entrusted to his uncle, Fortunato Magi, a pupil of his father; however, Giacomo showed neither inclination nor talent for music. His mother, determined to continue the family tradition, sent him to the local Istituo Musicale Pacini, where Carlo Angeloni — its director, who had also studied with Michele Puccini — became his teacher. After Angeloni's untiring patience had aroused interest, and then enthusiasm in his pupil, progress was rapid and he soon became a proficient pianist and organist. He began serving as a church organist in Lucca and environs when he was 14, and began composing when he was 17. After hearing *Aida* in Pisa in 1876, he resolved to win laurels as a dramatic composer. Having written mainly sacred music, it was self-evident that he needed further training after graduation from the Istituto (1880). With financial support from his granduncle, Dr. Nicolao Cer, and a stipend from Queen Margherita, he pursued studies with Antonio Bazzini and Amilcare Ponchielli at the Milan Cons. (1880–83). For his graduation, he wrote a *Capriccio sinfonico*, which was conducted by Faccio at a Cons. concert, eliciting unstinting praise from the critics. In the same year, Ponchielli introduced Puccini to the librettist Fontana, who furnished him the text of a 1-act opera; in a few weeks the score was finished and sent to the Zonzongo competition. It did not win the prize, but on May 31, 1884, *Le villi* was produced at the Teatro dal Verme in Milan, with gratifying success. Ricordi, who was present, considered the work sufficiently meritorious to commission the young composer to write a new opera for him; but 5 years elapsed before this work, *Edgar* (3 acts; text by Fontana), was produced at La Scala in Milan (April 21, 1889), scoring only a moderate success. By this time Puccini had become convinced that, in order to write a really effective opera, he needed a better libretto than Fontana had provided. Accordingly, he commissioned Domenico Oliva to write the text of *Manon Lescaut*; during the composition, however, Puccini and Ricordi practically rewrote the entire book, and in the publ. score Oliva's name is not mentioned. With *Manon Lescaut* (4 acts), first produced at the Teatro Regio in Turin on Feb. 1, 1893, Puccini won a veritable triumph, which was even surpassed by his next work, *La Bohème* (4 acts; text by Illica and Giacosa), produced at the same theater on Feb. 1, 1896. These 2 works not only carried their composer's name throughout the world, but also have found and maintained their place in the repertoire of every house. With fame came wealth, and in 1900 Puccini built at Torre del Lago, where he had been living since 1891, a magnificent villa. His next opera, *Tosca* (3 acts; text by Illica and Giacosa), produced at the Teatro Costanzi in Rome on Jan. 14, 1900, is Puccini's most dramatic work; it has become a fixture of the standard repertoire, and contains some of his best-known arias. At its premiere at La Scala on Feb. 17, 1904, *Madama Butterfly* (2 acts; text by Illica and Giacosa) was hissed. Puccini thereupon withdrew the score and made some slight changes (division into 3 acts, and addition of the tenor aria in the last scene). This revised version was greeted with frenzied applause in Brescia on May 28 of the same year. Puccini was now the acknowledged ruler of Verdi in the number of performances. The first performance of *Madame Butterfly* at the Metropolitan Opera in N.Y. (Feb. 11, 1907) took place in the presence of the composer, whom the management had invited especially for the occasion. It was then suggested that he write an opera on an American subject, the premiere to take place at the Metropolitan. He found his subject when he witnessed a performance of Belasco's *The Girl of the Golden West*; he commissioned C. Zangarini and G. Civinini to write the libretto, and in the presence of the composer the world premiere of *La Fanciulla del West* occurred, amid much enthusiasm, at the Metropolitan on Dec. 10, 1910; while it never equalled the success of his *Tosca* or *Madama Butterfly*, it returned to favor in the 1970s as a period piece. Puccini then brought out *La Rondine* (3 acts; Monte Carlo, March 27, 1917) and the 3 1-act operas *Il Tabarro* (after Didier Gold's *La Houppelande*), *Suor Angelica*, and *Gianni Schicchi* (all 1st perf. at the Metropolitan Opera, Dec. 14, 1918). His last opera, *Turandot* (after Gozzi), was left unfinished; the final scene was completed by Franco Alfano and performed at La Scala on April 25, 1926.

BIBL.: A. Brüggemann, *Madama Butterfly e l'arte di G. P.* (Milan, 1904); W. Dry, *G. P.* (London, 1906); F. Torrefranca, *G. P. e l'opera internazionale* (Turin, 1912); D. Parker, "A View of G. P.," *Musical Quarterly* (Oct. 1917); A. Weismann, *G. P.* (Munich, 1922); A. Bonaventura, *G. P.: L'Uomo, l'artista* (Livorno, 1924); A. Coeuroy, *La Tosca* (Paris, 1924); A. Fraccaroli, *La vita di G. P.* (Milan, 1925; also in Ger.); G. Marotti and F. Pagni, *G. P. intimo* (Florence, 1926); G. Adami, *Epistolario di G. P.* (Milan, 1928; Eng. tr., London, 1931); G. Gatti, "The Works of P.," *Musical Quarterly* (Jan. 1928); A. Neisser, *P.* (Leipzig, 1928); F. Salerno, *Le Donne pucciniane* (Palermo, 1928); R. Merlin, *P.* (Milan, 1930); R. Specht, *P.* (Berlin, 1931; Eng. tr., N.Y., 1933); W. Maisch, *P.s musikalische Formgebung* (Neustadt, 1934); G. Adami, *P.* (Milan, 1935; Ger. tr., 1943); M. Carner, "The Exotic Element in P.," *Musical Quarterly* (Jan. 1936); K. Fellerer, *G. P.* (Potsdam, 1937); V. Seligman, *P. among Friends* (correspondence; N.Y., 1938); F. Thiess, *P., Versuch einer Psychologie seiner Musik* (Berlin, 1950); G. Marek, *P.: A Biography* (N.Y., 1951); D. del Fiorentino, *Immortal Bohemian: An Intimate Memoir of G. P.* (N.Y., 1952); A. Machard, *Une Vie d'amour: P.* (Paris, 1954); L. Ricci, *P. interprete di se stesso* (Milan, 1954); V. Terenzio, *Ritratto di P.* (Bergamo, 1954); M. Carner, *P.* (London, 1958; 3rd ed., rev., 1992); E. Greenfield, *P.: Keeper of the Seal* (London, 1958); C. Sartori, *P.* (Milan, 1958); C. Paladini, *G. P.* (Flornece, 1961); C. Hopkinson, *A Bibliography of the Works of G. P.* (1974); W. Ashbrook, *The Operas of P.* (N.Y., 1968; 2nd ed., rev., 1985); D. Amy, *G. P.* (Paris, 1970); A. Monnosi, *P. a tu per tu* (Pisa, 1970); G. Tarozzi, *P.: La fine del bel canto* (Milan, 1972); N. Galli, *P. e la sua terra* (Lucca, 1974); G. Magri, *P. e le sue rime* (Milan, 1974); I. Lombardi, *P., ancora da scoprire* (Lucca, 1976); E. Siciliani, *P.* (Milan, 1976); W. Weaver, *P.: The Man and His Music* (N.Y., 1977); C. Casini, *G. P.* (Turin, 1978); L. Pinzauti, *P.* (Milan, 1978); H. Greenfield, *P.* (N.Y., 1980); C. Osborne, *The Complete Operas of P.* (London, 1981); M. Courtin, *Tosca de G. P.* (Paris, 1983); A. Bottero, *Le Donne di P.* (Lucca, 1984); M. Carner, *Tosca* (Cambridge, 1985); E. Krause, *P.* (Leipzig, 1985); D. Martino, *Metamorfosi del femminino nei libretti per P.* (Turin, 1985); A. Groos and R. Parker, *G. P.: "La Bohème"* (Cambridge, 1986); J. DiGaetani, *P., the Thinker: The Composer's Intellectual and Dramatic Development* (Bern and N.Y., 1987); M. Kaye, *The Unknown P.: A Historical Perspective on the Songs, including Little-Known Music from "Edgar" and "La Rondine," with Complete Music for Violin and Piano* (Oxford, 1987); G. Musco, *Musica e teatro in G. P.* (vol. I, Cortona, 1989); K. Berg, *G. P.s Opern: Music und Dramaturgie* (Kassel, 1991); R. Giazotto, *P. in Casa P.* (Lucca, 1992); G. Magri, *L'uomo P.* (Milan, 1992); P. Korfmacher, *Exotismus in G. P.s Turandot* (Cologne, 1993); W. Volpers, *G. P.s "Turandot:" Untersuchungen zum Text und zur musikalischen Dramaturgie* (Laaber, 1994); W. Weaver and S. Puccini, eds., *The P. Companion* (N.Y., 1994).

Pugliese, Michael (Gabriel), American percussionist and composer; b. Buffalo, N.Y., Sept. 26, 1956. He studied with Jan Williams at the State Univ. of N.Y. at Buffalo (B.F.A., 1979) and at the Manhattan School of Music (M.M., 1981), then pursued a career as an avant-garde percussionist. In 1982 he produced a 12-hour marathon of the music of John Cage at Cooper Union in N.Y.; also gave premiere performances of Cage's *Etudes Boreales*, *Ryoanji*, and *Three²*, and received their dedications. He was a core member of the Bowery Ensemble and the New

Music Consort, and founder of the Talking Drums, an experimental percussion trio. In 1985 he joined the Merce Cunningham Dance Co., with which he subsequently toured throughout the U.S., South America, Europe, and Asia. His compositions for Cunningham are *Peace Talks* (Berkeley, Calif., Sept. 22, 1989) for a Variety of Ethnic Percussion Instruments and Sitar, inspired by the concept of global union of socially and politically troubled nations, *Mixed Signals* for Four Marimbulas and Tape (Paris, 1991), and *Ice Breeze* for Frame Drums, Waterphones, and Chant (London, 1992). Other compositions include *June 22, 1978* for Percussion Quintet, 2 Narrators, and Tape (1978), *Not Jinxed* for 4 Marimbas, 4 Berimbaus, and Digital Delay (1991), *Traditions I* and *II* for Rocks, Glass, Metal, and MOOG Synthesizer (1995), and *Sound Scripts I* and *II* for Bottle Caps and Electronics (1995). Pugliese also appeared as a rock drummer, and made numerous rock arrangements, including one of Henry Mancini's *Peter Gunn* for Percussion Quartet.

Puig-Roget, Henriette, French organist, pianist, teacher, and composer; b. Bastia, Jan 9, 1910; d. Paris, Nov. 24, 1992. She studied with Philipp (piano), Dupré (organ), J. Gallon (harmony), Tournemire (chamber music), Emmanuel (music history), and Büsser (composition) at the Paris Cons., winning premiers prix in 1926 and 1930. In 1933 she won the Premier 2nd Prix de Rome. From 1934 to 1979 she was organist at l'Oratoire du Louvre in Paris. She also purused an active career as a pianist until 1975. She was "chef de chant" at the Paris Opéra (1937–40; 1946–57) and then was prof. of piano accompaniment and score reading at the Paris Cons. (1957–79). She wrote many piano books for children.

WORKS: BALLET: *Cathérinettes* (1937). **ORCH.:** *Montanyas del Rosello* for Organ and Orch. (Paris, April 6, 1933, composer soloist); *3 ballades françaises* (1935; Paris, Jan. 11, 1936); *Sinfonia andorrana* (1936); *Rythmes* (1936; Paris, Jan. 23, 1937); *Concerto sicilien* for Piano and Orch. (1943); *Concerto classique* for Cello and Orch. (1944); *Symphonie pour rire* (1947). **OTHER:** Organ pieces.

Putnam, Ashley (Elizabeth), American soprano; b. N.Y., Aug. 10, 1952. She studied flute at the Univ. of Mich., eventually turning to voice (B.M., 1974; M.M., 1975). After graduating, she was an apprentice with the Santa Fe Opera Co. In 1976 she made her operatic debut in the title role of Donizetti's *Lucia di Lammermoor* with the Virginia Opera Assn. in Norfolk. After winning 1st prize in the Metropolitan Opera Auditions and receiving the Weyerhauser Award (1976), she made her European debut as Musetta in Puccini's *La Bohème* at the Glyndebourne Festival (1978). On Sept. 15, 1978, she won accolades as Violetta in her N.Y. City Opera debut. In 1986 she made her first appearance at London's Covent Garden as Jenůfa. She sang Donna Elvira at her Metropolitan Opera debut in N.Y. in 1990. As a concert artist, she appeared with leading U.S. and European orchs., and also gave recitals.

Puyana, Rafael, Colombian harpsichordist; b. Bogotá, Oct. 14, 1931. He studied piano at the New England Cons. of Music in Boston, and harpsichord with Wanda Landowska in N.Y.; also had general music training at the Hartt College of Music in Hartford, Conn. He made a tour of Europe (1955); made his first appearances in N.Y. (1957) and London (1966); thereafter toured worldwide. His extensive repertory ranges from early music to contemporary scores.

Pylkkänen, Tauno Kullervo, Finnish composer; b. Helsinki, March 22, 1918; d. there, March 13, 1980. He studied composition with Palmgren, Madetoja, and Ranta at the Helsinki Academy of Music (1937–40); also studied musicology at the Univ. of Helsinki (M.A., 1941). He worked at the Finnish Broadcasting Co. (1942–61) and was artistic director of the Finnish National Opera (1960–70); lectured on opera history at the Sibelius Academy (from 1967). He was primarily an opera composer; his idiom was basically Romantic, with sporadic excursions into modernity.

WORKS: DRAMATIC: OPERAS: *Bathsheba Saarenmaalla* (Bathsheba at Saarenmaa; 1940; rev. 1958); *Mare ja hanen poikansa* (Mare and Her Son; 1943); *Simo Hurtta* (1948); *Sudenmorsian* (The Wolf's Bride), radio opera (1950); *Varjo* (The Shadow; 1952); *Ikaros* (1956–60); *Opri and Oleksi* (1957); *Vangit* (The Prisoners; 1964); *Tuntematon sotilas* (The Unknown Soldier; 1967). **BALLET:** *Kaarina Maununtytar* (Kaarina, Maunu's Daughter; 1960). **ORCH.:** *Introduction and Fugue* (1940); *Lapin kesa* (Summer in Lapland; 1941); *Kullervon sotaanlahto* (Kullervo Leaves for War; 1942); Sinfonietta (1944); Sym. No. 1 (1945); *Suite* for Oboe and Strings (1946); *Marathon*, overture (1947); *Symphonic Fantasy* (1948); *Ultima Thule* (1949); Cello Concerto (1950); *Symphonic Prelude* (1952). **CHAMBER:** *Notturno* for Violin and Piano (1943); String Quartet (1945); *Fantasia appassionata* for Cello and Piano (1954); *Trittico* for Clarinet, Violin, Viola, and Cello (1978). **VOCAL:** Cantatas; songs.

Quadri, Argeo, Italian conductor; b. Como, March 23, 1911. He studied piano, composition, and conducting at the Milan Cons. (graduated, 1933); then conducted opera throughout Italy. In 1956 he became a conductor at Covent Garden in London; was a regular conductor at the Vienna State Opera (1957–75).

Quaile, Elizabeth, Irish-American piano pedagogue; b. Omagh, Jan. 20, 1874; d. South Kent, Conn., June 30, 1951. She went to N.Y. and studied with Franklin Robinson; then devoted herself to teaching. From 1916 to 1919 she was head of the piano dept. of the David Mannes School; then went to Paris, where she studied piano with Harold Bauer. Returning to N.Y. in 1921, she founded, with Angela Diller, the Diller-Quaile School of Music. She publ. a number of highly successful piano teaching methods, some written by her alone (*First Book of Technical Exercises, A Pre-Czerny Book*, etc.), and some in collaboration with Diller. The books proved to be standard guides for piano students for many years.

Queffélec, Anne (Tita), French pianist; b. Paris, Jan. 17, 1948. She was the daughter of Henri and sister of Yann Queffélec, both noted writers. She received her initial training at the Paris Cons. with Lélia Gousseau (premier prix in piano, 1965) and Jean Hubeau (premier prix in chamber music performance, 1966); subsequently pursued studies with Brendel, Demus, and Badura-Skoda in Vienna. After capturing 1st prize at the Munich International Competition in 1968 and 5th prize at the Leeds International Competition in 1969, she toured widely at home and abroad; was a soloist with major orchs. of the world, and also was active as a recitalist and chamber music player. In addition to the French repertoire, she became particularly known for her performances of works by Mozart and Scarlatti.

Queler, Eve (née **Rabin**), American conductor; b. N.Y., Jan. 1, 1936. She studied in N.Y. with Bamberger at the Mannes College of Music, and took courses at the Hebrew Union School of Education and Sacred Music; after studying with Rosenstock on a Martha Baird Rockefeller Fund grant, she continued her training with Susskind and Slatkin in St. Louis and with Markevitch and Blomstedt in Europe. She made her conducting debut with *Cavalleria rusticana* in Fairlawn, N.J. (1966); then devoted herself mainly to conducting operas in concert with her own Opera Orch. of N.Y. (from 1967); led performances of rarely heard operas on both sides of the Atlantic, and also gave the U.S. premieres of many works, ranging from Donizetti to Richard Strauss. She also appeared as a guest conductor with several North American orchs. Queler was the first American woman to conduct such esteemed ensembles as the Philadelphia Orch., the Cleveland Orch., and the Montreal Sym. Orch.

Querol (Gavaldá), Miguel, Spanish musicologist and composer; b. Ulldecona, Tarragona, April 22, 1912. He studied music at the Benedictine Monastery of Monserrat (1926–36) and later in Barcelona with Juan Lamote de Grignon; continued his training at the univs. of Saragossa (1943), Barcelona (1944–45), and Madrid (Ph.D., 1948, with the diss. *La escuela estética catalana contemporánea*; publ. in Madrid, 1953). He was prof. of musicology at the Univ. of Barcelona (1957–70). He publ. *La música en las obras de Cervantes* (Barcelona, 1948) and *Breve historia de la música* (Madrid, 1955). Among his compositions are sacred music, chamber pieces, and piano works.

Quilico, Gino, Canadian baritone, son of **Louis Quilico**; b. N.Y., April 29, 1955. He received training from his parents, and then from James Craig and Constance Fischer at the Univ. of Toronto Opera Dept. On June 8, 1977, he made his operatic debut as Mr. Gobineau in *The Medium* with the COMUS Music Theatre in Toronto. In 1978 he sang Papageno in Milwaukee. He first appeared with the Canadian Opera Co. in 1979 singing Escamillo. Following additional studies at the École d'art lyrique of the Paris Opéra (1979–80), he made his debut with the company in Damase's *L'Héritière* in 1980 and sang with it for 3 seasons. In 1982 he made his British debut with the Scottish Opera at the Edinburgh Festival. He made his first appearance at London's Covent Garden as Gounod's Valentin in 1983. That same year he sang Massenet's Lescaut at his debut with the Opéra de Montréal, a role he also chose for his Metropolitan Opera debut in N.Y. in 1987. In 1988 he appeared as Dandini at the Salzburg Festival. He sang Riccardo in *I Puritani* in Rome in 1990. In 1991 he appeared in Corigliano's *The Ghosts of Versailles* at the Metropolitan Opera. Among his other roles are Monteverdi's Orfeo, Don Giovanni, Dr. Malatesta, and Posa.

BIBL.: R. Mercer, *The Q.s: Louis, G. & Lina: An Operatic Family* (Oakville, Ontario, 1991).

Quilico, Louis, notable Canadian baritone and teacher of Italian and French-Canadian descent, father of **Gino Quilico**; b. Montreal, Jan. 14, 1925. He was a solo chorister in the St.-Jacques Church Choir in Montreal and began his vocal studies with Frank Rowe. After training with Teresa Pediconi and Riccardo Stracciani at the Cons. de Santa Cecilia in Rome (1947–48), he returned to Montreal to study at the Cons. (1948–52) with Lina Pizzolongo (b. Montreal, Jan. 25, 1925; d. Toronto, Sept. 21, 1991), who became his wife in 1949, and with Singher. He completed his training at the Mannes College of Music in N.Y. (1952–55) with Singher and Emil Cooper. In 1954 he made his professional operatic stage debut with the Opera Guild of Montreal as Rangoni. In 1955 he won the Metropolitan Opera Auditions of the Air, but made his U.S. debut with the N.Y. City Opera on Oct. 10, 1955, as Germont. He made his European debut at the Spoleto Festival as Donizetti's Duca d'Alba in 1959. In 1960 he made his first appearance at London's Covent Garden as Germont, and sang there until 1963. In 1962 he sang for the first time at Moscow's Bolshoi Theater as Rigoletto. He made his debut at the Paris Opéra as Verdi's Rodrigo in 1963. In subsequent seasons, he sang regularly in Europe and with the Canadian Opera Co. On Feb. 10, 1972, Quilico made his Metropolitan Opera debut in N.Y. as Golaud, and thereafter sang there regularly. In 1991 he revealed a lighter touch when he sang Tony in *The Most Happy Fella* at the N.Y. City Opera. That same year he appeared as Rigoletto at the Opéra de Montréal, a role he essayed over 500 times. From 1970 to 1987 he taught at the Univ. of Toronto, and from 1987 to 1990 at the McGill Cons. in Montreal. In 1965 he received the Prix de musique Calixa-Lavallee and in 1974 he was made a Commander of the Order of Canada.

BIBL.: R. Mercer, *The Q.s: L., Gino & Lina: An Operatic Family* (Oakville, Ontario, 1991).

Quilter, Roger, English composer; b. Brighton, Nov. 1, 1877; d. London, Sept. 21, 1953. He received his primary education at Eton College; then studied with Iwan Knorr at the Hoch Cons. in Frankfurt am Main. He was particularly noted for his fine settings of Shakespeare's poems.

WORKS: *As You Like It,* incidental music to Shakespeare's play (1922); *Julia,* light opera (London, Dec. 3, 1936); *The Sailor and His Lass* for Soprano, Baritone, Chorus, and Orch. (1948); numerous song cycles.

BIBL.: T. Hold, *The Walled-in Garden: A Study of the Songs of R. Q.* (Rickmansworth, 1978); M. Pilkington, *Gurney, Ireland, Q. and Warlock* (London, 1989).

Quinet, Fernand, Belgian cellist, teacher, conductor, and composer; b. Charleroi, Jan. 29, 1898; d. Liège, Oct. 24, 1971. After training in theory in Charleroi, he studied with Edouard Jacobs (cello) and Léon Dubois (composition) at the Brussels Cons. (1913–15) before completing his training with d'Indy in Paris. In 1921 he won the Belgian Prix de Rome with his cantata *La guerre.* He played in the Pro Arte Quartet (1916–32), was director of the Charleroi Cons. (1924–38), and was prof. of harmony at the Brussels Cons. (1927–38). From 1938 to 1963 he was director of the Liège Cons. In 1948 he founded the Liège Sym. Orch., which he served as music director until 1965.

WORKS: ORCH.: *3 Symphonic Movements* (London, July 28, 1931). **CHAMBER:** Violin Sonata (1923); *Charade* for Piano Trio (1927); Viola Sonata (1928); *L'École buissoniere* for String Quartet (1930); Suite for 3 Clarinets (1930). **VOCAL:** Cantatas, including *La guerre* (1921); *Moralités-non-légendaires* for Voice and 18 Instruments (1930); songs.

Quinet, Marcel, Belgian composer and teacher; b. Binche, July 6, 1915; d. Woluwé-St. Lambert, Brussels, Dec. 16, 1986. He studied at the conservatories of Mons and Brussels with Leon Jongen, Raymond Moulaert, and Marcel Maas (1934–43); also took private composition lessons with Jean Absil (1940–45). In 1945 he won the Belgian Grand Prix de Rome with his cantata *La Vague et le Sillon.* He was on the staff of the Brussels Cons. (1943–79) and also taught at the Chapelle Musicale Reine Elisabeth (1956–59; 1968–71; 1973–74). In 1978 he was made a member of the Academie Royale de Belgique. His music is moderately modernistic in the amiable manner of the French school, with some euphoniously dissonant excrescences.

WORKS: DRAMATIC: *Les 2 Bavards,* chamber opera (1966); *La Nef des fous,* ballet (1969). **ORCH.:** *3 esquisses concertantes* for Violin and Orch. (1946); *Divertissement* (1946); *3 pièces* (1951; Salzburg, June 21, 1952); *Sinfonietta* (1953); *Variations élégiaques sur un thème de Rolland de Lassus* (1955); 3 piano concertos (1955, 1964, 1966); Variations (1956); *Serenade* for Strings (1956); *Impressions symphoniques* (1956); *Allegro de concert* (1958); *Divertimento* for Chamber Orch. (1958); *Concertino* for Flute, Celesta, Harp, and Strings (1959); Sym. (1960); *Concertino* for Oboe, Clarinet, Bassoon, and String Orch. (1960); *Ballade* for Clarinet and Strings (1961); Viola Concerto (1962–63); *Concerto grosso* for 4 Clarinets and Strings (1964); *Overture for a Festival* (1967); *Music* for Strings and Timpani (1971); *Mouvements* for Chamber Orch. (1973); *Esquisses symphoniques* (1973); *Gorgone* (1974); *Séquence* (1974); *Dialogues* for 2 Pianos and Orch. (1975); *Diptyque* for Chamber Orch. (1975); *Climats* for Chamber Orch. (1978); *Caractères* (1978; rev. 1983); *Métamorphoses* (1979); *Préludes* (1979); *Chromatismes* (1980); Concerto for Kettle Drums and Orch. (1981); *Concerto grosso* for 4 Saxophones and Orch. (1982); Concerto for 2 Pianos and Orch. (1983). **CHAMBER:** *8 petites pièces* for Wind Quintet (1946); 2 string trios (1948, 1969); Wind Quintet (1949); Violin Sonatina (1952); Piano Quartet (1957); String Quartet (1958); *Petite Suite* for 4 Clarinets (1959); *Sonate a 3* for Trumpet, Horn, and Trombone (1961); *Ballade* for Violin and Wind Quintet (1962); Wind Quartet (1964); Sonata for 2 Violins and Piano (1964); *Ballatella* for Trumpet or Horn or Trombone and Piano (1966); *Pochades* for 4 Saxophones (1967); Trio for Oboe, Clarinet, and Bassoon (1967); Flute Sonata (1968); *Polyphonies* for 3 Performers on 8 Wind Instruments (1971); *Novelettes* for 2 Pianos (1973); *Sept tankas* for Double or Triple Vocal Quartet and Piano (1978); *Terzetto* for Flute, Violin, and Harpsichord (1981); *Ébauches* for Saxophone Quartet (1984); solo piano pieces. **VOCAL:** 2 cantatas: *La Vague et le Sillon* (1945) and *Lectio pro Feria Sexta* (1973); *Hommage à Ravel* for Woman's Voice, Piano, Flute, and Cello (1985); songs.

Quintanar, Héctor, Mexican composer; b. Mexico City, April 15, 1936. He had lessons in music theory with Chávez, Halffter, and Galindo at the National Cons. in Mexico City (1959–64); also worked on problems of electronic music in N.Y. (1964), Paris (1967), and Mexico City (1968). Upon his return to Mexico, he supervised the construction of the country's first electronic music studio at the National Univ. (1970). He composed orch. works, chamber music, and vocal pieces, some of which utilized electronics.

Quiroga, Manuel, Spanish violinist and composer; b. Pontevedra, April 15, 1890; d. there, April 19, 1961. He studied at the Royal Cons. in Madrid and at the Paris Cons. He toured in Europe and in the U.S. with great success. After suffering a street accident in N.Y. in 1937 during one of his American tours, he was compelled to abandon public appearances; he then retired to Pontevedra. He composed some violin pieces and a "sainete," *Los amos del barrio* (Madrid, Sept. 7, 1938).

Quivar, Florence, black American mezzo-soprano; b. Philadelphia, March 3, 1944. She studied at the Philadelphia Musical

Academy, the Salzburg Mozarteum, and with Luigi Ricci in Rome. She was a member of the Juilliard Opera Theater in N.Y.; subsequently launched a successful concert career, appearing as soloist with the N.Y. Phil., the Cleveland Orch., the Philadelphia Orch., the Chicago Sym. Orch., and the Boston Sym. Orch. She made her Metropolitan Opera debut in N.Y. as Marina in *Boris Godunov* on Oct. 10, 1977; then sang there regularly, appearing in such roles as Jocasta in *Oedipus Rex*, Isabella in *L'Italiana in Algeri*, Fides in *Le Prophète*, Eboli in *Don Carlos*, Marfa in *Khovanshchina*, and Serena in *Porgy and Bess*. In 1983 she made her first appearance at the Salzburg Festival as a soloist in Mahler's 3rd Sym. with Mehta and the Israel Phil. She made her first operatic appearance there in 1989 as Ulrike. In 1991 she was a soloist in the *Gurrelieder* at the Promenade Concerts in London.

Raabe, Peter, German conductor and writer on music; b. Frankfurt an der Oder, Nov. 27, 1872; d. Weimar, April 12, 1945. He studied with Bargiel at the Berlin Hochschule für Musik and later continued his training at the Univ. of Jena (Ph.D., 1916). In 1894 he began a career as a theater conductor; from 1899 to 1903 he conducted the Netherlands Opera in Amsterdam, and from 1903 to 1907, the Volks-Symphonie-Konzerte in Munich; in 1907 he became court conductor in Weimar; in 1910 he was appointed curator of the Liszt Museum in Weimar; from 1920 to 1934 he was Generalmusikdirektor in Aachen. In 1935 he became head of the Reichsmusikkammer and the Deutscher Tonkünstlerverein; in these offices he was called upon to perform administrative tasks for the Nazi regime, including the racial restrictions of musicians. His co-workers presented him with *Von deutscher Tonkünst: Festschrift zu Peter Raabes 70. Geburtstag* (Leipzig, 1942; 2nd ed., rev., 1944). Raabe died just before the total collapse of the 3rd Reich, which he tried to serve so well. He left some scholarly and valuable writings, among them: *Grossherzog Carl Alexander und Liszt* (Leipzig, 1918); *Franz Liszt: Leben und Schaffen* (2 vols., Stuttgart, 1931; rev. ed. 1968 by his son Felix); *Die Musik im dritten Reich* (Regensburg, 1935); *Kulturwille im deutschen Musikleben* (Regensburg, 1936); *Deutsche Meister* (Berlin, 1937); *Wege zu Weber* (Regensburg, 1942); *Wege zu Liszt* (Regensburg, 1943); *Wege zu Bruckner* (Regensburg, 1944).

Raalte, Albert van, Dutch conductor; b. Amsterdam, May 21, 1890; d. there, Nov. 23, 1952. He studied at the Cologne Cons. with Bram Eldering (violin) and Baussnern (theory); later in Leipzig with Nikisch and Reger. He was a theater conductor in Brussels (1911) and Leipzig (1912; 1914–15), then at the Dutch National Opera in The Hague; formed his own opera enterprise there. He remained in the Netherlands during the German occupation; conducted the radio orch. at Hilversum; was sent to a concentration camp as a person with Jewish associations; after the liberation in 1945, he returned to his post at Hilversum, building the radio orch. to a high degree of efficiency.

Raasted, Niels Otto, Danish organist, conductor, and composer; b. Copenhagen, Nov. 26, 1888; d. there, Dec. 31, 1966. He studied at the Copenhagen Cons. (1909–12); then at the Leipzig Cons. with Reger, Straube, and Teichmüller (1913–14); returning to Denmark, he became organist at Copenhagen Cathedral; also conducted the Bach Soc. (1925–46).

WORKS: ORCH.: 3 syms. (1914, 1938, 1944); orch. suites, among them *Pictures from Finland* (1928) and *Hans Christian Andersen Suite* (1940); *Sinfonia da chiesa* (1944). **CHAMBER:** 3 string quartets (1914, 1918, 1920); 5 violin sonatas; 6 organ sonatas. **VOCAL:** *Saul,* oratorio (1923); 3 cantatas (all perf. on Copenhagen Radio): *Sangen om København* (June 27, 1934), *Thylands pris* (May 12, 1941), and *Kong Vaar* (Oct. 20, 1947).

Raäts, Jaan, Estonian composer; b. Tartu, Oct. 15, 1932. He studied with Saar (1952–54) and Eller (1954–57) at the Tallinn Cons. He was director of the music division of the Estonian Radio (1955–66); then served as music director of Estonian TV. His music possesses firm thematic lines animated by a motoric pulse.

WORKS: ORCH.: 8 syms. (1957, 1958, 1959, 1959, 1966, 1967, 1973, 1985); Concerto for Chamber Orch. (1961); 2 concertos for Violin and Chamber Orch. (1963, 1979); 2 piano concertos (1971, 1983); Concerto for 2 Pianos and Orch. (1986). **CHAMBER:** 5 string quartets; 4 piano trios; 3 piano quintets; Piano Sextet; various piano pieces, including 8 sonatas. **VOCAL:** *Karl Marx,* "declamatorio" for Narrator, Chorus, and Orch. (Tallinn, June 6, 1964).

Rabaud, Henri (Benjamin), noted French conductor, pedagogue, and composer; b. Paris, Nov. 10, 1873; d. there, Sept. 11, 1949. His father was Hippolyte Rabaud (1839–1900), prof. of cello at the Paris Cons., where Henri studied with Gédalge and Massenet (1893–94); won the Premier Grand Prix de Rome in 1894 with his cantata *Daphné.* In 1908 he became conductor at the Paris Opéra and at the Opéra-Comique; from 1914 to 1918 he was director of the Opéra. In 1918–19 he was engaged to conduct the Boston Sym. Orch.; then was appointed director of the Paris Cons. in 1922; he held this post until 1941.

WORKS: DRAMATIC: OPERAS: *La Fille de Roland* (Paris, March 16, 1904); *Le Premier Glaire* (Béziers, 1908); *Marouf, savetier du Caire* (Paris, May 15, 1914); *Antoine et Cléopâtre*, after Shakespeare (1916–17); *L'Appel de la mer* (Paris, April 10, 1924); *Le Miracle des loups* (Paris, Nov. 14, 1924); *Rolande et le mauvais garçon* (1933; Paris, May 28, 1934); *Le Jeu de l'amour et du hasard* (1948; Monte Carlo, 1954); incidental music and film scores. **ORCH.:** 2 syms. (1893, 1900); *La Procession nocturne*, symphonic poem (Paris, Jan. 15, 1899); *Divertissement sur des chansons russes* (1899); *Lamento* (1930); *Prelude and Toccata* for Piano and Orch. (1945). **CHAMBER:** String Quartet (1898); Trio for Oboe, Clarinet, and Bassoon (1949); piano pieces. **VOCAL:** *L'Été* for Soprano, Alto, Chorus, and Orch. (1895); *Job*, oratorio (1900); *Hymne à la France éternelle* for Chorus (1916); songs.

BIBL.: M. d'Ollone, *H. R.: Sa vie et son oeuvre* (Paris, 1958).

Rabe, Folke (Alvar Harald Reinhold), Swedish trombonist and composer; b. Stockholm, Oct. 28, 1935. He studied composition with V. Sölderholm, B. Wallner, Blomdahl, and Ligeti at the Stockholm Musikhögskolan (1957–64), where he also received training in trombone and music pedagogy. He began his career as a jazz musician while still a teenager; later was a member of the Culture Quartet (1963–73) and the New Culture Quartet (from 1983), which performed contemporary scores; was on the staff (1968–80) and served as program director (1977–80) of the Inst. for National Concerts; then was a producer with the Swedish Radio. He experimented with multimedia techniques; produced pieces of "vocal theater" with non-semantic texts.

WORKS: INTERMEDIA SHOWS: *Ship of Fools* (1983); *The World Museum* (1987); *Beloved Little Pig*, musical fairy tale for children (1986); film scores; incidental music. **ORCH.:** *Hep-Hep*, overture for Small Orch. (1966); *Altiplano* for Wind Orch. (1982); *All the lonely people*, concerto for Trombone and Chamber Orch. (1990). **CHAMBER:** Suite for 2 Clarinets (1957); *Bolos* for 4 Trombones (1962; in collaboration with J. Bark); *Impromptu* for Clarinet, Trombone, Cello, Piano, and Percussion (1962); *Pajazzo* for 8 Jazz Musicians (1964); *Polonaise* for 4 Trombones and Light (1965–66; in collaboration with J. Bark); *From the Myths of Time* for 3 Cellos, Gamelan, and Percussion (1966); *Pipe Lines* for 4 Trombones (1969); *Zug* for 4 Trombones (1970); *Shazam* for Trumpet (1984); *With Love* for Piano (1985); *Escalations* for Brass Quintet (1988). **VOCAL:** *7 Poems by Nils Ferlin* for Chorus (1958); *Notturno* for Mezzo-soprano, Flute, Oboe, and Clarinet (1959); *Pièce* for Speaking Chorus (Swedish, German, and Eng. versions, 1961; in collaboration with L. O'Mansson); *Souvenirs* for Reciter, Electric Organ, and Rhythm Section (1963); *Rondes* for Chorus (1964); *O. D.* for Men's Chorus (1965); *Joe's Harp* for Chorus (1970); *Tva Strofer* for Chorus (1980); *to love* for Chorus, after e.e. cummings (1984); songs. **OTHER:** *Eh??* for Electronics (1967); *To the Barbender* for Tape (1982); *New Construction* for Small Children, Electronics, and Various Sound Sources (1984); *Cyclone* for Electronics (1985).

Rabin, Michael, gifted American violinist; b. N.Y., May 2, 1936; d. there, Jan. 19, 1972. He was of a musical family; his father was a violinist in the N.Y. Phil., his mother a pianist. He studied with Ivan Galamian in N.Y. and made excellent progress; in his early youth, he appeared as a soloist with a number of American orchs.; made several European tours as a concert violinist, and also played in Australia. His sudden death at the age of 35 was a shock to American music lovers.

Rabinof, Benno, esteemed American violinist; b. N.Y., Oct. 11, 1908; d. Brevard, N.C., July 2, 1975. He studied privately with Küzdö, Kneisel, and Auer. He made his debut on Nov. 18, 1927, playing the Tchaikovsky Violin Concerto with members of the N.Y. Phil., conducted by Auer. In 1930 he played Glazunov's Violin Concerto, with Glazunov himself leading the Boston Sym. Orch. as guest conductor. With his wife, the pianist Sylvia Smith-Rabinof, he traveled extensively in Europe and America.

Racek, Jan, Czech musicologist; b. Bučovice, June 1, 1905; d. Brno, Dec. 5, 1979. He studied with Helfert at the Univ. of Brno (Ph.D., 1929, with the diss. *Idea vlasti, národa a slávy v dile B. Smetany* [The Idea of the Fatherland, Nation, and Glory in the Works of B. Smetana]; publ. in Brno, 1933; 2nd ed., aug., 1947); later received a D.Sc. degree (1957). He was director of the music archives of the Moravian Regional Museum (1930–48); also was a lecturer at the Univ. of Brno (from 1939) and prof. and director of the Brno dept. of ethnography and folk music of the Czech Academy of Sciences (1948–70). He served as ed. of the journal *Musikologie* and as general ed. of Musica Antiqua Bohemica.

WRITINGS: *Leoš Janáček* (Olomouc, 1938); *Slohové problémy italské monodie* (Problems of Style in Italian Monody; Prague and Brno, 1938; Ger. tr., 1965); ed. with L. Firkušný, *Janáčkovy feuilletony z Lidové Noviny* (Janáček's Feuilletons in the Lidové Noviny; Brno, 1938; 2nd ed., rev., 1958, as *Leoš Janáček: Fejetony z Lidových Noviny*; Ger. tr., 1962); *Leoš Janáček a současni moravšti skladatelé* (Leoš Janáček and Contemporary Moravian Composers; Brno, 1940); *Česká hudba od nejstarších dob do počátku 19. stoleti* (Czech Music from the Earliest Times to the Beginning of the 19th Century; Prague, 1949; 2nd ed., Aug., 1958); *Ruská hudba: Od nejstarších dob az po velkou řijnovou revoluci* (Russian Music from the Earliest Times up to the Great Revolution; Prague, 1953); *Beethoven a české země* (Beethoven in Bohemia and Moravia; Brno, 1964).

Rachmaninoff, Sergei (Vassilievich), greatly renowned Russian-born American pianist, conductor, and composer; b. probably in Oneg, April 1, 1873; d. Beverly Hills, March 28, 1943. He was of a musical family; his grandfather was an amateur pianist, a pupil of John Field; his father also played the piano; Rachmaninoff's *Polka* was written on a theme improvised by his father; his mother likewise played piano, and it was from her that he received his initial training at their estate, Oneg, near Novgorod. After financial setbacks, the family estate was sold and he was taken to St. Petersburg, where he studied piano with Vladimir Demiansky and harmony with Alexander Rubets at the Cons. (1882–85); acting on the advice of his cousin, Alexander Siloti, he enrolled as a piano student of Nikolai Zverev at the Moscow Cons. (1885); then entered Siloti's piano class and commenced the study of counterpoint with Taneyev and harmony with Arensky (1888). He met Tchaikovsky, who appreciated his talent and gave him friendly advice. He graduated as a pianist (1891) and as a composer (1892), winning the gold medal with his opera *Aleko*, after Pushkin. Then followed his Prelude in C-sharp minor (1892); publ. that same year, it quickly became one of the most celebrated piano pieces in the world. His 1st Sym., given in Moscow (1897), proved a failure, however. Discouraged, Rachmaninoff destroyed the MS, but the orch. parts were preserved; after his death, the score was restored and performed in Moscow (1945). In the meantime, Rachmaninoff launched a career as a piano virtuoso; also took up a career as a conductor, joining the Moscow Private Russian Orch. (1897). He made his London debut in the triple capacity of pianist, conductor, and composer with the Phil. Soc. (1899). Although he attempted to compose after the failure of his 1st Sym., nothing significant came from his pen. Plagued by depression, he underwent treatment by hypnosis with Nikolai Dahl, and then began work on his 2nd Piano Concerto. He played the first complete performance of the score with Siloti conducting in Moscow (Nov. 9, 1901); this concerto became the most celebrated work of its genre written in the 20th century, and its singular charm has never abated since; it is no exaggeration to say that it became a model for piano concertos by a majority of modern Russian composers, and also of semi-popular virtuoso pieces for piano and orch. written in America. On May 12, 1902, Rachmaninoff married his cousin Natalie Satina; they spent some months in Switzerland, then returned to Moscow. After conducting at Moscow's Bolshoi Theater (1904–06), he decided to spend most of his time in Dresden, where he composed his 2nd Sym., one of his most popular works. Having composed another major work, his 3rd Piano Concerto, he took it on his first tour of the U.S. in 1909. His fame was so great that he was offered the conductorship of the Boston Sym. Orch., but he declined; the offer was repeated in 1918, but once again he declined. He lived in Russia from 1910 until after the Bolshevik Revolution of Oct. 1917, at which time he left Russia with his family, never to return. From 1918 until 1939 he made annual tours of Europe as a pianist; also of the U.S. (from 1918 until his death), where he spent much of his time; he also owned a villa in Lucerne (1931–39), and it was there that he composed one of his most enduring scores, the *Rhapsody on a Theme of Paganini* (1934). In 1932 he was awarded the Gold Medal of the Royal Phil. Soc. of London. After the outbreak of World War II (1939), he spent his remaining years in the U.S. He became a naturalized American citizen a few weeks before his death, having made his last appearance as a pianist in Knoxville, Tenn., on Feb. 15, 1943.

Among Russian composers, Rachmaninoff occupies a very important place. The sources of his inspiration lie in the Romantic tradition of 19th-century Russian music; the link with Tchaikovsky's lyrical art is very strong; melancholy moods prevail and minor keys predominate in his compositions, as in Tchaikovsky's; but there is an unmistakable stamp of Rachmaninoff's individuality in the broad, rhapsodic sweep of the melodic line, and particularly in the fully expanded sonorities and fine resonant harmonies of his piano writing; its technical resourcefulness is unexcelled by any composer since Liszt. Despite the fact that Rachmaninoff was an émigré and stood in avowed opposition to the Soviet regime (until the German attack on Russia in 1941 impelled him to modify his stand), his popularity never wavered in Russia; after his death, Russian musicians paid spontaneous tribute to him. Rachmaninoff's music is much less popular in Germany, France, and Italy; on the other hand, in England and America it constitutes a potent factor on the concert stage.

WORKS: OPERAS: *Esmeralda* (1888; introduction to Act 1 and fragment of Act 3 only completed); *Aleko*, after Pushkin's *Tsigani* (The Gypsies; 1892; Moscow, May 9, 1893); *The Miserly Knight*, op. 24, after Pushkin (1903–05; Moscow, Jan. 24, 1906); *Francesca da Rimini*, op. 25, after Dante's *Inferno* (1900; 1904–05; Moscow, Jan. 24, 1906); *Monna Vanna*, after Maeterlinck (1907; piano score of Act 1 and sketches of Act 2 only completed; Act 1 orchestrated by I. Buketoff; concert perf., Saratoga, N.Y., Aug. 11, 1984). **ORCH.:** *Scherzo* in D minor (1887); Piano Concerto in C minor (1889; sketches only); 4 numbered piano concertos: No. 1 in F-sharp minor, op. 1 (1890–91; Moscow, March 17, 1892; rev. 1917), No. 2 in C minor, op. 18 (Moscow, Nov. 9, 1901), No. 3 in D minor, op. 30 (N.Y., Nov. 28, 1909), and No. 4 in G minor, op. 40 (1926; Philadelphia, March 18, 1927; rev. 1927, 1941); *Manfred*, symphonic poem (1890–91; not extant); Sym. (1897; sketches only); 3 numbered syms.: No. 1 in D minor, op. 13 (1895; St. Petersburg, March 27, 1897), No. 2 in E minor, op. 27 (1906–08; St. Petersburg, Feb. 8, 1908), and No. 3 in A minor, op. 44 (Philadelphia, Nov. 6, 1936; rev. 1938); *Prince Rostislav*, symphonic poem (1891); *The Rock*, fantasy (1893; Moscow, March 20, 1896); *Capriccio on Gypsy Themes* or *Capriccio bohémien*, op. 12 (1892, 1894); 2 episodes after Byron's *Don Juan* (1894; not extant); *The Isle of the Dead*, symphonic poem, op. 29, after Böcklin's painting (Moscow, May 1, 1909); *Rhapsody on a Theme of Paganini* for Piano and Orch., op. 43 (Baltimore, Nov. 7, 1934); *Symphonic Dances*, op. 45 (1940; Philadelphia, Jan. 3, 1941). **CHAMBER:** 2 numbered string quartets (1889, 2 movements only; c.1896, 2 movements only); *Romance* in A minor for Violin and Piano (c.1880–90); *Romance* in F minor for Cello and Piano (1890); *Melodie* in D major for Cello and Piano (c.1890; arranged by M. Altschuler, 1947); String Quintet (n.d.; not extant); *Trio élégiaque* in G minor for Piano Trio (1892); 2 pieces for Cello and Piano, op. 2 (1892): *Prélude* in F major (revision of a piano piece, 1891) and *Danse orientale* in A minor; *2 Morceaux de salon* for Violin and Piano, op. 6 (1893): *Romance* and *Danse hongroise*; *Trio élégiaque* in D minor for Piano Trio, op. 9, in memory of Tchaikovsky (1893; rev. 1907, 1917); Cello Sonata in G minor, op. 19 (1901). **PIANO:** *Song without Words* (c.1887); *3 Nocturnes* (1887–88); 4 pieces: *Romance, Prélude, Mélodie*, and *Gavotte* (1887); *Canon* (1890–91); 2 pieces for 6 Hands: *Waltz* (1890) and *Romance* (1891), *Prélude* (1891; rev. as *Prélude* for Cello and Piano, 1892), *Russian Rhapsody* for 2 Pianos (1891), *Morceaux de fantaisie* (1892; includes the famous *Prélude* in C-sharp minor), and *Romance* for Piano, 4-hands (c.1894); *Fantaisie-tableaux: Suite No. 1* for 2 Pianos, op. 5 (1893); *Morceaux de salon*, op. 10 (1893–94); *Romance* for Piano, 4-hands (c.1894); *6 Morceaux* for Piano, 4-hands, op. 11 (1894); *6 Moments musicaux*, op. 16 (1896); *Improvisations* (1896; in *4 Improvisations* in collaboration with Arensky, Glazunov, and Taneyev); *Morceaux de fantaisie* (1899); *Fughetta* (1899); *Suite No. 2* for 2 Pianos, op. 17 (1900–1901); *Variations on a Theme of Chopin*, op. 22 (1902–03); *10 Préludes*, op. 23 (1901–03); *Polka italienne* for Piano, 4-hands (c.1906); 2 sonatas: No. 1, op. 28 (1907) and No. 2, op. 36 (1913; rev. 1931); *13 Préludes*, op. 32 (1910); *Études-tableaux*, op. 33 (1911); *Polka V.R.*, on a theme by the composer's father, Vasily Rachmaninoff (1911); *Études-tableaux*, op. 39 (1916–17); *Oriental Sketch* (1917); *Prélude* (1917); Fragments in A-flat major (1917); *Variations on a Theme of Corelli*, op. 42 (1931). **VOCAL:** *Deus meus*, motet for 6 Voices (1890); *O Mother of God Vigilantly Praying* for 4 Voices (1893); *Chorus of Spirits* and *Song of the Nightingale* from *Don Juan* (c.1894); 6 choruses for Women's or Children's Voices, op. 15 (1895–96); *Panteley the Healer* (1901); *Spring*, cantata for Baritone, Chorus, and Orch., op. 20 (Moscow, March 24, 1902); *Liturgy of St. John Chrysostom*, op. 31 (Moscow, Nov. 25, 1910); *The Bells*, choral sym. for Soprano, Tenor, Baritone, Chorus, and Orch., op. 35, after Poe (St. Petersburg, Dec. 13, 1913); *All-Night Vigil*, op. 37 (1915); *3 Russian Songs* for Chorus and Orch., op. 41 (1926; Philadelphia, March 18, 1927); also 82 songs (1890–1916).

BIBL.: I. Lipayev, *S. R.* (Saratov, 1913); V. Belaiev, *S. R.* (Moscow, 1924; Eng. tr. in *Musical Quarterly*, July 1927); O. von Riesemann, *R.'s Recollections* (N.Y., 1934); W. Lyle, *R.: A Biography* (London, 1939); A. Solovtsov, *S. R.* (Moscow, 1947); J. Culshaw, *S. R.* (London, 1949); V. Seroff, *R.* (N.Y., 1950); A. Alexeyev, *S. R.* (Moscow, 1954); Z. Apetian, ed., *S.V. R.: Letters* (Moscow, 1955); S. Bertensson and J. Leyda, *S. R.: A Lifetime in Music* (N.Y., 1956; 2nd ed., 1965); Z. Apetian, ed., *Reminiscences of R.* (Moscow, 1957; 4th ed., aug., 1974); Y. Keldish, *R. and His Time* (Moscow, 1973); R. Threlfall, *S. R., His Life and Music* (London, 1973); P. Piggott, *R. Orchestral Music* (London, 1974); V. Bryantseva, *S.V. R.* (Moscow, 1976); G. Norris, *R.* (London, 1976; 2nd ed., rev., 1993); Z. Apetian, ed., *S. R.: Literary Heritage* (Moscow, 1978–80); R. Walker, *R.: His Life and Times* (Tunbridge Wells, 1980); R. Threlfall and G. Norris, *Catalogue of the Compositions of S. R.* (London, 1982); R. Palmieri, *S.V. R.: A Guide to Research* (London and N.Y., 1985); C. Poivre D'Arvor, *R., ou, La Passion au bout des doigts* (Monaco, 1986); M. Biesold, *S. R., 1873–1943: Zwischen Moskau und New York: Eine Künstlerbiographie* (Weinheim, 1991); B. Nikitin, *S. R.: Dve zhizni* (Moscow, 1993).

Račiūnas, Antanas, significant Lithuanian composer and pedagogue; b. Užliašiai, near Panevėzys, Sept. 17, 1905; d. Kaunas, April 3, 1984. He studied composition with J. Gruodis at the Kaunas Cons. (graduated, 1933) and with Boulanger and Koechlin in Paris (1936–39). He taught at the Kaunas Cons. (1933–36; 1939–49) and the Vilnius Cons. (1949–59). In 1965 he was made a People's Artist of the Lithuanian S.S.R. He wrote and produced the first opera in Lithuanian.

WORKS: OPERAS: *3 Talismen* (Kaunas, March 19, 1936); *Amber Shore* (1940); *Marite* (1953); *Sun City* (1965). **ORCH.:** 9 syms. (1933, 1946, 1951, 1960, 1961, 1966, 1969, 1970, 1974); 4 symphonic poems: *Evening in Vilnius* (1939), *The Secret of Lake*

Plateliu (1956), *Jurgenas and Ramune* (1958), and *Mother Pirčiupio* (1972); *Scenes of Lithuania*, suite (1955); 3 Pieces (1964); *Prelude and Joke* (1974); Piano Concerto (1976). **CHAMBER:** *Sonata-Fantasy* for Oboe and Piano (1963); Cello Sonatina (1965); Sonata for 2 Pianos (1967); Cello Sonata (1968); Suite for 2 Pianos and Percussion (1973); *Triptych* for Oboe and Piano (1973); Violin Sonata (1977); solo piano pieces. **VOCAL:** 2 cantatas (1943, 1949); *Liberated Lithuania*, oratorio (1945); many choruses; songs.

Radford, Robert, esteemed English bass; b. Nottingham, May 13, 1874; d. London, March 3, 1933. He was educated at London's Royal Academy of Music, taking voice lessons with Alberto Randegger. He made his operatic debut at Covent Garden in London in 1904 as the Commendatore in *Don Giovanni*; later sang Hagen and Hunding in the first English *Ring* cycle under Richter in London (1908). In 1921 he became a founder, with Beecham, of the British National Opera Co.; later became its director. In 1929 he was appointed to the faculty of his alma mater. His fame as an opera singer was great in England; in addition to singing opera, he greatly distinguished himself as a concert artist. His daughter, Winifred Radford (b. London, Oct. 2, 1901; d. Cheltenham, April 15, 1993), was a singer and teacher. She was closely associated with Bernac and Poulenc.

Radíc, Dušan, Serbian composer; b. Sombor, April 10, 1929. He studied at the Belgrade Academy of Music; then went to Paris, where he had private lessons with Milhaud and Messiaen. His music followed the cosmopolitan modernistic manner, Baroque in formal structure, dissonant in contrapuntal intricacies, and hedonistic in its utilitarian appeal.

WORKS: *Symphoniette* (1954); *Spisak* (Inventory), song cycle for 2 Women's Voices and 11 Instruments (Belgrade, March 17, 1954); *Balada o mesecu lutalici* (Ballad of the Errant Moon), ballet (Belgrade, Oct. 19, 1960); Concertino for Clarinet and Strings (1956); *Sinfonia* (1965–66); Piano Quintet; several cantatas; songs; theater music; film scores.

Radica, Ruben, Croatian composer and teacher; b. Split, May 19, 1931. He studied with Kelemen in Zagreb, Frazzi in Siena, and Leibowitz in Paris. In 1963 he was appointed to the faculty of the Zagreb Academy of Music; served as its dean (1981–85). He belongs to the avant-garde of Slovenian music; in 1961 he adopted the 12-tone method of composition.

WORKS: *Concerto grosso* (1957); *4 Dramatic Epigrams* for Piano and String Quartet (1959); *Concerto abbreviato* for Cello and Orch. (1960); *Lyrical Variations* for Strings (1961); *Formacije* (Formations) for Orch. (1963); *19 and 10, Interferences* for Narrator, Chorus, and Orch. (1965); *Sustajarnje* (Prostration) for Electric Organ and Orch. (1967); *Composition* for Ondes Martenot and Chamber Orch. (Graz, Sept. 26, 1968); *Extensio* for Piano and Orch. (1973); *Per se II* for Wind Quintet (1975); *Ka* for 2 Instrumental Groups and Synthesizer (1977); *Alla madrigalesca* for Chorus (1979); *Passion* for Baritone and 3 Instrumental Groups (1981); *Barocchiana* for Trumpet and Strings (1984).

Radnai, Miklós, Hungarian composer; b. Budapest, Jan. 1, 1892; d. there, Nov. 4, 1935. He studied violin, piano, and composition at the Budapest Academy of Music; continued his composition studies with Mottl in Munich (1911). In 1925 he was appointed director of the Budapest Opera. He wrote a textbook on harmony and contributed critical essays to publications. He wrote an opera, *Az infánsnő születésnapja*; a ballet, *The Birthday of the Infanta*, after Oscar Wilde (Budapest, April 26, 1918); *Symphony of the Magyars* for Chorus and Orch.; Violin Concerto; some chamber music.

Radó, Aladár, Hungarian composer; b. Budapest, Dec. 26, 1882; d. in battle near Belgrade, Sept. 7, 1914. He studied in Budapest and Berlin. He wrote 2 operas: *The Black Knight* (1911) and *Golem* (1912); Sym. (1909); *Hungarian Concerto* for Cello and Orch. (1909); 2 string quartets; String Quintet; publ. several albums of piano pieces and song cycles.

Radoux-Rogier (real name, **Radoux**), **Charles,** Belgian pedagogue, writer on music, and composer;b. Liège, July 30, 1877; d. there, April 30, 1952. He was the son of the composer and pedagogue Jean-Théodore Radoux (b. Liège, Nov. 9, 1835; d. there, March 20, 1911). He studied with his father at the Liège Cons., winning the Belgian Prix de Rome with his cantata *Geneviève de Brabant* (1907); was made a prof. of harmony there (1905); wrote music criticism and was active in folk-song research; served as inspector of music education (1930–42). His compositions included 2 operas: *Les Sangliers des Ardennes* (1905) and *Oudelette* (Brussels, April 11, 1912); orch. pieces; chamber music; piano pieces; choral works; folk song albums.

Radovanović, Vladan, Serbian composer; b. Belgrade, Sept. 5, 1932. He studied at the Belgrade Academy of Music. His early works were set in a neo-Classical style; later he annexed ultramodern techniques, including electronic effects. His *Urklang* for Mezzo-soprano and Chamber Orch. (Belgrade, March 14, 1962) deploys a counterpoint of instrumental colors, with the soloist singing wordlessly. Similarly wordless is his suite *Chorales, Intermezzi e Fuga* for Women's Chorus (Belgrade, May 16, 1962). His experimental period included such innovative works as *Sphaeroön* for 26 vocal parts, singing detached vowels (Belgrade, March 14, 1962), and *Pentaptych*, suite for Voice and 6 Instruments (Belgrade, April 22, 1964).

Rae, Allan, Canadian composer; b. Blairmore, Alberta, July 3, 1942. He studied arranging and theory at the Berklee School of Music in Boston (graduated, 1965) and took courses in electronic music at the Royal Cons. of Music of Toronto (1970–73); then was on its faculty (1973–74).

WORKS: MUSIC THEATER AND MULTIMEDIA: *An Approach to Improvisation* (n.d.); *Like Gods, Like Gods among Them* for 6 Speaking Voices, Chorus, Dancers, and Orch. (1973); *Mirror Mirror* (1974); *C.3.3.*, chamber opera (1988); incidental music. **ORCH.:** *Trip* (1970); *Wheel of Fortune* for Winds and Strings (1971); 3 syms.: No. 1, *In the Shadow of Atlantis* (1972), No. 2, *Winds of Change* (1978), and No. 3, *Alam-Al-Mithal* (1980); *The Hippopotamus* (1972); *A Crack in the Cosmic Turtle* for Jazz Group and Orch. (1975); *Image* (1975); Sonata for Clarinet and Strings (1976); Harp Concerto (1976); *4 Paintings of Salvador Dali*, concerto for Double Bass and String Orch. (1977); Concerto for Violin and String Orch. (1979); *Mirror of Galadriel* (1982). **CHAMBER:** 2 string quartets (1966, 1967); *A Day in the Life of a Toad* for Brass Quintet (1970); *Impressions* for Wind Quintet (1971); *Sleep Whispering* for Alto Flute, Piano, and Vibraphone (1971); 4 brass quartets for 2 Trumpets and 2 Trombones (1975); *Improvizations* for String Quartet (1977); *Whispering of the Nagual* for Flute, Clarinet, Trumpet, Trombone, Cello, Piano, and Percussion (1978); *Images No. 1* for Horn and Trumpet (1979), *No. 2* for Flute and Clarinet (1979), *No. 3* for Trumpet, Horn, and Trombone (1979), and *No. 4* for Flute, Clarinet, and Bassoon (1979); *Kiwani Owapi* (Dakota: Awakening of Earth) for Clarinet, 2 Pianos, and Percussion (1981); *Reflections* for Violin, Cello, and Piano (1981); *En passant* for 2 Marimbas (1982).

Rago, Alexis, Venezuelan composer; b. Caracas, May 25, 1930. He studied in Caracas and at the Peabody Cons. of Music in Baltimore; then took courses in piano and composition in Vienna and Rome; subsequently was director of the Aragua Cons. in his homeland.

WORKS: *3 escenas de ritos prohibidos* for Piano (1959); *Autantepuy*, symphonic poem (1962); *5 instantes* for Orch. (1968); *Mitica de sueños y cosmogonías* for Wind Quartet (Washington, D.C., June 25, 1968); *Guri*, symphonic poem on indigenous themes (1968); *Sincronismos, audiosonorrítmicos* (1969); piano suites; songs.

Rahbari, Alexander (actually, **Ali**), Iranian-born Austrian conductor; b. Varamin, May 26, 1948. After studying violin at the Tehran Cons., he went to Vienna to study conducting and composition at the Academy of Music, his principal mentors being Swarowsky, Osterreicher, and Einem. He was active as a violinist and conductor in Tehran, where he later was chief conductor of the Opera. In 1977 he went to Austria, becoming a naturalized Austrian citizen. After winning the Besançon conducting competition and a medal at the Geneva competition in 1978, he was invited to appear as a guest conductor with the Berlin Phil. in 1979; thereafter appeared as a guest conductor throughout Europe. In 1989 he became chief conductor of the Belgian Radio and TV Phil. in Brussels.

Rahn, John, American composer and music theorist; b. N.Y., Feb. 26, 1944. He studied bassoon at the Juilliard School of Music in N.Y. (diploma, 1967). He played in a number of ensembles (1960–70). After military service, he studied composition with Babbitt, Boretz, and Randall at Princeton Univ. (M.F.A., 1972; Ph.D., 1974, with the diss. *Lines [Of and About Music]*). He taught at the Univ. of Mich., Ann Arbor (1973–75); then joined the faculty of the Univ. of Wash. in Seattle (1975), where he became a prof. in 1984. He was associated with the journal *Perspectives of New Music* (from 1972); in 1983, became ed. In addition to his numerous articles on theory and computer applications, his *Basic Atonal Theory* (N.Y., 1980) has the unique distinction of being a lucid introduction to set theory.

WORKS: Sonata for Bassoon and Harpsichord (1967); *Alice* for Tape (1967); *Collaboration* for 5 Instruments (1967); *Epithalamium* for Piano (1968); *5 Forms* for Piano (1968); *Games* for Saxophone and String Quartet (1969); Quintet for Winds (1969); *Reductionist Variations* for Piano (1969); *Deloumenon* for Band (1970); *3 Titbits* for Clarinet and Cello (1970); *Counterparts* for Trumpet (1970); *Trois chants de Mère L'Oie* for Soprano and Piano (1971); *Hos Estin* for Chorus and Ensemble (1971); Trio for Clarinet, Cello, and Piano (1972); *Peanut Butter Defies Gravity* for Soprano and Piano (1973); *Breakfast* for Piano (1976); *Improvisations on a Synclavier of Corn* for Tape (1978); *Another Lecture* for Tape and Speaker (1980); *Out of Haydn* for Fortepiano (1981); *IRT 4/23* for Tape (1983); *Kali* for Computer-generated Tape (1986).

Raichev, Alexander, prominent Bulgarian composer and pedagogue; b. Lom, April 11, 1922. He studied composition with Vladigerov at the Bulgarian State Cons. in Sofia (1943–47); then took courses in composition with Kodály and Viski and in conducting with Ferencsik at the Budapest Academy of Music (1949–50); returning to Sofia, he taught at the Bulgarian State Cons. (from 1950), where he also served as rector (1972–79). His music makes use of innovative techniques that breathe new life into traditional genres and forms.

WORKS: DRAMATIC: OPERAS: *The Bridge* (Ruse, Oct. 2, 1965); *Your Presence* (Sofia, Sept. 5, 1969); *Alarm* (Sofia, June 14, 1974); *Khan Asparouch* (Ruse, March 9, 1981). **OPERETTA:** *The Nightingale of Orchid* (Sofia, March 7, 1963). **BALLETS:** *A Haidouk Epic* (Sofia, Feb. 13, 1953); *The Spring of the White-legged Maiden* (Sofia, Feb. 26, 1978). **ORCH.:** Piano Concerto (1947); 5 syms.: No. 1, *He Does Not Die*, sym.-cantata (1949), No. 2, *The New Prometheus* (1958), No. 3, *Strivings* (1966), No. 4 for Strings (1972), and No. 5 for Chamber Orch. (1972); *Sonata-Poem* for Violin and Orch. (1955); *Leninist Generations*, symphonic glorification (1970); *Radiant Dawn*, overture (1971); *Leipzig 33* (1972); Concerto (1978); *Balkan Rhapsody* (1983); overtures, including *Jubilee Overture* (1986) and *Levsky* (1988). **OTHER:** Chamber music; piano pieces. **VOCAL: ORATORIOS:** *Friendship* (1954); *Dimitrov Is Alive* (1954); *October 50* (1967); *Bulgaria—White, Green, Red* (1977); *Oratorio Meeting* (1984). **CANTATAS:** *My Dear Lassie* (1974); *Varna* (1979); *September Requiem* for Women's Chamber Chorus and Orch. (1973). Also choral works and songs.

Raichl, Miroslav, Czech composer; b. Náchod, Feb. 2, 1930. He studied composition with Bořkovec at the Prague Academy of Music, graduating in 1953. He subsequently devoted himself mainly to teaching and administrative work in the Union of Czechoslovak Composers.

WORKS: OPERA: *Fuente Ovejuna*, after Lope de Vega (1957; Prague, 1959). **ORCH.:** 2 syms. (1955; 1958–60); Cello Concerto (1955–56); *Revolutionary Overture* (1958); *Symfonietta* for Chamber Orch. (1976–77); *5 Dance Fantasies* (1981). **CHAMBER:** Piano Sonata No. 2 (1962). **VOCAL:** *Someone Was Playing on the Oboe* for Women's Chorus (1970); *Farewell Elegy*, concertant aria for Soprano and Chamber Orch. (1981–82); *3 Ends of Love* for Women's Chorus (1982).

Raimondi, Gianni, Italian tenor; b. Bologna, April 13, 1923. He was a student of Gennaro Barra-Carcacciolo and Ettore Campogalliani. In 1947 he made his operatic debut as the Duke of Mantua in Bologna, and then sang in other Italian opera centers. In 1953 he made appearances at the Stoll Theatre in London, at the Paris Opéra, and in Monte Carlo. In 1955 he joined Milan's La Scala. He made his U.S. debut in San Francisco in 1957. In 1959 he appeared in Vienna. In 1960 he sang in Munich. On Sept. 29, 1965, he made his Metropolitan Opera debut in N.Y. as Rodolfo, remaining on its roster until 1969. From 1969 to 1977 he sang at the Hamburg State Opera. He became well known for his roles in Rossini's operas, and also had success as Alfredo, Cavaradossi, Faust, Pollione, and Edgardo.

BIBL.: D. Rubboli, *G. R., felicemente tenore* (Parma, 1992).

Raimondi, Ruggero, notable Italian bass; b. Bologna, Oct. 3, 1941. He was a student of Pediconi (1961–62) and Piervenanzi (1963–65) at the Cons. di Santa Cecilia in Rome. In 1964 he made his operatic debut as Colline in Spoleto, and then sang at the Teatro La Fenice in Venice until 1969. In 1964 he made his first appearance in Rome as Procida. In 1968 he made his debut at Milan's La Scala as Timur in *Turandot*, and his London debut in a concert perf. of Donizetti's *Lucrezia Borgia*. He sang Don Giovanni at the Glyndebourne Festival in 1969. In 1970 he made his first appearance at the Salzburg Festival as a soloist in the Verdi *Requiem*. On Sept. 14, 1970, he made his Metropolitan Opera debut in N.Y. as Silva in *Ernani*, and subsequently made regular appearances there. He made his first appearance at London's Covent Garden as Verdi's Fiesco on Feb. 23, 1972. In 1978 he returned to the Salzburg Festival to make his operatic bow as Philip in *Don Carlos*. He sang at the Paris Opéra in 1979. In 1982 he appeared as Don Quichotte at the Vienna State Opera. In 1987 he sang Mozart's Count Almaviva in Chicago. He appeared in the opening concert at the new Opéra de la Bastille in Paris in 1989. In 1990 he sang Attila at Covent Garden. In 1992 he appeared as Scarpia in Rome. He returned to Covent Garden in 1994 as Rossini's Mosé. Raimondi's vocal resources are ably complemented by his stage deportment. Among his other distinguished roles are Boris Godunov, Méphistophélès, Sparafucile, Oroveso, and Ramfis.

Rainier, Priaulx, South African-born English composer and teacher; b. Howick, Natal, Feb. 3, 1903; d. Bessen-Chandesse, Auvergne, Oct. 10, 1986. After violin training at the South African College of Music in Cape Town (1913–20), she studied violin at the Royal Academy of Music in London, where she also took courses with McEwen; in 1937 she studied with Boulanger in Paris. From 1943 to 1961 she was a prof. of composition at the Royal Academy of Music.

WORKS: ORCH.: *Incantation* for Clarinet and Orch. (1933); *Sinfonia da camera* for Strings (1947; rev. version, London, Feb. 21, 1958); *Ballet Suite* (1950); *Phala-Phala*, dance concerto (1960–61; London, Jan. 17, 1961); Cello Concerto (1963–64; London, Sept. 3, 1964); *Aequora lunae* (1966–67; Cheltenham, July 18, 1967); *Trios and Triads* for 10 Trios and Percussion (1969–73); *Ploërmel* for Winds and Percussion (London, Aug. 13, 1973); Violin Concerto, *Due canti e finale* (1976–77; Edinburgh, Sept. 8, 1977); *Concertante* for Oboe, Clarinet, and Orch. (1977–80; London, Aug. 7, 1981). **CHAMBER:** String Quartet (1939); Suite for Clarinet and Piano (1943); Violin Sonata (1945); *6 Pieces* for Flute, Oboe, Clarinet, Horn, and Bassoon (1954); *Trio-Suite* for Piano Trio (1959); *Pastoral Triptych* for Oboe (1960); *Quanta* for Oboe and String Trio (1961–62); Suite for Cello (1963–65); String Trio (1965–66); *Grand Duo* for Cello and Piano (1980–82; London, May 30, 1983). **KEYBOARD: PIANO:** *Barbaric Dance Suite* (1949). **HARPSICHORD:** *Quinque* (1971). **ORGAN:** *Gloriana* (1972); *Primordial Canticles* (1974). **VOCAL:**

3 Greek Epigrams for Soprano and Piano (1937); *Dance of the Rain* for Tenor and Guitar (1948); *Cycle for Declamation* for Soprano, Tenor, or Baritone (1953); *Requiem* for Tenor and Chorus (1955–56); *The Bee Oracles* for Tenor or Baritone, Flute, Oboe, Violin, Cello, and Harpsichord (1969); *Ubunzima* for Tenor or Soprano and Guitar (1973); *Prayers from the Ark* for Tenor and Harp (1974–75).

BIBL.: J. Opie, *Come and Listen to the Stars: P. R.: A Pictorial Biography* (Penzance, 1988).

Raisa, Rosa (real name, **Raisa** or **Rose Burschstein**), outstanding Polish soprano; b. Bialystok, May 23, 1893; d. Los Angeles, Sept. 28, 1963. In order to escape the horrors of anti-Semitic persecution, she fled to Naples at the age of 14; on Lombardi's advice she entered the Cons. San Pietro a Majella, where she studied under Barbara Marchisio. She made her operatic debut as Leonora in Verdi's *Oberto, Conte di San Bonifacio* in Parma on Sept. 6, 1913; then sang 2 seasons at the Teatro Costanzi in Rome. In 1914 she made her first appearance at Covent Garden in London. She sang with increasing success in Rio de Janeiro, Montevideo, Sao Paulo, and Milan. In 1920 she married the baritone Giacomo Rimini, with whom she founded a singing school in Chicago in 1937. Raisa was one of the finest dramatic sopranos of her day, excelling in the Italian repertoire; she created the title role in Puccini's *Turandot* at Milan's La Scala (April 25, 1926), her husband taking the role of Ping.

Raitio, Pentti, Finnish composer and pedagogue; b. Pieksämäki, June 4, 1930. He studied composition with Kokkonen (1961–63) and Bergman (1963–66) at the Sibelius Academy in Helsinki, receiving his diploma in 1966; then was director of the Hyvinkää School of Music (from 1967). He was chairman of the Lahti Organ Festival (1981–85) and of the Assn. of Finnish Music Schools (from 1985).

WORKS: ORCH.: *"13"* (1964); *Audiendum* (1967); 5 Pieces for Strings (1975); *Petandrie* (1977); *Noharmus I* (1978) and *II* (1980); *Canzone d'autunno* (1982); Flute Concerto (1983); *Due figure* (1985); *Yoldia arctica* (1987). **CHAMBER:** Small Pieces for Brass Instruments (1974); Wind Quintet (1975); *Nocturne* for Violin and Piano (1977). **VOCAL:** *Joki* (The River), 7 songs for Soprano and 7 Instruments (1965); *Kuun tietä* (Along the Moonlit Path), 3 songs for Soprano and 4 Instruments (1965); *Orfilainen kuoro* (Orphean Chorus), 3 songs for Baritone and Men's Chorus (1966); 3 Songs for Baritone and String Quartet (1970); *Eräs kesäilta* (One Summer Evening) for Men's Chorus (1971); *Laulu* (Song) for Men's Chorus (1972); *Lemminkäinen kuokkavieraana Pohjolassa* for 2 Baritones and Men's Chorus (1978); *Katselen jokea* (I'm Looking at the River), 6 songs for Women's or Youth Chorus (1986).

Raitio, Väinö (Eerikki), Finnish composer; b. Sortavala, April 15, 1891; d. Helsinki, Sept. 10, 1945. He studied in Helsinki with Melartin and Furuhjelm and in Moscow with Ilyinsky; also in Berlin (1921) and Paris (1925–26). From 1926 to 1932 he taught at the Viipuri Music Inst. His music is programmatic in the Romantic manner, but there is a more severe strain in his pieces derived from Finnish legends. He was one of the earliest Finnish composers to embrace modern compositional techniques, being mainly influenced by Scriabin, German expressionism, and French Impressionism.

WORKS: DRAMATIC: OPERAS: *Jephtan tytär* (Jephtha's Daughter; 1929; Helsinki, 1931); *Prinsessa Cecilia* (1933; Helsinki, 1936); *Väinämöinen kosinta* (Väinämöinen's Courtship; 1935); *Lyydian kuningas* (The King of Lydia; 1937; Helsinki, 1955); *Kaksi kuningatarta* (2 Queens; 1937–40; Helsinki, 1945). **BALLET:** *Vesipatsas* (Waterspout; 1929). **ORCH.:** Piano Concerto (1915); *Poem* for Cello and Orch. (1915); *Symphonic Ballad* (1916); Sym. (1918–19); *Joutsenet* (The Swans; 1919); *Fantasia estatica*, symphonic poem (1921); *Antigone* (1921–22); *Kuutamo Jupiterissa* (Moonlight on Jupiter), symphonic tableau (1922); *Fantasia poetica*, symphonic poem (1923); *Felis domestica*, scherzo (1935); Concerto for Violin, Cello, and Orch. (1936); *Nocturne* for Violin and Orch. (1938); *Fantasy* for Cello, Harp, and Orch. (1942); *Le Ballet grotesque* (1943). **CHAMBER:** String Quartet; Piano Quintet; Violin Sonata; piano and organ works. **VOCAL:** *Pyramid* for Chorus and Orch. (1924–25).

Rajičić, Stanojlo, Serbian composer and pedagogue; b. Belgrade, Dec. 16, 1910. He studied composition (diplomas, 1934 and 1935) with Karel and Suk and piano (diploma, 1935) with Alois Sima at the Prague Cons.; then attended piano master classes of Hoffmeister in Prague and of Walter Kerschbaumer in Vienna. From 1937 to 1977 he was prof. of composition at the Belgrade Academy of Music. In 1950 he was elected a corresponding member and in 1958 a fellow of the Serbian Academy of Sciences and Arts, serving as secretary of its dept. of visual and musical arts (from 1964); also was elected a member of the Slovenian Academy of Sciences and Arts (1975). He received the Serbian State Prize (1968), the Gottfried von Herder Prize of Vienna (1975), and the Vuk Prize (1986). His early compositions are set in a radical idiom of atonal music, verging on dodecaphony, but later he adopted a national style derived from melorhythms of Serbian folk songs.

WORKS: DRAMATIC: OPERAS: *Simonida* (1956; Sarajevo, May 24, 1957); *Karadjordje* (1973; Belgrade, June 26, 1977); *Dnevnik jednog ludaka* (The Diary of a Madman; 1977; Belgrade, April 4, 1981); *Bele noći* (White Nights; 1983; Belgrade, April 14, 1985). **BALLET:** *Pod zemljom* (Under the Earth; 1940). **ORCH.:** 6 syms. (1935, 1941, 1944, 1946, 1959, 1967); 3 piano concertos (1940, 1942, 1950); 3 violin concertos (1941, 1946, 1950); 2 clarinet concertos (1943, 1962); Cello Concerto (1949); Bassoon Concerto (1969). **CHAMBER:** Piano Trio (1934); 2 string quartets (1938, 1939); piano pieces. **VOCAL:** *Magnovenja* (Moments), song cycle for Mezzo-soprano and Orch. (1964).

Rajna, Thomas, Hungarian-English pianist and composer; b. Budapest, Dec. 21, 1928. He studied composition and piano at the Franz Liszt Academy of Music in Budapest (1944–47), where his teachers were Kodály, Veress, and Weiner; in 1947 he went to London on a scholarship to study with Howells and others at the Royal College of Music, graduating in 1952. He taught at the Guildhall School of Music (1963–67) and the Univ. of Surrey (1967–70), and in 1970 was appointed a lecturer in piano at the Univ. of Cape Town in South Africa. As a pianist, he excels in performances of 20th-century music. His own works assume a classical mold, with distinctly modern contents in harmony and counterpoint.

WORKS: ORCH.: *Rhapsody* for Clarinet and Orch. (1948–50); *Suite* for Strings (1952–54); 2 piano concertos: No. 1 (1960–62; London, March 18, 1966) and No. 2 (1984); *Movements* for Strings (1962); *Cantilenas & Interludes* (London, Feb. 7, 1968); Harp Concerto (1990). **CHAMBER:** *Dialogues* for Clarinet and Piano (1947); String Quartet (1948); *Music* for Cello and Piano (1950); *Music* for Violin and Piano (1956–57); *Serenade* for 10 Winds, Percussion, Harpsichord, and Piano (1958). **VOCAL:** *2 Hebrew Prayers* for Chorus (1972–73); *4 Traditional African Lyrics* for Voice and Piano (1976).

Rajter, Ludovít, Slovak conductor and composer; b. Pezinok, July 30, 1906. After training in piano and cello in Bratislava, he studied with Franz Schmidt, Joseph Marx, Clemens Krauss, and Alexander Wunderer at the Vienna Academy of Music (1924–29), and with Dohnányi at the Budapest Academy of Music. From 1933 to 1945 he was a conductor of the Hungarian Radio in Budapest, and also was a prof. at the Academy of Music there from 1938 to 1945. He settled in Bratislava, where he was chief conductor of the Czech Radio from 1945 to 1950. From 1949 to 1976 he conducted the Slovak Phil., and concurrently was a prof. at the Bratislava Academy of Music. He also served again as chief conductor of the Czech Radio in Bratislava from 1968 to 1977. Among his works were a ballet; *Sinfonietta* (1929); *Divertimento* for Orch. (1932); chamber music; choral pieces.

Rakov, Nikolai, Russian composer; b. Kaluga, March 14, 1908; d. 1990. He studied violin in Moscow and composition at the

Moscow Cons. with Glière; in 1935 he joined its staff as a teacher of orchestration. He was also active as a violinist and conductor. In his compositions, he pursued the Romantic and nationalistic line of Russian music.

WORKS: ORCH.: 2 numbered syms. (1940, 1957); 2 violin concertos (1944, 1955); *Sinfonietta* (1958); Concertino for Violins and Strings (1959); Sym. for Strings (1962); *Concerto-Fantasy* for Clarinet and Orch. (1968); 4 piano concertos (1969, 1969, 1977, 1977). **CHAMBER:** 2 violin sonatas (1951, 1974); 2 oboe sonatas (1951, 1978); Flute Sonata (1970). **PIANO:** 15 sonatinas (1950–76); 2 sonatas (1959, 1973). **OTHER:** Numerous pieces for Russian folk instruments.

BIBL.: A. Solovtsov, *N. R.* (Moscow, 1958).

Raksin, David, remarkable American composer of film music; b. Philadelphia, Aug. 4, 1912. He studied piano in his childhood and also learned to play woodwind instruments from his father, a performer and conductor; when barely past puberty, he organized his own jazz band. In 1931 he entered the Univ. of Pa.; also studied composition privately with Isadore Freed (1934–35). In 1935 he went to Hollywood to assist Charlie Chaplin with the music for his film *Modern Times* (which he later orchestrated with Edward Powell); this provided Raksin a wonderful companionship with the great comedian. Raksin wrote a delectable piece of reminiscences, "Life with Charlie" (*Quarterly Journal of the Library of Congress*, Summer 1983). After a period of travel, he returned to work in the Hollywood film studios and to study with Schoenberg. He composed more than 100 film scores, some of which attained great popularity; his greatest success was the film theme song *Laura*, ingratiatingly melodious in its sinuous and convoluted pattern; it generated more than 400 different recordings. Apart from his activities as a composer and conductor, Raksin appeared as an actor and commentator in television programs. Using material from his film music, he composed several symphonic suites, among them *Forever Amber* and *The Bad and the Beautiful*. Other coruscating scores include *Force of Evil, Carrie, The Redeemer*, and *Separate Tables*, all of which are featured in *Wonderful Inventions* (Library of Congress, Washington, D.C., 1985). Raksin is the first member of his profession invited to deposit his film music in the collections of the Library of Congress in Washington, D.C. He also wrote incidental music for the theater, as well as purely symphonic and choral pieces, including a madrigal, *Simple Symmetries*. His orchestral *Toy Concertino* received many performances; at the request of Stravinsky, he made the original band instrumentation of *Circus Polka* for George Balanchine's production with the Barnum and Bailey Circus. In 1956 he joined the composition faculty of the Univ. of Southern Calif., where he also served on its faculty of the School of Public Administration (1968–89); he also taught film and television composition at the Univ. of Calif., Los Angeles (1970–92). He wrote, narrated, and conducted interviews for a three-year series of hour-long radio programs, "The Subject is Film Music." Raksin received an Elizabeth Sprague Coolidge Commission from the Library of Congress; the resulting composition, *Oedipus memneitai* (Oedipus Remembers) for Bass-Baritone Narrator/Soloist, 6-part Mixed Chorus, and Chamber Ensemble, text by the composer, was conducted by him at a special Founder's Day Concert, Oct. 30, 1986, in Washington, D.C. He conducted a concert of the music of his colleague Alex North with the Orquestra Sinfonica of Seville in May, 1991. In April, 1992, he received the Golden Soundtrack Award for Career Achievement from ASCAP, to whose Board of Directors he was subsequently elected; he also served as president of the Composers & Lyricists Guild of America (1962–70) and of the Society for the Preservation of Film Music (1992–95). He was Guest of Honor at the Ecrans Sonores Festival, Biarritz, France, where Nov. 18, 1993 was declared "David Raksin Day." Raksin completed a survey/study of transcriptions of Mussorgsky's *Picture at an Exhibition* (to date some 95 versions), compiled for eventual distribution in the CD/ROM medium. On Aug. 23, 1995, he conducted the U.S. Marine Band in transcriptions of 3 of his film pieces. He is featured in the documentary film "The Hollywood Sound," broadcast via PBS throughout the U.S. and Europe.

Ralf, Oscar (Georg), Swedish tenor, brother of **Torsten (Ivar) Ralf**; b. Malmö, Oct. 3, 1881; d. Kalmar, April 3, 1964. He studied with Forsell (1902–04) and Gillis Bratt (from 1905), and in Berlin and Munich. He began his career as a singer at Stockholm's Oscarsteatern, an operetta theater (1905–15); completing his studies with Bratt, he made his operatic debut as Siegmund at the Royal Opera in 1918; was a principal member of the company until 1940; also appeared as Siegmund at Bayreuth in 1927. He was best known for his roles in operas by Wagner and Verdi. He publ. an autobiography, *Tenoren han går i Ringen* (The Tenor Goes into the Ring; Stockholm, 1953).

Ralf, Richard, German composer; b. Karlsruhe, Sept. 30, 1897; d. Los Angeles, June 22, 1977. He studied piano as a child with his father, the choirmaster at the Karlsruhe Opera; later attended the Scharwenka Cons. in Berlin, graduating in 1914. Drafted into the German army in World War I, he suffered severe shell shock at the French front; returning to Berlin, he studied composition with Hugo Kaun. In 1946 he emigrated to the U.S., eventually settling in Los Angeles. His music follows the florid and emotional trend of post-Wagnerian Romanticism. Among his compositions were *Transcendental*, ballet (1921); Violin Sonata (1923); String Quartet (1924); Violin Concerto (1925); *Brothers Arise*, cantata (1959); *Symphonic Songs* for Mezzo-soprano and Orch. (1968).

Ralf, Torsten (Ivar), Swedish tenor, brother of **Oscar (Georg) Ralf**; b. Malmö, Jan. 2, 1901; d. Stockholm, April 27, 1954. He studied at the Stockholm Cons. and with Hertha Dehmlow in Berlin. He made his operatic debut as Cavaradossi in Stettin (1930); then sang in Chemnitz (1932–33) and Frankfurt am Main (1933–35). He was a member of the Dresden State Opera (1935–44), where he created the role of Apollo in Strauss's *Daphne* in 1938; was made a Kammersänger in 1936. He sang at London's Covent Garden (1935–39; 1948) and at the Teatro Colón in Buenos Aires (1946); made his Metropolitan Opera debut in N.Y. as Lohengrin on Nov. 26, 1945, and remained on its roster until 1948. He was best known for such roles as Walther von Stolzing, Tannhäuser, Parsifal, Otello, and Radames.

Ramey, Phillip, American writer on music and composer; b. Elmhurst, Ill., Sept. 12, 1939. He began playing the piano at 7 and composing at 17. After training in composition with A. Tcherepnin at the International Academy of Music in Nice (summer, 1959) and at DePaul Univ. in Chicago (B.A., 1962), he pursued graduate studies with Beeson at Columbia Univ. (M.A., 1965). He contributed numerous articles to magazines and wrote hundreds of notes for recordings. From 1977 to 1993 he was the annotator and program ed. of the N.Y. Phil. As a composer, he explored atonal and serial writing in several of his works. He later pursued a generally tonal course marked by complexity of style and form. His music for piano is thoroughly idiomatic.

WORKS: ORCH.: Concert Suite for Piano and Small Orch. (1962; rev. for Piano and Orch., 1983–84; N.Y., March 9, 1984); *Music* for Brass and Percussion (1964); *Orchestral Discourse* (1967); 3 piano concertos (1969–71; 1976; 1991–94); Concerto for Chamber Orch. (1974); Concerto for Horn and Strings for the 150th anniversary of the N.Y. Phil. (1987; rev. 1989; N.Y., April 22, 1993). **CHAMBER:** *Idyll* for Flute and Piano (1960; rev. 1984); *3 Caprices* for Horn (1960); Sonata for 3 Timpani (1961); *4 Bagatelles* for Percussion (1964); *Capriccio* for Percussion (1966); *Toccata Breve* for Percussion (1966); *Night Music* for Percussion (1967); *Commentaries* for Flute and Piano (1968); Suite for Violin and Piano (1971); *La Citadelle*, rhapsody for Oboe and Piano (1975; rev. 1980; also for Horn and Piano, 1994); *Arabesque* for Flute (1977); *Fanfare-Sonata* for Trumpet (1981); *Phantasm* for Flute and Violin or 2 Violins (1984); *Café of the Ghosts: Fantasy-Trio on a Moroccan Beggar's Song* for

Violin, Cello, and Piano (Sacramento, Calif., Nov. 6, 1992); *Rhapsody* for Cello (1992); Trio Concertant for Violin, Horn, and Piano (1993; Sacramento, Calif., Jan. 30, 1994); *Praeludium* for 5 Horns (1994). **PIANO:** *Incantations* (1960; rev. 1982); Suite (1960–63; rev. 1988); 6 sonatas (1961; 1966; 1968; 1968; 1974; 1987–88); *Diversions* (1966); *Toccata Giocosa* (1966); *2 Short Pieces* (1967); *Epigrams,* I (1967) and II (1986; N.Y., March 22, 1987); *Fantasy* (1969–72); *Doomsday Fragments* (1970); *Leningrad Rag: Mutations on Scott Joplin* (1972); *Night Song* (1973); *Memorial* (1977); *Mud Cat Rag* (1979); *Autumn Pastorale* (1980); *Echoes* (1981–82); *Cossack Variations* (1981–85); *Canzona* (1982); *Capriccio: Improvisation on a Theme from Youth* (1985; N.Y., April 29, 1986); 2 toccatas: No. 1 (1986; Fullerton, Calif., March 5, 1987) and No. 2 (1990; N.Y., Feb. 27, 1991); *Tangier Nocturne* (Chicago, April 25, 1989); *Canticle* for Piano, Left-hand (1989; N.Y., March 10, 1991); *Burlesque-Paraphrase on a Theme of Stephen Foster* (1990; N.Y., March 10, 1991); *Mirage* (1990); *Cantus Arcanus* (1990; N.Y., Feb. 27, 1991); *Tangier Portraits* (1991–94); *Color Etudes* (1994; Tangier, May 1995). **VOCAL:** *Cat Songs* for Soprano, Flute, and Piano (1962; rev. 1965); *7, They Are 7,* incantation for Bass-baritone and Orch. (1965); *Merlin's Prophecy* for High Voice and Piano (1966); *A Chemical Wedding* for High Voice and Piano (1974); *A William Blake Trilogy* for Soprano and Piano (1980); *Moroccan Songs to Words of Paul Bowles* for High Voice and Piano (1982–86).

Ramey, Samuel (Edward), outstanding American bass; b. Colby, Kansas, March 28, 1942. He attended Kansas State Univ., then studied voice with Arthur Newman at Wichita State Univ. (B.Mus., 1968); after singing with the Grass Roots Opera Co. in Raleigh, N.C. (1968–69), he continued his studies with Armen Boyajian in N.Y. He made his professional operatic debut as Zuniga in *Carmen* at the N.Y. City Opera (March 11, 1973), and within a few seasons established himself as its principal bass; also made guest appearances at the Glyndebourne Festival (1976), the Netherlands Opera in Amsterdam (1978), the Hamburg State Opera (1978), the Chicago Lyric Opera (1979), the San Francisco Opera (1979), Milan's La Scala (1981), and the Vienna State Opera (1981). From 1981 to 1989 he appeared in various Rossini roles in Pesaro. In 1982 he made his first appearance at London's Covent Garden as Mozart's Figaro. On Jan. 19, 1984, he made a brilliant debut at the Metropolitan Opera in N.Y. as Argante in Handel's *Rinaldo.* In 1987 he made his debut at the Salzburg Festival as Don Giovanni. He subsequently appeared with leading opera houses around the world, and was engaged as a soloist with the major orchs. Among his notable roles are Leporello, Don Giovanni, Figaro, Gounod's Méphistophélès, the 4 villains in *Les Contes d'Hoffmann,* Attila, Boito's Mefistofele, and Olin Blitch; he sang the role of Figaro for the sound-track recording of the award-winning film *Amadeus* (1984).

Ramin, Günther (Werner Hans), distinguished German organist, conductor, composer, and pedagogue; b. Karlsruhe, Oct. 15, 1898; d. Leipzig, Feb. 27, 1956. As a boy he sang in the Thomanerchor in Leipzig; he then studied organ with Straube, piano with Teichmüller, and theory with Krehl at the Leipzig Cons. In 1918 he was appointed organist of the Thomaskirche in Leipzig; he also was organist of the Gewandhaus concerts and a teacher at the Leipzig Cons. During the season 1933–34, he toured the U.S. as an organ virtuoso. He was also active as a conductor; he led the Lehrergesangverein in Leipzig (1922–35) and the Gewandhaus Choir (1933–34; 1945–51); from 1935 to 1943 he conducted the Phil. Choir in Berlin. In 1940 he became cantor of the Thomaskirche, where he sought to preserve the integrity of the Thomanerchor after the establishment of the German Democratic Republic. His compositions include an *Orgelchoral-Suite* and many other organ pieces, as well as chamber music and songs. He ed. several collections of organ works and publ. the manual *Gedanken zur Klärung des Orgelproblems* (Kassel, 1929; new ed., 1955). A vol. of his essays on Bach was ed. by D. Hellmann (Wiesbaden, 1973).

BIBL.: L. von Koerber, *Der Thomanerchor und sein Kantor* (Hamburg, 1954); E. Hasse, *Erinnerungen an G. R.* (Berlin, 1958); C. Ramin, *G. R.* (Freiburg im Breisgau, 1958); idem, *Weggefährten im Geiste Johann Sebastian Bachs: Karl Straube—G. R.: Zwei Thomaskantoren 1918–1956* (Darmstadt, 1981).

Ramírez, Luis Antonio, Puerto Rican composer and teacher; b. San Juan, Feb. 10, 1923. He studied in San Juan and at the Madrid Cons. (composition diploma, 1964). From 1968 he taught at the Puerto Rico Cons. of Music in San Juan.

WORKS: ORCH.: *Tres Homenages* for Strings (1962–65); *Sinfonietta* (1963); Suite (1966); *Balada Concierto* for Violin and Orch. (1967); *Fantasía Sobre un Mito Antillano* (1969); *Tres Piezas Breves* (1972); *Fragmentos,* 3 pieces (1973); 6 symphonic poems: No. 1, *Figuraciones* (1974), No. 2, *Rasgos y Perfiles* for Cello and Orch. (1977), No. 3, *Aire y Tierra* (1978), No. 4, *Ciclos* (1979), No. 5, *El Cuarto Rey Mago* (1983), and No. 6, *La Tierra escuchó tu Voz* (1984); *Suite para la Navidad* (1982); *Días sin Alborada* (1986); *Siete Episodios Históricos* (1986); *Elegía* for Strings (1987). **CHAMBER:** *Sonata Elegíaca* for Cello and Piano (1968); *Meditación a la Memoria de Segundo Ruíz Belvis* for Viola and Piano (1972); piano pieces. **VOCAL:** *Nueve Cantos Antillanos* for Soprano and Orch. (1975).

Ramón y Rivera, Luis Felipe, Venezuelan ethnomusicologist and composer; b. San Cristóbal, Aug. 23, 1913. He studied viola pedagogy at the Caracas Escuela Superior de Música (degree, 1934); returned to his native city to teach at the Escuela de Artes y Oficios de San Cristóbal (1939) and to found and direct the Táchira Music School (1940–50). He studied folklore and ethnomusicology with Carlo Vega at the Inst. of Musicology in Buenos Aires and with Isabel Aretz and Augusto Raúl Cortázar at the Colegio Libre de Estudios Superiores (1945–47); returned to Caracas as chief of musicology of the Servicio de Investigaciones Folklóricas Nacionales (1947), and then went back to Buenos Aires to direct the Americana Orch. (1948–52). In 1953 he became director of the National Inst. of Folklore of Venezuela in Caracas. He traveled extensively in South America; taught folklore and ethnomusicology at Venezuelan and foreign univs.; was president of the Venezuelan Soc. of Authors and Composers (1972–73). Ramón y Rivera's extensive fieldwork enabled him to make a comparative study of the music of the South American continent; he contributed greatly to the study of Venezuelan indigenous, folk, and popular music.

WRITINGS: *La polifonia popular de Venezuela* (Buenos Aires, 1949); *El joropo, baile nacional de Venezuela* (Caracas, 1953); *Cantos de trabajo del pueblo venezolano* (Caracas, 1955); *La música colonial profana* (Caracas, 1966); *Música indigena, folklorica y popular de Venezuela* (Buenos Aires, 1970); *La música afrovenezolana* (Caracas, 1971); *La musica popular de Venezuela* (Caracas, 1976).

Ramovš, Primož, Slovenian composer; b. Ljubljana, March 20, 1921. He studied composition with Slavko Osterc at his hometown's Academy of Music (1935–41), with Vito Frazzi in Siena (1941), and privately with Casella and Petrassi in Rome (1941–43). He was a librarian (1945–52) and chief librarian (1952–87) of the Slovenian Academy of Sciences and Art; was also a prof. at the Ljubljana Cons. (1948–52; 1955–64). The framework of his style of composition is neo-Classical, distinguished by great contrapuntal skill and ingenious handling of rich, dissonant sonorities; dodecaphony and aleatorality are sometimes employed.

WORKS: ORCH.: 3 numbered syms. (1940, 1943, 1948); 3 divertimentos (1941, 1942, 1944); Piano Concerto (1946); Concertino for Piano and Strings (1948); Concerto for 2 Pianos and Strings (1949); *Suite* for 2 Violins, Cello, and String Orch. (1950); Sinfonietta (1951); *Musique funèbre* (1955); *Chorale and Toccata* (1955); *Adagio* for Cello and String Orch. (1958); *Concerto piccolo* for Bassoon and Strings (1958); Trumpet Concertino (1960); *7 Compositions* for Strings (1960); Concerto for Violin, Viola, and Orch. (1961); *Koncertantza glasba* (Concertante Music) for Percussion and Orch. (1961); *Intrada* (1962);

Profiles (1964); *Vzporedja* (Parallels) for Piano and Strings (1965); *Odmevi* (Echoes) for Flute and Orch. (1965); *Antiparallels* for Piano and Orch. (1966; Zagreb, May 15, 1967); *Finale* (1966); *Portret* for Harp, Winds, Strings, and Percussion (1968); *Symphony 68* (Ljubljana, Oct. 27, 1968); *Nasprotja* (Contrasts) for Flute and Orch. (1969); Sym. for Piano and Orch. (1970); Cello Concerto (1974); Double Bass Concerto (1976); Bassoon Concerto (1978); *Triplum* (1980); Concerto for 2 Pianos and Orch. (1981); Organ Concerto (1983); *Concerto profano* for Organ and Orch. (1984); Trumpet Concerto (1985); *Kolovrat* for Strings (1986); Concerto for Violin, Cello, and Orch. (1988); *Pismo* (Letter; 1989); Triple Concerto for Oboe, Clarinet, Bassoon, and Orch. (1990); *Per aspera ad astra* (1991); *Celeia laboribus suis gaudens* for Strings (1993); *Zvočni svet* (Sonorous World) for 2 Pianos and Orch. (1993); *AS* (1994); *Živio SGŠ!* for Trumpet and Orch. (1994); *Simfonija Pietà* (1995). **CHAMBER:** Quartet for 4 Horns (1939); Wind Trio (1942); Trio for Flute, Trumpet, and Bassoon (1952); *Kontrasti* for Piano Trio (1961); *Eneafonia* for 9 Instruments (1963); *Fluctuations* for Chamber Ensemble (1964); *Prolog* for Flute, Clarinet, and Bassoon (1966); *Nihanja* (Oscillations) for Flute, Harp, Percussion, and Strings (1969); *Siglali* for Piano and 8 Instruments (1973); Quartet for Flute, Violin, Cello, and Harpsichord (1988); *Dilema* for Clarinet and Piano (1991); *Cum jibilo* for Brass Quintet (1992); *Discessus* for 9 Brass Instruments (1993); *Dovolj naj bo* (It must be enough) for Cello and Piano (1995); many compositions for solo instruments; piano pieces. **VOCAL:** Choruses; songs.

Rampal, Jean-Pierre (Louis), celebrated French flutist, conductor, and teacher; b. Marseilles, Jan. 7, 1922. He studied flute as a child with his father, 1st flutist in the Marseilles orch. and a prof. at the Cons.; then studied medicine until being drafted for military service by the German occupation authorities in 1943; when he learned that he was to be sent to Germany as a forced laborer, he went AWOL; subsequently attended flute classes at the Paris Cons., winning the premier prix in 5 months. He played solo flute in the orch. of the Vichy Opera (1946–50); concurrently began to tour, often in duo recitals with the pianist and harpsichordist Robert Veyron-Lacroix. He was solo flutist in the orch. of the Paris Opéra from 1956 to 1962, and also became a popular artist on the Paris Radio. He subsequently toured throughout the world with phenomenal success as a virtuoso, appearing as soloist with all the major orchs. and in innumerable recitals. In later years, he also appeared as a guest conductor. He taught at the Paris Cons., and gave master classes worldwide. His repertoire is vast, ranging from the Baroque masters to jazz, from the music of Japan to that of India, from arrangements to specially commissioned works. Of the last, such composers as Poulenc and Jolivet wrote pieces for him. Through his countless concerts and recordings, he did more than any other flutist of his time to bring his instrument into the mainstream of musical life. He was made a Chevalier of the Légion d'Honneur in 1966 and an Officier des Arts et Lettres in 1971. With D. Wise, he publ. *Music, My Love: An Autobiography* (N.Y., 1989).

Ran, Shulamit, Israeli pianist and composer; b. Tel Aviv, Oct. 21, 1949. She studied piano with Miriam Boskovich and Emma Gorochov and composition with Ben-Haim and Boskovich; then was a scholarship student at the America-Israel Cultural Foundation and the Mannes College of Music in N.Y. (graduated, 1967), her mentors being Reisenberg (piano) and Dello Joio (composition); continued piano studies with Dorothy Taubman and composition training with Ralph Shapey (1976). She made tours of the U.S. and Europe as a pianist; was artist-in-residence at St. Mary's Univ. in Halifax, Nova Scotia (1972–73); then taught at the Univ. of Chicago. She held a Guggenheim fellowship (1977); was a visiting prof. at Princeton Univ. (1987). In 1991 she became composer-in-residence of the Chicago Sym. Orch. Her 1st Sym. won the Pulitzer Prize in Music in 1991 and 1st prize in the Kennedy Center Friedheim awards in 1992.

WORKS: OPERA: *Between Two Worlds: The Dybbuk* (1994–95). **ORCH.:** *Capriccio* for Piano and Orch. (N.Y., Nov. 30, 1963); *Symphonic Poem* for Piano and Orch. (Jerusalem, Oct. 17, 1967); *10 Children's Scenes* (1970; arranged from a piano work); *Concert Piece* for Piano and Orch. (Tel Aviv, July 12, 1971); Piano Concerto (1977); *Concerto for Orchestra* (1986; N.Y., Feb. 1, 1987); Sym. No. 1 (1989–90; Philadelphia, Oct. 19, 1990); *Chicago Skyline* for Brass and Percussion (Chicago, Dec. 12, 1991); *Legends* (1992–93; Chicago, Oct. 7, 1993); *3 Fantasy Movements* for Cello and Orch. (Berkeley, Calif., Oct. 2, 1993; based on *3 Fantasy Pieces* for Cello and Piano, 1971); *Invocation* for Horn, Timpani, and Chimes (1994; Los Angeles, Feb. 15, 1995). **CHAMBER:** Quartet for Flute, Clarinet, Cello, and Piano (1967); *3 Fantasy Pieces* for Cello and Piano (1971; also as *3 Fantasy Movements* for Cello and Orch., 1993); *Double Vision* for Woodwind Quintet, Brass Quintet, and Piano (1976; Chicago, Jan. 21, 1977); *A Prayer* for Clarinet, Bass Clarinet, Bassoon, Horn, and Timpani (1981); 2 string quartets: No. 1 (1984) and No. 2 (1988–89; Chicago, Nov. 17, 1989); *Concerto da camera I* for Woodwind Quintet (1985) and *II* for Clarinet, String Quartet, and Piano (1987); *Mirage* for 5 Players (1990; N.Y., March 7, 1991); *Inscriptions* for Violin (Chicago, June 9, 1991). **PIANO:** *Structures* (1968); *Hyperbolae* (1976); *Sonata Waltzer* (1981–82); *Verticals* (1982). **VOCAL:** *Hatzvi Israel Eulogie* for Mezzo-soprano, Flute, Harp, and String Quartet (1968); *7 Japanese Love Poems* for Voice and Piano (1968); *O the Chimneys* for Mezzo-soprano, Ensemble, and Tape (1969); *Ensembles for 17* for Soprano and 16 Instruments (Chicago, April 11, 1975); *Apprehensions* for Voice, Clarinet, and Piano (1979); *Amichai Songs* for Mezzo-soprano, Oboe or English Horn, Viola da Gamba, and Harpsichord (1985); *Adonai Malach* for Cantor, Horn, Piccolo, Oboe, and Clarinet (1985).

Ranalow, Frederick (Baring), Irish baritone; b. Dublin, Nov. 7, 1873; d. London, Dec. 8, 1953. He became a chorister at St. Paul's Cathedral in London when he was 10. After training with Randegger at the Royal Academy of Music in London, he pursued a successful career as an oratorio singer. He also appeared with the Beecham Opera Co., winning praise for his Mozart's Figaro. In 1920 he sang Captain Macheath in Austin's revival of *The Beggar's Opera,* a role he sang on some 1,600 occasions.

Ranczak, Hildegard, Czech soprano; b. Vitkovice, Dec. 20, 1895; d. Munich, Feb. 19, 1987. She studied at the Vienna Cons. She made her operatic debut in Düsseldorf in 1918; remained there until 1923; then sang in Cologne (1923–25) and Stuttgart (1925–27). In 1927 she joined the Bavarian State Opera in Munich, where she appeared until 1944; sang there again from 1946 to 1949; also sang at Covent Garden in London, the Paris Opéra, the Rome Opera, and the Berlin State Opera. She created the role of Clairon in Richard Strauss's *Capriccio* in 1942.

Randall, J(ames) K(irtland), American composer; b. Cleveland, June 16, 1929. He studied at the Cleveland Inst. of Music (1934–47), Columbia Univ. (B.A., 1955), Harvard Univ. (M.A., 1956), and Princeton Univ. (M.F.A., 1958); among his teachers were Leonard Shure for piano and Elwell, Thad Jones, Sessions, and Babbitt for composition. He taught at Princeton Univ. (from 1958). From 1980 he produced various improvised performance pieces under the general name INTER/PLAY.

WORKS: *Slow Movement* for Piano (1959); *Improvisation on a Poem by e.e. cummings* for Soprano, Clarinet, Saxophone, Trumpet, Guitar, Piano or Soprano, and Piano (1960); *Pitch-derived Rhythm: 7 Demonstrations* for Flute, Clarinet, Piano, and 2 Cellos (1961–64); *Quartets in Pairs* for Computer (1964); *Mudgett: Monologues by a Mass Murderer* for Taped Violin and Computer (1965); *Lyric Variations* for Taped Violin and Computer (1968); *Quartersines* for Computer (1969); *Music for Eakins,* film score for Computer (1972); *. . . such words as it were vain to close . . .* for Piano (1974–76); *Troubador Songs* for Voice and Percussion (1977); *Meditation on Rossignol* for Piano (1978); *Soundscroll 2* for Piano (1978); *Greek Nickel I* and *II* for Piano (1979).

Randolph, David, American conductor; b. N.Y., Dec. 21, 1914. He studied at City College, N.Y. (B.S., 1936) and Teachers College, Columbia Univ. (M.A., 1941). From 1943 to 1947 he was assistant director of music of the U.S. Office of War Information. In 1943 he organized the Randolph Singers, which he conducted until 1972. In 1955 he founded the Masterwork Chorus and Orch., which he conducted until 1992; also led the St. Cecilia Chorus and Orch. and, from 1981, the Masterwork Chamber Orch. He taught conducting at the Dalcroze School (1947–50); was a prof. of music at the State Univ. of N.Y. College at New Paltz (1970–72), at Fordham Univ. (1972–73), and at Montclair State College (from 1973). He was also active as a radio music commentator. He publ. the book *This Is Music* (N.Y., 1964); also ed. The David Randolph Madrigal Series.

Rands, Bernard, remarkable English-born American composer; b. Sheffield, March 2, 1934. He studied piano and organ at home; at the age of 18, he entered the Univ. of Wales in Bangor, majoring in music and English literature. He also developed a passion for Celtic lore; in his student days he became a sort of polyglot, delving into the linguistic mysteries of Welsh, Irish, and Scottish vocables, and on the way acquiring a fluency in French, Italian, and Spanish. He also immersed himself in the hypergrammatical and ultrasyntactic glossolalia of James Joyce. After graduating from the Univ. of Wales (B.Mus., 1956; M.Mus., 1958), he took lessons in musicology with Vlad in Rome and studied composition with Dallapiccola in Florence (1958–60); also attended seminars in composition and conducting given by Boulez and Maderna at the Darmstadt summer courses in new music; later consulted with Berio in Milan on problems of electronic music. He was on the faculty of the Univ. of York (1968–75); then was engaged as a prof. of music at the Univ. of Calif. at San Diego, where he found the musical atmosphere particularly congenial to his innovative ideas; was a visiting prof. at the Calif. Inst. of the Arts in Valencia in 1984–85 while retaining his San Diego post. In 1989 he became prof. of music at Harvard Univ., where he was the Walter Bigelow Rosen Prof. of Music from 1993. He also taught at the Juilliard School in N.Y. In 1982–83 he held a Guggenheim fellowship. In 1983 he became a naturalized American citizen. He was awarded the Pulitzer Prize in Music in 1984 for his *Canti del sole* for Tenor and Orch. In 1989 he became composer-in-residence of the Philadelphia Orch.

The sources of Rand's music are astonishingly variegated, drawing upon religious, mystical, mathematical, and sonoristic premises. At one time he was preoccupied with Hinduism; these interests are reflected in his work *Aum*, a mantric word (*Om*) interpreted as having 3 sounds representing the triune stasis of Brahma, Vishnu, and Siva. Despite the complex nature of his compositions, he seems to encounter little resistance on the part of performers and audiences; his music possesses the rare quality of immediate communication. Several works reflect the scientific bent of his mind, as exemplified by *Formants*; there are mundane references in the titles of such works as *Memos* (*2B* and *2D*) and *Agenda*; other sets contain references to sports, as in *Wildtrack*. Then there are in his catalog educational pieces, such as *Sound Patterns*, designed to be interpreted by children and professional performers alike. His *Canti lunatici* penetrate the inner recesses of the human mind in a state of turbulence.

WORKS: MUSIC THEATER: *Memo 2B* for Trombone and Female Dancer (1980); *Memo 2D* for Trombone, String Quartet, and Female Dancer (1980). **ORCH.:** *Per esempio* (1968); *Wildtrack 1* (1969) and *2* (1973); *Agenda* (1969–70); *Mesalliance* for Piano and Orch. (1972); *Aum* for Harp and Orch. (1974); *Madrigali*, after Monteverdi/Berio (1977); *Le Tambourin*, 2 suites (both 1984); *Ceremonial 1* (1985), *2* (1986), and *3* (N.Y., March 18, 1991); *Requiescant* (1985–86); *Hiraeth* for Cello and Orch. (San Diego, Feb. 19, 1987); . . . *Body and Shadow* . . . (1988; Boston, Feb. 22, 1989); *Tre canzone senza parole* (Philadelphia, April 22, 1992); . . . *Where the Murmurs Die* . . . (N.Y., Dec. 9, 1993); Sym. (Los Angeles, Feb. 24, 1994); *Canzoni* (1995). **INSTRUMENTAL ENSEMBLE:** *Actions for 6* for Flute, Harp, 2 Percussion, Viola, and Cello (1962–63); *Formants 2—Labyrinthe* for Clarinet, Trombone, Piano, 2 Percussion, Viola, and Cello (1969–70); *Tableau* for Flute, Clarinet, Piano, Percussion, Viola, and Cello (1970); *déjà* for Flute, Clarinet, Piano, Percussion, Viola, and Cello (1972); *"as all get out"* (1972); *Response—Memo 1B* for Double Bass and Tape or 2 Double Basses (1973); *Cuaderno* for String Quartet (1974); *étendre* (1974); *Scherzi* for Clarinet, Piano, Violin, and Cello (1974); *Serenata 75* (1976); *Obbligato—Memo 2C* for Trombone and String Quartet (1980); *Serenata 85* for Flute, Harp, Violin, Viola, and Cello (1986); . . . *in the receding mist* . . . for Flute, Harp, Violin, Viola, and Cello (1988). **INSTRUMENTAL SOLO:** *Tre espressioni* for Piano (1960); *Formants 1—Les Gestes* for Harp (1965); *Memo 1* for Double Bass (1971), *2* for Trombone (1972), and *5* for Piano (1975). **VOICES AND INSTRUMENTS:** *Sound Patterns 1* for Voices and Hands (1967), *2* for Voices, Percussion, and Instruments (1967), and *3* for Voices (1969); *Ballad 1* for Mezzo-soprano and 5 Instruments (1970), *2* for Voice and Piano (1970), *3* for Soprano, Tape, and Bell (1973), and *4* for Voices and 20 Instruments (1980); *Canti lunatici* for Soprano and Orch. (1981); *Canti del sole* for Tenor and Orch. (1983–84); *Flickering Shadows* for Solo Voices and Instruments (1983–84); . . . *among the voices* . . . for Chorus and Harp (Cleveland, April 16, 1988).

Rangström, (Anders Johan) Ture, prominent Swedish conductor, music critic, and composer; b. Stockholm, Nov. 30, 1884; d. there, May 11, 1947. He studied counterpoint with Johan Lindegren in Stockholm (1903–04); then went to Berlin, where he took courses in singing with Hey and in composition with Pfitzner (1905–06); continued his vocal training with Hey in Munich (1906–08). He was a music critic for Stockholm's *Svenska Dagbladet* (1907–09), the *Stockholms Dagblad* (1910–14; 1927–30), and the *Nya Dagligt Allehanda* (1938–42); was conductor of the Göteborg Sym. Orch. (1922–25), and thereafter made guest conducting appearances in Scandinavia. His music is permeated with a lyrical sentiment, and his forms are rhapsodic; in his syms. he achieves great intensity by concentrated development of the principal melodic and rhythmic ideas; his songs are also notable.

WORKS: OPERAS: *Kronbruden* (The Crown Bride; 1915–16; 1st perf. in German as Die Kronbraut, Stuttgart, Oct. 21, 1919; 1st perf. in Swedish, Göteborg, March 25, 1936); *Middelalderlig* or *Medeltida* (1917–18; Göteborg, May 11, 1921); *Gilgamesj* (1943–44; unfinished; completed and orchestrated by J. Fernström; Stockholm, Nov. 20, 1952). **ORCH.:** *Dityramb* (1909); *Ballad* for Piano and Orch. (1909; rev. 1937); *Ett midsommarstycke* (1910); *En höstrång* (1911); *Havet sjunger* (1913); 4 syms.: No. 1, *August Strindberg in memoriam* (1914; Berlin, Jan. 4, 1922), No. 2, *Mitt Land* (My Country; Stockholm, Nov. 20, 1919), No. 3, *Sång under stjärnorna* (Song under the Stars; 1912; Stockholm, Jan. 8, 1930), and No. 4, *Invocatio* (Göteborg, Nov. 20, 1936); *Intermezzo drammatico*, suite for Small Orch. (1916); *Divertimento elegiaco*, suite for Strings (1918); *Partita* for Violin and Orch. (1933); *Vauxhall*, miniature suite (1937); *På nordisk sträng*, prelude (1941); *Vårhymn* (1942); *Festpreludium: Tempest, Youth, Poetry, and Song* (1944). **CHAMBER:** *Improvisata: Vårnätterna* for Violin and Piano (1904); *Ver sacrum* for Cello and Piano (1906–07); *String Quartet: Ein Nachtstück (Notturno) in E.T.A. Hoffmanns Manier* (1909); *Suite (No. 1) in modo antico* for Violin and Piano (1912) and *Suite No. 2 in modo barocco* for Violin and Piano (1921–22); piano pieces. **VOCAL:** Choral works; over 250 songs.

BIBL.: A. Helmer and S. Jacobsson, *T. R.: Life and Work* (Stockholm, 1987).

Ránki, Dezső, Hungarian pianist; b. Budapest, Sept. 8, 1951. He studied piano with Klára Máthé at the Bartók Cons. (1964–69) and at the Franz Liszt Academy of Music with Pál Kadosa and Ferenc Rados (1969–73). In 1969 he won the International Schumann Competition in Zwickau, and from that time toured with notable success. His repertoire encompasses the classics and the moderns; he particularly excels in the works of Béla Bartók.

Ránki, György, noted Hungarian composer; b. Budapest, Oct. 30, 1907. He studied composition with Kodály at the Budapest Academy of Music (1926–30) and ethnomusicology with Schaeffner in Paris (1938–39); then devoted himself to composition. He won the Erkel (1952, 1957) and Kossuth (1954) prizes; in 1963, was made a Merited Artist by the government; received the Bartók-Pásztory award (1987). He won distinction as a composer of both serious and popular works.

WORKS: DRAMATIC: *King Pomádé's New Clothes,* comic opera (1953–67); *The Tragedy of Man,* "mystery opera" (1970); *The Boatman of the Moon,* "opera-fantasy" (1979); *Terminal,* music drama (1988); also *3 Nights,* musical tragedy (1961), an operetta, much other theater music, and numerous film scores. **ORCH.:** *Aristophanes Suite* for Violin and String Orch. (1947–58); *Sword Dance* (1949); *Hungarian Dances from the 16th Century* (1950); *Don Quijote y Dulcinea,* 2 miniatures for Oboe and Small Orch. (1961); *Fantasy* for Piano and Orch., after woodcuts by Gyula Derkovits (1962); *Aurora tempestuosa,* prelude (1967); *Circus,* symphonic dance drama (1965); *Raga di notte* for Violin and Orch. (1974); 2 syms.: No. 1 (1977) and No. 2, *In Memoriam Zoltán Kodály* (1981); Concertino for Cimbalom, Xylophone, Timpani, Percussion, and String Quintet (1978); Viola Concerto (1979); *Divertimento* for Clarinet and Strings (1986). **CHAMBER:** *Serenata all'antiqua* for Violin and Piano (1956); *Pentaerophonia,* 3 pieces for Wind Quintet (1958); *Serenade of the 7-Headed Dragon* for Brass Septet (1980); String Quartet No. 1: *In Memoriam Béla Bartók* (1985); *The Tales of Father Goose,* musical joke for Brass Septet (1987); also piano pieces, including 3 sonatas (n.d., 1947, 1980). **VOCAL:** *1944,* oratorio for Baritone, Chorus, and Chamber Orch. (1967); *Cantus urbis* for 4 Soloists, Chorus, and Instrumental Ensemble (1972); *Leverkühn's Abschied,* monodrama for Tenor and 10 Instruments (1979); *Overture to the 21st Century* for Chorus and Orch. (1987); choruses; songs.

Rankin, Nell, American mezzo-soprano; b. Montgomery, Ala., Jan. 3, 1926. She studied voice with Jeanne Lorraine at the Birmingham Cons. of Music; continued her training with Karin Branzell in N.Y. (1945–49). In 1949 she made her operatic debut as Ortrud in *Lohengrin* at the Zürich Opera, of which she later became an active member; in 1950–51 she sang at the Basel Opera, and in 1951 appeared at La Scala, Milan. In 1951 she won the Metropolitan Opera Auditions of the Air and made her debut with it in N.Y. on Nov. 22, 1951, as Amneris; she then sang at Covent Garden in London (1953–54) and at the San Francisco Opera (1955). Subsequently she appeared at the Teatro Colón in Buenos Aires, in Mexico, and in Europe. Her best roles were Carmen, Azucena, Ortrud, Santuzza, and Maddalena.

Rankl, Karl, Austrian-born English conductor and composer; b. Gaaden, near Vienna, Oct. 1, 1898; d. Salzburg, Sept. 6, 1968. He was a pupil of Schoenberg and Webern in Vienna; from them he acquired a fine understanding of the problems of modern music. He occupied various positions as a chorus master and an opera coach in Vienna; served as assistant to Klemperer at the Kroll Opera in Berlin (1928–31); then conducted opera in Graz (1932–37) and at the German Theater in Prague (1937–39). At the outbreak of World War II, he went to England and later became a naturalized subject; was music director at Covent Garden in London (1946–51), the Scottish National Orch. in Glasgow (1952–57), and the Elizabethan Opera Trust in Sydney (1958–60). He composed an opera, *Deirdre of the Sorrows* (1951), which won the Festival of Britain prize but was not perf.; also 8 syms.; an oratorio, *Der Mensch*; and many choral works.

Ranta, Sulho, Finnish composer and writer on music; b. Peräseinäjoki, Aug. 15, 1901; d. Helsinki, May 5, 1960. He studied at the Univ. of Helsinki (M.A., 1925); took courses in composition with Melartin at the Helsinki Cons. (1921–24), and later in Germany, France, and Italy. Returning to Finland, he taught at the Sibelius Academy in Helsinki (1934–56); was also active as a music critic and theater conductor. He was ed. of a comprehensive biographical dictionary of Finnish composers, *Suomen Säveltäjiä* (Helsinki, 1945), and a general biographical survey of performers, *Sävelten Taitureita* (Helsinki, 1947). As a composer, he excelled in chamber music and songs.

WORKS: ORCH.: 4 syms.: No. 1, *Sinfonia programmatica* (1929–31), No. 2, *Sinfonia piccola* (1931–32), No. 3, *Sinfonia semplice* (1936), and No. 4, *Sinfonia dell'arte* (1947); *Tuntematon maa* (The Unknown Land) for Piano and Orch. (1930); 2 concertinos: No. 1 for Piano and Strings (1932) and No. 2 for Flute, Harp, Viola, and Strings (1934); *Kainuun kuvia* (Images boréales), suite (1933); *Concerto for Orchestra* (1938); *Kansansatu* (Folk Story), symphonic variations (1940). **CHAMBER:** Piano Trio (1923); *Suite symphonique* for Flute, Clarinet, Horn, String Quartet, and Piano (1926–28); Concertino for String Quartet (1935); piano pieces. **VOCAL:** *Sydärnen tie* (The Way of the Heart), cantata (1945–46); *Oratorio volgare* for Soloists, Chorus, and Orch. (1951); *Eksyneitten legioonalaisten rukous* (Prayer of the Lost Legionnaires) for 8 Soloists, Chorus, and Orch. (1956).

Rapchak, Lawrence, interesting American composer; b. Hammond, Ind., May 7, 1951. (His unusual name is explained by the Czech origin of his grandparents.) He studied piano in grade school and learned to read music by intelligent guesswork; from his earliest attempts at composition, he was greatly impressed by Shostakovich's 10th Sym.; he tried to write a similar work, which became his first symphonic composition; it was performed in Cleveland on June 3, 1967. In 1969 he entered regular classes in composition with Marcel Dick and Donald Erb at the Cleveland Inst. of Music; also had a course in conducting with James Levine. In the meantime, he taught himself to play drums and other percussion instruments; also led a student orch. He describes his music as having emphasis on contrasting colors with markedly propulsive rhythms.

WORKS: Sym. for Chamber Orch. (Cleveland, June 3, 1967); *2 Short Pieces* (1967); *4 Pieces for Orchestra* (1969); *Poem* for Oboe Ensemble (Cleveland, Dec. 1980); *Bifrost* (1981); *Lanterloo* (1981); *3 Rappaccini Rhapsodies* (1982); *Sky Dancers* (1983); *Magic Box* for Oboe, English Horn, and Orch. (1984); *Mesazoa* (1985); *Mystic Promenade* (St. Louis, Oct. 7, 1987); *Il concerto vetrina* for Bass Clarinet and Small Orch. (1988; Chicago, March 17, 1991); Violin Concerto (1988); *The Lifework of Juan Diaz,* based on a Ray Bradbury story (1988; Chicago, April 21, 1990, composer conducting); *Chasing the Sunset* (N.Y., April 28, 1989); *Sinfonia antiqua* (1989; Detroit, Feb. 7, 1991); *Aubade* (1990).

Rapee, Erno, Hungarian-American conductor, arranger, and composer; b. Budapest, June 4, 1891; d. N.Y., June 26, 1945. He studied at the National Cons. in Budapest (graduated, 1909). After conducting opera in Dresden and Katowice, he toured Mexico and South America as a pianist. In 1912 he settled in N.Y. as conductor of the Hungarian Opera Co. From 1917 he conducted for various film theaters, becoming closely associated with the Roxy (S.L. Rothafel) enterprises. He also was active as an arranger and composer for silent and then sound films. From 1927 he conducted at the new Roxy Theater, where he led weekly radio broadcasts of symphonic music. After a sojourn in Hollywood (1930–31), he returned to N.Y. as music director for NBC. He was music director at Radio City Music Hall from 1932, where he led numerous radio broadcasts.

Rapf, Kurt, Austrian composer; b. Vienna, Feb. 15, 1922. He studied piano, organ, and composition at the Vienna Academy of Music (1936–42). He was founder-conductor of the chamber music ensemble Collegium Musicum Wien (1945–56); was city music director in Innsbruck (1953–60); was president of the Austrian Composers' Union (1970–83).

WORKS: ORCH.: *Aphorismen* (1968); Violin Concerto (1971); 3 concertos for Chamber Orch.: No. 1, *Imaginations* (1971), No. 2, *Contrasts* (1972), and No. 3, *Remembrances* (1978); Piano Concerto (1973); *Concerto per viaggio* for Chamber Orch. (1975); *4 Orchestral Pieces* (1975); 2 syms. (1976,

1981); Concerto for Violin, Cello, and Orch. (1976); Organ Concerto (1977–84); *Leanda*, fantasy-overture (1979); Concerto for Organ and Strings (1979); *Concerto estivo* (1982); Concerto for Violin, Piano, and Orch. (1982); *Concerto for Orchestra* (1984). **CHAMBER:** *6 Pieces* for Wind Quintet (1963); *4 Impressions* for 9 Players (1966); Quintet for Harp and 4 Wind Instruments (1968); *Toccata, Adagio, and Finale* for Organ (1972); *3 Episodes* for Cello (1981–84); piano pieces. **VOCAL:** *Wiener Veduten*, 11 songs for Tenor and Orch. (1972); *Passio aeterna*, oratorio (1979).

Raphael, Günter (Albert Rudolf), German composer; b. Berlin, April 30, 1903; d. Herford, Oct. 19, 1960. His father, Georg Raphael, was music director of Berlin's St. Matthäi. He studied with Max Trapp (piano), Walter Fischer (organ), and Robert Kahn (composition) at the Berlin Hochschule für Musik (1922–25). He taught theory and composition at the Leipzig Cons. and at the Kirchenmusikalisches Institut (1926–34); after his works were banned by the Nazis, he lived in Meiningen and then in Sweden. Following the collapse of the 3rd Reich, he taught in Laubach (1945–48); taught theory and composition at the Duisburg Cons. (1949–53); was on the faculty of the Mainz Cons. (1956–58); served as prof. at the Cologne Hochschule für Musik (1957–60). His early works followed in the German Romantic tradition, but he later adopted a more contemporary idiom with excursions into serialism.

WORKS: ORCH.: 5 syms. (1926; 1932; 1942; 1942–47; 1953); *Theme, Variations, and Rondo* (1927); 2 violin concertos (1929, 1960); *Variations on a Scottish Folktune* (1930); Chamber Concerto for Violin and Chamber Orch. (1930); *Divertimento* (1932); Organ Concerto (1936); *Smetana Suite*, after Smetana's dances (1938); *Sinfonietta* (1938); *Symphonische Fantasie* for Violin and Strings (1940); *Jabonah*, ballet suite (1948); *Reger Suite* (1948); *Sinfonia breve* (1949); Concertino for Alto Saxophone and Chamber Orch. (1951); *Die vier Jahreszeiten* for Strings (1953); *Zoologica* (1958). **CHAMBER:** 2 clarinet quintets (1924); trios for Piano, Violin, and Cello (1925), Flute, Cello, and Piano (1938), Flute, Violin, and Viola (1940), 2 Violins and Viola (1941), and Clarinet, Cello, and Piano (1950); sonatas for Viola and Piano (1925, 1926), Flute and Piano (1925), Violin and Piano (1926, 1968), Cello and Piano (1926), Oboe and Piano (1933), and Violin and Organ (1934); 4 string quartets (1926, 1926, 1930, 1945); String Quintet (1927); 9 sonatas for Solo Instruments (1940–46); 6 duo sonatas for Various Instruments (1940–46); Woodwind Quintet (1945); piano pieces; organ music. **VOCAL:** Much choral music, including a cantata (1926), *Requiem* (1927–28), *Te Deum* (1930), *Busskantate* (1952), *Judica Kantate* (1955), and motets.

Rappold, Marie (née **Winterroth**), English soprano; b. London, c.1873; d. Los Angeles, May 12, 1957. The family moved to America when she was a child. She studied with Oscar Saenger in N.Y.; made her Metropolitan Opera debut there as Sulamith in *Die Königen von Saba* (Nov. 22, 1905); remained on its roster until 1909; then went to Europe. She was married to Dr. Julius Rappold, but divorced him and married **Rudolf Berger** in 1913. She had another period of singing at the Metropolitan Opera (1910–20) and later appeared in Chicago (1927–28); then settled in Los Angeles as a teacher.

Rascher, Sigurd (Manfred), German-born American saxophonist; b. Elberfeld, May 15, 1907. He studied at the Stuttgart Cons., and became proficient on the saxophone. In 1939 he went to the U.S., where he developed a fine concert career. He founded the Rascher Saxophone Quartet (1969); commissioned numerous works for his instrument, including pieces by Glazunov, Ibert, Martin, Milhaud, and Hindemith.

Raskin, Judith, noted American soprano; b. N.Y., June 21, 1928; d. there, Dec. 21, 1984. She studied at Smith College, graduating in 1949; took private voice lessons with Anna Hamlin in N.Y. Her stage career received an impetus on July 7, 1956, when she sang the title role in Douglas Moore's folk opera *The Ballad of Baby Doe*, premiered in Central City, Colo. In 1957 she became a member of the NBC-TV Opera; in 1959, joined the N.Y. City Opera. She made her Metropolitan Opera debut in N.Y. on Feb. 23, 1962, as Susanna in *Le nozze di Figaro*; sang there until 1972. She taught at the Manhattan School of Music and the 92nd Street "Y" School of Music in N.Y. from 1975; also at the Mannes College of Music there from 1976.

Rasmussen, Karl Aage, Danish composer, conductor, and teacher; b. Kolding, Dec. 13, 1947. He took courses in music history, theory, and composition at the Århus Cons. (graduated, 1971), where his principal mentors were Nørgård and Gudmundsen-Holmgreen. He taught at the Funen Cons. (1970–72); in 1971 he joined the faculty of the Århus Cons. as a lecturer, becoming a docent in 1979 and a prof. in 1988; also was a docent at the Royal Danish Cons. of Music in Copenhagen (1980–82). From 1973 to 1988 he was active with the Danish Radio; in 1975 he founded a chamber ensemble, the Elsinore Players, and in 1978 the NUMUS Festival, serving as its artistic director until 1985 and again from 1987 to 1990; in 1986 he founded the Danish Piano Theater. From 1987 to 1990 he was chairman of the Danish Arts Foundation. In addition to monographs on composers, he wrote much music criticism and contributed articles on music history to periodicals in his homeland and abroad. His music follows the cosmopolitan trends of pragmatic hedonism within neo-Classical formal structures.

WORKS: DRAMATIC: *Crapp's Last Tape*, opera (1967); *Jephta*, opera (1977); *Majakovskij*, scenic concert piece (1978); *The Story of Jonah*, musical radio play (1981); *Our Hoffmann*, musical play (1986); *The Sinking of the Titanic*, opera (1993; Jutland, May 4, 1994). **ORCH.:** *Symphony for Young Lovers* (1966); *Recapitulations* (1967); *Symphonie classique* (1968); *Anfang und Ende*, sym. (1972; Århus, Feb. 11, 1976); *Contrafactum* for Cello and Orch. (1979); *A Symphony in Time* (1982); *Movements on a Moving Line* (1987); *Sinking Through the Dream-Mirror*, concerto for Violin and 13 Instruments (1993). **CHAMBER:** *Protocol and Myth* for Accordion, Electric Guitar, and Percussion (1971); *Genklang* (Echo) for 3 Pianos (1 prepared, 1 mistuned) and Celesta (1972); *A Ballad of Game and Dream* for Chamber Ensemble (1974); *Berio Mask* for Chamber Ensemble (1977); *Encore: I (Lonesome)* for Guitar (1977), *II (Join)* for Guitar (1985), *III (Encore for Frances)* for Cello (1982), *IV (Match)* for Cello and Piano (1983), *V (Ich, nur . . .)* for Voice (1983), *VI (Chains)* for Clarinet (1983–85), *VII (Strain)* for Piano (1984), *VIII (Fugue)* for Clarinet, Vibraphone, and Piano (1983–84), and *IX (Beat)* for Silenced Percussion (1985); *Italian Concerto* for Chamber Ensemble (1981); *A Quartet of 5* for 2 Trumpets, Horn, and 2 Trombones (1982); *Solos and Shadows* for String Quartet (1983); *Surrounded by Scales* for String Quartet (Lerchenborg, Aug. 4, 1985); *Still* for String Quartet (1989); *Continuo* for Flute and Guitar (1991). **VOCAL:** *This Moment* for 3 Sopranos, Flute, and Percussion (1966); *Love Is in the World* for Voice, Guitar, and Percussion (1974–75); *Liederkreis* for Soprano, Tenor or Baritone, Flute, Clarinet, Vibraphone, and Piano (1986).

Rasse, François (Adolphe Jean Jules), Belgian violinist, conductor, teacher, and composer; b. Helchin, near Ath, Jan. 27, 1873; d. Brussels, Jan. 4, 1955. He studied violin with Ysaÿe at the Brussels Cons., winning the Belgian Grand Prix de Rome in 1899. From 1925 to 1938 he was director of the Liège Cons.

WORKS: DRAMATIC: OPERAS: *Déidamia* (1905); *Soeur Béatrice* (1938). **BALLET:** *Le maître à danser* (1908). **ORCH.:** *Symphonie romantique* (1901); *Symphonie mélodique* (1903); Violin Concerto (1906); *Symphonie rythmique* (1908); 3 tone poems: *Douleur* (1911), *Joie* (1925), and *Aspiration* (1946); *La Dryade* for Clarinet and Orch. (1943); *Lamento* for Cello and Orch. (1952). **CHAMBER:** 3 piano trios (1897, 1911, 1951); 2 string quartets (1906, 1950); Piano Quintet (1914); Piano Quartet (1941); piano pieces. **VOCAL:** Choral music; song cycles.

Rathaus, Karol, Polish-born American pedagogue and composer; b. Tarnopol, Sept. 16, 1895; d. N.Y., Nov. 21, 1954. He studied at the Vienna Academy of Music and the Univ. of Vienna (Ph.D., 1922) and in Berlin (1920–21; 1922–23). In 1932 he went to Paris, and in 1934 to London. In 1938 he settled in the U.S., becoming a naturalized American citizen in 1946. After a brief stay in Hollywood in 1939, during which he wrote some film scores, he settled in N.Y.; in 1940 he was appointed to the faculty of Queens College. He was highly respected as a teacher of composition. His own music, however, never attracted large audiences; always noble in purpose and design and masterly in technique, it reveals a profound feeling for European neo-Romanticism. In 1952 he rev. and ed. the orch. score to Mussorgsky's *Boris Godunov* on a commission from the Metropolitan Opera, which gave the new version on March 6, 1953.

WORKS: DRAMATIC: OPERA: *Fremde Erde* (Berlin, Dec. 10, 1930; also as a symphonic interlude, 1950). **BALLETS:** *Der letzte Pierrot* (1926; Berlin, May 7, 1927); *Le Lion amoureux* (1937). **INCIDENTAL MUSIC:** *Uriel Acosta* (1930; orch. suite, 1933; rev. 1947). **FILM MUSIC:** 17 scores, including *The Brothers Karamazov* (1931), *The Dictator* (1934), *Dame de pique* (1937), *Let Us Live* (1939), and *Out of Evil* (1950). **ORCH.:** 3 syms. (1921–22; 1923; 1942–43); *4 Dance Pieces* (1924); Piano Concertino (1925); *Overture* (1927); Suite for Violin and Chamber Orch. or Piano (1929); Suite (Liège, Sept. 6, 1930); *Allegro concertante* for Strings and Trumpet obbligato (1930); *Serenade* (1932); *Symphonic Movement* (1933); *Contrapuntal Triptych* (1934); *Jacob's Dream*, nocturne (1938); Piano Concerto (1939; Berkeley, Calif., Aug. 1, 1942); *Prelude and Gigue* (1939); *Music* for Strings (1941); *Polonaise symphonique* (1943; N.Y., Feb. 26, 1944); *Vision dramatique* (1945; Tel Aviv, April 4, 1948); *Salisbury Cove Overture* (1949); *Sinfonia concertante* (1950–51); *Intermezzo giocoso* for Woodwinds, Brass, and Percussion (1950–51); *Prelude* (1953; Louisville, June 5, 1954). **CHAMBER:** 5 string quartets (1921, 1925, 1936, 1946, 1954); 2 violin sonatas (1924, 1938); Clarinet Sonata (1927); *Little Serenade* for Clarinet, Bassoon, Trumpet, Horn, and Piano (1927); Trio for Violin, Clarinet, and Piano (1944); Piano Quintet (1948; unfinished); *Dedication and Allegro* for Violin and Piano (1949); *Rapsodia notturna* for Viola or Cello and Piano (1950); *Trio Serenade* for Piano Trio (1953); *Divertimento* for 10 Woodwinds (1954; unfinished). **KEYBOARD: PIANO:** Numerous pieces, including 4 sonatas (1920; 1920–24, rev. 1928; 1927; 1946). **ORGAN:** *Prelude and Toccata* (1933). **VOCAL:** *Song without Words* and *Fugue*, both for Chorus and Chamber Orch. (1928); *3 Calderon Songs* for Low Voice and Orch. or Piano (1931); *XXIII Psalm* for Tenor, Women's Chorus, and Orch. or Piano (1945); *O Juvenes*, academic cantata (1947); *Lament from "Iphigenia in Aulis" by Euripides* for Chorus and Horn (1947); *Diapason* for Baritone, Chorus, and Orch., after Dryden and Milton (1950); choruses; songs.

Rathburn, Eldon (Davis), Canadian composer; b. Queenstown, New Brunswick, April 21, 1916. He studied composition with Willan, organ with Peaker, and piano with Godden at the Toronto Cons. of Music (1938–39). From 1947 to 1976 he served as staff composer for the National Film Board; also taught film composition at the Univ. of Ottawa (1972–76). Among his film scores for documentaries are *The Romance of Transportation* (1952), *City of Gold* (1957), and *Labyrinth* (1967).

WORKS: ORCH.: *Symphonette* (1943; rev. 1946); *2 Cartoons* (1944, 1946); *Images of Childhood* (1949–50); *Overture to a Hoss Opera* (1952); *Nocturne* for Piano and Small Orch. (1953); *Overture burlesca* (1953); *Milk Maid Polka* (1956); *Gray City* (1960); *City of Gold*, suite from music to the film (1967); *Aspects of Railroads* (1969); *3 Ironies* for Solo Brass Quintet and Orch. (Hamilton, Ontario, Oct. 15, 1975); *Steelhenge*, Steel Band concerto (1975); *The Train to Mariposa* (1986). **CHAMBER:** *5 Short Pieces* for differing combinations of Winds, each piece having a separate title (1949–56); *In 3 Rounds* for Guitar and Double Bass (1971); *The Metamorphic 10* for Accordion, Mandolin, Banjo, Guitar, Double Bass, Harp, Piano, Celesta, and 3 Percussionists (1971); *2 Interplays* for Saxophone Quartet (1972); *Rhythmette* for 2 Pianos and Rhythm Band (1973); *The Nomadic 5*, brass quintet (1974); *Turbo* for Brass Quintet (1978); *The Rise and the Fall of the Steam Railroad* for Chamber Ensemble (1983); *Dorion Crossing*, trio for Clarinet, Cello, and Piano (1987); *2 Railoramas* for Woodwind Quintet (1990). **PIANO:** *Silhouette* for 2 Pianos (1936); *Black and White* (1970); *The Iron Horses of Delson* (1980); *6 Railroad Preludes* (1987).

Raţiu, Adrian, Romanian composer and musicologist; b. Bucharest, July 28, 1928. He studied at the Bucharest Cons. (1950–56) with Constantinescu (harmony), Negrea (counterpoint), Rogalski (orchestration), and Klepper (composition), and later attended the summer courses in new music in Darmstadt (1969). In 1962 he became a prof. at the Bucharest Cons. From 1968 he also was a member of the executive committee of the Union of Composers and Musicologists in Romania. His various writings on music appeared in many publications. Among his honors were composition prizes of the Union of Composers and Musicologists (1967, 1972, 1973, 1981, 1990, 1993) and the Enesco Prize of the Romanian Academy (1974). In his music, Raţiu combines accessible atonal writing with euphonious dissonance.

WORKS: ORCH.: 2 syms.: No. 1 (1961; Timişoara, Oct. 13, 1962) and No. 2 (1976–77; Timişoara, May 12, 1977); Concerto for Oboe, Bassoon, and Orch. (1962–63; Bucharest, Nov. 27, 1969); *Diptych* (1965; Timişoara, Dec. 10, 1966); *Studi* for Strings (1968; Bucharest, Dec. 15, 1986); *6 Images* (1971; Craiova, Oct. 19, 1974); Piano Concerto (1988; Bucharest, May 30, 1993). **CHAMBER:** 2 string quartets (1956; *Convergences II*, 1988); *Noctural Vision* for Viola and Piano (1964); *Partita* for Wind Quintet (1966); *Impressions* for Chamber Ensemble (1969); *Transfigurations*, quintet for Piano, Clarinet, Violin, Viola, and Cello (1974–75); Trio for Flute, Oboe, and Clarinet (1979–80); *Sonata a cinque* for Brass Quintet (1984); Sonata for Solo Violin (1985); *Alternations* for Clarinet and Bass Clarinet (1986); Trio for Piano, Clarinet, and Guitar or Vibraphone (1987); *Echoes* for Vibraphone and Marimba (1989); *Convergences III* for Flute, Oboe, and Bassoon (1991) and *IV* for Piano, Clarinet or Saxophone, and Percussion (1994); Violin Sonata (1991); piano pieces. **VOCAL:** 3 Madrigals for Chorus, after Shakespeare (1964); *Fragment of a Triumphal Arch for Beethoven* for Soprano, Clarinet, and Piano (1970); *Hommage à Erik Satie* for Voice and Piano (1994).

Ratner, Leonard Gilbert, American musicologist and composer; b. Minneapolis, July 30, 1916. He studied composition with Schoenberg at the Univ. of Calif. at Los Angeles, and musicology with Bukofzer and Elkus at the Univ. of Calif. at Berkeley (Ph.D., 1947). He also had composition lessons with Bloch and F. Jacobi. In 1947 he was appointed to the staff of Stanford Univ.; held a Guggenheim fellowship in 1962–63.

WORKS: *The Necklace*, chamber opera; Sym.; *Harlequin*, overture; 2 string quartets; Violin Sonata; Cello Sonata; Piano Sonata.

WRITINGS: *Music: The Listener's Art* (N.Y., 1957); *Harmony: Structure and Style* (N.Y., 1962); *Classic Music: Expression, Form, and Style* (N.Y., 1979); *Romantic Music: Sound and Syntax* (N.Y., 1992).

BIBL.: W. Allanbrook, J. Levy, and W. Mahrt, eds., *Conventions in Eighteenth- and Nineteenth-Century Music: Essays in Honor of L.G. R.* (Stuyvesant, N.Y., 1992).

Ratz, Erwin, Austrian musicologist; b. Graz, Dec. 22, 1898; d. Vienna, Dec. 12, 1973. He studied musicology with Adler at the Univ. of Vienna (1918–22), and also received training in composition from Schoenberg and Webern. In 1945 he became a prof. of theory at the Vienna Academy of Music. He served as president of the International Gustav Mahler Soc. from 1955, and was ed. of the complete critical edition of Mahler's works. He also ed. the critical editions of Beethoven's piano variations and Schubert's piano sonatas.

WRITINGS (all publ. in Vienna unless otherwise given): *Erkenntnis und Erlebnis des musikalischen Kunstwerks* (1950);

Einführung in die musikalische Formenlehre: Über Formprinzipien in den Inventionen und Fugen J.S. Bachs und ihre Bedeutung für die Kompositionstechnik Beethovens (1951; 3rd ed., 1973); *Die Originalfassung des Streichquartettes op. 130 von Beethoven* (1952); *Zur Chronologie der Klaviersonaten Franz Schuberts* (1955); *Gustav Mahler* (Berlin, 1957); F. Heller, ed., *Gesammelte Aufsätze* (1975).

Rattle, Sir Simon (Denis), brilliant English conductor; b. Liverpool, Jan. 19, 1955. He began playing piano and percussion as a child; appeared as a percussionist with the Royal Liverpool Phil. when he was 11, and was a percussionist in the National Youth Orch.; also took up conducting in his youth, and was founder-conductor of the Liverpool Sinfonia (1970–72); concurrently studied at the Royal Academy of Music in London (1971–74). After winning 1st prize in the John Player International Conductors' Competition (1974), he was assistant conductor of the Bournemouth Sym. Orch. and Sinfonietta (1974–76); made his first tour of the U.S. conducting the London Schools Sym. Orch. (1976). In 1977 he conducted at the Glyndebourne Festival; then was assistant conductor of the Royal Liverpool Phil. (1977–80) and the BBC Scottish Sym. Orch. in Glasgow (1977–80). He made his first appearance as a guest conductor of a U.S. orch. with the Los Angeles Phil. in 1979; was its principal guest conductor (from 1981); also appeared as a guest conductor with other U.S. orchs., as well as with those in Europe. In 1980 he became principal conductor of the City of Birmingham Sym. Orch.; led it on its first tour of the U.S. in 1988, the same year in which he made his U.S. debut as an opera conductor leading *Wozzeck* in Los Angeles. In 1990 he made his debut at London's Covent Garden conducting *The Cunning Little Vixen.* He was named music director of the City of Birmingham Sym. Orch. in 1991, which post he held until 1998. In 1987 he was made a Commander of the Order of the British Empire. He was knighted in 1994.

BIBL.: N. Wheen, "S. R.," *Ovation* (June 1985); N. Kenyon, *S. R.: The Making of a Conductor* (London, 1987).

Raugel, Félix, French conductor and musicologist; b. St.-Quentin, Nov. 27, 1881; d. Paris, Dec. 30, 1975. While attending the Lycée at Lille, he studied music with C. Queste and F. Lecocq; continued his studies in 1900 in Paris with H. Libert and at the Schola Cantorum with d'Indy. Together with E. Borrel, he founded in 1908 the Société Haendel for the cultivation of early music; was conductor of the Rheims Phil. (1926–62).

WRITINGS (all publ. in Paris): *Les Orgues de l'abbaye de Saint-Mihiel* (1919); *Les Organistes* (1923; 2nd ed., 1961); *Recherches sur les maîtres de l'ancienne facture française d'orgues: Les Lépine, les Cavaillé, Dom Bedos* (1925); *Les Grandes Orgues des églises de Paris et du Département de la Seine* (1926); *Palestrina* (1930); *Les Grandes Orgues de Notre-Dame* (1934); *Le Chant choral* (1948; 3rd ed., 1966); *L'Oratorio* (1948).

Rautavaara, Einojuhani (actually, **Eino Juhani**), prominent Finnish composer and pedagogue; b. Helsinki, Oct. 9, 1928. He took up piano lessons at 17 in Turku, and then went to Helsinki to study musicology at the Univ. (M.A., 1953). He also studied composition with Merikanto at the Sibelius Academy (1951–53), where he was awarded his diploma (1957). In 1955–56 he pursued his training with Persichetti at the Juilliard School of Music in N.Y., and with Sessions and Copland at the Berkshire Music Center in Tanglewood (summers, 1956–57). Following further training with Vogel in Ascona, Switzerland (1957), he completed his studies with Petzold in Cologne (1958). From 1957 to 1959 he taught at the Sibelius Academy. He was acting general manager of the Helsinki Phil. from 1959 to 1961. In 1965–66 he was principal of the Käpylä Music School in Helsinki. In 1966 he joined the faculty of the Sibelius Academy as a lecturer in composition, a position he held until 1976. He also held the Finnish State title of Arts Prof. from 1971 to 1976. From 1976 to 1988 he was prof. of composition at the Sibelius Academy. He served on the music panel of the Finnish Arts Council from 1989 to 1991. His autobiography, *Omakuva* (Self-Portrait), was publ. in 1989. In 1961 he was honored with the Arnold Bax Medal, in 1965 he received the International Sibelius Prize of the Wihuri Foundation in Helsinki, and in 1985 he won the Finnish State music prize. In 1975 he was made a member of the Royal Swedish Academy of Music in Stockholm and in 1983 he received an honorary doctorate from the Univ. of Oulu. An eclectic composer, Rautavaara has employed various musical techniques over the years, ranging the gamut from Gregorian chant to the 12-tone method and aleatory.

WORKS: DRAMATIC: OPERAS: *Kaivos* (The Mine; 1957–58; Finnish TV, April 10, 1963); *Apollo contra Marsyas,* comic opera-musical (1970; Helsinki, Aug. 30, 1973); *Runo 42, "Sammon ryöstö"* (The Abduction of Sampo), choral opera (1974–81; Helsinki, April 8, 1983); *Thomas* (1984–85; Joensuu, June 21, 1985); *Vincent* (1986–87; Helsinki, May 17, 1990); *Auringon talo* (The House of the Sun), chamber opera (1990; Lappeenranta, April 25, 1991). **MYSTERY PLAY:** *Marjatta matala neiti* (Marjatta, the Lowly Maiden; 1975; Espoo, Sept. 3, 1977). **BALLET:** *Kiusaukset* (The Temptations; 1969; Helsinki, Feb. 8, 1973). **ORCH.:** Suite for Strings (1952; based on the String Quartet No. 1); *Pelimannit* (The Fiddlers) for Strings (1952; orchestrated 1972; Helsinki, Nov. 11, 1973); *Divertimento* for Strings (1953); *A Requiem in Our Time* (1953; Cincinnati, May 10, 1954); *Epitaph for Béla Bartók* for Strings (1955; rev. 1986; Helsinki, July 27, 1987); 6 syms.: No. 1 (1956; Helsinki, Jan. 22, 1957; rev. 1988; Helsinki, Aug. 24, 1990), No. 2 (Helsinki, Oct. 11, 1957; rev. 1984; Helsinki, Feb. 16, 1985), No. 3 (1961; Helsinki, April 10, 1962), No. 4, *Arabescata* (Helsinki, Feb. 26, 1963), No. 5 (1985–86; Helsinki, May 14, 1986), and No. 6, *Vincentiana* (Helsinki, Oct. 29, 1992); *Praevariata* (1957; Strasbourg, June 1958); *Modificata* (1957; Helsinki, April 25, 1958); *Canto I* (1960; Helsinki, March 7, 1967), *II* (1960; Helsinki, Oct. 27, 1961), *III: A Portrait of the Artist at a Certain Moment* (Jyväskylä, June 27, 1972), and *IV* (1992; Kokkola, Oct. 9, 1993) for Strings; *Helsinki Fanfare* (Helsinki, June 12, 1967; rev. version, Helsinki, April 6, 1987); *Lahti Fanfare* (1967; Lahti, Nov. 1, 1968); *Anadyomene* (Helsinki, May 30, 1968); Cello Concerto (1968; Helsinki, Feb. 26, 1969); *A Soldier's Mass* (Helsinki, Nov. 20, 1968); 2 piano concertos: No. 1 (1969; Helsinki, May 29, 1970) and No. 2 (Munich, Oct. 19, 1989); *Dithyrambos* for Violin and Orch. (1970); *Helsinki Dancing* (Helsinki, Dec. 5, 1971); *Säännöllisiä Yksikköjaksoja Puolisäännöllisessä Tilanteessa* (Regular Sets of Elements in a Semi-regular Situation; 1971; Helsinki, April 19, 1972); *Cantus Arcticus,* concerto for Birds and Orch. (Oulu, Oct. 18, 1972); Flute Concerto (1973; Stockholm, May 4, 1974); *Ballad* for Harp and Strings (1973; Helsinki, Oct. 19, 1976; rev. version, Helsinki, May 19, 1981); *Annunciations,* concerto for Organ and Symphonic Wind Orch. (1976; Stockholm, Sept. 13, 1977); *Suomalainen myytti* (A Finnish Myth) for Strings (1977; Jyväskylä, April 29, 1978); *Angels and Visitations* (Helsinki, Nov. 22, 1978); *Fanfare for the Lahti World Athletics Championships 1978* (1978); *Pohjalainen Polska* (Ostrobothnian Polka; Vaasa, April 11, 1980); *Angel of Dusk,* double bass concerto (1980; Helsinki, May 6, 1981); *Hommage à Zoltán Kodály* for Strings (Helsinki, Dec. 16, 1982); *Hommage à Ferenc Liszt* for Strings (1989; Helsinki, Aug. 9, 1990). **CHAMBER:** 4 string quartets (1952; 1958, Helsinki, April 2, 1959; 1965; 1975); *Poytamusiikki Herttua Juhanalle* (Banqueting Music for Duke Juhana) for 4 Recorders (1954); *2 Preludes and Fugues* for Cello and Piano (1955); Quartet for Oboe and String Trio (1957; rev. 1965); Wind Octet (1962); Bassoon Sonata (1965–68); *Sonetto* for Clarinet and Piano (1969); Sonata for Solo Cello (1969); *Dithyrambos* for Violin and Piano (1970); *Ugrilainen Dialogi* for Violin and Cello (1973); *Variétude* for Violin (1974); Sonata for Flutes and Guitar (1975); *Music* for Upright Piano and Amplified Cello (1976); *Tarantara* for Trumpet (1976); *Polska* for 2 Cellos and Piano (1977); *Angel of Dusk,* concerto for Double Bass, 2 Pianos, and Percussionist (1980; rev. 1993); *Playgrounds for Angels* for 4 Trumpets, 4 Trombones, Horn, and Tuba (Helsinki, Sept. 12, 1981); *Fanfare for Emo* for 2 Trumpets and 2 Trombones (1983); Cello Sonata

(Helsinki, Sept. 16, 1991); *Fanfare for the 75th Anniversary of Finland's Independence 1992* for 4 Trumpets (Joensuu, June 14, 1992); piano pieces, including 2 sonatas (*Christus und die Fischer*, 1969; *The Fire Sermon*, 1970); organ music; guitar pieces. **VOCAL:** *5 Sonette an Orpheus*, song cycle for High, Medium, or Low Voice and Piano (1954–55; also for Medium Voice and Orch., 1960; Helsinki, April 14, 1961); *Die Liebenden*, song cycle for Voice and Piano (1958–59; also for High Voice and String Orch., 1960); *Itsenäisyyskantaatti* (Independence Cantata) for Soloists, Reciter, Chorus, and Orch. (Tampere, June 10, 1967); *True & False Unicorn* for 3 Reciters, Chamber Chorus, Ensemble, and Tape (1971; Holstebro, Denmark, March 25, 1974); *Vigilia* (Vigil Commemorating St. John the Baptist) for Soloists and Chorus (1971–72; part 1, Helsinki, Aug. 28, 1971; part 2, Helsinki, Sept. 9, 1972); *Elämän kirja* (A Book of Life), 11 songs for Soloists and Men's Chorus (1972; Helsinki, Feb. 5, 1975); *A Children's Mass* for Children's Chorus and String Orch. (Espoo, Dec. 20, 1973); *Kainuu*, cantata for Chorus, Reciter, and Percussionist (1975); *Magnificat* for Soloists and Chorus (1979); *Parantaja* (The Healer) for Reciter, Chorus, and Orch. (Helsinki, May 29, 1981); *Katedralen* (The Cathedral) for Soloists and Chorus (1983); *Katso Minun Kansani on Puu* (Behold, My People Are a Tree), independence cantata 1992 for Chorus and Orch. (1991–92; Joensuu, June 14, 1992). **TAPE:** *Number 1* and *2* (both 1980); *Heureka Music 1–2* (1989).

BIBL.: K. Aho, *E. R. sinfonikkona* (E. R. as Symphonist; Helsinki, 1988).

Rautio, Matti, Finnish composer and teacher; b. Helsinki, Feb. 25, 1922; d. Tampere, June 22, 1986. He studied at the Univ. of Helsinki (M.A., 1945); took courses in composition and piano at the Sibelius Academy in Helsinki (certificate, 1950), where he served on its faculty as a piano teacher (1947–64), senior theory teacher (from 1956), and director of the school music dept. (1966–70). In his works, he followed a median line of modern music, programmatic and utilitarian in the use of advanced techniques.

WORKS: *Divertimento 1* for Cello and Orch. or Piano (1955) and *2* for Cello and Piano (1972); *Sininen haikara* (The Blue Heron), suite from the ballet (1957); *Tanhumusiikkia* (Folk Dance Music) for Soprano, Baritone, Chorus, and Orch. (1960); Piano Concerto (1968–71).

Ravasenga, Carlo, Italian composer; b. Turin, Dec. 17, 1891; d. Rome, May 6, 1964. He studied violin, piano, and composition in Turin; then became active as a teacher and music ed. He wrote the operas *Una tragedia fiorentina*, after Oscar Wilde (Turin, 1916), and *Il giudizio di Don Giovanni* (1916); orch. suite, *Un giorno di festa* (1916); symphonic suite, *Giuditta e Oloferno*; *Variazioni pittoresche* for String Quartet; *Contrasto burlesco-sentimentale* for Piano; Violin Sonata; Piano Sonata.

Ravel, (Joseph) Maurice, great French composer; b. Ciboure, Basses-Pyrénées, March 7, 1875; d. Paris, Dec. 28, 1937. His father was a Swiss engineer, and his mother of Basque origin. The family moved to Paris when he was an infant. He began to study piano at the age of 7 with Henri Ghis and harmony at 12 with Charles-René. After further piano studies with Emile Descombes, he entered the Paris Cons. as a pupil of Eugène Anthiôme in 1889; won 1st medal (1891), and passed to the advanced class of Charles de Bériot; also studied harmony with Emile Pessard. He left the Cons. in 1895 and that same year completed work on his song *Un Grand Sommeil noir*, the *Menuet antique* for Piano, and the *Habanera* for 2 Pianos (later included in the *Rapsodie espagnole* for Orch.); these pieces, written at the age of 20, already reveal great originality in the treatment of old modes and of Spanish motifs; however, he continued to study; in 1897 he returned to the Cons. to study with Fauré (composition) and Gédalge (counterpoint and orchestration); his well-known *Pavane pour une infante défunte* for Piano was written during that time (1899). On May 27, 1899, he conducted the premiere of his overture *Shéhérazade* in Paris; some elements of this work were incorporated in his song cycle of the same name (1903). In 1901 he won the 2nd Prix de Rome with the cantata *Myrrha*; but ensuing attempts to win the Grand Prix de Rome were unsuccessful; at his last try (1905) he was eliminated in the preliminaries, and so was not allowed to compete; the age limit then set an end to his further effort to enter. Since 6 prizes all went to pupils of Lenepveu, suspicion of unfair discrimination was aroused; Jean Marnold publ. an article, "Le Scandale du Prix de Rome," in the *Mercure de France* (June 1905) in which he brought the controversy into the open; this precipitated a crisis at the Cons.; its director, Théodore Dubois, resigned, and Fauré took his place. By that time, Ravel had written a number of his most famous compositions, and was regarded by most French critics as a talented disciple of Debussy. No doubt Ravel's method of poetic association of musical ideas paralleled that of Debussy; his employment of unresolved dissonances and the enhancement of the diatonic style into pandiatonicism were techniques common to Debussy and his followers; but there were important differences: whereas Debussy adopted the scale of whole tones as an integral part of his musical vocabulary, Ravel resorted to it only occasionally; similarly, augmented triads appear much less frequently in Ravel's music than in Debussy's; in his writing for piano, Ravel actually anticipated some of Debussy's usages; in a letter addressed to Pierre Lalo and publ. in *Le Temps* (April 9, 1907), Ravel pointed out that at the time of the publication of his piano piece *Jeux d'eau* (1902) Debussy had brought out only his suite *Pour le piano*, which had contained little that was novel. In Paris, elsewhere in France, and soon in England and other European countries, Ravel's name became well known, but for many years he was still regarded as an ultramodernist. A curious test of audience appreciation was a "Concert des Auteurs Anonymes" presented by the Société Independante de Musique on May 9, 1911; the program included Ravel's *Valses nobles et sentimentales*, a set of piano pieces in the manner of Schubert; yet Ravel was recognized as the author. Inspired evocation of the past was but one aspect of Ravel's creative genius; in this style are his *Pavane pour une infante défunte, Le Tombeau de Couperin*, and *La Valse;* luxuriance of exotic colors marks his ballet *Daphnis et Chloé*, his opera *L'Heure espagnole*, the song cycles *Shéhérazade* and *Chansons madécasses*, and his virtuoso pieces for Piano *Miroirs* and *Gaspard de la nuit*; other works are deliberately austere, even ascetic, in their pointed classicism: the piano concertos, the Piano Sonatina, and some of his songs with piano accompaniment. His association with Diaghilev's Ballets Russes was most fruitful; for Diaghilev he wrote one of his masterpieces, *Daphnis et Chloé;* another ballet, *Boléro*, commissioned by Ida Rubinstein and performed at her dance recital at the Paris Opéra on Nov. 22, 1928, became Ravel's most spectacular success as an orch. piece.

Ravel never married, and lived a life of semi-retirement, devoting most of his time to composition; he accepted virtually no pupils, although he gave friendly advice to Vaughan Williams and to others; he was never on the faculty of any school. As a performer, he was not brilliant; he appeared as a pianist only in his own works, and often accompanied singers in programs of his songs; although he accepted engagements as a conductor, his technique was barely sufficient to secure a perfunctory performance of his music. When World War I broke out in 1914, he was rejected for military service because of his frail physique, but he was anxious to serve; his application for air service was denied, but he was received in the ambulance corps at the front; his health gave way, and in the autumn of 1916 he was compelled to enter a hospital for recuperation. In 1922 he visited Amsterdam and Venice, conducting his music; in 1923 he appeared in London; in 1926 he went to Sweden, England, and Scotland; in 1928 he made an American tour as a conductor and pianist; in the same year he received the degree of D.Mus. honoris causa at the Univ. of Oxford. In 1929 he was honored by his native town by the inauguration of the Quai Maurice Ravel. Shortly afterward, he began to experience difficulties in muscular coordination, and suffered from attacks of aphasia, symptoms indicative of a cerebral malady;

he underwent brain surgery on Dec. 19, 1937, but it was not successful; he died 9 days later.

WORKS: DRAMATIC: OPERAS: *L'Heure espagnole*, opera (1907–09; Paris, May 19, 1911); *L'Enfant et les sortilèges*, fantaisie lyrique (1920–25; Monte Carlo, March 21, 1925). **BALLETS:** *Ma Mère l'Oye* (1911; Paris, Jan. 21, 1912; based on the piano work with additional material); *Daphnis et Chloé* (1909–12; Paris, June 8, 1912); *Adélaïde, ou Le Langage des fleurs* (Paris, April 22, 1912; based on the *Valses nobles et sentimentales*); *Le Tombeau de Couperin* (Paris, Nov. 8, 1920; based on the piano work); *La Valse* (Paris, Dec. 12, 1920); *Boléro* (Paris, Nov. 22, 1928). **ORCH.:** *Shéhérazade*, ouverture féerique (1898; Paris, May 27, 1899); *Une Barque sur l'océan* (1906; based on the piano work); *Rapsodie espagnole* (Paris, March 15, 1908); *Pavane pour une infante défunte* (Paris, Dec. 25, 1910; based on the piano work); *Daphnis et Chloé*, 2 suites (1911, 1913); *Alborada del gracioso* (Paris, May 17, 1919; based on the piano work); *La Valse*, poème chorégraphique (Paris, Dec. 12, 1920); *Le Tombeau de Couperin* (Paris, Feb. 28, 1920; based on the piano work); *Tzigane*, rapsodie de concert for Violin and Orch. (Paris, Dec. 7, 1924; based on the work for Violin and Piano); *Menuet antique* (1929; based on the piano work); Piano Concerto in D for Left Hand Alone, written for Paul Wittgenstein (1929–30; Vienna, Nov. 27, 1931); Piano Concerto in G major (1929–31; Paris, Jan. 14, 1932). **CHAMBER:** Violin Sonata (1897); String Quartet in F major (1902–03); *Introduction et Allegro* for Harp, Flute, Clarinet, and String Quartet (1905; Paris, Feb. 22, 1907); Piano Trio (1914); *Le Tombeau de Claude Debussy* for Violin and Cello (1920); Sonata for Violin and Cello (1920–22); *Berceuse sur le nom de Gabriel Fauré* for Violin and Piano (1922); Violin Sonata (1923–27); *Tzigane*, rapsodie de concert for Violin and Piano (London, April 26, 1924). **PIANO:** *Sérénade grotesque* (c.1893); *Menuet antique* (1895); *Sites auriculaires* for 2 Pianos (1895–97): *Pavane pour une infante défunte* (1899) and *Jeux d'eau* (1901); *Sonatine* (1903–05); *Miroirs* (1904–05); *Gaspard de la nuit* (1908); *Menuet sur le nom d'Haydn* (1909); *Ma Mère l'Oye*, 5 "pièces enfantines" for Piano, 4-hands (written for Christine Verger, age 6, and Germaine Durant, age 10, and 1st perf. by them, Paris, April 20, 1910); *Valses nobles et sentimentales* (1911); *Prélude* (1913); *À la manière de . . . Borodin* (1913); *A la manière de . . . Chabrier* (1913); *Le Tombeau de Couperin* (1914–17); *Frontispiece* for 2 Pianos, 5-hands (1918); *La Valse* for 2 Pianos (1921; based on the orch. work); *Boléro* for 2 Pianos (1930; based on the orch. work). **VOCAL:** *Les Bayadères tournent légères* for Soprano, Chorus, and Orch. (1900); 3 cantatas, all for 3 Solo Voices and Orch.: *Myrrha* (1901), *Alcyone* (1902), and *Alyssa* (1903); *Tout est lumière* for Soprano, Chorus, and Orch. (1901); *La Nuit* for Soprano, Chorus, and Orch. (1902); *Matinée de Provence* for Soprano, Chorus, and Orch. (1903); *Manteau de fleurs* for Voice and Orch. (1903; based on the song for Voice and Piano); *Shéhérazade* for Mezzo-soprano and Orch. (1903; Paris, May 17, 1904); *Noël des jouets* for Voice and Orch. (1905; 2nd version, 1913; based on the song for Voice and Piano); *L'Aurore* for Tenor, Chorus, and Orch. (1905); *Chanson de la Mariée* and *Tout gai* for Voice and Orch. (1904–06; based on songs nos. 1 and 5 from the cycle *Cinq mélodies populaires grecques* for Voice and Piano); *Trois poèmes de Stéphane Mallarmé* for Voice, Piccolo, Flute, Clarinet, Bass Clarinet, Piano, and String Quartet (1913; Paris, Jan. 14, 1914); *Trois chansons* for Chorus (1914–15); *Deux mélodies hébraïques* for Voice and Orch. (1919; based on the songs for Voice and Piano); *Chanson hébraïque* for Voice and Orch. (1923–24; based on song no. 4 from the cycle *Chants populaires* for Voice and Piano); *Chansons madécasses* for Voice, Flute, Piano, and Cello (1925–26); *Don Quichotte à Dulcinée* for Baritone and Orch. (1932–33; Paris, Dec. 1, 1934); *Ronsard à son âme* for Voice and Orch. (1935; based on the song for Voice and Piano). **SONGS:** *Ballade de la Reine morte d'aimer* (c.1893); *Un Grand Sommeil noir* (1895); *Sainte* (1896); *Deux épigrammes de Clément Marot* (1896–99); *Chanson du rouet* (1898); *Si morne!* (1898); *Manteau de fleurs* (1903); *Shéhérazade* (1903; based on the work for Mezzo-soprano and Orch.); *Noël des jouets* (1905); *Cinq mélodies populaires grecques* (1904–06); *Histoires naturelles* (1906); *Les Grands Vents venus d'outremer* (1907); *Sur l'herbe* (1907); *Vocalise-étude en forme de habanera* (1907); *Tripatos* (1909); *Chants populaires* (1910); *Trois poèmes de Stéphane Mallarmé* (1913; based on songs for Voice and Various Instruments); *Deux mélodies hébraïques* (1914); *Trois chansons* (1914–15; based on the choral work); *Ronsard à son âme* (1923–24); *Chansons madécasses* (1926; based on the work for Voice, Flute, Piano, and Cello); *Rêves* (1927); *Don Quichotte à Dulcinée* (1932–33; based on the work for Baritone and Orch.). **OTHER:** Various arrangements, including a celebrated version of Mussorgsky's *Pictures at an Exhibition* for Orch. (Paris, Oct. 19, 1922, Koussevitzky conducting).

BIBL.: Roland-Manuel, *M. R. et son oeuvre* (Paris, 1914; 2nd ed., rev., 1926; Eng. tr., 1941); M. Morris, "M. R.," *Music & Letters* (July 1921); Roland-Manuel, "M. R.," *La Revue Musicale*, II/6 (1921); F. Shera, *Debussy and R.* (Oxford, 1925); special issue of *La Revue Musicale*, VI/8 (1925); W.-L. Landowski, *M. R., Sa vie, son oeuvre* (Paris, 1938; 2nd ed., 1950); Roland-Manuel, *À la gloire de R.* (Paris, 1938; 2nd ed., 1948; Eng. tr., 1947); special issue of *La Revue Musicale*, 187 (1938); V. Jankélévitch, *M. R.* (Paris, 1939; 2nd ed., 1956; Eng. tr., 2nd ed., 1959); P. Landormy, "M. R.," *Musical Quarterly* (Oct. 1939); R. Wild, ed., *M. R. par quelques-uns de ses familiers* (Paris, 1939); M. Goss, *Boléro: The Life of M. R.* (N.Y., 1940); M.-D. Calvocoressi, "R.'s Letters to Calvocoressi," *Musical Quarterly* (Jan. 1941); idem, "When R. Composed to Order," *Music & Letters*, XXII (1941); K. Akeret, *Studien zum Klavierwerk von M. R.* (Zürich, 1941); H. Jourdan-Morhange, *R. et nous* (Geneva, 1945); N. Demuth, *R.* (London, 1947); A. Machabey, *M. R.* (Paris, 1947); F. Onnen, *M. R.* (Stockholm, 1947); special issue of *Melos*, XIV/12 (1947); R. Malipiero, *M. R.* (Milan, 1948); L.-P. Fargue, *M. R.* (Paris, 1949); J. Bruyr, *M. R. ou Le Lyrisme et les sortilèges* (Paris, 1950); L. La Pegna, *R.* (Brescia, 1950); W. Tappolet, *M. R.: Leben und Werk* (Olten, 1950); V. Perlemuter and H. Jourdan-Morhange, *R. d'après R.* (Lausanne, 1953; Eng. tr., 1988, as *R. according to R.*); V. Seroff, *M. R.* (N.Y., 1953); M. Gerar and R. Chalupt, eds., *R. au miroir de ses lettres* (Paris, 1956); Roland-Manuel, "Lettres de M. R. et documents inédits," *Revue de Musicologie*, XXXVIII (1956); J. van Ackere, *M. R.* (Brussels, 1957); J. Geraedts, *R.* (Haarlem, 1957); R. de Fragny, *M. R.* (Lyons, 1960); R. Myers, *R.: Life and Works* (London, 1960); H. Stuckenschmidt, *M. R.: Variationen uber Person und Werk* (Frankfurt am Main, 1966; Eng. tr., 1969); A. Orenstein, "M. R.'s Creative Process," *Musical Quarterly* (Oct. 1967); P. Petit, *R.* (Paris, 1970); A. Orenstein, "Some Unpublished Music and Letters by M. R.," *Music Forum*, III (1973); idem, *R.: Man and Musician* (N.Y., 1975; new ed., 1991); R. Nichols, *R.* (London, 1977); H. Macdonald, "R.'s Unknown Choruses," *Musical Times* (Dec. 1983); S. Bress, "Le Scandale R. de 1905," *Revue Internationale de Musique Française*, 14 (1984); A. Orenstein, "R. and Falla: An Unpublished Correspondence, 1914–1933," *Music and Civilization: Essays in Honor of Paul Henry Lang* (N.Y., 1984); M. Marnat, ed., *M. R.: L'Hommage de La Revue musicale, decembre 1938* (Lyons, 1987); R. Nichols, *R. Remembered* (London and Boston, 1987); M. Rosenthal, *Satie, R., Poulenc: An Intimate Memoir* (Madras and N.Y., 1987); T. Hirsbrunner, *M. R.: Sein Leben, sein Werk* (Laaber, 1989); A. Orenstein, ed., *R.: Correspondance, écrits et entretiens* (Paris, 1989; Eng. tr., 1989, as *A R. Reader*); R. Beyer, *Organale Satztechniken in den Werken von Claude Debussy und M. R.* (Wiesbaden, 1992).

Raver, Leonard, American organist and teacher; b. Wenatchee, Wash., Jan. 8, 1927; d. N.Y., Jan. 29, 1992. He studied organ and piano in Tacoma, where he was active as a church organist. After moving to N.Y., he pursued a career as a recitalist and a teacher. His appearances as a soloist with the N.Y. Phil. led to his appointment as its organist in 1977, which position he retained until his death. While he displayed a fine command of the Baroque repertoire, he had a special flair for contemporary works. Among the composers he championed were Diamond, Persichetti, Rorem, and Read.

Rawsthorne, Alan, important English composer; b. Haslingden, May 2, 1905; d. Cambridge, July 24, 1971. He went to a dentistry school; did not begin to study music until he was 20, when he entered the Royal Manchester College of Music; later studied piano with Egon Petri in Berlin (1930–31). After returning to England in 1932, he occupied various teaching posts; then devoted himself mainly to composition, and succeeded brilliantly in producing music of agreeable, and to some ears even delectable, music. In 1961 he was made a Commander of the Order of the British Empire. His music is essentially a revival of the contrapuntal style of the past, without much harmonic elaboration; but the rhythms are virile and the melodies fluid, emanating from a focal point of tonality.

WORKS: BALLET: *Madame Chrysanthème* (London, April 1, 1955). **ORCH.:** Concerto for Clarinet and Strings (1936); *Symphonic Studies* (1938; Warsaw, April 21, 1939); 2 piano concertos: No. 1 (originally for Strings and Percussion, 1939; rescored for Full Orch., 1942) and No. 2 (London, June 17, 1951); 2 violin concertos: No. 1 (1940; sketches lost in an air raid; reconstructed 1943–48; Cheltenham, July 1, 1948) and No. 2 (London, Oct. 24, 1956); 4 overtures: *Street Corner* (1944), *Cortèges* (1945), *Hallé*, for the centennial of the Hallé Orch. (1958), and *Overture for Farnham* (1967); Concerto for Oboe and Strings (1947); Concerto for Strings (1949); 3 syms.: No. 1 (London, Nov. 15, 1950), No. 2, *Pastoral*, for Soprano and Orch. (Birmingham, Sept. 29, 1959), and No. 3 (Cheltenham, July 8, 1964); *Concertante pastorale* for Flute, Horn, and Strings (1951); *Improvisations on a Theme of Constant Lambert* (1960); Concerto for 10 Instruments (1962); *Divertimento* for Chamber Orch. (1962); *Elegiac Rhapsody* for Strings (1964); Cello Concerto (London, April 6, 1966); Concerto for 2 Pianos and Orch. (1968); *Theme, Variations and Finale* (1968); *Triptych* (1970). **CHAMBER:** *Concertante* for Violin and Piano (1935–62); Trio for Flute, Oboe, and Piano (1936); *Theme and Variations* for 2 Violins (1937); Viola Sonata (1938); *Theme and Variations* for String Quartet (1939); 3 string quartets (1939, 1954, 1965); Clarinet Quartet (1948); Cello Sonata (1949); Violin Sonata (1959); Piano Trio (1962); Quintet for Piano, Oboe, Clarinet, Horn, and Bassoon (1963); Quintet for Piano and Strings (1968); Oboe Quartet (1970); Suite for Flute, Viola, and Harp (1970); Quintet for Piano, Clarinet, Horn, Violin, and Cello (1971); *Elegy* for Guitar (1971; completed from composer's sketches by Julian Bream). **PIANO:** *Bagatelles* (1938); *The Creel* for 2 Pianos (1940); Sonatina (1948); *4 Romantic Pieces* (1953); *Ballade* (1967); *Theme with 4 Studies* (1971). **VOCAL:** *A Canticle of Man*, chamber cantata for Baritone, Chorus, Flute, and Strings (1952); *Practical Cats*, children's entertainment for Narrator and Orch., after T.S. Eliot (Edinburgh, Aug. 26, 1954); *Medieval Diptych* for Baritone and Orch. (1962); *Carmen Vitale*, cantata (London, Oct. 16, 1963); *Tankas of the 4 Seasons* for Tenor, Oboe, Clarinet, Bassoon, Violin, and Cello (1965); *The God in the Cave* for Chorus and Orch. (1967).

BIBL.: A. Poulton, ed., *A. R.: A Catalogue of His Music* (Kidderminster, 1984); A. Poulton, ed., *A. R.* (3 vols., Hindhead, 1984–86).

Raxach, Enrique, Spanish-born Dutch composer; b. Barcelona, Jan. 15, 1932. After studies with Nuri Aymerich, he attended the summer courses in new music in Darmstadt given by Messiaen, Boulez, Maderna, and Stockhausen (1959–66). In 1962 he settled in the Netherlands and in 1969 became a naturalized Dutch citizen. In his music, Raxach utilizes various contemporary modes of expression, including electronics.

WORKS: DRAMATIC: *Reflections Inside*, electronic ballet music (1992–94). **ORCH.:** *Polifonías* for Strings (1953–56); *6 Mouvements* (1955); *Metamorphose I* (1956), *II* (1958), and *III* for 15 Solo Instruments (1959); *Prometheus*, renamed *Poème* (1957–58); *Fluxión* for 17 Players (1962–63); *Syntagma* (1964–65); *Textures* (1965–66); *Equinoxial* for Winds, Percussion, Hammond Organ, and Double Basses (1967–68); *Inside Out* for Orch. and Tape ad libitum (1969); *Figuren in einer Landschaft* (1972–74); *Ad Marginem*, triple concerto for Flute, Violin, Viola, and Orch. (1974–75); *Erdenlicht* (1975); *Am Ende des Regenbogens* (1980); *Opus Incertum* for Large Chamber Orch. (1985); *Calles y sueños—in memoriam García Lorca* for Chamber Orch. (1986); *Codex Z* for Large Wind Orch. and Bambuso Sonore (Bamboo Organ) ad libitum (1991); Piano Concertino (1994–95). **CHAMBER:** 2 string quartets: No. 1, *Fases* (1961) and No. 2, with live electronics ad libitum (1971); *Imaginary Landscape* for Flute and Percussionist (1968); *Scattertime* for 6 Players (1971); *Chimaera* for Bass Clarinet and Tape (1974); *Aubade* for Percussion Quintet (1978); *The Hunting in Winter* for Horn and Piano (1979); *Careful with that . . .* for Clarinet and Percussionist (1982); *Chalumeau* for Clarinet Quartet (1982); *Ode* for Flute and String Trio (1982); *Vórtice* for 6 Bass and 3 Contrabass Clarinets (1983); *Antevísperas* for Saxophone Quartet (1986); *Asalto* for Saxophone and Piano (1986); *Obessum* for Bassoon and 9 Accordions (1988); *Danses Pythiques* for Harp (1992); *Decade* for Bass Clarinet and Accordion (1992). **KEYBOARD: PIANO:** *Ricercare* (1976); *12 Preludes* (1993–94). **ORGAN:** *Tientos* (1964–65); *The Looking Glass* (1967). **VOCAL:** *Pequeña Cantata* for Tenor and Small Ensemble (1952); *Fragmento II* for Soprano, Flute, and 2 Percussionists (1965–66); *Paraphrase* for Mezzo-soprano and 11 Players (1969); *Interface* for Chorus and Orch. (1971–72); *Sine Nomine* for Soprano and Orch. (1973); *Soirée musicale* for Women's Chorus, Bass Clarinet, and Orch. (1978); *. . . hub of ambiguity* for Soprano and 8 Players (1984); *Nocturno del hueco* for Chorus, Large Ensemble, and Tape (1990).

Ray, Don Brandon, American conductor and composer; b. Santa Maria, Calif., June 7, 1926. He studied composition in Los Angeles with John Vincent at the Univ. of Calif. (B.A., 1948) and with Ernst Kanitz at the Univ. of Southern Calif.; also studied conducting with Roger Wagner and Richard Lert. He composed orch. pieces; Protestant church services; incidental music to theatrical plays; *Symrock* (symphonic rock) for Orch. (1978).

Rea, John (Rocco), Canadian composer and teacher; b. Toronto, Jan. 14, 1944. He studied at Wayne State Univ. in Detroit (B.Mus., 1967). Following training in composition with Weinzweig and Ciamaga at the Univ. of Toronto (M.Mus., 1969), he studied with Babbitt and Westergaard at Princeton Univ. (Ph.D., 1978). In 1973 he became a teacher of composition and theory at McGill Univ. in Montreal, where he also was dean of the faculty of music (1986–91). He was composer-in-residence in Mannheim in 1984 and of the Incontri music festival in Terra di Siena in 1991. In his music, Rea has explored various genres and styles, and has utilized both Western and non-Western elements in a number of his scores.

WORKS: DRAMATIC: *The Days/Les Jours*, ballet (1969; suite, Toronto, July 11, 1974); *The Prisoners Play*, opera (Toronto, May 12, 1973); *Com-possession*, "daemonic afterimages in the theatre of transitory states" (1980). **ORCH.:** *Piece* for Chamber Orch. (1967; rev. 1971); *Hommage à Vasarely* (1977); *Vanishing Points* (1983); *Over Time* (1987); *Time and Again* (Montreal, March 1987). **CHAMBER:** *Sestina* for Chamber Ensemble (1968); *Fantaisies and/et Allusions* for Saxophone Quartet and Snare Drum (1969); *Anaphora I–IV* for Various Instruments (1970–74); *Jeux de scène*, fantaisie-hommage à Richard Wagner for Horn, Oboe, Cello, Piccolo, Flute, Piano, Marimba, 3 Glockenspiels, and Blacksmith's Anvil (1976; Vancouver, Feb. 27, 1977); *Les Blues d'Orphée* for Flute, Clarinet, Viola, Cello, and Piano (1981); *Le Dernière Sirène* for Ondes Martenot, Piano, and Percussion (1981); *Médiator ". . . pincer la musique aujourd'hui . . ."* for Chamber Ensemble (1981); *Treppenmusik* for Saxophone Quartet, 4 Clarinets, Violin, Viola, Cello, Double Bass, and Tape (1982); *Glide Reflexions* for 2 Clarinets and 2 Cellos (1984); *Les Raisons des forces mouvants* for Flute, Alto Flute, and String Quartet (1984); *Spin* for String Quartet and Piano (1984); *Some Time Later* for Electronic String Quartet (1986); *Big Apple Jam* for Saxophone Quartet and Tape (1987–91; Montreal, March 19, 1991); *Kubla Khan* for Chamber Ensemble (Waterloo, Ontario, May 1989). **PIANO:** *What You Will* for Piano 2- or 4-hands (1969); *Las Meninas* (1990–91).

VOCAL: *Prologue, Scene, and Movement* for Soprano, Viola, and 2 Pianos (1968); *Le Petit Livre des "Ravalets"* for 4 Narrators, Early Music Instruments, and Tape (1983); *Litaneia* for Chorus and Orch. (1984); *Offenes Lied* for 2 Sopranos and Clarinet (1986). **TAPE:** *S.P.I. 51* (1969); *STER 1.3* (1969).

Read, Gardner, eminent American composer, pedagogue, and writer on music; b. Evanston, Ill., Jan. 2, 1913. He studied at Northwestern Univ. (1930–32), with Hanson and Rogers at the Eastman School of Music in Rochester, N.Y. (B.M., 1936; M.M., 1937), with Pizzetti in Rome on a Cromwell Traveling Fellowship (1938–39), and with Copland at the Berkshire Music Center in Tanglewood (summer, 1941). In 1936 he won 1st prize in the American Composers' Contest of the N.Y. Phil. for his 1st Sym. and in 1943 he won the Paderewski Prize for his 2nd Sym. After teaching at the St. Louis Inst. of Music (1941–43) and the Kansas City Cons. (1943–45), he was head of the Cleveland Inst. of Music (1944–48). He subsequently was prof. of music and composer-in-residence at the Boston Univ. School for the Arts (1948–78). He publ. *Thesaurus of Orchestral Devices* (1953), *Music Notation: A Manual of Modern Practice* (1964), *Contemporary Instrumental Techniques* (1976), *Modern Rhythmic Notation* (1978), *Style and Orchestration* (1979), *Source Book of Proposed Music Notation Reform* (1987), *20th-Century Microtonal Notation* (1990), *Compendium of Modern Instrumental Techniques* (1993), and *Pictographic Score Notation* (1995). As a composer, Read has produced a substantial body of works notable for their mastery of orchestration and form.

WORKS: DRAMATIC: *Villon*, opera (1965–67); incidental music. **ORCH.:** *The Lotus-Eaters* (Interlochen, Mich., Aug. 12, 1932); *Sketches of the City* (1933; Rochester, N.Y., April 18, 1934); *The Painted Desert* (Interlochen, Mich., July 28, 1935); *Fantasy* for Viola and Orch. (1935); 4 syms.: No. 1 (1936; N.Y., Nov. 4, 1937), No. 2 (1942; Boston, Nov. 26, 1943), No. 3 (1948), and No. 4 (1951–59; Cincinnati, Jan. 30, 1970); *Prelude and Toccata* for Chamber Orch. (1936–37; Rochester, N.Y., April 29, 1937); Suite for Strings (N.Y., Aug. 5, 1937); *Passacaglia and Fugue* (Chicago, June 30, 1938); *Pan e Dafni* (1940); *American Circle* (Evanston, Ill., March 15, 1941); Overture No. 1 (Indianapolis, Nov. 6, 1943); *Night Flight* (Rochester, N.Y., April 27, 1944); Cello Concerto (1945); *Threnody* for Flute and Strings (Rochester, N.Y., Oct. 21, 1946); *Quiet Music* for Strings (1946; Washington, D.C., May 9, 1948; arranged for organ, 1950); *Partita* for Chamber Orch. (1946; Rochester, N.Y., May 4, 1947); *Bell Overture* (Cleveland, Dec. 22, 1946); *Pennsylvaniana* (1946–47; Pittsburgh, Nov. 21, 1947); *The Temptation of St. Anthony*, dance sym. (1947; Chicago, April 9, 1953); *Dance of the Locomotives* (Boston, June 26, 1948); *Arioso elegiaca* for Strings (1951); *Toccata giocosa* (1953; Louisville, March 13, 1954); *Vernal Equinox* (Brockton, Mass., April 12, 1955); *Jeux des timbres* (1963); *Sonoric Fantasia No. 2* for Violin and Chamber Orch. (1965; also for Violin and Piano) and *3* for Wind and Percussion (1971); Piano Concerto (1977); *Astral Nebulae* (1983). **CHAMBER:** *6 Intimate Moods* for Violin and Piano (1935–37); Suite for String Quartet (1936); Piano Quintet (1945; also as *Music* for Piano and Strings, 1946); *Sonata brevis* for Violin and Piano (1948); *Sound Piece* for Brass and Percussion (1949); *9 by 6* for 6 Winds (1950); *Sonoric Fantasia No. 1* for Celesta, Harp, and Harpsichord (1958) and *No. 4* for Organ and Percussion (1975–76); *Los dioses aztecas* for 6 Percussion (1959); *Petite suite* for Soprano Recorder, Alto Recorder, Piano, and Harpsichord (1963); *Invocation* for Trombone and Organ (1977); *Galactic Notes* for Organ and Percussion (1978); *Diabolic Dialogue* for Double Bass and 4 Timpani (1978–79); *Music for Chamber Winds* for Double Wind Quintet and Percussion (1980); *Phantasmagoria* for Oboe, Oboe d'Amore, English Horn, and Organ (1985–87; rev. 1988); *Fantasy-Toccata* for Harpsichord (1990); *5 Aphorisms* for Violin and Piano (1991). **KEYBOARD: PIANO:** *3 Satirical Sarcasms* (1934–35); *Driftwood Suite* (1942); *Sonata da chiesa* (1945; also for Organ and Brass Quintet, 1947); *6 Easy Pieces* (1947–48); *Touch Piece* (1949); *5 Polytonal Etudes* (1961–64); *Motives* (1980). **ORGAN:** *Passacaglia and Fugue* (1935–36; also for 2 Pianos, 1938–40); Suite (1949); *14 Preludes on Old Southern Hymns* (1950, 1960); *Variations on a Chromatic Ground* (1964); *And There Appeared Unto Them Tongues as of Fire* (1977). **VOCAL:** *4 Nocturnes* for Alto and Orch. (1934); *A Merry Madrigal* for Women's Voices (1934–35; also for Chorus, 1964); *From a Lute of Jade* for Mezzo-soprano and Chamber Orch. or Piano (1935–36); *The Golden Journey to Samarkand* for Soloists, Chorus, and Orch. (1936–39); *Songs for a Rainy Night* for Baritone and Piano or Orch. (1938–40; also for Chorus and Piano, 1953); *Songs to Children* for Mezzo-soprano and Piano (1947–49); *A Sheaf of Songs* for Mezzo-soprano and Piano (1949–50; also for Chorus and Piano, 1954); *The Prophet*, oratorio (1960; Boston, Feb. 23, 1977); *Haiku Seasons* for 4 Speakers and 5 Instruments (1970); *The Hidden Lute* for Soprano, Alto Flute, Percussion, and Harp (1979); other choral pieces and songs.

Reale, Paul, American composer and pianist; b. New Brunswick, N.J., March 2, 1943. He studied with Luening and Chou Wen-chung at Columbia Univ. (B.A., 1963; M.A., 1967) and with Rochberg and Crumb at the Univ. of Pa. (Ph.D., 1970). He joined the faculty of the Univ. of Calif. at Los Angeles in 1969, becoming a prof. in 1980. His works, which are mostly based in tonality, include a series of piano sonatas (Nos. 1–3, 1985; No. 5, 1988) and a number of comic stage works, including *We All Loved You, Jenny Jo* (1981) and *Uncle Sigmund Goes to the Opera* (1986). As a pianist, he toured Europe, South America, and China; from 1970, specialized in playing 20th-century American music. He also performed numerous guest lectures at the piano on 20th-century music and philosophy. Among his other compositions are *Dancer's Dream* for 9 Strings (1980), Cello Sonata (1982; rev. 1983), and Violin Concerto (1990).

Reaney, Gilbert, learned English musicologist; b. Sheffield, Jan. 11, 1924. He took courses in music and French at the Univ. of Sheffield (B.A., 1948; M.A., 1951, with the diss. *The Ballades, Rondeaux and Virelais Set to Music by Guillaume de Machaut*; B.Mus., 1951); also studied at the Sorbonne in Paris on a French government grant (1950–53). He was a research fellow at the Univs. of Reading (1953–56) and Birmingham (1956–59), and then a visiting prof. at the Univ. of Hamburg (1959–60); subsequently was assoc. prof. (1960–63) and prof. (from 1963) at the Univ. of Calif. at Los Angeles. He served as assistant ed. of *Musica Disciplina* (1956–93) and was general ed. of the Corpus Scriptorum de Musica series. His contributions to the latter include: with A. Gilles and J. Maillard, *P. de Vitry: Ars nova*, VIII (1964); *Willemus: Breviarium regulare musicae; Anon.: Tractatus de figuris; J. Torkesey: Declaratio trianguli et scuti*, XII (1966); with A. Gilles, *Anon.: Ars musicae mensurabilis secundum Franconem*, XV (1971); with A. Gilles, *Franco of Cologne: Ars cantus mensurabilis*, XVIII (1974); 3 anonymous 14th-century mensural treatises, XXX (1982); the mensural treatises of John Hothby and Thomas Walsingham, XXXI (1983); with H. Ristory, 4 mainly anonymous mensural treatises of the 13th to 14th centuries, XXXIV (1987). He also ed. *Early Fifteenth-Century Music* in the Corpus Mensurabilis Musicae series, XI/1–7 (1955–83). Among his other writings are *Ch. Jones, the Saint Nicholas Liturgy and Its Literary Relationships* (Berkeley and Los Angeles, 1963) and *Guillaume de Machaut* (London, 1971).

Reardon, John, American baritone; b. N.Y., April 8, 1930; d. Santa Fe, N.Mex., April 16, 1988. He studied at Rollins College (B.Mus., 1952); then took voice lessons with Martial Singher and Margaret Harshaw. He made his first appearance with the N.Y. City Opera on Oct. 16, 1954, as Falke in *Die Fledermaus*. He made his Metropolitan Opera debut in N.Y. on Sept. 28, 1965, as Count Tomsky in Tchaikovsky's *Queen of Spades*, remaining on its roster until 1977. He mastered an extensive repertoire, which included several roles in modern operas.

Rebner, Adolf, Austrian violinist and teacher, father of **Wolfgang Eduard Rebner**; b. Vienna, Nov. 21, 1876; d. Baden-Baden, June 19, 1967. He was a pupil of Grun at the Vienna

Cons. He settled in Frankfurt am Main in 1896, and from 1904 taught violin at the Hoch Cons. In 1921 he organized the Rebner String Quartet, with Hindemith as the violist, and gave numerous concerts with it, obtaining excellent success; with the advent of the Nazi regime in Germany, he went to Vienna; after the Anschluss, lived briefly in the U.S.; eventually returned to Europe and lived in Baden-Baden.

Rebner, Wolfgang Eduard, German pianist and composer, son of **Adolf Rebner**; b. Frankfurt am Main, Dec. 20, 1910. He studied at the Hoch Cons. in Frankfurt am Main; served as accompanist to Feuermann in the U.S. (1935–37) and South America. In 1955 he returned to Germany, and taught at the Richard Strauss Cons. in Munich. He composed some excellent chamber music and the orch. suites *Persönliche Noten* (1961) and *Aus Sudamerika* (1964).

Rechberger, Herman(n), Austrian-born Finnish recorder player, conductor, and composer; b. Linz, Feb. 14, 1947. He studied classical guitar at the Bruckner Cons. in Linz; after further training in Zürich and at the Brussels Cons., he settled in Finland in 1970 and became a naturalized citizen (1974); took courses with Osmo Lindeman (electronic music), Olli Ruottinen (recorder; teacher's diploma, 1973), Ivan Putilin (guitar; teacher's diploma, 1973), and Aulis Sallinen (composition; diploma, 1976) at the Sibelius Academy in Helsinki (1971–77), where he also received instruction in piano, violin, and oboe. He was active as a music teacher (1975–79); then was a producer of contemporary music for and director of the electronic music studio at the Finnish Radio (1979–84). He toured widely as a recorder player; also appeared as a conductor. In his own music, he employs the full arsenal of contemporary resources, experimenting in multimedia spectacles, with ample use of electronics.

WORKS: DRAMATIC: MULTIMEDIA AND RADIOPHONIC: *Naula* (The Nail) for Bass-baritone, Actors, Dancers, Slide Projection, and Instruments (1975–76); *Pekka Mikkosen nousu* (The Rise of Jonathan Smith), radiophonic piece for Narrator, Piano, Various Sound Sources, and Non-conventional Instruments (1976–78); *Tree-O* for Stage Equipment, Slide Projection, 3 Actors, and Lute (1976); *Publico concertante* for 6 to 30 Different Instruments, Audience, and Slides (1977); *Zin Kibaru*, multimedia piece for Young Performers (1977); *. . . i$mo*, multimedia piece for Sound Objects, Actor, Slide Projectors, Light Organ, Flute, Clarinet, Violin, Cello, Videotape, and Kinetic Wall (1982); *Magnus Cordius—Entries in a Diary*, radiophonic piece for Actors, Orch., Chorus, Early Instruments, Vocal Ensemble, and Tapes (1985); *Die Nonnen* (The Nuns), chamber opera (1987); also music for plays and television. **ORCH.:** Concerto for Guitar and Strings (1971); *Kaamos* for Strings and Timpani (1973); *Music for Under-developed Film* (1973); *Loitsut* (Charms) for High Soprano and Chamber Orch. (1974); *La macchina capricciosa* for Double Bassoon, Chamber Orch., and Optional Slides (1974–75); *Consort Music 1* for Recorders, Chamber Orch., and Tape (1974–76), *2* for Renaissance Instruments and Chamber Orch. (1977), and *5* (1985–86); *Himojen Puutarha* (The Garden of Delights; 1976–77); *Venezia, visioni per grande orchestra, diversi soli e nastro* (1985). **CHAMBER:** *Ylistyslaulu höyryveturille* (Ode to a Steam Locomotive) for Flute, Clarinet, Viola, and Cello (1971); *Mayenzeit one neidt* for Flute, Violin, Cello, Double Bass, Metronome, and Live Electronics (1974); *Meccanismo* for Flute, Clarinet, Violin, Cello, and Metronomes (1978); *Fragebogen* for Double Bassoon and Pedal Sounds (1979); *Consort Music 3* for 4 Trumpets, 4 Trombones, and Tuba (1980–81); *Almost 4 Seasons* for String Quartet (1981); *Consort on an Egg* for Renaissance Instruments (1985); *NCG 7293* for 2 to 4 Instrumentalists (1986); *tympanon* for 2X5 Tambourins and Cowbells (1987); works for solo instruments. **OTHER:** Choral music; pieces for solo tape and for tape and instruments; text scores; musical graphics.

Reda, Siegfried, German organist, pedagogue, and composer; b. Bochum, July 27, 1916; d. Mülheim, Dec. 13, 1968. He studied in Dortmund, and then with Pepping and Distler in Berlin. In 1946 he became director of the Essen Folkwang-Hochschule, where he also was prof. of organ and composition. From 1953 he also served as director of church music in Mülheim. Reda was an influential figure in progressive Protestant church music circles in Germany after World War II. In addition to his masterpiece, the Requiem for Soloists, Chorus, and Orch. (1963), he composed much other sacred choral music, as well as various liturgical organ works.

BIBL.: R. Webb, *S. R. (1916–1968)* (diss., Univ. of Cincinnati, 1974).

Redel, Kurt, German flutist and conductor; b. Breslau, Oct. 8, 1918. He studied at the Breslau Cons.; also conducting with C. Krauss. In 1939 he became a member of the Salzburg Mozarteum Orch.; in 1941 he joined the orch. of the Bavarian State Opera in Munich. From 1946 to 1953 he taught at the North West German Music Academy in Detmold. In 1953 he founded the Pro Arte Orch. of Munich, with which he toured widely.

Redlich, Hans F(erdinand), Austrian-born English conductor, musicologist, and composer; b. Vienna, Feb. 11, 1903; d. Manchester, Nov. 27, 1968. He studied piano and composition, but devoted his energies mainly to writing biographical and analytical books on composers; he was only 16 when he publ. an essay on Mahler. After taking courses at the Univs. of Vienna and Munich, he obtained his Ph.D. at the Univ. of Frankfurt am Main with the diss. *Das Problem des Stilwandels in Monteverdis Madrigalwerk* (publ. in Berlin, 1931; 2nd ed., aug., 1932, as *Claudio Monteverdi: I. Das Madrigalwerk*). He conducted opera in Mainz (1925–29); then lived in Mannheim. In 1939 he emigrated to England and in 1947 became a naturalized British subject. From 1941 to 1955 he conducted the Choral and Orch. Soc. in Letchworth and also was a lecturer for the extramural depts. of the Univs. of Cambridge and Birmingham. From 1955 to 1962 he was a lecturer at the Reid School of Music at the Univ. of Edinburgh; then was at the Univ. of Manchester (1962–68).

WRITINGS: *Gustav Mahler: Eine Erkenntnis* (Nuremberg, 1919); *Richard Wagner: Tristan und Isolde, Lohengrin, Parsifal* (London, 1948; 3rd ed., 1951); *Claudio Monteverdi: Leben und Werk* (Olten, 1949; Eng. tr., 1952); *Bruckner and Mahler* (London, 1955; 2nd ed., rev., 1963); *Alban Berg: Versuch einer Würdigung* (Vienna, 1957; condensed Eng. version, 1957, as *Alban Berg: The Man and His Music*).

Redman, Harry N(ewton), American teacher, composer, and painter; b. Mount Carmel, Ill., Dec. 26, 1869; d. Boston, Dec. 26, 1958. He received instruction in piano, violin, and theory at the New England Cons. of Music in Boston, his principal teacher being Chadwick; then was on its faculty (1897–1937). He subsequently devoted himself to painting; exhibited in Boston as late as 1957. He publ. a piano method and *A Pronouncing Dictionary of Musical Terms* (1901); wrote 4 string quartets, 2 violin sonatas, and other chamber works, songs, and piano pieces.

Reed, Alfred, American conductor, composer, and arranger; b. N.Y., Jan. 25, 1921. He studied theory and harmony with John Sacco and Paul Yartin. He enlisted in the U.S. Air Force during World War II and was assigned to the Army Air Force Band; upon discharge from military service, he enrolled at the Juilliard School of Music in N.Y. as a student of Vittorio Giannini; completed his training at Baylor Univ. (B.M., 1955; M.M., 1956). In 1948 he was appointed staff composer and arranger with NBC; later served in the same capacity with ABC. From 1953 to 1966 he conducted the Baylor Univ. Sym. Orch.; in 1966 he joined the music faculty at the Univ. of Miami, where he developed a unique music merchandising program; also conducted its sym. orch. (from 1980). He composed a great number of band pieces; also wrote a multitude of 3-minute musical sequences for sound-track library recordings.

Reed, H(erbert) Owen, American composer and music educator; b. Odessa, Mo., June 17, 1910. He was educated at the Univ. of Missouri (theory and composition, 1929–33), Louisiana

State Univ. (B.M. in theory, 1934; M.M. in composition, 1936; B.A. in French, 1937), and at the Eastman School of Music in Rochester, N.Y. (Ph.D. in composition, 1939), where his mentors included Hanson, Rogers, and McHose. He pursued further studies at the Berkshire Music Center in Tanglewood (summer, 1942) with Martinů, Copland, and Bernstein and in Colorado Springs (summer, 1947) with Roy Harris. Subsequently he studied folk music in Mexico (1948–49; 1960), the Caribbean (1976), and Scandinavia (1977), and also native American music in Arizona. In 1939 he joined the faculty of Michigan State Univ., where he was chairman of its theory and composition dept. until 1967; he then was chairman of music composition from 1967 until his retirement as prof. emeritus in 1976. In 1948–49 he held a Guggenheim fellowship and in 1960 a Huntington Foundation fellowship. His textbooks have been widely used. In his compositions, Reed generally has followed a tonal course with later diversions into nontonal pathways.

WRITINGS: *A Workbook in the Fundamentals of Music* (1947); *Basic Music* (1954); *Basic Music Workbook* (1954); *Composition Analysis Chart* (1958); with P. Harder, *Basic Contrapuntal Technique* (1964); *Basic Contrapuntal Workbook* (1964); with J. Leach, *Scoring for Percussion and the Instruments of the Percussion Section* (1969; rev. ed., 1979); with R. Sidnell, *The Materials of Music Composition* (3 vols., 1978, 1980, in progress).

WORKS: DRAMATIC: *The Masque of the Red Death*, ballet-pantomime (1936); *Michigan Dream*, renamed *Peter Homan's Dream*, folk opera (East Lansing, Mich., May 13, 1955; rev. 1959); *Earth Trapped*, chamber dance opera (1960; East Lansing, Mich., Feb. 24, 1962); *Living Solid Face*, chamber dance opera (1974; Brookings, S. Dak., Nov. 28, 1976); *Butterfly Girl and Mirage Boy*, chamber opera (East Lansing, Mich., May 1980). **ORCH.:** *Evangeline*, symphonic poem (Rochester, N.Y., March 30, 1938); 2 syms.: No. 1 (Rochester, N.Y., April 27, 1939) and No. 2, *La fiesta mexicana*, Mexican folk-song sym. (1968; also for Band, 1949); Overture (1940); *Symphonic Dance* (1942); Cello Concerto (1949); Overture for Strings (1961); *The Turning Mind* (1968); *Ut Re Mi* for Orch. and Taped or Live Men's Voices (1979; also for Wind Ensemble and Taped or Live Men's Voices, 1980). **BAND:** *Spiritual* (1947); *La fiesta mexicana*, Mexican folk-song sym. (1949; also for Orch., 1968); *Missouri Shindig* (1951); *Theme and Variations* (1954); *Renascence* (1959); *Che-ba-kun-ah* (Road of Souls) for Wind Ensemble and String Quartet (1959); *The Touch of the Earth* for Concert Band (1971; also for Solo Voices, Chorus, and Concert Band, 1972); *For the Unfortunate* for Concert Band and Tape or Chorus (1975); *Ut Re Mi* for Wind Ensemble and Taped or Live Men's Voices (1980; also for Orch. and Taped or Live Men's Voices, 1979); *The Awakening of the Ents* for Winds and Percussion (1985); *Of Lothlórien* for Winds and Percussion (1987). **CHAMBER:** String Quartet (1937); *Scherzo* for Clarinet and Piano (1947); *Symphonic Dance* for Piano and Woodwind Quintet (1954); *El Muchacho* for 7 Handbells and 3 Percussion (1965); *Fanfare for Remembrance* for 6 Trumpets, Flugelhorn, Percussionist, and Narrator (1986); piano pieces. **VOCAL:** *A Psalm of Praise* for Soprano and 7 Instruments (1937); *Wondrous Love* for Tenor and Woodwind Quintet (1948); *Ripley Ferry* for Women's Voices and Wind Septet (1958); *A Tabernacle for the Sun*, oratorio for Contralto, Chorus, Speaking Men's Chorus, and Orch. (1963); *Rejoice! Rejoice!* for Soloist, Chorus, Taped Chorus, Vibe or Bells, and Double Bass (1977); other choral pieces and songs.

Reed, William L(eonard), English composer, lecturer, and editor; b. London, Oct. 16, 1910. He studied at the Guildhall School of Music in London (1917–26), Dulwich College, London (1922–29), the Univ. of Oxford (M.A., 1934; B.Mus., 1936; M.Mus., 1939), and with Howells (composition) and Lambert (conducting) at the Royal College of Music in London (1934–36; 1st Cobbett Prize in composition, 1936). After World War II, he traveled widely in Europe, the U.S., and Asia; in 1961 settled in London, where he served as director of music at the Westminster Theatre Arts Centre (1967–80).

WORKS: MUSICALS: *The Vanishing Island* (Santa Barbara, Calif., 1955; in collaboration with G. Fraser); *Annie* (London, 1967); *High Diplomacy* (London, 1969; in collaboration with G. Fraser); *Love All* (London, 1978). **ORCH.:** *Recitative and Dance* (1934); *Jig* (1935); *Siciliana* (1935); *Pantomime* (1935); *Saraband* (1935); *Idyll* for Small Orch. (1935); *Waltz Fantasy* (1935); *Concert Rhapsody* for Viola and Orch. (1935); *6 Facets* (1936); *A Reflection* for Small Orch. (1936); *Scherzo* (1937); *2 Short Pieces* (1937); *Hornpipe* (1939); *Doctor Johnson's Suite* for Strings (1944); *Country Overture and Scherzo* for Strings (1944); *Mountain House*, suite (1949); *Concert Overture* (1950). **CHAMBER:** *Fantasy* for String Quartet (1936); *Tarantelle fantastique* for Piano and String Quartet (1943); *Waltz* for Piano and String Quartet (1944); 2 suites for Violin and Piano: No. 1 (1945) and No. 2, *On the Road* (1948); *The Top Flat*, suite for Viola and Piano (1947); *Rhapsody on Christmas Carols* for Violin and Piano (1951); piano pieces; organ works. **OTHER:** Vocal music.

WRITINGS (all publ. in London): *The Treasury of Christmas Music* (1950; 7th ed., 1978); *Music of Britain* (1952); *The Treasury of Easter Music* (1963); with G. Knight, *The Treasury of English Church Music* (5 vols., 1965); *The Second Treasury of Christmas Music* (1967); with E. Smith, *The Treasury of Vocal Music* (4 vols., 1969); *National Anthems of the World* (5th ed. with M. Cartledge, 1978; 6th and 7th eds. with M. Bristow, 1985, 1987).

Reese, Gustave, eminent American musicologist; b. N.Y., Nov. 29, 1899; d. Berkeley, Calif., Sept. 7, 1977. At N.Y. Univ. he studied jurisprudence (LL.B., 1921) and music (Mus.Bac., 1930); joined its faculty, teaching there during the periods 1927–33, 1934–37, and 1945–74; concurrently worked with G. Schirmer, Inc. (1924–45; from 1940 to 1945 was director of publications); was director of publications for Carl Fischer (1944–55). From 1933 to 1944 he was assoc. ed., and in 1944–45 ed., of the *Musical Quarterly*. In 1934 he was a co-founder of the American Musicological Soc.; was its president from 1950 to 1952, and remained its honorary president until his death. He gave numerous lectures at American univs.; also gave courses at the Juilliard School of Music in N.Y. An entire generation of American music scholars numbered among his students; he was widely regarded as a founder of American musicology as a science. He held a chair at the Graduate School of Arts and Science at N.Y. Univ., which gave him its "Great Teacher Award" in 1972 and its presidential citation on his retirement from active teaching in 1974; he then became a visiting prof. at the Graduate Center of the City Univ. of N.Y. He died while attending the congress of the International Musicological Soc. in Berkeley. Reese contributed a great number of informative articles to various American and European publications and music encyclopedias, but his most lasting achievement lies in his books, *Music in the Middle Ages* (N.Y., 1940; also in Italian, Florence, 1960) and *Music in the Renaissance* (N.Y., 1954; 2nd ed., rev., 1959), which have become classics of American music scholarship; he also brought out an interesting book that describes selected early writings on music not available in English, *Fourscore Classics of Music Literature* (N.Y., 1957).

BIBL.: J. LaRue, ed., *Aspects of Medieval and Renaissance Music: A Birthday Offering to G. R.* (N.Y., 1966; 2nd ed., 1978).

Reeser, (Hendrik) Eduard, distinguished Dutch musicologist; b. Rotterdam, March 23, 1908. He studied art history with Vogelsang and musicology with Smijers at the Univ. of Utrecht (Ph.D., 1939). He taught music history at the Rotterdam Cons. (1930–37) and musicology at the Univ. of Utrecht (1947–73); was also president of the Donemus Foundation (1947–57), the Maatschappij tot Bevordering der Toonkünst (1951–69), and the IMS (1972–77). He was made a member of the Royal Dutch Academy of Sciences (1961) and the Royal Academy of Sciences and Arts of Belgium (1973); was also made an honorary member of the Royal Musical Assn. in London (1974).

WRITINGS (all publ. in Amsterdam unless otherwise given): *De musikale handscriften van Alphons Diepenbrock* (1933); *Alphons Diepenbrock* (1935); *De zonen van Bach* (1941; Eng.

tr., 1946); *Musiekgeschiedenis in vogelvlucht* (1942; Eng. tr., 1946); *De Vereeniging voor Nederlandsche muziekgeschiedenis 1863–1943: Gedenboek* (1943); *De geschiedenis van de wals* (1947; Eng. tr., 1947); *Muziek in de gemeenschap der Kunsten* (Rotterdam, 1947); *Een eeuw Nederlandse muziek* (1950); ed. *Verzamelde geschriften van Alphons Diepenbrock* (Utrecht, 1950); *Music in Holland* (1959); ed. *Alphons Diepenbrock: Brieven en documenten* (2 vols., The Hague, 1962, 1967); *Gustav Mahler und Holland* (Vienna, 1980); *Ein Augsburger Musiker in Paris: Johann Gottfried Eckard* (Augsburg, 1985).

Refardt, Edgar, eminent Swiss musicologist and bibliographer; b. Basel, Aug. 8, 1877; d. there, March 3, 1968. He studied law and obtained the degree of Dr.Jur. in 1901. In 1915 he was appointed librarian and cataloguer of the musical collection of the Municipal Library of Basel; from 1921 to 1948 he was director of the Basel Orch. Society. He publ. valuable bibliographical works on Swiss music; also essays on various literary and musical subjects.

WRITINGS: *Hans Huber: Beiträge zu einer Biographie* (Leipzig, 1922); *Verzeichnis der Aufsätze zur Musik in den nichtmusikalischen Zeitschriften der Universitätsbibliothek Basel* (Leipzig, 1925); *Historisch-biographisches Musikerlexikon der Schweiz* (Leipzig and Zürich, 1928); *Hans Huber: Leben und Werk eines schweizer Musikers* (Zürich, 1944); *Theodor Fröhlich: Ein schweizer Musiker der Romantik* (Basel, 1947); *Johannes Brahms, Anton Bruckner, Hugo Wolf: Drei Wiener Meister des 19. Jahrhunderts* (Basel, 1949); *Musik in der Schweiz: Ausgewählte Aufsätze* (1952); H. Zehntner, ed., *Thematischer Katalog der Instrumentalmusik des 18. Jahrhunderts in den Handschriften der Universitätsbibliothek Basel* (Bern, 1952).

Refice, Licinio, Italian conductor, teacher, and composer; b. Patrica, near Rome, Feb. 12, 1883; d. while conducting his sacred play Santa Cecilia in Rio de Janeiro, Sept. 11, 1954. He studied organ and composition at Rome's Liceo di Santa Cecilia (diploma, 1910); after being ordained (1910), he taught at Rome's Scuola Pontificia Superiore di Musica Sacra (1910–50) and was maestro di cappella at S. Maria Maggiore (1911–47); toured Europe and North and South America as a conductor.

WORKS: OPERAS: *Cecilia* (1922–23; Rome, 1934); *Margherita da Cortona* (Milan, 1938). **VOCAL:** 4 oratorios: *La Cananea* (1910), *Maria Magdalena* (1914), *Martyrium S. Agnetis Virginis* (1919), and *Trittico Francescano* (1926); *La vedova di Naim,* cantata (1912); *Stabat Mater* (1917); *Te Deum* (1918); many other sacred works, including over 40 masses; secular songs.

BIBL.: E. Mucci, *L. R.* (Assisi, 1955); T. Onofri and E. Mucci, *Le composizioni di L. R.* (Assisi, 1966).

Regamey, Constantin, Swiss pianist and composer; b. Kiev (of a Swiss father and a Russian mother), Jan. 28, 1907; d. Lausanne, Dec. 27, 1982. He went to Poland in 1920 and took piano lessons with Turczyński (1921–25); then turned to linguistics and took courses in Sanskrit at the Univ. of Warsaw and later at L'École des Hautes Études in Paris, graduating in 1936. Returning to Poland, he taught Sanskrit at the Univ. of Warsaw (1937–39); concurrently he ed. periodicals on contemporary music. He was interned by the Germans during World War II, but managed to escape to Switzerland in 1944. He received an appointment to teach Slavic and oriental languages at the Univ. of Lausanne; also gave courses in Indo-European linguistics at the Univ. of Fribourg. However, he did not abandon his musical activities; he served as co-ed. of the *Revue Musicale de Suisse Romande* (1954–62); was president of the Assn. of Swiss Composers (1963–68) and a member of the executive board of the ISCM (1969–73). In 1978 he became partially paralyzed; he dictated the last pages of his last work, *Visions,* to Jean Balissat, a fellow composer, who also orchestrated the work. As a composer, he adopted free serial methods, without a doctrinaire adherence to formal dodecaphony. In 1963 he moderated his modernity and wrote music using free, often composite, techniques.

WORKS: DRAMATIC: *Don Robott,* opera (1970); *Mio, mein Mio,* fairy tale opera, after Bächli and Lindgren (1973). **ORCH.:** *Variazioni e tema* (1948); *Music* for Strings (1953); *Autographe* for Chamber Orch. (1962–66); *4 x 5,* concerto for 4 Quintets (Basel, May 28, 1964); *Lila,* double concerto for Violin, Cello, and Chamber Orch. (1976). **CHAMBER:** Quintet for Clarinet, Bassoon, Violin, Cello, and Piano (1944); String Quartet (1948). **VOCAL:** *7 chansons persanes* for Baritone and Chamber Orch., after Omar Khayyám (1942); *5 études* for Woman's Voice and Orch. (1955–56); *5 poèmes de Jean Tardieu* for Chorus (1962); *Symphonie des Incantations* for Soprano, Baritone, and Orch. (1967); *3 Lieder des Clowns* for Baritone and Orch. (1968; from the opera *Don Robott*); *Unidentity and Infinity* for Silent Narrator, Woman's Voice, and an unidentified number of Instruments (1969); *Alpha,* cantata for Tenor and Orch., to a Hindu text (1970); *Visions* for Baritone, Chorus, Orch., and Organ, after the life of the prophet Daniel (1978–79; orchestrated by J. Balissat).

WRITINGS: *Musique du XXe siècle: Présentation de 80 oeuvres pour orchestre de chambre* (Lausanne and Paris, 1966).

BIBL.: H. Jaccard, *Initiation à la musique contemporaine: Trois compositeurs vaudois: Raffaele d'Alessandro, C. R., Julien-François Zbinden* (Lausanne, 1955).

Reger, (Johann Baptist Joseph) Max(imilian), celebrated German composer; b. Brand, Upper Palatinate, Bavaria, March 19, 1873; d. Leipzig, May 11, 1916. His father, a schoolteacher and amateur musician, gave him instruction on the piano, organ, and various string instruments. In 1874 the family moved to Weiden, where he studied organ and theory with Adalbert Lindner; he then attended the teacher-training college; after visiting the Bayreuth Festival in 1888, he decided on a career in music. He went to Sondershausen to study with Riemann in 1890, and continued as his pupil in Wiesbaden (1890–93); was also active as a teacher of piano, organ, and theory (1890–96). Following military service, he returned to Weiden in 1898 and wrote a number of his finest works for organ. He went to Munich in 1901, first gaining general recognition as a pianist, and later as a composer; was prof. of counterpoint at the Königliche Akademie der Tonkünst (1905–06). Prominent compositions from this period included the Piano Quintet, op. 64 (1901–02), the Violin Sonata, op. 72 (1903), the String Quartet, op. 74 (1903–04), the *Variationen und Fuge über ein Thema von J.S. Bach* for Piano, op. 81 (1904), and the *Sinfonietta,* op. 90 (1904–05). He went to Leipzig as music director of the Univ. (1907–08) and as prof. of composition at the Cons. (from 1907). His fame as a composer was enhanced by his successful tours as a soloist and conductor in Germany and throughout Europe. While he continued to produce major chamber works and organ pieces, he also wrote such important orch. compositions as the *Variationen und Fuge über ein lustiges Thema von J.A. Hiller,* op. 100 (1907), the Violin Concerto, op. 101 (1907–08), the *Symphonischer Prolog zu einer Tragödie,* op. 108 (1908), the Piano Concerto, op. 114 (1910), and the *Variationen und Fuge über ein Thema von Mozart,* op. 132 (1914). As a result of having been awarded an honorary Ph.D. from the Univ. of Jena in 1908, he composed his most distinguished sacred work, the *Psalm C,* op. 106 (1908–09). He was called to Meiningen as conductor of the Court Orch. in 1911, assuming the title of Hofkapellmeister; was also Generalmusikdirektor (1913–14). He settled in Jena in 1915.

Reger was an extraordinarily gifted musician, widely respected as a composer, pianist, organist, conductor, and teacher. A master of polyphonic and harmonic writing, he carried on the hallowed Classical and Romantic schools of composition. Although he wrote major works in nearly every genre, his music has not found a place of permanence in the repertoire.

WRITINGS: *Beiträge zur Modulationslehre* (Leipzig, 1903; 24th ed., 1952).

WORKS: ORCH.: *Heroide,* symphonic movement (1889); *Castra vetera,* incidental music (1889–90); *Symphoniesatz* (1890; Dortmund, 1960); *Lyrisches Andante* for Strings (1898);

Scherzino for Horn and Strings (1899); *Elegie*, op. 26/1 (1899; arranged from a piano work); *2 Romanzen* for Violin and Orch., op. 50 (1900); *Variationen und Fuge über ein Thema von Beethoven*, op. 86 (1915; arranged from the work for 2 Pianos, 1904); *Sinfonietta*, op. 90 (Essen, Oct. 8, 1905); *Suite im alten Stil*, op. 93 (1916; arranged from the work for Violin and Piano, 1906); *Serenade*, op. 95 (1905–06); *Variationen und Fuge über ein lustiges Thema von J. A. Hiller*, op. 100 (Cologne, Oct. 15, 1907); Violin Concerto, op. 101 (Leipzig, Oct. 13, 1908); *Aria* for Violin and Chamber Orch., op. 103a (1908; arranged from the Suite for Violin and Piano, 1908); *Symphonischer Prolog zu einer Tragödie*, op. 108 (1908); Piano Concerto, op. 114 (Leipzig, Dec. 15, 1910); *Eine Lustspielouvertüre*, op. 120 (1911); *Konzert im alten Stil*, op. 123 (1912); *Eine romantische Suite*, op. 125 (1912); *4 Tondichtungen nach Arnold Böcklin*, op. 128 (Essen, Oct. 12, 1913); *Eine Ballettsuite*, op. 130 (1913); *Variationen und Fuge über ein Thema von Mozart*, op. 132 (1914; Berlin, Feb. 5, 1915; arranged from the work for 2 Pianos, 1914); *Eine vaterländische Ouvertüre*, op. 140 (1914); *Sinfonische Rhapsodie* for Violin and Orch., op. 147 (unfinished; completed by F. von Reuter).

CHAMBER: Scherzo for Flute and String Quartet (n.d.); String Quartet (1888–89); Violin Sonata, op. 1 (1890); Trio for Violin, Viola, and Piano, op. 2 (1891); Violin Sonata, op. 3 (1891); Cello Sonata, op. 5 (1892); Piano Quintet (1897–98); Cello Sonata, op. 28 (1898); Violin Sonata, op. 41 (1899); 4 sonatas for Violin, op. 42 (1900); 2 clarinet sonatas, op. 49 (1900); 2 string quartets, op. 54 (1900); *Caprice* for Cello and Piano (1901); Piano Quintet, op. 64 (1901–02); *Prelude and Fugue* for Violin (1902); *Romanze* for Violin and Piano (1902); *Petite caprice* for Violin and Piano (1902); *Albumblatt* for Clarinet or Violin, and Piano (1902); *Tarantella* for Clarinet or Violin and Piano (1902); *Allegretto grazioso* for Flute and Piano (1902); Violin Sonata, op. 72 (1903); String Quartet, op. 74 (1903–04); *Serenade* for Flute, Violin, and Viola, op. 77a (1904); String Trio, op. 77b (1904); Cello Sonata, op. 78 (1904); *Wiegenlied, Capriccio, and Burla* for Violin and Piano, op. 79d (1902–04); *Caprice, Kleine Romanze* for Cello and Piano, op. 79e (1904); Violin Sonata, op. 84 (1905); *Albumblatt*, romanze for Violin and Piano, op. 87 (1905); 7 sonatas for Violin, op. 91 (1905); *Suite im alten Stil* for Violin and Piano, op. 93 (1906; orchestrated 1916); Trio for Violin, Cello, and Piano, op. 102 (1907–08); Suite (*6 Vortragstücke*) for Violin and Piano, op. 103a (1908); 2 little sonatas for Violin and Piano, op. 103b (1909); *12 kleine Stücke nach eigenen Liedern* (from op. 76) for Violin and Piano, op. 103c (1916); Sonata for Clarinet or Viola and Piano, op. 107 (1908–09); String Quartet, op. 109 (1909); Piano Quartet, op. 113 (1910); Cello Sonata, op. 116 (1910); *Preludes and Fugues* for Violin, op. 117 (1909–12); Sextet for 2 Violins, 2 Violas, and 2 Cellos, op. 118 (1910); String Quartet, op. 121 (1911); Violin Sonata, op. 122 (1911); *Preludes and Fugues* for Violin, op. 131a (1914); *3 Duos (Canons und Fugen) im alten Stil* for 2 Violins, op. 131b (1914); 3 suites for Cello, op. 131c (1915); 3 suites for Viola, op. 131d (1915); Piano Quartet, op. 133 (1914); *Allegro* for 2 Violins (1914); Violin Sonata, op. 139 (1915); *Serenade* for Flute or Violin, Violin, and Viola, op. 141a (1915); String Trio, op. 141b (1915); Clarinet Quintet, op. 146 (1915); *Prelude* for Violin (1915); numerous pieces for piano and organ works.

VOCAL: 3 Choruses for Mixed Voices and Piano, op. 6 (1892); *Tantum ergo sacramentum* for 5 Voices (1895); *Hymne an den Gesang* for Men's Chorus and Orch. or Piano, op. 21 (1898); *Gloriabuntur in te omnes* for 4 Voices (1898); 7 Men's Choruses, op. 38 (1899); 3 Choruses, op. 39 (1899); *Maria Himmelsfreud!* (1899); 8 settings of *Tantum ergo*, op. 61a (1901); 4 settings of *Tantum ergo* for Women's or Men's Voices and Organ, op. 61b (1901); 4 settings of *Tantum ergo* for 4 Voices and Organ, op. 61c (1901); *8 Marienlieder*, op. 61d (1901); *4 Marienlieder* for Women's or Men's Voices and Organ, op. 61e (1901); *4 Marienlieder* for 4 Voices and Organ, op. 61f (1901); *6 Trauergesänge*, op. 61g (1901); *Palmsonntagmorgen* for 5 Voices (1902); *Gesang der Verklärten* for Mixed Voices and Orch., op. 71 (1903); 5 cantatas (1903–05); *10 Gesänge* for Men's Voices, op. 83 (1904, 1909); *Weihegesäng* for Chorus and Wind Orch. (1908); *Psalm C* for Chorus, Organ, and Orch., op. 106 (1908–09); *Geistliche Gesänge* for 5 Voices, op. 110 (1912); *Vater unser* for 12 Voices (1909); *3 Gesänge* for 4 Women's Voices, op. 111b (1909); *Die Nonnen* for Chorus and Orch., op. 112 (1909); *Die Weihe der Nacht* for Men's Voices and Orch., op. 119 (1911); *Lasset uns den Herren preisen* for 5 Voices (1911); *Römischer Triumphgesang* for Men's Voices and Orch., op. 126 (1912); *8 geistliche Gesänge* for 4 to 8 Voices, op. 138 (1914); *Abschiedslied* for 4 Voices (1914); *Requiem* for Soloists, Chorus, and Orch. (1914; 2nd movement unfinished); *2 Gesänge*, op. 144 (1915); *20 Responsorien* (1916); works for solo voice.

BIBL.: The *Sämtliche Werke* was publ. in Wiesbaden (38 vols., 1954–86). F. Stein ed. the *Thematisches Verzeichnis der im Druck erschienenen Werke von M. R. einschliesslich seiner Bearbeitungen und Ausgaben* (Leipzig, 1953). H. Rösner ed. a *M.-R.-Bibliographie* (Bonn, 1968). See also the following: R. Braungart, *M. R., Monographien Moderner Musiker*, II (Leipzig, 1907); V. Junk, *M. R. als Orchesterkomponist* (Leipzig, 1910); W. Fischer, *Über die Wiedergabe der Orgelkompositionen M. R.s* (Cologne, 1911); F. Rabich, *R.s Lieder: Eine Studie* (Langensalza, 1914); R. Eucken, *Persönliche Erinnerungen an M. R.* (Bielefeld, 1916); H. Poppen, *M. R.* (Leipzig, 1918; 3rd ed., 1947); H. Grabner, *R.s Harmonik* (Munich, 1920); R. Würz, ed., *M. R.: Eine Sammlung von Studien* (4 vols., Munich, 1920–23); K. Hasse, *M. R.: Mit R.s Schriften und Aufsätzen* (Leipzig, 1921); A. Lindner, *M. R.: Ein Bild seines Jugendlebens und künstlerischen Werdens* (Stuttgart, 1922; 3rd ed., 1938); G. Bagier, *M. R.* (Stuttgart and Berlin, 1923); E. Gatscher, *Die Fugentechnik M. R.s in ihrer Entwicklung* (Stuttgart, 1925); S. Kallenberg, *M. R.* (Leipzig, 1929); E. Reger, *Mein Leben mit und für M. R.* (Leipzig, 1930); P. Coenen, *M. R.s Variationsschaffen* (diss., Univ. of Berlin, 1935); E. Brand, *M. R. im Elternhaus* (Munich, 1938); F. Stein, *M. R.* (Potsdam, 1939); idem, *M. R.: Sein Leben in Bildern* (Leipzig, 1941; 2nd ed., 1956); A. Kalkoff, *Das Orgelschaffen M. R.s* (Kassel, 1950); special issue of the *Zeitschrift für Musik* (March 1953); G. Wehmeyer, *M. R. als Liederkomponist*, Kölner Beiträge zur Musikforschung, VIII (Regensburg, 1955); E. Otto, *M. R.: Sinnbild einer Epoche* (Wiesbaden, 1957); G. Sievers, *Die Grundlagen Hugo Riemanns bei M. R.* (Wiesbaden, 1967); M. Stein, *Der heitere R.* (Wiesbaden, 1969); H. Wirth, *M. R.* (Hamburg, 1973); K. Röhring, ed., *M. R. 1873–1973: Ein Symposion* (Wiesbaden, 1974); S. Popp and S. Shigihara, eds., *M. R.: Am Wendepunkt zur Moderne: Ein Bildband mit Dokumenten aus den Beständen des M.-R.-Instituts* (Bonn, 1987; Eng. tr., 1988, as *M. R. at the Turning Point to Modernism: An Illustrated Volume with Documents of the M. R. Institute*); W. Grim, *M. R.: A Bio-bibliography* (N.Y., 1988); R. Gadenbach, *M. R. und seine Zeit* (Laaber, 1991); H. Brauss, *M. R.'s Music for Solo Piano* (Edmonton, Alberta, 1994).

Rehfuss, Heinz (Julius), German-born Swiss, later American, bass-baritone; b. Frankfurt am Main, May 25, 1917; d. Buffalo, June 27, 1988. He studied with his father, Carl Rehfuss (1885–1946), a singer and teacher, and with his mother, Florentine Rehfuss-Peichert, a contralto. The family moved to Neuchâtel, and Rehfuss became a naturalized Swiss citizen. He made his professional debut in opera at Biel-Solothurn in 1938; then sang with the Lucerne Stadttheater (1938–39) and at the Zürich Opera (1940–52). He subsequently was active mainly in Europe and in America; became a naturalized American citizen; taught voice at the Montreal Cons. in 1961; in 1965 was on the faculty of the State Univ. of N.Y. at Buffalo; in 1970 was a visiting prof. at the Eastman School of Music in Rochester, N.Y. He also toured in Asia, giving vocal recitals in India and Indonesia. He was successful mainly in dramatic roles, such as Don Giovanni and Boris Godunov.

Rehm, Wolfgang, German musicologist; b. Munich, Sept. 3, 1929. He studied with Gurlitt and Zenck at the Univ. of Freiburg im Breisgau (Ph.D., 1952, with the diss. *Das Chanson-*

werk von Gilles Binchois); also studied theory and piano at the Hochschule für Musik in Freiburg im Breisgau. In 1954 he joined the publishing firm of Bärenreiter in Kassel, eventually becoming chief ed.; held that position until 1982. In 1960 he was named co-ed. (with Wolfgang Plath) of the *Neue Mozart-Ausgabe*, serving as chief ed. from 1981 to 1994.

Reich, Steve (actually, **Stephen Michael**), prominent American composer; b. N.Y., Oct. 3, 1936. He studied philosophy at Cornell Univ. (B.A., 1957), where he became fascinated with the theories of Ludwig Wittgenstein (a brother of the amputated pianist Paul Wittgenstein), who enunciated the famous tautological formula "Whereof one cannot speak thereof one must be silent." Reich in his music confuted this dictum by speaking loudly of tonalities and modalities which had remained in limbo for a millennium. He had a normal childhood; took piano lessons and also studied drumming with Roland Koloff, timpanist of the N.Y. Phil.; synchronously, he became infatuated with jazz and Bach by way of Stravinsky's stylizations. In N.Y. he took private composition lessons with Hall Overton and earned his living by driving a taxicab. From 1958 to 1961 he took courses with Bergsma and Persichetti at the Juilliard School of Music; later went to California, where he entered Mills College in Oakland in the classes of Milhaud and Berio (M.A., 1963); during this period, he became interested in electronic composition and African music. He launched his career as a composer with scores for the underground films *The Plastic Haircut* and *Oh Dem Watermelons* in 1963, utilizing tape sounds. His subsequent works for tape included *It's Gonna Rain* (1965) and *Come Out* (1966). He returned to N.Y. and in 1966 organized his own ensemble, Steve Reich and Musicians, which began as a trio with Arthur Murphy and Jon Gibson and eventually expanded into a duo-de-viginti multitude. With his work *4 Organs* for 4 Electric Organs and Maracas (1970), he first made an impact outside his small group of devotees. In the summer of 1970 Reich traveled to Accra, Ghana, where he practiced under the tutelage of indigenous drummers; this experience bore fruit with the composition *Drumming* (1971), which became quite popular. In 1973 he studied the Balinese gamelan with a native teacher at the American Soc. for Eastern Arts Summer Program at the Univ. of Wash. in Seattle. Becoming conscious of his ethnic heredity, he went to Jerusalem in 1976 to study the traditional forms of Hebrew cantillation. In 1974 he received grants from the NEA and from the N.Y. State Council on the Arts; was also invited to Berlin as an artist-in-residence. He subsequently received grants from the Martha Baird Rockefeller Foundation (1975, 1979, 1980, and 1981) and a 2nd grant from the NEA (1976). In 1978 he was awarded a Guggenheim fellowship. He publ. a book, *Writings about Music* (N.Y., 1974; French tr., Paris, 1981, as *Écrits et entretiens sur la musique*).

Slowly but surely Reich rose to fame; his group was invited to perform at the Holland Festival and at the radio stations of Frankfurt am Main and Stuttgart. His increasing success led to a sold-out house when he presented a concert of his works at N.Y.'s Carnegie Hall on Feb. 19, 1980. In 1986 he took his ensemble on a world tour. With his wife, the visual artist Beryl Korot, he created the documentary music video piece *The Cave*, which was first seen in Vienna on May 15, 1993. In 1994 he was elected a member of the American Academy of Arts and Letters. His music was astoundingly audacious; rather than continue in the wake of obsolescent modernism, inexorably increasing in complexity, he deliberately reduced his harmonic and contrapuntal vocabulary and defiantly explored the fascinating potentialities of repetitive patterns. This kind of technique has been variously described as minimalist (for it was derived from a minimum of chordal combinations), phase music (because it shifted from one chord to another, a note at a time), modular (because it was built on symmetric modules), and pulse music (because it derived from a series of measured rhythmic units). Another definition is simply "process," suggesting tonal progressions in flux. Etiologically, this type of composition is hypnopompic, for it creates a subliminal state between a strong dream and a sudden reality. Analytically, it represents a paradox, for it is uncompromisingly modern in its use of exotic instruments, infinitely challenging in its obdurate continuity, and yet elemental in the deliberate limitations of its resources. This system of composition is akin to serialism in its application of recurrent melodic progressions and periodic silences. Despite his apparent disregard for musical convention, or indeed for public taste, Reich likes to trace his musical ancestry to the sweetly vacuous homophony of the Ars Antiqua, with particular reference to the opaque works of the great master of the Notre Dame School of Paris, Perotin. He deliberately avoids fanciful titles in his works, preferring to define them by names of instruments, or numbers of musical parts. The extraordinary aspect of Reich's career is that by rejecting the conventional way of music making, and by thus infuriating the academics, he finds a direct avenue to the hearts, minds, and ears of the young.

WORKS: *Pitch Charts* for Any Instruments (1963); *Plastic Haircut*, film score for Tape (1963); *Music* for 3 or More Pianos or Piano and Tape (1964); *It's Gonna Rain* for Tape (1965); *Oh Dem Watermelons*, film score for 5 Voices and Piano (1965); *Come Out* for Tape (1966); *Melodica* for Tape (1966); *Reed Phase* for Soprano Saxophone and Tape (1966; N.Y., March 17, 1967); *My Name Is* for 3 or More Tape Recorders, Performers, and Audience (1967); *Piano Phase* for 2 Pianos and 2 Marimbas (1967); *Slow Motion Sound* for Tape (1967); *Violin Phase* for Violin and Tape or 4 Violins (1967); *Pendulum Music* for 3 or More Microphones, Amplifiers, and Loudspeakers (1968; N.Y., May 27, 1969); *4 Log Drums* for Phase Shifting Pulse Gate and 4 Log Drums (N.Y., May 27, 1969); *Pulse Music* for Phase Shifting Pulse Gate (N.Y., May 27, 1969); *4 Organs* for 4 Electric Organs and Maracas (1970); *Drumming* for 2 Women's Voices, Piccolo, 4 Pairs of Tuned Bongo Drums, 3 Marimbas, and 3 Glockenspiels (N.Y., Dec. 1971); *Clapping Music* for 2 Performers (1972); *Music for Mallet Instruments, Voices, and Organ* for 3 Women's Voices, 3 Marimbas, 3 Glockenspiels, Vibraphone, and Electric Organ (N.Y., May 12, 1973); *Music for Pieces of Wood* for 5 pairs of Tuned Claves (N.Y., May 12, 1973); *6 Pianos* (N.Y., May 12, 1973); *Music for 18 Musicians* for 4 Women's Voices, 2 Clarinets, 3 Marimbas, 2 Xylophones, Vibraphone, 4 Pianos, Maracas, Violin, and Cello (N.Y., April 24, 1976); *Music for a Large Ensemble* (1978; N.Y., Feb. 19, 1980); Octet for 2 Flutes, 2 Clarinets, 2 Bass Clarinets, 2 Pianos, 2 Violins, Viola, and Cello (Frankfurt am Main radio broadcast, June 21, 1979; rev. in collaboration with Robert Wilson as *8 Lines* for Chamber Orch., N.Y., Dec. 10, 1983); *Variations for Winds, Strings and Keyboards* (1979; N.Y., Feb. 19, 1980; orch. version, San Francisco, May 17, 1980); *My Name Is* for Tape (1980); *Tehillim* (Psalms) for 3 Sopranos, Alto, and Chamber Orch. (Houston, Nov. 21, 1981; orch. version, N.Y., Sept. 16, 1982); *Vermont Counterpoint* for Piccolo, Flute, Alto Flute, and Tape (1 performer, 10 parts on tape, N.Y., Oct. 1, 1982; also for 11 Flutes, N.Y., Dec. 10, 1983); *The Desert Music* for Small Amplified Chorus and Large Orch. (1983; Cologne, March 17, 1984); Sextet for 4 Percussion and 2 Pianos (1984–85); *Impact*, dance music (N.Y., Oct. 31, 1985); *New York Counterpoint* for Clarinet, Bass Clarinet, and Tape or Clarinets and Bass Clarinets (1985; N.Y., Jan. 20, 1986); *3 Movements* for Orch. (1985–86; St. Louis, April 3, 1986); *The 4 Sections* for Orch. (San Francisco, Oct. 7, 1987); *Electric Counterpoint* for Guitar and Tape (N.Y., Nov. 5, 1987); *Different Trains* for String Quartet and Tape (1988); *The Cave*, documentary music video piece (1989–93; Vienna, May 15, 1993); *Nagoya Marimbas* for 2 Marimbas (1994); *City Life* for 17 Performers with concrète urban sounds from 2 sampling keyboards (1994; Metz, March 7, 1995); *Proverb* for 3 Sopranos, 2 Tenors, 2 Vibraphones, and 4 Synthesizers (1995–1996).

BIBL.: W. Mertens, *American Minimal Music: La Monte Young, Terry Riley, S. R., Philip Glass* (London, 1991).

Reich, Willi, Austrian-born Swiss music critic and musicologist; b. Vienna, May 27, 1898; d. Zürich, May 1, 1980. He studied at the Univ. of Vienna, receiving his Ph.D. (1934) with the diss. *Padre Martini als Theoretiker und Lehrer*, also studied privately with Berg and Webern. He ed. a modern music magazine, *23—Eine Wiener Musikzeitschrift* (1932–37). In 1938 he settled in Switzerland; in 1948, became music critic of the *Neue Zürcher Zeitung*; in 1961, became a naturalized Swiss citizen. In addition to editing numerous documentary vols., he publ. the studies *Wozzeck: A Guide to the Words and Music of Alban Berg* (N.Y., 1932), *Alban Berg* (Vienna, 1937), *Romantiker der Musik* (Basel, 1947), *Alexander Tscherepnin* (Bonn, 1961; 2nd ed., 1970), *Alban Berg: Leben und Werk* (Zürich, 1963; Eng. tr., 1965), and *Arnold Schonberg oder der konservative Revolutionar* (Vienna, 1968; Eng. tr., 1971, as *Schoenberg: A Critical Biography*).

Reichwein, Leopold, Austrian conductor, teacher, and composer; b. Breslau, May 16, 1878; d. (suicide) Vienna, April 8, 1945. He was a theater conductor in Breslau, Mannheim, and Karlsruhe; then was on the staff of the Vienna Opera (1913–21), music director of the Gesellschaft der Musikfreunde in Vienna (1921–26), and music director in Bochum (1926–38); he returned to Vienna in 1938; conducted at the State Opera and taught conducting at the Academy of Music. He wrote the operas *Vasantasena* (Breslau, 1903) and *Die Liebenden von Kandahar* (Breslau, 1907); incidental music to Goethe's *Faust*; songs.

Reid, Cornelius L., American voice teacher and music scholar; b. Jersey City, N.J., Feb. 7, 1911. He was a member of the Trinity Church Choir in N.Y. (1920–25), and studied with Frederick Kurzweil and Ruth Kirch-Arndt at the N.Y. College of Music (1945–48); studied voice privately with George Mead (1929), Marie Wagner (1929–30), and Douglas Stanley (1934–37), and had coaching from Frieda Hempel (1930) and Povla Frijsh (1932–40). He taught voice privately in N.Y. (from 1934); also taught at Marymount College (1940–41) and at the General Theological Seminary there (1946–49); conducted various performing groups (1939–45) and gave master classes and lectures throughout the U.S. Reid authored 3 books defining his Functional vocal training: *Bel Canto: Principles and Practices* (Boston, 1950), *The Free Voice* (N.Y., 1965), and *Voice: Psyche and Soma* (N.Y., 1975); also compiled the important *Dictionary of Vocal Terminology* (N.Y., 1984).

Reif, Paul, Czech-American composer; b. Prague, March 23, 1910; d. N.Y., July 7, 1978. He played violin as a child; studied composition in Vienna with Richard Stöhr and Franz Schmidt, and conducting with Franz Schalk and Bruno Walter; also had lessons with Richard Strauss. In 1941 he emigrated to the U.S., and in 1942 joined the U.S. Intelligence Corps; while with the U.S. Army in North Africa, he set to music the soldiers' song *Dirty Gertie from Bizerte*, which was introduced by Josephine Baker in Algiers in April 1943. Upon his discharge in 1945, he was awarded the Croix de Guerre and the Purple Heart. Returning to the U.S., he composed various serious and light scores.

WORKS: *Triple City* for Chorus and Brass Ensemble (N.Y., April 16, 1963); *Requiem to War* for Chorus and Percussion (N.Y., May 20, 1963); *Birches* for Voice and Orch., after Robert Frost (N.Y., Feb. 2, 1965); *Letter from a Birmingham Jail* for Chorus and Piano, after Martin Luther King, Jr. (Washington, D.C., March 2, 1965); *Philidor's Defense* for Chamber Orch., inspired by the famous Philidor chess opening: 1. P-K4, P-K4; 2. N-KB3, P-Q3 (N.Y., April 10, 1965); 2 operas: *Mad Hamlet* (1965) and *Portrait in Brownstone* (N.Y., May 15, 1966); *Pentagram* for Piano (1969); *The Artist* (N.Y., April 17, 1972); *The Curse of Mauvais-Air* (N.Y., May 9, 1974); *5 Divertimenti* for 4 Strings (1969); *Episodes* for String Orch. (1972); Quintet for Clarinet, Viola, Piano, Percussion, and Folksinger (1974); *Duo for 3* for Clarinet, Cello, and Mezzo-soprano (1974); *America 1776–1876–1976* for Orch., Solo Guitar, Banjo, Electric Guitar, and Vocal Quartet (N.Y., Jan. 24, 1976).

Reimann, Aribert, German composer, pianist, and teacher; b. Berlin, March 4, 1936. He studied at the Berlin Hochschule für Musik (1955–60) with Otto Rausch (piano), Blacher (composition), and Pepping (counterpoint), and also took courses in musicology at the Univ. of Vienna (1958). In 1963 he received the Prix de Rome and studied at the Villa Massimo in Rome. In 1957 he made his debut as a pianist, becoming particularly known in later years as a sensitive accompanist. From 1971 he was a member of the Berlin Akademie der Künste. He also was a prof. at the Hamburg Hochschule für Musik (1974–83), and later at the Berlin Hochschule der Künste (1983). In 1976 he was made a member of the Bayerische Akademie der Schönen Künste in Munich and in 1985 of the Hamburg Freien Akademie der Künste. In 1986 he won the Prix de la composition musicale of the Prince Pierre Foundation of Monaco. He received the Frankfurt am Main music award in 1991. After adhering to the precepts of the 2nd Viennese School of composition, he abandoned orthodox serialism in favor of a compositional style in which linear elements were occasionally complemented by lyrical effusions.

WORKS: DRAMATIC: OPERAS: *Ein Traumspiel* (1963–64; Kiel, June 20, 1965); *Melusine* (1970; Schwetzingen, April 29, 1971); *Lear* (1976–78; Munich, July 9, 1978); *Die Gespenstersonate* (1983; Berlin, Sept. 25, 1984); *Troades* (1985; Munich, July 7, 1986); *Das Schloss* (1989–91; Berlin, Sept. 2, 1992). **BALLETS:** *Stoffreste* (1957; Essen, 1959); *Die Vogelscheuchen* (1969–70; Berlin, Oct. 7, 1970; orch. suite, 1970). **POÉME VISUEL:** *Chacun sa chimère* for Tenor and Orch. (1981; Düsseldorf, April 17, 1982). **ORCH.:** *Elegie* (1957; Darmstadt, April 5, 1963); Cello Concerto (1959; Berlin, March 23, 1961); *Monumenta* for Winds and Percussion (1960; Baden-Baden, Nov. 27, 1963); 2 piano concertos: No. 1 (1961; Berlin, Oct. 26, 1962) and No. 2 for Piano and 19 Players (1972; Nuremberg, Jan. 12, 1973); Sym., after the opera *Ein Traumspiel* (1964; Darmstadt, Sept. 12, 1976); *Rondes* for Strings (1967; Cologne, Jan. 25, 1968); *Loqui* (Saarbrücken, Dec. 5, 1969); *Variationen* (1975; Zürich, Jan. 13, 1976); *Sieben Fragmente* (1988); Double Concerto for Violin, Cello, and Orch. (1988–89; Hannover, Nov. 13, 1989); *9 Pieces* (1993; Houston, May 14, 1994). **CHAMBER:** *Canzoni e ricercari* for Flute, Viola, and Cello (1961); Cello Sonata (1963); *Nocturnos* for Cello and Harp (1965); *Reflexionen* for 7 Instruments (1966); *Invenzioni* for 12 Players (1979); *Solo* for Cello (1981); String Trio (1987). **KEYBOARD: PIANO:** Sonata (1957); *Spektren* (1967); *Variationen* (1979). **ORGAN:** *Dialogo I* (1963). **VOCAL:** *Ein Totentanz* for Baritone and Chamber Orch. (1960); *Hölderlin-Fragmente* for Soprano and Orch. (1963); *Epitaph* for Tenor and 7 Instruments (1965); *Verrà la morte*, cantata for Soloists, 2 Choruses, and Orch. (1966; Berlin, Feb. 28, 1967); *Nenia* for Speaker and Orch. (1967; Kassel, June 26, 1968); *Inane*, monologue for Soprano and Orch. (1968); *Fragmente aus Melusine* for Soprano, Baritone, and Orch. (1970); *Zyklus* for Baritone and Orch. (Nuremberg, April 15, 1971); *Lines* for Soprano and Chamber String Orch. (1973); *Wolkenloses Christfest*, requiem for Baritone, Cello, and Orch. (Landau, June 2, 1974); *Fragmente aus Lear* for Baritone and Orch. (1976–78; Zürich, April 29, 1980); *Unrevealed* for Baritone and String Quartet (1980; Berlin, Sept. 3, 1981); *Drei Lieder* for Soprano and Orch. (1980–82; Kiel, June 26, 1982); *Ein apokalyptisches Fragment* for Mezzo-soprano, Piano, and Orch. (Berlin, Sept. 27, 1987); song cycles and solo songs with piano.

Reimers, Paul, German-American tenor; b. Lunden, Schleswig-Holstein (of Danish parents), March 14, 1878; d. N.Y., April 14, 1942. He studied in Hamburg, where he made his stage debut as Max in *Der Freischütz* (1902); after further training with George Henschel in Scotland, Raimund von Zur Mühlen in London, and Jean Criticos in Paris, he devoted himself to a concert career; sang widely in Europe. In 1913 he went to America; gave programs of German lieder, and also performed songs of the modern French school. From 1924 he taught at the Juilliard School of Music in N.Y.

Reinberger, Jiří, Czech organist, teacher, and composer; b. Brünn, April 14, 1914; d. Prague, May 28, 1977. He was a student of Treglar (organ diploma, 1932) and of Petrželka (composition diploma, 1938) at the Brno Cons., and then of Novák (composition) in Prague (1938–40). He also studied organ with Widermann and in Leipzig with Ramin and Straube. After teaching at the Brno Cons. (1945), he settled in Prague as a teacher at the Cons. From 1951 he taught at the Academy of Musical Arts. He made tours of Europe as a recitalist, winning distinction for his performances of Bach and Czech composers. In 1964 he was made an Artist of Merit by the Czech government. Among his compositions were 2 syms. (1938, 1958), 3 organ concertos (1940, 1956, 1960), and a Cello Concerto (1962).

Reiner, Fritz (actually, **Frigyes**), eminent Hungarian-born American conductor; b. Budapest, Dec. 19, 1888; d. N.Y., Nov. 15, 1963. He studied piano with Thoman and composition with Koessler at the Royal Academy of Music in Budapest; concurrently took courses in jurisprudence at the Univ. of Budapest. In 1909 he made his debut in Budapest conducting *Carmen*. In 1910–11 he conducted at the Laibach Landestheater. He was conductor of the Volksoper in Budapest (1911–14) and of the Court (later State) Opera in Dresden (1914–21); also conducted in Hamburg, Berlin, Vienna, Rome, and Barcelona. In 1922 he was engaged as music director of the Cincinnati Sym. Orch.; was naturalized as a U.S. citizen in 1928. In 1931 he became a prof. of conducting at the Curtis Inst. of Music in Philadelphia; among his students were Leonard Bernstein and Lukas Foss. In 1936–37 he made guest appearances at London's Covent Garden; between 1935 and 1938 he was a guest conductor at the San Francisco Opera; from 1938 to 1948 he was music director of the Pittsburgh Sym. Orch.; then was a conductor at the Metropolitan Opera in N.Y. until 1953. He achieved the peak of his success as a conductor with the Chicago Sym. Orch., which he served as music director from 1953 to 1962, and which he brought up to the point of impeccably fine performance in both Classical and modern music. His striving for perfection created for him the reputation of a ruthless master of the orch.; he was given to explosions of temper, but musicians and critics agreed that it was because of his uncompromising drive toward the optimum of orch. playing that the Chicago Sym. Orch. achieved a very high rank among American symphonic organizations.

BIBL.: R. Potter, *F. R., Conductor, Teacher, Musical Innovator* (diss., Northwestern Univ., 1980); P. Hart, *R. R.: A Biography* (Evanston, Ill., 1994).

Reiner, Karel, prominent Czech composer and pianist; b. Žatec, June 27, 1910; d. Prague, Oct. 17, 1979. He studied law at the German Univ. in Prague (Dr.Jur., 1933) and musicology at the Univ. of Prague; attended Suk's master classes (1931) and A. Hába's courses in microtonal music (1934–35) at the Prague Cons. He was associated with E. Burian's improvisational theater in Prague (1934–38). Unable to leave Central Europe when the Nazis invaded Czechoslovakia, he was detained at Terezín, and later sent to the concentration camps of Dachau and Auschwitz, but survived, and after liberation resumed his activities as a composer and pianist. His earliest works were atonal and athematic; in 1935–36 he wrote a *Suite* and a *Fantasy* for quarter tone piano, and a set of 5 quarter-tone songs; after 1945 he wrote mostly traditional music; then returned to ultramodern techniques.

WORKS: DRAMATIC: OPERAS: *Pohádka o zakleté píseň* (Tale of an Enchanted Song; 1949); *Schustermärchen*, fairy tale opera (1972). **BALLET:** *Jednota* (Unity; 1933). **ORCH.:** Piano Concerto (1932); Violin Concerto (1937); *Concertante Suite* for Winds and Percussion (1947); *Divertimento* for Clarinet, Harp, Strings, and Percussion (1947); *3 Czech Dances* (1949); *Spring Prelude* (1950); *Motýli tady nežijí* (Butterflies Don't Live Here Anymore), 6 pictures, based on music to the film (1959–60; depicts the fate of Jewish children in the Terezín concentration camp); Sym. (1960); *Symphonic Overture* (1964); Concerto for Bass Clarinet, Strings, and Percussion (1966); *Concertante Suite* (1967); Bassoon Concertino (1969); *Promluvy* (Utterances) for Chamber Orch. (1975); *Music* for Strings (1975); *Introduction and Allegro (Diptych No. 2)* (1976); *Diptych No. 1* (1977); *3 Symphonic Movements* (1978). **CHAMBER:** 3 string quartets (1931, 1947, 1951); *7 Miniatures* for Wind Quintet (1931); *Dvanáct* (The 12), suite for Piano and Wind Quintet (1931); 2 nonets (Concerto, 1933; *Preambule*, 1974); *Sonata brevis* for Cello and Piano (1946); *4 Compositions* for Clarinet and Piano (1954); *3 Compositions* for Oboe and Piano (1955); *Elegie and Capriccio* for Cello and Piano (1957); Double Bass Sonata (1957); Violin Sonata (1959); *Small Suite* for 9 Wind Instruments (1960); *6 Bagatelles* for Trumpet and Piano (1962); *2 Compositions* for Oboe and Harp (1962); *4 Compositions* for Clarinet (1963); *6 Studies* for Flute and Piano (1964); Trio for Flute, Bass Clarinet, and Percussion (1964); Piano Trio (1965); *Suite* for Bassoon and Piano (1965); *Music* for 4 Clarinets (1965); *Črty* (Sketches) for Piano Quartet (1966–67); *Concert Studies* for Cymbalom (1967); *2 Compositions* for Saxophone and Piano (1967); *Concertante Sonata* for Percussion (1967); *Prolegomena* for String Quartet (1968); *4 Abbreviations* for Brass Quintet (1968); *Dua*, 5 compositions for 2 Flutes, 2 Oboes, 2 Clarinets, and 2 Trumpets, in any combination (1969); *Volne listy* (Loose Leaves) for Clarinet, Cello, and Piano (1969); *Formulas* for Trombone and Piano (1970); *Recordings* for Bassoon (1970); *Drawings* for Clarinet, Horn, and Piano (1970); *Maxims* for Flute Quartet (1970); *Tercetti* for Oboe, Clarinet, and Bassoon (1971); *Talks* for Wind Quintet (1971–72); *Akrostichon a Allegro* for Bass Clarinet and Piano (1972); *Duo* for 2 Quarter Tone Clarinets (1972); *Replicas* for Flute, Viola, and Harp (1973); *Sujets* for Guitar (1973); *Overtura ritmica* for Guitar (1974); *Strophes* for Viola and Piano (1975); *Portraits*, suite for String Trio (1977); *Dialogues* for 2 Flutes (1978); *Panels*, sextet for Brasses (1979). **PIANO:** *9 Merry Improvisations* (1928–29); *5 Jazz Studies* (1930); 3 sonatas (1931, 1942, 1961); *Minda-Minda*, 7 compositions (1937). **VOCAL:** *Bylo jim tisíc let* (It Was a Thousand Years since Then), cantata (1962); *Talks* for Baritone, Saxophone, and Flute (1979); songs.

Reinhard, Kurt, German ethnomusicologist; b. Giessen, Aug. 27, 1914; d. Wetzlar, July 18, 1979. He studied musicology and composition in Cologne (1933–35), and musicology and ethnology at the univs. in Leipzig and Munich under Huber, Ficker, and Ubbelohdé-Doering (1935–36); received a doctorate with a diss. on Burmese music (1938). He worked at the Staatliche Musikinstrumentensammlung in Berlin, then was director of the Berliner Phonogramm-Archiv (1948–68) and head of the dept. of music pedagogy at the Peterson Cons. (1947–52). In 1948 he began teaching at the Free Univ. in Berlin, where he completed a Habilitation on organology (1950); subsequently became prof. and head of the ethnomusicology dept. there (1957). His most important research focused on the folk and art music of Turkey.

WRITINGS: *Die Musik exotischer Völker* (Berlin, 1951); *Chinesische Musik* (Kassel, 1956); *Turkische Musik* (Berlin, 1962); *Einführung in die Musikethnologie* (Wölfenbuttel, 1968).

Reinhardt, Delia, German soprano; b. Elberfeld, April 27, 1892; d. Arlesheim, near Basel, Oct. 3, 1974. She studied with Strakosch and Hedwig Schako at the Hoch Cons. in Frankfurt am Main. She made her operatic debut in Breslau in 1913. In 1916 she joined the Munich Court (later Bavarian State) Opera, where she sang until 1923. She made her debut at the Metropolitan Opera in N.Y. on Jan. 27, 1923, as Sieglinde; then sang at the Berlin State Opera (1924–33); also made guest appearances at Covent Garden in London (1924–27; 1929). She was married to **Gustav Schützendorf**, and later to **Georges Sébastian**. Among her outstanding roles were Desdemona, Elsa, and Eva.

Reining, Maria, noted Austrian soprano; b. Vienna, Aug. 7, 1903; d. there, March 11, 1991. She studied at a business school, and was employed in the foreign exchange dept. of a Vienna bank before taking up singing. In 1931 she made her debut at the Vienna State Opera, remaining on its roster until 1933; then sang in Darmstadt (1933–35) and at the Bavarian State Opera in Munich (1935–37). In 1937 she rejoined the Vienna State Opera, continuing on its roster, with interruptions, until 1958; also appeared at the Salzburg Festivals (1937–41);

Toscanini engaged her to sing Eva in *Die Meistersinger von Nürnberg* in Salzburg under his direction in 1937; she also sang the role of the Marschallin in *Der Rosenkavalier* and the title role in *Arabella* by Richard Strauss. She was equally successful in soubrette roles and as a dramatic soprano. In 1938 she appeared with the Covent Garden Opera in London and with the Chicago Opera; in 1949, as the Marschallin with the N.Y. City Opera. She also sang at La Scala in Milan, and toured as a concert singer. In 1962 she became a prof. of singing at the Mozarteum in Salzburg.

Reinmar (real name, **Wochinz**), **Hans,** distinguished Austrian baritone; b. Vienna, April 11, 1895; d. Berlin, Feb. 7, 1961. He studied at the Vienna Academy of Music and in Milan. He made his operatic debut in 1919 in Olomouc as Sharpless; then sang in Nuremberg, Zürich, Dresden, and Hamburg; was a member of the Berlin Städtische Oper (1928–45; 1952–61), the Bavarian State Opera in Munich (1945–46; 1950–57), the Berlin State Opera (1948–52), and the Berlin Komische Oper (1952–61); also sang at the festivals in Bayreuth and Salzburg. He excelled in dramatic roles in Italian operas.

Reisenberg, Nadia, Russian-American pianist and pedagogue, sister of **Clara Rockmore**; b. Vilnius, July 14, 1904; d. N.Y., June 10, 1983. She was 9 when she commenced studies with Leonid Nikolayev at the St. Petersburg Cons. In 1920 she left the Soviet Union and toured in Poland, Latvia, Lithuania, and Germany. In 1922 she emigrated to the U.S. and continued her training with Alexander Lambert, and then with Josef Hofmann at the Curtis Inst. of Music in Philadelphia. On Dec. 17, 1922, she made her U.S. debut as soloist in Paderewski's *Fantaisie polonaise* with the N.Y. City Sym. Orch. with the composer in attendance. On Feb. 6, 1924, she made her N.Y. recital debut. In subsequent years, she toured as a soloist with orchs., as a recitalist, and as a chamber music player. In 1939 she was soloist in all the Mozart concerti on radio with Wallenstein and the WOR Sym. Orch. She devoted much of her time to teaching and served on the faculties of the Curtis Inst. of Music, the Mannes College, Queens College of the City Univ. of N.Y., and the Juilliard School. In 1964 she gave her farewell performance in N.Y. as soloist in Liszt's 2nd Piano Concerto. She possessed a fine technique and a lyrical expressivity.

BIBL.: A. and R. Sherman, eds., *N. R.: A Musician's Scrapbook* (College Park, Md., 1985).

Reiser, Alois, Czech-American composer; b. Prague, April 6, 1887; d. Los Angeles, April 4, 1977. He studied composition with Dvořák; also took cello lessons and toured Europe; later emigrated to the U.S. and played cello with the Pittsburgh Sym. Orch. and the N.Y. Sym. Orch. From 1918 to 1929 he was engaged as a theater conductor in N.Y.; in 1929 he settled in Hollywood, where he worked as a composer and conductor at film studios. His works adhere to the established style of European Romanticism; typical of these are *Slavic Rhapsody*, which he conducted in Los Angeles on March 8, 1931, and *Erewhon*, which he conducted there on Jan. 24, 1936. He composed a Cello Concerto, which he performed in Los Angeles on March 23, 1933; also a considerable amount of chamber music. He wrote an opera, *Gobi*, in which he painted in tones the great Asian desert; it had its first and last performance in N.Y. on July 29, 1923, and even then only in concert excerpts.

Reiss, Albert, German tenor; b. Berlin, Feb. 22, 1870; d. Nice, June 19, 1940. He was an actor before his voice was discovered by Pollini, after which he studied with Wilhelm Vilmar in Berlin, and later with Beno Stolzenburg and Julius Lieban. He made his operatic debut in Königsberg as Ivanov in *Zar und Zimmermann* (Sept. 28, 1897); then sang in various German towns; on Dec. 23, 1901, he made his American debut at the Metropolitan Opera in N.Y. in the minor roles of the Sailor and the Shepherd in *Tristan und Isolde;* remained on its roster until 1920; he won distinction there as David in *Die Meistersinger von Nürnberg* and Mime in the *Ring* cycle. In 1919 he returned to Berlin and sang at the Volksoper (1923–25). In 1938 he retired from the stage and lived in Nice.

Reisserová, Julie, Czech composer; b. Prague, Oct. 9, 1888; d. there, Feb. 25, 1938. She studied with J.B. Foerster; also with Roussel in Paris. Among her works are *Pastorale maritime* for Orch. (1933), *Esquisses* for Piano, and several albums of songs.

BIBL.: J. Vacková, *J. R.* (Prague, 1948).

Reizen, Mark (Osipovich), notable Russian bass; b. Zaytsevo, July 3, 1895; d. Moscow, Nov. 25, 1992. He was a pupil of Bugamelli at the Kharkov Cons. In 1921 he made his operatic debut as Pimen at the Kharkov Opera. After singing at the Kirov Theater in Leningrad (1925–30), he was a principal member of the Bolshoi Theater in Moscow (1930–54). As a guest artist, he sang with the Paris Opéra, the Berlin State Opera, the Dresden State Opera et al.; also toured widely as a concert artist. In 1985 he returned to the Bolshoi Theater to celebrate his 90th birthday, appearing as Gremin in *Evgeny Onegin.* He publ. a vol. of autobiographical notes (Moscow, 1980). Reizen possessed a voice of remarkable beauty, ably complemented by his assured stage deportment. Among his finest portrayals were Mozart's Don Basilio, Gounod's Méphistophélès, Boris Godunov, Philip II, Dosifey, and Ivan Susanin.

Reizenstein, Franz (Theodor), German-born English pianist, teacher, and composer; b. Nuremberg, June 7, 1911; d. London, Oct. 15, 1968. He studied piano with Leonid Kreutzer and composition with Hindemith at the Hochschule für Musik in Berlin (1930–34); with the advent of the anti-Semitic Nazi regime, he went to England; entered the Royal College of Music in London and studied with Lambert and Vaughan Williams (1934–36); then took private piano lessons with Solomon (1938–40). He was an instructor in piano at the Royal Academy of Music in London (1958–68), and from 1962 until his death, at the Royal Manchester College of Music. He wrote music of fine neo-Romantic quality.

WORKS: RADIO OPERAS: *Men against the Sea* (1949); *Anna Kraus* (1952). **ORCH.:** Cello Concerto (1936); *Prologue, Variations and Finale* for Violin and Orch. (1938; originally for Violin and Piano); 2 piano concertos: No. 1 (1941) and No. 2 (1956–61; London, June 7, 1961, composer soloist); *Cyrano de Bergerac*, overture (1951); *Serenade in F* for Wind Ensemble and Double Bass or for Small Orch. (1951); Violin Concerto (1953); Concerto for Strings (1966–67; London, Jan. 17, 1969). **CHAMBER:** Sonata for Solo Cello (1931; rev. 1967); *Theme, Variations and Fugue* for Clarinet Quintet (1932; rev. 1960); Wind Quintet (1934); *Divertimento* for String or Brass Quartet (1936–37); Oboe Sonatina (1937); *Partita* for Flute and String Trio (1938); Violin Sonata (1945); Cello Sonata (1947); Piano Quintet (1948); Trio for Flute, Oboe, and Piano (1949); *Fantasia concertante* for Violin and Piano (1956); Trio for Flute, Clarinet, and Bassoon (1963); *Concert Fantasy* for Viola and Piano (1956); Sonata for Solo Viola (1967); Sonata for Solo Violin (1968); 2 piano sonatas (1944, 1964). **VOCAL:** *Genesis*, oratorio (1958); *Voices of Night*, cantata (1950–51).

Rekašius, Antanas, Lithuanian composer; b. Pauvandene, Telsiu, July 24, 1928. He studied composition with Juzeliunas at the Lithuanian State Cons. in Vilnius (1954–59). He taught at the J. Gruodis Music School in Kaunas (1959–69). His music is cast in a highly advanced idiom incorporating aleatory and sonoristic techniques.

WORKS: DRAMATIC: OPERA-ORATORIO: *The Ballad of Light* (1969). **BALLETS:** *The Light of Happiness* (1959); *The Smouldering Cross* (1963); *Passions* (1968); *A Little Humming Fly*, children's ballet (1969). **ORCH.:** *Dramatic Poem* (1958); 5 syms. (1962; 1968; 1969; 1970; *Segments*, 1981); Concerto for Flute and Chamber Orch. (1971); *Metafonia* for Violin and Orch. (1972); *Diafonia* for Cello and Orch. (1972); *Sonnets* for Chamber Orch. (1974); *Epitaph and Poem* for Strings (1975); *Emanations*, concerto for Electric Cello and Chamber Ensemble (1981). **CHAMBER:** 4 string quartets (1954, 1974, 1976, 1980); 4

wind quintets (1974, 1976, 1978, 1980); 2 capriccios for Flute and Oboe (1974, 1976); Sonata for Solo Flute (1975); Sonata for Solo Oboe (1976); Sonata for Solo Clarinet (1976); Sonata for Solo Horn (1976). **VOCAL:** Song cycles; children's choruses.

Remedios, Alberto, English tenor; b. Liverpool, Feb. 27, 1935. He studied in Liverpool with Edwin Francis and later in London with Clive Carey at the Royal College of Music. He made his operatic debut as Tinca in *Il tabarro* at the Sadler's Wells Opera in London in 1957; made his first appearance at Covent Garden in London as Dimitri in *Boris Godunov* in 1965; sang at the Frankfurt am Main Opera (1968–70). He made his U.S. debut with the San Francisco Opera in 1973; made his Metropolitan Opera debut in N.Y. as Bacchus in *Ariadne auf Naxos* on March 20, 1976. He was highly successful as Lohengrin, Siegfried, and Siegmund; showed fine lyrical talent as Faust in Gounod's opera, and a dramatic flair in Verdi's Otello.

Remenkov, Stefan, Bulgarian composer; b. Silistra, April 30, 1923. He studied piano with Nenov and composition with Vladigerov and Stoyanov at the Bulgarian State Cons. in Sofia, graduating in 1950; later took a course with Khachaturian at the Moscow Cons.

WORKS: DRAMATIC: *The Unvanquished*, ballet (1960); *The Errors Are Ours*, operetta (1966); 2 children's operettas: *Ghanem* (1967) and *The Prince and the Pauper* (1973). **ORCH.:** 2 piano concertos (1953, 1970); *Prelude and Dance* for Strings (1957); 4 syms.: No. 1, *Children's Symphony* (1961), No. 2, *Symphony in the Classical Style* (1962), No. 3 (1965), and No. 4 (1968); Cello Concerto (1964); Concertino for Flute and Strings (1973); *Fantasy* for Violin and Orch. (1974). **CHAMBER:** Violin Sonata (1955); Nonet; 3 piano sonatas (1944, 1948, 1949).

Remington, Emory, American trombonist and pedagogue; b. Rochester, N.Y., Dec. 22, 1891; d. there, Dec. 11, 1971. He was a student of Gardell Simons, Edward Llewellyn, and Ernest Williams. From 1922 until his death he taught at the Eastman School of Music in his native city. He also was 1st trumpeter in the Rochester Phil. from 1923 to 1949. By adopting the larger-bore trombone with F-valve attachment, Remington proved highly influential as a teacher of the instrument.

Remoortel, Edouard van, Belgian conductor; b. Brussels, May 30, 1926; d. Paris, May 16, 1977. He studied at the Brussels Cons. and at the Geneva Cons.; also took courses in conducting with Guarnieri and Galliera at the Accademia Musicale Chigiana in Siena and privately with Josef Krips. From 1951 he was the principal conductor of the Orchestre National de Belgique in Brussels. In 1958 he was appointed music director of the St. Louis Sym. Orch., retaining this post until 1962. In 1965 he went to Monte Carlo as artistic consultant to the Orchestre National de l'Opera of Monaco, resigning in 1969.

Remy, Alfred, German-American writer on music and editor; b. Elberfeld, March 16, 1870; d. N.Y., Feb. 26, 1937. He emigrated to the U.S. in 1882; studied at the City College of N.Y. (B.A., 1890)); received private instruction in piano, violin, and theory (1890–96); completed his education at Columbia Univ. (M.A., 1905). He was music critic of *Vogue* and music ed. of *The Looker-On* (1895–97); taught music and modern languages at various N.Y. institutions (from 1896). He was music ed. of the *New International Encyclopaedia* (1901–30) and ed.-in-chief of the 3rd ed. of *Baker's Biographical Dictionary of Musicians* (1919).

Rendall, (Francis) Geoffrey, English organologist and librarian; b. Dulwich, Sept. 20, 1890; d. London, Dec. 3, 1952. He received training in clarinet at Charterhouse School and in classics at Cambridge (M.A., 1914). He was on the staff of the British Museum in London, where he later served as Keeper of Printed Books. Rendall was the author of the valuable study *The Clarinet* (London, 1954; 3rd ed., 1971).

Rendano, Alfonso, Italian pianist, teacher, and composer; b. Carolei, near Cosenza, April 5, 1883; d. Rome, Sept. 10, 1931. He studied in Caserta and then at the Naples Cons. (1863). After making his debut as a pianist in 1864, he pursued training with Thalberg in Naples (1866–67), with Mathias in Paris (1867), and with Reinecke and Richter at the Leipzig Cons. (1868). He successfully toured in Europe. After teaching at the Naples Cons. (1883) and at his own piano school (1883–86), he settled in Rome to teach privately. Rendano was the inventor of the pedale indipendente, which became known as the pedale Rendano. This 3rd pedal was placed between the standard 2 pedals of the piano with the intention of prolonging the vibration of single sounds or chords. He composed an opera, *Consuelo* (Turin, May 25, 1902), a Piano Concerto, a Piano Quintet, many piano pieces, and vocal works.

BIBL.: G. Puccio, *A. R.* (Rome, 1937); F. Perrino, "A. R.," *Rassegna musicale Curci*, XV (1961).

Renié, Henriette, eminent French harpist, pedagogue, and composer; b. Paris, Sept. 18, 1875; d. there, March 1, 1956. She studied with Alphonse Hasselmans at the Paris Cons.; received the premier prix for harp at the age of 11; then entered the classes of Lenepveu and Dubois in harmony and composition. She performed her own Harp Concerto at the Concerts Lamoureux in Paris on March 24, 1901. She taught at the Paris Cons.; among her students was Marcel Grandjany. Among her other works were *Pièce symphonique* for Harp and Orch.; *Légende et Danse caprice* for Harp and Orch.; numerous solo harp pieces; chamber music; songs.

Rennert, Günther, leading German opera producer and administrator; b. Essen, April 1, 1911; d. Salzburg, July 31, 1978. He was educated in Munich, Berlin, and Halle. From 1935 to 1939 he worked in Wuppertal, in Frankfurt am Main (with Walter Felsenstein), and in Mainz; then was chief producer in Königsberg (1939–42), at the Berlin Stadtische Oper (1942–44), and at the Bavarian State Opera in Munich (1945). In 1946 he became Intendant of the Hamburg State Opera, a post he held until 1956; then worked as a guest producer with several major opera houses, including La Scala in Milan and the Metropolitan Opera in N.Y. From 1967 to 1976 he was Intendant of the Bavarian State Opera in Munich. Through the consistent successes of his operatic productions in several cities under changing circumstances, Rennert acquired a reputation as one of the most competent members of his profession.

BIBL.: W. Schafer, *G. R., Regisseur in dieser Zeit* (Bremen, 1962).

Renz, Frederick, American harpsichordist and conductor; b. Buffalo, July 27, 1940. He studied at the State Univ. of N.Y. at Fredonia (graduated, 1962) and at Indiana Univ. (M.M. in conducting, 1964; M.M. in harpsichord, 1966); then studied harpsichord with Gustav Leonhardt on a Fulbright fellowship in Amsterdam (1967–69). After performing as a keyboard player with the N.Y. Pro Musica (1969–74), he founded his own Ensemble for Early Music in N.Y. (1974), with which he toured widely. His repertoire extends from the 12th to the early 19th century.

Repin, Vadim, Russian violinist; b. Novosibirsk, Aug. 31, 1971. He was a pupil of Zakhar Bron at the Novosibirsk Cons. When he was 11, he took 1st prize in the junior division of the Wieniawski competition in Poland. At age 13, he appeared with Yevgeny Kissen in the inaugural recital of the 1984 Tchaikovsky competition in Moscow, and subsequently made appearances in his homeland. In 1987 he made his British debut as soloist with the BBC Phil. at the Lichfield Festival. After capturing 1st prize in both the Tibor Varga (1988) and Queen Elisabeth of Belgium (1989) competitions, he toured extensively. During the 1990–91 season, he appeared as soloist with the Minnesota Orch., toured Germany with the London Phil., and gave recitals in Paris, London, Frankfurt am Main, and Salzburg. In 1991 he toured the U.S. and Germany with the State Sym. Orch. of Russia, and also made his North American recital debut at the Ravinia Festival in Chicago. In subsequent seasons, his tours took him all over the world. Repin's playing is a tribute to the time-honored Russian tradition of violin virtuosity, most notable for its seemingly effortless technical display and élan.

Resnik, Regina, American soprano, later mezzo-soprano; b. N.Y., Aug. 30, 1922. She studied in N.Y. She made her concert debut at the Brooklyn Academy of Music (Oct. 27, 1942); sang in opera in Mexico (1943); won an annual audition at the Metropolitan Opera in N.Y. in 1944, and appeared there as Leonora in *Il Trovatore* (Dec. 6, 1944); continued to sing there regularly, turning to mezzo-soprano roles in 1955. In 1953 she appeared in Bayreuth as Sieglinde; made her Covent Garden debut in London as Carmen in 1957, and sang there until 1972. She remained on the roster of the Metropolitan Opera until 1974. She was active as an opera producer from 1971. Among her finest roles were Mistress Quickly, Marina, Amneris, Herodias, and Clytemnestra. She also created the role of the Countess in Barber's *Vanessa* (1958).

Respighi, Ottorino, eminent Italian composer and teacher; b. Bologna, July 9, 1879; d. Rome, April 18, 1936. He studied violin with F. Sarti and composition with L. Torchi and G. Martucci at Bologna's Liceo Musicale (1891–1900). In 1900 he went to Russia, and played 1st viola in the orch. of the Imperial Opera in St. Petersburg; there he took lessons with Rimsky-Korsakov, which proved a decisive influence in Respighi's coloristic orchestration. From 1903 to 1908 he was active as a concert violinist; also played the viola in the Mugellini Quartet of Bologna. In 1913 he was engaged as a prof. of composition at Rome's Liceo (later Conservatorio) di Santa Cecilia; in 1924, was appointed its director, but resigned in 1926, retaining only a class in advanced composition; subsequently devoted himself to composing and conducting. He was elected a member of the Italian Royal Academy on March 23, 1932. In 1925–26 and again in 1932 he made tours of the U.S. as a pianist and a conductor. Respighi's style of composition is a highly successful blend of songful melodies with full and rich harmonies; he was one of the best masters of modern Italian music in orchestration. His power of evocation of the Italian scene and his ability to sustain interest without prolixity is incontestable. Although he wrote several operas, he achieved his greatest success with 2 symphonic poems, *Le fontane di Roma* and *I pini di Roma*, each consisting of 4 tone paintings of the Roman landscape; a great innovation for the time was the insertion of a phonograph recording of a nightingale into the score of *I pini di Roma*. His wife, Elsa Olivieri Sangiacomo Respighi (b. Rome, March 24, 1894; d. there, March 17, 1996, missing her 102nd birthday by 7 days), was his pupil; she wrote a fairy opera, *Fior di neve*; the symphonic poem *Serenata di maschere;* and numerous songs; was also a concert singer. She publ. a biography of her husband.

WORKS: DRAMATIC: OPERAS: *Re Enzo* (Bologna, March 12, 1905); *Semirama*, lyric tragedy (Bologna, Nov. 20, 1910); *Marie-Victoire* (1913–14; not perf.); *La bella dormente nel bosco* or *La bella addormentata nel bosco*, musical fairy tale (1916–21; Rome, April 13, 1922); *Belfagor*, lyric comedy (1921–22; Milan, April 26, 1923); *La campana sommersa*, after Hauptmann's *Die versunkene Glocke* (1923–27; Hamburg, Nov. 18, 1927); *Maria Egiziaca*, mystery play (1929–32; N.Y., March 16, 1932); *La fiamma* (1930–33; Rome, Jan. 23, 1934); a free transcription of Monteverdi's *Orfeo* (Milan, March 16, 1935); *Lucrezia* (1935; Milan, Feb. 24, 1937). **BALLETS:** *La Boutique fantasque*, on themes by Rossini (London, June 5, 1919); *Scherzo veneziano* (Rome, Nov. 27, 1920); *Belkis, Regina di Saba* (1930–31; Milan, Jan. 23, 1932). **ORCH.:** Piano Concerto (1902); Suite for Organ and Strings (1902–05); *Notturno* (1905); *Sinfonia drammatica* (1913–14); *Le fontane di Roma*, symphonic poem (1914–16; Rome, March 11, 1917); *Antiche arie e danze per liuto*, 3 sets, the 3rd for Strings (1916, 1923, 1931); *Ballata delle gnomidi* (1918–20; Rome, April 11, 1920); *Poema autunnale* for Violin and Orch. (1920–25); *Concerto gregoriano* for Violin and Orch. (1921; Rome, Feb. 5, 1922); *I pini di Roma*, symphonic poem (Rome, Dec. 14, 1924); *Concerto in modo misolidio* for Piano and Orch. (N.Y., Dec. 31, 1925, composer soloist); *Rossiniana*, suite from Rossini's piano pieces (1925); *Vetrate di chiesa*, symphonic impressions (Boston, Feb. 25, 1927); *Impressioni brasiliane*, symphonic suite (1927; São Paulo, June 16, 1928, composer conducting); *Trittico Botticelliano* for Chamber Orch. (1927); *Gli Uccelli*, suite for Small Orch. on themes by Rameau, B. Pasquini, and others (1927); *Toccata* for Piano and Orch. (1928); *Feste romane*, symphonic poem (1928; N.Y., Feb. 21, 1929); *Metamorphosen modi XII* (Boston, Nov. 7, 1930); *Concerto à 5* for Violin, Oboe, Trumpet, Double Bass, Piano, and Strings (1932). **BAND:** *Huntingtower Ballad* (Washington, D.C., April 17, 1932). **CHAMBER:** 11 pieces for Violin and Piano (1904–07); String Quartet in D major (1907); *Quartetto dorico* for String Quartet (1924); Violin Sonata (1917). **VOCAL:** *Il tramonto* for Mezzo-soprano and String Quartet, after Shelley (1917); *La Primavera*, cantata for Soloists, Chorus, and Orch. (1918–19; Rome, March 4, 1923); *Lauda per la Natività del Signore* for Soloists, Chorus, and Orch. (1928–30); 45 songs; 3 vocalises; arrangements.

BIBL.: R. de Rensis, *O. R.* (Turin, 1935); E. Respighi, *O. R.: Dati biografici ordinati* (Milan, 1954; abridged Eng. tr., 1962); *O. R.: Catalogo delle opere* (Milan, 1965); E. Battaglia, ed., *O. R.* (Turin, 1985); D. Bryant, ed., *Il Novecento musicale italiano: Tra neoclassicismo e neogoticismo: Atti del convegno di studi promosso dalla Fondazione Giorgio Cini per il 50° anniversario della scomparsa di O. R.* (Florence, 1988).

Rethberg, Elisabeth (real name, **Lisbeth Sattler**), outstanding German-American soprano; b. Schwarzenberg, Sept. 22, 1894; d. Yorktown Heights, N.Y., June 6, 1976. She studied at the Dresden Cons. and with Otto Watrin. She made her operatic debut as Arsena in *Der Zigeunerbaron* at the Dresden Court Opera (1915); continued to sing there when it became the State Opera in 1918. She then made her U.S. debut as Aida at the Metropolitan Opera in N.Y. on Nov. 22, 1922, remaining one of its most celebrated artists until her farewell performance there in that same role on March 6, 1942. She subsequently embarked on a grand concert tour with Ezio Pinza in the U.S., Europe, and Australia; their close association resulted in a lawsuit for alienation of affection brought by Pinza's wife against her, but the court action was not pursued. Throughout her operatic career, Rethberg sang in many of the major music centers in Italy; also appeared at the Salzburg Festivals and at London's Covent Garden (1925; 1934–39). She excelled in both the German and Italian repertoires; among her memorable roles were Mozart's Countess, Donna Anna, Pamina, Constanze, and Donna Elvira; Verdi's Aida, the 2 Leonoras, Amelia, Desdemona, and Maria Boccanegra; and Wagner's Eva, Elisabeth, Sieglinde, and Elsa; also created the title role in Strauss's *Die ägyptische Helena* (Dresden, June 6, 1928). Rethberg was married twice: first to Ernst Albert Dormann, and then to George Cehanovsky, whom she married in 1956.

BIBL.: H. Henschel and E. Friedrich, *E. R.: Ihr Leben und Künstlertum* (Schwarzenberg, 1928).

Réti, Rudolph (Richard), Hungarian-American music theorist, pianist, and composer; b. Užice, Serbia, Nov. 27, 1885; d. Montclair, N.J., Feb. 7, 1957. He studied at the Vienna Academy of Music and at the Univ. of Vienna. He took an early interest in new music and was one of the founders of the ISCM (Salzburg, 1922). In 1938 he went to the U.S.; in 1943 he married the Canadian pianist Jean Sahlmark; in 1950 they settled in Montclair, N.J. His compositions are marked by precise structure and fine stylistic unity. Among his works are *Symphonia mystica* (1951); *Triptychon* for Orch. (1953); Concertino for Cello and Orch. (1953); 2 piano concertos; Violin Sonata; several choruses and solo songs; piano pieces. An original music analyst, he wrote several books which contributed to the development of logical theory of modern music: *The Thematic Process in Music* (N.Y., 1952); *Tonality, Atonality, Pantonality* (N.Y., 1958); *Thematic Patterns in Sonatas of Beethoven* (ed. by D. Cooke, London, 1965).

Rettich, Wilhelm, German-born Dutch composer and conductor; b. Leipzig, July 3, 1892; d. Sinzheim bei Baden-Baden, Dec.

27, 1988. He studied at the Leipzig Cons. with Reger. He was in the German army in World War I and was taken prisoner by the Russians; sent to Siberia, he made his way to China after the Russian Revolution and eventually returned to Leipzig. He occupied various posts as a theater conductor; was music director of the local synagogue until 1933, when the advent of the Nazi regime forced him to leave Germany; he went to the Netherlands and became a naturalized Dutch citizen. In 1964 he returned to Germany and lived in Baden-Baden. As a composer, he excelled in symphonic and chamber music; wrote 3 syms.; Violin Concerto; Piano Concerto; much chamber music for various combinations; choral works; piano pieces and songs.

Reuss, August, German composer and teacher; b. Liliendorf bei Znaim, Moravia, March 6, 1871; d. Munich, June 18, 1935. He was a pupil of Thuille in Munich; after a brief activity as Kapellmeister in Augsburg (1906) and Magdeburg (1907), he lived in Berlin; then in Munich, where he taught at the Trapp Cons. (1927–29) and at the Akademie der Tonkünst (1929–35). His works, all in a late Romantic style, include an opera, *Herzog Philipps Brautfahrt* (Graz, 1909); orch. works, including the tone poems *Johannisnacht* (1903) and *Judith* (1903), *Sommeridylle* (1920), and a Piano Concerto (1924); and numerous chamber works, including a Piano Trio (1912), 2 string quartets (1906, 1914), and an Octet for 2 Oboes, 2 Clarinets, 2 Bassoons, and 2 Horns (1918).

Reuss-Belce, Luise, Austrian soprano; b. Vienna, Oct. 24, 1860; d. (found dead in a refugee train) Aibach, Germany, March 5, 1945. She studied voice in Vienna. She made her operatic debut as Elsa in *Lohengrin* in Karlsruhe (1881); then sang in Bayreuth (1882) and in Wiesbaden (1896–99); her subsequent appearances were at Covent Garden in London (1900) and at the Metropolitan Opera in N.Y., where she made her debut as Brünnhilde in *Die Walküre* (Feb. 11, 1902); then sang in Dresden (1903–11). In 1885 she married Eduard Reuss (b. N.Y., Sept. 16, 1851; d. Dresden, Feb. 18, 1911), a music pedagogue; after his death, she moved to Berlin, where she established a singing school. In 1913 she was appointed stage manager at the festival opera performances in Nuremberg; she was the first woman to occupy such a post in Germany.

Reuter, Rolf, German conductor; b. Leipzig, Oct. 7, 1926. He studied at the Academy for Music and Theater in Dresden. He conducted in Eisenach (1951–55); then was Generalmusikdirektor in Meiningen (1955–61). In 1961 he became a conductor at the Leipzig Opera, and subsequently served as its Generalmusikdirektor (1963–78). He was chief conductor of the Weimar State Orch. (1979–81). From 1981 to 1994 he was chief conductor and music director of the Komische Oper in East Berlin.

Reutter, Hermann, outstanding German composer and pedagogue; b. Stuttgart, June 17, 1900; d. Heidenheim an der Brenz, Jan. 1, 1985. He studied with Franz Dorfmüller (piano), Ludwig Mayer (organ), Karl Erler (voice), and Walter Courvoisier (composition) at the Munich Academy of Music (1920–23). He began his career as a pianist in 1923; made numerous concert tours with the singer Sigrid Onegin (1930–35), including 7 separate tours in the U.S. He taught composition at the Stuttgart Hochschule für Musik (1932–36); after serving as director of the Berlin Staatliche Hochschule für Musik (1936–45), he became a teacher of lieder and composition at the Stuttgart Staatliche Hochschule für Musik (1952), serving as its director (1956–66); then was prof. of music at the Munich Academy of Music. As a composer, Reutter followed the traditional line of German neo-Classicism, in which the basic thematic material, often inspired by German folk music, is arranged along strong contrapuntal lines, wherein a dissonant intervallic fabric does not disrupt the sense of immanent tonality. He excelled particularly in stage music and songs. He brought out an anthology of contemporary art songs, *Das zeitgenössische Lied* (4 vols., Mainz, 1969).

WORKS: OPERAS: *Saul* (Baden-Baden, July 15, 1928; rev. version, Hamburg, Dec. 21, 1947); *Der verlorene Sohn* (Stuttgart, March 20, 1929; rev. as *Die Rückkehr des verlorenen Sohnes*, Dortmund, 1952); *Doktor Johannes Faust* (1934–36; Frankfurt am Main, May 26, 1936; rev. version, Stuttgart, 1955); *Odysseus* (1940–42; Frankfurt am Main, Oct. 7, 1942); *Der Weg nach Freundschaft: Ballade der Landstrasse* (Göttingen, Jan. 25, 1948); *Don Juan und Faust* (Stuttgart, June 11, 1950); *Die Witwe von Ephesus* (1953; Cologne, June 23, 1954); *Die Brücke von San Luis Rey* (Frankfurt am Main Radio, June 20, 1954); *Hamlet* (Stuttgart, 1980); also *Der Tod des Empedokles*, scenic concerto (1965; Schwetzingen, May 29, 1966). **ORCH.:** 3 piano concertos (1925, 1929, 1944); Violin Concerto (c.1930); Concerto for 2 Pianos and Orch. (1949); *Prozession* for Cello and Orch. (1956); Sym. for Strings (1960). **OTHER:** Chamber music; piano pieces; choral works; about 200 songs.

BIBL.: H. Lindlar, ed., *H. R.: Werk und Wirken: Festschrift der Freunde* (Mainz, 1965).

Revelli, William D(onald), American band director and teacher; b. Spring Gulch, near Aspen, Colo., Feb. 12, 1902; d. Ann Arbor, July 16, 1994. The family moved to southern Illinois, near St. Louis, when he was an infant; he began to study the violin at the age of 5; later he was a pupil of Dominic Sarli. After graduating from the Chicago Musical College in 1922, he completed his education at the Columbia School of Music in Chicago (diploma in music education, 1925). In 1925 he became supervisor of music in Hobart, Ind., where he founded the high school band, which he in time built to national prominence, winning the high school band championship for 6 consecutive years. In 1935 he was made director of the Univ. of Mich. Band at Ann Arbor, and was also in charge of its wind instruments dept. Revelli's Symphonic Band toured the country many times and made several trips abroad under State Dept. auspices, most notably a 16-week tour in early 1961 that took it to the Soviet Union, Bulgaria, Turkey, Egypt, and other countries in the Middle East. In 1971 Revelli became director emeritus of the Univ. of Mich. Bands. As an instructor and promoter of bands within the U.S. academic system, Revelli continued the tradition of Fillmore and A.A. Harding. He was active as an ed., adviser, and administrator of various undertakings in the American band field; was also founder of the College Band Directors National Assn. (1941) and was its honorary life president. He received honorary doctoral degrees from 5 American univs.

BIBL.: G. Cavanagh, *W.D. R.: The Hobart Years* (diss., Univ. of Mich., 1971).

Révész, Géza, Hungarian psychologist; b. Siófek, Dec. 9, 1878; d. Amsterdam, Aug. 19, 1955. He studied experimental psychology at the Univ. of Göttingen (Ph.D., 1905). He taught psychology at the Univ. of Budapest (1906–20). In 1921 he settled in the Netherlands, where he became director of the Psychological Inst. of the Univ. of Amsterdam.

WRITINGS: *Zur Grundlegung der Tonpsychologie* (Leipzig, 1913); *Das frühzeitige Auftreten der Begabung und ihre Erkennung* (Leipzig, 1921); with Katz, *Musikgenuss bei Gehörlosen* (Leipzig, 1926); *Inleiding tot de muziekpsychologie* (Amsterdam, 1944; Ger. tr., Bern, 1946; Eng. tr., N.Y., 1953, as *Introduction to the Psychology of Music*). The book that attracted the most attention, and also put in doubt the efficacy of the author's method, was *Ervin Nyiregyházi. Psychologische Analyse eines musikalisch hervorragenden Kindes* (Leipzig, 1916; Eng. tr., London, 1925, as *The Psychology of a Musical Prodigy*), which analyzes the case of a talented Hungarian child pianist who had perfect pitch, could transpose at sight and commit to memory short musical phrases instantly; but examples cited in the book do not go beyond the capabilities of thousands of other musically gifted children.

Revueltas, Silvestre, remarkable Mexican composer; b. Santiago Papasquiaro, Dec. 31, 1899; d. Mexico City, Oct. 5, 1940. He began violin studies when he was 8 in Colima; then entered the Juárez Inst. in Durango at age 12; after studies with Tello (composition) and Rocabruna (violin) in Mexico City (1913–16), he took courses at St. Edward College in Austin, Texas

(1916–18), and with Sametini (violin) and Borowski (composition) at the Chicago Musical College (1918–20); returned to Chicago to study violin with Kochánski and Sevčik (1922–26). He was active as a violinist and conductor in Texas and Alabama (1926–28); was assistant conductor of the Orquesta Sinfónica de Mexico (1929–35); only then did he begin to compose. In 1937 he went to Spain, where he was active in the cultural affairs of the Loyalist government during the Civil War. His health was ruined by exertions and an irregular life-style, and he died of pneumonia. His remains were deposited in the Rotonda de los Hombres Ilustres in Mexico City on March 23, 1976, to the music of his *Redes* and the funeral march from Beethoven's *Eroica*. He possessed an extraordinary natural talent and an intimate understanding of Mexican music; he succeeded in creating works of great originality, melodic charm, and rhythmic vitality.

WORKS (all 1st perf. in Mexico City unless otherwise given): **BALLETS:** *El Renacuajo paseador* (1933; Oct. 4, 1940); *La Coronela* (unfinished; completed by Galindo and Huizar; Nov. 20, 1941). **ORCH.:** *Cuauhnahuac* (1931–32; June 2, 1933); *Esquinas* for Small Orch. (Nov. 20, 1931; also for Large Orch., 1933); *Ventanas* (1931; Nov. 4, 1932); *Alcancias* (1932); *Colorines* for Small Orch. (Aug. 30, 1932); *Ocho por Radio* for Small Orch. (Oct. 13, 1933); *Janitzio* (Oct. 13, 1933; rev. 1936); *Caminos* (July 17, 1934); *Planos*, "geometric dance" (Nov. 5, 1934); *Redes*, concert suite from the film score, for Small Orch. (1935; Barcelona, Oct. 7, 1937); *Homenaje a Federico García Lorca* for Small Orch. (1935; Madrid, Sept. 22, 1937); *Sensemayá* (Dec. 15, 1938; also for Voice and Small Orch., 1937); *Música para charlar*, concert suite from the film scores *El Indio* and *Ferro-carriles de Baja California* (Dec. 15, 1938); *La noche de los Mayas*, concert suite from the film score (1939); *Itinerarios* (1939); *Paisajes* (1940); *Troka* (1940). **CHAMBER:** 4 string quartets: No. 1 (1930), No. 2, *Magueyes* (1931), No. 3 (1931; recovered in 1984 and posthumously numbered), and No.4, *Música de feria* (1932; posthumously numbered); *3 Pieces* for Violin and Piano (1932); *Tocata sin fuga* for Violin and 7 Winds (1933); *Canto de guerra de los frentes leales* for 3 Trumpets, 3 Trombones, 2 Tubas, Percussion, and Piano (1938); *3 sonetas* for Chamber Ensemble (1940); *3 Little Serious Pieces* for Piccolo, Oboe, Trumpet, Clarinet, and Saxophone (1940). **VOCAL:** *Sensemayá* for Voice and Small Orch., based on an Afro-Cuban legend (1937; rev. for Large Orch. alone, Dec. 15, 1938); *Hora de junio* for Narrator and Orch. (1938); *Parias* for Soprano, Chorus, and Small Orch. (1940); many songs.

BIBL.: G. Contreras, *S. R.: Genio atormentado* (Mexico City, 1954).

Revutsky, Lev(ko Mikolaievich), Ukrainian composer; b. Irshavetz, near Poltava, Feb. 20, 1889; d. Kiev, March 31, 1977. He went to Kiev and studied with Glière at the Cons. (graduated, 1916). From 1924 to 1941 he taught at the Musico-Dramatic Inst. In 1957 he was elected to the Ukrainian Academy of Sciences. He composed music for the theater, films, and radio; 2 piano concertos (1914, 1934); 2 syms. (1916–21; 1926–27); choral pieces.

Rey, Cemal Reshid, Turkish pianist, conductor, teacher, and composer; b. Jerusalem, Sept. 24, 1904; d. Istanbul, Oct. 7, 1985. Of a distinguished family (his father was a poet and also served twice as minister of the interior in the Turkish government), he went to Paris at age 9 to study composition with Laparra; then continued his studies at the Geneva Cons.; returning to Paris, he took courses in piano with Long, composition with Fauré, and conducting with Derosse. In 1923 he settled in Constantinople and taught at the Cons.; from 1949 to 1969 he was principal conductor of the Istanbul Radio Orch. His music is imbued with Turkish melorhythms; many of his works are written on Turkish subjects.

WORKS: DRAMATIC: OPERAS: *Yann Marek* (1922); *Sultan Cem* (1923); *Zeybek* (1926); *Tchelebi* (1945); *Benli Hürmüz* (1965). **OPERETTA:** *Yaygara* (1969). **ORCH.:** *La Légende du Bebek* (Paris, Dec. 15, 1929); *Karagueuz*, symphonic poem (Paris, Feb. 14, 1932, composer conducting); *Scènes turques* (Paris, March 6, 1932); *Concerto chromatique* for Piano and Orch. (Paris, March 12, 1933, composer soloist); Violin Concerto (1939); 3 syms. (1941, 1950, 1968); *L'Appel*, symphonic poem (Paris, April 3, 1952, composer conducting); *Fatih* (1956); 3 symphonic scherzos (1958); *Colloque instrumental* for Flute, 2 Horns, Harp, and Strings (1957); *Variations on an Istanbul Folksong* for Piano and Orch. (1966). **OTHER:** Numerous arrangements of Turkish folk songs for various instrumental combinations; choruses; piano pieces.

Reynolds, Anna, English mezzo-soprano; b. Canterbury, Oct. 4, 1931. She studied piano at the Royal Academy of Music in London; then went to Italy for vocal lessons. She made her operatic debut in Parma in 1960 as Suzuki; subsequently sang in Vicenza (1961), Rome (1964), Spoleto (1966), Trieste (1967), and Venice (1969), and at La Scala in Milan (1973). She made her first appearance in England at Glyndebourne in 1962; sang at Covent Garden in London in 1967; also sang at Bayreuth (1970–76). She made her Metropolitan Opera debut in N.Y. as Flosshilde in *Das Rheingold* on Nov. 22, 1968, and returned there in 1975. She also sang widely as a concert artist and recitalist.

Reynolds, Roger (Lee), American composer and teacher; b. Detroit, July 18, 1934. He studied engineering physics (B.S.E., 1957) and was a student of Ross Lee Finney (composition; B.M., 1960; M.M., 1961) at the Univ. of Mich. in Ann Arbor; he was also a co-founder of the ONCE festival there in 1961. He also studied with Roberto Gerhard at the Univ. of Mich. in 1960, following him to the Berkshire Music Center in Tanglewood during the summer of 1961, and winning the Koussevitsky Prize there. In 1962–63 a Fulbright fellowship enabled him to work at the WDR electronic studio in Cologne. He held a Guggenheim fellowship in 1963–64. From 1966 to 1969 he was a fellow of the Inst. of Current World Affairs in Tokyo, where he was co-organizer of the Cross Talk concerts and the Cross Talk festival. He taught at the Univ. of Calif. at San Diego from 1969; he was founder-director of its Center for Music Experiment and Related Research (1971–77), and then chairman of the music dept. (1979–81). As a guest composer and lecturer, he was active in both the U.S. and abroad. In 1982 he was visiting prof. of composition at Yale Univ., and in 1992–93 was the Rothschild composer-in-residence at the Peabody Cons. of Music in Baltimore. In addition to his numerous articles on music, he publ. the studies *Mind Models: New Forms of Musical Experience* (1975), *A Searcher's Path: A Composer's Ways* (1987), and *A Jostled Silence: Contemporary Japanese Musical Thought* (serialized in *Perspectives of New Music*, XXX, 1 and 2, 1992, and XXXI, 2, 1993). In 1971 he received a National Inst. of Arts and Letters award. In 1975, 1978, 1979, and 1986 he held NEA grants. He won the Pulitzer Prize in Music in 1989 for his *Whispers Out of Time* for Strings. In 1990 he received a Suntory Foundation commission. In 1991–92 he received a Koussevitzky Foundation commission. In his music, Reynolds owes much to the examples set by Ives, Varèse, and Cage. He makes use of every resource available to the contemporary composer, from traditional instruments and voices to electronics and computer-generated sounds.

WORKS: DRAMATIC: *The Emperor of Ice Cream*, theater piece for 8 Voices, Piano, Contrabass, and Percussion (1962; concert version, N.Y., March 19, 1965; stage version, Rome, April 27, 1965; rev. 1974); *I/O* for 9 Women Vocalists, 9 Male Mimes, 2 Flutes, Clarinet, Projections, and Live Electronics (1970; Pasadena, Calif., Jan. 24, 1971); *A Merciful Coincidence (VOICESPACE II)*, music theater (Bourges, June 9, 1976); *The Tempest*, incidental music to Shakespeare's play, for Electroacoustic Sound, Voices, and Instruments (Lenox, Mass., July 30, 1980); *Ivanov*, incidental music to Chekhov's play, for Computer-processed Sound (1991; Mito, Japan, Jan. 1992). **ORCH.:** *Graffiti* (1964; Seattle, May 2, 1965); *Threshold* (1967; Tokyo, June 7, 1968); *". . . between . . ."* for Chamber Orch. and Live Electronics (1968; Chicago, March 10, 1970); *Only Now, and Again* for 23 Winds, Piano, and Percussion (Milwaukee, May 6,

1977); *Fiery Wind* (N.Y., Feb. 13, 1978); *Archipelago* for Chamber Orch. and Computer-generated Tape (1982–83; Paris, Feb. 15, 1983); *Transfigured Wind II* for Flute, Orch., and Computer-generated Tape (N.Y., June 4, 1984); *The Dream of the Infinite Rooms* for Cello, Orch., and Computer-generated Tape (1986; Cleveland, March 2, 1987); 3 syms.: *Symphony [Vertigo]* for Orch. and Tape (San Francisco, Dec. 9, 1987), *Symphony [Myths]* (Tokyo, Oct. 25, 1990), and *Symphony [The Stages of Life]* (1991–92; Los Angeles, April 4, 1993); *Whispers Out of Time* for Strings (Amherst, Mass., Dec. 11, 1988); *Dreaming* (1992; N.Y., Jan. 10, 1993); *Watershed III*, concerto for Percussion, Chamber Ensemble, and Real-time Computer Sound Spatialization (N.Y., Oct. 30, 1995). **CHAMBER:** *Situations* for Cello and Piano (1960); *Continuum* for Viola and Cello (1960); *Consequent* for Alto Flute, Violin, Bassoon, and Piano (1961); *Wedge* for Chamber Ensemble (1961); *Mosaic* for Flute and Piano (1961); *String Quartet No. 2* (1961); *Quick Are the Mouths of Earth* for Chamber Ensemble (1964–65; N.Y., Nov. 24, 1965); *Gathering* for Woodwind Quintet (1965; Amsterdam, July 12, 1966); *Ambages* for Flute (1965); *Ping* for Piano, Flute, Percussion, Slides, Films, Live Electronics, and Tape (Tokyo, June 5, 1968); *Traces* for Piano, Flute, Cello, Tape, and Live Electronics (N.Y., Dec. 17, 1968); *". . . from behind the unreasoning mask"* for Trombone, Percussion, and Tape (Las Vegas, Jan. 20, 1975); *The Promises of Darkness* for Chamber Ensemble (1975; N.Y., Jan. 8, 1976); *Less Than Two* for 2 Pianos, 2 Percussion, and Computer-generated Tape (1977–79; Washington, D.C., Feb. 23, 1979); *Shadowed Narrative* for Chamber Quartet (1977–82; N.Y., March 29, 1982); *". . . the serpent-snapping eye"* for Trumpet, Percussion, Piano, and Computer-generated Tape (1978; San Diego, Jan. 31, 1979); *Transfigured Wind I* for Flute (1983), *III* for Flute, Chamber Ensemble, and Computer-generated Tape (Los Angeles, June 22, 1984), and *IV* for Flute and Tape (N.Y., Feb. 10, 1985); *Aether* for Violin and Piano (Washington, D.C., Oct. 29, 1983); *Mistral* for 6 Brass, 6 Strings, and Amplified Harpsichord (1984; N.Y., Feb. 12, 1985); *Summer Island (Islands from Archipelago I)* for Oboe and Computer-generated Tape (1984); *Coconino . . . a shattered landscape* for String Quartet (London, Nov. 10, 1985); *The Behavior of Mirrors* for Guitar (N.Y., Feb. 9, 1986); *Autumn Island (Islands from Archipelago II)* for Marimba (Washington, D.C., Nov. 7, 1986); *Personae* for Violin, Chamber Ensemble, and Computer-generated Sound (N.Y., March 26, 1990); *Dionysus* for 8 Instruments (Bloomington, Ind., July 1, 1990); *Focus a beam, emptied of thinking, outward . . .* for Cello (1989; N.Y., Feb. 27, 1992); *Visions* for String Quartet (Tokyo, May 27, 1992); *Kokoro* for Violin (1992); *Ariadne's Thread* for String Quartet and Computer-generated Sound (Radio France, Paris, Dec. 2, 1994). **PIANO:** *Fantasy for Pianist* (Warsaw, Sept. 26, 1965); *Variation* (1988; N.Y., Dec. 3, 1991). **VOCAL:** *Sky* for Soprano, Alto Flute, Bassoon, and Harp (1961); *A Portrait of Vanzetti* for Narrator, Instruments, and Tape (1963); *Masks* for Chorus and Orch. (1965); *Blind Men* for Chorus, Brass, Piano, and Percussion (Tanglewood, Aug. 15, 1966); *Again* for 2 Sopranos, 2 Flutes, 2 Contrabasses, 2 Trombones, 2 Percussion, Tape, and Amplification (St.-Paul-de-Vence, France, July 20, 1970); *Compass* for Tenor, Bass, Cello, Contrabass, Projections, and Tape (1972–73; Los Angeles, March 16, 1973); *The Palace (VOICESPACE IV)* for Bass-baritone, Tape, and Staging (1978–80; La Jolla, Calif., Dec. 19, 1980); *Sketchbook (for "The Unbearable Lightness of Being")* for Alto, Piano, and Electronics (N.Y., May 14, 1985); *Not Only Night* for Soprano, Piccolo, Clarinet, Violin, Cello, Piano, and Tape (Los Angeles, Nov. 7, 1988); *Odyssey* for Soprano, Bass-baritone, 16 Instruments, Computer-processed Sound, and Lighting (1989–93; Paris, June 17, 1993); *last things, I think, to think about*, song cycle for Bass-baritone, Piano, and Computer-processed Sound, after John Ashbery (N.Y., Nov. 17, 1994). **OTHER:** *Still (VOICESPACE I)* for Electroacoustic Sound (1975); *Eclipse (VOICESPACE III)* FOR Computer-generated and Electroacoustic Sound (1979–80; also as a media piece, 1982); *Vertigo* for Computer-processed Sound (1985; also with synthesized video, 1986); *The Vanity of Words (VOICESPACE V)* for Computer-processed Sound (1986); *Versions/Stages I–IV* for Computer-processed Sound (1988–91) and *V* for Computer-generated Sound (1991).

BIBL.: G. Chase, *R. R.: Portrait of a Composer* (N.Y., 1982).

Reynolds, Verne (Becker), American composer, horn player, and teacher; b. Lyons, Kansas, July 18, 1926. He received training in violin, piano, and horn. He was a composition student at the Cincinnati Cons. of Music (B.M., 1950), of Burleigh at the Univ. of Wisc. (M.M., 1951), and of Howells at the Royal College of Music in London. After playing horn in the Cincinnati Sym. Orch. (1947–50), he was 1st horn in the Rochester (N.Y.) Phil. (1959–68). He taught at the Univ. of Wisc. (1950–53), the Indiana Univ. School of Music in Bloomington (1954–59), and the Eastman School of Music in Rochester, N.Y. (1959–95).

WORKS: ORCH.: Violin Concerto (1951); *Saturday with Venus*, overture (1953); *Celebration Overture* (1960); *Ventures* (1975); *Festival and Memorial Music* (1977); Concerto for Band (1980). **CHAMBER:** *Serenade* for 13 Winds (1958); Flute Sonata (1962); String Quartet (1967); *Concertare I* for Brass Quintet and Percussion (1968), *II* for Trumpet and Strings (1968), *III* for Wind Quintet and Piano (1969), *IV* for Brass Quintet and Piano (1971), and *V* for Chamber Ensemble (1976); Tuba Sonata (1968); Horn Sonata (1970); Violin Sonata (1970); Viola Sonata (1975); *Signals* for Trumpet, Tuba, and Brass (1976); *Events* for Trombone Choir (1977); *Scenes Revisited* for Wind Ensemble (1977); Trio for Horn, Trombone, and Tuba (1978); *Fantasy-Etudes I* for Trumpet and Piano (1979), *II* for Clarinet, Percussion, and Piano (1990), *III* for Euphonium or Tuba and Piano (1991), *IV* for Bassoon and Percussion (1992), and *V* for Horn and Piano (1992); Cello Sonata (1983); Quintet for Piano and Winds (1986); Brass Quintet (1987); Trio for Oboe, Horn, and Piano (1990); Clarinet Sonata (1994); piano pieces. **VOCAL:** *The Hollow Men* for Baritone, Men's Chorus, Brass Choir, and Percussion (1954); *Songs of the Season* for Soprano, Horn, and Piano (1988); *Letter to the World* for Soprano and Percussion (1994).

Řezáč, Ivan, Czech composer; b. Řevnice, Nov. 5, 1924; d. Prague, Dec. 26, 1977. He studied piano with Rauch and composition with Šín, Janeček, and Dobiáš at the Prague Academy, graduating in 1953; later he joined its faculty, becoming its vice-dean in 1961. In his music, he follows the type of optimistic lyricism made popular by Shostakovich.

WORKS: OPERA: *Pan Theodor Mundstock* (Mr. Theodor Mundstock; 1974). **ORCH.:** 3 piano concertos (1955, 1964, 1972); 2 syms. (1958, 1961); *Návrat* (The Return) for Cello and Orch. (1962); *Quadrature of the Heart* for String Quartet and Orch. (1975); *Vivace* for 67 Musicians (1977); *Montage* (1977). **CHAMBER:** 2 string quartets (1955, 1971); Cello Sonata (1956); Piano Trio (1958); *Nocturnes* for Violin and Piano (1959); *Torso of a Schumann Monument* for Viola and Piano (1963); Duo for Violin and Piano (1965); *6 Tales* for Cello and Guitar (1973); *Musica da camera* for Flute, Oboe, Violin, Viola, and Cello (1973). **PIANO:** 2 sonatas (1954, 1957); 2 sonatinas (1959, 1966); *Dry Points* (1962); *Sisyfona Neděle* (Sisyphus Sunday) (1972).

Rhené-Baton (real name, **René Baton**), French conductor and composer; b. Courseulles-sur-Mer, Calvados, Sept. 5, 1879; d. Le Mans, Sept. 23, 1940. He studied piano at the Paris Cons. and theory privately with Gédalge. He began his conducting career as a chorus master at the Opéra-Comique in Paris; then conducted various concert groups in Angers and Bordeaux; from 1916 to 1932 he was principal conductor of the Concerts Pasdeloup in Paris. He composed orch. pieces, chamber music, and a number of songs.

Rhodes, Jane (Marie Andrée), French mezzo-soprano; b. Paris, March 13, 1929. Following vocal studies, she made her debut as Marguerite in *La Damnation de Faust* in Nancy in 1953, which role she also chose for her first appearance at the Paris Opéra in 1958. On Nov. 15, 1960, she made her Metropolitan Opera debut in N.Y. as Carmen, returning to sing Salome in 1962. In 1961 she appeared at the Aix-en-Provence Festival and in 1968 at the Paris Opéra-Comique; also sang in various other French operatic centers, and in Buenos Aires and Tokyo. In 1966 she married **Roberto Benzi**. In addition to her French roles, Rhodes also essayed the roles of Tosca and Renata in Prokofiev's *The Fiery Angel.*

Rhodes, Phillip (Carl), American composer and teacher; b. Forest City, N.C., June 6, 1940. He studied composition with Iain Hamilton at Duke Univ. (B.A., 1962); took courses in composition with Martino and Powell and in theory with Schuller and Perle at Yale Univ. (M.M., 1963). He was composer-in-residence in Cicero, Ill. (1966–68), and Louisville (1969–72); taught at Amherst College (1968–69), the Univ. of Louisville (1969–72), and Carleton College in Northfield, Minn. (from 1974), where he was composer-in-residence and the Andrew W. Mellon Prof. of the Humanities. From 1985 to 1987 he served as president of the College Music Soc.

WORKS: DRAMATIC: OPERAS: *The Gentle Boy* (1979–80; rev. version, Tallahassee, June 12, 1987); *The Magic Pipe* (1989). **BALLET:** *About Faces* (1970). **ORCH.:** *4 Movements* for Chamber Orch. (1962); *Remembrance* for Symphonic Wind Ensemble (1966–67); *Divertimento* for Small Orch. (1971); *3 "B's"* for Youth Orch. (1971); Concerto for Bluegrass Band and Orch. (Louisville, Dec. 22, 1974); *Ceremonial Fanfare and Chorale* for 2 Brass Choirs (1977); *Adventure Fantasies* for Young Players for Wind Ensemble (1983–84); *Reels and Reveries,* variations (1991); works for band. **CHAMBER:** String Trio (1965; rev. 1973); *Museum Pieces* for Clarinet and String Quartet (1973); Quartet for Flute, Harp, Violin, and Cello (1975); *Fiddle Tunes* for Violin and Synthesized Strings (1995); pieces for solo instruments. **VOCAL:** *On the Morning of Christ's Nativity,* cantata for Soprano, Tenor, Wind Quintet, and Harp (1976); *Wind Songs* for Unison Children's Chorus and Orff Instruments (1979); *In Praise of Wisdom* for Chorus and Brass Choir (1982); *Dancing Songs* for Unison Children's Chorus and Orff Instruments (1985); *Nets to Catch the Wind* for Chorus and Percussion (1986); *Wedding Song* for Soprano, Violin, and Organ (1990); *Mary's Lullaby* for Soprano, Violin, and Organ (1993); *Chorale and Meditation (O Sacred Head Now Wounded)* for Women's Voices and Organ (1994).

Rhodes, Willard, distinguished American music educator and ethnomusicologist; b. Dashler, Ohio, May 12, 1901; d. Sun City, Ariz., May 15, 1992. He earned his A.B. and B.Mus. degrees from Heidelberg College in Tiffin, Ohio, both in 1922; then studied at the Mannes School of Music in N.Y. (1923–25) and at Columbia Univ. (M.A., 1925); went to Paris, where he took lessons in piano with Cortot and in composition with Boulanger (1925–27). From 1927 to 1935 he served as conductor with the American Opera Co., the Cincinnati Summer Opera Co., and with his own Rhodes Chamber Opera Co. He was director of music in the public schools of Bronxville, N.Y. (1935–37). In 1937 he was appointed to the faculty at Columbia Univ.; became prof. emeritus in 1969. He held the post of music consultant to the U.S. Bureau of Indian Affairs beginning in 1937, and was a founding member (1953) and first president (1956–58) of the Soc. for Ethnomusicology. It was in this connection that he accumulated a most valuable collection of Amerindian folk music, both notated and recorded (many pressings released by the Library of Congress). In 1961 he was elected president of the Soc. for Asian Music, and in 1968 of the International Folk Music Council; also was a Fellow of the African Studies Assn. and numerous other ethnomusicological organizations. He conducted field work in Rhodesia and Nyasaland (1957–58) and in South India (1965–66); was visiting prof. at various institutions.

Ribáry, Antal, Hungarian composer; b. Budapest, Jan. 8, 1924. He studied composition with Rezső Kokai at the Budapest Academy of Music (1943–47); later took lessons with Ferenc Szabó.

WORKS: DRAMATIC: OPERAS: *Lajos Király Válik* (The Divorce of King Louis; 1959); *Liliom* (1960). **BALLET:** *Fortunio* (1969). **ORCH.:** *Sinfonietta* (1956); Cello Concerto (1958); 11 syms. (1960–89); *Musica per archi* (1961); *Pantomime* (1962); Violin Concertino (1965); *Dialogues* for Viola and Orch. (1967); 3 piano concertos (1979, 1980, 1985); Violin Concerto (1987); *Funeral Music in Memory of Bohuslav Martinů* (1988). **CHAMBER:** 4 violin sonatas; 5 string quartets; 2 cello sonatas (1948, rev. 1973; 1968); String Quintet (1956); Viola Sonata (1958); *9 Miniatures* for String Quartet (1966); *5 Miniatures* for Wind Trio (1969); *Chamber Music* for 5 Instruments (1970); *Dialogues* for Flute and Piano (1971); *Fantasia* or *Fantasia Concertante* for Violin, Viola, and Cello (1973); *Sonata Fantasia* for Cello and Piano (1977–78); *Rhapsodietta* for Flute and Piano (1982); piano music, including 4 sonatas. **VOCAL:** Cantatas; *Metamorphosis* for Soprano, 3 Woodwinds, Piano, Vibraphone, 3 Bongos, 3 Gongs, and Strings (1966); *La Pâques à New York,* oratorio (1987); songs.

Ribaupierre, André de, Swiss violinist and pedagogue; b. Clarens, May 29, 1893; d. Rochester, N.Y., Jan. 17, 1955. He studied with his brother, Émile, and then with Gorski and Ysaÿe. At 17, he launched his career as a violinist. After teaching a master class at the Lausanne Cons. (1914–19), he went to Cincinnati to study once more with Ysaÿe. From 1921 to 1924 he was head of Ysaÿe's class, and also was a teacher at the Cleveland Inst. of Music from 1923 to 1929. He then returned to Switzerland and was founder-director of the Institut de Ribaupierre. He also was active as a chamber music player. Ribaupierre eventually settled in Rochester, N.Y., as head of the violin dept. at the Eastman School of Music.

Ricci, Ruggiero, celebrated American violinist; b. San Bruno, Calif., July 24, 1918. His musical education was lovingly fostered by his father, along with that of 6 of his siblings, every one of whom started out as a musician, and 2 of whom, the cellist Giorgio Ricci and the violinist Emma Ricci, achieved the rank of professional performer. Ruggiero studied violin with Louis Persinger, and made a sensational appearance at a public concert in San Francisco on Nov. 15, 1928, when he was 10 years old, with his teacher accompanying him at the piano. On Oct. 20, 1929, he played in N.Y.; he embarked on an international concert tour in 1932. He successfully negotiated the perilous transition from child prodigy to serious artist. He accumulated a formidable repertoire of about 60 violin concertos, including all the violin works of Paganini; ed. the newly discovered MS of Paganini's early Violin Concerto, presumed to have been composed c.1815, and gave its first N.Y. perf. with the American Sym. Orch. on Oct. 7, 1977; he also gave the first performances of violin concertos by several modern composers, among them Alberto Ginastera (1963) and Gottfried von Einem (1970). During World War II, he served as "entertainment specialist" with the U.S. Army Air Force. After the end of the war, he returned to the concert stage; made several world tours, which included South America, Australia, Japan, and Russia; he also gave master courses at the North Carolina School of the Arts, Indiana Univ., and the Juilliard School of Music in N.Y. He owns a 1734 Guarnerius del Ges violin. In 1978 he celebrated a "Golden Jubilee," marking half a century of his professional career.

Ricciarelli, Katia, Italian soprano; b. Rovigo, Jan. 18, 1946. She studied at the Venice Cons. She made her operatic debut as Mimi in Mantua in 1969; after winning the Giuseppe Verdi Award for Young Singers in Parma (1970) and the New Verdi Voices Contest (1971), she pursued a successful career in the major Italian music centers. She made her U.S. debut as Lucrezia in *I due Foscari* in Chicago (1972); her first appearance at London's Covent Garden was as Mimi (1974), a role she also chose for her Metropolitan Opera debut in N.Y. (April 11, 1975). In 1979 she made her debut in recital at the Salzburg Festival. In 1985 she sang Desdemona in Zeffirelli's film version of Verdi's *Otello.* In 1985–86 she sang Rossini roles in Pesaro, returning there in 1988. She appeared as Desdemona at the Metropolitan Opera and at Covent Garden in 1990. Among her other fine roles were Amelia Boccanegra, Suor Angelica, Luisa Miller, and Elisabeth de Valois.

Rich, Alan, muckraking American music critic; b. Boston, June 17, 1924. He pursued a pre-med course at Harvard Univ. (A.B., 1945), studied musicology with Bukofzer and Kerman at the Univ. of Calif. at Berkeley (M.A., 1952) and with Deutsch in Vienna (1952–53), and learned the rudiments of conducting from Gmeindl. He was assistant music critic of the *Boston Herald* (1944–45) and the *N.Y. Sun* (1947–48). Rich was a contributor to the *American Record Guide* (1947–61), the *Saturday Review* (1952–53), and *Musical America* (1955–61). After serving as assistant music critic of the *N.Y. Times* (1961–63), he was chief music critic and ed. of the *N.Y. Herald-Tribune* (1963–66). In 1966–67 he was music critic and ed. of the *N.Y. World-Journal-Tribune*, and then was a contributing ed. of *Time* magazine in 1967–68. From 1979 to 1983 he was music and drama critic, as well as arts ed., of *California* magazine, and then served as a contributing ed. to it (1983–85). After holding the post of general ed. of *Newsweek* magazine (1983–87), he was music critic of the *Los Angeles Herald-Examiner* (from 1987). In 1970, 1973, and 1974 he won ASCAP-Deems Taylor awards.

WRITINGS: *Careers and Opportunities in Music* (1964); *Music, Mirror of the Arts* (1969); *Simon & Schuster Listeners Guide to Music* (3 vols., 1980); *The Lincoln Center Story* (1984); *American Pioneers: Ives to Cage and Beyond* (London, 1995).

Richter, Hans (Johann Baptist Isidor), celebrated Austro-Hungarian conductor; b. Raab, Hungary, April 4, 1843; d. Bayreuth, Dec. 5, 1916. He was born into a musical family; his father, Anton Richter, was a composer and Kapellmeister at Raab Cathedral, and his mother, Josefine (née Czasensky) Richter, was an opera singer and vocal teacher. Richter was blessed with perfect pitch and was only 4 when he began piano lessons with his mother; he soon received instruction in organ and timpani, and also began to sing. In 1854 he was taken to Vienna to pursue academic studies at the Piaristengymnasium; he also was accepted as a chorister in the Imperial Chapel, where he sang until 1858. He then studied at the Cons. of the Gesellschaft der Musikfreunde (1858–62); his principal mentors there were Kleinecke (horn), Heissler (violin), Ramesch (piano), J. Hellmesberger (orchestral training), and Sechter (theory and composition). He continued his training with Kleinecke as an external student until 1865. In addition, he learned to play virtually every instrument in the orch., the harp excepted. While still attending to his studies, he gained experience as a player in various opera orchs. before serving as a horn player in the orch. of Vienna's Kärtnerthortheater (1862–66). In the meantime, he made his professional debut as a conductor in a concert in Raab on Sept. 19, 1865. Upon the recommendation of Heinrich Esser, Wagner invited Richter to Tribschen in 1866 to prepare the fair copy of his score to the opera *Die Meistersinger von Nürnberg*. Wagner was so satisfied with Richter's work that he secured the young musician's appointment as chorus master and répétiteur at the Munich Court Opera. Richter prepared the chorus for the premiere of *Die Meistersinger*, which was conducted by Han von Bülow on June 21, 1868. Later that year he was appointed court music director in Munich, but was dismissed from his post the following year after a dispute with the royal authorities over aspects of the staging of the premiere of *Das Rheingold*. With Wagner's approval, Richter conducted instead the Brussels premiere (in French) of *Lohengrin* on March 22, 1870, with notable success. In 1871 Richter became conductor of the Opera and Phil. concerts in Budapest, where he won distinction as both an operatic and symphonic conductor. In 1874 he was made the director of the Opera. In 1875 he was called to Vienna to assume the post of 1st Kapellmeister of the Court Opera, a position he retained until 1900. From 1875 to 1882, and again from 1883 to 1898, he was conductor of the Vienna Phil. At Wagner's invitation, he went to Bayreuth in 1876 to conduct the first complete staging of the *Ring* cycle at the opening of the Festival: *Das Rheingold* on Aug. 13, *Die Walküre* on Aug. 14, *Siegfried* on Aug. 16, and *Götterdammerung* on Aug. 17. In May 1877 Wagner invited Richter to share his conducting duties at the Royal Albert Hall in London. That same year Richter was made Vize-Hofkapellmeister of the Court Chapel in Vienna. In 1879 he returned to London to conduct a series of Orchestral Festival Concerts, which he subsequently led as the annual Richter Concerts from 1880 to 1902. In 1882 Richter conducted the first British performances of *Die Meistersinger* (May 30) and *Tristan und Isolde* (June 20) at the Theatre Royal, Drury Lane, London. His debut at London's Covent Garden followed on June 4, 1884, when he conducted *Die Meistersinger*. In 1884 he became conductor of the Gesellschaft der Musikfreunde in Vienna, a post he held until 1890. From 1885 to 1909 he was conductor of the Birmingham Triennial Music Festival. In 1887 he returned to Bayreuth, and between 1892 and 1912 conducted notable performances at 11 festivals there. In 1893 Richter accepted the conductorship of the Boston Sym. Orch., but was compelled to withdraw his acceptance when he learned from the Viennese authorities that he would lose his pension. Instead, he was made Imperial Hofkapellmeister that year, a title he retained until 1900. In 1895 Richter made his first appearance as a guest conductor with the Hallé Orch. in Manchester, and subsequently served as its conductor from 1899 to 1911. From 1903 to 1910 he conducted seasons of German opera at Covent Garden, and in 1908 conducted the first English-language performances of the *Ring* cycle there. On June 9, 1904, he conducted the inaugural concert of the London Sym. Orch., and then served as its principal conductor until 1911. After making his home in Bayreuth, Richter conducted his farewell performance at the Festival there with *Die Meistersinger* on Aug. 19, 1912. In addition to the honors bestowed upon him in his homeland, he was also honored in England with honorary doctorates in music by the Univs. of Oxford (1885) and Manchester (1902), and was made an Honorary Member, 4th class (1904) and Honorary Commander (1907) of the Royal Victorian Order. Richter's unstinting devotion to the composer's intentions, communicated via a flawless conducting technique, resulted in performances of great commitment and authority. He invariably conducted all his scores from memory. While his association with Wagner rendered his performances of the master of Bayreuth's works as authoritative, he also won great renown for his interpretations of Beethoven. He further distinguished himself as an outstanding champion of Mozart, Brahms, Bruckner, Tchaikovsky, Dvořák, and Elgar.

BIBL.: C. Fifield, *True Artist and True Friend: A Biography of H. R.* (Oxford, 1993).

Richter, Karl, distinguished German organist, harpsichordist, and conductor; b. Plauen, Oct. 15, 1926; d. Munich, Feb. 15, 1981. He studied organ, harpsichord, and conducting at the Dresden Kreuzschule; then took courses at the Leipzig Cons. with Rudolf Mauersberger, Gunther Ramin, and Karl Straube. In 1946 he became choirmaster of the Christuskirche in Leipzig; in 1947 he was named organist of Leipzig's Thomaskirche. In 1951 he settled in Munich; organized the Munich Bach Orch. and Choir, which brought him great acclaim; made many tours and numerous recordings with them; also appeared as a guest conductor in Europe. On April 18, 1965, he made his U.S. debut with them at N.Y.'s Carnegie Hall.

Richter, Marga, American composer; b. Reedsburg, Wis., Oct. 21, 1926. She was prepared for a musical career by her mother, Inez Chandler-Richter, a soprano; studied at the MacPhail School of Music in Minneapolis; in 1943 she entered the Juilliard School of Music in N.Y., where she studied piano with Tureck and composition with Persichetti and Bergsma, graduating in 1949 (M.S., 1951). She received 30 annual ASCAP awards (1966–95) and 2 grants from the NEA (1977, 1979). Her compositions reflect a pragmatic modern trend without rigid adherence to any particular doctrine or technique; the overriding concern is aural.

WORKS: BALLETS: *Abyss* (1964; Cannes, Feb. 5, 1965); *Bird of Yearning* (1967; as *Der Türm*, Cologne, Oct. 30, 1969; version for Piano, 1976). **ORCH.:** 2 piano concertos: No. 1 (1955) and No. 2, *Landscapes of the Mind I* (1968–74; Tucson, March 19, 1976, Masselos soloist); *Lament* for Strings (1956); *Aria and Toccata* for Viola and String Orch. (1956–57); *Variations on a Sarabande* (1959); *8 Pieces* (1961; originally for Piano); *Fragments* (1976); *Country Auction* for School Band (1976); *Blackberry Vines and Winter Fruit* (North Bennington, Vt., Oct. 17, 1976); *Music* for 3 Quintets and Orch. (1978–80); *Düsseldorf Concerto* for Solo Flute, Solo Viola, Harp, Percussion, and String Ensemble (1981–82; Salzburg, May 20, 1982); *Out of Shadows and Solitude* (1985; Chicago, Dec. 9, 1988); *Quantum Quirks of a Quick Quaint Quark* (1991; Brookville, N.Y., April 25, 1992); *. . . beside the still waters: Variations and Interludes*, concerto for Piano, Violin, Cello, and Orch. (1992; Greensboro, N.C., July 3, 1993). **CHAMBER:** *1 for 2 and 2 for 3* for Trombone Duet and Trio (1947; rev. 1974); Clarinet Sonata (1948); 2 string quartets (1950, withdrawn; 1958); *Ricercare* for Brass Quartet (1958); *Darkening of the Light* for Viola (1961; version for Cello, 1976); *Suite* for Violin and Piano (1964); *Landscapes of the Mind II* for Violin and Piano (1971) and *III* for Piano Trio (1979); *Pastorale* for 2 Oboes (1975); *Sonora* for 2 Clarinets and Piano (1981); *Seacliff Variations* for Piano, Violin, Viola, and Cello (1984); *Qhanri* (Snow Mountain), Tibetan variations for Cello and Piano (1988); *Obsessions* for Trombone (1990). **KEYBOARD: PIANO:** Sonata (1954–55); *Melodrama* for 2 Pianos (1958); *Variations on a Theme by Latimer* for Piano, 4-hands (1964); *Remembrances* (1971); *Requiem* (1976); *Exequy* (1980); *Quantum Quirks of a Quick Quaint Quark No. 3* (1993). **ORGAN:** *Quantum Quirks of a Quick Quaint Quark No. 2* (1992). **VOCAL:** *Do Not Press My Hands* for Vocal Sextet (1981); *Into My Heart*, 7 poems for Chorus, Oboe, Violin, Brass Sextet, and Percussion (1990); choruses; songs.

Richter, Nico (Max), Dutch composer; b. Amsterdam, Dec. 2, 1915; d. there, Aug. 16, 1945. He studied conducting with Scherchen; directed a student orch.; in Feb. 1942 he was arrested by the Nazis as a member of the Dutch Resistance, and spent 3 years in the Dachau concentration camp, which fatally undermined his health; he died shortly after liberation.

WORKS: DRAMATIC: *Amorijs*, chamber opera (1937); *Kannitverstan*, ballet. **ORCH.:** *Serenade*, sinfonietta for Flute, Oboe, Guitar, and Strings (1931–34); *Sinfonia-Divertimento* for Chamber Orch. (1936). **CHAMBER:** Concertino for Clarinet, Horn, Trumpet, Piano, and 2 Violins (1935); Trio for Flute, Viola, and Guitar (1935); *Serenade* for Flute, Violin, and Viola (1945; 2 extant movements reconstructed by Lex van Delden).

Richter, Sviatoslav (Teofilovich), outstanding Russian pianist; b. Zhitomir, March 20, 1915. Both his parents were pianists. He was engaged as a piano accompanist at the Odessa Opera, and developed exceptional skill in playing orch. scores at sight. He made his formal debut as a concert artist at the Odessa House of Engineers in 1934; entered the Moscow Cons. in 1937 as a student of Heinrich Neuhaus, graduating in 1947. He acquired a notable following even during his student years; in 1945 he made a stunning appearance at the All-Union Contest of Performances, and was awarded its highest prize. He received the Stalin Prize in 1949. In subsequent years, he played throughout the Soviet Union and Eastern Europe. During the Russian tour of the Philadelphia Orch. in 1958, Richter was soloist, playing Prokofiev's 5th Piano Concerto in Leningrad; he made several international concert tours, including visits to China (1957) and the U.S. (1960). Both in Russia and abroad he has earned a reputation as a piano virtuoso of formidable attainments. He is especially praised for his impeccable sense of style, with every detail of the music rendered with lapidary perfection. His performances of the Romantic repertoire have brought him great renown, and he has made notable excursions into the works of Debussy, Ravel, and Prokofiev as well; gave the first performances of Prokofiev's 6th, 7th, and 9th sonatas.

Richter-Haaser, Hans, respected German pianist and teacher; b. Dresden, Jan. 6, 1912; d. Braunschweig, Dec. 13, 1980. At age 13, he became a pupil of Hans Schneider at the Dresden Academy of Music, where he won the Bechstein Prize when he was 18. He made his debut in Dresden (1928), and thereafter performed throughout Germany. After his career was interrupted by World War II, he settled in Detmold and conducted the municipal orch. (1946–47); then was a prof. at the North West German Music Academy there (1947–62); concurrently pursued an international career; made his U.S. debut in N.Y. (1959). He was esteemed for his performances of the Classical and Romantic repertoire, winning high praise for his Beethoven. He also composed 2 piano concertos, chamber music, piano pieces, and songs.

Rickenbacher, Karl Anton, Swiss conductor; b. Basel, May 20, 1940. He received his training at the Berlin Städtisches Cons. (1962–66); his mentors in conducting were Karajan and Boulez. After serving as an assistant conductor at the Zürich Opera (1966–69), he was conductor of the Freiburg im Breisgau Opera (1969–74). From 1976 to 1985 he was Generalmusikdirektor of the Westhphalian Sym. Orch. in Recklinghausen. He also served as principal conductor of the BBC Scottish Sym. Orch. in Glasgow from 1977 to 1980. In 1983 he appeared for the first time as a guest conductor with the Berlin Phil. and at the Deutsche Oper in Berlin. In 1987 he made his debuts as a guest conductor with the Royal Phil. and the Philharmonia Orch. in London. After making his first appearances in the U.S. during the 1987–88 season, he was a guest conductor with many European and North American orchs. His repertoire embraces the classical, romantic, and modern repertoires.

Ricketts, Frederick J., English bandmaster and composer who used the pseudonym **Kenneth J. Alford**; b. London, Feb. 21, 1881; d. Reigate, Surrey, May 15, 1945. Trained first as an organist, Ricketts graduated from Kneller Hall, afterward serving his longest stint as bandmaster of the Royal Marines (1928–44). In Feb. 1914 he publ., under his pseudonym "Alford" (not to be confused with the American bandmaster and composer Harry L. Alford), his popular march *Col. Bogey*, epitomizing the steadily swinging and moderately paced English military march. *Col. Bogey* reached its height of fame when it was introduced into the film *The Bridge on the River Kwai* (1958).

Ridder, Anton de, Dutch tenor; b. Amsterdam, Feb. 13, 1929. He studied voice at the Amsterdam Cons. with Herman Mulder (1947–49) and with Jan Keyzer (1951–56). From 1956 to 1962 he was on the roster of the Karlsruhe Opera; then sang at the Gärtnerplatz Theater in Munich (1962–66). In 1965 he joined the Komische Oper in West Berlin. In 1969 he took part in the Salzburg Festival; also sang in Vienna and Hamburg. In 1972 he appeared at the Edinburgh Festival. He sang Florestan at the Glyndebourne Festival in 1979. In 1985 he again appeared at the Salzburg Festival. He was equally adept at lyric and dramatic tenor parts.

Ridderbusch, Karl, admired German bass; b. Recklinghausen, May 29, 1932. He was a student of Rudolf Schock at the Duisburg Cons. and of Clemens Kaiser-Breme in Essen. In 1961 he made his operatic debut in Münster. After singing in Essen (1963–65), he appeared with the Deutsche Oper am Rhein in Düsseldorf (from 1965). In 1967 he made his debut at the Bayreuth Festival as Titurel, and sang there regularly until 1976. He appeared for the first time in Paris in 1967. On Nov. 21, 1967, he made his Metropolitan Opera debut in N.Y. as Hunding, and returned there as Hans Sachs in 1976. In 1968 he appeared for the first time in Vienna and at the Salzburg Easter Festival. In 1971 he made his debut at London's Covent Garden. He also sang with many other leading opera houses and toured widely as a concert singer. He was especially noted for his Wagnerian roles. In addition to those already noted, he excelled as King Marke, Fafner, Hagen, and Daland. Among his esteemed non-Wagnerian roles were Rocco, Boris Godunov, Baron Ochs, and the Doktor in *Wozzeck*.

Rider-Kelsey, Corinne (née **Rider**), American soprano and teacher; b. near Batavia, N.Y., Feb. 24, 1877; d. Toledo, Ohio, July 10, 1947. She studied with Helen Rice at the Oberlin (Ohio) College Cons.; then with L. Torrens in Rockford, Ill., where she made her recital debut (1897); after further training with Toedt and his wife in N.Y., she became successful as a concert singer. She made her debut as a soloist in Handel's *Messiah* in St. Louis (Nov. 24, 1904); made her operatic debut as Micaëla at London's Covent Garden (July 2, 1908), but soon abandoned the opera stage to devote herself to a concert career. In 1926 she married the violinist and composer Lynnel Reed; they settled in Toledo, where she was active as a singer and a teacher.

BIBL.: L. Reed, *Be Not Afraid: Biography of Madame R. K.* (N.Y., 1955).

Řídký, Jaroslav, eminent Czech composer and teacher; b. Františkov, near Liberec, Aug. 25, 1897; d. Poděbrady, Aug. 14, 1956. He took courses in composition at the Prague Cons. (1919–23) with K. Jirák, J. Křička, and E.B. Foerster, continuing his training in Foerster's master class there (1923–26); also studied harp. He was 1st harpist in the Czech Phil. (1924–38); also was conductor of its choir (1925–30). He taught theory at the Prague Cons. (1928–48); was named a teacher (1946) and a prof. (1955) of composition at the Prague Academy of Music.

WORKS: ORCH.: *Sinfonietta* (1923); 7 syms: No. 1 (1924), No. 2 for Orch. and Cello obbligato (1925), No. 3 (1927), No. 4 for Chorus and Orch. (1928), No. 5 (1930–31), No. 6, *The Year 1938* (1938; unfinished), and No. 7 (1955); Violin Concerto (1926); *Overture* (1928–29); 2 cello concertos (1930, 1940); *Serenade* for Strings (1941); *Chamber Sinfonietta* (1944–45); Piano Concerto (1952); *Slavonic March* (1954). **CHAMBER:** 2 cello sonatas (1923; 1947–48); Clarinet Quintet (1926); 5 string quartets (1926, 1927, 1931, 1933, 1937); *Serenata appassionata* for Cello and Piano (1929); 2 nonets (1933–34; 1943); Wind Quintet (1945); *Joyous Sonatina* for Violin and Piano (1947); Piano Trio (1950–51); piano pieces. **VOCAL:** 2 cantatas: *A Winter Fairytale* (1936) and *To My Fatherland* (1941); choruses.

Ridout, Godfrey, Canadian composer, teacher, conductor, and writer on music; b. Toronto, May 6, 1918; d. there, Nov. 24, 1984. He studied at the Toronto Cons. with Charles Peaker (organ and counterpoint), Ettore Mazzoleni (conducting), Weldon Kilburn (piano), and Healey Willan (composition). He served on the faculties of the Toronto Cons. (from 1940) and the Univ. of Toronto (from 1948), retiring in 1982. He also was music director of the Eaton Operatic Soc. (1949–58), director of the Composers, Authors, and Publishers Assn. of Canada (1966–73), and a program annotator for the Toronto Sym. (1973–84). With T. Kenins, he ed. the vol. *Celebration* (Toronto, 1984). In his music, Ridout charted an eclectic path notable for its accessible style.

WORKS: DRAMATIC: *La Prima Ballerina*, ballet (1966; Montreal, Oct. 26, 1967); *The Lost Child*, television opera (1976). **ORCH.:** *Ballade No. 1* (1938; Toronto, May 29, 1939) and *No. 2* (1980) for Viola and Strings; *Festal Overture* (1939); *Comedy Overture* (1941); *Dirge* (1943); *2 Études* for Strings (1946; rev. 1951); *Esther*, dramatic sym. for Soprano, Baritone, Chorus, and Orch. (1951–52; Toronto, April 29, 1952); *Music for a Young Prince*, suite (1959); *Fall Fair* (N.Y., Oct. 24, 1961); *Overture to Colas et Colinette* (1964); *Partita academica* for Concert Band (1969); *Frivolités canadiennes*, after melodies of Joseph Vézina (1973); *Jubilee* (1973); Concerto Grosso No. 1 for Piano, Violin, and Strings (1974; Toronto, Jan. 18, 1975) and No. 2 for Brass Quintet and Orch. (1980); *George III, His Lament*, variations on an old British tune (1975); *Kid's Stuff* (1978); *No Mean City: Scenes from Childhood* (1983). **CHAMBER:** *Folk Song Fantasy* for Piano Trio (1951); *Introduction and Allegro* for Woodwind Quintet, Violin, and Cello (1968); *2 Dances* for Guitar (1976); *Tafelmusik* for Woodwind Ensemble (1976); *A Birthday Fantasy* for Flute, Clarinet, and Bassoon (1982); piano pieces; organ music. **VOCAL:** *Cantiones Mysticae No. 1* for Soprano and Orch. (N.Y., Oct. 16, 1953), *No. 2, The Ascension*, for Soprano, Trumpet, and Strings (Toronto, Dec. 23, 1962) and *No. 3, The Dream of the Rood*, for Baritone or Tenor, Chorus, Orch., and Organ (1972); *The Dance* for Chorus and Orch. (1960); *Pange lingua* for Chorus and Orch. (1960); *4 Sonnets* for Chorus and Orch. (1964); *In Memoriam Anne Frank* for Soprano and Orch. (Toronto, March 14, 1965); *When Age and Youth Unite* for Voice and/or Chorus and Orch. (1966); *Folk Songs of Eastern Canada* for Soprano and Orch. (1967); *The Seasons* for Tenor and Piano Quintet (1980); *Exile* for Narrator and 9 Instruments (1984).

Riegel, Kenneth, American tenor; b. Womelsdorf, Pa., April 29, 1938. He studied at the Manhattan School of Music in N.Y. and also at the Metropolitan Opera Studio. He made his operatic debut as the Alchemist in Henze's opera *König Hirsch* with the Santa Fe Opera in 1965; then sang with the Cincinnati Opera, the Houston Opera, the N.Y. City Opera, and others. On Oct. 22, 1973, he made his debut with the Metropolitan Opera in N.Y. as Iopas in *Les Troyens*. In 1977 he appeared at the Vienna State Opera, in 1978 at the Paris Opéra, in 1979 at Milan's La Scala, in 1981 at the Hamburg State Opera, in 1983 at the Deutsche Oper in Berlin, and in 1985 at London's Covent Garden. Thereafter he sang with many other opera houses. He also toured as a concert artist.

Rieger, Fritz, German conductor; b. Oberaltstadt, June 28, 1910; d. Bonn, Sept. 29, 1978. He was educated at the Prague Academy of Music, taking courses in piano with Langer, composition with Finke, and conducting with Szell. He conducted at the German Opera Theater in Prague (1931–38), the Bremen Opera (1939–41), and the Mannheim National Theater (1947–49). From 1949 to 1966 he was Generalmusikdirektor of the Munich Phil.; also conducted at the Bavarian State Opera in Munich. In 1972–73 he was chief conductor of the Melbourne Sym. Orch.; he also gave guest performances in Japan. In his programs, he gave considerable prominence to modern music.

Riegger, Wallingford (Constantin), outstanding American composer and teacher; b. Albany, Ga., April 29, 1885; d. N.Y., April 2, 1961. At an early age, he was taken by his family to Indianapolis, where he received his primary musical training at home; his father played violin, and his mother, piano. After his father took the family to N.Y. to pursue his business interests (1900), Wallingford learned to play the cello. He then began serious study with Goetschius (theory) and Schroeder (cello) at the Inst. of Musical Art; after graduating in 1907, he went to Berlin, where he studied cello with Robert Hausmann and Anton Hekking and composition with Max Bruch and Edgar Stillman-Kelley at the Hochschule für Musik (1907–10). In 1910 he made his debut as a conductor with Berlin's Blüthner Orch.; then returned to the U.S. and served as a cellist in the St. Paul (Minn.) Sym. Orch. (1911–14); returning to Germany, he worked as a vocal coach and assistant conductor at the operas in Würzburg (1914–15) and Königsberg (1915–16); then was again conductor of Berlin's Blüthner Orch. (1916–17) before returning to the U.S. He taught theory and cello at Drake Univ., Des Moines (1918–22); in 1922, received the Paderewski Prize for his Piano Trio; in 1924, was awarded the E.S. Coolidge Prize for his setting of Keats's *La Belle Dame sans merci*; in 1925, was given the honorary degree of D.Mus. by the Cincinnati Cons. He taught at the Inst. of Musical Art in N.Y. (1924–25) and at the Ithaca Cons. (1926–28); then settled in N.Y., where he became active as a composer and a participant in various modern music societies; took part in the development of electronic instruments (in association with Theremin), and learned to play an electric cello. His music is of a highly advanced nature; a master craftsman, he wrote in disparate styles with an equal degree of proficiency; used numerous pseudonyms for certain works (William Richards, Walter Scotson, Gerald Wilfring Gore, John H. McCurdy, George Northrup, Robert Sedgwick, Leonard Griegg, Edwin Farell, Edgar Long, etc.). After a long period of neglect on the part of the public and the critics, Riegger began to receive recognition; his 3rd Sym. was the choice of the N.Y.

Music Critics' Circle in 1948. He received further attention in 1957 when he was compelled to appear before the House Un-American Activities Committee to explain his self-proclaimed leftist and pro-Communist sympathies.

WORKS: DANCE: *Bacchanale* (1930; N.Y., Feb. 2, 1931); *Evocation* (N.Y., April 21, 1932; orchestrated 1948); *Frenetic Rhythms: 3 Dances of Daemoniacal Possession* (N.Y., Nov. 19, 1933); *New Dance* (Bennington, Vt., Aug. 3, 1935; also orch. and chamber versions); *Theater Piece* (1935; N.Y., Jan. 19, 1936); *With My Red Fires* (Bennington, Vt., Aug. 13, 1936); *Chronicle* (N.Y., Dec. 20, 1936); *The Cry* (Bennington, Vt., Aug. 7, 1936); *City Nocturne* (Bennington, Vt., Aug. 7, 1936); *4 Chromatic Eccentricities* (Bennington, Vt., Aug. 7, 1936; based on the *4 Tone Pictures* for Piano, 1932); *Candide* (N.Y., May 6, 1937); *Festive Rhythm* (Bennington, Vt., Aug. 13, 1937); *Trend* (Bennington, Vt., Aug. 13, 1937); *Case History No. . . .* (N.Y., Feb. 28, 1937); *Trojan Incident* (N.Y., April 21, 1938); *Machine Ballet* (Toronto, March 1938); *Fancy Fannie's Judgement Day* (1938; N.Y., Feb. 26, 1939); *Pilgrim's Progress* (N.Y., April 20, 1941).

ORCH.: *The Beggerman*, overture (1912; St. Paul, Minn., 1913; not extant); *Elegie* for Cello and Orch. (1916; Berlin, Feb. 6, 1917); *Triple Jazz: American Polonaise* (1922; N.Y., July 27, 1923); *Rhapsody: 2nd April* (1924–26; N.Y., Oct. 29, 1931); *Holiday Sketches* for Violin and Orch. (1927); *Study in Sonority* (Ithaca, N.Y., Aug. 11, 1927; orig. *Caprice* for 10 Violins); *Fantasy and Fugue* for Organ and Orch. (1930–31; N.Y., Dec. 5, 1932); *Dichotomy* for Chamber Orch. (Berlin, March 10, 1932); *Scherzo* for Chamber Orch. (1932; N.Y., Jan. 30, 1933; also for 2 Pianos); *Consummation* (1939; withdrawn and utilized in *Music for Orchestra*, 1952); *New Dance* (1940; Pittsburgh, Jan. 30, 1942; also for Band, N.Y., July 7, 1942; also dance and chamber versions); *Canon and Fugue* for Strings (1941; Berkeley, Calif., Aug. 1, 1942; also for Orch., 1941; N.Y., Feb. 14, 1944); *Passacaglia and Fugue* for Band (1942; N.Y., June 16, 1943; also for Orch., 1942; Washington, D.C., March 19, 1944); *Processional: Funeral March* for Band (1943; West Point, N.Y., Jan. 23, 1944; also for Orch., 1943; Moscow, July 3, 1945); 4 syms.: No. 1 (1944; N.Y., April 3, 1949; withdrawn), No. 2 (1945; withdrawn), No. 3 (1946–47; N.Y., May 16, 1948), and No. 4 (1956; Urbana, Ill., April 12, 1957); *Evocation* (Vancouver, British Columbia, Nov. 27, 1948; based on the dance piece, 1932); *Music for Brass Choir* for 10 Trumpets, 8 Horns, 10 Trombones, 2 Tubas, and Percussion (N.Y., April 18, 1949); *Music for Orchestra* (1952; N.Y., March 27, 1955; includes *Consummation* for Orch., 1939); *Prelude and Fugue* for Band (Louisville, May 5, 1953); *Variations* for Piano and Orch. (1952–53; Louisville, Feb. 23, 1954); *Variations* for 2 Pianos and Orch. (1952–54; Fish Creek, Wis., Aug. 1954); *Suite for Younger Orchestras* (1953; N.Y., April 26, 1954); *Dance Rhythms* (1954; Albany, Ga., March 4, 1955); *Overture* (1955; Cincinnati, Oct. 26, 1956); *Preamble and Fugue* (1955; Oklahoma City, March 18, 1956); *Festival Overture* (Boston, May 4, 1957); *Variations* for Violin and Orch. (1958; Louisville, April 1, 1959); *Quintuple Jazz* (Iowa City, May 20, 1959); *Sinfonietta* (1959); *Introduction, Scherzo, and Fugue* for Cello, Winds, and Timpani (Rochester, N.Y., Sept. 30, 1960; a revision of *Introduction and Fugue* for 4 Cellos, 1957); *Duo* for Piano and Orch. (1960).

CHAMBER: *Reverie* for Cello and Piano (1918); Piano Trio (1919–20); *Whimsy* for Cello or Violin and Piano (1920); *Meditation* for Cello or Violin and Piano (1927); *Suite* for Flute (1928–29); *3 Canons* for Woodwinds for Flute, Oboe, Clarinet, and Bassoon (1931); *Divertissement* for Flute, Cello, and Harp (1933); *New Dance* for 2 Pianos, or Piano, 4-hands, or Violin and Piano, or Solo Piano (1935; also orch. and band versions, 1940–42); *Music* for Voice and Flute (1936–37); 2 string quartets (1938–39; 1948); *Duos* for 3 Woodwinds for Flute, Oboe, and Clarinet (1943); Violin Sonatina (1947); Piano Quintet (1950–51); Nonet for Brass for 3 Trumpets, 2 Horns, 3 Trombones, and Tuba (1951); *Canon on a Ground Bass of Purcell* for Strings (1951); *Blaserquintett*, woodwind quintet (1952); Concerto for Piano and Woodwind Quintet (1953); *Variations* for Violin and Viola (1957); *Movement* for 2 Trumpets, Trombone, and Piano (1957); *Introduction and Fugue* for 4 Cellos (1957; rev. as *Introduction, Scherzo, and Fugue* for Cello, Winds, and Timpani, 1960); *Cooper Square* for Accordion (1958). **PIANO:** *Blue Voyage* (1927); *Scherzo* for 2 Pianos (1932; also for Chamber Orch., 1932); *4 Tone Pictures* (1932; dance version as *4 Chromatic Eccentricities*, 1932); *New and Old: 12 Pieces for Piano* (1944); *Variations* for 2 Pianos (1952–53).

VOCAL: *La Belle Dame sans merci* for Tenor, Women's Voices, and 7 Instruments (1921–24); *Eternity* for Women's Voices and 4 Instruments (1942); *From Some Far Shore* for 4 Voices and Piano or Organ (1946); *Easter Passacaglia: Ye Watchers and Ye Holy Ones* for 4 Voices and Piano or Organ (1946); *Little Sam: Little Black Sambo* for Narrator and Chamber Orch. (1946); *Who Can Revoke?* for 4 Voices and Piano (1948); *In Certainty of Song*, cantata for 4 Solo Voices, 4 Voices, and Piano or Chamber Orch. (1950); *Non vincit malitia: Evil Shall Not Prevail* for Antiphonal Chorus (1951); *A Child Went Forth* for 4 Voices and Oboe (1953); *A Shakespeare Sonnet* for Baritone, Chorus, and Piano or Chamber Orch. (1956); also solo songs; more than 700 arrangements of carols, anthems, and folk songs; several vols. of pedagogical works.

BIBL.: A. Weiss, "W. R.," in H. Cowell, ed., *American Composers on American Music* (Stanford, Calif., 1933); R. Goldman, "The Music of W. R.," *Musical Quarterly* (Jan. 1950); E. Carter, "W. R.," *American Composers Alliance Bulletin*, II/1 (1952); J. Schmoll, *An Analytical Study of the Principal Instrumental Compositions of W. R.* (diss., Northwestern Univ., 1954); R. Goldman, "W. R., Composer and Pedagog," *Etude*, LXXIV/8 (1956); P. Freeman, *The Compositional Technique of W. R. as Seen in Seven Major Twelve-tone Works* (diss., Eastman School of Music, 1963); D. Garwood, *W. R.: A Biography and Analysis of Selected Works* (diss., George Peabody College for Teachers, 1970); L. Ott, *An Analysis of the Later Orchestral Style of W. R.* (diss., Michigan State Univ., 1970); N. Savage, *Structure and Cadence in the Music of W. R.* (diss., Stanford Univ., 1972); S. Spackman, *W. R.: Two Essays in Musical Biography* (Brooklyn, N.Y., 1982); idem, "W. R. and the Modern Dance," *Musical Quarterly*, 4 (1985).

Rieti, Vittorio, Italian-born American composer and teacher; b. Alexandria, Egypt, Jan. 28, 1898; d. N.Y., Feb. 19, 1994. He studied with Frugatta in Milan; then took courses with Respighi and Casella in Rome, where he lived until 1940, when he emigrated to the U.S.; he became a naturalized American citizen on June 1, 1944. He taught at the Peabody Cons. of Music in Baltimore (1948–49), Chicago Musical College (1950–53), Queens College in N.Y. (1958–60), and N.Y. College of Music (1960–64). His style of composition represents an ingratiating synthesis of cosmopolitan modern tendencies.

WORKS: DRAMATIC: OPERAS: *Orfeo tragedia* (1928; withdrawn); *Teresa nel bosco* (1933; Venice, Sept. 15, 1934); *Don Perlimplin* (1949; Urbana, Ill., March 30, 1952); *Viaggio d'Europa*, radio opera (1954); *The Pet Shop* (1957; N.Y., April 14, 1958); *The Clock* (1959–60); *Maryam the Harlot* (1966). **BALLETS:** *L'Arca di Noè* (1923; only orch. suite extant); *Robinson et Vendredi* (1924); *Barabau* (London, Dec. 11, 1925); *Le Bal* (Monte Carlo, May 1929); *David triomphant* (Paris, May 1937); *Hippolyte* (1937); *The Night Shadow* (1941; N.Y., Feb. 1946); *Waltz Academy* (Boston, Oct. 1944); *The Mute Wife* (N.Y., Nov. 1944); *Trionfo di Bacco e Arianna*, ballet-cantata (1946–47; N.Y., Feb. 1948); *Native Dancer* (1959; based on the Sym. No. 5); *Conundrum* (1961); *A Sylvan Dream* (1965; Indianapolis, Oct. 1, 1982); *Scenes Seen* (1975; Indianapolis, March 25, 1976); *Verdiana* (1983; Indianapolis, Feb. 16, 1984); *Indiana* (1984; Indianapolis, Sept. 14, 1985); *Kaleidoscope* (1987; Indianapolis, April 30, 1988). **ORCH.:** Woodwind Concerto (1923; Prague, May 31, 1924); *Noah's Ark*, symphonic suite (1925); *2 Pastorali* for Chamber Orch. (1925); 3 piano concertos (1926; 1930–37; 1955); *Madrigale* for Chamber Orch. (1927); 2 violin concertos: No. 1, *Concerto napoletano* (1928; Paris, May 1930) and No. 2 (1969); 8 syms.: No. 1 (1929; Paris, Jan. 1930), No. 2 (1930; Brussels, April 1931), No. 3, *Sinfonietta* (Paris, May 1932), No 4,

Sinfonia tripartita (1942; St. Louis, Dec. 16, 1944), No. 5 (1945; Venice, Sept. 1947), No. 6 (1973; N.Y., Dec. 11, 1974), No. 7 (1977), and No. 8, *Sinfonia breve* (Lafayette, Ind., May 2, 1987); *Serenata* for Violin and Chamber Orch. (1931); 2 cello concertos: No. 1 for Cello and Chamber Orch. (1934) and No. 2 (1953); *Concerto du Loup* (1938); Partita for Harpsichord and Chamber Orch. (1946); Concerto for 2 Pianos and Orch. (1951); Harpsichord Concerto (1952–55; rev. 1972); *Introduction e gioco delle ore* (1953); *Dance Variations* for Strings (1956); *La fontaine*, suite (1968; N.Y., Nov. 1, 1969); *Concerto Triplo* for Violin, Viola, Piano, and Orch. (1971; N.Y., Jan. 27, 1973); Concerto for String Quartet and Orch. (1976; N.Y., Feb. 1, 1978); *Concertino pro San Luca* for 10 Instruments (1984); *Concertino Novello* for 10 Instruments (1986); *Congedo* for 12 Instruments (1987); *Enharmonic Variations* for Piano and Chamber Orch. (N.Y., Feb. 4, 1988). **CHAMBER:** Sonata for Flute, Oboe, Bassoon, and Piano (1924); 5 string quartets (1926, 1941, 1951, 1960, 1988); Woodwind Quintet (1957); Octet for Piano and 7 Instruments (1971); Piano Trio (1972); Piano Quartet (1973); *Allegretto alla croma* for Flute, Oboe, Clarinet, Bassoon, Strings, and Piano (1981); *Romanza lidica* for Clarinet and Piano (1984); Piano Quintet (1989); numerous works for solo piano; pieces for 2 pianos.

BIBL.: F. Ricci, *V. R.* (Naples, 1987).

Rifkin, Joshua, American musicologist, pianist, and conductor; b. N.Y., April 22, 1944. He studied with Persichetti at the Juilliard School of Music in N.Y. (B.S., 1964); with Gustave Reese at N.Y. Univ. (1964–66); at the Univ. of Göttingen (1966–67); and later with Mendel, Lockwood, Babbitt, and Oster at Princeton Univ. (M.F.A., 1969). He also worked with Stockhausen at Darmstadt (1961, 1965). From 1970 to 1982 he was on the faculty of Brandeis Univ. He led the Bach Ensemble from 1978. He is noted for his research in the field of Renaissance and Baroque music, but he became popular as a performer and explicator of ragtime.

Rignold, Hugo (Henry), English conductor; b. Kingston upon Thames, May 15, 1905; d. London, May 30, 1976. He studied violin in Winnipeg and in 1920 returned to England as a scholarship student at the Royal Academy of Music in London of Hans Wessely (violin), Lionel Tertis (viola), and Leon Goossens (oboe). After working as a violinist and bandleader, he served in the Royal Air Force during World War II, during which time he conducted the Cairo Sym. Orch. (1944). In 1947 he conducted at Sadler's Wells in London. From 1948 to 1954 he was principal conductor of the Liverpool Phil. In 1956, 1971–72, and 1973 he was resident guest conductor of the Cape Town Sym. Orch. He was music director of the Royal Ballet in London (1957–60) and of the City of Birmingham Sym. Orch. (1960–68).

Rihm, Wolfgang (Michael), German composer and teacher; b. Karlsruhe, March 13, 1952. He received training in composition with Eugen Velte at the Karlsruhe Hochschule für Musik (1968–72), with Stockhausen in Cologne (1972–73), and with Klaus Huber in Freiburg im Breisgau (1973–76). He also studied with Fortner and Searle, and received training in musicology with Eggebrecht in Freiburg im Breisgau. From 1970 he attended the summer courses in new music in Darmstadt, and then taught there from 1978. He taught at the Karlsruhe Hochschule für Musik (1973–78). After teaching in Munich (1981), he returned to the Karlsruhe Hochschule für Musik as a prof. (from 1985). In his music, Rihm embraced an atonal, post-expressionist path with occasional infusions of tonal writing.

WORKS: DRAMATIC: *Faust und Yorick*, chamber opera (1976; Mannheim, April 29, 1977); *Jakob Lenz*, chamber opera (1977–78; Hamburg, March 8, 1979); *Tutuguri*, ballet (1981–82; Berlin, Nov. 12, 1982); *Die Hamletmaschine*, music theater (1983–86; Mannheim, April 4, 1987); *Oedipus*, music theater (1986–87; Berlin, Oct. 4, 1987); *Die Eroberung von Mexico*, music theater (1987–91; Hamburg, Feb. 9, 1992); *Medea-Spiel*, dance theater (1988–89; Salzburg, April 6, 1989); *Séraphin*, music theater (Frankfurt am Main, Sept. 7, 1994). **ORCH.:** 4 syms.: No. 1 (1969; Hannover, Feb. 5, 1984), No. 2 (1975; Berlin, June 27, 1976), No. 3 for Soprano, Baritone, Chorus, and Orch. (1976–77; Berlin, Nov. 15, 1979), and No. 4, *Symphonie fleuve* (Hamburg, Nov. 6, 1994); *Adagio* for Strings (1969); *Magma* (1973); *Dis-Kontur* (1974; Stuttgart, Oct. 10, 1975); *Sub-Kontur* (1974–75; Donaueschingen, Oct. 26, 1976); *Lichtzwang* for Violin and Orch. "in memoriam Paul Celan" (1975–76; Royan, April 3, 1977); *Cuts and Dissolves* (1976; Paris, March 3, 1977); *Nachtordnung*, 7 pieces for 15 Strings (1976; Berlin, Sept. 19, 1977); *La Musique creuse le ciel* for 2 Pianos annd Orch. (1977–79; Cologne, Nov. 14, 1980); *Abgesangsszene No. 1* (Kassel, Nov. 8, 1979) and *No. 5* (1979; Kiel, Jan. 12, 1981); 3 waltzes: No. 1, *Sehnsuchtswalzer* (1979–81; Stuttgart, Oct. 23, 1981), No. 2, *Drängender Walzer* (1986–87; Frankfurt am Main, Feb. 21, 1987), and No. 3, *Brahmsliebewalzer* (1979–88; Flensburg, July 6, 1988); Viola Concerto (1979–83; Berlin, Nov. 13, 1983); *Doppelgesang No. 1* for Viola, Cello, and Orch. (1980; Baden-Baden, Jan. 18, 1984) and *No. 2* for Clarinet, Cello, and Orch. (1981–83; Hitzacker, Aug. 7, 1983); *Zeichen I* for 2 Soloists and 2 Orchs. (1981–85; Venice, Sept. 29, 1985); *Monodram* for Cello and Orch. (1982–83; Graz, Oct. 9, 1983) *Schattenstück* (1982–84; Karlsruhe, June 24, 1984); *Klangbeschreibung I* for Cello and Orch. (1982–87; Donaueschingen, Oct. 18, 1987) and *III* (1984–87; Donaueschingen, Oct. 18, 1987); *Gebild* for Piccolo Trumpet, 2 Percussionists, and 20 Strings (Zürich, May 15, 1983); *Chiffre II: Silence to be Beaten* (London, Nov. 30, 1983), *V* (Paris, Dec. 3, 1984), and *VII* (Frankfurt am Main, Sept. 15, 1985); *Spur* (1984–85; Saarbrücken, March 24, 1985); *Umriss* (1985–86; Berlin, May 5, 1986); *Compresenze* (1985–87; Cologne, June 4, 1987); *Unbenannt I* (Munich, May 23, 1986), *II* (Tokyo, Oct. 30, 1987), and *III* (1989–90; WDR, Cologne, March 23, 1990); *Blick* (1987–88; Freiburg im Breisgau, April 25, 1988); *Kein Firmament* for Chamber Orch. (Berlin, Oct. 29, 1988); *Ungemaltes Bild* (1988–90; Stockholm, May 17, 1990); *Ins offene . . .* (Glasgow, Sept. 22, 1990); *bildos/weglos* (1990–91); *La lugubre gondola/Das Eismeer* for 2 Orch. Groups and Piano "in memoriam Luigi Nono" (1990–92); *et nunc I* and *II* for Wind Orch. (both 1992); *Form/Zwei Formen* (1993–94). **CHAMBER:** Concerto for Piano and 8 Instruments (1969; Karlsruhe, Oct. 3, 1987); 9 string quartets: No. 1 (1970; Hamburg, June 15, 1987), No. 2 (1970), No. 3, *Im Innersten* (1976; Royan, April 3, 1977), No. 4 (1979–81; Badenweiler, Nov. 12, 1983), No. 5, *Ohne Titel* (1981–83; Brussels, Dec. 9, 1983), No. 6, *Blaubuch* (1984; Kassel, Oct. 26, 1985), No. 7, *Veranderungen* (1985; Darmstadt, June 1986), No. 8 (1988; Milan, Jan. 17, 1989), and No. 9 (1993); *Music-Hall Suite* for 8 Players (1979; Baden-Baden, April 1980); *Chiffre I* for Piano and 7 Instruments (1982; Saarbrücken, April 22, 1983), *III* for 12 Players (Karlsruhe, Dec. 7, 1983), *IV* for Bass Clarinet, Cello, and Piano (1983–84; Hamburg, Feb. 3, 1984), *VI* for 8 Players (Karlsruhe, April 12, 1985), and *VIII* for 8 Players (1985–88; Witten, April 23, 1988); *Musik* for 3 Strings (Darmstadt, July 31, 1978); *Canzona* for 4 Violas (Stuttgart, June 6, 1982); *Fremde Szene I* for Violin, Cello, and Piano (Salzburg, Aug. 17, 1982), *II* for Violin, Cello, and Piano (1983; Düsseldorf, June 8, 1984), and *III* for Violin, Cello, and Piano (1983; Gelsenkirchen, Nov. 21, 1984); Clarinet Quintet (London, June 29, 1988); *Kalt*, octet (Berlin, Feb. 16, 1991); *Sphere* for Piano, Winds, and Percussion (1992–94); *Antlitz* for Cello and Piano (1993); piano pieces; organ music. **VOCAL:** *Konzertarie*, "telepsychogramm" for Mezzo-soprano and Orch. (1975; Rome, June 28, 1989); *Abgesangsszene No. 2* for Medium Voice and Orch. (1979; Karlsruhe, Nov. 5, 1980), *No. 3* for Baritone and Orch. (1979–80; Freiburg im Breisgau, May 18, 1981), *No. 4* for Medium Voice and Orch. (1979; Berlin, Sept. 18, 1983), and *No. 5* for Mezzo-soprano, Baritone, and Orch. (1979–81; Berlin, Sept. 18, 1983); *Lowry-Lieder* for Voice and Orch. (1982–87); *Umsungen* for Baritone and 8 Instruments (1984); *Dies* for Soprano, Alto, Tenor, Baritone, 2 Speakers, Children's Chorus, Speaking Chorus, Mixed Chorus, Organ, and Orch. (1984; Vienna, Nov. 13, 1986); *Andere Schatten*, musical scene for Soprano, Mezzo-soprano, Baritone, Speaker, Chorus, and Orch. (Frankfurt am Main, Sept. 6, 1985); *Klangbeschrei-*

bung II for 4 Voices, 5 Brass, and 6 Percussion (1986–87; Donaueschingen, Oct. 18, 1987); *Mein Tod: Requiem in memoriam Jane S.* for Soprano and Orch. (1988–89; Salzburg, Aug. 16, 1990); *Frau/Stimme* for Soprano and Orch. (Donaueschingen, Oct. 22, 1989); *Geheimer Block* for 4 Soloists, Chorus, and Orch. (Frankfurt am Main, Aug. 27, 1989); *Abschiedsstücke* for Woman's Voice and Small Orch. (1993).

BIBL.: R. Urmetzer, *W. R.* (Stuttgart, 1988).

Říhovský, Vojtěch, Czech choirmaster and composer; b. Dub na Moravě, April 21, 1871; d. Prague, Sept. 15, 1950. He was trained in Prague at the Organ School, the Jan Ludvík Singing Inst., and the Arnošt Černý Music Inst. (1887–92). He served as a choirmaster in Dub na Moravě (1892–1902), Chrudim (1902–14), and at St. Ludmila in Prague (1914–36). He composed some 300 sacred works, as well as secular vocal works and instrumental pieces.

BIBL.: C. Russ, *R. als Kirchenkoponist* (Prague, 1913); V. Bathasar, *V. R.* (Prague, 1921); J. Dušek, *V. R. a jeho životní dílo* (V. R. and His Life's Work; Prague, 1933).

Riisager, Knudåge, prominent Danish composer; b. Port Kunda, Estonia, March 6, 1897; d. Copenhagen, Dec. 26, 1974. He went to Copenhagen and studied theory and composition with Otto Malling and Peder Gram, and violin with Peder Møller (1915–18). He also took courses in political science at the Univ. (1916–21; graduated, 1921) before pursuing musical studies with Roussel and Le Flem in Paris (1921–23), and later with Grabner in Leipzig (1932). He held a civil service position in Denmark (1925–50); was chairman of the Danish Composers' Union (1937–62) and director of the Royal Danish Cons. (1956–67). A fantastically prolific composer, he wrote music in quaquaversal genres, but preserved a remarkable structural and textural consistency while demonstrating an erudite sense of modern polyphony. He also had a taste for exotic and futuristic subjects. He publ. a collection of essays, *Det usynlige mønster* (The Unseemly Monster; Copenhagen, 1957), and a somewhat self-deprecatory memoir, *Det er sjovt at vaere lille* (It Is Amusing to Be Small; Copenhagen, 1967).

WORKS (all 1st perf. in Copenhagen unless otherwise given): **DRAMATIC: OPERA BUFFA:** *Susanne* (1948; Jan. 7, 1950). **BALLETS:** *Benzin* (1927; Dec. 26, 1930); *Cocktails-Party* (1929); *Tolv med Posten* (12 by the Mail), after H.C. Andersen (1939; Feb. 21, 1942); *Slaraffenland* (Fool's Paradise; 1940; Feb. 21, 1942; originally an orch. piece, 1936); *Qarrtsiluni*, on Eskimo themes (Feb. 21, 1942; originally an orch. piece, 1938); *Fugl fønix* (Phoenix; 1944–45; May 12, 1946); *Étude*, based on Czerny's studies (1947; Jan. 15, 1948); *Månerenen* (The Moon Reindeer; 1956; Nov. 22, 1957); *Stjerner* (1958); *Les Victoires de l'Amour* (1958; March 4, 1962); *Fruen fra havet* (Lady from the Sea; 1959; N.Y., April 20, 1960); *Galla-Variationer* (1966; March 5, 1967); *Ballet Royal* (May 31, 1967); *Svinedrengen* (The Swineherd; Danish TV, March 10, 1969). **ORCH.:** *Erasmus Montanus*, overture (1920; Göteborg, Oct. 15, 1924); *Suite Dionysiaque* for Chamber Orch. (1924); 5 syms.: No. 1 (1925; July 17, 1926), No. 2 (1927; March 5, 1929), No. 3 (Nov. 21, 1935), No. 4, *Sinfonia gaia* (Oct. 24, 1940), and No. 5, *Sinfonia serena* for Strings and Percussion (1949–50; Nov. 21, 1950); *Introduzione di traverso*, overture (1925); *Variations on a Theme of Mezangean* (1926); *T-DOXC*, "poème mécanique" (1926; Sept. 3, 1927); *Klods Hans* (1929); *Fastelavn* (Shrovetide), overture (1929–30); Suite for Small Orch. (1931); *Concerto for Orchestra* (1931; Dec. 7, 1936); Concertino for Trumpet and Strings (1933; March 2, 1934); *Primavera*, overture (1934; Jan. 31, 1935); *Slaraffenland*, 2 suites (1936, 1940; as a ballet, 1940); *Sinfonia concertante* for Strings (1937); *Partita* (1937); *Basta* (1938); *Qarrtsiluni* (1938; as a ballet, 1940); *Torgutisk dans* (1939); *Tivoli-Tivoli!* (Aug. 15, 1943); *Sommer-Rhapsodi* (1943; Jan. 30, 1944); *Bellman-Variationer* for Small Orch. (1945); *Sinfonietta* (Stockholm, Oct. 1, 1947); *Chaconne* (1949); *Archaeopteryx* (1949); *Variations on a Sarabande of Charles, Duke of Orleans, 1415* for Strings (1950); Violin Concerto (1950–51; Oct. 11, 1951); *Toccata* (1952); *Pro fistulis et fidibus* for Woodwinds and Strings (1952; March 2, 1953); *Rondo giocoso* for Violin and Orch. (June 18, 1957); *Burlesk ouverture* (1964); *Entrada-Epilogo* (May 19, 1971); *Bourrée*, ballet-variations (Danish Radio, March 7, 1972); *Trittico* for Woodwinds, Brass, Double Bass, and Percussion (Danish Radio, March 3, 1972); *Apollon* (Nov. 11, 1973). **CHAMBER:** 2 violin sonatas (1917, 1923); 6 string quartets (1918; 1920; 1922; 1925–26; 1932; 1942–43); Sonata for Violin and Viola (1919); Wind Quintet (1921); *Variations* for Clarinet, Viola, and Bassoon (1923); *Sinfonietta* for 8 Wind Instruments (1924); *Divertimento* for String Quartet and Wind Quintet (1925); Sonata for Flute, Violin, Clarinet, and Cello (1927); *Music* for Wind Quintet (1927); *Conversazione* for Oboe, Clarinet, and Bassoon (1932); Concertino for 5 Violins and Piano (1933); *Serenade* for Flute, Violin, and Cello (1936); Quartet for Flute, Oboe, Clarinet, and Bassoon (1941); *Divertimento* for Flute, Oboe, Horn, and Bassoon (1944); Sonatina for Piano Trio (1951); Sonata for 2 Violins (1951); String Trio (1955). **PIANO:** *4 épigrammes* (1921); Sonata (1931); *2 morceaux* (1933); Sonatina (1950); *4 Børneklaverstykker* (1964). **VOCAL:** *Dansk Salme* for Chorus and Orch. (1942; April 13, 1943); *Sang til Solen* for Mezzo-soprano, Baritone, Chorus, and Orch. (Sept. 25, 1947); *Sangen om det Uendelige (Canto dell'Infinito)* for Chorus and Orch. (1964; Sept. 30, 1965); *Stabat Mater* for Chorus and Orch. (1966; Danish Radio, Nov. 9, 1967); choruses; songs.

Riley, Terry (Mitchell), significant American composer and performer; b. Colfax, Calif., June 24, 1935. He studied piano with Duane Hampton at San Francisco State College (1955–57) and composition with Seymour Shifrin and William Denny at the Univ. of Calif. at Berkeley (M.A., 1961). In 1967 he was a creative assoc. at the Center for Creative and Performing Arts at the State Univ. of N.Y. in Buffalo. In 1970 he was initiated in San Francisco as a disciple of Pandit Pran Nath, the North Indian singer, and followed him to India. From 1971 to 1980 he was assoc. prof. at Mills College in Oakland, California. In 1979 he held a Guggenheim fellowship. In his music, Riley explores the extremes of complexity and gymnosophistical simplicity.

WORKS: CHAMBER OPERA: *The Saint Adolf Ring* (1992). **TAPE AND INSTRUMENTAL:** Trio for Violin, Clarinet, and Cello (1957); *Spectra* for 3 Winds and 3 Strings (1959); *Concert* for 2 Pianos and Tape (1960); *Earpiece* for 2 Pianos and Tape (1960); String Quartet (1960); String Trio (1961); *I Can't Stop No, Mescalin Mix*, and *She Moves* for Tape (1962–63); *In C* for Variable Ensemble, notated in fragments to be played any number of times at will in the spirit of aleatory latitudinarianism, all within the key of C major, with an occasional F sharp providing a trompe l'oreille effect (San Francisco, May 21, 1965); *Cadenza on the Night Plain* for String Quartet (1984); *Salome Dances for Peace* for String Quartet (1985–86); *The Room of Remembrance* for Vibraphone, Marimba, Piano, and Soprano Saxophone (1987); *Chanting the Light of Foresight* for Saxophone Quartet (1987); *The Crows Rosary* for Keyboard and String Quartet (1988); *The Jade Palace Orchestral Dances* for Orch. (1989; N.Y., Feb. 4, 1991); *Cactus Rosary* for Chamber Ensemble (1990); *The Sands*, concerto for String Quartet and Orch. (1991); N.Y., May 3, 1992); *June Buddhas*, concerto for Chorus and Orch. (1991; N.Y., Nov. 9, 1991); *4 Wölfli Sketches* for Chamber Ensemble (1992); *Ascension* for Guitar (1993); *El Hombre*, piano quintet (1993). **PIECES WITH SYNTHESIZER:** *Poppy Nogoods Phantom Band* (1966); *A Rainbow in Curved Air* (1968); *Genesis '70*, ballet (1970); *Chorale of the Blessed Day* for Voice and 2 Synthesizers or Piano and Sitar (1980); *Eastern Man* for Voice and 2 Synthesizers (1980); *Embroidery* for Voice and 2 Synthesizers or Piano, Synthesizer, Sitar, Tabla, and Alto Saxophone (1980); *Song from the Old Country* for Voice, Piano, Sitar, Tabla, String Quartet, and Synthesizer (1980); *G-Song* for Voice, String Quartet, and Synthesizer (1981); *Remember this oh Mind* for Voice and Synthesizer (1981); *Sunrise of the Planetary Dream Collector* for Voice, Synthesizer, and String Quartet (1981); *The Ethereal Time Shadow* for Voice and 2 Synthesizers (1982); *Offering to Chief Crazy Horse* for Voice and 2 Synthesizers (1982); *The Medicine Wheel* for Voice, Piano, Sitar, Tabla, String Quartet, and Synthesizer (1983); *Song of the Emerald Runner* for Voice, Piano, String Quartet, Sitar, Tabla, and Synthesizer (1983); also various improvisational pieces.

BIBL.: W. Mertens, *American Minimal Music: La Monte Young, T. R., Steve Reich, Philip Glass* (London, 1991).

Rilling, Helmuth, noted German organist, conductor, and pedagogue; b. Stuttgart, May 29, 1933. He studied at the Hochschule für Musik in Stuttgart (1952–55) and later took a course in organ with Fernando Germani at the Accademia di Santa Cecilia in Rome (1955–57); went to N.Y. to study conducting with Bernstein (1967). He founded the Stuttgart Gächinger Kantorei in 1954, which he conducted on numerous tours. He taught choral conducting and organ at the Kirchenmusikschule in Berlin-Spandau (1963–66); in 1966 he was appointed to the faculty of the Frankfurt am Main Hochschule für Musik. In 1965 he founded the Stuttgart Bach-Collegium, an instrumental ensemble to accompany his Gächinger Kantorei; made his first tour of the U.S. with it in 1968; in 1969 he succeeded Kurt Thomas as conductor of the Frankfurter Kantorei. He was founder–artistic director of the Oregon Bach Festival in Eugene (from 1970). He has acquired a distinguished reputation as both a performing musician and a teacher.

Rimini, Giacomo, Italian baritone and teacher; b. Verona, March 22, 1888; d. Chicago, March 6, 1952. He was trained at the Verona Cons. After making his operatic debut in Verona (1910), he sang in various Italian opera houses. In 1916 he joined the Chicago Opera. He also appeared at London's Covent Garden in 1933. In 1920 he married **Rosa Raisa**. They opened a singing school in Chicago in 1937.

Rimsky-Korsakov, Andrei (Nikolaievich), Russian musicologist, uncle of **Georgi (Mikhailovich) Rimsky-Korsakov**; b. St. Petersburg, Oct. 17, 1878; d. there (Leningrad), May 23, 1940. His father was the great Russian composer Nikolai (Andreievich) Rimsky-Korsakov (b. Tikhvin, near Novgorod, March 18, 1844; d. Liubensk, near St. Petersburg, June 21, 1908). He studied philology at the Univ. of St. Petersburg and later at the Univs. of Strasbourg and Heidelberg (Ph.D., 1903). Returning to Russia, he devoted his energies to Russian music history. In 1915 he began the publication of an important magazine, *Musikalny Sovremennik* (The Musical Contemporary), but the revolutionary events of 1917 forced suspension of its publication. He wrote a major biography of his father (5 vols., Moscow, 1933–46; vol. V ed. by his brother, Vladimir Rimsky-Korsakov); also ed. the 3rd to 5th eds. of his father's autobiography (Moscow, 1926, 1932, 1935) and publ. a study of Maximilian Steinberg (Moscow, 1928). He was married to **Julia Weissberg**.

Rimsky-Korsakov, Georgi (Mikhailovich), Russian musicologist and composer, nephew of **Andrei (Nikolaievich) Rimsky-Korsakov;** b. St. Petersburg, Dec. 26, 1901; d. there (Leningrad), Oct. 10, 1965. His grandfather was the great Russian composer Nikolai (Andreievich) Rimsky-Korsakov (b. Tikhvin, near Novgorod, March 18, 1844; d. Liubensk, near St. Petersburg, June 21, 1908). He was a student of Steinberg, Sokolov, Liapunov, and Nicolai at the St. Petersburg Cons. In 1927 he took his kandidat degree at the Leningrad Inst. of Theater and Music. From 1927 to 1962 he taught at the Leningrad Cons. In 1923 he founded a society for the cultivation of quarter tone music, and wrote some works in that system. He later experimented with electronic instruments, and was co-inventor of the Emeriton in 1930, which was capable of producing a complete series of tones at any pitch and of any chosen or synthetic tone color. He wrote solo pieces for the instrument. His other works include incidental music; film scores; Sym. (1925); Quintet for Clarinet, Horn, and String Trio (1925); 2 string quartets (1926, 1932); Octet for 2 Emeritons, 2 Clarinets, Bassoon, Violin, Viola, and Cello (1932); piano pieces, including 2 sonatas (1924, 1932); choral music.

Ringbom, Nils-Eric, Finnish violinist, music critic, music administrator, and composer; b. Turku, Dec. 27, 1907; d. Korpoström, Feb. 13, 1988. He studied at the Turku Academy (M.A., 1933) and at the Univ. of Helsinki (D.Mus., 1955, with the diss. *Über die Deutbarkeit der Tonkunst*; publ. in Helsinki and Wiesbaden, 1955); among his teachers were O. Andersson and L. Funtek. He played violin in the Turku Sym. Orch. (1927–28; 1930–33); was music critic of the *Svenska Pressen* (1933–44) and the *Nya Pressen* (1945–70); was assistant manager (1938–42) and manager (1942–70) of the Helsinki Phil.; served as artistic director of the Sibelius Festival (1951–60) and chairman of the Helsinki Festival (1966–70).

WRITINGS: *Helsingfors orkesterföretag 1882–1932* (Helsinki, 1932); *Säveltaide* (The Art of Music; Helsinki, 1945); *Sibelius* (Stockholm, 1948; Ger. tr., 1950; Eng. tr., 1954); *Musik utan normer* (Music without Norms; 1972); *Orkesterhovdingar* (1981).

WORKS: ORCH.: *Little Suite* (1933; rev. 1946); 5 syms. (1938–39; 1943–44; 1948; 1962; 1970). **CHAMBER:** Duo for Violin and Viola (1945); Wind Sextet (1951); String Quartet (1952); piano pieces. **VOCAL:** *Till livet* (To Life) for Chorus and String Orch. (1936); *Vandrerska* (The Wanderer) for Soprano and Orch. (1942); *Hymn till Helsingfors* for Chorus and Orch. (1949); songs.

Ringer, Alexander L(othar), American musicologist; b. Berlin (of Dutch parents), Feb. 3, 1921. He attended the Hollander Cons. in Berlin. In 1939 went to Amsterdam, where he studied composition with Henk Badings. In 1946 he emigrated to the U.S.; continued his education at the New School for Social Research in N.Y. (M.A., 1949) and at Columbia Univ. (Ph.D., 1955). He taught at the City College of N.Y. (1948–52), the Univ. of Pa. (1952–55), the Univ. of Calif., Berkeley (1955–56), and the Univ. of Okla. (1956–58). In 1958 he was appointed to the faculty of the Univ. of Ill. in Urbana; also was a regular guest lecturer at the Hebrew Univ. in Jerusalem. He contributed many articles to the *Musical Quarterly*; also publ. the study *Arnold Schoenberg: The Composer as Jew* (Oxford, 1990).

Rios, Waldo de los, Argentine composer, conductor, arranger, and pianist; b. Buenos Aires, Sept. 7, 1934; d. (of a self-inflicted gunshot wound) Madrid, March 29, 1977. He studied in Argentina with his mother, Martha de los Rios, a prominent Argentine folksinger; then had piano, composition, and conducting lessons at the National Academy of Music (graduated, 1954). He served in the Argentine military; concurrently made his first folk recordings with Columbia Records (1955). This and subsequent recordings of indigenous folk tunes arranged for sym. orch. were not well received, since Argentina was experiencing renewed interest in its folk music and was intent upon authenticity. In 1962 he emigrated to Spain, where he subsequently made it his mission to popularize the classics for the enlightenment of the masses; this he accomplished by selecting outstanding movements from large-scale, well-known works and, after condensing them to 3–5 minutes, arranging them for symphonic forces augmented by pop ensembles which included saxophone, drums, and Spanish and/or Latin percussion instruments. His rendition of Mozart's Sym. No. 40 became particularly popular. During the 1970s he was conductor-director of the Manuel de Falla Orch. and Chorus, with which he made numerous recordings, including *Sinfonias* (1971), *Operas* (1974), *Sinfonias for the 70's* (1975), *Concertos for the 70's* (1976), and *Corales* (1978). Among his legitimately original works was *South American Suite* (1957), based upon primitive melodies and rhythms of Paraguay, Argentina, Uruguay, and Peru, and scored for orch. augmented by guitars, Indian harp, and various native wind and percussion instruments.

Ristenpart, Karl, German conductor; b. Kiel, Jan. 26, 1900; d. Lisbon, Dec. 24, 1967. He studied at the Stern Cons. in Berlin and Vienna. In 1932 he became conductor of the Berlin Chamber Orch.; also led concerts with the Radio Orch. in Berlin. In 1946 he was named conductor of the Chamber Orch. of RIAS

(Radio in the American Sector of Berlin). In 1953 he became conductor of the Chamber Orch. of the Saar, a noted ensemble of the Saarland Radio in Saarbrucken; made many tours and recordings with this group.

Ristić, Milan, Serbian composer; b. Belgrade, Aug. 31, 1908; d. there, Dec. 20, 1982. He studied in Belgrade with Slavenski and in Prague with Alois Hába. A prolific composer, he wrote mostly instrumental music; his style ranged from neo-Romantic grandiosity to economic neo-Classicism, from epically declamatory diatonicism to expressionistically atonal melos. Some of his works were written in an explicit dodecaphonic technique; in some, he made use of quarter tones.

WORKS: ORCH.: 7 syms. (1941, 1951, 1961, 1966, 1967, 1968, 1972); Violin Concerto (1944); Piano Concerto (1954); *Suite giocosa* (1956); *Symphonic Variations* (1957); *Burleska* (1957); *7 Bagatelles* (1959); *Concerto for Orchestra* (1963); Clarinet Concerto (1964); *4 Movements* for Strings (1971). **CHAMBER:** 2 string quartets; Wind Quintet; Septet; Violin Sonata; Viola Sonata; 24 fugues for various instrumental combinations; Suite for 4 Trombones in quarter-tones.

Ritchie, Margaret (Willard), English soprano; b. Grimsby, June 7, 1903; d. Ewelme, Oxfordshire, Feb. 7, 1969. She studied at the Royal College of Music in London and with Plunket Greene, Agnes Wood, and Henry Wood. She established herself as a prominent concert artist early in her career, and also was the principal soprano of Frederick Woodhouse's Intimate Opera Co. Later she sang with the Sadler's Wells Opera in London (1944–47), at the Glyndebourne Festivals (1946–47), with the English Opera Group (from 1947), and at Covent Garden in London. From 1960 she taught voice in Oxford. She created the roles of Lucia in *The Rape of Lucretia* (1946) and of Miss Wordsworth in *Albert Herring* (1947). As a concert artist, she was much admired for her Schubert lieder recitals.

Ritchie, Stanley (John), Australian violinist and teacher; b. Yenda, New South Wales, April 21, 1935. He studied violin with Florent Hoogstoel at the New South Wales State Conservatorium of Music in Sydney (diploma, 1956); after receiving instruction in violin and chamber music from Jean Fournier and Sandor Vegh in Paris (1958–59), he went to the U.S. and continued his training with Joseph Fuchs at Yale Univ. (1959–60), Oscar Shumsky, and Samuel Kissell. He served as concertmaster of the N.Y. City Opera orch. (1963–65) and assoc. concertmaster of the Metropolitan Opera orch. (1965–70); was a member of the N.Y. Chamber Soloists (1970–73), founder of the early-music ensemble Aston Magna (1974), and 1st violin in the Philadelphia String Quartet (1975–81). With his wife, harpsichordist and fortepianist Elizabeth Wright, he performed in the Duo Geminiani (from 1974); was prof. of violin and director of the Baroque orch. at Indiana Univ. (from 1982) and a prof. at the Juilliard School in N.Y. (from 1984). He has championed the performance of early music on period instruments.

Rivier, Jean, French composer and pedagogue; b. Villemonble, July 21, 1896; d. La Penne sur Huveaune, Nov. 6, 1987. His early musical training was interrupted by his enlistment in the French army during World War I. His health was severely damaged as a result of mustard gas, and it was only after a long recuperation that he was able to enter the Paris Cons. in 1922 to study with Emmanuel (music history), J. Gallon (harmony), and Caussade (counterpoint and fugue; premier prix, 1926). He also studied cello with Bazelaire. In subsequent years, he was active with various contemporary music societies in Paris, including Triton, of which he was president (1936–40). From 1948 to 1966 he taught composition at the Paris Cons. In 1970 he was awarded the Grand Prix for music of the City of Paris. He formed a style of composition in which he effectively combined elements of French Classicism and Impressionism.

WORKS: OPERA: *Vénitienne* (Paris, July 8, 1937). **ORCH.:** Cello Concerto (1927); *Chant funèbre*, symphonic poem (1927); *Danse* (1928); *3 Pastorales* (1928; Paris, Feb. 7, 1929); *Ouverture pour un Don Quichotte* (1929); *Burlesque* for Violin and Orch. (1929); *Adagio* for Strings (1930; Paris, March 1, 1931); *Ouverture pour une opérette imaginaire* (1930); *5 Mouvements brefs* (1931); *Le Livre d'Urien* (1931); 8 syms.: No. 1 (1931; Paris, Jan. 29, 1933), No. 2 for Strings (1937), No. 3 for Strings (1937; Paris, Nov. 25, 1940), No. 4 for Strings (1947), No. 5 (1950; Strasbourg, June 24, 1951), No. 6, *Les Présages* (Paris, Dec. 11, 1958), No. 7, *Les Contrastes* (1961; Paris, Jan. 9, 1962), and No. 8 for Strings (1978); Viola or Alto Saxophone Concertino (1935; Paris, Feb. 15, 1936); *Musiques nocturnes* (1936); *Paysage pour une Jeanne d'Arc à Domrémy*, symphonic tableau (1936; Paris, Jan. 31, 1937); 2 piano concertos: No. 1 (1940) and No. 2, *Concerto breve*, for Piano and Strings (1953); Violin Concerto (1942); *Rapsodie provençale* (Aix-en-Provence, July 22, 1949); *Ouverture pour un drame* (1952); Concerto for Alto Saxophone, Trumpet, and Strings (1954); Concerto for Flute and Strings (Strasbourg, June 1956); *Musique pour un ballet* (1957); *Le Déjeuner sur l'herbe* (1958); Concerto for Clarinet and Strings (1958); Concerto for Bassoon and Strings (1963); Concerto for Brass, Timpani, and Strings (1963); *Drames*, symphonic movement (1966); *Résonances* (1966); *Triade* for Strings (1967); Concerto for Oboe and Strings (1967); Concerto for Trumpet and Strings (1970); *Lento doloroso* for Strings (1981). **CHAMBER:** 2 string quartets (1924, 1940); String Trio (1933); *Grave et presto* for Saxophone Quartet (1938); Duo for Flute and Clarinet (1968); *Climats* for Celesta, Vibraphone, Xylophone, Piano, and Strings (1968); *Capriccio* for Wind Quintet (1972); *Brilliances* for Brass Septet (1972); *Comme une tendre berceuse* for Flute and Piano (1984); *3* Movements for Clarinet and Piano (1985). **PIANO:** *Quatre Fantasmes* (1967); Sonata (1969); *Contrasts* (1981); *Stèle* (1982). **VOCAL:** *Psaume LVI* for Soprano, Chorus, and Orch. (1937); *Ballade des amants désespérés* for Chorus and Orch. (1945); *Requiem* for Mezzo-soprano, Bass, Chorus, and Orch. (1953); *Christus Rex*, oratorio for Contralto, Chorus, and Orch. (1966); *Dolor* for Chorus and Orch. (1973); choruses; songs.

Rizzi, Carlo, Italian conductor; b. Milan, July 19, 1960. He took courses in piano, conducting, and composition at the Milan Cons., and then studied conducting with Delman in Bologna (1984) and Ferrara at the Accademia Musicale Chigiana in Siena (1985). In 1982 he made his debut conducting Donizetti's *L'Ajo nell'imbarazzo, o Don Gregorio* at Milan's Angelicum. In 1985 he was 1st prize winner in the new Toscanini conducting competition in Parma, where he then conducted *Falstaff*; subsequently conducted throughout Italy. In 1988 he made his British debut at the Buxton Festival conducting *Torquato Tasso*, and in 1989 conducted *Il Barbiere di Siviglia* at the Australian Opera in Sydney and *Don Pasquale* at the Netherlands Opera in Amsterdam. He conducted *La Cenerentola* at London's Covent Garden in 1990. He was chosen to conduct *Il Trovatore* at the opening of the restored Teatro Carlo Felice in Genoa in 1991. In 1992 he made his first appearance at the Deutsche Oper in Berlin conducting *L'Italiana in Algeri*. Rizzi served as music director of the Welsh National Opera in Cardiff from 1992. In 1993 he made his first appearance in the U.S. as a guest conductor of the Chicago Sym. Orch. at the Ravinia Festival in Chicago. On Oct. 29, 1993, he made his Metropolitan Opera debut in N.Y. conducting *La Bohème*.

Roach, Max(well Lemuel), remarkable black American jazz drummer and composer; b. Elizabeth City, N.C., Jan. 10, 1924. He was taken to N.Y. as a child; after playing in a church drum-and-bugle corps, he was a drummer in his high school band; also sat in on jam sessions in various jazz haunts around the city. He began his professional career as a member of Dizzy Gillespie's quintet, becoming immersed in the bebop movement; after a stint with Benny Carter's band (1944–45), he joined Charlie Parker's quintet (1947) and became widely recognized as one of the most innovative drummers of his era. He also studied composition with John Lewis at the Manhattan School of Music. He then led his own groups (from 1949), perfecting his "hard-bop" style. With the trumpeter Clifford Brown, he was co-leader of an outstanding quintet (1953–56). In subsequent years he led various groups, including M'Boom Re, a percussion ensemble (from 1970). With his own quartet, he played throughout the U.S., Europe, and Japan (1976–77). He became a prof. of music at the Univ. of Mass. in Amherst (1972), where he instituted a jazz studies program. As a composer, he became best known for his *Freedom Now Suite* (1960), an expression of his solidarity with the U.S. civil rights movement. He also wrote and recorded the avant-garde scores *Force* (1976; dedicated to Mao Tse-tung) and *1 in 2—2 in 1* (1978). He was awarded an honorary Mus.D. degree from the New England Cons. of Music in Boston in 1982.

Robertson, Alec (actually, **Alexander Thomas Paul**), English writer on music and broadcaster; b. Southsea, June 3, 1892; d. Midhurst, Jan. 18, 1982. After studies at Bradfield College and the Royal Academy of Music in London (1910–13), he was active with the Gramophone Co. (1920–30); then entered the Collegio Beda in Rome (1930) and was ordained a priest (1934). After serving at Westminster Cathedral, he joined the Gramophone Dept. of the BBC (1940), where he was chief producer of music talks on the Home and Third Programmes, a position he held until 1952. He was also a reviewer (from 1932) and music ed. (1952–72) for the journal *Gramophone*. His autobiography was publ. as *More than Music* (London, 1961).

WRITINGS (all publ. in London unless otherwise given): *The Interpretation of Plainchant* (1937); *Brahms* (1939; 2nd ed., 1974); *Dvořák* (1945; 2nd ed., 1964); *Contrasts: The Arts and Religion* (1947); *How to Listen to Music* (1948); *Sacred Music* (1950); ed. *Chamber Music* (Harmondsworth, 1956; 4th ed., 1967); ed. with D. Stevens, *Pelican History of Music* (Harmondsworth, 1960–68); *Christian Music* (N.Y., 1961); *Music of the Catholic Church* (1961); ed. *G.B. S. on Music* (1962); *Requiem: Music of Mourning and Consolation* (1967); *Church Cantatas of J.S. Bach* (1972).

Robertson, David, American conductor and composer; b. Santa Monica, Calif., July 19, 1958. He received training in horn, viola, conducting, and composition; in 1976, became a student at the Royal Academy of Music in London; also attended the Hilversum conducting courses in 1979 and 1980, and concurrently studied privately with Kondrashin before attending the master class given by Kubelik in Lucerne in 1981. In 1980 he took 2nd prize at the Nicolai Malko Competition in Copenhagen, and then was an assistant at the Deutsche Oper am Rhein in Düsseldorf in 1981. He was a resident conductor of the Jerusalem Sym. Orch. from 1985 to 1987. In 1992 he became music director of the Ensemble InterContemporain in Paris. In addition to conducting contemporary scores in Paris, Robertson appeared as a guest conductor of the traditional repertoire with various European orchs. and in various opera houses. His compositions include Quartet for 4 Trombones (1978–79); *Ricercar I* for Harpsichord and Strings (1981), *II* for Brass Quintet (1983–84), and *III* for Trombone and Marimba (1984–86); an unfinished operatic trilogy: part 1, *Dangerous Children* (1989–90).

Robertson, Leroy, American composer and teacher; b. Fountain Green, Utah, Dec. 21, 1896; d. Salt Lake City, July 25, 1971. He studied in Provo; then in Boston with Chadwick and Converse at the New England Cons. of Music (diploma, 1923); subsequently went to Europe, where he took courses with Bloch in Switzerland, Leichtentritt in Berlin, and Toch. Returning to America, he studied at the Univ. of Utah (M.A., 1932) and later at the Univ. of Southern Calif. in Los Angeles (Ph.D., 1954). He was a prof. and chairman of the music dept. at Brigham Young Univ. in Provo (1925–48); then was chairman of the music dept. at the Univ. of Utah (1948–63). In 1947 his symphonic work *Trilogy* received the 1st prize of $25,000 in a contest sponsored by Henry H. Reichhold of Detroit; it was performed by the Detroit Sym. Orch. on Dec. 11, 1947, but despite the attendant publicity, the work was not successful, and there were few subsequent performances. Other works include: *The Book of Mormon*, oratorio (Salt Lake City, Feb. 18, 1953); *Prelude, Scherzo, Ricercare* for Orch. (1940); *Rhapsody* for Piano and Orch. (1944); *Punch and Judy Overture* (1945); Violin Concerto (1948); Piano Concerto (Salt Lake City, Nov. 30, 1966); Cello Concerto (1966); Piano Quintet (1933); String Quartet (1940; N.Y. Music Critics' Circle Award, 1944); *American Serenade* for String Quartet (1944); other chamber music; piano pieces; songs.

Robertson, Rae, Scottish pianist; b. Ardersier, Inverness, Nov. 29, 1893; d. Los Angeles, Nov. 4, 1956. He studied with F. Niecks at the Univ. of Edinburgh; then at the Royal Academy of Music in London with Matthay and F. Corder. He married **Ethel Bartlett**, with whom he gave numerous concerts in Europe and America as duo-pianists (from 1928). With her he ed. an Oxford Univ. Press series of works for 2 pianos.

Robertson, Stewart (John), Scottish conductor and pianist; b. Glasgow, May 22, 1948. He studied at the Royal Scottish Academy of Music in Glasgow (1965–69), the Univ. of Bristol (1969–70), the Vienna Academy of Music (1975), and the Salzburg Mozarteum (1977). His conducting mentors were Suitner and Swarowsky; also studied piano with Denis Matthews. In 1968–69 he was assistant chorus master of Glasgow's Scottish Opera and of the Edinburgh Festival. After serving as chorus master of the London City Singers (1970–72), he conducted at the Cologne Opera (1972–75). In 1975–76 he was music director of the Tanz Forum at the Zürich Opera, and then of the Scottish Opera Touring Co. (1976–79). From 1979 to 1982 he was music director of the Hidden Valley Chamber Orch. in California. From 1980 to 1988 he was assoc. conductor and director of the apprentice artists program of the Des Moines Metro Opera. In 1984–85 he was music director of the Mid-Columbia Sym. Orch., and in 1985–86 assistant conductor of the Oakland (Calif.) Sym. Orch. He subsequently was music director of the Santa Fe (N.M.) Sym. Orch. (from 1986) and of the Glimmerglass Opera in N.Y. (from 1987).

Robeson, Paul (Bustill), great black American bass and actor; b. Princeton, N.J., April 9, 1898; d. Philadelphia, Jan. 23, 1976. He first studied law (B.A., 1919, Rutgers Univ.; LL.B, 1923, Columbia Univ.). When his talent for singing and acting was discovered, he appeared in plays in the U.S. and England. He acted the part of Emperor Jones in Eugene O'Neill's play and of Porgy in the Negro folk play by Du Bose and Dorothy Heyward. In 1925 he gave his first Negro spiritual recital in N.Y.; then toured in Europe. In 1927 he scored an enormous success in the musical *Show Boat*, becoming deservedly famous for his rendition of *Ol' Man River*. In 1930 he appeared in the title role of Shakespeare's *Othello* in London. Returning to the U.S., he continued to give recitals, but his outspoken admiration for the Soviet regime from the 1940s on interfered with the success of his career. In 1952 he was awarded the International Stalin Peace Prize ($25,000). During the summer of 1958, he made an extensive European tour. He continued to sing abroad until he was stricken with ill health and returned to the U.S. in 1963. His autobiography was publ. as *Here I Stand* (London, 1958).

BIBL.: E. Robeson, *P. R., Negro* (N.Y., 1930); S. Graham, *P. R.: Citizen of the World* (N.Y., 1946); M. Seton, *P. R.* (London, 1958); E. Hoyt, *P. R.: The American Othello* (London, 1967); D. Gilliam, *P. R., All American* (N.Y., 1977); P. Dean, *P. R.* (Garden City, N.Y., 1978); S. Robeson, *The Whole World in His Hands: A Pictorial Biography of P. R.* (Secaucus, N.J., 1981); L. Davis, *A P. R. Research Guide* (Westport, Conn., 1983); C. Bell, *P. R.'s Last Days in Philadelphia* (Bryn Mawr, 1986).

Robin, Mado, French soprano; b. Yseures-sur-Creuse, near Tours, Dec. 29, 1918; d. Paris, Dec. 10, 1960. She studied voice with Giuseppe Podestà. She then began her career as a concert artist; made her operatic debut in 1945 as Gilda at the Paris Opéra; also sang at the Opéra-Comique; made guest appearances in Brussels, Liège, and San Francisco. She was best known for her performances in the roles of Lakmé and Lucia.

Robinson, Earl (Hawley), American composer; b. Seattle, July 2, 1910; d. in an automobile accident there, July 20, 1991. He studied with George McKay at the Univ. of Wash. (B.M. and teaching diploma, 1933), and then went to N.Y. (1934), where he completed his training with Copland and Eisler; was also active with the Workers Laboratory Theater and the Composers Collective of the Pierre Degeyter Club; it was during this period that he first gained notice via his topical songs. He won a Guggenheim fellowship (1942); was active in Hollywood as a composer for films until he was blacklisted during the McCarthy era; then returned to N.Y. and served as head of the music dept. at Elisabeth Irwin High School (1958–65). The film *The House I Live In* (1946) was inspired by his song of that title (1942), which won him an Academy Award in 1947.

WORKS: DRAMATIC: MUSIC DRAMA: *Song of Atlantis* (1983). **FOLK OPERAS:** *Sandhog* (1951–54); *David of Sassoon* (1978). **MUSICALS:** *Processional* (1938); *Sing for Your Supper* (1939); *1 Foot in America* (1962); *Earl Robinson's America* (1976); *Listen for the Dolphin,* children's musical (1981). **BALLET:** *Bouquet for Molly* (1949). Also film scores. **ORCH.:** *Good Morning* (1949); *A Country They Call Puget Sound,* tone poem for Tenor and Orch. (1956; rev. 1961); Banjo Concerto (1966–67); *The New Human,* piano concerto (1973); *To the Northwest Indians* for Narrator, Folk Instruments, and Orch. (1974). **VOCAL:** Cantatas; songs.

Robinson, Faye, prominent black American soprano; b. Houston, Nov. 2, 1943. She studied at Bennett College in Greensboro, N.C., Texas Southern Univ. in Houston, and North Texas State Univ. in Denton. After winning 1st prize in the San Francisco Opera Auditions, she made her debut as Micaëla in *Carmen* at the N.Y. City Opera on Sept. 2, 1972; was on its roster until 1979. She appeared with opera companies in Houston, Philadelphia, Pittsburgh, San Diego, and Washington, D.C.; also sang widely in Europe and appeared frequently at the Aix-en-Provence Festival from 1974; was a guest artist with the Paris Opéra, the Vienna State Opera, the Hamburg State Opera, the Frankfurt am Main Opera, the Bavarian State Opera in Munich, and others. She was also active as a concert artist. Her operatic roles include Donna Anna, Pamina, Constanze, Elvira in I Puritani, Gilda, Li, Violetta, the 4 principal soprano roles in *Les Contes d'Hoffmann,* and Gounod's Juliette; also sang in the premiere of Tippett's *The Mask of Time* (Boston, April 5, 1984).

Robinson, (Peter) Forbes, English bass; b. Macclesfield, May 21, 1926; d. London, May 13, 1987. He studied at Loughborough College; then went to Italy and took courses at the La Scala Opera School in Milan. He made his professional debut as Monterone at Covent Garden in London in 1954; later sang at the Aldeburgh Festival and the Edinburgh Festival, and with the English Opera Group, the English National Opera, the Teatro Colón in Buenos Aires, and the Zürich Opera. He had an extensive repertoire; his roles included Figaro, Boris Godunov, Don Giovanni, King Philip, Claggart in *Billy Budd,* and Tippett's King Priam, which role he created in 1962; also appeared widely as a concert artist.

Robinson, Michael Finlay, English musicologist; b. Gloucester, March 3, 1933. He was educated at the Univ. of Oxford (B.A., 1956; B.Mus., 1957; M.A., 1960; Ph.D., 1963, with the diss. *Neapolitan Opera, 1700–1780).* He taught at the Royal Scottish Academy of Music in Glasgow (1960–61), the Univ. of Durham (1961–65), and McGill Univ. in Montreal (1965–70). In 1970 he joined the faculty of the Univ. of Wales College in Cardiff, where he was senior lecturer (1975–91) and prof. (1991–94), and head of the music dept. (1987–94). He publ. *Opera Before Mozart* (1966), *Naples and Neapolitan Opera* (1972), and a thematic catalog of the works of Paisiello (2 vols., 1990, 1993).

Robinson, Ray, American writer on music and choral conductor; b. San Jose, Calif., Dec. 26, 1932. He learned to play the viola; studied at San Jose State College (B.A., 1956) and at Indiana Univ. in Bloomington (M.M., 1958; D.Mus.Ed., 1969, with the diss. *A History of the Peabody Conservatory*). He was an assoc. prof. of music and chairman of the division of fine arts at Cascade College in Portland, Oreg. (1959–63). From 1963 to 1966 he was dean of the Peabody Cons. of Music in Baltimore; then was its assoc. director (1966–69). From 1969 to 1987 he was president of Westminster Choir College in Princeton, N.J. His books include *The Choral Experience* (with A. Winold; 1976); *Choral Music: A Norton Historical Anthology* (1978); *Krzysztof Penderecki: A Guide to His Works* (1983); *A Study of the Penderecki St. Luke Passion* (with A. Winold; 1983); *John Finley Williamson: A Centennial Appreciation* (1987).

Robinson, Sharon, American cellist; b. Houston, Dec. 2, 1949. She studied at the North Carolina School of the Arts in Winston-Salem (graduated, 1968), the Univ. of Southern Calif. in Los Angeles (1968–70), and the Peabody Cons. of Music in Baltimore (B.M., 1974). In 1974 she made her formal debut in N.Y.; subsequently appeared as a solo artist and chamber music player. In 1975 she won the Levintritt Award. She married the violinist **Jaime Laredo** in 1976, with whom she joined that year with the pianist Joseph Kalichstein to form the Kalichstein-Laredo-Robinson Trio. They subsequently toured extensively in North America and Europe.

Robinson, Stanford, English conductor; b. Leeds, July 5, 1904; d. Brighton, Oct. 25, 1984. He studied with Boult at the Royal College of Music in London. He began his career on the staff of the BBC in London, where he organized its Wireless Chorus in 1924. After conducting other BBC choral groups, he served as conductor of the BBC Theatre Orch. (1932–46), assoc. conductor of the BBC Sym. Orch. (1946–49), conductor of the BBC Opera Orch. for broadcasting symphonic music (1949–52), and a BBC staff conductor (1952–66). In 1968–69 he was chief conductor of the Queensland Sym. Orch. in Brisbane, Australia. In 1972 he was made an Officer of the Order of the British Empire.

Robison, Paula (Judith), gifted American flutist; b. Nashville, Tenn., June 8, 1941. Her family went to Los Angeles when she was a child; there she studied piano, but then turned to the flute. After attending the Univ. of Southern Calif., she studied flute with Julius Baker at the Juilliard School of Music in N.Y. (graduated, 1963); continued her studies with Marcel Moyse at the Marlboro (Vt.) Festival and in N.Y., where she made her recital debut (1961). After sharing 1st prize in the Munich Competition (1964), she became the first American to capture the 1st prize for flute in the Geneva International Competition (1966). She became a member of the Chamber Music Soc. of Lincoln Center in 1969. With her husband, the violist Scott Nickrenz, she was made co-artistic director of chamber music at the Spoleto Festival of Two Worlds in Italy and Charleston, S.C. (1977), and at the Spoleto/Melbourne (Australia) Festival of Three Worlds (1986). She was also active as a teacher. She commissioned and gave the premieres of works by Leon Kirchner, Robert Beaser, Toru Takemitsu, and Oliver Knussen.

Robles, Marisa, Spanish harpist, teacher, and composer; b. Madrid, May 4, 1937. She was educated at the Madrid Cons., graduating in 1953. In 1954 she made her formal debut as soloist with the Orquesta Nacional de España in Madrid. In 1958 she joined the faculty of the Madrid Cons. After making her home in England in 1959, she became well known via television appearances. In 1963 she made her London concert debut, and subsequently appeared as a soloist with orchs. and as a recitalist throughout the world. From 1971 she also was a prof. of harp at the Royal College of Music in London. In 1991 and 1994 she was artistic director of the World Harp Festival.

Rocca, Lodovico, Italian composer; b. Turin, Nov. 29, 1895; d. there, June 25, 1986. He studied with Orefice at the Milan Cons.; also attended the Univ. of Turin. From 1940 to 1966 he was director of the Turin Cons.

WORKS: OPERAS: *La morte di Frine* (1917–20; Milan, April 24, 1937); *In terra di leggenda* (1922–23; Milan, Sept. 28, 1933); *Il Dibuk* (1928–30; Milan, March 24, 1934); *Monte Ivnor* (1936–38; Rome, Dec. 23, 1939); *L'uragano* (1942–51 Milan, Feb. 8, 1952). **ORCH.:** *Contrasti* (1919); *Aurora di morte*

(1920); *La foresta delle samodive* (1921); *L'alba del malato* (1922); *Le luci* (1923); *La cella azzurra* (1925); *Interludio epico* (1928). **VOCAL:** *Birib, Occhi di rana* for Voice and String Quartet (1937); *Schizzi francescani* for Tenor and 8 Instruments (1942); *Antiche iscrizioni* for Soloists, Chorus, and Orch. (1952; Rome, Feb. 6, 1953); songs.

BIBL.: M. Bruni, *L. R.* (Milan, 1963).

Rochberg, George, significant American composer and teacher; b. Paterson, N.J., July 5, 1918. He took courses in counterpoint and composition with Weisse, Szell, and Mannes at the Mannes College of Music in N.Y. (1939–42); after military service during World War II, he took courses in theory and composition with Scalero and Menotti at the Curtis Inst. of Music in Philadelphia (B.Mus., 1947); also studied at the Univ. of Pa. (M.A., 1948). He taught at the Curtis Inst. of Music (1948–54); was in Rome on Fulbright and American Academy fellowships (1950). In 1951 he became music ed. of the Theodore Presser Co. in Philadelphia, and soon after was made its director of publications. In 1960 he joined the faculty of the Univ. of Pa. as chairman of the music dept., a position he held until 1968; then continued on its faculty as a prof. of music, serving as Annenberg Prof. of the Humanities from 1979 until his retirement in 1983. He held 2 Guggenheim fellowships (1956–57; 1966–67); was elected to membership in the American Academy and Inst. of Arts and Letters (1985) and was made a fellow of the American Academy of Arts and Sciences (1986); was awarded honorary doctorates from the Univ. of Pa. (1985) and the Curtis Inst. of Music (1988). He publ. the study *The Hexachord and Its Relation to the Twelve-Tone Row* (Bryn Mawr, Pa., 1955). A collection of his writings was ed. by W. Bolcom as *The Aesthetics of Survival: A Composer's View of Twentieth-century Music* (Ann Arbor, 1984). In his style, he pursues the ideal of tonal order and logically justifiable musical structures; the most profound influence he experienced was that of Schoenberg and Webern; many of his early works follow the organization in 12 different notes; more recently, he does not deny himself the treasures of the sanctified past, and even resorts to overt quotations in his works of recognizable fragments from music by composers as mutually unrelated as Schutz, Bach, Mahler, and Ives, treated by analogy with the "objets trouvés" in modern painting and sculpture.

WORKS: DRAMATIC: *The Confidence Man*, opera, after Melville (Santa Fe, July 31, 1982); *Phaedra*, monodrama for Mezzo-soprano and Orch. (1974–75; Syracuse, N.Y., Jan. 9, 1976); incidental music to Ben Jonson's play *The Alchemist* (1965; N.Y., Oct. 13, 1968). **ORCH.:** *Night Music* (1948; N.Y., April 23, 1953; orig. the 2nd movement of the Sym. No. 1); *Capriccio* (1949; rev. 1957; orig. the 3rd movement of the Sym. No. 1); 6 syms: No. 1 (1st version in 3 movements, 1948–57; Philadelphia, March 28, 1958; 2nd version in 5 movements, including *Night Music* and *Capriccio*, 1971–77), No. 2 (1955–56; Cleveland, Feb. 26, 1959), No. 3 for Solo Voices, Chamber Chorus, Double Chorus, and Orch. (1966–69; N.Y., Nov. 24, 1970), No. 4 (Seattle, Nov. 15, 1976), No. 5 (1984; Chicago, March 13, 1986), and No. 6 (Pittsburgh, Oct. 16, 1987); *Cantio sacra* for Small Orch. (1954); *Cheltenham Concerto* for Flute, Oboe, Clarinet, Bassoon, Horn, Trumpet, Trombone, and Strings (1958); *Time-Span I* (St. Louis, Oct. 22, 1960; withdrawn) and *II* (1962; Buffalo, Jan. 19, 1964); *Apocalyptica* for Wind Ensemble (1964; Montclair, N.J., May 19, 1965); *Zodiac* (Cincinnati, May 8, 1965; orch. version of the *12 Bagatelles* for Piano, 1952); *Music for the Magic Theater* for 15 Instruments (1965); *Fanfares for Brass* (Philadelphia, March 17, 1968); *Imago mundi* (1973; Baltimore, May 8, 1974); Violin Concerto (1974; Pittsburgh, April 4, 1975); *Transcendental Variations* for Strings (1975; based on the String Quartet No. 3, 1972); Oboe Concerto (1983; N.Y., Dec. 13, 1984); Clarinet Concerto (1994–95). **CHAMBER:** 7 string quartets: No. 1 (1952; N.Y., Jan. 10, 1953), No. 2, with Soprano (1959–61; Philadelphia, April 30, 1962), No. 3 (N.Y., May 15, 1972), No. 4 (1977; Philadelphia, Jan. 20, 1979), No. 5 (1978; Philadelphia, Jan. 20, 1979), No. 6 (1978; Philadelphia, Jan. 20, 1979), and No. 7, with Baritone (1979; Ann Arbor, Jan. 27, 1980); Chamber Sym. for 9 Instruments (1953); *Serenate d'estate* for Flute, Harp, Guitar, and String Trio (1955); 2 piano trios (1963, 1985); *Contra mortem et tempus* for Flute, Clarinet, Piano, and Violin (1965; N.Y., May 15, 1972); Quintet for Piano and String Quartet (1975; N.Y., March 15, 1976); *Octet: A Grand Fantasia* for Flute, Clarinet, Horn, Piano, Violin, Viola, Cello, and Double Bass (N.Y., April 25, 1980); Trio for Clarinet, Horn, and Piano (1980); String Quintet (Philadelphia, Jan. 6, 1982); Quartet for Piano, Violin, Viola, and Cello (1983; Washington, D.C., June 18, 1985); *To the Dark Wood* for Woodwind Quintet (1985; Armidale, Australia, Oct. 3, 1986); Trio for Piano, Violin, and Cello (1985; Washington, D.C., Feb. 27, 1986); Violin Sonata (1988; Pasadena, Calif., April 10, 1989); *Ora Pro Nobis* for Flute and Guitar (1989–90); *Muse of Fire* for Flute and Guitar (1990; N.Y., Feb. 1991); *Summer 1990*, trio for Violin, Cello, and Piano (1990; Philadelphia, March 23, 1992); *American Banquet, Versions of American Popular Song* for Guitar (1991); *Sonata-Aria* for Cello and Piano (1992; Houston, Jan. 25, 1993). **PIANO:** *Book of Contrapuntal Pieces* (1940–77); *Variations on an Original Theme* (1941); *12 Bagatelles* (1952; also as *Zodiac* for Orch., 1965); *Sonata-fantasia* (1956); *Bartókiana* (1959); *Nach Bach* (1966; also for Harpsichord); *Carnival Music* (1969); *Partita-variations* (1976); *4 Short Sonatas* (1984). **VOCAL:** *David, the Psalmist* for Tenor and Orch. (1954); *Blake Songs* for Soprano and 8 Instruments (1961); *Passions according to the 20th Century* for Solo Voices, Chorus, Jazz Quintet, Brass Ensemble, Percussion, Piano, and Tape (1967; withdrawn); *Tableaux* for Soprano, 2 Actors, Small Men's Chorus, and 12 Instruments (1968); *Sacred Song of Reconciliation* for Bass-baritone and Chamber Orch. (1970); also a cappella choruses; songs.

BIBL.: J. Buccheri, *An Approach to Twelve-tone Music: Articulation of Serial Pitch Units in Piano Works of Schoenberg, Webern, Krenek, Dallapiccola, and R.* (diss., Univ. of Rochester, 1975); C. Sams, *Solo Vocal Writing in Selected Works of Berio, Crumb, and R.* (diss., Univ. of Wash., 1975); J. Smith, *The String Quartets of G. R.* (diss., Eastman School of Music, 1976); J. Reise, "R. the Progressive," *Perspectives of New Music*, XIX (1980–81); J. Dixon, *G. R.: A Bio-Bibliographic Guide to His Life and Works* (Stuyvesant, N.Y., 1991).

Roche, Jerome (Lawrence Alexander), English musicologist; b. Cairo, May 22, 1942; d. Durham, June 2, 1994. He studied at St. John's College, Cambridge (B.A., 1962; Mus.B., 1963); received his Ph.D. from the Univ. of Cambridge in 1968 with the diss. *North Italian Liturgical Music in the Early 17th Century*. In 1967 he became a lecturer at the Univ. of Durham. He publ. the books *Palestrina* (London, 1972) and *The Madrigal* (London, 1972; 2nd ed., 1990); with his wife, Elizabeth, he brought out a useful reference source, *A Dictionary of Early Music from the Troubadours to Monteverdi* (London, 1981); also publ. *Lassus* (Oxford, 1982) and *North Italian Church Music in the Age of Monteverdi* (Oxford, 1984).

Rocherolle, Eugénie, American composer; b. New Orleans, Aug. 24, 1936. After piano studies in childhood, she pursued training in piano and composition at Sophie Newcomb College of Tulane Univ. She also received training from Boulanger in Paris. In addition to composing, she was also active as a pianist, teacher, and lyricist. Her compositions are unabashedly Romantic in nature. Among her works are *America, My Home* for Chorus and Concert Band (1976), for the U.S. Bicentennial, *The New Colossus* for Chorus and Concert Band (1986), for the 100th anniversary of the Statue of Liberty, various choral pieces, and much piano music.

Rockefeller, Martha Baird, American pianist and music patroness; b. Madera, Calif., March 15, 1895; d. N.Y., Jan. 24, 1971. She studied at Occidental College in Los Angeles and the New England Cons. of Music in Boston (graduated, 1917); received instruction in piano from Schnabel in Berlin. After touring with Dame Nellie Melba (1918), she appeared as a soloist with leading orchs. and as a recitalist until her retirement in 1931. In later years she devoted herself to musical philanthropy; after the death of her 3rd husband, John D. Rockefeller, Jr., she organized the Martha Baird Rockefeller Fund for Music (1962); by the time it was dissolved in 1982, it had dispensed grants of some $9,000,000 to individuals and organizations.

Rockmore, Clara, Russian-born American theremin player, sister of **Nadia Reisenberg**; b. Vilnius, March 9, 1911. She received piano lessons as a small child, and at the age of 4 entered the Imperial Cons. of Music in St. Petersburg (1915–17); subsequently settled in N.Y., where she studied violin with Auer (1925–28) and theremin with Leon Theremin, its inventor (1932–34). She thereafter devoted herself to a career as a theremin player; gave a public demonstration of the instrument (which, incidentally, plays without being touched) in a concert at N.Y.'s Town Hall on Oct. 30, 1934, which included a rendition of Franck's formidable Violin Sonata. She subsequently appeared as a soloist with major orchs. and as a recitalist. In 1977 Rockmore made a historically significant recording, *The Art of the Theremin—Clara Rockmore*. With the rekindling of interest in the instrument in the 1980s, she became something of a celebrity; at the instigation of filmmaker and theremin enthusiast Steve Martin, her ancient instrument was repaired by Robert Moog and subsequently appeared as the subject of a CBS-TV documentary program entitled *The Art of the Theremin*.

Rodan (real name, **Rosenblum**), **Mendi,** Romanian-born Israeli conductor; b. Iaşi, April 17, 1929. He studied in Bucharest at the Academy of Music (1945–47) and the Arts Inst. (1947–49), then conducted various ensembles in Romania. He settled in Israel (1960) and became a naturalized citizen (1961); was chief conductor of the Israel Broadcasting (later Jerusalem) Sym. Orch. (1963–72) and founder-conductor of the Jerusalem Chamber Orch. (1965–69), with which he toured Europe, the U.S., and the Far East; was also made a teacher (1962) and a prof. (1973) at Jerusalem's Rubin Academy of Music, where he later was director. He was music director of the Israel Sinfonietta in Beersheba (from 1977) and chief conductor of the Orchestre National de Belgique in Brussels (1983–89). In 1993 he became co-conductor of the Israel Phil. in Tel Aviv.

Rode, Wilhelm, German bass-baritone; b. Hannover, Feb. 17, 1887; d. Icking, near Munich, Sept. 2, 1959. He studied in Hannover. He made his operatic debut in 1908 as the Herald in *Lohengrin* in Erfurt; then sang in Bremerhaven (1912–14), Breslau (1914–21), and Stuttgart (1921–22). He was a leading member of the Bavarian State Opera in Munich (1922–30), the Vienna State Opera (1930–32), and the Deutsches Opernhaus in Berlin (1932–45), where he also served as Intendant (1935–45); also appeared at London's Covent Garden and in other European opera houses. A member of the Nazi party, he was compelled to give up his career at the close of World War II. He became best known for his roles in Wagner's operas.

Rodgers, Richard (Charles), celebrated American composer of popular music; b. Hammels Station, Long Island, N.Y., June 28, 1902; d. N.Y., Dec. 30, 1979. He began piano lessons when he was 6; studied at Columbia Univ. (1919–21) and at the Inst. of Musical Art in N.Y. (1921–23), receiving instruction in the latter from Krehbiel and Goetschius. He collaborated with the lyricist Lorenz Hart in a series of inspired and highly popular musical comedies: *The Girl Friend* (1926); *A Connecticut Yankee* (1927); *On Your Toes* (1936); *Babes in Arms* (1937); *I Married an Angel* (1938); *The Boys from Syracuse* (1942). After Hart's death in 1943, Rodgers became associated with Oscar Hammerstein II. Together they wrote the greatly acclaimed musical *Oklahoma!* (1943; Pulitzer Prize, 1944), followed by a number of no less successful productions: *Carousel* (1945); *Allegro* (1947); *South Pacific* (1949; Pulitzer Prize, 1950); *The King and I* (1951); *Me and Juliet* (1953); *Pipe Dream* (1955); *The Flower Drum Song* (1958); *The Sound of Music* (1959). After Hammerstein's death in 1960, Rodgers wrote his own lyrics for his next musical, *No Strings* (1962); then followed *Do I Hear a Waltz?* (1965) to the lyrics of Stephen Sondheim. His autobiography was publ. as *Musical Stages* (N.Y., 1975). See *The Rodgers and Hart Song Book* (N.Y., 1951) and H. Simon, ed., *The Rodgers and Hammerstein Song Book* (N.Y., 1958; 2nd ed., rev., 1968).

BIBL.: D. Taylor, *Some Enchanted Evenings: The Story of R. and Hammerstein* (N.Y., 1953); D. Ewen, *R. R.* (N.Y., 1957; 2nd ed., rev., 1963, as *With a Song in His Heart*); *R. R. Fact Book* (N.Y., 1965; new ed. with supplement, 1968); M. Kaye, *R. R.: A Comparative Analysis of His Songs with Hart and Hammerstein Lyrics* (diss., New York Univ., 1969); E. Mordden, *R. & Hammerstein* (N.Y., 1992).

Rodrigo, Joaquín, noted Spanish composer and teacher; b. Sagunto, Valencia, Nov. 22, 1901. He lost his sight as a child but revealed an innate talent for music and was sent to Paris, where he studied with Dukas at the Schola Cantorum; returned to Madrid in 1939, where the Manuel de Falla chair was created for him at the Univ. in 1947. His music is profoundly imbued with Spanish melorhythms; his *Concierto de Aranjuez* for Guitar and Orch. (1939) became famous.

WORKS: DRAMATIC: *Pavana real*, ballet (1955); *El hijo fingido*, zarzuela (1964); *La azuzena de Quito*, opera (1965). **ORCH.:** *Juglares* (1923); *Concierto de Aranjuez* for Guitar and Orch. (1939; Barcelona, Nov. 9, 1940); *Concierto heróico* for Piano and Orch. (1942; Lisbon, April 5, 1943); *Concierto de estío* for Violin and Orch. (1943; Lisbon, April 11, 1944); *Concierto in modo galante* for Cello and Orch. (Madrid, Nov. 4, 1949); *Concierto serenata* for Harp and Orch. (1952); *Fantasía para un gentilhombre* for Guitar and Orch. (1954); *Sones en la Giralda* for Harp and Orch. (1963); *Concierto Andaluz* for 4 Guitars (1967); *Concierto-madrigal* for 2 Guitars and Orch. (1968); *Dos danzas españoles* (1969); *Palillos y panderetas* (1982); *Concierto para una fiesta* for Guitar and Orch. (1982). **CHAMBER:** *Sonata Pimpante* for Violin and Piano (1966); *Sonata a la española* for Guitar (1969); *Pájaros de primavera* for Guitar (1972); piano pieces. **VOCAL:** *Cantico de San Francisco de Asis* for Chorus and Orch. (1986); choruses.

BIBL.: F. Sopeña, *J. R.* (Madrid, 1946; 2nd ed., rev., 1970); A. Iglesias, *J. R.: Su música para piano* (Madrid, 1965); V. Vaya Pia, *J. R.: Su vida y su obra* (Madrid, 1977); V. Kamhi de Rodrigo, *De la mano de J. R.: Historia de nuestra vida* (Madrid, 1986; Eng. tr., 1992, as *Hand in hand with J. R.: My Life at the Maestro's Side*); *90 aniversario de J. R.* (1992).

Rodríguez (Amador), Augusto (Alejandro), Puerto Rican conductor and composer; b. San Juan, Feb. 9, 1904. After studying literature at the Univ. of Puerto Rico, he pursued music training at Harvard Univ. with E.B. Hill, Piston, and Leichtentritt (1933–34). Returning to San Juan, he was on the faculty of the Univ. of Puerto Rico (1934–70); organized its chorus, which achieved a high degree of excellence; gave a concert with it in N.Y. in 1949. He publ. choral works, piano pieces, and songs.

Rodriguez, Robert Xavier, American composer; b. San Antonio, June 28, 1946. He studied with Hunter Johnson and Kent Kennan at the Univ. of Texas in Austin (B.M., 1967; M.M., 1969), Stevens and Dahl at the Univ. of Southern Calif. in Los Angeles (D.M.A., 1975), Druckman at the Berkshire Music Center in Tanglewood, and Boulanger in Paris; also attended master classes given by Maderna and Carter. He taught at the Univ. of Southern Calif. (1973–75) and at the Univ. of Texas in Dallas (from 1975); held a Guggenheim fellowship (1976); was composer-in-residence of the Dallas Sym. Orch. (1982–85).

WORKS: DRAMATIC: OPERAS: *Le Diable amoureux* (1978; orch. suite, 1978); *Suor Isabella* (1982; Boston, May 3, 1984); *Tango*, chamber opera (1985); *Monkey See, Monkey Do*, children's opera (1986); *Frida* (1990); *The Old Majestic* (1991). **BALLETS:** *Estampie* (1980); *Meta-4* (1993). **ORCH.:** *Adagio* for 7 Winds and Strings (1967); 3 piano concertos (1968; 1972; 1973–74); *Lyric Variations* for Oboe, 2 Horns, and Strings (1970); *Sinfonia concertante* for Saxophone, Harpsichord, and Chamber Orch. (1974); *Favola concertante* for Violin, Cello, and Strings (1975); *Frammenti musicali* for Flute or Violin and Strings (1978); *Favola Boccaccesca* (1979); *Oktoechoes*, concerto for Octet and Orch. (1983; Dallas, May 4, 1984); *Trunks: A Circus Story* for Narrator and Orch. (1983); *7 Deadly Sins* for Wind Ensemble and Percussion (1984); *A Colorful Symphony* for Narrator, Orch., and Optional Visual Effects, for children (1987; Indianapolis, May 3, 1988); *Invocation of Orpheus*, trumpet concerto (1989); *A Gathering of Angels*, bolero (1989); *Ursa: 4 Seasons* for Double Bass and Strings (San Antonio, Nov. 29, 1990); *Piñata* (1990); *Máscaras* for Cello and Orch. (1994). **CHAMBER:** 2 piano trios (1970, 1971); Sonata for Soprano Saxophone or Clarinet and Piano (1972); *Toccata* for Guitar Quartet (1975); *Variations* for Violin and Piano (1975); *Quodlibet on Medieval Tunes* for Instruments (1978); *Semi-suite* for Violin and Piano (1980–81; originally for Piano, 4-hands; also for Violin and Orch., or Violin, Clarinet, Piano, and Percussion, 1984); *Les Niais Amoureux* for Quartet (1989); *3 Lullabies* for Guitar (1993). **PIANO:** *For Piano I–II* (1972); *Serbelloni Birthday Rag* (1976; arranged for Orch., 1977); *Fantasia Lussuriosa* (1989). **VOCAL:** Cantata for Soprano, Chorus, and Orch. (1972); *Canto*, cantata for Soprano, Tenor, Piano, Cello, and Orch. (1973); *Transfigurationis mysteria* for 3 Solo Voices, Narrator, Chorus, and Orch. (1978); *Praline and Fudge* for Baritone and Piano, to texts from cookbooks (1979); *Adoración Ambulante*, folk mass for Tenor, Bass, Chorus, Children's Chorus, Mariachi Band, Dancers, Puppets, Slides, Fireworks, Orch., and Audience Participation (1994); *Scrooge*, concert scene from "A Christmas Carol" for Bass-baritone, Chorus, and Orch. (El Paso, Texas, Dec. 9, 1994).

Rodriguez, Santiago, talented Cuban-American pianist; b. Cardenas, Feb. 16, 1952. He settled in the U.S. when he was 8 and pursued training in New Orleans, at the Univ. of Texas, and at the Juilliard School in N.Y. He made his debut at age 9 with the New Orleans Phil.; in 1975 he won 1st prize at the Univ. of Maryland Piano Competition, and in 1981 shared 2nd prize at the Van Cliburn Piano Competition. In 1982 he was awarded an Avery Fisher Career Grant, and in 1986 was honored as the first recipient of the Shura Cherkassky Recital Award of N.Y.'s 92nd St. Y. Rodriguez has appeared widely as a soloist with orchs. and as a recitalist, both in the U.S. and abroad. He also taught at the Univ. of Maryland at College Park. He is a versatile virtuoso whose expansive and intriguing repertoire includes not only standard works but works by Busoni, Mrs. H.H.A. Beach, Castelnuovo-Tedesco, Hanson, Ginastera, Shchedrin, and others.

Rodzinski, Artur, eminent Polish-born American conductor; b. Spalato, Dalmatia, Jan. 1, 1892; d. Boston, Nov. 27, 1958. He studied jurisprudence at the Univ. of Vienna; at the same time, he took lessons in piano with Sauer, composition with Schreker, and conducting with Schalk. He made his conducting debut in Lwów in 1920; subsequently conducted at the Warsaw Opera. In 1926 he was appointed assistant conductor to Stokowski with the Philadelphia Orch.; concurrently he was head of the opera and orch. depts. at the Curtis Inst. of Music; in 1929 he was appointed conductor of the Los Angeles Phil.; after 4 seasons there, he was engaged as conductor of the Cleveland Orch., where he introduced the novel custom of presenting operas in concert form; on Jan. 31, 1935, he conducted the American premiere of Shostakovich's controversial opera *Lady Macbeth of the District of Mtzensk*. He became a naturalized American citizen in 1932. In 1943 he received his most prestigious appointment as conductor of the N.Y. Phil., but his independent character and temperamental ways of dealing with the management forced him to resign amid raging controversy in the middle of his 4th season (Feb. 3, 1947); almost immediately he was engaged as conductor of the Chicago Sym. Orch., but there, too, a conflict rapidly developed, and the management announced after a few months of the engagement that his contract would not be renewed, stating as a reason that his operatic ventures using the orch. were too costly. After these distressing American experiences, Rodzinski conducted mainly in Europe; in the autumn of 1958 he received an invitation to conduct at the Lyric Opera in Chicago, but after 3 performances of *Tristan und Isolde* (Nov. 1, 7, and 10), a heart ailment forced him to cancel his remaining appearances; he died in a Boston hospital.

BIBL.: H. Rodzinski, *Our Two Lives* (N.Y., 1976).

Roesgen-Champion, Marguerite, Swiss harpsichordist and composer; b. Geneva, Jan. 25, 1894; d. Paris, June 30, 1976. She studied composition with Bloch and Jaques-Dalcroze at the Geneva Cons., but devoted herself mainly to harpsichord playing, giving numerous recitals in Europe. Her own works are couched in the neo-Romantic vein; she wrote *Faunesques* for Orch. (Paris, 1929); *Concerto moderne* for Harpsichord and Orch. (Paris, Nov. 15, 1931, composer soloist); *Aquarelles*, symphonic suite (Paris, Nov. 26, 1933); Harp Concerto (Paris, March 28, 1954); 5 harpsichord concertos (1931–59), including No. 1, *Concerto moderne* (Paris, Nov. 15, 1931, composer soloist); *Concerto romantique* for Piano and Orch. (1961); a number of pieces for flute in combination with the harpsichord and other instruments; a curious piece for Piano, 4-hands, entitled *Spoutnik* (1971).

Rogalski, Theodor, Romanian conductor, teacher, and composer; b. Bucharest, April 11, 1901; d. Zürich, Feb. 2, 1954. He was a student of Gheorghe Cucu (theory), Castaldi (composition), and Cuclin (music history) at the Bucharest Cons. (1919–20), of Karg-Elert (conducting and composition) at the Leipzig Cons. (1920–23), and of d'Indy (composition) and Ravel (orchestration) in Paris (1924). Returning to Bucharest, he was conductor of the Radio Sym. Orch. (1930–51), and then of the Phil.: he also was prof. of orchestration at the Cons. (from 1950). In 1923 and 1926 he was awarded the Enesco Prize for composition. In 1953 he was made a Merited Artist by the Romanian government. His music was permeated by the spirit of Romanian folk melos, while his harmony and orchestration revealed coloristic infusions.

WORKS: BALLET: *Fresque antique* (1923). **ORCH.:** Rondo (1921); *2 Dansuri româneşti* (1926; Bucharest, Jan. 20, 1927); *2 Symphonic Sketches* (1929; Bucharest, May 11, 1930); *2 Capricii* (1932); *3 Dansuri româneşti* (1950; Bucharest, May 27, 1951). **CHAMBER:** *Crépuscule* for Violin and Piano (1922); *Frühlingsnacht* for 2 Violins and Viola (1922); String Quartet (1923); *Esquisse* for Violin and Piano (1923); *Sonet* for Violin and Piano (1924); *Porumbel* for Violin (1925); *La chef* for String Quartet (1928); piano pieces, including a Sonata (1919). **VOCAL:** Many songs with orch. or piano.

Rogatis, Pasqual de. See **De Rogatis, Pascual.**

Rogé, Pascal, French pianist; b. Paris, April 6, 1951. He entered the Paris Cons. at age 11 and made his debut as a soloist at the same age in Paris; his principal teacher was L. Descaves, and he graduated with premiers prix in piano and chamber music (1966); then studied with Julius Katchen (1966–69). In 1969 he made his London debut; after winning joint 1st prize in the Long-Thibaud Competition in Paris in 1971, he pursued a successful international career.

Roger-Ducasse, Jean (-Jules Aimable), French composer and teacher; b. Bordeaux, April 18, 1873; d. Le-Taillan-Médoc, near Bordeaux, July 19, 1954. He studied at the Paris Cons. with Fauré (composition), Pessard (harmony), Gédalge (counterpoint), and de Bériot. In 1902 he won the 2nd Prix de Rome for the cantata *Alcyone*. In 1909 he was appointed inspector of singing in the Paris schools; subsequently was a prof. of ensemble at the Paris Cons.; from 1935 to 1940, taught composition there; then retired to Bordeaux. His first work to be played in public was a *Petite suite* for Orch. (Paris, March 5, 1898). He adopted a pleasing style of Impressionism; his symphonic pieces enjoyed considerable success, without setting a mark for originality. His autobiography was publ. in *L'Écran des musiciens* (1930).

WORKS: DRAMATIC: *Orphée*, mimodrama (1913; St. Petersburg, Jan. 31, 1914); *Cantegril*, comic opera (1930; Paris, Feb. 9, 1931). **ORCH.:** *Variations plaisantes sur un thème grave* (Paris, Jan. 24, 1909); *Suite française* (1909); *Prélude d'un ballet*

(1910); *Le Joli Jeu de furet*, scherzo (1911); *Nocturne de printemps* (Paris, Feb. 14, 1920); *Symphonie sur la Cathédrale de Reims* (unfinished); *Le Petit Faune* (Bordeaux, May 22, 1954). **CHAMBER:** Piano Quartet (1899–1912); String Quartet (1900–1909). **VOCAL:** *Au Jardin de Marguerite* for Soloists, Chorus, and Orch. (1901–05); *Sarabande* for Voices and Orch. (1911); *Sur quelques vers de Virgile* for Chorus and Orch.; songs. **OTHER:** Pedagogical works.

BIBL.: L. Ceillier, *R.-D.* (Paris, 1920); *Catalogue de l'oeuvre de R.-D.* (Bordeaux, 1955).

Rogers, Bernard, distinguished American composer and pedagogue; b. N.Y., Feb. 4, 1893; d. Rochester, N.Y., May 24, 1968. He began piano lessons when he was 12; after leaving school at 15, he was employed in an architectural firm while training in architecture at Columbia Univ.; subsequently received instruction in theory from Hans van den Berg, composition from Farwell, and harmony and composition from Bloch in Cleveland; returning to N.Y., he continued his studies with Goetschius at the Inst. of Musical Art (1921); later held a Guggenheim fellowship (1927–29), which made it possible for him to train with Bridge in England and Boulanger in Paris. He first won recognition as a composer with his orch. work *To the Fallen* (1918; N.Y., Nov. 13, 1919), on the strength of which he received a Pulitzer Traveling Scholarship. He taught at the Cleveland Inst. of Music (1922–23), the Hartt School of Music in Hartford, Conn. (1926–27), and the Eastman School of Music in Rochester, N.Y. (1929–67), where he also served as chairman of the composition dept. In 1947 he was elected to membership in the National Inst. of Arts and Letters. He publ. a valuable manual, *The Art of Orchestration* (N.Y., 1951).

WORKS (all 1st perf. in Rochester, N.Y., unless otherwise given): **OPERAS:** *Deirdre* (1922); *The Marriage of Aude* (May 22, 1931); *The Warrior* (1944; N.Y., Jan. 11, 1947); *The Veil* (Bloomington, Ind., May 18, 1950); *The Nightingale* (1954). **ORCH.:** *To the Fallen* (1918; N.Y., Nov. 13, 1919); *The Faithful*, overture (1922); *Soliloquy No. 1* for Flute and Strings (1922) and *No. 2* for Bassoon and Strings (Oct. 18, 1938); *In the Gold Room* (1924); *Pastorale* for 11 Instruments (1924); *Fuji in the Sunset Glow* (1925); *Hamlet*, prelude (1925); 5 syms.: No. 1, *Adonais* (1926; April 29, 1927), No. 2 (1928; Oct. 24, 1930), No. 3, *On a Thanksgiving Song* (1936; Oct. 27, 1937), No. 4 (1940; May 4, 1948), and No. 5, *Africa* (1958; Cincinnati, Jan. 30, 1959); *3 Japanese Dances* (1933; May 3, 1934); *2 American Frescoes* (1934); *Once upon a Time*, 5 fairy tales for Small Orch. (April 4, 1935); *The Supper at Emmaus* (April 29, 1937); *Fantasy* for Flute, Viola, and Strings (1937; April 25, 1938); *The Song of the Nightingale*, suite (1939; Cincinnati, March 21, 1940); *The Colors of War* (Oct. 25, 1939); *The Dance of Salome* (April 25, 1940); *The Plains* for Small Orch. (1940; N.Y., May 3, 1941); *Invasion* (N.Y., Oct. 17, 1943); *Anzacs* (1944); *Elegy in Memory of Franklin D. Roosevelt* (1945; N.Y., April 11, 1946); *Characters from Hans Christian Andersen* for Small Orch. (April 28, 1945); *Amphitryon Overture* (1946; N.Y., March 10, 1947); *Elegy* for Small Orch. (1947); *The Silver World* for Small Orch. (1949); *The Colors of Youth* (1951); *Portrait* for Violin and Orch. (1952); *Fantasy* for Horn, Timpani, and Strings (1952; Feb. 20, 1955); *Dance Scenes* (Louisville, Oct. 28, 1953); *Variations on a Song by Mussorgsky* (1960); *New Japanese Dances* (1961); *Allegory* for Small Orch. (1961); *Apparitions* (1967). **CHAMBER:** *Mood* for Piano Trio (1918); 2 string quartets (1918, 1925); *The Silver World* for Flute, Oboe, and Strings (1950); String Trio (1953); *Ballade* for Bassoon, Viola, and Piano (1959); Violin Sonata (1962). **VOCAL: CHORUS AND ORCH.:** *The Raising of Lazarus* (1928); *The Exodus* (1931); *The Passion*, oratorio (1942; Cincinnati, May 12, 1944); *A Letter from Pete*, cantata (1947); *The Prophet Isaiah*, cantata (1950); *The Light of Man*, oratorio (1964). **SOLO VOICE AND ORCH.:** *Arab Love Songs* for Soprano and Orch. (1927); *Horse Opera* for Narrator and Orch. (1948); *Leaves from the Tale of Pinocchio* for Narrator and Orch. (1951); *Psalm LXVIII* for Baritone and Orch. (1951); *The Musicians of Bremen* for Narrator and 13 Instruments (1958); *Aladdin* for Narrator and Wind Ensemble (1965). **OTHER VOCAL:** *Psalm XCIX* for Chorus and Organ (1945); *Response to Silent Prayer* for Chorus (1945); *Hear My Prayer, O Lord* for Soprano, Chorus, and Organ (1955); *Psalm XVIII* for Men's Voices and Piano (1963); *Psalm LXXXIX* for Baritone, Chorus, and Piano (1963); *Faery Song* for Women's Voices (1965); *Dirge for 2 Veterans* for Chorus and Piano (1967); *Psalm CXIV* for Chorus and Piano (1968).

BIBL.: H. Hanson, "B. R.," *Modern Music*, XXII (1945); D. Diamond, "B. R.," *Musical Quarterly* (April 1947); S. Dershan, *Orchestration in the Orchestral Works of B. R.* (diss., Univ. of Rochester, 1975); D. Intili, *Text-Music Relationships in the Large Choral Works of B. R.* (diss., Case Western Reserve Univ., 1977); F. Koch, *Reflections on Composing: Four American Composers: Elwell, Shepherd, R., Cowell* (Pittsburgh, 1983).

Rogers, Nigel (David), English tenor, conductor, and teacher; b. Wellington, Shropshire, March 21, 1935. He studied at King's College, Cambridge (1953–56), in Rome (1957), in Milan (1958–59), and with Hüsch at the Munich Hochschule für Musik (1959–64). He became a singer with the Studio der frühen Musik in Munich in 1961 and later acquired a fine reputation as an interpreter of Baroque music. He was a prof. of singing at the Royal College of Music in London (from 1978) and founded the vocal ensemble Chiaroscuro for the performance of Italian Baroque music (1979).

Rogg, Lionel, eminent Swiss organist, harpsichordist, pedagogue, and composer; b. Geneva, April 21, 1936. He studied at the Geneva Cons. with Charles Chaix (harmony, counterpoint, and composition), Pierre Segond (organ; 1st prize, 1956), and André Perret and Nikita Magaloff (piano; 1st prize, 1957), and then with André Marchal in Paris. From 1960 he was a prof. at the Geneva Cons. After performing all of Bach's organ works in a series of recitals at Victoria Hall in Geneva in 1961, he toured throughout the world as an organ and harpsichord virtuoso. He also gave master classes in keyboard interpretation and publ. a course on organ improvisation. Rogg's exhaustive repertoire ranges from Bach and Buxtehude to Hindemith and Ligeti. He is especially known as a master of improvisation. Among his compositions are an Organ Concerto (1992) and numerous solo organ pieces; piano music; vocal scores, including a Missa Breves for Chorus and Orch. and a cantata.

Rogister, Jean (François Toussaint), Belgian violist, pedagogue, and composer; b. Liège, Oct. 25, 1879; d. there, March 20, 1964. He studied violin, viola, horn, and composition at the Liège Cons.; was head of the viola classes there (1900–1945) and at the Brussels Cons. (1945–48); played in various orchs.; was also founder of the Liège Quartet (1925), with which he toured extensively. His style of composition followed the precepts of Cesar Franck, but upon occasion he introduced into his music some modernistic impressionistic sonorities.

WORKS: LYRIC DRAMA: *Lorsque minuit sonna* (1930). **ORCH.:** *Fantaisie concertante* for Viola and Orch. (1910); Viola Concerto (1914); Cello Concerto (1917); Trombone Concerto (1919); *Destin* (1919); *La Fiancée du lutin* (1920); *Poème* for Violin and Orch. (1920); *Nuit d'Avril* (1921); *Paysage* (1923); 3 syms.: No. 1 (1927), No. 2, *Symphonie wallonne* (1931–32), and No. 3 for String Quartet and Orch. (1942–43); *Fantaisie burlesque sur un thème populaire* (1928); *La Lune et les peupliers* (1932); *Impression de mai* for Violin and Orch. (1935); Suite for Flute and Chamber Orch. (1949); *Jeux symphoniques* (1952); *Hommage à César Franck* (1955); *Adagio* for 2 String Ensembles (1960). **CHAMBER:** 8 string quartets (1902, 1914, 1921, 1926, 1927, 1928, 1931, 1940); *Symphonie intime* for String Quartet, Double Bass, Flute, Clarinet, and Bassoon (1929); Quintet for Harpsichrod, 2 Quintons, Viola d'Amore, and Viola da Gamba (1934); *Esquisse dramatique* for String Quartet (1935); Wind Quintet (1947). **VOCAL:** *The Bells*, oratorio for Soprano and 8 Instruments, after Edgar Allan Poe (1924); *Requiem* for Chorus and Orch. (1944; Liège, March 24, 1946); choruses; songs.

BIBL.: J. Servais, *J. R.: Un Musicien du coeur* (1972).

Rögner, Heinz, German conductor; b. Leipzig, Jan. 16, 1929. He studied piano with Hugo Steuer, viola with Gutschlicht, and conducting with Egon Bölsche at the Hochschule für Musik in Leipzig. He was a conductor at the German National Theater in Weimar (1951–54); then led the opera school at the Hochschule für Musik in Leipzig (1954–58). From 1958 to 1962 he was chief conductor of the Great Radio Orch. in Leipzig; from 1962 to 1973 he was Generalmusikdirektor of the State Opera in East Berlin. In 1973 he became chief conductor of the (East) Berlin Radio Sym. Orch.; also appeared as a guest conductor in Europe. He served as music director of the Yomiuri Nippon Sym. Orch. in Tokyo (1985–91).

Rogowski, Ludomir (Michal), Polish composer and conductor; b. Lublin, Oct. 3, 1881; d. Dubrovnik, March 14, 1954. He was a student of Noskowski (composition) and Mlynarski (conducting) at the Warsaw Cons., and then of Nikisch and Riemann in Leipzig. In 1909 he went to Vilnius as director of the Organ School. He also founded the Vilnius Sym. Orch. in 1910. From 1912 to 1914 he was a theater conductor in Warsaw. In 1926 he settled in Dubrovnik. In 1938 he was awarded the Polish State Music Prize.

WORKS: DRAMATIC: OPERAS: *Tamara* (1918); *Un Grand Chagrin de la petite Ondine* (1919); *La Sérénade inutile* (1921); *Królewicz Marko* (1930). **BALLETS:** *Bajka* (1922); *Kupala* (1925). **ORCH.:** *Images ensoleillées* (1918); *Villafranca* (1919); 7 syms. (1921, 1936, 1940, 1943, 1947, 1949, 1951); *Les Saisons* (1933); *Les Sourires* (1933); *Poéme du travail* (1936); *Fantômes* (1937); 4 rhapsodies on Slavonic themes (1945); *Dubrovnik Impressions* (1950). **OTHER:** 2 string quartets; choral arrangements of Slavonic songs.

Roig, Gonzalo, Cuban conductor and composer; b. Havana, July 20, 1890; d. there, June 13, 1970. He played violin in theater orchs. In 1922 he organized the Orquesta Sinfónica de la Habana. He wrote zarzuelas, among which *Cecilia Valdés* enjoyed considerable success. In 1912 he wrote the song *Quiereme mucho*, which became a popular hit.

Rojo Olalla, Casiano, Spanish organist, choirmaster, and writer on music; b. Hacinas, Aug. 5, 1877; d. Burgos, Dec. 4, 1931. He studied at the Santo Domingo de Silos monastery in Burgos, where he became a Benedictine monk (1896); later pursued studies with Pothier in Belgium. He was active as an organist and choirmaster; became an authority on Gregorian chant; publ. a valuable manual, *Método de canto gregoriano* (Valladolid, 1906); also wrote *Manual de canto gregoriano* (Silos, 1908); *Cantus Lamentationum* (Bilbao, 1917); *Antiphonarium Mozarabicum de la Catedral de León* (with G. Prado; León, 1928); and *El Canto mozárabe* (with G. Prado; Barcelona, 1929).

Rokseth, Yvonne (née **Rihouët**), eminent French musicologist; b. Maisons-Laffitte, near Paris, July 17, 1890; d. Strasbourg, Aug. 23, 1948. She studied at the Paris Cons., with d'Indy and Roussel at the Schola Cantorum, and with Pirro at the Sorbonne; received her doctorat és lettres in 1930 with the diss. *La Musique d'orgue au XVe siècle et au début du XVIe* (publ. in Paris, 1930). She was a librarian at the Cons. and the Bibliothèque Nationale (1934–37); then was made maître de conférences at the Univ. of Strasbourg (1937); after serving in the Resistance during World War II, she rejoined its faculty as prof. of musicology. She ed. the valuable *Polyphonies du XIIIe siècle: Le Manuscrit H 196 de la Faculté de médecine de Montpellier* (4 vols., Paris, 1935–39); also publ. a biography of Grieg (Paris, 1933) and other vols.

Roland, Claude-Robert, Belgian composer, organist, conductor, and teacher; b. Pont-de-Loup, Dec. 19, 1935. He studied composition at the Music Academy in Châtelet and at the conservatories of Mons, Liège, Paris, and Brussels with Froidebise, C. Schmit, R. Bernier, Messiaen, and Defossez; also took a course in conducting with Scherchen. He was an organist in churches in various Belgian cities (1955–67); was director of the Music Academy at Montignies-le-Tilleul (1966–75); in 1972, was appointed to the staff of the Brussels Cons.

WORKS: ORCH.: *Recherche* (1956); *Indicatif 1* for 12 Strings (1957); *Sinfonia scolastica pour les bouffons de la Reine* (1961); *Serenade* for Chamber Orch. (1961); Organ Concerto (1963); *Rossignolet du bois* (1971). **CHAMBER:** *Sonance* for String Quartet (1956); *2 sonances* for Piano (1956, 1960); *Sonance* for Clavichord (1959); *Chansons et reveries* for Violin and Piano (1962); *Ballade* for Violin and Piano (1966); *Prélude, Fugue et Rondo a 5* for Wind Quintet (1967); *Sonancelle* for Guitar (1967); *Prelude, Fugue et Commentaires* for 4 Clarinets (1971); *Faits-divers* for Horn and Piano (1981); *Thriller* for Trumpet and Piano (1985); *De profundis* for Tuba and Piano (1985).

Roland-Manuel (real name, **Roland Alexis Manuel Lévy**), French composer and writer on music; b. Paris, March 22, 1891; d. there, Nov. 1, 1966. He was a pupil of Roussel and d'Indy; also studied privately with Ravel. In 1947 he became a prof. at the Paris Cons. In his compositions, he adopted the French neo-Classical style, close to Roussel's manner; however, he became best known as a perspicacious critic, publishing, in Paris, 3 vols. on Ravel: *Maurice Ravel et son oeuvre* (1914; 2nd ed., rev., 1926; Eng. tr., 1941), *Maurice Ravel et son oeuvre dramatique* (1928), and *À la gloire Maurice Ravel* (1938; 2nd ed., 1948; Eng. tr., 1947); also monographs on Satie (1916), Honegger (1925) and Falla (1930).

WORKS: DRAMATIC: *Isabelle et Pantalon*, opéra-bouffe (Paris, Dec. 11, 1922); *Le Diable amoureux*, light opera (1929); *L'Écran des jeunes filles*, ballet (Paris, May 16, 1929); *Elvire*, ballet on themes of Scarlatti (Paris, Feb. 8, 1937). **OTHER:** *Jeanne d'Arc*, oratorio (1937); Piano Concerto (1938); *Cantique de la sagesse* for Chorus and Orch. (1951).

Rolandi, Gianna, gifted American soprano; b. N.Y., Aug. 16, 1952. Her first contact with opera came through her mother, herself a singer, and by the age of 15 she had already become acquainted with much of the operatic repertoire. She then enrolled at the Curtis Inst. of Music in Philadelphia (B.M., 1975). While still a student there, she was contracted to sing at the N.Y. City Opera, with which she made an impressive debut as Olympia in *Les Contes d'Hoffmann* (Sept. 11, 1975). On Dec. 26, 1979, she made her Metropolitan Opera debut in N.Y. as Sophie in *Der Rosenkavalier*. In 1981 she made her European debut at the Glyndebourne Festival singing Zerbinetta. In 1982 she sang the title role in a televised production of *Lucia di Lammermoor* with the N.Y. City Opera, receiving flattering notices from the press. She scored an outstanding success as Bianca in Rossini's *Bianca e Falliero* at its U.S. premiere at the Greater Miami Opera in 1987. In 1989 she appeared as Cimarosa's Curiazio at the Rome Opera. In 1993 she sang Despina in Chicago. She was married to **Andrew Davis**.

Roldán, Amadeo, Cuban violinist, conductor, and composer; b. Paris (of Cuban parents), July 12, 1900; d. Havana, March 2, 1939. He studied violin at the Madrid Cons. with Fernández Bordas, graduating in 1916; won the Sarasate Violin Prize; subsequently studied composition with Conrado del Campo in Madrid and with Pedro Sanjuán. In 1921 he settled in Havana; in 1924, became concertmaster of the Orquesta Filarmónica; in 1925, assistant conductor; in 1932, conductor. He was prof. of composition at the Cons. (from 1935). In his works, he employed with signal success the melorhythms of Afro-Cuban popular music; as a mulatto, he had an innate understanding of these elements.

WORKS: BALLET: *La Rebambaramba*, employing a number of Cuban percussion instruments (1927–28; suite, Havana, Aug. 12, 1928). **ORCH.:** *Obertura sobre têmas cubanos* (Havana, Nov. 29, 1925); *El Milagro de Anaquillé* (Havana, Sept. 22, 1929); *3 Toques* for Chamber Orch. (1931). **CHAMBER:** *Rítmica* Nos. 1–4 for Piano and Wind Quintet, and Nos. 5 and 6 for Percussion Ensemble. **VOCAL:** *Danza negra* for Voice and 7 Instruments (1929); *Motivos de son* for Voice and 9 Instruments (1930).

Rolfe Johnson, Anthony, English tenor; b. Tackley, Nov. 5, 1940. He was a student of Ellis Keeler at the Guildhall School of Music in London, and later of Vera Rozsa. He gained experience singing in the chorus and appearing in small roles at the Glyndebourne Festivals between 1972 and 1976. In 1973 he made his formal operatic debut with the English Opera Group in *Iolanta.* In 1978 he made his first appearance with the English National Opera in London as Don Ottavio. He sang Tamino with the Welsh National Opera in Cardiff in 1979. In 1983 he appeared as Aschenbach at Glasgow's Scottish Opera. In 1987 he made his first appearance at the Salzburg Festival in Schmidt's *Das Buch mit sieben Siegeln.* On Dec. 22, 1988, he made his debut at London's Covent Garden as Jupiter in Handel's *Semele.* In 1990 he returned to the Salzburg Festival to sing his first operatic role there, Monteverdi's Orfeo. From 1990 he served as director of singing at the Britten-Pears School in Snape, but also continued his singing career. In 1994 he appeared as Peter Grimes in the reopening of the Glyndebourne Festival and sang Aschenbach at the Metropolitan Opera in N.Y. As a concert artist, he received many engagements with leading orchs. in Europe and North America.

Roll, Michael, English pianist; b. Leeds, July 17, 1946. He received his training from Fanny Waterman. In 1958 he made his formal debut as soloist in the Schumann Concerto under Sir Malcolm Sargent's direction at London's Royal Festival Hall. After winning 1st prize in the Leeds competition in 1963, he made regular appearances as soloist with the principal British orchs.; later toured with British orchs. in Europe and the Far East. In 1974 he made his U.S. debut with Colin Davis and the Boston Sym. Orch. In subsequent years, he appeared not only as a soloist with various orchs. but as a recitalist. In 1992 he made his N.Y. recital debut. He was married to **Juliana Markova**.

Rolland, Romain, famous French author and musicologist; b. Clamecy, Nièvre, Jan. 29, 1866; d. Vézelay, Yonne, Dec. 30, 1944. He was educated in Paris at the École Normale Supérieure (1886–89), the École de Rome (1889–91), and the Sorbonne (doctorat és lettres, 1895, with the diss. *Les Origines du théâtre lyrique moderne: L'Histoire de l'opéra en Europe avant Lully et Scarlatti*; publ. in Paris, 1895; 4th ed., 1936). He then was a prof. of music history at the École Normale Supérieure until becoming the first prof. of music history at the Sorbonne (1903); was also director of the École des Hautes Sociales (1903–09). In 1900 he organized the first international congress for the history of music in Paris, and read a paper on *Les Musiciens italiens en France sous Mazarin et "l'Orfeo" de Luigi Rossi* (publ. 1901); with J. Combarieu, he ed. the transactions and the papers read as *Documents, mémoires et voeux* (1901). In 1901 he founded, with J. Combarieu (ed.), P. Aubry, M. Emmanuel, L. Laloy, and himself as principal contributors, the fortnightly *Revue d'Histoire et Critique Musicales.* From 1913 he resided in Switzerland, but in 1938 returned to France and took up his residence at Vézelay.

Rolland's writings exhibit sound scholarship, broad sympathy, keen analytical power, well-balanced judgment, and intimate acquaintance with the musical milieu of his time. The book by which he is most widely known is *Jean-Christophe,* a musical novel remarkable for its blending of historical accuracy, psychological and aesthetic speculation, subtle psychological analysis, and romantic interest; it won him the Nobel Prize in literature (1915). The 1st vol. was publ. in 1905, the last (10th) in 1912 (Eng. tr., N.Y., 1910–13). Rolland's other works include *Paris als Musikstadt* (1904; in Strauss's series *Die Musik*; rewritten and publ. in French as *Le Renouveau in Musiciens d'aujourd'hui*); *Beethoven* (Paris, 1903; 3rd ed., 1927, as *La Vie de Beethoven*; Eng. tr., 1969); *La Vie de Haendel* (Paris, 1906; 2nd ed., 1910; Eng. tr., 1916; rev. and enl. by F. Raugel, 1974); *Voyage musical au pays du passé* (1920; Eng. tr., 1922); *Beethoven: Les Grandes Époques créatrices* (4 vols., Paris, 1928–45; Eng. tr., 1964); *Goethe et Beethoven* (1930; Eng. tr., 1931); *Beethoven: Le Chant de la Résurrection* (1937; on the *Missa solemnis* and the last sonatas); essays in various journals he collected and publ. in 2 vols. as *Musiciens d'autrefois* (1908; 6th ed., 1919; Eng. tr., 1915) and *Musiciens d'aujourd'hui* (1908; 8th ed., 1947; Eng. tr., 1914); D. Ewen, ed., *Essays on Music* (a selection from some of the above books; N.Y., 1948).

BIBL.: P. Seippel, *R. R.: L'Homme et l'oeuvre* (Paris, 1913); S. Zweig, *R. R.: Der Mann und das Werk* (Frankfurt am Main, 1921; Eng. tr., N.Y., 1921); J. Bonnerot, *R. R., Sa vie, son oeuvre* (Paris, 1921); E. Lerch, *R. R. und die Erneuerung der Gesinnung* (Munich, 1926); M. Lob, *Un Grand Bourguignon, R. R.* (Auxerre, 1927); C. Sénéchal, *R. R.* (Paris, 1933); M. Doisy, *R. R.* (Brussels, 1945); R. Argos, *R. R.* (Paris, 1950); W. Starr, *A Critical Bibliography of the Published Writings of R. R.* (Evanston, Ill., 1950); J. Robichez, *R. R.* (Paris, 1961); E. Bondeville, *R. R. à la recherche de l'homme dans la création artistique* (Paris, 1966).

Roller, Alfred, influential Austrian stage designer and painter; b. Vienna, Oct. 2, 1864; d. there, June 21, 1935. He studied painting at the Vienna Academy. Roller became closely associated with Mahler at the Vienna Court Opera. With Gustav Klimt, Egon Schiele, Oskar Kokoschka et al., he founded the Vienna Sezession, a group of artists whose ideals were at variance with the established orthodoxy of the day. His ideal as a stage designer was to integrate the elements of space, color, and light in an effort to harmonize stage decors with the music and stage action. His slogan, "space, not pictures," embodied his attempt to discard naturalism in opera productions in favor of a new symbolism. In his production of *Tristan und Isolde* (1903), which inaugurated his 30-year tenure as chief designer at the Vienna Opera, he allowed a different color to symbolize the mood of each act. The subtle lighting effects he achieved prompted one reviewer to declare "here is the conception of the music of light." His Wagner productions, which continued with the first 2 parts of the *Ring,* set new standards throughout Europe. They also had a strong influence on later productions at Bayreuth. In his production of *Don Giovanni* (1905), he introduced his "Roller towers," focal points in a stylized stage picture which, remaining on stage throughout the opera, served different purposes as the action progressed. He was also active in Berlin, Salzburg, and Bayrueth. He designed the Dresden premiere productions of *Elektra* (1909) and *Der Rosenkavalier* (1911). His subtle and harmonious use of color was also in evidence for the premiere production of *Die Frau ohne Schatten* (Vienna, 1919). Roller taught at the Vienna School of Arts and Crafts for 25 years.

Rollin, Jean, French composer; b. Paris, Aug. 3, 1906; d. Bayeux, Calvados, Aug. 30, 1977. He studied composition at the Paris Cons. with N. Gallon, and musicology with Pirro and Masson. His works included Concerto for Piano and Strings (1947); Violin Concerto (1950); Double Bass Concerto (1951); 2 syms. (1953, 1958); *Gringoué,* opera (1965); chamber music; songs.

Rolnick, Neil (Burton), American composer and teacher; b. Dallas, Oct. 22, 1947. After studying English literature at Harvard Univ. (B.A., 1969), he studied composition with Adams and Imbrie at the San Francisco Cons. of Music (1973–74) and with Felciano and Wilson at the Univ. of Calif. at Berkeley (M.A., 1976; Ph.D., 1980); he also studied with Milhaud at the Aspen (Colo.) Music School and received training in computer music from Chowning at Stanford Univ. (summer, 1976). He pursued research at IRCAM in Paris (1977–79). Rolnick has performed with various ensembles, including Dogs of Desire, a "multimedia orch. of the future," which he co-founded, in 1994, with David Alan Miller. He has received numerous awards, grants, and fellowships, including a Fulbright fellowship (1989) for travel to Yugoslavia and a Rockefeller Foundation grant (1994) for extended residence at the Bellagio Center in Italy; in 1995 he worked in Japan on a fellowship from the Asian Cultural Council. From 1981 he taught at the Rensselaer Polytechnic Inst. in Troy, N.Y. In 1994, with Paul Lansky and Joel Chadabe, he founded the Electronic Music Foundation in Albany, N.Y.

WORKS: *Massachusetts F* for String Quartet, Percussion, and Piano (1974); *Empty Mirror* for Tape (1975); *Hell's Bells* for Tape (1975); *Newsical Muse*, live electronic music for radio (Berkeley, KPFA-FM Radio, June 4, 1975); *SF Hack* for Tape and Percussion (1975; in collaboration with M. Haller; also for Video); *Memory* for Tape (1976); *Thank You, Thelonius* for Trumpet, Trombone, Cello, Marimba, and Cimbalom (1976); *Video Songs* for Tape (1976); *A Po-sy, a Po-sy* for Tenor, Violin, Double Bass, Percussion, and Tape, to texts by Charles Olson (1976; rev. 1981); *Blue Monday* for Soprano, Flute, Clarinet, Saxophone, Violin, Cello, and Percussion (1977; rev. for 13 Instruments and Synthesizer, 1983); *Ever-livin' Rhythm* for Percussion and Tape (1977); *Wondrous Love* for Trombone and Tape (1979); *Blowing* for Flute (1980); *No Strings* for 12 Winds, 2 Pianos, 4 Percussion, and Organ (1980); *Lao Tzu's Blues* for Tenor and Piano (1981); *Loopy* for Synthesizer (1982); *Real Time* for Synthesizer and 13 Instruments (1983); *The Original Child Bomb Song* for Soprano and Synthesizer (1983); *A La Mode* for 8 Instruments and Synthesizer (1985); *The Master Speed* for Chorus, Instruments, and Synthesizer (1985); *What Is The Use?*, film music (1985); *A Robert Johnson Sampler* for Computer (1987); *Melting Pot*, video work (1987; in collaboration with J. Sturgeon); *Vocal Chords* for Jazz Singer, Digital Delay, and Sampler (1988); *Drones and Dances* for Chamber Orch. and Synthesizer (1988); *Balkanization* for Computer (1988); *I Like It* for 2 Singers and Computer (1989); *ReRebong* for Gamelan and Computer (1989); *Macedonian Air Drumming* for Computer with Air Drum MIDI Controllers (1990); *Sanctus*, electronic film score (1990); *ElectriCity* for Flute, Clarinet, Violin, Cello, Synthesizer, Sampler, and Digital Processing (1991); *Nerve Us* for Computer (1992); *Requiem Songs for the Victims of Nationalism* for 2 Singers, Percussion, and Computer (1993); *Heat: The Rise and Fall of Isabella Rico* for 2 Singers, Amplified Chamber Orch., and Video (1994); *An Irish Peace* for Variable Instruments (1994); *HomeGame* for 2 Actors, 5 Instruments, Interactive Video, and Computer-mediated Story Generation (1994–95).

Rolón, José, Mexican composer and teacher; b. Ciudad Gusmán, Jalisco, June 22, 1883; d. Mexico City, Feb. 3, 1945. He studied in Paris with Moszkowski, and later with Boulanger and Dukas. In Mexico he was active as a teacher. He composed a symphonic suite, *Zapotlán* (1895; reorchestrated 1925; Mexico City, Nov. 4, 1932); Sym. (1918–19); symphonic poem, *Cuauhtémoc* (1929; Mexico City, Jan. 10, 1930); Piano Concerto (1935; Mexico City, Sept. 4, 1942); chamber music; many effective piano pieces; songs.

Roman, Stella (real name, **Florica Vierica Alma Stela Blasu**), Romanian-American soprano; b. Cluj, March 25, 1904; d. N.Y., Feb. 12, 1992. She was a student of Pfeiffer in Cluj, Cosma, Vulpescu, and Pessione in Bucharest, Narducci and Poli-Randaccio in Milan, and Baldassare-Tedeschi and Ricci in Rome. In 1932 she made her operatic debut in Piacenza. In 1940 she made her first appearance at Milan's La Scala as the Empress in *Die Frau ohne Schatten*. On Jan. 1, 1941, she made her Metropolitan Opera debut in N.Y. as Aida. She remained on its roster until 1950, becoming best known for such roles as Gioconda, Amelia, Leonora in *Il Trovatore*, Desdemona, and Tosca.

Romberg, Sigmund, famous Hungarian-born American composer; b. Nagykanizsa, July 29, 1887; d. N.Y., Nov. 9, 1951. He studied at the Univ. of Bucharest and in Vienna (with Heüberger). In 1909 he went to the U.S. as an engineer; later became a naturalized American citizen; settled in N.Y. in 1913 and devoted himself to composing for the theater. He composed over 70 operettas, including *The Midnight Girl* (Feb. 23, 1914); *The Blue Paradise* (with E. Eysler; N.Y., Aug. 5, 1915); *Maytime* (N.Y., Aug. 16, 1917); *Blossom Time* (on Schubert's melodies; N.Y., Sept. 29, 1921); *The Rose of Stamboul* (March 7, 1922); *The Student Prince* (N.Y., Dec. 2, 1924); *The Desert Song* (N.Y., Nov. 30, 1926); *My Maryland* (N.Y., Sept. 12, 1927); *The New Moon* (Sept. 19, 1928); *Up in Central Park* (N.Y., Jan. 27, 1945).

BIBL.: E. Arnold, *Deep in My Heart* (a biography in the form of a novel, N.Y., 1949); J. Koegel, *The Film Operettas of S. R.* (thesis, Calif. State Univ., 1984).

Romero, family of famous Spanish-American guitarists constituting a quartet known as Los Romeros:

Celedonio Romero (b. Málaga, March 2, 1918; d. San Diego, May 8, 1996) pursued a career as a soloist in Spain; he served as mentor to each of his 3 sons, **Celin** (b. Málaga, Nov. 23, 1940), **Pepe** (b. Málaga, March 8, 1944), and **Angel** (b. Málaga, Aug. 17, 1946); they eventually appeared together as a guitar quartet, playing engagements throughout Spain. The family emigrated to the U.S. in 1958 and made their first tour of the country in 1961; billed as "the royal family of the guitar," they toured with great success worldwide. In addition to making their own arrangements and transcriptions, they commissioned works from various composers, including Joaquín Rodrigo and Federico Moreno Torroba.

Ronald, Sir Landon (real name, **Landon Ronald Russell**), English pianist, conductor, and composer; b. London, June 7, 1873; d. there, Aug. 14, 1938. He was a son of the composer Henry Russell and brother of the impresario Henry Russell. He entered the Royal College of Music in London, where he studied composition with Parry and also attended the classes of Stanford and Parratt. He first embarked on a concert career as a pianist, but soon turned to conducting light opera and summer sym. concerts; was conductor of the New Sym. Orch. of London (1909–14) and of the Scottish Orch. in Glasgow (1916–20). He served as principal of the Guildhall School of Music and Drama in London (1910–38). He was knighted in 1922. He composed an operetta, *A Capital Joke*; a ballet, *Britannia's Realm* (1902; for the coronation of King Edward VII); and a scenic spectacle, *Entente cordiale* (1904; to celebrate the triple alliance of Russia, France, and England); about 300 songs. He publ. 2 autobiographical books: *Variations on a Personal Theme* (London, 1922) and *Myself and Others* (London, 1931).

Roncaglia, Gino, Italian musicologist and composer; b. Modena, May 7, 1883; d. there, Nov. 27, 1968. He studied composition with Sinigaglia; devoted himself to musical biography.

WRITINGS: *Giuseppe Verdi* (Naples, 1914; 2nd ed., rev., 1940, as *L'ascensione creatice di Giuseppe Verdi*; 3rd ed., 1951); *La Rivoluzione musicale italiana* (Milan, 1928); *Rossini l'olimpico: Vita e opere* (Milan, 1946; 2nd ed., 1953); *Invito alla musica* (Milan, 1946; 4th ed., 1958); *Invito all' opera* (Milan, 1949; 4th ed., 1958); *La Cappella musicale del Duomo di Modena* (Florence, 1957); *Galleria verdiana: Studi e figure* (Milan, 1959).

Ronga, Luigi, eminent Italian musicologist; b. Turin, June 19, 1901; d. Rome, Sept. 11, 1993. After obtaining an arts degree from the Univ. of Turin, he went to Dresden to pursue his training in musicology. In 1930 he received his libera docenza. In 1926 he became a prof. at the Palermo Cons. In 1930 he settled in Rome, where he was a teacher at the Accademia di Santa Cecilia and at the Pontifico Istituto di Musica Sacra. He then was a lecturer (1938–50) and subsequently a prof. (1950–71) at the Univ. of Rome. He was ed. of *Rassegna musicale* (1928–29) and *Rivista musicale italiana* (1954–55).

WRITINGS: *Per la critica wagneriana* (Turin, 1928); *Gerolamo Frescobaldi, organista vaticano, nella storia della musica strumentale* (Turin, 1930); *Lezioni di storia della musica* (2 vols., Rome, 1933, 1935; new ed., 1991); *Rossini* (Florence, 1939); *Lineamenti del romanticismo musicale* (Rome, 1943); *La musica nell'antichità* (Rome, 1945); *Claude Debussy e l'impressionismo musicale* (Rome, 1946); *Il dramma musicale di Richard Wagner* (Rome, 1947); *Arte e gusto nella musica, dell'ars nova a Debussy* (Milan, 1956); *Bach, Mozart, Beethoven: Tre problemi critici* (Venice, 1956); *The Meeting of Poetry and Music* (N.Y., 1956); *La musica nell'età barocca* (Rome, 1959); *Il linguaggio musicale romantico* (Rome, 1960); *L'esperienza storica della musica* (Bari, 1960); *Introduzione a "La Diana schernita" di Cornacchioli* (Rome, 1961); *La musica europa nella* *seconda metà dell'Ottocento* (Rome, 1961); *Storia della musica* (2 vols., Rome, 1962–63).

BIBL.: *Scritti in onore di L. R.* (Milan and Naples, 1973).

Ronnefeld, Peter, German conductor and composer; b. Dresden, Jan. 26, 1935; d. Kiel, Aug. 6, 1965. He studied with Blacher in Berlin and Messiaen in Paris. After winning the Hilversum conducting competition in 1955, he was assistant conductor at the Vienna State Opera (1958–61); served as chief conductor at the Theater der Stadt Bonn (1961–63); then was Generalmusikdirektor in Kiel from 1963 until his death. As a conductor, he specialized in modern music, but he also excelled in the Romantic repertoire; his own opera, *Die Ameise* (Düsseldorf, Oct. 21, 1961), had a fine reception. He also wrote a chamber opera, *Nachtausgabe* (Salzburg, 1956); 2 ballets, *Peter Schlemihl* (1955–56) and *Die Spirale* (1961); Concertino for Flute, Clarinet, Horn, Bassoon, and Strings (1950); *Sinfonie '52* (1952); *Rondo* for Orch. (1954); *2 Episodes* for Chamber Orch. (1956); cantata, *Quartar* (1958); chamber music; songs.

Rooley, Anthony, English lutenist and teacher; b. Leeds, June 10, 1944. He received training in guitar at the Royal Academy of Music in London (1965–68), but was self-taught as a lutenist. From 1969 to 1971 he taught at the Royal Academy of Music, and later gave courses in Japan, Italy, and Switzerland as well as in England. With James Tyler, he founded the Consort of Musicke in 1969, an ensemble devoted to the performance of Renaissance music. From 1972 he was its sole director, and led it on many tours of Europe, the Middle East, and North America. In later years, he also was active as a stage director of early music and was co-director of the early music recording label Musica Oscura. He publ. the vols. *A New Varietie of Lute Lessons* (1975), *The Penguin Book of Early Music* (1976), and *Performance: Revealing the Orpheus Within* (1990).

Roos, Robert de, Dutch composer; b. The Hague, March 10, 1907; d. there, March 18, 1976. He was a student of Wagenaar (composition) at the Royal Cons. of Music in The Hague. After further studies in Paris (1926–34) with Koechlin, Roland-Manuel, and Milhaud (composition), Philipp (piano), and Monteux (conducting), he completed his training in his homeland with Dresden. He was a cultural attaché at the Dutch embassy in Paris (1947–56), and then was first secretary for press and cultural affairs for the Dutch embassies in Caracas (1957–62), London (1962–67), and Buenos Aires (1967).

WORKS: DRAMATIC: *Kaartspel* (Card Game), ballet (1930); *Landelijke Comedie* (Pastoral Comedy), dance pantomime (1937–39); incidental music. **ORCH.:** *5 Études* for Piano and Small Orch. (1929); *Mouvement symphonique* (1930); Violin Concertino (1939); *Danses* for Flute and Small Orch. (1940); Viola Concerto (1941–42); *Sinfonietta* (1943); 3 sinfonias: No. 1, *Sinfonia romantica: Museum-Symphonie* for Chamber Orch. (1943), No. 2 (1952), and No. 3, *Sinfonia in 2 moti* for Strings (1968); Piano Concerto (1943–44); *Quo Vadis*, suite (1947); *Variations sérieuses sur un thème ingénu* (1947); 2 violin concertos (1949–50; 1956–58); *Suggestioni* (1961); *Composizioni* (1962); *Musica* for Violins, Cellos, and Double Basses (1971); *Rapsodie e Danza* for 2 Flutes and Orch. (1972–73). **CHAMBER:** Sextet for Piano and Winds (1935); 7 string quartets (1941; 1942; 1944–45; 1945–49; 1951; 1969–70; *Quartettino*, 1970); Sonata for Solo Violin (1943); *Introduction, Adagio, and Allegro* for 2 Violins (1945); Violin Sonata (1946); *Capriccio* for Clarinet and Piano (1952); *Distrazioni* for Violin and Piano (1953); *3 pezzi senza nome* for Piano Quartet (1958); Trio for 2 Violins and Cello (1965); *4 per 2* for Oboe and Viola (1966); *Incontri* for Wind Quintet (1966); *Incidenze* for Flute, Cello or Viola da Gamba, and Harpsichord (1966–67); Piano Trio (1968); *2 moti lenti* for 2 Violins and Cello (1970); *4 pezzi* for Wind Trio (1970–71). **VOCAL:** Chamber oratorio (1928); *Lyrische suite* for Chorus and Small Orch. (1938); *Adam in ballingschap* for 2 Narrators, 2 Flutes, 2 Horns, and Strings (1944); *De getemde Mars* for Chorus and Orch. (1948); *Postrema Verba*, cantata for Baritone, Chorus, and 25 Instruments (1969); *2 Songs* for Baritone and Instruments (1971); *3 Romantic Songs* for Soprano and Orch. (1975).

Roosenschoon, Hans, Dutch-born South African composer; b. The Hague, Dec. 17, 1952. He was taken in infancy to Pretoria, where he studied at the Cons. (1969–71; 1974–75). Following further training with Paul Patterson at the Royal Academy of Music in London (1977–78), he returned to South Africa and pursued studies at the Univs. of Stellenbosch (M.Mus., 1989) and Cape Town (D.Mus., 1991). In 1976 he joined the staff of the South African Broadcasting Corp. in Johannesburg, later serving it in Cape Town as production manager for music from 1980 to 1995. In his output, Roosenschoon has demonstrated an adept handling of various styles, both traditional and contemporary. In some of his works, he explores the use of African elements and electronics.

WORKS: ORCH.: *Tablo* (1976); Sinfonietta (1976); *Katutura* (1977); *Palette* for Strings (1977; Johannesburg, April 24, 1978); *'n Saaier het uitgegaan om te saai . . .* (1978); *Mosaiek* (1978); *Ghomma* (1980; Johannesburg, July 2, 1983); *Ikonografie* (1983; Cape Town, Nov. 2, 1989); *Anagram* (1983; Cape Town, May 29, 1984); *Timbila* for Chopi Xylophone Ensemble and Orch. (Grahamstown, July 12, 1985); *Architectura* (Johannesburg, Oct. 8, 1986); *Horizon, Night-Sky, and Landscape* for Strings (Bloemfontein, June 18, 1987); *Chronicles* (Grahamstown, July 10, 1987); *Clouds Clearing* for Strings (1987; Cape Town, July 16, 1994); *Mantis*, ballet suite (Johannesburg, Oct. 22, 1988); *Circle of Light* (Cape Town, March 9, 1989); *Die Sonnevanger* (1990; Cape Town, Sept. 11, 1992); *The Magic Marimba* (Cape Town, Oct. 10, 1991); *do-re-mi-fabriek* (Johannesburg, Nov. 29, 1992); Trombone Concerto (1994–95). **CHAMBER:** Suite for Oboe and Piano (1973); *Bepeinsing* for Cello and Piano (1973); *Toccatino* for Piano Quartet (1973); *Makietie* for Brass Quintet (London, Dec. 1, 1978); String Quartet (1995). **KEYBOARD: PIANO:** *Drie Klavierstuck* (1972); *Goggaboek* (1972); Sonatina (1974; Johannesburg, May 13, 1977); *Credo* (1975; Johannesburg, May 13, 1977); *Fingerprints* (Johannesburg, Nov. 1, 1989). **ORGAN:** Double Fugue (1975); Chorale Prelude (1978; Durban, Aug. 5, 1979); Chorale Prelude (1978; Durban, Aug. 5, 1979). **VOCAL:** *Ekstase* for Chorus and Orch. (1975); *Cantata on Psalm 8* for Chorus and Orch. (1976; Johannesburg, July 7, 1977); *Ars Poetica* for Baritone, Double Chorus, and Orch. (Johannesburg, Oct. 9, 1979); *Psalm 23* for Chorus (1979); *Firebowl* for Chorus (1980; Windhoek, May 21, 1986); *Does the noise in my head bother you?* for 2 Choruses, Pop Group, and Orch. (Cape Town, July 29, 1988); *Prayer of St. Richard: Thanks be to Thee* for Chorus (Johannesburg, Nov. 18, 1990); *Miserere* for Men's Chorus (1991); *Ko, lat ons sing* for Double Chorus (Stellenbosch, June 18, 1993); *Mbira* for Chorus (1994). **ELECTRONIC:** *Kataklisme* (1980; Johannesburg, July 4, 1983); *Helios* (1984; Grahamstown, July 6, 1985); *If Music Be* (1984; Cape Town, Nov. 21, 1985); *Narcissus* (1985).

Roosevelt, J(oseph) Willard, American composer, pianist, and teacher; b. Madrid, Jan. 16, 1918. He was the grandson of President Theodore Roosevelt. He studied at Harvard College (1936–38), at the Longy School of Music in Cambridge, Mass. (1936–38; 1940–41), with Boulanger in Paris and Gargenville (1938–39), at the N.Y. College of Music (composition and piano diplomas, 1947), and at the Hartt College of Music in Hartford, Conn. (B.Mus., 1959; M.Mus., 1960). In addition to his appearances as a pianist, he lectured on music at Columbia Univ. (1961), Fairleigh-Dickinson Univ. (1964–67), and the N.Y. College of Music (1967–68).

WORKS: OPERA: *And the Walls Came Tumbling Down* (1974–76). **ORCH.:** Piano Concerto (1948; rev. 1983); Cello Concerto (1963); *Amistad, homenaje al gran Morel-Campos*, overture (1965). **BAND:** *The Twinkle in His Eye*, in memory of the composer's father, Kermit Roosevelt (1979; rev. 1993). **CHAMBER:** *Song and Dance Suite* for Oboe, Clarinet, and Viola (1991); Suite for Viola (1992); *Fanfare for Sagamore Hill* for Brass Quintet (Oyster Bay, N.Y., July 4, 1993); Trio for Clarinet, Cello, and Piano (1993). **PIANO:** *Theme and Variations*

(1948; rev. version, Long Island, N.Y., March 28, 1995, composer pianist). **VOCAL:** *War Is Kind* for Soloists and Small Orch. (1976; rev. for Soprano, Narrator, Oboe, String Quartet, and Piano, 1992; N.Y., Jan. 1993); *Hopkins Suite* for Baritone, Speaker, and Piano, after Gerard Manley Hopkins (1991); solo songs.

Rootham, Cyril (Bradley), English organist, teacher, and composer; b. Bristol, Oct. 5, 1875; d. Cambridge, March 18, 1938. He studied music with his father, Daniel Rootham (1837–1922); won classical and musical scholarships at St. John's College, Cambridge (B.A., 1897; Mus.B., 1900; M.A., 1901; Mus.Doc., 1910); finished at the Royal College of Music in London under Stanford, Parratt, and Barton. He was organist (from 1901) and a lecturer (from 1913) at St. John's College, Cambridge; also conductor of the Univ. Musical Soc. there (1912–36). His career as a composer was very much bound to the musical life of Cambridge. He brought out his opera, *The 2 Sisters*, there on Feb. 14, 1922; also wrote *For the Fallen* for Chorus and Orch. (1919) and *Brown Earth* (London, March 14, 1923). His 2nd Sym., *Revelation* (with a choral ending), was performed posthumously by the BBC, March 17, 1939. Other works include *Pan*, rhapsody for Orch. (1912); String Quintet (1909); String Quartet (1914); Septet for Viola, Flute, Oboe, Clarinet, Bassoon, Horn, and Harp (1930); Piano Trio (1931).

Ropartz, Joseph Guy (Marie), French conductor, teacher, and composer; b. Guingamp, Côtes-du-Nord, June 15, 1864; d. Lanloup-par-Plouha, Côtes-du-Nord, Nov. 22, 1955. He entered the Paris Cons. as a pupil of Dubois and Massenet; then took lessons in organ and composition from Franck, who remained his chief influence in composition. From 1894 to 1919 he was director of the Cons. and conductor of the sym. concerts at Nancy; from 1919 to 1929 he conducted the Municipal Orch. and was director of the Cons. in Strasbourg.

WORKS: DRAMATIC: OPERA: *Le Pays* (1910; Nancy, Feb. 1, 1912). **BALLETS:** *Prélude dominical et 6 pièces à donner pour chaque jour de la semaine* (1929); *L'Indiscret* (1931). **INCIDENTAL MUSIC TO:** *Pêcheur d'Islande* (1891); *Oedipe à Colonne* (1914). **ORCH.:** *La Cloche des morts* (1887); *Les Landes* (1888); *Marche de Fête* (1888); *5 pièces brèves* (1889); *Carnaval* (1889); *Sérénade* (1892); *Dimanche breton* (1893); 5 syms.: No. 1 (1894), No. 2 (1900), No. 3 for Chorus and Orch. (1905), No. 4 (1910), and No. 5 (1944); *À Marie endormie* (1912); *La Chasse du prince Arthur* (1912); *Soir sur les Chaumes* (1913); *Divertissement* (1915); *Rapsodie* for Cello and Orch. (Paris, Nov. 3, 1928); *Concerto for Orchestra* (1930); *Sérénade champêtre* (1932; Paris, Feb. 24, 1934); *Bourrées bourbonnaises* (1939); *Petite symphonie* for Chamber Orch. (1943). **CHAMBER:** 6 string quartets (1893, 1912, 1925, 1934, 1940, 1951); 2 cello sonatas (1904, 1918); 3 violin sonatas (1907, 1917, 1927); Piano Trio (1918); String Trio (1935). **PIANO:** *Dans l'ombre de la montagne* (1913); *Musiques au jardin* (1917); *Croquis d'été* (1918); *Croquis d'automne* (1929); *Jeunes filles* (1929). **VOCAL:** 5 motets (1900); *Requiem* for Soloists, Chorus, and Orch. (Paris, April 7, 1939); *De Profundis* for Solo Voice, Chorus, and Orch. (1942); masses; songs.

BIBL.: F. Lamy, *J. G.-R., l'homme et l'oeuvre* (Paris, 1948); L. Kornprobst, *J. G.-R.* (Strasbourg, 1949); *Livre du centenaire de J. G.-R.* (Paris, 1966).

Rorem, Ned, brilliant American composer, pianist, and writer; b. Richmond, Ind., Oct. 23, 1923. His father, C. Rufus Rorem, was a medical economist, and his mother, Gladys Miller Rorem, was a civil rights activist. Following piano lessons as a youth, he entered the American Cons. in Chicago in 1938 to study harmony with Sowerby. After further training with Nolte at Northwestern Univ. (1940–42) and Scalero at the Curtis Inst. of Music in Philadelphia (1942–44), he went to N.Y. and received private lessons in orchestration from Virgil Thomson (1944) and then pursued training in composition with Wagenaar at the Juilliard School of Music (B.S., 1946; M.S., 1948). During the summers of 1946 and 1947, he studied with Copland at the Berkshire Music Center in Tanglewood. In 1949 he went to Paris, where he rapidly absorbed French musical culture and mastered the French language. After a sojourn in Morocco (1949–51), he lived in Paris until 1957, where he found a patroness in Vicomtesse Noailles and moved in the circle of modern French composers. In 1951 he received a Fulbright fellowship and in 1957 a Guggenheim fellowship. From 1959 to 1961 he was composer-in-residence at the State Univ. of N.Y. at Buffalo. In 1965 he became a prof. of composition at the Univ. of Utah, where he later was composer-in-residence (until 1967). He received an award from the National Inst. of Arts and Letters in 1968. In 1971 and 1975 he received ASCAP-Deems Taylor awards for his outstanding achievements as a writer. In 1976 he won the Pulitzer Prize in Music for his *Air Music* for Orch. In 1978 he received a 2nd Guggenheim fellowship. In 1980 he became a teacher of composition at the Curtis Inst. of Music. In 1980, 1982, 1985, and 1990 he served as composer-in-residence at the Santa Fe Chamber Music Festival. Rorem is one of America's most distinguished and original compositional craftsmen. A born linguist, he has a natural feeling for vocal line and for prosody of text. He is without question one of the finest composers of art songs America has produced. An elegant stylist in French as well as in English, he has publ. various books recounting with gracious insouciance his encounters in Paris and N.Y.

WORKS: DRAMATIC: OPERAS: *Cain and Abel* (1946); *A Childhood Miracle* (1952; N.Y., May 10, 1955); *The Robbers* (1956; N.Y., April 14, 1958); *Miss Julie* (N.Y., Nov. 4, 1965; rev. 1978; N.Y., April 5, 1979); *3 Sisters Who Are Not Sisters* (1968; Philadelphia, July 24, 1971); *Bertha* (1968; N.Y., Nov. 26, 1973); *Fables*, 5 short operas (1970; Martin, Tenn., May 21, 1971); *Hearing* (1976; N.Y., March 15, 1977; arranged from a song cycle, 1966). **MUSICAL COMEDY:** *The Ticklish Acrobat* (1958). **BALLETS:** *Lost in Fear* (1945); *Death of the Black Knight* (1948); *Ballet for Jerry* (1951); *Melos* (1951); *Dorian Gray* (1952); *Early Voyagers* (1959); *Excursions* (1965). Also incidental music. **ORCH.:** *Overture for G.I.'s* for Band (1944); 3 piano concertos: No. 1 (1948; withdrawn), No. 2 (1950), and No. 3, *Piano Concerto in 6 Movements* (1969; Pittsburgh, Dec. 3, 1970); Overture (1949); 3 syms.: No. 1 (1950), No. 2 (La Jolla, Calif., Aug. 5, 1956), and No. 3 (1958; N.Y., April 16, 1959); *Design* (1953; Louisville, May 29, 1955); *Sinfonia* for Wind Orch. (Pittsburgh, July 14, 1957); *Eagles* (1958; Philadelphia, Oct. 23, 1959); *Pilgrims* for Strings (1958; N.Y., Jan. 30, 1959); *Ideas* (1961); *Lions (A Dream)* (1963; N.Y., Oct. 28, 1965); *Water Music* for Clarinet, Violin, and Orch. (1966; Oakland, Calif., April 9, 1967); *Air Music* (1974; Cincinnati, Dec. 5, 1975); *Assembly and Fall* (Raleigh, N.C., Oct. 11, 1975); *Sunday Morning* (1977; Saratoga, N.Y., Aug. 25, 1978); *Remembering Tommy* for Cello, Piano, and Orch. (1979; Cincinnati, Nov. 13, 1981); Organ Concerto (Portland, Maine, March 19, 1985); String Sym. (Atlanta, Oct. 31, 1985); Violin Concerto (Springfield, Mass., March 30, 1985); *Frolic*, fanfare (Houston, April 12, 1986); *A Quaker Reader* for Chamber Orch. (N.Y., Oct. 9, 1988; orchestration of 8 of 11 pieces from the organ works, 1976); *Fantasy and Polka* (1988; Evian, France, May 20, 1989); Concerto for Piano, Left hand, and Orch. (1991; Philadelphia, Feb. 4, 1993); English Horn Concerto (1992; N.Y., Jan. 27, 1994); *Triptych*, 3 pieces for Chamber Orch. (Bexley, Ohio, Oct. 4, 1993). **CHAMBER:** *Concertino da Camera* for Harpsichord and 7 Instruments (1947; Minneapolis, Oct. 10, 1993); 3 string quartets (1947, withdrawn; 1950; 1991); *Mountain Song* for Flute and Piano (1949); Violin Sonata (1949); *3 Slow Pieces* for Cello and Piano (1950, 1959, 1970; N.Y., Oct. 8, 1977); *11 Studies* for 11 Players (Buffalo, May 17, 1960); Trio for Flute, Cello, and Piano (1960); *Lovers* for Harpsichord, Oboe, Celli, and Percussion (N.Y., Dec. 15, 1964); *Day Music* for Violin and Piano (1971; Ames, Iowa, Oct. 15, 1972); *Night Music* for Violin and Piano (1972; Washington, D.C., Jan. 12, 1973); *Solemn Prelude*, fanfare for Brass (N.Y., May 1973); *Book of Hours* for Flute and Harp (1975; N.Y., Feb. 29, 1976); *Sky Music* for Harp (Albuquerque, June 1976); *Romeo and Juliet* for Flute and Guitar (1977; N.Y., March 1, 1978); *After Reading*

Shakespeare for Cello (1980; N.Y., March 15, 1981); Suite for Guitar (Cuyahoga Falls, Ohio, July 25, 1980); *Winter Pages*, quintet for Clarinet, Bassoon, Violin, Cello, and Piano (1981; N.Y., Feb. 14, 1982); *Dances* for Cello and Piano (1983; Detroit, May 5, 1984); *Picnic on the Marne*, 7 waltzes for Alto Saxophone and Piano (N.Y., Feb. 14, 1984); *The End of Summer* for Clarinet, Violin, and Piano (1985; Bombay, March 26, 1986); *Scenes from Childhood*, septet for Oboe, Horn, Piano, and String Quartet (Santa Fe, Aug. 11, 1985); *Bright Music* for Flute, 2 Violins, Cello, and Piano (1987; Bridgehampton, N.Y., Aug. 6, 1988); *Fanfare and Flourish* for 2 Trumpets, 2 Trombones, and Organ (N.Y., Oct. 16, 1988); *Diversions* for Brass Quintet (1989; Nantucket, Mass., July 11, 1990); *Spring Music* for Violin, Cello, and Piano (1990; N.Y., Feb. 8, 1991). **KEYBOARD: PIANO:** Sonata for Piano, 4-hands (1943); 3 sonatas (1948, 1949, 1954); *A Quiet Afternoon* (1948); *Toccata* (1948); *Barcarolles* (1949); Suite for 2 Pianos (1949); *Sicilienne* for 2 Pianos (1950); *Burlesque* (1955); *Slow Waltz* (1958); *8 Etudes* (1975; Washington, D.C., March 13, 1976); *Song and Dance* (1986; College Park, Md., July 12, 1987); *For Shirley* for Piano, 4-hands (1989). **ORGAN:** *Fantasy and Toccata* (1946); *Pastorale* (1950); *A Quaker Reader* (1976; N.Y., Feb. 2, 1977; 8 movements orchestrated for Chamber Orch., 1988); *Views from the Oldest House* (1981; Washington, D.C., June 29, 1982); *Organbook I* (N.Y., Oct. 30, 1989), *II* (1989; Nantucket, Mass., July 7, 1990) and *III* (1989; Nantucket, Mass., July 7, 1990). **HARPSICHORD:** *Spiders* (1968; Waterloo, Ontario, July 23, 1969). **VOCAL:** *The 70th Psalm* for Chorus and Wind Ensemble (Washington, D.C., Aug. 1943); *The Long Home* for Chorus and Orch. (1946); *Mourning Scene from Samuel* for Voice and String Quartet (1947); *A Sermon on Miracles* for Voice, Chorus, and Strings (Boston, Nov. 30, 1947); *6 Irish Poems* for Voice and Orch. (1950); *The Poet's Requiem* for Soprano, Chorus, and Orch. (1955; N.Y., Feb. 15, 1957); *Miracles of Christmas* for Chorus and Organ or Piano (1959); *King Midas*, cantata for Voice(s) and Piano (1961; N.Y., March 11, 1962); *2 Psalms and a Proverb* for Chorus and 5 Strings (1962); *Lift Up Your Heads (The Ascension)* for Chorus, Wind Ensemble, and Timpani (1963; Washington, D.C., May 7, 1964); *Laudemus Tempus Actum* for Chorus and Orch. or Piano (1964); *Letters from Paris* for Chorus and Small Orch. (1966; Ann Arbor, April 25, 1969); *Prosper for the Votive Mass of the Holy Spirit* for Chorus and Organ (1966); *Sun* for Soprano and Orch. (1966; N.Y., July 1, 1967); *Praises for the Nativity* for 4 Soloists, Chorus, and Organ (1970); *Ariel* for Soprano, Clarinet, and Piano (Washington, D.C., Nov. 26, 1971); *Little Prayers* for Soprano, Baritone, Chorus, and Orch. (1973; Sioux City, Iowa, April 20, 1974); *Missa Brevis* for 4 Soloists and Chorus (1973; Cleveland, June 17, 1974); *Serenade on 5 English Poems* for Voice, Violin, Viola, and Piano (1975; Akron, May 23, 1976); *The Santa Fe Songs* for Medium Voice, Violin, Viola, Cello, and Piano (Santa Fe, July 27, 1980); *After Long Silence* for Voice, Oboe, and String Orch. (Miami, June 11, 1982); *A Whitman Cantata* for Men's Chorus, 12 Brass, and Timpani (N.Y., Sept. 11, 1983); *An American Oratorio* for Tenor, Chorus, and Orch. (1984; Pittsburgh, Jan. 4, 1985); *Pilgrim Strangers* for 6 Men's Voices (N.Y., Nov. 16, 1984); *Homer*, 3 scenes from *The Iliad*, for Chorus and 8 Instruments (1986; Lancaster, Pa., April 12, 1987); *The Death of Moses* for Chorus and Organ (1987; N.Y., Jan. 29, 1988); *The Schuyler Songs* for Voice and Orch. (1987; Fargo, N.Dak., April 23, 1988); *Te Deum* for Chorus, 2 Trumpets, 2 Trombones, and Organ (Indianapolis, July 19, 1987); *Goodbye My Fancy*, oratorio for Alto, Baritone, Chorus, and Orch. (1988; Chicago, Nov. 8, 1990); *The Auden Poems* for Voice, Violin, Cello, and Piano (1989; Santa Fe, July 29, 1990); *Swords and Plowshares* for 4 Soloists and Orch. (1990; Boston, Nov. 14, 1991); *Songs of Sadness* for Voice, Guitar, Cello, and Clarinet (N.Y., Oct. 30, 1994); *Present Laughter* for Chorus, 4 Brasses, and Piano (1995); numerous other choral pieces, both sacred and secular; song cycles; solo songs.

WRITINGS (all publ. in N.Y.): *The Paris Diary of Ned Rorem* (1966; reprint, 1983, with *The New York Diary*, as *The Paris and New York Diaries*); *The New York Diary* (1967; reprint, 1983, with *The Paris Diary of Ned Rorem*, as *The Paris and New York Diaries*); *Music from the Inside Out* (1967); *Music and People* (1968); *Critical Affairs: A Composer's Journal* (1970); *Pure Contraption: A Composer's Essays* (1973); *The Final Diary, 1961–1972* (1974; reprint, 1983, as *The Later Diaries of Ned Rorem*); *An Absolute Gift: A New Diary* (1977); *Setting the Tone: Essays and a Diary* (1983); *The Nantucket Diary of Ned Rorem, 1973–1985* (1987); *Settling the Score: Essays on Music* (1988); *Knowing When to Stop: A Memoir* (1994).

BIBL.: A. McDonald, *N. R.: A Bio-Bibliography* (Westport, Conn., 1989).

Ros-Marbá, Antoni, Spanish conductor; b. Barcelona, April 2, 1937. He studied at the Barcelona Cons., and later with Celibidache at the Accademia Musicale Chigiana in Siena and Martinon in Düsseldorf. After making his debut in Barcelona (1962), he conducted in Europe, the U.S., Mexico, and Israel. He was conductor of the Orquesta Sinfónica de Radio Televisión Española in Madrid (1966–68) and of the Orquesta Ciudad de Barcelona (1967–78). He was chief conductor of the Orquesta Nacional de España in Madrid (1979–81); served as principal conductor of the Netherlands Chamber Orch. (1979–85) and again as conductor of the Orquesta Ciudad de Barcelona (1981–86). In 1989 he became music director of the Teatro Real in Madrid.

Rosand, Aaron, gifted American violinist and pedagogue; b. Hammond, Ind., March 15, 1927. A child prodigy, he made his formal debut at age 9 in a recital at Chicago's Civic Opera House, sharing the occasion with Jan Peerce, who was also making his Chicago debut. After studies with P. Marinus Paulsen (1935–39) and Leon Sametini (1940–44), he completed his training with Zimbalist at the Curtis Inst. of Music in Philadelphia (1944–48). He made his N.Y. debut in a Town Hall recital (1948); following his European debut in Copenhagen (1955), he pursued an international career as a virtuoso. He taught at the Curtis Inst. of Music (from 1981). A charismatic performer, blessed with a singing tone supported by an extraordinary technique, he established himself as a champion of the Romantic repertoire. In addition to the standard literature, he has consistently sought out rarely heard compositions by Spohr, Godard, Wieniawski, Lalo, Vieuxtemps, and many others for performance at his concerts.

Rosbaud, Hans, eminent Austrian conductor; b. Graz, July 22, 1895; d. Lugano, Dec. 29, 1962. He studied at the Hoch Cons. in Frankfurt am Main. He was director of the Hochschule für Musik in Mainz (1921–30); also conducted the City Orch. there; served as 1st Kapellmeister of the Frankfurt am Main Radio and of the Museumgesellschaft concerts (1928–37); then was Generalmusikdirektor in Münster (1937–41) and in Strasbourg (1941–44); subsequently was appointed Generalmusikdirektor of the Munich Phil. (1945). In 1948 he became chief conductor of the Sym. Orch. of the Southwest Radio in Baden-Baden, and in 1957, music director of the Tonhalle Orch. in Zürich. He particularly distinguished himself as a conductor of modern works. He conducted the first performance of Schoenberg's *Moses und Aron* (concert perf., Hamburg, 1954); also conducted its first stage performance (Zürich, 1957).

BIBL.: J. Evans, *H. R.: A Bio-Bibliography* (N.Y., 1992).

Rose, Bernard (William George), English organist, conductor, musicologist, and composer; b. Little Hallingbury, Hertfordshire, May 9, 1916. He studied with Alcock at the Royal College of Music in London (1933–35); subsequently was an organ scholar at St. Catharine's College, Cambridge, where his principal mentors were Middleton and Dent (B.A., 1938; Mus.B., 1939). He then was organist (1939–57), teacher (1946–55), and lecturer (1955–81) at Queen's College, Oxford; was also made a supernumerary Fellow (1949) and an official Fellow (1954) there, obtaining his D.Mus. (1955). He served as organist, Informator choristarum, and Fellow at Magdalen College, Oxford (1957–81), where he also was vice-president (1973–75). Throughout his career he was active as a conductor, being mainly known for his choral performances. He was president of the Royal College of Organists (1974–76). In 1980 he was made an Officer of the Order of the British Empire. He prepared numerous eds. of English works ranging from the 16th to the 18th century; also composed a number of sacred works.

Rose, Jerome, noted American pianist and teacher; b. Los Angeles, Aug. 12, 1938. He was a pupil of Adolf Baller at the San Francisco Cons. (1952–56), making his debut at the age of 15 with the San Francisco Sym. Orch.; studied piano and chamber music with Shure at the Mannes College of Music in N.Y. (B.S., 1960; M.S., 1961); also with Serkin at the Marlboro (Vt.) School of Music (1956, 1965). In 1961 he captured 1st prize at the Busoni Competition in Bolzano, and then pursued an international career. In 1981 he organized the International Festival of the Romantics in London. In 1986 he organized the Franz Liszt Celebration in Washington, D.C., and was also awarded the Franz Liszt Medal by the Hungarian government. He was artist-in-residence at Bowling Green (Ohio) State Univ. (from 1963); also visiting artist-in-residence at the Univ. of Mich. in Ann Arbor (1984–85). Rose has won special praise for his performances of the Romantic repertoire; in addition to his compelling readings of Liszt, he gives fine interpretations of Beethoven, Schübert, Schumann, and Chopin. He is pianist-author of the film *For the Young Virtuoso: A Piano Masterclass with Jerome Rose* (1987).

Rose, Leonard (Joseph), eminent American cellist and pedagogue; b. Washington, D.C., July 27, 1918; d. White Plains, N.Y., Nov. 16, 1984. He began to study the cello at age 10; enrolled at the Miami Cons. when he was 11, and continued his training with Walter Grossman; then went to N.Y. to study with his cousin, Frank Miller; subsequently received a scholarship to the Curtis Inst. of Music in Philadelphia, where he completed his studies with Felix Salmond (1934–38). He was assistant 1st cellist of the NBC Sym. Orch. in N.Y. (1938–39); then was 1st cellist of the Cleveland Orch. (1939–43), and also served as head of the cello depts. at the Cleveland Inst. of Music and the Oberlin (Ohio) Cons. In 1943 he became 1st cellist of the N.Y. Phil.; appeared at his concerto debut with it at Carnegie Hall on Jan. 29, 1944; resigned his post in 1951 and embarked upon a brilliant career as a virtuoso of the 1st rank in appearances as a soloist with the world's great orchs.; also gave recitals and appeared in numerous chamber music settings, later serving as a member of the renowned Istomin-Stern-Rose Trio (from 1961). He taught at the Juilliard School of Music in N.Y. (1947–51; 1962–84) and at the Curtis Inst. of Music (1951–62). Among his notable pupils were Stephen Kates, Lynn Harrell, and Yo-Yo Ma.

Rösel, Peter, outstanding German pianist and teacher; b. Dresden, Feb. 2, 1945. He began training in his youth. In 1963 he won 2nd prize in the International Schumann Competition in Zwickau; he was then chosen by the German Democratic Republic's Ministry of Culture for further training at the Moscow Cons., where he studied with Dmitri Bashkirov and Lev Oborin, graduating in 1969. In 1978 he made a highly successful tour of the U.S. as piano soloist with the Gewandhaus Orch. of Leipzig. He became a prof. at the Dresden Hochschule für Musik in 1985. Apart from a brilliant technique, Rosel has a Romantic sensitivity characteristic of the Russian mode of instrumental playing; his repertoire is comprehensive, ranging from Mozart to Prokofiev.

BIBL.: H.-P. Müller, *P. R.: Für Sie porträtiert* (Leipzig, 1986).

Rosell, Lars-Erik, Swedish composer, teacher, and organist; b. Nybro, Aug. 9, 1944. He studied organ (1962–68) and then was a composition student of Ingvar Lidholm at the Stockholm Musikhögskolan (1968–72); then taught counterpoint there (from 1973). He was also active as an organist, becoming well known for his advocacy of contemporary scores. In his music, he often requires improvisation from performers.

WORKS: *Moments of a Changing Sonority* for Harpsichord, Hammond Organ, and Strings (1969); *Terry Riley* for 3 Pianos (1970); *Twilight* for Chamber Ensemble (1970); *Dorian Mode* for Piano, Vibraphone, Clarinet, Cello, and Trombone (1971); *3 Psaltarpsalmer* for Chorus and Instruments (1971); *Poem in the Dark* for Mezzo-soprano, Flute, Trombone, Double Bass, and Percussion, after Sachs (1972); *Efter syndafallet*, dramatic scene for Soprano, Alto, Baritone, and Instrumental Ensemble, after Arthur Miller's play *After the Fall* (Stockholm, Feb. 15, 1973); *Nattesang*, chamber opera (Copenhagen, Dec. 15, 1974); *Visiones prophetae*, biblical scene for Soloists, 3 Choruses, Wind Orch., Harp, Organ, and 2 Double Basses (Lund, June 27, 1974); *Musik* for Cello and String Orch. (Stockholm, March 4, 1975); *Expando* for Orch. (1976); *Reflections* for Trombone and Organ (1979); *Ordens kalla*, scenic cantata (Stockholm, Nov. 7, 1980); *Stages* for 7 Instruments (1980); *Tillfalligt avbrott*, chamber opera (Stockholm, Dec. 12, 1981); Organ Concerto (Stockholm, Nov. 25, 1982); *Amedee*, chamber opera (1983–85); String Quartet (1989); Viola Sonata (1989); *Fantasie concertante* for Cello and Orch. (1992); Overture for Organ (1993); *Musica dolce* for Flute (1994).

Rosen, Charles (Welles), erudite American pianist, teacher, and writer on music; b. N.Y., May 5, 1927. He began piano studies when he was only 4. Between the ages of 7 and 11 he studied at the Juilliard School of Music in N.Y., and then took piano lessons with Moriz Rosenthal and Hedwig Kanner-Rosenthal (1938–44). He continued his training with the latter (1944–52) and also received lessons in theory and composition from Karl Wiegl. He concurrently studied music history at Princeton Univ. (B.A., 1947; M.A., 1949), where he took his Ph.D. in Romance languages in 1951. In 1951 he made his debut in N.Y., and subsequently appeared as a soloist with major orchs. and as a recitalist. He was assistant prof. of modern languages at the Mass. Inst. of Technology (1953–55). In 1971 he became prof. of music at the State Univ. of N.Y. at Stony Brook. In 1976–77 he also was the Ernest Bloch Prof. of Music at the Univ. of Calif. at Berkeley. As a pianist, Rosen has garnered notable distinction for his insightful interpretations of Bach, Beethoven, and Debussy, and for his traversal of such 20th-century composers as Schoenberg, Webern, Boulez, and Carter. He has contributed brilliant articles on various subjects to various publications. In 1972 he received the National Book Award for his distinguished vol. *The Classical Style: Haydn, Mozart, Beethoven* (N.Y., 1971). His subsequent books included *Arnold Schoenberg* (N.Y., 1975), *Sonata Forms* (N.Y., 1980; 2nd. ed., rev., 1988), *Frontiers of Meaning: Three Informal Lectures on Music* (N.Y., 1994), and *The Romantic Generation* (Cambridge, Mass., 1995).

Rosen, Jerome (William), American clarinetist, teacher, and composer; b. Boston, July 23, 1921. He studied at New Mexico State Univ. in Las Cruces, and with William Denny and Sessions at the Univ. of Calif. at Berkeley (M.A., 1949); then, as recipient of a Ladd Prix de Paris, he went to Paris, where he continued his studies with Milhaud and also obtained a diploma as a clarinetist (1950). Upon his return to the U.S., he became a teacher at the Univ. of Calif. at Davis (1952); was made an assoc. prof. (1957) and a prof. (1963); also served as director of its electronic music studio; was made prof. emeritus (1988).

WORKS: DRAMATIC: OPERA: *Emperor Norton of the U.S.A.* (1990). **CHAMBER OPERA:** *Calisto and Melibea* (1978; Davis, Calif., May 31, 1979). **MUSICAL PLAY:** *Emperor Norton Lives!* (1976). **DANCE SATIRES:** *Search* (1953); *Life Cycle* (1954). **ORCH.:** Saxophone Concerto (1957; Sacramento, Calif., Jan. 24, 1958); *5 Pieces* for Band (1960); *Sounds and Movements* (1963); Concerto for Clarinet, Trombone, and Band (1964); *Synket Concerto* (1968); *3 Pieces* for 2 Recorders and Orch. (1972); Clarinet Concerto (1973; Sacramento, Calif., Dec. 4, 1976); *3 Waltzes* for Saxophone and Band (1995). **CHAMBER:** Woodwind Quintet (1949); Sonata for Clarinet and Cello (1950); 2 string quartets (1953, 1965); Clarinet Quintet (1959); *Serenade* for Clarinet and Percussion (1967); Quintet for Saxophone and String Quartet (1974); *Serenade* for Clarinet and Violin (1977); *Play Time I* for Clarinet and Double Bass (1981) and *II* for Clarinet and String

Quartet (1981). **VOCAL:** *13 Ways of Looking at a Blackbird,* song cycle for Soprano and Piano (1951); *Serenade* for Soprano and Saxophone (1964); *Chamber Music* for Women's Voices and Harp (1975); *Campus Doorways* for Chorus and Orch. (1978); *White-Haired Lover,* song cycle for Baritone, Flute, Clarinet, String Quartet, and Piano (1985); *Love Poems,* song cycle for Man's and Woman's Speaking Voices, Flute, Clarinet, String Quartet, and Piano (1988).

Rosen, Max, Romanian-born American violinist; b. Dorohoi, April 11, 1900; d. N.Y., Dec. 16, 1956. He was taken to the U.S. as an infant and studied with David Mannes in N.Y. In 1912 he went to Germany, where he had lessons with Auer. He made his debut in Dresden, Nov. 16, 1915, and his American debut with the N.Y. Phil. (Jan. 12, 1918); then made tours of the U.S. (1918–21) and Europe (1921–26); subsequently appeared as a recitalist in N.Y. until his retirement there as a teacher in 1946.

Rosen, Nathaniel (Kent), American cellist and teacher; b. Altadena, Calif., June 9, 1948. He studied at Pasadena City College (1965–67) and with Piatigorsky at the Univ. of Southern Calif. in Los Angeles (Mus.B., 1971). He made his debut as a soloist with the Los Angeles Phil. in 1969, and in 1970 won the Piatigorsky Award of the Violoncello Soc. of N.Y., which led to his N.Y. debut at Carnegie Recital Hall. He was an assistant prof. at Calif. State Univ. at Northridge (1970–76); also was principal cellist of the Los Angeles Chamber Orch. (1970–76) and of the Pittsburgh Sym. Orch. (1977–79). In 1978 he became the first American cellist to capture the Gold Medal at the Tchaikovsky Competition in Moscow; subsequently toured throughout the globe. He was a prof. at the Manhattan School of Music in N.Y. (1981–88) and at the Univ. of Illinois at Urbana-Champaign (1988–94). In 1994 he rejoined the faculty of the Manhattan School of Music.

Rosenberg, Hilding (Constantin), important Swedish composer and teacher; b. Bosjökloster, Ringsjön, Skåne, June 21, 1892; d. Stockholm, May 19, 1985. He studied piano and organ in his youth, and then was active as an organist. He went to Stockholm in 1914 to study piano with Andersson; then studied composition with Ellberg at the Stockholm Cons. (1915–16), and later took a conducting course there. He made trips abroad from 1920; then studied composition with Stenhammer and conducting with Scherchen. He was a répétiteur and assistant conductor at the Royal Opera in Stockholm (1932–34); also appeared as a guest conductor in Scandinavia and later in the U.S. (1948), leading performances of his own works; likewise was active as a teacher, numbering Bäck, Blomdahl, and Lidholm among his students. Rosenberg was the foremost Swedish composer of his era. He greatly influenced Swedish music by his experimentation and stylistic diversity, which led to a masterful style marked by originality, superb craftsmanship, and refinement.

WORKS: DRAMATIC: OPERAS: *Resa till Amerika* (Journey to America; Stockholm, Nov. 24, 1932; orch. suite, Stockholm, Sept. 29, 1935); *Spelet om St. Örjan,* children's opera (1937; rev. 1941); *Marionetter* (1938; Stockholm, Feb. 14, 1939; 2 suites for Small Orch., 1926; overture and dance suite, 1938); *De två konungadöttrarna* (The 2 Princesses), children's opera (Swedish Radio, Stockholm, Sept. 19, 1940); *Lycksalighetens o* (The Isle of Bliss; 1943; Stockholm, Feb. 1, 1945; *Vindarnas musik* for Orch. from the opera, 1943); *Josef och hans bröder* (Joseph and His Brothers), opera-oratorio, after Thomas Mann (1946–48; Swedish Radio, Stockholm: part 1, May 30, 1946; part 2, Dec. 19, 1946; part 3, Sept. 9, 1947; part 4, Jan. 23, 1948; *Partita* for Orch. from the opera-oratorio, 1948); *Kaspers fettisdag* (Kasper's Shrove Tuesday), chamber opera (1953; Swedish Radio, Stockholm, Feb. 28, 1954); *Porträtett* (The Portrait), radio opera after Gogol (1955; Swedish Radio, Stockholm, March 22, 1956; rev. 1963); *Hus med dubbel ingång* (The House with 2 Doors), lyric comedy after Calderón (1969; Stockholm, May 24, 1970). **BALLETS:** *Eden* (1946; based on the Concerto No. 1 for Strings, 1946); *Salome* (1963; Stockholm, Feb. 28, 1964; based on the *Metamorfosi sinfoniche Nos. 1* and *2,* 1963); *Sönerna* (The Sons; Swedish TV, Stockholm, Dec. 6, 1964; based on the *Metamorfosi sinfoniche No. 3,* 1964); *Babels torn* (The Tower of Babel; 1966; Swedish TV, Stockholm, Jan. 8, 1968; based on the Sym. for Wind and Percussion, 1966). **PANTOMIME:** *Yttersta domen* (The Last Judgment; 1929; not perf.; 2 preludes and 2 suites for Orch. from the pantomime, 1929). **MELODRAMAS:** *Prometheus och Ahasverus* (Swedish Radio, Stockholm, April 27, 1941); *Djufars visa* (Djufar's Song; Swedish Radio, Stockholm, Dec. 18, 1942; suite for Orch. from the melodrama, 1942). **INCIDENTAL MUSIC TO:** Plays and films.

ORCH.: *Adagio* (1915); Syms.: No. 1 (1917; rev. 1919; Göteborg, April 5, 1921; rev. 1922–71; Stockholm, May 18, 1974), No. 2, *Sinfonia grave* (1928–35; Göteborg, March 27, 1935), No. 3 (Swedish Radio, Stockholm, Dec. 11, 1939; orig. subtitled *De fyra tidsåldrarna* [The 4 Ages of Man], with text from Rolland's novel *Jean Christoph;* rev. 1952), No. 4, *Johannes uppenbarelse* (The Revelation of St. John), for Baritone, Chorus, and Orch. (Swedish Radio, Stockholm, Dec. 6, 1940), No. 5, *Hortulanus* or *Örtagårdsmästaren* (The Keeper of the Garden), for Alto, Chorus, and Orch. (Swedish Radio, Stockholm, Oct. 17, 1944), No. 6, *Sinfonia semplice* (1951; Gavle, Jan. 24, 1952), Sym. for Wind and Percussion (1966; Göteborg, Oct. 27, 1972; music also used in the ballet *Babels torn,* 1966), No. 7 (Swedish Radio, Stockholm, Sept. 29, 1968), and No. 8, *In candidum,* for Chorus and Orch. (1974; Malmö, Jan. 24, 1975); *3 fantasistycken* (1918; Göteborg, 1919); *Sinfonia da chiesa No. 1* (1923; Stockholm, Jan. 16, 1925; rev. 1950) and *No. 2* (1924; Stockholm, Jan. 20, 1926); 2 violin concertos: No. 1 (1924; Stockholm, May 8, 1927) and No. 2 (1951; Stockholm, March 25, 1952); *Suite on Swedish Folk Tunes* for Strings (Swedish Radio, Stockholm, Sept. 13, 1927); Threnody for Stenhammar *(Sorgemusik)* (1927); Trumpet Concerto (1928; Stockholm, Jan. 16, 1929); *Overtura piccola* (1934); *Symphonie Concertante* for Violin, Viola, Oboe, Bassoon, and Orch. (1935; Göteborg, Jan. 1936); 2 cello concertos: No. 1 (1939) and No. 2 (1953; Swedish Radio, Stockholm, April 25, 1954); *Adagio funèbre* (1940); *I bergakungens sal* (In the Hall of the Mountain King), suite (1940); Viola Concerto (1942; Swedish Radio, Stockholm, Feb. 11, 1943); 4 concertos for Strings: No. 1 (1946; Swedish Radio, Stockholm, July 6, 1947; music used in the ballet *Eden,* 1946), No. 2 (n.d.), No. 3 (n.d.), and No. 4 (1966; Stockholm, Sept. 14, 1968); *Overtura bianca-nera* (1946); Concerto No. 2 (1949; Malmö, Jan. 12, 1950) and No. 3, *Louisville* (1954; Louisville, March 12, 1955; rev. 1968) for Orch.; Piano Concerto (1950; Göteborg, March 14, 1951); *Ingresso solenne del premio Nobel* (1952); *Variations on a Sarabande* (1953); *Riflessioni* No. 1 (1959; Swedish Radio, Stockholm, April 24, 1965), No. 2 (1960; Swedish Radio, Stockholm, March 2, 1962), and No. 3 (1960) for Strings; *Dagdrivaren (The Sluggard)* for Baritone and Orch. (1962; Stockholm, Oct. 28, 1964); *Metamorfosi sinfoniche* Nos. 1 to 3 (1963–64; music from Nos. 1 and 2 used in the ballet *Salome,* 1963; music from No. 3 used in the ballet *Sönerna,* 1964); various suites, preludes, partitas, etc.

CHAMBER: String quartets: No. 1 (1920; Stockholm, March 6, 1923), No. 2 (1924; Stockholm, March 6, 1925), No. 3, *Quartetto pastorale* (1926; Göteborg, April 3, 1932), No. 4 (1939; Stockholm, Nov. 2, 1942), No. 5 (1949; Stockholm, May 23, 1950), No. 6 (Stockholm, May 25, 1954), No. 7 (1956; Swedish Radio, Stockholm, Nov. 13, 1958), No. 8 (1956; Swedish Radio, Stockholm, Dec. 20, 1958), No. 9 (1956; Swedish Radio, Stockholm, March 17, 1959), No. 10 (1956; Swedish Radio, Stockholm, May 12, 1959), No. 11 (1956; Swedish Radio, Stockholm, Oct. 23, 1959), and No. 12, *Quartetto riepilogo* (1956; Swedish Radio, Stockholm, Dec. 11, 1959); Trio for Flute, Violin, and Viola (1921); 3 sonatas for Solo Violin (1921; 1953; 1963, rev. 1967); 2 violins sonatas (1926, 1940); Trio for Oboe, Clarinet, and Bassoon (1927); *Taffelmusik* for Piano Trio or Chamber Orch. (1939); Wind Quintet (1959); Sonata for Solo Flute (1959); Sonata for Solo Clarinet (1960); numerous piano works.

VOCAL: ORATORIOS: *Den heliga natten* (The Holy Night; Swedish Radio, Stockholm, Dec. 27, 1936); *Perserna* (The Persians; 1937; not perf.); *Huvudskalleplats* (Calvary), for Good Friday (Swedish Radio, Stockholm, April 15, 1938; rev. 1964–65); *Svensk lagsaga* (Swedish Radio, Stockholm, Feb. 24, 1942); *Hymnus* (1965; Swedish Radio, Stockholm, July 24, 1966). **CANTATAS:** *Julhymn av Romanus* (Swedish Radio, Stockholm, Dec. 25, 1941); Cantata for the National Museum (1942; Swedish Radio, Stockholm, June 1, 1943); *Lyrisk svit* (Göteborg, Oct. 2, 1954); *Hymn to a University* (1967; Lund, June 13, 1968). Also choruses and songs.

BIBL.: M. Pergament, *H. R., a Giant of Modern Swedish Music* (Stockholm, 1956); P. Lyne, *H. R.: Catalogue of Works* (Stockholm, 1970).

Rosenblum, Mathew, American composer; b. N.Y., March 19, 1954. He studied at the New England Cons. of Music in Boston (B.M., 1977; M.M., 1979) and Princeton Univ. (M.F.A., 1981); in 1980 he won the Rockefeller Foundation Contemporary American Chamber Works award; also received grants and awards from BMI (1978), the New Jersey State Council on the Arts (1981), the Inst. of Contemporary American Music (1981), the American Composers Alliance (1987), and the N.Y. Foundation for the Arts (1989); was artist-in-residence at the MacDowell Colony, the Djerassi Foundation, and Yaddo. His recent works use hybrid tuning systems which combine both just- and equal-tempered intervals.

WORKS: *Harp Quartet* for Alto Flute/Flute, Bass Clarinet/Clarinet, Viola, and Harp (N.Y., Dec. 8, 1980); *Cascades* for Violin (1982; Glassboro, N.J., April 30, 1983); *Le Jon Ra* for 2 Cellos (1983; N.Y., April 24, 1987); *Continental Drift* for Horn, Percussion, and 2 Keyboards (San Francisco, Sept. 26, 1988); *Circadian Rhythms* for Cello, Percussion, and 2 Keyboards (N.Y., June 6, 1989; also for Clarinet, Harp, Synthesizer, and 2 Percussion; Oslo, Sept. 24, 1990).

Rosenboom, David (Charles), American composer, performer, designer and maker of electronic instruments, and teacher; b. Fairfield, Iowa, Sept. 9, 1947. He took courses in composition and electronic and computer music at the Univ. of Ill. at Urbana, where his principal mentors were Gordon Binkerd, Salvatore Martirano, Kenneth Gaburo, and Lejaren Hiller; also studied theory, conducting, physics, computer science, and experimental psychology. In 1967–68 he was a creative assoc. at the Center for Creative and Performing Arts at the State Univ. of N.Y. at Buffalo and artistic coordinator of the Electric Circus in N.Y.; also in N.Y., was co-founder and president of the Neurona Co., a research and development firm for electronics in the arts (1969–71). From 1972 to 1979 he taught at York Univ. in Toronto; concurrently served as director of the Laboratory of Experimental Aesthetics at the Aesthetic Research Center of Canada, where he pursued studies in information processing as it relates to aesthetics; his studies resulted in several musical works. With D. Buchla, he developed the Touché, a computerized keyboard instrument, during his period as a software developer with Buchla's firm in Berkeley, California (1979–80). In 1979 he joined the faculty of Mills College in Oakland, California, where he was assoc. prof. of music and director of the Center for Contemporary Music (from 1983); also was head of the music dept. (from 1984), holder of the Darius Milhaud Chair in Music (from 1988), and prof. of music (1989–90) there. From 1981 to 1984 he also taught at the San Francisco Art Inst. In 1990 he became dean of music at the Calif. Inst. of the Arts. He wrote a number of articles on contemporary music for various journals and publications; ed. the book *Biofeedback and the Arts: Results of Early Experiments* (1975) and brought out the vol. *Selected Articles 1968–1982* (1984); also publ. a Leonardo monograph, *Extended Musical Interface with the Human Nervous System: Assessment and Prospectus* (1990). His music is generally experimental in nature, explorative of unique notation systems, improvisation, and extended instrumental techniques. He designed and co-developed H(ierarchical)M(usic)(Specification)L(anguage), a widely used programmimg language for interactive computer music systems (1987).

WORKS: *Contrasts* for Violin and Orch. (1963); *Caliban upon Setebos* for Orch. (1966); *The Brandy of the Damned*, theater piece, with Electronic Tape (1967); *How Much Better if Plymouth Rock Had Landed on the Pilgrims* for Variable Ensembles, Electronics, and Outdoor Environments (1969–72); *On Being Invisible* for Soloist, with Computer-assisted Brain Signal Analysis and Electronic Music System, Touch Sensors, and Small Acoustic Sources (1976–77); *In the Beginning: I (Electronic)* for Soloist, with Computer-assisted Electronic Music System (1978), *II (Quartet)* for 2 or 4 Cellos and 2 Violas, Trombone, and Percussion (1979), *III (Quintet)* for Woodwind Quintet (1979), *Etude I (Trombones)* for any number of Trombones (1979), *IV (Electronic)* for Soloist, with Computer-assisted Electronic Music System (1980), *Etude II* (Keyboards/Mallets/Harps) for 2, 4, 6, or 8 Players (1980), *Etude III (Piano and 2 Oranges)* for Piano (1980), and *V (The Story)* for Chamber Orch., Film or Video, and Synthetic Speech (1980); *Future Travel* for Piano, Violin, and Computer Music System (1982; rev. 1987); *Champ Vital (Life Field)*, trio for Violin, Piano, and Percussion (1987); *Systems of Judgment*, tape collage (1987); *2 Lines*, duets for Melodic Instruments (1989); *Predictions, Confirmations, and Disconfirmations* for Piano, Computer Software, and Automatically Responding Instruments (1991); *Extended Trio* for Improvising Trio, Computer Software, and Computer Music Systems (1992; in collaboration with C. Haden and T. Sankaran); *It Is About To . . . Sound*, interactive computer media installation utilizing the music of John Cage and 36 other composers (1993; in collaboration with M. Coniglio and S. Mosko); *On Being Invisible II: Hypatia Speaks to Jefferson in a Dream*, multimedia performance piece (1994–95); *Brave New World: Music for the Play* for Computer Music System (1995); also film music; improvisational pieces; sound sculptures; many other works.

Rosenfeld, Paul (Leopold), American author and music critic; b. N.Y., May 4, 1890; d. there, July 21, 1946. He studied at Yale Univ. (B.A., 1912) and at Columbia Univ. School of Journalism (Litt.B., 1913). He then associated himself with progressive circles in literature and music; wrote music criticism for *The Dial* (1920–27); contributed also to other literary and music magazines. Although not a musician by training, Rosenfeld possessed a penetrating insight into musical values; he championed the cause of modern American music. He collected the most significant of his articles in book form: *Musical Portraits* (on 20 modern composers; 1920); *Musical Chronicle*, covering the N.Y. seasons 1917–23 (1923); *An Hour with American Music* (1929); *Discoveries of a Music Critic* (1936). Analects from his articles were publ. as *Musical Impressions* (N.Y., 1969).

BIBL.: J. Mellquist and L. Wiese, eds., *P. R., Voyager in the Arts* (N.Y., 1948); B. Mueser, *The Criticism of New Music in N.Y.: 1919–1929* (City Univ. of N.Y., 1975); C. Silet, *The Writings of P. R.: An Annotated Bibliography* (N.Y., 1981).

Rosenman, Leonard, American composer; b. N.Y., Sept. 7, 1924. He studied with local teachers; later took courses with Sessions, Dallapiccola, and briefly with Schoenberg. His main mundane occupation is that of a movie composer; he wrote the scores for such commercially notable films as *East of Eden*, *Rebel without a Cause*, and *The Chapman Report*; also compiled music for television programs, among them *The Defenders* and *Marcus Welby, M.D.* But he is also the composer of a number of highly respectable musical works, among them a Violin Concerto and the challenging score *Foci* for 3 Orchs. His *Threnody on a Song of K. R.* (written to the memory of his wife, Kay Rosenman), a set of orch. variations on her original melody, was performed by the Los Angeles Phil., under the composer's direction, May 6, 1971. Among his later compositions are *Foci I* for Orch. (1981; rev. 1983) and *Chamber Music 5* for Piano and 6 Players (1979).

Rosenshein, Neil, American tenor; b. N.Y., Nov. 27, 1947. He studied at Wilkes College in Wilkes-Barre, Pa. (1967), and with Jennie Tourel and others at N.Y.'s Juilliard School (1969). He made his operatic debut as Count Almaviva in *Il Barbiere di Siviglia* in Cocoa Beach, Fla. (1972); his first appearance in Europe was as Tom Rakewell in *The Rake's Progress* with the Netherlands Opera in Amsterdam (1982). He made frequent appearances with the major U.S. and European opera houses thereafter, and also sang with the leading orchs. On June 2, 1986, he made his Covent Garden debut in London as Lensky in *Eugene Onegin.* He made his Metropolitan Opera debut in N.Y. as Alfredo in *La Traviata* on Nov. 19, 1987. In 1988 he sang in the premiere of Argento's *The Aspern Papers* in Dallas. On Dec. 19, 1991, he created the role of Leon in Corigliano's *The Ghosts of Versailles* at the Metropolitan Opera. In 1994 he appeared in Santa Fe as Cavaradossi. Among his other roles are Belmonte in *Die Entführung aus dem Serail,* Tamino in *Die Zauberflöte,* Oberon, Werther, Alfred in *Die Fledermaus,* Alfonso in Korngold's *Violanta,* and the title role in Stravinsky's *Oedipus Rex.*

Rosenstock, Joseph, Polish-born American conductor; b. Kraków, Jan. 27, 1895; d. N.Y., Oct. 17, 1985. He studied in Kraków and at the Vienna Cons.; also received instruction from Franz Schreker. He was assistant conductor at the Stuttgart Opera (1919–20); was a conductor (1920–22) and Generalmusikdirektor (1922–25) at the Darmstadt Opera; then was Generalmusikdirektor at the Wiesbaden Opera (1927–29). On Oct. 30, 1929, he made his Metropolitan Opera debut in N.Y. conducting *Die Meistersinger von Nürnberg*; returning to Germany, he became Generalmusikdirektor at the Mannheim National Theater in 1930. As a Jew, he was removed from his post by the Nazis in 1933; he then conducted the Judisches Kulturbund in Berlin until 1936. He went to Tokyo to become conductor of the Nippon Phil. (1936); as an alien, he lost his post and was removed to Karuizawa with the Japanese attack on Pearl Harbor in 1941; after his liberation in 1945, he returned to Tokyo to help reorganize musical life under the U.S. occupation forces. In 1946 he settled in the U.S.; became a naturalized citizen in 1949. He became a conductor at the N.Y. City Opera in 1948, and subsequently was its general director (1952–56); after serving as music director of the Cologne Opera (1958–60), he conducted at the Metropolitan Opera in N.Y. (1960–69). His wife was **Herta Glaz**.

Rosenthal, Harold (David), English music editor and critic; b. London, Sept. 30, 1917; d. there, March 19, 1987. He received his B.A. degree from Univ. College, London, in 1940. In 1950 he launched, with the Earl of Harewood, the magazine *Opera* and was its ed. (1953–86). He was archivist of the Royal Opera House in London (1950–56). Rosenthal contributed to many European and American music journals, and also wrote numerous biographical entries on singers for *The New Grove Dictionary of Music and Musicians* (1980). In 1983 he was made an Officer of the Order of the British Empire. His publications, all publ. in London, included *Sopranos of Today* (1956), *Two Centuries of Opera at Covent Garden* (1958), ed. with J. Warrack, *The Concise Oxford Dictionary of Opera* (1964; 2nd ed., rev., 1979), and *Covent Garden: A Short History* (1967). He ed. *The Opera Bedside Book* (1965) and *The Mapleson Memoirs* (1966); also wrote an autobiography, *My Mad World of Opera* (1982).

Rosenthal, Manuel (actually, **Emmanuel**), French composer and conductor; b. Paris (of a French father and a Russian mother), June 18, 1904. He studied violin and composition at the Paris Cons. (1918–23); also took some lessons with Ravel. He was co-conductor of the Orchestre National de la Radiodiffusion in Paris from 1934 until his mobilization as an infantryman at the outbreak of World War II in 1939; after being held as a prisoner of war in Germany (1940–41), he was released and returned to France, where he became active in the Résistance. After the liberation, he served as chief conductor of the French Radio orch. (1944–47); made his first tour of the U.S. in 1946; in 1948, was appointed instructor in composition at the College of Puget Sound in Tacoma, Wash. In 1949 he was engaged as conductor of the Seattle Sym. Orch.; was dismissed summarily for moral turpitude in Oct. 1951 (the soprano who appeared as soloist with the Seattle Sym. Orch. under the name of Mme. Rosenthal was not his legal wife). In 1962 he was appointed prof. of conducting at the Paris Cons.; was conductor of the Liège Sym. Orch. (1964–67). He made his belated Metropolitan Opera debut in N.Y. on Feb. 20, 1981, conducting a triple bill of Ravel's *L'Enfant et les sortilèges,* Poulenc's *Les Mamelles de Tirésias,* and Satie's *Parade*; returned there in subsequent seasons with notable success. Rosenthal publ. the books *Satie, Ravel, Poulenc: An Intimate Memoir* (Madras and N.Y., 1987) and *Musique dorable* (Paris, 1994). In 1992 he received the Grand Prix for music of the City of Paris.

WORKS: DRAMATIC: *Rayon des soieries,* comic opera (1926–28); *Un baiser pour rien,* ballet (1928–29); *Les Bootleggers,* musical comedy (1932; Paris, May 2, 1933); *La Poule noire,* musical comedy (1934–37; Paris, 1937); *Gaîté parisienne,* ballet after Offenbach (Monte Carlo, April 5, 1938); *Que le diable l'emporte,* ballet (1948); *Les Femmes au tombeau,* lyric drama (1956); *Hop, signor!,* lyric drama (1957–61). **ORCH.:** *Sérénade* (1927); *Les Petits Métiers* (1933; St. Louis, March 3, 1936); *Jeanne d'Arc* (1934–36); *La Fête du vin,* choreographic poem (1937; N.Y., Dec. 5, 1947, composer conducting); *Musique de table,* suite (1941; N.Y., Oct. 10, 1946); *Noce villeageoise* (1941); *Symphonies de Noël* (1947); *Magic Manhattan* (1948); Sym. (1949); *Offenbacchiana* (1953); *Rondes françaises* (1955); *2 Études en camaïeu* for Strings and Percussion (1969); *Aeolus* for Wind Quintet and Orch. (1970). **CHAMBER:** Sonatine for 2 Violins and Piano (1923); *Saxophone-Marmelade* for Alto Saxophone and Piano (1929); *Les Soirées du petit Juas* for String Quartet (1942); piano pieces. **VOCAL:** *Saint-François d'Assise* for Reciter, Chorus, Orch., and Vibraphone (1936–39; Paris, Nov. 1, 1944, composer conducting); *Cantate pour le temps de la Nativité* for Soprano, Chorus, and Orch. (1943–44); *Missa Deo Gratias* for Soloists, Chorus, and Orch. (1953); choruses; songs.

BIBL.: D. Saudinos, *M. R., une vie* (Paris, 1992).

Rosenthal, Moriz, famous Austrian pianist; b. Lemberg, Dec. 17, 1862; d. N.Y., Sept. 3, 1946. He studied piano at the Lemberg Cons. with Karol Mikuli, who was a pupil of Chopin; in 1872, when he was 10 years old, he played Chopin's Rondo in C for 2 Pianos with his teacher in Lemberg. The family moved to Vienna in 1875, and Rosenthal became the pupil of Joseffy, who inculcated in him a passion for virtuoso piano playing, which he taught according to Tausig's method. Liszt accepted Rosenthal as a student during his stay in Weimar and Rome (1876–78). After a hiatus of some years, during which Rosenthal studied philosophy at the Univ. of Vienna, he returned to his concert career in 1884, and established for himself a reputation as one of the world's greatest virtuosos; was nicknamed (because of his small stature and great pianistic power) "little giant of the piano." Beginning in 1888 he made 12 tours of the U.S., where he became a permanent resident in 1938. He publ. (with L. Schytte) a *Schule des höheren Klavierspiels* (Berlin, 1892). He was married to **Hedwig Kanner-Rosenthal**.

Rosing, Vladimir, Russian-American tenor and opera director; b. St. Petersburg, Jan. 23, 1890; d. Los Angeles, Nov. 24, 1963. He studied voice with Jean de Reszke. He made his operatic debut in St. Petersburg in 1912; gave a successful series of recitals in programs of Russian songs in London between 1913 and 1921. In 1923 he was appointed director of the opera dept. at the Eastman School of Music in Rochester, N.Y.; founded an American Opera Co., which he directed in a series of operatic productions in the English language. In 1939 he went to Los Angeles as organizer and artistic director of the Southern Calif. Opera Assn.

BIBL.: R. Rosing, *V. R.: Musical Genius, an Intimate Biography* (Manhattan, Kansas, 1993).

Roslavetz, Nikolai (Andreievich), remarkable Russian composer; b. Suray, near Chernigov, Jan. 5, 1881; d. Moscow, Aug. 23, 1944. He studied violin with his uncle and theory with A.M. Abaza in Kursk; then studied violin with Jan Hřímalý, and composition with Ilyinsky and Vassilenko, at the Moscow Cons., graduating in 1912; won the Silver Medal for his cantata *Heaven and Earth*, after Byron. A composer of advanced tendencies, he publ. in 1913 an atonal Violin Sonata, the first of its kind by a Russian composer; his 3rd String Quartet exhibits 12-tone properties. He ed. a short-lived journal, *Muzykalnaya Kultura*, in 1924, and became a leading figure in the modern movement in Russia. But with a change of Soviet cultural policy toward socialist realism and nationalism, Roslavetz was subjected to severe criticism in the press for persevering in his aberrant ways. To conciliate the authorities, he tried to write operettas; then was given an opportunity to redeem himself by going to Tashkent to write ballets based on Uzbek folk songs; he failed in all these pursuits. But interest in his music became pronounced abroad, and posthumous performances were arranged in West Germany.

WORKS: ORCH.: 2 symphonic poems: *Man and the Sea*, after Baudelaire (1921) and *End of the World*, after Paul Lafargue (1922); Sym. (1922); Violin Concerto (1925). **CHAMBER:** *Nocturne* for Harp, Oboe, 2 Violas, and Cello (1913); 3 string quartets (1913, 1916, 1920); *3 Dances* for Violin and Piano (1921); Cello Sonata (1921); 3 piano trios; 4 violin sonatas; 5 piano sonatas. **VOCAL:** *October*, cantata (1927).

BIBL.: D. Gojowy, "N.A. R., ein früher Zwölftonkomponist," *Die Musikforschung*, XXII (1969).

Rösler, Endre, Hungarian tenor; b. Budapest, Nov. 27, 1904; d. there, Dec. 13, 1963. He studied in Budapest and with De Lucia and Garbin in Italy. In 1927 he made his operatic debut as Alfredo at the Budapest Opera, where he was a principal member for some 30 years. Subsequently he sang comprimario roles there. At the apex of his career, he appeared as a guest artist with other European opera houses and also pursued a concert career. From 1953 until his death he taught at the Budapest Academy of Music. He was especially esteemed for his roles in Mozart's operas.

BIBL.: P. Varnai, *R. E.* (Budapest, 1969).

Rosner, Arnold, American composer and teacher; b. N.Y., Nov. 8, 1945. He studied mathematics at the State Univ. of N.Y. at Buffalo, and composition with Leo Smit, Allen Sapp, and Lejaren Hiller (Ph.D., 1972). He subsequently taught at various schools, including Kingsborough Community College (from 1983). His music is couched formally in a neo-Classical idiom, but he freely admits melodic, harmonic, and contrapuntal methods of the modern school of composition.

WORKS: OPERA: *The Chronicle of 9* (1984). **ORCH.:** 6 syms. (1961, 1961, 1963, 1964, 1973, 1976); *5 Mystical Pieces* for English Horn, Harp, and Strings (1967; later rev. as *5 Meditations*); *6 Pastoral Dances* (1968); *A Gentle Musicke* for Flute and Strings (1969); *A Mylai Elegy* (1971); 2 concerti grossi (1974, 1979); *5 Ko-ans* (1976); *Responses, Hosanna and Fugue* for Harp and Strings (1977); *Nocturne* (1978); *Tragedy to Queen Jane* (1982); *From the Diaries of Adam Czerniakow* for Narrator and Orch. (1986); *Trinity* for Symphonic Band (1988). **CHAMBER:** 5 string quartets (1962, 1963, 1965, 1972, 1975); Sonata for Flute and Cello (1962); 3 piano sonatas (1963, 1970, 1978); Violin Sonata (1963); Woodwind Quintet (1964); Concertino for Harp, Harpsichord, Celesta, and Piano (1968; rev. 1988); Cello Sonata (1968); Sonata for Oboe or Violin and Piano (1972); *Musique de clavecin* for Harpsichord (1974); Brass Quintet (1978); Horn Sonata (1979); *Sonatine d'amour* for Harpsichord (1987); *A Plaintive Harmony* for Horn (1988). **VOCAL: CHORAL:** Masses (1967, 1971, 1974); *Requiem* (1973); *Magnificat* (1979); *Let Them Praise* for Boys' Chorus (1984). **SONGS:** *3 Elegiac Songs* (1973); *Nightstone* (1979); *Besos sin Cuento*, 6 songs for Low Voice, Flute, Viola, and Harp (1989).

Ross, Hugh (Cuthbert Melville), English-born American organist, choral conductor, and teacher; b. Langport, Aug. 21, 1898; d. N.Y., Jan. 20, 1990. He studied at the Royal College of Music in London and at New College, Oxford (D.Mus.); his principal mentors were Mengelberg and Vaughan Williams. In 1921 he went to Winnipeg as conductor of its Male Voice Choir; in 1922 he founded that city's Phil. Choir, and in 1923 its Orchestral Club, which later became the Winnipeg Sym. Orch. In 1927 he settled in N.Y. as conductor of the Schola Cantorum, which post he held until 1971; also appeared as a guest conductor throughout North America. He taught at the Manhattan School of Music (from 1930); was also chairman of the choral dept. at the Berkshire Music Center at Tanglewood (1941–62). In 1949 he became a naturalized American citizen. He championed contemporary works.

Ross, Scott, American harpsichordist and organist; b. Pittsburgh, March 1, 1951; d. Assas, France, June 14, 1989. He went to France in his youth and entered the Nice Cons. in 1965 to study organ with René Saorgin and harpsichord with Huguette Grémy-Chauliac, taking the premier prix on the latter instrument in 1968. In 1969 he entered the Paris Cons. and studied harpsichord with Robert Veyron-Lacroix. Upon completing his training there in 1971, he pursued further studies in harpsichord with Kenneth Gilbert and was awarded a diplôme supérieur in 1972. In 1971 he captured 1st prize in the Bruges competition. In 1973 he became a prof. at Laval Univ. in Quebec, remaining primarily active in France as a harpsichordist and organist. Ross was held in high regard for his insightful interpretations of 17th- and 18th-century music, especially the works of Bach, Scarlatti, and composers of the French school.

Ross, Walter (Beghtol), American composer; b. Lincoln, Nebr., Oct. 3, 1936. He studied music at the Univ. of Nebr., receiving an M.Mus. in 1962; then composition with Robert Palmer and conducting with Husa at Cornell Univ. (D.M.A., 1966). In 1967 he was appointed to the music faculty of the Univ. of Virginia. Much of his music is inspired by American themes.

WORKS: OPERA: *In the Penal Colony* (1972). **ORCH.:** Concerto for Brass Quintet and Orch. (1966); 2 trombone concertos (1970, 1982); 2 syms.: No. 1, *A Jefferson Symphony*, for Tenor, Chorus, and Orch. (Charlottesville, Va., April 13, 1976) and No. 2 for Strings (1994); Concerto for Wind Quintet and String Orch. (1977); *Nocturne* for Strings (1980); Concerto for Bassoon and Strings (1983); Concerto for Oboe, Harp, and Strings (1984); *Overture to the Virginian Voyage* (1986); Concerto for Flute, Guitar, and Orch. (1987); *Sinfonietta Concertante* for Strings (1987); Concerto for Euphonium, Symphonic Brass, and Timpani (1988); *Fantastic Dances* for Strings (1990); *Mosaics*, piano concerto (1991); *Scherzo Festivo* (1992); *A Celebration of Dances* (1993); Clarinet Concerto (1994); many works for band. **CHAMBER:** *Cryptical Triptych* for Trombone and Piano (1968); *5 Dream Sequences* for Percussion Quartet and Piano (1968); *Canzona I* (1969) and *II* (1979) for 4 Trumpets, 4 Horns, 4 Trombones, 2 Euphoniums, 2 Tubas, and 3 Percussion, *III* for 12 Horns (1986), and *IV* for 4 Trumpets, 4 Horns, 4 Trombones, 2 Tubas, Timpani, and 2 Percussion (1989); 3 wind quintets (1974, 1985, 1989); String Trio (1978); Violin Sonata (1981); Suite No. 1 for Chamber Ensemble (1983); 3 brass trios (1985, 1986, 1986); Brass Quintet No. 1 (1987); *Oil of Dog* for Brass Quintet and Actor (1988); *Shapes in Bronze* for 2 Euphoniums and 2 Tubas (1992); *Summer Dances* for Oboe and Marimba (1992); *Contrasts!* for 12 Euphoniums (1992); *Harlequinade* for Flute, Oboe, Clarinet, Horn, Bassoon, and Piano (1994). **OTHER:** Numerous vocal works.

Rosseau, Norbert (Oscar Claude), Belgian composer; b. Ghent, Dec. 11, 1907; d. there, Nov. 1, 1975. He played violin as a child; his family emigrated to Italy in 1921, and he studied piano with Silvestri and composition with Respighi at the Accademia di Santa Cecilia in Rome (1925–28). His early works are cast in a traditional style of European modernism; later he halfheartedly experimented with dodecaphony and electronics.

WORKS: DRAMATIC: OPERAS: *Sicilenne* (1947); *Les Violons du prince* (1954). **BALLET:** *Juventa* (1957). **ORCH.:** *Suite Agreste* (1936); *H_2O*, symphonic poem (1938; Liège, June 24, 1939); 2 concertos (1948, 1963); 2 syms.: No. 1 (1953) and No. 2, *Sinfonia sacra*, for Soloists, Chorus, and Orch. (1960–63); *Suite concertante* for String Quintet, Winds, Harpsichord, and

Timpani (1959); Concerto for Wind Quintet and Orch. (1961); *Variations* (1963); Viola Concerto (1964); *Sonata a 4* for 4 Violins and Strings (1966); Horn Concerto (1967). **CHAMBER:** Violin Sonatina (1949); *3 jouets* for Oboe, Clarinet, and Bassoon (1955); Wind Quintet (1955); Clarinet Sonatina (1956); String Quartet (1956); Trio for Flute, Cello, and Piano (1956); *Rapsodie* for Flute, Bassoon, and Piano (1958); *Serenade à Syrinx* for Flute, Violin, Cello, and Harp (1959); Concertino for Piano, Double String Quartet, and Double Bass (1963); *Pentafonium* for Viola, Cello, Flute, Oboe, and Harpsichord (1964); *Diptique* for String Quartet (1971); *Dialogue* for Flute, Oboe, Viola, and Piano (1971); Piano Quartet (1975). **VOCAL:** *Inferno*, oratorio after Dante (1940); *L'An mille*, dramatic ode (1946); *Incantations*, cantata (1951); *Maria van den Kerselare*, Flemish oratorio (1952); *Zeepbellen*, chamber cantata, with Children's Chorus (1958); *Il Paradiso terrestre*, oratorio after Dante (1968).

Rossellini, Renzo, Italian composer and teacher; b. Rome, Feb. 2, 1908; d. Monte Carlo, May 14, 1982. He studied composition in Rome with Setaccioli and Sallustio; also took courses in orchestration with Molinari. In 1940 he was appointed prof. of composition at the Rome Cons., and in 1956 at the Accademia di Santa Cecilia in Rome. In 1973 he was named artistic director at the Opera at Monte Carlo. He publ. 2 books of autobiographical content, *Pagine di un musicista* (Bologna, 1964) and *Addio del passato* (Milan, 1968).

WORKS: DRAMATIC: OPERAS: *Alcassino e Nicoletta* (1928–30); *La guerra* (Rome, Feb. 25, 1956); *Il vortice* (Naples, Feb. 8, 1958); *Uno sguardo del ponte* (Rome, March 11, 1961); *L'Avventuriere* (Monte Carlo, Feb. 2, 1968); *La Reine morte* (Monte Carlo, 1973). **BALLETS:** *La danza di Dassine* (San Remo, Feb. 24, 1935); *Poemetti pagani* (Monte Carlo, 1963); *Il Ragazzo e la sua ombra* (Venice, 1966). Also film music. **ORCH.:** *Suite in 3 tempi* (1931); *Stornelli della Roma bassa* (1946); *Ut unum sint* (Miami, Oct. 20, 1963).

Rossi, Mario, eminent Italian conductor; b. Rome, March 29, 1902; d. there, June 29, 1992. He studied at the Rome Cons. (graduated, 1925). He was deputy conductor of the Augusteo Orch. in Rome (1926–36) and resident conductor of the Maggio Musicale Orch. in Florence (1936–44); subsequently was chief conductor of the RAI Orch. in Turin (1946–69); also appeared as a guest conductor in Europe. He became especially well known for his performances of contemporary music.

Rossi-Lemeni, Nicola, Italian bass; b. Constantinople (of an Italian father and a Russian mother), Nov. 6, 1920, d. Bloomington, Ind., March 12, 1991. He was educated in Italy; studied law and planned a diplomatic career. In 1943 he decided to become a professional singer, but World War II interfered with his plans, and his debut as Varlaam in Venice did not take place until May 1, 1946. He first sang in the U.S. as Boris Godunov with the San Francisco Opera (Oct. 2, 1951); sang at the Metropolitan Opera in N.Y. in 1953–54. In 1980 he joined the faculty of Indiana Univ. in Bloomington. He married **Virginia Zeani** in 1958. Besides the regular operatic repertoire, he sang a number of roles in modern works, such as Wozzeck.

Rössl-Majdan, Hildegard, Austrian contralto; b. Moosbierbaum, Jan. 21, 1921. She was educated at the Vienna Academy of Music. In 1946 she launched her career as a concert singer; also appeared at the Vienna State Opera, Milan's La Scala, London's Covent Garden, and other European opera houses; sang at the festivals in Salzburg, Edinburgh, and Aix-en-Provence; later was active as a voice teacher.

Rössler, Ernst Karl, German organist and composer; b. Pyritz, Pomerania, Oct. 18, 1909; d. Königsfeld, Aug. 19, 1980. He studied organ and was active mainly in organ building and church music. He lectured on composition for organ in Lübeck and Freiburg im Breisgau; publ. *Klangfunktion und Registrierung* (Kassel, 1952) and several other papers concerning organ registration. He composed some sacred choruses and numerous organ pieces.

Rossum, Frederik (Leon Hendrik) van, Belgian composer and teacher of Dutch descent; b. Elsene, Brussels, Dec. 5, 1939. He took Belgian citizenship when he was 18; studied composition with Souris and Quinet at the Brussels Cons. (1956–62); won a Premier Grand Prix de Rome for his *Cantate de la Haute Mer* (1965). He taught piano at the Brussels Cons. (1965–68); then became prof. of counterpoint at the Liège Cons. (1968); served as prof. of analysis at the Brussels Cons. (from 1971); also was director of the Watermael-Bosvoorde Academy of Music.

WORKS: *Petite pièce* for Clarinet and Piano (1961); Piano Sonata (1963); *Capriccio* for Wind Quintet (1963); Sinfonietta (1964); *Cantata sacrée* for Chorus, Strings, and Harpsichord (1966); *12 Miniatures* for Piano or Orch. (1967); *Divertimento* for Strings (1967); *Sinfonie concertante* for Horn, Piano, Percussion, and Orch. (1968); *Graffiti* for Violin and Piano (1968); *Duetto* for Cello and Piano (1968); *Pyrogravures* for Wind Quintet (1968); *Threni* for Mezzo-soprano and Orch. (1969); *Der Blaue Reiter* for Orch., in homage to German expressionistic painters (1971); *Epitaph* for Strings (1972); Piano Quintet (1972); *Rétrospection* for Soprano, Contralto, Chorus, 2 Pianos, and Percussion (1973); *Réquisitoire* for Brass and Percussion (1973); Piano Concerto (1975); *Petite suite réactionnaire* for Orch. (1975); *De soldaat Johan*, television opera (1975–76); 2 violin concertos (1979; 1985–89); *Polyptyque* for Orch. (1986); piano pieces.

Rostal, Max, Austrian-born English violinist and pedagogue; b. Teschen, Silesia, Aug. 7, 1905; d. Bern, Aug. 6, 1991. He studied violin with Arnold Rosé in Vienna and with Carl Flesch in Berlin, where he also took courses in composition with Emil Bohnke and Mátyás Seiber at the Hochschule für Musik; then was a prof. there (1930–33). In 1934 he left Nazi Germany; eventually went to London and became a naturalized British subject. He was a prof. at the Guildhall School of Music (1944–58), the Cologne Cons. (1957), and the Bern Cons. (1958). In 1977 he was made a Commander of the Order of the British Empire. He was especially noted for his performances of contemporary music.

Rostand, Claude, French writer on music; b. Paris, Dec. 3, 1912; d. Villejuif, Oct. 9, 1970. He studied literature and law at the Sorbonne in Paris; also received private instruction from Edouard Mignan, Marc Vaubourgoin, Jacques Février, and Norbert Dufourcq. He was active as a music critic; organized a modern music society in Paris, Musique d'Aujourd'hui (1958); served as vice-president of the ISCM (from 1961).

WRITINGS: *L'Oeuvre de Gabriel Fauré* (Paris, 1945); *La Musique française contemporaine* (Paris, 1952); dialogues with Milhaud, Poulenc, Markevitch, and others; biographies of Brahms (2 vols., Paris, 1954–55), Liszt (Paris, 1960; Eng. tr., 1970), Hugo Wolf (Paris, 1967), and Webern (1969); *Dictionnaire de la musique contemporaine* (Lausanne, 1970).

Rostropovich, Leopold, Russian cellist and teacher, father of **Mstislav (Leopoldovich) Rostropovich**; b. Voronezh, March 9, 1892; d. Orenburg, July 31, 1942. He studied cello with his father, Vitold Rostropovich. In addition to giving concerts, he served as a prof. at the Azerbaijan Cons. (1925–31); then lived in Moscow; after the outbreak of the Nazi-Soviet war in 1941, he moved to Orenburg.

Rostropovich, Mstislav (Leopoldovich), famous Russian cellist and conductor, son of **Leopold Rostropovich**; b. Baku, March 27, 1927. A precocious child, he began cello studies with his father at an early age; also had piano lessons from his mother. In 1931 the family moved to Moscow, where he made his debut when he was 8; continued his training at the Central Music School (1939–41); then studied cello with Kozolupov and composition with Shebalin and Shostakovich at the Moscow Cons. (1943–48); subsequently studied privately with Prokofiev. He won the International Competition for Cellists in Prague in 1950, and the next year made his first appearance in the West in Florence. A phenomenally successful career ensued. He made his U.S. debut at N.Y.'s Carnegie Hall in 1956, winning extraordinary critical acclaim. He became a teacher (1953) and a prof. (1956) at the Moscow Cons., and also a prof. at the Leningrad Cons. (1961). A talented pianist, he frequently appeared as accompanist to his wife, **Galina Vishnevskaya**, whom he married in 1955. In 1961 he made his first appearance as a conductor. As his fame increased, he received various honors, including the Lenin Prize in 1963 and the Gold Medal of the Royal Phil. Soc. of London in 1970. In spite of his eminence and official honors, however, he encountered difficulties with the Soviet authorities, owing chiefly to his spirit of uncompromising independence. He let the dissident author Aleksandr Solzhenitsyn stay at his dacha near Moscow, protesting the Soviet government's treatment of the Nobel prize winner for literature in a letter to *Pravda* in 1969. Although the letter went unpubl. in his homeland, it was widely disseminated in the West. As a result, Rostropovich found himself increasingly hampered in his career by the Soviet Ministry of Culture. His concerts were canceled without explanation, as were his wife's engagements at the Bolshoi Theater. Foreign tours were forbidden, as were appearances on radio, television, and recordings. In 1974 he and his wife obtained permission to go abroad, and were accompanied by their 2 daughters. He made a brilliant debut as a guest conductor with the National Sym. Orch. in Washington, D.C. (March 5, 1975); his success led to his appointment as its music director in 1977. Free from the bureaucratic annoyances of the U.S.S.R., he and his wife publicized stories of their previous difficulties at home in Russia. Annoyed by such independent activities, the Moscow authorities finally stripped them both of their Soviet citizenship as "ideological renegades." The Soviet establishment even went so far as to remove the dedication to Rostropovich of Shostakovich's 2nd Cello Concerto. The whole disgraceful episode ended when the Soviet government, chastened by perestroika, restored Rostropovich's citizenship in Jan. 1990, and invited him to take the National Sym. Orch. to the U.S.S.R. Besides conducting the American orch. there, Rostropovich appeared as soloist in Dvořák's Cello Concerto. His return to Russia was welcomed by the populace as a vindication of his principles of liberty. A symbolic linguistic note: the difficult-to-pronounce first name of Rostropovich, which means "avenged glory," is usually rendered by his friends and admirers as simply Slava, that is, "glory." In 1993 he took the National Sym. Orch. on another visit to Russia and on Sept. 26 conducted it in a special concert in Moscow's Red Square in commemoration of the 100th anniversary of the death of Tchaikovsky. In 1994 he stepped down as the orch.'s music director and was named life-time conductor laureate.

Rostropovich is duly recognized as one of the greatest cellists of the century, a master interpreter of both the standard and the contemporary literature. To enhance the repertoire for his instrument, he commissioned and premiered numerous scores, including works by Prokofiev, Shostakovich, Britten, Piston, and Foss. As a conductor, he proved himself an impassioned and authoritative interpreter of the music of the Russian national and Soviet schools of composition. He organized the 1st Rostropovich International Cello Competition in Paris in 1981 and the Rostropovich Festival in Snape, England, in 1983. He was made an Officer of the French Légion d'honneur in 1982, and received an honorary knighthood from Queen Elizabeth II of England in 1987. In 1993 he was awarded the Japanese Praemium Imperiale. He received the Polar Music Prize of Sweden in 1995.

BIBL.: T. Gaidamovich, M. R. (Moscow, 1969); J. Roy, *R., Gainsbourg et Dieu* (Paris, 1992); S. Khentova, *R.* (St. Petersburg, 1993); C. Samuel, *M. R. and Galina Vishnevskaya: Russia, Music, and Liberty: Conversations with Claude Samuel* (Portland, Oreg., 1995).

Rosvaenge (real name, **Rosenving-Hansen**), **Helge,** esteemed German tenor; b. Copenhagen (of German parents), Aug. 29, 1897; d. Munich, June 19, 1972. He studied in Copenhagen and Berlin. He made his operatic debut as Don José in Neustrelitz in 1921; then sang in Altenburg (1922–24), Basel (1924–26), and Cologne (1926–29). He distinguished himself as a member of the Berlin State Opera (1929–44); also sang in Vienna and Munich. He appeared at the Salzburg (1933, 1937) and Bayreuth (1934, 1936) festivals; made his debut at London's Covent Garden as Florestan in 1938. After World War II, he again sang in Berlin and Vienna; made a concert tour of the U.S. in 1962. In his prime, he was compared to Caruso as a practitioner of bel canto. He excelled in the operas of Mozart; was also noted for his portrayals of Radames, Manrico, Huon, and Calaf. He publ. the autobiographical booklets *Skratta Pajazza* (*Ridi, Pagliaccio*; Copenhagen, 1945); *Mach es besser, mein Sohn* (Leipzig, 1962); and *Leitfaden für Gesangsbeflissene* (Munich, 1964).

BIBL.: F. Tassie, *H. R.* (Augsburg, 1975).

Rota (real name, **Rinaldi**), **Nino,** brilliant Italian composer; b. Milan, Dec. 3, 1911; d. Rome, April 10, 1979. He was a precocious musician; at the age of 11 he wrote an oratorio which had a public performance, and at 13 composed a lyric comedy in 3 acts, *Il Principe porcaro*, after Hans Christian Andersen. He entered the Milan Cons. in 1923, and took courses with Delachi, Orefici, and Bas; after private studies with Pizzetti (1925–26), he studied composition with Casella at the Accademia di Santa Cecilia in Rome, graduating in 1930; later went to the U.S., and enrolled in the Curtis Inst. of Music in Philadelphia, studying composition with Scalero and conducting with Reiner (1931–32). Returning to Italy, he entered the Univ. of Milan to study literature, gaining a degree in 1937. He taught at the Taranto music school (1937–38); then was a teacher (from 1939) and director (1950–78) at the Bari Liceo Musicale. His musical style demonstrates a great facility, and even felicity, with occasional daring excursions into the forbidding territory of dodecaphony. However, his most durable compositions are related to his music for the cinema; he composed the sound tracks of a great number of films of the Italian director Federico Fellini covering the period from 1950 to 1979.

WORKS: DRAMATIC: OPERAS: *Il Principe porcaro* (1925); *Ariodante* (Parma, Nov. 5, 1942); *Torquemada* (1943; rev. version, Naples, Jan. 24, 1976); *I 2 timidi*, radio opera (Italian Radio, 1950; stage version, London, March 17, 1952); *Il cappello di paglia di Firenzi* (1946; Palermo, April 2, 1955); *La scuola di guida* (Spoleto, 1959); *Lo scoiattolo in gamba* (Venice, Sept. 16, 1959); *La notte di un nevrastenico*, opera buffa (concert version, Turin, July 9, 1959; stage version, Milan, Feb. 8, 1960); *Aladino e la lampada magica* (Naples, Jan. 14, 1968); *La visita meravigliosa*, after H.G. Wells (Palermo, Feb. 6, 1970); *Napoli milionaria* (Spoleto, June 22, 1977). **BALLETS:** *La rappresentazione di Adamo ed Eva* (Perugia, Oct. 5, 1957); *La strada* (after the 1954 Fellini film of the same name; Milan, 1965; rev. 1978); *La Molière imaginaire* (Paris, 1976). **FILM SCORES:** For films by Fellini, including *Lo sceicco bianco* (*The White Sheik*, 1950); *I vitelloni* (1953); *La strada* (1954); *Il bidone* (1955); *Notti di Cabiria* (1957); *La dolce vita* (1959); part of *Boccaccio 70* (1962); *Otto de mezza* (*8 1/2*; 1963); *Giulietta degli spiriti* (*Juliet of the Spirits*, 1965); *Satyricon* (1969); *The Clowns* (1971); *Fellini Roma* (1972); *Amarcord* (1974); *Casanova* (1977); *Orchestra Rehearsal* (1979). His scores for other directors include Cass's *The Glass Mountain* (1950); De Filippo's *Napoli milionaria* (1950); Vidor's *War and Peace* (1956); Visconti's *Le notti bianche* (1957), *Rocco e i suoi fratelli* (1960), and *Il gattopardo* (*The Leopard*; 1963); Zeffirelli's *The Taming of the Shrew* (1966) and *Romeo e Giulietta* (1968); Bondarchuk's *Waterloo* (1969); Coppola's *The Godfather I* (1972) and *II* (1974); Harvey's *The Abdication* (1974); Wertmuller's *Love and Anarchy* (1974); Guillermin's *Death on the Nile* (1978); Monicelli's *Caro Michele* (1978); and Troell's *Hurricane* (1979). **ORCH.:** *Balli* (1932); *Serenata* (1932); 3 syms. (1936–39; 1938–43; 1957); *Sinfonia sopra una canzone d'amore* (1947–72); Harp Concerto (1948); *Variazioni sopra un tema gioviale* (1954); *Concerto festivo* (1958); 2 piano concertos (1960; *Piccolo mondo antico*, 1979); *Concerto soirée* for Piano and Orch.; *Fantasia sopra 12-note del*

"Don Giovanni" di Mozart for Piano and Orch. (1961); Concerto for Strings (1964); Trombone Concerto (1968); *Divertimento concertante* for Double Bass and Orch. (1968–69); Cello Concerto (1973); *Castel del Monte* for Horn and Orch. (1975–76); Bassoon Concerto (1974–77); *The Godfather Suite* (from the films; Buffalo, Nov. 5, 1976). **CHAMBER:** *Invenzioni* for String Quartet (1933); Viola Sonata (1934); *Canzona* for 11 Instruments (1935); Quintet for Flute, Oboe, Viola, Cello, and Harp (1935); Violin Sonata (1937); Sonata for Flute and Harp (1937); Trio for Flute, Violin, and Piano (1958); Nonet (1958); *Elegy* for Oboe and Piano (1959); Sonata for Organ and Brass (1968). **KEYBOARD: PIANO:** *Variazioni e fuga sul nome B-A-C-H* (1950); *15 Preludes* (1964). **ORGAN:** Sonata (1965). **VOCAL: ORATORIOS:** *L'infanzia di S. Giovanni Battista* (1923); *Mysterium Catholicum* (1962); *La vita di Maria* (1970); *Roma capomunni* (1972); *Rabelaisiana* (1978); also 3 masses (1960–62); songs.

Roters, Ernst, German composer; b. Oldenburg, July 6, 1892; d. Berlin, Aug. 25, 1961. He was a student of Moritz Mayer-Mahr (piano), Leichtentritt (theory), and Georg Schumann (composition) at Berlin's Klindworth-Scharwenka Cons., and then devoted himself mainly to composition. He wrote an opera, *Die schwarze Kammer* (Darmstadt, 1928), incidental music to plays, radio scores, 3 piano concertos, chamber music, and songs.

Roth, Daniel, distinguished French organist and pedagogue; b. Mulhouse, Oct. 31, 1942. He studied with Marie-Claire Alain and Maurice Duruflé at the Paris Cons., making his recital debut in Paris at the age of 20; won the Grand Prix de Chartres (1971). He was deputy organist (1963–72) and organist (1972–85) at Sacré-Coeur in Paris, prof. of organ at the Marseilles Cons. (1973–79), and artist-in-residence of the National Shrine of the Immaculate Conception and chairman of the organ dept. at the Catholic Univ. of America in Washington, D.C. (1974–76). He became organist of St.-Sulpice in Paris in 1985. From 1988 he also was a prof. at the Saarbrücken Hochschule für Musik. In 1986 he was made a Chevalier de l'ordre des Arts et des Lettres. He made many tours of Europe; also appeared widely in North America.

Roth, Feri, Hungarian-American violinist and teacher; b. Zvolen, Czechoslovakia, July 18, 1899; d. Los Angeles, May 7, 1969. He studied at the Royal Academy of Music in Budapest. He organized the Budapest String Quartet (1923), with which he toured Europe; then emigrated to the U.S. and formed the Roth Quartet (1928; with Jenö Antal, Ferenc Molnar, and Janos Scholz), which made an American debut at the Pittsfield Music Festival, Sept. 21, 1928. In 1946 he was appointed prof. of violin and chamber ensemble at the Univ. of Calif. at Los Angeles, a post he held until his death.

Rothenberger, Anneliese, esteemed German soprano; b. Mannheim, June 19, 1924. After vocal study with Erika Müller at the Mannheim Hochschule für Musik, she made her operatic debut in Koblenz in 1943. From 1946 to 1957 and again from 1958 to 1973 she was a member of the Hamburg State Opera; also had engagements in Düsseldorf, Salzburg, Edinburgh, and Aix-en-Provence. In 1958 she joined the Vienna State Opera; also sang at La Scala in Milan and in Munich. On Nov. 18, 1960, she made a notable debut at the Metropolitan Opera in N.Y. as Zdenka in *Arabella*, and remained on its roster until 1966. She was one of the most versatile singers of her generation, capable of giving congenial renditions of soprano roles in operas of Mozart and Verdi. She also gave excellent performances of the challenging role of Marie in Berg's *Wozzeck*. She further distinguished herself in the even more demanding role of Lulu in Berg's opera. She publ. an autobiography, *Melodie meines Lebens* (Munich, 1972).

Rother, Artur (Martin), German conductor; b. Stettin, Oct. 12, 1885; d. Aschau, Sept. 22, 1972. He studied piano and organ with his father; also attended the Univs. of Tübingen and Berlin. In 1906 he became a répétiteur at the Wiesbaden Opera; was an assistant at the Bayreuth Festivals (1907–14); from 1927 to 1934 he was Generalmusikdirektor in Dessau; in 1938 he went to Berlin as a conductor at the Deutsches Opernhaus, where he remained until 1958; was also chief conductor of the Berlin Radio (1946–49).

Rothier, Léon, French bass and teacher; b. Rheims, Dec. 26, 1874; d. N.Y., Dec. 6, 1951. He studied at the Paris Cons. with Crosti (singing), Lherie (opéra comique), and Melchissedec (opera), winning 1st prizes in all 3 classes upon graduation. He made his operatic debut as Jupiter in Gounod's *Philemon et Baucis* at the Opéra-Comique in Paris in 1899, remaining there until 1903; then was active in Marseilles (1903–07), Nice (1907–09), and Lyons (1909–10). On Dec. 10, 1910, he made his American debut at the Metropolitan Opera in N.Y. as Méphistophélès; remained on its roster until 1939 and then devoted himself to recitals. He taught at the Volpe Inst. in N.Y. (from 1916); also privately after his retirement from the stage.

Rothmüller, (Aron) Marko, Croatian baritone and teacher; b. Trnjani, Dec. 31, 1908; d. Bloomington, Ind., Jan. 20, 1993. He studied in Zagreb; then took lessons in singing with Franz Steiner in Vienna, and also had lessons in composition with Alban Berg. He made his operatic debut as Ottokar in *Der Freischütz* at the Schiller Theater in Hamburg-Altona in 1932; was a member of the opera in Zagreb (1932–34) and Zürich (1935–47); was with the Covent Garden Opera in London (1939; 1948–55). He sang with the N.Y. City Opera (1948–52); also at the Glyndebourne and Edinburgh festivals (1949–52); made his debut at the Metropolitan Opera in N.Y. on Jan. 22, 1959, as Kothner in *Die Meistersinger von Nürnberg*; appeared there again in 1960 and 1964. He taught at the Indiana Univ. School of Music in Bloomington from 1955 to 1979. He was distinguished in Wagnerian roles; also sang leading roles in modern works, including Wozzeck in Berg's opera. He wrote some chamber music and songs. Rothmüller publ. an interesting vol., *Die Musik der Juden* (Zürich, 1951; Eng. tr., London, 1953; 2nd ed., rev., 1967).

Röttger, Heinz, German conductor and composer; b. Herford, Westphalia, Nov. 6, 1909; d. Dessau, Aug. 26, 1977. He studied in Munich at the Academy of Music (1928–31) and took courses in musicology at the Univ. (Ph.D., 1937, with the diss. *Das Formproblem bei Richard Strauss*; publ. in Berlin, 1937). He served as music director of the Stralsund City Theater (1948–51), Generalmusikdirektor in Rostock (1951–54), and chief conductor of the Dessau Landestheater (from 1954).

WORKS: DRAMATIC: OPERAS: *Bellmann* (1946); *Phaëton* (1957); *Der Heiratsantrag* (1959); *Die Frauen von Troja* (1961); *Der Weg nach Palermo* (1965); *Spanisches Capriccio* (1976). **BALLETS:** *. . . und heller wurde jeder Tag* (1964); *Der Kreis* (1964). **ORCH.:** 2 syms. (1939; *Dessauer Sinfonie*, 1966–67); 2 violin concertos (1942, 1970); Piano Concerto (1950); Cello Concerto (1962); Viola Concerto (1966). **OTHER:** Chamber music; piano pieces.

Rotzsch, Hans-Joachim, German tenor and choral conductor; b. Leipzig, April 25, 1929. He studied at the Leipzig Hochschule für Musik, where his principal teachers were Günther Ramin, Amadeus Webersinke, and Johannes Weyrauch; also studied voice with Fritz Polster. In 1961 he joined the faculty of the Leipzig Hochschule für Musik; in 1963 he became director of the choral program at the Univ. of Leipzig. He was named cantor of the Thomaskirche of Leipzig in 1972; also conducted the Neues Bachisches Collegium Musicum. He distinguished himself as a soloist in Bach's passions, oratorios, and cantatas as well as in the capacity of choral conductor. During the 1984–85 and 1985–86 seasons, he conducted a series of performances of Bach's works at Leipzig's Thomaskirche and Gewandhaus in commemoration of the 300th anniversary of the master's birth.

Rouget, Gilbert, French ethnomusicologist; b. Paris, July 9, 1916. He studied at the Sorbonne in Paris under André Schaeffner and

Constantin Brăiloiu (1935–42). He joined the ethnomusicology dept. at the Musée de l'Homme in 1941, succeeding Schaeffner as director in 1965; also became director of research at CNRS in 1972. During expeditions to equatorial and western Africa (1946–70), he made 3 films in collaboration with J. Rouch: *Sortie des novices de Sakpata; Batteries dogon: Éléments pour une étude des rhythmes*; and *Danses des reines a Porto-Novo.* His field of study focuses on the music of Africa, particularly that of southern Benin; he has collected many recordings and written a number of articles, the originality and scholarship of which have made substantial contributions to African ethnomusicology.

Rouleau, Joseph (Alfred Pierre), admired Canadian bass and teacher; b. Matane, Quebec, Feb. 28, 1929. He went to Montreal and studied with Édouard Woolley and Albert Cornellier, and then at the Cons. with Martial Singher (1949–52). In 1951 he made a concert tour of eastern Canada. After further training with Mario Basiola and Antonio Narducci in Milan (1952–54), he made his first major appearance in opera as Colline at the New Orleans Opera in 1955. In 1956 he sang Verdi's King Philip II in Montreal. On April 23, 1957, he made his debut at London's Covent Garden as Colline, and continued to make appearances there for some 20 seasons. He made his first appearance at the Paris Opéra as Raimondo in 1960. In 1965–66 he toured Australia with Joan Sutherland's operatic enterprise. In 1967 he sang Basilio with the Canadian Opera Co., and returned there as Ramfis in 1968. In the latter year, he also made his debut at the N.Y. City Opera as Méphistophélès. In subsequent years, he sang with various North American and European opera companies. He also was engaged as a soloist with leading orchs. on both sides of the Atlantic. On April 13, 1984, he made his Metropolitan Opera debut in N.Y. as the Grand Inquisitor. His esteemed portrayal of Boris Godunov in Montreal in Feb. 1988 was telecast by the CBC. From 1980 he taught at the Montreal Cons. In 1967 he won the Prix de musique Calixa-Lavallée. He was made an Officer of the Order of Canada in 1977. In 1990 he was awarded the Prix Denise-Pelletier.

Rouse, Christopher (Chapman), American composer; b. Baltimore, Feb. 15, 1949. He studied with Richard Hoffman at the Oberlin (Ohio) College Cons. of Music (B.Mus., 1971). After private lessons with George Crumb (1971–73), he completed his training with Karel Husa at Cornell Univ. (D.M.A., 1977). He taught at the Univ. of Mich. (1978–81) and at the Eastman School of Music in Rochester, N.Y. (from 1981), where he was a prof. (from 1991). In 1985–86 he was composer-in-residence of the Indianapolis Sym. Orch., and then of the Baltimore Sym. Orch. from 1986 to 1989. In 1990 he held a Guggenheim fellowship. In 1993 he was awarded the Pulitzer Prize in Music for his Trombone Concerto.

WORKS: ORCH.: *The Infernal Machine* (1980; Evian, France, May 9, 1981); *Gorgon* (Rochester, N.Y., Nov. 15, 1984); Double Bass Concerto (1985; Buffalo, Feb. 25, 1988); *Phantasmata* (1985; St. Louis, Oct. 25, 1986); *Phaethon* (1986; Philadelphia, Jan. 8, 1987); 2 syms.: No. 1 (1986; Baltimore, Jan. 21, 1988) and No. 2 (1994; Houston, March 2, 1995); *Jagannath* (1987; Houston, Sept. 22, 1990); *Iscariot* for Chamber Orch. (St. Paul, Minn., Oct. 28, 1989); *Concerto per Corde* for Strings (N.Y., Nov. 28, 1990); Trombone Concerto (1991; N.Y., Dec. 30, 1992); Violin Concerto (1991); Cello Concerto (1992; Los Angeles, Jan. 23, 1994); Flute Concerto (1993). **CHAMBER:** *Liber Daemonum* for Organ (1980); 2 string quartets (1982; Aspen, Colo., July 23, 1988); *Rotae Passionis* for Chamber Ensemble (1982; Boston, April 8, 1983). **VOCAL:** *Mitternachtlieder* for Baritone and Chamber Ensemble (1979); *Karolju* for Chorus and Orch. (1990; Baltimore, Nov. 7, 1991).

Roussakis, Nicolas, Greek-born American composer and teacher; b. Athens, June 10, 1934; d. N.Y., Oct. 23, 1994. He emigrated to the U.S. in 1949 and became a naturalized citizen in 1956; attended Columbia Univ. (B.A., 1956; M.A., 1960; D.M.A., 1975), where he studied with Luening, Beeson, Cowell, Weber, Shapey, and Jarnach. He received a Fulbright grant for study in Germany (1961–63); attended seminars of Boulez, Berio, Ligeti, and Stockhausen in Darmstadt. Upon his return to the U.S., he became active with contemporary music groups. He taught at Columbia Univ. (1968–77) and at Rutgers, the State Univ. of N.J. (from 1977). His works are marked by an aggressive modernity of idiom, but are satisfyingly playable and surprisingly pleasurable even to untutored ears. They include *Night Speech* for Chorus and Percussion (1968); *Short Pieces* for 2 Flutes (1969); Concertino for Percussion and Woodwinds (1973); *Ode and Cataclysm* for Orch. (1975); *Ephemeris* for String Quartet (1979); *Fire and Earth and Water and Air* for Orch. (1980–83); *Pas de deux* for Violin and Piano (1985); *Trigono* for Trombone, Vibraphone, and Drums (1986); *The God Abandons Antony*, cantata for Narrator, Chorus, and Orch. (1987); *Hymn to Apollo* for Small Orch. (1989); *To Demeter*, for Orch. (1994; N.Y., Oct. 29, 1995); piano pieces; choruses.

Rousseau, Eugene, noted American saxophonist and pedagogue; b. Blue Island, Ill., Aug. 23, 1932. He studied clarinet at the Chicago Musical College (B.M.B., 1953), oboe at Northwestern Univ. (M.M., 1954), and saxophone at the Paris Cons. (1960–61); completed his academic training at the Univ. of Iowa (Ph.D., 1962, with the diss. *Clarinet Instructional Materials from 1732 to circa 1825*). In 1965 he made his Carnegie Recital Hall debut in N.Y.; was the first saxophonist to give solo recitals in London, Amsterdam, Vienna, and Berlin (1967) and in Paris (1968); also appeared as a soloist with orchs. in the U.S., Europe, and the Far East. In 1969 he was co-founder of the World Saxophone Congress. He taught at Luther College in Iowa (1956–59), Central Missouri State Univ. (1962–64), and the Univ. of Iowa (1964); in 1964 he joined the faculty of the Indiana Univ. School of Music, where he was chairman of the woodwind dept. (1966–73), a prof. (1972–88), and Distinguished Prof. (from 1988). He was also a guest prof. at the Vienna Hochschule für Musik (1981–82), Arizona State Univ. (1984), and the Prague Cons. (1985). He publ. a *Method for Saxophone* (2 vols., 1973, 1977).

Rousseau, Marcel (-Auguste-Louis), French composer, son of **Samuel-Alexandre Rousseau**; b. Paris, Aug. 18, 1882; d. there, June 11, 1955. He studied with his father, then entered the Paris Cons. as a student of Lenepveu; won the Deuxième Premier Grand Prix de Rome with the cantata *Maia* (1905); later added his father's first name to his own, and produced his works as Samuel-Rousseau. In 1947 he was elected to the Académie des Beaux-Arts.

WORKS: DRAMATIC: OPERAS (all 1st perf. in Paris): *Tarass Boulba* (Nov. 22, 1919); *Le Hulla* (March 9, 1923); *Le Bon Roi Dagobert* (Dec. 5, 1927); *Kerkeb* (April 6, 1951). **BALLETS:** *Promenade dans Rome* (Paris, Dec. 7, 1936); *Entre 2 rondes* (Paris, April 27, 1940). **ORCH.:** *Tableaux: Solitude triste* and *Impression dolente*, etc.

Roussel, Albert (Charles Paul Marie), outstanding French composer and teacher; b. Tourcoing, Département du Nord, April 5, 1869; d. Royan, Aug. 23, 1937. Orphaned as a child, he was educated by his grandfather, mayor of his native town, and after the grandfather's death, by his aunt. He studied academic subjects at the College Stanislas in Paris and music with the organist Stoltz; then studied mathematics in preparation for entering the Naval Academy; at the age of 18, he began his training in the navy; from 1889 to Aug. 1890 he was a member of the crew of the frigate *Iphigénie*, sailing to Indochina. This voyage was of great importance to Roussel, since it opened for him a world of oriental culture and art, which became one of the chief sources of his musical inspiration. He later sailed on the cruiser *Dévastation*; received a leave of absence for reasons of health, and spent some time in Tunis; was then stationed in Cherbourg, and began to compose there. In 1893 he was sent once more to Indochina. He resigned from the navy in 1894 and went to Paris, where he began to study music seriously with Gigout. In 1898 he entered the Schola Cantorum in Paris as a pupil of d'Indy; continued this study until 1907, when he was already 38 years old, but at the same time he was entrusted with a class in counterpoint, which he conducted at the Schola Cantorum from 1902 to 1914; among his students were Satie, Golestan, Le Flem, Roland-Manuel, Lioncourt, and Varèse. In 1909 Roussel and his wife, Blanche Preisach-Roussel, undertook a voyage to India, where he became acquainted with the legend of the queen Padmavati, which he selected as a subject for his famous opera-ballet. His choral sym. *Les Évocations* was also inspired by this tour. At the outbreak of World War I in 1914, Roussel applied for active service in the navy but was rejected, and volunteered as an ambulance driver. After the Armistice of 1918, he settled in Normandy and devoted himself to composition. In the autumn of 1930 he visited the U.S.

Roussel began his work under the influence of French Impressionism, with its dependence on exotic moods and poetic association. However, the sense of formal design asserted itself in his symphonic works; his Suite (1926) signalizes a transition toward neo-Classicism; the thematic development is vigorous, and the rhythms are clearly delineated, despite some asymmetrical progressions; the orchestration, too, is in the Classical tradition. Roussel possessed a keen sense of the theater; he was capable of fine characterization of exotic or mythological subjects, but also knew how to depict humorous situations in lighter works.

WORKS (all 1st perf. in Paris unless otherwise given): **DRAMATIC:** *Le marchand de sable qui passe*, incidental music (Le Havre, Dec. 16, 1908); *Le festin de l'araignée*, ballet-pantomime (1912; April 3, 1913); *Padmâvatî*, opera-ballet (1914–18; June 1, 1923); *La naissance de la lyre*, lyric opera (1923–24, July 1, 1925); *Sarabande*, ballet music (June 16, 1927); *Bacchus et Ariane*, ballet (1930; May 22, 1931; 2 orch. suites: No. 1, April 2, 1933; No. 2, Feb. 2, 1934); *Le testament de la tante Caroline*, opéra-bouffe (1932–33; Olomouc, Nov. 14, 1936); *Aenéas*, ballet (Brussels, July 31, 1935); Prelude to Act 2 of *Le quatorze juillet*, incidental music (July 14, 1936); *Elpénor* for Flute and String Quartet, radio music (n.d.). **ORCH.:** *Marche nuptiale* (1893); *Résurrection*, symphonic prélude (May 17, 1904); *Vendanges* (1904; April 18, 1905; not extant); 4 syms.: No. 1, *Le poème de la forêt* (1904–06; 1st complete perf., Brussels, March 22, 1908), No. 2 (1919–21; March 4, 1922), No. 3 (1929–30; Boston, Oct. 24, 1930), and No. 4 (1934; Oct. 19, 1935); *Évocations* (1910–11; May 18, 1912); *Pour une fête de printemps*, symphonic poem (1920; Oct. 29, 1921); Suite (1926; Boston, Jan. 21, 1927); Concerto for Small Orch. (1926–27; May 5, 1927); Piano Concerto (1927; June 7, 1928); *Little Suite* (April 11, 1929); *A Glorious Day* for Military Band (1932; July 1933); Sinfonietta for Strings (Nov. 19, 1934); *Rapsodie flamande* (Brussels, Dec. 12, 1936); Cello Concertino (1936; Feb. 6, 1937). **CHAMBER:** *Fantaisie* for Violin and Piano (1892; not extant); *Andante* for Violin, Viola, Cello, and Organ (1892; not extant); Horn Quintet (Feb. 2, 1901); 1 unnumbered violin sonata (May 5, 1902); 2 numbered violin sonatas: No. 1 (1907–08; Oct. 9, 1908; rev. 1931) and No. 2 (1924; Oct. 15, 1925); Piano Trio (1902; April 14, 1904; rev. 1927); *Divertissement* for Wind Quintet and Piano (April 10, 1906); *Impromptu* for Harp (April 6, 1919); *Fanfare pour un sacre païen* for Brass and Drums (1921; April 25, 1929); *Joueurs de flûte* for Flute and Piano (1924; Jan. 17, 1928); *Ségovia* for Guitar (Madrid, April 25, 1925); *Sérénade* for Flute, Violin, Viola, Cello, and Harp (Oct. 15, 1925); Duo for Bassoon and Cello or Double Bass (1925; Dec. 23, 1940); Trio for Flute, Viola, and Cello (Oct. 29, 1929); String Quartet (1931–32; Brussels, Dec. 9, 1932); *Andante and Scherzo* for Flute and Piano (Milan, Dec. 17, 1934); *Pipe* for Flageolet and Piano (1934); String Trio (1937); *Andante* for Oboe, Clarinet, and Bassoon (Nov. 30, 1937). **KEYBOARD: PIANO:** *Des heures passant* (1898); *Conte à la poupée* (1904); *Rustiques* (1904–06; Feb. 17, 1906); Suite (1909–10; Jan. 28, 1911); Sonatine (1912; Jan. 18, 1913); *Petit canon perpétuel* (1913); *Doute* (1919; May 5, 1920); *L'accueil des muses (in memoriam Debussy)* (1920; Jan. 24, 1921); *Prélude and Fugue* (1932–34; Feb. 23, 1935); 3 pieces (1933; April 14, 1934). **ORGAN:** *Prélude and Fughetta* (1929; May 18, 1930). **VOCAL:** 2 madrigals for Chorus (1897; May 3, 1898); *Deux mélodies* for Voice and Piano or Orch. (1919; orch. version, Dec. 9, 1928); *Madrigal aux muses* for Women's Voices (1923; Feb. 6, 1924); *Deux poèmes de Ronsard* for Voice and Flute (No. 1, May 15, 1924; No. 2, May 28, 1924); *Le bardit de francs* for Men's Voices, Brass, and Percussion ad libitum (1926; Strasbourg, April 21, 1928); *Psalm LXXX* for Tenor, Chorus, and Orch. (1928; April 25, 1929); many songs for Voice and Piano. N. Labelle ed. a *Catalogue raisonné de l'oeuvre d'Albert Roussel* (Louvain-la-Neuve, 1992).

BIBL.: L. Vuillemin, *A. R. et son oeuvre* (Paris, 1924); A. Hoérée, *A. R.* (Paris, 1938); N. Demuth, *A. R.: A Study* (London, 1947); R. Bernard, *A. R.: Sa vie, son oeuvre* (Paris, 1948); M. Pincherle, *A. R.* (Geneva, 1957); B. Deane, *A. R.* (London, 1961); J. Eddins, *The Symphonic Music of A. R.* (diss., Florida State Univ., 1967); A. Surchamp, *A. R.* (Paris, 1967); R. Follet, *A. R.: A Bio-Bibliography* (Westport, Conn., 1988); M. Kelkel and M. Cusin, *Colloque international A. R., 1869–1937 (1987: Lyon, France and Saint-Etienne, Loire, France* (Paris, 1989).

Rousselière, Charles, French tenor; b. St. Nazaire, Jan. 17, 1875; d. Joue-les-Tours, May 11, 1950. He studied at the Paris Cons. He made his operatic debut in 1900 as Samson at the Paris Opéra, where he sang until 1912; also sang with the Monte Carlo Opera (1905–14), creating roles in Mascagni's *Amica*, Saint-Saëns's *L'Ancêtre*, and Fauré's *Pénélope*; also sang the role of Julien in Charpentier's opera at its first performance at the Opéra-Comique in Paris. He made his debut at the Metropolitan Opera in N.Y. as Romeo on Nov. 26, 1906, but remained on its roster for only 1 season. He made guest appearances at La Scala in Milan, the Teatro Colón in Buenos Aires, in Palermo, etc.

Rousset, Christophe, remarkable French harpsichordist; b. Avignon, April 12, 1961. Following training with André Raynaud and Huguette Dreyfus at the Schola Cantorum in Paris, he was a student of Kenneth Gilbert before completing his studies with Bob van Asperen (harpsichord), the Kuijken brothers and Lucy van Dael (chamber music), and Leonhardt (interpretation) at the Royal Cons. of Music at The Hague (soloist diploma, 1983). In 1983 he took 1st prize in the Bruges harpsichord competition, and then launched a global career. From 1992 he also was active with his own Les Talons Lyriques ensemble. Rousset has won critical accolades for his extraordinary command of the harpsichord repertory. He particularly excells in the music of the French school, giving particularly outstanding performances of Couperin and Rameau.

Routh, Francis (John), English pianist, organist, conductor, writer on music, and composer; b. Kidderminster, Jan. 15, 1927. He studied at King's College, Cambridge (1948–51), at the Royal Academy of Music in London (1951–53), and with Seiber. He was founder and artistic director of the Redcliffe Concerts (from 1964), with which he presented works by British composers of the past and present.

WORKS: ORCH. (all 1st perf. in London unless otherwise given): Violin Concerto (1965; April 25, 1968); *Dialogue* for Violin and Orch. (May 20, 1969); Double Concerto for Violin, Cello, and Orch. (May 11, 1970); Sym. (1973; Dublin, July 22, 1975); Cello Concerto (1973; May 20, 1974); Piano Concerto (1976; Sept. 26, 1977); *Scenes* (1978); Oboe Concerto (1984); *Poème fantastique* (1987); Suite for Strings (1992); Suite for Strings (1992). **CHAMBER:** *Dance Suite* for String Quartet (1967); Sonata for Solo Cello (1971); Piano Quartet (1971); *Serenade* for String Trio (1972); Cello Sonata (1975); Oboe Quartet (1977); *Concerto for Ensemble I* (1981), *II* (1983), and *III* (1991); *Dance Interludes* for Flute and Guitar (1987); *Fantasy Duo* for Violin and Piano (1990); Clarinet Quintet (1994); piano pieces; organ works. **VOCAL:** *Ode to the Evening Star* for Chorus (1966); *Spring Night*, concert aria for Mezzo-soprano and Orch. (1971; March 13, 1972); *The Death of Iphigenia* for Soprano and 13 Instruments (1972); *On a Deserted Shore* for Soloists, Chorus,

2 Pianos, and 2 Percussion (1975); *Vocalise* for Soprano, Clarinet, Violin, Cello, and Piano (1979); *Love's Fool* for Soprano, Flute, and Guitar (1980); *Woefully Arranged* for Soloists, Chorus, and Orch. (1990); solo songs.

WRITINGS: *The Organ* (1958); *Contemporary Music: An Introduction* (1968); *Contemporary British Music* (1972); *Early English Organ Music* (1973); with others, *Patronage of the Creative Artist* (1974); *Stravinsky* (1975).

Routley, Erik (Reginald), English clergyman, organist, teacher, writer on music, and composer; b. Brighton, Oct. 31, 1917; d. Nashville, Tenn., Oct. 8, 1982. He studied classics at Magdalen College, Oxford (1936–40; B.A., 1940) and theology at Mansfield College, Oxford (1940–43). In 1943 he was made a minister in the Congregational Church of England and Wales, and then pursued his education at Oxford (B.D., 1946; Ph.D., 1952, with the diss. *An Historical Study of Christian Hymnology: Its Development and Discipline;* publ. as *The Music of Christian Hymnody,* London, 1957). In 1948 he became director of music at Mansfield College. After serving as a minister in Edinburgh (1959–67) and Newcastle upon Tyne (1967–75), he was prof. of church music at Westminster Choir College in Princeton, N.J. (from 1975). He also appeared as an organ recitalist. From 1964 he was ed. of the Studies in Church Music series. Routley was a composer mainly of sacred music.

WRITINGS: (all publ. in London unless otherwise given): *The Church and Music: An Enquiry into the History, the Nature and the Scope of Christian Judgment of Music* (1950; 2nd ed., rev., 1967); with K. Parry, *Companion to Congregational Praise* (1953); *The English Carol* (1958); *Ecumenical Hymnody* (1959); *Hymns Today and Tomorrow* (N.Y., 1964); *Twentieth Century Church Music* (1964); *Words, Music and the Church* (Nashville, Tenn., 1968); *The Musical Wesleys* (1969).

BIBL.: R. Leaver, ed., *Duty and Delight: R. Remembered. A Memorial Tribute to E. R. (1917–1982)* (1985).

Rowen, Ruth Halle, American music educator; b. N.Y., April 5, 1918. She studied at Barnard College (B.A., 1939) and with Mitchell, Lang, Hertzmann, and Moore at Columbia Univ. (M.A., 1941; Ph.D., 1948). She was director of the education dept. of Carl Fischer, Inc. (1954–63), then taught at the City College of N.Y. (1963–67) and at the graduate school of the City Univ. of N.Y. (from 1967). She wrote *Early Chamber Music* (N.Y., 1949; new ed., 1974) and *Music through Sources and Documents* (Englewood Cliffs, N.J., 1978).

Rowicki, Witold, Polish conductor and composer; b. Taganrog, Russia, Feb. 26, 1914; d. Warsaw, Oct. 1, 1989. He studied violin with Malawski and composition with Piotrowski and Wallek-Walewski at the Kraków Cons. (graduated as a violinist, 1938); then studied with Rudolf Hindemith, the brother of Paul Hindemith (1942–44). Although he made his conducting debut in 1933, he pursued a career as a violinist until the end of World War II. In 1945 he helped organize the Polish Radio Sym. Orch. in Katowice, which he conducted until 1950; then in 1950 he reorganized the Warsaw Phil., which he conducted until 1955, at which time he opened the orch.'s new home and oversaw the renaming of the orch. as the National Phil. before resigning his post. From 1958 to 1977 he was again the conductor of the National Phil.; then was chief conductor of the Bamberg Sym. Orch. (1982–85). He became widely known for his promotion of contemporary Polish music. He wrote syms., other orch. works, chamber music, and songs.

BIBL.: L. Terpilowski, *W. R.* (Kraków, 1961).

Rowley, Alec, English pianist, teacher, and composer; b. London, March 13, 1892; d. Weybridge, Jan. 11, 1958. He was a pupil of Corder at the Royal Academy of Music in London. From 1920 he taught at London's Trinity College of Music. He also was active as a recitalist. He composed a *Rhapsody* for Viola and Orch. (1936), 2 piano concertos (both 1938), an Oboe Concerto, 2 trios for Flute, Oboe and Piano (1930), a String Quartet (1932), numerous piano pieces, and some vocal music.

Roxburgh, Edwin, English composer, oboist, conductor, and teacher; b. Liverpool, Nov. 6, 1937. He studied composition with Howells at the Royal College of Music in London, with Nono and Dallapiccola in Italy, and with Boulanger in France; completed his education at St. John's College, Cambridge. He was principal oboist in the Sadler's Wells Opera orch. in London (1964–67), then prof. of composition and founder-director of the 20th-century performance studies dept. at the Royal College of Music (from 1967); also appeared as an oboist and was conductor of the 20th Century Ensemble of London. With L. Goossens, he publ. *The Oboe* (London, 1976). He composed a number of finely crafted orch., chamber, and vocal works, his idiomatic writing for woodwinds being particularly admirable.

WORKS: DRAMATIC: *Abelard,* opera; *The Tower,* ballet (1964). **ORCH.:** *Variations* (1963); *Montage* (1977); *7 Tableaux,* trumpet concerto (1979); *Prelude* (1981); *Saturn* (1982); *Serenata* for Strings (1983); *Tamesis* for Chamber Orch. (1983). **CHAMBER:** *Movements* for String Quartet (1961); Quartet for Flute, Clarinet, Violin, and Cello (1964); *Music 3* for String Trio (1966); *Dithyramb I* for Clarinet and Percussion (1972) and *II* for Piano and 3 Percussion (1972); *Nebula I* for Clarinet Choir (1974) and *II* for Wind Quintet (1974); *At the Still Point of the Turning World* for Amplified Oboe and Electronics (1978); *Hexham Tropes* for Oboe, Oboe d'Amore, Bassoon, and Harpsichord (1979); Wind Quintet No. 2 (1983); Quartet for Flute, Violin, Viola, and Cello (1984); *Voyager* for 3 Oboes, 3 English Horns, and 3 Bassoons (1989); piano pieces. **VOCAL:** *Recitative after Blake* for Contralto and String Quintet or String Orch. (1961); *Night Music* for Soprano and Orch. (1969); *How Pleasant to Know Mr. Lear* for Narrator and Chamber Orch. (1971); *A Scottish Fantasy* for Soprano, Violin, and String Orch. (1973); *A Portrait of e e cummings* for 2 Narrators, Violin, and Orch. (1974); *The Rock,* oratorio for Soloists, Chorus, Children's Chorus, and Orch. (1979); *et vitam venturi saeculi* for Chorus (1983); other choruses; songs.

Roy, Klaus George, Austrian-born American composer, writer, and program annotator; b. Vienna, Jan. 24, 1924. He went to the U.S. in 1940 and became a naturalized American citizen in 1944. He studied at Boston Univ. with Geiringer (B.Mus., 1947) and at Harvard Univ. with Davison, Kinkeldey, Merritt, and Piston (M.A., 1949). In 1945–46 he served as an officer in education and information with U.S. Army General Headquarters in Tokyo. From 1948 to 1957 he was employed as a librarian and instructor at Boston Univ.; also wrote music criticism for the *Christian Science Monitor* (1950–57). From 1958 to 1988 he was program annotator and ed. of the Cleveland Orch.; also taught at the Cleveland Inst. of Art (from 1975) and served as adjunct prof. at the Cleveland Inst. of Music (1986–94), which bestowed upon him an honorary doctorate in music (1987). A perspicacious collection of his writings appeared as *Not Responsible for Lost Articles: Thoughts and Second Thoughts from Severance Hall (1958–1988)* (Cleveland, 1993). He writes compositions in a variety of genres, all extremely pleasing to the ear.

WORKS: Duo for Flute and Clarinet (1947); Trombone Sonata (1950–51); *St. Francis' Canticle of the Sun* for Chorus and Viola (Boston, Nov. 5, 1951); *The Clean Dispatch of Dying,* song cycle for Soprano and Piano (1951); *Christopher-Suite* for Piano or Harpsichord (1953); *Lie Still, Sleep Becalmed* for Chorus (1954); *Sterlingman,* chamber opera (WGBH-TV, Boston, April 18, 1957); *Nostalgicon,* 9 retrospective pieces for Piano (1964–65); *Inaugural Fantasia* for Organ (1965); *Chorale-Variants on an Appalachian Ballad* for Orch. (1965; Cleveland, April 3, 1966); *Serenade* for Cello (Cleveland, May 15, 1968); *Lunar Modulations* for Children's Chorus and Percussion (Cuyahoga Falls, Ohio, July 19, 1969); *7 Brief Sermons on Love* for Soprano and Organ (1972); *A New Song* for Chorus, Speaking Chorus, and Organ (1973); *Retrospective '15–'50* for Violin and Piano (1974; rev. 1983); *Winter Death Songs,* 7 haiku for Low Voice and Piano (1982); *Songs of Alexias* for Low Voice and Piano (1982); *Zoopera: The Enchanted Garden* (Cleveland, Sept. 2, 1983); *Cheaper by the Dozen,* 12 flute duets (1985);

Miracles Are Not Ceased, scena for Soprano and Oboe (1985); *The Illuminated Fountain* for Soprano and Oboe (1993).

Royce, Edward, American composer and teacher; b. Cambridge, Mass., Dec. 25, 1886; d. Stamford, Conn., July 7, 1963. He studied at Harvard Univ. (B.A., 1907), later at the Stern Cons. in Berlin. In 1913 he founded the music dept. at Middlebury College in Vermont; was head of the theory dept. at the Ithaca Cons. (1916–21); from 1923 to 1947 he was a prof. of theory at the Eastman School of Music in Rochester, N.Y. He composed 2 tone poems: *The Fire Bringers* (Rochester, April 23, 1926) and *Far Ocean* (Rochester, June 3, 1929); piano pieces; songs.

Rozanov, Sergei (Vasilievich), Russian clarinetist and pedagogue; b. Ryazan, July 5, 1870; d. Moscow, Aug. 31, 1937. He settled in Moscow and studied with Zimmermann at the Cons. (1886–90). After playing in several opera orchs. (1891–94), he was a member (1894–97) and then 1st clarinetist (1897–1929) in the orch. of the Bolshoi Theater. He also pursued a solo career. From 1916 until his death he taught at the Cons. He wrote studies on the schools of clarinet playing (Moscow, 1947; 7th ed., 1968) and the principles of teaching wind instruments (Moscow, 1955). He also prepared transcriptions of various works for clarinet.

Rozhdestvensky, Gennadi (Nikolaievich), eminent Russian conductor, son of **Nikolai Anosov**; b. Moscow, May 4, 1931. He studied piano with Oborin and conducting with his father at the Moscow Cons.; graduated in 1954. From 1951 to 1961 he served as assistant conductor at the Bolshoi Theater in Moscow, and from 1964 to 1970 was its principal conductor. From 1961 to 1974 he was chief conductor of the All-Union Radio and TV Sym. Orch. in Moscow; also was chief conductor of the Stockholm Phil. (1975–77), the BBC Sym. Orch. in London (1978–81), and the Vienna Sym. Orch. (1981–83). In 1982 he founded and became chief conductor of the State Symphonic Orch. of the Soviet Ministry of Culture in Moscow. In 1991 he renamed it the Soviet Phil., and then later that year the State Symphonic Kapelle of Moscow. He conducted it at its U.S. debut in N.Y. on Feb. 4, 1992. From 1991 he also served as chief conductor of the Royal Stockholm Phil. He married **Viktoria Postnikova** in 1969. He is distinguished by his encompassing interest in new music; he conducted notable performances of works by Soviet composers, particularly Prokofiev and Shostakovich, as well as by Stravinsky, Schoenberg, Berg, Milhaud, Honegger, and Poulenc. Rozhdestvensky publ. a technical treatise on conducting (Leningrad, 1974) and a collection of essays on his thoughts on music (Moscow, 1975).

Rózsa, Miklós, brilliant Hungarian-American composer; b. Budapest, April 18, 1907; d. Los Angeles, July 27, 1995. He studied violin in childhood with Lajos Berkovits. After training at the Leipzig Cons. with Straube and Grabner, he went to Paris in 1931 and established himself as a composer. In 1935 he went to London. In 1940 he emigrated to the U.S., and settled in Hollywood; was on the staff of MGM (1948–62); also taught at the Univ. of Southern Calif. in Los Angeles (1945–65). His autobiography was publ. as *Double Life* (London, 1982). His orch. and chamber music is cast in the advanced modern idiom in vogue in Europe between the 2 world wars; neo-Classical in general content, it is strong in polyphony and incisive rhythm; for his film music, he employs a more Romantic and diffuse style, relying on a Wagnerian type of grandiloquence. He won Oscars for his film scores to *Spellbound* (1945), *A Double Life* (1947), and *Ben-Hur* (1959).

WORKS: FILM SCORES: *Knight without Armour* (1937); *The Four Feathers* (1939); *The Thief of Bagdad* (1940); *Lydia* (1941); *That Hamilton Woman* (1941); *Jacare* (1942); *Jungle Book* (1942); *5 Graves to Cairo* (1943); *Double Indemnity* (1944); *The Lost Weekend* (1945); *Spellbound* (1945); *The Killers* (1946); *The Strange Love of Martha Ivers* (1946); *Brute Force* (1947); *A Double Life* (1947); *The Naked City* (1948); *The Secret beyond the Door* (1948); *Madame Bovary* (1949); *The Asphalt Jungle* (1950); *Quo vadis?* (1951); *Ivanhoe* (1952); *Plymouth Adventure* (1952); *Julius Caesar* (1953); *The Story of Three Loves* (1953); *Knights of the Round Table* (1954); *Lust for Life* (1956); *A Time to Love and a Time to Die* (1958); *Ben-Hur* (1959); *El Cid* (1961); *King of Kings* (1961); *The V.I.P.s* (1963); *The Green Berets* (1968); *The Private Life of Sherlock Holmes* (1970); *The Golden Voyage of Sinbad* (1974); *Providence* (1977); *Time after Time* (1979); *Eye of the Needle* (1981); *Dead Men Don't Wear Plaid* (1982). **ORCH.:** *Rhapsody* for Cello and Orch. (1929); *Variations on a Hungarian Peasant Song* for Violin and Orch. (1929; also for Violin and Piano); *North Hungarian Peasant Songs and Dances* for Violin and Orch. (1929; also for Violin and Piano); *Symphony in 3 Movements* (1930; rev. 1993); *Scherzo* (1930; originally a movement of the preceding); *Serenade* for Small Orch. (1932; rev. 1946 as *Hungarian Serenade*); *Theme, Variations, and Finale* (1933; rev. 1943); Concerto for Strings (1943; Los Angeles, Dec. 28, 1944; rev. 1957); *The Vintner's Daughter*, 12 variations on a French Folk Song (1955; also for Piano, 1953); Violin Concerto (Dallas, Jan. 5, 1956; Jascha Heifetz soloist); *Overture to a Symphony Concert* (1957); *Notturno ungherese* (1964); *Sinfonia concertante* for Violin, Cello, and Orch. (1966); Piano Concerto (1966; Los Angeles, April 6, 1967); Cello Concerto (1969); *Tripartita* (1973); Viola Concerto (1979; Pittsburgh, May 4, 1984; Pinchas Zukerman, soloist). **CHAMBER:** Trio-Serenade for Violin, Viola, and Cello (1927); Piano Quintet (1928); Duo for Violin and Piano (1931); Duo for Cello and Piano (1931); Sonata for 2 Violins (1933; rev. 1973); 2 string quartets (1950, 1981); Flute Sonata (1983); Sonata for Solo Clarinet (N.Y., Jan. 14, 1987); various works for piano. **VOCAL:** Choral works; songs.

BIBL.: C. Palmer, *M. R.: A Sketch of His Life and Work* (N.Y., 1975).

Rozsnyai, Zoltán, Hungarian conductor; b. Budapest, Jan. 29, 1927; d. San Diego, Sept. 10, 1990. He was educated at the Franz Liszt Academy of Music, where his teachers included Bartók, Kodály, and Dohnányi; also took courses at the Technical Univ. and at the Pazmany Peter Univ. of Sciences in Budapest; completed his musical training at the Univ. of Vienna. He was conductor of the Phil. Orch. in Miskolc (1948–50); then conducted the Debrecen Opera (1950–53); later led several Hungarian orchs. He left Hungary after the abortive revolution of 1956 and went to the U.S. In 1957 he organized the Philharmonia Hungarica; toured with it in 1958. He was an assistant conductor of the N.Y. Phil. (1962–63); then was music director of the Cleveland Phil. (1965–68) and the San Diego Sym. (1967–71). In 1976 he became music director of the Golden State Opera Co. in Los Angeles; in 1978, became music director of the Knoxville (Tenn.) Sym. Orch., which post he retained until 1985.

Różycki, Ludomir, Polish composer and pedagogue; b. Warsaw, Nov. 6, 1884; d. Katowice, Jan. 1, 1953. He was a student of his father and Zawirski (piano), and of Noskowski (composition) at the Warsaw Cons., graduating with honors in 1903; then completed his training with Humperdinck in Berlin (1905–08). In 1908 went to Lemberg as conductor at the Opera and as a piano teacher at the Cons. After another Berlin sojourn (1914–20), he went to Warsaw as conductor of the Opera. In 1926 he helped to found the Polish Composers Union and served as its first president. From 1930 to 1945 he was a prof. at the Warsaw Cons., and then from 1945 at the Katowice Cons. He was highly regarded in Poland as a national composer of stature; his style of composition was a successful blend of German, Russian, and Italian ingredients, yet the Polish characteristics were not obscured by the cosmopolitan harmonic and orch. dress.

WORKS: DRAMATIC: OPERAS: *Boleslaw Śmialy* (Boleslaw the Bold; 1908; Lemberg, Feb. 11, 1909); *Meduza* (1911; Warsaw, Oct. 22, 1912); *Eros i Psyche* (1916; in German, Breslau, March 10, 1917); *Casanova* (1922; Warsaw, June 8, 1923); *Beatrix Cenci* (1926; Warsaw, Jan. 30, 1927); *Mlyn diabelski* (The Devilish Mill; 1930; Poznań, Feb. 21, 1931). **OPERETTA:** *Lili* *chce śpiewac* (Lile Wants to Sing; 1932; Poznań, March 7, 1933). **BALLETS:** *Pan Twardowski* (1920; Warsaw, May 9, 1921); *Apollo i dziewczyna* (Apollo and the Maiden; 1937). **ORCH.:** *Stańczyk*, symphonic scherzo (1903); symphonic poems: *Bolesław Smiały* (1906); *Pan Twordowski* (1906); *Anhelli* (1909); *Król Koftua* (1910); *Mona Lisa Gioconda* (1911); *Pietà* (1942); *Warszawa wyzwolona* (Warsaw Liberated; 1950); 2 piano concertos (1918, 1942); Violin Concerto (1944). **CHAMBER:** Violin Sonata (1903); Cello Sonata (1906); Piano Quintet (1913); String Quartet (1916); piano pieces. **VOCAL:** Choral music; song cycles.

BIBL.: A. Wieniawski, *L. R.* (Warsaw, 1928); M. Kaminski, *L. R.* (Katowice, 1951); J. Kański, *L. R.* (Kraków, 1955).

Rubbra, (Charles) Edmund, notable English composer and teacher; b. Northampton, May 23, 1901; d. Gerard's Cross, Feb. 13, 1986. His parents were musical, and he was taught to play the piano by his mother. He left school when he was 14 and was employed in various factories; at the same time, he continued to study music by himself, and attempted some composition; received a scholarship to study composition at Reading Univ. in 1920, and then entered the Royal College of Music in London in 1921, taking courses with Holst (composition), R.O. Morris (harmony and counterpoint), and Evlyn and Howard Jones (piano); also received some instruction from Vaughan Williams there before completing his studies in 1925. He taught at the Univ. of Oxford (1947–68) and at the Guildhall School of Music and Drama in London (from 1961). In 1960 he was made a Commander of the Order of the British Empire. He compensated for a late beginning in composition by an extremely energetic application to steady improvement of his technique; finally elaborated a style of his own, marked by sustained lyricism and dynamic Romanticism; his harmonic language often verged on polytonality. He publ. the books *Holst: A Monograph* (Monaco, 1947), *Counterpoint: A Survey* (London, 1960), and *Casella* (London, 1964).

WORKS: DRAMATIC: *Bee-Bee-Bei*, opera (1933); *Prism*, ballet (1938). **ORCH.:** *Double Fugue* (1924); *Triple Fugue* (1929); *Sinfonia concertante* for Piano and Orch. (1934; London, Aug. 10, 1943); *Rhapsody* for Violin and Orch. (1934); 11 syms.: No. 1 (1935–37; London, April 30, 1937), No. 2 (1937; London, Dec. 16, 1938; rev. 1951), No. 3 (1939; Manchester, Dec. 15, 1940), No. 4 (1941; London, Aug. 14, 1942), No. 5 (1947–48; London, Jan. 26, 1949), No. 6 (London, Nov. 17, 1954), No. 7 (Birmingham, Oct. 1, 1957), No. 8, *Hommage à Teilhard de Chardin* (1966–68; London, Jan. 5, 1971), No. 9, *Sinfonia sacra, the Resurrection*, for Soprano, Alto, Baritone, Chorus, and Orch. (1971–72), No. 10, *Sinfonia da camera* (1974; Middlesborough, Jan. 8, 1975), and No. 11 (1978–79; London, Aug. 20, 1980); *Soliloquy* for Cello and Orch. (London, Jan. 1, 1945); Viola Concerto (London, April 15, 1953); Piano Concerto (1956); Violin Concerto (1959). **CHAMBER:** *Fantasy* for 2 Violins and Piano (1925); 3 violin sonatas (1925, 1931, 1967); *Lyric Movement* for String Quartet and Piano (1929); 4 string quartets (1933, rev. 1956; 1952; 1962–63; 1976–77); Cello Sonata (1946); *The Buddha*, suite for Flute, Oboe, Violin, Viola, and Cello (1947); 2 piano trios (1950, 1970); Oboe Sonata (1958); various piano pieces. **VOCAL:** Many choral works; songs.

BIBL.: R. Grover, *The Music of E. R.* (Aldershot, 1993).

Rubin, Marcel, Austrian composer; b. Vienna, July 7, 1905; d. there, May 12, 1995. He studied piano with Richard Robert, theory of composition with Richard Stöhr, and counterpoint and fugue with Franz Schmidt at the Vienna Academy of Music; simultaneously attended courses in law. In 1925 he went to Paris, where he took private lessons with Milhaud. He was back in Vienna in 1931 to complete his studies in law, and in 1933 received his degree of Dr.Juris. After the Nazi Anschluss of Austria in 1938, Rubin, being a non-Aryan, fled to Paris, but was interned as an enemy alien; after France fell in 1940, he made his way to Marseilles. Convinced that only the Communists could efficiently oppose fascism, he became a member of the illegal Austrian Communist party in exile; in 1942 he went to Mexico and remained there until 1946; returned to Vienna in 1947. His music followed the modernistic models of Parisianized Russians and Russianized Frenchmen, with a mandatory hedonism in "new simplicity." Although he studied works of Schoenberg, Berg, and Webern with great assiduity and wrote articles about them, he never adopted the method of composition with 12 tones in his own music.

WORKS: DRAMATIC: *Die Stadt*, dance piece (1932; rev. 1980); *Kleider machen Leute*, comic opera (1966–69; Vienna, Dec. 14, 1973). **ORCH.:** 10 syms. (1927, rev. 1957; 1937, rev. 1974; 1939, rev. 1962; 1943–45, rev. 1971; 1964–65; 1973–74, rev. 1983; 1977; 1980; 1984; 1986); *Ballade* (1948); *Rondo-Burleske* (1960); *Drei Komodianten*, little suite (1963); *Sonatine* (1965); *Sinfonietta* for Strings (1966); *Pastorale* for Strings (1970); Double Bass Concerto (1970); Trumpet Concerto (1971–72); Bassoon Concerto (1976; Vienna, Aug. 23, 1977); *Hymnen an die Nacht* (1982; Vienna, April 18, 1985). **CHAMBER:** String Quartet No. 1 (1926; rev. 1961); Trio for Strings (1927; rev. 1962); *Sonatine* for Oboe and Piano (1927); Cello Sonata (1928); *Divertimento* for Piano Trio (1966–67); *Serenade* for 5 Brass (1971); Violin Sonata (1974); Clarinet Quintet (1985). **PIANO:** 3 sonatas (1925, rev. 1974; 1926–27; 1928). **VOCAL:** *Ein Heiligenstädter Psalm* for Baritone, Chorus, and Orch., after Beethoven's Heiligenstädt Testament (1977; Vienna, March 7, 1978); *Licht über Damaskus*, oratorio for 4 Soloists, Chorus, Organ, and Orch. (1987–88).

BIBL.: H. Krones, *M. R.* (Vienna, 1975).

Rubinstein, Arthur (actually, **Artur**), celebrated Polish-born American pianist; b. Łódź, Jan. 28, 1887; d. Geneva, Dec. 20, 1982. He was a product of a merchant family with many children, of whom he alone exhibited musical propensities. He became emotionally attached to the piano as soon as he saw and heard the instrument. At the age of 7, on Dec. 14, 1894, he played pieces by Mozart, Schubert, and Mendelssohn at a charity concert in Łódź. His first regular piano teacher was one Adolf Prechner. He was later taken to Warsaw, where he had piano lessons with Alexander Różycki; then went to Berlin in 1897 to study with Heinrich Barth; also received instruction in theory from Robert Kahn and Max Bruch. In 1900 he appeared as soloist in Mozart's A-major Concerto, K.488, in Potsdam; he repeated his success that same year when he played the work again in Berlin under Joachim's direction; then toured in Germany and Poland. After further studies with Paderewski in Switzerland (1903), he went to Paris (1904), where he played with the Lamoureux Orch. and met Ravel, Dukas, and Thibaud. He also played the G-minor Piano Concerto by Saint-Saëns in the presence of the composer, who commended him. The ultimate plum of artistic success came when Rubinstein received an American contract. He made his debut at Carnegie Hall in N.Y. on Jan. 8, 1906, as soloist with the Philadelphia Orch. in his favorite Saint-Saëns concerto. His American tour was not altogether successful, and he returned to Europe for further study. In 1915 he appeared as soloist with the London Sym. Orch. During the season 1916–17, he gave numerous recitals in Spain, a country in which he was to become extremely successful; from Spain he went to South America, where he also became a great favorite; he developed a flair for Spanish and Latin American music, and his renditions of the piano works of Albéniz and Falla were models of authentic Hispanic modality. Villa-Lobos dedicated to Rubinstein his *Rudepoema*, regarded as one of the most difficult piano pieces ever written. Symbolic of his cosmopolitan career was the fact that he maintained apartments in N.Y., Beverly Hills, Paris, and Geneva. He was married to Aniela Mlynarska in 1932. Of his 4 children, 1 was born in Buenos Aires, 1 in Warsaw, and 2 in the U.S. In 1946 he became a naturalized American citizen. On June 11, 1958, Rubinstein gave his first postwar concert in Poland; in 1964 he played in Moscow, Leningrad, and Kiev. In Poland and in Russia he was received with tremendous emotional acclaim. But he forswore any appearances in Germany as a result of the Nazi extermination of the members of his family during World War

II. On April 30, 1976, at the age of 89, he gave his farewell recital in London.

Rubinstein was one of the finest interpreters of Chopin's music, to which his fiery temperament and poetic lyricism were particularly congenial. His style of playing tended toward bravura in Classical compositions, but he rarely indulged in mannerisms; his performances of Mozart, Beethoven, Schumann, and Brahms were particularly inspiring. In his characteristic spirit of robust humor, he made jokes about the multitude of notes he claimed to have dropped, but asserted that a worse transgression against music would be pedantic inflexibility in tempo and dynamics. He was a bon vivant, an indefatigable host at parties, and a fluent, though not always grammatical, speaker in most European languages, including Russian and his native Polish. In Hollywood, he played on the sound tracks for the films *I've Always Loved You* (1946), *Song of Love* (1947), and *Night Song* (1947). He also appeared as a pianist, representing himself, in the films *Carnegie Hall* (1947) and *Of Men and Music* (1951). A film documentary entitled *Artur Rubinstein, Love of Life* was produced in 1975; a 90-minute television special, *Rubinstein at 90,* was broadcast to mark his entry into that nonagenarian age in 1977; he spoke philosophically about the inevitability of dying. He was the recipient of numerous international honors: a membership in the French Académie des Beaux Arts and the Légion d'Honneur, and the Order of Polonia Restituta of Poland; he held the Gold Medal of the Royal Phil. Soc. of London and several honorary doctorates from American institutions of learning. He was a passionate supporter of Israel, which he visited several times. In 1974 an international piano competition bearing his name was inaugurated in Jerusalem. On April 1, 1976, he received the U.S. Medal of Freedom, presented by President Ford. During the last years of his life, he was afflicted with retinitis pigmentosa, which led to his total blindness; but even then he never lost his joie de vivre. He once said that the slogan "wine, women, and song" as applied to him was 80% women and only 20% wine and song. And in a widely publicized interview he gave at the age of 95 he declared his ardent love for Annabelle Whitestone, the Englishwoman who was assigned by his publisher to help him organize and edit his autobiography, which appeared as *My Young Years* (N.Y., 1973) and *My Many Years* (N.Y., 1980). He slid gently into death in his Geneva apartment, as in a pianissimo ending of a Chopin nocturne, ritardando, morendo . . . Rubinstein had expressed a wish to be buried in Israel; his body was cremated in Switzerland; the ashes were flown to Jerusalem to be interred in a separate emplacement at the cemetery, since the Jewish law does not permit cremation.

BIBL.: B. Gavoty, *A. R.* (Geneva, 1955; Eng. tr., 1956); D. Vroon, "An Appreciation: A. R.," *Le Grand Baton* (Dec. 1983; with complete discography by D. Manildi).

Rubinstein, Beryl, American pianist, teacher, and composer; b. Athens, Ga., Oct. 26, 1898; d. Cleveland, Dec. 29, 1952. He studied piano with his father and Alexander Lambert; toured the U.S. as a child (1905–11); then went to Berlin to study with Busoni and Vianna da Motta. He was appointed to the faculty of the Cleveland Inst. of Music in 1921; became its director in 1932. He wrote an opera, *The Sleeping Beauty,* to a libretto by John Erskine (Juilliard School of Music, N.Y., Jan. 19, 1938); 32 piano studies; 3 dances for Piano; transcriptions from Gershwin's *Porgy and Bess.* He conducted his orch. *Scherzo* with the Cleveland Orch. on March 17, 1927; performed his Piano Concerto with the same orch. on Nov. 12, 1936.

Rubio (Calzón), Samuel, Spanish musicologist; b. Posada de Omano, Oct. 20, 1912; d. Madrid, March 15, 1986. He entered the Augustinian order and was active in various monasteries. He received instruction in philosophy, theology, Gregorian chant, and other subjects, and later went to Rome to study sacred music and musicology at the Pontificio Instituto di Musica Sacra (1952–55) and musicology with Anglès at the Univ. (Ph.D., 1967, with the diss. *Cristóbal de Morales*; publ. in El Escorial, 1969). After serving as organist and choirmaster at the Escorial (1939–59; 1971–72), he was prof. of musicology at the Madrid Cons. (from 1972). He was the ed. of the collected works of Juan de Anchieta and Juan Navarro.

WRITINGS: *In XVI centenario nativitatis Sancti Patris Augustini: XXIV cantica sacra in honorem S. P. Augustini ex auctoribus antiquis et hodiernis* (Bilbao, 1954); *La politonía clásica* (El Escorial, 1956; Eng. tr., 1972); *Catalogo del archivo de música del monasteria de San Lorenzo el Real de El Escorial* (Cuenca, 1976); *Antonio Soler: Catálogo Crítico* (Cuenca, 1980).

Rübner, Cornelius. See **Rybner, Cornelius.**

Rübsam, Wolfgang, German organist and teacher; b. Giessen, Oct. 16, 1946. He studied at Southern Methodist Univ. in Dallas (M.Mus., 1970); took lessons with Helmut Walcha at the Frankfurt am Main Staatliche Hochschule für Musik, where he graduated with an artist diploma in 1971; he subsequently studied with Marie-Claire Alain in Paris (1971–74). In 1974 he joined the faculty of Northwestern Univ. He made extensive tours as an organ virtuoso.

Rubsamen, Walter (Howard), renowned American musicologist; b. N.Y., July 21, 1911; d. Los Angeles, June 19, 1973. He studied flute with Barrère in N.Y. and musicology at Columbia Univ. with Lang (B.A., 1933); then attended classes of Ursprung and Ficker at the Univ. of Munich; received his doctorate there with the diss. *Pierre de la Rue als Messenkomponist* (1937). Returning to the U.S., he was appointed to the music faculty at the Univ. of Calif., Los Angeles, obtaining a full professorship in 1955; was chairman of the music dept. (1965–73). He ed. the *Opera omnia* of Pierre de La Rue for the American Inst. of Musicology and brought out a German 16th-century *Magnificat on Christmas Carols* (N.Y., 1971); contributed a number of informative articles on ballad opera in England and on Renaissance composers to various American and European publications.

WRITINGS: *Literary Sources of Secular Music in Italy c.1500* (Berkeley, Calif., 1943); with D. Heartz and H.M. Brown, *Chanson and Madrigal, 1480–1530* (Cambridge, Mass., 1964).

Rudel, Julius, prominent Austrian-born American conductor; b. Vienna, March 6, 1921. Following training at the Vienna Academy of Music, he emigrated to the U.S. in 1938 and became a naturalized American citizen in 1944. He completed his studies at the Mannes School of Music in N.Y. In 1943 he joined the staff of the N.Y. City Opera as a répétiteur. On Nov. 25, 1944, he made his conducting debut there with *Der Zigeunerbaron,* and subsequently remained closely associated with it. From 1957 to 1979 he served as its music director. During his innovative tenure, he programmed an extensive repertoire of standard, non-standard, and contemporary operas. He made a special effort to program operas by American composers. He also was music director of the Caramoor Festival in Katonah, N.Y., and the Wolf Trap Farm Park for the Performing Arts in Vienna, Virginia. He was the first music director of the Kennedy Center in Washington, D.C. (1971–74). On. Oct. 7, 1978, he made his Metropolitan Opera debut in N.Y. conducting *Werther,* and continued to make occasional appearances there in subsequent years. He also appeared as a guest conductor of operas in San Francisco, Chicago, London, Paris, Berlin, Munich, Milan, Hamburg, and Buenos Aires. After serving as music director of the Buffalo Phil. from 1979 to 1985, he concentrated on a career as a guest conductor around the world. In 1969 the Julius Rudel Award for young conductors was established in his honor.

Ruders, Poul, Danish composer; b. Ringsted, March 27, 1949. He began piano and organ lessons in childhood, and later pursued training in organ at the Royal Danish Cons. of Music in Copenhagen (graduated, 1975). Although he had a few orchestration lessons there, he was mainly autodidact as a composer. From 1975 he was active as a Lutheran church organist and choirmaster. Later he devoted much time to composition and guest lecturing. In 1991 he was a guest lecturer at Yale Univ. He received the Charles Heidseick Award of the Royal Phil. Soc. of London in 1991. In his music, Ruders has been particularly cognizant of all styles of music, from the Baroque to the popular genres. His works are notable for their startling juxtapositions and superimpositions of various styles and techniques.

WORKS: OPERA: *Tycho* (1985–86; Århus, May 16, 1987). **ORCH.:** *Pavane* (1971); *Etudes* (1974); *Capriccio pian'e forte* (Odense, Sept. 5, 1978); *Recitatives and Arias*, piano concerto (1978; Buffalo, April 1, 1979); 2 violin concertos: No. 1 (1981; Copenhagen, Oct. 16, 1982) and No. 2 (1990–91); *Manhattan Abstraction* (1982); *Thus Saw St. John* (1984); Concerto for Clarinet and Twin Orch. (1985); *Jubileephony* (1986); *Drama Trilogy I: Dramaphonia* for Piano and Orch. (1987), *II: Monodrama* for Percussionist and Orch. (1988), and *III: Polydrama* for Cello and Orch. (1988); Sym., *Himmelhoch Jauchzend-zum Tode betrubt* (1989); *Psalmodies* for Guitar and Orch. (1989); *Tundra* (1990); *The Second Night Shade* (1991); *Gong* (1992); *Concerto in Pieces (A Latterday "Young Person's Guide to the Orchestra")* (1994–95); Viola Concerto (Copenhagen, April 21, 1995); Piano Concerto (1995). **CHAMBER:** 3 string quartets (1972; 1979; *Motet*, 1979); *Bravour-Studien* for Cello (1976); *Wind-Drumming* for Wind Quintet and 4 Percussionists (1979); *4 Compositions* for 9 Instruments (1980); *Diferencias* for 7 Instruments (1980); *Carnival* for Electric Alto Flute and Foot Bongos (1980); *Cha Cha Cha* for Percussion (1981); *Greeting Concertino* for 8 Instruments (1982); *4 Dances in 1 Movement* for Chamber Ensemble (1983); *Vox im Rama* for Clarinet, Electric Violin, and Piano (1983); *Alarm* for Percussion (1983); *Tattoo for 1* for Clarinet (1984); *Tattoo for 3* for Clarinet, Cello, and Piano (1984); *Corpus cum Figuris* for Chamber Ensemble (1985); *Break-Dance* for Piano, 2 Trumpets, and 3 Trombones (1985); *Cembal d'Amore* for Harpsichord and Piano (1986); *Nightshade* for Chamber Ensemble (1987); *Throne* for Clarinet and Piano (1988); *Variations* for Violin (1989); *De Profundis* for 2 Pianos and Percussion (1990); *Towards the Precipice* for Percussion (1990); piano pieces, including 2 sonatas (*Dante Sonata*, 1970; 1982); organ music. **VOCAL:** *Stabat Mater* for Chorus, Piano, and Organ (1973); *Pestilence Songs* for Soprano, Guitar, and Saloon Piano (1975); *glOriA* for Chorus and 12 Brasses (1981); 3 motets for Chorus (1981, 1985, 1988); *The City in the Sea* for Contralto and Orch. (1990).

Rudhyar, Dane (real name, **Daniel Chennevière**), French-born American composer, painter, and mystical philosopher; b. Paris, March 23, 1895; d. San Francisco, Sept. 13, 1985. He changed his name in 1917 to Rudhyar, derived from an old Sanskrit root conveying the sense of dynamic action and the color red, astrologically related to the zodiacal sign of his birth and the planet Mars. He studied philosophy at the Sorbonne in Paris (baccalaureat, 1911), and took music courses at the Paris Cons. In composition he was largely self-taught; he also achieved a certain degree of proficiency as a pianist; developed a technique that he called "orchestral pianism." In 1913 the publisher Durand commissioned him to write a short book on Debussy, with whom he briefly corresponded. At the same time, he joined the modern artistic circles in Paris. In 1916 he went to America; became a naturalized American citizen in 1926. His "dance poems" for Orch., *Poèmes ironiques* and *Vision végétale*, were performed at the Metropolitan Opera in N.Y. (April 4, 1917). In 1918 he visited Canada; in Montreal he met the pianist Alfred Laliberté, who was closely associated with Scriabin, and through him Rudhyar became acquainted with Scriabin's theosophic ideas. In Canada he also publ. a collection of French poems, *Rapsodies* (Toronto, 1918). In 1920 he went to Hollywood to write scenic music for *Pilgrimage Play, The Life of Christ*, and also acted the part of Christ in the prologue of the silent film version of *The Ten Commandments* produced by Cecil B. DeMille. In Hollywood he initiated the project of "Introfilms," depicting inner psychological states on the screen through a series of images, but it failed to receive support and was abandoned. Between 1922 and 1930 he lived in Hollywood and N.Y.; was one of the founding members of the International Composers Guild in N.Y. In 1922 his orch. tone poem *Soul Fire* won the $1,000 prize of the Los Angeles Phil.; in 1928 his book *The Rebirth of Hindu Music* was publ. in Madras, India. After 1930 Rudhyar devoted most of his time to astrology. His first book on the subject, *The Astrology of Personality* (1936), became a standard text in the field; it was described by Paul Clancy, the pioneer in the publication of popular astrological magazines, as "the greatest step forward in astrology since the time of Ptolemy." A new development in Rudhyar's creative activities took place in 1938 when he began to paint, along nonrepresentational symbolistic lines; the titles of his paintings (*Mystic Tiara, Cosmic Seeds, Soul and Ego, Avatar*, etc.) reflect theosophic themes. His preoccupations with astrology left him little time for music; about 1965 he undertook a radical revision of some early compositions, and wrote several new ones; was also active as a lecturer.

The natural medium for Rudhyar's musical expression was the piano; his few symphonic works were mostly orchestrations of original piano compositions. In his writing for piano, he built sonorous chordal formations supported by resonant pedal points, occasionally verging on polytonality; a kinship with Scriabin's piano music was clearly felt, but Rudhyar's harmonic idiom was free from Scriabin's Wagnerian antecedents. Despite his study of oriental religions and music, Rudhyar did not attempt to make use of Eastern modalities in his own music. He lived his last years in Palo Alto, California, and kept active connections with the world of theosophy; he also orchestrated his early piano works. Before his death his wife asked him whom he expected to meet beyond the mortal frame; he replied, "Myself."

WORKS: ORCH.: *3 poèmes ironiques* (1914); *Vision végétale* (1914); *The Warrior*, symphonic poem for Piano and Orch. (1921; Palo Alto, Dec. 10, 1976); *Sinfonietta* (1927); *Syntonies* in 4 sections: *To the Real* (1920), *The Surge of Fire* (1921), *Ouranos* (1927), and *The Human Way* (1927); *Tripthong* for Piano and Orch. (1948; rev. 1977); *Thresholds* (1954); *Dialogues* for Chamber Orch. (1977; San Francisco, May 23, 1982); *Cosmic Cycle* (1981). **CHAMBER:** *3 Melodies* for Flute, Cello, and Piano (1919); *3 Poems* for Violin and Piano (1920); *Solitude* for String Quartet (1950); Piano Quintet (1950); *Barcarolle* for Violin and Piano (1955); *Alleluia* for Carillon (1976); *Nostalgia* for Flute, Piano, and Strings (1977); 2 string quartets (*Advent*, 1978; *Crisis and Overcoming*, 1979). **PIANO:** *3 poèmes* (1913); *Mosaics*, tone cycle in 8 movements on the life of Christ (1918); *Syntony* (1919–34; rev. 1967); *9 Tetragrams* (1920–67)); *Pentagrams* (1924–26); *3 Paeans* (1925); *Granites* (1929); *Transmutation* (1976); *Theurgy* (1976); *Autumn and 3 Cantos* (1977); *Epic Poem* (1979); *Rite of Transcendence* (1981). **SONGS:** *3 chansons de Bilitis* (1919); *3 poèmes tragiques* (1918); *3 invocations* (1939).

WRITINGS: *Claude Debussy et son oeuvre* (Paris, 1913); *Art as Release of Power* (N.Y., 1930); *The Astrology of Personality* (N.Y., 1936; 2nd ed., 1979); *The Practice of Astrology* (Amsterdam, 1967; N.Y., 1970); *The Planetarization of Consciousness* (Amsterdam, 1970; N.Y., 1972); *The Astrological Houses* (N.Y., 1972); *Culture, Crisis and Creativity* (Wheaton, Ill., 1977); *The Astrology of Transformation* (Wheaton, 1980); *The Magic of Tone and the Art of Music* (Boulder, Colo., 1982); *The Rhythm of Wholeness* (Wheaton, 1983).

BIBL.: A. Morang, *D. R., Pioneer in Creative Synthesis* (N.Y., 1939); *D. R.: A Brief Biography* (Berkeley, Calif., 1972).

Rüdinger, Gottfried, German composer; b. Lindau, Aug. 23, 1886; d. Gauting, near Munich, Jan. 17, 1946. He was a student in theology; took courses in composition with Reger at the Leipzig Cons. (1907–09); in 1910 he settled in Munich and began teaching privately; taught at the Academy of Music there from 1920. He composed industriously in many genres; brought out a "peasant play-opera," *Die Tegernseer im Himmel*, and several children's operas, including *Benchtesgadener Sagenspiel, Musikantenkomodie*, and *König Folkwart*; also 2 syms.; 2 violin concertos; Cello Concerto; much choral and chamber music, and a number of instructive piano pieces. His pieces for small brass ensembles, in the style of old town piper music, are especially attractive.

Rudnicki, Marian (Teofil), Polish conductor and composer; b. Kraków, March 7, 1888; d. Warsaw, Dec. 31, 1944. He conducted operetta in Kraków (1916–19) and later at the Warsaw Municipal Opera. He wrote mostly theater music; also composed choral works and solo songs.

Rudnytsky, Antin, Polish-American pianist, conductor, and composer; b. Luka, Galicia, Feb. 7, 1902; d. Toms River, N.J., Nov. 30, 1975. He studied piano with Schnabel and Petri, composition with Schreker, and musicology with Curt Sachs in Berlin; received his Ph.D. at the Univ. of Berlin in 1926. In 1927 he went to Russia, where he conducted opera in Kharkov and Kiev; then was conductor of the Lwów Opera (1932–37). In 1937 he emigrated to the U.S.; toured with his wife, the singer Maris Sokil, as her piano accompanist. He composed 3 syms. (1936, 1941, 1942); a Cello Concerto (1942); an opera, *Dovbush* (1937); some ballet music; miscellaneous pieces for instrumental ensembles; piano works.

Rudolf, Max, eminent German-born American conductor and teacher; b. Frankfurt am Main, June 15, 1902; d. Philadelphia, Feb. 28, 1995. He began his musical training when he was 7. He studied cello with Maurits Frank, piano with Eduard Jung, and composition with Bernhard Sekles, and also learned to play the organ and the trumpet. In 1921–22 he attended the Univ. of Frankfurt am Main. In 1922 he became a répétiteur at the Freiburg im Breisgau Opera, where he made his conducting debut in 1923. After working as a répétiteur at the Darmstadt Opera (1923–25), he returned there to hold its post of 1st conductor from 1927 to 1929. From 1929 to 1935 he conducted at the German Theater in Prague. In 1929–30 he appeared as a guest conductor of the Berlin Phil. In 1935 he went to Göteborg, where he made appearances as a conductor with both the radio orch. and the orch. society. In 1940 he emigrated to the U.S. and in 1945 became a naturalized American citizen. He conducted the New Opera Co. in N.Y. before joining the staff of the Metropolitan Opera in N.Y. in 1945. On Jan. 13, 1946, he made his first appearance as a conductor at the Metropolitan Opera in a Sunday night concert. His formal debut followed on March 2, 1946, when he conducted *Der Rosenkavalier*. From 1950 to 1958 he served as artistic administrator of the Metropolitan Opera, and also was active as a conductor there. In 1958 he became music director of the Cincinnati Sym. Orch., a position he retained with distinction until 1969. In 1966 he led it on a world tour and in 1969 on a major tour of Europe. He also served as music director of the Cincinnati May Festival in 1963 and again from 1967 to 1970. From 1970 to 1973 he was head of the opera and conducting depts. at the Curtis Inst. of Music in Philadelphia. In 1973–74 he was principal conductor of the Dallas Sym. Orch., and he also returned to the Metropolitan Opera as a conductor during this time. In 1976–77 he was music advisor of the New Jersey Sym. Orch. In subsequent years, he made occasional appearances as a guest conductor with American orchs. From 1983 he again taught at the Curtis Inst. of Music. In 1988 he received the 1st Theodore Thomas Award for his services to music. He publ. the widely used vol. *The Grammar of Conducting: A Comprehensive Guide to Baton Technique and Interpretation* (N.Y., 1950; 3rd. ed., 1994, with the assistance of Michael Stern). As was to be expected, Rudolf displayed a mastery of baton technique. In his interpretations, he excelled in unmannered performances of the great Austro-German masterpieces.

Rudziński, Witold, Polish composer and pedagogue; b. Siebież, Lithuania, March 14, 1913. He studied with Szeligowski at the Vilnius Cons. (1928–36) and attended the Univ. of Vilnius (1931–36); went to Paris, where he took composition lessons with Boulanger and Koechlin (1938–39); upon his return, he taught at the Vilnius Cons. (1939–42) and the Łódź Cons. (1945–47); settled in Warsaw and served as director of the Opera (1948–49) and as a prof. at the Cons. (from 1957). He wrote a biography of Moniuszko (2 vols., Kraków, 1955, 1961), a study on the technique of Bartók (Kraków, 1965), and an exposition on musical rhythm (2 vols., 1987), among other works.

WORKS: OPERAS: *Janko muzykant* (Janko the Musician; 1948–51; Bytom, June 20, 1953); *Komendant Paryza* (The Commander of Paris; 1955–58; Poznań, 1960); *Odprawa posłów greckich* (The Departure of Greek Emissaries; Kraków, 1962); *Sulamita* (The Shulamite; 1964); *The Yellow Nightcap* (1969); *Chlopi* (The Peasants; 1972; Warsaw, June 30, 1974); *The Ring and the Rose* (1982). **ORCH.:** Piano Concerto (1936); 2 syms. (1938, 1944); *Divertimento* for Strings (1940); *Uwertura baltycka* (Baltic Overture; 1948); *Parades*, suite (1958); *Music Concertante* for Piano and Chamber Orch. (1959); *Musica profana* for Flute, Clarinet, Trumpet, and Strings (1960); *Obrazy Świętokrzyskie* (Pictures from the Holy-Cross Mountains; 1965); *Concerto Grosso* for Percussion and 2 String Orchs. (1970; Poznań, March 29, 1973); *Uwertura góralska* (Mountain Overture; 1970). **CHAMBER:** Trio for Flute, Oboe, and Piano (1934); Clarinet Sonatina (1935); 2 string quartets (1935, 1943); Violin Sonata (1937); Viola Sonata (1946); Nonet (1947); Quintet for Flute and Strings (1954); *Variations and Fugue* for Percussion (1966); *Preludes* for Clarinet, Viola, Harp, and Percussion (1967); *Polonaise-Rapsodie* for Cello and Piano (1969); *Fantazja góralska* (Mountain Fantasia) for Guitar (1970); *Proverbia latina* for Harpsichord (1974); *Duo Concertante* for Percussion (1976); *Sonata Pastorale* for Violin and Piano (1976); Harpsichord Sonata (1978); piano pieces. **VOCAL:** *2 portraits de femmes* for Voice and String Quartet (1960); 2 oratorios: *Gaude Mater Polonia* for Narrator, 3 Soloists, Chorus, and Orch. (1966) and *Lipce* for Chorus and Chamber Orch. (1968); *Chlopska droga* (Peasants' Road), cantata (1952); *Dach świata* (The Roof of the World) for Narrator and Orch. (1960); *To Citizen John Brown*, concertino for Soprano, Flute, Horn, Cello, Piano, and Percussion (1972); *The Nike of the Vistula*, war ballads and scenes for Narrator, 4 Soloists, Chorus, and Orch. (1973); songs.

Rudzinski, Zbigniew, Polish composer and teacher; b. Czechowice, Oct. 23, 1935. After attending the Univ. of Warsaw (1956), he pursued training in composition with Perkowski at the Warsaw Academy of Music (diploma, 1960); completed his studies in Paris and the Netherlands. He served as chief of the music dept. of the Warsaw Documentary Film Studio (1960–67); then was a prof. (from 1973) of composition at the Chopin Academy of Music in Warsaw, where he also was vice-rector (1981–83).

WORKS: CHAMBER OPERA: *Manekiny* (The Mannequins; Wroclaw, Oct. 29, 1981). **ORCH.:** *Contra fidem* (1964); *Moments musicaux I–III* (1965–68); Sym. for Men's Chorus and Orch. (1969); *Muzyka nova* (Night Music; 1970). **CHAMBER:** Sonata for 2 String Quartets, Piano, and Kettledrums (1960); String Trio (1964); *Impromptu* for 2 Pianos, 3 Cellos, and Percussion (1966); Quartet for 2 Pianos and Percussion (1969); Piano Sonata (1975); *Campanella* for Percussion Ensemble (1977); *Trytony* (Tritons) for Percussion Ensemble (1979–80). **VOCAL:** *Epigrame* for Flute, Chorus, and Percussion (1962); *Requiem ofiarom wojen* (Requiem for the Victims of the Wars) for Chorus and Orch. (1971); *Kséiga godzin* (The Book of Hours), 5 Romantic songs for Mezzo-soprano and Piano Trio (1983); *To nie sa sny* (These are not dreams), 6 songs for Mezzo-soprano and Piano (1987).

Rufer, Josef (Leopold), Austrian music scholar; b. Vienna, Dec. 18, 1893; d. Berlin, Nov. 7, 1985. He studied composition with Zemlinsky, and then with Schoenberg in Vienna (1919–22). He was assistant to Schoenberg at the Prussian Academy of Arts in Berlin (1925–33); from 1928, was also active as a music critic. From 1947 to 1950 he ed. (with Stuckenschmidt) the monthly music magazine *Stimmen*; then taught at the Free Univ. (from 1950) and at the Hochschule für Musik (1956–69) in Berlin. He publ. *Die Komposition mit zwölf Tönen* (Berlin, 1952; Eng. tr., 1954, as *Composition with 12 Notes Related Only to One*

Another), *Musiker über Musik* (Darmstadt, 1955), *Das Werk Arnold Schönbergs* (Kassel, 1959; Eng. tr., 1962, as *The Works of Arnold Schoenberg*), and *Technische Aspekte der Polyphonie in der 1. Hälfte des 20. Jahrhunderts* (Ghent, 1969).

Ruffo, Titta (real name, **Ruffo Cafiero Titta**), famous Italian baritone; b. Pisa, June 9, 1877; d. Florence, July 5, 1953. He found it convenient to transpose his first and last names for professional purposes. He studied with Persichini at the Accademia di Santa Cecilia in Rome, then with Casini in Milan. He made his operatic debut in Rome as the Herald in *Lohengrin* (1898); then sang in South America; returning to Italy, he appeared in all the principal theaters; also sang in Vienna, Paris, and London. He made his American debut in Philadelphia as Rigoletto (Nov. 4, 1912) with the combined Philadelphia-Chicago Opera Co., and then sang in Chicago (1912–14; 1919–27); his first appearance with the Metropolitan Opera was as Figaro in *Il Barbiere di Siviglia* (N.Y., Jan. 19, 1922). He left the Metropolitan in 1929 and returned to Rome. In 1937 he was briefly under arrest for opposing the Mussolini regime; then went to Florence, where he remained until his death. His memoirs appeared as *La mia parabola* (Milan, 1937; rev. 1977, by his son). A renowned dramatic artist, he excelled in roles from Verdi's operas; was also an outstanding Figaro, Hamlet, Tonio, and Scarpia.

BIBL.: M. Barrenechea, *T. R.: Notas de psicologia artistica* (Buenos Aires, 1911); A. Farkas, ed., *T. R.: An Anthology* (Westport, Conn., 1984).

Ruggles, Carl (actually, **Charles Sprague**), remarkable American composer; b. Marion, Mass., March 11, 1876; d. Bennington, Vt., Oct. 24, 1971. He learned to play violin as a child; then went to Boston, where he took violin lessons with Felix Winternitz and theory with Josef Claus; later enrolled as a special student at Harvard Univ., where he attended composition classes of John Knowles Paine. Impressed with the widely assumed supremacy of the German school of composition (of which Paine was a notable representative), Ruggles Germanized his given name from Charles to Carl. In 1907 he went to Minnesota, where he organized and conducted the Winona Sym. Orch. (1908–12). In 1917 he went to N.Y., where he became active in the promotion of modern music; was a member of the International Composers Guild and of the Pan American Assn. of Composers. He later taught composition at the Univ. of Miami (1938–43). Ruggles wrote relatively few works, which he constantly revised and rearranged, and they were mostly in small forms. He did not follow any particular modern method of composition, but instinctively avoided needless repetition of thematic notes, which made his melodic progressions atonal; his use of dissonances, at times quite strident, derived from the linear proceedings of chromatically inflected counterpoint. A certain similarity with the 12-tone method of composition of Schoenberg resulted from this process, but Ruggles never adopted it explicitly. In his sources of inspiration, he reached for spiritual exaltation with mystic connotations, scaling the heights and plumbing the depths of musical expression. Such music could not attract large groups of listeners and repelled some critics; one of them remarked that the title of Ruggles's *Sun-Treader* ought to be changed to *Latrine-Treader*. Unable and unwilling to withstand the prevailing musical mores, Ruggles removed himself from the musical scene; he went to live on his farm in Arlington, Vt., and devoted himself mainly to his avocation, painting; his pictures, mostly in the manner of Abstract Expressionism, were occasionally exhibited in N.Y. galleries. In 1966 he moved to a nursing home in Bennington, where he died at the age of 95. A striking revival of interest in his music took place during the last years of his life, and his name began to appear with increasing frequency on the programs of American orchs. and chamber music groups. His MSS were recovered and publ.; virtually all of his compositions have been recorded.

WORKS: *Mood* for Violin and Piano (c.1918); *Toys* for Voice and Piano (1919); *Men and Angels* (*Men* for Orch., 1920–21; *Angels* for 6 Muted Trumpets, 1920–21; perf. as *Men and Angels*, N.Y., Dec. 17, 1922; *Angels* rev. for 4 Trumpets and 3 Trombones, 1938, and perf. in Miami, April 24, 1939); *Vox clamans in deserto* for Soprano and Chamber Orch. (1923; N.Y., Jan. 13, 1924); *Men and Mountains* for Chamber Orch. (N.Y., Dec. 7, 1924; rev. for Large Orch., N.Y., March 19, 1936; rev. 1941); *Portals* for 13 Strings (1925; N.Y., Jan. 24, 1926; rev. for String Orch., 1929; rev. 1941 and 1952–53); *Sun-Treader* for Large Orch. (1926–31; Paris, Feb. 25, 1932, N. Slonimsky conducting); *Evocations*, 4 chants for Piano (1937, 1943; N.Y., Jan. 9, 1943; rev. 1954; orch. version, N.Y., Feb. 3, 1971); *Organum* for Large Orch. (1944–47; N.Y., Nov. 24, 1949; also arranged for 2 Pianos, 1946–47); *Exaltation*, hymn tune for "congregation in unison" and Organ (1958); also several unfinished works.

BIBL.: C. Seeger, "C. R.," *Musical Quarterly* (Oct. 1932); L. Harrison, *About C. R.* (Yonkers, N.Y., 1946); T. Peterson, *The Music of C. R.* (diss., Univ. of Wash., 1967); N. Archabal, *C. R.: Composer and Painter* (diss., Univ. of Minnesota, 1975); J. Tenney, "The Chronological Development of C. R.' Melodic Style," *Perspectives of New Music*, XVI/1 (1977); M. Ziffrin, *C. R.: Composer, Painter, and Storyteller* (Urbana, Ill., 1994).

Ruhnke, Martin, German musicologist; b. Köslin, June 14, 1921. He studied with Blume at the Univ. of Kiel (Ph.D., 1954, with the diss. *Joachim Burmeister: Ein Beitrag zur Musiklehre um 1600*; publ. in Kassel, 1955). After serving as an assistant lecturer at the Free Univ. in Berlin (1954–60), he completed his Habilitation there in 1961 with his *Beiträge zu einer Geschichte der deutschen Hofmusikkolegien im 16. Jahrhundert* (publ. in Berlin, 1963). In 1964 he became prof. of musicology at the Univ. of Erlangen. As an authority on Telemann, he served as general ed. of the complete critical edition of that composer's works (from 1960) and as ed. of *Georg Philipp Telemann: Thematisch-Systematisches Verzeichnis seiner Werke: Instrumentalwerke* (2 vols., Kassel, 1984, 1992). From 1968 to 1974 he was president of the Gesellschaft für Musikforschung. He was president of the Internationalen Telemann-Gesellschaft from 1991.

BIBL.: W. Hirschmann et al., eds., *Festschrift M. R.: Zum 65. Geburtstag* (Stuttgart, 1986).

Ruiter, Wim de, Dutch composer, organist, and teacher; b. Heemstede, Aug. 11, 1943. He studied organ with Piet Kee in Amsterdam (1963–69) and composition with Ton de Leeuw there (1968–74). He taught at the Zwolle Cons. (1973–77) and the Amsterdam Cons. (from 1973). With another Dutch organist, he gave successful concerts of duo-organ music, 4 hands, 4 feet.

WORKS: ORCH.: *Re* (Utrecht, Sept. 14, 1975); *3 Pieces* (1977); *Spectrum* (1978); *Allegro, adagio en variaties* (1980); *Theme, Variations, and Finale* (1985); Accordion Concerto (1987; rev. 1988). **CHAMBER:** *Solo* for Flute (1969); *Music* for 2 Double Basses (1969); Quartet for 2 Violas and 2 Cellos (1970); Quartet for Flute, Bass Clarinet, Vibraphone, and Piano (1970); *2 Quartets Together* (1970; a joining together of the previous 2 quartets); 3 string quartets (1972, 1974, 1984); *Thick & Thin* for Organ, 4 hands, 4 feet (1975); *Tall & Small* for Treble Recorder (1975); *Off & On* for 4 Bass Clarinets (1976); *To Be or Not to Be* for 12 Wind Instruments and Vibraphone (1976); Quintet for 5 Flutes and Tape (1976; in collaboration with Jacques Bank); Quartet for Recorders (1977); Flute Quartet No. 2 (1986); *Pastorale* for Bass Clarinet and Tape (1994). **VOCAL:** *Situations* for 16 Voices (1970); *Hoplopoia* for Chorus and Orch. (1973); choral works; songs.

Runnicles, Donald, Scottish conductor; b. Edinburgh, Nov. 16, 1954. He was educated at the univs. of Edinburgh and Cambridge, and also studied at the London Opera Centre. In 1980 he became a répétiteur at the Mannheim National Theater, where he then was a conductor (1984–87); then was conductor in Hannover (1987–89). From 1989 to 1992 he was Generalmusikdirektor in Freiburg im Breisgau. He also conducted at the Metropolitan Opera in N.Y. (from 1988), the San Francisco Opera (from 1990), the Vienna State Opera (from 1990), and the Glyndebourne Festival (from 1991). In 1992 he became music director of the San Francisco Opera. In 1994 he scored an outstanding success at the Edinburgh Festival conducting Mahler's 8th Sym. Runnicles conducts left-handed.

Rúnólfsson, Karl Ottó, Icelandic trumpeter, teacher, and composer; b. Reykjavík, Oct. 24, 1900; d. there, Nov. 29, 1970. He studied in Copenhagen (1926–27) and with Mixa and Urbancic at the Reykjavík College of Music (1934–39). He was active with brass bands; played 1st trumpet in the Icelandic Sym. Orch. (1950–55); taught at the Reykjavík College of Music (1939–64). He wrote a set of Icelandic songs for Voice and Orch. (1938); *Esja*, sym. (1968); choral works on Icelandic themes; Trumpet Sonata; Violin Sonata.

Rupnik, Ivan, Serbian composer; b. Belgrade, Aug. 29, 1911. He studied in Ljubljana; later in Vienna with Berg. His early works are in a neo-Romantic vein, with expressionistic overtones; later he abjured modern devices and began writing music for the masses, in conformity with socialist ideology. His cantata, *Song of the Dead Proletarians*, which he conducted in Belgrade on Dec. 14, 1947, is an epitome of programmatic realism. He also wrote 2 syms., several overtures (*Romantic Overture; Youth Overture*), ethnic symphonic works (*Musical Impressions from Istria; A Peasant Evening Party*), and a *Hymn of Peace*.

Rupp, Franz, German-American pianist and teacher; b. Schongau, Feb. 24, 1901; d. N.Y., May 27, 1992. He received his training at the Munich Akademie der Tonkunst. In 1920 he made his first tour of the U.S. with Willy Burmester, and subsequently acquired a distinguished reputation as an accompanist to Fritz Kreisler. In 1938 he settled in the U.S. and was accompanist to Marian Anderson until her retirement in 1965. He continued to perform regularly until his farewell appearance at the Lockenhaus Festival in Austria in 1985. He was also active as a teacher at the Curtis Inst. of Music in Philadelphia.

Rusconi, Gerardo, Italian composer; b. Milan, Feb. 1, 1922; d. there, Dec. 23, 1974. He studied at the Parma Cons. He began his career as a composer by writing light music for the stage, radio, and the films; then undertook more serious genres of music. He composed *La moglie di Lot* for Soprano, Horn, and Piano (1962); *Concerto breve* for Horn and Strings (1965); *3 musiche* for Flute and Piano (1967); *Moments* for Orch. in memory of Martin Luther King (1968); *L'appuntamento*, opera (1971); numerous transcriptions and harmonizations of popular songs.

Rush, Loren, American composer; b. Fullerton, Calif., Aug. 23, 1935. He studied piano, bassoon, and double bass; played bassoon in the Oakland Sym. Orch. and double bass in the Richmond Sym. Orch.; also was a drummer. He studied composition with Erickson at San Francisco State College (B.A., 1957); upon graduation, organized the Loren Rush Jazz Quartet; enrolled at the Univ. of Calif. at Berkeley, studying composition with Imbrie, Shifrin, Denny, and Cushing (M.A., 1960), and completed his training at Stanford Univ. (D.M.A., 1960). He was active in various new-music ventures; was chairman of the composition dept. at the San Francisco Cons. (1967–69); taught at Stanford Univ. (from 1967), where he served as assoc. director of the Center for Computer Research in Music and Acoustics (from 1975). In his works, he applies a whole spectrum of modern techniques, including serialism, spatial distribution, controlled improvisation, and pointillistic exoticism. He is married to **Janis Mattox**.

WORKS: *5 Japanese Poems* for Soprano, Flute, Clarinet, Viola, and Piano (1959); *Serenade* for Violin and Viola (1960); String Quartet (1960–61); *Mandala Music*, improvisation for a group, inspired by the oriental geometrization of the cosmos and an important symbol in Jungian psychology (1962); *Hexahedron* for Piano, notated on all 6 surfaces of a large cube (1964); *Nexus 16* for Chamber Orch. (1964); *Dans le sable* for Soprano, Narrator, 4 Altos, and Chamber Orch. (1967–68; also for Large Orch., 1970); *Soft Music, Hard Music* for 3 Amplified Pianos (1969–70); *The Cloud Messenger* for Orch. (1966–70); *Oh, Susanna* for Piano (1970); *A Little Traveling Music* for Amplified Piano and 4-track Tape (1971–73); *I'll See You in My Dreams* for Amplified Orch. and Tape (1973); *Song and Dance* for Orch. and 4-track Tape (1975); *The Digital Domain* for Tape (1983; in collaboration with J. Mattox).

Rushton, Julian (Gordon), English musicologist; b. Cambridge, May 22, 1941. He studied at the Guildhall School of Music and Drama in London (1959–60), Trinity College, Cambridge (B.A., 1963), and Magdalen College, Oxford (B.Mus., 1965; M.A., 1967; Ph.D., 1970, with the diss. *Music and Drama at the Academie royale de musique, Paris, 1774–1789*). He taught at the Univ. of East Anglia (1968–74) and at the Univ. of Cambridge (1974–81); was West Riding Prof. of Music and head of the music dept. at the Univ. of Leeds (from 1982). He ed. *W.A. Mozart: Don Giovanni* (Cambridge, 1981) and *W.A. Mozart: Idomeneo* (Cambridge, 1993); publ. *The Musical Language of Berlioz* (Cambridge, 1983) and *Classical Music: A Concise History* (London, 1986).

Russell, (George) Alexander, American organist and composer; b. Franklin, Tenn., Oct. 2, 1880; d. Dewitt, N.Y., Nov. 24, 1953. The son of a Presbyterian minister, he studied at home; his mother, Felicia Putnam Russell (a direct descendant of General Israel Putnam of Revolution fame), taught him piano; the family moved to Texas, where he studied academic subjects; entered the College of Fine Arts of Syracuse Univ., studying organ with George A. Parker and composition with William Berwald, where he took his B.Mus. in 1901; subsequently studied in Europe with Leopold Godowsky and Harold Bauer (piano), and with Widor (organ). Returning to America in 1908, he toured as accompanist to various artists; from 1910 to 1952, was associated with the Auditorium concerts at Wanamaker's department store in N.Y.; was also director of music at Princeton Univ. (1917–35). He wrote a number of organ works, piano pieces, songs, and partsongs.

BIBL.: J. Howard, *Studies of Contemporary American Composers: A. R.* (N.Y., 1925).

Russell, William (real name, **Russell William Wagner**), American composer; b. Canton, Mo., Feb. 26, 1905. When he began to study music he eliminated his patronymic as possibly invidious, and placed his first Christian name as a surname. He was fascinated with the sounds of drums, and wrote music almost exclusively for percussion instruments; his first important work in this category was the *Fugue for 8 Percussion Instruments* (1932). Another work of importance was *3 Dance Movements* (N.Y., Nov. 22, 1933); the scoring is for tone clusters and piano strings activated with a fork, and a cymbal sounded by drawing the teeth of a saw across its edge; the ensemble also includes a bottle which must be broken at the climax. His other percussion works include *Ogou Badagri* (1933; based on Voodoo rites); *3 Cuban Pieces* (1935); *Made in America* (1936; the scoring calls for firecrackers); *March Suite* (1936); Concerto for Trumpet and Percussion (1937). Giving up composition, he moved to New Orleans in 1940, and from 1944 to 1957 he recorded historic jazz on his own label; from 1958 he was the jazz-archive curator at Tulane Univ. As late as age 85 he continued playing violin with the New Orleans Ragtime Orch. For a retrospective concert of his works in N.Y. on Feb. 24, 1990, he broke his compositional silence by writing a percussion *Tango* to accompany his *3 Dance Movements*; the concert included the premiere performances of his Trumpet Concerto and *Ogou Badagri*.

Russo, William (Joseph), American composer and teacher; b. Chicago, June 25, 1928. He studied privately with Lennie Tristano (composition and improvisation, 1943–46), John J. Becker (composition, 1953–55), and Karel B. Jirák (composition and conducting, 1955–57). He was a trombonist and chief composer-arranger with the Stan Kenton Orch. (1950–54); then worked with his own groups in N.Y. and London. He taught at the School of Jazz in Lenox, Mass. (summers, 1956–57), and at the Manhattan School of Music (1958–61). In 1965 he joined the faculty of Columbia College in Chicago; also was a Distinguished Visiting Prof. of Composition at the Peabody Inst. in Baltimore (1969–71), a teacher at Antioch College (1971–72), and composer-in-residence of the city and county of San Francisco (1975–76). He publ. *Composing for the Jazz Orchestra* (Chicago, 1961; 2nd ed., 1973), *Jazz: Composition and Orchestration* (Chicago, 1968; 2nd ed., 1974), and *Composing Music: A New Approach* (Chicago, 1988). Russo's expertise as a composer-arranger has led him to create a number of remarkable third-stream scores.

WORKS: DRAMATIC: OPERAS: *John Hooton* (1961; BBC, London, Jan. 1963); *The Island* (1963); *Land of Milk and Honey* (1964); *Antigone* (1967); *Aesop's Fables*, rock opera (N.Y., Aug. 17, 1972); *A General Opera* (1976); *The Payoff*, cabaret opera (Chicago, Feb. 16, 1984); *A Cabaret Opera* (1985; alternate forms as *The Alice B. Toklas Hashish Fudge Review*, N.Y., Dec. 8, 1977; Paris Lights, N.Y., Jan. 24, 1980, and *The Shepherds' Christmas*, Chicago, Dec. 1979); *Dubrovsky* (1988); *The Sacrifice* (1990). **BALLETS:** *The World of Alcina* (1954; rev. 1962); *Les Deux Errants* (Monte Carlo, April 1956); *The Golden Bird* (Chicago, Feb. 17, 1984); other stage pieces; film music. **ORCH.:** *Allegro* for Concert Band (1957; N.Y., July 18, 1961); 2 syms.: No. 1 (1957) and No. 2, *Titans* (1958; N.Y., April 16, 1959); *Newport Suite* (Newport, R.I., July 4, 1958; rev. for Jazz Orch., 1960); *Concerto grosso* for Saxophone Quartet and Concert Band (N.Y., July 29, 1960); Cello Concerto (1962); *3 Pieces* for Blues Band and Orch. (Ravinia Festival, July 7, 1968); *Street Music: A Blues Concerto* (1975; San Francisco, May 19, 1976); *Urban Trilogy* (1981; Los Angeles, March 13, 1982). **JAZZ ORCH.:** *Solitaire*, with Strings (1949); 2 suites: No. 1 (1952; rev. 1962) and No. 2 (1951–54; rev. 1962); *4 Pieces* (1953–54); *The 7 Deadly Sins* (1960); *Variations on an American Theme* (1960; Kansas City, Mo., Feb. 4, 1961); *The English Concerto*, with Violin (Bath, June 11, 1963); *America 1966* (Ravinia Festival, Aug. 3, 1966); *The New Age Suite* (1984); *For My Friend* (1991); *The Horn Blower* (1991); *The Garden of Virtue* (1993). **CHAMBER:** *21 Etudes* for Brass Instruments (1959); Violin Sonata (1986); *Memphis* for Alto Saxophone and 9 Instruments (Memphis, Tenn., April 21, 1988); *Women* for Harmonica, Piano, and String Quartet (1990); piano pieces. **VOCAL: ROCK CANTATAS:** *The Civil War* (1968); *David* (1968); *Liberation* (1969); *Joan of Arc* (1970); *The Bacchae* (1972); *Song of Songs* (1972). **OTHER CANTATAS:** *Im Memoriam* for Jazz Orch. (Los Angeles, March 7, 1966); *Songs of Celebration* for 5 Solo Voices, Chorus, and Orch. (1971; Baltimore, Feb. 21, 1973; rev. version, San Francisco, May 18, 1975); *The Touro Cantata* (N.Y., April 4, 1988). **OTHER VOCAL:** *Talking to the Sun*, song cycle theater piece (Chicago, March 5, 1989); *Listen Beneath* for Soprano, Jazz Contralto, and Orch. (1992); *In Memoriam, Hermann Conaway* for Mezzo-soprano, Tenor, Baritone, and 11 Instruments (1994); choruses; songs.

Russolo, Luigi, Italian inventor, painter, and composer; b. Portogruaro, April 30, 1885; d. Cerro di Laveno, Varese, Feb. 4, 1947. In 1909 he joined the futurist movement of Marinetti; formulated the principles of "art of noises" in his book, *L'arte dei rumori* (Milan, 1916); constructed a battery of noise-making instruments ("intonarumori"), with which he gave concerts in Milan (April 21, 1914) and Paris (June 18, 1921), creating such a commotion in the concert hall that on one occasion a group of outraged concertgoers mounted the stage and physically attacked Russolo and his fellow noisemakers. The titles of his works sing the glory of the machine and of urban living: *Convegno dell'automobili e dell'aeroplani, Il Risveglio di una citta*, and *Si pranza sulla terrazza dell'Hotel.* In his "futurist manifesto" of 1913, the noises are divided into 6 categories, including shrieks, groans, clashes, explosions, etc. In 1929 he constructed a noise instrument which he called "Russolophone." Soon the novelty of machine music wore out, the erstwhile marvels of automobiles and airplanes became commonplace, and the future of the futurists turned into a yawning past; Russolo gradually retreated from cultivation of noise and devoted himself to the most silent of all arts, painting. His pictures, influenced by the modern French school, and remarkable for their vivid colors, had several successful exhibitions in Paris and N.Y. The text of Russolo's manifesto is reproduced, in an Eng. tr., in N. Slonimsky's *Music since 1900* (N.Y., 1937; 5th ed., rev., 1994).

BIBL.: M. Zanovello Russolo, *R.: L'uomo, l'artista* (Milan, 1958); R. Payton, *The Futurist Musicians: Francesco Balilla Pratella and L. R.* (diss., Univ. of Chicago, 1974); G. Maffina, *L. R. e l'arte dei rumori* (Turin, 1978).

Rutkowski, Bronislaw, Polish organist, teacher, and composer; b. Komaje, near Vilnius, Feb. 27, 1898; d. Leipzig, June 1, 1964. He studied organ with Handschin and theory with Kalafati and Vitols at the St. Petersburg Cons. After further training with Surzýnski (organ), Rytel and Statkowski (theory), and Melcer (conducting) at the Warsaw Cons. (graduated, 1924), he completed his studies in Paris (1924–26) with Vierne (organ) and Pirro (aesthetics). From 1926 to 1939 he taught at the Warsaw Cons., and then at the Kraków Cons. from 1946, where he was rector from 1955 until his death. He made tours as a recitalist throughout Europe. Among his works were choral pieces and organ music.

Rutter, John (Milford), well-known English conductor and composer; b. London, Sept. 24, 1945. He was educated at Clare College, Cambridge (B.A., 1967; Mus.B., 1968; M.A., 1970), where he was later director of music (1975–79); among his teachers was David Willcocks, with whom he co-edited several choral collections, including 3 in the Carols for Choirs series (Oxford, 1970–80); he also taught through the Open Univ. (1975–88). In 1981 he founded the Cambridge Singers, subsequently conducting them in an extensive repertoire; in 1990 he conducted their Carnegie Hall debut in N.Y.; in 1984 he established Collegium Records, a label dedicated to their performances. His compositions and arrangements are numerous and accessible, and feature an extensive catalog of choral works that are frequently performed in Britain and the U.S.

WORKS: *The Falcon* for Chorus and Orch. (1969); *Fancies* for Chorus and Chamber Orch. (1972); *Partita* for Orch. (1973); *Gloria* for Chorus, Brass Ensemble, Percussion, and Organ (1974; for Orch., 1988); *Bang!*, children's opera (1975); *Canticles of America* for Chorus and Orch. (1976); *Beatles' Concerto* for 2 Pianos and Orch. (1977); *The Reluctant Dragon* for Voices and Chamber Orch. (1978); *Suite antique* for Flute, Harpsichord, and Strings (1979); *Reflections* for Piano and Orch. (1979); *The Piper of Hamelin*, children's opera (1980); *The Wind in the Willows* for Voices and Chamber Orch. (1981); *Requiem* for Soprano and Chorus (1985); *Te Deum* for Chorus and Various Accompaniments (1988); *Magnificat* for Soprano, Chorus, and Ensemble (1990).

Ruwet, Nicolas, French linguist and musical analyst; b. Saive, Belgium, Dec. 31, 1932. He studied Romance philology at the Univ. of Liège, with Lévi-Strauss and Benveniste at the École Pratique des Hautes Études in Paris, and with Jakobson and Chomsky at the Mass. Inst. of Technology; also studied music privately. In 1968 he became prof. of linguistics at the Univ. of Paris at Vincennes. Although not primarily a musician, he has been a fundamental thinker in the semiology of music, contributing important articles which were reprinted in his *Langage, musique, poésie* (Paris, 1972). His multi-leveled system for analyzing musical syntax, "distributional analysis," has been a central influence in the work of Nattiez and his followers.

Ruyneman, Daniel, Dutch composer; b. Amsterdam, Aug. 8, 1886; d. there, July 25, 1963. He began his study of music relatively late. He received training in piano from De John and in composition from Zweers at the Amsterdam Cons. (1913–16). In 1918 he was a co-founder of the Nederlansche Vereeniging voor Moderne Scheppende Toonkunst, which became the Dutch section of the ISCM in 1922. In 1930 he organized the Netherlands Soc. for Contemporary Music, serving as president until 1962; ed. its journal, *Maandblad voor Hedendaagse Muziek* (1930–40), until it was suppressed during the Nazi occupation of the Netherlands; was general secretary of the ISCM (1947–51). Ruyneman made a special study of Javanese instruments and introduced them in some of his works. He was naturally attracted to exotic subjects with mystic connotations and coloristic effects; also worked on restoration of early music; in 1930 he orchestrated fragments of Mussorgsky's unfinished opera *The Marriage*, and added his own music for the missing acts of the score.

WORKS: DRAMATIC: OPERAS: *De gebroeders Karamasoff* (1928); *Le Mariage* (1930). **INCIDENTAL MUSIC:** *De Clown*, "psycho-symbolic" play (1915). **ORCH.:** 2 syms.: No. 1, *Symphonie brève* (1927), and No. 2, *Symphony 1953* (1953; Utrecht, March 14, 1956); *Musica per orchestra per una festa Olandese* (1936); *Concerto for Orchestra* (1937); Piano Concerto (1939); Violin Concerto (1940; Amsterdam, Feb. 23, 1943); *Partita* for Strings (1943); *Amphitryon*, overture (1943); *Amatarasu* (Ode to the Sun Goddess), on a Japanese melody, for Chamber Ensemble (1953); *Gilgamesj*, Babylonian epos (1962). **CHAMBER:** 3 violin sonatas (No. 2, 1914; No. 3, 1956); *Klaaglied van een Slaaf* for Violin and Piano (1917); *Hiëroglyphs* for 3 Flutes, Celesta, Harp, Cup-bells, Piano, 2 Mandolins, and 2 Guitars (1918; the unique cup-bells, which some claim were cast by J. Taylor & Co., Loughborough, England, and which others claim were found by the composer in a London junk shop, were destroyed in a Rotterdam air raid in 1940, and perfs. of the work since then have substituted a vibraphone); Violin Sonata (1925); *Divertimento* for Flute, Clarinet, Horn, Violin, and Piano (1927); Clarinet Sonata (1936); *4 tempi* for 4 Cellos (1937); *Sonatina in modo antiquo* for Cello and Piano (1939); *Sonata da camera* for Flute and Piano (1942); String Quartet (1946); *Nightingale Quintet* for Winds (1949); *4 chansons Bengalies* for Flute and Piano (1950); Sonatina for Flute and Piano or Harpsichord (1951); Oboe Sonatina (1952); *Reflexions II* for Flute, Viola, and Guitar (1959), *III* for Flute, Violin, Viola, Cello, and Piano or Harpsichord (1960–61; reconstructed by R. du Bois), and *IV* for Wind Quintet (1961); *3 Fantasies* for Cello and Piano or Harpsichord (1960). **PIANO:** *3 Pathematologieën* (1915); 2 sonatinas (1917, 1954); Sonata (1931); *Kleine Sonata* (1938); *5 sonatines mélodiques pour l'enseignement moderne du piano* (1947). **VOCAL:** *Sous le pont Mirabeau* for Women's Chorus, Flute, Harp, and String Quartet (1917); *De Roep* (The Call), a color spectrum of wordless vowel sounds for Chorus (1918); *Sonata*, on wordless vowel sounds, for Chamber Chorus (1931); *4 Liederen* for Tenor and Small Orch. (1937); *Die Weise von Liebe und Tod des Kornets Christoph Rilke* for Narrator and Piano (1946; orchestrated 1951); *Ancient Greek Songs* for Baritone or Bass, Flute, Oboe, Cello, and Harp (1954); *5 Melodies* for Voice and Piano (1957); *3 chansons de Maquisards condamnes* for Alto or Baritone, and Orch. (1957); *Reflexions I* for Soprano, Flute, Guitar, Viola, Vibraphone, Xylophone, and Percussion (1958–59).

BIBL.: A. Petronio, *D. R. et son oeuvre* (Liège, 1922).

Ruzicka, Peter, German composer and Intendant; b. Düsseldorf, July 3, 1948. Following training in piano, oboe, and composition at the Hamburg Cons. (1963–68), he studied law and musicology in Munich, Hamburg, and Berlin (Ph.D., 1977). He was Intendant of the (West) Berlin Radio Sym. Orch. from 1979 to 1987. In 1988 he became Intendant of the Hamburg State Opera and State Phil. Orch. He was made a fellow of the Bavarian Academy of Fine Arts in Munich in 1985 and of the Free Academy of Arts in Hamburg in 1987. In his compositions, Ruzicka has followed a determined contemporary path which is reflected in his capable handling of various avant-garde techniques in whatever genre he chooses to explore.

WORKS: DRAMATIC: *Outside-Inside*, radiophonic piece (Radio Bremen/Bavarian Radio, June 10, 1972; also as an expanded music theater piece, Augsburg, Aug. 18, 1972). **ORCH.:** *Antifone-Strofe* for 25 Solo Strings and Percussion (Göttingen, Oct. 23, 1970); *Sinfonia* for 25 Solo Strings, 16 Vocalists, and Percussion (1970–71; Stuttgart, Sept. 25, 1971; rev. version, Berlin, Nov. 20, 1974); *Versuch*, 7 pieces for Strings (1970–74; Stuttgart, Oct. 11, 1975); *Metastrofe* for 87 Instrumentalists (Berlin, May 4, 1971); *In processo di tempo* for 26 Instrumentalists and Cello (1971; Hilversum, Sept. 11, 1972); *Feed Back* for 4 Orch. Groups (Donaueschingen, Oct. 21, 1972); *Torso* (Cologne, Dec. 7, 1973); *Einblendungen* (1973–77; Hannover, Dec. 1, 1977); *Befragung*, 5 pieces (1974; Paris, Oct. 30, 1975); *Emanazione*, variations for Flute and 4 Orch. Groups (1975; Berlin, Jan. 13, 1976); *Abbrüche* (1977–78; Düsseldorf, April 20, 1978); *Annäherung und Stille*, 4 fragments after Schumann for Piano and 42 Strings (Interlaken, Aug. 23, 1981); *... den Impuls zum Weitersprechen erst empfinge* for Viola and Orch. (1981; Saarbrücken, June 1, 1982); *Satyagraha* (1984; Hamburg, Oct. 16, 1985); *Fünf Bruchstücke* (1984–87; Berlin, Feb. 15, 1988); *Metamorphosen über ein Klangfeld von Joseph Haydn* (Cologne, Oct. 5, 1990); *... das Gesegnete, das Verfluchte*, 4 sketches (1991; Munich, Nov. 27, 1992); *Tallis* (Kiel, Aug. 11, 1993); *... Inseln, randlos ...* for Violin, Chamber Chorus, and Orch. (1994). **CHAMBER:** *Drei Szenen* for Clarinet (1967; Hamburg, Feb. 27, 1970); *Ausgeweidet die Zeit ...*, 3 night pieces for Piano (1969; Spoleto, July 1, 1971); Sonata for Solo Cello (1969; Hamburg, Feb. 27, 1970); 3 string quartets: No. 1 (1969–70; Hamburg, Feb. 27, 1970; rev. version, Kiel, Nov. 20, 1970), No. 2, *... fragment ...* (1970; Stuttgart, June 18, 1974), and No. 3, *... über ein Verschwinden* (1992; Cologne, April 5, 1993); *Movimenti* for Harpsichord (1969–70; Hamburg, June 12, 1974); *Stress* for 8 Percussion Groups (Munich, April 13, 1972); *Zeit* for Organ (Kassel, April 3, 1975); *Z-Zeit* for Organ (1975; Bremen, May 13, 1976); *Stille* for Cello (Erlangen, Nov. 28, 1976); *Seboniana* for 3 Flutes, 1 Player (Marktbreit, Sept. 29, 1979); *Préludes* for Piano (Neumünster, Aug. 16, 1987); *Klangschatten* for String Quartet (Vienna, Nov. 18, 1991). **VOCAL:** *Esta Noche*, funeral music for the victims of the Vietnam War, for Alto or Tenor, Flute, English Horn, Viola, and Cello (1967; Hamburg, April 18, 1968); *Todesfuge* for Alto, Speaker, Chamber Ensemble, and Tape (1968–69; Hamburg, Feb. 27, 1970); *Elis* for Mezzo-soprano, Oboe or Oboe d'amore, and Orch. (1969; Leverkusen, April 9, 1970); *Gestalt und Abbruch* for Voices (Donaueschingen, Oct. 21, 1979); *... der die Gesänge zerschlug* for Baritone and Chamber Ensemble (Berlin, Sept. 3, 1985); *Vier Gesänge nach Fragmenten von Nietzsche* for Mezzo-soprano and Piano (1992; Savonlinna, July 13, 1993). **OTHER:** *DE ... /MUSAC* for Variable Ensemble (1971); *Bewegung* for Tape (1972).

Růžička, Rudolf, Czech composer and pedagogue; b. Brno, April 25, 1941. After attending the Brno Cons. (1958–62), he studied composition with Theodor Schaefer and Miloslav Ištvan (1962–67) and Miloslav Kabeláč (1967–69) at the Janáček Academy of Music and Dramatic Arts (1967–69). In 1969 he joined the faculty of the latter, where he taught courses in electroacoustic and computer composition. As a prominent figure in avant-garde circles, Růžička became suspect in the eyes of the rigid Communist regime. All the same, he persevered in his activities with various avant-garde groups at home and abroad. In 1970 his *Gurges* won 1st prize in the Musica Nova competition in Brno and in 1984 his *Tibia I* received 1st prize in the Marcel Josse competition in Paris. Following the collapse of the Communist regime in 1989, Růžička assumed an even greater prominence among the avant-garde of his homeland and abroad. While he has composed various works in the traditional genres, he has become best known for his use of computers in producing innovations in the forms and structures of his works.

WORKS: ORCH.: *Suite of Ancient Dances* (1964); *Cosmic Symphony* for Organ and Orch. (1971); Concertante Sym. for Chamber String Orch. (1972); *Symphonic Concerto* for Violin and Orch. (1972); *Festive Overture* (1973); Sym. No. 4 (1974); Concerto for Double Bass and Strings (1978); Double Concerto for Oboe, Trumpet, and Orch. (1981); *Festive Music* for Brass Ensemble (1985). **CHAMBER:** *Divertimento* for 2 Flutes and Piano (1960); *Miniatures* for Flute and Piano (1962); Trio for Flute, Viola, and Harp (1963); *Sonata aleatoria* for Organ,

Piano, and Percussion (1963); *Sonata nuova* for Cello and Piano (1967); *Contaminationi* for Bass Clarinet and Piano (1968); *Sonata triste* for Trombone and Piano (1972); String Quartet No. 2 (1972); *Sonata bravura* for Violin or Viola or Cello and Piano (1973); Sextet No. 2 for Flute, Oboe, and String Quartet (1975); Wind Quintet No. 2 (1975); *Divertimento* for 4 Horns (1979); Suite No. 3 for Clarinet (1980); *Nomos I* for Flute and Guitar (1981), *II* for English Horn or Flute or Oboe or Clarinet or Saxophone (1982), and *III* for Harp (1983); Quartet for 4 Saxophones (1986); *Musica giocosa* for Chamber Ensemble (1987); Chamber Concerto No. 1 for Oboe or Clarinet and Brass Quintet (1988) and No. 2 for Flute and Viola Ensemble (1988); *Fulmen* for Percussion (1991). **VOCAL:** *Morning Song*, cantata for Chorus and Orch. (1958); *Anna* for Reciter, Alto, Flute, and Harp (1966); *Cantilena Ae Ae Ae* for Chorus (1970); *Homage to Apollo* for Soprano, Alto, Chamber Chorus, Flute, Oboe and Harp (1974); *Olympic Songs* for Reciter, Bass-baritone, Chamber Chorus, and Chamber Orch. (1976); *Eirene* for Mixed or Men's or Children's Chorus (1977); *Auletike* for Chorus and Oboe or Flute (1977); *Femis* for Medium Voice and Instruments (1979); *Ode to Aphrodite* for Soprano and Harp (1982); *The Aeolian Harp* for Medium Voice, Harp, and Percussion (1989). **OTHER:** *Electronia A* for Alto, Chamber Orch., and Electronics (1964), *B* for Chamber Chorus, Chamber Orch., and Electronics (1965), and *C* for Electronics (1966); *Timbri* for Wind Quintet and Electroacoustics (1967); *Deliciae* for Double Bass and Electroacoustics (1968); *Gurges* for Spatial Electroacoustics (1968); *Anthroporea* for Spatial Electroacoustics (1969); *Aphorisms* for Reciter and Electroacoustics (1969); *Mavors* for Electroacoustics (1970); *Discordia* for Electronics (1970); *Cantata Ai Ai A* for Mezzo-soprano, Bass-Baritone, Chamber Chorus, Chamber Orch., and Electroacoustics (1971); *Tibia* for Flute and Electroacoustics (1972); Concertino for Harp and Electroacoustics (1973); *Arcanum* for Electroacoustics (1974); *Malefica* for Mezzo-soprano, Flute, Clarinet, Viola, Harpsichord or Piano, and Electroacoustics (1974); *Paean* for Trombone and Electroacoustics (1976); *Tibia I* for Saxophone and Electroacoustics (1984); *Rota* for Piano or Harpsichord and Electroacoustics (1985); Suite No. 6 for Synthesizer (1986); *Celula* for Electroacoustics (1986); *Bucina* for Trumpet and Electroacoustics (1988); *Parabola* for Synthesizer (1989); *Rosa sepulcreti* for Baritone and Electroacoustics (1989); Chamber Concerto No. 3 for Synthesizer and Chamber Orch. (1990); *Crucifixion I* for Computer (1992).

Růžičková, Zuzana, Czech harpsichordist and teacher; b. Plzeň, Jan. 14, 1928. She studied at the Prague Academy of Music. In 1956 she won the Munich International Competition. She was a member of the Prague Chamber Soloists (1962–67), which she co-founded with the conductor Vaclav Neumann. In 1962 she joined the faculty of the Prague Academy of Music. She appeared in duo recitals with Josef Suk from 1963. In 1969 she was named an Artist of Merit. In 1952 she married **Viktor Kalabis**.

BIBL.: B. Berkovec, *Z. R.* (Prague, 1972).

Rychlík, Jan, Czech composer; b. Prague, April 27, 1916; d. there, Jan. 20, 1964. He studied with Řídký at the Prague Cons. (1939–45) and in his master classes there (1945–46). A practical musician, he played in dance orchs., experimented with modern techniques, and was active as a music critic; he wrote a book on jazz and one on valveless brass instruments.

WORKS: *Symphonic Overture* (1944); *Suite* for Wind Quintet (1946); *Concert Overture* (1947); *Partita giocosa* for Wind Orch. (1947); Trio for Clarinet, Trumpet, and Bassoon (1948); *Divertimento* for 3 Double Basses (1951); *Études* for English Horn and Piano (1953); String Trio (1953); *4 Partitas* for Flute (1954); *Chamber Suite* for String Quartet (1954); *Arabesques* for Violin and Piano (1955); *Burlesque Suite* for Clarinet (1956); *Serenade* for Wind Octet (1957); Wind Quintet (1960); *Hommagi gravicembalistici* for Harpsichord (1960); *African Cycle I–V* for 8 Winds and Piano (1961; Prague, June 29, 1962); *Relazioni* for Alto Flute, English Horn, and Bassoon (1964); music for films and plays.

Rychlik, Józef, Polish composer; b. Kraków, May 12, 1946. He graduated in composition from the Kraków State College of Music. He composed *Symphonic Music I* for 2 String Quartets and 2 Pianos (1969) and *II* for Chamber Ensemble (1969); *Ametrio* for Flute, Violin, and Cello (1971); *Spatial Sequences* for 22 Players (1971); *"000"* for Chamber Group and any Wind Instrument Solo (1972); *Sketches* for Organ and Orch. (1972); *Plenitudo temporis* for Orch. (1974); *Peutêtre*, graphic composition for any Solo Instrument, or Voice, or Dancer, or Ballet Group, with ad libitum Tape (1974); *Podtytul sen Eurydyki II* for Woman's Voice and Tape (1982).

Ryelandt, Joseph, Belgian composer and teacher; b. Bruges, April 7, 1870; d. there, June 29, 1965. He studied composition with Edgar Tinel. Thanks to a personal fortune (he was a baron), he did not have to earn a living by his music. He was director of the Bruges Cons. (1924–45) and a teacher at the Ghent Cons. (1929–39). He lived a very long life (obiit aet. 95) and composed much music.

WORKS: DRAMATIC: *La Parabole des vierges*, spiritual drama (1894); *Sainte Cécile*, lyrical drama (1902). **ORCH.:** 5 syms. (1897, 1904, 1908, 1913, 1934); *Gethsemani*, symphonic poem (1908); *Patria*, overture (1917). **CHAMBER:** 7 violin sonatas; 4 string quartets; 3 cellos sonatas; 2 piano quintets; 2 piano trios; Viola Sonata; Horn Sonata; 11 piano sonatas; organ music. **VOCAL:** 5 oratorios: *Purgatorium* (1904), *De Komst des Heren* (1906–07), *Maria* (1910), *Agnus Dei* (1913–15), and *Christus Rex* (1921–22); *Te Deum* for Soli, Chorus, and Orch. (1927); 7 cantatas; songs.

Rypdal, Terje, Norwegian composer and jazz and rock guitarist; b. Oslo, Aug. 23, 1947. He took up the piano at age 5 and the guitar at 13; subsequently studied musicology at the Univ. of Oslo and was a composition student of Mortensen at the Oslo Cons. (1970–72) and of George Russell, who introduced him to his Lydian Concept of tonal organization. Rypdal was active as a performer with his own pop band, the Vanguards, and later with his group, Dreams; also worked with Russell's sextet and big band. In 1969 he became a member of the Jan Garbarek Quartet. His long association with jazz and rock had significant impact upon his approach to composition. Whether composing in a serial or tonal mode, Rypdal's music relfects a penchant for utilizing late romantic, jazz, and avant-garde elements.

WORKS: DRAMATIC: *Orfeus*, opera (1971); *Freden*, opera (1976); incidental music. **ORCH.:** *Capriccio* for Strings (1970); Double Bass Concerto (1973); 5 syms. (1973, 1977, 1981, 1986, 1992); *Tumulter* for Percussion and Orch. (1973); *Krystaller* for Alto Flute and Orch. (1973); Horn Concerto (1977); *Julemusikk* for Strings (1978); Piano Concerto (1979); *In Autumn* for Electric Guitar, Trumpet, and Orch. (1979); *Undisonus* for Violin and Orch. (1979–81); *Shadows* for Oboe, 4 Trombones, Percussion, and Strings (1980); *Hulter til Bulter* for Percussion and Orch. (1980); *Modulation* for Harmonica and Orch. (1980); *A.B.C. or Adventure-Bedtime Story-Celebration* for Accordion and Orch. (1981); *Labyrint* (1982); *Vilanden*, symphonic poem (1982); *Telegram* for Chamber Orch. (1982); *Imagi* for Cello and Big Band (1983–84); *Patina* for Cello and Orch. (1984); *Buldur og Brak* for Symphonic Band (1986); *Lirum Larum* for Electric Guitar, 2 Rock Bands, Symphonic Band, Chorus, and Orch. (1987); *Det blå Folket* (1987); *Over Fjorden* for Symphonic Band (1989); *The Vanguardian* for Jazz Guitar and Orch. (1989); *Soleis* for Pan Flute and Orch. (1990); *Q.E.D.* (1991); *Hip som Happ* (1991); *Déja-vu* for Soprano Saxophone, Bass Clarinet, Baritone Saxophone, and Strings (1991); *Adagio von Mozart* (1991); Double Concerto for 2 Electric Guitars and Orch. (1992). **CHAMBER:** String Quartet (1970); Wind Quintet (1973); *Whenever I Seem to Be Far Away* for Electric Guitar, Strings, Oboe, and Clarinet (1974); *Unfinished Highballs* for Jazz Quartet (1976); *Concerto ECM* for Electric Guitar, 8 Cellos, Keyboards, and Percussion (1982); *Enigma* for 2 Trumpets, Horn, Trombone, and Tuba (1982); *10 X 10* for Improvisation Ensemble (1983); *Vidare* for Acoustic or Electric Violin (1984);

Crooner Songs for Clarinet, Trumpet, Violin, Keyboards, and Percussion (1986); *Troll* for Electric Guitar, Flute, Clarinet, Violin, Cello, and Keyboards (1986); *Passion* for Harpsichord or Synthesizer, Vibraphone, and Fretless Electric Bass Guitar (1987); *The Illuminator* for Electric Guitar, Percussion, Winds, Brass, Double Bass, and Keyboards (1987); *Drømmespinn* for Oboe, 2 Violins, Viola, Cello, and Double Bass (1988); *Arktik* for Electric Guitar or Alto Flute, Trumpet, Synthesizer, Double Bass, and Percussion (1988); *Sesam* for Clarinet, Trombone, and Piano or Synthesizer (1989); *Inntil Vidare* for Violin, Trumpet, Electric Guitar, Bass Guitar, and Percussion (1990); *Largo* for Electric Guitar, Strings, and Percussion (1991); *Détente* for Flute, Clarinet, 2 Violins, Viola, Cello, and 2 Synthesizers (1992); *Fire* for Violin, Oboe, Viola, and Cello (1992); *The Big Bang II* for Oboe or English Horn, Cello, Double or Electric Bass, Synthesizer, Percussion, and Electric Guitar (1992); *Time* for English Horn, Cello, Double Bass, Synthesizer, Percussion, and Guitar (1993). **VOCAL:** *Eternal Circulation* for Soprano, Chorus, and Orch. (1970); *Spegling* for Mezzo-soprano and Orch. (1981); *Ineo* for Chorus, Electric Guitar, and Orch. (1983); *Vardøger* for Men's Chorus (1984); *Metamorphosis* for Women's Chorus (1984); *The Big Bang* for Women's Chorus and Chamber Ensemble (1990).

Rysanek, Leonie, distinguished Austrian soprano; b. Vienna, Nov. 14, 1926. She studied at the Vienna Cons. with Rudolf Grossmann, whom she later married. She made her operatic debut as Agathe in *Der Freischütz* in Innsbruck in 1949; then sang at Saarbrücken (1950–52). She first attracted notice when she appeared as Sieglinde at the Bayreuth Festival in 1951; became a member of the Bavarian State Opera in Munich in 1952, and went with it to London's Covent Garden in 1953, where she sang Danae; in 1954 she joined the Vienna State Opera; also sang in various other major European opera houses. On Sept. 18, 1956, she made her U.S. debut as Senta at the San Francisco Opera; later made a spectacular appearance at the Metropolitan Opera in N.Y. on Feb. 5, 1959, when she replaced Maria Callas in the role of Lady Macbeth in Verdi's opera on short notice; she continued to sing there with notable distinction for some 35 years. She received the Lotte Lehmann Ring from the Vienna State Opera in 1979. In 1984 she toured Japan with the Hamburg State Opera. In 1986 she appeared as Kostelnička in *Jenůfa* in San Francisco. She sang Kabanicha in *Kat'á Kabanová* in Los Angeles in 1988. In 1990 she appeared as Herodias at the Deutsche Opera in Berlin. In 1992 she sang the Countess in *The Queen of Spades* in Barcelona, a role she repeated for her farewell appearance at the Metropolitan Opera on Jan. 2, 1996. Her younger sister Lotte Rysanek (b. Vienna, March 18, 1928) attained a fine reputation in Vienna as a lyric soprano.

BIBL.: P. Dusek, and P. Schmidt, *L. R.: 40 Jahre Operngeschichte* (Hamburg, 1990).

Rytel, Piotr, Polish composer and teacher; b. Vilnius, Sept. 20, 1884; d. Warsaw, Jan. 2, 1970. He studied with Michalowski and Noskowski at the Warsaw Cons.; in 1911, was appointed a prof. of piano, and in 1918 a prof. of harmony there. He was director of the Sopot State College of Music (1956–61).

WORKS: OPERAS: *Ijola* (1927; Warsaw, Dec. 14, 1929); *Koniec Mesjasza* (1935–36); *Krzyzowcy* (1940–41); *Andrzej z Chelmna* (1942–43). **BALLETS:** *Faun i Psyche* (1931); *Śląski pierścień* (The Silesian Ring; 1956). **ORCH.:** Piano Concerto (1907); 5 symphonic poems: *Grazyna* (1908; rev. 1954), *Poemat* (1910), *Korsarz*, after Byron (The Corsair; 1911), *Sen Dantego* (The Dream of Dante; 1911), and *Legenda o sw. Jerzym* (The Legend of St. George; 1918); 3 syms.: No. 1 (1909), No. 2, *Mickiewiczowska* (in honor of the Polish poet Mickiewicz) for Tenor, Chorus, and Orch. (1949), and No. 3 for Tenor and Orch. (1950–51); Violin Concerto (1950); *Sinfonia concertante* for Flute, Clarinet, Horn, Harp, and Orch. (1960). **CHAMBER:** *Romance* for Clarinet and Piano (1948); *Variations* for Clarinet and Piano (1957).

Rzewski, Frederic (Anthony), American pianist, teacher, and avant-garde composer; b. Westfield, Mass., April 13, 1938. He studied counterpoint with Thompson and orchestration with Piston at Harvard Univ. (B.A., 1958) and continued his studies with Sessions and Babbitt at Princeton Univ. (M.F.A., 1960); then received instruction from Dallapiccola in Florence on a Fulbright scholarship (1960–61) and from Carter in Berlin on a Ford Foundation grant (1963–65). With Curran and Teitelbaum, other similarly futuroscopic musicians, he founded the M.E.V. (Musica Elettronica Viva) in Rome in 1966; was active as a pianist in various avant-garde settings; played concerts with the topless cellist Charlotte Moorman; also devoted much time to teaching. In 1977 he became prof. of composition at the Liège Cons. As a composer, he pursues the shimmering distant vision of optimistic, positivistic anti-music. He is furthermore a granitically overpowering piano technician, capable of depositing huge boulders of sonoristic material across the keyboard without actually wrecking the instrument.

WORKS: DRAMATIC: *The Persians,* music theater (1985); *Chains,* 12 television operas (1986); *The Triumph of Death,* stage oratorio (1987–88). **ORCH.:** *Nature morte* for 25 Instruments (1965); *A Long Time Man* for Piano and Orch. (1979); *The Price of Oil* for 2 Speakers, Winds, and Percussion (1980); *Satyrica* for Jazz Band (River Falls, Wis., April 27, 1983); *Una breve storia d'estate* for 3 Flutes and Small Orch. (1983). **INSTRUMENTAL:** Octet for Flute, Clarinet, Trumpet, Trombone, Piano, Harp, Violin, and Double Bass (1961–62); *For Violin* (1962); *Speculum Dianae* for 8 Instruments (1964); *Les Moutons de Panurge* for Variable Ensemble (1969); *Last Judgement* for 1 or More Trombones (1969); *Attica* for Narrator and Variable Ensemble (1972); *Coming Together* for Narrator and Variable Ensemble (1972); *What Is Freedom?* for 6 Instruments (1974); *13 Instrumental Studies* (1977); *Song and Dance* for Flute, Bass Clarinet, Vibraphone, and Electric Bass (1977); *To the Earth* for Speaking Percussionist (1985); *The Lost Melody* for Clarinet, Piano, and 2 Percussion (1989); *Whang Doodles,* trio for Violin, Piano, and Percussion (Chicago, Aug. 20, 1990); *Crusoe* for 4 to 12 Performers (1993); *Histories,* saxophone quartet (1993); *Whims* for Marimba and String Quartet (1993). **PIANO:** *Preludes* (1957); *Poem* (1959); Sonata for 2 Pianos (1960); *Study I* (1960) and *II* (1961); *Falling Music* for Amplified Piano and Tape (1971); *Variations on No Place to Go but Around* (1974); *The People United Will Never Be Defeated,* 36 variations on the Chilean song *El pueblo unido jamas sera vencido!* (1975); *4 pieces* (1977); *4 North American Ballads* (1978–79); *Squares* (1979); *Winnsboro Cotton Mill Blues* for 2 Pianos (1980); *A Machine* for 2 Pianos (1984); Sonata (1991); *De Profundis* (1992). **OTHER:** *Spacecraft* (his magnum opus; 1967; "plan for spacecraft" publ. in *Source,* 3, 1968); *Impersonation,* audiodrama (1967); *Requiem* (1968); *Symphony for Several Performers* (1968).

S

Saar, Louis Victor (Franz), Dutch pianist, teacher, and composer; b. Rotterdam, Dec. 10, 1868; d. St. Louis, Nov. 23, 1937. He studied with Rheinberger in Munich (1886–89); lived in Vienna, Leipzig, and Berlin; in 1894 he went to the U.S.; taught music at various schools in N.Y. He was a member of the faculty at the Cincinnati College of Music (1906–17), the Chicago Musical College (1917–33), and the St. Louis Inst. of Music (1934–37). He wrote the orch. pieces *From the Mountain Kingdom of the Great Northwest* (1922) and *Along the Columbia River* (1924), but became best known for his choral works, songs, and violin and piano pieces.

Saar, Mart, Estonian composer; b. Vastemõisa, Livonia, Sept. 16, 1882; d. Tallinn, Oct. 28, 1963. He was a pupil of Louis Homilius, Rimsky-Korsakov, and Liadov at the St. Petersburg Cons. (1901–11). He was active as a folk-song collector, critic, and teacher in Dorpat, Reval (Tallinn), and Hüpassare; also taught composition at the Tallinn Cons. (1943–56). He was one of Estonia's leading composers; wrote orch. music, choral works, including cantatas and many songs, and much piano music.

BIBL.: K. Leichter, *M. S.* (Tallinn, 1964); V. Rumessen, ed., *M. S. sõnas ja pildis* (M. S. in Words and Pictures; Tallinn, 1973).

Saariaho, Kaija (Anneli), significant Finnish composer; b. Helsinki, Oct. 14, 1952. She was a student of Heininen at the Sibelius Academy in Helsinki (1976–81), and also attended the Univ. of Industrial Arts in Helsinki. She pursued training with Ferneyhough and Huber at the Freiberg im Breisgau Hochschule für Musik (diploma, 1983), and also attended the summer courses in new music in Darmstadt (1980, 1982) and worked in computer music at IRCAM in Paris (1982). From 1983 to 1986, and again from 1988 to 1992, she held a Finnish government artist's grant. In 1986 she won the Kranichstein Prize in Darmstadt. She received the Prix Italia in 1988. In 1988–89 she held a composition fellowship at the Univ. of Calif. at San Diego. In 1989 she received the Austrian TV's Ars Electronica. Saariaho has followed an advanced compositional path in which she makes use of tape, live electronics, and computers. Her works are often of striking individuality and communicative power.

WORKS: DRAMATIC: *Maa,* ballet (Helsinki, Oct. 31, 1991); several tape music scores for theater. **ORCH.:** *Verblendungen* for Orch. and Tape (1982–84; Helsinki, April 10, 1984); *Du Cristal* (1989–90; Helsinki, Sept. 5, 1990); . . . *à la Fumée* (1990; Helsinki, March 20, 1991); *Graal Théâtre* for Violin and Orch. (1994; London, Aug. 29, 1995). **CHAMBER:** *Canvas* for Flute (1978); *Yellows* for Horn and Percussion (1980); *Im Traume* for Cello and Piano (1980); *Laconisme de l'aile* for Flute (1982; Freiburg im Breisgau, March 1, 1983); *Jardin Secret II* for Harpsichord and Tape (1984; Savonlinna, July 12, 1986) and *III: Nymphéa* for String Quartet and Live Electronics (N.Y., May 20, 1987); *Lichtbogen* for Chamber Ensemble and Live Electronics (1985–86; Paris, May 13, 1986); *Io* for Chamber Ensemble, Tape, and Live Electronics (1986–87; Paris, July 27, 1987); *Petals* for Cello and Optional Electronics (Bremen, May 20, 1988); *Oi kuu* for Bass Clarinet and Cello (Warsaw, Sept. 15, 1990; also for Bass Flute and Cello); *Amers* for Cello, Chamber Ensemble, and Live Electronics (London, Dec. 8, 1992); *NoaNoa* for Flute and Electronics (Darmstadt, July 23, 1992); *Près* for Cello and Electronics (Strasbourg, Nov. 10, 1992); *6 Japanese Gardens* for Percussion and Electronics (1993); *Solar* for Chamber Ensemble (Antwerp, Oct. 26, 1993); *Nocturne* for Violin (Helsinki, Feb. 16, 1994); *Trois Rivières* for Percussion Quartet and Electronics (Strasbourg, Sept. 25, 1994); *Folia* for Double Bass and Electronics (Lyons, March 23, 1995). **VOCAL:** *Bruden* (The Bride), song cycle for Soprano, 2 Flutes, and Percussion (1977); *Jing* for Soprano and Cello (1979); *Nej och inte* (No and not), 3 songs for Women's Quartet or Chorus (1979); *Suomenkielinen sekakuorokappale* (A Piece for Mixed Chorus in the Finnish Language; 1979); *Preludi-Tunnustus-Postludi* (Prelude-Confession-Postlude) for Soprano and Prepared Grand Piano (1980); *Study for Life* for Woman's Voice, Dancer, Tape, and Light (1980); *Kolme Preludia* (3 Preludes) for Soprano and Organ (1980); . . . *sah den Vögeln* for Soprano, Flute, Oboe, Cello, and

Prepared Piano (1981); *Ju lägre solen* for Soprano, Flute, and Guitar (1982; Freiburg im Breisgau, March 1, 1983; rev. 1985 as *Adjö*); *Piipää* for 2 Singers, Tape, and Live Electronics (1987); *Grammaire des Rêves* for Soprano, Alto, 2 Flutes, Harp, Viola, and Cello (1988; Paris, March 20, 1989); *From the grammar of dreams* for 2 Sopranos (Huddersfield, Nov. 24, 1988); *Nuits, adieux* for 4 Voices and Live Electronics (Witten, May 11, 1991); *Caliban's Dream* for Baritone, Guitar, Mandolin, Harp, and Double Bass (Brussels, March 13, 1993). **ELECTRONIC:** *Stilleben* (1987–88).

Sabaneyev, Leonid (Leonidovich), Russian writer on music and composer; b. Moscow, Oct. 1, 1881; d. Antibes, May 3, 1968. He studied with Taneyev at the Moscow Cons.; also took a course in mathematics at the Univ. of Moscow. In 1920 he joined the board of the newly organized Moscow Inst. of Musical Science. In 1926 he left Russia and eventually settled in France. He was an energetic promoter of modern music, and a friend of Scriabin, about whom he wrote a monograph, which would have been important if his account of Scriabin's life and ideology could be trusted; he compromised himself when he wrote a devastating review of Prokofiev's *Scythian Suite* at a concert that never took place. His books in Eng. comprised *Modern Russian Composers* (N.Y., 1927) and *Music for the Films* (London, 1935). His compositions included the ballet, *L'Aviatrice* (Paris, 1928); *Flots d'azur*, symphonic poem (1936); *The Revelation*, oratorio (1940); 2 piano trios (1907, 1924); Violin Sonata (1924); piano pieces; songs.

Sabata, Victor de. See **De Sabata, Victor.**

Sabin, Wallace Arthur, English organist and composer; b. Culworth, Dec. 15, 1860; d. Berkeley, Calif., Dec. 8, 1937. He studied with M.J. Monk at Banbury and T.W. Dodds at Oxford, where he obtained a degree at Queen's College (1890). He emigrated to the U.S. and settled in San Francisco, where he was organist at St. Luke's (1894–1906), Temple Emanu-El (1895–1937), and the First Church of Christ, Scientist (1906–37). He composed the music to the plays *St. Patrick at Tara* (1906) and *The Twilight of the Kings* (1918), many part songs for men's voices, and sacred music.

BIBL.: R. Rinder, *Tribute to W.A. S.* (San Francisco, 1938).

Sacco, P(atrick) Peter, American composer, tenor, and teacher; b. Albion, N.Y., Oct. 25, 1928. He was born into a musical family and began touring as a child pianist and boy soprano at an early age. Following studies at the Eastman Preparatory School in Rochester, N.Y. (1941–44), he pursued training with Vivian Major and William Willett at the State Univ. of N.Y. at Fredonia (B.M., 1950). During military service, he continued his studies with Wolfgang Niederste-Schee in Frankfurt am Main (1950–52). After his discharge, he completed his training with Barlow, Rogers, and Hanson at the Eastman School of Music in Rochester, N.Y. (M.M., 1954; D.Mus., 1958). From 1959 until his retirement in 1980 he taught at San Francisco State Univ. He also pursued an active career as a concert artist. In his music, Sacco adhered to traditional harmony but developed an ingenious chromatic method of expression.

WORKS: CHAMBER OPERA: *Mr. Vinegar* (1966–67; Redding, Calif., May 12, 1967). **ORCH.:** 3 syms.: No. 1 (1955; Oklahoma City, Dec. 17, 1958), No. 2, *Symphony of Thanksgiving* (1965–76; San Francisco, March 23, 1976), and No. 3, *Convocation Symphony* (Redding, Calif., June 1, 1968); *4 Sketches on Emerson Essays* for Wind Ensemble (1963); Piano Concerto (1964; San Francisco, April 4, 1968); Violin Concerto (1969–74; Walnut Creek, Calif., April 24, 1974); band music. **CHAMBER:** Clarinet Quintet (1956); String Quartet (1966). **PIANO:** 2 sonatas (1951, 1965); 4 sonatinas (1962–63); *Variations on Schubert's "An die Musik"* for Piano, 4-hands (1981). **VOCAL:** 3 oratorios: *Jesu* (Grand Rapids, Mich., Dec. 3, 1956), *Midsummer Dream Night* (San Francisco, June 15, 1961), and *Solomon* (San Francisco, Dec. 12, 1976); cantatas; choruses; anthems; many solo songs.

Sacher, Paul, respected Swiss conductor and philanthropist; b. Basel, April 28, 1906. He studied with Weingartner (conducting) at the Basel Cons. and with Karl Nef (musicology) at the Univ. of Basel. In 1926 he founded the Basel Chamber Orch., which specialized in playing works from the pre-Classical and contemporary periods; in 1928 he also organized the Basel Chamber Choir. In 1933 he founded the Schola Cantorum Basiliensis; was also director of the Collegium Musicum in Zürich from 1941. His Schola Cantorum Basiliensis was amalgamated with Basel's Cons. and Musikschule to form the Musikakademie der Stadt Basel, which he directed from 1954 to 1969. He appeared as a guest conductor in many European cities; made his U.S. debut as a guest conductor with the Collegiate Chorale in N.Y. (April 3, 1955). In 1934 he married Maja Stehlin, widow of Emmanuel Hoffmann, whose father founded the Hoffmann-La Roche pharmaceutical firm, makers of the drugs Valium and Librium. Through his wife's fortune, Sacher was able to pursue his goal of commissioning works from the leading composers of the 20th century; in all, he commissioned over 200 works, including scores by Stravinsky, Bartók, Strauss, Honegger, Hindemith, Martin, Britten, Henze, and Boulez, many of which received their premieres under his direction. In 1983 he purchased the entire Stravinsky archive in N.Y. for $5,250,000. In 1986 the Paul Sacher Foundation building was opened in Basel; it houses the archives of Stravinsky, Webern, Martin, and Maderna, as well as of Sacher.

BIBL.: E. Lichtenhahn and T. Seebass, eds., *Musik Handschriften aus der Sammlung P. S.: Festschrift zu P. S.s siebzigstem Geburtstag* (Basel, 1976); M. Rostropovich, ed., *Dank an P. S.* (Zürich, 1976).

Sachs, Curt, eminent German musicologist; b. Berlin, June 29, 1881; d. N.Y., Feb. 5, 1959. While attending the Gymnasium in Berlin, he studied piano and composition with L. Schrattenholz and clarinet with Rausch; entered the Univ. there, where he studied music history with Oskar Fleischer, and also art history (Ph.D., 1904). He was active as an art historian until 1909 while receiving instruction in musicology from Kretzschmar and Wolf; then devoted himself to musicology, specializing in the history of musical instruments. In 1919 he became director of Berlin's Staatliche Instrumenten Sammlung; also taught at the Univ. of Berlin, the Staatliche Hochschule für Musik, and the Akademie für Kirchen- und Schulmusik. In 1933 he was compelled to leave Germany; went to Paris as chargé de mission at the Musée de l'Homme; was a visiting prof. at the Sorbonne. In 1937 he settled in the U.S.; was a prof. of music at N.Y. Univ. (1937–53); also was consultant to the N.Y. Public Library (1937–52), adjunct prof. at Columbia Univ. (from 1953), and president of the American Musicological Soc. (1949–50).

WRITINGS: *Musikgeschichte der Stadt Berlin bis zum Jahre 1800* (1908); *Musik und Oper am kurbrandenburgischen Hof* (1910); *Reallexikon der Musikinstrumente* (1913); *Handbuch der Musikinstrumentenkunde* (1920; 2nd ed., 1930); *Die Musikinstrumente des alten Ägyptens* (1921); *Katalog der Staatlichen Instrumentensammlung* (1922); *Das Klavier* (1923); *Die modernen Musikinstrumente* (1923); *Geist und Werden der Musikinstrumente* (1929); *Vergleichende Musikwissenschaft in ihren Grundzügen* (1930); *Eine Weltgeschichte des Tanzes* (1933; Eng. tr., 1937); *Les Instruments de musique de Madagascar* (1938); *The History of Musical Instruments* (1940); *The Rise of Music in the Ancient World* (1943); ed. *The Evolution of Piano Music* (1944); *The Commonwealth of Art* (1946); *Our Musical Heritage* (1948; 2nd ed., 1955); *Rhythm and Tempo: A Study in Music History* (1953).

BIBL.: G. Reese and R. Brandel, eds., *The Commonwealth of Music, in Honor of C. S.* (N.Y., 1965).

Sachs, Joel, American pianist, conductor, and musicologist; b. New Haven, Conn., Dec. 19, 1939. He studied piano with Ray Lev and theory with Sam DiBonaventura and David Kraehenbuehl; in 1957, entered Harvard College, majoring in chemistry and physics, but eventually turned to music, studying with Piston, Thompson, Pirotta, and Ward; also took piano lessons with

Miklos Schwalb in Boston and with Rosina Lhévinne in N.Y. In 1961 he received a fellowship for travel in Europe; after appearances as a pianist in London in 1963, he returned to the U.S. to study musicology at Columbia Univ., completing his Ph.D. in composition in 1968. He joined similarly inclined musicians and scholars to form Continuum, a group devoted to the exploration of new music; gave concerts with it in the U.S. and Europe, attaining a considerable reputation for excellence. He also taught and was active as coordinator of contemporary music (from 1985) at the Juilliard School in N.Y. In 1993 he founded the new Juilliard Ensemble, a chamber orchestra devoted to new music. Through the years he gave several hundred concerts and lectures dealing with 20th-century music; also directed radio performances in Europe dedicated to the works of Ives and Webern. In purely musicological pursuits, particularly valuable are his detailed writings on the works of J.N. Hummel, for which he had the cooperation of Hummel's descendants.

Sachse, Leopold, German-American bass, opera producer, and administrator; b. Berlin, Jan. 5, 1880; d. Englewood, N.J., April 3, 1961. He studied at the Cologne Cons.; then in Vienna. In 1902 he joined the Strasbourg Opera as a baritone; then was Intendant in Münster (1907), Halle (1914–19), and at the Hamburg Opera (1922–33), where he produced a number of contemporary works. He was forced to leave his homeland by the Nazis and settled in the U.S.; was a producer at the Metropolitan Opera in N.Y. (1935–55); taught stage technique at the Juilliard Graduate School in N.Y. (1936–43); was a stage director at the N.Y. City Opera (from 1945); founded his own Opera in English Co. (1951).

Sack (real name, **Weber**), **Erna,** German soprano; b. Berlin, Feb. 6, 1898; d. Mainz, March 2, 1972. She studied in Prague and with O. Daniel in Berlin. She made her operatic debut as a contralto at the Berlin Städtische Oper (1925); then turned to coloratura soprano roles and sang in Bielefeld (1930–32), Wiesbaden (1932–34), and Breslau (1934–35); subsequently, in 1935, joined the Dresden State Opera, where she was chosen to create the role of Isotta in Strauss's *Die schweigsame Frau*; appeared with the company as Zerbinetta under Strauss's direction during its visit to London's Covent Garden in 1936. In 1937 she sang opera in Chicago and made a concert tour of the U.S.; also appeared in opera in Milan, Paris, Vienna, Salzburg, and other major European music centers. After World War II, she made an extensive world tour as a concert singer (1947–52); again gave concerts in the U.S. (1954–55). In 1966 she settled in Wiesbaden.

Sadai, Yizhak, Bulgarian-born Israeli composer and teacher; b. Sofia, May 13, 1935. He emigrated to Israel in 1949 and studied with Haubenstock-Ramati and Boscovich at the Tel Aviv Academy of Music (1951–56). In 1966 he joined the music staff of the Univ. of Tel Aviv.

WORKS: OPERA: *Trial* (1979). **ORCH.:** *Ricercare symphonique* (1956); *Serenade* for Winds (1956); *Nuances* for Chamber Orch. (1964); *Canti Fermi* for Orch. and Synthesizer (1986). **CHAMBER:** *Interpolations* for Harpsichord and String Quartet (1960); *Aria da Capo* for 6 Instruments and 2 Tape Recorders (1965); *Registers* for Violin and Piano (1967); *From the Diary of a Percussionist* for Percussion Player and Tape (1971); *Anamorphoses* for String Quartet (1982); *Antiphonies* for Chamber Ensemble (1986); *Reprises* for Nonet (1986). **VOCAL:** *Divertimento* for Alto, Flute, Viola, and Piano (1954); 3 cantatas: *Ecclesiastes* (1956), *Hazvi Israel* (1957), and *Psychoanalysis* (1958); *Préludes a Jérusalem* for Voice and Instruments (1968). **TAPE:** *The Interrupted Prayer* (1975).

Sadie, Julie Anne (née **McCormack**), American cellist and writer on music; b. Eugene, Oreg., Jan. 26, 1948. She was educated at the Univ. of Oregon (B.Mus., 1970) and Cornell Univ. (M.A., 1973; Ph.D., 1978). She was active as a cellist and viola da gambist, and later as a player on the Baroque cello. From 1974 to 1976 she taught at the Eastman School of Music in Rochester, N.Y. In 1978 she married **Stanley Sadie** and settled in London, where she lectured at King's College, Univ. of London (1982) and at the Royal College of Music (1986–88). In addition to articles in various journals, she publ. the vols. *The Bass Viol in French Baroque Chamber Music* (1980), *Everyman Companion to Baroque Music* (1991), and, with R. Samuel, *The New Grove Dictionary of Women Composers* (1994).

Sadie, Stanley (John), eminent English writer on music and lexicographer; b. London, Oct. 30, 1930. He studied music privately with Bernard Stevens (1947–50) and then with Dart, Hadley, and Cudworth at Cambridge (B.A. and Mus.B., 1953; M.A., 1957; Ph.D., 1958, with the diss. *British Chamber Music, 1720–1790*). He was on the staff of Trinity College of Music in London (1957–65); from 1964 to 1981, was a music critic on the staff of the *Times* of London. In 1967 he became the ed. of the *Musical Times*, which position he retained until 1987. A distinguished scholar, he wrote the following monographs (all publ. in London): *Handel* (1962); *Mozart* (1966); *Beethoven* (1967; 2nd ed., 1974); *Handel* (1968); and *Handel Concertos* (1972); also publ. numerous articles in British and American music journals. With Arthur Jacobs, he ed. *The Pan Book of Opera* (London, 1964; rev. ed. as *Opera: A Modern Guide*, N.Y., 1972; new ed., 1984). In 1969 he was entrusted with the formidable task of preparing for publication, as ed.-in-chief, a completely new ed. of *Grove's Dictionary of Music and Musicians*; after 11 years of labor, *The New Grove Dictionary of Music and Musicians* was publ. in London in 1980; this 6th ed., in 20 vols., reflected the contributions of more than 2,400 scholars throughout the world, and was accorded a premier place of honor among the major reference sources of its kind. He also ed. *The New Grove Dictionary of Musical Instruments* (1984) and was co-ed., with H. Wiley Hitchcock, of *The New Grove Dictionary of American Music* (4 vols., 1986). With A. Hicks, he ed. the vol. *Handel Tercentenary Collection* (Ann Arbor, 1988). He also ed. *The Grove Concise Dictionary of Music* (1988; U.S. ed., 1988, as *The Norton/Grove Concise Encyclopedia of Music*) and *The New Grove Dictionary of Opera* (4 vols., 1992). He likewise ed. *Wolfgang Amadè Mozart: Essays on His Life and His Music* (Oxford, 1995). He served as ed. of the Master Musicians series from 1976. In 1981 he received the honorary degree of D.Litt. from the Univ. of Leicester and was made an honorary member of the Royal Academy of Music, London. In 1982 he was made a Commander of the Order of the British Empire. In 1978 he married **Julie Anne Sadie**.

Sadra, I Wayan, significant Indonesian composer, performer, and writer on music; b. Denpasar, Bali, Aug. 1, 1953. He attended the local high school cons., Konservatori Karawitan (KOKAR; graduated, 1972), where he specialized in traditional Balinese music, particularly *gender wayang* (music for the Balinese shadow play). In 1973–74 he worked with the well-known experimental Indonesian choreographer Sardono W. Kusumo; after touring with his group in Europe and the Middle East, Sadra settled in Jakarta, where he studied painting and taught Balinese gamelan at Institut Kesenian Jakarta (IKJ, Jakarta Fine Arts Inst.; 1975–78); also taught Balinese music at the Indonesian Univ. (1978–80), and experimental composition, Balinese gamelan, and music criticism at Sekolah Tinggi Seni Indonesia Surakarta (STSI, National College of the Arts; from 1983), where he earned a degree in composition (1988); concurrently wrote new music criticism for various Indonesian newspapers, including *Suara Karya* and *Bali Post*. He appeared widely as a performer with traditional Indonesian ensembles; performed throughout Indonesia and Europe, and in Singapore, Japan, Hong Kong, Australia, and Seoul. In 1988 he was keynote speaker at the national Pekan Komponis (Composers' Festival) in Jakarta; in 1989, appeared in California at the Pacific Rim Festival; in 1990, was a featured participant at Composer-to-Composer in Telluride, Colo. Concurrent with the development of Indonesia's national identity has come an increase of national new-music festivals, increased interaction among artists from different regions, and the greater degree of individual freedom to create autonomous music; all have contributed to the emergence of a distinct Indonesian aesthetic and a contemporary art music. Sadra is one of the outstanding young composers to emerge from this period, and his works have contributed much to the development of "musik kontemporer," "komposisi," and "kreasi baru" ("new creations"). He is also concerned with the social context of performance, considering audience development as important as the development of new works. His compositions are often scored for unusual combinations of instruments. In an experimental piece performed at the Telluride Inst., raw eggs were thrown at a heated black panel; as the eggs cooked and sizzled, they provided both a visual and sonic element for the closing of the piece. He also proposed to the mayor of Solo, Central Java, a new work entitled *Sebuah Kota Yang Bermain Musik* (A City That Plays Music), wherein the entire population of the city would make sounds together for a specified 5 minutes; the proposal was not accepted, but Sadra hopes for its realization in the future.

WORKS: *Nadir* for Gong Kebyar (1977); *Lanyad* for Gong Kebyar (1978); *Lad-Lud-an* for Knobbed Gongs from Reong and Terompong, 4 Kempul, Gong, 8 Kendang, 2 Suling, Gentorak, Ceng-Ceng, and Rebab (1981); *Gender* for Javanese Gender, 2 Balinese Gender, and Visual Elements, including Shadow Puppets (1982); *Sekitar 12–14 Menit* for Javanese Gamelan (1987); *Karya spontan* (Spontaneous Creation), accompaniment for Theater Perampok, for Saluang (Sumatran end-blown flute), Gender, Bumbung, and Kenong (1988); *Stay a Maverick* for Javanese Gamelan, Balinese Suling, and Sunda nese Kecapi (1989); *Terus dan Terus* (On and On) for Balinese Drum, Javanese Drum, and Drone Instruments (1989). **DANCE ACCOMPANIMENT:** *Kicaka* for Gender Wayang, Suling Gambuh, Reong, Terompong, and Kendang (1976); *Gatotkaca-Sraya* for Gong Kebyar (1980); *Mecanda* (for children's improvised dance) for Genggong, Ceng-Ceng Kopyak, Tambur, and Gong Kebyar (1981); *Kusalawa* (1984); *Drebah* (1987); *Buhin*, collaborative improvisation for Triplex (Masonite board), Milk Cans Suling Gambuh, Balinese Drums, Gentorak, Knobbed Gongs, Rebab, and Slentem (1983); O-A-E-O for Voices, Flexotone, Kemanak, Suling, Rebab, Kendang, and Javanese Gamelan (1988); *Aku* for Street Musicians, Suling, Singers, and Drums (1990).

Saenger, Gustav, American music editor and arranger; b. N.Y., May 31, 1865; d. there, Dec. 10, 1935. He studied violin with Leopold Damrosch and others. He was an orch. violinist; then conducted theater orchs. in N.Y.; in 1897 he was engaged as an arranger for Carl Fischer, Inc., and in 1909 became ed.-in-chief of Fischer's publs.; also edited the Fischer periodicals *Metronome* (from 1900) and the *Musical Observer* (1904–29). Besides a vast number of arrangements, he publ. pieces for violin and piano (*5 Silhouettes*; *3 Concert Miniatures*; etc.); also *New School of Melody*.

Saenger, Oscar, American singing teacher; b. Brooklyn, Jan. 5, 1868; d. Washington, D.C., April 20, 1929. He sang in church as a boy; studied voice with J. Bouhy at the National Cons. in N.Y., where he taught (1889–97). He made his operatic debut with the Hinrichs Grand Opera Co. in 1891; after a brief tour in Germany and Austria, he returned to America and devoted himself entirely to teaching. Among his students were many well-known singers, including Marie Rappold, Paul Althouse, and Mabel Garrison.

Saenz, Pedro, Argentine composer; b. Buenos Aires, May 4, 1915. He studied piano with Alberto Williams and theory with Arturo Palma. In 1948 he went to Paris, where he took lessons with Honegger, Milhaud, and Rivier. Returning to Buenos Aires, he occupied numerous teaching and administrative posts in educational institutions. Among his compositions were *Movimientos sinfónicos* for Orch. (1963); Piano Quintet (1942); String Trio (1955); *Divertimento* for Oboe and Clarinet (1959); *Capriccio* for Harpsichord and String Quartet (1966); numerous piano pieces and songs.

Saeverud, Harald (Sigurd Johan), prominent Norwegian composer, father of **Ketil Hvoslef** (real name, **Saeverud**); b. Bergen, April 17, 1897; d. Siljustøl, March 27, 1992. He studied theory at the Bergen Music Academy with B. Holmsen (1915–20) and with F.E. Koch at the Hochschule für Musik in Berlin (1920–21); took a course in conducting with Clemens Krauss in Berlin (1935). In 1953 he received the Norwegian State Salary of Art (a government life pension for outstanding artistic achievement). He began to compose very early, and on Dec. 12, 1912, at the age of 15, conducted in Bergen a program of his own symphonic pieces. His music was permeated with characteristically lyrical Scandinavian Romanticism, with Norwegian folk melos as its foundation; his symphonic compositions are polyphonic in nature and tonal in essence, with euphonious dissonant textures imparting a peculiarly somber character.

WORKS: DRAMATIC: *The Rape of Lucretia*, incidental music to Shakespeare's play (1935; also a *Lucretia Suite* for Orch., 1936); *Peer Gynt*, incidental music to Ibsen's play (1947; Oslo, March 2, 1948; also as 2 orch. suites and a piano suite); *Olav og Kari*, dance scene (1948); *Ridder Blåskjeggs mareritt* (Bluebeard's Nightmare), ballet (Oslo, Oct. 4, 1960). **ORCH.:** 9 syms.: No. 1, in 2 symphonic fantasias (1916–20; Bergen, 1923), No. 2 (1922; Bergen, Nov. 22, 1923; rev. 1934; Oslo, April 1, 1935), No. 3 (1925–26; Bergen, Feb. 25, 1932), No. 4 (Oslo, Dec. 9, 1937), No. 5, *Quasi una fantasia* (Bergen, March 6, 1941), No. 6, *Sinfonia dolorosa* (1942; Bergen, May 27, 1943), No. 7, *Salme* (Psalm; Bergen, Sept. 1, 1945), No. 8, *Minnesota* (Minneapolis, Oct. 18, 1958), and No. 9 (Bergen, June 12, 1966); *Ouverture Appassionata* (1920; retitled 2nd fantasia of his Sym. No. 1); *50 Small Variations* (1931); Oboe Concerto (1938); *Divertimento No. 1* for Flute and Strings (1939); *Syljetone* (The Bride's Heirloom Brooch) for Chamber Orch. or Piano (1939); *Rondo amoroso* for Chamber Orch. or Piano (1939); *Gjaetlevise-Variasjoner* (Shepherd's Tune Variations) for Chamber Orch. (1941); *Siljuslåtten* (Countryside Festival Dance; 1942; also for Piano); *Galdreslåtten* (The Sorcerer's Dance; 1942); *Romanza* for Violin and Orch. or Piano (1942); *Kjempeviseslåtten* (Ballad of Revolt; 1943; also for Piano); Piano Concerto (1948–50); Violin Concerto (1956); *Allegria (Sinfonia concertante)* (1957); Bassoon Concerto (1963); *Mozart-Motto-Sinfonietta* (1971). **CHAMBER:** *20 Small Duets* for Violins (1951); 3 string quartets (1970, 1975, 1978); *Pastorale* (Indian Summer) for Cello (1978). **PIANO:** *5 Capricci* (1918–19); Sonata (1921); *Tunes and Dances from Siljustøl* (5 vols., 1943–46); 6 sonatinas (1948–50); *Fabula gratulatorum* (1973).

BIBL.: C. Baden, *H. S. 80 år* (Oslo, 1977).

Saeverud, Ketil. See **Hvoslef, Ketil.**

Sagaev, Dimiter, Bulgarian composer and teacher; b. Plovdiv, Feb. 27, 1915. He was a student of Stoyanov and Vladigerov at the Bulgarian State Cons. in Sofia (graduated, 1940), where he then taught. His music is Romantic in essence and national in its thematic resources.

WORKS: DRAMATIC: OPERAS: *Under the Yoke* (1965); *Samouil* (1975). **BALLETS:** *The Madara Horseman* (1960); *Orpheus* (1978). Also incidental music. **ORCH.:** *Youth Suite* (1952); *Sofia*, symphonic poem (1954); *3 Bulgarian Symphonic Dances* (1956); 2 violin concertos (1963, 1964); Viola Concerto (1963); 2 oboe concertos (1964, 1991); 7 syms. (1964, 1977, 1979, 1980, 1981, 1982, 1987); Flute Concerto (1974); Cello Concerto (1977); Concerto for Wind Orch. (1981); Clarinet Concerto (1983); Horn Concerto (1986); Trumpet Concerto (1989); Piano Concerto (1992). **CHAMBER:** 7 string quartets (1945, 1962, 1962, 1963, 1966, 1967, 1968); 2 wind quintets (1961, 1962); Trio for Flute, Violin, and Piano (1974); Quartet for Flute, Viola, Harp, and Piano (1975); Clarinet Sonata No. 3 (1989). **VOCAL:** *In the Name of Freedom*, oratorio (1969); *The Shipka Epic* (1977); *The Artist*, oratorio (1987); songs.

Saikkola, Lauri, Finnish violinist and composer; b. Vyborg, March 31, 1906. He studied violin at the local music school (1919–28) and composition privately with Akimov and Funtek (1930–34). He was a violinist in the Viipuri (Vyborg) Phil. (1923–34) and the Helsinki Phil. (1934–65). His extensive compositional output followed along traditional lines.

WORKS: OPERAS: *Taivaaseen menija*, radio opera (1950);

Ristin (1957–58). **ORCH.:** *1500m.* (1933); *Lasten maailmasta* for Strings (1933); 10 syms. (1938, 1946, 1949, 1951, 1958, 1982, 1984, 1984, 1985, 1989); *Pieni elegia* for Strings (1939); *Kuvia Karjalasta* (1940–46); *Pieni sävelmä* for Strings (1946); *Canzone* for Strings (1948); *Overtura del dramma* (1949); *Music* for Strings (1950); Violin Concerto (1952); *Concerto da camera* for Piano and Chamber Orch. (1957); *Musica sinfonica* (1966); Concertino for Clarinet and Strings (1968); *Raasepori* (1971); *Concerto miniaturo* for Viola and Strings (1979); 12 sinfoniettas (1983–90); *Tripartita* for Strings (1984). **CHAMBER:** 5 string quartets (1931, 1938, 1983, 1984, 1985); *Divertimento* for Wind Quartet (1968); Wind Quintet (1968); *Notturno* for Violin and Piano (1977); piano pieces. **VOCAL:** *Laulusarja* for Soprano and Orch. (1946); *Kevät merellä* for Tenor or Soprano and Orch. (1977); *Unen kaivo* for Voice and Orch. (1985); many mixed and men's choral pieces; numerous pieces for Voice and Piano.

Saint-Foix, (Marie-Olivier-) Georges (du Parc Poulain), Comte de, eminent French musicologist; b. Paris, March 2, 1874; d. Aix-en-Provence, May 26, 1954. He studied law at the Sorbonne and concurrently attended classes in theory with d'Indy and had violin lessons (diploma, 1906) at the Schola Cantorum in Paris. His principal, and most important, publ. was *Wolfgang-Amédée Mozart, sa vie musicale et son oeuvre, de l'enfance à la pleine maturité* (5 vols., Paris, 1912–46; vols. 1–2 with T. de Wyzewa); also publ. *Les Symphonies de Mozart* (Paris, 1932; 2nd ed., 1948; Eng. tr., London, 1947).

Saint-George, George, noted English viola d'amore player; b. Leipzig (of English parents), Nov. 6, 1841; d. London, Jan. 5, 1924. He studied piano, violin, and theory in Dresden and Prague; his violin teacher, Moritz Mildner of Prague, had a fine viola d'amore, which he lent to Saint-George for practicing; he made such progress on this little-used instrument that he decided to adopt it as a specialty. About 1862 he settled in London and became a manufacturer of string instruments; gave performances on the Welsh crwth for the "Hon. Soc. Cymmrodorion"; also played the viola d'amore in duos with his son, Henry Saint-George (b. London, Sept. 26, 1866; d. there, Jan. 30, 1917), who assisted him on the viola da gamba.

Saint-Marcoux, Micheline Coulombe, Canadian composer and teacher; b. Notre-Dame-de-la-Doré, Quebec, Aug. 9, 1938; d. Montreal, Feb. 2, 1985. After training with François Brassard (piano and harmony) in Jonquière, Quebec (1956–58), she went to Montreal and pursued studies with Yvonne Hubert (piano), Françoise Aubut (theory), and Claude Champagne (composition) at the École Vincent-d'Indy (B.Mus., 1962). She continued her training with Tremblay and Pépin at the Montreal Cons., taking the premier prix in composition in 1967. That same year, she won the Prix d'Europe for her orch. score *Modulaire.* In 1968 she went to Paris and studied electronic music with the Groupe de recherches musicales of the ORTF and received training from Schaeffer at the Cons. She also studied privately with Amy and Guézec. In 1969 she was a founder of the Groupe international de musique electroacoustique de Paris. In 1971 she returned to Montreal and helped organize the Ensemble Polycousmie, which was dedicated to experimenting with electronic techniques in combination with percussion and dance. From 1971 to 1984 she taught at the Montreal Cons. In a number of her works, she applied serial techniques.

WORKS: DRAMATIC: *Tel qu'en Lemieux,* film score (1973); *Comment Wang-Fô fut sauvé,* incidental music (1983); *Transit,* musical theater (1984). **ORCH.:** *Modulaire* for Orch. and Ondes Martenot (1967; Montreal, March 31, 1968); *Hétéromorphie* (1969; Montreal, April 14, 1970); *Luminance* (1978). **CHAMBER:** *Évocations doranes* for Piccolo, 3 Flutes, Oboe, and Clarinet (1964); Flute Sonata (1964); String Quartet (1966); *Équation I* for 2 Guitars (1968); *Séquences* for 2 Ondes Martenot and Percussion (1968; rev. 1973); *Trakadie* for Percussion and Tape (1970); *Épisode II* for 3 Percussion (1972); *Genesis* for Wind Quintet (1975); *Miroirs* for Harpsichord and Tape (1975); *Regards* for 3 Winds, Harp, Piano, Percussion, 3 Strings, and Tape (1978); *Mandala I* for Flute, Oboe, Cello, Piano, and Percussion (1980); *Intégration I* for Cello (1980) and *II* for Violin (1980); *Composition I* for Horn (1981); *Horizon I* for Flute (1981) and *II* for Oboe (1981); *Étreinte* for 3 Ondes Martenot (1984). **PIANO:** *Suite Doréane* (1961); *Variations* (1963); *Kaleidoscope* (1964); *Assemblages* (1969); *Mandala II* (1980). **VOCAL:** *Chanson d'automne* for Soprano or Tenor, Flute, Violin and Piano (1963; rev. 1966); *Wing Tra La* for Chorus and 6 Performers (1964); *Makazoti* for 8 Voices, 4 Winds, 2 Strings, and Percussion (1971); *Alchera* for Mezzo-soprano, 8 Instruments, Tape, and Lights (1973); *Ishuma* for Soprano and 9 Instruments (1974); *Moments* for Soprano, Flute, Viola, and Cello (1977); *Gésode I* for Soprano and Piano (1981) and *II* for Tenor and Piano (1981). **ELECTROACOUSTIC:** *Bernavir* (1970); *Arksalalartôq* (Paris, Feb. 26, 1971); *Contrastances* (1971); *Moustieres* (1971); *Zones* (1972); *Constellation I* (1980).

Saint-Requier, Léon, French choral conductor, teacher, and composer; b. Rouen, Aug. 8, 1872; d. Paris, Oct. 1, 1964. He went to Paris and studied with d'Indy, Guilmant, and Bordes. He taught harmony at the Schola Cantorum (1900–1934) and at the École Cesar Franck (1934–44); was active as a choral conductor at various Paris churches; ed. the collection Palestrina (sacred songs of the 16th, 17th, and 18th centuries). He composed a Christmas motet, *Il est né le divin enfant,* using some folk melodies (1924); the oratorio *La Mort du doux Jésus* (1932); *Messe de grande louange* (1946); *Le Sermon sur la montagne* (1949); *Messe de St. Jean Apôtre* (1957); other religious works.

Saint-Saëns, (Charles-) Camille, celebrated French composer; b. Paris, Oct. 9, 1835; d. Algiers, Dec. 16, 1921. His widowed mother sent him to his great-aunt, Charlotte Masson, who taught him to play piano. He proved exceptionally gifted, and gave a performance in a Paris salon before he was 5; at 6, he began to compose; at 7, he became a private pupil of Stamaty; so rapid was his progress that he made his pianistic debut at the Salle Pleyel on May 6, 1846, playing a Mozart concerto and a movement from Beethoven's C minor Concerto, with Orch. After studying harmony with Pierre Maleden, he entered the Paris Cons., where his teachers were Benoist (organ) and Halévy (composition). He won the 2nd prize for organ in 1849, and the 1st prize in 1851. In 1852 he competed unsuccessfully for the Grand Prix de Rome, and failed again in a 2nd attempt in 1864, when he was already a composer of some stature. His *Ode à Sainte Cécile* for Voice and Orch. was awarded the 1st prize of the Société Sainte-Cécile (1852). On Dec. 11, 1853, his 1st numbered sym. was performed; Gounod wrote him a letter of praise, containing a prophetic phrase regarding the "obligation de devenir un grand maitre." From 1853 to 1857 Saint-Saëns was organist at the church of Saint-Merry in Paris; in 1857 he succeeded Léfebure-Wély as organist at the Madeleine. This important position he filled with distinction, and soon acquired a great reputation as virtuoso on the organ and a master of improvisation. He resigned in 1876, and devoted himself mainly to composition and conducting; also continued to appear as a pianist and organist. From 1861 to 1865 he taught piano at the École Niedermeyer; among his pupils were André Messager and Gabriel Fauré. Saint-Saëns was one of the founders of the Société Nationale de Musique (1871), established for the encouragement of French composers, but withdrew in 1886 when d'Indy proposed to include works by foreign composers in its program. In 1875 he married Marie Truffot; their 2 sons died in infancy; they separated in 1881, but were never legally divorced; Madame Saint-Saëns died in Bordeaux on Jan. 30, 1950, at the age of 95. In 1891 Saint-Saëns established a museum in Dieppe (his father's birthplace), to which he gave his MSS and his collection of paintings and other art objects. On Oct. 27, 1907, he witnessed the unveiling of his own statue (by Marqueste) in the court foyer of the opera house in Dieppe. He received many honors: in 1868 he was made a Chevalier of the Legion of Honor; in 1884, Officer; in 1900, Grand-Officer; in 1913, Grand-Croix (the highest rank). In 1881 he was elected to the Institut de France; he was also a member of many foreign organizations; received an honorary Mus.D. degree at the Univ. of Cambridge. He visited the U.S. for the first time in 1906; was a representative of the French government at the Panama-Pacific Exposition in 1915 and conducted his choral work *Hail California* (San Francisco, June 19, 1915), written for the occasion. In 1916, at the age of 81, he made his first tour of South America; continued to appear in public as conductor of his own works almost to the time of his death. He took part as conductor and pianist in a festival of his works in Athens in May 1920. He played a program of his piano pieces at the Saint-Saëns museum in Dieppe on Aug. 6, 1921. For the winter he went to Algiers, where he died.

The position of Saint-Saëns in French music was very important. His abilities as a performer were extraordinary; he aroused the admiration of Wagner during the latter's stay in Paris (1860–61) by playing at sight the entire scores of Wagner's operas; curiously, Saint-Saëns achieved greater recognition in Germany than in France during the initial stages of his career. His most famous opera, *Samson et Dalila,* was produced in Weimar (1877) under the direction of Eduard Lassen, to whom the work was suggested by Liszt; it was not performed in France until nearly 13 years later, in Rouen. He played his 1st and 3rd piano concertos for the first time at the Gewandhaus in Leipzig. Solidity of contrapuntal fabric, instrumental elaboration, fullness of sonority in orchestration, and a certain harmonic saturation are the chief characteristics of his music, qualities that were not yet fully exploited by French composers at the time, the French public preferring the lighter type of music. However, Saint-Saëns overcame this initial opposition, and toward the end of his life was regarded as an embodiment of French traditionalism. The shock of the German invasion of France in World War I made him abandon his former predilection for German music, and he wrote virulent articles against German art. He was unalterably opposed to modern music, and looked askance at Debussy; he regarded later manifestations of musical modernism as outrages, and was outspoken in his opinions. That Saint-Saëns possessed a fine sense of musical characterization, and true Gallic wit, is demonstrated by his ingenious suite *Carnival of the Animals,* which he wrote in 1886 but did not allow to be publ. during his lifetime. He also publ. a book of elegant verse (1890).

WORKS: DRAMATIC (all 1st perf. in Paris unless otherwise given): **OPERAS:** *La Princesse jaune* (June 12, 1872); *Le Timbre d'argent* (Feb. 23, 1877); *Samson et Dalila* (Weimar, Dec. 2, 1877); *Étienne Marcel* (Lyons, Feb. 8, 1879); *Henry VIII* (March 5, 1883); *Proserpine* (March 16, 1887); *Ascanio* (March 21, 1890); *Phryné* (May 24, 1893); *Frédégonde* (Dec. 18, 1895); *Les Barbares* (Oct. 23, 1901); *Hélène* (Monte Carlo, Feb. 18, 1904); *L'Ancêtre* (Monte Carlo, Feb. 24, 1906); *Déjanire* (Monte Carlo, March 14, 1911). **BALLET:** *Javotte* (Lyons, Dec. 3, 1896). **INCIDENTAL MUSIC TO:** *Antigone* (Nov. 21, 1893); *Parysatis* (Béziers, Aug. 17, 1902); *Andromaque* (Feb. 7, 1903); *La Foi* (Monte Carlo, April 10, 1909); *On ne badine pas avec l'amour* (Feb. 8, 1917). **FILM SCORE:** *L'Assassinat du Duc de Guise* (Nov. 16, 1908).

ORCH.: Overture to a comic opera (c.1850); *Scherzo* for Small Orch. (c.1850); 5 syms.: A major (c.1850), No. 1 in E-flat major, op. 2 (Paris, Dec. 18, 1853), F major, *Urbs Roma* (1856; Paris, Feb. 15, 1857), No. 2 in A minor, op. 55 (Leipzig, Feb. 20, 1859), and No. 3, *Organ,* in C minor, op. 78 (London, May 19, 1886); *Ouverture d'un opéra comique inachevé,* op. 140 (1854); *Tarantelle* for Flute, Clarinet, and Orch., op. 6 (1857); 5 piano concertos (all 1st perf. with the composer as soloist): No. 1, op. 17 (1858; Leipzig, Oct. 26, 1865), No. 2, op. 22 (Paris, May 6, 1868), No. 3, op. 29 (Leipzig, Nov. 25, 1869), No. 4, op. 44 (Paris, Oct. 31, 1875), and No. 5, *Egyptian,* op. 103 (Paris, June 3, 1896); 3 violin concertos: No. 1, op. 20 (1859; Paris, April 4, 1867), No. 2, op. 58 (1858; Paris, Feb. 13, 1880), and No. 3, op. 61 (1880; Paris, Jan. 2, 1881); *Introduction and Rondo capriccioso* for Violin and Orch., op. 28 (1863); Suite, op. 49 (1863); *Spartacus Overture* (1863); *Marche héroïque,* op. 34 (1871); *Romance* for Flute or Violin and Orch., op. 37 (1871); *Le Rouet d'Omphale,* op. 31 (Paris, Jan. 9, 1872); 2 cello concertos: No. 1, op. 33 (1872; Paris, Jan. 19, 1873) and No. 2, op. 119 (1902; Paris, Feb. 5, 1905); *Phaéton,* op. 39 (Paris, Dec. 7, 1873); *Romance* for Horn or Cello and Orch., op. 36 (1874); *Romance* for Violin and Orch., op. 48 (1874); *Danse macabre,* op. 40 (1874; Paris, Jan. 24, 1875); *La Jeunesse d'Hercule,* op. 50 (Paris, Jan. 28, 1877); *Suite algérienne,* op. 60 (Paris, Dec. 19, 1880); *Morceau de concert* for Violin and Orch., op. 62 (1880); *Une Nuit à Lisbonne,* op. 63 (1880; Paris, Jan. 23, 1881); *Jota aragonese,* op. 64 (1880); *Rapsodie d'Auvergne,* op. 73 (1884); *Wedding Cake* for Piano and Orch., op. 76 (1885); *Le Carnaval des animaux* (1886; Paris, Feb. 26, 1922); *Havanaise* for Violin and Orch., op. 83 (1887); *Morceau de concert* for Horn and Orch., op. 94 (1887); *Rapsodie bretonne,* op. 7 bis (1891); *Africa* for Piano and Orch., op. 89 (Paris, Oct. 25, 1891); *Sarabande et Rigaudon,* op. 93 (1892); *Marche du couronnement,* op. 117 (c.1902); *Caprice andalous* for Violin and Orch., op. 122 (1904); *Trois tableaux symphoniques d'après La foi,* op. 130 (1908); *Morceau de concert* for Harp and Orch., op. 154 (1918); *Cyprès et Lauriers* for Organ and Orch., op. 156 (1919); *Odelette* for Flute and Orch., op. 162 (1920); also works for Band.

CHAMBER: 2 piano quartets (1853, 1875); Piano Quintet, op. 14 (1855); *Caprice brillant* for Piano and Violin (1859); Suite for Piano and Cello, op. 16 (1862); 2 piano trios, opp. 18 and 92 (1863, 1892); *Sérénade* for Piano, Organ, Violin, and Viola or Cello, op. 15 (1866; also for Orch.); *Romance* for Piano, Organ, and Violin, op. 27 (1868); *Les Odeurs de Paris* for 2 Trumpets, Harp, Piano, and Strings (c.1870); *Berceuse* for Piano and Violin, op. 38 (1871); 2 cello sonatas, opp. 32 and 123 (1872, 1905); *Allegro appassionato* for Cello and Piano, op. 43 (1875; also for Cello and Orch.); *Romance* for Piano and Cello, op. 51 (1877); Septet for Piano, Trumpet, and Strings, op. 65 (1881); *Romance* for Piano and Horn, op. 67 (1885); 2 violin sonatas, opp. 75 and 102 (1885, 1896); *Caprice sur des airs danois et russes* for Piano, Flute, Oboe, and Clarinet, op. 79 (1887); *Chant saphique* for Piano and Cello, op. 91 (1892); *Fantaisie* for Harp, op. 95 (1893); *Barcarolle* for Violin, Cello, Organ, and Piano, op. 108 (1897); 2 string quartets, opp. 112 and 153 (1899, 1918); *Fantaisie* for Violin and Harp, op. 124 (1907); *La Muse et le poète* for Violin, Cello, and Piano, op. 132 (1910; also for Violin, Cello, and Orch.); *Triptyque* for Piano and Violin, op. 136 (1912); *Élégie* for Piano and Violin, op. 143 (1915); *Cavatine* for Piano and Trombone, op. 144 (1915); *L'Air de la pendule* for Piano and Violin (c.1918); *Prière* for Organ and Violin or Cello, op. 158 (1919); *Élégie* for Piano and Violin, op. 160 (1920); Oboe Sonata, op. 166 (1921); Clarinet Sonata, op. 167 (1921); Bassoon Sonata, op. 168 (1921); piano pieces.

VOCAL: Sacred pieces, including *Oratorio de Noël* for Solo Voices, Chorus, String Quartet, Harp, and Organ, op. 12 (1858), *Veni Creator* for Chorus and Organ ad libitum (1858), and *Le Déluge,* oratorio for Solo Voices, Chorus, and Orch., op. 45 (1875; Paris, March 5, 1876); secular choral works; song cycles (*Mélodies persanes* [1870], *La Cendre rouge* [1914], etc.); about 100 solo songs; also cadenzas to Mozart's piano concertos K.482 and 491, and to Beethoven's 4th Piano Concerto and Violin Concerto; made various transcriptions and arrangements.

For a complete list of his works, see the Durand *Catalogue général et thématique des oeuvres de Saint-Saëns* (Paris, 1897; rev. ed., 1909).

WRITINGS (all publ. in Paris unless otherwise given): *Notice sur Henri Reber* (1881); *Harmonie et mélodie* (1885; 9th ed., 1923); *Charles Gounod et le "Don Juan" de Mozart* (1893); *Problèmes et mystères* (1894; rev. ed., aug., 1922, as *Divagations sérieuses*); *Portraits et souvenirs* (1899; 3rd ed., 1909); *Essai sur les lyres et cithares antiques* (1902); *Quelques mots sur "Prosperpine"* (Alexandria, 1902); *École buissonnière: Notes et souvenirs* (1913; abr. Eng. tr., 1919); *Notice sur Le Timbre d'argent* (Brussels, 1914); H. Bowie, ed., *On the Execution of Music, and Principally of Ancient Music* (San Francisco, 1915); *Au courant de la vie* (1916); *Germanophile* (1916); *Les idées de M. Vincent d'Indy* (1919); F. Rothwell, tr., *Outspoken Essays on Music* (London and N.Y., 1922).

BIBL.: C. Bellaigue, *M. C. S.-S.* (Paris, 1889); C. Kit and P. Loanda, *Musique savante. Sur la musique de M. S.-S.* (Lille, 1889); Blondel, *C. S.-S. et son cinquantenaire artistique* (Paris, 1896); O. Neitzel, *C. S.-S.* (Berlin, 1899); E. Solenière, *C. S.-S.* (Paris, 1899); special S.-S. issue of *Le Monde Musical* (Oct. 31, 1901); E. Baumann, *Les Grandes Formes de la musique: L'Oeuvre de S.-S.* (Paris, 1905; new ed., 1923); special S.-S. issue of *Musica* (June 1907); L. Auge de Lassus, *S.-S.* (Paris, 1914); J. Bonnerot, *C. S.-S.* (Paris, 1914; 2nd ed., 1922); J. Montargis, *C. S.-S.* (Paris, 1919); *Funerailles de S.-S.* (collection of speeches, Paris, 1921); J. Chantavoine, *L'Oeuvre dramatique de C. S.-S.* (Paris, 1921); A. Hervey, *S.-S.* (London, 1921); W. Lyle, *C. S.-S., His Life and Art* (London, 1923); G. Servières, *S.-S.* (Paris, 1923; 2nd ed., 1930); A. Dandelot, *S.-S.* (Paris, 1930); J. Handschin, *C. S.-S.* (Zürich, 1930); J. Normand, *S.-S.* (1930); L. Schneider, *Une Heure avec S.-S.* (1930); J. Langlois, *C. S.-S.* (Moulins, 1934); R. Dumanine, *Les Origines normandes de C. S.-S.* (Rouen, 1937); R. Fauchois, *La Vie et l'oeuvre prodigieuse de C. S.-S.* (Paris, 1938); J. Chantavoine, *C. S.-S.* (Paris, 1947); J. Harding, *S.-S. and His Circle* (London, 1965); S. Ratner, *The Piano Works of C. S.-S.* (diss., Univ. of Mich., 1972); D. Fallon, *The Symphonies and Symphonic Poems of C. S.-S.* (diss., Yale Univ., 1973); E. Harkins, *The Chamber Music of S.-S.* (diss., N.Y. Univ., 1976); M. Stegemann, *C. S.-S. und das französische Solokonzert von 1850 bis 1920* (Mainz, 1984; Eng. tr., 1991); R. Smith, *S.-S. and the Organ* (N.Y., 1992).

Saito, Hideo, Japanese cellist, conductor, and music educator; b. Tokyo, May 23, 1902; d. there, Sept. 18, 1974. He was a cello student of Julius Klengel in Leipzig (1923–27) and of Feuermann in Berlin (1930). Returning to Japan, he played cello in the Nihon Sym. Orch., and studied conducting with Rosenstock. He was a co-founder of the Toho Music School in Tokyo, where he taught cello, conducting, and academic music courses. Among his students was Seiji Ozawa, who came to regard Saito's influence as a major factor in his own career.

Sakač, Branimir, Croatian composer and teacher; b. Zagreb, June 5, 1918; d. there, Dec. 29, 1979. He received training at the Zagreb Academy of Music (graduated, 1941), and later taught there. He adopted a purely structural method of composition, using highly dissonant contrapuntal combinations within strict neo-Classical forms.

WORKS: *Serenade* for String Orch. (1947); *Simfonija o mrtvom vojniku* (Sym. of the Dead Soldiers; 1951); Chamber Sym. (1953); Sonata for Solo Violin (1953); *Aleatory Prélude* for Piano and Tape (1961); *Episode* for Orch. and Tape (1963); *Study I* for Piano and Percussion (1963) and *II* for Piano (1964); *Structure I* for Chamber Ensemble (1965); *Prostori* (Spaces) for Orch. and Tape (1965); *Syndrome* for Chamber Orch. (1966); *Solo I* for Violin and Chamber Orch. (1968); *Doppio* for String Quartet (1968); *Omaggio—Canto della Commedia* for 7 Soli, Chorus, Violin, and Percussion (1969); *Attitudes* for Cello and Piano (1969–70); *Turm-Musik* (Tower Music) for Orch. (1970); *Ad litteram* for Piano (1970); *Bellatrix-Alleluia*, cycle of 5 pieces; *Bellatrix-Alleluia* for Voices and Ensemble, *Sial* for Chamber Ensemble and Folk Instruments, *Umbrana* for 12 Voices, *Synthana* for Tape, and *Matrix-Symphony* for 3 Voices and Orch. (1970–73); *Barasou* (Ballad of Rats and Mice) for Voice and Chamber Ensemble (1971); *Scena* for Chamber Ensemble (1971); *Songelu* for Light Projections, Actor, and Ensemble (1972); *A Play* for Chamber Ensemble (1973); *Ariel* for Piano (1979).

Salabert, Francis, French music publisher; b. Paris, July 27, 1884; d. in an airplane accident at Shannon, Ireland, Dec. 28, 1946. The Editions Salabert was founded by his father, Edouard Salabert (b. London, Dec. 1, 1838; d. Paris, Sept. 8, 1903), in 1896; Francis took over from his ailing father in 1901. A professional musician and composer in his own right, he made a series of practical arrangements for small orch. of numerous classical and modern works, which were widely used. Editions Salabert expanded greatly through the purchase of the stock of orch. and other music of the firms Gaudet (1927), Mathot (1930), Senart (1941), Rouart-Lerolle (1942), and Deiss (1946). On the death of Francis Salabert, his widow assumed the directorship.

Salas Viú, Vicente, Spanish-born Chilean musicologist; b. Madrid, Jan. 29, 1911; d. Santiago, Chile, Sept. 2, 1967. He studied piano and theory at the Madrid Cons. (1928–30); also received instruction in composition from his brother-in-law, Rodolfo Halffter, and from Falla. He wrote for various literary and musical publs. until 1939, when he emigrated to Chile; became a prof. of music history at the National Cons. in Santiago. He was founder-ed. of the *Revista Musical Chilena* (1945); was director of the Instituto de Investigaciones Musicales (from 1947). He publ. a very valuable book, *La creación musical en Chile* 1900–1950 (Santiago, 1952), in 2 sections, embracing a general account of musical activities in Chile and detailed biographies of 40 Chilean composers; also *La última luz de Mozart* (Santiago, 1949) and *Momentos decisivos en la música* (Buenos Aires, 1957).

Salazar, Adolfo, eminent Spanish musicologist; b. Madrid, March 6, 1890; d. Mexico City, Sept. 27, 1958. He studied with Falla and Perez Casas; then went to Paris, where he completed his training with Ravel. He was ed.-in-chief of the *Revista Musical Hispano-Americana* (1914–18) and music critic of Madrid's *El Sol* (1918–36); was founder and later secretary of the Sociedad Nacional de Música (1915–22). During the final period of the Spanish Civil War, he was cultural attaché at the Spanish embassy in Washington, D.C. (1938–39); then settled in Mexico City as a writer and teacher, serving on the faculties of the Colegio de México (from 1939) and the National Cons. (from 1946). Salazar was also a composer; wrote 3 symphonic works: *Paisajes, Estampas*, and *Don Juan de los Infernos*; songs to words by Verlaine; piano pieces.

WRITINGS: *Música y músicos de hoy* (Madrid, 1928); *Sinfonía y ballet* (Madrid, 1929); *La música contemporánea en España* (Madrid, 1930); *La música actual en Europa y sus problemas* (Madrid, 1935); *El siglo romántico* (Madrid, 1935; new ed., 1955, as *Los grandes compositores de la época romántica*); *La música en el siglo XX* (Madrid, 1936); *Música y sociedad en el siglo XX* (Mexico City, 1939); *Las grandes estructuras de la música* (Mexico City, 1940); *La rosa de los vientos en la música europea* (Mexico City, 1940; reissued in 1954 as *Conceptos fondamentales en la historia de la música*); *Forma y expresión en la música: Ensayo sobre la formación de los géneros en la música instrumental* (Mexico City, 1941); *Introducción en la música actual* (Mexico City, 1941); *Los grandes periodos en la historia de la música* (Mexico City, 1941); *Poesía y música en lengua vulgar y sus antecedientes en la edad media* (Mexico City, 1943); *La música en la sociedad europea* (4 vols., Mexico City, 1942–46); *La música moderna* (Buenos Aires, 1944; Eng. tr., 1946, as *Music in Our Time*); *Música, instrumentos y danzas en las obras de Cervantes* (Mexico City, 1948); *La danza y el ballet* (Mexico City, 1949); *La música, como proceso histórico de su invención* (Mexico City, 1950); *J.S. Bach* (Mexico City, 1951); *La música de España* (Buenos Aires, 1953).

Salazar, Manuel, Costa Rican tenor; b. San José, Jan. 3, 1887; d. there, Aug. 6, 1950. He was trained in Italy and N.Y. In 1913 he made his operatic debut in Vicenza as Edgardo, and then sang in various Italian opera houses. After appearing in Havana (1917), he toured North America with the San Carlo Opera Co. On Dec. 31, 1921, he made his Metropolitan Opera debut in N.Y. as Alvaro, and remained on its roster until 1923. Among his other roles were Radames, Andrea Chénier, and Canio.

Salerno-Sonnenberg, Nadja, gifted American violinist of Russian-Italian descent; b. Rome, Jan. 10, 1961. After violin lessons with Antonio Marchetti, her mother took her to the U.S., where she continued her training with Jascha Brodsky at the Curtis Inst. of Music in Philadelphia (1969–75). In 1975 she went to N.Y. to pursue studies with Dorothy DeLay at the Juilliard School; after winning the Naumburg Competition in 1981, she dropped out of Juilliard sans diploma to launch an independent career. On Feb. 6, 1982, she made her N.Y. recital debut at Alice Tully Hall. In 1983 she was awarded an Avery Fisher Career Grant. Her nonconformist persona, highlighted by her impassioned stage deportment and disdain for conventional attire, have made her a popular media figure. All the same, she reveals a genuine talent in her virtuosic performances of the violin literature. She publ. the vol. *Nadja, On My Way* (N.Y., 1989).

Salignac, Thomas (real name, **Eustace Thomas**), French tenor, opera director, and teacher; b. Générac, near Nîmes, March 19, 1867; d. Paris, 1945. He studied in Marseilles and with Duvernoy at the Paris Cons. In 1893 he became a member of the Paris Opéra-Comique. On Dec. 11, 1896, he made his debut at the Metropolitan Opera in N.Y. as Don José, remaining on its roster for that season and again from 1898 to 1903. He also sang at London's Covent Garden (1897–99; 1901–04) and again at the Paris Opéra-Comique (1905–14). He sang in the premieres of operas by Laparra, Leroux, Milhaud, and Widor, and in the private premiere of Falla's *El retablo de Maese Pedro* (1923). In 1913–14 he was director of the Nice Opera, and later of an opéra comique company which toured North America in 1926. He was founder-ed. of the journal *Lyrica* (1922–39), and a teacher at the American Cons. in Fontainebleau (1922–23) and at the Paris Cons. (from 1924).

Sallinen, Aulis, prominent Finnish composer; b. Salmi, April 9, 1935. He studied under Merikanto and Kokkonen at the Sibelius Academy in Helsinki (1955–60). He was managing director of the Finnish Radio Sym. Orch. in Helsinki (1960–70); also taught at the Sibelius Academy (1963–76); held the government-bestowed title of Professor of Arts for Life (from 1981), the first such appointment. In 1979 he was made a member of the Royal Swedish Academy of Music in Stockholm. With Penderecki, he was awarded the Withuri International Sibelius Prize in 1983. In his music, he uses modern techniques, with a prevalence of euphonious dissonance and an occasional application of serialism.

WORKS: DRAMATIC: OPERAS: *Ratsumies* (The Horseman; 1973–74; Savonlinna, July 17, 1975); *Punainen viiva* (The Red Line; 1976–78; Helsinki, Nov. 30, 1978); *Kuningas lähtee Ranskaan* (The King Goes Forth to France; 1983; Savonlinna, July 7, 1984; in Eng., London, April 1, 1987); *Kullervo* (1986–88; Los Angeles, Feb. 25, 1992); *The Palace* (1993; Savonlinna, July 26, 1995). **BALLETS:** *Variations sur Mallarmé* (1967; Helsinki, 1968); *Midsommernatten* (Atlanta, March 29, 1984; based on the Sym. No. 3); *Himlens hemlighet* (Secret of Heavens; Swedish TV, Oct. 20, 1986; based on the syms. Nos. 1, 3, and 4). **ORCH.:** *2 Mythical Scenes* (1956); Concerto for Chamber Orch. (1959–60); *Variations* (1963); *Mauermusik* (1962); *14 Juventas Variations* (1963); *Metamorphoses* for Piano and Chamber Orch. (1964); Violin Concerto (1968); *Chorali* for 32 Wind Instruments, 2 Percussion, Harp, and Celesta (1970); 6 syms.: No. 1 (Helsinki, Dec. 2, 1971), No. 2, *Symphonic Dialogue*, for Percussion and Orch. (1972; Norrköping, Feb. 25, 1973), No. 3 (Helsinki, April 8, 1975), No. 4 (Turku, Aug. 9, 1979), No. 5, *Washington Mosaics* (Washington, D.C., Oct. 10, 1985), and No. 6, *From a New Zealand Diary* (1989–90); *Chamber Music I* for Strings (1975), *II* for Alto Flute and Strings (1975–76), and *III: The Nocturnal Dances of Don Juanquixote* for Cello and String Orch. (Naantali, June 15, 1986); Cello Concerto (1976); *Shadows*, prelude (Washington, D.C., Nov. 30, 1982); *Fanfare* for Brass and Percussion (Houston, May 17, 1986); *Sunrise Serenade* for 2 Trumpets, Piano, and Strings (1989); Flute Concerto (Helsinki, March 8, 1995). **CHAMBER:** 5 string quartets: No. 1 (1958), No. 2, *Canzona* (1960), No. 3, *Some Aspects of Peltoniemi Hintrik's Funeral March* (1969; also for String Orch.), No. 4, *Quiet Songs* (1971), and No. 5, *Pieces of Mosaic* (1983); *Elegy for Sebastian Knight* for Cello (1964); *Quattro per quattro* for Oboe or Flute or Clarinet, Violin, Cello, and Harpsichord (1964–65); *Cadenze* for Violin (1965); *Notturno* for Piano (1966); *Quatre études* for Violin and Piano (1970); *Chaconne* for Organ (1970); Sonata for Solo Cello (1971); *Metamorfora* for Cello and Piano (1974); *Canto and Ritornello* for Violin (1975); *Echoes from a Play* for Oboe and String Quartet (1990); *From a Swan Song* for Cello and Piano (1991). **VOCAL:** *Suite grammaticale* for Children's Chorus and Chamber Orch. (1971); *4 Dream Songs* for Soprano and Orch. (1972); *Songs from the Sea* for Children's Chorus (1974); *Dies Irae* for Soprano, Bass, Men's Chorus, and Orch. (1978); *Song around a Song* for Children's Chorus (1980); *The Iron Age: Suite* for Soprano, Children's Chorus, Mixed Chorus, and Orch. (1983); *The Beaufort Scale*, humoresque for Chorus (1984); *Songs of Life and Death*, cantata for Baritone or Mezzo-soprano, Chorus, and Orch. (1994–95).

BIBL.: J. Parsons, "A. S.," *Musical Times* (Nov. 1980); R. Henderson, "A. S.: Singing of Man," ibid. (April 1987).

Salmanov, Vadim (Nikolaievich), Russian composer and teacher; b. St. Petersburg, Nov. 4, 1912; d. there (Leningrad), Feb. 27, 1978. He studied piano with his father and theory with Akimenko. He studied composition with Gnessin at the Leningrad Cons. (1936–41); was head of its composition dept. (1947–51), and a teacher (1951–65) and a prof. (from 1965). His early works are marked by broad Russian melodism, with the harmonic structure following the models of Prokofiev and Shostakovich; after 1960 he adopted more advanced techniques, including dodecaphony.

WORKS: BALLET: *The Man* (1960). **ORCH.:** *Little Symphony* for Strings (1941); *The Forest*, symphonic picture (1948); *Russian Capriccio* (1950); *Slavic Dance* (1952); *Poetic Pictures*, symphonic suite (1952); 4 syms. (1952, 1959, 1963, 1976); Sonata for Piano and Strings (1961); *Children's Symphony* (1962); 2 violin concertos (1964, 1974); *Nights in the Big City* for Violin and Chamber Orch. (1969); *Monologue* for Cello and Chamber Orch. (1972). **CHAMBER:** 6 string quartets (1945; 1947, rev. 1958; 1961; 1963; 1968; 1971); 2 violin sonatas (1945, 1962); 2 piano trios (1946, 1949); Piano Quartet (1947). **VOCAL:** *Soja*, symphonic poem for Voice and Orch. (1951); *The 12*, oratorio, after Alexander Blok (1957); 2 cantatas: *Ode to Lenin* (1970) and *The Scythians*, after Alexander Blok (1973); choruses; songs, including *Spain Is in My Heart* for Mezzo-soprano and Piano (1962).

BIBL.: M. Aranovsky, *V.N. S.* (Leningrad, 1961).

Salmen, Walter, respected German musicologist; b. Paderborn, Sept. 20, 1926. He began musicological training with Besseler at the Univ. of Heidelberg and also took organ and composition lessons with Poppen, Fortner, and Peterson; continued musicological study at the Univ. of Münster (Ph.D., 1949, with the diss. *Das deutsche Tenorlied bis zum Lochamer Liederbuch*) and completed his Habilitation at the Univ. of Saarbrücken in 1958 with his *Der fahrende Musiker im europäischen Mittelalter* (Kassel, 1960). He became a research assistant at the Deutsches Volksliedarchiv in Freiburg im Briesgau in 1950; then was made prof. (1963) and research fellow (1964) at the Univ. of Saarbrücken; after serving as prof. and director of the musicological inst. at the Univ. of Kiel (1966–73), he was engaged as prof. and director of the musicological inst. at the Univ. of Innsbruck, positions he held until 1993. He ed. the Müller-Blattau Festschrift (Saarbrücken, 1960), *Beiträge zur Musikanschauung im 19. Jahrhundert* (Regensburg, 1965), *Kieler Schriften zur Musikwissenschaft* (Kassel, 1967–74), *Der Sozialstatus des Berufsmusikers vom 17. bis 19. Jahrhundert* (Kassel, 1971), *Innsbrucker Beitrage zur Musikwissenschaft* (Innsbruck, 1977–), *The Social Status of the Professional Musician from the Middle Ages to the 19th Century* (N.Y., 1983), and *Der musikalische Satz* (Innsbruck, 1987).

WRITINGS: *Das Lochamer Liederbuch* (Leipzig, 1951); *Die Schichtung der mittelalterlichen Musikkultur in der ostdeutschen Grenzlage* (Kassel, 1954); *Das Erbe des ostdeutschen Volksgesanges: Geschichte und Verzeichnis seiner Quellen und Sammlungen* (Würzburg, 1956); *Johann Friedrich Reichardt* (Freiburg, 1963); *Geschichte der Musik in Westfalen* (Kassel, 1963–67); *Geschichte der Rhapsodie* (Freiburg im Breisgau, 1966); *Haus- und Kammermusik: Privates Musizieren im gesellschaftlichen Wandel zwischen 1600 und 1900* (Leipzig,

1969); *Musikgeschichte Schleswig-Holsteins von der Frühzeit bis zur Reformation* (Neumünster, 1972); *Musikleben im 16. Jahrhundert* (Leipzig, 1976); *Bilder zur Geschichte der Musik in Österreich* (Innsbruck, 1983); *Musiker im Porträt* (Munich, 1983); *Der Spielmann im Mittelalter* (Innsbruck, 1983); *Das Konzert: Eine Kulturgeschichte* (Munich, 1988); *Tänze im 17. und 18. Jahrhundert* (Leipzig, 1988); *Tanz im 19. Jahrhundert* (Leipzig, 1989); *Jüdische Musikanten und Tänzer vom 13. bis 20. Jahrhundert: "—denn die Fiedel macht das Fest"* (Innsbruck, 1991).

BIBL.: M. Fink, R. Gstrein, and G. Mössmer, eds., *Musica Privata: Festschrift für W. S. zum 65. Geburtstag* (Innsbruck, 1992).

Salmenhaara, Erkki (Olavi), Finnish composer and musicologist; b. Helsinki, March 12, 1941. He studied at the Sibelius Academy in Helsinki with Kokkonen (diploma, 1963); then went to Vienna, where he took lessons with Ligeti (1963); then pursued his education with Tawaststjerna at the Univ. of Helsinki (Ph.D., 1970), where he taught (from 1963). He was chairman of the Society of Finnish Composers (1974–76). His music is often inspired by literary works; he favors unusual combinations of instruments, including electronics, and makes use of serial techniques in dense, fastidious sonorities.

WORKS: OPERA: *Portugalin nainen* (The Woman of Portugal; 1970–72; Helsinki, Feb. 4, 1976). **ORCH.:** 4 syms.: No. 1, *Crescendi* (1962; Helsinki, Jan. 11, 1963; rev. 1963), No. 2 (1963; Helsinki, Jan. 17, 1964; rev. 1966), No. 3 (Turku, Dec. 5, 1963; rev. 1964), and No. 4, *Nel mezzo del cammin di nostra vita* (1971–72; Helsinki, Oct. 13, 1972); *Le Bateau ivre* (Helsinki, June 1, 1965; rev. 1966); *Suomi—Finland*, "unsymphonic poem" (1966; Helsinki, Oct. 31, 1967); *La Fille en mini-jupe* (1967; Helsinki, Feb. 13, 1968); *Canzonetta per archi* (1971; Savonlinna, July 10, 1972); *Illuminations* (1971); Horn Concerto (1973; Oslo, Oct. 3, 1974); *Canzona per piccola orchestra* (Kuopio, July 26, 1974); *Poema* for Violin or Viola or Cello and String Orch. (1975; Graz, May 28, 1976); *Introduction and Chorale* for Organ and Orch. (Helsinki, Dec. 1, 1978); *Lamento per orchestra d'archi* (Kokkola, Aug. 26, 1979); Concerto for 2 Violins and Orch. (1980; Helsinki, Sept. 21, 1982); *Adagio* for Strings (1981; Porvoo, June 13, 1982; also for Oboe and Piano or Organ); *Adagietto* (1981; Finnish Radio, Dec. 23, 1982); *Sinfonietta per archi* (1985; Kokkola, Feb. 16, 1986); Cello Concerto (1983–87; Lahti, March 25, 1988). **CHAMBER:** 2 cello sonatas (1960, rev. 1969; 1982); *Elegy I* for 3 Flutes, 2 Trumpets, and Double Bass (1963) and *II* for 2 String Quartets (1963); Quintet for Wind Instruments (1964); Quartet for Flute, Violin, Viola, and Cello (1971); Sonatine for 2 Violins (1972); String Quartet No. 1 (1977); Sonatine for Flute and Guitar (1981); Violin Sonata (1982); Sonatella for Piano, 4-hands (1983); *Introduction and Allegro* for Clarinet or Viola, Cello, and Piano (1985); various pieces for Solo Instrument. **VOCAL:** *Requiem profanum* (Helsinki, May 24, 1969); *Lintukoto* (Isle of Bliss) for Baritone, Soprano, and Orch. (1990); choral pieces; song cycles.

Salmhofer, Franz, Austrian conductor, operatic administrator, and composer; b. Vienna, Jan. 22, 1900; d. there, Sept. 22, 1975. He studied composition with Schreker and Schmidt at the Vienna Academy of Music and musicology with Guido Adler at the Univ. of Vienna. In 1929 he became conductor at the Vienna Burgtheater, for which he composed incidental music, ballets, and operas; he resigned in 1939; from 1945 to 1955, was director at the Vienna State Opera; then was director of the Vienna Volksoper (1955–63). In 1923 he married the pianist Margit Gál.

WORKS: DRAMATIC: OPERAS: *Dame im Traum* (Vienna, Dec. 26, 1935); *Iwan Sergejewitsch Tarassenko* (Vienna, March 9, 1938); *Das Werbekleid* (Salzburg, Dec. 5, 1943); *Dreikönig* (1945; Vienna, 1970). **BALLETS:** *Das lockende Phantom* (1927); *Der Taugenichts in Wien* (1930); *Österreichische Bauernhochzeit* (1933); *Weihnachtsmarchen* (1933). Also incidental music to about 300 plays. **ORCH.:** *Der Ackermann und der Tod*, overture (1922); Trumpet Concerto (1922); *Kammersuite* for 16 Instruments (Vienna, May 10, 1923); *Der geheimnisvolle Trompeter*, symphonic poem for Narrator and Orch. (1924); Cello Concerto (1927); 2 syms. (1948, 1955); Violin Concerto (1950); *Symphonic Prologue* (1966). **CHAMBER:** 6 string quartets; Piano Quartet; String Trio; Viola Sonata; Cello Sonata; piano pieces. **VOCAL:** Songs.

Salminen, Matti, notable Finnish bass; b. Turku, July 7, 1945. He studied at the Sibelius Academy in Helsinki and with Luigi Rossi in Rome. In 1966 he joined the Finnish National Opera in Helsinki, where he sang his first major role, Verdi's Philip II, in 1969. From 1972 to 1979 he was principal bass of the Cologne Opera. In 1973 he sang Fafner at Milan's La Scala and Glinka's Ivan Susanin in Wexford. He made his first appearance at London's Covent Garden as Fasolt in 1974. From 1975 he sang at the Savonlinna Festival. In 1976 he made his debut at the Bayreuth Festival as Hunding. On Jan. 9, 1981, he made his Metropolitan Opera debut in N.Y. as King Marke. He appeared as Boris Godunov in Zürich in 1985. In 1990 he sang Hunding at the Metropolitan Opera. His performances in operas by Mozart, Wagner, and Verdi have been much admired.

BIBL.: P. Tuomi-Nikula, *Kuningasbasso: M. S.* (Porvoo, 1994).

Salmond, Felix (Adrian Norman), distinguished English cellist and pedagogue; b. London, Nov. 19, 1888; d. N.Y., Feb. 19, 1952. He studied at the Royal College of Music in London with W.E. Whitehouse, and in Brussels with Edouard Jacobs. He made his debut in London (1909), accompanied at the piano by his mother, Mrs. Norman Salmond. He was the soloist in the premiere of Elgar's Cello Concerto, under Elgar's direction, in London on Oct. 27, 1919; after a European tour, he settled in America (debut, N.Y., March 29, 1922); was head of the cello dept. at the Curtis Inst. of Music in Philadelphia (1925–42) and taught at the Juilliard Graduate School of Music in N.Y. (from 1924). He enjoyed a reputation as a fine chamber music player and an excellent teacher; was the mentor of Orlando Cole, Leonard Rose, Bernard Greenhouse, and many other cellists of distinction.

Salomon, (Naphtali) Siegfried, Danish cellist and composer; b. Copenhagen, Aug. 3, 1885; d. there, Oct. 29, 1962. He studied with Rudinger, Malling, and Bondesen at the Copenhagen Cons. (1899–1902), Klengel in Leipzig, and Le Flem in Paris. Returning to Copenhagen, he was principal cellist in the Tivoli Orch. (from 1903) and a cellist in the Royal Orch. (1907–56). He also pursued a solo career. He wrote an opera, *Leonora Christina* (1926); 2 syms. (1916, 1920); Violin Concerto (1916); 2 cello concertos (1922, 1958); Piano Concerto (1947); 6 string quartets and other chamber music; piano pieces; songs.

Salonen, Esa-Pekka, spirited Finnish conductor and composer; b. Helsinki, June 30, 1958. He entered the Sibelius Academy in Helsinki as a horn pupil of Holgar Fransman in 1973, taking his diploma in 1977; then studied composition with Rautavaara and conducting with Panula; subsequently studied with Donatoni in Siena, attended the Darmstadt summer course, and finally received instruction from Castiglioni in Milan (1980–81). After appearances as a horn soloist, he took up conducting; was a guest conductor throughout Scandinavia, and later extended his activities to include Europe. In 1984 he made his U.S. debut as a guest conductor with the Los Angeles Phil. He became principal conductor of the Swedish Radio Sym. Orch. in Stockholm in 1984; led it on a tour of the U.S. in 1987; also served as principal guest conductor of the Oslo Phil. (from 1984) and the Philharmonia Orch. in London (from 1985). In 1989 he was appointed music director of the Los Angeles Phil., which tenure began in 1992. In his music, Salonen tends toward pragmatic aural accessibility, employing fairly modern techniques while preserving the formal centrality of traditional tonality.

WORKS: ORCH.: *Apokalyptische Phantasie* for Brass Band and Tape (1978); *Boutade* for Violin, Cello, Piano, and Orch. (1979); *. . . auf den ersten Blick und ohne zu wissen* (a quotation from Kafka's *The Trial*) for Alto Saxophone and Orch. (1980–81); *Giro* (1981); *Mimo II* (1992). **CHAMBER:** *Horn Music I* for Horn and Piano (1976) and *II* for 6 Horns, Percussion, and Electronic Tape (1979); Cello Sonata (1976–77); *Nachtlieder* for Clarinet and Piano (1978); *Sets* for Brass Quintet (1978); *Prologue* for Oboe, Violin, Cello, and Percussion (1979); *Goodbye* for Violin and Guitar (1979–80); *Meeting* for Clarinet and Harpsichord (1982); Wind Quintet (1982); *YTA 1* for Flute (1982) and *YTA 2* for Piano (1985). **VOCAL:** *Aubades* for Flute, Soprano, and Strings (1977–78).

Salonen, Sulo (Nikolai), Finnish organist and composer; b. Pyhtää, Jan. 27, 1899; d. Porvoo, May 21, 1976. He was a pupil of Furuhjelm and Palmgren at the Helsinki Cons. (1917–22; 1926–29). He then was organist in Jacobstad (1929–48) and Sibbo (1952–64).

WORKS: *Passion Cantata* (1942); *Viisauden ylistys* (In Praise of Wisdom) for Narrator, Voices, and Instruments (1961); *Requiem* (1962); Wind Quintet (1962); String Trio (1971); 2 string quartets (1971, 1972); *Cum jubilo* for Chorus, Organ, and Percussion (Helsinki, Jan. 24, 1974); about 50 motets; numerous organ pieces.

Salter, Lionel (Paul), English conductor, pianist, harpsichordist, and writer on music; b. London, Sept. 8, 1914. He studied at the Royal College of Music in London and at the Univ. of Cambridge with Dent and Ord (B.A., 1935; B.Mus., 1936); then returned to the Royal College of Music, where he studied conducting with Lambert and piano with Benjamin. He began his career working in radio and television in London; in 1945 he became assistant conductor of the BBC Theatre Orch.; from 1948 he held administrative posts with the BBC; retired in 1974. His books include *Going to a Concert* (London, 1950), *Going to the Opera* (London, 1955), *The Musician and His World* (London, 1963), and *Music and the 20th-Century Media* (with J. Bornoff; Florence, 1972); he also compiled a useful *Gramophone Guide to Classical Music and Recordings.*

Salter, Mary Elizabeth (née **Turner**), American soprano and composer; b. Peoria, Ill., March 15, 1856; d. Orangeburg, N.Y., Sept. 12, 1938. She studied in Burlington, Iowa, and in Boston. She sang in Boston and N.Y. churches (1874–93); she married Sumner Salter (1856–1944) in 1881, with whom she settled in Williamstown, Mass. She composed until her 80th year; among her compositions were the song cycles *Love's Epitome, A Night in Naishapur, Lyrics from Sappho*, and *From Old Japan*; also about 80 songs (*The Cry of Rachel, The Pine Tree, Für Musik, Die stille Wasserrose*, etc.); duets; some part songs; church music.

Saltzmann-Stevens, Minnie, American soprano; b. Bloomington, Ill., March 17, 1874; d. Milan, Jan. 25, 1950. She studied voice with Jean De Reszke in Paris. She made her operatic debut as Brünnhilde in the English version of the *Ring des Nibelungen* at London's Covent Garden in 1909; she continued to sing there until 1913; also appeared at the Bayreuth Festivals of 1911 and 1913. From 1911 to 1914 she sang with the Chicago Grand Opera. Her other roles included Kundry, Isolde, and Sieglinde.

Salva, Tadeáš, Slovak composer; b. Lúčky, near Ružonberok, Oct. 22, 1937; d. Bratislava, Jan. 3, 1995. Following early training with Viliam Kostka, he studied cello, accordion, and piano at the Žilina Cons. (1953–58). During this time, he also took composition lessons with Zimmer in Bratislava. He continued his composition studies with Moyzes and Cikker at the Bratislava Academy of Music and Drama (1958–60). Subsequently he completed his composition training with Szabelski in Katowice and Lutosławski in Warsaw. From 1965 to 1968 he was head of the music dept. of the Czech Radio in Košice. He then was a dramaturg for the Czech TV in Bratislava (1965–77) and the Slovak Folk Artistic Ensemble (1977–88). In his music, Salva embraced sonorism with occasional excursions into aleatory procedures.

WORKS: DRAMATIC: *Margita a Besná*, television opera (1971); *The Weeping*, radio opera (1977); *Reminiscor*, ballet-opera (1982). **ORCH.:** Cello Concerto (1966); *Burlesca*, concerto for Violin and Chamber Ensemble (1970); *Étude* (1972); Concertante Sym. (1978); *Musica in memoriam Arthur Honegger* for Trumpet, Bass, Organ, and Strings (1978); *Rhapsody* for Violin and Orch. (1981); *Symfonia pastoralis* (1983); *12 Symphonic Préludes* (1987); *Ballad Symphony* (1989); *Liturgical Chamber Symphony* (1989); *Slovak Concerto Grosso No. 5* for Violin, English Horn, Bass Clarinet, Organ, and Strings (1989); *Slovak Liturgical Concerto Grosso* for Strings (1994). **CHAMBER:** 4 string quartets (1959, 1962, 1973, 1988); *Ballad* for Violin (1974); *Musica . . . Musica* for Brass and Winds (1979); *Fairy Tales about Magic Violins Playing Themselves* for Violin, Piano, and Percussion (1979); *Variations in memoriam J. Ježek* for Flute, Clarinet, Double Bass, Piano, and Percussion (1982); *Slovak Rhapsody No. 1* for Clarinet, Trumpet, Cimbalom, and Percussion (1984); *Impressions* for Horn and Piano (1986); *Étude* for 3 Violins and Tape (1987); *Slovak Concerto Grosso No. 3* for Clarinet, Cello, and Organ (1988) and *No. 4* for Flute, Clarinet, Violin, Cello, and Piano (1988); *Saxofoniada* for 4 Saxophones (1988); *3 Arias* for Cello and Piano (1990); piano pieces; organ music. **VOCAL:** Concerto for Reciter, 4 Men's Voices, Clarinet, and Percussion (1964); *Requiem aeternam* (1967); *Ballad-Fantasia* for Soprano, Piano, and Orch. (1971); *Wedding Ballad* for Soprano, Alto, Chorus, Bass Clarinet, Viola, Double Bass, and Flute (1972); *Elegies* for Soprano, Reciter, Chorus, and Chamber Ensemble (1972); *Good Morning, My Deceased Ones* for Soprano and Men's Chorus (1973); *Slovak Concerto Grosso No. 1* for Alto, Baritone, and Folk Instruments (1978) and *No. 2* for Soprano, Bass, and Chamber Ensemble (1981); *Aria* for Soprano, Alto, Tenor, Bass, and Piano (1980); *Mechúrik-Koščúrik and his Friends* for Soloists, Women's Chorus, and Orch. (1983); *The Purest Love*, cantata (1984); *Slovak Song of Songs*, oratorio for Soprano, Bass, Chorus, Organ, and Orch. (1987); *Slovak Vocal Concerto Grosso* for Soprano, Alto, Tenor, Bass, and Chorus (1993).

Salviucci, Giovanni, Italian composer; b. Rome, Oct. 26, 1907; d. there, Sept. 4, 1937. He studied with Respighi and Casella; also took courses in law at the Univ. of Rome. He then taught at the Istituto Muzio Clementi in Rome and wrote music criticism for the *Rassegna Nazionale*. He developed a fine style of instrumental writing; his works were performed by Italian orchs. with increasing frequency, but his early death cut short his promising career. His Overture in C-sharp minor (1932) received a national prize.

WORKS: ORCH.: *La Tentazione e la preghiera*, symphonic poem (1931); *Sinfonia italiana* (1932; Rome, Feb. 25, 1934); Overture in C-sharp minor (1932); Sinfonia da camera (1933); *Introduzione, Passacaglia e Finale* (1934). **CHAMBER:** String Quartet (1932); *Serenata* for 9 Instruments (1937). **VOCAL:** *Psalm of David* for Soprano and Chamber Orch. (Rome, 1935); *Alcesti* for Chorus and Orch., after Euripides (1937); songs.

BIBL.: F. Ballo, "Musicisti del nostro tempo: G. S.," *Rassegna Musicale* (Jan. 1937); G. Arledler, *Prospettive critiche su G. S.* (diss., Univ. of Bologna, 1974).

Salzedo (actually, **Salzédo**), **(Léon) Carlos,** eminent French-born American harpist, pedagogue, and composer; b. Arcachon, April 6, 1885; d. Waterville, Maine, Aug. 17, 1961. He studied at the Bordeaux Cons. (1891–94), winning the premier prix in piano; then entered the Paris Cons., where his father, Gaston Salzedo, was a prof. of singing; studied with Charles de Bériot (piano), gaining the premier prix in 1901, and with Hasselmans (harp), also receiving the premier prix. He began his career as a concert harpist upon graduation; traveled all over Europe (1901–05); was solo harpist of the Association des Premiers Prix de Paris in Monte Carlo (1905–09). In 1909 he settled in N.Y.; was 1st harpist in the orch. of the Metropolitan Opera (1909–13). In 1913 he formed the Trio de Lutèce (from Lutetia, the ancient name for Paris), with Georges Barrère (flute) and Paul Kéfer (cello). In 1921 he was co-founder, with Edgard

Varèse, of the International Composers' Guild in N.Y., with the aim of promoting modern music; this organization presented many important contemporary works; in the same year, he founded a modern music magazine, *Eolian Review*, later renamed *Eolus* (discontinued in 1933). He became a naturalized American citizen in 1923. He taught at the Inst. of Musical Art in N.Y., and the Juilliard Graduate School of Music; organized and headed the harp dept. at the Curtis Inst. of Music in Philadelphia. In 1931 he established the Salzedo Harp Colony at Camden, Maine, for teaching and performing during the summer months. Salzedo introduced a number of special effects, and publ. special studies for his new techniques; designed a "Salzedo Model" harp, capable of rendering novel sonorities (Eolian flux, Eolian chords, gushing chords, percussion, etc.). His own compositions are rhythmically intricate and contrapuntally elaborate and require a virtuoso technique. He publ. *Modern Study of the Harp* (N.Y., 1921; 2nd ed., 1948), *Method for the Harp* (N.Y., 1929), and *The Art of Modulating* (with L. Lawrence; N.Y., 1950).

WORKS: *3 morceaux* for Harp (1913); *Terres enchantées* or *The Enchanted Isle*, symphonic poem for Harp and Orch. (1918; Chicago, Nov. 28, 1919, composer soloist); *5 Poetical Studies* for Harp (1918); *3 Poems* for Soprano, 6 Harps, and 3 Wind Instruments (1919); *Bolmimerie* for 7 Harps (1919); *4 Preludes to the Afternoon of a Telephone* for 2 Harps (1921); Harp Sonata (1922); *3 Poems by Mallarmé* for Soprano, Harp, and Piano (1924); 2 harp concertos: No. 1 for Harp and 7 Wind Instruments (1925–26; N.Y., April 17, 1927, composer soloist) and No. 2 (n.d.; orchestration completed by R.R. Bennett); *Pentacle*, 5 pieces for 2 Harps (1928); *Préambule et Jeux* for Harp, 4 Wind Instruments, and 5 String Instruments (Paris, 1929); *Scintillation* for Harp (1936); *Panorama*, suite for Harp (1937); *Suite* for Harp (1943); *10 Wedding Presents* for Harp (1946–52); *Prélude fatidique* for Harp (1954); various other works; many transcriptions for Harp.

BIBL.: S. Archambo, *C. S. (1885–1961): The Harp in Transition* (diss., Univ. of Kansas, 1984).

Salzer, Felix, distinguished Austrian-born American music theorist and pedagogue; b. Vienna, June 13, 1904; d. N.Y., Aug. 12, 1986. He studied musicology with Guido Adler at the Univ. of Vienna (Ph.D., 1926, with the diss. *Die Sonatenform bei Schubert*); concurrently studied theory and analysis with Weise and Schenker; later received a conducting diploma from the Vienna Academy of Music (1935). With O. Jonas, he was founder-ed. of the journal *Der Dreiklang* (1937–39). He emigrated to the U.S. in 1939 and became a naturalized American citizen in 1945; taught at N.Y.'s Mannes College of Music (1940–56), serving as its executive director (1948–55); was again a teacher there (1962–81); was also a prof. of music at Queens College of the City Univ. of N.Y. (from 1963). He was a leading "Schenkerian" theorist and was instrumental in bringing the views of his teacher to the attention of American musicians; his own contribution was in the expansion and application of Schenker's concepts (previously restricted to a narrow range of tonal music) to Renaissance, medieval, and some 20th-century music. He publ. a number of important books on music theory: *Sinn und Wesen der abendländischen Mehrstimmigkeit* (Vienna, 1935); *Structural Hearing* (2 vols., N.Y., 1952; new ed., N.Y., 1962); *Counterpoint in Composition: The Study of Voice Leading* (with C. Schachter; N.Y., 1969); ed. (with William Mitchell) *Music Forum* (N.Y., from 1967), a hardcover periodical.

Salzman, Eric, versatile American composer, writer on music, editor, teacher, and pioneer of new music theater; b. N.Y., Sept. 8, 1933. His maternal grandfather, Louis Klenetzky, was a song-and-dance performer in the Yiddish theater and his mother, Frances Klennett Salzman, a founder-director of a children's music-theater company. He studied composition and theory in N.Y. with Mark Lawner while still in high school; then studied composition at Columbia Univ. with Luening, Ussachevsky, Mitchell, and Beeson (B.A., 1954) and at Princeton Univ. with Sessions, Babbitt, Kim, and Cone (M.F.A., 1956); in addition, he took courses in musicology with Strunk, Mendel, and Pirotta. In 1956–58 he was in Rome on a Fulbright fellowship for study with Petrassi at the Accademia di Santa Cecilia; also attended courses of Stockhausen, Scherchen, Maderna, and Nono at Darmstadt (summer, 1957). Returning to the U.S., he was a music critic for the *N.Y. Times* (1958–62) and the *N.Y. Herald Tribune* (1964–67); from 1984 to 1991 he was ed. of the *Musical Quarterly* and from 1962 to 1964 and again from 1968 to 1972 music director of the Pacifica Radio station WBAI-FM in N.Y., where he founded the Free Music Store. He taught at Queens College of the City Univ. of N.Y. (1967–68); also lectured at N.Y. Univ., Yale Univ., Brooklyn College, Hunter College, Instituto Torquato di Tella in Buenos Aires, the Banff Centre for the Arts et al. Salzman has long been active in creating new music theater for contemporary performing arts; he founded and was artistic director, in N.Y., of the Electric Ear (at Electric Circus; 1967–68), New Image of Sound (1968–71), Quog Music Theater (1970–82), and Music Theater/New York (from 1993); also was founder and artistic director of the American Music Theater in Philadelphia (1982–93); his works for Quog Music Theater include *Ecolog*, music theater work for television (1971; in collaboration with J. Cassen), *Helix* for Voice, Percussion, Clarinet, and Guitar (1972), *Voices*, a capella radio opera (1972), *Saying Something* (1972–73), and *Biograffiti* (1972–73). From 1975 to 1990 he produced and directed some 2 dozen recordings (2 receiving Grammy Award nominations, a Prix Italia, and an Armstrong Award), featuring works by Weill, Partch, and Bolcom et al., as well as his own music; also produced numerous programs for public radio. He is the composer, author, and/or adaptor of more than 24 music-theater works; in all capacities, he merges the most advanced techniques in mixed media with ideas and forms derived from popular music and theater. He made a significant reconstruction and adaptation for the American Music Theater Festival of the long-unperformed Gershwin/Kaufman *Strike Up the Band* (1984) and the Kurt Weill/Alan Jay Lerner *Love Life* (1990), and a translation/adaptation of a French music-theater piece, *Jumelles*, by James Giroudon, Pierre Alain Jaffrennou, and Michel Rostain (as *The Silent Twins*, London Opera Festival, June 17, 1992). In 1994 he commenced work on a new music theater piece commissioned by the National Theater in Quimper, France. His writings include *Twentieth Century Music: An Introduction* (Englewood Cliffs, N.J., 1967; 3rd ed., rev., 1988; tr. into Spanish, Portuguese, Hungarian, and Japanese), *Making Changes: A Practical Guide to Vernacular Harmony* (with M. Sahl; N.Y., 1977), and *The New Music Theater* (Oxford, 1998). Salzman is also a seasoned and enthusiastic ornithologist and has contributed writings on natural history to various publs. He is married to the environmentalist Lorna Salzman, with whom he has twin daughters, Eva, a poet resident in England, and Stephanie, a music-theater and pop song lyricist and composer.

WORKS: String Quartet (1955); Flute Sonata (1956); *Night Dance* for Orch. (1957); Songs for Voice and Piano, after Whitman (1955–57); *Cummings Set* for Voice and Piano (1958; also for Orch., 1962); *Partita* for Violin (1958); *Inventions* for Orch. (1957–58); *In Praise of the Owl and the Cuckoo* for Soprano, Guitar, Violin, and Viola (1963–64); *Larynx Music*, verses for Soprano, Guitar, and 4-track Tape (1966–67); *Verses* for Guitar (1967); *Foxes and Hedgehogs*, verses and cantos for 4 Voices and 2 Instrumental Groups with Sound Systems, after John Ashbery (N.Y., Nov. 30, 1967); *Queens Collage*, academic festival overture for Tape (1966); *The Peloponnesian War*, mime-dance theater piece (1967–68; in collaboration with D. Nagrin); *Wiretap* for Tape (1968); *Feedback*, multimedia participatory environmental work for Live Performers, Visuals, and Tape (1968; in collaboration with S. Vanderbeek); *The Nude Paper Sermon* for Actor, Renaissance Consort, Chorus, and Electronics, after Stephen Wade and John Ashbery (1968–69); *Can Man Survive?*, environmental multimedia piece for the centennial of the American Museum of Natural History (1969–71); *Strophe/Antistrophe* for Keyboard and Tape (1969; rev. 1971); *The 10 Qualities* and 3 Madrigals for Chorus (1970–71); *Fantasy on Lazarus* for

String Orch. (1974); *The Conjurer*, music theater work (1975; in collaboration with M. Sahl); *Accord*, music theater piece for Accordion (1975); *Stauf*, music theater piece, after *Faust* (1976; rev. 1987; in collaboration with M. Sahl); *Civilization and Its Discontents*, music theater comedy (1977; in collaboration with M. Sahl); *Noah*, music theater miracle (N.Y., Feb. 10, 1978; in collaboration with M. Sahl); *The Passion of Simple Simon* (1979; in collaboration with M. Sahl); *Boxes*, music theater piece (1982–83; in collaboration with M. Sahl); *Variations on Sacred Harp Hymn Tunes* for Harpsichord (1982); *Big Jim & the Small-time Investors*, music theater piece, after N. Jackson (1985–86; rev. 1990); *Toward a New American Opera*, mixed-media piece (1985); *Birdwalk* for Tape and Optional Keyboard (1986); *Signals*, structure for conducted improvisation for Any Number of Vocal or Instrumental Performers (1988); *The Last Words of Dutch Schultz* (1995–96; in collaboration with V. Vasilevski); *Body Language* for Singers, Dancers, Violin, Piano, and Accordion (1995–96; in collaboration with M. Sahl).

BIBL.: S. Krantz, *Science & Technology in the Arts: A Tour Through the Realm of Science/Art* (N.Y., 1974); J. Quinn, "Divine Dissatisfaction: Reinventing Opera," *Seven Arts* (Philadelphia, 1993).

Samaroff, Olga (née **Hickenlooper**), American pianist and educator; b. San Antonio, Aug. 8, 1882; d. N.Y., May 17, 1948. She studied as a child with her mother and grandmother (Mrs. L. Grünewald, a former concert pianist); subsequently studied in Paris (with Delaborde), Baltimore (with Ernest Hutcheson), and Berlin (with Ernst Jedliczka). She made her concert debut in N.Y. (Jan. 18, 1905) with the N.Y. Sym. Soc.; appeared with other orchs. in the U.S. and Europe; gave joint recitals with Kreisler, Zimbalist, and other violinists. She was music critic for the *N.Y. Evening Post* (1927–29); was on the faculties of the Philadelphia Cons. and the Juilliard School of Music in N.Y. (1924–48); among her outstanding students were Eugene List, Rosalyn Tureck, William Kapell, and Alexis Weissenberg. In 1911 she married **Leopold Stokowski**; they divorced in 1923. Her autobiography was publ. as *An American Musician's Story* (N.Y., 1939); she also publ. *The Layman's Music Book* (N.Y., 1935; 2nd ed., rev., 1947, as *The Listener's Music Book*), *The Magic World of Music* (N.Y., 1936), and *A Music Manual* (N.Y., 1937).

BIBL.: D. Pucciani, *O. S. (1882–1948), American Musican and Educator* (diss., N.Y. Univ., 1979).

Samazeuilh, Gustave (Marie Victor Fernand), French writer on music and composer; b. Bordeaux, June 2, 1877; d. Paris, Aug. 4, 1967. He studied music with Chausson and at the Paris Schola Cantorum with d'Indy; also took some lessons from Dukas. In his music, he absorbed the distinct style of French Impressionism, but despite the fine craftsmanship of his work, performances were few and far between. He publ. the studies *Paul Dukas* (Paris, 1913; 2nd ed., 1936) and *Ernest Chausson: Musicien de mon temps* (Paris, 1947); also ed. *Écrits de Paul Dukas sur la musique* (Paris, 1948).

WORKS: ORCH.: *Étude symphonique* (1906); *Nuit* (Paris, March 15, 1925); *Naiades au soir* (Paris, Oct. 18, 1925); *Sérénade* (1926); *Gitanes* (1931); *L'Appel de la danse* (1946). **CHAMBER:** Violin Sonata (1903); String Quartet (1911); *Esquisse d'Espagne* for Flute and Piano (1914); *Luciole* for Clarinet and Piano (1934); *Suite en trio* for Strings (1938); *Cantabile e capriccio* for String Quartet (1948); many transcriptions for piano of orch. works by d'Indy, Debussy, Franck, and Fauré. **CHORUS AND ORCH.:** *Le Sommeil de Canope* (1908); *Chant d'Espagne* (Paris, Jan. 10, 1926); *Le Cercle des heures* (Paris, Feb. 17, 1934).

BIBL.: J. Poupard, *Entretiens avec G. S.* (Paris, 1962).

Saminsky, Lazare, Russian-American composer, conductor, and writer on music; b. Valegotsulova, near Odessa, Nov. 8, 1882; d. Port Chester, N.Y., June 30, 1959. He studied mathematics and philosophy at the Univ. of St. Petersburg, and composition with Rimsky-Korsakov and Liadov and conducting with N. Tcherepnin at the St. Petersburg Cons. (graduated, 1910). He emigrated to the U.S. in 1920, settling in N.Y.; in 1923 he was a co-founder of the League of Composers; served as music director of Temple Emanu-El in N.Y. (1924–56), where he founded the annual Three Choirs Festival (1926). He was married to an American writer, Lillian Morgan Buck, who died in 1945; in 1948 he married the American pianist Jennifer Gandar. He wrote an autobiography, *Third Leonardo* (MS, 1959). In his compositions, he followed the Romantic tradition; Hebrew subjects and styles play an important part in some of his music.

WORKS: DRAMATIC: *The Gagliarda of a Merry Plague*, opera ballet (1924; N.Y., Feb. 22, 1925); *The Daughter of Jephta*, opera ballet (1928); *Julian, the Apostate Caesar*, opera (1933–38). **ORCH.:** *Vigiliae*, symphonic triptych (1912; Moscow, Feb. 20, 1913, composer conducting); 5 syms.: No. 1, *Of the Great Rivers*, in "E-Frimoll" (free minor mode) (1914; Petrograd, Feb. 25, 1917, composer conducting), No. 2, *Symphonie des sommets* (1918; Amsterdam, Nov. 16, 1922), No. 3, *Symphony of the Seas* (1924; Paris, June 1925, composer conducting), No. 4 (1926; Berlin, April 19, 1929, composer conducting), and No. 5, *Jerusalem, City of Solomon and Christ*, for Chorus and Orch. (1929–30; N.Y., April 29, 1958); *Lament of Rachel*, ballet suite (Boston, March 3, 1922); *Venice*, "poem-serenade" for Chamber Orch. (Berlin, May 9, 1928); *Ausonia*, suite (1930; Florence, Feb. 24, 1935); *To a New World* (1932; N.Y., April 16, 1951); *3 Shadows* (1935; N.Y., Feb. 6, 1936); *Pueblo, A Moon Epic* (1936; Washington, D.C., Feb. 17, 1937); *Stilled Pageant* (1937; Zürich, Aug. 1938); *East and West*, suite for Violin and Orch. (1943). **VOCAL:** *Litanies of Women* for Voice and Chamber Orch. (1925; Paris, May 21, 1926); *Eon Hours*, suite of 4 rondos for 4 Voices and 4 Instruments (1935; N.Y., Nov. 28, 1939); *Requiem*, in memory of Lillian M. Saminsky (N.Y., May 20, 1946); *A Sonnet of Petrarch* for 3 Voices and 3 Instruments (1947); several Hebrew services. **OTHER:** Piano pieces.

WRITINGS: *Music of Our Day* (N.Y., 1932; 2nd ed., rev. and aug., 1939); *Music of the Ghetto and the Bible* (N.Y., 1934); *Living Music of the Americas* (N.Y., 1949); *Physics and Metaphysics of Music and Essays on the Philosophy of Mathematics* (The Hague, 1957); *Essentials of Conducting* (N.Y., 1958).

BIBL.: D. de Paoli et al., *L. S.: Composer and Civic Worker* (N.Y., 1930); A. Weisser, ed., "L. S.'s Years in Russia and Palestine: Excerpts from an Unpublished Autobiography," *Musica Judaica*, II (1977–78).

Sammarco, (Giuseppe) Mario, Italian baritone; b. Palermo, Dec. 13, 1868; d. Milan, Jan. 24, 1930. He studied singing with Antonio Cantelli, making a successful debut as Valentine in Faust in Palermo (1888); then sang in Brescia, Madrid, Lisbon, Brussels, Moscow, Warsaw, Berlin, and Vienna. After his London appearance as Scarpia in Tosca at Covent Garden in 1904, he sang there every season until the outbreak of World War I in 1914. He made his American debut as Tonio (Feb. 1, 1908) at the Manhattan Opera House in N.Y.; from 1910 to 1913 he sang with the Chicago Grand Opera; retired from the operatic stage in 1919 and later settled in Milan as a teacher. He was one of the finest verismo singers of his time.

Sammons, Albert (Edward), esteemed English violinist and pedagogue; b. London, Feb. 23, 1886; d. Southdean, Sussex, Aug. 24, 1957. He received some instruction from his father and others in London, but was mainly autodidact. He began his professional career at age 11, making his solo debut at 20. He was 1st violinist of the London String Quartet (1907–16); was also concertmaster of Beecham's Orch. (1908–13), Diaghilev's Ballets Russes orch. (from 1911), and the orch. of the Phil. Soc. (from 1913). In subsequent years, he appeared as a soloist with various orchs. in England, becoming well known as a champion of the Elgar Violin Concerto; Delius dedicated his Violin Concerto to Sammons, who ed. its violin part and was soloist in its premiere (London, Jan. 30, 1919). For a quarter of a century he gave duo recitals with the pianist William Murdoch, often playing premieres of British scores. He served as a prof. at the Royal College of Music in London. In 1944 he was made a Commander of the Order of the British Empire. He also composed; his *Phantasy Quartet* for Strings was awarded the Cobbett Prize. He publ. *The Secret of Technique in Violin Playing* (London, 1916) and *Violin Exercises for Improving the Bowing Technique by Means of the Tone Perfecter* (London, 1930).

Samosud, Samuil (Abramovich), prominent Russian conductor and teacher; b. Tiflis, May 14, 1884; d. Moscow, Nov. 6, 1964. He studied cello at the Tiflis Cons. (graduated, 1906). After playing cello in various orchs., he went to St. Petersburg, where he was a conductor at the Maryinsky Theater (1917–19) and artistic director of the Maly Theater (1918–36); then settled in Moscow and was artistic director of the Bolshoi Theater (1936–43), the Stanislavsky-Nemirovich-Danchenko Music Theater (1943–50), and the Moscow Phil. and the All-Union Radio orch. (1953–57); also taught conducting at the Leningrad Cons. (1929–36), being made a prof. in 1934. In 1937 he was made a People's Artist of the U.S.S.R. He conducted premieres of a number of works by Soviet composers, including Shostakovich's opera *The Nose* (1930) and Prokofiev's 7th Sym. (1952).

Sams, Eric, English writer on music; b. London, May 3, 1926. He was educated at Corpus Christi College, Cambridge (1947–50; B.A., 1950); later he was awarded his Ph.D. (1972). He worked in Army cryptanalysis (1947–50), and then was in the British civil service (1950–78). In 1976–77 he was a visiting prof. at McMaster Univ. in Hamilton, Ontario, Canada. Sams is an expert in codes and ciphers. His work was detailed in the television film *Code and Cipher in Music* (1989). He contributed articles and reviews to various publications. His valuable books comprise *The Songs of Hugo Wolf* (London, 1961; 3rd ed., rev. and enl., 1993), *The Songs of Robert Schumann* (London, 1969; 3rd ed., rev. and enl., 1993), and *Brahms Songs* (London, 1972).

Samuel, Gerhard, German-born American conductor, composer, and pedagogue; b. Bonn, April 20, 1924. He studied violin in his youth. In 1939 he emigrated to the U.S. and in 1943 became a naturalized American citizen. He studied conducting with Hermann Genhart at the Eastman School of Music in Rochester, N.Y. (B.S., 1945), composition with Hindemith at Yale Univ. (M.M., 1947), and conducting with Koussevitzky at the Berkshire Music Center at Tanglewood (summers, 1946–47). After playing violin in the Rochester Phil. (1941–45) and conducting on Broadway (1948–49), he was a violinist and assoc. conductor with the Minneapolis Sym. Orch. (1949–59). He also was music director of the Collegium Musicum and the Minneapolis Civic Opera (1949–59). From 1959 to 1971 he was music director of the Oakland (Calif.) Sym. Orch. He also was music director of the San Francisco Ballet (1960–70), as well as the Oakland Chamber Orch. and the Cabrillo Festival (1962–66). From 1970 to 1973 he was assoc. conductor of the Los Angeles Phil. He also was on the faculty of the Calif. Inst. of the Arts in Valencia from 1972 to 1976. In 1976 he became director of orchestral activities at the Univ. of Cincinnati College-Cons. of Music, where he was music director of its Philharmonia Orch. He also was music director of the Cincinnati Chamber Orch. from 1983 to 1991. As a guest conductor, he appeared with orchs. throughout North America and abroad. In 1994 he won the Alice M. Ditson Award. In his compositions, Samuel has pursued a contemporary path.

WORKS: DRAMATIC: *Agam*, ballet music (1982); *Nicholas and Conception*, ballet (1987). **ORCH.:** *Looking at Orpheus Looking* (1971); *Into Flight From* (1972); *Requiem for Survivors* (1974); *Cold When the Drum Sounds for Dawn* (1975); *On a Dream* for Viola and Orch. (1977); *Out of Time*, short sym. (1978); *Chamber Concerto in the Shape of a Summer* for Flute, 3 Percussion, and Strings (1981); Double Concerto for Viola, Violin, and Orch. (1983); *Before Webern* (1983); *Lucille's Wave* (1984); *As Imperceptibly as Grief* (1987); *Apollo and Hyacinth* (1989); Soprano Saxophone Concerto (1990); *Outcries and Consolations* (1990); *Auguri* (1993); *Tragic Scene* (1994); *Transformations* for Violin and Strings (1994). **CHAMBER:** *3 Hymns to Apollo* for Cello and 7 Instrumentalists (1973); *Beyond McBean* for Violin and 13 Instrumentalists (1975); *Au Revoir to Lady R* for Clarinet, Cello, and Percussion (1976); 2 string quartets (1978, 1981); *Pezzo Serioso* for 2 Tubas and Percussion (1978); *Circles* for 3 Percussion (1979); *Put Up My Lute* for Cello and 3 Percussion (1979); *Aftermath* for Clarinet and 3 Percussion (1983); *Nocturne on an Impossible Dream* for Violin, Clarinet, Piano, 2 Percussion, Violin, Viola, Cello, and Bass (1986); *The Naumburg Cadenza* for Violin (1990); *Dirge for John Cage* for Bassoon and Percussion (1992); *Left-Over Mirrors* for 3 Flutes, 3 Horns, and 3 Percussion (1992); *Music for 4* for Violin, Clarinet, Cello, and Piano (1992); *After a Dirge* for Flute, Bassoon, and 3 Percussion (1993). **VOCAL:** *12 on Death and No* for Tenor, Chorus, and Orch. (1968); *The Relativity of Icarus* for Contralto or Baritone and 8 Instrumentalists (1970); *To an End* for Chorus and Orch. (1972); *And Marsyas* for Mezzo-soprano and 10 Instrumentalists (1974; rev. 1989); *Sun-Like* for Soprano and Chamber Ensemble (1975); *Fortieth Day* for Soprano, Narrator, and 7 Instrumentalists (1976); *Paul Blake—Ikon Maker* for Soprano and 8 Instrumentalists (1979); *What of My Music* for Soprano, 3 Percussion, and String Bass Ensemble (1979); *The Emperor and the Nightingale* for Soprano, Bass-baritone, String Bass, and 3 Percussion (1980); *On the Beach at Night Alone* for Chorus, Clarinet, and Strings or Organ (1980); *3 Minor Desperations* for Mezzo-soprano and Orch. (1980); *Traumbild* for Soprano, Tenor, and Orch. (1983); *Mid-Autumn Moon* for Mezzo-soprano or Baritone and 5 Instrumentalists (1988); *This Heart That Broke So Long . . .* for Soprano or Tenor and Piano (1991).

Samuel, Harold, distinguished English pianist and pedagogue; b. London, May 23, 1879; d. there, Jan. 15, 1937. He studied at the Royal College of Music in London with Dannreuther (piano) and Stanford (composition); later was on its faculty. He was particularly distinguished as an interpreter of Bach; in 1921 he gave 6 successive Bach recitals in London and a similar cycle in N.Y.; toured the U.S. regularly from 1924. He wrote a musical comedy, *Hon'ble Phil*, songs, and piano pieces.

Samuel, Léopold, Belgian composer; b. Brussels, May 5, 1883; d. there, March 10, 1975. He studied with Edgar Tinel at the Brussels Cons. and took courses in Berlin, winning the Belgian Prix de Rome with his cantata *Tycho-Brahé* (1911). He later served as inspector of music education in Belgium (1920–45) and was made a member of the Belgian Royal Academy (1958). His works follow in a late Romantic style, with pronounced impressionistic elements.

WORKS: OPERAS: *Ilka* (1919); *La Sirène au pays des hommes* (1937). **ORCH.:** *Morceaux de concert* for Cello and Orch. (1908); *Petite suite fantasque* (1945). **CHAMBER:** String Quintet (1909); Piano Trio (1920); 3 string quartets (1941, 1942, 1948); *Pièce à 5* for Flute, String Trio, and Harp (1954); *Invocation* for Cello and Piano (1959). **VOCAL:** Songs.

Samuel-Holeman, Eugène, Belgian pianist, conductor, and composer; b. Brussels, Nov. 3, 1863; d. there, Jan. 25, 1942. He was the son of the composer and teacher Adolphe (-Abraham) Samuel (b. Liège, July 11, 1824; d. Ghent, Sept. 11, 1898). After studying piano and theory at the Ghent Cons., he was active as a pianist and conductor, pursuing his career primarily in France. He wrote an opera, *Un vendredi saint en Zélande;* monodrama, *La jeune fille à la fenêtre* (1904); Sym.; Harp Concerto; chamber music; songs.

Samuel-Rousseau, Marcel. See **Rousseau, Marcel.**

Sánchez de Fuentes, Eduardo, important Cuban composer and educator; b. Havana, April 3, 1874; d. there, Sept. 7, 1944. He studied music with Ignacio Cervantes and Carlos Anckermann. He occupied an influential position in the artistic affairs of Cuba. He wrote 5 operas and many other works, but is known outside Cuba chiefly by his popular song "Tú," which he publ. at the age of 18.

WORKS: OPERAS (all 1st perf. in Havana): *El náufrago*, after Tennyson's *Enoch Arden* (1900; Jan. 31, 1901); *La dolorosa* (April 23, 1910); *Doreya* (1917; Feb. 7, 1918); *El caminante*

(1921); *Kabelia*, after a Hindu legend (June 22, 1942). **ORCH.:** *Temas del patio*, symphonic prelude; *Anacaona*, symphonic poem (1928). **VOCAL:** *Bocetos cubanos* for Soprano, Women's Chorus, and Orch. (1922); songs. **OTHER:** Piano pieces.

WRITINGS (all publ. in Havana): *El folklore en la música cubana* (1923); *Folklorismo* (1928); *Viejos ritmos cubanos* (1937).

BIBL.: M. Guiral, *Un gran musicógrafo y compositor cubano: E. S.d.F.* (Havana, 1944); O. Martínez, *E. S.d.F.: In Memoriam* (Havana, 1944).

Sandberg, Mordecai, Romanian-born American composer and music theorist; b. in Romania, Feb. 4, 1897; d. Toronto, Dec. 28, 1973. As a child, he studied violin with a Gypsy violinist-conductor, composing the overture *Demosthenes* while still in his teens. He pursued training in music in Vienna while attending the Univ. there as a medical student (M.D., 1921). From 1922 to 1938 he was active as both a physician and a composer in Jerusalem, where he founded the local branch of the ISCM and the Inst. of New Music; in 1930 he served as contributing ed. of the Hebrew monthly music journal *Hallel*. In 1929–30 he pursued research on acoustics in Germany; also lectured at the Berlin Hochschule für Musik and publ. an essay on his music theories as *Die Musik der Menschheit: Die Tondifferenzierung und ihre Bedeutung*. In 1938 he lectured on microtones at the Congress of Music and Life in London. He went to the U.S. in 1939 and later settled in N.Y., where several of his works were premiered, including *Ezkerah* (I Remember; 1952), an oratorio "dedicated to the memory of all victims of persecution, oppression, and hatred." From 1970 until his death he taught at York Univ. in Toronto. Sandberg was an original and prolific composer. He was one of the earliest explorers of microtonal music, originating his own "Universal Tonal System" using microtones based on a synthesis of Oriental and Western scales. To facilitate the writing and performance of microtonal music, he designed a refined notational system and several instruments, including 2 harmoniums—one bichromatic with quarter tones (1926) and one with 12th and 16th tones (1929), both built by Straube. He composed orch. works, including 5 syms., a Concerto for Clarinet and Strings, and a Concerto for Oboe, Viola, and Orch.; much chamber music, including sextets, quintets, quartets, and sonatas for cello, piano, violin, viola, and organ; numerous sacred and secular vocal works, including 15 oratorios, among them *Ruth* (N.Y., May 22, 1949) and *Ezkerah* (N.Y., April 22, 1952); *Shelomoh*, symphonic tetralogy for Soloists, Chorus, and Orch.; *Jerusalem*, cantata (N.Y., Nov. 10, 1943); *Hebrew Spirituals and Prayer for Peace* (N.Y., Jan. 16, 1946). His major achievement was his *Symphonic Psalms*, settings of the entire book of Psalms, among them *Pilgrim Songs* (Psalms 128, 130, and 134; N.Y., Jan. 16, 1946), *Songs of Ascent* (Psalms 126, 131, and 132; N.Y., June 17, 1947), and *Psalm 51* (N.Y., May 30, 1987).

Sandberger, Adolf, eminent German musicologist; b. Würzburg, Dec. 19, 1864; d. Munich, Jan. 14, 1943. He studied composition in Würzburg and Munich (1881–87) and musicology in Munich and Berlin (1883–87); obtained his Ph.D. in 1887 at the Univ. of Würzburg with the diss. *Peter Cornelius* (publ. in Leipzig, 1887) and completed his Habilitation in 1894 at the Univ. of Munich with his *Beiträge zur Geschichte der Bayerischen Hofkapelle unter Orlando di Lasso* (Vols. 1 and 3 publ. in Leipzig, 1894–95; Vol. 2 not publ.). In 1889 he was appointed head of the music dept. at the Bavarian Hofbibliothek in Munich; also was a reader (1900–1904) and a prof. (1904–30) at the Univ. of Munich. He was ed. of Denkmaler der Tonkunst in Bayern (1900–1931) and the *Neues Beethoven-Jahrbuch* (1924–42); with F. Haberl, he also ed. Breitkopf & Härtel's monumental edition of the complete works of Lassus (1894–1927). Sandberger was one of the most important teachers of musicology in Germany; he formulated the basic principles of 20th-century musical bibliography. Among his writings were *Emmanuel Chabriers Gwendoline* (Munich, 1898), *Über zwei ehedem Wolfgang Mozart zugeschriebene Messen* (Munich, 1907), and *Ausgewählte Aufsätze zur Musikgeschichte* (Munich, 1921–24). He was also a composer; wrote 2 operas, choral pieces, chamber works, songs, etc.

BIBL.: T. Kroyer, ed., *Festschrift zum 50. Geburtstag A. S.* (Munich, 1918).

Sandby, Hermann, Danish cellist and composer; b. Kundby, March 21, 1881; d. Copenhagen, Dec. 14, 1965. After training in Copenhagen, he was a student of Hugo Becker (cello) and Iwan Knorr (composition) in Frankfurt am Main (1895–1900). He gave concerts in Europe before playing in the Philadelphia Orch. (1912–16). After living in N.Y. (1916–30), he returned to Denmark.

WORKS: DRAMATIC: Stage music. **ORCH.:** Cello Concerto (1915; Philadelphia, Feb. 5, 1916); 5 syms. (1930–54); *Pastorale d'automne* (1937); *Serenade* for Strings (1940); *Nordische Rhapsodie* (1954); Violin Concerto; Triple Concerto for Violin, Viola, Piano, and Orch. **CHAMBER:** 4 string quartets (1907–36); String Quintet (1936); Piano Quintet (1938); Piano Trio (1940); piano pieces. **VOCAL:** Songs.

Sanderling, Kurt, eminent German conductor, father of **Thomas Sanderling**; b. Arys, Sept. 9, 1912. Following private studies, he joined the Berlin Städtische Oper as a répétiteur (1931). Being Jewish, he left Nazi Germany and made his way to the Soviet Union (1936); was a conductor with the Moscow Radio Orch. (1936–41) and the Leningrad Phil. (1941–60). He then was chief conductor of the (East) Berlin Sym. Orch. (1960–77). From 1964 to 1967 he was chief conductor of the Dresden State Opera. He also filled a number of engagements as a guest conductor in Western Europe and America.

BIBL.: H. Bitterlich, *K. S.: für Sie portratiert* (Leipzig, 1987).

Sanderling, Thomas, German conductor, son of **Kurt Sanderling;** b. Novosibirsk, Russia, Oct. 2, 1942. He studied at the Leningrad Cons. and at the Hanns Eisler Hochschule für Musik in East Berlin. In 1962 he made his conducting debut with the (East) Berlin Sym. Orch. After serving as music director in Sondershausen (1963–64) and Reichenbach (1964–66), he was music director in Halle (from 1966). In 1978 he became permanent guest conductor of the (East) Berlin State Opera. In 1979 he made a highly successful debut at the Vienna State Opera conducting *Die Zauberflöte*, and subsequently was engaged by many major opera houses and orchs. in Europe and abroad. From 1984 to 1986 he was artistic director of the Amsterdam Phil. He was music director of the Osaka Sym. Orch. from 1992.

Sanders, Robert L(evine), American organist, conductor, music educator, and composer; b. Chicago, July 2, 1906; d. Delray Beach, Fla., Dec. 26, 1974. He studied at the Bush Cons. of Music in Chicago (Mus.B., 1924; Mus.M., 1925); in 1925 he went to Rome on a fellowship of the American Academy there, and studied composition with Respighi; later was in Paris, where he took lessons with Guy de Lioncourt. Returning to America in 1929, he joined the faculty of the Chicago Cons.; was also organist at the First Unitarian Church; from 1938 to 1947 he was dean of the School of Music at Indiana Univ. in Bloomington; from 1947 to 1973 he taught at Brooklyn College of the City Univ. of N.Y.

WORKS: BALLET: *L'Ag'ya* (1943). **ORCH.:** Violin Concerto (1932–36); *Scenes of Poverty and Toil* (1934–35; perf. as *The Tragic Muse*, Chicago, Jan. 30, 1936, composer conducting); 3 Little Syms. (1936–37; 1953; 1963); Sym. for Concert Band (1942–43). **CHAMBER:** Piano Trio (1926); Brass Quintet (1942); Brass Quartet (1949); Brass Trio (1958); various sonatas; piano pieces; organ music. **VOCAL:** *The Mystic Trumpeter* for Narrator, Baritone, Chorus, and Orch., after Walt Whitman (1939–41); *Song of Myself* for Reciter, Soprano, Chorus, Brass, and Percussion, after Walt Whitman (1966–70; N.Y., April 19, 1970); choruses; hymns.

Sanders, Samuel, American pianist; b. N.Y., June 27, 1937. He attended Hunter College (B.A., 1959), and studied the art of accompaniment with Sergius Kagen and piano with Irwin Freundlich at the Juilliard School of Music in N.Y. (M.S., 1961); also pursued studies with Martin Canin and Boulanger. He made his debut as a recitalist at N.Y.'s Town Hall at age 12; after winning a prize as a piano accompanist at the Tchaikovsky Competition in Moscow (1966), he became well known as an accompanist to many major artists; was also active as a chamber music player. In 1963 he joined the faculty of the Juilliard School of Music; was also a prof. at the State Univ. of N.Y. in Purchase (1972–79). He founded the Cape and Islands Chamber Music Festival in 1980 and the Musica Camerit of N.Y.'s Hebrew Arts School in 1983. Although he underwent a heart transplant in 1990, he was able to eventually resume his career.

Sandi, Luis, Mexican conductor, teacher, and composer; b. Mexico City, Feb. 22, 1905. He studied violin with Rocabruna (1923–30) and composition with Campa and Mejía (1925–31) at the National Cons. of Mexico City. He conducted a chorus at the Cons. (1922–35); in 1937 he founded the Coro de Madrigalistas and conducted it until 1965. He was a prof. of music in primary schools (1924–32) and chief of the Music Section of the Secretariat of Public Education (1933–65). He publ. *Introducción al estudio de la música: Curso completo* (Mexico City, 1923; 2nd ed., 1956) and a collection of articles as *De música y otras cosas* (Mexico City, 1969).

WORKS: DRAMATIC: OPERAS: *Carlota* (Mexico City, Oct. 23, 1948); *La señora en su balcón* (1964). **BALLETS:** *Día de difuntos* (1938); *Bonampak* (1948; Mexico City, Nov. 2, 1951); *Coatlicue* (1949). **ORCH.:** *El venado* (1932; Mexico City, Oct. 28, 1938); *Sonora* (1933); *Suite banal* for Small Orch. (1936); *Norte* (Mexico City, Aug. 15, 1941); Flute Concertino (1944); *Tema y Variaciones* (1944); *Esbozos sinfónicos* (1951); *4 Miniatures* (1952); *América,* symphonic poem (1965); Sym. No. 2 (1979). **CHAMBER:** String Quartet (1938); *La hoja de plata* for Instruments (1939); *Fátima,* suite for Guitar (1948); *Cuatro momentos* for String Quartet (1950); *Hoja de album* for Cello and Piano (1956); Cello Sonatina (1958); Quintet (1960); Sonatina for Solo Violin (1967); Violin Sonata (1969); *4 piezas* for Recorders (1977); piano pieces. **VOCAL:** *Las troyanas* for Chorus and Instruments (1936); *Gloria a los héroes,* cantata (1940); *La suave patria,* cantata (1951); choruses; songs.

BIBL.: C. Chávez, "L. S.," *Nuestra Música* (July 1949).

Sándor, Arpád, Hungarian-born American pianist, cousin of **György Sándor**; b. Budapest, June 5, 1896; d. there, Feb. 10, 1972. He studied with Bartók and Kodály at the Royal Academy of Music in Budapest, graduating in 1914. He toured the U.S. as an accompanist in 1922; wrote art and music criticism for the *Berliner Tageblatt* (1926–33); then settled in the U.S. and became a naturalized American citizen (1943); toured widely as an accompanist to leading artists, including Jascha Heifetz and Lily Pons.

Sándor, György, admired Hungarian-born American pianist and teacher, cousin of **Arpád Sándor**; b. Budapest, Sept. 21, 1912. He studied at the Royal Academy of Music in Budapest with Bartók (piano) and Kodály (composition). After making his debut in Budapest (1930), he toured in Europe before settling in the U.S. (1939); became a naturalized American citizen (1943). After World War II, he played in major music centers of the world. He also taught at Southern Methodist Univ. in Dallas (1956–61); then was director of graduate studies in piano at the Univ. of Mich. in Ann Arbor (1961–81); subsequently taught at the Juilliard School in N.Y. (from 1982). He won particular distinction as an interpreter of the music of Bartók, Kodály, and Prokofiev; was soloist in the premiere of Bartók's 3rd Piano Concerto (Philadelphia, Feb. 8, 1946). He made brilliant transcriptions of Dukas's *L'Apprenti sorcier* and Shostakovich's *Danse russe.* He publ. *On Piano Playing: Motion, Sound, and Expression* (N.Y., 1981).

Sandoval, Miguel, Guatemalan-American pianist, conductor, and composer; b. Guatemala City, Nov. 22, 1903; d. N.Y., Aug. 24, 1953. He settled in the U.S. in 1925, where he was active as a conductor and pianist. He wrote a symphonic poem, *Recuerdos en un paseo,* and publ. numerous piano works and songs in a Latin American vein.

Sandström, Sven-David, Swedish composer and teacher; b. Borensberg, Oct. 30, 1942. He studied art history and musicology at the Univ. of Stockholm (1963–67); attended composition classes with Lidholm at the Stockholm Musikhögskolan (1967–72); also took special courses in advanced techniques of composition with Norgard and Ligeti. In 1981 he joined the faculty of the Stockholm Musikhögskolan. In 1983 he served as chairman of the Swedish section of the ISCM. In his early works he made use of quarter-tone tuning. Later he turned to tonal and modal writing.

WORKS: DRAMATIC: *Stark såsom döden* (Strong like Death), church opera (Stockholm, April 18, 1978); *Hasta o älskade brud* (Hasta, O Beloved Bride), chamber opera (1978); *Kejsaren Jones* (Emperor Jones), after O'Neill (1980); *Ett drömspel* (The Dreamplay), incidental music to Strindberg's play (1980); *Amos,* church opera (1981); *Slottet det vita,* opera (1981–82; Stockholm, Feb. 12, 1987); *Admorica,* ballet (1985); *Den elfte gryningen,* ballet (Stockholm, Nov. 4, 1988); ballet music (1991). **ORCH.:** *Bilder* (Pictures) for Percussion and Orch. (Norrköping, April 17, 1969); *Intrada* for Wind Instruments, Strings, and Percussion (1969); *17 Bildkombinationen* (17 Picture Combinations) for Wind Instruments, Percussion, and Strings (1969); *In the Meantime* for Chamber Orch. (1970); *Sounds* for 14 Strings (1970); *To You* (Arvika, Aug. 15, 1970); *Around a Line* for Wind Instruments, Piano, Percussion, and Strings (1971); *Through and Through* (1972; Stockholm, Feb. 1, 1974); *Con tutta forza* for 41 Wind Instruments and 6 Percussionists (Stockholm, Oct. 28, 1976); *Culminations* (Swedish Radio, Feb. 22, 1977); *Agitato* for Piano and Orch. (1978); *The Rest Is Dross* for Strings (1979); Flute Concerto (1980; Stockholm, Oct. 24, 1983); *Lonesome,* guitar concerto (1982–83; Malmö, May 18, 1983); Concerto for Violin and String Orch. (1985; Orebro, Jan. 18, 1986); *A Day—The Days* (1987); Overture (Stockholm, June 18, 1987); *Invigningsfanfar* for the 50th anniversary of the Swedish Radio (Swedish Radio, Oct. 14, 1988); Cello Concerto (1989; Stockholm, March 2, 1990); Piano Concerto (1990; Helsingborg, Jan. 31, 1991); *Pieces of Pieces* (1992); *Vattenmusik 1* and *2* for Wind Band (1992); Percussion Concerto (1993); *First-pieces,* overture (1994); *Symphonic Piece* for Orch. and Men's Chorus (1994). **CHAMBER:** *Music* for 5 String Instruments (1968); Sonata for Solo Flute (1968); *Combinations* for Clarinet (1960); Concertato for Clarinet, Trombone, Cello, and Percussion (1969); String Quartet (1969); *Disturbances* for 6 Brasses (1970); *Disjointing* for Trombone (1970); *Jumping Excursions* for Clarinet, Cello, Trombone, and Cymbal (1970); *Mosaic* for String Trio (1970); *Under the Surface* for 6 Trombones (1971); *Concentration* for 8 Wind Instruments and 4 Double Basses (1971); *Closeness* for Clarinet (1973); *. . . And All the Flavors Around,* 6 pieces for Violin, Piano, Clarinet, and Flute (1973); *6 Character Pieces* for Flute, Oboe, Bassoon, 2 Violins, Double Bass, and Percussion (1973); *Convergence* for Bassoon (1973); *Inside* for Bass Trombone and Piano (1974); *Metal, Metal* for 4 Percussionists (1974); *In the Shadow of . . .* for Piano, Cello, and Percussion (1974); *Ratio* for Tuba and Bass Drum (1974); *Utmost* for Wind Quintet, Trumpet, Trombone, Tuba, and Percussion (London, Nov. 10, 1975); *Effort* for Cello (1977); *Break This Heavy Chain That Does Freeze My Bones Around* for 2 Bassoons (1979); *Within* for 8 Trombones and Percussion ad libitum (1979); *Drums* for Timpani and 4 Percussionists (1980); *Behind* for String Quartet (1981); *The Last Fight* for Percussion (1984); *Sax Music* for Saxophone Quartet (1985); *Chained* for Percussion Ensemble (1986); *The Slumberous Mass* for 4 Trombones (1987); *Dance III* for 3 Cellos (1988); *Pieces of Wood* for 6 Percussionists (1992). **KEYBOARD: PIANO:** *Concentration II* for 2 Pianos (1972); *High Above* (1972); *5 Duets* for Piano (1973); *Introduction—Out of Memories—Finish* for 2 Pianos (1981). **ORGAN:** *The Way* (1973); *Openings* (1975); *Libera me* (1980). **VOCAL:** *Invention* for 16 Voices (1969); *Lamento* for 3 Choral Groups and 4 Trombones (1971); *Visst?* for Soprano, 2 Choruses, Wind

Instruments, Pop Orch., and Violin Group (1971; Mellerud, April 23, 1972); *Just a Bit* for Soprano, Bassoon, Violin, and Harp (1972); *Birgitta-Music I* for Speaking and Singing Groups, Orch., Renaissance Ensemble, Organ, and Folk Musicians and Dancers (Vadstena, June 23, 1973); *Dilecte mi (Canticum canticorum)*, motet for Men's and Women's Choruses (1974); *Expression* for Amplified Mezzo-soprano, Cello, Piano, 4-hands, and Tape (1976); *A Cradle Song/The Tyger*, 2 poems for Chorus, after William Blake (1978); *Spring—Introduction—Earth's Answer*, 3 poems for Chorus, after William Blake (1978); *Tystnaden* (Silence) for Tenor, Narrator, and 14 String Instruments (1979); *Requiem: De ur alla minnen fallna* (Requiem: Mute the Bereaved Memories Speak) for 4 Soloists, Mixed Chorus, Children's Chorus, Orch., and Tape (1979; Stockholm, Feb. 19, 1982); *Agnus Dei* for Chorus (1980); *Our Peace*, motet for 3 Choruses and 3 Organs (1983); *Missa brevis* for Chorus (1984); *Ut över slätten med en doft av hav*, cantata for Soloists, Chorus, and Orch. (1984); *Convivere* for 5 Singers and 6 Instrumentalists (1985); *Kantat till Filharmonin* for Soloists, Chorus, and Orch. (1985); *Stille etter Gud* for 3 Choruses (1986); *24 romantiska etyder* for Chorus (1988); *Mass and Psaltery Psalm* for Soli, Chorus, Brass Quintet, and 2 Organs (1992); *High Mass* for Chorus, Organ, and Orch. (1993–94); *Nobelmusik* for Chorus, Brass Quintet, and Organ (1994).

Sandvik, Ole Mørk, respected Norwegian musicologist; b. Hedemarken, May 9, 1875; d. Holmenkollen, near Oslo, Aug. 5, 1976. He received training for careers in teaching (1895) and theology (graduated, 1902); also studied music with his father and Gudbrand Bøhn, and in Germany (1913); took his Ph.D. in 1922 at the Univ. of Christiania. He taught at Christiania's (Oslo's) Hegdehaugen School (1913–45) and gave courses in church music at the Seminary for Practical Theology at the Univ. of Christiania (Oslo; 1916–45). He was founder of the Norwegian Musicological Soc., serving as ed. of its yearbook (1937–72).

WRITINGS: *Norsk kirkenmusikk og densilder* (Christiania, 1918); *Folkemusik i Gudbrandsdalen* (Christiania, 1919; 2nd ed., 1948); *Norsk folkemusik: Saerlig Østlandsmusikken* (Christiania, 1921); with G. Schjelderup, *Norges musikhistorie* (Christiania, 1921–22); ed. with H. Panum and W. Behrend, *Illustreret musikleksikon* (Copenhagen, 1924–26; new ed., 1940); *Graduale for den norske kirke* (Oslo, 1925; 2nd ed., 1957); with J. Gleditsch et al., *Koralbok for den norske kirke* (Oslo, 1926); *Liturgisk musikk til minnegudstjenester på 900-års-jubileet Olsok* 1930 (Oslo, 1930); *Norsk koralhistorie* (Oslo, 1930); *Kingotona* (Oslo, 1941); *Vesperale for den norske kirke* (Oslo, 1941); *Gregoriansk sang* (Oslo, 1945); *Ludwig M. Lindeman og folkemelodien: Ein kilderstudie* (Oslo, 1950); *Setesdalsmelodier* (Oslo, 1952); *Norske religiose folketoner* (Oslo, 1960–64); *"Springleiker" i norske bygdier* (Oslo, 1967); ed. with O. Gaukstad, *David Monrad Johansen i skrift og tale* (Oslo, 1968).

BIBL.: *Festschrift til O.M. S.s, 70 års dagen 1875–9. Mai 1945* (Oslo, 1945).

Sandvold, Arild (Edvin), eminent Norwegian organist, choral conductor, teacher, and composer; b. Christiania, June 2, 1895; d. there (Oslo), Aug. 15, 1984. He studied at the Christiania Cons. and with Straube in Leipzig. He made Christiania the center of his activities, where he was active as an organist from 1914, later serving as cathedral organist and subsequently canon at Var Frelsers Church (1933–66). From 1917 to 1969 he taught organ at the Cons. He was conductor of the Caecilia Choral Soc. from 1928 to 1957. In 1956 the Norwegian government awarded him an annual stipend. He composed mainly sacred works, including cantatas. His most ambitious score was his *Misjonskantate* (Mission Cantata; 1942; orchestrated 1967). He also wrote many organ pieces. Sandvold greatly influenced the course of 20th-century Norwegian sacred music.

Sanjuán, Pedro, Spanish-born American conductor, teacher, and composer; b. San Sebastián, Nov. 15, 1886; d. Washington, D.C., Oct. 18, 1976. He studied composition with Turina. After conducting in Europe, he went to Havana, where he organized the Havana Phil. (1926); was also a teacher of composition there, numbering Roldán, Caturla, and other Cuban composers among his pupils. After a sojourn in Madrid (1932–36), he again conducted the Havana Phil. (1939–42); in 1942 he was appointed prof. of composition at Converse College in Spartanburg, S.C. In 1947 he became a naturalized American citizen.

WORKS: ORCH.: *Rondo fantástico* (Havana, Nov. 29, 1926); *Castilla*, suite (Havana, June 12, 1927); *Sones de Castilla* for Small Orch.; *La Macumba*, "ritual sym." (St. Louis, Dec. 14, 1951, composer conducting); *Antillean Poem* for Band (N.Y., Aug. 11, 1958, composer conducting); *Symphonic Suite* (Washington, D.C., May 9, 1965). **OTHER:** Choral works; piano pieces.

Sanjust, Filippo, Italian stage designer and opera director; b. Rome, Sept. 9, 1925; d. there, Nov. 29, 1992. He studied architecture in Rome and at Princeton Univ. before turning to stage design. In 1958 Visconti chose him as designer for his staging of *Don Carlos* at London's Covent Garden, and thereafter they collaborated successfully on various productions, including *Il Trovatore* at Covent Garden (1964) and *Le Nozze di Figaro* in Rome (1964) and at the Metropolitan Opera in N.Y. (1968). Henze chose Sanjust as designer for the premieres of his *Der junge Lord* in Berlin in 1965 and for his *The Bassarids* at the Salzburg Festival in 1966. From 1969 Sanjust combined work as a stage designer with opera directing. Among his most distinguished productions were *Ariadne auf Naxos* (1976) and *Falstaff* (1980) in Vienna, *L'incoronazione di Poppea* (1979) in Brussels, and *Simon Boccanega* (1980) at Covent Garden.

Sanromá, Jesús María, brilliant Puerto Rican pianist; b. Carolina (of Catalonian parents), Nov. 7, 1902; d. San Juan, Oct. 12, 1984. At the age of 14, he was sent to the U.S. by the governor of Puerto Rico; he studied piano with Antoinette Szumowska at the New England Cons. of Music in Boston; in 1920, won the Mason & Hamlin piano prize; then studied with Cortot (in Paris) and Schnabel (in Berlin). From 1926 to 1944 he was pianist of the Boston Sym. Orch.; he taught at the New England Cons. of Music (1930–41); gave annual concerts in the U.S., Canada, and South America; also played in Europe. In 1951 he was appointed chairman of the music dept. at the Univ. of Puerto Rico; he was head of the piano dept. at the Puerto Rico Cons. of Music (1959–80). He excelled particularly as an interpreter of contemporary music; gave the premieres of Piston's Concertino (1937) and Hindemith's Concerto (1947).

BIBL.: E. Belava, *El niño S.: Biografia mínima* (San Juan, 1952; 2nd ed., 1962).

San Sebastián, Padre José Antonio de. See **Donostia, José Antonio de.**

Santa Cruz (Wilson), Domingo, eminent Chilean composer and music educator; b. La Cruz, near Quillota, July 5, 1899; d. Santiago, Jan. 6, 1987. He studied jurisprudence at the Univ. of Chile; then entered diplomatic service; was 2nd secretary of the Chilean legation in Spain (1921–24); received his musical training with Enrique Soro in Santiago and with Conrado del Campo in Madrid. Returning to Chile, he devoted himself to musical administration, teaching, and composition; from 1928 to 1953 he served as a prof. at the National Cons. in Santiago; was acting dean (1932–33) and dean (1933–51; 1962–68) of the faculty of fine arts at the Univ. of Chile. His role in the promotion of musical culture in Chile was of great importance. In his works, he followed the cosmopolitan traditions of neo-Classical music; made use of identifiable Chilean melodies in but a few of his compositions.

WORKS (all 1st perf. in Santiago unless otherwise given): **ORCH.:** *5 piezas breves* for Strings (May 31, 1937); *Variaciones* for Piano and Orch. (June 25, 1943); *Sinfonia concertante* for Flute, Piano, and Strings (Nov. 29, 1945); 4 syms.: No. 1 for Strings, Celesta, and Percussion (1945–46; May 28, 1948; rev. 1970), No. 2 for Strings (Nov. 26, 1948), No. 3 for Contralto and Orch. (Washington, D.C., May 9, 1965), and No. 4 (1968).

CHAMBER: 3 string quartets (1930; 1946–47; 1959); piano pieces. **VOCAL:** *Cantata de los ríos de Chile* for Chorus and Orch. (1941; Nov. 27, 1942); *Egloga* for Soprano, Chorus, and Orch. (1949; Nov. 24, 1950); *Cantares de la pascua* for Women's Voices (1949; Dec. 7, 1950); *Canciones del mar*, song cycle (1955); *Endechas* for Tenor and 8 Instruments (1957); *Oratio Ieremiae prophetae* for Chorus and Orch. (1970).

BIBL.: Special issue of *Revista Musical Chilena* (Dec. 1951).

Santi, Nello, Italian conductor; b. Adria, Sept. 22, 1931. He studied at the Padua Liceo Musicale and with Coltro and Pedrollo. In 1951 he made his debut conducting *Rigoletto* in Padua, and then conducted in various Italian opera houses. From 1958 he was a regular conductor at the Zürich Opera. In 1960 he made his first appearance at London's Covent Garden conducting *La Traviata.* That same year he made his debuts at the Vienna State Opera and the Salzburg Festival. He made his Metropolitan Opera debut in N.Y. on Jan. 25, 1962, conducting *Un ballo in maschera.* He remained on its roster until 1965, and then conducted there regularly from 1976. As a guest conductor, he led operatic performances in Milan, Paris, Berlin, Munich, Florence, Naples, Geneva, and other European music centers. He also appeared as a guest conductor with many European orchs. In 1986 he became chief conductor of the Basel Radio Sym. Orch. In 1988 he conducted *Aida* in the first arena production in London at Earl's Court. He has won particular distinction for his performances of the Italian operatic repertoire.

Santini, Gabriele, Italian conductor; b. Perugia, Jan. 20, 1886; d. Rome, Nov. 13, 1964. After studies in Perugia and Bologna, he conducted opera in Rio de Janeiro, Buenos Aires, N.Y., and Chicago. From 1925 to 1929 he was Toscanini's assistant at La Scala in Milan; then was a conductor (1929–33) and artistic director (1944–47) at the Rome Opera.

Santoliquido, Francesco, Italian composer; b. San Giorgio a Cremano, Naples, Aug. 6, 1883; d. Anacapri, Aug. 26, 1971. He studied at the Liceo di Santa Cecilia in Rome; graduated in 1908; in 1912 he went to live in Hammamet, a village in Tunisia, spending part of each year in Rome; in 1933 he made his home in Anacapri. Many of his compositions contain melodic inflections of Arabian popular music. He publ. *Il Dopo-Wagner, Claudio Debussy e Richard Strauss* (Rome, 1909; 2nd ed., 1922); also books of verse; wrote short stories in Eng. His 3rd wife was the pianist and teacher Ornella (née Puliti) Santoliquido (b. Florence, Sept. 4, 1906; d. there, Nov. 11, 1977); she studied with Brugnoli; after receiving her diploma at the Florence Cons., she continued her training with Casella in Rome and Cortot in Paris; was a teacher at the Rome Cons. (1939–71); played in chamber-music concerts; became an advocate of contemporary music.

WORKS: DRAMATIC: OPERAS: *La Favola di Helga* (Milan, Nov. 23, 1910); *Ferhuda* (Tunis, Jan. 30, 1919); *L'Ignota* (1921; not perf.); *La porta verde*, musical tragedy (Bergamo, Oct. 15, 1953). **BALLET:** *La Bajadera dalla maschera gialla* (1917). **ORCH.:** *Crepuscolo sul mare* (Nuremberg, Jan. 19, 1909, composer conducting); *Acquarelli* (1914; Rome, April 11, 1923); *Il profumo delle oasi sahariane* (1915; Tunis, April 17, 1918); 2 syms. (1916; c.1927); *La sagra dei morti*, heroic elegy for the victims of World War I (1920); *Grotte di Capri* (1925; rev. 1943); *Preludio e Burlesca* for Strings (1938); *Alba di gloria sul passo Uarièu*, symphonic prelude (1939; Rome, Nov. 13, 1940); *Santuari asiatici*, symphonic sketches (1952). **CHAMBER:** Violin Sonata (1924); String Quartet (1931); *Aria antica* for Cello and Piano; *Chiarita lunare* for Violin and Piano; *2 pezzi* for 5 Wind Instruments. **PIANO:** *Piccola ballata*; *2 acquaforti tunisine.* **VOCAL:** Song cycle after P. Louÿs; *Messa facile* for Chorus.

Santoro, Claudio, distinguished Brazilian composer, conductor, and teacher; b. Manáos, Nov. 23, 1919; d. Brasília, March 27, 1989. He studied at the Rio de Janeiro Cons. and received training from Guerra and Koellreutter. In 1946 he held a Guggenheim fellowship. In 1947 he received a French scholarship and pursued his studies in Paris with Boulanger and Eugène Bigot. He was awarded the Lili Boulanger Prize in 1948. In 1965 he held a Ford Foundation scholarship and was active in Berlin. From 1970 to 1978 he taught at the Univ. of Heidelberg-Mannheim. In 1979 he settled in Brasília, where he was a conductor at the Univ. and of the orch. of the National Theater until his death. He also appeared as a guest conductor in South America and Europe. In his earliest works, he composed mainly in the 12-tone manner. After a period in which he wrote in an accessible style, he returned to advanced techniques, including aleatory.

WORKS: BALLETS: *A fábrica* (1947); *Anticocos* (1951); *O café* (1953); *Icamiabas* (1959); *Zuimaaluti* (1960); *Prelúdios* (1962). **ORCH.:** 14 syms.: No. 1 (1940), No. 2 (1945), No. 3 (Rio de Janeiro, Dec. 20, 1949), No. 4, *Da paz* (Rio de Janeiro, Oct. 30, 1945), No. 5 (Rio de Janeiro, March 28, 1956), No. 6 (Paris, May 1, 1963), No. 7, *Brasília* (1960), No. 8 (1963), No. 9 (1982), No. 10 (1982), No. 11 (1984), No. 12 (1985), No. 13 (1986), and No. 14 (1987); *Variations on a 12-tone Row* (1945); *Ponteio* for Strings (Rio de Janeiro, June 19, 1945); 2 violin concertos (1951, 1958); *Chôro* for Saxophone and Orch. (Rio de Janeiro, June 20, 1952); 3 piano concertos (1953, 1959, 1960); *Abertura tragica* (1958); Cello Concerto (1961; Washington, D.C., May 12, 1965); *Asymptotic Interactions* (1969). **CHAMBER:** 5 violin sonatas (1940–57); String Trio (1941); Flute Sonata (1941); 7 string quartets (1943–65); 4 cello sonatas (1943–63); Oboe Sonata (1943); Trumpet Sonata (1946); *Diagrammas cíclicos* for Piano and Percussion (1966); *Mutations I–VI* for Various Instruments (1968–72); *Antistruktur* for Harp and Cello (1970). **PIANO:** 25 preludes (1957–63). **VOCAL:** *Ode to Stalingrad* for Chorus and Orch. (1947); *Berlin, 13 de agôsto* for Narrator, Chorus, and Orch. (1962); *Agrupamento a 10* for Voice and Chamber Orch. (1966).

BIBL.: V. Mariz, *C. S.* (Rio de Janeiro, 1994).

Santos, (José Manuel) Joly Braga, Portuguese conductor and composer; b. Lisbon, May 14, 1924; d. there, July 18, 1988. He studied composition with Luis de Freitas Branco at the Lisbon Cons. (1934–43), conducting with Scherchen at the Venice Cons. (1948), electronic music at the Gavessano (Switzerland) Acoustic Experimental Studio (1957–58), and composition with Mortari at the Rome Cons. (1959–60). He conducted the Oporto Radio Sym. Orch. (1955–59); subsequently was active as a guest conductor. His music represents a felicitous fusion of Portuguese Renaissance modalities and folk rhythms.

WORKS: DRAMATIC: OPERAS: *Viver ou morrer* (To Live or to Die), radio opera (1952); *Mérope* (Lisbon, May 15, 1959); *Trilogia das Barcas* (1969; Lisbon, May, 1970). **BALLETS:** *Alfama* (1956); *A nau Catrineta* (1959); *Encruzilhada* (1968). **ORCH.:** 3 symphonic overtures (1945, 1947, 1954); 6 syms.: No. 1 (1946), No. 2 (1948), No. 3 (1949), No. 4 (1950), No. 5, *Virtus Lusitaniae* (1966), and No. 6 for Soprano, Chorus, and Orch. (1972); *Nocturno* for Strings (1947); Concerto for Strings (1951); *Variações sinfónicas sobre un theme de l'Alentejano* (1952); Viola Concerto (1960); *Divertimento* for Chamber Orch. (1961); *3 esboços sinfónicos* (3 Symphonic Sketches; 1962); *Sinfonietta* for Strings (1963); Double Concerto for Violin, Cello, String Orch., and Harp (1965); *Variações concertantes* for Harp and Strings (1967); Piano Concerto (1973); *Variações* (1976). **CHAMBER:** *Nocturno* for Violin and Piano (1942); 2 string quartets (1944, 1956); Violin Sonata (1945); Piano Quartet (1957). **VOCAL:** *Requiem à memória de Pedro de Freitas Branco* for Soloists, Chorus, and Orch. (1964); *Ode à música* for Chorus and Orch. (1965); choruses.

Sanzogno, Nino, Italian conductor and composer; b. Venice, April 13, 1911; d. Milan, May 4, 1983. He studied at the Venice Cons. (graduated, 1932), pursuing his training with Malipiero (composition) in Venice and Scherchen (conducting) in Brussels. He began his career as a violinist in the Guarneri Quartet. In 1937 he became conductor at the Teatro La Fenice in Venice, and he also conducted the Gruppo Strumentale Italiano (1938–39). In 1939 he made his first appearance at Milan's La

Scala, returning there as a conductor in subsequent years. In 1955 he conducted Cimarosa's *Il matrimonio segreto* at the first performance given at Milan's Piccola Scala. He took the company to the Edinburgh Festival in 1957. As a guest conductor, he appeared with principal Italian, European, and North and South American opera houses. In addition to his performances of works from the standard repertoire, he became particularly known for his advocacy of contemporary composers, among them Petrassi, Malipiero, Milhaud, Berio, Hartmann, and Poulenc. He composed a Viola Concerto (1935), a Cello Concerto (1937), symphonic poems and other orch. pieces, chamber music, and other works.

Sapelnikov, Vasili, Russian pianist and composer; b. Odessa, Nov. 2, 1867; d. San Remo, March 17, 1941. He was a pupil of L. Brassin and Sophie Menter at the St. Petersburg Cons.; in 1888, made his debut at Hamburg with Tchaikovsky's First Piano Concerto, under the composer's direction; then made tours throughout Europe; after living in Russia (1916–22), he settled in the West. He wrote an opera, *Der Khan und sein Sohn*, and piano pieces.

Saperton, David, American pianist and teacher; b. Pittsburgh, Oct. 29, 1889; d. Baltimore, July 5, 1970. He received his first instruction on the piano from his grandfather, a former tenor at the Brünn Opera, while his father, a physician and former concert bass, superintended his theoretical studies. At the age of 10, he made his first public appearance with an orch. in Pittsburgh; in 1905 he gave a recital in N.Y.; from 1910 to 1912 he toured Germany, Austria, Hungary, Italy, Russia, and Scandinavia. In 1924 he joined the piano faculty of the Curtis Inst. of Music in Philadelphia.

Sapp, Allen Dwight, Jr., American composer and pedagogue; b. Philadelphia, Dec. 10, 1922. He studied composition with Piston and Thompson and music history with Davison at Harvard Univ. (B.A., 1942), and then pursued private training in composition with Copland and Boulanger. Following military service during World War II, he returned to Harvard Univ. to complete his education (M.A., 1949). He was on the staff of Harvard Univ. (1948–58), and then taught at Wellesley College (1958–61). From 1961 to 1975 he was on the faculty of the Univ. of Buffalo (later the State Univ. of N.Y. at Buffalo). He was a faculty member at Florida State Univ. from 1975 to 1978. He served as dean (1978–80) and as prof. of composition (from 1978) at the Univ. of Cincinnati College-Cons. of Music. In his early compositions, Sapp wrote in a neo-Classical vein. From 1949 he experimented with serial techniques but within tonal frames of reference.

WORKS: ORCH.: *Andante* (1941; N.Y., April 18, 1942); Concertino for Piano and Chamber Orch. (1942); 2 suites: No. 1 (1949) and No. 2 (1952–56; Buffalo, Dec. 8, 1968); *The Double Image* (1957; Buffalo, May 28, 1967); *The Women of Trachis*, overture (Boston, Nov. 27, 1960); *June* for Wind Quintet and Strings (Boston, June 14, 1961); *Colloquies I* for Piano and Strings (1963; Buffalo, Feb. 23, 1964); *Imaginary Creatures: A Bestiary for the Credulous* for Harpsichord and Chamber Orch. (1981; Cincinnati, March 21, 1982); *Xenón Ciborium* (1982–85; Cincinnati, Oct. 11, 1986); *The Cheektowaga and Tonawanda Divisions* for Wind Orch. (1983; 1st complete perf., Cincinnati, March 7, 1984); *The 4 Winds* for Wind Orch. (1984; Boulder, Colo., Feb. 27, 1985); *Cincinnati Morality and Consolation* for Wind Orch. (1985; Cincinnati, May 21, 1986). **CHAMBER:** Cello Sonata (1941–42); 4 violin sonatas: No. 1 (1942–43; N.Y., June 21, 1945), No. 2 (1948), No. 3 (1960), and No. 4 (1981; Buffalo, Dec. 10, 1982); Viola Sonata (1948; rev. version, Cincinnati, Oct. 29, 1986); Piano Trio (1949); 4 string quartets (1951, 1981, 1981, 1981); *Chaconne* for Violin and Organ (1953); *6 Ricercare* for Viols (1956); String Trio (1957); *6 Variations on the Hymn Tune Durant* for Flute, Oboe, English Horn, and Bassoon (1960); *Variations on A solis ortus cardine* for Oboe, Horn, 2 Violins, Viola, Cello, and Contrabass (Buffalo, Dec. 9, 1962); *Irregular Polygon* for String Quartet (1973); *Nocturne* for Cello (1978); *Colloquies II* for Piano, Flute, and Viola (1978; rev. 1982), *III* for Piano and 10 Winds (1981; Cincinnati, April 25, 1982), *IV: The Lament of Adonis* for Cello and Piano (1984; Cincinnati, May 14, 1985), *V: The Cage of All Bright Knocks* for Alto Flute and Piano (Cincinnati, Nov. 14, 1986), and *VI: Socrates and Phaedrus Speak of Love by the Banks of the Ilissus* for Oboe and Piano (1988; Cincinnati, Jan. 10, 1990); *Taylor's 9* for Percussion Ensemble (Cincinnati, Oct. 9, 1981); *Sirius: Stella Canis; The Companion of Sirius: The Serious Companion* for Tuba and Piano (1984); *A Garland for Anna* for Violin (1984); *13 Anti-Strophes* for Cello and Piano (1985); *Romance* for Violin (1985); *Fantasia* for Violin and Piano (1986; Cincinnati, Feb. 20, 1987); *To Be Played Softly . . .* for Violin, Viola, and Cello (Cincinnati, June 13, 1987). **KEYBOARD: PIANO:** 10 sonatas (1941; 1954–56, rev. 1957; 1957; 1957; 1980; 1980; 1980; 1985, rev. 1986; 1989; 1989); 3 sonatas for Piano, 4-hands (1944, 1981, 1981); 2 sonatinas (1945, 1957); Suite (1949); *4 Dialogues* for 2 Pianos (1954–55); *7 Bagatelles* (1956); *4 Impromptus* (1957); *Up in the Sky* (1983–84); *Eaux-Fortes* for Piano Duet (1984); *Aquarelles* for Piano Duet (1984); *A Bestiary*, 25 preludes (1989). **ORGAN:** *Epithalamium* (1986). **VOCAL:** *The Marriage Song* for Chorus and Chamber Orch. (1948); *5 Landscapes* for Chorus (1950); *The Lady and the Lute* for Soprano and Piano (1952); *7 Epigrams (Both Sweet and Sour)* for Bass and Piano (1952; Cambridge, Mass., April 25, 1958); *The Little Boy Lost* for Chorus and Instrumental Ensemble (1953); *A Maiden's Complaint in Springtime* for Chorus, Winds, and Strings (1959–60; Wellesley, Mass., April 17, 1960); *7 Songs of Carew* for High Voice and Piano (1961, 1982; Cincinnati, April 24, 1985); *Canticum Novum Pro Pace* for Men's Chorus and Wind Quintet (1962; Buffalo, March 31, 1963); *Crennelations* for Tenor and Orch. (1982; Cincinnati, Feb. 26, 1983); *Moral Maxims: 30 Songs for 30 Years* for High Voice and Piano (1982; Cincinnati, May 5, 1987); *Illusions and Affirmations* for Bass and String Orch. (1982); *Affliction* for Mezzo-soprano and Piano (1983); *A Set of 12 Canons* for 2 Sopranos, Tenor, and Chamber Group (Cincinnati, Dec. 10, 1987); *Anoia* for Soprano, Flute, Clarinet, Violin, and Cello (Cincinnati, Feb. 13, 1988); *Dix chansons sphériques* for Soprano and Piano (Cincinnati, Oct. 28, 1989).

Sarabia, Guillermo, Mexican baritone; b. Mazatlán, Aug. 30, 1936; d. Amsterdam, Sept. 19, 1985. He studied with Herbert Graf, Ria Ginster, Dusolina Giannini, and Carl Ebert in Zürich at the Opera Studio and Cons. After making his operatic debut as Doktor Faust in Detmold (1965), he sang in various German opera houses. On May 5, 1973, he made his Metropolitan Opera debut in N.Y. as Amonasro. In 1976 he made his first appearance at the N.Y. City Opera as the Dutchman. His guest appearances took him to Vienna, Berlin, London, Paris, and Milan. He made his last appearance in the U.S. as Falstaff with Solti and the Chicago Sym. Orch. in 1985, shortly before his death. Among his other roles were Pizzaro, Rigoletto, Scarpia, and Wozzeck.

Saradzhev, Konstantin, Armenian conductor and pedagogue; b. Derbent, Oct. 8, 1877; d. Yerevan, July 22, 1954. He studied violin with Hřímalý at the Moscow Cons. (graduated, 1898). After further training with Ševčík in Prague (1900), he studied conducting with Nikisch in Leipzig (1904–08). He began his conducting career in Moscow, where he championed the cause of Soviet composers. From 1922 to 1935 he also was prof. of conducting at the Cons. He then settled in Yerevan, where he was artistic director of the Opera and Ballet Theater. He also was director of the Cons. (from 1939) and principal conductor of the Phil. (1941–44). In 1946 he was made a People's Artist of the Armenian S.S.R.

Sárai, Tibor, Hungarian composer and teacher; b. Budapest, May 10, 1919. He studied composition with Kadosa and violin with Sándor at the Franz Liszt Academy of Music in Budapest (diploma, 1942). In 1948 he became secretary general of the Union of Hungarian Musicians; after serving as head of the music dept. of the Hungarian Ministry of Culture (1949–50), he held that position with the Hungarian Radio (1950–53). From

1953 to 1959 he taught at the Béla Bartók Cons. in Budapest; then was a prof. at the Franz Liszt Academy of Music (1959–80). He was also secretary general of the Assn. of Hungarian Musicians (1959–78); likewise was vice-president (1975–77) and secretary general (1980–82) of the International Music Council of UNESCO. In 1959 he was awarded the Erkel Prize and in 1975 the Kossuth Prize. In 1988 he was made a Merited Artist by the Hungarian government. In his compositions, he adheres to the national Hungarian tradition, enhanced by a free use of euphonious dissonances.

WORKS: ORCH.: *Serenade* for Strings (1946); *Tavaszi concerto* (Spring Concerto) for Flute, Viola, Cello, and String Orch. (1955); *6 Scenes* from the dance play *János vitéz* (1956–57); 3 syms. (1965–67; 1972–73; 1987); *Musica* for 45 Strings (1970–71); *Epitaph in Memory of Ferenc Szabó* (1974); *Notturno* (1977–78); *Autumn Concerto* for Violin, Cello, Horn, Trumpet, and Orch. (1984). **CHAMBER:** 3 string quartets (1958; 1971; 1980–82); *Lassu es friss* for Violin and Piano (1958); Quartet for Flute, Violin, Viola, and Cello (1961–62); *Studio* for Flute and Piano (1964); Sonata for Solo Violin (1990); piano pieces. **VOCAL:** *Variations on a Theme of Peace*, oratorio for Soloists, Chorus, and Orch. (1961–64); *De profundis*, cantata for Tenor and Wind Quintet (1968); *Diagnosis '69* for Tenor and Orch. (1969); *Future Questioning* for Alto, Baritone, Men's Chorus, and Orch. (1971); *Christ or Barabbas* for Tenor, Baritone, Bass, Chorus, and Orch. (1976–77); *Scena* for Soprano and Bassoon (1980); songs.

Saraste, Jukka-Pekka, Finnish conductor; b. Helsinki, April 22, 1956. He studied violin and conducting at the Sibelius Academy in Helsinki, obtaining diplomas in both subjects in 1979; then made his debut as a conductor with the Helsinki Phil. in 1980. After winning the Nordic conducting competition in 1981, he appeared as a guest conductor throughout Scandinavia. In 1983 he made his first tour of the U.S. as co-conductor (with Okko Kamu) of the Helsinki Phil.; his British debut followed in 1984, when he appeared as a guest conductor of the London Sym. Orch. at a Promenade concert in London; he also made his German debut as a guest conductor with the Munich Phil. In 1985 he was named principal guest conductor of the Finnish Radio Sym. Orch. in Helsinki. He toured Australia in 1986. In 1987 he took the Finnish Radio Sym. Orch. to England, during which tour he conducted all the Sibelius syms. at the Brighton Festival; that same year, he was promoted to chief conductor of the orch. and became principal conductor of the Scottish Chamber Orch. in Glasgow. In 1994 he became music director of the Toronto Sym.

Sargeant, Winthrop, prominent American music critic; b. San Francisco, Dec. 10, 1903; d. Salisbury, Conn., Aug. 15, 1986. He studied violin in San Francisco with Arthur Argiewicz and with Lucien Capet in Paris; took composition lessons with Albert Elkus in San Francisco and with Carl Prohaska in Vienna. He played the violin in the San Francisco Sym. Orch. (1922–24), the N.Y. Sym. Orch. (1926–28), and the N.Y. Phil. (1928–30). He then devoted himself to musical journalism; was on the editorial staff of *Musical America* (1931–34); was music critic of the *Brooklyn Daily Eagle* (1934–36); served as music ed. of *Time* magazine (1937–39); also wrote essays on various subjects for *Time* (1939–45); subsequently was roving correspondent for *Life* magazine (1945–49) and music critic for the *New Yorker* (1947–72), continuing as a contributor to the latter until his death. He evolved a highly distinctive manner of writing: professionally solid, stylistically brilliant, and ideologically opinionated; he especially inveighed against the extreme practices of the cosmopolitan avant-garde. He publ. *Jazz: Hot and Hybrid* (N.Y., 1938; 3rd ed., N.Y., 1975); *Geniuses, Goddesses, and People* (N.Y., 1949); *Listening to Music* (N.Y., 1958); *In Spite of Myself: A Personal Memoir* (N.Y., 1970); *Divas: Impressions of Today's Sopranos* (N.Y., 1973).

Sargent, Sir (Harold) Malcolm (Watts), eminent English conductor; b. Stamford, Lincolnshire, April 29, 1895; d. London, Oct. 3, 1967. He studied organ at the Royal College of Organists in London; then was articled to Keeton, organist of Peterborough Cathedral (1912–14); subsequently served in the infantry during World War I. He made his first major conducting appearance on Feb. 3, 1921, in Leicester, leading the Queen's Hall Orch. of London in his own composition, *Allegro impetuoso: An Impression on a Windy Day.* He then went to London, where he conducted the D'Oyly Carte Opera Co. and Diaghilev's Ballets Russes; from 1928 he was conductor-in-chief of the Royal Choral Soc. From 1929 to 1940 he was conductor of the Courtauld-Sargent Concerts in London. He toured Australia in 1936, 1938, and 1939, and Palestine in 1937. He was conductor-in-chief and musical adviser of the Hallé Orch. of Manchester (1939–42); then was principal conductor of the Liverpool Phil. (1942–48). In 1945 he made his American debut with the NBC Sym. Orch. in N.Y.; then made appearances in Europe, Australia, and Japan. He was knighted in 1947. From 1950 to 1957 he was chief conductor of the BBC Sym. Orch. in London; led this ensemble on several European tours. From 1948 to 1966 he also served as chief conductor of the London Promenade Concerts. He took the London Phil. on an extensive Far Eastern tour in 1962; also led the Royal Phil. to the Soviet Union and the U.S. in 1963. His performances of the standard repertoire were distinguished for their precision and brilliance; he championed the music of Elgar, Vaughan Williams, Walton, and other English composers throughout his career. A commemorative stamp with his portrait was issued by the Post Office of Great Britain on Sept. 1, 1980.

BIBL.: C. Reid, *M. S.: A Biography* (London, 1968).

Sargon, Simon, Indian-born American pianist and composer; b. Bombay (of Sephardic, Russian-Jewish, and Indian descent), April 6, 1938. He took private piano lessons with Horszowski; studied theory at Brandeis Univ. (B.A., 1959) and composition with Persichetti at the Juilliard School of Music in N.Y. (M.S., 1962); also took a course with Milhaud at the Aspen (Colo.) School of Music. He was a teacher at Sarah Lawrence College in Bronxville, N.Y. (1965–68), at the Rubin Academy of Music in Jerusalem (1971–74), where he served as head of the voice dept., and at Hebrew Univ. in Jerusalem (1973–74). In 1974 he was appointed music director at Temple Emanu-El in Dallas.

WORKS: DRAMATIC: *Thirst*, chamber opera, after Eugene O'Neill (Jerusalem, Dec. 17, 1972); *A Voice Still and Small*, children's musical play (Dallas, Dec. 6, 1981); *Saul, King of Israel*, opera (1990). **ORCH.:** Sym., *Holocaust*, for Baritone, Men's Chorus, and Orch. (1985); *Questings*, horn concerto (1987). **VOCAL:** 3 cantatas: *Elul: Midnight* (Dallas, Sept. 17, 1976), *Flame of the Lord* (Dallas, May 31, 1977), and *Visions of Micah* (Dallas, April 30, 1980); *Not by Might*, oratorio, after the Books of the Maccabees (Dallas, Dec. 16, 1979); temple services; songs.

Sari, Ada (real name, **Jadwiga Szajerowa**), Polish soprano; b. Wadowice, near Kraków, June 29, 1886; d. Ciechocinek, July 12, 1968. She studied in Milan. After appearances in Rome, Naples, Trieste, and Parma, she joined the Warsaw Opera; made extensive tours in Europe, South America, and the U.S.; later taught voice in Warsaw.

Sárközy, István, Hungarian composer and teacher; b. Erzsébetfalva, Nov. 26, 1920. He was a student of Farkas and Szatmári, and of Kodály and Viski at the Budapest Academy of Music. From 1957 to 1960 he was ed.-in-chief for music with Editio Musica Budapest. In 1959 he became a teacher of theory at the Budapest Academy of Music.

WORKS: DRAMATIC: *Az új traktorállomás* (The New Tractor Station), ballet (1949); *Liliomfi*, musical play (1950); *Szelistyei asszonyok* (The Women of Szelistye), opera (1951); folk dance plays; incidental music. **ORCH.:** Concerto grosso (1943; rev. 1969 as *Ricordanze I*); *To Youth* (1953); Sinfonia concertante for Clarinet and 24 Strings (1963; also for Clarinet, 24 Strings, and 12 Winds, 1964); *Concerto semplice: Ricordanze II* for Violin and Orch. (1973); *Confessioni* for Piano and Orch. (1979). **CHAMBER:** *Sonata da camera* for Flute and Piano (1964); *Ciaccona* for Cello (1967); Chamber Sonata for Clarinet and Piano (1969);

Psaume et jeu, wind quartet (1970); *Ricordanze III*, string quartet (1977). **PIANO:** *12 Variations* (1945); Sonatina for 2 Pianos (1950). **VOCAL:** *A walesi bárdok* (The Bards of Wales) for Baritone and Orch. (1942–43); *Munkások* (Workers) for Bass and Orch. (1947); *Vörös Rébék* for Mezzo-soprano and Orch. (1947); *12 Balkan Folksongs* for Soprano and Chamber Orch. (1949); *Óda Sztálinhoz* (Ode to Stalin), cantata for Chorus and Orch. (1949); *Ifjúság*, suite for Chorus and Orch. (1952); *Júlia énekek* (Julia Songs), chamber cantata for Tenor, Chorus, and 4 Instruments (1958); *Reng már a föld . . .* (The Earthquake Approaches), cantata for Baritone, Chorus, and Orch. (1967); *Aki szegény . . .* (He Who is Poor) for Soprano, Chorus, and Orch. (1967); *Ypsilon háború* ("Y" War), comedy oratorio for 10 Solo Singers, Vocal Quintet, Flute, Clarinet, String Quintet, and Harpsichord (1971); choruses; solo songs.

Sarly, Henry, Belgian composer; b. Tirlemont, Dec. 28, 1883; d. Brussels, Dec. 3, 1954. He studied with his father and with Huberti, Tinel, Gilson, and Du Bois at the Brussels Cons.; in 1921 he became inspector of musical education in Belgian schools. He composed a number of attractive pieces, among them *Scènes brabançonnes* for Orch.; Piano Quintet; *Poème* for Piano Trio; Violin Sonata; numerous piano pieces and songs. He also publ. a manual, *Cours théorique et pratique d'harmonie.*

Sárosi, Bálint, Hungarian ethnomusicologist; b. Csikrákos, Jan. 1, 1925. He was educated in Csolszereda, and took a doctorate in Hungarian and Romanian philology in Budapest (1948); also received diplomas in musicology (1956) and composition (1958) at the Budapest Academy of Music, where his teachers included Kodály. He worked in Kodály's group for folk-music research at the Hungarian Academy of Sciences in 1958; in 1974 he became director of the folk-music dept. of the Academy's Inst. for Musicology. His fieldwork includes trips to Ethiopia (1965) and Armenia (1972); his most important research is in the field of instrumental folk music.

WRITINGS: *Die Volksmusikinstrumente Ungarns* (Leipzig, 1967); *Cigányzene* (Gypsy Music; Budapest, 1971; Eng. tr., 1978); *Zenei anyanyelvünk* (Our Own Musical Vernacular; Budapest, 1973).

Sartori, Claudio, eminent Italian music scholar and bibliographer; b. Brescia, April 1, 1913; d. Milan, March 11, 1994. He received an arts degree in 1934 from the Univ. of Pavia with a thesis in music history; then studied with Gerold at the Univ. of Strasbourg and with Vittadini at the Pavia Cons. He served as an assistant librarian at the Bologna Cons. (1938–42); in 1943 he was appointed prof. of Italian literature there; in 1967 he assumed a similar professorship at the Milan Cons. He founded and became director of the Ufficio Ricerche Musicali in 1965; its aim was to conduct a thorough codification of Italian musical sources, providing information on all MSS and publ. music in Italy before 1900, on all publ. librettos in Italy down to 1800, and on all literature on music in Italy. In addition to this invaluable compilation, he also served as ed.-in-chief of *Dizionario Ricordi della musica e dei musicisti* (Milan, 1959). In 1983 he was made a corresponding member of the American Musicological Soc.

WRITINGS: *Il R. Conservatorio di Musica G.B. Martini di Bologna* (Florence, 1942); *Bibliografia delle opere musicali stampate da Ottaviano Petrucci* (Florence, 1948; later continued as "Nuove conclusive aggiunte alla 'Bibliografia del Petrucci'," *Collectanea Historiae Musicae*, I, 1953); *Bibliografia della musica strumentale italiana stampata in Italia fino al 1700* (2 vols., Florence, 1952 and 1968); *Monteverdi* (Brescia, 1953); *Catalogo delle musiche della Cappella del Duomo di Milano* (Milan, 1957); *Riccardo Malipiero* (Milan, 1957); *Casa Ricordi 1808–1958* (Milan, 1958); *Dizionario degli editori musicali italiani* (Florence, 1958); *Giacomo Puccini a Monza* (Monza, 1958); *Puccini* (Milan, 1958); ed. *Puccini Symposium* (Milan, 1959); *Assisi: La Cappella della Basilica di S. Francesco: Catalogo del fondo musicale nella Biblioteca comunale di Assisi* (Milan, 1962); ed. *L'enciclopedia della musica* (Milan, 1963–64); *Commemorazione di Ottaviano de' Petrucci* (Fossombrone, 1966); *Giacomo Carissimi: Catalogo delle opere attribuite* (Milan, 1975); ed., with F. Lesure, *Bibliografia della musica italiana vocale profana pubblicata dal 1500 al 1700* (Geneva, 1978).

Sáry, László, Hungarian composer; b. Győr, Jan. 1, 1940. He studied at the Budapest Academy of Music with Szervánszky; after graduation in 1966, he helped to found the Budapest New Music Studio (1970). His works represent various contemporary trends, ranging from the music of Christian Wolff to the American minimalists.

WORKS: ORCH.: *Canzone solenne* (1970); *Immaginario No. 1* (1971); *Diana búcsúja* (Diana's Farewell) for Chamber Orch. (1976); *Music* for 24 Strings and 24 Winds: *Hommage à Szervánszky* (1977); *Párhuzamos mozgások* (Parallel Movements) for Chamber Orch. (1981); *In memoriam Igor Stravinsky* for 24 Wind Instruments (1981); *Hyperion sorsdala* (Hyperion's Song of Destiny) for 24 String Instruments (1985–86); *Tükörképek* (Mirror Images) for 24 Strings and 24 Winds (1986); *Polyphonie* for 18 Strings and 10 Winds (1986); *7 Movements* for Saxophone, Harp, Percussion, and 14 Strings (Budapest, Nov. 19, 1994). **CHAMBER ENSEMBLE:** *Polyrhythmia* for 100 Bells and 10 Players (1979); *Discussions* (1980); *Pentagram* for 5 Percussion Groups and Prepared Piano (1982); *Előjáték és hat miniatűr* (Prelude and Six Miniatures) for 5 Percussion Groups (1982); *Hölderlin tornya* (Hölderlin's Tower; 1985); *Az ismétlődő ötös* (Fives Repeated; 1985). **CHAMBER:** *Variazioni* for Clarinet and Piano (1965); *Catacoustics* for 2 Pianos (1967); *Pezzo concertato* for Flute and Piano (1967); *Fluttuazioni* for Violin and Piano (1967); *Incanto* for 5 Saxophones (1969); *Versetti* for Organ and Percussion (1970); *Sonanti No. 2* for Flute and Percussion (1970); *Image* for Clarinet, Cello, and Piano (1972); *Az ég virágai* (Flowers of Heaven) for 1 to 4 Pianos (1973); *Oda egy feketerigó halálára* (Ode on the Death of a Blackbird) for Brass Quintet (1982); *Egy akkordsor forgatókönyve* (Scenario of a Series of Chords) for Piano(s) and Flute(s) (1982); *Kettős végtelen* (Double Infinity) for 2 Cimbaloms (1986); String Quartet in 4 Movements with Piano in the 4th movement (1986); *In All Eternity* for String Quartet (1986); *Az elhagyott kert éneke* (Song of the Deserted Garden) for String Quartet and Alto Flute (1986); *és a Nap?* (and the Sun?) for String Quartet (1986); *Variations* for String Quartet (1986–88); also works for Solo Instruments; pieces for Unspecified Instruments. **VOCAL:** *Lamento* for 5 Voices (1965); *Három madrigál* (3 Madrigals) for 5 Voices or Chamber Chorus (1966); *Quartetto* for Soprano, Flute, Violin, and Cimbalom (1968); *Incanto* for 5 Voices (1969); Cantata No. 1 for Soprano, Chamber Chorus, and Instrumental Ensemble (1969); *Hommage aux ancêtres* for 6 Voices, 3 Trumpets, and 3 Trombones (1970); *Psalmus* for Soprano and Melody Instrument (1972); *In sol* for 4-part Vocal Ensemble (1975); *Lied in lyd* for Alto, Bass, and Chamber Chorus (1975); *Hangok fehérben* (Voices in White) for Chamber Chorus (1975); *Variációk 14 hang fölött* (Variations on 14 Pitches) for Soprano and Piano (1975); *Dob és tánc* (Drum and Dance) for 24-part Women's Chorus (1975); *A hangzók változásai* (Mutations of the Sounds of Speech) for Soli, Chorus, and Strings (1979); *Socrates utolsó tanítása* (Socrates's Last Teaching) for Soprano and Piano (1980); *Imitatio homophona* for Soprano and 3 Identical Instruments (1982); *Hold-ének* (Moon-Song) for Soprano, Bass, and Chorus (1982); *Kánon a felkelő naphoz* (Canon to the Rising Sun) for 4- or 6-part Chorus of Equal Voices or Instrumental Ensemble (1982); *Magnificat* for Soprano and Melody Instrument (1982; rev. 1986). **OTHER:** Collaborative works, including *Hommage à Dohnányi* for Chamber Ensemble (1979; with Z. Jeney, B. Dukay, and L. Vidovszky).

Sás (Orchassal), Andrés, French-born Peruvian composer; b. Paris, April 6, 1900; d. Lima, July 25, 1967. He went to Brussels, where he studied harmony at the Anderlecht Academy, violin with Marchot, chamber music with Miry, and music history with Closson at the Cons., and counterpoint and fugue privately with Imbert. In 1924 he was engaged by the Peruvian government to teach violin at the National Academy of Music in Lima;

in 1928 he returned temporarily to Belgium; the following year, he settled in Lima permanently. He married the Peruvian pianist Lily Rosay, and with her established the Sás-Rosay Academy of Music. He became profoundly interested in Peruvian folk music, and collected folk melodies; made use of many of them in his own compositions.

WORKS: DRAMATIC: BALLETS: *La señora del pueblo* (Viña del Mar, Chile, Jan. 20, 1946); *El hijo pródigo* (1948). **INCIDENTAL MUSIC TO:** Molière's *Le Malade imaginaire* (1943). **ORCH.:** *Canción india* (1927); *3 estampas del Perú* (1936); *Poema indio* (1941); *Sueño de Zamba* (1943); *Danza gitana* (1944); *La patrona del pueblo* (1945); *La parihuana* (1946); *Las seis edades de la Tía Conchita* (1947); *La leyenda de la Isla de San Lorenzo* (1949); *Fantasía romántica* for Trumpet and Orch. (1950). **CHAMBER:** *Recuerdos* for Violin and Piano (also for Orch.; 1927); *Rapsodia peruana* for Violin and Piano (also for Orch.; 1928); *Sonata-Fantasia* for Flute and Piano (1934); String Quartet (1938); *Cantos del Peru* for Violin and Piano (1941). **PIANO:** *Aires y Danzas del Peru* (2 albums, 1930 and 1945); *Suite peruana* (1931); *Himno y Danza* (1935); *Sonatina peruana* (1946). **VOCAL:** Numerous choruses and songs.

Sass, Sylvia, Hungarian soprano; b. Budapest, July 21, 1951. She was a student of Olga Revghegyi at the Budapest Academy of Music; later in her career she received some lessons from Callas. In 1971 she made her operatic debut as Frasquita at the Hungarian State Opera in Budapest, where she subsequently sang many major roles. In 1972 she appeared as Violetta at the Bulgarian State Opera in Sofia. She made her first appearance at the Hamburg State Opera as Fiodiligi in 1975, the same year she made her debut at Glasgow's Scottish Opera as Desdemona. In 1976 she sang Giselda at her debut at London's Covent Garden and appeared as Violetta in Aix-en-Provence. On March 12, 1977, she made her Metropolitan Opera debut in N.Y. as Tosca. In 1979 she appeared in recital at London's Wigmore Hall. In subsequent years, she sang in opera and concert in many major music centers. Among her other operatic roles were Donna Elvira, Countess Almaviva, Donna Anna, Lady Macbeth, Turandot, Salome, and Bartók's Judith. Her concert repertoire extended from Bach to Messiaen.

Sassoli, Ada, Italian harpist and teacher; b. Bologna, Sept. 25, 1886; d. Rome, Dec. 3, 1946. She studied at the Bologna Cons.; then entered the class of A. Hasselmans at the Paris Cons., winning the premier prix for harp playing in 1902. She toured with Melba in England and Australia (1904–05); made several tours of the U.S.; later was prof. of harp at the Santa Cecilia Cons. in Rome.

Satie, Erik (Alfred-Leslie), celebrated French composer who elevated his eccentricities and verbal virtuosity to the plane of high art; b. Honfleur, May 17, 1866; d. Paris, July 1, 1925. He received his early musical training from a local organist, Vinot, who was a pupil of Niedermeyer; at 13 he went to Paris, where his father was a music publisher, and received instruction in harmony from Taudou and in piano from Mathias; however, his attendance at the Cons. was only sporadic between 1879 and 1886. He played in various cabarets in Montmartre; in 1884 he publ. a piano piece which he numbered, with malice aforethought, op. 62. His whimsical ways and Bohemian manner of life attracted many artists and musicians; he met Debussy in 1891; joined the Rosicrucian Society in Paris in 1892 and began to produce short piano pieces with eccentric titles intended to ridicule modernistic fancies and Classical pedantries alike. Debussy thought highly enough of him to orchestrate 2 numbers from his piano suite *Gymnopédies* (1888). Satie was almost 40 when he decided to pursue serious studies at the Paris Schola Cantorum, taking courses in counterpoint, fugue, and orchestration with d'Indy and Roussel (1905–8). In 1898 he had moved to Arcueil, a suburb of Paris; there he held court for poets, singers, dancers, and musicians, among whom he had ardent admirers. Milhaud, Sauguet, and Désormière organized a group, which they called only half-facetiously "École d'Arcueil," in honor of Satie as master and leader. But Satie's eccentricities were not merely those of a Parisian poseur; rather, they were adjuncts to his aesthetic creed, which he enunciated with boldness and total disregard for professional amenities (he was once brought to court for sending an insulting letter to a music critic). Interestingly enough, he attacked modernistic aberrations just as assiduously as reactionary pedantry, publishing "manifestos" in prose and poetry. Although he was dismissed by most serious musicians as an uneducated person who tried to conceal his ignorance of music with persiflage, he exercised a profound influence on the young French composers of the first quarter of the 20th century; moreover, his stature as an innovator in the modern idiom grew after his death, so that the avant-garde musicians of the later day accepted him as inspiration for their own experiments; thus "space music" could be traced back to Satie's *musique d'ameublement*, in which players were stationed at different parts of a hall playing different pieces in different tempi. The instruction in his piano piece *Vexations*, to play it 840 times in succession, was carried out literally in N.Y. on Sept. 9, 1963, by a group of 5 pianists working in relays overnight, thus setting a world's record for duration of any musical composition. When critics accused Satie of having no idea of form, he publ. *Trois Morceaux en forme de poire*, the eponymous pear being reproduced in color on the cover; other pieces bore self-contradictory titles, such as *Heures séculaires et instantanées* and *Crépuscule matinal de midi*; other titles were *Pièces froides, Embryons desséchés, Prélude en tapisserie, Préludes flasques (pour un chien), Descriptions automatiques*, etc. In his ballets, he introduced jazz for the first time in Paris; at the performance of his ballet *Relâche* (Nov. 29, 1924), the curtain bore the legend "Erik Satie is the greatest musician in the world; whoever disagrees with this notion will please leave the hall." He publ. a facetious autobiographical notice as *Mémoires d'un amnésique* (1912); N. Wilkins tr. and ed. *The Writings of Erik Satie* (London, 1980).

WORKS: DRAMATIC: *Geneviève de Brabant*, marionette opera (1899); *Le Piège de Méduse*, lyric comedy (1913); *Parade*, ballet (Paris, May 18, 1917); *Mercure*, ballet (Paris, June 15, 1924); *Relâche*, ballet (Paris, Nov. 29, 1924). Also incidental music to *Le Fils des étoiles* (1891; prelude reorchestrated by Ravel, 1913), *Le Prince de Byzance* (1891), *Le Nazaréen* (1892), *La Porte heroïque du ciel* (1893), and *Pousse l'Amour* (1905). **ORCH.:** *Jack in the Box* (1900; orchestrated by Milhaud, 1920); *En habit de cheval* (1911); *Cinq Grimaces* (1914); *Trois petites pièces montées* (1919; also for Piano, 4-hands, 1920); *La belle excentrique* (1920). **CHAMBER:** *Choses vues à droite et à gauche (sans lunettes)* for Violin and Piano (1914). **PIANO:** 3 Sarabandes (1887–88; orchestrated by Caby); *Trois Gymnopédies* (1888; Nos. 1 and 3 orchestrated by Debussy, 1896; No. 2 orchestrated by H. Murrill and by Roland–Manuel); *Trois Gnossiennes* (1890; orchestrated by Lanchbery; No. 3 orchestrated by Poulenc, 1939); *Trois Préludes* from *Le Fils des étoiles* (1891; orchestrated by Roland-Manuel); *9 Danses gothiques* (1893); *Quatre Préludes* (1893; Nos. 1 and 3 orchestrated by Poulenc, 1939); *Prélude de la Porte héroïque du ciel* (1894; orchestrated by Roland-Manuel, 1912); *2 Pièces froides* (1897); *Valse, Je te veux* (c.1900; arranged for Violin and Orch.; also arranged for Orch. by C. Lambert); *3 Nouvelles Pièces froides* (n.d.); *Le Poisson rêveur* (1901; arranged for Piano and Orch. by Caby); *Trois Morceaux en forme de poire* for Piano, 4-hands (1903; orchestrated by Désormière); *Douze Petits Chorals* (c.1906); *Passacaille* (1906); *Prélude en tapisserie* (1906); *Aperçus désagréables* for Piano, 4-hands (1908–12); *Deux Rêveries nocturnes* (1910–11); *En habit de cheval* for Piano, 4-hands (1911); *Trois Véritables Préludes flasques (pour un chien)* (1912); *3 Descriptions automatiques* (1913); *3 Embryons desséchés* (1913); *3 Croquis et agaceries d'un gros bonhomme en bois* (1913); *3 Chapitres tournés en tous sens* (1913); *3 Vieux Séquins et vieilles cuirasses* (1913); *Enfantines* (1913); *6 Pièces de la période 1906–13; 21 Sports et divertissements* (1914); *Heures séculaires et instantanées* (1914); *Trois Valses du precieux degoûté* (1914; orchestrated by Greenbaum); *Avant-*

dernières pensées (1915); *Parade*, suite for Piano, 4-hands, after the ballet (1917); *Sonatine bureaucratique* (1917); *5 Nocturnes* (1919); *Premier Menuet* (1920). **VOCAL:** *Trois Mélodies de 1886* for Voice and Piano (1886); *Messe des Pauvres* for Chorus and Organ or Piano (1895; orchestrated by D. Diamond, 1960); *Trois Poèmes d'amour* for Voice and Piano (1914); *Trois Mélodies* for Voice and Piano (1916); *Socrate* for 4 Sopranos and Chamber Orch. (1918; Paris, Feb. 14, 1920); *Ludions*, 5 songs for Voice and Piano (1923).

BIBL.: C. van Vechten, "E. S.," Interpreters and Interpretations (N.Y., 1917); R. Chennevière, "E. S. and the Music of Irony," *Musical Quarterly* (Oct. 1919); W. Roberts, "The Problem of S.," *Music & Letters* (Oct. 1923); 2 special issues of the *Revue Musicale* (March 1924; June 1925); W. Dankert, "Der Klassizismus E. S.s und seine geistesgeschichtliche Stellung," *Zeitschrift für Musikwissenschaft* (Nov. 1929); P.-D. Templier, *E. S.* (Paris, 1932); D. Milhaud, "Notes sur E. S.," *Les Oeuvres nouvelles* (vol. 6, N.Y., 1946); R. Myers, *E. S.* (London, 1948); A. Rey, *E. S.* (Paris, 1974); G. Wehmeyer, *E. S.* (Berlin, 1974); M. Brendel, *E. S.* (1982); V. Lajoinie, *E. S.* (Lausanne, 1985); J.-J. Barbier, *Au piano avec E. S.* (Paris, 1986); M. Rosenthal, *S., Ravel, Poulenc: An Intimate Memoir* (Madras and N.Y., 1987); A. Gillmor, *E. S.* (Boston, 1988); R. Orledge, *S. the Composer* (Cambridge, 1990); N. Perloff, *Art and the Everyday: Popular Entertainment and the Circle of E. S.* (Oxford, 1991); O. Volta, *S. et la danse* (Paris, 1992); G. Wehmeyer, *E. S.: Bilder und Dokumente* (Munich, 1992); R. Orledge, *S. Remembered* (Portland, Oreg., 1995).

Satoh, Sômei, Japanese composer; b. Sendai, Jan. 19, 1947. Born into a musical family, he was self-educated in composition. In the late 1960s he began experimenting in music, producing multimedia scores. In 1983–84 he lived in N.Y. on a Rockefeller Foundation scholarship. His music, ethereally static and subtley metered in the non-Western tradition, seeks to reproduce the inner voices of elements and beings.

WORKS: *Litania* for 1 or 2 Pianos and Tape or Digital Delay (1973); *Hymn for the Sun* for 2 Pianos and Digital Delay (1975); *Cosmic Womb* for 1 or 2 Pianos and Tape or Digital Delay (1975); *Incarnation I* for Piano, Marimba, and Harp (1977) and *II* for Piano and Digital Delay (1978); *The Heavenly Spheres Are Illuminated by Light* for Soprano, Piano, and Percussion (1979); *Birds in Warped Time I* for Shakuhachi, Sangen, and 20-String Koto (1980) and *II* for Violin and Piano (1980); *Lyra* for 2 Harps, Percussion, and Strings (1980); *Sumeru I* for Percussion and Strings (1982) and *II* for Tubular Bells, Piano, and Strings (1985); *A Journey Through Sacred Time* for Shō, 2 Harps, Percussion, and Strings (1983); *Naohi* for Piano (1983); *Hikari* (Light) for Trumpet and Piano (1986); *Shirasagi* (A White Heron) for String Quartet (1987); *Stabat Mater*, operatic oratorio for Soprano and Chorus (1987); *Uzu* (Vortex) for Flute, Clarinet, Piano, Harp, and Percussion (1988); *Toki No Mon* (A Gate into Infinity) for Violin, Piano, and Percussion (1988); *Homa* for Soprano and String Quartet or String Orch. (1988); *Ruika* (Miserere) for Cello and String Orch. (1990); *Toward the Night* for String Quartet or String Orch. (1991); *Kami No Miuri* (Gods Sells His Own Body) for Mezzo-soprano and 7 Instruments (1991); *Recitative* for Accordion (1991); *Burning Meditation* for Baritone, Harp, Tubular Bells, and String Quartet (1993; rev. version, N.Y., Dec. 19, 1995); *Lanzarote* for Soprano Saxophone and Piano (1993); pieces for Japanese instrumental ensembles; tape music.

Satz, Ilya, Russian composer; b. Chernobyl, Kiev Oblast, April 30, 1875; d. Moscow, Dec. 24, 1912. He studied cello in Kiev; then took lessons in composition with Taneyev in Moscow. He traveled in Europe in 1900; then made a tour as a cellist through Siberia. He returned to Moscow in 1903; in 1905 he became music director of the Studio of the Moscow Art Theater, and wrote incidental music for new plays, including Maeterlinck's *Blue Bird* and Andreyev's *A Man's Life*; also composed ballet music for Salome's dance; the ballet *The Goat-Footed (The Dance of the Satyrs)* was reorchestrated and prepared for performance by Glière. Satz had a talent for the grotesque; a lack of technique prevented his development into a major composer. A memorial vol., *Ilya Satz*, with articles by Glière and several members of the Moscow Art Theater, was publ. in Moscow in 1923.

Sauer, Emil (Georg Konrad) von, eminent German pianist and pedagogue; b. Hamburg, Oct. 8, 1862; d. Vienna, April 27, 1942. He studied with Nikolai Rubinstein in Moscow (1879–81), and Liszt in Weimar (1884–85). He made numerous European tours; played in the U.S. in 1898–99 and 1908. From 1901 to 1907, and again from 1915, he was a prof. at the Meisterschule für Klavierspiel in Vienna; from 1908 to 1915 he lived in Dresden; he appeared in concerts until 1936, and then retired to Vienna. He was ennobled for his services to music. He wrote 2 piano concertos, 2 piano sonatas, and many studies for piano; ed. the complete works of Brahms and pedagogical works of Pischna, Plaidy, Kullak, and others. He publ. an autobiography, *Meine Welt* (Stuttgart, 1901).

Sauguet, Henri (real name, **Jean Pierre Poupard**), French composer; b. Bordeaux, May 18, 1901; d. Paris, June 22, 1989. He assumed his mother's maiden name as his own. He was a pupil of Vaubourgois in Bordeaux and of Canteloube in Montauban. In 1922 he went to Paris, where he studied with Koechlin; became associated with Satie, and formed a group designated as the École d'Arcueil (from the locality near Paris where Satie lived). In conformity with the principles of utilitarian music, he wrote sophisticated works in an outwardly simple manner; his first conspicuous success was the production of his ballet *La Chatte* by Diaghilev in 1927. He was elected a member of the Académie des Beaux Arts in 1976. He was the author of *La Musique, ma vie* (Paris, 1990).

WORKS: DRAMATIC: OPERAS: *Le Plumet du colonel* (Paris, April 24, 1924); *La Chartreuse de Parme* (1927–36; Paris, March 16, 1939; rev. 1968); *La Contrebasse* (1930; Paris, 1932); *La Gageure imprévue* (1942; Paris, July 4, 1944); *Les Caprices de Marianne* (Aix-en-Provence, July 20, 1954); *Le Pain des autres* (1967–74); *Boule de suif* (Lyons, 1978); *Tistou les pouces verts* (Paris, 1980). **BALLETS:** *La Chatte* (Monte Carlo, April 30, 1927); *Paul et Virginie* (Paris, April 15, 1943); *Les Mirages* (Paris, Dec. 15, 1947); *Cordelia* (Paris, May 7, 1952); *L'As de coeur* (1960); *Paris* (1964); *L'Imposteur ou Le Prince et le mendiant* (1965). **ORCH.:** 3 piano concertos (1934; 1948; 1961–63); 4 syms.: No. 1, *Expiatoire*, in memory of innocent war victims (1945; Paris, Feb. 8, 1948), No. 2, *Allégorique* (1949), No. 3, *INR* (1955), and No. 4, *Du troisième âge* (1971); *Orphée* for Violin and Orch. (Aix-en-Provence, July 26, 1953); *Mélodie concertante* for Cello and Orch. (1963); *The Garden Concerto* for Harmonica and Orch. (1970); *Reflets sur feuilles* for Harp, Piano, Percussion, and Orch. (1979). **CHAMBER:** 3 string quartets (1926, 1948, 1979); *Divertissement de chambre* for Flute, Clarinet, Viola, Cello, and Piano (1931); Suite for Clarinet and Piano (1935); *Golden Suite* for Brass (1963); *Sonatine bucolique* for Alto Saxophone and Piano (1964); *Sonatine aux bois* for Oboe and Piano (1971); *Oraisons* for Organ and 4 Saxophones (1976); *Alentours saxophoniques* for Alto Saxophone, Winds, and Piano (1976); *Ne moriatur in aeternum* "in memoriam André Jolivet" for Trumpet and Organ (1979); *Sonate d'église* for Organ and String Quintet (1985); *Musique pour Cendrars* for Piano and String Quintet (1986); piano pieces. **VOCAL:** *La Voyante*, cantata for Woman's Voice and 11 Instruments (1932); *Petite Messe pastorale* for 2 Voices and Organ (1934); *Le Cornette*, ballade for Bass and Orch. (1951); *Plus loin que la nuit et le jour*, cantata for Chorus (1960); *L'oiseau a vu tout cela*, cantata for Baritone and String Orch. (1960); *Chant pour une ville meurtrie*, oratorio (1967); *Messe jubilatoire* for Tenor, Bass, and String Quartet (1983); songs.

BIBL.: M. Schneider, *H. S.* (Paris, 1959); F.-Y. Bril, *H. S.* (Paris, 1967); D. Austin, *H. S.: A Bio-Bibliography* (N.Y., 1991).

Saunders, Arlene, American soprano and teacher; b. Cleveland, Oct. 5, 1935. She studied at Baldwin-Wallace College and in N.Y. She made her operatic debut as Rosalinde with the

National Opera Co. in 1958; won the Vercelli Vocal Competition and made her European debut as Mimi at Milan's Teatro Nuovo in 1961; that same year, she appeared as Giorgetta in *Il tabarro* at the N.Y. City Opera. In 1964 she joined the Hamburg State Opera, where she subsequently sang regularly and was made a Kammersängerin in 1967; also appeared as Pamina at the Glyndebourne Festival (1966), as Louise at the San Francisco Opera (1967), as the creator of the title role in Ginastera's *Beatrice Cenci* at the Opera Soc. in Washington, D.C. (Sept. 10, 1971), as Eva in her Metropolitan Opera debut in N.Y. (April 2, 1976), and as Minnie at London's Covent Garden (1980); in 1985 she made her farewell appearance in opera as the Marschallin at the Teatro Colón in Buenos Aires. She taught at Rutgers, the State Univ. of New Jersey (from 1987), and at the Abraham Goodman School in N.Y. (from 1987). Among her other roles were Sieglinde, Nedda, Desdemona, Tosca, and Santuzza.

Saunders, Russell, eminent American organ pedagogue; b. Montezuma, Iowa, Oct. 24, 1921; d. Rochester, N.Y., Dec. 6, 1992. He was a student of Frank Jordan at Drake Univ., where he received the degrees of B.Mus.Ed. (1948), M.M. in organ (1949), and an honorary D.Mus. (1977); also studied organ with Arthur Foister at Syracuse Univ. and on a Fulbright grant in Germany with Helmut Walcha (1953–54). From 1948 to 1967 he taught organ and church music at Drake Univ., and then at the Eastman School of Music in Rochester, N.Y., from 1967 until his death. Early in his Eastman years, Saunders gave up public performance and devoted himself to the study of historical performance practices; became an acknowledged authority and appeared frequently as a lecturer and master teacher at workshops and conferences.

BIBL.: K. Snyder, ed., *The Organist as Scholar: Essays in Memory of R. S.* (Stuyvesant, N.Y., 1994).

Savage, Henry W(ilson), American impresario; b. New Durham, N.H., March 21, 1859; d. Boston, Nov. 29, 1927. He started in business as a real estate operator in Boston, where he took control of the Castle Square Opera House by default in 1894; founded his own company there to present opera in English in 1895, and subsequently gave performances in Chicago, N.Y., and other cities; with Maurice Grau, he produced opera in English at the Metropolitan Opera in N.Y. (1900). His Henry Savage Grand Opera Co. toured throughout the U.S. with an English-language production of *Parsifal* in 1904–05; subsequently made successful tours with Puccini's *Madama Butterfly* (1906) and *La fanciulla del West* (1911), and Lehár's *Die lustige Witwe* (1907).

Savín, Francisco, Mexican conductor and composer; b. Mexico City, Nov. 18, 1929. He studied piano in Mexico City with José Velásquez (1944–53) and took conducting lessons with Scherchen and composition with Rodolfo Halffter (1955–56); continued his studies at the Prague Academy of Music, and also had composition lessons with Janeček (1957–59). He was an assistant conductor of the Mexican National Sym. Orch. (1959–62) and principal conductor of the Xalapa Sym. Orch. (1963–67); was then director of the National Cons. of Music in Mexico City (1967–70); led conducting workshops there (from 1973).

WORKS: ORCH.: *Metamorfosis* (1962); *Concreción* for Electronic Organ and Orch. (1969). **CHAMBER:** *2 formas plásticas* for Wind Quintet (1964, 1965); *Quasar 1* for Electronic Organ, Tape, and Percussion (1970). **VOCAL:** *Quetzalcoátl,* symphonic poem for 2 Narrators and Orch. (1957); *3 líricas* for Mezzo-soprano, Flute, Clarinet, Viola, Percussion, and Piano (1966); *Monología de las Delicias* for 4 Women's Voices and Orch. (1969).

Savine, Alexander, Serbian-American conductor, teacher, and composer; b. Belgrade, April 26, 1881; d. Chicago, Jan. 19, 1949. He studied in Belgrade with S. Mokranjac, and later studied voice at the Vienna Cons. with Pauline Lucca. He was an opera conductor in Berlin (1905–07); taught voice at the Musical Academy in Winnepeg, Canada (1908–12); settled in the U.S.; was director of the opera dept. at the Inst. of Musical Art in N.Y. (1922–24); in 1929 he moved to Chicago. In 1914 he married **Lillian Blauvelt**. He wrote the opera *Xenia* (Zürich, May 29, 1919); 4 symphonic poems; choruses; songs.

Sawallisch, Wolfgang, eminent German conductor; b. Munich, Aug. 26, 1923. He began piano study when he was 5; later pursued private musical training with Ruoff, Haas, and Sachse in Munich before entering military service during World War II (1942); then completed his musical studies at the Munich Hochschule für Musik. In 1947 he became répétiteur at the Augsburg Opera, making his conducting debut there in 1950; then was Generalmusikdirektor of the opera houses in Aachen (1953–58), Wiesbaden (1958–60), and Cologne (1960–63); also conducted at the Bayreuth Festivals (1957–61). From 1960 to 1970 he was chief conductor of the Vienna Sym. Orch.; made his first appearance in the U.S. with that ensemble in 1964; also was Generalmusikdirektor of the Hamburg State Phil. (1961–73). From 1970 to 1980 he was chief conductor of the Orchestre de la Suisse Romande in Geneva; from 1971, also served as Generalmusikdirektor of the Bavarian State Opera in Munich, where he was named Staatsoperndirektor in 1982. In 1990 he was named music director of the Philadelphia Orch., which position he assumed in 1993. That same year, he took it on an acclaimed tour of China. He appeared as a guest conductor with a number of the world's major orchs. and opera houses. A distinguished representative of the revered Austro-German tradition, he has earned great respect for his unostentatious performances; he has also made appearances as a sensitive piano accompanist to leading singers of the day. His autobiography appeared as *Im Interesse der Deutlichkeit: Mein Leben mit der Musik* (Hamburg, 1988). He also publ. *Kontrapunkt—Herausforderung Musik* (Hamburg, 1993).

BIBL.: H. Krellmann, ed., *Stationen eines Dirigenten, W. S.* (Munich, 1983).

Saxton, Robert (Louis Alfred), English composer and teacher; b. London, Oct. 8, 1953. He was a student of Elisabeth Lutyens (1970–74), of Robin Holloway at St. Catherine's College, Cambridge (1972–75; B.A.), of Robert Sherlaw Johnson at Worcester College, Oxford (1975–76; B.Mus.), and of Luciano Berio (1976–77). In 1979 he became a teacher at the Guildhall School of Music in London, where he headed its composition dept. from 1990. His music reveals fine craftsmanship and harmonic invention.

WORKS: OPERA: *Caritas* (1990–91; Huddersfield, Nov. 1991). **ORCH.:** *Reflections of Narziss and Goldmund* (1975); *Choruses to Apollo* (1980); *Traumstadt* (1980); *The Ring of Eternity* (1982–83; London, Aug. 24, 1983); *Concerto for Orchestra* (London, Aug. 13, 1984); *The Circles of Light* (1985–86); Viola Concerto (Cheltenham, July 9, 1986); *Variation on "Sumer is icumen in"* (1987); *In the Beginning* (1987; London, Jan. 30, 1988); *Birthday Music for Sir William Glock* for Small Orch. (1988; London, Feb. 13, 1989); *Elijah's Violin* (1988; London, Feb. 13, 1989); *Music to Celebrate the Resurrection of Christ* (1988; BBC–TV, March 26, 1989); Violin Concerto (1989; Leeds, June 29, 1990); *Psalm: A Song of Ascents* for Trumpet and Orch. (1992; London, Jan. 23, 1993); Cello Concerto (1992–93; London, March 18, 1993); Sym. for Soprano, Baritone, and Orch. (1993–95). **CHAMBER:** *Krystallen* for Flute and Piano (1973); *Echoes of the Glass Bead Game* for Wind Quintet (1975); *Poems for Mélisande* for Flute and Piano (1977); *Arias* for Oboe and Piano (1977); *Study for a Sonata* for Flute, Oboe, Cello, and Harpsichord (1977); *Toccata* for Cello (1978); *Canzona in memoriam Igor Stravinsky* for Flute, Oboe, Clarinet, Horn, Harp, and String Trio (1978); *Processions and Dances* for Flute, Oboe, Piano, Harp, and String Trio (1981); *Piccola musica per Luigi Dallapiccola* for Flute, Oboe, Viola, Cello, and Piano or Celesta (1981); *Chiaroscuro* for Percussion (1981); *Fantasiestück* for Accordion (1982); *The Sentinel of the Rainbow* for Flute, Clarinet, Piano, Violin, and Cello (London, Oct. 24, 1984); *Night Dance* for Guitar (1986); Fanfare for Brass and Percussion (1987); *Paraphrase on Mozart's Idomeneo* for Wind Octet

(1990–91; Glyndebourne, June 15, 1991); *Invocation, Dance and Meditation* for Viola and Piano (Litchfield, July 5, 1991); *Fantasia* for String Quartet (1994); Piano Quintet (1994–95). **PIANO:** *Ritornelli and Intermezzi* (1972); *2 Pieces* (1976); *Sonatas* for 2 Pianos (1977); *Sonata: In Memory of Bêla Bartók* (1981); *Chacony* for Piano, Left-hand (1988). **VOCAL:** *La Promenade d'Automne* for Soprano, Flute, Clarinet, Percussion, Piano, and String Trio (1972); *Where Are You Going To, My Pretty Maid?* for Soprano, Flute, Clarinet, Harp, Guitar, Violin, and Cello (1973); *What Does the Song Hope For?* for Soprano, Flute, Oboe, Clarinet, Piano, String Trio, and Tape (1974); *Brise Marine* for Soprano, Piano, and Tape (1976); *Cantata* [No. 1] *on Poems of Hölderlin* for Tenor, Countertenor, and Piano (1979), No. 2 for Tenor, Oboe, and Piano (1980), and No. 3 for 2 Sopranos and Tape Delay (1981); *Eloge* for Soprano, Flute, Oboe, Clarinet, Horn, Piano, and String Quartet (1980); *Chaconne* for Double Chorus (1981); *Child of Light* for Sopranos and Organ (1984); *I Will Awake the Dawn* for Double Chorus (1986–87); *Rex gloriae* for Women's Voices and Organ (1988); *At the Round Earth's Imagined Corners* for Chorus (1992); *Prayer to a Child* for Soprano and 2 Clarinets (1992); *O Sing Unto the Lord a New Song* for Chorus and Organ (1993); *Canticum Luminis* for Soprano, Chorus, and Orch. (1994; Cambridge, March 11, 1995).

Sayão, Bidú (actually, **Balduina de Oliveira**), noted Brazilian soprano; b. Niteroi, near Rio de Janeiro, May 11, 1902. She studied with Elena Teodorini in Rio de Janeiro, and then with Jean de Reszke in Vichy and Nice. Returning to Brazil, she gave her first professional concert in Rio de Janeiro in 1925; in 1926 she sang the role of Rosina in *Il Barbiere di Siviglia* at the Teatro Municipal there. She made her American debut on Dec. 29, 1935, in a recital in N.Y. On Feb. 13, 1937, she sang Manon at her Metropolitan Opera debut in N.Y., earning enthusiastic reviews; remained on its roster until 1952. She retired in 1958. Her finest performances were in lyric roles in bel canto operas; especially memorable were her interpretations of Violetta, Gilda, and Mimi. She also showed her versatility in coloratura parts, such as Lakmé; in France, she was described as "a Brazilian nightingale." She also sang vocal parts in several works of her great compatriot Villa-Lobos. She was a recipient of numerous honors from European royalty, and of the Palmes Academiques from the French government; in 1972 she was decorated a Commandante by the Brazilian government.

Saygun, Ahmed Adnan, Turkish teacher and composer; b. Izmir, Sept. 7, 1907; d. Istanbul, Jan. 6, 1991. He studied composition in Paris with Borrel at the Cons. and with Le Flem and d'Indy at the Schola Cantorum; returning to Turkey in 1931, he taught at the Istanbul Cons. (1936–39); accompanied Bartók on a music-ethnological trip through Anatolia (1936). From 1964 he taught composition at the State Cons. in Ankara and from 1972 at the Istanbul State Cons. He wrote operas, including *Tasbebek* (Ankara, Dec. 27, 1934) and *Kerem* (1947; Ankara, March 1, 1953); also the oratorio *Yunus Emre* (Ankara, May 25, 1946), 4 syms. (1953, 1955, 1961, 1973), a Piano Concerto (1956), a Violin Concerto (1967), and chamber pieces.

Saylor, Bruce (Stuart), American composer and teacher; b. Philadelphia, April 24, 1946. He studied composition with Weisgall and Sessions at the Juilliard School of Music in N.Y. (B.Mus., 1968; M.S., 1969). In 1969–70 he held a Fulbright grant and pursued his training with Petrassi at the Accademia di Santa Cecilia in Rome. In 1970 he entered the Graduate School of the City Univ. of N.Y. and studied composition with Perle and theory with Salzer, taking his Ph.D. in 1978. He taught at Queens College of the City Univ. of N.Y. (1970–76) and at N.Y. Univ. (1976–79). In 1979 he returned to Queens College, where he became a prof. at the Aaron Copland School of Music. He also served on the faculty of the Graduate School of the City Univ. of N.Y. from 1983. From 1992 to 1994 he was composer-in-residence of the Lyric Opera of Chicago, which gave the premiere of his opera *Orpheus Descending* on June 10, 1994. He received grants from the NEA (1976, 1978), the Ives scholarship (1976) and an award (1983) from the American Academy and Inst. of Arts and Letters, a Guggenheim fellowship (1982–83), and the Ingram Merrill Foundation Award (1991). He is married to the mezzo-soprano Constance Beavon, who has performed many of his vocal works.

WORKS: DRAMATIC: *My Kinsman, Major Molineux*, opera (Pittsburgh, Aug. 28, 1976); *Cycle*, dance piece (Chilmark, Mass., July 27, 1978; rev. version, Chilmark, Mass., July 24, 1980); *Inner World Out*, dance piece (Chilmark, Mass., Aug. 30, 1978); *Wildfire*, dance piece (Chilmark, Mass., Aug. 29, 1979; rev. version as *Wildfire II*, N.Y., April 2, 1985); *The Waves*, 3 dramatic monologues for Mezzo-soprano and 5 Instruments (Chilmark, Mass., Aug. 27, 1981; rev. version, Paris, Nov. 18, 1985); *Spill*, dance piece (N.Y., May 10, 1984); *Voices from Sandover*, incidental music (N.Y., May 23, 1989); *Orpheus Descending*, opera (Chicago, June 10, 1994). **ORCH.:** *Cantilena* for Strings (N.Y., May 1965); *Notturno* for Piano and Orch. (1969); *Turns and Mordents*, flute concerto (New Haven, Conn., March 6, 1977); *Symphony in 2 Parts* (1980; Houston, Feb. 6, 1981); *Archangel* for Antiphonal Brass Quartet and Orch. (San Francisco, May 20, 1990); *Supernova* for Concert Band (Lancaster, Pa., Nov. 6, 1992). **CHAMBER:** Woodwind Quintet (1965; Sunnyside, N.Y., March 21, 1992); Suite for Viola (1967); Duo for Violin and Viola (Rome, May 12, 1970); *Conductus* for 3 Winds, 3 Strings, and Percussion (Rome, May 1970); *Firescreen* for Flute, Cello, and Piano (N.Y., Nov. 1, 1979); *St. Ulmo's Fire* for Flute and Harp (N.Y., March 16, 1980); *Fire-Flaught* for Flute, Bassoon, and Harp (1982); *State Trumpets* for Organ and Brass (Lattingtown, N.Y., Sept. 23, 1982; also for Organ); *Carillon Te Deum* for Bells (Ithaca, N.Y., June 29, 1983); Fanfare for Double Brass Quintet (N.Y., Nov. 14, 1983); *Soggetti I* for Flute (Paris, Nov. 18, 1985) and *II* for Flute and Harpsichord (N.Y., May 11, 1986); *Electra: A translation* for Viola, Contrabass, and Piano (Minneapolis, May 11, 1986); Trio for Clarinet, Viola, and Piano (Washington, D.C., June 20, 1989); *Fanfares and Echoes* for Horn and String Trio (Paris, Nov. 28, 1992). **KEYBOARD: PIANO:** *5 Short Pieces* (1965–67; N.Y., April 16, 1969); *Saltarello* (Paris, Nov. 18, 1981); *Quattro Passi* (1991; N.Y., Sept. 16, 1992). **ORGAN:** *Ricercare and Sinfonia* (1965, 1969; N.Y., Aug. 22, 1971); *State Trumpets* (Rome, May 22, 1983; also for Organ and Brass). **VOCAL:** *5 Songs from "Whispers of Heav'nly Death"* for Soprano and String Quartet (1965–67); *To Winter* and *To Autumn* for Soloists, Chorus, and Orch. (1968); *3 Collects* for Mezzo-soprano and Organ (1968); *Benedictus es* for Chorus and Organ (1969); *2 Yiddish Folksongs* for Tenor, Chorus, and Piano, 4-hands (1969); *Lyrics* for Soprano and Violin (1970; N.Y., Nov. 13, 1971); *Loveplay* for Mezzo-soprano, Flute, and Viola (N.Y., Nov. 18, 1975; also for Voice, Flute, and Cello, N.Y., Jan. 30, 1977); *4 Psalms* for Voice and Flute (1976–78); *Songs from Water Street* for Mezzo-soprano, Viola, and Piano (Washington, D.C., May 10, 1980); *Swimming by Night* for Mezzo-soprano, Viola, and Piano (1980; N.Y., Jan. 25, 1982); *Te Deum* for Chorus and Organ (N.Y., Oct. 23, 1982); *5 Old Favorites* for Voice, Flute, and Piano (1983; N.Y., Jan. 22, 1984); *It Had Wings* for Voice and Piano (Rome, April 12, 1984; also for Voice and Orch., N.Y., Nov. 3, 1991); *Psalm 23* for Voice and Oboe (McLean, Va., Aug. 17, 1985; also for Chorus and Instruments obbligato (N.Y., Nov. 15, 1987); *See You in the Morning* for Soprano and 6 Instruments (N.Y., Feb. 22, 1987); *Mass of the Holy Trinity* for Congregation, Chorus, Organ, and Brass (Paris, June 14, 1987); *Jubilate Fantasy* for Soprano, Chorus, and Orch. (Paris, Dec. 19, 1990); *Behold that Star* for Soprano and String Quartet (Paris, Dec. 19, 1990); *Star of Wonder*, Christmas cantata for Soprano, Children's Chorus, String Quartet, and Harp (Paris, Dec. 19, 1990); *3 Spirituals* for Soprano and Chorus (Paris, Dec. 19, 1990); *The Star Song* for Mezzo-soprano, Chorus, and Orch. (Rome, Sept. 25, 1992); *Honor, Honor*, spiritual for Soprano and Chorus (N.Y., May 3, 1993; also for Voice and Piano, Chicago, Aug. 11, 1993); *Angels* for Mezzo-soprano, Flute, Cello, and Piano (N.Y., May 11, 1993); *Canticle of Blessing* for Chorus, Brass, Percussion, and Organ (Flushing, N.Y., May 17, 1994); *In Praise of Jerusalem* for Chorus, 3 Brass Ensembles, and Organ (1994); *Song of Ascent* for

Chorus, 3 Trumpets, and Organ (1994; Chicago, Jan. 29, 1995); *Magnificat* for Voice, Flute, and Guitar (Chicago, Feb. 13, 1995); *By the Power of Your Love* for 3 Women's Voices and Chorus (Chicago, March 12, 1995).

Scacciati, Bianca, Italian soprano; b. Florence, July 3, 1894; d. Brescia, Oct. 15, 1948. She studied in Milan. She made her operatic debut there as Marguerite in *Faust* in 1917. She rapidly asserted herself as one of the most impressive dramatic sopranos in Italy; sang for many seasons at La Scala in Milan; also made successful appearances at Covent Garden in London, at the Paris Opéra, and at the Teatro Colón in Buenos Aires. She was particularly noted for her interpretation of the title role of Puccini's *Turandot.*

Scalero, Rosario, eminent Italian pedagogue and composer; b. Moncalieri, near Turin, Dec. 24, 1870; d. Settimo Vittone, near Turin, Dec. 25, 1954. After training at the Turin Liceo Musicale, he studied violin with Sivori in Genoa and Wilhelmj in London; subsequently studied general subjects with Mandyczewski in Vienna. He taught violin in Lyons (1896–1908); then went to Rome as a teacher of theory at the Accademia di Santa Cecilia; was also founder-director of the Società del Quartetto (1913–16) and a high commissioner for examinations at the conservatories of Naples, Rome, and Parma. From 1919 to 1928 he was chairman of the theory and composition dept. at N.Y.'s David Mannes School; also taught at the Curtis Inst. of Music in Philadelphia (1924–33; 1935–46), where his students included Samuel Barber, Gian Carlo Menotti, and Lukas Foss. He wrote a Violin Concerto; *Neapolitan Dances* for Violin and Piano; chamber music; sacred songs; etc.

Scarmolin, (Anthony) Louis, Italian-American composer; b. Schio, July 30, 1890; d. Union City, N.J., July 13, 1969. He went to the U.S. as a boy; graduated from the N.Y. College of Music in 1907; served in the U.S. Army during World War I; then lived in Union City, N.J. He wrote 6 operas and several symphonic poems and overtures; also *Miniature Symphony* (Cleveland, Feb. 7, 1940).

Scarpini, Pietro, Italian pianist, teacher, and composer; b. Rome, April 6, 1911. He studied at the Accademia di Santa Cecilia in Rome. He made his concert debut in 1936; then gave recitals in Europe and in the U.S.; from 1940 to 1967 he taught at the Florence Cons.; in 1967 he joined the faculty of the Milan Cons. He specialized in the modern repertoire of piano music; wrote a Piano Concerto and a Piano Quintet; also made an arrangement for 2 pianos of Mahler's 10th Sym.

Scelsi, Giacinto (actually, **Conte Giacinto Scelsi di Valva**), remarkable Italian composer; b. La Spezia, Jan. 8, 1905; d. Rome, Aug. 9, 1988. He was descended from a family of the nobility. He received some guidance in harmony from Giacinto Sallustio; after studies with Egon Koehler in Geneva, he completed his formal training with Walter Klein in Vienna (1935–36), where he became interested in the Schoenbergian method of writing music outside the bounds of traditional tonality; at the same time, he became deeply immersed in the study of the musical philosophy of the East, in which the scales and rhythms are perceived as functional elements of the human psyche. As a result of these multifarious absorptions of ostensibly incompatible ingredients, Scelsi formulated a style of composition that is synthetic in its sources and pragmatic in its artistic materialization. His works began to have a considerable number of performances in Italy and elsewhere, most particularly in the U.S. A curious polemical development arose after his death, when an Italian musician named Vieri Tosatti publ. a sensational article in the *Giornale della Musica,* declaring "I was Giacinto Scelsi." He claimed that Scelsi used to send him thematic sections of unfinished compositions, usually in the 12-tone system, for development and completion, using him as a ghostwriter. So many of such "improvisations" did Scelsi send to Tosatti that the latter had 2 other musicians to serve as secondary "ghosts," who, in turn, comfirmed their participation in this peculiar transaction. The matter finally got to the court of public opinion, where it was decided that the works were genuine compositions by Scelsi, who improvised them on his electric piano, and merely ed. for better effect by secondary arrangers.

WORKS: ORCH.: *Rotative* for 3 Pianos, Winds, and Percussion (1930); *Rapsodia romantica* (1931); *Sinfonietta* (1932); *Preludio e fuga* (1938); *Ballata* for Cello and Orch. (1945); *Quattro pezzi (su una nota sola)* for Chamber Orch. (1959); *Hurqualia* (1960); *Aiôn* (1961); *Chukrum* for Strings (1963); *Hymnos* for Organ and 2 Orchs. (1963); *Anagamin* for 12 Strings (1965); *Anahit* for Violin and 18 Instruments (1965); *Oboi* for 16 Strings (1966); *Natura renovatur* for 11 Strings (1967). **CHAMBER:** 4 string quartets (1944, 1961, 1963, 1964); 5 divertimenti for Violin (1952, 1954, 1955, 1955, 1956); Suite for Flute and Clarinet (1953); *Preghiera per un' ombra* for Clarinet (1954); *Pwyll* for Flute (1954); *Tre studi* for Clarinet (1954); *Coelocanth* for Viola (1955); *Hykos* for Flute and Percussion (1955); *Ixor* for Clarinet or Soprano Saxophone (1956); *Quattro pezzi* for Horn (1956); *Quattro pezzi* for Trumpet (1956); *Tre pezzi* for Soprano Saxophone or Bass Trumpet (1956); *Rucke di Guck* for Piccolo and Oboe (1957); *Tre pezzi* for Trombone (1957); *Trilogy* for Cello (1957–65); *Elegia per Ty* for Viola and Double Bass (1958); *I presagi* for 10 Instruments (1958); Trio for Violin, Viola, and Cello (1958); *Kya* for Clarinet and 7 Instruments (1959); *Xnoybis* for Violin (1964); Duo for Violin and Cello (1965); *Ko-Lho* for Flute and Clarinet (1966); *Ko-Tha* for Guitar and Percussion (1967); *Okanagon* for Harp, Tam-tam, and Double Bass (1968); *Praham II* for 9 Instruments (1973); *En maintenant, c'est à vous de jouer* for Cello and Double Bass (1974); *Voyages* for Cello (1974); *Dharana* for Double Bass and Cello (1975); *Kshara* for 2 Double Basses (1975). **PIANO:** 11 suites (c.1929–56); *6 pièces* (1930–40); *4 poems* (1936–39); *24 Préludes* (1936–40); *Hispania* (1939); 4 sonatas (n.d., 1939, 1939, 1941); *Quattro illustrazioni* (1953); *Cinque incantesimi* (1953); *Action music* (1955); *Aitsi* for Amplified Piano (1974). **VOCAL:** *Perdus* for Woman's Voice and Piano (1937); *La Nascita del verbo* for Chorus and Orch. (1948; Brussels, June 28, 1950); *Yamaon* for Bass and 5 Instruments (1954–58); *Tre canti popolari* for Chorus (1958); *Tre canti sacri* for Chorus (1958); *Hô* for Soprano (1960); *Wo-Ma* for Bass (1960); *Khoom* for Soprano and 6 Instruments (1962); *Lilitu* for Woman's Voice (1962); *Taiagarù* for Soprano (1962); *Yliam* for Women's Chorus (1964); *Uaxuctum* for Chorus and Orch. (1966); *TKRDG* for 6 Men's Voices, Amplified Guitar, and 2 Percussionists (1968); *Konx-om-pax* for Chorus and Orch. (1969); *Ogloudoglou* for Voice and Percussion (1969); *3 Latin Prayers* for Man's or Woman's Voice or Chorus (1970); *Pranam I* for Voice and 12 Instruments (1972); *Canti del capricorno* for Woman's Voice, Another Voice, and Instruments (1972–73); *Sauh I* and *II* for 2 Women's Voices or Voice and Tape (1973); *Manto per quattro* for Voice, Flute, Trombone, and Cello (1974); *Pfhat* for Chorus and Orch. (1974); *Litanie* for 2 Women's Voices or Woman's Voice and Tape (1975); *Maknongan* for Bass (1976).

BIBL.: A. Cremonese, *G. S.: Prassi compositiva e riflessione teorica fino alla metà anni '40* (Palermo, 1992).

Schadewitz, Carl, German choral conductor, teacher, and composer; b. St. Ingbert, Jan. 23, 1887; d. Reppendorf, near Kitzingen, March 27, 1945. He studied in Würzburg, where he was active for most of his life as a choral conductor and teacher. He was a prolific composer; his works include a musical fairy tale, *Johannisnacht*; a "Romantic" oratorio, *Kreislers Heimkehr*; an opera, *Laurenca*; a tone poem, *Heldengedenken* (1943); a number of songs, of which the cycle *Die Heimat* (1934) is outstanding; much chamber music; choruses.

BIBL.: A. Maxsein, *C. S.* (Würzburg, 1954).

Schaefer, Theodor, Czech composer and teacher; b. Telč, Jan. 23, 1904; d. Brno, March 19, 1969. He studied with Kvapil at the Brno Cons. (1922–26) and with Novák at the Prague Cons. (1926–29). Upon graduation, he taught at the Palacký Univ. at Olomouc, the Brno Cons. (1948–59), and at the Janáček Academy of Music in Brno (1959–69). He was an advocate of a so-called diathematic principle of constructing themes using fragments of preceding thematic units.

WORKS: DRAMATIC: *Maugli*, children's opera (1932); *Legenda o štěstí* (Legend of Happiness), ballet (1952). **ORCH.:** 2 unnumbered syms. (1926; 1955–61); Violin Concerto (1932–33); *Wallachian Serenade* (1936); Piano Concerto (1937–43); *Jánošík*, balladic overture (1939); *Diathema* for Viola and Orch. (1955–56); *The Barbarian and the Rose* for Piano and Orch. (1957–58); *Diathema* (1957–58); *Rhapsodic Reportage* (1960). **CHAMBER:** 3 string quartets (1929; 1941; 1944–45); Wind Quintet (1935–36); *Divertimento mesto* for Wind Quintet and String Trio (1946); *Cikánovy housle* (Gypsy Violin), 4 movements for Violin and Piano (1960). **PIANO:** *Etudes* (1936–37); *Theme with Variations* (1936). **VOCAL:** *Milostné balady* (Love Ballads) for Voice and Piano, commemorating the destruction of Lidice by the Nazis (1943); *Winter Cantata* for Soprano, Chorus, and Orch. (1943–45); *Bithematikon* for Baritone and Piano (1967).

Schaeffer, Boguslaw (Julien), outstanding Polish composer, pianist, pedagogue, writer on music, stage manager, and playwright; b. Lwów, June 6, 1929. He studied violin in Opole; then went to Kraków, where he took courses in composition with Malawski at the State High School of Music and in musicology with Jachimecki at the Jagiello Univ. (1949–53); later received instruction in advanced techniques from Nono (1959). In 1963 he became prof. of composition at the Kraków Cons.; served as prof. of composition at the Salzburg Mozarteum (from 1986). In 1967 he founded the periodical *Forum Musicum*, devoted to new music; in addition to his writings on music, he was active as a playwright from 1955; he was the most widely performed playwright in Poland from 1987 to 1995, winning an award at the Wroclaw Festival of Contemporary plays in 1987 and in 5 subsequent years. All of his plays were publ. in 3 vols. and were translated into 16 languages. As a composer, he received many awards, and numerous concerts of his works were presented in Poland and abroad. In 1995 he was made an honorary member of the Polish Soc. of Contemporary Music. He is married to **Mieczyslawa Janina Hanuszewska-Schaeffer**. Their son, Piotr (Mikolaj) Schaeffer (b. Kraków, Oct. 1, 1958), is a music journalist. Schaeffer's earliest compositions (*19 Mazurkas* for Piano, 1949) were inspired by the melorhythms of Polish folk songs, but he made a decisive turn in 1953 with his *Music for Strings: Nocturne*, which became the first serial work by a Polish composer; he devised a graphic and polychromatic optical notation indicating intensity of sound, proportional lengths of duration, and position of notes in melodic and contrapuntal lines, with the components arranged in binary code; he also wrote music in the "third stream" style, combining jazz with classical procedures. In 1960 he invented topophonical music in a tone-color passacaglia form in his *Topofonica* for 40 Instruments. In 1966 he created so-called idiomatic music by using various stylistic categories, including early jazz, neo-Classicism, entertainment music, and indeterminate music (e.g. *Howl*). In 1967 he introduced his own rhythmic system, built on metric-tempo proportions. In 1970 he began using synthesizers and computers. Many of his chamber scores, such as *Quartet 2+2*, utilize indeterminacy. He experimented by introducing ideas of philosophers such as Heraclitus, Spinoza, Bergson, and Heidegger in his music called *Heraklitiana, Spinoziana* et al. In his music for and with actors, he uses mixed media procedures. With his *Missa elettronica* (1975), he charted a bold course in sacred music. Schaeffer is regarded as one of the foremost composers of microtonal scores. *Three Short Pieces* for Orch. (1951) and *Music* for String Quartet (1954) are notable examples of his early microtonal works in which he uses a 24-tone row with 23 different microtonal intervals. In 1979 he introduced a new kind of instrumentation in which the disposition of instruments totally changes many times, thus utilizing various changing orchs.; in his Organ Concerto the disposition of instruments changes 53 times. Each of his orch. works and concertos follows this new disposition, sometimes very specifically, as in his *Musica ipsa* (1962). In his orch. works, he utilizes precisely calculated textures. Many of his works are inspired by paintings and literature. There are great influences of his theatrical praxis on his music. He uses electronic and computer media in a free and poetic manner.

WORKS: DRAMATIC: *TIS-MW-2*, metamusical audiovisual spectacle for Actor, Mime, Ballerina, and 5 Musicians (1962–63; Kraków, April 25, 1964); *TIS GK*, stage work (1963); *Audiences I–V* for Actors (1964); *Howl*, monodrama for Narrator, 2 Actors, Ensemble of Instrumentalists, and Ensemble of Performers, after Alan Ginsberg (1966; Warsaw, March 1, 1971); *Quartet* for 4 Actors (1966; Athens, Sept. 15, 1979); *Hommage à Czyzewski* for Ensemble of Stage and Musical Performers (1972); *Vaniniana* for 2 Actors, Soprano, Piano, Cello, and Electronic Sources (1978; Lecce, Oct. 24, 1985); *Teatrino fantastico* for Actor, Violin, and Piano, with Multimedia and Tape (Brussels, Nov. 17, 1983); *Liebesblicke*, opera (1990). **PLAYS (WITH ORIGINAL MUSIC):** *Anton Webern* (1955); *Eskimos' Paradise* (1964; the same as his *Audience III*); *Scenario* for 3 Actors (1970); *Mroki* (Darknesses; 1979); *Zorza* (Dawn; 1981); *Grzechy starosci* (Sins of Old Age; 1985); *Kaczo* for 2 Actors and an Actress (1987); *Ranek* (Daybreak; 1988).

ORCH.: 3 piano concertos (*4 movimenti*, 1957; 1967; 1988); *Tertium datur*, treatise for Harpsichord and Chamber Orch. (1958; Warsaw, Sept. 19, 1960); *Equivalenze sonore*, concerto for Percussion Chamber Orch. (1959); *Concerto breve* for Cello and Orch. (1959); *Joint Constructions* for Strings (1960); *Topofonica* for 40 Instruments (1960); *Little Symphony: Scultura* (1960; Warsaw, Sept. 29, 1965); *Concerto per sei e tre* for a changing Solo Instrument (Clarinet, Saxophone, Violin, Cello, Percussion, and Piano) and 3 Orchs. (1960; Katowice, Nov. 7, 1962); *Musica* for Harpsichord and Orch. (Venice, April 25, 1961); *Kody* (Codes) for Chamber Orch. (Warsaw, Sept. 19, 1961); Violin Concerto (1961–63); *Course "J"* for Jazz Ensemble and Chamber Sym. Orch. (Warsaw, Oct. 28, 1962); *Musica ipsa* for an Orch. of Deep Instruments (Warsaw, Sept. 20, 1962); *Collage and Form* for 8 Jazz Musicians and Orch. (1963; Urbana, Ill., March 19, 1967); *S'alto* for Saxophone and Chamber Orch. of Soloists (Zagreb, May 13, 1963); *Collage* for Chamber Orch. (1964); *Symfonia: Muzyka orkiestrowa* (1967); *Jazz Concerto* for Jazz Ensemble of 12 Instruments and Orch. of Flutes, Bassoons, Trumpets, Trombones, and Low Strings (1969; Boston, Oct. 30, 1976); *Texts* (1971); *Experimenta* for Pianist (on 2 pianos) and Orch. (1971; Poznań, April 27, 1972); *Confrontations* for Solo Instrument and Orch. (1972); Sym. in 9 movements for Large Orch. and 6 Solo Instruments (1973; Wroclaw, Sept. 18, 1978); tentative music for 159 Instruments (1973; 7 versions: for 1, 5, 9, 15, 19, 59, and 159 instruments); *Harmonies and Counterpoints* (2 overtures: *Warsaw Overture*, 1975; Warsaw, Sept. 10, 1975, and *Romuald Traugutt*, 1975; Warsaw, Sept. 20, 1977); *Gravesono* for Orch. of Wind and Percussion Instruments (1977); *Kesukaan* for 13 Strings (1978; Rzeszow, April 8, 1983); *Jangwa* for Double Bass and Orch. (1979); *Maah* for Orch. and Tape (1979); *Heideggeriana* for 11 Instruments (1979; Warsaw, Nov. 22, 1988); *5 Introductions and an Epilogue* for Small Chamber Orch. (1981); *Entertainment Music* for Orch. of Wind and Percussion Instruments (1981); Guitar Concerto (Rzeszow, March 9, 1984); Accordion Concerto (1984); Concerto for Organ, Violin, and Orch., *B-A-C-H* (1984; Nuremberg, July 5, 1985); Concerto for Flute, Harp, and Orch. (1986); Concerto for Saxophone (Soprano, Alto, and Tenor) and Orch. (1986); Concerto for Violin, Gasab-violin, English Horn, 2 Oboes, and Orch. (Kraków, June 10, 1986); *Sinfonia* (1988; Opole, March 19, 1993); Concerto for Jazz Percussion, Piano, and Orch. (1988; Kraków, June 23, 1993); Concerto for 2 Pianos, 8-hands, and Orch. (1988); Double Concerto for 2 Violins and Orch. (1988; Warsaw, March 21, 1995); *blueS No. 5* for Piano and Orch. (1992; Warsaw, March 21, 1995); Sym. No. 6 (1993); Clarinet Concerto (Kraków, April 3, 1995); Concerto for Violin, Piano, and Orch. (1995); Sym. No. 7 (1995).

CHAMBER: Sonata for Solo Violin (1955; Warsaw, April 24, 1983); *Permutations* for 10 Instruments (1956); *Extremes* for 10

Instruments, a score without notes (1957); 5 string quartets (1957, 1964, 1971, 1973, 1986); *Monosonata* for 6 String Quartets subdivided into 3 uneven groups (1959; Vienna, June 19, 1961); Concerto for String Quartet (1959); *Montaggio* for 6 Players (1960); *Azione a due* for Piano and 11 Instruments (1961; Stuttgart, June 6, 1971); *Imago musicae* for Violin and 9 Interpolating Instruments (1961); Quartet for 2 Pianists and 2 Optional Performers (1965); *Przeslanie* (Transmissions) for Cello and 2 Pianos (1965); Trio for Flute, Harp, Viola, and Tape (1966); Quartet for Oboe and String Trio (1966); Piano Trio (1969); *Heraklitiana* for 10 Solo Instruments and Tape (1970); *Mare*, concertino for Piano and 9 Instruments (1971); *Estratto* for String Trio (1971; Kraków, April 7, 1987); *Variants* for Wind Quintet (1971); *Sgraffito* for Flute, Cello, Harpsichord, and 2 Pianos (1971); *Free Form No. 1* for 5 Instruments and *No. 2, Evocazioni*, for Double Bass (both 1972); *blueS No. 2* for Instrumental Ensemble (1972); *Dreams of Schäffer* for an Ensemble of Performers, after Ionesco (1972; Kraków, April 14, 1975); *Spinoziana* for an Ensemble of Performers (1977); *Berlin '80/I (Tornerai)* for Piano, Syn-lab, Electronic Media, and Tape (West Berlin, Oct. 2, 1980) and *II (In jener Zeit)* for Piano, Syn-lab, Electronic Media, and Tape (West Berlin, Oct. 3, 1980); Concerto for Saxophone Quartet (1980); Octet for Wind Instruments and Double Bass (1980); *Addolorato* for Violin and Tape (1983; Kraków, Feb. 22, 1988); *Gasab* for Gasab-violin and Piano Accompaniment (Brussels, Nov. 16, 1983); *Schpass* (Nonet) for 3 Oboists (1986; Kraków, Feb. 22, 1988); *Kwaiwa* for Violin and Computer (1986; Kraków, Feb. 22, 1988); *Little Concerto* for Violin and 3 Oboes (1987; Kraków, Feb. 22, 1988). **KEYBOARD: PIANO:** *16 Models* (1956–84); Concerto for 3 Pianos (1972); *blueS No. 1* for 2 Pianos and Tape (1972; Wroclaw, April 21, 1977), *No. 3* for 2 Pianos (1978), *and No. 4* for 2 Pianos and Tape (audiovisual; 1980); *Open Music Nos. 2, 3*, and *4* for Piano and Tape (1983); *Acontecimiento* for 3 Pianos and Computer (1988). **ORGAN:** 4 sonatas (*Spring*, 1985; *Summer*, 1985; *Autumn*, 1986; *Winter*, 1986).

VOCAL: *Expressive Aspects* for Soprano and Flute (1963); *Music for MI* for Voice, Vibraphone, 6 Narrators, Jazz Ensemble, and Orch. (1963); *Media* for Voices and Instruments (1967); *Bergsoniana* for Soprano, Flute, Piano, Horn, Double Bass, and Piano (1972); *Missa elettronica* for Boy's Chorus and Tape (1975; Warsaw, Sept. 23, 1976; also for Mixed Chorus and Tape); *Miserere* for Soprano, Chorus, Orch., and Tape (1978); *Te Deum* for Solo Voices, Vocal Ensemble, and Orch. (1979); *Stabat Mater* for Soprano, Alto, Chorus, Strings, and Organ (1983); *Missa sinfonica* for Soprano, Violin, Soprano Saxophone, and Orch. (Katowice, April 25, 1986).

TAPE: *Symphony: Electronic Music* (1964–66).

WRITINGS: *Maly informator muzyki XX wieku* (Little Lexicon of Music of the 20th Century; Kraków, 1958; new ed., 1987); *Nowa muzyka, problemy współczesnej techniki kompozytorskiej* (New Music: Problems of Contemporary Technique in Composing; Kraków, 1958; new ed., 1969); *Klasycy dodekafonii* (Classics of Dodecaphonic Music; 2 vols., Kraków, 1961, 1964); *Leksykon kompozytorów XX wieku* (Lexicon of 20th-century Composers; 2 vols., Kraków, 1963, 1965); *W kręgu nowej muzyki* (In the Sphere of New Music; Kraków, 1967); *Dźwieki i znaki* (Sounds and Signs: Introduction to Contemporary Composition; Warsaw, 1969); *Muzyka XX wieku, Tworcy i problemy* (Music of the 20th Century, Composers and Problems; Kraków, 1975); *Wstęp do kompozycji* (Introduction to Composition; in Polish and Eng.; Kraków, 1976); *Dzieje muzyki* (History of Music; Warsaw, 1983); *Dzieje kultury muzycznej* (History of Music Culture; Warsaw, 1987); *Kompozytorzy XX wieku* (Composers of the 20th Century; 2 vols., Kraków, 1988, 1990).

BIBL.: J. Hodor and B. Pociej, *B. S. and His Music* (Glasgow, 1975); L. Stawowy, *B. S.: Leben, Werk, Bedeutung* (Innsbruck, 1993).

Schaeffer, Pierre, French acoustician, composer, and novelist; b. Nancy, Aug. 14, 1910; d. Aix-en-Provence, Aug. 19, 1995. Working in a radio studio in Paris, he conceived the idea of arranging a musical montage of random sounds, including outside noises. On April 15, 1948, he formulated the theory of *musique concrète*, which was to define such random assemblages of sounds. When the magnetic tape was perfected, Schaeffer made use of it by rhythmic acceleration and deceleration, changing the pitch and dynamics and modifying the nature of the instrumental timbre. He made several collages of elements of "concrete music," among them *Concert de bruits* (1948) and (with P. Henry) *Symphonie pour un homme seul* (1950); he also created an experimental opera, *Orphée 53* (1953). He incorporated his findings and ideas in the publ. *A la recherche de la musique concrète* (Paris, 1952) and in *Traité des objects sonores* (Paris, 1966). Eventually he abandoned his acoustical experimentations and turned to literature. He publ. both fictional and quasi-scientific novels, among them *Traité des objets musicaux* (1966); *Le Gardien de volcan* (1969); *Excusez-moi si je meurs* (1981); *Prélude, Chorale et Fugue* (1983).

BIBL.: M. Pierret, *Entretiens avec P. S.* (Paris, 1969); S. Brunet, *P. S.* (Paris, 1970).

Schaeffner, André, French musicologist and ethnomusicologist; b. Paris, Feb. 7, 1895; d. there, Aug. 11, 1980. He studied composition with d'Indy at the Schola Cantorum (1921–24), ethnology with M. Mauss at the Institut d'Ethnologie (1932–33), religious science at the École Pratique des Hautes Études (1934–37; diploma, 1940), and archeology with S. Reinach at the École du Louvre in Paris. In 1929 he founded the ethnological dept. at the Musée de l'Homme in Paris, which he headed until 1965. Between 1931 and 1958 he led 6 scientific excursions in Africa. From 1958 to 1961 he was president of the Société Française de Musicologie. He also took great interest in modern music and in lexicography; in addition to editing the French edition of Riemann's *Musiklexikon (Dictionnaire de musique*, Paris, 1931), he brought out the books *Le jazz* (with A. Coeuroy; Paris, 1926), a monograph on Stravinsky (Paris, 1931), *Origines des instruments de musique* (Paris, 1936; new ed., 1994), *Les Kissi: Une Société noire et ses instruments de musique* (Paris, 1951), and *Segalen et Claude Debussy* (with A. Joly-Segalen; Monaco, 1961). His *Le sistre et le hochet: Musique, théâtre et danse dans les sociétés africaines* was publ. posthumously (Paris, 1990). A Festschrift was publ. in his memory in 1982.

Schäfer, Dirk, eminent Dutch composer, pianist, and pedagogue; b. Rotterdam, Nov. 23, 1873; d. Amsterdam, Feb. 16, 1931. He studied in Rotterdam and Cologne. After a European concert tour, he settled in Amsterdam, where he was active as a pianist and teacher. I. Schäfer-Dumstorff ed. his *Het klavier* (Amsterdam, 1942).

WORKS: ORCH.: *Suite pastorale* (1903); *Rhapsodie javanaise* (1904). **CHAMBER:** Piano Quintet (1901); 4 violin sonatas (1901–09); Cello Sonata (1909); String Quartet (1922); many piano pieces. **VOCAL:** Songs.

Schafer, R(aymond) Murray, Canadian composer, writer, and educator; b. Sarnia, Ontario, July 18, 1933. After obtaining his Licentiate from the Royal Schools of Music (1952), he studied with Alberto Guerrero (piano), Greta Kraus (harpsichord), Arnold Walter (musicology), and John Weinzweig (composition) at the Royal Cons. of Music of Toronto (1952–55). He pursued studies in languages, literature, and philosophy on his own, and then lived in Vienna (1956–57). After receiving some lessons from Peter Racine Fricker in England, he returned to Toronto in 1961 and served as director of the Ten Centuries Concerts. From 1963 to 1965 he was artist-in-residence at Memorial Univ., and from 1965 to 1975 taught at Simon Fraser Univ. In 1972 he founded the World Soundscape Project for the purpose of exploring the relationship between people and their acoustic world. As the self-styled "father of acoustic ecology," he campaigned against the "sonic sewers" of modern urban life caused by noise pollution. In 1974 he held a Guggenheim fellowship and in 1987 received the Glenn Gould Award. In addition to his many books on music, he also wrote literary works and was active as a visual artist. Over the years, Schafer has utilized various contemporary techniques in his compositions. His explorations into ancient and modern languages, literature, and philosophy are reflected in many of his works. In his later scores, he made use of Eastern philosophy and religion.

WRITINGS: *British Composers in Interview* (London, 1963); *The Composer in the Classroom* (Toronto, 1965); *Ear Cleaning: Notes for an Experimental Music Course* (Toronto, 1967); *The New Soundscape* (Toronto, 1969); *The Book of Noise* (Vancouver, 1970); *When Words Sing* (Scarborough, Ontario, 1970); *The Public of the Music Theatre: Louis Riel—A Case Study* (Vienna, 1972); *The Rhinoceros in the Classroom* (London, 1975); *E.T.A. Hoffmann and Music* (Toronto, 1975); *Creative Music Education* (N.Y., 1976); ed. and commentator, *Ezra Pound and Music: The Complete Criticism* (N.Y., 1977); *On Canadian Music* (Bancroft, Ontario, 1984); *Dicamus et Labyrinthos: A Philologist's Notebook* (Bancroft, Ontario, 1984); *The Thinking Ear: Complete Writings on Music Education* (Toronto, 1986); *Patria and the Theatre of Confluence* (Indian River, Ontario, 1991).

WORKS: DRAMATIC: *Loving* or *Toi*, opera (1963–65; 1st complete perf., Toronto, March 11, 1978); *Patria*, cycle of 12 musical/theatrical pieces (1966–in progress); *Jonah*, theater piece (1979); *Apocalypsis*, musical/theatrical pageant (London, Oct. 28, 1980). **ORCH.:** *In Memoriam: Alberto Guerrero* for Strings (1959); *Partita* for Strings (1961); *Canzoni for Prisoners* (1962); Untitled Composition No. 1 for Small Orch. (1963) and No. 2 for Full Orch. (1963); *Statement in Blue* for Youth Orch. (1964); *Son of Heldenleben* for Orch. and Tape (Montreal, Nov. 13, 1968); *No Longer Than Ten (10) Minutes* (1970; rev. 1972); *East* for Small Orch. (1972); *North/White* for Orch. and Snowmobile (Vancouver, Aug. 17, 1973); *Train* for Youth Orch. (1976); *Cortège* for Small Orch. (1977); Flute Concerto (Montreal, Oct. 8, 1984); *Ko wo kiku* (Listen to the Incense; 1985); *Dream Rainbow Dream Thunder* (1986); Concerto for Harp, Orch., and Tape (1987); Concerto for Guitar and Small Orch. (1989); *Scorpius* (1990; Toronto, March 25, 1991); *The Darkly Splendid Earth: The Lonely Traveller* for Violin and Orch. (Toronto, April 17, 1991). **CHAMBER:** Concerto for Harpsichord and 8 Winds (1954); Sonatina for Flute and Harpsichord or Piano (1958); *Minimusic* for Any Combination of Instruments or Voices (1967); 6 string quartets (1970; *Waves*, 1976; 1981; 1989; *Rosalind*, 1989; 1993); *Music for Wilderness Lake* for 12 Trombones and Small Rural Lake (1979); *Theseus* for Harp and String Quartet (1983); *Le Cri de Merlin* for Guitar and Tape (1987). **VOCAL:** *Minnelieder* for Mezzo-soprano and Woodwind Quintet (1956; also for Mezzo-soprano and Orch., 1987); *Protest and Incarceration* for Mezzo-soprano and Orch. (1960); *Brébeuf*, cantata for Baritone and Orch. (1961); *5 Studies on Texts by Prudentius* for Soprano and 4 Flutes (1962); *Threnody* for Chorus, Orch., and Tape (1966; rev. 1967); *Lustro*, part 1: *Divan i Shams i Tabriz* for 6 Solo Voices, Orch., and Tape (1969; rev. 1970), 2: *Music for the Morning of the World* for Voice and Tape (1970), and 3: *Beyond the Great Gate of Light* for 6 Solo Voices, Orch., and Tape (1972); *Enchantress* for Voice, Exotic Flute, and 8 Cellos (1971); *In Search of Zoroaster* for Man's Voice, Chorus, Percussion, and Organ (1971); *Miniwanka or the Moments of Water* for Women's Voices or Chorus (1971); *Adieu Robert Schumann* for Alto and Orch. (1976); *The Garden of the Heart (The Thousand and One Nights)* for Alto and Orch. (1980); *Snowforms* for Women's Voices (1981; rev. 1983); *A Garden of Bells* for Chorus (1983); *Letters from Mignon* for Mezzo-soprano and Orch. (1987); *The Death of the Buddha* for Chorus, Gongs, and Bell Tree (1989); *Gitanjali* for Soprano and Small Orch. (1990; Ottawa, May 14, 1992). **OTHER:** *Kaleidoscope* for Tape (1967); *Harbour Symphony* for Fog Horns (1983).

Schalk, Franz, noted Austrian conductor; b. Vienna, May 27, 1863; d. Edlach, Sept. 2, 1931. He studied with Bruckner at the Vienna Cons.; after making his debut in Liberec (1886), he conducted in Reichenbach (1888–89), Graz (1889–95), and Prague (1895–98), and at the Berlin Royal Opera (1899–1900). He subsequently concentrated his activities in Vienna, where he conducted at the Court Opera (from 1900); when it became the State Opera in 1918, he was named its director; after sharing that position with R. Strauss (1919–24), he was sole director until 1929. He was a regular conductor with the Vienna Phil. from 1901 until his death; also was conductor of the Gesellschaft der Musikfreunde (1904–21). On Dec. 14, 1898, he made his Metropolitan Opera debut in N.Y. conducting *Die Walküre*, but remained on the roster for only that season. He also conducted *Ring* cycles at London's Covent Garden in 1898, 1907, and 1911; likewise conducted at the Salzburg Festivals. He devoted part of his time to teaching conducting in Vienna. A champion of Bruckner, he ed. several of his syms., even recomposing his 5th Sym. While Schalk's eds. were well-intentioned efforts to obtain public performances of Bruckner's scores, they are now totally discredited. L. Schalk ed. his *Briefe und Betrachtungen* (Vienna, 1935). His brother, the Austrian pianist, teacher, and writer Josef Schalk (b. Vienna, March 24, 1857; d. there, Nov. 7, 1900), also defended Bruckner's music; publ. *Anton Bruckner und die moderne Musikwelt* (1885).

Schall, Richard, German musicologist; b. Dortmund, Dec. 3, 1922. He studied at the Univ. of Marburg (Ph.D., 1946, with the diss. *Hugo Kaun: Leben und Werk, 1863–1932: Ein Beitrag zur Musik der Jahrhundertwende*; publ. in Regensburg, 1948); also received instruction in theory from H. Gebhard-Elsass and in conducting from H. von Waltershausen, and later attended the library school of the Bavarian State Library in Munich, where he took the senior librarian's examination (1956). From 1962 to 1986 he was musicological adviser to the Bavarian Radio, for which he prepared various publications. He contributed numerous articles to *Die Musik in Geschichte und Gegenwart*; also served as ed. of the *Quellenkataloge zur Musikgeschichte* (Wilhelmshaven, from 1966), the *Taschenbücher zur Musikwissenschaft* (Wilhelmshaven, from 1969), *Veröffentlichungen zur Musikforschung* (Wilhelmshaven, from 1972), and *Paperbacks on Musicology* (N.Y., from 1980). His writings are of value for the bibliography of German musicology.

Scharrer, August, German composer and conductor; b. Strasbourg, Aug. 18, 1866; d. Weiherhof, near Furth, Oct. 24, 1936. After studies in Strasbourg and Berlin, he was a theater conductor in Karlsruhe (1897–98) and Regensburg (1898–1900); from 1914 to 1931 he conducted the Phil. Soc. of Nuremberg. He wrote an opera, *Die Erlösung* (Strasbourg, Nov. 21, 1895); overtures; chamber music; choruses; songs.

Scharrer, Irene, English pianist and teacher; b. London, Feb. 2, 1888; d. there, Jan. 11, 1971. She studied with Matthay at the Royal Academy of Music in London. After making her London debut in 1904, she toured throughout England and Europe; made her first visit to the U.S. in 1925. In addition to appearing as a soloist with orchs., recitalist, and chamber-music artist, she gave duo recitals with her cousin, Dame Myra Hess, with whom she gave her farewell perf. in London in 1958. She also engaged in teaching.

Schat, Peter, significant Dutch composer; b. Utrecht, June 5, 1935. He was a student of Baaren at the Utrecht Cons. (1952–58), of Seiber in London (1959), and of Boulez in Basel (1960–62). Settling in Amsterdam, he was active with the Studio for Electro-Instrumental Music (from 1967), and with the Amsterdam Electric Circus (from 1973). After teaching at the Royal Cons. of Music in The Hague (1974–83), he devoted himself fully to composition. In his early works, he followed a diligent serialist path. Later he combined serial and tonal elements in his works. Finally, he experimented with a method of 12 tonalities related only to each other as formulated in his "tone clock" (1982). In his "tone clock," Schat distinguishes between 12 trichords, one being the natural trichord, which are interrelated through their steering principle. This expansive harmonic and melodic method points the way to a new tonal system. He explained his system in the book *De Toonklok, Essays en gesprekken over muziek* (Amsterdam, 1984; Eng. tr., 1993).

WORKS: DRAMATIC: *Labyrint*, a kind of opera (1964; Amsterdam, June 23, 1966); *Reconstructie*, a morality (Amsterdam,

June 29, 1969; in collaboration with L. Andriessen, R. de Leeuw, M. Mengelberg, and J. van Vlijmen); *Het vijde seizoen* (The 5th Season), music theater (1973); *Houdini*, circus opera (1974–76; Amsterdam, Sept. 29, 1977); *I am Houdini*, ballet (1976); *Aap verslaat de knekelgeest* (Monkey Subdues the White-Bone Demon), strip opera (1980); *Symposion*, opera (1989). **ORCH.:** *Mozaïeken* (Mosaics; 1959); *Concerto da camera* (1960); *Entelechie I* for 5 Instrumental Groups (1960–61); *Dansen uit het Labyrint* (Dances from the Labyrinth; 1963); *Clockwise and anti-clockwise* for 16 Winds (1967); *On Escalation* for 6 Percussionists and Orch. (1968); *Thema* for Oboe and Orch. (1970); 2 syms.: No. 1 (1978; rev. 1979) and No. 2 (1983; rev. 1984); *Serenade* for 12 Strings (1984); *De hemet* (The Heavens; 1990); *Opening* (1991); *Études* for Piano and Orch. (1992); *Préludes* for Flute and Small Orch. (1993). **CHAMBER:** *Introduction and Adagio* for String Quartet (1954); Septet for Flute, Oboe, Bass Clarinet, Horn, Cello, Piano, and Percussion (1956); Octet for Flute, Oboe, Clarinet, Bassoon, Horn, 2 Trumpets, and Trombone (1958); *2 Pieces* for Flute, Violin, Trumpet, and Percussion (1959); *Improvisations and Symphonies* for Wind Quintet (1960); *Signalement* for 6 Percussionists and 3 Double Basses (1961); *Hypothema* for Recorders (1969). **KEYBOARD: PIANO:** *Inscripties* (1959); *Anathema* (1969); *Polonaise* (1981). **ORGAN:** *Passacaglia and Fugue* (1954). **VOCAL:** *Cryptogamen*, 5 songs for Baritone and Orch. (1959); *The Fall* for 16 Voices (1960); *Entelechie II* for Mezzo-soprano and 10 Instruments (1961); *Stemmen uit het Labyrint* (Voices from the Labyrinth) for Alto, Tenor, Basso Profondo, and Orch. (1963); *Koren uit het Labyrint* (Choruses from the Labyrinth) for Chorus and Orch. (1964); *Scènes uit het Labyrint* (Scenes from the Labyrinth) for Reciter, Alto, Tenor, Bass, Chorus, and Orch. (1964); *Improvisaties uit het Labyrint* (Improvisations from the Labyrinth) for 3 Singers and 4 Instrumentalists (1964); *To You* for Mezzo-soprano, Amplified Instruments, and Electronics (1972); *Het vijde seizoen* (The 5th Season), cantata for Soprano and Chamber Ensemble (1973); *Canto General*, "in memoriam Salvador Allende," for Mezzo-soprano, Violin, and Piano (1974); *Mei '75, een lied van bevrijding* (May '75, a Song of Liberation) for Mezzo-soprano, Baritone, Chorus, and Orch. (1975); *Houdini Symphony* for Soprano, Mezzo-soprano, Tenor, Baritone, Chorus, and Orch. (1976); *De briefscène* (The Letter Scene) for Soprano, Tenor, and Orch. or Piano (1976); *Kind en kraai* (Child and Crow), song cycle for Soprano and Piano (1977); *Adem* (Breath) for Chamber Chorus (1984); *For Lenny* for Tenor and Piano (for Leonard Bernstein's 70th birthday; 1988); *De Trein* (The Train) for 5 Men's Voices and Orch. (1989). **OTHER:** *Banden uit het Labyrint* (Tapes from the Labyrinth), electronic music (1965); *The Aleph*, electronic music (1965); *The Tone Clock* for Mechanical Clock (1987); *Alarm* for Carillon and Ringing Bells ad libitum (1994).

Schaub, Hans (actually, **Siegmund Ferdinand**), German music critic, teacher, and composer; b. Frankfurt am Main, Sept. 22, 1880; d. Hanstedt, near Marburg, Nov. 12, 1965. He studied at the Frankfurt am Main Hoch Cons. with Iwan Knorr (theory) and Carl Friedberg (piano), with Arnold Mendelssohn in Darmstadt, and with Humperdinck in Berlin; also took lessons with Richard Strauss. He taught at the Breslau Cons. (1903–06); was on the faculty of Benda's Cons. and served as ed. of the *Deutsche Musikerzeitung* in Berlin (1906–16). After working as a music critic and pedagogue in Hamburg (1916–51), he settled in Hanstedt. Among his compositions were *Passacaglia* for Orch. (1928); *3 Intermezzi* for Small Orch.; *Capriccio* for Violin and Piano; *Den Gefallenen*, cantata (1940); *Deutsches Te Deum*, oratorio (1942).

Schaum, John W., American piano pedagogue; b. Milwaukee, Jan. 27, 1905; d. there, July 19, 1988. He studied at Milwaukee State Teachers College, at Marquette Univ. (B.M., 1931), and at Northwestern Univ. (M.M., 1934). He established a successful piano teaching class in Milwaukee and publ. several piano methods and many collections of piano pieces that sold an enormous number of copies: *The Schaum Piano Course* (9 vols.); *The Schaum Adult Piano Course* (3 vols.); *The Schaum Duet Albums* (2 vols.); also theory books: *The Schaum Theory Lessons* (2 vols.) and *The Schaum Note Spellers* (2 vols.).

Schech, Marianne, German soprano; b. Geitau, Jan. 18, 1914. She was educated in Munich. She made her operatic debut in Koblenz in 1937; then sang in Munich (1939–41), Düsseldorf (1941–44), and at the Dresden State Opera (1944–51); also sang with the Bavarian State Opera in Munich. In 1956 she was named a Kammersängerin. On Jan. 22, 1957, she made her debut at the Metropolitan Opera in N.Y. as Sieglinde in *Die Walküre;* also made guest appearances in London, Vienna, and Hamburg. She retired from the stage in 1970 and devoted herself mainly to teaching.

Scheff, Fritzi, famous Austrian soprano; b. Vienna, Aug. 30, 1879; d. N.Y., April 8, 1954. She studied with her mother, the singer Anna Jäger; after further training with Schröder-Hanfstängl in Munich, she completed her studies at the Frankfurt am Main Cons. She made her operatic debut as Martha in Frankfurt am Main (1896), and soon adopted her mother's maiden name of Scheff for professional purposes. After singing at the Munich Hofoper (1897–1900), she made her Metropolitan Opera debut in N.Y. as Marzellina in *Fidelio* (Dec. 28, 1900), and remained on its roster until 1903; concurrently sang at London's Covent Garden. She later shifted to light opera, and it was in this field that she became famous. She created the role of Fifi in Victor Herbert's operetta *Mlle. Modiste* (Trenton, N.J., Oct. 7, 1905); her singing of Fifi's waltz song "Kiss Me Again" became a hallmark of her career. She also found success as a dramatic actress, becoming particularly well known for her appearance in *Arsenic and Old Lace*. Her 3 marriages (to Baron Fritz von Bardeleben, the American writer John Fox, Jr., and the singer George Anderson) ended in divorce.

Scheidl, Theodor, Austrian baritone and teacher; b. Vienna, Aug. 3, 1880; d. Tübingen, April 22, 1959. He was trained in Vienna. After making his debut there at the Volksoper in *Lohengrin* (1910), he sang in Olmütz (1911–12) and Augsburg (1913). He was a member of the Stuttgart Opera (1913–21) and of the Berlin State Opera (1921–32). He also appeared at the Bayreuth Festivals, most notably as Klingsor (1914), Amfortas (1924–25), and Kurwenal (1927). In 1932 he joined the German Theater in Prague. In 1937 he became a prof. of voice at the Munich Hochschule für Musik. He settled in Tübingen as a teacher in 1944.

Scheidt, family of German singers, all siblings:

(1) Selma vom Scheidt, soprano; b. Bremen, Sept. 26, 1874; d. Weimar, Feb. 19, 1959. She was a pupil of Heinrich Böllhoff in Hamburg, and later of Theodor Bertram. In 1891 she made her operatic debut as Agathe in Elberfeld. After singing in Essen (1892–94) and Düsseldorf (1894–95), she appeared in Aachen, Bonn, and Berlin. In 1900 she joined the Weimar Opera, where she sang for some 25 years.

(2) Julius vom Scheidt, baritone; b. Bremen, March 29, 1877; d. Hamburg, Dec. 10, 1948. He made his operatic debut in Cologne in 1899, and sang there until 1916. After appearing at the Berlin Deutsches Opernhaus (1916–24), he sang at the Hamburg Opera (1924–30). He subsequently taught voice.

(3) Robert vom Scheidt, baritone; b. Bremen, April 16, 1879; d. Frankfurt am Main, April 10, 1964. He studied at the Cologne Cons. In 1897 he made his operatic debut at the Cologne Opera, singing there until 1903. From 1903 to 1912 he sang at the Hamburg Opera, and in 1904 at the Bayreuth Festival. He was a member of the Frankfurt am Main Opera from 1912 to 1940, singing in the premieres of Schreker's *Die Gezeichneten* (1918) and *Der Schatzgräber* (1920), and of Egk's *Die Zaubergeige* (1935).

Schein, Ann, American pianist; b. White Plains, N.Y., Nov. 10, 1939. She studied with Glenn Gunn in Washington, D.C., Mieczyslaw Munz at the Peabody Cons. of Music in Baltimore, Artur Rubinstein (1961–63), and Dame Myra Hess (1961–65).

She made her London debut in a recital in 1958; after appearing as a soloist with the N.Y. Phil. and making her Carnegie Hall recital debut in 1962, she toured widely. In 1968 she organized the People-to-People Music Committee in an effort to encourage amicable relations between nations via the art of music. She taught at the Peabody Cons. (from 1980) and the Aspen (Colo.) School of Music (from 1984). Her husband is the violinist Earl Carlyss. In addition to her performances of Chopin, she has won accolades for her interpretations of works by contemporary composers.

Scheinpflug, Paul, German violinist, conductor, and composer; b. Loschwitz, near Dresden, Sept. 10, 1875; d. Memel, March 11, 1937. He studied violin with Rappoldi and composition with Draeseke at the Dresden Cons. In 1898 he went to Bremen as concertmaster of the Phil. and conductor of the Liederkranz; then was conductor of the Königsberg Musikverein (1909–14); conducted the Blüthner Orch. in Berlin (1914–19); was music director in Duisburg (1920–28) and of the Dresden Phil. (1929–33).

WORKS: OPERA: *Das Hofkonzert* (1922). **ORCH.:** *Frühlung* (1906); *Lustspiel-Ouvertüre* (1909); *Bundes-Ouverture* (1918); *Serenade* for Cello, English Horn or Viola, Harp, and Strings (1937); *Ein Sommertagebuch* (1937); *Nokturno* (1937). **CHAMBER:** Piano Quartet (1903); Violin Sonata (1908); String Quartet (1912); String Trio (1912). **VOCAL:** Men's choruses; songs.

Schelle, Michael, American composer and teacher; b. Philadelphia, Jan. 22, 1950. He studied theater at Villanova Univ. (B.A., 1971), then pursued musical training at Butler Univ. (B.M., 1974), at the Hartt School of Music of the Univ. of Hartford (M.M., 1976), with Copland (1976–77), and with Argento at the Univ. of Minnesota (Ph.D., 1980). From 1979 he taught at Butler Univ., where he also was composer-in-residence from 1981. He received grants from the NEA, the Rockefeller Foundation, BMI, ASCAP et al., and in 1989 was named distinguished composer of the year by the Music Teachers National Assn. Many major American orchs. have commissioned and premiered his scores, including those of Indianapolis, Detroit, Buffalo, Cleveland, Seattle, Milwaukee, and Cincinnati. He was also a guest composer at Capital Univ. in Columbus, Ohio (1991), the Univ. of Southern Calif. in Los Angeles (1994), and Sam Houston State Univ. in Huntsville, Texas (1995), among others.

WORKS: CHAMBER OPERA: *Soap Opera* (1988; Indianapolis, June 9, 1989). **ORCH.:** *Lancaster Variations* (1976); *Masque—A Story of Puppets, Poets, Kings, and Clowns* (1977); *El Medico* (1977); *Pygmies I* for Youth Orch. and Tape (1982) and *II* for Youth Orch. and Speaker (1983); Oboe Concerto (1983; Indianapolis, Jan. 6, 1984); *Swashbuckler!* (1984); Concerto for 2 Pianos and Orch. (1987; Indianapolis, Jan. 14, 1988); *Blast!* (1991); *Spirits* (1993); *Giant* (1993); *Centennimania I* for the 100th anniversary of the Cincinnati Sym. Orch. (1994). **SYMPHONIC BAND/LARGE WIND ENSEMBLE:** *King Uba* (1980); *Cliff Hanger March* (1984); *7 Steps from Hell* (1985); *Guttersnipe* (1993); *Centennimania II: When Hell Freezes Over* for the 100th anniversary of the Butler Univ. School of Music (Indianapolis, Oct. 6, 1995). **CHAMBER:** *Song without Words* for Piano Trio (1977); Chamber Concerto for Violin and 3 Players (1978); *Music for the Last Days of Strindberg* for 9 Players (1979); Double Quartet for 8 Winds (1980); *Cry Wolf!* for Piano, Cello, and 5 Percussionists (1981); *Rattlesnake!* for Percussionist and Auxiliary Percussionists (1982); *Blue Plate Special* for Tuba and Auxiliary Percussion (1983); *Music for the Alabama Kid* for 8 Players (1984); *Play Us Chastity on Your Violin*, chamber concerto for Violin and 13 Players (1984); *Howl!* for Clarinet and 4 Players (1986); *Daydream* for 6 Players or Actors (1988); *Musica Magnetizzare* for Piano and 4 Players (1988); *Racing with Rabbits* for Percussionist (1988); piano pieces. **VOCAL:** *The Wife Wrapt in Wether's Skin* for Men's Chorus (1974); *Cantus Matrimonium* for Chorus, Organ, and Instruments (1976); *Katzenmusik* for Baritone and 6 Players, after T.S. Eliot's *Old Possum's Book of Practical Cats* (1976); *Caroleluia* for Chorus (1978); *Swanshite—Letters to Strindberg from Harriet Bosse*, song cycle for Soprano and Piano (1980); *Golden Bells* for Chorus and Orch. (1983; completion of an unfinished work by N. Dinerstein); *Deus Angelis* for Chorus and Organ (1987); *Kidspeace* for Voices and Orch. (1987); *Oboe Darkness* for Youth Chorus, Oboe, and Percussion (1987); *6 Seasonal Anthems* for Chorus and Organ (1987); *Struwwelpeter*, song cycle for Tenor and Piano (1991).

Schelling, Ernest (Henry), American conductor, composer, and pianist; b. Belvidere, N.J., July 26, 1876; d. N.Y., Dec. 8, 1939. He first appeared in public as a child prodigy, playing the piano at the age of 4½ at the Academy of Music in Philadelphia. He was then sent to Paris in 1882, where he studied at the Cons. with Mathias until 1885; later received instruction from Moszkowski, Leschetizky, H. Huber, K. Barth, and finally Paderewski in Morges, Switzerland (1898–1902). Extended tours in Europe (from Russia to Spain) followed; he also toured in South America. Returning to the U.S. in 1905, he devoted most of his energies to conducting and composing. He conducted the N.Y. Phil. Young People's Concerts (1924–39); was conductor of the Baltimore Sym. Orch. (1936–38); also made frequent appearances as a conductor in Europe. He was elected a member of the National Inst. of Arts and Letters in 1913.

WORKS: ORCH.: Sym. (n.d.); *Légende symphonique* (1904; Philadelphia, Oct. 31, 1913); *Suite fantastique* for Piano and Orch. (1905; Amsterdam, Oct. 10, 1907); *Impressions from an Artist's Life*, symphonic variations for Piano and Orch. (1913; Boston, Dec. 31, 1915, composer soloist); Violin Concerto (Providence, R.I., Oct. 17, 1916, Fritz Kreisler soloist); *A Victory Ball*, symphonic poem after Noyes (Philadelphia, Feb. 23, 1923); *Morocco*, symphonic tableau (N.Y., Dec. 19, 1927, composer conducting). **CHAMBER:** Violin Sonata (n.d.); *Divertimenti* for Piano Quintet (1925); piano pieces.

BIBL.: T. Hill, *E. S. (1876–1939): His Life and Contributions to Music Education through Educational Concerts* (diss., Catholic Univ. of America, 1970).

Schenck, Andrew (Craig), American conductor; b. Honolulu, Jan. 7, 1941; d. Baltimore, Feb. 19, 1992. He was educated at Harvard Univ. (B.A., 1962) and Indiana Univ. (Mus.M., 1968); pursued training in conducting with Bernstein at the Berkshire Music Center in Tanglewood, Monteux in Hancock, Maine, and in Germany on a Fulbright scholarship (1962–63), subsequently winning 1st prize in the Besançon conducting competition. He was assistant conductor of the Honolulu Sym. Orch. (1970–73) and the Baltimore Sym. Orch. (1973–80), and then founder-music director of the Baltimore Chamber Opera (1980–84). After serving as a resident conductor of the San Antonio Sym. Orch. (1986–88), he was music director of the Nassau (N.Y.) Sym. Orch. and the Atlantic Sinfonietta of N.Y. Schenck made a special effort to program American music at his concerts, both with his own orchs. and as a guest conductor with the Pittsburgh Sym. Orch., the Chicago Sym. Orch., the London Sym. Orch. et al.

Schenk, Erich, eminent Austrian musicologist; b. Salzburg, May 5, 1902; d. Vienna, Oct. 11, 1974. He studied theory and piano at the Salzburg Mozarteum and musicology with Sandberger at the Univ. of Munich (Ph.D., 1925, with the diss. *Giuseppe Antonio Paganelli: Sein Leben und seine Werke*; publ. in Salzburg, 1928); completed his Habilitation at the Univ. of Rostock in 1929 with his *Studien zur Triosonate in Deutschland nach Corelli*; subsequently founded its musicology dept. (1936). From 1940 until his retirement in 1971 he was a prof. of musicology at the Univ. of Vienna. He was particularly esteemed for his studies of Baroque and Classical music. In 1947 he revived the Denkmäler der Tonkunst in Österreich series, overseeing its progress until 1972. In 1955 he also took over the valuable *Studien zur Musikwissenschaft.* Festschrifts honored him on his 60th (Vienna, 1962) and 70th (Kassel, 1975) birthdays.

WRITINGS: *Johann Strauss* (Potsdam, 1940); *Musik in Kärnten* (Vienna, 1941); *Beethoven zwischen den Zeiten* (Bonn,

1944); *950 Jahre österreichische Musik* (Vienna, 1946); *Kleine wiener Musikgeschichte* (Vienna, 1946); *W.A. Mozart: Eine Biographie* (Vienna, 1955; Eng. tr., 1960, as *Mozart and His Time*; 2nd Ger. ed., aug., 1975, as *Mozart: Sein Leben, seine Welt*); *Ausgewählte Aufsätze: Reden und Vorträge* (Vienna, 1967); ed. *Beethoven-Studien* (Vienna, 1970).

Schenker, Heinrich, outstanding Austrian music theorist; b. Wisniowczyki, Galicia, June 19, 1868; d. Vienna, Jan. 13, 1935. He studied jurisprudence at the Univ. of Vienna (Dr.Jur., 1890); concurrently took courses with Bruckner at the Vienna Cons. He composed some songs and piano pieces; Brahms liked them sufficiently to recommend Schenker to his publisher Simrock. For a while Schenker served as accompanist of the baritone Johannes Messchaert; then returned to Vienna and devoted himself entirely to the development of his theoretical research; gathered around himself a group of enthusiastic disciples who accepted his novel theories, among them Otto Vrieslander, Hermann Roth, Hans Weisse, Anthony van Hoboken, Oswald Jonas, Felix Salzer, and John Petrie Dunn. He endeavored to derive the basic laws of musical composition from a thoroughgoing analysis of the standard masterworks. The result was the contention that each composition represents a horizontal integration, through various stages, of differential triadic units derived from the overtone series. By a dialectical manipulation of the thematic elements and linear progressions of a given work, Schenker succeeded in preparing a formidable system in which the melody is the "Urlinie" (basic line), the bass is "Grundbrechung" (broken ground), and the ultimate formation is the "Ursatz" (background). The result seems as self-consistent as the Ptolemaic planetary theory of epicycles. Arbitrary as the Schenker system is, it proved remarkably durable in academia; some theorists even attempted to apply it to modern works lacking in the triadic content essential to Schenker's theories.

WRITINGS: *Ein Beitrag zur Ornamentik als Einführung zu Ph.E. Bachs Klavierwerke* (Vienna, 1904; 2nd ed., rev., 1908; Eng. tr. in *Music Forum*, IV, 1976); *Neue musikalische Theorien und Fantasien*: I. *Harmonierlehre* (Stuttgart, 1906; Eng. tr., ed. by O. Jonas, Chicago, 1954); II. *Kontrapunkt* in 2 vols., *Cantus Firmus und zweistimmiger Satz* (Vienna, 1910), and *Drei- und mehrstimmiger Satz, Übergänge zum freien Satz* (Vienna, 1922); Eng. tr. of both vols. by J. Thymn, N.Y., 1987; III. *Der freie Satz* (Vienna, 1935; new ed. by O. Jonas, 1956; Eng. tr. by E. Oster, 1979); *Beethovens Neunte Sinfonie* (Vienna, 1912; Eng. tr., ed. by J. Rothgeb, New Haven, 1992); *Der Tonwille* (a periodical, 1921–24); *Beethovens Fünfte Sinfonie* (Vienna, 1925); *Das Meisterwerk in der Musik* (3 vols., Vienna, 1925, 1926, 1930); *Fünf Urlinie-Tafeln* (Vienna, 1932; 2nd ed., rev., 1969 as *Five Graphic Music Analyses by F. Salzer*); *Johannes Brahms: Oktaven und Quinten* (Vienna, 1933).

BIBL.: W. Riezler, "Die Urlinie," *Die Musik* (April 1930); I. Citkowitz, "The Role of H. S.," *Modern Music*, 11 (1933); O. Jonas, *Das Wesen des musikalischen Künstwerks* (Vienna, 1934; 2nd ed., rev., 1973 as *Einführung in die Lehre H. S.s*; Eng. tr., 1982); A. Katz, "H. S.'s Method of Analysis," *Musical Quarterly* (July 1935); R. Sessions, "H. S.'s Contribution," *Modern Music*, 12 (1953); A. Waldeck and N. Broder, "Musical Synthesis as Expounded by H. S.," *Musical Mercury* (Dec. 1935); A. Katz, *Challenge to Musical Tradition* (N.Y., 1945); W. Mann, "S.'s Contribution to Music Theory," *Music Review*, X (1949); F. Salzer, *Structural Hearing* (N.Y., 1952; 2nd ed., 1962); F. Salzer and C. Schachter, *Counterpoint in Composition: The Study of Voice Leading* (N.Y., 1969): L. Laskowski, ed., *H. S.: An Annotated Index to His Analyses of Musical Works* (N.Y., 1978); A. Whittall, "S. and the Prospects for Analysis," *Musical Times* (Sept. 1980); A. Forte and S. Gilbert, *An Introduction to S.ian Analysis* (London, 1982); W. Pastille, "H. S., Anti-Organicist," *19th Century Music* (Summer 1984); D. Beach, "The Current State of S.ian Research," *Acta Musicologica*, LVII (1985); F.-E. von Cube, *The Book of the Musical Artwork: An Interpretation of the Musical Theories of H. S.* (Lewiston, N.Y., 1988); H. Siegel, ed., *S. Studies* (Cambridge, 1989); A. Cadwallader, ed., *Trends in S.ian Research* (N.Y., 1990); D. Neumeyer and S. Tepping, *A Guide to S.ian Analysis* (Englewood Cliffs, N.J., 1992).

Scherchen, Hermann, eminent German conductor, father of **Tona Scherchen**; b. Berlin, June 21, 1891; d. Florence, June 12, 1966. He was mainly self-taught in music; learned to play the viola and joined the Blüthner Orch. in Berlin at age 16; then was a member of the Berlin Phil. (1907–10). He worked with Schoenberg (1910–12), and toured as a conductor (1911–12); became conductor of the Riga Sym. Orch. in 1914, but with the outbreak of World War I that same year, he was interned in Russia. After the Armistice, he returned to Berlin and founded the Neue Musikgesellschaft in 1918; also ed. the periodical *Melos* (1920–21). He was conductor of the Frankfurt am Main Museumgesellschaft concerts (1922–28) and Generalmusikdirektor in Königsberg (1928–33); also conducted at many contemporary-music festivals. With the advent of the Nazi regime in 1933, he settled in Switzerland, where he had conducted the concerts of the Winterthur Musikkollegium from 1922; continued in this capacity until 1947. He also conducted the Zürich Radio Orch. (from 1933), serving as its director (1944–50). He was ed. of the Brussels periodical *Musica Viva* (1933–36). Scherchen founded the Ars Viva Orch. (1939) and that same year an annual summer school for conductors. After World War II, he resumed his extensive European guest conducting engagements. On Oct. 30, 1964, he made his long-awaited U.S. debut, as a guest conductor with the Philadelphia Orch. He distinguished himself as a scholarly exponent of modern music; conducted many premieres of ultramodern works; publ. a valuable manual, *Lehrbuch des Dirigierens* (Leipzig, 1929; Eng. tr., 1933, as *Handbook of Conducting*; 6th ed., 1949); also publ. *Vom Wesen der Musik* (Zürich, 1946; Eng. tr., 1947, as *The Nature of Music*); *Musik für Jedermann* (Winterthur, 1950). J. Lucchesi ed. his *Werke und Briefe* (Berlin, 1991 et seq.).

BIBL.: M. Kreikle, *H. S. 1891–1966: Phonographie: Deutsche Rundfunkproduktionen, Industrietonträger, Eigenaufnahmen* (Frankfurt am Main, 1992).

Scherchen, Tona, Swiss-born French composer, daughter of **Hermann Scherchen**; b. Neuchâtel, March 12, 1938. She was taken to China at age 12 by her mother, the Chinese composer Hsia Shu-sien, who was her first mentor in theory, composition, and classical Chinese music (from 1952). She studied basic Western theory and the Chinese instrument P'i p'a at the conservatories in Shanghai and Peking (1957–60). Upon returning to Europe, she studied composition with Henze at the Salzburg Mozarteum (1961–63). She continued her training in Paris with Pierre Schaeffer at the Centre de Recherche Musicale (1963), and also received instruction in analysis from Messiaen at the Cons. (1963–64), where she won a premier prix; then had private lessons with Ligeti in Vienna (1966–67). In 1972 she settled in France and later became a naturalized French citizen. In 1991 she was awarded the Prix Italia. In addition to works for traditional instruments, she has produced electronic and multimedia scores. In all her works, her Eastern heritage has remained a powerful resource and inspiration.

WORKS: DRAMATIC: *Tzan-Shen*, ballet (1970–71; version of *Shen* for Percussion, 1968); *Éclats obscurs*, radiophonic piece, after St.-John Perse (1982). **MULTIMEDIA:** *Between* (1978–86); *Cancer, solstice '83* (1983–87); *Fuite?* (1987); *Le Jeu de Pogo*, radiophonique film piece (1989–91). **ORCH.:** *Tzang* for Chamber Orch. (1966); *Khouang* (1966–68); *Tao* for Viola and Orch. (1971); *Vague-T'ao* (1974–75); *"S . . ."* for Chamber Orch. (1975); *Oeil de chat* (1976–77); *L'Invitation au voyage* for Chamber Orch. (1977); *Lô* for Trombone and 12 Strings (1978–79); *L'Illégitime* for Orch. and Tape (1985–86). **CHAMBER:** *In, Sin*, 2 pieces for Flute (1965); *Hsun* for 6 Instruments (1968); *Shen* for 6 Percussionists or Percussion Orch. (1968; ballet version as *Tzan-Shen*, 1970–71); *Tzoue*, trio for Clarinet or Flute, Cello or Double Bass, and Harpsichord (1970; also as a multimedia piece, 1980); *Yun-Yu* for Violin or Viola and Vibraphone (1972); *Bien* for 12 Instruments (1972–73); *Tjao-Houen* for 9 Instruments (1973); *Ziguidor* for Wind Quintet

(1977); *Tzing* for Brass Quintet (1979); *Tarots* for Harpsichord and 7 Instruments (1981–82); *Lustucru* for Variable Ensemble (1983). **VOCAL:** *Wai* for Mezzo-soprano and String Quartet (1966–67); *Tzi* for 16-voice Chorus (1969–70); *La Larme de crocodile* for Voice (1977).

Scheremetiev, Alexander. See **Sheremetiev, Alexander.**

Schering, Arnold, eminent German music historian; b. Breslau, April 2, 1877; d. Berlin, March 7, 1941. His father was a merchant; the family moved to Dresden, where Schering began to take violin lessons with Blumner. In 1896 he went to Berlin, where he studied violin with Joachim, hoping to start a concert career; he organized a tour with the pianist Hinze-Reinhold, but soon gave up virtuoso aspirations, and in 1898 entered classes in musicology with Fleischer and Stumpf at the Univ. of Berlin; then took courses with Sandberger at the Univ. of Munich and with Kretzschmar at the Univ. of Leipzig, obtaining his Ph.D. in 1902 with the diss. *Geschichte des Instrumental- (Violin-) Konzerts bis A. Vivaldi* (publ. in Leipzig, 1905; 2nd ed., 1927); subsequently completed his Habilitation there in 1907 with his *Die Anfänge des Oratoriums* (publ. in an aug. ed. as *Geschichte des Oratoriums*, Leipzig, 1911). He devoted himself to teaching and musical journalism; from 1904 to 1939 he was ed. of the *Bach-Jahrbuch*. From 1909 to 1923 he taught at the Leipzig Cons.; from 1915 to 1920 he was prof. of the history and aesthetics of music at the Univ. of Leipzig; then was prof. of music at the Univ. of Halle (1920–28); subsequently was prof. of musicology at the Univ. of Berlin (1928–41). In 1928 he became president of the Deutsche Gesellschaft für Musikwissenschaft. In his voluminous publications, he strove to erect an infallible system of aesthetic principles derived from musical symbolism and based on psychological intuition, ignoring any contradictions that ensued from his axiomatic constructions. In his book *Beethoven in neuer Deutung*, publ. in 1934 at the early dawn of the Nazi era, he even attempted to interpret Beethoven's music in terms of racial German superiority, alienating many of his admirers. But in his irrepressible desire to establish an immutable sequence of historic necessity, he compiled an original and highly informative historical tabulation of musical chronology, *Tabellen zur Musikgeschichte*, which was publ. in 1914 and went through several eds.

WRITINGS: *Musikalische Bildung und Erziehung zum musikalischen Hören* (Leipzig, 1911; 4th ed., 1924); *Tabellen zur Musikgeschichte* (Leipzig, 1914; 4th ed., 1934; 5th ed., 1962, by H.J. Moser); *Aufführungspraxis alter Musik* (Berlin, 1931); *Geschichte der Musik in Beispielen* (Leipzig, 1931; 2nd ed., 1954; Eng. tr., 1950); *Beethoven in neuer Deutung* (Berlin, 1934); *Beethoven und die Dichtung* (Berlin, 1936); *Johann Sebastian Bachs Leipziger Kirchenmusik* (Leipzig, 1936; 2nd ed., 1954); *Von grossen Meistern der Musik* (Leipzig, 1940); *Das Symbol in der Musik* (ed. by W. Gurlitt; Berlin, 1941); *Über Kantaten J.S. Bachs* (ed. by F. Blume; Berlin, 1942; 2nd ed., 1950); *Vom musikalischen Künstwerk* (ed. by F. Blume; Berlin, 1949; 2nd ed., 1951); *Humor, Heldentum, Tragik bei Beethoven* (Strasbourg, 1955).

BIBL.: H. Osthoff, ed., *Festschrift A. S. zum 60. Geburtstag* (Berlin, 1937).

Scherman, Thomas (Kielty), American conductor; b. N.Y., Feb. 12, 1917; d. there, May 14, 1979. He was a son of Harry Scherman, founder and president of the Book-of-the-Month Club; attended Columbia Univ. (B.A., 1937); then studied piano with Vengerova, theory with Weisse, and conducting with Bamberger, Rudolf, and Klemperer, whose assistant he became in conducting a chamber orch. composed of European refugees at the New School for Social Research in N.Y. (1939–41). He subsequently served in the U.S. Army (1941–45), reaching the rank of captain in the Signal Corps. In 1947 he became assistant conductor of the National Opera in Mexico City; that same year, he organized in N.Y. the Little Orch. Society for the purposes of presenting new works, some of them specially commissioned, and of reviving forgotten music of the past; he also gave performances of operas in concert versions. He terminated the seasons of the Little Orch. Soc. in 1975, but organized the New Little Orch. Soc. to present children's concerts; these he continued to lead until his death.

Schermerhorn, Kenneth (de Witt), American conductor; b. Schenectady, N.Y., Nov. 20, 1929. He studied conducting with Richard Burgin at the New England Cons. of Music in Boston (graduated, 1950); also took courses at the Berkshire Music Center at Tanglewood, where he won the Koussevitzky Prize. His first important engagement was as conductor of the American Ballet Theater in N.Y. (1957–67); also was assistant conductor of the N.Y. Phil. (1960–61). He was music director of the New Jersey Sym. Orch. in Newark (1963–68) and the Milwaukee Sym. Orch. (1968–80); then was general music director of the American Ballet Theater in N.Y. (from 1982) and also music director of the Nashville (Tenn.) Sym. Orch. (from 1983) and the Hong Kong Phil. (1984–88). In 1975 he married **Carol Neblett**.

Schibler, Armin, Swiss composer; b. Breuzlingen, Nov. 20, 1920; d. Zürich, Sept. 7, 1986. He went to Zürich and studied with Frey and Müller, and then with Burkhard (1942–45). After further training in England (1946), he attended the summer courses in new music in Darmstadt (1949–53) and profited from studies with Fortner, Krenek, Leibowitz, and Adorno. He taught music at the Zürich Real- und Literargymnasium from 1944. His music represented an eclectic synthesis of various 20th-century compositional techniques.

WORKS: DRAMATIC: *Der spanische Rosenstock*, opera (1947–50; Bern, April 9, 1950); *Der Teufel im Winterpalais*, opera (1950–53); *Das Bergwerk von Falun*, opera (1953); *Die späte Sühne*, chamber opera (1953–54); *Die Füsse im Feuer*, opera (Zürich, April 25, 1955); *Blackwood & Co.*, musical burlesque (1955–58; Zürich, June 3, 1962); *La Folie de Tristan*, music theater (1980); *Antonie und die Trompete*, chamber musical (1981); *Amadeus und der graue Bote*, chamber opera (1982–85); *Königinnen von Frankreich*, musical chamber-comedy (1982–85); *Schlafwagen Pegasus*, chamber opera (1982–85); *Sansibar oder Die Rettung*, music theater (1984–86). **BALLETS:** *Der Raub des Feuers* (1954); *Die Gefangene*, chamber ballet (1957); *Ein Lebenslauf*, chamber ballet (1958); *Selene und Endymion* (1959–60); *Die Legende von der drei Liebespfändern* (1975–76); *La Naissance d'Eros* (1985). **RADIO PIECES:** *Das kleine Mädchen mit den Schwefelhölzchen*, melodrama (1955; rev. 1965); *Orpheus: Die Unwiederbringlichkeit des Verlorenen* (1967–68); *The Point of Return* (1971–72); *. . . später als du denkst* (1973); *. . . der da geht . . .* (1974); *Epitaph auf einen Mächtigen* (1974–75). **ORCH.:** Concertino for Piano and Chamber Orch. (1943); *Fantasy* for Viola and Small Orch. (1945); *Fantasy* for Oboe, Harp, and Small Orch. (1946); 4 syms.: No. 1 (1946), No. 2 (1952–53), No. 3 (Winterthur, Nov. 13, 1957), and No. 4, *Sechs Orchesterstücke* (1968); *Symphonic Variations* (1950); *Concertante fantasie* for Cello and Orch. (1951); Horn Concerto (1956); Trombone Concerto (1957); *Concerto breve* for Cello and Strings (1958–59); Violin Concerto (1959–60); 2 percussion concertos (1959–60; 1962–63); Trumpet Concerto (1960–61); *Metamorphoses ebrietatis* (1962–63); Piano Concerto (1962–68); Bassoon Concerto (1966–67); *Concerto 77* for Orch., Big Band, Jazz-Rock Group, and Tape (1976–77); *Konzertante Fantasie*, alto saxophone concerto (1978); *Dialogues concertants*, harp concerto (1985). **CHAMBER:** Sonata for Solo Flute (1944); 5 string quartets (1945; 1951; 1958; 1961–62; 1975); *Konzertantes Duo* for Violin and Piano (1949–51); *Kaleidoskop* for Wind Quintet (1954); *Ballade* for Viola and Piano (1957); *Epitaph, Furioso und Epilog* for Flute, Violin, Viola, and Cello (1958); *Recitativi e Danze* for 2 Violins, Viola, and 2 Cellos (1962–64); *Fantaisie concertante* for Harp (1964); *Pantomimes solitaires* for Violin and Piano (1964); *Anspielungen* for Clarinet and Piano (1972); *Quatuor sonore pour un quatuor de corps*, saxophone quartet (1980); piano pieces; organ music. **VOCAL:** 5 oratorios: *Media in vita* for 4 Soloists, Mixed Chorus, Men's Chorus, and Orch. (1958–59), *Der Tod Enkidus* for Choruses and Orch. (1970–72), *Der Tod des Einsiedlers* for Soloists, Chorus, and Chamber Ensemble (1975), *Messe für die gegenwärtige Zeit* for 2 Soloists, Youth Chorus, 2 Pianos, and Jazz-rock Group (1979–80), and *De Misterio* for Speaking Voice, Man's Voice, and Orch. (1982); *Huttens letzte Tage* for Voice and Orch. (1966–67); *Iter Montanum* for Voice, Piano, and String Orch. (1983–84).

BIBL.: K. Wörner, *A. S.: Werk und Persönlichkeit* (Amriswil, 1953); H.-R. Metzger, *A. S., 1920–1986* (2 vols., Zürich, 1990–91).

Schick, George, Czech-American conductor; b. Prague, April 5, 1908; d. N.Y., March 7, 1985. He studied at the Prague Cons. He was assistant conductor at the Prague National Theater from 1927 until 1938. He settled in the U.S. in 1939; was conductor of the San Carlo Opera (1943); from 1948 to 1950 he was conductor of the Little Sym. of Montreal; from 1950 to 1956 he was assoc. conductor of the Chicago Sym. Orch. He was a conductor at the Metropolitan Opera in N.Y. (1958–69); then served as president of the Manhattan School of Music in N.Y. (1969–76).

Schickele, Peter, American composer and musical humorist; b. Ames, Iowa, July 17, 1935. He was educated at Swarthmore College (B.A., 1957) and studied composition with Harris in Pittsburgh (1954), Milhaud at the Aspen (Colo.) School of Music (1959), and Persichetti and Bergsma at the Juilliard School of Music in N.Y. (M.S., 1960). After serving as composer-in-residence to the Los Angeles public schools (1960–61), he taught at Swarthmore College (1961–62) and at the Juilliard School of Music (from 1962). He rocketed to fame at N.Y.'s Town Hall on April 24, 1965, in the rollicking role of the roly-poly character P.D.Q. Bach, the mythical composer of such outrageous travesties as *The Civilian Barber, Gross Concerto for Divers Flutes* (featuring a Nose Flute and a Wiener Whistle to be eaten during the perf.), *Concerto for Piano vs. Orchestra, Iphigenia in Brooklyn, The Seasonings, Pervertimento for Bagpipes, Bicycles & Balloons, No-No Nonette, Schleptet, Fuga Meshuga, Missa Hilarious, Sanka Cantata, Fantasie-Shtick*, and the opera *The Abduction of Figaro* (Minneapolis, April 24, 1984). He publ. *The Definitive Biography of P.D.Q. Bach (1807–1742?)* (N.Y., 1976). In 1967 he organized a chamber-rock-jazz trio known as Open Window, which frequently presented his serious compositions; among these are several orch. works, vocal pieces, film and television scores, and chamber music. In later years, he was host of his own radio program, "Schickele Mix."

Schidlowsky, León, Chilean composer; b. Santiago, July 21, 1931. He studied in Santiago at the National Cons. (1940–47), and also took courses in philosophy and psychology at the Univ. of Chile (1948–52), and had private lessons in composition with Focke and in harmony with Allende-Blin; then went to Germany for further studies (1952–55). Returning to Chile, he organized the avant-garde group Agrupación Tonus for the propagation of new techniques of composition. He taught at the Santiago Music Inst. (1955–63) and served as prof. of composition at the Univ. of Chile (1962–68), then held a Guggenheim fellowship (1968). In 1969 he emigrated to Israel, where he was appointed to the faculty of the Rubin Academy of Music. In his music, he adopts a serial technique, extending it into fields of rhythms and intensities; beginning in 1964, he superadded aleatory elements, using graphic notation.

WORKS: OPERA: *Die Menschen* (1970). **ORCH.:** *Tríptico* (1959); *Eróstrato* for Percussion Orch. (1963); *Nueva York*, dedicated to "my brothers in Harlem" (Washington, D.C., May 9, 1965); *Kadish* for Cello and Orch. (1967); *Epitaph for Hermann Scherchen* (1967); *Babi Yar* for Strings, Piano, and Percussion (1970); *Serenata* for Chamber Orch. (1970); *Arcanas* (1971); *Constellation II* for Strings (1971); *Prelude to a Drama* (1976); *Images* for Strings (1976); *Lux in Tenebris* (1977); *Tel Aviv* (1978–83); *Trilogy* (1986); *Ballade* for Violin and Orch. (1986); *Elegy* (1988); *Laudatio* (1988); *Kaleidoscope* (1989); *Prelude* (1990); *Polyphony IV* (1991); *Exhortatio* (1991); *I Will Lay Mind Hand Upon My Mouth* (1994). **CHAMBER:** *Elegía* for Clarinet and String Quartet (1952); Trio for Flute, Cello, and Piano (1955); *Cuarteto mixto* for Flute, Clarinet, Violin, and Cello (1956); Concerto for 6 Instruments (1957); *In memoriam* for Clarinet and Percussion (1957); *4 Miniatures* for Flute, Oboe, Clarinet, and Bassoon (1957); *Soliloquios* for 8 Instruments (1961); *Visiones* for 12 Strings (1967); String Quartet (1967); Wind Quintet (1968); *Eclosión* for 9 Instruments (1967); *6 Hexáforos* for 6 Percussionists (1968); Sextet (1970); *Kolot* for Harp (1971); *Meshulash* (Triangle) for Piano Trio (1971); *Voices* for Harp (1972); *Invention* for Flute and Piano (1975); Piano Quartet (1988); String Quartet (1988); *Shadows II* for Chamber Ensemble (1990); *Trio-in Memoriam Luigi Nono* for Viola, Cello, and Double Bass (1990); *Sealed Room* for 12 Instruments (1991). **PIANO:** *6 Miniatures*, after paintings by Klee (1952); *8 Structures* (1955); *5 Pieces* (1956); *Actus* (1972); *Trilogy* for 2 Pianos (1990); *Toccata* (1990). **VOCAL:** *Requiem* for Soprano and Chamber Orch. (1954); *Caupolicán*, epic narrative for Narrator, Chorus, 2 Pianos, Celesta, and Percussion Orch. (1958); *Oda a la tierra* for 2 Narrators and Orch. (1958–60); *La Noche de Cristal*, sym. for Tenor, Men's Chorus, and Orch., commemorating the martyrdom of Jews on the Nazi "crystal night" (1961); *Invocación* for Soprano, Narrator, Percussion, and String Orch. (1964); *Amereida* (consisting of *Memento, Llaqui*, and *Ecce Homo*) for Narrator and Orch. (1965–72); *Jeremias* for 8 Mixed Voices and String Orch. (1966); *Rabbi Akiba*, scenic fantasy for Narrator, 3 Soloists, Children's and Mixed Choruses, and Orch. (1972); *Hommage à Neruda* for Chorus and Orch. (1975); *Adieu* for Mezzo-soprano and Chamber Orch. (1982); *Amerindia*, a pentology: *I: Prologue* for Orch. (1982), *II: Los Heraldos Negros* for Narrator, Harp, Piano, Percussion, and String Orch. (1983), *III: Sacsahuaman* for Winds and Percussion (1983), *IV: Yo Vengo a Hablar* for Narrator and Orch. (1983), and *V: Era e Crepusculo de la Iguana* for Narrator and Orch. (1985); *Missa in nomine Bach* for Chorus and 8 Instruments (1984); *Laude* for Chorus and Orch. (1984); *Missa-dona nobis pacem* for Chorus (1987); *Chanson* for Voice and Tam-tam (1988); *Carrera* for Narrator and Orch. (1991); *Silvestre Revueltas*, oratorio for Narrator, 9 Voices, and Chamber Orch. (1994); *Am Grab Kafka's* for Woman Singer Playing Crotales (1994).

BIBL.: M. Grebe, "L. S., síntesis de su trayectoria creativa," *Revista Musical Chilena* (1968); W. Elias, *L. S.* (Tel Aviv, 1978).

Schiedermair, Ludwig, eminent German musicologist; b. Regensburg, Dec. 7, 1876; d. Bensberg, near Cologne, April 30, 1957. He studied in Munich with Sandberger and Beer-Walbrunn; received his Ph.D. at the Univ. of Erlangen in 1901 with the diss. *Die Künstlerische Bestrebungen am Hofe des Kurfürsten Ferdinand Maria von Bayern*; studied further with Riemann at the Univ. of Leipzig and with Kretzschmar at the Univ. of Berlin; completed his Habilitation in 1906 at the Univ. of Marburg with his *Simon Mayr: Beiträge zur Geschichte der Oper um die Wende des 18. und 19. Jahrhunderts* (publ. in Leipzig, 1907–10), where he then taught (1906–11); then went to the Univ. of Bonn (1911), where he was a reader (1915–20) and a prof. (1920–45). He was founder-director of the Beethoven Archives in Bonn; was made president of the Deutsche Gesellschaft für Musikwissenschaft (1937) and chairman of the music section of the Deutsche Akademie (1940). A Festschrift was publ. in honor of his 60th (Berlin, 1937) and 80th (Cologne, 1956) birthdays.

WRITINGS: *Gustav Mahler* (Leipzig, 1901); *Bayreuther Festspiele im Zeitalter des Absolutismus* (Leipzig, 1908); *Die Briefe Mozarts und seiner Familie* (5 vols., Munich, 1914; vol. 5 is an iconography); *W.A. Mozarts Handschrift* (Bückeburg, 1919; facsimiles); *Einführung in das Studium der Musikgeschichte* (Munich, 1918; new ed., Bonn, 1947); *Mozart* (Munich, 1922; 2nd ed., Bonn, 1948); *Der junge Beethoven* (Leipzig, 1925; 4th ed., 1970); *Beethoven: Beiträge zum Leben und Schaffen* (Leipzig, 1930; 3rd ed., 1943); *Die deutsche Oper* (Leipzig, 1930); *Die Gestaltung weltanschaulicher Ideen in der Vokalmusik Beethovens* (Leipzig, 1934); *Musik am Rheinstron* (Cologne, 1947); *Musikalische Begegnungen; Erlebnis und Erin-*

nerung (Cologne, 1948); *Deutsche Musik im Europäischen Raum* (Münster, 1954).

BIBL.: J. Kross, "L. S.," *Bonner Gelehrte* (1968).

Schierbeck, Poul (Julius Ouscher), distinguished Danish organist, pedagogue, and composer; b. Copenhagen, June 8, 1888; d. there, Feb. 9, 1949. He studied composition with Nielsen and Laub; also received instruction from Paul Hellmuth, Henrik Knudsen, and Frank van der Stucken. He was organist at Copenhagen's Skovshoved Church (1916–49) and a teacher of composition and instrumentation at the Royal Danish Cons. of Music (1931–49). In 1947 he was made a member of the Royal Swedish Academy of Music in Stockholm.

WORKS: OPERA: *Fête galante* (1923–30; Copenhagen, Sept. 1, 1931). **ORCH.:** Sym. (1916–21; Göteborg, Feb. 15, 1922, Nielsen conducting); *Natten* (The Night), symphonic scene for Piano and Orch. (1938); *Andante doloroso* for Strings (1942). **VOCAL:** Many cantatas; numerous choral works; songs, including the sets *Nakjaelen* (1921) and *Alverden gaar omkring* (The World Goes Round; 1938). **OTHER:** Chamber music; organ chorales.

BIBL.: O. Mathisen, *P. S.* (diss., Univ. of Copenhagen, 1972).

Schiff, András, distinguished Hungarian pianist; b. Budapest, Dec. 21, 1953. He studied piano as a child with Elizabeth Vadasz in Budapest, where he made his debut at 9; then entered the Franz Liszt Academy of Music at 14, continuing his studies with Kadosa; also studied with George Malcolm in London. After winning prizes at the Tchaikovsky Competition in Moscow in 1974 and at the Leeds Competition in 1975, he embarked upon an international career. He made his U.S. debut at N.Y.'s Carnegie Hall as soloist with the visiting Franz Liszt Chamber Orch. of Budapest in 1978; then settled in the West (1979). He first gained recognition for his insightful and intellectually stimulating interpretations of the music of Bach; also was a distinguished interpreter of Mozart, Beethoven, Schubert, Schumann, and Chopin. On Oct. 19, 1989, he made his Carnegie Hall recital debut in N.Y. In 1993 he played a cycle of the complete piano sonatas of Schubert as part of the Schubertiade at N.Y.'s 92nd Street Y.

Schiff, Heinrich, prominent Austrian cellist and conductor; b. Gmunden, Nov. 18, 1951. He first studied piano; then took cello lessons with Tobias Kühne in Vienna and later with André Navarra in Detmold. After winning prizes in competitions in Geneva, Vienna, and Warsaw, he was a soloist with the Vienna Phil., the Concertgebouw Orch. in Amsterdam, the Stockholm Phil., the BBC Sym. Orch., and the Royal Phil. in London; also concertized in Toronto and Montreal. He made his U.S. debut as soloist in the Dvořák Cello Concerto with Sir Colin Davis and the Cleveland Orch. at the Blossom Music Center (Aug. 21, 1981); also appeared in Australia, Israel, and Japan. He maintains a comprehensive repertory, ranging from Vivaldi to such contemporary works as Henze's concerto, written for him; also performs rarely-heard scores, including 2 concertos by Vieuxtemps, which he discovered. His playing is marked by assured technical resources and mellowness of tone. Schiff has also appeared as a conductor; in 1990 he became artistic director of the Northern Sinfonia in Newcastle upon Tyne.

Schifrin, Lalo (Boris), Argentine-American pianist, conductor, and composer; b. Buenos Aires, June 21, 1932. He studied music at home with his father, the concertmaster of the Teatro Colón orch.; subsequently studied harmony with Juan Carlos Paz; won a scholarship to the Paris Cons. in 1950, where he received guidance from Koechlin, and took courses with Messiaen. He became interested in jazz, and represented Argentina at the International Jazz Festival in Paris in 1955; returning to Buenos Aires, he formed his own jazz band, adopting the bebop style. In 1958 he went to N.Y., and later was pianist with Dizzy Gillespie's band (1960–62); composed for it several exotic pieces, such as *Manteca, Con Alma*, and *Tunisian Fantasy*, based on Gillespie's *Night in Tunisia*. In 1963 he wrote a ballet, *Jazz Faust*. In 1964 he went to Hollywood, where he rapidly found his métier as composer for the films and television; among his scores are *The Liquidator* (1966), *Cool Hand Luke* (1967), *The Fox* (1967), *The Amityville Horror* (1978), *The Sting II* (1983), and *Bad Medicine* (1985). He also experimented with applying the jazz idiom to religious texts, as, for instance, in his *Jazz Suite on Mass Texts* (1965). He achieved his greatest popular success with the theme-motto for the television series *Mission: Impossible* (1966–73), in 5/4 time, for which he received 2 Grammy awards. His adaptation of modern techniques into mass media placed him in the enviable position of being praised by professional musicians. His oratorio *The Rise and Fall of the Third Reich*, featuring realistic excerpts and incorporating an actual recording of Hitler's speech in electronic amplification, was brought out at the Hollywood Bowl on Aug. 3, 1967. His other works include a Suite for Trumpet and Brass Orch. (1961); *The Ritual of Sound* for 15 Instruments (1962); *Pulsations* for Electronic Keyboard, Jazz Band, and Orch. (Los Angeles, Jan. 21, 1971); *Madrigals for the Space Age*, in 10 parts, for Narrator and Chorus (Los Angeles, Jan. 15, 1976); *Capriccio* for Clarinet and Strings (Los Angeles, Nov. 5, 1981); Guitar Concerto (1984); *Songs of the Aztecs* for Soloist and Orch. (Teotihuacan, Mexico, Oct. 29, 1988); 2 piano concertos, including No. 2, *Concerto of the Americas* (Washington, D.C., June 11, 1992). He served as music director of the newly-organized Paris Phil from 1988.

Schillinger, Joseph (Moiseievich), Russian-born American music theorist and composer; b. Kharkov, Aug. 31, 1895; d. N.Y., March 23, 1943. He studied at the St. Petersburg Cons. with Tcherepnin, Wihtol, and others. He was active as a teacher, conductor, and administrator in Kharkov (1918–22), Moscow, and Leningrad (1922–28). In 1928 he emigrated to the U.S. and became a naturalized American citizen in 1936; settled in N.Y. as a teacher of music, mathematics, and art history as well as his own system of composition based on rigid mathematical principles; taught at the New School for Social Research, N.Y. Univ., and Columbia Univ. Teachers College; also gave private lessons. Among his pupils were Tommy Dorsey, Vernon Duke, George Gershwin, Benny Goodman, Oscar Levant, and Glenn Miller. Schillinger publ. a short vol. of musical patterns, *Kaleidophone: New Resources of Melody and Harmony* (N.Y., 1940). L. Dowling and A. Shaw ed. and publ. his magnum opus, *The Schillinger System of Musical Composition* (2 vols., N.Y., 1941; 4th ed., 1946); this was followed by *The Mathematical Basis of the Arts* (N.Y., 1948) and *Encyclopedia of Rhythm* (N.Y., 1966). Schillinger was also a composer; his works include *March of the Orient* for Orch. (Leningrad, May 12, 1926); *First Airphonic Suite* for Theremin and Orch. (Cleveland, Nov. 28, 1929; Leo Theremin soloist); *North-Russian Symphony* (1930); *The People and the Prophet*, ballet (1931); piano pieces; songs; etc.

BIBL.: H. Cowell, "J. S. as Composer," *Music News*, XXXIV/3 (1947); V. Duke, "Gershwin, S., Dukelsky: Some Reminiscences," *Musical Quarterly* (Jan. 1947); F. Schillinger, *J. S.: A Memoir by His Wife* (N.Y., 1949); D. Augestine, *Four Theories of Music in the United States, 1900–1950: Cowell, Yasser, Partch, S.* (diss., Univ. of Texas, 1979); J. Burk, "S.'s Double Equal Temperament System," in E. Asmus, ed., *The Pyschology and Acoustics of Music: A Collection of Papers* (Lawrence, Kansas, 1979).

Schillings, Max von, German composer and conductor; b. Duren, April 19, 1868; d. Berlin, July 24, 1933. While attending the Gymnasium at Bonn, he studied violin with O. von Königslow, and piano and composition with K.J. Brambach. He then entered the Univ. of Munich, where he studied law, philosophy, literature, and art. He became associated with Richard Strauss, and under his influence decided to devote himself entirely to music. In 1892 he was engaged as assistant stage director at the Bayreuth Festival; in 1902 he became chorus master. He went to Stuttgart in 1908 as assistant to the Intendant at the Royal Opera, and then was its Generalmusikdirektor (1911–18); upon the inauguration of its new opera theater, he was ennobled as von Schillings; was Intendant of the Berlin State Opera (1919–25). He made several visits as a conductor to the U.S. In 1923 he married **Barbara Kemp**. As a composer, he trailed in the path of Wagner, barely avoiding direct imitation.

WORKS: OPERAS: *Ingwelde* (Karlsruhe, Nov. 13, 1894); *Der Pfeifertag* (Schwerin, Nov. 26, 1899; rev. 1931); *Moloch* (Dresden, Dec. 8, 1906); *Mona Lisa* (Stuttgart, Sept. 26, 1915). **ORCH.:** 2 Phantasiestücke: *Dem Andenken seiner Mutter* (1883) and *Aus dem Jahre* (1890); 2 symphonische Phantarien: *Meergruss* and *Seemorgen* (1895); *Ein Zwiegesprach*, tone poem for Violin, Cello, and Orch. (1896); *Symphonischer Prolog zu Sophokles Ödipus* (1900); *Musik zu Aeschylos Orestie* (1901); *Musik zu Goethes Faust*, part 1 (1908; rev. and aug., 1915); Violin Concerto (1910); *Festlicher Marsch* for Military Band (1911); *Tanz der Blumen* for Small Orch. (1930). **CHAMBER:** String Quartet (1887; rev. 1906); Improvisation for Violin and Piano (1895); Piano Quintet (1917); piano pieces. **VOCAL:** Choral pieces; songs.

BIBL.: R. Louis, *M. S.* (Leipzig, 1909); A. Richard, *M. S.* (Munich, 1922); W. Raupp, *M. v.S.: Der Kampf eines deutschen Künstlers* (Hamburg, 1935); J. Geuenich and K. Strahn, eds., *Gedenkschrift M. v.S. zum 100. Geburtstag* (Düren, 1968).

Schindler, Kurt, German-American conductor, music editor, and composer; b. Berlin, Feb. 17, 1882; d. N.Y., Nov. 16, 1935. He studied piano with Ansorge and composition with Bussler and others in Berlin; took additional theory lessons in Munich with Thuille. He then was briefly assistant conductor to Richard Strauss in Berlin and to Mottl in Munich; in 1904 he emigrated to America and, after serving as an assistant chorus master at the Metropolitan Opera in N.Y., was engaged as a reader, ed., and critic for G. Schirmer (1907), remaining with the firm for about 20 years. In 1909 he founded the MacDowell Chorus, which became the Schola Cantorum of N.Y. in 1912. Schindler conducted it until 1926 in programs including his choral arrangements of folk songs of various nations. Among his valuable folk song eds. are *A Century of Russian Song from Glinka to Rachmaninoff* (N.Y., 1911); *Songs of the Russian People* (Boston, 1915); *Masters of Russian Song* (1917); *Sixty Russian Folk-Songs for One Voice* (N.Y., 1918–19); and *Folk Music and Poetry of Spain and Portugal* (N.Y., 1941); also ed. the anthology *The Development of Opera: From its Earliest Beginnings to the Masterworks of Gluck* (1913).

Schiøler, Victor, Danish pianist and conductor; b. Copenhagen, April 7, 1899; d. there, Feb. 17, 1967. He studied with his mother, Augusta Schiøler (1868–1946); then with Ignaz Friedman and Artur Schnabel. He made his debut in 1914; from 1919, toured in Europe; made his first American tour in 1948–49. He was also active as a conductor in Denmark.

Schiørring, Nils, Danish musicologist; b. Copenhagen, April 8, 1910. He studied musicology with Abrahamsen and Larsen at the Univ. of Copenhagen (M.A., 1933); concurrently took lessons in cello from L. Jensen. He completed his musicological training at the Univ. of Copenhagen (Ph.D., 1950, with the diss. *Det 16. og 17. århundredes verdslige danske visesang*; publ. in Copenhagen, 1950). He worked at the Copenhagen Music History Museum (1932–53); also wrote music criticism and served as ed. of *Dansk musiktidsskrift* (1943–45) and *Dansk årbog for musikforskning* (with S. Sorensen; from 1961). In 1950 he joined the faculty of the Univ. of Copenhagen, retiring in 1980.

WRITINGS (all publ. in Copenhagen): *Billeder fra 125 aars musikliv (1827–1952)* (1952); *Selma Nielsens Viser* (1956); *Allemande og fransk ouverture* (1957); *Musikkens vije* (1959; 2nd ed., 1964); ed. with S. Kragh-Jacobsen, *August Bournonville: Lettres à la maison de son enfance* (1969–70); with N. Jensen, *Deutschdänische Begegnungen um 1800: Künst, Dichtung, Musik* (1974); *Musikkens Historie i Danmark* (1978).

Schiøtz, Aksel (Hauch), famous Danish tenor, baritone, and pedagogue; b. Roskilde, Sept. 1, 1906; d. Copenhagen, April 19, 1975. His father was an architect, and he urged Schiøtz to follow an academic career; accordingly, he enrolled at the Univ. of Copenhagen in language studies (M.A., 1929). He also studied singing, first at the Danish Royal Opera School in Copenhagen, and later with John Forsell in Stockholm. He made his concert debut in 1938; his operatic debut followed in 1939 as Ferrando in *Così fan tutte* at the Royal Danish Theater in Copenhagen, and he soon gained wide recognition as a Mozartian and as a lieder artist. In 1946 he made appearances in England; in 1948 he visited the U.S. His career was tragically halted when he developed a brain tumor in 1950, which led to an impairment of his speech; however, he regained his capacities as a singer and gave concerts as a baritone. From 1955 to 1958 he taught voice at the Univ. of Minnesota; from 1958 to 1961, was a prof. of voice at the Royal Cons. of Music and the Univ. of Toronto; from 1961 to 1968, at the Univ. of Colo.; and from 1968, at the Royal Danish School of Educational Studies in Copenhagen. In 1977 a memorial fund was formed in the U.S. to preserve his memory by granting scholarships in art songs. He publ. *The Singer and His Art* (N.Y., 1969).

BIBL.: G. Schiøtz, *Kunst og Kamp: Gerd og A. S.* (Copenhagen, 1951).

Schipa, Tito (actually, **Raffaele Attilio Amadeo**), famous Italian tenor; b. Lecce, Jan. 2, 1888; d. N.Y., Dec. 16, 1965. He studied with A. Gerunda in Lecce and with E. Piccoli in Milan, and began his career as a composer of piano pieces and songs; then turned to singing, and in 1910 made his operatic debut at Vercelli in *La Traviata*. After numerous appearances in Europe, he was engaged by the Chicago Opera (1919–32); made his first appearance with the Metropolitan Opera in N.Y. on Nov. 23, 1932, as Nemorino in *L'elisir d'amore*; continued to sing with the Metropolitan until 1935, then again in 1941. Schipa made extensive tours of Europe and South America, as well as in the U.S. He retired from the operatic stage in 1954, but continued to give concerts until late in life. Among his greatest roles were Des Grieux in *Manon*, the Duke of Mantua, Don Ottavio, and Werther. He wrote an operetta, *La Principessa Liana* (1935); a Mass (1929); several songs; also wrote a book, *Si confessi* (Genoa, 1961).

Schipper, Emil (Zacharias), Austrian bass-baritone; b. Vienna, Aug. 19, 1882; d. there, July 20, 1957. He studied in Vienna and with Guarino in Milan. He made his operatic debut at the German Theater in Prague in 1904 as Telramund; then sang in Linz (1911–12), at the Vienna Volksoper (1912–15), the Bavarian Court (later State) Opera (1916–22), and the Vienna State Opera (1922–28); also made guest appearances at Covent Garden in London (1924–28), in Chicago (1928–29), and in Salzburg (1930; 1935–36). His finest roles were in operas by Wagner and R. Strauss. He was married to **Maria Olczewska**.

Schippers, Thomas, greatly gifted American conductor; b. Kalamazoo, Mich., March 9, 1930; d. N.Y., Dec. 16, 1977. He played piano in public at the age of 6, and was a church organist at 14. He studied piano at the Curtis Inst. of Music in Philadelphia (1944–45) and privately with Olga Samaroff (1946–47); subsequently attended Yale Univ., where he took some composition lessons from Hindemith. In 1948 he won 2nd prize in the contest for young conductors organized by the Philadelphia Orch. He then took a job as organist at the Greenwich Village Presbyterian Church in N.Y.; joined a group of young musicians in an enterprise called the Lemonade Opera Co., and conducted this group for several years. On March 15, 1950, he conducted the N.Y. premiere of Menotti's opera *The Consul*; also conducted the television premiere of his *Amahl and the Night Visitors* (N.Y., Dec. 24, 1951). On April 9, 1952, he made his first appearance at the N.Y. City Opera conducting Menotti's *The Old Maid and the Thief*, remaining on its roster until 1954. On March 26, 1955, he led the N.Y. Phil. as guest conductor. On Dec. 23, 1955, he made his debut at the Metropolitan Opera in N.Y. conducting *Don Pasquale*; conducted there regularly in subsequent seasons. From 1958 to 1976 he was associated with Menotti at the Spoleto Festival of Two Worlds. Other engagements included appearances with the N.Y.

Phil., which he accompanied in 1959 to the Soviet Union as an alternate conductor with Leonard Bernstein. In 1962 he conducted at La Scala the premiere of Manuel de Falla's cantata *Atlantida*. In 1964 he conducted at the Bayreuth Festival. He was a favorite conductor for new works at the Metropolitan Opera; conducted the first performance of Menotti's opera *The Last Savage* and the opening of the new home of the Metropolitan with Samuel Barber's *Antony and Cleopatra* (Sept. 16, 1966); he also conducted the first production at the Metropolitan of the original version of Mussorgsky's *Boris Godunov* (1974). In 1970 he was appointed music director of the Cincinnati Sym. Orch., one of the few American-born conductors to occupy a major sym. orch. post; was also a prof. at the Univ. of Cincinnati College-Cons. of Music (from 1972). There was an element of tragedy in his life. Rich, handsome, and articulate, he became a victim of lung cancer, and was unable to open the scheduled season of the Cincinnati Sym. Orch. in the fall of 1977; in a gesture of gratitude for his work, the management gave him the title of conductor laureate; he bequeathed a sum of $5,000,000 to the orch. His wife died of cancer in 1973. When he conducted *La forza del destino* at the Metropolitan Opera on March 4, 1960, the baritone Leonard Warren collapsed and died on the stage.

Schirmer, Ernest Charles, American music publisher; b. Mt. Vernon, N.Y., March 15, 1865; d. Waban, Mass., Feb. 15, 1958. After serving as business manager (1891–1902) and partner (1902–17) of the Boston Music Co., he founded the E.C. Schirmer Music Co. in 1921. It published the Concord Series, the Choral Repertory of the Harvard Univ. Glee Club, Radcliffe, Vassar, and Wellesley College Choral Music, the Polyphonic and "A Cappella" Libraries, the St. Dunstan Edition of Sacred Music, and treatises on harmonic analysis, musical theory, and music appreciation. The firm enjoyed a world market for its publications, with agencies in London and Hamburg.

Schirmer, G., Inc., one of the leading American music publishing firms. It was an outgrowth of the business founded in N.Y. in 1848 by Kerksieg & Breusing, of which Gustav Schirmer became manager in 1854. With another employee, Bernard Beer, he took over the business in 1861, and the firm became known as "Beer & Schirmer." In 1866 he became the sole owner, establishing the house of "G. Schirmer, Music Publishers, Importers and Dealers." After his death in 1893, the firm was incorporated under the management of his sons, Rudolph Edward Schirmer and Gustave Schirmer. Rudolph Schirmer died in 1919, and was succeeded by his nephew Gustave Schirmer, 3rd, who was president until 1921. W. Rodman Fay was president (1921–29). Carl Engel served as president from 1929 to 1944, with the exception of 1933, when Hermann Irion held the office. Gustave Schirmer, 3rd, was again president from 1944 until 1957. He was succeeded by Rudolph Tauhert (1957–72). Until 1880, the business was located at 701 Broadway in N.Y.; then it was moved to 35 Union Square, and in 1909 was transferred to a 7-story building at 3 East 43rd St. It remained at that address until 1960, when it was moved to 609 5th Ave., and its retail store relocated at 4 East 49th St. In 1969 G. Schirmer, Inc. was acquired by Macmillan, Inc., and in 1973 the executive offices were moved to 866 3rd Ave.; in 1995 they were moved to 1633 Broadway. In 1973 Schirmer Books was founded as a division of Macmillan Publ. Co., Inc., taking over the publication of books on music for college, trade, and professional/reference markets, while G. Schirmer continued publication of musical works. In 1986 the latter was sold to Music Sales Corp. of N.Y. The N.Y. firm also maintained branches in Cleveland (until 1962) and in Los Angeles (until 1967). In 1892 the firm began publ. of the Library of Musical Classics, notable for careful editing and general typographical excellence; with its didactic Latin motto, "Musica laborum dulce lenimen," it became a familiar part of musical homes. In the same year was launched the Collection of Operas, a series of vocal scores with original text and Eng. tr.; another series, The Golden Treasury, was begun in 1905. Schirmer's Scholastic Series, containing pedagogical works, began publ. in 1917. Among other laudable initiatives was the American Folk-Song Series, offering authentic folk material. The firm entered the field of musical lexicography in 1900 when it publ. *Baker's Biographical Dictionary of Musicians*, ed. by Theodore Baker. A 2nd ed. appeared in 1905. Alfred Remy was ed. of the 3rd edition (1919). The 4th edition was ed. by Carl Engel (1940). Nicolas Slonimsky brought out a Supplement in 1949, and then ed. the 5th edition (1958) and the Supplements of 1965 and 1971; he subsequently ed. the 6th (1978), 7th (1984), and 8th (1992) editions. Theodore Baker also compiled and ed. *A Dictionary of Musical Terms* (G. Schirmer, N.Y., 1895; many reprints) and *Pronouncing Pocket-Manual of Musical Terms* (1905; more than a million copies sold). In 1915 the *Musical Quarterly* was founded under the editorship of O.G. Sonneck; its subsequent editors have been Carl Engel (1929–44), Gustave Reese (1944–45), Paul Henry Lang (1945–72), Christopher Hatch (1972–77), Joan Peyser (1977–84), Eric Salzman (1984–91), and Leon Botstein (from 1992). It has publ. articles by the foremost scholars of Europe and the U.S.; beginning in 1989, it was publ. by the Oxford Univ. Press. The music catalog of G. Schirmer, Inc. comprises tens of thousands of publs., ranging from solo songs to full orch. scores. Particularly meritorious is the endeavor of the publishers to promote American music; the firm has publ. works by Ernest Bloch, Charles Loeffler, Charles Griffes, Walter Piston, Roy Harris, William Schuman, Samuel Barber, Gian Carlo Menotti, Paul Creston, Leonard Bernstein, Elliott Carter, Henry Cowell, Norman Dello Joio, Morton Gould, Virgil Thomson, Milton Babbitt, Gunther Schuller, and many others; it also took over some works of Charles Ives. Among European composers, the works of Arnold Schoenberg, Gustav Holst, and Benjamin Britten are included in the Schirmer catalogue, as well as a number of works by modern Russian composers.

Schirmer, Ulf, German conductor; b. Eschenhausen, near Bremen, Jan. 8, 1959. He received training in composition from Ligeti and in conducting from Horst Stein and Dohnányi. After working as a répétiteur at the Mannheim National Theater (1980), he was named to that position at the Vienna State Opera (1981). He was assistant to Maazel (1982) and Stein (1983) at the Bayreuth Festival, and then conducted at the Vienna State Opera (1984–86), where he subsequently served as 1st conductor (1986–88). From 1988 to 1991 he was Generalmusikdirektor in Wiesbaden. He appeared as a guest conductor at the Salzburg Festival (1989), with the Vienna Phil. (1992), at Milan's La Scala (1993), and with the Berlin Phil. (1993), among others. In 1995 he became chief conductor of the Danish National Radio Sym. Orch. in Copenhagen.

Schiske, Karl (Hubert Rudolf), distinguished Austrian composer and pedagogue; b. Raab, Feb. 12, 1916; d. Vienna, June 16, 1969. He studied at the New Vienna Cons. (1932–38) and received training in piano with Roderich Bass and Julius Varga, and in harmony and counterpoint with Ernst Kanitz. After taking diplomas in composition (1939) and piano (1940) at the Vienna Academy of Music, he pursued his academic training at the Univ. of Vienna (Ph.D., 1942, with the diss. *Zur Dissonanzanwendung in den Symphonien Anton Bruckners*). In 1952 he became a teacher of composition at the Vienna Academy of Music, and was granted the title of prof. in 1954. In 1966–67 he also was a visiting prof. at the Univ. of Calif. at Riverside. Among his honors were the music prize of the City of Vienna (1950), the Austrian State Prize (1952), and the Great Austrian State Prize (1967). Schiske was highly influential as a teacher. His compositional technique was curiously synthetic, and yet invariably logical, containing elements of early polyphony and contemporary serialism.

WORKS: ORCH.: *Vorspiel* (1937–38); Piano Concerto (1938–39); 2 concertos for Strings (1940–41; 1945); Trumpet Concerto (1939–40); 5 syms. (1941–42; 1947–48; 1950–51; 1955; 1965); *Tanzrondo* (1942); *Kammerkonzert* (1949); Violin Concerto (1952); *Synthese* (1958); *Divertimento* for Chamber Orch. (1963; also for 10 Instruments). **CHAMBER:** 2 string quartets (1936–37; 1945); Sextet for Clarinet, String Quartet, and Piano

(1937); 3 suites for 2 Recorders (1941, 1945, 1949); Violin Sonata (1943–44); Quintet for Flute, Oboe, Clarinet, Horn, and Bassoon (1945); *Musik* for Clarinet, Trumpet, and Viola (1947–48); *Drei Stücke für Gloria* for Violin (1951); Sonatine for Violin, Cello, and Piano (1951–52); Trio Sonata for 3 Melody Instruments or Organ (1954); *Dialog* for Cello and Piano (1967). **KEYBOARD: PIANO:** *Kleine Suite* (1935); *Thema, 8 Variationen und Doppelfuge* (1935–36); Sonata (1936); *Rhapsodie* (1945); *Tanzsuite* (1945); Sonata for Piano, 4-hands (1949); *Drei Stücke nach Volksweisen* (1951); *Étudensuite* (1951); Sonatine (1953). **ORGAN:** *Variationen über ein eigenes Thema* (1938); *Toccata* (1951–52); Choral-Partita (1957). **VOCAL:** *Reitjagd*, cantata for Baritone, Chorus, and Orch. (1938); *Vom Tode*, oratorio for Soprano, Alto, Tenor, Bass, Chorus, Orch., and Organ (1946); *Candada* for Soprano, Chorus, and Orch. (1956); *Missa: Cunctipotens genitor Deus* for Chorus and Organ ad libitum (1954); choruses; songs.

Schiuma, Alfredo, Argentine composer; b. Buenos Aires, July 1, 1885; d. there, July 24, 1963. He studied with Romaniello in Buenos Aires, and later established his own music school there. He wrote several operas in a singable Italianate idiom for Buenos Aires: *Amy Robsart*, based on Walter Scott's novel *Kenilworth* (April 24, 1920); *La Sirocchia* (April 23, 1922); *Tabaré* (Aug. 6, 1925); *Las virgenes del sol* (June 20, 1939); *La infanta* (Aug. 12, 1941); also 4 syms. (1928–57); a symphonic tableau, *Pitunga* (Buenos Aires, March 31, 1929); symphonic sketch, *Los Incas* (Buenos Aires, April 26, 1931); choruses; chamber music; songs.

Schlesinger, Kathleen, Irish musicologist; b. Hollywood, near Belfast, June 27, 1862; d. London, April 16, 1953. She was educated in Switzerland; then settled in England; became interested in musical instruments. She publ. *The Instruments of the Modern Orchestra* (2 vols., London, 1910). Her chief work was *The Greek Aulos* (London, 1939), not only containing a description of ancient Greek instruments, but also propounding an original theory of the formation of Greek modes, which aroused much controversy; the weight of learned opinion inclined against her hypotheses.

Schlick, Barbara, admired German soprano; b. Würzburg, July 21, 1943. She studied at the Würzburg Hochschule für Musik, with Lohmann in Wiesbaden, and with Wesselmann in Essen. In 1966 she joined Adolf Scherbaum's Baroque ensemble as a soloist, and began to sing widely in Europe. In 1972 she toured North America as soloist with Paul Kuentz and his chamber orch. In subsequent years, she appeared as a concert artist and established a strong reputation as an exponent of early music. From 1979 she also sang in Baroque and classical operas, appearing in Munich, Göttingen, Bern, St. Gallen, and Hamburg. She also taught at the Würzburg Hochschule für Musik.

Schloezer, Boris de, renowned Russian-French writer on music; b. Vitebsk, Dec. 20, 1881; d. Paris, Oct. 7, 1969. He studied music in Brussels and Paris; returning to Russia, he devoted himself to a profound study of philosophy, aesthetics, and theory. His sister, Tatiana Schloezer, was the 2nd wife of Scriabin, and Schloezer became a close friend of Scriabin, who confided to him his theosophic and musical ideas. In 1920 he emigrated to France, where he continued his literary activities in the Russian émigré press and in French literary magazines. He publ. a monograph on Scriabin in Russian (vol. 1, Berlin, 1923; French tr., Paris, 1975; Eng. tr. by N. Slonimsky, Berkeley and Los Angeles, 1987; vol. II not completed); other books include *Igor Stravinsky* (Paris, 1929) and *Introduction à J.S. Bach* (Paris, 1947). He also wrote a philosophical fantasy, *Mon nom est personne* and *Rapport secret*, depicting a distant planet whose inhabitants achieved immortality and divinity through science.

BIBL.: *B. d.S.* (Paris, 1981).

Schlusnus, Heinrich, eminent German baritone; b. Braubach am Rhein, Aug. 6, 1888; d. Frankfurt am Main, June 18, 1952. He studied voice in Frankfurt am Main and Berlin. He made his operatic debut as the Herald in *Lohengrin* at the Hamburg Opera on Jan. 1, 1914; was then on its roster for the 1914–15 season; he subsequently sang in Nuremberg (1915–17), then was a leading member of the Berlin Royal (later State) Opera, remaining there until 1945; also appeared in Chicago (1927–28), Bayreuth (1933), and Paris (1937). He was renowned as a lieder artist.

BIBL.: E. von Naso and A. Schlusnus, *H. S., Mensch und Sänger* (Hamburg, 1957).

Schlüter, Erna, German contralto, later soprano; b. Oldenburg, Feb. 5, 1904; d. Hamburg, Dec. 1, 1969. She made her operatic debut as a contralto in Oldenburg in 1922. Turning to soprano roles, she sang in Mannheim (1925–30) and Düsseldorf (1930–40). From 1940 to 1956 she was a member of the Hamburg State Opera. On Nov. 26, 1947, she made her Metropolitan Opera debut in N.Y. as Isolde, remaining on the roster for one season. In 1948 she appeared at the Salzburg Festival as Beethoven's Leonore. She also made guest appearances at London's Covent Garden, the Vienna State Opera, in Amsterdam, and in Brussels. Her most famous role was Elektra.

Schmid, Erich, Swiss conductor and composer; b. Balsthal, Jan. 1, 1907. He began his studies at the Solothurn teachers training college. Following musical instruction from Max Kaempfert and Hermann Suter, he pursued his training at the Hoch Cons. in Frankfurt am Main (1928–30) and won the Frankfurt am Main Mozart Prize. In 1930–31 he completed his studies with Schoenberg at the Prussian Academy of Arts in Berlin. After appearing with the Hessian Radio in Frankfurt am Main (1931–33), he was music director in Glarus (1934–49). From 1949 to 1957 he was chief conductor of the Zürich Tonhalle Orch., and from 1949 to 1975 was conductor of the Gemischter Chor in Zürich. He was chief conductor of the Beromünster Radio Orch. in Zürich from 1957 to 1970. As a guest conductor, he appeared with various European orchs. From 1978 to 1984 he was principal guest conductor of the City of Birmingham Sym. Orch. Schmid was esteemed for his championship of modern music.

WORKS: ORCH.: *3 Stücke* (1930); Suite No. 1 for Wind Orch. and Percussion (1931). **CHAMBER:** 2 sonatinas: No. 1 for Piano and Violin (1929) and No. 2, *Zwei Sätze*, for Violin and Piano (1932–34); String Quartet (1930–31); Trio for Clarinet, Cello, and Piano (1931); *Notturno* for Bass Clarinet, Violin, and Cello (1935); *Rhapsodie* for Clarinet and Piano (1936); *Mura*, trio for Flute, Violin, and Cello (1955). **PIANO:** *6 Stücke* (1932); *Widmungen* (1933–35); *5 Bagatellen* (1943). **VOCAL:** Suite for Mezzo-soprano and Chamber Orch. (1929–36); 4 choruses (1930–40); 3 songs (1938–41).

Schmid, Ernst Fritz, eminent German musicologist; b. Tübingen, March 7, 1904; d. Augsburg, Jan. 20, 1960. He studied violin, viola, and viola d'amore at the Munich Academy of Music; took private lessons in theory and conducting; then studied musicology at the Univs. of Munich (with Sandberger), Freiburg im Breisgau (with Gurlitt), Tübingen (with Hasse), and Vienna (with Haas, Orel et al.); received his Ph.D. from the Univ. of Tübingen in 1929 with the diss. *Carl Philipp Emanuel Bach und seine Kammermusik* (publ. in Kassel, 1931); completed his Habilitation as a Privatdozent in musicology at the Univ. of Graz in 1934 with his *Joseph Haydn: Ein Buch von Vorfahren und Heimat des Meisters* (publ. in Kassel, 1934). He became a prof. at the Univ. of Tübingen in 1935; also founded the Schwabisches Landesmusikarchiv; he left Tübingen in 1937 to devote himself to private research. During World War II, he served in the German army. In 1948 he founded the Mozartgemeinde, and in 1951 the German Mozartgesellschaft. In 1954 he became academic director of the Neue Mozart Ausgabe; from 1955 he oversaw the publ. of the new critical ed. of Mozart's complete works, the *Neue Ausgabe Sämtlicher Werke*. In addition to his valuable research on Mozart, he discovered the private music collection of Emperor Franz II in Graz in 1933; this important collection is now housed in Vienna's Nationalbibliothek.

WRITINGS: *Wolfgang Amadeus Mozart* (Lübeck, 1934; 3rd ed., 1955); *Die Orgeln der Abtei Amorbach* (Buchen, 1938); ed. *Ein schwäbisches Mozartbuch* (Lorch and Stuttgart, 1948); *Musik am Hofe der Fürsten von Löwenstein-Wertheim-Rosenberg, 1720–1750* (Würzburg, 1953); *Musik an den schwäbischen Zollernhöfen der Renaissance* (Kassel, 1962).

BIBL.: W. Fischer et al., eds., *In memoriam E.F. S., 1904–1960: Ein Gedenkblatt für seine Angehörigen und Freunde* (Recklinghausen, 1961).

Schmid, Heinrich Kaspar, German composer and teacher; b. Landau an der Isar, Bavaria, Sept. 11, 1874; d. Munich, Jan. 8, 1953. He studied with Thuille and Bussmeyer at the Munich Academy of Music (1899–1903). In 1903 he went to Athens, where he taught music at the Odeon; in 1905 he returned to Munich and was on the faculty of the Academy of Music until 1921; then was director of the Karlsruhe Cons. (1921–24) and of the Augsburg Cons. (1924–32). His eyesight failed him and he was totally blind during the last years of his life. As a composer, he followed the Romantic tradition of the Bavarian School; he wrote a great number of lieder, and composed singspiels in a folklike manner, as well as choruses and chamber music.

BIBL.: H. Roth, *H.K. S.* (Munich, 1921); W. Zentner, "H.K. S.," *Neue Musikzeitschrift* (Aug.–Sept. 1949).

Schmidl, Carlo, Italian music publisher and lexicographer; b. Trieste, Oct. 7, 1859; d. there, Oct. 7, 1943. He was the son and pupil of the Hungarian composer Antonio (actually, Anton) Schmidl (1814–80). In 1872 he entered the employ of the music publisher Vicentini, and in 1889 he established his own business at Trieste; also directed the Leipzig branch of the Ricordi Co. (1901–06). He compiled and publ. an important biographical music dictionary, *Dizionario universale dei musicisti* (Milan, 1887–89; 2nd ed., 1926–29; supplement, 1938; 3rd ed., 1938), containing scrupulously accurate data on Italian musicians, exact dates of performance of major works, and other information testifying to independent research. Schmidl also wrote biographies of Schumann (1890) and G.S. Mayr (1901).

Schmidt, Annerose, German pianist; b. Wittenberg, Oct. 5, 1936. She studied with her father for 12 years, making her debut in Wittenberg when she was 9; then completed her training with Hugo Steurer at the Leipzig Hochschule für Musik (1953–58). In 1954 she was awarded a diploma at the International Chopin Competition in Warsaw, and in 1956 captured 1st prize at the International Robert Schumann Competition in Zwickau. She toured in both Eastern and Western Europe, appearing with the Gewandhaus Orch. of Leipzig, the Dresden State Orch., the Royal Phil. of London, the Concertgebouw Orch. of Amsterdam, and the Residentie Orch. of The Hague; also appeared at festivals in Salzburg, the Netherlands, Prague, Edinburgh, Berlin, Dresden, and Warsaw. In 1980 she made her U.S. debut as soloist with Kurt Masur and the Gewandhaus Orch. at Carnegie Hall in N.Y. She became a prof. at the East Berlin Hochschule für Musik in 1986. While best known for her performances of Bach, Mozart, Beethoven, Schumann, Chopin, and Brahms, Schmidt also plays contemporary works, including those of Siegfried Matthus and Wolfgang Rihm.

Schmidt, Franz, important Austrian composer and pedagogue; b. Pressburg, Dec. 22, 1874; d. Perchtoldsdorf, near Vienna, Feb. 11, 1939. He began his musical training with the Pressburg Cathedral organist, Maher; in 1888 his family settled in Vienna, where he had piano lessons from Leschetizky and also studied composition with Bruckner, theory with Fuchs, and cello with Hellmesberger at the Cons. (from 1890). He was a cellist in the orch. of the Vienna Court Opera (1896–1911); also taught cello at the Cons. of the Gesellschaft der Musikfreunde (1901–08) and was prof. of piano (1914–22) and of counterpoint and composition (from 1922) at the Vienna Staatsakademie; also served as director (1925–27); subsequently was director of the Vienna Hochschule für Musik (1927–31). In 1934 he was awarded an honorary doctorate from the Univ. of Vienna. After his retirement in 1937, Schmidt received the Beethoven Prize of the Prussian Academy in Berlin. His 2nd wife, Margarethe Schmidt, founded the Franz Schmidt-Gemeinde in 1951. Schmidt's music is steeped in Viennese Romanticism; the works of Bruckner and Reger were particularly influential in his development, but he found an original voice in his harmonic writing. Although he is regarded in Austria as a very important symphonic composer, his music is almost totally unknown elsewhere. Outside his homeland, he remains best known for his orch. suite, *Zwischenspiel aus einer unvollständigen romantischen Oper* (Vienna, Dec. 6, 1903), taken from his opera *Notre Dame* (1902–04; Vienna, April 1, 1914). Among his other significant works are 4 syms.: No. 1 (1896–99; Vienna, Jan. 25, 1902), No. 2 (1911–13; Vienna, Dec. 3, 1913), No. 3 (Vienna, Dec. 2, 1928), and No. 4 (1932–33; Vienna, Jan. 10, 1934); a Piano Concerto for Piano, Left-hand and Orch., for Paul Wittgenstein (1923; Vienna, Feb. 2, 1924); and the oratorio *Das Buch mit Sieben Siegeln* (1935–37; Vienna, June 15, 1938). He also composed 2 string quartets (1925, 1929) and other chamber works, 2 piano sonatas, and much organ music.

BIBL.: A. Liess, *F. S.: Sein Leben und Schaffen* (Graz, 1951); C. Nemeth, *F. S.: Ein Meister nach Brahms und Bruckner* (Vienna, 1957); R. Scholz, *F. S. als Orgelkomponist* (Vienna, 1971); N. Tschulik, *F. S.* (Vienna, 1972; Eng. tr., 1980); H. Truscott, *The Music of F. S.*: vol. I, *The Orchestral Music* (London, 1985); T. Leibnitz, *Österreichische Spätromantiker: Studien zu Emil Nikolaus von Rezniček, Joseph Marx, F. S., und Egon Kornauth* (Tutzing, 1986); T. Corfield, *F. S. (1874–1939): A Discussion of his Style with Special Reference to the Four Symphonies and "Das Buch mit sieben Siegeln"* (N.Y. and London, 1989); G. Gruber, *F. S. als Rektor der Fachhochschule für Musik und darstellende Kunst in Wien (1927–1931)* (Vienna, 1989); M. Gailit, *Das Orgelsoloschaffen von F. S. (1874–1939)* (Vienna, 1990); R. Schuhenn, *F. S.s oratorische Werke: Zur Entstehungsgeschichte des "Buches mit sieben Siegeln" und der "Deutschen Auferstehung"* (Vienna, 1990).

Schmidt, Joseph, Romanian tenor; b. Bavideni, Bukovina, March 4, 1904; d. Zürich, Nov. 16, 1942. He studied at the Berlin Cons. In 1928 he began his career as a radio singer and won great popularity in Germany. In 1933 he went to Belgium; in 1938 was briefly in America; then settled in Switzerland, where he died in an internment camp. His voice was regarded as of great lyric expressiveness, but being almost a dwarf (he stood only 4 feet, 10 inches in height), he was unable to appear in opera.

BIBL.: A. Fassbind, *J. S.: Ein Lied Geht um die Welt: Spuren einer Legende* (Zürich, 1992).

Schmidt, Ole, Danish conductor and composer; b. Copenhagen, July 14, 1928. He studied at the Royal Danish Cons. of Music in Copenhagen (1947–55) and received training in conducting from Albert Wolff, Celibidache, and Kubelik. From 1959 to 1965 he was conductor of the Royal Danish Opera and Ballet in Copenhagen. After serving as chief conductor of the Hamburg Sym. Orch. (1970–71), he was a guest conductor of the Danish Radio Sym. Orch. in Copenhagen (from 1971). He also appeared as a guest conductor throughout Europe. Following his first appearance as a guest conductor of the BBC Sym. Orch. in London in 1977, he appeared as a guest conductor of all the BBC regional orchs. From 1979 to 1985 he was chief conductor of the Århus Sym. Orch. In 1980 he made his U.S. debut as a guest conductor of the Oakland (Calif.) Sym. Orch. From 1986 to 1989 he was chief guest conductor of the Royal Northern College of Music in Manchester, England. In 1989–90 he was interim conductor of the Toledo (Ohio) Sym. Orch.

WORKS: DRAMATIC: *Bag taeppet*, ballet (Copenhagen, Oct. 9, 1954); *Feber*, ballet (Copenhagen, Oct. 8, 1957); *Chopiniana*, ballet (Copenhagen, Feb. 2, 1958); *Ballet* (1959; Copenhagen, April 27, 1961); *Udstilling*, opera (Copenhagen, Dec. 5, 1969); *Jeanne d'Arc*, music for C.T. Dreyer's silent film of 1927 (Los Angeles, May 27, 1983); *Dyrefabler og Fabeldyr*, musical fairy tale (Copenhagen, April 26, 1987); *Harald og Tine*, musical

(Århus, Sept. 9, 1988). **ORCH.:** 2 piano concertos: No. 1 for Piano and Chamber Orch. (1951) and No. 2 for Piano and Strings (1954); *Elegi* for Oboe and Strings (1955); Sym. (1956); *Pièce concertante* for Trumpet, Trombone, and Orch. (1957); 2 accordion concertos (*Symphonic Fantasy and Allegro*, 1958; 1962); Suite for Flute and Chamber Orch. (1960); *Briol* (1962); Concerto for Horn and Chamber Orch. (1966); Concert Overture (1966); *2 mobiler* for Winds, Percussion, and Piano (1970); Violin Concerto (1971); Tuba Concerto (1975); *Tango Grosso* (Copenhagen, Sept. 14, 1975); Guitar Concerto (1976); *Dansk-Faerøsk Fanfare* (1977; rev. 1992); Sinfonietta for 3 Quintets (1977); Duo concertante for Flugelhorn, Tuba, and Orch. (1981); *Festouverture* for Wind Orch. (1984); *Hommage à Stravinsky* for Wind Orch. (Århus, May 23, 1985); Concerto for Flute and Strings (Århus, Nov. 27, 1985); *Renaessancedans* (1986); *Rapsodi* for Violin and Orch. (1988); *Pneumafonikon* (1992); *Øresundssymfoni* (1994; collaborative piece). **CHAMBER:** 5 string quartets (1954, 1963, 1965, 1969, 1977); Quartet for 2 Trumpets, Trombone, and Tuba (1955); *Divertimento* for Violin, Cello, Viola, and Piano (1956); Octet for Flute, Oboe, Clarinet, Bassoon, 2 Violins, Viola, and Cello (1960); 2 accordion toccatas (1960, 1963); *Fanfare, Intrada, and Gigue* for 7 Players (1967); *Festmusik* for Organ, 3 Trumpets, 3 Trombones, and 2 Timpani (1975); *Raxallo*, quintet for 2 Trumpets, Horn, Trombone, and Tuba (1976); Tuba Sonata (1976); *Fragmenter og samtaler* for 2 Trumpets, Horn, Trombone, and Tuba (1976); 2 accordion dialogues (1977, 1992); *Tube and Bones* for 3 Trombones and Tuba (1982); *Blå strå* for Flute, Violin, Viola, and Cello (1986); *Jahreszeiten* for Oboe and Organ (1989); *Karnak* for Trombone and Piano (1990); Wind Quintet (1991); Trio Sonata for 2 Trumpets and Organ (1992); Viola Sonata (1992–93); piano pieces.

Schmidt, Trudeliese, German mezzo-soprano; b. Saarbrücken, Nov. 7, 1941. She received her training in Saarbrücken and Rome. In 1965 she made her operatic debut as Hansel in Saarbrücken. In 1969 she became a member of the Deutsche Oper am Rhein in Düsseldorf. From 1971 she appeared in various German music centers, and in 1974 toured Japan with the Bavarian State Opera of Munich. She sang Dorabella at the Glyndebourne Festival in 1976. In subsequent years, she appeared in leading European music centers. In 1985 she was a soloist in Mozart's *Coronation Mass* with Karajan and the Vienna Phil. at a special concert at the Vatican in Rome for Pope John Paul II. Among her prominent roles are Cherubino, Rossini's Isabella, Weber's Fatima, and Strauss's Octavian and Composer.

Schmidt-Görg, Joseph, eminent German musicologist; b. Rüdinghausen, near Dortmund, March 19, 1897; d. Bonn, April 3, 1981. He studied musicology with Schiedermair and Schmitz at the Univ. of Bonn (Ph.D., 1926, with the diss. *Die Messen des Clemens non Papa*; completed his Habilitation there in 1930 with his *Die Mitteltontemperatur*). He became Schiedermair's assistant in the Beethoven Archives in Bonn in 1927; later served as director of the archives (1946–72); concurrently lectured on musicology at the Univ. of Bonn (1930–65). On his 70th birthday, he was presented with a Festschrift under the friendly Latin title *Colloquium amicorum* (Bonn, 1967), containing a catalogue of his writings. His publs. include *Unbekannte Manuskripte zu Beethovens weltlicher und geistlicher Gesangsmusik* (Bonn, 1928), *Katalog der Handschriften des Beethoven-Hauses und Beethoven-Archivs Bonn* (Bonn, 1935), *Nicolas Gombert: Leben und Werk* (Bonn, 1938), and *Ludwig van Beethoven* (with H. Schmidt; Bonn, 1969; Eng. tr., N.Y., 1970).

Schmidt-Isserstedt, Hans, respected German conductor; b. Berlin, May 5, 1900; d. Holm-Holstein, near Hamburg, May 28, 1973. He studied composition with Schreker at the Berlin Hochschule für Musik; also took courses at the Univs. of Berlin, Heidelberg, and Münster. In 1923 he became a répétiteur at the Wuppertal Opera; after conducting opera in Rostock (1928–31) and Darmstadt (1931–33), he held the post of 1st conductor at the Hamburg State Opera (1935–43); then joined the Deutsche Oper in Berlin, where he was made Generalmusikdirektor in 1944. In 1945 he was mandated by the British occupation authorities with the direction of the music section of the Hamburg Radio; he organized the North German Radio Sym. Orch., which he led with notable distinction until his retirement in 1971; was also chief conductor of the Stockholm Phil. (1955–64). He appeared widely as a guest conductor; also conducted at Covent Garden in London and at the Bavarian State Opera in Munich. He was especially admired for his cultured performances of the Austro-German repertoire.

Schmieder, Wolfgang, noted German music librarian; b. Bromberg, May 29, 1901; d. Fürstenfeldbruck, Nov. 8, 1990. He studied musicology with Kroyer and Moser, German philology and literature with F. Panzer and F. von Waldberg, and art history with C. Neumann at the Univ. of Heidelberg (Ph.D., 1927, with the diss. *Zur Melodiebildung in Liedern von Neidhart von Reuental*); then was an assistant lecturer in its musicology dept. (1927–30); subsequently studied library science with M. Bollert at the Sachsischen Landesbibliothek in Dresden and with O. Glauning at the Univ. of Leipzig Library. He was librarian of the Technische Hochschule in Dresden (1931–33); then went to Leipzig as head of the archives of Breitkopf & Härtel (1933–42). In 1946 he founded the music dept. of the City and Univ. Library in Frankfurt am Main, which he headed until 1963. He was presented a Festschrift on his 70th birthday in 1971, *Quellenstudien zur Musik*, ed. by K. Dorfmuller and G. von Dadelsen. Of his numerous publications, of fundamental importance is his exhaustive *Thematisch-systematisches Verzeichnis der musikalischen Werke von Johann Sebastian Bach: Bach-Werke-Verzeichnis* (Leipzig, 1950; 5th ed., rev., 1990); also valuable is *Musikalische alte Drücke bis etwa 1750* (with G. Hartweig; 2 vols., Wolfenbüttel, 1967).

Schmitt, Camille, Belgian organist, pedagogue, and composer; b. Aubange, March 30, 1908; d. Limelette, May 11, 1976. He studied at the Brussels Cons. (1928–37). He was an organist in France and Belgium (1923–29; 1940–48), a prof. at the Liège Cons. (1947–66), and director of the French Section of the Brussels Cons. (1966–73). In 1961 he married **Jacqueline Fontyn**.

WORKS: ORCH.: *Triptyque angevin* (1941); *Psaume* (1942); Sinfonietta (1943); *Rapsodie* (1944); *Préludes joyeux* (1945; Copenhagen, June 2, 1946); Piano Concerto (1955); *Métamorphoses* (1963); *Contrepoints* (1965); *Polyphonies* (1966); *Alternances* (1970). **CHAMBER:** Wind Quintet (1943); Trio for Oboe, Clarinet, and Bassoon (1945); String Quartet (1948); *Prélude* for Clarinet and Piano (1952); *Dialogue* for Violin and Piano (1953); *Métamorphoses* for Cello and Piano (1961); Quartet for 4 Clarinets (1964); *Burlesques* for Flute, Oboe, Clarinet, and Bassoon (1965); *Contrepoints* for Wind Quintet (1965); *Polyphonies* for Wind Quintet (1969); *Polyphonies* for Saxophone Quartet (1970). **PIANO:** *Polyphonies* (1966); *Histoire pour Pierre* (1970). **VOCAL:** *Psautier* for Alto, Piano, Oboe, Clarinet, and Bassoon (1946); *La Halte des heures*, cantata for Voice and Piano (1959); choruses.

Schmitt, Florent, outstanding French composer; b. Blâmont, Meurthe-et-Moselle, Sept. 28, 1870; d. Neuilly-sur- Seine, near Paris, Aug. 17, 1958. He studied piano with H. Hess and harmony with G. Sandré at the Nancy Cons. (1887–89); then entered the Paris Cons., where he took courses in harmony with Dubois and Lavignac, fugue with Gédalge, and composition with Massenet and Fauré; won the 2nd Prix de Rome with his cantata *Frédégonde* (1897) and the Grand Prix de Rome with his cantata *Sémiramis* (1900). He spent the years 1901–04 in the Villa Medicis in Rome, sending to the Académie several important instrumental and choral works; then traveled in Germany, Austria, Hungary, and Turkey. In 1906 he returned to Paris, where he served as a member of the executive committee of the Société Musicale Indépendante from its foundation in 1909; was also a member of the Société Nationale de Musique. He became an influential music critic, writing regularly for *Le*

Temps (1919–39); was also director of the Lyons Cons. (1922–24). In 1936 he was elected to Dukas's place in the Institut; also became a Commander of the Légion d'honneur. Schmitt spent his formative years in the ambience of French symbolism in poetry and Impressionism in music, and he followed these directions in his programmatically conceived orch. music; he nonetheless developed a strong, distinctive style of his own, mainly by elaborating the contrapuntal fabric of his works and extending the rhythmic design to intricate, asymmetrical combinations; he also exploited effects of primitivistic percussion, in many respects anticipating the developments of modern Russian music. The catalogue of his works is very long; he continued to compose until his death at the age of 87.

WORKS: DRAMATIC: BALLETS: *La Tragédie de Salomé* (Paris, Nov. 9, 1907; orch. suite, Paris, Jan. 8, 1911); *Le Petit Elfe Ferme-l'oeil*, after Hans Christian Andersen (Paris, Feb. 29, 1924); *Oriane la sans-égale* (Paris, Jan. 7, 1938). **INCIDENTAL MUSIC TO:** *Antoine et Cléopâtre*, after Shakespeare (Paris, June 14, 1920); *Reflets* (Paris, May 20, 1932). **ORCH.:** *En été* (1894); *Musiques de plein-air* (1897–99); *Le Palais hanté*, after Poe (1900–1904); *3 rapsodies* (1903–04); *Scherzo vif* for Violin and Orch. (1903–10); *Feuillets de voyage* (1903–13); *Reflets de l'Allemagne*, suite (1905); *Sélamlik*, symphonic poem for Military Band (1906); *Puppazzi*, suite (1907); *Légende* for Viola or Saxophone and Orch. (1918); *Mirages: Tristesse de Pan, La Tragique Chevauchée* (1921); *Fonctionnaire MCMXII: Inaction en musique* (1924; Paris, Jan. 16, 1927); *Danse d'Abisag* (1925); *Salammbô*, after Flaubert (1925); *Ronde burlesque* (1927; Paris, Jan. 12, 1930); *Çhançunik* (humorous phonetic spelling of Sens unique, i.e., "one-way street"; Paris, Feb. 15, 1930); *Symphonie concertante* for Piano and Orch. (Boston, Nov. 25, 1932, composer soloist); *Suite sans esprit de suite* (1937; Paris, Jan. 29, 1938); *Branle de sortie* (1938; Paris, Jan. 21, 1939); *Janiana*: Sym. for Strings (score entitled Sym. No. 2; 1941; Paris, May 1, 1942); *Habeyssée* for Violin and Orch. (phonetic representation of "ABC," as pronounced in French; Paris, March 14, 1947); Sym. (1957; Strasbourg, June 15, 1958). **CHAMBER:** *Scherzo-pastorale* for Flute and Piano (1889); *4 pièces* for Violin and Piano (1901); Piano Quintet (1901–08); *Andante et Scherzo* for Harp and String Quartet (1906); *Lied et Scherzo* for Double Wind Quintet (1910); *Sonate libre en deux parties enchainées* for Violin and Piano (1919); *Suite en rocaille* for Flute, Violin, Viola, Cello, and Harp (1934); *Sonatine en trio* for Flute, Clarinet, and Harpsichord (1935); *Minorités* for Flute, Violin, and Piano (1938); *Hasards* for Violin, Viola, Cello, and Piano (1939); *A tours d'anches* for Flute, Clarinet, Bassoon, and Piano (1939); Quartet for Saxophones (1941); String Trio (1944); Quartet for Flutes (1944); String Quartet (1945–48). **PIANO:** *Musiques intimes* (2 sets, 1890–1900 and 1898–1904); *Soirs*, 10 preludes (n.d.); *Ballade de la neige* (1896); *Pièces romantiques* (1900–1908); *Nuits romaines* (1901); *3 danses* (1935; also for Orch.); *Clavecin obtempérant*, suite (1945). **VOCAL:** *Tristesse au Jardin* for Voice and Orch. (1897–1908); *Musique sur l'eau* for Voice and Orch. (1898); *Danse des Devadasis* for Voice, Chorus, and Orch. (1900–1908); *Psaume XLVII* for Soprano, Chorus, Orch., and Organ (1904; Paris, Dec. 27, 1906); *Chant de guerre* for Tenor, Men's Chorus, and Orch. (1914); *Kerob-Shal* for Tenor and Orch. (1920–24); *Fête de la lumière* for Soprano, Chorus, and Orch. (1937); *L'Arbre entre tous* for Chorus and Orch. (1939); *A contre-voix* for Chorus (1943); other choruses; motets; solo songs.

BIBL.: P. Ferroud, *Autour de F. S.* (Paris, 1927); Y. Hucher, *F. S., L'homme et l'artiste* (Paris, 1953); Y. Hucher and M. Raveau, *L'Oeuvre de F. S.* (Paris, 1960).

Schmitt-Walter, Karl, German baritone; b. Gernersheim am Rhein, Dec. 23, 1900; d. Kreuth, Oberbayern, Jan. 14, 1985. He studied in Nuremberg and Munich. He made his operatic debut in 1921 in Oberhausen; then sang in Nuremberg, Saarbrücken, and Dortmund; was a member of the Wiesbaden Opera (1929–34), the Berlin Deutsche Oper (1934–50), and the Bavarian State Opera in Munich (1950–61); also sang at Bayreuth and Salzburg. In 1957 he became a prof. of voice at the Munich Academy of Music.

Schmitz, (Franz) Arnold, German musicologist; b. Sablon, near Metz, July 11, 1893; d. Mainz, Nov. 1, 1980. He took courses in musicology, history, and philosophy at the Univs. of Bonn, Munich, and Berlin; his principal mentors were Friedlaender, Kroyer, Sandberger, Schiedermair, and Wolf; received his Ph.D. in 1919 from the Univ. of Bonn with the diss. *Untersuchungen über des jungen Schumann Anschauungen vom musikalischen Schaffen*; completed his Habilitation there in 1921. He taught there (1921–28) and at the Dortmund Cons. (1925–29), then at the Univs. of Breslau (1929–39) and Mainz (1947–61); he served as rector at the latter (1953–54; 1960–61); later taught at the Univ. of Basel (1965–67).

WRITINGS: *Beethovens "zwei Prinzipe"* (Berlin, 1923); *Beethoven: unbekannte Skizzen und Entwürfe* (Bonn, 1924); *Das romantische Beethovenbild* (Berlin, 1927); *Die Bildlichkeit der wortgebundenen Musik J.S. Bachs* (Mainz, 1950).

Schmitz, Elie Robert, eminent French pianist and pedagogue; b. Paris, Feb. 8, 1889; d. San Francisco, Sept. 5, 1949. He studied at the Paris Cons. with Diémer, winning the premier prix. In 1908 he toured as accompanist of Slezak, Emma Eames, and other celebrated singers. In 1912 he organized in Paris the Assn. des Concerts Schmitz, which he led until 1914. In 1919 he toured the U.S. as a pianist; in 1920 he founded the Franco-American Music Soc. in N.Y. (incorporated in 1923 as Pro Musica), of which he was president from its inception; toured again in the U.S. and Europe (1921–29), and in the Orient (1929–30; 1932–33); eventually settled in San Francisco as a teacher. He publ. a book on his system of piano study, *The Capture of Inspiration* (N.Y., 1935; 2nd ed., 1944), and a valuable technical analysis with commentary, *The Piano Works of Claude Debussy* (N.Y., 1950).

Schmitz, Eugen, German musicologist; b. Neuburg an der Donau, Bavaria, July 12, 1882; d. Leipzig, July 10, 1959. He studied musicology with Sandberger and Kroyer at the Univ. of Munich (Ph.D., 1905, with the diss. *Der Nürnberger Organist Johann Staden: Beiträge zur Würdigung seiner musikgeschichtlichen Stellung*; extracts publ. in Leipzig, 1906); then completed his Habilitation there in 1909 with his *Beiträge zur Geschichte der italienischen Kammerkantate im 17. Jahrhundert* (publ. in Leipzig, 1914, as *Geschichte der Kantate und des geistlichen Konzerts I. Theil: Geschichte der weltlichen Solokantate*; 2nd ed., 1955, as *Geschichte der weltlichen Solokantate*). He wrote music criticism in Dresden; taught music at the Dresden Technische Hochschule (1916–39). From 1939 to 1953 he was director of the Musikbibliothek Peters in Leipzig.

WRITINGS: *Hugo Wolf* (Leipzig, 1906); *Richard Strauss als Musikdramatiker: eine ästhetische-kritische Studie* (Munich, 1907); *Richard Wagner* (Leipzig, 1909; 2nd ed., 1918); *Harmonielehre als Theorie: Aesthetik und Geschichte der musikalischen Harmonik* (Munich, 1911); *Palestrina* (Leipzig, 1914; 2nd ed., 1954); *Musikästhetik* (Leipzig, 1915; 2nd ed., 1925); *Orlando di Lasso* (Leipzig, 1915; 2nd ed., 1954); *Klavier, Klaviermusik und Klavierspiel* (Leipzig, 1919); *Richard Wagner: Wie wir ihn heute sehen* (Dresden, 1937); *Schuberts Auswirkung auf die deutsche Musik bis zu Hugo Wolf und Bruckner* (Leipzig, 1954); *Unverwelkter Volksliedstil: J.A.P. Schulz und seine "Lieder im Volkston"* (Leipzig, 1956).

Schmuller, Alexander, Russian violinist and teacher; b. Mozyr, Dec. 5, 1880; d. Amsterdam, March 29, 1933. He was a pupil of Ševčik, Hřimaly, and Auer. From 1908 he taught at the Stern Cons. in Berlin, and from 1914 at the Amsterdam Cons. For several years, he gave concerts with Max Reger, whose music he was one of the first to champion; made many concert tours in Europe and the U.S.

Schnabel, Artur, celebrated Austrian-born American pianist and pedagogue, father of **Karl Ulrich Schnabel**; b. Lipnik, April 17, 1882; d. Axenstein, Switzerland, Aug. 15, 1951. He first studied with Hans Schmitt and made his debut at 8; then studied with Leschetizky in Vienna (1891–97). He went to Berlin in 1900; there he married the contralto Therese Behr (1905), with whom he frequently appeared in recitals; he also played in recitals with leading musicians of the day, including Flesch, Casals, Feuermann, Huberman, Primrose, and Szigeti; likewise gave solo recitals in Europe and the U.S., presenting acclaimed cycles of the Beethoven sonatas; taught at the Berlin Hochschule für Musik (from 1925). After the advent of the Nazi regime in 1933, he left Germany and settled in Switzerland; taught master classes at Lake Como and recorded the first complete set of the Beethoven sonatas. With the outbreak of World War II in 1939, he went to the U.S.; became a naturalized American citizen in 1944; taught at the Univ. of Mich. (1940–45); then returned to Switzerland. Schnabel was one of the greatest pianists and pedagogues in the history of keyboard playing; eschewing the role of the virtuoso, he concentrated upon the masterworks of the Austro-German repertoire with an intellectual penetration and interpretive discernment of the highest order; he was renowned for his performances of Beethoven and Schubert; prepared an edition of the Beethoven piano sonatas. He was also a composer. A renewed interest in his music led to the recording of several of his compositions in the 1980s. In his works, he pursued an uncompromisingly modernistic idiom, thriving on dissonance and tracing melodic patterns along atonal lines.

WORKS: ORCH.: Piano Concerto (1901); 3 syms.: No. 1 (1937–38; Minneapolis, Dec. 13, 1946), No. 2 (1941–42; London recording studio, July 18–20, 1988), and No. 3 (1948); *Rhapsody* (1946; Cleveland, April 15, 1948). **CHAMBER:** Piano Quintet (1916); 5 string quartets (1918; 1921; 1923–24; 1924; 1940); Sonata for Solo Violin (1919); String Trio (1925); Sonata for Solo Cello (1931); Violin Sonata (1935); Piano Trio (1945); *Duodecimet* for Wind Quintet, Bass Clarinet, Trumpet, String Trio, Double Bass, and Percussion (1950; unfinished; completed and orchestrated by R. Leibowitz). **PIANO:** *3 Pieces* (1896); *3 Pieces* (1906); *Dance Suite* (1921); Sonata (1922); *Piano Piece in 7 Movements* (1936); *7 Pieces* (1947). **VOCAL:** *Aussöhnung* for Voice and Piano (1902); *Notturno* for Voice and Piano (1914); *2 Pieces* for Chorus and Orch. (1943).

WRITINGS: *Reflections on Music* (Manchester, 1933; N.Y., 1934); *Music and the Line of Most Resistance* (Princeton, N.J., 1942); *My Life and Music* (London, 1961).

BIBL.: C. Saerchinger, *A. S.* (London, 1957); K. Wolff, *The Teaching of A. S.* (London, 1972); H. Goldsmith, "S. the pianist," *Musical Times* (June 1989); M. Swed, "S. the composer," ibid.

Schnabel, Karl Ulrich, German-American pianist, teacher, and composer, son of **Artur Schnabel;** b. Berlin, Aug. 6, 1909. He was a student of Leonid Kreutzer (piano) and Paul Juon (composition) at the Prussian State Academy of Music in Berlin (1922–26). After making his debut in Berlin in 1926, he toured in Europe. From 1935 to 1940 he made duo appearances with his father. On Feb. 23, 1937, he made his U.S. debut in N.Y., where he settled in 1939. With his wife, Helen (née Fogel) Schnabel, he toured extensively in duo recitals from 1940 until her death in 1974. From 1980 he appeared in duo recitals with Joan Rowland. In addition to his many tours around the globe, he devoted much time to teaching. He was the author of *Modern Technique of the Pedal* (N.Y., 1950). He also composed pieces for piano, 4-hands.

Schnebel, Dieter, eminent German composer; b. Lahr, March 14, 1930. At 10, he began piano lessons with Wilhelm Siebler. After further piano instruction from Wilhelm Resch in Villingen (1945–49), he studied theory and music history with Erich Doflein at the Freiburg im Breisgau Hochschule für Musik (1949–52). He also attended the summer courses in new music in Darmstadt beginning in 1950. He completed his studies at the Univ. of Tübingen (1952–56), where he took courses in theology, philosophy, and musicology, receiving his doctorate with a thesis on Schoenberg's dynamics. From 1963 to 1970 he taught religion in Frankfurt am Main, and then religion and music in Munich from 1970 to 1976. He also devoted increasing attention to his career as a composer. In 1976 he was a prof. of experimental music and musicology at the Berlin Hochschule für Musik. In 1991 he was made a member of the Berlin Akademie der Künste. The complex construction of his early works gave way in 1968 to simpler forms intended for wider audiences; in 1984 he began a "third period" of major forms as collections of traditions and innovation, first the mass (*Miss [Dahlemer Messe]*), then the symphony (*Sinfonie X*) and opera (*Majakovskis Tod*; Venice, Sept. 1996). Among his writings are *Mauricio Kagel: Musik, Theater, Film* (1970), *Denkbare Musik: Schriften 1952–72* (1972), *MO-NO: Musik zum Lesen* (1973), and *Anschläge-Ausschläge: Texte zur Neuen Musik* (1994). In his music, Schnebel follows a conceptually sophisticated and highly avant-garde course in which he makes use of such unusual materials as vocal noise, breath, and graphics.

WORKS: MUSIC THEATER: *ki-no (Räume 1)* (1963–67; Munich, July 10, 1967); *Maulwerke* (1968–74; Donaueschingen, Oct. 20, 1974); *Körper-Sprache* (1979–80; Metz, Nov. 20, 1980); *Jowaegerli (Tradition IV, 1)* (1982–83; Baden-Baden, June 26, 1983); *Zeichen-Sprache* (1987–89; Berlin, April 12, 1989); *Chili (Tradition IV, 2)* (1989–91; Hamburg, May 12, 1991). **ORCH.:** *Versuche I–IV* (1953–56; rev. 1964; 1st complete perf., Stuttgart, Sept. 14, 1973); *Webern-Variationen (Re-Visionen I, 3)* for Chamber Orch. (1972; Paris, Oct. 20, 1973); *Canones* (1975–77; rev. 1993–94; Ludwigshafen, March 6, 1995); *Orchestra* (1974–77; Cologne, Jan. 20, 1978); *Schubert-Phantasie (Re-Visionen I, 5)* (1978; Frankfurt am Main, March 16, 1979; rev. 1989); *Thanatos-Eros (Tradition III, 1)* (1979–82; Graz, Nov. 5, 1982; rev. version, Berlin, April 12, 1985); *Sinfonie-Stücke* (1984–85; Hamburg, June 23, 1985); *Mahler-Moment (Re-Visionen II, 4)* for Strings (1985; Zürich, April 4, 1986); *Sinfonie X* for Orch., Alto, and Tape (1987–92; Donaueschingen, Oct. 18, 1992); *Mozart-Moment (Re-Visionen II, 3)* for Small Orch. (1988–89; Frankfurt am Main, June 16, 1989); *Verdi-Moment (Re-Visionen II, 5)* (Frankfurt am Main, June 16, 1989); *Janáček-Moment (Re-Visionen II, 1)* (1991–92; Hamburg, May 22, 1992); *inter* for Small Orch. (Frankfurt am Main, Sept. 3, 1994). **CHAMBER:** *Analysis (Versuche I)* for String Instrument and Percussion (1953; Brussels, Dec. 12, 1964); *Stücke* for String Quartet (1954–55; Rome, June 1968); *anschläge-ausschläge (Modelle No. 5)* for Flute, Cello, and Harpsichord (1965–66; Zürich, Jan. 5, 1970); *In motu proprio (Tradition I)* for 7 Cellos or 7 Clarinets (Paris, Oct. 24, 1975); *Drei-Klange (Räume 4)* for Chamber Ensemble (1976–77; Bremen, Dec. 12, 1977); *B-Dur-Quintett (Tradition II, 1)* for 2 Violins, Viola, Cello, and Piano (1976–77; Darmstadt, April 17, 1978); *Handwerke-Blaswerke I* for Wind Player, String Player, and Percussionist (1977; Frankfurt am Main, April 16, 1978); *Rhythmen (aus Schulmusik)* for Percussion (1977; Munich, June 20, 1978); *Pan* for Flute and Cello (1978; Zürich, Jan. 25, 1980; rev. version, Lahr, April 21, 1988); *Beethoven-Symphonie (Re-Visionen I, 2)* for Chamber Ensemble (1985; Essen, April 14, 1988); *5 Inventionen* for Cello (1987; Stuttgart, May 3, 1988); *Marsyas* for Bass Clarinet and Percussion (Munich, Nov. 22, 1987); *Circe* for Harp (San Felice, June 1988); *Sisyphos* for 2 Winds (Leipzig, Nov. 26, 1990); *4 Stücke* for Violin and Piano (Frankfurt am Main, Sept. 24, 1991); *Languido* for Bass Flute and Live Electronics (1992–93; Graz, Oct. 9, 1993). **KEYBOARD: PIANO:** *espressivo (Modelle No. 2)* (1961–63; Munich, April 16, 1964); *concert sans orchestre (Modelle No. 3)* (1964; Zürich, June 13, 1970); *Bagatellen* (1986; Bonn, Jan. 17, 1987); *Monotonien* for Piano and Live Electronics (1988–89; Munich, Oct. 28, 1993). **ORGAN:** *Zwischenfugen (Tradition V, 1)* (1979–82; Essen, April 26, 1986). **VOCAL:** *Für Stimmen (. . . missa est)* for Chorus (1956–69); *Das Urteil* for Chorus, Orch., and Tape (1959; rev. version, Hannover, Aug. 31, 1990); *Glossolalie 6 (Projekte IV)* for 3 to 4 Speakers and for 3 to 4 Instrumentalists (1960–61; Paris, Oct. 21, 1966); *Bach-Contrapuncti (Re-Visionen I, 1)* for Chorus (1972–76); *Wagner-Idyll (Re-Visionen I, 4)* for Voice and Chamber Ensemble (Berlin, Sept. 9, 1980); *Lieder ohne Worte (Tradition III, 3)* for Voice and 2 Instruments (1980–86; Münster, Feb. 14, 1987); *5*

Geistliche Lieder von Bach for Voice and Small Orch. (1984; Cologne, Oct. 12, 1985); *Missa (Dahlemer Messe)* for 4 Soloists, Chorus, Orch., and Organ (1984–87; Berlin, Nov. 11, 1988); *Metamorphosenmusik* for Voice and Chamber Ensemble (1986–87; Aachen, Jan. 10, 1990); *Schumann-Moment (Re-Visionen II, 2)* for Voices, Harp, and Percussion (Frankfurt am Main, June 16, 1989); *Chili* for 3 Speakers, 4 Singers, and Chamber Ensemble (1989–91); *Lamento di Guerra* for Mezzo-soprano and Organ or Synthesizer (Berlin, Sept. 29, 1991); *Mit diesen Händen* for Voice and Cello (Cologne, Dec. 14, 1992); *Kaschnitz-Gedichte* for Speaker and Piano (Tutzing, Nov. 25, 1994). **OTHER:** Tape pieces; graphic and conceptual works.

BIBL.: H.-K. Metzger and R. Riehn, eds., *D. S.* (Munich, 1980); W. Grünzweig, G. Schröder, and M. Supper, eds., *S. 60.* (Hofheim, 1990).

Schneerson, Grigori, eminent Russian musicologist; b. Eniseisk, Siberia, March 13, 1901; d. Moscow, Feb. 6, 1982. He was the son of a political exile under the tsarist regime; went to Moscow as a youth, and studied piano at the Cons. with Medtner and Igumnov. From 1939 to 1948 he was in charge of the music dept. of the Society for Cultural Relations with Foreign Nations; from 1948 to 1961, was head of the foreign section of the monthly *Sovietskaya Muzyka,* and from 1954 to 1966, ed. the bibliographic series Foreign Literature of Music. A remarkably gifted linguist, he mastered several European languages and undertook a study of Chinese. In his polemical writings he displayed wit and sarcasm in attacking the extreme manifestations of Western modernism, but preserved scholarly impartiality in analyzing the music of all genres and styles. He was a Member Correspondent of the Academy of the Arts of the German Democratic Republic (1968), Honorary Member of the Accademia di Scienze, Lettere, Arti (1976), and a recipient of the Bernier Prize of the Académie des Beaux-Arts, Paris (1976). Among his writings, all publ. in Moscow, were monographs on Khachaturian (1957; Eng. tr., 1959) and Ernst Busch (1962; rev. 1964), a study of French music in the 20th century (1964; rev. 1970), and a vol. of articles on foreign music (1974). He also ed. a vol. on Shostakovich (1976).

Schnéevoigt, Georg (Lennart), prominent Finnish conductor; b. Vyborg, Nov. 8, 1872; d. Malmö, Nov. 28, 1947. He received training in cello in Helsinki, with Karl Schröder in Sondershausen, and with Julius Klengel in Leipzig. He then continued his musical studies in Brussels, Dresden, and with Robert Fuchs in Vienna. Returning to Helsinki, he served as principal cellist in the Phil. (1895–98; 1899–1903) and as a cello teacher at the Music Inst. In 1901 he launched his conducting career in Riga. From 1904 to 1908 he was conductor of the Kaim Orch. in Munich. After conducting the Kiev Sym. Orch. (1908–09), he was conductor of the Riga Sym. Orch. (1912–14). He also conducted the Helsinki Sym. Orch. (1912–14); in 1914 it merged with Kajanus's Helsinki Phil. to form the Helsinki City Orch. with Schnéevoigt as co-conductor (1916–32). From 1932 to 1941 Schnéevoigt was its sole conductor. He also was conductor of the Stockholm Konsertförening (1915–21), founder-conductor of the Christiania (later Oslo) Phil. (1919–27), conductor in Düsseldorf (1924–26), of the Los Angeles Phil. (1927–29), and of the Riga Opera (1929–32). Subsequently he conducted in Malmö. In 1907 he married the pianist and teacher Sigrid Ingeborg Sundgren (b. Helsinki, June 17, 1878; d. Stockholm, Sept. 14, 1953). She studied at the Helsinki Music Inst. (1886–94) and with Busoni in Berlin (1894–97). From 1901 she taught at the Helsinki Music Inst. She also appeared as a soloist with orchs., often under the direction of her husband, and as a recitalist.

Schneider, (Abraham) Alexander, Russian-born American violinist, conductor, and teacher; b. Vilnius, Oct. 21, 1908; d. N.Y., Feb. 2, 1993. He enrolled in the Vilnius Cons. at 10 and in the Frankfurt an Main Hochschule für Musik at 16; at the latter he studied violin with Adolf Rebner; later took lessons with Carl Flesch in Berlin. While still in his teens, he became concertmaster of the Frankfurt am Main Museumgesellschaft Orch.; was also active in Saarbrücken and Hamburg. In 1932 he became 2nd violinist in the Budapest Quartet, with which he toured widely. He settled in the U.S. in 1938, and remained with the Budapest Quartet until 1944; then played in the Albeneri Trio and the N.Y. Quartet, and also conducted chamber orch. concerts. In 1945 he received the Elizabeth Sprague Coolidge Medal for eminent services to chamber music. In 1950 he persuaded Casals to come out of retirement and honor the 200th anniversary of Bach's death with a festival in Prades; he continued to work with Casals in subsequent years, organizing the Casals Festival in San Juan, Puerto Rico, in 1957. He founded his own quartet in 1952, and was again a member of the Budapest Quartet from 1955 until it disbanded in 1967. In later years he gave increasing attention to conducting, leading both chamber groups and major orchs.; he was also active as a teacher. In 1988 he received a Kennedy Center Honor for his services to music.

Schneider, Marius, distinguished German musicologist; b. Hagenau, July 1, 1903; d. Marquartstein, July 10, 1982. He studied philology and musicology at the Univs. of Strasbourg and Paris, then trained with Wolf at the Univ. of Berlin (Ph.D., 1930, with the diss. *Die Ars nova des XIV. Jahrhunderts in Frankreich und Italien*; publ. in Wolfenbüttel, 1931); his Habilitation was rejected there after Nazi intervention in 1937, but was subsequently accepted by the Univ. of Cologne after the collapse of the Third Reich (1955). He was Hornbostel's assistant at the Berlin Phonogramm-Archiv (1932–34), and then was its director. After serving in the armed forces during World War II, he went to Barcelona in 1944 as founder-director of the ethnomusicology dept. at the Spanish Inst. of Musicology. He taught at the Consejo Superior de Investigaciones Cientificas at the Univ. of Barcelona (1947–55); then taught comparative musicology and ethnomusicology at the Univ. of Cologne (1955–68); subsequently was on the faculty of the Univ. of Amsterdam (1968–70). He made valuable contributions to musicology, the philosophy of music, and the history of musical structures. A Festschrift was publ. in his honor (Regensburg, 1977).

WRITINGS: *Geschichte der Mehrstimmigkeit: Historische und phänomenologische Studien*: I, *Die Naturvölker*; II, *Die Anfänge in Europa* (Berlin, 1934–35; 2nd ed., 1968, with vol. III, *Die Kompositionsprinzipien und ihre Verbreitung*); *El origen musical de los animales-simbolos en la mitología y la escultura antiguas: Ensayo histórico-etnográfico sobre la subestructura totemística y megalítica de las altas culturas y su supervivencia en el folklore español* (Barcelona, 1946); *La danza de espadas y la tarantela: Ensayo musicológico, etnográfico y arqueológico sobre los ritos medicinales* (Barcelona, 1948); *Singende Steine: Rhythmus-Studien an drei kalantanischen Kreuzgängen romanischen Stils* (Kassel, 1955); *Die Natur des Lobgesangs* (Basel, 1964); ed. *Aussereuropäische Folklore und Kunstmusik* (Cologne, 1972); ed. *Studien zur Mittelmeermusik*: I, *Die tunesische Nuba ed Dhil* (Regensburg, n.d.).

Schneider, Max, eminent German musicologist; b. Eisleben, July 20, 1875; d. Halle, May 5, 1967. He studied musicology at the Univ. of Leipzig with Riemann and Kretzschmar, and harmony and composition with Jadassohn; continued his musicological training at the Univ. of Berlin (Ph.D., 1917), where he was a librarian (1904–07); then was assistant librarian at the Royal Library (1907–14). He conducted in Halle (1897–1901); also taught at the Church Music Inst. in Berlin; then was a prof. at the Univs. of Breslau (1915–28) and Halle (1928–60). He publ. *Beiträge zu einer Anleitung Clavichord und Cembalo zu spielen* (Strasbourg, 1934) and *Beiträge zur Musikforschung* (vol. I, Halle, 1935). He did useful work in compiling miscellaneous bio-bibliographical materials in music; ed. numerous important bibliographical surveys; also ed. the works of Heinrich Schütz. He enjoyed a well-merited reputation in Germany as a thorough scholar. He was honored 3 times by Festschrifts: H. Zingel, ed., *Festschrift Max Schneider zum 60. Geburtstag* (Halle, 1935), W. Vetter, ed., *Festschrift Max Schneider zum 80. Geburtstag* (Leipzig, 1955), and W. Siegmund-Schulze, ed., *Festschrift Max Schneider zum 85. Geburtstag* (Leipzig, 1960).

Schneiderhan, Wolfgang (Eduard), noted Austrian violinist and pedagogue; b. Vienna, May 28, 1915. He studied violin mainly in Prague with Ševčik and Pisek; later with Julius Winkler in Vienna. He was concertmaster of the Vienna Sym. Orch. (1933–37); then of the Vienna Phil. (1937–51); concurrently was 1st violinist in his own Scheiderhan Quartet. From 1951 he made tours of Europe as a soloist with the major orchs. He taught at the Salzburg Mozarteum (1938–56) and at the Vienna Academy of Music (1939–50); was on the faculty of the Lucerne Cons. (from 1949). With Rudolf Baumgartner, he helped to found the Lucerne Festival Strings in 1956. He married **Irmgard Seefried** in 1948. He was best known for his performances of the Viennese classics and contemporary music.

BIBL.: F. Fassbind, *W. S., Irmgard Seefried: Eine Künstler- und Lebensgemeinschaft* (Bern, 1960); *W. S. zum 60. Geburtstag* (Wiesbaden, 1975).

Schneider-Trnavský, Mikuláš, Slovak choral conductor and composer; b. Trnava, May 24, 1881; d. Bratislava, May 28, 1958. He studied in Budapest, Vienna, and Prague. He was choirmaster of the cathedral of St. Mikuláš in Trnava (1909–58); was named a National Artist in 1956. He publ. several valuable collections of Slovak folk songs, arranged with piano accompaniment: *Sbierka slovenských ludových piesní* (2 vols., 1905–10); *Sbierka slovenských národných piesní* (5 sections, Bratislava, 1930; new ed., Prague, 1935–40); *50 Slovakische Volkslieder* (Bratislava, 1943). He also publ. a book of memoirs, *Usmevy a slzy* (Smiles and Tears; Bratislava, 1959).

WORKS: *Bellarosa*, operetta (1941); *Dumka and Dance* for Orch. (1905); *Comedy Overture* (1930–31); *Symphony of Recollections* (1956); Violin Sonata (1905); Slovak Sonatina for Piano (1938); church music, including several masses; songs.

BIBL.: J. Samko, *M. S.-T.-phol'ad na život a dielo* (Bratislava, 1965).

Schneidt, Hanns-Martin, German organist, conductor, pedagogue, and composer; b. Kitzingen, Dec. 6, 1930. He studied at the Thomasschule in Leipzig with Gunther Ramin; also took courses in choral music in Munich and served as a church organist there. In 1955 he became director of the Church Music School in Berlin; was also conductor of the Berlin Bach-Collegium and Choir, as well as cantor and organist at the Church of St. John the Evangelist. In 1963 he became conductor of the Wuppertal City Orch.; it became the Wuppertal Sym. Orch. in 1976, and he continued as its conductor until 1985; also held the post of Generalmusikdirektor for the city of Wuppertal (1975–85). He was prof. of conducting at the Hamburg Hochschule für Musik (from 1971). In 1984 he became conductor of the Munich Bach Choir. He wrote a number of choral works.

Schnittke, Alfred (Garrievich), prominent Russian composer of German descent; b. Engels, near Saratov, Nov. 24, 1934. He studied piano in Vienna (1946–48), where his father was a correspondent of a German-language Soviet newspaper; then took courses in composition with Golubev and in instrumentation with Rakov at the Moscow Cons. (1953–58); after serving on its faculty (1962–72), he devoted himself fully to composition. He pursued many trips abroad, and in 1981 was a guest lecturer at the Vienna Hochschule für Musik and Darstellende Künst. In 1981 he was elected a member of the Bayerische Akademie der Schönen Künste. In 1985 he survived a serious heart attack. In 1988 and again in 1991 he suffered debilitating strokes. After writing in a conventional manner, he became acutely interested in the new Western techniques, particularly in serialism and "sonorism," in which dynamic gradations assume thematic significance; soon he became known as one of the boldest experimenters in modernistic composition in Soviet Russia.

WORKS: DRAMATIC: OPERAS: *Odinnadtsataya Zapoved* (The 11th Commandment; 1962; unfinished); *Historia von D. Johann Fausten* (1989–93); *Zhizn's idiotom* (Life With an Idiot; 1990–91; Amsterdam, April 13, 1992); *Gesualdo* (1993–94). **BALLETS:** *Labirinti* (Labyrinths; 1971; Leningrad, June 7, 1978); *Zhyoltïy zvuk* (Yellow Sound), after Kandinsky (Saint Bomme, France, 1974); *Sketches*, after Gogol (1984; Moscow, Jan. 16, 1985; in collaboration with E. Denisov, S. Gubaidulina, and G. Rozhdestvensky); *Peer Gynt*, after Ibsen (1986; Hamburg, Jan. 1989). Also incidental music to plays and many film scores.

ORCH.: 4 violin concertos: No. 1 (1957; rev. 1962; Moscow, Nov. 29, 1963), No. 2 for Violin and Chamber Orch. (1966; Leningrad, Feb. 20, 1968), No. 3 for Violin and Chamber Orch. (1978; Moscow, Jan. 29, 1979), and No. 4 (1982; West Berlin, Sept. 11, 1984); Piano Concerto (1960); *Poem about Cosmos* (1961); *Music* for Chamber Orch. (1964); *Music* for Piano and Chamber Orch. (1964); *. . . pianissimo . . .* (1967–68; Donaueschingen, Oct. 19, 1969); Sonata for Violin and Chamber Orch. (1968; Moscow, Feb. 5, 1986; chamber orch. version of Sonata No. 1 for Violin and Piano); Double Concerto for Oboe, Harp, and Strings (1970–71; Zagreb, May 1972); 8 syms.: No. 1 (1969–72; Gorky, Feb. 9, 1974), No. 2, *St. Florian*, for Chamber Chorus and Orch. (1979; London, April 23, 1980), No. 3 (Leipzig, Nov. 5, 1981), No. 4 for Tenor, Alto, Chorus, and Orch. or Chamber Orch. (Moscow, April 12, 1984), No. 5, *Concerto Grosso No. 4/Symphony No. 5* (1987–88; Amsterdam, Nov. 10, 1988), No. 6 for Chamber Orch. (1991–92), No. 7 (1993; N.Y., Feb. 10, 1994), and No. 8 (1993–94; Stockholm, Nov. 11, 1994); *In memoriam* (1972–78; Moscow, Dec. 20, 1979; orch. version of Piano Quintet); 6 concerti grossi: No. 1 for 2 Violins, Prepared Piano, Harpsichord, and Strings (Leningrad, March 21, 1977), No. 2 for Violin, Cello, and Orch. (West Berlin, Sept. 11, 1982), No. 3 for 2 Violins and Chamber Orch. (Moscow, April 20, 1985), No. 4, *Concerto Grosso No. 4/Symphony No. 5* (1987–88; Amsterdam, Nov. 10, 1988), No. 5 for Violin, Piano, and Orch. (1990–91; N.Y., May 2, 1991), and No. 6 for Piano and Orch. (1993); Concerto for Piano and Strings (Leningrad, Dec. 10, 1979); *Passacaglia* (1979–80; Baden-Baden, Nov. 8, 1981); *Gogol Suite* (from incidental music to *The Dead Souls Register*, London, Dec. 5, 1980); *Ritual* (Novosibirsk, March 15, 1985); *(K)ein Sommernachstraum* ([Not] A Midsummer Night's Dream; Salzburg, Aug. 12, 1985); Viola Concerto (1985; Amsterdam, Jan. 6, 1986); 2 cello concertos: No. 1 (Munich, May 7, 1986) and No. 2 (1989); *Quasi una Sonata* for Violin and Chamber Orch. (1987; chamber orch. version of Sonata No. 2 for Violin and Piano); Trio Sonata for Chamber Orch. (1987; chamber orch. version of String Trio); *4 Aphorisms* (West Berlin, Sept. 18, 1988); *Monologue* for Viola and String Orch. (Bonn, June 4, 1989); Concerto for Piano, 4-hands, and Chamber Orch. (1989; Moscow, April 27, 1990); *5 Fragments on Pictures by Hieronymus Bosch* (London, Nov. 11, 1994).

CHAMBER: 2 violin sonatas: No. 1 (1963) and No. 2, *Quasi una Sonata* (1968); *Dialogue* for Cello and 7 Instruments (1965); 4 string quartets (1966, 1980, 1983, 1989); *Serenade* for Violin, Clarinet, Double Bass, Piano, and Percussion (1968); *Canon in memoriam Igor Stravinsky* for String Quartet (1971); *Suite in Old Style* for Violin and Piano or Harpsichord (1972); Piano Quintet (1972–76; orchestrated as *In memoriam*); *Hymnus I* for Cello, Harp, and Timpani (1974), *II* for Cello and Double Bass (1974), *III* for Cello, Bassoon, Harpsichord, and Bells or Timpani (1975), and *IV* for Cello, Double Bass, Bassoon, Harpsichord, Harp, Timpani, and Bells (1976; all 1st perf. Moscow, May 26, 1979); *Praeludium in memoriam Dmitri Shostakovich* for 2 Violins or 1 Violin and Tape (1975); *Cantus Perpetuus* for Keyboards and Percussion (1975); *Moz-Art* for 2 Violins (1976); *Mozart à la Haydn* for 2 Violins, 2 Small String Ensembles, Double Bass, and Conductor (1977); 2 cello sonatas (1978, 1994); *Stille Musik* for Violin and Cello (1979); *Polyphonic Tango* for Ensemble (1979); *Moz-Art* for Oboe, Harpsichord, Harp, Violin, Cello, and Double Bass (1980); Septet (1981–82); *Lebenslauf* for 4 Metronomes, 3 Percussionists, and Piano (1982); *A Paganini* for Violin (1982); *Schall und Hall* for Trombone and Organ (1983); String Trio (1985; new version for Chamber Orch. as Trio-Sonata); Piano Quartet (1988); *Klingende buchstaben* for Cello (1988); *3 × 7* for Clarinet, Horn, Trombone, Harpsichord, Violin, Cello, and Double Bass (1989); *Moz-Art à la Mozart* for 8 Flutes and Harpsichord (1990). **PIANO:** *Prelude and Fugue* (1963); *Improvisation and Fugue*

(1965); *Variations on a Chord* (1965); *4 Pieces* (1971); *Dedication to Stravinsky, Prokofiev, and Shostakovich* for Piano, 6-hands (1979); 2 sonatas (1987–88; 1990).

VOCAL: *Nagasaki*, oratorio for Mezzo-soprano, Chorus, and Orch. (1958); *Songs of War and Peace*, cantata for Soprano, Chorus, and Orch. (1959); *3 Poems* for Mezzo-soprano and Piano (1965); *Voices of Nature* for 10 Women's Voices and Vibraphone (1972); *Requiem* for 3 Sopranos, Alto, Tenor, Chorus, and 8 Instrumentalists, after stage music to Schiller's *Don Carlos* (1975; Budapest, Oct. 8, 1977); *Der Sonnengesang des Franz von Assisi* for 2 Choruses and 6 Instruments (1976); *3 Madrigals* for Soprano and 5 Instruments (Moscow, Nov. 10, 1980); *3 Scenes* for Soprano and Instrumental Ensemble (1980); *Minnesang* for 52 Voices (1980–81; Graz, Oct. 21, 1981); *Seid nüchtern und wachet . . .*, cantata for 4 Soloists, Chorus, and Orch., after the version of the Faust legend publ. in 1587 under the title *Historia von D. Johann Fausten* and commissioned by the Vienna Choral Academy on the occasion of its 125th anniversary (1st perf. as *Faust Cantata*, Vienna, June 19, 1983); Concerto for Chorus (1984–85); *Busslieder* for Chorus (Moscow, Dec. 26, 1988); *Eroffnungsvers zum ersten Festspielsonntag* for Chorus (Lockenhaus, July 2, 1989).

BIBL.: D. Shulgin, *Gody neizvestnosti A. S.: Besedy s kompozitorom* (Moscow, 1993).

Schnoor, Hans, distinguished German writer on music; b. Neumünster, Oct. 4, 1893; d. Bielefeld, Jan. 15, 1976. He studied with Riemann and Schering at the Univ. of Leipzig, where he received his Ph.D. with the diss. *Das Buxheimer Orgelbuch* in 1919. He was a music critic in Dresden and Leipzig (1922–26); then music ed. of the *Dresdner Anzeiger* (1926–45). He was an authority on the life and music of Weber.

WRITINGS: *Musik der germanischen Völker im XIX. und XX. Jahrhundert* (Breslau, 1926); with G. Kinsky and R. Haas, *Geschichte der Musik in Bildern* (Leipzig, 1929; Eng. tr., 1930); *Weber auf dem Welttheater* (Dresden, 1942; 4th ed., 1963); *Weber: Ein Lebensbild aus Dresdner Sicht* (Dresden, 1947); *400 Jahre deutscher Musikkultur: Zum Jubiläum der Staatskapelle und zur Geschichte der Dresdner Oper* (Dresden, 1948); *Geschichte der Musik* (1953); *Weber: Gestalt und Schöpfung* (Dresden, 1953; 2nd ed., rev., 1974); *Oper, Operette, Konzert: Ein praktisches Nachschlagsbuch* (Gutersloh, 1955); ed. *Bilderatlas zur Musikgeschichte* (Brussels, 1960; 2nd ed., 1963); *Harmonie und Chaos* (Munich, 1962); *Musik und Theater ohne eigene Dach* (Hagen, 1969); *Die Stunde des Rosenkavalier* (Munich, 1969).

Schock, Rudolf (Johann), German tenor; b. Duisburg, Sept. 4, 1915; d. Duren-Gürzenich, Nov. 13, 1986. He studied in Cologne, Hannover, and with Robert von der Linde and Laurenz Hofer in Berlin. At the age of 18, he joined the chorus of the Duisburg Opera. In 1937 he made his operatic debut in Braunschweig, where he sang until 1940. After singing in Hannover (1945) and at the Berlin State Opera (1946), he was a member of the Hamburg State Opera (1947–56), with which company he visited the Edinburgh Festival (1952). In 1948 he made his first appearance at the Salzburg Festival as Idomeneo and in 1951 his debut at the Vienna State Opera. In 1959 he made his Bayreuth Festival debut as Walther von Stolzing. He also appeared in operetta. Among his other roles were Tamino, Florestan, Max in *Der Freischütz*, and Bacchus in *Ariadne auf Naxos*. His autobiography was publ. as *Ach ich hab' in meinem Herzen* (Berlin and Munich, 1985).

Schoeck, Othmar, eminent Swiss pianist, conductor, and composer; b. Brunnen, Sept. 1, 1886; d. Zürich, March 8, 1957. He was the son of the painter Alfred Schoeck; went to Zürich, where he took courses at the Industrial College before pursuing musical training with Attenhofer, Freund, Hegar, and Kempter at the Cons. (from 1905); after further studies with Reger in Leipzig (1907–08), he returned to Zürich and conducted the Aussersihl Men's Chorus (1909–15), the Harmonie Men's Chorus (1910–11), and the Teachers' Chorus (1911–17); then was conductor of the St. Gallen sym. concerts (1917–44). Schoeck was one of the most significant Swiss composers of his era; he won his greatest renown as a masterful composer of songs, of which he wrote about 400. He also was highly regarded as a piano accompanist and a conductor. Among his many honors were an honorary doctorate from the Univ. of Zürich (1928), the 1st composer's prize of the Schweizerische Tonkünstlerverein (1945), and the Grand Cross of Merit and Order of Merit of the Federal Republic of Germany (1956). In 1959 the Othmar Schoeck Gesellschaft was founded to promote the performance of his works.

WORKS: DRAMATIC: OPERAS: *Don Ranudo de Colibrados*, op. 27 (1917–18; Zürich, April 16, 1919); *Venus*, op. 32 (1919–20; Zürich, May 10, 1922); *Penthesilea*, op. 39 (1924–25; Dresden, Jan. 8, 1927); *Massimilla Doni*, op. 50 (1934–35; Dresden, March 2, 1937); *Das Schloss Dürande*, op. 53 (1938–39; Berlin, April 1, 1943); other stage works. **ORCH.:** *Serenade* for Small Orch., op. 1 (1906–07); *Eine Ratcliff-Ouvertüre* (1907); *Concerto quasi una fantasia* for Violin and Orch., op. 21 (1911–12); *Praeludium*, op. 48 (1932); *Sommernacht* for Strings, op. 58 (1945); *Suite* for Strings, op. 59 (1949); Cello Concerto, op. 61 (1947); *Festlicher Hymnus*, op. 64 (1951); Horn Concerto, op. 65 (1951). **CHAMBER:** 3 violin sonatas (1908, 1909, 1931); 2 string quartets (1912–13; 1923); 2 clarinet sonatas (1916; 1927–28); piano pieces. **CHORAL:** *'s Seeli* for Men's Chorus (1906–07); *5 Lieder* (1906–15); *Sehnsucht* for Men's Chorus (1909); *Der Postillon* for Tenor, Men's Chorus, and Piano or Orch., op. 18 (1909); *Dithyrambe* for Double Chorus and Orch., op. 22 (1911); *Wegelied* for Men's Chorus, and Piano or Orch., op. 24 (1913); *Trommelschläge* for Chorus and Orch., op. 26 (1915); *Die Drei* for Men's Chorus (1930); *Cantata* for Baritone, Men's Chorus, and Instruments, op. 49 (1933); *Für ein Gesangfest im Frühling* for Men's Chorus and Orch., op. 54 (1942); *Nachruf* (1943); *Zimmerspruch* for Men's Chorus (1947); *Vision* for Men's Chorus, Brass, Percussion, and Strings, op. 63 (1950); *Maschinenschlacht* for Men's Chorus, op. 67a (1953); *Gestutze Eiche* for Men's Chorus, op. 67b (1953); numerous works for Solo Voice with instrumental accompaniment; about 400 songs, including cycles.

BIBL.: H. Corrodi, ed., *O. S.: Festgabe . . . zum 50. Geburtstag* (Erlenbach and Zürich, 1936); special issues of *Schweizerische Musikzeitung/Revue Musicale Suisse*, LXXXIII (1943) and XCVI (1956); W. Vogel, *Wesenszüge von O. S.s Liedkunst* (Zürich, 1950); idem, *Thematisches Verzeichnis der Werke von O. S.* (Zürich, 1956); F. Kienberger, *O. S.: Eine Studie* (Zürich, 1975); S. Tiltmann-Fuchs, *O. S.s Liederzyklen für Singstimme und Orchester* (Regensburg, 1976); D. Puffet, *The Song Cycles of O. S.* (Stuttgart and Bern, 1982).

Schoemaker, Maurice, Belgian composer; b. Anderlecht, near Brussels, Dec. 27, 1890; d. Brussels, Aug. 24, 1964. He studied harmony with Théo Ysaÿe, counterpoint with Michel Brusselmans, fugue with Martin Lunssens, and composition and orchestration with Paul Gilson. He was one of 8 Gilson pupils to form, in 1925, the Groupe des Synthétistes, whose aim was to promote modern music. He held administrative posts in various Belgian musical organizations.

WORKS: DRAMATIC: OPERAS: *Swane* (1933); *Arc-en-ciel* (1937); *De Toverviool* (1954). **RADIO PLAYS:** *Sire Halewijn* (1935); *Médée la magicienne* (1936); *Philoctetes* (1942). **BALLETS:** *Breughel-Suite* (1928); *Pan* (1937). **ORCH.:** *Le Facétieux Voyage* (1914); *Récit, Aria et Final* for Violin and Orch. (1920); *Pan*, prelude (1921); *Feu d'artifice* for Wind Orch. (1922); *2 fantasques* (1924); *Sinfonia da camera* (1929); *Légende de Sire Halewijn*, symphonic poem (1930); *Rapsodie flamande* (1931); *Variations on a Popular Song* (1937); *Sinfonia breve* (1938); *Pièce concertante* for Trombone and Orch. (1939); *Variazioni* for Horn and Orch. (1941); *Mouvement symphonique* (1942); *Scènes espagnoles* (1943); *2 danses flamandes* (1944); Sym. (1946); Bassoon Concerto (1947); *Ouverture romane* (1947); *Marillac l'Epée*, dramatic prologue (1949). **CHAMBER:** Piano Trio (1934); Piano Sonata (1934); Sonata for Solo Cello (1940);

Suite champêtre for Oboe, Clarinet, and Bassoon (1940); String Quartet (1945); *Variations miniatures* for String Trio (1949); *Morceau de concert* for Trombone and Piano (1949); *Tombeau de Chopin* for 2 Pianos (1949); *Sonata du souvenir* for Cello and Piano (1953); *La Cage des oiseaux* for 4 Clarinets (1961).

Schoenberg (originally, **Schönberg**), **Arnold (Franz Walter),** great Austrian-born American composer whose new method of musical organization in 12 different tones related only to one another profoundly influenced the entire development of modern techniques of composition; b. Vienna, Sept. 13, 1874; d. Los Angeles, July 13, 1951. He studied at the Realschule in Vienna; learned to play the cello, and also became proficient on the violin. His father died when Schoenberg was 16; he took a job as a bank clerk to earn a living; an additional source of income was arranging popular songs and orchestrating operetta scores. Schoenberg's first original work was a group of 3 piano pieces, which he wrote in 1894; it was also about that time that he began to take lessons in counterpoint from Alexander Zemlinsky, whose sister he married in 1901. He also played cello in Zemlinsky's instrumental group, Polyhymnia. In 1897 Schoenberg wrote his 1st String Quartet, in D major, which achieved public performance in Vienna on March 17, 1898. About the same time, he wrote 2 songs with piano accompaniment which he designated as op. 1. In 1899 he wrote his first true masterpiece, *Verklärte Nacht*, set for string sextet, which was first performed in Vienna by the Rosé Quartet and members of the Vienna Phil. on March 18, 1902. It is a fine work, deeply imbued with the spirit of Romantic poetry, with its harmonic idiom stemming from Wagner's modulatory procedures; it remains Schoenberg's most frequently performed composition, known principally through its arrangement for string orch. About 1900 he was engaged as conductor of several amateur choral groups in Vienna and its suburbs; this increased his interest in vocal music. He then began work on a choral composition, *Gurre-Lieder*, of monumental proportions, to the translated text of a poem by the Danish writer Jens Peter Jacobsen. For grandeur and opulence of orchestral sonority, it surpassed even the most formidable creations of Mahler or Richard Strauss; it calls for 5 solo voices, a speaker, 3 men's choruses, an 8-part mixed chorus, and a very large orch. Special music paper of 48 staves had to be ordered for the MS. He completed the first 2 parts of *Gurre-Lieder* in the spring of 1901, but the composition of the remaining section was delayed by 10 years; it was not until Feb. 23, 1913, that Franz Schreker was able to arrange its complete performance with the Vienna Phil. and its choral forces.

In 1901 Schoenberg moved to Berlin, where he joined E. von Wolzogen, F. Wedekind, and O. Bierbaum in launching an artistic cabaret, which they called Überbrettl. He composed a theme song for it with trumpet obbligato, and conducted several shows. He met Richard Strauss, who helped him to obtain the Liszt Stipendium and a position as a teacher at the Stern Cons. He returned to Vienna in 1903 and formed friendly relations with Gustav Mahler, who became a sincere supporter of his activities; Mahler's power in Vienna was then at its height, and he was able to help him in his career as a composer. In March 1904 Schoenberg organized with Alexander Zemlinsky the Vereinigung Schaffender Tonkünstler for the purpose of encouraging performances of new music. Under its auspices he conducted on Jan. 26, 1905, the first performance of his symphonic poem *Pelleas und Melisande*; in this score occurs the first use of a trombone glissando. There followed a performance on Feb. 8, 1907, of Schoenberg's *Kammersymphonie*, op. 9, with the participation of the Rosé Quartet and the wind instrumentalists of the Vienna Phil.; the work produced much consternation in the audience and among critics because of its departure from traditional tonal harmony, with chords built on fourths and nominal dissonances used without immediate resolution. About the same time, he turned to painting, which became his principal avocation. In his art, as in his music, he adopted the tenets of Expressionism, that is, freedom of personal expression within a self-defined program. Schoenberg's reputation as an independent musical thinker attracted to him such progressive-minded young musicians as Alban Berg, Anton von Webern, and Egon Wellesz, who followed Schoenberg in their own development. His 2nd String Quartet, composed in 1908, which included a soprano solo, was his last work that carried a definite key signature, if exception is made for his *Suite* for Strings, ostentatiously marked as in G major, which he wrote for school use in America in 1934. On Feb. 19, 1909, Schoenberg completed his piano piece op. 11, no. 1, which became the first musical composition to dispense with all reference to tonality. In 1910 he was appointed to the faculty of the Vienna Academy of Music; in 1911 he completed his important theory book *Harmonielehre*, dedicated to the memory of Mahler; it comprises a traditional exposition of chords and progressions, but also offers illuminating indications of possible new musical developments, including fractional tones and melodies formed by the change of timbre on the same note. In 1911 he went again to Berlin, where he became an instructor at the Stern Cons. and taught composition privately. His *5 Orchesterstücke*, first perf. in London on Sept. 3, 1912, under Sir Henry Wood's direction, attracted a great deal of attention; the critical reception was that of incomprehension, with a considerable measure of curiosity. The score was indeed revolutionary in nature, each movement representing an experiment in musical organization. In the same year, Schoenberg produced another innovative work, a cycle of 21 songs with instrumental accompaniment, entitled *Pierrot Lunaire*, and consisting of 21 "melodramas," to German texts translated from verses by the Belgian poet Albert Giraud. Here he made systematic use of *Sprechstimme*, with a gliding speech-song replacing precise pitch (not an entire innovation, for Engelbert Humperdinck had applied it in his incidental music to Rosmer's play *Königskinder* in 1897). The work was given, after some 40 rehearsals, in Berlin on Oct. 16, 1912, and the reaction was startling, the purblind critics drawing upon the strongest invective in their vocabulary to condemn the music.

Meanwhile, Schoenberg made appearances as conductor of his works in various European cities (Amsterdam, 1911; St. Petersburg, 1912; London, 1914). During World War I, he was sporadically enlisted in military service; after the Armistice, he settled in Mödling, near Vienna. Discouraged by his inability to secure performances for himself and his associates in the new music movement, he organized in Vienna, in Nov. 1918, the Verein für Musikalische Privataufführungen (Society for Private Musical Performances), from which critics were demonstratively excluded, and which ruled out any vocal expression of approval or disapproval. The organization disbanded in 1922. About that time, Schoenberg began work on his *Suite* for Piano, op. 25, which was to be the first true 12-tone piece consciously composed in that idiom. In 1925 he was appointed prof. of a master class at the Prussian Academy of Arts in Berlin. With the advent of the beastly Nazi regime, the German Ministry of Education dismissed him from his post as a Jew. As a matter of record, Schoenberg had abandoned his Jewish faith in Vienna on March 25, 1898, by being baptized in the Protestant Dorotheer Community (Augsburger Konfession); 35 years later, horrified by the hideous persecution of Jews at the hands of the Nazis, he was moved to return to his ancestral faith and was reconverted to Judaism in Paris on July 24, 1933. With the rebirth of his hereditary consciousness, he turned to specific Jewish themes in works such as *Survivor from Warsaw* and *Moses und Aron*. Although Schoenberg was well known in the musical world, he had difficulty obtaining a teaching position; he finally accepted the invitation of Joseph Malkin, founder of the Malkin Cons. of Boston, to join its faculty. He arrived in the U.S. on Oct. 31, 1933. After teaching in Boston for a season, he moved to Hollywood. In 1935 he became a prof. of music at the Univ. of Southern Calif. in Los Angeles, and in 1936 accepted a similar position at the Univ. of Calif. at Los Angeles, where he taught until 1944, when he reached the mandatory retirement age of 70. On April 11, 1941, he became a naturalized American citizen. In 1947 he received the Award of Merit for Distinguished Achievements from the National Inst. of Arts and Letters. In the U.S. he changed the original spelling of his name from Schönberg to Schoenberg.

In 1924 Schoenberg's creative evolution reached the all-important point at which he found it necessary to establish a new governing principle of tonal relationship, which he called the "method of composing with 12 different notes related entirely to one another." This method was adumbrated in his music as early as 1914, and is used partially in his *5 Klavierstücke*, op. 23, and in his *Serenade*, op. 24; it was employed for the first time in its integral form in the piano *Suite*, op. 25 (1924); in it, the thematic material is based on a group of 12 different notes arrayed in a certain pre-arranged order; such a tone row was henceforth Schoenberg's mainspring of thematic invention; development was provided by the devices of inversion, retrograde, and retrograde inversion of the basic series; allowing for transposition, 48 forms were obtainable in all, with counterpoint and harmony, as well as melody, derived from the basic tone row. Immediate repetition of thematic notes was admitted; the realm of rhythm remained free. As with most historic innovations, the 12-tone technique was not the creation of Schoenberg alone but was, rather, a logical development of many currents of musical thought. Josef Matthias Hauer rather unconvincingly claimed priority in laying the foundations of the 12-tone method; among others who had elaborated similar ideas at about the same time with Schoenberg was Jef Golyscheff, a Russian émigré who expounded his theory in a publication entitled "12 Tondauer-Musik." Instances of themes consisting of 12 different notes are found in the *Faust Symphony* of Liszt and in the tone poem *Also sprach Zarathustra* of Richard Strauss in the section on Science. Schoenberg's great achievement was the establishment of the basic 12-tone row and its changing forms as foundations of a new musical language; using this idiom, he was able to write music of great expressive power. In general usage, the 12-tone method is often termed "dodecaphony," from Greek dodeca, "12," and phone, "sound." The tonal composition of the basic row is devoid of tonality; an analysis of Schoenberg's works shows that he avoided using major triads in any of their inversions, and allowed the use of only the 2nd inversion of a minor triad. He deprecated the term "atonality" that was commonly applied to his music. He suggested, only half in jest, the term "atonicality," i.e., absence of the dominating tonic. The most explicit work of Schoenberg couched in the 12-tone idiom was his *Klavierstück*, op. 33a, written in 1928–29, which exemplifies the clearest use of the tone row in chordal combinations. Other works that present a classical use of dodecaphony are *Begleitungsmusik zu einer Lichtspielszene*, op. 34 (1929–30); Violin Concerto (1934–36); and Piano Concerto (1942). Schoenberg's disciples Berg and Webern followed his 12-tone method in general outlines but with some personal deviations; thus, Berg accepted the occasional use of triadic harmonies, and Webern built tone rows in symmetric groups. Other composers who made systematic use of the 12-tone method were Egon Wellesz, Ernst Krenek, René Leibowitz, Roberto Gerhard, Humphrey Searle, and Luigi Dallapiccola. As time went on, dodecaphony became a lingua franca of universal currency; even in Russia, where Schoenberg's theories were for many years unacceptable on ideological grounds, several composers, including Shostakovich in his last works, made use of 12-tone themes, albeit without integral development. Ernest Bloch used 12-tone subjects in his last string quartets, but he refrained from applying inversions and retrograde forms of his tone rows. Stravinsky, in his old age, turned to the 12-tone method of composition in its total form, with retrograde, inversion, and retrograde inversion; his conversion was the greatest artistic vindication for Schoenberg, who regarded Stravinsky as his most powerful antagonist, but Schoenberg was dead when Stravinsky saw the light of dodecaphony.

Schoenberg's personality was both heroic and egocentric; he made great sacrifices to sustain his artistic convictions, but he was also capable of engaging in bitter polemics when he felt that his integrity was under attack. He strongly opposed the claims of Hauer and others for the priority of the 12-tone method of composition, and he vehemently criticized in the public press the implication he saw in Thomas Mann's novel *Doktor Faustus*, in which the protagonist was described as the inventor of the 12-tone method of composition; future historians, Schoenberg argued, might confuse fiction with facts, and credit the figment of Mann's imagination with Schoenberg's own discovery. He was also subject to superstition in the form of triskaidecaphobia, the fear of the number 13; he seriously believed that there was something fateful in the circumstance of his birth on the 13th of the month. Noticing that the title of his work *Moses und Aaron* contained 13 letters, he crossed out the 2nd "a" in Aaron to make it 12. When he turned 76 and someone remarked facetiously that the sum of the digits of his age was 13, he seemed genuinely upset, and during his last illness in July 1951, he expressed his fear of not surviving July 13; indeed, he died on that date. Schoenberg placed his MSS in the Music Division of the Library of Congress in Washington, D.C.; the remaining materials were deposited after his death at the Schoenberg Inst. at the Univ. of Southern Calif. in Los Angeles. Schoenberg's centennial in 1974 was commemorated worldwide. A Journal of the Schoenberg Institute began publ. in 1976, under the editorship of Leonard Stein.

Schoenberg's personality, which combined elements of decisive affirmation and profound self-negation, still awaits a thorough analysis. When he was drafted into the Austrian armed forces during World War I (he never served in action, however) and was asked by the examiner whether he was the "notorious" modernist composer, he answered "someone had to be, and I was the one." He could not understand why his works were not widely performed. He asked a former secretary to Serge Koussevitzky why the Boston Sym. Orch. programs never included any of his advanced works; when the secretary said that Koussevitzky simply could not understand them, Schoenberg was genuinely perplexed. "Aber, er spielt doch Brahms!" he said. To Schoenberg, his works were the natural continuation of German classical music. Schoenberg lived in Los Angeles for several years during the period when Stravinsky was also there, but the two never made artistic contact. Indeed, they met only once, in a downtown food market, where they greeted each other, in English, with a formal handshake. Schoenberg wrote a satirical canon, *Herr Modernsky*, obviously aimed at Stravinsky, whose neo-Classical works ("ganz wie Papa Bach") Schoenberg lampooned. But when Schoenberg was dead, Stravinsky said he forgave him in appreciation of his expertise in canonic writing.

In his private life, Schoenberg had many interests; he was a fairly good tennis player, and also liked to play chess. In his early years in Vienna, he launched several theoretical inventions to augment his income, but none of them ever went into practice; he also designed a set of playing cards. The MSS of arrangements of Viennese operettas and waltzes he had made in Vienna to augment his meager income were eventually sold for large sums of money after his death. That Schoenberg needed money but was not offered any by an official musical benefactor was a shame. After Schoenberg relocated to Los Angeles, which was to be his final destination, he obtained successful appointments as a prof. at the Univ. of Southern Calif. and eventually at the Univ. of Calif., Los Angeles. But there awaited him the peculiar rule of age limitation for teachers, and he was mandatorily retired when he reached his seventieth year. His pension from the Univ. of Calif., Los Angeles, amounted to $38 a month. His difficulty in supporting a family with growing children became acute and eventually reached the press. He applied for a grant from the munificent Guggenheim Foundation, pointing out that since several of his own students had received such awards, he was now applying for similar consideration, but the rule of age limitation defeated him there as well. It was only after the Schoenberg case and its repercussions in the music world that the Guggenheim Foundation cancelled its offensive rule. Schoenberg managed to square his finances with the aid of his publishing income, however, and, in the meantime, his children grew up. His son Ronald (an anagram of Arnold) eventually became a city judge, an extraordinary development for a Schoenberg!

WORKS: DRAMATIC: *Erwartung*, monodrama, op. 17 (1909; Prague, June 6, 1924, Gutheil-Schoder mezzo-soprano, Zemlinsky conducting); *Die glückliche Hand*, drama with music, to Schoenberg's own libretto, op. 18 (1910–13; Vienna, Oct. 14, 1924, Stiedry conducting); *Von Heute auf Morgen*, opera, op. 32 (1928–29; Frankfurt am Main, Feb. 1, 1930, W. Steinberg conducting); *Moses und Aron*, biblical drama, to Schoenberg's own libretto (2 acts composed 1930–32; 3rd act begun in 1951, but not completed; radio perf. of Acts 1 and 2, Hamburg, March 12, 1954, Rosbaud conducting; stage perf., Zürich, June 6, 1957, Rosbaud conducting).

ORCH.: *Frülings Tod*, symphonic poem (fragment, 1898; Berlin, March 18, 1984, R. Chailly conducting); *Pelleas und Melisande*, symphonic poem, after Maeterlinck, op. 5 (1902–03; Vienna, Jan. 26, 1905, composer conducting); *Kammersymphonie No. 1* for 15 Instruments, op. 9 (1906; Vienna, Feb. 8, 1907; arranged for Orch., 1922; new version for Orch., op. 9b, 1935); *5 Orchester-Stücke*, op. 16 (1909; London, Sept. 3, 1912, Sir Henry Wood conducting; rev. 1922 and 1949); *3 Little Pieces* for Chamber Orch. (1911; Berlin, Oct. 10, 1957); *Variations*, op. 31 (1926–28; Berlin, Dec. 2, 1928, Furtwängler conducting); *Begleitungsmusik zu einer Lichtspielszene*, op. 34 (1929–30; Berlin, Nov. 6, 1930, Klemperer conducting); *Suite* in G major for Strings (1934; Los Angeles, May 18, 1935, Klemperer conducting); Violin Concerto, op. 36 (1934–36; Philadelphia, Dec. 6, 1940, Krasner soloist, Stokowski conducting); 2nd Chamber Sym., op. 38a (1906–16 and 1939; N.Y., Dec. 15, 1940, Stiedry conducting; op. 38b is an arrangement for 2 Pianos, 1941–42); Piano Concerto, op. 42 (1942; N.Y., Feb. 6, 1944, Steuermann pianist, Stokowski conducting); *Theme and Variations* for Wind Band, op. 43a (1943; arranged for Orch., op. 43b, Boston, Oct. 20, 1944, Koussevitzky conducting).

CHAMBER: 1 unnumbered string quartet in D major (1897; Vienna, March 17, 1898); 4 numbered string quartets: No. 1, in D minor, op. 7 (1904–05; Vienna, Feb. 5, 1907), No. 2, in F-sharp minor, op. 10, with Voice (Vienna, Dec. 21, 1908, Rosé Quartet, Gutheil Schoder mezzo-soprano; arranged for String Orch., 1929), No. 3, op. 30 (Vienna, Sept. 19, 1927, Kolisch Quartet), and No. 4, op. 37 (1936; Los Angeles, Jan. 9, 1937, Kolisch Quartet); *Verklärte Nacht*, sextet for Strings, op. 4 (1899; Vienna, March 18, 1902; arranged for String Orch., 1917; rev. 1943; perf. as the ballet *The Pillar of Fire*, N.Y., April 8, 1942); *Ein Stelldichein* for Oboe, Clarinet, Violin, Cello, and Piano (1905); *Die eiserne Brigade*, march for String Quartet and Piano (1916); *Weihnachtsmusik* for 2 Violins, Cello, Harmonium, and Piano (1921); *Serenade* for Clarinet, Bass Clarinet, Mandolin, Guitar, Violin, Viola, and Cello, op. 24 (4th movement with a sonnet by Petrarch for Baritone; 1920–23; Donaueschingen, July 20, 1924); Quintet for Flute, Oboe, Clarinet, Horn, and Bassoon, op. 26 (Vienna, Sept. 13, 1924); *Suite* for 2 Clarinets, Bass Clarinet, Violin, Viola, Cello, and Piano, op. 29 (1925–26; Paris, Dec. 15, 1927); *Ode to Napoleon* for String Quartet, Piano, and Reciter, after Byron (1942; also a version with String Orch., N.Y., Nov. 23, 1944, Rodzinski conducting); String Trio, op. 45 (1946; Cambridge, Mass., May 1, 1947); *Phantasy* for Violin, with Piano Accompaniment (Los Angeles, Sept. 13, 1949). **KEYBOARD: PIANO:** *3 Klavierstücke*, op. 11 (1909; Vienna, Jan. 14, 1910; rev. 1924); *6 kleine Klavierstücke*, op. 19 (1911; Berlin, Feb. 4, 1912); *5 Klavierstücke*, op. 23 (1920–23); *Suite*, op. 25 (1921–23); *Klavierstück*, op. 33a (1928–29; Hamburg, Jan. 30, 1931); *Klavierstück*, op. 33b (1931). **ORGAN:** *Variations on a Recitative*, op. 40 (1941; N.Y., April 10, 1944).

VOCAL: CHORAL: *Gurre-Lieder* for Soli, Chorus, and Orch. (1900–03 and 1910–11; Vienna, Feb. 23, 1913, Schreker conducting); *Friede auf Erden*, op. 13 (1907; Vienna, Dec. 9, 1911, Schreker conducting); 4 pieces for Chorus, op. 27 (1925); *3 Satires*, op. 28 (1925); 3 German folk songs (Vienna, Nov. 1929); 6 pieces for Men's Chorus, op. 35 (1929–30; Frankfurt am Main, Nov. 29, 1931, F. Schmidt conducting); *Kol Nidre* for Speaker, Chorus, and Orch., op. 39 (Los Angeles, Oct. 4, 1938, composer conducting); *Genesis*, prelude for Orch. and Chorus (Los Angeles, Jan. 11, 1945); *A Survivor from Warsaw* for Narrator, Chorus, and Orch., op. 46 (1947; Albuquerque, Nov. 4, 1948); 3 German folk songs for Chorus, op. 49 (1948); *Dreimal tausend Jahre* for Chorus, op. 50a (Fylkingen, Sweden, Oct. 29, 1949); *De Profundis* for Chorus, after a Hebrew text, op. 50b (1950; Cologne, Jan. 29, 1954); *Modern Psalm* for Chorus, Speaker, and Chorus, after the composer (unfinished; Cologne, May 29, 1956, Sanzogno conducting). The oratorio *Die Jakobsleiter*, begun in 1917, was left unfinished; a performing version was prepared by Winfried Zillig, and given for the first time in Vienna on June 16, 1961. **SONGS:** 2 songs, op. 1 (1898); 4 songs, op. 2 (1899); 7 Chansons, *Brettl-Lieder* (1901); *Nachtwandler* for Soprano, Piccolo, Trumpet, Side Drum, and Piano (1901); 6 songs, op. 3 (1899–1903); 8 songs, op. 6 (1903–05); 6 songs, op. 8 (nos. 2, 5, and 6 for Orch., Prague, Jan. 29, 1914, Zemlinsky conducting); 2 ballads, op. 12 (1907); 2 songs, op. 14 (1907–08); cycle of 15 poems after Stefan George's *Das Buch der hängenden Gärten* (1908–09; Vienna, Jan. 14, 1910); *Herzgewächse* for Soprano, Celesta, Harmonium, and Harp, after Maeterlinck, op. 20 (1911); *Pierrot Lunaire*, 21 poems for Sprechstimme, Piano, Flute/Piccolo, Clarinet/Bass Clarinet, Violin/Viola, and Cello, after Albert Giraud, op. 21 (Berlin, Oct. 16, 1912, A. Zehme soloist, composer conducting); 4 songs, op. 22 (with Orch.; 1913–16; Frankfurt am Main, Feb. 21, 1932, Rosbaud conducting); *Lied der Waldtaube* for Mezzo-soprano and Chamber Ensemble (1922; arranged from *Gurre-Lieder*); 3 songs, op. 48 (1933; London, June 5, 1952).

ARRANGEMENTS AND TRANSCRIPTIONS: 2 chorale preludes by Bach, for Large Orch.: No. 1, *Komm, Gott, Schöpfer, Heiliger Geist*, and No. 2, *Schmücke dich, O liebe Seele* (N.Y., Dec. 12, 1922); *Prelude and Fugue* in E-flat major for Organ by Bach, for Large Orch. (1928; Vienna, Nov. 10, 1929, Webern conducting); Piano Quartet No. 1, in G minor, op. 25, by Brahms, for Orch. (1937; Los Angeles, May 7, 1938, Klemperer conducting); also a Cello Concerto, transcribed from a Harpsichord Concerto by G.M. Monn (1932–33; London, Dec. 7, 1935, Feuermann soloist); Concerto for String Quartet and Orch. after Handel's Concerto Grosso, op. 6, No. 7 (1933; Prague, Sept. 26, 1934, Kolisch Quartet); etc.

WRITINGS: *Harmonielehre* (Vienna, 1911; 3rd ed., rev., 1922; abr. Eng. tr., 1947, as *Theory of Harmony*; complete Eng. tr., 1978); *Models for Beginners in Composition* (N.Y., 1942; 3rd ed., rev., 1972, by L. Stein); *Style and Idea* (N.Y., 1950; enl. ed. by L. Stein, London, 1975); *Structural Functions of Harmony* (N.Y., 1954; 2nd ed., rev., 1969, by L. Stein); *Preliminary Exercises in Counterpoint*, ed. by L. Stein (London, 1963); *Fundamentals of Musical Composition*, ed. by L. Stein (London, 1967); also numerous essays in German and American publs.

BIBL.: COLLECTED WORKS, SOURCE MATERIAL: J. Rufer and his successors are preparing a complete ed. of his works, *A. S.: Sämtliche Werke* (Mainz, 1966–). Rufer also compiled an annotated catalogue, *Das Werk A. S.s* (Kassel, 1959; Eng. tr., 1962; 2nd Ger. ed., rev., 1975). I. Vojtch ed. vol. I of the *Gesammelte Schriften* (Frankfurt am Main, 1976).

See also the following: Special issue of *Der Merker*, II/17 (1911); *A. S.: Mit Beiträgen von Alban Berg, Paris von Gutersloh . . .* (essays by 11 admirers; Munich, 1912); E. Wellesz, "S. and Beyond," *Musical Quarterly* (Jan. 1916); idem, *A. S.* (Leipzig, 1921; Eng. tr., rev., London, 1925); C. Gray, "A. S., A Critical Study," *Music & Letters* (Jan. 1922); E. Stein, *Praktischer Leitfaden zu S.s Harmonielehre* (Vienna, 1923); P. Stefan, *A. S.: Wandlung, Legende, Erscheinung, Bedeutung* (Vienna, 1924); *A. S. zum 60. Geburtstag* (articles by friends and pupils; Vienna, 1934); H. Wind, *Die Endkrise der bürgerlichen Musik und die Rolle A. S.s* (Vienna, 1935); R. Hill, "S.'s Tone-Rows and the Tonal System of the Future," *Musical Quarterly* (Jan. 1936); M. Armitage, ed., *A. S.* (contains essays by Sessions, Krenek, E.

Stein, C. Engel, Klemperer, P. Pisk, P. Stefan et al.; also 2 by Schoenberg: "Tonality and Form" and "Problems of Harmony"; N.Y., 1937); H. Jalowetz, "On the Spontaneity of S.'s Music," *Musical Quarterly* (Oct. 1944); D. Milhaud, "To A. S. on His Seventieth Birthday: Personal Recollections," ibid.; R. Sessions, "S. in the United States," *Tempo,* no. 9 (1944; rev. in *Tempo,* no. 103, 1972); P. Gradenwitz, "The Idiom and Development in S.'s Quartets," *Music & Letters,* XXVI (1945); R. Leibowitz, *S. et son école* (Paris, 1947; Eng. tr., 1949); D. Newlin, *Bruckner, Mahler, S.* (N.Y., 1947; rev. ed., 1978); W. Rubsamen, "S. in America," *Musical Quarterly* (Oct. 1951); H. Stuckenschmidt, *A. S.* (Zürich, 1951; 2nd ed., rev., 1957; Eng. tr., 1959); G. Perle, "S.'s Later Style," *Music Review,* XIII (1952); J. Rufer, *Die Komposition mit zwölf Tönen* (Berlin, 1952; Eng. tr., 1954, as *Composition with 12 Notes Related to One Another*); L. Rognoni, *Espressionismo e dodecafonia* (Turin, 1954; 2nd ed., rev., 1966, as *La scuola musicale di Vienna*); H. Keller, "S.'s 'Moses and Aron'," *Score,* no. 21 (1957); T. Tuttle, "S.'s Compositions for Piano Solo," *Music Review,* XVIII (1957); K. Wörner, *Gotteswort und Magie* (Heidelberg, 1959; Eng. tr., rev., 1963, as *S.'s "Moses and Aron"*); M. Kassler, *The Decision of A. S.'s Twelve-Note-Class-System and Related Systems* (Princeton, 1961); H. Pauli, "Zu S.s 'Jakobsleiter'," *Schweizerische Musikzeitung/Revue Musicale Suisse,* CII (1962); G. Perle, *Serial Composition and Atonality: An Introduction to the Music of S., Berg and Webern* (Berkeley, 1962; 5th ed., rev., 1982); W. Rogge, *Das Klavierwerke A. S.s* (Regensburg, 1964); P. Friedheim, "Rhythmic Structure in S.'s Atonal Compositions," *Journal of the American Musicological Society,* XIX (1966); J. Meyerowitz, *A. S.* (Berlin, 1967); B. Boretz and E. Cone, eds., *Perspectives on S. and Stravinsky* (Princeton, 1968); G. Krieger, *S.s Werke für Klavier* (Göttingen, 1968); A. Payne, *S.* (London, 1968); W. Reich, *A. S., oder Der konservative Revolutionär* (Vienna, 1968; Eng. tr., 1971); R. Brinkmann, *A. S.: Drei Klavierstücke Op. 11* (also includes bibliography of publ. writings; Wiesbaden, 1969); R. Leibowitz, *S.* (Paris, 1969); D. Rexroth, *A. S. als Theoretiker der tonalen Harmonik* (Bonn, 1971); J. Maegaard, *Studien zur Entwicklung des dodekaphonen Satzes bei A. S.* (Copenhagen, 1972); A. Whittall, *S. Chamber Music* (London, 1972); E. Freitag, *A. S. in Selbstzeugnissen und Bilddokumenten* (Reinbek, 1973); J. Samson, "S.'s 'Atonal' Music," *Tempo,* no. 109 (1974); E. Steiner, "S.'s Quest: Newly Discovered Works from His Early Years," *Musical Quarterly* (Oct. 1974); H. Stuckenschmidt, *S.: Leben, Umwelt, Werk* (Zürich, 1974; Eng. tr., 1976, as *S.: His Life, World and Work*); C. Rosen, *A. S.* (N.Y., 1975); G. Schubert, *S.s frühe Instrumentation* (Baden-Baden, 1975); M. Macdonald, *S.* (London, 1976); D. Newlin, *S. Remembered: Diaries and Recollections (1938–76)* (N.Y., 1980); W. Bailey, *Programmatic Elements in the Works of A. S.* (Ann Arbor, 1983); W. Jakobik, *A. S.: die Verräumlichte Zeit* (Regensburg, 1983); J. Christensen, "The Spiritual and the Material in S.'s Thinking," *Music & Letters* (Oct. 1984); J. Hahl-Koch, ed., *A. S./Wassily Kandinsky: Letters, Pictures and Documents* (London, 1984); P. Franklin, The Idea of Music: S. and Others (London, 1985); G. Bauer, *A Contextual Approach to S.'s Atonal Works: Self Expression, Religion, and Music Theory* (diss., Wash. Univ., 1986); J. Brand, C. Hailey, and D. Harris, eds., *The Berg-S. Correspondence* (N.Y., 1986); E. Smaldone, *Linear Analysis of Selected Posttonal Works of A. S.: Toward an Application of Schenkerian Concepts to Music of the Posttonal Era* (diss., City Univ. of N.Y., 1986); J. Smith, *S. and His Circle: A Viennese Portrait* (N.Y., 1986); J. Straus, "Recompositions by S., Stravinsky, and Webern," *Musical Quarterly,* no.3 (1986); E. Haimo, "Redating S.'s Passacaglia for Orchestra," *Journal of the American Musicological Society* (Fall 1987); D. Lambourn, "Henry Wood and S.," *Musical Times* (Aug. 1987); M. Mäckelmann, *S.: Fünf Orchesterstücke op. 16* (Munich, 1987); J. and J. Christensen, *From A. S.'s Literary Legacy: A Catalog of Neglected Items* (Warren, Mich., 1988); W. Frisch, "Thematic Form and the Genesis of S.'s D-Minor Quartet, Opus 7," *Journal of the American Musicological Society* (Summer 1988); G. Beinhorn, *Das Groteske in der Musik: A. S.s Pierrot Lunaire* (Pfaffenweiler, 1989); G. Biringer, *Registral and Temporal Influences on Segmentation and Form in S.'s Twelve-Tone Music* (diss., Yale Univ., 1989); R. Boestfleisch, *A. S.s frühe Kammermusik: Studien unter besonderer Berücksightigung der ersten beiden Streichquartette* (Frankfurt am Main, 1990); E. Haimo, *S.'s Serial Odyssey: The Evolution of his Twelve-Tone Method, 1914–1928* (Oxford, 1990); A. Ringer, *A. S.: The Composer as Jew* (Oxford, 1990); M. Sichardt, *Die Entstehung der Zwölftonmethode A. S.s* (Mainz, 1990); A. Trenkamp and J. Suess, eds., *Studies in the S.ian Movement in Vienna and the United States: Essays in Honor of Marcel Dick* (Lewiston, N.Y., 1990); W. Thomson, *S.'s Error* (Philadelphia, 1991); J. Dunsby, *S.: Pierrot lunaire* (Cambridge, 1992); B. Meier, *Feschichtliche Signaturen der Musik bei Mahler, Strauss und S.* (Hamburg, 1992); S. Milstein, *A. S.: Notes, Sets, Forms* (Cambridge, 1992); N. Nono-Schoenberg, ed., *A. S., 1874–1951: Lebensgeschichte in Begegnungen* (Klagenfurt, 1992); W. Frisch, *The Early Works of A. S., 1893–1908* (Berkeley, 1993); C. Sterne, *A. S.: The Composer as Numerologist* (Lewiston, N.Y., 1993); C.-S. Mahnkopf, *Gestalt und Stil: S.s Erste Kammersymphonie und ihr Umfeld* (Kassel and N.Y., 1994).

Schoen-René, Anna, German-American singing teacher; b. Koblenz, Jan. 12, 1864; d. N.Y., Nov. 13, 1942. She studied singing with Pauline Viardot-García. She appeared in opera before settling in the U.S., where she taught in Minneapolis and then at the Juilliard School of Music in N.Y. She publ. a book of memoirs, *America's Musical Heritage* (N.Y., 1941).

Schöffler, Paul, distinguished German bass-baritone; b. Dresden, Sept. 15, 1897; d. Amersham, Buckinghamshire, Nov. 21, 1977. He studied in Dresden, Berlin, and Milan. In 1925 he made his operatic debut at the Dresden State Opera as the Herald in *Lohengrin*; continued on its roster until 1938, then was a member of the Vienna State Opera until 1965. He also sang at London's Covent Garden (1934–39; 1949–53), the Bayreuth Festivals (1943–44; 1956), and the Salzburg Festivals (1938–41; 1947; 1949–65). He made his Metropolitan Opera debut in N.Y. on Jan. 26, 1950, as Jokanaan in *Salome*; continued to sing there, with interruptions, until 1956, returning in 1963 to sing one of his finest roles, Hans Sachs; remained on its roster until 1965, when he went to England. His other notable roles included Figaro, Don Giovanni, the Dutchman, Kurwenal, Scarpia, and Hindemith's Cardillac and Mathis der Maler; he also created the role of Jupiter in the first stage perf. of Strauss's *Die Liebe der Danae* (1952) and Einem's Danton (1947).

BIBL.: H. Christian, *P. S.: Versuch einer Würdigung* (Vienna, 1967).

Scholes, Percy (Alfred), eminent English writer on music; b. Leeds, July 24, 1877; d. Vevey, Switzerland, July 31, 1958. (He pronounced his name "Skoles.") He took his B.Mus. at the Univ. of Oxford in 1908, and his doctorat ès lettres from the Univ. of Lausanne (1934) for his study of Puritans and music. He began his career as a church organist; in 1907, founded the Home Music Study Union, and until 1921 ed. its *Music Student* (later *Music Teacher*); also wrote for the *Evening Standard* (1913–20), *Observer* (1920–27), and the *Radio Times* (1923–29). He lived in Switzerland (1928–40); then made his home in England (1940–57) until returning to Switzerland. He received many honors, including the degrees of D.Mus. (1943) and D.Litt. (1950) from the Univ. of Oxford, and D.Litt. (1953) from the Univ. of Leeds; was made an Officer of the Order of the British Empire in 1957. A writer of great literary attainments and stylistic grace, he succeeded in presenting music "appreciation" in a manner informative and stimulating to the layman and professional alike.

WRITINGS: *Everyman and His Music* (1917); *An Introduction to British Music* (1918); *The Listener's Guide to Music* (1919; 10th ed., 1942); *Music Appreciation: Why and How?* (1920; 4th ed., 1925); *The Book of the Great Musicians* (3 vols., 1920); *New Works by Modern British Composers* (2 series, 1921, 1924); *The Beginner's Guide to Harmony* (1922); *The Listener's History of Music* (3 vols., 1923–28; 4th ed., 1933); *Crotchets* (1924); *Learn-*

ing to Listen by Means of the Gramophone (1925); *Everybody's Guide to Broadcast Music* (1925); *The Appreciation of Music by Means of the Pianola and Duo Art* (1925); *A Miniature History of Music* (1928); *The Columbia History of Music through Eye and Ear* (5 albums of records with accompanying booklets; 1930–39; eds. in Japanese and Braille); *Music and Puritanism* (Vevey, 1934); *The Puritans and Music in England and New England* (London, 1934); *Music: The Child and the Masterpiece* (1935; American ed., *Music Appreciation: Its History and Technics*); *Radio Times Music Handbook* (1935; 3rd ed., 1936; American ed. as *The Scholes Music Handbook*, 1935); *The Oxford Companion to Music* (1938; 9th ed., rev., 1955; rev. and aug. by D. Arnold as *The New Oxford Companion to Music*, 2 vols., 1983); *God Save the King: Its History and Romance* (1942; new ed. as *God Save the Queen! The History and Romance of the World's First National Anthem*, 1954); *The Mirror of Music, 1844–1944, A Century of Musical Life in Britain as Reflected in the Pages of the "Musical Times"* (1947); *The Great Dr. Burney* (2 vols., 1948); *Sir John Hawkins: Musician, Magistrate, and Friend of Johnson* (1952); *The Concise Oxford Dictionary of Music* (1952; 3rd ed., rev., 1980 by M. Kennedy; rev. and aug. ed., 1985 by Kennedy as *The Oxford Dictionary of Music*; 2nd ed., rev., 1994); *The Oxford Junior Companion to Music* (1954; 2nd ed., rev., 1979).

Schollum, Robert, Austrian composer, writer on music, and teacher; b. Vienna, Aug. 22, 1913; d. there, Sept. 30, 1987. He was a student at the Vienna Academy of Music and at the New Vienna Cons. He also received training from Marx and Lustgarten (theory and composition), Lafite (piano and organ), and Nilius (conducting). From 1959 to 1982 he taught voice at the Vienna Academy of Music. He was president of the Austrian Composers Union from 1965 to 1970, and again in 1983. In 1961 he was awarded the Austrian State Prize for composition and in 1971 the prize of the City of Vienna. After World War II, the influence of impressionism on his music was replaced by dodecaphony, aleatory, and timbre display.

WRITINGS (all publ. in Vienna unless otherwise given): *Musik in der Volksbildung* (1962); *Egon Wellesz* (1964); *Die Wiener Schule: Entwicklung und Ergebnis* (1969); with J. Fritz et al., *Das kleine Wiener Jazzbuch* (Salzburg, 1970); *Singen als menschliche Kundgebung: Einführung in die Arbeit mit den "Singblattern zur Musikerziehung"* (1970); *Das Österreichische Lied des 20. Jahrhunderts* (Tutzing, 1977); *Vokale Aufführungspraxis* (1983).

WORKS: DRAMATIC: *Der Tote Mann*, musical comedy (1936–38); *Mirandolina*, musical comedy (1950); *Der Biedermann Elend*, opera (1962). **ORCH.:** *Dance Suite* (1933); *17 Intermezzi on Folk Songs* (1934–35); *Romance* for Violin and Orch. (1942); *Festive Capriccio* (1943); 3 violin concertos: No. 1 (1944), No. 2 (1961; Vienna, Feb. 1, 1963), and No. 3 (1979–81; Vienna, Feb. 26, 1982); *Admonter Dance* (1945); Clarinet Concerto (1948); *Sonata* (1949); *Serenade* (1949–52); Piano Concerto (1950); Cello Concerto (1953–55); 6 syms.: No. 1 (1954–55; Vienna, March 26, 1976), No. 2 (1955–59; Linz, Oct. 28, 1963), No. 3 (1962; Vienna, May 6, 1966), No. 4 (1966–67; Vienna, Jan. 26, 1968), No. 5, *Venetianische Ergebnisse* (1969; Vienna, Jan. 23, 1970), and No. 6 (1986; Vienna, Feb. 12, 1987); *Toccata* (1957); *Dialogue* for Horn and Strings (1958); *Contures* for Strings (1958); *Game* (1970–71); *Exclamation* (1973); *Seestück* for Piano and Orch. (1974–79; Vienna, May 23, 1980); *Epitaph for Hingerichtete* (1976); *Konzertstück, Fanfares* (Linz, Sept. 8, 1984). **CHAMBER:** Bassoon Sonata (1949); Viola d'Amore Sonata (1949); 2 string quartets (1949; 1966–67); Viola Sonata (1950); Trio for Flute, Bassoon or Cello, and Piano (1951); Violin Sonata (1953); *Chaconne* for Viola and Piano (1955); Octet (1959); Suite for Trumpet and Piano (1964); Trio for Oboe, Clarinet, and Piano (1965); *2 Pieces* for Clarinet and Piano (1966); Alto Flute Sonata (1968); Oboe Sonata (1970); *5 Pieces* for Wind Quintet (1970–71); *Die Ameisen* for Cello and Piano (1973–74); Wind Quintet (1975); *Adagio* for Cello and Piano (1981); several sonatinas and Konzertstücken; piano pieces; organ music. **VOCAL:** Choral pieces; songs.

Schönbach, Dieter, German composer; b. Stolp-Pommern, Feb. 18, 1931. He studied at the Freiburg im Briesgau Hochschule für Musik with Bialas and Fortner (1949–59). He was music director of the Bochum theater (1959–73). His style of composition is quaquaversal. He wrote the first genuine multimedia opera, *Wenn die Kälte in die Hütten tritt, um sich bei den Frierenden zu wärmen, weiss einer "Die Geschichte von einem Feuer"* (Kiel, 1968); his other works include *Farben und Klänge*, in memory of Kandinsky, for Orch. (1958); Piano Concerto (1958); *Canticum Psalmi Resurrectionis* (Rome, June 13, 1959); *Kammermusik* for 14 Instruments (1964); *Hoquetus* for 8 Wind Instruments (1964); 4 chamber music pieces, each titled *Canzona da sonar* (1966–67); *Atemmusik* for Fifes, Whistles, and some other "breath" Instruments (1969); *Hymnus 2*, multimedia show (Munich, 1972); *Come S. Francesco II*, chamber spectacle for Speaker, Dancer, Chamber Orch., and Multivision (1979).

Schönberg, Arnold (Franz Walter). See **Schoenberg (Schonberg), Arnold (Franz Walter).**

Schonberg, Harold C(harles), eminent American music critic; b. N.Y., Nov. 29, 1915. He studied at Brooklyn College (B.A., 1937) and at N.Y. Univ. (M.A., 1938). He served in the army (1942–46); then was on the staff of the *N.Y. Sun* (1946–50); he was appointed to the music staff of the *N.Y. Times* in 1950; was senior music critic from 1960 until 1980. In 1971 he was the first music critic to be honored with the Pulitzer Prize in criticism. In his concert reviews and feature articles, he reveals a profound knowledge of music and displays a fine journalistic flair without assuming a posture of snobbish aloofness or descending to colloquial vulgarity. His intellectual horizon is exceptionally wide; he is well-versed in art, and can draw and paint; he is a chess aficionado and covered knowledgeably the Spassky-Fischer match in Reykjavík in 1972 for the *N.Y. Times.* He publ. in N.Y.: *Chamber and Solo Instrument Music* (1955); *The Collector's Chopin and Schumann* (1959); *The Great Pianists* (1963; 2nd ed., rev., 1987); *The Great Conductors* (1967); *Lives of the Great Composers* (1970; 2nd ed., 1981); *Facing the Music* (1981); *The Glorious Ones: Classical Music's Legendary Performers* (1985); *Horowitz: His Life and Music* (1992).

Schönberg, Stig Gustav, Swedish organist and composer; b. Västra Husby, May 13, 1933. He studied at the Stockholm Musikhögskolan (1953–60), where he graduated with diplomas as a music teacher, organist, and choirmaster; his composition mentors were Larsson and Blomdahl; also studied theory with Erland von Koch and Valdemar Söderholm; also organ with Flors Peeters in Belgium. He was active as a church organist and toured as a recitalist.

WORKS: BALLET: *Madeleine och Conrad* (1967; rev. 1972). **ORCH.:** *Intermezzo* (1958); *Introduktion och Allegro* for Strings (1958–59); Concerto for Organ and Strings (1962); *Sinfonia aperta* (1965); 3 concertinos for Strings (1966); *Fantasia* for Strings (1967); *Concitato* (1968); *Impromptu visionario* (1972); Concerto for 2 Flutes and Strings (1976); Sym. No. 2 (1977); Concerto for Organ and Orch. (1982); Concerto for Organ and Brass Orch. (1986–87); Bassoon Concerto (1992). **CHAMBER:** 7 string quartets (1961–84); *Madrigaler* for 2 Trumpets and 2 Trombones (1962); *Intrada* for 2 Trumpets, 2 Trombones, and Organ (1963); Sonata for Flute and Organ (1963); Trio for Flute, Violin, and Cello (1967); 2 violin sonatas (1964, 1967); *Vad Ijus over griften*, intrada for Organ and Brass Ensemble (1971); *Liten fantasi* for 2 Trumpets (1973); Flute Sonata (1974); *Pastoral* for Horn and Organ (1979); *Air* for Viola and Organ (1982); Sonata for Cello and Organ (1984); *Poème memorial* for Viola, and Piano or Organ or Harpsichord (1985); *Sonata all ricercata* for Violin and Organ (1989); piano pieces and organ music. **VOCAL:** Various works for Soloists, Chorus, and Instrument(s), including *Regina coeli* (1973), *Cantata gloriae* (1975), *Missa coralis* (1983), *Missa da pacem* (1985), and *Missa brevis* (1994); choruses; songs.

Schöne, Lotte (real name, **Charlotte Bodenstein**), admired Austrian-born French soprano; b. Vienna, Dec. 15, 1891; d.

Paris, Dec. 22, 1977. She studied in Vienna. She made her debut at the Vienna Volksoper in 1912, and continued to appear there until 1917; then sang at the Vienna Court (later State) Opera (1917–26); also at the Berlin Städtische Oper (1926–33); made many appearances at the Salzburg Festivals (1922–35). After leaving Germany in 1933, she went to Paris, became a naturalized French citizen, and made guest appearances at the Opéra and the Opéra-Comique; she was compelled to go into hiding during the Nazi occupation, but resumed her career after the liberation, and sang in Berlin in 1948; she retired in 1953. Among her many notable roles were Cherubino, Papagena, Susanna, Despina, Pamina, Zerlina, Sophie, Mimi, Liù, and Mélisande.

Schöne, Wolfgang, German baritone; b. Bad Gandersheim, Feb. 9, 1940. He received his vocal training at the Hochschules für Musik in Hannover and Hamburg (diploma, 1969), his principal teacher being Naan Pöld. He took prizes in competitions in Berlin, Bordeaux, 's-Hertogenbosch, and Rio de Janeiro, and was active as a concert artist. In 1970 he launched his operatic career with engagements at the Württemberg State Opera in Stuttgart, the Hamburg State Opera, and the Vienna State Opera. In 1973 he became a member of the Württemberg State Opera, where he was honored as a Kammersänger in 1978; also was a guest artist in Geneva, Salzburg, Cologne, Florence, and Paris. As a concert singer, he garnered extensive engagements in Europe and the Americas, appearing with many notable orchs. and as a recitalist. Among his operatic roles are Don Giovanni, Guglielmo, Count Almaviva, Eugene Onegin, Wolfram, Amfortas, Golaud, Mamdryka, and Tom in Henze's *The English Cat,* which role he created at the Schwetzingen Festival in 1981.

Schönherr, Max, Austrian conductor, musicologist, and composer; b. Marburg an der Drau, Nov. 23, 1903; d. Mödling, near Vienna, Dec. 13, 1984. He studied with Hermann Frisch in Marburg and Roderich von Mojsisovics at the Graz Cons.; later studied musicology at the Univ. of Vienna (Ph.D., 1970). After conducting at the Graz Landestheater (1924–28), he settled in Vienna as a conductor with the Theater an der Wien and Stadttheater (1929–33), the Volksoper (1933–38), and the Austrian Radio (1931–68), where he won distinction for his idiomatic readings of light Viennese scores. He composed much light music in a stylish manner, and also made effective arrangements of scores by the Viennese Strausses et al. He publ. *Carl Michael Ziehrer: Sein Werk, sein Leben, seine Zeit* (Vienna, 1974), *Lanner, Strauss, Ziehrer: Synoptic Handbook of the Dances and Marches* (Vienna, 1982), and with E. Brixel, *Karl Komzák: Vater, Sohn, Enkel: Ein Beitrag zur Rezeptionsgeschichte der Österreichischen Popularmusik* (Vienna, 1989). A Lamb ed. the vol. *Unterhaltungsmusik aus Österreich: Max Schönherr in seinen Erinnerungen und Schriften (Light Music from Austria: Reminiscences and Writings of Max Schönherr)* (in Ger. and Eng., N.Y., 1992).

Schöning, Klaus, German radio producer and writer on music; b. Rastenburg, Feb. 24, 1936. After univ. studies in Munich, Göttingen, and Berlin, he worked in the theater; in 1961 he began a lengthy association with the Westdeutscher Rundfunk (WDR) of Cologne, where he is producer, director, and chief ed. of the WDR Studio for Acoustic Art, an international workshop for audio art and research that he established. He commissioned and produced over 1,000 radio broadcasts for the WDR and other international radio stations; was a pioneer in the reorientation of the German Horspiel in the late 1960s, his main programs being "New Hörspiel," "Composers as Hörspielmakers," and "Ars Acustica." Among the composers from whom he has commissioned works are John Cage, Alvin Curran, Pauline Oliveros, Alison Knowles, Charles Amirkhanian, Jackson Mac Low, and Joan La Barbara. With support from the WDR and the Goethe Inst., he also developed a transcontinental link for acoustic art, Acustica International; in 1985 he was artistic director of the 1st Acustica International Festival (Cologne), and, in 1990, of the Sound Art Festival and 2nd Acustica International Festival (N.Y. and Montreal). He was the producer of the first Satellite Soundsculptures with *Earbridge Köln—San Francisco* (1987) and *Soundbridge Köln—Kyoto* (1993) by Bill Fontana. In 1993 he was curator of sound installation with radio compositions by John Cage at the Venice Biennale and in 1993–94 at the Museum of Contemporary Art in San Francisco and the Guggenheim Museum in N.Y. He has won numerous awards for his productions, including the Prix Italia, Prix Futura, Karl-Sczuka-Preis, Hörspielpreis der Kriegsblinden, and Premio Ondas; in 1983 he received the Berliner Kunstpreis for Film/Radio/TV and in 1993 the Medienkunstpreis of the Zentrum für Kunst- und Medientechnologie in Karlsruhe. He also lectured extensively in Germany, France, and the U.S.; was curator of the exhibition "American Audio Art on WDR" at the Whitney Museum of Art in N.Y. (1990). Among his numerous publications are *John Cage: Roaratorio: Ein irischer Circus über Finnegans Wake* (1982), *Geschichte und Typologie des Hörspiels* (7 vols., 1988–90), and *1. Acustica International: Komponisten als Hörspielmacher* (1990); he also produced the CD-anthology *Ars Acustica* (1992).

Schønwandt, Michael, Danish conductor; b. Copenhagen, Sept. 10, 1953. After training in musicology at the Univ. of Copenhagen (B.Mus., 1975), he studied conducting and composition at the Royal Academy of Music in London (1975–77). In 1977 he made his conducting debut in Copenhagen, and subsequently appeared as a guest conductor with various European orchs. After conducting opera at the Royal Danish Theater in 1979, he appeared as a guest conductor at London's Covent Garden, the Paris Opéra, and the Stuttgart Opera. In 1981 he became music director of the Collegium Musicum in Copenhagen. He was also principal guest conductor of the Théâtre Royal de la Monnaie in Brussels (1984–87), the Nice Opera (1987–91), and the Danish Radio Sym. Orch. in Copenhagen (from 1989). From 1990 he was permanent conductor at the Vienna State Opera and, from 1992, music director of the Berlin Sym. Orch.

Schönzeler, Hans-Hubert, German conductor and musicologist; b. Leipzig, June 22, 1925. He went to Australia as a youth, and studied conducting with Goossens at the New South Wales Conservatorium of Music in Sydney; later traveled in Europe, where he received further instruction in conducting with Kubelik, with Zecchi in Hilversum, and with Kempen in Siena. He eventually made his home in London, where he led the 20th-Century Ensemble (1957–62). In 1967 he was appointed deputy chief conductor of the West Australian Sym. Orch. in Perth, while continuing his appearances as a guest conductor in Europe. He publ. *Bruckner* (London and N.Y., 1970; rev. ed., 1978), *Dvořák* (London, 1984), *Furtwängler* (London, 1987), and *Zu Bruckners IX. Symphonie: die Krakauer Skizzen/Bruckner's 9th Symphony: the Cracow Sketches* (Vienna, 1987).

Schoop, Paul, Swiss-American composer; b. Zürich, July 31, 1909; d. Los Angeles, Jan. 1, 1976. He studied piano in Paris with Cortot and Casadesus, and in Berlin with Schnabel; also composition with Dukas in Paris, and with Hindemith and Schoenberg in the U.S. He settled in Los Angeles, and wrote music for films; also composed a comic opera, *The Enchanted Trumpet*; a symphonic poem, *Fata Morgana*; ballet scores for productions of his sister, Trudi Schoop, a modern dancer.

Schorr, Friedrich, renowned Hungarian-American bass-baritone; b. Nagyvarád, Sept. 2, 1888; d. Farmington, Conn., Aug. 14, 1953. He studied law at the Univ. of Vienna, and also took private lessons in singing. He appeared with the Chicago Grand Opera (1912); then was a member of the opera companies in Graz (1912–16), Prague (1916–18), Cologne (1918–23), and of the Berlin State Opera (1923–31); also sang Wotan at Bayreuth (1925–31), and appeared at London's Covent Garden (1925–33). He made his Metropolitan Opera debut in N.Y. as Wolfram on Feb. 14, 1924, and continued as a member until his farewell performance as the Wanderer in *Siegfried* on March 2,

1943. Schorr is generally recognized as the foremost Wagnerian bass-baritone of his era; he also sang roles in operas by Beethoven, Strauss, Verdi, and Puccini, and appeared in the U.S. premieres of Krenek's *Jonny Spielt Auf* (Daniello; 1929) and Weinberger's *Schwanda* (title role; 1931) at the Metropolitan Opera.

Schouwman, Hans, Dutch pianist, singer, and composer; b. Gorinchem, Aug. 8, 1902; d. The Hague, April 8, 1967. After training from Peter van Anrooy, he was active as a recitalist accompanying himself at the piano. He also devoted much time to composition.

WORKS: ORCH.: *5 Sketches* for Clarinet and Small Orch. (1942); Suite for Amateur Orch. (1958); *De Prinses op de erwt* (1965). **CHAMBER:** 2 oboe sonatinas (1940, 1944); *Aubade en Barcarolle* for Clarinet and Piano (1944); Trio for Clarinet, Bassoon, and Piano (1944); *Romance en Humoreske* for Bassoon and Piano (1944); *4 Pieces* for Flute and Piano (1944); *2 Legends* for Horn and Piano (1944); *Nederlandse suite* for Wind Quintet (1953); *3 Preludes* for Piano, Left-hand (1959). **VOCAL:** *3 danswijzen* (3 Dance Tunes) for Voice, 2 Flutes, Strings, and Percussion (1938); *Friesland,* 4 songs for Voice and Orch. (1945); *Memento mori* for Alto, Chorus, and Small Orch. (1947); *Notturno* for Mezzo-soprano, Cello, and Piano (1949); *Om de kribbe* for Soprano, Contralto, Women's Chorus, and Piano (1952); vocal duets; solo songs; arrangements.

Schrade, Leo, eminent German musicologist; b. Allenstein, Dec. 13, 1903; d. Spéracédès, Alpes-Maritimes, Sept. 21, 1964. He studied with Hermann Halbig at the Univ. of Heidelberg (1923–27), with Sandberger at the Univ. of Munich, and with Kroyer at the Univ. of Leipzig (Ph.D., 1927, with the diss. *Die ältesten Denkmäler der Orgelmusik als Beitrag zu einer Geschichte der Toccata*; publ. in Münster, 1928); completed his Habilitation in 1929 at the Univ. of Königsberg. He taught at the Univs. of Königsberg (1928–32) and Bonn (from 1932). In 1937 he emigrated to the U.S.; was on the faculty of Yale Univ. (1938–58), where he taught music history; in 1958 he was appointed to the music faculty of the Univ. of Basel. He was also the Charles Eliot Norton Lecturer at Harvard Univ. in 1962–63. He was founder-ed. of the Yale Studies in the History of Music and the Yale Collegium Musicum series (1947–58); was co-ed. of the *Journal of Renaissance and Baroque Music* (1946–47), *Annales musicologiques* (1953–64), and the *Archiv für Musikwissenschaft* (1958–64); served as an ed. of the series Polyphonic Music in the Fourteenth Century (vols. 1–3, 1956; vol. 4, 1958).

WRITINGS: *Beethoven in France: The Growth of an Idea* (New Haven, 1942); *Monteverdi: Creator of Modern Music* (N.Y., 1950; 2nd ed., 1964); *Bach: The Conflict Between the Sacred and the Secular* (N.Y., 1954); *W.A. Mozart* (Bern and Munich, 1964); *Tragedy in the Art of Music* (Cambridge, Mass., 1964).

BIBL.: *Musik und Geschichte: L. S. zum sechzigsten Geburtstag* (Cologne, 1963; Eng. tr., 1965, as *Music and History: L. S. on the Occasion of His 60th Birthday*); *L. S. in memoriam* (Bern and Munich, 1966); E. Lichtenhahn, ed., *L. S.: De scientia musicae studia atque orationes* (Bern and Stuttgart, 1967); W. Arlt et al., eds., *Gattungen der Musik in Einzeldarstellungen: Gedenkschrift für L. S.* (Bern and Munich, 1973).

Schrader, Barry, American composer; b. Johnstown, Pa., June 26, 1945. He received degrees at the Univ. of Pittsburgh in English literature (B.A., 1967) and in musicology (M.A., 1970); also served as an organist at Heinz Chapel. In 1969–70 he studied electroacoustic techniques with Subotnick. In 1970 he moved to Los Angeles and attended the Calif. Inst. of the Arts (M.F.A. in composition, 1971); later joined its faculty. From 1975 to 1978 he also taught at Calif. State Univ. at Los Angeles. He organized a series of electroacoustic music programs under the name "Currents," held in Los Angeles from 1973 to 1979; also participated in many electronic music festivals in other countries. In 1984 he became the first president of the Soc. for Electro-Acoustic Music in the U.S. He publ. *Introduction to Electro-Acoustical Music* (Englewood Cliffs, N.J., 1982). Most of his music is for electronic sound; in his *Bestiary* (1972–74), Schrader explored the potentialities of synthesizing new timbres; in his *Trinity* (1976), he transmuted given timbres to more complex sonorities; in his *Lost Atlantis,* he essayed a programmatic use of electronic sound. He also experimented in combining live music with electronic resources, as in his work *Moon-Whales and other Moon Songs* (1982–83).

WORKS: *Signature for Tempo* for Soprano and Piano (1966); *Serenade* for Tape (1969); *Incantation* for Tape (1970); *Sky Ballet* for Sound Environment (1970); *Elysium* for Harp, Dancers, Tape, and Projections (1971); *Bestiary* for Tape (1972–74); *Trinity* for Tape (1976); *Lost Atlantis* for Tape (1977); *Moon-whales and Other Moon Songs* for Soprano and Tape (1982–83); *Electronic Music Box I* for Sound Installation (1983), *II* (1983), and *III* (1984); *TWO: Square Flowers Red: SONGS* (1990); also many film scores, including *Death of the Red Planet* (1973), *Heavy Light* (1973), *Exploratorium* (1975), *Mobiles* (1978), *Along the Way* (1980), and *Galaxy of Terror* (1981).

Schramm, Hermann, German tenor; b. Berlin, Feb. 7, 1871; d. Frankfurt am Main, Dec. 14, 1951. He made his operatic debut in Breslau in 1895 as Gomez in Kreutzer's *Die Nachtlager von Granada.* From 1896 to 1900 he sang at the Cologne Opera. In 1899 he appeared at London's Covent Garden and at the Bayreuth Festival (debut as David). From 1900 to 1933 he was a member of the Frankfurt am Main Opera, where he created the role of the chancellor in Schreker's *Der Schatsgräber* (1920). Schramm was hailed as the finest David and Mime of his era.

Schramm, Margit, German soprano; b. Dortmund, July 21, 1935; d. Munich, May 12, 1996. She was educated at the Dortmund Cons., and made her debut at Saarbrücken in 1956. She sang in Koblenz (1957–58), in Munich at the Gärtnerplatz Theater (1959–64), in Berlin at the Theater des Westens (1965–66), and in the municipal theaters in Dortmund (1967). In 1968 she joined the ensemble of the State Theater in Wiesbaden. Her repertoire of German and Austrian operettas was vast and impressive.

Schreiber, Frederick (actually, **Friedrich**), Austrian-American organist, choirmaster, and composer; b. Vienna, Jan. 13, 1895; d. N.Y., Jan. 15, 1985. He studied piano, cello, and composition in Vienna. After teaching at the Cons. there (1927–38), he emigrated to N.Y. and was organist and choirmaster of the Reformed Protestant Church (1939–58). Among his orch. works are 7 syms. (1927–57); *The Beatitudes,* symphonic trilogy for Orch. and Chorus (1950); *Christmas Suite* (1967); *Images* (1971); *Contrasts* (1972); 2 piano concertos; Cello Concerto; 2 violin concertos; *Variations on a German Folksong* (1974); numerous choral pieces; chamber music, including 2 string quintets, 7 string quartets, Piano Quartet, and 3 piano trios; much organ music.

Schreier, Peter (Max), esteemed German tenor and conductor; b. Meissen, July 29, 1935. He sang in the Dresdner Kreuzchor. He gained a taste for the theater when he appeared as one of the 3 boys in *Die Zauberflöte* at Dresden's Semper Opera House (1944). He received private vocal lessons from Polster in Leipzig (1954–56), and then with Winkler in Dresden; also took courses at the Hochschule für Musik there (1956–59); concurrently worked at the studio of the Dresden State Opera, where he appeared as Paolino in *Il matrimonio segreto* (1957); made his official debut there as the 1st Prisoner in *Fidelio* (1959), and went on to become a regular member of the company in 1961. In 1963 he joined the Berlin State Opera, and became one of its principal artists; he also made guest appearances with opera houses throughout Eastern Europe and the Soviet Union; likewise sang in London (debut as Ferrando with the visiting Hamburg State Opera, 1966) and at the Salzburg Festivals (from 1967), the Vienna State Opera (from 1967), the Metropolitan Opera in N.Y. (debut as Tamino, Dec. 25, 1967),

La Scala in Milan (1969), and the Teatro Colón in Buenos Aires (1969). His roles in Mozart's operas brought him critical acclaim; he was also a distinguished oratorio and lieder artist, excelling in a repertoire that ranged from Bach to Orff. In 1970 he launched a second, equally successful career as a conductor. In 1964 he was honored with the title of Kammersänger. He publ. the book *Aus meiner Sicht: Gedanken und Erinnerungen* (ed. by M. Meier; Vienna, 1983).

BIBL.: G. Schmiedel, *P. S.: Für Sie portratiert* (Leipzig, 1976); W.-E. von Lewinski, *P. S.: Interviews, Tatsachen, Meinungen* (Munich, 1992).

Schreker, Franz, eminent Austrian conductor, pedagogue, and composer; b. Monaco (of Austrian parents), March 23, 1878; d. Berlin, March 21, 1934. His father, the court photographer, died when he was 10; the family went to Vienna, where he studied with Arnold Rosé; also received instruction in composition from Robert Fuchs at the Cons. (1892–1900). He first gained notice as a composer with his pantomime *Der Geburtstag der Infantin* (Vienna, Aug. 1908); that same year he founded the Phil. Chorus, serving as its conductor until 1920. He won great distinction with his opera *Der ferne Klang* (Frankfurt am Main, Aug. 18, 1912); outstanding among his later operas were *Die Gezeichneten* (Frankfurt am Main, April 25, 1918) and *Der Schatzgräber* (Frankfurt am Main, Jan. 21, 1920). After teaching composition at the Vienna Academy of Music (1912–20), he settled in Berlin as director of the Hochschule für Musik. Being of Jewish birth, he became a target of the rising Nazi movement; in 1931 he withdrew from performance his opera *Christophorus* in the face of Nazi threats; his last opera, *Der Schmied von Gent,* was premiered in Berlin on Oct. 29, 1932, in spite of Nazi demonstrations. Schreker was pressured into resigning his position at the Hochschule für Musik in 1932, but that same year he was given charge of a master class in composition at the Prussian Academy of Arts; he lost this position when the Nazis came to power in 1933. Shortly afterward, he suffered a major heart attack, and spent the remaining months of his life in poor health and reduced circumstances. As a composer, Schreker led the neo-Romantic movement in the direction of Expressionism, emphasizing psychological conflicts in his operas; in his harmonies, he expanded the basically Wagnerian sonorities to include many devices associated with Impressionism. He exercised considerable influence on the German and Viennese schools of his time, but with the change of direction in modern music toward economy of means and away from mystical and psychological trends, Schreker's music suffered a decline after his death.

WORKS: DRAMATIC: OPERAS (all but the 1st to his own librettos): *Flammen* (c.1900; concert perf., Vienna, April 24, 1902); *Der ferne Klang* (1901–10; Frankfurt am Main, Aug. 18, 1912); *Das Spielwerk und die Prinzessin* (1909–12; Frankfurt am Main and Vienna, March 15, 1913; rev. as *Das Spielwerk,* 1916; Munich, Oct. 30, 1920); *Die Gezeichneten* (1913–15; Frankfurt am Main, April 25, 1918); *Der Schatzgräber* (1915–18; Frankfurt am Main, Jan. 21, 1920); *Irrelohe* (1919–23; Cologne, March 27, 1924); *Christophorus, oder Die Vision einer Oper* (1924–27; Freiburg im Breisgau, Oct. 1, 1978); *Der singende Teufel* (1924–28; Berlin, Dec. 10, 1928); *Der Schmied von Gent* (1929–32; Berlin, Oct. 29, 1932). **PANTOMIME:** *Der Geburtstag der Infantin* for Strings (Vienna, Aug. 1908; rev. as *Spanisches Fest* for Orch., 1923). **DANCE ALLEGORY:** *Der Wind* for Clarinet and Piano Quartet (1908). **BALLET:** *Rokoko* (1908; rev. as *Ein Tanzspiel,* 1920). **ORCH.:** *Love Song* for Strings and Harp (1895; not extant); *Intermezzo* for Strings (1900; included in the *Romantische Suite,* 1902); *Romantische Suite* (1902; includes the *Intermezzo* for Strings, 1900); *Ekkehard,* overture (1902); *Phantastische Ouverture* (1902); *Festwalzer und Walzerintermezzo* (1908); *Vorspiel zu einem Drama* (1913; used as a prelude to his opera *Die Gezeichneten*); *Kammersymphonie* for 23 Solo Instruments (1916; Vienna, March 12, 1917); *Kleine Suite* for Chamber Orch. (1928; Breslau, Jan. 17, 1929); *4 Little Pieces* (1930); *Vorspiel zu einer grossen Oper* (1933; Baden-Baden, March 11, 1958; symphonic fragments from an unfinished opera, *Memnon*). **CHAMBER:** Violin Sonata (1897); piano pieces. **VOCAL:** *Der Holdstein* for Soprano, Bass, Chorus, and Orch. (c.1898); *Psalm CXVI* for Women's Chorus, Orch., and Organ (1900); *Schwanengesang* for Chorus and Orch. (1902); *Fünf Gesänge* for Alto or Bass and Orch. (c.1921; based on the song cycle, 1909); *Vom ewigen Leben* for Voice and Orch. (1927; based on *Zwei lyrische Gesänge,* 1924); some unaccompanied choral pieces; songs.

BIBL.: P. Bekker, *F. S.: Studie zur Kritik der modernen Oper* (Berlin, 1919; 2nd ed., 1983); special issue of *Musikblätter des Anbruch,* ii/1–2 (1920); R. Hoffmann, *F. S.* (Leipzig and Vienna, 1921); J. Kapp, *F. S.: Der Mann und sein Werk* (Munich, 1921); F. Bayerl, *F. S.s Opernwerk* (Erlangen, 1928); *S.-Heft* (Berlin, 1959); G. Neuwirth, *F. S.* (Vienna, 1959); H. Bures-Schreker, *El caso S.* (Buenos Aires, 1969; rev. Ger. tr. with H. Stuckenschmidt and W. Oehlmann as *F. S.,* Vienna, 1970); G. Neuwirth, *Die Harmonik in der Oper "Der ferne Klang" von F. S.* (Regensburg, 1972); F. Heller, ed., *Arnold Schönberg—F. S.: Briefwechsel* (Tutzing, 1974); O. Kolleritsch, ed., *F. S. am Beginn der neuen Musik, Studien zur Wertungsforschung,* XI (Graz, 1978); R. Ermen, ed., *F. S. (1878–1934) zum 50. Todestag* (Aachen, 1984); M. Brzoska, *F. S.s Oper "Der Schatzgräber"* (Stuttgart, 1988); C. Hailey, *F. S.: His Life, Times, and Music* (Cambridge, 1993).

Schröder, Hanning, German composer; b. Rostock, July 4, 1896; d. Berlin, Oct. 16, 1987. He was a medical student; concurrently he took violin lessons with Havemann in Berlin and composition with Weismann in Freiburg im Breisgau; then took a course in musicology with W. Gurlitt. In 1929 he married the musicologist Cornelia Auerbach (b. Breslau, Aug. 24, 1900); they remained in Germany under the Nazi regime, but were barred from professional work for their act of human charity in giving shelter to a Jewish couple in their Berlin apartment. After the fall of the Third Reich, they resumed their careers.

WORKS: *Hänsel und Gretel,* children's Singspiel (Berlin, Dec. 23, 1952); *Musik* for Recorder (1954), and similar solo works for Viola, Cello, Violin, and Bassoon; *Divertimento* for 5 Wind Instruments (1957); *Divertimento* for Viola and Cello (1963); *Metronome 80* for Violin (1969); Nonet for Wind Quintet, Violin, Viola, Cello, and Double Bass (1970); *Varianten* for Flute and Orch. (1971).

Schröder, Jaap, distinguished Dutch violinist and pedagogue; b. Amsterdam, Dec. 31, 1925. He studied violin at the Amsterdam Cons. and in Paris; also attended classes in musicology at the Sorbonne. He then served as concertmaster of the Hilversum Radio Chamber Orch., and was a member of the Netherlands String Quartet. In 1975 he founded the Quartetto Esterhazy, which gave performances of music from the Classical era on period instruments; it was dissolved in 1981. He subsequently served as music director and concertmaster of the Academy of Ancient Music in London. In 1982 he was appointed visiting music director of the Smithsonian Chamber Players in Washington, D.C.

Schrøder, Jens, Danish conductor; b. Bielsko, Poland, Nov. 6, 1909; d. Ålborg, Aug. 10, 1991. He studied at the Prague Academy of Music. After conducting in various Danish cities, he was chief conductor of the Municipal Theater (1942–75) and the Sym. Orch. (1942–80) in Ålborg; he also was a guest conductor with the Danish Radio Sym. Orch. and the Royal Danish Orch. in Copenhagen. In 1980 he was made a Knight of the Dannebrog Order (1st Grade) for his services to Danish music.

Schröder-Feinen, Ursula, German soprano; b. Gelsenkirchen, July 21, 1936. She studied voice with Maria Helm in Gelsenkirchen, and took courses at the Essen Folkwangschule. She sang in the chorus of the Gelsenkirchen Opera (1958), where she made her operatic debut as Aida in 1961, and remained on its roster until 1968; then sang with the Deutsche Opera am Rhein in Düsseldorf (1968–72). On Dec. 4, 1970, she made her Metropolitan Opera debut in N.Y. as Chrysothemis in *Elektra*; also sang at Bayreuth, Salzburg, Milan, and Berlin. She retired in 1979. Schröder-Feinen was a versatile singer whose repertoire included major dramatic roles in German and Italian opera.

Schryock, Buren, American composer and conductor; b. Sheldon, Iowa, Dec. 13, 1881; d. San Diego, Jan. 20, 1974. At the age of 7, he moved to West Salem, Oreg., where he studied music and played organ in a church. He occupied various teaching posts in Michigan, Texas, Nebraska, and California; was conductor of the San Diego Sym. Orch. (1913–20) and the San Diego Opera (1920–36).

WORKS: OPERAS: *Flavia* (1930–46); *Mary and John* (1948); *Nancy and Arthur* (1951); *Malena and Nordico* (1954); *Tanshu and Sanchi* (1955). **OTHER:** Sym.; chamber music; piano pieces.

Schub, André-Michel, French-born American pianist; b. Paris, Dec. 26, 1952. He was taken to N.Y. as an infant and was taught piano by his mother; then became a pupil of Jascha Zayde. After attending Princeton Univ. (1968–69), he studied with Rudolf Serkin at the Curtis Inst. of Music in Philadelphia (1970–73). In 1974 he won 1st prize in the Naumburg competition and in 1977 the Avery Fisher Prize; after winning 1st prize in the Van Cliburn competition in 1981, he pursued an international career. His brilliant virtuoso technique is matched by a sensitive temperament; he shines in the Classic and Romantic repertoire.

Schubel, Max, American composer; b. N.Y., April 11, 1932. He was educated at N.Y. Univ. (graduated, 1953); his composition teachers were Charles Haubiel in N.Y. and Frank Martin. In 1960 he formed OPUS ONE, an independent recording company dedicated to producing non-commercial concert and electronic music; in 1982 its headquarters was moved to a small cabin he built on a remote mountain in the Catskills. From 1954 Schubel spent much of his time on his small island in Moosehead Lake, Maine, where he became interested in environmental protection and self-sufficient living; developed skills in recycling, composting, raising chickens, and developing non-electrical sources of power and water. As a composer, he received 2 NEA awards (1974, 1982) and a Ford Foundation Recording Grant (1971); also was in residence at the MacDowell Colony, the Wurlitzer Foundation, Ossabaw Island, and Wolf Trap.

WORKS: ORCH.: *Fracture* (1969); *Divertimento* for Piano, Trumpet, and Chamber Orch. (1980; rev. 1987); *Guale* (1984); *Punch and Judie* for Chamber Orch. (1980); *Scherzo* (1987); *SuperScherzo* for Chamber Orch. (1988–89). **CHAMBER:** *Insected Surfaces*, concerto for Clarinet, Cello, Bass, Harpsichord, and Piano (1965); *Exotica* for Cello and Harpsichord (1967); 2 string quartets (1968, 1980); *Zing and ZipZap* for Chamber Ensemble (1986); *The Spoors of Time* for Viola and Piano (1986); Septet (1988); *Dragondust* for Clarinet and Piano (1988); String Quintet (1989); Trio for Violin, Cello, and Piano (1989). **PIANO:** *Everybody's Favourite Rag* (1979); *Miraplex* (1979); *B Natural* for Prepared Piano (1980); *Stable Turner* (1981); *Klish Klash* for Prepared Piano (1982); *Dragonseed* (1986).

Schubert, Richard, German tenor; b. Dessau, Dec. 15, 1885; d. Oberstaufen, Oct. 12, 1959. He studied with Rudolf von Milde. In 1909 he made his operatic debut as a baritone in Strasbourg. Following further training from Milde and Hans Nietan in Dresden, he turned to tenor roles and sang in Nuremberg (1911–13) and Wiesbaden (1913–17). From 1917 to 1935 he was a member of the Hamburg Opera, where he became well known for his Wagnerian roles. He also created the role of Paul in Korngold's *Die tote Stadt* there in 1920. As a guest artist, he sang at the Vienna State Opera (1920–29) and in Chicago (1921–22).

Schüchter, Wilhelm, German conductor; b. Bonn, Dec. 15, 1911; d. Dortmund, May 27, 1974. He studied conducting with Abendroth and composition with Jarnach at the Cologne Hochschule für Musik. He then conducted opera at Würzburg (1937–40), and served as assistant to Karajan in Aachen (1940–42); also conducted at the Berlin Städtische Oper (1942–43). In 1947 he was appointed to the post of 1st conductor of the North German Radio Sym. Orch. in Hamburg. After serving as principal guest conductor of the NHK Sym. Orch. in Tokyo (1958–61), he settled in Dortmund as Generalmusikdirektor in 1962; was named artistic director of its Städtische Oper in 1965, and conducted the inaugural production at its new opera house in 1966. He acquired a fine reputation as a Wagnerian interpreter.

Schudel, Thomas (Michael), American-born Canadian composer and teacher; b. Defiance, Ohio, Sept. 8, 1937. He studied composition with Marshal Barnes, and received training in bassoon at Ohio State Univ. (B.Sc., 1959; M.A., 1961); then studied composition with Bassett and Finney at the Univ. of Mich. (D.M.A., 1971). In 1964 he joined the faculty of the Univ. of Regina in Saskatchewan; also was principal bassoonist in the Regina Sym. Orch. (1964–67; 1968–70); became a naturalized Canadian citizen in 1974. In 1972 his 1st Sym. won 1st prize in the City of Trieste International Competition for symphonic composition.

WORKS: CHILDREN'S OPERETTA: *The Enchanted Cat* (1992). **ORCH.:** 2 syms.: No. 1 (1971; Trieste, Oct. 20, 1972) and No. 2 (1983); *Variations* (1977); *Winterpiece* for Chamber Orch. and Dancers (1979); *Elegy and Exaltation* for Concert Band (1984); Concerto for Piccolo, String Orch. or String Quintet, and Percussion (1988); Concerto for Alto Trombone and Chamber Orch. (1990); *A Tangled Web* for Chamber Orch. (1993); *Sinfonia Concertante* for Saxophone Quartet and Wind Ensemble (1994). **CHAMBER:** *Set No. 2* for Wind and Brass Quintets (1963); Violin Sonata (1966); *String Quartet 1967* (1967); *Chanson and Minuet* for Oboe and Piano (1977); Trio for 3 Percussionists (1977); *Triptych* for Chamber Wind Ensemble (1978); *Richter 7.8* for 12 Tubas or Low Brass (1979); *4 by 2* for Horn and Marimba (1980); *Etchings* for Horn and Piano (1985); *Incantations* for Double Bass and Percussion (1986); *Intermezzo* for Flute and Clarinet (1987); *Dialogues* for Trombone and Percussion (1987); *Bagatelle* for 2 Flutes (1987); *Pentagram* for Saxophone Quartet and Percussionist (1987); *2 Images* for Alto Saxophone and Piano (1988); *5 Pastels* for Oboe and Percussionist (1990); *Prairie Winds* for Flute and Piano (1991); *Trigon* for 2 Saxophones and Percussionist (1992); solo pieces; piano works. **VOCAL: CHORAL:** *Psalm 23* (1968); *Acquainted with the Night* (1980); *Fire and Ice* (1980); *Desert Places* (1980); *A Dream within a Dream* (1985); *Ale* (1985); *Eldorado* (1985); *Pick Up the Earth* (1994); *Gold and Rose* (1994); *Another Love Poem* (1994). **OTHER VOCAL:** *Queer Cornered Cap* for Mezzo-soprano, Flute, and Marimba (1982); *A.C.T.S.* for Narrator, Flute, Oboe, Clarinet, Double Bass, and Percussion (1986); *Edging Out* for Soprano, Flute, Oboe, and Vibraphone (1987); *An Emily Dickinson Folio* for Soprano, Flute, Oboe, Clarinet, Viola, Vibraphone, and Piano (1991); songs.

Schuh, Willi, eminent Swiss music critic and musicologist; b. Basel, Nov. 12, 1900; d. Zürich, Oct. 4, 1986. He studied music in Aarau with Kutschera and Wehrli, in Bern with Papst, and in Munich with Courvoisier and Beer-Walbrunn. He took courses in art history and musicology in Munich with Sandberger and in Bern with Kurth; in 1927 he received his Ph.D. from the Univ. of Bern with the diss. *Formprobleme bei Heinrich Schütz* (publ. in Leipzig, 1928). In 1928 he was engaged as music critic of the *Neue Zurcher Zeitung*; was its music ed. from 1944 until 1965; was also ed.-in-chief of the *Schweizerische Musikzeitung* (1941–68). He also taught music history and harmony in Winterthur, in St. Gall, and at the Zürich Cons. He was made an honorary member of the Schweizerischer Tonkünstlerverein in 1969 and of the Schweizerische Musikforschende Gesellschaft in 1971. He was an ed. of the *Schweizer Musikerlexikon* (Zürich, 1964). Several of his writings were republished in *Kritiken und Essays* (4 vols.: vol. 1, *Über Opern von Richard Strauss*, Zürich, 1947; vol. 2, *Zeitgenössische Musik*, Zürich, 1947; vol. 3, *Schweizer Musik der Gegenwart*, Zürich, 1948; vol.

4, *Von neuer Musik*, Zürich, 1955); also *Umgang mit Musik: Über Komponisten, Libretti und Bilder* (Zürich, 1970; 2nd ed., 1971). He was the ed. of *Die Briefe Richard Wagners an Judith Gautier* (Zürich, 1936); *Ferruccio Busoni: Briefe an seine Frau* (Zürich, 1936); *Hugo von Hofmannsthal's Beethoven* (Vienna, 1937; 2nd ed., 1949); with H. Ehinger and E. Refardt, *Schweizer Musikbuch* (Zürich, 1939); *Richard Strauss: Betrachtungen und Erinnerungen* (Zürich, 1949; Eng. tr., 1955; 2nd Swiss ed., rev., 1957); *Hugo von Hofmannsthal: Briefwechsel* (Zürich, 1952; Eng. tr., 1961; 4th Swiss ed., rev., 1970); *Richard Strauss: Briefe an die Eltern* (Zürich, 1954); *Igor Strawinsky: Leben und Werk, von ihm selbst* (Zürich and Mainz, 1957); *Richard Strauss und Stefan Zweig: Briefwechsel* (Frankfurt am Main, 1957; Eng. tr., 1977, as *A Confidential Matter: The Letters of Richard Strauss and Stefan Zweig 1931–1935*); with G. Kende, *Richard Strauss und Clemens Krauss: Briefwechsel* (Munich, 1963; 2nd ed., 1964); *Richard Strauss und Willi Schuh: Briefwechsel* (Zürich, 1969). His publ. writings include *Othmar Schoeck* (Zürich, 1934); *In memoriam Richard Strauss* (Zürich, 1949); *Danae oder Die Vernunftheirat* (Frankfurt am Main, 1952); *Renoir und Wagner* (Zürich, 1959); *Ein paar Erinnerungen an Richard Strauss* (Zürich, 1964); *Hugo von Hofmannsthal und Richard Strauss: Legende und Wirklichkeit* (Munich, 1964); *Der Rosenkavalier: Vier Studien* (Olten, 1968); *Richard Strauss: Jugend und frühe Meisterjahre: Lebenschronik 1864–98* (the authorized biography; Zürich, 1976; Eng. tr., 1982, as *Richard Strauss: A Chronicle of the Early Years 1864–98*).

Schüler, Johannes, German conductor; b. Vietz, Neumark, June 21, 1894; d. Berlin, Oct. 3, 1966. He received his training at the Berlin Hochschule für Musik. After conducting opera in Gleiwitz (1920–22), Königsberg (1922–24), and Hannover (1924–28), he was music director in Oldenburg (1928–32) and Essen (1933–36). From 1936 to 1949 he conducted at the Berlin State Opera, where he was granted the titles of Staatskapellmeister and Generalmusikdirektor. He then was Generalmusikdirektor in Hannover from 1949 to 1960, where he conducted a number of contemporary operas.

Schulhoff, Ervín, Czech composer and pianist; b. Prague, June 8, 1894; d. in the concentration camp in Wülzburg, Bavaria, Aug. 18, 1942. He was the great-grandnephew of the noted Bohemian pianist, teacher, and composer Julius Schulhoff (b. Prague, Aug. 2, 1825; d. Berlin, March 13, 1898). He was a student of Kaan at the Prague Cons. (1904–06), of Thern in Vienna, and of Reger at the Leipzig Cons. (1908–10) before completing his training at the Cologne Cons. (1911–14). In 1913 he won the Mendelssohn Prize for piano and in 1918 for composition. Following military service during World War I, he was active in Germany (1919–23), where he became involved in left-wing avant-garde circles. During this period, he was attracted to Dadaism and jazz. His music of this period also reveals the influence of Schoenberg and Stravinsky. Upon returning to Prague, he taught piano privately and later was on the faculty of the Cons. (1929–31). As a pianist, he was a champion of the quarter tone music of Alois Hába and his disciples. After composing works along expressionist and neo-Classical lines, Schulhoff embraced the tenets of proletarian art in the early 1930s. He also became a member of the Communist Party, a decision that placed him in peril after the Nazi occupation in 1939. When the Nazis attacked the Soviet Union in 1941, Schulhoff was arrested and imprisoned in Prague. Later that year he was sent to the concentration camp in Wülzburg, where he died of tuberculosis.

WORKS: DRAMATIC: *Ogelala*, ballet (1922–24; Dessau, Nov. 21, 1925); *Náměsíčná* (The Sleepwalker), dance grotesque (1925; Oxford, July 24, 1931); *Le bourgeois gentilhomme*, music for Molière's play (1926); *Plameny* (Flames), tragicomedy (1927–29; Brno, Jan. 27, 1932). **ORCH.:** 2 piano concertos (1913, 1923); *Joyful Overture* (1913); *32 Variations on an Original 8-bar Theme* (1919); Suite for Chamber Orch. (1921); 8 syms.: No. 1 (1925), No. 2 (1932; Prague, April 24, 1935), No. 3 (1935), No. 4, *Spanish*, for Baritone and Orch. (1936–37), No. 5 (1938), No. 6, *Symphony of Freedom*, for Chorus and Orch. (1940–41; Prague, May 5, 1946), No. 7, *Eroica* (1941; unfinished), and No. 8 (1942; unfinished); Double Concerto for Flute, Piano, and Orch. (1927); *Festive Overture* (1929); Concerto for String Quartet and Wind Orch. (1930; Prague, Nov. 9, 1932). **CHAMBER:** 2 violin sonatas (1913, 1927); Cello Sonata (1914); Sextet for 2 Violins, 2 Violas, and 2 Cellos (1920–24); *Bass Nightingale* for Contrabassoon (1922); *5 Pieces* for String Quartet (1923); 2 string quartets (1924, 1925); Duo for Violin and Cello (1925); Concertino for Flute, Viola, and Double Bass (1925); *Divertissement* for Oboe, Clarinet, and Bassoon (1926); Sonata for Solo Violin (1927); Flute Sonata (1927); *Hot Sonata* for Alto Saxophone and Piano (1930). **PIANO:** *Variations on an Original Theme* (1913); *9 Little Round Dances* (1914); *10 Variations on "Ah vous dirais-je, Maman"* (1914); *5 Grotesques* (1917); 1 unnumbered sonata (1918); 3 numbered sonatas (1924, 1926, 1927); *5 Burlesques* (1918); *3 Waltzes* (1918); *5 Humoresques* (1919); *5 Arabesques* (1919); *5 Pictures* (1919); *10 Themes* (1920); *Ironies*, 6 pieces for Piano, 4-hands (1920); *Partita* (1920); *11 Inventions* (1921); *Rag Music* (1922); *6 Family Matters* (1923); 2 suites (1925, 1926); *Esquisses de Jazz* (1927); *Hot Music* (1928); *Suite dansante en jazz* (1931); *Studien*, 2 pieces (1936). **VOCAL:** *3 Songs* for Alto and Piano (1914); *Krajiny* (Landscapes), 5 songs for Mezzo-soprano and Orch. (1918–19); *Menschheit* for Alto and Orch. (1919); *Serious Songs* for Baritone, 4 Winds, and Percussion (1922); *H.M.S. Royal Oak*, jazz oratorio for Reciter, Jazz Singer, Chorus, and Symphonic Jazz Orch. (1930; Brno Radio, Feb. 12, 1935); *Manifest*, cantata after *The Communist Manifesto* of Marx and Engels, for 4 Soloists, Double Chorus, Children's Chorus, and Wind Orch. (1932–33; Prague, April 5, 1962); *1917*, song cycle for Voice and Piano (1933).

BIBL.: V. Stará, *E. S.: Vzpomínky, studie a dokumenty* (E. S.: Recollections, Studies and Documents; Prague, 1958); O. Pukl, *Konstanty, dominanty a varianty S.ova skladebného stylu* (The Constants, Dominants and Variants of S.'s Compositional Style; Prague, 1986).

Schuller, Gunther (Alexander), significant American composer, conductor, and music educator; b. N.Y., Nov. 22, 1925. He was of a musical family; his paternal grandfather was a bandmaster in Germany before emigrating to America; his father was a violinist with the N.Y. Phil. He was sent to Germany as a child for a thorough academic training; returning to N.Y., he studied at the St. Thomas Choir School (1938–44); also received private instruction in theory, flute, and horn. He played in the N.Y. City Ballet orch. (1943); then was 1st horn in the Cincinnati Sym. Orch. (1943–45) and the Metropolitan Opera orch. in N.Y. (1945–49). At the same time, he became fascinated with jazz; he played the horn in a combo conducted by Miles Davis; also began to compose jazz pieces. He taught at the Manhattan School of Music in N.Y. (1950–63), the Yale Univ. School of Music (1964–67), and the New England Cons. of Music in Boston, where he greatly distinguished himself as president (1967–77). He was also active at the Berkshire Music Center at Tanglewood as a teacher of composition (1963–84), head of contemporary-music activities (1965–84), artistic co-director (1969–74), and director (1974–84). In 1984–85 he was interim music director of the Spokane (Wash.) Sym. Orch.; then was director of its Sandpoint (Idaho) Festival. In 1986 he founded the Boston Composers' Orch. In 1988 he was awarded the 1st Elise L. Stoeger Composer's Chair of the Chamber Music Soc. of Lincoln Center in N.Y. In 1975 he organized Margun Music to make available unpubl. American music. He founded GunMar Music in 1979. In 1980 he organized GM Recordings. He publ. the manual *Horn Technique* (N.Y., 1962; 2nd ed., 1992) and the very valuable study *Early Jazz: Its Roots and Musical Development* (3 vols., N.Y., 1968 et seq.). A vol. of his writings appeared as *Musings* (N.Y., 1985). In his multiple activities, he tried to form a link between serious music and jazz; he popularized the style of "cool jazz" (recorded as Birth of the Cool). In 1957 he launched the slogan "third stream" to designate the combination of classical forms with improvisatory elements of jazz as a synthesis of disparate, but not necessarily incompatible, entities, and wrote fanciful pieces in this synthetic style; in many of these, he worked in close cooperation with John Lewis of the Modern Jazz Quartet. As part of his investigation of the roots of jazz, he became interested in early ragtime and formed, in 1972, the New England Cons. Ragtime Ensemble; its recordings of Scott Joplin's piano rags in band arrangement were instrumental in bringing about the "ragtime revival." In his own works he freely applied serial methods, even when his general style was dominated by jazz. He received honorary doctorates in music from Northwestern Univ. (1967), the Univ. of Ill. (1968), Williams College (1975), the New England Cons. of Music (1978), and Rutgers Univ. (1980). In 1967 he was elected to membership in the National Inst. of Arts and Letters, and in 1980 to the American Academy and Inst. of Arts and Letters. In 1989 he received the William Schuman Award of Columbia Univ. In 1991 he was awarded a MacArthur Foundation grant. In 1994 he won the Pulitzer Prize in Music for his orch. work, *Of Reminiscences and Reflections* (1993), composed in memory of his wife who died in 1992.

WORKS: DRAMATIC: OPERAS: *The Visitation* (Hamburg, Oct. 12, 1966); *The Fisherman and His Wife*, children's opera (Boston, May 7, 1970); *A Question of Taste* (Cooperstown, N.Y., June 24, 1989). **BALLET:** *Variants* for Jazz Quartet and Orch. (1960; N.Y., Jan. 4, 1961). **FILM SCORES:** *Automation* (1962); *Journey to the Stars* (1962); *Yesterday in Fact* (1963). **TELEVISION SCORES:** *Tear Drop* (1966); *The 5 Senses*, ballet (1967).

ORCH.: 2 horn concertos: No. 1 (1944; Cincinnati, April 6, 1945, composer soloist) and No. 2 (1976; Budapest, June 19, 1978); Cello Concerto (1945; rev. 1985); *Suite* for Chamber Orch. (1945); *Vertige d'Eros* (1945; Madison, Wis., Oct. 15, 1967); *Symphonic Study* (1947–48; Cincinnati, May 1949); *Dramatic Overture* (1951; Darmstadt, Aug. 1954); *Recitative and Rondo* for Violin and Orch. (1953; Chicago, July 16, 1967; also for Violin and Piano); *Symphonic Tribute to Duke Ellington* (1955; Lenox, Mass., Aug. 19, 1976); *Little Fantasy* (Englewood, N.J., April 7, 1957); *Contours* for Chamber Orch. (1958; Cincinnati, Dec. 31, 1959); *Spectra* (1958; N.Y., Jan. 14, 1960); Concertino for Jazz Quartet and Orch. (1959; Baltimore, Jan. 2, 1960); *7 Studies on Themes of Paul Klee* (Minneapolis, Nov. 27, 1959); *Capriccio* for Tuba and Orch. (1960); *Contrasts* for Wind Quintet and Orch. (1960; Donaueschingen, Oct. 22, 1961); *Journey to the Stars* (Toledo, Ohio, Dec. 1, 1962); *Movements* for Flute and Strings (Dortmund, May 29, 1962); 2 piano concertos: No. 1 (Cincinnati, Oct. 29, 1962) and No. 2 (1981; Mainz, Nov. 24, 1982); *Composition in 3 Parts* (Minneapolis, March 29, 1963); *Diptych* for Brass Quintet and Band (1963; also for Brass Quintet and Orch.; Ithaca, N.Y., March 22, 1964); *Meditation* for Band (Greensboro, N.C., March 7, 1963); *Threnos* for Oboe and Orch. (Cologne, Nov. 29, 1963); *5 Bagatelles* (Fargo, N.Dak., March 22, 1964); *American Triptych: 3 Studies in Textures* (New Orleans, March 9, 1965); Sym. (Dallas, Feb. 8, 1965); 2 concertos: No. 1, *Gala Music* (Chicago, Jan. 20, 1966) and No. 2 (Washington, D.C., Oct. 12, 1976); *5 Etudes* (1966; New Haven, March 19, 1967); *Triplum I* (N.Y., June 28, 1967) and *II* (Baltimore, Feb. 26, 1975); *Colloquy* for 2 Pianos and Orch. (Berlin, June 6, 1968); Double Bass Concerto (N.Y., Jan. 27, 1968); *Fanfare for St. Louis* (St. Louis, Jan. 24, 1968); *Shapes and Designs* (Hartford, April 26, 1969); *Consequents* (New Haven, Dec. 16, 1969); *Museum Piece* for Renaissance Instruments and Orch. (Boston, Dec. 11, 1970); *Concerto da camera* for Chamber Orch. (1971; Rochester, N.Y., April 24, 1972); *Capriccio stravagante* (San Francisco, Dec. 6, 1972); *3 Nocturnes* (Interlochen, July 15, 1973); *4 Soundscapes—Hudson Valley Reminiscences* (1974; Poughkeepsie, N.Y., March 7, 1975); 2 violin concertos: No. 1 (Lucerne, Aug. 25, 1976) and No. 2 (1991); *Deai—Encounters* for 7 Voices and 3 Orchs. (Tokyo, March 17, 1978); Contrabassoon Concerto (1978; Washington, D.C., Jan. 16, 1979); Trumpet Concerto (Jefferson, N.H., Aug. 25, 1979); *Eine kleine Posaunenmusik* for Trombone and Orch. (Norfolk, Conn., July 18, 1980); *Music for a Celebration* for Chorus, Audience, and Orch. (Springfield, Mass., Sept. 26, 1980); *In Praise of Winds* for Large Wind Orch. (Ann Arbor, Feb. 13, 1981); Alto Saxophone Concerto (1983; Pittsburgh, Jan. 18, 1984); *Concerto quarternio* for Violin, Flute, Oboe, Trumpet, and Orch. (N.Y., Nov. 21, 1984); *Concerto festivo* for Brass Quintet and Orch. (Trier, Nov. 29, 1984); *Jubilee Musik* (Dayton, March 7, 1984); Bassoon Concerto, *Eine kleine Fagottmusik* (Washington, D.C., May 17, 1985); *Farbenspiel*, concerto (Berlin, May 8, 1985); Viola Concerto (New Orleans, Dec. 17, 1985); Concerto for String Quartet and Orch. (Madison, Wis., Feb. 20, 1988); Flute Concerto (Chicago, Oct. 13, 1988); *On Winged Flight*, divertimento for Band (Tallahassee, Fla., March 4, 1989); *Chamber Symphony* (Cleveland, April 16, 1989); Concerto for Piano, 3-hands (2 Pianos) and Chamber Orch. (1989; Springfield, Ill., Jan. 19, 1990); *Ritmica Melodia Armonia* (1992); *Of Reminiscences and Reflections* (Louisville, Dec. 2, 1993); *The Past is Present* (1993; Cincinnati, March 25, 1994); Organ Concerto (Calgary, Oct. 14, 1994).

CHAMBER: *Romantic Sonata* for Clarinet, Horn, and Piano (1941; rev. 1983); *Suite* for Woodwind Quintet (1945); *3 hommages* for Horn or 2 Horns and Piano (1942–46); *Fantasia concertante No. 1* for 3 Oboes and Piano (1947) and *No. 2* for 3 Trombones and Piano (1947); Quartet for 4 Double Basses (1947); *Perpetuum mobile* for 4 Horns, and Bassoon or Tuba (1948); Trio for Oboe, Horn, and Viola (1948); Oboe Sonata (1948–51); *Duo Sonata* for Clarinet and Bass Clarinet (1948–49); *Fantasy* for Cello (1951); *5 Pieces* for 5 Horns (1952); *Recitative and Rondo* for Violin and Piano (1953; also for Violin and Orch.); 3 string quartets (1957, 1965, 1986); Woodwind Quintet (1958); *Fantasy Quartet* for 4 Cellos (1959); *Fantasy* for Harp (1959); *Lines and Contrasts* for 16 Horns (1960); *Double Quintet* for Wind and Brass Quintets (1961); *Music* for Brass Quintet (1961); *Fanfare* for 4 Trumpets and 4 Trombones (1962); *Music* for Carillon (1962; also arranged for other instruments); *Studies* for Horn (1962); *Little Brass Music* for Trumpet, Horn, Trombone, and Tuba (1963); *Episodes* for Clarinet (1964); *Aphorisms* for Flute and String Trio (1967); *5 Moods* for 4 Tubas (1973); *Sonata serenata* for Clarinet, Violin, Cello, and Piano (1978); Octet (1979); Piano Trio (1983); *On Light Wings* for Piano Quartet (1984); Sextet for Bassoon, Piano, and String Quartet (1986); *The Sandpoint Rag* for Ragtime Ensemble (1986; also for Brass Sextet); *Chimeric Images* for Chamber Group (1988); *A Bouquet for Collage* for Clarinet, Flute, Violin, Cello, Piano, and Percussion (1988); Horn Sonata (1988); *5 Impromptus* for English Horn and String Quartet (1989); *Hommage à Rayechla* for 8 Cellos or Multiples Thereof (1990); *A Trio Setting* for Clarinet, Violin, and Piano (1990); Brass Quintet No. 2 (1993); Sextet for Piano, Left-hand, and Woodwind Quintet (1994). **PIANO:** *Sonata/Fantasia* (Boston, March 28, 1993).

VOCAL: *O Lamb of God* for Chorus and Optional Organ (1941); *O Spirit of the Living God* for Chorus and Optional Organ (1942); *6 Renaissance Lyrics* for Tenor and 7 Instruments (1962); *Journey into Jazz* for Narrator, Jazz Quintet, and Orch. (Washington, D.C., May 30, 1962); *5 Shakespearean Songs* for Baritone and Orch. (1964); *Sacred Cantata* for Chorus and Chamber Orch. (1966); *The Power within Us*, oratorio for Baritone, Narrator, Chorus, and Orch. (1971); *Poems of Time and Eternity* for Chorus and 9 Instruments (1972); *Thou Art the Son of God*, cantata for Chorus and Chamber Ensemble (1987); songs.

BIBL.: J. Tassel, "G. S.: Composer, Conductor and Musical Conscience," *Ovation* (Nov. 1985); N. Carnovale, *G. S.: A Bio-Bibliography* (Westport, Conn., 1987).

Schulthess, Walter, Swiss conductor and composer; b. Zürich, July 24, 1894; d. there, June 23, 1971. He studied with Andreae in Zürich, Courvoisier in Munich, and Ansorge in Berlin; in 1918, settled in Zürich. As a composer, he excelled in lyric songs, in a style resembling Othmar Schoeck's. He also wrote a Violin Concertino (1921), *Serenade* for Orch. (1921), *Symphonische Variationen* for Cello and Orch. (1926), and various chamber works, including a String Quartet (1921), 2 violin sonatas (1921, 1922), and *3 Capricen nach Paganini* for Violin and Piano (1923); also wrote piano pieces, choruses, and lieder. He married **Stefi Geyer** in 1919.

Schultz, Svend (Simon), Danish composer, pianist, and conductor; b. Nykøbing Falster, Dec. 30, 1913. He received training in piano and composition at the Copenhagen Cons. (1933–38), where his principal mentor was Schierbeck. After serving as music critic for *Politiken* (1942–49), he was a choral conductor with the Danish Radio in Copenhagen (from 1949). He also appeared as a pianist and conductor of his own works throughout Europe. His music is neo-Classical in style and is characterized by simplicity of form and a cumulative rhythmic drive.

WORKS: DRAMATIC: OPERAS: *Bag kulisserne* (Behind the Scenes; 1946; Copenhagen, May 26, 1949); *Solbadet* (The Sunbath; 1947; Århus, Nov. 26, 1949); *Kaffehuset* (The Coffee House; 1948); *Høst* (Harvest; 1950); *Bryllupsrejsen* (The Honeymoon; 1951); *Hyrdinden og skorstensfejeren* (The Shepherdess and the Chimney Sweep), puppet opera (1953); *Tordenvejret* (The Thunderstorm; 1954); *Hosekraemmeren* (The Stocking Peddler; 1955; rev. 1985; Århus, May 4, 1990); *The Marionettes*, puppet opera (1957); *Dommer Lynch* (Judge Lynch; 1959); *Konen i muddergrøften* (The Woman in the Muddy Ditch), comic television opera (1964; Danish TV, April 18, 1965); *Lykken og forstanden*, children's opera (1973). **CHAMBER OPERETTA:** *Den kåde Donna* (Copenhagen, Aug. 30, 1957). **MUSICAL CHURCH PLAY:** *Eva* (1968). **ORCH.:** *Serenade* for Strings (1940); 7 syms. (1941, 1949, 1955, 1957, 1960, 1962, 1973); Piano Concerto (1943); *Storstrømsbroen* (The Storstroem Bridge; 1951); *Introduction and Rondo* for Piano and Orch. (Danish Radio, Nov. 8, 1964); *2 Variations: Nocturne and Aubade* (1965); *Northern Overture* (1975); *Pale make* (1981); Concertino for Clarinet and Strings (1982); Harp Concertino (1986); *Hommage à Rossini* (1986); *Garde-Gratulation* for Wind Orch. (1992). **CHAMBER:** 6 string quartets (1939, 1940, 1940, 1961, 1962, 1975); 2 piano trios (1942, 1963); Flute Quartet (1961); *Romantic Trio* for Piano Trio (1961); Quartet for Flute, Violin, Viola, and Cello (1962); Clarinet Quintet (1965); *Music for Wind Players* for Flute, Trumpet, Clarinet, Percussion, Vibraphone, and Piano (1966); *Quintetto per Nefertite* for Flute, Violin, Viola, Cello, and Piano (1985). **PIANO:** Sonata (1931); 2 sonatinas (1940, 1950). **VOCAL:** *Job*, oratorio (1945); *Sankt Hans Nat* for Soloists, Chorus, and Orch. (1953); *Hymn* for Chorus and Orch. (Copenhagen, March 13, 1957); *Hr. Mortens klosterrov* (Morten's Pillage of the Monastery) for Soloists, Chorus, and Chamber Orch. (1958; Copenhagen, Oct. 13, 1960); *3 Pastorales* for Soloists, Chorus, and Orch. (Danish Radio, May 28, 1962); *The 4 Temperaments* for Women's Chorus, Men's Chorus, and Orch. (Hillerød, Nov. 15, 1974); *Jul*, cantata (1981); *It Is Perfectly True*, scene for Soloists, Chorus, and Clarinet (1982).

Schultze, Norbert, German composer; b. Braunschweig, Jan. 26, 1911. He studied piano, conducting, and composition at the Cologne Staatliche Hochschule für Musik; after studying theatrical arts in Cologne and Munich (1931), he was active as an actor and composer in a student cabaret, *Vier Nachrichter*, in Munich (1931–32); then conducted opera in Heidelberg (1932–33) and Darmstadt (1933–34); later was a composer for stage, films, and television; was head of his own music publishing business (from 1953). He wrote the operas *Schwarzer Peter* (Hamburg, 1936) and *Das kalte Herz* (Leipzig, 1943); television opera, *Peter der dritte* (1964); operetta, *Regen in Paris* (Nuremberg, 1957); 3 pantomimes: *Struwwelpeter* (Hamburg, 1937), *Max und Moritz* (Hamburg, 1938), and *Maria im Walde* (Vienna, 1940); but his chief claim to fame was a sentimental song, *Lili Marleen* (1938), which became immensely popular during World War II among both German and Allied soldiers after it was broadcast from the German-occupied Belgrade in 1941; it was tr. into 27 languages. For some of his works he used the names Frank Norbert, Peter Kornfeld, and Henri Iversen.

Schulze, Hans-Joachim, distinguished German musicologist; b. Leipzig, Dec. 3, 1934. He studied musicology in Leipzig at the Hochschule für Musik (1952–54) and with Serauky, Eller, and Besseler at the Karl Marx Univ. (1954–57); completed his education at the Univ. of Rostock (Ph.D., 1979, with the diss. *Studien zur Bach-Überlieferung im 18. Jahrhundert*; publ. in Leipzig, 1984). In 1957 he became a research assistant at the Leipzig Bach Archive, where he later served as deputy director (1974–79); with C. Wolff, he was co-ed. of the *Bach-Jahrbuch* (from 1975). He was made head research fellow of the Nationale Forschungs- und Gedenkstatten Johann Sebastian Bach in Leipzig in 1979, and was appointed director of the Leipzig Bach Archive in 1986. He was a lecturer at the Martin Luther Univ. in Halle-Wittenberg (1987–88), and has lectured as a visiting prof. in univs. in Europe and the U.S. A devoted scholar of Bach, Schulze is a respected authority in his field.

WRITINGS: Ed. with W. Neumann, *Schriftstücke von der Hand Johann Sebastian Bachs, Bach-Dokumente*, I (Leipzig, 1963); ed. *Fremdschriftliche und gedruckte Dokumente zur Lebensgeschichte Johann Sebastian Bachs 1685–1750, Bach-Dokumente*, II (Leipzig, 1969); ed. *Dokumente zum Nachwirken Johann Sebastian Bachs 1750–1800, Bach-Dokumente*, III (Leipzig, 1972); *Johann Sebastian Bach: Leben und Werk in Dokumenten* (Leipzig, 1975); ed. with C. Wolff, *Bach Compendium: Analytisch-bibliographisches Repertorium der Werke Johann Sebastian Bachs* (5 vols., Leipzig and Dresden, 1985 et seq.).

Schuman, William (Howard), eminent American composer, music educator, and administrator; b. N.Y., Aug. 4, 1910; d. there, Feb. 15, 1992. He began composing at 16, turning out a number of popular songs; also played in jazz groups. He took courses at N.Y. Univ.'s School of Commerce (1928–30) before turning decisively to music and taking private lessons in harmony with Max Persin and in counterpoint with Charles Haubiel (1931) in N.Y. After attending summer courses with Wagenaar and Schmid at N.Y.'s Juilliard School (1932–33), he pursued his education at Teacher's College of Columbia Univ. (B.S., 1935; M.A., 1937); also studied conducting at the Salzburg Mozarteum (summer, 1935) and composition with Harris, both at the Juilliard School (summer, 1936) and privately (1936–38). He came to the attention of Koussevitzky, who conducted the premieres of his *American Festival Overture* (1939), 3rd Sym. (1941; received the 1st N.Y. Music Critics' Circle Award), *A Free Song* (1943; received the 1st Pulitzer Prize in Music), and the Sym. for Strings (1943); Rodzinski conducted the premiere of his 4th Sym. (1942). After teaching at Sarah Lawrence College (1935–45), he served as director of publications of G. Schirmer, Inc. (1945–52) and as president of the Juilliard School of Music (1945–62), where he acquired a notable reputation as a music educator; he subsequently was president of Lincoln Center for the Performing Arts in N.Y. (1962–69). He was chairman of the MacDowell Colony (from 1973) and the first chairman of the Norlin Foundation (1975–85). The recipient of numerous honors, he held 2 Guggenheim fellowships (1939–41), was elected a member of the National Inst. of Arts and Letters (1946) and the American Academy of Arts and Letters (1973), was awarded the gold medal of the American Academy and Inst. of Arts and Letters (1982), won a 2nd, special Pulitzer Prize (1985), and received the National Medal of Arts (1987) and a Kennedy Center Honor (1989). Columbia Univ. established the William Schuman Award in 1981, a prize of $50,000 given to a composer for lifetime achievement; fittingly, Schuman was its first recipient. His music is characterized by great emotional tension, which is maintained by powerful asymmetric rhythms; the contrapuntal structures in his works reach a great degree of complexity and are saturated with dissonance without, however, losing the essential tonal references. In several of his works, he employs American melorhythms, but his general style of composition is cosmopolitan, exploring all viable techniques of modern composition.

WORKS: DRAMATIC: OPERA: *The Mighty Casey* (1951–53; Hartford, Conn., May 4, 1953; rev. as the cantata *Casey at the Bat*, Washington, D.C., April 6, 1976). **BALLETS:** *Undertow* (N.Y., April 10, 1945); *Night Journey* (Cambridge, Mass., May 3,

1947); *Judith* (1949; Louisville, Jan. 4, 1950); *Voyage for a Theater* (N.Y., May 17, 1953; withdrawn); *The Witch of Endor* (N.Y., Nov. 2, 1965; withdrawn). **FILM SCORES:** *Steeltown* (1941); *The Earth Is Born* (1959).

ORCH.: *Potpourri* (1932; withdrawn); 10 syms.: No. 1 for 18 Instruments (1935; N.Y., Oct. 21, 1936; withdrawn), No. 2 (1937; N.Y., May 25, 1938; withdrawn), No. 3 (Boston, Oct. 17, 1941), No. 4 (1941; Cleveland, Jan. 22, 1942), No. 5, Sym. for Strings (Boston, Nov. 12, 1943), No. 6 (1948; Dallas, Feb. 27, 1949), No. 7 (Boston, Oct. 21, 1960), No. 8 (N.Y., Oct. 4, 1962), No. 9, *Le fosse ardeatine* (1968; Philadelphia, Jan. 10, 1969), and No. 10, *American Muse* (1975; Washington, D.C., April 6, 1976); Piano Concerto (1938; rev. 1942; N.Y., Jan. 13, 1943); *American Festival Overture* (Boston, Oct. 6, 1939); *Newsreel*, in 5 Shots for Concert Band (1941; also for Orch., N.Y., July 15, 1942); *Prayer in Time of War* (Pittsburgh, Feb. 26, 1943); *William Billings Overture* (1943; N.Y., Feb. 17, 1944; withdrawn); *Variations on a Theme by Eugene Goossens* (No. 5 of 10 variations, each by a different composer; 1944; Cincinnati, March 23, 1945); *Circus Overture: Side Show* (1944; for Small Orch., Philadelphia, July 20, 1944; for Full Orch., Pittsburgh, Jan. 7, 1945); *Undertow*, choreographic episodes from the ballet (Los Angeles, Nov. 29, 1945); Violin Concerto (1947; Boston, Feb. 10, 1950; rev. 1954; N.Y., Feb. 26, 1956; rev. 1958–59; Aspen, Colo., Aug. 9, 1959); *George Washington Bridge* for Concert Band (Interlochen, Mich., July 30, 1950); *Credendum, Article of Faith* (Cincinnati, Nov. 4, 1955); *New England Triptych* (Miami, Oct. 28, 1956); *Chester Overture* for Concert Band from *New England Triptych* (1956); *When Jesus Wept* for Concert Band from *New England Triptych* (1958); *A Song of Orpheus* for Cello and Orch. (1961; Indianapolis, Feb. 17, 1962; arranged for Cello and Chamber Orch. in collaboration with J. Goldberg, 1978); *Variations on "America"* after the organ work by Ives (1963; N.Y., May 20, 1964; also for Band, 1968); *The Orchestra Song* (1963; N.Y., April 11, 1964; also for Band as *The Band Song*); *Philharmonic Fanfare* for Concert Band (N.Y., Aug. 10, 1965; withdrawn); *Dedication Fanfare* for Concert Band (St. Louis, July 4, 1968); *To Thee Old Cause* for Oboe, Brass, Timpani, Piano, and Strings (N.Y., Oct. 3, 1968); *In Praise of Shahn*, canticle (1969; N.Y., Jan. 29, 1970); *Anniversary Fanfare* for Brass and Percussion (1969; N.Y., April 13, 1970); *Voyage for Orchestra* (Rochester, N.Y., Oct. 27, 1972); *Prelude for a Great Occasion* for Brass and Percussion (Washington, D.C., Oct. 1, 1974); *Be Glad Then, America* for Concert Band from *New England Triptych* (1975); *3 Colloquies* for Horn and Orch. (1979; N.Y., Jan. 24, 1980); *American Hymn* (1980; St. Louis, Dec. 24, 1982; also for Band).

CHAMBER: *Canon and Fugue* for Piano Trio (1934; withdrawn); 2 pastorales: No. 1 for Alto and Clarinet, or 2 Violas, or Violin and Cello (1934), and No. 2 for Flute, Oboe, and Clarinet; or Flute, Violin, and Clarinet (1934; withdrawn); 5 string quartets: No. 1 (N.Y., Oct. 21, 1936; withdrawn), No. 2 (1937), No. 3 (1939; N.Y., Feb. 27, 1940), No. 4 (Washington, D.C., Oct. 28, 1950), and No. 5 (1987; N.Y., June 21, 1988); *Quartettino* for 4 Bassoons (1939); *Amaryllis*, variations for String Trio (Washington, D.C., Oct. 31, 1964; also for String Orch.); *XXV Opera Snatches* for Trumpet (1978; N.Y., Jan. 10, 1979); *Night Journey* for Various Instruments, after the ballet (1980; Albany, N.Y., Feb. 27, 1981); *American Hymn* for Brass Quintet (1980; N.Y., March 30, 1981); *Dances* for Wind Quintet and Percussion (1984; N.Y., Oct. 1, 1985). **PIANO:** *3-score Set* (1943); *Voyage* (1953); *3 Piano Moods* (1958).

VOCAL (all for a cappella Mixed Chorus unless otherwise given): *God's World* for Voice and Piano (1932); *4 Canonic Choruses* (1932–33; N.Y., May 3, 1935); *Pioneers!* for 8-part Chorus (1937; Princeton, N.J., May 23, 1938; withdrawn); *Choral Etude* (1937; N.Y., March 16, 1938); *Prologue* for Chorus and Orch. (N.Y., May 7, 1939); *Prelude* for Soprano and Women's or Mixed Chorus (1939; N.Y., April 24, 1940); *This Is Our Time*, secular cantata No. 1 for Chorus and Orch. (N.Y., July 4, 1940); *Requiescat* for Women's or Mixed Chorus and Piano (N.Y., April 4, 1942); *Holiday Song* for Women's Voices or Mixed Chorus and Piano (1942; N.Y., Jan. 13, 1943; also for Voice and Piano); *A Free Song*, secular cantata No. 2 for Chorus and Orch. (1942; Boston, March 26, 1943); *Orpheus and His Lute* for Voice and Piano (1944; also for Cello and Orch. as *A Song of Orpheus*, 1961); *Te Deum* (1944; Cambridge, Mass., April 1945); *Truth Shall Deliver* for Men's Chorus (New Haven, Conn., Dec. 7, 1946); *The Lord Has a Child* for Mixed or Women's Chorus or Voice and Piano (1956); *5 Rounds on Famous Words* (Nos. 1–4, 1956; No. 5, 1969); *Carols of Death* (1958; Canton, N.Y., March 20, 1959); *Deo ac veritati* for Men's Chorus (Hamilton, N.Y., April 19, 1963); *Declaration Chorale* (1971; N.Y., April 30, 1972); *Mail Order Madrigals* (1971; Ames, Iowa, March 12, 1972); *To Thy Love*, choral fantasy on old English rounds for 3-part Women's Chorus (1973); *Concerto on Old English Rounds* for Viola, Women's Chorus, and Orch. (Boston, Nov. 29, 1974); *The Young Dead Soldiers* for Soprano, Horn, Woodwinds, and Strings (1975; Washington, D.C., April 6, 1976); *Casey at the Bat*, cantata for Soprano, Baritone, Chorus, and Orch. (Washington, D.C., April 6, 1976; revision of the opera *The Mighty Casey*); *In Sweet Music* for Mezzo-soprano, Flute, Viola, and Harp (N.Y., Oct. 29, 1978; based on the song *Orpheus and His Lute*, 1944); *Time to the Old* for Voice and Piano (1979); *Esses: Short Suite for Singers on Words Beginning with S* (Ithaca, N.Y., Nov. 13, 1982); *Perceptions* (1982; Greenwich, Conn., Jan. 9, 1983); *On Freedom's Ground: An American Cantata* for Baritone, Chorus, and Orch., for the rededication of the Statue of Liberty (1985; N.Y., Oct. 28, 1986).

BIBL.: L. Bernstein, "W. S.," *Modern Music*, XIX (1942); A. Frankenstein, "W. S.," ibid., XXII (1944–45); N. Broder, "The Music of W. S.," *Musical Quarterly* (Jan. 1945); F. Schreiber and V. Persichetti, *W. S.* (N.Y., 1954); S. Keats, "W. S.," *Stereo Review*, XXXII/6 (1974); H. Hitchcock, "W. S.: Musical All-American," *Keynote* (Aug. 1980); C. Rouse, *W. S.: Documentary* (N.Y., 1980); P. Dickinson, "W. S.: An American Symphonist at 75," *Musical Times* (Aug. 1985); D. Hall, "A Bio-Discography of W. S.," *Ovation* (Aug. and Sept. 1985); J. Clark, "W. S. on His Symphonies: An Interview," *American Music* (Fall 1986).

Schumann, Camillo, German organist and composer, brother of **Georg (Alfred) Schumann**; b. Königstein, March 10, 1872; d. Gottleuba, Dec. 29, 1946. He learned the rudiments of music from his father; then studied with Jadassohn and Reinecke at the Leipzig Cons. After further study with Adolf Bargiel in Berlin (1894–96), he became organist at the Eisenach church. For some years before his death, he lived in retirement at Gottleuba. He was a prolific composer, especially noted for his organ works; he also wrote 6 cantatas, 3 piano trios, 5 cello sonatas, 2 clarinet sonatas, 2 violin sonatas, and 30 albums of piano pieces.

Schumann, Elisabeth, celebrated German-born American soprano; b. Merseburg, June 13, 1888; d. N.Y., April 23, 1952. She studied in Dresden, Berlin, and Hamburg. She made her operatic debut at the Hamburg Opera on Sept. 2, 1909, as the Shepherd in *Tannhäuser*, remained on its roster until 1919. In the meantime, she made her American debut at the Metropolitan Opera in N.Y. on Nov. 20, 1914, as Sophie in *Der Rosenkavalier*, one of her most famous roles; sang there only one season (1914–15). From 1919 to 1938 she was a principal member of the Vienna State Opera. In 1921 she made a concert tour of the U.S. with Richard Strauss. After the Anschluss in 1938, she settled in the U.S. and taught at the Curtis Inst. of Music in Philadelphia. She became a naturalized American citizen in 1944. She publ. *German Song* (London, 1948). Among her finest roles were Blondchen, Zerlina, Susanna, Adele, and Sophie; she also was renowned as an incomparable lieder artist.

BIBL.: E. Puritz, *The Teaching of E. S.* (1956); D. Shawe-Taylor, "Lotte Lehmann and E. S.: A Centenary Tribute," *Musical Times* (Oct. 1988); G. Puritz, *E. S.: A Biography* (London, 1993).

Schumann, Georg (Alfred), German conductor and composer, brother of **Camillo Schumann**; b. Königstein, Oct. 25, 1866; d. Berlin, May 23, 1952. He studied with his father, the town music director, and with his grandfather, a cantor; then took courses in Dresden and at the Leipzig Cons. with Reinecke and Jadassohn; received the Beethoven Prize in 1887. He conducted a choral society in Danzig (1890–96) and the Bremen Phil. (1896–99). In 1900 he settled in Berlin, where he was made conductor of the Singakademie; was made a member of the Akademie der Künste in 1907, teaching a master class in composition (1913–45); was elected its president in 1934.

WORKS: *Zur Karnevalszeit,* orch. suite; *Liebesfrühling,* overture; *Lebensfreude,* overture; 2 syms.; 2 violin sonatas; 2 piano quintets; Cello Sonata; Piano Trio; Piano Quartet; *Ruth,* oratorio (1909); other choral works, with Orch.: *Amor und Psyche, Totenklage, Sehnsucht,* and *Das Tranenkrüglein*; numerous songs; piano pieces.

BIBL.: P. Hielscher, *G. S.* (Leipzig, 1906); H. Biehle, *G. S.* (Münster, 1925).

Schumann, Walter, American composer; b. N.Y., Oct. 8, 1913; d. Minneapolis, Aug. 21, 1958. He studied law and music at the Univ. of Southern Calif. in Los Angeles. He became associated with radio shows and composed music for films; wrote an opera, *John Brown's Body* (Los Angeles, Sept. 21, 1953). He contributed the famous ominously syncopated theme to the television show *Dragnet,* based on the initial 3 notes of the minor scale.

Schumann-Heink, Ernestine (née **Rössler**), famous Austrian-born American contralto and mezzo-soprano; b. Lieben, near Prague, June 15, 1861; d. Los Angeles, Nov. 17, 1936. Her father was an officer in the Austrian army; her mother, an Italian amateur singer. In 1872 she was sent to the Ursuline Convent in Prague, where she sang in the church choir; after lessons from Marietta von Leclair in Graz, she made her first public appearance there as soloist in Beethoven's 9th Sym. (1876); made her operatic debut at the Dresden Court Opera (Oct. 15, 1878) as Azucena, where she sang until 1882; also continued her studies with Karl Krebs, Franz Wüllner, and others. From 1883 to 1897 she was a member of the Hamburg Opera; appeared with the company on its visit to London's Covent Garden in 1892, where she sang Erda, Fricka, and Brangäne. She was a regular singer at the Bayreuth Festivals from 1896 to 1914; appeared at Covent Garden (1897–1901); also sang with the Berlin Royal Opera. She made her U.S. debut as Ortrud in Chicago on Nov. 7, 1898, a role she chose for her Metropolitan Opera debut in N.Y. on Jan. 9, 1899; canceled her contract with the Berlin Royal Opera in order to remain a member of the Metropolitan Opera (until 1903; then appeared intermittently until 1932); created the role of Klytemnestra in *Elektra* (Dresden, Jan. 25, 1909); made her last operatic appearance as Erda at the Metropolitan on March 11, 1932. She became a naturalized American citizen in 1908. During the last years of her life, she was active mainly as a teacher. Her operatic repertoire included about 150 parts; her voice, of an even quality in all registers, possessed great power, making it peculiarly suitable to Wagnerian roles. She was married in 1882 to Ernst Heink of Dresden, from whom she was later divorced; in 1893 she married the actor Paul Schumann in Hamburg; he died in 1904; she assumed the names of both Schumann and Heink. Her 3rd husband was a Chicago lawyer, William Rapp, Jr., whom she married in 1905 and then subsequently divorced (1914).

BIBL.: M. Lawton, *S.-H., The Last of the Titans* (N.Y., 1928); J. Howard, *Madame E. S.-H.: Her Life and Times* (Sebastopol, Calif., 1990).

Schünemann, Georg, eminent German musicologist and music educator; b. Berlin, March 13, 1884; d. there (suicide), Jan. 2, 1945. He studied at the Stern Cons. in Berlin; played flute in various orchs. in Berlin; then took courses in musicology with Kretzschmar, Friedlaender, Wolf, and others at the Univ. of Berlin; also studied German literature and philosophy there, receiving his Ph.D. in 1907 with the diss. *Geschichte des Dirigierens* (publ. in Leipzig, 1913). In 1919 he joined the faculty of the Univ. of Berlin; was appointed deputy director of the Berlin Hochschule für Musik in 1920, and director in 1932; later held the post of director of the State Musical Instrument Collections. In 1935 he was appointed director of the music division of the Prussian State Library. He took his own life during the darkest stages of World War II.

WRITINGS: *Das Lied der deutschen Kolonisten in Russland* (Berlin, 1923); *Die Musica des Listhenius* (Berlin, 1927); *Geschichte der deutschen Schulmusik* (Leipzig, 1928; 2nd ed., 1931); *Die Musikerziehung,* I: *Die Musik in Kindheit und Jugend, Schule und Volk* (Leipzig, 1930); *C.F. Zelter, der Begründer der preussischen Musikpflege* (Berlin, 1932); *Führer durch die deutsche Chorliteratur* (2 vols., Wolfenbüttel, 1935–36); ed. *Musiker-Handschriften von Bach bis Schumann* (facsimile ed., Berlin, 1936; rev. and publ. in an Eng. tr. by W. Gerstenberg and M. Hürimann, 1968); *C.F. Zelter, Der Mensch und sein Werk* (Berlin, 1937); *Die Violine* (Hamburg, 1940); *Geschichte der Klaviermusik* (Hamburg, 1940; 2nd ed., rev. by H. Gerigk, 1953; 3rd ed., 1956); *Die Singakademie zu Berlin* (Regensburg, 1941); ed. *Ludwig van Beethovens Konversationshefte* (not complete; 3 vols., Berlin, 1941–43).

BIBL.: E. Preussner, "G. S.," *Die Musikforschung,* I (1948).

Schunk, Robert, German tenor; b. Neu-Isenburg, Jan. 5, 1948. He was a pupil of Martin Grundler at the Frankfurt Hochschule für Musik. In 1973 he made his operatic debut as Jack in *The Midsummer Marriage* in Karlsruhe, where he sang until 1975; then appeared in Bonn (1975–77), Dortmund (1977–79), and at the Bayreuth Festivals (from 1977), where he was heard as Siegmund, Melot, Erik, and Walther in *Tannhäuser.* As a guest artist, he appeared in operas in Hamburg, Munich, Vienna, Cologne, Berlin, Geneva, Chicago, and San Francisco. He made his debut at the Metropolitan Opera in N.Y. as Florestan on Dec. 10, 1986. In 1987 he sang for the first time at London's Covent Garden as the Emperor in *Die Frau ohne Schatten.* His other roles include Don Carlos, Weber's Max, Hoffmann, Walther von Stolzing, and Parsifal.

Schuricht, Carl, distinguished German conductor; b. Danzig, July 3, 1880; d. Corseaux-sur-Vevey, Switzerland, Jan. 7, 1967. He studied at home, his father being an organ manufacturer and his mother a pianist. He then took lessons with Humperdinck at the Hochschule für Musik in Berlin, and later in Leipzig with Reger. He began his career conducting in various provincial theaters. In 1911 he became music director in Wiesbaden, and in 1942 principal guest conductor of the Dresden Phil. He made numerous guest conducting appearances in various European music centers, and also conducted in the U.S. for the first time in 1927. After falling out of favor with the Nazis in 1944, he fled to Switzerland, which remained his home until his death. In 1946 he reopened the Salzburg Festival; continued to conduct there and in France. In 1956 he took the Vienna Phil. on its first U.S. tour, sharing his duties with André Cluytens. In 1957 he conducted at the Ravinia Festival with the Chicago Sym. Orch. and at the Tanglewood Festival with the Boston Sym. Orch.; in subsequent years, he regularly conducted the Berlin and Vienna Phils.; also was a frequent guest conductor of the Stuttgart Radio Sym. Orch. He also composed, wrote orch. music, piano pieces, and songs. As a conductor, Schuricht was one of the last representatives of the Austro-German tradition. After concentrating on contemporary music in his early years, he turned to the great masterworks of the Austro-German repertory, his interpretations being noted for their freedom and beauty of expression.

BIBL.: B. Gavoty, *C. S.* (Geneva, 1955).

Schurmann (Schürmann), (Eduard) Gerard, pianist, conductor, and composer of Dutch and Hungarian descent; b. Kertosono, Dutch East Indies, Jan. 19, 1924. His father was an employee at a sugar factory in Java; his mother was a pianist who had studied with Bartók at the Budapest Academy of Music. As war clouds gathered over Southeastern Asia, Schurmann was sent to England in 1937; he went to school in London, and after matriculation joined the Royal Air Force, serving in aircrews on active flying duty. While still in uniform, he gave piano recitals; studied piano with Kathleen Long and composition with Alan Rawsthorne. During his travels in Italy, he took lessons in conducting with Ferrara. The government of the Netherlands offered him the position of cultural attaché at the Dutch Embassy in London; being fluent in the Dutch language, which was his mother tongue in the Dutch East Indies, he accepted. Later, he moved to the Netherlands, where he was active with the radio in Hilversum. He developed a successful career in London as a pianist, conductor, and composer. In 1981 he settled in Hollywood, where he became active as a film composer; also traveled widely as a guest conductor, presenting a comprehensive repertory ranging from Haydn to contemporary composers, including his own works. The structure of Schurmann's music is asymptotic toward tonality; melodic progressions are linear, with the fundamental tonic and dominant often encasing the freely atonal configurations, while dodecaphony assumes the adumbrative decaphonic lines, with 2 notes missing in the tone row. The harmonic texture is acrid, acerbic, and astringent; the styptic tendency is revealed in his predilection for dissonant minor seconds and major sevenths treated as compound units; yet after the needed tension is achieved, the triadic forms are introduced as a sonic emollient. Thanks to this versatility of application, Schurmann achieves a natural felicity in dealing with exotic subjects; his proximity to gamelan-like pentatonicism during his adolescence lends authentic flavor to his use of pentatonic scales; remarkable in his congenial treatment is the set *Chuench'i*, to Eng. trs. of 7 Chinese poems. On the other hand, his intimate knowledge of Eng. music and history enables him to impart a true archaic sentiment to his opera-cantata based on the medieval poem *Piers Plowman*. Schurmann is self-critical in regard to works of his which he deems imperfect; thus, he destroyed his Piano Concerto, which he had played under prestigious auspices with the London Sym. Orch. conducted by Sir Adrian Boult in Cambridge in April 1944.

WORKS: OPERA: *Piers Plowman*, opera-cantata after William Langland (Gloucester Cathedral, Aug. 22, 1980). **ORCH.:** *6 Studies of Francis Bacon*, comprising *Figures in a Landscape, Popes, Isabel, Crucifixion, George and the Bicycle*, and *Self-Portrait* (1968; Dublin, Jan. 7, 1969); *Variants* (1970; Guildford, March 8, 1971); *Attack and Celebration* (1971); Piano Concerto (1972–73; Portsmouth, Nov. 21, 1973); Violin Concerto (1975–78; Liverpool, Sept. 26, 1978); *The Garden of Exile*, cello concerto (1989–90); *Concerto for Orchestra* (1994–95). **CHAMBER:** Violin Sonata (1943); 2 string quartets (1943, 1946); *Duo* for 2 Violins (1950); Wind Quintet (1964; rev. 1976); *Fantasia* (1968); Flute Sonatina (1968); *Serenade* for Violin (1969); *Duo* for Violin and Piano (1984); Quartet for Piano and Strings (1986). **PIANO:** Sonata (1943); *Rotterdam*, suite for 2 Pianos (1944); *Bagatelles* (1945); *Contrasts* (1973); *Leotaurus* (1975); *2 Ballades* (1981–83). **VOCAL:** *Pacific*, 3 songs (1943); *5 Facets* (London, Jan. 20, 1946, Peter Pears tenor, Benjamin Britten pianist); *9 poems of William Blake* (1956); *Chuench'i*, cycle of 7 songs from the Chinese for Voice and Orch. (1966; Harrogate, Aug. 10, 1969); *Summer Is Coming*, madrigal (1970); *The Double Heart*, cantata for Voices (1976); *9 Slovak Folk Songs* for High Voice and Piano or Orch. (1988).

Schuster, Bernhard, German music publisher and composer; b. Berlin, March 26, 1870; d. there, Jan. 13, 1934. After studies in piano, organ, and violin, he was active as a theater conductor. In 1901 he founded the fortnightly review *Die Musik*, which from its inception ranked with the foremost musical journals of Germany; was its ed.-in-chief until 1933. In 1905 he founded the publishing house Schuster und Loeffler (Berlin and Leipzig), which brought out a number of important works on music (the business was acquired by the Stuttgart Deutsche Verlags-Anstalt in 1922). He wrote the operas *Der Jungbrunnen* (Karlsruhe, 1920) and *Der Dieb des Glucks* (Wiesbaden, March 10, 1923); Sym.; String Quartet; sacred choruses; songs.

Schützendorf, family of German musicians, all brothers:

(1) Guido Schützendorf, bass; b. Vught, near 's-Hertogenbosch, the Netherlands, April 22, 1880; d. in Germany, April 1967. He studied at the Cologne Cons. He sang with the German Opera Co., with which he toured the U.S. (1929–30); also sang under the name Schützendorf an der Mayr.

(2) Alfons Schützendorf, bass-baritone; b. Vught, May 25, 1882; d. Weimar, Aug. 1946. He studied in Cologne and with Borgatti in Milan. He sang at the Bayreuth Festivals (1910–12) and at London's Covent Garden (1910); taught at the Essen Folkwangschule (1927–31) and in Berlin (from 1932). He was esteemed for such roles as Wotan, Klingsor, and Telramund.

(3) Gustav Schützendorf, baritone; b. Cologne, 1883; d. Berlin, April 27, 1937. He studied at the Cologne Cons. and in Milan. He made his operatic debut as Don Giovanni in Düsseldorf (1905); after singing in Berlin, Wiesbaden, and Basel, he was a member of the Bavarian Court Opera (later State Opera) in Munich (1914–20) and the Berlin State Opera (1920–22); made his Metropolitan Opera debut in N.Y. as Faninal on Nov. 17, 1922, and remained on its roster until 1935. He married **Grete Stückgold** in 1929.

(4) Leo Schützendorf, bass-baritone; b. Cologne, May 7, 1886; d. Berlin, Dec. 31, 1931. He studied with D'Arnals in Cologne. He made his operatic debut in Düsseldorf (1908); sang in Krefeld (1909–12), Darmstadt (1913–17), Wiesbaden (1917–19), and Vienna (1919–20) and at the Berlin State Opera (1920–29), where he created the role of Wozzeck (Dec. 14, 1925); among his other roles were Faninal, Beckmesser, and Boris Godunov.

Schuyler, Philippa Duke, black American pianist and composer; b. N.Y., Aug. 2, 1931; d. in a helicopter crash in Da Nang Bay, Vietnam, May 9, 1967. By the age of 12, she had written the whimsical *Cockroach Ballet* for Piano and had become the youngest member of ASCAP; at the age of 14, she appeared as piano soloist with the N.Y. Phil. at Lewisohn Stadium in a program that included the scherzo from her "fairy-tale symphony," *Rumpelstiltskin* (July 13, 1946); made her Town Hall debut in N.Y. on May 12, 1953. She traveled to Africa, Europe, South America, and Asia under the auspices of the State Dept., playing command performances for such leaders as Emperor Haile Selassie of Ethiopia and the Queen of Malaya. Of mixed race (her mother was from a wealthy white Texas family; her father, George Schuyler, was the black novelist and newspaper ed.), she was a founder of the Amerasian Foundation to aid children fathered by American soldiers in Vietnam. Most of her more than 60 compositions were for solo piano, many with humorous titles, some inspired by her travels; few were publ. Her last completed composition, *Nile Fantasia* for Piano and Orch., was performed posthumously (N.Y., Sept. 24, 1967). She wrote 5 books about her life and travels: *Adventures in Black and White* (N.Y., 1960), *Who Killed the Congo* (N.Y., 1963), *Jungle Saints: Africa's Heroic Catholic Missionaries* (Rome, 1962), *Kingdom of Dreams* (with her mother, Josephine Schuyler; N.Y., 1966), and *Good Men Die* (N.Y., 1969). Her funeral at St. Patrick's Cathedral in N.Y. received extensive press coverage. In recognition of her musical and literary precocity, Mayor Fiorello LaGuardia declared June 19, 1940, Philippa Schuyler Day at the N.Y. World's Fair.

BIBL.: J. Schuyler, *Philippa the Beautiful American: The Travelled History of a Troubadour* (N.Y., 1969); R. Fisher, "Two Black Prodigies on the Concert Stage," *Musical Prodigies* (N.Y., 1973); K. Talalay, "P.D. S., Pianist/Composer/Writer," *The Black Perspective in Music* (1982).

Schuyt, Nico(laas), Dutch composer; b. Alkmaar, Jan. 2, 1922; d. Amsterdam, Jan. 25, 1992. He received training from Jacob van Domselaer (piano and harmony), Eberhard Rebling (piano), and Willem Hijstek (theory) before completing his studies with Bertus van Lier (composition; 1949–52). From 1964 he was active with Donemus in Amsterdam.

WORKS: ORCH.: Concerto for Youth Orch. (1952–53); *Réveil* (1955); *Corteggio* (1958); *Sinfonia divertente* for Small Orch. (1958); Sonatina for Youth Chamber Orch. (1961); Sonata (1964); *Discorsi capricciosi* for Small Orch. (1965); *Hymnus* for Small Orch. (1966); *Greetings from Holland* for Small Orch.

(1970); *Quasi in modo de valzer* (1973); *Discorsi, discorsi . . .* for Wind Orch. (1979); *Festa seria* (1980); *Down to the Shades* (1985; rev. 1986); *Discorsi ariosi* for Wind Orch. (1988). **CHAMBER:** *Sonata a tre* for Oboe, Bassoon, and Piano (1953–54); *5 Dramatic Nocturnes* for Flute and Piano (1954); *Quatuor de ballet* for Clarinet, Trumpet, Percussion, and Piano (1962); *De belevenissen van Strip-Thijs* for Clarinet, Trumpet, Percussion, and Piano (1962); *Allegro and Passacaglia* for Violin and Piano (1965); *Alla notturna* for 2 Oboes, Oboe d'Amore, and English Horn (1971); *Furies for 4* for Piano Quartet (1975); *Atalanta* for Flute, Violin, Cello, and Harp (1986); piano music. **VOCAL:** *Arkadia* for Mezzo-soprano, Viola, and Cello (1966); *Naar de maan* (To the Moon) for Women's Chorus, Mixed Chorus, and Orch. (1967–68).

Schwann, William (Joseph), pioneering American discographer; b. Salem, Ill., May 13, 1913. He began his career as an organist and choir director in Louisville (Ky.) churches (1930–35); also studied at the Univ. of Louisville (B.A., 1935), Boston Univ. (1935–37), and Harvard Univ. (1937–39), where his teachers included E.B. Hill, Leichtentritt, Merritt, Piston, and Woodworth; also received private organ instruction from E. Power Biggs. He was a music critic for the *Boston Herald* (1937–41), and also ran his own record shop in Cambridge (1939–53). In 1949 he launched his Schwann Record Catalog, the first monthly compilation of available recordings in the world; an invaluable source, it expanded over the years to include not only long-playing records but also tapes and compact discs; special compilations were also issued from time to time. Among Schwann's numerous accolades are honorary D.Mus. degrees from the Univ. of Louisville (1969) and the New England Cons. of Music in Boston (1982).

Schwantner, Joseph, American composer and teacher; b. Chicago, March 22, 1943. He studied classical guitar and composed jazz pieces in his youth before pursuing his training with Bernard Dieter at the American Cons. of Music in Chicago (B.M., 1964) and with Donato and Stout at Northwestern Univ. (M.M., 1966; D.M., 1968). In 1965, 1966, and 1968 he received BMI Student Composer awards. In 1970 he won the 1st Charles Ives Scholarship of the American Academy of Arts and Letters. He taught at the Eastman School of Music in Rochester, N.Y. (from 1970), where he then was a prof. of composition (from 1980). He also was composer-in-residence of the St. Louis Sym. Orch. (1982–85), the Cabrillo Music Festival (1992), and the Sonoklect New Music Festival (1993). In 1974, 1977, 1979, and 1988 he received NEA composer fellowship grants. He held a Guggenheim fellowship in 1978. In 1979 he won the Pulitzer Prize in Music for his orch. score *Aftertones of Infinity.* In 1981 he received a 1st-prize Kennedy Center Freidheim Award. His early works followed the dictates of serialism, but he eventually developed an eclectic style, incorporating tonal materials into harmonically complex works. Interested in new colors, textures, and timbres, he often employs tonalities produced by a wide spectrum of musical instruments.

WORKS: BALLET: *Through Interior Worlds* (Seattle, Oct. 9, 1992; concert version, Nashville, Tenn., Oct. 7, 1994). **ORCH.:** *Modus Caelestis* (1973); *And the Mountains Rising Nowhere* (1977); *Aftertones of Infinity* (1978; N.Y., Jan. 29, 1979); *From a Dark Millennium* (1981); *Distant Runes and Incantations* for Piano and Chamber Orch. (Pasadena, Calif., June 1, 1984); *Someday Memories* (1984; St. Louis, May 16, 1985); *A Sudden Rainbow* (1984; St. Louis, Jan. 31, 1986); *Toward Light* (1986; Canton, Ohio, March 15, 1987); *From Afar,* fantasy for Guitar and Orch. (1987; N.Y., Jan. 8, 1988); Piano Concerto (N.Y., July 8, 1988); *Freeflight* (1989); *A Play of Shadows,* fantasy for Flute and Orch. (N.Y., April 16, 1990); Percussion Concerto (1991; N.Y., Jan. 6, 1995). **CHAMBER:** *Diaphonia Intervallum* for Alto Saxophone and Chamber Ensemble (1965); *Chronicon* for Bassoon and Piano (1968); *Consortium I* for Flute, Clarinet, Violin, Viola, and Cello (1970) and *II* for Flute, Clarinet, Violin, Cello, Piano, and Percussion (1971); *Elixir* for Flute and 5 Players (1974); *Autumn Canticles* for Violin, Cello, and Piano (1974); *In Aeternum* for Cello and 4 Players (1975); *Canticle of the Evening Bells* for Flute and 12 Players (1976); *Wind Willow, Whisper* for Chamber Ensemble (1980); *Through Interior Worlds* for Chamber Ensemble (1981); *Music of Amber* for Flute, Clarinet, Violin, Cello, Percussion, and Piano (1981); *Velocities* for Marimba (1990). **VOCAL:** *Wild Angels of the Open Hills,* song cycle for Soprano, Flute, Harp, and Chamber Ensemble (1977); *Sparrows* for Soprano and Chamber Ensemble (1979); *2 Poems of Agueda Pizarro* for Voice and Piano (1981); *New Morning for the World: Daybreak of Freedom* for Speaker and Orch., after Martin Luther King, Jr. (1982); *Magabunda (Witchnomad),* song cycle for Soprano and Orch. (1983); *Dreamcaller,* song cycle for Soprano, Violin, and Chamber Orch. (St. Paul, Minn., May 11, 1984).

Schwartz, Elliott (Shelling), American composer, teacher, and writer on music; b. N.Y., Jan. 19, 1936. He studied composition with Luening and Beeson at Columbia Univ. (A.B., 1957; M.A., 1958; Ed.D., 1962); also had private instruction in piano from Alton Jones and in composition from Creston; likewise studied composition at the Bennington (Vt.) Composers Conference (summers, 1961–66). After teaching at the Univ. of Mass. in Amherst (1960–64), he joined the faculty of Bowdoin College in Brunswick, Maine (1964); was assoc. prof. (1970–75) and then prof. (from 1975) and chairman of its music dept. (1975–87); also held appointments as Distinguished Univ. Visiting Prof. (1985–86) and part-time prof. of composition (1989–92) at Ohio State Univ., and as visiting Bye fellow at Robinson College, Cambridge, England (1993). He was vice president of the American Music Center (1982–88), chairman of the American Soc. of Univ. Composers (1984–88), and president of the College Music Soc. (1989–90). In his compositions, he develops the Satiesque notions of unfettered license leading to a completely unbuttoned state.

WRITINGS: *The Symphonies of Ralph Vaughan Williams* (Amherst, Mass., 1964); ed. with B. Childs, *Contemporary Composers on Contemporary Music* (N.Y., 1967); *Electronic Music: A Listener's Guide* (N.Y., 1973; 2nd ed., rev., 1976); *Music: Ways of Listening* (N.Y., 1982); with D. Godfrey, *Music Since 1945: Issues, Materials, and Literature* (N.Y., 1993).

WORKS: DRAMATIC: *Elevator Music* for Any Instruments (1967); *Areas* for Flute, Clarinet, Violin, Cello, Trombone, Piano, and 2 to 4 Dancers (1968); *Gibson Hall* for Keyboards and Synthesizer (1969); Music for Soloist and Audience (1970); *Telly* for 5 Woodwind or Brass, 4 Percussion, 3 Television Sets, and Tape (1972); *A Dream of Beats and Bells* for Piano and Audience (1977); *California Games* for 4 to 6 Players, Tape, and Audience (1978); *Radio Games,* duet for Performers in a Radio Studio and Audience (1980). **ORCH.:** *Music* for Orch. and Tape (1965); *Texture* for Chamber Orch. (1966); *Magic Music* for Piano and Orch. (1968); *Island* (1970); *Dream Overture* (1972); *The Harmony of Maine* for Synthesizer and Orch. (1974); *Eclipse III* for Chamber Orch. (1975); *Janus* for Piano and Orch. (1976); *Chamber Concerto I* for Double Bass and 15 Instruments (1977) and *III* for Piano and Small Orch. (1977); *Zebra* for Youth Orch. and Tape (1981); *Celebrations/Reflections: A Time Warp* (1985); *4 Ohio Portraits* (Columbus, Ohio, April 12, 1986); *Timepiece 1794* for Chamber Orch. (1994); *Equinox: Concerto for Orchestra* (1994). **CHAMBER:** Oboe Quartet (1963); Trio for Flute, Cello, and Piano (1964); *Music for Napoleon and Beethoven* for Trumpet, Piano, and 2 Tapes (1969); Septet for Voice, Piano, and 5 Instruments (1969); *Eclipse I* for 10 Instruments (1971); Octet (1972); *Echo Music II* for Wind Quartet and Tape (1974); *A Bowdoin Anthology* for Narrator, Instruments, and Tape (1976); *Chamber Concerto II* for Clarinet and 9 Instruments (1977), *IV* for Saxophone and 10 Instruments (1981), and *V* for Bassoon, Strings, and Piano (1992); *Bellagio Variations* for String Quartet (1980); *Octagon* for 8 Percussion (1984); *Purple Transformation* for Wind Ensemble (1987); *Memorial in 2 Parts* for Violin and Piano (1988); *Northern Pines* for 2 Oboes, Clarinet, 2 Horns, and Piano (1988); *Palindromes* for Cello and Percussion (1989); *A Garden for RKB* for Violin, Clarinet, and Piano (1990); *Elan* for Flute, Clarinet, Violin, Cello, and Piano (1991); *Rows Garden* for Woodwind Quintet (1993); *Spaces* for Piano and Percussion (1995).

Schwartz, Francis, American composer, teacher, and music critic; b. Altoona, Pa., March 10, 1940. He studied piano with Lonny Epstein, theory with Giannini, and chamber music with Persinger at the Juilliard School of Music in N.Y. (B.S., 1961; M.S., 1962) and with Daniel Charles at the Univ. of Paris (Ph.D. in musical aesthetics, 1981). In 1965 he went to Puerto Rico; was music critic of the *San Juan Star* (1966–81); concurrently taught at the Univ. of Puerto Rico, where he was later chairman of the music dept. (1971–80) and Director of Cultural Affairs (1981–86); was also composer-in-residence at the Centro de Investigaciones de Communición Masiva y Tecnología in Buenos Aires (1975) and visiting prof. of experimental music at the Univ. of Paris (1977–78). He wrote with María Luisa Muñoz the book *El mundo de la música* (1982). Schwartz was a key figure in the introduction of contemporary music in Puerto Rico and the proliferation of the avant-garde in Paris; in Puerto Rico, he was active with Grupo Fluxus and the 2nd Biennal of Contemporary Music; among his prestigious commissions was the "Commande d'État" from the French government to compose a work for the group 2E2M. In 1986 he was made a Chevalier of the Order of the Arts and Letters of France. His compositions employ a broad range of avant-garde techniques; in many, he cultivates multimedia forms, in which music, stage, and electronics are combined.

WORKS: DRAMATIC: *Auschwitz* for Tape, Lights, Odors, and Movement (San Juan, May 15, 1968); *My Name's Caligula, What's Yours?* for 3 Actor-Instrumentalists (1970; N.Y., March 3, 1975)); *Geo-flux*, electronic ballet (1974); *Time, Sound, and the Hooded Man* for Actors, Tape, and Videotape (Buenos Aires, July 16, 1975); Is There Sex in Heaven? (1976); *Hommage à K . . .* (1978); *Mon oeuf* for Tape, Videotape, Odors, Sculpture, and Audience (1979); *Musique pour Juvisi* for Tape, Videotape, and Synthesizer (1979; in collaboration with C. Miereanu); *Cosmos* (1980); *La guerra de las flores* (1982). **ORCH.:** *Plegaria* (1973); *Yo protesto* (San Juan, March 23, 1974); *The Tropical Trek of Tristan Trimble* (1975); *Amistad III* (1979); *Un sourire festif* (1981); *Gestos* for Orch. and Audience (1983); *Fantasía de la Libertad* (1986). **CHAMBER:** *Ergo sum* for Flute and Tape (1979); *Eros by Any Other Name* for Double Bass and Piano (1983); *I've Got (Poly) Rhythm* for Guitar, Body Percussion, and Vocal Sounds (1984); *Quasi una Sonatina . . . devero* for Violin and Piano (1985); *Que reine la Paz* for 4 Guitars (1987); *El Trango del último momento* for Piano or Harpsichord (1988); *Trio para Edgar Allan Poe* for Violin, Cello, and Piano (1988). **VOCAL:** *Canibal-Caliban* for Voice and Variable Ensemble (1976); *4 + 3 = Paris VIII*, didactic music for Voice, Violin, Guitar, Alto Saxophone, Trumpet, Trombone, and Percussion (1978); *Grimaces* for Voice, Flute, Alto Saxophone, Double Bass, Percussion, Tape, and Audience (1984); *Tres canciones para el futuro* for Flute or Oboe, Soprano or Tenor, 2 Percussion, and Audience (1985); *The night of the fiery angels* for Flute, Oboe, Clarinet, Horn, and Audience (1987); *Dos Canciones sobre textos de Schopenhauer* for Soprano and Synthesizer (1988); *Dulce Libertad* for Soprano, Violin, Cello, and Piano (1988); *El Sueño de Bolivar* for Soprano, Clarinet, Violin, and Piano (1988); other songs with Instruments or Tape.

Schwarz, Boris, distinguished Russian-born American violinist, teacher, and musicologist; b. St. Petersburg, March 26, 1906; d. N.Y., Dec. 31, 1983. He went to Berlin as a youth; at the age of 14, made his debut as a violinist in Hannover, accompanied at the piano by his father, Joseph Schwarz. He took violin lessons with Flesch in Berlin (1922–25) and Thibaud and Capet in Paris (1925–26); subsequently took courses in musicology with Sachs, Schering, and Wolf at the Univ. of Berlin (1930–36). In 1936 he emigrated to the U.S., becoming a naturalized American citizen in 1943. He completed his musicological studies with Lang at Columbia Univ. (Ph.D., 1950, with the diss. *French Instrumental Music Between the Revolutions, 1789–1830*; publ. in N.Y., 1950; 2nd ed., rev., 1983). After serving as concertmaster of the Indianapolis Sym. Orch. (1937–38) and playing in the NBC Sym. Orch. in N.Y. (1938–39), he was a prof. of music at Queens College of the City Univ. of N.Y. (1941–76), where he founded (1945) the Queens College Orch. Soc., conducting annual concerts of symphonic and choral music; also was chairman of its music dept. (1948–51; 1952–55). In 1959–60 he held a Guggenheim fellowship. A trilingual writer, he was fluent in Russian, German, and English; contributed numerous articles, mostly on Russian music, to *The New Grove Dictionary of Music and Musicians* (1980) and to various music journals. His valuable study, *Music and Musical Life in Soviet Russia, 1917–1970* (N.Y., 1972; 2nd ed., rev., 1983), was highly critical of certain aspects of the musical situation in Russia; it won an award from ASCAP as the best book on music criticism. His 2nd book, *Great Masters of the Violin* (N.Y., 1983), is valuable for its accuracy of documentation.

BIBL.: M. Brown, ed., *Russian and Soviet Music: Essays for B. S.* (Ann Arbor, 1984).

Schwarz, Gerard (Ralph), esteemed American conductor; b. Weehawken, N.J., Aug. 19, 1947. He commenced trumpet lessons when he was 8; after attending the National Music Camp in Interlochen, Mich. (summers, 1958–60), he studied at N.Y.'s High School of Performing Arts; also received trumpet instruction from William Vacchiano (1962–68), and completed his training at the Juilliard School (B.S., 1972). He played in the American Brass Quintet (1965–73) and the American Sym. Orch. in N.Y. (1966–72); also made appearances as a conductor. After serving as co-principal trumpet of the N.Y. Phil. (1972–75), he pursued a conducting career. He was music director of the Waterloo Festival in Stanhope, N.J., and of its music school at Fairleigh Dickinson Univ. (from 1975), of the 92nd St. Y Chamber Sym. (later N.Y. Chamber Sym.) in N.Y. (from 1977), and of the Los Angeles Chamber Orch. (1978–86). He also appeared widely as a guest conductor; one such engagement, at the Mostly Mozart Festival in N.Y. in 1980, led to his appointment as its music adviser in 1982; he then served as its music director (from 1984). He also was music adviser (1983–85) and principal conductor (from 1985) of the Seattle Sym. Orch. In 1989 he received the Alice M. Ditson Award for Conductors. In 1993 he stepped down as music director of the Waterloo Festival. From 1993 to 1996 he was artistic advisor of the Tokyu Bunkamura, a Tokyo cultural center. Schwarz is duly recognized as one of America's outstanding conductors, and a musician of uncommon attainments. He has won especial critical accolades for his discerning and innovative programs; his vast repertoire ranges from early music to the contemporary era.

Schwarz, Hanna, German mezzo-soprano; b. Hamburg, Aug. 15, 1943. She studied in Hamburg, Hannover, and Essen. In 1970 she made her operatic debut as Maddalena in *Rigoletto* in Hannover. In 1973 she became a member of the Hamburg State Opera. She sang with the Bavarian State Opera in Munich for the first time in 1974. In 1975 she made her debut at the Bayreuth Festival as Flosshilde in *Das Rheingold*, and continued to sing there during the next decade. In 1977 she made her U.S. debut as Fricka in *Das Rheingold* at the San Francisco Opera, and also appeared as Preziosilla at the Paris Opéra. In 1978 she sang Cherubino at the Deutsche Oper in Berlin. On Feb. 24, 1979, she appeared as Countess Geschwitz in the first complete performance of *Lulu* at the Paris Opéra. That same year she also made her debut at the Salzburg Festival as a soloist in Beethoven's 9th Sym. In 1980 she sang for the first time at London's Covent Garden as Waltraute and returned to the Salzburg Festival to sing Juana in a concert performance of Krenek's *Karl V.* In 1992 she made her first operatic stage appearance at the Salzburg Festival when she sang Herodias. As a concert artist, she sang widely in Europe and North America.

Schwarz, Joseph, German baritone; b. Riga, Oct. 10, 1880; d. Berlin, Nov. 10, 1926. He studied in Berlin with Alexander Heinemann, and then continued his training at the Vienna

Cons. In 1900 he made his operatic debut in *Aida* in Linz. Following engagements in Riga, Graz, and St. Petersburg, he sang in Vienna, principally at the Volksoper and then at the Court Opera (1909–15). From 1915 he was a principal member of the Berlin Royal (later State) Opera. He also sang at the Chicago Opera (1921–25) and at London's Covent Garden as Rigoletto (1924).

Schwarz, Paul, Austrian tenor; b. Vienna, June 30, 1887; d. Hamburg, Dec. 24, 1980. He sang in Bielitz and Vienna (1909–12). From 1923 to 1933 he was a member of the Hamburg Opera, where he gained success in buffo roles. He made guest appearances in Berlin, Paris, Amsterdam, and London (Covent Garden debut as Monostatos, 1936). During World War II, he lived in the U.S. After the War, he resumed his career in Europe, singing until 1949.

Schwarz, Rudolf, Austrian-born English conductor; b. Vienna, April 29, 1905; d. London, Jan. 30, 1994. He studied violin. He joined the Düsseldorf Opera as a répétiteur (1923), and then made his conducting debut there (1924); subsequently was a conductor at the Karlsruhe Opera (1927) until being removed in 1933 by the Nazis as a Jew. After serving as music director of the Judischer Kulturbund in Berlin (1936–39), he was imprisoned (1939–40), and then interred at the Belsen concentration camp (1943–45). Following his liberation, he settled in England, becoming a naturalized British subject in 1952. He was conductor of the Bournemouth Municipal Orch. (1947–51) and music director of the City of Birmingham Sym. Orch. (1951–57); after serving as chief conductor of the BBC Sym. Orch. in London (1957–62), he was principal conductor (1964–67) and artistic director (1967–73) of the Northern Sinfonia in Newcastle upon Tyne. He was made a Commander of the Order of the British Empire in 1973.

Schwarz, Vera, Austrian soprano; b. Zagreb, July 10, 1889; d. Vienna, Dec. 4, 1964. She studied voice and piano in Vienna, where she appeared in operettas. She went to Hamburg in 1914 and to Berlin in 1917; toured in South America. In 1939 she went to Hollywood, where she became a vocal instructor; in 1948 she returned to Austria; gave courses at the Mozarteum in Salzburg. Her best roles were Carmen and Tosca.

Schwarzkopf, Dame (Olga Maria) Elisabeth (Friederike), celebrated German-born English soprano; b. Jarotschin, near Posen, Dec. 9, 1915. She studied with Lula Mysz-Gmeiner at the Berlin Hochschule für Musik; made her operatic debut as a Flower Maiden in Parsifal at the Berlin Stadtische Oper (April 17, 1938); then studied with Maria Ivogun while continuing on its roster, appearing in more important roles from 1941. In 1942 she made her debut as a lieder artist in Vienna, and also sang for the first time at the State Opera there as Zerbinetta, remaining on its roster until the Nazis closed the theater in 1944. Having registered as a member of the German Nazi Party in 1940, Schwarzkopf had to be de-Nazified by the Allies after the end of World War II. In 1946 she rejoined the Vienna State Opera and appeared as Donna Elvira during its visit to London's Covent Garden in 1947; subsequently sang at Covent Garden regularly until 1951. In 1947 she made her first appearance at the Salzburg Festival as Susanna; also sang regularly at Milan's La Scala (1948–63). Furtwängler invited her to sing in his performance of the Beethoven 9th Sym. at the reopening celebrations of the Bayreuth Festival in 1951. She then created the role of Anne Trulove in Stravinsky's *The Rake's Progress* in Venice on Sept. 11, 1951. On Oct. 25, 1953, she gave her first recital at N.Y.'s Carnegie Hall; made her U.S. operatic debut as the Marschallin with the San Francisco Opera on Sept. 20, 1955. On Oct. 13, 1964, she made her belated Metropolitan Opera debut in N.Y. in the same role, continuing on its roster until 1966. In 1975 she made a farewell tour of the U.S. as a concert singer. She married **Walter Legge** in 1953 and became a naturalized British subject. She ed. his memoir, *On and Off the Record* (N.Y., 1982; 2nd ed., 1988). In 1992 she was made a Dame Commander of the Order of the British Empire. In addition to her acclaimed Mozart and Strauss roles, she was also admired in Viennese operetta. As an interpreter of lieder, she was incomparable.

BIBL.: A. Sanders and J. Steane, *E. S.: A Career on Record* (Portland, Oreg., 1996).

Schweinitz, Wolfgang von, German composer; b. Hamburg, Feb. 7, 1953. After studies with Esther Ballou at the American Univ. in Washington, D.C. (1968–69), he pursued his training with Ernst Klussmann (1971–73) and György Ligeti (1973–75) at the Hamburg Hochschule für Musik. In 1975–76 he worked at the Center for Computer Research in Music and Acoustics at Stanford Univ. in Calif. He was a resident at the German Academy in Rome in 1978–79. In 1986 he won the 1st annual Schneider-Schott prize for young German composers. In 1988 he received the Plöner Hindemith-Preis. Schweinitz established his name as a composer with his song cycle *Papiersterne* (1980–81), which premiered at the Berlin Festival on Sept. 22, 1981. His most ambitious score is the "azione musicale" *Patmos* (1986–89), a complete setting of the book of *Revelation.* It was first performed in Munich on April 28, 1990.

WORKS: DRAMATIC: *Patmos,* "azione musicale" (1986–89; Munich, April 28, 1990). **ORCH.:** 2 syms. (1973, 1974); *Mozart-Variationen* (1976); Piano Concerto (1979); Konzertouvertüre (1979–80; Darmstadt, July 5, 1980); . . . *wir aber singen,* symphonic cycle for Cello and Orch. (I, Kiel, Sept. 6, 1992; II, Hagen, Sept. 5, 1995; III, 1996). **CHAMBER:** String Quartet (1977); *Adagio* for English Horn, Basset Horn, Horn, and Bassoon (1983); *Englische Serenade* for 2 Clarinets, 2 Bassoons, and 2 Horns (1984; Hamburg, March 27, 1985); *Musik* for 4 Saxophones (1985; Witten, April 27, 1986); *Morgenlied* for Flute (1990); *Franz* [Schubert] *and Morton* [Feldman] *Singing Together in Harmony (With the Lord Himself Enjoying His Bells,* 12 stanzas for Violin, Cello, and Piano (1993–94). **KEYBOARD: PIANO:** *3 Etudien* (1983–84; Hamburg, Feb. 24, 1984). **ORGAN:** *7 Patmos Souvenirs* (1990). **VOCAL:** *Die Brücke* for Tenor, Baritone, and Small Orch. (1978); *Papiersterne,* song cycle for Mezzo-soprano and Piano (1980–81; Berlin, Sept. 22, 1981); *Mass* for Soloists, Chorus, and Orch. (1981–83; Berlin, July 8, 1984); *6 Alte Lieder* for Children's Chorus, 2 Soprano Recorders, 2 Alto Recorders, 2 Trumpets, and Percussion (1984).

Schweitzer, Albert, famous Alsatian theologian, philosopher, medical missionary, organist, and music scholar; b. Kaysersberg, Jan. 14, 1875; d. Lambaréné, Gabon, Sept. 4, 1965. He studied piano as a child with his father, a Lutheran pastor; then began organ studies at 8, his principal mentors being Eugen Munch in Mulhouse, Ernst Munch in Strasbourg, and Widor in Paris. He pursued training in philosophy (Ph.D., 1899) and theology (Ph.D., 1900) at the Univ. of Strasbourg; also received instruction in theory from Jacobsthal in Strasbourg and in piano from Philipp and M. Jäell in Paris. In 1896 he became organist of the Bach Concerts in Strasbourg; also joined the faculty of the Univ. there in 1902, where he also completed his full medical course (M.D., 1912); concurrently was organist of the Bach Soc. in Paris (1905–13). In 1913 he went to Lambaréné in the Gabon province of French Equatorial Africa, and set up a jungle hospital, which subsequently occupied most of his time and energy. However, he continued to pursue his interest in music, theology, and philosophy, making occasional concert tours as an organist in Europe to raise funds for his hospital work among the African natives. In 1952 he was awarded the Nobel Peace Prize, the only professional musician to hold this prestigious award. His philosophical and theological writings had established his reputation as one of the foremost thinkers of his time. In the field of music he distinguished himself as the author of one of the most important books on Bach, greatly influencing the interpretation of Bach's music, and contributing to the understanding of Bach's symbolic treatment of various musical devices. He ed. *J.S. Bach: Complete Organ Works: A Critico-practical Edition* (N.Y.; vols. I–V, 1912–14, with C. Widor; vols. VI–VIII, 1954–67, with E. Nies-Berger).

WRITINGS: *Eugène Munch, 1857–1898* (Mulhouse, 1898); *J.S. Bach, le musicien-poète* (Paris, 1905; aug. Ger. eds., 1908, 1915; Eng. tr. by E. Newman, 2 vols., Leipzig, 1911); *Deutsche und französische Orgelbaukunst und Orgelkunst* (Leipzig, 1906; 2nd ed., 1927); *Aus meiner Kindheit und Jugendzeit* (Bern and Munich, 1924; Eng. tr., 1924, as *Memoirs of Childhood and Youth*); *Aus meinem Leben und Denken* (Leipzig, 1931; Eng. tr., 1933); also various theological and philosophical books. A complete German ed. of his writings was ed. by R. Grabs (5 vols., Munich, 1974).

BIBL.: C. Campion, *A. S.: Philosopher, Theologian, Musician, Doctor* (N.Y., 1928); J. Regester, *A. S.: The Man and His Work* (N.Y., 1931); M. Ratter, *A. S.* (London, 1935; rev. ed., 1950); G. Sutherland, "The S.ian Heresy," *Music & Letters*, XXIII (1942); A. Roback, ed., *The A. S. Jubilee Book* (Cambridge, Mass., 1946); H. Hagedorn, *Prophet in the Wilderness: The Story of A. S.* (N.Y., 1947); O. Kraus, *A. S.: His Work and His Philosophy* (N.Y., 1947); G. Seaver, *A. S.: The Man and His Mind* (London, 1947); R. Grabs, *A. S.: Weg und Werk eines Menschenfreundes* (Berlin, 1953); R. Sonner, *S. und die Orgelbewegung* (Colmar, 1955); W. Picht, *The Life and Thought of A. S.* (N.Y., 1965); E. Jacobi, *A. S. und die Musik* (Wiesbaden, 1975); S. Hanheide, *Johann Sebastian Bach im Verständis A. S.s* (Munich, 1990); K. and A. Bergel, eds., *A. S. and Alice Ehlers: A Friendship in Letters* (Lanham, Md., 1991); H. Schützeichel, *Die Konzerttätigkeit A. S.s* (Bern, 1991); idem, *Die Orgel im Leben und Denken A. S.s* (Kleinblittersdorf, 1991); M. Murray, *A. S., Musician* (Aldershot, 1994).

Schwerkė, Irving, American writer on music; b. Appleton, Wis., July 21, 1893; d. Neenah, Wis., Nov. 3, 1975. He studied at Charleston (S.C.) College and the Univ. of Wisc.; in 1920, went to Europe, continuing his education at the Univ. of Madrid, and taking piano lessons with Rosenthal. He went to Paris in 1921, where he was active as a pianist, teacher, and a music and drama critic for the Paris *Tribune* (until 1934) and a Paris correspondent of the *Musical Digest* of N.Y. (1922–29), the *Musical Courier* of N.Y. (1932–41), the *Nuova Italia musicale* of Rome, and the *Musical Times* of London; organized the first European festival of American music in Bad Homburg (1931). In 1941 he settled in Wisconsin as a teacher and writer. In 1954 the French government made him a Chevalier of the Légion d'honneur. He publ. *Kings Jazz and David* (Paris, 1927), *Alexandre Tansman: compositeur polonais* (Paris, 1931), and *Views and Interviews* (Paris, 1936). He contributed an account of his Paris years in H. Ford's *The Left Bank* (University Park, Pa., 1973).

Schwertsik, Kurt, Austrian composer, horn player, and teacher; b. Vienna, June 25, 1935. He studied composition with Marx and Schiske at the Vienna Academy of Music (1949–57), where he also received training in horn. From 1955 to 1959 he played horn in the Niederösterreichisches Tonkünstler-Orch. in Vienna. With Cerha, he founded the new music ensemble "die reihe" in Vienna in 1958. He continued his training with Stockhausen in Darmstadt and Cologne (1959–62), and held a bursary with the Austrian Cultural Inst. in Rome (1960–61). From 1962 to 1968 he again played horn in the Niederösterreichisches Tonkünstler-Orch. He also studied analysis with Polnauer (1964–65). While serving as a visiting teacher of composition at the Univ. of Calif. at Riverside (1966), he pursued his studies in analysis with Jonas. In 1968 he became a horn player in the Vienna Sym. Orch. He also taught composition at the Vienna Cons. from 1979. A skillful and imaginative composer, he explores in his works many new paths in synthesizing the traditional with the contemporary.

WORKS: DRAMATIC: *Der lange Weg zur grossen Mauer*, opera (1974; Ulm, May 13, 1975); *Walzerträume (. . . als das Tanzen noch geholfen hat)*, ballet (1976; Cologne, Feb. 16, 1977; also as the ballet or set of 3 orch. suites, *Wiener Chronik 1848*, 1976–77); *Ur-Faust*, music to Goethe's play (1976; Mattersburg, Feb. 2, 1977); *Kaiser Joseph und die Bahnwärters-Tochter*, music to Herzmanovsky-Orlando's play (1977); *Das Märchen von Fanferlieschen Schönefusschen*, opera (1982; Stuttgart, Nov. 24, 1983); *Macbeth*, dance theater (Heidelberg, Feb. 10, 1988); *Die verlorene Wut*, Singspiel (ORF, Dec. 26, 1989); *Das Friedensbankett*, operetta (1990); *Frida Kahlo*, ballet (1991; Bremen, Feb. 8, 1992); *Ulrichslegende*, music for an opera (1992); *Café Museum oder die Erleuchtung*, opera (Deutschlandsberg, Oct. 9, 1993); *Nietzsche*, ballet (1994); *Der ewige Frieden*, operetta (1994; Bonn, Jan. 8, 1995). **ORCH.:** 4 syms.: No. 1, *. . . für Audifax und Abachum* (1963–70), No. 2, *Draculas Haus- und Hofmusik: Eine transsylvanische Symphonie* for Strings (1968), No. 3, *Symphonie im Mob-Stil* (1971), and No. 4, *Irdische Klänge* (Vienna, April 16, 1980); Alphorn Concerto "in the Celtic manner" (1975; Vienna, May 15, 1977); Violin Concerto (Graz, Oct. 9, 1977); *Epilog zu Rosamunde* (Vienna, May 31, 1978); *Tag- und Nachtweisen* (Salzburg, Aug. 25, 1978); Concerto for Guitar and Small Orch. (1979); *Instant Music* for Flute and Wind Orch. (1981; Vienna, Nov. 28, 1982; rev. 1983); *Der irdischen Klänge 2. Teil, nämlich Fünf Naturstücke* (1984; Vienna, Dec. 4, 1985); Timpani Concerto, *Irdische Klänge 4* (1987–88; Vienna, July 5, 1988); Double Bass Concerto, *ein emfindsames Konzert* (Heidelberg, April 29, 1989); *Mit den Riesenstiefeln, Irdische Klänge 5* (1991; Vienna, April 24, 1992); *Uluru (in mitten der Irdischen Klänge)* (Vienna, Nov. 19, 1992); *Baumgesänge* (Vienna, Nov. 16, 1992). **CHAMBER:** Horn Sonata (1952); *Duo and Double* for Violin and Piano (1957); Trio for Violin, Horn, and Piano (1960); String Quartet (1961); *Salotto romano* for 12 Bass Instruments (1961); *Liebesträume* for 7 Instruments (1963); *Eichendorff Quintet* for Winds (1964); *Proviant* for Wind Sextet (1965); *5 Nocturnes* for Cello and Piano (1966); *Querschnitt durch eine Operette* for Wind Quintet (1966); *Österreichisches Quodlibet* for Chamber Ensemble (Montreal, April 28, 1967); *Musik vom Mutterland Mu* for 11 Instruments (1974); *Skizzen und Entwürfe* for String Quartet (Hamburg, Sept. 13, 1974); *Twilight Music: A Celtic Serenade* for Octet (1976; Hall, Aug. 25, 1977); *Kleine Blaumusik* for 2 Trumpets and 2 Trombones (Graz, Oct. 16, 1977); *Bagatellen* for Piano Trio (Vienna, Dec. 12, 1979); *Sotto Voce: Gedämpfte Unterhaltung* for Flute, Violin, Cello, and Guitar (South German Radio, Stuttgart, Oct. 3, 1980); *Blechpartie im neuesten Geschmack* for Brass Quintet (Innsbruck, Nov. 8, 1982; rev. 1986); *Fantasy Piece* for Trumpet and Piano (1982); *Hornpostille*, 4 pieces for 4 Horns (Vienna, Sept. 1983); *Neues von Eu-Sirius* for 2 Violins and Viola (Vienna, Oct. 2, 1988); *Am Ende Steht ein Marsch* for Wind Octet (Vienna, March 4, 1991); *3 späte Liebeslieder* for Cello and Piano (Vienna, Oct. 17, 1992); *Möbelmusik-Klassich* for 2 Violins, Viola, and Double Bass (1993); *Wake* for String Quartet (1994). **VOCAL:** *Shâl-i-mâr*, 7 songs for Baritone and Orch. (1962–72; rev. version, Vienna, Oct. 24, 1992); *Stückwerk* for Soprano and Chamber Orch. (1966; Vienna, Jan. 30, 1967); *Kurt Schwertsiks lichte Momente* for Singers and Instrumentalists (1971); *Brautigan Songbook* for Voice and Piano (1971); *Manchmal vertrödelt Christa S. den Tag* for Voice and Instrumentalists (1975); *Ich sein Blumenbein*, 11 songs for Voice and Piano (Vienna, June 1980; also for Voice, Guitar, and Keyboards); *Starckdeutsche Lieder und Tänze* for Baritone and Orch. (1980–82; Vienna, Feb. 13, 1986); *Kurze Geschichte der Bourgeoise* for Chorus (1981); *. . . & was ist dann Friede?*, 6 songs for Voice and Guitar (1983); *Starker Tobak*, cantata for Soprano and 7 Instruments (Vienna, Sept. 13, 1983); *Iba di gaunz oaman Fraun*, 8 songs for Soprano, Piano, Bass, and Drums (1983; Vienna, Jan. 1984); *Cinq chansons cryptiques* for Voice and Piano (1985; Vienna, June 1986); *Gute Nacht, Guten Morgen*, 8 songs for Voice and Piano (1985; Vienna, Oct. 26, 1986); *Das Leben*, 8 songs for Mezzo-soprano and Celtic Naturehorn (Bregrenz, Aug. 21, 1986); *Gedichte an Ljuba*, 5 songs for Voice and Piano (1986; Vienna, Feb. 5, 1987); *Es friert zuweilen auch den Geist* for Voice and Piano (1991); *Human Existence* for Soprano and Ensemble (Dartington, Aug. 17, 1992); *Singt meine Schwäne* for Soprano and Ensemble (Dartington, Aug. 17, 1992); *Der Herr weis was der Wil* for Soprano and Ensemble (Dartington, Aug. 17, 1992); *The Fox and the Magpie* for Tenor, Baritone, Soprano Saxophone, Horn, Bassoon, and Piano (Syndey, July 18, 1994).

Schwieger, Hans, German-born American conductor; b. Cologne, June 15, 1906. He studied in Cologne. He was assistant conductor at the Berlin State Opera (1927–30), at the Kassel Opera (1930–31), in Mainz (1932–33), and in Danzig (1936–37). In 1937 he went to Japan, where he conducted the Tokyo Sym. Orch. In 1938 he settled in the U.S.; became a naturalized American citizen in 1944. He organized and conducted the Southern Sym. Orch. in Columbia, S.C. (1938–41); then was conductor of the Fort Wayne Phil. (1944–48). From 1948 to 1971 he was conductor of the Kansas City (Mo.) Phil.; then filled engagements as a guest conductor in Europe.

Sciarrino, Salvatore, Italian composer; b. Palermo, April 4, 1947. He was 12 when he began to compose under the tutelage of Antonino Titione; also received some guidance from Evangelisti. After studies with Turi Belfiore (1964), he attended Evangelisti's electronic music sessions at the Accademia di Santa Cecilia in Rome (1969). He taught at the Milan Cons. (from 1974); also served as artistic director of the Teatro Comunale in Bologna (1977–80). His music reveals an innovative approach to traditional forms; in some works he utilizes aleatoric procedures.

WORKS: OPERAS: *Amore e Psiche* (Milan, March 2, 1973); *Aspern* (Florence, June 8, 1978); *Cailles en sarchophage* (Venice, Sept. 26, 1979); *Vanitas* (Milan, Dec. 11, 1981); *Lohengrin* (Milan, Jan. 15, 1983); *Perseo e Andromeda* (1990; Stoccardo, Jan. 27, 1991). **ORCH.:** *Berceuse* (1967; Venice, Sept. 13, 1969); *Da a da da* (Venice, Sept. 12, 1970); *Sonata da camera* (Rome, Oct. 31, 1971); *Grande sonata da camera* (1971; Paris, Feb. 21, 1972); *Rondo* for Flute and Orch. (1972; Naples, April 6, 1973); *Romanza* for Viola d'Amore and Orch. (Florence, Oct. 20, 1973); *Variazioni* for Cello and Orch. (Saarbrücken, May 23, 1974); *Clair de lune* for Piano and Orch. (Milan, Feb. 12, 1976); *Il paese senz'alba* (Naples, June 19, 1977); *Che sai guardiano, della notte?* for Clarinet and Small Orch. (Paris, June 19, 1979); *Autoritratto nella notte* (Lugano, March 17, 1983); Violin Concerto, *Allegoria della notte* (Rome, Oct. 1, 1985); *Sul poemi concentrici I, II,* and *III* (RAI, Turin, April 8, 1988); *Lettura da lontano* for Double Bass and Orch. (Milan, Oct. 21, 1989). **CHAMBER:** *Quartetto II* for String Quartet (1967); . . . *Da un divertimento* for 10 Instruments (1970); *Arabesque* for 2 Organs (1971); *2 Studies* for Cello (1974); 2 piano trios (1975, 1986); 2 quintets (1976, 1977); *Ai limiti della notte* for Viola (1979; also for Cello); *Fauno che fischia a un merlo* for Flute and Harp (1980); *Introduzione all'oscuro* for Instruments (1981); *Nox apud Orpheum* for 2 Organs and Instruments (1982); *Codex purpureus I* for String Trio (1983); *Codex purpureus II* for 2 Violins, Viola, Cello, and Piano (1984); *La canzone di ringraziamento* for Flute (1985); *Esplorazione del bianco III* for Jazz Ensemble (1986); *Il motivo degli oggetti di vetro* for 2 Flutes and Piano (1987); *Il silenzio degli oracoli* for Wind Quintet (1989); also piano pieces, including 3 sonatas (1976, 1983, 1986). **VOCAL:** *Aka aka to I, II,* and *III* for Soprano and 12 Instruments (1968); *Il paese senza tramonto* for Soprano and Orch. (Montepulciano, Aug. 14, 1977); *12 canzoni da battello* for Soprano and Instruments (1977); *Kindertotenlied* for Soprano, Tenor, and Small Orch. (1978; Venice, Oct. 7, 1979); *Un'immagine di Arpocrate* for Chorus, Piano, and Orch. (Donaueschingen, Oct. 19, 1979); *Flos florum* for Chorus and Orch. (Turin, April 30, 1981); *Efebo con radio* for Voice and Orch. (Florence, May 28, 1981); *Rose, Liz* for Voice and 5 Instruments (1984); *Morte di Borromini* for Narrator and Orch. (Milan, Oct. 18, 1988); *Due Arie marine* for Mezzo-soprano and Electronics (Turin, Oct. 27, 1990).

Scimone, Claudio, Italian conductor, musicologist, and music educator; b. Padua, Dec. 23, 1934. He studied conducting with Zecchi, Mitropoulos, and Ferrara. In 1959 he founded the noted chamber orch. I Solisti Veneti (in Padua), and made numerous tours with it, presenting works from the Baroque to the avant-garde. He also acquired a fine reputation as a scholar specializing in Italian music; supervised a modern ed. of the works of Giuseppe Tartini, and prepared a complete edition of Rossini. He taught at the Venice Cons. (1961–67) and the Verona Cons. (1967–74); then was a teacher and director of the Padua Cons. (1974–83). In addition to numerous articles for various music journals, he publ. *Segno, Significato, Interpretazione* (1970).

Sciutti, Graziella, Italian soprano, opera producer, and teacher; b. Turin, April 17, 1927. She received her training at the Accademia di Santa Cecilia in Rome. In 1951 she made her debut as Lucy in Menotti's *The Telephone* at the Aix-en-Provence Festival. In 1954 she sang for the first time at the Glyndebourne Festival as Rosina, and she returned there until 1959. She sang Carolina in *Il Matrimonio Segreto* at the opening of the Piccola Scala in Milan in 1955. From 1956 she appeared at La Scala in Milan. She made her debut at London's Covent Garden in 1956 as Oscar, and made appearances there until 1962. In 1958 she made her first appearance at the Salzburg Festival as Despina, and continued to sing there until 1966. In 1961 she made her U.S. debut as Susanna at the San Francisco Opera. After her career as a soubrette exponent ended, she devoted herself to producing opera in Glyndebourne, at Covent Garden, in N.Y., Chicago, and other opera centers. From 1986 she also ran her own music academy in Florence.

Scott, Charles Kennedy, English conductor and composer; b. Romsey, Nov. 16, 1876; d. London, July 2, 1965. He studied organ at the Brussels Cons., taking 1st prize (1897). In 1898 he settled in London; in 1904 he established the Oriana Madrigal Society, in 1919 the Phil. Choir, and in 1922 the Euterpe String Players. He publ. *Madrigal Singing* (London, 1907; 2nd ed., enl., 1931), *Word and Tone: An English Method of Vocal Technique* (2 vols., London, 1933), and *The Fundamentals of Singing* (London, 1954).

Scott, Cyril (Meir), remarkable English composer; b. Oxton, Cheshire, Sept. 27, 1879; d. Eastbourne, Dec. 31, 1970. He was a scion of a cultural family; his father was a classical scholar, his mother a fine amateur musician. Having displayed a natural penchant for music as a child, he was sent to Frankfurt am Main at age 12 to study with Uzielli and Humperdinck, remaining there for a year and a half before returning to England; he once again went to Frankfurt am Main in 1895 to study piano and theory with Iwan Knorr. In 1898 he went to Liverpool as a teacher. In 1900 Hans Richter conducted Scott's *Heroic Suite*, in Liverpool and Manchester; also in 1900, his 1st Sym. was played in Darmstadt; his overture *Pelléas and Mélisande* was performed in Frankfurt am Main. His 2nd Sym. (1902) was given at a Promenade Concert in London on Aug. 25, 1903. (It was later converted into *3 Symphonic Dances*.) His setting of Keats's *La Belle Dame sans merci* for Baritone, Chorus, and Orch. was premiered in London in 1916. His opera *The Alchemist* (1917), for which he wrote his own libretto, was premiered in Essen on May 28, 1925. In 1920 Scott traveled to the U.S. and played his 1st Piano Concerto with the Philadelphia Orch. under Stokowski (Nov. 5, 1920). However, Scott acquired fame mainly as a composer of some exotically flavored piano pieces, of which *Lotus Land* became a perennial favorite; Fritz Kreisler arranged it for violin and piano, and played it repeatedly at his concerts. Other popular piano pieces were *Danse negre, Chinese Serenade, Russian Dance, Sphinx, Autumn Idyll, Berceuse, Little Russian Suite, Indian Suite, Spanish Dance*, and most particularly the ingratiating suite *Impressions of the Jungle Book*, after Kipling. He also wrote over 100 songs. In all these pieces, Scott showed himself a master of musical miniature; he wrote in a distinctly modern idiom, very much in the style of French Impressionism; employed sonorous parallel progressions of unresolved dissonant chords; made frequent use of the whole-tone scale. His writing for piano is ingratiating in its idiomatic mastery; his harmonious modalities exude an aura of perfumed euphony. Among his other works are: 2 more operas, *The Saint of the Mountain* (1925) and *Maureen O'Mara* (1946); 3 ballets, *The Incompetent Apothecary* (1923), *Karma* (1926), and *The Masque of the Red Death* (1932); *Christmas Overture* (London, Nov. 13, 1906); *La Princesse Maleine*, symphonic poem (London, Aug. 22, 1907); 3 violin concertos (1927, c.1935, c.1935); Cello Concerto (1931); Harpsichord Concerto (1937); Sym. No. 3, *The Muses* (1939); Oboe Concerto (1946); Sinfonietta for Strings, Organ, and Harp (1954); *Neapolitan Rhapsody* for Orch. (1960); Sinfonietta for Strings (1962); numerous overtures and suites; *Nativity Hymn* for Chorus and Orch. (1913); *The Ballad of Fair Helen of Kirkconnel* for Baritone and Orch. (1925); *Rima's Call to the Birds* for Soprano and Orch. (1933); *Let Us Now Praise Famous Men* for Chorus and Orch. (1935); *Ode to Great Men* for Tenor and Orch. (1936); *Hymn of Unity* for Solo Voices, Chorus, and Orch. (1946); more than 100 songs; Piano Quartet (1900); 4 string quartets (1920, 1958, 1960, 1968); 3 piano trios (1920, 1950, 1957); 2 piano quintets (1924, 1952); 2 string trios (1931, 1949); Cello Sonata (1950); Clarinet Quintet (1953); Flute Sonata (1961); 3 piano sonatas (1910, 1932, 1956); 160 other piano pieces. From his early youth, Scott was attracted to occult sciences, and was a believer in the reality of the supernatural; he publ. books and essays on music as a divinely inspired art, and inveighed violently against jazz as the work of Satan. Among his books, all publ. in London, are *The Philosophy of Modernism in Its Connection with Music* (1917); *The Initiate Trilogy* (1920, 1927, 1935); *My Years of Indiscretion* (1924); *The Influence of Music on History and Morals: A Vindication of Plato* (1928); *Music: Its Secret Influence through the Ages* (1933; aug. ed., 1958); *An Outline of Modern Occultism* (1935); *The Christian Paradox* (1942); an autobiographical vol., *Bone of Contention* (1969); also 2 books on medical matters: *Medicine, Rational and Irrational* (1946) and *Cancer Prevention* (1968).

BIBL.: A. Hull, *C. S.: Composer, Poet and Philosopher* (London, 1918; 3rd ed., 1921); I. Parrott, *C. S. and his Piano Music* (London, 1992).

Scott, Francis George, Scottish composer; b. Hawick, Roxburghshire, Jan. 25, 1880; d. Glasgow, Nov. 6, 1958. He studied humanities at the Univ. of Edinburgh, Moray House College of Education in Edinburgh, and the Univ. of Durham (B.M., 1909); also took theory lessons with a local organist, and later pursued training with Roger-Ducasse. After a period as a school teacher, he was a lecturer in music at Jordanhill College in Glasgow (1925–46). Scott was at his best as a composer of songs; publ. *Scottish Lyrics* for Voice and Piano (5 vols., London and Glasgow, 1922–39) and *35 Scottish Lyrics and Other Poems* (Glasgow, 1949); also wrote *The Ballad of Kynd Kittok* for Baritone and Orch. (1934), *Renaissance*, overture (1937; Glasgow, Jan. 14, 1939), *The Seven Deadly Sinnes*, dance suite for Orch. (1941), and *Lament for the Heroes* for String Orch. (1941). Scott had a number of ardent admirers in England, among them the poet Hugh MacDiarmid and the composer Kaikhosru Sorabji, who in their exuberant encomiums place him in the ranks of Schubert and Schumann as a songwriter.

BIBL.: M. Lindsay, "The Scottish Songs of F.G. S.," *Music & Letters*, XXVI (1945); H. MacDiarmid, *F.G. S.: An Essay on his 75th Birthday* (Edinburgh, 1955).

Scott, Marion (Margaret), English violinist and writer on music; b. London, July 16, 1877; d. there, Dec. 24, 1953. She studied at the Royal College of Music in London. In 1911 she organized, with Gertrude Eaton, the Soc. of Women Musicians; was ed. of the *RCM Magazine* (1936–44). She specialized in Haydn research, giving special attention to his string quartets; also publ. *Beethoven* (London, 1934; rev. ed. by J. Westrup, 1947) and *Mendelssohn* (London, 1938).

BIBL.: R. Hughes, "M. S.'s Contribution to Musical Scholarship," *RCM Magazine*, I (1954).

Scott, Stephen, American composer and performer; b. Corvallis, Oreg., Oct. 10, 1944. He studied with Homer Keller at the Univ. of Oregon (B.A., 1967) and with Paul Nelson at Brown Univ. (M.A., 1969); also studied African music in Ghana, Tanzania, and Zimbabwe (1970). In 1969 he began teaching at Colorado College in Colorado Springs, where he founded the Pearson Electronic Sound Studio (1969) and the New Music Ensemble (1972). Scott's compositions are built around gentle repetitions and gradual rhythmic changes. In 1977 he developed a "bowed piano" technique for up to 10 players, resulting in his recording *New Music for Bowed Piano* (1984).

WORKS: Woodwind Quintet (1967); *5 Ferlinghetti Poems* for Narrator, Voices, and Tape (1969); *Traffic Jam* for Unspecified Ensemble (1970); *Baby Ben* for Ensemble (1971); *Suspended Animation* for 2 Pianos, 2 Harpsichords, and Tape Delay (1972); *Glacier Music* for Woodwind Quintet and Tape Delay (1973); *Variations on an American Folk Tune* for Orch. and Tape (1973); *Monophonies and Euphonies* for Wind Ensemble (1974); *American Pie* for Voices and Ensemble (1976); *Barney's Piece* for Ensemble (1977); *Rauschpfanpfare* for 3 Rauschpfeiffen (1979); *3-piece Suitcase*, sound sculpture (1979); *Ceremonial Music* for Brass (1979); *The Orphan*, incidental music (1980); *The Things Which Are Seen* for Tenor, Chorus, Synthesizer, and Orch. (1981); *Resonant Resources* for Bowed Piano (1983); *Ta ta logy* for Voices (1984); many works for Bowed Piano, including *Music I* (1977), *II* (1978), and *III* (1979), *Arcs* (1980; rev. 1984), and *Rainbows* (1981).

Scott, Tom (actually, **Thomas Jefferson**), American folksinger and composer; b. Campbellsburg, Ky., May 28, 1912; d. N.Y., Aug. 12, 1961. He studied violin with an uncle. He played in dance bands and also wrote songs; then went to Hollywood, where he took theory lessons with Antheil; subsequently studied with Harrison Kerr and Riegger.

WORKS: OPERA: *The Fisherman* (1956). **ORCH.:** *Song with Dance* (1932); *Plymouth Rock* (1938); *Hornpipe and Chantey* (1944); Sym. No. 1 (Rochester, N.Y., Oct. 22, 1946); *From the Sacred Harp* (1946); *Johnny Appleseed* (N.Y., March 1, 1948); *Lento* for Saxophone and Strings (1953). **CHAMBER:** 2 string quartets (1944, 1956); *Emily Dickinson Suite* for Violin and Harp (1955). **VOCAL:** *Ballad of the Harp Weaver* for Narrator, Harp, Chorus, and String Quartet (N.Y., Feb. 22, 1947); also chanteys for chorus; solo songs; arrangements of folk songs.

BIBL.: J. Ringo, "Some Notes on T. S.'s Music," *American Composers Alliance Bulletin* (Winter 1957; with a list of works).

Scotti, Antonio, celebrated Italian baritone; b. Naples, Jan. 25, 1866; d. there, Feb. 26, 1936. He studied with Ester Trifari-Paganini in Naples. He made his operatic debut in Naples (March 1889) as Cinna in Spontini's *La Vestale*; then sang elsewhere in Italy, Russia, Spain, and South America. He made his London debut at Covent Garden on June 8, 1899, as Don Giovanni, and appeared in the same role with the Metropolitan Opera in N.Y. (Dec. 27, 1899). He remained with the Metropolitan for 33 years; made his farewell appearance on Jan. 20, 1933. He also toured in America with his own company. He possessed great histrionic ability, and was especially noted for his dramatic roles (Scarpia, Rigoletto, Falstaff, Don Giovanni, and Iago).

Scotto, Renata, famous Italian soprano; b. Savona, Feb. 24, 1933. She commenced music study in Savona at age 14; when she was 16, she went to Milan for vocal training with Emilio Ghirardini, then with Merlini, and finally with Mercedes Llopart. She made her debut as Violetta in Savona in 1952. After winning a national vocal competition in 1953, she made her formal debut as Violetta at Milan's Teatro Nuovo; then joined Milan's La Scala, where she sang secondary roles until being called upon to replace Maria Callas as Amina during the company's visit to the Edinburgh Festival in 1957. She made her U.S. debut at the Chicago Lyric Opera on Nov. 2, 1960, as Mimi, a role she also chose for her Metropolitan Opera debut in N.Y. on Oct. 13, 1965. She scored a brilliant success with her portrayal of Mimi in the Metropolitan Opera production of *La Bohème* in the "Live from Lincoln Center" telecast on PBS (March 15, 1977); thereafter she was a stellar figure in the U.S. opera scene; also toured widely as a recitalist. In later years she was active as an opera director, producing *Madama Butterfly* at the Metropolitan Opera in 1986. She sang her final performance there as Cio-Cio-San in 1987. In 1995 she sang the Marshallin at the Spoleto Festival U.S.A. in Charleston, S.C. Among her other fine roles were Lucia, Gilda, Elena in *I Vespri Siciliani,* Norma, Manon Lescaut, and Luisa Miller. She publ. the book *Scotto: More than a Diva* (with O. Riva; N.Y., 1984).

BIBL.: B. Tosi, *R. S.: Voce di due mondi* (Venice, 1990).

Scovotti, Jeanette, American soprano; b. N.Y., Dec. 5, 1936. She received her training in N.Y. at the High School of Music and Art, and at the Juilliard School of Music. She began her career singing in concerts. In 1960 she appeared as Despina with the New England Opera Theater in Boston. After singing at the Santa Fe Opera, she appeared as Blondchen at the San Francisco Opera. On Nov. 15, 1962, she made her Metropolitan Opera debut in N.Y. as Adele, and remained on its roster until 1966. She also appeared at the Teatro Colón in Buenos Aires (1963–65). From 1966 to 1977 she sang with the Hamburg State Opera. In 1977 she appeared in the U.S. premiere of Glinka's *Ruslan and Ludmila* in Boston. Among her other roles of note were Zerlina, Rosina, Gilda, Lucia, Aminta in *Die schweigsame Frau,* the Italian Singer in *Capriccio,* and the title role in Krenek's *Sardakai.*

Scriabin, Alexander (Nikolaievich), remarkable Russian composer whose solitary genius had no predecessors and left no disciples, father of **Marina Scriabine**; b. Moscow, Jan. 6, 1872; d. there, April 27, 1915. His father was a lawyer; his mother, Lyubov Petrovna (née Shchetinina), was a talented pianist who had studied with Leschetizky at the St. Petersburg Cons.; his mother died of tuberculosis when he was an infant, and his father remarried and spent the rest of his life in the diplomatic service abroad. Scriabin was reared by an aunt, who gave him initial instruction in music, including piano; at 11 he began regular piano lessons with Georgi Conus, and at 16 became a pupil of Zverev; in 1885 he commenced the study of theory with Taneyev. When he entered the Moscow Cons. in 1888, he continued his studies with Taneyev, and also received instruction in piano with Safonov. He practiced assiduously, but never became a virtuoso pianist; at his piano recitals, he performed mostly his own works. Graduating with a gold medal from Safonov's class, Scriabin remained at the Moscow Cons. to study fugue with Arensky, but failed to pass the required test and never received a diploma for composition. Upon leaving the Cons. in 1892, he launched a career as a concert pianist. By that time he had already written several piano pieces in the manner of Chopin; the publisher Jurgenson brought out his opp. 1, 2, 3, 5, and 7 in 1893. In 1894 Belaieff became his publisher and champion, financing his first European tour in 1895; on Jan. 15, 1896, Scriabin gave a concert of his own music in Paris. Returning to Russia, he completed his first major work, a Piano Concerto, and was soloist in its first performance on Oct. 23, 1897, in Odessa. In the same year, he married the pianist Vera Isakovich. They spent some time abroad; on Jan. 31, 1898, they gave a joint recital in Paris in a program of Scriabin's works. From 1898 to 1903 Scriabin taught piano at the Moscow Cons. His first orch. work, *Rêverie,* was conducted in Moscow by Safonov on March 24, 1899; he also conducted the first performance of Scriabin's 1st Sym. (March 29, 1901). Scriabin's 2nd Sym. was brought out by Liadov in St. Petersburg (Jan. 25, 1902). After the death of Belaieff in 1904, Scriabin received an annual grant of 2,400 rubles from the wealthy Moscow merchant Morosov, and went to Switzerland, where he began work on his 3rd Sym., *Le Poème divin*; it had its first performance in Paris on May 29, 1905, under the direction of Arthur Nikisch. At that time Scriabin separated from Vera Isakovich and established a household with Tatiana Schloezer, sister of the music critic Boris de Schloezer, who subsequently became Scriabin's close friend and biographer. In Dec. 1906 he appeared as a soloist with Modest Altschuler and the Russian Sym. Soc. in N.Y.; also gave recitals of his works there and in other U.S. music centers. Tatiana Schloezer joined him in N.Y. in Jan. 1907, but they were warned by friends familiar with American mores of the time that charges of moral turpitude might be brought against them, since Scriabin had never obtained a legal divorce from his 1st wife and Tatiana Schloezer was his common-law wife. There was no evidence that such charges were actually contemplated, but to safeguard themselves against such a contretemps, they went to Paris in March 1907. Altschuler continued to champion Scriabin's music, and on Dec. 10, 1908, gave the world premiere with his Russian Sym. Orch. of Scriabin's great work *Le poème de l'extase*; the first Russian performance followed in St. Petersburg (Feb. 1, 1909). In the spring of 1908, Scriabin met Serge Koussevitzky, who became one of his most ardent supporters, both as a conductor and as a publisher. He gave Scriabin a 5-year contract with his newly established publishing firm Editions Russes, with a generous guarantee of 5,000 rubles annually. In the summer of 1910, Koussevitzky engaged Scriabin as soloist on a tour in a chartered steamer down the Volga River, with stopovers and concerts at all cities and towns of any size along the route. Scriabin wrote for Koussevitzky his most ambitious work, *Promethée,* or *Poème du feu,* with an important piano part, which featured the composer as soloist at its premiere in Moscow (March 15, 1911). The score also included a color keyboard (*clavier à lumière* or, in Italian, *luce*) intended to project changing colors according to the scale of the spectrum, which Scriabin devised (for at that time he was deeply immersed in the speculation about parallelism of all arts in their visual and auditory aspects). The construction of such a color organ was, however, entirely unfeasible at the time, and the premiere of the work was given without luce. A performance with colored lights thrown on a screen was attempted by Altschuler at Carnegie Hall in N.Y. on March 20, 1915, but it was a total failure. Another attempt was made in Moscow by Safonov after Scriabin's death, but that, too, was completely unsuccessful. The crux of the problem was that the actual notes written on a special staff in the score had to be translated into a color spectrum according to Scriabin's visualization of corresponding colors and keys (C major was red, F-sharp major was bright blue, etc.). Perhaps the nearest approximation to Scriabin's scheme was the performance of *Promethée* by the Univ. of Iowa Sym. Orch. on Sept. 24, 1975, under the direction of James Dixon, with a laser apparatus constructed by Lowell Cross; previously, the American pianist Hilde Somer made use of the laser to accompany her solo piano recitals of Scriabin's works, without attempting to follow the parallelism of sounds and colors envisioned by Scriabin, but nonetheless conveying the idea underlying the scheme. The unique collaboration between Scriabin and Koussevitzky came to an unfortunate end soon after the production of *Promethée*; Scriabin regarded Koussevitzky as the chief apostle of his messianic epiphany, while Koussevitzky believed that it was due principally to his promotion that Scriabin reached the heights in musical celebrity; to this collision of 2 mighty egotisms was added a trivial disagreement about financial matters. Scriabin left Koussevitzky's publishing firm, and in 1912 signed a contract with Jurgenson, who guaranteed him 6,000 rubles annually. In 1914 Scriabin visited London and was soloist in his Piano Concerto and in *Prometheus* at a concert led by Sir Henry Wood (March 14, 1914); he also gave a recital of his own works there (March 20, 1914). His last public appearance was in a recital in Petrograd on April 15, 1915; upon his return to Moscow, an abscess developed in his lip, leading to blood poisoning; he died after a few days' illness. His 3 children (of the union with Tatiana Schloezer) were legitimized at his death. His son Julian, an exceptionally gifted boy, was accidentally drowned at the age of 11 in the Dnieper River at Kiev (June 22, 1919); Julian's 2 piano preludes, written in the style of the last works of his father, were publ. in a Scriabin memorial vol. (Moscow, 1940).

Scriabin was a genuine innovator in harmony. After an early period of strongly felt influences (Chopin, Liszt, and Wagner), he gradually evolved in his own melodic and harmonic style, marked by extreme chromaticism; in his piano piece *Désir,* op. 57 (1908), the threshold of polytonality and atonality is reached; the key signature is dispensed with in his subsequent works; chromatic alterations and compound appoggiaturas create a harmonic web of such complexity that all distinction between consonance and dissonance vanishes. Building chords by fourths rather than by thirds, Scriabin constructed his "mystic chord" of 6 notes (C, F-sharp, B-flat, E, A, and D), which is the harmonic foundation of *Promethée*. In his 7th Piano Sonata (1913) appears a chordal structure of 25 notes (D-flat, F-flat, G, A, and C, repeated in 5 octaves), which was dubbed "a 5-story chord." These harmonic extensions were associated in Scriabin's mind with theosophic doctrines; he aspired to a universal art in which the impressions of the senses were to unite with religious experience. He made plans for the writing of a "Mysterium," which was to accomplish such a synthesis, but only the text of a preliminary poem (*L'Acte préalable*) was completed at his death. Scriabin dreamed of having the "Mysterium" performed as a sacred action in the Himalayas, and actually made plans for going to India; the outbreak of World War I in 1914 put an end to such a project. Scriabin's fragmentary sketches for *L'Acte préalable* were arranged in 1973 by the Russian musician Alexander Nemtin, who supplemented this material with excerpts from Scriabin's 8th Piano Sonata, *Guirlandes*, and Piano Preludes, op. 74; the resulting synthetic score was performed in Moscow on March 16, 1973, under the title *Universe*; a species of color keyboard was used at the performance, projecting colors according to Scriabin's musical spectrum.

WORKS: ORCH.: Piano Concerto, op. 20 (1896; Odessa, Oct. 23, 1897, composer soloist); Symphonic Poem (1896–97); *Rêverie*, op. 24 (1898; Moscow, March 24, 1899); *Andante* for Strings (1899); 3 syms.: No. 1, op. 26 (1899–1900; Moscow, March 29, 1901), No. 2, op. 29 (1901; St. Petersburg, Jan. 25, 1902), and No. 3, op. 43, *Le divin poème* (1902–04; Paris, May 29, 1905); *Le poème de l'extase*, op. 54 (1905–08; N.Y., Dec. 10, 1908); *Promethée*, or *Poème du feu*, op. 60 (1908–10; Moscow, March 15, 1911, composer soloist). **CHAMBER:** *Romance* for Horn and Piano (1890); 2nd Variation for *Variations on a Russian Theme* for String Quartet (1899; in collaboration with 9 other composers). **PIANO:** *Canon* (1883); *Nocturne* in A-flat major (1884); *Valse* in F minor, op. 1 (1885); *Sonate-fantaisie* (1886); *Valse* in G-sharp minor (1886); *Valse* in D-flat major (1886); *Variations on a Theme by Mlle. Egorova* (1887); 11 sonatas: in E-flat major (1887–89), op. 6 (1892), op. 19, *Sonata-Fantasy* (1892–97), op. 23 (1897–98), op. 30 (1903), op. 53 (1907), op. 62 (1911), op. 64, *Messe blanche* (1911), op. 66 (1913), op. 68, *Messe noire* (1913), and op. 70 (1913); 3 Pieces, op. 2 (1887–89); *Feuillet d'album* in A-flat major (1889); *10 Mazurkas*, op. 3 (1889); *Mazurka* in F major (1889?); *Mazurka* in B minor (1889?); *Fantasy* for 2 Pianos (1889?); *Allegro appassionato*, op. 4 (1892; based on the 1st movement of the Sonata in E-flat major); *2 Nocturnes*, op. 5 (1890); *Deux impromptus à la Mazur*, op. 7 (1892); *Douze études*, op. 8 (1894); 2 Pieces for Piano, left-hand, op. 9 (1894); *2 Impromptus*, op. 10 (1894); *24 Préludes*, op. 11 (1888–96); *2 Impromptus*, op. 12 (1895); *6 Préludes*, op. 13 (1895); *2 Impromptus*, op. 14 (1895); *5 Préludes*, op. 15 (1895–96); *5 Préludes*, op. 16 (1894–95); *7 Préludes*, op. 17 (1895–96); *Allegro de concert*, op. 18 (1896); *Polonaise*, op. 21 (1897); *4 Préludes*, op. 22 (1897); *9 Mazurkas*, op. 25 (1899); *2 Préludes*, op. 27 (1900); *Fantaisie*, op. 28 (1900); *4 Préludes*, op. 31 (1903); *Deux poèmes*, op. 32 (1903); *4 Préludes*, op. 33 (1903); *Poème tragique*, op. 34 (1903); *3 Préludes*, op. 35 (1903); *Poème satanique*, op. 36 (1903); *4 Préludes*, op. 37 (1903); *Valse*, op. 38 (1903); *4 Préludes*, op. 39 (1903); *2 Mazurkas*, op. 40 (1902–03); *Poème*, op. 41 (1903); *Huit études*, op. 42 (1903); *Deux poèmes*, op. 44 (1905); 3 Pièces, op. 45 (1904–05); *Scherzo*, op. 46 (1905); *Quasi-valse*, op. 47 (1905); *4 Préludes*, op. 48 (1905); 3 Pièces, op. 49 (1905); *Feuille d'album* (1905); 4 Pieces, op. 51 (1906); 3 Pieces, op. 52 (1906); 4 Pieces, op. 56 (1907); 2 Pieces, op. 57 (1907); *Feuillet d'album*, op. 58 (1910); 2 Pieces, op. 59 (1910); *Poème-nocturne*, op. 61 (1911); *Deux poèmes*, op. 63 (1911); *Trois études*, op. 65 (1912); *2 Préludes*, op. 67 (1912–13); *Deux poèmes*, op. 69 (1913); *Deux poèmes*, op. 71 (1914); *Vers la flamme*, op. 72 (1914); *Deux danses*, op. 73 (1914); *5 Préludes*, op. 74 (1914).

BIBL.: L. Sabaneyev, "Prometheus von S.," *Der blaue Reiter* (Munich, 1912; 2nd ed., 1965; Eng. tr., 1974); G. Clutsam, "The Harmonies of S.," *Musical Times*, LIV (1913); I. Lipayev, *A.N. S.* (Moscow, 1913); R. Newmarch, "S. and Contemporary Russian Music," *Russian Review*, II (1913); idem, "Prometheus: The Poem of Fire," *Musical Times*, LV (1914); E. Gunst, *S. and His Work* (Moscow, 1915); V. Karatigin, *S.* (Petrograd, 1915); special issues of *Musikalnyi Sovremennik*, IV (1915) and V (1916); A. Hull, *A Great Russian Tone-poet: S.* (London, 1916; 2nd ed., 1927); idem, "The Pianoforte Works of S.," *Musical Times*, LVII (1916); idem, "S.'s Scientific Derivation of Harmony versus Empirical Methods," *Proceedings of the Musical Association*, XLIII (1916–17); idem, "A Survey of the Pianoforte Works of S.," *Musical Quarterly* (Oct. 1916); A. Koptyayev, *A.N. S.* (Petrograd, 1916); L. Sabaneyev, *S.* (Moscow, 1916; 2nd ed., 1923); M. Montagu-Nathan, *Handbook to the Piano Works of A. S.* (London, 1917; 2nd ed., 1922); I. Glebov, *S.* (Petrograd, 1921); B. de Schloezer, "S.," *La Revue Musicale*, II (1921); I. Lapshin, *S.'s Intimate Thoughts* (Petrograd, 1922); L. Sabaneyev, *A.N. S.* (Moscow, 1922; 2nd ed., 1923); B. Asafiev, *S. 1871–1915* (Petrograd, 1923); L. Sabaneyev, ed., *Pisma A.N. S.a* (letters; Moscow,1923); B. de Schloezer, *A. S. lichnost mysteriya* (A. S., Character of Mystery; vol. I, Berlin, 1923; Fr. tr., Paris, 1975; Eng. tr., by N. Slonimsky, Berkeley and Los Angeles, 1987; vol. II not completed); A. Swan, *S.* (London, 1923); H. Antcliffe, "The Significance of S.," *Musical Quarterly*, X (1924); V. Yakovlev, *A.N. S.* (Moscow, 1925); E. von Tidebohl, "Memories of S.'s Volga Tour (1910)," *Monthly Musical Record*, LVI (1926); L. Sabaneyev, "S. and the Idea of a Religious Art," *Musical Times*, LXXII (1931); M. Cooper, "S.'s Mystical Beliefs," *Music & Letters*, XVI (1935); P. Dickenmann, *Die Entwicklung der Harmonik bei A. S.* (Bern and Leipzig, 1935); M. Metshik, *A. S.* (Moscow, 1935); A. Nikolayev, *A. S.* (Moscow, 1940); N. Rimskaya-Korsakova, "Rimsky-Korsakov i S.," *Sovetskaya musika*, No. 5 (1950); L. Danilevich, *A.N. S.* (Moscow, 1953); B. de Schloezer, "A. S.," *Musique russe*, II (Paris, 1953); H. Boegner, *Die Harmonik der späten Klavierwerke S.s* (diss., Univ. of Munich, 1955); R. Wood, "S. and His Critics," *Monthly Musical Record*, LXXXVI (1956); R. Myers, "S.: A Reassessment," *Musical Times*, XCVIII (1957); D. Blagoy, *Etyudi S.a* (Moscow, 1963); C. von Gleich, *Die sinfonischen Werke von A. S.* (Bilthoven, 1963); H. Forster, *Die Form in den symphonischen Werken von A.N. S.* (diss., Univ. of Leipzig, 1964); P. Dickinson, "S.'s Later Music," *Music Review*, XXVI (1965); M. Mikhailov, *A.N. S.* (Moscow, 1966); V. Dernova, *S.'s Harmony* (Leningrad, 1968; Eng. tr. and commentary by R. Guenther, diss., Catholic Univ. of America, 1979); F. Bowers, *S.: A Biography of the Russian Composer* (2 vols., Palo Alto, 1969); V. Delson, *S.* (Moscow, 1971); W. Evrard, *S.* (Paris, 1972); E. Kaufman, *The Evolution of Form and Technique in the Late Works of S.* (diss., Yale Univ., 1972); H. Steger, *Der Weg der Klaviersonaten bei A. S.* (Munich, 1972); F. Bowers, *The New S.: Enigma and Answers* (N.Y., 1973); S. Pavchinsky and V. Zuckerman, eds., *A.N. S.* (Moscow, 1973); H. Steger, *Materialstrukturen in den fünf späten Klaviersonaten A. S.s* (Regensburg, 1977); G. Eberle, *Zwischen Tonalität und Atonalität: Studien zur Harmonik A. S.s* (Munich, 1978); M. Kelkel, *A. S., sa vie, l'ésotérisme et la langage musical dans son oeuvre* (Paris, 1978); H. Macdonald, *S.* (London, 1978); M. Brown, "S. and Russian 'Mystic' Symbolism," *19th Century Music* (July 1979); E. Rudakova and A. Kandinsky, *A.N. S.* (Moscow, 1979); O. Kolleritsch, ed., *A. S.* (Graz, 1980); I. Belza, *A.N. S.* (Moscow, 1983); H. Metzger and R. Riehn, eds., *A. S. und die S.isten, Musik Konzepte*, Nos. 32–33 (Munich, 1983) and Nos. 37–38 (Munich, 1984); S. Schibli, *A. S. und seine Musik: Grenzuberschreitungen eines prometheischen Geistes* (Munich, 1983); G. Perle, "S.'s Self-Analyses," *Musical Analysis*, III (1984); M. Cooper, "A. S. and the Russian Renaissance," *Slavonic and Western Music: Essays for Gerald Abraham* (Ann Arbor and Oxford, 1985); J. Baker, *The Music of A. S.* (New Haven, 1986); A. Pople, *S. and Stravinsky 1908–1914: Studies in Theory and Analysis* (N.Y. and London, 1989); L. Verdi, *A. S., tra musica e filosofia* (Florence, 1991).

Scriabine, Marina, Russian-French music scholar and composer, daughter of **Alexander (Nikolaievich) Scriabin**; b. Moscow, Jan. 30, 1911. After her father's death, she lived with her mother in Kiev and Moscow; when her mother died, she went to Belgium to live with her maternal grandmother; in 1927 she settled in Paris. She studied at the École Nationale des Arts Décoratifs and designed art posters; studied theory with Leibowitz. In 1950 she joined the Radiodiffusion Française and worked in electronic techniques; composed a *Suite radiophonique* (1951); also a ballet, *Bayalett* (1952), and some chamber music. In 1967 she received a doctorate in aesthetics for her thesis *Répresentation du temps et de l'intemporalité dans les arts plastiques figuratifs*. She publ. *Problèmes de la musique moderne* (in collaboration with her uncle, Boris de Schloezer; Paris, 1959; also in Spanish, 1960); *Le Langage musical* (Paris, 1963); *Le Miroir du temps* (Paris, 1973). She contributed the biographical entry on Scriabin for the *Encyclopédie de la musique* (Paris, 1961); wrote an introduction to Schloezer's book on Scriabin, in French (Paris, 1975).

Scribner, Norman (Orville), American organist, conductor, and composer; b. Washington, D.C., Feb. 25, 1936. He studied organ with Paul Callaway and theory with Walter Spencer Huffman at the Peabody Cons. of Music in Baltimore (B.Mus., 1961). In 1960 he was appointed director of music of St. Alban's Episcopal Church in Washington, D.C.; was also a staff keyboard artist with the National Sym. Orch. (1963–67). In 1965 he founded the all-volunteer Choral Arts Soc. of Washington, D.C.; in 1971 he founded the Norman Scribner Choir. He served on the faculties of American Univ. (1960–63) and George Washington Univ. (1963–69). He composed a Sextet for Winds and Piano (1975); *The Nativity*, choral cantata (1975); *The Tide Pool*, song cycle for Mezzo-soprano and Orch. (1977); *Laudate Dominum*, choral cantata (1979); *I Hear America Singing*, choral suite (1979); *Nicholas*, musical show (1980).

Sculthorpe, Peter (Joshua), eminent Australian composer and teacher; b. Launceston, Tansmania, April 29, 1929. He studied at the Univ. of Melbourne Conservatorium of Music (B.Mus., 1951) and with Wellesz and Rubbra at Wadham College, Oxford (1958–60). In 1963 he joined the faculty of the Univ. of Sydney, where he later served as prof. of composition. He also was composer-in-residence at Yale Univ. while on a Harkness Fellowship (1966–67) and a visiting prof. at the Univ. of Sussex (1972–73). In 1970 he was made a Member and in 1977 an Officer of the Order of the British Empire. He was awarded the Silver Jubilee Medal in 1977. In 1980 he received an honorary doctor of letters degree from the Univ. of Tasmania, and in 1989 he received the same from the Univ. of Sussex; that same year he also received an honorary doctor of music degree from the Univ. of Melbourne. He was elected a fellow of the Australian Academy of the Humanities in 1991. Schulthorpe rejected such modern compositional methods as atonality and serialism to pursue an independent course. He has found inspiration in aboriginal Australian music, as well as in the music of Asia, particularly Japanese and Balinese music. In all of his music, one finds a discerning musicianship, mastery of resources, and inventiveness.

WORKS: DRAMATIC: *Sun Music*, ballet (Sydney, Aug. 2, 1968; based on the *Sun Music* series); *Rites of Passage*, theater piece (1972–73); *Quiros*, television opera (ABC National TV, July 1, 1982). **ORCH.:** *Irkanda IV* for Violin, Percussion, and Strings (Melbourne, Aug. 5, 1961); *Small Town* (Hobart, Dec. 13, 1963; rev. 1976); *Sun Music I* (London, Sept. 30, 1965), *II: Ketjak* (1966; rev. version, Sydney, Feb. 22, 1969), *III: Anniversary Music* (1967), and *IV* (Melbourne, May 29, 1967); *From Tabuh Tabuhan* (1968); *Music for Japan* (Melbourne, May 25, 1970); *Overture for a Happy Occasion* (Launceston, Nov. 16, 1970); *Lament* for Strings (Wollongong, May 26, 1976; also for Cello and Strings, Sydney, Sept. 22, 1991); *Port Essington* for String Trio and String Orch. (Sydney, Aug. 18, 1977); *Mangrove* (Sydney, April 27, 1979); *Cantares* for Chamber Orch. (1979; Sydney, Jan. 17, 1980); Piano Concerto (1983); 2 sonatas for Strings: No. 1 (1983) and No. 2 (Brighton, May 19, 1988); *Little Suite* for Strings (Sydney, Sept. 22, 1983); *Sun Song* (Perth, Oct. 20, 1984); *Earth Cry* (Adelaide, Aug. 22, 1986); *Autumn Song* for Strings (1986; also for Chorus, 1968); *Kakadu* (Aspen, Colo., July 24, 1988); *Nourlangie*, concerto for Guitar, Percussion, and Strings (Brisbane, Oct. 24, 1989); *Little Nourlangie* for Organ and Orch. (Sydney, June 6, 1990); *From Uluru* (1991); *Nangaloar* (Aspen, Colo., July 14, 1991); *Awake Glad Heart!* for 2 Trumpets, Cello, and Strings (1992; arranged from *The Birthday of Thy King* for Chorus, 1988); *Memento mori* (1992–93; Perth, July 2, 1993). **BAND:** *Burke and Willis Suite* for Symphonic Band (Melbourne, Nov. 11, 1985; also for Brass Band, Adelaide, March 3, 1986). **CHAMBER:** 11 string quartets: No. 1 (1947), No. 2 (1948), No. 3 (1949), No. 4 (1950), No. 5, *Irkanda II* (1959), No. 6 (1964–65; Sydney, April 1, 1965), No. 7, *Red Landscape* (Norfolk, Va., July 29, 1966), No. 8, *String Quartet Music* (1968; London, Jan. 15, 1970), No. 9 (Sydney, Oct. 17, 1975), No. 10 (San Francisco, April 8, 1983), and No. 11, *Jabiru Dreaming* (Adelaide, March 10, 1990); *The Loneliness of Bunjil* for String Trio (1954; London, Nov. 30, 1960; rev. 1964); *Irkanda I* for Violin (Melbourne, June 30, 1955) and *III* for Piano Trio (1961); Sonata for Viola and Percussion (Attingham Park, July 1960); *Tabuh Tabuhan* for Wind Quintet and Percussion (Adelaide, March 20, 1968); *Dream* for Any Instruments and Any Number of Players (Sydney, Sept. 22, 1970); *How the Stars Were Made* for 4 Percussionists (Canberra, Oct. 4, 1971); *Alone* for Violin (1976); *Landscape II* for Amplified Piano and String Trio (Sydney, April 27, 1978); *Little Serenade* for String Quartet (1978); *Requiem* for Cello (Mittagong, April 14, 1979); *Tailitnama Song* for 5 Players (1981); *Dhilile* for 4 Percussionists (1981; Adelaide, March 7, 1990); *Songs of Sea and Sky* for Clarinet and Piano (New Haven, Conn., Oct. 15, 1987; also for Flute and Piano); *Sun Song* for 4 Percussionists (Paris, June 1, 1989); *Threnody (In memoriam Stuart Challender)* for Cello (Sydney, Feb. 20, 1991); *Tropic* for 6 Players (Brighton, May 23, 1992); *Dream Tracks* for Clarinet, Violin, and Piano (San Diego, Oct. 31, 1992); *From Saibai* for Violin and Piano (Penrith, April 3, 1993). **PIANO:** *2 Easy Pieces* (1958, 1968); *Callabonna* (1963; Melbourne, July 30, 1989); *Landscape I* for Amplified Piano and Tape (Perth, Feb. 28, 1971); *Night Pieces* (Perth, Feb. 28, 1971); *Koto Music I* and *II* for Amplified Piano and Tape (1976); *4 Pieces* for Piano Duet (Sydney, April 28, 1979); *Mountains* (1980; Sydney, July 4, 1981); *Nocturnal* (1983). **VOCAL:** *Sun Music* for Chorus, Piano, and Percussion (Adelaide, March 13, 1966); *Morning Song for the Christ Child*, carol for Chorus (1966); *Sea Chant* for Unison Voices and Orch. (1968; Melbourne, June 1975); *Autumn Song* for Chorus (1968; also for String Orch., 1986); *Love 200* for 2 Singers, Rock Band, and Orch. (Sydney, Feb. 14, 1970); *The Song of Tailitnama* for High Voice, 6 Cellos, and Percussion (1974; also for Medium Voice and Piano, 1984; Sydney, Sept. 9, 1986); *Child of Australia* for Soprano, Speaker, Chorus, and Orch. (Sydney, Jan. 26, 1988); *The Birthday of Thy King*, carol for Chorus (Cambridge, Dec. 24, 1988; also arranged as *Awake Glad Heart!* for 2 Trumpets, Cello, and Strings, 1992).

BIBL.: M. Hannan, *P. S.: His Music and Ideas 1929–1979* (Brisbane, 1982); D. Hayes, *P. S.: A Bio-Bibliography* (Westport, Conn., 1993).

Seaman, Christopher, English conductor; b. Faversham, Kent, March 7, 1942. He studied at King's College, Cambridge (M.A., 1963) and received training in conducting at the Guildhall School of Music in London. In 1964 he became principal timpanist of the London Phil. In 1968 he was made assistant conductor of the BBC Scottish Sym. Orch. in Glasgow, and then was its principal conductor from 1971 to 1977. From 1973 to 1979 he was also principal conductor of the Northern Sinfonia in Newcastle upon Tyne. In 1978 he became principal conductor of the Robert Mayer children's concerts in London. From 1979 to 1983 he was chief guest conductor of the Utrecht Sym. Orch. In 1987 he became conductor-in-residence of the Baltimore Sym. Orch. In 1993 he became music director of the Naples (Fla.) Phil.

Search, Frederick Preston, American cellist, conductor, and composer; b. Pueblo, Colo., July 22, 1889; d. Carmel Valley, Calif., Nov. 1, 1959. After studying cello in Jena (from 1901), he returned to the U.S. and continued his training with Adamowski at the New England Cons. of Music in Boston (1903–04) and with Lino Mattioli and Georg Rogovoy at the Cincinnati College Cons. of Music (1904–07); then studied cello with Klengel, conducting with Nikisch, and composition with Reger, Schreck, Hofmann, and Sitt at the Leipzig Cons. (1907–11); also played cello in the Gewandhaus Orch. in Leipzig (1910–12). On his return to the U.S., he was conductor of the Mare Island Naval Training Station orch. and band (1918–19) and the orch. of the Hotel Del Monte in Del Monte, Calif. (1920–32); after further tours as a recitalist (1932, 1934), he served as conductor of the Federal Symphonic Band in San Francisco (1936–40). In 1923 he married the pianist and composer Opal Piontkowski Heron.

WORKS: ORCH.: 4 syms.: No. 1, in D major (1913), No. 2, in G minor (1938; Oakland, Calif., Feb. 23, 1940), No. 3, in B minor (1931), and No. 4, in B-flat major, *Roan Stallion* (1941); Cello Concerto (1932; Monterey, Aug. 22, 1933); *Korkle* (1932; Oakland, Calif., Aug. 4, 1936); *Exhilaration*, overture (1933; San Francisco, Jan. 9, 1936); *Holly, A Jolly Suite* (1934); *Oriental Dance* for Cello and Orch. (1934); *Rhapsody* (1934; San Francisco, April 30, 1936); *Sinfonietta* (1938); *Suite* for Saxophone and Orch. (1939); *Romanze* for Cello or Viola and Orch. (San Francisco, Sept. 20, 1939; transcription of the 3rd string quartet); *Jollity* for Trumpet and Orch. (1957); *Quicksilver* for Flute and Orch. (1957); *Polly* (1958). **BAND:** *Courageous* (1936); *Carmelita* (1938); *Kathleen* (1938); *Romantic Overture* (1938); *Sweet Dreams* (1938); *Woodland Sketch* (1938); *March militaire* (1939); *Minuet* (1939); *Reverie* (1939). **CHAMBER:** 4 string quartets (1910; 1915; 1932, rev. 1942; 1935); *Reverie of the Garda-See* for Violin or Cello and Piano (1911); *Romance* for Cello and Piano (1912); *Etude* for Cello (1913); *Aria* for Cello and Piano (1914); Cello Sonata (1914); *Elegie* for Piano Trio (1920); *Amara* for Saxophone and Piano (1930; also for Band, 1937); Septet (1936); *Jamesburg Quintet* (1937); *Chinese Dance* for Woodwind Quintet (1957). **VOCAL:** *The Bridge Builders* for Soloists, Chorus, and Orch. (1937).

Searle, Humphrey, distinguished English composer, teacher, and writer on music; b. Oxford, Aug. 26, 1915; d. London, May 12, 1982. He studied classical literature at Oxford (1933–37) and music at the Royal College of Music in London (1937), where his teachers were John Ireland and R.O. Morris. In 1937 he went to Vienna, where he took private lessons with Webern; this study proved to be a decisive influence in Searle's own compositions, which are imbued with the subtle coloristic processes peculiar to the 2nd Viennese School of composition. He served in the British army during World War II, and was stationed in Germany in 1946. Returning to London, he engaged in various organizations promoting the cause of modern music. He was honorary secretary of the Liszt Society (1950–62); was an adviser on music for the Sadler's Wells Ballet (1951–57). In 1964–65 he was composer-in-residence at Stanford Univ. in California; after serving as a prof. at the Royal College of Music in London (1965–76), he was composer-in-residence at the Univ. of Southern Calif. in Los Angeles (1976–77). In 1968 he was made a Commander of the Order of the British Empire. Although Searle's method of composing included some aspects of the 12-tone method, he did not renounce tonal procedures, and sometimes applied purely national English melodic patterns. As a writer, he became particularly well known for his writings on Liszt.

WORKS: DRAMATIC: OPERAS: *The Diary of a Madman* (Berlin, Oct. 3, 1958); *The Photo of the Colonel* (Frankfurt am Main, June 3, 1964); *Hamlet* (1964–68; Hamburg, March 5, 1968). **BALLETS:** *Noctambules* (1956); *The Great Peacock* (1957–58); *Dualities* (1963). **ORCH.:** 2 suites for Strings (1942, 1943); 2 piano concertos (1944, 1955); *Fuga giocosa* (1948); 5 syms.: No. 1 (1953), No. 2 (1956–58), No. 3 (1958–60; Edinburgh, Sept. 3, 1960), No. 4 (Birmingham, Nov. 8, 1962), and No. 5 (Manchester, Oct. 7, 1964); *Scherzi* for Small Orch. (1964); *Sinfonietta* (1968–69); *Zodiac Variations* for Small Orch. (1970); *Labyrinth* (1971); *Tamesis* (1979). **CHAMBER:** Bassoon Quintet (1945); *Intermezzo* for 11 Instruments (1946); Quartet for Clarinet, Bassoon, Violin, and Viola (1948); *Passacaglietta in nomine Arnold Schoenberg* for String Quartet (1949); *Gondoliera* for English Horn and Piano (1950); *Suite* for Clarinet and Piano (1956); *3 Movements* for String Quartet (1959); *Il penseroso e L'allegro* for Cello and Piano (1975). **VOCAL:** *Gold Coast Customs* for Speaker, Men's Chorus, and Orch. (1947–49); *The Shadow of Cain* for Speakers, Men's Chorus, and Orch. (1951); *Jerusalem* for Speakers, Tenor, Chorus, and Orch. (1970); *Kubla Khan* for Tenor, Chorus, and Orch. (1973); *Rhyme Rude to My Pride* for Men's Voices (1974); *My Beloved Spake* for Chorus and Organ (1976); *Dr. Faustus* for Solo Voices, Chorus, and Orch. (1977).

WRITINGS (all publ. in London): *The Music of Liszt* (1954; 2nd ed., 1966); *Twentieth Century Counterpoint* (1954); *Ballet Music: An Introduction* (1958; 2nd ed., rev., 1973); with R. Layton, *Twentieth-Century Composers 3: Britain, Scandinavia and the Netherlands* (1972).

Seashore, Carl Emil, Swedish-American psychologist; b. Morlunda, Jan. 28, 1866; d. Lewiston, Idaho, Oct. 16, 1949. He was taken to the U.S. as a child; studied at Gustavus Adolphus College in Minn. (B.A., 1891), and pursued the study of psychology at Yale Univ. (Ph.D., 1895), where he was an assistant in its psychological laboratory (1895–97). He joined the faculty of the Univ. of Iowa in 1902, where he was head of its psychology dept. and its psychological laboratory (from 1905). He devised a widely used method for measuring musical talent ("Seashore Test") through special measurements of his own invention (audiometer, tonoscope, chronograph, etc.).

WRITINGS: *Measures of Musical Talent* (N.Y., 1919; 2nd ed., rev., 1939 with D. Lewis and J. Saetveit as *Seashore Measures of Musical Talents*; 3rd ed., rev., 1960); ed. *Psychology of the Vibrato in Voice and Instrument* (Iowa City, 1936); *Psychology of Music* (N.Y., 1938); *In Search of Beauty in Music: A Scientific Approach to Musical Aesthetics* (N.Y., 1947).

BIBL.: Special issue of *Iowa Studies in Psychology: Psychological Monographs*, XXXIX/2 (1929); W. Miles, "C.E. S., 1866–1949," *Biographical Memoirs*, National Academy of Sciences, XXIX (N.Y., 1956).

Sébastian, Georges (real name, **György Sebestyén**), Hungarian-born French conductor; b. Budapest, Aug. 17, 1903; d. Le Hauteville, Yvelines, April 12, 1989. He studied with Bartók, Kodály, and Weiner at the Budapest Academy of Music (graduated, 1921); then received instruction in conducting from Walter in Munich (1922–23). He conducted at the Hamburg Opera (1924–25) and with the Leipzig Gewandhaus Orch. (1925–27). After serving as principal conductor at Berlin's Städtische Oper (1927–31), he went to Moscow as music director of the Radio and as a conductor with the Phil. In 1938 he went to the U.S.; was conductor of the Scranton (Pa.) Phil. (1940–45); also conducted in South America. In 1946 he settled in Paris, where he conducted at the Opéra and the Opéra-Comique; also appeared with the Orchestre National de France. Sébastian became well known for his championship of the Romantic repertoire. He conducted complete cycles of the Brucker and Mahler syms. in France.

Sebestyén, János, esteemed Hungarian harpsichordist, organist, and pedagogue; b. Budapest, March 2, 1931. He was an organ pupil of Ferenc Gergely at the Budapest Academy of Music (graduated, 1956). He toured as a harpsichord and organ virtuoso in Europe, the U.S., and the Far East. He was founder-director of the harpsichord dept. at the Budapest Academy of Music (from 1970). In 1982 he was made a Merited Artist by the Hungarian government. In 1983, 1988, and 1993 he served as president of the jury of the Liszt International Organ Competition in Budapest.

Sebök, György, Hungarian pianist; b. Szeged, Nov. 2, 1922. He first studied piano in Szeged; then went to the Franz Liszt Academy of Music in Budapest, where he studied composition with Kodály and chamber music with Leo Weiner. In 1949 he was appointed to the faculty of the Bartók Cons. in Budapest; in 1952 he won the Liszt Prize. During the Hungarian turmoil in 1956 he went to Paris, and later settled in the U.S. In 1962 he was appointed prof. of piano at the Indiana Univ. School of Music in Bloomington; continued to travel widely, visiting South Africa and Japan as a pianist and pedagogue.

Secunda, Sholom, Russian-born American composer; b. Alexandria, near Kherson, Sept. 4, 1894; d. N.Y., June 13, 1974. His family went to the U.S. in 1907. He took music lessons with Goetschius and Bloch at the Inst. of Musical Art in N.Y., graduating in 1917. He became a naturalized American citizen in 1923. In 1932 he became a founder of the Society of Jewish Composers, Publishers and Songwriters, which was absorbed by Broadcast Music, Inc. in 1940. From 1916 to 1973 he was associated with the Yiddish Theater in N.Y., for which he wrote over 40 operettas; most of these hardly made any impression outside ethnic circles, but one song, *Bei mir bist du schön*, from the operetta *I Would if I Could* (1933), made an unexpected splash even among gentiles, and was sung, in the original Yiddish, by the Andrews Sisters, Rudy Vallee, July Garland, and Kate Smith, becoming one of the most popular songs worldwide. Secunda sold the copyright in 1937 for $30; he regained it in 1961, but never made any appreciable sum of money from it; a legal hassle with the author of the lyrics, Jacob Jacobs, further depleted Secunda's income. Other songs from his operettas were often taken as traditional; among these, *Dona, Dona, Dona*, from the operetta *Esterke* (1940), was recorded by Joan Baez. He also wrote some Jewish service music.

BIBL.: V. Secunda, *Bei Mir Bist Du Schön: The Story of S. S.* (N.Y., 1982).

Seefried, Irmgard, outstanding German soprano; b. Köngetried, Bavaria, Oct. 9, 1919; d. Vienna, Nov. 24, 1988. She received her early musical instruction from her father; then studied voice at the Augsburg Cons., graduating in 1939. She made her professional operatic debut as the Priestess in *Aida* at the Aachen Stadttheater (Nov. 8, 1940); her first appearance at the Vienna State Opera followed as Eva in *Die Meistersinger von Nürnberg* (May 2, 1943); Richard Strauss chose her for the role of the Composer in *Ariadne auf Naxos* at his 80th birthday celebration there (1944). She subsequently sang in Salzburg, Edinburgh, Berlin, Paris, London, and Buenos Aires. On Nov. 20, 1953, she made her Metropolitan Opera debut in N.Y. as Susanna in *Le nozze di Figaro*. She was made a Kammersängerin of the Vienna State Opera in 1947; was named an honorary member in 1969. In 1948 she married **Wolfgang Schneiderhan**.

BIBL.: F. Fassbind, *Wolfgang Schneiderhan, I. S.: Eine Künstler- und Lebensgemeinschaft* (Bern, 1960).

Seeger, Charles (Louis), eminent American musicologist, ethnomusicologist, teacher, and composer, father of **Pete(r) Seeger**; b. Mexico City (of American parents), Dec. 14, 1886; d. Bridgewater, Conn., Feb. 7, 1979. He was educated at Harvard Univ. (graduated, 1908). After conducting at the Cologne Opera (1910–11), he returned to the U.S. as chairman of the music dept. of the Univ. of Calif. at Berkeley (1912–19), where he gave the first classes in musicology in the U.S. (1916); then taught at N.Y.'s Inst. of Musical Art (1921–33) and the New School for Social Research (1931–35); at the latter, he gave the first classes (with Henry Cowell) in ethnomusicology in the U.S. (1932); was also active in contemporary music circles, as a composer and a music critic. He served as a technical adviser on music to the Resettlement Administration (1935–38), as deputy director of the Federal Music Project of the Works Progress Administration (1938–41), and as chief of the music division of the Pan-American Union (1941–53) in Washington, D.C.; was also a visiting prof. at Yale Univ. (1949–50). He subsequently was a research musicologist at the Inst. of Ethnomusicology at the Univ. of Calif. at Los Angeles (1960–70), and then taught at Harvard Univ. (from 1972). He was a founder and chairman (1930–34) of the N.Y. Musicological Soc., which he helped to reorganize as the American Musicological Soc. in 1934; was its president (1945–46) and also president of the American Soc. for Comparative Musicology (1935) and the Soc. for Ethnomusicology (1960–61; honorary president from 1972). Seeger also was instrumental (with Cowell and Joseph Schafer) in the formation of the N.Y. Composers' Collective (1932); since he was profoundly interested in proletarian music throughout the 1930s, he wrote on the need for a revolutionary spirit in music for such publications as *The Daily Worker*; he also contributed songs under the name Carl Sands to *The Workers Song Books* (1934 and 1935). Two of his essays are of especial historical interest: "On Proletarian Music" (*Modern Music*, XI/3 [1934]), which lamented the dearth of folk songs in the work of professional musicians, and "Grassroots for American Composers" (*Modern Music*, XVI [1938–40]), which, by shedding earlier Marxist rhetoric, had wide influence on the folk movement in the 1950s. Since many of his compositions were destroyed by fire at Berkeley in 1926, his extraordinary contribution to American music rests upon his work as a scholar whose uniquely universalist vision for the unification of the field of musicology as a whole continues to challenge the various, sometimes contentious contributing factions of musicology, ethnomusicology, and comparative musicology. He was also a noted teacher; one of his most gifted students, **Ruth (Porter) Crawford**, became his 2nd wife. In addition to Pete(r) Seeger, 2 other of his children became musicians: Mike (Michael) Seeger (b. N.Y., Aug. 15, 1933) was a folksinger and instrumentalist; after learning to play various folk instruments on his own, he became active in promoting the cause of authentic folk music of the American Southeast; became widely known for his expertise as a banjo player; with John Cohen and Tom Paley, he organized the New Lost City Ramblers in 1958; then founded the Strange Creek Singers in 1968. Peggy (actually, Margaret) Seeger (b. N.Y., June 17, 1935) was a folksinger, songwriter, and song collector; studied both classical and folk music; after further training at Radcliffe College, she became active as a performer; settled in England in 1956, becoming a naturalized subject in 1959; became a leading figure in the folk-music revival.

WRITINGS: With E. Stricklen, *Harmonic Structure and Elementary Composition* (Berkeley, 1916); *Music as Recreation* (Washington, D.C., 1940); with R. Crawford Seeger, J. Lomax, and A. Lomax, *Folk Song: USA* (N.Y., 1947; 2nd ed., rev., 1975); *Music and Society: Some New World Evidence of Their Relationship* (Washington, D.C., 1953); *Studies in Musicology, 1935–1975* (Berkeley, 1977); ed. *Essays for a Humanist: An Offering to Klaus Wachsmann* (N.Y., 1977); A. Pascarella, ed., *Studies in Musicology II, 1929–1979* (Berkeley, 1994).

BIBL.: A. Pescatello, *C. S.: A Life in American Music* (Pittsburgh, 1992).

Seeger, Horst, German musicologist; b. Erkner, near Berlin, Nov. 6, 1926. He began his training at the Berlin Hochschule für Musik (1950–55); then studied musicology at Humboldt Univ. in Berlin, where he received his Ph.D. in 1958 with the diss. *Komponist und Folklore in der Musik des 20. Jahrhunderts.* He was chief dramaturg of the (East) Berlin Komische Oper (1960–73); from 1973 to 1983 he served as Intendant of the Dresden State Opera. His books include *Wolfgang Amadeus Mozart* (Leipzig, 1956); *Kleines Musiklexikon* (Berlin, 1958); *Joseph Haydn* (Leipzig, 1961); *Der kritische Musikus: Musikkritiken aus zwei Jahrhunderten* (Leipzig, 1963); *Musiklexikon* (Leipzig, 1966); *Wir und die Musik* (Berlin, 1968); *Opern-Lexikon* (Berlin, 1978; 3rd ed., rev., 1987).

Seeger, Pete(r), noted American folksinger, songwriter, and political activist, son of **Charles (Louis) Seeger**; b. Patterson, N.Y., May 3, 1919. He studied sociology at Harvard Univ. before turning to folk music; taking up the banjo, he became active as a traveling musician; with Lee Hays and Millard Lampell, he organized the Almanac Singers in 1941, and subsequently appeared before union and political audiences; then joined the Weavers in 1949, with which he became well known via Leadbelly's "Goodnight Irene." His political activism was targeted by the House Committee on Un-American Activities, which cited him for contempt of Congress in 1956; in spite of his being blacklisted, he pursued his career and his commitment to various causes. A leading figure in the folk-song revival of the late 1950s, he won notable success with his songs "Where Have All the Flowers Gone?" and "If I Had a Hammer. "In all, he wrote over 100 songs, many of which became popular via his many tours through the U.S. and abroad. He wrote manuals for the 5-string banjo (1948; 3rd ed., rev., 1961) and the 12-string guitar (with J. Lester; 1965). J. Schwartz ed. a collection of his essays as *The Incompleat Folksinger* (1972). In 1994 he received a Kennedy Center honor.

SONG COLLECTIONS (all publ. in N.Y.): Ed. with W. Guthrie, *The People's Songbook* (1948); ed. *The Caroler's Songbag* (1952); ed. *American Favorite Ballads* (1961); *The Goofing Off Suite* (1961); *The Bells of Rhymney* (1964); *Bits and Pieces* (1965); *Oh Had I a Golden Thread* (1968); *Pete Seeger on Record* (1971).

BIBL.: D. Dunaway, *How Can I Keep from Singing? P. S.* (N.Y., 1981; new ed., 1990).

Seeger, Ruth Crawford. See **Crawford (Seeger), Ruth Porter.**

Segal, Uri, Israeli conductor; b. Jerusalem, March 7, 1944. He studied violin and conducting at the Rubin Cons. in Jerusalem; then went to London and enrolled as a conducting student at the Guildhall School of Music (1966–69); later in Siena. In 1969 he won 1st prize in the Mitropoulos Competition in N.Y.; served as Leonard Bernstein's assistant with the N.Y. Phil. (1969–70); subsequently developed a fine career conducting major orchs. in Europe and America. He was principal conductor of the Philharmonia Hungarica in Marlkreis Recklinghausen (1979–84) and of the Bournemouth Sym. Orch. (1980–82). In 1989 he became music director of the Chautauqua (N.Y.) Sym. Orch. and chief conductor of the Century Orch. Osaka in Japan.

Segerstam, Leif (Selim), Finnish conductor and composer; b. Vaasa, March 2, 1944. He studied violin and conducting (diplomas in both, 1963) and also took courses in composition with Fougstedt, Kokkonen, and Englund at the Sibelius Academy in Helsinki. He then was a student of Persinger (violin), Overton and Persichetti (composition), and Morel (conducting) at the Juilliard School of Music in N.Y., where he took his diploma (1964) and postgraduate diploma (1965); in the summer of 1964 he also attended Susskind's conducting course at the Aspen (Colo.) Music School. After conducting at the Finnish National Opera in Helsinki (1965–68), he became a conductor at the Royal Theater in Stockholm in 1968; he was made its principal conductor in 1970 and its music director in 1971. In 1972–73 he held the post of 1st conductor at the Deutsche Oper in Berlin. In 1973–74 he was general manager of the Finnish National Opera. He was chief conductor of the Austrian Radio Sym. Orch. in Vienna (1975–82) and the Finnish Radio Sym. Orch. in Helsinki (1977–87), and also was Generalmusikdirector of the State Phil. in Rheinland-Pfalz (1983–89). From 1989 to 1995 he was chief conductor of the Danish National Radio Sym. Orch. in Copenhagen. In 1995 he became music director of the Royal Theater in Stockholm. Segerstam is one of the most prolific composers of his era. He composes in what he describes as a "freely pulsative" style. Among his works are 8 violin concertos (1967–93); 2 piano concertos (1977, 1981); 19 syms. (1977–94); 8 cello concertos (1981–93); a series of *Thoughts* for Orch. (1987–96); 27 string quartets (1962–90); 4 string trios (1977–91); many other chamber pieces; piano music; organ pieces; many songs.

Segovia, Andrés, Marquis of Salobreia, great Spanish guitarist and teacher; b. Linares, near Jaen, Feb. 21, 1893; d. Madrid, June 2, 1987. He took up the guitar at a very early age; his parents opposed his choice of instrument and saw to it that he received lessons in piano and cello instead, all to no avail; while taking courses at the Granada Inst. of Music, he sought out a guitar teacher; finding none, he taught himself the instrument; later studied briefly with Miguel Llobet. He made his formal debut in Granada at the age of 16; then played in Madrid in 1912, at the Paris Cons. in 1915, and in Barcelona in 1916; toured South America in 1919. He made his formal Paris debut on April 7, 1924; his program included a work written especially for him by Roussel, entitled simply *Segovia.* He made his U.S. debut at N.Y.'s Town Hall on Jan. 8, 1928; subsequently toured all over the world, arousing admiration for his celebrated artistry wherever he went. He did much to reinstate the guitar as a concert instrument capable of a variety of expression; made many transcriptions for the guitar, including one of Bach's *Chaconne* from the Partita No. 2 for Violin. He also commissioned several composers to write works for him, including Ponce, Turina, Castelnuovo-Tedesco, Moreno-Torroba, Villa-Lobos, and Tansman. He continued to give concerts at an advanced age; made appearances in 1984 in celebration of the 75th anniversary of his professional debut. He received many honors during his long career; a commemorative plaque was affixed in 1969 to the house where he was born, honoring him as the "hijo predilecto de la ciudad." In 1981 King Juan Carlos of Spain made him Marquis of Salobreia; that same year the Segovia International Guitar Competition was founded in his honor. In 1985 he was awarded the Gold Medal of the Royal Phil. Society of London. He wrote *Andrés Segovia: An Autobiography of the Years 1893–1920* (N.Y., 1976).

BIBL.: V. Borri, *The S. Technique* (N.Y., 1972); G. Wade, *S.: A Celebration of the Man and His Music* (London, 1983); G. Wade, *Maestro S.* (London, 1986).

Seiber, Mátyás (György), significant Hungarian-born English composer; b. Budapest, May 4, 1905; d. in an automobile accident in Kruger National Park, Johannesburg, South Africa, Sept. 24, 1960. Of a musical family, he learned to play the cello at home; later entered the Budapest Academy of Music, where he studied composition with Kodály (1919–24). During the following years, he traveled as a member of a ship's orch. on a transatlantic liner; visited Russia as a music journalist. From 1928 to 1933 he taught composition at the Frankfurt am Main Hoch Cons.; was the cellist in the Lenzewski Quartet, which specialized in modern music; then was again in Budapest. The catastrophic events in Germany and the growing Nazi influence in Hungary forced him to emigrate to England in 1935, where he quickly acquired a group of loyal disciples; was co-founder of the Society for the Promotion of New Music (1942) and founder-conductor of the Dorian Singers (1945); taught at Morely College (from 1942). His early music followed the national trends of the Hungarian School; later he expanded his melodic resources to include oriental modes and also jazz, treated as folk music; by the time he arrived in England, he had added dodecaphony to his oeuvre, though he used it in a very personal, lyrical manner, as in his cantata *Ulysses* and his 3rd String Quartet. He publ. the books *Schule für Jazz-Schlagzeug* (Mainz, 1929) and *The String Quartets of Béla Bartók* (London, 1945).

WORKS: DRAMATIC: *Eva spielt mit Puppen,* opera (1934); 2 operettas; *The Invitation,* ballet (London, Dec. 30, 1960); over 25 film scores, including Orwell's *Animal Farm.* **ORCH.:** *Besardo Suite* No. 1 (1940) and No. 2 for Strings (1941); *Transylvanian Rhapsody* (1941); *Pastorale and Burlesque* for Flute and Strings (1941–42); *Fantasia concertante* for Violin and String Orch. (1943–44; London, Dec. 3, 1945); *Notturno* for Horn and Strings (1944); Concertino for Clarinet and Strings (1951; London, May 11, 1954); *Elegy* for Viola and Small Orch. (1955); *3 Pieces* for Cello and Orch. (1956); *Improvisations* for Jazz Band and Sym. Orch. (London, June 2, 1959; in collaboration with J. Dankworth). **CHAMBER:** 3 string quartets (1924; 1934–35; *Quartetto Lirico,* 1948–51); *Sarabande and Gigue* for Cello and Piano (1924); *Sonata da camera* for Violin and Cello

(1925); *Serenade* for 2 Clarinets, 2 Bassoons, and 2 Horns (1925); *Divertimento* for Clarinet and String Quartet (1928); *2 Jazzolettes* for 2 Saxophones, Trumpet, Trombone, Piano, and Percussion (1929, 1933); *4 Hungarian Folksongs* for 2 Violins (1931); *Fantasy* for Cello and Piano (1940); *Fantasia* for Flute, Horn, and String Quartet (1945); *Andantino and Pastorale* for Clarinet and Piano (1949); *Concert Piece* for Violin and Piano (1953–54); *Improvisation* for Oboe and Piano (1957); *Permutazioni a cinque* for Wind Quintet (1958); Violin Sonata (1960); piano pieces. **VOCAL:** *Ulysses*, cantata for Tenor, Chorus, and Orch., after James Joyce (1946–47; London, May 27, 1949); *4 French Folksongs* for Soprano and Strings (1948); *Faust* for Soprano, Tenor, Chorus, and Orch. (1949); *Cantata secularis* for Chorus and Orch. (1949–51); *3 Fragments from "A Portrait of the Artist as a Young Man,"* chamber cantata for Narrator, Wordless Chorus, and Instrumental Ensemble, after James Joyce (1957); *More Nonsense* for Baritone, Violin, Guitar, Clarinet, and Bass Clarinet, after E. Lear (1957); songs with orch. or instrumental accompaniment; folk song arrangements.

Seidel, Jan, Czech composer; b. Nymburk, Dec. 25, 1908. He was first attracted to architecture and graphic art; attended Alois Hába's classes in quarter-tone composition at the Prague Cons. (1936–40); then took private lessons in theory with J.B. Foerster for a more traditional musical training. He was a composer, conductor, and pianist in E.F. Burian's Theater; acted as artistic adviser to the recording firm Esta (1938–45) and the Gramophone Corp. (1945–53); was chief of the Opera of the National Theater (1958–64); then served as dramatic adviser there. In 1976 he was made a National Artist by the Czech government. His String Quartet No. 2 is in the quarter tone system, but most of his music is based on folk-song tradition according to the doctrine of socialist realism.

WORKS: OPERA: *Tonka Šibenice* (Tonka the Gallows; 1964). **ORCH.:** Sym. No. 1, *Prologue* (1942); 2 oboe concertos (1955); 2 orch. suites from the film *The Piper of Strakonice* (1956, 1958); *Lovecká sinfonietta* (Hunting Sinfonietta) for Horn and Small Orch. (1965–66; Prague, March 14, 1973); Concerto for Flute, Strings, and Piano (1966); *Giocosa* (1972). **CHAMBER:** 4 string quartets: No. 1, with Soprano (1930), No. 2, with Narrator (1940), No. 3, *Chrysanthemums* (1943), and No. 4 (1944); 2 wind quintets (1941, 1946); Violin Sonata (1950). **VOCAL:** 3 cantatas: *Call to Battle* (1946), *May Prelude* (1952), and *Message to the Living* (1953); also numerous patriotic choruses and songs.

Seidel, Toscha, Russian-born American violinist and teacher; b. Odessa, Nov. 17, 1899; d. Rosemead, Calif., Nov. 15, 1962. He began to play the violin as a small child, and took lessons with Max Fiedelmann in Odessa; subsequently studied with Alexander Fiedelmann in Berlin, and then became a pupil of Auer at the St. Petersburg Cons. He made his U.S. debut at N.Y.'s Carnegie Hall on April 14, 1918; settled in the U.S., becoming a naturalized American citizen in 1924; made many tours in Europe and the U.S.; also played in Australia. He suffered an irreversible mental illness and was confined to a sanatorium in California for several years before his death.

Seidl, Arthur, German writer on music; b. Munich, June 8, 1863; d. Dessau, April 11, 1928. He studied with Spitta and Bellermann in Berlin; completed his training at the Univ. of Leipzig (Ph.D., 1887, with the diss. *Vom Musikalisch-Erhabenen: Prolegomena zur Ästhetik der Tonkunst*; publ. in 1887; 2nd ed., 1907). He was music critic of Munich's *Neueste Nachrichten* (1899–1903).

WRITINGS: *Zur Geschichte des Erhabenheitsbegriffs seit Kant* (1889); *Hat Richard Wagner eine Schule hinterlassen?* (1892); with W. Klatte, *Richard Strauss: Eine Charakterstudie* (1896); *Moderner Geist in der deutschen Tonkunst* (1901; 2nd ed., 1913); *Wagneriana* (3 vols., 1901–02); *Moderne Dirigenten* (1902); *Kunst und Kultur* (1902); *Die Hellerauer Schulfeste und die "Bildungsanstalt Jaques-Dalcroze"* (1912); *Straussiana* (1913); *Ascania. Zehn Jahre in Anhalt* (1913); *Richard Wagners "Parsifal"* (1914); *Neue Wagneriana* (3 vols., 1914); *Hans Pfitzner* (1921); *Neuzeitliche Tondichter und zeitgenössische Tonkünstler* (2 vols. 1926).

BIBL.: L. Frankenstein, *A. S.* (Regensburg, 1913); B. Schuhmann, ed., *Musik und Kultur. Festschrift zum 50. Geburtstag A. S.s* (1913).

Seiffert, Max, eminent German musicologist; b. Beeskow an der Spree, Feb. 9, 1868; d. Schleswig, April 13, 1948. He studied musicology with Philipp Spitta at the Univ. of Berlin (Ph.D., 1891, with the diss. *J.P. Sweelinck und seine direkten deutschen Schüler*, publ. in Leipzig, 1891). He was ed.-in- chief of *Sammelbände der Internationalen Musik-Gesellschaft* (1903–14); with J. Wolf and M. Schneider, he ed. the *Archiv für Musikwissenschaft* (1918–26); also taught at Berlin's Hochschule für Musik and at the Akademie für Kirchen- und Schulmusik (from 1909). He served as provisional director of the Fürstliches Forschungsintitut für Musikwissenschaft in Bückeburg (from 1921); after it became the Staatliches Institut für deutsche Musikforschung in Berlin in 1935, he served as its director until 1942. He publ. *Geschichte der Klaviermusik* (Berlin, 1899–1901), nominally the 3rd ed. of Weitzmann's history, but actually a new and valuable study. He contributed many editions to the Denkmäler Deutscher Tonkunst series (1892–1927); also ed. the works of Sweelinck (12 vols., 1895–1901). Festschrifts were publ. in his honor for his 70th (1938) and 80th (1948) birthdays.

Seinemeyer, Meta, admired German soprano; b. Berlin, Sept. 5, 1895; d. Dresden, Aug. 19, 1929. She studied with Nikolaus Rothmühl and Ernst Grenzebach in Berlin. She made her operatic debut there in *Orphée aux enfers* at the Deutsches Opernhaus (1918), where she continued to sing until 1925; also toured the U.S. with the German Opera Co. (1923–24); then was a member of the Dresden State Opera (from 1925); also appeared in South America (1926), at the Vienna State Opera (1927), and at London's Covent Garden (1929). She married the conductor Frieder Weissmann on her deathbed. Her voice possessed a silken quality and a natural expressiveness; she was particularly esteemed for her roles in operas by Wagner, Verdi, Puccini, and Strauss.

Šejna, Karel, Czech conductor; b. Zálezly, Nov. 1, 1896; d. Prague, Dec. 17, 1982. He studied double bass with F. Cerný at the Prague Cons. (1914–20); also took private lessons in composition with K.B. Jirák. In 1921 he joined the Czech Phil. in Prague as principal double bass; later appeared as a conductor with it; in 1937 he was appointed its 2nd conductor; was its artistic director in 1949–50; then 2nd conductor again from 1950 until 1965; subsequently appeared with it as a guest conductor. He was particularly esteemed for his congenial interpretations of Czech music. In 1960 he was made an Artist of Merit by the Czech government.

Sekles, Bernhard, German conductor, composer, and teacher; b. Frankfurt am Main, March 20, 1872; d. there, Dec. 8, 1934. He studied with Knorr and Uzielli at the Hoch Cons. in Frankfurt am Main, where he became a prof. of theory in 1896. From 1923 to 1933 he was director of the Cons.

WORKS: DRAMATIC: OPERAS: *Scheherazade* (Mannheim, Nov. 2, 1917); *Die zehn Küsse* (1926). **BALLETS:** *Der Zwerg und die Infantin* (1913); *Die Hochzeit des Faun* (1921). **ORCH.:** *Aus den Garten der Semiramis*, symphonic poem; *Die vier Temperamente*, Sym.; *Sommergedicht*; *Kleine Suite*; *Serenade* for 11 Instruments. **CHAMBER:** *Passacaglia und Fuge* for String Quartet; Trio for Clarinet, Cello, and Piano; Violin Sonata; piano music. **VOCAL:** Songs.

Selig, Robert Leigh, American composer; b. Chicago, Jan. 29, 1939; d. Cambridge, Mass., Jan. 15, 1984. He studied at Northwestern Univ., and later (1966–67) took doctoral courses at Boston Univ., where he studied with Gardner Read. He held Guggenheim fellowships twice, in 1971 and in 1977. In 1968 he was appointed to the faculty at the New England Cons. of Music in Boston.

WORKS: *Mirage* for Trumpet and String Orch. (1967); *Variations* for Brass Quintet (1967); *Islands* for Chorus and Chamber Orch. (1968); Concerto for Rock Group and Orch. (1969); *Rhapsody* for Flute, Violin, and Clarinet (1970); *Orestes: Flight into Fury* for Trumpet and Piano (1970); Quartet for Voice, Flute, Cello, and Percussion (1971); Sym. for Woodwind Quintet (1971); *Chocorua*, opera for Voice, Chorus, and Chamber Orch. (1972); *Pometacomet, 1676* for Band (1974–75); *Survival Fragments* for Soprano and Piano (1976); Sonata, *3 Cryptic Portraits* for Piano (1977); *Music* for Brass Instruments (1977); *Reflections from a Back Window* for Piano (1980); *After the Ice* for Soprano and Piano (1981).

Sellars, Peter, provocative American theater producer; b. Pittsburgh, Sept. 27, 1957. His fascination with the stage began at age 10, when he began working with a puppet theater; he then attended Harvard Univ., where his bold theatrical experiments resulted in his expulsion from student theater groups. He gained wide notice when he produced Gogol's *The Inspector General* for the American Repertory Theater in Cambridge, Mass., in 1980. During the 1981–82 season, he staged a highly controversial mounting of Handel's *Orlando*, in which the protagonist is depicted as an astronaut. In 1983 he became director of the Boston Shakespeare Co. and in 1984 of the American National Theater Co. at the Kennedy Center in Washington, D.C. In 1987, at the Houston Grand Opera, he produced John Adam's opera *Nixon in China*, which he then mounted in other U.S. cities and at the Holland Festival in 1988; that same year, he jolted the Glyndebourne Festival with his staging of Nigel Osborne's *Electrification of the Soviet Union*. He oversaw the Los Angeles Festival in 1990. That same year he became artistic advisor of the Boston Opera Theatre. His staging of *Pelléas et Mélisande* in Amsterdam in 1993 concentrated on the contemporary themes of sex and violence.

BIBL.: M. Gray, "P. S.: Opera's Enfant Terrible Reaches Mark Two," *Ovation* (Sept. 1988).

Selva, Blanche, French pianist and teacher; b. Brive, Jan. 29, 1884; d. St. Amand, Tallende, Puy-de-Dome, Dec. 3, 1942. She studied piano at the Paris Cons., and took courses in composition with d'Indy at the Paris Schola Cantorum. She was one of the strongest propagandists of modern French music early in the 20th century; she presented programs of piano works by Debussy, Ravel, and others; also became a proponent of Czech music. She taught at the Schola Cantorum (1901–22); then at the Strasbourg Cons. and Prague Cons. She publ. several books dealing with piano technique; her compendium, *L'Enseignement musical de la technique du piano* (4 vols., Paris, 1922) is valuable; also publ. disquisitions on musical form: *La Sonate* (Paris, 1913); *Quelques mots sur la sonate* (Paris, 1914); *Les Sonates de Beethoven* (Barcelona, 1927); also a monograph on Déodat de Séverac (Paris, 1930).

Selvaggi, Rito, Italian composer and pedagogue; b. Noicattaro di Bari, May 22, 1898; d. Zoagli (Genoa), May 19, 1972. He studied piano and composition at the Liceo Musicale in Pesaro, and later took lessons with Busoni. He was a prof. at the Parma Cons. (1934–38), then director of the Palermo Cons. (1938–58) and the Pesaro Cons. (1959–68). He composed the operas *Maggiolata veneziana* (Naples, 1929) and *Santa Caterina de Siena* (1947); the music drama *Eletta* (1947); the oratorio *Estasi francescana* (1926); a "trittico sinfonico," *La Natività di Gesù* (1935); *Sonata drammatica* for Viola and Piano (1954); *Elegie* for Cello, Chorus, and Orch., in memory of Toscanini (1957); numerous choruses and piano transcriptions of Classical syms.

Sembach (real name, **Semfke**), **Johannes,** German tenor; b. Berlin, March 9, 1881; d. Bremerhaven, June 20, 1944. He studied in Vienna and with Jean de Reszke in Paris. In 1900 he made his operatic debut at the Vienna Court Opera. From 1905 to 1913 he was a member of the Dresden Court Opera, where he appeared as a Wagnerian and also created the role of Aegisthus in Strauss's *Elektra* (1909). On Nov. 26, 1914, he made his Metropolitan Opera debut in N.Y. as Parsifal, remaining on its roster until 1917; was again on its roster during the 1920–22 seasons. His guest engagements also took him to London, Paris, and South America. In 1925 he settled in Berlin as a voice teacher.

Semeonova, Nedyalka, Bulgarian violinist and teacher; b. Khaskovo, Dec. 2, 1901; d. Paris, March 14, 1959. A child prodigy, she studied at a very early age with her father. Following concerts in the U.S. (1913), she pursued training in Dresden with Auer, Rapoldi, and Havemann, and later with Auer in N.Y. (1921–23). Following a successful N.Y. debut in 1923, she toured throughout Europe, the U.S., India, and the Far East. In 1932 she returned to Bulgaria but continued to make tours. From 1946 she also taught violin at the Bulgarian State Cons. in Sofia.

Semkow, Jerzy, prominent Polish conductor; b. Radomsko, Oct. 12, 1928. He studied at the Univ. of Kraków (1946–50) and at the Leningrad Cons. (1951–55). After serving as assistant conductor of the Leningrad Phil. (1954–56), he conducted at Moscow's Bolshoi Theater (1956–58); also continued his training with Kleiber in Prague, Serafin in Rome, and Walter in Vienna. He was artistic director and chief conductor of the Warsaw National Opera (1959–62); then was chief conductor of the Royal Danish Theater in Copenhagen (1966–76). In 1968 he made his U.S. debut as a guest conductor of the Boston Sym. Orch. He served as music director of the St. Louis Sym. Orch. (1976–79), artistic director of the RAI orch. in Rome (1979–83), and music adviser and principal conductor of the Rochester (N.Y.) Phil. (1985–89). His guest conducting engagements took him all over the world. He is especially admired for his performances of Polish and Russian scores, particularly of works from the late Romantic era.

Sender (Barayón), Ramon, Spanish-born American poet, novelist, writer on music, and composer; b. Madrid, Oct. 29, 1934. He was sent to the U.S. in 1939 as a Spanish Civil War refugee. After studies in piano with Copeland (1948–52) and in composition with Carter, he took courses at the Accademia di Santa Cecilia in Rome (1952–53); also had private lessons with Haieff. Returning to the U.S., he had lessons with Shapero and Cowell; also studied at Brandeis Univ. (1953–54) and at the San Francisco Cons. of Music (B.Mus., 1962). In 1962 he co-founded (with Morton Subotnick) the San Francisco Tape Music Center, which gave important first performances of works by Oliveros, Riley, Reich, and others; while serving as its co-director, he continued his composition studies with Milhaud at Mills College in Oakland, California (M.A., 1965), where the Tape Music Center was moved in 1966. In 1966 Sender moved to Sonoma, California, where he undertook research into acoustic vocalizations and comparative religions; also taught hatha-yoga, meditation, and mantric chant at the Morning Star Range, a shelter for Haight-Ashbury youth; in 1969 he became co-music director of Wheeler's Ranch. He wrote a series of essays on the Open Land Movement (*The Open Land Church*, 1971; etc.); also taught courses in electronic music composition at Sonoma State Univ. (1971); traveled to South America and to India, where he studied yoga and Sanskrit. From 1976 to 1980 he served as assistant director of the Occidental Community Choir. In addition to his work as a composer, Sender devoted much time to writing essays, novels, and poetry; among his literary works are *Zero Weather* (1980) and *Death in Zamora, a Son's Search for His Mother* (1984). In 1983 he received an NEA grant for creative prose; from 1981 to 1984 he wrote book and music reviews for the *San Francisco Chronicle*.

WORKS: *Kore* for 2-channel Tape and Liquid Projections (1961); *Balances* for Amplified and Prepared String Trio and String Bass, and Mixer Console (1962); Violin Sonata (1962); *Time Fields*, study in multiple, simultaneous rhythms for Piano, Cello, String Bass, Oboe, Clarinet, and Percussion (1963); *City Scape*, a 6-hour work for approximately 10 Actor-Musicians, House, 2 Parks, and 2 Trucks (1963; in collaboration with A. Martin and K. Dewey); *Information* for 2 Pianos and Narrator

(1963); *Transformation,* theater piece (1963; in collaboration with M. Subotnick and R. Levine); *Desert Ambulance* for Accordion, 2-channel Tape, Movie, Slides, and Liquid Projections (1964; in collaboration with A. Martin); *In the Garden* for 2-channel Tape, Viola, Clarinet, and Visual Score (1965; in collaboration with A. Martin); *Loopy Gamelan on C, "O 'C' Can You Say,"* for Children's Chorus and 4 Cassette Recorders loaded with Loopies (1976); *Great[10] Grandpa Lemuel's Death-Rattle Reincarnation Blues* for Amplified Accordion and Dixieland Band with Ampex PR-10 Tape Duplicator (or equivalent) (1981); *Our Mother the Earth* for Chorus, after Tewa Pueblo Indians (1983); *I Have a Dream* for Chorus, after Martin Luther King, Jr. (1984).

Sendrey, Albert Richard, American composer, son of **Aladár Szendrei**; b. Chicago, Dec. 26, 1911. He studied in Leipzig, Paris, and London. He was an arranger for film companies in Paris (1935–37) and London (1937–44) before settling in Hollywood in 1944. Among his original works are *Oriental Suite* for Orch. (1935); 3 syms.; piano pieces; cello pieces.

Sendrey, Alfred. See **Szendrei, Aladár.**

Senilov, Vladimir, Russian composer; b. Viatka, Aug. 8, 1875; d. Petrograd, Sept. 18, 1918. He was a student of jurisprudence at the Univ. of St. Petersburg; went to Leipzig, where he studied with Hugo Riemann (1895–1901); returning to Russia, he studied composition with Rimsky-Korsakov and Glazunov at the St. Petersburg Cons., graduating in 1906. His works include a lyric drama, *Vasili Buslayev,* and an opera, *Hippolytus,* after Euripides; also the symphonic poems *In Autumn, Mtziri, Pan,* and *The Scythians*; 3 string quartets; choral pieces; songs.

Senn, Kurt Wolfgang, Swiss organist, pedagogue, and music editor; b. Szczakow, Poland, March 11, 1905; d. Bern, June 25, 1965. He studied at the Basel Cons. and with Straube in Leipzig (1923–29). He was organist in Elgg and Thalwil (1929–38), and also taught at the Zürich Academy of Music. From 1938 until his death he was organist at the Bern Cathedral. He also taught church music at the Univ. and organ at the Cons. in Bern. As a recitalist, Senn made many tours. He ed. many scores for performance.

Serafin, Tullio, eminent Italian conductor; b. Rottanova de Cavarzere, Venice, Sept. 1, 1878; d. Rome, Feb. 2, 1968. He studied at the Milan Cons. He made his conducting debut in Ferrara in 1898. In 1901 Toscanini engaged him as one of his assistant conductors at La Scala in Milan. Later he was principal conductor of La Scala (1909–14; 1917–18); from 1924 to 1934 he was a conductor at the Metropolitan Opera in N.Y. In 1934 he became chief conductor and artistic director of the Rome Opera, a post he retained until 1943; then was engaged as artistic director of La Scala (1946–47). From 1956 to 1958 he conducted at the Chicago Lyric Opera; in 1962 he was named artistic adviser of the Rome Opera. He was especially authoritative in the Italian operatic repertoire. As an artistic adviser, he helped launch the careers of Maria Callas and several other noted artists. He publ. (with A. Toni) 2 vols. on the history of Italian opera, *Stile, tradizioni e convenzioni del melodramma italiano del Settecento e del l'Ottocento* (Milan, 1958–64).

BIBL.: T. Celli and G. Pugliese, *T. S.: Il patriarca del melodramma* (Venice, 1985).

Serato, Arrigo, Italian violinist and pedagogue; b. Bologna, Feb. 7, 1877; d. Rome, Dec. 27, 1948. He began his training with his father, the cellist Francesco Serato (1843–1919), then studied with Federico Sarti at the Bologna Cons. (diploma, 1894). He was mainly active as a chamber music player; formed the Trio Bolognese with Sarti and Gustavo Tofano, and the Quartetto Bolognese with Sarti, Massarenti, and Angelo Consolini; then settled in Berlin, where he took a course in violin study with Joachim, and was also a member of Joachim's string quartet. He returned to Italy in 1915, and taught master classes at the Accademia di Santa Cecilia in Rome (1926–48); also taught postgraduate courses at the Accademia Chigiana in Siena.

BIBL.: A. Della Corte, *A. S. violinista* (Siena, 1950).

Serauky, Walter (Karl-August), eminent German musicologist; b. Halle, April 20, 1903; d. there, Aug. 20, 1959. He studied musicology in Halle and with Schering at the Univ. of Leipzig (Ph.D., 1929, with the diss. *Die musikalische Nachahmungsästhetik im Zeitraum von 1700 bis 1850*; publ. in Münster, 1929); completed his Habilitation in 1932 at the Univ. of Halle, where he subsequently served as a prof. (from 1940); then was director of the musicological inst. at the Univ. of Leipzig (from 1949), which post he shared with Besseler (from 1956). He contributed valuable essays to various German publications; also publ. *Samuel Scheidt in seinen Briefen* (Halle, 1937) and *G.F. Händel: Sein Leben, sein Werk* (Kassel and Leipzig, 1956–58).

Serebrier, José, Uruguayan-American conductor and composer; b. Montevideo, Dec. 3, 1938. He began to conduct at the age of 12; went to the U.S. in 1950; studied composition with Giannini at the Curtis Inst. of Music in Philadelphia (1956–58) and conducting with Dorati in Minneapolis; also took conducting lessons with Monteux at his summer residence in Maine. He subsequently conducted guest engagements in the U.S., South America, and Europe; gave the first performance in Poland of the 4th Sym. of Charles Ives. He was assoc. conductor of the American Sym. Orch. in N.Y. (1962–67), composer-in-residence of the Cleveland Orch. (1968–70), and music director of the Cleveland Phil. (1968–71). He was principal guest conductor of the Adelaide Sym. Orch. (from 1982); was founder and artistic director of the International Festival of the Americas (1984). In 1969 he married **Carole Ann Farley**.

WORKS: Quartet for Saxophones (1955); *Pequeña música* for Wind Quintet (1955); Sym. No. 1 (1956); *Momento psicologico* for String Orch. (1957); *Suite canina* for Wind Trio (1957); Sym. for Percussion (1960); *The Star Wagon* for Chamber Orch. (1967); *Nueve* for Double Bass and Orch. (1970); *Colores mágicos,* variations for Harp and Chamber Orch., with "Synchrona" images (Washington, D.C., May 20, 1971); *Preludio fantastico y danza magica* for 5 Percussion (1973); Violin Concerto (1992); band music.

Sereni, Mario, Italian baritone; b. Perugia, March 25, 1928. He studied at the Accademia di Santa Cecilia in Rome; also in Siena with Mario Basiola. He made his debut at the Florence May Festival in 1953, and then sang throughout Italy. In 1956 he sang at the Teatro Colón in Buenos Aires. He made his Metropolitan Opera debut in N.Y. on Nov. 9, 1957, as Gérard in *Andrea Chénier*; subsequently sang there for some 2 decades in such roles as Amonasro, Belcore, Germont, Marcello, and Sharpless; also sang in London, Vienna, Milan, Chicago, Houston, Dallas, and other opera centers.

Sérieyx, Auguste (Jean Maria Charles), French teacher, writer on music, and composer; b. Amiens, June 14, 1865; d. Montreux, Feb. 19, 1949. He studied in Paris at the Schola Cantorum with Gédalge and d'Indy where he taught composition (1900–1914). He collaborated with d'Indy on his monumental *Cours de composition* (3 vols., Paris, 1897–1933); publ. *Les Trois États de la tonalité* (Paris, 1910) and *Cours de grammaire musicale* (Paris, 1925). His compositions include both sacred and secular vocal works, a Violin Sonata, piano pieces, and songs.

BIBL.: J. Matthey, *Inventaire de fonds musical A. S.* (Lausanne, 1974).

Serkin, Peter (Adolf), outstanding American pianist, son of **Rudolf Serkin**; b. N.Y., July 24, 1947. At age 11, he enrolled at the Curtis Inst. of Music in Philadelphia, where he studied with Horszowski, Luvisi, and his father (graduated, 1964). He made his debut as a soloist with Schneider and a chamber orch. at the Marlboro (Vt.) Music Festival (1958); later studied there with the flutist Marcel Moyse, and also received additional piano training from Karl Ulrich Schnabel. He made his N.Y. debut as a soloist with Schneider and his chamber orch. (Nov. 29, 1959); his N.Y. recital debut followed (March 27, 1965). In 1973 he formed the group Tashi ("good fortune" in Tibetan) with clarinetist Richard Stoltzman, violinist Ida Kavafian, and cellist Fred Sherry; the group toured extensively, giving performances of contemporary music in particular. After leaving the group in 1980, Serkin renewed his appearances as a soloist and recitalist. While he championed modern music, he acquired a distinguished reputation as an interpreter of both traditional and contemporary scores. He excels in works by Mozart, Beethoven, Schubert, Brahms, Stravinsky, Schoenberg, Messiaen, Takemitsu, Peter Lieberson, and others. He also made appearances as a fortepianist. In 1983 he was awarded the Premio of the Accademia Musicale Chigiana in Siena. In 1992 he joined the faculty of the Curtis Inst. of Music in Philadelphia.

Serkin, Rudolf, eminent Austrian-born American pianist and pedagogue of Russian descent, father of **Peter (Adolf) Serkin**; b. Eger, March 28, 1903; d. Guilford, Vt., May 8, 1991. He studied piano with Richard Robert and composition with Joseph Marx and Schoenberg in Vienna. He made his debut as a soloist with Oskar Nedbal and the Vienna Sym. Orch. at age 12; his career began in earnest with his Berlin appearance with the Busch Chamber Orch. in 1920; thereafter he performed frequently in joint recitals with Adolf Busch, whose daughter he married in 1935. He made his U.S. debut in a recital with Busch at the Coolidge Festival in Washington, D.C., in 1933; then made a critically acclaimed appearance as a soloist with Toscanini and the N.Y. Phil. (Feb. 20, 1936). In 1939 he became a naturalized U.S. citizen. After World War II, he pursued an international career; appeared as a soloist with all the major orchs. of the world, gave recitals in the leading music centers, and played in numerous chamber music settings. In 1939 he was appointed head of the piano dept. at the Curtis Inst. of Music in Philadelphia; was its director from 1968 to 1976. In 1950 he helped to establish the Marlboro (Vt.) Music Festival and school, and subsequently served as its artistic director. In 1985 he celebrated his 70th anniversary as a concert artist. He received the Presidential Medal of Freedom in 1963; in 1988 he was awarded the National Medal of Arts. The authority and faithfulness of his interpretations of the Viennese classics placed him among the masters of the 20th century.

Serly, Tibor, Hungarian-born American violist, conductor, teacher, music theorist, and composer; b. Losonc, Nov. 25, 1901; d. London, Oct. 8, 1978. His family moved to the U.S. in 1905, and he became a naturalized American citizen in 1911. He received his early musical training from his father, Lajos Serly, founder of the first Hungarian theater in N.Y. and his own Hungarian-German opera company; then returned to Hungary, where he enrolled in the Royal Academy of Music in Budapest; there he took courses with Koessler, Hubay, Bartók, and Kodály (graduated, 1925). Upon his return to the U.S., he was a violist in the Cincinnati Sym. Orch. (1926–27); then was a violinist (1928–35) and assistant conductor (1933–35) with the Philadelphia Orch.; subsequently was a violinist in the NBC Sym. Orch. in N.Y. (1937–38). After studying conducting with Scherchen in Europe (1934), he led various concerts in N.Y.; was primarily active as a private teacher from 1938. When Bartók settled in the U.S. in 1940, Serly became his closest friend and adviser; after Bartók's death in 1945, Serly completed the last 17 measures of Bartók's 3rd Piano Concerto, and totally reconstructed and orchestrated Bartók's Viola Concerto from 13 unnumbered MS pages. In 1948 he devised a system of composition called Modus Lascivus. Although the medieval Modus Lascivus was synonymous with the C-major scale, Serly expanded its connotation to include enharmonic modulation. He wrote the treatises *A Second Look at Harmony* (1965), *Modus Lascivus: The Road to Enharmonicism* (1976), and *The Rhetoric of Melody* (with N. Newton; 1978). Shortly before his death, he arranged Bartók's Viola Concerto for cello and orch.

WORKS: BALLETS: *Mischchianza* (1937); *Ex Machina* (1943); *Cast Out* (1973). **ORCH.:** *Transylvania Rhapsody* (1926); Viola Concerto (1929); 2 syms.: No. 1 (1931; Budapest, May 13, 1935, composer conducting) and No. 2 for Winds, Brass, and Percussion (1932); *6 Dance Designs* (1932–33; Budapest, May 13, 1935); *The Pagan City*, symphonic poem (1932–38; in collaboration with J. Klenner); *Transylvanian Suite* for Chamber Orch. (1935); *Sonata concertante* for Strings (1935–36); *Colonial Pageant* and *Alarms and Excursions*, 2 suites (1936–37); *Midnight Madrigal* for Trumpet and Orch. (1939); Concerto for 2 Pianos and Orch. (1943–58); *American Elegy*, based on *Taps* (1945); *Rhapsody* for Viola and Orch. (1946–48; N.Y., Feb. 27, 1948); *Miniature Suite* for 12 Winds and Percussion (1947; revision of a discarded *Rhapsody* of 1927); *American Fantasy of Quodlibets* (1950); Concerto for Trombone and Chamber Orch. (1952–54); *Lament: Homage to Bartók* (1955); Concerto for Violin, Winds, and Orch. (1953–58; Portland, Oreg., Nov. 30, 1978); *Symphonic Variations* for Audience and Orch. (1956); String Sym. (1956–58); *Little Christmas Cantata* for Audience and Orch. (1957); *Symphony in 4 Cycles* for Strings (1960); *Concertino 3 × 3* for Piano and Chamber Orch. (1964–65; Syracuse, N.Y., Jan. 13, 1967); *Canonic Fugue in 10 Voices on 10 Tones* for Strings (1971; Portland, Oreg., June 5, 1977); *Music* for 2 Harps and Strings (1976). **CHAMBER:** Violin Sonata (1923); String Quartet (1924); Sonata for Solo Violin (1947); Trio for Clarinet, Violin, and Piano (1949); *Chorale in 3 Harps* (1967); *Rondo Fantasy in Stringometrics* for Violin and Harp (1969); piano pieces, including *40 Piano Études in Modus Lascivus* (1946–60; 1st complete perf. by his 2nd wife, Miriam Molin, N.Y., May 4, 1977). **VOCAL:** *4 Songs from Chamber Music* for Soprano and Orch., after James Joyce (1926); *Strange Story* for Mezzo-soprano and Orch., after E. Wylie (1927); *Anniversary Cantata on a Quodlibet* for Voices and Small Orch. (1966); *Consovowels 1–5*: No. 1 for Soprano (1968), Nos. 2 and 3 for Soprano and Clarinet (1970, 1971), and Nos. 4 and 5 for Soprano and Violin (both 1974).

Sermilä, Jarmo (Kalevi), Finnish trumpeter and composer; b. Hämeenlinna, Aug. 16, 1939. He was active as a jazz musician before studying at the Hämeenlinna School of Music; subsequently received composition instruction from Marttinen and Kokkonen at the Sibelius Academy in Helsinki (diploma, 1975) and from Kovaříček in Prague; concurrently pursued training in musicology and literature at the Univ. of Helsinki (M.A., 1975). He was artistic director of the Finnish Radio's Experimental Music Studio in Helsinki (1973–79); also was composer-in-residence for the city of Hameenlinna (1977–82). He also pursued a career as a trumpeter, performing in both classical and jazz settings. His compositions, which range from aleatory to jazz pieces, employ various contemporary means.

WORKS: BALLET: *The Wolf Bride*, electroacoustic ballet (1980). **ORCH.:** *Early Music* for Strings (1971); *Pentagram* for Trumpet and Orch. (1972); *Mimesis 2* (1974); *Cornologia* for 24 to 44 Horns (1975); *Counterbass* for Double Bass and String Orch. (1975); *Manifesto* (1977); *Time Machine* for 4 Trumpets, 4 Trombones, 4 Horns, Baritone Horn, Tuba, and 4 Percussion (1977); *A Circle of the Moon* for Oboe and Orch. (1979); *LABOR!* (1982); *Due divertimenti* for Oboe, Trumpet, and Strings (1983); *Transformations* for Strings (1984); *La Place Revisitée* for Flute or Alto Flute, Clarinet or Bass Clarinet, 2 Percussionists, Strings, and Tape (1984); *Rilievo 4* for Small Orch. (1989). **CHAMBER:** *Monody* for Horn and Percussion (1970); *Homage to EV* for 2 Horns, 2 Trumpets, 3 Trombones, and 2 Percussionists (1971); *Crisis* for Clarinet, 2 Violins, Viola, and Cello (1972); *Colors & Contrasts* for Flute, Violin, and Piano (1976); *Thus I Saw This* for Flute, Oboe, Clarinet, Bassoon, and Horn (1977); *Invocation* for English Horn, Baritone, and Tape (1978); *Dissimilitudes* for 2 Violins, 2 Violas, and 2 Cellos (1980); *A Canonized Reflection* for 2 Flutes, 2 Oboes, 2 Clarinets, 2 Horns, 2 Trumpets, 2 Trombones, and 2 Percussionists (1980); *The Mythic Man* for 5 Percussionists (1982); *The Sermon* for Trumpet and 4 Reciters (1983); *A Prague Thoroughfare* for Electric Guitar, 2 Violins, Viola, and Cello (1983); *. . . and an elk was formed by Hiisi* for 2 Trombones, 2 Percussionists, and Tape (1984); *Jean-Eduard en face du fait accompli* for Soprano, Alto, Tenor, and Baritone Saxophones (1986); *Movimenti e ritornelli* for 2 Violins, Viola, and Cello (1986); *Ego 1* for Violin, Double Bass, and Accordion (1988); *Final Conclusion* for Trumpet and Tape (1988); *Ego 2* for Accordion, Flute, and Guitar (1990); *Das Gebläse* for Horn (1993). **OTHER:** Vocal works; electroacoustic music; jazz pieces.

Serocki, Kazimierz, prominent Polish composer; b. Toruń, March 3, 1922; d. Warsaw, Jan. 9, 1981. He studied piano with Szpinalski and composition with Sikorski at the Łódž Cons. (graduated, 1946); then received further training in composition from Boulanger and in piano from Lévy in Paris (1947–48). He was active as a pianist in Poland (1946–51); formed, with Tadeusz Baird and Jan Krenz, the modernistic Group '49, dedicated to the cause of the avant-garde; in 1956 he was one of the organizers of the audaciously futuristic "Warsaw Autumn" Festivals. In the interim he toured as a concert pianist. In his early music, he fell into the fashionable neo-Classical current strewn with tolerable dissonances and spiked with bristling atonalities; experimented with Webernized dodecaphonies before molding his own style of composition, an amalgam of pragmatic serialism and permissible aleatory procedures, while maintaining an air of well-nigh monastic nominalism in formal strictures and informal structures; in some pieces, he made incursions into the exotic field of American jazz.

WORKS: ORCH.: *Symphonic Scherzo* (1948); *Triptych* for Chamber Orch. (1949); *4 tańce ludowe* (4 People's Dances) for Chamber Orch. (1949); *Romantic Concerto* for Piano and Orch. (1950); 2 syms.: No. 1 (1952) and No. 2, *Symphony of Songs,* for Soprano, Baritone, Chorus, and Orch. (Warsaw, June 11, 1953); Trombone Concerto (1953); *Sinfonietta* for 2 String Orchs. (1956); *Musica concertante* for Chamber Orch. (1958); *Episodes* for Strings and 3 groups of Percussion (1958–59); *Segmenti* for 12 Winds, 6 Strings, Piano, Celesta, Harpsichord, Guitar, Mandolin, and 58 Percussion Instruments (1960–61); *Symphonic Frescoes* (1963); *Forte e piano* for 2 Pianos and Orch. (1967; Cologne, March 29, 1968); *Dramatic Story* (1968–71; Warsaw, Sept. 23, 1971); *Fantasia elegiaca* for Organ and Orch. (1971–72; Baden-Baden, June 9, 1972); Sonatina for Trombone and Orch. (1972–73; Strasbourg, Dec. 19, 1975); *Concerto alla cadenza* for Recorder and Orch. (1975); *Ad Libitum,* 5 pieces (1976; Hamburg, Sept. 17, 1977); *Pianophonie* for Piano, Electronic Sound Transformation, and Orch. (1976–78; Metz, Nov. 18, 1978). **CHAMBER:** Suite for 4 Trombones (1953); *Continuum,* sextet for 123 Percussion Instruments manipulated by 6 Multimanual Percussionists (1965–66); *Swinging Music* for Clarinet, Trombone, Cello or Double Bass, and Piano (1970); *Phantasmagoria* for Piano and Percussion (1970–71); *Impromptu fantastique* for 6 Flutes, Mandolins, Guitars, Percussionists, and Piano (1973–74). **PIANO:** Sonatina (1952); Sonata (1955); *A piacere* (1963). **VOCAL:** *3 melodie Kurpiowskie* (3 Melodies from Kurpie) for 6 Sopranos, 6 Tenors, and Chamber Orch. (1949); 2 cantatas: *Mazowsze* (1950) and *Murarz warszawski* (1951); *Serce nocy* (Heart of the Night), cycle for Baritone and Piano (1956); *Oczy powietrza* (Eyes of the Wind), cycle for Soprano and Orch. or Piano (1957–58); *Niobe* for 2 Narrators, Chorus, and Orch. (1966); *Poezje* (Poems) for Soprano and Chamber Orch. (1968–69).

Seroen, Berthe, Belgian-born Dutch soprano and teacher; b. Mechelen, Nov. 27, 1882; d. Amsterdam, April 17, 1957. She was trained at the Brussels Cons. After giving concerts in Belgium and France, she made her operatic debut in Antwerp in 1908 at the Flemish Opera as Elisabeth in *Tannhäuser.* She later sang at the Théâtre Royal de la Monnaie in Brussels. In 1914 she settled in Holland and pursued a career as a concert artist. She taught at the Rotterdam Cons. (from 1927), and at the conservatories in Amsterdam and Utrecht (from 1937). Seroen was particularly admired for her performances of contemporary Dutch and French art songs.

BIBL.: W. Paap, "B. S.," *Mens en melodie,* XIII (1957).

Seroff, Victor, Russian-born American writer on music; b. Batumi, Caucasus, Oct. 14, 1902; d. N.Y., May 10, 1979. He studied law at the Univ. of Tiflis; then took piano lessons with Moriz Rosenthal in Vienna and Theodore Szanto in Paris. He eventually settled in N.Y. and became a naturalized American citizen.

WRITINGS (all publ. in N.Y.): *Dmitri Shostakovich: The Life and Background of a Soviet Composer* (1943); *The Mighty Five: The Cradle of Russian National Music* (1948); *Rachmaninoff* (1950); *Maurice Ravel* (1953); *Debussy, Musician of France* (1956); *Hector Berlioz* (1967); *Prokofiev: A Soviet Tragedy* (1968); *Mussorgsky* (1968); *Franz Liszt* (1970).

BIBL.: M. Werner, *To Whom It May Concern: The Story of V.I. S.* (N.Y., 1931).

Serrano y Ruiz, Emilio, Spanish conductor, teacher, and composer; b. Vitoria, March 13, 1850; d. Madrid, April 8, 1939. He studied at the Madrid Cons., and taught piano and composition there (1870–1920); also conducted sym. concerts in Madrid. He wrote 5 operas: *Mitridates* (Madrid, 1882), *Doña Juana la Loca* (Madrid, 1890), *Irene de Otranto* (Madrid, Feb. 17, 1891), *Gonzalo de Córdoba* (Madrid, Dec. 6, 1898), and *La Maja de Rumbo* (Buenos Aires, Sept. 24, 1910); also a zarzuela, *La bejarana* (in collaboration with F. Alonso); Sym. (1887); Piano Concerto (1904); String Quartet (1908); songs.

Serres, Louis (Arnal) de, French composer and teacher; b. Lyons, Nov. 8, 1864; d. Néronde, Loire, Dec. 25, 1942. He studied at the Paris Cons. with Taudou (harmony) and Franck (organ). He joined the faculty of the Schola Cantorum in 1900; when the institution was reorganized in 1935 as the École César Franck, he became its director. His compositions include *Les Heures claires* for Voice and Orch.; *Les Caresses* for Orch.; choruses, motets, and songs.

Sessions, Roger (Huntington), eminent American composer and teacher; b. Brooklyn, Dec. 28, 1896; d. Princeton, N.J., March 16, 1985. He studied music at Harvard Univ. (B.A., 1915); took a course in composition with Parker at the Yale School of Music (B.M., 1917); then took private lessons with Bloch in Cleveland and N.Y.; this association was of great importance for Sessions; his early works were strongly influenced by Bloch's rhapsodic style and rich harmonic idiom verging on polytonality. He taught theory at Smith College (1917–21); then was appointed to the faculty of the Cleveland Inst. of Music, first as assistant to Bloch, then as head of the dept. (1921–25). He lived mostly in Europe from 1926 to 1933, supporting himself on 2 Guggenheim fellowships (1926, 1927), an American Academy in Rome fellowship (1928), and a Carnegie Foundation grant (1931); also was active with Copland in presenting the Copland-Sessions Concerts of contemporary music in N.Y. (1928–31), which played an important cultural role at that time. His subsequent teaching posts included Boston Univ. (1933–35), the New Jersey College for Women (1935–37), Princeton Univ. (1935–44), and the Univ. of Calif. at Berkeley (1944–53); returned to Princeton as Conant Professor of Music in 1953 and as co-director of the Columbia-Princeton Electronic Music Center in N.Y. in 1959; subsequently taught at the Juilliard School of Music in N.Y. (1965–85); also was Bloch Prof. at Berkeley (1966–67) and Norton Prof. at Harvard Univ. (1968–69). In 1938 he was elected a member of the National Inst. of Arts and Letters, in 1953 of the American Academy of Arts and Letters, and in 1961 of the American Academy of Arts and Sciences. In 1974 he received a special citation of the Pulitzer Award Committee "for his life's work as a distinguished American composer." In 1982 he was awarded a 2nd Pulitzer Prize for his *Concerto for Orchestra* (1979–81). In his compositions, Sessions evolved a remarkably compact polyphonic idiom, rich in unresolvable dissonances and textural density, and yet permeated with true lyricism. In his later works, he adopted a *sui generis* method of serial composition. The music of Sessions is decidedly in advance of his time; the difficulty of his idiom, for both performers and listeners, creates a paradoxical situation in which he is recognized as one of the most important composers of the century, while actual performances of his works are exasperatingly infrequent.

WORKS: DRAMATIC: OPERAS: *Lancelot and Elaine* (1910); *The Fall of the House of Usher* (1925; unfinished); *The Trial of Lucullus* (Berkeley, April 18, 1947); *Montezuma* (1941–63; West

Berlin, April 19, 1964). **INCIDENTAL MUSIC TO:** L. Andreyev's *The Black Maskers* (Northampton, Mass., June 1923; orch suite, 1928; Cincinnati, Dec. 5, 1930); Volkmüller's *Turandot* (Cleveland, May 8, 1925). **ORCH.:** Sym. in D major (1917); 9 numbered syms.: No. 1 (Boston, April 22, 1927), No. 2 (1944–46; San Francisco, Jan. 9, 1947), No. 3 (1955–57; Boston, Dec. 6, 1957), No. 4 (1958; Minneapolis, Jan. 2, 1960), No. 5 (Philadelphia, Feb. 7, 1964), No. 6 (Newark, N.J., Nov. 19, 1966), No. 7 (Ann Arbor, Mich., Oct. 1, 1967), No. 8 (N.Y., May 2, 1968), and No. 9 (1975–78; Syracuse, Jan. 17, 1980); *Nocturne* (1921–22); *3 Dirges* (1933; withdrawn); Violin Concerto (1930–35; Chicago, Jan. 8, 1940); Piano Concerto (N.Y., Feb. 10, 1956); *Divertimento* (1959–60; Honolulu, Jan. 9, 1965); *Rhapsody* (Baltimore, March 18, 1970); Concerto for Violin, Cello, and Orch. (N.Y., Nov. 5, 1971); Concertino for Chamber Orch. (Chicago, April 14, 1972); *Concerto for Orchestra* (1979–81; Boston, Oct. 23, 1981). **CHAMBER:** Piano Trio (1916); 3 violin sonatas (1916; 1953; 1981, unfinished); *Pastorale* for Flute (1927; not extant); 2 string quartets: No. 1 (1936; Washington, D.C., April 1937) and No. 2 (Madison, Wisc., May 28, 1951); Duo for Violin and Cello (1942); String Quintet (1957–58; N.Y., Nov. 23, 1959); 6 Pieces for Cello (1966; N.Y., March 31, 1968); *Canons (to the Memory of Igor Stravinsky)* for String Quartet (1971); Duo for Violin and Cello (1978; unfinished). **KEYBOARD: PIANO:** 3 sonatas: No. 1 (1927–30; N.Y., May 6, 1928), No. 2 (1946; N.Y., March 1947), and No. 3 (1964–65; Berkeley, Calif., March 1969); *4 Pieces* for Children (1935–39); *Pages from a Diary*, later titled *From My Diary* (1937–39); *5 Pieces* (1975); *Waltz* (1977–78). **ORGAN:** *3 Chorale Preludes* (1924–26); *Chorale* (1938). **VOCAL:** *Romauldo's Song* for Soprano and Orch. (Northampton, Mass., June 1923); *On the Beach at Fontana* for Soprano and Piano (1930); *Turn, O Libertad* for Chorus and Piano, 4-hands or 2 Pianos (N.Y., April 1944); *Idyll of Theocritus* for Soprano and Orch. (1953–54; Louisville, Jan. 14, 1956); *Mass* for Unison Chorus (1955; N.Y., April 1956); *Psalm CXL* for Soprano and Organ (Princeton, N.J., June 1963; also for Soprano and Orch., Boston, Feb. 11, 1966); *When Lilacs Last in the Dooryard Bloom'd*, cantata for Soprano, Alto, Baritone, Chorus, and Orch. (1964–70; Berkeley, Calif., May 23, 1971); *3 Choruses on Biblical Texts* for Chorus and Orch. (1971–72; Amherst, Mass., Feb. 8, 1975).

WRITINGS: *The Musical Experience of Composer, Performer, Listener* (Princeton, N.J., 1950); *Harmonic Practice* (N.Y., 1951); *Reflections on the Music Life in the United States* (N.Y., 1956); *Questions about Music* (Cambridge, Mass., 1970); E. Cone, ed., *Roger Sessions on Music: Collected Essays* (Princeton, N.J., 1979); A. Olmstead, ed., *Correspondence of Roger Sessions* (Ithaca, N.Y., 1992).

BIBL.: M. Brunswick, "American Composers, X: R.H. S.," *Modern Music*, X (1932–33); M. Schubart, "R. S.: Portrait of an American Composer," *Musical Quarterly* (April 1946); A. Imbrie, "R. S.: In Honor of his 65th Birthday," *Perspectives of New Music*, i/1 (1962); E. Schweitzer, *Generation in String Quartets of Carter, S., Kirchner, and Schuller* (diss., Eastman School of Music, 1965); E. Cone, "In Honor of R. S.," *Perspectives of New Music*, X/2 (1972); A. Imbrie, "The Symphonies of R. S.," *Tempo*, No. 103 (1972); L. Wright and A. Bagnall, "R.H. S.: A Selective Bibliography and a Listing of His Compositions," *Current Musicology*, 15 (1973); R. Henderson, *Tonality in the Pre-serial Instrumental Music of R. S.* (diss., Eastman School of Music, 1974); A. Olmstead, "R. S.: A Personal Portrait," *Tempo*, No. 127 (1978); C. Oja, "The Copland-S. Concerts," *Musical Quarterly*, LXV (1979); H. Gleason and W. Becker, "R. S.," *20th-century American Composers* (Bloomington, Ind., 2nd ed., rev., 1981); M. Campbell, *The Piano Sonatas of R. S.: Sequel to a Tradition* (diss., Peabody Inst., 1982); C. Gagne and T. Caras, "R. S.," in *Soundpieces: Interviews with American Composers* (Metuchen, N.J., 1982); S. Kress, *R. S., Composer and Teacher: A Comparative Analysis of R. S.'s Philosophy of Educating Composers and his Approach to Composition in Symphonies Nos. 2 and 8* (diss., Univ. of Florida, 1982); C. Mason, *A Comprehensive Analysis of R. S.'s Opera Montezuma* (diss., Univ. of Ill., Urbana, 1982); F. Prausnitz, *R. S.: A Critical Biography* (London, 1983); O. Daniel, "R. S.," *Ovation* (March 1984); R. Meckna, *The Rise of the American Composer-Critic: Aaron Copland, R. S., Virgil Thomson, and Elliott Carter in the Periodical "Modern Music," 1924–1946* (diss., Univ. of Calif., Santa Barbara, 1984); A. Olmstead, *R. S. and his Music* (Ann Arbor, 1985); idem, *Conversations with R. S.* (Boston, 1986); M. Nott, "R. S.'s Fugal Studies with Ernest Bloch: A Glimpse into the Workshop," *American Music* (Fall 1989).

Šesták, Zdeněk, Czech composer and musicologist; b. Citoliby, near Louny, Dec. 10, 1925. He received training in composition from Hlobil and Krejčí at the Prague Cons. (1945–50) and in musicology at the Charles Univ. in Prague (1945–50). In addition to composing, Šesták devoted much time to researching the musical history of Citoliby and its leading composers of the past, Václav Jan Kopřiva and his son Karel Blažej Kopřiva. Their works, along with other 18th-century composers of the region, are showcased in Šesták's anthology of recordings entitled *Hudba citolibských mistrů 18. století* (Music of the Citoliby Masters of the 18th Century, 1968 and 1985). In his own music, Šesták has followed the path of Czech modernism without straying from accessible modes of expression.

WORKS: ORCH.: 6 syms.: (*Epitaph*, 1961; 1970; 1971; 1973; *Chronos*, 1978; *Eternal Heart's Unrest*, 1979); *Symphonic Fantasie* (1966); Concerto for Strings (1974); *Sonata Sinfonica* for Winds, Bell, and Kettledrums (1976); *Actualisation of an Instant*, symphonic variations (1980); *Sursum Corda*, concerto for Violin, Winds, Harp, Celesta, Gong, and Kettledrums (1981); *Meditations of Socrates*, viola concerto (1982); *Fatum*, vocal-symphonic fragment after Sophocles (1983); *Memoria*, symphonic fresco (1983). **CHAMBER:** 9 string quartets (n.d.; n.d.; *Acroasis*, 1974; *Known Voice*, 1975; *Labyrinth of Soul*, 1976; *Variations of Mácha*, 1993; *Soliloquy*, 1994; 1995); Concerto for Flute, Oboe, Clarinet, Horn, and Bassoon (1964); *Divertimento Concertante* for 5 Winds (1966); *5 Virtuoso Inventions* for Bassoon (1966); Sonata for 2 Clarinets (1967); *Music* for Oboe (1967); *3 Metamorphoses* for Flute (1968); *Musica tripartita* for Clarinet (1968); *Concentus musicus*, string quintet (1975); *Partita profana* for 2 Oboes, English Horn, and 2 Bassoons (1976); *Euterpé* for Oboe and Piano (1977); *Sonata da camera* for 2 Oboes, 2 Clarinets, 2 Horns, and 2 Bassoons (1978); *Evocationes paschales* for Trumpet and Organ (1992); *Dies laetitiae*, sonata for Trumpet and Organ (1993). **VOCAL:** Cycle of 6 sacred cantatas for Voices (1972–93); 3 choral cycles (*Hommage à Apollinaire*, 1972; *Portrait of the Poet Konstantin Biebl*, 1974; *Pushkinian Vigils*, 1978); *Manon Lescaut*, chamber cantata for Soprano, Tenor, Chorus, Viola, and Piano (1975); other cantatas; 16 song cycles for Voice and Piano; children's songs.

Seter, Mordecai, Russian-born Israeli composer; b. Novorossiysk, Feb. 26, 1916; d. Tel Aviv, Aug. 8, 1994. He went to Palestine in 1926, where he studied with J. Weinberg and R. Burstein-Arber; then traveled to Paris, where he received instruction in piano from Lévy and in theory from Dandelot (1932–34), completing his training with Dukas (1934–35) and Boulanger (1935–37) at the École Normale de Musique. Returning to Palestine, he taught at the Rubin Academy of Music at the Univ. of Tel Aviv (from 1951); was a prof. there from 1972 until his retirement as prof. emeritus in 1985. In 1962 he received the Prix d'Italie, in 1965 the Israel State Prize, and in 1983 the A.C.U.M. Prize. His works were marked by the eastern Mediterranean style and techniques of composition.

WORKS: DRAMATIC: BALLETS: *Pas de deux* or *Women in Tent* (ballet version of the *Ricercar*, 1956); *Midnight Vigil, Rhapsody on Yemenite Themes* (1958); *The Legend of Judith* (1962); *Part Real, Part Dream* (ballet version of the *Fantasia concertante*, 1964); *Jephthah's Daughter* (ballet version of sym. score, 1965); *Stone of Destiny* (1974). **RADIOPHONIC ORATORIO:** *Midnight Vigil* (1962; concert version of the ballet; Jerusalem, July 16, 1963). **ORCH.:** *Elegy* for Viola or Clarinet and Orch. or Piano (1954); *Ricercar* for Violin, Viola, Cello, and String Ensemble (1956); *Variations* (1959); *Fantasia concertante* for Chamber Orch. (1965); Sinfonietta (1966); *Yemenite Suite* for Chamber

Orch., with optional Voice (1966); *Meditation* (1967); *Rounds* for Chamber Orch. (1967–68); *Requiem* for Oboe, Piano, and Strings (1970). **CHAMBER:** *Partita* for Violin and Piano (1951); Sonata for 2 Violins (1952); Sonata for Solo Violin (1953); *Diptyque* for Wind Quintet (1955); *Chamber Music 1970*, 6 works for different instrumental combinations (1970); *Concertante* for Violin, Oboe, Horn, and Piano (1973); 2 piano quartets (1973–81; 1982); Piano Trio (1973); Woodwind Trio (1974); Quintet for Violin, Cello, Flute, Horn, and Piano (1975); *Ensemble* for 6 Instruments (1975); *Solo and Tutti* for Clarinet and String Quartet (1976); 4 string quartets (1976–77); *The Double* for Clarinet and Piano (1986); *Post Scriptum* for String Quartet (1986). **PIANO:** Sonata (1982); *Triptyque I, II*, and *III* (all 1985); *Contrasts* (1987). **VOCAL:** *Sabbath Cantata* for Soloists, Chorus, and String Orch. (1940); *Jerusalem* for Chorus and Orch. (1966); *Saperi* for Chorus, Percussion, Piano, and Strings (1968).

Ševčik, Otakar, noted Czech violinist and pedagogue; b. Horaždowitz, March 22, 1852; d. Písek, Jan. 18, 1934. He studied violin with his father; then at the Prague Cons. with Anton Bennewitz. From 1870 to 1873 he was concertmaster of the Mozarteum in Salzburg; held a similar post in the Theater an der Wien in Vienna. He was a prof. at the Prague Cons. (1892–1906); after teaching privately in Písek, he was prof. of violin at the Vienna Academy of Music (1909–18), and then taught at the Prague Master School (1919–21); also gave master classes in the U.S. (1920, 1924, 1931), London (1932), and elsewhere. His method, in contradistinction to the usual diatonic system, is founded on chromatic progressions, especially valuable in securing both accuracy and facility. His most famous pupils were Jan Kubelík, Efrem Zimbalist, and Erica Morini. He wrote many pieces for solo violin.

WRITINGS: *Schule der Violine-Technik* (1881); *Schule der Bogentechnik* (1895); *Lagenwechsel und Tonleiter-Vorstudien* (1895); *Triller-Vorstudien und Ausbildung des Finger-Anschlages* (1901); *Doppelgriff-Vorstudien in Terzen, Sexten, Oktaven und Dezimen* (1901); *Violine-Schule für Anfänger* (1904–08).

BIBL.: V. Nopp, *Profesor O. S.: Žvot a dílo* (Professor O. S.: Life and Work; Brno, 1948); O. Ševl and J. Dostál, eds., *O. S.* (Prague, 1953).

Séverac, (Marie-Joseph-Alexandre) Déodat de, French composer; b. Saint Félix de Caraman en Lauragais, Haute-Garonne, July 20, 1872; d. Céret, Pyrénées-Orientales, March 24, 1921. He studied piano with his father, a painter and music lover, then in Toulouse at the Dominican College of Sorèze, at the Univ. (law), and at the Cons. (1893–96); also took courses with d'Indy and Magnard (composition), Blanche Selva and Albéniz (piano), Guilmant (organ), and Bordes (choral conducting) at the Paris Schola Cantorum. After completing his training (1907), he divided his time between Paris and his native town, devoting himself mainly to composition. His works are notable for their Gallic refinement.

WORKS: DRAMATIC: OPERAS: *Le Coeur du moulin* (1903–08; Paris, Dec. 8, 1909); *Héliogabale* (Béziers, Aug. 21, 1910); *La Fille de la terre* (Coursan, July 1913); *Le Roi pinard* (1919). **INCIDENTAL MUSIC TO:** L. Damard's *Le Mirage* (1905); M. Navarre's *Muguetto* (Tarn, Aug. 13, 1911); E. Verhaeren's *Hélène de Sparthe* (Paris, May 5, 1912). **ORCH.:** 4 symphonic poems: *L'Automne* for Voice and Orch. (1900), *L'Hiver* for Voice and Orch. (1900), *Nymphes au crépuscule* (1901), and *Les Grenouilles qui demandent un roi* (1909–21); *Didon et Enée*, suite (1903); *Tryptique* (1903–04). **CHAMBER:** *Sérénade au clair de lune* for Flute or Oboe, Piano, Harp, and String Quintet (1890; rev. 1919); Piano Quintet (1898); *Les Muses sylvestres*, suite for 5 Woodwinds and String Quartet (1908); *Le Parc aux cerfs* for Oboe, String Quintet, and Piano (1909); piano pieces; organ music. **VOCAL:** Choral works; arrangements of early folk songs.

BIBL.: W. Roberts, "D. d.S.," *Music & Letters*, III (1922); B. Selva, *D. d.S.* (Paris, 1930); P. Landormy, "D. d.S.," *Musical Quarterly* (April 1934); E. Brody, *The Piano Works of D. d.S.: A Stylistic Analysis* (diss., N.Y. Univ., 1964); *Centenaire D. d.S.* (Paris, 1972).

Severinsen, Doc (actually, **Carl Hilding**), American trumpeter, bandleader, conductor, and teacher; b. Arlington, Oregon, July 7, 1927. He studied cornet with his father and with Benny Baker. After playing lead trumpet in the big bands of Charlie Barnet, Tommy Dorsey, and Benny Goodman, he joined the staff of NBC in 1949 and appeared regularly on television. He became assistant conductor of Skitch Henderson's orch. on Johnny Carson's "Tonight" television show in 1962, and from 1967 to 1992 was the music director. He also worked with his own groups in concert and nightclub settings, made many recordings, and was active in brass clinics and workshops for young musicians. He likewise appeared as a trumpet virtuoso and conductor with various American orchs. In 1993 he was named principal pops conductor of the Minnesota Orch. in Minneapolis. While perhaps best known for his work in popular music, he has not forsaken the performance of more serious music. On Sept. 24, 1992, he was soloist in the premiere of Zwilich's Trumpet Concerto in San Diego.

Severn, Edmund, English-American composer and teacher; b. Nottingham, Dec. 10, 1862; d. Melrose, Mass., May 14, 1942. In 1866 his father, a violinist, settled in Hartford, Conn.; Severn studied violin with him and with Bernhard Listemann in Boston; then composition with Chadwick in Boston and with P. Scharwenka in Berlin. He wrote 2 symphonic poems: *Lancelot and Elaine* (1898) and *Eloise and Abelard* (1915); a suite, *From Old New England* (originally for Violin and Piano, 1912; orch. version, Springfield, Mass., May 17, 1919); *Song Celestial* for Orch. (1912); Violin Concerto (N.Y., Jan. 7, 1916); choral works; songs.

Sevitzky (real name, **Koussevitzky**), **Fabien,** Russian-born American conductor, nephew of **Serge (Alexandrovich) Koussevitzky**; b. Vishny Volochok, Sept. 29, 1891; d. Athens, Feb. 2, 1967. He studied double bass at the St. Petersburg Cons., where he graduated with its gold medal (1911). He then played in orchs., made appearances as a soloist, and began his conducting career. His uncle, who was already a celebrated double bass player himself, suggested that he adopt a truncated form of the last name, and he complied to avoid a family quarrel. In 1922–23 he played in the orch. of the Warsaw Opera and in the Warsaw Phil. With his wife, the Russian singer Maria Koussevitzky, he went to Mexico in 1923; then emigrated to the U.S., becoming a naturalized American citizen in 1928. He played in the Philadelphia Orch. (1923–30); organized the Philadelphia Chamber String Sinfonietta in 1925, and led several ensembles in Boston from 1930. He then was music director of the Indianapolis Sym. Orch. (1937–55), the Univ. of Miami Sym. Orch. (1959–65), and the Greater Miami Phil. (1965–66). He died while on a visit to Athens to conduct the State Orch.

Seymour, John Laurence, American composer; b. Los Angeles, Jan. 18, 1893; d. San Francisco, Feb. 1, 1986. He studied piano at the Univ. of Calif. at Berkeley (B.A. in music, 1917; M.A. in Slavic languages, 1919); received instruction in piano and theory from Fannie Charles Dillon and in violin from Leila Fagge; then took courses in composition with Pizzetti and Bohgen in Italy and with d'Indy in Paris (1923–28); later obtained his Ph.D. in English literature in 1940 from the Univ. of Calif. at Berkeley with the diss. *Drama and Libretto*. He lectured there on opera and drama (1928–36), and also served as chairman of the theater dept. of Sacramento Junior College; later was a librarian at Southern Utah College in Cedar City (1969–85). His opera, *In the Pasha's Garden*, was premiered at the Metropolitan Opera in N.Y. on Jan. 24, 1935, and won the David Bispham Memorial Award.

WORKS: DRAMATIC: OPERAS: *Les précieuses ridicules* (1920); *In the Pasha's Garden* (1934; N.Y., Jan. 24, 1935); *Ramona* (Provo, Utah, Nov. 11, 1970); *Ollanta, el Jefe Kolla* (1977). **OPERETTAS:** *Bachelor Belles* (1922); *Hollywood Madness* (1936); *The Devil and Tom Walker* (1942). **MUSICALS:** *Ming Toy* (1949); *The Lure and the Promise* (1960). **OTHER:**

Piano Concerto; String Quartet; 2 string trios; sonatas for various instruments; piano pieces; songs; etc.

Sgouros, Dimitris, gifted Greek pianist; b. Athens, Aug. 30, 1969. He enrolled in the Athens Cons., where he found a mentor in Maria Herogiorgiou-Sigara; later took lessons with Stewart Gordon in Baltimore and Guy Johnson at the Royal Academy of Music in London; subsequently pursued training in mathematics at the Univ. of Athens. He won the UNICEF Competition in 1980. His musical prowess was evident in his youth: he was only 7 when he made his public debut in Piraeus, and at the age of 12 he appeared as soloist in the Rachmaninoff 3rd Piano Concerto with Rostropovich and the National Sym. Orch. at Carnegie Hall in N.Y. He made his London debut at 13, and subsequently performed as a soloist with many major orchs. and as a recitalist.

Sgrizzi, Luciano, Italian harpsichordist; b. Bologna, Oct. 30, 1910; d. Monte Carlo, Sept. 11, 1994. He learned to play the piano as a child and was awarded a diploma from the Accademia Filarmonica in Bologna. He pursued training in piano and harmony at the Bologna Cons. (1920–21), and also studied organ and composition. Following studies in organ and composition with Ferrari-Trecate at the Parma Cons. (1927–31), he completed his training with Bertelin in Paris. Although he made appearances as a pianist from the days of his youth, he turned to the harpsichord and clavichord in 1948 and subsequently gave numerous recitals. He championed the vast collection of harpsichord sonatas by Domenico Scarlatti. His repertoire embraced numerous works by Italian and French composers. He edited many performing eds., ranging from Monteverdi to Pergolesi.

Shafran, Daniel (Borisovich), remarkable Russian cellist; b. Petrograd, Jan. 13, 1923. He studied cello with his father, Boris Shafran, who was an eminent cellist. He received 1st prize at the 1937 All-Union competition for string players in Moscow; continued his training with Alexander Stirmer at the Leningrad Cons. (graduated, 1950); won the Prague International Cello Competition (1950). He played through Russia, and later made tours throughout the world with great success. In 1955 he was made a People's Artist of the R.S.F.S.R.

BIBL.: I. Yampolsky, *D. S.* (Moscow, 1973).

Shaham, Gil, American violinist; b. Urbana, Ill., Feb. 19, 1971. He was taken to Israel as a child by his parents; began violin training at age 7 with Samuel Bernstein at the Rubin Academy of Music and later was a pupil in Jerusalem of Haim Taub. In 1980 he began working with Dorothy DeLay and Jens Ellerman at the Aspen (Colo.) Music School. He made his debut as soloist in 1981 with Alexander Schneider and the Jerusalem Sym. Orch. After capturing 1st prize in the Claremont competition in Israel (1982), he continued his training on scholarship at N.Y.'s Juilliard School with DeLay and Hyo Kang. In 1990 he received the Avery Fisher Career Grant. He made his Carnegie Hall recital debut in N.Y. on Jan. 23, 1992. In subsequent seasons, Shaham appeared internationally as a soloist with major orchs. and as a recitalist. His repertoire embraces scores extending from Paganini to Samuel Barber.

Shallon, David, Israeli conductor; b. Tel Aviv, Oct. 15, 1950. He studied composition and conducting with Sheriff, then completed his conducting studies with Swarowsky at the Vienna Academy of Music (1973–75). He was an assistant to Bernstein in Europe (1974–79), and also made appearances as a guest conductor with major European orchs. and opera houses. Shallon led the premiere of Gottfied von Einem's controversial opera *Jesu Hochzeit* in Vienna in 1980. He made his U.S. debut as a guest conductor with the San Francisco Sym. in 1980. From 1987 to 1993 he was Generalmusikdirektor of the Düsseldorf Sym. Orch. He was music director of the Jerusalem Sym. Orch. from 1993.

Shamo, Igor, talented Ukrainian composer; b. Kiev, Feb. 21, 1925; d. there, Aug. 17, 1982. He studied medicine in Kiev; after World War II, studied composition with Liatoshinsky at the Kiev Cons., graduating in 1951. Many of his works, numbering some 200, used native instruments such as the bayan and the bandura, and the lyrics extolled Soviet youth and the Soviet system. In 1975 he received the Shevchenko State Prize of the Ukrainian SSR and became a National Artist of the Ukraine.

WORKS: DRAMATIC: Film scores. **ORCH.:** *Symphonic Dances* (1949); Piano Concerto (1951); *Festival Suite* (1954); *Moldavian Poem—Rad o diya* (1956); 3 syms. (1964, 1968, 1975); *Komsomol Overture* (1967); *Theatrical Kaleidoscope* (1968); *Evening Music* (1971); *Morning Music* (1975); Flute Concerto (1975); Concerto for Bayan and Strings (1980); Sinfonietta-Concerto for Chamber Orch. (1980). **CHAMBER:** Piano Trio (1947); 5 string quartets (1955–80); Piano Quintet (1958); piano pieces. **VOCAL:** *Lenin*, cantata-oratorio (1980); choruses.

BIBL.: L. Efremova, *I. S.* (Moscow, 1958).

Shanet, Howard, American conductor; b. N.Y., Nov. 9, 1918. He studied cello with Evsei Beloussoff; played in the National Orch. Assn., under the direction of Barzin; later studied conducting with Rudolph Thomas and Stiedry, and at the Berkshire Music Center in Tanglewood with Koussevitzky; took composition lessons with Weisse, Dessau, Martinů, Lopatnikoff, and Honegger. He completed his academic studies at Columbia Univ. (A.B., 1939; A.M., 1941). He taught at Hunter College in N.Y. (1941–42). After serving in the U.S. Army as a warrant officer and bandleader (1942–46), he again taught at Hunter College (1946–53); also was on the staff at the Berkshire Music Center (summers, 1949–52); in 1953 he was appointed to the faculty of Columbia Univ. and as conductor of the Univ. Orch. and assistant (later full) prof. of music, which led to his designation as Director of Music Performance in 1978; in 1989 he was named Professor Emeritus. He served as assistant conductor of the N.Y. City Sym. (1947–48), conductor of the Huntington (W.Va.) Sym. Orch. (1951–53), and a guest conductor with the Israel Phil. (1950) and the N.Y. Phil. (1951, 1959). In 1977 he received the presidential citation of the National Federation of Music Clubs and a certificate of distinguished service from the Inst. of International Education; in 1990 he was invited by the College of Physicians and Surgeons of Columbia Univ. to give the Dean's Distinguished Lecture in the Humanities, the first musician to be accorded that honor. He composed *Allegro Giocoso* for String Quartet (1942; also for String Orch., 1987); *A War March* for Military Band (1944); *Introduction and Fugue* for Flute, Clarinet, and Bassoon (1947); *2 Canonic Pieces* for 2 Clarinets (1947); *Variations on a Bizarre Theme* for Orch. (1960); arr. and reconstructed the score *Night of the Tropics* by Gottschalk (1955). He publ. an "adult education book," *Learn to Read Music* (N.Y., 1956; tr. into Norwegian, 1972, Italian, 1975, and Spanish, 1981); a fundamental documentary vol., *Philharmonic: A History of New York's Orchestra* (N.Y., 1975); ed. and wrote a critical introduction for *Early Histories of the New York Philharmonic*, containing reprints of books by Krehbiel, Huneker, and Erskine (N.Y., 1978). He also publ. authoritative articles on such varied subjects as Bach's transpositions, Bizet's suppressed sym., and (in *The New Grove Dictionary of American Music*) the development of orchs. in the U.S.

Shankar (Lakshminarayana), Indian singer, composer, arranger, producer, and violinist; b. Madras, April 26, 1950. He first studied voice, violin, and drumming at home with his father, V. Lakshminarayana (d. Dec. 3, 1990), and mother, L. Seethlakshmi; then went to the U.S., where he earned his Ph.D. at Wesleyan Univ. in Middletown, Conn. (1974). With the English-Irish composer Caroline, he formed the pop group the Epidemics in 1980, bringing together in its performances and recordings a variety of genres, including classical Indian, folk, pop, and Western; is also active with his own Indian classical group, Shankar. He invented the Ten String Stereophonic Double Violin, a double-bodied instrument that, when both necks are played simultaneously, is capable of producing all the tones of the orch. string family; when the necks are played separately, the strings of the one not played respond sympathetically. The instrument made its debut in Shankar's *Ragam*

Tanam Pallavi Ragam Hemmavthi for Double Violin and South and North Indian Drums (1980), which appeared on the album *Who's to Know*; other albums include *Palghat Mani Tyer* (2 vols.), *Pancha Nadai Pallavi*, and *Eye Catcher*. He also provided film scores for *The Last Temptation of Christ* (1989) and *Jacob's Ladder* (1990). Shankar has appeared widely at festivals promoting a variety of social causes; he performed at the United Nations Peace Day Festival in N.Y. (1987), festivals in support of the Schizophrenia Research Foundation in India (1989–91), and the Tibet Alive for World Peace concert (1991). His other compositions include *Himmalaya* for Vocalists and Double Violin (1981) and the song *Never Take No for an Answer* (1985).

Shankar, Ravi, famous Indian sitarist, teacher, and composer; b. Varanasi, Uttar Pradesh, April 7, 1920. He revealed a notable talent as a musician and dancer in childhood. After some training from his brother, Uday Shankar, he accompanied him to Paris in 1930 to further his education. Returning to India, he pursued his musical training with Ustad Allauddin Khan in Maihar (1936). After World War II, Shankar became active as a performer. He also served as director of the instrumental ensemble of All-India Radio from 1949 to 1956. In 1956–57 he toured Europe and the U.S., and subsequently performed extensively in both East and West. In 1962 he became founder-director of the Kinnara School of Music in Bombay. His numerous sitar recitals in the West did much to foster an appreciation for Indian music. He publ. a memoir, *My Music, My Life* (N.Y., 1968). E. Barnett ed. *Ravi Shankar: Learning Indian Music, a Systematic Approach* (1981).

WORKS: DRAMATIC: *Ghanashyam* (A Broken Branch), opera-ballet (1989); several ballets; film scores, including the trilogy *Pather Panchali* (1955), *Aparajito* (1956), and *Apur Sansar* (1959); television music. **OTHER:** 2 sitar concertos (1971, 1976); instrumental pieces; songs.

Shapero, Harold (Samuel), American pianist, teacher, and composer; b. Lynn, Mass., April 29, 1920. After piano lessons with Eleanor Kerr, he studied composition with Slonimsky at the Malkin Cons. in Boston (1936–37), Krenek (1937), Piston at Harvard Univ. (1938–41), Hindemith at the Berkshire Music Center at Tanglewood (summers, 1940–41), and Boulanger at the Longy School (1942–43). In 1941 he received the American Prix de Rome for his *9-Minute Overture*. He held Naumburg (1942), Guggenheim (1947, 1948), and Fulbright (1948) fellowships. In addition to his appearances as a pianist, he taught at Brandeis Univ. (from 1952), where he was founder-director of its electronic music studio. In some of his early scores, Shapero employed dodecaphonic techniques. On the whole, his music adhered to an austere Classical pattern, without excluding a highly emotional melodic line. His exceptional mastery of contrapuntal technique secured clarity of intermingled sonorities in his chamber music.

WORKS: ORCH.: *9-Minute Overture* (1940; N.Y., June 8, 1941); *Serenade* for Strings (1945); *Symphony for Classical Orchestra* (1947; Boston, Jan. 30, 1948); *Sinfonia: The Travelers Overture* (1948); *Concerto for Orchestra* (1950); *Credo* (Louisville, Oct. 19, 1955); *Lyric Dances* (1955); *On Green Mountain* for Jazz Ensemble (1957; also for Orch., 1981); *Partita* for Piano and Small Orch. (1960). **CHAMBER:** String Trio (1938); *3 Pieces for 3 Pieces* for Flute, Clarinet, and Bassoon (1939); Trumpet Sonata (1940); String Quartet (1941); Violin Sonata (1942); *3 Improvisations* (1968), *3 Studies* (1969), and *4 Pieces* (1970) for Piano and Synthesizer. **PIANO:** Sonata for Piano, 4-hands (1941); 4 sonatas (1944, 1944, 1944, 1948); *Variations* (1947); *American Variations* (1950). **VOCAL:** *4 Baritone Songs* (1942); *2 Psalms* for Chorus (1952); *Hebrew Cantata* for Soprano, Alto, Tenor, Baritone, Chorus, Flute, Trumpet, Violin, Harp, and Organ (1954); *2 Hebrew Songs* for Tenor and Piano (1970; also for Tenor, Piano, and String Orch., 1980).

Shapey, Ralph, American conductor, teacher, and composer; b. Philadelphia, March 12, 1921. He studied violin with Zeitlin and composition with Wolpe; served as assistant conductor of the Philadelphia National Youth Administration Sym. Orch. (1938–47). In 1954 he founded and became music director of the Contemporary Chamber Players of the Univ. of Chicago, with which he presented new works; in 1963–64 he taught at the Univ. of Pa., and then was made prof. of music at the Univ. of Chicago in 1964; after serving as Distinguished Prof. of Music at the Aaron Copland School of Music at Queens College of the City Univ. of N.Y. (1985–86), he resumed his duties at the Univ. of Chicago, retiring as prof. emeritus in 1991. Disappointed by repeated rejections of his works by performers and publishers, Shapey announced in 1969 that he would no longer submit his works to anyone for performance or publication. However, in 1976 he had a change of heart and once more gave his blessing to the performance and publication of his works. In 1982 he became a MacArthur Fellow. In 1989 he was elected a member of the American Academy and Inst. of Arts and Letters. On Nov. 21, 1991, he conducted the premiere of his *Concerto Fantastique* with the Chicago Sym. Orch. In 1992 the judges of the Pulitzer Prize in Music awarded him its prize for this score, but then the Pulitzer Prize board rejected its own judges' decision and denied Shapey the honor. The ensuing scandal did little to enhance the reputation of the Pulitzer Prize in Music. In 1993 Shapey was honored with the Paul Fromm Award. In 1994 he was elected a member of the American Academy of Arts and Sciences. His music employs serialistic but uncongested procedures in acrid counterpoint, while formally adhering to neo-Classical paradigms.

WORKS: ORCH.: *Fantasy for Symphony Orchestra* (1951); Sym. No. 1 (1952); Concerto for Clarinet and Chamber Ensemble (1954; Strasbourg, June 9, 1958); *Challenge—The Family of Man* (1955); *Ontogeny* (1958; Buffalo, May 1, 1965); *Invocation*, concerto for Violin and Orch. (1958; N.Y., May 24, 1968); *Rituals* (1959; Chicago, May 12, 1966); Double Concerto for Violin, Cello, and Orch. (1983; N.Y., Jan. 24, 1984); *Groton: 3 Movements* for Young Orchestra (1984); *Symphonie concertante* (1985); Concerto for Piano, Cello, and String Orch. (1986); *Concerto Fantastique* (1989; Chicago, Nov. 21, 1991). **CHAMBER:** 9 string quartets (1946; 1949; 1950–51; 1953; 1957–58; 1963; 1972; 1993; 1995); Piano Quintet (1946–47); Violin Sonata (1949–50); Oboe Sonata (1951–52); Quartet for Oboe, Violin, Viola, and Cello (1952); Cello Sonata (1953); Piano Trio (1953–55); *Evocation* for Violin, Piano, and Percussion (1959; N.Y., March 26, 1960); *De Profundis* for Double Bass, Piccolo or Flute, Oboe or English Horn, Clarinet or Bassoon, and Clarinet or Alto Saxophone (1960); *Movements* for Woodwind Quintet (1960); Chamber Symphony for 10 Instruments (1962); *Convocation* for Chamber Ensemble (1962); Piece for Violin, 7 Instruments, and Percussion (1962); Brass Quintet (1963); String Trio (1965; 2nd movement for Solo Violin as Sonata No. 1, 1972); *Partita* for Violin, 11 Instruments, and 2 Percussion (1966); *Partita-fantasy* for Cello, 14 Instruments, and Percussion (1966); *3 for 6* for Chamber Ensemble (1979); Concerto Grosso for Woodwind Quintet (1981); *Discourse II* for Violin, Clarinet, Cello, and Piano (1983); *Concertante I* for Trumpet and 10 Performers (1984) and *II* for Alto Saxophone and 14 Performers (1987); *Soli* for Solo Percussion (1985); *Kroslish Sonate* for Cello and Piano (1985); *Variations* for Viola and 9 Performers (1987); *Intermezzo* for Dulcimer and Piano or Celesta (1990); Duo for 2 Wind Players (1991); *Movement of Varied Moments for Two* for Flute and Vibraphone (1991); Trio for Violin, Cello, and Piano (1992); Trio Concertante for Violin, Piano, and Percussion (1992); *Inventions* for Clarient and Percussion (1992); *Dinosaur Annex* for Violin and Vibraphone Marimba (1993); *Constellations for Bang on A Can All-Stars* for Chamber Ensemble (1993); *Rhapsody* for Cello and Piano (1993); *Evocation IV* for Violin, Cello, Piano, and Percussion (1994); also piano pieces and organ works. **VOCAL:** Cantata for Soprano, Tenor, Bass, Narrator, Chamber Orch., and Percussion (1951; rev. as String Quartet No. 5, 1957–58); *Soliloquy* for Narrator, String Quartet, and Percussion (1959); *Dimensions* for Soprano and 23 Instruments (1960); *Incantations* for Soprano and 10 Instruments

(1961); *Praise*, oratorio for Bass-baritone, Double Chorus, and Chamber Ensemble (1962–71; Chicago, Feb. 28, 1976); *Songs of Eros* for Soprano, Orch., and Tape (1975); *The Covenant for Soprano*, Chamber Orch., and Tape (1977); *Song of Songs* for Soprano, Chamber Orch., and Tape: *I* (1979), *II* (1980), and *III* (1980); *In Memoriam Paul Fromm* for Soprano, Baritone, and 9 Performers (1987); *Centennial Celebration* for Soprano, Mezzo-sorpano, Tenor, Baritone, and 12 Players (1991).

Shapleigh, Bertram, American pianist, cellist, writer on music, and composer; b. Boston, Jan. 15, 1871; d. Washington, D.C., July 2, 1940. He studied composition with G.E. Whiting and Chadwick at the New England Cons. of Music in Boston (graduated, 1891); also received instruction from MacDowell; studied medicine at Vermont Medical College (M.D., 1893). After giving a series of lecture-recitals in the U.S., he went to Europe (1898); lived in England from 1902 until his return in 1917 to the U.S., where he was active as a lecturer and writer on music; became a specialist in oriental music. His compositions, which include 2 suites (*Ramayana* and *Gur Amir*, both 1908), a *Symphonic Prelude*, 2 syms., and *Poem* for Cello and Orch., are in a Romantic vein. The Bertram Shapleigh Foundation was founded in Washington, D.C., after his death.

Shaporin, Yuri (Alexandrovich), significant Russian composer; b. Glukhov, Ukraine, Nov. 8, 1887; d. Moscow, Dec. 9, 1966. He studied law, and graduated from the Univ. of St. Petersburg in 1912; also studied at the St. Petersburg Cons. with Sokolov (composition), graduating in 1918. He wrote theatrical music in Leningrad; moved to Moscow in 1936, where he served as a prof. at the Cons. (from 1939). His masterpiece is the opera *The Decembrists*, which occupied him for over 30 years.

WORKS: DRAMATIC: *Polina Gyebl*, opera (1925; rev. and enl. as *The Decembrists*, 1925–53; Moscow, June 23, 1953); about 80 theater scores; much film music. **ORCH.:** *The Flea*, comic suite (1928). **VOCAL:** *On the Field of Kolikovo*, sym.-cantata for Solo Voices, Chorus, and Orch. (1918–39; Moscow, Nov. 18, 1939); Sym. for Chorus, Orch., Band, and Piano (1928–33; Moscow, May 11, 1933); *A Tale of the Battle for the Russian Land*, oratorio for Solo Voices, Chorus, and Orch. (Moscow, April 18, 1944); songs. **PIANO:** 2 sonatas (1924, 1926).

BIBL.: E. Grosheva, *Y.S.: I evo oratorii* (Moscow, 1947); idem, *Y.A. S.* (Moscow, 1957); I. Martynov, *Y. S.* (Moscow, 1966).

Sharp, Cecil (James), English folk music collector and editor; b. London, Nov. 22, 1859; d. there, June 23, 1924. He studied mathematics and music at Uppingham and Clare College, Cambridge. In 1882 he settled in Adelaide, where he worked in a bank and practiced law, becoming assoc. to the Chief Justice of Southern Australia; in 1889 he resigned from the legal profession and took up a musical career. He was assistant organist of the Adelaide Cathedral, and co-director of the Adelaide College of Music. In 1892 he returned to England; was music instructor of Ludgrove School (1893–1910) and principal of the Hampstead Cons. (1896–1905). At the same time, he became deeply interested in English folk songs; publ. a *Book of British Songs for Home and School* (1902); then proceeded to make a systematic survey of English villages with the aim of collecting authentic specimens of English songs. In 1911 he established the English Folk Dance Society; also was director of the School of Folk Song and Dance at Stratford-upon-Avon. During World War I he was in the U.S., collecting folk music in the Appalachian Mountains, with a view to establishing their English origin. In 1923 he received the degree of M.M. honoris causa from the Univ. of Cambridge. In 1930 the "Cecil Sharp House" was opened in London as headquarters of the English Folk Dance Soc. (amalgamated with the Folk Song Soc. in 1932).

WRITINGS (all publ. in London): *English Folk-song: Some Conclusions* (1907; 2nd ed., 1936; 4th ed., 1965, by M. Karpeles); *Folk-singing in Schools* (1912); *Folk-dancing in Elementary and Secondary Schools* (1912); with A. Oppe, *The Dance: An Historical Survey of Dancing in Europe* (1924).

FOLKSONG EDITIONS (all publ. in London): *Folk Songs from Somerset* (1904–09); with S. Baring-Gould et al., *Songs of the West* (1905); with S. Baring-Gould, *English Folk Songs for Schools* (1905); with H. MacIlwaine and G. Butterworth, *The Morris Book* (1907–13); with G. Butterworth, *Morris Dance Tunes* (1907–24); with G. Butterworth and M. Karpeles, *The Country Dance Book* (1909–22); *Country Dance Tunes* (1909–22); *English Folk-carols* (1911); *The Sword Dances of Northern England* (1911–13; 2nd ed., 1950–51, by M. Karpeles); with O. Campbell, *English Folk-songs from the Southern Appalachians* (1917; 2nd ed., 1932; 3rd ed., 1960, by M. Karpeles); *Folk-songs of English Origin Collected in the Appalachian Mountains* (1919–21); M. Karpeles, ed., *Cecil Sharp's Collection of English Folk Songs* (1973).

BIBL.: W. Shaw, "C. S. and Folk Dancing," *Music & Letters* (Jan. 1921); A. Fox Strangways and M. Karpeles, *C. S.* (London, 1933; 2nd ed., 1955; rev. by Karpeles as *C. S.: His Life and Work*, 1967).

Sharp, Elliott, American electric guitarist and composer; b. Cleveland, March 1, 1951. He studied anthropology at Cornell Univ. (1969–71); then took degrees in music at Bard College (B.A., 1973), where he studied ethnomusicology with Roswell Rudd and composition with Elie Yarden and Boretz, and at the State Univ. of N.Y. at Buffalo (M.A., 1977), where he studied ethnomusicology with Charles Keil and composition with Hiller. In 1980 he formed Carbon, one of N.Y.'s most innovative "downtown" ensembles; in late 1989 its flexible instrumentation included, in addition to electric harp, keyboards, and drums, "slabs"—homemade instruments made of wood and long metal strips that produce both ethereal harmonics and percussive sounds when struck with drumsticks. Since he is well versed in both science and physics, Sharp employs mathematical formulas and relationships in his works; he tends toward micro-rhythms, what he calls "layers of resonating rhythms that groove hard and cause a certain type of turbulence," which led one reviewer to describe his music as "urban rāgas." His musical aims are often political; some works utilize sampled voices of politicians, while Sharp sees the flexible organization and improvisatory performance style of Carbon itself as an implicit expression of his own social and political ideas.

WORKS: *Innosense* for 3 Musicians and Tapes (N.Y., Oct. 22, 1981); *Crowds and Power* for 21 Musicians (N.Y., Oct. 15, 1982); *Haka* for 4 Musicians (Washington, D.C., Oct. 12, 1983); *Marco Polo's Argali* for 10 Musicians (N.Y., March 1, 1985); *Sili/Contemp/Tation* for 3 Musicians (N.Y., April 4, 1986); *Self-Squared Dragon* for 9 Musicians (Zürich, Feb. 5, 1986); *Re/Iterations* for Orch. (N.Y., June 23, 1986); *Tessalation Row* for String Quartet (N.Y., July 11, 1986); *20 Below* for 6 Keyboards (N.Y., April 1, 1987); *Mansereel* for 4 Musicians (Philadelphia, Oct. 2, 1987); *Larynx* for 13 Musicians (N.Y., Nov. 13, 1987); *Hammer Anvil Stirrup* for String Quartet (Pori, Finland, July 15, 1988); *Jump Cut* for 4 Musicians (Troy, N.Y., Dec. 5, 1988); *Ferrous* for 5 Musicians (N.Y., Nov. 30, 1989); *Deception* for 6 Musicians and Film (N.Y., Feb. 8, 1990).

Sharrow, Leonard, noted American bassoonist and pedagogue; b. N.Y., Aug. 4, 1915. He studied at the Inst. of Musical Art in N.Y. (1932–35). He was 1st bassoonist in the National Sym. Orch. in Washington, D.C. (1935–37); then played in the NBC Sym. Orch. in N.Y. (1937–41); subsequently was 1st bassoonist in the Buffalo Phil. (1946), Detroit Sym. Orch. (1946–47), NBC Sym. Orch. (1947–51), Chicago Sym. Orch. (1951–64), and Pittsburgh Sym. Orch. (1977–87). He taught at the Juilliard School of Music in N.Y. (1948–51), Roosevelt College in Chicago (1952–55), the Indiana Univ. School of Music in Bloomington (1964–77), the Aspen (Colo.) Music School (from 1967), and the New England Cons. of Music in Boston (1986–89). He also toured as a bassoon virtuoso and chamber music player. As a teacher, he was mentor to several generations of bassoonists. He publ. eds. of works by Corelli, Vivaldi, Handel, Boismortier, Weber, Hummel, J.A. Koželuh et al.

Shaw (real name, **Shukotoff**), **Arnold,** American composer, writer, editor, lecturer, and music executive; b. N.Y., June 28, 1909; d. Las Vegas, Sept. 26, 1989. He was of Russian-Jewish descent. He majored in English literature at the City College of N.Y. (B.S., 1929) and Columbia Univ. (M.A., 1931). In his college years he was a campus radical, active particularly in the Anti-Fascist Assn. of the Staffs of the City College. As such, he was listed as "subversive" by some right-wing political organizations. He made a living by composing and teaching music at the New School for Social Research in N.Y., the Univ. of Calif. at Los Angeles, and the Univ. of Nevada in Reno and Las Vegas, where in 1985 he founded the Popular Music Research Center. In order to protect himself against would-be political factions, he changed his name from the Russian-sounding Shukotoff to the more common name Shaw. Among the various positions he occupied was that of music executive with the Dutchess Music Corp. (1950–53), Hill and Range Songs (1953–55), and the Edward B. Marks Music Corp. (1955–66); at these companies he promoted such popular singers as Rod McKuen, Burt Bacharach, and Elvis Presley. He wrote numerous articles and books; received the ASCAP-Deems Taylor Award (1968, 1979); ed., with L. Dowling, *The Schillinger System of Musical Composition* (N.Y., 1941; 4th ed., 1946); and publ. a novel, *The Money Song* (N.Y., 1953). His compositions include the musical *They Had a Dream* (1976), some snappy piano pieces, and songs.

WRITINGS (all publ. in N.Y.): Ed. with L. Dowling, *The Schillinger System of Musical Composition* (1941; 4th ed., 1946); *Lingo of Tin Pan Alley* (1950) *Belafonte: An Unauthorized Biography* (1960); *Sinatra: Twentieth-Century Romantic* (1968); *The Rock Revolution* (1969); *The World of Soul: Black America's Contribution to the Pop Music Scene* (1970); *The Street That Never Slept: New York's Fabled 52nd Street* (1971; reprint, 1977, as *52nd Street, the Street of Jazz*); *The Rockin' 50s: The Decade That Transformed the Pop Music Scene* (1974); *Honkers and Shouters: The Golden Years of Rhythm and Blues* (1978); *Dictionary of American Pop Rock: From Blue Suede Shoes to Blondie* (1982); *Sinatra, the Entertainer* (1982).

Shaw, Geoffrey (Turton), English organist, music educator, and composer, brother of **Martin (Edward Fallas) Shaw**; b. London, Nov. 14, 1879; d. there, April 14, 1943. He was a chorister at St. Paul's Cathedral in London and studied at Gonville and Caius College, Cambridge (B.A., 1901; Mus.B., 1902). From 1902 to 1910 he was music master at Gresham's School, Holt. In 1920 he was named his brother's successor as organist at St. Mary's, Primrose Hill, London. He also served as inspector of music to the Board of Education from 1928 until his retirement in 1942. In 1932 he was awarded the honorary Lambeth degree of D.Mus. In 1947 the Geoffrey Shaw Memorial Fund was established to assist musically talented children. He composed a ballet, *All at Sea*, orch. works, and chamber pieces.

Shaw, George Bernard, famous Irish dramatist; b. Dublin, July 26, 1856; d. Ayot St. Lawrence, England, Nov. 2, 1950. Before winning fame as a playwright, he was active as a music critic in London, writing for the *Star* under the name of "Corno di Bassetto" (1888–89) and for the *World* (1890–94). In 1899 he publ. *The Perfect Wagnerite*, a highly individual socialistic interpretation of the *Ring of the Nibelung*. His criticisms from the *World* were reprinted as *Music in London* (3 vols., 1932; new ed., 1950); those from the *Star* as *London Music in 1888–89* (London and N.Y., 1937); selected criticisms were ed. by E. Bentley (N.Y., 1954). Shaw's play *Arms and the Man* was made into an operetta, *The Chocolate Soldier*, by Oskar Straus (1908); his *Pygmalion* was converted into a highly successful musical comedy under the title *My Fair Lady*, with a musical score by Frederick Loewe (1956).

BIBL.: W. Irvine, "G.B. S.'s Musical Criticism," *Musical Quarterly* (July 1946).

Shaw, Martin (Edward Fallas), English organist and composer, brother of **Geoffrey (Turton) Shaw**; b. London, March 9, 1875; d. Southwold, Sussex, Oct. 24, 1958. He was a pupil at the Royal College of Music in London; played organ in various churches in London. In 1900 he founded the Purcell Operatic Society in London. He was made an Officer of the Order of the British Empire in 1955. He composed the operas *Mr. Pepys* (London, Feb. 11, 1926) and *The Thorn of Avalon* (1931); also incidental music; sacred works; some 100 songs; etc. He publ. *The Principles of English Church Music Composition* (London, 1921) and *Up to Now* (autobiography; London, 1929). Among his eds., all publ. in London, are *Songs of Britain* (with F. Kidson; 1913), *The English Carol Book* (with P. Dearmer; 1913–19), *The League of Nations Song Book* (with P. Dearmer; 1921), *Songs of Praise* (with P. Dearmer and R. Vaughan Williams; 1925; 2nd ed., aug., 1931), and *The Oxford Book of Carols* (1928; 25th ed., rev., 1964).

BIBL.: E. Routley, *M. S.: A Centenary Appreciation* (London, 1975).

Shaw, Robert (Lawson), distinguished American conductor; b. Red Bluff, Calif., April 30, 1916. He came from a clerical family; his father and his grandfather were clergymen; his mother sang in church choirs. He studied at Pomona College (1934–38), where he conducted its Glee Club. In 1938 Fred Waring asked him to help organize the Fred Waring Glee Club, and Shaw conducted it until 1945. In 1941 he founded his own Collegiate Chorale in N.Y., which he led in diversified programs of choral music, old and new, until 1954. In 1944 he was awarded a Guggenheim fellowship. He taught choral conducting at the Berkshire Music Center at Tanglewood (summers, 1946–48), and concurrently at the Juilliard School of Music in N.Y. In 1946 he made his debut as a sym. conductor with the Naumburg Orch. in N.Y. In 1948 he founded the Robert Shaw Chorale, which he conducted with notable success for 20 seasons. Eager to acquire more experience as an orch. conductor, he studied conducting with Monteux in San Francisco and Rodzinski in N.Y. in 1950. From 1953 to 1958 he conducted summer concerts of the San Diego Sym. Orch. In 1956 he led the Robert Shaw Chorale through a tour of 15 countries of Europe, including Russia, and the Middle East, under the auspices of the State Dept. In 1964 the Robert Shaw Chorale gave concerts in South America. For his Chorale, Shaw commissioned several choral works from contemporary composers, including Bartók, Milhaud, Britten, Barber, and Copland. Beginning in 1956 he was co-director of the Alaska Festival of Music in Anchorage. From 1956 to 1967 he served as assoc. conductor with Szell and the Cleveland Orch. In 1967 he became music director of the Atlanta Sym. Orch., and by dint of talent and perseverance brought it to a high degree of excellence. In 1977 he conducted it at the gala concert for President Carter's inauguration in Washington, D.C., and in 1988 he took it to Europe. After retiring from his post in 1988, he was accorded the titles of music director emeritus and conductor laureate. He then was active as director of the new inst. named in his honor at Emory Univ. In 1991 he received a Kennedy Center Honor. In 1992 President Bush awarded him the National Medal of Arts. In 1995 he took part as both conductor and reciter in the 50th anniversary concert of the Atlanta Sym. Orch. in a program later telecast to the nation by PBS.

BIBL.: J. Mussulman, *Dear People . . . R. S.: A Biography* (Bloomington, Ind. and London, 1979); M. Shakespeare, "R. S. Remembers," *Ovation* (May 1988).

Shaw, (Harold) Watkins, English musicologist and teacher; b. Bradford, April 3, 1911. He studied history at Wadham College, Oxford (B.A., 1932); then took courses in musicology with Colles and R.O. Morris at the Royal College of Music in London (1932–33); received the D.Litt in the faculty of music from the Univ. of Oxford (1967). In 1949 he was appointed lecturer at the Worcester College of Education; from 1971 until his retirement in 1980, he served as keeper of the Parry Room Library at the Royal College of Music. In 1985 he was made an Officer of the Order of the British Empire. Among his publs. are *The Three Choirs Festival, c. 1713–1953* (1954), *The Story of Han-*

del's "Messiah," 1741–1784 (London, 1963), *A Textual and Historical Companion to Handel's "Messiah"* (London, 1965), *The Organists and Organs of Hereford Cathedral* (Hereford, 1976); *The Succession of Organists of the Chapel Royal and the Cathedrals of England and Wales from c.1538: Also of the Organists of the Collegiate Churches of Westminster and Windsor, Certain Academic Choral Foundations, and the Cathedrals of Armagh and Dublin* (Oxford, 1991); also ed. *Sir Frederick Ouseley and St Michael's, Tenbury* (Birmingham, 1988).

Shawe-Taylor, Desmond (Christopher), eminent Irish music critic; b. Dublin, May 29, 1907; d. Wimborne, Nov. 1, 1995. He was educated at Oriel College, Oxford (1926–30). Through the years he contributed literary and musical criticism to various newspapers and periodicals. After service in World War II, he was engaged as music critic of the New Statesman in 1945, retaining his post until 1958; from 1950 to 1958 he also served as phonograph record reviewer for the *Observer.* In 1958 he was named music critic of the *Sunday Times*; he retired in 1983; also was a guest critic for the *New Yorker* (1973–74). He was made a Commander of the Order of the British Empire in 1965. His writings are notable for their unostentatious display of wide learning. He publ. the vol. *Covent Garden for the World of Music Series* (London, 1948); also, with Edward Sackville-West, *The Record Guide* (London, 1951, and later rev. eds.). He contributed a number of insightful biographies of singers to *The New Grove Dictionary of Music and Musicians* (1980).

Shchedrin, Rodion (Konstantinovich), brilliant Russian composer; b. Moscow, Dec. 16, 1932. His father was a music theorist and writer. After piano lessons in childhood, he attended the music and then choral schools (1948–51) attached to the Moscow Cons.; subsequently took courses in piano with Yakov Flier and composition with Yuri Shaporin at the Cons. (1951–55), where he subsequently taught (1965–69). Following graduation, he achieved great recognition within the accepted Soviet establishment; wrote about current trends in Soviet music in official publications; held several significant posts within the Composer's Union, including chairman of the Russian Federation section (from 1974); received many awards, and was made a People's Artist of the U.S.S.R. (1981). In 1964, 1968, and 1986 he visited the U.S. on cultural-exchange programs. His music has wide appeal, artfully employing numerous pseudo-modernistic devices; particularly interesting among his compositions are the aleatoric 2nd Sym., the prepared encore for the 1st Piano Concerto, and his ballets *Anna Karenina* and *Carmen Suite,* which incorporate music by earlier composers (Tchaikovsky and Bizet, respectively). He was married to the ballerina Maya Plisetskaya, for whom he wrote several ballets.

WORKS (all 1st perf. in Moscow unless otherwise given): **DRAMATIC: OPERAS:** *Not for Love Alone* (Dec. 25, 1961; version for Chamber Orch., 1971); *Dead Souls,* after Gogol (1976; June 7, 1977). **BALLETS:** *The Little Humpback Horse* (1955; March 4, 1960); *Carmen Suite* (April 20, 1967); *Anna Karenina* (1971; June 10, 1972); *The Seagull* (1979; rev. 1980). Also incidental music to plays and film scores. **ORCH.:** 4 piano concertos: No. 1 (Nov. 7, 1954; rev. version, May 5, 1974), No. 2 (1966; Jan. 5, 1967), No. 3 (1973; May 5, 1974), and No. 4, *Sharp Keys* (1991; Washington, D.C., June 11, 1992); 2 suites from *The Little Humpback Horse* (1955, 1965); 2 syms.: No. 1 (Dec. 6, 1958) and No. 2, *25 Preludes* (April 11, 1965); 2 concertos: No. 1, *The Naughty Limericks* (Warsaw, Sept. 1963) and No. 2, *Ringing Bells* (1967; N.Y., Jan. 11, 1968); Suite from *Not for Love Alone* (1964); *Symphonic Fanfares,* festive overture (Nov. 6, 1967); *Anna Karenina,* Romantic music (Oct. 24, 1972); *The Nursery,* transcription of Mussorgsky's song cycle (Stockholm, March 5, 1972); *Solemn Overture* (Dec. 1982); *Music for the Town of Kothen* for Chamber Orch. (1985); *Geometry of Sound* for 18 Soloists (Cologne, April 28, 1987); *Sotte voce,* cello concerto (London, Nov. 8, 1994); *Kristallene Gusli* (Moscow, Nov. 21, 1994). **CHAMBER:** 2 string quartets (1951, 1954); Suite for Clarinet and Piano (1951); Piano Quintet (1952); Chamber Suite for 20 Violins, Harp, Accordion, and 2 Double Basses (1961); *The Frescoes of Dionysus* for Nonet (1981); *Musical Offering* for Organ, 3 Flutes, 3 Bassoons, and 3 Trombones (Oct. 21, 1983); *Musical Offering* for Organ and Wind Instruments (1985); *Echo Sonata* for Solo Violin (Cologne, April 28, 1987). **PIANO:** 2 Études (1949); *Festivity on a Collective Farm* (1951); 9 Pieces (1952–61); *Variations on a Theme of Glinka* (1957); *Toccatina* (1958); Sonata (1962); *24 Preludes and Fugues* (1970); *Polyphonic Book* (1972); *Notebook for Youth* (1982); numerous other solo pieces. **VOCAL:** *Ukrainian Night Is Quiet* (1950); 13 Russian Folk Songs (1950); 12 Choruses (1950–70); *Song and Ditties of Varvara* (1961); *Bureaucratiade,* cantata based upon rules of a boarding house (1963; Feb. 24, 1965); *3 Solfège Exercises* (1965); *2 Laments* (1965); *Poetica,* concerto for Narrator, Woman Soloist, Chorus, and Orch. (Feb. 24, 1968); *Lenin Lives in the People's Heart* (1969; Feb. 6, 1970); *The Song of Pugachev* (1981); 6 Stanzas from *Eugene Onegin* (1981); Concertino for Chorus (1982); *Prayer* for Chorus and Orch. (Moscow, March 7, 1991); *Long Life* for Chorus, Piano, and 3 Percussionists (1991).

Shchelokov, Viacheslav (Ivanovich), Russian trumpet pedagogue and composer; b. Sloboda Elan, near Tzaritzin, Dec. 11, 1904; d. Sverdlovsk, Jan. 4, 1975. He studied trumpet with Mikhail Tabakov and composition with Alexander Alexandrov and Anatoly Alexandrov at the Moscow Cons. (graduated, 1931). In 1931 he became a teacher of trumpet at the Tchaikovsky Music School in Sverdlovsk. He was a teacher (1935–47) and a prof. (1947–75) of trumpet at the Cons. of the Urals, where he also served as director (1951–53) and chairman of the wind instrument dept. (1954–75).

WORKS: ORCH.: 10 trumpet concertos (1928, 1945, 1945, 1947, 1955, 1958, 1967, 1967, 1968, 1974); *Poem Captain Gastello* (1942); *Victory March* (1945); *Festival of Victory* (1951); *Children's Concerto* for Trumpet and Orch. (1967). **CHAMBER:** *Comical Procession* for Trumpet and Piano (1947); *Pioneer Suite* for Trumpet and Piano (1954); *Poem* for Trumpet and Piano (1958); *Study Etudes* for Trumpet (3 vols., 1964–65); other trumpet pieces.

BIBL.: B. Manzhora, *V.I. S.* (Sverdlovsk, 1968).

Shcherbachev, Vladimir (Vladimirovich), Russian composer; b. Warsaw, Jan. 24, 1889; d. Leningrad, March 5, 1952. He studied at the St. Petersburg Cons. with Maximilian Steinberg and Liadov, graduating in 1914. From 1924 to 1931 he was a prof. of composition at the Leningrad Cons. He wrote an opera, *Anna Kolosova* (1939); 5 syms.: No. 1 (1913; Petrograd, Nov. 5, 1916), No. 2 (1922–24; Leningrad, Dec. 14, 1924), No. 3 (1926–31; Leningrad, Feb. 4, 1932, composer conducting), No. 4, *History of the Izhorsky Factory* (1932–34; partial perf., Leningrad, May 28, 1934; 1st complete perf., Radio Leningrad, Dec. 23, 1935; 1st public perf., Leningrad, Jan. 21, 1936), and No. 5, *Russkaya* (1942–48; Leningrad, Dec. 21, 1948; rev. version, Kiev, Oct. 21, 1950); music for films; the orch. suite from one of them, *The Thunderstorm,* became popular in Russia; he further wrote *A Fairy Tale* for Orch. (Petrograd, Dec. 20, 1915); Nonet (1917); numerous piano works; songs.

BIBL.: G. Orlov, *V.V. S.* (Leningrad, 1959).

Shebalin, Vissarion (Yakovlevich), Russian composer; b. Omsk, June 11, 1902; d. Moscow, May 28, 1963. He studied at the Moscow Cons. with Miaskovsky (1923–28); then began teaching there; in 1935, was appointed prof. of composition there; from 1942 to 1948, was its director. On Feb. 10, 1948, by resolution of the Central Committee of the Communist Party, he was condemned (along with Shostakovich, Prokofiev, Miaskovsky, and others) for adhering to a "decadent formalism" in composition; but these strictures were removed in a corrective declaration of May 28, 1958, "restoring the dignity and integrity of Soviet composers." In addition to his original compositions, Shebalin also completed Mussorgsky's unfinished opera *The Fair at Sorotchintsy,* using only Mussorgsky's own material (Leningrad, Dec. 21, 1931; version with supplementary materials, Moscow, March 19, 1952).

WORKS: DRAMATIC: OPERAS: *The Taming of the Shrew*, after Shakespeare (concert version, Oct. 1, 1955; stage version, Kuibishev, May 25, 1957); *Sun over the Steppe* (Moscow, June 9, 1958). **BALLETS:** *Festival* (1958; unfinished); *Reminiscences of a Bygone Day* (1961). **MUSICAL COMEDY:** *Bridegroom from the Embassy* (Sverdlovsk, Aug. 1, 1942). **ORCH.:** 5 syms.: No. 1 (1925; Leningrad, Nov. 13, 1926), No. 2 (1929), No. 3 (1934; Moscow, Feb. 11, 1944), No. 4 (1935; Moscow, Feb. 27, 1936), and No. 5 (Moscow, Oct. 9, 1962); *Overture on Mari Themes* (1926); Horn Concertino (1930; rev. 1959); Violin Concertino (1931); 3 suites (1935; 1935, rev. 1961; 1963); *Variations on Russian Folk Songs* (1940); Violin Concerto (Leningrad, Oct. 29, 1940); *Russian Overture* (1941); Sinfonietta (1949); Cello Concerto (1950). **CHAMBER:** 9 string quartets (1923, 1934, 1939, 1940, 1942, 1943, 1947, 1960, 1963); Piano Trio (1924); Viola Sonata (1954); Violin Sonata (1958); Cello Sonata (1960); Guitar Sonatina (1963); also several piano sonatas. **VOCAL:** *Lenin*, symphonic poem for Soloists, Chorus, and Orch. (1931; Leningrad, Jan. 21, 1934; rev. 1959); *Moscow*, cantata (Moscow, Dec. 14, 1946); songs.

BIBL.: I. Boelza, *V. S.* (Moscow, 1945); I. Boelza and V. Protopopov, eds., *V.Y. S.: Articles, Reminiscences, Materials* (Moscow, 1970); V. Protopopov, ed., *V.Y. S.: Literary Heritage* (Moscow, 1975).

Sheinfeld, David, American composer and violinist; b. St. Louis, Sept. 20, 1906. He began violin training as a child, then studied harmony and counterpoint in Chicago; subsequently was a student of Respighi in Rome (1929–31). After pursuing his career in Chicago (1931–44), he studied conducting with Monteux; then played in the Pittsburgh Sym. Orch. (1944–45) and the San Francisco Sym. Orch. (1945–71). In 1993 he received an award from the American Academy of Arts and Letters. In his compositions from 1962, he combined tonal and atonal writing.

WORKS: ORCH.: *Adagio and Allegro* (1946; San Francisco, March 14, 1947); *Concerto for Orchestra* (1949; San Francisco, Feb. 20, 1951); *Fantasia* for Trumpet, Piano, Percussion, and Strings (1951); Violin Concerto (1955; Philadelphia, April 23, 1965); Concerto for Woodwinds and Chamber Orch. (1957; San Francisco, Jan. 14, 1958); *Etudes* (1959; Pittsburgh, Nov. 18, 1960); *Dialogues* for Chamber Orch. (Philadelphia, Oct. 26, 1966); *Confrontations* for Electric Guitar, Electric Violin, Saxophone, and Orch. (1969; Oakland, Calif., Jan. 20, 1970); *Time Warp* for Electric Instruments and Orch. (1972; San Francisco, Jan. 24, 1973); *Dreams and Fantasies* (1981; San Francisco, May 5, 1982); 2 syms.: No. 1, *Polarities* (1991) and No. 2 (1995). **CHAMBER:** Sonata for Solo Violin (1950); *Serenade* for 6 Instruments (1961); *Patterns* for Harp (1962); *4 Pieces* for Cello (1964); *Duo* for Viola and Harp (1965); *Memories of Yesterday and Tomorrow* for 3 Players (1971); *Elegiac Sonorities* for Organ (1973); *Dualities* for Harp (1976); 2 string quartets (1978, 1994); *Threnody* for Violin (1981). **VOCAL:** *The Earth Is a Sounding Board* for Small Chorus and Orch. (1978).

Shekhter, Boris (Semyonovich), Russian composer and teacher; b. Odessa, Jan. 20, 1900; d. Moscow, Dec. 16, 1961. After studies at the Odessa Cons. (graduated, 1922), he entered the Moscow Cons., studying composition with Vasilenko and Miaskovsky (graduated, 1929). In 1940 he became a prof. at the Ashkhabad Cons.

WORKS: OPERAS: *1905 god* (The Year 1905; 1935; rev. 1955; in collaboration with A. Davidenko); *Yusup i Akhmet* (1941; Ashkhabad, June 12, 1942; in collaboration with A. Kuliyev); *Pushkin v Mikhailovskom* (1955). **ORCH.:** 5 syms. (1929; 1943; 1944–45; 1947; 1951, rev. 1952–53); *Turkmenia*, suite based on Central Asian themes (1932; Florence, April 4, 1934); Piano Concerto (1932); *Rhapsody* (1935). **OTHER:** Cantatas; choruses; piano pieces; songs.

Shelley, Howard (Gordon), English pianist and conductor; b. London, March 9, 1950. He studied piano in childhood and was only 10 when he appeared on British television; subsequently studied at the Royal College of Music in London (1967–71), his principal mentors being Harold Craxton, Kendall Taylor, Lamar Crowson, and Ilona Kabos. In 1971 he received the Dannreuther Concerto Prize and the Silver Medal of the Worshipful Company of Musicians; also made his formal debut at London's Wigmore Hall. In 1972 he made his first appearance at London's Promenade Concerts, a televised event that launched his international career. After marrying the pianist Hilary Macnamara in 1975, he made duo appearances with her as well as continuing his solo career. In 1983 he played all the solo piano works of Rachmaninoff for the first time in a cycle at Wigmore Hall. After making his debut as a conductor with the London Sym. Orch. in 1985, he pursued a dual career as pianist and conductor. From 1990 to 1992 he was assoc. conductor of the London Mozart Players; served as its principal guest conductor from 1992. In addition to such masters as Mozart, Schubert, Chopin, Schumann, Rachmaninoff, Vaughan Williams, and Hindemith, Shelley has championed the piano music of contemporary composers, including Sir Michael Tippett, Howard Ferguson, Peter Dickinson, and Edward Cowie.

Shelton, Lucy (Alden), American soprano; b. Pomona, Calif., Feb. 25, 1944. She studied at Pomona College (B.A., 1965) and with Gladys Miller at the New England Cons. of Music in Boston (M.M., 1968); completed her training with DeGaetani at the Aspen (Colo.) School of Music. While a member of the Jubal Trio, she shared in winning the Naumburg Competition in 1977, and then won it on her own in 1980. She sang with the Waverly Consort, the N.Y. Pro Musica, and the 20th Century Consort of the Smithsonian Institution, and also pursued a career as a touring solo artist. In 1989 she sang the role of Jenifer in the Thames TV production of Tippett's *Midsummer Marriage* in England. While she has become closely associated with the performance of contemporary music, her repertoire ranges across the entire spectrum of music.

Sheng, Bright, remarkable Chinese composer; b. Shanghai, Dec. 6, 1955. He began piano lessons when he was 5; after graduating from high school, he worked as a pianist and timpanist in a dance company in Chinhai, near Tibet, where he began to study Chinese folk music. After China's Cultural Revolution, he entered the Shanghai Cons. (1976), where he earned an undergraduate degree in composition. In 1982 he followed his parents to the U.S., where he attended Queens College at the City Univ. of N.Y. and Columbia Univ.; his teachers included Chou-Wen Chung, Davidovsky, Perle, and Weisgall. Sheng received numerous awards, both in China and the U.S., including NEA grants, a Guggenheim fellowship, and awards from the American Academy and Inst. of Arts and Letters. His works have been championed by such eminent artists as Peter Serkin, who commissioned his *MY SONG* (1988), and Gerard Schwarz, who has given many premiere performances of his orch. pieces. His *H'UN (Lacerations): In Memoriam 1966–1976* was the 1st runner-up for the 1989 Pulitzer Prize in Music. Sheng appeared throughout the U.S. as a lecturer. After serving as composer-in-residence of the Chicago Lyric Opera, for which he wrote the opera *The Song of Majnun* (1992) with a libretto by Andrew Porter on an Islamic legend, he held that post with the Seattle Sym. Orch. (1992–94). He also orchestrated Leonard Bernstein's *Arias and Barcarolles*, which received its premiere performance under the direction of Leonard Slatkin in N.Y. on Dec. 6, 1990. Like so many refugees of China's cultural upheaval, Sheng strives to find the personal means to integrate the disparate musical styles of China and the West.

WORKS: OPERA: *The Song of Majnun* (1992). **ORCH.:** *3 Pieces* (1981; Shanghai, July 1, 1982); *Adagio* for Chamber Orch. (N.Y., March 7, 1987); *H'UN (Lacerations): In Memoriam 1966–1976* (1987; N.Y., April 16, 1988); *Prelude* (Houston, Nov. 1994). **CHAMBER:** Trio for Flute, Harp, and Cello (1982); *3 Pieces* for Flute (1982; N.Y., Nov. 8, 1985); *5 Pieces* for Oboe and Cello (1983; N.Y., Feb. 20, 1986); 2 string quartets: No. 1 (1984; N.Y., Nov. 11, 1985) and No. 2 (1984; Tanglewood, Aug. 21, 1985); *Shao* for Oboe, Violin, Cello, and Piano (N.Y., April

1986); *3 Pieces* for Viola and Piano (1986; N.Y., Jan. 15, 1987); *4 Movements* for Piano Trio (1990). **PIANO:** *Suite* (Aspen, Aug. 23, 1984); *MY SONG* (1988; N.Y., 1989). **VOCAL:** *4 Poems from the Tang Dynasty* for Mezzo-soprano and Piano (1984; Tanglewood, Aug. 23, 1985); *5 Chinese Folk Songs* for Tenor and Piano (N.Y., Sept. 21, 1985); *3 Poems from the Sung Dynasty* for Soprano and Chamber Orch. (1985; N.Y., March 26, 1986); *3 Chinese Love Songs* for Soprano, Viola, and Piano (Tanglewood, Aug. 26, 1988); *3 Chinhai Folk Songs* for Chorus and Orch. (Boston, Oct. 28, 1989).

Shenshin, Alexander (Alexeievich), Russian conductor, teacher, and composer; b. Moscow, Nov. 18, 1890; d. there, Feb. 14, 1944. He studied philology at the Univ. of Moscow; later took music lessons with Gretchaninoff and Glière. He subsequently taught music in Moscow, and also conducted occasional sym. concerts. His music is cast in a style reminiscent of Liadov; the elements of exotic musical patterns are noticeable. He composed an opera, *O T'ao* (1925); 2 ballets: *Ancient Dances* (1933) and *Story of Carmen* (1935); a song cycle, *From Japanese Anthologies*; numerous songs to German poems.

BIBL.: V. Belaiev, *A.A. S.* (Moscow, 1929).

Shepherd, Arthur, eminent American composer and pedagogue; b. Paris, Idaho, Feb. 19, 1880; d. Cleveland, Jan. 12, 1958. He studied with G. Haessel; in 1892, entered the New England Cons. of Music in Boston, where he studied piano with Dennee and Carl Faelten, and composition with Goetschius and Chadwick. In 1897 he went to Salt Lake City, where he was active as a teacher and as conductor of the Salt Lake Sym. Orch. He returned to Boston in 1908, and became a prof. of harmony and counterpoint at the New England Cons. of Music (until 1917; again in 1919–20). In 1917 he joined the U.S. Army, and was bandmaster of the 303rd Field Artillery in France. He settled in Cleveland, where he was assistant conductor (1920–26) and program annotator (1920–30) of its orch., prof. at Western Reserve Univ. (1927–50), and music critic of the *Cleveland Press* (1928–31). In 1938 he was elected to membership in the National Inst. of Arts and Letters. A composer of national tendencies, Shepherd wrote in a grand Romantic manner, derived from an intense feeling for American melos. He publ. a valuable handbook, *The String Quartets of Beethoven* (Cleveland, 1937).

WORKS: ORCH.: 3 overtures: *The Nuptials of Attila, Ouverture joyeuse* (1902), *The Festival of Youth* (1915), and *Overture to a Drama* (1919; Cleveland, March 27, 1924); *Fantaisie humoresque* for Piano and Orch. (Boston, Feb. 8, 1918); 2 syms.: No. 1, *Horizons* (Cleveland, Dec. 15, 1927) and No. 2 (1939; Cleveland, March 7, 1940); *Choreographic Suite* (Cleveland, Oct. 22, 1931); *Fantasy on Down East Spirituals* (Indianapolis, Nov. 2, 1946); Violin Concerto (1946–47); *Theme and Variations* (Cleveland, April 9, 1953). **BAND:** *Hilaritas*, overture (1942). **CHAMBER:** 2 violin sonatas (1914, 1927); 5 string quartets (1926, 1933, 1936, 1944, 1955); Piano Quintet (1940); *Praeludium salutatorium* for Flute, Oboe, Horn, Bassoon, Violin, Viola, and Cello (1942); *Divertissement* for Flute, Oboe, Clarinet, Bassoon, and Horn (1943). **PIANO:** 2 sonatas in F minor (1907, 1929). **VOCAL:** *The City in the Sea* for Baritone, Double Chorus, and Orch. (1913); *Song of the Sea Wind* for Women's Voices and Piano (1915); *He Came All So Still* for Women's Voices (1915); *Deck Thyself My Soul* for Chorus and Organ (1918); *Triptych* for Voice and String Quartet (1926); *Song of the Pilgrims* for Tenor, Double Chorus, and Orch. (1932); *Ballad of Trees and the Master* for Chorus (1935); *Invitation to the Dance* for Chorus and Orch. or 2 Pianos (1936); *Grace for Gardens* for Chorus (1938); *Build Thee More Stately Mansions* for Women's Voices (1938); *Psalm XLII* for Chorus and Orch. (1944); *Drive On* for Baritone and Chorus (1946); *A Psalm of the Mountains* for Chorus and Orch. or Piano (1956); songs.

BIBL.: R. Loucks, *A. S.: American Composer* (Provo, Utah, 1980).

Shere, Charles, American writer on music and composer; b. Berkeley, Calif., Aug. 20, 1935. He was reared on a small farm in Sonoma County, where he attended high school and learned to play wind instruments; after graduating from the Univ. of Calif. at Berkeley with a degree in English (1960), he studied composition with Erickson privately and at the San Francisco Cons. of Music, and also studied conducting with Samuel (1961–64); also studied art, on which he later wrote and lectured extensively. From 1964 to 1967 he was music director of Berkeley's KPFA-FM; also was active at San Francisco's KQED-TV (1967–73), an instructor at Mills College in Oakland (1973–84), and art and music critic for the Oakland *Tribune* (1972–88). He was co-founder, publisher, ed., and a major contributor to *EAR*, a monthly new-music tabloid magazine. He is married to Lindsey Remolif Shere, the famed pastry chef of Chez Panisse in Berkeley. Shere describes his early compositions, many notated in open form and scored for unspecified or variable ensembles, as "rural and contemplative rather than urban and assertive in nature"; his later works utilize more conventional notation, his shift from pen-and-ink to computer-generated notation coinciding with a greater use of rhythmic conventions, as in the ostinatos in the finales of his *Symphony in 3 Movements* (1988), Concerto for Violin with Harp, Percussion, and Small Orchestra (1985), and *Sonata: Bachelor Machine* (1989). Among his publications are *,Even Recently Cultural HIstory, Five Lectures for the 1980s* (Lebanon, New Hampshire, 1995), *Thinking Sound Music: The Life and Work of Robert Erickson* (Berkeley, 1995), and *Everbest Ever: Letters from Virgil* (Berkeley, 1995).

WORKS: OPERAS: *The Box of 1914* (1980; San Francisco, Jan. 29, 1981); *The Bride Stripped Bare by Her Bachelors, Even* (partial perf., Oakland, Dec. 1, 1984); *Ladies Voices*, chamber opera for 3 Sopranos and 6 Instruments (Berkeley, Oct. 30, 1987). **ORCH.:** Small Concerto for Piano and Orch. (1964; Aptos, Calif., Aug. 22, 1965); *Nightmusic* for Diminished Orch. (1967; Oakland, Jan. 24, 1982, K. Nagano conducting); *Soigneur de gravité (de l'orgue pour orchestre)* (1972); *Music for Orchestra (Symphony)* (Kensington, Calif., Oct. 28, 1976, composer conducting); *Tongues for Poet* (speaking in tongues), Chamber Orch., and Tape (San Francisco, May 6, 1978); Concerto for Violin, Harp, Percussion, and Small Orchestra (1985; Aptos, Calif., July 21, 1990); *Symphony in 3 Movements* (1988; Berkeley, April 28, 1989, K. Nagano conducting). **CHAMBER:** *Fratture* for 7 Instruments (1962; Osaka, Dec. 23, 1963); *Ces désirs du quatuor* for any 4 Musicians (1965); Quartet No. 2 for 3 to 5 or 6 Musicians (1966); *Screen*, Quartet No. 3 for 4 to 6 Strings (1969); Quartet No. 7, *Like a piece of silvered glass*, for Flute, English Horn, Clarinet, and Bassoon (1970); *Handler of Gravity* for Organ and Optional Chimes (1971); *Parergon to Woodwind Quintet* for English Horn, Bass Clarinet, and Bassoon (1974); String Quartet No. 1 (Oakland, Calif., May 10, 1980); Trio for Violin, Piano, and Percussion (Berkeley, Calif., Nov. 24, 1996). **PIANO:** *Sonata: Bachelor Machine* (1989; San Francisco, July 25, 1990). **VOCAL:** *Certain Phenomena of Sound* for Soprano and Violin (1983; San Francisco, Feb. 11, 1984); *Requiem with Oboe* for 8 Voices or Double Chorus and Oboe (San Francisco, June 11, 1985); *I Like It to Be a Play* for Tenor, Baritone, Bass, and String Quartet (San Francisco, Feb. 6, 1989). **TAPE:** *Ces désirs du vent des gregoriens* for Tape (1967).

Sheridan, Margaret, Irish soprano; b. Castlebar, County Mayo, Oct. 15, 1889; d. Dublin, April 16, 1958. She was a student of William Shakespeare at the Royal Academy of Music in London (1909–11) and of Alfredo Martino in Italy. In 1918 she made her operatic debut in *La bohème* in Rome. She sang at London's Covent Garden (1919; 1925–26; 1928–30) but pursued her career principally in Italy. In 1931 she settled in Dublin as a singing teacher. She was esteemed for her roles in Puccini's operas.

Sheriff, Noam, Israeli conductor, composer, and pedagogue; b. Tel Aviv, Jan. 7, 1935. He studied composition with Ben-Haim (1949–57), conducting with Markevitch at the Salzburg Mozarteum (1955), philosophy at the Hebrew Univ. in Jerusalem (1955–59), and composition with Blacher at the

Berlin Hochschule für Musik (1960–62). In 1955 he won the 1st Josef Krips prize of the Israel Phil. conducting competition. He returned there in 1959 and won the conducting competition outright. In the meantime, he was founder-conductor of the Hebrew Univ. Sym. Orch. (1955–59). From 1963 to 1983 he taught composition, orchestration, and conducting at the Rubin Academies of Music in Jerusalem and Tel Aviv. He was music director of the Kibbutz Chamber Orch. from 1970 to 1982, and also was assoc. conductor of the Israel Chamber Orch. (1971–73). From 1983 to 1986 he taught orchestration at the Cologne Hochschule für Musik, and then was on the faculty of the Rubin Academy of Music in Jerusalem (1986–88). In 1989 he became music director of the Israel Sym. Orch., Rishon LeZion. He also was a prof. at the Univ. of Tel Aviv's Rubin Academy of Music from 1991, where he was head of the orch. conducting dept. In his music, Sheriff has adroitly fused Western and Eastern elements in scores made notable by their command of orchestration and form.

WORKS: DRAMATIC: *Destination 5*, ballet music (1961); *Psalms of Jerusalem*, ballet (1982); *The Sorrows of Job*, opera (1990); *Gesualdo*, chamber opera (1996). **ORCH.:** *Festival Prelude* (1957); *Song of Degrees* (1959); *Music* for Chamber Orch. (1961); *Heptaprisms* (1965); *Metamorphoses on a Galliard* for Chamber Orch. (1967); *Chaconne* (1968); *2 Epigrams* for Chamber Orch. (1968); *Sonata* for Chamber Orch. (1973); *Essay* for Strings (1977); *Prayers* for Strings (1983); Violin Concerto (1984); *La Folia Variations* (1984); *Mechaye Hametim* (Revival of the Dead), sym. for Soloists, Choruses, and Orch. (1985); *A Vision of David* for Narrator and Orch. (1986); Concerto for Cello and Chamber Orch. (1987); Piano Concerto (1994). **CHAMBER:** Piano Sonata (1961); *Confession* for Cello (1966); *Invention* for Flute (1966); String Quartet (1969–82); *Mai Ko Mashma Lan* for Harp and String Quartet (1976); *Trey-Assar*, dodekalog for 12 Cellos (1978); *Meeting for 6* for 6 Cellos (1985–86). **VOCAL:** *Adhrei* for Alto and Chamber Group (1961); *Sephardic Passion* for Soli and Orch. (1992); songs.

Sherman, Norman (Morris), American bassoonist, teacher, and composer; b. Boston, Feb. 25, 1926. He studied composition in Boston with Roslyn Brogue Henning and at Boston Univ. (1946–50), where he also received instruction in bassoon from Ernst Panenka; subsequently attended Messiaen's analysis class at the Paris Cons. (1950). He was principal bassoonist with the Winnipeg Sym. Orch. (1957–61), the Residentie Orch. in The Hague (1961–69), the National Arts Centre Orch. in Ottawa (1969–73), the Israel Radio Orch. (1973–74), and the Kingston (Ont.) Sym. Orch. (from 1974); also taught bassoon and chamber music at the Queen's Univ. in Kingston (from 1974).

WORKS: BALLET: *The Red Seed* (1950). **ORCH.:** *Sinfonia concertante* for Bassoon and Strings (1950; Winnipeg, Jan. 19, 1961); *2 Pieces* (1952–62); *Through the Rainbow and/or Across the Valley* (1966–67; Rotterdam, April 25, 1968); *Thesis* (Kingston, March 23, 1975); *Canadian Summer* (1976); *Icthyon* for 13 Strings (1979); *The 2-Bit Dance Hall* (1980); *Garden of Love* for Strings, Brass, and Percussion (1988). **BAND:** *The Pioneers* (1982). **CHAMBER:** Concerto for Flute, Clarinet, Horn, Bassoon, and Piano (1948); *Traditions* for Flute, Oboe, Clarinet, and Bassoon (1948); *The Reunion* for Flute, Violin, Viola, and Cello (1971; CBC, Feb. 4, 1979); *Quadron* for String Quartet (Kingston, July 15, 1976); *Quintessant* for Flute, Oboe, Clarinet, Horn, and Bassoon (Kingston, May 11, 1977); *Bouquet* for Piano or Celesta, Clarinet, and 3 Percussion (1978); *Entretien* for Flute and Bassoon (1981); *Euphoria* for Flute, Clarinet, Horn, Bassoon, and Percussion (1983); *Tango* for Flute, Horn, Viola, and Cello (1984); *La Bodega* for Flute and Guitar (1987); piano pieces. **VOCAL:** *The Events of November 10, 1812* for Narrator and Orch. (1978).

Sherman, Russell, American pianist and pedagogue; b. N.Y., March 25, 1930. He took instruction in piano with Steuermann (1941–55); earned a degree in humanities at Columbia Univ. (B.A., 1949). On Nov. 17, 1945, he made his formal debut in a recital in N.Y., and then pursued a modest concert career while devoting himself mainly to teaching. In 1967 he became chairman of the piano dept. of the New England Cons. of Music in Boston. He was active in promoting contemporary music in chamber ensembles in the Boston area. His performances won praise for their discernment and spontaneity. In 1975 a N.Y. recital attracted attention and quickened interest in his career; in 1978 he performed in Paris and London, and was a soloist with the leading orchs. of Europe. In 1986 he joined the faculty of the Juilliard School in N.Y. On March 28, 1993, he played the premiere of Gunther Schuller's *Sonata/Fantasia* in Boston.

Sherry, Fred (Richard), American cellist and conductor; b. Montrose, N.Y., Oct. 27, 1948. He studied cello with Leonard Rose and Channing Roberts, and chamber music with Felix Galimir at the Juilliard School of Music in N.Y. (1965–69). In 1968 he won the Young Concert Artists competition, which led to his solo debut at N.Y.'s Carnegie Recital Hall in 1969. With Richard Fritz, he organized the new-music group Speculum Musicae in 1971, remaining with it until 1978; was also a founding member of the chamber group Tashi in 1973. In 1989 he became artistic director of the Chamber Music Soc. of Lincoln Center in N.Y., which position he resigned in 1991.

Shibata, Minao, Japanese composer; b. Tokyo, Sept. 29, 1916; d. there, Feb. 2, 1996. He studied science at the Univ. of Tokyo (graduated, 1939) and music with Saburo Moroi (1940–43). From 1959 to 1969 he taught at the Tokyo National Univ. of Fine Arts and Music.

WORKS: OPERAS: *Strada a Roma*, radio opera (1961); *Forgotten Boys* (1990). **ORCH.:** Sinfonia (Tokyo, Dec. 12, 1960); *Consort* for Orch. and Tape (1972–73); *Metaphor* for 27 Japanese Instruments (1975); *Yūgaku* for Orch. and Tape (1977); *Diaphonia* for Orch. and Tape (1979); *U235 and the Peace of Mankind* (1983); *Metafonia* (1984); *Antifonia* (1989). **CHAMBER:** 2 string quartets (1943, 1947); *Classical Suite* for Violin and Piano (1953); *Essay* for 3 Trumpets and 3 Trombones (1965); *Imagery* for Marimba (1969); *Display '70 I* (1969) and *II* (1970) for Ryûteki, Marimba, Percussion, and Tape; *Concerto for 8* for 8 Flutes (1971); *Trimurti* for Flute, Violin, Keyboard, and Electronics (1973–74); *Ashirai* for 6 Percussionists (1980). **KEYBOARD: PIANO:** Sonata (1943); *2 Improvisations* (1957, 1968); *Generation* (1981). **ORGAN:** *Diferencias* (1983). **VOCAL:** *Symbology* for Soprano and Chamber Orch. (1953); *Black Portrait* for Soprano and Chamber Orch. (1954); *3 Poems on Katsue Kitazono* for Soprano and Chamber Orch. (1954–58); *Black Distance* for Soprano and Chamber Orch. (1958); *The Street* for Chorus and 4 Percussion (1960); *Poem Recited in the Night* for Soprano and Chamber Orch. (1963); *L'Oiseau noir en soliel Levant* for Narrator, 6 Soloists, Piano, Percussion, and Synthesizer (1986). **OTHER:** *Musique concrète* for Tape (1955); *Improvisation* for Electronic Sound (1968).

Shicoff, Neil, American tenor; b. N.Y., June 2, 1949. He began vocal training with his father, a cantor; then studied at the Juilliard School in N.Y. After singing Narroboth in Salome in Washington, D.C., he appeared as Ernani at the Cincinnati May Festival in 1975. On Oct. 15, 1976, he made his Metropolitan Opera debut in N.Y. as Rinuccio in *Gianni Schicchi*, returning there in subsequent seasons as the Duke in *Rigoletto*, Rodolfo, Werther, Hoffmann, Romeo, and Massenet's *Des Grieux*. He also sang at London's Covent Garden (debut as Pinkerton, 1978), the Chicago Lyric Opera (debut as Rodolfo, 1979), the San Francisco Opera (debut as Edgardo, 1981), and the Paris Opéra (debut as Romeo, 1981). In 1988 he sang Macduff in the BBC production of *Macbeth*. In 1990 he made his debut in Barcelona as Hoffmann. In 1993 he appeared at Covent Garden as Pinkerton. He also toured as a concert artist. In 1978 he married the soprano Judith Haddon.

Shifrin, David, American clarinetist and teacher; b. N.Y., Jan. 2, 1950. He studied at the High School of Performing Arts in N.Y. (1964–65), the Interlochen (Mich.) Arts Academy (1965–67), and the Curtis Inst. of Music in Philadelphia (artist diploma, 1971; B.M., 1973). He played clarinet in the Cleveland Orch., the Los Angeles Chamber Orch., the Dallas Sym. Orch., the Honolulu Sym. Orch., and the American Sym. Orch. in N.Y. As a soloist, he appeared with various orchs. in the U.S. and abroad, and was also very active as a recitalist and chamber music artist. He was artistic director of Chamber Music Northwest in Portland, Oreg. (from 1980). In 1987 he was awarded an Avery Fisher Career Grant. He was then a member (from 1989) and artistic director (from 1992) of the Chamber Music Soc. of Lincoln Center in N.Y. He taught at the Cleveland Inst. of Music (1974–76), the Univ. of Mich. (1976–82), the Univ. of Southern Calif. in Los Angeles (1982–87), the Juilliard School in N.Y. (1987–90), and at the Yale Univ. School of Music (from 1987). In addition to his performances of the standard clarinet literature, Shifrin has commissioned scores from several American composers, among them Stephen Albert and Ezra Laderman.

Shifrin, Seymour, American composer and teacher; b. N.Y., Feb. 28, 1926; d. Boston, Sept. 26, 1979. After studies at N.Y.'s High School of Music and Art, he received private instruction from Schuman (1942–45); continued his training at Columbia Univ. (B.A., 1947), where he completed his graduate study in composition with Luening (M.A., 1949); then pursued additional training with Milhaud in Paris on a Fulbright scholarship (1951–52). He held 2 Guggenheim fellowships (1956, 1960). Shifrin taught at Columbia Univ. (1949–50), City College of the City Univ. of N.Y. (1950–51), the Univ. of Calif. at Berkeley (1952–66), and at Brandeis Univ. (1966–79). He wrote music of high chromatic consistency, with finely delineated contrapuntal lines often resulting in sharp dissonance.

WORKS: ORCH.: *Music for Orchestra* (1948); *Chamber Symphony* (1952–53); *3 Pieces* (1958; Minneapolis, Jan. 8, 1960). **CHAMBER:** Cello Sonata (1948); 5 string quartets (1949; 1962; 1965–66; 1966–67; 1971–72); *Serenade* for Oboe, Clarinet, Horn, Viola, and Piano (1954); *Concert Piece* for Violin (1959); *In eius memoriam* for Flute, Clarinet, Violin, Cello, and Piano (1967–68); *Duo* for Violin and Piano (1969); Piano Trio (1974); *The Nick of Time* for Flute, Clarinet, Percussion, Piano Trio, and Double Bass (1978). **PIANO:** *4 Cantos* (1948); *Composition* (1950); *Trauermusik* (1956); *The Modern Temper* for Piano, 4-hands (1959); *Fantasy* (1961); *Responses* (1973); *Waltz* (1977). **VOCAL:** *Cantata to Sophoclean Choruses* for Chorus and Orch. (1957–58; Boston, May 2, 1984); *Odes of Chang* for Chorus, Piano, and Percussion (1963); *Satires of Circumstance* for Mezzo-soprano, Flute, Clarinet, Violin, Cello, Double Bass, and Piano (1964); *Chronicles* for 3 Male Soloists, Chorus, and Orch. (1970; Boston, Oct. 27, 1976); *A Renaissance Garland* for Soprano, Tenor, Recorders, Viols, Lute, and Percussion (1975); *Five Last Songs* for Soprano and Piano (1979; also for Soprano and Chamber Orch. as completed by M. Boykan).

Shilkret, Nat(haniel), American conductor, arranger, and composer; b. N.Y., Dec. 25, 1889; d. Franklin Square, Long Island, N.Y., Feb. 18, 1982. He studied composition with Pietro Floridia. He played the clarinet in the Russian Sym. Orch. in N.Y., the N.Y. Phil., the N.Y. Sym. Orch., and the Metropolitan Opera orch., as well as in bands led by Sousa, Pryor, and E.F. Goldman. In 1916 he became music director of the Victor Talking Machine Co., and created the Victor Salon Orch. in 1924, for which he made numerous arrangements, recordings, and radio broadcasts. In 1935 he went to Hollywood, where he became active as a film score arranger and composer. He wrote a symphonic poem, *Skyward* (1928), a Trombone Concerto (1942), various descriptive pieces for orch., chamber music, and numerous songs; also commissioned Schoenberg, Stravinsky, Toch, Milhaud, Castelnuovo-Tedesco, and Tansman to write a movement each for a biblical cantata, *Genesis* (1947), to which he himself contributed a movement.

Shiloah, Amnon, Israeli ethnomusicologist; b. Lanus, Argentina (of Syrian parents), Sept. 28, 1928. He went to Israel in 1941 to study flute with Uri Toeplitz at the Rubin Academy of Music in Jerusalem; later studied flute at the Paris Cons. (1954–58), and also took courses with Corbin and Chailley at the Sorbonne Inst. of Musicology. He returned to Israel as flutist of the Israel Broadcasting Sym. Orch. (1959–60); studied Hebrew and Arab literature at Hebrew Univ. in Jerusalem (M.A., 1960); subsequently earned his Ph.D. at the Sorbonne (1963, with the diss. *La Perfection des connaissances musicales,* a study of Arab theory; publ. in Paris, 1972). As head of the folklore dept. of the Israel Broadcasting Authority, Shiloah undertook extensive fieldwork in Jewish and Arab music (1965–69); also directed the Jewish music center at Hebrew Univ. (1967–71), where he was head of the musicology dept. (1970–75) and a prof. (from 1973). He co-edited the periodical *Yuval;* also produced records of Jewish and Eastern Christian music. His research focuses on the literature of Arab and Hebrew theory in addition to contemporary musics of both cultures.

WRITINGS: *Caractéristiques de l'art vocale arabe du Moyen-Âge* (Tel Aviv, 1963); *Kit'ey ham-musika baz-zohar* (Musical Passages in the Zohar; Jerusalem, 1977); *The Epistle on Music of the Ikhwan al-Safa* (Tel Aviv, 1978).

Shimizu, Osamu, Japanese composer; b. Osaka, Nov. 4, 1911; d. Tokyo, Oct. 29, 1986. He studied traditional Japanese instruments; also took courses in theory and composition with Hashimoto and Hosokawa at the Tokyo Music School (1936–39). He was active in the music dept. of Tokyo Radio; also wrote articles on music.

WORKS: DRAMATIC: OPERAS: *The Tale of the Mask-Maker Shuzenji* (Osaka, Nov. 4, 1954); *The Charcoal Princess* (Osaka, Nov. 1, 1956); *The Man Who Shoots at the Blue Sky* (Osaka, Nov. 26, 1956); *Gauche, the Violoncellist* (Osaka, Oct. 11, 1957); *The Singing Skeleton* (Osaka, March 15, 1962); *Shunkan, the Exile* (Osaka, Nov. 18, 1964); *The Merciful Poet,* operetta (1965); *Muko Erabi* (The Marriage Contest), comic opera (Los Angeles, Oct. 3, 1968); *Daibutsu-Kaigen* (The Great Image of Buddha), historic opera on the inauguration of the bronze statue of Buddha on April 9, A.D. 752 (Tokyo, Oct. 2, 1970); *Ikuta Gawa* (The River Ikuta; Tokyo, Nov. 10, 1971). **BALLETS:** *The Sun* (1955); *The Crane* (1956); *The Earth* (1957); *Araginu* (1958); *Fire in the Field* (1962); *Love Poems* (1966). **ORCH.:** *Ballad* for Violin and Orch. (1941); *Dance Suite on the Themes of Flowers* (1944); *Poème* for Flute and Orch. (1950); *4 Movements on Indian Melodies* (1950); 3 syms.: No. 1 (Tokyo, Dec. 8, 1951), No. 2 (1957), and No. 3 (1961); Suite (1953); *Taiheiraku* (1971). **CHAMBER:** String Quartet (1940); *Ballad* for Flute and Piano (1940); Quartet for Flute, Oboe, Clarinet, and Bassoon (1958). **VOCAL:** *Olympic Hymn,* for the opening of the Olympic Games (Tokyo, Oct. 10, 1964); numerous cantatas, including *Ren-nyo* (Tokyo, April 8, 1948), *La Paix* (Tokyo, April 22, 1949), and *Hymn to Dengyo-Daishi* (1966); much choral music; many songs.

Shimoyama, Hifumi, Japanese composer; b. Aomoriken, June 21, 1930. He studied with Y. Matsudaira. In his music, he followed a determined contemporary path.

WORKS: DRAMATIC: *Halley's Comet (Fulfillment of a 76-Year Vow),* radiophonic piece (1981). **ORCH.:** *Reflections* for 3 Groups of Strings (1967; Hamburg, June 27, 1969); *Zone* for 16 Strings (1970); *Fümon* for Chamber Orch. and Tape (1974); *Saikyo* (1981); Cello Concerto (1984); *Yugenism* (1988). **CHAMBER:** Violin Sonata (1956); String Quartet (1959); *Structure* for 4 Players (1961); *Dialog* for Cello and Piano (1962) and *1* to *3* for 2 Guitarists (1963, 1971, 1984); *2 Ceremonies* for Cello (1969, 1971); *Exorcism* for 5 Strings (1970); *MSP* for Violin and Piano (1972); *Wave* for Cello, Strings, Harp, Piano, and Percussion (1972); *Transmigration I* for Percussion and Double Bass (1973) and *II* for Shakuhachi, Cello, and Harp (1984); *Poem* for Cello, Piano, and Tape (1974); *Kaisho* for Organ and Percussion (1982); *Meditation* for Cello and Piano (1983); *Fümon IV* for Percussion and Tape (1984) and *V* for Clarinet, Horn, Trombone, Cello, Double Bass, Percussion, and Tape (1992); *Cube* for 8 Cellos and Timpani (1985); *The Da I* (1985) and *II* (1991) for 4 Percussionists; *Emanation* for Alto Saxophone and Percussion (1986); *Mirage* for Cello and Percussion (1989); *Ichigo* *no Tsukikage* for Koto, Cello, and Tape (1989–90); *Aira* for Cello (1990); *Gamma* for Guitar and String Trio (1990). **VOCAL:** *Breath* for Chorus, Percussion, Piano, and 3 Horns (1971; Tokyo, Nov. 9, 1972); *Voices* for 3 Soloists and 2 Percussionists (1985); *Catalysis III* for Soprano and Tuba (1991).

Shinohara, Makota, Japanese composer and teacher; b. Osaka, Dec. 10, 1931. He was a student of Ikenouchi at the Tokyo National Univ. of Fine Arts and Music (1952–54), of Messiaen at the Paris Cons. (1954–59), of Zimmermann at the Cologne Hochschule für Musik (1962–64), and of Stockhausen in Cologne (1962–65). He then worked at the Univ. of Utrecht electronic music studio (1965–66) and at the Columbia-Princeton Electronic Music Studio in N.Y. (1971–72). After serving as a prof. of Japanese music at McGill Univ. in Montreal (1978), he settled in the Netherlands in 1979 as a composer and teacher.

WORKS: ORCH.: *Solitude* (1961); *Visione II* (1970); *Egalisation* (1975); *Liberation* for Strings (1977); *Cooperation* for 8 Japanese and 8 Western Instrumentalists (1990; rev. version, Zürich, Sept. 16, 1991). **CHAMBER:** Violin Sonata (1958); *8 pièces concertante* for Trumpet and Piano (1959); *Obsession* for Oboe and Piano (1960); *Alternance* for 6 Percussionists (1961–62); *Consonance* for Flute, Horn, Cello, Harp, Vibraphone, and Marimba (1967); *Reflexion* for Oboe (1970); *Rencontre* for Percussion and Tape (1972); *Tayutai* for Koto, Percussion, and Voice (1972); *Kyudo* for Shakuhachi and Harp (1973); *Passage* for Stereophonically-Amplified Bass Flute (1980; rev. 1986); *Play* for 9 Winds (1982; rev. 1985); *Turns* for Chamber Ensemble (1984); *Evolution* for Cello (1986); piano pieces; organ music. **VOCAL:** *Personnage* for Man's Voice, Tape, and Optional Pantomime and Color Lighting (1968); *Ways of Dreams* for Chorus, Japanese Instruments, and Chamber Orch. (1992). **OTHER:** Tape pieces.

Shirinsky, Vasili (Petrovich), Russian violinist, conductor, teacher, and composer; b. Ekaterinodar, Jan. 17, 1901; d. Mamontovka, near Moscow, Aug. 16, 1965. He studied violin with D. Krein and composition with Miaskovsky at the Moscow Cons.; then played in orchs.; in 1923 he joined the Moscow Cons. Quartet as 2nd violin. Concurrently, he was active as conductor with the Moscow Radio Orch. (1930–32) and the Opera Theater Orch. (1932–36); was a teacher (1939–49) and a prof. (1949–65) at the Moscow Cons. In 1944 he was made a People's Artist of the R.S.F.S.R. He wrote 2 operas, *Pyer i Lyus* (1943–46) and *Ivan the Terrible* (1951–54); Violin Concerto (1921); 2 syms. (1936, 1938); Harp Concerto (1957); 6 string quartets (1923, 1925, 1929, 1940, 1953, 1958); piano pieces, including Sonata (1929), 98 fugues (1937–63), and 24 preludes (1962); incidental music for theatrical plays; film scores; choruses. His music adheres to the principles of socialist conservatism, emphasizing playability and tonal coherence; it was met with appreciation by the Soviet critics, but its performances were few and far between. His brother, Sergei Shirinsky (b. Ekaterinodar, July 18, 1903; d. Moscow, Oct. 18, 1974), was a cellist, who promoted in his programs the cause of Soviet music; he also made arrangements of various works by Classical and Romantic composers.

Shirley, George (Irving), black American tenor and teacher; b. Indianapolis, April 18, 1934. He was educated at Wayne State Univ. in Detroit, and then received vocal training from Thelmy Georgi in Washington, D.C. and Cornelius Reid in N.Y. He made his operatic debut as Eisenstein in *Die Fledermaus* with the Turnau Opera Players in Woodstock, N.Y. (1959). In 1960 he won the American Opera Auditions and in 1961 the Metropolitan Opera Auditions; following appearances in Europe, he made his Metropolitan Opera debut in N.Y. as Ferrando on Oct. 24, 1961, and continued to sing there until 1973, as well as with other U.S. opera companies; in addition, he sang at Glyndebourne, Covent Garden in London, and La Scala in Milan. He created the role of Romilayu in Kirchner's *Lily* (N.Y., April 14, 1977). In 1992 he was made the Joseph Edgar Maddy Distinguished Univ. Prof. of Music at the Univ. of Mich.

Shirley-Quirk, John (Stanton), distinguished English baritone; b. Liverpool, Aug. 28, 1931. (His hyphenated name is composed of the place-name Shirley, in Derbyshire, where his ancestors lived, and the Celtic appellation in the Manx language, used on the channel Isle of Man.) He studied voice with Roy Henderson, and at the same time took courses in chemistry and physics at the Univ. of Liverpool. He made his operatic debut as the Doctor in *Pelléas et Mélisande* at the Glyndebourne Festival (1961); then was a leading member of the English Opera Group (1964–76), where he became well known for his roles in Britten's operas; created all 7 baritone roles in Britten's *Death in Venice* (June 16, 1973). In 1973 he sang at London's Covent Garden; then made his Metropolitan Opera debut in N.Y. as the Traveler in *Death in Venice* on Oct. 18, 1974. On July 7, 1977, he created the role of Lev in Tippett's *The Ice Break* at Covent Garden. He also toured widely as a concert artist. In 1975 he was made a Commander of the Order of the British Empire.

Shishov, Ivan, Russian composer; b. Novocherkassk, Oct. 8, 1888; d. Moscow, Feb. 6, 1947. He studied composition with Koreshchenko at the Phil. Society in Moscow, and also took courses in choral polyphony with Kastalsky and in form and orchestration with G. Conus, graduating in 1914. He subsequently conducted choral groups and taught at the Moscow Cons. (1925–31). He wrote the opera *Painter Serf* (Moscow, March 24, 1929); 2 syms. (1925, 1933); a Requiem in memory of Lenin (1925); a symphonic poem, *In the Desert* (1920); a festive overture, *Song of Victory* (1942; anticipating the victory over Nazi Germany by 3 years); piano pieces; choruses; more than 300 songs; arrangements of Russian folk songs.

Shmueli, Herzl, Israeli musicologist; b. Constantinople, Nov. 8, 1920. He began studying violin at 7 and piano at 10; in 1933, went to Palestine, where he studied violin with P. Ginzburg (until 1934); later attended the Tel Aviv Cons. (1944–48) while studying theory and composition with Boskovich; subsequently studied musicology with Cherbuliez, composition and history with Hindemith at the Univ. of Zürich, and acoustics at the Zürich Eidgenössische Technische Hochschule für Musik (1949–53); received his Ph.D. from the Univ. of Zürich (1953, with the diss. *Higgajon Bechinnor: Betrachtungen zum Leierspiel des Jehudaa Ben-Arie Mosscato, Rabbi zu Mantua*; publ. in Tel Aviv, 1954). He returned to Tel Aviv to teach at the Music Teachers' Seminary (from 1953), where he served as director (1955–66); concurrently taught at the Tel Aviv Academy of Music. When the dept. of musicology of the Univ. of Tel Aviv was founded in 1966, he joined its faculty, subsequently becoming a prof. and dept. chairman (1971); also was chairman of the Israeli Musicological Soc. (1968–71). Shmueli directed a series of programs on music for Israeli Instructional TV, and spoke throughout Israel before many non-academic audiences; his research centers on Israeli song and art music, in addition to music of the early Romantics and of England in the 17th and 19th centuries. His writings, all publ. in Tel Aviv, include *Umanut harmusica* (Musical Craft; 1955), *Toldot hamak'hela* (History of the Choir; 1963), and *Hazemer hayisraeli* (Israeli Song; 1971).

Shnitke, Alfred. See **Schnittke, Alfred.**

Shoemaker, Carolie J., American composer and multidisciplinary performance artist; b. Kennewick, Wash., April 9, 1963. She studied composition with William O. Smith and Diane Thome, and voice with Montserrat Alavedra at the Univ. of Wash. (B.F.A., 1989). She conducted lifelong studies in violin, voice, drama, dance, literary arts, linguistics, electronic music, and composition. Her work emphasizes the interaction of language and music and brings together such aural and visual elements as speech, narration, movement, tape, electronics, and live music into a synergistic whole. Many of her compositions are scored for variable ensemble and involve structured improvisation.

WORKS: *The Elephant's Child* for Narrator and Brass Quintet (1987); *Stitch in Time* for Voice and Tape (1988); *Classified Info* for Mixed Instruments and Newspaper (1989); *Crackdown* for Tape with Optional Live Sung/Spoken Performance (1989);

Extended Forcast for Voice, String Quartet, and Bass Viol (1989); *Lagan Tide* for Tape, Mixed Instruments, and Voice (1989); *Bedtime Stories* for Voice over Variable Solo, or Group Ensemble with Electronics (1990); *Yo(u) Tarzan* for Voice, Sequenced Electronics, and Tape (1990).

Shostakovich, Dmitri (Dmitrievich), preeminent Russian composer of the Soviet generation, whose style and idiom of composition largely defined the nature of new Russian music, father of **Maxim Shostakovich**; b. St. Petersburg, Sept. 25, 1906; d. Moscow, Aug. 9, 1975. He was a member of a cultured Russian family; his father was an engineer employed in the government office of weights and measures; his mother was a professional pianist. Shostakovich grew up during the most difficult period of Russian revolutionary history, when famine and disease decimated the population of Petrograd. Of frail physique, he suffered from malnutrition; Glazunov, the director of the Petrograd Cons., appealed personally to the Commissar of Education, Lunacharsky, to grant an increased food ration for Shostakovich, essential for his physical survival. At the age of 9, he commenced piano lessons with his mother; in 1919 he entered the Petrograd Cons., where he studied piano with Nikolayev and composition with Steinberg; graduated in piano in 1923, and in composition in 1925. As a graduation piece, he submitted his 1st Sym., written at the age of 18; it was first performed by the Leningrad Phil. on May 12, 1926, under the direction of Malko, and subsequently became one of Shostakovich's most popular works. He pursued postgraduate work in composition until 1930. His 2nd Sym., composed for the 10th anniversary of the Soviet Revolution in 1927, bearing the subtitle *Dedication to October* and ending with a rousing choral finale, was less successful despite its revolutionary sentiment. He then wrote a satirical opera, *The Nose*, after Gogol's whimsical story about the sudden disappearance of the nose from the face of a government functionary; here Shostakovich revealed his flair for musical satire; the score featured a variety of modernistic devices and included an interlude written for percussion instruments only. *The Nose* was premiered in Leningrad on Jan. 12, 1930, with considerable popular acclaim, but was attacked by officious theater critics as a product of "bourgeois decadence," and quickly withdrawn from the stage. Somewhat in the same satirical style was his ballet *The Golden Age* (1930), which included a celebrated dissonant *Polka*, satirizing the current disarmament conference in Geneva. There followed the 3rd Sym., subtitled *May First* (Leningrad, Jan. 21, 1930), with a choral finale saluting the International Workers' Day. Despite its explicit revolutionary content, it failed to earn the approbation of Soviet spokesmen, who dismissed the work as nothing more than a formal gesture of proletarian solidarity. Shostakovich's next work was to precipitate a crisis in his career, as well as in Soviet music in general; it was an opera to the libretto drawn from a short story by the 19th-century Russian writer Leskov, entitled *Lady Macbeth of the District of Mtsensk*, and depicting adultery, murder, and suicide in a merchant home under the czars. It was premiered in Leningrad on Jan. 22, 1934, and was hailed by most Soviet musicians as a significant work comparable to the best productions of Western modern opera. But both the staging and the music ran counter to growing Soviet puritanism; a symphonic interlude portraying a scene of adultery behind the bedroom curtain, orchestrated with suggestive passages on the slide trombones, shocked the Soviet officials present at the performance by its bold naturalism. After the Moscow production of the opera, *Pravda*, the official organ of the Communist party, publ. an unsigned (and therefore all the more authoritative) article accusing Shostakovich of creating a "bedlam of noise." The brutality of this assault dismayed Shostakovich; he readily admitted his faults in both content and treatment of the subject, and declared his solemn determination to write music according to the then-emerging formula of "socialist realism." His next stage production was a ballet, *The Limpid Brook* (Leningrad, April 4, 1935), portraying the pastoral scenes on a Soviet collective farm. In this work he tempered his dissonant idiom, and the subject seemed eminently fitting for the Soviet theater; but it, too, was condemned in *Pravda*, this time for an insufficiently dignified treatment of Soviet life. Having been rebuked twice for 2 radically different theater works, Shostakovich abandoned all attempts to write for the stage, and returned to purely instrumental composition. But as though pursued by vengeful fate, he again suffered a painful reverse. His 4th Sym. (1935–36) was placed in rehearsal by the Leningrad Phil., but withdrawn before the performance when representatives of the musical officialdom and even the orch. musicians themselves sharply criticized the piece. Shostakovich's rehabilitation finally came with the production of his 5th Sym. (Leningrad, Nov. 21, 1937), a work of rhapsodic grandeur, culminating in a powerful climax; it was hailed, as though by spontaneous consensus, as a model of true Soviet art, classical in formal design, lucid in its harmonic idiom, and optimistic in its philosophical connotations. The height of his rise to recognition was achieved in his 7th Sym. He began its composition during the siege of Leningrad by the Nazis in the autumn of 1941; he served in the fire brigade during the air raids; then flew from Leningrad to the temporary Soviet capital in Kuibishev, on the Volga, where he completed the score, which was premiered there on March 1, 1942. Its symphonic development is realistic in the extreme, with the theme of the Nazis, in mechanical march time, rising to monstrous loudness, only to be overcome and reduced to a pathetic drum dribble by a victorious Russian song. The work became a musical symbol of the Russian struggle against the overwhelmingly superior Nazi war machine; it was given the subtitle *Leningrad Symphony*, and was performed during World War II by virtually every orch. in the Allied countries. Ironically, in later years Shostakovich intimated that the sym. had little or nothing to do with the events of the siege of Leningrad but actually with the siege of Russia in the grip of the dehumanizing and tyrannical Stalinist regime. After the tremendous emotional appeal of the Leningrad Symphony, the 8th Sym., written in 1943, had a lesser impact; the 9th, 10th, and 11th syms. followed (1945, 1953, 1957) without attracting much comment; the 12th Sym. (1960–61), dedicated to the memory of Lenin, aroused a little more interest. But it was left for his 13th Sym. (Leningrad, Dec. 18, 1962) to create a controversy which seemed to be Shostakovich's peculiar destiny; its vocal 1st movement for solo bass and men's chorus, to words by the Soviet poet Yevtushenko, expressing the horror of the massacre of Jews by the Nazis during their occupation of the city of Kiev, and containing a warning against residual anti-Semitism in Soviet Russia, met with unexpected criticism by the chairman of the Communist party, Nikita Khrushchev, who complained about the exclusive attention in Yevtushenko's poem to Jewish victims, and his failure to mention the Ukrainians and other nationals who were also slaughtered. The text of the poem was altered to meet these objections, but the 13th Sym. never gained wide acceptance. There followed the remarkable 14th Sym. (1969), in 11 sections, scored for voices and orch., to words by Federico García Lorca, Apollinaire, Rilke, and the Russian poet Kuchelbecker. Shostakovich's 15th Sym., his last (premiered in Moscow under the direction of his son Maxim on Jan. 8, 1972), demonstrated his undying spirit of innovation; the score is set in the key of C major, but it contains a dodecaphonic passage and literal allusions to motives from Rossini's *William Tell Overture* and the Fate Motif from Wagner's *Die Walküre*. Shostakovich's adoption, however limited, of themes built on 12 different notes, a procedure that he had himself condemned as anti-musical, is interesting both from the psychological and sociological standpoint; he experimented with these techniques in several other works; his first explicit use of a 12-tone subject occurred in his 12th String Quartet (1968). Equally illuminating is his use in some of his scores of a personal monogram, D.S.C.H. (for D, Es, C, H in German notation, i.e., D, E-flat, C, B). One by one, his early works, originally condemned as unacceptable to Soviet reality, were returned to the stage and the concert hall; the objectionable 4th and 13th syms. were publ. and recorded; the operas *The Nose* and *Lady Macbeth of the District of Mtzensk* (renamed *Katerina Izmailova*, after the name of the heroine) had several successful revivals.

Shostakovich excelled in instrumental music. Besides the 15 syms., he wrote 15 string quartets, a String Octet, Piano Quintet, 2 piano trios, Cello Sonata, Violin Sonata, Viola Sonata, 2 violin concertos, 2 piano concertos, 2 cello concertos, 24 preludes for Piano, 24 preludes and fugues for Piano, 2 piano sonatas, and several short piano pieces; also choral works and song cycles. What is most remarkable about Shostakovich is the unfailing consistency of his style of composition. His entire oeuvre, from his first work to the last (147 opus numbers in all), proclaims a personal article of faith. His idiom is unmistakably of the 20th century, making free use of dissonant harmonies and intricate contrapuntal designs, yet never abandoning inherent tonality; his music is teleological, leading invariably to a tonal climax, often in a triumphal triadic declaration. Most of his works carry key signatures; his metrical structure is governed by a unifying rhythmic pulse. Shostakovich is equally eloquent in dramatic and lyric utterance; he has no fear of prolonging his slow movements in relentless dynamic rise and fall; the cumulative power of his kinetic drive in rapid movements is overwhelming. Through all the peripeties of his career, he never changed his musical language in its fundamental modalities. When the flow of his music met obstacles, whether technical or external, he obviated them without changing the main direction. In a special announcement issued after Shostakovich's death, the government of the U.S.S.R. summarized his work as a "remarkable example of fidelity to the traditions of musical classicism, and above all, to the Russian traditions, finding his inspiration in the reality of Soviet life, reasserting and developing in his creative innovations the art of socialist realism, and in so doing, contributing to universal progressive musical culture." His honors, both domestic and foreign, were many: the Order of Lenin (1946, 1956, 1966), People's Artist of the U.S.S.R. (1954), Hero of Socialist Labor (1966), Order of the October Revolution (1971), honorary Doctor of the Univ. of Oxford (1958), Laureate of the International Sibelius Prize (1958), and Doctor of Fine Arts from Northwestern Univ. (1973). He visited the U.S. as a delegate to the World Peace Conference in 1949, as a member of a group of Soviet musicians in 1959, and to receive the degree of D.F.A. from Northwestern Univ. in 1973. A postage stamp of 6 kopecks, bearing his photograph and an excerpt from the Leningrad Symphony, was issued by the Soviet Post Office in 1976 to commemorate his 70th birthday. A collected edition of his works was publ. in Moscow (42 vols., 1980–).

WORKS: DRAMATIC: OPERAS: *The Nose*, op. 15 (1927–28; Leningrad, Jan. 12, 1930); *Lady Macbeth of the District of Mtsensk*, op. 29 (1930–32; Leningrad, Jan. 22, 1934; rev. as *Katerina Izmaylova*, op. 114, 1956–63; Moscow, Jan. 8, 1963); *The Gamblers* (1941–42; unfinished; Leningrad, Sept. 18, 1978). **OPERETTA:** *Moskva, Cheryomushki*, op. 105 (1958; Moscow, Jan. 24, 1959). **BALLETS:** *The Golden Age*, op. 22 (Leningrad, Oct. 26, 1930); *Bolt*, op. 27 (Leningrad, April 8, 1931); *The Limpid Brook*, op. 39 (Leningrad, April 4, 1935). **INCIDENTAL MUSIC:** *The Bedbug*, op. 19 (Moscow, Feb. 13, 1929); *The Shot*, op. 24 (Leningrad, Dec. 14, 1929; not extant); *Virgin Soil*, op. 25 (Leningrad, May 9, 1930; not extant); *Rule, Britannia!*, op. 28 (Leningrad, May 9, 1931); *Conditionally Killed*, op. 31 (Leningrad, Oct. 20, 1931); *Hamlet*, op. 32 (Moscow, March 19, 1932); *The Human Comedy*, op. 37 (Moscow, April 1, 1934); *Hail, Spain*, op. 44 (Leningrad, Nov. 23, 1936); *King Lear*, op. 58a (1940; Leningrad, March 24, 1941); *Native Country*, op. 63 (Moscow, Nov. 7, 1942); *Russian River*, op. 66 (Moscow, Dec. 1944); *Victorious Spring*, op. 72 (1945; Moscow, May 1946). **FILM SCORES:** *New Babylon*, op. 18 (1928–29); *Alone*, op. 26 (1930–31); *Golden Mountains*, op. 30 (1931); *Counterplan*, op. 33 (1932); *The Tale of the Priest and His Worker Blockhead*, op. 36 (1933–34; unfinished; rev. as a comic opera by S. Khentova, 1980); *Love and Hatred*, op. 38 (1934); *The Youth of Maxim*, op. 41 (1934); *Girl Friends*, op. 41a (1934–35); *The Return of Maxim*, op. 45 (1936–37); *Volochayev Days*, op. 48 (1936–37); *The Vyborg District*, op. 50 (1938); *Friends*, op. 51 (1938); *The Great Citizen*, op. 52 (1937); *The Man with a Gun*, op. 53 (1938); *The Great Citizen*, op. 55 (1938–39); *The Silly Little Mouse*, op. 56 (1939; unfinished); *The Adventures of Korzinkina*, op. 59 (1940; not extant); *Zoya*, op. 64 (1944); *Simple People*, op. 71 (1945); *The Young Guard*, op. 75 (1947–48); *Pirogov*, op. 76 (1947); *Michurin*, op. 78 (1948); *Encounter at the Elbe*, op. 80 (1948); *The Fall of Berlin*, op. 82 (1949); *Belinsky*, op. 85 (1950); *The Unforgettable Year 1919*, op. 89 (1951); *Song of the Great Rivers (Unity)*, op. 95 (1954); *The Gadfly*, op. 97 (1955); *The First Echelon*, op. 99 (1955–56); *Five Days—Five Nights*, op. 111 (1960); *Hamlet*, op. 116 (1963–64); *A Year is a Lifetime*, op. 120 (1965); *Sofia Perovskaya*, op. 132 (1967); *King Lear*, op. 137 (1970).

ORCH.: *Scherzo*, op. 1 (1919); *Theme and Variations*, op. 3 (1921–22); *Scherzo*, op. 7 (1923–24); 15 syms.: No. 1, op. 10 (1924–25; Leningrad, May 12, 1926), No. 2, *To October*, with Bass and Chorus in the finale, op. 14 (Leningrad, Nov. 5, 1927), No. 3, *The First of May*, with Chorus in the finale, op. 20, (1929; Leningrad, Jan. 21, 1930), No. 4, op. 43 (1935–36; Moscow, Dec. 30, 1961), No. 5, op. 47 (Leningrad, Nov. 21, 1937), No. 6, op. 54 (Leningrad, Nov. 5, 1939), No. 7, *Leningrad*, op. 60 (1941; Kuibishev, March 1, 1942), No. 8, op. 65 (Moscow, Nov. 3, 1943), No. 9, op. 70 (Leningrad, Nov. 3, 1945), No. 10, op. 93 (Leningrad, Dec. 17, 1953), No. 11, *The Year 1905*, op. 103 (Moscow, Oct. 30, 1957), No. 12, *The Year 1917*, op. 112, dedicated to the memory of Lenin (Leningrad, Oct. 1, 1961), No. 13, *Babiy Yar*, with Bass and Men's Chorus, op. 113 (Moscow, Dec. 18, 1962), No. 14 for Soprano, Bass, Strings, and Percussion, op. 135 (Leningrad, Sept. 29, 1969), and No. 15, op. 141 (1971; Moscow, Jan. 8, 1972); 2 Pieces for E. Dressel's opera *Der arme Columbus*, op. 23 (1929); 2 piano concertos: No. 1 for Piano, Trumpet, and Strings, op. 35 (Leningrad, Oct. 15, 1933) and No. 2, op. 102 (Moscow, May 10, 1957); *5 Fragments*, op. 42 (1935); *Solemn March* for Military Band (1942); 2 violin concertos: No. 1, op. 77 (1947–48; Leningrad, Oct. 29, 1955) and No. 2, op. 129 (Moscow, Sept. 13, 1967); *3 Pieces for Orchestra* (1947–48); *Festive Overture*, op. 96 (1954); 2 cello concertos: No. 1, op. 107 (Leningrad, Oct. 4, 1959) and No. 2, op. 126 (Moscow, Sept. 25, 1966); *Novorossiisk Chimes: The Flame of Eternal Glory* (1960); *Overture on Russian and Khirghiz Folk Themes*, op. 115 (1963; Moscow, Oct. 10, 1965); *Funeral-Triumphal Prelude in Memory of the Heroes of the Battle of Stalingrad*, op. 130 (1967); *October*, symphonic poem, op. 131 (Moscow, Sept. 26, 1967); *March of the Soviet Militia* for Military Band, op. 139 (1970); also 27 suites from various works (1927–65).

CHAMBER: 2 piano trios: No. 1, op. 8 (1923) and No. 2, op. 67 (Leningrad, Nov. 14, 1944); 3 Pieces for Cello and Piano, op. 9 (1923–24; not extant); 2 Pieces for String Octet, op. 11 (1924–25); Cello Sonata, op. 40 (Leningrad, Dec. 25, 1934); 15 string quartets: No. 1, op. 49 (Leningrad, Oct. 10, 1938), No. 2, op. 68 (Leningrad, Nov. 14, 1944), No. 3, op. 73 (Moscow, Dec. 16, 1946), No. 4, op. 83 (1949; Moscow, Dec. 3, 1953), No. 5, op. 92 (1952; Moscow, Nov. 13, 1953), No. 6, op. 101 (Leningrad, Oct. 7, 1956), No. 7, op. 108 (Leningrad, May 15, 1960), No. 8, op. 110 (Leningrad, Oct. 2, 1960), No. 9, op. 117 (Moscow, Nov. 20, 1964), No. 10, op. 118 (Moscow, Nov. 10, 1964), No. 11, op. 122 (Leningrad, May 28, 1966), No. 12, op. 133 (Moscow, Sept. 14, 1968), No. 13, op. 138 (Leningrad, Dec. 13, 1970), No. 14, op. 142 (Leningrad, Nov. 12, 1973), and No. 15, op. 144 (Leningrad, Nov. 15, 1974); 3 Pieces for Violin (1940); Piano Quintet, op. 57 (Moscow, Nov. 23, 1940); Violin Sonata, op. 134 (1968; Moscow, May 3, 1969); Viola Sonata, op. 147 (Leningrad, Oct. 1, 1975). **PIANO:** *Minuet, Prelude, and Intermezzo* (1919–20; unfinished); *Murzilka* (n.d.); *8 Preludes*, op. 2 (1918–20); *5 Preludes* (1919–21); *3 Fantastic Dances*, op. 5 (1920–22); Suite for 2 Pianos, op. 6 (1922); 2 sonatas: No. 1, op. 12 (Leningrad, Dec. 12, 1926) and No. 2, op. 61 (Moscow, June 6, 1943); *Aphorisms*, op. 13 (1927); *24 Preludes*, op. 34 (1932–33); *Children's Notebook*, op. 69 (1944–45); *Merry March* for 2 Pianos (1949); *24 Preludes and Fugues*, op. 87 (1950–51; Leningrad, Dec. 23, 1952); Concertino for 2 Pianos, op. 94 (1953).

VOCAL: CHORAL: *The Oath to the People's Commissar* for Bass, Chorus, and Piano (1941); *Poem of the Motherland*, cantata for Mezzo-soprano, Tenor, 2 Baritones, Bass, Chorus, and Orch., op. 74 (1947); *Song of the Forests*, oratorio for Tenor, Bass, Boy's Chorus, Mixed Chorus, and Orch., op. 81 (Leningrad, Nov. 15, 1949); *10 Poems* for Chorus and Boy's Chorus, op. 88 (1951); *10 Russian Folksong Arrangements* for Soloists, Chorus, and Piano (1951); *The Sun Shines on our Motherland*, cantata for Boy's Chorus, Mixed Chorus, and Orch., op. 90 (1952); *2 Russian Folksong Arrangements* for Chorus, op. 104 (1957); *Little Paradise*, cantata for 4 Basses, Small Chorus, and Piano (c.1960; Washington, D.C., Jan. 12, 1989); *The Execution of Stepan Razin* for Bass, Chorus, and Orch., op. 119 (Moscow, Dec. 28, 1964); *Loyalty*, 8 ballads for Men's Chorus, op. 136 (1970). **SOLO VOICE:** *2 Fables of Krilov* for Mezzo-soprano and Orch., op. 4 (1922; Moscow, Sept. 16, 1981); *6 Romances on Texts of Japanese Poets* for Tenor and Orch., op. 21 (1928–32); *4 Romances* for Bass and Piano, op. 46 (1936–37; Nos. 1 to 3 orchestrated); *6 Romances* for Bass and Piano, op. 62 (1942; orchestrated as opp. 62a and 140); *Patriotic Song* (1943); *Song About the Red Army* (1943; in collaboration with A. Khachaturian); *From Jewish Folk Poetry* for Soprano, Alto, Tenor, and Piano, op. 79 (1948; orchestrated as op. 79a); *2 Romances* for Man's Voice and Piano, op. 84 (1950); 4 Songs for Voice and Piano, op. 86 (1951); *4 Monologues* for Bass and Piano, op. 91 (1952); *Greek Songs* for Voice and Piano (1952–53); *5 Romances: Songs of our Days* for Bass and Piano, op. 95 (1954); *There Were Kisses* for Voice and Piano (1954); *Spanish Songs* for Mezzo-soprano and Piano, op. 100 (1956); *Satires: Pictures of the Past* for Soprano and Piano, op. 109 (1960); *5 Romances* for Bass and Piano, op. 121 (1965); *Preface to the Complete Collection of My Works and Reflections on this Preface* for Bass and Piano, op. 123 (1966); *7 Romances on Poems of A. Blok* for Soprano, Violin, Cello, and Piano, op. 127 (1967); *Spring, Spring* for Bass and Piano, op. 128 (1967); *6 Romances* for Bass and Chamber Orch., op. 140 (1971); *6 Poems of Marina Tsvetayeva* for Alto and Piano, op. 143 (1973; orchestrated as op. 143a); *Suite* for Bass and Piano, op. 145 (1974; orchestrated as op. 145a); *4 Verses of Captain Lebyadkin* for Bass and Piano, op. 146 (1975).

OTHER: Orchestrations of several works, including Mussorgsky's *Boris Godunov* (1939–40), *Khovanshchina* (1958), and *Songs and Dances of Death* (1962).

BIBL.: N. Slonimsky, "D.D. S.," *Musical Quarterly* (Oct. 1942); V. Seroff, *D. S.: The Life and Background of a Soviet Composer* (N.Y., 1943); M. Sahlberg-Vatchnadze, *S.* (Paris, 1945); I. Martinov, *D. S.* (Moscow, 1946; 2nd ed., 1956; Eng. tr., 1947); L. Danilevich, *D. S.* (Moscow, 1958); M. Sabinina, *D. S.* (Moscow, 1959); G. Orlov, *Simfonii S.s* (Moscow, 1961–62); H. Brockhaus, *D. S.* (Leipzig, 1962; 2nd ed., abr., 1963); M. Sabinina, *Simfonizm S.a* (Moscow, 1965); K. Laux, *D. S., Chronist seines Volkes* (Berlin, 1966); G. Orlov, *D. S.* (Leningrad, 1966); L. Danilevich, ed., *D. S.* (Moscow, 1967); G. Ordzhonokidze, ed., *D. S.* (Moscow, 1967); N. Kay, *S.* (London, 1971); P. Buske, *D. S.* (Berlin, 1975); special issues of *Sovetskaya Musika* (1976, 1981); L. Tretyakova, *D. S.* (Moscow, 1976); M. MacDonald, *D. S.: A Complete Catalogue* (London, 1977); H. Ottaway, *S. Symphonies* (London, 1978); R. Blokker, *The Music of D. S.: The Symphonies* (London, 1978); S. Khentova, *S. v Petrograde-Leningrade* (Leningrad, 1979; 2nd ed., 1979); G. Norris, "S.'s *The Nose*," *Musical Times*, CXX (1979); M. Shaginyan, *D. S.* (On S.; Moscow, 1979); S. Volkov, ed., *Testimony: The Memoirs of D. S.* (London and N.Y., 1979); L. Fay, "S. Versus Volkov: Whose Testimony?," *Russian Review*, XXXIX (1980); N. Lukyanova, *D.D. S.* (Moscow, 1980); G. Norris, "Bitter Memories: The S. Testimony," *Musical Times*, CXXI (1980); D. and L. Sollertinsky, *Pages from the Life of D. S.* (N.Y., 1980); D. Hulme, *D. S.: Catalogue, Bibliography and Discography* (Muir of Ord, 1982; 2nd ed., 1991); C. Norris, ed., *S.: The Man and His Music* (London, 1982); E. Roseberry, *S.: His Life and Times* (Tunbridge Wells and N.Y., 1982); F. Streller, *D. S.* (Leipzig, 1982); J. Devlin, *S.* (Borough Green, 1983); D. Gojowy, *D. S. mit Selbstzeugnissen und Bilddokumenten* (Reinbek bei Hamburg, 1983); J. Hubard, *The First Five Symphonies of D. S.* (diss., Ball State Univ., 1984); B. Schwarz, "S., Soviet Citizen and Anti-Stalinist," *Music and Civilization: Essays in Honor of Paul Henry Lang* (N.Y., 1984); J. Braun, "The Double Meaning of Jewish Elements in D. S.'s Music," *Musical Quarterly*, LXXI, No. 1 (1985); D. Fanning, *The Breath of a Symphonist: S.'s Tenth* (London, 1988); K. Kopp, *Form und Gehalt der Symphonien des D. S.* (Bonn, 1990); I. MacDonald, *The New S.* (Boston, 1990); G. Wolter, *D. S., eine sowjetische Tragödie: Rezeptionsgeschichte* (Frankfurt am Main, 1991); E. Wilson, *S.: A Life Remembered* (London, 1994); D. Fanning, ed., *S. Studies* (Cambridge, 1995).

Shostakovich, Dmitri, Russian pianist, son of **Maxim** and grandson of **Dmitri (Dmitrievich) Shostakovich**; b. Moscow, Aug. 9, 1961. He studied piano with Elena Khoven. He made his debut as a soloist with the State Academic Sym. Orch. in 1978 in Moscow; also toured Italy in 1979. In April 1981 he was soloist with the U.S.S.R. State Radio Orch. during its tour of West Germany, conducted by his father, who then decided not to return to Russia; both applied for resident visas for the U.S., which were granted. In Sept. 1981 he joined his father and Mstislav Rostropovich in a series of concerts with the National Sym. Orch. of Washington, D.C., in celebration of the 75th anniversary of the birth of his grandfather. In subsequent years he also appeared with other U. S. and European orchs.

Shostakovich, Maxim, Russian conductor, son of **Dmitri (Dmitrievich)** and father of **Dmitri Shostakovich**; b. Leningrad, May 10, 1938. He studied piano at the Moscow Cons. with Yakov Flier, and conducting with Gauk and Rozhdestvensky. In 1963 he became assistant conductor of the Moscow Sym. Orch., and in 1966, of the U.S.S.R. State Orch., which he accompanied on its U.S. tour in 1969; then was its principal conductor from 1971 until he defected during the orch.'s tour of West Germany in 1981. He and his son then settled in the U.S. On Memorial Day 1981 he conducted the National Sym. Orch. of Washington, D.C., in a special concert on the West Lawn of the U.S. Capitol; subsequently appeared as a guest conductor throughout North America, Europe, and the Far East. He was principal conductor of the Hong Kong Phil. (1983–85), artistic director of the Hartford (Conn.) Sym. Orch. (1985–86), and music director of the New Orleans Sym. Orch. (1986–91). He has become best known for his obviously authentic interpretations of his father's works.

Shtogarenko, Andrei (Yakovlevich), Ukrainian composer and pedagogue; b. Noviye Kaidaki, near Ekaterinoslov, Oct. 15, 1902; d. Kiev, Sept. 25, 1992. He studied with Bogatyrev at the Kharkov Cons. (graduated, 1936). From 1954 to 1968 he was director of the Kiev Cons., where he also was a prof. from 1960. In 1972 he was made a People's Artist of the U.S.S.R.

WORKS: DRAMATIC: Film scores. **ORCH.:** 3 syms. (1947, rev. 1958; 1965, rev. 1970; 1971); *Partisan Sketches* (1957); Violin Concerto (1969); Piano Concertino (1972); Violin Concertino (1972). **OTHER:** *Lenin Walks the Planet*, choral sym. (1958); cantatas; songs; chamber music; piano pieces.

BIBL.: A. Znosco-Borovsky, *A. S.* (Kiev, 1947; 2nd ed., 1951); M. Borvoyk, *A. Y. S.* (Kiev, 1961); G. Vynogradov, *A. S.* (Kiev, 1973).

Shuard, Amy, English soprano; b. London, July 19, 1924; d. there, April 18, 1975. She studied at London's Trinity College of Music. Her principal vocal instructors were Ivor Warren, Ernst Urbach, Gustav Sachs, and Eva Turner. In 1948 she gave a series of lecture-recitals in South Africa, and then made her operatic debut as Aida in Johannesburg in 1949. Returning to London, she sang at the Sadler's Wells Opera until 1955. From 1954 to 1974 she was a principal member of London's Covent Garden. She also sang in Italy, Vienna, Bayreuth, San Francisco, and Buenos Aires. In 1966 she was made a Commander of the

Order of the British Empire. Her most acclaimed role was Turandot, but she also won admiration for her Brünnhilde, Sieglinde, Lady Macbeth, Santuzza, Elektra, Káta Kabanová, and Jenůfa.

Shulman, Alan, American cellist, teacher, and composer; b. Baltimore, June 4, 1915. He studied cello with Salmond at the Peabody Cons. of Music in Baltimore, and composition with Wagenaar at the Juilliard School of Music in N.Y., graduating in 1937. He was a member of the NBC Sym. Orch. in N.Y. (1937–42; 1945–54); also was a teacher at Sarah Lawrence College and at the Juilliard School of Music.

WORKS: ORCH.: *Theme and Variations* for Viola and Orch. (N.Y., Feb. 17, 1941); *Pastorale and Dance* for Violin and Orch. (N.Y., July 15, 1944); Cello Concerto (1948; N.Y., April 13, 1950); *Waltzes* (1949); *A Laurentian Overture* (1951; N.Y., Jan. 7, 1952); *Popocatepetl*, symphonic picture (1952). **CHAMBER:** *Rendezvous* for Clarinet and Strings (1946); *Threnody* for String Quartet (1950); *Suite Miniature* for Octet of Cellos (1956); *Suite* for Cello (1950); *Top Brass* for 12 Brass Instruments (Portland, Oreg., April 25, 1958); *4 Diversions* for a Pride of Cellos (Philadelphia, April 6, 1975); numerous short works for Violin, for Cello, for Piano, etc.

Shumsky, Oscar, esteemed American violinist, conductor, and pedagogue; b. Philadelphia, March 23, 1917. He commenced violin lessons at an early age and made his debut with Stokowski and the Philadelphia Orch. as a soloist in Suk's *Fantasy* for Violin and Orch. when he was only 8 (March 27, 1925); that same year he began private lessons with Auer, and then continued training with him at the Curtis Inst. of Music in Philadelphia (1928–30), where he subsequently studied with Zimbalist (1930–36). After further private studies with Zimbalist (1936–38), he played in the NBC Sym. Orch. in N.Y. (1939–42); also was 1st violinist in the Primrose Quartet, and appeared as a soloist with the leading U.S. orchs.; later was solo violinist with the Bach Aria Group. In 1959 he made his debut as a conductor with the Canadian National Festival Orch.; then was music director of the Canadian Stratford Festival (1959–67). In 1942 he became a teacher at the Peabody Cons. of Music in Baltimore; in 1953 he joined the staff of the Juilliard School of Music in N.Y.; also taught at the Curtis Inst. of Music (1961–65) and at the Yale School of Music (from 1975). He gave up teaching in 1981 to concentrate on his performance activities. His son, Eric Shumsky (b. Port Chester, N.Y., Dec. 7, 1953), is a violist who appeared frequently with his father in chamber music concerts.

Shure, Leonard, respected American pianist and teacher; b. Los Angeles, April 10, 1910; d. Nantucket, Mass., Feb. 28, 1995. He was a pupil of Artur Schnabel at the Berlin Hochschule für Musik (graduated, 1928). He made his recital debut in Berlin in 1927; after serving as Schnabel's teaching assistant (1928–33), he made his U.S. debut in Boston in 1933; subsequently appeared as soloist with many U.S. orchs., as a recitalist, and as a chamber music artist. He served on the faculties of the Longy School of Music in Cambridge, Mass., the New England Cons. of Music in Boston, the Mannes College of Music in N.Y., the Cleveland Inst. of Music, the Univ. of Texas in Austin, and Boston Univ., numbering among his pupils David del Tredici, Gilbert Kalisch, Gary Karr, Ursula Oppens, and Pinchas Zukerman. He was particularly admired for his performances of Beethoven, Schubert, and Brahms.

Siagian, Rizaldi, significant Indonesian performer, composer, and ethnomusicologist; b. Medan, North Sumatra, early 1950s. He played drums and guitar, and also sang in urban pop groups in the late 1960s, then became interested in traditional Sumatran music; studied at the Univ. of North Sumatra (B.A., 1982) and at San Diego State Univ. (M.A., 1985, with a thesis on South Indian drumming); then returned to Indonesia to head the ethnomusicology program at Universitas Sumatera Utara (U.S.U., Univ. of North Sumatra). He participated in various independent music groups; in 1981 he appeared at London's Royal Albert Hall with the group Ansambel Bukit Barisan, and in 1989 directed a performance at the National Palace in Jakarta. In 1987 he served as artistic director for the performance of North Sumatran music for the Cultural Festival Celebration of North Sumatra and in The Hague. In 1991 he was engaged to lead a group of Batak musicians from the Lake Toba area of North Sumatra on a tour of the U.S. as part of its "Festival of Indonesia." As a composer, Siagian was first active as an arranger of popular music (1970–80); in 1986 he began composing works that combined modern and traditional musical elements, his intent being to reintegrate North Sumatran traditional instruments into the musical life of North Sumatra and Indonesia. An example of such compositional "conservation" is his resurrection of the Gambus (plucked lute), as in his *Gambus Menjelang Magrib* for Gambus, Voice, Frame Drum, Harmonium, and Violin, and in his *Gambus Kehendak in 7* and *Gambus Binal*, both for Gambus, Malaysian Drum, Taganing, Gong, Lonceng, Harmonium, Violin, Hasapi, Tube Zither, and Voice. He also composed *Lebah*, a dance accompaniment for Tube Zither, Drum, Shawm, Slit Drum, Cymbal, and Voice.

Sibelius, Jean (actually, **Johan Julius Christian**), great Finnish composer whose music, infused with the deeply felt modalities of national folk songs, opened a modern era of Northern musical art; b. Hämeenlinna, Dec. 8, 1865; d. Järvenpää, Sept. 20, 1957. The family name stems from a Finnish peasant named Sibbe, traced back to the late 17th century; the Latin noun ending was commonly added among educated classes in Scandinavia. Sibelius was the son of an army surgeon; from early childhood, he showed a natural affinity for music. At the age of 9, he began to study piano; then took violin lessons with Gustaf Levander, a local bandmaster. He learned to play violin well enough to take part in amateur performances of chamber music. In 1885 he enrolled at the Univ. of Helsingfors (Helsinki) to study law, but abandoned it after the first semester. In the fall of 1885, he entered the Helsingfors Cons., where he studied violin with Vasiliev and Csillag; he also took courses in composition with Wegelius. In 1889 his String Quartet was performed in public, and produced a sufficiently favorable impression to obtain for him a government stipend for further study in Berlin, where he took lessons in counterpoint and fugue with Albert Becker. Later he proceeded to Vienna for additional musical training, and became a student of Robert Fuchs and Karl Goldmark (1890–91). In 1892 he married Aino Järnefelt. From then on, his destiny as a national Finnish composer was determined; the music he wrote was inspired by native legends, with the great Finnish epic *Kalevala* as a prime source of inspiration. On April 28, 1892, his symphonic poem *Kullervo*, scored for soloists, chorus, and orch., was first performed in Helsingfors. There followed one of his most remarkable works, the symphonic poem entitled simply *En Saga*, that is, "a legend"; in it he displayed to the full his genius for variation forms, based on a cumulative growth of a basic theme adorned but never encumbered with effective contrapuntal embellishments. From 1892 to 1900 he taught theory of composition at the Helsingfors Cons. In 1897 the Finnish Senate granted him an annual stipend of 3,000 marks. On April 26, 1899, he conducted in Helsingfors the premiere of his 1st Sym. He subsequently conducted the first performances of all of his syms., the 5th excepted. On July 2, 1900, the Helsingfors Phil. gave the first performance of his most celebrated and most profoundly moving patriotic work, *Finlandia*. Its melody soon became identified among Finnish patriots with the aspiration for national independence, so that the czarist government went to the extreme of forbidding its performances during periods of political unrest. In 1901 Sibelius was invited to conduct his works at the annual festival of the Allgemeiner Deutscher Tonkünstlerverein at Heidelberg. In 1904 he settled in his country home at Järvenpää, where he remained for the rest of his life; he traveled rarely. In 1913 he accepted a commission for an orch. work from the American music patron Carl Stoeckel, to be performed at the 28th annual Festival at Norfolk, Conn.

For it he contributed a symphonic legend, *Aalotaret* (Nymphs of the Ocean; later rev. as *The Oceanides*). He took his only sea voyage to America to conduct its premiere on June 4, 1914; on that occasion he received the honorary degree of Mus.D. from Yale Univ. Returning to Finland just before the outbreak of World War I, Sibelius withdrew into seclusion, but continued to work. He made his last public appearance in Stockholm, conducting the premiere of his 7th Sym. on March 24, 1924. He wrote 2 more works after that, including a score for Shakespeare's *The Tempest* and a symphonic poem, *Tapiola*; he practically ceased to compose after 1927. At various times, rumors were circulated that he had completed his 8th Sym., but nothing was forthcoming from Järvenpää. One persistent story was that Sibelius himself decided to burn his incomplete works. Although willing to receive journalists and reporters, he avoided answering questions about his music. He lived out his very long life as a retired person, absorbed in family interests; in some modest ways he was even a *bon vivant*; he liked his cigars and his beer, and he showed no diminution in his mental alertness. Only once was his peaceful life gravely disrupted; this was when the Russian army invaded Finland in 1940; Sibelius sent an anguished appeal to America to save his country, which by the perverse fate of world politics became allied with Nazi Germany. But after World War II, Sibelius cordially received a delegation of Soviet composers who made a reverential pilgrimage to his rural retreat. Honors were showered upon him; festivals of his music became annual events in Helsinki; in 1939 the Helsinki Cons. was renamed the Sibelius Academy in his honor; a postage stamp bearing his likeness was issued by the Finnish government on his 80th birthday; special publications—biographical, bibliographical, and photographic—were publ. in Finland. Artistically, too, Sibelius attained the status of greatness rarely vouchsafed to a living musician; several important contemporary composers paid him homage by acknowledging their debt of inspiration to him, Vaughan Williams among them. Sibelius was the last representative of 19th-century nationalistic Romanticism. He stayed aloof from modern developments, but he was not uninterested in reading scores and listening to performances on the radio of works of such men as Schoenberg, Prokofiev, Bartók, and Shostakovich.

The music of Sibelius marked the culmination of the growth of national Finnish art, in which Pacius was the protagonist, and Wegelius a worthy cultivator. Like his predecessors, he was schooled in the Germanic tradition, and his early works reflect German lyricism and dramatic thought. He opened a new era in Finnish music when he abandoned formal conventions and began to write music that seemed inchoate and diffuse but followed a powerful line of development by variation and repetition; a parallel with Beethoven's late works has frequently been drawn. The thematic material employed by Sibelius is not modeled directly on known Finnish folk songs; rather, he re-created the characteristic melodic patterns of folk music. The prevailing mood is somber, even tragic, with a certain elemental sweep and grandeur. His instrumentation is highly individual, with long songful solo passages, and with protracted transitions that are treated as integral parts of the music. His genius found its most eloquent expression in his syms. and symphonic poems; he wrote relatively little chamber music, and only in his earlier years. His only opera, *The Maid in the Tower* (1896), to a text in Swedish, was never publ. He wrote some incidental music for the stage; the celebrated *Valse triste* was written in 1903 for *Kuolema*, a play by Arvid Järnefelt, brother-in-law of Sibelius.

WORKS: DRAMATIC: OPERA: *Jungfrun i tornet* (The Maid in the Tower; Helsinki, Nov. 7, 1896). **INCIDENTAL MUSIC:** Overture, op. 10, and Suite, op. 11, to *Karelia* (Helsinki, Nov. 13, 1893); *King Kristian II*, op. 27, for a play by A. Paul (Helsinki, Feb. 28, 1898, composer conducting); *Kuolema* (Death) for Strings and Percussion, op. 44, for a play by Arvid Järnefelt (Helsinki, Dec. 2, 1903, composer conducting); *Pelléas et Mélisande*, op. 46, for Maeterlinck's play (Helsinki, March 17, 1905, composer conducting); *Belshazzar's Feast*, op. 51, for a play by H. Procopé (Helsinki, Nov. 7, 1906, composer conducting); *Svanevhit* (Swanwhite), op. 54, for Strindberg's play (Helsinki, April 8, 1908, composer conducting); *Ödlan* (The Lizard) for Violin and String Quintet, op. 8, for a play by M. Lybeck (1909; Helsinki, April 6, 1910, composer conducting); *Jedermann* for Chorus, Piano, Organ, and Orch., op. 83, for Hofmannsthal's play (Helsinki, Nov. 5, 1916); *The Tempest*, op. 109, for Shakespeare's play (1925; Copenhagen, March 16, 1926). **OTHER:** *Näcken* (The Watersprite), 2 songs with Piano Trio, for a play by Wennerberg (1888); The Language of the Birds, a wedding march for A. Paul's play *Die Sprache der Vögel* (1911); *Scaramouche*, op. 71, "tragic pantomime" after the play by P. Knudsen and M. Bloch (1913; Copenhagen, May 12, 1922).

ORCH.: *Andantino and Menuetto* for Clarinet, 2 Cornets, 2 Horns, and Baritone (1890–91); *Overture* in E major (1890–91); *Scène de ballet* (1891); *En Saga*, tone poem, op. 9 (1891–92; Helsinki, Feb. 16, 1893; rev. 1901–02; Helsinki, Nov. 2, 1909); *Menuetto* (1894); *Skogsrået* (The Wood Nymph), tone poem, op. 15 (1894); *Vårsång* (Spring Song), tone poem, op. 16 (Vaasa, June 21, 1894); *4 Legends*, op. 22 (all 1st perf. in Helsinki, April 13, 1896, composer conducting): No. 1, *Lemminkäinen and the Maidens of the Island* (1895; rev. 1897 and 1939), No. 2, *The Swan of Tuonela* (1893; rev. 1897 and 1900), No. 3, *Lemminkäinen in Tuonela* (1895; rev. 1897 and 1939), and No. 4, *Lemminkäinen's Homeward Journey* (1895; rev. 1897 and 1900); *King Kristian II*, suite from the incidental music, op. 27 (1898); *Scènes historiques*, op. 25, I (1899; rev. 1911); *Finlandia*, tone poem, op. 26 (1899; rev. 1900; Helsinki, July 2, 1900, Kajanus conducting); 7 syms.: No. 1, in E minor, op. 39 (Helsinki, April 26, 1899, composer conducting), No. 2, in D major, op. 43 (Helsinki, March 8, 1902, composer conducting), No. 3, in C major, op. 52 (1904–07; Helsinki, Sept. 25, 1907, composer conducting), No. 4, in A minor, op. 63 (1909–11; Helsinki, April 3, 1911, composer conducting), No. 5, in E-flat major, op. 82 (Helsinki, Dec. 8, 1915, Kajanus conducting; rev. version, Helsinki, Dec. 14, 1916; rev. version, Helsinki, Nov. 24, 1919), No. 6, in D minor, op. 104 (Helsinki, Feb. 19, 1923, composer conducting), and No. 7, in C major, op. 105 (Stockholm, March 24, 1924, composer conducting); *Björneborgarnas March* (1900); *Cortège* (1901); Overture in A minor (Helsinki, March 3, 1902, composer conducting); *Romance* in C major for Strings, op. 42 (1903; Turku, March 1904, composer conducting); Concerto in D minor for Violin and Orch., op. 47 (1903–04; Helsinki, Feb. 8, 1904; Viktor Nováček soloist, composer conducting; rev. version, Berlin, Oct. 19, 1905; Karl Halir soloist, R. Strauss conducting); *Cassazione*, op. 6 (1904); *Pelléas et Mélisande*, suite from the incidental music, op. 46 (1905); *Pohjola's Daughter*, symphonic fantasia, op. 49 (St. Petersburg, Dec. 29, 1906, composer conducting); *Belshazzar's Feast*, suite from the incidental music, op. 51 (1906; Helsinki, Sept. 25, 1907); *Pan and Echo*, dance intermezzo, op. 53 (1906); *Nightride and Sunrise*, tone poem, op. 55 (1907; St. Petersburg, Jan. 1909); *Svanevhit* (Swanwhite), suite from the incidental music, op. 54 (1908); *In Memoriam*, funeral march, op. 59 (1909; Helsinki, April 3, 1911); *The Dryad*, tone poem (1910), and *Dance Intermezzo* (1907), op. 45; *Rakastava* (The Lover) for Strings and Percussion, op. 14 (1911); *Scènes historiques*, op. 66, II (1912); 2 serenades for Violin and Orch., op. 69: No. 1, in D major (1912) and No. 2, in G minor (1913); *The Bard*, tone poem, op. 64 (1913; rev. 1914); *Aallottaret* (Nymphs of the Ocean), tone poem, op. 73 (1914; 2nd version as *The Oceanides*, 1914; the latter 1st perf. at the Norfolk [Conn.] Festival, June 4, 1914, composer conducting); 2 pieces for Violin or Cello, and Orch., op. 77 (1914); *2 Humoresques* for Violin and Orch., op. 87 (1917); *4 Humoresques* for Violin and Orch., op. 89 (also numbered as 3–6 in continuation of the preceding; 1917); *Promootiomarssi* (Academic March) (1919); 3 pieces, op. 96: No. 1, *Valse lyrique* (1920), No. 2, *Autrefois, Scène pastorale* for 2 Voices and Orch. (1919), and No. 3, *Valse chevaleresque* (1920); *Suite mignonne* for 2 Flutes and Strings, op. 98a (1921); *Suite champêtre* for Strings, op. 98b (1921); *Suite caractéris-*

tique for Harp and Strings, op. 100 (1922); *The Tempest*, concert version of the incidental music, op. 109 (1925); *Tapiola*, tone poem, op. 112 (N.Y., Dec. 26, 1926, W. Damrosch conducting); *Andante festivo* for Strings and Percussion (1930?; also for String Quartet, 1922); Suite for Violin and Strings, op. 117 (n.d.; Lahti, Dec. 8. 1990).

CHAMBER: *Vattendroppar* (Water Drops) for Violin and Cello (1875–76); *Menuetto* in F major for 2 Violins and Piano (1883); Trio in G major for 2 Violins and Piano (1883); *Andantino* in C major for Cello and Piano (1884?); 2 quartets for 2 Violins, Cello, and Piano: D minor (1884) and C minor (1891); 4 piano trios: A minor (1884?), A minor (1886), D major, *Korpo* (1887), and C major, *Lovisa* (1888); 2 violin sonatas: A minor (1884) and F major (1889); *Andante grazioso* for Violin and Piano (1884–85); 4 string quartets: E-flat major (1885), A minor (1889), B-flat major, op. 4 (1890), and D minor, op. 56, *Voces intimae* (1909); *Allegro* in D major for Piano Trio (1886); *Andante cantabile* for Violin and Piano (1887); *Andante molto* in F minor for Cello and Piano (1887?); *Fantasia* for Cello and Piano (1887?); Quartet in G minor for Violin, Cello, Harmonium, and Piano (1887?); *Scherzo* for Violin, Cello, and Piano, 4-hands (1887?); *Tempo di valse* in G minor for Cello and Piano (1887?); *Theme and Variations* in D minor for Cello (1887?); *Andantino* in G minor for Piano Trio (1887–88); *Allegretto* in C major for Violin and Piano (1888?); *Allegretto* in E-flat major for Violin and Piano (1888?); *Andante-Allegro* in A major for Piano Quintet (1888?); *Moderato maestoso* for Violin and Piano (1888?); *Romance and Epilogue* for Violin and Cello, op. 2 (1888; rev. 1911); Suite (Sonata) in D minor for Violin and Piano (1888?); *Theme and Variations* in C-sharp minor for String Quartet (1888); *Theme and Variations* in G minor for String Quartet (1888–89); Suite (Trio) in A major for String Trio (1889); *Tempo di valse* in F-sharp minor for Cello and Piano, *Lulu Waltz* (1889); Quintet in G minor for Piano and Strings (1890); Rondo for Viola and Piano (1893); *Malinconia* for Cello and Piano, op. 20 (1900); 2 pieces for Violin or Cello and Piano, op. 77: No. 1, *Laetare anima mea. Cantique* (1914–15) and No. 2, *Devotion* (1915); 4 pieces for Violin or Cello and Piano, op. 78: No. 1, *Impromptu* (1915), No. 2, *Romance* (1915), No. 3, *Religioso* (1917), and No. 4, *Rigaudon* (1915); 6 pieces for Violin and Piano, op. 79: No. 1, *Souvenir* (1915?), No. 2, *Tempo di menuetto* (1915), No. 3, *Danse caractéristique* (1916), No. 4, *Sérénade* (1916), No. 5, *Danse Idyll* (1917), and No. 6, *Berceuse* (1917); Violin Sonata in E major, op. 80 (1915); 5 pieces for Violin and Piano, op. 81: No. 1, *Mazurka* (1915), No. 2, *Rondino* (1917), No. 3, *Valse* (1917), No. 4, *Aubade* (1918), and No. 5, *Menuetto* (1918); *Novelette* for Violin and Piano, op. 102 (1922); *Andante festivo* for String Quartet (1922; also for Strings and Percussion, 1930?); *5 Danses champêtres* for Violin and Piano, op. 106 (1925); 4 pieces for Violin and Piano, op. 115 (1929): No. 1, *On the Heath*, No. 2, *Ballade*, No. 3, *Humoresque*, and No. 4, *The Bells*; 3 pieces for Violin and Piano, op. 116 (1929): No. 1, *Scène de danse*, No. 2, *Danse caractéristique*, and No. 3, *Rondeau romantique*. **KEYBOARD: PIANO:** More than 150 pieces (1890–1929). **ORGAN:** 2 pieces, op. 111: No. 1, *Intrada* (1925) and No. 2, *Sorgmusik Surusoitto* (Funeral Music; 1931).

VOCAL: *Kullervo*, symphonic poem for Soprano, Baritone, Men's Chorus, and Orch., op. 7 (Helsinki, April 28, 1892); *Rakastava* (The Lover) for Men's Chorus, op. 14 (1893; Helsinki, April 28, 1894); *Laulu Lemminkäiselle* (A Song for Lemminkäinen) for Men's Chorus and Orch., op. 31, No. 1 (1896); *Har du mod?* (Have You Courage?) for Men's Chorus and Orch., op. 31, No. 2 (1904); *Atenarnes sång* (The Song of the Athenians) for Men's Voices, Winds, and Percussion, op. 31, No. 3 (Helsinki, April 26, 1899); *Tulen synty* (The Origin of Fire) for Baritone, Men's Chorus, and Orch., op. 32 (Helsinki, April 9, 1902, composer conducting; rev. 1910); *Vapautettu kuningatar* (The Liberated Queen), cantata for Chorus and Orch., op. 48 (Helsinki, May 12, 1906); *Luonnotar* (Spirit of Nature), tone poem for Soprano and Orch., op. 70 (1910; Gloucester, Sept. 10, 1913); *Oma maa* (Our Native Land), cantata for Chorus and Orch., op. 92 (1918); *Jordens sång* (Song of the Earth), cantata for Chorus and Orch., op. 93 (1919); *Maan virsi* (Hymn of the Earth), cantata for Chorus and Orch., op. 95 (Helsinki, June 1920, composer conducting); *Väinön virsi* (Väinö's Song) for Chorus and Orch., op. 110 (Helsinki, June 28, 1926, Kajanus conducting); *Masonic Ritual Music* for Men's Voices, Piano, and Organ, op. 113 (1927–46; rev. 1948); also numerous other choral works, and more than 100 songs composed between 1891 and 1918.

BIBL.: K. Flodin, *Finska musiker* (Helsinki, 1900); R. Newmarch, *J. S.: A Finnish Composer* (Leipzig, 1906); E. Furuhjelm, *J. S.: Hans tondikting och drag ur hans liv* (Borgå, 1916); W. Niemann, *J. S.* (Leipzig, 1917); C. Gray, *S.* (London, 1931; 2nd ed., 1945); K. Ekman, *J. S.: En konstnärs liv och personlighet* (Stockholm, 1935; Eng. tr., 1935, as *J. S.: His Life and Personality*; 4th Swedish ed., 1959); C. Gray, *S.: The Symphonies* (London, 1935); A. Meyer, "S.: Symphonist," *Musical Quarterly* (Jan. 1936); B. de Törne, *S.: A Close-Up* (London, 1937); R. Newmarch, *J. S.: A Short History of a Long Friendship* (Boston, 1939; 2nd ed., 1945); H. Askeli, "A Sketch of S. the Man," *Musical Quarterly* (Jan. 1940); B. Sandberg, *J. S.* (Helsinki, 1940); E. Arnold, *Finlandia: The Story of S.* (N.Y., 1941; 2nd ed., 1951); E. Roiha, *Die Symphonien von J. S.: Eine formanalytische Studie* (Jyväskylä, 1941); I. Krohn, *Der Formenbau in den Symphonien von J. S.* (Helsinki, 1942); E. Tanzberger, *Die symphonischen Dichtungen von J. S. (Ein inhalt sund formanalytische Studie)* (Würzburg, 1943); S. Levas, *J. S. ja hänen Ainolansa* (Helsinki, 1945; 2nd ed., 1955); M. Similä, *Sibeliana* (Helsinki, 1945); B. de Törne, *S., i närbild och samtal* (Helsinki, 1945; 2nd ed., 1955); G. Abraham, ed., *S.: A Symposium* (London, 1947; 2nd ed., 1952); I. Hannikainen, *S. and the Development of Finnish Music* (London, 1948); N.-E. Ringbom, *S.* (Stockholm, 1948; Eng. tr., Norman, Okla., 1954); V. Helasvuo, *S. and the Music of Finland* (Helsinki, 1952; 2nd ed., 1957); O. Anderrson, *J. S. i Amerika* (Åbo, 1955); S. Parmet, *S. symfonier* (Helsinki, 1955; Eng. tr., 1959, as *The Symphonies of S.: A Study in Musical Appreciation*); L. Solanterä, *The Works of J. S.* (Helsinki, 1955); H. Johnson, *J. S.* (N.Y., 1959); E. Tanzberger, *J. S.: Eine Monographie* (Wiesbaden, 1962); F. Blum, *J. S.: An International Bibliography on the Occasion of the Centennial Celebrations, 1965* (Detroit, 1965); R. Layton, *S.* (London, 1965; 3rd ed., rev., 1983); E. Tawaststjerna, *J. S.* (5 vols., Helsinki, 1965–88; Eng. tr. by R. Layton, 1976–); R. Layton, *The World of S.* (London, 1970); B. James, *The Music of J. S.* (East Brunswick, N.J.; London; and Mississauga, Ontario; 1983); E. Salmenhaara, *J. S.* (Helsinki, 1984); F. Dahlström, *The Works of J. S.* (Helsinki, 1987); T. Howell, *J. S.: Progressive Techniques in the Symphonies and Tone Poems* (N.Y., 1989); special issue of *Finnish Music Quarterly*, 3–4 (1990); K. Kilpeläinen, *The J. S. Musical Manuscripts at Helsinki University Library: A Complete Catalogue* (Wiesbaden, 1991); E. Tawaststerjna, *J. S.: Aren 1865–1893* (Helsinki, 1992); J. Hepokoski, *S.: Symphony No. 5* (Cambridge, 1993); V. Murtomaki, *Symphonic Unity: The Development of Formal Thinking in the Symphonies of S.* (Helsinki, 1993); G. Schlüter, *The Harold E. Johnson J. S. Collection at Butler University: A Complete Catalogue* (Indianapolis, 1993); G. Goss, *J. S. and Olin Downes: Music, Friendship, Criticism* (Boston, 1995).

Siciliani, Alessandro, Italian conductor and composer; b. Florence, June 5, 1952. He received training in piano, conducting, and composition at the Milan Cons. and the Accademia di Santa Cecilia in Rome, his principal conducting mentor being Ferrara. He conducted opera throughout Italy, including Rome, Naples, and Palermo; also conducted opera in Barcelona, Marseilles, Nice, Liège, N.Y., Philadelphia, and New Orleans. In 1988 he conducted for the first time at the Metropolitan Opera in N.Y., leading the double bill of *Cavalleria Rusticana* and *Pagliacci*; also appeared as a symphonic conductor with leading orchs. throughout Europe, the U.S., and the Far East. In 1988 he became principal guest conductor of the Teatro Colón in Buenos Aires, and of the Teatro Municipal in São Paulo. He was music advisor (1991–92) and music director (from 1992) of the Columbus (Ohio) Sym. Orch. Among his compositions are a ballet, *L'Amour Peintre*; orch. works; an oratorio, *Giona*; a cantata; etc.

Sicilianos, Yorgos, Greek composer; b. Athens, Aug. 29, 1922. He studied harmony with Varvoglis at the Hellenic Cons. and with Sklavos at the Athens Cons. (until 1943); then went to Rome, where he took a course with Pizzetti at the Accademia di Santa Cecilia (1951–53); supplemented his music education at the Paris Cons. (1953–54), where he studied with Milhaud and Aubin. He received a Fulbright scholarship to continue his training with Piston at Harvard Univ., Blacher at the Berkshire Music Center at Tanglewood, and Persichetti at the Juilliard School of Music in N.Y. (1955–56). Upon his return to Greece, he occupied various educational and administrative posts; was head of music services for the National Broadcasting Inst. (1960–61; 1979); taught at Pierce College in Athens (from 1967). His style of composition is classical in format, pandiatonic in harmony, and intricately polyphonic in contrapuntal and fugal developments.

WORKS: BALLETS: *The Pearl* (1957); *Tanagra* for 2 Pianos and Percussion (Athens, April 21, 1958; orch. version, Athens, Feb. 5, 1962); *Bacchantes* (Athens, Jan. 11, 1960). **ORCH.:** Sym. (1941–47); Sym. No. 1 (1955–56; N.Y., March 1, 1958); *Prelude and Dance* (Athens Radio, Sept. 1, 1948); *The Revelation of the Fifth Seal*, symphonic poem (1951; Athens, May 11, 1952); Concertino for 5 Winds and Strings (Rome, June 9, 1953); *Concerto for Orchestra* (Athens, Nov. 28, 1954); *Synthesis* for 2 String Orchs. and Percussion (Athens, Nov. 26, 1962; based on the String Quartet No. 3, 1957–62); Cello Concerto (1963); *Variations on 4 Rhythmical Themes* (1963); *Perspectives* for 4 Orch. Groups (1966); *Episodia* for 17 Instruments (1964–67); *Antiphona* for Strings, Brass, and Percussion (1976). **CHAMBER:** 4 string quartets (1951; 1954–55; 1957–62; 1967); *Study* for Tuba (1974); *Schemata* for 6 Percussion (1976). **PIANO:** 3 sonatas (1939); *8 Children's Miniatures* (1963); (8) *Études compositionnelles* (1972–73; rev. as 6 études for Piano and Orch., 1975). **VOCAL:** *Stasimon II* for Mezzo-soprano, Women's Voices, and Orch. (1965); *Episodes II* for Double Chorus, Piano, Double Bass, Percussion, and Tape (1971); *Epitaphion: in memoriam Nikos Marangopoulos* for Chorus, Children's Voices, Narrator, and Orch. (1971); *Parable* for Chorus, Flute, Tuba, Percussion, and Tape (1973); *6 Songs* for Mezzo-soprano or Baritone and Piano (1975); *Moonlight Sonata*, cantata for Mezzo-soprano, Clarinet, Viola, and Guitar (1976–77).

Sidarta, Otok Bima, active Indonesian composer, teacher, dancer, painter, and journalist; b. Yogyakarta, Java, May 18, 1960. He was born into an artistic family; his father, Bagong Kussudiarja, is a famous choreographer and painter, and his brother, Djaduk Ferianto, a well-known composer. Sidarta studied dance at his father's Pusat Latihan Tari (PLT, Center for Dance Study; 1967) and at Pamulangan Beksa Nyayogyakarta (PBN, 1979), founded by the important choreographer/dancer Romo Sasminta Mardawa; also studied music at the Yogyakarta high school cons., Sekolah Menengah Karawitan Indonesia (SMKI). From 1980 to 1984 he was active in California; appeared at World Music Festivals at the Calif. Inst. of the Arts in Valencia (1981) and in San Diego (1982); also participated in the Asian Pacific Culture Festival at Loyola Marymount Univ. (1983) and in the activities of the Indonesian Cultural Center, both in Los Angeles. In 1984 he returned to Indonesia, where he founded the group Kelompok Musik Sempu (KMS), which took 1st place in the "best creativity" category at the Acoustic Music Competition (1984); taught dance and music in Sumatra (1985) and in Kuala Lumpur (1986), following a tour to Malaysia; also was active at his father's Padepokan Seni Bagong Kussudiarja (PSBK, Residential Art Center) in Yogyakarta. In 1987 he participated in the ASEAN workshop on Liturgy and Music in Manila; also performed his own *Meja, meja* (Table, table) at a PSBK concert, "Experimental Arts I," and collaborated on and performed in the collective composition *Antara Tugu Ngejaman* with his brother at the national Pekan Komponis (Composers Festival) in Jakarta. He also founded a group that specialized in children's songs, Sanggar Dolanan Anak-anak Among Siswa. After touring with his father's group in Seoul, Japan, Hong Kong, Singapore, and Malaysia (1988), he founded Pusat Latihan Karawitan Yogyakarta (PLK, Center for the Study of [Javanese] Music). In 1989 he founded and coordinated the first composition festival in Yogyakarta for new music using Javanese gamelan, "Lomba Komposisi Karawitan I," in cooperation with PSBK and the Yogyakarta Arts Council. Sidarta's musical innovations include the addition to the gamelan of hand-held percussion instruments (such as bells, triangles, and claves), as well as the development of new percussion techniques, including placing hanging gongs horizontally on cloth and striking them muted. He also created a personal drumming style that combines Javanese, Sundanese, and original elements. He composed for various venues; from 1984 he created pieces for dance accompaniment, alone and collectively, which included *Kebangkitan Nasional, Lintasan Sejarah (ABRI)* (Armed Forces) and *Sendratari Kelahiran*; also created works for folk theater, known as ketoprak, which were performed in art centers and on Indonesian National TV (TVRI) in Yogyakarta and Jakarta. His compositions for Javanese gamelan include *Meja, meja* (1987), *Antara Tugu Ngejaman* (with Djaduk Ferianto), and *Sang Pahlawan, Lesehan, Sibab*, and *511* (all 1988). Among his popular songs is *Kemuning* (1983). He was also active as a choreographer, numbering among his dance works *Sasap* (1978); *GothakGathuk* (1979); *Kelahiran* (1981); *Gerka Suara Nusantara* (1981); *Gaung Kaputren, Santyang*, and *Kasonangane* (all 1985); and *Lima Alit* (1988). From 1975 he was active as a painter; his works have been exhibited in Bali and at the Indonesian Consulate in Los Angeles.

Sidlin, Murray, American conductor; b. Baltimore, May 6, 1940. He was a student of Galkin and Cheslock (theory) and Harold Rherig (trumpet) at the Peabody Cons. of Music in Baltimore (B.A., 1962; M.M., 1968), of Celibidache (conducting) at the Accademia Musicale Chigiana in Siena (summers, 1961–62), and of Grout and Husa at Cornell Univ. (1963–65). In 1970–71 he was assistant conductor at the Aspen (Colo.) Music Festival. After working with Barzin and the National Orchestral Assn. in N.Y. (1971), he was assistant conductor of the Baltimore Sym. Orch. (1971–73). From 1973 to 1977 he was resident conductor of the National Sym. Orch. in Washington, D.C. From 1977 to 1988 he was music director of the New Haven (Conn.) Sym. Orch. He also was music director of the Tulsa Phil. (1978–80). From 1978 to 1993 he served as director of the Aspen Music Festival conducting fellowship program. He also was music director of the Long Beach (Calif.) Sym. Orch. from 1980 to 1988. From 1987 to 1992 he was conductor of the American Music Concerts for Chevron Corp. In 1994 he became resident conductor of the Oregon Sym. Orch. in Portland.

Siegel, Jeffrey, American pianist; b. Chicago, Nov. 18, 1942. He was a student of Ganz at the Chicago Musical College, and later of Rosina Lhévinne and Kabos at the Juilliard School in N.Y. (D.M.A., 1971). In 1958 he made his debut as a soloist with the Chicago Sym. Orch. In 1968 he captured the Silver Medal at the Queen Elisabeth of Belgium Competition in Brussels. In subsequent years, he appeared as a soloist with major American and European orchs., and also toured widely as a recitalist. His vast repertoire ranges from Mozart to Dutilleux.

Siegl, Otto, Austrian composer, conductor, and pedagogue; b. Graz, Oct. 6, 1896; d. Vienna, Nov. 9, 1978. He was a pupil of Mojsisovics, Kroemer, Kunzel, and Kornauth at the Graz Schule des Steiermärkischen Musikverein (1901–15; 1918–20). In 1921–22 he was a violinist in the Vienna Sym. Orch., and then was assistant conductor of the Graz Opera (1922–24). After serving as music director in Paderborn and Herford, as a choral conductor in Essen and Bielefeld, and as a theory teacher in Hagen, he was a teacher (1933–35) and a prof. (1935–48) at the Cologne Hochschule für Musik. He also was conductor of the chorus at the Univ. and of the Gürzenich choir of Cologne (1934–48).

Returning to Vienna, he taught theory at the Academy of Music (from 1948), where he later was head of the theory and conducting depts. (from 1955), and served as a prof. (1958–67). In 1957 he received Austria's Great State Prize for music.

WORKS: ORCH.: Flute Concerto (1955); Cello Concerto (1957); 2 syms. (1958, 1959); Chamber Concerto for Piano and Orch. (1960); Concerto for Clarinet and Strings (1968). **CHAMBER:** 4 cello sonatas (1923, 1923, 1924, 1967); 5 string quartets (*Burleskes*, 1924; 1924; 1932; 1941; *Festliches*, 1956); 2 viola sonatas (1925, 1938); 2 violin sonatas (1925, 1940); 2 string quintets (1940, 1954); Trio for Clarinet, Cello, and Piano (1959); *Quintet-Serenade* for Clarinet, Bassoon, Violin, Viola, and Cello (1961); Sonata for Clarinet and Cello (1965); 2 clarinet sonatas (1965, 1968); Flute Sonata (1968). **VOCAL:** *Missa Mysterium magnum* for Chorus (1926); *Eines Menschen Lied*, cantata for Soloists, Chorus, and Orch. (1931); *Klingendes Jahr*, cantata for Soprano, Men's Chorus, Piano, and String Orch. (1933); *Missa parva* for Soloists, Chorus, and Orch. (1953); *Wort und Wunder*, cantata for Soprano, Chorus, and Orch. (1955); *Missa humilitatis* for Soloists, Chorus, Organ, and Orch. (1959); *Stern des Lebens*, oratorio for Soloists, Chorus, Organ, and Orch. (1959).

BIBL.: W. Trienes, *O. S.* (Mülheim, 1956); W. Suppan, *O. S.* (Vienna, 1966).

Siegmeister, Elie, significant American composer and teacher, whose works reflected the national moods and preoccupations from early social trends to universal concepts; b. N.Y., Jan. 15, 1909; d. Manhasset, N.Y., March 10, 1991. He took piano lessons as a youth with Emil Friedberger; in 1925 he entered Columbia Univ. and studied theory and composition with Seth Bingham (B.A., 1927); also took private lessons in counterpoint with Riegger; after training with Boulanger in Paris (1927–32), he received instruction in conducting from Stoessel at the Juilliard School of Music in N.Y. (1935–38). He was active with the Composers Collective of N.Y., for which he wrote songs under the name L.E. Swift; was a founder of the American Composers Alliance in 1937; was founder-conductor of the American Ballad Singers (1939–46), which he led in performances of American folk songs. He felt strongly that music should express the social values of the people; in his early songs, he selected texts by contemporary American poets voicing indignation at the inequities of the modern world; he also gave lectures and conducted choruses at the revolutionary Pierre Degeyter (composer of the *Internationale*) Club in N.Y. As a result of his multiple musical experiences, Siegmeister developed an individual style of composition ranging from the populist American manner to strong modernistic sonorities employing a sort of euphonious dissonance with intervallic stress on minor seconds, major sevenths, and minor ninths. In his syms. and chamber music, he organized this dissonant idiom in self-consistent modern formulations, without, however, espousing any of the fashionable doctrines of composition, such as dodecaphony. The subject matter of his compositions, especially in the early period, was marked by a strongly national and socially radical character, exemplified by such works as *American Holiday, Ozark Set, Prairie Legend, Wilderness Road,* and *Western Suite*, the last achieving the rare honor of being performed by Toscanini. Siegmeister did not ignore the homely vernacular; his Clarinet Concerto is a brilliant realization of jazz, blues, and swing in a classically formal idiom. Siegmeister achieved an important position as an educator; he taught at Brooklyn College (1934), the New School for Social Research (1937–38), the Univ. of Minnesota (1948), and Hofstra Univ. (1949–76), where he also was composer-in-residence (from 1966); in 1976 he became prof. emeritus. He received numerous commissions and awards; held a Guggenheim fellowship in 1978 and in 1990 was elected a member of the American Academy and Inst. of Arts and Letters. In accepting this honor, he stated his *profession de foi* as first formulated in 1943: "My aim is to write as good music as I can that will at the same time speak the language of all our people."

WORKS: DRAMATIC: OPERAS: *Darling Corie* (1952; Hempstead, N.Y., Feb. 18, 1954); *Miranda and the Dark Young Man* (1955; Hartford, Conn., May 9, 1956); *The Mermaid of Lock No. 7* (Pittsburgh, July 20, 1958); *Dublin Song* (St. Louis, May 15, 1963; rev. version as *The Plough and the Stars*, Baton Rouge, La., March 16, 1969); *Night of the Moonspell* (Shreveport, La., Nov. 14, 1976); *The Marquesa of O* (1982); *Angel Levine* (N.Y., Oct. 5, 1985); *The Lady of the Lake* (N.Y., Oct. 5, 1985). **OTHER DRAMATIC:** *Doodle Dandy of the USA*, play with music (N.Y., Dec. 26, 1942); *Sing Out, Sweet Land*, musical (Hartford, Conn., Nov. 10, 1944); *Fables from the Dark Woods*, ballet (Shreveport, April 25, 1976). Also incidental music; film scores, including *They Came to Cordura* (1959).

ORCH.: *American Holiday* (1933); *Abraham Lincoln Walks at Midnight* (1937); *Ozark Set* (1943; Minneapolis, Nov. 7, 1944); *Prairie Legend* (1944; N.Y., Jan. 18, 1947); *Wilderness Road* (1944; Minneapolis, Nov. 9, 1945); *Western Suite* (N.Y., Nov. 24, 1945); *Sunday in Brooklyn* (N.Y., July 21, 1946); *Lonesome Hollow* (1946; Columbus, Ohio, 1948); 8 syms.: No. 1 (N.Y., Oct. 30, 1947; rev. 1972), No. 2 (1950; N.Y., Feb. 25, 1952; rev. 1971), No. 3 (1957; Oklahoma City, Feb. 8, 1959), No. 4 (1967–70; Cleveland, Dec. 6, 1973), No. 5, *Visions of Time* (1971–75; Baltimore, May 4, 1977), No. 6 (1983; Sacramento, Nov. 4, 1984), No. 7 (1986), and No. 8 (1989; Albany, N.Y., March 30, 1990); *Summer Night* (1947; N.Y., Sept. 27, 1952); *From My Window* (1949; also for Piano); *Divertimento* (1953; Oklahoma City, March 28, 1954); Clarinet Concerto (Oklahoma City, Feb. 3, 1956); Flute Concerto (1960; Oklahoma City, Feb. 17, 1961); *Theater Set*, after the film score *They Came to Cordura* (1960; Rochester, N.Y., May 8, 1969); *Dick Whittington and His Cat* for Narrator and Orch. (1966; Philadelphia, Feb. 10, 1968); *5 Fantasies of the Theater* (1967; Hempstead, N.Y., Oct. 18, 1970); Piano Concerto (1974; Denver, Dec. 3, 1976; rev. 1982); *Shadows and Light: Homage to 5 Paintings* (Shreveport, La., Nov. 9, 1975); *Double Concerto: An Entertainment* for Violin, Piano, and Orch. (Columbia, Md., June 25, 1976); Violin Concerto (1977–83; Oakland, Calif., Jan. 29, 1985); *Fantasies in Line and Color: 5 American Paintings* (1981); *From These Shores: Homage to 5 American Authors* (1986; Merillville, Ind., Feb. 13, 1990); *Figures in the Wind* (1990); also works for Band.

CHAMBER: *Nocturne* for Flute and Piano (1927); *Prelude* for Clarinet and Piano (1927); *Contrasts* for Bassoon and Piano (1929); 3 string quartets (1935, 1960, 1973); *Down River* for Alto Saxophone and Piano (1939); 6 violin sonatas (1951, 1965, 1965, 1971, 1975, 1988); *Song for a Quiet Evening* for Violin and Piano (1955); *Fantasy and Soliloquy* for Cello (1964); Sextet for Brass and Percussion (1965); *American Harp* for Harp (1966); *Declaration* for Brass and Timpani (1976); *Summer* for Viola and Piano (1978); *Ten Minutes* for 4 Players for Wind Quartet (N.Y., Jan. 15, 1989). **PIANO:** *Theme and Variations No. 1* (1932) and *No. 2* (1967); *Toccata on Flight Rhythms* (1937); 5 sonatas: No. 1, *American* (1944), No. 2 (1964), No. 3 (1979), No. 4, *Prelude, Blues, and Toccata* (1980), and No. 5 (1987; N.Y., Jan. 15, 1988); *Sunday in Brooklyn* (1946); *3 Moods* (1959); *On This Ground* (1971); *3 Studies* (1982); also 4 vols. of educational pieces (1951–77).

VOCAL: CHORAL: *Heyura, Ding, Dong, Ding* (1935–70); *John Henry* (1935); *American Ballad Singers Series* (1943); *American Folk Song Choral Series* (1953); *I Have a Dream*, cantata for Baritone, Narrator, Chorus, and Orch., after Martin Luther King, Jr. (1967; Omaha, Oct. 7, 1968); *A Cycle of Cities* for Soprano, Tenor, Chorus, and Orch. (Wolf Trap, Va., Aug. 8, 1974); *Cantata for FDR* for Baritone, Chorus, and Wind Ensemble (1981; Denver, May 5, 1982); *Sing Unto the Lord a New Song* for Chorus and Organ (1981). **SONGS AND SONG CYCLES** (all for Solo Voice and Piano unless otherwise given): *Cortège for Rosenbloom* (1926); *4 Robert Frost Songs* (1930); *The Strange Funeral in Braddock* (1933; also for Baritone and Orch., 1938); *3 Elegies for García Lorca* (1938); *Johnny Appleseed* for Solo Voice (1940; also for Chorus, 1940); *Nancy Hanks* (1941); *For My Daughters* (1952); *Madam to You* (1964); *The Face of War*

(1966; also for Voice and Orch., 1967–68; N.Y., May 24, 1968); *Songs of Experience* (1966; rev. for Alto or Bass, Viola, and Piano, 1977); 11 songs to words by e.e. cummings (1970); *Songs of Innocence* (1972); *City Songs* (1977); *3 Minute Songs* (1978); *Brief Introduction to the Problems of Philosophy* (1979); *Ways of Love* for Voice and Chamber Orch. (1983; N.Y., Jan. 15, 1984); *Bats in My Belfry* (1990); *4 Langston Hughes Songs* (1990); *Outside My Window* (1990).

WRITINGS: Ed. with O. Downes, *A Treasury of American Song* (N.Y., 1940; 3rd ed., 1984); *The Music Lover's Handbook* (N.Y., 1943; rev., 1973, as *The New Music Lover's Handbook*; new ed., 1983); *Work and Sing* (N.Y., 1944); *Invitation to Music* (Irvington-on-Hudson, 1961); *Harmony and Melody* (2 vols.; Belmont, Calif., 1965–66).

BIBL.: J. Gallagher, *Structural Design and Motivic Unity in the 2nd, 3rd, and 4th Symphonies of E. S.* (diss., Cornell Univ., 1982); C. Oja, "Composer with a Conscience: E. S. in Profile," *American Music* (Summer 1988).

Siegmund-Schultze, Walther, German musicologist; b. Schweinitz, July 6, 1916; d. Halle, March 6, 1993. He studied musicology with Arnold Schmitz at the Univ. of Breslau (Ph.D., 1940, with the diss. *Mozarts Vokal- und Instrumentalmusik in ihren motivisch-thematischen Beziehungen*); he completed his Habilitation at the Univ. of Halle with his *Untersuchungen zum Brahms Stil und Brahms Bild* in 1951. In 1954 he became a lecturer at the Univ. of Halle; in 1956 he was made a prof. of musicology, director of the musicological faculty, and dean of the philosophy faculty. He was noted for his studies of 18th-century music; his analysis of the styles of Bach, Handel, and Mozart is interesting as an example of Marxist theories applied to music.

WRITINGS: *Die Musik Bachs* (Leipzig, 1953); *Georg Friedrich Händel: Leben und Werk* (Leipzig, 1954; 3rd ed., 1962); *Mozarts Melodik und Stil: Eine Studie* (Leipzig, 1957); *Lehrbriefe für das Fernstudium: Die Musik der Klassik* (Halle, 1964); *Georg Friedrich Händel: Thema mit 20 Variationen* (Halle, 1965); *Die Hauptvertreter der bürgerlichen Musikkultur im 20. Jahrhundert* (Halle, 1966–67); *Johannes Brahms: Eine Biographie* (Leipzig, 1966; 2nd ed., 1974); *Die Musik der sozialistischen Länder (ausser DDR)* (Halle, 1967); *Ziele und Aufgaben der sozialistischen Musikerziehung* (Leipzig, 1967; 3rd ed., 1975); *Die Bach-Händel-Epoche* (Halle, 1968); *Das Musikschaffen der DDR* (Halle, 1969); *Ludwig van Beethoven: Eine Biographie* (Leipzig, 1975; 2nd ed., 1977); *Johann Sebastian Bach* (Leipzig, 1976); *Wolfgang Amadeus Mozart, 1756–1791: Eine kleine Biographie gewidmet allen Freunden von Michaelstein im Mozartjahr 1991* (Michaelstein, 1991).

Siems, Margarethe, outstanding German soprano; b. Breslau, Dec. 30, 1879; d. Dresden, April 13, 1952. She studied with Orgeni. She made her debut at the Prague May Festival in 1902, and that same year joined the Prague Opera; in 1908 she joined the Dresden Court (later State) Opera, where she was a leading dramatic coloratura soprano until 1920; Strauss chose her to create the roles of Chrysothemis in *Elektra* (Jan. 25, 1909) and the Marschallin in *Der Rosenkavalier* (Jan. 26, 1911) there, and also Zerbinetta in *Ariadne auf Naxos* in Stuttgart (Oct. 25, 1912). In 1913 she made her London debut at Covent Garden. She retired from the operatic stage in Breslau in 1925 but continued to sing in concerts; taught at the Berlin Cons. (1920–26), and then in Dresden and Breslau. In addition to her roles in Strauss's operas, she gained renown for her performances in the operas of Bellini, Donizetti, Verdi, and Wagner.

Siepi, Cesare, admired Italian bass; b. Milan, Feb. 10, 1923. He studied at the Milan Cons. He made his operatic debut as Sparafucile in Schio, near Vicenzo (1941); appeared as Zaccaria in *Nabucco* in Verona (1945) and at his La Scala debut in Milan (1946), where he was a principal artist until 1958; also appeared with the company during its 1950 visit to London's Covent Garden, where he was a regular singer from 1962 to 1973. On Nov. 6, 1950, he made his Metropolitan Opera debut in N.Y. as Philip II in *Don Carlos*, remaining on its roster until 1973; also sang in other major opera houses on both sides of the Atlantic. An esteemed cantante artist, he excelled in the operas of Mozart and Verdi.

Sierra, Roberto, Puerto Rican composer; b. Vega Baja, Oct. 9, 1953. He began musical training at the Puerto Rico Cons. of Music and at the Univ. of Puerto Rico (graduated, 1976); then pursued studies in London at the Royal College of Music and the Univ. (1976–78), at the Inst. of Sonology in Utrecht (1978), and with Ligeti at the Hamburg Hochschule für Musik (1979–82). He was assistant director (1983–85) and director (1985–86) of the cultural activities dept. at the Univ. of Puerto Rico, then dean of studies (1986–87) and chancellor (1987–89) at the Puerto Rico Cons. of Music. From 1989 to 1992 he was composer-in-residence at the Milwaukee Sym. Orch. In 1992 he became an assistant prof. at Cornell Univ.

WORKS: DRAMATIC: *El Mensajero de Plata*, chamber opera (1984); *El Contemplado*, ballet (1987). **ORCH.:** *Polaeizaciones* for 2 Orch. Groups (1979); *Jubilo* (1985); *Cuatro ensayos orquestales* (1986); *Glosas* for Piano and Orch. (1987); *Descarga* (1988; Milwaukee, Sept. 28, 1989); *Préambulo* (Milwaukee, Sept. 28, 1989); *SASIMA* (San Antonio, Feb. 22, 1990); *Idilio* (1990); *A Joyous Overture* (1991); *Concierto Evocativo* for Horn and Orch. (1991); *Tropicalia* (Milwaukee, Nov. 14, 1991); *Of Discoveries* for 2 Guitars and Orch. (Chautauqua, N.Y., July 3, 1992); *Imágenes*, concerto for Violin, Guitar, and Orch. (1993); *Concierto Caribe* for Flute and Orch. (1993); *Evocaciones*, violin concerto (Pittsburgh, Dec. 1, 1994); *Ritmo* (1995); *Saludo* (1995); Concertino for Chamber Orch. and Tape (N.Y., Dec. 15, 1995). **CHAMBER:** *Tiempo Muerto* for String Quartet (1978; London, Feb. 7, 1986); *Salsa on the C String* for Cello and Piano (1981); *Seis piezas fáciles* for 2 Violins (1982); *Bongo-O* for Percussion (1982); *Salsa* for Wind Quintet (1983); *Cinco bocetos* for Clarinet (1984); *Concierto Nocturnal* for Harpsichord, Flute, Clarinet, Oboe, Violin, and Cello (1985); *Memorias Tropicales* for String Quartet (1985); *El sueño de Antonia* for Clarinet and Percussion (1985); *Toccata y Lamento* for Guitar (1987); *Essays* for Wind Quintet (1987); *Mano a mano* for 2 Percussionists (1987); *Introducción y Descarga* for Piano, Brass Quintet, and Percussion (1988); *Tributo* for Harp, Flute, Clarinet, and String Quartet (1988); *Trio Tropical* for Violin, Cello, and Piano (1992); *Segunda Crónica del Descubrimiento* for Flute and Guitar (1992); *Tercera Crónica del Descubrimiento* for Flute and Guitar (1992); *Tres Fantasías* for Clarinet, Cello, and Piano (1994); *Ritmorroto* for Clarinet (1995). **KEYBOARD: PIANO:** *Descarga en sol* (1981); *Vestigios Rituales* for 2 Pianos (1984); *Tres inventos* (1987); *2 X 3* for 2 Pianos (1994). **HARPSICHORD:** *Tres miniaturas* (1982); *Con salsa* (1984). **VOCAL:** *Cantos populares* for Chorus (1983); *Doña Rosíta* for Mezzo-soprano and Wind Quintet (1985); *Invocaciones* for Voice and Percussion (1986); *Glosa a la sombra . . .* for Mezzo-soprano, Viola, Clarinet, and Piano (1987); *Bayoán*, oratorio for Soprano, Baritone, and Orch. (1991; N.Y., Oct. 14, 1994). **OTHER:** *entre terceras* for 2 Synthesizers and Computer (1988).

Sieveking, Martinus, Dutch pianist and teacher; b. Amsterdam, March 24, 1867; d. Pasadena, Calif., Nov. 26, 1950. He studied piano with his father. He began his career as an accompanist; traveled with Adelina Patti on her tour of England (1891–92); then settled in the U.S. In 1915 he established his own piano school in N.Y. and announced a new method which guaranteed to achieve virtuosity in 24 months; not very successful in N.Y., he went to California, where he found a fertile field for his quick road to virtuosity for everybody.

Sigtenhorst-Meyer, Bernhard van den, Dutch composer; b. Amsterdam, June 17, 1888; d. The Hague, July 17, 1953. He studied at the Amsterdam Cons.; later in Vienna and Paris. He settled in The Hague as a composer and writer.

WRITINGS: *Jan Pieterszoon Sweelinck en zijn instrumentale muziek* (The Hague, 1934; 2nd ed., 1946); *De vocale muziek van Jan Pieterszoon Sweelinck* (The Hague, 1948).

WORKS: 2 string quartets (1919, 1944); Sonata for Solo Cello (1926); 2 violin sonatas (1926, 1938); *6 Miniatures* for Oboe and Piano (1926–46); 2 piano sonatas (1922, 1925); 3 piano sonatinas (1928, 1930, 1948); other piano pieces, including *La Vieille Chine* (1916), *Les Oiseaux* (1917), and *Le Monde de contesbleus* (2 albums; 1926–28).

Sigurbjörnsson, Thorkell, prominent Icelandic composer, pedagogue, and administrator; b. Reykjavík, July 16, 1938. He studied at the Reykjavík College of Music (1948–57); then had lessons in composition with R.G. Harris at Hamline Univ. in St. Paul, Minn. (B.A., 1959), and in electronic music with Hiller and composition with Gaburo at the Univ. of Illinois in Urbana (M.M., 1961); then attended sessions in Nice and Darmstadt (1962). Returning to Reykjavík, he founded the modern group Musica Nova; taught at the Reykjavík College of Music (from 1962), becoming a full prof. in 1969; also was active with the Icelandic State Radio (1966–69). In 1973 he was a creative assoc. at the State Univ. of N.Y. at Buffalo, and in 1975 was a research musician at the Univ. of Calif. in La Jolla. He served as secretary (1969–85) and president (1985–88) of the Icelandic Soc. of Composers. In addition to his work as a composer, pedagogue, and broadcaster, he also appeared as a pianist and conductor.

WORKS: DRAMATIC: *Composition in 3 Scenes*, chamber opera (1964); *Apaspil*, children's opera (1966); *Rabbi*, children's opera (1968); *Thorgeirsboli* (The Bull-man), ballet (1971). **ORCH.:** *Flökt* (Fluctuations; 1961); *Cadenza and Dance* for Violin and Orch. (1967); *Ymur* (1969); *Ys og Thys* (Much Ado), overture (1970); *Laeti* for Orch. and Orch. on Tape (1971); *Mistur* (1972); *Haflög* (1973); *Nidur*, double bass concerto (1974); *Bükolla*, clarinet concerto (1974); *Albumblatt* (1975); *Eurydice* for Flute and Orch. (1978); *Sequences*, violin concerto (1981); *Ulisse ritorna*, cello concerto (1981); *Columbine*, divertimento for Flute and Strings (Falun, Sweden, Dec. 5, 1982); *Diaphony* (1984); Triple Concerto for Violin, Cello, Piano, and Orch. (1984); *Longate*, concerto for Flute, Strings, and Percussion (1984); *Trifonia* (1990). **CHAMBER:** *Víxl* (Rotation) for Violin, Clarinet, Cello, and Duplicate Instruments on Tape (1962); *Hässelby-Quartet*, string quartet (1968); *Kisum* for Clarinet, Viola, and Piano (1970); *Intrada* for Clarinet, Viola, and Piano (1970); *Happy Music* for Brass Ensemble (1971); *Dáik* for Clarinet, Cello, and Synthesizer (1973); *Hylling* (Homage) for Flute, Cello, Piano, Percussion, Tape, and Audience (1974); *4 Better or Worse* for Flute, Clarinet, Cello, and Piano (1975); *Copenhagen Quartet* for String Quartet (1977); *The Pied Piper* for Flute and String Trio (1978); *Bergabesk* for Woodwind Quintet (1979); *Ra's Dozen* for 12 Flutes (1980); *Tema senza variazioni* for Clarinet, Cello, and Piano (1981); *Saman* for 2 Flutes, 2 Oboes, 2 Clarinets, 2 Bassoons, 2 Horns, and Piano (1983); *Drift* for Clarinet and Piano (1984); *Hot Spring Birds* for Flute, Guitar, and Cello (1984); *Hoquetus minor* (Minor Hiccups) for Harpsichord and Percussion (1987); *6 Icelandic Folksongs* for Flute, Violin, and Cello (1988); *Bird of Fate* for Clarinet and String Quartet (1989); *Music from the Court of Thora* for Alto Saxophone, Vibraphone, Harpsichord, and Electric Bass Guitar (1990); Duo for Violin and Cello (1990); *6 Icelandic Folksongs* for Clarinet, Cello, and Piano (1991); *Gövertimento* for Flute, Oboe, Clarinet, Horn, Bassoon, and Piano (1991); *Usamo* for Organ, Percussion, and Strings (1992). **VOCAL:** *Ballade* for Tenor, Flute, Viola, and Guitar (1960); *Leikar* for Chorus and Orch. (1961); *Solstice* for Soprano, Alto, Baritone, Flute, Marimba, and Double Bass (1976); *The Last Flower* for Children's Chorus and Children's Orch. (1983); *A Poem About Settlement* for Tenor and Chamber Orch. (1987); *The Coming* for Chorus (1988); *A Birthday Song: Ruv at 60* for Chorus and Orch. (1990).

Sigwart, Botho (real name, **Sigwart Botho, Count of Eulenburg**), German pianist, musicologist, and composer; b. Berlin, Jan. 10, 1884; d. from wounds received in battle, Galicia, June 2, 1915. He was the son of the German diplomat and poet Count Phillip of Eulenburg. He studied piano in Vienna and musicology at the Univ. of Munich (Ph.D., 1907, with the diss. *Erasmus Widmann*); completed his studies with Reger in Leipzig (1908–09). In 1909 he married the concert singer Helene Staegemann. He wrote a number of piano pieces, a String Quartet, and several melodramas.

Siki, Béla, distinguished Hungarian pianist and teacher; b. Budapest, Feb. 21, 1923. He studied with Dohnányi and Leo Weiner at the Budapest Academy of Music; later took lessons with Lipatti in Geneva. In 1945 he made his debut in Budapest; in 1947 he won the Concours International d'Exécutions Musicales in Geneva; then made tours of Australia, Japan, South America, and the U.S. In 1965 he became a prof. of piano at the Univ. of Wash. in Seattle, and in 1980 at the Univ. of Cincinnati College-Cons. of Music. He wrote *Piano Repertoire: A Guide to Interpretation and Performance* (N.Y., 1981). He became especially known for his authoritative performances of the works of Liszt and Bartók.

Siklós (real name, **Schönwald**), **Albert,** Hungarian cellist, musicologist, pedagogue, and composer; b. Budapest, June 26, 1878; d. there, April 3, 1942. He changed his name to Siklós in 1910. He studied law, and later took courses with Koessler at the Budapest Academy of Music, graduating in 1901; he taught at the Academy from 1910, and gradually became one of its most respected teachers. He was a prolific composer, but few of his works were publ., and there were virtually no performances outside Hungary. He publ. a number of instructive books; also a music dictionary (1923).

WORKS: DRAMATIC: OPERAS: *Knight Fulkó* (1896); *The House of Moons* (1926; Budapest, Dec. 21, 1927). **BALLET:** *The Mirror* (Budapest, March 28, 1923). **ORCH.:** 2 cello concertos (1895, 1902); 3 sym. (1896; *Anlauf*, 1896; 1901); *Symphonie aetherique* for 12 Double Basses (1899); Violin Concerto (1899); overtures; suites. **OTHER:** Chamber music; vocal works; piano pieces; organ music.

Sikorski, Kazimierz, Swiss-born Polish composer and pedagogue, father of **Tomasz Sikorski**; b. Zürich (of Polish parents), June 28, 1895; d. Warsaw, June 23, 1986. He studied composition with Szopski at the Chopin Music High School in Warsaw (graduated, 1919); took courses in philosophy at the Univ. of Warsaw (graduated, 1921) and then pursued musicology training with Chybiński at the Univ. of Lwów; completed his musical studies in Paris (1925–27; 1930). He taught at the Łódž Cons. (1947–54) and the Warsaw Cons. (1951–57), serving as director of the latter (1957–66). Among his many students were Bacewicz, Panufnik, Palester, Serocki, and his own son. He publ. *Instrumentoznawstwo* (The Study of Instruments; Warsaw, 1932; 3rd ed., 1975), *Harmonia* (Harmony; 3 vols., Kraków, 1948–49; 4th ed., 1972), and *Kontrapunkt* (Counterpoint; 3 vols., Kraków, 1953–57).

WORKS: ORCH.: *Suite* for Strings (1917); 6 syms. (1918; 1921; 1953; 1969; 1978–79; 1983); Clarinet Concerto (1947); Concerto for Horn and Small Orch. (1948); *Popular Overture* (1954); Flute Concerto (1957); Concerto for Trumpet, Strings, 4 Timpani, Xylophone, and Tam-tam (1959); *6 Old Polish Dances* for Small Orch. (1963); *Concerto Polyphonique* for Bassoon and Orch. (1965); Oboe Concerto (1967); Trombone Concerto (1973). **CHAMBER:** 3 string quartets; String Sextet. **VOCAL:** Choruses.

Sikorski, Tomasz, Polish composer and pianist, son of Kazimierz Sikorski; b. Warsaw, May 19, 1939; d. there, Nov. 13, 1988. He studied piano with Drzewiecki and composition with his father at the Warsaw Cons.; then took lessons with Boulanger in Paris. As a pianist, he emphasized new music in his programs. His own compositions were in an advanced idiom.

WORKS: RADIO OPERA: *Przygody Sindbada zeglaraza* (The Adventures of Sinbad the Sailor; 1971). **ORCH.:** *Concerto breve* for Piano, 24 Winds, and 4 Percussionists (1965); *Sequenza I* (1966); *Holzwege* (1972); *Étude* (1972); *Music in Twilight* for Piano and Orch. (1978); *Strings in the Earth* for 15

Strings (1979–80); *Self-portrait* (1983); *Autoritratto* for 2 Pianos and Orch. (1983); *La Notte* for Strings (1984); *Omaggio per quattro pianoforti ed orchestra in memoriam Borges* (1987). **CHAMBER:** *Echoes 2 quasi improvvisazione* for 1 to 4 Pianos, Percussion, and Tape (1961–63); *Architectures* for Piano, Winds, and Percussion (1965); *Intersections* for 36 Percussion Instruments (1968); *Homophony* for 4 Trumpets, 4 Horns, 4 Trombones, Piano, and 2 Gongs (1968); *For Strings* for 3 Violins and 3 Violas (1970); *Bez tytulu* (Untitled) for Piano, Clarinet, Trombone, and Cello (1972); *Other Voices* for Winds and Percussion (1975); *Das Schweigen der Sirenen* for Cello (1986). **PIANO:** *Sonant* (1967); *Diafonia* for 2 Pianos (1969); *Zerstreutes Hinausschauen* (1971); *Listening Music* for 2 Pianos (1973). **VOCAL:** *Antyfony* for Soprano without Text, Piano, Horn, Chimes, 2 Gongs, 2 Tam-tams, and Tape (1963); *Prologues* for Women's Chorus, 2 Pianos, 4 Flutes, 4 Horns, and 4 Percussionists (1964); *Vox humana* for Chorus, 12 Brasses, 2 Pianos, 4 Gongs, and 4 Tam-tams (1971); *Music from Afar* for Chorus and Orch. (1974); *Sickness Unto Death* for Narrator, 2 Pianos, 4 Trumpets, and 4 Horns (1976).

Silja, Anja, remarkable German soprano; b. Berlin, April 17, 1935. Her grandmother was the singer Paula Althof; at the age of 8, she began vocal training with her grandfather, Egon van Rijn; gave a solo recital in Berlin at the age of 10. In 1956 she sang Rosina at the Berlin Städtische Opera; after appearing at the Braunschweig State Theater (1956–58), she sang at the Württemberg State Theater in Stuttgart (1958), at the Frankfurt am Main Opera (1960–63), and at the Bayreuth Festivals (from 1965). In 1968 she made her U.S. debut as Senta with the Chicago Lyric Opera; her Metropolitan Opera debut followed in N.Y. as Leonore in *Fidelio* on Feb. 26, 1972. In subsequent years, she made appearances with leading North American and European opera houses; also sang in concerts with major orchs. She later was also active as an opera producer. However, she continued to make appearances in opera. In 1995 she gave a stunning portrayal of Janaček's Elina Makropulos at the Glyndebourne Festival and at the London Proms. The breadth of her repertoire is commanding. Wagner's grandson Wieland coached her in the Wagnerian roles, among them Elisabeth, Elsa, Eva, and Senta, which she performed at Bayreuth. She also sang the roles of Salome and Elektra in Strauss's operas, of Marie and Lulu in Berg's operas, and of the sole character in Schoenberg's *Erwartung*. As a matter of course, she mastered the majority of standard soprano roles. She married **Christoph von Dohnányi**, under whose baton she sang in both operatic and concert settings.

Silk, Dorothy (Ellen), English soprano; b. King's Norton, Worcestershire, May 4, 1883; d. Alvechurch, Worcestershire, July 30, 1942. She studied in Birmingham and with Johannes Ress in Vienna. She pursued a fine career as a concert artist, appearing in London and at major English festivals. She also made forays into opera. In addition to her performances of works by English composers, she programmed the music of Schütz and other rarely heard composers.

Sills, Beverly (real name, **Belle Miriam Silverman**), celebrated American soprano and operatic administrator; b. N.Y., May 25, 1929. At the age of 3, she appeared on the radio under the cute nickname "Bubbles," and won a prize at a Brooklyn contest as "the most beautiful baby of 1932." At 4, she joined a Saturday morning children's program, and at 7 she sang in a movie. At 10, she had a part on the radio show "Our Gal Sunday." Her natural thespian talent and sweet child's voice soon proved to be valuable financial assets. She did a commercial advertising Rinso White soap, and appeared on an early television program, "Stars of the Future." She began formal vocal studies with Estelle Liebling when she was 7; also studied piano with Paolo Gallico; in Public School 91 in Brooklyn she was voted most "likely to succeed." In 1947 she made her operatic debut as Frasquita in *Carmen* with the Philadelphia Civic Opera; then toured with several operas companies, and sang with the San Francisco Opera (1953) and the N.Y. City Opera (1955), quickly establishing herself at the latter as one of its most valuable members. She extended her repertoire to embrace modern American operas, including the title role of Douglas Moore's *The Ballad of Baby Doe*; she also sang in the American premiere of Luigi Nono's avant-garde opera *Intolleranza 1960*. She was a guest singer at the Vienna State Opera and in Buenos Aires in 1967, at La Scala in Milan in 1969, and at Covent Garden in London and the Deutsche Oper in Berlin in 1970. She made her first appearance with the Metropolitan Opera as Donna Anna in a concert production of *Don Giovanni* on July 8, 1966, at the Lewisohn Stadium in N.Y.; her formal debut with the Metropolitan took place at Lincoln Center in N.Y. as Pamira in *Le Siège de Corinthe* on April 7, 1975. At the height of her career, she received well-nigh universal praise, not only for the excellence of her voice and her virtuosity in coloratura parts, but also for her intelligence and erudition, rare among the common run of operatic divas. She became general director of the N.Y. City Opera in 1979, and made her farewell performance as a singer in 1980. She showed an uncommon administrative talent; during her tenure with the N.Y. City Opera, she promoted American musicians and broadened the operatic repertoire. In 1988 she retired from her post with the N.Y. City Opera. In 1994 she was named chairwoman of Lincoln Center. In her personal life, she suffered a double tragedy; one of her 2 children was born deaf, and the other was mentally retarded. In 1972 she accepted the national chairmanship of the Mothers' March on Birth Defects. She publ. *Bubbles: A Self-portrait* (N.Y., 1976; 2nd ed., rev., 1981, as *Bubbles: An Encore*) and *Beverly: An Autobiography* (N.Y., 1987). She received (deservedly so) honorary doctorates from Harvard Univ., N.Y. Univ., and the Calif. Inst. of the Arts. On Nov. 22, 1971, she was the subject of a cover story in *Time*. In 1980 she was awarded the U.S. Presidential Medal of Freedom. Her most notable roles included Cleopatra in Handel's *Giulio Cesare*, Lucia, Elisabeth in *Roberto Devereux*, Anna Bolena, Elvira in *I puritani*, and Maria Stuarda.

BIBL.: M. Kerby, *B. S.: America's Own Opera Star* (N.Y., 1989); B. Paolucci, *B. S.* (N.Y., 1990).

Siloti, Alexander, eminent Russian pianist, pedagogue, and conductor; b. near Kharkov, Oct. 9, 1863; d. N.Y., Dec. 8, 1945. He studied piano with Zverev and Nikolai Rubinstein at the Moscow Cons., and theory there with Tchaikovsky (1876–81), winning the gold medal. He made his debut as a pianist in Moscow in 1880; then made a tour in Germany; Liszt accepted him as a student in 1883, and Siloti continued his study with him in Weimar until Liszt's death in 1886. Returning to Russia, he was a prof. of piano at the Moscow Cons. (1888–91); among his students was Rachmaninoff (his 1st cousin). Between 1891 and 1900 he lived in Germany, France, and Belgium; returned to Russia in 1901 and conducted the concerts of the Moscow Phil. Soc. during the 1901–02 season; in 1903 he organized his own orch. in St. Petersburg; these concerts acquired great cultural importance; Siloti invited Mengelberg and Mottl as guest conductors, and Rachmaninoff, Casals, and Chaliapin as soloists. In 1915 he began a series of popular free concerts, and in 1916 started a Russian Musical Fund to aid indigent musicians. In 1919 he left Russia; in 1922 he settled in N.Y., where he was active principally as a teacher but continued to appear as a soloist with American orchs.; from 1925 to 1942 he was on the faculty of the Juilliard School of Music. He publ. a collection of piano pieces which he ed., with indications of fingering and pedaling; also arranged and ed. concertos by Bach and Vivaldi. He publ. a book of reminiscences of Liszt (St. Petersburg, 1911; Eng. tr., Edinburgh, 1913).

Silva, Luigi, Italian-born American cellist and pedagogue; b. Milan, Nov. 13, 1903; d. N.Y., Nov. 29, 1961. He was of a musical family; his father was a vocal teacher; his mother a singer. He studied music at home; then took cello lessons with Arturo Bonucci in Bologna and composition with Respighi in Rome. He played in the Quartetto di Roma (1930–39). In 1939 he emigrated to the U.S.; became a naturalized American citizen in 1945. On April 5, 1941, he made his N.Y. debut in a joint recital with Leopold Mannes; with the latter and Vittorio Brero, he performed with the Mannes Trio (from 1949). He served as chairman of the cello and chamber music depts. at the Eastman School of Music in Rochester, N.Y. (1941–49); then taught at the Mannes College of Music (1949–61), the Yale Univ. School of Music (1951–58), the Juilliard School of Music (1953–61), and the Hewitt School (1956–61). He made transcriptions for cello of works by Paganini, Boccherini, and other Italian composers; ed. Bach's unaccompanied cello suites.

Silva, Oscar da, Portuguese pianist, teacher, and composer; b. Paranhos, near Oporto, April 21, 1870; d. Oporto, March 6, 1958. He studied at the Lisbon Cons.; in 1892 he went to Leipzig, where he had lessons with Reinecke and Clara Schumann. Returning to Portugal in 1910, he devoted himself mainly to teaching, acquiring a very high reputation as a piano pedagogue. From 1932 to 1952 he lived in Brazil; then returned to Portugal. He wrote an opera, *Dona Mecia* (Lisbon, July 4, 1901); a symphonic poem, *Alma crucificada*; chamber music; songs; effective piano pieces.

BIBL.: A. Pinto, *Musica moderna portuguesa e os seus representantes* (Lisbon, 1930).

Silver, Charles, French composer; b. Paris, April 16, 1868; d. there, Oct. 10, 1949. He studied with Dubois and Massenet at the Paris Cons., winning the Grand Prix de Rome in 1891 with the cantata *L'Interdit*. He wrote the operas *La Belle au bois dormant* (Marseilles, 1902); *Le Clos* (Paris, 1906); *Myriane* (Nice, 1913); *La Mégère apprivoisée* (Paris, Jan. 30, 1922); *La Grand-mère* (Oct. 7, 1930); *Quatre-vingt-treize* (Paris, Jan. 24, 1936); also orch. works, songs, etc.

Silver, Sheila, talented, prolific, and original American composer; b. Seattle, Wash., Oct. 3, 1946. She studied at the Univ. of Wash. in Seattle (1964–65), then went to Paris for a course at the Inst. for European Studies (1966–67); returned to the U.S. to earn her B.A. degree at the Univ. of Calif. at Berkeley (1968), and then enrolled at the Paris Cons. (1968). She further took courses at the Hochschule für Musik in Stuttgart, where her mentors were Ligeti and Karkoschka. Shuttling back to the U.S. once more, she studied with Shifrin, Berger, and Shapero at Brandeis Univ., completing her Ph.D. in composition there in 1976; she also attended the summer courses in new music in Darmstadt (1970), and studied with Druckman at the Berkshire Music Center at Tanglewood (summer, 1972). There followed a number of grants that enabled her to travel to London and to Italy, where she was awarded the Prix de Rome at the American Academy. The list of awards she has received is most impressive. In 1979 she was appointed instructor in composition at the State Univ. of N.Y. at Stony Brook. During all of her peregrinations, she continued to compose productively; her mature style may be described as enlightened dissonance devoid of ostensible disharmonies.

WORKS: OPERA: *The Thief of Love*, after a Bengali tale (1986). **ORCH.:** *Galixidi* (Seattle, Wash., March 1977); *Shirat Sarah* (Song of Sarah) for Strings (Hartford, Conn., Jan. 1987); *Dance of Wild Angels* for Chamber Orch. (1990). **CHAMBER:** String Quartet (Boston, Dec. 1977); *Dynamis* for Horn (Rome, May 1979); *Theme and Variations* for Bowed Vibraphone (N.Y., April 1981); *Dance Converging* for Viola, Horn, Piano, and Percussion (1987); *G Whiz*, etude for 2 Violins and Marimba (N.Y., May 1988); *Window Waltz* for Bass Clarinet, Horn, Strings, Harpsichord, Piano, and Percussion (N.Y., May 1988); Cello Sonata (N.Y., Nov. 1988). **PIANO:** *Fantasy Quasi Theme and Variations* (Washington, D.C., April 1981); *Oh, Thou Beautiful One* (1989). **VOCAL:** *Canto* for Baritone and Chamber Ensemble, after Ezra Pound's "Canto XXXIX" about Ulysses (1979); *Chariessa* for Soprano and Orch., after Sappho (Rome, June 1980; also for Soprano and Piano, 1978); *2 Elizabethan Songs* for Chorus (N.Y., Sept. 1982); *Ek Ong Kar* for Chorus (N.Y., Feb. 1983).

Silveri, Paolo, Italian baritone; b. Ofena, near Aquila, Dec. 28, 1913. He studied in Milan and at the Accademia di Santa Cecilia in Rome. In 1939 he made his operatic debut as Schwarz in *Die Meistersinger von Nürnberg*. After singing bass roles, he turned to baritone roles after successfully appearing as Germont in Rome in 1944. In 1946 he sang Marcello, Scarpia, and Rossini's Figaro with the Teatro San Carlo of Naples during its visit to London's Covent Garden. He continued to sing at Covent Garden until 1952, both with the resident company and with the visiting La Scala company of Milan as Rigoletto, Count Luna, Amonasro, and Iago. He sang Don Giovanni and Renato with the Glyndebourne company during its visit to the Edinburgh Festival (1948, 1949). From 1949 to 1955 he sang regularly at La Scala. On Nov. 20, 1950, he made his Metropolitan Opera debut in N.Y. as Don Giovanni. He remained on its roster until 1953, singing such roles as Tonio, Marcello, Germont, Escamillo, Rigoletto, and Scarpia. He then pursued his career in Europe. In 1959 he sang the tenor role of Otello in Dublin but then resumed his career as a baritone. His farewell performance took place at the Camden Festival in 1967 as Donizetti's Israele. From 1970 he taught voice in Rome.

Silverstein, Joseph, distinguished American violinist and conductor; b. Detroit, March 21, 1932. He received his early instruction in violin from his father; then studied with V. Reynolds and Zimbalist at the Curtis Inst. of Music in Philadelphia (1945–50) and later with Gingold and Mischakoff. He played in the Houston Sym. Orch., Denver Sym. Orch., and Philadelphia Orch. before joining the Boston Sym. Orch. in 1955, where he was concertmaster (1962–83) and assistant conductor (1971–83). Having won the Queen Elisabeth of Belgium competition (1959) and the Naumburg Foundation Award (1960), he made solo appearances while retaining his Boston posts; was also chairman of the violin faculty of the Berkshire Music Center and a teacher at Boston Univ. He appeared as guest conductor with various U.S. orchs. Silverstein served as interim music director of the Toledo (Ohio) Sym. Orch. (1979–80) and principal guest conductor of the Baltimore Sym. Orch. (1981–83). He then was music director of the Utah Sym. Orch. in Salt Lake City (1983–98) and the Chautauqua (N.Y.) Sym. Orch. (from 1987). In 1994–95 he also was music adviser of the Louisville Orch. As both a violinist and conductor, he impressed his auditors by his technical expertise and musical integrity.

Silvestri, Constantin, esteemed Romanian-born English conductor and composer; b. Bucharest, June 13, 1913; d. London, Feb. 23, 1969. He studied piano as a child, making his debut at age 10; after taking courses in piano and composition (with Jora) at the Bucharest Cons., he was active as a pianist. In 1930 he made his debut as a conductor with the Bucharest Radio Sym. Orch.; was a conductor with the Bucharest Opera (from 1935) and music director of the Bucharest Phil. (1947–53); also taught conducting at the Bucharest Cons. (from 1948). In 1956 he went to Paris, and in 1957 settled in England, becoming a naturalized British subject in 1967. In 1961 he became principal conductor of the Bournemouth Sym. Orch., which he led with distinction until his death; took it on a European tour in 1965. In 1963 he made his debut at London's Covent Garden conducting *Khovanshchina*. He was an impassioned if sometimes willful interpreter of the classics. He composed mostly in small forms in an unpretentious, neo-Baroque manner.

WORKS: ORCH.: *Jocuri populare româneşti din Transilvania* (1929; Bucharest, March 10, 1933); *3 Pieces* for Strings (1933; rev. 1950; Bucharest, Jan. 7, 1951); *Prelude and Fugue* (1955; Bucharest, Nov. 1956). **CHAMBER:** 2 string quartets (1935, 1947); *Sonata breve* for Clarinet and Bassoon (1938; rev. 1957); Violin Sonata (1939); Oboe Sonata (1939); Harp Sonata (1940); piano pieces, including sonatas, suites, and sonatinas. **VOCAL:** Songs.

Silvestrov, Valentin (Vasilievich), Russian composer; b. Kiev, Sept. 30, 1937. He studied with Liatoshinsky at the Kiev Cons. (1958–64). He began to compose in a boldly experimental idiom of Western provenance; wrote piano pieces in the strict 12-tone technique. Although severely reprimanded in the Soviet press, he was not forcibly restrained from continuing to write music in a modernistic manner. After the demise of the Soviet regime, he encountered no obstructive criticism to his chosen means of compositional expression.

WORKS: ORCH.: 4 syms.: No. 1 (1963), No. 2 for Flute, Percussion, Piano, and Strings (1965), No. 3 (1966), and No. 4 for Brass Instruments and Strings (1976); *Monodia* for Piano and Orch. (1965); *Spectrum* for Chamber Orch. (1965); *Meditation* for Cello and Chamber Orch. (1972). **CHAMBER:** Piano Quintet (1961); *Quartetto piccolo* for String Quartet (1961); Trio for Flute, Trumpet, and Celesta (1962); *Mysteries* for Alto Flute and Percussion (1964); *Projections* for Harpsichord, Vibraphone, and Bells (1965); *Drama* for Violin, Cello, and Piano (1971); String Quartet (1974). **PIANO:** *Variations* (1958); Sonatina (1959); Sonata (1960); *Signals* (1962); *Serenade* (1962). **VOCAL:** Songs.

Simándy, Jószef, Hungarian tenor; b. Budapest, Sept. 18, 1916. He studied with Emilia Posszert at the Budapest Academy of Music. After singing in the Budapest Opera chorus (from 1940), he made his operatic debut as Don José at the Szeged National Theater in 1946. In 1947 he became a member of the Budapest Opera, where he was its principal heroic tenor until 1973. From 1956 to 1960 he also appeared at the Bavarian State Opera in Munich. Among his finest roles were Lohengrin, Walther von Stolzing, Radames, and Otello.

Simeonov, Konstantin (Arsenievich), Russian conductor; b. Koznakovo, June 20, 1910; d. Kiev, Jan. 3, 1987. He began a career as a singer; then studied conducting at the Leningrad Cons. with Alexander Gauk. He subsequently appeared as a guest conductor throughout the Soviet Union; served as chief conductor of the Ukrainian Theater of Opera and Ballet in Kiev (1961–66); then occupied a similar post at the Kirov Theater of Opera and Ballet in Leningrad (1966–75); he resumed his Kiev post in 1975. He also appeared as a guest conductor abroad.

Similä, Martti, Finnish conductor and composer; b. Oulu, April 9, 1898; d. Lahti, Jan. 9, 1958. He studied in Finland, then in Paris and London. He conducted the Helsinki Opera (1927–44) and the Municipal Orch. of Lahti. He made 2 tours in the U.S. as a pianist, in 1923 and 1926; was again in the U.S. in 1957 to lead a memorial concert of the music of Sibelius with the N.Y. Phil. (Dec. 8, 1957). He wrote the book, *Sibeliana* (Helsinki, 1945); also composed orch. music.

Simionato, Giulietta, outstanding Italian mezzo-soprano; b. Forli, May 12, 1910. She studied with Locatello and Palumbo in Rovigo; won the bel canto competition in Florence in 1933, and then returned there to sing in the premiere of Pizzetti's *Orsèolo* (May 5, 1935). In 1939 she joined Milan's La Scala, remaining on its roster as one of its principal artists until 1966. In 1947 she made her British debut as Cherubino at the Edinburgh Festival; her first appearance at London's Covent Garden followed, as Adalgisa in 1953. In 1954 she made her U.S. debut at the Chicago Lyric Opera. On Oct. 26, 1959, she made her first appearance at the Metropolitan Opera in N.Y. as Azucena; sang there again in 1960 and 1962. She gave her farewell stage performance as Servilia in *La clemenza di Tito* at Milan's Piccola Scala in 1966. A distinguished coloratura artist, Simionato excelled in the operas of Rossini, Donizetti, Bellini, and Verdi.

BIBL.: J.-J. Hanine Vallaut, *G. S.: Come Cenerentola divenne regina* (n.p., 1987).

Simmons, Calvin (Eugene), gifted black American conductor; b. San Francisco, April 27, 1950; d. (drowned) Connery Pond, east of Lake Placid, N.Y., Aug. 21, 1982. He was the son of a longshoreman and a gospel singer. He joined the San Francisco Boys' Choir at age 11, where he received conducting lessons from its conductor, Madi Bacon; then went to the Cincinnati College-Cons. of Music, where he studied conducting with Max Rudolf (1968–70); when Rudolf was appointed to the faculty of the Curtis Inst. of Music in Philadelphia, Simmons joined him there (1970–72); he also took piano lessons with Serkin. He served as a rehearsal pianist and assistant conductor under Adler at the San Francisco Opera (1968–75), where he made his formal debut conducting *Hänsel und Gretel* in 1972. In 1975 he made his British debut at the Glyndebourne Festival. He was assistant conductor of the Los Angeles Phil. and music director of the Young Musicians Foundation orch. (1975–78). In 1979 he was appointed music director of the Oakland (Calif.) Sym. Orch. Before his tragic death in a canoeing accident, he appeared as a guest conductor with increasing success throughout North America. He made his Metropolitan Opera debut in N.Y. in 1978 and his N.Y. City Opera debut in 1980.

Simon, Abbey, distinguished American pianist and teacher; b. N.Y., Jan. 8, 1922. He studied with Saperton and Hofmann at the Curtis Inst. of Music in Philadelphia (1932–41); also took lessons with Godowsky in N.Y. In 1941 he won the Naumberg Award and then launched a major career, appearing as a soloist with the leading U.S. orchs.; made his first tour of Europe in 1949, and subsequently traveled all over the world. He taught at the Indiana Univ. School of Music in Bloomington (1960–74), the Juilliard School in N.Y. (from 1977), and the Univ. of Houston (from 1977). A master of the repertory from Beethoven to Rachmaninoff, he evolved a grand bravura style of pianistic virtuosity in which no technical difficulties seem to exist, no tempi are too fast, no nuance is too subtle.

Simon, Alicja, Polish musicologist; b. Warsaw, Nov. 13, 1879; d. Łódź, May 23, 1957. She studied in Warsaw, Berlin, and Zürich; then received instruction in musicology from Kretzschmar and Wolf at the Univ. of Berlin (1904–09), where she also took courses in philosophy, psychology, and history; subsequently completed her training at the Univ. of Zürich (Ph.D., 1914, with the diss. *Polnische Elemente in der deutschen Musik bis zur Zeit der Wiener Klassiker*, publ. in Zürich, 1916). She worked in Berlin (1920–23) and Geneva (1923–24); went to the U.S., and worked on the staff of the Library of Congress in Washington, D.C. (1924–28); then returned to Poland. She was a reader (1945–54) and a prof. (1954–57) at the Univ. of Łódź. She publ. a study on the Polish songwriters (Warsaw, 1936; 2nd ed., enl., 1939).

Simon, Geoffrey, Australian conductor; b. Adelaide, July 3, 1946. He was educated at the Univ. of Melbourne (1964–68), the Juilliard School in N.Y. (1968–69), and Indiana Univ. in Bloomington (1969–72); also was a student in conducting of Ferrara in Hilversum (1972), Swarowsky in Ossiach, Austria (1973–75), Markevitch in France (1974), and Kempe in London (1974–75). He was assistant conductor of the South Melbourne Sym. Orch. (1966–68), and then music director of the Bloomington (Ind.) Sym. Orch. (1969–72). Returning to London, he was music director of the Australian Sinfonia (1975–79) and the Zemel Choir (1975–78); after conducting and teaching at the Univ. of Wisc. in Milwaukee (1978–82) and at North Texas State Univ. in Denton (1982–84), he was music director of the Albany (N.Y.) Sym. Orch. (1987–89). In 1991 he became artistic director of Cala Records in London, with which he recorded rarely heard scores from both the past and present; concurrently served as artistic advisor and principal conductor of the Sacramento (Calif.) Sym. Orch. in 1993–94, becoming its music director in 1994. His guest conducting engagements have taken him around the globe.

Simon, James, German musicologist and composer; b. Berlin, Sept. 29, 1880; d. in the Auschwitz concentration camp about Oct. 14, 1944. He studied piano with Ansorge and composition with Bruch in Berlin. From 1907 to 1919 he taught at the Klindworth-Scharwenka Cons. in Berlin. He left Germany shortly after the advent of the Nazi regime in 1933, and lived in Zürich; then moved to Amsterdam, where the Hitlerite wave engulfed him after the Nazi invasion of the Netherlands. He was deported to Theresienstadt on April 5, 1944, and from there, on Oct. 12, 1944, was sent to Auschwitz, where he was put to death a few days later. His opera, *Frau im Stein*, was premiered in Stuttgart in 1925; he also wrote a Sym.; Piano Concerto; Sextet for Piano and Wind Instruments; choruses; many songs.

Simon, Stephen (Anthony), American conductor; b. N.Y., May 3, 1937. He studied piano with Joel Rosen; then enrolled at the Yale Univ. School of Music; also took courses in choral conducting with Hugh Ross and Julius Herford. In 1963 he became music director of the Westchester Orch. Soc.; from 1970 to 1974 he was music director of the Handel Soc. in N.Y., and then of the Handel Festival in Washington, D.C. (from 1977).

Simoneau, Léopold, eminent Canadian tenor, pedagogue, and administrator; b. St.-Flavien, near Quebec City, May 3, 1916. He was a student of Émile Larochelle in Quebec City (1939–41) and of Salvator Issaurel in Montreal (1941–44). In 1941 he made his operatic debut as Hadji in *Lakmé* with the Variétés lyriques in Montreal. In 1943 he sang Don Curzio at the Montreal Festival. After winning the Prix Archambault in 1944, he studied with Paul Althouse in N.Y. (1945–47). He also pursued his career, winning extraordinary success as Ferrando and Tamino in Montreal in 1945. During this period, he also sang in the U.S. In 1949 he made his Paris debut as Mireille at the Opéra-Comique; he continued to sing there, as well as at the Opéra, until 1954. In 1953 he made his first appearance at Milan's La Scala. In 1954 he sang with the Vienna State Opera on its visit to London. He soon acquired a notable reputation as a Mozartian. He also sang widely in the U.S. and Canada as a soloist with the leading orchs. and as a recitalist. On Oct. 18, 1963, he made his Metropolitan Opera debut in N.Y. as Ottavio, but remained on its roster for only that season. In 1964 he chose Ottavio as his farewell to the operatic stage at the Place des arts in Montreal. He sang for the last time in public as a soloist in *Messiah* with the Montreal Sym. Orch. on Nov. 24, 1970. From 1963 to 1967 he taught at the Montreal Cons. In 1967 he became deputy head of the music division of the Ministry of Cultural Affairs of Quebec. In 1971 he served as the first artistic director of the Opéra du Quebec. He taught at the San Francisco Cons. of Music from 1972, and also at the Banff School of Fine Arts from 1973 to 1976. In 1982 he settled in Victoria, British Columbia, and founded Canada Opera Piccola. In 1946 he married **Pierrette Alarie.** In 1959 they were the first recipients of the Prix de musique Calixa-Lavallée. In 1971 he was made an Officer of the Order of Canada. The French government made him an Officier of the Ordre des arts des lettres in 1990.

BIBL.: R. Maheu, *Pierrette Alarie, L. S.: Deux voix, un art* (Montreal, 1988).

Simonetti, Achille, Italian-English violinist and composer; b. Turin, June 12, 1857; d. London, Nov. 19, 1928. He began violin lessons with Francesco Bianchi; after training with Eugenio Cavallini at the Milan Cons. (1872–73), he returned to Turin to study violin with Giuseppe Gamba and composition with Carlo Pedrotti; then continued his violin training with Sivori in Genoa, and finally studied violin with Danda and composition with Massenet at the Paris Cons. (1881–83). In 1887 he settled in England, where he toured with Maria Roze and Benno Schönberger. He lived in London from 1891; was a member of the London Trio (1901–12) and a prof. of violin at the Irish Royal Academy of Music (1912–19). He was greatly esteemed as both a soloist and chamber music artist. An early champion of the Brahms Violin Concerto, he wrote a cadenza for the work, which he introduced in Dresden (Dec. 11, 1896). He composed numerous pieces for solo violin; his *Madrigale* became world famous.

Simon-Girard, Juliette, French soprano; b. Paris, May 8, 1859; d. Nice, Dec. 1959. She made her debut at the Folies-Dramatiques in Paris, where she created the principal role in *Les Cloches de Cornevilles* on April 19, 1877; then sang at the premieres of *La Fille du Tambour-major* (1879), *Fanfan la tulipe* (1882), and many other operettas; she became particularly successful in Offenbach's repertoire. She married the tenor Nicolas Simon, known as Simon-Max (1855–1923); divorced him in 1894, and married the comedian Huguenet; then retired to Nice.

Simonis, Jean-Marie, Belgian composer; b. Mol, Nov. 22, 1931. He studied composition with Stekke, Souris, Louel, and Quinet, and conducting with Defossez at the Brussels Cons.; taught there (from 1969) and at the Uccles Academy of Music (from 1971).

WORKS: RADIO OPERA: *Gens de maison* (1962). **ORCH.:** *Introduction et Danse* for Chamber Orch. (1963); *3 esquisses symphoniques* (1964); *Sinfonia da camera* for Strings (1966); *L'Automne,* symphonic poem (1967); *Scherzetto* for Chamber Orch. (1968); *Evasions* (1982); *Cantilène* for Violin and Orch. (1985); *Espressioni* (1988). **CHAMBER:** *3 Pieces* for 4 Clarinets (1965); *Duetti* for Viola and Piano (1968); *Impromptu* for Cello (1968–69); *Séquences* for Clarinet and Piano (1969); *Suggestions* for Flute and 4 Percussionists (1970); *Boutades* for 4 Saxophones (1971); *Résonances* for Percussion and Piano (1979); *Introit et Graduel* for String Quartet and Organ (1984); *Fantasia a due* for Violin and Piano (1986). **PIANO:** *Étude de Concert* (1963); *Mouvements* for 2 Pianos (1971); *Historiettes* (1972); *Impromptu* (1973); *2 animations* (1973); *2 pastourelles* (1973); *Evocations* (1974); *Incantations* (1980). **VOCAL:** *3 Motets* for Soprano, Chorus, and Orch. (1961); *3 Lagu Dolanan* for Soprano and Percussion (1969).

Simonov, Yuri (Ivanovich), prominent Russian conductor; b. Saratov, March 4, 1941. He received training in violin at a Saratov music school, where he made his debut as a conductor of the school orch. when he was only 12. He pursued his studies with Kramarov (viola) and Rabinovich (conducting) at the Leningrad Cons. (1956–68), where he made his formal conducting debut as a student in 1963. In 1966 he won 1st prize in the U.S.S.R. conducting competition and in 1968 took 1st prize in the Accademia di Santa Cecilia conducting competition in Rome. He was conductor of the Kislovodsk Phil. (1967–69) and assistant conductor to Mravinsky and the Leningrad Phil. (1968–69). In 1969 he made his debut at the Bolshoi Theater in Moscow conducting *Aida.* From 1970 to 1985 he was chief conductor of the Bolshoi Theater, where he established a notable reputation for his idiomatic performances of the Russian masterworks. He also restored Wagner's operas to the active repertoire after a hiatus of some 40 years. He conducted the company on acclaimed tours abroad, including visits to Paris, Vienna, N.Y. (Metropolitan Opera, *War and Peace,* 1975), Milan, Washington, D.C., and Japan. During these years, he also appeared as a conductor with the leading Russian orchs. at home and on tours abroad. In 1982 he made his first appearance with a Western opera company when he made his debut at London's Covent Garden with *Eugene Onegin.* He returned to Covent Garden in 1986 to open the season with *La Traviata.* He also appeared with most of the major British orchs. During the 1991–92 season, he conducted the Junge Deutsche Philharmonie and the Buenos Aires Phil. on tours of Europe. He made his debut at the Hamburg State Opera conducting *Don Carlo* during the 1992–93 season. In 1994 he became music director of the Orchestre national de Belgique in Brussels.

Simonsen, Rudolph (Hermann), eminent Danish music historian and composer; b. Copenhagen, April 30, 1889; d. there, March 28, 1947. He studied piano with Agnes Adler and theory with Otto Malling at the Copenhagen Cons. (1907–09), completing his piano studies with Teresa Carreño and Anders Rachlew; also earned a law degree from the Univ. of Copenhagen (1912). He taught at the Copenhagen Cons. from 1916, succeeding Nielsen as director in 1931. Although his compositions reveal the influence of Nielsen, he succeeded in producing works of distinction and individuality, but it is as a compiler of books on music culture and philosophy that he is best known.

WORKS: ORCH.: Piano Concerto (Copenhagen, Nov. 15, 1915); 4 syms.: No. 1, *Zion* (Göteborg, Feb. 4, 1920), No. 2, *Hellas* (Berlin, Sept. 23, 1921), No. 3, *Roma* (1923; Copenhagen, March 5, 1928), and No. 4, *Danmark* (1925; Copenhagen, April 4, 1931). **CHAMBER:** Piano Quintet (1908); 2 string quartets (1923, 1925); Clarinet Quintet (1929). **VOCAL:** Works for Chorus and Orch.; songs.

WRITINGS (all publ. in Copenhagen): *Musikkultur* (1927); *Musikhistoriske hovedstrømninger* (1930); *Alenmenneskelige vaerdier: Plato-Spinoza-Goethe* (1940); *Sub specie aeternitatis* (1942); *Musikhistorisk kompendium* (1946).

BIBL.: *Mindeskrift om R. S.* (Copenhagen, 1949).

Simovich, Roman, outstanding Ukrainian composer; b. Sniatin, Feb. 28, 1901; d. Lwów, July 30, 1984. He studied piano and composition with Novák at the Prague Cons. (1933–36). He taught at the Lisenko Institutes in Drogobych and Stanislav (1936–44) and at the Lwów Cons. (from 1944), where he became a prof. in 1963. He was made an Honored Artist of the Ukraine in 1954. His compositions were firmly rooted in the history and lore of the western Ukraine.

WORKS: BALLET: *Sopilka Dovbusha* (1948). **ORCH.:** 7 syms. (*Gutsulska*, 1945; *Lemkovsk*, 1947; *Springtime*, 1951; *Heroic*, 1954; *Celestial*, 1955; 1965; 1972); 3 suites; 6 symphonic poems; 4 overtures: *Carnival* (1936), *Youth* (1958), *Ceremonial* (1966), and *Bombastic* (1967); Flute Concerto (1953); Piano Concerto (1971). **CHAMBER:** 2 piano trios (1929, 1935); 2 string quartets (1929, 1950); solo piano pieces. **VOCAL:** 4 vocal symphonic poems: *The Shawl* (1933), *The Word* (1946), *In the Carpathians* (1949), and *The Flowers of Happiness and Freedom* (1959).

BIBL.: A. Tereshchenko, *R. S.* (Kiev, 1973).

Simpson, Robert (Wilfred Levick), English composer and writer on music; b. Leamington, March 2, 1921. He studied composition with Howells in London (1942–46) and received his Mus.D. from the Univ. of Durham in 1951. He joined the staff of the BBC as a music producer in 1951, resigning in 1980. He was awarded the Carl Nielsen Gold Medal of Denmark in 1956 and the Bruckner Medal in 1962. In his compositions, Simpson has pursued a tonal path.

WORKS: INCIDENTAL MUSIC TO: Ibsen's *The Pretenders* (1965); Milton's *Samson Agonistes* (1974). **ORCH.:** 11 syms.: No. 1 (1951; Copenhagen, June 11, 1953), No. 2 (1955; Cheltenham, July 16, 1957), No. 3 (1962; Birmingham, March 14, 1963), No. 4 (1970–72; Manchester, April 26, 1973), No. 5 (1972; London, May 3, 1973), No. 6 (1976; London, April 8, 1980), No. 7 (1977), No. 8 (1981; London, Nov. 10, 1982), No. 9 (1985; Poole, April 8, 1987), No. 10 (1988), and No. 11 (1990); Violin Concerto (1959; Birmingham, Feb. 25, 1960); Piano Concerto (Cheltenham, July 14, 1967); Flute Concerto (1989); Cello Concerto (1991). **BRASS BAND:** *Canzona* (1958); *Energy* (1971); *Volcano* (1979); *The 4 Temperaments* (1983); *Introduction and Allegro on a Bass by Max Reger* (1987); *Vortex* (1989). **CHAMBER:** 15 string quartets (1952, 1953, 1954, 1973, 1974, 1975, 1977, 1979, 1982, 1983, 1984, 1987, 1989, 1990, 1991); *Canzona* for Brass (1958); *Variations and Fugue* for Recorder and String Quartet (1958); Trio for Clarinet, Cello, and Piano (1967); Quartet for Clarinet and Strings (1968); Quartet for Horn, Violin, Cello, and Piano (1975); Quintet for Clarinet, Bass Clarinet, and String Trio (1981); Trio for Horn, Violin, and Piano (1984); Violin Sonata (1984); String Trio (1987); String Quintet (1987); Trio for Violin, Cello, and Piano (1988–89). **KEYBOARD: PIANO:** Sonata (1946); *Variations and Finale on a Theme by Haydn* (1948); Sonata for 2 Pianos (1980); *Variations and Finale on a Theme of Beethoven* (1990). **ORGAN:** *Eppur si muove: Ricercar e Passacaglia* (1985). **VOCAL:** *Media morte in vita sumus* for Chorus, Brass, and Timpani (1975); *Tempi* for Chorus (1985).

WRITINGS (all publ. in London unless otherwise given): *Carl Nielsen, Symphonist* (1952; 2nd ed., rev., 1979); *Bruckner and the Symphony* (1963); *Sibelius and Nielsen* (1965); *The Essence of Bruckner: An Essay towards the Understanding of his Music* (1966; 3rd ed., rev., 1992); ed. *The Symphony* (Harmondsworth, vol. I, 1966; 2nd ed., 1972; vol. II, 1967); *Beethoven Symphonies* (1970); *The Proms and Natural Justice* (1981).

BIBL.: R. Johnson, *R. S.: 50th Birthday Essays* (London, 1971); S. Johnson, "R. S.'s Ninth," *Musical Times* (April 1987); R. Matthew-Walker, ed., *The Symphonies of R. S.* (London, 1991).

Sims, Ezra, innovative American composer; b. Birmingham, Ala., Jan. 16, 1928. After training at Birmingham Southern College (B.A., 1947) and with G. Ackley Brower at the Birmingham Cons. of Music (1945–48), he was a student of Porter at the Yale Univ. School of Music (B.Mus., 1952). While serving in the U.S. Army, he studied Chinese at its language school (1953). Following his discharge, he pursued his musical training with Kirchner and Milhaud at Mills College in Oakland, Calif. (M.A., 1956). In 1962–63 he was active at the NHK electronic music studio in Tokyo. From 1968 to 1978 he was music director of the New England Dinosaur Dance Theatre. He taught at the New England Cons. of Music in Boston from 1976 to 1978. From 1977 to 1981 he was president of the Dinosaur Annex Music Ensemble. In 1992–93 he was a guest lecturer at the Salzburg Mozarteum. In 1962 he held a Guggenheim fellowship, and in 1976 and 1978 NEA fellowships. In 1985 he received an award from the American Academy of Arts and Letters. He held a Fulbright research grant in 1992. Sims began to compose tape music early in his career. In 1971 he devised a microtonal system utilizing an assymetrical mode of 18 (later 24) pitches, taken from and made transposable within a 72-note division of the octave, or an unaltered diatonicism. In 1988 he also began to use computer elements in some of his instrumental music.

WORKS: MICROTONAL: ORCH.: *Longfellow Sparrow* (1976); *Y^{r}Obed^{t}Servt* (1977; rev. 1981); *Pictures for an Institution* for Chamber Orch. (1983); *Night Unto Night* (1984); *Concert Piece* for Viola, Flute, Clarinet, Cello, and Small Orch. (1990; Cambridge, Mass., March 1, 1992). **CHAMBER:** String Octet (1964); string quartets nos. 2 (1974) and 4 (1984); *and, as I was saying . . .* for Viola (1979); *All Done From Memory* for Violin (1980); *2 for 1* for Violin and Viola (1980); Sextet for Clarinet, Alto Saxophone, Horn, Violin, Viola, and Cello (1981); *Phenomena* for Flute, Clarinet, Violin, Viola, and Cello (1981); Quartet for Flute, Violin, Viola, and Cello (1982); *This Way to the Egress or Manners Makyth Man* for Violin, Viola, and Cello (1983); Quintet for Clarinet, 2 Violins, Viola, and Cello (1987); *Solo in 4 Movements* for Cello (1987); *Flight* for Flute and Electronics (1989); *Night Piece* for Flute, Clarinet, Viola, Cello, and Electronics (1989); Duo for Flute and Cello (1992). **QUARTER TONE:** *Sonate Concertante* for Strings and/or Other Instruments (1961); String Quartet No. 3 (1962). **VOCAL:** *In Memoriam Alice Hawthorne* for Tenor, Baritone, Narrator, 4 Clarinets, Horn, and Marimba 4-hands or 2 Marimbas (1967); *Celebration of Dead Ladies* for Voice, Alto Flute, Basset Clarinet, Viola, Cello, and Percussion (1976); *Elegie-nach Rilke* for Soprano, Flute, Clarinet, Violin, Viola, and Cello (1976); *Aeneas on the Saxophone* for Chorus, 2 Clarinets, Horn, Trombone, Viola, and Double-Bass (1977); *Come Away* for Mezzo-soprano, Viola, Clarinet, Alto Flute, Horn, Trombone, and Double Bass (1978); *The Conversions* for Chorus (1985). **MUSIC USING 12-NOTE EQUAL DIVISION OF THE OCTAVE: ORCH.:** *Le Tombeau d'Albers* (1959). **CHAMBER:** Cello Sonata (1959); String Quartet (1959); *Slow Hiccups* for 2 Equal Melody Instruments (1975). **PIANO:** Sonatine (1957); *Buchlein for Lyon* (1962). **VOCAL:** *Chanson d'aventure* for Tenor and Harpsichord or Piano (1951; rev. 1975); *Chamber Cantata on Chinese Poems* for Tenor, Flute, Clarinet, Viola, Cello, and Harpsichord (1954); *2 Folk Songs* for Baritone and Piano (1958); *3 Songs* for Tenor and Orch. (1960); *The Bewties of the Futeball* for Children's Chorus, Optional Recorders, Piano, and Metal Idiophones (1974); *What God Is Like To Him I Serve?* for Chorus (1976). **TAPE:** *Sakoku*, music for a television drama (NHK-TV, Tokyo, April 1963); *McDowell's Fault, or The 10th Sunday After Trinity* (1968); *Commonplace Book or A Salute to Our American Container Corp.* (1969); *A Frank Overture. 4 Dented Interludes. And Coda* (1969); *Warts and All* (1969); *Clement Wenceslaus Lothaire Nepomucene, Prince Metternich (1773–1859): In Memoriam* (1970); *Elina's Piece* (1970); *Real Toads* (1970); *Where the Wild Things Are* (1973).

Sims, Jon Reed, American conductor; b. Smith Center, Kansas, May 6, 1947; d. (of AIDS) San Francisco, July 16, 1984. He studied piano and horn, and was drum major of his high school band; later attended Wichita State Univ. (B.Mus. and B.A., 1969) and Indiana Univ. (M.Mus., 1972). He studied eurhythmics at the Dalcroze School in N.Y.; arts administration at San Francisco's Golden Gate Univ.; dance in N.Y., Chicago, and San Francisco; and horn and composition (with Milhaud). He taught in Chicago (1972–74) and San Francisco (1974–78). In 1978 he founded the San Francisco Gay Freedom Day Marching Band & Twirling Corps, which made its debut performance at the Gay Pride Day parade that same year; founded in rapid succession the San Francisco Gay Men's Chorus (Nov. 1978), the Golden Gate Performing Arts (an administrative organization, March 1979), Lambda Pro Musica, and the San Francisco Lesbian & Gay Men's Community Chorus; directed the San Francisco Band & Corps until early 1982. Sims's dream was to create a nationwide network of gay and lesbian instrumental and choral ensembles; the San Francisco chorus toured the U.S. in 1981, a public gesture that caused the founding of ensembles nationwide. Gay and lesbian choruses appeared in quick succession in Los Angeles (July 12, 1979), Seattle (Nov. 1979), and Chicago. The first meeting of what was to become GALA (Gay and Lesbian Assn. [of choruses]; Chicago, June 1981) included directors and ensemble founders Jerry Carlson (Chicago Gay Men's Chorus; later director of the Los Angeles Gay Men's Chorus; d. of AIDS, Nov. 1987), Dennis Coleman (Seattle Men's Chorus), Richard Garrin (Chicago's Windy City Gay Chorus), Dick Kramer (San Francisco Gay Men's Chorus), Gary Miller (N.Y. City Gay Men's Chorus), and Susan Schleef (Chicago's Artemis Singers). The first West Coast conference of GALA included 9 choruses (1982); the first national conference, with 11 choruses (N.Y., 1983), was followed by conferences with 17 (Minneapolis, 1986) and 43 choruses (Seattle, 1989); in 1990 GALA boasted a membership of 88 choruses situated throughout North America and Europe. Most GALA choruses are made up of gay men, although there are a number of lesbian and mixed-voice ensembles; many additional lesbian groups are not GALA members. Following Sims's example, gay and lesbian musical organizations have grown remarkably in number, size, and sophistication; they are important examples of communal expression in American gay and lesbian culture.

Šín, Otakar, eminent Czech music theorist and composer; b. Rokytno, Moravia, April 23, 1881; d. Prague, Jan. 21, 1943. He studied composition with V. Novák at the Prague Cons., where he was appointed a prof. of theory in 1920. He publ., in Prague, the textbooks *Uplná nauka o harmonii na základě melodie a rytmu* (A Complete Harmony Course on the Basis of Melody and Rhythm; 1922; 6th ed., rev., 1949), *Nauka o kontrapunktu, imitaci a fuge* (Counterpoint, Imitation and Fugue; 1936; 2nd ed., 1945), and *Všeobecná nauka o hudbě* (A General Music Course; 1949; completed by F. Bartoš and K. Janeček).

WORKS: ORCH.: 2 symphonic poems: *Tillotama* (1908) and *King Menkera* (1916–18); *Radio Overture* (1936); *3 Czech Dances* for Orch. (1939; also for Nonet). **CHAMBER:** 2 string quartets (1923; 1926–28); Cello Sonata (1934); *Small Suite* for Violin and Piano (1937); *Hunting*, festive greeting for Horns (1938); numerous piano pieces. **VOCAL:** Choruses; songs.

BIBL.: K. Janeček, *O. S.* (Prague, 1944).

Sinclair, Monica, English mezzo-soprano; b. Evercreech, Somerset, March 23, 1925. She studied voice with Marcus Thomson and piano with Harold Craxton at the Royal Academy of Music (1942–44), and voice with Arnold Smith, piano with Olive Bloom, and accompaniment with Charles Lofthouse at the Royal College of Music (1944–48) in London. In 1948 she made her operatic debut as Suzuki with the Carl Rosa Opera Co., a role she also chose for her debut at London's Covent Garden in 1949, where she sang until 1967. In 1954 she appeared as Ragonde in *Le Comte Ory* with the Glyndebourne company during its visit to the Edinburgh Festival, and she continued to make appearances with the Glyndebourne company until 1960. She also made frequent appearances with the Handel Opera Soc. On March 14, 1972, she made her Metropolitan Opera debut in N.Y. as Berkenfield in *La Fille du Régiment.* She was best known for her roles in operas by Lully, Mozart, Rossini, and Strauss.

Sinding, Christian (August), celebrated Norwegian composer; b. Kongsberg, Jan. 11, 1856; d. Oslo, Dec. 3, 1941. He studied first with L. Lindeman in Norway, then at the Leipzig Cons. (1874–78) with Schradieck (violin), Jadassohn (theory), and Reinecke (orchestration); a government stipend enabled him to continue his studies in Germany, and he spent 2 years (1882–84) in Munich, Berlin, and Dresden; there he wrote his first opera, *Titandros*, much influenced by Wagner. On Dec. 19, 1885, he gave a concert of his works in Oslo; during another stay in Germany, his Piano Quintet was played in Leipzig, with Brodsky and Busoni among the performers (Jan. 19, 1889); Erika Lie-Nissen played his Piano Concerto in Berlin (Feb. 23, 1889). He publ. a number of piano pieces in Germany; of these, *Frühlingsrauschen* became an international favorite. His opera to a German text, *Der heilige Berg* (1914), was not successful. In 1915 he received a life pension of 4,000 crowns "for distinguished service"; on his 60th birthday (1916), the Norwegian government presented him with a purse of 30,000 crowns, a mark of appreciation for "the greatest national composer since Grieg." He was invited by George Eastman to teach at the Eastman School of Music in Rochester, N.Y., during the academic season 1921–22; after this journey, he lived mostly in Oslo. He continued to compose, and toward the end of his life wrote in larger forms; his 3rd Sym. was conducted by Nikisch with the Berlin Phil. in 1921, and his 4th Sym. was performed on his 80th birthday in Oslo (1936). His works aggregate to 132 opus numbers. Most of his music is of a descriptive nature; his lyric pieces for piano and his songs are fine examples of Scandinavian Romanticism, but the German inspiration of his formative years is much in evidence; he was chiefly influenced by Schumann and Liszt.

WORKS: OPERAS: *Titandros* (1884; not perf); *Der heilige Berg* (1912; Dessau, April 19, 1914). **ORCH.:** 4 syms.: No. 1 (1880–82; Christiania, March 25, 1882), No. 2 (1903–04; Berlin, March 22, 1907), No. 3 (1920; Berlin, Jan. 10, 1921), and No. 4, *Vinter og vår* (1921–36; Oslo, Jan. 11, 1936); *Episodes chevaleresques* (1888); *Rondo infinito* (1886; rev. 1897); Piano Concerto (Berlin, Feb. 23, 1889); 3 violin concertos (1898, 1901, 1917); *Legende* for Violin and Orch. (1900); *Romanze* for Violin and Orch. (1910); *Abendstimmung* for Violin and Orch. (1915). **CHAMBER:** Piano Quintet (1882–84); 2 string quartets (1884, 1904); 3 piano trios (1893, 1902, 1908); 4 violin sonatas (1894, 1895, 1905, 1909); *Scènes de la vie* for Violin and Piano (1900); *Cantus doloris*, variations for Violin and Piano (1906); *Nordische Ballade* for Cello and Piano (1911); etc. **PIANO:** Sonata (1909); *Fatum*, variations (1909); *5 Stücke*, op. 24 (1894); *7 Stücke*, op. 25 (1895); *6 Stücke*, op. 31 (1896); *6 Stücke*, op. 32 (1896; No. 3 is the celebrated *Frühlingsrauschen*); *6 Charakterstücke*, op. 33 (1896; contains *A la Menuetto* and *Standchen*); *6 Charakterstücke*, op. 34 (1896; contains *Chanson*); *6 Klavierstücke* (1899; contains *Humoresque*); *Mélodies mignonnes* (1900); *4 morceaux de salon* (1900; contains *Sérénade*); etc. **VOCAL:** About 250 songs, including *Alte Weisen* (1886), *Lieder und Gesange* (1888; contains *Viel Träume* and *Ein Weib*), *Galmandssange* (1893; contains *Mainat*), and *Nyinger* (1908); several cantatas and other choral works. A complete list of Sinding's works was publ. by Ö. Gaukstad in *Norsk Musikkgranskning arbok* (Oslo, 1938).

Singer, George, Czech-born Israeli conductor and composer; b. Prague, Aug. 6, 1908; d. Tel Aviv, Sept. 30, 1980. He studied piano at the Prague Academy of Music with Schulhoff and composition with Zemlinsky. He made his first appearance as an opera conductor in Prague in 1926. In 1930 he received an engagement at the Hamburg Opera, returning to Prague in 1934. When the Nazis invaded Czechoslovakia in 1939, he, being Jewish, was compelled to take refuge in Tel Aviv, where he established himself favorably as a conductor. He also accepted engagements as a conductor in Russia and in the U.S., where he led the N.Y. City Opera in 1968. Back in Israel, he gave performances of several works of local composers. He was known for his phenomenal facility in sight-reading, performing works perfectly at first reading on the piano and conducting every nuance of an orch. score. He composed some orch pieces.

Singher, Martial (Jean-Paul), noted French baritone and pedagogue; b. Oloron-Ste. Marie, Aug. 14, 1904; d. Santa Barbara, Calif., March 10, 1990. He received his education as a public-school teacher in Dax, and at the École Normale de Toulouse and the École Normale Supérieure de St. Cloud. He then studied voice with André Gresse at the Paris Cons. (premier prix for singing, 1929; premier prix for opera and opéra-comique singing, 1930; Grand Prix Osiris de l'Institute de France, 1930); also studied voice with Juliette Fourestier. He made his operatic debut in Amsterdam as Orestes in *Iphigénie en Tauride* on Nov. 14, 1930; then joined the Paris Opéra, remaining with it until 1941; also sang at the Opéra-Comique. On Jan. 10, 1940, he married Margareta Busch, daughter of the conductor Fritz Busch. He went to the U.S. in 1941; made his Metropolitan Opera debut in N.Y. on Dec. 10, 1943, as Dapertutto in *Les Contes d'Hoffmann*; subsequently sang the roles of the Count in *Le nozze di Figaro*, Lescaut in *Manon*, and all 4 baritone roles in *Les Contes d'Hoffmann*; remained on the roster, with some interruptions, until 1959. He also sang with the leading orchs. of the U.S., and appeared widely in song recitals. He was on the faculty of the Mannes College of Music in N.Y. (1951–62) and the Curtis Inst. of Music in Philadelphia (1955–68); then was director of the voice and opera dept., and was the opera producer at the Music Academy of the West in Santa Barbara (1962–81). His students included Donald Gramm, John Reardon, James King, Louis Quilico, Judith Blegen, Benita Valente, and Jeannine Altmeyer. He was a particularly distinguished interpreter of the French operatic and song repertoire. He wrote a book useful to vocalists aspiring to an operatic career, *An Interpretive Guide to Operatic Arias: A Handbook for Singers, Coaches, Teachers, and Students* (1983).

Singleton, Alvin (Elliot), black American composer; b. N.Y., Dec. 28, 1940. He took courses in composition and music education at N.Y. Univ. (B.M., 1967), then continued his study of composition with Powell and Wyner at Yale Univ. (M.M.A., 1971). He received a Fulbright fellowship to study with Petrassi in Rome at the Accademia di Santa Cecilia (1971–72), and in 1981 was awarded an NEA grant. From 1985 to 1988 he served as composer-in-residence of the Atlanta Sym. Orch.; in 1988 he was appointed composer-in-residence at Spelman College in Atlanta.

WORKS: OPERA: *Dream Sequence '76* (1976). **ORCH.:** *Kwitana* for Piano, Double Bass, Percussion, and Chamber Ensemble (1974); *Again* for Chamber Orch. (1979); *A Yellow Rose Petal* (1982); *Shadows* (1987); *After Fallen Crumbs* (1988); *Sinfonia Diaspora* (Portland, Oreg., May 5, 1991); *Even Tomorrow* (Birmingham, Ala., Oct. 11, 1991); *56 Blows (Quis Custodiet Custodies?)*, based on the Rodney King beating by the Los Angeles police (1992; Philadelphia, Jan. 13, 1994); *Blueskonzert* for Piano and Orch. (Houston, Sept. 30, 1995). **CHAMBER:** Woodwind Quintet (1969); *Argoru I* for Piano (1970), *II* for Cello (1970), *III* for Flute (1971), *IV* for Viola (1978), *V* for Bass Clarinet (1984), and *VI* for Marimba (1989). **VOCAL:** *Messa* for Soprano, Chorus, Flute, 2 Guitars, Electric Organ, Cello, and Double Bass (1975); *Necessity Is a Mother*, wordless drama (1981); *Between Sisters* for Soprano, Piano, Alto Flute, and Vibraphone (1990).

Sinigaglia, Leone, Italian composer; b. Turin, Aug. 14, 1868; d. there, May 16, 1944. He was a pupil at the Turin Cons., studying with Giovanni Bolzoni; later studied in Vienna (1894–1900) with Mandyczewski, and in Prague with Vysoka and Dvořák (1900–1901). His first successful work was a violin concerto (1900) dedicated to Arrigo Serato, who played it with considerable success in the principal cities of Germany. His early works were much influenced by Brahms and Dvořák; then he turned for inspiration to the music of his native Piedmont, and in this field achieved a lasting reputation. Toscanini conducted in Turin the premiere of Sinigaglia's suite *Danze piemontesi*, on popular themes (May 14, 1905); later Sinigaglia publ. a collection of songs (6 albums), *Vecchie canzoni populari del Piemonte*; another work in the folk-song manner is the symphonic suite *Piemonte* (1909; Utrecht, Feb. 16, 1910); he further wrote *Le Baruffe Chiozzotte*, an overture to Goldoni's comedy (Utrecht, Dec. 21, 1907); *Rapsodia piemontese* for Violin and Orch. (1900); *Romanze* for Violin and Orch. (1899); *Variations on a Theme of Brahms* for String Quartet (1901); *Serenade* for String Trio (1906); Cello Sonata (1923).

BIBL.: E. Desderi, "L. S.," *Rivista Musicale Italiana*, XLVII (1946); L. Rognoni, "L. S.," *Musicisti piemontesi e liguri*, Chigiana, XVI (1959); C. Mosso and E. Bassi, eds., *L. S., Torino, 1868–1944: Primo centenario della nascita* (Turin, 1968).

Sinopoli, Giuseppe, distinguished Italian conductor and composer; b. Venice, Nov. 2, 1946. He studied organ and harmony as a youth in Messina, then took courses in harmony and counterpoint at the Venice Cons.; also studied medicine at the Univ. of Padua (degree in psychiatry, 1971) while concurrently studying composition privately with Donatoni in Paris; then took a course in conducting with Swarowsky at the Vienna Academy of Music. He organized the Bruno Maderna Ensemble in 1975, and conducted it in performances of contemporary music; was also active as a teacher. After a successful engagement as a guest conductor at the Teatro La Fenice in Venice in 1976, he appeared at the Deutsche Oper in Berlin (1980), the Hamburg State Opera (1980), and the Vienna State Opera (1982). On May 3, 1983, he made his Covent Garden debut in London, conducting *Manon Lescaut*; his Metropolitan Opera debut followed in N.Y. on March 11, 1985, when he led a performance of *Tosca*. He served as chief conductor of the Orchestra dell'Accademia Nazionale di Santa Cecilia in Rome (1983–87); also was principal conductor of the Philharmonia Orch. of London (1984–94). In 1990 he became Generalmusikdirektor of the Deutsche Oper in Berlin, but abruptly resigned that same year after disagreements with its Intendant, Götz Friedrich. In 1992 he became chief conductor of the Dresden State Orch. and Opera. His training as a psychiatrist led him to probe deeply into the scores he conducted, often resulting in startlingly revealing but controversial interpretations. As a composer, he pursues contemporary modes of expression.

WORKS: OPERA: *Lou Salome* (Munich, May 10, 1981; also 2 suites: No. 1 for Soli, Chorus, and Orch., 1981, and No. 2 for Orch., 1985). **ORCH.:** *Opus Daleth* (1970); *Opus Ghimel* for Chamber Orch. (1971); Piano Concerto (1974–75); *Tombeau d'Armor I* (1975) and *II* (1977). **CHAMBER:** *Numquid et unum* for Flute and Harpsichord (1970); String Quintet (1970); *Numquid* for Chamber Ensemble (1972); Chamber Concerto for Piano and Instrumental Ensemble (1977–78). **PIANO:** Sonata (1973–75). **VOCAL:** *Opus Shir*, cantata (1971); *Symphonie imaginaire* for Soloists, Chorus, Piano, and Orch. (1973); *Souvenirs à la Mémoire* for Solo Voices and Chamber Orch. (1973–74); *Requiem Hashshirim* for Chorus (1975–76).

BIBL.: D. Stearns, "The Psychodynamics of S.," *Ovation* (March 1989).

Siohan, Robert (-Lucien), French conductor, composer, and writer on music; b. Paris, Feb. 27, 1894; d. there, July 16, 1985. He studied at the Paris Cons. (1909–22). In 1929 he founded the Concerts Siohan, which he conducted until 1936; was chorus master at the Paris Opéra (1931–46); from 1948 to 1962 he was an instructor in solfège and sight-reading at the Paris Cons.; subsequently served as inspector-general of music in the Ministry of Culture. He received his doctorate at the Sorbonne in Paris in 1954 with the diss. *Théories nouvelles de l'homme* (publ. as *Horizons sonores*, Paris, 1956). Among his compositions are the opera *Le saut dans les etoiles* (1926–27); *Cantique au frère soleil* for Soloists, Chorus, and Orch. (1926); Violin Concerto (1928); Piano Concerto (1939); String Quartet (1922); *Gravitations* for Viola and Piano (1952). He publ. *Stravinsky* (Paris, 1959; Eng. tr., London, 1966) and *Histoire du public musical* (Lausanne, 1967); also numerous articles in French and German publs.

Sipilä, Eero (Aukusti), Finnish composer and teacher; b. Hailuoto, July 27, 1918; d. Kajaani, May 18, 1972. He studied in Helsinki at the Church Music Inst. (graduated, 1943) and the Sibelius Academy (organ diploma, 1945); then taught at the Kajaani training college (1945–72).

WORKS: String Trio (1952); *Partita* for Wind Quartet (1955); *Super flumina Babylonis* and *Miserere,* 2 motets for Chorus (1963); *Te Deum Laudamus* for Alto, Baritone, Chorus, and Orch. (1969); *Fugue and Chaconne* for Strings (1969); *Lux aeterna* for String Quartet (1972); *Composition* for Orch. (Kajaani, May 8, 1973); song cycles; organ music.

Siqueira, José (de Lima), Brazilian conductor and composer; b. Conceição, June 24, 1907. After training in saxophone and trumpet from his father, he studied with Paulo Silva, Francisco Braga, and Burle Marx at the National School of Music in Rio de Janeiro; much later he studied with Aubin, Bigot, Chailley, and Messiaen in Paris (1954). In 1940 he founded the Orquesta Sinfónica Brasileira in Rio de Janeiro, for which he served as music director until 1944. In 1948 he founded the Orquesta Sinfónica de Rio de Janeiro. He also appeared as a guest conductor abroad.

WORKS: DRAMATIC: *A compadecida,* opera (1959; Rio de Janeiro, Dec. 20, 1961); *Gimba,* drama (1960); *O carnaval Caricoa,* theater piece (1965). **ORCH.:** 4 syms. (1933, 1951, 1954, 1956); *Alvorada brasileira,* symphonic poem (1936); *4 poemas indígenas* (1944); Cello Concerto (1952); 3 piano concertos (1955, 1965, 1966); 5 suites (1955–70); Violin Concerto (1957). **CHAMBER:** 3 string quartets (1933, 1963, 1963); 2 violin sonatas (1949, 1952); Wind Quintet (1962); piano pieces. **VOCAL:** *Candomblé,* oratorio (Rio de Janeiro, Dec. 20, 1957); *Encantamento da Magia Negra,* motet (1957); songs.

Širola, Božidar, distinguished Croatian musicologist and composer; b. Žakanj, Dec. 20, 1889; d. Zagreb, April 10, 1956. He studied mathematics and physics at the Univ. of Zagreb. After training in composition from Ivan Zajc, he studied musicology with Robert Lach at the Univ. of Vienna (Ph.D., 1921, with the diss. *Das istrische Volkslied*). He taught mathematics and physics in Zagreb secondary schools, and also was active as a lecturer, critic, ethnomusicologist, and organologist. From 1935 to 1941 he was director of the secondary school of music at the Zagreb Academy of Music, and then was director of the Ethnographic Museum. After Tito consolidated his control of Yugoslavia in 1945, Širola devoted himself to private research. He was a noted authority on Croatian folk music. As a composer, he became best known for his operas and songs.

WRITINGS (all publ. in Zagreb): *Pregled povijesti hrvatske muzike* (Survey of the History of Croatian Music; 1922); with M. Gavazzi, *Muzikološki rad Etnografskog muzeja u Zagrebu* (Musicological Works of the Ethnographic Museum in Zagreb; 1931); *Fućkalice: Sviraljke od kore svježeg drveta* (Fućkalice: Wind Instruments Made From the Bark of Green Wood; 1932); *Sopile i zurle* (Sopilas and Zurlas; 1932); *Sviraljke s udarnim jezičkom* (Wind Instruments with a Beating Reed; 1937); *Hrvatska narodna glazba* (Croatian Folk Music; 1940; 2nd ed., 1942); *Hrvatska umjetnička glasba: Odabrana poglavlja iz povijesti hrvatske glazbe* (Croatian Art Music: Selected Chapters of a History of Croatian Music; 1942).

WORKS: DRAMATIC: OPERAS: *Stanac* (1915); *Citara i bubanj* (The Cittern and the Drum; 1929); *Grabancijaš* (The Student of the Black Arts; 1935); *Mladi gospodin* (The Young Gentleman; 1940); *Kameni svatovi* (The Stone Wedding Guests; 1954). **MELODRAMAS:** *Iz Danteova "Ruja"* (From Dante's "Paradiso"; 1912); *Putnik* (The Traveller; 1919); *Otmica* (The Abduction; 1922); *Šuma Striborova* (1923); *Kameni svatovi* (1935). **OPERETTAS:** *Z Griča na Trešnjevku* (1931); *Mecena* (1934). Also ballets and incidental music. **ORCH.:** *Novela od Stanac* (The Story of Stanac), overture (1912); *Symphonic Scherzo* (1912); *Svećana uvertira* (Festival Overture; 1920); *Concerto da camera* for 2 Flutes and Chamber Orch. (1927); *Koncertna uvertira* (1927); *Romanca* for Violin and Strings (1939); *Scherzo i ricercar* for Violin and Strings (1939); *Sinfonietta* for Strings (1939); Sym. (1945); *Sinfonia concertante* for Piano and Orch. (1952); Violin Concerto (1953). **CHAMBER:** 13 string quartets (*Medimurski,* 1920; *Bodulski,* 1933; 1946; 1946; 1951; 1951; 1951; 1952; *Nizozemski,* 1953; 1955; 1955; 1955; 1955); 3 piano trios (1934, 1937, 1939); Suite for Violin and Harpsichord or Piano (1940); Cello Sonata (1952); 2 violin sonatas (1952, 1955); Rondo for Trumpet and Piano (1954); piano pieces. **VOCAL:** 6 oratorios (1924, 1926, 1928, 1928, 1929, 1931); choruses; song cycles.

Sitkovetsky, Dmitry, esteemed Russian-born American violinist and conductor; b. Baku, Sept. 27, 1954. He was born into a distinguished family of musicians. His father was the violinist Julian Sitkovetsky and his mother the pianist **Bella Davidovich.** He was taken to Moscow to study at the Central Music School (1961–72). In 1966 he won 1st prize in the Concertino Praha Competition in Prague. After further training with Yankelevich and Bezrodny at the Moscow Cons. (1972–77), he completed his studies with Galamian at the Juilliard School in N.Y. (1977–79). In 1979 he captured 1st prize in the Fritz Kreisler Competition in Vienna, which led to an auspicious appearance as a soloist with the Berlin Phil. in 1980. He made his U.S. debut as a soloist with the Chicago Sym. Orch. in 1983; that same year he was awarded an Avery Fisher Career Grant. In 1985 he appeared for the first time at the Salzburg Festival as a soloist with the Polish Chamber Orch. In 1986 he played at the London Promenade Concerts. In 1988 he was a soloist with the N.Y. Phil. He toured as a soloist with Leppard and the Indianapolis Sym. Orch. on their visit to many of the major European music centers in 1993. That same year Sitkovetsky became artistic director of the Seattle International Music Festival. In addition to his numerous engagements as a soloist with the world's principal orchs., he has appeared frequently as a recitalist. He has also given duo concerts with his mother. He likewise has devoted a portion of his career to conducting. His repertoire ranges from Bach to Prokofiev. He prepared and conducted a highly effective transcription of Bach's *Goldberg Variations* for String Ensemble.

Sitsky, Larry, Australian pianist, teacher, and composer; b. Tientsin, China (of Russian parents), Sept. 10, 1934. He was improvising on the piano and writing music by the age of 10; in 1951 his family went to Australia, where he studied piano with Winifred Burston and composition with Raymond Hanson at the New South Wales State Conservatorium of Music in Sydney (1951–55); after further piano training with Petri in San Francisco (1958–61), he taught piano at the Queensland State Conservatorium (1961–65); then was head of keyboard studies (1966–78) and composition and musicology (from 1981) at the Canberra School of Music. He undertook official exchange visits as a composer to Russia (1977) and to the People's Republic of China (1983), where he was the first composer from the West to make an official visit since the 1950s; also appeared as a pianist in China (1945–51). In 1989–90 he was composer-in-residence at the Univ. of Cincinnati College-Cons. of Music. He specializes in late Romantic and early 20th-century scores, showing preference for the music of Busoni. He publ. *Busoni and the Piano: The Music, the Writings, the Recordings: A Complete Survey* (Westport, Conn., 1986), *The Classical Reproducing Piano Roll: A Catalogue-Index* (2 vols., Westport, Conn., 1990), and *Music of the Repressed Russian Avant-Garder, 1900–1929* (Westport, Conn., 1994); also made transcriptions and ed. some of Busoni's scores for publication. Sitsky's own music is advanced, although it makes no systematic use of particular devices.

WORKS: OPERAS: *Fall of the House of Usher* (Hobart Festival, Aug. 1965); *Lenz* (1969–70; Sydney, March 1974); *The Fiery*

Tales, after Chaucer and Boccaccio (1975); *Voices in Limbo*, radio opera (1977); *The Golem* (1980; Sydney, Oct. 14, 1993; orch. extracts as *Songs and Dances* and *9 Orchestral Interludes*, 1984). **ORCH.:** *4 Orchestral Pieces*, cycle of individually titled works that may be performed separately (1966–74); 3 violin concertos: No. 1, *Mysterium Cosmographicum*, with Women's Voices (1971), No. 2, *Gurdjieff* (1983), and No. 3, *I Ching: The 8 Trigrams* (1987); Concerto for Wind Quintet and Orch. (Sydney, April 3, 1971); Concerto for Trombone, Keyboards, and Percussion, *Kundalini* (1981–82); Concerto for Clarinet and Strings, *Santana* (1981); Guitar Concerto (1984); *Concerto for Orchestra* (completion and realization of Busoni's *Fantasia Contrappuntistica*; 1984); Piano Concerto (1991); Cello Concerto (1993). **CHAMBER:** Sonata for Solo Violin (1959); 2 sonatas for Solo Flute (1959; *The 14 Days of Bardo Thodol*, 1979). Wind Quartet (1963); *Sinfonia* for 10 Players (1964; also as a TV ballet, *The Dark Refuge*); Sonata for 2 Guitars (1968); 3 string quartets (1969; *13 Concert Studies*, 1981; 1993); 6 trios (1969–93); *Fantasia No. 3* for Trumpet and String Ensemble, in memory of Don Banks (1980); *Zuqerq* for Clarinet and Bongos (1984); *Diabolus in Musica* for 4 Percussionists (1986); *The Secret Gates of the House of Osiris* for Flute, Viola, Cello, and Piano (1987); *The Phantom Drummer of Tedworth* for Percussionist (1990); other chamber works; various piano pieces. **VOCAL:** *Concert Aria* for Low Voice, Ensemble, Tape, and Synthesizer (1972); *7 Orchestral Songs* for Low Voice and Orch. (1979); *De Profundis* for Baritone, 2 String Quartets, and Percussion (1982); *Deep in My Hidden Country*, cantata for Soprano, Flute, Cello, Piano, and Percussion (1983–84); solo songs.

BIBL.: "L. S.: Interview," *Musica Viva Bulletin* (Sept./Dec. 1984).

Sixta, Jozef, Slovak composer and teacher; b. Jičín, May 12, 1940. He was a student of Očenaš at the Cons. (1955–60) and of Moyzes at the Academy of Music and Drama (1960–64) in Bratislava, and later worked with Messiaen and Jolivet in Paris (1971). After teaching at the Cons. (1964–76), he taught at the Academy of Music and Drama in Bratislava. In 1987 and 1990 he won the Ján Levoslav Bella prize. In his works, Sixta has utilized serialism and aleatory with judicious handling of harmonic, chordal, and melodic writing.

WORKS: ORCH.: Suite for Strings (1960); *3 Compositions* for Small Orch. (1963); Sym. (1964); *Asynchrony* (1968); *Punctum contra punctum* (1971); *4 Orchestral Pieces* (1979). **CHAMBER:** Quintet for Flute, Oboe, Clarinet, Bassoon, and Piano (1961); 2 string quartets (1965, 1983); *Variations* for 13 Instruments (1967); Nonet for 4 Strings and 5 Winds (1970); Quartet for 4 Flutes (1972); *Recitative* for Violin (1974); Octet for 2 Flutes, 2 Oboes, 2 Clarinets, and 2 Bassoons (1977); Trio for 2 Oboes and English Horn (1980); Trio for Clarinet, Cello, and Piano (1981); *Music for 4 Players* for Oboe, Clarinet, Bassoon, and Clavichord or Harpsichord (1988). **PIANO:** *Phantasia* (1962); *Solo* (1973); Sonata (1985); *Concertante Étude* (1986; also for Harpsichord).

Skalkottas, Nikos (actually, **Nikolaos**), greatly talented Greek composer; b. Chalkis, island of Euboea, March 8, 1904; d. Athens, Sept. 19, 1949. He studied violin with his father, with his uncle, and with a nonrelated violinist at the Athens Cons. (1914–20). In 1921 he went to Berlin, where he continued his violin studies with Hess at the Hochschule für Musik (until 1923); then took lessons in theory with Jarnach (1925–27). The greatest influence on Skalkottas' creative life was Schoenberg, with whom he studied in Berlin (1927–31); Schoenberg, in his book *Style and Idea*, mentions Skalkottas as one of his most gifted disciples. Skalkottas eagerly absorbed Schoenberg's instruction in the method of composition with 12 tones related only to one another, but in his own music applied it in a very individual manner, without trying to imitate Schoenberg's style. In Berlin, Skalkottas also received some suggestions in free composition from Kurt Weill (1928–29). He returned to Athens and earned his living by playing violin in local orchs., but continued to compose diligently, until his early death from a strangulated hernia. His music written between 1928 and 1938 reflects Schoenberg's idiom; later works are tonally conceived, and several of them are in the clearly ethnic Greek modalities, set in the typical asymmetric meters of Balkan folk music. After his death, a Skalkottas Soc. was formed in Athens to promote performances and publications of his works; about 110 scores of various genres are kept in the Skalkottas Archives in Athens.

WORKS: DRAMATIC: *I lygery kai o charos* (The Maiden and Death), ballet (1938; Athens, May 10, 1940; rev. version, Athens, March 23, 1947); *Me tou mayoa ta maya* (The Spell of May), incidental music (1943–44; orchestrated 1949; London, May 30, 1961); *Henry V*, incidental music to Shakespeare's play (1947–48; not extant). **ORCH.:** 1 unnumbered symphonic suite (1928; not extant); 2 numbered symphonic suites: No. 1 (1935; London, April 28, 1973) and No. 2 (1944; orchestrated 1946–49; London, Jan. 31, 1966); Concerto for Winds and Orch. (1929; Berlin, May 20, 1930; not extant); *Little Suite* for Violin and Chamber Orch. (1929; Berlin, April 6, 1930; not extant); Concerto for Piano, Violin, and Chamber Orch. (Berlin, April 6, 1930; not extant); 3 piano concertos: No. 1 (1931), No. 2 (1937–38; Hamburg, Oct. 12, 1953), and No. 3 (1938–39; London, July 9, 1969); *36 elliniki chori (36 greichische Tänze)* (1931–36; reorchestrated, 1948–49); Concertino for 2 Pianos and Orch. (1935; Geneva, June 15, 1952); Violin Concerto (1937–38; Hamburg, May 14, 1962); Cello Concerto (1938; not extant); Concerto for Violin, Viola, Winds, and Double Basses (1939–40; London, July 7, 1969); *10 Musical Sketches* for Strings (1940; Athens, Nov. 6, 1952; also for String Quartet); *Little Suite* for Strings (1942; Zürich, Aug. 30, 1953); *I epistrophi tou Odyssevs* (The Return of Ulysses), overture (1942–43; London, June 23, 1969; also for 2 Pianos, 1943–44); Double Bass Concerto (1942–43); Concerto for 2 Violins and Orch. (1944–45); *Klassiki symphonia* for Winds and Double Basses (1947); Sinfonietta (1948); Piano Concertino (1948); *Mikri chorevtiki suita: 4 chori ya balleto* (Kleine Tanz-Suite: 4 Tanze für Ballett; 1948–49; Athens, May 2, 1949); *Dance Suite* (1948–49); *Nocturne-divertimento* for Xylophone and Orch. (1949); *I thalassa* (The Sea; 1949). **CHAMBER:** 2 string trios (1924, not extant; 1935; Athens, March 20, 1954); 1 unnumbered string quartet (1924; not extant); 4 numbered string quartets: No. 1 (1928; Berlin, June 19, 1929), No. 2 (1929; Athens, Nov. 27, 1930; not extant), No. 3 (1935; Oxford, July 3, 1965), and No. 4 (1940; London, July 13, 1969); Sonata for Solo Violin (1925); 2 violin sonatas (1928, not extant; 1940); *Evkoli mousiki* (Easy Music) for String Quartet (1929; Athens, Nov. 27, 1930; not extant); 4 violin sonatinas (1929, only 2nd movement extant; 1929; 1935; 1935); Octet for Flute, Clarinet, Bassoon, Trumpet, Trombone, and Piano Trio (1929; not extant); Octet for Woodwind Quartet and String Quartet (Berlin, June 2, 1931); Piano Trio (1936); *Der Marsch der kleinen Soldaten, Rondo, Nachstück, Kleiner Choral und Fuge* for Violin and Piano (1937–38); Suite for Cello and Piano (1937–38; not extant); Duo for Violin and Viola (1938); *8 Variationen über ein griechisches Volksthema* for Piano Trio (1938; Athens, March 31, 1950); *9 Greek Dances* for String Quartet (1938–47); *Gavotte, Scherzo, Menuetto cantato* for Violin and Piano (1939); Concertino for Oboe and Piano (1939); *Scherzo* for Piano Quartet (1939–40); 2 quartets for Oboe, Bassoon, Trumpet, and Piano (1940–42; Bamberg, June 15, 1968); Concertino for Trumpet and Piano (1940–42); *6 Greek Dances* for Violin and Piano (1940–47); *Largo* for Cello and Piano (1941–42); *Sonata concertante* for Bassoon and Piano (1943); *Mikri serenate (Kleine Serenade)* for Cello and Piano (1945); *Bolero* for Cello and Piano (1945); *3 Greek Folksongs* for Violin and Piano (1945–46); *2 Little Suites* for Violin and Piano (1946, 1949); *4 parties* for Violin and Cello (1947); Cello Sonatina (1949); *Zarte Melodie* for Cello and Piano (1949). **PIANO:** 2 suites for 2 Pianos (1924–25); Sonatina (1927); *15 Little Variations* (1927); 4 suites (1936, 1940, 1940, 1940); 32 pieces (1940–41). **VOCAL:** Choral piece (1930; not extant); 3 songs for Voice and Piano (1932–38); *Kapote* (Sometime) for Soprano or Baritone and Piano (1938–39); *16 Songs* for Mezzo-soprano and Piano (1941; London, March 18, 1962); *To fengari* (The Moon) for Soprano and Piano (1941–42); *To tragoudi tou kleidona* (The Locksmith's Song) for 2 Sopranos and 2 Mezzo-sopranos (1943–44).

Škerjanc, Lucijan Marija, Slovenian pianist, conductor, teacher, writer on music, and composer; b. Graz, Dec. 17, 1900; d. Ljubljana, Feb. 27, 1973. He studied composition in Vienna with Marx and in Paris with d'Indy. He became a music teacher in Ljubljana in 1922, where he was a teacher of composition at the Cons. (1926–40) and at the Academy of Music (1940–70), serving as rector of the latter (1945–47). He was conductor of the Glasbena Matica orch. society (1925–45), and director of the Slovene Philharmonia (1950–55). Much of his music reflects neo-Romantic trends, with some impressionistic colors; in later works he also utilized 12-note techniques.

WORKS: ORCH.: 2 violin concertos (1927, 1944); 5 syms. (1931, 1938, 1940, 1941, 1943); Piano Concerto (1940); Bassoon Concerto (1953); Harp Concerto (1954); Concerto for Clarinet, Strings, Percussion, and Harp (1958); Flute Concerto (1962); Concerto for Piano, Left-hand, and Orch. (1963). **CHAMBER:** 5 string quartets (1917, 1921, 1925, 1935, 1945); Wind Quintet (1925); Piano Trio (1935); String Quintet (1945); *Concertone* for 4 Cellos (1954); other chamber works; piano pieces. **VOCAL:** Songs.

Škerl, Dane, Slovenian composer; b. Ljubljana, Aug. 26, 1931. He studied with Škerjanc at the Ljubljana Academy of Music, graduating in 1952; then took courses in electronic music in Cologne. He taught at the Sarajevo Academy of Music (1960–70); in 1970 he was appointed to the faculty of the Ljubljana Academy of Music.

WORKS: BALLETS: *Kontrasti* (Contrasts; 1967); *Grozdanin kikot* (1969). **ORCH.:** Concertino for Violin and String Orch. (1948); *Prelude and Scherzo* for Clarinet and Strings (1948); Concertino for Piano and Strings (1949); 5 syms. (1951, 1963, 1965, 1970, 1972); *Serenade* for Strings (1952); *Concerto for Orchestra* (1956); *Rolo* (1959); *Inventions* for Violin and Strings (1960); *18 Etudes* for Strings (1960); *5 Compositions* for Clarinet and Strings (1961); *Contrasts* (1962); Clarinet Concerto (1963); *Little Suite* (1965); *7 Bagatelles* for Strings (1966); *Improvvisazione concertante* for Horn, Viola, and Chamber Orch. (1968); Trombone Concerto (1970). **CHAMBER:** *4 Miniatures* for Flute, Bassoon, and Piano (1957); *Prelude and Scherzo* for Violin, Clarinet, and Piano (1959); *Skica* (Sketch) for Violin and Piano (1964); *3 Improvisations* for Flute, Cello, and Piano (1966); piano pieces. **VOCAL:** *Moj dom* (My House), cantata (1962).

Skilton, Charles Sanford, American composer and teacher; b. Northampton, Mass., Aug. 16, 1868; d. Lawrence, Kansas, March 12, 1941. He first studied in Germany; after graduating from Yale Univ. (B.A., 1889), he studied in N.Y. with Harry Rowe Shelley (organ) and Dudley Buck (composition); then at the Berlin Hochschule für Musik with Bargiel (1891–93). From 1893 to 1896 he was director of music at the Salem (N.C.) Academy and College, and conducted the local orch. there; then filled a similar post at the State Normal School in Trenton, N.J. (1897–1903); in 1903 he was engaged as a prof. of organ and theory at the Univ. of Kansas, Lawrence, where he remained most of his life. He made a detailed study of Indian music, and introduced Indian motifs into the traditional forms of the suite and fantasy. His opera *Kalopin* (1927) received the David Bispham Memorial Medal in 1930.

WORKS: OPERAS: *Kalopin* (1927); *The Sun Bride* (NBC, April 17, 1930); *The Day of Gayomair* (1936). **ORCH.:** *Suite Primeval*, on Indian melodies, in 2 parts: *2 Indian Dances* (originally for String Quartet, 1915; Minneapolis, Oct. 29, 1916) and part II (Minneapolis, Nov. 13, 1921); *Autumn Night* (Detroit, Dec. 11, 1930); *Shawnee Indian Hunting Dance* (Detroit, Dec. 11, 1930); *A Carolina Legend*, symphonic poem; *Mt. Oread*, overture. **CHAMBER:** *2 Indian Dances* for String Quartet (1915; orchestrated as part 1 of *Suite Primeval*); Violin Sonatina (1923); String Quartet (1938). **KEYBOARD: PIANO:** *3 Indian Sketches* (1919); *Shawnee Indian Hunting Dance* (1929). **ORGAN:** *American Indian Fantasy* (1926; also for Orch., 1932). **VOCAL:** *The Witch's Daughter*, cantata (1918); *The Guardian Angel*, oratorio (1925); *From Forest and Stream* for Women's Chorus (1930).

BIBL.: J. Howard, *C.S. S.* (N.Y., 1929); J. Smith, *C.S. S. (1868–1941), Kansas Composer* (thesis, Univ. of Kansas, 1979).

Skinner, Ernest M(artin), American organ builder; b. Clarion, Pa., Jan. 15, 1866; d. Duxbury, Mass., Nov. 27, 1960. He was the founder of the Ernest M. Skinner Co., organ builders, originally of Dorchester, later of Methuen, Mass. Until 1905 the business was carried on by Skinner himself; it was then incorporated, with Skinner as president. From 1917 to 1932 he was technical director of the Skinner Organ Co., which in 1932 was merged with the Aeolian Co. of Garwood, N.J., and became the Aeolian-Skinner Organ Co. He was especially successful in the construction of organ pipes reproducing the exact tone color of the various woodwind instruments and the French horn; among several important inventions is the "duplex windchest," by means of which the stops of 2 manuals are made interchangeable, and the arrangement of placing the stops on swinging sides. The Skinner Co. built the organ in the National Cathedral at Washington, D.C. He publ. *The Modern Organ* (1915; 6th ed., 1945) and *The Composition of the Organ* (1947).

BIBL.: D. Holden, *The Life and Work of E.M. S.* (Richmond, Va., 1985).

Sklavos, George, Greek composer and teacher; b. Brailov, Romania (of Greek parents), Aug. 20, 1888; d. Athens, March 19, 1976. He studied with Armand Marsick at the Athens Cons., where he was an instructor (1913–68). He devoted himself chiefly to the musical theater.

WORKS: DRAMATIC: OPERAS: *Niovi* (1919); *Lestenisa* (1923; Athens, March 14, 1947); *Kassiani* (1929–36; Athens, Oct. 30, 1959); *Krino st' akroyali* (Lily at the Seashore; 1937–41); *Amphitryon* (1955–60); *St' Ai Yorghi to panyghiri* (At St. George's Fair; 1961–62). Also incidental music. **ORCH.:** *Aetos* (Eagle; 1922); *Arcadian Suite* (1922); *Cretan Fantasy* (1922); *Heroiko poiema* (1926); *2 idylls* (1928); *Nissiotikos gamos* (Marriage on a Greek Island; 1937). **VOCAL:** Choruses; songs.

Sköld, (Karl) Yngve, Swedish composer; b. Vallby, April 29, 1899; d. Stockholm, Dec. 6, 1992. He studied piano and composition in Stockholm (1915–18), then in Brno (1920–22) and Prague (1922). From 1938 to 1964 he was librarian of the Swedish Composers' Society. His music blends Nordic Romanticism with subdued modernity.

WORKS: ORCH.: 4 syms. (1915, 1937, 1949, 1968); 3 piano concertos (1917, 1946, 1968); *Suite concertante* for Viola and Orch. (1936); *Sinfonia di chiesa* (1939); Violin Concerto (1941); Cello Concerto (1947); Double Concerto for Violin, Cello, and Orch. (1950); *Divertimento* (1951). **CHAMBER:** Cello Sonata (1927); 4 string quartets (1930, 1955, 1965, 1974); Quintet for 2 Flutes, Cello, and Piano (1958); Sonata for Viola and Organ (1962); Concertino for 5 Winds, Timpani, and Strings (1963); *Divertimento* for Violin, Viola, and Cello (1971); *Trio domestico* for Piano Trio (1974). **PIANO:** 2 sonatas (1963); Sonatina (1970).

Skriabin, Alexander (Nikolaievich). See **Scriabin, Alexander (Nikolaievich).**

Skrowaczewski, Stanislaw, eminent Polish-born American conductor and composer; b. Lwów, Oct. 3, 1923. His father was a brain surgeon; his mother, a fairly good pianist. A precocious *wunderkind* even for a fabled land of child prodigies, he composed an orch. overture at the age of 8, played a piano recital at 11, and performed Beethoven's 3rd Piano Concerto at 13, conducting the orch. from the keyboard. He studied composition and conducting at the Lwów Cons. and also physics, chemistry, and philosophy at the Univ. of Lwów. The oppressive Nazi occupation of Poland interrupted his studies, and a bomb exploded in the vicinity of his house, causing an injury to his hands that interfered with his further activities as a concert pianist. After World War II, he went to Kraków to study composition with Palester and conducting with Bierdiajew. In 1947 he received a French government scholarship which enabled him to study composition with Boulanger and conducting with Kletzki in Paris. He then conducted the Wroclaw Orch. (1946–47), the State Silesian Phil. in Katowice (1949–54), the Kraków Phil. (1954–56), and the National Phil. in Warsaw (1956–59). In 1956 he won 1st prize in the international conducting competition in Rome. On Dec. 4, 1958, he made his American debut as a guest conductor of the Cleveland Orch., scoring an impressive success. In 1960 he was named music director of the Minneapolis Sym. Orch. (renamed the Minnesota Orch. in 1968), and asserted his excellence both as a consummate technician of the baton and a fine interpreter of the classic and modern repertoire. In 1966 he became a naturalized American citizen. In the interim, he appeared as a guest conductor throughout the world. As an opera conductor, he made his Metropolitan Opera debut in N.Y. on Jan. 8, 1970, with *Die Zauberflöte*. In 1979 he resigned as music director of the Minnesota Orch., and was made its conductor emeritus. He was principal conductor and musical adviser of the Hallé Orch. in Manchester from 1984 to 1990; also served as music adviser of the St. Paul (Minn.) Chamber Orch. (1987–88).

WORKS: DRAMATIC: BALLET: *Ugo and Parisina* (1949). Also theater and film music. **ORCH.:** 4 syms.: No. 1 (1936), No. 2 (1945), No. 3, *Symphony for Strings* (1947), and No. 4 (1954); *Overture 1947* (1947); *Music at Night*, extracts from the ballet, *Ugo and Parisina* (1949–51); English Horn Concerto (Minneapolis, Nov. 21, 1969); *Ricercari notturni* for Saxophone and Orch. (1977; Minneapolis, Jan. 19, 1978); Clarinet Concerto (1981); Violin Concerto (Philadelphia, Dec. 12, 1985); Fanfare (1987); Triple Concerto for Violin, Clarinet, Piano, and Orch. (1991); *Gesualdo di Venosa*, arrangement of 6 madrigals for Chamber Orch. (1992). **CHAMBER:** 4 string quartets; Trio for Clarinet, Bassoon, and Piano (1982–84); *Fantasie per quattro* for Clarinet, Violin, Cello, and Piano (1984); *Fantasie per sei* for Oboe, Violin, Viola, Cello, Bass, and Piano (Atlanta, April 16, 1989); String Trio (1990); *Fantasie per tre* for Flute, Oboe, and Cello (1992); 6 piano sonatas. **OTHER:** Theater music; film scores; songs.

Slatkin, Felix, American violinist and conductor, father of **Leonard (Edward) Slatkin**; b. St. Louis, Dec. 22, 1915; d. Los Angeles, Feb. 8, 1963. He studied violin with Zimbalist and conducting with Reiner at the Curtis Inst. of Music in Philadelphia. He was a member of the St. Louis Sym. Orch. (1931–37). In 1937 he went to Los Angeles, where he played in film studio orchs. In 1947 he organized the Hollywood String Quartet, which gave regular performances until it was dissolved in 1961. He also was active as a conductor, especially in programs of light music. In 1939 he married the cellist Eleanor Aller Slatkin (b. N.Y., May 20, 1917; d. Los Angeles, Oct. 12, 1995). She studied with her father and at the Juilliard School of Music in N.Y. At the age of 12 she played at N.Y.'s Carnegie Hall. She was principal cellist in the Warner Brothers studio orch. in Hollywood from 1939 to 1963, and also was a member of the Hollywood String Quartet. From 1968 to 1970 she was head of the string dept. at DePaul Univ. in Chicago.

Slatkin, Leonard (Edward), prominent American conductor, son of **Felix Slatkin**; b. Los Angeles, Sept. 1, 1944. He received musical training in his youth, studying violin, viola, piano, and conducting, as well as composition with Castelnuovo-Tedesco; after attending Indiana Univ. (1962) and Los Angeles City College (1963), he received valuable advice from Susskind at the Aspen (Colo.) Music School (1964); then studied conducting with Morel at the Juilliard School of Music in N.Y. (Mus.B., 1968). In 1968 he joined the St. Louis Sym. Orch. as assistant conductor to Susskind, and was successively named assoc. conductor (1971), assoc. principal conductor (1974), and principal guest conductor (1975). He made his European debut in London as a guest conductor with the Royal Phil. in 1974. He was music adviser of the New Orleans Phil. (1977–80); also music director of the Minnesota Orch. summer concerts (from 1979). In 1979 he became music director of the St. Louis Sym. Orch.; took it on a major European tour in 1985. In 1990 he also became music director of the Great Woods Performing Arts Center in Mansfield, Mass., the summer home of the Pittsburgh Sym. Orch., and in 1991 of the Blossom Music Center, the summer home of the Cleveland Orch. On Oct. 10, 1991, he made his Metropolitan Opera debut in N.Y. conducting *La Fanciulla del West*. In 1992 he was awarded the Elgar Medal. He was named music director designate of the National Sym. Orch. in Washington, D.C., in 1994. After completing his tenure with the St. Louis Sym. Orch. in 1996, he thereafter served as its laureate conductor. In 1996 he assumed his new post as music director of the National Sym. Orch. He appeared widely as a guest conductor of major orchs., both in North America and Europe, demonstrating particular affinity for works of the 19th and 20th centuries.

Slavenski (real name, **Štolcer**), **Josip,** outstanding Croatian composer and teacher; b. Čakovec, May 11, 1896; d. Belgrade, Nov. 30, 1955. He studied with Kodály in Budapest and with Novák in Prague. He taught at the Zagreb Cons. (1923–24); then settled in Belgrade, where he taught at the Stankovič Music School; subsequently was a teacher (1937–45) and a prof. (1945–55) at the Academy of Music. About 1930 he adopted the name Slavenski, which he used exclusively in his publ. works. A musician of advanced ideas, he attempted to combine Slavic melodic and rhythmic elements with modern ingredients; he experimented with nontempered scales and devised a "natural" scale of 53 degrees to the octave. His significance was only fully recognized in his homeland after his death.

WORKS: DRAMATIC: Incidental music; film scores. **ORCH.:** *Nocturne* (1916; rev. 1920); *Chaos* (1918–32); *Prasimfonia* ("protosymphony") for Organ, Piano, and Orch. (1919–26); *Balkanophonia*, suite (1927; Berlin, Jan. 25, 1929); Violin Concerto (1927); 2 suites (1929, 1935); *Religiophonia (Simfonija orijenta)* for Solo Voices, Chorus, and Orch. (1934); *Muzika za film* (1936); Muzika for Chamber Orch. (1938); *4 balkanske igre* (4 Balkan Dances; 1938); *Simfonijski epos* (1944–46); Piano Concerto (1951; unfinished). **CHAMBER:** 4 string quartets (1923; *Lyric*, 1928; 1938; c.1949, arr. from the *4 Balkan Dances* for Orch., 1938); *Slavenska*, violin sonata (1924); *Sonata religiosa* for Violin and Organ (1925); Wind Quintet (1930); Piano Trio (1930); piano pieces. **VOCAL:** *Pesme moje majik* (Songs of My Mother) for Alto and String Quartet (1944); choral pieces.

Slavický, Klement, Czech composer; b. Tovačov, Sept. 22, 1910. He entered the Prague Cons. in 1927 to study composition with Jirák, and also received training there in conducting, piano, and viola. His advanced training was also completed there as a student of Suk and Talich (1931–33). He subsequently worked at the Czech Radio in Prague. His 1st Sinfonietta was awarded the prize of the Czech Academy of Sciences and Arts in 1941. In spite of the notable success of his *3 Compositions* for Piano at the Prague Spring Festival in 1947, the Communist regime branded his music as formalistic in 1949 and in 1951 he was forced to leave the Czech Radio. When he refused to join the Communist Party, he was expelled from the Union of Czech Composers and spent many years working outside official musical life. However, his music continued to be heard. With the Soviet-bloc invasion of Czechoslovakia in 1968, Slavický's music was banned for the next decade. His 4th Sinfonietta, *Pax hominibus in universo orbi*, dedicated to the United Nations in honor of its 40th anniversary in 1985, was awarded the U.N. Gold Commemorative Medal. When the Communist regime finally recognized his talent with its title of National Artist in 1989, Slavický refused to accept the title. With the collapse of the Communist regime later that year, he emerged as a respected elder statesman of Czech musical life. In his music, Slavický has generally written scores notable for their technical complexity and assured handling of instrumental resources. On occasion he has also utilized Moravian folk melos.

WORKS: ORCH.: *Fantasy* for Piano and Orch. (1931); 4 sinfoniettas: No. 1 (1940), No. 2 (1962), No. 3, *Concerto for Orchestra* (1980), and No. 4, *Pas hominibus in universo orbi*, for Strings, Keyboard, Percussion, Voice, Reciter, and Organ (1984); *Moravian Dance Fantasies* (1951); *Rhapsodic Variations* (1953). **CHAMBER:** 2 string quartets (1932, 1972); *2 Compositions* for Cello and Piano (1936); Trio for Oboe, Clarinet, and Bassoon (1937); Suite for Oboe and Piano (1959); *Partita* for Violin (1963); *Intermezzi Mattutini* for Flute and Harp (1965); *Trialog* for Violin, Clarinet, and Piano (1966); *Capriccio* for Horn and Piano (1967); *Musica monologica* for Harp (1973); *Poem and Rondo* for Cello and Piano (1973); Violin Sonata, *Friendship* (1974); *Sentenze* for Trombone and Piano (1976); *Playing in 2 and 3* for Young Violinists (1986); *Rhapsody* for Viola (1987); *Musica* for Horn (1988). **KEYBOARD: PIANO:** *3 Compositions* (1947); Sonata, *Meditation on Life* (1958); *On the Black and White* (1958); *Piano and Youth* (1958); *12 Small Études* (1964); *Études and Essays* (1965); Suite for Piano, 4-hands (1968); *A Song for the Homeland and Furiat* for Piano, 4-hands (1971). **HARPSICHORD:** *3 Studies* (1983). **VOCAL:** *To Nature* for High Voice and Orch. (1942); *Lidice* for Double Men's Chorus (1945); *Šohajé*, Moravian love songs for Women's Chorus (1948; rev. 1950–51); *Madrigals* for Chamber Chorus (1959); *Psalms* for Soprano, Alto, Tenor, Bass, Chorus, and Organ (1970); *A Path Towards the Light*, dramatic fresco for Tenor, Reciter, and Men's Chorus (1980); *The Homeland* for Chorus (1982); other choral pieces and songs.

Slawson, Wayne, American composer and music theorist; b. Detroit, Dec. 29, 1932. He studied at the Univ. of Mich. (B.A. in mathematics, 1955; M.A. in composition, 1959) and Harvard Univ. (Ph.D. in psychoacoustics, 1965). He was a computer programmer and systems analyst with the U.S. Air Force, the Rand Corp. in Santa Monica, Calif. (1955–57), and the Mitre Corp. in Bedford, Mass. (1959–62), specializing in speech synthesis. He taught at Yale Univ. (1967–72), the Univ. of Pittsburgh (1972–86; prof. from 1984), and the Univ. of Calif. at Davis (from 1986), where he directed the Computer and Electronic Music Studio. He composed MUCH, electronic music from various sources, with Robert Morris (1971–74); developed the music and speech synthesis programs MUSE (1961) and SYNTAL (1969–89); publ. numerous articles on theory and psychoacoustics, his monograph *Sound Color* (Berkeley, 1985) seeking to systematize timbre for analytical and compositional purposes.

WORKS: ORCH.: *Motions* (1973); *Match* (1994). **CHAMBER:** *5 Turns for 10* for Variable Ensemble (1970); *Pieces* for String Quartet (1970; rev. and aug. as *Limits*, 1977); *Reflections* for Cello and Piano (1975; rev. and aug. as *Rereflections*, 1988); *Variations* for 2 Violins (1977); *Triad* for Clarinet, Horn, and Cello (1984); *Quick Trick* for String Quartet (1987); *Interpolation of Dance* for String Quartet (1992). **VOCAL:** *Music for an Ordination* for Organ and Chorus (1963); *Pity . . . Not* for Chorus (1974); *Omaggio a Petrarca* for Chorus (1975); *Minglings* for Men's Chorus (1976); *Warm Shades*, octet for Singers and Woodwinds (1993). **COMPUTER:** *Colors* (1981); *Greetings* (1985); *Quatrains Miniatures I–V* (1985); *Swapper I* (1989; rev. and aug. as *If These 2 Tolled*, 1990). **TAPE:** *Wishful Thinking about Winter* (1967); *Death, Love, and the Maiden* (1975); *poor flesh and trees, poor stars and stones* (1977).

Sleeper, Henry Dike, American organist, music educator, and composer; b. Patten, Maine, Oct. 9, 1865; d. Winter Park, Fla., Jan. 28, 1948. He studied at Harvard Univ. and the Hartford Theological Seminary (graduated, 1891); although ordained as a Congregational minister, he turned to music and studied with J.K. Paine, Clarence Eddy, and Frederick Root. After teaching at various colleges and at the Univ. of Wisc., he was a teacher (1898–1924) and head of the music dept. (1902–24) at Smith College; also was active as a church organist (from 1895). He wrote orch. pieces, partsongs, and an organ suite.

Slenczynska, Ruth, American pianist of precocious talent; b. Sacramento, Calif., Jan. 15, 1925. Her father, a violinist, subjected her to severe discipline when her musical talent was revealed in early childhood; she was only 4 when she began piano lessons with Alma Schmidt-Kennedy; played in public in Berlin at 6 years and with an orch. in Paris at 11. She made a sensation and was acclaimed by European critics as a prodigy of nature; she took lessons with Petri, Schnabel, Cortot, and others in Europe and America, and even played for Rachmaninoff, who became interested in her destiny. However, she developed psychological difficulties with her father, whose promotion of her career became obsessive, and had to cease public appearances; when she played concerts at the age of 15, the critics characterized her performances as mechanical reproductions of the music, seemingly without any personal projection. She then withdrew from public performances; after taking a degree in psychology at the Univ. of Calif. at Berkeley (1954), she resumed her career; also taught at Southern Illinois Univ. at Edwardsville (1964–90). She publ. a book of memoirs (with L. Biancolli), *Forbidden Childhood* (N.Y., 1957), in which she recounted the troubles of a child prodigy's life; she also brought out a pedagogical ed., *Music at Your Fingertips. Aspects of Pianoforte Technique* (with A. Lingg; N.Y., 1961).

Slezak, Leo, famous Austrian tenor; b. Mährisch-Schönberg, Moravia, Aug. 18, 1873; d. Egern am Tegernsee, Bavaria, June 1, 1946. He studied with Adolf Robinson; as a youth, sang in the chorus of the Brunn Opera, making his operatic debut there as Lohengrin (March 17, 1896), one of his finest roles. He appeared with the Berlin Royal Opera (1898–99); in 1901 he became a member of the Vienna Opera, where he was active until 1926; also performed frequently in Prague, Milan, and Munich. He made his London debut with marked acclaim as Lohengrin, May 18, 1900, at Covent Garden; not satisfied with his vocal training, he went to Paris, where he studied with Jean de Reszke in 1907. He appeared in America for the first time as Otello with the Metropolitan Opera in N.Y. (Nov. 17, 1909); remained with the company until 1913. He returned to the Vienna Opera as a guest artist, making his farewell appearance in *Pagliacci* on Sept. 26, 1933. Slezak also toured widely as a recitalist of impeccable taste; also made some appearances in films. He was a man of great general culture, and possessed an exceptionally sharp literary wit, which he displayed in his reminiscences, *Meine sämtlichen Werke* (1922) and *Der Wortbruch* (1927); both were later combined in a single vol. (1935; Eng. tr. as *Songs of Motley: Being the Reminiscences of a Hungry Tenor*, London, 1938); he also publ. *Der Rückfall* (1940). A final book of memoirs, *Mein Lebensmärchen*, was publ. posthumously (1948). His son, the film actor Walter Slezak, publ. Slezak's letters, *Mein lieber Bub. Briefe eines besorgten Vaters* (Munich, 1966), and *What Time's the Next Swan?* (N.Y., 1962), alluding to the possibly apocryphal story of the swan failing to arrive in time during one of his father's performances as Lohengrin, thus prompting the non-Wagnerian query from the hapless hero.

BIBL.: L. Kleinenberger, *L. S.* (Munich, 1910); J. Dennis, "L. S.," *Record Collector*, XV (1964).

Slobodianik, Alexander, brilliant Russian pianist; b. Kiev, Sept. 5, 1941. He studied at the Moscow Cons. with Gornostaeva, graduating in 1964. In 1966 he received 4th prize at the Tchaikovsky Competition in Moscow. He subsequently undertook numerous concert tours in Russia and abroad. He was particularly successful during his American tours in the 1970s. Like most Russian pianists who venture abroad, he astounds by his unlimited technical resources, but he is also appreciated for the romantic elan of his playing.

Slobodskaya, Oda, esteemed Russian soprano; b. Vilnius, Dec. 10, 1888; d. London, July 29, 1970. She studied at the St. Petersburg Cons. She made her operatic debut as Lisa in *The Queen of Spades* at the Maryinsky Theater there in 1917. She also sang the regular repertoire there, including the roles of Marguerite in *Faust* and *Aida*. She emigrated in 1922; sang in Paris, at La Scala in Milan, and in Buenos Aires; eventually settled in London; sang Venus in *Tannhäuser* at Covent Garden in 1932. She developed an active career in England, establishing herself as an authoritative interpreter of Russian songs in recital; she also joined the faculty of the Guildhall School of Music and proved a sympathetic and effective voice teacher.

BIBL.: M. Leonard, *S.: A Biography of O. S.* (London, 1978).

Slonimsky, Nicolas (actually, **Nikolai Leonidovich**), legendary Russian-born American musicologist of manifold endeavors, uncle of **Sergei (Mikhailovich) Slonimsky**; b. St. Petersburg, April 27, 1894; d. Los Angeles, Dec. 25, 1995. A self-described failed *wunderkind,* he was given his first piano lesson by his illustrious maternal aunt Isabelle Vengerova, on Nov. 6, 1900, according to the old Russian calendar. Possessed by inordinate ambition, aggravated by the endemic intellectuality of his family of both maternal and paternal branches (novelists, revolutionary poets, literary critics, university professors, translators, chessmasters, economists, mathematicians, inventors of useless artificial languages, Hebrew scholars, speculative philosophers), he became determined to excel beyond common decency in all these doctrines; as an adolescent, wrote out his future biography accordingly, setting down his death date as 1967, but survived. He enrolled in the St. Petersburg Cons. and studied harmony and orchestration with 2 pupils of Rimsky-Korsakov, Kalafati and Maximilian Steinberg; also tried unsuccessfully to engage in Russian journalism. After the Revolution he made his way south; was a rehearsal pianist at the Kiev Opera, where he took some composition lessons with Glière (1919); then was in Yalta (1920), where he earned his living as a piano accompanist to displaced Russian singers, and as an instructor at a dilapidated Yalta Cons.; thence proceeded to Turkey, Bulgaria, and Paris, where he became secretary and piano-pounder to Serge Koussevitzky. In 1923 he went to the U.S.; became coach in the opera dept. of the Eastman School of Music in Rochester, N.Y., where he took an opportunity to study some more composition with the visiting prof. Selim Palmgren, and conducting with Albert Coates; in 1925 he was again with Koussevitzky in Paris and Boston, but was fired for insubordination in 1927. He learned to speak polysyllabic English and began writing music articles for the *Boston Evening Transcript* and the *Christian Science Monitor*; ran a monthly column of musical anecdotes of questionable authenticity in *Etude* magazine; taught theory at the Malkin Cons. in Boston and at the Boston Cons.; conducted the Pierian Sodality at Harvard Univ. (1927–29) and the Apollo Chorus (1928–30). In 1927 he organized the Chamber Orch. of Boston with the purpose of presenting modern works; with it he gave first performances of works by Charles Ives, Edgar Varèse, Henry Cowell, and others. He became a naturalized American citizen in 1931. In 1931–32 he conducted special concerts of modern American, Cuban, and Mexican music in Paris, Berlin, and Budapest under the auspices of the Pan-American Assn. of Composers, producing a ripple of excitement; he repeated these programs at his engagements with the Los Angeles Phil. (1932) and at the Hollywood Bowl (1933), which created such consternation that his conducting career came to a jarring halt. From 1945 to 1947 he was, by accident (the head of the dept. had died of a heart attack), lecturer in Slavonic languages and literatures at Harvard Univ. In 1962–63 he traveled in Russia, Poland, Yugoslavia, Bulgaria, Romania, Greece, and Israel under the auspices of the Office of Cultural Exchange at the U.S. State Dept., as a lecturer in native Russian, ersatz Polish, synthetic Serbo-Croatian, Russianized Bulgarian, Latinized Romanian, archaic Greek, passable French, and tolerable German. Returning from his multinational travels, he taught variegated musical subjects at the Univ. of Calif., Los Angeles; was irretrievably retired after a triennial service (1964–67), ostensibly owing to irreversible obsolescence and recessive infantiloquy; but, disdaining the inexorable statistics of the actuarial tables, continued to agitate and even gave long-winded lecture-recitals in institutions of dubious learning. In 1987 he received a Guggenheim fellowship. In 1991 he was inducted as an honorary member of the American Academy and Inst. of Arts and Letters for his manifold contributions to music. As a composer, he cultivated miniature forms, usually with a gimmick, e.g., *Studies in Black and White* for Piano (1928; orchestrated as *Piccolo Divertimento*; Los Angeles Phil. New Music Group, Oct. 17, 1983) in "mutually exclusive consonant counterpoint," a song cycle, *Gravestones,* to texts from tombstones in an old cemetery in Hancock, N.H. (1945), and *Minitudes,* a collection of 50 quaquaversal piano pieces (1971–77). His only decent orch. work is *My Toy Balloon* (1942), a set of variations on a Brazilian song, which includes in the score 100 colored balloons to be exploded *fff* at the climax. He also conjured up a *Möbius Strip-Tease,* a perpetual vocal canon notated on a Möbius band to be revolved around the singer's head; it had its first and last performance at the Arrière-Garde Coffee Concert at UCLA, on May 5, 1965, with the composer officiating at the piano non-obbligato. A priority must be conceded to him for writing the earliest singing commercials to authentic texts from the *Saturday Evening Post* advertisements, among them *Make This a Day of Pepsodent, No More Shiny Nose,* and *Children Cry for Castoria* (1925). More "scholarly," though no less defiant of academic conventions, is his *Thesaurus of Scales and Melodic Patterns* (1947), an inventory of all conceivable and inconceivable tonal combinations, culminating in a mind-boggling "Grandmother Chord" containing 12 different tones and 11 different intervals. Beset by a chronic itch for novelty, he coined the term "pandiatonicism" (1937), which, *mirabile dictu,* took root and even got into reputable reference works, including the 15th ed. of the *Encyclopaedia Britannica.* In his quest for trivial but not readily accessible information, he blundered into the muddy field of musical lexicography; publ. *Music since 1900,* a chronology of musical events, which actually contains some beguiling serendipities (N.Y., 1937; 5th ed., rev., 1994); took over the vacated editorship (because of the predecessor's sudden death during sleep) of Thompson's *International Cyclopedia of Music and Musicians* (4th to 8th eds., 1946–58) and accepted the editorship of the 5th, 6th, 7th, and 8th eds. of the prestigious *Baker's Biographical Dictionary of Musicians* (N.Y., 1958, 1978, 1984, 1992). He also abridged this venerable vol. into *The Concise Baker's Biographical Dictionary of Musicians* (N.Y., 1988). In 1978 he mobilized his powers of retrospection in preparing an autobiography, *Failed Wunderkind,* subtitled *Rueful Autopsy* (in the sense of self-observation, not dissection of the body); the publishers, deeming these titles too lugubrious, renamed it *Perfect Pitch* (N.Y., 1988). He also translated Boris de Schloezer's biography of Scriabin from the original Russian (Berkeley and Los Angeles, 1987), which was followed by his *Lectionary of Music,* a compendium of articles on music (N.Y., 1988). His other writings include *Music of Latin America* (N.Y., 1945; several reprints; also in Spanish, Buenos Aires, 1947); *The Road to Music,* ostensibly for children (N.Y., 1947); *A Thing or Two about Music* (N.Y., 1948; inconsequential; also lacking an index); *Lexicon of Musical Invective,* a random collection of pejorative reviews of musical masterpieces (N.Y., 1952); numerous articles for encyclopedias; also a learned paper, *Sex and the Music Librarian,* valuable for its painstaking research; the paper was delivered by proxy, to tumultuous cachinnations, at a symposium of the Music Library Assn., at Chapel Hill, N.C., Feb. 2, 1968. R. Kostelanetz ed. a collection of his writings as *Nicolas Slonimsky: The First Hundred Years* (N.Y., 1994). His much-lamented death, just 4 months before his 102nd birthday, brought to a close one of the most remarkable careers in the annals of 20th-century music.

BIBL.: H. Cowell, "N. S.," *American Composers on American Music* (Stanford, Calif., 1933; cf. reciprocally, N. Slonimsky, "Henry Cowell," ibid.); C. Nott, "The Many-Sided Musical Mind of N. S.," *Ovation* (July 1984); L. Weschler, "N. S.," *The New Yorker* (Nov. 17 and 24, 1986); R. Kostelanetz, "Conversation with N. S. about His Composing," *Musical Quarterly,* No. 3 (1990).

Slonimsky, Sergei (Mikhailovich), greatly talented Russian composer, nephew of **Nicolas (Nikolai Leonidovich) Slonimsky**; b. Leningrad, Aug. 12, 1932. A member of a highly intellectual family (his father was a well-known Soviet author;

his paternal grandfather, an economist, the author of the first book on Karl Marx in the Russian language; his father's maternal uncle was a celebrated Russian ed. and literary critic; his father's maternal aunt was the noted piano teacher Isabelle Vengerova), he studied at the Leningrad Cons., taking composition with Boris Arapov and Orest Evlakhov (graduated, 1955) and piano with Vladimir Nilsen (graduated, 1956); he also took courses in musicology with F. Rubtzov (folk music) and N. Uspensky (polyphonic analysis). While a student, he wrote a fairy-tale suite, *Frog-Princess*, and in 1951 composed a string quartet on Russian folk motifs. In 1959 he was appointed to the faculty of the Leningrad Cons. For further study of folk music he traveled into the countryside, in the rural regions of Pskov and Novgorod. Concurrently, he explored the technical modalities of new music, in the tradition of Soviet modernism, evolving a considerable complexity of texture in a framework of dissonant counterpoint, while safeguarding the tonal foundation in triadic progressions. Some of his works, such as his opera *Virineya*, represent a contemporary evolution of the Russian national school of composition, broadly diatonic and spaciously songful; his other works tend toward ultramodern practices, including polytonality, microtonality, dodecaphony, tone-clusters, amplified sound, prepared piano, electronic sonorism, aleatory proceedings, and spatial placement of instruments. His *Concerto for Orchestra* employs electronically amplified guitars and solo instruments; even more advanced is his *Antiphones* for String Quartet, employing non-tempered tuning and an "ambulatory" setting, in which the players are placed in different parts of the hall and then walk, while playing, en route to the podium; the piece is especially popular at modern music festivals. A prolific composer, he has written 10 syms. and a remarkably varied catalogue of chamber music pieces which he produces with a facility worthy of Rossini. He also has an easy hand with choral works. Although his natural impulse tends towards the newest sound elements, he proves remarkably successful in gathering and transforming folk motifs and rhythms, as in his Novgorod choruses, composed for the American Festival of Soviet Music of 1988. The most unusual subject, for a Soviet composer, was an opera based on the life and death of the Catholic Queen of Scotland, Mary Stuart. Mary Stuart was first performed in Kuibishev on Oct. 1, 1983, and then subsequently performed in Leningrad and in Leipzig (1984). It was then selected for a gala production at the Edinburgh Festival in Scotland, where it was given on Aug. 22, 1986, by the Leningrad Opera in a performance in the Russian language. The score utilizes authentic Scottish folk songs, suitably arranged in modern harmonies, as well as original themes in the pentatonic scale. The opera received the prestigious Glinka Prize in 1983. Slonimsky encountered considerable difficulties in producing his chamber opera, *The Master and Margarita*, after a novel by Bulgakov, because the subject had to do with mystical religious events. The Soviet authorities delayed its production for nearly 15 years. Finally, with a liberal change in the political climate, the opera was performed, first in East Germany, and, eventually and to considerable acclaim, in Leningrad, on Dec. 1, 1989. Practically all of Slonimsky's music, including the operas, has been publ. Apart from his work as a composer and teacher, he contributes music criticism to Russian magazines; he also publ. a valuable analytic survey of the symphonies of Prokofiev (Leningrad, 1976).

WORKS: DRAMATIC: OPERAS: *Virineya* (Leningrad, Sept. 30, 1967); *The Master and Margarita*, chamber opera, after Bulgakov (1973; Leningrad, Dec. 1, 1989); *Mary Stuart*, opera-ballad (1978–80; Kuibishev, Jan. 31, 1981); *Hamlet* (1992). **BALLET:** *Icarus* (1962–69; Moscow, May 29, 1971). Also incidental music and film scores.

ORCH.: *Carnival Overture* (1957); 10 syms.: No. 1 (1958; Leningrad, March 11, 1962), No. 2 (1977; Leningrad, Sept. 21, 1979), No. 3 (Leningrad, Dec. 15, 1982), No. 4, dedicated to the memory of his father (Kuibishev, Oct. 1, 1983), No. 5 (1983; Kuibishev, Oct. 1, 1984), No. 6 (1983; Leningrad, June 21, 1986), No. 7 (1984; Leningrad, June 21, 1986), No. 8 for Chamber Orch. (Vilnius, Sept. 30, 1985), No. 9 (Leningrad, Feb. 18, 1989), and No. 10 (1992); *Choreographic Miniatures* (1964); *Concerto buffo* (1964–65; Leningrad, April 28, 1966); Concerto for Sym. Orch., 3 Electric Guitars, and Solo Instruments (1973; Leningrad, Feb. 9, 1974); *Dramatic Song* (1974); *Festive Music* for Balalaika, Castanets, and Orch. (1975); *Symphonic Motet* (1976); *Quiet Music* (1981; Leningrad, March 7, 1982); *Concerto primaverile* for Violin and String Orch. (Vilnius, Oct. 8, 1983, Sergei Stadler soloist).

CHAMBER: String Quartet on Russian Themes (1951); 2 Pieces for Viola and Piano (1956); Suite for Viola and Piano (1959); Sonata for Solo Violin (1960); *Chromatic Flute and Humoresque* for Flute (1961); 3 Pieces for Cello (1964); *Dialogues* for Wind Quintet (1964); *Antiphones* for String Quartet (1968); *Sonatina allegro* for Horn and Piano (1974); *Monologue and Toccata* for Clarinet and Piano (1974); *Solo espressivo* for Oboe (1975); *Exotic Suite* for 2 Violins, 2 Electric Guitars, Saxophone, and Percussion (1976; Leningrad, Nov. 3, 1978); *Legend* for Domra and Piano (1976); *Merry Rondo* for Domra and Piano (1976); *Novgorod Dance* for Clarinet, Trombone, Cello, Piano, and Percussion (1980); *Rondo*, on a theme by Gounod, for Trumpet and Piano (1980); *Musica lirica* for Flute, Violin, and Harpsichord (1981); *Dithyramb* for Cello Ensemble and Piano (1982); *In the World of Animals*, children's suite for Cello and Piano (1982); Suite (Seattle, July 1990). **KEYBOARD: PIANO:** Sonata (1962); *Three Graces*, suite (1964); *Children's Pieces* (1970); *Coloristic Fantasy* (1972); *Tiny Pieces* for children (1973); *Serenade from a Musical*, street song (1976); *Round Dance and Merry Rumba* (1977); *Charlie Chaplin Whistles On* (1978); *Cat's Lullaby* (1978); *Hungarian March* for Piano, 4-hands (1980); *Intermezzo in Memory of Brahms* (1980); *Travel Suite* (1981); *Romantic Waltz* (1982); *Variations on a Theme by Mussorgsky* (1984); 3 pieces: *Jump Rope, Blues*, and *Metro* (1984); *24 Preludes and Fugues* (1993). **ORGAN:** *Pastorale and Toccata* (1961); *Chromatic Poem* (1969); *Round Dance and Fugue* (1976); *Rondo-Humoresque* (1979).

VOCAL: *Songs of Freedom*, on Russian folk motifs, for Mezzo-soprano, Baritone, and Piano (1957); *Spring has arrived*, vocal cycle for Voice and Piano, after Japanese poets (1958); *Polish Stanzas*, vocal cycle, after the Polish poet Anthoni Slonimski, 1st cousin of the composer's father (1963); *Lyric Stanzas*, vocal cycle for Voice and Piano (1964); *Voice from the Chorus*, cantata, after Alexander Blok (1964); *Farewell to a Friend* for Voice and Piano (1966); *Monologues* for Soprano, Oboe, Horn, and Harp (1967); *2 Russian Songs* for Chorus (1968); *6 Songs*, after Anna Akhmatova (1969); *Northern Landscapes* for Chorus (1969); *Merry Songs* for Voice and Piano (1971); *Choral Games* for Children's Chorus, Boy Soloist, and 2 Percussion Instruments (1972); *Evening Music* for Chorus (1973); *4 Songs*, after Osip Mandelstam (1974); *10 Songs*, after Anna Akhmatova (1974); *4 Russian Songs* for Chorus (1974); *Virineya*, suite-oratorio from the opera of the same name (1974); *Pesnoborka* (Sing-Chorus) for Contralto, Flute, Oboe, Trumpet, Balalaika, Accordion, 3 Electric Guitars, Castanets, and Vibraphone, on Russian folk songs (1975); *Songs of the Troubadours*, vocal cycle on old French ballads for Soprano, Tenor, 4 Recorders, and Lute (1975); *Songs of Songs* for Soprano, Tenor, Chorus, Oboe, Horn, and Harp (1975); *Bashkir Girl's Song* for Voice, Flute, and 2 Bongos (1977); *Quiet Flows the Don* for Chorus, to words of old Cossack chants, after Sholokhov's novel (1977); *2 Poems* for Chorus, after Pushkin (1979); Suite from the opera *Mary Stuart* for Chorus and Orch. (1980); *2 Songs* for Mezzo-soprano and Piano, after Alexander Blok (1980); *White Night* for Chorus (1980); *Morning Song* for Children's Chorus and Snare Drum (1981); *Strophes of Dhammapada* for Soprano, Harp, and Percussion, after the classic Buddhist epic (1983; Leningrad, Feb. 21, 1984); *Song of Leningrad* for Bass, Chorus, and Orch. (1983); *Little Triptych* for Chorus (1983); *2 Vocalises* for Soprano and Mezzo-soprano (1983); *Railroad* for Chorus, Trumpet, Piano, and Percussion (1983); *White Night in Leningrad* for Chorus (1983); *4 Strophes* for Chorus, after Sophocles' *Oedipus Colonus* (1983).

BIBL.: A. Milka, *S. S.* (Leningrad, 1976).

Slovák, Ladislav, Slovak conductor; b. Bratislava, Sept. 9, 1919. He studied organ and conducting at the Bratislava Cons. (1938–45) and conducting with Talich at the Bratislava Academy of Music (1949–53). He was music director of Bratislava Radio (from 1949), where he founded and conducted its choir; after serving as an assistant to Mravinsky and the Leningrad Phil. (1953–55), he returned to Bratislava as conductor of the Radio Orch. (1955–61); then was chief conductor of the Slovak Phil. there (1961–81) and of the Prague Sym. Orch. (1972–76). In 1964 he was made an Artist of Merit and in 1977 a National Artist by the Czech government.

Smallens, Alexander, Russian-born American conductor; b. St. Petersburg, Jan. 1, 1889; d. Tucson, Ariz., Nov. 24, 1972. He was taken to the U.S. as a child; became a American naturalized citizen in 1919. He studied at the Inst. of Musical Art and the College of the City of N.Y. (B.A., 1909); then took courses at the Paris Cons. (1909). He was assistant conductor of the Boston Opera (1911–14); accompanied the Anna Pavlova Ballet Co. on a tour of South America (1915–18); then was on the staff of the Chicago Opera (1919–23) and of the Philadelphia Civic Opera (1924–31); from 1927 to 1934 he was assistant conductor of the Philadelphia Orch., and from 1947 to 1950, was music director at Radio City Music Hall in N.Y. In 1934 he conducted the premiere of Gershwin's *Porgy and Bess* in Boston; conducted it on a European tour in 1956. He retired in 1958.

Smalley, Roger, English pianist, composer, and teacher; b. Swinton, Manchester, July 26, 1943. He studied piano with Antony Hopkins and composition with Peter Racine Fricker and John White at the Royal College of Music in London (1961–65); also took private composition lessons with Goehr and attended Stockhausen's Cologne course for new music (1965). With Tim Souster, he founded the contemporary music ensemble Intermodulation, with which he toured extensively in Europe until 1976. In 1968 he became the first artist-in-residence at King's College, Cambridge; in 1974 he was named musician-in-residence at the Univ. of Western Australia, where he became a research fellow (1976) and then senior lecturer. As a pianist, he consistently champions avant-garde music. His compositions are steeped in electronic and aleatory techniques.

WORKS: MUSIC THEATER: *William Derrincourt*, entertainment for Baritone, Men's Chorus, and Instrumental Ensemble (1978; Perth, Aug. 31, 1979); *The Narrow Road to the Deep North*, "journey" for Baritone and 6 Players (London, Nov. 29, 1983). **ORCH.:** *Variations* for Strings (1964); *Gloria Tibi Trinitas* (1965; rev. 1969; Liverpool, Sept. 30, 1969); *Beat Music* for Percussion, Electric Organ, Viola, Soprano Saxophone, and Orch. (London, Aug. 13, 1971); *Strata* for 15 Solo Strings (1971; London, Feb. 19, 1973); *Konzertstück* for Violin and Orch. (Perth, Feb. 23, 1980); Sym. (1981; London, Aug. 25, 1982); Piano Concerto (Swansea, Aug. 11, 1985); *Strung Out* for 13 Solo Strings (Perth, Feb. 20, 1988). **CHAMBER:** String Sextet (1964); *Missa Parodia II*, nonet (1967); *Pulses* for Brass, Percussion, and Live Electronics (1969; rev. 1986); *Zeitebenen* for Live Electronic Ensemble and Tape (1973); *Echo II* for Cello and Stereo Tape-delay System (1978), *III* for Trumpet and Stereo Tape-delay System (1978), and *IV* for Horn and Stereo Tape-delay System (1983); String Quartet (1979); *Movement* for Flute and Piano (1976–80); *Impulses* for Flute, Trombone, Percussion, Piano, Synthesizer, and Cello (1986); *Ceremony I* for Percussion Quartet (1987); various piano pieces. **VOCAL:** Choral music.

BIBL.: J. Thönell, ed., *Poles Apart: The Music of R. S.* (Perth, 1994).

Smend, Friedrich, eminent German musicologist; b. Strasbourg, Aug. 26, 1893; d. Berlin, Feb. 10, 1980. He studied theology at the Univs. of Strasbourg, Tübingen, Marburg, and Münster (Ph.D., 1921, with the diss. *Die Acta-Berichte über Bekehrung des Paulus nach ihrem Quellenwert*). He was employed at the Univ. of Münster Library (1921–23) and at the Prussian State Library in Berlin (1923–45); was a teacher (1945–46), director of the library (1946–58), a prof. (1949–58), and rector (1954–57) at the Kirchliche Hochschule in Berlin. In 1951 he received an honorary doctorate in theology from the Univ. of Heidelberg and in 1954 an honorary doctorate in philosophy from the Univ. of Mainz. He was an authority on the life and music of Bach.

WRITINGS: *Luther und Bach* (Berlin, 1947); *J.S. Bachs Kirchen-Kantaten* (Berlin, 1947–49; 2nd ed., 1950); *Johann Sebastian Bach bei seinem Namen gerufen* (Kassel and Basel, 1950); *Bach in Köthen* (Berlin, 1951); *Goethes Verhältnis zu Bach* (Berlin and Darmstadt, 1955); *Bach Studien: Gesammelte Reden und Aufsätze* (Kassel, 1969).

BIBL.: *Festschrift für F. S. zum 70. Geburtstag dargebracht von Freunden und Schülern* (Berlin, 1963); A. Durr, "F. S. (1893–1980)," *Die Musikforschung*, XXXIII (1980); R. Tatlow, "J.S. Bach and the Baroque Paragram: A Reappraisal of F. S.'s Number Alphabet Theory," *Music & Letters* (May 1989).

Smendzianka, Regina, Polish pianist and teacher; b. Torún, Oct. 9, 1924. She studied at the Pomerian Cons. in Torún, with Sztompka at the Torún Cons., and with Drzewiecki at the Kraków State College of Music (1945–48). After making her formal debut as soloist with the Kraków Phil. in 1947, she toured widely in Europe, the U.S., and the Far East. In 1964 she joined the faculty of the Warsaw Academy of Music, where she later was rector (1972–73) and a prof. (from 1977). Her exhaustive repertoire ranges from Bach to contemporary composers.

Smetáček, Václav, noted Czech oboist, conductor, and teacher; b. Brunn, Sept. 30, 1906; d. Prague, Feb. 18, 1986. He studied oboe with Ladislav Skuhrovský, composition with Jaroslav Křička, and conducting with Metod Doležil and Pavel Dědeček at the Prague Cons. (1922–30); also took courses in musicology and aesthetics at the Charles Univ. in Prague (Ph.D., 1933). In 1928 he founded the Prague Wind Quintet, remaining with it until 1955; was also oboist in the Czech Phil. (1930–33). He conducted the Radio Orch. (1934–43) and the Hlahol Choir (1934–46) in Prague; became chief conductor of Prague's FOK Sym. Orch. in 1942; it became the Prague Sym. Orch. in 1952, and he continued to lead it until 1972; he also appeared widely as a guest conductor. He taught at Prague's Cons. and Academy of Music (1945–66). In 1962 he was made an Artist of Merit and in 1976 a National Artist by the Czech government. He was best known for his performances of Czech music, both traditional and contemporary.

BIBL.: L. Šíp, *V. S.* (Prague, 1957).

Smeterlin, Jan, Polish-born English pianist; b. Bielsko, Feb. 7, 1892; d. London, Jan. 18, 1967. He was a child prodigy, making his public debut at the age of 8; after studies with Godowsky in Vienna, he toured throughout Europe and the U.S. (from 1930), eventually settling in London just before the outbreak of World War II; became a naturalized British subject. He was praised for his congenially Romantic interpretations of Chopin's music; celebrated his 50th anniversary as a concert artist at London's Wigmore Hall in 1951.

Smijers, Albert(us Antonius), eminent Dutch musicologist; b. Raamsdonksveer, July 19, 1888; d. Huis ter Heide, near Utrecht, May 15, 1957. He studied music with Averkamp at the Amsterdam Cons.; was trained for the priesthood and was ordained in 1912; then entered the school for church music at Klosterneuburg; later took a course in musicology with Adler at the Univ. of Vienna (Ph.D., 1917, with the diss. *Karl Luython als Motettenkomponist*; publ. in Amsterdam, 1923). He taught at Beekvliet Seminary in Amsterdam until 1929, then at the Amsterdam Cons. (1929–33); in 1930 he was appointed prof. of musicology at the Univ. of Utrecht; formed the Inst. of Musicology there. He brought out 7 vols. of the anthology *Van Ockeghem tot Sweelinck* (Amsterdam, 1939–56); in collaboration with C. Van den Borren and others, he publ. *Algemeene Muziekgeschiedenis* (Utrecht, 1938; 4th ed., 1947); ed. the collected works of Josquin Des Prez (Amsterdam, 1921–56) and Obrecht (Vols. I–III, Amsterdam, 1953–56).

Smirnov, Dmitri (Alexeievich), outstanding Russian tenor; b. Moscow, Nov. 19, 1882; d. Riga, April 27, 1944. He sang in a church choir as a youth; then studied voice with Dodonov and others in Moscow. On Feb. 3, 1903, he made his debut as Gigi in Esposito's *Camorra* at Moscow's Hermitage Theater. In 1904 he was accepted as a member of the Bolshoi Theater there, but interrupted his career by traveling to Paris and Milan for further voice training. Returning to Moscow in 1906, he sang again at the Bolshoi Theater; from 1910 he appeared also with the Maryinsky Opera Theater in St. Petersburg. During the same period, he took part in the famous Russian Seasons in Paris. On Dec. 30, 1910, he made his debut at the Metropolitan Opera in N.Y. in the role of the Duke of Mantua in *Rigoletto*, remaining with the company until 1912; then sang with the Boston Opera (1911); after a tour of Latin America, he appeared at London's Drury Lane (1914) and other European theaters. Although he lived mostly abroad, he revisited Russia in 1926 and 1928 as a guest artist. He later appeared mostly in solo recitals; was also active as a voice teacher; taught at the Athens Cons. and in Riga. In Russia he was regarded as one of the finest lyric tenors of his time, often compared to Caruso; as a bel canto singer, he was praised by Russian and European critics. Apart from the Russian repertoire, in which he excelled, he made a deep impression in such lyrico-dramatic roles as Faust, Don José, Canio, and Rodolfo.

Smirnov, Dmitri, Russian composer; b. Minsk, Nov. 2, 1948. After training in Frunze, he studied at the Moscow Cons. (1967–72) with Nikolai Sidelnikov (composition), Edison Denisov (orchestration), and Yuri Kholopov (analysis). He also received private instruction from Philip Gershkovich. From 1973 to 1980 he was an ed. with the publishing firm Soviet Composer. In 1993 he became a prof. and composer-in-residence at the Univ. of Keele in England. In 1972 he married **Elena Firsova.** While thoroughly grounded in various contemporary styles and techniques, Smirnov has found great inspiration in the tonal world of late Romanticism. He has also been much influenced by the poetry and painting of William Blake, and has set a number of his works to music.

WORKS: DRAMATIC: *Tiriel*, opera (1983–85; Freiburg im Breisgau, Jan. 28, 1989); *The Lamentations of Thel*, opera (1985–86; London, June 9, 1989); film scores. **ORCH.:** *2 Ricercares* for Strings (1963–83; Moscow, April 11, 1983); 2 piano concertos: No. 1 (1971; Moscow, June 21, 1972) and No. 2 (Moscow, Dec. 25, 1978); Clarinet Concerto (1974; rev. 1977); *Pastorale* (1975; Leningrad, Feb. 14, 1977); Triple Concerto for Alto Saxophone, Double Bass, Piano, and Orch. (Moscow, Dec. 26, 1977); *Fanfares*, symphonic poem (1978); 3 syms.: No. 1, *The Seasons (in Memory of William Blake)* (1980; Riga, Oct. 8, 1981), No. 2 for 4 Singers, Chorus, and Orch. (1982), and No. 3 (1995); *Tiriel-Prologue* (1983); *Mozart Variations* (1987; Moscow, Feb. 2, 1988); Concerto for Violin and 13 Strings (1990); Cello Concerto (1992); *The Moony Space* (1994). **CHAMBER:** *Monologue* for Clarinet (1968); 2 violin sonatas: No. 1 (1969; Moscow, April 20, 1970; rev. 1971) and No. 2 (Moscow, Dec. 26, 1979); *2 Fugues* for Violin (1970); String Trio (1970; Moscow, Feb. 28, 1971); *Cradle Song* for Oboe and Piano (1972); 4 string quartets: No. 1 (1973), No. 2 (Moscow, Oct. 22, 1985), No. 3 (1993), and No. 4 (1993); *Trio Sacrum* for Percussion (1974); *The Melancholic Minute* for Clarinet and Piano (1975); *Preparations* for Clarinet and Piano (1975); *Canon-Humoresque* for 3 Saxophones (1975); Sonata for Flute and Harp (Moscow, Oct. 6, 1975); *Mirages* for Saxophone Quartet (1975; Moscow, May 6, 1976); *Lyrical Composition* for Flute, Oboe, Violin, Cello, and Harpsichord (1975; Moscow, May 11, 1977); *Solo* for Harp (Limburg, Aug. 1976); Bassoon Sonata (1977; Moscow, Jan. 30, 1978); *3 Dances* for Xylophone (1977); 2 piano trios: No. 1 (1977; Moscow, Oct. 11, 1980) and No. 2 (1992); Cello Sonata (1978; Moscow, Feb. 24, 1979); *2 Pieces* for Harp (1978); *9 Children's Pieces* for Horn and Piano (1979); *Children's Concerto* for Cello and Piano (1980); *Dirge Canons in memoriam Igor Stravinsky* for 13 Players (Moscow, Dec. 14, 1981); *Serenade* for Oboe, Saxophone, and Cello (Moscow, May 25, 1981); *3 Equale* for 4 Instruments (1981); *Ballade* for Alto Saxophone and Piano (Moscow, April 14, 1982); *Forest Pictures* for Harp (1982); *The Farewell Song* for Viola and Harp (Moscow, Oct. 4, 1982); *Fantasia* for Saxophone Quartet (1982; Moscow, Dec. 12, 1983); *Tiriel* for Baritone Saxophone and Piano (1983; Moscow, April 25, 1984); *Tiriel* for Cello and Piano (1984; Kishinev, March 5, 1987); *Music Greeting to H. S.* for Trumpet (Hamburg, Oct. 16, 1985); *Partita* for Violin (1985; N.Y., Dec. 7, 1987); *Epitaph to Emil Gilels* for Piano and Organ (1985); *7 Melancholic Waltzes* for Alto Saxophone and Piano (1985; Kiev, Feb. 22, 1986); *Thel-Prologue* for Chamber Ensemble (1985); *2 Moods* for Guitar (1987); *The Moonlight Story* for Piccolo, Bass Clarinet, Violin, Viola, Cello, and Double Bass (1988; London, June 8, 1989); *The Evening Song* for Alto or Tenor Saxophone and Piano (1990); *Trinity Music* for Clarinet, Violin, and Piano (1990); *Jacob's Ladder* for Chamber Ensemble (1990; London, April 17, 1991); *Job's Studies* for Clarinet (1992); *The River of Life* for Chamber Ensemble (1992); *Prayer* for Trumpet and Organ (1992); *Threnody* for Trumpet and Organ (1992); *Orcades* for Flute (1992); Piano Quintet (1992); *Dies Irae* for Recorder (1994). **KEYBOARD: PIANO:** *12 Melancholic Waltzes* (1965–85); *2 Pieces* (1966); 3 sonatas (1967, 1980, 1992); *5 Little Pieces* (1968); *Magic Casket* (1969–85); *2 Magic Quadrates* (1971); Toccata (1972); *9 Pieces* (1979); *Suite in Baroque Style* (1980; also for Harpsichord); *Epitaph* (1985; also for Organ); *2 Intermezzi* (1987); *The 7 Angels of William Blake* (1988); *The Angels of Albion* (1991); *Magic Music Box*, 50 children's pieces (1993). **ORGAN:** *Diptych* (1992). **VOCAL:** *The Handful of Sand* for Voice and 12 Players (1967; rev. 1983; also for Voice and Piano); *2 Choruses* (1968); *12 Chorales* for Chorus (1968–72); *The Ominous Stink* for Bass, Chorus, and Orch. (1969–70); *6 Poems by Alexander Blok* for Voice and Orch. (1972); *Eternal Refuge* for Voice, Organ, Strings, and Percussion (1972; rev. 1981); *6 Haiku of Kabajasi Issa* for Voice, Flute, and Piano (1973); *Cantata in memoriam Pablo Neruda* for Soprano, Tenor, Chorus, Strings, and Percussion (1974); *The Sorrow of Past Days* for Voice, Flute, Violin, Cello, and Percussion (1976); *The Seasons* for Voice, Flute, Viola, and Harp (1979); *The Night Rhymes* for Voice and Orch. (1982); *The Visions of Coleridge* for Voice, Flute, Clarinet, Horn, Percussion, and String Quintet (1987); *Songs of Love and Madness* for Voice, Clarinet, Celesta, Harp, and String Trio (1988); *8-line Poems* for Voice, Flute, Horn, Harp, and String Trio (1989); *A Song of Liberty* for Soprano, Alto, Tenor, Bass, Chorus, and Orch. (1991); *Short Poems* for Soprano and Ensemble (1991); *3 Blake Songs* for Soprano and Ensemble (1991); *Ariel Songs* for Countertenor, 2 Recorders, Cello, and Harpsichord (1993); *The Lamb* for Voice and Ensemble (1995); many solo songs for Voice and Piano.

Smit, Leo, Dutch composer; b. Amsterdam, May 14, 1900; d. in the concentration camp in Auschwitz, 1943. He studied piano (diploma, 1922) and took courses in composition (diploma, 1924) with Zweers and Dresden at the Amsterdam Cons., where he taught analysis and harmony (1924–27); after a sojourn in Paris (1927–33), he returned to Amsterdam as a music teacher. He was arrested by the Nazi occupiers in 1943 and sent to the concentration camp at Westerbork in the Netherlands, and eventually perished in Auschwitz. His music was greatly influenced by the contemporary French school.

WORKS: BALLET: *Schemselnihar* (1929). **ORCH.:** *Introduction to Teirlinck's play "De Vertraagde Film"* for Chamber Orch. (1923); *Silhouetten*, suite for Orch.; Harp Concertino (1933); Sym. (1934–36); Concerto for Piano and Wind Orch. (1937); *Forlane en Rondeau* (orch. by Godfried Devreese); Concertino for Cello and Small Orch. (1937); Concerto for Viola and Strings (1940). **CHAMBER:** Quintet for Flute, Violin, Viola, Cello, and Harp (1928); Sextet for Piano and Wind Quintet (1933); *Suite* for Oboe and Cello (1938); Trio for Clarinet, Viola, and Piano (1938); Flute Sonata (1943). **PIANO:** *2 hommages* (Sherlock Holmes and Remington) for Piano (1928–30); *Divertimento* for Piano, 4-hands (1940).

Smit, Leo, American pianist and composer; b. Philadelphia, Jan. 12, 1921. He studied piano with Vengerova at the Curtis Inst. of Music in Philadelphia (1930–32); took lessons in composition with Nabokov (1935). He made his debut as a pianist at Carnegie Hall in N.Y. in 1939; then made tours of the U.S.; also taught at Sarah Lawrence College (1947–49), at the Univ. of Calif. at Los Angeles (1957–63), and at the State Univ. of N.Y. at Buffalo (from 1962); likewise served as director of the Monday Evening Concerts in Los Angeles (1957–63) and as composer-in-residence at the American Academy in Rome (1972–73) and at Brevard Music Center (1980). His style of composition is neo-Classical, marked by a strong contrapuntal fabric; the influence of Stravinsky, with whom he had personal contact, is particularly pronounced here.

WORKS: DRAMATIC: OPERAS: *The Alchemy of Love* (1969); *Magic Water* (1978). **MELODRAMA:** *A Mountain Eulogy* (1975). **BALLETS:** *Yerma* (1946); *Virginia Sampler* (N.Y., March 4, 1947; rev. 1960). **ORCH.:** *The Parcae*, overture (Boston, Oct. 16, 1953); 3 syms.: No. 1 (1956; Boston, Feb. 1, 1957), No. 2 (1965), and No. 3 (1981); *Capriccio* for Strings (Ojai, Calif., May 23, 1958; rev. 1974); Piano Concerto (1968; rev. 1980); *4 Kookaburra Marches* for Orch. and Tape (1972); *Symphony of Dances and Songs* (1981); *Variations* for Piano and Orch. (1981). **CHAMBER:** Sextet for Clarinet, Bassoon, and Strings (1940); *Invention* for Clarinet and Piano (1943); *In Woods* for Oboe, Harp, and Percussion (1978); *Delaunay Pochoirs*, 3 pieces for Cello and Piano (1980); Sonata for Solo Cello (1982); *Flute of Wonder*, 3 pieces for Flute and Piano (1983); *Tzadik* for Saxophone Quartet (1983), 12 Instruments (1984), String Quartet (1984), and Piano Trio (1985); *Exequy* for String Trio (1985); piano pieces, including a Sonata for Piano, 4-hands (1987). **VOCAL:** *Academic Graffiti* for Voice, Clarinet, Cello, Piano, and Percussion, after W.H. Auden (1959); choruses; solo songs and song cycles.

Smith, Carleton Sprague, distinguished American musicologist; b. N.Y., Aug. 8, 1905; d. Washington, Conn., Sept. 19, 1994. He was educated at Harvard Univ. (M.A., 1928) and at the Univ. of Vienna (Ph.D., 1930, with the diss. *Die Beziehungen zwischen Spanien und Oesterreich im 17. Jahrhundert*). Returning to the U.S., he was an instructor in history at Columbia Univ. (1931–35), then at N.Y. Univ. (1939–67); he also served as chief of the Music Division at the N.Y. Public Library (1931–43; 1946–59). A linguist, he lectured in South America, in Spanish and Portuguese, on the social history of the U.S.; a skillful flutist, he often took part in concerts of early and new music.

BIBL.: I. Katz, M. Kuss, and R. Wolfe, eds., *Libraries, History, Diplomacy, and the Performing Arts: Essays in Honor of C.S. S.* (Stuyvesant, N.Y., 1991).

Smith, Chas, American composer and performer; b. West Brookfield, Mass., March 15, 1948. He began playing piano at the age of 8; played guitar in rock bands (1964–69), and attended N.Y.'s Utica College (1967) and studied jazz composition and arranging at the Berklee School of Music in Boston (1969–70). He studied composition with Powell, Subotnick, Budd, Brown, and Tenney at the Calif. Inst. of the Arts in Valencia (B.F.A., 1975; M.F.A., 1977), where he performed with Michael Le Donne-Bhennet, Michael Jon Fink, and William Hawley at galleries and performance spaces under such ensembles as Ronin, C33, 100 Miles of Sheep Jokes, and Stilllife (1975–80). The Chas Smith Ensemble, formed in 1985, made appearances in various Los Angeles venues. His recordings include *Stilllife* (1981), *Santa Fe* (1982), and *Nakadai* (1987); also played on records by Harold Budd, Jim Fox, and Carole Caroompas and appeared in several rock videos that feature his extensive tattoos, of which he is justly proud; also performed in a number of film soundtracks, including *The Lost Boys* and *Less than Zero*. Smith performs chiefly on the pedal steel guitar, but also plays other stringed instruments, keyboards, and electronics; his music consists of austere meditations on very slowly evolving chords in the Lydian mode. He is a certified welder.

WORKS: *Ontolosis* for Electronics (1974); *Triactus* for Electronics (1975); *Mirage* for Voices, Bells, and Mallet Instruments (1977); *Santa Fe, October 68*, and *After*, all for Pedal Steel Guitar (1979–82); *Scicura* for 2 Pianos, 3 Vibraphones, Marimba, and Wind Instruments (1975; also arranged for Dobro and Pedal Steel Guitar, 1982); *Beatrix* for Pedal Steel Guitar (1983); *James Tenney* for Pedal Steel Guitar (1984); *Nakadai* for Multitrack Pedal Steel Guitar (1985); *A Judas Within: Seduction and Betrayal* for Vibraphone, Marimba, Hammer Dulcimer, Pedal Steel Guitar, Microtonal Chimes, Bowed Rods, and Small Metal Objects (1985–86); *Hollister* for Pedal Steel Guitar (1986).

Smith, Curtis O(tto) B(ismarck) Curtis-. See **Curtis-Smith, Curtis O(tto) B(ismarck).**

Smith, Cyril (James), English pianist and teacher; b. Middlesbrough, Aug. 11, 1909; d. London, Aug. 2, 1974. He was a pupil of Herbert Fryer at the Royal College of Music in London. He made his formal debut as a soloist in the Brahms 2nd Piano Concerto in Birmingham (1929). In 1937 he married the pianist Phyllis Sellick, with whom he often appeared in works for 2 pianos from 1941; during a visit to the Soviet Union in 1956, he suffered a stroke that incapacitated his left arm; they subsequently gave concerts for piano, 3-hands (from 1957). He taught at the Royal College of Music (1934–74). In 1971 he was made an Officer of the Order of the British Empire. His autobiography was appropriately titled *Duet for Three Hands* (London, 1958). At the apex of his career, he won particular distinction for his performances of Rachmaninoff; he later commissioned new works and arrangements for piano, 3-hands.

Smith, David Stanley, American conductor, music educator, and composer; b. Toledo, Ohio, July 6, 1877; d. New Haven, Conn., Dec. 17, 1949. He studied with Horatio Parker at Yale Univ., graduating in 1900. He then took courses in composition with Thuille in Munich and Widor in Paris. Upon his return to the U.S., he obtained a Mus.B. degree at Yale (1903) and was appointed an instructor at the Yale Univ. School of Music; in 1916 he became a prof. there; in 1920 was appointed dean of the School of Music, retiring in 1946. He was conductor of the New Haven Sym. Orch. from 1920 to 1946. In 1910 he was elected a member of the National Inst. of Arts and Letters. His compositions were cast in a conservative mold.

WORKS: OPERA: *Merrymount* (1914). **ORCH.:** 4 syms.: No. 1 (1910), No. 2 (1917), No. 3 (1928; Cleveland, Jan. 8, 1931, composer conducting), and No. 4 (1937; Boston, April 14, 1939, composer conducting); *Prince Hal*, overture (New Haven, Dec. 1912); *Impressions*, suite (1916); *Fête galante*, fantasy for Flute and Orch. (N.Y., Dec. 11, 1921); *Epic Poem* (1926; Boston, April 12, 1935, composer conducting); *Sinfonietta* for Strings (1931); *1929: A Satire* (1932; N.Y., Nov. 15, 1933); *Requiem* for Violin and Orch. (1939); *Credo*, symphonic poem (1941); 4 Pieces for Strings (1943); *The Apostle*, symphonic poem (1944). **CHAMBER:** 10 string quartets (1899–1938); *Sonata Pastorale* for Oboe and Piano (1918); Violin Sonata (1923); *Flowers* for 10 Instruments (1924); Piano Quintet (1927); String Sextet (1931); piano pieces, including a Sonata (1929). **VOCAL:** *Rhapsody of St. Bernard* for Solo Voices, Chorus, and Orch. (1915); *The Vision of Isaiah* for Soprano, Tenor, Chorus, and Orch. (1927); *The Ocean* for Bass, Chorus, and Orch. (1945); song cycles.

BIBL.: B. Tuthill, "D.S. S.," *Musical Quarterly* (Jan. 1942); E. Goode, *D.S. S. and his Music* (diss., Univ. of Cincinnati, 1978).

Smith, Gregg, American conductor and composer; b. Chicago, Aug. 21, 1931. He studied composition with Leonard Stein, Lukas Foss, and Ray Moreman and conducting with Fritz Zweig at the Univ. of Calif. at Los Angeles (M.A., 1956). In 1955 in Los Angeles he founded the Gregg Smith Singers, a chamber choir, with which he toured and recorded extensively; from 1970, was active with it in N.Y. He also taught at Ithaca College, the State Univ. of N.Y. at Stony Brook, the Peabody Cons. of Music in Baltimore, Barnard College, and the Manhattan School of Music in N.Y. His repertoire extends from early music to works by contemporary American composers. He ed. the Gregg Smith Choral Series; wrote much vocal music, including 2 operas, choral works, songs, and pieces for chamber orch.

Smith, Hale, black American composer; b. Cleveland, June 29, 1925. He studied piano with Dorothy Price and composition with Marcel Dick at the Cleveland Inst. of Music (B.Mus., 1950; M.Mus., 1952); went to N.Y. in 1958 and was active as a music ed. for publishers, as a jazz arranger, and as a teacher; later was a prof. at the Univ. of Conn. in Storrs (1970–84). His output is remarkable for its utilization of serial procedures with jazz infusions; wrote musical scores for Dizzy Gillespie, Ahmad Jamal, Eric Dolphy, and Abby Lincoln, and worked in various capacities for Quincy Jones, Clark Terry, Oliver Nelson, Miriam Makeba, and Hugh Masekela.

WORKS: CHAMBER OPERA: *Blood Wedding* (1953). **ORCH.:** *Orchestral Set* (1952; rev. 1968); *Contours* (Louisville, Oct. 17, 1961); *By Yearning and By Beautiful* for Strings (1964); *Music* for Harp and Orch. (1972); *Ritual and Incantations* (1974); *Innerflexions* (N.Y., Sept. 2, 1977). **CHAMBER:** Duo for Violin and Piano (1953); Cello Sonata (1955); *Epicedial Variations* for Violin and Piano (1956); *3 Brevities* for Flute (1960); *Introductions, Cadenzas and Interludes* for 8 Players (1974); *Variations* for 6 Players (1975); *Variations a due* for Cello, Alto Saxophone, and Flute or Saxophone, or Clarinet ad libitum (1984). **PIANO:** *Evocation* (1966); *Anticipations, Introspections and Reflections* (1971). **VOCAL:** *5 Songs* for Voice and Violin (1956); *2 Love Songs of John Donne* for Soprano and 9 Instruments (1958); *Comes Tomorrow,* jazz cantata for Chorus and Accompaniment (1972; rev. 1977); *Toussaint L'Ouverture 1803* for Chorus and Piano (1977); *Symphonic Spirituals* for Soprano and Orch. (1979); *Meditations in Passage* for Soprano, Baritone, and Piano or Orch. (1980).

BIBL.: M. Breda, *H. S.: Biographical and Analytical Study of the Man and His Music* (diss., Univ. of Southern Miss., Harrisburg, 1975).

Smith, Jennifer (Mary), English soprano; b. Lisbon, July 13, 1945. She received training in Lisbon, where she made her operatic debut as the Heavenly Voice in *Don Carlos* in 1968. After settling in London in 1971, she completed her studies with Winifred Radford and Pierre Bernac. In 1979 she appeared as Mozart's Countess Almaviva with the Welsh National Opera in Cardiff; subsequently sang with the Scottish Opera in Glasgow, the Kent Opera, and the English National Opera in London. In 1982 she sang Alphise in the first staging of Rameau's *Les Boréades* at the Aix-en-Provence Festival. In 1988 she made her U.S. debut in N.Y. as Cybele in Lully's *Atys.* In 1991 she appeared as the Queen of the Night in Toronto. Smith won extraordinary praise for her performances with principal British early music orchs. and ensembles. She also scored remarkable success in appearances as a soloist with orchs. and as a recitalist abroad.

Smith (real name, **Vielehr**), **Julia (Frances),** American pianist, composer, and writer on music; b. Denton, Texas, Jan. 25, 1911; d. N.Y., April 27, 1989. She studied at North Texas State Univ. (graduated, 1930), then took courses in piano with Carl Friedberg and received instruction in composition at the Juilliard School of Music in N.Y. (diploma, 1939); also studied at N.Y. Univ. (M.A., 1933; Ph.D., 1952). She was the pianist of the all-women Orchestrette of N.Y. (1932–39); made tours of the U.S., Latin America, and Europe; taught at the Hartt School of Music in Hartford, Conn. (1941–46).

WRITINGS: *Aaron Copland: His Work and Contribution to American Music* (N.Y., 1955); *Master Pianist: The Career and Teaching of Carl Friedberg* (N.Y., 1963); *Directory of American Women Composers* (Indianapolis, 1970).

WORKS: OPERAS: *Cynthia Parker* (1938; Denton, Feb. 16, 1940; rev. 1977); *The Stranger of Manzano* (1943; Dallas, May 6, 1947); *The Gooseherd and the Goblin* (1946; N.Y., Feb. 22, 1947); *Cockcrow* (1953; Austin, Texas, April 22, 1954); *The Shepherdess and the Chimney Sweep* (1963; Fort Worth, Texas, Dec. 28, 1967); *Daisy* (Miami, Nov. 3, 1973). **ORCH.:** *Episodic Suite* (1936); Piano Concerto (1938; rev. 1971; Dallas, Feb. 28, 1976; arr. for 2 Pianos, 1971); *Folkways Symphony* (1948); *Remember the Alamo* for Symphonic or Full Band and Optional Narrator and Chorus (1965; in collaboration with C. Vashaw). **CHAMBER:** Piano trio, *Cornwall* (1955); String Quartet (1964); Suite for Wind Octet (1980); piano pieces. **VOCAL:** *Our Heritage* for Double Chorus and Orch. (1958); *Prairie Kaleidoscope,* song cycle for Soprano and String Quartet (1982).

Smith, Lawrence Leighton, American conductor and pianist; b. Portland, Oreg., April 8, 1936. He studied piano with Ariel Rubstein in Portland and then with Leonard Shure in N.Y.; enrolled in Portland State Univ. (B.S., 1956) and at the Mannes College of Music in N.Y. (B.M., 1959). In 1964 he received 1st prize at the Mitropoulos International Conducting Competition in N.Y.; was then assistant conductor at the Metropolitan Opera in N.Y. (1964–67). He was music director of the Westchester (N.Y.) Sym. Orch. (1967–69) and principal guest conductor of the Phoenix (Ariz.) Sym. Orch. (1971–73); also was music director of the Austin (Tex.) Sym. Orch. (1972–73). He served as music director of the Oregon Sym. Orch. in Portland (1973–80) and of the San Antonio Sym. Orch. (1980–85); also was artistic adviser and principal guest conductor of the North Carolina Sym. Orch. in Raleigh (1980–81) and music director of the Louisville Orch. (1983–94) and of the Music Academy of the West in Santa Barbara (from 1985). In addition to his appearances as a conductor in the U.S. and abroad, he continued to perform as a pianist, especially as an accompanist.

Smith, Leland (Clayton), American bassoonist, clarinetist, teacher, computer music publisher, and composer; b. Oakland, Calif., Aug. 6, 1925. He was a student of Milhaud (composition) at Mills College in Oakland, Calif. (1941–43; 1946–47), of Sessions (composition) and Bukofzer (musicology) at the Univ. of Calif. at Berkeley (M.A., 1948), and of Messiaen at the Paris Cons. (1948–49). After teaching at the Univ. of Calif. at Berkeley (1950–51), Mills College (1951–52), and the Univ. of Chicago (1952–58), he joined the faculty of Stanford Univ. in 1958 and was a prof. there from 1968 until his retirement in 1992. He was one of the founders and director of Stanford's computer music center, and he also served as an advisor to IRCAM in Paris. He pioneered in the development of a computer music publishing system he named SCORE. In 1971 he published what is believed to have been the first score ever printed entirely by a computer without added hand work. Since that time, he has perfected his system to such a high level of excellence that most of the principal music publishers of the world have chosen his SCORE system for their prestige publications. He later worked on projects to use his SCORE system and the Internet for complete music distribution systems. In addition to his lectures on the use of computers in both composing and printing, he publ. the *Handbook of Harmonic Analysis* (1963). In his compositions, Smith has traversed a modern course in which serial procedures are often utilized with occasional excursions into explorations of computer-generated sounds.

WORKS: OPERA: *Santa Claus* (Chicago, Dec. 9, 1955). **ORCH.:** Sym. (1951); *Concerto for Orchestra* (1956); *Divertimento* No. 2 for Chamber Orch. (1957). **CHAMBER:** Trumpet Sonata (1947); Trio for Flute, Cello, and Piano (1947); Trio for Violin, Trumpet, and Clarinet (1948); *Divertimento* No. 1 for 5 Instruments (1949); Woodwind Quintet (1951); 2 Duets for Clarinet and Bassoon (1953); Sonata for Heckelphone or Viola and Piano (1953); String Trio (1953); Quintet for Bassoon and Strings (1956); Trio for Oboe, Clarinet, and Bassoon (1960); Quartet for Horn, Violin, Cello, and Piano (1961); *Orpheus* for Guitar, Harp, and Harpsichord (1967); piano pieces. **VOCAL:** 2 motets (1948, 1954); *3 Pacifist Songs* for Soprano and Piano (1951–58); *Advice to Young Ladies* for Women's Voices, Clarinet, Violin, and Cello (1963); *Dona nobis pacem* for Chorus and Chamber Ensemble (1964); *Machines of Loving Grace* for Narrator, Bassoon, and Computer (1970).

Smith, (Joseph) Leo(pold), English-born Canadian cellist, teacher, writer on music, and composer; b. Birmingham, Nov. 26, 1881; d. Toronto, April 18, 1952. A child prodigy, he made his debut at the Birmingham Town Hall at age 8. Following instruction from Priestly in Birmingham and Fuchs in Manchester, he studied at the Royal Manchester College of Music and the Univ. of Manchester (Mus.B., 1902). He played in the Hallé Orch. in Manchester and in the Covent Garden orch. in London before emigrating to Canada in 1910. In 1911 he joined the faculty of the Toronto Cons. and served as the cellist in the Cons. Trio and later the Cons. String Quartet (1929–41). From 1932 to 1940 he was 1st cellist in the Toronto Sym. Orch., a post he also held in the Toronto Phil. In 1927 he joined the faculty of the Univ. of Toronto, where he was a prof. from 1938 to 1950. From 1950 until his death, he was the chief music critic of the *Toronto Globe and Mail*. In addition to serving as contributing ed. of the *Toronto Conservatory Quarterly Review* (1918–35), he publ. the books *Musical Rudiments* (Boston, 1920), *Music of the 17th and 18th Centuries* (Toronto, 1931), and *Elementary Part-Writing* (Oakville, Ontario, 1939). Smith utilized Canadian folk tunes in his compositions, although the English character of his music remained predominent. Among his works were orch. pieces, chamber music, piano pieces, many songs, and folk song arrangements.

BIBL.: P. McCarthy, *L. S.: A Biographical Sketch* (Toronto, 1956).

Smith, Leonard B(ingley), American cornetist, trumpeter, conductor, arranger, and composer; b. Poughkeepsie, N.Y., Sept. 5, 1915. After training with Ernest S. Williams, he studied at the N.Y. Military Academy, the Ernest Williams School of Music, N.Y. Univ., and the Curtis Inst. of Music in Philadelphia. He was first trumpeter in the Detroit Sym. Orch. (1936–42), and concurrently played during the summers with the Goldman Band in N.Y. In 1942 he enlisted in the U.S. Navy, serving as cornet soloist with the U.S. Navy Band in Washington, D.C. In 1946 he became founder-conductor of the Detroit Concert Band, which became one of the leading ensembles of its kind in the U.S. He composed and arranged numerous works for band, and also publ. the manual *The Treasury of Scales* (1952).

Smith, Moses, American music critic; b. Chelsea, Mass., March 4, 1901; d. Boston, July 27, 1964. He studied law at Harvard Univ. (graduated, 1924) and also music. He was music critic of the *Boston American* (1924–34) and of the *Boston Evening Transcript* (1934–39); then was music director of the Columbia Phonograph Co. (1939–42). In 1947 he publ. a controversial biography of Koussevitzky, who brought a libel suit for $1,000,000 against Smith and his publisher, claiming that the book described him as "generally incompetent, brutal to the musicians and a poseur." The suit, however, was dismissed.

BIBL.: K. DeKay, "Koussevitzky and His Biographers," *Koussevitzky Recordings Society*, newsletter, Vol. II, No. 1 (1988).

Smith, Patrick J(ohn), American music critic, author, and editor; b. N.Y., Dec. 11, 1932. He was educated at Princeton Univ. (A.B., 1955). He then pursued a career as a music critic, contributing articles to *High Fidelity, Musical America, Musical Quarterly*, and the *Musical Times*. From 1965 to 1985 he was book ed. of *Musical America*; also served as N.Y. music correspondent to the *Times* of London. He was president of the Music Critics Assn. (1977–81); was director of the Opera-Musical Theater Program of the NEA (from 1985). In 1988 he was appointed ed.-in-chief of *Opera News*. He publ. *The Tenth Muse, A Historical Study of the Opera Libretto* (N.Y., 1970) and *A Year at the Met* (N.Y., 1983).

Smith, Ronald, English pianist, writer on music, and composer; b. London, Jan. 3, 1922. He won the Sir Michael Costa Scholarship for composition and studied at the Royal Academy of Music in London, later completing his training in Paris. In 1942 he made his debut at a London Promenade concert. In 1951 he made his debut on the Continent as a soloist with Ansermet and the Orchestre de la Suisse Romande in Geneva, and subsequently appeared as a soloist with many orchs. He toured Australia in 1975, 1977, 1981, and 1983, the Far East in 1977, the U.S. and Canada in 1982, 1983, and 1987, and Russia in 1985. As a leading interpreter of the music of Alkan, he gave an Alkan centenary concert at London's Wigmore Hall in 1988. He also championed the music of Beethoven, Schubert, Chopin, Liszt, and the Russian masters of the 19th century. He publ. the major study *Alkan, Vol. I: The Enigma* (London, 1976) and *Alkan, Vol. II: The Music* (London, 1978). Among his other writings were *Alkan, The Man and His Music* (London, 1975) and *Alkan in Miniature* (London, 1978). He composed several orch. works.

Smith, William O(verton), American clarinetist, composer, and teacher; b. Sacramento, Calif., Sept. 22, 1926. He took up the clarinet as a child. After attending the Juilliard School of Music in N.Y. (1945–46), he pursued his training with Milhaud at Mills College in Oakland, Calif. (1946–47) and with Sessions at the Univ. of Calif. at Berkeley (B.A., 1950; M.A., 1952). He performed with various jazz musicians, including Dave Brubeck. He also played much contemporary music. Smith held the Prix de Paris (1951–53), the American Prix de Rome (1957), and a Guggenheim fellowship (1960). After teaching at the Univ. of Calif. at Berkeley (1952–53), the San Francisco Cons. of Music, and the Univ. of Southern Calif. in Los Angeles (1954–60), he was on the faculty of the Univ. of Wash. in Seattle (1966–88). In his extensive catalog of works, Smith has applied a variety of quaquaversal elements, from jazz to dodecaphony to electronics.

WORKS: ORCH.: Concerto for Trombone and Chamber Orch. (1949); Suite for Concert Band (1954); Concerto for Clarinet and Combo (1957); Concerto for Jazz Soloist and Orch. (1962); *Interplay* for Jazz Combo and Orch. (1964); *Tangents* for Clarinet and Orch. (1965); *Quadri* for Jazz Combo and Orch. (1968); *Agate* for Jazz Soloist and Jazz Orch. (1974); *Theona* for Jazz Combo and Orch. (1975); *Ecco!* for Clarinet and Orch. (1979); *Mu* for Clarinet and Small Orch. (1978); Concerto for Clarinet and Small Orch. (1985); *East Wind* for Wind Ensemble (1990); *Blue Shades* for Clarinet and Wind Ensemble (1993). **CHAMBER:** Clarinet Sonata (1948); Quintet for Clarinet and String Quartet (1950); 2 string quartets (1952, 1969); 2 trios for Clarinet, Violin, and Piano (1957, 1984); Quartet for Clarinet, Violin, and Piano (1958); *Explorations* for Jazz Combo and Tape (1963); *Ambiente* for Jazz Ensemble (1970); *Jazz Set* for Flute and Clarinet (1974); *Chronos* for String Quartet (1975); *Janus* for Trombone and Jazz Ensemble (1977); *Eternal Truths* for Wind Quintet (1979); *Pente* for Clarinet and String Quartet (1983); *Oni* for Clarinet, Keyboard, Percussion, and Electronics (1986); *Slow Motion* for Electric Clarinet and Computer Graphics (1987); *Illuminated Manuscript* for Wind Quintet and Computer Graphics (1987); *Serenade* for Clarinet, Violin, and Cello (1989); *Piccolo Concerto* for Flute, Clarinet, Violin, Cello, and Piano (1991); *Jazz Set* for Violin and Wind Quintet (1991); *Jazz Fantasy* for Jazz Improvisors and String Quartet (1992); *Ritual* for Clarinet, Viola, Percussion, Tape, and Projections (1992); *86910* for Clarinet and Digital Delay (1993); *Soli* for Flute, Clarinet, Violin, and Cello (1993); *Studies* for 2 Clarinets and Computers (1994). **VOCAL:** *My Father Moved Through Dooms of Love* for Chorus and Orch. (1955); *Songs to Myself Alone* for Soprano and Percussion (1970); *1* for Chorus and 6 Instruments (1975); *3* for Soprano, Clarinet, Trombone, and Dancer (1975); *Ilios* for Chorus, Winds, and Dancers (1977); *Manadala I* for Voices and Instruments (1977); *Intermission* for Soprano, Chorus, and Instruments (1978); *Enchantments* for Women's Voices and Flute (1983); *Sudana* for Voices and Oboe (1985); *Psyche* for Voices and Viola (1987); *Alleluia* for Chorus and/or Instruments (1990).

Smith Brindle, Reginald, English composer, teacher, and writer on music; b. Bamber Bridge, Lancashire, Jan. 5, 1917. He studied architecture before serving as a captain in the Royal Engineers (1940–46). He then studied music at the Univ. College of North Wales in Bangor (1946–49; B.Mus.; later Mus.D.), and subsequently with Pizzetti at the Accademia di Santa Cecilia in Rome (1949–52; composition diploma). He also studied privately with Dallapiccola in Florence (1949; 1952–53).

From 1956 to 1961 he was active with the RAI. In 1957 he joined the faculty of the Univ. College of North Wales, serving as a prof. there from 1967 to 1970. From 1970 to 1985 he was prof. of music at the Univ. of Surrey in Guildford. In addition to his many articles in journals, he publ. the books *Serial Composition* (1966), *Contemporary Percussion* (1970), *The New Music* (1975), and *Musical Composition* (1980). He utilized serial techniques in his scores until about 1970, all the while varying his style. Thereafter his path proved ever more eclectic as he refined his personal idiom of musical expression.

WORKS: OPERA: *The Death of Antigone* (1969). **ORCH.:** Concertino for Guitar and Chamber Orch. (1951); 2 syms. (1954, 1990); *Variations on a Theme by Dallapiccola* (1955); *An Epitaph for Alban Berg* (1955); *Symphonic Variations* (1957); *Cosmos* (1959); *Via Crucis* (1960); *Homage to H.G. Wells* (1960); Clarinet Concerto (1962); *Creation Epic* (1964); *Apocalypse* (1970); *Fons Bonitatis II* (1973); Guitar Concerto (1977); *Le Chant du Monde* (1984); *Recordando el gran maestro* (1987); *Grande Chaconne* (1993). **CHAMBER:** *3 Pieces* for Guitar and Piano (1956); *10-String Music* for Guitar and Cello (1957); *5 Sketches* for Violin and Guitar (1957); *String Quartet Music* (1958); Concerto for 5 Instruments and Percussion (1960); *Segments and Variants* for Wind Quintet (1965); *Andromeda* for Flute (1966); *Orion M42* for Percussion (1967); *Auriga* for Percussion (1967); *Concerto Breve Omnis Terra* for 8 Guitars and Percussion (1971); *Tubal Cain's Heritage* for Trombone and Piano (1973); *Concerto de angelis* for 4 Guitars (1973); *Concerto CumJubilo* for 3 Guitars (1974); *The Walls of Jericho* for Tuba (1975); *The Pillars of Karnak* for 4 Guitars (1979); *Las doces cuerdas* for 2 Guitars (1989); numerous solo guitar pieces. **ORGAN:** Organ Sym. (1979); *Missa de spiritus flammis* (1980); *Regina caeli* (1986); *The Harmonies of Peace* (1986); *Inner Refrains* (1988); *The Firmament Beyond* (1988).

Smither, Howard E(lbert), distinguished American musicologist; b. Pittsburg, Kansas, Nov. 15, 1925. He studied at Hamline Univ. in St. Paul, Minn. (A.B., 1950), and at Cornell Univ. with Grout and Austin (M.A., 1952; Ph.D., 1960, with the diss. *Theories of Rhythm in the Nineteenth and Twentieth Centuries, with a Contribution to the Theory of Rhythm for the Study of Twentieth Century Music*); also attended classes of Rudolf von Ficker at the Univ. of Munich (1953–54). He taught at the Oberlin Cons. of Music (1955–60), the Univ. of Kansas (1960–63), and Tulane Univ. (1963–68); in 1968 he was appointed a prof. of music at the Univ. of North Carolina at Chapel Hill; served as president of the American Musicological Soc. (1981–82). His major work is the valuable study *A History of the Oratorio* (3 vols., Chapel Hill, 1977–87); also contributed to *The New Grove Dictionary of Music and Musicians.*

Smithers, Don (LeRoy), American music historian, trumpeter, cornett player, and wind player; b. N.Y., Feb. 17, 1933. He studied at Hofstra Univ. (B.S., 1957), attended seminars in musicology at N.Y. Univ. (1957–58), took courses in Renaissance and Reformation history at Columbia Univ. (1958), and completed his training in music history at the Univ. of Oxford (Ph.D., 1967, with the diss. *The Baroque Trumpet: Instruments and Music c.1600–1700*). In 1965 he co-founded and became the first music director of the Oxford Pro Musica. He also gave many performances as a Baroque trumpeter, cornett player, and Renaissance wind player. After teaching at Syracuse Univ. (1966–75), he taught at the Royal Cons. of Music in The Hague (1975–80). In addition to his numerous articles in books and journals, he publ. *The Music and History of the Baroque Trumpet Before 1721* (1973) and *Number, Symbolism, and Allegory in the Late Works of Johann Sebastian Bach* (1975).

Smits van Waesberghe, Jos(eph Maria Antonius Franciscus), prominent Dutch musicologist; b. Breda, North Brabant, April 18, 1901; d. Amsterdam, Oct. 9, 1986. He studied at several Jesuit seminaries; became a priest; in addition to his training in philosophy (1922–26) and theology (1930–35), he also studied music with Louis van Tulder, Marius Monnikendam, and Johan Winnubst. He taught at Canisius College in Nijmegen (1935–37), Ignatius College in Amsterdam (1937–43), the Rotterdam Cons. (1939–43), the Amsterdam Cons. (1944–46), and the Univ. of Amsterdam, where he was a Privatdozent in music and medieval theory (1945–57) and a prof. (1957–71). He served as general secretary of the Koninklije Nederlandse Toonkunstenaars Vereniging (1945–48), founder-secretary of the Nederlandse Toonkunstenaars Raad (from 1948), and president of the Gregoriusvereniging (1958–67).

WRITINGS: *Klokken en klokkengieten in de middeleeuwen* (Tilburg, 1937); *Muziekgeschiedenis der middeleeuwen* (Tilburg, 1936–42); *Het Gregoriaans* (Amsterdam, 1943; Eng. tr., 1946); *Muziek en drama in de middeleeuwen* (Amsterdam, 1943; 2nd ed., 1954); *De uitzonderlijke plaats van de Ars Musica in de ontwikkeling der wetenschappen gedurende de eeuw der Karolingers* (The Hague, 1947); *Handleiding voor het lezen der neumletters van St. Gallen* (Tilburg, 1947); *School en muziek in de Middeleeuwen* (Amsterdam, 1949); *Melodieleer* (Amsterdam, 1950; Eng. tr., 1954); *Cymbala: Bells in the Middle Ages* (Rome, 1951); *De musico et musico-paedogogico Guidone Aretino* (Florence, 1953); *Oud-Nederlands paasspel* (Bussum, 1953); *Het toonkunstenaarsboek van Nederland* (Amsterdam, 1956); with P. Fischer and C. Maas, *The Theory of Music from the Carolingian Era up to 1400* (1961); *Musikerziehung* (Leipzig, 1969); *De muzische mens: Zijn motoriek* (Amsterdam, 1971).

BIBL.: *Organicae voces: Festschrift J. S.v.W. angeboten anlässlich seines 60. Geburtstages* (Amsterdam, 1963); *Diapason, de omnibus: Ausgewählte Aufsätze von J. S.v.W.: Festgabe zu seinem 75. Geburtstag* (Buren, 1976).

Smyth, Dame Ethel (Mary), eminent English composer; b. London, April 22, 1858; d. Woking, Surrey, May 8, 1944. She became a pupil of Reinecke and Jadassohn at the Leipzig Cons. in 1877, but soon turned to Heinrich von Herzogenberg for her principal training, following him to Berlin; her String Quintet was performed in Leipzig in 1884. She returned to London in 1888; presented her orchestral *Serenade* (April 26, 1890) and an overture, *Antony and Cleopatra* (Oct. 18, 1890). Her prestige as a composer rose considerably with the presentation of her *Mass* for Solo Voices, Chorus, and Orch. at the Albert Hall (Jan. 18, 1893). After that she devoted her energies to the theater. Her first opera, *Fantasio*, to her own libretto in German, after Alfred de Musset's play, was premiered in Weimar on May 24, 1898; this was followed by *Der Wald* (Berlin, April 9, 1902), also to her own German libretto; it was premiered in London in the same year, and then performed in N.Y. by the Metropolitan Opera on March 11, 1903. Her next opera, *The Wreckers*, was her most successful work; written originally to a French libretto, *Les Naufrageurs*, it was first performed in a German version as *Strandrecht* (Leipzig, Nov. 11, 1906); the composer herself tr. it into Eng., and it was staged in London on June 22, 1909; the score was revised some years later, and produced at Sadler's Wells, London, on April 19, 1939. She further wrote a comic opera, *The Boatswain's Mate* (London, Jan. 28, 1916); a one-act opera, described as a "dance-dream," *Fête galante* (Birmingham, June 4, 1923); and the opera *Entente cordiale* (Bristol, Oct. 20, 1926). Other works are a Concerto for Violin, Horn, and Orch. (London, March 5, 1927); *The Prison* for Soprano, Bass Chorus, and Orch. (London, Feb. 24, 1931); 2 string quartets (1884; 1902–12); Cello Sonata (1887); Violin Sonata (1887); 2 trios for Violin, Oboe, and Piano (1927); choral pieces, including *Hey Nonny No* for Chorus and Orch. (1911) and *Sleepless Dreams* for Chorus and Orch. (1912); songs; etc. Her music never overcame the strong German characteristics, in the general idiom as well as in the treatment of dramatic situations on the stage. At the same time, she was a believer in English national music and its potentialities. She was a militant leader for woman suffrage in England, for which cause she wrote *The March of the Women* (1911), the battle song of the WSPU After suffrage was granted, her role in the movement was officially acknowledged; in 1922 she was made a Dame Commander of the Order of the British Empire. She publ. a number of books in London, mostly autobiographical in nature: *Impressions That Remained* (2 vols., 1919; new ed., 1945); *Streaks of Life* (1921); *As Time Went On* (1936); *What Happened Next* (1940); also some humorous essays and reminiscences, *A Three-legged Tour in Greece* (1927); *A Final Burning of Boats* (1928); *Female Pipings in Eden* (1934); *Beecham and Pharaoh* (1935); *Inordinate (?) Affection* (1936).

BIBL.: K. Dale, "D. E. S.," *Music & Letters*, XXV (1944); C. St. John, *E. S.: A Biography* (N.Y., 1959); L. Collis, *Impetuous Heart: The Story of E. S.* (London, 1984).

Sobinov, Leonid (Vitalievich), celebrated Russian tenor; b. Yaroslavl, June 7, 1872; d. Riga, Oct. 14, 1934. He was an offspring of a middle-class family with peasant roots (his grandfather was an emancipated serf). He studied law at the Univ. of Moscow, where he also sang in a student choir. In 1892 he began to study voice with Dodonov and appeared professionally in a traveling Italian opera company in Moscow without interrupting his univ. study (1893–94); he graduated in law in 1894, and was appointed assistant advocate to a Moscow lawyer. Turning decisively to singing, he made his debut at the Bolshoi Theater in Moscow in 1897, and retained his connection with it during almost his entire career. In 1901 he also joined the Imperial Maryinsky Theater in St. Petersburg. His successes on the European stage were no less outstanding; he sang at La Scala in Milan (1904–06); from 1909 he also appeared in London, Paris, and Berlin. He was eloquent in the roles of Alfredo in *La Traviata*, Des Grieux in *Manon*, and Faust in Gounod's opera. His performance of Lensky in *Eugene Onegin* remained an unsurpassed model of Russian operatic lyricism. In his solo recitals he could squeeze the last fluid ounce out of Tchaikovsky's melancholy songs. No wonder that he was idolized by Russian audiences, particularly among the young and female; a whole tribe of "Sobinovites" appeared, and long queues formed before his concerts, willing to stand in line for hours in the hope of obtaining scarce tickets. He served as director of the Bolshoi Theater in 1917–18. In 1918–19 he gave recitals in and around Kiev, N. Slonimsky serving occasionally as his accompanist. He retired from the stage in 1924.

BIBL.: M. Lvov, *L. S.* (Moscow, 1951).

Socor, Matei, Romanian composer; b. Iaşi, Sept. 28, 1908; d. Bucharest, May 30, 1980. He studied theory with Castaldi at the Bucharest Cons. (1927–29) and composition with Karg-Elert at the Leipzig Cons. (1930–33). He then was active as a composer and teacher in his homeland.

WORKS: OPERA: *Conu Leonida fata cu reactiunea* (1976; Bucharest, Dec. 28, 1978). **ORCH.:** Concerto for Clarinet, Horn, Cello, and Orch. (1939); *Passacaglia* for Cello and Chamber Orch. (1944; also for Violin or Cello and Piano); Violin Concerto (1955). **CHAMBER:** Piano Sonata (1932); Concerto for Oboe, Clarinet, Bassoon, Violin, Viola, Cello, and Piano (1936); Wind Sextet (1968). **VOCAL:** *Mama*, poem for Mezzo-soprano, Chorus, and Orch. (1949); choruses; songs.

Söderblom, Ulf, Finnish conductor; b. Turku, Feb. 5, 1930. He received his training from Swarowsky at the Vienna Academy of Music (graduated, 1957). In 1957 he made his debut as a conductor at the Finnish National Opera in Helsinki, where he subsequently conducted regularly. From 1973 to 1993 he was its music director. During his long tenure, he became particularly known for his championship of contemporary operas. In 1983 he took the Finnish National Opera to the U.S. for performances at the Metropolitan Opera in N.Y. He also appeared as a guest conductor with many orchs. in Finland and abroad. On Feb. 25, 1992, he conducted the premiere of Sallinen's *Kullervo* at the Los Angeles Opera.

Söderlind, Ragnar, Norwegian composer; b. Oslo, June 27, 1945. He was a student of Baden (counterpoint), Hukvari (conducting), and Ulleberg (horn) at the Oslo Cons. (1966–67), of Bergman and Kokkonen (composition) at the Sibelius Academy in Helsinki (1967–68), and of Fladmoe (conducting) at the Oslo Cons. (graduate degree, 1976). For all practical purposes, he was autodidact in composition. Söderlind eschewed the predominant avant-garde course blazed by his contemporaries to embrace a style akin to the new Romanticist persuasion. Programmatic elements are found in several of his scores.

WORKS: DRAMATIC: *Esther and the Blue Serenity*, opera (1971–72); *Hedda Gabler*, symphonic/choreographic drama (1978); *Kristin Lavransdatter*, ballet (1982); *Victoria*, ballet music (1985–86); *Rose og Ravn*, opera (1989). **ORCH.:** *Jølsterslått* (1962–63); *Preludium* (1964–65); *Rokkomborre*, symphonic poem (1967); *Polaris*, symphonic vision (1967–69); *Trauermusik* (1968); *Fantasia borealis* (1969); *Sinfonia minimale* for Youth Orch. (1971); *International Rhapsody* (1971–72); *2 Pieces from the Desert* for Oboe and Small Orch. (1973–75); 4 syms.: No. 1 for Soprano and Orch. (1975–79), No. 2, *Sinfonia breve* (1981), No. 3, *Les illuminations symphonique*, for Soprano, Baritone, and Orch. (1984), and No. 4 (1991); *Amor et labor*, symphonic poem (1979); Sinfonietta for Brass and Percussion (1981–88); *Kom Havsvindar, Kom!*, symphonic poem (1982); *Toccata brillante over "Seier'n er Vår"* (1984); *Eystradalir*, nostalgic rhapsody (1984); *Ecstasy* for Strings (1988); Violin Concerto (1986–87); *The Hour of Love*, tone poem from the ballet *Victoria* (1990). **CHAMBER:** *Elegia I* for Cello (1966) and *II* for Violin (1966); *Intermezzo* for Percussionist (1967); *La poema battutta* for Percussion (1973); *2 Pieces from the Desert: A Study in Arabian Music* for Oboe and Piano (1973); String Quartet (1975); Quintet for 2 Trumpets, Horn, Trombone, and Tuba (1982); organ music, including *Ciacona* (1976–77) and *Preludium funebre* (1991). **VOCAL:** *Pietá* for Voice and String Orch. (1965–77); *Körsbärsblommor* for Baritone, Flute, English Horn, Cello, and 2 Percussion (1967–71); *La mort des pauvres* for Men's Chorus, Percussion, and 4 Trombones ad libitum (1969); *Vaer Utålmodig, Menneske* for Children's or Women's Chorus and Orch. (1977); *Olavs Hymne* (Olav's Hymn) for Voice, Chorus, and Orch. for the 80th birthday of King Olav I (1983); *Septemberlys* for Voice and Orch. (1983); *Nasadiya/Upphavshymnia* for 3 Choruses and Instrumental Ensemble (1984); *Pasjonskantate* for 2 Soloists, Chorus, and Orch. (1989); *Tranströmer-Svit* for Voice, Piano, 2 Percussion, and String Orch. (1991).

Soderlund, Gustav Frederic, Swedish-American music scholar, teacher, and composer; b. Göteborg, Jan. 25, 1881; d. Rochester, N.Y., Nov. 28, 1972. He studied piano and theory in Sweden. After teaching at the Valparaiso Cons. in Chile (1908–16), he settled in the U.S.; taught at the Univ. of Kansas (1919–27) and at the Eastman School of Music in Rochester, N.Y. (1928–47).

WORKS: ORCH.: *Nocturne* (1918); *Svithiod*, symphonic poem (1928); *Serenade* (1929); *Festival Symphony* (1942); *Suite* for Small Orch. (1965). **OTHER:** Chamber music; piano pieces.

WRITINGS: *Examples Illustrating the Development of Melodic Line and Contrapuntal Style from Greek Melody to Mozart* (Rochester, N.Y., 1932); *Examples of Gregorian Chant and Works by Orlandus Lassus and Giovanni Pierluigi Palestrina* (Rochester, N.Y., 1937; 3rd ed., 1946); *Direct Approach to Counterpoint in 16th Century Style* (N.Y., 1947).

Sodero, Cesare, Italian-American conductor and composer; b. Naples, Aug. 2, 1886; d. N.Y., Dec. 16, 1947. He studied with Alessandro Longo (piano) and Martucci (composition) at the Naples Cons. In 1907 he emigrated to the U.S. and settled in N.Y.; was a music director of the Edison Phonograph Co., the National Broadcasting Co., and the Mutual Broadcasting Co.; conducted the San Carlo Grand Opera Co. and the Philadelphia Grand Opera. He wrote an opera, *Ombre russe* (Venice, June 19, 1930); ballets; chamber music.

Söderström (-Olow), (Anna) Elisabeth, prominent Swedish soprano; b. Stockholm, May 7, 1927. She studied voice with Andreyeva von Skilondz in Stockholm; also took courses in languages and literary history at the Univ. of Stockholm, and received a thorough musical education at the Stockholm Royal Opera School. She made her operatic debut as Bastienne in

Mozart's *Bastien und Bastienne* at the Drottningholm Court Theater in Stockholm in 1947; became a member of the Royal Opera there in 1950. She made her first appearance in Salzburg as Ighino in Pfitzner's *Palestrina* in 1955; then at the Glyndebourne Festival as the Composer in *Ariadne auf Naxos* in 1957, becoming one of its most noted singers. She made her Metropolitan Opera debut in N.Y. as Susanna in *Le nozze de Figaro* on Oct. 30, 1959, and remained on its roster until 1964; subsequently pursued her career mainly in Europe until returning to the U.S. in 1977 to sing the title role in *Kat'a Kabanova* at the San Francisco Opera; returned to the Metropolitan Opera in 1983 as Ellen Orford in *Peter Grimes.* In 1988 she sang in the premiere of Argento's *The Aspern Papers* in Dallas. In 1990 she was appointed artistic director of the Drottningholm Court Theater. In 1991 she was awarded the Stora Culture Prize. Her extraordinary command of languages made her an outstanding concert and lieder artist, both in Europe and in North America. Among her notable roles were Fiordiligi, Tatyana, Sophie, Marie in *Wozzeck*, the Countess in *Capriccio*, Jenůfa, Emilia Marty in *The Makropoulos Affair*, and the Governess in *The Turn of the Screw.* She publ. a lighthearted autobiography, *I Min Tonart* (1978; Eng. tr., 1979, as *In My Own Key*).

Sofronitzky, Vladimir (Vladimirovich), esteemed Russian pianist and teacher; b. St. Petersburg, May 8, 1901; d. Moscow, Aug. 29, 1961. He studied with A. Lebedeva-Geshevich and A. Mikhailovsky in Warsaw, where he began his career while still a child; completed his training with Nikolayev at the Petrograd Cons. (graduated, 1921). He then toured throughout Europe; also was a prof. at the Leningrad Cons. (1936–42) and the Moscow Cons. (1942–61). He was greatly praised for his interpretations of Chopin and Scriabin; his performances of Liszt, Schumann, and Rachmaninoff were also notable.

BIBL.: V. Delson, *V. S.* (Moscow, 1959); Ya. Milstein, ed., *Vospominaniya o Sofronitskom* (Reminiscences of S.; Moscow, 1970).

Sohal, Naresh (Kumar), Indian composer; b. Harsipind, Punjab, Sept. 18, 1939. He took courses in science and mathematics at Punjab Univ. In 1962 he settled in England and pursued training in harmony and counterpoint at the London College of Music (1965) and in composition with Jeremy Dale Roberts (1965–66); then conducted research on micro-intervals under Alexander Goehr.

WORKS: ORCH.: *Asht Prahar* (1965; London, Jan. 17, 1970); Concerto for Harmonica, Percussion, and Strings (1966); *Aalaykhyam I* (1970; London, Nov. 27, 1971) and *II* (1972; London, Feb. 5, 1973); *Indra-Dhanush* (1973); *Dhyan I* for Cello and Small Orch. (1974); *Tandavva Nritya: Dance of Destruction and Re-creation* (1984). **CHAMBER:** *Hexand* for 6 Players (1971); *Octal* for 8 Players (1972); *Hexahedron* for 6 Players (1975); 2 brass quintets (1981, 1983). **VOCAL:** *Kavita I* for Soprano and 8 Players (1970), *II* for Soprano, Flute, and Piano (1972), and *III* for Soprano and Electric Double Bass (1972); *Surya* for 5 Soloists, Chorus, Flute, and 3 Percussion (1970); *Inscape* for 6 Solo Voices, Flute, Percussion, and Electronics (1979); *The Wanderer* for Baritone, Chorus, and Orch. (1981; London, Aug. 23, 1982); *From Gitanjali* for Bass-baritone and Orch. (N.Y., Sept. 12, 1985).

Söhngen, Oskar, learned German theologian and musicologist; b. Hottenstein, Dec. 5, 1900; d. Berlin, Aug. 28, 1983. He studied philosophy and theology (Ph.D., 1922) at the Univ. of Bonn; took courses in philosophy and theology (licentiae, 1924) at the Univ. of Marburg, where he also received instruction in musicology from Stephani. He was a priest in Cologne (1926–32), then an adviser to the Evangelical Church Synod (1932–33; 1935–69); also taught at the Berlin Hochschule für Musikerziehung und Kirchenmusik (1935–59). He devoted his efforts to the study and promotion of liturgical music; was an ed. of the journal *Kunst und Kirche.*

WRITINGS: *Pfarrer und Kirchenmusiker: Sinn und Richtlinien einer Arbeitsgemeinschaft* (Kassel, 1933); *Die neue Kirchenmusik: Wandlungen und Entscheidungen* (Berlin, 1937); ed. with C. Mahrenholz, *Handbuch zum Evangelischen Kirchengesangbuch* (Berlin, 1953); *Kämpfende Kirchenmusik: Die Bewährungsprobe der evangelischen Kirchenmusik im Dritten Reich* (Kassel and Basel, 1954); *Theologische Grundlagen der Kirchenmusik* (Kassel, 1958); *Wandel und Beharrung* (Berlin, 1965); *Theologie der Musik* (Kassel, 1967); *Erneuerte Kirchenmusik: Eine Streitschrift* (Göttingen, 1975).

Sojo, Vicente Emilio, Venezuelan conductor, pedagogue, ethnomusicologist, and composer; b. Guatire, Dec. 8, 1887; d. Caracas, Aug. 11, 1974. He studied music at the Academia de Bellas Artes in Caracas (1910). In 1921 he became a prof. of theory at the Escuela Superior de Música in Caracas. In 1937 he founded the Orquesta Sinfónica Venezuela and the choral ensemble Orfeón Lamas, which became of prime importance in the musical culture of Venezuela. Sojo was also active in national ethnomusicology; he collected and harmonized several hundred Venezuelan folk songs and church hymns of the colonial period. He composed mainly sacred music, motets, and organ pieces.

BIBL.: R. Fernández, *V.E. S.* (Caracas, 1968).

Sokola, Miloš, Czech composer; b. Bučovice, Moravia, April 18, 1913; d. Malé Kyšice, Sept. 27, 1976. He studied composition with Petrželka and violin with O. Vávra at the Brno Cons. (1929–38); had further composition studies at the Prague Cons. with Novák (1938–40) and Kříčka (1942–44). From 1942 to 1973 he was a violinist in the Prague National Theater orch.

WORKS: OPERA: *Marnotratný syn* (The Prodigal Son; 1948; Olomouc, 1963). **ORCH.:** *9 Variations on a Theme by Vítězslava Kaprálová* (1952; Prague, Feb. 17, 1957; from Kaprálová's *April Preludes*); Violin Concerto (1952); *Devátý květen* (The Ninth of May), symphonic poem (1960); Concerto for Organ and Strings (1971); Piano Concertino (1972). **CHAMBER:** 5 string quartets (1944; with Solo Tenor, 1946; 1955; 1964; 1971); Violin Sonata (1972); Wind Quintet (1973). **KEYBOARD: PIANO:** *5 Miniatures* (1931); Sonata (1946); *Valses* (1953); *12 Preludes* (1954); *Suite* for Piano, Left-hand (1972). **ORGAN:** *Toccata quasi Passacaglia* (1964); *B-A-C-H Studies* (1972); *Andante cantabile* (1973).

Sokoloff, Nicolai, Russian-born American conductor; b. near Kiev, May 28, 1886; d. La Jolla, Calif., Sept. 25, 1965. He was taken to the U.S. as a child, and studied violin with Loeffler in Boston; played violin in the Boston Sym. Orch. In 1907 he went to Europe to complete his studies. After serving as concertmaster of the Russian Sym. Orch. in N.Y., he decided to settle in the U.S. in 1914 and became a naturalized American citizen; became music director of the San Francisco Phil. in 1914, then served as the first music director of the Cleveland Orch. (1918–33). He was director of the Federal Music Project (1935–38) and music director of the Seattle Sym. Orch. (1938–40); later was music director of the La Jolla Arts Assn.

Solares, Enrique, Guatemalan pianist and composer; b. Guatemala City, July 11, 1910. He studied piano with Salvador Ley in Guatemala and composition with Moulaert in Brussels, Kříčka in Prague (1936–39), and Casella in Rome (1939–42). He returned to Guatemala in 1943 and taught piano; then was a consular officer in Guatemalan embassies in Rome, Brussels, Madrid, and Paris. His early compositions are set in Baroque forms; later he experimented with serial techniques.

WORKS: *Ricercare sobre el nombre de BACH* for Strings (1941); *Toccatina* for Guitar (1946); *Partita* for Strings (1947); Sonata for Solo Violin (1958); *Fantasia* for Guitar (1959); *Idea con 15 Deformaciones* for Piano (1962); *7 Traversuras* for Piano (1969); *12 Microtransparencias* for Piano (1970).

Soler, Josep, Catalan composer; b. Barcelona, March 25, 1935. He studied composition with Leibowitz in Paris (1959) and with Taltabull in Barcelona (1960–64). In 1977 he was appointed to the staff of the Barcelona Cons.

WORKS: OPERAS: *Agamemnon* (1960); *Edipo y Iocasta* (1972; Barcelona, Oct. 30, 1974); *Jesús de Nazaret* (1974–78).

ORCH.: *Danae* for Strings (1959; rev. 1969; Lisbon, June 23, 1977); *Orpheus* for Piano and Orch. (1965; rev. 1974); *Quetzalcoatl* for Flute and Chamber Orch. (1966); 2 syms.: *The Solar Cycle I* (1967) and *II* (1969; rev. 1977); *Diaphonia* for 17 Wind Instruments (1968); Piano Concerto (1969); Cello Concerto (1973); *Requiem* for Percussion and Orch. (1974–75; Kassel, Sept. 18, 1977); *Apuntava l'alba* (1975; Barcelona, Feb. 5, 1976). **CHAMBER:** Trio for 2 Violins and Piano (1961); Piano Trio (1964); 3 string quartets (1966, 1971, 1975); *Lachrymae* for 11 Instruments (1967); String Trio (1968); *Musica triste* for Guitar (1968); Concerto for Harpsichord, Oboe, English Horn, Bass Clarinet, Viola, and Cello (1969); *Sounds in the Night* for 6 Percussionists (1969); *Inferno* for Chamber Ensemble (1970); *Tanido de Falsas* for Guitar and Percussion (1971); *Noche oscura* for Organ and Percussion (1971); *Harmonices mundi*, in 3 vols.: No. 1 for Piano, and Nos. 2 and 3 for Organ (1977). **VOCAL:** *Cantata Ioel Prophetae*, chamber cantata (1960); *3 Erotic Songs* for Chorus (1976); *Shakespeare Lieder* for Tenor and Orch. (1976–77); songs.

Sollberger, Harvey (Dene), American flutist, conductor, teacher, and composer; b. Cedar Rapids, Iowa, May 11, 1938. He studied composition with Philip Bezanson and Eldon Obrecht at the Univ. of Iowa (B.A., 1960) and also received instruction in flute from Betty Bang Mather; completed his training in composition with Beeson and Luening at Columbia Univ. (M.A., 1964); held 2 Guggenheim fellowships (1969, 1973). With Charles Wuorinen, he founded the Group for Contemporary Music in N.Y. in 1962; appeared regularly with it as a flutist and conductor; also toured as a flutist and conductor in the U.S. and Europe. He served on the faculties of Columbia Univ. (1965–83), the Manhattan School of Music (1971–83), the Philadelphia College of the Performing Arts (1980–82), and the Indiana Univ. School of Music (1983–92), where he also directed its new-music ensemble. In 1992 he became a prof. of music at the Univ. of Calif. at San Diego. His music reveals an imaginatively applied serial method.

WORKS: *Grand Quartet* for Flutes (1962); *2 Oboes Troping* (1963); *Chamber Variations* for 12 Players and Conductor (1964); *Music for Sophocles' Antigone*, electronic music (1966); *Fanfare Mix Transpose*, electronic music (1968); *As Things Are and Become* for String Trio (1969; rev. 1972); *Musica transalpina*, 2 motets for Soprano, Baritone, and 9 Players (1970); *Elegy for Igor Stravinsky* for Flute, Cello, and Piano (1971); *The 2 and the 1* for Amplified Cello and 2 Percussionists (1972); *Folio*, 11 pieces for Bassoon (1974–76); *Sunflowers* for Flute and Vibraphone (1976); *Flutes and Drums* for 8 Flutes, 8 Percussionists, and 4 Double Basses (1977); *Music for Prepared Dancers* for Dancers, Flute, Violin, and Percussion (1978); *6 Quartets* for Flute and Piano (1981); *The Humble Heart/CAT Scan* for Woodwind Quintet (1982); *Interrupted Night* for 5 Instruments (1983); *Killapata/Chaskapata* for Solo Flute and Flute Choir (1983); *Double Triptych* for Flute and Percussion (1984); *3 or 4 Things I Know about the Oboe*, chamber concerto for Oboe and 13 Players (1986); *original substance/manifests/traces* for Flute, Harp, Guitar, Piano, and Percussion (1987); *Persian Golf* for Strings (1987); *Quodlibetudes* for Flute (1988); *Aurelian Echoes* for Flute and Alto Flute (1989); *. . . from winter's frozen stillness*, trio for Violin, Cello, and Piano (1990); *Passages* for Soloists, Chorus, and Orch. (1990); *Mutable Duo* for Flute, Clarinet, Violin, Cello, Piano, and Percussion (1991); *The Advancing Moment* for Flute, Clarinet, Violin, Cello, Piano, and Percussion (1993); *CIAO, Arcosanti!* for 8 Instruments (1994); *In Terra Aliena* for 5 Soloists and Orch. (1995).

Sollertinsky, Ivan (Ivanovich), brilliant Russian musicologist and music critic; b. Vitebsk, Dec. 3, 1902; d. Novosibirsk, Feb. 11, 1944. He studied Hispanic philosophy at the Univ. of Petrograd (1919–24) and drama at the Inst. for the History of the Arts (graduated, 1923), subsequently pursuing postgraduate courses (1926–29); also took conducting lessons with Malko. He was active as a lecturer and music critic in Leningrad, where he later taught at the Cons. (from 1936). He showed profound understanding of the problems of modern music and was one of the earliest supporters of Shostakovich; publ. numerous articles dealing with Soviet music in general; M. Druskin ed. 4 vols. of his writings (Leningrad, 1946; 1956, 2nd ed., 1963; 1973; 1973).

BIBL.: L. Mikheeva, *I.I. S.* (Leningrad, 1988).

Solomon (actually, **Solomon Cutner**), outstanding English pianist; b. London, Aug. 9, 1902; d. there, Feb. 2, 1988. He studied with Mathilde Verne, making a sensational debut as a child prodigy as soloist in Tchaikovsky's 1st Piano Concerto in London (June 30, 1911); later studied in Paris with Lévy and Dupré, and then resumed his career in 1923, adopting his first name for his concert engagements. In 1926 he made his U.S. debut, and in subsequent years toured all over the world as a soloist with orchs., recitalist, and chamber music artist. His remarkable career was cut short at the height of his interpretative powers when he was stricken by an incapacitating illness in 1955. In 1946 he was made a Commander of the Order of the British Empire. His performances of the classics were particularly esteemed; he eschewed virtuosity for its own sake, opting instead for intellectually insightful and unmannered interpretations of the highest order.

Solomon, Izler, American conductor; b. St. Paul, Minn., Jan. 11, 1910; d. Fort Wayne, Ind., Dec. 6, 1987. He took violin lessons with Myron Poliakin in Philadelphia and Michael Press in N.Y.; then studied at Michigan State College (1928–31). He made his debut as a conductor with the Lansing (Mich.) Civic Orch. on March 17, 1932; led that orch. until 1936; then conducted the Illinois Sym. Orch. (1936–42) and the Columbus (Ohio) Phil. (1941–49); was guest conductor of the Israel Phil. during its American tour in 1951. His major post, which established his reputation, was as music director of the Indianapolis Sym. Orch. (1956–75), which he brought to a level of excellence. In his programs he included many modern American works. In 1976 he suffered a stroke, which ended his career.

Solomon, Maynard (Elliott), American recording executive and writer on music; b. N.Y., Jan. 5, 1930. He was educated in N.Y. at the High School of Music and Art and at Brooklyn College (A.B., 1950); then pursued postgraduate studies at Columbia Univ. (1950–51). He was co-founder and co-owner of the Vanguard Recording Soc., Inc., of N.Y. (1950–86); was on the faculty of the City Univ. of N.Y. (1979–81) and served as a visiting prof. at the State Univ. of N.Y. at Stony Brook (1988–89), Columbia Univ. (1989–90), Harvard Univ. (1991–92), and Yale Univ. (1994–95). In 1978 and 1989 he won ASCAP-Deems Taylor Awards. He contributed many articles on Beethoven, Schubert, and other composers to the *Musical Quarterly, Music & Letters, 19th Century Music, Beethoven Studies*, the *Beethoven-Jahrbuch*, the *Journal of the American Musicological Society*, and other publications, and also served as assoc. ed. of *American Imago*. He ed. "Beethoven's Tagebuch 1812–1818," in *Beethoven Studies 3* (London, 1982).

WRITINGS: *Marxism and Art* (1973); *Beethoven* (1977); *Myth, Creativity and Psychoanalysis* (1978); *Beethoven Essays* (1988); *Mozart: A Life* (1994).

Solomon, Yonty, South African-born English pianist and teacher; b. Cape Town, May 3, 1938. He was a pupil of Cameron Taylor at the Univ. of Cape Town (B.Mus., 1958). In 1963 he won the Beethoven International Award and settled in London, where he continued his training with Dame Myra Hess. He later studied with Agosti in Rome and Rosen in the U.S. He appeared as a soloist with orchs. in Europe, North America, South Africa, and Israel, and also gave recitals. Solomon was also active as a prof. at the Royal College of Music and gave various master classes in other locales. In addition to the standard piano literature, he championed many composers of the modern age, among them Janáček, Ives, Schoenberg, Prokoviev, Sorabji, Bennett, and Josephs.

Soloviev-Sedoy, Vasili (Pavlovich), Russian composer; b. St. Petersburg, April 25, 1907; d. Moscow, Dec. 2, 1979. He learned to play the balalaika, guitar, and piano before pursuing studies at the Mussorgsky Music School (1929–31) and the Leningrad Cons. (1931–36). He was active as a pianist, playing improvisations on the radio and accompanying exercises in the Leningrad Studio of Creative Gymnastics. During World War II, he organized a series of theatrical productions for the Soviet army. He was a member of the Supreme Soviet in the 3rd, 4th, and 5th congresses. In 1975 he was awarded the order of Hero of Socialist Labor. He was regarded in Russia as one of the most expert composers of Soviet songs, some of which acquired immense popularity; one of them, "Moscow Nights," became a musical signature of daily news broadcasts on the Soviet radio. In all, he wrote over 700 songs. He was able to synthesize the melos of Russian folk songs with revolutionary ballads and marching rhythms. His other works include an opera, several operettas, the ballet *Taras Bulba* (Leningrad, Dec. 12, 1940; rev. 1953), a few orch. pieces, film scores, and piano music.

BIBL.: A. Sokhor, *V.P. S.-S.* (Leningrad and Moscow, 1952; 2nd ed., 1967); Yu. Kremlyov, *V.P. S.-S.: Ocherk zhizni i tvorchestva* (V.P. S.-S.: Outline of His Life and Work; Leningrad, 1960).

Solti, Sir Georg (actually, **György**), eminent Hungarian-born English conductor; b. Budapest, Oct. 21, 1912. He began to study the piano when he was 6, making his first public appearance in Budapest when he was 12; at 13, he enrolled there at the Franz Liszt Academy of Music, studying piano with Dohnányi and, briefly, with Bartók; took composition courses with Kodály. He graduated at the age of 18, and was engaged by the Budapest Opera as a répétiteur; also served as an assistant to Bruno Walter (1935) and Toscanini (1936, 1937) at the Salzburg Festivals. On March 11, 1938, he made a brilliant conducting debut at the Budapest Opera with Mozart's *Le nozze di Figaro*; however, the wave of anti-Semitism in Hungary under the reactionary military rule forced him to leave Budapest (he was Jewish). In 1939 he went to Switzerland, where he was active mainly as a concert pianist; in 1942 he won the Concours International de Piano in Geneva; finally, in 1944, he was engaged to conduct concerts with the orch. of the Swiss Radio. In 1946 the American occupation authorities in Munich invited him to conduct *Fidelio* at the Bavarian State Opera; his success led to his appointment as its Generalmusikdirektor, a position he held from 1946 to 1952. In 1952 he became Generalmusikdirektor in Frankfurt am Main, serving as director of the Opera and conductor of the Museumgesellschaft Concerts. He made his U.S. debut with the San Francisco Opera on Sept. 25, 1953, conducting *Elektra*; later conducted the Chicago Sym. Orch., the N.Y. Phil., and at the Metropolitan Opera in N.Y., where he made his first appearance on Dec. 17, 1960, with *Tannhäuser*. He was then engaged as music director of the Los Angeles Phil., but the project collapsed when the board of trustees refused to grant him full powers in musical and administrative policy. In 1960–61 he was music director of the Dallas Sym. Orch. In the meantime, he made his Covent Garden debut in London in 1959; in 1961 he assumed the post of music director of the Royal Opera House there, retaining it with great distinction until 1971. In 1969 he became music director of the Chicago Sym. Orch., and it was in that capacity that he achieved a triumph as an interpreter and orch. builder, so that the "Chicago sound" became a synonym for excellence. He showed himself an enlightened disciplinarian and a master of orch. psychology, so that he could gain and hold the confidence of the players while demanding from them the utmost in professional performance. Under his direction the Chicago Sym. Orch. became one of the most celebrated orchs. in the world. He took it to Europe for the first time in 1971, eliciting glowing praise from critics and audiences; subsequently led it on a number of acclaimed tours there; also took it to N.Y. for regular appearances at Carnegie Hall. He held the additional posts of music adviser of the Paris Opéra (1971–73) and music director of the Orch. de Paris (1972–75), which he took on a tour of China in 1974; he served as principal conductor and artistic director of the London Phil. from 1979 to 1983; was then accorded the title of conductor emeritus. During all these years, he retained his post with the Chicago Sym. Orch., while continuing his appearances as a guest conductor with European orchs. In 1983 he conducted the *Ring* cycle at the Bayreuth Festival, in commemoration of the 100th anniversary of the death of Richard Wagner. Solti retained his prestigious position with the Chicago Sym. Orch. until the close of the 100th anniversary season in 1990–91, and subsequently held the title of Laureate Conductor. In 1992–93 he served as artistic director of the Salzburg Festival. In 1968 he was made an honorary Commander of the Order of the British Empire; in 1971 he was named an honorary Knight Commander of the Order of the British Empire. In 1972 he became a British subject and was knighted, assuming the title of Sir Georg. In 1992 he was awarded Germany's Grosses Verdienstskreuz mit Stern und Schulterband. In honor of his 80th birthday in 1992 the Vienna Phil. awarded him the first Hans Richter Medal. In 1993 President Clinton awarded him the National Medal of Arts and he was accorded honors at the Kennedy Center in Washington, D.C. Solti is generally acknowledged as a superlative interpreter of the symphonic and operatic repertoire. He is renowned for his performances of Wagner, Verdi, Mahler, Richard Strauss, and other Romantic masters; he also conducts notable performances of Bartók, Stravinsky, Schoenberg, and other composers of the 20th century. His recordings received innumerable awards.

BIBL.: W. Furlong, *Season with S.: A Year in the Life of the Chicago Symphony* (N.Y. and London, 1974); P. Robinson, *S.* (London, 1979); J. von Rhein, "S. at Seventy-five," *Ovation* (Nov. 1987).

Soltys, Adam, Polish pedagogue and composer, son of **Mieczyslaw Soltys**; b. Lemberg, July 4, 1890; d. there (Lwów), July 6, 1968. He studied with his father, and later with Georg Schumann in Berlin; also took courses in musicology at the Univ. of Berlin with Kretzschmar and Johannes Wolf (Ph.D., 1921). Returning to Poland, he served as director of the Lwów Cons. (1930–39) and again after World War II. His compositions include 2 syms. (1927, 1946); the symphonic poems *Slowanie* (1949), *O pokoj* (About Peace; 1953), and *Z gór i dolin* (From Mountains and Valleys; 1960); numerous teaching pieces for violin and for piano.

Soltys, Mieczyslaw, Polish conductor, teacher, and composer, father of **Adam Soltys**; b. Lemberg, Feb. 7, 1863; d. there (Lwów), Nov. 12, 1929. He studied in Lemberg and Paris. Returning to Lemberg in 1899, he was director of the Cons. and of the Musical Society; also wrote music criticism.

WORKS: OPERAS: *Rzeczpospolita Babińska* (Republic of Babin; 1894; Lemberg, April 27, 1905); *Panie Kochanku* (1890; Lwów, May 3, 1924) *Opowieść kresowa* or *Opowieść ukraińska* (A Ukraine Story; 1909; Lemberg, March 8, 1910); *Nieboska komedia* (1925). **OTHER:** 2 syms.; 3 symphonic poems; *Concerto religioso* for Piano and Orch.; oratorios; choruses; piano pieces; songs; organ music.

Solum, John (Henry), American flutist and teacher; b. New Richmond, Wis., May 11, 1935. He studied flute with William Kincaid in Philadelphia (1953–58) and was a student at Princeton Univ. (B.A., 1957); he also received instruction in harmony, counterpoint, composition, and musicology. He made his debut in 1953. In 1957 he appeared as a soloist with the Philadelphia Orch. In 1959 he made his N.Y. recital debut. In subsequent years, he toured all over the world as a soloist with orchs., as a chamber music artist, and as a recitalist. He taught at Vassar College (1969–71). After teaching at Indiana Univ. (1973) and the Oberlin (Ohio) College Cons. of Music (1976), he again taught at Vassar College (from 1977). From 1979 to 1989 he was co-director of the Bath (England) Summer School of Baroque Music. He also was active with the Connecticut Early Music Festival from 1982. His repertoire ranges from Bach, Handel, Telemann, and Vivaldi to Honegger, Ibert, Jolivet, and Sir Malcolm Arnold.

Solzhenitsyn, Ignat, Russian pianist; b. Moscow, Sept. 23, 1972. He is the son of the great novelist Aleksandr Solzhenitsyn. He accompanied his family in exile while still an infant, settling in Vermont; began piano lessons at age 9 with Chonghyo Shin. After further studies with Luis Battle, he went to London in 1987 to pursue training with Maria Curcio and at the Purcell School of Music; subsequently studied piano with Gary Graffman at the Curtis Inst. of Music in Philadelphia, where he also received training in conducting. He was only 11 when he began appearing as a soloist with orchs. and as a recitalist in the U.S. In 1989 he made his London debut. After appearing as soloist in Shostakovich's 1st Piano Concerto with Rostropovich and the National Sym. Orch. on its tour in Alaska in 1992, he accompanied them to Moscow in 1993, receiving critical acclaim. He also played throughout the Continent, in Japan, and in Central America. In 1994 he was awarded an Avery Fisher Career Grant.

Somary, Johannes (Felix), American organist, conductor, and composer; b. Zürich (of American parents), April 7, 1935. He was taken to the U.S. as a child, and received his musical training at Yale College (B.A., 1957) and with Quincy Porter and Keith Wilson at the Yale Univ. School of Music (M.M., 1959). In 1961 he founded the Amor Artis Chorale and Orch., which he conducted in much Baroque music; led the U.S. premieres of Handel's *Esther* in 1961, *Theodora* in 1963, and *Susanna* in 1965; also was a guest conductor in the U.S. and Europe. From 1971 he was chairman of the arts and music dept. at the Horace Mann School in N.Y. He also was conductor of the Fairfield County Chorale (from 1975), the Great Neck Choral Soc. (from 1982), and the Taghkanic Chorale (from 1992). He composed orch. works, choral pieces, songs, and chamber music.

Somer, (Ruth) Hilde, Austrian-born American pianist; b. Vienna, Feb. 11, 1922; d. Freeport, Bahamas, Dec. 24, 1979. She studied with her mother; in 1938 the family went to the U.S. and she enrolled at the Curtis Inst. of Music in Philadelphia as a student of Serkin; also took private lessons with Arrau. She cultivated modern works; commissioned piano concertos from John Corigliano, Jr. (San Antonio, April 7, 1968) and Antonio Tauriello (Washington, D.C., June 29, 1968), the 2nd Piano Concerto by Alberto Ginastera (Indianapolis, March 22, 1973), and a "spatial concerto" by Henry Brant (Tucson, Ariz., Nov. 16, 1978). She also gave a series of concerts of piano music by Scriabin, with color images projected upon the screen to suggest Scriabin's own ideas of a synthesis of sounds and colors.

Somers, Harry (Stewart), outstanding Canadian composer and pianist; b. Toronto, Sept. 11, 1925. He studied piano with Dorothy Hornfelt (1939–41), Reginald Godden (1942–43), Weldon Kilburn (1945–48), and E.R. Schmitz (1948) in Toronto; also attended classes in composition with John Weinzweig (1941–43; 1945–49); then studied with Milhaud in Paris (1949–50). Returning to Canada, he eked out a meager living as a music copyist, finally receiving commissions in 1960; also became active as a broadcaster. In 1972 he was made a Companion of the Order of Canada. His historical opera, *Louis Riel*, was performed at the Kennedy Center in Washington, D.C., on Oct. 23, 1975, as part of America's Bicentennial celebration. His musical idiom is quaquaversal, absorbing without prejudice ancient, national, and exotic resources, from Gregorian chant to oriental scales, from simple folkways to electronic sound, all handled with fine expertise.

WORKS: DRAMATIC: *The Fool*, chamber opera for 4 Soloists and Chamber Orch. (1953; Toronto, Nov. 15, 1956); *The Homeless Ones*, television operetta (CBC-TV, Toronto, Dec. 31, 1955); *The Fisherman and His Soul*, ballet (Hamilton, Nov. 5, 1956); *Ballad*, ballet (Ottawa, Oct. 29, 1958); *The House of Atreus*, ballet (1963; Toronto, Jan. 13, 1964); *Louis Riel*, historical opera (Toronto, Sept. 23, 1967); *Improvisation*, theater piece for Narrator, Singers, Strings, any number of Woodwinds, 2 Percussionists, and Piano (Montreal, July 5, 1968); *And*, choreography for Dancers, Vocal Soloists, Flute, Harp, Piano, and 4 Percussionists (CBC-TV, Toronto, 1969); *Death of Enkidu: Part I*, chamber opera, after the epic of Gilgamesh (Toronto, Dec. 7, 1977); *Mario and the Magician*, opera (1991). **ORCH.:** *Scherzo* for Strings (1947); 3 piano concertos: No. 1 (Toronto, March, 1949), No. 2 (Toronto, March 12, 1956), and No. 3 (1994–95); *North Country* for Strings (Toronto, Nov. 10, 1948); *Suite* for Harp and Chamber Orch. (Toronto, Dec. 11, 1952); *The Case of the Wayward Woodwinds* for Chamber Orch. (1950); Sym. No. 1 (1951; Toronto, April 27, 1953); *Passacaglia and Fugue* (1954); *Little Suite for String Orchestra on Canadian Folk Songs* (1955); *Fantasia* (Montreal, April 1, 1958); *Lyric* (Washington, D.C., April 30, 1961); *5 Concepts* (1961; Toronto, Feb. 15, 1962); *Movement* (CBC-TV, Toronto, March 4, 1962); *Stereophony* (Toronto, March 19, 1963); *The Picasso Suite*, light music for Small Orch. (1964; Saskatoon, Feb. 28, 1965); *Those Silent Awe-filled Spaces* (Ottawa, Feb. 2, 1978); *Variations* for Strings (1979); *Elegy, Transformation, Jubilation: In Memoriam Four Suicides* (1981); *Concertante* for Violin, String Orch., and Percussion (1982); Guitar Concerto (1984). **CHAMBER:** 3 string quartets (1943, 1950, 1959); *Suite* for Percussion (1947); *Mime* for Violin and Piano (1948); *Rhapsody* for Violin and Piano (1948); Wind Quintet (1948); Trio for Flute, Violin, and Cello (1950); 2 violin sonatas (1953, 1955); *Movement* for Wind Quintet (1957); Sonata for Solo Guitar (1959); *Theme and Variations* for any combination of Instruments (1964); *Music* for Violin (1974); *Movement* for String Quartet (1982); *Fanfare to J.S. B.* for Brass Quintet (1984); *11 Miniatures* for Oboe and Piano (1994). **PIANO:** *Strangeness of Heart* (1942); *Flights of Fancy* (1944); 5 sonatas (*Testament of Youth*, 1945; 1946; 1950; 1950; 1957); *3 Sonnets* (1946); *Solitudes* (1947); *4 Primitives* (1949); *12 × 12*, fugues (1951). **VOCAL:** *5 Songs for Dark Voice* for Contralto and Orch. (Stratford, Ontario, Aug. 11, 1956); *At the Descent from the Cross* for Bass and 2 Guitars (1962); *12 Miniatures* for Soprano, Recorder or Flute, Viola da Gamba, and Spinet (1963); *Crucifixion* for Chorus, English Horn, 2 Trumpets, Harp, and Percussion (1966); *Kuyas* for Soprano, Flute, and Percussion (1967; adapted from Louis Riel); *Kyrie* for Soloists, Chorus, Flute, Oboe, Clarinet, Cello, 3 Trumpets, Piano, and 6 Percussionists (1970–72); *Voiceplay* for Male or Female Singer/Actor (Toronto, Nov. 14, 1972; Cathy Berberian, soloist); *Zen, Yeats and Emily Dickinson* for Female and Male Narrators, Soprano, Flute, Piano, and Tape (1975); *Churachurum* for Chorus, Flute, Harp, Piano, 4 Percussion, and 8 Loudspeakers (1985); choruses; songs.

BIBL.: B. Cherney, *H. S.* (Toronto, 1975).

Somervell, Sir Arthur, English music educator and composer; b. Windermere, June 5, 1863; d. London, May 2, 1937. He studied the classics at King's College, Cambridge (B.A., 1883), where he also took courses in music with Stanford; after further training at the Berlin Hochschule für Musik (1883–85), he studied at the Royal College of Music in London (1885–87); then received private instruction from Parry. He taught at the Royal College of Music (1893–1901); then was active as an inspector of music. He was knighted in 1929. He was at his best as a composer of vocal music.

WORKS: ORCH.: *Normandy*, symphonic variations (1912); *Thalassa*, sym. (1912); *Highland Concerto* for Piano and Orch. (1921); Violin Concerto (1932). **VOCAL: CHORAL:** 2 Masses (1891, 1907); *Joan of Arc* (1893); *Ode to the Sea* (1897); *Ode on the Intimations of Immortality* (1907); *Christmas*, cantata (1926). Also song cycles. **OTHER:** Piano pieces; numerous educational pieces for schools.

Somfai, László, Hungarian musicologist; b. Jászladány, Aug. 15, 1934. He studied at the Budapest Academy of Music as a student of Szabolcsi and Bartha; received his Ph.D. there in 1959. He served as a music librarian at the National Széchényi Library (1958–62); in 1963 he joined the staff of the Bartók Archives (from 1969 known as the Inst. of Musicology of the Hungarian Academy of Sciences); became its director in 1972. He also taught at the Budapest Academy of Music (from 1969; prof. from 1980) and was ed. of the archive series Documenta Bartókiana (from 1972).

WRITINGS: *Haydn als Opernkapellmeister: Die Haydn-Dokumente der Esterházy-Opernsammlung* (with D. Bartha; Budapest and Mainz, 1960); *Joseph Haydn: Sein Leben in zeitgenössischen Bildern* (Budapest and Kassel, 1966; Eng. tr., 1969); *Anton Webern* (Budapest, 1968); *The Keyboard Sonatas of Joseph Haydn: Instruments and Performance Practice, Genres and Styles* (Chicago, 1994); *Béla Bartók: Composition, Concepts, and Autograph Sources* (Berkeley, 1996).

Somigli, Franca (real name, **Maria Bruce Clark**), American-Italian soprano; b. Chicago, March 17, 1901; d. Trieste, May 14, 1974. She was a pupil of Malatesta, Votto, and Storchio in Milan. After making her operatic debut as Mimi in Rovigo (1926), she sang at Milan's La Scala (1933–44), in Chicago (debut as Maddalena in *Andrea Chénier*, 1934), in Rome (1934–43), at the Salzburg Festivals (1936–39), at Buenos Aires's Teatro Colón (1936–39), and at the Metropolitan Opera in N.Y. (debut as Cio-Cio-San, March 8, 1937). She was married to **Giuseppe Antonicelli**. Among her most prominent roles were Kundry, Sieglinde, Fedora, the Marschallin, Arabella, and Salome.

Sommer, Vladimír, Czech teacher and composer; b. Dolní Jiřetín, near Most, Feb. 28, 1921. He studied composition with Janeček at the Prague Cons. (1942–46) and with Bořkovec at the Prague Academy of Music (1946–50). He was music ed. of foreign broadcasts of Radio Prague (1953) and then was creative secretary of the Czech Composers Union (1953–56); taught at the Prague Academy of Music (1953–60) and then at the Charles Univ. in Prague (from 1960), where he was a prof. of theory from 1968 until his retirement in 1987. His music is crafted in a fine, expressive manner.

WORKS: ORCH.: Violin Concerto (Prague, June 13, 1950); *Antigone*, overture (1956–57); Cello Concerto (1956–59); 3 syms.: No. 1, *Vokální symfonie*, for Narrator, Mezzo-soprano, Chorus, and Orch., after Dostoyevsky, Kafka, and Cesare Pavese (1957–59; rev. 1963; Prague, March 12, 1963), No. 2, *Anno mundi ardenti*, for Piano, Timpani, and Strings (1968), and No. 3, *Sinfonia concertante*, for 2 Violins, Viola, Cello, and Chamber Orch. (1968). **CHAMBER:** Sonata for 2 Violins (1948; also for Violin and Viola); 3 string quartets (1950; 1955; 1960–66); Piano Sonata (1954–56). **VOCAL:** *Cantata on Gottwald* for Baritone, Chorus, and Orch. (Prague, Nov. 20, 1949); *Černý Muž* (The Black Man), symphonic poem for Tenor, Bass, and Orch. (1964); *Sinfonia da Requiem: Vokální symfonie No. 2* for Soli, Chorus, and Orch. (1978); songs.

Sommerfeldt, Øistein, Norwegian composer; b. Christiania, Nov. 25, 1919. He studied theory and composition in Paris with Boulanger (1950–56). He was active as a music critic and composer in Oslo.

WORKS: ORCH.: 3 suites (1956; based on Grieg's *Dances* for Piano, op. 72); *Miniature Suite* (1958; rev. 1972); *Miniature Overture* (1960); *Adagio, Scherzo, and Finale* (1969); *Sinfonia "La Betulla"* (1974); *Mot en Lengsel*: Piano Concerto in 1 Movement (1976–77); *Intrada*, symphonic prelude (1980); *Eika*, symphonic prelude (1981–83). **CHAMBER:** *Divertimento* for Flute (1960; rev. 1969); *Divertimento* for Bassoon (1960; rev. 1973); *Transformation*, audio-visual score for Chamber Group and Tape (1970); *Divertimento* for Trumpet (1971); Violin Sonata (1971); *Elegy* for Trumpet and Organ (1971); *Suite* for Piano Trio (1973); *Divertimento* for Oboe (1974). **PIANO:** 5 sonatinas (1956, 1960, 1968, 1970, 1972). **VOCAL:** *Hafrsfjord* for Narrator and Orch. (1972); *3 Lyrical Scenes* for Tenor or Soprano and Orch. (1973).

BIBL.: *Festskrift til O. S.: Til 70-årsdagen 25. november 1989* (Oslo, 1989).

Somogi, Judith, American conductor; b. N.Y., May 13, 1937; d. Rockville Centre, N.Y., March 23, 1988. She studied violin, piano, and organ at the Juilliard School of Music in N.Y. (M.M., 1961); attended courses at the Berkshire Music Center in Tanglewood; later was an assistant to Schippers at the Spoleto Festival and to Stokowski at the American Sym. Orch. in N.Y. In 1974 she made a successful debut with the N.Y. City Opera conducting *The Mikado*, and subsequently conducted in San Francisco, San Diego, San Antonio, and Pittsburgh. She made her European debut in Saarbrücken in 1979. After conducting *Madama Butterfly* at the Frankfurt am Main Opera in 1981, she held its position of 1st conductor from 1982 to 1987.

Somogyi, László, Hungarian conductor; b. Budapest, June 25, 1907; d. Geneva, May 20, 1988. He learned to play the violin; after training in composition with Kodály at the Budapest Academy of Music (1930–34), he studied conducting with Scherchen in Brussels (1935). He was a violinist in the Budapest Concert Orch. (1930–39), and then was founder-conductor of the Goldmark Sym. Orch. in Budapest (1939–43), a Jewish ensemble; subsequently he was chief conductor of the Municipal Sym. Orch. (1945–51) and the Sym. Orch. of the Hungarian Radio (1951–56) in Budapest, and also was prof. of conducting at the Academy of Music there (1949–56). In succeeding years, he lived abroad and toured as a guest conductor throughout Europe and the U.S. before serving as music director of the Rochester (N.Y.) Phil. (1964–69).

Sondheim, Stephen (Joshua), brilliant American composer and lyricist; b. N.Y., March 22, 1930. Of an affluent family, he received his academic education in private schools; composed a school musical at the age of 15. He then studied music at Williams College, where he wrote the book, lyrics, and music for a couple of college shows; graduated magna cum laude in 1950. In quest of higher musical learning, he went to Princeton Univ., where he took lessons in modernistic complexities with Babbitt and acquired sophisticated techniques of composition. He made his mark on Broadway when he wrote the lyrics for Bernstein's *West Side Story* (1957). His first success as a lyricist-composer came with the Broadway musical *A Funny Thing Happened on the Way to the Forum* (1962), which received a Tony award. His next musical, *Anyone Can Whistle* (1964), proved unsuccessful, but *Company* (1970), for which he wrote both lyrics and music, established him as a major composer and lyricist on Broadway. There followed *Follies* (1971), for which he wrote 22 pastiche songs; it was named best musical by the N.Y. Drama Critics Circle. His next production, *A Little Night Music*, with the nostalgic score harking back to the turn of the century, received a Tony, and its leading song, "Send in the Clowns," was awarded a Grammy in 1976. This score established Sondheim's characteristic manner of treating musicals; it is almost operatic in conception, and boldly introduces dissonant counterpoint *à la moderne.* In 1976 he produced *Pacific Overtures*, based on the story of the Western penetration into Japan in the 19th century, and composed in a stylized Japanese manner, modeled after the Kabuki theater; he also wrote the score to the musical *Sunday in the Park with George*, inspired by the painting by Georges Seurat entitled *Sunday Afternoon on the Island of La Grande Jatte* (1982; N.Y., May 1, 1984), which received the Pulitzer Prize for drama in 1985. In 1987 his musical *Into the Woods*, based on 5 of the Grimm fairytales, scored a popular success on Broadway. It was followed by the musical *Assassins* in 1990. In 1992 he was selected to receive the National Medal of Arts, but he rejected the medal by stating that to accept it would be an act of hypocrisy in light of the controversy over censorship and funding of the NEA. After the inauguration of Bill Clinton as president in 1993, Sondheim accepted the National Medal of Arts and was honored at the Kennedy Center in Washington, D.C. His musical *Passion* was premiered in N.Y. on April 28, 1994.

BIBL.: C. Zadan, *S. & Co.* (N.Y., 1974; 2nd ed., rev., 1994); T. Adler, "The Musical Dramas of S. S.: Some Critical Approaches," *Journal of Popular Culture*, XII (1978–79); M. Adams, *The Lyrics of S. S.: Form and Function* (diss., Northwestern Univ., 1980); D. Cartmell, *S. S. and the Concept Musical* (diss., Univ. of Calif., Santa Barbara, 1983); S. Wilson, *Motivic, Rhythmic, and Harmonic Procedures of Unification in S. S.'s "Company" and "A Little Night Music"* (diss., Ball State Univ., 1983); T. Sutcliffe, "S. and the Musical," *Musical Times* (Sept. 1987); J. Gordon, *Art*

Isn't Easy: The Achievement of S. S. (Carbondale, Ill., 1990; rev. ed., 1992); S. Banfield, *S.'s Broadway Musicals* (Ann Arbor, 1993); M. Gottfried, *S.* (N.Y., 1993).

Sonneck, Oscar G(eorge) T(heodore), eminent American musicologist; b. Jersey City, N.J., Oct. 6, 1873; d. N.Y., Oct. 30, 1928. He attended the Gelehrtenschule in Kiel (1883–89) and the Kaiser Friedrich Gymnasium in Frankfurt am Main (1889–93), where he also took piano lessons with James Kwast; attended the Univ. of Heidelberg and received instruction in musicology from Sandberger at the Univ. of Munich (1893–97); studied composition privately with Melchior and Ernest Sachs in Munich; took courses in composition and orchestration with Iwann Knorr in Frankfurt am Main and in conducting with Carl Schroder at the Sondershausen Cons. (1897–98). After doing research in Italy in 1899, he returned to the U.S. to pursue his interest in early American music. From 1902 to 1917 he was chief of the Music Division of the Library of Congress in Washington, D.C. He then became director of the Publishing Dept. of G. Schirmer in N.Y., managing ed. of the *Musical Quarterly* (of which he had been ed. since its founding in 1915), and personal representative of the president, Rudolph E. Schirmer; in 1921 he became vice-president of G. Schirmer. He took a leading part in the formation of the Society for the Publication of American Music, and of the Beethoven Assn. in N.Y. Under Sonneck's administration, the Music Division of the Library of Congress became one of the largest and most important music collections in the world. His writings, exhibiting profound and accurate scholarship and embodying the results of original research, laid a real foundation for the scientific study of music in the U.S.; his elaborate catalogues, issued by the Library of Congress, are among the most valuable contributions to musical bibliography. The Sonneck Soc., an organization designed to encourage the serious study of American music in all its aspects, was established in 1975 and named after Sonneck in recognition of his achievements in this area. He was also a composer and a poet; wrote symphonic pieces; a String Quartet; *Rhapsody and Romanze* for Violin and Piano; some vocal works and piano pieces. He publ. 2 vols. of poems: *Seufzer* (1895) and *Eine Totenmesse* (1898).

WRITINGS: *Protest gegen den Symbolismus in der Musik* (Frankfurt am Main, 1897); *Classification: Class M, Music: Class ML, Literature of Music: Class MT, Musical Instruction: Adopted December, 1902: as in force April, 1904* (Washington, D.C., 1904; 2nd ed., rev., 1917; 3rd ed., 1957); *A Bibliography of Early Secular American Music* (Washington, D.C., 1905; 2nd ed., rev. and enl., 1945 by W. Upton); *Francis Hopkinson, the First American Poet-Composer (1737–1791) and James Lyon, Patriot, Preacher, Psalmodist (1735–1794): Two Studies in Early American Music* (Washington, D.C., 1905); *Early Concert-life in America (1731–1800)* (Leipzig, 1907); *Dramatic Music: Catalogue of Full Scores in the Collection of the Library of Congress* (Washington, D.C., 1908; 2nd ed., 1917); *Report on "The Star-Spangled Banner," "Hail Columbia," "America," "Yankee Doodle"* (Washington, D.C., 1909; 2nd ed., rev. and enl., 1914); *Orchestral Music Catalogue: Scores* (Washington, D.C., 1912); with J. Gregory, *Catalogue of Early Books on Music (before 1800)* (Washington, D.C., 1913); *Catalogue of Opera Librettos Printed before 1800* (Washington, D.C., 1914); with W. Whittlesey, *Catalogue of First Editions of Stephen C. Foster (1826–1864)* (Washington, D.C., 1915); *Early Opera in America* (N.Y., 1915); *Suum cuique: Essays in Music* (N.Y., 1916); *Catalogue of First Editions of Edward MacDowell (1861–1908)* (Washington, D.C., 1917); *Miscellaneous Studies in the History of Music* (N.Y., 1921); *Beethoven: Impressions of Contemporaries* (N.Y., 1926); *Beethoven Letters in America* (N.Y., 1927).

BIBL.: H. Putnam and R. Goldmark, "Remarks at the Funeral Services for O.G. S.," *Musical Quarterly* (Jan. 1929); C. Engel, "O.G. S.," ibid. (Jan. 1939); O. Kinkeldey, "O.G.T. S.," *Notes*, XI (1953–54); G. Chase, "The Significance of O. S.: A Centennial Tribute," *Yearbook for Inter-American Musical Research*, IX (1973); H. Wiley Hitchcock, *After 100 [!] Years: The Editorial Side of S.* (Washington, D.C., 1974; with complete list of writings and compositions compiled by I. Lowens); W. Lichtenwanger, ed., *O. S. and American Music* (Urbana, Ill., 1983).

Sonninen, Ahti, Finnish composer; b. Kuopio, July 11, 1914; d. Helsinki, Aug. 27, 1984. Following graduation from the Kajaani training college, he took courses in theory and composition with Palmgren, Merikanto, Ranta, and Funtek at the Sibelius Academy in Helsinki (1939–47). He taught elementary school (1936–43), then taught in the school music dept. of the Sibelius Academy (from 1957). He followed the tenets of international musical modernism in his technique of composition, but also adhered to subjects from Finnish folklore.

WORKS: DRAMATIC: *Merenkuninkaan tytär* (Daughter of Neptune), opera (1949); *Pessi and Illusia*, ballet (1952); *Ruususolmu* (Wreath of Roses), ballet (1956); *Karhunpeijaiset* (Feast to Celebrate the Killing of a Bear), ritual opera (1968); *Se* (It), ballet farce (Helsinki, Feb. 24, 1972); *Haavruuva* (Lady of the Sea), opera (1971); film scores. **ORCH.:** *East Karelian Suite* (1942); Violin Concerto (1943–45); Piano Concerto (1944–45); *Symphonic Sketches* (1947); *Preludio festivo* (1953); *Under Lapland's Sky*, suite (1954); *Pezzo pizzicato* (1954–55); *Rhapsody* (1957); *4 Partitas* for Strings (1958); *Prelude and Allegro* for Trumpet, Trombone, and Orch. (1961); *Reactions* for Chamber Orch. (1961). **CHAMBER:** *Conference* for Clarinet, Horn, Trumpet, and Trombone (1954); *Theses* for String Quartet (1968); *Divertimento* for Wind Quintet (1970). **PIANO:** 5 suites: *In the Big City* (1954), *White Pepper* (1970), *Black Pepper* (1970), *Koli* (1970), and *3 Characters* (1971). **VOCAL:** *7 Songs to Hungarian Folk Poems* for Soprano and Orch. (1939–41); *Midsummer Night* for Soprano and Orch. (1946); *El amor pasa* for Soprano, Flute, and Orch. (1953); *Smith of the Heavens* for Baritone and Orch. (1957); *The Karelian Wedding* for Voice, Chorus, Flute, Accordion, Percussion, Harpsichord, and Tape (1965); *Highway Requiem* for Soprano, Baritone, Chorus, and Orch. (1970); *Forging of the Golden Virgin* for Voices, 2 Percussionists, and Tape (1971); *Finnish Messiah* for Soloists, Mixed and Children's Choruses, and Orch. (1972); *In the Court of the Lamb*, suite for Soloists, Chorus, and Orch. (1972); about 15 cantatas and 100 choruses; about 70 songs with piano.

Sonzogno, Giulio Cesare, Italian composer; b. Milan, Dec. 24, 1906; d. there, Jan. 23, 1976. He was related to the family of the music publishers Sonzogno. He studied cello and composition in Milan; composed mostly for the stage.

WORKS: DRAMATIC: OPERAS: *Regina Uliva* (Milan, March 17, 1949); *I Passeggeri* (1961); *Il denaro del Signor Arne* (1968); *Boule de suif*, after Maupassant (1970); *Mirra* (1970). **BALLET:** *L'amore delle tre melarancie* (Milan, Feb. 1, 1936).

Soomer, Walter, German bass-baritone; b. Liegnitz, March 12, 1878; d. Leipzig, Aug. 1955. He was a student of Hermann Stoeckert and Anna Uhlig in Berlin. In 1902 he made his operatic debut in Kolmar. After singing in Halle (1902–06), he was a member of the Leipzig Opera (1906–27). He also appeared at the Bayreuth Festivals (1906; 1908–14; 1924–25). On Feb. 18, 1909, he made his Metropolitan Opera debut in N.Y. as Wolfram, remaining on its roster until 1911. From 1911 to 1915 he sang in Dresden. In 1927 he became director of his own vocal and opera school in Leipzig. Soomer was best known as a Wagnerian, singing such roles as Hans Sachs, Wotan, Gurnemanz, Kurwenal, and Amfortas.

Soot, Fritz (actually, **Friedrich Wilhelm**), distinguished German tenor; b. Wellesweiler-Neunkirchen, Saar, Aug. 20, 1878; d. Berlin, June 9, 1965. He first pursued a career as an actor in Karlsruhe (1901–07); then studied voice with Scheidemantel in Dresden. He made his operatic debut with the Dresden Court Opera as Tonio in *La Fille du régiment* in 1908, remaining on its roster until 1918; during his tenure there, he sang in the first performance of *Der Rosenkavalier* as the Italian Singer. His subsequent engagements were in Stuttgart (1918–22), at the Berlin State Opera (1922–44; 1946–52), and at the Berlin Stadtische Oper (1946–48). He sang in the premieres of Berg's *Wozzeck*, as well as in works by Pfitzner and Schreker; he excelled in such Wagnerian roles as Tristan, Siegmund, and Siegfried.

Sopeña (Ibáñez), Federico, noted Spanish musicologist; b. Valladolid, Jan. 25, 1917; d. Madrid, May 22, 1991. He studied in Bilbao and Madrid; later obtained a doctorate in theology at the Università Gregoriana in Rome. He was active as a music critic; from 1951 to 1956, was director of the Madrid Cons.; was also the founder and publisher of the music magazine *Música.* He publ. (in Madrid) a number of useful monographs of Spanish composers, including *Joaquín Turina* (1943; 2nd ed., 1952) and *Joaquín Rodrigo* (1946; 2nd ed., rev. 1970); also *Historia de la música* (1946; 5th ed., 1974); *La música europea contemporánea* (1952); *Historia de la música española contemporánea* (1958; 2nd ed., 1967); *Música y literatura* (1974).

Sopkin, Henry, American conductor; b. N.Y., Oct. 20, 1903; d. Stanford, Calif., March 1, 1988. He was reared in Chicago, where he earned degrees in violin at the American Cons. of Music. He was head of its instrumental dept. and also taught at Woodrow Wilson College; in 1944 he became conductor of the Atlanta Youth Sym. Orch., which served as the foundation of the Atlanta Sym. Orch. in 1945, which he conducted until 1966; then taught briefly at the Calif. Inst. of the Arts in Valencia.

Soproni, József, Hungarian composer and pedagogue; b. Sopron, Oct. 4, 1930. He studied with Viski at the Budapest Academy of Music (1949–56). In 1957 he became a teacher at the Béla Bartók School in Budapest. In 1962 he joined the faculty of the Budapest Academy of Music, where he was a prof. from 1977. From 1988 to 1994 he served as its rector.

WORKS: OPERA: *Antigone* (1987). **ORCH.:** Concerto for Strings (1953); Viola Concerto (1967); 2 cello concertos (1967, 1984); *Eklypsis* (1969); 5 syms.: No. 1 (1975), No. 2, *The Seasons* (1977), No. 3, *Sinfonia da Requiem,* for Soloists, Chorus, and Orch. (1979–80), No. 4 for Strings and 3 Winds (1994), and No. 5 (1995); Concertino for Flute, Clarinet, Cimbalom, and Orch. (1976); Violin Concerto (1982–83); *Comments on a Theme by Handel* (1985); *3 Pieces* (1987–88). **CHAMBER:** Viola Sonatina (1958); 10 string quartets (1958–94); *Musica da camera No. 1* for Piano Trio (1963) and *No. 2, Capricorn Music,* for Violin, Clarinet, Cello, and Piano (1976); Flute Sonata (1971); *Concerto da camera* for 12 Instruments (1972); Horn Sonata (1976); *Tre pezzi* for Flute and Cimbalom (1977); *6 Bagatelles* for Wind Quintet (1977); *4 Pieces* for Saxophone and Piano (1978); *Late Summer Caprices* for Violin, Viola, Cello, and Piano (1978); *Episodi ritornanti* for 2 Cimbaloms (1979); 2 violin sonatas (1979, 1980); Piano Quintet (1990). **KEYBOARD: PIANO:** *4 Bagatelles* (1957); *7 Piano Pieces* (1963); *Incrustations* (1970); *Invenzioni sul B-A-C-H* (1971); *Note Pages* (4 books, 1974–78); *Quattro intermezzi* (1976). **ORGAN:** *Meditatio con toccata* (1959); *Livre d'orgue,* 9 pieces (1994). **VOCAL:** *Carmina polinaesiana,* cantata for Women's Chorus and Chamber Ensemble (1963); *Ovidii metamorphoses,* cantata for Soprano, Chorus, and Orch. (1965); *De aetatibus mundi carmina,* cantata for Soprano, Baritone, Chorus, and Orch. (1968); *Magnificat* for Soloists, Chorus, and Orch. (1989); *Missa Scarbantiensis* for Soloists, Chorus, and Orch. (1991); *Missa choralis* for Soloists, Chorus, and Orch. (1992); *Missa super B-A-C-H* for Chorus, Organ, Trumpet, and Trombone (1992); *Litaniae Omnium Sanctorum* for Soloists, Chorus, and Orch. (1993); *Psalm XXIX* for Chorus, Organ, Trumpet, and Trombone (1993); *Missa Gurcensis* for Chorus and Chamber Ensemble (1994); choruses; song cycles.

Sorabji, Kaikhosru Shapurji (actually, **Leon Dudley**), remarkable English pianist, writer on music, and composer of unique gifts; b. Chingford, Aug. 14, 1892; d. Wareham, Dorset, Oct. 14, 1988. His father was a Parsi, his mother of Spanish-Sicilian descent. He was largely self-taught in music; after appearing with notable success as a pianist in London, Paris, Vienna (1921–22), Glasgow, and Bombay, he gave up the concert platform and began writing on music. Through sheer perseverance and an almost mystical belief in his demiurgic powers, he developed an idiom of composition of extraordinary complexity, embodying within the European framework of harmonies the Eastern types of melodic lines and asymmetrical rhythmic patterns, and creating an enormously intricate but architectonically stable edifice of sound. His most arresting work is his magisterial *Opus Clavicembalisticum,* completed in 1930, taking about 5 hours to play and comprising 3 parts with 12 subdivisions, including a theme with 49 variations and a passacaglia with 81 variations; characteristically, the score is dedicated to "the everlasting glory of those few men blessed and sanctified in the curses and execrations of those many whose praise is eternal damnation." Sorabji gave its premiere in Glasgow under the auspices of the Active Society for the Propagation of Contemporary Music on Dec. 1, 1930. Wrathful at the lack of interest in his music, Sorabji issued in 1936 a declaration forbidding any performance of his works by anyone anywhere; since this prohibition could not be sustained for works actually publ., there must have been furtive performances of his piano works in England and the U.S. by fearless pianists. Sorabji eventually mitigated his ban, and in 1975 allowed the American pianist Michael Habermann to perform some of his music; in 1976 he also gave his blessing to the English pianist Yonty Solomon, who included Sorabji's works in a London concert on Dec. 7, 1976; on June 16, 1977, Solomon gave in London the first performance of Sorabji's 3rd Piano Sonata. Gradually, Sorabji's music became the cynosure and the lodestone of titanically endowed pianists. Of these, the most Brobdingnagian was the Australian pianist Geoffrey Madge, who gave the second complete performance in history of *Opus Clavicembalisticum* at the 1982 Holland Festival in Utrecht; he repeated this feat at the first American performance of the work at the Univ. of Chicago on April 24, 1983; 2 weeks later he played it in Bonn. True to his estrangement from the human multitudes and music officials, Sorabji took refuge far from the madding crowd in a castle he owned in England; a notice at the gate proclaimed: Visitors Unwelcome. Yet as he approached his 90th birthday, he received at least 2 American musicians who came to declare their admiration, and allowed them to photocopy some of his MSS.

WORKS: ORCH.: 8 indefinitely numbered piano concertos (1915–16; 1916–17; 1917; 1918; 1922; *Simorg-Anka,* 1924; 1924–25; 1927); *Chaleur* (1920); *Opusculum* (1923); *Symphonic Variations* for Piano and Orch. (1951–55); *Opus Clavisymphonicum* for Piano and Orch. (1957–59); *Opusculum Claviorchestrale* for Piano and Orch. (1973–75). **CHAMBER:** 2 piano quintets: No. 1 (1920) and No. 2 (1949–53); *Concertino non Grosso* for 4 Violins, Viola, 2 Cellos, and Piano (1968); *Il tessuto d'Arabeschi* for Flute and String Quartet (1979; Philadelphia, May 2, 1982). **KEYBOARD: PIANO:** 6 sonatas: No. 0 (1917), No. 1 (1919), No. 2 (1920), No. 3 (1922), No. 4 (1928–29), and No. 5, *Opus Archimagicum* (1934–35); 2 pieces: *In the Hothouse* and *Toccata* (1918, 1920); *Fantaisie espagnole* (1919); *Prelude, Interlude and Fugue* (1920–22); *3 Pastiches*: on Chopin, Bizet, and Rimsky-Korsakov (1922); *Le Jardin parfumé* (1923); *Variations and Fugue on "Dies Irae"* (1923–26); *Valse-Fantaisie (Hommage à Johann Strauss)* (1925); *Fragment* (1926; rev. 1937); *Djâmî,* nocturne (1928); 4 toccatas: No. 1 (1928), No. 2 (1933–34), No. 3 (1957), and No. 4 (1964–67); *Opus Clavicembalisticum* (Glasgow, Dec. 1, 1930, composer soloist); *Symphonic Variations* (1935–37); 6 solo syms.: No. 1, *Tantrik* (1938–39), No. 2 (1954), No. 3 (1959–60), No. 4 (1962–64), No. 5, *Symphonia Brevis* (1973–75), and No. 6, *Symphonia Magna* (1975–76); *Gulistan,* nocturne (1940); *100 Transcendental Studies* (1940–44); *St. Bertrand de Comminges: "He Was Laughing in the Tower"* (1941); *Concerto per suonare da me solo* (1946); *Sequentia Cyclica on "Dies Irae"* (1949); *Un nido di scatole* (1954); *Passeggiata veneziana* (1956); *Rosario d'arabeschi* (1956); *Fantasiettina* (1961); *Symphonic Nocturne* (1977–78); *Il grido del gallino d'oro* (1978–79); *Evocazione nostalgicaVilla Tasca* (1979); *Opus secretum* (1980–81); *Passeggiata arlecchinesca* (1981–82). **ORGAN:** 3 solo syms.: No. 1 (1924), No. 2 (1929–32), and No. 3 (1949–53). **VOCAL:** Sym. No. 1 for

Orch., Chorus, Organ, and Piano (1921–22); *5 sonetti del Michelangelo Buonarroti* for Voice and Chamber Orch. (1923; Toronto, Feb. 2, 1980); *Jâmî*, sym. for Orch., Baritone, Chorus, Organ, and Piano (1942–51); *Symphonic High Mass* for Orch., Solo Voices, Chorus, Organ, and Piano (1955–61); songs.

WRITINGS: *Around Music* (London, 1932); *Mi contra fa: The Immoralisings of a Machiavellian Musician* (London, 1947).

BIBL.: A. Browne, "The Music of K. S.," *Music & Letters* (Jan. 1930); E. Rubbra, "S.'s Enigma," *Monthly Musical Record* (Sept. 1932); B. Posner, *S.* (diss., Fordham Univ., N.Y., 1975); P. Rapoport, "S. and the Computer," *Tempo*, no. 117 (1976); idem, *Opus Est: 6 Composers from Northern Europe* (London, 1978, and N.Y., 1979); idem, ed., *S.: A Critical Celebration* (Aldershot, 1992).

Sørensen, Bent, Danish composer; b. Borup, July 18, 1958. He studied with Nordholm in Copenhagen (1983–87), and also had lessons with Nørgård. After composing in a tonal style, Sørensen embraced a highly personal contemporary means of expression. His Violin Concerto, *Sterbende Gärten* (1992–94), won the Nordic Council Music Prize in 1996. Among his other works are *Lacrimae* for Orch. (1985); 3 string quartets (*Alman*, 1984; *Adieu*, 1986; *Angel's Music*, 1988); piano pieces; vocal music, including *Cyprianus* for 3 Women's Voices, 2 Clarinets, and Percussion (1983) and *Pop Sange* for Tenor and Piano (1990).

Sørensen, Søren, distinguished Danish musicologist, organist, and harpsichordist; b. Copenhagen, Sept. 20, 1920. He studied organ with Viderø at the Copenhagen Cons. (diploma, 1943) and musicology with Abrahamsen and Larsen at the Univ. of Copenhagen (M.A., 1943; Ph.D., 1958, with the diss. *Diderich Buxtehudes vokale kirkemusik*; publ. in Copenhagen, 1958). In 1943, with L. Friisholhm, he founded Copenhagen's Collegium Musicum, a chamber ensemble with which he made frequent appearances as an organist and harpsichordist; also was organist at Holmens Church (1947–58). He was prof. of musicology and chairman of the musicologial inst. at the Univ. of Århus (from 1958); was co-ed. of the *Dansk Årbog for Musikforskning* (from 1961). Among his many administrative positions were the chairmanships of the Danish Soc. of Organists and Choirmasters (1953–59), the Carl Nielsen Soc. (from 1966), the Danish Council for Research in the Humanities (from 1974), and the State Council of Music Education (from 1986). In 1982 he was awarded Hungary's Bartók Medal. He won notable distinction as an authority on 17th-century music, most particularly that of Buxtehude.

WRITINGS: *Kirkens liturgi* (Copenhagen, 1952; 2nd ed., 1969); ed. with B. Hjelmbor, *Natalicia musicologica Knud Jeppesen* (Copenhagen, 1962); *Renaissancebegrebet i musikhistorien* (Århus, 1964); *Das Buxtehudebild im Wandel der Zeit* (Lübeck, 1973); *Kobenhavns Drengekor gennem 50 år* (Copenhagen, 1974); ed. *Gads musikleksikon* (Copenhagen, 1976; 2nd ed., 1987).

Sörenson, Torsten, Swedish organist, teacher, and composer; b. Grebbestad, April 25, 1908; d. Uddevalla, Dec. 29, 1992. He began his training at the Stockholm Musikhögskolan (diplomas as a music teacher and church musician, 1934, and as an organist, 1936). After studies with Torsten Ahlberg (counterpoint) in Göteborg (1936–39), he studied composition with Rosenberg (1942) and Orff (1949). From 1935 he was a church organist in Göteborg, later serving at the Oscar Fredrik Church (1946–75); he also taught theory at the Göteborg Musikhögskolan (1954–76). He composed a number of fine works, ranging from large forces to lieder.

WORKS: ORCH.: Sinfonietta for Strings (1946; rev. 1957); Concerto for Organ and Strings (1952); Sym. for Chamber Orch. (1956); *Sinfonia da chiesa* 1 (1958) and 2 (1964–69) for Strings; Concerto for Flute, Strings, and Percussion (1976). **CHAMBER:** 2 trios for Flute, Clarinet, and Oboe (1949, 1959); Sonata for Solo Viola (1956); 3 sonatas for Solo Flute (1962, 1964, 1966); 2 string quartets (1970; *Due contrasti*, 1983); Brass Quintet (1970); *Divertimento* for Flute, Oboe, Violin, and Viola (1976); *Quintafonia* for 5 Instrumentalists (1979); *Sonans* for Piano and Organ (1983); Violin Sonata (1985); *Pezzo d'amore* for Viola d'Amore and 4 Violas (1986). **PIANO:** Sonata (1956); *Svart-Vitt* (Black and White), 24 pieces (1975); *Dygnets fyra tider*, 4 studies (1975–79); *Floriad*, 15 pieces (1981–82); *Två sånger* (1988). **VOCAL:** *Den underbara Kvarnan* for Baritone and Orch. (1936; rev. 1958); *Hymn om Kristus*, cantata (1950); *Hymnarium*, 56 motets for 1 to 6 Voices and Instruments (1957–62); *Laudate nomen Domini* for Chorus, 17 Winds, and Percussion (1972); *En sang om Herrens boninger* for Soprano, 2 Choruses, and Orch. (1975); *Gud är här tillstädes*, cantata (1978).

Soresina, Alberto, Italian composer and teacher; b. Milan, May 10, 1911. He studied with Paribeni and Bossi at the Milan Cons., graduating in 1933; then took a course in composition in Siena with Frazzi. He subsequently was on the faculty of the Milan Cons. (1947–60) and the Turin Cons. (1963–66); then again at the Milan Cons. (from 1967).

WORKS: OPERAS: *Lanterna rossa* (1942); *Cuor di cristallo* (1942); *L'amuleto* (Bergamo, Oct. 26, 1954); *Tre sogni per Marina* (1967). **ORCH.:** *Trittico Wildiano* (1939); *Il Santo*, symphonic poem (1940); *2 notturni* for Harp and Strings (1946); *Divertimento* (1956). **CHAMBER:** Concertino for Viola, Cello, and Piano (1953); *Sonatina serena* for Violin and Piano (1956); piano pieces. **VOCAL:** Several works for Voice and Orch., including *La Fanciulla mutata in rio* (1939).

Soriano, Gonzalo, Spanish pianist; b. Alicante, March 14, 1913; d. Madrid, April 14, 1972. He studied with Cabiles in Madrid, and later with Cortot and Landowska at the Paris Cons. He made his debut in Alicante in 1929; pursued an active career in Europe; also gave concerts in the U.S. and the Far East. He was particularly noted for his congenial performances of Spanish music.

Soro (Barriga), Enrique, prominent Chilean composer, pedagogue, and pianist; b. Concepción, July 15, 1884; d. Santiago, Dec. 2, 1954. He was a son of the Italian composer José Soro Sforza, with whom he studied piano and theory; played in public as a small child. He was granted a stipend by the government of Chile for study in Italy; entered the Milan Cons. at 14; graduated in 1904 with a grand prize in composition. Returning to Chile in 1905, he was appointed inspector of musical education in primary schools; in 1906 he joined the faculty of the Santiago Cons.; from 1919 to 1928 he was its director. He traveled as a pianist; gave concerts in Europe and South America; also publ. a number of works. In 1948 he was awarded the Premio Nacional de Arte.

WORKS: ORCH.: *Andante appassionato* (1915); *Danza fantastica* (1916); *Suite sinfónica*, No. 1, *Pensamientos intimos* (1918) and No. 2 (Santiago, May 9, 1919, composer conducting); *Impresiones líricas* for Piano and Strings (1919); Piano Concerto (1919); *Sinfonía romántica* (1920); *3 preludios sinfónicos* (Santiago, July 18, 1936); *Aires chilenos* (Santiago, 1942); *Suite en estilo antiguo* (Santiago, May 28, 1943). **CHAMBER:** String Quartet (1904); Piano Quintet (1919); Piano Trio (1926); Violin Sonata; Cello Sonata. **PIANO:** 3 sonatas (1920, 1923, 1942); piano pieces in a salon genre, some of them based on Chilean melorhythms.

BIBL.: L. Giarda, *Analytische Studie über S. 2. Sonate für Violine und Klavier A moll, das Quartett A dur und das Klavierquintett* (Santiago, 1919); V. Salas Viú, *La creación musical en Chile 1900–1951* (Santiago, 1953).

Sotin, Hans, notable German bass; b. Dortmund, Sept. 10, 1939. He was a student of F.W. Hetzel and then of Dieter Jacob at the Dortmund Hochschule für Musik. In 1962 he made his operatic debut as the Police Commissioner in *Der Rosenkavalier* in Essen. After joining the Hamburg State Opera in 1964, he quickly became one of its principal members singing not only traditional roles but creating new roles in works by Blacher, Einem, Penderecki et al. His success led to his being made a

Hamburg Kammersänger. In 1970 he made his first appearance at the Glyndebourne Festival as Sarastro. He made his debut at the Chicago Lyric Opera as the Grand Inquisitor in *Don Carlos* in 1971. That same year he sang for the first time at the Bayreuth Festival as the Landgrave, where he subsequently returned with success in later years. On Oct. 26, 1972, he made his Metropolitan Opera debut in N.Y. as Sarastro. From 1973 he sang at the Vienna State Opera. He made his debut at London's Covent Garden as Hunding in 1974. In 1976 he sang for the first time at Milan's La Scala as Baron Ochs. He also appeared as a soloist with the leading European orchs. In 1986 he returned to Covent Garden as Baron Ochs. In 1988 he sang Lodovico in *Otello* at the Metropolitan Opera. In 1992 he appeared as the Landgrave in Berlin. His portrayals of Tannhäuser, Lohengrin, and Gurnemanz at the 1993 Bayreuth Festival elicited critical accolades. In addition to his varied operatic repertoire, Sotin has won distinction for his concert repertoire, most particularly of the music of Bach, Haydn, Beethoven, and Mahler.

Soukupová, Věra, Czech mezzo-soprano; b. Prague, April 12, 1932. She was a student in Prague of Kadeřábek and Mustanová-Linková. In 1957 she made her debut at the J.K. Tyl Theater in Plzeň, where she sang until 1960. From 1960 to 1963 she was a member of the Prague National Theater. After capturing 1st prize in the Rio de Janeiro competition in 1963, she pursued a major career as an opera and concert singer. In 1966 she sang at the Bayreuth Festival. She made her first appearance in Hamburg in 1968. Thereafter she sang with major European opera houses and at major festivals. She became particularly known for her idiomatic performances of roles in 19th- and 20th-century Czech operas.

Souliotis, Elena, Greek soprano and mezzo-soprano; b. Athens, May 28, 1943. She studied in Buenos Aires with Alfredo Bonta, Jascha Galperin, and Bianca Lietti, and in Milan with Mercedes Llopart. In 1964 she made her operatic debut as Santuzza at the Teatro San Carlo in Naples. In 1965 she made her U.S. debut as Elena in Boito's *Mefistofele* in Chicago. In 1966 she sang Abigaille in *Nabucco* at Milan's La Scala, appeared as Luisa Miller in Florence, and made her N.Y. debut as Anna Bolena in a concert performance at Carnegie Hall. Her London debut followed in 1968 as Abigaille in a concert performance. She returned to London in 1969 to make her Covent Garden debut as Lady Macbeth, and continued to sing there until 1973. In subsequent years, she sang in various European operatic centers. Among her other roles were Norma, Gioconda, Manon Lescaut, Desdemona, Leonora in *Il Trovatore*, and Aida.

Šourek, Otakar, Czech writer on music; b. Prague, Oct. 1, 1883; d. there, Feb. 15, 1956. He was trained as an engineer, and although he was employed in the Prague City Council works dept. (1907–39), music was his avocation. He wrote music criticism for several publications, including Prague's *Venkov* (1918–41). However, it was as an authority on the life and music of Dvořák that he gained distinction; he devoted fully 40 years to Dvořák research, and served as the first ed. of the composer's collected works.

WRITINGS: *Život a dílo Antonína Dvořáka* (The Life and Works of Dvořák; 4 vols., Prague, 1916–33; vols. I–II, 3rd ed., 1955–56; vols. III–IV, 2nd ed., 1957–58; in Ger. as *Dvořák: Leben und Werk*, one vol., abr. by P. Stefan, Vienna, 1935; Eng. tr. by Y. Vance as *Anton Dvořák*, N.Y., 1941); *Dvořák's Werke: Ein völlstandiges Verzeichnis in chronologischer, thematischer und systematischer Anordnung* (Berlin, 1917; rev. Czech ed., Prague, 1960); *Výlety pana Broučka* (Mr. Brouček's Excursions; Prague, 1920); *Dvořákovy symfonie* (Prague, 1922; 3rd ed., 1948; abr. ed. in Ger. in *Antonín Dvořák Werkanalysen I, Orchesterwerke*, Prague, 1954, and in Eng. in *The Orchestral Works of Antonín Dvořák*, Prague, 1956); *Antonín Dvořák* (Prague, 1929; 4th ed., 1947; Eng. tr., Prague, 1952, as *Antonín Dvořák: His Life and Work*); *Dvořákova citanka* (A Dvořák Reader; Prague, 1929; 3rd ed., 1946; Eng. tr., Prague, 1954); *Dvořák ve vzpomínkach a dopisech* (Prague, 1938; 9th ed., 1951; Eng. tr., Prague, 1954, as *Dvořák: Letters and Reminiscences*; Ger. tr., 1955; Russian tr., 1964); *Smetanova Ma vlast* (Prague, 1940); *Antonín Dvořák přátelům doma* (Dvořák to His Friends at Home; 395 letters; Prague, 1941); *Antonín Dvořák a Hans Richter* (Letters to Richter; Prague, 1942); *Dvořákovy skladby komorni* (Prague, 1943; 2nd ed., 1949; abr. ed. in Ger. in *Antonín Dvořák Werkanalysen II, Kammermusik*, Prague, 1954, and in Eng. in *The Chamber Music of Antonín Dvořák*, Prague, 1956); *Dvořákovy skladby orchestralni* (2 vols., Prague, 1944 and 1946; abr. ed. in Ger. in *Antonín Dvořák Werkanalysen I, Orchesterwerke*, Prague, 1954, and in Eng. in *The Orchestral Works of Antonín Dvořák*, Prague, 1956); *Komorni skladby Bedřicha Smetany* (Smetana's chamber works; Prague, 1945); *Rudolf Karel* (Prague, 1947).

BIBL.: F. Oeser, "O. Š.," *Musica* (April 1956).

Souris, André, prominent Belgian conductor, musicologist, and composer; b. Marchienne-au-Pont, Hainaut, July 10, 1899; d. Paris, Feb. 12, 1970. He studied at the Brussels Cons. (1911–18) with Lunssens (harmony) and Closson (music history), and privately with Gilson (composition). In 1925 he began teaching at the Royal Cons. in Brussels; in 1927 he won the Prix Rubens, and traveled to Italy, France, and Austria; conducted the Belgian Radio Orch. (1937–46); from 1949 to 1964 he was a prof. of harmony at the Royal Cons. in Brussels. He was the founder of the quarterly music review *Polyphonie* (1947–54). He collaborated with R. Vannes on the *Dictionnaire des musiciens (compositeurs)* (Brussels, 1947); also ed. works by various composers. His compositions reflect the influence of the French avant-garde of the period between the 2 World Wars; in a few of his later works, he adopted serialism.

WORKS: DRAMATIC: Theater music; radio and film scores. **ORCH.:** *Soliloque* for Strings and Percussion (1923); *Scherzo* (1923); *Musique (Collage)* (1928); *Rêverie* (1931); *Danceries de la Renaissance* (1932); *Canzone* (1932); *Hommage à Babeuf* for Wind Orch. (1934); *Fanfare et scherzo* for Winds and Percussion (1937); *Burlesque* (1938); *Symphonies* (1939); *Suite de danceries No. 2* for Wind Orch. (1943); *Danses mosanes* (1943); *4 Fantasies* for Strings (1960); *Ouverture pour une arlequinade* (1962). **CHAMBER:** *Fantasque* for 4 Instruments (1916); *Fugue* for String Quartet (1917); *2 petits poèmes* for Violin and Piano (1917); *Hymne à l'automne* for Violin and Piano (1919); *Bagatelle* for Violin and Piano (1923); *Berceuse* for Violin and Piano (1924); *Choral, marche et galop* for 2 Trumpets and 2 Trombones (1925); *Burlesque* for Trumpet and Piano (1931); *Fatrasie* for Violin and Piano (1934); *Rengaines* for Woodwind Quintet (1937); *Suite de danceries No. 3* for 2 Trumpets, Horn, and Trombone (1944); *Concert flamand* for Woodwind Quartet (1965); *3 pièces anciennes* for Violin and Viola (1969). **PIANO:** *Improvisation* (1917); Sonatine (1920); *Echos de Spa* (1934). **VOCAL:** *3 poèmes japonais* for Soprano and String Quartet (1916); *Avertissement* for 3 or 5 Narrators and Percussion (1926); *Quelques airs de Clarisse Juranville* for Alto and 8 Instruments or Piano Quintet (1928); *Alleluia* for Voice and 9 Instruments (1928); *Pastorales wallonnes* for Soprano, Alto, Tenor, Bass, and Orch. (1942); *Comptines pour enfants sinistres* for Soprano, Mezzo-soprano, Violin, Clarinet, and Piano (1942); *8 chansons enfantines* for Voice and Orch. (1943); *La légende de St. Nicolas* for Voice, Celesta, and Orch. (1943); *Le marchand d'images*, rustic cantata for 2 Speakers, Soprano, Alto, Tenor, Bass, Chorus, and Orch., after popular Walloon songs (1944–65); *L'autre voix* for Soprano, Flute, Clarinet, Violin, Cello, and Piano (1948); *5 laude* for Soprano, Alto, Tenor, Bass, and Chorus (1961); *Motet* for 6 Solo Voices and Orch. (1961); *Triptyque pour un violon* for Speaker, Mezzo-soprano, 2 Altos, 2 Baritones, Bass, Organ, and Percussion (1963); choruses; solo songs.

Sousa, John Philip, famous American bandmaster and composer; b. Washington, D.C., Nov. 6, 1854; d. Reading, Pa., March 6, 1932. He was the son of a Portuguese father and a German mother. He studied violin and orchestration with John Esputa, Jr., and violin and harmony with George Felix Benkert in Washington, D.C.; also acquired considerable proficiency on wind instruments. After playing in the Marine Band (1868–75), he was active in theater orchs.; in 1876 he was a violinist in the special orch. in Philadelphia conducted by Offenbach during his U.S. tour. In 1880 he was appointed director of the Marine Band, which he led with distinction until 1892. He then organized his own band and led it in its first concert in Plainfield, N.J., on Sept. 26, 1892. In subsequent years he gave successful concerts throughout the U.S. and Canada; played at the Chicago World's Fair in 1893 and at the Paris Exposition in 1900; made 4 European tours (1900, 1901, 1903, and 1905), with increasing acclaim, and finally a tour around the world, in 1910–11. His flair for writing band music was extraordinary; the infectious rhythms of his military marches and the brilliance of his band arrangements earned him the sobriquet "The March King"; particularly celebrated is his march *The Stars and Stripes Forever,* which became famous all over the world; in 1987 a bill was passed in the U.S. Congress and duly signed by President Ronald Reagan making it the official march of the U.S.. During World War I, Sousa served as a lieutenant in the Naval Reserve. He continued his annual tours almost to the time of his death. He was instrumental in the development of the Sousaphone, a bass tuba with upright bell, which has been used in bands since the 1890s.

WORKS (in alphabetical order): **DRAMATIC: OPERETTAS:** *The American Maid* (1909; Rochester, N.Y., Jan. 27, 1913); *The Bride Elect* (New Haven, Conn., Dec. 28, 1897); *El Capitan* (1895; Boston, April 13, 1896); *The Charlatan* (Montreal, Aug. 29, 1898); *Chris and the Wonderful Lamp* (New Haven, Conn., Oct. 23, 1899); *Desirée* (1883; Washington, D.C., May 1, 1884); *The Free Lance* (1905; Springfield, Mass., March 26, 1906); *The Irish Dragoon* (1915; unfinished); *Katherine* (1879); *The Queen of Hearts* (1885; Washington, D.C., April 12, 1886); *The Smugglers* (Washington, D.C., March 25, 1882). Also incidental music.

MARCHES: *Across the Danube* (1877); *America First* (1916); *Anchor and Star* (1918); *Ancient and Honorable Artillery Company* (1924); *The Atlantic City Pageant* (1927); *The Aviators* (1931); *The Beau Ideal* (1893); *The Belle of Chicago* (1892); *Ben Bolt* (1888); *The Black Horse Troop* (1924); *Bonnie Annie Laurie* (1883); *Boy Scouts of America* (1916); *The Bride Elect* (1897); *Bullets and Bayonets* (1918); *El Capitan* (1896); *A Century of Progress* (1931); *The Chantyman's March* (1918); *The Charlatan* (1898); *The Circumnavigators Club* (1931); *Circus March* (n.d.); *Columbia's Pride* (1914); *Comrades of the Legion* (1920); *Congress Hall* (1882); *Corcoran Cadets* (1890); *The Crusader* (1888); *Daughters of Texas* (1929); *The Dauntless Battalion* (1922); *The Diplomat* (1904); *The Directorate* (1894); *Esprit de Corps* (1878); *The Fairest of the Fair* (1908); *The Federal* (1910); *Flags of Freedom* (1918); *La Flor de Sevilla* (1929); *Foshay Tower Washington Memorial* (1929); *The Free Lance* (1906); *From Maine to Oregon* (1913); *The Gallant Seventh* (1922); *George Washington Bicentennial* (1930); *The Gladiator* (1886; the 1st work to sell a million copies); *Globe and Eagle* (1879); *The Glory of the Yankee Navy* (1909); *Golden Jubilee* (1928); *The Golden Star* (1919); *The Gridiron Club* (1926); *Guide Right* (1881); *Hail to the Spirit of Liberty* (1900); *Hands Across the Sea* (1899); *Harmonica Wizard* (1930); *The High School Cadets* (1890); *Homeward Bound* (n.d.); *The Honored Dead* (1876); *Imperial Edward* (1902); *In Memoriam* (1881; for the assassinated President Garfield); *The Invincible Eagle* (1901); *Jack Tar* (1903); *Kansas Wildcats* (1931); *Keeping Step with the Union* (1921); *King Cotton* (1895); *The Lambs' March* (1914); *The Legionnaires* (1930); *The Liberty Bell* (1893); *Liberty Loan* (1917); *The Loyal Legion* (1890); *Magna Carta* (1927); *The Man Behind the Gun* (1899); *Manhattan Beach* (1893); *March of the Mitten Men* (1923); *March of the Pan-Americans* (1915); *March of the Royal Trumpets* (1892); *Marquette University March* (1924; on receiving an honorary D.M., Nov. 16, 1923); *Mikado March* (1885); *The Minnesota March* (1927); *Mother Goose* (1883); *Mother Hubbard March* (1885); *National Fencibles* (1888); *The National Game* (1925; for the 50th anniversary of the National League of baseball); *The Naval Reserve* (1917); *New Mexico* (1928); *The New York Hippodrome* (1915); *Nobles of the Mystic Shrine* (1923); *The Northern Pines* (1931); *The Occidental* (1887); *Old Ironsides* (1926); *On Parade* (1892); *On the Campus* (1920); *On the Tramp* (1879); *Our Flirtations* (1880); *The Pathfinder of Panama* (1915); *Pet of the Petticoats* (1883); *The Phoenix March* (1875); *The Picador* (1889); *Powhatan's Daughter* (1907); *President Garfield's Inauguration March* (1881); *The Pride of Pittsburgh* (1901); *The Pride of the Wolverines* (1926); *Prince Charming* (1928); *The Quilting Party March* (1889); *Recognition March* (c.1880); *Resumption March* (1879); *Review* (1873; his 1st publ. march); *Revival March* (1876); *Riders for the Flag* (1927); *The Rifle Regiment* (1886); *Right Forward* (1881); *Right—Left* (1883); *The Royal Welch Fusiliers* (No. 1, 1929; No. 2, 1930); *Sable and Spurs* (1918); *Salutation* (1873); *The Salvation Army* (1930); *Semper Fidelis* (1888); *Sesquicentennial Exposition March* (1926); *Solid Men to the Front* (1918); *Sound Off* (1885); *The Stars and Stripes Forever* (1896; made the official march of the U.S. by act of Congress, 1987); *The Thunderer* (1889); *Transit of Venus* (1883); *The Triton* (1892); *Triumph of Time* (1885); *Universal Peace* (probably 1925); *University of Illinois* (1929); *University of Nebraska* (1928); *USAAC March* (1918); *U.S. Field Artillery* (1917); *The Victory Chest* (1918); *The Volunteers* (1918); *The Washington Post* (1889); *Wedding March* (1918); *The White Plume* (1884); *The White Rose* (1917); *Who's Who in Navy Blue* (1920); *The Wildcats* (1930 or 1931); *Wisconsin Forward Forever* (1917); *The Wolverine March* (1881); *Yorktown Centennial* (1881).

OTHER: Suites for Band; overtures; descriptive pieces; instrumental solos; orch. works; about 76 songs, ballads, hymns; many arrangements and transcriptions.

WRITINGS: AUTOBIOGRAPHICAL: *Through the Years with Sousa* (1910); *Marching Along* (1928). **MANUALS:** *The Trumpet and Drum* (1886); *National Patriotic and Typical Airs of All Lands* (1890). **NOVELS:** *The Fifth String* (1902); *Pipetown Sandy* (1905); *The Transit of Venus* (1919).

BIBL.: M. Simon, *J.P. S., the March King* (N.Y., 1944); A. Lingg, *J.P. S.* (N.Y., 1954); K. Berger, *The March King and His Band* (N.Y., 1957); R. Goldman, "The Great American Composers: J.P. S.," *HiFi Stereo Review* (July 1967); J. Smart, *The S. Band: A Discography* (Washington, D.C., 1970); W. Stacy, *J.P. S. and His Band Suites: An Analytic and Cultural Study* (diss., Univ. of Colo., 1972); P. Bierley, *J.P. S.: American Phenomenon* (N.Y., 1973; 2nd ed., rev., 1986); idem, *J.P. S.: A Descriptive Catalog of His Works* (Urbana, Ill., 1973; 2nd ed., rev. and aug., 1984, as *The Works of J.P. S.*); J. Newsom, ed., *Perspectives on J.P. S.* (Washington, D.C., 1983); W. Mitziga, *The Sound of S.: J.P. S. Compositions Recorded* (Chicago, 1986).

Souster, Tim(othy Andrew James), avant-garde English composer; b. Bletchley, Buckinghamshire, Jan. 29, 1943; d. Cambridge, March 1, 1994. He studied with Rose, Lumsden, and Wellesz at the Univ. of Oxford (B.A., 1964; B.Mus., 1965); in 1964 he attended courses in new music given by Stockhausen and Berio in Darmstadt; received private instruction from Bennett (1965). He was a music producer for the BBC (1965–67); after serving as composer-in-residence at King's College, Cambridge (1969–71), he was a teaching assistant to Stockhausen in Cologne (1971–73); later was a research fellow in electronic music at the Univ. of Keele (1975–77); in 1988–89 he was chairman of the Assn. of Professional Composers. He became one of the most articulate exponents of serial, aleatory, and combinatorial ideas, in which electronic media are employed in conjunction with acoustical performances by humans; he expounded these ideas in his writings in the *Listener, Tempo,* and other progressive publications. In 1969 he was a cofounder (with Roger Smalley) of the Intermodulation Group, with the aim of presenting works by congenial composers and experimenters; it disbanded in 1976 and he then formed a new group, OdB.

WORKS: *Songs of the Seasons* for Soprano and Viola (1965); *Poem in Depression* for Soprano, Flute, Viola, Cello, and Piano (1965); *Parallels* for 2 Percussion Players (1966); *Metropolitan*

Games for Piano Duet (1967); *Titus Groan Music* for Wind Quintet, Electronics, and Magnetic Tape (1969); *Chinese Whispers* for Percussion and 3 Electronic Synthesizers (1970); *Waste Land Music* for Soprano Saxophone, Modulated Piano, Modulated Organ, and Electronic Synthesizer (London, July 14, 1970); *Triple Music II* for 3 Orchs. (London, Aug. 13, 1970); *Song of an Average City* for Small Orch. and Tape (1974); *Afghan Amplitudes* for Keyboards and Synthesizers (1976); Sonata for Cello and Ensemble (1979); *Mareas* for 4 Amplified Voices and Tape (1981); *Paws 3D* for Orch. (1984); *Le Souvenir de Maurice Ravel* for Septet (1984); *Hambledon Hill* for Amplified String Quartet (1985); Concerto for Trumpet, Live Electronics, and Orch. (1988).

Soustrot, Marc, French conductor; b. Lyons, April 15, 1949. He studied at the Lyons Cons. (1962–69) and then was a student at the Paris Cons. (1969–76) of Paul Bernard (trombone), Christian Lardé (chamber music), Claude Ballif (analysis), and Manuel Rosenthal and Georges Tzipine (conducting). In 1974 he won the Rupert conducting competition in London, and was Previn's assistant with the London Sym. Orch. from 1974 to 1976. In 1975 he won the Besançon conducting competition. He was made 2nd conductor of l'Orchestre Philharmonique des Pays de la Loire in Angers in 1976, and then was its music director from 1978. From 1986 to 1990 he concurrently served as artistic director of the Nantes Opera. As a guest conductor, Soustrot appeared with various orchs. and opera houses in Europe.

Southern, Eileen, black American musicologist; b. Minneapolis, Feb. 19, 1920. The Norwegian pianist Meda Zarbell Steele supervised her studies at Chicago Musical College and helped her obtain scholarships at the Univ. of Chicago, where she studied with Scott Goldwaite and Sigmund Levarie (B.A., 1940; M.A., 1941, with the thesis *The Use of Negro Folksong in Symphonic Music*). She then taught at Prairie View State College (1941–42), Southern Univ. (1943–45; 1949–51), Alcorn State College (1945–46), Claflin Univ. (1947–49), and secondary schools in N.Y. (1954–60). Simultaneously she pursued her own studies of medieval and Renaissance music; enrolled at N.Y. Univ. in the classes of Reese and Bernstein, and wrote her diss., *The Buxheim Organ Book* (Ph.D., 1961; publ. 1963). She gave courses in Renaissance music at Brooklyn College (1960–68) and York College (1968–75); also founded the journal *Black Perspective in Music* (1973), which she ed. until 1991. She was prof. of music and chairman of the dept. of Afro-American studies at Harvard Univ. (1975–86). In addition to her articles in journals, she was a contributor to *The New Grove Dictionary of Music and Musicians* (1980) and *The New Grove Dictionary of American Music* (1986). In 1991 she was made an honorary member of the American Musicological Soc.

WRITINGS: *The Music of Black Americans: A History* (N.Y., 1971; 2nd ed., 1984); *Readings in Black American Music* (N.Y., 1971; 2nd ed., 1983); *Biographical Dictionary of Afro-American and African Musicians* (Westport, Conn., 1982); *Afro-American Traditions in Song: An Annotated Bibliography* (1990).

BIBL.: J. Wright and S. Floyd, Jr., *New Perspectives on Music: Essays in Honor of E. S.* (Detroit, 1992).

Souzay, Gérard (real name, **Gérard Marcel Tisserand**), distinguished French baritone; b. Angers, Dec. 8, 1918. He studied voice with Pierre Bernac, Claire Croiza, Vanni Marcoux, and Lotte Lehmann, and was a student at the Paris Cons. (1940–45). He made his recital debut in Paris in 1945, his U.S. debut in a recital at N.Y.'s Town Hall in 1950, and his operatic debut as Count Robinson in Cimarosa's *Il Matrimonio segreto* at the Aix-en-Provence Festival in 1957. He made his Metropolitan Opera debut in N.Y. as Count Almaviva in *Le nozze di Figaro* on Jan. 21, 1965. In subsequent years, he toured extensively, mainly as a recitalist. In 1985 he joined the faculty of the Indiana Univ. School of Music in Bloomington; taught at the Univ. of Texas in Austin in 1986. Souzay won renown as a concert artist; after Bernac, he was esteemed as the foremost interpreter of French art songs; equally acclaimed were his performances of German lieder, which received encomiums from German critics and audiences.

BIBL.: M. Morris, *The Recorded Performances of G. S.: A Discography* (N.Y., 1991).

Sowande, Fela (actually, **Olufela**), Nigerian composer; b. Oyo, May 29, 1905; d. Ravenna, Ohio, March 13, 1987. He studied music in Lagos; then went to London, where he played in a combo in nightclubs; at the same time he took courses at London Univ. and the Trinity College of Music. He served in the Royal Air Force during World War II. In 1944 he composed an *African Suite* for Strings; returned to Nigeria in 1953; in 1957 he received a grant from the State Dept. to travel in the U.S.; was again in the U.S. in 1961, on a Rockefeller grant, and on June 1, 1961, conducted a group of members of the N.Y. Phil. in Carnegie Hall in a program of his own compositions, among them *Nigerian Folk Symphony.* Upon returning to Nigeria, he joined the staff of the Univ. College at Ibadan. In his music he pursued the goal of cultural integration of native folk material with Western art forms.

Sowerby, Leo, remarkable American composer and organist; b. Grand Rapids, Mich., May 1, 1895; d. Fort Clinton, Ohio, July 7, 1968. He studied piano with Calvin Lampert and theory with Arthur Andersen in Chicago; also had sporadic lessons with Grainger. He learned to play the organ without a teacher, and yet developed a virtuoso technique that enabled him to hold prestigious appointments as a church organist. He was extremely precocious; on Jan. 17, 1917, he presented himself in Chicago in a program grandiloquently billed "Leo Sowerby: His Music," which included such ambitious works as a Piano Concerto, with the composer at the keyboard; a Cello Concerto; and symphonic pieces. During World War I, he served as a bandmaster in the U.S. Army. He completed his musical studies at the American Cons. in Chicago (M.M., 1918). In 1921 he received the American Prix de Rome, the first of its kind to be awarded for composition; he spent 3 years at the American Cons. in Rome. Returning to Chicago, he served as a teacher of composition at the American Cons. (1925–62); also was organist and choirmaster at the Episcopal Cathedral of St. James (1927–62); then was founder-director of the College of Church Musicians at the National Cathedral in Washington, D.C. (1962–68). In 1935 he was elected to membership in the National Inst. of Arts and Letters. In 1946 he won the Pulitzer Prize in Music for his *Canticle of the Sun.* Sowerby never attempted to discover new ways of making music; his style was eclectic in the positive sense of the word, selecting what appeared to be the best in various doctrines and styles. Hindemith's invidious reference to Sowerby as the 4th B in music, a "sour B," is not appropriate, for Sowerby's music is anything but sour; he certainly knew how to build up sonorous masses, particularly in his vocal compositions.

WORKS: ORCH.: Violin Concerto (1913; rev. 1924); *The Sorrow of Mydath*, symphonic poem (1915); *Rhapsody on British Folk Tunes* (1915); *Comes Autumn Time*, overture (Chicago, Jan. 17, 1917); 2 cello concertos: No. 1 (Chicago, Jan. 17, 1917) and No. 2 (1929–34; N.Y., April 2, 1935); 2 piano concertos: No. 1, with Soprano obbligato (Chicago, Jan. 17, 1917; rev., 1919, without soprano) and No. 2 (1932; Boston, Nov. 30, 1936); *The Irish Washerwoman*, transcription (Chicago, Jan. 17, 1917); *Money Musk*, transcription (1917); *A Set of 4: Suite of Ironics* (Chicago, Feb. 15, 1918); Concerto for Harp and Small Orch. (1919); 5 syms.: No. 1 (Chicago, April 7, 1922), No. 2 (Chicago, March 29, 1929), No. 3 (Chicago, March 6, 1941), No. 4 (Boston, Jan. 7, 1949, Koussevitzky conducting), and No. 5 (1964); *King Estmere*, ballad for 2 Pianos and Orch. (Rome, April 8, 1923); *Rhapsody* for Chamber Orch. (1922); *From the Northland* (Rome, May 27, 1924); *Synconata and Monotony* for Jazz Orch. (1924, 1925; Chicago, Oct. 11, 1925); *Medieval Poem* for Organ and Orch. (Chicago, April 20, 1926); *Prairie*, symphonic poem (Interlochen, Mich., Aug. 11, 1929); *Passacaglia, Interlude and Fugue* (1931–32); *Sinfonietta* for Strings (1933–34); *Theme in Yellow*, after Sandburg (1937); Concerto in

C for Organ and Orch. (Boston, April 22, 1938, E. Power Biggs soloist); *Concert Overture* (1941); *Poem* for Viola and Orch. or Organ (1941); *Fantasy on Hymn Tunes* (1943); *Classic Concerto* for Organ and Strings (1944); *Portrait: Fantasy in Triptych* (1946; Indianapolis, Nov. 21, 1953); *Concert Piece* for Organ and Orch. (1951); *All on a Summer's Day* (1954; Louisville, Jan. 8, 1955); untitled work (Concerto No. 2) for Organ and Orch. (1967–68). **CHAMBER:** Quartet for Violin, Cello, Horn, and Piano (1911); 3 unnumbered piano trios (in D, undated; 1911; 1953); 5 unnumbered violin sonatas (in E, 1912, rev. 1916; in G, undated; in B-flat, 1922; in A, *Fantasy Sonata*, 1944; in D, 1959); 2 unnumbered cello sonatas (1912, 1920); Sonata for Solo Violin (1914); *Serenade* for String Quartet (1916); Wind Quintet (1916); Trio for Flute, Viola, and Piano (1919); 2 string quartets (1923–24; 1934–35; both MSS lost); *Pop Goes the Weasel* for Wind Quintet (1927); *Chaconne* for Trombone and Piano (1936); Clarinet Sonata (1938); *Poem* for Viola and Organ (1941); Trumpet Sonata (1945); *Ballade* for English Horn and Organ (1949); *Fantasy* for Trumpet and Organ (1962); *Suite* for Oboe and Piano (1963); *Triptych of Diversions* for Organ, 2 Violins, Double Bass, Oboe, and Percussion (1962); *Dialog* for Organ and Piano (1967); an undated Horn Trio. **KEYBOARD: PIANO:** 2 sonatas (1912; 1948, rev. 1965); *Florida*, suite (1929); Suite (1959); Suite for Piano, 4-hands (1959). **ORGAN:** Sonata (1914–17); Sym. (1930); *Suite* (1934); *Church Sonata* (1956); *Sinfonia brevis* (1965); *Bright, Blithe and Brisk* (1967); *Passacaglia* (1967). **VOCAL:** *A Liturgy of Hope* for Soprano, Men's Chorus, and Organ (1917); an untitled oratorio after the Book of Psalms (1924); *The Vision of Sir Launfal*, cantata after James Lowell (1925); *Great Is the Lord* for Chorus, Orch., and Organ (1933); *Forsaken of Man* for Chorus and Organ (1939); *Song for America* for Chorus and Orch. (1942); *The Canticle of the Sun* for Chorus and Orch., after St. Francis (1944; N.Y., April 16, 1945); *Christ Reborn*, cantata for Chorus and Organ (1950; Philadelphia, Nov. 1, 1953); *The Throne of God* for Chorus and Orch. (1956; Washington, D.C., Nov. 18, 1957); *The Ark of the Covenant*, cantata for Chorus and Organ (1959); *Solomon's Garden*, cantata for Tenor, Chorus, and Chamber Orch. (1964); *La Corona* for Chorus and Orch. (1967); numerous anthems, songs, etc.

BIBL.: "L. S.: A Symposium of Tribute," *Music: the A.G.O. and R.C.C.O. Magazine*, II/10 (1968); M. Guiltinan, *The Absolute Music for Piano Solo by L. S.* (diss., Univ. of Rochester, 1977); *L. S.: A Short Biography and a Complete List of His Compositions* (Chicago, 1979); D. Bading, *L. S.'s Works for Organ with Orchestra or Ensemble* (thesis, Univ. of Kansas, 1983).

Soyer, Roger (Julien Jacques), French bass; b. Paris, Sept. 1, 1939. He began his training with Daum, and then studied with Jouatte and Musy at the Paris Cons., where he won premiers prix in singing (1962) and opera (1963). In 1962 he made his debut at the Piccola Scala in Milan as Poulenc's Tiresias. From 1963 he sang at the Paris Opéra. In 1964 he appeared as Pluto in Monteverdi's *Orfeo* at the Aix-en-Provence Festival, where he sang with much success in subsequent years. In 1968 he made his U.S. debut in Miami as Friar Lawrence in *Roméo et Juliette*, and also appeared at the Wexford Festival in England in *La Jolie Fille*. He made his Metropolitan Opera debut in N.Y. in one of his finest roles, Don Giovanni, on Nov. 16, 1972. He also chose that role for his first appearance at the Edinburgh Festival in 1973. In subsequent years, he sang with principal European opera houses and festivals. He also appeared widely as a concert artist. Among his other admired roles were Don Basilio, Méphistophélès, Ferrando, Colline, and Sulpice.

Spadavecchia, Antonio (Emmanuilovich), Russian composer; b. Odessa, June 3, 1907; d. Moscow, Feb. 7, 1988. He was of Italian descent. After training with Shebalin at the Moscow Cons. (graduated, 1937), he completed his studies with Prokofiev (1944).

WORKS: DRAMATIC: OPERAS: *Ak-Buzat* (The Magic Steed; Ufa, Nov. 7, 1942; rev. 1952; in collaboration with Zaimov); *Khozyaka gostinitis* (The Inn Hostess; Moscow, April 24, 1949); *Khozhdeniye po mukam* (Pilgrimage of Sorrows; Perm, Dec. 29, 1953); *Ovod* (The Gadfly; Perm, Nov. 8, 1957); *Braviy soldat Shveky* (1963); *Yukki* (1970); *Ognenniye godi* (Ordeal by fire; 1971). **BALLETS:** *Vragie* (Enemies; Moscow, May 20, 1938); *Bereg schastya* (The Shore of Happiness; Moscow, Nov. 6, 1948; rev. 1955). Also musical comedies, incidental music, and film scores. **ORCH:** *Dzangar*, symphonic suite (1940); *Heroic Overture on Bashkir Songs* (Ufa, Nov. 6, 1942); Piano Concerto (1944). **CHAMBER:** *Romantic Trio* for Violin, Cello, and Piano (1937); String Quartet (1937); *Elegie* for Cello and Piano (1955). **VOCAL:** Songs.

Spaeth, Sigmund, American writer on music; b. Philadelphia, April 10, 1885; d. N.Y., Nov. 11, 1965. He studied piano and violin with A. Bachmann; then attended Haverford College (B.A., 1905; M.A., 1906) and Princeton Univ. (Ph.D., 1910, with the diss. *Milton's Knowledge of Music*; publ. in Princeton, N.J., 1913). He was music ed. of the *N.Y. Evening Mail* (1914–18), education director of the American Piano Co. (1920–27), and president of the National Assn. of American Composers and Conductors (1934–37). Spaeth lectured widely on music, gave popular talks on the radio, was active in musical journalism, and held various posts in educational organizations. He ed. the valuable collections *Read 'em and Weep* (1926; rev. 1945) and *Weep Some More, My Lady* (1927).

WRITINGS (all publ. in N.Y. unless otherwise given): *The Common Sense of Music* (1924); *The Art of Enjoying Music* (1933; rev. 1949); *Music for Everybody* (1934); *Great Symphonies* (Garden City, N.Y., 1936; 2nd ed., rev., 1952); *Stories behind the World's Great Music* (1937); *Music for Fun* (1939); *Great Program Music* (1940); *A Guide to Great Orchestral Music* (1943); *At Home with Music* (Garden City, N.Y., 1945); *A History of Popular Music in America* (1948); *Dedication: The Love Story of Clara and Robert Schumann* (N.Y., 1950); *Opportunities in Music Careers* (1950; 2nd ed., rev., 1966); *Fifty Years with Music* (1959); *The Importance of Music* (1963).

Spalding, Albert, esteemed American violinist; b. Chicago, Aug. 15, 1888; d. N.Y., May 26, 1953. He studied violin with Ulpiano Chiti in Florence and with Juan Buitrago in N.Y. before entering the Bologna Cons. at the age of 14; subsequently received further violin training from Augustin Lefort at the Paris Cons., and studied composition with Antonio Scontrino in Florence. He made his public debut in Paris on June 6, 1905, and his American debut as a soloist with the N.Y. Sym. Orch. on Nov. 8, 1908. Beginning in 1919, he made annual tours of the U.S. and acquired the reputation of a fine artist, even though not necessarily a contagiously flamboyant one. He also made appearances in Europe. On June 20, 1950, he gave his farewell performance in N.Y. In 1926 he was elected to the National Inst. of Arts and Letters and in 1937 to the American Academy of Arts and Letters. He gave the U.S. premieres of the violin concertos of Dohnányi, Elgar, and Barber. His own works include an orch. suite, 2 violin concertos, a String Quartet, a Violin Sonata, various violin pieces, songs, and piano pieces. He publ. an autobiography, *Rise to Follow* (N.Y., 1943), and a fictionalized biography of Tartini, *A Fiddle, a Sword, and a Lady* (N.Y., 1953).

Spani, Hina (real name, **Higinia Tunon**), Argentine soprano; b. Puán, Feb. 15, 1896; d. Buenos Aires, July 11, 1969. She studied in Buenos Aires and Milan. She made her operatic debut at La Scala in Milan in 1915 as Anna in Catalani's *Loreley*; also sang in Turin, Naples, and Parma; made many appearances at the Teatro Colón in Buenos Aires (1915–40). From 1946 she taught voice in Buenos Aires, and from 1952 served as director of the School of Music at the Univ. of Buenos Aires. She was highly regarded as a dramatic soprano; her repertoire included more than 70 roles.

Spano, Robert, American conductor and pianist; b. Conneaup, Ohio, May 7, 1961. He studied conducting with Robert Baustian at the Oberlin (Ohio) College Cons. of Music, where he also received training in piano, violin, and composition; later completed his conducting studies with Max Rudolf at the Curtis Inst. of Music in Philadelphia. In 1989 he became music director of the Opera Theater at Oberlin College. From 1990 to 1993 he was assistant conductor of the Boston Sym. Orch.; subsequently toured widely as a guest conductor of major orchs. throughout North America, Europe, and Asia. In 1994 he received the Seaver/NEA conductors award. During the 1994–95 season, he made his debut at London's Covent Garden conducting *Billy Budd.* He was music director designate (1995–96) and then music director (from 1996) of the Brooklyn Phil.

Sparnaay, Harry, prominent Dutch bass clarinetist; b. Amsterdam, April 14, 1944. He played tenor saxophone in the Bohemia Jazz Quintet and later in the Theo Deken Orch.; studied clarinet at the Amsterdam Cons., where he eventually turned to the bass clarinet. He had over 100 works written for him (as a soloist or for his chamber duo, Fusion Moderne, which was formed in 1971 with the pianist Polo de Haas) by Berio, Goeyvaerts, Hrisanidis, Kunst, Logothetis, Raxach, Straesser, and others; played in contemporary music festivals.

Spasov, Ivan, Bulgarian composer; b. Sofia, Jan. 17, 1934. He studied composition with Vladigerov at the Bulgarian State Cons. in Sofia (1951–56) and later with Sikorski and Wislocki at the Warsaw Cons.; subsequently devoted himself mainly to teaching and composing. Spasov composed in an advanced style.

WORKS: ORCH.: *Sonata concertante* for Clarinet and Orch. (1959); 3 syms. (1960, 1975, 1978); *Micro-Suite* for Chamber Orch. (1963); *Dances* (1964); *2 Bulgarian Melodies* (1968, 1970); *Competition* for 22 Winds (1969; Plovdiv, May 10, 1973); Cello Concerto (1974); Piano Concerto (1976); *Firework* (1980); Violin Concerto (1980). **CHAMBER:** Clarinet Sonata (1959); Viola Sonata (1960); *Bagatelles* for Flute and Harp (1964); *Episodes* for 4 Instrumental Groups (1965); *Movements I* for 12 Strings (1966) and *II* for 12 Strings and 3 Bagpipes (1968); *10 Groups* for Hunting Horn and Piano (1965); *Musique pour des amis* for String Quartet and Jazz Quartet (1966); String Quartet No. 1 (1973); Cello Sonata (1980); Piano Trio (1981). **PIANO:** *Games* (1964); *The Art of the Seria* (3 notebooks; 1968, 1969, 1970). **VOCAL:** *Plakat,* oratorio (1958); *Monologues of a Lonely Woman,* monodrama for Soprano, Women's Chorus, Chamber Ensemble, and Tape (1976); *Canti lamentosi* for 2 Sopranos and Chamber Orch. (1979); *23 Lines from Emily Dickenson* for Soprano and Instrumental Ensemble (1989).

Speaks, Oley, American baritone and song composer; b. Canal Winchester, Ohio, June 28, 1874; d. N.Y., Aug. 27, 1948. He studied singing with Emma Thursby and composition with Max Spicker and W. Macfarlane. He sang at various churches in N.Y. (1898–1906); then devoted himself entirely to concert singing and composition. He wrote some of the most popular songs in the American repertoire of his day: *On the Road to Mandalay* (1907), *Morning* (1910), *To You* (1910), *Sylvia* (1914), and *The Prayer Perfect* (1930).

Spelman, Timothy (Mather), American composer; b. Brooklyn, Jan. 21, 1891; d. Florence, Italy, Aug. 21, 1970. He studied with H.R. Shelley in N.Y. (1908), W.R. Spalding and E.B. Hill at Harvard Univ. (1909–13), and Walter Courvoisier at the Munich Cons. (1913–15); he returned to the U.S. in 1915 and was active as director of a military band. After 1918 he went back to Europe with his wife, the poetess Leolyn Everett, settling in Florence. He returned to the U.S. in 1935; in 1947 he went back to Florence. His music was performed more often in Europe than in America; indeed, his style of composition is exceedingly European, influenced by Italian Romanticism and French Impressionism.

WORKS: DRAMATIC: *Snowdrop,* pantomime (Brooklyn, 1911); *The Romance of the Rose,* "wordless fantasy" (Boston, 1913; rev., St. Paul, Minn., Dec. 4, 1915); *La Magnifica,* music drama after Leolyn Everett-Spelman (1920); *The Sea Rovers,* opera (1928); *The Sunken City,* opera (1930); *Babakan,* fantastic comedy (1935); *The Courtship of Miles Standish,* opera after Longfellow (1943). **ORCH.:** *Saint's Days,* suite in 4 movements, including *Assisi, the Great Pardon of St. Francis* (Boston, March 26, 1926); *The Outcasts of Poker Flat,* symphonic poem after Bret Harte (1928); Sym. (1935; Rochester, N.Y., Oct. 29, 1936); *Jamboree,* "pocket ballet" (1945); Oboe Concerto (1954). **CHAMBER:** *5 Whimsical Serenades* for String Quartet (1924); *Le Pavillion sur l'eau* for Flute, Harp, and Strings (1925); *Eclogue* for 10 Instruments (1926); String Quartet (1953); piano pieces, including a sonata (1929). **VOCAL:** *Pervigilium Veneris* for Soprano, Baritone, Chorus, and Orch. (1929; Paris, April 30, 1931); *I Love the Jocund Dance* for Women's Voices and Piano (1938); choruses; songs.

Spencer, Émile-Alexis-Xavier, French composer; b. Brussels, May 24, 1859; d. Nanterre, Seine, May 24, 1921. He studied piano in Brussels. In 1881 he went to Paris, where he found his métier as a composer for vaudeville; he was credited with about 4,000 chansonettes, which were popularized by famous singers, among them Yvette Guilbert. His chanson *Jambes de bois* was used by Stravinsky in *Petrouchka* under the impression that it was a folk song; when Spencer brought an action for infringement on his authorship, Stravinsky agreed to pay him part of the royalties for performances.

Spencer, Robert, English lutenist, guitarist, singer, and teacher; b. Ilford, May 9, 1932. He studied lute with Walter Gerwig and Julian Bream (1955) and voice at the Guildhall School of Music in London (1956). Following additional studies at the Dartington School of Music (from 1956), he married the mezzo-soprano Jill Nott-Bower in 1960 and thereafter appeared with her in recitals. He also was a lutenist with the Julian Bream Consort (from 1960) and the Deller Consort (from 1974). He likewise served as prof. of lute at the Royal Academy of Music in London. His repertoire embraces works from the Renaissance to the contemporary era.

Spendiarov, Alexander (Afanasii), significant Armenian composer; b. Kakhovka, Crimea, Nov. 1, 1871; d. Yerevan, May 7, 1928. He studied violin as a child; in 1896 he went to St. Petersburg and took private lessons with Rimsky-Korsakov. In his works, he cultivated a type of Russian orientalism in which the elements of folk songs of the peripheral regions of the old Russian Empire are adroitly arranged in the colorful harmonies of the Russian national school. His best work in this manner was an opera, *Almast,* the composition of which he undertook a decade before his death. It was completed and orchestrated by Maximilian Steinberg, and performed posthumously in Moscow on June 23, 1930. Other works were: *The 3 Palm Trees,* a symphonic tableau (1905); *Crimean Sketches* for Orch. (1903–12); *2 Songs of the Crimean Tatars* for Voice and Orch. (1915; Moscow, Dec. 25, 1927); *Études d'Eriwan,* on Armenian melodies (1925). A complete ed. of his works was publ. in Yerevan (1943–71).

BIBL.: A. Shaverdian, *A. S.* (Moscow, 1929); G. Tigranov, *A. S.* (Yerevan, 1953); idem, *A. S.* (Moscow, 1959; 2nd ed., 1971); R. Atadjan, *A. S.* (Yerevan, 1971).

Sperry, Paul, American tenor; b. Chicago, April 14, 1934. He studied psychology at Harvard Univ., then attended the Sorbonne in Paris; returning to the U.S., he took courses at the Harvard Business School. He then decided upon a career in music, and proceeded to take vocal lessons from a number of coaches, among them Olga Ryss, Michael Trimble, Randolph Mickelson, Martial Singher, Pierre Bernac, Jennie Tourel, and Hans Hotter. He made his debut at Alice Tully Hall in N.Y. on Oct. 8, 1969, then toured throughout the U.S. and Europe. He became chiefly known for his performances of contemporary scores. From 1989 to 1992 he served as president of the American Music Center in N.Y.

Spialek, Hans, Austrian-American orchestrator, arranger, and composer; b. Vienna, April 17, 1894; d. N.Y., Nov. 20, 1983. He took courses at the Vienna Cons. He was drafted into the Austrian army during World War I and taken prisoner by the Russians. In Russia his musical abilities were duly appreciated, and after the Russian Revolution he was given a job at the Bolshoi Theater in Moscow as assistant stage manager (1918–20); concurrently studied at the Cons. with Glière; later he conducted sym. orchs. in Bessarabia (1920–22). He married a Russian singer, Dora Boshoer. In 1923 he went to Germany, and in 1924 reached the U.S. He earned his living as a music copyist; he also supplied orch. interludes and entr'acte music, showing such expertise at organizing the raw materials of American musicals that even before he could master the American tongue he intuitively found the proper instrumentation for the text; and he could work fast to meet the deadlines. Altogether he orchestrated 147 shows, among them 5 by Cole Porter and 11 by Richard Rodgers and Lorenz Hart. With Robert Russell Bennett, he became one of the most reliable arrangers on Broadway. He also composed some orch. works in the approved Broadway style, with such idiosyncratic titles as *The Tall City* (1933) and *Manhattan Watercolors* (1937).

Spiegel, Laurie, American composer, innovator in computer-music technology, computer artist, and writer; b. Chicago, Sept. 20, 1945. She taught herself mandolin, then guitar and banjo in her youth; majored in social sciences at Shimer College in Mt. Carroll, Ill. (B.A., 1967), before switching to the lute and also studying composition with Michael Cjakowski, Persichetti, and Druckman at the Juilliard School in N.Y. (1969–72) and then at Brooklyn College of the City Univ. of N.Y. (M.A., 1975), where she also studied American music with H. Wiley Hitchcock and Richard Crawford; received additional training in philosophy at the Univ. of Oxford, in classical guitar from John W. Duarte in London, in Renaissance and Baroque lute from Fritz Rikko, and in computer music from Emmanuel Ghent and Max Mathews at Bell Labs (1973–79). She taught composition and/or directed electronic- and computer-music studios at Bucks County Community College in Newton, Pa. (1971–75), Aspen (Colo.) Music School (summers, 1971–73), the Cooper Union for the Advancement of Science and Art in N.Y. (1979–81), and N.Y. Univ. (1982). Throughout the 1970s, she worked as a composer and music ed. for film and television and also created computer-generated visual art and computer-animation software based on her music software. She served as a consultant to firms involved in information- and signal-processing technology, being a designer of computer systems and software for musical composition and performance; her program *Music Mouse—An Intelligent Instrument* (1986) is widely known and used. In addition to her electronic and computer scores, she has composed works for traditional media. Her realization of Kepler's *Harmony of the Planets* was sent into space as the first cut in the recording *Sounds of Earth* on each of the 2 *Voyager* spacecrafts in 1977. Her articles on such topics as music and computers, software design and applications, analogies between the musical and visual arts, and music in the media have appeared in a variety of publications; in 1977–78 she served as co-ed. (with Beth Anderson) of *EAR* magazine, a monthly tabloid devoted to the promulgation of new musical ideas. Spiegel has most recently been associated with the revival of Romanticism, tonality, and folk modalities and with the development of visual music, interactive process composition, algorithmic composition, logic-based intelligent instruments, and the use of computers as a performance instrument, compositional tools, and means of distributing music.

WORKS: COMPUTER OR ELECTRONIC: *Orchestras* (1971); *A Tombeau* (1971); *Sojourn* (1971); *Before Completion* (1971); *Mines* (1971); *Harmonic Spheres* (1971); *Return to Zero* (1972); *Sediment* (1972); *Rāga* (1972); *Sunsets* (1973); *Introit* (1973); *2 Fanfares* (1973); *Purification* (1973); *Water Music* (1974); *A Meditation* (1974); *Appalachian Grove* (1974); *The Unquestioned Answer* (1974; also for Harp, 1981); *The Orient Express* (1974); *Pentachrome* (1974); *Patchwork* (1974; rev. 1976); *The Expanding Universe* (1975); *Drums* (1975); *Clockworks* (1975); *Voyages* (1976; rev. with video, 1978); *Music for a Garden of Electronic Delights* (1976); *A Folk Study* (1976); *Kepler's Harmony of the Planets* (1977); Concerto for Digital Synthesizer (1977); *5 Short Visits to Different Worlds* (1977); *An Acceleration* (1978); *Voices Within* (1979); *2 Nocturnes* (1980); *Modes* (1980); *A Quadruple Canon* (1980); *A Canon* (1980); *Phantoms* (1980); *Nomads* (1981); *A Harmonic Algorithm* (1981); *A Cosmos* (1982); *Progression* (1982); *Idea Pieces* (1983); *Harmonic Rhythm* (1983); *Immersion* (1983); *3 Modal Pieces* (1983); *Over Time* (1984); *Cavis Muris* (1986); *Passage* (1987). **OTHER:** *A Deploration* for Flute and Vibraphone (1970); *An Earlier Time* for Guitar (1972); *Waves*, dance piece (1975); *Music for Dance*, dance-video piece (1975); *East River*, dance piece (1976); *Escalante*, ballet (1977); *Evolutions*, music with video (1977); *A Living Painting*, silent visual study (1979); *Hearing Things* for Chamber Orch. (1983); *Over Time*, dance piece (1984); *A Stream* for Mandolin (1984); *Gravity's Joke*, dance piece (1985); *Rain Pieces*, dance suite (1985); *All Star Video*, music for videotape by Nam June Paik (1985); *Song without Words* for Guitar and Mandolin (1986); *Cavis Muris* (1986); *Passage* (1987); *A Harmonic Algorithm* (1988; from the projected *A Musical Offering*); *3 Sonic Spaces* (1989); *Returning East and After the Mountains* (N.Y., Oct. 10, 1990); *3 Movements* for Harpsichord (1990); also computer versions of pieces for Piano or Guitar; incidental music; film and video scores.

Spiegelman, Joel (Warren), American pianist, harpsichordist, conductor, and composer; b. Buffalo, N.Y., Jan. 23, 1933. He studied at the Yale School of Music (1949–50), the Univ. of Buffalo (B.A., 1953), the Longy School of Music at Cambridge, Mass. (1953–54), and Brandeis Univ., where he attended the classes of Shapero, Fine, and Berger (1954–56; 1960–61; M.F.A.); also studied with Boulanger privately in Paris and took courses at the Cons. there (1956–57). He taught at the Longy School of Music (1961–62), Brandeis Univ. (1961–66), and Sarah Lawrence College (from 1966), where he was director of its Studio for Electronic Music and Sound Media. He made tours as a harpsichordist; was director of the N.Y. Electronic Ensemble (1970–73) and conductor of the Russian Orch. of the Americas (1976–79). His output as a composer reveals an eclectic bent.

WORKS: *Ouverture de Saison 1958* for 2 Harps, 2 Flutes, Piano, and Celesta (1958); *2 Fantasies* for String Quartet (1963, 1974); *Kusochki* (Morsels) for Piano, 4-hands (1966); *3 Miniatures* for Clarinet and Piano (1972); *Chamber Music* for Piano Quartet and Percussion (1973); *Midnight Sun* for Oboe and Tape (1976); *A Cry, a Song, a Dance* for Strings (1978); *How Lovely is Thy Dwelling Place* for Bass, Chorus, and Organ (1982); *Astral Dimensions II—Metamorphosis* for Piano, Violin, and Cello (1983; rev. 1984); *Cicada Images: Moltings* for Soprano, Flute, Piano, Pipa, Erhu, and Percussion (1983).

Spies, Claudio, Chilean-born American teacher, conductor, and composer; b. Santiago, March 26, 1925. He settled in the U.S. in 1942 and became a naturalized American citizen in 1966; in 1942 he entered the New England Cons. of Music in Boston and in 1943 became a pupil of Boulanger at the Longy School of Music in Cambridge, Mass.; received private instruction from Shapero (1944–45) and attended the conducting class at the Berkshire Music Center in Tanglewood (summer, 1946); pursued his musical training with Fine, Hindemith, Tillman Merritt, Piston, and Thompson at Harvard Univ. (A.B., 1950), completing his graduate studies there under Piston and Gombosi (M.A., 1954). He was an instructor at Harvard Univ. (1954–57) and a lecturer at Vassar College (1957–58); was assistant prof. (1958–64), assoc. prof. (1964–69), and prof. (1969) at Swarthmore College, where he also conducted its orch. (1958–69); was visiting assoc. prof. at Princeton Univ. (1966–67), returning there as prof. in 1970. In 1950–51 he held a John Knowles Paine Traveling Fellowship and in 1956 received the Lili Boulanger Memorial Fund Award; also received the Brandeis Univ. Creative Arts Award (1967) and an NEA fellowship (1975).

WORKS: ORCH.: *Music for a Ballet* (1955); *Tempi* for 14 Instrumentalists (1962); *LXXXV, Eights and Fives* for Strings and Clarinets (1967). **CHAMBER:** *Canon* for 4 Flutes (1959); *Canon* for Violas (1961); *Viopiacem,* duo for Viola and Keyboard Instruments (1965); *Times 2* for Horns (1968); *Half-time* for Clarinet and Trumpet (1981); *Dreimal Sieben . . .* for Oboe and Piano (1991); *Insieme* for Flute and Violin (1994); *Beisammen* for 2 Oboes or English Horns (1994). **PIANO:** *Impromptu* (1963); *Bagatelle* (1970); *A Between-Birthdays Bagatelle for Roger Sessions's 80th-81st* (1977); *Ein Aggregats-Walzer* (1978); *Bagatelle* (1979); *Verschieden* (1980); *Jahrhundertwalzer* (1981). **VOCAL:** *Il cantico de frate solo* for Bass and Orch. (1958); *Proverbs on Wisdom* for Men's Voices, Organ, and Piano (1964); *7 Enzensberger-Lieder* for Baritone, Clarinet, Horn, Cello, and Percussion (1972); *Rilke: Ruhmen* for Soprano, Clarinet, Trumpet, and Piano (1981); *7 Sonnets* for Soprano, Bass, Clarinet, Bass Clarinet, and String Trio (1989).

Spies, Leo, German conductor and composer; b. Moscow, June 4, 1899; d. Ahrenshoop an der Ostsee, May 1, 1965. He studied with Oskar von Riesemann (1913–15), then continued his training with Schreyer in Dresden and with Kahn and Humperdinck at the Berlin Hochschule für Musik (1916–17). He worked as a répétiteur and conductor in German theaters and with the Universum Film AG; then was in Berlin as conductor of the ballet at the State Opera (1928–35) and the Deutsche Opernhaus (1935–44); subsequently was director of studies and conductor at the Komische Oper (1947–54). In 1956 he was awarded the National Prize of the German Democratic Republic. His compositions followed Romantic lines.

WORKS: DRAMATIC: BALLETS: *Apollo und Daphne* (1936); *Der Stralauer Fischzug* (1936); *Seefahrt* (1937); *Die Sonne lacht* (1942); *Pastorale* (1943); *Die Liebenden von Verona* (1944); *Don Quijote* (1944). Also incidental music. **ORCH.:** *Saltabile* for Strings (1929); Cello Concerto (1940); *Divertimento notturno* for Piano and Orch. (1941); *Fröhliche Ouvertüre* (1951); *Trauermusik* (1951); Violin Concerto (1953); *Orchesterfantasie "Friedrich Engels"* (1955); 2 syms. (1957, 1961); Viola Concerto (1961); *Festmusik* (1964). **CHAMBER:** 2 string quartets (1939, 1961); *Divertimento goldoniano* for 9 Instruments (1939); *Serenade* for 6 Winds, Harp, Percussion, and Double Bass (1946); Sonata for 3 Violins (1958); Trio for 2 Cellos and Piano (1959); 2 sonatas for Wind Quintet (1959, 1963); *Rustikale Fantasien* for 9 Instruments (1962); piano pieces, including 3 sonatas (1917, 1938, 1963). **VOCAL:** Cantatas; choruses; lieder; mass songs.

Spiess, Ludovic, Romanian tenor; b. Cluj, May 13, 1938. He studied in Braşov, Bucharest, and with Antonio Narducci in Milan (1965–66). In 1962 he made his operatic debut as the Duke of Mantua in Galaţi. After singing at the Bucharest Operetta Theater (1962–64), he made his first appearance at the Bucharest Opera as Cavaradossi in 1964, where he subsequently sang regularly. In 1967 he made his debut at the Salzburg Festival as Dmitri in *Boris Godunov.* In 1968 he made his first appearances in Zürich as Radames and at the Vienna State Opera as Dalibor. He sang Calaf at the Verona Arena in 1969. On June 3, 1971, he made his Metropolitan Opera debut in N.Y. as Manrico. He sang Radames at his Covent Garden debut in London in 1973. He also appeared with many other opera houses in Europe and North and South America. Among his other roles were Florestan, Lohengrin, Otello, Don José, and Rodolfo.

Spilka, František, Czech choral conductor, pedagogue, and composer; b. Štěken, Nov. 13, 1887; d. Prague, Oct. 20, 1960. He studied at the Prague Cons. with Stecker, Knittl, and Dvořák. In 1918 he was appointed administrative director of the Prague Cons. He established the Prague Teachers' Choral Society in 1908, of which he remained choirmaster until 1921, and gave concerts with it in France and England; later directed the Prague singing ensemble Smetana. Spilka developed, together with Ferdinand Vach, a new approach to choral performance, emphasizing sound color.

WORKS: OPERAS: *Stará práva* (Ancient Rights; 1915; Prague, June 10, 1917); *Cain or The Birth of Death* (1917). **ORCH.:** *Rhapsody* (1896); Overture (1897). **CHAMBER:** *6 Sonnets* for Violin and Piano (1944); *Rhapsodic Sonata* for Cello and Piano (1946); numerous piano pieces. **VOCAL:** *Jan Hus at the Stake,* oratorio (1907); *Miller's Journeyman,* cantata (1947); choruses; songs.

Spink, Ian (Walter Alfred), noted English musicologist; b. London, March 29, 1932. He studied at London's Trinity College of Music (B.Mus., 1952) and pursued postgraduate studies at the Univ. of Birmingham (diss., 1957–58, *The English Declamatory Ayre, c. 1620–60*). He served as an overseas examiner for Trinity College of Music (1958–60), then was senior lecturer at the Univ. of Sydney (1962–69); subsequently was head of the music dept. of Royal Holloway College at the Univ. of London (from 1969), where he was a reader (1971–74) and a prof. (from 1974); also was dean of the Faculty of Arts (1973–75; 1983–85) and of the Faculty of Music (1974–78). A learned authority on English lute songs, he ed. the valuable collection English Songs, 1625–1660 for the Musica Britannica series, XXXIII (1971); also authored *An Historical Approach to Musical Form* (London, 1967) and *English Song: Dowland to Purcell* (London, 1974; rev. 1986), and ed. Vol. 3, *The Seventeenth Century,* in *The Blackwell History of Music in Britain* (1992).

Spinner, Bob (actually, **Robert Channing**), American dulcimer player; b. Elk Rapids, Mich., Oct. 25, 1932; d. in an automobile accident near there, Oct. 1, 1990. He was born with perfect pitch and built his first hammer dulcimer at the age of 12; as a teen, was known as an exceptional player throughout northern Michigan, one of the traditional homes of the instrument, where he performed at community venues. He played banjo, fiddle, piano, and the cymbalom, and performed Hungarian music on both the dulcimer and the cymbalom; played at the Indiana State Fair in 1952, whereupon he was invited to Indiana Univ. to assist with research and restoration of its dulcimer collection. He appeared on the recorded collection *The American Hammer Dulcimer* (1977) and was taped for the Univ. of Mich. video archive. Spinner was a mentor to numerous dulcimer players, among them Michael Masley, Thomas Bauer, and Paul Gifford; also was co-founder of the Everett Dulcimer Club. He owned more than 20 instruments; a favorite was an unusual and partly damaged instrument made by John Brown of Torch Lake Village in 1880, which went with him to his grave.

Spinner, Leopold, Austrian composer; b. Lemberg (Galicia), April 26, 1906; d. London, Aug. 12, 1980. He studied at the Univ. of Vienna with Adler, von Ficker, and Lach (Ph.D., 1931, with the diss. *Das Rezitativ in der romantischen Oper bis Wagner*); also studied composition with Pisk (1930) and Webern (1935–38). He settled in London in 1938. He received the Hertzka Prize (1933) and the Henri-le-Boeuf Prize (1936) for his compositions. Most of his works are set in the serial mode. His paper "The Abolition of Thematicism" was publ. posthumously in *Tempo* (Sept. 1983).

WORKS: ORCH.: Sym. for Small Orch. (1933); *Passacaglia* for Winds and Piano Trio (1934; Brussels, April 29, 1936); Concerto for Piano and Chamber Orch. (1948; Paris, May 13, 1949); Violin Concerto (1955); *Concerto for Orchestra* (1957); *Ricercata* (1965); Chamber Sym. (1979; BBC, April 15, 1985). **CHAMBER:** 3 string quartets (1935, 1941, 1952); Violin Sonata (1936); Piano Quintet (1937); Piano Trio (1950); Suite for Clarinet and Piano (1956); Clarinet Sonata (1961); Quintet for Clarinet, Horn, Bassoon, Guitar, and Double Bass (1963). **PIANO:** *Fantasy* (1954); *5 Inventions* (1958). **VOCAL:** *Die Sonne sinkt,* cantata (1952); *6 Canons on Irish Folk Songs* for Chorus (1963); many songs.

BIBL.: D. Drew and L. S., "12 Questions for L. S.," *Tempo* (Dec. 1971); M. Graubart, "The Music of L. S.," ibid. (June 1974); idem, "L. S.'s Later Music," ibid. (Sept. 1974); idem, "L. S.: The Final Phase," ibid. (Sept. 1981); R. Bush, "L. S.," *Österreichische Musik Zeitschrift,* No. 10 (1982); D. Drew, "S., 'Die Reihe,' and Thematicism," *Tempo* (Sept. 1983); R. Bush, "L. S.: A List of His Works," ibid. (Sept. 1985).

Spisak, Michal, eminent Polish composer; b. Dabrowa Górnicza, Sept. 14, 1914; d. Paris, Jan. 29, 1965. He studied violin and composition at the Katowice Cons. (diplomas in both, 1937), and composition with Sikorski in Warsaw (1935–37). He completed his training with Boulanger in Paris, where he lived for the rest of his life although he continued to be closely associated with his homeland. In 1964 he was awarded the Polish Composers' Union Prize. He was greatly influenced by Boulanger and by the music of Stravinsky.

WORKS: OPERA: *Marynka* (1955). **ORCH.:** *Serenade* (1939); Concertino for Strings (1942); *Aubade* for Small Orch. (1943); *Allegro de Voiron* (1943); Bassoon Concerto (1944; Copenhagen, June 2, 1947); *Toccata* (1944); *Suite* for Strings (1945); Piano Concerto (1947); *2 Symphonies concertante* (1947, 1956); *Etudes* for Strings (1948); *Divertimento* for 2 Pianos and Orch. (1948); Sonata for Violin and Orch. (1950); Trombone Concertino (1951); *Divertimento* (1951); *Andante and Allegro* for Violin and Orch. (1954); *Concerto giocoso* for Chamber Orch. (1957); Oboe Concerto (1962); Violin Concerto (Katowice, Jan. 30, 1976). **CHAMBER:** Quartet for Oboe, 2 Clarinets, and Bassoon (1938); Sonatina for Oboe, Clarinet, and Bassoon (1946); Violin Sonata (1946); Wind Quintet (1948); *Duetto concertante* for Viola and Bassoon (1949); String Quartet (1953); *Suite* for 2 Violins (1957); *Improvvisazione* for Violin and Piano (1962). **PIANO:** Concerto for 2 Solo Pianos (1942); other pieces. **VOCAL:** Choruses; songs.

Spitzmüller (-Harmersbach), Alexander, Freiherr von, Austrian composer; b. Vienna, Feb. 22, 1894; d. Paris, Nov. 12, 1962. His father was the last finance minister of Austria-Hungary. He studied law at the Univ. of Vienna (D.Jur., 1919); later took lessons in composition with Alban Berg and Hans Apostel. In 1928 he went to Paris, where he taught at the Schola Cantorum; also was active in radio broadcasting and as a music critic. In 1959 he was awarded the music prize of the city of Vienna. His early works are in the neo-Classical vein; eventually he followed the method of composition with 12 tones, following its usage by Berg and Webern.

WORKS: DRAMATIC: OPERA: *Der Diener zweier Herren* (1958). **BALLETS:** *Le premier amour de Don Juan* (1954); *L'impasse* (1956); *Die Sackgasse* (1957); *Le journal* (1957); *Construction humaine* (1959). **ORCH.:** *Sinfonietta ritmica* (1933); 2 piano concertos (1937, 1953); Sym. (1939); *Der 40. Mai,* suite for Chamber Orch. (1941; Amsterdam, June 12, 1948); *3 hymnes à la Paix* (1947); Sym. for Strings (1954). **OTHER:** Chamber music; choral works.

Spivacke, Harold, eminent American musicologist and librarian; b. N.Y., July 18, 1904; d. Washington, D.C., May 9, 1977. He studied at N.Y. Univ. (B.A., 1923; M.A., 1924) and at the Univ. of Berlin (Ph.D., 1933, with the diss. *Über die objektive und subjektive Tonintensität*); while in Berlin, he took private lessons with d'Albert and Leichtentritt as an American-German Students Exchange Fellow and an Alexander von Humboldt Stiftung Fellow. Returning to the U.S., he joined the staff of the Music Division of the Library of Congress in Washington, D.C., first as assistant chief (1934–37), then as chief (1937–72). He also held numerous advisory positions with the Dept. of State, UNESCO et al. As chief of the Music Division of the Library of Congress, he was responsible for the acquisition of many important MSS by contemporary composers, including a large collection of Schoenberg's original MSS. He also commissioned works from contemporary composers for the Coolidge Foundation at the Library of Congress. He publ. some valuable bibliographical papers, among them *Paganiniana* (Washington, D.C., 1945). In 1939 he was chairman of the Organizing Committee of the National Music Council, and until 1972 was Archivist and a member of the Executive Committee of the Council.

Spivakov, Vladimir, Russian violinist and conductor; b. Ufa, Sept. 12, 1944. He studied with Veniamin Sher at the music school of the Leningrad Cons. (1956–60), and with Yankelevich at the Moscow Cons. (graduated, 1967); also received instruction in conducting. He won prizes in various competitions, including the prestigious Long-Thibaud in Paris (3rd, 1965), the Paganini in Genoa (2nd, 1967), the Montreal (1st, 1969), and the Tchaikovsky in Moscow (2nd, 1970). On Feb. 2, 1975, he made his N.Y. debut. In 1979 he made his debut as a conductor with the Chicago Sym. Orch. at the Ravinia Festival; that same year, he founded the Moscow Virtuosi, with which he appeared both as violinist and conductor throughout the world.

Spivakovsky, Tossy, outstanding Russian-American violinist; b. Odessa, Feb. 4, 1907. He studied with Arrigo Serato and Willy Hess at the Berlin Hochschule für Musik. He made his concert debut there at the age of 10; toured Europe (1920–33) and Australia (1933–39). In 1940 he settled in the U.S. and made his N.Y. debut that same year at N.Y.'s Town Hall; then appeared with major American orchs. He taught at the Juilliard School in N.Y. (from 1974). A brilliant virtuoso, his repertory ranged from the classics to contemporary works. As a teacher, he advocated new bowing techniques which proved controversial.

BIBL.: G. Yost, *The S. Way of Bowing* (Pittsburgh, 1949); S. and S. Applebaum, "T. S.," *The Way They Play* (Vol. I, Neptune City, N.J., 1972).

Spoorenberg, Erna, Dutch soprano; b. Yogyakarta, Java, April 11, 1926. She studied in Hilversum and Amsterdam. She made her debut in an appearance with Radio Hilversum in 1947. In 1958 she became a leading member of the Netherlands Opera in Amsterdam. She made occasional appearances at various European music centers, but principally was associated with the musical life of the Netherlands; made her first appearance at the Vienna State Opera in 1949 and her U.S. debut in N.Y. in 1967. She was especially esteemed for her roles in operas by Mozart and for her portrayal of Mélisande. She also pursued a successful career as a concert singer.

Spratlan, Lewis, American composer and teacher; b. Miami, Sept. 5, 1940. He studied composition with Wyner, Schuller, and Powell at Yale Univ. (B.A., 1962; M.M., 1965); then studied with Rochberg and Sessions at the Berkshire Music Center in Tanglewood (1966); held a Guggenheim fellowship (1980–81). He taught at Bay Path Junior College (1965–67), Pennsylvania State Univ. (1967–70), and at Amherst College (from 1970), where he was made a prof. in 1980; also served as chairman of its music dept. (1977–80; 1984; 1985–88; 1992; 1994).

WORKS: DRAMATIC: *Life is a Dream,* opera (1975–77); *Unsleeping City,* dance music (1967). **ORCH.:** 2 Pieces (1971); *Penelope's Knees,* double concerto for Alto Saxophone, Double Bass, and Chamber Orch. (1986); *Apollo and Daphne Variations* (1987; Kislovodsk, Russia, Oct. 4, 1989). **CHAMBER:** *Flange* for 14 Instruments (1965); *Serenade* for 6 Instruments (1970); *Trope-Fantasy* for Oboe, English Horn, and Harpsichord (1970); *Summer Music* for Oboe, Horn, Violin, Cello, and Piano (1971); Woodwind Quintet (1971); *Dance Suite* for Clarinet, Violin, Guitar, and Harpsichord (1973); *Fantasy* for Piano and Chamber Ensemble (1973); *Coils* for Flute, Clarinet, Violin, Viola, Cello, Percussion, and Piano (1980); *Diary Music II* for Chamber Ensemble (1981); String Quartet (1982); *When Crows Gather* for 3 Clarinets, Violin, Cello, and Piano (1986); *A Fanfare for the Tenth* for String Quartet (1988); *Hung Monophonies* for Oboe and 11 Instruments (1990); *Night Music* for Violin, Clarinet, and Percussion (1991); Concertino for Violin, Cello, and Double Bass (1995). **VOCAL:** *Missa brevis* for Men's Chorus and Winds (1965); *Cantata Domine* for Men's Chorus, Winds, and Tape (1968); *Structures after Hart Crane* for Tenor, Piano, and Tape (1968); *Moonsong* for Chorus and Ensemble (1969); *3 Carols on Medieval Texts* for Chorus and Ensemble (1971); *3 Ben Jonson Songs* for Soprano, Flute, Violin, and Cello (1974); *Night Songs* for Soprano, Tenor, and Orch. (1976); *Celebration* for Chorus and Orch. (1984); *Wolves* for Soprano, Flute, Clarinet, and Piano (1988); *In Memoriam* for Soloists, Chorus, and Orch. (1993); *A Barred Owl* for Baritone and 5 Instruments (1994). **OTHER:** Electronic pieces.

Springer, Max, German writer on music and composer; b. Schwendi, Württemberg, Dec. 19, 1877; d. Vienna, Jan. 20, 1954. He attended the Univ. of Prague, and studied music with Klička. In 1910 he was appointed prof. of Gregorian choral singing and organist in the section for church music of the Klosterneuburg Academy, retiring shortly before his death. He publ. *Die Kunst der Choralbegleitung* (1907; Eng. tr., 1908) and manuals on liturgical choral singing; *Graduale Romanum* in modern notation (1930); *Kontrapunkt* (Vienna, 1936). He composed 4 syms. and a great deal of church music, including 8 masses.

Sprongl, Norbert, Austrian composer; b. Obermarkersdorf bei Retz, April 30, 1892; d. Mödling, near Vienna, April 26, 1983. He studied at the Vienna Cons. (graduated, 1933) with J. Marx (composition), N. Kahrer (piano), and R. Lach (theory). Following the development of a style of "free dissonance" modeled after Bartók and Hindemith, he wrote 166 works.

WORKS: ORCH.: 5 piano concertos (1935, 1938, 1952, 1953, 1975); 4 syms. (1941, 1956, 1964, 1969); *Passacaglia* for Piano and Strings (1945); Concerto for Mandolin, Lute, Guitar, and Orch. (1953); 2 violin concertos (1955, 1968); Concerto for Viola, Piano, and Orch. (1960); 2 partitas (1962, 1966); Concerto for Flute, Guitar, and Orch. (1965). **CHAMBER:** Cello Sonata (1937); 2 double bass sonatas (1944, 1960); 2 clarinet sonatas (1948, 1960); Viola Sonata (1955); Viola d'Amore Sonata (1957); Oboe Sonata (1960); Trio for Violin, Guitar, and Double Bass (1964).

BIBL.: R. Stockhammer, *N. S.* (Vienna, 1977).

Spross, Charles Gilbert, American pianist, organist, and composer; b. Poughkeepsie, N.Y., Jan. 6, 1874; d. there, Dec. 23, 1961. He studied piano with X. Scharwenka in N.Y.; also studied organ with various teachers. For nearly 40 years, he was an organist at various churches in Poughkeepsie, Paterson, N.J., N.Y., etc.; was accompanist to celebrated singers (Fremstad, Schumann-Heink, Nordica, Emma Eames et al.). He wrote some 450 works, including 250 songs, 5 sacred cantatas, and chamber music.

Šrámek, Vladimír, Czech composer; b. Kosiče, March 3, 1923. He was a student of Picha at the Prague Cons. After working in the music division of the National Museum in Prague, he joined the staff of the Opera at the National Theater in Prague. In 1977 he became ed. of music at the FILIA. In his early works, Šrámek composed in a traditional style. Later he embraced avant-garde techniques. In his orch. score *The Astronauts* (1959), he introduced the Monophon, an electronic device of his own creation.

WORKS: DRAMATIC: *Driver to Aristofana*, opera (1955); *Flower of Cobalt*, radio opera (1963); *The Pit*, pantomime (1963); *Spectrum I* (1964), *II* (1964), and *III* (1965), music theater; *Light of the World*, pantomime (1964); *The Last Forest*, musical television play (1965). **ORCH.:** *Comedy* for Winds and Percussion (1957); *The Astronauts* (1959); *Metamorphoses I–VII* for Various Instrumental Groups (1961–63); *Swiss Diary* (1966); *Catastrophic Account* (1966); *Delta 12* (1986). **CHAMBER:** Suite for Trombone and Piano (1953); Recorder Sonatina (1955); Suite for Accordion, 2 Clarinets, Trumpet, and Bassoon (1958); *Study* for Flute and Piano (1960); *Tempi* for String Quartet (1960); *Metra symmetrica* for Flute, Oboe, Clarinet, Bassoon, and Horn (1961); *Rondo* for Flute, Oboe, Clarinet, Bassoon, 2 Horns, and 2 Trombones (1961); *Prodomos* for Flute, Bass Clarinet, Trumpet, and Violin (1962); *The Laughter* for Tape-Speaker, Flute, Piano, and Percussion (1962); *Proportioni* for Viola (1964); *Dialogue* for Violin and Viola (1965); *Kaleidoscope* for Violin, Viola, and Cello (1965); *Anticomposizione* for Violin, Viola, and Cello (1966); *Circulus perpetuus* for Flute, Oboe, and Clarinet (1975); Nonetto (1982); *5 Pieces* for 2 Violins, Viola, and Cello (1984); *The Puppet Show Music*, quintet for Flute, Oboe, Clarinet, Bassoon, and Horn (1985); Trio for Oboe, Clarinet, and Bassoon (1986); *Masques*, quintet for Flute, Oboe, Clarinet, Bassoon, and Horn (1986); Quartet for Flute, Oboe, Clarinet, and Bassoon (1986). **OTHER:** *The City*, electronic music (1959); *Sonnet for Sonnet Duo*, electronic music (1966); *The Play* for Monophon (1966).

Srebotnjak, Alojz, Slovenian composer and pedagogue; b. Postojna, June 27, 1931. He studied with Škerjanc at the Ljubljana Academy of Music (1953–58), with Porrena in Rome (1958–59), with Fricker in London (1960–61), and in Paris (1963). After teaching at the Ljubljana Pedagogical Academy (1964–70), he was a prof. of composition at the Ljubljana Academy of Music (1970–95). In his works, Srebotnjak has made effective use of various modern techniques, including atonality and serialism.

WORKS: DRAMATIC: *The Trumpet and the Devil*, ballet (1980; orch. suite, 1983); incidental music; film scores. **ORCH.:** *Music* for Strings (1955; rev. 1982); *Sinfonietta in due tempe* (1958); *Monologues* for Flute, Oboe, Horn, and Strings (1962); *Kraška Suite* (1964); *Antifona* (1964); *Episodes* (1967); Harp Concerto (1971); Violin Concerto (1975); *Slovenica* (1976); *Macedonian Dances* for Strings (1976; also for Orch. or 2 Oboes, 2 Clarinets, 2 Bassoons, and Percussion); *Balade* (1977); *Naturae vox* (1981); *Slovenian Folk Dances* for Strings (1982; also for Orch. or Violin and Piano); *Rapsodica* for Strings (1988). **CHAMBER:** 3 violin sonatinas (1954, 1966, 1968); *Allegro, Corale 3 Passacaglia* for String Quartet (1954); *Fantasia Notturna* for 3 Violins, Clarinet, and Harp (1957); *5 Préludes* for Harp (1960); *Serenata* for Flute, Clarinet, and Bassoon (1961); *6 Pieces* for Bassoon and Piano (1963); *Diary* for Piano Trio (1972); *Lamento* for Chamber Ensemble (1976); *Naif*, collage for Instrumental Group (1977); *Macedonica*, collage for Instrumental Group (1978); *Spray*, collage for Instrumental Group (1981); *Improvisation After Tartini* for Violin (1991). **PIANO:** *Invenzione variata* (1961); *Variations on a Theme by Marij Kogoj* (1984); *The Folk Music Player—Folk Melodies* (1988); *Variations on a Theme by Slavko Osterc* (1990). **VOCAL:** *Mother* for Voice and Strings (1955); *Letters* for Soprano and Harp (1956); *War Pictures* for Tenor, Viola, Percussion, and Piano (1957); *Requiem for a Hostage* for Chorus, Harp, Timpani, and Tam-tam (1963); *Micro Songs* for Voice and Chamber Ensemble (1964); *Ecstasy of Death* for Baritone, Chorus, and Orch. (1965); *A Naive Orpheus* for Chorus and Chamber Ensemble (1973); *Dark Stars, Brighten Up!*, cantata for Baritone, Trumpet, Harp, Timpani, and String Orch. (1989); *Sonnets* for Tenor and Piano (1991); *The Poet's Portrait* for Tenor and Piano (1993); other choral works and songs.

Srnka, Jiří, Czech composer; b. Pisek, Aug. 19, 1907; d. Prague, Jan. 31, 1982. He took violin lessons at the Prague Cons. under A. Mařák and J. Feld (1922–24); then studied composition there with Šín (1924–28) and Novák (1928–32); had instruction in quarter tone music with Alois Hába (1927–28; 1934–37). He was an assistant conductor and violinist with J. Ježek's Liberated Theater in Prague (1929–35); then became interested in film music; produced over 120 film scores. From 1950 to 1953 he taught classes in film music at the Academy of Musical Arts in Prague.

WORKS: DRAMATIC: Over 120 film scores. **ORCH.:** *Symphonic Fantasy* (1932); Violin Concerto (1957; Olomouc, Sept. 23, 1958); *Historical Pictures from the Pisek Region* for Amateur String Orch. (1961); *Partita* for Violin and Chamber Orch. (1962); Piano Concerto (1968); Concerto for Flute, Strings, and Piano (1974; Prague, March 8, 1975); *Nocturne* for Strings (1975); *Echo of Songs of the Prachen Region* (1976); *Sinfonietta* (1977); *Mater Dolorosa* for Flute, Harp, and Strings (1977); *Lyrical Symphony* (1979). **CHAMBER:** 2 string quartets (1928, 1936); Wind Quartet (1928); *Suite* for Violin and Piano (1929); String Quintet (1930); *3 Pieces* for Violin and Piano (1961); *Léto budiž pochváleno* (Summer Be Thou Praised) for String Quartet (1980); *Byl tichý letní večer* (There Was a Quiet Summer Evening) for String Quartet (1980); Nonet (1981). **PIANO:** Suite (1933); *Fantasy* (1934); *2 Quarter-Tone Pieces* (1936); *3 Pieces* (1936). **VOCAL:** Songs.

Šrom, Karel, Czech composer, writer on music, and administrator; b. Pilsen, Sept. 14, 1904; d. Prague, Oct. 21, 1981. He studied composition with Jan Zelinka and Karel Hába in Prague (1919–25); also took courses in law at the Univ. (Jur.Dr., 1927). He wrote music criticism (1928–45) and served as head of the music dept. of the Czech Radio (1945–51).

WRITINGS (all publ. in Prague): *Orchestr a dirigent* (1960); *Záhudbí* (Beyond Music; 1965); *Karel Ančerl* (1968).

WORKS: ORCH.: 2 syms. (1930, 1951); *Plivník* (The Gnome), scherzo (1953); *Vzdech na bruslích* (A Sigh on Skates), symphonic allegretto (1957); *Hayaya,* suite for adults and children (1961); Piano Concerto (1961); *Etudes* (1970); *Mala* for Chamber Orch. (1972). **CHAMBER:** Violin Sonata (1920); 3 string quartets (1923, 1941, 1966); *Scherzo* Trio for String Trio (1943); *Vynajitka* (Fairytale) for Nonet (1952); *Etudes* for Nonet (1959); Concertino for 2 Flutes and String Quintet or String Orch. (1971). **PIANO:** *Whiles,* trifles (1942); 7 *Pieces* (1942); *Black Hour,* cycle (1965).

St. Clair, Carl, American conductor; b. Hochheim, Texas, June 5, 1952. He studied opera and orch. conducting with Walter Ducloux at the Univ. of Texas in Austin, and later worked with Bernstein and Masur. After serving as a conducting fellow at the Tanglewood Music Center (summer, 1985), he was assistant conductor of the Boston Sym. Orch. from 1986 to 1990. He also was music director of the Ann Arbor (Mich.) Sym. Orch. (1985–92) and of the Cayuga Chamber Orch. in Ithaca, N.Y. (1986–91). In 1990 he won the NEA/Seaver Conducting Award. From 1990 he was music director of the Pacific Sym. Orch. in Santa Ana, California. He also appeared as a guest conductor throughout North America, Europe, and the Far East.

Stabile, Mariano, prominent Italian baritone; b. Palermo, May 12, 1888; d. Milan, Jan. 11, 1968. He studied voice at the Accademia di Santa Cecilia in Rome. He made his operatic debut as Amonasro in Palermo (1909). For a number of seasons he sang in provincial opera houses in Italy. The turning point in his career came when he was engaged by Toscanini to sing Falstaff in Verdi's opera at La Scala (Dec. 26, 1921). He triumphed and the role became his major success; he sang it more than 1,000 times. His guest engagements took him to London's Covent Garden (1926–31), the Salzburg Festivals (1935–39), the Glyndebourne Festivals (1936–39), again in London (1946–49), and the Edinburgh Festival (1948). He retired in 1960. Among his other notable roles were Don Giovanni, Mozart's and Rossini's Figaro, Don Alfonso, Dr. Malatesta, Iago, Rigoletto, and Scarpia.

Stäblein, Bruno, distinguished German musicologist; b. Munich, May 5, 1895; d. Erlangen, March 6, 1978. He studied musicology with Sanderberger and Kroyer at the Univ. of Munich (Ph.D., 1918, with the diss. *Musicque de Joye: Studien zur Instrumentalmusik des 16. Jahrhunderts*); later completed his Habilitation at the Univ. of Erlangen in 1946 with his *Hymnestudien.* He was a theater conductor in Innsbruck, Coburg, and Regensburg, where he was also active as an adviser in musical studies. He was a prof. and chairman of the seminars in musicology at the Univ. of Erlangen (1956–63); in 1967 he was appointed director of the Society for Bavarian Music History. He ed. the important collection Monumenta Monodica Medii Aevi (Kassel, 1956–70); contributed a number of informative articles on the music of the Middle Ages and the Renaissance; ed. reprints of documentary materials pertaining to these epochs. A Festschrift in his honor, issued for his 70th birthday, contains a complete list of his publs. (Kassel, 1967).

Stäbler, Gerhard, German organist, teacher, and composer; b. Wilhelmsdorf, near Ravensburg, July 20, 1949. He studied at the North West German Music Academy in Detmold (1968–70) and with Nicolaus Huber (composition) and Gerd Zacher (organ) at the Essen Folkwang Hochschule (1970–76); also attended courses with Stockhausen, Schnebel, Kagel, and Ligeti. In 1982 he won the Cornelius Cardew Memorial Prize in London. He taught at the Essen Folkwang Hochschule from 1982 to 1984, and again from 1989. In 1983 and 1986 he worked at the Stanford Univ. computer music center. From 1985 he toured widely in Europe and the U.S. as an organist in programs ranging from Bach and Bull to Ligeti, Cage, and himself. He also gave lectures and taught. From 1986 he worked with Aktiv Musik, a touring concert/lecture series. In 1989 he oversaw "Actik Musik '89" in N.Y. In 1991 he co-founded the Gesellschaft für neue Musik Ruhr. He made a concert and lecture tour of Japan and Korea in 1991. In 1992 he was composer-in-residence at Northwestern Univ. in Chicago, and returned there as a guest prof. in 1993. In 1994 he was awarded a Japan Foundation scholarship; in 1995 he made concert and lecture tours in Brazil and Japan. In his music, Stäbler has charted his own avant-garde, and even radical, course. All the same, he has attempted to reestablish a working relationship with the public. His work is infused with a political and social consciousness.

WORKS: *Dämpfe,* 5-fold chamber music (1968–70); *Mo-ped* for Organ and Motorcycle (1970–71); *drüber . . .* for 8 Active Screamers, Cello, Synthesizer, and Tape (1972–73); *Gehörsmassage* for Active Audience (1973); *Cage-Mix,* arrangement with Animal Voices (1973–74); *Suchen nach . . .*, experiments with historical materials for Various Ensembles (1976–80); *Drei Lieder zu Gedichten von Gert Udo Jerns* for Voice, Drum, and Piano (1979–82); *Hitlerchoräle IV–VI* for Chorus and Electronic Organ (1980); *. . . fürs Vaterland,* 3 songs for Instruments, Voices, and Speaking Chorus (1981–82); *Reisegepäck,* traveling works (1981–84); *Den Toten von Sabra und Chatila* for Voice, Flute, Oboe, Clarinet, and Piano (1982; rev. for Flute, Oboe, Clarinet, Trombone, and Piano, 1988); *Das Sichere ist nicht sicher,* spiraling rondo for 8 Instruments and Tape (1982); *Windows: Elegien* for Chamber Ensemble (1983; various other versions, 1983–85); *Schatten wilder Schmerzen* for Orch. (1984–85); *Die Spieldose* for Percussion, Tape, and Visual Media (1984–85); *California Dreams: Lullaby (poisoned), Shooting Stars, Soul Trap,* and *Crack of Dawn* for Accordion (1986); *Hart auf Hart,* improvisatory music for Ensemble (1986); *rasend still* for Euphonium or Trumpet (1986); *Warnung mit Liebeslied* for Harp, Accordion, and Percussion (1986); *Mit wachen Sinnen* for Chorus and Drums (1986–87); *Ruck-VERSCH[ei]BEN Zuck* for Accordion and Orch. (1986–88); *. . . strike the ear . . .* for String Quartet (1987–88); *auf dem Seil, auf scharf gespanntem Seil* for Flute, Violin, Trombone, and Piano (1987–88); *fallen, fallen . . . und liegen und fallen* for Soprano or Alto, Accordion, Tuba, and Tape (1988–89); *Nachbeben und Davor* for Cello and Accordion (1988–89); *Oktober* for Flute, Violin, and Double Bass (1989); *Affiliert* for Ensemble (1989–90); *Den Müllfahrern von San Francisco* for 17 Instruments (1989–90); *Co—wie Kobalt* for Double Bass and Orch. (1989–90); *. . . Im Spalier . . .* for Brass Quintet (1990); *Ungaretti Lieder* for Mezzo-soprano or Baritone and Percussion (1990); *Zeitsprünge* for Accordion and Percussion (1990); *Sunde. Fall. Beil.,* opera, after Dumas' *Catherine Howard* (1990–91; Munich, May 16, 1992); *Traum 1/9/92* for Saxophone, Cello, Piano, and Ensemble (1992); *Cassandracomplex,* music theater, after Christa Wolf (1993–94); *Beppu,* "Thoughts on 3 Haiku by Matsuo Basho," for Trumpet and Percussion (1994; also for Trombone or Tuba and Percussion); *[Apparat]* for Chorus, Clarinet, Accordion, Double Bass, and 3–6 Percussion (1994–95); *Karas. Krähen.* for Tape (1994–95; also for Vocalists, Sho or Accordion, Double Bass, Percussion, and Tape); *Winter, Blumen* for Countertenor, Violin, Viola, Cello, and Double Bass (1995).

Stachowski, Marek, Polish composer; b. Piekary Śląskie, March 21, 1936. He studied theory and composition with Penderecki at the Kraków Cons. (1963–66); then taught there and at the Jagiellonian Univ. in Kraków, remaining on the faculty of the latter until 1979. In 1993 he became rector of the Kraków Cons. His music is both constructivistically impressionistic and sonoristically coloristic.

WORKS: ORCH.: *Musica con una battuta del tam-tam* for Tam-tam and Strings (1968); *Sequenze concertanti* (1968); *Irisation* (Graz, Oct. 23, 1970); *Solemn Music* (1973; Warsaw, Sept.

27, 1974); *Poème sonore* (1975; Monchengladbach, June 24, 1976); *Divertimento* for Strings (1978); *Choreia* (1980); *Capriccio* (1983); Concerto for Clarinet and Strings (1988); Chamber Concerto (1989); *From the Book of Night* (1990). **CHAMBER:** *Chamber Music* for Flute, Harp, and Percussion (1965); 2 string quartets (1965, 1972); *Audition* for Flute, Cello, and Piano (1970); *Extensions*, 3 pieces for 1, 2, or 3 Performers on Piano (1971–74); *Quartetto da ingresso* for String Quartet (1980); *Musique en quatre scènes pour clarinette et quatuor à cordes* (1987); *Sonata per archi* (1991); *3 Intermezzos* for String Trio (1993–94). **VOCAL:** *Pieć zmysłów i rósa* (5 Senses and the Rose) for Voice, Flute, Horn, Trombone, and Marimbaphone (1964); *Lines of Dylan Thomas* for 2 Choruses and Orch. (1967); *Neusis II* for 2 Choral Groups, Percussion, Cello, and Double Bass (1968); *Chant de l'espoir* for Narrator, Soprano, Baritone, Chorus, Boy's Chorus, and Orch., after Eluard (1969); *Words* for Soprano, Bass, Chorus, and Orch. (1971); *Thakurian Songs* for Chorus and Orch. (1974); *Birds* for Soprano and Ensemble (1976); *Sapphic Odes* for Mezzo-soprano and Orch. (1985).

Stacy, Thomas, American English-horn player; b. Little Rock, Ark., Aug. 18, 1938. He received his training at the Eastman School of Music in Rochester, N.Y. After graduating in 1960, he made his formal debut as a soloist with the Minneapolis Sym. Orch., with which he subsequently was solo English horn. In 1972 he became solo English horn in the N.Y. Phil. He also toured as an English-horn soloist, appearing with many American orchs. Stacy was soloist in the premieres of the English-horn concertos of Skrowaczewski (Minneapolis, Nov. 21, 1969), Persichetti (N.Y., Nov. 17, 1977), and Rorem (N.Y., Jan. 27, 1994).

Stade, Frederica von. See **Von Stade, Frederica.**

Stader, Maria, noted Hungarian-born Swiss soprano; b. Budapest, Nov. 5, 1911. She studied voice with Keller in Karlsruhe, Durigo in Zürich, Lombardi in Milan, and T. Schnabel in N.Y.; won the Geneva International Competition (1939). After a brief career as an opera singer, she devoted herself to a distinguished concert career after World War II; toured extensively in Europe, North America, and the Far East; following her retirement in 1969, she was active as a teacher. She was particularly esteemed as an interpreter of Mozart, in both operatic and concert settings.

Stadlmair, Hans, Austrian conductor and composer; b. Neuhofen an der Krems, May 3, 1929. He received his musical training in Linz and Vienna; eventually settled in Munich. In 1956 he founded the Munich Chamber Orch., with which he traveled on numerous tours in Europe, the U.S., South America, Africa, and Asia. He served as its music director until 1995. As a composer, he wrote mostly instrumental works, in a neo-Baroque manner, among them a Toccata for Strings and Harpsichord (1966), a Trumpet Concerto with Strings (1967), and *Sinfonia serena* for Strings (1970); he also wrote some choral pieces.

Staempfli, Edward, Swiss composer, pianist, and conductor; b. Bern, Feb. 1, 1908. He received training in composition from Jarnach and Maler in Cologne (1929–30) and Dukas in Paris (1930), and in conducting from Scherchen in Brussels (1935). After living in Paris (1930–39), he returned to Switzerland. He went to Heidelberg in 1951 before settling in Berlin in 1954. He made occasional appearances as a pianist and conductor, usually in hs own works. His early music reflected his Parisian sojourn, but later he embraced 12-tone writing.

WORKS: DRAMATIC: OPERAS: *Ein Traumspiel* (1943); *Medea* (1954); *Caligula* (1981–82). Also several ballets. **ORCH.:** 4 piano concertos (1932, 1933, 1954, 1963); 4 violin concertos (1936, 1939, 1941, 1990); 6 syms. (1938–88); Concerto for 2 Pianos and Orch. (1940); *Praeludim und Variationen über ein Tessiner Volkslied* (1945); *Mouvements concertantes* (1947); *Epitaphe pour Paul Eluard* (1954); *Fantasie* for Strings (1955); *Strophen* (1958); *5 Nachstücke* (1961); *Musik* for 16 Strings (1968); *Tripartita* for 3 Pianos and 23 Winds (1969); *Satze und Gegensatze* for Vibraphone, Piano, Percussion, and 15 Strings (1972); Concerto for Horn, Trumpet, Trombone, and Orch. (1984); *Helles Licht und spate Schatten* (1988); Cello Concerto (1991); *Ornamente III* (1992). **CHAMBER:** 6 string quartets (1926–62); Quartet for Flute and String Trio (1932); 2 piano trios (1932, 1956); Wind Quintet (1934); 2 string trios (1937, 1984); Wind Trio (1949); *Ornamente I* for 2 Flutes, Celesta, and Percussion (1960) and *III* for Oboe, Saxophone, Marimbaphone, Percussion, and Harp (1983); Trio for Violin, Clarinet, and Piano (1985); Duo for Alto Flute and Cello (1987); Quintet for Flute, Violin, Viola, Cello, and Piano (1988); *Why not?*, quartet for Alto Saxophone, Trumpet, Vibraphone, and Piano (1990); Quintet for 2 Violins, Viola, Cello, and Double Bass (1992); piano pieces. **VOCAL:** Oratorios; cantatas; choruses; songs.

Stahlman, Sylvia, American soprano; b. Nashville, Tenn., March 5, 1933. She studied voice at the Juilliard School of Music in N.Y. She then went to Europe and pursued her budding career under a suitably Italianate pseudonym, Giulia Bardi; made her debut in Brussels in 1951; then sang regularly in Frankfurt am Main (1954–72). In 1956, under her own name, she joined the N.Y. City Opera; then sang at San Francisco (1958) and Chicago (1960). She also toured as a concert artist.

Stainov, Petko, Bulgarian composer; b. Kazanluk, Dec. 1, 1896; d. Sofia, June 25, 1977. Despite an almost complete loss of sight at age 5, he learned to play piano by ear; studied composition with Wolf and piano with E. Münch in Braunschweig and Berlin (1920–24). Returning to Sofia, he taught piano at the Inst. for the Blind (1927–41); then was director of the National Opera (1941–44) and of the Inst. for Music of the Bulgarian Academy of Sciences (from 1948).

WORKS: ORCH.: *Thracian Dances* (1925–26); *Legend*, symphonic poem (1927; Sofia, Jan. 1, 1928); *Balkan*, overture (1936); 2 syms. (1945, 1948); *Youth Concert Overture* (1952). **VOCAL:** Numerous choruses and choral ballads.

BIBL.: V. Krastev, *P. S.* (Sofia, 1957).

Stalvey, Dorrance, American composer; b. Georgetown, S.C., Aug. 21, 1930. He studied clarinet and general music subjects at the College of Music in Cincinnati (M.M., 1955). Prior to his late twenties, his interest was primarily in jazz improvisation. In composition he was wholly self-taught, and thanks to that developed an independent style marked by quaquaversal contrapuntal and harmonic techniques vivified by asymmetrical rhythms. He embraced a variegated career of teaching, composing, and management. He lectured on music history, theory, and analysis, off and on, at various schools; was an assistant prof. (1972–77) and then full prof. (1977–80) in composition at the Immaculate Heart College in Los Angeles. In 1971 he assumed the post of artistic director of the Monday Evening Concerts in Los Angeles, and since 1981 has been music director for the Los Angeles County Museum of Art. He also was active as a radio commentator and conductor. Stalvey received several awards from ASCAP and other musical organizations. His compositions had frequent performances, and astonishingly good reviews from habitually fatigued critics for his special spatial effects in multifarious multimedia productions.

WORKS: *Celebration-Principium* for Brass and Percussion (1967); *Points-Lines-Circles* for Clarinet, Double Bass, Harp, Guitar, and Percussion (1968); *In Time and Not* for Multimedia Ensembles (1970); *Togethers I* for Guitar and Tape (1970), *II* for Percussion and Tape (1970), and *III* for Clarinet and Tape (1970); *Celebration-Sequents I* for Various Instruments (1973), *II* (1976), and *IV* (1980); *Agathlon* for Modern Dance and Instruments (1978); *Ex Ferus* for 6 Cellos or String Sextet (1982); *Pound Songs* for Soprano and Instruments (1985); *Dualities* for Guitar, Soprano, and Instruments (1986–87); *String Quartet 1989* (1989); *Exordium/Genesis/Dawn* for 6 Players (1990). Also theatrical multi-lectures; chamber works (with and without tape); piano solos; composite compositions compounded of combinations of original numbers.

Stam, Henk (actually, **Hendrikus Gerardus**), Dutch composer, conductor, teacher, and writer on music; b. Utrecht, Sept. 26, 1922. He studied instrumentation with Hendrik Andriessen and piano with Jan Wagenaar and André Jurres at the Utrecht Cons.; later studied musicology at the Univ. of Utrecht and composition with Fortner in Germany. He taught at the music school in Deventer (1948–54); was director at the music schools in Zeeland (1954–61) and Rotterdam (1962–72).

WORKS: 5 piano sonatinas (1943, 1946, 1946, 1947, 1953); *2 Rispetti* for Baritone and String Orch. (1944); 3 string quartets (1947, 1948, 1949); *Histoire de Barbar*, 8 pieces for Piano (1949); *Cassation*, pantomime for 3 Dancers, Violin, Flute, Cello, Trombone, Mezzo-soprano, Baritone, Speaking Voice, and Chamber Orch. (1949); Violin Sonata (1950); Sonata for Solo Violin (1951); *Suite* for Violin and Piano (1953); *Ouverture Michiel de Ruyter* (1957); Cello Sonata (1966); *Tropic* for Flute, Oboe, and Piano (1972); Flute Sonata (1972); *Klachte der Prinsesse van Oranjen* for Chorus and 3 Trumpets ad libitum (1973); *Sonata concertante* for Cello and Piano (1982); *Berceuse pour B.* for Cello and Piano (1983); choruses.

Standage, Simon, English violinist, conductor, and teacher; b. High Wycombe, Buckinghamshire, Nov. 8, 1941. He studied at Bryanston School and the Univ. of Cambridge; subsequently took private lessons with Ivan Galamian in N.Y. (1967–69). Upon his return to England, he became an assoc. member of the London Sym. Orch. and sub-concertmaster of the English Chamber Orch. In 1973 he was appointed principal violin of the English Concert and concertmaster of the Richard Hickox Orch. and City of London Sinfonia. In 1981 he founded the Salomon String Quartet. In 1983 he was appointed teacher of Baroque violin at the Royal Academy of Music. In 1990 he founded with Richard Hickox the Collegium Musicum 90 of London. He became assoc. director of the Academy of Ancient Music in London in 1991. In 1993 he was made prof. of Baroque violin at the Dresden Academy of Early Music.

Standford, Patric (actually, **John Patric Standford Gledhill**), English composer and teacher; b. Barnsley, Feb. 5, 1939. He was a student of Edmund Rubbra and Raymond Jones at the Guildhall School of Music in London (1961–63); after receiving the Mendelssohn Scholarship in 1964, he continued his studies with Malipiero in Italy and with Lutoslawski. He taught at the Guildhall School of Music (1968–80) and also served as chairman of the Composer's Guild of Great Britain (1977–79). He was director of the music school at Bretton Hall College (Univ. of Leeds) in Wakefield (1980–93). In 1983 he was awarded the Ernest Ansermet prize of Geneva for his 3rd Sym.

WORKS: DRAMATIC: OPERA: *Villon* (1972–85). **BALLETS:** *Celestial Fall* (1968; orch. suite, 1971); *Reflections* (1980). **ORCH.:** 6 syms.: No. 1, *The Seasons* (1971–72), No. 2, *Christus-Requiem* for 4 Soloists, Narrator, Chorus, Children's Chorus, and Orch. (1971–72; rev. 1980), No. 3, *Toward Paradise* for Chorus and Orch. (1982; Geneva, June 11, 1986), No. 4, *Taikyoku* for 2 Pianos and Percussion (1975–79), No. 5, with Soprano Solo (Manchester, Jan. 24, 1986), and No. 6 (1995); *Saracinesco*, symphonic poem (1966); *Notte*, poem for Chamber Orch. (1968); *Antitheses* for 15 Strings (1971); Cello Concerto (1974); Violin Concerto (1975); *Variations* (1977; arranged from the Piano Variations, 1969); Piano Concerto (1979); *Dialogues* for Cimbalom and Chamber Orch. (1981); *Folksongs* for Strings (3 sets, 1982, 1985, 1986); *Rage* (1993). **CHAMBER:** 3 string quartets (1965, 1973, 1992); *Suite française*, 4 pieces for Wind Quintet (1964); *4 Cartoons* for Oboe, Clarinet, and Bassoon (1984); Concertino for Piano, Oboe, and String Trio (1986); *Suite humoresque* for Piano, Oboe, Clarinet, and Bassoon (1987); Piano Quartet (1988); *Divertimento* for Violin and Piano (1989). **PIANO:** *Variations* (1969); Sonata (1979–80); *Faeries* (1987); *3 Nocturnes* (1991). **VOCAL:** 3 motets: *In memoriam Benjamin Britten* for Chorus (1976–77), *Mass* for Chorus and Brass Band (1980), and *O sacrum convivium* for Chorus (1985); *Mass of Our Lady and St. Rochus* for Chorus (1988); *The Inheritor* for Tenor and String Quartet (1992); *A Messiah Reborn* for 4 Soloists, Chorus, and Orch., after Handel (1993).

Stanford, Sir Charles Villiers, eminent Irish organist, conductor, pedagogue, and composer; b. Dublin, Sept. 30, 1852; d. London, March 29, 1924. Brought up in an intellectual atmosphere, he was a diligent student in his early youth; studied piano, organ, violin, and composition with Michael Quarry at St. Patrick's Cathedral, and with Robert Stewart and Joseph Robinson at the Royal Irish Academy of Music in Dublin; in 1862, was sent to London, where he studied piano with Ernst Pauer and composition with Arthur O'Leary. In 1870 he entered Queen's College, Cambridge, as a choral scholar (B.A., 1874); then studied composition with Reinecke in Leipzig (1874–76) and with Kiel in Berlin (1876); was awarded the M.A. degree from Cambridge (1877). In 1883 he was appointed prof. of composition at the Royal College of Music and conductor of the orch. there; in 1887 he also became a prof. of music at Cambridge, holding both positions until his death; he was conductor of the Leeds Festivals from 1901 to 1910, and appeared as guest conductor of his own works in Paris, Berlin, Amsterdam, and Brussels; from 1885 to 1902 he conducted the London Bach Choir. He was knighted in 1902. He was an extremely able and industrious composer in a distinctly Romantic style, yet unmistakably national in musical materials, both Irish and English. In recent years there has been renewed interest in and appreciation of his music, both in England and abroad.

WORKS: DRAMATIC: OPERAS: *The Veiled Prophet of Khorassan* (1877; Hannover, Feb. 6, 1881); *Savonarola* (Hamburg, April 18, 1884); *The Canterbury Pilgrims* (London, April 23, 1884); *Lorenza* (c.1894; not perf.); *Shamus O'Brian* (London, March 2, 1896); *Christopher Patch (The Barber of Bath)* (c.1897; not perf.); *Much Ado about Nothing* (London, May 30, 1901); *The Critic, or An Opera Rehearsed* (London, Jan. 14, 1916); *The Traveling Companion* (1919; amateur perf., Liverpool, April 30, 1925; professional perf., Bristol, Oct. 25, 1926). Also incidental music. **ORCH.:** 7 syms.: No. 1 (1876; London, March 8, 1879), No. 2, *Elegiac* (1880; Cambridge, March 7, 1882, composer conducting), No. 3, *Irish* (London, May 17, 1887), No. 4 (1888; Berlin, Jan. 14, 1889, composer conducting), No. 5, *L'Allegro ed il Penseroso* (1894; London, March 20, 1895, composer conducting), No. 6, "In honour of the life-work of a great artist: George Frederick Watts" (1905; London, Jan. 18, 1906), and No. 7 (1911; London, Feb. 22, 1912); *Suite* for Violin and Orch. (Berlin, Jan. 14, 1889; Joachim, soloist); 3 piano concertos (1896, 1915, 1919); *6 Irish Rhapsodies* (1901–c.1923); *Overture in the Style of a Tragedy* (1904); 2 violin concertos (1904, 1918); *Irish Concertino* for Violin, Cello, and Orch. (1919); *Variations* for Violin and Orch. (1921; also for Violin and Piano). **CHAMBER:** 4 violin sonatas (c.1880, 1893, c.1898, 1919); 3 piano trios (1889, 1899, 1918); 8 string quartets (c.1891–c.1919); 2 string quintets (1903, c.1903); various piano pieces, including 5 sonatas (1917–21); organ music. **VOCAL:** *Eden*, oratorio (Birmingham, 1891); *Mass* (London, 1893); *Requiem* (Birmingham, 1897); *Te Deum* (Leeds, 1898); *Stabat Mater* (Leeds, 1907); numerous other works, including *2 Magnificats* (1872, 1873), anthems, services, choruses, song cycles, and solo songs.

WRITINGS (all publ. in London): *Studies and Memories* (1908); *Musical Composition: A Short Treatise for Students* (1911; 6th ed., 1950); *Brahms* (1912); *Pages from an Unwritten Diary* (1914); *Interludes: Records and Reflections* (1922).

BIBL.: J. Porte, *Sir C.V. S.* (London and N.Y., 1921); T. Dunhill, "C.V. S.: Some Aspects of his Life and Works," *Proceedings of the Musical Association*, LIII (1927–28); J. Fuller Maitland, *The Music of Parry and S.* (Cambridge, 1934); H. Plunket Greene, *C.V. S.* (London, 1935); F. Hudson, "C.V. S.: nova bibliographica," *Musical Times*, CIV (1963); idem, "A Catalogue of the Works of C.V. S. (1852–1924)," *Music Review*, XXV (1964); idem, "C.V. S.: nova bibliographica II," *Musical Times*, CV (1964); idem, "C.V. S.: nova bibliographica III," ibid., CVIII (1967); idem, "A Revised and Extended Catalogue of the Works of C.V. S.

(1852–1924)," *Music Review*, XXXVII (1976); G. Norris, *S., the Cambridge Jubilee and Tchaikovsky* (Newton Abbot, 1980).

Stanislav, Josef, Czech composer and pedagogue; b. Hamburg, Jan. 22, 1897; d. Prague, Aug. 5, 1971. He went in his youth to Prague, where he took lessons in composition with Jeremiáš and Foerster and in piano with Mikeš and Veselý; completed his training in the Cons. master classes of Novák in composition (1922) and of Hoffmeister in piano (1929); also studied with Nejedlý at the Univ. He joined the Czech Communist party and was active in various left-wing organizations. His music was banned during the German occupation, but after the liberation in 1945, he played a prominent role in Czech musical life; was a prof. at the Prague Academy of Music (from 1948) and director of the ethnographical and folklore inst. of the Czech Academy of Sciences (from 1953).

WORKS: *Symfonické vypravovani* (Symphonic Narration; n.d.); *Rudoarmějská symfonie* (Red Army Sym.; 1942); Viola Sonata (1920); 3 piano sonatas (1921, 1929, 1944); Viola Sonata (1933); String Quartet (1935); several cantatas; choruses; songs; incidental music.

WRITINGS: *O té lidové a vážné hudbě a lidových hudebnících* (Folk Music, Art Music, and Folk Musicians; Prague, 1939); *Hudebni kultura, umění a život* (Musical Culture, Art, and Life; Prague, 1940); *Ludvík Kuba* (Prague, 1963).

Stanislavsky (real name, **Alexeiev**), **Konstantin (Sergeievich),** famous Russian actor and theater and opera director; b. Moscow, Jan. 17, 1863; d. there, Aug. 7, 1938. He received practical experience by performing in and directing operettas in his family's private theater; studied voice with Komisarzhevsky, but gave up all hope of a career in opera when his voice proved inadequate. Then, with Nemirovich-Danchanko, he founded the Moscow Art Theater in 1898; it became an innovative setting for both stage plays and operas. In 1918 he founded the Bolshoi Theater Opera Studio, which became an independent studio in 1920; it was named the Stanislavsky Opera Theater in his honor in 1926. The Stanislavsky method as applied to opera concentrates upon the musical score as the guiding force of a production, allowing all elements to evolve naturally to present a realistic work of art. He wrote several books on his theater methods.

BIBL.: G. Kristi, *Rabota Stanislavskovo v opernom teatre* (S.'s Work in the Opera Theater; Moscow, 1952); I. Vinogradskaya, ed., *Zhizn i tvorchestvo K.S. Stanislavskovo: Letopis* (The Life and Work of K.S. S.: A Chronicle; Moscow, 1973); E. Hapgood, ed., *S. on Opera* (N.Y., 1975).

Stapp, Olivia, American soprano; b. N.Y., May 31, 1940. She studied at Wagner College in Staten Island, N.Y. (B.A.) and received vocal training from Oren Brown in N.Y. and Ettore Campogalliani and Rodolfo Ricci in Italy. In 1960 she made her debut as Beppe in *L'Amico Fritz* at the Spoleto Festival, and then appeared in various operatic centers in Europe and the U.S. In 1972 she made her first appearance at the N.Y. City Opera as Carmen, and subsequently sang there with fine success. In 1981 she appeared as Elvira in *Ernani* in Barcelona. She sang Norma in Montreal and Lady Macbeth at the Paris Opéra in 1982. On Dec. 7, 1982, she made her Metropolitan Opera debut in N.Y. as Lady Macbeth. In 1983 she appeared as Turandot at Milan's La Scala. She again sang Lady Macbeth in Geneva and in Venice in 1986. In 1990 she appeared as Shostakovich's Katerina Ismailova in Hamburg. Among her other prominent roles were Lucrezia Borgia, Aida, Elektra, and Tosca.

Starer, Robert, esteemed Austrian-born American composer and pedagogue; b. Vienna, Jan. 8, 1924. He entered the Vienna Academy of Music at 13 and studied piano with Victor Ebenstein. Shortly after the Anschluss in 1938, he went to Jerusalem and pursued his training at the Cons. with Rosowsky, Tal, and Partos (until 1943). After service in the British Royal Air Force (1943–46), he emigrated to the U.S. and became a naturalized American citizen in 1957. He pursued postgraduate studies under Jacobi at the Juilliard School of Music in N.Y. (1947–49) and studied with Copland at the Berkshire Music Center in Tanglewood (summer, 1948). From 1949 to 1974 he taught at the Juilliard School of Music; he also taught at the N.Y. College of Music (1959–60) and the Jewish Theological Seminary in N.Y. (1962–63). In 1963 he became an assoc. prof. of music at Brooklyn College of the City Univ. of N.Y., where he was made a full prof. in 1966 and a Distinguished Prof. in 1986. He retired in 1991. He publ. the vol. *Rhythmic Training* (1969) and the autobiography *Continuo: A Life in Music* (1987). In 1957 and 1963 he held Guggenheim fellowships, and he also received grants from the NEA and the Ford Foundation. In 1994 he was elected to membership in the American Academy of Arts and Letters. Starer's music reflects his grounding in the 20th-century Viennese tradition and his study of Arabic scales and rhythms. In some of his works, he utilized aleatory techniques and collage. His output is particularly distinguished by its craftsmanship.

WORKS: DRAMATIC: OPERAS: *The Intruder* (N.Y., Dec. 4, 1956); *Pantagleize* (1967; N.Y., April 7, 1973); *Apollonia* (1978). **MUSICAL MORALITY PLAY:** *The Last Lover* (1974; Katonah, N.Y., Aug. 2, 1975). **BALLETS:** *The Story of Esther* (1960); *The Dybbuk* (1960); *Samson Agonistes* (1961); *Phaedra* (1962); *The Sense of Touch* (1967); *The Lady of the House of Sleep* (1968); *Holy Jungle* (N.Y., April 2, 1974). **ORCH.:** *Fantasy for Strings* for Violin, Viola, Cello, and String Orch. (1945); 3 piano concertos (1947, 1953, 1972); 3 syms. (1950, 1951, 1969); *Prelude and Rondo Giocoso* (1953); *Concerto a tre* for Clarinet, Trumpet, Trombone, and Strings (1954); *Ballade* for Violin and Orch. (1955); Concerto for Viola, Strings, and Percussion (1958; Geneva, July 3, 1959); *Samson Agonistes*, symphonic poem after the ballet (1963); *Mutabili (Variants for Orchestra)* (1965); Concerto for Violin, Cello, and Orch. (1967; Pittsburgh, Oct. 11, 1968); *6 Variations with 12 Notes* (1967); Violin Concerto (1979–80; Boston, Oct. 16, 1981); *Concerto à quattro* for Solo Woodwind and Chamber Orch. (1983); *Hudson Valley Suite* (1984); *Serenade* for Trombone, Vibraphone, and Strings (1984); *Symphonic Prelude* (1984); Cello Concerto (N.Y., May 7, 1988). **CHAMBER:** String Quartet (1947); *5 Miniatures* for Brass (1948); *Prélude* for Harp (1948); Cello Sonata (1951); *Dirge* for Brass Quartet (1956); *Serenade* for Brass (1956); *Dialogues* for Clarinet and Piano (1961); *Variants* for Violin and Piano (1963); Trio for Clarinet, Cello, and Piano (1964); Woodwind Quartet (1970); *Colloquies* for Flute and Piano (1974); *Mandala* for String Quartet (1974); *Profiles in Brass* for Brass (1974); *Annapolis Suite* for Harp and Brass Quintet (1982); *6 Preludes* for Guitar (1984); Piano Trio (1985); *Kaaterskill Quartet* (1987); Duo for Violin and Piano (Washington, D.C., Nov. 18, 1988); *Angel Voices* for Brass and Organ (Bergen, May 29, 1989); Clarinet Quintet (1992); *Episodes* for Viola, Cello, and Piano (1992; Hartford, Conn., Jan. 23, 1993); *Dialogues* for Flute and Harp (N.Y., March 23, 1993). **PIANO:** 3 sonatas: No. 1 (1949), No. 2 (1965), and No. 3 (N.Y., Nov. 27, 1994); *Fantasia concertante* (1959); *Sketches in Color I* (1963) and *II* (1973); *Evanescents* (1975); *4 Seasonal Pieces* (1985); *The Ideal Self* (1985). **VOCAL:** Concertino for 2 Voices or 2 Instruments, Violin, and Piano (1948); *5 Proverbs on Love* for Chorus (1950); *Kohelet* for Soprano, Baritone, Chorus, and Orch. (1952); *Ariel: Visions of Isaiah* for Soprano, Baritone, Chorus, and Orch. or Piano and Organ (1959); *Joseph and His Brothers* for Narrator, Soprano, Tenor, Baritone, Chorus, and Orch. (1966); *Images of Man* for Soprano, Mezzo-soprano, Tenor, Baritone, Chorus, Flute, Horn, Cello, Harp, and Percussion (1973); *Journals of a Songmaker* for Soprano, Baritone, and Orch. (1975); *The People, Yes* for Chorus and Orch. (1976); *Anna Margarita's Will* for Soprano, Flute, Horn, Cello, and Piano (1979); *Transformations* for Soprano, Flute or Clarinet, and Piano (1980); *Voices of Brooklyn* for Solo Voices, Chorus, and Band (1980–84); *Night Thoughts* for Chorus and Synthesizer (1990); *Proverbs for a Son* for Chorus (1991); various other choral pieces and songs. **OTHER:** Many band pieces and didactic works.

Starker, János, renowned Hungarian-born American cellist and pedagogue; b. Budapest, July 5, 1924. He made his first public appearance when he was only 6 and at 7 studied cello with Adolf Cziffer at the Budapest Academy of Music and made his solo debut there at the age of 11. After graduating, he served as 1st cellist of the Budapest Opera orch. (1945–46), but decided to leave Hungary; he emigrated to the U.S. in 1948; became a naturalized American citizen in 1954. He held the positions of 1st cellist in the Dallas Sym. Orch. (1948–49), the Metropolitan Opera Orch. in N.Y. (1949–53), and the Chicago Sym. Orch. (1953–58); subsequently he embarked upon a solo career. In 1958 he was appointed a prof. of music at the Indiana Univ. School of Music in Bloomington, where he was named Distinguished Prof. of Music in 1965. As a soloist, he achieved renown in performances of Bach's unaccompanied cello suites; also devoted much attention to modern music; promoted cello works of Kodály and gave first performances of works by Messiaen, Peter Mennin, Miklós Rozsa, and others. He publ. *An Organized Method of String Playing* (1961).

Starokadomsky, Mikhail, Russian composer; b. Brest-Litovsk, June 13, 1901; d. Moscow, April 24, 1954. He studied composition with Miaskovsky at the Moscow Cons., graduating in 1928. He remained in Moscow, where he became a prof. of orchestration. His works follow the traditional line of Russian nationalism, but several of his early orch. scores are purely neo-Classical, and in this respect parallel the European developments. He was once known in his homeland for his songs for children.

WORKS: DRAMATIC: OPERA: *Sot* (1933); **OPERETTAS:** *3 Encounters* (1942); *The Gay Rooster* (1944); *The Sun Flower* (1947). **ORCH.:** *Concerto for Orchestra* (Paris, June 22, 1937); Violin Concerto (Moscow, March 20, 1939). **OTHER:** Chamber music; numerous songs.

Staryk, Steven, Canadian violinist and teacher; b. Toronto, April 28, 1932. He studied at the Royal Cons. of Music of Toronto and with Mischakoff, Shumsky, and Schneider in N.Y. (1950–51). He played in the Toronto Sym. Orch. (1950–52) and the CBC Sym. Orch. (1952–56). In 1956 he took 2nd prizes in the Geneva Competition and the Carl Flesch Competition in London. He was concertmaster of the Royal Phil. in London (1956–60) and of the Concertgebouw Orch. in Amsterdam (1960–63), where he concurrently taught at the Amsterdam Cons.; then was concertmaster of the Chicago Sym. Orch. (1963–67) and a teacher at Northwestern Univ. and the American Cons. He was a prof. at the Oberlin (Ohio) College Cons. of Music (1968–72). Returning to Canada, he was head of the string dept. at the Community Music School of Greater Vancouver (1972–75). From 1975 to 1987 he was a teacher at the Royal Cons. of Music of Toronto. He also taught at the Univ. of Western Ontario (1977–79) and at the Univ. of Toronto (1978–87). From 1982 to 1987 he was likewise concertmaster of the Toronto Sym. In 1987 he became a teacher at the Univ. of Wash. in Seattle.

Steber, Eleanor, eminent American soprano; b. Wheeling, W.Va., July 17, 1914; d. Langhorne, Pa., Oct. 3, 1990. She studied singing with her mother; then with William Whitney at the New England Cons. of Music in Boston (Mus.B., 1938) and with Paul Althouse in N.Y. She won the Metropolitan Opera Auditions of the Air in 1940; made her debut with the Metropolitan Opera in N.Y. as Sophie in *Der Rosenkavalier* on Dec. 7, 1940, and remained with the company until 1962; altogether she appeared 286 times in N.Y. and 118 times on tour; she sang 28 leading roles in an extremely large repertoire. She performed brilliantly in the roles of Donna Anna in *Don Giovanni*, Pamina in *Die Zauberflöte*, and the Countess in *Le nozze di Figaro*, as well as in other Mozart operas; her other roles were Violetta, Desdemona, Marguerite, Manon, Mimi, and Tosca; in Wagner's operas she sang Eva in *Die Meistersinger von Nürnberg* and Elsa in *Lohengrin*; she also performed the challenging part of Marie in Berg's opera *Wozzeck*. She sang the title role in the premiere of Samuel Barber's opera *Vanessa* on Jan. 15, 1958. After several years of absence from the Metropolitan Opera, she took part in the final gala performance in the old opera building on April 16, 1966. Her European engagements included appearances at Edinburgh (1947), Vienna (1953), and the Bayreuth Festival (1953). After partial retirement in 1962, she was head of the voice dept. at the Cleveland Inst. of Music (1963–72); taught at the Juilliard School in N.Y. and at the New England Cons. of Music (both from 1971); also at the American Inst. of Music Studies in Graz (1978–80; 1988). She established the Eleanor Steber Music Foundation in 1975 to assist young professional singers. With R. Beatie, she publ. the study *Mozart Operatic Arias* (N.Y., 1988). Her autobiography, written in collaboration with M. Sloat, was publ. posthumously (Ridgewood, N.J., 1992).

Štědroň, Bohumír, eminent Czech musicologist, brother of **Vladimír** and uncle of **Miloš Štědroň**; b. Vyžkov, Oct. 30, 1905; d. Brno, Nov. 24, 1982. He studied theory with Josef Blatný (1925–28) and piano with Vilém Kurz (1926–28); also took courses in history and geography at the Univ. of Brno (graduated, 1929), where he attended Helfert's lectures in musicology; after further training in Italy (1931), he returned to the Univ. of Brno to take his Ph.D. in 1934 with the diss. *Sólové chrámové kantáty G. B. Bassaniho* (G.B. Bassani's Solo Church Cantatas) and to complete his Habilitation in 1945 with his *Chrámová hudba v Brně v XVIII. století* (Church Music in Brno in the XVIIIth Century). He taught music education at a teacher-training college (1931–39), and also was an assistant to Helfert (1932–38); then taught music history at the Brno Cons. (1939–45; 1950–52); in 1945 he became a teacher at the Univ. of Brno, where he subsequently was made assistant lecturer in 1950, lecturer in 1955, and prof. in 1963. He was an authority on the life and music of Janáček. In addition to his important books, he contributed many articles to scholarly journals.

WRITINGS: *Leoš Janáček a Luhačovice* (Leoš Janáček and Luhačovice; Luhacovice, 1939); *Leoš Janáček ve vzpominkách a dopisech* (Prague, 1945; rev. Ger. tr., 1955; rev. Eng. tr., 1955, as Leoš Janáček: Letters and Reminiscences); *Josef Bohuslav Foerster a Moravia* (Brno, 1947); ed. with G. Černušák and Z. Nováček, *Československý hudebni slovnik osob a instituci* (Czechoslovak Music Dictionary of Places and Institutions; Prague, 1963–65); *Vitežlav Novák v obrazech* (Vitežlav Novák in Pictures; Prague, 1967); *Zur Genesis von Leoš Janáček's Oper Jenůfa* (Brno, 1968; 2nd ed., rev., 1971); *Leoš Janáček: K jeho lidskému a uměleckému profilu* (Leoš Janáček: Personal and Artistic Profile; Prague, 1976).

BIBL.: *Sbornik praci filosofické fakulty brněnské univerzitě* (Brno, 1967; dedicated to S. on his 60th birthday).

Štědroň, Miloš, significant Czech composer and musicologist, nephew of **Bohumír** and **Vladimír Štědroň**; b. Brno, Feb. 9, 1942. He studied musicology with Racel, Vysloužil, and his uncle Bohumír at the Univ. of Brno (Ph.D., 1967); also studied composition at the Janáček Academy of Music in Brno (1965–70). After working in the music dept. of Brno's Moravian Museum (1963–72), he taught theory at the Univ. of Brno (from 1972). Among his books is a monograph on Monteverdi (Prague, 1985) and a study on Josef Berg (Brno, 1992). He contributed important articles to various journals, many of which deal with the music of Janáček. His own works range from traditional scores to pieces utilizing jazz and pop elements or tape.

WORKS: DRAMATIC: OPERAS: *Aparát* (The Apparatus), chamber opera after Kafka's *In the Penal Colony* (1967); *Kychýnské starosti* (1977); *Josef Fouché-Chameleon* (1984). **BALLETS:** *Justina* (1969); *Ballet macabre* (1986). **ORCH.:** *Moto balladico* (1968); *Quiet Platform* (1969); Concerto for Double Bass and Strings (1971); *To the Memory of Gershwin* for Piano and Jazz Orch. (1971); *Diagram* for Piano and Jazz Orch. (1971); *Music for Ballet* for Chamber Orch. (1972); *Kolo* (Wheel), sym. in memory of Yugoslav partisans of World War II (1971–72); Cello Concerto (1975); *Sette Villanelle* for Cello and Strings (1981); *Musica concertante* for Bassoon and Strings (1986); *Lammento* for Viola and Orch. (1987). **CHAMBER:** *Via crucis* for Flute, Bass Clarinet, Piano, Harpsichord, and Percussion (1964); *Dyptich* for Bass Clarinet, Piano, Strings, and Percussion (1967); *Lai* for Bass Clarinet and Timpani (1967); *Utis II* for Bass Clarinet and Tape (1967); *Util II* for Bass Clarinet, Piano, and Tape (1968); *O, Sancta Caecilia* for Double Bass and Tape

(1968); *Musica ficta* for Wind Quintet (1968); *Duplum* for Bass Clarinet and Double Bass (1968); *Free Landino Jazz* for Bass Clarinet and Piano (1968); *Affeti graziosi* for Violin and Piano (1969); *Saluti musicali* for Bass Clarinet and Piano (1969); *4 Together (Everyman for Himself)* for Bass Clarinet, Piano, and Jazz Combo (1969); String Quartet (1970); *Seikilos z Moravy* (Seikilos from Moravia) for Bass Clarinet and Piano (1978; in collaboration with A. Parsch); *Old and New Renaissance Poems* for Bass Clarinet, Piano, Strings, and Drums (1980); *Trium vocum* for Flute, Cello, and Drums (1984); *Danze, Canti e lamenti* for String Quartet (1986); solo pieces; piano works. **VOCAL:** *Agrafon* for Madrigal Chorus, Renaissance Instruments, and Jazz Ensemble (1968); *Mourning Ceremony*, cantata for Chorus, Trumpet, Oboe, and Church Bell (Czech Radio, Feb. 21, 1969); Vocal Sym. for Soprano, Bass-baritone, and Orch. (1969); *Verba*, cantata for Chorus and 2 Trumpets (1969); *Jazz trium vocum*, free jazz for Chorus and Jazz Ensemble (1972); *Dolorosa gioia*, madrigal-cantata (1975); *Attendite, populi*, cantata for Chorus and Drums (1982); *Conversations, Tunes, Desires* for Tenor, Lute, and Viola da Gamba (1986); *Ommaggio a Gesualdo: Death of Dobrovský*, cantata-oratorio for 2 Solo Voices, Chorus, and Orch. (1988).

Štědroň, Vladimír, Czech composer, brother of **Bohumír** and uncle of **Miloš Stědroň**; b. Vyškov, March 30, 1900; d. Brno, Dec. 12, 1982. He studied law at the Univ. of Prague; simultaneously took lessons in composition with Foerster, Novák, and Suk at the Prague Cons. (1919–23); then studied musicology with Helfert at the Univ. of Brno. He served for many years as a judge, but found time to compose; later was in Prague as a teacher at the Academy of Music, the Univ., and the Cons. (1951–60). His music is couched in an unassuming style inspired by native folk songs.

WORKS: ORCH.: *Fidlovacka*, overture (1916); *Fantastic Scherzo* (1920); *Illusions*, symphonic poem (1936); *Janka*, polka (1962); *Moto balladico* (1967). **CHAMBER:** 2 string quartets (1920; 1940–45); *Variation Fantasy* for String Quartet (1923); *Little Domestic Suite* for 2 Violins and Viola (1937); *Monologe* for Flute (1967); *Monologe* for Horn (1969).

Steel, Christopher (Charles), English composer and teacher; b. London, Jan. 15, 1939; d. Cheltenham, Dec. 31, 1991. He studied composition with John Gardner at the Royal Academy of Music in London (1957–61) and with Harald Genzmer at the Staatliche Hochschule für Musik in Munich (1961–62). He taught at Cheltenham College Junior School (1963–66); was assistant director (1966–68) and director (1968–81) of music at Bradfield College, also serving as an instructor; taught at North Hennepin Community College in Brooklyn Park, Minn. (1977–78); accepted private students from 1982.

WORKS: OPERAS: *The Rescue*, chamber opera (1974); *The Selfish Giant* for Baritone and Children (Westclife-on-Sea, July 1981); *The Angry River*, chamber opera for 7 Soloists, Chorus, and Orch. (1989). **ORCH.:** 7 syms., including No. 3, *A Shakespeare Symphony* for Baritone, Chorus, and Orch. (1967), No. 4 (Manchester, Nov. 2, 1983), No. 5, *Romantic Symphony* (Manchester, Oct. 21, 1986), and No. 6, *Sinfonia sacra* for Soprano, Baritone, Chorus, and Orch. (Sheffield, Nov. 22, 1985); Concerto for Organ and Chamber Orch. (1967); Concerto for String Quartet and Orch. (1968); *Overture Island* (1968); *Odyssey*, suite for Concert Brass Band (1973); *6 Turner Paintings*, suite (1974); *Apollo and Dionysus* (1983); *The City of God and the Garden of Earthly Delights* (Reading, April 12, 1986); Cello Concerto (1988); *Sinfonietta Concertante No. 1* for Organ and Strings (1989) and *No. 2* for Small Orch. (1990); *Serenata Concertante* for Trumpet and Strings or Organ (1991). **VOCAL:** 4 cantatas: *Gethsemane* (1964), *Mary Magdalene* (1967), *Paradise Lost* (1972), and *Jerusalem* (1972); Mass (1968); *Piping Down the Valleys Wild*, song cycle for Baritone and Piano (1971); *Passion and Resurrection According to St. Mark* for Soloists, Chorus, and Chamber Orch. (1978); *The Path of Creation* for Baritone, Oboe, Soloists, Chorus, and Orch. (1984); anthems. **OTHER:** Chamber music, piano pieces, and organ works.

Stefan (actually, **Stefan-Grünfeldt**), **Paul,** Austrian writer on music; b. Brünn, Nov. 25, 1879; d. N.Y., Nov. 12, 1943. He settled in Vienna, where he studied law (doctorate, 1904), philosophy, and art history at the Univ.; also received instruction in theory with Hermann Grädener and Schoenberg. He was employed as a municipal functionary, and at the same time became associated with the modern group of musicians in Vienna; ed. the progressive music periodical *Musikblätter des Anbruch* (1921–38), and was a founder of the Ansorge-Verein (1903) and the ISCM (1922). After the Anschluss in 1938, he went to Switzerland, and later to Lisbon, eventually emigrating to the U.S. in 1941.

WRITINGS: *Gustav Mahler* (Munich, 1910; 7th ed., 1921; Eng. tr., N.Y., 1913); *Das neue Haus: ein Halbjahrhundert Weiner Opernspeil* (Vienna, 1919); *Die Feindschaft gegen Wagner* (Regensburg, 1919); *Neue Musik und Wien* (Leipzig, 1921); *Arnold Schönberg: Wandlung, Legende, Erscheinung, Bedeutung* (Vienna, 1924); *Franz Schubert* (Berlin, 1928); *Geschichte der Wiener Oper* (Vienna, 1932); *Arturo Toscanini* (Vienna, 1936; Eng. tr., N.Y., 1936; Italian tr., Milan, 1937); *Bruno Walter* (Vienna, 1936); *Georges Bizet* (Zürich, 1952).

Stefánsson, Fjölnir, Icelandic composer; b. Reykjavík, Oct. 9, 1930. He studied cello and took theory lessons with Jon Thorarinsson at the Reykjavík Music School, graduating in 1954; then went to England, where he studied composition with Seiber (1954–58). Returning to Iceland, he taught at his alma mater (1958–68); later was headmaster of the Kópavogur School of Music. He composed a Trio for Flute, Clarinet, and Bassoon (1951); Violin Sonata (1954); Duo for Oboe and Clarinet (1974); *Koplon* for Orch. (1979); Sextet for Flute, Clarinet, Bassoon, Horn, Violin, and Cello (1983); numerous arrangements of Icelandic folk songs for chorus.

Steffek, Hanny (actually, **Hannelore**), Austrian soprano; b. Biala, Galicia, Dec. 12, 1927. She received her training at the Vienna Academy of Music and the Salzburg Mozarteum. In 1949 she made her concert debut at the Salzburg Festival, and returned there in 1950 to make her operatic debut in a minor role in *Die Zauberflöte*. She also sang in Graz and Frankfurt am Main, and then was a member of the Bavarian State Opera in Munich (1957–72). In 1959 she made her debut at London's Covent Garden as Sophie. From 1964 to 1973 she sang at the Vienna State Opera. In 1965 she appeared with the visiting Bavarian State Opera at the Edinburgh Festival singing Christine in the first British performance of *Intermezzo*. She also sang with various other European opera houses. In addition to her noted portrayal of Christine, she was admired for such roles as Despina, Blondchen, Papagena, and Ilia. She also was highly successful in Viennese operetta.

Steffen, Wolfgang, German composer; b. Neuhaldensleben, April 28, 1923; d. Berlin, Dec. 4, 1993. He studied at the Berlin Cons. (1946–49) and with Tiessen at the Hochschule für Musik there (1949–53); after graduation, he devoted himself principally to the promotion of new music. He was active as a conductor (1947–59); was an honorary and guest prof. at the Berlin Staatliche Hochschule der Künste (from 1974). In 1978 he won the Australian composition prize and in 1979 the Johann Wenzel Stamitz Prize.

WORKS: ORCH.: *Serenade* for Flute and Strings "im alten Stil" (1948); *Sinfonietta* for Strings (1949); *Tanzerische Impression I* for Piano and Orch. (1950) and *II* for Piano, Percussion, and Orch. (1970); *Intrada seria* (1953); *Meditations de la nuit* (1954); *Aus dem Lebensbuch eines Tanzers* (1954); Piano Concerto (1955); Violin Concerto (1966); *Polychromie* for Piano and 10 Instruments (1970; also for Piano and Orch., 1971); *Klangsegmente* for Cymbal, Harp, Harpsichord, and Orch. (1973–74); *Sinfonia da camera* (1976); Chamber Concerto (1978); Concerto for 6 Flutes and Orch. (1979–83); Concertino for Piano and 9 Instruments or Chamber Orch. (1984); *GOSLAR*, symphonic poem (1991). **CHAMBER:** Trio for Oboe, Flute, and Bassoon (1947); *Theme with 8 Variations* for String Quartet

(1948); Trio for Clarinet, Cello, and Piano (1959); *Diagram* for Viola or Cello and Piano (1965); Wind Quintet (1966); *Jeu* for Violin and Piano (1967); Trio for Flute, Cello, and Piano (1970); *Triplum 72* for Flute, Piano, and Percussion (1972); *Tetraphonie* for Flute Ensemble (1974); *Trilogie 75* for Bandoneon, Flute, and Percussion (1975); *Music* for Piano and 7 Players (1975); *Meditation* for Violin (1981); Duo for Cello and Accordion (1982); *Piece* for Clarinet (1983); String Trio (1983); *Duo Serenade* for Flute and Piano (1987); *Klangdialog* for Mandolin and Guitar (1989); *Klangspiele* for 6 to 7 Percussionists (1991). **PIANO:** *Fantasy* (1947); Sonata (1955); *Reihenproportionen* (1961); *Notturno* for 4-hands (1968); *Les Spirales* (1969); *Introversion* (1982); *Music* (1985). **VOCAL:** *Nachtwachen* for Chorus, Flute, Oboe, Clarinet, and String Quintet (1954); *Hermann-Hesse-Zyklus* for Chorus, Clarinet, Viola, and Piano (1955); *Botschaft*, oratorio (1975–76); *Augenblicke* for Chorus (1986); *Kantate nach Gedichten von Gertrud Kolmar* for Soprano, Chorus, and 6 Instruments (1987); *Bilder von Algina* for Baritone or Bass-baritone and Piano (1987; also for Baritone, Piano, and Orch., 1989); songs.

Steglich, Rudolf, eminent German musicologist; b. Rats-Damnitz, Feb. 18, 1886; d. Scheinfeld, July 8, 1976. He studied musicology with Sandberger at the Univ. of Munich, with Wolf at the Univ. of Berlin, and with Riemann at the Univ. of Leipzig (Ph.D., 1911, with the diss. *Die Quaestiones in Musica und ihr mutmasslicher Verfasser Rudolf von St. Trond* (1070–1138); publ. in Leipzig, 1911); completed his Habilitation in 1930 at the Univ. of Erlangen with his *Die elementare Dynamik des musikalischen Rhythmus* (publ. in Leipzig, 1930). He was in the German army during World War I; then was active as music critic of the Hannover *Anzeiger* (1919–29); in 1929 he was appointed to the faculty of the Univ. of Erlangen; retired in 1956. He was ed. of the *Händel-Jahrbuch* (1928–33) and of the *Archiv für Musikforschung* (1936–40); ed. the Hallische Händel-Ausgabe (with M. Schneider; from 1955), works by Bach's sons, early German song collections, etc. Steglich was an authority on music of the 18th and 19th centuries.

WRITINGS: *J.S. Bach* (Potsdam, 1935); *Mozarts Flügel klingt wieder* (Nuremberg and Salzburg, 1937); *Robert Schumanns Kinderszenen* (Kassel, 1949); *Wege zu Bach* (Regensburg, 1949); *Über die 'kantable Art' der Musik J.S. Bachs* (Zürich, 1958); *Georg Friedrich Händel* (Wilhelmshaven, 1960); *Tanzrhythmus in der Musik J.S. Bachs* (Wolfenbüttel and Zürich, 1962).

Stehle, Adelina, outstanding Austrian soprano; b. Graz, 1860; d. Milan, Dec. 24, 1945. She studied in Milan. She made her operatic debut in Broni in 1881 as Amina; then sang in Bologna, Florence, and Venice. In 1890 she joined La Scala in Milan, where she created roles in *Falstaff* as Nanetta, in *Guglielmo Ratcliff* as Maria, and others; also sang in Berlin, Vienna, St. Petersburg, South America, and the U.S. After her marriage to the Italian tenor Edoardo Garbin, she appeared under the name of Stehle Garbin.

Stehman, Jacques, Belgian composer, music critic, and teacher; b. Brussels, July 8, 1912; d. Heist-aan-Zee, May 20, 1975. He studied piano with Del Pueyo, composition with Absil, and orchestration with Gilson at the Brussels Cons. He then was active as music critic for *Le soir*; was made a prof. of practical harmony (1954) and of music history (1968) at the Brussels Cons.; also taught at the Chapelle Musicale Reine Elisabeth. His music is cautiously modernistic, with engaging touches of jazz.

WORKS: ORCH.: *Symphonie de poche* (1950); *Musique de mai* for Strings (1961); *Dialogues* for Harp and Small Orch. (1964); *Escapades* for Piano and Strings (1965–72); Piano Concerto (1965–72); *Lamento* for Cello and Piano (1947). **PIANO:** *Burlesques en 6 formes* (1934); *Colloque* for 2 Pianos (1943); *3 rythmes* for 2 Pianos (1955); *Montmartre* for 2 Pianos (1975). **VOCAL:** *Melos* for Mezzo-soprano, Flute, and Strings (1968); songs.

Steiger, Rand, American composer and conductor; b. N.Y., June 18, 1957. He attended N.Y.'s High School of Music and Art (1972–75), then studied percussion and composition (with Tanenbaum) at the Manhattan School of Music (B.Mus., 1980); attended the Calif. Inst. of the Arts, where he studied with Brown, Mosko, Powell, and Subotnick (M.F.A., 1982); also studied at Yale Univ. with Carter, Druckman, Jolas, and Martino (1981) and at IRCAM in Paris (1982). He taught at the Univ. of Costa Rica (1984–85), the Calif. Inst. of the Arts (1982–87), and the Univ. of Calif. at San Diego (from 1987). He was the first Composer Fellow of the Los Angeles Phil. (1987–88). His works include *Dialogues II* for Marimba and Orch. (1979–80); *Brave New World* for Voices and Electronics (1980); *Quintessence* for 6 Instruments (1981); *Currents Caprice*, electronic film score (1982); *Kennedy Sketches* for Marimba and Vibraphone (1982); *In Nested Symmetry* for 15 Instruments and Electronics (1982); *Hexadecathlon* for Horn and 7 Instruments (1984); *Fanfare erafnaF* for Double Chamber Orch. (1985); *Tributaries* for Chamber Orch. (1986); *Tributaries for Nancarrow* for 6 Computer-controlled Pianos (1987); Double Concerto for Piano, Percussion, and Double Chamber Orch. (1987); *Druckman Tributary* for 11 Instruments (1988); *ZLoops* for Clarinet, Piano, and Percussion (1989); *Mozart Tributary* for Clarinet Quintet (1991); *The Burgess Shale* for Orch. (1991). Steiger has conducted and directed new-music performances by SONOR of the Univ. of Calif. at San Diego and the Los Angeles Phil. New Music Group. He is perhaps best known as a member of the Calif. E.A.R. Unit, a highly respected new-music ensemble established at the Calif. Inst. of the Arts in 1981. Other members include cellist Erika Duke-Kirkpatrick (b. Los Angeles, Aug. 1, 1956), who studied with Cesare Pascarella (1971–82) and at the Calif. Inst. of the Arts (B.F.A., 1978; M.F.A., 1982), where she later taught (from 1987); among composers who have written works for her are Subotnick, La Barbara, Powell, and Mosko; she performed as a soloist and in ensembles in the U.S., South America, and Europe. Pianist Lorna Ellen Eder (b. Aberdeen, Wash., April 2, 1953) studied at the Univ. of Puget Sound in Tacoma, Wash. (1971–73), Wash. State Univ. in Pullman (B.Mus., 1975), with Leonid Hambro at the Calif. Inst. of the Arts (M.F.A., 1980), and with Bruno Seidlhofer in Vienna (1975–77). She was a staff accompanist at the Calif. Inst. of the Arts (1980–84); played with the Santa Clarita Chamber Players (1985–90) and in duo recitals with Eugene Fodor (1984–86). Composer, percussionist, and performance artist Art(hur) Jarviven (b. Ilwaco, Wash., Jan. 27, 1956) studied at Ohio Univ. (B.Mus., 1978) and the Calif. Inst. of the Arts (M.F.A., 1981); had percussion lessons from Guy Remonko, John Bergamo, Karen Ervin, and Ruth Underwood, and composition lessons with Subotnick, Brown, and Mosko. He performed with the Los Angeles Phil. New Music Group and the performance-art ensemble Le Momo; also worked with Steve Reich and Frank Zappa. His satiric works, which involve poetry, theater, visual media, and various musical styles, have been performed throughout the U.S.; these include *Vote of Confidence* for Percussion Trio (1979); *Through Birds, through Fire, but Not through Glass* for Percussion Quartet (1979); *Soluble Furniture* for Piano (1980); *Mercury at Right Angles* for Celesta (1980); *Viscous Linings* for Celesta, Viola, Bass Clarinet, and Percussion (1981); *Prosthesis*, false piece for anything or nothing (1981); *Raison d'etre* for Marimba and Vibraphone (1981); *Carbon* for Bass Clarinet (1982); *Deductible Rooms* for Marimba (1982); *Adult Party Games from the Leisure Planet* for Various Ensembles (1985); *Ivan, Where Are You Running To* for 9 Players and Tape (1985); *Electric Jesus* for Juvenile Pianist and Large Ensemble (1985); *Mass Death of a School of Small Herring* for Chamber Orch. (1986); *A Book of 5 Rings* for Pianos and Percussion (1986); *Egyptian 2-Step* for Ensemble (1986); *The 7 Golden Vampires* for 2 Pianos (1987); *35 1/2 Minutes for Gaylord Mowrey* for Piano, Video, and Refreshments (1987); *Goldbeater's Skin* for Clarinet (1987; other versions, 1988); *The Queen of Spades, parts I–III* for 2 Electronic Harpsichords and Percussion (1988–90); *The 15 Fingers of Doctor Wu* for Oboe (1987); *Murphy-Nights* for Ensemble (1989); *The Vul-*

ture's Garden for 4 Players (1990). Percussionist Amy Knoles (b. Milwaukee, Sept. 10, 1959) studied at the Univ. of Wisc. (1977–79) and at the Calif. Inst. of the Arts (B.F.A., 1982), where she later taught. Among the composers whose works she has premiered are Powell, Subotnick, Chatham, and Tower. Violinist and vocalist Robin Lorentz (b. Seattle, Dec. 19, 1956) studied at the Cornish School of Music, the Univ. of Wash. (1977–78), and with Emanuel Zetlin and Yoko Matsuda at the Calif. Inst. of the Arts (B.F.A., 1980); taught at the Kirk Cons. of Music in Pasadena, Calif., and at the Aspen Music Festival (1989, 1990). She was concertmaster for the Ojai Festival (1986, 1988), and assoc. concertmaster for both the San Diego Chamber Players (1988) and the Los Angeles Phil. New Music Group (1987, 1988, 1990). She has performed with the Sterling Consort (1987–90) and the Ensemble of Santa Fe (from 1985). Her solo recording credits include works for television and film, in Irish, Cajun, bluegrass, jazz, and pop-rock styles. She joined the E.A.R. Unit in 1983. Clarinetist and saxophonist Jim Rohrig (b. Long Beach, Calif., Nov. 30, 1954) studied at the Univ. of Southern Calif. (B.A., 1977) and at the Calif. Inst. of the Arts (M.F.A., 1981; advanced certificate, 1983), where he also taught (1982–83); his teachers included Mitchell Lurie, Michelle Zukovsky, and Douglas Masek. He was a co-founder of the E.A.R. Unit. He has recorded works by Subotnick, La Barbara et al., and is an active member of the performance-art ensemble Le Momo. He has composed incidental music for the stage and has directed and ed. film and video, including those of E.A.R. Unit performances. His in-progress projects include a film documentary of Nicolas Slonimsky. Flutist Dorothy Stone (b. Kingston, Pa., June 7, 1958) studied at the Manhattan School of Music (B.Mus., 1980) and at the Calif. Inst. of the Arts (M.F.A., 1982), her teachers including Harold Bennett, Harvey Sollberger, Thomas Nyfenger, Julius Baker, and Ann Deiner Giles; gave first performances of works by Boulez, Cage, Ferneyhough, and Carter; numerous composers have composed works for her, including Babbitt, Steiger, and Mosko. She composed Wizard Ball for Flute and Electronics, which won several awards. Stone is artistic director and administrative manager of the E.A.R. Unit. She is married to **Stephen Mosko**.

Stein, Erwin, Austrian conductor and editor; b. Vienna, Nov. 7, 1885; d. London, July 19, 1958. He studied composition with Schoenberg in Vienna (1906–10) and became Schoenberg's early champion. From 1910 to 1914 he conducted various theater orchs. in Austria and Germany; returning to Vienna, he was a member, with Schoenberg, Berg, and Webern, of the famous Verein für musikalische Privataufführungen (Soc. for Musical Private Performances), which excluded music critics from attendance (1920–22). He then became an ed. for Universal Edition in Vienna, where he was instrumental in bringing out works by the composers of the Second Viennese School. From 1924 to 1930 he ed. the journal *Pult und Taktstock.* He also conducted a tour with a Vienna group named Pierrot Lunaire Ensemble. After the Anschluss in 1938, he went to London and joined the music publ. firm of Boosey & Hawkes. He contributed a fundamental paper on Schoenberg's method of composition with 12 tones, "Neue Formprinzipien," publ. in *Anbruch* (1924). He publ. a selective collection of Schoenberg's letters (Mainz, 1958; Eng. tr., London, 1964); a collection of essays, *Orpheus in New Guises* (London, 1953); his theoretical monograph *Musik, Form und Darstellung* was publ. posthumously, first in Eng. as *Form and Performance* (London, 1962) and later in German (Munich, 1964).

Stein, Fritz (actually, **Friedrich Wilhelm**), German musicologist; b. Gerlachsheim, Baden, Dec. 17, 1879; d. Berlin, Nov. 14, 1961. He studied theology in Karlsruhe, then took courses in musicology with P. Wolfrum in Heidelberg; subsequently went to Leipzig, where he studied various subjects with Krehl, Nikisch, Riemann, and Straube; completed his musicological training at the Univ. of Heidelberg (Ph.D., 1910, with the diss. *Zur Geschichte der Musik in Heidelberg*; publ. in 1912; new ed., 1921, as *Geschichte des Musikwesens in Heidelberg bis zum Ende des 18. Jahrhunderts*). He went to Jena in 1906 as music director of the Univ. and city organist; in 1913 he was appointed prof. of musicology at the Univ.; was in the German army during World War I and directed a male chorus for the troops at the front. He became a reader in musicology at the Univ. of Kiel in 1920, then was a prof. from 1928 to 1933; in 1933 he became director of the Hochschule für Musik in Berlin, holding this position to the end of World War II in 1945. He achieved notoriety when he discovered in the library of the Univ. of Jena the parts of a sym. marked by an unknown copyist as a work by Beethoven. The sym. became famous as the "Jena Symphony" and was hailed by many as a genuine discovery; the score was publ. by Breitkopf & Härtel in 1911, and performances followed all over the world; Stein publ. his own exegesis of it as "Eine unbekannte Jugendsymphonie Beethovens?" in the *Sammelbände der Internationalen Musik-Gesellschaft* (1911). Doubts of its authenticity were raised, but it was not until 1957 that H.C. Robbins Landon succeeded in locating the original MS, proving that the "Jena Symphony" was in reality the work of Friedrich Witt (1770–1837). Stein publ. a monograph on Max Reger (Potsdam, 1939) and *Max Reger: Sein Leben in Bildern* (a pictorial biography; Leipzig, 1941; 2nd ed., 1956); brought out a thematic catalogue of Reger's works (Leipzig, 1934; definitive ed., 1953); ed. works by Johann Christian Bach, Telemann, Handel, Beethoven, etc.; contributed essays to numerous learned publs. A Festschrift was publ. in his honor on his 60th birthday (1939).

Stein, Horst (Walter), German conductor; b. Elberfeld, May 2, 1928. He studied at the Hochschule für Musik in Cologne, and at age 23 was engaged as a conductor at the Hamburg State Opera; then was on the staff of the State Opera in East Berlin (1955–61). He was deputy Generalmusikdirektor at the Hamburg State Opera (1961–63); after serving as Generalmusikdirektor of the Mannheim National Theater (1963–70), he returned to the Hamburg State Opera as Generalmusikdirektor (1972–77); also was Generalmusikdirektor with the Hamburg State Phil. (1973–76). He subsequently was chief conductor of the Orchestre de la Suisse Romande in Geneva (1980–85), the Bamberg Sym. Orch. (from 1985), and the Basel Sym. Orch. (1987–94). He made many guest conducting appearances in Europe and in North and South America.

Stein, Leon, American composer, teacher, and conductor; b. Chicago, Sept. 18, 1910. He studied violin at the American Cons. in Chicago (1922–27), and theory at Crane Junior College in Chicago (1927–29); took private lessons in composition with Sowerby, in orchestration with DeLamarter, and in conducting with Stock and Lange (1937–40); also studied at De Paul Univ. (B.M., 1931; M.M., 1935; Ph.D., 1949; diss. publ. as *The Racial Thinking of Richard Wagner*, 1950), where he served on its faculty (1931–78); served as dean of its school of music (1966–76); also was director of the Inst. of Music of the College of Jewish Studies (1952–59) and was a conductor of various community orchs. He publ. *Structure and Style: The Study and Analysis of Musical Form* (Evanston, Ill., 1962; 3rd ed., rev. and enl., 1979) and *Anthology of Musical Forms* (Evanston, Ill., 1962). In 1982 he received Chicago's Hall of Fame Award. His music is academic, but not devoid of occasional modernities.

WORKS: DRAMATIC: OPERAS: *The Fisherman's Wife* (1953–54; St. Joseph, Mich., Jan. 10, 1955); *Deirdre*, after Yeats (1956; Chicago, May 18, 1957). **BALLETS FOR PIANO:** *Exodus* (Chicago, Jan. 29, 1939); *Doubt* (Chicago, Jan. 21, 1940). **ORCH.:** *Prelude and Fugue* (1935); *Passacaglia* (1936); *Sinfonietta* for Strings (1938); Violin Concerto (1938–39; Chicago, Dec. 3, 1948); 4 syms.: No. 1 (1940), No. 2 (1942), No. 3 (1950–51), and No. 4 (1975); *3 Hassidic Dances* (1940–41; Chicago, April 13, 1942); *Triptych on 3 Poems of Walt Whitman* (1943; Chicago, March 29, 1949); *Great Lakes Suite* for Small Orch. (1943–44); *Rhapsody* for Flute, Harp, and Strings (1954; Chicago, Nov. 8, 1955); *Adagio and Rondo Ebraico* (1957); *A Festive Overture* (1959); *Then Shall the Dust Return* (1971); Cello Concerto (1977; Chicago, June 11, 1983); Concerto for

Clarinet and Percussion Ensemble (1979); *Nexus* for Wind Ensemble (1983); *Aria Hebraique* for Oboe and Strings (1984; Los Angeles, April 10, 1994); Concerto for Oboe and Strings (1986; Chicago, Jan. 29, 1988). **CHAMBER:** Sonata for 2 Violins (1931); Violin Sonata (1932); 5 string quartets (1933, 1962, 1964, 1964, 1967); Woodwind Quintet (1936); *12 Preludes* for Violin and Piano (1942–49); Trio for 3 Trumpets (1953); Quintet for Saxophone and String Quartet (1957); Sextet for Alto Saxophone and Wind Quintet (1958); solo sonatas for Violin (1960), Flute (1968), Horn (1969), Trombone (1969), Trumpet (1969), Bassoon (1969), Oboe (1969), Bass (1970), and Cello (1970); *Trio Concertante* for Saxophone, Violin, and Piano (1961); *Suite* for Saxophone Quartet (1962); Tenor Saxophone Sonata (1967); Trio for Alto Saxophone, Clarinet, and Piano (1969); *3 Pieces* for Clarinet (1969); *Rhapsody* for Alto Saxophone (1969); Suite for Brass Quintet (1975); Quintet for Harp and String Quartet (1976); *Introduction and Rondo* for Flute and Percussion (1977); Suite for Woodwind Quintet (1978); *Rhapsody* for Cello (1979); Suite for Violin, Viola, and Cello (1980); *Dance ebraico* for Cello and Piano (1982); *Duo Concertante* for Bassoon or Violin and Marimba (1988); Trio Concertante for Violin, Saxophone or Cello, and Piano (1993); numerous solo works and various piano pieces. **VOCAL:** *The Lord Reigneth*, cantata for Tenor, Women's Chorus, and Orch. (1953); choral pieces; songs.

Stein, Leonard, eminent American music scholar; b. Los Angeles, Dec. 1, 1916. He attended Los Angeles City College (1933–36) and studied piano privately with Richard Buhlig (1936–39); enrolled in the class of composition and musical analysis with Schoenberg at the Univ. of Southern Calif. (1935–36) and at the Univ. of Calif. at Los Angeles (1936–42); from 1939 to 1942 he was Schoenberg's teaching assistant; received the degrees of B.A. (1939) and M.M. (1941) from the Univ. of Calif. at Los Angeles, and his D.M.A. from the Univ. of Southern Calif. (1965); was the recipient of a Guggenheim fellowship (1965–66). He taught at Occidental College (1946–48); Los Angeles City College (1948–60); Pomona College (1961–62); Univ. of Calif. at Los Angeles (1962–64); Claremont Graduate School (1963–67); Univ. of Calif. at San Diego (1966); and Calif. State College at Dominguez Hills (1967–70); in 1970 he was appointed a member of the music faculty of the Calif. Inst. of the Arts; in 1975 he became adjunct prof. in the School of Music at the Univ. of Southern Calif. in Los Angeles. In 1975 he was elected director of the Arnold Schoenberg Inst. of the Univ. of Southern Calif., and editorial director of the *Journal of the Arnold Schoenberg Institute.* Stein retired in 1991. In addition to his musicological work, he also made occasional appearances as a pianist and conductor. He contributed a number of articles on the proper performance of piano works by Schoenberg; was a member of the editorial board of the complete works of Schoenberg. He ed. Schoenberg's *Nachtwandler* (1969); Piano Concerto (1972); *Ode to Napoleon Bonaparte* (1973); *Brettl-Lieder* (1974); ed. and completed Schoenberg's pedagogical works: *Preliminary Exercises in Counterpoint* (1963); *Models for Beginners in Composition* (rev. of the text, 1972); *Structural Functions of Harmony* (rev., 1969); *Style and Idea. Selected Writings of Arnold Schoenberg* (London, 1975; received the 1976 ASCAP award).

Stein, Richard Heinrich, German music theorist and composer; b. Halle, Feb. 28, 1882; d. Santa Brigida, Canary Islands, Aug. 11, 1942. He studied law and music; received his Ph.D. from the Univ. of Erlangen in 1911 with the diss. *Die psychologischen Grundlagen der Wundtschen Ethik.* From 1914 to 1919 he lived in Spain; from 1920 to 1932 he taught in Berlin. In 1933 he settled in the Canary Islands. He was a composer of experimental tendencies; his *2 Konzertstücke* for Cello and Piano, op. 26 (1906), was the first composition containing quarter tones to be publ. In 1909 he wrote a brochure giving a detailed exposition of his quarter-tone system, and in 1914 he built a quarter-tone clarinet. He composed about 100 piano pieces and about 50 songs; *Scherzo fantastico* for Orch.; publ. the books *La música moderna* (Barcelona, 1918; in Spanish and German), *Grieg* (1921), and *Tschaikowsky* (1927).

Steinbauer, Othmar, Austrian violinist, conductor, teacher, instrument maker, and composer; b. Vienna, Nov. 6, 1895; d. Altenburg, Sept. 5, 1962. He studied violin at the Vienna Academy of Music. He founded the Chamber Concert Soc. of Vienna, playing and conducting works of the modern Viennese School. He publ. a theoretical treatise, *Das Wesen der Tonalität* (Munich, 1928). In 1938 he founded the Musikschule der Stadt Wien. After 1945 he devoted himself mainly to manufacturing new instruments; constructed a violin specially adapted for easy performance by amateurs. His own music is quite conservative.

Steinberg, Maximilian (Osseievich), significant Russian composer and pedagogue; b. Vilnius, July 4, 1883; d. Leningrad, Dec. 6, 1946. He was a student at the Univ. of St. Petersburg (graduated, 1907) and of Rimsky-Korsakov (composition), Liadov (harmony), and Glazunov (instrumentation) at the St. Petersburg Cons. (graduated, 1908). In 1908 he married Rimsky-Korsakov's daughter and became a teacher of theory and composition at the St. Petersburg Cons. From 1917 to 1931 he was dean of its faculty of composition, and later was its acting rector from 1934 to 1939. Many composers who became prominent in the Soviet era were his pupils. His early compositions reflected the influence of his teachers, but he gradually evolved a personal style distinguished by rhapsodic eloquence with some touches of French Impressionism.

WORKS: BALLET: *Metamorphoses* (2nd part perf. in Paris, June 2, 1914). **ORCH.:** 4 syms.: No. 1 (1907), No. 2 (St. Petersburg, Nov. 27, 1909), No. 3 (Leningrad, March 3, 1929, composer conducting), and No. 4, *Turksib* (Leningrad, Dec. 2, 1933); *In Armenia* (Leningrad, Dec. 24, 1940); Violin Concerto (1946). **CHAMBER:** 2 string quartets; piano pieces. **VOCAL:** *La Princesse Maleine* for Women's Chorus and Orch. (1916); *Heaven and Earth* for 6 Soloists and Orch. (1918); songs. **OTHER:** Arrangements of works by other composers.

BIBL.: A. Rimsky-Korsakov, *M. S.* (Moscow, 1928); V. Bogdanov-Berezovsky, *M. S.* (Moscow, 1947).

Steinberg, (Carl) Michael (Alfred), German-born American music critic; b. Breslau, Oct. 4, 1928. He went to England in 1939 and to the U.S. in 1943, becoming a naturalized American citizen in 1950; studied music at Princeton Univ. (A.B., 1949; M.F.A., 1951); then was in Italy (1952–54). Returning to North America, he taught at Princeton Univ., Hunter College, Manhattan School of Music, Univ. of Saskatchewan, Smith College, Brandeis Univ., Boston Univ., and (from 1968) the New England Cons. of Music in Boston. In 1964 he was appointed music critic of the *Boston Globe.* His criticisms, utterly disrespectful of the most sacrosanct musical personalities, aroused periodic outbursts of indignation among outraged artists, aggrieved managers, and chagrined promoters. In 1969 several Boston Sym. Orch. players petitioned the management to banish him from their concerts. Then, in a spectacular peripeteia, he left the Boston Globe in 1976 and was appointed director of publs. for the Boston Sym. Orch. In 1979 he assumed the position of artistic adviser and publications director of the San Francisco Sym., subsequently serving as its program annotator from 1989. He also was artistic advisor of the Minnesota Orch. in Minneapolis (1989–92) and program annotator of the N.Y. Phil. (from 1995). He publ. *The Symphony: A Listener's Guide* (Oxford, 1995).

Steinberg, Pinchas, American conductor; b. N.Y., Feb. 12, 1945. He studied violin in N.Y., then pursued musical training at Tanglewood and at Indiana Univ. In 1967 he became a conductor at the Chicago Lyric Opera; in 1971 he conducted in Berlin; subsequently conducted opera in Frankfurt am Main, Stuttgart, Hamburg, London, Paris, and San Francisco. From 1985 to 1989 he was Generalmusikdirektor in Bremen. In 1989 he became chief conductor of the Austrian Radio Sym. Orch. in Vienna.

Steinberg, William (actually, **Hans Wilhelm**), eminent German-born American conductor; b. Cologne, Aug. 1, 1899; d. N.Y., May 16, 1978. He studied piano and violin at home; conducted his own setting for chorus and orch. of a poem from Ovid's *Metamorphoses* in school at the age of 13; then took lessons in conducting with Hermann Abendroth, in piano with Lazzaro Uzielli, and in theory with Franz Bölsche at the Cologne Cons., graduating in 1920, with the Wüllner Prize for conducting. He subsequently became assistant to Otto Klemperer at the Cologne Opera, and in 1924 became principal conductor. In 1925 he was engaged as conductor of the German Theater in Prague; in 1929 he was appointed Generalmusikdirektor of the Frankfurt am Main Opera, where he brought out several modern operas, including Berg's *Wozzeck*. With the advent of the Nazi regime in 1933, he was removed from his position and became conductor for the Jewish Culture League, restricted to Jewish audiences. In 1936 he left Germany and became one of the conductors of the Palestine Orch., which he rehearsed and prepared for Toscanini, who subsequently engaged him as an assistant conductor of the NBC Sym. Orch. in N.Y. in 1938. His career as an orch. conductor was then connected with major American orchs. He became a naturalized American citizen in 1944. He was music director of the Buffalo Phil. (1945–52); in 1952 he was appointed music director of the Pittsburgh Sym. Orch.; concurrently, he served as music director of the London Phil. (1958–60) and of the Boston Sym. Orch. (1969–72); he retired from his Pittsburgh post in 1976. He also made many guest conducting appearances with major U.S. and European orchs. His performances were marked by impeccable taste and fidelity to the music; in this respect he was a follower of the Toscanini tradition.

Steinberg, Ze'ev (Wolfgang), German-born Israeli violist and composer; b. Düsseldorf, Nov. 27, 1918. He studied with Eldering in Cologne (1933). In 1934 he emigrated to Palestine, where he studied viola and composition with Partos (1940–42). He then became a violist in the Palestine Sym. Orch. (later the Israel Phil.) in Tel Aviv; in 1957, became the violinist in the New Israeli String Quartet; from 1969 to 1972, was a lecturer at the Tel Aviv Academy of Music. His compositions present an agreeable blend of oriental melos, asymmetrical rhythms, and sharp atonal progressions in dissonant counterpoint.

WORKS: Sonata for 2 Violas (1955–56); 3 string quartets (1959; 1969; 1981–82); *6 Miniatures* for Cello and Piano (1961); *4 Bagatelles* for 2 Recorders (1962); *2 concerti da camera*: No. 1 for Viola and String Orch. (1962) and No. 2 for Violin and 8 Instruments (1966); *Purim Variations* on a nursery song for Horn and String Trio (1963); *The Story of Rahab and the Spies*, biblical cantata (1969); *Festive Prologue* for Flute, Oboe, and String Trio (1969); *2 Songs without Words* for Viola, String Quartet, and String Orch. (1970); *a little suite for a big flute* for Bass Flute in C (1972); *Variations and Dance* for Violin (1976); *Prelude and Fughetta* for Flute, Viola, and Harp (1977); *4 Pieces* for Orch. (1985); *7 Pieces* for 11 Instruments (1987); arrangements of works by Vivaldi, Bach, Schubert, and others.

Steiner, Emma, American composer and conductor; b. 1850; d. N.Y., Feb. 27, 1928. Her grandfather led the Maryland 16th Brigade, which won the battle of North Point (near Fort McHenry, Baltimore) on Sept. 13, 1814, enabling Francis Scott Key to finish the last stanza of *The Star-Spangled Banner*. She wrote 7 light operas, plus ballets, overtures, and songs; purportedly she was also the first woman ever to receive payment for conducting. Conried, the manager of the Metropolitan Opera, is said to have declared that he would have let her conduct a performance had he dared to put a woman armed with a baton in front of a totally male orch. According to unverifiable accounts, she conducted 6,000 performances of 50 different operas. She also organized an Emma R. Steiner Home for the Aged and Infirm Musicians at Bay Shore, Long Island. On Feb. 28, 1925, she conducted a concert at the Metropolitan Opera to commemorate the 50th anniversary of her first appearance as conductor. Her works, of different genres and light consistency, aggregate more than 200 opus numbers.

Steiner, Max(imilian Raoul Walter), Austrian-born American composer; b. Vienna, May 10, 1888; d. Los Angeles, Dec. 28, 1971. He studied at the Vienna Cons. with Fuchs and Gradener, and also had some advice from Mahler. At the age of 14, he wrote an operetta. In 1904 he went to England; in 1911 he proceeded to Paris. In 1914 he settled in the U.S.; after conducting musical shows in N.Y., he moved in 1929 to Hollywood, where he became one of the most successful film composers. His music offers a fulsome blend of lush harmonies artfully derived from both Tchaikovsky and Wagner, arranged in a manner marvelously suitable for the portrayal of psychological drama on the screen. Among his film scores, of which he wrote more than 200, are *King Kong* (1933), *The Charge of the Light Brigade* (1936), *Gone with the Wind* (1939), and *The Treasure of Sierra Madre* (1948).

BIBL.: G. Lazarou, *M. S. and Film Music: An Essay* (Athens, 1971).

Steinert, Alexander Lang, American pianist, conductor, composer, and arranger; b. Boston, Sept. 21, 1900; d. N.Y., July 7, 1982. He was the son of a piano manufacturer; studied at Harvard Univ., graduating in 1922; then took private lessons in composition with Loeffler in Boston, and with Koechlin and d'Indy in Paris. He lived much of his time in Europe; was active as a conductor and arranger in Hollywood. His music bears the imprint of the French modern school.

WORKS: ORCH.: *Nuit méridionale* (Boston, Oct. 15, 1926); *Leggenda sinfonica* (Rome, 1930); *Concerto sinfonico* for Piano and Orch. (Boston, Feb. 8, 1935, composer soloist); *Rhapsody* for Clarinet and Orch. (1945); *The Nightingale and the Rose* for Speaker and Orch. (Philadelphia, March 31, 1950). **CHAMBER:** Violin Sonata; Piano Trio; piano pieces. **VOCAL:** Songs.

Steingruber, Ilona, Austrian soprano; b. Vienna, Feb. 8, 1912; d. there, Dec. 10, 1962. She studied piano before taking up vocal training at the Vienna Academy of Music. She sang in performances broadcast by the Austrian Radio (1939–42); made her operatic debut in Tilsit (1942); after World War II, she toured as a concert artist; also sang at the Vienna State Opera (1948–51); then taught in Darmstadt. In 1946 she married **Friedrich Wildgans**.

Steinhardt, Milton, American musicologist; b. Miami, Okla., Nov. 13, 1909; d. Lawrence, Kansas, June 30, 1994. After preliminary study at the Univ. of Kansas, he took courses at the Akademie der Tonkunst in Munich, and had violin lessons with Maurice Hewitt in Paris. Returning to the U.S., he enrolled in the Eastman School of Music in Rochester, N.Y. (B.M., 1936; M.M., 1937); then attended courses of Kinkeldey at Cornell Univ. and Sachs and Reese at N.Y. Univ. (Ph.D., 1950, with the diss. *Jacobus Vaet and His Motets*; publ. in East Lansing, Mich., 1951). He was a lecturer at Michigan State Univ. (1948–50), Ohio Univ. (1950–51), and the Univ. of Kansas (1951–75). He ed. the works of Jacobus Vaet for Denkmäler der Tonkunst in Österreich (vols. 98, 100, 103/104, 108/109, 113/114, 116) and the motets of P. de Monte in 7 vols. (1975–86) for the New Complete Edition publ. in Louvain.

Steinitz, (Charles) Paul (Joseph), English organist and conductor; b. Chichester, Aug. 25, 1909; d. Oxted, April 22, 1988. He studied at the Royal Academy of Music in London, and also privately with George Oldroyd. He then served as church organist in Ashford, Kent (1933–42). In 1947 he organized the South London Bach Soc.; this choral group later became noteworthy under the name of the London Bach Soc. He also served as organist and choirmaster at the Church of St. Bartholomew-the-Great in London (1949–61). In 1969 he founded the Steinitz Bach Players, which he conducted on tours. In 1945 he became a prof. at the Royal Academy of Music in London; also taught at Goldsmiths' College, Univ. of London (1948–76). He publ. *Bach's Passions* (London, 1979). In 1985 he was made a member of the Order of the British Empire.

Steinpress, Boris (Solomonovich), erudite Russian musicologist; b. Berdyansk, Aug. 13, 1908; d. Moscow, May 21, 1986. He studied piano with Igumnov at the Moscow Cons., graduating in 1931, and took a postgraduate course there in musicology with Ivanov-Boretsky, completing it in 1936; was a member of its faculty (1931; 1933–36); in 1938 he received the title of candidate of fine arts for his diss. on Mozart's *Le nozze di Figaro.* He taught at the Urals Cons. in Sverdlovsk (1936–37; 1942–43); served as head of the music history dept. of the Central Correspondence Inst. for Musical Education (1939–41), and was senior lecturer and dean of the faculty of history and theory (from 1940). In 1942 he joined the Communist Party. Although engaged primarily in musical encyclopedic work, Steinpress also composed; his patriotic songs were popular in the U.S.S.R. during World War II. From 1938 to 1940 and from 1943 to 1959 he was chief contributor to the music section of the *Great Soviet Encyclopedia.* His publications are particularly important in musical biography; he decisively refuted the legend of Salieri's poisoning Mozart. His biography of Aliabiev clarifies the story of Aliabiev's life and his internal exile on the false charge of murder in a duel. With I. Yampolsky, he ed. an extremely valuable and accurate one-vol. encyclopedic musical dictionary (Moscow, 1959; 2nd ed., 1966); also with Yampolsky he compiled a useful brief dictionary for music lovers (Moscow, 1961; 2nd ed., 1967). In 1963 he publ. a partial vol. of a monumental work on opera premieres covering the period 1900–40, giving exact dates and names of theaters for all opera productions worldwide.

Steinway & Sons, celebrated family of German-American piano manufacturers. The founder of the firm was Heinrich Engelhard Steinweg (b. Wolfshagen, Germany, Feb. 15, 1797; d. N.Y., Feb. 7, 1871; in 1864 he Anglicized his name to Henry E. Steinway). He learned cabinetmaking and organ building at Goslar, and in 1818 entered the shop of an organ maker in Seesen, also becoming church organist there. From about 1820 he became interested in piano making and worked hard to establish a business of his own. He built his first piano in 1836. In 1839 he exhibited one grand and 2 square pianos at the Braunschweig State Fair, winning the gold medal. The Revolution of 1848 caused him to emigrate to America with his wife, 2 daughters, and 4 of his 5 sons: Charles (actually, Christian Karl Gottlieb; b. Seesen, Jan. 4, 1829; d. there, March 31, 1865); Henry (actually, Johann Heinrich Engelhard; b. Seesen, Oct. 29, 1830; d. N.Y., March 11, 1865); William (actually, Johann Heinrich Wilhelm; b. Seesen, March 5, 1835; d. N.Y., Nov. 30, 1896); and (Georg August) Albert (b. Seesen, June 10, 1840; d. N.Y., May 14, 1877). The management of the German business at Seesen was left in charge of the eldest son, (Christian Friedrich) Theodore (b. Seesen, Nov. 6, 1825; d. Braunschweig, March 26, 1889). The family arrived in N.Y. on June 29, 1850, and for about 2 years father and sons worked in various piano factories there. On March 5, 1853, they established a factory of their own under the above firm name, with premises on Varick St. In 1854 they won a gold medal for a square piano at the Metropolitan Fair in Washington, D.C. Their remarkable prosperity dates from 1855, when they took 1st prize for a square over-strung piano with cast-iron frame (an innovation then) at the N.Y. Industrial Exhibition. In 1856 they made their first grand, and in 1862 their first upright. Among the numerous honors subsequently received may be mentioned 1st prize at London, 1862; 1st grand gold medal of honor for all styles at Paris, 1867 (by unanimous verdict); diplomas for "highest degree of excellence in all styles" at Philadelphia, 1876. In 1854 the family name (Steinweg) was legally changed to Steinway. In 1865, upon the death of his brothers Charles and Henry, Theodore gave up the Braunschweig business and became a full partner in the N.Y. firm; he built Steinway Hall on 14th St., which, in addition to the offices and retail warerooms, housed a concert hall that became a leading center of N.Y. musical life. In 1925 headquarters were established in the Steinway Building on 57th St. Theodore was especially interested in the scientific aspects of piano construction and made a study of the acoustical theories of Helmholtz and Tyndall, which enabled him to introduce important improvements. He returned to Germany in 1870. On May 17, 1876, the firm was incorporated and William was elected president; he opened a London branch in 1876, and established a European factory at Hamburg in 1880. In the latter year he also bought 400 acres of land on Long Island Sound and established there the village of Steinway (now part of Long Island City), where since 1910 the entire manufacturing plant has been located. Control and active management of the business, now the largest of its kind in the world, has remained in the hands of the founder's descendants. Theodore E. Steinway (d. N.Y., April 8, 1957), grandson of Henry E. Steinway, was president from 1927; also a stamp collector, he was honored by Liechtenstein with his portrait on a postage stamp on Sept. 7, 1972; in 1955 he was succeeded by his son, Henry Steinway. The firm was sold to CBS in 1972, although the Steinway family continued to be closely associated with the business. In 1985 CBS sold the firm to Steinway Musical Properties. In 1988 Steinway & Sons celebrated its 135th anniversary with a special concert in N.Y. and the unveiling of its 500,000th piano. In 1995 the firm was purchased by the Selmer Co.

BIBL.: O. Floersheim, *W. S.* (Breslau, 1894); E. Hubbard, *The Story of the S.s* (East Aurora, N.Y., 1911); T. Steinway, *People and Pianos* (N.Y., 1953; 2nd ed., 1961); C. Ehrlich, *The Piano: A History* (London, 1976); C. Hoover, "The S.s and their Pianos in the Nineteenth Century," *Journal of the American Musical Instrument Society,* VII (1981).

Stekke, Léon, Belgian composer and teacher; b. Soignies, Oct. 12, 1904; d. Anderlecht, near Brussels, Jan. 24, 1970. He studied with Joseph Jongen and Paul Gilson in Brussels. From 1942 until his death he taught at the Royal Cons. in Brussels.

WORKS: OPERA: *Les Cornes du Croissant* (Brussels, 1952). **ORCH.:** *Fantaisie-rapsodie*; *Burlesco* for Oboe and Orch.; Trumpet Concerto (Brussels, 1948); *Fantaisie élégiaque* for English Horn and Orch.; *Poème sylvestre* for Horn and Orch.; *Impression de cinéma* for Bassoon and Orch.; *Variations* for Trombone and Orch. **VOCAL:** 2 cantatas: *Héro et Léandre* (1931); *La Légende de St.-Hubert* (1933); songs.

Stella, Antonietta, Italian soprano; b. Perugia, March 15, 1929. She studied voice with Aldo Zeetti in Perugia. She made her operatic debut in Rome as Leonore in *La forza del destino* in 1951; in 1953 she sang at La Scala in Milan; further engagements were at Covent Garden in London (1955) and at the Vienna State Opera. She made her American debut at the Metropolitan Opera in N.Y. on Nov. 13, 1956, as Aida; after remaining on its roster until 1960, she pursued her career in Europe.

Stemper, Frank, American pianist and composer; b. Milwaukee, Oct. 19, 1951. He studied at the Univ. of British Columbia in Vancouver (B.Mus., 1975), the State Univ. of N.Y. at Stony Brook (M.A., 1978), and the Univ. of Calif. at Berkeley (Ph.D., 1981); also with Betsy Jolas at the Paris Cons. (1981, 1983). He was a studio technician at the Univ. of Calif. at Berkeley's Electronic Music Studio (1979–81) and guest composer at the Computer Music Project at the Univ. of Ill. at Urbana (1987; 1988); also appeared as a pianist in classical, jazz, and big-band settings. His music fuses postwar serial techniques with jazz elements.

WORKS: ORCH.: Violin Concerto (1978); *Hoye's Tribute* for Winds (Carbondale, Ill., Oct. 1, 1988). **CHAMBER:** Trio for Oboe, Clarinet, and Bassoon (1974; Vancouver, March 27, 1975); *Off Center to the Left* for Percussion Quartet (1977; Stony Brook, N.Y., Oct. 19, 1978); *Humble Cake* for Flute, Clarinet, Bass Clarinet, Violin, and Cello (1977; Stony Brook, N.Y., April 24, 1978); String Quartet (1982; Carbondale, Ill., March 29, 1988); Double Wind Trio for Oboe, Bassoon, and Piano (1983); *Chameleon* for Clarinet, String Trio, and Piano (Los Angeles, May 13, 1984); *Dreams* for Woodwind Quintet (1984; Bucharest, Feb. 17, 1987); *Memories from Euphoria* for Guitar and Harpsichord (1986); *2nd Diary* for Clarinet and Piano (1986; Urbana, Ill., April 3, 1988); *Some Things* for Flute, Clarinet, Violin, Cello, and Piano

(1987; St. Louis, March 25, 1988); works for Solo Instruments. **VOCAL:** *Written in Response to a Request for a Manifesto on Music, 1952* for Chorus (1980; Berkeley, April 15, 1981); *Seamaster* for Soprano and Chamber Orch. (1981; Milwaukee, May 13, 1983); *My Breakfast with Ronald* for Soprano, Clarinet, and Piano (Raleigh, N.C., March 10, 1985).

Stenhammar, (Karl) Wilhelm (Eugen), eminent Swedish pianist, conductor, and composer; b. Stockholm, Feb. 7, 1871; d. there, Nov. 20, 1927. His father was the Swedish composer Per Ulrik Stenhammar (b. Törnvalla, Feb. 20, 1828; d. Stockholm, Feb. 8, 1875). He began to play the piano and to compose in childhood; attended Richard Andersson's music school and then studied theory with Joseph Dente and organ with Heintze and Lagergren (1888–89); passed the organists' examination privately (1890); later pursued theory lessons with Emil Sjörgren and Andreas Hallén; completed his piano training with Heinrich Barth in Berlin (1892–93). He subsequently toured as a pianist, appearing as a soloist and frequently with the Aulin Quartet. His first large work for Solo Voices, Chorus, and Orch., *I rosengård* (In a Rose Garden; 1888–89; after K.A. Melin's collection of fairy tales, *Prinsessan och svennen*), was performed in Stockholm on Feb. 16, 1892, attracting considerable attention; his love for the theater prompted him to compose 2 music dramas, *Gildet på Solhaug* (1892–93) and *Tirfing* (1897–98), neither of which was successful; he did, however, compose much outstanding incidental music. He made his conducting debut with a performance of his overture *Excelsior!* in 1897. After serving as artistic director of the Phil. Soc. (1897–1900), the Royal Theater (1 season), and the New Phil. Soc. (1904–6) in Stockholm, he went to Göteborg as artistic director of the Orch. Soc.; during his tenure (1906–22), he elevated the musical life of the city; then returned to Stockholm, where he again took charge of the Royal Theater (1924–25) before ill health compelled him to retire. Stenhammar's early compositions reflect his preoccupation with the Romantic movement; the influence of Wagner and Liszt is quite perceptible, but he later developed an individual style based on his detailed study of Classical forms. His ability to absorb and transmute authentic folk melodies is a notable characteristic of many of his works. Among his most outstanding scores are the 2nd Sym., the 2nd Piano Concerto, the Serenade for Orch., several of his string quartets, his choral pieces, and a number of his songs.

WORKS: DRAMATIC: OPERAS: *Gildet på Solhaug* (The Feast at Solhaug), op. 6, after Ibsen (1892–93; 1st perf. in Ger. as *Das Fest auf Solhaug*, Stuttgart, April 12, 1899; 1st perf. in Swedish, Stockholm, Oct. 31, 1902); *Tirfing*, op. 15 (Stockholm, Dec. 9, 1898). **INCIDENTAL MUSIC TO:** Strindberg's *Ett drömspel*; H. Bergman's *Lodolezzi sjunger*, Tagore's *Chitra*; Shakespeare's *Romeo and Juliet*. **ORCH.:** 2 piano concertos: No. 1 (1893; Stockholm, March 17, 1894) and No. 2, op. 23 (1904–7; Göteborg, April 15, 1908); *Excelsior!*, overture, op. 13 (1896); 2 syms.: No. 1 (Stockholm, Dec. 1903) and No. 2, op. 34 (1911–15; Göteborg, April 22, 1915); *2 sentimentala romanser* for Violin and Orch., op. 28 (1910); Serenade, op. 31 (1911–13; rev. 1919). **CHAMBER:** 6 string quartets: No. 1, op. 2 (1894), No. 2, op. 14 (1896), No. 3, op. 18 (1897–1900), No. 4, op. 24 (1905–09), No. 5, op. 29 (1910), and No. 6, op. 35 (1916); Violin Sonata, op. 19 (1899–1900). **PIANO:** 2 sonatas (1890, 1895); *3 fantasier*, op. 11 (1895); *Sensommarnätter*, op. 33 (1914). **VOCAL:** *I rosengård* for Solo Voices, Chorus, and Orch. (1888–89); *Norrland* for Men's Voices, Mixed Chorus, and Orch.; *3 körvisor till dikter av J.P. Jacobsen* for Chorus (c.1890); *Snöfrid* for Solo Voices, Chorus, and Orch., op. 5 (1891); *Florez och Blanzeflor* for Baritone and Orch., op. 3 (1891); *Ur idyll och epigram av J.L. Runeberg* for Mezzo-soprano and Orch., op. 4a (1893); *Ett folk* for Baritone, Chorus, and Orch., op. 22 (1904–05); *Midvinter* for Chorus and Orch., op. 24 (1907); *Folket i Nifelhem Vårnatt* for Chorus and Orch., op. 30 (1911–12); *Sangen* for Solo Voices, Chorus, and Orch., op. 44 (1921); also *Ithaka* for Baritone and Orch., op. 21; *4 Stockholmsdikter*, op. 38; other songs.

BIBL.: S. Broman, "W. S.: A Survey," *Music Review* (May 1947); B. Wallner, "W. S. och kammarmusiken," *Svensk Tidskrift för Musikforskning*, XXXIV (1952), XXXV (1953), and XLIII (1961); J. Rabe, "En musikalisk dagbok av W. S.," ibid., XL (1958); special issue of *Musikrevy*, XXVI/6 (1971); H. Connor, "W. S.," in A. Aulin and H. Connor, *Svensk musik* (Stockholm, 1974); B. Wallner, *W. S. och hans tid* (3 vols., Stockholm, 1991).

Stenzl, Jürg (Thomas), prominent Swiss musicologist; b. Basel, Aug. 23, 1942. He began instruction in recorder and violin in 1949 in Bern; then studied the oboe with Huwiler at the Bern Cons. in 1961; attended the Univ. of Bern as a student of musicology with Geering and Dickenmann (Ph.D., 1968, with the diss. *Die vierzig Clausulae der Handschrift Paris, Bibliothèque Nationale, latin 15139 [Saint Victor-Clauselae]*; publ. in Bern, 1970); he also worked with Chailley at the Univ. of Paris (1965) and later completed his Habilitation at the Univ. of Fribourg (1974), where he was a prof. from 1980 to 1992. He was engaged as a visiting prof. at the Univs. of Geneva (1976–77; 1979–80), Neuchâtel (1982), Bern (1986–87), and Basel (1987–88); subsequently served at the Technical Univ. in Berlin (1988–89). In 1992–93 he was artistic director of Universal Edition in Vienna. He was secretary of the Société Suisse de Musicologie (1972–80) and ed. of the *Schweizerische Musikzeitung* (1975–83); contributed valuable articles and music criticism to various publications, including *Sohlmans Musiklexikon* (1975–79) and *The New Grove Dictionary of Music and Musicians* (1980); was author of *Von Giacomo Puccini zu Luigi Nono: Italienische Musik, 1922–1952: Faschismus, Resistenza, Republik* (Buren, 1990). His expertise ranges from the Middle Ages to contemporary music.

Štěpán, Václav, Czech pianist, pedagogue, and writer on music; b. Pečky, near Kolín, Dec. 12, 1889; d. Prague, Nov. 24, 1944. He studied musicology with Nejedlý at the Univ. of Prague (graduated, 1913), and then took courses at the German Univ. of Prague and in Berlin; also studied piano with Josef Čermák in Prague (1895–1908), and later with James Kwast in Berlin and Blanche Selva in Paris. He was active as a pianist from 1908; also taught aesthetics (from 1919) and later piano at the Prague Cons. He was an authority on Suk and Novák; a collection of his major articles on these composers appeared as *Novak à Suk* (Prague, 1945); also publ. *Symbolika z příbuzné zjevy v programni hudbě* (Symbolism and Related Phenomena in Program Music; Prague, 1915). He composed some vocal, chamber, and piano pieces but abandoned composition when he was 30.

Stepanian, Aro (Levoni), Armenian composer; b. Elizavetpol, April 24, 1897; d. Yerevan, Jan. 9, 1966. He studied with Gnessin in Moscow (1923–27) and with Shcherbachev and Kushnarian at the Leningrad Cons. (1926–30). He then settled in Yerevan, where he served as president of the Armenian Composers' Union (1938–48). He was one of the leading Armenian composers of his generation.

WORKS: OPERAS: *Brave Nazar* (1934; Yerevan, Nov. 29, 1935); *David of Sasun* (1936); *At the Dawn* (1937); *Nune* (1947); *Heroine* (1950). **ORCH.:** 3 syms. (1943, 1945, 1953); 2 piano concertos (1947, 1955); Viola Concerto (1955); Rhapsody for Piano and Orch. (1962). **CHAMBER:** 4 string quartets; 2 violin sonatas; Cello Sonata. **VOCAL:** Numerous choruses and songs.

BIBL.: M. Kazakhian, *A. S.* (Yerevan, 1962); G. Tigranov, *A. S.* (Moscow, 1967).

Stephan, Rudi, German composer; b. Worms, July 29, 1887; d. in battle near Tarnopol, Galicia, Sept. 29, 1915. He studied counterpoint with Sekles at the Hoch Cons. in Frankfurt am Main (1905), then went to Munich, where he received instruction in composition from Rudolf Louis and in piano from Heinrich Schwartz (1906–08); also studied philosophy at the Univ. His output is marked by a secure command of harmony and counterpoint with a fine feeling for orch. color. Stephan's tragic death was greatly lamented.

WORKS: OPERA: *Die ersten Menschen* (1911–14; Frankfurt am Main, July 1, 1920). **ORCH.:** *Musik für Orchester* (1912; Jena, June 6, 1913); *Musik für Geige und Orchester* (Berlin, Oct. 10, 1913). **CHAMBER:** *Musik für sieben Saiteninstrumente* (2 violins, viola, cello, double bass, harp, and piano; 1911; Danzig, May 30, 1912). **VOCAL:** *Liebeszauber* for Tenor and Orch. (1909–10; Munich, Jan. 16, 1911; withdrawn; rev. for Baritone and Orch., 1913); 18 songs (1908–14).

BIBL.: K. Holl, *R. S.: Studie zur Entwicklungsgeschichte der Musik am Anfang des 20. Jahrhunderts* (Saarbrücken, 1920; 2nd ed., 1922); A. Machner, *R. S.s Werk* (diss., Univ. of Breslau, 1943); idem, "Zwischen gestern und heute: Ein Wort für R. S.," *Musica*, VIII (1954); A. McCredie, "The Munich School and R. S. (1887–1915): Some Forgotten Sources and Byways of Musical Jugendstil and Expressionism," *Music Review*, XXIX (1968); R. Blackburn, "R. S.: An Unfulfilled Talent?," *Musical Times* (July 1987).

Stephan, (Gustav-Adolf Carl) Rudolf, learned German musicologist; b. Bochum, April 3, 1925. He studied in Heidelberg, receiving instruction in violin at the Cons., in theory with Fortner at the Inst. of Protestant Church Music, and in musicology with Besseler and in philosophy with Jaspers and Hofmann at the Univ. He subsequently studied at the Univ. of Göttingen, where he took courses in philosophy with Hartmann and in musicology with Gerber (Ph.D., 1950, with the diss. *Die Tenores der Motetten Ältesten Stils*); completed his Habilitation there in 1963 with his *Antiphonar-Studien*, and then served on its faculty as a lecturer (1966–67). From 1967 to 1990 he was a prof. at the Free Univ. of Berlin, being made prof. emeritus in 1990. In 1981 he was a visiting prof. at the Univ. of Vienna. He served as editorial director of both the Schönberg-Gesamtausgabe and the Berg-Gesamtausgabe, and as president of the Institut für Neu Musik und Musikerziehung in Darmstadt (1970–76) and of the Gesellschaft für Musikforschung (1980–89). He has written valuable articles on topics ranging from medieval music to Hindemith for a variety of publications.

WRITINGS: *Musik* (Frankfurt am Main, 1957); *Neue Musik* (Göttingen, 1958; 2nd ed., 1973); *Gustav Mahler: Vierte Symphonie G-Dur* (Munich, 1966); *Alexander Zemlinsky: Ein unbekannter Meister der Wiener Schule* (Kiel, 1978); *Gustav Mahler: Zweite Symphonie C-Moll* (Munich, 1979); *Gustav Mahler: Werk und Interpretation* (Cologne, 1979); *Vom musikalischen Denken* (Mainz, 1985); *Alban Berg: Violinkonzert (1935)* (Munich, 1988); *Die Wiener Schule* (Darmstadt, 1989); A. Riethmüller, ed., *Musiker der Moderne* (Laaber, 1995).

Stephani, Hermann, German musicologist and composer; b. Grimma, June 23, 1877; d. Marburg, Dec. 3, 1960. He studied at the Leipzig Cons. with Jadassohn and Reinecke, and at the Univ. of Munich with Lipps and Sandberger; obtained his Ph.D. there in 1902 with the diss. *Das Erhabene, insonderheit in der Tonkunst, und das Problem der Form* (publ. in Leipzig, 1903; 2nd ed., 1907). In 1921 he was appointed to the faculty of the Univ. of Marburg; taught musicology there until 1946. His scholarly publications include: *Der Charakter der Tonarten* (Habilitationsschrift, Univ. of Marburg, 1921; publ. in Regensburg, 1923); *Grundfragen des Musikhörens* (Leipzig, 1925); *Das Vierteltonproblem* (Leipzig, 1925); *Polare Harmonik bei Beethoven* (Leipzig, 1927); *Das Problem des Orgelstils* (Essen, 1942). He advocated a reform in score notation through the exclusive use of the G clef with octave indications ("Einheitspartitur") and ed. Schumann's *Manfred* overture using this system (1905). He wrote about 100 opus numbers, mostly vocal works; also contrapuntal pieces for various combinations of instruments; ed. works by Handel, Weber et al. A Festschrift was presented to him on his 70th birthday (Regensburg, 1947).

Stephens, John (Elliott), American conductor and composer; b. Washington, D.C., Nov. 6, 1929. He studied at the Catholic Univ. of America in Washington, D.C. (B.M., 1959; M.M., 1962; D.M.A., 1972); also had lessons in 20th-century conducting with Boulez at the Basel Academy of Music (certificate, 1969), and studied composition privately with Wuorinen, Shapey, and Brant. He founded and was music director of the American Camerata for New Music in Washington, D.C., with which he appeared widely and made numerous recordings; taught at George Washington Univ. (1963–74), Catholic Univ. (1967–68), American Univ. (1976–83), and the Univ. of the District of Columbia (from 1983). He produced for radio the acclaimed educational series "New Sounds for Young Ears."

WORKS: String Quartet (1959); *Concert Piece* for Jazz Band (1960); Sym. in 1 Movement (1962); Sextet for Woodwind Quintet and Piano (1963); Chamber Sym. (1964); *Inventions* for Treble Instruments (1965); *Concert Music* for Flutes and Piano (1970); *Cantata* for Narrator, Chamber Chorus, Baritone, Boy's Chorus, and Chamber Ensemble (1972); Songs for Soprano, Flute, Harp, and Strings (1975); *Inventions* for Clarinet (1978); *Creations* for Trombone and String Quartet (1982); *3 for 4* for Harp, Flute/Piccolo, Viola, and Trombone (1984); Double Concerto for Flute, Oboe, Strings, Percussion, and Harp (1988).

Steptoe, Roger (Guy), English composer, teacher, and pianist; b. Winchester, Hampshire, Jan. 25, 1953. He studied at the Univ. of Reading (B.A., 1974) and received training in composition from Alan Bush at the Royal Academy of Music in London (1974–76). After serving as composer-in-residence at Charterhouse School, Surrey (1976–79), he was a prof. of composition at the Royal Academy of Music (1980–91), where he served as administrator of its International Composers Festivals (1986–93). In 1993 he became artistic director of the Landmark Festivals Assn. He also was active as a pianist.

WORKS: OPERA: *King of Macedon* (Surrey, Oct. 18, 1979). **ORCH.:** *2 Miniatures* for Strings (1977; Oxford, May 29, 1982); *Sinfonia concertante* for Violin, Viola, Cello, and Strings (1981; London, June 26, 1982); Concerto for Oboe and Strings (1982; Crewe, Jan. 10, 1984); Concerto for Tuba and Strings (1983; London, Oct. 27, 1986); *Rapsodia sinfonica*, concerto for Violin and Orch. (1987); Sym. (1988); Concerto for Clarinet and Strings (1989); Organ Concerto (1990); Cello Concerto (1991); *Cheers!* (1993). **CHAMBER:** 2 string quartets: No. 1 (1976; London, Jan. 5, 1977) and No. 2 (1985; Aberystwyth, May 5, 1986); Suite for Cello (1977); *Study* for Violin (1978); *2 Impromptus* for Clarinet (1978); Quintet for Clarinet and Strings (1980); *Study* for Guitar (1981); *The Knight of the Sun* for Brass Quintet (1982); *3 Pieces* for Viola and Piano (1982); 2 violin sonatas (1983, 1986); *2 Studies* for Bassoon and Piano (1983); *4 Sonnets* for Brass Quintet (1984); Quartet for Oboe and Strings (1988; Berlin, April 18, 1989); Duo for Oboe and Harp (1991); Piano Trio (1993). **PIANO:** *3 Preludes* (1976); 2 sonatas (1979, 1988); *Equinox* (1981). **VOCAL:** *2 Madrigals* for Chorus (1976): *2 Introits* for Chorus and Organ (1977, 1985); *The Looking Glass* for Soprano, Oboe, and Piano (1980); *Chinese Lyrics*: set 1 for Soprano and Piano (1982) and set 2 for Mezzo-soprano or Countertenor and Piano (1983); *Another Part of the Forest*, scena for 4 Voices and Piano (1983); *In Winter's Cold Embraces Dye*, cantata for Mezzo-soprano, Tenor, Chorus, and Orch. (1985); *Elegy on the Death and Burial of Cock Robin* for Countertenor and 11 Solo Strings (1988); *Life's Unquiet Dream* for Baritone, Chorus, and Chamber Orch. (1992); *The Passionate Shepherd to his Love* for Children's Voices and Piano (1992); *3 Sonnets to Delia* for Baritone and Piano (1993).

Stern, Isaac, outstanding Russian-born American violinist; b. Kremenetz, July 21, 1920. He was taken to the U.S. as an infant and was trained in music by his mother, who was a professional singer. He studied violin at the San Francisco Cons. (1928–31), then with Louis Persinger; also studied with Naoum Blinder (1932–37). On Feb. 18, 1936, he made his orch. debut as soloist in the Brahms Concerto with Monteux and the San Francisco Sym. Orch.; his N.Y. debut followed on Oct. 11, 1937. After further training in San Francisco, he returned to N.Y. and gave a notably successful concert on Feb. 18, 1939; his Carnegie Hall debut there on Jan. 8, 1943, was a triumph. In 1947 he toured Australia; made his European debut at the

Lucerne Festival in 1948; subsequently appeared regularly with American and European orchs.; in 1956 he made a spectacularly successful tour of Russia. In 1961 he organized a trio with the pianist Eugene Istomin and the cellist Leonard Rose, which toured widely until Rose's death. In 1986 he celebrated the 50th anniversary of his orch. debut. He received various honors; in 1979 he was made an Officer of the Legion d'honneur of France, in 1984 he received the Kennedy Center Honors Award, in 1987 was given the Wolf Prize of Israel, and in 1992 he received the Presidential Medal of Freedom. Stern belongs to the galaxy of virtuoso performers to whom fame is a natural adjunct to talent and industry; he is also active in general cultural undertakings, and is an energetic worker for the cause of human rights.

BIBL.: J. Wechsberg, "Profiles: I. S.," *New Yorker* (June 5, 1965).

Sternberg, Constantin, Russian-American pianist, teacher, and composer; b. St. Petersburg, July 9, 1852; d. Philadelphia, March 31, 1924. He studied piano with Moscheles at the Leipzig Cons., and later had lessons with Theodor Kullak; also visited Liszt at Weimar. He toured Russia as a concert pianist; in 1880 he emigrated to the U.S. In 1890 he established the Sternberg School of Music in Philadelphia, and was its director until his death. He was greatly esteemed as a piano teacher. He wrote some 200 salon pieces for piano, and *Danses cosaques* for Violin; publ. *Ethics and Aesthetics of Piano Playing* (N.Y., 1917) and *Tempo Rubato and Other Essays* (N.Y., 1920).

Sternberg, Erich Walter, German-born Israeli composer; b. Berlin, May 31, 1891; d. Tel Aviv, Dec. 15, 1974. He studied law at the Univ. of Kiel (graduated, 1918), and then received training in composition from Leichtentritt and in piano from Praetorius in Berlin. In 1932 he emigrated to Palestine. In 1936 he was a co-founder of the Palestine Orch. (later the Israel Phil.). Many of his works were inspired by biblical subjects.

WORKS: DRAMATIC: *Dr. Dolittle*, children's opera (1937; orch. suite, 1941); *Pacificia, the Friendly Island*, opera for "children and others" (1972–74). **ORCH.:** *Overture to a Comedy* (1932); *Quodlibet* (1935); *Amcha* (Thy People), suite (1936); *Joseph and His Brothers*, suite for Strings (1937); *The 12 Tribes of Israel*, variations (Tel Aviv, May 3, 1942); *Shema Israel* (Hear, O Israel; 1947); *Höre Israel* (1948); *Contrapuntal Study* (1955); *Tewat Noah* (Noah's Ark; 1960). **CHAMBER:** 2 string quartets (1924, 1926); Violin Sonata (1955); Piano Trio; Wind Quintet. **VOCAL:** *The Story of David and Goliath* for Baritone and Orch. (1927); *Kol nidrei* for Baritone and Orch. (1927); *Halochem ha'amitz* (The Garland Soldier) for Baritone and Orch. (1930); *Ami* (My People) for Soprano and Orch. (1945); *Shirim mukdamim* (Early Songs) for Soprano and Orch. (1946); *Ha'orev* (The Raven) for Baritone and Orch. (1949); *Sichot haruach* (Dialogues with the Wind) for Alto and Orch. (1955); *Hachalil bamerchakim* (The Distant Flute) for Alto and Flute (1958); *Shirei neziñt* (Songs of Resignation) for Baritone and Orch. (1958); *Songs of Hafis* for Voice and Orch. (1959); *Techiat Israel* (The Resurrection of Israel), oratorio (1959); *Tefilot* (Prayers of Humility) for Contralto and Chamber Orch. (1962); *The Sacrifice of Isaac* for Soprano and Orch. (1965); *Love Songs* for Chorus and Orch. (1968); *The Wretched* for Baritone and String Orch. (1969); *My Brother Jonathan* for Chorus and String Orch. (1969); about 100 solo songs.

Sternberg, Jonathan, American conductor; b. N.Y., July 27, 1919. He studied at the Juilliard School of Music (1929–31), N.Y. Univ. (B.A., 1939; graduate study, 1939–40), and the Manhattan School of Music (1946); took conducting lessons with Monteux at his summer school (1946, 1947). In 1947 he made his conducting debut with the Vienna Sym. Orch.; then toured extensively as a guest conductor in Europe, North America, and the Far East. He was music director of the Royal Flemish Opera in Antwerp (1961–62), the Harkness Ballet in N.Y. (1966–68), and the Atlanta Opera and Ballet (1968–69); then was a visiting prof. of conducting at the Eastman School of Music in Rochester, N.Y. (1969–71), a prof. of music at Temple Univ. (1971–89), and a lecturer at Chestnut Hill College (from 1989).

Sternefeld, Daniël, Belgian conductor, teacher, and composer; b. Antwerp, Nov. 27, 1905; d. Brussels, June 2, 1986. He studied flute and theory at the Antwerp Cons. (1918–24); then composition with Gilson and conducting with van der Stücken (1928); subsequently took lessons in conducting with Paumgartner, Krauss, and Karajan at the Mozarteum in Salzburg. He was a flutist in the orch. of the Royal Flemish Opera in Antwerp (1929–38); then was its 2nd conductor (1938–44) and principal conductor (1944–48); subsequently was chief conductor of the Belgian Radio and Television Orch. in Brussels (1948–72); also appeared as a guest conductor in Europe and South America. He taught conducting at the Antwerp Cons. (1949–71).

WORKS: DRAMATIC: OPERA: *Mater Dolorosa* (1934; Antwerp, 1935). **BALLETS:** *Pierlala* (1937); *Antverpia* (1975); *Rossiniazata* (1982). Also incidental music to various plays. **ORCH.:** *Variations symphoniques* (1928); *Elégie* (1931); *Suite de vieilles chansons flamandes et wallonnes* for Chamber Orch. (1934); 2 syms.: No. 1 (1943) and No. 2, *Bruegelsymfonie* (1981–83); *Frère Jacques*, variations for Brass and Percussion (1955); *Divertimento* for Wind Orch. (1980); *Waaier* (1984). **CHAMBER:** *Étude-passacaglia* for Harp (1979); Quintet for Flute, Oboe, Clarinet, Bassoon, and Horn (1986).

Sternfeld, F(riedrich) W(ilhelm), Austrian-born English musicologist; b. Vienna, Sept. 25, 1914; d. Brightwell-cum-Sotwell, near Wallingford, Jan. 13, 1994. He took courses with Lach and Wellesz at the Univ. of Vienna (from 1933); then pursued his training with Schrade at Yale Univ. (Ph.D., 1943, with the diss. *Goethe and Music*); held a Guggenheim fellowship (1954). He taught at Wesleyan Univ. (1940–46) and Dartmouth College (1946–56); also was a member of the Inst. for Advanced Studies at Princeton Univ. (1955). In 1956 he joined the faculty of the Univ. of Oxford, where he served as a reader in music history (1972–81). He also became a naturalized British subject. He was ed. of *Renaissance News* (1946–54) and of the *Proceedings of the Royal Musical Association* (1957–62); publ. the books *Goethe's Relationship to Music: A List of References* (N.Y., 1954), *Music in Shakespearean Tragedy* (London, 1963; 2nd ed., 1967), *Songs from Shakespeare's Tragedies* (London, 1964), and *The Birth of Opera* (Oxford, 1993). He also ed. *A History of Western Music* (London, 1973); with Wellesz, the 7th vol. of *The New Oxford History of Music: The Age of Enlightenment 1745–1790* (Oxford, 1973); and with others, *Essays on Opera and English Music in Honour of Sir Jack Westrup* (Oxford, 1975).

Steuermann, Edward (actually, **Eduard**), eminent Polish-American pianist, pedagogue, and composer; b. Sambor, near Lemberg, June 18, 1892; d. N.Y., Nov. 11, 1964. He studied piano with Vilém Kurz in Lemberg and with Busoni in Berlin (1911–12), and theory with Schoenberg (1912–14); also took some composition lessons with Humperdinck. Returning to Poland, he taught at the Paderewski School in Lwów, and concurrently at the Jewish Cons. in Kraków (1932–36). In 1936 he emigrated to the U.S. He taught at the Philadelphia Cons. (1948–63) and at the Juilliard School of Music in N.Y. (1952–64); also gave summer classes at the Salzburg Mozarteum (1953–63) and in Darmstadt (1954; 1957–60). As a recitalist and soloist with major orchs., Steuermann was an ardent champion of new music, particularly of Schoenberg; gave the first performance of Schoenberg's Piano Concerto (1944); made excellent arrangements for piano of Schoenberg's operatic and symphonic works, among them *Erwartung, Die glückliche Hand, Kammersymphonie No. 1*, and the Piano Concerto; received the Schoenberg Medal from the ISCM in 1952. Although he did not follow Schoenberg's method of composition with 12 tones with any degree of consistency, his music possesses an expressionistic tension that is characteristic of the 2nd Viennese School.

WORKS: ORCH.: *Variations* (1958); *Music for Instruments*

(1959–60); Suite for Chamber Orch. (1964). **CHAMBER:** 7 *Waltzes* for String Quartet (1946); Piano Trio (1954); *Improvisation and Allegro* for Violin and Piano (1955); String Quartet, *Diary* (1960–61); *Dialogues* for Violin (1963). **PIANO:** Sonata (1926); Suite (1952). **VOCAL:** *Brecht-Lieder* for Contralto (1945); *3 Choirs* (1956); Cantata for Chorus and Orch., after Kafka (1964); other songs. **BIBL.:** A. Ani Netto, *E. S.: Um esboço de figura* (São Paulo, 1991).

Stevens, Bernard (George), English composer; b. London, March 2, 1916; d. Great Maplestead, Essex, Jan. 2, 1983. He studied composition with Dent and Rootham at Cambridge (1934–37) and with Morris and Jacob at the Royal College of Music in London (1937–40), where he was named a prof. of composition in 1948; received his Mus.D. from the Univ. of Cambridge in 1968. He wrote a number of works for various instrumental combinations; his music adheres to traditional concepts of harmony, while the programmatic content is often colored by his radical political beliefs.

WORKS: ORCH.: Violin Concerto (1943); *Ricercar* for Strings (1944); *A Symphony of Liberation* (1945); Cello Concerto (1952); Piano Concerto (1955); Sym. No. 2 (1964); *Choriamb* (1968); *Introduction, Variations and Fugue on a Theme of Giles Farnaby* (1972). **CHAMBER:** Trio for Violin, Horn, and Piano (1966); *Suite* for 6 Instruments (1967); *The Bramble Briar* for Guitar (1974); piano pieces. **VOCAL:** 3 cantatas: *The Harvest of Peace* (1952), *The Pilgrims of Hope* (1956), and *Et resurrexit* (1969); *The Turning World* for Baritone, Chorus, and Orch. (1971).

BIBL.: B. Stevens, ed., *B. S. and His Music: A Symposium* (White Plains, N.Y., 1989).

Stevens, Delores (Elaine), American pianist and teacher; b. Kingman, Kansas, Jan. 29, 1930. She studied with Gordon Terwilliger (1946–48) and Jan Chiapusso (1948–52) at the Univ. of Kansas (B.M., 1952) and also had private study at the Music Academy of the West with Ernst von Dohnányi and Joanna Graudan. From 1968 to 1980 she was a pianist in the Montagnana Trio, which commissioned some 28 works by contemporary composers, including Daniel Lentz, Barney Childs, Per Nørgård et al.; toured with the ensemble in the U.S., England, and Scandanavia (1971–90). She was a founding member of Tandem, a piano/percussion duo; also performed extensively as a soloist, giving premieres of Poul Ruders' Sonata No. 2, Arne Nordheim's *Listen*, and Per Nørgård's *Turn*; toured in the U.S. (1988–95), Japan (1990), Japan (1992, with the Daniel Lentz Group), and Spain (1993). From 1971 she also was a member of the Monday Evening Concerts Ensemble in Los Angeles and pianist and director of the Da Camera Players. She taught at the Calif. Inst. of the Arts, Mount St. Mary's College, and at Calif. State Univ. at Dominguez Hills, where she also served as director of piano studies; in 1987 she joined the faculty of the American String Teachers Assn. Chamber Music Inst. From 1988 to 1997 she received annual Solo Touring Grants from the Calif. Arts Council.

Stevens, Denis (William), distinguished English violinist, musicologist, and conductor; b. High Wycombe, Buckinghamshire, March 2, 1922. He studied music with R.O. Morris, Egon Wellesz, and Hugh Allen at Jesus College, Oxford (M.A., 1947). He played violin and viola in the Philharmonia Orch. of London (1948–49); then was a program planner in the music dept. of the BBC (1949–54). He served as a visiting prof. of music at Cornell Univ. (1955) and Columbia Univ. (1956), and taught at the Royal Academy of Music in London (1956–61). He subsequently was a visiting prof. at the Univ. of Calif. at Berkeley (1962) and at Pa. State Univ. (1963–64). He was prof. of musicology at Columbia Univ. (1964–76). He was also a visiting prof. at the Univ. of Calif. at Santa Barbara (1974) and at the Univ. of Wash. at Seattle (1976–77). As a conductor, he was cofounder of the Ambrosian Singers in 1952 and served as president and artistic director of the Accademia Monteverdiana from 1961; in his programs, he emphasized early polyphonic works. He ed. several important collections, including *The Mulliner Book*, vol. I in the Musica Britannica series (1951; 3rd ed., rev., 1962); *Early Tudor Organ Music*, in the Early English Church Music series (1969); and works by Monteverdi. He was made a Commander of the Order of the British Empire in 1984.

WRITINGS: *The Mulliner Book: A Commentary* (London, 1952); *Tudor Church Music* (N.Y., 1955; 3rd ed., 1966); *Thomas Tomkins 1572–1656* (London, 1957; 2nd ed., 1967); ed. *A History of Song* (London, 1960; 2nd ed., 1970); co-ed., with A. Robertson, *The Pelican History of Music* (3 vols., Harmondsworth, 1960–68); *Plainsong Hymns and Sequences* (London, 1965); *Claudio Monteverdi: Sacred, Secular and Occasional Music* (N.Y., 1977); ed. and tr. *The Letters of Claudio Monteverdi* (London, 1980; rev. ed., 1995); ed. *Ten Renaissance Dialogues* (Seven Oaks, 1981); T. Lewis, ed., *Musicology in Practice: Collected Essays*, Vol. I, 1948–1970 (N.Y., 1987).

Stevens, Halsey, significant American composer, teacher, and writer on music; b. Scott, N.Y., Dec. 3, 1908; d. Long Beach, Calif., Jan. 20, 1989. He studied composition with William Berwald at Syracuse Univ. (B.M., 1931; M.M., 1937) and with Bloch at the Univ. of Calif. at Berkeley (1944). He taught at Syracuse Univ. (1935–37) and Dakota Wesleyan Univ. (1937–41); was a prof. and director of the College of Music at Bradley Polytechnic Inst. in Peoria, Ill. (1941–46), and then a prof. at the Univ. of Redlands (1946). In 1946 he joined the faculty of the Univ. of Southern Calif. in Los Angeles, serving in various capacities until his retirement as prof. emeritus in 1976. He was a visiting prof. at Pomona College (1954), the Univ. of Wash. (1958), Yale Univ. (1960–61), the Univ. of Cincinnati (1968), and Williams College (1969). His music is above all a monument of sonorous equilibrium; melodies and rhythms are coordinated in a fine melorhythmic polyphony; dissonances are emancipated and become natural consorts of triadic harmony. Tonality remains paramount, while a stream of coloristic passages contributes to the brilliance of the instrumental texture. Stevens wrote only "absolute" music, without resort to the stage; there are no operas or ballets in his creative catalog. He does not apply conventional modernistic devices in his music, designed at its culmination to please the aural sense. Apart from composition, Stevens took great interest in the autochthonous music of the peoples of the earth; he was particularly fascinated by the fieldwork that Bartók undertook in gathering authentic folk songs of southeastern Europe. He mastered the Hungarian language, retraced Bartók's travels, and assembled materials on Bartók's life; the result was his exemplary biography, *The Life and Music of Béla Bartók* (N.Y., 1953; 2nd ed., rev., 1964; 3rd ed., rev., 1993, by M. Gillies). Stevens received numerous grants and honors; he held 2 Guggenheim fellowships (1964–65; 1971–72), a grant from the NEA (1976), and the Abraham Lincoln Award of the American Hungarian Foundation (1978).

WORKS: ORCH.: 3 syms.: No. 1 (1945; San Francisco, March 7, 1946, composer conducting; rev., Los Angeles, March 3, 1950), No. 2 (1945; N.Y., May 17, 1947), and No. 3 (1946); *A Green Mountain Overture* (Burlington, Vt., Aug. 7, 1948; rev. 1953); *Triskelion* (a figure with 3 branches; 1953; Louisville, Feb. 27, 1954); *Sinfonia breve* (Louisville, Nov. 20, 1957); *Symphonic Dances* (San Francisco, Dec. 10, 1958); Cello Concerto (1964; Los Angeles, May 12, 1968); *Threnos: In Memoriam Quincy Porter* (1968); Concerto for Clarinet and Strings (Denton, Texas, March 20, 1969); Double Concerto for Violin, Cello, and String Orch. (Los Angeles, Nov. 4, 1973); Viola Concerto (1975). **CHAMBER:** Piano Trio No. 2 (1945); Quintet for Flute, Violin, Viola, Cello, and Piano (1945; Middlebury, Vt., Aug. 30, 1946); Suite for Clarinet and Piano (1945; rev. 1953); Bassoon Sonata (1949); String Quartet No. 3 (1949): *3 Hungarian Folk Songs* for Viola and Piano (1950); Viola Sonata (1950); Horn Sonata (1953); Trumpet Sonata (1956); Piano Trio No. 3 (1954); *Sonatina piacevole* for Alto Recorder or Flute and Keyboard (1956); Septet for Clarinet, Bassoon, Horn, 2 Violas, and 2 Cellos (Urbana, Ill., March 3, 1957); *Divertimento* for 2 Violins

(1958–66); Suite for Viola and Piano (1959); Bass Tuba Sonatina (1960); *12 Slovakian Folk Songs* for 2 Violins (1962); Cello Sonata (1965); Oboe Sonata (1971); *Quintetto "Serbelloni"* for Woodwinds (1972); also works for solo instruments. **PIANO:** 3 sonatas (1933–48); *Partita* (1954); *6 preludes* (1956); *Ritratti* (1960); *Fantasia* (1961); numerous other pieces. **VOCAL:** *The Ballad of William Sycamore* for Chorus and Orch. (Los Angeles, Oct. 6, 1955); *2 Shakespeare Songs* for Voice, Flute, and Clarinet (1959); *A Testament of Life* for Tenor, Bass, Chorus, and Orch. (1959); *4 Canciones* for Voice and Piano (1961); *Magnificat* for Chorus and String Orch. (1962); *7 Canciones* for Voice and Piano (1964); *Campion Suite* for Chorus (1967); *Te Deum* for Chorus, Brass Septet, Organ, and Timpani (1967); *Chansons courtoises* for Chorus (1967); *Songs from the Paiute* for Chorus, 4 Flutes, and Timpani (1976).

Stevens, Horace (Ernest), Australian bass-baritone; b. Melbourne, Oct. 26, 1876; d. there, Nov. 18, 1950. He studied at St. Kilda in Melbourne, and then sang as a lay clerk at St. Paul's Cathedral in Melbourne. In 1919 he made his London debut in a Queen's Hall concert, and subsequently became a popular favorite at major English festivals. He also sang in oratorios in the U.S. and appeared with the British National Opera Co. and other English companies. Stevens was particularly successful as a concert artist, excelling as Elijah. In opera he won accolades for his Wagnerian roles.

Stevens, John (Edgar), distinguished English musicologist; b. London, Oct. 8, 1921. He studied classics (1940–41) and English (B.A., 1948) at Magdalene College, Cambridge; then pursued training with Dart at the Univ. there (Ph.D., 1953, with the diss. *Early Tudor Song Books*); served on the univ. faculty as a teacher of English (1952–74), reader in English and music history (1974–78), and prof. of medieval and Renaissance English (from 1978). He was made a Commander of the Order of the British Empire in 1980. An erudite scholar, he contributed greatly to the understanding of music from the medieval and Renaissance periods. In addition to his books and articles, he ed. works for the Musica Britannica series. His writings include *Music and Poetry in the Early Tudor Court* (London, 1961; 2nd ed., rev., 1979), *Medieval Romance* (London, 1973), and *Words and Music in the Middle Ages* (London, 1986).

Stevens, Risë, noted American mezzo-soprano; b. N.Y., June 11, 1913. The original family surname was Steenberg. She studied voice with Orry Prado; after graduating from high school, she sang minor roles with the N.Y. Opera-Comique Co. The enterprise soon went bankrupt, and for a while she had to earn her living by dress modeling, before she was offered free singing lessons by Anna Schoen-René at the Juilliard School of Music. She was subsequently sent to Salzburg to study with Marie Gutheil-Schoder at the Mozarteum, and later entered classes in stage direction with Herbert Graf. In 1936 she was engaged by Szell for the Prague Opera as a contralto; she prepared several roles from standard operas, coaching with George Schick. She went on a tour to Cairo, Egypt, with a Vienna opera group, and then sang at the Teatro Colón in Buenos Aires. She made her American debut as Octavian in *Der Rosenkavalier* with the Metropolitan Opera in Philadelphia on Nov. 22, 1938. She greatly extended her repertoire, and added Wagnerian roles to her appearances with the Metropolitan. On Jan. 9, 1939, she married in N.Y. the Czech actor Walter Surovy, who became her business manager. In 1939 she sang at the Glyndebourne Festival in England; on Oct. 12, 1940, she appeared with the San Francisco Opera as Cherubino; in 1941 she joined Nelson Eddy in a film production of the operetta *The Chocolate Soldier*, and in 1944 acted in the movie *Going My Way*, in which she sang the Habanera from *Carmen*; on Dec. 28, 1945, she appeared as Carmen at the Metropolitan Opera, scoring a fine success. Carmen became her most celebrated role; she sang it 75 times with the Metropolitan. She remained with the Metropolitan until 1961. On March 24, 1954, she appeared for the first time at La Scala in Milan. She retired from the stage in 1964. In 1975 she joined the teaching staff at the Juilliard School in N.Y. She also served as president of the Mannes College of Music in N.Y. (1975–78).

BIBL.: K. Crichton, *Subway to the Met: R. S.' Story* (N.Y., 1959).

Stevenson, Robert (Murrell), erudite American musicologist, educator, composer, and pianist; b. Melrose, N.Mex., July 3, 1916. He studied at the Univ. of Texas, El Paso (A.B., 1936); then went to N.Y. to study piano with Ernest Hutcheson at the Juilliard School of Music; subsequently entered Yale Univ., studying composition with David Stanley Smith and musicology with Leo Schrade (M.Mus., 1939). In 1939 he had 23 private lessons in composition with Stravinsky in Cambridge, Mass., and in 1940 he took private piano lessons with Artur Schnabel in N.Y.; then attended classes in composition with Hanson at the Eastman School of Music in Rochester, N.Y. (Ph.D., 1942); he later had regular music courses at Harvard Univ. (S.T.B., 1943). He also took graduate degrees in theology from the Harvard Divinity School and the Theological Seminary at Princeton Univ. (Th.M., 1949). He served as chaplain with the U.S. Army (1942–46); received the Army Commendation Ribbon; remained in service as a reserve officer until 1953. He then went to the Univ. of Oxford in England, where he took courses in musicology with Jack Allan Westrup (B.Litt., 1954). While thus occupied, he pursued an active career as a concert pianist; gave his first N.Y. recital on Jan. 5, 1942; gave another recital there on March 20, 1947; in both he included his own compositions; he played in London on Oct. 7, 1953. He taught music at the Univ. of Texas, El Paso from 1941 to 1943 and in 1949; lectured on church music at Westminster Choir College in Princeton, N.J., from 1946 to 1949. In 1949 he was appointed to the music faculty at the Univ. of Calif., Los Angeles; was made a prof. of music in 1961; was named faculty research lecturer in 1981. In 1955–56 he was a visiting assistant prof. at Columbia Univ.; also was a visiting prof. at Indiana Univ. in Bloomington (1959–60) and at the Univ. of Chile in Santiago (1965–66). A widely informed musical scientist, he gave courses at the Univ. of Calif. on music appreciation, special seminars on individual composers, and a highly popular course in 1983 on rock-'n'-roll music. He also presented piano recitals as part of the curriculum. A master of European languages, he concentrated his scholarly energy mainly on Latin American, Spanish, and Portuguese music, both sacred and secular, and his publications on these subjects are of inestimable value; he is also an investigative explorer of Italian Renaissance music. He contributed more than 400 articles to *The New Grove Dictionary of Music and Musicians*, and numerous articles on the Baroque period and on American composers to *Die Musik in Geschichte und Gegenwart*; was its American ed. from 1967 to the completion of the last fascicle of its supplement. He held numerous grants, fellowships, and awards from learned societies: was a recipient of a Gulbenkian Foundation fellowship (1953–54); a Carnegie Foundation Teaching Award (1955–56); Fulbright research awards (1958–59; 1964; 1970–71); Ford Foundation fellowships (1966, 1981); a National Endowment for Humanities fellowship (1974); and a fellowship from the American Philosophical Soc. He was a contributor, beginning in 1976, to the *Handbook of Latin American Studies* at the Library of Congress; from 1978 was ed. of and principal contributor to *Inter-American Music Review*. The versatility of his contributions on various subjects is indeed extraordinary. Thus, he publ. several articles containing materials theretofore unknown about Liszt's piano concerts in Spain and Portugal. He ed., transcribed, and annotated *Vilancicos portugueses for Portugaliae Musica XXIX* (Lisbon, 1976); contributed informative articles dealing with early American composers, South American operas, sources of Indian music, and studies on Latin American composers to the *Musical Quarterly, Revista Musical Chilena, Journal of the American Musicological Society, Ethnomusicology*, and *Inter-American Music Review*. His avowed mission in his work is "to rescue the musical past of the Americas." The honors bestowed upon him, especially in the

Spanish-speaking world, are many. In 1988 the Organization of American States created the Robert Stevenson Prize in Latin American Musicology. In April 1990 he was awarded a gold medal in ceremonies at the Prado Museum in Madrid, presided over by the King of Spain, and in Dec. of that year was inducted as an honorary member into the Sociedad Española de Musicologica. Also in 1990, the Sociedad Argentina de Musicologia made him an honorary member, and he was honored by the Comisión Nacional de Cultura de Venezuela. In coordination with the quincentennial of the discovery of America in 1992, Stevenson's book *Spanish Cathedral Music in the Golden Age* (1961) was publ. in Madrid in a Spanish tr. as *La música en las catedrales de España durante el siglo do oro.* Among other assorted distinctions, the mayor of El Paso, Texas (where Stevenson had resided from age 2 to 18), presented him with a scroll making him an honorary citizen. Stevenson's compositions are marked by kinetic energy and set in vigorous and often acrid dissonant counterpoint. His symphonic *2 Peruvian Preludes* were performed by Stokowski with the Philadelphia Orch. on June 28, 1962; the score was later expanded into *3 preludias peruanos* and first performed in Mexico City, on July 20, 1963, with Luis Herrera de la Fuente conducting. Other works include *Nocturne in Ebony* and *A Texas Suite* for Orch.; Clarinet Sonata; 3 piano sonatas: *A Cambridge Sonata, A Manhattan Sonata,* and *A New Haven Sonata.* He also wrote *Coronation Concerto* for Organ and *A Sandburg Cantata* for Chorus.

WRITINGS: *Music in Mexico. A Historical Survey* (N.Y., 1952); *Patterns of Protestant Church Music* (Durham, N.C., 1953); *La musica en la catedral de Sevilla, 1478–1606; Documentos para su estudio* (Los Angeles, 1954; Madrid, 1985); *Music before the Classic Era* (London, 1955; 2nd ed., 1958); *Cathedral Music in Colonial Peru* (Lima, 1959); *The Music of Peru: Aboriginal and Viceroyal Epochs* (Washington, D.C., 1960); *Juan Bermudo* (The Hague, 1960); *Spanish Music in the Age of Columbus* (The Hague, 1960); *Music Instruction in Inca Land* (Baltimore, 1960); *Spanish Cathedral Music in the Golden Age* (Berkeley, Calif., 1961; Spanish tr., Madrid, 1992); *Mexico City Cathedral Music, 1600–1750* (Washington, D.C., 1964); *Protestant Church Music in America* (N.Y., 1966); *Music in Aztec and Inca Territory* (Berkeley, 1968); *Renaissance and Baroque Musical Sources in the Americas* (Washington, D.C., 1970); *Foundations of New World Opera, with a Transcription of the Earliest Extant American Opera, 1701* (Lima, 1973); *Christmas Music from Baroque Mexico* (Berkeley, 1974); *Latin American Colonial Music Anthology* (Washington, D.C., 1975); *A Guide to Caribbean Music History* (Lima, 1975); *Antologia de la musica postuguesa 1490–1680* (Lisbon, 1984).

Stevenson, Ronald, English pianist and composer; b. Blackburn, Lancashire, March 6, 1928. He studied piano as a child; began to compose at 14; took courses in composition at the Royal Manchester College of Music (1945–48); later studied at the Accademia di Santa Cecilia in Rome on an Italian government scholarship (1955). Returning to England, he was appointed lecturer at the Univ. of Edinburgh (in the Extra-Mural Dept.) in 1962; was on the music staff at the Univ. of Cape Town (South Africa) from 1963 to 1965. A fervent intellectual, he contributed cultured articles to the *Listener* and other publications; engaged in a thoroughgoing bio-musical tome on Busoni, with whose art he felt a particular kinship; publ. a book, *Western Music: An Introduction* (London, 1971). He adheres to neo-Baroque polyphony; a formidable exemplar is his *Passacaglia on DSCH* for Piano, a Brobdingnagian set of variations in 3 parts, 80 minutes long, derived from the initial D of the first name and the first 3 letters of the last name of Dmitri Shostakovich, in German notation (D; S = Es = E-flat; C; H = B), first performed by Stevenson himself in Cape Town, Dec. 10, 1963. Other works include: *Anger Dance* for Guitar (1965); *Triptych*, on themes from Busoni's opera *Doktor Faust*, for Piano and Orch. (Piano Concerto No. 1; Edinburgh, Jan. 6, 1966, composer soloist); *Scots Dance Toccata* for Orch. (Glasgow, July 4, 1970); *Peter Grimes Fantasy* for Piano, on themes from Britten's opera (1971); *Duo-Sonata* for Harp and Piano (1971); Piano Concerto No. 2 (1972); *Ben Dorian*, choral sym. (1973); Violin Concerto, *The Gipsy* (1973); *Corroboree for Grainger* for Piano and Wind Band (1987); *St. Mary's May Song* for Soprano and Strings (1988); *Voces Vagabundae* for String Quartet (1990); numerous settings for voice and piano and for chorus of Scottish folk songs; transcriptions of works of Purcell, Bach, Chopin, Berlioz, Busoni, Paderewski, Delius, Britten, Berg, Pizzetti, Grainger, and many others.

BIBL.: M. MacDonald, *R. S.: A Musical Biography* (Edinburgh, 1989).

Stewart, Reginald (Drysdale), Scottish conductor, pianist, and music educator; b. Edinburgh, April 20, 1900; d. Montecito, Calif., July 8, 1984. After training from H.T. Collinson, choirmaster at St. Mary's Anglican Cathedral in Edinburgh, he studied with Arthur Friedheim and Mark Hambourg in Toronto, and then with Boulanger and Philipp in Paris. From 1921 to 1924 he taught at the Canadian Academy of Music. He also began a career as a pianist and conductor in Canada. From 1929 to 1931 he conducted his own radio orch. From 1933 to 1941 he was conductor of the Toronto Bach Choir, and from 1934 to 1941 was conductor of the Toronto Promenade Sym. Concerts. During these years, he also appeared as a guest conductor and a pianist in Canada and the U.S. From 1941 to 1958 he was head of the Peabody Cons. of Music in Baltimore. He also was music director of the Baltimore Sym. Orch. from 1942 to 1952. In 1962 he joined the faculty of the Music Academy of the West in Santa Barbara, where he later served as head of its piano dept. His career was highlighted in the PBS documentary film *An Evening with Reginald Stewart* (Sept. 28, 1983).

Stewart, Thomas (James), distinguished American baritone; b. San Saba, Texas, Aug. 29, 1928. He studied electrical engineering in Waco; later went to N.Y., where he became a student of Mack Harrell at the Juilliard School of Music. He made his debut there in 1954 as La Roche in *Capriccio* by Richard Strauss; then sang with the N.Y. City Opera and the Chicago Opera in bass roles. In 1957 he received a Fulbright grant and went to Berlin; was engaged as a baritone with the Städtische Oper; made his debut there as the Don Fernando in *Fidelio* on March 28, 1958; remained on its roster until 1964; also sang regularly at London's Covent Garden (1960–78) and at the Bayreuth Festivals (1960–75). He made his Metropolitan Opera debut in N.Y. on March 9, 1966, as Ford in Verdi's *Falstaff*; in 1981 he sang the title role in the American premiere of Reimann's *Lear* with the San Francisco Opera. His other roles were Don Giovanni, Count di Luna in *Il Trovatore*, Escamillo in *Carmen*, Iago in *Otello*, and Wotan. In 1955 he married **Evelyn Lear**, with whom he often appeared in opera and concert settings.

Stibilj, Milan, Slovenian composer; b. Ljubljana, Nov. 2, 1929. He studied composition with Karol Pahor at the Ljubljana Academy of Music (1956–61) and with Kelemen at the Zagreb Academy of Music (1962–64); took courses in electronic music at the Univ. of Utrecht (1966–67). He composes in an advanced idiom, exploring the techniques of integral serial organization of musical parameters.

WORKS: ORCH.: *Koncertantna glasba* (Concertante Music) for Horn and Orch. (1959); *Skladbe* (Composition) for Horn and Strings (1959); *Slavcek in vrtnica* (The Nightingale and the Rose), symphonic poem (1961); *Skladja* (Congruences) for Piano and Orch. (1963); *Impressions* for Flute, Harp, and String Quintet or String Orch. (1963); *Verz* (1964); *Indian Summer* for Chamber Orch. (1974). **CHAMBER:** *Anekdote* for Piano (1957); *Sarabanda* for 4 Clarinets (1960); *Assimilation* for Violin (1965); *Contemplation* for Oboe and String Quintet (1966); *Condensation* for Trombone, 2 Pianos, and Percussion (1967); *Zoom* for Clarinet and Bongos (1970). **VOCAL:** *Epervier de ta faiblesse, Domine* for Narrator and 5 Percussionists (1964); *Apokatastasis, Slovenian Requiem* for Tenor, Chorus, and Orch. (1967).

Stich-Randall, Teresa, admired American soprano; b. West Hartford, Conn., Dec. 24, 1927. She received her training at the Hartt School of Music in Hartford and at Columbia Univ. In 1947 she made her operatic debut as Gertrude Stein in the premiere of Thomson's *The Mother of Us All* in N.Y. She was chosen to create the title role in Luening's *Evangeline* in N.Y. in 1948. She then was engaged to sing with Toscanini and the NBC Sym. Orch. in N.Y. After winning the Lausanne competition in 1951, she made her European operatic debut that year as the Mermaid in *Oberon* in Florence. In 1951–52 she sang at the Basel Opera. In 1952 she made her first appearance at the Salzburg Festival and at the Vienna State Opera. In 1955 she made her debut at the Chicago Lyric Opera as Gilda. From 1955 she appeared regularly at the Aix-en-Provence Festivals. On Oct. 24, 1961, she made her Metropolitan Opera debut in N.Y. as Fiordiligi, remaining on its roster until 1966. She also sang widely in the U.S. and Europe as a concert artist. Her success in Vienna led her to being the first American to be made an Austrian Kammersängerin in 1962. She retired in 1971. Stich-Randall was especially esteemed for her roles in Mozart's operas.

Stiedry, Fritz, eminent Austrian-born American conductor; b. Vienna, Oct. 11, 1883; d. Zürich, Aug. 9, 1968. He studied jurisprudence in Vienna and took a course in composition with Mandyczewski. Mahler recommended him to Schuch in Dresden, and he became his assistant conductor (1907–08); he subsequently was active as a theater conductor in the German provinces, and in Prague. He conducted at the Berlin Opera (1916–23); then led the Vienna Volksoper (1923–25). After traveling as a guest conductor in Italy, Spain, and Scandinavia (1925–28), he returned to Berlin as conductor of the Städtische Oper (1929–33). With the advent of the Nazi regime in 1933, he went to Russia, where he conducted the Leningrad Phil. (1934–37). In 1938 he emigrated to the U.S. and became a naturalized American citizen; conducted the New Friends of Music Orch. in N.Y.; on Nov. 15, 1946, he made his Metropolitan Opera debut in N.Y. conducting *Siegfried*, remaining on its roster as one of its most distinguished conductors until 1958. As a conductor, he championed the 2nd Viennese School of composition. He was a close friend of Schoenberg; conducted first performances of his opera *Die glückliche Hand* in Vienna (1924) and his 2nd Chamber Sym. in N.Y. (1940). He also gave fine performances of the operas of Wagner and Verdi.

Stignani, Ebe, esteemed Italian mezzo-soprano; b. Naples, July 11, 1904; d. Imola, Oct. 6, 1974. She studied voice with Agostino Roche at the Naples Cons. She made her operatic debut as Amneris at the Teatro San Carlo in Naples (1925); then joined Milan's La Scala in 1926, winning great distinction for her roles in Italian operas as well as Gluck's Orfeo, Brangane, and Ortrud. She made guest appearances at London's Covent Garden, winning success as Amneris (1937, 1939, 1955), Azucena (1939, 1952), and Adalgisa (1952, 1957); also sang in San Francisco (1938, 1948). In 1958 she made her operatic farewell as Azucena at London's Drury Lane.

Still, William Grant, eminent black American composer; b. Woodville, Miss., May 11, 1895; d. Los Angeles, Dec. 3, 1978. His father was bandmaster in Woodville; after his death when Still was in infancy, his mother moved the family to Little Rock, Ark., where she became a high school teacher. He grew up in a home with cultured, middle-class values, and his stepfather encouraged his interest in music by taking him to see operettas and buying him operatic recordings; he was also given violin lessons. He attended Wilberforce College in preparation for a medical career, but became active in musical activities on campus; after dropping out of college, he worked with various groups, including that of W.C. Handy (1916); then attended the Oberlin (Ohio) College Cons. During World War I, he played violin in the U.S. Army; afterward returned to work with Handy, and became oboist in the Shuffle Along orch. (1921); then studied composition with Varèse, and at the New England Cons. of Music in Boston with Chadwick. He held a Guggenheim fellowship in 1934–35; was awarded honorary doctorates by Howard Univ. (1941), Oberlin College (1947), and Bates College (1954). Determined to develop a symphonic type of Negro music, he wrote an *Afro-American Symphony* (1930). In his music he occasionally made use of actual Negro folk songs, but mostly he invented his thematic materials. He married the writer Verna Arvey, who collaborated with him as librettist in his stage works.

WORKS: DRAMATIC: OPERAS: *Blue Steel* (1934); *Troubled Island* (1941); *A Bayou Legend* (1940; PBS, 1981); *A Southern Interlude* (1943); *Costaso* (1950); *Mota* (1951); *The Pillar* (1956); *Minette Fontaine* (1958); *Highway 1, U.S.A.* (1962; Miami, May 13, 1963). **BALLETS:** *La Guiablesse* (1927); *Sahdji* (1930); *Lennox Avenue* (1937); *Miss Sally's Party* (1940). **INCIDENTAL MUSIC:** *The Prince and the Mermaid* (1965). **ORCH.:** *Darker America* (1924; Rochester, N.Y., Nov. 21, 1927); *From the Black Belt* (1926); *From the Journal of a Wanderer* (Rochester, N.Y., May 8, 1929); 5 syms.: No. 1, *Afro-American Symphony* (1930; Rochester, N.Y., Oct. 29, 1931), No. 2 in G minor, *Song of a New Race* (Philadelphia, Dec. 19, 1937), No. 3 (1945; discarded; new No. 3, *The Sunday Symphony*, 1958), No. 4, *Autochthonous* (1947; Oklahoma City, March 18, 1951), and No. 5, *Western Hemisphere* (revision of discarded No. 3, 1945; Oberlin, Ohio, Nov. 9, 1970); *Africa* (1930); *A Deserted Plantation* (1933); *Kaintuck (Kentucky)* for Piano and Orch. (1935; Rochester, N.Y., Jan. 16, 1936); *Dismal Swamp* (Rochester, N.Y., Oct. 30, 1936); *Beyond Tomorrow* (1936); *Ebon Chronicle* (Fort Worth, Nov. 3, 1936); *Can'tcha Line 'em* (1940); *Old California* (1941); *Pages from Negro History* (1943); *In Memoriam: The Colored Soldiers Who Died for Democracy* (1943; N.Y., Jan. 5, 1944); *Fanfare for American War Heroes* (1943); *Poem* (Cleveland, Dec. 7, 1944); *Festive Overture* (1944; Cincinnati, Jan. 19, 1945); *Fanfare for the 99th Fighter Squadron* for Winds (1945); *Archaic Ritual* (1946); *Wood Notes* (1947; Chicago, April 22, 1948); *Danzas de Panama* for Strings (1948; also for String Quartet); *Ennanga* for Harp and Orch. or Flute and Strings (1956); *The American Scene* (1957); *Little Red Schoolhouse* (1957); *The Peaceful Land* (1960); *Patterns* (1960); *Los alnados de España* (1962); *Preludes* for Strings, Flute, and Piano (1962); *Threnody in Memory of Jan Sibelius* (1965); *Miniature Overture* (1965); *Choreographic Prelude* for Strings, Flute, and Piano (1970). **CHAMBER:** Suite for Violin and Piano (1943); *Pastorela* for Violin and Piano (1946); *4 Folk Suites* for Flute, Clarinet, Oboe, Bassoon, Strings, and Piano (1962); *Vignettes* for Oboe, Bassoon, and Piano (1962); piano pieces. **VOCAL:** *Plain Chant for Americans* for Baritone and Orch. (N.Y., Oct. 23, 1941); *Caribbean Melodies* for Chorus, Piano, and Percussion (1941); *Wailing Woman* for Soprano and Chorus (1946); many songs. **OTHER:** Band pieces; arrangements of spirituals.

BIBL.: V. Arvey, *W.G. S.* (N.Y., 1939); R. Simpson, *W.G. S.: The Man and His Music* (diss., Michigan State Univ., 1964); M. Hudgins, "An Outstanding Arkansan: W.G. S.," *Arkansas Historical Quarterly* (Winter 1965); R. Haas, ed., *W.G. S. and the Fusion of Cultures in American Music* (Los Angeles, 1972); F. Douglass, "A Tribute to W.G. S.," *Black Perspective in Music* (Spring 1974); "A Birthday Offering to W.G. S. upon the Occasion of His 80th Anniversary," ibid. (May 1975); A. Arvey, *In One Lifetime* (Fayetteville, Ark., 1984).

Stillman-Kelley, Edgar. See **Kelley, Edgar Stillman.**

Stillman, Mitya, Russian-American violist and composer; b. Ilyintza, near Kiev, Jan. 27, 1892; d. N.Y., April 11, 1936. He studied composition with Glière and violin and viola with Pulikovsky at the Kiev Cons. After the Russian Revolution, he emigrated to the U.S. (1920); played viola in the Detroit Sym. Orch. and in the CBS Sym. Orch. As a composer, he developed a strong individual style in a peculiarly compact contrapuntal technique. He wrote 8 string quartets, of which No. 7 received a posthumous 1st-prize award from the NBC Guild as the best chamber music work for 1936 (N.Y., Jan. 1, 1937). He also wrote some programmatic orch. pieces, among them

Dnieprostroy (1933); *Yalta Suite* for String Trio; *Cyprus* for Strings, Woodwinds, and Percussion; etc.

Stilwell, Richard (Dale), outstanding American baritone; b. St. Louis, May 6, 1942. After studying English at Anderson (Ind.) College, he appeared as Silvio in *Pagliacci* with the St. Louis Grand Opera (1962); then studied voice with F. St. Leger and P. Mathen at the Indiana Univ. School of Music in Bloomington (B.A., 1966) and with D. Ferro in N.Y. On April 7, 1970, he made a successful debut as Pelléas with the N.Y. City Opera. In 1973 he made his British debut as Ulysses in *Il ritorno d'Ulisse in Patria* at the Glyndebourne Festival. He was chosen to create the role of Constantine in Pasatieri's *The Seagull* (Houston, 1974) and the title role in Pasatieri's *Ines de Castro* (Baltimore, 1976). On Oct. 15, 1976, he made his Metropolitan Opera debut in N.Y. as Guglielmo in *Così fan tutte*; scored a major success there as Billy Budd in 1978; also appeared at the Paris Opéra, the Netherlands Opera, the Chicago Lyric Opera, the Washington (D.C.) Opera Soc., and the Berlin Deutsche Oper; likewise sang in concerts with the major U.S. orchs. In 1988 he sang in the premiere of Argento's The Aspern Papers in Dallas. In 1990 he appeared as Sharpless in Lyons. He sang Don Alfonso in Seattle in 1992. In addition to his remarkable portrayal of Pelléas, he also excels as Papageno, Don Giovanni, Figaro in *Il Barbiere di Siviglia*, Don Pasquale, Eugene Onegin, Rodrigo in *Don Carlos*, and Ford in *Falstaff*.

Stock, David (Frederick), American composer and conductor; b. Pittsburgh, June 3, 1939. He studied composition with Lopatnikoff and Haieff, musicology with Dorian, and trumpet at Carnegie-Mellon Univ. (B.F.A., 1962; M.F.A., 1963); took courses with Boulanger, Fournet, and Vaurebourg-Honegger at the École Normale de Musique in Paris (1960–61); attended the Berkshire Music Center at Tanglewood (summer, 1964); engaged in advanced studies with Berger at Brandeis Univ. (M.F.A., 1973). He played trumpet in several orchs.; taught at the Cleveland Inst. of Music (1964–65), Brandeis Univ. (1966–68), and the New England Cons. of Music in Boston (1968–70). From 1970 to 1974 he taught at Antioch College and conducted its chamber orch., and also served as chairman of its music dept, (1971–74). In 1974 he held a Guggenheim fellowship. In 1975 he became conductor of the Pittsburgh New Music Ensemble. He also taught at Carnegie-Mellon Univ. (1976–77) and conducted the Carnegie Sym. Orch. (1976–82); taught at the Univ. of Pittsburgh (1978–86) and Duquesne Univ. (from 1987), where he was later a prof. of music and conductor of the Duquesne Contemporary Ensemble. In 1987–88 he was composer-in-residence of the Pittsburgh Sym. Orch. He received NEA fellowships (1974, 1976, 1978, 1983) and various commissions. His compositions are written in a gratefully accessible style.

WORKS: ORCH.: *Divertimento* (1957); *Capriccio* for Small Orch. (1963); *Symphony in 1 Movement* (1963); *Flashback* (1968); *Inner Space* (1973); *Triflumena* (1978); *Zohar* (1978); *The Philosopher's Stone* for Violin and Chamber Orch. (1980); *A Joyful Noise* (1983; Pittsburgh, May 23, 1985); *Parallel Worlds* for Chamber Orch. (1984); *American Accents* for Chamber Orch. (1984; Los Angeles, Oct. 12, 1985); *Back to Bass-ics* for Strings (1985); *On the Shoulders of Giants* (1986); *Rockin' Rondo* (1987); *Quick Opener* for Chamber Orch. (1987); *Tekiah* for Trumpet and Chamber Orch. (1987); *Fast Break* (1988); *Kickoff* (1990); *Fanfarria* (1993); *Power Play* (1993); *String Set* for Chamber Orch. (1993); *Available Light* for Chamber Orch. (1994). **WIND ENSEMBLE:** *Nova* for Band (1974); *The Body Electric* for Amplified Contrabass, Winds, and Percussion (1977); *The 'Slibert Stomp* (1985); *Evensong* for English Horn and Wind Orch. (1985); *No Man's Land* for Wind Sym. (1988); *The Winds of Summer* for Saxophone and Band (1989); *Earth Beat* for Timpani and Wind Sym. (1992). **CHAMBER:** 3 string quartets (1962–94); *Shadow Music* for 5 Percussion and Harp (1964; rev. 1979); *Serenade* for 5 Instruments for Flute, Clarinet, Horn, Viola, and Cello (1964); Quintet for Clarinet and Strings (1966); *Triple Play* for Piccolo, Contrabass, and Percussion (1970); *Dreamwinds* for Woodwind Quintet (1975); *Night Birds* for 4 or More Cellos (1975); *Icicles* for Piccolo, Oboe, and Clarinet (1976); *Brass Rubbing* for 6 Trumpets (1976); *Pentacles* for Brass Quintet (1978); *Starlight* for Clarinet and Percusion (1979); *Night* for Clarinet, Violin, and Cello (1980); *Persona* for Clarinet, Violin, Cello, Piano, and Percussion (1980); *Keep the Change* for Any 5 Treble Clef Instruments (1981); *Speaking Extravagantly* for String Quartet (1981); *Sulla Spiaggia* for Alto Flute, English Horn, Bass Clarinet, Electric Piano, and Percussion (1985); *Yerusha* for Clarinet and 7 Players (1986); *Partners* for Cello and Piano (1988); *Sunrise Sarabande* for Recorder Quartet (1988); *Sax Appeal* for Saxophone Quartet (1990); *Sonidos de la Noche* for Clarinet, Violin, Cello, and Piano (1994). **VOCAL:** *Scat* for Soprano, Flute, Bass Clarinet, Violin, and Cello (1971); *Spirits* for Chorus or Soloists, Harp and/or Electric Piano, and Percussion (1976); *Upcountry Fishing* for Voice and Violin (1982); *Dor L'Dor* for Chorus (1990); *Beyond Babylon* (1994).

Stock, Frederick (actually, **Friedrich August**), respected German-born American conductor; b. Jülich, Nov. 11, 1872; d. Chicago, Oct. 20, 1942. He was first trained in music by his father, a bandmaster; then studied violin with G. Japha and composition with Wüllner, Zöllner, and Humperdinck at the Cologne Cons. (1886–91). From 1891 to 1895 he was a violinist in the Cologne municipal orch. In 1895 he was engaged as a violist in Theodore Thomas's newly organized Chicago Orch., becoming his assistant conductor in 1901; following Thomas's death in 1905, he inherited the orch., which took the name of the Theodore Thomas Orch. in 1906; it became the Chicago Sym. Orch. in 1912, with Stock serving as its conductor until his death, the 1918–19 season excepted. In 1919 he became a naturalized American citizen. As a conductor, Stock was extremely competent, even though he totally lacked that ineffable quality of making orch. music a vivid experience in sound; but he had the merit of giving adequate performances of the classics, of Wagner, and of the German Romantic school. He also programmed several American works, as long as they followed the Germanic tradition. The flowering of the Chicago Sym. Orch. was to be accomplished by his successors Reiner and Solti. Stock was also a composer; wrote 2 syms., a Violin Concerto (Norfolk Festival, June 3, 1915, E. Zimbalist soloist, composer conducting), and some chamber music.

BIBL.: P. Otis, *The Chicago Symphony Orchestra* (Chicago, 1925); W. Holmes, "F. S.," *Le Grand Baton*, VI/2 (1969).

Stockhausen, Karlheinz, outstanding German composer; b. Modrath, near Cologne, Aug. 22, 1928. He was orphaned during World War II and was compelled to hold various jobs to keep body and soul together; all the same, he learned to play the piano, violin, and oboe; then studied piano with Hans Otto Schmidt-Neuhaus (1947–50), form with H. Schröder (1948), and composition with Frank Martin (1950) at the Cologne Staatliche Hochschule für Musik; also took courses in German philology, philosophy, and musicology at the Univ. of Cologne. After studies in Darmstadt (1951), he received instruction in composition from Messiaen in Paris (1952); subsequently studied communications theory and phonetics with Werner Meyer-Eppler at the Univ. of Bonn (1954–56). He was active at the electronic music studio of the West German Radio in Cologne (from 1953); also was a lecturer at the Internationalen Ferienkurse für Musik in Darmstadt (until 1974) and was founder-artistic director of the Cologne Kurse für Neue Musik (1963–68); likewise served as prof. of composition at the Cologne Hochschule für Musik (1971–77). He was made a member of the Swedish Royal Academy (1970), the Berlin Academy of Arts (1973), and the American Academy and Inst. of Arts and Letters (1979); also was made a Commandeur dans l'Ordre des Arts et des Lettres of France (1985) and an honorary member of the Royal Academy of Music in London (1987). He investigated the potentialities of *musique concrète* and partly incorporated its techniques into his own empiric method of composition, which from the very first included highly complex contrapuntal conglomerates with uninhibited applications of non-euphonious dissonance as well as recourse to the primal procedures of obdurate iteration of single tones; all this set in the freest of rhythmic patterns and diversified by constantly changing instrumental colors with obsessive percussive effects. He further perfected a system of constructivist composition, in which the subjective choice of the performer determines the succession of given thematic ingredients and their polyphonic simultaneities, ultimately leading to a totality of aleatory procedures in which the ostensible application of a composer's commanding function is paradoxically reasserted by the inclusion of prerecorded materials and by recombinant uses of electronically altered thematic ingredients. He evolved energetic missionary activities in behalf of new music as a lecturer and master of ceremonies at avant-garde meetings all over the world; having mastered the intricacies of the English language, he made a lecture tour of Canadian and American Univs. in 1958; in 1965, was a visiting prof. of composition at the Univ. of Pa.; was a visiting prof. at the Univ. of Calif. at Davis in 1966–67; in 1969, gave highly successful public lectures in England that were attended by hordes of musical and unmusical novitiates. Stockhausen is a pioneer of "time-space" music, marked by a controlled improvisation, and adding the vectorial (i.e., directional) parameter to the 4 traditional aspects of serial music (pitch, duration, timbre, and dynamics), with performers and electronic apparatuses placed in different parts of the concert hall; such performances, directed by himself, were often accompanied by screen projections and audience participation; he also specified the architectural aspects of the auditoriums in which he gave his demonstrations. His annotations to his own works were publ. in the series entitled *Texte* (6 vols., Cologne, 1963–88). See also R. Maconie, ed., *Stockhausen on Music: Lectures and Interviews* (London and N.Y., 1989).

WORKS: *Chöre für Doris* (1950); *Drei Lieder* for Contralto and Chamber Orch. (1950); *Choral* (1950); Violin Sonatine (1951); *Kreuzspiel* for Oboe, Bass Clarinet, Piano, and 3 Percussion (1951); *Formel* for Orch. (1951); *Etude*, concrete music (1952); *Spiel* for Orch. (1952); *Schlagtrio* for Piano and Kettledrums (1952); *Punkte* for Orch. (1952; rev. 1962); *Kontra-Punkte* for 10 Instruments (Cologne, May 26, 1953); *Klavierstücke I–IV* (1952–53); *Studie I* (1953) and *II* (1954), electronic music; *Klavierstücke V–X* (1954–55); *Zeitmasse* for 5 Woodwinds (1955–56); *Gruppen* for 3 Orchs. (1955–57; Cologne, March 24, 1959); *Klavierstücke XI* (1956); *Gesang der Junglinge*, electronic music, after the Book of Daniel, dealing with the ordeal of 3 monotheistic Hebrew youths in the Babylonian fiery furnace, scored for 5 groups of loudspeakers surrounding the audience (Cologne, May 30, 1956); *Zyklus* for Percussion (1959); *Carré* for 4 Orchs. and Choruses (Hamburg, Oct. 28, 1960); *Refrain* for 3 Performers (1959); *Kontakte* for Electronics (1959–60); *Kontakte* for Electronics, Piano, and Percussion (Cologne, June 11, 1960); *Originale*, music theater (1961); *Momente* for Soprano, 4 Choruses, and 13 Instrumentalists (1962–64); *Plus-Minus* for Clarinet, Trombone, Cello, and 3 Pianos (1963; Warsaw, Sept. 25, 1968); *Mikrophonie I* for 6 Performers (1964) and *II* for 12 Singers, Hammond Organ, 4 Ring Modulators, and Tape (1965); *Mixtur* for Orch., Sinus Generator, and Ring Modulator (1964); *Stop* for Orch. (1965); *Solo* for Melody Instrument (1965–66); *Telemusik*, electronic music (1966; Warsaw, Sept. 23, 1968); *Adieu* for Wind Quintet (1966); *Hymnen*, electronic and concrete music (Cologne, Nov. 30, 1967); *Prozession* for Ensemble (1967); *Stimmung* for 6 Vocalists (1968); *Kurzwellen* for 6 Performers (1968); *Aus den Sieben Tagen*, 15 pieces in graphic notation for various ensembles (1968); *Spiral* for Soloist and Short-wave Transmitter (1968); *Für kommende Zeiten*, 17 texts of "intuitive music" (1968–70); *Dr. K.-Sextett* (1969); *Fresco* for 4 Orchs. (1969); *Pole* for 2 Performers or Singers, and Short-wave Transmitter (1969–70); *Expo* for 3 Instrumentalists or Singers and Short-wave Transmitter (1969–70); *Mantra* for 2 Pianos (Donaueschingen, Oct. 18, 1970); *Sternklang*, "park music" for 5 Groups (1971); *Trans* for Orch. (1971); *Alphabet für Liège*, 13 musical pictures for Soloist and Duo Performers (1972); *"Am Himmel wandre ich . . . ,"* Indian lieder for 2 Soloists and Orch. (Donaueschingen, Oct. 20, 1974); *Herbstmusik* for 4 Performers (1974); *Musik im Brauch* for Percussion and Musical Clocks (1975); *"Atmen gibt das Leben . . . ,"* choral opera with Orch. or Tape (1975–77); *Sirius*, electronic music, dedicated to American pioneers on earth and in space (1975–77); *Tierkreis* for Various Instruments and Voices (4 versions, 1975–81); *Harlekin* for Clarinet (1975); *Amour*, 5 pieces for Clarinet (1976); *Jubilaum* for Orch. (1977; N.Y., Sept. 10, 1981); *In Freundschaft* for 11 Solo Instruments (1977); *Licht*, projected cycle of 7 operas, 1 for each day of the week: *Dienstag aus Licht* (1977–91); *Donnerstag aus Licht* (1978–80; Milan, April 3, 1981); *Samstag aus Licht* (1981–83; Milan, May 25, 1984); *Montag aus Licht* (1985–88; Milan, May 7, 1988).

BIBL.: K. Wörner, *K. S., Werk und Wollen* (Cologne, 1963; Eng. tr. as *S., Life and Work*, London, 1973); C. Cardew, *S. Serves Imperialism*, a rambling diatribe by a disenchanted follower who became a militant Maoist (London, 1974); J. Cott, *S., Conversations with the Composer* (N.Y., 1973, and London, 1974); J. Harvey, *The Music of S.* (London, 1975); R. Maconie, *S.* (London, 1976); B. Sullivan and M. Manion, *S. in Den Haag* (The Hague, 1983); H.-J. Nagel, ed., *S. in Calcutta* (Calcutta, 1984); P. Britton, "S.'s Path to Opera," *Musical Times* (Sept. 1985); M. Tannenbaum, *Intervisto sul genio musicale* (Rome, 1985; Eng. tr., 1987, as *Conversations with S.*); *S.: 60. Geburtstag: 22. August 1988* (n.p., 1988); M. Kurtz, *S.: Eine Biographie* (Kassel and Basel, 1988; Eng. tr., 1992, as *S.: A Biography*); C. von Blumröder, *Die Grundlegung der Musik K. S.s* (Stuttgart, 1993).

Stockhoff, Walter William, American composer; b. St. Louis, Nov. 12, 1876; d. there, April 1, 1968. He was largely autodidact, and began to compose early in life. In his music he was influenced mainly by German Romantic composers, but his thematic material was distinctly American. In some of his early piano music he made use of modernistic devices, such as the whole-tone scale, cadential triads with the added sixth, etc. Busoni wrote an enthusiastic article about him (1915) in which he described him as one of America's most original composers. The orch. version of his piano suite *To the Mountains* was premiered under the title *American Symphonic Suite* (Frankfurt am Main, Dec. 10, 1924). Several of his piano works and some chamber music were publ. Other works include *5 Dramatic Poems* for Orch. (1943); Piano Sonata; *Metamorphoses* for Piano; etc.

Stockmann, (Christine) Doris, German ethnomusicologist; b. Dresden, Nov. 3, 1929. She studied piano, opera production, and music theory at the Dresden Hochschule für Musik (1947–49) and musicology with Dräger, Meyer, and Vetter at Humboldt Univ. in Berlin; then studied ethnography, folklore, and linguistics with Steinitz there, taking her doctorate in 1958 with the diss. *Der Volksgesang in der Altmark* (publ. in Berlin, 1962). She became scientific assistant in ethnomusicology at the Inst. for German Folklore of the Academy of Sciences in Berlin (1953); lectured at Humboldt Univ. (1967–68) and at the Univs. in Uppsala (1965) and Göteborg (1969). She publ. extensively, alone and with her husband, **Erich Stockmann**, on German and European folk music, particularly in their medieval and contemporary forms.

Stockmann, Erich, German ethnomusicologist; b. Stendal, March 10, 1926. He studied musicology and German at the Univ. of Greifswald (1946–49) and musicology with Dräger, Meyer, and Vetter at Humboldt Univ. in Berlin (Ph.D., 1953, with the diss. *Der musikalische Sinn der elektro-akustischen Musikinstrumente*). After serving as ethnomusicologist at the Inst. for German Folklore of the Academy of Sciences in Berlin, he became a lecturer in ethnomusicology and organology at Humboldt Univ. (1957). He was largely responsible for the development of the ethnomusicological research center of the Berlin Academy of Sciences, leading its first expedition to collect folk music in Albania (1957). He ed. several series, including the Handbüchern der Europäischen Volksmusikinstrumente (Leipzig, 1967 et seq.), Annual Bibliography of European Ethnomusicology (Bratislava, 1967 et seq.), and Studia Instrumentorum Musicae Popularis (Stockholm, 1969 et seq.); also publ. extensively, alone and with his wife, **Doris Stockmann**, on European folk music and instruments.

Stoessel, Albert (Frederic), distinguished American violinist, conductor, teacher, and composer; b. St. Louis, Oct. 11, 1894; d. (fatally stricken while conducting the premiere of Walter Damrosch's Dunkirk) N.Y., May 12, 1943. He began his musical studies in St. Louis; then received training in violin with Willy Hess and in theory with Kretzschmar at the Berlin Hochschule für Musik, where he also studied conducting. In 1914 he appeared as a violin soloist in Berlin; after touring in Europe, he returned to St. Louis and performed as a soloist there. During World War I he was a military bandmaster in the U.S. Army (1917–19), serving as director of the school for bandmasters of the American Expeditionary Force in France. Returning to the U.S., he appeared as a violin soloist with the Boston Sym. Orch. and toured with Caruso in 1920. He settled in N.Y. in 1921 as Walter Damrosch's successor as conductor of the Oratorio Soc.; also was named director of music at the Chautauqua Institution (1923) and conductor of the Worcester (Mass.) Music Festival (1925); likewise appeared widely as a guest conductor. In 1923 he founded the music dept. at N.Y. Univ., which he headed until 1930; was director of the opera and orch. depts. at the Juilliard Graduate School (from 1927), where he conducted a number of premieres of American works. He was elected a member of the National Inst. of Arts and Letters in 1931. He publ. *The Technic of the Baton* (N.Y., 1920; 2nd ed., rev. and enl., 1928).

WORKS: *5 Miniatures* for Violin and Piano (1917); *Suite antique* for 2 Violins and Piano (1917; arranged for 2 Violins and Chamber Orch.); Violin Sonata (1919); *Hispania Suite* for Piano (1920; arranged for Orch., 1927); *Cyrano de Bergerac*, symphonic portrait (1922); *Flitting Bats* for Violin and Piano (1925); *Concerto Grosso* for Piano obbligato and Strings (1935); *Early Americana*, orch. suite (1935); *Garrick*, opera (1936; N.Y., Feb. 24, 1937); choral works; songs; piano pieces; transcriptions.

BIBL.: C. McNaughton, *A. S., American Musician* (diss., N.Y. Univ., 1957).

Stoeving, (Carl Heinrich) Paul, German-American violinist, teacher, and composer; b. Leipzig, May 7, 1861; d. N.Y., Dec. 24, 1948. He studied violin in Leipzig and in Paris. He toured as a soloist in Russia and Scandinavia; taught at the Guildhall School of Music in London (from 1896). In 1914 he emigrated to the U.S. and was employed as a violin teacher in New Haven and N.Y. He wrote the "song-play" *Gaston and Jolivette* and some violin music of considerable insignificance, but his publications on violin technique have a certain pragmatic value; among them are *The Art of Violin Bowing* (London, 1902); *The Story of the Violin* (London, 1904); *The Mastery of the Bow and Bowing Subtleties* (N.Y., 1920); *The Violin, Cello and String Quartet* (N.Y., 1927); *The Violin: Its Famous Makers and Players* (Boston, 1928).

Stogorsky, Alexander, Russian cellist, brother of **Gregor Piatigorsky**; b. Ekaterinoslav, Feb. 26, 1910. Piat is "5" in Russian and sto is "100." A story goes that when Gregor Piatigorsky became world famous, his lesser brother changed his name to Stogorsky to avoid confusion, but observed that he was 20 times as good since 100 is 20 times 5. He studied cello at the Moscow Cons. with Mark Yampolsky; subsequently taught at the Gorky Cons. (1946–54) and at the Minsk Cons. (1954–62). As a solo cellist, he gave first performances of concertos by Mosolov and Zolotarev.

Stöhr, Richard, Austrian-American pedagogue and composer; b. Vienna, June 11, 1874; d. Montpelier, Vt., Dec. 11, 1967. He studied medicine in Vienna (M.D., 1898), but then turned to music and studied with Robert Fuchs and others at the Vienna Cons. In 1903 he was appointed instructor in theory there, and during his long tenure had many pupils who later became celebrated (Artur Rodzinski, Erich Leinsdorf et al.). In 1938 he was compelled to leave Vienna and settled in the U.S., where he taught at the Curtis Inst. of Music in Philadelphia (1939–42); then taught music and German at St. Michael's College in Winooski, Vt. (1943–50). He wrote 4 operas; 4 syms.; *Vermont Suite* for Orch. (1954); much chamber music; piano pieces. He publ. a popular manual, *Praktischer Leitfaden der Harmonielehre* (Vienna, 1909; 21st ed., 1963); also *Praktischer Leitfaden des Kontrapunkts* (Hamburg, 1911) and *Musikalische Formenlehre* (Leipzig, 1911; rev. 1933, as *Formenlehre der Musik*); *Modulationslehre* (1932).

BIBL.: H. Sittner, *R. S., Mensch, Musiker, Lehrer* (Vienna, 1965).

Stoin, Elena, Bulgarian ethnomusicologist, daughter of **Vassil Stoin**; b. Samokov, April 12, 1915. She graduated from the Bulgarian State Academy of Music in Sofia (1938), then taught music in various schools until 1945; became research assistant at the Ethnographical Museum in Sofia (1946) and also worked in the folk-music dept. of the Music Inst. of the Bulgarian Academy of Sciences (from 1950), becoming a senior research fellow (1970). She lectured widely in Eastern Europe on Bulgarian folk music; her folk-song collections include *Sbornik narodini pesni ot Samokov i Samokovsko* (Collection of Folk Songs from Samokov and the Samokov Region; Sofia, 1975), to which her father had contributed.

Stoin, Vassil, Bulgarian ethnomusicologist, father of **Elena Stoin**; b. Samokov, Dec. 5, 1880; d. Sofia, Dec. 5, 1938. He taught himself violin at the age of 10; after graduating from the seminary in Samokov (1897), he taught in neighboring villages until 1907, meanwhile recording folk songs. He studied at the Brussels Cons. (1907–10) and taught music in Sofia, Samokov, and other regions (1911–22), organizing and conducting choirs and orchs. He taught in several schools in Sofia (1922–25), and began lecturing on folk music at the Bulgarian State Academy of Music, becoming a prof. in 1927 and director in 1931. He founded the folk-music dept. of the National Ethnographic Museum (1926). Stoin was one of the first ethnomusicologists to study Bulgarian folk song, transcribing over 9,000 songs and publishing several collections; he laid a foundation for future studies, particularly those of his daughter. His books include *Hypothèse sur l'origine bulgare de la diaphome* (Sofia, 1925), *Balgarskata narodna muzika, metrika i ritmika* (Bulgarian Folk Music, Meter, and Rhythm; Sofia, 1927), and *Bulgarska narodna muzika* (Bulgarian Folk Music; Sofia, 1956).

Stojanović, Peter Lazar, Yugoslav violinist, teacher, and composer; b. Budapest, Sept. 6, 1877; d. Belgrade, Sept. 11, 1957. He studied violin with Hubay at the Budapest Cons. and with J. Grun at the Vienna Cons., where he also received training in composition. In 1913 he established his own school for advanced violin playing in Vienna. In 1925 he settled in Belgrade and became a prof. at the Stankovic Music School; was its director from 1925 to 1928; from 1937 to 1945 he was a prof. of violin at the Belgrade Academy of Music. He publ. *Schule der Skalentechnik* for Violin. His works include the operas *A Tigris* (The Tiger; Budapest, Nov. 14, 1905), *Das Liebchen am Dache* (Vienna, May 19, 1917), and *Der Herzog von Reichsstadt* (Vienna, Feb. 11, 1921); 2 ballets; 2 symphonic poems: *Heldentod* (1918) and *Sava* (1935); 7 violin concertos; 2 cello concertos; 2 viola concertos; Flute Concerto; Horn Concerto; chamber music, including a Piano Trio, a Piano Quartet, and a Piano Quintet.

Stojowski, Sigismund (actually, **Zygmunt Denis Antoni**), noted Polish-born American pianist, pedagogue, and composer; b. Strzelce, May 14, 1869; d. N.Y., Nov. 5, 1946. He was a pupil of Zeleński in Kraków and of Diémer (piano) and Delibes (composition) at the Paris Cons. (1887–89), winning 1st prize for piano playing and composition; later he took a course with Paderewski. He remained in Paris until 1906, when he emigrated to the U.S. as head of the piano dept. at the Inst. of Musical Art in N.Y. (until 1912); later held a similar position at the Von Ende School of Music in N.Y.; taught at the Juilliard Summer School for several years. He became a naturalized American citizen in 1938. In his prime he was extremely successful as a concert pianist, and in his later years was greatly esteemed as a pedagogue.

WORKS: ORCH.: 2 piano concertos: No. 1 (Paris, 1891, composer soloist) and No. 2, *Prologue, Scherzo and Variations* (London, June 23, 1913, composer soloist); Sym. (1899); Violin Concerto (1900); *Romanza* for Violin and Orch. (1901); *Rapsodie symphonique* for Piano and Orch. (1904); Cello Concerto (1922). **OTHER:** Chamber works, including a Piano Quintet, 2 cello sonatas, and 2 violin sonatas; piano pieces; choral works.

Stoker, Richard, English composer and author; b. Castleford, Yorkshire, Nov. 8, 1938. He attended the Huddersfield School of Music and School of Art in Yorkshire (1953–58) and studied with Eric Fenby. After further training with Berkeley at the Royal Academy of Music in London (1958–62), he completed his studies with Boulanger in Paris (1962–63). From 1963 to 1987 he taught composition at the Royal Academy of Music. He also was ed. of the journal *Composer* (1969–80). He publ. the autobiographical vols. *Open Window—Open Door* (1985) and *Between the Lines* (1994). His other writings include novels *Tanglewood* (1993) and *Diva* (1995), as well as a collection of short stories (1995). Stoker has composed in various genres producing scores of both a serious and more popular nature. He has utilized a modified serial technique in some of his works, but tonal elements are always in evidence.

WORKS: DRAMATIC: *Johnson Preserv'd*, opera (1966; London, July 4, 1967); *My Friend—My Enemy*, ballet (1970); *Garden Party*, ballet (1973); *Thérèse Raquin*, opera (1979); *Prospero's Magic Island*, musical (1980); film and television scores. **ORCH.:** *Antic Hay*, overture (1960); *A Purcell Suite* (1960); *Petite Suite* for Small Orch. (1961); *Serenade* (1964); *4 Countries*, suite for Strings (1965); *French Suite* for Strings (1966); *Feast of Fools*, overture (1967); *Little Symphony* for Youth Orch. (1969); *Chorale* for Strings (1970); *Antiphons and Responses* for Recorder Consort and Orch. (1972); *Movement from Bouquet for Lennox* (1979); *Variations, Passacaglia, and Fugue* for Strings (1980); Piano Concerto (1983); *Locations* for Strings (1990); *Chinses Canticle* (1992). **CHAMBER:** 3 string quartets (1961, 1964, 1968); Wind Quintet (1962); 2 violin sonatas (1962, 1970); 3 piano trios (1963, 1968, 1974); Terzetto for Clarinet, Viola, and Piano (1964); Sextet (1965); *Litany, Sequence, and Hymn* for Brass Quartet (1968); *Sinfonia for Sax* for Saxophone Quartet (1969); *Polemics* for Oboe and String Trio (1970); Trio Sonata for Flute, Violin, and Organ or Piano (1972); Sonata for 2 Guitars (1975); Concerto for 2 Guitars and Tape (1976); Duo for Cello and Piano (1978); *Ostinato* for Guitar and Cello (1993); *Partita* for Mandolin and Harp (1993); piano pieces, including 2 sonatas (1962, 1992); organ music, including an Organ Sym. (1969). **VOCAL:** *Ecce Homo*, cantata for Speaker, Tenor, Baritone, Chorus, and Orch. (1964); *Proverbs* for Chorus and Organ or Ensemble (1970); *Benedictus* for Chorus and Orch. or Organ (1972); *The Scholars* for Voice and Ensemble (1992); numerous choruses and solo songs.

Stokes, Eric (Norman), iconoclastic American composer and teacher; b. Haddon Heights, N.J., July 14, 1930. He studied at Lawrence College (B.Mus., 1952) and with Carl McKinley and Francis Judd Cooke at the New England Cons. of Music (M.Mus., 1956); completed his education with Argento and Fetler at the Univ. of Minnesota (Ph.D., 1964), where he taught (from 1961; prof. from 1977); founded its electronic music laboratory and contemporary music ensemble, 1st Minnesota Moving and Storage Warehouse Band (1971). Stokes has been variously described as a crusty, eccentric, wonderfully humorous, very healthy and resourceful American composer of gentle, witty, lyrically accessible music, with a taste for folkloric Americana and a "Whitmanesque" ear. Some of his works (i.e., the series *Phonic Paradigms*) call for unusual instruments that produce unforeseen effects; his *Rock & Roll (Phonic Paradigm I)* (1980) is executed by 5 players hitting rocks together and rolling them across the floor.

WORKS: DRAMATIC: OPERAS: *Horspfal* (1969); *Happ or Orpheus in Clover* (1977); *The Jealous Cellist & Other Acts of Misconduct* (1979); *Itaru the Stonecutter* (1982); *The Further Voyages of the Santa Maria* (1984); *Apollonia's Circus* (1984). Also musicals and theater pieces, including *The Shake of Things to Come (Phonic Paradigm V)* for Mime and 3 Percussionists (1983) and *We're Not Robots, You Know* for Vocal Quintet and Optional Matching Vocal Quintet and Instrumental Ensemble (1986; Banff, Canada, Dec. 1990). **ORCH.:** *A Center Harbor Holiday* (1963); *On the Badlands—Parables* for Chamber Orch. (1972); *5 Verbs of Earth Encircled* for Chamber Orch. (1973); *The Continental Harp and Band Report* (1974–75); *The Spirit of Place among the People* for Chamber Orch. (1977); Syms.: Book I (1979), Book II (1981), and Book III, *Captains on the War against Earth* (Kansas City, Mo., Jan. 5, 1990); *Prairie Drum* for Chamber Orch. (1981); *Concert Music* for Piano and Orch. (1982); *The Greenhouse Effect* (1983); *Stages (Homage to Kurt Weill)* (Wales, Aug. 27, 1988). **CHAMBER:** Trio for Clarinet, Cello, and Piano (1955; rev. 1963); *Expositions on Themes by Henry David Thoreau* for Flute, Oboe, Trumpet, Horn, Violin, Cello, Piano, Accordion or Organ, and Percussion (1970); *Circles in a Round* for Piano and Optional Tape (1972); *Rock & Roll (Phonic Paradigm I)* for 5 Performers, Rocks, and Found Objects (1980); *Spring Song (Phonic Paradigm II)* for 5 Performers, Springs, and Found Objects (1980); Wind Quintet No. 2 (1981); *Tintinnabulary (Phonic Paradigm IV)* for Tape (1983); *Brazen Cartographies* for Brass Quintet (Philadelphia, Nov. 6, 1988); *The Lyrical Pickpocket* for Flute (Piccolo and Alto), Oboe (English Horn), Bassoon, and Piano (Toy Piano) (Minneapolis, March 25, 1990). **VOCAL:** *Smoke and Steel* for Tenor, Men's Chorus, and Orch. (Boston, May 14, 1958; rev. 1989); *The River's Minute by the Far Brook's Year* for Narrator, Chorus, and Orch. (1981); *Peppercorn Songs* for Chorus, Piano, and Optional Instrumental Ensemble (1984); *Firecho* for 5 or More Voices and Optional Percussion (Minneapolis, Aug. 23, 1987); solo songs.

Stokowski, Leopold (Anthony), celebrated, spectacularly endowed, and magically communicative English-born American conductor; b. London (of a Polish father and an Irish mother), April 18, 1882; d. Nether Wallop, Hampshire, Sept. 13, 1977. He attended Queen's College, Oxford, and the Royal College of Music in London, where he studied organ with Stevenson Hoyte, theory with Walford Davies, and composition with Sir Charles Stanford. At the age of 18, he obtained the post of organist at St. James, Piccadilly. In 1905 he went to America and served as organist and choirmaster at St. Bartholomew's in N.Y.; he became a naturalized American citizen in 1915. In 1909 he was engaged to conduct the Cincinnati Sym. Orch.; although his contract was for 5 years, he obtained a release in 1912 in order to accept an offer from the Philadelphia Orch. This was the beginning of a long and spectacular career as a sym. conductor; he led the Philadelphia Orch. for 24 years as its sole conductor, bringing it to a degree of brilliance that rivaled the greatest orchs. in the world. In 1931 he was officially designated by the board of directors of the Philadelphia Orch. as music director, which gave him control over the choice of guest conductors and soloists. He conducted most of the repertoire by heart, an impressive accomplishment at the time; he changed the seating of the orch., placing violins to the left and cellos to the right. After some years of leading the orch. with a baton, he finally dispensed with it and shaped the music with the 10 fingers of his hands. He emphasized the colorful elements in the music; he was the creator of the famous "Philadelphia sound" in the strings, achieving a well-nigh bel canto quality. Tall and slender, with an aureole of blond hair, his figure presented a striking contrast with his stocky, mustachioed German predecessors; he was the first conductor to attain the status of a star comparable to that of a film actor. Abandoning the proverbial ivory tower in which most conductors dwelt, he actually made an appearance as a movie actor in the film *One Hundred Men and a Girl*. In 1940 he agreed to participate in the production of Walt Disney's celebrated film *Fantasia*, which featured both live performers and animated characters; Stokowski conducted the music and in one sequence engaged in a bantering colloquy with Mickey Mouse. He was lionized by the Philadelphians; in 1922 he received the Edward Bok Award of $10,000 as "the person who has done the most for Philadelphia." He was praised in superlative terms in the press, but not all music critics approved of his cavalier treatment of sacrosanct masterpieces, for he allowed himself to alter the orchestration; he doubled some solo passages in the brass, and occasionally introduced percussion instruments not provided in the score; he even cut out individual bars that seemed to him devoid of musical action. Furthermore, Stokowski's own orch. arrangements of Bach raised the pedantic eyebrows of professional musicologists; yet there is no denying the effectiveness of the sonority and the subtlety of color that he succeeded in creating by such means. Many great musicians hailed Stokowski's new orch. sound; Rachmaninoff regarded the Philadelphia Orch. under Stokowski, and later under Ormandy, as the greatest with which he had performed. Stokowski boldly risked his popularity with the Philadelphia audiences by introducing modern works. He conducted Schoenberg's music, culminating in the introduction of his formidable score Gurrelieder on April 8, 1932. An even greater gesture of defiance of popular tastes was his world premiere of *Amériques* by Varèse on April 9, 1926, a score that opens with a siren and thrives on dissonance. Stokowski made history by joining the forces of the Philadelphia Orch. with the Philadelphia Grand Opera Co. in the first American performance of Berg's masterpiece *Wozzeck* (March 31, 1931). The opposition of some listeners was now vocal; when the audible commotion in the audience erupted during his performance of Webern's Sym., he abruptly stopped conducting, walked off the stage, then returned only to begin the work all over again. From his earliest years with the Philadelphia Orch., Stokowski adopted the habit of addressing the audience, to caution them to keep their peace during the performance of a modernistic score, or reprimanding them for their lack of progressive views; once he even took to task the prim Philadelphia ladies for bringing their knitting to the concert. In 1933 the board of directors took an unusual step in announcing that there would be no more "debatable music" performed by the orch.; Stokowski refused to heed this proclamation. Another eruption of discontent ensued when he programmed some Soviet music at a youth concert and trained the children to sing the Internationale. Stokowski was always interested in new electronic sound; he was the first to make use of the Theremin in the orch. in order to enhance the sonorities of the bass section. He was instrumental in introducing electrical recordings. In 1936 he resigned as music director of the Philadelphia Orch.; he was succeeded by Eugene Ormandy, but continued to conduct concerts as co-conductor of the orch. until 1938. From 1940 to 1942 he took a newly organized All-American Youth Orch. on a tour in the U.S. and in South America. During the season 1942–43 he was assoc. conductor, with Toscanini, of the NBC Sym. Orch.; he shared the season of 1949–50 with Mitropoulos as conductor of the N.Y. Phil.; from 1955 to 1960 he conducted the Houston Sym. Orch. In 1962 he organized in N.Y. the American Sym. Orch. and led it until 1972; on April 26, 1965, at the age of 83, he conducted the orch. in the first complete performance of the 4th Sym. of Charles Ives. In 1973 he went to London, where he continued to make recordings and conduct occasional concerts; he also appeared in television interviews. He died in his sleep at the age of 95; rumor had it that he had a contract signed for a gala performance on his 100th birthday in 1982. Stokowski was married 3 times: his 1st wife was **Olga Samaroff**, whom he married in 1911; they were divorced in 1923; his 2nd wife was Evangeline Brewster Johnson, heiress to the Johnson and Johnson drug fortune; they were married in 1926 and divorced in 1937; his 3rd marriage, to Gloria Vanderbilt, produced a ripple of prurient newspaper publicity because of the disparity in their ages; he was 63, she was 21; they were married in 1945 and divorced in 1955. Stokowski publ. *Music for All of Us* (N.Y., 1943), which was translated into the Russian, Italian, and Czech languages.

BIBL.: E. Johnson, ed., *S.: Essays in Analysis of His Art* (London, 1973); P. Robinson, *S.* (N.Y., 1977); A. Chasins, *L. S.: A Profile* (N.Y., 1979); O. Daniel, *S.: A Counterpoint of View* (N.Y., 1982); P. Opperby, *L. S.* (Tunbridge Wells and N.Y., 1982); W. Smith, *The Mystery of L. S.* (Rutherford, N.J., 1990).

Stoliarsky, Piotr (Solomonovich), significant Russian violin pedagogue; b. Lipovets, near Kiev, Nov. 30, 1871; d. Sverdlovsk, April 29, 1944. He began his violin training with his father, then studied with S. Barcewica at the Warsaw Cons. and with E. Mlynarski and Josef Karbulka at the Odessa Music School (graduated, 1898). He played violin in the Odessa Opera orch. (1898–1914); also taught in his own music school (from 1911); in 1920 he joined the faculty of the Odessa Cons., where he was made a prof. in 1923; opened another school for talented youths that was the first of its kind in the Soviet Union (1933). His role in musical pedagogy was similar to that of Auer in training students from limited backgrounds to attain international stature as virtuosi; among his notable pupils were Oistrakh, Gilels, and Milstein.

Stoltzman, Richard (Leslie), outstanding American clarinetist; b. Omaha, July 12, 1942. He began clarinet lessons when he was 8 and gained experience playing in local jazz settings with his father, an alto saxophonist. He then studied mathematics and music at Ohio State Univ. (B.Mus., 1964); also studied clarinet with Robert Marcellus; after studies at Yale Univ. (M.Mus., 1967), he completed his clarinet training with Harold Wright at the Marlboro Music School and with Kalman Opperman in N.Y.; pursued postgraduate studies at Columbia Univ.'s Teachers College (1967–70). He played in many concerts at Marlboro; also founded the group Tashi ("good fortune" in Tibetan) with pianist Peter Serkin, violinist Ida Kavafian, and cellist Fred Sherry in 1973, and toured widely with the group; likewise taught at the Calif. Inst. of the Arts (1970–75). He made his N.Y. solo recital debut in 1974; after being awarded the Avery Fisher Prize in 1977, he pursued an international career as a virtuoso; appeared as soloist with major orchs., as a chamber music artist, and as a solo recitalist. In 1982 he became the first clarinetist ever to give a solo recital at N.Y.'s Carnegie Hall. In 1986 he received the Avery Fisher Artist Award. In 1989 he made his debut at the London Promenade Concerts as soloist in the Mozart Clarinet Concerto. He maintains an extensive repertoire, ranging from the classics to the avant-garde, and including popular music genres; he has also commissioned works and made his own transcriptions.

Stolz, Robert (Elisabeth), noted Austrian conductor and composer; b. Graz, Aug. 25, 1880; d. Berlin, June 27, 1975. His father was the conductor and pedagogue Jacob Stolz and his mother the pianist Ida Bondy; after initial studies with them, he was a pupil of R. Fuchs at the Vienna Cons. and of Humperdinck in Berlin. He became a répétiteur in Graz in 1897; after serving as 2nd conductor in Marburg an der Drau (1898–1902), he was 1st conductor in Salzburg (1902–03) and at the German Theater in Brünn (1903–05). From 1905 to 1917 he was chief conductor of the Theater an der Wien, where he conducted the premieres of many Viennese operettas. He became successful as a composer of popular songs in the Viennese tradition; his first success as an operetta composer came with his *Der Tanz ins Glück* (Vienna, Oct. 18, 1921). In 1924 he went to Berlin, where he eventually won success as a composer for film musicals. His disdain for the Nazi regime led him to leave Germany in 1936 and then Austria in 1938, but not before he helped to smuggle numerous Jews out of the clutches of the Nazis prior to leaving for Paris in 1938. In 1940 he went to the U.S. and was active as a conductor and as a composer for Hollywood films. In 1946 he returned to Vienna, where he conducted and composed until his last years. He possessed an extraordinary facility for stage music and composed about 65 operettas and musicals in a typical Viennese manner; of these the most famous is *2 Herzen im 3/4 Takt* or *Der verlorene Walzer* (Zürich, Sept. 30, 1933). Other operettas are: *Die lustigen Weiber von Wien* (Munich, 1909); *Das Glücksmädel* (1910); *Das Lumperl* (Graz, 1915); *Lang, lang, ist's her* (Vienna, March 28, 1917); *Die Tanzgräfin* (Vienna, May 13, 1921); *Mädi* (Berlin, April 1, 1923); *Ein Ballroman oder Der Kavalier von zehn bis vier* (Vienna, Feb. 29, 1924); *Eine einzige Nacht* (Vienna, Dec. 23, 1927); *Peppina* (1931); *Wenn die kleinen Veilchen bluhen* (The Hague, April 1, 1932); *Venus im Seide* (Zürich, Dec. 10, 1932); *Der verlorene Walzer* (Zürich, Sept. 30, 1933); *Gruzi* (Zürich, 1934); *Frühling im Prater* (Vienna, Dec. 22, 1949); *Karneval in Wien* (1950); *Trauminsel* (Bregenz, July 21, 1962); *Frühjahrs-Parade* (Vienna, March 25, 1964). He wrote about 100 film scores and nearly 2,000 lieder. His other works include waltzes, marches, and piano pieces. After he was forced to leave Austria, he composed a funeral march for Hitler (at a time when Hitler was, unfortunately, very much alive).

BIBL.: G. Holm, *Im Dreivierteltakt durch die Welt* (Linz, 1948); W.-D. Brümmel and F. van Booth, *R. S.: Melodie eines Lebens* (Stuttgart, 1967); O. Herbrich, *R. S.: König der Melodie* (Vienna and Munich, 1975).

Stolze, Gerhard, German tenor; b. Dessau, Oct. 1, 1926; d. Garmisch-Partenkirchen, March 11, 1979. He studied voice in Dresden and Berlin. He made his operatic debut as Augustin Moser in *Die Meistersinger von Nürnberg* at the Dresden State Opera in 1949. From 1951 he made regular appearances at the Bayreuth Festivals; also sang at the Vienna State Opera, and from 1953 to 1961 at the Berlin State Opera. He established his reputation as a Wagnerian singer, but also sang leading parts in German contemporary operas, including *Satan in Martin's Le Mystère de la Nativité* (1960).

Stone, Carl, innovative American composer and performer; b. Los Angeles, Feb. 10, 1953. He studied with Tenney and Subotnick at the Calif. Inst. of the Arts in Valencia (B.F.A., 1975). He served as music director of KPFK Radio in Los Angeles (1978–81) and as director of Meet the Composer/California (from 1981); in 1985, was co-artistic director of the 7th New Music America Festival. Among his awards are an NEA grant (1981–82), tour support awards from the Calif. Arts Council (1984–90), and annual ASCAP awards (from 1985); in 1989 he was funded by the Asian Cultural Council for 6 months' residence in Japan. From 1992 to 1995 he served as president of the American Music Center. Stone composes exclusively electroacoustic music, often employing natural sounds and occasional fragments of familiar pieces, as in his *Sonali* (1988; *Die Zauberflöte*), *Hop Ken* (1987; Mussorgsky's *Pictures at an Exhibition*), and Shing Kee (1986; recording of a Japanese pop star singing a Schubert lied); Stone inscrutably manipulates his Macintosh computer in solo performances to create sensuous, playful, and often enigmatic real-time compositions. He is also an ethnic foods enthusiast (see J. Gold, "Carl Stone: Between Bytes," in *Los Angeles Times*, Aug. 19, 1990), naming many of his pieces after favorite restaurants. He has performed extensively in the U.S., Canada, Europe, Asia, Australia, South America, and the Near East; among choreographers who have used his music are Bill T. Jones, Ping Chong, and Blondell Cummings. His *Ruen Pair* (1993) was created as part of a (Paul Dresher) consortium commission from the Meet the Composer/*Reader's Digest* Fund; his untitled collaborative work with Kuniko Kisanuki for Electronics and Dancer (1995) was commissioned by the Aichi-ken Cultural Center in Nagoya, Japan.

WORKS: TAPE: *LIM* (1975); *Maneeya* (1976); *Sukothai* (1979); *Unthaitled* (1979); *Chao Praya* (1980); *A Tip* (1980); *Thoughts in Stone* (1980); *Woo Lae Oak* (1980); *Jang* (1983). **ELECTRONICS:** *Busobong* (1980); *Kuk II Kwan* (1981); *Green Card March* (1981); *Dong II Jang* (1982); *Vault*, soundtrack (1982); *Woo Lae Oak* (1982); *Hama* (1983); *Torung* (1983); *Fanfare for Pershing Square* (1984); *Ho Ban* for Piano and Electronics (1984; also for Solo Piano, 1990); *Spalding Gray's Map of LA*, soundtrack (1984); *Mae Yao* (in 2 parts; 1984; also for Electronics and Percussion, 1989); *Rime* (1984); *Se Jong* (1984); *Shibucho* (1984); *Wave-Heat* (1984); *Everett & Jones* (1985); *Pho Bác* (1985); *Chia Heng* (1986); *Kappa* (1986); *Imae* (1986); *Samanluang* (1986); *Shing Kee* (1986); *Thanh My* (1986); *Vim* (1986); *Audible Structure* (1987); *Hop Ken* (1987; also for Electronics and Percussion, 1989); *Wall Me Do* (1987); *Amaterasu* (1988); *Amaterasu's Dance* (1988); *Jang Toh* (1988); *Mae* (1988); *Nekai* (1988); *Sonali* (1988); *Zang* (1988); *Zhang Toh* (1988); *Gadberry's* (1989; also for Electronics and Percussion); *Jakuzure* (1989; also *Jakuzure II* for Koto and Electronics and *Jakuzure III* for Flute and Electronics, 1991); *Keika* (1989); *Kokami* (1989); *Kong Joo* (1989; also for Electronics and Percussion); *She Gol Jib* (1989); *Chao Nue* (1990); *Mom's* (1990); *Banteay Srey* (1991); *Janken Pon* (1991); *Noor Mahal* (1991); *Recurring Cosmos* (in 2 parts; 1991; also as a soundtrack); *Rezukuja* for Bass Marimba and Electronics (1991); *She Gol Jib* for Flute and Electronics (1991); *Dur-Pars*, soundtrack (1993); *Ruen Pair* for Violin, Clarinet, 2 Keyboards, Marimba, Drums, and Computer (1993); *Mae Ploy* for String Quartet and Electronics (1994); *Nyala* for Electronics (1995); an untitled collaborative work (with Kuniko Kisanuki) for Electronics and Dancer (1995); *Sudi Mampir* for Electronics (1995); *Wei-fun* for Audio Samples and Computer-generated Images (1996); *Music for the Noh Project* for Electronics and Noh Musicians (1996).

Stone, Kurt, German-American musicologist; b. Hamburg, Nov. 14, 1911; d. Wilmington, N.C., June 15, 1989. He studied music in Hamburg and Copenhagen. He went to N.Y. in 1938 as a teacher at the Dalcroze School of Music; also worked for various music publishers from 1942; contributed knowledgeable articles on modern music and composers to various periodicals. With his wife, he ed. *The Writings of Elliott Carter* (1977); publ. *Music Notation in the Twentieth Century: A Practical Guide* (1980).

Storchio, Rosina, Italian soprano; b. Venice, May 19, 1876; d. Milan, July 24, 1945. She studied at the Milan Cons.; then made her operatic debut at Milan's Teatro del Verme as Micaëla in *Carmen* in 1892. In 1895 she made her first appearance at Milan's La Scala as Sophie in *Werther*; in 1897 she sang in the premiere of Leoncavallo's *La Bohème* in Venice; returning to Milan, she appeared in the title role of Leoncavallo's *Zaza* at the Teatro Lirico in 1900; then appeared at La Scala (from 1902), where she sang in the premieres of several operas, including the title role of *Madama Butterfly* (Feb. 7, 1904); continued to appear there until 1918. After a series of tours in South America and in Europe, she was briefly engaged at N.Y.'s Manhattan Opera House and at the Chicago Grand Opera (1920–21); then retired from the stage. She was paralyzed during the last years of her life as a result of an apoplectic stroke.

Storck, Karl G(ustav) L(udwig), Alsatian writer on music; b. Dürmenach, April 23, 1873; d. Olsberg, Westphalia, May 9, 1920. He studied at the Univs. of Strasbourg and Berlin (Ph.D., 1895). He wrote music criticism for the *Deutsche Zeitung* (Berlin). He publ. a unique ed., *Musik und Musiker in Karikatur und Satire* (Oldenburg, 1911), richly illustrated by numerous reproductions of caricatures on musical subjects; other publications include: *Der Tanz* (1903); *Geschichte der Musik* (1904; 6th ed., 1926); *Das Opernbuch* (1905; 44th printing, 1946); *Die Kulturelle Bedeutung der Musik* (1906); *Mozart: Sein Leben und Schaffen* (1908; 2nd ed., 1923); *Musik-Politik* (1911); *Emil Jaques-Dalcroze: Seine Stellung und Aufgabe in unserer Zeit* (1912).

Story, Liz, American pianist and composer; b. Los Angeles, Oct. 28, 1956. She began playing piano at an early age, tackling

Mozart's 11th concerto at the age of 11; when she was in high school, her family moved to Germany, where she studied languages, philosophy, and poetry. On returning to the U.S., she studied at Hunter College (1977) and the Juilliard School in N.Y. (1978–79); heard jazz pianist Bill Evans, and recognized her own interest in improvisation. She began studying with Sanford Gold, returning to Los Angeles to study at the Univ. of Calif. and at the Dick Grove Music Workshops (1980–81). Her compositions are in reality new-age improvisations with impassioned gestures; among her recordings are *Solid Colors* (1982), *Unaccountable Effect* (1985), *Part of Fortune* (1986), and *Escape of the Circus Ponies* (1990).

Stout, Alan (Burrage), significant American composer and teacher; b. Baltimore, Nov. 26, 1932. He studied composition with Henry Cowell at the Peabody Cons. of Music in Baltimore and took courses at Johns Hopkins Univ. (B.S., 1954); sporadically had composition lessons with Riegger in N.Y. (1951–56); pursued postgraduate studies at the Univ. of Copenhagen (1954–55); then had lessons with John Verrall at the Univ. of Wash. (1958–59), acquiring an M.A. in music and in Swedish language. From 1959 to 1962 he was employed in the music dept. of the Seattle Public Library; in 1963 he was appointed to the music faculty of Northwestern Univ.; in 1973 he was a visiting lecturer at the Stockholm Musikhögskolan. Besides his primary activities as a composer and a teacher, he also performed valuable service in editing (with some conjectural reconstruction) fragmentary pieces by Ives, to prepare them for practical performance.

WORKS: ORCH.: *3 Hymns* (1953–54); *Intermezzo* for English Horn, Percussion, and Strings (1954); *Pietà* for String or Brass Orch. (1957); 4 syms.: No. 1 (1959), No. 2 (1951–66; Chicago, Aug. 4, 1968), No. 3 for Soprano, Men's Chorus, and Orch. (1959–62), and No. 4 (1962–71; Chicago, April 15, 1971); *Serenity* for Solo Cello or Bassoon, Percussion, and Strings (1959); *Ricercare and Aria* for Strings (1959); *Movements* for Violin and Orch. (1962; Fish Creek, Wis., Aug. 17, 1966); *Fanfare for Charles Seeger* (1972); *Pulsar* for 3 Brass Choirs and Timpani (1972); *Nimbus* for 18 Strings (1979); *Pilvia* (1983). **CHAMBER:** 10 string quartets (1952–53; 1952; 1954; 1954; 1957; 1959; 1960; 1960; 1962; 1962); *Solemn Prelude* for Trombone and Organ (1953); Quintet for Clarinet and String Quartet (1958); *Triptych* for Horn and Organ (1961); *Suite* for Flute and Percussion (1962); *Toccata* for Saxophone and Percussion (1965); Cello Sonata (1966); *Music* for Oboe and Piano (1966); *Music* for Flute and Harpsichord (1967); *2 Movements* for Clarinet and String Quartet (1968); *Recitative, Capriccio and Aria* for Oboe, Harp, and Percussion (1970); *Suite* for Saxophone and Organ (1973); Concertino for Clarinet and Chamber Ensemble (1978); *Meditation* for Tenor Saxophone and Organ (1982); Brass Quintet (1984). **KEYBOARD: PIANO:** *Varianti* (1962); *Fantasia* (1962); Suite (1964–67); Sonata for 2 Pianos (1975); *Waltz* (1977). **ORGAN:** *8 Chorales* (1960); *Study in Densities and Durations* (1966–67); *3 Chorales* (1967); *Study in Timbres and Interferences* (1977); *Study in Timbres and Interferences* for Fully Mechanical Organ (1978). **VOCAL:** *2 Hymns* for Tenor and Orch. (1953); *Passion*, oratorio (1953–75; Chicago, April 15, 1976); *Die Engel* for Soprano, Flute, Piano, Percussion, and Brass (1957); *2 Ariel Songs* for Soprano and Chamber Ensemble (1957); *Elegiac Suite* for Soprano and Strings (1959–61); *Laudi* for Soprano, Baritone, and Small Orch. (1961); *Canticum canticorum* for Soprano and Chamber Ensemble (1962); *George Lieder* for High Baritone and Orch. (1962; rev. 1965 and 1970; Chicago, Dec. 14, 1972); *Christmas Poem* for Soprano and Chamber Ensemble (1962); *Prologue*, oratorio (1963–64); *Nattstycken* (Nocturnes) for Narrator, Contralto, and Chamber Ensemble (Chicago, Nov. 10, 1970); *Dialogo per la Pascua* for Soloists, Chorus, and 8 Instruments (1973); *O Altitudo* for Soprano, Women's Chorus, Solo Flute, and Instrumental Ensemble (1974); *5 visages de Laforgue* for Voice and Chamber Orch. (1978); *Triptych* for Soloists, Children's Chorus, and Orch. (1981); choruses, including *The Great Day of the Lord*, with Organ (1956).

Stoutz, Edmond de, Swiss conductor; b. Zürich, Dec. 18, 1920. He studied law at the Univ. of Zürich; then took courses in piano, cello, oboe, percussion, and composition at the Zürich Hochschule für Musik; later pursued training in Salzburg and Vienna. He began his career as a cellist in various ensembles in Zürich; then founded the Zürich Chamber Orch. (1954), with which he toured widely as a conductor; in 1962 he also founded the Zürich Concert Choir. In his programs, he invariably included works by contemporary composers.

Stoyanov, Veselin, Bulgarian composer; b. Shumen, April 20, 1902; d. Sofia, June 29, 1969. He studied piano with his brother Andrei Stoyanov at the Sofia Cons, graduating in 1926; then went to Vienna, where he studied with Joseph Marx and Franz Schmidt. In 1937 he was appointed prof. at the Cons. in Sofia; was director of the Cons. in 1943–44 and from 1956 to 1962.

WORKS: DRAMATIC: OPERAS: *Jensko zarstwo* (Kingdom of Women; Sofia, April 5, 1935); *Salambo* (Sofia, May 22, 1940); *Hitar Petar* (The Wise Peter; 1952; Sofia, 1958). **BALLET:** *Papessa Joanna* (1966; Sofia, Oct. 22, 1968). **ORCH.:** *Capriccio* (1934); *Bai Ganju* (Uncle Ganju), grotesque suite (1941); 3 piano concertos (1942, 1953, 1966); *Karwawa pessen* (Bloody Song; 1947); Violin Concerto (1948); Cello Concerto (1960); 2 syms.: No. 1 (1962) and No. 2, *Weliki Preslaw* (The Great Preslaw; 1969). **CHAMBER:** 3 string quartets (1933, 1934, 1935); Violin Sonata (1934); also piano works, including a Sonata (1930), Suite (1931), and *3 Pieces* (1956). **VOCAL:** *Da bade den* (Let There Be Day), cantata (1952); choral works.

Stracciari, Riccardo, Italian baritone; b. Casalecchio di Reno, near Bologna, June 26, 1875; d. Rome, Oct. 10, 1955. He studied with Ulisse Masetti in Bologna, where he made his operatic debut as Marcello in 1898. He was a member of La Scala in Milan (1904–06); also sang at Covent Garden in London (1905). He made his debut at the Metropolitan Opera in N.Y. on Dec. 1, 1906, as Germont *père*; remained on the roster until 1908; then returned to Europe, continuing his career there and in South America. He returned to the U.S. to sing with the Chicago Opera (1917–19) and in San Francisco (1925); continued to make appearances in Italy until 1944; also was active as a teacher from 1926, his most eminent student being Boris Christoff. He sang all the major baritone roles in the operatic repertoire, his most famous being Rossini's Figaro, which he sang more than 900 times.

Straesser, Joep, Dutch composer and teacher; b. Amsterdam, March 11, 1934. He studied musicology at the Univ. of Amsterdam (1952–55); then took organ lessons with Van der Horst (1956–59) and theory lessons with Felderhof (1959–61) at the Amsterdam Cons.; also received instruction in composition from Ton de Leeuw (1960–65). He was a church organist (1953–61). From 1962 to 1989 he taught at the Utrecht Cons.

WORKS: *5 Close-ups* for Piano (1960–61; rev. 1973); *Music* for Oboe Quartet (1962); *Psalmus* for Men's Chorus, Winds, and Percussion (1963); *22 Pages* for Wind Orch., Percussion, and 3 Men's Voices, after John Cage essays (Hilversum, Sept. 14, 1965); String Quartet No. 2 (1966); *Chorai* for 48 Strings and Percussion (1966; Hilversum, Sept. 14, 1967; re-composed in 1974 for Full Orch. and retitled *Chorai Revisited*); *Duet* for 2 Cellos (1967); *Seismograms* for 2 Percussionists (1967; rev. 1979); *Adastra*, music for ballet (1967); *Summer Concerto* for Oboe and Chamber Orch. (1967; Graz, Oct. 24, 1969); *Ramasasiri* (Traveling Song) for Soprano, Flute, Vibraphone, Piano, and 2 Percussionists, on texts in the Papuan language (1967–68); *Musique pour l'homme* for Soprano, Alto, Tenor, Bass, and Orch. (1968; Amsterdam, Dec. 9, 1968); *Missa* for Chorus and Wind Instruments (1969); *Intersections I* for Wind Quintet and 5 Instrumental Groups spatially positioned (1969), *II* for 100 or More Musicians (1970; Amsterdam, April 3, 1971; except for percussionists, all orch. members improvise freely), *III* for Piano (1971), *IV* for Oboe, Violin, Viola, and Cello (1972), *V (A Saxophone's World)* for 4 Saxophones (1974; rev. 1979), and *V-2* for Bass Clarinet and Piano (1975); *Sight-Seeing*

I, II, III for Flute and Prepared Piano (1969), *IV* for Double Bass (1970), and *V (Spring Quartet)* for String Quartet (1971); *Emergency Case* for Flute, Piano, and Percussion (1970); *Enclosures* for Winds and Percussion (1970; as a ballet, Rotterdam, Oct. 3, 1971); *Eichenstadt und Abendstern*, 6 songs for Soprano and Piano (1972); *Encounters* for Bass Clarinet and 6 Percussionists (1973); *Chorai Revisited* for Orch. (1975); *Intervals I* for Chamber Chorus, Flute, Cello, and Harp (1975–76), *II* for Chorus and Instruments (1979), and *III: Longing for the Emperor*, 5 songs for Soprano, Clarinet, Mandolin, Guitar, Percussion, Viola, and Double Bass, after early Japanese texts (1981); *3 Psalms* for Chorus and Organ (1976); *"Just a moment . . ."* for Piano Trio (1978); *"Just a moment again . . ."* for Piano, 2 Percussion, and Strings (1978); *Fusian a six*, symphonic music (1980); *Signals and Echoes* for Bass Clarinet and Orch. (1982); *Winter Concerto* for Soprano Saxophone and Orch. (1984); *Ueber Erich M.*, Singspiel (1985–86); *Verzauberte Lieder* for Chorus and Orch. (1986); *Triplum* for Violin, Viola, and Cello (1986); *Faites vos jeux* for Organ (1986); *Motetus* for Chorus (1987); Chamber Concerto I for Cello, Winds, Harp, and Percussion (1991), II for Harp and Chamber Orch. (1993), and III for Flute and Chamber Orch. (1993); Sym. No. 3 (1992).

Strang, Gerald, inventive American composer; b. Claresholm, Canada, Feb. 13, 1908; d. Loma Linda, Calif., Oct. 2, 1983. He studied at Stanford Univ. (B.A., 1928) and at the Univ. of Southern Calif. in Los Angeles (Ph.D., 1948); also took private lessons in composition with Toch and Schoenberg, and served as Schoenberg's assistant at the Univ. of Calif. at Los Angeles (1936–38). He taught at Long Beach City College (1938–43; 1945–58); in 1958 he founded the music dept. at San Fernando Valley State College (later Calif. State Univ.) at Northridge, where he taught until 1965; then was chairman of the music dept. at Calif. State Univ. at Long Beach (1965–69); subsequently taught electronic music at the Univ. of Calif. (1969–74). His music is strongly formal, with a unifying technical idea determining the content. An intelligent, energetic, and astute musical technician, he experimented successfully with the new resources available in the fields of acoustics, electronics, and computers; he was also active as an ed. of modern works and was for many years an assoc. of Henry Cowell in editing Cowell's *New Music Quarterly*. The titles of his compositions give clues to their formative semiotics; thus his piano piece *Mirrorrorrim* is an obvious palindrome or cancrizans. His series of *4 Synclavions* is an electronic synthesis of keyboard variations. Similarly suggestive are his various pieces bearing such titles as *Compusitions* (= computerized compositions) and *Synthions* (= synthetic ions). Strang was also active in the field of acoustics, and served as a consultant on some 25 newly built auditoriums in California and elsewhere.

WORKS: ORCH.: Suite for Chamber Orch. (1934–35); 2 syms. (1938–42; 1946–47); *Canzonet* for Strings (1942); *Overland Trail* (1943); Overture (1943); Concerto Grosso (1950); Cello Concerto (1951). **CHAMBER:** Clarinet Sonatina (1932); Quintet for Clarinet and Strings (1933); String Quartet (1934); *Percussion Music* for 3 Percussion (1935); *Divertimento* for 4 Woodwinds or Strings (1948); Violin Sonata (1949); Flute Sonata (1951); *Variations* for 4 Woodwinds or Strings (1956); piano pieces. **OTHER:** Tape and electronic pieces.

BIBL.: M. Berman, *G. S.: Composer, Educator, Acoustician* (thesis, Calif. State Univ., Long Beach, 1977); L. Stein, "G. S. (1908–1983)," *Journal of the Arnold Schoenberg Institute*, VII (1983).

Stransky, Josef, Bohemian conductor; b. Humpoletz, near Deutschbrod, Sept. 9, 1872; d. N.Y., March 6, 1936. While studying medicine (M.D., Univ. of Prague, 1896), he also studied music in Leipzig with Jadassohn and in Vienna with R. Fuchs, Bruckner, and Dvořák. In 1898 he was engaged by A. Neumann as 1st Kapellmeister at the Landestheater in Prague; in 1903 he went in a similar capacity to the Stadttheater in Hamburg; in 1910 he resigned from the Hamburg opera to devote himself to concert work; in the autumn of 1911 became Mahler's successor as conductor of the N.Y. Phil. Soc.; a position he held until 1923. A bequest of $1,000,000 to the society (by Joseph Pulitzer, 1912) enabled Stransky to carry out successfully the sweeping reforms instituted by his illustrious predecessor (chief of which was a system of daily rehearsals during the season of 23 weeks). In 1924 he gave up his musical career and spent the rest of his life as an art dealer. He wrote an operetta, *Der General*, which was produced in Hamburg; orch. works; instrumental pieces; songs.

BIBL.: H. Shanet, *Philharmonic: A History of New York's Orchestra* (Garden City, N.Y., 1975).

Straram, Walther, French conductor; b. London (of French parents), July 9, 1876; d. Paris, Nov. 24, 1933. He was educated in Paris. He played violin in Paris orchs.; then was choirmaster at the Opéra-Comique there; later traveled to America as assistant to André Caplet at the Boston Opera Co. Returning to Paris, he established the Concerts Straram, which enjoyed a fine reputation. He conducted the first performance of Ravel's *Bolero* for Ida Rubinstein (dance recital, Nov. 22, 1928).

Strassburg, Robert, American conductor, teacher, and composer; b. N.Y., Aug. 30, 1915. He studied composition with Marion Bauer at N.Y. Univ.; then enrolled at Harvard Univ. (M.A., 1950). He was conductor and founder of the All-Miami Youth Sym. (1957–60). In 1961 he joined the faculty of the Univ. of Judaism in Los Angeles; from 1966 he was on the faculty of Calif. State College. His works include *4 Biblical Statements* for Strings (1946); *Fantasy and Allegro* for Violin and Orch. (1947); *Torah Sonata* for Piano (1950); *Chelm*, folk opera (1956); *Tropal Suite* for Strings (1967). He is the author of a monograph, *Ernest Bloch, Voice in the Wilderness* (Los Angeles, 1977).

Stratas, Teresa (real name, **Anastasia Stratakis**), outstanding Canadian soprano; b. Toronto, May 26, 1938. She was born into a family of Greek immigrant restaurateurs. At 12, she began voice training and, at 13, appeared on the radio singing pop songs. In 1954 she entered the Royal Cons. of Music of Toronto to study with Irene Jessner, and in 1959 was awarded her Artist Diploma. In 1958 she sang Nora in Vaughan Williams' *Riders to the Sea* in Toronto. On Oct. 13, 1958, she made her professional operatic debut as Mimi at the Toronto Opera Festival. In 1959 she was a co-winner in the Metropolitan Opera Auditions, which led to her debut with the company in N.Y. on Oct. 28, 1959, as Poussette in *Manon*. She continued to sing at the Metropolitan, winning her first notable success as Liù in 1961. On Aug. 19, 1961, she created the title role in Peggy Glanville-Hicks' *Nausicaa* in Athens. On June 18, 1962, she made her debut at Milan's La Scala as Queen Isabella in the posthumous premiere of Falla's *L'Atlántida*. She appeared as Desdemona in *Otello* at Expo '67 in Montreal in 1967. In 1974 she starred as Salome in the film version conducted by Karl Böhm. On May 28, 1979, she sang the title role in the first performance of the complete version of Berg's *Lulu* in Paris. She sang Violetta in Zeffirelli's film version of *La Traviata* in 1983. In 1986 she appeared on Broadway in *Rags*. On Dec. 19, 1991, she sang Marie Antoinette in the premiere of Corigliano's *The Ghosts of Versailles* at the Metropolitan Opera. In 1992 she appeared as Mélisande in Chicago. Stratas was made an Officer of the Order of Canada in 1972. A film portrait of her was made by Harry Rasky as *StrataSphere*. Stratas' remarkable lyric voice made her interpretations of such roles as Cherubino, Zerlina, Lisa in *The Queen of Spades*, Marguerite in *Faust*, Micaëla, Liù, and Weill's Jenny particularly memorable.

BIBL.: H. Rasky, *S.: An Affectionate Tribute* (Oxford, 1989).

Strategier, Herman, Dutch composer, organist, and teacher; b. Arnhem, Aug. 10, 1912; d. Doorwerth, Oct. 26, 1988. He studied music with his father, a church organist, and with H. Andriessen. He succeeded his father as organist at St. Walpurgis at Arnhem in 1935, but the church was destroyed in war action in 1944. He taught at the Inst. for Catholic Church Music in Utrecht (1939–63); also taught there at the Cons. and at the Univ., and likewise at the Univ. of Rotterdam. He was notable mainly as a composer of liturgical music of the Roman Catholic rite.

WORKS: ORCH.: *Divertimento* for Strings and 4 Winds (1937); Flute Concerto (1943); *Haarlem-suite* (1945–47); *Ramiro-suite* (1946); Piano Concerto (1947–48); Sym. No. 1 (1949); Clarinet Concertino (1950); *Musique pour faire plaisir* for Strings (1950); *Intrada sinfonica* (1954); *Rondo giocoso* (1955); *Rapsodia elegiaca* (1956); *Turandot-suite* (1956); *Kadullen Varieties* for Flute, Bassoon, and Strings (1958); *Triptych* for Piano and Wind Orch. (1960); Accordion Concerto (1969); *Concertante Speelmuziek* for Flute, Bassoon, and Orch. (1970); *Intrada festiva* (1976); Sonatine (1978); Basset Horn Concerto (1981); *Cassation* (1983). **CHAMBER:** 3 string quartets (1935, 1936, 1937); *3 pieces* for Oboe and String Quartet (1937); Sextet for Piano and Wind Quintet (1951); Suite for Harp (1961); Quartet for Flute, Violin, Viola, and Cello (1968); *Curven* for Accordion and String Quartet (1970); *Divertissement* for Oboe, Clarinet, and Bassoon (1970); Suite for Piano and Harpsichord (1973); Piano Trio (1974); *Sonata da camera* for Flute, Oboe, Violin, Viola, Cello, and Piano (1978); *5 Pieces* for Harp (1986). **KEYBOARD: PIANO:** Suite for Piano, 4-hands (1945); Sonata (1948); Sonatina (1951); *Tema con variazioni* for Piano, 4-hands (1952); *Elegie* (1954); *4 pièces brèves* for Piano, 4-hands (1973); *3 Speelmuziekjes* (1974); *6 études* (1974); *Zes preludes* (1986). **ORGAN:** *Preludium, Intermezzo and Theme with Variations* (1939); *Ritornello capriccioso* (1944); *Toccatina* (1951); *Chaconne* (1955); *Voluntary* (1975). **VOCAL:** *Stabat Mater* for Chorus and Small Orch. (1939); *Septem cantica* for Mezzo-soprano and Piano (1941); *4 Drinkleideren* for Baritone and Orch. (1945); *Van der mollenfeeste*, old ballad for Chorus and Small Orch. (1947–48); *Henric van Veldeke* for Narrator, Baritone, and Orch. (1952); *5 Minneliederen* for Middle Voice, Flute, and Small String Orch. (1952); *Koning Swentibold*, oratorio (1955); *Arnhemsche Psalm* for Narrator, Soloists, Chorus, and Orch. (1955); *Rembrandt Cantata* (1956); *Requiem* for Chorus, Wind Quintet, and Strings (1961); *Ballade van de Maagd van Wognum* for Chorus and Orch. (1965); *Plaisanterie* for Chorus and Orch. (1966); *Te Deum* for Soprano, Alto, Chorus, and Orch. (1967); *Colloquia familiaria* for Soprano, Chorus, and String Orch. (1969); *Zoo, Buddingh'zoo* for Baritone, Chorus, and Small Orch. (1970); *Ligeia or The Shadow Out of Time* for Chorus, Flute, 6 Percussionists, Organ, and Harp (1973); *De hond* (De Schoolmeester) for Children's Chorus and Orch. (1979); *Hasseltsch meilied* for Chorus and Orch. (1981); *Lof van Walcheren* for Chorus and Orch. (1982); *Hazerswoude* for Chorus and Orch. (1984); choruses; songs.

Stratton, George (Robert), English violinist and pedagogue; b. London, July 18, 1897; d. there, Sept. 4, 1954. He studied in London at the Guildhall School of Music. He was concertmaster of the London Sym. Orch. (1933–52); also organized the Stratton String Quartet (1925–42), which became the Aeolian String Quartet, and was a founding member of the Reginald Paul Piano Quartet (1932–42); served as prof. of violin at the Royal College of Music in London (from 1942). With A. Frank, he publ. *The Playing of Chamber Music* (London, 1935).

Straube, (Montgomery Rufus) Karl (Siegfried), prominent German organist, choral conductor, and pedagogue; b. Berlin, Jan. 6, 1873; d. Leipzig, April 27, 1950. He was a scion of an established ecclesiastical family; his father was an organist and instrument maker in Berlin; his mother was an Englishwoman who was a piano student of Sir Julius Benedict. He studied organ with his father, Dienel, Reimann, and others in Berlin, where he became deputy organist at the Kaiser-Wilhelm-Gedächtniskirche in 1895. From 1897 to 1902 he was organist at the Cathedral of Wesel; in 1902 he became organist at the Thomaskirche in Leipzig; in 1903 he was appointed conductor of the Bachverein there, and in 1907 became a prof. at the Cons. and organist ex officio at the Gewandhaus. In 1918 he became cantor at the Thomaskirche. At his suggestion the Gewandhaus Chorus and the Bachverein were united in 1919, and he conducted the combined choir until 1932. He conducted the Handel Festival in 1925, leading to the formation of the Handel Soc. In his teaching, he followed the great tradition of Leipzig organists, traceable to Bach. Among Straube's numerous collections of organ and choral pieces are *Alte Orgelmeister* (1904); *45 Choralvorspiele alter Meister* (1907); *Alte Meister des Orgelspiels* (2 vols., 1929); *Ausgewahlte Gesänge des Thomanerchors* (1930); he brought out eds. of several works of Bach, Handel, and Liszt. His *Briefe eines Thomaskantors* was publ. posthumously (Stuttgart, 1952).

BIBL.: J. Wolgast, *K. S.* (Leipzig, 1928); *K. S. zu seinem 70. Geburtstag* (Leipzig, 1943); G. Hartmann, *K. S. und seine Schule: "Das Ganze ist ein Mythos"* (Bonn, 1991).

Straus, Oscar (Nathan), noted Austrian-born French operetta composer and conductor; b. Vienna, March 6, 1870; d. Bad Ischl, Jan. 11, 1954. (His name was spelled "Strauss" on his birth certificate; he cut off the 2nd *s* to segregate himself from the multitudinous musical Strausses.) He studied privately in Vienna with A. Prosnitz and H. Gradener, and with Max Bruch in Berlin. From 1893 to 1900 he conducted at various theaters in Austria and Germany. In 1901 he became conductor of the artistic cabaret Uberbrettl in Berlin, and wrote a number of musical farces for it. He remained in Berlin until 1927; then lived in Vienna and Paris; on Sept. 3, 1939, he became a naturalized French citizen. In 1940 he went to America; lived in N.Y. and Hollywood until 1948, when he returned to Europe. He was one of the most successful composers of Viennese operettas. His most celebrated production was *Der tapfere Soldat*, based on G.B. Shaw's play *Arms and the Man* (Vienna, Nov. 14, 1908; in N.Y. as *The Chocolate Soldier*, Nov. 13, 1909; London, Sept. 10, 1910; numerous perfs. all over the world). Other operettas were: *Die lustigen Nibelungen* (Vienna, Nov. 12, 1904); *Hugdietrichs Brautfahrt* (Vienna, March 10, 1906); *Ein Walzertraum* (Vienna, March 2, 1907; rev. 1951); *Didi* (Vienna, Oct. 23, 1909); *Das Tal der Liebe* (Berlin and Vienna, simultaneously, Dec. 23, 1909); *Mein junger Herr* (Vienna, Dec. 23, 1910); *Die kleine Freundin* (Vienna, Oct. 20, 1911); *Love and Laughter* (London, 1913); *Rund um die Liebe* (Vienna, Nov. 9, 1914; in N.Y. as *All around Love*, 1917); *Die himmelblaue Zeit* (Vienna, Feb. 21, 1914); *Die schöne Unbekannte* (Vienna, Jan. 15, 1915; in N.Y. as *My Lady's Glove*, 1917); *Der letzte Walzer* (Berlin, Feb. 12, 1920); *Mariette, ou Comment on écrit l'histoire* (Paris, Oct. 1, 1928); *Eine Frau, die weiss was sie will* (Berlin, Sept. 1, 1932); *Drei Walzer* (Zürich, Oct. 5, 1935); *Die Musik kommt* (Zürich, 1948; rev. as *Ihr erster Walzer*, Munich, May 16, 1952); *Božena* (Munich, May 16, 1952). Among his other works were ballets, film scores, orch. music, chamber pieces, choruses, about 500 cabaret songs, and piano pieces.

BIBL.: B. Grun, *Prince of Vienna: The Life, the Times, and the Melodies of O. S.* (London, 1955); F. Mailer, *Weltburger der Musik: Eine O.-S.-Biographie* (Vienna, 1985).

Strauss, Richard (Georg), great German composer and distinguished conductor, one of the most inventive music masters of the modern age, son of Franz (Joseph) Strauss; b. Munich, June 11, 1864; d. Garmisch-Partenkirchen, Sept. 8, 1949. Growing up in a musical environment, he studied piano as a child with August Tombo, harpist in the Court Orch.; then took violin lessons from Benno Walter, its concertmaster, and later received instruction from the court conductor, Friedrich Wilhelm Meyer. According to his own account, he began to improvise songs and piano pieces at a very early age; among such incunabula was the song *Weihnachtslied*, followed by a piano dance, *Schneiderpolka*. On March 30, 1881, his first orch. work, the Sym. in D minor, was premiered in Munich under Hermann Levi. This was followed by the Sym. in F minor, premiered on Dec. 13, 1884, by the N.Y. Phil. under Theodore Thomas. Strauss also made progress as a performing musician; when he was 20 years old, Hans von Bülow engaged him as assistant conductor of his Meiningen Orch. About that time, Strauss became associated with the poet and musician Alexander Ritter, who introduced him to the "music of the future," as it was commonly called, represented by orch. works of Liszt and operas by Wagner.

In 1886 Strauss received an appointment as the 3rd conductor of the Court Opera in Munich. On March 2, 1887, he conducted in Munich the first performance of his symphonic fantasy, *Aus Italien.* This was followed by the composition of his first true masterpiece, the symphonic poem *Don Juan,* in which he applied the thematic ideas of Liszt; he conducted its premiere in Weimar on Nov. 11, 1889; it became the first of a series of his tone poems, all of them based on literary subjects. His next tone poem of great significance in music history was *Tod und Verklärung*; Strauss conducted it for the first time in Eisenach on June 21, 1890, on the same program with the premiere of his brilliant *Burleske* for Piano and Orch., featuring Eugen d'Albert as soloist. There followed the first performance of the symphonic poem *Macbeth,* which Strauss conducted in Weimar on Oct. 13, 1890. In these works, Strauss established himself as a master of program music and the most important representative of the nascent era of musical modernism; as such, he was praised extravagantly by earnest believers in musical progress and damned savagely by entrenched traditionalists in the press. He effectively adapted Wagner's system of leading motifs (leitmotifs) to the domain of symphonic music. His tone poems were interwoven with motifs, each representing a relevant programmatic element. Explanatory brochures listing these leading motifs were publ. like musical Baedekers to guide the listeners. Bülow, ever a phrasemaker, dubbed Strauss "Richard the 3rd," Richard the 1st being Wagner but no one worthy of direct lineage as Richard the 2nd in deference to the genius of the master of Bayreuth.

Turning to stage music, Strauss wrote his first opera, *Guntram,* for which he also composed the text; he conducted its premiere in Weimar on May 10, 1894, with the leading soprano role performed by Pauline de Ahna; she was married to Strauss on Sept. 10, 1894, and remained with him all his life; she died on May 13, 1950, a few months after Strauss himself. While engaged in active work as a composer, Strauss did not neglect his conducting career. In 1894 he succeeded Bulow as conductor of the Berlin Phil., leading it for a season. Also in 1894 he became assistant conductor of the Munich Court Opera; he became chief conductor in 1896. In 1896–97 he filled engagements as a guest conductor in European music centers. His works of the period included the sparkling *Till Eugenspiegels lustige Streiche* (Cologne, Nov. 5, 1895), *Also sprach Zarathustra,* a philosophical tone poem after Nietzsche (Frankfurt am Main, Nov. 27, 1896, Strauss conducting), and *Don Quixote,* variations with a cello solo, after Cervantes (Cologne, March 8, 1898). In 1898 Strauss became a conductor at the Berlin Royal Opera; in 1908 he was made its Generalmusikdirektor, a position he held until 1918. He conducted the first performance of his extraordinary autobiographical tone poem *Ein Heldenleben* in Frankfurt am Main on March 3, 1899; the hero of the title was Strauss himself, while his critics were represented in the score by a cacophonous charivari; for this exhibition of musical self-aggrandizement, he was severely chastised in the press. There followed his first successful opera, *Feuersnot* (Dresden, Nov. 21, 1901).

In June 1903 Strauss was the guest of honor of the Strauss Festival in London. It was also in 1903 that the Univ. of Heidelberg made him Dr.Phil., *honoris causa.* For his first visit to the U.S., he presented to the public the premiere performance of his *Symphonia domestica* at Carnegie Hall in N.Y. on March 21, 1904. The score represented a day in the Strauss household, containing an interlude describing, quite literally, the feeding of the newly born baby. The reviews in the press reflected aversion to such a musical self-exposure. There followed his opera *Salome,* to the German tr. of Oscar Wilde's play. Schuch led its premiere in Dresden on Dec. 9, 1905. *Salome* had its American premiere at the Metropolitan Opera in N.Y. on Jan. 22, 1907; the ghastly subject, involving intended incest, 7-fold nudity, and decapitation followed by a labial necrophilia, administered such a shock to the public and the press that the Metropolitan Opera took it off the repertoire after only 2 performances. Scarcely less forceful was Strauss's next opera, *Elektra,* to a libretto by the Austrian poet and dramatist Hugo von Hofmannsthal, in which the horrors of matricide were depicted with extraordinary force in unabashedly dissonant harmonies. Schuch conducted its premiere in Dresden on Jan. 25, 1909.

Strauss then decided to prove to his admirers that he was quite able to write melodious operas to charm the musical ear; this he accomplished in his next production, also to a text of Hofmannsthal, *Der Rosenkavalier,* a delightful opera-bouffe in an endearing popular manner; Schuch conducted its premiere in Dresden on Jan. 26, 1911. Turning once more to Greek mythology, Strauss wrote, with Hofmannsthal again as librettist, a short opera, *Ariadne auf Naxos,* which he conducted for the first time in Stuttgart on Oct. 25, 1912. In June 1914 Strauss was awarded an honorary D.Mus. degree from the Univ. of Oxford. His next work was the formidable, and quite realistic, score *Eine Alpensinfonie,* depicting an ascent of the Alps, and employing a wind machine and a thunder machine in the orch. to illustrate an Alpine storm. Strauss conducted its first performance with the Dresden Court Orch. in Berlin on Oct. 28, 1915. Then, again with Hofmannsthal as librettist, he wrote the opera *Die Frau ohne Schatten* (Vienna, Oct. 10, 1919), using a complex plot, heavily endowed with symbolism.

In 1917 Strauss helped to organize the Salzburg Festival and appeared there in subsequent years as conductor. In 1919 he assumed the post of co-director with Franz Schalk of the Vienna State Opera, a position he held until 1924. In 1920 he took the Vienna Phil. on a tour of South America; in 1921 he appeared as a guest conductor in the U.S. For his next opera, *Intermezzo* (Dresden, Nov. 4, 1924), Strauss wrote his own libretto; then, with Hofmannsthal once more, he wrote *Die ägyptische Helena* (Dresden, June 6, 1928). Their last collaboration was *Arabella* (Dresden, July 1, 1933).

When Hitler came to power in 1933, the Nazis were eager to persuade Strauss to join the official policies of the 3rd Reich. Hitler even sent him a signed picture of himself with a flattering inscription, "To the great composer Richard Strauss, with sincere admiration." Strauss kept clear of formal association with the Führer and his cohorts, however. He agreed to serve as president of the newly organized Reichsmusikkammer on Nov. 15, 1933, but resigned from it on July 13, 1935, ostensibly for reasons of poor health. He entered into open conflict with the Nazis by asking Stefan Zweig, an Austrian Jew, to provide the libretto for his opera *Die schweigsame Frau*; it was duly produced in Dresden on June 24, 1935, but then taken off the boards after a few performances. His political difficulties grew even more disturbing when the Nazis found out that his daughter-in-law was Jewish. Zweig himself managed to escape Nazi horrors, and emigrated to Brazil, but was so afflicted by the inhumanity of the world that he and his wife together committed suicide.

Strauss valiantly went through his tasks; he agreed to write the *Olympische Hymne* for the Berlin Olympic Games in 1936. On Nov. 5, 1936, he was honored with the Gold Medal of the Royal Phil. Soc. in London; the next day he conducted the visiting Dresden State Opera in a performance of his *Ariadne auf Naxos* at Covent Garden. For his next opera, he chose Joseph Gregor as his librettist; with him Strauss produced *Daphne* (Dresden, Oct. 15, 1938), which was once more a revival of his debt to Greek mythology. For their last collaboration, Strauss and Gregor produced the opera *Die Liebe der Danae,* also on a Greek theme. Its public dress rehearsal was given in Salzburg on Aug. 16, 1944, but by that time World War II was rapidly encroaching on devastated Germany, so that the opera did not receive its official premiere until after Strauss's death. The last opera by Strauss performed during his lifetime was *Capriccio.* Its libretto was prepared by the conductor Clemens Krauss, who conducted its premiere in Munich on Oct. 28, 1942. Another interesting work of this period was Strauss's Horn Concerto No. 2, first performed in Salzburg on Aug. 11, 1943.

During the last weeks of the war, Strauss devoted himself to the composition of *Metamorphosen*, a symphonic work mourning the disintegration of Germany; it contained a symbolic quotation from the funeral march from Beethoven's *Eroica* Sym. He then completed another fine score, the Oboe Concerto. In Oct. 1945 he went to Switzerland.

In Oct. 1947 Strauss visited London for the Strauss Festival and also appeared as a conductor of his own works. Although official suspicion continued to linger regarding his relationship with the Nazi regime, he was officially exonerated of all taint on June 8, 1948. A last flame of creative inspiration brought forth the deeply moving *Vier letzte Lieder* (1948), for Soprano and Orch., inspired by poems of Herman Hesse and Eichendorff. With this farewell, Strauss left Switzerland in 1949 and returned to his home in Germany, where he died at the age of 85. Undeniably one of the finest master composers of modern times, Strauss never espoused extreme chromatic techniques, remaining a Romanticist at heart. His genius is unquestioned as regards his tone poems from *Don Juan* to *Ein Heldenleben* and his operas from *Salome* to *Der Rosenkavalier*, all of which have attained a permanent place in the repertoire, while his *Vier letzte Lieder* stand as a noble achievement of his Romantic inspiration. In 1976 the Richard-Strauss-Gesellschaft was organized in Munich.

WORKS: DRAMATIC: OPERAS: *Guntram*, op. 25 (1892–93; Hoftheater, Weimar, May 10, 1894, composer conducting; rev. version, with score cut by one 3rd, 1934–39; Deutsches Nationaltheater, Weimar, Oct. 29, 1940); *Feuersnot*, op. 50 (1900–1901; Hofoper, Dresden, Nov. 21, 1901, Ernst von Schuch conducting); *Salome*, op. 54 (1903–05; Hofoper, Dresden, Dec. 9, 1905, Schuch conducting); *Elektra*, op. 58 (1906–08; Hofoper, Dresden, Jan. 25, 1909, Schuch conducting); *Der Rosenkavalier*, op. 59 (1909–10; Hofoper, Dresden, Jan. 26, 1911, Schuch conducting); *Ariadne auf Naxos* "zu spielen nach dem *Bürger als Edelmann* des Molière," op. 60 (1911–12; Hoftheater, Stutt gart, Oct. 25, 1912, composer conducting; rev. version, with prologue, 1916; Hofoper, Vienna, Oct. 4, 1916, Franz Schalk conducting); *Die Frau ohne Schatten*, op. 65 (1914–18; Staatsoper, Vienna, Oct. 10, 1919, Schalk conducting); *Intermezzo*, op. 72 (1918–23; Staatsoper, Dresden, Nov. 4, 1924, Fritz Busch conducting); *Die ägyptische Helena*, op. 75 (1923–27; Staatsoper, Dresden, June 6, 1928, Fritz Busch conducting; rev. version, 1932–33; Festspielhaus, Salzburg, Aug. 14, 1933); *Arabella*, op. 79 (1929–32; Staatsoper, Dresden, July 1, 1933, Clemens Krauss conducting; rev. version, Munich, July 16, 1939); *Die schweigsame Frau*, op. 80 (1933–34; Staatsoper, Dresden, June 24, 1935, Karl Böhm conducting); *Friedenstag*, op. 81 (1935–36; Nationaltheater, Munich, July 24, 1938, Krauss conducting); *Daphne*, op. 82 (1936–37; Staatsoper, Dresden, Oct. 15, 1938, Böhm conducting); *Die Liebe der Danae*, op. 83 (1938–40; public dress rehearsal, Festspielhaus, Salzburg, Aug. 16, 1944, Krauss conducting; official premiere, Festspielhaus, Salzburg, Aug. 14, 1952, Krauss conducting); *Capriccio*, op. 85 (1940–41; Bayerische Staatsoper, Munich, Oct. 28, 1942, Krauss conducting). **BALLETS AND OTHER DRAMATIC WORKS:** *Romeo und Julia*, incidental music to Shakespeare's drama (Nationaltheater, Munich, Oct. 23, 1887); *Josephslegende*, op. 63 (1912–14; Opéra, Paris, May 14, 1914, composer conducting); *Der Bürger als Edelmann*, incidental music to Hofmannsthal's version of Molière's drama, op. 60 (1917; Deutsches Theater, Berlin, April 9, 1918); *Schlagobers*, op. 70 (1921–22; Staatsoper, Vienna, May 9, 1924, composer conducting); *Verklungene Feste*, after Couperin (1940; Nationaltheater, Munich, April 5, 1941, Krauss conducting); *Des Esels Schatten*, comedy for music (1949; Hellbrunn Castle, near Salzburg, July 31, 1982, Ernst Märzendorfer conducting).

ORCH.: Overture for the Singspiel *Hochlands Treue* (1872–73); *Festmarsch* in E-flat major, op. 1 (1876; Munich, March 26, 1881, Franz Strauss conducting); Concert Overture in B minor (1876); Serenade in G major (1877); Overture in E major (1878); *Romanze* in E-flat major for Clarinet and Orch. (1879); Overture in A minor (1879); Sym. in D minor (1880; Munich, March 30, 1881, Hermann Levi conducting); Violin Concerto in D minor, op. 8 (1880–82; Vienna, Dec. 5, 1882, Benno Walter violinist, composer pianist; official premiere, Leipzig, Feb. 17, 1896, Alfred Krasselt violinist, composer conducting); Serenade in E-flat major for 13 Wind Instruments, op. 7 (1881; Dresden, Nov. 27, 1882, Franz Wüllner conducting); Horn Concerto No. 1 in E-flat major, op. 11 (1882–83; Meiningen, March 4, 1885, Gustav Leinhos soloist, Hans von Bülow conducting); Overture in C minor (Munich, Nov. 28, 1883, Levi conducting); *Romanze* in F major for Cello and Orch. (1883); *Lied ohne Worte* in E-flat major (1883); Sym. in F minor, op. 12 (1883–84; N.Y., Dec. 13, 1884, Theodore Thomas conducting); Suite in B-flat major for 13 Wind Instruments, op. 4 (Munich, Nov. 18, 1884, composer conducting); *Der Zweikampf—Polonaise* in B-flat major for Flute, Bassoon, and Orch. (1884); *Festmarsch* in D major (1884; Munich, Jan. 8, 1885, Franz Strauss conducting; rev. 1888); *Burleske* in D minor for Piano and Orch. (1885–86; Eisenach, June 21, 1890, Eugen d'Albert soloist, composer conducting); *Aus Italien*, symphonic fantasy, op. 16 (1886; Munich, March 2, 1887, composer conducting); *Macbeth*, tone poem after Shakespeare's drama, op. 23 (1886–88; rev. 1889–90; Weimar, Oct. 13, 1890, composer conducting; rev. 1891); *Don Juan*, tone poem after Lenau, op. 20 (1888–89; Weimar, Nov. 11, 1889, composer conducting); *Tod und Verklärung*, tone poem, op. 24 (1888–89; Eisenach, June 21, 1890, composer conducting); *Festmarsch* in C major (Munich, Feb. 1, 1889, Franz Strauss conducting); Fanfare for A.W. Iffland's drama *Der Jäger* (1891); *Festmusik* "Lebende Bilder" for the golden wedding anniversary of the Grand Duke and Duchess of Weimar (Weimar, Oct. 8, 1892, composer conducting); *Till Eulenspiegels lustige Streiche, nach alter schelmenweise—in Rondeauform*, op. 28 (1894–95; Cologne, Nov. 5, 1895, Wüllner conducting); *Also sprach Zarathustra*, tone poem after Nietzsche, op. 30 (1895–96; Frankfurt am Main, Nov. 27, 1896, composer conducting); *Don Quixote, fantastische Variationen über ein Thema ritterlichen Charakters* for Cello and Orch., op. 35 (1896–97; Cologne, March 8, 1898, Wüllner conducting); *Ein Heldenleben*, tone poem, op. 40 (1897–98; Frankfurt am Main, March 3, 1899, composer conducting); *Symphonia domestica*, op. 53 (1902–03; N.Y., March 21, 1904, composer conducting); *Zwei Militärmärsche*, op. 57 (1906; Berlin, March 6, 1907, composer conducting); *Feierlicher Einzug der Ritter des Johanniter-Ordens* for Brass and Timpani (1909); *Festliches Präludium* for Orch. and Organ, op. 61 (for the dedication of the Konzerthaus, Vienna, Oct. 19, 1913, Ferdinand Löwe conducting); *Eine Alpensinfonie*, op. 64 (1911–15; Berlin, Oct. 28, 1915, composer conducting); *Der Bürger als Edelmann*, suite, op. 60 (1918; Vienna, Jan. 31, 1920, composer conducting); *Tanzsuite aus Klavierstücken von François Couperin* for Small Orch. (Vienna, Feb. 17, 1923, Krauss conducting); *Wiener Philharmoniker Fanfare* for Brass and Timpani (Vienna, March 4, 1924); *Fanfare zur Eröffnung der Musikwoche der Stadt Wien im September 1924* for Brass and Timpani (Vienna, Sept. 14, 1924); *Parergon zur Symphonia domestica* for Piano, Left-hand, and Orch., op. 73 (1924; Dresden, Oct. 16, 1925, Paul Wittgenstein soloist, Fritz Busch conducting); *Militärmarsch* in F major for the film *Der Rosenkavalier* (1925; Dresden, Jan. 10, 1926, composer conducting); *Panathenäenzug, symphonische Etüden in Form einer Passacaglia* for Piano, Left-hand, and Orch., op. 74 (1927; Vienna, March 11, 1928, Wittgenstein soloist, Schalk conducting); *Vier sinfonische Zwischenspiele aus Intermezzo* (BBC, London, May 24, 1931); *München*, "ein Gelegenheitswalzer" (for the film *München*, 1939; Munich, May 24, 1939; rev. 1945 as *München*, "ein Gedächtniswalzer"; Vienna, March 31, 1951); *Festmusik zur Feier des 2600 jährigen Bestehens des Kaiserreichs Japan*, op. 84 (Tokyo, Dec. 7, 1940); *Divertimento, Klavierstücke von Couperin* for Small Orch., op. 86 (1940–41; Vienna, Jan. 31, 1943, Krauss conducting); Horn Concerto No. 2 in E-flat major (1942; Salzburg, Aug. 11, 1943, Gottfried Freiberg soloist, Böhm conducting); *Festmusik der Stadt Wien* for Brass and Timpani (1943; 2nd version as *Fanfare der Stadt Wien*, 1943; Vienna, April 9, 1943, composer conducting); Sonatina No. 1 in F major, "Aus der Werkstatt eines Invaliden," for 16 Wind Instruments (1943; Dresden, June 18, 1944, Karl Elmendorff conducting); *Erste Walzerfolge aus Der Rosenkavalier* (1944; London, Aug. 4, 1946, Erich Leinsdorf conducting); *Metamorphosen* for 23 Solo Strings (1945; Zürich, Jan. 25, 1946, Paul Sacher conducting); Sonatina No. 2 in E-flat major, "Fröhlische Werkstatt," for 16 Wind Instruments (1944–45; Winterthur, March 25, 1946, Hermann Scherchen conducting); Oboe Concerto in D major (1945–46; Zürich, Feb. 26, 1946, Marcel Saillet soloist, Volkmar Andreae conducting); *Symphonische Fantasie aus Die Frau ohne Schatten* (1946; Vienna, June 26, 1947, Böhm conducting); *Duett-Concertino* for Clarinet, Bassoon, Strings, and Harp (1947; Radio Svizzera Italiana, Lugano, April 4, 1948); *Symphonisches Fragment aus Josephslegende* (1948; San Antonio, Feb. 26, 1949, Max Reiter conducting).

CHAMBER: String Quartet in A major, op. 2 (1880; Munich, March 14, 1881); Cello Sonata in F major, op. 6 (1880–83; Nuremberg, Dec. 8, 1883); Piano Quartet in C minor, op. 13 (1883–84; Weimar, Dec. 8, 1885); Violin Sonata in E-flat major, op. 18 (1887; Munich, Oct. 3, 1888); Allegretto in E major for Violin and Piano (1948). **PIANO:** *5 Klavierstücke*, op. 3 (1880–81); Sonata in B minor, op. 5 (1880–81); *5 Stimmungsbilder*, op. 9 (1882–84).

VOCAL: CHORAL: Chorus for *Elektra of Sophocles* (1881); *Wanderers Sturmlied* for Chorus and Orch., op. 14 (1884; Cologne, March 8, 1887, composer conducting); *Taillefer* for Soprano, Tenor, Baritone, Chorus, and Orch., op. 52 (Heidelberg, Oct. 26, 1903, composer conducting); *Bardengesang* for Men's Chorus and Orch., op. 55 (1905; Dresden, Feb. 6, 1906); *Deutsche Motette* for Soprano, Alto, Tenor, Bass, and Chorus, op. 62 (Berlin, Dec. 2, 1913); *Die Tageszeiten* for Men's Chorus and Orch., op. 76 (Vienna, July 21, 1928); *Olympische Hymne* for Chorus and Orch. (1934; Berlin, Aug. 1, 1936, composer conducting); *Die Göttin im Putzzimmer* for Chorus (1935; Vienna, March 2, 1952, Krauss conducting); *An dem Baum Daphne*, epilogue to *Daphne*, for Chorus (1943; Vienna, Jan. 5, 1947, Felix Prohaska conducting). **SONGS** (source of text precedes date of composition): *Weihnachtslied* (C. Schubart; 1870); *Einkehr* (Uhland; 1871); *Winterreise* (Uhland; 1871); *Waldkonzert* (J. Vogel; 1871?); *Der böhmische Musikant* (O. Pletzsch; 1871?); *Herz, mein Herz* (E. Geibel; 1871); *Der müde Wanderer* (A. Hoffman von Fallersleben; 1873?); *Husarenlied* (von Fallersleben; 1873?); *Der Fischer* (Goethe; 1877); *Die Drossel* (Uhland; 1877); *Lass ruhn die Toten* (A. von Chamisso; 1877); *Lust und Qual* (Goethe; 1877); *Spielmann und Zither* (T. Körner; 1878); *Wiegenlied* (von Fallersleben; 1878); *Abend- und Morgenrot* (von Fallersleben; 1878); *Im Walde* (Geibel; 1878); *Der Spielmann und sein Kind* (von Fallersleben; 1878; orchestrated); *Nebel* (Lenau; 1878?); *Soldatenlied* (von Fallersleben; 1878?); *Ein Röslein zog ich mir im Garten* (von Fallersleben; 1878?); *Waldegesang* (Geibel; 1879); *In Vaters Garten heimlich steht ein Blümchen* (Heine; 1879); *Die erwachte Rose* (F. von Sallet; 1880); *Begegnung* (O. Gruppe; 1880); *John Anderson, mein Lieb* (Burns; F. Freiligrath, tr.; 1880); *Rote Rosen* (K. Stieler; 1883); *Acht Lieder aus Letzte Blätter*, op. 10 (H. von Gilm; 1885): *Zueignung* (orchestrated, 1940), *Nichts, Die Nacht, Die Georgine, Geduld, Die Verschwiegenen, Die Zeitlose*, and *Allerseelen*; *Wer hat's gethan?* (Gilm; 1885); *Fünf Lieder*, op. 15 (1884–86): *Madrigal* (Michelangelo), *Winternacht* (Schack), *Lob des Leidens* (Schack), *Aus den Liedern der Trauer (Dem Herzen ähnlich)* (Schack), and *Heimkehr* (Schack); *Sechs Lieder*, op. 17 (Schack; 1885–87): *Seitdem dein Aug' in meines schaute, Ständchen, Das Geheimnis, Aus den Liedern der Trauer (Von dunklem Schleier umsponnen), Nur Muth!*, and *Barkarole*; *Sechs Lieder aus Lotusblattern*, op. 19 (Schack; 1885–88): *Wozu noch, Mädchen, soll es frommen, Breit über mein Haupt dein schwarzes Haar, Schön sind, doch kalt die Himmelssterne, Wie sollten wir geheim sie halten, Hoffen und wieder versagen*, and *Mein Herz ist stumm, mein Herz ist kalt*; *Schlichte Weisen*, op. 21 (F. Dahn; 1887–88): *All' mein Gedanken, mein Herz und mein Sinn, Du meines Herzens Krönelein, Ach Lieb, ich muss nun scheiden, Ach weh, mir unglückhaften Mann*, and *Die Frauen sind oft fromm und still*; *Mädchen-blumen*, op. 22 (Dahn): *Kornblumen* (1888), *Mohnblumen* (1888), *Efeu* (1886–88), and *Wasserrose* (1886–88); *Zwei Lieder*, op. 26 (Lenau; 1891): *Frühlingsgedränge* and *O wärst du mein*; *Vier Lieder*, op. 27 (1894): *Ruhe, meine Seele* (K. Henckell; orchestrated, 1948), *Cäcilie* (Hart; orchestrated, 1897), *Heimliche Aufforderung* (J. Mackay), and *Morgen* (Mackay; orchestrated, 1897); *Drei Lieder*, op. 29 (Bierbaum; 1895): *Traum durch die Dämmerung, Schlagende Herzen*, and *Nachtgang*; *Wir beide wollen springen* (Bierbaum; 1896); *Drei Lieder*, op. 31: *Blauer Sommer* (Busse; 1896), *Wenn* (Busse; 1895), and *Weisser Jasmin* (Busse; 1895); added song, *Stiller Gang* (Dehmel; 1895); *Fünf Lieder*, op. 32 (1896): *Ich trage meine Minne* (Henckell), *Sehnsucht* (Liliencron), *Liebeshymnus* (Henckell; orchestrated, 1897), *O süsser Mai* (Henckell), and *Himmelsboten* (Des Knaben Wunderhorn); *Vier Gesänge*, op. 33, for Voice and Orch.: *Verfuhrung* (Mackay; 1896), *Gesang der Apollopriesterin* (E. von und zu Bodman; 1896), *Hymnus* (1896), and *Pilgers Morgenlied* (Goethe; 1897); *Vier Lieder*, op. 36: *Das Rosenband* (Klopstock; orchestrated, 1897), *Für funfzehn Pfennige* (Des Knaben Wunderhorn; 1897), *Hat gesagt—bleibt's nicht dabei* (Des Knaben Wunderhorn; 1898), and *Anbetung* (Rückert; 1898); *Sechs Lieder*, op. 37: *Glückes genug* (Liliencron; 1898), *Ich liebe dich* (Liliencron; 1898; orchestrated, 1943), *Meinem Kinde* (Falke; 1897; orchestrated, 1897), *Mein Auge* (Dehmel; 1898; orchestrated, 1933), *Herr Lenz* (Bodman; 1896), and *Hochzeitlich Lied* (A. Lindner; 1898); *Fünf Lieder*, op. 39 (1898): *Leises Lied* (Dehmel), *Junghexenlied* (Bierbaum), *Der Arbeitsmann* (Dehmel), *Befreit* (Dehmel; orchestrated, 1933), and *Lied an meinen Sohn* (Dehmel); *Fünf Lieder*, op. 41 (1899): *Wiegenlied* (Dehmel; orchestrated, 1916), *In der Campagna* (Mackay), *Am Ufer* (Dehmel), *Bruder Liederlich* (Liliencron), and *Leise Lieder* (Morgenstern); *Drei Lieder*, op. 43 (1899): *An Sie* (Klopstock), *Muttertändelei* (G. Bürger; orchestrated, 1900), and *Die Ulme zu Hirsau* (Uhland); *Zwei grössere Gesänge*, op. 44, for Voice and Orch. (1899): *Notturno* (Dehmel) and *Nächtlicher Gang* (Rückert); *Weihnachtsgefühl* (Greif; 1899); *Funf Lieder*, op. 46 (Rückert): *Ein Obdach gegen Sturm und Regen* (1900), *Gestern war ich Atlas* (1899), *Die sieben Siegel* (1899), *Morgenrot* (1900), and *Ich sehe wie in einem Spiegel* (1900); *Fünf Lieder*, op. 47 (Uhland; 1900): *Auf ein Kind, Des Dichters Abendgang* (orchestrated, 1918), *Rückleben, Einkehr*, and *Von den sieben Zechbrüdern*; *Fünf Lieder*, op. 48 (1900): *Freundliche Vision* (Bierbaum; orchestrated, 1918), *Ich schwebe* (Henckell), *Kling!* (Henckell), *Winterweihe* (Henckell; orchestrated, 1918), and *Winterliebe* (Henckell; orchestrated, 1918); *Acht Lieder*, op. 49: *Waldseligkeit* (Dehmel; 1901; orchestrated, 1918), *In goldener Fülle* (P. Remer; 1901), *Wiegenliedchen* (Dehmel; 1901), *Das Lied des Steinklopfers* (Henckell; 1901), *Sie wissen's nicht* (O. Panizza; 1901), *Junggesellenschwur* (*Des Knaben Wunderhorn*; 1900), *Wer lieben will* (C. Mündel; 1901), and *Ach, was Kummer, Qual und Schmerzen* (Mündel; 1901); *Zwei Gesänge*, op. 51, for Voice and Orch.: *Das Thal* (Uhland; 1902) and *Der Einsame* (Heine; 1906); *Sechs Lieder*, op. 56: *Gefunden* (Goethe; 1903), *Blindenklage* (Henckell; 1903–06), *Im Spätboot* (Meyer; 1903–06), *Mit deinen blauen Augen* (Heine; 1903–06), *Frühlingsfeier* (Heine; 1903–06; orchestrated, 1933), and *Die heiligen drei Könige aus Morgenland* (Heine; 1903–06; orchestrated, 1906); *Der Graf von Rom* (no text; 1906); *Krämerspiegel*, op. 66 (A. Kerr; 1918): *Es war einmal ein Bock, Einst kam der Bock als Bote, Es liebte einst ein Hase, Drei Masken sah ich am Himmel stehn, Hast due ein Tongedicht vollbracht, O lieber Künstler sei ermahnt, Unser Feind ist, grosser Gott, Von Händlern wird die Künst bedroht, Es war mal eine Wanze, Die Künstler sind die Schöpfer, Die Händler und die Macher*, and *O Schöpferschwarm, o Händlerkreis*; *Sechs Lieder*, op. 67 (1918): 1, *Lieder der Ophelia* (Shakespeare; K. Simrock, tr.): *Wie erkenn ich mein Treulieb vor andern nun?, Guten Morgen, 's ist Sankt Valentinstag*, and *Sie trugen ihn auf der Bahre bloss*; 2, *Aus den Buchern des Unmuts der Rendsch Nameh* (Goethe): *Wer wird von der Welt verlangen, Hab' ich euch denn je geraten*, and *Wanderers Gemütsruhe*; *Sechs Lieder*, op. 68 (Brentano; 1918): *An die Nacht, Ich wollt' ein Sträusslein binden, Säusle, liebe Myrthe, Als mir dein Lied erklang*, and *Amor* (all 5 orchestrated,

1940); *Lied der Frauen* (orchestrated, 1933); *Fünf kleine Lieder,* op. 69 (1918): *Der Stern* (A. von Arnim), *Der Pokal* (Arnim), *Einerlei* (Arnim), *Waldesfahrt* (Heine), and *Schlechtes Wetter* (Heine); *Sinnspruch* (Goethe; 1919); *Drei Hymnen von Friedrich Hölderlin,* op. 71, for Voice and Orch. (1921): *Hymne an die Liebe, Rückkehr in der Heimat,* and *Die Liebe; Durch allen Schall und Klang* (Goethe; 1925); *Gesänge des Orients,* op. 77 (Bethge, tr.; 1928): *Ihre Augen* (Hafiz), *Schwung* (Hafiz), *Liebesgeschenke* (*Die chinesische Flöte*), *Die Allmächtige* (Hafiz), *Huldigung* (Hafiz); and *Wie etwas sei leicht* (Goethe; 1930); *Vom künftigen Alter,* op. 87 (Rückert; 1929); *Erschaffen und Beleben* (Goethe; 1922); *Und dann nicht mehr* (Rückert; 1929); *Im sonnenschein* (Rückert; 1935); *Zugemessne Rhythmen* (Goethe; 1935); *Das Bachlein,* op. 88 (1933; orchestrated, 1935); *Blick vom oberen Belvedere* (J. Weinheber; 1942); *Sankt Michael* (Weinheber; 1942); *Xenion* (Goethe; 1942); *Vier letzte Lieder* for Voice and Orch. (1948): *Frühling* (Hesse), *September* (Hesse), *Beim Schlafengehen* (Hesse), and *Im Abendrot* (Eichendorff) (London, May 22, 1950, Kirsten Flagstad soloist, Wilhelm Furtwängler conducting); *Malven* (B. Knobel; 1948; N.Y., Jan. 10, 1985). **SPEAKER AND PIANO:** *Enoch Arden,* after Tennyson, op. 38 (Munich, March 24, 1897); *Das Schloss am Meer,* after Uhland (Berlin, March 23, 1899).

ARRANGEMENTS, ETC.: Strauss prepared a cadenza for Mozart's C-minor Piano Concerto, K.491 (1885); arranged Gluck's *Iphigénie en Tauride* (1899; Hoftheater, Weimar, June 9, 1900); made a new version of Beethoven's *Die Ruinen von Athen* with Hugo von Hofmannsthal (Staatsoper, Vienna, Sept. 20, 1924, composer conducting); made a new version of Mozart's *Idomeneo* with Lothar Wallerstein (1930; Staatsoper, Vienna, April 16, 1931, composer conducting).

BIBL.: WORKS, SOURCE MATERIAL: There is no complete ed. of Strauss's works. The standard thematic catalog was prepared by E.H. Mueller von Asow, *R. S.: Thematisches Verzeichnis* (3 vols., Vienna, 1954–74). Many of his writings may be found in W. Schuh, ed., *R. S.: Betrachtungen und Erinnerungen* (Zürich, 1949; Eng. tr., N.Y., 1953; 2nd Ger. ed., rev., 1957). The major bibliographical source is *R.-S.-Bibliographie* (2 vols., Vienna; Vol. I, 1882–1944, ed. by O. Ortner, 1964; Vol. II, 1944–1964, ed. by G. Brosche, 1973). Other sources include the following: R. Specht, *R. S.: Vollständiges Verzeichnis der im Druck erschienen Werke* (Vienna, 1910); J. Kapp, *R. S. und die Berliner Oper* (Berlin, 1934–39); E. Wachten, *R. S., geboren 1864: Sein Leben in Bildern* (Leipzig, 1940); R. Tenschert, *Anekdoten um R. S.* (Vienna, 1945); idem, *R. S. und Wien: Eine Wahlverwandtschaft* (Vienna, 1949); E. Roth, ed., *R. S.: Bühnenwerk* (text in Ger., Eng., and French; London, 1954); W. Schuh, *Das Bühnenwerke von R. S. in den unter Mitwirkung des Komponisten geschaffenen letzten Münchner Inszenierungen* (Zürich, 1954); F. Trenner, *R. S.: Dokumente seines Lebens und Schaffens* (Munich, 1954); R. Petzoldt, *R. S.: Sein Leben in Bildern* (Leipzig, 1962); F. Dostal, ed., *Karl Böhm: Begegnung mit R. S.* (Vienna, 1964); F. Grasberger and F. Hadamowsky, eds., *R.-S.-Ausstellung zum 100. Geburtstag* (Vienna, 1964); F. Hadamowsky, *R. S. und Salzburg* (Salzburg, 1964); W. Schuh, *Ein paar Erinnerungen an R. S.* (Zürich, 1964); W. Schuh and E. Roth, eds., *R. S.: Complete Catalogue* (London, 1964); W. Thomas, *R. S. und seine Zeitgenössen* (Munich, 1964); F. Grasberger, *R. S.: Höbe Kunst, erfülltes Leben* (Vienna, 1965); W. Deppisch, *R. S. in Selbstzeugnissen und Bilddokumenten* (Reinbek, 1968); F. Grasberger, *R. S. und die Wiener Oper* (Vienna, 1969); A. Jefferson, *R. S.* (London, 1975); F. Trenner, *Die Skizzenbücher von R. S. aus dem R.-S.-Archiv in Garmisch* (Tutzing, 1977); idem, *R. S. Werkverzeichnis* (Vienna, 1985).

CORRESPONDENCE: F. Strauss, ed., *R. S.: Briefwechsel mit Hugo von Hofmannsthal* (Berlin, 1925; Eng. tr., N.Y., 1927); *R. S. et Romain Rolland: Correspondance, fragments de journal* (Paris, 1951; Eng. tr., 1968); F. von Schuch, *R. S., Ernst von Schuch und Dresdens Oper* (Leipzig, 1952; 2nd ed., 1953); W. Schuh, ed., *R. S. und Hugo von Hofmannsthal: Briefwechsel: Gesamtausgabe* (Zürich, 1952; 2nd ed., rev., 1955; Eng. tr., 1961, as *A Working Friendship: The Correspondence between R. S. and Hugo von Hofmannsthal*); idem, ed., *R. S.: Briefe an die Eltern 1882–1906* (Zürich, 1954); W. Schuh and F. Trenner, eds., "Hans von Bülow/R. S.: Briefwechsel," *R. S. Jahrbuch 1954* (Eng. tr. publ. separately in London, 1955); R. Tenschert, ed., *R. S. und Joseph Gregor: Briefwechsel 1934–1949* (Salzburg, 1955); W. Schuh, ed., *R. S., Stefan Zweig: Briefwechsel* (Frankfurt am Main, 1957; Eng. tr., 1977, as *A Confidential Matter: The Letters of R. S. and Stefan Zweig 1931–1935*); D. Kämper, ed., *R. S. und Franz Wüllner im Briefwechsel* (Cologne, 1963); G. Kende and W. Schuh, eds., *R. S., Clemens Krauss: Briefwechsel* (Munich, 1963; 2nd ed., 1964); A. Ott, ed., *R. S. und Ludwig Thuille: Briefe der Freundschaft 1877–1907* (Munich, 1969); W. Schuh, ed., *R. S.: Briefwechsel mit Willi Schuh* (Zürich, 1969).

BIOGRAPHICAL: A. Seidl and W. Klatte, *R. S.: Eine Charakterskizze* (Prague, 1896); G. Brecher, *R. S.: Eine monographische Skizze* (Leipzig, 1900); E. Urban, *R. S.* (Berlin, 1901); R. Batka, *R. S.* (Charlottenburg, 1908); E. Newman, *R. S.* (London, 1908); M. Steinitzer, *R. S.* (Berlin, 1911; final ed., enl., 1927); H. Finck, *R. S.: The Man and His Works* (Boston, 1917); R. Specht, *R. S. und sein Werk* (2 vols., Leipzig, 1921); R. Muschler, *R. S.* (Hildesheim, 1924); S. Kallenberg, *R. S.: Leben und Werk* (Leipzig, 1926); J. Cooke, *R. S.: A Short Biography* (Philadelphia, 1929); W. Hutschenruyter, *R. S.* (The Hague, 1929); E. Gehring, ed., *R. S. und seine Vaterstadt: Zum 70. Geburtstag am 11. Juni 1934* (Munich, 1934); F. Gysi, *R. S.* (Potsdam, 1934); W. Brandl, *R. S.: Leben und Werk* (Wiesbaden, 1949); E. Bücken, *R. S.* (Kevelaer, 1949); K. Pfister, *R. S.: Weg, Gestalt, Denkmal* (Vienna, 1949); C. Rostand, *R. S.* (Paris, 1949; 2nd ed., 1965); O. Erhardt, *R. S.: Leben, Wirken, Schaffen* (Olten, 1953); E. Krause, *R. S.: Gestalt und Werk* (Leipzig, 1955; 3rd ed., rev., 1963; Eng. tr., 1964); I. Fabian, *R. S.* (Budapest, 1962); H. Kralik, *R. S.: Weltbürger der Musik* (Vienna, 1963); W. Panofsky, *R. S.: Partitur eines Lebens* (Munich, 1965); G. Marek, *R. S.: The Life of a Non-Hero* (N.Y., 1967); A. Jefferson, *The Life of R. S.* (Newton Abbot, 1973); M. Kennedy, *R. S.* (London, 1976; 2nd ed., rev., 1983; rev. and aug., 1995); W. Schuh, *R. S.: Jugend und Meisterjahre: Lebenschronik 1864–98* (Zürich, 1976; Eng. tr. as *R. S.: A Chronicle of the Early Years 1864–98,* Cambridge, 1982); K. Wilhelm, *R. S. persönlich: Eine Bildbiographie* (Munich, 1984).

CRITICAL, ANALYTICAL: G. Jourissenne, *R. S.: Essai critique et biographique* (Brussels, 1899); E. Urban, *S. contra Wagner* (Berlin, 1902); O. Bie, *Die moderne Musik und R. S.* (Berlin, 1906); L. Gilman, *S.' Salome: A Guide to the Opera* (N.Y., 1906); J. Manifarges, *R. S. als Dirigent* (Amsterdam, 1907); E. Schmitz, *R. S. als Musikdramatiker: Eine aesthetisch-kritische Studie* (Munich, 1907); E. von Ziegler, *R. S. und seine dramatischen Dichtungen* (Munich, 1907); P. Bekker, *Das Musikdrama der Gegenwart* (Stuttgart, 1909); E. Fischer-Plasser, *Einführung in die Musik von R. S. und Elektra* (Leipzig, 1909); G. Gräner, *R. S.: Musikdramen* (Berlin, 1909); F. Santoliquido, *Il dopo-Wagner: Claude Debussy e R. S.* (Rome, 1909); O. Hübner, *R. S. und das Musikdrama: Betrachtungen über den Wert oder Unwert gewisser Opernmusiken* (Leipzig, 1910); E. Hutcheson, *Elektra by R. S.: A Guide to the Opera with Musical Examples from the Score* (N.Y., 1910); M. Steinitzer, *S.iana und Anderes* (Stuttgart, 1910); H. Daffner, *Salome: Ihre Gestalt in Geschichte und Künst* (Munich, 1912); A. Seidl, *S.iana: Aufsätze zur R.S.—Frage auf drei Jahrzehnten* (Regensburg, 1913); F. Dubitzky, "R. S.' Kammermusik," *Die Musik,* XIII (1913–14); E. Thilo, "R. S. als chorkomponist," ibid.; M. Steinitzer, *R. S. in seiner Zeit, mit einem Abdruck der auf der S.woche zu Stuttgart im. Kgl. Hoftheater gehaltenen Rede und einem Bildnis* (Leipzig, 1914; 2nd ed., 1922); O. Bie, *Die neuere Musik bis R. S.* (Leipzig, 1916); L. Gilman, "R. S. and His Alpine Symphony," *North American Review,* XXIV (1919); H. Scherchen, "Tonalitätsprinzipund die Alpen-Symphonie von R. S.," *Melos,* 1 (1920); H. von Waltershausen, *R. S.: Ein Versuch* (Munich, 1921); R. Rosenzweig, *Zur Entwicklungsgeschichte des S.'schen Musikdramas* (diss., Univ. of Vienna, 1923); H. Windt, "R. S. und die Atonalität," *Die Musik,* XVI (1923–24); W. Schrenk, *R. S. und die neue Musik* (Berlin, 1924); K. Westphal, "Das musikdramatische Prinzip bei R. S.," *Die Musik,* XIX (1926–27); E. Blom, *The Rose*

Cavalier (London, 1930); T. Armstrong, *S.' Tone Poems* (London, 1931); G. Röttger, *Die Harmonik in R. S.' Der Rosenkavalier: Ein Beitrag zur Entwicklung der romantische Harmonik nach Richard Wagner* (diss., Univ. of Munich, 1931); M. Steinitzer, "R. S.' Werke für Klavier," *Die Musik*, XXIV (1931–32); E. Wachten, *Das psychotechnische Formproblem in den Sinfonischen Dichtungen von R.S. (mit besonderer Berücksichtigung seiner Bühnenwerk)* diss., Univ. of Berlin, 1932; publ. in an abr. ed., Berlin, 1933); K.-J. Krüger, *Hugo von Hofmannsthal und R. S.: Versuch einer Deutung des künstlerisschen Weges Hugo von Hofmannsthals, mit einem Anhang; erstmalige Veröffentlichung der bischer ungedruckten einzigen Vertonung eines Hofmannsthalschen Gedichtes durch R. S.* (Berlin, 1935); H. Röttger, *Das Formproblem bei R. S. gezeigt an der Oper Die Frau ohne Schatten, mit Einschluss von Guntram und Intermezzo* (diss., Univ. of Munich, 1935; publ. in an abr. ed., Berlin, 1937); J. Gregor, *R. S.: Der Meister der Oper* (Munich, 1939; 2nd ed., 1942); G. Becker, *Das Problem der Oper an Hand von R. S.' Capriccio* (diss., Univ. of Jena, 1944); R. Tenschert, *Dreimal sieben Variationen über das Thema R. S.* (Vienna, 1944; 2nd ed., 1945); O. Gatscha, *Librettist und Komponist: Dargestellt an den Opern R. S.'* (diss., Univ. of Vienna, 1947); A. Pryce-Jones, *R. S.: Der Rosenkavalier* (London, 1947); W. Schuh, *Über Opern von R. S.* (Zürich, 1947); F. Trenner, *Die Zusammenarbeit von Hugo von Hofmannsthal und R. S.* (diss., Univ. of Munich, 1949); D. Lindner, *R. S./Joseph Gregor: Die Liebe der Danae: Herkunft, Inhalt und Gestaltung eines Opernwerkes* (Vienna, 1952); R. Schopenhauer, *Die antiken Frauengestalten bei R. S.* (diss., Univ. of Vienna, 1952); G. Hausswald, *R. S.: Ein Beitrag zur Dresdener Operngeschichte seit 1945* (Dresden, 1953); W. Wendhausen, *Das stilistische Verhältnis von Dichtung und Musik in der Entwicklung der musikdramatischen Werke R. S.'* (diss., Univ. of Hamburg, 1954); G. Kende, *R. S. und Clemens Krauss: Eine Künstlerfreundschaft und ihre Zusammenarbeit an Capriccio (op. 85): Konversationsstück für Musik* (Munich, 1960); N. Del Mar, *R. S.: A Critical Commentary on His Life and Works* (3 vols., London, 1962, 1969, and 1972; reprint with corrections, 1978); A. Jefferson, *The Operas of R. S. in Britain, 1910–1963* (London, 1963); A. Natan, *R. S.: Die Opern* (Basel, 1963); A. Berger, *R. S. als geistige Macht: Versuch eines philosophischen Verständnisses* (Gisch, 1964); L. Lehmann, *Five Operas and R. S.* (N.Y., 1964; publ. in London, 1964, as *Singing with R. S.*); W. Mann, *R. S.: A Critical Study of the Operas* (London, 1964); K. Pörnbacher, *Hugo von Hofmannsthal/R. S.: Der Rosenkavalier* (Munich, 1964); W. Schuh, *Hugo von Hofmannsthal und R. S.: Legende und Wirklichkeit* (Munich, 1964); A. Goléa, *R. S.* (Paris, 1965); R. Gerlach, *Tonalität und tonale Konfiguration im Oeuvre von R. S.: Analysen und Interpretationen als Beiträge zum Verständnis von tonalen Problemen und Formen in sinfonischen Werken und in der "Einleitung" und ersten Szene des Rosenkavalier* (diss., Univ. of Zürich, 1966; publ. as *Don Juan und Rosenkavalier*, Bern, 1966); R. Schäfer, *Hugo von Hofmannsthals Arabella* (Bern, 1967); W. Gruhn, *Die Instrumentation in den Orchesterwerken von R. S.* (diss., Univ. of Mainz, 1968); W. Schuh, *Der Rosenkavalier: 4 Studien* (Olten, 1968); J. Knaus, *Hugo von Hofmannsthal und sein Weg zur Oper Die Frau ohne Schatten* (Berlin, 1971); W. Schuh, ed., *Hugo von Hofmannsthal, R. S.: Der Rosenkavalier: Fassungen, Filmszenarium, Briefe* (Frankfurt am Main, 1971); A. Abert, *R. S.: Die Opern: Einführung und Analyse* (Hannover, 1972); A. Jefferson, *The Lieder of R. S.* (London, 1972); W. Colson, *Four Last Songs by R. S.* (diss., Univ. of Ill., 1974); D. Daviau and G. Buelow, *The "Ariadne auf Naxos" of Hugo von Hofmannsthal and R. S.* (Chapel Hill, 1975); B. Peterson, *Ton und Wort: The Lieder of R. S.* (Ann Arbor, 1979); K. Forsyth, *Ariadne auf Naxos by Hugo von Hofmannsthal and R. S.: Its Genesis and Meaning* (Oxford, 1982); R. Hartmann, *R. S.: The Staging of His Operas and Ballets* (Oxford, 1982); R. Schlötter, *Musik und Theater im "Rosenkavalier" vom R. S.* (Vienna, 1985); H. Wajemann, *Die Chorkompositionen von R. S.* (Tutzing, 1986); G. Splitt, *R. S. 1933–1935: Ästhetik und Musikpolitik zu Beginn der nationalsozialistischen Herrschaft* (Pfaffenweiler, 1987); C. Osborne, *The Complete Operas of R. S.* (London, 1988); A. Garlington, Jr., "R. S.'s *Vier letzte Lieder*: The Ultimate opus ultimum," *Musical Quarterly*, 73/1 (1989); E.-M. Axt, *Musikalische Form als Dramaturgie: Prinzipien eines Spätstils in der Oper "Friedenstag" von R. S. und Joseph Gregor* (Munich, 1989); B. Gilliam, *R. S.'s Elektra* (Oxford, 1991); D. Greene, *Listening to S. Operas: The Audience's Multiple Standpoints* (N.Y., 1991); W. Krebs, *Der Wille zum Rausch: Aspekte der musikalischen Dramaturgie von R. S.' "Salome"* (Munich, 1991); B. Gilliam, ed., *R. S. and His World* (Princeton, 1992); idem, ed., *R. S.: New Perspectives on the Composer and His Work* (Durham, N.C., 1992); B. Meier, *Geschichtliche Signaturen der Musik bei Mahler, S. und Schönberg* (Hamburg, 1992); A. Unger, *Welt, Leben und Kunst als Themen der "Zarathustra-Kompositionen" von R. S. und Gustav Mahler* (Frankfurt am Main, 1992); J. Williamson, *S.: Also sprach Zarathustra* (Cambridge, 1993).

Stravinsky, Igor (Feodorovich), great Russian-born French, later American composer, one of the supreme masters of 20th-century music, whose works exercised the most profound influence on the evolution of music through the emancipation of rhythm, melody, and harmony, son of **Feodor (Ignatievich)** and father of **(Sviatoslav) Soulima Stravinsky**; b. Oranienbaum, near St. Petersburg, June 17, 1882; d. N.Y., April 6, 1971. He was brought up in an artistic atmosphere; he often went to opera rehearsals when his father sang, and acquired an early love for the musical theater. He took piano lessons with Alexandra Snetkova, and later with Leokadia Kashperova, who was a pupil of Anton Rubinstein; but it was not until much later that he began to study theory, first with Akimenko and then with Kalafati (1900–1903). His progress in composition was remarkably slow; he never entered a music school or a cons., and never earned an academic degree in music. In 1901 he enrolled in the faculty of jurisprudence at Univ. of St. Petersburg, and took courses there for 8 semesters, without graduating; a fellow student was Vladimir Rimsky-Korsakov, a son of the composer. In the summer of 1902 Stravinsky traveled in Germany, where he met another son of Rimsky-Korsakov, Andrei, who was a student at the Univ. of Heidelberg; Stravinsky became his friend. He was introduced to Rimsky-Korsakov, and became a regular guest at the latter's periodic gatherings in St. Petersburg. In 1903–04 he wrote a piano sonata for the Russian pianist Nicolai Richter, who performed it at Rimsky-Korsakov's home. In 1905 he began taking regular lessons in orchestration with Rimsky-Korsakov, who taught him free of charge; under his tutelage, Stravinsky composed a Sym. in E-flat major; the 2nd and 3rd movements from it were performed on April 27, 1907, by the Court Orch. in St. Petersburg, and a complete performance of it was given by the same orch. on Feb. 4, 1908. The work, dedicated to Rimsky-Korsakov, had some singularities and angularities that showed a deficiency of technique; there was little in this work that presaged Stravinsky's ultimate development as a master of form and orchestration. At the same concert, his *Le Faune et la bergère* for Voice and Orch. had its first performance; this score revealed a certain influence of French Impressionism. To celebrate the marriage of Rimsky-Korsakov's daughter Nadezhda to the composer Maximilian Steinberg on June 17, 1908, Stravinsky wrote an orch. fantasy entitled *Fireworks*. Rimsky-Korsakov died a few days after the wedding; Stravinsky deeply mourned his beloved teacher and wrote a funeral song for Wind Instruments in his memory; it was first performed in St. Petersburg on Jan. 30, 1909. There followed a *Scherzo fantastique* for Orch., inspired by Maeterlinck's book *La Vie des abeilles*. As revealed in his correspondence with Rimsky-Korsakov, Stravinsky had at first planned a literal program of composition, illustrating events in the life of a beehive by a series of descriptive sections; some years later, however, he gratuitously denied all connection of the work with Maeterlinck's book.

A signal change in Stravinsky's fortunes came when the famous impresario Diaghilev commissioned him to write a work for the Paris season of his company, the Ballets Russes. The result was the production of his first ballet masterpiece, *The Firebird*, staged by Diaghilev in Paris on June 25, 1910. Here he created music of extraordinary brilliance, steeped in the colors of Russian fairy tales. There are numerous striking effects in the score, such as a glissando of harmonics in the string instruments; the rhythmic drive is exhilarating, and the use of asymmetrical time signatures is extremely effective; the harmonies are opulent; the orchestration is coruscating. He drew 2 orch. suites from the work; in 1919 he reorchestrated the music to conform to his new beliefs in musical economy; in effect he plucked the luminous feathers off the magical firebird, but the original scoring remained a favorite with conductors and orchs. Stravinsky's association with Diaghilev demanded his presence in Paris, which he made his home beginning in 1911, with frequent travels to Switzerland. His 2nd ballet for Diaghilev was *Pétrouchka*, premiered in Paris on June 13, 1911, with triumphant success. Not only was the ballet remarkably effective on the stage, but the score itself, arranged in 2 orch. suites, was so new and original that it marked a turning point in 20th-century music; the spasmodically explosive rhythms, the novel instrumental sonorities, with the use of the piano as an integral part of the orch., the bold harmonic innovations in employing 2 different keys simultaneously (C major and F-sharp major, the "Pétrouchka Chord") became a potent influence on modern European composers. Debussy voiced his enchantment with the score, and young Stravinsky, still in his 20s, became a Paris celebrity. Two years later, he brought out a work of even greater revolutionary import, the ballet *Le Sacre du printemps* (Rite of Spring; Russian title, *Vesna sviashchennaya*, literally Spring the Sacred); its subtitle was "Scenes of Pagan Russia." It was premiered by Diaghilev with his Ballets Russes in Paris on May 29, 1913, with the choreography by Nijinsky. The score marked a departure from all conventions of musical composition; while in Petrouchka the harmonies, though innovative and dissonant, could still be placed in the context of modern music, the score of *Le Sacre du printemps* contained such corrosive dissonances as scales played at the intervals of major sevenths and superpositions of minor upon major triads with the common tonic, chords treated as unified blocks of sound, and rapid metrical changes that seemingly defied performance. The score still stands as one of the most daring creations of the modern musical mind; its impact was tremendous; to some of the audience at its first performance in Paris, Stravinsky's "barbaric" music was beyond endurance; the Paris critics exercised their verbal ingenuity in indignant vituperation; one of them proposed that *Le Sacre du printemps* should be more appropriately described as *Le Massacre du printemps*. On May 26, 1914, Diaghilev premiered Stravinsky's lyric fairy tale *Le Rossignol*, after Hans Christian Andersen. It too abounded in corrosive discords, but here it could be explained as "Chinese" music illustrative of the exotic subject. From 1914 to 1918 he worked on his ballet *Les Noces* (Russian title, *Svadebka*; literally, Little Wedding), evoking Russian peasant folk modalities; it was scored for an unusual ensemble of chorus, soloists, 4 pianos, and 17 percussion instruments.

The devastation of World War I led Stravinsky to conclude that the era of grandiose Romantic music had become obsolete, and that a new spirit of musical economy was imperative in an impoverished world. As an illustration of such economy, he wrote the musical stage play *L'Histoire du soldat*, scored for only 7 players, with a narrator. About the same time, he wrote a work for 11 instruments entitled *Ragtime*, inspired by the new American dance music. He continued his association with Diaghilev's Ballets Russes in writing the ballet *Pulcinella*, based on themes by Pergolesi and other 18th-century Italian composers. He also wrote for Diaghilev 2 short operas, *Renard*, to a Russian fairy tale (Paris, May 18, 1922), and *Mavra*, after Pushkin (Paris, June 3, 1922). These 2 works were the last in which he used Russian subjects, with the sole exception of an orch. *Scherzo à la russe*, written in 1944. Stravinsky had now entered the period usually designated as neo-Classical. The most significant works of this stage of his development were his Octet for Wind Instruments and the Piano Concerto commissioned by Koussevitzky. In these works, he abandoned the luxuriant instrumentation of his ballets and their aggressively dissonant harmonies; instead, he used pandiatonic structures, firmly tonal but starkly dissonant in their superposition of tonalities within the same principal key. His reversion to old forms, however, was not an act of ascetic renunciation but, rather, a grand experiment in reviving Baroque practices, which had fallen into desuetude. The Piano Concerto provided him with an opportunity to appear as soloist; Stravinsky was never a virtuoso pianist, but he was able to acquit himself satisfactorily in such works as the Piano Concerto; he played it with Koussevitzky in Paris on May 22, 1924, and during his first American tour with the Boston Sym. Orch., also under Koussevitzky, on Jan. 23, 1925. The Elizabeth Sprague Coolidge Foundation commissioned him to write a pantomime for string orch.; the result was *Apollon Musagète*, given at the Library of Congress in Washington, D.C., on April 27, 1928. This score, serene and emotionally restrained, evokes the manner of Lully's court ballets. He continued to explore the resources of neo-Baroque writing in his *Capriccio* for Piano and Orch., which he performed as soloist, with Ansermet conducting, in Paris, on Dec. 6, 1929; this score is impressed by a spirit of hedonistic entertainment, harking back to the *style galant* of the 18th century; yet it is unmistakably modern in its polyrhythmic collisions of pandiatonic harmonies. Stravinsky's growing disillusionment with the external brilliance of modern music led him to seek eternal verities of music in ancient modalities. His well-nigh monastic renunciation of the grandiose edifice of glorious sound to which he himself had so abundantly contributed found expression in his opera-oratorio *Oedipus Rex*; in order to emphasize its detachment from temporal aspects, he commissioned a Latin text for the work, even though the subject was derived from a Greek play; its music is deliberately hollow and its dramatic points are emphasized by ominous repetitive passages. Yet this very austerity of idiom makes *Oedipus Rex* a profoundly moving play. It had its first performance in Paris on May 30, 1927; its stage premiere took place in Vienna on Feb. 23, 1928. A turn to religious writing found its utterance in Stravinsky's *Symphony of Psalms*, written for the 50th anniversary of the Boston Sym. Orch. and dedicated "to the glory of God." The work is scored for chorus and orch., omitting the violins and violas, thus emphasizing the lower instrumental registers and creating an austere sonority suitable to its solemn subject. Owing to a delay of the Boston performance, the world premiere of the *Symphony of Psalms* took place in Brussels on Dec. 13, 1930. In 1931 he wrote a Violin Concerto commissioned by the violinist Samuel Dushkin, and performed by him in Berlin on Oct. 23, 1931. On a commission from the ballerina Ida Rubinstein, he composed the ballet *Perséphone*; here again he exercised his mastery of simplicity in formal design, melodic patterns, and contrapuntal structure. For his American tour he wrote *Jeu de cartes*, a "ballet in 3 deals" to his own scenario depicting an imaginary game of poker (of which he was a devotee). He conducted its first performance at the Metropolitan Opera in N.Y. on April 27, 1937. His concerto for 16 instruments entitled *Dumbarton Oaks*, named after the Washington, D.C., estate of Mr. and Mrs. Robert Woods Bliss, who commissioned the work, was first performed in Washington, on May 8, 1938; in Europe it was played under the noncommittal title Concerto in E-flat; its style is hermetically neo-Baroque. It is germane to note that in his neo-Classical works Stravinsky began to indicate the key in the title, e.g., *Serenade* in A for Piano (1925), Concerto in D for Violin and Orch. (1931), Concerto in E-flat (*Dumbarton Oaks*, 1938), Sym. in C (1938), and Concerto in D for String Orch. (1946).

With World War II engulfing Europe, Stravinsky decided to seek permanent residence in America. He had acquired French citizenship on June 10, 1934; in 1939 he applied for American citizenship; he became a naturalized American citizen on Dec. 28, 1945. To celebrate this event, he made an arrangement of the *Star-Spangled Banner*, which contained a curious modulation into the subdominant in the coda. He conducted it with the Boston Sym. Orch. on Jan. 14, 1944, but because of legal injunctions existing in the state of Massachusetts against intentional alteration, or any mutilation, of the national anthem, he was advised not to conduct his version at the 2nd pair of concerts, and the standard version was substituted. In 1939–40 Stravinsky was named Charles Eliot Norton lecturer at Harvard Univ.; about the same time, he accepted several private students, a pedagogical role he had never exercised before. His American years form a curious panoply of subjects and manners of composition. He accepted a commission from the Ringling Bros. to write a *Circus Polka* "for a young elephant." In 1946 he wrote *Ebony Concerto* for a swing band. In 1951 he completed his opera *The Rake's Progress*, inspired by Hogarth's famous series of engravings, to a libretto by W.H. Auden and C. Kallman. He conducted its premiere in Venice on Sept. 11, 1951, as part of the International Festival of Contemporary Music. The opera is a striking example of Stravinsky's protean capacity for adopting different styles and idioms of composition to serve his artistic purposes; *The Rake's Progress* is an ingenious conglomeration of disparate elements, ranging from 18th-century British ballads to cosmopolitan burlesque. But whatever transmutations his music underwent during his long and productive career, he remained a man of the theater at heart. In America he became associated with the brilliant Russian choreographer Balanchine, who produced a number of ballets to Stravinsky's music, among them his *Apollon Musagète*, Violin Concerto, Sym. in 3 movements, *Scherzo à la russe*, *Pulcinella*, and *Agon*. It was in his score of *Agon* that he essayed for the first time to adopt the method of composition with 12 tones as promulgated by Schoenberg; *Agon* (the word means "competition" in Greek) bears the subtitle "ballet for 12 tones," perhaps in allusion to the dodecaphonic technique used in the score. Yet the 12-tone method had been the very antithesis of his previous tenets. In fact, an irreconcilable polarity existed between Stravinsky and Schoenberg even in personal relations. Although both resided in Los Angeles for several years, they never met socially; Schoenberg once wrote a canon in which he ridiculed Stravinsky as Herr Modernsky, who put on a wig to look like "Papa Bach." After Schoenberg's death, Stravinsky became interested in examining the essence of the method of composition with 12 tones, which was introduced to him by his faithful musical factotum Robert Craft; Stravinsky adopted dodecaphonic writing in its aspect of canonic counterpoint as developed by Webern. In this manner he wrote his *Canticum sacrum ad honorem Sancti Marci nominis*, which he conducted at San Marco in Venice on Sept. 13, 1956. Other works of the period were also written in a modified 12-tone technique, among them *The Flood*, for Narrator, Mime, Singers, and Dancers, presented in a CBS-TV broadcast in N.Y. on June 14, 1962; its first stage performance was given in Hamburg on April 30, 1963.

Stravinsky was married twice; his 1st wife, Catherine Nosenko, whom he married on Jan. 24, 1906, and who bore him 3 children, died in 1939; on March 9, 1940, Stravinsky married his longtime mistress, Vera, who was formerly married to the Russian painter Serge Sudeikin. She was born Vera de Bosset in St. Petersburg, on Dec. 25, 1888, and died in N.Y. on Sept. 17, 1982, at the age of 93. An ugly litigation for the rights to the Stravinsky estate continued for several years between his children and their stepmother; after Vera Stravinsky's death, it was finally settled in a compromise, according to which 2/9 of the estate went to each of his 3 children and a grandchild and 1/9 to Robert Craft. The value of the Stravinsky legacy was spectacularly demonstrated on Nov. 11, 1982, when his working draft of *Le Sacre du printemps* was sold at an auction in London for the fantastic sum of $548,000. The purchaser was Paul Sacher, the Swiss conductor and philanthropist. Even more fantastic was the subsequent sale of the entire Stravinsky archive, consisting of 116 boxes of personal letters and 225 drawers containing MSS, some of them unpubl. Enormous bids were made for it by the N.Y. Public Library and the Morgan Library, but they were all outbid by Sacher, who offered the overwhelming purse of $5,250,000, which removed all competition. The materials were to be assembled in a specially constructed 7-story Sacher Foundation building in Basel, to be eventually opened to scholars for study.

In tribute to Stravinsky as a naturalized American citizen, the U.S. Postal Service issued a 2-cent stamp bearing his image to mark his centennial in 1982, an honor theretofore never granted to a foreign-born composer (the possible exception being Victor Herbert, but his entire career was made in America).

Few composers escaped the powerful impact of Stravinsky's music; ironically, it was his own country that had rejected him, partly because of the opposition of Soviet ideologues to modern music in general, and partly because of Stravinsky's open criticism of Soviet ways in art. But in 1962 he returned to Russia for a visit, and was welcomed as a prodigal son; as if by magic, his works began to appear on Russian concert programs, and Soviet music critics issued a number of laudatory studies of his works. Yet it is Stravinsky's early masterpieces, set in an attractive colorful style, that continue to enjoy favor with audiences and performers, while his more abstract and recursive scores are appreciated mainly by specialists.

WORKS: DRAMATIC: *L'Oiseau de feu* (The Firebird), ballet (Paris Opéra, June 25, 1910; 3 suite versions: 1911, 1919, and 1945; 2 sections arranged for Violin and Piano, 1926); *Pétrouchka*, ballet (Paris, June 13, 1911, Monteux conducting; rev. 1946; excerpts officially designated as a "suite" in 1946); *Le Sacre du printemps*, ballet, "scenes of pagan Russia" (1911–13; Paris, May 29, 1913, Monteux conducting; 1st concert perf., Moscow, Feb. 18, 1914, Serge Koussevitzky conducting; 1st Paris concert perf., April 5, 1914, Monteux conducting); *Le Rossignol*, "lyric tale" in 3 acts, after Hans Christian Andersen (1908–14; Paris Opéra, May 26, 1914, Monteux conducting; in 1917 the 2nd and 3rd acts were scored as a ballet, *Le Chant du rossignol*; Paris Opéra, Feb. 2, 1920; also, in 1917, fragments from the 2nd and 3rd acts were used for a symphonic poem under the same title); *Renard*, burlesque chamber opera (1915–16; Paris, May 18, 1922); *L'Histoire du soldat*, ballet with Narrator and 7 Instrumentalists (Lausanne, Sept. 28, 1918; concert suite with original instrumentation, London, July 20, 1920, Ansermet conducting; also *Petite suite* for Violin, Clarinet, and Piano extracted from the score, 1919); *Pulcinella*, ballet "after Pergolesi" with solos, trios, and a duet for Soprano, Tenor, and Bass (Paris Opéra, May 15, 1920; an orch. suite was extracted from it in 1922, and 1st perf. in Boston, Dec. 22, 1922, rev. 1947; 2 chamber pieces, Suite italienne); *Mavra*, comic opera, after Pushkin (Paris Opéra, June 3, 1922); *Les Noces* (The Wedding), ballet-cantata, subtitled "choreographic Russian scenes," revision for Soloists, Chorus, 4 Pianos, and 17 Percussion Instruments (1921–23; Paris, June 13, 1923; orig. scored with Full Orch., 1914–17); *Oedipus Rex*, opera-oratorio, after Sophocles (concert perf., Paris, May 30, 1927; 1st stage perf., Vienna, Feb. 23, 1928; rev. 1948); *Apollon Musagète*, classic ballet for String Orch. (Washington, D.C., April 27, 1928; rev. 1947); *Le Baiser de la fée*, ballet on themes of Tchaikovsky (Paris Opéra, Nov. 27, 1928; in 1934 several sections were collected for an independent symphonic piece called *Divertimento*; entire ballet rev. 1950); *Perséphone*, melodrama in 3 parts for Female Narrator, Tenor, Chorus, and Orch., after André Gide (1933; Paris Opéra, April 30, 1934; rev. 1949); *Jeu de cartes*, "ballet in 3 deals" (1935–37; N.Y., April 27, 1937); *Orpheus*, ballet (1946–47; N.Y., April 28, 1948); *The Rake's Progress*, opera after Hogarth's engravings, with libretto by W.H. Auden and C. Kallman (1948–51; Venice, Sept. 11, 1951, composer conducting); *Agon*, ballet for 12 Dancers (1954–57; Los Angeles, June 17, 1957); *Noah and the Flood*, also called *The Flood*, biblical spectacle narrated, mimed, sung, and danced (CBS-TV, N.Y., June 14, 1962; 1st stage perf., Hamburg, April 30, 1963).

ORCH.: Sym. in E-flat major, op. 1 (1905–07; 1st partial perf., 2nd and 3rd movements only, St. Petersburg, April 27, 1907; 1st complete perf., St. Petersburg, Feb. 4, 1908; rev. version, Montreux, Switzerland, April 2, 1914); *Scherzo fantastique*, op. 3 (1907; St. Petersburg, Feb. 6, 1909); *Fireworks*, op. 4 (St. Petersburg, June 17, 1908; reorchestrated and 1st perf. in St. Petersburg, Jan. 22, 1910); *Chant funèbre* for Wind Instruments, on the death of Rimsky-Korsakov (1908; St. Petersburg, Jan. 30, 1909; score lost); *Le Chant du rossignol*, symphonic poem (from the opera *Le Rossignol*; Geneva, Dec. 6, 1919); *Symphonies of Wind Instruments*, in memory of Debussy (1918–20; London, June 10, 1921; rev. 1945–47); 2 suites for Small Orch.: No. 1 (1917–25; orch. arrangement of Nos. 1–4 of the *5 pièces faciles* for Piano, 4-hands: Andante, Napolitana, Española, and Balalaika) and No. 2 (1921; orch. arrangement of *3 pièces faciles* and No. 5 of *5 pièces faciles* for Piano, 4-hands: March, Waltz, Polka, and Galop); Concerto for Piano, with Wind Instruments, Double Basses, and Percussion (Paris, May 22, 1924; rev. 1950); *Capriccio* for Piano and Orch. (Paris, Dec. 6, 1929; rev. 1949); 4 études: *Danse, Excentrique, Cantique*, and *Madrid* (1928; orch. arrangement of 3 pieces for String Quartet, and Étude for Pianola; Berlin, Nov. 7, 1930; rev. 1952); Concerto in D for Violin and Orch. (Berlin, Oct. 23, 1931; adapted in 1940 for Balanchine's ballet *Balustrade*); *Divertimento* (sections of the ballet *Le Baiser de la fée*, combined in 1934); *Praeludium* for Jazz Ensemble (1936–37; rev. 1953; Los Angeles, Oct. 19, 1953); Concerto in E-flat, *Dumbarton Oaks*, for Chamber Orch. (Washington, D.C., May 8, 1938); Sym. in C (1938–40; Chicago, Nov. 7, 1940); *Tango*, arrangement by Felix Günther of the piano piece (Philadelphia, July 10, 1941, Benny Goodman conducting; Stravinsky's own orchestration, 1953; Los Angeles, Oct. 19, 1953); *Danses concertantes* for Chamber Orch. (Los Angeles, Feb. 8, 1942); *Circus Polka* for Piano (commissioned by the Ringling Bros. Circus, to accompany the elephant numbers; arranged for Band by David Raksin, 1942; arranged by Stravinsky for sym. orch. and conducted by him with the Boston Sym. Orch., Cambridge, Mass., Jan. 13, 1944); *4 Norwegian Moods* (1942; Cambridge, Mass., Jan. 13, 1944, composer conducting); Sym. in 3 movements (1942–45; N.Y., Jan. 24, 1946); *Ode*, in 3 parts (Boston, Oct. 8, 1943); *Scènes de ballet* (orig. composed for Billy Rose's Broadway show *The Seven Lively Arts*, which opened in Philadelphia, Nov. 24, 1944; rev. for concert performance and 1st perf. in N.Y., Feb. 3, 1945); *Scherzo à la russe* (1944; San Francisco, March 22, 1946; orig. for Big Jazz Band); *Ebony Concerto* for Clarinet and Swing Band (1945; N.Y., March 25, 1946); Concerto in D for String Orch., *Basler* (1946; Basel, Jan. 21, 1947); *Greeting Prelude* ("Happy Birthday," written for Monteux's 80th birthday; Boston, April 4, 1955); *Movements* for Piano and Orch. (1958–59; N.Y., Jan. 10, 1960); *Tres Sacrae Cantiones* for Chamber Orch., after Gesualdo (1957–59); *Monumentum pro Gesualdo di Venosa ad CD Annum*, instrumental surrealization of 3 madrigals by Gesualdo for 4 Wind Instruments, 8 Brass, and Strings (Venice, Sept. 27, 1960); *Variations: Aldous Huxley, In Memoriam* (1963–64; Chicago, April 17, 1965; as a ballet, N.Y., March 31, 1966); *Canon*, from finale of *The Firebird*, in memory of Monteux (Toronto, Dec. 16, 1965).

CHAMBER: 3 pieces for String Quartet (1914); *Ragtime* for 11 Instruments (1918; London, April 27, 1920); *Petite suite* for Violin, Clarinet, and Piano (1919; arranged from *L'Histoire du soldat*); 3 pieces for Clarinet (Lausanne, Nov. 8, 1919); Concertino for String Quartet (1920; rev. for 12 Instruments, 1952); Octet for Wind Instruments (Paris, Oct. 18, 1923); *Duo concertant* for Violin and Piano (Berlin, Oct. 28, 1932); *Russian Dance* for Violin and Piano, from *Pétrouchka* (1932); *Suite italienne* No. 1 for Cello and Piano, and No. 2 for Violin and Piano (both from *Pulcinella*; 1932, 1934); *Pastorale* for Violin, Oboe, English Horn, Clarinet, and Bassoon (1933; arrangement of vocal *Pastorale*); *Divertimento* for Violin and Piano, based on material from *Le Baiser de la fée* (1934); *Élégie* for Violin and Viola (1944); Septet for Piano, and String and Wind Instruments (1952; Washington, D.C., Jan. 24, 1954); *Epitaphium for Prince Max of Fürstenberg* for Flute, Clarinet, and Harp (Donaueschingen, Oct. 17, 1959); Double Canon for String Quartet (1959); 8 instrumental miniatures for 15 Players (Toronto, April 29, 1962; instrumentation of *Les Cinq Doigts* for Piano); *Fanfare for a New Theater* for 2 Trumpets (N.Y., April 19, 1964). **PIANO:** 2 sonatas (1903–04; 1924); 4 Études, op. 7 (1908); *Le Sacre du printemps* for Piano, 4-hands (1912); *3 pièces faciles* for Piano, 4-hands (1915); *5 pièces faciles* for Piano, 4-hands (1917); Étude for Pianola (1917); *Piano-Rag-Music* (1919); 3 movements from *Pétrouchka* (1921); *Les Cinq Doigts* (1920–21); *Serenade* in A (1925); Concerto for 2 Solo Pianos (1931–35; Paris, Nov. 21, 1935); *Tango* (1940); *Circus Polka* (1942); Sonata for 2 Pianos (Edgewood College of the Dominican Sisters, Madison, Wis., Aug. 2, 1944).

VOCAL: *Le Faune et la bergère* for Mezzo-soprano and Orch. (1906; St. Petersburg, Feb. 4, 1908); *Pastorale*, "song without words" for Soprano and Piano (1908; also for Soprano, Oboe, English Horn, Clarinet, and Bassoon, 1923); *2 Poems of Verlaine* for Baritone and Piano (1910; with Orch., 1951); *2 Poems of Balmont* for High Voice and Piano (1911; also with Chamber Orch., 1954); *Le Roi des étoiles* (Zvezdoliki), cantata for Men's Chorus and Orch. (1912; Brussels Radio, April 19, 1939); 3 poems from the Japanese for Soprano, 2 Flutes, 2 Clarinets, Piano, and String Quartet (1912–13); *Pribaoutki* (Peasant Songs) for Voice and 8 Instruments (1914; Vienna, June 6, 1919); *The Saucer*, 4 Russian songs for Women's Voices (1914–17; as *4 Russian Peasant Songs*, with 4 Horns added, 1954); *Berceuses du chat*, suite of 4 songs for Woman's Voice and 3 Clarinets (1915–16; Vienna, June 6, 1919); *Paternoster* for Chorus (1926); *Symphony of Psalms* for Chorus and Orch. (Brussels, Dec. 13, 1930); *Credo* for Chorus (1932); *Ave Maria* for Chorus (1934); *Tango* for Wordless Voice and Piano (1940); *Babel* for Male Narrator, Men's Chorus, and Orch. (1944; Los Angeles, Nov. 18, 1945; 7th and final movement of *Genesis Suite*, in collaboration with Schoenberg, Shilkret, Tansman, Milhaud, Castelnuovo-Tedesco, and Toch; Mass for Men's and Boy's Voices and 10 Wind Instruments (1944–48; Milan, Oct. 27, 1948); Cantata on 4 poems by anonymous English poets of the 15th and 16th centuries for Soprano, Tenor, Women's Chorus, and 5 Instruments (Los Angeles, Nov. 11, 1952); 3 songs from William Shakespeare for Mezzo-soprano, Flute, Clarinet, and Viola (1953; Los Angeles, March 8, 1954); *In Memoriam Dylan Thomas* for Tenor, String Quartet, and 4 Trombones (Hollywood, Sept. 20, 1954); *4 Russian Songs* for Soprano, Flute, Guitar, and Harp (1954); *Canticum sacrum ad honorem Sancti Marci nominis* for Tenor, Baritone, Chorus, and Orch. (Venice, Sept. 13, 1956, composer conducting); arrangement for Chorus and Orch. of J.S. Bach's *Choral-Variationen über das Weihnachtslied "Vom Himmel hoch da komm' ich her"* (Ojai, May 27, 1956, Robert Craft conducting); *Threni*, on Lamentations of Jeremiah from the Vulgate, for 6 Solo Voices, Chorus, and Orch. (Venice, Sept. 23, 1958); *A Sermon, a Narrative and a Prayer*, cantata for Speaker, Alto, Tenor, Chorus, and Orch. (1960–62; Basel, Feb. 23, 1962); *The Dove Descending Breaks the Air*, anthem, after T.S. Eliot (Los Angeles, Feb. 19, 1962, Craft conducting); *Elegy for J.F.K.* for Mezzo-soprano or Baritone, 2 Clarinets, and Corno di Bassetto (Los Angeles, April 6, 1964); *Abraham and Isaac*, sacred ballad for Baritone and Chamber Orch., after Hebrew texts (1962–64; Jerusalem, Aug. 23, 1964); *Introitus (T.S. Eliot in Memoriam)* for 6 Men's Voices, Harp, Piano, Timpani, Tam-tams, Viola, and Double Bass (Chicago, April 17, 1965); *Requiem Canticles* for 4 Vocal Soloists, Chorus, and Orch. (Princeton, N.J., Oct. 8, 1966); *The Owl and the Pussycat* for Voice and Piano, after Lear (Los Angeles, Oct. 31, 1966).

NONDESCRIPT: *Do Not Throw Paper Towels in Toilet* for Treble Voice Unaccompanied, to text from poster in men's room at Harvard Univ. (dated Dec. 16, 1939).

WRITINGS: *Chroniques de ma vie* (2 vols., Paris, 1935; Eng. tr., 1936, as *Chronicles of My Life*); *Poetique musicale*, the Charles Eliot Norton Lectures at Harvard Univ. (Paris, 1946; Eng. tr., 1948, as *Poetics of Music*); with R. Craft, 6 vols. of revelatory autobiographical publications: *Conversations with Igor Stravinsky* (N.Y., 1958), *Memories and Commentaries* (N.Y., 1959), *Expositions and Developments* (N.Y., 1962), *Dialogues and a Diary* (N.Y., 1963), *Themes and Episodes* (N.Y., 1967), and *Ret-*

rospections and Conclusions (N.Y., 1969); *Themes and Conclusions,* amalgamated and ed. from *Themes and Episodes* and *Retrospections and Conclusions* (1972); also R. Craft, ed., *Stravinsky: Selected Correspondence* (2 vols., N.Y., 1982 and 1984).

A sharp debate raged, at times to the point of vitriolic polemical exchange, among Stravinsky's associates as to the degree of credibility of Craft's reports in his dialogues, or even of the factual accounts of events during Stravinsky's last years of life. Stravinsky was never a master of the English language; yet Craft quotes him at length as delivering literary paragraphs of impeccable English prose. Craft admitted that he enhanced Stravinsky's actual words and sentences (which were never recorded on tape), articulating the inner, and at times subliminal, sense of his utterances. Craft's role was made clear beyond dispute by Stravinsky himself, who, in a letter to his publishing agent dated March 15, 1958, urged that the title of the book be changed to *Conversations with Igor Stravinsky* by Robert Craft, and emphatically asserted that the text was in Craft's language, and that in effect Craft "created" him.

BIBL.: C. Wise, "Impressions of I. S.," *Musical Quarterly* (April 1916); R. Chennevière, "The Two Trends of Modern Music in S.'s Works," *Musical Quarterly* (April 1919); B. de Schloezer, *I. S.* (Paris, 1926); A. Casella, *S.* (Rome, 1926); J. Vainkop, *I. S.* (Leningrad, 1927); V. Belaiev, *I. S.'s Les Noces: An Outline* (London, 1928); I. Glebov, *S.* (Leningrad, 1929); C. Ramuz, *Souvenirs sur I. S.* (Paris, 1929; rev. ed., Lausanne, 1946); P. Collaer, *S.* (Brussels, 1930); E. White, *S.'s Sacrifice to Apollo* (London, 1930); H. Fleischer, *S.* (Berlin, 1931); A. Schaeffner, *I. S.* (Paris, 1931); J. Handschin, *I. S.* (Zürich, 1933); E. Evans, *The Firebird and Pétrouchka* (London, 1933); D. de Paoli, *I. S.* (Turin, 1934); M. Blitzstein, "The Phenomenon of S.," *Musical Quarterly* (July 1935); M. Armitage, ed., *S., a compendium of articles* (N.Y., 1936); *S.*, special issue of *La Revue Musicale* (May-June 1939); A. Kall, "S. in the Chair of Poetry," *Musical Quarterly* (July 1940); S. Babitz, "S.'s Symphony in C," *Musical Quarterly* (Jan. 1941); M. Fardell, *S. et les Ballets Russes* (Nice, 1941); G. Malipiero, *S.* (Venice, 1945); A. Casella, *S.* (Brescia, 1947, different from his 1926 book); E. White, *S.: A Critical Survey* (London, 1947; N.Y., 1948); T. Stravinsky, *Le Message d'I. S.* (Lausanne, 1948; Eng. tr. as *The Message of I. S.*, London, 1953); A. Tansman, *I. S.* (Paris, 1948; Eng. tr., 1949); E. Corle, ed., *I. S.* (N.Y., 1949, a compendium of articles, some of them reprinted from M. Armitage's 1936 collection); M. Lederman, ed., *S. in the Theater* (N.Y., 1949); F. Onnen, *S.* (Stockholm, 1949; Eng. tr.); R. Myers, *Introduction to the Music of S.* (London, 1950); W.H. Auden et al., *I. S.* (Bonn, 1952); H. Strobel, *I. S.* (Zürich, 1956; Eng. tr., 1956, as *S.: Classic Humanist*); special issue of *Score* for S.'s 75th birthday (London, 1957); *I. S.: A Complete Catalogue of His Published Works* (London, 1957); H. Kirchmeyer, *I. S.: Zeitgeschichte im Persönlichkeitsbild* (Regensburg, 1958); R. Vlad, *S.* (Rome, 1958; Eng. tr., London, 1960; 3rd ed., 1979); R. Siohan, *S.* (Paris, 1959; Eng. tr., London, 1966); F. Herzfeld, *I. S.* (Berlin, 1961); special issue of the *Musical Quarterly* on S.'s 80th birthday (July 1962); *S. and the Dance: A Survey of Ballet Productions, 1910–1962* (N.Y. Public Library, 1962); P. Lang, ed., *S.: The Composer and His Works* (London, 1966); E. White, *S.: The Composer and His Works* (Berkeley, Calif., 1966; 2nd ed., 1979); special S. issue of *Tempo* (Summer 1967); A. Boucourechliev, ed., *S.* (Paris, 1968); *The Rite of Spring: Sketches, 1911–1913* (London, 1969); A. Dobrin, *I. S.: His Life and Time* (London, 1970); B. Boretz and E. Cone, eds., *Perspectives on Schoenberg and S.* (N.Y., 1972); P. Horgan, *Encounters with S.* (N.Y., 1972; rev. ed., 1989); L. Libman, *And Music at the Close: S.'s Last Years, A Personal Memoir* (N.Y., 1972); D. De Lerma, *I. S., 1882–1971, A Practical Guide to Publications of His Music* (N.Y., 1974); T. Stravinsky, *Catherine and I. S.: A Family Album* (N.Y., 1973); B. Yarustovsky, ed., *I. S.: Articles and Materials* (Moscow, 1973); V. Stravinsky and R. Craft, *S.* (N.Y., 1975); idem, *S. in Pictures and Documents* (N.Y., 1976); L. Morton, "Footnotes to S.'s Studies: *Le Sacre du printemps*," *Tempo* (1979); R. Taruskin, "Russian Folk Melodies in The Rite of Spring," *Journal of the American Musicological Society* (1980); A. Boucourechliev, *I. S.* (Paris, 1982; Eng. tr., 1987); P. Griffiths, *I. S.: The Rake's Progress* (Cambridge, 1982); H. Keller and M. Cosman, *S. Seen and Heard* (London, 1982); A. Schouvaloff and V. Borovsky, *S. on Stage* (London, 1982); C. Joseph, *S. and the Piano* (Ann Arbor, 1983); S. Karlinsky, "S. and Russian Pre-Literate Theater," *19th Century Music* (Spring 1983); M. Ruskin, *I. S.: His Personality, Works and Views* (Cambridge, 1983); V. Scherliess, *I. S. und seine Zeit* (Laaber, 1983); P. van den Toorn, *The Music of I. S.* (London, 1983); J. Pasler, ed., *Confronting S.: Man, Musician, and Modernist* (Berkeley, 1986); J. Straus, "Recompositions by Schoenberg, S., and Webern," *Musical Quarterly*, 3 (1986); E. Haimo and P. Johnson, eds., *S. Retrospectives* (Lincoln, Nebr., 1987); J. Kobler, *Firebird: A Biography of S.* (N.Y., 1987); P. van den Toorn, *S. and the Rite of Spring: The Beginnings of a Musical Language* (Berkeley, 1987); R. Craft, "The Rite: Counterpoint and Choreography," *Musical Times* (April 1988); S. Walsh, *The Music of S.* (London and N.Y., 1988); L. Andriessen and E. Schönberger, *The Apollonian Clockwork: On S.* (Oxford, 1989); A. Pople, *Skryabin and S. 1908–1914: Studies in Theory and Analysis* (N.Y. and London, 1989); C. Goubault, *I. S.* (Paris, 1991); V. Stemann, *Das epische Musiktheater bei S. und Brecht: Studien zur Geschichte und Theorie* (N.Y., 1991); P. Stuart, *I. S.—the Composer in the Recording Studio: A Comprehensive Discography* (N.Y., 1991); C. Migliaccio, *I balletti di I. S.* (Milan, 1992); G. Vinay, ed., *S.* (Bologna, 1992); S. Walsh, *S.: Oedipus Rex* (Cambridge, 1993).

Stravinsky, (Sviatoslav) Soulima, Russian-American pianist, teacher, and composer, son of **Igor (Feodorovich) Stravinsky;** b. Lausanne, Sept. 23, 1910; d. Sarasota, Fla., Nov. 28, 1994. He received training in piano from Philipp and in theory and composition from Boulanger in Paris. In 1934 he made his Paris debut as a pianist, and subsequently established himself as an authoritative interpreter of his father's piano music. In 1939 he joined the French Army and remained in France during World War II. In 1948 he settled in the U.S., where he appeared as soloist in his father's works with his father conducting. From 1950 to 1978 he taught piano at the Univ. of Ill. School of Music. Among his compositions were several chamber pieces, including 3 string quartets and a Cello Sonata. He prepared eds. of various Mozart piano concertos, for which he also composed cadenzas.

Street, Tison, American composer; b. Boston, May 20, 1943. He studied violin with Einer Hansen in Boston (1951–59) and composition with Kirchner and Del Tredici at Harvard Univ. (B.A., 1965; M.A., 1971). He was a composer-in-residence at the Marlboro Music Festival (1964, 1965, 1966, 1972) and a visiting lecturer at the Univ. of Calif., Berkeley (1971–72); taught at Harvard Univ. (1979–82). He was the recipient of an award from the National Inst. of the American Academy of Arts and Letters (1973), the Rome Prize Fellowship (1973), and grants from the NEA (1978) and the Guggenheim Foundation (1981).

WORKS: ORCH.: *Adagio in E-flat* for Oboe and Strings (1977); *Montsalvat* for Orch. (1980); *Variations on a Ground* for Organ and Orch. (1981). **CHAMBER:** String Trio (1963); *Variations* for Flute, Guitar, and Cello (1964); String Quartet (1972); String Quintet (1974; rev. 1976); *Piano Phantasy* (1975); *3 Pieces* for consort of Viols and Harpsichord (1977); *John Major's Medley* for Guitar (1977); *Arias* for Violin and Piano (1978). **PIANO:** *Romanza* (1989). **VOCAL:** *6 Odds and Ends from "So Much Depends"* for Voices and Diverse Instruments (1964–73).

Strehler, Giorgio, Italian opera director; b. Trieste, Aug. 14, 1921. He studied at the Accademia di Filodrammatici in Milan. In 1940 he launched an acting career and in 1943 directed his first theater production. With Paolo Grassi, he founded the Piccolo Teatro in Milan in 1947, the same year he staged his first opera, *La Traviata.* In 1955 he helped organize the Piccola Scala in Milan, where he was regularly engaged as an opera director; also worked at Milan's La Scala. In 1956 he staged a remarkable production of *Die Dreigroschenoper* at the Piccola Scala, winning the praise of Brecht. Strehler first gained wide notice outside Italy with his production of *Die Entführung aus dem Serail* at the Salzburg Festival in 1965. While he continued to work regularly in Milan, he became closely associated with the Théâtre de l'Europe at the Odéon in Paris. Strehler's background as an actor was instrumental in forging his vision of the serious and comic elements of theatrical scores; his productions of Mozart and Verdi have been particularly acclaimed. Conversations on his works with the drama critic Ugo Ronfani were publ. as *Io, Strehler* (Milan, 1986).

BIBL.: F. Battistini, *G. S.* (Rome, 1980).

Streich, Rita, noted German soprano; b. Barnaul, Russia, Dec. 18, 1920; d. Vienna, March 20, 1987. She studied with Erna Berger, Maria Ivogün, and Willi Domgraf-Fassbänder. She made her operatic debut as Zerbinetta in Aussig in 1943; from 1946 she sang with the Berlin State Opera; in 1951 she joined the Berlin Städtische Oper. She also appeared in Vienna, Bayreuth, Salzburg, and Glyndebourne; made her U.S. debut as Zerbinetta with the San Francisco Opera in 1957. In 1974 she became a prof. at the Folkwang-Hochschule in Essen. She was a leading interpreter of parts in Mozart operas.

Strelnikov, Nikolai, Russian composer; b. St. Petersburg, May 14, 1888; d. there (Leningrad), April 12, 1939. He studied composition with Liadov in St. Petersburg. In 1922 he became music director of the Young People's Theater in Leningrad. He wrote 2 operas, *A Fugitive* (Leningrad, May 26, 1933) and *Count Nulin*, after Pushkin (1935); but he is chiefly remembered for his operettas: *The Black Amulet* (Leningrad, 1927); *Luna-Park* (Moscow, 1928); *The Heart of a Poet* (Leningrad, 1934); *Presidents and Bananas* (1939). Other works include a Piano Concerto, choruses, and chamber music. He also publ. monographs on several Russian composers.

Strens, Jules, Belgian organist and composer; b. Ixelles, near Brussels, Dec. 5, 1892; d. there, March 19, 1971. He studied with Gilson. In 1925 was one of 8 founders of the Group des Synthétistes (all Gilson pupils), endeavoring to establish a modern style of composition within the formal categories of early music; was active mainly as an organist.

WORKS: OPERAS: *Le Chanteur de Naples* (1937); *La Tragédie d'Agamemnon* (1941). **ORCH.:** *Gil Blas*, symphonic variations (1921); *Les Elfes*, symphonic poem (1923); *Danse funambulesque* (1925); *Rapsodie tzigane* (1927); *Fantaise concertante* for Piano and Orch. (1938); *Symphonie Sylvestre* for Soli, Chorus, and Orch. (1939); Violin Concerto (1951); Concerto for Organ and Strings (1958). **CHAMBER:** Piano Trio (1920); 4 string quartets (1925, 1929, 1933, 1935); Cello Sonata (1926); String Sextet (1935); Wind Quintet (1943); Quartet for 4 Horns (1950); *Suite* for 4 Horns (1951); Viola Sonata (1954); Trio for Oboe, Clarinet, and Bassoon (1954); Piano Quartet (1955); also piano pieces; organ pieces. **VOCAL:** Songs.

Stresemann, Wolfgang, German conductor and orchestral Intendant; b. Dresden, July 20, 1904. His father, Gustav Stresemann, was the distinguished chancellor and foreign minister of the Weimar Republic. He was educated in Berlin, Heidelberg, and Erlangen (Dr.Jur., 1928); also studied music in Berlin. After the Nazis came to power (1933), he left Germany and eventually settled in the U.S. He served as assistant conductor of the National Orch. Assn. in N.Y. (1939–45); then conducted the Toledo (Ohio) Orch. (1949–55). He returned to Germany and held the post of Intendant of the (West) Berlin Radio Sym. Orch. (1956–59). In 1959 he assumed the prestigious post of Intendant of the Berlin Phil., with Herbert von Karajan as its artistic director. He retired in 1978, only to be recalled to his post in 1984 during the so-called Karajan affair, when the chief conductor and the musicians of the orch. locked horns in a bitter artistic dispute. After serving as mediator, Stresemann continued as Intendant until retiring for a second time in 1986. He wrote an informative history of the Berlin Phil., *The Berlin Philharmonic from Bülow to Karajan: Home and History of a World-Famous Orchestra* (in German and Eng.; Berlin, 1979); likewise publ. *Eine Lanze für Felix Mendelssohn* (Berlin, 1984) and *Ein seltsamer Mann: Erinnerungen an Herbert von Karajan* (Frankfurt am Main, 1991). He also composed some orch. music and songs.

Strickland, Lily (Teresa), American composer; b. Anderson, S.C., Jan. 28, 1887; d. Hendersonville, N.C., June 6, 1958. She studied at Converse College in Spartanburg, S.C. (1901–04) and then with Albert Mildenberg, William Henry Humiston, Daniel Gregory Mason, and Percy Goetschius at the Inst. of Musical Art in N.Y.; also received private lessons from Alfred John Goodrich. She married J. Courtney Anderson of N.Y. in 1912; traveled in the Orient between 1920 and 1930, and spent several years in India; then returned to the U.S. Among her works were several operettas, including *Jewel of the Desert* (1933) and *Laughing Star of Zuni* (1946), orch. suites, the sacred cantata *St. John the Beloved* (1930), many piano suites, and numerous songs.

BIBL.: A. Howe, *L. S.: Her Contribution to American Music in the Early Twentieth Century* (diss., Catholic Univ. of America, 1968).

Strickland, William, American conductor; b. Defiance, Ohio, Jan. 25, 1914; d. Westport, Conn., Nov. 17, 1991. He attended the choir school of the Cathedral of St. John the Divine in N.Y. He was founder-conductor of the National Youth Administration Sinfonietta in N.Y. (1940–41), and then of the Nashville (Tenn.) Sym. Orch. (1946–51). After serving as conductor of the Oratorio Soc. of N.Y. (1955–59), he toured as a guest conductor in the U.S. and abroad as an advocate of American music.

Striegler, Kurt, German conductor, teacher, and composer; b. Dresden, Jan. 7, 1886; d. Wildthurn, near Landau, Aug. 4, 1958. He studied with Draeseke at the Dresden Cons. He became répétiteur at the Dresden Opera in 1905, and then conductor there in 1912; was associated with the company until 1945, and also taught at the Dresden Hochschule für Musik (1905–45). In 1945 he became director of the Coburg Cons. He went to Munich in 1950. He wrote the operas *Der Thomaskantor* and *Hand und Herz* (Dresden, 1924); 4 syms.; Violin Concerto; Cello Concerto; *Scherzo* for 7 Kettledrums and Orch.; much chamber music; numerous choruses; songs and piano pieces.

Stringfield, Lamar (Edwin), American flutist, conductor, and composer; b. Raleigh, N.C., Oct. 10, 1897; d. Asheville, N.C., Jan. 21, 1959. He served in the U.S. Army during World War I; after the Armistice, he studied theory with Goetschius and flute with Barrère at the Inst. of Musical Art in N.Y.; also took lessons in conducting with Chalmers Clifton. In 1930 he organized the Inst. of Folk Music at the Univ. of North Carolina, and conducted its orch.; was conductor of the Knoxville (Tenn.) Sym. Orch. (1946–47), then of the Charlotte Sym. Orch. (1948–49). The source material of his compositions is largely derived from the folk songs of the U.S. South. He learned the trade of printing and was able to publ. his own works. He wrote *America and Her Music* (Chapel Hill, 1931) and a *Guide for Young Flutists* (MS, c.1945; included in the Nelson diss. listed in the bibliography below).

WORKS: DRAMATIC: *The 7th Queue*, ballet (1928); *The Mountain Song*, opera (1929); *Carolina Charcoal*, musical folk comedy (1951–53). **ORCH.:** *The Desert Wanderer*, overture for Band (1921); *Tango* for Small Orch. (1921); *Valse triste* (1921); *Mountain Suite* for Band (1922); *Indian Legend* (1923); *Asheville Kiwana's March* for Band (1924); *Squaw Dance* (1925); *From the Southern Mountains* (1927); *From a Negro Melody* for Chamber Orch. (1928); *At the Factory*, symphonic fantasy (1929); *Negro Parade* (1931); *The Legend of John Henry*, symphonic ballad (1932); *Moods of a Moonshiner* (1934); *From the Blue Ridge*, symphonic sketches (1936); *Peace*, symphonic poem (1942); *Mountain Dawn* for Flute and Strings (1945); *Georgia Buck* for Band (1949). **CHAMBER:** *Mountain Echoes* for Flute and Harp (1921); *Indian Sketches* for Flute and String Quartet (1922); *Mountain Sketches* for Flute, Cello, and Piano

(1923); *Fugue* for String Quartet (1924); *Concert Fugue* for String Quartet (1924); *The Ole Swimmin' Hole* for Flute, Viola, and Cello (1924); Suite for Oboe and Flute (1925); *Elegy* for Cello and Piano (1930); Quintet for Clarinet, Flute, Oboe, Bassoon, and Horn (1932); *A Mountain Episode* for String Quartet (1933); *Dance of the Frogs* for Chamber Ensemble (1939). **VOCAL:** *Fly Low, Vermillion Dragon* for Voice and Orch. (1925); *The Vagabond's Prayer* for Baritone and String Quartet (1925); *On a Moonbeam* for Voice, Piano, and Flute (1938); *Peace*, cantata for Chorus and Orch. or Organ (1949); *About Dixie* for Chorus and Orch. (1950); songs.

BIBL.: D. Nelson, *The Life and Works of L. S. (1897–1959)* (diss., Univ. of North Carolina, 1971).

Stringham, Edwin John, American music educator and composer; b. Kenosha, Wis., July 11, 1890; d. Chapel Hill, N.C., July 1, 1974. He studied at Northwestern Univ. and at the Cincinnati Cons.; in 1920 he went to Italy, where he took lessons in composition with Respighi. Returning to the U.S., he occupied teaching posts at the Denver College of Music (1920–29), Teachers College of Columbia Univ. (1930–38), Juilliard School of Music in N.Y. (1930–45), and Queens College of the City Univ. of N.Y. (1938–46). In 1948 he settled in Chapel Hill. He publ. the books *Listening to Music Creatively* (N.Y., 1943; rev. ed., 1959) and *Creative Harmony and Musicianship* (with H.A. Murphy, N.Y., 1951).

WORKS: ORCH.: *Visions*, symphonic poem (1924); *The Ancient Mariner*, after Coleridge (Denver, March 16, 1928); Sym. No. 1 (Minneapolis, Nov. 15, 1929); *Fantasy on American Folk Tunes* for Violin and Orch. (1942). **OTHER:** Chamber music; songs.

Strobel, Heinrich, eminent German musicologist, music critic, and administrator; b. Regensburg, May 31, 1898; d. Baden-Baden, Aug. 18, 1970. He studied musicology with Sandberger and Kroyer and theory with H.K. Schmidt at the Univ. of Munich (Ph.D., 1922, with the diss. *Johann Wilhelm Hässlers Leben und Werke*). He was music critic of the *Thüringer Allgemeine Zeitung* in Erfurt (from 1921) and of the *Börsenkurier* (1927–33) and *Tageblatt* (1934–38) in Berlin; also was the ed. of *Melos* (1933–34) and of the *Neue Musikblatt* (1934–39). In 1939 he went to Paris; in 1946 he returned to Germany and again became ed. of *Melos*; that same year, he also was made director of music at the South West Radio in Baden-Baden; in 1956 he became chairman of the ISCM. He devoted himself energetically to the cause of modern music; wrote numerous articles on the subject; promoted programs of avant-garde composers on the radio and at various festivals in Germany.

WRITINGS: *Paul Hindemith* (Mainz, 1928; 3rd ed., enl., 1948); *Claude Debussy* (Zürich, 1940; 5th Ger. ed., 1961; French ed., Paris, 1942); *Igor Stravinsky* (Zürich, 1956; Eng. tr., 1956, as *Stravinsky: Classic Humanist*).

Strobel, Otto, German musicologist; b. Munich, Aug. 20, 1895; d. Bayreuth, Feb. 23, 1953. He studied at the Univ. of Munich (Ph.D., 1924, with the diss. *Richard Wagner über sein Schaffen: Ein Beitrag zur "Künstlerasthetek"*; publ. in Munich, 1924). After working as an archivist of the Wahnfried Archives in Bayreuth (from 1932), he was director of the short-lived Richard Wagner Forschungsstätte (1938). He publ. *Richard Wagner: Skizzen und Entwürfe zur Ring-Dichtung* (Munich, 1930); *Genie am Werk: Richard Wagners Schaffen und Wirken im Spiegel eigenhandschriftlicher Urkunden: Führer durch die einmalige Ausstellung einer umfassenden Auswahl von Schätzen aus dem Archiv des Hauses Wahnfried* (Bayreuth, 1933; 2nd ed., rev., 1934); *Richard Wagner: Leben und Schaffen: Eine Zeittafel* (Bayreuth, 1952).

Stroe, Aurel, Romanian composer; b. Bucharest, May 5, 1932. He studied harmony with Negrea, composition with Andricu, and orchestration with Rogalski at the Bucharest Cons. (1951–56); had a course in electronic music in Munich (1966) and attended the annual summer courses in new music given in Darmstadt (1966–69) by Kagel, Ligeti, and Stockhausen. In 1962 he joined the faculty of the Bucharest Cons.; also worked at the Bucharest Computing Center (1966–69). His early music is rooted in folklore, but in his later period he experimented with sonoristic constructions, some of which were put together by computerized calculations.

WORKS: DRAMATIC: OPERAS: *Ça n'aura pas le Prix Nobel* (Această piesă nu va primi premiul Nobel; 1969; Kassel, Nov. 28, 1971); *De Ptolemaeo*, mini-opera for Tape (1970); *Aristophane: La Paix* (1972–73); *Orestia II* (Purtatoarele de prinoase), chamber opera (1974–77; Bucharest, Nov. 14, 1978). **MUSIC THEATER:** *Agamemnon (Orestia I)* (1979–81; Bucharest, March 1, 1983). **ORCH.:** Concerto for Strings (1956; Bucharest, Dec. 22, 1957); *Uvertură burlescă* (1961); *Arcade* for 11 Instrumental Formations (1962); *Muzică de concert* for Piano, Percussion, and Brass (1964–65; Cluj, April 2, 1966); *Laudes I* for 28 Strings (1966) and *II* for 12 Instrumental Formations (1968); *Canto I* (1967) and *II* (1971) for 12 Instrumental Formations; Clarinet Concerto (1974–75). **CHAMBER:** Trio for Oboe, Clarinet, and Bassoon (1953); 2 piano sonatas (1955, 1984); *Rêver, c'est desengrener les temps superposés II* for Clarinet, Cello, and Harpsichord (1970); String Quartet (1972); *Quintandre*, quintet for Flute, Oboe, Clarinet, Bassoon, and Horn (1984); *Anamorphoses canoniques* for 3 Flutes, Clarinet, Clavichord, Trombone, Cello, and Tape (1984). **VOCAL:** *Chipul păcii*, chamber cantata for Mezzo-soprano, Chorus, and Chamber Orch. (1959); *Monumentum I* for Men's Voices and Orch. (1961) and *II* for Mezzo-soprano, Percussion, Double Bass, and Tape (1982); *Numai prin timp poate fi timpul cucerit* (Only through Time, Time Is Conquered) for Baritone, Organ, 4 Trombones, and 4 Gongs, after T.S. Eliot (1965); *Il giardino delle Strutture + Rime de Michelangelo* for Baritone, Trombone, Violin, Viola, Cello, Harpsichord, and Tape (1975); various solo songs.

Strohm, Reinhard, German musicologist; b. Munich, Aug. 4, 1942. He studied with Georgiades at the Univ. of Munich and Dahlhaus at Berlin's Technical Univ. (Ph.D., 1971, with the diss. *Italienische Opernarien des fruhen Settecento [1720–1730]*, 2 vols., Cologne, 1976). He was assistant ed. of the Richard-Wagner-Ausgabe (1970–81); also lectured on music at King's College, Univ. of London (1975–83); then was prof. of music history at Yale Univ. (from 1983). In 1990 he rejoined the faculty of King's College, where he served as director of its Inst. for Advanced Musical Studies from 1991. He publ. several valuable books, among them *Music in Late Medieval Bruges* (1985), *Essays on Handel and Italian Opera* (1985), *Music in Late Medieval Europe* (1987), and *The Rise of European Music, 1380–1500* (1993).

Strong, George Templeton, American composer; b. N.Y., May 26, 1856; d. Geneva, June 27, 1948. He was the son of the N.Y. lawyer G.T. Strong, who was also a music-lover, and whose diary, expressing his dislike of Liszt and Wagner, was publ. in 1952. From him, and from his mother, who was an amateur pianist, Strong received his first training. In 1879 he went to Leipzig, where he studied with Jadassohn. He entered the Liszt circle at Weimar, and became an adherent of program music; from 1886 to 1889 he lived in Wiesbaden, where he became friendly with MacDowell; he returned briefly to America, and taught theory at the New England Cons. in Boston (1891–92); then went back to Europe and settled in Switzerland. He expressed his indignation at the lack of recognition of American composers in their own country; most performances of his works took place in Switzerland. In 1930 he donated many of his original MSS to the Library of Congress in Washington, D.C. Toscanini performed his orch. suite *Die Nacht* with the NBC Sym. Orch. in N.Y. on Oct. 21, 1939; his other symphonic suite, *Une Vie d'artiste* for Violin and Orch., was presented at the 20th festival of the Assn. des Musiciens Suisses at Zürich in June 1920; he also wrote 3 syms.: No. 1, *In den Bergen*, No. 2, *Sintram*, and No. 3, *An der See*; and the symphonic poems *Undine* and *Le Roi Arthur*.

BIBL.: P. Scholes, "An American Composer: G.T. S.," *Music Student*, VII (1915); J. Matthey, *Inventaire du fonds musical*

G.T. S. (Lausanne, 1973); V. Lawrence, *S. on Music: The New York Music Scene in the Days of G.T. S., 1836–1875: Vol. I: Resonances, 1836–1850* (Oxford and N.Y., 1988).

Strouse, Charles (Louis), American composer; b. N.Y., June 7, 1928. He studied at the Eastman School of Music in Rochester, N.Y., and later took private lessons in composition with Copland and Boulanger, under whose guidance he wrote some ambitious instrumental music. He was mainly active as a composer for Broadway and films; with the lyricist Lee Adams (b. Mansfield, Ohio, Aug. 14, 1924), he wrote the musicals *Bye Bye Birdie* (N.Y., April 16, 1960) and *Applause* (N.Y., March 30, 1970), both of which won Tony awards. His other musicals include *Golden Boy* (N.Y., Oct. 20, 1964), after a play by Clifford Odets, and *Annie* (N.Y., April 21, 1977). He also composed a Piano Concerto and other orch. pieces and a String Quartet.

Strube, Gustav, German-American violinist, conductor, music educator, and composer; b. Ballenstedt, March 3, 1867; d. Baltimore, Feb. 2, 1953. He was taught the violin by his father, and later by Brodsky at the Leipzig Cons.; was a member of the Gewandhaus Orch. of Leipzig until 1891, when he emigrated to America. He was a violinist in the Boston Sym. Orch. from 1891 to 1913; also conducted the Boston Pops Orch. (1898; 1900–1902; 1905–12); then taught theory and conducting at the Peabody Cons. in Baltimore (from 1913), where he also was its director (1916–46). In 1916 he was appointed conductor of the newly organized Baltimore Sym. Orch., which he led until 1930. He publ. a useful manual, *The Theory and Use of Chords: A Textbook of Harmony* (Boston, 1928).

WORKS: OPERA: *Ramona*, later renamed *The Captive* (1916). **ORCH.:** Sinfonietta (1922); 2 violin concertos (1924, 1930); Sym., *Lanier*, after Sidney Lanier (Washington, D.C., March 17, 1925, composer conducting); *Symphonic Prologue* (Baltimore, April 24, 1927, composer conducting); *Americana* (1930); *Harz Mountains*, symphonic poem (1940); *Peace Overture* (1945). **CHAMBER:** 2 string quartets (1923, 1936); 2 violin sonatas (1923); Viola Sonata (1924); Cello Sonata (1925); Piano Trio (1925); Quintet for Wind Instruments (1930).

Strunk, (William) Oliver, distinguished American musicologist; b. Ithaca, N.Y., March 22, 1901; d. Grottaferrata, Italy, Feb. 24, 1980. He studied at Cornell Univ. (1917–19); in 1927 took a course in musicology with Otto Kinkeldey there; then entered the Univ. of Berlin to study musicology with J. Wolf (1927–28). Returning to America, he served as a member of the staff of the Music Division at the Library of Congress in Washington, D.C. (1928–34), and then was head of its music division (1934–37). In 1937 he was appointed to the faculty of Princeton Univ.; after retirement in 1966, he lived mostly in Italy. He was a founding member of the American Musicological Soc., serving as the first ed. of its journal (1948) and as its president (1959–60), then was director of Monumenta Musicae Byzantinae (1961–71). He publ. *State and Resources of Musicology in the U.S.* (Washington, D.C., 1932) and the extremely valuable documentary *Source Readings in Music History* (N.Y., 1950). Collections of his writings were publ. as *Essays on Music in the Western World* (N.Y., 1974) and *Essays on Music in the Byzantine World* (N.Y., 1977).

BIBL.: H. Powers, ed., *Studies in Music History: Essays for O. S.* (Princeton, N.J., 1968).

Stücken, Frank Van Der. See **Van Der Stücken, Frank.**

Stückenschmidt, Hans Heinz, eminent German music critic and writer on music; b. Strasbourg, Nov. 1, 1901; d. Berlin, Aug. 15, 1988. He studied violin, piano, and composition. He was chief music critic of Prague's *Bohemia* (1928–29) and of the *Berliner Zeitung am Mittag* (1929–34); also was active as a lecturer on contemporary music. In 1934 he was forbidden to continue journalism in Germany, and went to Prague, where he wrote music criticism until 1941, when his activities were stopped once more by the occupation authorities; then was drafted into the German army. In 1946 he became director of the dept. for new music of the radio station RIAS in Berlin; also was a lecturer (1948–49), reader (1949–53), and prof. (1953–67) of music history at the Technical Univ. there. With Josef Rufer, he founded and ed. the journal *Stimmen* (Berlin, 1947–49).

WRITINGS: *Arnold Schönberg* (Zürich and Freiburg im Breisgau, 1951; 2nd ed., 1957; Eng. tr., 1960); *Neue Musik zwischen den beiden Kriegen* (Berlin and Frankfurt am Main, 1951); *Strawinsky und sein Jahrhundert* (Berlin, 1957); *Schöpfer der neuen Musik* (Frankfurt am Main, 1958); *Boris Blacher* (Berlin, 1963); *Oper in dieser Zeit* (Velber, 1964); *Johann Nepomuk David* (Wiesbaden, 1965); *Maurice Ravel: Variationen über Person und Werk* (Frankfurt am Main, 1966; Eng. tr., 1968); *Ferruccio Busoni. Zeittafel eines Europaers* (Zürich, 1967; Eng. tr., 1970); *Twentieth Century Music* (London, 1968; Ger. original, 1969); *Twentieth Century Composers* (London, 1970; Ger. original, 1971); *Schönberg: Leben, Umwelt, Werk* (Zürich, 1974; Eng. tr., 1976); *Die Musik eines halben Jahrhunderts: 1925–1975* (Munich, 1976); *Schöfer klassischer Musik: Bildnisse und Revisionen* (Berlin, 1983).

BIBL.: W. Burde, ed., *Aspekte der neuen Musik: Professor H.H. S. zum 65. Geburtstag* (Kassel, 1968).

Stückgold, Grete (née **Schneidt**), German soprano; b. London (of a German father and an English mother), June 6, 1895; d. Falls Village, Conn., Sept. 13, 1977. She studied voice with **Jacques Stückgold**, whom she married (divorced in 1928); later married **Gustav Schützendorf**. She commenced her career as a concert and oratorio singer; made her operatic debut in Nuremberg in 1917; joined the Berlin State Opera in 1922. On Nov. 2, 1927, she made her Metropolitan Opera debut in N.Y. as Eva in *Die Meistersinger von Nürnberg*; she continued to make appearances there until 1939; also sang in San Francisco, Philadelphia, and Chicago. She later taught voice at Bennington (Vt.) College.

Stückgold, Jacques, Polish singing teacher; b. Warsaw, Jan. 29, 1877; d. N.Y., May 4, 1953. He studied in Venice; taught voice in Germany (1899–1903), where **Grete** (née **Schneidt**) **Stückgold** became his pupil and wife (divorced, 1928); settled in N.Y. in 1933. He publ. *Der Bankrott der deutschen Gesangskunst* and *Über Stimmbildungskunst.*

Stucky, Steven (Edward), American composer, teacher, conductor, and writer on music; b. Hutchinson, Kansas, Nov. 7, 1949. He received training in composition from Richard Willis at Baylor Univ. (B.M., 1971) and from Husa, Phillips, and Palmer at Cornell Univ. (M.F.A., 1973; D.M.A., 1978). He also studied conducting with Daniel Sternberg. After serving as a visiting assistant prof. at Lawrence Univ. in Appleton, Wis. (1978–80), he taught at Cornell Univ. (from 1980), later serving as a prof. and chairman of the music dept. there (from 1991). He also was composer-in-residence of the Los Angeles Phil. (1988–91), and then was its new music advisor. His study *Lutoslawski and His Music* (Cambridge, 1981) won the ASCAP-Deems Taylor Award. He also won the ASCAP-Victor Herbert Prize (1974), 1st prize of the American Soc. of Univ. Composers (1975), and fellowships from the NEA (1978), the American Council of Learned Societies (1979), the NEH (1979), and the Guggenheim Foundation (1986). Stucky's music is marked by rewarding craftsmanship, technical expertise, and a remarkable command of color and form.

WORKS: ORCH.: *Prelude and Toccata* (1969); 4 syms.: No. 1 (1972), No. 2 (1974), No. 3 (1976), and No. 4, *Kennigar* (1977–78; Terre Haute, Ind., Sept. 25, 1980); *Transparent Things: In Memoriam V. N.* (Appleton, Wis., May 11, 1980); Double Concerto for Violin, Oboe or Oboe d'Amore, and Chamber Orch. (1982–85; Tallahassee, March 9, 1985; rev. 1989); *Dreamwaltzes* (Minneapolis, July 17, 1986); *Concerto for Orchestra* (1986–87; Philadelphia, Oct. 27, 1988); *Threnos* for Wind Ensemble (1987–88; Ithaca, N.Y., March 6, 1988); *Son et lumière* (Baltimore, May 18, 1988); *Angelus* (1989–90; N.Y., Sept. 27, 1990); *Impromptus* (1989–91; St. Louis, April 26, 1991); *Anniversary Greeting* (Baltimore, May 2, 1991); *Fanfare for Los Angeles* (1993; Los Angeles, March 4, 1994); *Fanfare for Cincin-*

nati (1993; Cincinnati, March 10, 1995); *Ancora* (1994; Los Angeles, Oct. 6, 1995); *Fanfares and Arias* for Wind Ensemble (1994; Boulder, Colo., Feb. 22, 1995); Concerto for 2 Flutes and Orch. (1994; Los Angeles, Feb. 23, 1995). **CHAMBER:** *4 Bagatelles* for String Quartet (1969); Duo for Viola and Cello (1969); *Movements* for Cello Quartet (1970); *Divertimento* for Clarinet, Piano, and Percussion (1971); Quartet for Clarinet, Viola, Cello, and Piano (1973); *Notturno* for Alto Saxophone and Piano (Ithaca, N.Y., Sept. 19, 1981); *Varianti* for Flute, Clarinet, and Piano (1982; Ithaca, N.Y., Jan. 30, 1983); *Boston Fancies* for Flute, Clarinet, Percussion, Piano, Violin, Viola, and Cello (Cambridge, Mass., Nov. 15, 1985); *Serenade* for Wind Quintet (1989–90). **VOCAL:** *2 Holy Sonnets of Donne* for Mezzo-soprano, Oboe, and Piano (Waco, Tex., Oct. 14, 1982); *Sappho Fragments* for Mezzo-soprano, Flute, Clarinet, Percussion, Piano, Violin, and Cello (Syracuse, N.Y., Nov. 1, 1982); *Voyages* for Voice and Wind Orch. (1983–84; New Haven, Conn., Dec. 7, 1984); *4 Poems of A.R. Ammons* for Baritone, Flute, Clarinet, Horn, Viola, Cello, and Double Bass (1992; Syracuse, N.Y., March 28, 1993). **OTHER:** *Funeral Music for Queen Mary*, transcription and elaboration of music by Purcell for Wind Orch. (Los Angeles, Feb. 6, 1992).

Studer, Cheryl, American soprano; b. Midland, Mich., Oct. 24, 1955. She received her training in Ohio, at the Univ. of Tenn., and from Hans Hotter at the Vienna Hochschule für Musik. After appearing in concerts in the U.S., she made her debut at the Bavarian State Opera in Munich as Mařenka in *The Bartered Bride* in 1980. From 1983 to 1985 she sang at the Darmstadt Opera. In 1984 she made her U.S. operatic debut as Micaëla at the Chicago Lyric Opera. From 1985 she sang at the Deutsche Oper in Berlin. She made her Bayreuth Festival debut in 1985 as Elisabeth in *Tannhäuser.* In 1986 she sang Pamina at her debut at the Paris Opéra. In 1987 she made her first appearance at London's Covent Garden as Elisabeth, and also sang at Milan's La Scala. She made her Metropolitan Opera debut in N.Y. in 1988 as Micaëla, and subsequently sang there with success. In 1989 she made her first appearance at the Salzburg Festival as Chrysothemis. In 1990 she sang Elsa at the Vienna State Opera. She appeared as Giuditta at the Vienna Volksoper in 1992. On May 4, 1994, she made her Carnegie Hall recital debut in N.Y. She has won particular distinction for such Strauss roles as Salome, the Empress in *Die Frau ohne Schatten,* and Daphne. Among her other admired roles are Donna Anna, Lucia, Aida, and Singlinde.

Stumpf, (Friedrich) Carl, eminent German psychologist, acoustician, and musicologist; b. Wiesentheid, Lower Franconia, April 21, 1848; d. Berlin, Dec. 25, 1936. He studied philosophy and theology at the Univ. of Würzburg, and philosophy and natural sciences at the Univ. of Göttingen, where he took his Ph.D. (1870) and completed his Habilitation (1873). He was a prof. of philosophy at the Univs. of Würzburg (1873–79), Prague (1879–84), Halle (1884–89), Munich (1889–93), and Berlin (1893–1928). In 1893 he founded the Psychological Inst. in Berlin; its purpose was a scientific analysis of tonal psychology as it affected musical perception; but, realizing the utterly speculative and arbitrary premises of his theories, he revised them, and proposed the concepts of Konkordanz and Diskordanz to describe the relative euphony of triads and chords of several different notes. With his pupils Hornbostel and Abraham, he founded the Berlin Phonogrammarchiv in 1900. Stumpf publ. *Beiträge zur Akustik und Musikwissenschaft* (1898–1924), which incorporated his evolving theories, and, with Hornbostel, issued the *Sammelbände für vergleichende Musikwissenschaft* (1922–23); also contributed numerous articles to scholarly publications.

WRITINGS: *Tonpsychologie* (2 vols., Leipzig, 1883, 1890; reprint, Hilversum, 1965); *Geschichte des Konsonanzbegriffs* (Munich, 1901); *Die Anfänge der Musik* (Leipzig, 1911); *Die Sprachlaute. Experimentell-phonetische Untersuchungen nebst einem Anhang über Instrumentalklänge* (Berlin, 1926).

BIBL.: *Festscrift für C. S.* (Berlin, 1919); *C. S. zum 75. Geburtstag* (Berlin, 1923); E. Schumann, "Die Förderung der Musikwissenschaft durch die akustisch-psychologische Forschung C. S.s," *Archiv für Musikwissenschaft,* V (1923); C. Sachs, "Zu C. S.s achtzigstem Geburtstag," *Zeitschrift für Musikwissenschaft,* 10 (1927–28); N. Hartmann, *Gedächtnisrede C. S.* (Berlin, 1937).

Stupka, František, Czech conductor; b. Tedrazice, Jan. 18, 1879; d. Prague, Nov. 24, 1965. He studied violin with Sevčik at the Prague Cons., graduating in 1901. He then went to Russia, where he became a violin teacher at the Odessa Cons. He left Russia after the Revolution; served as 2nd conductor of the Czech Phil. in Prague (1919–39); also was a guest conductor with various European orchs. He specialized in the repertoire of Czech composers.

Stürmer, Bruno, German conductor, teacher, and composer; b. Freiburg im Breisgau, Sept. 9, 1892; d. Bad Homburg, May 19, 1958. He studied piano at the Karlsruhe Cons.; then organ and composition with Wolfrum at the Univ. of Heidelberg, and musicology with Sandberger and Kroyer at the Univ. of Munich. He taught piano in Karlsruhe (1917–22); then was a theater conductor in Remscheid, Essen, and Duisburg (1922–27); in 1927 he founded a music school in Homburg; then was a conductor of choral societies in Kassel and elsewhere (until 1945). He composed in a distinctly modern manner. In addition to numerous vocal works, he wrote concertos and much chamber music. He publ. the book *Frisch fröhlich woll'n wir singen* (Cologne, 1956).

Sturzenegger, (Hans) Richard, Swiss cellist, teacher, and composer; b. Zürich, Dec. 18, 1905; d. Bern, Oct. 24, 1976. He studied cello with Fritz Reitz at the Zürich Cons., and then continued his training in Paris (1924–27) with Alexanian and Casals (cello) and Boulanger (harmony and counterpoint). He completed his training in Berlin (1929–35) with Feuermann (cello) and Toch (composition), during which time he served as solo cellist of the Dresden Phil. From 1935 to 1949 he played in the Bern String Quartet, and from 1935 to 1963 he was solo cellist of the Bern Musikgesellschaft. He also taught cello and chamber music at the Bern Cons. From 1954 to 1963 he likewise taught cello in Zürich. In 1963 he became director of the Bern Cons.

WORKS: OPERA: *Atalante* (1963–68). **ORCH.:** 4 cello concertos (1933, 1937, 1947, 1974); *Triptychon* (1951); *3 Gesänge Davids* for Violin and Orch. (1963); *Fresco* for Strings (1965). **CHAMBER:** Sonata for Solo Cello (1934); String Trio (1937); 2 string quartets (1940, 1974); Cello Sonata (1950); *Elegie* for Cello, Oboe, Harp, Viola, Cello, and Double Bass (1950); Piano Trio (1964). **VOCAL:** *Chorale Fantasy* for Contralto, Strings, Trumpet, and Drums (1941); *Cantico di San Francesco* for Chorus, Strings, and Harp (1945); *Richardis,* festival music for Chorus, Wind Orch., and Organ (1949).

BIBL.: *R. S., Werkverzeichnis* (Zürich, 1970); E. Hochuli, ed., *Variationen: Festgabe für R. S. zum siebzigsten Geburtstag* (Bern, 1975).

Stutschewsky, Joachim, Russian-born Israeli cellist, pedagogue, ethnomusicologist, and composer; b. Romny, Feb. 7, 1892; d. Tel Aviv, Nov. 14, 1982. He received his early education at a music school in Kherson; as a youth, played cello in various orchs. in southern Russia; then studied cello with J. Klengel and orch. playing with H. Sitt at the Leipzig Cons. (1909–12). After playing in the Jena Quartet, he was active as a performer, teacher, and editor in Zürich (1914–24) and Vienna (1924–38), where he entered the circle of Schoenberg, Berg, and Webern. Together with the violinist Rudolf Kolisch, he formed the Wiener Streichquartett (later known as the Kolisch String Quartet). With the usurpation of Austria by the Nazi hordes in 1938, Stutschewsky emigrated to Palestine, and eventually became a naturalized Israeli citizen. From 1939 to 1948 he served as inspector of music in the cultural section of the Jewish National Council. In his early compositions, he followed median modern techniques; then began a study of Jewish folklore in diaspora, and wrote music of profound racial feeling, set in the framework of advanced harmonies. He also contributed to the study of cello techniques and to ethnomusicology.

WRITINGS: *Die Kunst des Cellospiels* (Vols. 1–2, Mainz, 1929; Vols. 3–4, Vienna, 1938); *Mein Weg zur jüdischen Musik* (Vienna, 1935); *Musika yehudit* (Jewish Music; Tel Aviv, 1946); *The Cello and Its Masters: History of Cello Playing* (MS, 1950); *Klezmerim* (Tel Aviv, 1959); *Musical Folklore of Eastern Jewry* (Tel Aviv, 1959); *Korot hayav shel musikai yehudi* (The Life of a Jewish Musician; Tel Aviv, 1975).

WORKS: ORCH.: Concertino for Clarinet and Strings (1958); *Fantasy* for Oboe, Harp, and Strings (1959); *Safed,* symphonic poem (1960); *Israel,* symphonic suite (1964; Tel Aviv, May 7, 1973). **CHAMBER:** *Dreykut* for Cello and Piano (1924); Duo for Violin and Cello (1940); *Hassidic Suite* for Cello and Piano (1946); *Legend* for Cello and Piano (1952); *Israeli Dances* for Flute, Cello, and Piano (1953); *Verschollene Klänge* for Flute, String Quartet, and Percussion (1955); *Hassidic Fantasy* for Clarinet, Cello, and Piano (1956); Piano Trio (1956); *5 Pieces* for Flute (1956); String Quartet (1956); *Terzetto* for Oboe, Clarinet, and Bassoon (1959); String Trio (1960); Wind Sextet (1960); *Israeli Suite* for Cello and Piano (1962); *Monologue* for Clarinet (1962); *3 Pieces* for Bassoon (1963); *Moods* for Oboe (1963); *Impressions* for Clarinet and Bassoon (1963); *Soliloquy* for Viola (1964); *3 Miniatures* for 2 Flutes (1964); *Kol Kore* (Calling Voice) for Horn (1965); *Fragments* for 2 Clarinets (1966); *4 Movements* for Wind Quintet (1967); *3 for 3,* 3 pieces for 3 Cellos (1967); Woodwind Quintet (1967); *Visions* for Flute (1968); *Thoughts and Feelings* for Violin (1969); *Prelude and Fugue* for 2 Trumpets and 2 Trombones (1969); *Monologue* for Trombone (1970); *Dialogues variés* for 2 Trumpets (1970); *Imaginations* for Flute, Violin, Cello, and Piano (1971); *Kol Nidrei* for Cello and Piano (1972); *The Rabbi's Nigun* for Cello and Piano (1974); *Sine nomine* for Cello (1975); *2 Pieces* for Double Bass (1975). **PIANO:** *Palestinian Sketches* (1931); *Israeli Landscapes* (1949); *4 Inattendus* (1967); *Splinters* (1975). **VOCAL:** *Songs of Radiant Sadness,* cantata for Soloists, Chorus, Speaking Chorus, and Orch. (1958); *Jemama baschimscha* (24 Hours in the Looking Glass), chamber cantata for Narrator, 2 Sopranos, and 6 Instruments (1960). **OTHER:** Numerous arrangements for cello of works by Mozart, Tartini, and Boccherini.

BIBL.: *J. S.'s 70th Anniversary: Catalogue of Works* (Tel Aviv, 1971).

Subirá (Puig), José, eminent Spanish musicologist; b. Barcelona, Aug. 20, 1882; d. Madrid, Jan. 5, 1980. He studied piano and composition at the Madrid Cons. and simultaneously qualified for the practice of law (Dr.Jur., 1923); then held various government posts in Madrid while pursuing musicological research. In 1952 he was elected a member of the Real Academia de Bellas Artes de San Fernando in Madrid. Apart from his scholarly pursuits, he publ. a novel, *Su virginal pureze* (1916), and a historical account, *Los Españoles en la guerra de 1914–1918* (4 vols.).

WRITINGS: *Enrique Granados* (Madrid, 1926); *La música en la Casa de Alba* (Madrid, 1927); *La participación musical en el antiguo teatro español* (Barcelona, 1930); *Tonadillas teatrales inéditas: Libretos y partituras* (Madrid, 1932); *"Celos aun del aire matan": Opera del siglo XVII, texto de Calderón y música de Juan Hidalgo* (Barcelona, 1933); *La tonadilla escénica: Sus obras y sus autores* (Barcelona, 1933); *Historia de la música teatral en España* (Barcelona, 1945); with H. Anglès, *Catálogo musical de la Biblioteca Nacional de Madrid* (Barcelona, 1946–51); *La ópera en los teatros de Barcelona* (Barcelona, 1946); *Historia de la música Salvat* (Barcelona, 1947; 3rd ed., enl., 1958); *Historia y ancedotario del Teatro Real* (Madrid, 1949); *El compositor Iriarte (1750–1791) y el cultivo español del melólogo (melodrama)* (Barcelona, 1949–50); *La música, etapas y aspectos* (Barcelona, 1949); *El teatro del Real palacio (1849–1851), con un bosquejo preliminar sobre la música palatina desde Felipe V hasta Isabel II* (Madrid, 1950); *Historia de la música española e hispanoamericana* (Barcelona, 1958); *Temas musicales madrileños* (Madrid, 1971).

Subono, Blacius, popular Indonesian composer and dhalang (shadow puppet master), brother of **Yohanes Subowo**; b. Klaten, Central Java, Feb. 3, 1954. He was born into an artistic family, the 7th of 9 children who all became successful artists. He began his music studies at 6, often accompanying his father, the shadow puppet master Yusuf Kiyatdiharjo; at 12, began to perform alone. While at the high school cons. Konservatori Karawitan (KOKAR), he helped to create a new form of puppet theater, *wayang kancil,* featuring a cast of animal characters and new musical arrangements; at the college cons. Akademi Seni Karawiten Indonesia (A.S.K.I., later Sekolah Tinggi Seni Indonesia [S.T.S.I.]) Surakarta, he was encouraged by its director, S.D. Humardani, to try his hand at musical experimentation. He composed several new works, including another wayang innovation, *wayang sandosa*; in 1983 he attended the national Pekan Komponis Muda (Young Composer's Festival) in Jakarta. He received numerous commissions and invitations to perform the 9-hour *wayang kulit*; performed and lectured in France (1982), Singapore (1982), England and Spain (1984), and Canada and the U.S. (1986); in 1990 he lectured at Simon Fraser Univ. in Vancouver, where he composed his first work with an English text. Subono's output includes popular songs with gamelan accompaniment as well as experimental scores, i.e., 1 for a chamber ensemble made up of only very high-pitched instruments (*griting rasa*), 1 for a wide range of knobbed gongs (*swara pencon*), and several unrealized pieces for very large chorus. His publications concerning musical accompaniment for the new, intensified style of *wayang kulit* called *pakeliran padat* include *Iringan Pakeliran Dewasa Ini* (1981), *Kuliah Letihan Tabuh Iringan Pakeliran Padat di ASKI Surakarta* (1984), and *Evaluasi Garap Iringan Pakeliran Padat* (1987).

WORKS (all for Central Javanese gamelan): **EXPERIMENTAL:** *Swara Pencon I* (1983) and *II* (1986); *Griting Rasa* (1989). **DANCE:** *Komposisi Hitam Putih* (1980); *Rudrah* (1981); *Bisma Gugur* (1982); *Ronggolawe Gugur* (1982); *Kusumo Asih* (1983); *Anila Prahastho* (1985); *Bhagawatgita* (1985); *Gathutkaca Burisrawa* (1985); *Jemparingan* (1985); *Anoman Kataksini* (1986); *Rahwana Gandrung* (1987). **SHADOW PUPPET THEATER (PAKELIRAN PADAT):** *Kangsa Lena* (1983); *Kilat Buana* (1984); *Duryudana Gugur* (1985); *Gandamana Tundhung* (1985). **DANCE OPERA (WAYANG ORANG):** *Seno Kridho* (1984). **MODERN SHADOW PUPPET THEATER (WAYANG SANDOSA):** *Karna Tandhing* (1982); *Dewa Ruci* (1983); *Ciptaning* (1984). **SONGS:** *Pungjir* (1974); *Kidang Kencana* (1980); *Surakarta Lejer Budaya* (1982); *Solo Berseri* (1985); *Gotong Royong* (1985); *Bingung* (1986); *Air Minum* (1987); *Palinglih* (1987); *Sukaharja Papanku* (1987); *Urip Prasaja* (1987); also scripts for puppet theater with animal characters only (*wayang kancil*) and for dance opera (*wayang orang*).

Subotnick, Morton, American composer and teacher; b. Los Angeles, April 14, 1933. He studied at the Univ. of Denver (B.A., 1958) and with Milhaud and Kirchner at Mills College in Oakland, Calif. (M.A., 1960); then was a fellow of the Inst. for Advanced Musical Studies at Princeton Univ. (1959–60). He taught at Mills College (1959–66), N.Y. Univ. (1966–69), and the Calif. Inst. of the Arts (from 1969); also held various visiting professorships and composer-in-residence positions. In 1979 he married **Joan La Barbara**. His compositions run the gamut of avant-garde techniques, often with innovative use of electronics; his *Silver Apples of the Moon* (1967) became a classic. In 1995, working with programmer Mark Coniglio at the Institute for Studies in the Arts at Arizona State Univ. in Tempe, he completed *Making Music,* an interactive CD-ROM composition program for children; his *All My Hummingbirds Have Alibis,* an "imaginary ballet" set to a series of Max Ernst's paintings for Flute, Cello, Midi Piano, Midi Mallets, and Electronics (1991), was also later converted into a critically appraised CD-ROM.

WORKS: DRAMATIC: OPERA: *Jacob's Room* (Philadelphia, April 20, 1993). **INCIDENTAL MUSIC TO:** Genet's *The Balcony* (1960); Shakespeare's *King Lear* (1960); Brecht's *Galileo* (1964) and *The Caucasian Chalk Circle* (1965); Büchner's *Danton's Death* (1966). **ORCH.:** *Play! No. 2* for Orch. and Tape (1964); *Lamination No. 1* for Orch. and Tape (1968) and *No. 2* for Chamber Ensemble and Electronics (1969); *Before the Butterfly* for 7 Solo Instruments and Orch. (1975; Los Angeles, Feb. 26, 1976); *2 Butterflies* for Amplified Orch. (1975); *Place* (1978); *Axolotl* for Cello, Chamber Orch., and Electronics (1982); *Liquid Strata* for Piano, Orch., and Electronics (1982); *The Key to Songs* for Chamber Orch. and Synthesizer (1985); *In 2 Worlds*, concerto for Saxophone, Electronic Wind Controller, and Orch. (1987–88); *And the Butterflies Began to Sing* for YCAMS and Chamber Ensemble (1988). **MIXED MEDIA:** *Mr. and Mrs. Discobolos* for Clarinet, Violin, Cello, Narrator-Mime, and Tape (1958); *Sound Blocks* for Narrator, Violin, Cello, Xylophone, Marimba, Tape, and Lights (1961); *Mandolin* for Viola, Tape, and Film (1963); *Play! No. 1* for Wind Quintet, Tape, and Film (1963), *No. 3* for Piano, Tape, and Film (1964), and *No. 4* for 4 Actors, Performers, Piano, Vibraphone, Cello, and 2 Films (1965); *4 Butterflies* for Tape and 3 Films (1973); *The Double Life of Amphibians*, theater piece (1984). **VOCAL:** *2 Life Histories* for Man's Voice, Clarinet, and Electronics (1977); *Last Dream of the Beast* for Woman's Voice and Electronics (1978); *Jacob's Room* for Voice and String Quartet (1984; San Francisco, Jan. 11, 1985). **INSTRUMENTAL:** *Prelude No. 1 (The Blind Owl)* for Piano and *No. 2 (The Feast)* for Piano (both 1956); Viola Sonata (1959); String Quartet (1960); Sonata for Piano, 4-hands (1960); *Serenade No. 1* for Flute, Clarinet, Vibraphone, Mandolin, Cello, and Piano (1960) and *No. 2* for Clarinet, Horn, Percussion, and Piano (1962); *10* for 10 Instruments (1963–76); *The Tarot* for Chamber Ensemble (1965); *The Fluttering of Wings* for String Quartet (1982). **INSTRUMENTAL AND ELECTRONICS:** *Preludes Nos. 3 and 4* for Piano and Tape (1962–65); *Serenade No. 3* for Flute, Clarinet, Violin, Piano, and Tape (1963); *Liquid Strata* for Piano and Electronics (1977); *Parallel Lines* for Piccolo, 9 Instruments, and Electronics (1978); *Passages of the Beast* for Clarinet and Electronics (1978); *The Wild Beasts* for Trombone, Piano, and Electronics (1978); *After the Butterfly* for Trumpet, 7 Instruments, and Electronics (1979); *The 1st Dream of Light* for Tuba, Piano, and Electronics (1979); *Ascent into Air* for 10 Instruments and Electronics (1981); *An Arsenal of Defense* for Viola and Electronics (1982); *Tremblings* for Violin, Piano, and Electronics (1983); *All My Hummingbirds Have Alibis* for Flute, Cello, Midi Piano, Midi Mallets, and Electronics (1991). **TAPE:** *The 5-legged Stool* (1963); *Parades and Changes* (1967); *Silver Apples of the Moon* (1967); *Realty I* and *II* (1968); *The Wild Bull* (1968); *Touch* (1969); *Sidewinder* (1971); *Until Spring* (1975); *Ice Floe* (1978); *A Sky of Cloudless Sulphur* (1978); *Sky with Clouds* (1978).

BIBL.: H. Whipple, "Beasts and Butterflies: M. S.'s Ghost Scores," *Musical Quarterly* (Oct. 1983).

Subowo, Yohanes, Indonesian dancer and composer, brother of Blacius Subono; b. Klaten, Central Java, Jan. 1, 1960. He was born into an artistic family (his 8 older siblings were professional artists), and although he wanted to join the army, he was persuaded by his father, the shadow puppet master (dhalang) Yusuf Kiyatdiharjo, to pursue a career in the arts. After studying dance and composition at Institute Seni Indonesia (I.S.I., National Arts Inst.; graduated, 1986), he joined its dance faculty. In 1982 he began experimenting with instruments other than those of the Javanese gamelan; made small instruments from bamboo, tuning them to the gamelan, using cowbells, tin roofing sheets, and whistles made from bamboo and coconut leaves; also transposed music using techniques from Javanese gamelan to such Western instruments as electronic keyboards. In some compositions, he imposes strict limitations on pitch and/or instrumentation and also experiments with such extended vocal techniques as having singers sing into bamboo tubes or bronze pot-gongs. His compositions borrow their structures from jazz, rock, and Western Classical styles, while drawing on African and popular Indonesian music; these include *Orak-Arik*, *Lesung* (1981), *Gobyog* (1982), *Kentongan*, *Patmo* (1982), and *Tanggung* (1984), variously scored for Javanese gamelan, found objects, farm tools, and electronic and original instruments. He also experimented with sounds generated by devices attached to a dancer's body. In 1985 he toured England as both a dancer and a musician.

Suchoff, Benjamin, distinguished American music educator and musicologist; b. N.Y., Jan. 19, 1918. He studied at Cornell Univ. (B.S., 1940); then took courses in composition with Vittorio Giannini at the Juilliard School of Music in N.Y. (1940–41). After serving in the U.S. Army in Europe and Asia in World War II, he resumed his studies, first at Juilliard (1946–47) and then at N.Y. Univ. (M.A., 1949; Ed.D., 1956, with the diss. *Guide to Bartók's Mikrokosmos*; publ. in London, 1957; 3rd ed., N.Y., 1982). From 1950 to 1978 he was administrator of music at Hewlett-Woodmere Union Free School on Long Island, where he also taught electronic music. From 1973 to 1984 he was adjunct prof. of arts and letters at the State Univ. of N.Y. at Stony Brook; also was director of its special collections and of the Center for Contemporary Arts and Letters, where he guided the fortunes of the COMMPUTE Program, a consortium of institutions active in research and development of computer-oriented music studies. In 1953 he became curator of the N.Y. Bartók Archive. From 1968 until the death of Bartók's widow in 1982 he was successor-trustee of the Bartók estate. In 1992 he became adjunct prof. in the dept. of ethnomusicology and systematic musicology at the Univ. of Calif., Los Angeles. He is the ed. of the N.Y. Bartók Archive edition of Bartók's writings in English trs. in its Studies in Musicology series; also is ed. of its edition of Bartók's compositions, known as *The Archive Edition*. He also publ. *A Musician's Guide to Desktop Computing* (N.Y., 1993) and *Bartók: The Concerto for Orchestra: Understanding Bartók's World* (N.Y., 1995).

Suchoň, Eugen, significant Slovak composer and pedagogue; b. Pezinok, Sept. 25, 1908; d. Bratislava, Aug. 5, 1993. He studied piano and composition with Kafenda at the Bratislava School of Music (1920–28); then took a course in advanced composition with V. Novák at the Master School of the Prague Cons. (1931–33). He taught composition at the Bratislava Academy of Music (1933–48) and music education at the Univ. of Bratislava (1949–60); was a prof. of theory there from 1959 to 1974; in 1971 he was appointed prof. at the College of Music and Dramatic Art in Bratislava. In 1958 he was named National Artist of the Republic of Czechoslovakia. He was one of the creators of the modern Slovak style of composition, based on authentic folk motifs and couched in appropriately congenial harmonies.

WORKS: OPERAS: *Krútňava* (The Whirlpool; 1941–49; Bratislava, Dec. 10, 1949); *Svätopluk* (1952–59; Bratislava, March 10, 1960). **ORCH.:** *Fantasy and Burlesque* for Violin and Orch. (originally a *Burlesque*, 1933; the *Fantasy* was added in 1948); *Balladic Suite* for Orch. or Piano (1935); *Metamorphoses*, symphonic variations (1951–52); *6 Pieces* for String Ensemble or String Quartet (1955–63); *Sinfonietta rustica* (1956); *Rhapsodic Suite* for Piano and Orch. (1965); *Kaleidoscope*, 6 cycles for Strings, Percussion, and Piano (1967–68); *Symphonic Fantasy on B-A-C-H* for Organ, Strings, and Percussion (1971); Clarinet Concertino (1975); *Prielom Symphony* (1976). **CHAMBER:** Violin Sonata (1930); String Quartet (1931; rev. 1939); *Serenade* for Wind Quintet (1931); Piano Quartet (1932–33); Violin Sonatina (1937); *Poème macabre* for Violin and Piano (1963); piano pieces, including a *Toccata* (1973). **VOCAL:** *Nox et solitudo* for Soprano, and Small Orch. or Piano (1933); *Carpathian Psalm*, cantata (1937–38); *Ad astra*, 5 songs for Soprano and Small Orch. (1961); *Contemplations* for Narrator and Piano (1964).

BIBL.: E. Zavarský, *E. S.* (Bratislava, 1955); J. Kresánek, *Národný umelec E. S.* (National Artist E. S.; Bratislava, 1961).

Suchý, František, Czech teacher, conductor, and composer; b. Březové Hory u Příbrami, April 21, 1891; d. Prague, June 13, 1973. He studied at the local teaching inst. (1906–10); after studies with Horník and Stecker at the Prague Cons. (1913–14), he received lessons in conducting from Nikisch in Leipzig (1914–16); subsequently was active as a teacher, conductor, and composer.

WORKS: DRAMATIC: OPERAS: *Lásky div* (The Wonder of Love; 1923); *Havéři* (The Miners; 1947–57). **BALLET:** *Porcelánové království* (The Porcelain Kingdom; 1922). **ORCH.:** *Rokoková suita* (Rococo Suite) for Small Orch. (1931); *Stříbrné město* (The Silver Town), sym. (1935). **OTHER:** Choruses; songs; piano pieces.

Suchý, František, Czech oboist, pedagogue, and composer; b. Libina u Šumperka, April 9, 1902; d. Brno, July 12, 1977. He studied oboe with Wagner and composition with Kvapil at the Brno Cons. (graduated, 1927); then attended Novák's master classes at the Prague Cons. (until 1937). He was 1st oboist in the Brno Radio Orch. (1927–47); then was a prof. of oboe at the Cons. and a prof. of oboe and theory at the Academy in Brno.

WORKS: OPERA: *Maryla* (1956). **ORCH.:** Flute Concerto (1939); *Baroque Concerto* for Violin and Orch. (1944); 4 syms. (1946, 1950, 1957, 1962); Oboe Concerto (1948); *Vysočina* (Uplands), symphonic suite (1957). **CHAMBER:** Oboe Sonatina (1927); 2 wind quintets (1928, 1958); Wind Sextet (1960); various sonatas. **VOCAL:** *V. Gethsemané*, oratorio (1933); cantatas; songs;

Suckling, Norman, English pianist, teacher, writer on music, and composer; b. London, Oct. 24, 1904. He received his academic education at Queen's College, Oxford, specializing in French literature. He was assistant master at Liverpool Collegiate School (1925–43); then was a lecturer in French language and literature at King's College, Newcastle upon Tyne, in the Federal Univ. of Durham (1943–70). While thus occupied, he developed sufficient mastery of the piano to give concerts, at which he presented programs of modern French music. He publ. a monograph on Gabriel Fauré (London, 1946) and several books on French literature; also contributed articles on English and French composers to the Listener and other literary publications. His compositions are mostly in small forms; his songs are particularly fine.

WORKS: *Introduction and Scherzo* for String Quartet (1923); *Ode* for Violin and Piano (1925); *A Vision of Avalon*, chamber opera (1928); *A Cycle of Shakespeare Sonnets* for Tenor, Violin, and Piano (1928); Violin Sonata (1928); *Man in the Beginning*, ballet (1934); *Berceuse élégiaque* for Clarinet and Piano, to commemorate a pet kitten, and written for the composer's 1st wife (1943); *Pastorale saugrenue* for Flute and Bassoon (1944); *Variations on a Theme of Rameau* for Flute and Piano (1947); many songs to words by English poets.

Sugár, Rezső, Hungarian composer and teacher; b. Budapest, Oct. 9, 1919; d. there, Sept. 22, 1988. He was a pupil of Kodály at the Budapest Academy of Music (1937–42). He taught in Budapest at the Béla Bartók Cons. (1949–68); from 1968 to 1980 he taught at the Academy of Music.

WORKS: BALLET: *Ácisz és Galatea* (Acis and Galatea; 1957; rev. 1961 as *A tenger lánya* [The Daughter of the Sea]). **ORCH.:** *Divertimento* for Strings (1948); *Rondo* for Piano and Strings (1952); *Concerto in Memoriam Béla Bartók* (1962); *Metamorfosi* (1966); *Partita* for Strings (1967); *Variation Symphony* (1970); *Epilogue* (1974); Concertino for Chamber Orch. (1976); *Pastorale e rondo* (1978). **CHAMBER:** *Serenade* for 2 Violins and Viola (1943); Violin Sonata (1946); 3 string quartets (1947, 1950, 1969); *Frammenti musicali*, sextet for Piano and Wind Quintet (1958); *Rhapsody* for Cello and Piano (1959); also *Baroque Sonatina* for Piano (1943–46). **VOCAL: ORATORIOS:** *Hunyadi: Hősi ének* (Hunyadi: Heroic Song; 1951); *Paraszti háború* (Peasant War; 1976); *Savonarola* (1979). **CANTATA:** *Kőmíves Kelemen* (Kelemen, the Mason; 1958). Also numerous choral pieces; songs.

Suggia, Guilhermina, gifted Portuguese cellist; b. Oporto, June 27, 1888; d. there, July 31, 1950. She was a child prodigy and made her first public appearance at age 7; became 1st cellist in the Oporto Orch. when she was 12. Under the patronage of the Queen of Portugal, she was sent to Leipzig in 1904 to study with Julius Klengel; in 1905 she joined the Gewandhaus Orch. there. In 1906 she began studies with Casals; they subsequently lived and toured together, although they were never legally married; she appeared in concerts as Mme. Casals-Suggia until they parted company in 1912. Shortly afterward she settled in London, where she continued to appear in concerts until 1949, when she went back to Portugal. She was greatly appreciated for her fine musicianship as well as virtuosity. In 1923 Augustus John painted her portrait, which became famous.

BIBL.: F. Pombo, *G. S. ou o violoncelo luxuriante* (Porto, 1993).

Suitner, Otmar, Austrian conductor; b. Innsbruck, May 16, 1922. He studied piano at the Innsbruck Cons. and then piano with Ledwinka and conducting with Krauss at the Salzburg Mozarteum (1940–42). In 1945 he conducted at the Innsbruck Landestheater; was then music director in Remscheid (1952–57) and Generalmusikdirektor in Ludwigshafen (1957–60). From 1960 to 1964 he served as Generalmusikdirektor of the Dresden State Opera and Dresden State Orch.; from 1964 to 1971, conducted at the East Berlin State Opera, and from 1974 to 1991 was its Generalmusikdirektor. He also conducted in America; was a guest conductor with the San Francisco Opera.

Suk (I), Josef, eminent Czech violinist, pedagogue, and composer, grandfather of **Josef Suk (II)**; b. Křečovice, Jan. 4, 1874; d. Benešov, near Prague, May 29, 1935. He received training in piano, violin, and organ from his father, Josef Suk (1827–1913), the Křečovice school- and choirmaster; then took courses in violin with Bennewitz, in theory with Foerster, Knittl, and Stecker, and in chamber music with Wihan at the Prague Cons. (1885–91); after graduating in 1891, he pursued additional training in chamber music with Wihan and in composition with Dvořák at the Cons. (1891–92). In 1898 he married Dvořák's daughter Otilie. He began his career playing 2nd violin in Wihan's string quartet, which became known as the Czech Quartet in 1892; he remained a member of it until his retirement in 1933. He also was a prof. of composition at the Prague Cons. (from 1922), where he was head of its master classes; also served as its rector (1924–26; 1933–35). Suk's early works were greatly influenced by Dvořák; in later years his lyrical Romantic style evolved into an individual style characterized by polytonal writing and harmonic complexity bordering on atonality.

WORKS: INCIDENTAL MUSIC: *Radúz a Mahulena* for Alto, Tenor, Reciters, Chorus, and Orch., op. 13 (Prague, April 6, 1898; rev. 1912); *Pod jabloní* (Beneath the Apple Tree) for Alto, Reciters, Chorus, and Orch., op. 20 (1900–1901; rev. 1911, 1915; Prague, Jan. 31, 1934).

ORCH. (all 1st perf. in Prague unless otherwise given): *Fantasie* for Strings (1888; Jan. 29, 1940); *Smuteční pochod* (Funeral March; 1889; rev. 1934; June 3, 1935); *Dramatická overtura*, op. 4 (1891–92; July 9, 1892); *Serenade* for Strings, op. 6 (1892; Feb. 25, 1894); *Pohádka zimního večera* (Tale of a Winter's Evening), overture after Shakespeare, op. 9 (1894; April 7, 1895; rev. 1918, 1925); 2 syms.: No. 1 in E major, op. 14 (1897–99; Nov. 25, 1899) and No. 2, *Asrael*, op. 27 (1905–06; Feb. 3, 1907); *Pohádka* (Fairy Tale), suite from *Radús a Mahulena*, op. 16 (1899–1900; Feb. 7, 1901); *Fantasie* for Violin and Orch., op. 24 (1902–03; Jan. 9, 1904); *Fantastické scherzo*, op. 25 (1903; April 18, 1905); *Praga*, symphonic poem, op. 26 (Pilsen, Dec. 18, 1904); *Pohádka léta* (A Summer Fairy Tale), symphonic poem, op. 29 (1907–09; Jan. 26, 1909); *Zrání* (The Ripening), symphonic poem, op. 34 (1912–17; Oct. 30, 1918); *Meditace na staročeský chorál "Svatý Vaclave"* (Meditation on an Old Czech Chorale "St. Wenceslas") for Strings, op. 35a (1914; also for String Quartet); *Legenda o mrtvých vítězích* (Legend of the Dead Victors), op. 35b (1919–20; Oct. 24, 1924); *V nový život* (Toward a New Life), march, op. 35c (June 27, 1920; also for Piano Duet); *Pod Blaníkem* (Beneath Blanik), march (1932; orchestrated by J. Kalaš; Jan. 26, 1934).

CHAMBER: *Polka* for Violin (1882); String Quartet (1888); *Fantasy* for String Quartet and Piano ad libidum (1888); Piano Quartet, op. 1 (1891); Piano Trio, op. 2 (1889; rev. 1890–91); *Balada* for String Quartet (1890); *Balada* for Cello and Piano, op. 3/1 (1890); *Serenade* for Cello and Piano, op. 3/2 (c.1898); *Balada* for Violin and Piano (1890); *Melodie* for 2 Violins (1893); Piano Quintet, op. 8 (1893); String Quartet, op. 11 (1896; last movement rev. 1915 and left as an independent work); 4 Pieces for Violin and Piano, op. 17 (1900); *Elegie: Pod dojmen Zeyerova Vyšehradu* (Under the Impression of Zeyer's Vyšehrad) for Violin, Cello, String Quartet, Harmonium, and Harp, op. 23 (1902; also for Piano Trio); String Quartet, op. 31 (1911); *Meditace na staročeský chorál "Svatý Václave"* (Meditation on an Old Czech Chorale "St. Wenceslas") for String Quartet, op. 35a (1914; also for String Orch.); *Bagatelle: S kyticí v ruce* (Carrying a Bouquet) for Flute, Violin, and Piano (1917); *Sousedská* for 5 Violins, Double Bass, Cymbals, Triangle, and Large and Small Drums (1935). **PIANO:** Sonata (1883); *Overture* (1884–85); *Polonaise* (1886–87); *Jindřichohradecký cyklus* (Jindřichův Hradec Suite; 1886–87); Fugue (1888); *Tři písně beze slov* (3 Songs without Words; 1891); *Fantaisie-polonaise*, op. 5 (1892); 6 pieces, op. 7 (1891–93); *Capriccietto* (1893); *Humoreska* (1894); *Lístek do památníku* (Album Leaf; 1895); *Nálady* (Moods), op. 10 (1895); 8 pieces, op. 12 (1895–96); Sonatina, op. 13 (1897; rev. as Suite, op. 21, 1900); *Vesnická serenáda* (Village Serenade; 1897); *Jaro* (Spring), op. 22a (1902); *Letni dojmy* (Summer Moods), op. 22b (1902); *O matince* (About Mother), op. 28 (1907); *Psina španělská* (Spanish Joke; 1909); *Životem a snem* (Things Lived and Dreamt), op. 30 (1909); *Ukolébavky*, op. 33 (1910–12); *O přátelství* (Friendship), op. 36 (1920).

VOCAL: *Křečovická mše* (Křečovice Mass) for Chorus, Strings, and Organ (1888–89); *Epilog* for Soprano, Baritone, Bass, 2 Choruses, and Orch., op. 37 (1920–33; Dec. 20, 1933); men's choruses; songs.

BIBL.: J. Kvt, ed., *J. S.: Život a dilo: Studie a vzpomínsky* (J. S.: Life and Works: Studies and Reminiscences; Prague, 1935); idem, *J. S.* (Prague, 1936); J. Šach, ed., *J. S.: Vzpomínková mozaika* (J. S.: A Mosaic of Reminiscences; Prague, 1941); V. Štěpán, *Novák a S.* (Prague, 1945); J. Květ, ed., *Živá slova J.a S.a* (In J. S.'s Own Words; Prague, 1946); O. Filipovský, *Klavirni tvorba J.a S.a* (J. S.'s Piano Works; Plzen, 1947); J. Květ, *J. S.* (Prague, 1947); J. Berkovec, *J. S. (1874–1935): Život a dilo* (J. S. [1874–1935]: Life and Works; Prague, 1956; 2nd ed., 1962; rev. and abr. ed., 1968, as *J. S.*; Eng., Ger., French, and Russian trs., 1968); J. Květ, *J. S. v obrazech* (J. S. in Pictures; Prague, 1964); Z. Sádecký, *Lyrismus v tvorbě J.a S.a* (Lyricism in J. S.'s Works; Prague, 1966); M. Svobodová, *J. S.: Tematický Katalog* (Jinočany, 1993).

Suk (II), Josef, outstanding Czech violinist, grandson of **Josef Suk (I)**; b. Prague, Aug. 8, 1929. His great-grandfather was the great Czech composer Antonin (Leopold) Dvořák (b. Mühlhausen, Sept. 8, 1841; d. Prague, May 1, 1904). He was only a child when he commenced violin lessons with Jaroslav Kocián, who remained his teacher until the latter's death in 1950; Suk also studied at the Prague Cons. (until 1951) and then with M. Hlouňová and A. Plocek at the Prague Academy of Music (1951–53). He made his public debut in 1940; later played in the orch. of the Prague National Theater; also was a member of the Prague Quartet (1951–52). In 1952 he founded the Suk Trio with the pianist Jan Panenka and the cellist Josef Chuchro, and toured widely with it; his interest in chamber music led him to form a duo with Zuzana Růžičkova in 1963; he was also a member of a trio with Julius Katchen and Janos Starker (1967–69). In 1959 he made a grand tour as soloist to 3 continents with the Czech Phil. On Jan. 23, 1964, he made his U.S. debut with the Cleveland Orch., and subsequently appeared as soloist with other American orchs. In 1964 he received a Czech State Prize; in 1970 he was made an Artist of Merit and in 1977 was named a National Artist of Czechoslovakia.

Suk, Váša (Václav; Viacheslav Ivanovich), noted Russian conductor and composer of Czech parentage; b. Kladno, Nov. 16, 1861; d. Moscow, Jan. 12, 1933. He studied violin at the Prague Cons. and composition privately with Fibich. He was concertmaster of the Kiev Opera orch. (1880–82) and a violinist in the Bolshoi Theater orch. in Moscow (1882–87); in 1885 he launched a conducting career, and subsequently appeared throughout Russia; was a conductor of the Bolshoi Theater (1906–32) and principal conductor of the Stanislavsky Opera Theater in Moscow (from 1927). He was appreciated in Russia for his thoroughness in drilling the singers and the orch.; achieved a fine reputation as an operatic conductor. He wrote an opera, *Lord of the Forests*, which he conducted in Kharkov on Feb. 16, 1900; also composed a symphonic poem, *Jan Huss* (Moscow, March 12, 1933); a Serenade for String Orch.; piano pieces; songs.

BIBL.: I. Remezov, *V.I. S.* (Moscow and Leningrad, 1951).

Sukegawa, Toshiya, Japanese composer; b. Sapporo, July 15, 1930. He studied with Ikenouchi from 1951; graduated in composition from the Univ. of Arts in Tokyo in 1957.

WORKS: TELEVISION OPERA: *Pôra no Hiroba* (1959). **ORCH.:** *Passacaglia* (1954); *Partita* (1960); *Legend* (1965). **CHAMBER:** String Quartet (1956); *Music* for Flute, Clarinet, Violin, Cello, Percussion, and Piano (1958); Wind Quintet (1962); *5 Metamorphoses* for Viola and Piano (1966); *3 Parts* for 5 Flute Players (1967); *3 Scenes* for Jushichigen, 3 Violins, and Viola (1969); *A Projection* for Marimba, Piccolo, Trombone, Piano, and Percussion (1969); *5 Pieces after Paul Klee* for Marimba (1973); *Song of the Wind* for Tape (1980); *Les Jours passants*, trio for Flute, Violin, and Harpsichord (1982); *Eternal Morning* for Tape (1983); *Mirror* for 2 Flutes (1984); *The Berin Strait* for Tape (1986); *Blue Mountain* for Synthesizer and Tape (1987); *La Folia 2 (From the Galaxy Far Away)* for Synthesizer (1988). **PIANO:** Sonata (1958); *Divertimento* for 2 Pianos (1958); *Tapestry* (1966–68); *5 Symbolic Pictures* (1972); *Sequenza* (1985); *Komoriuta* (1986). **VOCAL:** *The White World* for Chorus and Piano (1971); *Eika* for Chorus and Japanese Percussion (1972).

Sukerta, Pande Made, innovative Indonesian composer, writer on Balinese music, and teacher; b. Tekakula, Singaraja, Bali, 1953. He studied at the high school music cons. in Denpasar, specializing in the rebab (bowed double-stringed fiddle); in 1973 he entered the Akademi Seni Karawitan Indonesia (A.S.K.I.) Surakarta, where he was founding director of various Balinese gamelan groups; also was active as a performer of *eksperimen karawitan baru*, a style of experimental music played on traditional instruments. After graduating in 1979, he joined the faculty at A.S.K.I. (later Sekolah Tinggi Seni Indonesia [S.T.S.I.]), where he led improvisation workshops wherein students explored the sonic potential of both gamelan and "found" instruments. He participated in Jakarta's Young Choreographers' Festival (1978) and at the national Pekan Komponis Muda (Young Composers' Festival; 1979, 1981, 1984); his *Asanawali* for Balinese Gamelan and Chorus was heard at EXPO '86 in Vancouver as part of the 1st International Gamelan Festival on a program of the Vancouver Sym. Orch., which included works by Debussy and Colin McPhee. In 1989 he was one of 7 composers commissioned to create new works for a recording project of the American Gamelan Inst. in Hanover, N.H. He toured in France, Denmark, Italy, Switzerland, Iran, Australia, Canada, and the U.S. Sukerta's works are variously scored for Balinese and Javanese gamelans and "found" instruments and often include improvisatory aspects; his *Mana 689* (1989) makes use of drums from Java, Sunda, and Sumatra, as well as bottles, marbles, a chanting priest, and screaming children (2 of his own 4). Other works include *Malam, Demung, Gora Suara* (1981), and *Saik 789* (1989). He is also a prolific writer, numbering among his publications an extended essay on the process of composition, an encyclopedia of Balinese instruments, and transcriptions of melodies from the archaic Balinese ensemble Gambuh.

WRITINGS (all publ. in Surakarta): *Gending-gending Semar Pegulingan Saih Pitu* (1977); *Rebaban Karawitan Bali* (1979);

Gending-gending Gong Gede; Gamelan Gong Gede di Desa Batur (1986; notation and drawings of instruments and cases).

Šulek, Stjepan, prominent Croatian violinist, conductor, teacher, and composer; b. Zagreb, Aug. 5, 1914; d. there, Jan. 16, 1986. He studied violin with Huml at the Zagreb Academy of Music; was largely self-taught in composition, although he succeeded in becoming a composer of considerable merit. He was active as a violinist; became best known as a conductor; conducted the Zagreb Radio Chamber Orch. on many tours of Europe; was prof. of composition at the Zagreb Academy of Music (from 1945). His compositions reveal a strong individual profile.

WORKS: OPERAS: *Koriolan*, after Shakespeare (Zagreb, Oct. 12, 1958); *Oluja* (The Tempest), after Shakespeare (Zagreb, Nov. 28, 1969). **ORCH.:** 6 syms. (1944, 1946, 1948, 1954, 1963, 1966); *Scientiae et arti*, festive prologue (1966); 4 piano concertos (1949, 1951, 1963, 1970); Cello Concerto (1950); Violin Concerto (1951); Bassoon Concerto (1958); Viola Concerto (1959); Clarinet Concerto (1967); Horn Concerto (1972); Organ Concerto (1974). **OTHER:** *Zadnji Adam* (The Last Adam), cantata (1964); songs; piano pieces.

BIBL.: K. Šipuš, *S. Š.* (Zagreb, 1961).

Sultan, Grete, German-born American pianist; b. Berlin, June 21, 1906. She was reared in a musical family; studied with Kreutzer at the Berlin Hochschule für Musik (1922–25) and later with Fischer, Arrau, and Buhlig. She established herself as a pianist of both Classical and contemporary works in Berlin before going to the U.S. in 1941; she toured widely, giving all-Bach, all-Beethoven, all-Schubert, and all-contemporary programs; made her N.Y. debut in 1947. She became associated with Cowell, with whom she gave performances of works by Schoenberg and Stravinsky; settling in N.Y., she met John Cage, who became a lifelong friend and assoc.; they often appeared in concerts together, and Cage wrote his *Etudes australes*, a chance-determined set of 32 etudes based on star maps, for her; she performed it throughout the U.S. and Europe and in Japan. In 1968–69 she gave a series of programs at N.Y.'s Town Hall under its Jonathan Peterson Lectureship Fund. Sultan's performances, which continue well into her 80s, are always critically acclaimed, her alacrity, sensitivity, and uncompromising directness uniquely enhancing the disparate works she programs; most recently she has championed the works of Ben Weber and Tui St. George Tucker. She was praised by Arrau, who saw her as following ". . . in the footsteps of the greatest women keyboard masters—Landowska, Haskil, Hess—blessed with musical purity and inwardness, reinforced by mind as well as soul."

Sumac, Yma (real name, **Emperatriz Chavarri**), Peruvian-born American singer of a phenomenal diapason, whose origin is veiled in mystical mist; b. Ichocan, Sept. 10, 1927. She was reared in the Andes; it is credible that she developed her phenomenal voice of 5 octaves in range because her lungs were inflated by the necessity of breathing through oxygen at the high altitude. However that might be, she married Moises Vivanco, who was an arranger for Capitol Records and who launched her on a flamboyant career as a concert singer; with him and their cousin, Cholito Rivero, she toured South America as the Inca Taky Trio (1942–46); then settled in the U.S. and became a naturalized American citizen in 1955. She was billed by unscrupulous promoters as an Inca princess, a direct descendant of Atahualpa, the last emperor of the Incas, a Golden Virgin of the Sun God worshipped by the Quechua Indians. On the other hand, some columnists spread the scurrilous rumor that she was in actuality a Jewish girl from Brooklyn whose real name was Amy (retrograde of Yma) Camus (retrograde of Sumac). But Sumac never spoke with a Brooklyn accent. She exercised a mesmeric appeal to her audiences, from South America to Russia, from California to Central Europe; expressions such as "miraculous" and "amazing" were used by Soviet reviewers during her tour of Russia in 1962; "supersonic vocal skill" was a term applied by an American critic. Her capacity did not diminish with age; during her California appearances in 1984 and again in 1988 she still impressed audiences with the expressive power of her voice.

Sumera, Lepo, esteemed Estonian composer; b. Tallinn, May 8, 1950. He was educated at the Tallinn State Cons. (1968–73), where he subsequently was a prof. (from 1976) and chairman of its composition dept. (1988–89); also attended summer courses in new music in Darmstadt (1988–89). He was a recording supervisor for Estonian Radio (1973–78). From 1989 to 1990 he was deputy minister of culture and from 1990 minister of culture for the Republic of Estonia. He received many Estonian Music Prizes for best composition of the year, including those for his film scores (1978), his Sym. No. 1 (1982), his Sym. No. 2 (1985), and his *Saare Piiga laul merest* (The Island Maiden; 1989).

WORKS: DRAMATIC: *Anselmi lugu*, ballet (1977–78); *Ja'st'eritsa*, ballet (1986–88); *Saare Piiga laul merest* (The Island Maiden), *Linda matab Kalevit* (Linda Buries Kalev), and *Linda soome Tuuslar* (Linda Becomes Stone), multimedia dance drama for Chamber Chorus, Actors, and Shaman Drum (1988); also more than 40 scores for film, television, animation, and theater. **ORCH.:** *In Memoriam* (1972); *Music* for Chamber Orchestra (1977–78; Tallinn, June 30, 1979); *Olūpiamuusika* (Olympic Music; 1981); 3 syms.: No. 1 (1980; Tallinn, Oct. 10, 1981), No. 2 (Tallinn, April 4, 1984), and No. 3 (Tallinn, Oct. 9, 1988); *Pikseloits* (Thunder Incantation; 1983); Piano Concerto (1989); *Open(r)ing* (1989); *Music for Glasgow* for Synthesizers and Chamber Orch. (1989); *Musik für Karlsruhe im Barockstil* for Strings and Harp (1989). **CHAMBER:** *Mäng punkpillidele* for Wind Quintet (1976); *Kaks pala sooloviiulile* for Violin (1977); *Malera Kasuku*, trio for Violin, Cello, and Piano (1977); *Sarvelugu* for Horn (1977);*Pantomiim* for Renaissance Instruments (1980); *Quasi improvisata* for Violin and Piano (1983); 2 capriccios for Clarinet (1984); *Valss* for Violin and Piano (1985); *For Boris Björn Bagger and Friend* for Flute and Guitar (1988); *From 59'22" to 42'49"* for Guitar and Prerecorded Tape (1989); *The Borders* for Acoustic and Amplified Instruments (1990). **PIANO:** *Ostinato-variations* (1967); *Fughetta and Postludium* (1972); *Pianissimo* (1976); *2 Pieces from the Year 1981*: No. 1 and No. 2, *Pardon, Fryderyk!* (1980); *The Butterfly Who Woke Up in Winter* (1982); *The Sad Toreador or The One Who Is Wiser Concedes* (1984). **VOCAL:** *Elust ja surmast*, cantata for Chorus and Orch. (1975); *Seenekantaat* (Mushroom Cantata), Part II, *Timor* (Dangerous; 1980; Tallinn, Feb. 7, 1981), Part III, *Carmen autumnus* (Tallinn, April 23, 1982), and Part IV, *Luxuria* (1983); *Laulupea tuli*, cantata (1985); *Kui tume veel kauaks ka sinu maa* for Chorus (1985).

Suñol (y Baulenas), Gregoria María, learned Spanish ecclesiastic and music scholar; b. Barcelona, Sept. 7, 1879; d. Rome, Oct. 26, 1946. He became a Benedictine monk at Montserrat Abbey in 1895; was ordained a priest in 1902, and then served as choirmaster there (1907–28). In 1930 he went to Rome as director of the Istituto Pontifico di Musica Sacra; was made abbot of Ste. Cecilia in Montserrat in 1943. He publ. the valuable books *Método completo de canto gregoriano según la escuela de Solesmes* (8 eds., 1905–43; also in French, Ger., Eng., Italian, and Portuguese) and *Introducctió a la paleografia musical gregoriana* (Montserrat, 1925; rev. French ed., Tournai, 1935, with R. Renaudin).

Sun Ra (real name, **Herman Blount**), innovative black American jazz pianist, electric keyboardist, bandleader, and composer; b. Birmingham, Ala., May 1914; d. there, May 30, 1993. He learned to play the piano and first gained notice as a member of Fletcher Henderson's orch. (1946–47); then went to Chicago, where he became a prominent figure in the avant-garde jazz scene. In 1956 he founded his own band, which was variously known as Solar Arkestra, Intergalactic Myth-Science Arkestra, Space Arkestra, etc.; later was active in N.Y. and Philadelphia; also toured throughout the U.S. and Europe; was a featured artist on the "Saturday Night Live" television show

(1976). Compositionally, he developed an abrasive and complex style in which avant-garde techniques are combined with electronic resources.

Suolahti, Heikki, Finnish composer; b. Helsinki, Feb. 2, 1920; d. there, Dec. 27, 1936. He studied at the Helsinki Cons. His tragically premature death at the age of 16 moved Sibelius to say that "Finland lost one of her greatest musical talents." Suolahti composed a few fine works, including a Violin Concerto, written at the age of 14, and a *Sinfonia piccola,* which he composed at 15 and which was performed in Helsinki after his death; also left some songs.

Supervia, Conchita, famous Spanish mezzo-soprano; b. Barcelona, Dec. 9, 1895; d. London, March 30, 1936. She studied at the Colegio de las Damas Negras in Barcelona. She made her operatic debut with a visiting opera company at the Teatro Colón in Buenos Aires on Oct. 1, 1910, in Stiattesi's opera *Blanca de Beaulieu.* She then sang in the Italian premiere of *Der Rosenkavalier* in Rome in 1911, as Carmen in Bologna in 1912, and as a member of the Chicago Opera (1915–16). She appeared frequently at La Scala in Milan from 1924; also sang in other Italian music centers, and at London's Covent Garden (1934–35). She endeared herself to the Italian public by reviving Rossini's operas *L'Italiana in Algeri* and *La Cenerentola*; she also attracted favorable critical attention by performing the part of Rosina in *Il Barbiere di Siviglia* in its original version as a coloratura contralto. In 1931 she married the British industrialist Sir Ben Rubenstein. She died as a result of complications following the birth of a child.

Supičić, Ivo, Yugoslav musicologist; b. Zagreb, July 18, 1928. He studied piano at the Zagreb Academy of Music, graduating in 1953; worked with C.N.R.S. in Paris (1960–63) while studying musicology at the Sorbonne (Ph.D., 1962, with the diss. *Elementi sociologije muzike*; publ. in an aug. ed., N.Y., 1987, as *Music in Society: A Guide to the Sociology of Music*). He taught at the musicology dept. of the Zagreb Academy of Music (from 1964) and then at Harvard Univ. (1967–68); served on the editorial board of the journals *Acta Musicologica* and *Arti Musices*; also was ed. of the *International Review of the Aesthetics and Sociology of Music.* His numerous publications focus on sociological aspects of music, especially that of the 20th century. In addition to his valuable diss., he also publ. *La Musique expressive* (Paris, 1957). S. Tuksar ed. a Festschrift in his honor (Zagreb, 1993).

Suppan, Wolfgang, Austrian musicologist; b. Irdning, Aug. 5, 1933. He studied clarinet, violin, piano, and theory at the Graz Hochschule für Musik and musicology with Federhofer and Marx at the Univ. of Graz (Ph.D., 1959, with the diss. *Heinrich Eduard Joseph von Lannoy [1787–1853]: Leben und Werke*). He worked in Freiburg im Breisgau at the East German Folklore Inst. (1961–63) and as director of the music dept. of the Folk Song Archive (1963–71). He completed his Habilitation at the Univ. of Mainz in 1971. He became a prof. and director of the Ethnomusicological Inst. of the Graz Hochschule für Musik in 1974. His research focuses on European folk music and music education.

WRITINGS: *Hanns Holenia: Eine Würdigung seines Lebens* (Graz, 1960); *Steirisches Musiklexikon* (Graz, 1962–66); *Volkslied: Seine Sammlung und Erforschung* (Stuttgart, 1966; 2nd ed., 1974); *Lexikon des Blasmusikwesens* (Freiburg im Breisgau, 1971; 2nd ed., 1976).

Suratno, Nano, prolific Indonesian composer, known as **Nano S.**; b. Pasar Kemis Tarogong, West Java, April 4, 1944. He earned degrees from the Akademi Seni Tari Indonesia (A.S.T.I.) Bandung (1978) and Sekolah Tinggi Seni Indonesia (S.T.S.I.) Surakarta (1989); also studied with Daeng Sutikna (music), Syafei (literature), Tjetje Somantri (choreography and dance), and, especially, Mang Koko (music). He formed his own dance company and then performed with Koko's group, Ganda Mekar. He began composing experimental works for degung, a traditional Sundanese chamber ensemble of tuned gongs, drums, and bamboo flute; in 1979 his *Sangkuriang* was performed at the important national festival Pekan Komponis Muda (Young Composers' Festival); he also began composing highly expressive instrumental music ("karawitan total"), and in 1985 mounted *Umbul-umbul,* involving 75 players in a mixture of over 15 Sundanese styles, on Indonesian TV. Nano S. sees many of his songs as a means of making traditional music more accessible to Sundanese youths; he often recasts classical melodies in forms that conform to popular music styles of the West. Even in his more experimental instrumental works, which he calls "musik total" or "musik murni" (i.e., "absolute" music), he neither borrows from foreign sources nor uses diatonic tuning; while such works have not yet found a place in the standard repertoire of Sunda, audiences abroad have been receptive; in 1989, on a commission from the American Gamelan Inst. in Hanover, N.H., he composed and recorded *Jemplang Polansky,* inspired by his confusion upon listening to the computer music of Larry Polansky, and *Galura* (Emotion; 1988), an instrumental solo piece for kecapi (plucked zither). In 1986 he toured in Canada and the U.S.; after appearing in Japan (1988), he became a guest lecturer and composer at the Univ. of Calif. at Santa Cruz (1989). In 1990 he directed the touring program "Sunda: From Village to City," presented in the U.S. at its Festival of Indonesia. Nano S. is best known in Indonesia as a song composer; his texts are often about young love, cast in the regional language of Sundanese, modern Indonesian, or English. More than 200 audiotapes of his works have been released, several of them distributed by the American Gamelan Inst. Among his publications are a book of songs, *Haleuang Tondang* (Bandung, 1975), and *Mengolah Seni Pertunjukan Sebagai Media Penergangan* (Development of the Performing Arts as an Information Medium; 1989); also some 15 operetta librettos. In 1978 he married the Indonesian singer Dheniarsah; their home in Bandung is a fertile international meeting ground for artists of all disciplines.

WORKS: *Ki Lagoni,* operetta (1967); *Raja Kecit,* operetta (1974); *Bubat* for Degung (1978); *Sangkuriang* for Gamelan (1979); *Sekar Manis* for 4 Kecapi (1980); *Anjeun* for Degung (1986); *Kalangkang* for Degung (1986); *Kangen* for Degung (1987); *Kalangkang* for Jaipongan (1987; also for Western Band [1987] and Kliningan Wanda Anyar [1988]); *Tibelat* for Pop Sunda (1988); *Cinta* for Pop Degung (1988); *Galura* for Kecapi (1988); *Jemplang Polansky* for Mixed Ensemble (1989); *Love Smir/Parkir* for Gamelan (1990); *Warna* for Gamelan (1990); *Karesman* for Gamelan (1990); many songs.

Surdin, Morris, Canadian composer; b. Toronto, May 8, 1914; d. there, Aug. 19, 1979. He learned to play piano, violin, cello, horn, and trombone; studied composition with Gesensway in Philadelphia (1937) and with Brant in N.Y. (1950). He worked as a music arranger for the CBC and CBS. From 1954 he worked in Canada, primarily in scoring for musicals, radio, television, and films.

WORKS: DRAMATIC: *The Remarkable Rocket,* ballet, after Oscar Wilde (1960–61); *Look Ahead,* musical comedy (1962); *Wild Rose,* opera-musical (1967). **ORCH.:** *4 X Strings* for Strings (1947); *Credo* (1950); *Inheritance* for Wind Quartet and Strings (1951); *Concert Ballet* (1955); *Incident I* for Strings (1961); Concerto for Mandolin and Strings (1961–66); *5 Shades of Brass* for Trumpet and Orch. (1961); 2 concertos for Free-bass Accordion: No. 1 (1966; Toronto, Jan. 29, 1967) and No. 2, with Strings, Electric Guitar, and Percussion (1977); *2 Solitudes* for Horn or English Horn and Strings (1967); *Formula I* and *II* for Concert Band (1968–69); *Horizon* for Strings (1968); *Short! No. 1* for Piano and Strings (1969) and *No. 2* for Piano, Wind Quartet, and Strings (1969); *6 Pieces in Search of a Sequence* for Solo Instruments and Strings (1969–78); *Alteration I* for Piccolo and Strings (1970) and *II* for Strings (1970); *Terminus* for Oboe, Bassoon, and Strings (1972); *B'rasheet* (In the Beginning) for Mandolin, Clarinet, and Strings (Toronto, June 15, 1974); *Eine kleine "Hammer-Klapper" Musik* for Chamber Orch. (1976);

Berceuse for Horn and Chamber Orch. (1977); *A Group of 6* for Strings in 1st position (1977); *5 for 4* for Strings in 1st position (1977); *Who's on Bass?* for Strings (1977); Violin Concerto (1978). **CHAMBER:** Suite for Viola and Piano (1954); *Carol Fantasia* for Brass (1955); *Incident II* for Woodwinds, Horns, and Harp (1961); *Elements* for 2 Violins, Double Bass, and Harpsichord (1965); *Matin* for Wind Quartet (1965); *Arioso* for 4 Cellos (1966); String Quartet (1966); Trio for Saxophones (1968); *Piece* for Wind Quintet (1969); *Serious I–XVI* for Accordion (1969–73); *Trinitas in Morte* for 3 Oboes, Bassoon, 3 Horns, Timpani, 8 Cellos, and 2 Double Basses (1973); *Sly'd Trombones I & II* for Trombone and Bass Trombone or Trombone Ensemble (1975); *Heritage I–IV* for Varying Brass Quartets (1975–79); *Landscapes*, sonatina for Harp (1978); *2 fabliaux* for Cello (1979). **PIANO:** *Naiveté*, 6 pieces (1962); *Poco Giocoso Variations* (1966); *In Search of Form I* and *II* (1970); *Fragmentations I–III* (1972). **VOCAL:** *A Spanish Tragedy* for Soprano and Orch. (1955); *Suite canadienne* for Chorus and Orch. (1970); *Feast of Thunder* for Soloists, Men's Chorus, and Orch. (1972); *Music Fair* for Soprano, Cello, and Harp (1975); Quartet for Trio for Low Voice, Cello, and Harp (1976); *Pegleg's Fiddle* for Men's Chorus, Solo Violin, Mandolin Orch., Piano, and Percussion (1977); *Leave It Be* for Bass, Chorus, and Orch. (1977; based on the musical comedy *Look Ahead*).

Surette, Thomas Whitney, American music educator; b. Concord, Mass., Sept. 7, 1861; d. there, May 19, 1941. He studied piano with Arthur Foote and composition with J.K. Paine at Harvard Univ. (1889–92), but failed to obtain a degree. Deeply interested in making musical education accessible and effective in the U.S., he founded the Concord Summer School of Music in 1915, which continued to operate until 1938; with A.T. Davison, he ed. The Concord Series of educational music, which found a tremendously favorable acceptance on the part of many schools, particularly in New England; the series provided an excellent selection of good music which could be understood by most music teachers and performed by pupils. He was also largely responsible for the vogue of music appreciation courses that swept the country and spilled over into the British Isles. He publ. *The Appreciation of Music* (with D.G. Mason; 5 vols., of which vols. 2 and 5 were by Mason alone; N.Y., 1907; innumerable subsequent printings), and, on a more elevated plane, *Course of Study on the Development of Symphonic Music* (Chicago, 1915) and *Music and Life* (Boston, 1917); he also publ. popular articles on music and musicians, notable for their lack of discrimination and absence of verification of data. He was also a composer of sorts; wrote 2 light operas, *Priscilla, or The Pilgrim's Proxy*, after Longfellow (Concord, March 6, 1889; had more than 1,000 subsequent perfs. in the U.S.), and *The Eve of Saint Agnes* (1897), and a romantic opera, *Cascabel, or The Broken Tryst* (Pittsburgh, May 15, 1899).

BIBL.: C. Heffernan, *T.W. S.: Musician and Teacher* (diss., Univ. of Mich., 1962).

Suriano, Francesco. See **Soriano, Francesco.**

Surinach, Carlos, Spanish-born American composer and conductor; b. Barcelona, March 4, 1915. He studied in Barcelona with Morera (1936–39) and later with Max Trapp in Berlin (1939–43). Returning to Spain in 1943, he was active mainly as a conductor. In 1951 he went to the U.S.; became a naturalized American citizen in 1959. Surinach was a visiting prof. of music at Carnegie-Mellon Inst. in Pittsburgh in 1966–67. He won particular success as a composer for the dance.

WORKS: DRAMATIC: OPERA: *El Mozo que casó con mujer brava* (Barcelona, Jan. 10, 1948). **BALLETS:** *Monte Carlo* (Barcelona, May 2, 1945); *Ritmo jondo* (1953); *Embattled Garden* (1958); *Acrobats of God* (1960); *David and Bathsheba* (1960); *Apasionada* (1962); *Los renegados* (1965); *Venta quemada* (1966); *Agathe's Tale* (1967); *Suite española* (1970); *Chronique* (1974); *The Owl and the Pussycat* (1978); *Blood Wedding* (1979). **ORCH.:** 3 syms.: No. 1, *Passacaglia-Symphony* (Barcelona, April 8, 1945, composer conducting), No. 2 (Paris Radio, Jan. 26, 1950, composer conducting), and No. 3, *Sinfonía chica* (1957); *Sinfonietta flamenca* (1953; Louisville, Jan. 9, 1954); *Feria mágica*, overture (Louisville, March 14, 1956); *Concerto for Orchestra* (1959); *Symphonic Variations* (1962); *Drama Jondo*, overture (1964); *Melorhythmic Dramas* (1966); *Las trompetas de los serafines*, overture (1973); Piano Concerto (1973); Harp Concerto (1978); Concerto for Strings (1978); Violin Concerto (1980); *Symphonic Melismas* (Miami, Oct. 10, 1993). **OTHER:** Chamber music; piano pieces; guitar music; choral works; songs.

Susa, Conrad, American composer; b. Springdale, Pa., April 26, 1935. He studied theory with Lopatnikoff, musicology with Dorian, counterpoint with Leich, flute with Goldberg, and cello with Eisner at the Carnegie Inst. of Technology in Pittsburgh (B.F.A., 1957); completed his training in composition with Bergsma and Persichetti at the Juilliard School of Music in N.Y. (M.S., 1961). In 1959 he became composer-in-residence at the Old Globe Theatre in San Diego, where he was active for over 30 years; also was music director of the APA-Phoenix Repertory Co. in N.Y. (1961–68) and the American Shakespeare Festival in Stratford, Conn. (1969–71); also was dramaturge at the Eugene O'Neill Center in Connecticut (from 1986).

WORKS: DRAMATIC: OPERAS: *Transformations* (Minnesota Opera, May 5, 1973); *Black River* (Minnesota Opera, Nov. 1, 1975); *The Love of Don Perlimplin* (1983); *Dangerous Liaisons* (San Francisco, Sept. 10, 1994). Also incidental music; television scores. **OTHER:** *A Sonnet Voyage*, sym. (1963); chamber music; numerous choral works, including *Dawn Greeting* (1976), *The Chanticleer's Carol* (1982), and *Earth Song* (1988); keyboard pieces.

Susskind (originally, **Süsskind**), **(Jan) Walter,** distinguished Czech-born English conductor; b. Prague, May 1, 1913; d. Berkeley, Calif., March 25, 1980. He studied composition with Suk and Karel Hába and piano with Hoffmeister at the Prague Cons.; also studied conducting with Szell at the German Academy of Music in Prague, where he made his debut as a conductor in 1934 with *La Traviata* at the German Opera; also was pianist with the Czech Trio (1933–38). After the German occupation in 1938, he went to London, where he continued to serve as pianist with the exiled Czech Trio until 1942; became a naturalized British subject in 1946. He was music director of the Carl Rosa Opera Co. in London (1943–45); then went to Glasgow in that capacity with the Scottish Orch. in 1946, remaining with it after it became the Scottish National Orch. in 1950. After serving as music director of the Victoria Sym. Orch. in Melbourne (1953–55), he was music director of the Toronto Sym. Orch. (1956–65), the Aspen (Colo.) Music Festival (1962–68), the St. Louis Sym. Orch. (1968–75), and the Mississippi River Festival in Edwardsville, Ill. (1969–75); also taught at the Univ. of Southern Ill. (1968–75). His last position was that of music adviser and principal guest conductor of the Cincinnati Sym. Orch. from 1978 until his death. Susskind was a highly accomplished conductor, being a technically secure and polished musician. He also composed; among his works are 4 songs for Voice and String Quartet (Prague, Sept. 2, 1935); *9 Slovak Sketches* for Orch.; *Passacaglia* for Timpani and Chamber Orch. (St. Louis, Feb. 24, 1977).

Sutanto, Indonesian composer with radical tendencies; b. Magelang, Central Java, Feb. 5, 1954. He studied with Jack Body at the Akademi Musik Indonesia (A.M.I., a Western music cons. in Yogyakarta), and appeared with him in piano concerts; also studied psychology and literature. He founded a cultural center, Ritus Paguyuban (Inst. of Arts and Cultural Studies), in his native Magelang, and later initiated construction of a center near Candi Mendhut (on the road to Borododur), where he resides. Sutanto calls himself a "social engineer" rather than a composer; arranges day-long conglomerations of performing groups (martial arts, folk music, and trance dance) from neighboring villages and from the more urban Magelang (experimental ensembles). In 1989 he created *Wayang Imaginasi*, a shadow puppet play without shadows or puppets—as the puppet master tells the story and the gamelan plays, a painter stands at intervals and paints characters onto the screen. His works have been played in Indonesia as well as in England, Australia, and New Zealand; his *Sketsa Ide* (1979) was performed at the national festival, Pekan Komponis Muda. He is also active as a journalist and critic.

WORKS: *Proses* (1977); *Apa* (1979); *Sketsa Ide* for Chamber Orch., Percussion, and Pumps (1979); *Musik Opera*, consisting of *Blues in My Shoes* for 2 Guitars, Piano, and Vocalists, *Waras Vs Gila, Pegawai Sinting* (1981), and *Suara Orang-orang Luka dan Lebaran '82* for Tape (musique concrète) and 50 Dancers (July 23, 1982); *Ritus Paguyban* for 9 Ensembles totaling 74 Players; *Senam Flute* (1986); *Wayang Imaginasi* (1989).

Suter, Robert, Swiss composer and teacher; b. St. Gallen, Jan. 30, 1919. In 1937 he entered the Basel Cons., where he received instruction in piano from Paul Baumgartner, in theory from Gustav Güldenstein, Walter Müller von Kulm, and Ernst Mohr, and in composition from Walther Geiser; later took private composition lessons with Wladimir Vogel (1956). He taught at the Bern Cons. (1945–50) and at the Basel Academy of Music (1950–84).

WORKS: DRAMATIC: *Konrad von Donnerstadt*, musical fairy tale (1950; Basel, May 5, 1954); *Der fremde Baron*, musical comedy (1951; Basel, March 23, 1952). **ORCH.:** *Kleines konzert* for Piano and Chamber Orch. (St. Gallen, Nov. 17, 1948); Suite for Strings (Basel, Sept. 13, 1949); *Petite suite* (1953; Geneva, Dec. 8, 1956); *Impromptu* (1956; Basel, May 11, 1957); *Variationssatz über Schnitter Tod* (1958; Basel, Dec. 2, 1959); *Lyrische Suite* for Chamber Orch. (1959; Lugano, April 29, 1960); *Fantasia* for Clarinet, Harp, and Strings (Zürich, Oct. 6, 1965); *Sonata* (1967; Basel, Feb. 22, 1968); *Epitaffio* for Winds, Strings, and Percussion (Lucerne, Sept. 7, 1968); *Trois nocturnes* for Viola and Orch. (1968–69; Basel, March 19, 1970); *Airs et Ritournelles* for Percussion and Instrumental Group (1973; Basel, April 17, 1974); *Jour de fête* for Winds (Grenchen, Dec. 7, 1975); *Musik* (1975–76; Basel, May 25, 1977); *Sinfonia facile* (Basel, Aug. 26, 1977); *Conversazioni concertanti* for Saxophone, Vibraphone, and Strings (1978; Zürich, March 2, 1979); *L'Art pour l'art* (1979; Basel, June 6, 1980); Concerto Grosso (1984; Lugano, March 7, 1985); *Mouvements* for Winds (1985; Bern, April 3, 1986); *Gruezi* for Winds (Geneva, May 29, 1987); *Capriccio*, concerto for Marimba, Piano, and Orch. (1990–91). **CHAMBER:** 2 string quartets (1952, 1988); Flute Sonata (1954); *Estampida* for Percussion and 7 Instruments (1960); *Serenata* for 7 Instruments (1963–64); Fanfares et Pastorales for 2 Horns, Trumpet, and Trombone (1965); *Pastorale d'hiver* for 5 Instruments (1972); Sonata for Violin, Cello, and Piano (1975); *Jeux à quatre* for Saxophone Quartet (1976); *Music* for Brass (1980–81); *Small Talk* for Flute and Guitar (1984); *Ceremonie* for 6 Percussion (1984); Sextet for 2 Violins, 2 Violas, and 2 Cellos (1987); *Pulsation* for Percussionist (1990); 5 Duos for Violin and Viola (1992); also piano works. **VOCAL:** *Geisha-Lieder* for Soprano, Chorus, and 6 Instruments (1943); *Musikalisches Tagebuch No. 1* for Alto and 6 Instruments (1946) and *No. 2* for Baritone and 7 Instruments (1950); *Ballade von den Seeraeubern* for Men's Chorus and Instruments (1952); *Jedem das Seine* for Women's Chorus (1955); *Heilige Leier, sprich, sei meine Stimme*, chamber cantata for Soprano, Flute, and Guitar (1960); *Ballade von des Cortez Leuten* for Speaker, Chorus, Speaking Chorus, and Chamber Orch. (1960); *Ein Blatt aus Sommerlichen Tagen* for Women's Chorus (1965–66); *Die sollen loben den Namen des Herrn*, motet (1971); *Drei Geistliche Sprüche* (1971); *. . . aber auch lobet den Himmel* for Tenor, Baritone, Bass, Men's Chorus, Children's Chorus, and Instrumental Ensemble (1976); *Der abwesende Gott* for Soprano, Tenor, Speaker, 2 Choruses, Speaking Chorus, and Orch. (1978); *Marcia funèbre* for 3 Sopranos, Tape, and Orch. (1980–81; Zürich, Sept. 1982); *Vergänglichkeit der Schoenheit* for Countertenor, Tenor, Baritone, and 18 Baroque Instruments (1982–83); *Bhalt du mi Allewyyl lieb* for Children's Chorus and Wind Ensemble (1986).

BIBL.: D. Larese and J. Wildberger, *R. S.* (Amriswil, 1967).

Sutermeister, Heinrich, prominent Swiss composer; b. Feuerthalen, Aug. 12, 1910; d. Vaux-sur-Morges, March 16, 1995. He received training in music history from Karl Nef and in piano from Charlotte Schrameck, and also took courses in philology at the Univs. of Basel and Paris (1930–31). After further studies with Walter Courvoisier (harmony and counterpoint) and Hugo Röhr (conducting) at the Munich Akademie der Tonkunst (1931–34), he returned to Switzerland and devoted himself principally to composition. He also was president of the Swiss Copyright Soc. (1958–80) and a teacher of composition at the Hannover Hochschule für Musik (1963–75). In 1965 he won the opera prize of the City of Salzburg and in 1967 the prize of the Swiss Composers Union. In 1977 he was made a member of the Bavarian Akademie der Schönen Künste in Munich. In his music, Sutermeister placed prime importance upon the composer's responsibility to communicate directly with his listeners. While he utilized discordant combinations of sounds as a legitimate means of expression, he rejected what he considered artificial doctrines and opted instead for an effective and melodic style of wide appeal.

WORKS: DRAMATIC: OPERAS: *Die schwarze Spinne*, radio opera (1935; Bern Radio, Oct. 15, 1936; 1st stage perf., St. Gallen, March 2, 1949); *Romeo und Julia* (1938–40; Dresden, April 13, 1940; orch. suite, Berlin, April 9, 1941); *Die Zauberinsel* (1941–42; Dresden, Oct. 31, 1942); *Niobe* (1943–45; Zürich, June 22, 1946); *Raskolnikoff* (1945–47; Stockholm, Oct. 14, 1948); *Der rote Stiefel* (1949–51; Stockholm, Nov. 22, 1951); *Titus Feuerfuchs, oder Liebe, Tücke und Perücke*, burlesque opera (1956–58; Basel, April 14, 1958); *Seraphine, oder Die stumme Apothekerin*, opera buffa (Swiss TV, Zürich, June 10, 1959; 1st stage perf., Munich, Feb. 25, 1960); *Das Gespenst von Canterville*, television opera (1962–63; ZDF, Sept. 6, 1964); *Madame Bovary* (Zürich, May 26, 1967); *Der Flaschenteufel*, television opera (1969–70; ZDF, 1971); *Le Roi Bérenger* (1981–83; Munich, July 22, 1985). **BALLETS:** *Das Dorf unter dem Gletscher* (1936; Karlsruhe, May 2, 1937); *Max und Moritz* (Bern Radio, 1951). **ORCH.:** 2 divertimentos: No. 1 for Strings (1936; Basel, May 28, 1937) and No. 2 (1959–60; Lausanne, Nov. 21, 1960); *Lieder und Tänze* for Little String Orch. (1939); 3 piano concertos: No. 1 (1943; Dresden, April 14, 1944), No. 2 (1953; Hamburg, Oct. 17, 1954), and No. 3 (1961–62; Bern, Dec. 6, 1990); *Die Alpen* for Orch. and Speaker Obbligato (Bern, May 11, 1948); *Marche fantasque* (Bern, Oct. 1950); 2 cello concertos: No. 1 (1954–55; Zürich, June 19, 1956) and No. 2 (1973; Geneva, Nov. 27, 1974); *Poème funèbre: En memoire de Paul Hindemith* for Strings (Lucerne, Aug. 26, 1965); *Sérénade pour Montreux* for 2 Oboes, 2 Horns, and Strings (Montreux, Sept. 17, 1970); Clarinet Concerto (1975; Geneva, Jan. 19, 1979); *Quadrifoglio*, concerto for Flute, Oboe, Clarinet, Bassoon, and Orch. (Bern, Dec. 1, 1977); *Aubade pour Morges* for Small Orch. (1980). **CHAMBER:** *Capriccio* for Clarinet (1947); 2 serenades: No. 1 for 2 Clarinets, Trumpet, and Bassoon (1949) and No. 2 for Flute, Oboe, Clarinet, Bassoon, Horn, and Trumpet (1961); *Gavottte de Concert* for Piano and Trumpet (1958); *Modeste Mignon* for 10 Wind Instruments (1974; Hannover, Oct. 1975); Concertino for Piano and Wind Quintet (Chicago, March 21, 1994). **PIANO:** *12 Inventionen* (1934); *Bergsommer* (1941); Sonatina (1948); *Hommage à Arthur Honegger* (1955); *Winterferien* (1977). **VOCAL:** *Sieben Liebesbriefe* for Tenor and Orch. (1935); 8 cantatas: No. 1, *Andreas Gryphius*, for Chorus (1935–36; Zürich, March 20, 1938), No. 2 for Alto, Chorus, and 2 Pianos (1944; Zürich, May 18, 1946), No. 3, *Dem Allgegenwärtigen*, for Soprano, Bass-baritone, Chorus, and Orch. (1957–58; Duisburg, June 8, 1958), No. 4, *Das Hohelied*, for Soprano, Baritone, Chorus, and Orch. (1960; Amriswil, June 30, 1962), No. 5, *Der Papagei aus Kuba*, for Chorus and Chamber Orch. (1961; Bern, March 5, 1962), No. 6, *Erkennen und Schaffen*, for Soprano, Baritone, Chorus, and Orch. (1963; Lausanne, April 30, 1964), No. 7, *Sonnenhymne des Echnaton*, for Men's Chorus, 2 Horns, 3 Trumpets, 2 Trombones, Tuba, Piano, and Percussion (1965; Lucerne, May 1967), and No. 8, *Omnia ad*

Unum, for Baritone, Chorus, and Orch. (1965–66; Hannover, Nov. 18, 1966); *Vier Lieder* for High Voice and Piano (1945); *Der 70. und 86. Psalm* for Alto and Organ (1947); *Missa* for Chorus (1948); *Zwei Barocklieder* for Vocal Quartet and Chorus (1953); *Missa da Requiem* for Soprano, Baritone, Chorus, and Orch. (RAI, Rome, Dec. 21, 1953); *Drei Lieder* for Men's Chorus (1961); *Vier Lieder* for Baritone, Violin, Flute, Oboe, Bassoon, and Harpsichord (1967; also for Baritone and Piano); *Zwei Männerchöre* (1968); *Der Kaiser von China* for Men's Chorus (1969); *Drei Lieder* for Children's Chorus and Piano (1970); *Ecclesia* for Soprano, Bass, Chorus, and Orch. (1973–74; Lausanne, Oct. 19, 1975); *Te Deum 1975* for Soprano, Chorus, and Orch. (1974; Zürich, Nov. 25, 1975); *Consolatio philosophiae* for High Voice and Orch. (1977; Geneva, Feb. 21, 1979); *Sechs Liebesbriefe* for Soprano and Orch. (Geneva, Aug. 13, 1980); *Gloria* for Soprano, Chorus, and Orch. (1988).

BIBL.: D. Larese, *H. S.* (Amriswil, 1972).

Suthaus, (Heinrich) Ludwig, eminent German tenor; b. Cologne, Dec. 12, 1906; d. Berlin, Sept. 7, 1971. He received his training in Cologne. In 1928 he made his operatic debut as Walther von Stolzing in Aachen. After singing in Essen (1931–33) and Stuttgart (1933–41), he was a member of the Berlin State Opera (1941–49). In 1943 he made his debut at the Bayreuth Festival as Walther von Stolzing, and sang there again in 1944, 1956, and 1957. From 1948 to 1961 he was a member of the Berlin Städtische Oper, and then of its successor, the Deutsche Oper, from 1961 to 1965. In 1949 he appeared as the Emperor in *Die Frau ohne Schatten* at the Teatro Colón in Buenos Aires. He made his U.S. debut as Aegisthus at the San Francisco Opera in 1953, and that same year made his Covent Garden debut in London as Tristan. Suthaus was one of the outstanding Heldentenors of his day. In addition to his Wagnerian roles, he also excelled as Beethoven's Florestan, Tchaikovsky's Hermann, Verdi's Otello, and Janáček's Števa.

Sutherland, Dame Joan, celebrated Australian soprano; b. Sydney, Nov. 7, 1926. She first studied piano and voice with her mother; at age 19, she commenced vocal training with John and Aida Dickens in Sydney, making her debut there as Dido in a concert performance of *Dido and Aeneas* in 1947; then made her stage debut there in the title role of Judith in 1951; subsequently continued her vocal studies with Clive Carey at the Royal College of Music in London; also studied at the Opera School there. She made her Covent Garden debut in London as the 1st Lady in *Die Zauberflöte* in 1952; attracted attention there when she created the role of Jenifer in *The Midsummer Marriage* (1955) and as Gilda (1957); also appeared in the title role of Alcina in the Handel Opera Soc. production (1957). In the meantime, she married **Richard Bonynge** (1954), who coached her in the *bel canto* operatic repertoire. After making her North American debut as Donna Anna in Vancouver (1958), she scored a triumph as Lucia at Covent Garden (Feb. 17, 1959). From then on she pursued a brilliant international career. She made her U.S. debut as Alcina in Dallas in 1960. Her Metropolitan Opera debut in N.Y. as Lucia on Nov. 26, 1961, was greeted by extraordinary acclaim. She continued to sing at the Metropolitan and other major opera houses on both sides of the Atlantic; also took her own company to Australia in 1965 and 1974; during her husband's music directorship with the Australian Opera in Sydney (1976–86), she made stellar appearances with the company. On Oct. 2, 1990, she made her operatic farewell in *Les Huguenots* in Sydney. Sutherland was universally acknowledged as one of the foremost interpreters of the *bel canto* repertoire of her time. She particularly excelled in roles from operas by Rossini, Bellini, and Donizetti; was also a fine Handelian. In 1961 she was made a Commander of the Order of the British Empire and in 1979 was named a Dame Commander of the Order of the British Empire. In 1992 she was honored with the Order of Merit. With her husband, she publ. *The Joan Sutherland Album* (N.Y., 1986).

BIBL.: R. Braddon, *J. S.* (London, 1962); E. Greenfield, *J. S.* (London, 1972); B. Adams, *La Stupenda: A Biography of J. S.* (London, 1981); Q. Eaton, *S. & Bonynge: An Intimate Biography* (N.Y., 1987); M. Oxenbould, *J. S.: A Tribute* (1991); N. Major, *J. S.: The Authorized Biography* (Boston, 1994).

Sutherland, Margaret (Ada), Australian pianist, teacher, and composer; b. Adelaide, Nov. 20, 1897; d. Melbourne, Aug. 12, 1984. She was a student of Edward Goll (piano) and Fritz Hart (composition) at the Marshall Hall Cons. in Melbourne (1914), and then she pursued her training at the Univ. of Melbourne Conservatorium. In 1916 she launched her career as a pianist. In 1923 she went to Europe to study, receiving additional training in Vienna and London. In 1935 she returned to Australia and pursued a pioneering role in new music circles as a pianist, teacher, and composer. In 1970 she was made an Officer of the Order of the British Empire. She was at her best as a composer of chamber music.

WORKS: DRAMATIC: *Dithyramb*, ballet (1937); *A Midsummer Night's Dream*, incidental music to Shakespeare's play (1941); *The Young Kabbarli*, opera (1964). **ORCH.:** *Pavan* (1938); *Prelude and Jig* for Strings (1939); *Suite on a Theme of Purcell* (1939); Piano Concertino (1940); Concerto for Strings (1945); *Homage to J. Sebastian* (1947); *Pastoral* (1947); *Walking Tune* (1947); *4 Symphonic Concepts* (1949); *Bush Ballad* (1950); *The Haunted Hills* (1950); *Open Air Piece* (1953); Violin Concerto (1954); *Concerto Grosso* (1955); *Outdoor Overture* (1958); *3 Temperaments* (1958); *Movement* (1959); Concertante for Oboe, Strings, and Percussion (1961); *Fantasy* for Violin and Orch. (1962). **CHAMBER:** Violin Sonata (1925); Trio for Clarinet, Viola, and Piano (1934); *Fantasy Sonatina* for Saxophone and Piano (1935); *House Quartet* for Clarinet or Violin, Viola, Horn or Cello, and Piano (1936); *Rhapsody* for Violin and Piano (1938); 3 string quartets (1939; *Discussion*, 1954; 1967); *Ballad and Nocturne* for Violin and Piano (1944; later separated); Clarinet Sonata (1944); *Adagio and Allegro Giocoso* for 2 Violins and Piano (1945); Clarinet or Viola Sonata (1949); Trio for Oboe and 2 Violins (1951–56); *Contrasts* for 2 Violins (1953); Quartet for English Horn and String Trio (1955); *6 Bagatelles* for Violin and Viola (1956); Oboe or Violin Sonatina (1957); *Little Suite* for Wind Trio (1957–60); *Divertimento* for String Trio (1958); *Fantasy* for Violin and Piano (1960); Quartet for Clarinet and Strings (1967). **PIANO:** *Burlesque* for 2 Pianos (1927); *Holiday Tunes* (1936); 2 suites (1937, 1938); *Miniature Sonata* (1939); *6 Profiles* (1945–46); *Canonical Piece* for 2 Pianos (1957); Sonata (1966); *Extension* (1967); *Chiaroscuro I* and *II* (1968); *Valse Descants* (1968); *Voices I* and *II* (1968). **VOCAL:** Choral pieces; songs; arrangements of old Australian bush ballads.

Sutro, Rose Laura (b. Baltimore, Sept. 15, 1870; d. there, Jan. 11, 1957) and **Ottilie** (b. Baltimore, Jan. 4, 1872; d. there, Sept. 12, 1970), American duo-pianists. They were the daughters of Otto Sutro, an art patron and founder of the Baltimore Oratorio Soc. Both began piano lessons with their mother, and in 1889 were sent to Berlin to continue their studies. They made a spectacular debut in London on July 13, 1894; their first American appearance took place in Brooklyn on Nov. 13, 1894, followed by a tour of the U.S. Returning to Europe, they won fresh laurels, and were invited to play before Queen Victoria. Max Bruch wrote his Concerto for 2 Pianos and Orch. expressly for them, and they gave its premiere with the Philadelphia Orch. on Dec. 29, 1916.

Suwardi (Soewardi), Aloysius, respected Indonesian composer, performer, teacher, and experimental-instrument maker; b. Sukoharjo, Central Java, June 21, 1951. He studied in Surakarta at the Konservatori Karawitan (KOKAR, high school cons.), then at the Akademi Seni Karawitan Indonesia (A.S.K.I., college cons.), graduating in 1981 with the thesis *The Construction of Suling in Central Java*; subsequently taught classical music there (Sekolah Tinggi Seni Indonesia/S.T.S.I.). In 1974 he became involved in new music circles and subsequently participated in new music festivals throughout Indonesia. He developed a fine reputation as a player of traditional gamelan music and as a gamelan tuner and restorer; he is often called upon to repair and/or retune Javanese gamelan throughout Indonesia, Europe, and the U.S. In 1986–87 he was a Fulbright visiting scholar to the U.S., teaching at several Midwest univs. As a composer, Suwardi is best known for works that make use of his own experimental instruments; his instrument innovations include placing the bronze keys of the gender on motor-driven resonators, developing a giant-sized gambang (wooden xylophone) inspired by the log xylophones of Africa, and designing and building a kind of water suling wherein the air goes through a tube and into a tin can of water before passing, modified, into a bamboo tube with finger holes. Among his compositions are *Ngalor-Ngidul* (1982; in collaboration with Rustopo and Suparno), *Gender* (1984), *Sebuah Process* (1984), and *Saksake* (1988). He is one of the few Indonesian composers to have been invited twice (1984, 1988) to the Pekan Komponis Muda, a national young composers' festival held annually in Jakarta.

Suzuki, Shin'ichi, influential Japanese music educator and violin teacher; b. Nagoya, Oct. 18, 1898. He was the son of Masakichi Suzuki (1859–1944), a maker of string instruments and the founder of the Suzuki Violin Seizo Co. He studied violin with Ko Ando in Tokyo and with Karl Klinger in Berlin (1921–28); upon his return to Japan, he formed the Suzuki Quartet with 3 of his brothers; also made appearances as a conductor with his own Tokyo String Orch. He became president of the Teikoku Music School in 1930; subsequently devoted most of his time to education, especially the teaching of children. He maintained that any child, given the right stimuli under proper conditions in a group environment, could achieve a high level of competence as a performer. In 1950 he organized the Saino Kyoiku Kenkyu-kai in Matsumoto, where he taught his method most successfully. In subsequent years, his method was adopted for instruction on other instruments as well. He made many tours of the U.S. and Europe, where he lectured and demonstrated his method. See K. Selden, translator, *Where Love Is Deep: The Writings of Shin-ichi Suzuki* (St. Louis, 1982).

BIBL.: C. Cook, *S. Education in Action* (N.Y., 1970); E. Mills and T. Murthy, eds., *The S. Conception: An Introduction to a Successful Method for Early Music Education* (Berkeley, 1973).

Suzuki, Yukikazu, Japanese composer; b. Tokyo, Feb. 11, 1954. He studied with Hara Hoiroshi, Shishido Mutsuo, Matsumura Teizo, and Mayuzumi Toshiro at the Tokyo National Univ. of Fine Arts and Music (degree, 1984). In 1978 he was awarded 1st prize in the Japan Music Competition, and in 1979 5th prize in the International Contemporary Composer's Conference.

WORKS: ORCH.: *Climat* (1978); *Ode* (1990); *The River of Forest and Stars* for Hichiriki and Orch. (1992). **CHAMBER:** Oboe Sonata (1976); *Kyō-in* for 6 Players (1977); *Symphonic Metamorphoses* for Piano (1980); *Kundarini* for Contrabass (1981); Quintet for Piano, 2 Violins, Viola, and Cello (1987). **VOCAL:** *Utsukushi i mono nitsuite*, suite for Chorus (1982); *Sound of Sea*, suite for Chorus (1989).

Svanholm, Set (Karl Viktor), celebrated Swedish tenor; b. Vasterås, Sept. 2, 1904; d. Saltsjö-Duvnäs, near Stockholm, Oct. 4, 1964. He was first active as a church organist in Tillberga (1922–24) and Säby (1924–27). After training at the Royal Cons. in Stockholm (1927–29), he was precentor at St. James's Church in Stockholm. He then pursued vocal studies with Forsell at the Royal Cons. Opera School (1929–30). In 1930 he made his operatic debut in the baritone role of Silvio at the Royal Theater in Stockholm. In 1936 he made his debut there as a tenor singing Radames, and subsequently was one of the Royal Theater's most eminent members until 1956. In 1938 he appeared as Walther von Stolzing at the Salzburg Festival, and also sang at the Vienna State Opera that year. In 1941–42 he sang at Milan's La Scala. He made his Bayreuth Festival debut as Siegfried in 1942. He appeared as Tristan in Rio de Janeiro and as Lohengrin in San Francisco in 1946, and continued to sing in the latter city until 1951. On Nov. 15, 1946, he made his Metropolitan Opera debut in N.Y. as Siegfried. During his 10 seasons at the Metropolitan, he appeared in 105 performances and 17 roles. He was acclaimed not only for his Wagnerian heldentenor roles, but also for such roles as Florestan, Herod, Eisenstein, and Aegisth. His farewell to the Metropolitan came on March 4, 1956, when he sang Parsifal. From 1948 to 1957 he also appeared at London's Covent Garden. He served as director of the Royal Theater in Stockholm from 1956 to 1963.

Švara, Danilo, Slovenian conductor and composer; b. Ricmanje, near Trieste, April 2, 1902; d. Ljubljana, April 25, 1981. He studied piano with Troste in Vienna (1920–22); pursued training in politics and law at the Univ. of Frankfurt am Main (1922–25) and concurrently took piano lessons from Malata and studied conducting with Scherchen; attended the Frankfurt am Main Hochschule für Musik (1927–30), where he took courses in composition with Sekles, in conducting with von Schmiedel and Rottenberg, and in stage direction with Wallerstein. He began his career as répétiteur and conductor at the Ljubljana Opera in 1925; later conducted there regularly, serving as its director (1957–59); also wrote music criticism and taught conducting at the Ljubljana Academy of Music. His compositions are cast in a modern idiom.

WORKS: DRAMATIC: OPERAS: *Kleopatra* (1937); *Veronika Deseniska* (1943); *Slovo od mladosti* (Farewell to Youth; 1952); *Ocean* (1963). **BALLET:** *Nina* (1962). **ORCH.:** 3 syms. (1933, 1935, 1947); *Valse interrompue* (1948); *Sinfonia da camera in modo istriano* (1954); *Concerto grosso dodecafono* (1961); 2 suites (1962); *Dodekafonia*: I, *Duo concertante* for Flute, Harpsichord, and Orch. (1967), II, Violin Concerto (1966), III, Oboe Concerto (1966), IV, *Symposium* for Oboe, Viola, Harp, and Orch. (1968), and V, Clarinet Concerto (1969). **OTHER:** Chamber music; piano pieces; choral music; songs.

Svéd, Sândor, Hungarian baritone; b. Budapest, May 28, 1904; d. Vienna, June 9, 1979. He studied violin at the Budapest Cons.; then went to Milan for vocal studies with Sammarco and Stracciari. He made his operatic debut as Count Luna in Budapest in 1930; was a member of the Vienna State Opera (1936–39); also sang at Covent Garden in London and the Salzburg Festival. On Dec. 2, 1940, he made his debut under the name of Alexander Sved at the Metropolitan Opera in N.Y. as Renato in *Un ballo in maschera*; he remained on its roster until 1948, and then returned for the 1949–50 season. He subsequently sang in Rome, in Paris, and at the Bayreuth Festival; also made appearances with the Budapest Opera, and later toured as a concert singer. In 1956 he went to Stuttgart as a vocal teacher.

Sveinsson, Atli Heimer, Icelandic composer, teacher, conductor, and administrator; b. Reykjavík, Sept. 21, 1938. After studying piano at the Reykjavík College of Music, he took courses in theory and composition with Raphael, Petzold, and Zimmermann at the Cologne Staatliche Hochschule für Musik (1959–62). He also attended composition courses in Darmstadt and Cologne under Stockhausen and Pousseur, and took a course in electronic music in Bilthoven under Koenig. Upon returning to Reykjavík, he played a prominent role in Iceland's musical life. In addition to composing prolifically, he was active as a radio producer, conductor, and organizer. He also taught at the College of Music. From 1972 to 1983 he served as chairman of the Soc. of Icelandic Composers. In 1976 he won the Nordic Council Music Prize for his Flute Concerto. In his music, he has developed a style along Romantic-Expressionistic lines.

WORKS: DRAMATIC: *The Silken Drum*, opera (Reykjavík, June 6, 1982); *Vikivaki*, television opera (1989–90); *Dernier Amour*, chamber opera (1992). **ORCH.:** *Hlými* for Chamber Orch. (1963); *Tautophony* (1967); *Tengsl* (1970); *Flower Shower* (1973); *Hreinn: Gallery sum 1974* (1974); Flute Concerto (1975); Bassoon Concerto, *Trobar Clus* (1980); Trombone Concerto, *Jubilus* (1984); *Recitation* for Piano and Chamber Orch. (1984); *Dreamboat*, concerto for Violin, Harpsichord, and Orch. (1987); *A Gledistundu* for Chamber Orch. (1989); *Röckerauschen, Bruit des Robes* for Chamber Orch. (1993). **CHAM-**

BER: *Xanties* for Flute and Piano (1975); Septet (1976); *Plutot Blanche Qu'azurée* for Clarinet, Cello, and Piano (1976); *21 Sounding Minutes* for Flute (1980); *Precious Dances* for Guitar, Flute, Clarinet, Cello, and Piano (1983); *Bicentennial* for String Quartet (1984); Trio for Violin, Cello, and Piano (1985); Quartet for 4 Flutes (1991); *Tanzfiguren* for Accordion and Wind Quintet (1992); piano pieces; organ music. **VOCAL:** *Aria* for Soprano and 5 Instruments (1977); *Autumn Pictures* for Chorus, 2 Violins, Cello, and Accordion (1982); *The Night on Our Shoulders* for Soprano, Alto, Women's Chorus, and Orch. (1986); *Opplaring* for Soprano and Winds (1991); many choral pieces and songs. **OTHER:** *Ode to the Stone* for Piano, Reciter, and Projector (1983).

Svetlanov, Evgeny (Feodorovich), prominent Russian conductor and composer; b. Moscow, Sept. 6, 1928. He studied composition with Mikhail Gnessin and piano with Mariya Gurvich at the Gnessin Inst. in Moscow (graduated, 1951); took courses in composition with Shaporin and in conducting with Gauk at the Moscow Cons. (graduated, 1955). In 1953 he made his debut as a conductor with the All-Union Radio orch. in Moscow; was a conductor at the Bolshoi Theater there from 1955, serving as its chief conductor (1962–64). In 1965 he was appointed chief conductor of the State Sym. Orch. of the U.S.S.R.; from 1979 he was a principal guest conductor of the London Sym. Orch. Following the collapse of the Soviet Union in 1991, the U.S.S.R. State Sym. Orch. became the Russian State Sym. Orch. Svetlanov retained his position as its chief conductor, and also served as chief conductor of the Residentie Orch. in The Hague from 1992. He also made appearances as a pianist. In 1968 he was named a People's Artist of the U.S.S.R.; in 1972 he was awarded the Lenin Prize and in 1975 the Glinka Prize. He has won particular distinction for his compelling performances of the Russian repertoire. He wrote a Sym. (1956); *Siberian Fantasy* for Orch. (1953); Piano Concerto (1951); incidental music for plays; film scores. He is married to **Larissa Avdeyeva**.

BIBL.: L. Krylova, *E. S.* (Moscow, 1986).

Sviridov, Georgi (Vasilevich), Russian composer and pianist; b. Fatezh, near Kursk, Dec. 16, 1915. After studies in Kursk (1929–32), he was a student of Yudin (composition) at the Leningrad Central Music College (1932–36) and of Shostakovich (composition and orchestration) at the Leningrad Cons. (graduated, 1941). From 1945 he made appearances as a pianist but devoted much time to composition. In 1970 he was made a People's Artist of the U.S.S.R. His *Oratorio pathétique* (1959) was one of the most successful works by a Soviet composer as per the tenets of socialist realism.

WORKS: DRAMATIC: *Othello*, incidental music to Shakespeare's play (1944); *Twinling Lights*, operetta (1951); film scores. **ORCH.:** Sym. for Strings (1940); *Music* for Chamber Orch. (1964). **CHAMBER:** String Quartet (1945); many piano pieces. **VOCAL:** *The Decembrists*, oratorio (1955); *Oratorio pathétique* (1959); *Poem About Lenin* for Bass, Chorus, and Orch. (1960); *5 Songs About Our Fatherland* for Voices, Chorus, and Orch. (1967); numerous solo songs.

BIBL.: D. Frishman, ed., *G. S.* (Moscow, 1971); A. Sokhor, *G. S.* (Moscow, 1972).

Svoboda, Tomáš, Czech-American composer; b. Paris (of Czech parents), Dec. 6, 1939. His father was the renowned mathematician Antonin Svoboda. After the outbreak of World War II, his family went to Boston, where he began piano lessons as a child; in 1946 he went with his family to Prague and studied at the Cons. with Hlobil, Kabeláč, and Dobiáš (1954–62), graduating with degrees in composition, conducting, and percussion; he was only 17 when his 1st Sym. was premiered by the Prague Sym. Orch. Following further training at the Prague Academy of Music (1962–64), he settled in the U.S. and pursued graduate studies with Dahl and Stevens at the Univ. of Southern Calif. in Los Angeles (1966–69). In 1971 he became a teacher of composition, theory, and percussion at Portland (Oreg.) State Univ. His music is marked by broad melodic lines in economically disposed harmonies; there are elements of serialism in chromatic episodes.

WORKS: THEATER: Incidental music to D. Seabrook's play *The Clockmaker* (1986). **ORCH.:** *Scherzo* for 2 Euphonias and Orch. (1955; Prague, Sept. 3, 1958); 6 syms.: No. 1, *of Nature* (1956; Prague, Sept. 7, 1957; rev. 1984; Portland, Oreg., March 10, 1985), No. 2 (1964), No. 3 for Organ and Orch. (1965), No. 4, *Apocalyptic* (1975; Portland, Oreg., Feb. 19, 1978), No. 5, *in Unison* (1978; Portland, Oreg., Nov. 13, 1988), and No. 6 for Clarinet and Orch. (1991; Portland, Oreg., April 26, 1992); *In a Linden's Shadow*, symphonic poem for Organ and Orch. (1958); *Dramatic Overture* (Prague Radio, Sept. 18, 1959); *6 Variations* for Violin and String Orch. (1961); *Christmas Concertino* for Harp and Chamber Orch. (1961); Suite for Bassoon, Harpsichord, and Strings (1962; Prague, April 11, 1963); *Étude* for Chamber Orch. (1963); *3 Pieces* (1966; Sacramento, Calif., March 30, 1967); Concertino for Oboe, Brass Choir, and Timpani (1966; Los Angeles, March 21, 1968); *Reflections* (1968; Toronto, March 21, 1972); *Sinfoniette (à la Renaissance)* (Jacksonville, Oreg., Aug. 14, 1972); *Labyrinth* for Chamber Orch. (1974); *Prelude and Fugue* for Strings (1974); 2 piano concertos: No. 1 (Portland, Oreg., Nov. 17, 1974) and No. 2 (1989); Violin Concerto (1975; Jacksonville, Oreg., Aug. 15, 1976); *Overture of the Season* (Bend, Oreg., Oct. 6, 1978); *Nocturne (Cosmic Sunset)* (Sunriver, Oreg., Aug. 20, 1981); *Eugene Overture (Festive)* (Eugene, Oreg., Sept. 24, 1982); *Ex libris* (Louisville, Dec. 3, 1983); *Serenade* (Sarasota, Fla., March 24, 1984); Concerto for Chamber Orch. (1986; Portland, Oreg., Sept. 9, 1988); *Dance Suite* (Jacksonville, Oreg., Aug. 8, 1987); *3 Cadenzas* for Piano and Orch. (Boston, March 29, 1990); *Swing Dance* (1992; Billings, Mont., Aug. 29, 1993); *Meditation* for Oboe and Strings (1993); Marimba Concerto (1994; Portland, Oreg., March 26, 1995). **CHAMBER:** *Evening Negro Songs and Dances* for Piano and 2 Percussionists (1956); 2 string quartets (1960, 1995); *Baroque Quintet* for Flute, Oboe, Clarinet, Cello, and Piano (1962); Trio for Oboe, Bassoon, and Piano (1962); Septet for Bassoon, Harpsichord, and String Quintet (1962); *Divertimento* for 7 Instruments (1967); *Parabola* for Clarinet, Violin, Viola, Cello, and Piano (1971); Trio for Flute, Oboe, and Bassoon (1979); *Passacaglia and Fugue* for Violin, Cello, and Piano (1981); Trio for Electric Guitar, Piano, and Percussion (1982); Trio Sonata for Electric Guitar, Vibraphone, and Piano (1982); Brass Quintet (N.Y., Nov. 22, 1983); Violin Sonata (1984); Trio for Violin, Cello, and Piano (1984); Chorale in E-flat ("homage to Aaron Copland") for Clarinet, Violin, Viola, Double Bass, and Piano (N.Y., May 10, 1985); *Legacy* for Brass Septet (1988); *Military Movements* for Guitar and Harpsichord (1991); *Theme and Variations* for Flute, Clarinet, and Piano (1992); Duo for Xylophone and Marimba (1993); Quartet for 4 Horns (1993); *Arab Dance* for Synthesizer (1994); also piano music, including 2 sonatas (1967, 1985), and organ pieces. **VOCAL:** *44th Sonnet of Michelangelo* for Alto and Instrumental Ensemble (1967); *Separate Solitude* for Chorus and 2 Clarinets (1973; Portland, Oreg., March 2, 1976); *Celebration of Life*, cantata for Soprano, Tenor, Chorus, Instrumental Ensemble, and Tape, after Aztec poetry (Portland, Oreg., Oct. 31, 1976); *Chorale Without Words* for Chorus and Piano (1984; N.Y., March 16, 1986); *Festival* for Men's Chorus (Portland, Oreg., Sept. 9, 1987); *Haleluya* for Men's Chorus (1990); *Summer Fragments* for Soprano and Piano (1992).

Swan, Alfred (Julius), Russian-born English-American musicologist, educator, and composer; b. St. Petersburg (of English parents), Oct. 9, 1890; d. Haverford, Pa., Oct. 2, 1970. After attending a German-language school in St. Petersburg, he studied at the Univ. of Oxford (B.A., 1911; M.A., 1934); also took courses in composition at the St. Petersburg Cons. (1911). During the Russian Civil War, he served with the American Red Cross in Siberia (1918–19); then emigrated to the U.S.; taught at the Univ. of Virginia (1921–23) and was head of the music depts. at Swarthmore College and Haverford College (1926–58).

His specialty was Russian music. Swan wrote a Trio for Flute, Clarinet, and Piano (1932); 2 violin sonatas (1913, 1948); 4 piano sonatas (1932–46); several albums of songs. He ed. *Songs from Many Lands* (1923) and *Recueil de chansons russes* (1936); also contributed articles to many journals.

WRITINGS: *Scriabin* (London, 1923); *Music 1900–1930* (N.Y., 1930); *The Music Director's Guide to Musical Literature* (N.Y., 1941); *Russian Music and Its Sources in Chant and Folk-song* (N.Y., 1973).

Swann, Frederick (Lewis), American organist; b. Lewisburg, W.Va., July 30, 1931. He studied at the Northwestern Univ. School of Music in Evanston, Ill. (Mus.B., 1952), and at the School of Sacred Music of the Union Theological Seminary (M. of Sacred Mus., 1954). He was organist (1958–82) and director of music (1966–82) at the Riverside Church in N.Y.; also was chairman of the organ dept. at the Manhattan School of Music (1972–82); then was director of music and organist at the Crystal Cathedral in Garden Grove, Calif. (from 1983). He made many recital tours of the U.S., Canada, and Europe.

Swanson, Howard, black American composer; b. Atlanta, Aug. 18, 1907; d. N.Y., Nov. 12, 1978. He grew up in Cleveland, where he began piano lessons at 9. As a youth, he earned a living by manual labor on the railroad and as a postal clerk. He entered the Cleveland Inst. of Music at the age of 20, enrolling in evening courses with Herbert Elwell (graduated, 1937); obtained a stipend to go to Paris, where he studied composition with Boulanger (1938–40). Returning to the U.S., he took a job with the Internal Revenue Service (1941–45). In 1952 he received a Guggenheim fellowship that enabled him to go back to Paris, where he lived until 1966 before settling permanently in N.Y. Swanson's songs attracted the attention of such notable singers as Marian Anderson and William Warfield, who sang them on tours. He achieved signal success with his *Short Symphony* (Sym. No. 2, 1948), a work of simple melodic inspiration, which received considerable acclaim at its first performance by the N.Y. Phil., conducted by Mitropoulos (Nov. 23, 1950). In 1952 it won the Music Critics' Circle Award.

WORKS: ORCH.: 3 syms.: No. 1 (1945; N.Y., April 28, 1968), No. 2, *Short Symphony* (1948; N.Y., Nov. 23, 1950), and No. 3 (N.Y., March 1, 1970); *Night Music* for Strings and Wind Quintet (1950); *Music* for Strings (1952); *Concerto for Orchestra* (1954; Louisville, Jan. 9, 1957); Piano Concerto (1956); *Fantasy Piece* for Soprano Saxophone or Clarinet and Strings (1969); *Threnody for Martin Luther King, Jr.* for Strings (1969). **CHAMBER:** *Nocturne* for Violin and Piano (1948); Suite for Cello and Piano (1949); *Soundpiece* for Brass Quintet (1952); *Vista No. 2* for String Octet (1969; Washington, D.C., Feb. 18, 1986); Cello Sonata (N.Y., May 13, 1973); Trio for Flute, Oboe, and Piano (1975). **PIANO:** 3 sonatas (1948; 1970; 1974, unfinished); *2 Nocturnes* (1967). **VOCAL:** *Songs for Patricia* for Soprano and Strings or Piano (1951); *Nightingales* for Men's Voices (1952); *We Delighted, My Friend* for Chorus (1977); 30 songs for Voice and Piano, including *The Negro Speaks of Rivers* (1942), *The Junk Man* (1946), *Ghosts in Love* (1950), and *The Valley* (1951).

BIBL.: E. Ennett, *An Analysis and Comparison of Selected Piano Sonatas by Three Contemporary Black Composers: George Walker, H. S., and Roque Cordero* (diss., N.Y. Univ., 1973); D. Baker, L. Belt, and H. Hudson, eds., *The Black Composer Speaks* (Metuchen, N.J., 1978); R. Spearman, "The Joy of Langston Hughes and H. S.," *Black Perspective in Music*, IX (1981).

Swarowsky, Hans, noted Austrian conductor and pedagogue; b. Budapest, Sept. 16, 1899; d. Salzburg, Sept. 10, 1975. He studied in Vienna with Schoenberg and Webern, with whom he formed a friendly association; he also was in close relationship with Richard Strauss. He occupied posts as opera conductor in Hamburg (1932), Berlin (1934), and Zürich (1937–40); after conducting the Kraków orch. (1944–45), he was conductor of the Vienna Sym. Orch. (1946–48) and the Graz Opera (1947–50); from 1957 to 1959 he was conductor of the Scottish National Orch. in Glasgow; from 1959, appeared mainly as guest conductor of the Vienna State Opera. He became especially well known as a pedagogue; was head of the conducting class at the Vienna Academy of Music from 1946, where his pupils included Claudio Abbado and Zubin Mehta. As a conductor, he demonstrated notable command of a large symphonic and operatic repertoire, ranging from Haydn to the 2nd Viennese School. He was also a highly competent ed. of music by various composers; also tr. a number of Italian librettos into German. M. Huss ed. his book *Wahrung der Gestalt* (Vienna, 1979).

Swarthout, Gladys, American mezzo-soprano; b. Deepwater, Mo., Dec. 25, 1900; d. Florence, July 7, 1969. She received her training at the Bush Cons. in Chicago. In 1924 she made her operatic debut as the Shepherd in *Tosca* with the Chicago Civic Opera. In 1925 she sang Carmen with the Ravinia Opera Co. in Chicago. On Nov. 15, 1929, she made her Metropolitan Opera debut in N.Y. as La Cieca; she sang that role there often until her farewell in 1945. She was particularly admired for her Carmen and Mignon, but she also sang Adalgisa, Maddalena, and Preziosilla with success. She also sang Carmen in Chicago (1939) and San Francisco (1941), and made appearances in films. Swarthout's career was ended by a severe heart attack, and in 1954 she settled in Florence. Her autobiography appeared as *Come Soon, Tomorrow* (N.Y., 1945). Swarthout was admired for the warmth of her vocal technique.

Swayne, Giles (Oliver Cairnes), English composer; b. Stevenage, June 30, 1946. He began composing as a teenager, receiving encouragement from his cousin, Elizabeth Maconchy; then pursued training with Leppard and Maw at the Univ. of Cambridge (1963–68); subsequently studied piano with Gordon Green and composition with Birtwistle, Bush, and Maw at the Royal Academy of Music in London (1968–71); later attended Messiaen's classes in composition in Paris (1976–77). In 1982 he visited West Africa to study the music of the Jola people of Senegal and The Gambia. In common with many other British composers of his generation, he resolutely eschewed musical gourmandise in favor of writing music in an avant-garde, yet accessible style.

WORKS: DRAMATIC: *A World Within*, ballet for Tape (Stoke-on-Trent, June 2, 1978); *Le Nozze di Cherubino*, opera (1984; London, Jan. 22, 1985). **ORCH.:** *Orlando's Music* (1974; Liverpool, Feb. 3, 1976); *Charades* for School Orch. (1975); *Pentecost Music* (1977; Manchester, April 8, 1981); Sym. for Small Orch. (London, June 1, 1984); *Naaotwa Lala* (Manchester, Dec. 4, 1984); *The Song of Leviathan* (London, Oct. 10, 1988). **CHAMBER:** *4 Lyrical Pieces* for Cello and Piano (1970; Aldeburgh, June 16, 1971); 3 string quartets: No. 1 (1971), No. 2 (1977; Manchester, Oct. 30, 1978), and No. 3 (1992–93); *Paraphrase on a Theme of Tallis* for Organ (1971); *Canto* for Guitar (1972); *Canto* for Piano (1973); *Canto* for Violin (1973); *Synthesis* for 2 Pianos (1974); *Canto* for Clarinet (1975); *Duo* for Violin and Piano (1975); Suite for Guitar (1976); *Freewheeling* for Viola, Baryton, and Cello (Kuhmo Festival, Finland, July 25, 1980); *Canto* for Cello (1981); *Rhythm-Study I* for 2 Xylophone Players and 2 Marimba Players (1982) and *II* for Percussion Group (1982); *A Song for Haddi* for Flute, Clarinet, Viola, Cello, Double Bass, and Percussion (Bath Festival, June 4, 1983); *into the light* for 7 Players (1986); *PP* for 14 Players (1987); *Tonos* for Flute, Harp, Violin, Viola, and Cello (1987); *Songlines* for Flute and Guitar (1987); *A Memory of Sky* for Brass Quintet (1988). **VOCAL:** *The Good Morrow*, cycle of 5 settings of John Donne for Mezzo-soprano and Piano (1971); *Cry* for 28 Amplified Solo Voices (1979; The Hague, Oct. 22, 1982); *Count-Down* for 16-part Chorus and 2 Percussion Players (1981; Merton Festival, Yorkshire, May 23, 1982); *Magnificat* for Chorus (1982); *god-song* for Mezzo-soprano, Flute, Trombone, Cello, and Piano (1985–86); *Nunc Dimittis* for Chorus and Organ (1986); *O Magnum Mysterium* for Boy's Voices and Organ (1986); *Veni creator I* and *II* for Chorus and Organ (1987); *No Quiet Place* for Children's Voices, String Trio, and Xylophones (1989); *No*

Man's Land for Chorus and Ensemble (1990); *Circle of Silence* for 6 Voices (1991); *The Song of the Tortoise* for Narrator, Children's Voices, Chorus, and Orch. (1992); *The Owl and the Pussycat* for Narrator and 7 Instruments (1993).

Sweet, Sharon, American soprano; b. N.Y., Aug. 16, 1951. She was a student at the Curtis Inst. of Music in Philadelphia and of Marinka Gurewich in N.Y. Following appearances as a recitalist in Philadelphia, she sang Aida in a concert performance in Munich (1985). In 1986 she made her formal operatic debut as Elisabeth in *Tannhäuser* at the Dortmund Opera. In 1987 she joined the Deutsche Oper in Berlin, with which she toured Japan; also appeared as Elisabeth de Valois at the Paris Opéra and the Hamburg State Opera. Other engagements during the 1987–88 season included appearances at the Salzburg Festival and the Vienna State Opera. In 1989 she made her U.S. operatic debut as Aida at the San Francisco Opera, which role she also sang in Dallas in 1992. On Oct. 21, 1993, she sang Lina in the first staging of Verdi's *Stiffelio* by the Metropolitan Opera in N.Y. She also toured as a concert artist.

Swensen, Joseph, American conductor, violinist, and composer; b. N.Y., Aug. 4, 1960. His parents were musicians, and at a very young age he began piano lessons with his mother; at age 5 he took up the violin, and later the viola, clarinet, and tuba. When he was 7 he entered the Juilliard School in N.Y. on a piano scholarship, but at 10 enrolled in the violin class of DeLay, remaining her student until 1982; also received instruction in conducting from Berglund, Foster, Mester, and Mueller, and in composition from Diamond and Persichetti. After completing his studies with DeLay, he pursued a career as a violin virtuoso, appearing as a soloist with leading orchs. in North America and Europe; also appeared as a recitalist and chamber music player. Although he first appeared as a conductor at age 15, it was not until much later that he pursued conducting as a career; as an adult, Swenson held guest conducting engagements throughout North America and in Europe and Israel. His most important composition is *Ghazal* for Cello, 5 Women's Voices, and Orch. (1992); he also orchestrated Mahler's Piano Quartet.

Swenson, Ruth Ann, American soprano; b. Bronxville, N.Y., Aug. 25, 1959. She studied at the Academy of Vocal Arts in Philadelphia. In 1981 and 1982 she won the San Francisco Opera Auditions, which led to her professional opera debut with the company in 1983 as Despina. In subsequent seasons, she appeared there as Gounod's Juliette, Handel's Dorinda, Meyerbeer's Ines, Verdi's Nannetta and Gilda, and Donizetti's Adina. In 1988 she made her first appearance at the Lyric Opera in Chicago as Nannetta. She made her debut at the Opéra de la Bastille in Paris as Mozart's Susanna in 1990. On Jan. 27, 1991, she sang in the gala concert commemorating the 200th anniversary of Mozart's death with Raymond Leppard conducting the N.Y. Phil. in a program telecast live to the nation over PBS. She sang Mozart's Constanze at her debuts at the Munich and Schwetzingen festivals, and at the Cologne Opera in 1991. On Sept. 24, 1991, she made her Metropolitan Opera debut in N.Y. as Mozart's Zerlina; returned there as Gilda in 1992, as Adina and Zerbinetta in the 1992–93 season, and as Rosina and Susanna in the 1993–94 season. In 1993 she won the Richard Tucker Music Foundation Award and made her debut at the Berlin State Opera as Gilda. During the 1994–95 season, she returned to the Lyric Opera in Chicago as Anne Trulove. As a concert artist, she sang in principal North American and European music centers. Among her other operatic roles are Cleopatra in Handel's *Giulio Cesare*, Lucia, Martha, and Massenet's Manon.

Swift, Richard, American composer, teacher, and writer on music; b. Middlepoint, Ohio, Sept. 24, 1927. He studied with Grosvenor Cooper, Leonard Meyer, and Leland Smith at the Univ. of Chicago (M.A., 1956). In 1956 he joined the faculty of the Univ. of Calif. at Davis, retiring as prof. of music emeritus in 1991; also was chairman of the music dept. (1963–71); in 1977 he was a visiting prof. at Princeton Univ. He held editorial positions with the journal *19th Century Music* (from 1981); also contributed articles to various other journals and to reference works. In his compositions, he applies a variety of functional serial techniques, including electronic and aleatory devices.

WORKS: DRAMATIC: OPERA: *The Trial of Tender O'Shea* (Davis, Calif., Aug. 12, 1964). Also incidental music to various plays. **ORCH.:** *A Coronal* (1954; Louisville, Ky., April 14, 1956); 2 concertos for Piano and Chamber Ensemble (1961, 1980); *Extravaganza* (1961); Concerto for Violin and Chamber Orch. (Oakland, Calif., May 28, 1968); *Tristia* (1967; Oakland, Calif., April 20, 1968); Sym. (1970); *Prime* for Alto Saxophone and Chamber Ensemble (1973); *Some Trees* (1982). **CHAMBER:** String Trio (1954–55); *Study* for Cello (1955); 6 string quartets (1955; 1958; 1964; 1973; 1981–82; 1991–92); *Serenade concertante I* for Piano and Wind Quintet (1956) and *II* for Clarinet, Violin, Cello, and Piano (1985); *Stravaganza I–X* for various instrumentations (1956–85); Clarinet Sonata (1957); Trio for Clarinet, Cello, and Piano (1957); Sonata for Solo Violin (1957); *Music for a While I* for Violin, Viola, and Harpsichord (1965), *II* for 3 Instruments (1969), *III* for Violin and Harpsichord (1975), *IV* for String Quartet (1991), and *V* for Viola and Piano (1993–94); *Thrones* for Alto Flute and Contrabass (1966); Trio for Violin, Cello, and Piano (1976); *Some Versions of Paraphrase* for Violin, Clarinet, and Piano (1987); *In the Country of the Blue*, piano trio No. 2 for Violin, Cello, and Piano (1988); *A Stitch in Time* for Guitar (1989); *In Arcadia* for Clarinet and String Trio (1994); piano pieces. **OTHER:** Many vocal works.

Swoboda, Henry, Czech conductor; b. Prague, Oct. 29, 1897; d. Rossiniere, Switzerland, Aug. 13, 1990. He studied at the Cons. (with Talich) and at the German Univ. (Ph.D.) in Prague, and with Richard Robert in Vienna. He was an assistant conductor at the Opera (1921–23) and a conductor of the Radio (1931–38) in Prague; then went to the U.S., where he conducted for record companies and eventually devoted himself to teaching.

Syberg, Franz (Adolf), Danish organist and composer; b. Kerteminde, July 5, 1904; d. there, Dec. 11, 1955. His father was the painter Fritz Syberg. He took courses with Karg-Elert in Leipzig (1923–28) and studied organ with Peter Thomson in Copenhagen (organists' examination, 1932); then returned to Kerteminde as an organist. His small but finely crafted output was influenced by Nielsen.

WORKS: DRAMATIC: Incidental music. **ORCH.:** Concertino for Oboe and Strings (1932); *Sinfonietta* (1934); *Adagio* for Strings (1938); Sym. (1939). **CHAMBER:** String Quartet (1930–31); Quintet for Flute, Clarinet, and String Trio (1931); String Trio (1933); Wind Quintet (1940); organ pieces.

Sychra, Antonín, Czech aesthetician; b. Boskovice, June 9, 1918; d. Prague, Oct. 21, 1969. He studied musicology with Helfert at the Univ. of Brno; then continued his training at the Univ. of Prague (Ph.D., 1946); subsequently completed his Habilitation (1952) and received his D.Sc. (1959) there. After lecturing at the Education Research Inst. in Prague, he was made a lecturer (1948), dean (1950), and prof. (1951) at the Prague Academy of Music; also lectured on aesthetics and music history at the Univ. of Prague (from 1952), where he was director of the aesthetics dept. (from 1959). His work, which reveals his preoccupation with a Marxist approach to music and aesthetics, was productive for its contribution to musical semantics. Among his publications are *Stranická hudební kritika: Spolutvůrce nove hudby* (Party Music Criticism: A Co-creator of New Music; Prague, 1951; Ger. tr., 1953), *O hudbu zítřka* (The Music of Tomorrow; Prague, 1952), *Oestetické vychově* (Aesthetic Education; with O. Chlup; Prague, 1956), and *Hudba a slovo z experimentálního hlediska* (Music and Word—an Experimental Approach; with K. Sedláček; Prague, 1962).

Sydeman, William (Jay), American composer; b. N.Y., May 8, 1928. He studied at the Mannes College of Music in N.Y. with Salzer and Travis (B.S., 1955) and with Franchetti at the Hartt School of Music in Hartford, Conn. (M.M., 1958); also had sessions with Sessions and Petrassi. He taught at the Mannes College of Music (1959–70) and at Rudolph Steiner College in Fair Oaks, Calif. (1980–82). His early style of composition tended toward atonal Expressionism invigorated by spasmodic percussive rhythms in asymmetrically arranged meters. In his later works, he moved toward tonal scores with elements of folk, pop, and jazz infusions.

WORKS: DRAMATIC: OPERA: *Aria da capo* (1982). **INCIDENTAL MUSIC:** *Encounters* (1967); *Anti-Christ* (1981); *A Winter's Tale* (1982). **ORCH.:** *Orchestral Abstractions* (1958; N.Y., Jan. 10, 1962); *Study* No. 1 (1959), No. 2 (1963), and No. 3 (1965); *Oecumenicus*, concerto (1964); Concerto for Piano, 4-hands, and Orch. (1967); *5 Movements* for Winds (1973). **CHAMBER:** Woodwind Quintet (1959–61); Quartet for Flute, Clarinet, Piano, and Violin (1963); Duo for Trumpet and Percussion (1965); *Trio montagnana* for Clarinet, Cello, and Piano (1972); *Fugue* for String Quartet or Ensemble, with Optional Soprano (1975); 18 duos for 2 Violins (1976); *Long Life Prayer* for Violin and Speaker (1978); many other works. **VOCAL:** *Lament of Elektra* for Alto, Chorus, and Chamber Orch. (1964); *In memoriam: J.F. Kennedy* for Narrator and Orch. (1966); *Full Circle* for 3 Solo Voices, Clarinet, Trombone, Percussion, Organ, and Cello (1971); *Love Songs Based on Japanese Poems* for Soprano, Flute, and Violin (1978); *Calendar of the Soul* for Multi-chorus (1982).

Sygiètynski, Tadeusz, Polish conductor and arranger; b. Warsaw, Sept. 24, 1896; d. there, May 19, 1955. He studied in Lwów with Roman Statkowski and Henryk Melcer; later took courses with Reger in Leipzig and with Schoenberg in Vienna. In 1949 he organized the Mazowsze State Song and Dance Ensemble for the purpose of popularizing Polish folk music; toured with it in the Far East and in Western Europe with considerable acclaim. He made numerous arrangements of Polish folk songs for this group; in 1951 he received a state prize, and later was awarded the Banner of Labor by the State Council of Poland.

Sykes, James (Andrews), American pianist and pedagogue; b. Atlantic City, N.J., July 10, 1908; d. Hanover, N.H., July 26, 1985. He studied at Princeton Univ. (A.B., 1930) and at the Eastman School of Music in Rochester, N.Y. (M.A., 1933); also took courses at the Dalcroze School of Music in N.Y. and at the Austro-American Cons. in Mondsee, Austria. On Feb. 20, 1938, he made his Town Hall debut in N.Y.; made a world tour in 1945 under the sponsorship of the USO, and later performed in West Germany (1954), Central and South America (1960), and the Far and Middle East (1965) under the auspices of the U.S. State Dept. He was dean of the Lamont School of Music in Denver (1933–35); after serving as chairman of the music depts. at Colorado College (1935–46) and Colgate Univ. (1947–53), he was prof. of music at Dartmouth College (1953–73). He specialized in the performance of modern American music.

Symonds, Norman, Canadian clarinetist, saxophonist, and composer; b. near Nelson, British Columbia, Dec. 23, 1920. He took up the clarinet as a teenager and played in a dixieland band. After training in clarinet, piano, theory, and harmony at the Toronto Cons. (1945–48), he studied composition with Delamont. Between 1949 and 1966 he was active as a clarinetist, alto and baritone saxophonist, and as an arranger with Toronto dance bands. He also led his own jazz octet from 1953 to 1957. Symonds was one of Canada's early champions of the "3rd stream" idiom. In addition to scores composed in this manner, he also wrote works in an Expressionist vein.

WORKS: DRAMATIC: *Age of Anxiety*, radio play (1959); *Opera for 6 Voices*, radio opera (1962); *Tensions*, ballet (1966); *Man, Inc.*, mixed media piece (1970); *"Charnisay Versus LaTour"* or *The Spirit of Fundy*, opera (1972); *Laura and the Lieutenant*, musical play for children (1974); *The Canterville Ghost*, music theater (1975); *Lady of the Night*, opera (1977); *Episode at Big Quill*, radio theater (1979); *The Fall of the Leaf*, oratorical music drama (1982); *Sylvia*, music theater (1990). **ORCH.:** Concerto Grosso for Jazz Quintet and Orch. (1957); *The Age of Anxiety Suite* for Jazz Orch. (1958); *Autumn Nocturne* for Tenor Saxophone and Strings (1960); *Elegy* for Strings (1962); *Pastel Blue* for Strings (1963); *The Nameless Hour* for Improvising Soloist and Strings (1966); *The Democratic Concerto* for Jazz Quartet and Orch. (Winnipeg, Dec. 14, 1967); *Impulse* (Toronto, March 18, 1969); *3 Atmospheres* (1970); *Maya* (1973); *Big Lonely* (1975; rev. 1978); *Forest and Sky* (1977); *The Gift of Thanksgiving* (1980); *Spaces I: The River* for Strings (1980); *Sylvia*, "adult fairy tale" for Jazz Soloists and Jazz Ensemble (1982); *On an Emerald Sea* (1983); *The Eyes of Bidesuk* for Amplified Accordion and Jazz Orch. (1987); *From the Eye of the Wind* (1987; Toronto, Jan. 1, 1988). **CHAMBER:** *Fugue* for Reeds and Brass (1952); 2 concertos for Jazz Octet (1955, 1956); *Fugue for Shearing* for Piano and Jazz Ensemble (1957); *A 6 Movement Suite for 10 Jazz Musicians plus 4 Songs and Incidental Music* for Voice and Jazz Tentet (1959); *Fair Wind* for Jazz Ensemble (1965); *A Diversion* for Brass Quintet (1972); *Bluebeard Lives* for String Quintet and Tape (1975); Quintet for Clarinet and Synthesizers (1977); *Elegance* for Percussion (1982); *Salt Wind White Bird* for 4 Flutes (1984). **VOCAL:** *Deep Ground, Long Waters* for Medium Voice, Flute, and Piano (1972); *At the Shore: A Sea Image* for Chorus and Percussion (1976); *4 Images of Nature* for Chorus, Bass, and Percussion (1976); *Harvest Choral* for Chorus (1979); *Lullaby* for Chorus (1979); *Pity the Children* for Chorus (1979); *Lady Elegance* for Medium Voice and Piano (1986).

Synowiec, Ewa (Krystyna), Polish pianist, composer, painter, and writer; b. Kraków, April 12, 1942. She studied piano with Ludwik Stefanski at the Kraków Academy of Music (graduated, 1967) and with Susanne Roche and Vlado Perlemuter in Paris (1967–68); later studied composition with Boguslaw Schaeffer in Kraków. She toured widely as a pianist from 1948 to 1978. After serving on the faculty of the Kraków Academy of Music (1966–75), she taught piano and composition at the Gdansk Academy of Music, where she later was made a prof. in 1991; also was a member of the Grupa Krakówska from 1985. A versatile artist, she won recognition for both her musical and her non-musical gifts; in addition to composing in traditional forms, she has produced over 100 musical graphics that have been performed or exhibited in many European cities.

WORKS: ORCH.: *Schizofonia* (1971); *72* for 72 Instruments (1972); *Fantasy* for Trumpet and Orch. (1973); *Syntonia* for 58 String Instruments (1976); Concerto for Strings (1978); *Spiegelspiel* (1981); *Trivium* for Flute or Marimba and Orch. (1983); *Une Saison en enfer* (1983). **CHAMBER:** String Quartet No. 1 (1966); *Little Wind Quintet* (1967); String Trio (1967); *1 & 11* for Cello and 11 Saxophones (1968); *Quartettino* for Strings (1969); *Play* for 3 to 6 Trumpets (1972); *Serial* for Flute (1973); *Plus ça change—plus c'est la même chose* for String Sextet (1973); *Natura morta I* for 3 Instruments (1974), *II* for 9 Instruments (1974), *III, UDMSW* for 6 Instruments (1975), and *IV* for 3 Instruments (1976); *Da camera* for Flute, Violin, and Cello (1977); *Sinfonietta da camera* for 10 to 15 Players (1980); *Arboretum* for 2 Violins, 2 Violas, and 2 Cellos (1980); Sonata for Solo Violin (1980); Concertino for 3 Solo Instruments and 12 Strings (1980); *Abra . . .* for Oboe and English Horn (1986). **KEYBOARD: PIANO:** *Open Form* (1966); 2 sonatas (1969, 1981); *Change* for Piano, 4-hands (1972); *Alternative I* for 1 or 2 Pianos (1978) and *II* for Harpsichord or Piano (1979); *Pianoptikum* (1986). **HARPSICHORD:** *Quasimodo* (1985). **VOCAL:** *Psalm XXII* for Voice, Flute, Violin, and Celesta (1967); *Dedication*, 5 songs for Chorus (1983); song cycle on the 12 months of the year for Alto and Piano, to words by the composer (French version, Zürich, Dec. 6, 1987; Polish version, 1988). **OTHER:** Over 100 musical graphic scores.

Syukur, Slamet Abdul, important Indonesian composer, performer, and teacher; b. Surabaya, East Java, June 30, 1935. He studied piano (1944–52), then attended the Sekolah Musik Indonesia (S.M.I.) Yogyakarta (1952–56). He was a founding member (1957–61) and president (1961–62) of Pertemuan

Musik Surabaya, the first music society formed by the Indonesians after the liquidation of the former Dutch Muziek-Kunstkring; then went to Paris and studied organology with Chambure and analysis with Messiaen at the Cons. (1962–63); also earned degrees in piano (1965) and composition (1967) at the École Normale de Musique; in 1967–68, took part in Schaffer's Group de Recherches Musicales de l'ORTF. Syukur is among the many Indonesian composers who, after training in Europe, returned to play an important role in the development of contemporary music in Indonesia while remaining internationally active. From 1976 to 1987 he was a lecturer at the Institut Kesenian Jakarta (I.K.J., Jakarta Arts Inst.), where he also served as head of its music dept. (1981–83); from 1977 to 1981 he was head of the music committee of the Jakarta Arts Council, for which he organized a Festival of Contemporary French Music, the first such series given in Southeast Asia. In 1987 he joined the faculty at the Institut Seni Indonesia (I.S.I., National Arts Inst.); also lectured throughout Java, and from 1975 participated in workshops organized by the Eduard van Beinum Stichting and the Gaudeamus Foundation on the problems of geographic and historical musical acculturation. In 1989 he received a grant from the French government to conduct research on the influence of the Javanese gamelan on the aesthetic of Debussy. Syukur lives in Jakarta, where he founded in 1990 the Forum Musik Jakarta, an Indonesian Soc. for Contemporary Music that also serves as an information and educational center.

WORKS: *Point-Contre* for Vocalizing Trumpet, Percussion, and Harp (1969); *Parenthesis I–II* for Dancer, Prepared Piano, Suspended Chair, and Lighting, *IV* for 2 Electric Guitars, Percussion, Organ, Prepared Piano, 2 Dancers, Painter, Flute, Violin, and Cello (1973), and *VI* for 2 Guitars, Percussion, Children's Toys, Flute, Comedian (with a deep voice), Choreography, and Dancer's Voice; *Laticrak*, electroacoustic music for Dancers (1974); *Angklung* for Voices and Angklung (1975); *Kangen* for 3 Shakuhachi, Kokyu, and Traditional Japanese Percussion (1986); *Cucuku-Cu* for Guitar (1989); *Ji-Lala-Ji* for Flute and Percussion (1989); *Suara* for Piano (1990).

Szabados, Béla Antal, Hungarian pedagogue and composer; b. Pest, June 3, 1867; d. there (Budapest), Sept. 15, 1936. He studied with Erkel and Volkmann. He became an accompanist and coach at the Academy of Music and Dramatic Art (1888); in 1893 he was made a piano teacher and coach at the reorganized Academy of Music, where he was promoted to prof. of singing in 1920; in 1922 he became director of the dept. for the training of profs. of singing; served as head of the National Cons. from 1927. He wrote 2 operas: *Maria* (Budapest, Feb. 28, 1905; in collaboration with Arpád Szendy) and *Fanny* (Budapest, Feb. 16, 1927); 11 musical comedies; 4 string quartets; a Psalm; several song cycles; also publ. several vocal manuals. His brother, Karóly Szabados (b. Pest, Jan. 28, 1860; d. there [Budapest], Jan. 25, 1892), was a pianist, conductor, and composer who studied with Liszt, Erkel, and Volkmann; became conductor at the Klausenburg National Theater (1880) and then assistant conductor at the Royal Hungarian Opera in Budapest. His most successful score was the ballet *Vióra* (1891).

Szabelski, Boleslaw, Polish organist, teacher, and composer; b. Radoryż, near Lublin, Dec. 3, 1896; d. Katowice, Aug. 27, 1979. After studies with Lysakowski in Kiev (1915), he took courses in organ with Surzyński and in composition with Szymanowski and Statkowski at the Warsaw Cons. He made tours as an organist; also was prof. of organ and composition at the Kraków Cons. (1929–39; 1954–57). He wrote in a traditional style until turning to serial techniques in 1958.

WORKS: ORCH.: 5 syms. (1926; 1934, with Soprano and Chorus; 1951; 1956; 1968, with chorus and organ); Suite (1938); *Sinfonietta* for Strings and Percussion (1946); *Solemn Overture* (1953); *Concerto grosso* (1954); Piano Concertino (1955); *3 Sonnets* (1958); *Verses* for Piano and Orch. (1961); *Preludes* for Chamber Orch. (1963); Flute Concerto (1964); Piano Concerto (1978). **CHAMBER:** 2 string quartets (1935, 1956); Organ Sonata (1943); *Aphorisms "9"* for Chamber Ensemble (1962). **VOCAL:** *Heroic Poem* for Chorus and Orch. (1952); *Improvisations* for Chorus and Chamber Orch. (1959); *Nicolaus Copernicus*, oratorio (Poznań, April 2, 1976); *The Wola Redoubt* for 3 Soloists and Orch. (Warsaw, Nov. 5, 1976).

Szabó, Ferenc, distinguished Hungarian composer and teacher; b. Budapest, Dec. 27, 1902; d. there, Nov. 4, 1969. He studied with Kodály, Siklós, and Leo Weiner at the Budapest Academy of Music (1922–26). In 1926 he became aligned with the labor movement in Hungary and joined the outlawed Communist party in 1927; in 1932 he went to Russia, where he became closely associated with the ideological work of the Union of Soviet Composers. In 1944 he returned to Hungary as an officer in the Red Army; then was prof. of composition (1945–67) and director (1958–67) of the Budapest Academy of Music. He was awarded the Kossuth Prize in 1951 and 1954, and in 1962 was named an Eminent Artist of the Hungarian People's Republic. His music initially followed the trends of Central European modernism, with strong undertones of Hungarian melorhythms, but later he wrote music in the manner of socialist realism; his choruses are permeated with the militant spirit of the revolutionary movement.

WORKS: DRAMATIC: *Lúdas Matyi*, ballet (Budapest, May 16, 1960); *Légy jó mindhalálig* (Be Faithful until Death), opera (1968–69; completed by A. Borgulya; Dec. 5, 1975). **ORCH.:** *Suite* for Chamber Orch. (1926; rev. as *Sérénade oubliée*, 1964); *Class Struggle*, symphonic poem (Moscow, April 27, 1933); *Sinfonietta* for Russian National Instruments (1935); *Lyrical Suite* for Strings (1936); *Moldavian Rhapsody* (1940); *Hazatérés* (Homecoming), concerto (1948); *Számadás* (Summary), symphonic poem (1949); *Emlékeztető* (Memento), sym. (1952). **CHAMBER:** 2 string quartets (1926, 1962); Trio for 2 Violins and Viola (1927); Sonata for Solo Cello (1929); 2 sonatas for Solo Violin (1930); *Sonata alla rapsodia* for Clarinet and Piano (1964). **PIANO:** *Toccata* (1928); *8 Easy Piano Pieces* (1933); 3 sonatas (1940; 1947; 1957–61); *Felszabadult melódiák* (Melodies of Liberation), cycle of pieces (1949). **VOCAL:** *Meghalt Lenin* (Lenin is Dead), cantata (1933); *Föltámadott a tenger* (In Fury Rose the Ocean), oratorio (Budapest, June 15, 1955); *Vallomás* (Declaration) for Chorus, Brass, and Percussion (1967); choruses.

BIBL.: A. Pernye, *S. F.* (Budapest, 1965); J. Maróthy, *S. F. indulása* (Budapest, 1970).

Szabolcsi, Bence, eminent Hungarian music scholar; b. Budapest, Aug. 2, 1899; d. there, Jan. 21, 1973. He studied jurisprudence at the Univ. of Budapest; concurrently was a student of Kodály, Weiner, and Siklós at the Budapest Academy of Music (1917–21) and of Abert at the Univ. of Leipzig, where he received his Ph.D. in 1923 with the diss. *Benedetti und Saracini: Beiträge zur Geschichte der Monodie.* He was a prof. of music history at the Budapest Academy of Music from 1945 until his death. He was ed. of the Hungarian music periodical *Zenei Szemle* (with D. Bartha) from 1926 to 1929. With A. Toth, he brought out a music dictionary in the Hungarian language (1930–31); publ. a history of music (Budapest, 1940; 5th ed., 1974), a monograph on Beethoven (Budapest, 1944; 5th ed., 1976), and a number of valuable papers in various European magazines. His greatest contribution as a scholar is found in his valuable study *A melódia története* (A History of Melody; Budapest, 1950; 2nd ed., 1957; Eng. tr., 1965); also made valuable contributions to research on the life and works of Béla Bartók. On his 70th birthday he was presented with a Festschrift, ed. by Bartha, *Studia musicologica Bence Szabolcsi septuagenario* (Budapest, 1969). Of his writings on Bartók, the most important are *Bartók: Sa vie et son oeuvre* (Budapest, 1956; 2nd ed., 1968), *Béla Bartók* (Leipzig, 1968), and *Béla Bartók, Musiksprachen* (Leipzig, 1972). Two of his books were publ. in Eng.: *The Twilight of Ferenc Liszt* (Budapest, 1959) and *A Concise History of Hungarian Music* (Budapest, 1964).

Szalonek, Witold (Jozef), Polish composer; b. Czechowice, March 2, 1927. He studied with Woytowicz at the Katowice State College of Music (1949–56); attended summer courses in new music at Darmstadt (1960) and had a course in analysis with Boulanger in Paris (1962–63). Returning to Poland, he taught at the Katowice State College of Music (from 1967); also was on the faculty of the West Berlin Hochschule für Musik (from 1973).

WORKS: ORCH.: *Pastorale* for Oboe and Orch. or Piano (1952); *Toccata polyphonica* for Strings (1954); *Symphonic Satire* (1956); Flute Concertino (1962); *Les Sons* for Orch., without Violins and Cellos (1965); *Mutations* for Chamber Orch. (1966); Concerto for Strings (1971–75); *Musica concertante* for Double Bass and Orch. (1977); *Little B-A-C-H Symphony* for Piano and Orch. (1981). **CHAMBER:** Trio for Flute, Clarinet, and Bassoon (1952); Cello Sonata (1958); *Arabesques* for Violin and Piano (1964); *4 Monologues* for Oboe (1966); *Proporzioni I* for Flute, Viola, and Harp (1967), *II* for Flute, Cello, and Piano or Harp (1967–70), and *III* for Violin, Cello, and Piano (1977); *Improvisations sonoristiques* for Clarinet, Trombone, Cello, and Piano (1968); *Mutanza* for Piano (1968); *1 + 1 + 1 + 1* for 1, 2, 3, or 4 String Instruments (1969); *Århus Music* for Wind Quintet (1970); *3 Sketches* for Harp (1972); *Connections* for Wind Quintet, 4 Strings, and Piano (1972); *Piernikiana* for Tuba (1977); Trio for Oboe, Clarinet, and Bassoon (1978); *Take the game . . .* for 6 Percussionists (1981); *Alice's Unknown Adventures in the Fairy Land of Percussion* for Percussionist (1981); *D. P.'s 5 Ghoulish Dreams* for Alto Saxophone (1985); *Inside? Outside?* for Bass Clarinet and String Quartet (1988); *Toccata e corale* for Organ (1988; also for Piano, 1990); *Elegy on a Friend's Death* for Clarinet and Piano (1989); *7 Epigrammes modernes* for Saxophone, after Hoffnung (1993). **VOCAL:** *Suite kurpienne* for Contralto and 9 Instruments (1955); *Wyznania* (Confessions), triptych for Narrator, Chorus, and Chamber Orch. (1959); *Ziemio mila* (O, Pleasant Earth), cantata for Voice and Orch. (1969); *Silver Prelude and Prayer*, diptych for Chorus (1993).

Szalowski, Antoni, Polish-born French composer; b. Warsaw, April 21, 1907; d. Paris, March 21, 1973. He studied composition (with K. Sikorski) and piano and conducting at the Warsaw Cons., graduating in 1930; continued his studies with Boulanger in Paris (1931–36), where he then lived until his death, becoming a naturalized French citizen in 1968. His finely crafted works follow in the neo-Classical tradition with a diverting infusion of French elegance.

WORKS: BALLETS: *Zaczarowana oberza* (The Enchanted Inn; 1943–46; Warsaw, Feb. 7, 1962); *La Femme têtue* (1958). **ORCH.:** *Symphonic Variations* (1928); Piano Concerto (1930); Overture (1936); Sym. (1939); *Sinfonietta* (1940); Concerto for Strings (1942); Violin Concerto (1949–54); *Tryptyk* (1950); Concertino for Flute and Strings (1951); Suite (1952); *Partita* for Strings (1954); *La Danse* (1957); *Moto perpetuo* (1958); Concerto for Oboe, Clarinet, Bassoon, and Orch. (1958); *The Resurrection of Lazarus*, symphonic poem (1960); *Intermezzo* (1961); *Allegretto* for Bassoon and Orch. (1962); *Berceuse pour Clemantine* (1964); *Music* for Strings (1970); *6 Sketches* (1972). **CHAMBER:** 4 string quartets (1928, 1934, 1936, 1956); Clarinet Sonatina (1936); Oboe Sonatina (1946); Wind Quintet (1954); *Divertimento* for Oboe, Clarinet, and Bassoon (1955); *2 Pieces* for Ondes Martenot (1967); piano pieces, including a Sonata (1933). **VOCAL:** Songs.

BIBL.: Special issue of *Ruch Muzyczny*, XVII/10 (1973).

Szász, Tibor, Hungarian-born American pianist and teacher; b. Cluj, Romania, June 9, 1948. He began formal study at 13 with Elisa Ciolan and made his public orch. debut at 16; a laureate of the Georges Enesco International Piano Competition (1967), he subsequently appeared with leading orchs. throughout Romania. He was sentenced to prison during the Ceausescu regime but was granted refugee status; emigrated to the U.S. in 1970, obtaining citizenship in 1980. He made his N.Y. solo debut at Carnegie Recital Hall in 1977; subsequently studied with Leon Fleisher and Theodore Lettvin at the Univ. of Mich. (D.M.A., 1983). He taught at the Univ. of Dayton (1984–87), and in 1987 became pianist-in-residence at Duke Univ. in Durham, N.C. A musician of extraordinary sensitivity and intelligence, Szász has appeared as a recitalist, chamber artist, and soloist with orchs. throughout the U.S. and Europe in a repertoire ranging from Couperin to Messiaen; he has also lectured widely, given master classes, and publ. articles on Liszt and Beethoven.

Sze, Yi-Kwei, Chinese bass-baritone; b. Shanghai, June 1, 1919. He received his musical training at the Shanghai Cons.; then emigrated to the U.S., where he studied with Alexander Kipnis. He toured widely in Europe, South America, and Asia.

Székely, Endre, Hungarian composer; b. Budapest, April 6, 1912; d. there, April 14, 1989. He studied with Siklós at the Budapest Academy of Music (1933–37), then joined the outlawed Communist party, and was active as a conductor and composer with various workers' choral groups; ed. the periodicals *Éneklö Munkás* (The Singing Worker) and *Éneklö Nép* (The People Sing). In 1960 he was appointed to the faculty of the Budapest Training College for Teachers.

WORKS: DRAMATIC: OPERAS: *Vizirózsa* (Water Rose; 1959; Budapest Radio, 1962); *Kőzene* (Stone Music; 1981). **OPERETTA:** *Aranycsillag* (The Golden Star; Budapest, 1951). **ORCH.:** 3 suites: No. 1 for Small Orch. (1947), No. 2 for Strings (1961), and No. 3 for Full Orch. (1965); Sym. (1956); *Rhapsody* for Violin and Orch. (1956); *Partita* for Strings (1957); Concerto for Piano, Percussion, and Strings (1958); *Sinfonia concertante* for Violin, Piano, and Chamber Orch. (1960–61); Concerto for 8 Solo Instruments and Orch. (1964); *Partita* (1965); *Fantasma* (1969); Trumpet Concerto (1971); *Riflessioni*, concerto for Cello and Orch. (1973); *Humanisation* for Chamber Ensemble and Tape (1974); *Concerto in memoriam Webern* for Horn and Orch. (1976); Violin Concerto (1979; rev. 1987); *Rapsodia* for Piano and Orch. (1985); *Wave Motions* (1987); Concerto Grosso for Harpsichord and Strings (1987). **CHAMBER:** String Trio (1943); 3 wind quintets (1952, 1961, 1966); 5 string quartets (1953, 1958, 1962, 1972, 1981); *Rhapsody* for Viola and Piano (1956); 2 wind trios (1958, 1959); *Capriccio* for Flute and Piano (1961); *Chamber Music for 8* (1963); *Chamber Music for 3* (1965); *Musica notturna* for Piano, Wind Quintet, and String Quintet (1967); Trio for Percussion, Piano, and Cello (1968–69); *Musica da camera* for Double Bass, Flute, Percussion, and Piano (1978); Horn Sonata (1980); *HaBem Music* for Saxophone and Percussion (1983); Clarinet Sonata (1984); *Quartetto per tromboni* (1988); also 4 piano sonatas (1952, 1962, 1972, 1988). **VOCAL:** 3 oratorios: *Dózsa György* (1959; rev. 1974), *Nenia* (1968–69), and *Justice in Jerusalem* (1986); *Meditations* for Tenor and Orch. (1961–62); *Maqamat* for Soprano and Chamber Ensemble (1970); choruses; songs.

Székely, Mihály, noted Hungarian bass; b. Jászberény, May 8, 1901; d. Budapest, March 6, 1963. He studied in Budapest. He made his operatic debut as Weber's Hermit at the Budapest Municipal Theater in 1923; that same year, he made his first appearance at the Budapest Opera as Ferrando in *Il Trovatore*, remaining on its roster until his death; also made guest appearances throughout Europe. On Jan. 17, 1947, he sang the role of Hunding in *Die Walküre* at his Metropolitan Opera debut in N.Y.; continued on the roster until 1948, and then returned for the 1949–50 season. He subsequently sang in Europe, appearing at the Glyndebourne Festival, the Holland Festival, the Bavarian State Opera in Munich, and other music centers. He was renowned for such roles as Sarastro, Osmin, King Marke, Boris Godunov, Rocco, and Bluebeard.

BIBL.: P. Várnai, *S. M.* (Budapest, 1967).

Szekelyhidy, Ferenc, Hungarian tenor; b. Tövis, April 4, 1885; d. Budapest, June 27, 1954. He received vocal training in Klausenburg. In 1909 he became a member of the Budapest Opera, where he sang both lyric and dramatic roles with success. He also toured widely as an oratorio and recital artist.

Szelényi, István, Hungarian composer and musicologist; b. Zólyom, Aug. 8, 1904; d. Budapest, Jan. 31, 1972. He studied at the Budapest Academy of Music with Kodály. He toured as a concert pianist (1928–30); returning to Budapest, he taught at the Cons. (from 1945), later serving as its director; also taught at the Academy of Music (1956–72); ed. the journal *Új Zenei Szemle* (1951–56). In 1969 he was awarded the Erkel Prize.

WRITINGS (all publ. in Budapest): *Rendszeres modulációtan* (Methodical Theory of Modulation; 1927; 2nd ed., 1960); *A zenetörténet és bölcselettörténet kapcsolatai* (The Interrelations of the History of Music and That of Philosophy; 1944); *Liszt élete képekben* (Liszt's Life in Pictures; 1956); *A romantikus zene harmóniavilága* (The Harmonic Realm of Romantic Music; 1959); *A magyar zene története* (The History of Hungarian Music; 1965); *A népdalharmonizálás alapelvei* (Principles of Folk-Song Harmonization; 1967).

WORKS: DRAMATIC: PANTOMIMES: *A tékozlo fiú* (The Prodigal Son; 1931); *Babiloni vásár* (The Fair at Babylon; 1931). **OPERETTA:** *Hidavatás* (1936). **ORCH.:** Sym. No. 1 (1926); Violin Concerto (1930); *Ouverture activiste* (1931); Triple Concerto for Violin, Cello, Piano, and Wind Orch. (1933); *Géptánc—Munkatánc* (Machine Dance—Work Dance; 1942); *Az ösök nyomában* (In the Footsteps of the Ancestors), sym. for Strings (1946); *Egy gyár szimfóniája* (Symphony for a Factory; 1946–47); *Hommage à Bartók* (1947); Violin Concertino (1947–48); Suite for Strings (1952); *Summa vitae* for Piano and Orch. (1956); *Concerto da camera* (1963); *Dance Suite* for Strings (1964); Piano Concertino (1964); *Variations concertants* for Piano and Orch. (1965); Piano Concerto (1969). **CHAMBER:** 2 sonatas for Solo Violin (1925, 1934); Flute Sonata (1926); 4 string quartets (1927, 1928, 1929, 1964); 2 piano trios (1934, 1962); Sonata for 4 Violins (1946); Sonatina for 2 Violins (1963); *Sinfonietta a tre* for 3 Violins (1964); *3 Dialogues* for Violin and Cello (1965); *Chamber Music* for 2 Trumpets, 2 Horns, and 2 Trombones (1966). **PIANO:** 7 sonatas (1924–69); Sonatina (1960); *Toccata* (1964); *Musical Picture Book* (1967). **VOCAL:** Oratorios, including *Virata* (1935), *Spartacus* (1960), *10 Days That Shook the World* (1964), and *Pro Pace* (1968); choral works; songs.

Szeligowski, Tadeusz, notable Polish composer and pedagogue; b. Lemberg, Sept. 12, 1896; d. Poznań, Jan. 10, 1963. He studied piano with Kurz in Lemberg (1910–14) and composition with Wallek-Walewski in Kraków, where he also took a doctorate in law at the Univ.; after further studies with Boulanger in Paris (1929–31), he taught in Poznań (1932–39; 1947–62) and in Warsaw (1951–62). From 1951 to 1954 he served as president of the Polish Composers' Union.

WORKS: DRAMATIC: OPERAS: *Bunt Żaków* (Rebellion of Clerks; Wroclaw, July 14, 1951); *Krakatuk*, after E.T.A. Hoffmann (1955; Gdansk, Dec. 30, 1956); *Theodor gentleman* (1960; Wroclaw, 1963). **BALLETS:** *Paw i dziewczyna* (The Peacock and the Maiden; 1948; Wroclaw, Aug. 2, 1949); *Mazeppa* (1957; Warsaw, 1959). **ORCH.:** *Kaziuki*, suite (1928); *Concerto for Orchestra* (1932); Clarinet Concerto (1932); *Epitaph for Karol Szymanowski* for Strings (1937); Piano Concerto (1941; Kraków, May 17, 1946); *Suita lubelska* for Small Orch. (1945); *Nocturne* (1947); *Burlesque Overture* (1952). **CHAMBER:** 2 string quartets (1929, 1934); *Nocturne* for Cello and Piano (1945); *Orientale* for Cello and Piano (1945); Wind Quintet (1950); Flute Sonata (1953); *Air grave et air gai* for English Horn and Piano (1954); Piano Trio (1956). **PIANO:** Sonatina (1940); Sonata (1949). **VOCAL:** *Triptych* for Soprano and Orch. (1946); *Kantata o sporcie* for Voice, Chorus, and Orch. (1947); *Wesele lubelskie* (Lublin Wedding), suite for Soprano, Chorus, and Small Orch. (1948); *Rapsod* for Soprano and Orch. (1949); *Panicz i dziewczyna* (The Young Squire and the Country Girl), musical dialogue for Soprano, Baritone, Chorus, and Orch. (1949); *Karta serc* (The Charter of Hearts), cantata (1952); *Renegade*, ballad for Bass and Orch. (1953); songs.

BIBL.: *T. S.: W 10 rocznice śmierci* (T. S.: On the 10th Anniversary of His Death; Gdańsk, 1973).

Szell, George (actually, **György**), greatly distinguished Hungarian-born American conductor; b. Budapest, June 7, 1897; d. Cleveland, July 30, 1970. His family moved to Vienna when he was a small child. He studied piano with Richard Robert and composition with Mandyczewski; also composition in Prague with J.B. Foerster. He played a Mozart piano concerto with the Vienna Sym. Orch. when he was 10 years old, and the orch. also performed an overture of his composition. At the age of 17, he led the Berlin Phil. in an ambitious program which included a symphonic work of his own. In 1915 he was engaged as an assistant conductor at the Royal Opera of Berlin; then conducted opera in Strasbourg (1917–18), Prague (1919–21), Darmstadt (1921–22), and Düsseldorf (1922–24). He held the position of 1st conductor at the Berlin State Opera (1924–29); then conducted in Prague and Vienna. He made his U.S. debut as guest conductor of the St. Louis Sym. Orch. in 1930. In 1937 he was appointed conductor of the Scottish Orch. in Glasgow; he was also a regular conductor with the Residentie Orkest in The Hague (1937–39). He then conducted in Australia. At the outbreak of war in Europe in 1939 he was in America, which was to become his adoptive country by naturalization in 1946. His American conducting engagements included appearances with the Los Angeles Phil., NBC Sym. Orch., Chicago Sym. Orch., Detroit Sym. Orch., and Boston Sym. Orch. In 1942 he was appointed a conductor of the Metropolitan Opera in N.Y., where he received high praise for his interpretation of Wagner's music dramas; remained on its roster until 1946. He also conducted performances with the N.Y. Phil. in 1944–45. In 1946 he was appointed conductor of the Cleveland Orch., a post which he held for 24 years; he was also music adviser and senior guest conductor of the N.Y. Phil. from 1969 until his death. He was a stern disciplinarian, demanding the utmost exertions from his musicians to achieve tonal perfection, but he was also willing to labor tirelessly at his task. Under his guidance, the Cleveland Orch. rose to the heights of symphonic excellence, taking its place in the foremost rank of world orchs. Szell was particularly renowned for his authoritative and exemplary performances of the Viennese classics, but he also was capable of outstanding interpretations of 20th-century masterworks.

BIBL.: R. Marsh, *The Cleveland Orchestra* (Cleveland and N.Y., 1967); H.C. Robbins Landon, "In Memoriam: G. S., 1897–1970," *Ovation* (July 1985).

Szeluto, Apolinary, fecund Russian-Polish composer; b. St. Petersburg, July 23, 1884; d. Chodziez, Aug. 22, 1966. He studied with Exner at the Saratov Cons. and with Statkowski and Noskowski at the Warsaw Cons. (1902–05); then received instruction in piano from Godowsky in Berlin (1905–08); also took courses in law in Warsaw and Dorpat. He was active as a pianist (1909–31), then devoted himself to composition. In association with Szymanowski, Fitelberg, and Rózycki, he formed a progressive musical group, Young Poland. He wrote a number of syms. in piano score; only 10 were orchestrated. His music is ultra-Romantic in its essence; most of his works bear descriptive titles. Several of them are inspired by contemporary political and military events.

WORKS: ORCH.: 28 syms., of which 18 exist without complete orchestration: No. 1, *Academic* (1920), No. 2, *Spontaneous* (1938), No. 3, *Impressionistic* (1942), No. 4, *Romantic* (1942), No. 5, *Majestic Room* (1942), No. 6, *Birth of Stalingrad* (1943), No. 7, *Revolutionary* (1943), No. 8, *Resurrection* (1942), No. 9, *Elegiac* (1943), No. 10, *Oriental* (1944), No. 11, *Iberian* (1944), No. 12, *Nordic* (1944), No. 13, *Samurai* (1943–46), No. 14, *Neapolitan* (1943), No. 15, *Los Angeles American* (1944), No. 16, *Fate* (1946), No. 17, *Kujawska Region* (1946), No. 18, *Litewska*, No. 19, *Slaska*, No. 20, *Kupiowska*, No. 21, *Podhalanska*, No. 22, *To the Building of a Communist People's Union*, Nos. 23–28 without titles; 5 piano concertos (1937, 1939, 1940, 1943, 1948); Violin Concerto (1942–48); Cello Concerto (1942); some 32 other orch. works. **OTHER:** 9 ballets; 14 chamber music pieces; 18 choral works; (purportedly) 78 operas; conservatively counting, 205 piano pieces; maybe 165 songs.

BIBL.: J. Kański, "A. S.: 1884–1966," *Ruch Muzyczny* (1967); J. Dobrowoski, "Katalog utworow fortepianowych Apolinarego Szeluty," *Muzyka* (1973).

Szendrei, Aladár, Hungarian-American conductor, musicologist, and composer who Americanized his name to **Alfred Sendrey**; b. Budapest, Feb. 29, 1884; d. Los Angeles, March 3, 1976. He studied with Koessler at the Budapest Academy of Music (1901–05) and later took courses in musicology at the Univ. of Leipzig (Ph.D., 1932). After serving as a theater conductor in Germany, he went to the U.S., where he conducted opera in Philadelphia and Chicago (1911–12); appeared with N.Y.'s Century Co. (1913–14). He returned to Europe in 1914; served in the Austrian army during World War I; after the Armistice, conducted opera in Leipzig (1918–24) and sym. concerts there (1924–32). In 1933 he left Germany and went to Paris, where he conducted at Radiodiffusion Française; he also taught conducting; Charles Munch took private lessons in conducting with him (1933–40); after the fall of Paris, Szendrei emigrated to the U.S. and settled in Los Angeles. He was prof. of Jewish music at the Univ. of Judaism in Los Angeles (1962–73).

WORKS: DRAMATIC: OPERA: *Der türkisenblaue Garten* (Leipzig, Feb. 7, 1920). **BALLET:** *Danse d'odalisque.* **ORCH.:** *Hungarian Overture* (1904); Sym. (1923). **CHAMBER:** Piano Quintet (1925). **VOCAL:** *Stabat Mater* for 8 Solo Voices and Chorus (1905).

WRITINGS: *Rundfunk und Musikpflege* (Leipzig, 1931); *Dirigierkunde* (Leipzig, 1932; 3rd ed., 1956); *Bibliography of Jewish Music* (N.Y., 1951); *David's Harp: A Popular History of the Music in Biblical Times* (N.Y., 1964); *Music in Ancient Israel* (N.Y., 1969); *The Music of the Jews in the Diaspora (up to 1800)* (N.Y., 1969); *Music in the Social and Religious Life of Antiquity* (Canbury, N.J., 1974).

BIBL.: I. Katz, "Alfred Sendrey (1884–1976): In Memoriam," *Musica Judaica,* i (1975–76).

Szenkar, Eugen (actually, **Jenő**), Hungarian conductor; b. Budapest, April 9, 1891; d. Düsseldorf, March 28, 1977. He studied music with his father, a prominent organist; later attended classes at the Academy of Music in Budapest. He conducted at the German Theater in Prague (1911–13), the Budapest Volksoper (1913–15), the Salzburg Mozarteum (1915–16), in Altenburg (1916–20), the Frankfurt am Main Opera (1920–23), the Berlin Volksoper (1923–24), and the Cologne Opera (1924–33). With the advent of the Nazi regime, as a Jew he was forced to leave Germany in 1933; lived in Russia until 1937; subsequently conducted the Brazilian Sym. Orch. in Rio de Janeiro (from 1944). He returned to Germany in 1950; was Generalmusikdirektor in Düsseldorf from 1952 to 1960.

Szervánszky, Endre, Hungarian composer and teacher; b. Kistétény, Dec. 27, 1911; d. Budapest, June 25, 1977. He received training in clarinet as a child, and then was a student of F. Förster (clarinet; 1922–27) and Siklós (composition; 1931–36) at the Budapest Academy of Music. After teaching at the National Cons. in Budapest (1942–48), he taught at the Academy of Music (from 1948). In 1951 and 1955 he received the Kossuth Prize, in 1953 and 1954 he was awarded the Erkel Prize, and in 1972 he was made a Merited Artist by the Hungarian government. His works followed in the path marked out by Kodály and Bartók.

WORKS: DRAMATIC: *Napkeleti mese* (Oriental Tale), dance play (1948–49); incidental music; film scores. **ORCH.:** *Divertimento I* for Strings (1939), *II* for Small Orch. (1942), and *III* for Strings (1942–43); 2 suites (1944–45; 1948); Sym. (1946–48); *Serenade* for Strings (1947–48); *Rhapsody* (1950); *Serenade* for Clarinet and Orch. (1950–51); Flute Concerto (1953); *Variations* (1964); Clarinet Concerto (1965). **CHAMBER:** 2 string quartets (1936–37; 1956–57); *20 Little Duets* for 2 Violins (1942); Violin Sonata (1945); *25 Duos* for 2 Violins (1946); Clarinet Quintet (1948); Trio for Oboe, Clarinet, and Bassoon (1950); Trio for Flute, Violin, and Viola (1951); Flute Sonatina (1951); 2 wind quintets (1953, 1957); *5 Concert Études* for Flute (1956); Suite for 2 Flutes (1956); *2 Duos* for 2 Flutes (1972). **PIANO:** Sonatina (1940); Sonatina for Piano Duet (1950). **VOCAL:** *Requiem* for Chorus and Orch. (1963); cantatas; choruses; songs.

Szeryng, Henryk, celebrated Polish-born Mexican violinist and pedagogue; b. Zelazowa Wola, Sept. 22, 1918; d. Kassel, March 3, 1988. He commenced piano and harmony training with his mother when he was 5, and at age 7 turned to the violin, receiving instruction from Maurice Frenkel; after further studies with Flesch in Berlin (1929–32), he went to Paris to continue his training with Thibaud at the Cons., graduating with a premier prix in 1937. On Jan. 6, 1933, he made his formal debut as soloist in the Brahms Concerto with the Warsaw Phil. With the outbreak of World War II in 1939, he became official translator of the Polish prime minister Wladyslaw Sikorski's government-in-exile in London; later was made personal government liaison officer. In 1941 he accompanied the prime minister to Latin America to find a home for some 4,000 Polish refugees; the refugees were taken in by Mexico, and Szeryng, in gratitude, settled there himself, becoming a naturalized citizen in 1946. Throughout World War II, he appeared in some 300 concerts for the Allies. After the war, he pursued a brilliant international career; was also active as a teacher. In 1970 he was made Mexico's special adviser to UNESCO in Paris. He celebrated the 50th anniversary of his debut with a grand tour of Europe and the U.S. in 1983. A cosmopolitan fluent in 7 languages, a humanitarian, and a violinist of extraordinary gifts, Szeryng became renowned as a musician's musician by combining a virtuoso technique with a probing discernment of the highest order.

Szidon, Roberto, Brazilian pianist of Hungarian descent; b. Porto Alegre, Sept. 21, 1941. He gave a concert in his native city at the age of 9; later studied in N.Y. with Arrau. He then toured in the U.S., South America, and Europe as soloist with the leading orchs. and in recitals. Szidon was especially successful as a champion of the Romantic repertoire.

Szigeti, Joseph, eminent Hungarian-born American violinist and teacher; b. Budapest, Sept. 5, 1892; d. Lucerne, Feb. 19, 1973. He began his studies at a local music school; while still a child, he was placed in the advanced class of Hubay at the Budapest Academy of Music; then made his debut in Berlin at age 13. He made his first appearance in London when he was 15; subsequently toured England in concerts with Busoni; then settled in Switzerland in 1913; was a prof. at the Geneva Cons. (1917–25). He made an auspicious U.S. debut playing the Beethoven Concerto with Stokowski and the Philadelphia Orch. at N.Y.'s Carnegie Hall (Dec. 15, 1925); thereafter he toured the U.S. regularly while continuing to appear in Europe. With the outbreak of World War II, he went to the U.S. (1940), becoming a naturalized American citizen in 1951. After the end of the war, he resumed his international career; settled again in Switzerland in 1960, and gave master classes. Szigeti was an artist of rare intellect and integrity; he eschewed the role of the virtuoso, placing himself totally at the service of the music. In addition to the standard repertoire, he championed the music of many 20th-century composers, including Stravinsky, Bartók, Ravel, Prokofiev, Honegger, Bloch, and Martin. He wrote the books *With Strings Attached* (N.Y., 1947), *A Violinist's Notebook* (London, 1965), and *Szigeti on the Violin: Improvisations on a Violinist's Themes* (N.Y., 1969).

Szokolay, Sándor, Hungarian composer and teacher; b. Kunágota, March 30, 1931. He studied with Szabó (1950–52) and Farkas (1952–56) at the Budapest Academy of Music (graduated, 1957), concurrently teaching at the Municipal Music School (1952–55); then was music reader and producer for the Hungarian Radio (1955–59) and a teacher (1959–66) and prof. (from 1966) at the Budapest Academy of Music. He received the Erkel Prize (1960, 1965) and the Kossuth Prize (1966); in 1976 he was made a Merited Artist and in 1986 an Outstanding Artist by the Hungarian government. In 1987 he received the Bartók-Pásztory Award.

WORKS: DRAMATIC: OPERAS: *Vérnász* (Blood Wedding; Budapest, Oct. 30, 1964); *Hamlet* (1965–68; Budapest, Oct. 19, 1968); *Sámson* (Budapest, Oct. 23, 1973); *Ecce homo,* passion opera (1984); *Szávitri* (1987–89); also 2 children's operas. **BALLETS:** *Orbán és as ördög* (Urban and the Devil; 1958); *Az iszonyat balladája* (The Ballad of Terror; 1960); *Tetemrehivás* (Ordeal of the Bier; 1961–71); *Az áldozat* (The Victim; 1971). **ORCH.:** *Concert Rondo* for Piano and Strings (1955); Violin Concerto (1956–57); Piano Concerto (1958); *Ballata sinfonica* (1967–68); Trumpet Concerto (1968); *Archaikus nyitány* (Archaic Overture; 1977); *Rapszódia* for Chamber Orch. (1978); Concertino for Alto Flute, Flute, Piccolo, Strings, and Harpsichord (1981); *Concerto for Orchestra* (1982). **CHAMBER:** *Gyermek-kvartett* (Quartet for Children) for 2 Violins, Cello, and Piano (1954); Sonata for Solo Violin (1956); 2 string quartets (1972, 1982); *Sirató és kultikus tánc* (Lament and Ritual Dance) for Cimbalom, Celesta, Piano, and Harp (1974); *Miniature per ottoni* for Brass Sextet (1976); *Alliterációk* (Alliterations) for Brass Quintet (1977); *Játek a hangközökkel* (Playing with Intervals) for 5 Cimbalom Duos (1978); Sonata for Solo Cello (1979); *Polimorfia* (Polymorphy) for Violin, Cello, and Harpsichord or Piano (1980); *Hommage à Bartók*, divertimento for Brass Quintet (1981); *Gregorián változatok* (Gregorian Variations), 5 miniatures for Brass Quintet (1983); *Variáció egy sirató-dallamra* (Variations on a Lament Melody) for 6 Percussionists (1986). **VOCAL:** *Vizimesék* (Water Tales), children's cantata for Soprano, Children's Chorus, and Chamber Orch. (1957); *Világok vetélkedése* (Rivalry of Worlds), cantata for Soprano, Alto, Baritone, Chorus, and Orch. (1959); *Istár pokoljárása* (Isthar's Descent to Hell), oratorio for Soprano, Alto, Baritone, Bass, Chorus, and Orch. (1960–61); *Néger kantáta* (Negro Cantata) for Alto, Chorus, and Orch. (1962); *Deploration: Concerto da requiem* for Piano, Chorus, and Orch. in memory of Francis Poulenc (1964); *Vitézi ének* (Song of Heroes), cantata for Alto, Bass, Men's Chorus, and Orch. (1970); *Ódon ének* (Ancient Song), cantata for Chorus, Woodwind, Horns, Kettledrum, Harp, and Strings (1972); *Kantáta a gályarabok emlékére* (Cantata in Memory of Galley Slaves) for Narrator, Baritone, Chorus, Organ, and Orch. (1975); *Libellus ungaricus*, cantata for Soprano, Alto, Tenor, Baritone, Bass, Chorus, Organ, and Orch. (1979); *Confessio Augustana*, cantata for Baritone, Chorus, Organ, and Orch. (1980); *Luther-Kantate* for Baritone, Chorus, Chamber Orch., and Organ (1983); *Aeternitas temporis*, cantata for Soprano and String Quartet (1988).

Szőllősy, András, Hungarian composer and musicologist; b. Szászváros, Transylvania, Feb. 27, 1921. He studied with Kodály and Viski at the Budapest Academy of Music (1939–44) and took courses in musicology at the Univ. of Budapest (Ph.D., 1943); completed his training in composition with Petrassi at the Accademia di Santa Cecilia in Rome (1947–48). He was a prof. of music history and theory at the Budapest Academy of Music (from 1950). In 1971 he received the Erkel Prize, in 1985 the Kossuth Prize, and in 1986 the Bartók-Pásztory Award. He was made an Artist of Merit (1972) and an Outstanding Artist (1982) of the Hungarian People's Republic; in 1987 the French government made him a Commandeur de l'Ordre des Arts et Lettres. His music draws upon modern resources cast along traditional lines. He publ. a study on Honegger (Budapest, 1960) and ed. the writings of Bartók.

WORKS: BALLETS: *Oly korban éltem* (Improvisations on Fear; 1963); *Pantomime* (1965; based on *Tre pezzi* for Flute and Piano, 1964); *Diminuendo* (1977; based on *Transfigurazione* for Orch., 1972); *A tűz fiai* (Sons of Fire; 1977). **ORCH.:** 5 concertos: No. 1 for Strings, Brass, Piano, and Percussion (1959), No. 2 (destroyed), No. 3 for 16 Strings (1968; Vienna, Nov. 23, 1969), No. 4 for Small Orch. (Gyor, April 13, 1970), and No. 5, *Lebellet* (1975; Budapest, May 27, 1976); *Musica per orchestra (In memoriam Zoltán Kodály)* (1972; Vienna, Sept. 22, 1973); *Transfigurazioni* (Budapest, July 1, 1972); *Musica concertante* for Chamber Orch. (Zagreb, May 18, 1973); *Preludio, Adagio e Fuga* (1973); *Sonorità* (1974; Budapest, Sept. 29, 1975); Concerto for Harpsichord and 16 Strings (1978); *Pro somno Igoris Stravinsky quieto* for Chamber Orch. (Budapest, Nov. 17, 1978); *Tristia (Maros Lament)* for 16 Strings (1983); *Canto d'autunno* (1986; Swansea, Jan. 16, 1987); Violin Concerto (1994–95). **CHAMBER:** *Tre pezzi* for Flute and Piano (Darmstadt, July 18, 1964); *Musiche per ottoni*, 20 pieces for 3 Trumpets, 3 Trombones, and Tuba (1975); *A Hundred Bars for Tom Everett* for Bass Trombone and 3 Bongos (1980; Cambridge, Mass. Jan. 17, 1982); *Suoni di tromba* for Trumpet and Piano (1983; London, May 28, 1984); Trombone Quartet (1986); String Quartet (1988; Orlando, July 30, 1989); *4 Little Pieces* for Recorder and Piano (1991); *Elegia* for Wind Quintet and String Quintet (1993; Berlin, May 30, 1994). **PIANO:** *Old Hungarian Dance* for Piano Duet (1956); *Paessaggio con morti* (1987; Orkney Islands, June 18, 1988). **VOCAL:** *Night in Kolozsvár*, elegy for Voice and Wind Quintet (1955); *Restless Autumn*, cantata for Baritone and Piano (1955); *Fabula Phaedri* for Vocal Sextet (Budapest, Nov. 23, 1982); *In Pharisaeos* for Chorus and Trumpet (1982); *Planctus Mariae* for Women's Chorus (1982); *Miserere* for Vocal Sextet (1984; Brighton, May 10, 1985); *Fragments* for Mezzo-soprano, Flute, and Viola (Budapest, April 26, 1985).

Szönyi, Erzsébet, Hungarian composer and music educator; b. Budapest, April 25, 1924. She studied piano and composition at the Budapest Academy of Music, graduating in 1947; then went to Paris, where she took courses at the Cons. with Aubin and Messiaen; also took private lessons in composition with Boulanger. Returning to Budapest, she taught at the Academy of Music from 1948 to 1981. In 1959 she was awarded the Erkel Prize. She played a major role in promoting Kodály's educational methods in Hungary and elsewhere. Her writings include *A zenei írás-olvasás módszertana* (Methods of Musical Reading and Writing; 4 vols., Budapest, 1953–65; Eng. tr., 1972) and a study on Kodály's teaching methods (Budapest, 1973; numerous trs.).

WORKS: OPERAS: *Dalma* (1952); *The Stubborn Princess* (1955); *Firenzei tragédie* (1957); *The Little Bee with the Golden Wing* (1974); *A Gay Lament* (1979); *The Truth-telling Shepherd* (1979); *Break of Transmission* (1980); *Elfrida* (1985). **ORCH.:** 2 divertimentos (1948, 1951); Organ Concerto (1958); *Musica festiva* (1964); *3 Ideas in 4 Movements* for Piano and Orch. (1980). **CHAMBER:** Trio for Oboe, Clarinet, and Bassoon (1958); Trio Sonata for Violin, Cello, and Piano (1965); Double Bass Sonata (1982); *Evocatio* for Piano and Organ (1985). **PIANO:** 2 sonatinas (1944, 1946); Sonata (1953). **VOCAL:** Oratorios; cantatas; choruses.

Sztompka, Henryk, Polish pianist and pedagogue; b. Boguslawce, April 4, 1901; d. Kraków, June 21, 1964. He studied with Turczyński at the Warsaw Cons. (diploma, 1926) and with Paderewski in Morges, Switzerland (1928–32); he also took courses in philosophy at the Univ. of Warsaw. After making his formal debut in Paris in 1932, he made tours of Europe and South America. From 1945 he taught at the Kraków State College of Music. He was the author of a monograph on Arthur Rubinstein (Kraków, 1966). Sztompka became best known as an interpreter of Chopin.

Szulc, Józef Zygmunt, Polish pianist and composer; b. Warsaw, April 4, 1875; d. Paris, April 10, 1956. He studied at the Warsaw Cons. with Noskowski; then took piano lessons in Paris with Moszkowski. He remained in Paris as a piano teacher; then turned to composition of light operas. His first work in this genre, *Flup* (Brussels, Dec. 19, 1913), was successful and had numerous performances in Europe; he continued to produce operettas at regular intervals; the last one was *Pantoufle* (Paris, Feb. 24, 1945). He also wrote a ballet, *Une Nuit d'Ispahan* (Brussels, Nov. 19, 1909), overtures, chamber music, and piano pieces.

Szweykowski, Zygmunt M(arian), eminent Polish musicologist; b. Kraków, May 12, 1929. He was a pupil of Chybiński at the Univ. of Poznań (graduated, 1951) and of Chomiński at the Univ. of Kraków (Ph.D., 1964, with the diss. *Technika koncertujaca w polskiej muzyce wokalnmo-instrumentalnej okresu baroku* [Concerto Technique in Polish Vocal-Instrumental Music of the Baroque]; Eng. tr. in *Studia Hieronymo Feicht septuage-*

nario dedicata, Kraków, 1967, and in Polish Musicological Studies, I, 1977); completed his Habilitation at the latter in 1976 with his *Musica moderna w ujęciu Marka Scacchiego* (Musica Moderna as Conceived by Marco Scacchi; publ. in Kraków, 1977, with Eng. summary). After serving as Chybiński's assistant at the Univ. of Poznań (1950–53), he went to Kraków as ed. of Polskie Wydawnictwo Muzyczne (1954–61); also taught at the Univ. (from 1954), becoming head of its musicological dept. (1971–74; from 1979); was made a prof. in 1988. Szweykowski is a respected scholar of the Baroque era in Polish music history. He founded Źródła do Historii Muzyki Polskiej in 1960 and ed. various works in Wydawnictwo Dawnej Muzyki Polskiej; also contributed valuable articles to Polish and foreign journals and other publications.

WRITINGS: *Kultura wokalna XVI-wiecznej Polski* (The Vocal Culture of XVI-century Poland; Kraków, 1957); ed. *Z dziejów polskiej kultury muzycznej* (From the History of Polish Musical Culture; Kraków, 1958); *Katalog tematyczny rekopísmiennych zabytków dawnej muzyki w Polsce* (Thematic Catalog of Early Music Manuscripts in Poland; Kraków, 1969).

Szymanowski, Karol (Maciej), eminent Polish composer; b. Timoshovka, Ukraine, Oct. 6, 1882; d. Lausanne, March 28, 1937. The son of a cultured landowner, he grew up in a musical environment. He began to play the piano and compose very early in life. His first teacher was Gustav Neuhaus in Elizavetgrad; in 1901 he went to Warsaw, where he studied harmony with Zawirski and counterpoint and composition with Noskowski until 1904. With Fitelberg, Rózycki, and Szeluto, he founded the Young Polish Composer's Publishing Co. in Berlin, which was patronized by Prince Wladyslaw Lubomirski; the composers also became known as Young Poland in Music, publishing new works and sponsoring performances for some 6 years. Among the works the group publ. was Szymanowski's op. 1, 9 Piano Preludes (1906). He was greatly influenced by German Romanticism, and his first major orch. works reveal the impact of Wagner and Strauss. His 1st Sym. was premiered in Warsaw on March 26, 1909; however, he was dissatisfied with the score, and withdrew it from further performance. In 1911 he completed his 2nd Sym., which demonstrated a stylistic change from German dominance to Russian influences, paralleling the harmonic evolution of Scriabin; it was played for the first time in Warsaw on April 7, 1911. After a Viennese sojourn (1911–12) and a trip to North Africa (1914), he lived from 1914 to 1917 in Timoshovka, where he wrote his 3rd Sym.; he appeared in concert with the violinist Paul Kochański in Moscow and St. Petersburg, giving first performances of his violin works; it was for Kochański that he composed his violin triptych, *Mythes (La Fontaine d'Aréthuse;* in this cycle is one of his best-known compositions). About this time, his music underwent a new change in style, veering toward French Impressionism. During the Russian Revolution of 1917, the family estate at Timoshovka was ruined, and Szymanowski lost most of his possessions. From 1917 to 1919 he lived in Elizavetgrad, where he continued to compose industriously, despite the turmoil of the Civil War. After a brief stay in Bydgoszcz, he went to Warsaw in 1920. In 1920–21 he toured the U.S. in concerts with Kochański and Rubinstein. Returning to Warsaw, he gradually established himself as one of Poland's most important composers. His international renown also was considerable; his works were often performed in Europe, and figured at festivals of the ISCM. He was director of the Warsaw Cons. (1927–29) and reorganized the system of teaching along more liberal lines; was rector of its successor, the Warsaw Academy of Music (1930–32). His *Stabat Mater* (1925–26) produced a profound impression, and his ballet-pantomime *Harnasie* (1923–31), based on the life and music of the Tatra mountain dwellers, demonstrated his ability to treat national subjects in an original and highly effective manner. In 1932 he appeared as soloist in the first performance of his 4th Sym., *Symphonie concertante* for Piano and Orch., at Poznań, and repeated his performances in Paris, London, and Brussels. In April 1936, greatly weakened in health by chronic tuberculosis, he attended a performance of his *Harnasie* at the Paris Opéra. He spent his last days in a sanatorium in Lausanne. Szymanowski developed into a national composer whose music acquired universal significance.

WORKS: DRAMATIC: *Loteria na mezós* (The Lottery for Men), operetta (1908–09; not perf.); *Hagith*, op. 25, opera (1913; Warsaw, May 13, 1922); *Mandragora*, op. 43, pantomime (Warsaw, June 15, 1920); *Król Roger* (King Roger), op. 46, opera (1918–24; Warsaw, June 19, 1926); *Kniaź Patiomkin* (Prince Potemkin), op. 51, incidental music to T. Micínski's play (Warsaw, March 6, 1925); *Harnasie*, op. 55, ballet-pantomime (1923–31; Prague, May 11, 1935).

ORCH.: *Salome* for Soprano and Orch., op. 6 (c.1907; reorchestrated 1912); *Concert Overture*, op. 12 (1904–05; Warsaw, Feb. 6, 1906; reorchestrated 1912–13); 4 syms.: No. 1, op. 15 (1906–07; Warsaw, March 26, 1909), No. 2, op. 19 (1909–10; Warsaw, April 7, 1911; reorchestrated with the collaboration of G. Fitelberg, 1936; rev. version by S. Skrowaczewski, Minneapolis, Oct. 14, 1967), No. 3, *Pieśń o nocy* (Song of the Night) for Tenor, Soprano, Chorus, and Orch., op. 27 (1914–16; London, Nov. 24, 1921), and No. 4, *Symphonie concertante* for Piano and Orch., op. 60 (Poznań, Oct. 9, 1932, composer soloist); *Penthesilea* for Soprano and Orch., op. 18 (1908; Warsaw, March 18, 1910; reorchestrated 1912); *Pieśni milosne Hafiza* (Love Songs of Hafiz) for Voice and Orch., op. 26 (1914; Paris, June 23, 1925; arranged from op. 24, 1911); *Pieśni księźnicki z baśni* (Songs of a Fairy-Tale Princess) for Voice and Orch., op. 31 (Warsaw, April 7, 1933; arranged from the songs of 1915); 2 violin concertos: No. 1, op. 35 (1916; Warsaw, Nov. 1, 1922) and No. 2, op. 61 (Warsaw, Oct. 6, 1933); *Demeter* for Alto, Women's Chorus, and Orch., op. 37b (1917; reorchestrated 1924; Warsaw, April 17, 1931); *Agave* for Alto, Women's Chorus, and Orch., op. 39 (1917); *Pieśni muezina szalonego* (Songs of the Infatuated Muezzin) for Voice and Orch., op. 42 (1934; arranged from the songs of 1918); *Slopiewnie* for Voice and Orch., op. 46b (1928; arranged from the version for Voice and Piano of 1921); *Stabat Mater* for Soprano, Alto, Baritone, Chorus, and Orch., op. 53 (1925–26; Warsaw, Jan. 11, 1929); *Veni Creator* for Soprano, Chorus, Orch., and Organ, op. 57 (Warsaw, Nov. 7, 1930); *Litania do Marii Panny* (Litany to the Virgin Mary) for Soprano, Women's Chorus, and Orch., op. 59 (1930–33; Warsaw, Oct. 13, 1933).

CHAMBER: Violin Sonata, op. 9 (1904; Warsaw, April 19, 1909); Piano Trio, op. 16 (1907; destroyed); *Romance* for Violin and Piano, op. 23 (1910; Warsaw, April 8, 1913); *Nocturne and Tarantella* for Violin and Piano, op. 28 (1915); *Mity* (Myths) for Violin and Piano, op. 30 (1915); 2 string quartets: No. 1, op. 37 (1917; Warsaw, April 1924) and No. 2, op. 56 (1927; Paris, 1929); *3 Paganini Caprices* for Violin and Piano, op. 40 (Elizavetgrad, April 25, 1918); *Kolysanka* (Lullaby): *La Berceuse d'Aïtacho Enia* for Violin and Piano, op. 52 (1925). **PIANO:** *9 Preludes*, op. 1 (1900); *Variations*, op. 3 (1903); *4 Studies*, op. 4 (1902); 3 sonatas: No. 1, op. 8 (1904; Warsaw, April 19, 1907), No. 2, op. 21 (Berlin, Dec. 1, 1911), and No. 3, op. 36 (1917); *Wariacje na polski temat ludowy* (Variations on a Polish Theme), op. 10 (1904; Warsaw, Feb. 6, 1906); *Fantasy*, op. 14 (1905; Warsaw, Feb. 9, 1906); *Prelude and Fugue* (1905–09); *Metopy* (Metopes), op. 29 (1915); *12 Studies*, op. 33 (1916); *Maski* (Masques), op. 34 (St. Petersburg, Oct. 12, 1916); *20 Mazurkas*, op. 50 (1924–25); *Valse romantique* (1925); *4 Polish Dances* (1926); *2 Mazurkas*, op. 62 (1933–34; London, Nov. 1934).

VOCAL: About 100 songs.

WRITINGS: *Wychowawcza rola kultury muzycznej w spoleczenstwie* (The Educational Role of Musical Culture in Society; Warsaw, 1931); T. Bronowicz-Chylińska, ed., *Z pism* (From the Writings; Kraków, 1958; selected essays).

BIBL.: Z. Jachimecki, "K. S.," *Musical Quarterly* (Jan. 1922); A. Tansman, "K. S.," *Revue Musicale* (May 1922); Z. Jachimecki, *K. S.: Zarys dotychczasowej twórczości* (K. S.: An Outline of His Output; Kraków, 1927); special issue of *Muzyka Polska* (1937); S. Golachowski, *K. S.* (Warsaw, 1948; 2nd ed., 1956); S.

Lobaczewska, *K. S.: Zycie i twórczośc (1882–1937)* (K. S.: Life and Work [1882–1937]; Kraków, 1950); T. Bronowicz-Chylińska, ed., *S. K.: Z listow* (S. K.: From the Letters; Kraków, 1957); J. Chomiński, *Studia nad twórczóscia K.a S.ego* (Kraków, 1969); A. Wightman, *The Music of K. S.* (diss., Univ. of York, 1972); J. Samson, *The Music of S.* (London, 1980); A. Wightman, "S. and Joyce," *Musical Times* (Oct. 1982); C. Palmer, *S.* (London, 1983); M. Bristiger et al., eds., *K. S. in seiner Zeit* (Munich, 1984); Z. Sierpiński, ed., and E. Harris, tr., *K. S.: An Anthology* (Warsaw, 1986); A. Wightman, "S. and Islam," *Musical Times* (March 1987); J. Samson, "S. and Polish Nationalism," ibid. (March 1990); T. Chylińska, *K. S.: His Life and Works* (Los Angeles, 1993); S. Downes, *S. as Post-Wagnerian: The Love Songs of Hafiz, op. 24* (N.Y., 1994).

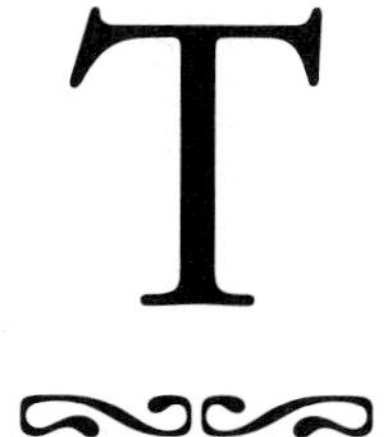

Tabachnik, Michel, Swiss conductor and composer; b. Geneva, Nov. 10, 1942. He received training in piano, composition, and conducting at the Geneva Cons. After attending the summer courses in new music given by Pousseur, Stockhausen, and Boulez in Darmstadt (1964), he served as assistant to Boulez in Basel. He was conductor of the Gulbenkian Foundation Orch. in Lisbon (1973–75), the Lorraine Phil. in Metz (1975–81), and the Ensemble Européen de Musique Contemporaine in Paris (1976–77). As a guest conductor, he appeared with principal orchs. of the world. He became particularly known for his interpretations of contemporary music. His compositions followed along advanced lines.

WORKS: OPERA: *La Légende de Haïsha* (Paris, Nov. 1989). **ORCH.:** *Supernova* for 16 Instruments (1967); *Fresque* for 33 Instruments (1969); *Invention à 16 voix* for 12 Instruments (1972); *Mondes* for 2 Orchs. (1972); *Sillages* for Strings (1972); *Movimenti* (1973); *Les Imaginaires* (1974); *Les Perseides* (1975); *Cosmogonie pour une rose* (1979–81); Piano Concerto (1989); *Le Cri de Mohim* (1990); *Evocation* (1992). **CHAMBER:** *D'autres Sillages* for 8 Percussion and Tape (1972); *Argile* for 4 Percussion (1974). **VOCAL:** *l'arch* for Soprano and Chamber Orch. (1982); *Le Pacte des Onze* for Soloists, Choruses, Orch., and Tape (1983).

Tabakov, Mikhail, Ukrainian trumpeter and pedagogue; b. Odessa, Jan. 6, 1877; d. Moscow, March 9, 1956. He studied at the Odessa Cons. He then went to Moscow and was engaged as a member of the Bolshoi Theater Orch. (1897–1938, with interruptions); also played in Koussevitzky's orch. (1910–17). In 1922 he became a member and manager of the conductorless orch. Persimfans (abbreviation of the Russian words Pervyi Symfonicheskii Ansambl, i.e., 1st Symphonic Ensemble), remaining with it until 1932. He devoted himself to teaching trumpet. He publ. the book *Progressivnaya shkola dlya trubi* (Progressive School for Trumpet; Moscow, 1946).

Tabuteau, Marcel, outstanding French oboist and pedagogue; b. Compiegne, July 2, 1887; d. Nice, Jan. 4, 1966. He studied oboe with Georges Gillet at the Paris Cons.; won a premier prix at the age of 17. In 1905 he went to the U.S., where he played in the N.Y. Sym. Orch. until 1914; also was a member of the orch. of the Metropolitan Opera (from 1908). In 1915 Stokowski engaged him as 1st oboist in the Philadelphia Orch., where he remained until 1954; he was also on the faculty of the Curtis Inst. of Music in Philadelphia (from 1924).

Tacchino, Gabriel, French pianist and teacher; b. Cannes, Aug. 4, 1934. He was a student of Jean Batalla, Jacques Févier, Marguerite Long, and Francis Poulenc at the Paris Cons. (1947–53), graduating with a premier prix in 1953. He took 1st prize in the Viotti competition in Vercelli (1953), 2nd prize in the Busoni competition in Bolzano (1954), co-2nd prize with Malcolm Frager in the Geneva competition (1955), 1st prize in the Casella competition in Naples (1956), and 4th prize in the Long-Thibaud competition in Paris (1957). Thereafter he pursued an international career as a soloist with orchs. and as a recitalist. In 1975 he became a prof. at the Paris Cons. He distinguished himself as an interpreter of the Classical and Romantic repertoire, but won particular notice for his championship of the music of Poulenc.

Tachezi, Herbert, Austrian organist, harpsichordist, and teacher; b. Wiener Neustadt, Feb. 12, 1930. He studied organ with Alois Forer, composition with Alfred Uhl, and musicology with Otto Siegl at the Vienna Academy of Music; also attended the Univ. of Vienna. In 1958 he joined the faculty of the Vienna Academy of Music, where he taught organ and composition; in 1972 he was made a prof. there (it became the Hochschule für Musik in 1970). He appeared regularly as an organist and harpsichordist with the Concentus Musicus in Vienna from 1964; was named organist of Vienna's Hofmusikkapelle in 1974. He toured widely as a recitalist in Europe and the U.S.

Taddei, Giuseppe, noted Italian baritone; b. Genoa, June 26, 1916. He studied in Rome, where he made his debut at the Teatro Reale dell'Opera as the Herald in *Lohengrin* in 1936; sang there until he was drafted into the Italian army in 1942. After World War II, he appeared at the Vienna State Opera (1946–48); made his London debut at the Cambridge Theatre in 1947 and his Salzburg Festival debut in 1948. He sang at Milan's La Scala (1948–51; 1955–61) and at London's Covent Garden (1960–67); also appeared in San Francisco, Chicago, and other music centers. On Sept. 25, 1985, at the age of 69, he made his long-awaited debut at the Metropolitan Opera in N.Y. as Falstaff. In 1986 he appeared as Scarpia at the Vienna State Opera. He sang Falstaff in Stuttgart in 1990. He excelled in both lyrico-dramatic and buffo roles.

Tagliabue, Carlo, noted Italian baritone; b. Mariano Comense, Jan. 12, 1898; d. Monza, April 5, 1978. He studied with Gennai and Guidotti. He made his debut as Amonasro in 1922 in Lodi. After singing in Italian provincial opera houses, he joined La Scala in Milan in 1930; continued to appear there regularly until 1943, and again from 1946 to 1953; also sang in Florence and Rome, at the Teatro Colón in Buenos Aires, and at Covent Garden in London (1938, 1946). On Dec. 2, 1937, he made his Metropolitan Opera debut in N.Y. as Amonasro; continued on its roster until 1939. He retired in 1960. He was a distinguished interpreter of Verdi and a fine Wagnerian.

Tagliaferro, Magda, Brazilian pianist and pedagogue; b. Petrópolis, Jan. 19, 1893; d. Rio de Janeiro, Sept. 9, 1986. She studied at the São Paulo Cons. before going to Paris to continue her training at the Cons. there (graduated with a premier prix, 1907); also received private lessons from Cortot. In 1908 she launched her concert career and also was active as a teacher; after teaching a master class at the Paris Cons. (1937–39), she pursued her career in the Americas; from 1949 she was again active in Paris. Her concert career lasted for over 75 years; she made numerous appearances in recitals in the U.S., the last one in 1980; gave a London recital in 1983 at the age of 90. In her prime, she was known for her sensitive readings of the French repertoire; she also gave the premiere of Villa-Lobos's *Momoprecoce* for Piano and Orch. (1929).

Tagliapietra, Gino, Italian pianist, teacher, and composer; b. Ljubljana, May 30, 1887; d. Venice, Aug. 8, 1954. He studied piano with Julius Epstein in Vienna and with Busoni in Berlin. In 1906 he was appointed to the faculty of the Liceo Benedetto Marcello in Venice; retired in 1940. His compositions include a fiaba musicale, *La bella addormentata* (Venice, March 11, 1926); Piano Concerto (1913); *Variazioni a fantasia* for Piano and Strings (1930); *Requiem* (1923), and various choral works; Violin Sonata (1937); songs; many piano pieces and various didactic works. He ed. *Antologia di musica antica e moderna per il pianoforte* (Milan, 1931–32) and *Raccolta di composizioni dei secoli XVI e XVII* (Milan, 1937).

BIBL.: F. Vadala, *G. T.* (diss., Univ. of Messina, 1976).

Tagliavini, Ferruccio, prominent Italian tenor; b. Reggio Emilia, Aug. 14, 1913; d. there, Jan. 28, 1995. He received his training from Brancucci in Parma and Bassi in Florence. In 1938 he won 1st prize for voice at the Maggio Musicale in Florence, where he made his operatic debut as Rodolfo in Oct. of that year. He then sang in various Italian opera houses. In 1942 he became a member of Milan's La Scala, where he sang with distinction until 1953. In 1946 he toured South America and made his U.S. operatic debut as Rodolfo in Chicago. He made his Metropolitan Opera debut in N.Y. on Jan. 10, 1947, again as Rodolfo, and remained on its roster until 1954. In 1961–62 he was again on the roster of the Metropolitan Opera. Among the roles he sang there were Count Almaviva, Edgardo, the Duke of Mantua, Alfredo, Cavaradossi, and Nemorino. In 1948–49 and again in 1952 he appeared at the San Francisco Opera. In 1950 he sang Nemorino with the visiting La Scala company at London's Covent Garden, and returned there in 1955–56. After retiring from the operatic stage as Werther in Venice in 1965, he made some appearances as a concert artist. In 1941 he married **Pia Tassinari.**

BIBL.: U. Bonafini, *F. T.: L'uomo, la voce* (Reggio Emilia, 1993).

Tagliavini, Luigi Ferdinando, distinguished Italian organist, harpsichordist, and musicologist; b. Bologna, Oct. 7, 1929. He studied organ at the Bologna Cons. and with Marcel Dupré at the Paris Cons. (1947–52); also studied at the Univ. of Padua, receiving his Ph.D. there in 1951 with the diss. *Studi sui testi delle cantate sacre J.S. Bach* (publ. in Padua, 1956). He taught organ at the G.B. Martini Cons. in Bologna (1952–54); also was head of its library (1953–60); concurrently he served as a prof. of organ at the Monteverdi Cons. in Bolzano (1954–64); from 1964 he was on the faculty of the Parma Cons. In 1959 he joined the staff of the Univ. of Bologna; from 1965 he taught music history at the Univ. of Fribourg. With R. Lunelli, he founded the journal *L'organo* in 1960; also served as ed. of Monumenti di Musica Italiana. He is an authority on organ restoration. With O. Mischiati, he ed. *Un anonimo trattato francese di arte organaria del sec. XVIII* (Bologna, 1974).

Tailleferre (real name, **Taillefesse**), **(Marcelle) Germaine,** fine French composer; b. Parc-St.-Maur, near Paris, April 19, 1892; d. Paris, Nov. 7, 1983. She studied harmony and solfège with H. Dallier (premier prix, 1913), counterpoint with G. Caussade (premier prix, 1914), and accompaniment with Estyle at the Paris Cons.; also had some informal lessons with Ravel. She received recognition as the only female member of the group of French composers known as Les Six (the other members were Honegger, Milhaud, Poulenc, Auric, and Durey). Her style of composition was pleasingly, teasingly modernistic and feministic (Jean Cocteau invoked a comparison with a young French woman painter, Marie Laurencin, saying that Tailleferre's music was to the ear what the painter's pastels were to the eye). Indeed, most of her works possess a fragile charm of unaffected *joie de jouer la musique.* She was married to an American author, Ralph Barton, in 1926, but soon divorced him and married a French lawyer, Jean Lageat. She visited the U.S. in 1927 and again in 1942. In 1974 she publ. an autobiographical book, *Mémoires à l'emporte pièce.*

WORKS: DRAMATIC: *Le Marchand d'oiseaux*, ballet (Paris, May 25, 1923); *Paris-Magie*, ballet (Paris, June 3, 1949); *Dolorès*, operetta (1950); *Il était un petit navire*, lyric satire (Paris, March 1951); *Parfums*, musical comedy (1951); *Parisiana*, opéra-comique (1955); *Monsieur Petit Pois achète un château*, opéra bouffe (1955); *Le Bel ambitieux*, opéra bouffe (1955); *La Pauvre Eugénie*, opéra bouffe (1955); *La Fille d'opéra*, opéra bouffe (1955); *La Petite Sirène*, chamber opera (1957); *Mémoires d'une bergère*, opéra bouffe (1959); *Le Maître*, chamber opera (1959). **ORCH.:** Piano Concerto (1919); Harp Concertino (1926; Cambridge, Mass., March 3, 1927); *Overture* (Paris, Dec. 25, 1932); Concertino for Flute, Piano, and Orch. (1952); *La Guirlande de Campra* (1952). **CHAMBER:** *Image* for Piano, Flute, Clarinet, String Quartet, and Celesta (1918); *Jeux de plein air* for 2 Pianos (1918); String Quartet (1918); 2 violin sonatas (1921, 1951); *Pastorale* for Violin and Piano (1921); *Pastorale* for Flute and Piano (1939); Harp Sonata (1954); *Partita* for 2 Pianos and Percussion (1964); *4 Pièces* for Flute, Oboe, Clarinet, Trumpet, and Piano (1973). **VOCAL:** *Chansons françaises* for Voice and Instruments (Liège, Sept. 2, 1930); Concerto for 2 Pianos, Voice, and Orch. (Paris, May 3, 1934); *Cantate du Narcisse* for Voice and Orch. (1937); Concertino for Soprano and Orch. (1953); *Concerto des vaines paroles* for Baritone and Orch. (1956).

BIBL.: J. Roy, *Le groupe des six: Poulenc, Milhaud, Honegger, Auric, T., Durey* (Paris, 1994); R. Shapiro, *G. T.: A Bio-Bibliography* (Westport, Conn., 1994).

Tajčević, Marko, Serbian choral conductor, music critic, teacher, and composer; b. Osijek, Jan. 29, 1900; d. Belgrade, July 19, 1984. He studied in Zagreb, Prague, and Vienna. In 1945 he was appointed a prof. at the Belgrade Academy of Music, retiring in 1966. He was primarily a folklore composer and was at his best in his sacred and secular choral works derived from regional folk songs. He also wrote songs and piano pieces, including *7 Balkan Dances* for Piano (1927), a set of brilliant stylizations of Serbian melorhythms.

BIBL.: D. Despić, *M. T.* (Belgrade, 1972).

Tajo, Italo, Italian bass and teacher; b. Pinerolo, April 25, 1915; d. Cincinnati, March 29, 1993. He studied at the Turin Cons. He made his operatic debut as Fafner at the Teatro Regio in Turin in 1935; then was a member of the Rome Opera (1939–48) and of La Scala in Milan (1940–41; 1946–56). He made his U.S. debut in Chicago in 1946. On Dec. 28, 1948, he appeared at the Metropolitan Opera in N.Y. as Don Basilio in *Il barbiere di Siviglia*; remained on its roster until 1950; also sang with the San Francisco Opera (1948–50; 1952–53; 1956); then appeared on Broadway and in films. In 1966 he was appointed prof. at the Univ. of Cincinnati College-Cons. of Music. He returned to the Metropolitan Opera after an absence of 30 years in 1980, and delighted audiences in buffo roles; made his operatic farewell there as the Sacristan in *Tosca* on April 20, 1991. He was equally adept in dramatic and buffo roles from the standard repertory, and also proved himself an intelligent interpreter in contemporary operas by Milhaud, Malipiero, Pizzetti, and even Nono.

Takács, Jenő, Hungarian pianist, ethnomusicologist, teacher, and composer; b. Siegendorf, Sept. 25, 1902. He studied composition with Marx and Gál at the Vienna Cons.. He taught at the Cairo Cons. (1927–32) and at the Univ. of the Philippines (1932–34); pursued ethnological research in the Philippines before again teaching in Cairo (1934–36). From 1940 to 1942 he taught at the Music School at Szombathely; then was director of the Pécs Cons. (1942–48); after teaching piano at the Univ. of Cincinnati College-Cons. of Music (1952–71), he retired to his birthplace. In 1962 he was awarded the Austrian State Prize. Reflecting his background of travel and residence in many different countries, his music contains elements of Hungarian, oriental, American, and cosmopolitan idioms.

WORKS: BALLETS: *Nile Legend* (1937–39; Budapest, May 8, 1940); *Narcissus* (1939); *The Songs of Silence* (1967). **ORCH.:** 2 piano concertos (1932, 1937); *Philippine Suite* (1934); *Tarantella* for Piano and Orch. (1937); *Antiqua Hungarica* (1941); *Partita* for Guitar and Orch. (1950). **CHAMBER:** *Gumbri*, oriental rhapsody for Violin and Piano (1930); Trombone Sonata (1957); Wind Quintet (1961–62); *Homage to Pan* for 4 Pianos (1968); *Essays in Sound* for Clarinet (1968); *2 Fantastics* for Alto Saxophone and Piano (1969); *Musica reservata* for Double Bass and Piano (1969); *Tagebuch-Fragmente* for 2 Pianos (1973); Octet (1974–75).

Takahashi, Aki, innovative Japanese pianist, sister of **Yuji Takahashi**; b. Kakamura, Sept. 6, 1944. She studied first with her mother, then with Yutaka Ito, (Miss) Ray Lev, and George Vásárhelyi at the Tokyo Univ. of the Arts (M.A., 1969). She made her public debut in Tokyo in 1970; her European debut followed in 1972. While acknowledged for her classical musicianship, she is particularly lauded for her imaginative interpretations of contemporary music; among the composers who have written works for her are Cage, Rzewski, Yuasa, Feldman, and Satoh. Her recording career is also distinguished; her *Aki Takahashi Piano Space* (20 works, including those by Berio, Boulez, Cage, Stockhausen, Webern et al.) earned her the Merit Prize at the Japan Art Festival in 1973. Her series of Satie concerts performed in Tokyo (1975–77) heralded the so-called "Satie Boom" in Japan and resulted in her editing and recording the composer's complete piano works; other noteworthy recordings include *Triadic Memories* (Feldman), *Planetary Folklore* (Mamoru Fujieda), *Eonta* (Xenakis), and *L'Histoire de Babar* (Poulenc). Her *Hyper Beatles* (1990–) features arrangements of Beatles songs by internationally recognized composers. In addition to performing throughout Europe, Japan, and the U.S., Takahashi also devoted time to teaching; she was artist-in-residence at the State Univ. of N.Y. at Buffalo (1980–81) and a guest prof. at the Calif. Inst. of the Arts in Valencia (1984). She received the 1st Kenzo Nakajima prize (1982) and the 1st Kyoto Music Award (1986). In 1983 she became director of the "New Ears" concert series in Yokohama.

Takahashi, Yuji, Japanese composer and pianist, brother of **Aki Takahashi**; b. Tokyo, Sept. 21, 1938. He studied composition with Shibata and Ogura at the Toho School of Music in Tokyo (1954–58); then went to Berlin and trained in electronics as a student of Xenakis (1963–65); also studied computer music in N.Y. and attended the summer courses at the Berkshire Music Center at Tanglewood (1966–68). He was a member of the Center for Creative and Performing Arts at the State Univ. of N.Y. in Buffalo (1968–69). In his music, he follows the stochastic procedures as practiced by Xenakis. He also has acquired considerable renown as a pianist in programs of avant-garde music.

WORKS: *Phonogène* for 2 Instruments and Tape (1962); *Chromamorphe I* for Violin, Double Bass, Flute, Trumpet, Horn, Trombone, and Vibraphone (1963) and *II* for Piano (1964); *6 Stoicheia (Elements in Succession)* for 4 Violins (1965); *Bridges I* for Electric Harpsichord or Piano, Amplified Cello, Bass Drum, and Castanets (1967) and *II* for 2 Oboes, 2 Clarinets, 2 Trumpets, and 3 Violas (1968); *Rosace I* for Amplified Violin (1967) and *II* for Piano (1967); *Operation Euler* for 2 or 3 Oboes (1967); *Metathèse* for Piano (1968); *Prajna Paramita* for 4 Voices, each in one of 4 Instrumental Ensembles (1969); *Orphika* for Orch. (Tokyo, May 28, 1969); *Yé Guèn* for Tape (1969); *Nikité* for Oboe, Clarinet, Trumpet, Trombone, Cello, and Double Bass (1971); *Kagahi* for Piano and 30 Instruments (Ojai, Calif., May 30, 1971); *Michi-Yuki* for Chorus, 2 Percussionists, and Electric Cello (1971); *Corona Borealis* for Piccolo, Oboe, Clarinet, Bassoon, and Horn (1971); *Tadori* for Tape (1972).

Takata, Saburô, Japanese composer and teacher; b. Nagoya, Dec. 18, 1913. He studied with Nobutkoki and Pringsheim at the Tokyo Music School (graduated, 1939). He was a prof. at the Kunitachi Music College in Tokyo (from 1953); also served as president of the Japanese Society for Contemporary Music (1963–68).

WORKS: OPERA: *Aoki-ōkami* (The Dark Blue Wolf; 1970–72; Tokyo, Oct. 15, 1972). **ORCH.:** *Ballade Based on a Folk Song from Yamagata (Fantasy and Fugue)* (Tokyo, Nov. 15, 1941; rev. 1965); *Seasons*, suite (1942); *Ballade* for Violin and Orch. (1943; Tokyo, Jan. 13, 1945); *The New Earth and Man* (1944); *2 Rhapsodies* (both 1945). **CHAMBER:** Octet for Clarinet, Bassoon, Horn, Trumpet, and String Quartet (1939); *Prelude and Fugue* for String Quartet (1940); Violin Sonata (1948–49); Cello Sonatina (1949–50); Suite for Flute, Oboe, 2 Clarinets, and Bassoon (1951); *Marionette*, suite for String Quartet (1954); *Fantasy* for String Quartet (1968). **KEYBOARD: PIANO:** 2 sonatas (1935, 1941); *5 Preludes* (1947). Also organ pieces. **VOCAL:** *Wordless Tears*, cantata for Narrator, Soprano, Baritone, Chorus, and Orch. (Tokyo, March 27, 1964); choruses; songs.

Takeda, Yoshimi, Japanese conductor; b. Yokohama, Feb. 3, 1933. He was educated at the Tokyo Univ. of the Arts (graduated, 1958); then went to the U.S. on a fellowship to work with George Szell and the Cleveland Orch. (1962–64). In 1964 he became assoc. conductor of the Honolulu Sym. Orch.; in 1970 he was appointed music director of the Albuquerque (later New Mexico) Sym. Orch., a position he held until 1985; in addition, he was music director of the Kalamazoo Sym. Orch. (from 1974). He also appeared as a guest conductor with major orchs. in North America, Europe, and Japan.

Takemitsu, Tōru, prominent Japanese composer; b. Tokyo, Oct. 8, 1930; d. there, Feb. 20, 1996. He studied composition privately with Yasuji Kiyose. In 1951, jointly with Yuasa and others, he organized in Tokyo the Jikken Kōbō (Experimental Workshop), with the aim of creating new music that would combine traditional Japanese modalities with modernistic procedures. In 1970 he designed the "Space Theater" for Expo '70 in Osaka, Japan. In 1975 he was a visting prof. at Yale Univ. In 1981 he served as regent lecturer at the Univ. of Calif. at San

Diego. He lectured at Harvard Univ., Boston Univ., and Yale Univ. in 1983, and also was composer-in-residence of the Colorado Music Festival that same year. In 1984 he was composer-in-residence at the Aldeburgh Festival. He received numerous honors; in 1979 he was made an honorary member of the Akademie der Künste of the German Democratic Republic, in 1984 he was elected an honorary member of the American Academy and Inst. of Arts and Letters, and in 1985 he received L'Ordre des Arts et des Lettres of the French government. In 1994 he received the Grawemeyer Award of the Univ. of Louisville for his *Fantasma/Cantos* for Clarinet and Orch. His music belies Kipling's famous asseveration that East is East and West is West, and never the twain shall meet, for Takemitsu performed through music just this kind of interpenetration; in an Oriental way, it is often formed from short motifs played out as floating dramas, subtle and exotic, through which Takemitsu seeks "to achieve a sound as intense as silence"; and on the Western side, he employs every conceivable technique developed by the European and American modernists. He publ. *Confronting Silence: Selected Writings* (tr. and ed. by Y. Kakudo and G. Galsow; Berkeley, 1995).

WORKS: ORCH.: *Requiem* for Strings (1957; Tokyo, June 20, 1958); *Solitude sonore* (1958); *Ki No Kyoku* (Music of Trees; 1961); *Arc*, Part I (1963) and Part II (1964–66) for Piano and Orch.; *Arc* for Strings (1963; from the 3rd movement of *Arc*, Part I); *Textures* for Piano and Orch. (1964; 1st movement of *Arc*, Part II); *The Dorain Horizon* for 17 Strings in 2 groups (1966; San Francisco, Feb. 1967, Copland conducting); *November Steps* for Biwa, Shakuhachi, and Orch. (N.Y., Nov. 9, 1967); *Green* (*November Steps II*; Tokyo, Nov. 3, 1967); *Asterism* for Piano and Orch. (1968; Toronto, Jan. 14, 1969); *Eucalypts I* for Flute, Oboe, Harp, and Strings (Tokyo, Nov. 16, 1970); *Winter* (Paris, Oct. 29, 1971); *Corona* for 22 Strings (1971); *Cassiopeia* for Solo Percussion and Orch. (Chicago, July 8, 1971); *Gemeaux* for Oboe, Trombone, and 2 Orchs. with separate conductors (1971–72); *Autumn* for Biwa, Shakuhachi, and Orch. (1973); *Gitimalya* (Bouquet of Songs) for Marimba and Orch. (Rotterdam, Nov. 1975); *Quatrain* for Violin, Cello, Clarinet, Piano, and Orch. (Tokyo, Sept. 1, 1975); *Marginalia* (Tokyo, Oct. 20, 1976); *A Flock Descends into the Pentagonal Garden* (San Francisco, Nov. 30, 1977); *In an Autumn Garden* for Gagaku Orch. (1979); *Far Calls. Coming Far!* for Violin and Orch. (Tokyo, May 24, 1980); *Dreamtime* (1981; ballet version, The Hague, May 5, 1983); *Toward the Sea II* for Alto Flute, Harp, and Strings (1981); *Star-Isle* (1982); *Rain Coming* for Chamber Orch. (1982); *To the Edge of Dream* for Guitar and Orch. (Liège, March 12, 1983); *Orion and Pleiades* for Cello and Orch. (1984); *Vers, l'arc-en-ciel, Palma* for Guitar, Oboe d'amore, and Orch. (Birmingham, England, Oct. 2, 1984); *riverrun* for Piano and Orch. (1984; Los Angeles, Jan. 10, 1985); *Dream/Window* (1985); *I Hear the Water Dreaming* for Flute and Orch. (Indianapolis, April 3, 1987); *Nostalgia—In Memory of Andrei Tarkovsky* for Violin and Strings (1987); *Twill by Twilight—In Memory of Morton Feldman* (1988); *Tree Line* for Chamber Orch. (1988); Viola Concerto (1989); *From Me Flows What You Call Time* for Percussion Quintet and Orch. (N.Y., Oct. 19, 1990); *Fantasma/Cantos* for Clarient and Orch. (1991); *Ceremonial* for Shō and Orch. (Matsumoto, Sept. 5, 1992). **CHAMBER:** *Son calligraphie I–III* for Double String Quartet (1958, 1958, 1963); *Mask* for 2 Flutes (1959); *Landscape 1* for String Quartet (1961); *Ring* for Flute, Terz-guitar, and Lute (1961); *Sacrifice* for Flute, Lute, and Vibraphone (1962); *Valeria* for Violin, Cello, Guitar, Electric Organ, and 2 Piccolos obbligato (1962); *Hika* for Violin and Piano (1966); *Cross Talk* for 2 Bandoneons and Tape (1968); *Stanza II* for Harp (1971) and *III* for Solo Oboe, or Oboe and Shō (1971); *Eucalypts II* for Flute, Oboe, and Harp (1970); *Seasons* in versions for 1 or 4 Percussionists (1970); *Voice* for Flute (1971); *Munari by Munari* for Percussion (1972); *Distance* for Oboe or Oboe and Shō (1972); *Voyage* for 3 Biwas (1973); *Folios* for Guitar (1973); *Garden Rain* for 4 Trumpets, 3 Trombones, Bass Trombone, Horn, and Tuba, separated into 2 groups (1974); *Waves* for Clarinet, Horn, 2 Trumpets, and Percussion (1976); *Bryce* for Flute, 2 Harps, Marimba, and Percussion (1976); *Quatrain II* for Clarinet, Violin, Cello, and Piano (1976); *Waterways* for Piano, Clarinet, Violin, Cello, 2 Harps, and 2 Vibraphones (1978); String Quartet No. 1, *A Way a Lone* (1980); *Toward the Sea* for Alto Flute and Guitar (1981); *Rain Tree* for 3 Percussionists or 3 Keyboard Players (1981); *Rain Spell* for Flute, Clarinet, Harp, Piano, and Vibraphone (1982); *Rocking Mirror Daybreak* for Violin Duo (1983); *From far beyond Chrysanthemums and November Fog* for Violin and Piano (1983); *Entretemps* for Oboe and String Quartet (1986); *Rain Dreaming* for Harpsichord (1986); *All in Twilight* for Guitar (1987); *Signals from Heaven: I, Day Signal* and *II, Night Signal* for Chamber Ensemble (1987). **PIANO:** *2 Lentos* (1950); *Undisturbed Rest* (1952–59); *Piano Distance* (1961); *Corona* for Pianist(s) (1962); *For Away* (1973); *Les Yeux clos* (1979); *Rain Tree Sketch I* (1981) and *II: In memoriam Olivier Messiaen* (1992). **VOCAL:** *Tableau noir* for Narrator and Orch. (1958); *Coral Island* for Soprano and Orch. (1962); *Wind Horse* for Women's Chorus (1962); *Stanza I* for Piano, Guitar, Harp, Vibraphone, and Woman's Voice (1968); *Crossing* for 12 Women's Voices, Guitar, Harp, Piano, Vibraphone, and 2 Orchs. (1969); *Grass* for Men's Chorus (1982); *Uta* for Chorus (1983); *Handmade Proverbs—4 pop songs* for 6 Men's Voices (1987). **TAPE:** *Sky, Horse and Death* (1954); *Static Relief* (1955); *Vocalism A-1* (1956); *Water Music* (1960); *Quiet Design* (1960); *Kwaidan* (1966; rev. of music from the film); *Toward* (1970). **OTHER:** Music for films, including *Hara-Kiri* (1962), *Woman in the Dunes* (1964), *Kwaidan* (1964), and *Empire of Passion* (1978).

BIBL.: N. Ohtake, *Creative Sources for the Music of T. T.* (Aldershot, 1993).

Taktakishvili, Otar (Vasilievich), Russian composer and teacher; b. Tiflis, July 27, 1924; d. there (Tbilisi), Feb. 22, 1989. He studied at the Tbilisi Cons., graduating in 1947; was on its faculty as a teacher of choral literature (from 1947) and of counterpoint and instrumentation (from 1959), serving as its rector (1962–65); was a prof. (from 1966). In 1974 he was made a People's Artist of the U.S.S.R. In 1982 he was awarded the Lenin Prize. His music is imbued with the characteristic melorhythms of the Caucasus; he had a natural knack for instrumental color.

WORKS: DRAMATIC: OPERAS: *Mindia* (Tbilisi, July 23, 1961); *Sami novela* (3 Stories; 1967); *Chikor* (1972); *Mtvaris Motatseba* (The Abduction of the Moon; 1976). Also film scores. **ORCH.:** Cello Concerto (1947); 2 syms. (1949, 1953); 3 overtures (1950, 1951, 1955); 2 symphonic poems: *Samgori* (1950) and *Mtsyri* (1956); 2 piano concertos: No. 1 (Tbilisi, Nov. 15, 1951) and No. 2 (1973); Trumpet Concerto (1954); *Humoresque* for Chamber Orch. (1963). **OTHER:** Oratorios; cantatas; choruses; songs; piano pieces.

BIBL.: L. Polyakova, *O. T.* (Moscow, 1956); L.V. Polyakova, *O. T.* (Moscow, 1979).

Taktakishvili, Shalva (Mikhailovich), Russian conductor, teacher, and composer; b. Kvemo-Khviti, Aug. 27, 1900; d. Tbilisi, July 18, 1965. He studied at the Tiflis Cons. He then taught theory at the Batumi Music School, of which he was a cofounder; then served as conductor at Tbilisi Radio; from 1952 to his death, conducted the Georgian State Orch.

WORKS: OPERAS: *Rassvet* (Sunrise; 1923); *Deputat* (The Delegate; 1939); *Otarova vdnova* (1942). **ORCH.:** *The Year 1905*, symphonic poem (1931); Cello Concerto (1932); 2 overtures (1944, 1949). **CHAMBER:** 2 string quartets (1930, 1933); Violin Sonata (1952); numerous piano pieces. **VOCAL:** Choruses; songs.

BIBL.: P. Hukua, *S. T.* (Tbilisi, 1962).

Tal, Josef (real name, **Joseph Gruenthal**), prominent German-born Israeli composer, pianist, conductor, and pedagogue; b. Pinne, near Posen, Sept. 18, 1910. He took courses with Tiessen, Hindemith, Sachs, Trapp, and others at the Berlin Staatliche Hochschule für Musik (1928–30). In 1934 he emigrated to Palestine, settling in Jerusalem as a teacher of piano and composition at the Cons. in 1936; when it became the Israel Academy of

Music in 1948, he served as its director (until 1952); also lectured at the Hebrew Univ. (from 1950), where he was head of the musicology dept. (1965–70) and a prof. (from 1971); likewise was director of the Israel Center of Electronic Music (from 1961). He appeared as a pianist and conductor with the Israel Phil. and with orchs. in Europe. In 1971 he was awarded the State of Israel Prize and was made an honorary member of the West Berlin Academy of Arts; in 1975 he received the Arts Prize of the City of Berlin, and in 1982 he became a fellow of its Inst. for Advanced Studies. His autobiography was publ. as *Der Sohn des Rabbiners: Ein Weg von Berlin nach Jerusalem* (Berlin, 1985). A true musical intellectual, Tal applies in his music a variety of techniques, being free of doctrinal introversion and open to novel potentialities without fear of public revulsion. Patriotic Hebrew themes often appear in his productions.

WORKS: DRAMATIC: *Saul at Ein Dor*, opera concertante (1957); *Amnon and Tamar*, opera (1961); *Ashmedai*, opera (1968; Hamburg, Nov. 9, 1971); *Massada 967*, opera (1972; Jerusalem, June 17, 1973); *Die Versuchung*, opera (1975; Munich, July 26, 1976); *Else-Hommage*, chamber scene for Mezzo-soprano, Narrator, and 4 Instruments (1975); Scene from Kafka's diaries for Soprano or Tenor Solo (1978); *Der Turm*, opera (1983; Berlin, Sept. 19, 1987); *Der Garten*, chamber opera (1987; Hamburg, May 29, 1988); *Die Hand*, dramatic scene for Soprano and Cello (1987); *Josef*, opera (1993–95; Tel Aviv, June 27, 1995). **ORCH.:** 3 piano concertos: No. 1 (1944), No. 2 (1953), and No. 3 for Tenor and Orch. (1956); *Reflections* for Strings (1950); 6 syms.: No. 1 (1953), No. 2 (1960), No. 3 (Tel Aviv, July 3, 1978), No. 4, *Hayovel* (Jubilee), for the 50th anniversary of the Israel Phil. (1985; Tel Aviv, Jan. 3, 1987); No. 5 (1990–91; Berlin, Feb. 29, 1992), and No. 6 (1991; Eschede, June 19, 1992); Viola Concerto (1954); *Hizayon Hagigi* (Festive Vision; 1959); Concerto for Cello and Strings (1961); Double Concerto for Violin, Cello, and Chamber Orch. (1970); *Dmut* (Shape) for Chamber Orch. (1975); Concerto for Flute and Chamber Orch. (1977); Concerto for 2 Pianos and Orch. (1980); Concerto for Clarinet and Chamber Orch. (1980); *Dance of the Events* (1981; rev. 1986); *Imago* for Chamber Orch. (1982); *Symphonic Fanfares* (1986). **CHAMBER:** *Kina* (Lament) for Cello and Harp (1950); Violin Sonata (1952); Oboe Sonata (1952); 3 string quartets (1959, 1964, 1976); Viola Sonata (1960); Woodwind Quintet (1966); *Fanfare* for 3 Trombones and 3 Trumpets (1968); Trio for Violin, Cello, and Piano (1974); Piano Quartet (1982); *Chamber Music* for Soprano Recorder, Marimba, and Harpsichord (1982); Duo for Oboe and English Horn (1992); Quartet for Tenor Saxophone, Violin, Viola, and Cello (1994). **KEYBOARD: PIANO:** Sonata (1950); *5 Inventions* (1956); *5 Densities* (1975); *Essay I, II*, and *III* (1986–89). Also organ pieces. **VOCAL:** *Yetsi'at Mitsrayim* (Exodus), choreographic poem for Baritone and Orch. (1946); *The Mother Rejoices*, symphonic cantata for Chorus, Piano, and Orch. (1949); *Succoth Cantata* for Soloists, Chorus, and Chamber Orch. (1955); *Mot Moshe* (The Death of Moses), Requiem for Soloists, Chorus, Orch., and Tape (1967); *Misdar hanoflim* (Parade of the Fallen), cantata for Soprano, Baritone, Chorus, and Orch. (1968); *Song* for Baritone or Alto, Flute, Horn, 2 Tom-toms, and Piano (1971); *Sus Ha'ets* (The Wooden Horse) for Soloists, Chorus, and Electronics (1976); *Bechol nafshecha* (With All Thy Soul), cantata for 3 Sopranos, Baritone, Boy's Chorus, Mixed Chorus, Brass, and Strings (1978); *Halom ha'igulim* (Dream of the Circles) for Baritone, Chorus, and 4 Instruments (1985); *Laga'at makom* (Touch a Place) for Voice and Chorus (1987); *Bitter Line* for Baritone and Chamber Ensemble (1992); *Wars Swept Through Here* for Baritone and 12 Players (1991); *Psalms* for Narrator, Chorus, and Orch. (1992); songs. **TAPE:** *Exodus II*, ballet (1954); Piano Concertos Nos. 4 to 6 for Piano and Tape (1962, 1964, 1970); *Ranges of Energy*, ballet (1963); *From the Depth of the Soul*, ballet (1964); Concerto for Harpsichord and Tape (1964; rev. 1977); *Ashmedai*, overture to the opera (1970); *Variations*, choreographic piece (1970); Concerto for Harp and Tape (1971; rev. 1980); *Min Hametsar Karati Yah* (I Called Upon the Lord in My Distress; 1971); *Frequencies 440–462: Hommage à Boris Blacher* (1972); *Backyard*, choreographic piece (1977).

BIBL.: W. Elias, *J. T.* (Tel Aviv, 1987).

Talbot (real name, **Munkittrick**), **Howard,** English conductor and composer; b. Yonkers, N.Y., March 9, 1865; d. Reigate, Sept. 12, 1928. He was taken to England at the age of 4, and studied at the Royal College of Music in London under Parry, Bridge, and Gladstone. From 1900 he was active as a conductor in various London theaters. He was a prolific composer of light operas, all produced in London; his greatest success was *A Chinese Honeymoon* (1899); his last work was *The Daughter of the Gods* (1929). Other operettas included *Monte Carlo* (1896); *3 Little Maids* (1902); *The Blue Moon* (1905); *The White Chrysanthemum* (1905); *The Girl behind the Counter* (1906); *The 3 Kisses* (1907); *The Belle of Brittany* (1908); *The Arcadians* (1909); *A Narrow Squeak* (1913); *The Pearl Girl* (1913); *A Lucky Miss* (1914); *A Mixed Grill* (1914); *The Light Blues* (1915).

Talbot, Michael (Owen), English musicologist; b. Luton, Jan. 4, 1943. He was educated at the Royal College of Music in London and at Clare College, Cambridge (Mus.B., 1963; Ph.D., 1968). In 1968 he joined the faculty of the Univ. of Liverpool as a lecturer in music, subsequently serving there as senior lecturer (1979–83), reader (1983–86), and the James and Constance Alsop Prof. of Music (from 1986). His articles have appeared in various journals; also publ. the studies *Vivaldi* (1978; 4th ed., rev., 1993), *Albinoni: Leben und Werk* (1980), *Tomaso Albinoni: The Venetian Composer and His World* (1990), and *Benedetto Vinaccesi: A Musician in Brescia and Venice in the Age of Corelli* (1994).

Talich, Václav, eminent Czech conductor; b. Kroměříž, May 28, 1883; d. Beroun, March 16, 1961. He received his early musical training from his father, Jan Talich (1851–1915), a choirmaster and music teacher; then studied violin with Mařák and Ševčik and chamber music with Kàan at the Prague Cons. (1897–1903). He was concertmaster of the Berlin Phil. (1903–04) and of the orch. of the Odessa Opera (1904–05); then taught violin in Tiflis (1905–06). He conducted the Slovenian Phil. in Ljubljana (1908–12); also took courses in composition with Reger and Sitt and in conducting with Nikisch at the Leipzig Cons.; also studied with Vigna in Milan. He was then opera conductor at Pilsen (1912–15). Talich held the post of 2nd conductor (1918–19) of the Czech Phil. in Prague, and subsequently served as its chief conductor from 1919 to 1931; in 1931–33 he was conductor of the Konsertforeningen in Stockholm; then in 1933 returned as chief conductor of the Czech Phil. (until 1941), which he brought to a high degree of excellence. He was director and conductor of the National Theater in Prague from 1935 to 1944, when the theater was closed by the Nazis; with the defeat of the Nazis, he resumed his activities there but was dismissed in 1945 after disagreements with the state authorities; he was recalled in 1947, but was dismissed once more in 1948 after conflicts with the new Communist regime. He then moved to Bratislava, where he conducted the Slovak Phil. (1949–52); returned as guest conductor of the Czech Phil. (1952–54); retired from concert appearances in 1954. He also taught conducting in Prague and Bratislava; among his pupils were Ančerl and Mackerras. He was renowned for his idiomatic performances of the Czech repertory. He was made a National Artist in 1957.

BIBL.: O. Šourek, ed., *V. T.* (Prague, 1943); V. Pospíšil, *V. T.: Několik kapitol o díle a životě českého umělce* (V. T.: Some Chapters on the Life and Work of a Czech Artist; Prague, 1961); H. Masaryk, ed., *V. T.: Dokument života a díla* (V. T.: A Document of His Life and Work; Prague, 1967); M. Kuna, *V. T.* (Prague, 1980).

Tallat-Kelpša, Juozas, Lithuanian conductor, teacher, and composer; b. Kalnujai, Jan. 1, 1889; d. Vilnius, Feb. 5, 1949. He studied cello at the Vilnius Music School before completing his music education at the St. Petersburg Cons. (1907–16). In 1920 he settled in Kaunas and founded its Opera, which he conducted until 1941 and again from 1944 to 1948. He also taught at the music school (1920–33) and at the Cons. (from 1933). In 1948 he was awarded the Stalin Prize. He wrote instrumental works, piano pieces, and choral songs, and also prepared folk song arrangements.

Talley, Marion, American soprano; b. Nevada, Mo., Dec. 20, 1906; d. Los Angeles, Jan. 3, 1983. She sang in churches in Kansas City, Mo., and at 16 appeared in *Mignon* there. Following training from Frank La Forge in N.Y., she completed her studies in Europe. On Feb. 17, 1926, she made her Metropolitan Opera debut in N.Y. as Gilda and created a stir as an American find. However, her success was short-lived. She sang at the Metropolitan for only 3 seasons and then made sporadic opera and recital appearances. In 1936 she sang on the radio and then returned to opera in 1940, but her career soon waned.

Talma, Louise (Juliette), American composer and teacher; b. Arcachon, France, Oct. 31, 1906; d. Yaddo, N.Y., Aug. 13, 1996. She studied at the Inst. of Musical Art in N.Y. (1922–30) and took courses at N.Y. Univ. (B.M., 1931) and at Columbia Univ. (B.Mus., 1933); took piano lessons with Philipp and composition with Boulanger in Fontainebleau (summers, 1926–39). She taught at Hunter College (1928–79); was the first American to teach at the Fontainebleau School of Music (summers, 1936–39; 1978; 1981–82). She received 2 Guggenheim fellowships (1946, 1947); was the first woman composer to be elected to the National Inst. of Arts and Letters in 1974. In her music, she adopted a strongly impressionistic style. She publ. *Harmony for the College Student* (1966) and *Functional Harmony* (with J. Harrison and R. Levin, 1970).

WORKS: OPERA: *The Alcestiad* (1955–58; Frankfurt am Main, March 1, 1962). **ORCH.:** *Toccata* (1944; Baltimore, Dec. 20, 1945); *Dialogues* for Piano and Orch. (1963–64; Buffalo, Dec. 12, 1965). **CHAMBER:** String Quartet (1954); Violin Sonata (1962); *Summer Sounds* for Clarinet, 2 Violins, Viola, and Cello (1969–73); *The Ambient Air* for Flute, Violin, Cello, and Piano (1980–83); *Studies in Spacing* for Clarinet and Piano (1982). **PIANO:** 2 sonatas (1943; 1944–55); *Passacaglia and Fugue* (1955–62); *Textures* (1977). **VOCAL: CHORAL:** *The Divine Flame*, oratorio (1946–48); *La corona*, 7 sonnets (1954–55); *A Time to Remember* for Chorus and Orch. (1966–67); *Voices of Peace* for Chorus and Strings (1973); *Mass for the Sundays of the Year* (1984). **WITH SOLO VOICE:** *Terre de France*, song cycle for Soprano and Piano (1943–45); *All the Days of My Life*, cantata for Tenor, Clarinet, Cello, Piano, and Percussion (1963–65); *The Tolling Bell* for Baritone and Orch. (1967–69); *Diadem*, song cycle for Tenor and Piano or 5 Instruments (1978–79); *Variations on 13 Ways of Looking at a Blackbird* for Soprano or Tenor and Flute or Oboe or Violin and Piano (1979).

BIBL.: R. Ericson, "Celebrating L. T.," *N.Y. Times* (Feb. 4, 1977); S. Teicher, "L. T.: Essentials of her style as seen through the Piano Works," *The Musical Woman: An International Perspective 1983* (Westport, Conn., 1984).

Talmi, Yoav, Israeli conductor; b. Kibbutz Merhavia, April 28, 1943. He studied at the Rubin Academy of Music in Tel Aviv (diploma, 1965) and at the Juilliard School of Music in N.Y. (1965–68); also studied conducting with Susskind at the Aspen (Colo.) School of Music (summer, 1966), Maderna in Salzburg (summer, 1967), Fournet in Hilversum (summer, 1968), and Leinsdorf at the Berkshire Music Center at Tanglewood (summer, 1969), where he won the Koussevitzky Memorial Conducting Prize. He was assoc. conductor of the Louisville Orch. (1968–70), music director of the Kentucky Chamber Orch. (1969–71), and co-conductor of the Israel Chamber Orch. (1970–72). After serving as artistic director of Arnhem's Het Gelders Orch. (1974–80) and as principal guest conductor of the Munich Phil. (1979–80), he returned to the Israel Chamber Orch. as its music director in 1984; also appeared widely as a guest conductor. He was music director-designate (1989–90) and music director (1990–96) of the San Diego Sym. Orch. In 1994 he served as artistic advisor of the Waterloo (N.J.) Festival.

Taltabull, Cristòfor, Catalan composer and pedagogue; b. Barcelona, July 28, 1888; d. there, May 1, 1964. He studied piano with Granados and composition with Pedrell. In 1908 he went to Germany, where he took lessons with Reger. In 1912 he went to Paris, where he was an accompanist to singers, a proofreader for the publisher Durand, and a music copyist; he also composed popular songs for vaudeville and wrote film music. After the outbreak of World War II in 1939, he returned to Barcelona, where he became a teacher of composition. Many important Spanish composers of the younger generation were his pupils. As a composer, he was particularly successful in songs to French and Catalan texts. His style of composition is impressionistic, mainly derived from Debussy; he had a delicate sense of color and rhythm; thematically, most of his music retains Spanish, or Catalan, melorhythmic characteristics.

Talvela, Martti (Olavi), remarkable Finnish bass; b. Hiitola, Feb. 4, 1935; d. Juva, July 22, 1989. He received training at the Lahti Academy of Music (1958–60). After winning the Finnish lieder competition in 1960, he studied voice with Carl Martin Ohmann in Stockholm. He made his operatic debut there at the Royal Theater as Sparafucile in *Rigoletto* in 1961. He made his first appearance at the Bayreuth Festival in 1962 as Titurel; that same year, joined the Deutsche Oper in Berlin, where he sang leading bass roles. In 1968 he made his U.S. debut in a recital at Hunter College in N.Y. He made his Metropolitan Opera debut in N.Y. as the Grand Inquisitor in *Don Carlos* on Oct. 7, 1968; appeared there in succeeding years with increasing success, being especially acclaimed for his dramatic portrayal of Boris Godunov. From 1972 to 1980 he served as artistic director of the Savonlinna Festival. He was to have assumed the post of artistic director of the Finnish National Opera in Helsinki in 1992, but death intervened. In 1973 he received the Pro Finlandia Award and the Finnish State Prize. A man of towering dimensions (6'7"), his command of the great bass roles was awesome. Among his outstanding portrayals, in addition to Boris Godunov, were Hagen, Hunding, Gurnemanz, the Commendatore, and Sarastro. He also was effective in contemporary roles.

Tamberg, Eino, Estonian composer and pedagogue; b. Tallinn, May 27, 1930. He studied composition with E. Kapp at the Tallinn Cons., graduating in 1953. He then was a music supervisor with the Estonian Radio; was a teacher (from 1967) and a prof. (from 1983) at the Tallinn Cons. In 1975 he was made a People's Artist of the Estonian SSR.

WORKS: DRAMATIC: OPERAS: *The House of Iron* (Tallinn, July 15, 1965); *Cyrano de Bergerac* (1974; Tallinn, July 2, 1976); *Flight* (1982; Tallinn, Dec. 30, 1983); *Creatures*, chamber opera (1992). **BALLETS:** *Ballet-Symphony* (1959; Schwerin, March 10, 1960); *The Boy and the Butterfly* (Tallinn, Nov. 30, 1963); *Joanna tentata* (1970; Tallinn, Jan. 23, 1971). **ORCH.:** Concerto Grosso (1956; Moscow, July 10, 1957); *Symphonic Dances* (Riga, Dec. 22, 1957); *Toccata* (1967); Trumpet Concerto (Tallinn, Nov. 21, 1972); 3 syms.: No. 1 (1978; Tallinn, Jan. 27, 1979), No. 2 (Tallinn, Oct. 23, 1986), and No. 3 (Tallinn, Nov. 12, 1989); Violin Concerto (Tallinn, Oct. 17, 1981); Alto Saxophone Concerto (1987; Tallinn, May 6, 1988); *Journey* for Strings (1990; Toronto, May 15, 1991); *Prelude* (Tallinn, May 15, 1993); *Nocturne* (1994); *Music* for Percussion and Orch. (1994; Tallinn, March 23, 1995). **CHAMBER:** String Quartet (1958); *5 Pieces* for Oboe and Piano (1970); 2 wind quintets (1975, 1984); *Waiting* for Alto Flute, Clarinet, Percussion, Violin, and Cello (1991); *Musica triste* for Flute, Vibraphone, and Strings (1991); *Music for 5* for 5 Instruments (1992); *A Play for 5 in 4 Acts* for Saxophone Quartet and Percussion (1994); piano pieces. **VOCAL:** *Moonlight Oratorio* for 2 Narrators, Soprano, Baritone, Chorus, and Orch. (1962; Tartu, Feb. 17, 1963); *Fanfares of Victory*, cantata for Bass, Chorus, and Orch. (1975); *Amores*, oratorio for Vocal Soloists, Chorus, and Orch. (1981; Tallinn, March 27, 1983); Concerto for Mezzo-soprano and Orch. (1985; Tallinn, Sept. 15, 1986); *Night Songs* for Mezzo-soprano, Flute, Violin, and Guitar (1992); other songs.

Tamkin, David, Russian-American composer; b. Chernigov, Aug. 28, 1906; d. Los Angeles, June 21, 1975. He was taken to the U.S. as an infant; the family settled in Portland, Oreg., where he studied violin with Henry Bettman, a pupil of Ysaÿe; took lessons in composition with Bloch. In 1937 he settled in Los Angeles; from 1945 to 1966 he was principal composer at Universal Pictures in Hollywood. His music is deeply permeated with the melodic and rhythmic elements of the Hassidic Jewish cantillation. His magnum opus is the opera *The Dybbuk* (1928–31; N.Y., Oct. 4, 1951); also wrote the opera *The Blue Plum Tree of Esau* (1962), 2 string quartets, a Woodwind Sextet, and several choruses.

Tan, Margaret Leng, significant Singaporean-American pianist; b. Penang, Malaysia, Dec. 12, 1945. She was educated in Singapore; at 16, went to N.Y., where she studied with Adele Marcus at the Juilliard School, becoming the first woman to graduate with the D.Mus. degree (1971). Tan specializes in new Asian and American music, evolving a highly individual approach to performance wherein sound, choreography, and theater assume equal significance; she has worked closely with such composers as John Cage, Alvin Lucier, William Duckworth, Lois V Vierk, Somei Satoh et al. in defining her role as the world's premiere string piano virtuoso. She became particularly known for her interpretive command of the works of Cage, giving performances throughout Europe, the U.S., and Asia; also appeared in PBS American Masters documentaries on Cage (1990) and Jasper Johns (1989). During the 1990–91 season, she presented retrospective performances of Cage's music in conjunction with retrospective exhibitions of Johns' paintings at the Walker Art Center in Minneapolis, the Whitney Museum of American Art in N.Y., the Hayward Gallery in London, and the Center for Fine Arts in Miami; she also performed for Cage exhibitions at the Neue Pinakothek (Munich 1991), "Il Suono rapido delle Cose (Cage & Company)" at the 45th Venice Biennale (1993), and at the Guggenheim Museum's "Rolywholyover A Circus" and related "Citycircus" events (1994). In 1984 she received an NEA Arts Solo Recitalist award (1984) and in 1988 an Asian Cultural Council grant for contemporary music research in Japan. In 1987 she appeared with the Brooklyn Phil., and in 1991 made her debut with the N.Y. Phil. Among her critically acclaimed recordings are *Litania: Margaret Leng Tan Plays Somei Satoh* (1988), *Sonic Encounters: The New Piano* (1989; with works by Cage, Hovhaness, Crumb, Satoh, and Ge Gan-ru), and *Daughters of the Lonesome Isle* (1994). From 1993 she developed a repertory for the toy piano through commissions and transcriptions. Tan also is a regular contributor to *Piano Today.* She currently resides in Brooklyn, N.Y., with 2 dogs, 3 Steinways, and 9 toy pianos.

Tan, Melvyn, talented Singaporean fortepianist and harpsichordist; b. Singapore, Oct. 13, 1956. He went to England, where he entered the Yehudi Menuhin School in Surrey when he was 12; later pursued training at the Royal College of Music in London. His principal mentors were Perlemuter and Boulanger. After commencing his career as a pianist, he took up the fortepiano and harpsichord in 1980; he subsequently appeared in the major British music centers, and in 1985 made his first tour of the U.S. In 1987 he won critical accolades as soloist in a series of Beethoven concerts, with Roger Norrington conducting the London Classical Players. In 1990 he toured in France, Germany, Japan, and Australia, and also played at N.Y.'s Carnegie Hall.

Tanabe, Hisao, Japanese musicologist and composer; b. Tokyo, Aug. 16, 1883; d. there, March 5, 1984. His mother played and taught Japanese instruments; he began learning the violin at the Tokyo Music School in 1903. While studying physics at the Univ. of Tokyo (1904–07), he took courses in composition with Noël Peri; also had postgraduate studies in acoustics (1907–10) and studied Japanese music and dance with Shōhei Tanaka. He taught acoustics, music history, and theory at the Toyo Music School (1907–35) and the Imperial Music Bureau (1919–23); also taught Japanese music history at Kokugakuin Univ. (1923), the Univ. of Tokyo (1930), Waseda Univ. (1947), and Musashino College of Music (1949). In 1936 Tanabe founded and served as the first president of the Soc. for Research in Asiatic Music; his field studies included collections of music from Korea (1921), Formosa and the Ryuku Islands (1922), northern China (1923), and the Pacific Islands (1934). He was a pioneer among modern Japanese musicologists; his writings and lectures on European music were important for its introduction into Japan in the early 20th century. He publ. nearly 50 books on a variety of musical subjects, especially oriental music and acoustics. He also performed widely, both European and Japanese music, and composed a number of works. He publ. his autobiography as *Tanabe Hisao jijoden* (2 vols., 1981, 1982). After his death, the Soc. for Research in Asiatic Music instituted the Tanabe Hisao Prize.

WRITINGS: *Nippon ongaku kōwa* (Lectures on Japanese Music; 1919); *Toyô ongakushi* (History of Oriental Music; 1930); *Ongaku riron* (Theories of Music; 1929; rev. 1956); *Ongaku onkyogaku* (Acoustics of Music; 1951); also ed. *Nihon ongakushû* (Collection of Japanese Music in Staff Notation; 1931) and *Kinsei Nihon ongakushû* (Collection of Modern Japanese Music in Staff Notation; 1931).

Tanaka, Karen, Japanese composer; b. Tokyo, April 7, 1961. She began formal composition studies at the age of 10; following training with Miyoshi at the Toho Gakuen School of Music in Tokyo (1982–86), she studied with Murial in Paris at IRCAM (1986–88); then had advanced instruction at the Banff Centre for the Arts in Alberta, Canada (1989), and was a pupil of Berio in Florence (1990–91). From 1991 to 1993 she worked at IRCAM. Her music aggressively explores the structure of sound.

WORKS: ORCH.: *Prismes* (Tokyo, Oct. 16, 1984); *Anamorphose* for Piano and Orch. (1985–87; Amsterdam, Sept. 13, 1987); *Hommage en cristal* for Piano and Strings (1991); *Initium* for Orch. and Live Electronics (1992–93; Tokyo, June 23, 1993). **CHAMBER:** *Tristesse* for Flute, Violin, and Piano (1983); *Monodrama* for Flute (1984); *Lilas* for Cello (1988); *Metallic Crystal* for Metallic Percussion, Computer, and Live Electronics (1992); *Polarization* for 2 Percussionists (1994). **KEYBOARD: PIANO:** *Solid Crossing* for 2 Pianos (1986); *Crystalline* (1988). **HARPSICHORD:** *Jardin des herbes* (1988). **VOCAL:** Quartet for Soprano, Violin, Viola, and Cello (1984).

Tanaka, Toshimitsu, Japanese composer and teacher; b. Aomori, July 17, 1930. He was a student at the Kunitani Music College (graduated, 1951), and then taught there.

WORKS: ORCH.: *Gunzo* (1979); *Pathos* (1981); *Sadlo Concerto* for Marimba and Orch. (1990). **CHAMBER:** Violin Sonata (1957); 2 string quartets (1962, 1988); *Tamanna* for 2 Pianos and Percussion (1967); Suite for Marimba, 7 Strings, and 2 Percussionists (1971); *Earthen Vessel* for Percussion Ensemble (1982); *Locus* for Percussion (1983); *Blue Ladder* for Synthesizer (1984); *Aoi Kizahashi* for Synthesizer (1984); *Persona* for Marimba and Percussion Ensemble (1990); piano pieces. **VOCAL:** *Magic Festival in the Mountain Crease* for Chorus, Ryûteki, and Various Types of Wadaiko (1968); *Epic "Wolf Boy"* for Soprano, Shamisen, Shakuhachi, Wadaiko, and Strings (Tokyo, Nov. 27, 1968); *The Grave,* requiem for Chorus and Orch. (Tokyo Radio, Nov. 5, 1972); *Kodai Sanka* for Chorus and Percussion Ensemble (1987); choruses; songs.

Tan Dun, significant Chinese composer; b. Si Mao, central Hunan Province, Aug. 18, 1957. While working among peasants during the Chinese Cultural Revolution, he began collecting folk songs. After playing viola in the Beijing Opera orch. (1976–77), he entered the recently reopened Central Cons. in Beijing in 1978 to study composition (B.A.; M.A.). In the 1980s he attended guest lectures given by Goehr, Henze, Crumb et al. In 1983 his String Quartet won a prize in Dresden, the first international music prize won by a Chinese composer since 1949. His Western compositional leanings led to a 6-month ban on performances or broadcasts of his music soon thereafter. In

1986 he settled in N.Y., where he accepted a fellowship at Columbia Univ. and studied with Chou Wen-Chung, Mario Davidovsky, and George Edwards. His early works are romantic and florid; after 1982, they reveal a progressing advancement of dissonance and sophistication, while retaining Chinese contexts. Many of his compositions require instrumentalists to vocalize in performance.

WORKS: DRAMATIC: *9 Songs*, ritual opera for 20 Singers/Performers (N.Y., May 12, 1989); *Marco Polo*, opera (1993–94). **ORCH.:** *Li Sao*, sym. (1979–80); Piano Concerto (1983); *Symphony in 2 Movements* (1985); *On Taoism* (1985; Hong Kong, June 28, 1986); *Out of Beijing Opera* for Violin and Orch. (1987); *Orchestral Theatre I: Xun* (1990), *II: Re* (1992), and *III: Red* (1994); *Death and Fire: Dialogue with Paul Klee* (1991–92; Glasgow, March 27, 1993); *Yi*, cello concerto (1993–94). **CHAMBER:** *Feng Ya Song*, string quartet (1982); *8 Colors* for String Quartet (1986–88); *In Distance* for Piccolo, Harp, and Bass Drum (1987); *Elegy: Snow in June*, concerto for Cello and 4 Percussionists (1991); *Circle with 4 Trios, Conductor, and Audience* (1992); *Lament: Autumn Wind* for Any 6 Instruments, Any Voice, and Conductor (1993). **PIANO:** *5 Pieces in Human Accent* (1978); *Traces* (1989; rev. 1992); *R;Beatles* (1990); *CAGE* (1993). **VOCAL:** *Fu* for 2 Sopranos, Bass, and Ensemble (1982); *Silk Road* for Soprano and Percussion (1989).

Tanev, Alexander, Bulgarian composer and teacher; b. Budapest (of Bulgarian parents), Oct. 23, 1928. He studied law at the Univ. of Sofia (1946–50) and composition with Veselin Stoyanov at the Bulgarian State Cons. in Sofia (graduated, 1957). He was a teacher of composition at the latter institution (from 1970), and dean of the faculty of composition and conductor (from 1986). He also served as secretary of the Union of Bulgarian Composers (1972–76).

WORKS: DRAMATIC: *Prasnik v Tsaravets* (Festival of Tsaravets), ballet (1968); *Gramada*, music drama (1977). **ORCH.:** Sinfonietta (1959); *Youth Concerto* for Violin and Strings (1969); *Rondo concertante* for Trombone and Orch. (1971); Concerto for Brass and Percussion (1972); *Builder's Music* for 2 Pianos and Orch. or Percussion (1974); *Divertimento concertante* for Piano and Orch. (1976); *Capriccio* for Symphonic and Wind Orchs. (1986); Concerto for Strings (1988). **VOCAL:** 3 oratorios: *Annals of Freedom* for Soloists, Chorus, and Orch. (1975–76), *Testament* for Bass, Reader, Chorus, Children's Chorus, and Orch. (1977–78), and *Native Land* for Bass, Reader, Chorus, Children's Chorus, and Orch. (1984–85); *The Way Is Fearful but Glorious*, symphonic poem for Bass-baritone and Orch. (1979); 3 cantatas: *In Praise of the Song about Damiancho* for Women's Chorus and 2 Pianos (1981), *In Praise of the Rila Monastery* for Bass, Men's Chorus, and Orch. (1982), and *The Song of Songs* for Tenor, Bass, and Orch. (1983); song cycles. **OTHER:** Chamber music; piano pieces.

Tangeman, Nell, American mezzo-soprano; b. Columbus, Ohio, Dec. 23, 1917; d. Washington, D.C., Feb. 15, 1965. She studied violin at Ohio State Univ. (M.A., 1937) and received vocal instruction at the Cleveland Inst. of Music and from Fritz Lehmann, Schorr, and Matzenauer in N.Y. In 1945 she made her debut as a soloist in *Das Lied von der Erde* with Goossens and the Cincinnati Sym. Orch. In 1948 she made her N.Y. recital debut, and then spent a year studying in Italy on a Fulbright scholarship. She created the role of Mother Goose in Stravinsky's *The Rake's Progress* in Venice in 1951. In subsequent years, she sang throughout the U.S. and Europe in a repertoire extending from the 16th century to the contemporary era.

Tango, Egisto, Italian conductor; b. Rome, Nov. 13, 1873; d. Copenhagen, Oct. 5, 1951. He studied engineering before pursuing musical training at the Naples Cons. He made his debut as an opera conductor in Venice (1893), then conducted at La Scala in Milan (1895) and at Berlin (1903–08). He conducted at the Metropolitan Opera in N.Y. (1909–10), in Italy (1911–12), and in Budapest (1913–19), where he gave the earliest performances of stage works by Bartók. From 1920 to 1926 he was active in Germany and Austria. In 1927 he settled in Copenhagen. He was distinguished for the technical precision and interpretative clarity of his performances.

Tansman, Alexandre, Polish-born French pianist, conductor, and composer; b. Łódź, June 12, 1897; d. Paris, Nov. 15, 1986. He studied at the Łódź Cons. (1902–14); then pursued training in law and philosophy at the Univ. of Warsaw; also received instruction in counterpoint, form, and composition from Rytel in Warsaw. In 1919 he went to Paris, where he appeared as a soloist in his own works (Feb. 17, 1920). In 1927 he appeared as a soloist with the Boston Sym. Orch., and then played throughout Europe, Canada, and Palestine. He later took up conducting; made a tour of the Far East (1932–33). After the occupation of Paris by the Germans in 1940, he made his way to the U.S.; lived in Hollywood, where he wrote music for films; returned to Paris in 1946. His music is distinguished by a considerable melodic gift and a vivacious rhythm; his harmony is often bitonal; there are some impressionistic traits that reflect his Parisian tastes.

WORKS: DRAMATIC: OPERAS: *La Nuit kurde* (1925–27; Paris Radio, 1927); *La toisson d'or*, opéra bouffe (1938); *Sabbataï Zevi, le faux Messie*, lyric fresco (1953; Paris, 1961); *Le serment* (1954; Brussels, March 11, 1955); *L'usignolo di Boboli* (1962); *Georges Dandin*, opéra comique (1974). **BALLETS:** *Sextuor* (Paris, May 17, 1924); *La Grande Ville* (1932); *Bric-à-Brac* (1937); *Train de nuit* (London, 1950); *Les Habits neufs du roi* (Venice, 1959); *Resurrection* (Nice, 1962). **ORCH.:** *Danse de la sorcière* (Brussels, May 5, 1924); 7 syms.: No. 1 (1925; Boston, March 18, 1927), No. 2 (1926), No. 3, *Symphonie concertante* (1931), No. 4 (1939), No. 5 (1942; Baltimore, Feb. 2, 1943), No. 6, *In memoriam* (1943), and No. 7 (1944; St. Louis, Oct. 24, 1947); 2 sinfoniettas: No. 1 (Paris, March 23, 1925) and No. 2 (1978); *Ouverture symphonique* (1926; Paris, Feb. 3, 1927); 2 piano concertos: No. 1 (Paris, May 27, 1926, composer soloist) and No. 2 (Boston, Dec. 28, 1927, composer soloist); Suite for 2 Pianos and Orch. (Paris, Nov. 16, 1930); Viola Concerto (1936); Violin Concerto (1937); *Fantaisie* for Violin and Orch. (1937); *Fantaisie* for Cello and Orch. (1937); *Rapsodie polonaise* (St. Louis, Nov. 14, 1941); *Études symphoniques* (1943); Guitar Concertino (1945); *Ricercari* (St. Louis, Dec. 22, 1949); Concerto (1954); Capriccio (Louisville, March 6, 1955); Clarinet Concerto (1958); Cello Concerto (1963); *Dyptique* for Chamber Orch. (1969); *Stèle: In memoriam Igor Stravinski* (1972); *Elégie (à la mémoire de Darius Milhaud)* (1976); *Les Dix Commandements* (1979). **CHAMBER:** 8 string quartets (1917–56); Violin Sonata (1919); *Danse de la sorcière* for Woodwind Quintet and Piano (1925; a version of the ballet); Flute Sonata (1925); Cello Sonata (1930); String Sextet (1940); *Divertimento* for Oboe, Clarinet, Trumpet, Cello, and Piano (1944); *Suite baroque* (1958); *Symphonie de chambre* (1960); *Musique à six* for Clarinet, String Quartet, and Piano (1977); *Musique* for Clarinet and String Quartet (1983). **PIANO:** *20 pièces faciles polonaises* (1924); 5 sonatas; mazurkas, and other Polish dances; *Sonatine transatlantique* (1930; also for Orch., Paris, Feb. 28, 1931; used by Kurt Jooss for his ballet *Impressions of a Big City*, Cologne, Nov. 21, 1932); *Pour les enfants*, 4 albums. **VOCAL:** *Ponctuation française* for Voice and Small Orch. (1946); *Psaumes 118, 119, and 120* for Tenor, Chorus, and Orch. (1961); *Apostrophe à Zion*, cantata for Chorus and Orch. (1977); *8 Stèles de Victor Segalen* for Voice and Chamber Orch. (1979).

WRITINGS: *Stravinsky* (Paris, 1948; Eng. tr., 1949, as *Igor Stravinsky: The Man and His Music*).

BIBL.: R. Petit, "A. T.," *Revue Musicale* (Feb. 1929); I. Schwerke, *A. T., compositeur polonais* (Paris, 1931).

Tapper, Thomas, American music educator; b. Canton, Mass., Jan. 28, 1864; d. White Plains, N.Y., Feb. 24, 1958. He studied in the U.S. and Europe. He ed. the *Music Record and Review* (1901–07) and the *Musician* (1905–07); then taught at N.Y. Univ. (1908–12); was lecturer at the Inst. of Musical Art (1905–24); also filled other editorial and educational positions. He publ. *The Music Life* (1891); *The Education of the Music Teacher* (1914);

Essentials in Music History (1914; with P. Goetschius); *The Melodic Music Course* (28 vols.; with F.H. Ripley); *Harmonic Music Course* (7 vols.); *The Modern Graded Piano Course* (19 vols.); *Music Theory and Composition* (6 vols.); *From Palestrina to Grieg* (Boston, 1929; 2nd ed., 1946). His wife, Bertha Feiring Tapper (b. Christiania, Norway, Jan. 25, 1859; d. N.Y., Sept. 2, 1915), was a pianist; she studied with Agathe Backer-Gröndahl in Norway and with Leschetizky in Vienna. She went to America in 1881; taught piano at the New England Cons. in Boston (1889–97) and at the Inst. of Musical Art in N.Y. (1905–10); she ed. 2 vols. of Grieg's piano works; publ. piano pieces and songs. She married Tapper on Sept. 22, 1895.

Tappolet, Willy, Swiss writer on music; b. Lindau, near Zürich, Aug. 6, 1890; d. Chêne-Bongeries, Feb. 24, 1981. He studied at the Univ. of Zürich (Ph.D., 1917, with the diss. *Heinrich Weber*, publ. in Zürich, 1918); completed his Habilitation at the Univ. of Geneva in 1938 with his *La Notation musicale et son influence sur la pratique de la musique du moyen-âge a nos jours* (publ. in Neuchâtel, 1945); was a reader on its faculty (1955–60). He wrote articles for various music journals; further publ. monographs on Honegger (in Ger., Zürich and Leipzig, 1933; in French, Neuchâtel, 1939; rev. ed., in Ger., 1954; in French, 1957) and on Ravel (Olten, 1950).

Tappy, Eric, Swiss tenor; b. Lausanne, May 19, 1931. He studied with Fernando Carpi at the Geneva Cons. (1951–58), Ernst Reichert at the Salzburg Mozarteum, Eva Liebenberg in Hilversum, and Boulanger in Paris. In 1959 he made his concert debut as the Evangelist in Bach's *St. Matthew Passion* in Strasbourg. His operatic stage debut followed in 1964 as Rameau's Zoroastre at the Paris Opéra-Comique. After singing in Geneva (1966) and Hanover (1967), he made his debut at London's Covent Garden as Mozart's Tito in 1974. He made his U.S. debut in 1974 as Don Ottavio at the San Francisco Opera, where he returned to sing Poppea and Idomeneo in 1977–78. In 1980 he appeared as Tito in Rome. He retired in 1982. Tappy was esteemed for the extraordinary range of his concert and operatic repertoire, which ranged from early music to the avant-garde.

Taranov, Gleb (Pavlovich), Ukrainian composer and teacher; b. Kiev, June 15, 1904; d. there, Jan. 25, 1989. He studied composition with Mikhail Chernov at the Petrograd Cons. (1917–19) and composition with Glière and Liatoshinsky and conducting with Blumenfield and Malko at the Kiev Cons. (1920–25). He served on the faculty of the Kiev Cons. (1925–41; 1944–74). In 1957 he was named Honored National Artist of the Ukraine. His works were cast in the accepted Soviet mold, with emphasis on the celebration of historical events.

WORKS: OPERA: *The Battle on the Ice*, depicting the victory of Alexander Nevsky over the Teutonic Knights at Lake Peipus on April 5, 1242 (1943; rev. 1979). **ORCH.:** Concerto Grosso (1936; rev. 1976); 9 syms. (1943; 1947; 1949, for Orch. of Native Instruments; 1957; *Antifascism*, 1963; "In Memory of Prokofiev" for Strings, 1964; *Heroic*, 1967; *Shushenskaya*, 1969; *The Banner of Victory*, 1974); 5 suites (1950, 1955, 1961, 1964, 1965); 2 symphonic poems: *David Guramishvili* (1953) and *Fire in the Hangar* (1958); *The 1st in Outer Space*, scherzo-poem (1961); *Overture to Memory* (1965); *New Express* (1977). **CHAMBER:** 2 string quartets (1929, 1945); *Enthusiastic Sextet* for Piano and Strings (1945); Woodwind Quintet (1959); works for Solo Instruments. **VOCAL:** Choruses; songs.

BIBL.: M. Mikhailov, *G.P. T.* (Kiev, 1963); S. Miroshnichenko, *G. T.* (Kiev, 1976).

Tăranu, Cornel, Romanian composer and teacher; b. Cluj, June 20, 1934. He was a student of Toduţă and Muresianu at the Cluj Cons. (1951–57), and he then joined its faculty. He also studied with Boulanger and Messiaen in Paris (1966–67) and attended the summer courses in music given by Ligeti and Maderna in Darmstadt (1968, 1969, 1972). His music is austerely formal, with atonal sound structures related through continuous variation with permissible aleatory interludes.

WORKS: OPERA: *Secretul lui Don Giovanni* (The Secret of Don Giovanni; Cluj, July 8, 1970). **ORCH.:** Sym. for Strings (1957); 4 numbered syms.: No. 1, *Sinfonia brevis* (Cluj, Nov. 17, 1962), No. 2, *Aulodica* (1975–76; Cluj, April 8, 1976), No. 3, *Signes* (Cluj, Sept. 25, 1984), and No. 4, *Ritornele* (Cluj, Oct. 9, 1987); *Secvenţe* (Sequences) for Strings (1960); *Simetrii* (Symmetries; 1964; Cluj, Jan. 15, 1966); *Incantaţii* (Incantations; 1965; Cluj, Jan. 15, 1966); Piano Concerto (1966; Cluj, May 29, 1967); *Intercalări* (Intercalations) for Piano and Orch. (1967–69; Cluj, Dec. 13, 1969); *Sinfonietta giocasa* for Strings (1968); *Alternanţe* (Alternations; 1968; Bucharest, May 29, 1969); *Racorduri* (Transitions) for Chamber Orch. (1971); *Cîntec lung* for Clarinet, Piano, and Strings (1974; Bern, April 18, 1975); *Ghirlande* (Garlands; 1979; also for Chamber Ensemble); *Prolegomene II* for Strings and Piano (1982); *Sonata rubato II* for Oboe, Piano, and Strings (1988); *Miroirs* for Saxophone and Chamber Orch. (1990; Cluj, Nov. 15, 1991). **CHAMBER:** String Trio (1952); *Poem-Sonata* for Clarinet and Piano (1954); Cello Sonata (1960); Flute Sonata (1961); Oboe Sonata (1963); *3 Pieces* for Clarinet and Piano (1964); *Dialogues for 6* for Flute, Clarinet, Trumpet, Vibraphone, Percussion, and Piano (1966); *Resonances I* for Guitar (1977) and *II* for Guitar and String Quartet (1978); *Offrande* (Gifts) *I* for Flute and 2 Percussion Groups (1978), *II* for Flute, 2 Percussion Groups, String Quintet, and Piano (1978), and *III* for 4 Flutes, Piano, and Percussion (1988); *Prolegomene I* for String Quartet and Piano (1981); Sonata for Clarinet and Percussion (1985); Sonata for Solo Double Bass (1986); *Sonata rubato I* for Oboe (1986); *Sempre ostinato I* for Soprano Saxophone or Clarinet (1986) and *II* for Saxophone or Clarinet and 7 Instruments (1986–88); Sonata for Solo Viola (1990); Sonata for Solo Cello (1992); *Mosaiques* for Saxophone or Clarinet and Ensemble (1992). **PIANO:** *Sonata Ostinato* (1961); *Contrastes I* (1962) and *II* (1963); *Dialogues II* (1967). **VOCAL:** *Ebauche* for Voice, Clarinet, Violin, Viola, Cello, and Piano (1966–68); *Le Lit de Procruste* (The Bed of Procustes) for Baritone, Clarinet, Viola, and Piano (1968–70); *Orfeu* (Orpheus) for Baritone and Chamber Ensemble (1985); *Chansons sans réponse* for Baritone, Narrator, Clarinet, Piano, and Strings (1986–88); *Hommage à Paul Célan* for Mezzo-soprano, Bass, and Chamber Ensemble (1989); *Dedications* for Bass, Narrator, Small Chorus, and Ensemble (1991); cantatas.

Tardos, Béla, Hungarian composer; b. Budapest, June 21, 1910; d. there, Nov. 18, 1966. He studied with Kodály at the Budapest Academy of Music (1932–37). Upon graduation, he was active as a concert manager and music publisher. He composed much choral music for mass singing employing the modalities of Hungarian folk songs.

WORKS: COMIC OPERA: *Laura* (1958, rev. 1964; Debrecen, Dec. 11, 1966). **ORCH.:** Overture (1949); Suite (1950); Piano Concerto (1954); *Overture to a Fairy Tale* (1955); Sym., in memory of the victims of fascism (1960); *Fantasy* for Piano and Orch. (1961); Violin Concerto (1962); *Evocatio* (1964). **CHAMBER:** Wind Octet (1935); Piano Quartet (1941); 3 string quartets (1947, 1949, 1963); *Improvisations* for Clarinet and Piano (1960); *Prelude and Rondo* for Flute and Piano (1962); *Quartettino-Divertimento* for 4 Wind Instruments (1963); *Cassazione* for Harp Trio (1963); Violin Sonata (1965); piano pieces. **VOCAL:** 8 cantatas: *A város peremén* (At the Outskirts of the City; 1944; 2nd version, 1958), *Rolád susog a lomb* (The Leaves Whisper About You; 1949), *Májusi kantáta* (May Cantata; 1950), *A béke napja alatt* (Under the Sun of Peace; 1953), *Hajnali dal* (Morning Song; 1953), *Dózsa feje* (Dózsa's Head; 1958), *Szabadság született* (Liberty Has Been Born; 1960), and *Az új Isten* (The New Gold, 1966); choruses; songs.

BIBL.: P. Várnai, *T. B.* (Budapest, 1966).

Tariol-Baugé, Anne, French singer; b. Clermont-Ferrand, Aug. 28, 1872; d. Asnières, near Paris, Dec. 1, 1944. She made her operatic debut in Bordeaux; then went to Russia; returning to France, she sang in Toulouse and Nantes; then settled in Paris, where she appeared mainly in light opera. She sang the title role at the premiere of Messager's opera *Véronique* at the

Bouffes-Parisiens (Dec. 10, 1898); distinguished herself especially in Offenbach's operettas. She was married to the baritone Alphonse Baugé.

Tarp, Svend Erik, Danish composer; b. Thisted, Jutland, Aug. 6, 1908; d. Copenhagen, Oct. 19, 1994. He studied theory with Jeppesen and music history with Simonson at the Copenhagen Cons. (1929–31); then was on its faculty (1936–42); concurrently lectured at the Univ. of Copenhagen (1939–47) and the Royal Theater Opera School (1936–40); subsequently was an administrator with Edition Dania (1941–60).

WORKS: DRAMATIC: OPERAS: *Princessen i det Fjerne* (The Princess at a Distance, 1952; Copenhagen, May 18, 1953); *9,90,* burlesque television opera (Copenhagen, Aug. 12, 1962). **BALLETS:** *Skyggen* (The Shadow, after Hans Christian Andersen, 1941–44; Copenhagen, April 1, 1960); *Den detroniserede dyretoemmer* (The Dethroned Tamer; Copenhagen, Feb. 5, 1944). Also film scores. **ORCH.:** Sinfonietta for Chamber Orch. (1931); Violin Concertino (1931); Flute Concertino (1937); *Orania,* suite (1937); *Mosaique,* miniature suite (1937); *Comedy Overture No. 1* (1939) and *No. 2* (1950); Piano Concerto (1943); 10 syms.: No. 1, *Sinfonia devertente* (1945), No. 2 (1948), No. 3, *Sinfonia quasi una fantasia* (1958), No. 4 (1975), No. 5 (1975), No. 6 (1976), No. 7 (1977), No. 8 for Girl's Chorus and Orch. (1989), No. 9 (1991), and No. 10 (1992); *Pro defunctis,* overture (1945); *Partita* (1947); *The Battle of Jericho,* symphonic poem (1949); *Preludio patetico* (1952); *Divertimento* (1954); *Scandinavian Design* (1955); *Lyrical Suite* (1956); *Little Dance Suite* (1964); *Little Festival Overture* (1969). **CHAMBER:** *Serenade* for Flute, Clarinet, and String Trio (1930); *Serenade* for Flute and String Trio (1936); Duet for Flute and Viola (1941); String Quartet (1973). **PIANO:** Sonata (1950); other pieces. **VOCAL:** *Te Deum* for Chorus and Orch. (1938); *Christmas Cantata* for Narrator, Baritone, Chorus, Organ, and Orch. (1946); songs.

Tarr, Edward H(ankins), distinguished American trumpeter, teacher, and musicologist; b. Norwich, Conn., June 15, 1936. He studied the trumpet in Boston with Voisin (1953) and in Chicago with Herseth (1958–59); then studied musicology with Schrade in Basel (1959–64). He subsequently was active both as a trumpet virtuoso and a musicologist; in 1967 he organized the Edward H. Tarr Brass Ensemble, with which he performed Renaissance and Baroque music on original instruments and on modern replicas. From 1968 to 1970 he taught at the Rheinische Musikschule in Cologne; in 1972 he was appointed to the faculty of the Schola Cantorum Basiliensis in Basel as a teacher of cornett and natural trumpet; also taught trumpet at the Basel Cons. (from 1974) and served as conservator of the Trumpet Museum in Bad Sackingen (from 1985). He contributed numerous articles on trumpet playing to various publications, and publ. the book *Die Trompete* (Bern, 1977; 2nd ed., 1978; Eng. tr., 1988). He also ed. a number of trumpet works, including a complete edition of the trumpet music of Torelli.

Taruskin, Richard, influential American musicologist and music critic; b. N.Y., April 2, 1945. He was educated at Columbia Univ., where he took his Ph.D. in historical musicology (1975); also held a Fulbright-Hayes traveling fellowship, which enabled him to conduct research in Moscow (1971–72). In 1975 he became an assistant prof. at Columbia Univ.; then was assoc. prof. there (1981–87). In 1985 he was a visting prof. at the Univ. of Pa. and in 1987 he was the Hanes-Willis visiting prof. at the Univ. of N.C. at Chapel Hill. In 1986 he was made an assoc. prof. at the Univ. of Calif. at Berkeley, subsequently becoming a prof. there in 1989. He held a Guggenheim fellowship in 1986. In 1987 he was awarded the Dent Medal of England. In 1989 he received the ASCAP-Deems Taylor Award. He contributed many valuable articles on Russian music and composers to *The New Grove Dictionary of Opera* (1992); also contributed articles and/or reviews to the Journal of *Musicology,* the *Journal of the American Musicological Society, Notes, 19th Century Music,* the *N.Y. Times,* the *New Republic,* and other publications. In addition to his ed. and commentary of Busnoys's *The Latin-Texted Works* (2 vols., N.Y., 1990), he publ. the books *Opera and Drama in Russia* (Ann Arbor, 1981; new ed., 1994), *Musorgsky: Eight Essays and an Epilogue* (Princeton, N.J., 1993), *Stravinsky and the Russian Traditions: A Biography of the Works Through Mavra* (2 vols, Berkeley and Los Angeles, 1995), and *Text and Act: Essays on Music and Performance* (N.Y., 1995).

Tassinari, Pia, Italian soprano and mezzo-soprano; b. Modigliana, Sept. 15, 1903; d. Faenza, May 15, 1995. She received her musical training in Bologna and Milan. She made her operatic debut as Mimi at Castel Monferrato in 1929; then sang at La Scala in Milan (1931–37; 1945–46) and at the Rome Opera (1933–44; 1951–52). She made her American debut at the Metropolitan Opera in N.Y. on Dec. 26, 1947, as Tosca. Although she began her career as a soprano, in later years she preferred to sing mezzo-soprano parts. Her repertoire included both soprano and mezzo-soprano roles, e.g., Mimi, Tosca, Manon, and Marguerite, and also Amneris and Carmen. She was married to **Ferruccio Tagliavini**.

Tate, Jeffrey, talented English conductor; b. Salisbury, April 28, 1943. Although a victim of spina bifida, he pursued studies at the Univ. of Cambridge and at St. Thomas's Medical School; then attended the London Opera Centre (1970–71). He was a member of the music staff at the Royal Opera, Covent Garden, London (1971–77); also served as an assistant conductor at the Bayreuth Festivals (1976–80). In 1978 he made his formal conducting debut with Carmen at the Göteborg Opera; on Dec. 26, 1980 he made his first appearance at the Metropolitan Opera in N.Y. conducting Berg's *Lulu*; his debut at Covent Garden followed with *La clemenza di Tito* on June 8, 1982. He appeared as a guest conductor at the Cologne Opera (1981), the Geneva Opera (1983), the Paris Opéra (1983), the Hamburg State Opera (1984), the San Francisco Opera (1984), the Salzburg Festival (1985), and the Vienna State Opera (1986). In 1983 he made his first appearance with the English Chamber Orch., being named its principal conductor in 1985; led it on tours abroad, including one to the U.S. in 1988. In 1986 he also became principal conductor at Covent Garden. In 1990 he was made a Commander of the Order of the British Empire. He was chief conductor of the Rotterdam Phil. from 1991 to 1994. His extensive operatic and concert repertoire encompasses works from the Classical to the contemporary era.

Tate, Phyllis (Margaret Duncan), English composer; b. Gerrards Cross, Buckinghamshire, April 6, 1911; d. London, May 27, 1987. She was a student of Harry Farjeon at the Royal Academy of Music in London (1928–32), and then devoted herself fully to composition. In 1935 she married **Alan Frank.** She was a composer of fine craftsmanship, excelling in works for voices and small ensembles.

WORKS: DRAMATIC: *The Lodger,* opera (1959–60; London, July 14, 1960); *Dark Pilgrimage,* television opera (1963); *Scarecrow,* operetta (1982). **ORCH.:** Cello Concerto (1933); *Valse lointaine* for Small Orch. (1941); *Prelude, Interlude, and Postlude* for Chamber Orch. (1942); Saxophone Concerto (1944); *Occasional Overture* (1955); *Illustrations* for Brass Band (1969); *Panorama* for Strings (1977). **CHAMBER:** Sonata for Clarinet and Cello (1947; Salzburg, June 23, 1951); String Quartet (1952; rev. 1982); *Air and Variations* for Violin, Clarinet, and Piano (1958); *Variegations* for Viola (1970); *The Rainbow and the Cuckoo* for Oboe, Violin, Viola, and Cello (1974); *Sonatina pastorale* for Harmonica and Harpsichord (1974); *Seasonal Sequence* for Viola and Piano (1977); *3 Pieces* for Clarinet (1979); *Prelude, Aria, Interlude, Finale* for Clarinet and Piano (1981). **PIANO:** *Explorations around a Troubadour Song* (1973); *Lyric Suite* for 2 Pianos (1973). **VOCAL:** *Nocturne* for Soloists, String Quartet, Double Bass, Bass Clarinet, and Celesta (1946); *Choral Scene from the Bacchae* for Chorus and Optional Organ (1953); *The Lady of Shalott* for Tenor and Chamber Ensemble (1956); *Witches and Spells* for Chorus (1959); *A Victorian Garland* for Soprano, Contralto, Horn, and Piano (1965); 7

Lincolnshire Folk Songs for Chorus and Ensemble (1966); *Gravestones* for Voice (1966); *A Secular Requiem* for Chorus, Organ, and Orch. (1967); *Apparitions* for Tenor, Harmonica, and Piano Quintet (1968); *Coastal Ballads* for Baritone and Instruments (1969); *To Words by Joseph Beaumont* for Women's Chorus (1970); *Serenade to Christmas* for Mezzo-soprano, Chorus, and Orch. (1972); *Creatures Great and Small* for Mezzo-soprano, Guitar, Double Bass, and Percussion (1973); *2 Ballads* for Mezzo-soprano and Guitar (1974); *Songs of Sundrie Kinds* for Tenor and Lute (1975); *St. Martha and the Dragon* for Narrator, Soloists, Chorus, and Orch. (1976); *Scenes from Kipling* for Baritone and Piano (1976); *All the World's a Stage* for Chorus and Orch. (1977); *Compassion* for Chorus and Orch. or Organ (1978); *Scenes from Tyneside* for Mezzo-soprano, Clarinet, and Piano (1978); *The Ballad of Reading Gaol* for Baritone, Organ, and Cello (1980).

Tattermuschová, Helena, Czech soprano; b. Prague, Jan. 28, 1933. She was a pupil of Vlasta Linhartová at the Prague Cons. In 1955 she made her operatic debut as Musetta in Ostrava. In 1959 she became a member of the Prague National Theater, where she won esteem for her portrayals of roles in operas by Mozart, Smetana, Janáček, Puccini, and Strauss. She also toured with the company abroad and made guest appearances in various European opera houses. She also pursued a concert career.

Taub, Robert (David), American pianist; b. New Brunswick, N.J., Dec. 25, 1955. He studied composition with Babbitt at Princeton Univ. (B.A., 1977) and piano with Lateiner at the Juilliard School in N.Y. (M.M., 1978; D.M.A., 1981). On Oct. 29, 1981, he made his N.Y. recital debut at Alice Tully Hall. Thereafter he toured North and South America, Europe, and the Far East. In addition to the piano literature of the early, Classical, and Romantic eras, he has explored the music of Scriabin, Persichetti, and Babbitt with success.

Taube, Michael, Polish-born Israeli conductor, teacher, and composer; b. Łódź, March 13, 1890; d. Tel Aviv, Feb. 23, 1972. He studied at the Leipzig Cons. and with Neitzel (piano), Strässer (composition), and Abendroth (conducting) in Cologne. In 1918 he founded the Bad Godesberg Concert Soc. In 1924 he became a conductor at the Berlin Städtische Oper, and also was founder-conductor of the his own chamber orch. and choir (from 1926). In 1935 he emigrated to Palestine. After appearing as a conductor with the Palestine Sym. Orch., he founded the Ramat Gan Chamber Orch., which he took on tours abroad. He also appeared as a guest conductor in Europe and was active as a teacher of voice and conducting. Taube composed orch. pieces and chamber music.

Tauber, Richard, eminent Austrian-born English tenor; b. Linz, May 16, 1891; d. London, Jan. 8, 1948. He was the illegitimate son of the actor Richard Anton Tauber; his mother was a soubrette singer. He was christened Richard Denemy after his mother's maiden name, but he sometimes used the last name Seiffert, his mother's married name. He took courses at the Hoch Cons. in Frankfurt am Main and studied voice with Carl Beines in Freiburg im Breisgau. He made his operatic debut at Chemnitz as Tamino in *Die Zauberflöte* (March 2, 1913) with such success that he was engaged in the same year at the Dresden Court Opera; made his first appearance at the Berlin Royal Opera as Strauss's Bacchus in 1915, and later won particular success in Munich and Salzburg for his roles in Mozart's operas. About 1925 he turned to lighter roles, and won remarkable success in the operettas of Lehár. He made his U.S. debut on Oct. 28, 1931, in a N.Y. recital. In 1938 he settled in England, where he appeared as Tamino and Belmonte at London's Covent Garden. In 1940 he became a naturalized British subject. He wrote an operetta, *Old Chelsea*, taking the leading role at its premiere (London, Feb. 17, 1943). He made his last American appearance at Carnegie Hall in N.Y. on March 30, 1947.

BIBL.: H. Ludwigg, ed., *R. T.* (Berlin, 1928); D. Napier-Tauber (his 2nd wife), *R. T.* (Glasgow, 1949); W. Korb, *R. T.* (Vienna, 1966); C. Castle and D. Napier-Tauber, *This Was R. T.* (London, 1971).

Taubman, Howard, American music and drama critic; b. N. Y., July 4, 1907; d. Sarasota, Fla., Jan. 8, 1996. He studied at Cornell Univ. (A.B., 1929). He joined the staff of the *N.Y. Times* in 1929, where he was its music ed. (1935–55), music critic (1955–60), drama critic (1960–66), and critic-at-large (1966–72).

WRITINGS: *Opera: Front and Back* (N.Y., 1938); *Music as a Profession* (N.Y., 1939); *Music on My Beat* (N.Y., 1943); *The Maestro: The Life of Arturo Toscanini* (N.Y., 1951); *How to Build a Record Library* (N.Y., 1953; new ed., 1955); *How to Bring Up Your Child to Enjoy Music* (Garden City, N.Y., 1958); *The Making of the American Theater* (N.Y., 1965; rev. in *Musical Comedy*, XII, 1967); *The New York Times Guide to Listening Pleasure* (N.Y., 1968); *The Pleasure of their Company: A Reminiscence* (Portland, Oreg., 1994).

BIBL.: L. Weldy, *Music Criticism of Olin Downes and H. T. in "The New York Times," Sunday Edition, 1924–29 and 1955–60* (diss., Univ. of Southern Calif., 1965).

Taucher, Curt, German tenor; b. Nuremberg, Oct. 25, 1885; d. Munich, Aug. 7, 1954. He studied with Heinrich Hermann in Munich. He made his operatic debut as Faust in Augsburg in 1908; then sang in Chemnitz (1911–14) and Hannover (1915–20). In 1920 he joined the Dresden State Opera, remaining there until 1934; during his tenure there, he created the role of Menelaus in Strauss's opera *Die Äegyptische Helena*. On Nov. 23, 1922, he sang the role of Siegmund in *Die Walküre* at his Metropolitan Opera debut in N.Y.; continued on its roster until 1927. He made guest appearances at Covent Garden in London (1932), at the Berlin State Opera, and at the Bavarian State Opera in Munich. He was noted for his roles in Wagner's operas.

Tauriello, Antonio, Argentine composer and conductor; b. Buenos Aires, March 20, 1931. He studied piano with Paul Spivak and Walter Gieseking, and composition with Alberto Ginastera. While still a youth, he was engaged to conduct opera and ballet at the Teatro Colón in Buenos Aires. He often appeared in the U.S. as an opera rehearsal coach, working at the Lyric Opera in Chicago, the Opera Soc. in Washington, D.C., and the N.Y. City Opera in the 1960s. In the 1970s he led Verdi opera festivals in San Diego. His early works, several of which were suppressed, were in a neo-Classical mold. His works composed after 1962 embrace the foundations of the international avant-garde.

WORKS: OPERA: *Les Guerres Picrocholines* (1969–70). **ORCH.:** *Obertura Sinfonica* (1951); *Serenade* (1957); *Música I* for Trumpet and Strings (1958), *II* for Clarinet and Instruments (1961), and *III* for Piano and Orch. (1966); *Ricercari 1 à 6* (1963); 2 serenatas (1964, 1966); *Transparencias* for 6 Instrumental Groups (1964; Washington, D.C., May 12, 1965); *Canti* for Violin and Orch. (1967); *Ilinx* for Clarinet and Orch. (1968); Piano Concerto (Washington, D.C., June 29, 1968); *Mansión de Tlaloc* (1969). **CHAMBER:** 4 piano sonatinas (1954); *Plany* for Organ (1968); *Suavissimo* for 2 Pianos (1969); *Al Aire Libre* for Trombone and Percussion (1969); *Signos de los Tiempos* for Quintet or Sextet (1969); *Aria* for Flute and Instruments (1970).

Tausinger, Jan, Romanian-born Czech conductor, teacher, and composer; b. Piatra Neamt, Nov. 1, 1921; d. Prague, July 29, 1980. He studied composition with Cuclin, Jora, and Mendelsohn at the Bucharest Cons., graduating in 1947; then went to Prague, where he had lessons in conducting with Ančerl; concurrently took courses in advanced harmony with Alois Hába and Bořkovec at the Prague Academy of Music (1948–52). He was active as a conductor of radio orchs. in Bucharest, Ostrava, and Plzeň; also taught at the Ostrava Cons., where he was director (1952–58); after working for the Czech Radio in Prague (1969–70), he served as director of the Prague Cons. His music was greatly diversified in style, idiom, and technique, ranging from neo-Classical modalities to integral dodecaphony; he made use of optical representational notation when justified by the structure of a particular piece.

WORKS: DRAMATIC: *Dlouhá noc* (The Long Night), ballet (1966); *Ugly Nature*, opera, after Dostoyevsky (1971). **ORCH.:** *Suite in the Old Style* (1946–47); Sym. No. 1, *Liberation* (1952); Violin Concerto (1962–63); *Confrontazione I* and *II* (1964); *Concertino meditazione* for Viola and Chamber Ensemble (1965); *Praeludium, Sarabande and Postludium* for Winds, Harp, Piano, and Percussion (1967); *Musica evolutiva* for Chamber Orch. (1967; Zagreb, Nov. 24, 1971); *Improvisations*, in honor of Bach, for Piano and Orch. (1970); *Sinfonia slovacca* (1979). **CHAMBER:** Violin Sonata (1954); *Partita* for Viola and Piano (1957–58); 2 string trios (1960, 1965); 4 string quartets (1961; 1966; 1970; *Structures*, 1972); *Colloquium* for 4 Wind Instruments (1964); Trio for Violin, Viola, and Guitar (1965); *Le avventure* for Flute and Harp (1965); *Canto di speranza* for Piano Quartet (1965); *Happening* for Piano Trio, based on proclamation of J. Shweik (1966); *De rebus musicalibus* for Flute, Bass Clarinet, Vibraphone, Piano, and Percussion (1967); *Sonatina emancipata* for Trumpet and Piano (1967); Brass Quintet (1968); *Hommage à Ladislav Černý* for Viola and Piano (1971); *"On revient toujours . . . ,"* suite for Violin and Piano (1974); *"Comme il faut,"* sonatina for Oboe and Piano (1974); *Hukvaldy Nonet* (1974); *"Au dernier amour . . . ,"* suite-sonata for Cello and Piano (1974–75); *Non-isosceles* for Flute, Cello, and Piano (1975); Clarinet Sonata (1975); *4 Evocations* for Flute, Viola, Cello, and Piano (1976); *Sketches*, 2nd nonet (1976); *Reminiscences*, 3rd nonet (1976); Sextet for Wind Quintet and Piano (1976); *7 Microchromophonies* for Clarinet, Viola, and Piano (1977); *4 Nuances* for Flute, Harp, Violin, Viola, and Cello (1978). **PIANO:** Sonata (1948–50); *10 Dodecaphonic Studies* (1972). **VOCAL:** *A Prayer* for Soprano and Chamber Orch. (1965); *Čmáranice po nebi* (Scrawling in the Sky) for Soprano, Flute, Bass Clarinet, Piano, and Percussion, after Khlebnikov, an early Russian futurist (1967); *Noc* (The Night), musical collage for Soprano, Chorus, Orch., and Guitar, after Pushkin (1967); *Správná věc* (The Right Thing), symphonic picture for Tenor, Baritone, Chorus, and Orch., after Mayakovsky (1967); *Duetti compatibili: Zerot Point* for Soprano and Viola (1971) and *Starting Point* for Soprano and 2 Violins (1979–80); *Ave Maria* for Narrator, Soprano, and Orch. (Prague, Oct. 17, 1972); *Sinfonia bohemica* for Bass, Men's Chorus, Trumpet, Harpsichord, and Orch. (1973–75); choruses.

Tavares, Hekel, Brazilian composer; b. Rio de Janeiro, Sept. 16, 1896; d. there, Aug. 8, 1969. He was the son of a wealthy plantation owner and, working in the fields, acquired intimate knowledge of native folk songs. Without benefit of formal education, he wrote instrumental and vocal music in large forms; his works include a Piano Concerto, based on urban and rural dance forms; another significant work on Brazilian themes is a Violin Concerto. The bulk of his compositions consists of popular songs.

Tavener, John (Kenneth), remarkable English composer; b. London, Jan. 28, 1944. He was a student of Berkeley at the Royal Academy of Music in London (1961–65) and of Lumsdaine (1965–67). In 1960 he became organist at St. John's, Kensington. From 1969 he served as a prof. of music at Trinity College of Music in London. Tavener's use of total serialism and electronics has been effectively demonstrated in many of his works. After his conversion to the Greek Orthodox faith in 1976, the spiritual and even mystical elements in his output grew apace as he created an important body of both sacred and secular works marked by expert craftsmanship.

WORKS: DRAMATIC: *The Cappemakers*, music drama (Alfriston, June 14, 1964; based on the choral piece); *Thérèse*, opera (1973–76; London, Oct. 1, 1979); *A Gentle Spirit*, chamber opera (1976–77; Bath, June 6, 1977); *Eis Thanaton* (1986; Cheltenham, July 5, 1987); *Mary of Egypt*, chamber opera (1990–91). **ORCH.:** Piano Concerto (1962–63; London, Dec. 6, 1963); Chamber Concerto (1965; London, Oct. 22, 1966; rev. version, London, June 12, 1968); *Variations on 3 Blind Mice* (1972; BBC-TV, Feb. 1, 1973); *Palintropes* for Piano and Orch. (1978–79; Birmingham, March 1, 1979); *Towards the Son: Ritual Procession* (Cheltenham, July 12, 1982); *The Protecting Veil* for Cello and Strings (1987); *The Repentant Thief* for Clarinet, Percussion, Timpani, and Strings (1990; London, Sept. 19, 1991); *Eternal Memory* for Cello and Ensemble (1992); *Theophany* (1994). **CHAMBER:** *Grandma's Footsteps* for Oboe, Bassoon, Horn, 5 Music Boxes, and Double String Quartet (1967–68; London, March 14, 1968); *In memoriam Igor Stravinsky* for 2 Alto Flutes, Organ, and Handbells (1971); *Greek Interlude* for Flute and Piano (Little Missenden, Oct. 10, 1979); *Trisagion* for Brass Quintet (1981; Huddersfield, Nov. 25, 1985); *Little Missenden Calm* for Oboe, Clarinet, Bassoon, and Horn (Little Missenden, Oct. 13, 1984); *Chant* for Guitar (London, May 17, 1984); *The Hidden Treasure* for String Quartet (1989; Keele, Feb. 1991); *Threnos* for Cello (1990); *The Last Sleep of the Virgin* for String Quartet and Handbells (1991). **KEYBOARD: PIANO:** *Palin* (1977; London, Nov. 24, 1980); *My Grandfather's Waltz* for Piano Duet (1980); *Mandoodles* (1982); *In Memory of Cats* (1986; London, Jan. 31, 1988). **ORGAN:** *Mandelion* (1981; Dublin, June 27, 1982). **VOCAL:** *3 Holy Sonnets* for Baritone, 2 Horns, 2 Trombones, Strings, and Tape (1962); *3 Sections from T.S. Eliot's The 4 Quartets* for High Voice and Piano (1963–64; London, Nov. 11, 1965); *The Cappemakers* for 2 Narrators, 10 Soloists, Men's Chorus, and Orch. (1964; rev. as a music drama, 1965); *Cain and Abel* for Soloists and Orch. (1965; London, Oct. 22, 1966); *The Whale* for Mezzo-soprano, Baritone, Chorus, Children's Chorus, Speakers, 6 Actors, Organ, Orch., and Tape (1965–66; London, Jan. 24, 1968); *Introit for March 27, the Feast of St. John Damascene* for Soprano, Alto, Chorus, and Orch. (1967–68; London, March 27, 1968); *3 Surrealist Songs* for Mezzo-soprano, Tape, and Piano (1967–68; BBC, March 21, 1968); *In Alium* for Soprano, Organ, Piano, and Strings (London, Aug. 12, 1968); *Celtic Requiem* for Soprano, Chorus, Children's Chorus, and Ensemble (London, July 16, 1969); *Coplas* for Soloists, Chorus, and Tape (Cheltenham, July 9, 1970); *Nomine Jesu* for Mezzo-soprano, Chorus, Ensemble, and 5 Speaking Voices (Dartington, Aug. 14, 1970); *Responsorium in memory of Annon Lee Silver* for 2 Sopranos, Chorus, and 2 Optional Flutes (Birmingham, Sept. 20, 1971); *Ma fin est mon commencement* for Tenor Chorus and Instruments (London, April 23, 1972); *Canciones españoles* for 2 Sopranos or Countertenors, 2 Flutes, Organ, and Harpsichord (London, June 8, 1972); *Little Requiem for Father Malachy Lynch* for Chorus, 2 Flutes, Trumpet, Organ, and Strings (Winchester, July 29, 1972); *Ultimos ritos* for Soprano, Alto, Tenor, Bass, 5 Choruses, and Orch. (1972; Haarlem, June 22, 1974); *Requiem for Father Malachy* for 2 Countertenors, Tenor, 2 Baritones, Bass, and Orch. (London, June 10, 1973); *Canticle of the Mother of God* for Soprano and Chorus (1976; Rye, April 22, 1977); *Lamentation, Last Prayer and Exaltation* for Soprano and Handbells or Piano (1977; Rye, April 28, 1978); *Kyklike Kinēsis* for Soprano, Cello, Chorus, and Orch. (1977; London, March 8, 1978); *6 Russian Folksongs* for Soprano and 8 Instruments (1977; London, Jan. 15, 1978); *The Liturgy of St. John Chrysostom* for Chorus (London, May 6, 1978); *The Immurement of Antigone* for Soprano and Orch. (1978; London, March 30, 1979); *Akhmatova: Requiem* for Soprano, Baritone, and Orch. (1979–80; Edinburgh, Aug. 20, 1980); *6 Abbasid Songs* for Tenor, 3 Flutes, and Percussion (1979–80; Snape, June 18, 1980); *Sappho: Lyrical Fragments* for 2 Sopranos and Strings (1980; London, April 25, 1981); *Risen!* for Chorus and Orch. (Bedford, Oct. 19, 1981); *The Great Canon of St. Andrew of Crete* for Chorus (1981); *Prayer for the World* for 16 Solo Voices (London, Oct. 11, 1981); *Funeral Ikos* for Chorus (1981); *Doxa* for Chorus (London, Sept. 12, 1982); *Lord's Prayer* for Chorus (London, Sept. 12, 1982); *The Lamb* for Chorus (Winchester, Dec. 22, 1982); *He Hath Entered the Heaven* for Trebles and Optional Handbells (1982; Oxford, Jan. 16, 1983); *To a Child Dancing in the Wind* for Soprano, Flute, Harp, and Viola (Little Missenden, Oct. 16, 1983); *Mini Song Cycle for Gina* for Soprano and Piano (1984; London, April 3, 1986); *Ikon of Light* for Chorus and String Trio

(Cheltenham, July 8, 1984); *Orthodox Vigil Service* for Chorus and Handbells (1984; Oxford, May 17, 1985); *A Nativity* for Women's Chorus (1984; London, Dec. 1987); *16 Haiku of Seferis* for Soprano, Tenor, Percussion, Bells, and Strings (St. David's, Wales, May 16, 1984); *Angels* for Chorus and Organ (Basingstoke, Nov. 3, 1985); *Love Bade Me Welcome* for Chorus (Winchester, June 28, 1985); *2 Hymns of the Mother of God* for Chorus (Winchester, Dec. 14, 1985); *Ikon of St. Cuthbert of Lindisfarne* for Chorus (1986; Durham, March 20, 1987); *Magnificat and Nunc Dimittis (Collegium Regale)* for Chorus (1986; Cambridge, April 24, 1987); *Meditation on the Light* for Countertenor, Guitar, and Handbells (1986); *Panikhida* for Chorus (London, June 21, 1986); *Akathist of Thanksgiving* for Soloists, Chorus, Bells, Percussion, and Strings (1986–87; London, Nov. 21, 1988); *Prayer (for Szymanowski)* for Bass and Piano (1987); *Wedding Prayer* for Chorus (London, April 1987); *Many Years* for Chorus (Frinton-on-Sea, Aug. 22, 1987); *Acclamation* for Chorus (Canterbury, Dec. 8, 1987); *God is With Us* for Chorus and Organ (Winchester, Dec. 22, 1987); *Hymn to the Holy Spirit* for Chorus (1987; London, June 30, 1988); *The Tyger* for Chorus (1987); *Apolytikion for St. Nicholas* for Chorus (1988); *The Call* for Chorus (Northampton, Sept. 23, 1988); *Ikon of St. Seraphim* for Baritone, 4 Basses, Chorus, Violin, and Orch. (St. Endellion, Aug. 7, 1988); *Let Not the Prince Be Silent* for 2 Antiphonal Choruses (1988; Sherborne, May 1989); *The Uncreated Eros* for Treble and Chorus (1988); *Lament of the Mother of God* for Soprano and Chorus (1988; Norwich, June 28, 1989); *Today the Virgin* for Chorus (London, Dec. 27, 1989); *Eonia* for Chorus (1989; Cork, May 6, 1990); *Psalm 121* for Chorus (1989; London, July 8, 1990); *Resurrection* for Soloists, Actors, Chorus, Men's Chorus, and Orch. (1989; Glasgow, April 17, 1990); *Thunder Entered Her: A Divine Allegory* for Chorus, Organ, Men's Chorus, and Handbells (1990; St. Albans, June 15, 1991); *Ikon the Trinity* for Chorus (1990); *Do Not Move* for Chorus (1990); *A Christmas Round* for Chorus (1990); *We Shall See Him As He Is* for Soprano, Tenor, Chorus, Organ, 2 Trumpets, Timpani, and Strings (1991–92); *The Child Lived* for Soprano and Ensemble (1992); *Wedding Greeting* for Tenor and Chorus (1992); *Hymns of Paradise* for Bass, Chorus, and Strings (1992–93); *The Apocalypse* for Soprano, Mezzo-soprano, Tenor, Countertenor, Bass, Chorus, Children's Chorus, and Orch. (1993–94; London, Aug. 14, 1994).

Tavrizian, Mikhail (Arsenievich), Armenian conductor; b. Baku, May 27, 1907; d. Yerevan, Oct. 17, 1957. He studied viola (diploma, 1932) and conducting with Gauk (diploma, 1934) at the Leningrad Cons. After playing viola in the Maly Opera orch. in Leningrad (1928–35), he pursued a conducting career. From 1938 he was principal conductor of the Yerevan Opera and Ballet Theater, where he conducted the premieres of many Armenian works. He also was active as a sym. conductor. In 1956 he was made a People's Artist of the U.S.S.R.

Tawaststjerna, Erik (Werner), eminent Finnish musicologist; b. Mikkeli, Oct. 10, 1916; d. Helsinki, Jan. 22, 1993. He studied piano with Hannikainen and Bernhard at the Helsinki Cons. (1934–44), with Leygraf in Stockholm, with Neuhaus in Moscow (1946), and with Cortot and Gentil in Paris (1947); later pursued musicological studies at the Univ. of Helsinki (Mag.Phil., 1958; Ph.D., 1960). After a brief career as a concert pianist, he devoted himself to musicology; was a prof. at the Univ. of Helsinki (1960–83).

WRITINGS (all publ. in Helsinki unless otherwise given): *Sibeliuksen pianosävellykset ja muita esseitä* (Sibelius's Piano Works; 1955; Eng. tr., 1957); *Sergei Prokofjevin ooppera Sota ja rauha* (Sergei Prokofiev's War and Peace; 1960); *Jean Sibelius* (5 vols., 1965–88; Eng. tr. by R. Layton, 1976–); *Esseitä ja arvosteluja* (Essays and Criticism; 1976); *Voces intimae: Minnesbilder från barndomen* (1990); *Scenes historiques: Kirjoituksia vuosilta 1945–58* (Helsingissä, 1992); *Jean Sibelius: Aren 1865–1893* (1992).

BIBL.: E. Salmenhaara, ed., *Juhlakirja E. T.lle* (Helsinki, 1976).

Taylor, Cecil (Percival), black American jazz pianist and composer; b. N.Y., March 15, 1933. He began piano lessons at age 5; was improvising and composing by the age of 8; later studied percussion. He studied harmony and composition at the N.Y. College of Music; subsequently studied composition at the New England Cons. of Music in Boston; also immersed himself in the Boston jazz scene. He then worked with his own combos in N.Y.; first appeared at the Newport Jazz Festival (1957); gained a name for himself as a performer in the off-Broadway production of Jack Gelber's The Connection (1959). He made his first tour of Europe in 1962, and then played in many jazz centers on both sides of the Atlantic; performed at N.Y.'s Carnegie Hall in 1977. He made a number of remarkable recordings, including *Into the Hot* (1961), *Unit Structures* (1966), *Silent Tongues* (1975), *The Cecil Taylor Unit* (1978), and *3 Phasis* (1978). His digitally agile piano style and penchant for extended improvisation made him an important figure in avant-garde jazz circles in his time.

Taylor, Clifford, American composer and teacher; b. Avalon, Pa., Oct. 20, 1923; d. Abington, Pa., Sept. 19, 1987. He studied composition with Lopatnikoff at the Carnegie-Mellon Univ. in Pittsburgh, and with Fine, Hindemith, Piston, and Thompson at Harvard Univ. (M.A., 1950). He taught at Chatham College in Pittsburgh (1950–63); in 1963 he joined the faculty of Temple Univ. in Philadelphia.

WORKS: OPERA: *The Freak Show* (1975). **ORCH.:** *Theme and Variations* (1951); *Concerto Grosso* for Strings (1957); 3 syms.: No. 1 (1958), No. 2 (1965; Philadelphia, Dec. 16, 1970), and No. 3 (1978); Concerto for Organ and Chamber Orch. (1963); *Sinfonia Seria* for Concert Band, Flute, and Baritone Horn (1965); Piano Concerto (1974). **CHAMBER:** Violin Sonata (1952); String Quartet for Amateurs (1959); Trio for Clarinet, Cello, and Piano (1959–60); 2 string quartets (1960, 1978); *Concert Duo* for Violin and Cello (1961); Duo for Saxophone and Trombone (1965); *Movement* for 3 for Violin, Cello, and Piano (1967); *Serenade* for Percussion Ensemble (1967); *5 Poems* for Oboe and 5 Brasses (1971). **PIANO:** 2 sonatas (1952, 1978); *Fantasia and Fugue* (1959); *30 Ideas* (1972); *36 More Ideas* (1976). **VOCAL:** Numerous a cappella choruses, including choral settings of Western Pennsylvania folk songs (1958) and *A Pageant of Characters from William Shakespeare* for Chorus and Soloists (1964); songs.

Taylor, (Joseph) Deems, greatly popular American composer and writer on music; b. N. Y., Dec. 22, 1885; d. there, July 3, 1966. He graduated from N.Y. Univ. (B.A., 1906); studied harmony and counterpoint with Oscar Coon (1908–11). After doing editorial work for various publishers and serving as war correspondent for the *N.Y. Tribune* in France (1916–17), he was music critic for the *N.Y. World* (1921–25), ed. of *Musical America* (1927–29), and music critic for the *N.Y. American* (1931–32). He was an opera commentator for NBC (from 1931); was intermission commentator for the N.Y. Phil. national broadcasts (1936–43); also served as director (1933–66) and president (1942–48) of ASCAP. In 1924 he was elected a member of the National Inst. of Arts and Letters and in 1935 of the American Academy of Arts and Letters. In 1967 the ASCAP-Deems Taylor Award was created in his memory for honoring outstanding writings on music. Following the success of his orch. suite *Through the Looking-Glass,* after Lewis Carroll's tale (1923), he was commissioned by Walter Damrosch to compose a symphonic poem, *Jurgen* (1925). Meanwhile, 2 widely performed cantatas, *The Chambered Nautilus* and *The Highwayman,* had added to his growing reputation, which received a strong impetus when his opera *The King's Henchman,* to a libretto by Edna St. Vincent Millay and commissioned by the Metropolitan Opera, was premiered in that house on Feb. 17, 1927. Receiving 14 performances in 3 seasons, it established a record for American opera at the Metropolitan Opera, but it was surpassed by Taylor's next opera, *Peter Ibbetson* (Feb. 7, 1931); this attained 16 performances in 4 seasons. These successes, however, proved ephemeral, and the operas were allowed to lapse into unmerited desuetude.

WORKS: DRAMATIC: OPERAS: *The King's Henchman* (1926; N.Y., Feb. 17, 1927); *Peter Ibbetson* (1929–30; N.Y., Feb. 7, 1931); *Ramuntcho* (Philadelphia, Feb. 10, 1942); *The Dragon* (N.Y., Feb. 6, 1958); also a comic opera, *Cap'n Kidd & Co.* (1908), a musical play, *The Echo* (1909), an operetta, *The Breath of Scandal* (1916), and incidental music. **ORCH.:** *The Siren Song*, symphonic poem (1912; N.Y., July 18, 1922); *Through the Looking-Glass* for Chamber Orch. (1917–19; N.Y., Feb. 18, 1919; for Full Orch., 1921–22; N.Y., March 10, 1923); *Jurgen*, symphonic poem (N.Y., Nov. 19, 1925; rev. 1926 and 1929); *Circus Day* for Jazz Orch. (1925; orchestrated by F. Grofé for Full Orch., 1933); *Marco Takes a Walk* (N.Y., Nov. 14, 1942); *A Christmas Overture* (N.Y., Dec. 23, 1943); *Elegy* (1944; Los Angeles, Jan. 4, 1945); *Restoration Suite* (Indianapolis, Nov. 18, 1950). **CHAMBER:** *The Portrait of a Lady*, rhapsody for 10 Instruments (1919); piano pieces. **VOCAL:** *The Chambered Nautilus*, cantata for Chorus and Orch. (1914); *The Highwayman*, cantata for Baritone, Mixed Voices, and Orch. (1914); song cycles; solo songs.

WRITINGS (all publ. in N.Y.): *Of Men and Music* (1937); *The Well Tempered Listener* (1940); *Walt Disney's Fantasia* (1940); ed., *A Treasury of Gilbert and Sullivan* (1941); *Music to My Ears* (1949); *Some Enchanted Evenings: The Story of Rodgers and Hammerstein* (1953).

BIBL.: J. Howard, *D. T.* (N.Y., 1927; 2nd ed., 1940).

Taylor, Janis (actually, **Janice Kathleen** née **Schuster**), American-born Canadian mezzo-soprano; b. Westfield, N.Y., March 10, 1946. She studied piano and clarinet before going to Montreal in 1967. In 1972 she became a naturalized Canadian citizen. Following vocal studies with Bernard Diamant, she studied with Lina and Antonio Narducci, Stevenson Barrett, Gérard Souzay, and Danielle Valin. In 1971 she made her recital debut in Montreal. Her orch. debut followed in 1973 as a soloist in *Messiah* with the Toronto Sym. She made her operatic debut as the Queen in Somer's *The Fool* at the Stratford (Ontario) Festival in 1975, and thereafter appeared with various Canadian and American opera houses. In 1979 she made her U.S. orch. debut as a soloist in *Messiah* with the National Sym. Orch. in Washington, D.C. Her European operatic stage debut came that same year when she appeared in Shostakovich's *Lady Macbeth of the District of Mtzensk* at the Spoleto Festival. In 1980 she made her first appearance as an orch. soloist in Europe in *Messiah* with the RAI Orch. in Milan. She sang Handel's Alessandro in a concert performance in N.Y.'s Carnegie Hall in 1985. In 1989 she made her London debut as a soloist in Verdi's *Requiem* with the London Sym. Orch. In 1990 she was the center of attention when she starred in Schoenberg's *Erwartung* at the Holland Festival in Amsterdam. Taylor has won particular distinction for her varied concert repertoire, being especially admired for her performances of the music of Mahler.

Tchaikowsky, André, Polish pianist and composer; b. Warsaw, Nov. 1, 1935; d. Oxford, June 26, 1982. Most of his family fell victim to the Nazis, but he and his grandmother were hidden by a Catholic family in Warsaw (1942–45). After the liberation, he studied piano at the Łódź State Music School (1945–47) and with Emma Tekla Altberg at the Warsaw Cons. (1947–48); then took an advanced piano course with Lazare Lévy at the Paris Cons. (premier prix, 1950); subsequently studied piano with Stanislaw Szpinalski and composition with Kazimierz Sikorski at the Warsaw Cons. (1950–55); made his debut as a pianist in 1955. He went to Paris to study composition with Boulanger (1957), and then to England to continue his studies with Musgrave and later with Hans Keller. Although he continued to make appearances as a pianist, he gave increasing attention to his work as a composer from 1960. An eccentric to the end, he bequeathed his skull to the Royal Shakespeare Co. for use in the graveside scene in *Hamlet* ("Alas, poor André, A fellow of infinite jest"); it made its debut in 1984.

WORKS: OPERA: *The Merchant of Venice* (1960–82). **ORCH.:** Violin Concerto (1950); Flute Concerto (1950); 2 piano concertos (1953, 1971); Clarinet Concerto (1953); Sym. (1958). **CHAMBER:** Sonata for Viola and Clarinet (1954); *Concerto classico* for Violin (1957); Clarinet Sonata (1959); Octet (1961); 2 string quartets (1967, 1975); *Trio notturno* (1978); piano pieces. **OTHER:** Vocal music.

Tchaikovsky, Boris (Alexandrovich), Russian composer; b. Moscow, Sept. 10, 1925; d. Feb. 1996. He studied at the Moscow Cons. with Shostakovich, Shebalin, and Miaskovsky (1941–49). His later works made use of expanded tonality.

WORKS: DRAMATIC: OPERA: *The Star* (1949; unfinished). Also much music for films, radio, and plays. **ORCH.:** *Procession* (1946); 3 syms.: No. 1 (1947; Moscow, Feb. 7, 1962), No. 2 (Moscow, Oct. 17, 1967), and No. 3, Sevastopol (1980; Moscow, Jan. 25, 1981); *Slavonic Rhapsody* (1951); *Sinfonietta* for Strings (1953); *Fantasia on Russian Folk Themes* (1954); *Capriccio on English Themes* (1954); Clarinet Concerto (1957); Overture (1957); Cello Concerto (1964); Chamber Sym. (Moscow, Oct. 27, 1967); Violin Concerto (1969; Moscow, April 25, 1970); Concerto for Piano, 2 Horns, Side Drum, Bass Drum, and Strings (Kaunas, Oct. 17, 1971); *Theme and 8 Variations* (1973; Dresden, Jan. 23, 1974); *6 Studies* for Strings and Organ (1976; Leningrad, Jan. 30, 1979). **CHAMBER:** Piano Trio (1953); 6 string quartets (1954, 1961, 1967, 1972, 1974, 1976); String Trio (1955); Cello Sonata (1957); Violin Sonata (1959); Suite for Cello (1960); Piano Quintet (1962); *Partita* for Cello and Chamber Ensemble (1966). **PIANO:** 2 sonatas (1944, 1952); Sonatina (1946); Sonata for 2 Pianos (1973). **VOCAL:** *Signs of the Zodiac*, cantata for Soprano, Harpsichord, and Strings (1974; Leningrad, Jan. 29, 1976); *The Last Spring*, song cycle for Mezzo-soprano, Flute, Clarinet, and Piano (1980); songs.

Tchakarov, Emil, Bulgarian conductor; b. Burgas, June 29, 1948; d. Paris, Aug. 4, 1991. He received his training at the Bulgarian State Cons. in Sofia, where he conducted its youth orch. (1965–72). From 1968 to 1970 he also was conductor of the Bulgarian TV Chamber Orch. After capturing 3rd prize in the Karajan Competition (1971), he pursued training in conducting with Ferrara (1972) and Jochum (1974). In 1974 he became conductor of the Plovdiv State Phil. On Sept. 27, 1979, he made his Metropolitan Opera debut in N.Y. conducting *Eugene Onegin*, and remained on its roster until 1983. In 1985–86 he was chief conductor of the Flanders Phil. in Antwerp. As a guest conductor, he appeared in many music centers around the globe.

Tcherepnin, Alexander (Nikolaievich), distinguished Russian-born American pianist, conductor, and composer, son of **Nikolai (Nikolaievich)** and father of **Serge (Alexandrovich)** and **Ivan (Alexandrovich) Tcherepnin**; b. St. Petersburg, Jan. 20, 1899; d. Paris, Sept. 29, 1977. He studied piano as a child with his mother; was encouraged by his father in his first steps in composition, but did not take formal lessons with him. He composed a short comic opera when he was 12, and a ballet when he was 13; then produced a number of piano works; composed 14 piano sonatas before he was 19. In 1917 he entered the Petrograd Cons., where he studied theory with Sokolov, and piano with Kobiliansky, but remained there only one school year; then joined his parents in a difficult journey to Tiflis during the Civil War; he took lessons in composition there with Thomas de Hartmann. In 1921 the family went to Paris, where he continued his studies, taking lessons in piano with Philipp and in composition with Vidal. In 1922 he played a concert of his own music in London; in 1923 he was commissioned by Anna Pavlova to write a ballet, *Ajanta's Frescoes*, which she produced in London with her troupe. Tcherepnin progressed rapidly in his career as a pianist and a composer; he played in Germany and Austria; made his first American tour in 1926. Between 1934 and 1937 he made two journeys to the Far East; gave concerts in China and Japan; numerous Chinese and Japanese composers studied with him; he organized a publishing enterprise in Tokyo for the publication of serious works by young Japanese and Chinese composers. He married a Chinese pianist, Lee Hsien-Ming. Despite his wide travels, he maintained his principal residence in Paris, and remained there during World War II. He resumed his concert career in 1947; toured the U.S. in 1948. In 1949 he and his wife joined the faculty of De Paul Univ. in Chicago, and taught there for 15 years. In the meantime, his music became well known; he appeared as a soloist in his piano concertos with orchs. in the U.S. and Europe. He became a naturalized American citizen in 1958. In 1967 he made his first visit to Russia after nearly a half century abroad. He was elected a member of the National Inst. of Arts and Letters in 1974. In his early works, he followed the traditions of Russian Romantic music; characteristically, his Piano Sonata No. 13, which he wrote as a youth, is entitled *Sonatine romantique.* But as he progressed in his career, he evolved a musical language all his own; he derived his melodic patterns from a symmetrically formed scale of 9 degrees, subdivided into 3 equal sections (e.g. C, D, E-flat, E, F-sharp, G, G-sharp, A-sharp, B, C); the harmonic idiom follows a similar intertonal formation; his consistent use of such thematic groupings anticipated the serial method of composition. Furthermore, he developed a type of rhythmic polyphony, based on thematic rhythmic units, which he termed "interpunctus." However, he did not limit himself to these melodic and rhythmic constructions; he also explored the latent resources of folk music, both oriental and European; he was particularly sensitive to the melorhythms of Russian national songs. A composer of remarkable inventive power, he understood the necessity of creating a communicative musical language, and was primarily concerned with enhancing the lyric and dramatic qualities of his music. At the same time, he showed great interest in new musical resources, including electronic sound.

WORKS: DRAMATIC: OPERAS: *Ol-Ol* (1925; Weimar, Jan. 31, 1928; rev. 1930); *Die Hochzeit der Sobeide* (1930; Vienna, March 17, 1933); *The Farmer and the Nymph* (Aspen, Colo., Aug. 13, 1952). **BALLETS:** *Ajanta's Frescoes* (London, Sept. 10, 1923); *Training* (Vienna, June 19, 1935); *Der fahrende Schüler mit dem Teufelsbannen* (1937; score lost during World War II; reconstructed, 1965); *Trepak* (Richmond, Va., Oct. 10, 1938); *La Légende de Razine* (1941); *Le Déjeuner sur l'herbe* (Paris, Oct. 14, 1945); *L'Homme à la peau de léopard* (Monte Carlo, May 5, 1946; in collaboration with A. Honegger and T. Harsányi); *La Colline des fantômes* (1946); *Jardin persan* (1946); *Nuit kurde* (Paris, 1946); *La Femme et son ombre* (Paris, June 14, 1948); *Aux temps des tartares* (Buenos Aires, 1949); *Le gouffre* (1953). **ORCH.:** 6 piano concertos: No. 1 (1919–20; Monte Carlo, 1923), No. 2 (1923; Paris, Jan. 26, 1924), No. 3 (1931–32; Paris, Feb. 5, 1933), No. 4 (1947; retitled *Fantasia*), No. 5 (Berlin, Oct. 13, 1963), and No. 6 (1965; Lucerne, Sept. 5, 1972); Overture (1921); *Rhapsodie georgienne* for Cello and Orch. (1922); *Concerto da camera* for Flute, Violin, and Chamber Orch. (1924); 4 syms.: No. 1 (Paris, Oct. 29, 1927), No. 2 (1947–51; Chicago, March 20, 1952), No. 3 (1952; Indianapolis, Jan. 15, 1955), and No. 4 (1957; Boston, Dec. 5, 1958); *Mystère* for Cello and Chamber Orch. (Monte Carlo, Dec. 8, 1926); *Magna mater* (1926–27; Munich, Oct. 30, 1930); Concertino for Violin, Cello, Piano, and Strings (1931); *Russian Dances* (Omaha, Feb. 15, 1934); *Suite georgienne* for Piano and Strings (1938; Paris, April 17, 1940); *Evocation* (1948); Harmonica Concerto (1953; Venice, Sept. 11, 1956); Suite (1953; Louisville, May 1, 1954); *Divertimento* (Chicago, Nov. 14, 1957); *Symphony-Prayer* (1959; Chicago, Aug. 19, 1960); *Serenade* for Strings (1964); *Russian Sketches* (1971); *Musica sacra* for Strings (Lourdes, April 28, 1973). **CHAMBER:** *Ode* for Cello and Piano (1919); 2 string quartets (1922, 1926); Violin Sonata (1922); 3 cello sonatas (1924, 1925, 1926); Piano Trio (1925); Piano Quintet (1927); *Elegy* for Violin and Piano (1927); *Le Violoncelle bien temperé,* 12 preludes for Cello with Piano, 2 with Drum (Berlin, March 23, 1927); *Mouvement perpetuel* for Violin and Piano (1935); Kettledrum Sonatina (1939); *Sonatine sportive* for Bassoon or Saxophone and Piano (1939); *Andante* for Tuba and Piano (1939): Trio for Flutes (1939); Quartet for Flutes (1939); *Marche* for 3 Trumpets (1939); Suite for Cello (1946); *Sonata da chiesa* for Viola da Gamba and Organ (1966); Quintet for 2 Trumpets, Horn, Trombone, and Tuba (1972); Woodwind Quintet (1976); Duo for 2 Flutes (1977). **KEYBOARD: PIANO:** *10 bagatelles* (1913–18); *Scherzo* (1917); *Sonatine romantique* (1918); 2 sonatas (1918, 1961); *Feuilles libres* (1920–24); *Toccata* (1921); *5 arabesques* (1921); *9 inventions* (1921); *2 novelettes* (1922); *4 préludes nostalgiques* (1922); *6 études de travail* (1923); *Message* (1926); *Entretiens* (1930); *Études de piano sur la gamme pentatonique* (1935); *Autour des montagnes russes* (1937); *Badinage* (1942); *Le Monde en vitrine* (1946); 12 Preludes (1952); 8 Pieces (1954). **HARPSICHORD:** Suite (1966). **VOCAL: CANTATAS:** *Vivre d'amour* (1942); *Pan Kéou* (Paris, Oct. 9, 1945); *Le Jeu de la Nativité* (Paris, Dec. 30, 1945); *Les Douze* for Narrator, Strings, Harp, Piano, and Percussion (Paris, Nov. 9, 1947); *Vom Spass und Ernst,* folksong cantata for Voice and Strings (1964); *The Story of Ivan the Fool,* with Narrator (London, Dec. 24, 1968); *Baptism Cantata* for Chorus and Orch. (1972). **OTHER VOCAL:** *Lost Flute,* 7 songs on poems translated from the Chinese, for Narrator and Piano (1954); several albums of songs to poems in Russian, French, and Chinese.

BIBL.: W. Reich, *A. Tscherepnine* (Bonn, 1959; 2nd ed., rev., 1970); N. Slonimsky, "Al. T., Septuagenarian," *Tempo* (Jan. 1969); C.-J. Chang, *A. T., His Influence on Modern Chinese Music* (diss., Columbia Univ. Teachers College, 1983); P. Ramey, "A. T.," *Ovation* (May 1984); E. Arias, *A. T.: A Bio-Bibliography* (Westport, Conn., 1988).

Tcherepnin, Ivan (Alexandrovich), French-born American composer of Russian descent, son of **Alexander (Nikolaievich)** and brother of **Serge (Alexandrovich) Tcherepnin**; b. Issy-les-Moulineaux, near Paris, Feb. 5, 1943. He studied composition with his father at home and at the Académie Internationale de Musique in Nice; also had piano lessons with his mother. He went to the U.S. and became a naturalized American citizen (1960); continued his studies with Thompson and Kirchner at Harvard Univ. (B.A., 1964; M.A., 1969); received the John Knowles Paine Travelling Fellowship to pursue training in electronic music with Stockhausen and Pousseur in Cologne and in conducting with Boulez (1965); likewise studied electronic techniques in Toronto (1966). He taught at the San Francisco Cons. and at Stanford Univ. (1969–72), where he served as co-director, with Chowning, of its new-music ensemble, Alea II; then was assoc. prof. and director of the electronic music studio at Harvard Univ. (from 1972). In 1989 he traveled to China, where he performed and gave lectures in Shanghai and Beijing. In 1996 he won the Grawemeyer Award at the Univ. of Louisville. From 1984 his work has been evenly divided between electronic and instrumental pieces; his Rhythmantics series uses digital sampling techniques and temporal displacement to explore areas of rhythmic pattern formation. His instrumental works, generally more referential, draw on musical resources ranging from gagaku and gamelan to Western tonal structures.

WORKS: ORCH.: *Le Va et le vient* (1978); Concerto for Oboe and Orch. or Wind Orch. (1980; rev. 1988); *New Consonance* for Strings (1983); *Solstice* for Chamber Orch. (1983); *Status* for Wind Orch. (1986); *Constitution* for Narrator and Wind Orch. (1987); *Concerto for 2 Continents* for Synthesizer and Wind Orch. (1989); *Carillona* for Wind Orch. (1993); *Dialogue Between the Moon and Venus as Overheard by an Earthling* for Wind Orch. (1994); Double Concerto for Violin, Cello, and Orch. (Cambridge, Mass., June 3, 1995). **CHAMBER:** *Suite progressive* for Flute, Cello, and Timpani (1959); *Deux entourages pour un thème russe* for Horn or Ondes Martenot, Piano, and Percussion (1961); *Suite Mozartienne* for Flute, Clarinet, and Bassoon (1962); *Cadenzas in Transition* for Clarinet, Flute, and Piano (1963); *Sombres lumières* for Flute, Guitar, and Cello (1965); *Wheelwinds* for 9 Wind Instruments (1966); *Explorations* for Flute, Clarinet, String Trio, Piano, and Optional Live Electronics (1985); *Trio Fantasia* for Violin, Cello, and Piano (1985); *Fanfare for Otto Hall* for 3 Trumpets and 4 Horns (1991); *7 Fanfares* for 3 Trumpets (1995). **PIANO:** *4 Pieces from Before* (1959–62); *Beginnings* (1963); *2 Reminiscences* (1968);

Silent Night Mix for 2 Pianos (1969); *3 Pieces* for 2 Pianos (1970–72); *12 Variations on Happy Birthday* (1970–80); *Fêtes* (1975); *Valse éternelle: "The 45 R.P.M."* (1977); *Summer Nights* (1980). **WITH ELECTRONICS:** *AC-DC (Alternating Currents)* for 8 Percussionists and Tape (1967); *Rings* for String Quartet and Ring Modulators (1969); *Light Music* for 4 Instrumental Groups, 4 Sound-activated Strobe Lights, Photocells, Electronics, and Tape (1970); *Les Adieux* for 3 Voices, 14 Instruments, Electronics, Tape, and Colored Lights (1971); *Globose Floccose* for Brass Quintet, String Quartet, Electronics, and Tape (1973); *Set, Hold, Clear, and Squelch* for Oboe, Frequency Follower, Electronics, and Tape (1976); *Santur Opera* for Santur, Electronics, Actors, and Projections (1977; rev. 1994 as *Santur Opera II, the Sequel*); *Flores musicales* for Oboe, Violin, Cello, Psalter, and Electronics (1979); *5 Songs* for Contralto, Flute, and Electronics (1979); *Cantilenas/Hybrids* for Violin and Electronics (1983); *New Rhythmantics* for String Quartet and Electronics (1985); *Explorations* for Flute, Clarinet, String Trio, Piano, and Optional Electronics (1985); *New Rhythmantics IV* for String Quartet, Trumpet, and Electronics (1987); *The Creative Act* for 4 Performers and Live Electronics (1990); also solo pieces for Tape. **VOCAL:** *And so it Came to Pass*, cantata for Soprano, Tenor, Chorus, and Orch. (1991).

Tcherepnin, Nikolai (Nikolaievich), noted Russian conductor, pedagogue, and composer, father of **Alexander (Nikolaievich) Tcherepnin**; b. St. Petersburg, May 15, 1873; d. Issy-les-Moulineaux, near Paris, June 26, 1945. He was a student of Rimsky-Korsakov at the St. Petersburg Cons. (1895–98); in 1905 he was appointed to its faculty; taught orchestration and conducting; Prokofiev was among his students. In 1908 he became a conductor at the Marinsky Theater and the Imperial Opera in St. Petersburg; was conductor of the initial season of the Ballets Russes in Paris in 1909. After the Russian Revolution in 1917, he served as director of the Tiflis Cons. (1918–21); then settled in Paris, where he was director of the Russian Cons. (1925–29; 1938–45). His music embodies the best elements of the Russian national school; it is melodious and harmonious; lyrical and gently dynamic; in some of his works, there is a coloristic quality suggesting French impressionistic influence.

WORKS: DRAMATIC: OPERAS: *Svat* (1930); *Vanka* (1932; Belgrade, 1935). **BALLETS:** *Le pavillon d'Armide* (St. Petersburg, Nov. 25, 1907); *Narcisse et Echo* (Monte Carlo, April 26, 1911); *Le Masque de la Mort Rouge* (Petrograd, Jan. 29, 1916); *Dionysus* (1922); *Russian Fairy Tale* (1923); *Romance of the Mummy* (1924). **ORCH.:** *Prelude* to Rostand's play *La Princesse lointaine* (1897); *Fantaisie dramatique* (1903); *Le Royaume enchanté*, symphonic tableau (1904); Piano Concerto (1907). **CHAMBER:** *Poème lyrique*; *Cadence fantastique; Un Air ancien* for Flute and Piano; *Pièce calme* for Oboe and Piano; *Pièce insouciante* for Clarinet and Piano; *Variations simples* for Bassoon and Piano; *Fanfare* for Trumpet and Piano; String Quartet; Quartet for Horns; *Divertissement* for Flute, Oboe, and Bassoon. **PIANO:** *14 esquisses sur les images d'un alphabet russe* (orch. version of 8, Boston, Nov. 27, 1931); *Primitifs; Pièces de bonne humeur; Pièces sentimentals.* **VOCAL:** Liturgical music of the Russian Orthodox rite, including masses a cappella; *Pilgrimage and Passions of the Virgin Mary* (Paris, Feb. 12, 1938); over 200 songs; realization and completion of Mussorgsky's opera *The Fair at Sorochinsk* (Monte Carlo, March 17, 1923).

Tcherepnin, Serge (Alexandrovich), French-born American composer and electronic musical instrument inventor of Russian descent, son of **Alexander (Nikolaievich)** and brother of **Ivan (Alexandrovich) Tcherepnin**; b. Issy-les-Moulineaux, near Paris, Feb. 2, 1941. He studied violin as a child; was taken to the U.S. in 1949 and became a naturalized American citizen in 1950; studied theory with his father and received instruction in harmony from Boulanger; took courses with Billy Jim Layton and Kirchner at Harvard Univ. (B.A., 1965), attended Princeton Univ. (1963–64), and completed his training with Eimert, Stockhausen, Nono, Earle Brown, and Boulez in Europe. He was director of the electronic music studio at N.Y. Univ. (1968–70), and was a teacher of composition at the Valencia (Calif.) School of Music (from 1970) and at Dartington Hall in England (summers, 1979–80). He invented the Serge, a modular synthesizer, which was manufactured by his own company (from 1974).

WORKS: *Inventions* for Piano (1960); String Trio (1961); *Kaddish* for Narrator, Flute, Oboe, Clarinet, Piano, 2 Percussion, and Violin (1962); *Figures-grounds* for 7 to 77 Instruments (1964); *2 Tapes: Giuseppe's Background Music I–II* for 4-track Tape (1966); *2 More Tapes: Addition and Subtraction* for 2-track Tape (1966); *Morning After Piece* for Saxophone and Piano (1966); *Quiet Day at Bach* for Instrument and Tape (1967); *Piece of Wood* for Performers, Actor, and Composer (1967); *Piece of Wood with Weeping Woman* for Musicians, Women, Stagehand, and Tape (1967); *Film* for Mixed Media (1967); *"Hat" for Joseph Beuys* for Actor and Tape (1968); *For Ilona Kabos* for Piano (1968); *Definitive Death Music* for Amplified Saxophone and Instrumental Ensemble (1968); *Paysages électroniques*, film score (1977); *Samba in Aviary*, film score (1978).

Tchesnokov, Pavel, Russian composer; b. near Voskresensk, Oct. 24, 1877; d. Moscow, March 14, 1944. He studied at the Moscow Cons. with Vasilenko, graduating in 1917; also took courses with Sergei Taneyev and Ippolitov-Ivanov. He devoted himself exclusively to choral composition, both secular and sacred; from 1920, was prof. of choral conducting at the Moscow Cons. He publ. a manual for choral singing (Moscow, 1940).

Tear, Robert, distinguished Welsh tenor and conductor; b. Barry, Glamorgan, March 8, 1939. He was a choral scholar at King's College, Cambridge, where he graduated in English (1957–61); received vocal instruction from Julian Kimbell. He became a lay vicar at St. Paul's Cathedral in London in 1960; also was active with the Ambrosian Singers. In 1963 he made his operatic debut as Quint in Britten's *The Turn of the Screw* with the English Opera Group in London, where he made regular appearances until 1971; also sang at London's Covent Garden, where he created the role of Dov in Tippett's *The Knot Garden* in 1970; was chosen to sing the role of the Painter in the first complete performance of Berg's *Lulu* in Paris in 1979. He made guest appearances with various opera houses at home and abroad; also won particular renown as a concert artist; after making his debut as a conductor in Minneapolis in 1985, he appeared as a guest conductor with many orchs. In 1986 he was appointed to the International Chair of Vocal Studies at the Royal Academy of Music in London. In 1984 he was made a Commander of the Order of the British Empire. His autobiography was publ. as *Tear Here* (London, 1990).

Tebaldi, Renata, celebrated Italian soprano; b. Pesaro, Feb. 1, 1922. Her mother, a nurse, took her to Langhirano after the breakup of her marriage to a philandering cellist. Renata was stricken with poliomyelitis when she was 3. After initial vocal training from Giuseppina Passani, she studied with Ettore Campogaliani at the Parma Cons. (1937–40) and with Carmen Melis at the Pesaro Cons. (1940–43). She made her operatic debut in Rovigo as Elena in Boito's *Mefistofele* in 1944. In 1946 Toscanini chose her as one of his artists for the reopening concert at La Scala in Milan, and she subsequently became one of its leading sopranos. She made her first appearance in England in 1950 with the visiting La Scala company at London's Covent Garden as Desdemona; also in 1950 she sang Aida with the San Francisco Opera. On Jan. 31, 1955, she made her Metropolitan Opera debut in N.Y. as Desdemona in Verdi's *Otello*; she continued to appear regularly there until 1973. She toured Russia in 1975 and 1976. Her repertoire was almost exclusively Italian; she excelled in both lyric and dramatic roles; was particularly successful as Violetta, Tosca, Mimi, and Madame Butterfly. She also sang the role of Eva in *Die Meistersinger von Nürnberg*. On Nov. 3, 1958, she was the subject of a cover story in *Time* magazine.

BIBL.: K. Harris, *R. T.: An Authorized Biography* (N.Y., 1974).

Tebaldini, Giovanni, Italian conductor, music scholar, and composer; b. Brescia, Sept. 7, 1864; d. San Benedetto del Tronto, May 11, 1952. He studied with Ponchielli, Panzini, and

Amelli at the Milan Cons. (1883–85) and with Haller and Haberl at the Regensburg School for Church Music (1888). He served as maestro of the Schola Cantorum at San Marco in Venice (1889–93), maestro di cappella at the Basilica of S. Antonio in Padua (1894–97), and director of the Parma Cons. (1897–1902). After teaching at the Cons. di San Pietro a Majella in Naples (1925–30), he went to Genoa, where he was appointed director of the Ateneo Musicale (1931). His specialty was Italian sacred music, but he gained sensational prominence when he publ. an article provocatively entitled "Telepatia musicale" (*Rivista Musicale Italiana*, March 1909), in which he cited thematic similarities between the opera *Cassandra* (1905) by the relatively obscure Italian composer Vittorio Gnecchi and *Elektra* by Richard Strauss, written considerably later, implying a "telepathic" plagiarism on the part of Strauss. However, the juxtaposition of musical examples from both operas proved specious and failed to support Tebaldini's contention.

WRITINGS: *La musica sacra in Italia* (Milan, 1894); *Gasparo Spontini* (Recanati, 1924); *Ildebrando Pizzetti* (Parma, 1931); also *Metodo teorico pratico per organo* (with Enrico Bossi; Milan, 1897).

BIBL.: M. Horwath, "T., Gnecchi and Strauss," *Current Musicology*, No. 16 (1970).

Teed, Roy (Norman), English pianist, organist, teacher, and composer; b. Herne Bay, Kent, May 18, 1928. He studied composition with Lennox Berkeley, piano with Virginia McLean, and harmony and counterpoint with Paul Steinitz at the Royal Academy of Music in London (1949–53); from 1966 to 1992 he was on its faculty; also taught at the Colchester Inst. Music School (1966–79).

WORKS: OPERA: *The Overcoat* (1988–93). **ORCH.:** Piano Concerto (1952); *Festival Suite* for Cello and String Orch. (1958); *Around the Town*, comedy march (1962); *Music for a Ballet*, suite (1975); *A Celebration Overture*, for Sir Lennox Berkeley's 80th birthday (1983); Concertino for Treble Recorder and Strings (1984); Overture (1989). **CHAMBER:** *Introduction and Scherzo* for Flute, Oboe, and Piano (1960); Quartet for Flute and Strings (1961); *Serenade* for 10 Winds (1982); Trio for Violin, Cello, and Piano (1985); *Sextet Variations* for Clarinet, Bassoon, Horn, Violin, Viola, and Cello (1987); *Elegy, Scherzo, and Trio* for Trumpet and Piano (1988); *Rondo with Variations* for Violin and Piano (1991); *Concert Piece* for Oboe and Piano (1994); Violin Sonata (1994); organ works. **VOCAL:** *5 Funny Songs* for Medium Voice and Clarinet or Piano or Orch. (1954); *So Blest a Day*, Christmas cantata (1960); *The Pied Piper* for Soloists, Chorus, and Orch. (1961); *The Jackdaw of Rheims*, narrative cantata (1964); *The Pardoner's Tale* for Baritone, Chorus, and Orch. (1966); 2 sets of *5 Epitaphs*, humorous song cycles (1969, 1978); *Music of the Seasons* for Baritone, Chorus, and Orch. (1980); *Music Fills the Air* for Chorus (1984); *A Trip to the Zoo*, 23 songs for Very Young Singers and Piano or Orch. (1987); *Psalm 89* for Chorus and Organ (1993); *6 Poems* for Medium Voice and Piano or Strings (1994); *5 Love Poems* for Tenor and Piano or Piano Quintet (1995); other choral pieces and songs; carols.

Teichmüller, Robert, German pianist and teacher; b. Braunschweig, May 4, 1863; d. Leipzig, May 6, 1939. He studied piano with his father and with Reinecke at the Leipzig Cons., where from 1897 until his death he taught piano; was made a prof. in 1908. With K. Hermann, he publ. *Internationale moderne Klaviermusik* (Leipzig, 1927).

BIBL.: A. Baresel, *R. T. als Mensch und Künstler* (Leipzig, 1922); idem, *R. T. und die Leipziger Klaviertradition* (Leipzig, 1934).

Te Kanawa, Dame Kiri, brilliant New Zealand soprano; b. Gisborne, March 6, 1944. Her father was an indigenous Maori who traced his ancestry to the legendary warrior Te Kanawa; her mother was Irish. She attended Catholic schools in Auckland, and was coached in singing by a nun. She was sent to Melbourne to compete in a radio show; won 1st prize in the Melbourne Sun contest. In 1966 she received a grant for study in London with Vera Rozsa. She made her operatic debut at the Camden Festival in 1969 in Rossini's *La Donna del Lago*; first appeared at London's Covent Garden in a minor role that same year, and then as the Countess in *Le nozze di Figaro* in 1971. She made her U.S. debut in the same role with the Santa Fe Opera in 1971; it became one of her most remarkable interpretations. She sang it again with the San Francisco Opera in 1972. A proverbial *coup de théâtre* in her career came on Feb. 9, 1974, when she was called upon to substitute at a few hours' notice for the ailing Teresa Stratas in the part of Desdemona in Verdi's *Otello* at the Metropolitan Opera in N.Y.; it was a triumphant achievement, winning for her unanimous praise. She also sang in the film version of *Le nozze di Figaro*. In 1977 she appeared as Pamina in *Die Zauberflöte* at the Paris Opéra. On Dec. 31, 1977, she took the role of Rosalinde in a Covent Garden production of *Die Fledermaus*, which was televised to the U.S. She excelled equally as a subtle and artistic interpreter of lyric roles in Mozart's operas and in dramatic representations of Verdi's operas. Among her other distinguished roles were the Marschallin and Arabella. She also won renown as a concert artist. In later years she expanded her repertoire to include popular fare, including songs by Cole Porter and Leonard Bernstein's *West Side Story*. Hailed as a prima donna assoluta, she pursued one of the most successful international operatic and concert careers of her day. In 1981 she sang at the royal wedding of Prince Charles and Lady Diana Spencer in London, a performance televised around the globe. In 1973 she was made an Officer of the Order of the British Empire; in 1982 she was named a Dame Commander of the Order of the British Empire.

BIBL.: D. Fingleton, *K. T.K.* (N.Y., 1983).

Telmányi, Emil, Hungarian-Danish violinist, conductor, and pedagogue; b. Arad, June 22, 1892; d. Holte, June 12, 1988. He took courses in violin, conducting, and composition at the Royal Academy of Music in Budapest. In 1911 he made his Berlin debut as a violinist, and subsequently made tours of Europe and North America. He first played in Copenhagen in 1912, and soon settled in Denmark. In 1919 he made his debut as a conductor in Copenhagen; he taught at the Århus Cons. (1940–69) and toured with his own Telmányi Quintet (from 1959). In 1970 he settled in Holte as a conductor and teacher. He supervised the construction of a curved bow for playing Bach's violin works, which became known as the Vega bow (1954). In 1918 he married Anne Marie Nielsen, a daughter of Carl Nielsen; in 1936 he married the pianist Annette Schiøler.

Temianka, Henri, distinguished Polish-born American violinist, conductor, and pedagogue; b. Greenock, Scotland (of Polish parents), Nov. 19, 1906; d. Los Angeles, Nov. 7, 1992. He studied violin with Blitz in Rotterdam (1915–23), W. Hess at the Berlin Hochschule für Musik (1923–24), and Boucherit in Paris (1924–26); completed his training with Flesch (violin) and Rodzinski (conducting) at the Curtis Inst. of Music in Philadelphia (graduated, 1930). In 1932 he made his N.Y. recital debut at Town Hall, and then gave recitals in Paris and London; was concertmaster of the Scottish Orch. in Glasgow (1937–38) and of the Pittsburgh Sym. Orch. (1941–42). In 1945 he became a naturalized American citizen. In 1946 he founded the Paganini String Quartet, serving as 1st violinist until it disbanded in 1966; in 1961 he founded the Calif. Chamber Sym. Orch., with which he toured extensively; in 1982 he organized the Baroque Virtuosi from its ranks. He served as a prof. at the Univ. of Calif. at Santa Barbara (1960–64) and at Calif. State Univ. at Long Beach (1964–76); also gave master classes. In addition to articles on violin technique, he publ. a book of reminiscences as *Facing the Music* (N.Y., 1973). He was equally esteemed as a violin soloist and chamber player, conductor, and teacher.

Temirkanov, Yuri, outstanding Russian conductor; b. Nalchik, Dec. 10, 1938. He received his training at the Leningrad Cons., where he graduated as a violinist in 1962 and as a conductor in 1965. In 1965 he made his first appearance as a conductor at the Leningrad Opera. After capturing 1st prize in the All-Union Conductors' Competition in 1966, he appeared as a guest conductor with many Russian orchs. and opera houses. From 1968 to 1976 he was music director of the Leningrad Sym. Orch. He also appeared as a guest conductor abroad, making his Salzburg Festival debut in 1971 with the Vienna Phil. In 1977 he made his London debut as a guest conductor with the Royal Phil., and subsequently appeared with the major British orchs. From 1977 to 1988 he was artistic director of the Kirov Opera and Ballet, which he also led on tours. In 1978 he made a tour of the U.S. In 1979 he was named principal guest conductor of the Royal Phil. In 1988 he became chief conductor of the Leningrad (later St. Petersburg) Phil. In 1992 he was made principal conductor of the Royal Phil. while retaining his position in St. Petersburg. During the 1992–93 season, he conducted the St. Petersburg Phil. on a tour of Europe and Japan and the Royal Phil. on a tour of the U.S. and Germany. Temirkanov has won particular renown for his brilliant and idiomatic performances of works from the Russian repertoire.

Temperley, Nicholas, English-born American musicologist; b. Beaconsfield, Aug. 7, 1932. He studied at Eton College (1945–51), at the Royal College of Music in London (1951–52), and at King's College, Cambridge (B.A., 1955; Mus.B., 1956; Ph.D., 1959, with the diss. *Instrumental Music in England, 1800–1850*); then was a postdoctoral fellow at the Univ. of Ill. (1959–61). He was an assistant prof. at the Univ. of Cambridge (1961–66); after serving as an assistant prof. at Yale Univ. (1966–67), he was an assoc. prof. (1967–72) and a prof. (from 1972) at the Univ. of Ill., where he also was chairman of the musicology dept. (1972–75; again from 1992). In 1977 he became a naturalized American citizen. He served as ed. of the *Journal of the American Musicological Society* (1978–80); also ed. the *Symphonie fantastique* for the New Berlioz Edition, XVII (Kassel, 1972), *English Songs, 1800–1860* in *Musica Britannica*, XLIII (1979), *The London Pianoforte School (1766–1860)* (with G. Bush; 20 vols., N.Y., 1984–87), and *Haydn's The Creation* (London, 1987; with authentic Eng. text). His books include *The Music of the English Parish Church* (2 vols., 1979); *The Romantic Age*, vol. 5 of *The Athlone History of Music in Britain* (1981); and *Fuguing Tunes in the Eighteenth Century* (with C. Manns; 1983).

Templeton, Alec (Andrew), blind Welsh-born American pianist and composer; b. Cardiff, July 4, 1909; d. Greenwich, Conn., March 28, 1963. He studied at Worcester College and in London at the Royal College of Music and at the Royal Academy of Music. He was only 12 when he began to appear on the BBC, remaining with it until 1935. He went to the U.S. in 1935 as a member of Jack Hylton's jazz band; became a naturalized American citizen in 1941. He was extremely successful as a radio pianist, especially with his humorous musical sketches, parodies, etc., such as *Bach Goes to Town, Mozart Matriculates*, etc. He also wrote some more ambitious works, including *Concertino lirico* (1942) and *Gothic Concerto* for Piano and Orch (N.Y., Dec. 19, 1954, composer soloist). With R. Baumel, he publ. *A. T.'s Music Boxes* (N.Y., 1958).

Tenney, James (Carl), highly influential American pianist, conductor, teacher, and composer; b. Silver City, N.Mex., Aug. 10, 1934. He studied engineering at the Univ. of Denver (1952–54) before devoting himself to music; received instruction in piano from Steuermann at the Juilliard School of Music in N.Y. (1954–55), took courses in piano and composition at Bennington (Vt.) College (B.A., 1958), and worked with Gaburo, Hiller, and Partch at the Univ. of Ill. (M.Mus., 1961); was also associated with Chou Wen-chung, Ruggles, and Varèse (1955–65). He was active as a performer with the Steve Reich and Philip Glass ensembles; concurrently conducted research at the Bell Laboratories (with Max Matthews; 1961–64), Yale Univ. (1964–66), and the Polytechnic Inst. of Brooklyn (1966–70). He taught at the Calif. Inst. of the Arts (1970–75), the Univ. of Calif. at Santa Cruz (1975–76), and York Univ. in Toronto (from 1976). As both a performer and a scholar, he is a prominent advocate of contemporary music; is also a notable authority on Ives and Nancarrow. He publ. *A History of Consonance and Dissonance* (N.Y., 1988).

WORKS: ORCH.: *Essay* for Chamber Orch. (1957); *Quiet Fan for Erik Satie* (1970); *Clang* (1972); *Chorales* (1974); *Rune* for Percussion Ensemble (1988). **CHAMBER:** *Seeds* for Flute, Clarinet, Bassoon, Horn, Violin, and Cello (1956; rev. 1962); *13 Ways of Looking at a Blackbird* for Tenor, 2 Flutes, Violin, Viola, and Cello, or for Bass, Alto, Flute, Oboe, Viola, Cello, and Double Bass (1958; rev. 1971); *String Complement* for Strings (1964); *Quintext* for String Quartet and Double Bass (1972); *In the Aeolian Mode* for Prepared Piano and Variable Ensemble (1973); *3 Pieces* for Drum Quartet (1974–75); *Harmonia* Nos. 1 to 6 for Various Ensembles (1976–81); *Saxony* for Saxophones and Tape Delay (1978); *3 Indigenous Songs* for 2 Piccolos, Alto Flute, Bassoon, and Percussion (1979); Septet for 6 Electric Guitars and Double Bass (1981); *Glissade* for Viola, Cello, Double Bass, and Tape Delay (1982); *Voice(s)* for Women's Voice(s), Instrumental Ensemble, and Multiple Tape Delay (1982); *Koan* for String Quartet (1984); *Water on the mountain . . . Fire in heaven* for 6 Electric Guitars (1985); *Changes: 64 Studies* for 6 Harps (1985); numerous works for Solo Instruments, including *Spectral Canon for Conlon Nancarrow* for Player Piano (1974); *Critical Band* for Ensemble (1988); *Cognate Canons* for String Quartet and 2 Percussionists (1995). **COMPUTER OR TAPE:** *Collage No. 1: Blue Suede* for Tape (1961); *Analog No. 1: Noise Study* for Computer (1961); *Stochastic Quartet*: String Quartet for Computer or Strings (1963); *Dialogue* for Computer (1963); *Ergodos II* for Computer (1964); *Fabric for Che* for Computer (1967); *For Ann (rising)* for Computer (1969). **OTHER:** Vocal pieces; theater works.

Tennstedt, Klaus, brilliant German conductor; b. Merseburg, June 6, 1926. He studied piano, violin, and theory at the Leipzig Cons. In 1948 he became concertmaster in Halle an der Saale, beginning his career as a conductor there in 1953; after serving as a conductor at the Dresden State Opera (1958–62), he was conductor in Schwerin (1962–71); also appeared as a guest conductor throughout East Germany, Eastern Europe, and the Soviet Union. In 1971 he settled in the West; after guest engagements in Sweden, he served as Generalmusikdirektor of the Kiel Opera (1972–76). In 1974 he made a remarkable North American debut as a guest conductor with the Toronto Sym. Orch., and also appeared with the Boston Sym. Orch., which led to numerous engagements with other major U.S. orchs. In 1976 he made his British debut as a guest conductor of the London Sym. Orch. He was chief conductor of the North German Radio Sym. Orch. in Hamburg (1979–81); was also principal guest conductor of the Minnesota Orch. in Minneapolis (1979–83). From 1980 to 1983 he was principal guest conductor of the London Phil., and then served as its principal conductor from 1983 until a diagnosis of throat cancer compelled him to give up his duties in 1987. He continued to make guest appearances in subsequent seasons. On Dec. 14, 1983, he made his Metropolitan Opera debut in N.Y. conducting *Fidelio.* In 1994 his worsening health compelled him to announce that he would no longer conduct in public. His appearances around the globe elicited exceptional critical acclaim; he was ranked among the foremost interpreters of the Austro-German repertoire of his day.

Tenschert, Roland, Austrian musicologist; b. Podersam, Bohemia, April 5, 1894; d. Vienna, April 3, 1970. He studied at the Leipzig Cons. (1913–15) and received instruction in musicology from Adler at the Univ. of Vienna (Ph.D., 1921); also studied composition with Schoenberg and conducting with L. Kaiser. He was librarian at the Salzburg Mozarteum (1926–31) and prof. of music history at the Vienna Academy of Music (from 1945).

WRITINGS: *Mozart: Ein Künstlerleben in Bildern und Dokumenten* (Leipzig, 1931); *Mozart* (Leipzig, 1931); *Joseph Haydn* (Berlin, 1932); *Musikerbrevier* (Vienna, 1940); *Mozart: Ein Leben* *für die Oper* (Vienna, 1941); *Dreimal sieben Variationen über das Thema Richard Strauss* (Vienna, 1944; 2nd ed., 1945); *Frauen um Haydn* (Vienna, 1946); *Salzburg und seine Festspiele* (Vienna, 1947); *Vater Hellmesberger: ein Kapitel Wiener Musikerhumor* (Vienna, 1947); *Richard Strauss und Wien, Eine Wahlverwandtschaft* (Vienna, 1949); *Wolfgang Amadeus Mozart* (Salzburg, 1951; Eng. tr., 1952); *Christoph Willibald Gluck: der grosse Reformer der Oper* (Olten and Freiburg im Breisgau, 1951).

BIBL.: *E. Tenschert, Musik als Lebensinhalt* (Vienna, 1971; contains a list of writings).

Teodorini, Elena, Romanian soprano; b. Craiova, March 25, 1857; d. Bucharest, Feb. 27, 1926. She studied piano with Fumagalli and voice with Sangiovanni at the Milan Cons.; also received vocal instruction from G. Stephănescu at the Bucharest Cons. In 1877 she commenced her career with appearances in Italian provincial theaters as a contralto, but her voice gradually changed to a mezzo-soprano of wide range. She made her debut at Milan's La Scala as Gounod's Marguerite on March 20, 1880; subsequently sang in various South American music centers; was particularly associated with the Italian Opera and the National Opera in Bucharest. In 1904 she retired from the operatic stage and became a teacher in Paris; after teaching in Buenos Aires (1909–16) and Rio de Janeiro (1916–23), she settled in Bucharest. Her most notable pupil was Bidú Sayão. Among her prominent roles were Rosina, Donna Anna, Amelia, Lucrezia Borgia, Amneris, and Gioconda. In 1964 the Romanian government issued a postage stamp in her honor bearing her stage portrait.

BIBL.: V. Cosma, *Cîtăreata E. T.* (Bucharest, 1962).

Terényi, Ede, Romanian composer and teacher of Hungarian descent; b. Tîrgu-Mureş, March 12, 1935. He studied at the Tîrgu-Mureş music college (1942–52) and with Jodál and Demian at the Cluj Cons. (1952–58); was on the latter's faculty from 1960. In his compositions, he applies a variety of modernistic resources.

WORKS: ORCH.: Concertino for Strings, Organ, and Electronics (1958; rev. 1969); *Pasărea măiastră* (The Wonderful Bird), symphonic variations (1965; Cluj, June 11, 1967); 5 syms.: No. 1, *Brâncusiană* (1965; rev. 1986), No. 2 for Strings, *In memoriam Bakfark* (1978), No. 3 for 2 Percussionists (1978), No. 4, *Hofgreff* (1982; rev. 1986), and No. 5 for Strings and Timpani (1984); Piano Concerto (1969); *Musică în Do,* concerto grosso (Cluj, Dec. 11, 1979); 6 neo-Baroque concertos: No. 1 for Flute and Chamber Orch., *Vivaldiana* (Cluj, May 27, 1983), No. 2 for Oboe and Chamber Orch., *Suită franceză* (1984), No. 3 for Trumpet and Chamber Orch., clarino concerto (1984), No. 4 for Cello and Chamber Orch., *Rapsodi barocă* (1984; Cluj, March 20, 1985), No. 5 for Harp and Chamber Orch., *Capriccio grazioso* (Cluj, Oct. 10, 1985), and No. 6 for Viola and Chamber Orch., *Rapsodisme händeliene* (1985). **CHAMBER:** 2 preludes for Flute (1962, 1966); 2 string quartets (1974, 1984); *Sonatina burletta* for Cello and Piano (1975); *Dansuri galante,* suite for Flute, Oboe, Harpsichord, and Cello (1977); 2 violin sonatas (1980, 1985); Sonata for 2 Percussionists (1980); Sonata for Solo Violin (1985); 2 percussion quartets (*Swinging Music,* 1985; *Hommage à Coltrane,* 1986); piano pieces; organ music. **VOCAL:** Cantata No. 1: *In memoriam* for Tenor or Soprano and Piano (1964; rev. and orchestrated as *In memoriam József Attila,* Cluj, May 19, 1968); *Terzine de Dante,* scenic cantata for Baritone, Trombone, and Piano (1971–72); *Micropantomimes* for Mezzo-soprano and Piano (1981).

Terfel, Bryn, outstanding Welsh bass-baritone; b. Pantglas, Nov. 9, 1965. He was a student of Arthur Reckless and Rudolf Piernay at the Guildhall School of Music in London (1984–89), winning the Kathleen Ferrier Memorial Scholarship (1988) and the Gold Medal (1989). After winning the Lieder Prize at the Cardiff Singer of the World Competition in 1989, he made his operatic debut as Guglielmo with the Welsh National Opera in Cardiff in 1990. In 1991 he sang Mozart's Figaro at his first appearance with the English National Opera in London, which role he also sang that same year at his U.S. debut in Santa Fe. In 1992 he appeared for the first time at the Salzburg Easter Festival as the Spirit Messenger in *Die Frau ohne Schatten*; that same year he also made his Salzburg Festival debut as Jochanaan and his first appearance at London's Covent Garden as Massetto. In 1993 he made his debut with the Lyric Opera of Chicago as Donner and at the Vienna State Opera as Mozart's Figaro; also appeared as Verdi's Ford with the Welsh National Opera. In 1994 he returned to the Vienna State Opera as Offenbach's 4 villains, at Covent Garden as Mozart's Figaro, and at the Salzburg Festival as Leporello. In 1994 he made an impressive appearance in the closing night gala concert of the 100th annivesary season of the London Promenade Concerts as soloist with Andrew Davis and the BBC Sym. Orch. His highly acclaimed Metropolitan Opera debut in N.Y. followed on Oct. 19, 1994, as Mozart's Figaro. On Oct. 24, 1994, he made his N.Y. recital debut at Alice Tully Hall. In 1995 he returned to the Lyric Opera of Chicago and at the Metropolitan Opera as Leporello. In addition to his operatic repertoire, Terfel has won a wide following for his concert engagements, in a repertoire extending from Bach to Walton.

Ternina, Milka, outstanding Croatian soprano; b. Doljnji, Moslavina, Dec. 19, 1863; d. Zagreb, May 18, 1941. She studied with Ida Winterberg in Zagreb and then with Gansbacher at the Vienna Cons. (1880–82). She made her operatic debut as Amelia in *Un ballo in maschera* in Zagreb (1882); then sang in Leipzig (1883–84), Graz (1884–86), and Bremen (1886–89). In 1889 she appeared as a guest artist at the Hamburg Opera, joining its roster in 1890; also was a member of the Munich Court Opera (1890–99), where she distinguished herself as a Wagnerian singer. She was engaged by Walter Damrosch for his German Opera Co. in N.Y., and made her American debut as Elsa in *Lohengrin* in Boston on March 4, 1896; also appeared at Covent Garden, London, as Isolde (June 3, 1898); after a series of successes at the Bayreuth Festivals (1899), she made her Metropolitan Opera debut in N.Y. as Elisabeth on Jan. 27, 1900, and sang there until 1904 (1902–03 season excepted); she sang Tosca at the American premiere (Feb. 4, 1901) and Kundry in *Parsifal* (Dec. 24, 1903). She made her farewell stage appearance as Sieglinde in Munich on Aug. 19, 1906. In subsequent years, she was active as a teacher, giving instruction at the Inst. of Musical Art in N.Y. and later in Zagreb, where she was the mentor of Zinka Milanov. She was renowned for her portrayals of Isolde and Beethoven's Leonore.

Terry, Charles Sanford, eminent English music scholar; b. Newport Pagnell, Buckinghamshire, Oct. 24, 1864; d. Westerton of Pitfodels, near Aberdeen, Nov. 5, 1936. He studied history at Clare College, Cambridge (1883–86). In 1890 he became a lecturer in history at Durham College of Science, Newcastle upon Tyne; joined the faculty of the Univ. of Aberdeen, 1898; from 1903 to 1930, held the Burnett-Fletcher chair of history there, and occupied himself with historical research; at the same time, he devoted much of his energy to the study of Bach and his period. His biography of Bach (London, 1928; 2nd ed., rev., 1933; 6th ed., 1967) places Bach's life within historical perspective with a fine discernment; it became a standard in the literature on Bach in English. Other books and eds. dealing with Bach included: *Bach's Chorals* (Cambridge, 1915–21); *Joh. Seb. Bach: Cantata Texts, Sacred and Secular, with a Reconstruction of the Leipzig Liturgy of his Period* (London, 1926); *The Origin of the Family of Bach Musicians* (London, 1929); *Bach: The Historical Approach* (1930); *Bach's Orchestra* (1932; 4th ed., 1966); *The Music of Bach: An Introduction* (1933). To the Musical Pilgrim series he contributed analyses of the B-minor Mass (1924), the cantatas and oratorios (1925), the Passions (1926), and the Magnificat, Lutheran masses, and motets (1929). He also ed. *Coffee and Cupid (The Coffee Cantata): An Operetta by Johann Sebastian Bach* (London, 1924) and *The Four-part Chorals of J.S. Bach* (London, 1929; 2nd ed., 1964). He also wrote a biography of Johann Christian Bach (1929; 2nd ed., rev., 1967 by H.C. Robbins Landon).

Terry, Sir R(ichard) R(unciman), noted English organist, choirmaster, and music scholar; b. Ellington, Northumberland, Jan. 3, 1865; d. London, April 18, 1938. In 1890 he was appointed organist and music master at Elstow School; from 1892 to 1896, was organist and choirmaster at St. John's Cathedral, Antigua, West Indies; from 1896 to 1901, was at Downside Abbey. There he attracted attention by his revival of the Catholic church music of early English masters (Byrd, Tallis, Tye, Morley, Mundy, White, Fayrfax et al.); from 1901 to 1924, he was organist and director of music at Westminster Cathedral. He was chairman of the committee appointed to prepare the Eng. supplement of the Vatican Antiphonary, and music ed. of the *Westminster Hymnal* (London, 1912; 3rd ed., rev., 1916; 7th ed., 1937), the official Roman Catholic hymnal for England. He was knighted in 1922. Besides masses, motets, and other church music, he composed *48 Old Rhymes with New Tunes* (1934). He ed. *The Shanty Book* (2 vols.; 1921; 1926); *Old Christmas Carols* (1923); *Hymns of Western Europe* (with Davies and Hadow; 1927); *Salt Sea Ballads* (1931); *A Medieval Carol Book* (1932); *200 Folk Carols* (1933); *Calvin's First Psalter [1539], harmonized* (1932); also the collections of 16th-century music *Downside Masses and Downside Motets, Motets Ancient and Modern,* and many separate works by early Eng. composers. He wrote the books *Catholic Church Music* (1907), *On Music's Borders* (1927), *A Forgotten Psalter and Other Essays* (1929), *The Music of the Roman Rite* (1931), and *Voodooism in Music and Other Essays* (1934).

BIBL.: H. Andrews, *Westminster Retrospect: A Memoir of Sir R. T.* (London, 1948); E. Roche, "'Great Learning, fine scholarship, impeccable taste': a fiftieth anniversary tribute to Sir R. T. (1865–1938)," *Early Music* (May 1988).

Tertis, Lionel, eminent English violist and teacher; b. West Hartlepool, Dec. 29, 1876; d. London, Feb. 22, 1975. He studied violin at the Leipzig Cons. and at the Royal Academy of Music in London. He took up the viola at 19 and became active as a chamber music artist; served as principal violist in the Queen's Hall Orch. (1900–1904), and in Beecham's orch. (1909); eventually became one of the most renowned violists in Europe. In 1901 he became prof. of viola at the Royal Academy of Music, where he was director of its ensemble class (1924–29). In 1936 he retired from his concert career, but in later years made occasional appearances; his farewell performance was given at the age of 87. In 1950 he was made a Commander of the Order of the British Empire. He prepared many transcriptions for his instrument and also commissioned various works from noted English composers. He wrote *Beauty of Tone in String Playing* (London, 1938) and the autobiographical *Cinderella No More* (London, 1953; 2nd ed., rev. and enl., 1974, as *My Viola and I: A Complete Autobiography*). He designed the Tertis viola (16 3/49), which is described in *Music & Letters* (July 1947).

Tervani, Irma, Finnish mezzo-soprano; b. Helsinki, June 4, 1887; d. Berlin, Oct. 29, 1936. She received her primary training with her mother, the soprano Emmy Strömer-Ackté; then studied voice in Paris and Dresden. She made her operatic debut with the Dresden Court Opera in 1908 as Dalila, remaining on its roster until 1932. She gained renown through her appearance in the role of Carmen opposite Caruso in Frankfurt am Main in 1910.

Terzakis, Dimitri, Greek composer and teacher; b. Athens, March 12, 1938. He studied composition with Iannis Papaioannou at the Hellenic Cons. in Athens (1957–64); then pursued studies with Bernd Alois Zimmermann at the Cologne Hochschule für Musik (diploma, 1970); also studied Byzantine music and at Mount Athos. He was co-founder of the Greek Soc. for Contemporary Music (1966). He lectured on Byzantine music and instrumentation at the Robert Schumann Inst. in Düsseldorf (from 1974), where he taught composition at the Hochschule für Musik (1987–93). From 1990 he taught composition at the Bern Hochschule für Musik and from 1994 he was prof. of composition at the Leipzig Hochschule für Musik. In 1980 he founded the International Inst. of Research on the Relations Between Occidental and Southeast-European Music in Nauplia, Greece. Terzaki's music steers a resolute course in the cosmopolitan avant-garde, leaving no tonal stone unturned; ancestral Grecian ethos is present, however, both in the titles and in the modalities of his output. In 1994 he began to compose monophonic scores.

WORKS: OPERAS: *Torquemada* (1974–76); *Circus Universal,* chamber opera (1975); *Hermes* (1983–84). **ORCH.:** *Ikona* for Strings (1963); Oboe Concerto (1968); *Chroai* (1970); *Transcriptions télégraphiques* (1971); *Kosmogramm* (1974); *Tropi* (1975); *Prooimion in Ethods C* for Chamber Orch. (1979); *Lachesis* (1984–85); Violin Concerto (1985–86); *Per aspera ad Astra* (1989–90); *Ikaros-Daidalos* for Saxophone Quartet and Brass Orch. (1990); Alto Saxophone Concerto (1994–95). **CHAMBER:** Septet for 7 Flutes (1965–66); Trio for Guitar, Cello, and Percussion (1966); 4 string quartets (1969; 1976; 1981–82; 1990); *Stixis II* for Clarinet (1973); Brass Quintet (1983); Saxophone Quartet (1986); Octet (1988); *Trias,* piano trio (1989); *Rabasso* for Saxophone Quartet, Viola, Cello, and Double Bass (1991–92); *Der Hölle Nachklang I* for Alto Saxophone and Piano (1992); *Jeux* for Recorder and Guitar (1993); Trio for Flute, Bass Clarinet, and Piano (1993); *Sonetto* for Viola and Piano (1993). **VOCAL:** *Okeaniden* for Chorus and Orch. (1967); *Ikos* for Chorus (1968); *Nuances* for Soprano and Tape (1970); *X* for Baritone and Ensemble (1971); *Karawassia* for 6 Singers (1971–72); *Ethos B* for Soprano and 3 Instruments (1972); *Stichiron* for Chorus and Brass (1972); *Passionen,* oratorio (1978–79); *Erotikon* for Soprano and 3 Instruments (1979); *6 Monologe* for Soprano and Orch. (1985); *Das sechste Siegel* for Chorus and Ensemble (1987); *Apokryphen* for Narrator, Soprano, and Chamber Ensemble (1988–89); *Der Hölle Nachklang II* for Soprano and Organ (1992–93); *Daphnis und Chloe* for Soprano and Viola (1994); *Lieder ohne Worte* for Soprano (1994). **ELECTRONIC:** *Ichochronos I* (1967).

Teschemacher, Margarete, German soprano; b. Cologne, March 3, 1903; d. Bad Wiesse, May 19, 1959. She was trained in Cologne. After making her operatic debut in Cologne as Micaela (1924), she sang in Aachen (1925–27), Dortmund (1927–28), Mannheim (1928–31), and Stuttgart (1931–34). From 1935 to 1946 she was a member of the Dresden State Opera, where Strauss chose her to create his Daphne in 1938. She also made appearances at London's Covent Garden (debut as Pamina, 1931) and at Buenos Aires's Teatro Colón (1934). From 1947 to 1952 she sang in Düsseldorf. Among her other roles were Donna Elvira, Countess Almaviva, Sieglinde, Senta, Jenůfa, and Arabella.

Tess (real name, **Tesscorolo**), **Giulia,** noted Italian mezzo-soprano, later soprano; b. Verona, Feb. 9, 1889; d. Milan, March 17, 1976. She studied with Bottagisio in Verona. She made her operatic debut as a mezzo-soprano in 1904 in Prato; later sang soprano roles after being encouraged by Battistini. In 1922 she was invited by Toscanini to sing at La Scala in Milan, where she created the role of Jaele in Pizzetti's *Debora e Jaele.* She continued to sing there with great distinction until 1936; then was director of stage craft at the Florence Centro di Avviamento al Teatro Lirico (1940–42), at the Bologna Cons. (1941–46), and at the La Scala opera school (from 1946). Her students included Tagliavini and Barbieri; she also produced opera at La Scala and other Italian opera houses. She was married to the conductor Giacomo Armani (1868–1954). In addition to the Italian repertoire, she gained distinction as an interpreter of roles by Richard Strauss, excelling as Salome and Elektra.

Tessier, André, French musicologist; b. Paris, March 8, 1886; d. there, July 2, 1931. He studied law, history of art, and other subjects; then devoted himself to musicology; took his diploma at the École du Louvre (1921). He was archivist in the Ministry of Fine Arts; also ed. of the *Revue de Musicologie.* He ed. the complete works of Chambonnières (with P. Brunold; 1925), and Denis Gaultier's *Rhétorique des Dieux* (facsimile, 1932; transcription, 1933). He was the author of a book on Couperin (Paris, 1926); prepared materials for the complete ed. of Couperin's works, but died before his work was finished. A complete list of his writings was publ. by A. Schaeffner in *Revue de Musicologie* (Dec. 1953).

Tetrazzini, Eva, Italian soprano, sister of **Luisa Tetrazzini**; b. Milan, March, 1862; d. Salsomaggiore, Oct. 27, 1938. She studied with Ceccherini in Florence, where she made her operatic debut in 1882 as Marguerite in *Faust.* She sang Desdemona in Verdi's *Otello* at its first American production (N.Y., April 16, 1888). On May 15, 1887, she married the conductor Cleofonte Campanini. She sang with the Manhattan Opera in N.Y. in 1908; then returned to Italy.

Tetrazzini, Luisa (actually, **Luigia**), celebrated Italian soprano, sister of **Eva Tetrazzini**; b. Florence, June 28, 1871; d. Milan, April 28, 1940. She learned the words and music of several operas by listening to her sister; then studied at the Liceo Musicale in Florence with Ceccherini. She made her operatic debut as Inez in *L'Africaine* in Florence (1890); then sang in Europe and traveled with various opera companies in South America. In 1904 she made her U.S. debut at the Tivoli Opera House in San Francisco. She made her London debut at Covent Garden as Violetta on Nov. 2, 1907. She was then engaged by Hammerstein to sing with his Manhattan Opera House in N.Y., where she sang Violetta on Jan. 15, 1908; she remained with the company until it closed in 1910; subsequently appeared for a single season at the Metropolitan Opera (1911–12), making her debut there on Dec. 27, 1911, as Lucia. After singing at the Chicago Grand Opera (1911–13), she toured as a concert artist. She made the first broadcast on the British radio in 1925; her last American appearance was in N.Y. in 1931. She then taught in Milan. Her fame was worldwide, and her name became a household word, glorified even in food, as in Turkey Tetrazzini. She publ. *My Life of Song* (London, 1921) and *How to Sing* (N.Y., 1923). She acquired a great fortune, but died in poverty.

Tetzlaff, Christian, German violinist; b. Hamburg, April 29, 1966. He began violin lessons at age 6 with Maren Tanke, and then pursued training with Evelyn Distler at the Hamburg Hochschule für Musik. At 14, he made his debut as soloist in the Brahms Violin Concerto in Hamburg. He then studied with Uwe-Martin Haiberg at the Lübeck Hochschule für Musik, where he also received training in theory and composition. In 1984 he took 2nd prize at the Munich Competition; then held a scholarship for further study with Walter Levin at the Univ. of Cincinnati-College Cons. of Music (1985–86). In 1988 he won particular notice as soloist in the Schoenberg Violin Concerto with Celibidache and the Munich Phil. at the Berlin Festival, and then made his U.S. orch. debut in the same work with Dohnányi and the Cleveland Orch.; thereafter he was engaged as a soloist with the foremost orchs. of the world and also toured extensively as a recitalist and chamber music artist, appearing throughout Europe (1992–93) and then widely in North America (1994–95). Tetzlaff has won merited praise for his fine musicianship in which he displays a remarkable balance between virtuosity and refinement of expression. In addition to his performances of the standard literature, he frequently performs works by such 20th-century masters as Schoenberg, Stravinsky, Janáček, Ravel, Bartók, and Hartmann.

Teyte (real name, **Tate**), **Dame Maggie,** distinguished English soprano; b. Wolverhampton, April 17, 1888; d. London, May 26, 1976. She studied in London; then was a pupil of Jean de Reszke in Paris (1903–07). In 1906 she made her debut at a Mozart Festival in France under her real name. In order to ensure correct pronunciation of her name in France, she changed the original spelling Tate to Teyte. She made her operatic debut as Tyrcis in Offenbach's *Myriame et Daphne* in Monte Carlo in 1907; was very successful as a concert singer in Paris, and appeared with Debussy at the piano; Debussy also selected her as successor to Mary Garden in the role of Mélisande (1908). She sang at the Paris Opéra-Comique (1908–10), with Beecham's Opera Co. in London (1910–11), with the Chicago Opera Co. (1911–14), and with the Boston Grand Opera Co. (1914–17). She made appearances at London's Covent Garden (1922–23; 1930; 1936–38); then sang in operetta and musical comedies in London; later devoted herself mainly to French song recitals there. In 1951 she made her farewell appearance in opera as Purcell's Belinda in London; gave her last concert there in 1955. She was made a Chevalier of the French Légion d'honneur in 1957 and a Dame Commander of the Order of the British Empire in 1958. In addition to her famous portrayal of Mélisande, she won notable distinction for such roles as Cherubino, Blondchen, Marguerite, Nedda, Madama Butterfly, and Mimi; she also created the Princess in Holst's *The Perfect Fool.* She had 2 indifferent husbands and 2 prominent lovers: Sir Thomas Beecham in London and Georges Enesco in Paris. She publ. a book of memoirs, *Star on the Door* (London, 1958).

BIBL.: G. O'Connor, *The Pursuit of Perfection, A Life of M. T.* (N.Y., 1979).

Thalben-Ball, Sir George (Thomas), Australian-born English organist, choirmaster, teacher, and composer; b. Sydney, June 18, 1896; d. London, Jan. 18, 1987. He was a student of Parry, Stanford, and Davies at the Royal College of Music in London. At the age of 16, he was made a Fellow of the Royal College of Organists in London. He served as acting organist (1919–23) and as organist and choirmaster (1928–81) at the Temple Church in London, and also was a teacher at the Royal College of Music. From 1949 to 1983 he likewise served as city and Univ. organist in Birmingham. In 1967 he was made a Commander of the Order of the British Empire and in 1982 he was knighted. Among his compositions were choral works and organ music.

BIBL.: J. Rennert, *G. T.-B.* (Newton Abbot and London, 1979).

Thebom, Blanche, American mezzo-soprano; b. Monessen, Pa., Sept. 19, 1918. She studied singing with Margaret Matzenauer and Edyth Walker in N.Y. She made her concert debut there in 1941 and her operatic debut, with the Metropolitan Opera, as Fricka on Dec. 14, 1944; remained on its roster until 1959, and sang there again from 1960 to 1967; also sang in various opera houses in America and Europe, with increasing success. In 1967 she was appointed head of the Southern Regional Opera Co. in Atlanta; it folded in 1968; in 1980 she was appointed director of the opera workshop of San Francisco State Univ. Among her best roles were Ortrud, Azucena, Amneris, Laura in *La Gioconda*, and Carmen.

Theodorakis, Mikis (actually, **Michael George**), Greek composer; b. Chios, July 29, 1925. He studied at the Athens Cons. During the German occupation of his homeland, he was active in the resistance; after the liberation, he joined the Left but was arrested and deported during the civil war. In 1953 he went to Paris and studied with Messiaen; soon after he began to compose. After returning to Greece in 1961, he resumed his political activities and served as a member of Parliament in 1963. Having joined the Communist Party, he was arrested after the military coup in 1967 and incarcerated. During this period, he wrote the music for the film *Z*, dealing with the police murder of the Socialist politician Gregory Lambrakis in Salonika in 1963. The film and the music were greatly acclaimed in Europe and America, and the fate of Theodorakis became a cause célèbre. Yielding to pressure from international public opinion, the military Greek government freed Theodorakis in 1970. In 1972 he quit the Communist Party and was active in the United Left; returning to the Communist Party, he served in Parliament in 1981 and again in 1985–86 before quitting it once more. In 1989 he became an ambassador of conservatism in Greece, going so far as to enter the race for the legislature on the New Democracy ticket; with 416 like-minded painters, writers, musicians, singers, and actors, Theodorakis signed his name to a manifesto (Nov. 3, 1989) condemning the divisive policies of the former Socialist government of Andreas Papandreou; he also ended 4 years of musical silence by appearing on an Athens stage before a crowd of 70,000 people, singing songs of protest and love in the name of national unity. From 1990 to 1992 he served in the Greek government as a Minister without Portfolio. In 1993 he became general director of the orch. and chorus of the Greek State Radio in Athens. His 4-vol. autobiography was publ. in Athens (1986–88).

WORKS: DRAMATIC: OPERAS: *Kostas Kariotakis* (1985); *Zorbas*, ballet-opera (1988); *Medea* (1990); *Elektra* (1993). **BALLETS:** *Carnaval* (1953; rev. as *Le Feu aux Poudres*, 1958); *Les Amants de Teruel* (1958); *Antigone* (1958); *Antigone II* (1971); *Elektra* (1976); *Mythologie* (1976); *Zorba* (1976); *7 danses grecques* (1982). Also incidental music to various dramas; film scores, including *Zorba the Greek* (1962) and *Z* (1973). **ORCH.:** *Assi-Gonia* (1945–50); *Oedipus Tyrannus* (1946; also for Strings, 1955); 8 syms., including No. 1 (1948–50), No. 2 for Piano, Children's Chorus, and Orch. (1958), No. 3 for Soprano, Chorus, and Orch. (1980), No. 4 for 2 Soloists, Chorus, and Orch. (1986), No. 7 for 4 Soloists, Chorus, and Orch. (1983), and No. 8, *Canto Olympico* (1991); 3 suites: No. 1 for Piano and Orch. (1954), No. 2 for Chorus and Orch. (1956), and No. 3 for Soprano, Chorus, and Orch. (1956); Piano Concerto (1957). **CHAMBER:** Trio for Violin, Cello, and Piano (1947); Flute Sextet (1948); 2 violin sonatinas (1955, 1958); various piano pieces. **VOCAL:** *L'Amour et la mort* for Mezzo-soprano and String Orch. (1948); *Axion Esti* for 2 Baritones, Speaker, Chorus, and Orch. (1960); *Épiphanie Averof* for Soloist, Chorus, and Piano (1968); *Canto General*, oratorio for 2 Soloists, Chorus, and Orch. (1971–74); *Sadoukeon Passion*, cantata for Tenor, Baritone, Bass, Speaker, Chorus, and Orch. (1982); *Phaedra*, 12 songs for 2 Soloists, Chorus, and Orch. (1983); *Requiem* for 4 Soloists, Chorus, and Children's Chorus (1984); *Dionysos*, religious drama for Voice, Chorus, and Chamber Ensemble (1984); also choruses and songs.

BIBL.: J. Coubard, *M. T.* (Paris, 1969); G. Giannaris, *M. T.: Music and Social Change* (London, 1973); G. Host, *T.: Myth and Politics in Modern Greek Music* (Amsterdam, 1981).

Theremin (real name, **Termen**; pronounced in Russian with the accent on the last syllable; Gallicized as Thérémin; Anglicized as Theremin, with the accent on the first syllable), **Leon,** Russian inventor of the space-controlled electronic instrument that bears his name; b. St. Petersburg, Aug. 15, 1896; d. Moscow, Nov. 3, 1993. He studied physics and astronomy at the Univ. of St. Petersburg; also cello and theory. He continued his studies in physics at the Petrograd Physico-Technical Inst.; in 1919 he became director of its Laboratory of Electrical Oscillators. On Aug. 5, 1920, he gave a demonstration there of his Aetherophone, which was the prototype of the Thereminovox; also gave a special demonstration of it for Lenin, who at the time was convinced that the electrification of Russia would ensure the success of communism. In 1927 he demonstrated his new instruments in Germany, France, and the U.S., where, on Feb. 28, 1928, he obtained a patent for the Thereminovox. On April 29, 1930, at Carnegie Hall in N.Y., he presented a concert with an ensemble of 10 of his instruments, also introducing a space-controlled synthesis of color and music. On April 1, 1932, in the same hall, he introduced the first electrical sym. orch., conducted by Stoessel and including Theremin fingerboard and keyboard instruments. He also invented the Rhythmicon, for playing different rhythms simultaneously or separately (introduced by Henry Cowell), and an automatic musical instrument for playing directly from specially written musical scores (constructed for Percy Grainger). With the theorist Joseph Schillinger, Theremin established an acoustical laboratory in N.Y.; also formed numerous scientific and artistic associations, among them Albert Einstein, who was himself an amateur violinist. Einstein was fascinated by the relationships between music, color, and geometric and stereometric figures; Theremin provided him a work space to study these geometries, but he himself took no further interest in these correlations, seeing himself "not as a theorist, but as an inventor." More to Theremin's point were experiments made by Stokowski, who tried to effect an increase in sonority among certain instrumental groups in the Philadelphia Orch., particularly in the double basses. These experiments had to be abandoned, however, when the players complained of deleterious effects upon their abdominal muscles, which they attributed to the electronic sound waves produced by the Thereminovox. In 1938 Theremin decided to return to Russia. He soon had difficulties with the Soviet government, which was suspicious of his foreign contacts. He was convicted of anti-Soviet propaganda and was imprisoned for 7 years in Magadan, Siberia. During his imprisonment, he did research for the Soviet government. His invention of a miniature electronic eavesdropping instrument led to a secret award of the Stalin Prize and his release. In subsequent years, he was active in research for the KGB. In 1964 he became a prof. of acoustics at the Moscow Cons. After Harold C. Schonberg wrote an article on him for the *N.Y. Times* in 1967, Theremin lost his professorship because of the unwanted publicity. He later worked in an electronics institute in Moscow. With the advent of new liberal policies in the U.S.S.R., he was able to travel abroad, appearing in Paris and in Stockholm in 1989. Among his American students from the 1930s, he especially commended Clara Rockmore, a well-known Thereminist. His career was surveyed in Steven M. Martin's British television documentary "The Electronic Odyssey of Leon Theremin" (1993).

BIBL.: H. Schonberg, "Music: L. T.," *N.Y. Times* (April 26, 1967); O. Mattis, "Entretien inédit avec Lev Termin," *La Revue Musicale* (Feb. 1991); S. Montague, "Rediscovering L. T.," *Tempo* (June 1991).

Thibaud, Jacques, celebrated French violinist; b. Bordeaux, Sept. 27, 1880; d. in an airplane crash near Mt. Cemet, in the French Alps, en route to French Indochina, Sept. 1, 1953. He began his training with his father and made his debut at age 8 in Bordeaux; at 13, he entered the Paris Cons. as a pupil of Martin Marsick, graduating with the premier prix in 1896. Obliged to earn his living, he played the violin at the Café Rouge in Paris, where he was heard by the conductor Colonne, who offered him a position in his orch.; in 1898 he made his debut as a soloist (with Colonne) with such success that he was engaged for 54 concerts in Paris in the same season. Subsequently he appeared in all the musical centers of Europe, and from 1903 visited America numerous times. With his 2 brothers, a pianist and a cellist, he formed a trio, which had some success; but this was discontinued when he joined Alfred Cortot and Pablo Casals in a famous trio (1930–35). With Marguerite Long, he founded the renowned Long-Thibaud competition in 1943. His playing was notable for its warmth of expressive tone and fine dynamics; his interpretations of Beethoven ranked very high, but he was particularly authoritative in French music.

BIBL.: J.-P. Dorian, ed., *Un Violon parle: Souvenirs de J. T.* (Paris, 1947).

Thibaudet, Jean-Yves, talented French pianist; b. Lyons, Sept. 7, 1961. When he was 5, he entered the Lyons Cons., where he was a pupil of Herrenschmidt and Bossard; after winning its gold medal in 1974, he pursued training with Descaves, Gianoli, Hubeau, and Ciccolini at the Paris Cons. (1974–81), taking premiers prix in piano and chamber music (1977). In 1978 he won the silver medal at the Busoni Competition in Bolzano; then took 2nd prize at the Casadesus Competition in Cleveland (1979) and at the Tokyo Competition (1980); in 1981 he won the Young Concert Artists International Auditions in N.Y., and subsequently pursued a fine international career. In 1989 he gave a recital at N.Y.'s Lincoln Center. His brilliance as a technician is complemented by his Gallic sensitivity; in addition to his notable interpretations of the French repertoire, he has won accolades for his performances of the masterworks of the 19th and 20th centuries.

Thibault, Geneviève (La Comtesse Hubert de Chambure), French musicologist; b. Neuilly-sur-Seine, May 20, 1902; d.

Strasbourg, Aug. 31, 1975. She went to Paris and studied piano with L. Lévy (1919–20), harmony and counterpoint with Eugene Cools (1915–20), and fugue and organ with Boulanger (1917–23); also took courses at the Sorbonne (diplôme d'Études Supérieurs, 1920); later completed her musicological training with Pirro at the École des Hautes Études (diploma, 1952). She became engaged in business, but continued her great interest in musical research; assembled a fine private library, containing rare eds. of Renaissance music, which she opened to research scholars; initiated the Société de Musique d'Autrefois in 1925, for the purpose of presenting concerts of early music performed on early instruments; from 1955 she lectured at the Sorbonne. Her contributions to musicology include: with L. Perceau, *Bibliographie des poésies de P. de Ronsard mises en musique au XVIe siècle* (Paris, 1941); with F. Lesure, *Bibliographie des éditions d'Adrien Le Roy et Robert Ballard (1551–1598)* (Paris, 1955; supplement in *Revue de Musicologie*, XL, 1957); with A. Berner and J. van der Meer, *Preservation and Restoration of Musical Instruments* (London, 1967).

Thielemann, Christian, German conductor; b. Berlin, April 1, 1959. He received training in Berlin. In 1979 he became an assistant to Karajan in Berlin and Salzburg. After working in opera houses in Gelsenkirchen, Karlsruhe, Hannover, and Düsseldorf (1982–85), he served as Generalmusikdirektor in Nuremburg (1988–92). In 1991 he conducted at the San Francisco Opera and at the Deutsche Oper in Berlin. He conducted at the Hamburg State Opera in 1992, the same year he made his Metropolitan Opera debut in N.Y. conducting *Der Rosenkavalier*. In 1995 he appeared as a guest conductor with the N.Y. Phil. From 1997 he was Generalmusikdirektor of the Deutsche Oper in Berlin.

Thienen, Marcel van, French composer and sculptor; b. Paris, Oct. 3, 1922. He studied in Paris, receiving instruction in violin at the École Normale de Musique and at the Cons. (graduated, 1940); also studied composition at the Cons. Russe. After serving as director of the Haiti Cons. (1954–57), he returned to Paris and founded an electronic music studio; in the mid-1960s he turned to sculpture.

WORKS: *Le Ferroviaire*, opera-farce (1951); *Petite symphonie sur le temps* (1944); *Petite suite digestive* (1951); several pieces for various instruments under the generic title *Amusette*; *Le Damné* for Soprano, Baritone, Men's Chorus, Electronic Music, and Orch. (1962); songs with orch. accompaniment.

Thill, Georges, distinguished French tenor; b. Paris, Dec. 14, 1897; d. Draguignan, Oct. 17, 1984. He studied at the Paris Cons. and with Fernando De Lucia in Naples. Returning to Paris, he sang at the Opéra-Comique; made his first appearance at the Opéra as Nicias in *Thaïs* (Feb. 4, 1924), and continued to sing there regularly until 1940. He appeared at London's Covent Garden (1928, 1937); made his Metropolitan Opera debut in N.Y. as Romeo (March 20, 1931), remaining on the company's roster until 1932. His farewell appearance was as Canio at the Opéra-Comique in 1953. His outstanding roles included Don José, Romeo, Julien in *Louise*, Aeneas, and Samson; he was also a fine singer of Italian and German roles.

BIBL.: R. Mancini, *G. T.* (Paris, 1966); A. Segond, *Album G. T.* (Aix-en-Provence, 1991).

Thilman, Johannes Paul, German composer and pedagogue; b. Dresden, Jan. 11, 1906; d. there, Jan. 29, 1973. He was a pupil of Hindemith, Grabner, and Scherchen; also studied at the Dresden Technical Univ. During the Nazi era (1933–45) he was declared an unacceptable composer, and it was only after the fall of the 3rd Reich that he was permitted to pursue his career in earnest. He was founder-director of the "New Music in Dresden" concert series (1947–51); he also taught at the Univ. of Dresden, and later was prof. of composition at the Dresden Hochschule für Musik (from 1965). He publ. *Probleme der neuen Polyphonie* (1949), *Neue Musik: Polemische Beiträge* (1950), and *Musikalische Formenlehre* (1952). Among his compositions are 7 syms. and other orch. works, much chamber music, choral works, piano pieces, and numerous works for school and domestic use.

Thiriet, Maurice, French composer; b. Meulan, May 2, 1906; d. Puys, near Dieppe, Sept. 28, 1972. He began his training at the Paris Cons. with Charles Silver, and later studied with Koechlin (counterpoint and fugue) and Roland-Manuel (composition and orchestration). He was a composer of much dramatic music.

WORKS: DRAMATIC: *Le Bourgeois de Falaise*, opéra-bouffe (1933; Paris, June 21, 1937); *La Véridique Histoire du docteur* (1937); *La Locandiera*, opéra-comique (1959); 16 ballets; film scores; radio music. **ORCH.:** *Le Livre pour Jean* (1927–29); *Poème* for Chamber Orch. (1935); *Rapsodie sur des thèmes incas* (Lyons, Jan. 20, 1936); *Introduction, chanson et ronde* for Harp and Orch. (1936); *Les Visiteurs du soir*, suite (1947); *Afriques* (1949); *Danceries françaises* for Strings (1957); Concerto for Flute and Strings (1959). **CHAMBER:** *4 Pièces* for Violin and Piano (1943); *Lai et virelais* for String Trio (1956); *Suite en trio* for Flute, Viola, and Harp (1956); piano pieces. **VOCAL:** *Oedipe-Roi*, oratorio for Men's Chorus and Orch. (1940–41); *6 Poèmes lyriques du vieux Japon* for Soprano and Orch. (1968); choruses; songs.

Thomán, István, Hungarian pianist and pedagogue; b. Homonna, Nov. 4, 1862; d. Budapest, Sept. 22, 1940. He studied with Erkel and Volkmann in Budapest (1882–85); then was a pupil of Liszt there and in Weimar and Rome. He taught at the Royal Academy of Music in Budapest (1888–1906). He was greatly esteemed as a teacher; among his students were Dohnányi and Bartók. He publ. a collection of technical piano studies in 6 vols., and also composed songs and piano pieces. His wife, Valerie Thomán (b. Budapest, Aug. 16, 1878; d. there, Sept. 8, 1948), was a renowned concert singer, who gave early performances of works by Kodály and Bartók; their daughter Mária Thomán (b. Budapest, July 12, 1899; d. there, Feb. 25, 1948), a pupil of Hubay, Vecsey, and Flesch, was a fine violinist who toured throughout Europe.

Thomas, Augusta Read, American composer; b. Glen Grove, N.Y., April 24, 1964. She was a student of Karlins and Stout at Northwestern Univ. (1983–87) and of Druckman at Yale Univ. (M.M., 1988) before completing postgraduate studies at the Royal Academy of Music in London (1988–89). She received numerous awards and honors, among them ASCAP prizes (1987–91), NEA fellowships (1988, 1992), a Guggenheim fellowship (1989), the International Orpheus Prize for Opera of Spoleto, Italy (1994), and the Charles Ives Fellowship (1994). In addition to composing, she taught at the Eastman School of Music in Rochester, N.Y.

WORKS: DRAMATIC: *Ligeia*, chamber opera (1991–94); *Conquering the Fury of Oblivion*, theatrical oratorio (1994–95). **ORCH.:** *Glow in the Light of Darkness* for Chamber Orch. (1983); *Tunnel at the End of Light* for Piano and Orch. (1984); *Sonnet from the Daybreak Moon* (1986); *Moon and Light* for Trumpet and Orch. (1987); *Under the Sun* (1987); *Glass Moon* (1988; Philadelphia, Dec. 14, 1990); *Sunset of Empire* (1988); *Crystal Planet* (1989); *. . . to the light unseen . . .* for Flute and Strings (1989); *Wind Dance* (1989; N.Y., July 27, 1990); *Haiku* for Violin, Cello, and Chamber Orch. (1990; N.Y., April 28, 1991); *Vigil* for Cello and Chamber Orch. (Cleveland, Nov. 4, 1990); *Overture Concertante* (1990); *Air and Angels* (Washington, D.C., Sept. 10, 1992); *Cathedral Summer* for Violin and Orch. (1992); *Sinfonia Concertante* for Soprano Saxophone and Orch. (1992); *Ancient Chimes* (1993); *Night's Midsummer Blaze*, triple concerto for Flute, Viola, Harp, and Orch. (Louisville, Nov. 18, 1993); *Fantasy* for Piano and Chamber Orch. (1993–94); *Echo Echo* for Trombone Quartet and Chamber Orch. (1994–95). **CHAMBER:** *Fantasy on 2 Klee Studies* for Cello (1988); Sonata for Solo Trumpet (1989); *Karumi* for Flute (1990); *Chant* for Cello and Piano (1990–91); *Angel Chant* for Piano Trio (1991); *Nocturne* for String Quartet and Mezzo-soprano (1993–94). **PIANO:** *Whites* (1988).

Thomas, David (Lionel Mercer), English bass; b. Orpington, Kent, Feb. 26, 1943. He was educated at St. Paul's Cathedral Choir School, King's School, Canterbury, and King's College, Cambridge. He first gained recognition as a soloist with Rooley's Consort of Musicke, Hogwood's Academy of Music, and other early music groups in England; subsequently appeared throughout Europe. In 1982 he made his U.S. debut at the Hollywood Bowl. In later years, he pursued an international career, specializing in the Baroque and Classical concert and operatic repertoires. He won particular distinction for his performances of works by Monteverdi, Purcell, Bach, Handel, and Mozart.

Thomas, Jess (Floyd), American tenor; b. Hot Springs, S.Dak., Aug. 4, 1927; d. San Francisco, Oct. 11, 1993. After studying psychology at the Univ. of Nebr. and at Stanford Univ., he turned to singing; had formal study with Otto Schulman. He made his formal operatic debut as Malcolm at the San Francisco Opera in 1957, then continued his training with Emmy Seiberlich in Germany. He was a member of the Karlsruhe Opera (1958–61); sang Parsifal at the Bayreuth Festival (1961) and appeared in other German music centers. On Dec. 11, 1962, he made his Metropolitan Opera debut in N.Y. as Walter von Stolzing. In 1963 he joined the Bavarian State Opera in Munich, and was honored with the title of Kammersänger; also made guest appearances in Salzburg, Vienna, London's Covent Garden, and other major opera centers.

Thomas, John Charles, American baritone; b. Meyersdale, Pa., Sept. 6, 1891; d. Apple Valley, Calif., Dec. 13, 1960. He studied at the Peabody Cons. of Music in Baltimore. From 1913 he sang in musical comedy in N.Y. He made his operatic debut as Amonasro in Washington, D.C. (March 3, 1924). In 1925 he made his European operatic debut as King Herod in Massenet's *Hérodiade* at the Théâtre Royal de la Monnaie in Brussels, where he sang until 1928; made his Covent Garden debut in London as Valentin in *Faust* (June 28, 1928). He then sang opera in Philadelphia (1928), San Francisco (1930, 1943), and Chicago (1930–32; 1934–36; 1939–42); made his Metropolitan Opera debut in N.Y. as the elder Germont on Feb. 2, 1934, and remained on the company's roster until 1943. Throughout these years, he toured widely in the U.S. as a concert artist; also appeared regularly on the "Bell Telephone Hour" radio program. Among his other roles were Rossini's Figaro, Scarpia, and Strauss's Jokanaan.

Thomas (Sabater), Juan Maria, Spanish organist and composer; b. Palma, Majorca, Dec. 7, 1896; d. there, May 4, 1966. He studied with Daniel, Mas y Serracant, and Huré. He was organist at the Palma Cathedral (from 1914); founded the Capella Classica (1932), with which he toured worldwide. He publ. the study *Don Manuel de Falla en la isla* (Palma, 1947); composed choral works, songs, organ music, and piano pieces.

Thomas, (Georg Hugo) Kurt, prominent German choral conductor, pedagogue, and composer; b. Tönning, May 25, 1904; d. Bad Oeynhausen, March 31, 1973. He studied organ with Straube, piano with Teichmüller, and composition with Grabner at the Leipzig Cons., and composition with A. Mendelssohn in Darmstadt. He taught theory and composition at the Leipzig Cons. (1925–34), and was conductor of the choir at the Inst. of Church Music in Leipzig (1928–34); then was a prof. at the Berlin Hochschule für Musik (1934–39). He went to Frankfurt am Main as director of the Musisches Gymnasium (1939–45) and as Kantor of the Dreikönigskirche (1945–56); also was a prof. at the North West German Music Academy in Detmold (1947–55). After serving as director of the Leipzig Thomaskantorei and of the Thomasschule (1955–61), he resumed his post with the Frankfurt am Main Dreikönigskirche and also became conductor of the Cologne Bach Soc.; taught choral conducting at the Lübeck Academy of Music (from 1969). He publ. the important manual *Lehrbuch der Chorleitung* (3 vols., Leipzig, 1935–48; Eng. tr., 1971, as *The Choral Conductor*). Among his compositions were many choral works, including a Mass (1925), *Passionsmusik nach den Evangelisten Markus, Weihnachts-Oratorium, Auferstehungs-Oratorium,* cantatas, Psalms, and motets; several orch. works, including a Piano Concerto; chamber music, organ pieces, and songs.

BIBL.: M. Kluge, ed., *Chorezienbung und neue Musik: Für K. T. zum 65. Geburtstag* (Wiesbaden, 1969); N. Bethke, *K. T.: Studien zu Leben und Werk* (Kassel, 1989).

Thomas, Michael Tilson, greatly talented American conductor; b. Los Angeles, Dec. 21, 1944. A grandson of Boris and Bessie Thomashefsky, founders of the Yiddish Theater in N.Y., he was brought up in a cultural atmosphere; he studied at the Univ. of Southern Calif. in Los Angeles, where he received instruction in composition with Dahl; he also studied with the pianist John Crown and the harpsichordist Alice Ehlers; concurrently took courses in chemistry. He acquired his conductorial skill by practical work with the Young Musicians Foundation Debut Orch., which he led from 1963 to 1967. He served as pianist in the master classes of Heifetz and Piatigorsky at the Univ. of Southern Calif. in Los Angeles; also conducted at the Monday Evening Concerts, where he presented first performances of works by Stravinsky, Copland, Boulez, and Stockhausen. In 1966 he attended master classes at the Bayreuth Festival; in 1967 he was assistant conductor to Boulez at the Ojai Festival; he conducted there also in 1968, 1969, and 1973. As a conducting fellow at the Berkshire Music Center at Tanglewood in the summer of 1968, he won the Koussevitzky Prize. The turning point in his career was his appointment in 1969 as assistant conductor of the Boston Sym. Orch.; he was the youngest to receive such a distinction with that great ensemble. He was spectacularly catapulted into public notice on Oct. 22, 1969, when he was called upon to conduct the 2nd part of the N.Y. concert of the Boston Sym. Orch., substituting for its music director, William Steinberg, who was taken suddenly ill. In 1970 he was appointed assoc. conductor of the Boston Sym. Orch., and then was a principal guest conductor there with Colin Davis from 1972 to 1974. From 1971 to 1979 he was music director of the Buffalo Phil.; served as music director of the N.Y. Phil. Young People's Concerts (1971–76). He was a principal guest conductor of the Los Angeles Phil. (1981–85). From 1986 to 1989 he was music director of the Great Woods Performing Arts Center in Mansfield, Mass., the summer home of the Pittsburgh Sym. Orch. He served as artistic advisor of the New World Sym. in Miami (from 1987). In 1988 he became principal conductor of the London Sym. Orch. In 1993 he was named music director designate of the San Francisco Sym., and in 1995 he stepped down from his position with the London Sym. Orch. to take up his duties there. From 1995 he also held the title of principal guest conductor of the London Sym. Orch. In 1993 he received the Alice M. Ditson Award for his services to American music. From 1994 he served as music director of the Ojai (Calif.) Festival. He has also appeared widely as a guest conductor throughout North America and Europe. His repertoire is exhaustive, ranging from the earliest masters to the avant-garde. He is also an excellent pianist. Above all, he is a modern musician, energetic, pragmatically proficient, and able to extract the maximum value of the music on hand.

Thommessen, Olav Anton, imaginative Norwegian composer and teacher; b. Oslo, May 16, 1946. He studied composition with Bernhard Heiden at the Indiana Univ. School of Music in Bloomington (B.M., 1969), where he also attended the lectures of Xenakis; continued his training in Warsaw, and then pursued studies in electronic music with Werner Kaegi and Otto Laske at the Instituut voor Sonologie at the Univ. of Utrecht. In 1973 he joined the faculty of the Norwegian State Academy of Music in Oslo. In his compositions, he utilizes Western and non-Western elements in a contemporary style mainly within the tonal tradition.

WORKS: DRAMATIC: *Hermaphroditen* (The Hermaphrodite), chamber opera comprising the following 6 works: *Det Hemmelige Evangeliet* (The Secret Gospel; Bergen, May 24, 1976), *Hermaphroditen* (1975; Vadstena, Sweden, July 28,

1976), *Et Konsert-Kammer* (A Concert-Chamber; 1971; Warsaw, Feb. 6, 1972), *Ekko av et ekko* (Echo of an Echo; Malmö, Oct. 26, 1980), *Gjensidig* (Mutually; 1973; Luleå, Sweden, July 4, 1974), and *Overtonen* (The Overtone; Bergen, May 31, 1977); *Melologer og Monodramaer* (Wordless Chamber Opera; Vadstena, July 20, 1982); *Hertuginnen dør* (The Duchess Dies), chamber opera (1987); incidental music. **ORCH.:** *Vårlosning* (Thaw; Bloomington, Ind., May 8, 1969); *Opp-Ned* (Up-Down; 1972–73; Oslo, March 23, 1973); *Stabsarabesk* (1974; orchestrated by A. Bukkvoll as *Barbaresk*, 1974–77; Trondheim, March 24, 1977); *Et Glassperlespill* (A Glass Bead Game), comprising the following 6 works: *Pedagogisk Ouverture* (Pedagogical Overture) for Narrator and Strings (1979–80; Oslo, Feb. 13, 1981), *Makrofantasi over Griegs a-moll Konsert* (Macrofantasy on Grieg's A-minor Concerto; 1980; Bergen, Jan. 14, 1982), *Hinsides neon* (Beyond Neon), post-commercial sound sculptures for Horn and Orch. (1981; Minneapolis, Sept. 22, 1982), *Korsymfoni over Beethoven Åttende* for Chorus and Orch. (1980), *Gjennom prisme* (Through a Prism), double concerto for Cello, Organ, and Orch. (1984; Norwegian Radio, Jan. 1989), and *Ekstranummer over Verdis Dies Irae: Apotheose* (Encore on Verdi's Dies Irae: Apotheosis) for Chorus and Orch. (1979–80); *Fra Oven* (From Above), concerto for Synthesizer and Orch. (1986; Stavanger, Sept. 16, 1987); *Trusselen mot lyset* (The Threat Toward the Light; 1986); *The Great Attractor*, "cadenza accompagnata" for Violin and Orch. (Oslo, Aug. 4, 1988); *The 2nd Creation*, orch. drama for Trumpet and Orch. (Oslo, Sept. 15, 1988); *Music for a Futurist Feature* for Symphonic Band (1990); *2 Instrumental Madrigals*, sinfonietta (1990–91); *Cassation 1*, sinfonietta (1994). **CHAMBER:** Violin Sonata (1966); Duo Sonata for Cello and Piano (1968); 2 string quartets (1969, 1970); *Kvadratspill I* (1972) and *II* (1974) for 4 Percussionists; *Stanza* for Clarinet (1975); *S 15* for Vihuela, Renaissance Lute or Guitar, Alto Guitar, and Small Percussion (1976); *Nok en til* (Yet Another) for Woodwind Quintet (1977); *Vennligst godta min hørsel* (Please Accept My Ears) for Violin and Piano (1981); *Blokkfuglen* (The Block-bird) for Alto or Tenor Recorder (1981); *Scherzofonia/Scherzofrenia* for Violin, Cello, and Piano (Bergen, March 6, 1982); *Gratias Agimus* for Trumpet and Piano (1983); *Minia-Teks-Tur* for Tuba and Percussion (1985); *Rhapsodia improvizata* for 2 Cellos (1985); *Smaragd tavlen* (The Emerald Tablet) for 2 Pianos and 2 Percussion (1985); *L'Éclat approchant* for Piano, Harpsichord, and Synthesizer (1986); *Tibil* for Organ and Synthesizer (1986); Piano Sonata (1986); *Bellow-Canto* for 2 Accordions (1989); *The Phantom of Light* for Cello and 2 Woodwind Quintets (1990); *Étude-Cadenza* for Cello (1994); *Cassation 2* for Saxophone (1995). **VOCAL:** *Maldoror/Hunhaien* for 2 Vocal Actors and 4 Percussionists (1974); *Stabat Mater speciosa* for Chorus (1977); *Elfuglen* (The Electric Bird) for Soprano and Electronics (1980); *Sjelen, Lyttende—En gnostisk kantate* (The Ears of the Mind—A Gnostic Cantata) for Soprano, Reciter, 2 Cellos, Double Bass, Organ, and 2 Percussion (1984); *Gratias agimus* for Soprano and Piano (1988); *Woven in Stems*, symphonic song for Soprano and Strings (1991); *Near the Comet Head*, orch. drama for Viola, Alto, Women's Chorus, and Orch. (1993–94).

Thompson, John Winter, American organist, teacher, and composer; b. Leland, Mich., Dec. 21, 1867; d. St. Charles, Ill., March 8, 1951. After graduating from the Oberlin (Ohio) Cons. (1890), he studied at the Leipzig Cons. with Schreck (1893–94); returned to Europe to study with Bonnet and Sinding (1921–22). He taught at Knox College, Galesburg, Ill. (from 1890), serving as a prof. (1909–38); also was organist at the Central Congregational Church in Galesburg (1890–1926) and toured as a recitalist. He publ. textbooks on harmony (1923) and counterpoint (1925); composed organ works, motets, and anthems.

Thompson, Oscar, American music critic and editor; b. Crawfordsville, Ind., Oct. 10, 1887; d. N.Y., July 3, 1945. He was educated at the Univ. of Wash., Seattle; also studied music with G. Campanari and others. He took up journalism and in 1919 joined the staff of *Musical America*, later becoming assoc. ed. and finally ed. (1936–43). He was music critic for the *N.Y. Evening Post* (1928–34); from 1937 to his death he was music critic for the *N.Y. Sun*. In 1928 he established the first class in music criticism in the U.S. at the Curtis Inst. of Music in Philadelphia; he also gave courses at Columbia Univ. and the N.Y. College of Music. In 1939 he brought out *The International Cyclopedia of Music and Musicians* in one vol. of more than 2,000 pages, with feature articles by eminent authorities; it went through 11 eds. and reprints. He wrote the books *Practical Musical Criticism* (1934); *How to Understand Music* (1935; 2nd ed., enl., 1958); *Tabulated Biographical History of Music* (1936); *The American Singer* (1937); *Debussy, Man and Artist* (1937); ed. *Plots of the Operas* (1940) and *Great Modern Composers* (1941), both vols. being extracts from the *Cyclopedia*.

Thompson, Randall, eminent American composer and pedagogue; b. N.Y., April 21, 1899; d. Boston, July 9, 1984. He was a member of an intellectual New England family; studied at Lawrenceville School in N.J., where his father was an English teacher; began taking singing lessons and received his rudimentary music training from the organist Francis Cuyler Van Dyck. When he died, Thompson took over his organ duties in the school. Upon graduation, he went to Harvard Univ., where he studied with Walter Spalding, Edward Burlingame Hill, and Archibald T. Davison (B.A., 1920; M.A., 1922). In 1920–21 he had some private lessons in N.Y. with Bloch. In 1922 he submitted his orch. prelude *Pierrot and Cothurnus*, inspired by the poetical drama *Aria da Capo* by Edna St. Vincent Millay, for the American Prix de Rome, and received a grant for residence in Rome; he conducted it there at the Accademia di Santa Cecilia on May 17, 1923. Encouraged by its reception, he proceeded to compose industriously, for piano, for voices, and for orch. He returned to the U.S. in 1925. From 1927 to 1929 he taught at Wellesley College, and again from 1936 to 1937; in 1929 he was appointed a lecturer in music at Harvard Univ.; in 1929–30 he held a Guggenheim fellowship. On Feb. 20, 1930, his 1st Sym. had its premiere in Rochester, N.Y., with Howard Hanson conducting, and on March 24, 1932, Hanson conducted in Rochester the first performance of Thompson's 2nd Sym., which was destined to become one of the most successful symphonic works by an American composer; it enjoyed repeated performances in the U.S. and also in Europe. Audiences found the work distinctly American in substance; the unusual element was the inclusion of jazz rhythms in the score. Equally American and equally appealing, although for entirely different reasons, was his choral work *Americana*, to texts from Mencken's satirical column in his journal, the *American Mercury*. There followed another piece of Americana, the nostalgic choral work *The Peaceable Kingdom*, written in 1936, and inspired by the painting of that name by the naturalistic fantasist Edward Hicks; for it, Thompson used biblical texts from the Prophets. Another piece for chorus, deeply religious in its nature, was *Alleluia* (1940), which became a perennial favorite in the choral literature; it was first performed at Tanglewood, Mass., at the inaugural session of the Berkshire Music Center, on July 8, 1940. In 1942 Thompson composed his most celebrated piece of choral writing, *The Testament of Freedom*, to words of Thomas Jefferson; it was first performed with piano accompaniment at the Univ. of Virginia on April 13, 1943. A version with orch. was presented by the Boston Sym. Orch. on April 6, 1945. With this work Thompson firmly established his reputation as one of the finest composers of choral music in America. But he did not limit himself to choral music. His 1st String Quartet in D minor (1941) was praised, as was his opera, *Solomon and Balkis*, after Kipling's *The Butterfly That Stamped*, a parody on Baroque usages, broadcast over CBS on March 29, 1942. In 1949 Thompson wrote his 3rd Sym., which was presented at the Festival of Contemporary American Music at Columbia Univ. in N.Y. on May 15, 1949. Thompson's subsequent works were an orch. piece, *A Trip to Nahant* (1954), a *Requiem* (1958), an opera, *The Nativity According to St. Luke* (1961), *The Passion According to St. Luke* (1965), the cantata *The Place of the Blest* (1969), and *A Concord Cantata* (1975). During all this time, he did not neglect his educational activities; he taught at the Univ. of Calif. at Berkeley (1937–39); the Curtis Inst. of Music in Philadelphia, where he served as director from 1939 to 1941; the School of Fine Arts at the Univ. of Virginia (1941–46); Princeton Univ. (1946–48); and Harvard Univ. (1948–65), where he retired as prof. emeritus in 1965. He also publ. a book, *College Music* (N.Y., 1935). In 1938 he was elected a member of the National Inst. of Arts and Letters; in 1959 he was named "Cavaliere ufficiale al merito della Repubblica Italiana." In his compositions, Thompson preserved and cultivated the melodious poetry of American speech, set in crystalline tonal harmonies judiciously seasoned with euphonious discords, while keeping resolutely clear of any modernistic abstractions.

WORKS: DRAMATIC: OPERAS: *Solomon and Balkis*, after Kipling's *The Butterfly That Stamped* (CBS, N.Y., March 29, 1942; 1st stage perf., Cambridge, Mass., April 14, 1942); *The Nativity According to St. Luke* (Cambridge, Mass., Dec. 13, 1961). **BALLET:** *Jabberwocky* (1951). **INCIDENTAL MUSIC TO:** *Torches* (1920); *Grand Street Follies* (N.Y., June 25, 1926; not extant); *The Straw Hat* (N.Y., Oct. 14, 1926); *The Battle of Dunster Street* (1953). **ORCH.:** *Pierrot and Cothurnus* (1922; Rome, May 17, 1923); *The Piper at the Gates of Dawn*, symphonic prelude (Rome, May 27, 1924); *Jazz Poem* for Piano and Orch. (Rochester, N.Y., Nov. 27, 1928); 3 syms.: No. 1 (1929; Rochester, N.Y., Feb. 20, 1930), No. 2 (1931; Rochester, N.Y , March 24, 1932), and No. 3 (1947–49; N.Y., May 15, 1949); *A Trip to Nahant*, symphonic fantasy (1953–54; Philadelphia, March 18, 1955). **CHAMBER:** *All on a Summer's Eve: Song* for Violin or Cello and Piano (1917); Septet for Flute, Clarinet, String Quartet, and Piano (1917); Quintet for Flute, Clarinet, Viola, Cello, and Piano (1920); *Scherzino* for Piccolo, Violin, and Viola (1920); *The Wind in the Willows* for String Quartet (1924); Suite for Oboe, Violin, and Viola (1940); 2 string quartets (1941, 1967); Trio for 3 Double Basses, a dinner-piece in honor of Koussevitzky (1949); *Katie's Dance* for Instrument (1969); *Wedding Music: A Wedding in Rome* for String Quartet and Double Bass ad libitum (1971); *Fuga a tre* for Instrument (1977). **PIANO:** *Allegro* (1918); *Indianola Variations*, 7 variations for 2 Pianos (1918; Nos. 2, 4, and 5 by L. Mannes). 2 scherzos (1921, 1921); *Varied Air* (1921–22); 2 sonatas (1922; 1922–23); Suite (1924); *The Boats were Talking* (1925); *Mazurka* (1926); *Song after Sundown* (1935); *Little Prelude* (1935); also *20 Chorale Preludes, 4 Inventions, and a Fugue* for Keyboard Instrument (1947–59). **VOCAL:** *The Last Invocation* for Chorus (1922); *5 Odes of Horace* for Chorus and Piano or Orch. (1924; Lauro, Italy, May 16, 1925); *2 Amens* for Chorus (Montclair, N.J., Feb. 26, 1927); *Pueri hebraeorum* for Women's Chorus (Wellesley, Mass., Feb. 5, 1928); *Rosemary* for Women's Chorus (1929; N.Y., Dec. 18, 1930); *Americana* for Chorus and Piano or Orch., after Mencken's journal, the *American Mercury* (N.Y., April 3, 1932); *The Peaceable Kingdom* for Chorus, inspired by a painting of Edmund Hicks (Cambridge, Mass., March 3, 1936); *Tarantella: Do you Remember an Inn, Miranda?* for Men's Chorus (New Haven, Conn., Nov. 12, 1937); *The Lark in the Morn* for Chorus (Berkeley, Calif., Dec. 2, 1938); *Alleluia* for Chorus (Lenox, Mass., July 8, 1940); *The Testament of Freedom* for Men's Chorus and Piano or Orch., after Thomas Jefferson (Charlottesville, Va., April 13, 1943; with orch., Boston, April 6, 1945); *Noel* for Chorus (1947); *Now I Lay me down to Sleep* for Women's Chorus (1947); *The Last Words of David* for Chorus and Piano or Orch. (with orch., Lenox, Mass., Aug. 12, 1949); *Felices ter: Horace Ode for A.T. Davison* for Chorus (1953); *Mass of the Holy Spirit* for Chorus (1955–56; Cambridge, Mass., March 22, 1957); *Ode to the Virginian Voyage* for Chorus and Piano or Orch. (1956–57; Williamsburg, Va., April 1, 1957); *Requiem* for Double Chorus (1957–58; Berkeley, Calif., May 22, 1958); *Glory to God in the Highest* for Chorus (1958); *The Gate of Heaven* for Women's Chorus (Hollins College, Va., Feb. 22, 1959; also for Mixed Chorus and for Men's Chorus); *Frostiana* for Chorus and Piano, after Robert Frost (Amherst, Mass., Oct. 18, 1959; also with orch., Cambridge, Mass., April 23, 1965); *The Lord is my Shepherd* for Women's Chorus and Piano, Organ, or Harp (1962; N.Y., May 1964); *The Best of Rooms* for Chorus (Evanston, Ill., April 7, 1963); *A Feast of Praise*, cantata for Chorus, Brass Choir, and Harp or Piano (Stanford, Calif., Aug. 11, 1963); *Hymn: Thy Book Falls Open* for Chorus and Organ or Band (1964); *The Passion According to St. Luke*, oratorio for Soloists, Chorus, and Orch. (1964–65; Boston, March 28, 1965); *A Psalm of Thanksgiving*, cantata for Chorus, Children's Chorus, and Orch., Piano, or Organ (Boston, Nov. 15, 1967); *The Eternal Dove* for Chorus (1968; Cambridge, Mass., May 18, 1970); *The Place of the Blest*, cantata for Women's Chorus and Piano or Chamber Orch. (N.Y., March 2, 1969); *2 Herbert Songs* for Chorus (N.Y., Oct. 25, 1970); *The Mirror of St. Anne* for Chorus (1972); *Farewell* for Chorus (Merrick, N.Y., March 4, 1973); *A Hymn for Scholars and Pupils* for Women's Chorus, Chamber Orch., and Organ (Washington, Conn., June 8, 1973; also for Chorus, Flute, 2 Trumpets, Trombone, Tuba, Organ, and Strings, Raleigh, N.C., Nov. 11, 1973); *A Concord Cantata* for Chorus and Orch., for the bicentennial of Concord, Mass. (Concord, Mass., May 2, 1975); various songs.

BIBL.: Q. Porter, "American Composers, XVIII, R. T.," *Modern Music*, XIX (1942); E. Forbes, "The Music of R. T.," *Musical Quarterly* (Jan. 1949); E. Forbes, J. Haar, A. Mann, and R. Thompson, "The Choral Music of R. T.," *American Choral Review*, XVI/4 (1974); B. McGilvray, *The Choral Music of R. T., an American Eclectic* (diss., Univ. of Missouri, Kansas City, 1979); C. Benser and D. Urrows, *R. T.: A Bio-Bibliography* (Westport, Conn., 1986).

Thomson, Bryden, Scottish conductor; b. Ayr, July 16, 1928; d. Dublin, Nov. 14, 1991. He studied at the Royal Scottish Academy of Music in Glasgow and at the Hochschule für Musik in Hamburg, his principal mentors being Schmidt-Isserstedt and Markevitch. He was assistant conductor of the BBC Scottish Orch. (1958–62) and assoc. conductor of the Scottish National Orch. (1966–68) in Glasgow. From 1968 to 1973 he was principal conductor of the BBC Northern Sym. Orch. in Manchester; then was music director of the Ulster Orch. in Belfast (1977–85); also was principal conductor of the BBC Welsh Sym. Orch. in Cardiff (1978–82) and the R(adio) T(elefis) E(ireann) Sym. Orch. in Dublin (1984–87). In 1988 he returned to the Scottish National Orch. as its principal conductor, becoming well known for his championship of British music.

Thomson, César, eminent Belgian violinist and teacher; b. Liège, March 17, 1857; d. Bissone, near Lugano, Aug. 21, 1931. He entered the Liège Cons. at the age of 7, where he began his training with Dupuis; won the Gold Medal at 11; he subsequently studied with Vieuxtemps, Léonard, Wieniawski, and Massart. In 1873 he entered the service of Baron Paul von Derwies in Lugano; in 1879 he became concertmaster of Bilse's orch. in Berlin; in 1882 he became prof. of violin at the Liège Cons.; then in 1898 at the Brussels Cons., where he founded a celebrated string quartet (with Lamoureux, Vanhout, and Jacobs). In 1914 he settled in Paris as a prof. at the Cons. In 1924 he visited America; taught at the Cons. of Ithaca, N.Y., and at the Juilliard School of Music, N.Y., returning to Europe in 1927. He was a famous violin teacher, emphasizing perfection of technical and expressive performance, rather than bravura. He made arrangements for the violin of various works by early Italian composers.

BIBL.: H. Timerman, *How to Produce a Beautiful Tone on the Violin . . . in Accordance with the Principles of C. T.* (N.Y., 1923).

Thomson, Virgil (Garnett), many-faceted American composer of great originality and a music critic of singular brilliance; b. Kansas City, Mo., Nov. 25, 1896; d. N.Y., Sept. 30, 1989. He began piano lessons at age 12 with local teachers; received instruction in organ (1909–17; 1919) and played in local churches; took courses at a local junior college (1915–17; 1919), then entered Harvard Univ., where he studied orchestration with E.B. Hill and became assistant and accompanist to A.T.

Davison, conductor of its Glee Club; also studied piano with Heinrich Gebhard and organ with Wallace Goodrich in Boston. In 1921 he went with the Harvard Glee Club to Europe, where he remained on a John Knowles Paine Traveling Fellowship to study organ with Boulanger at the Paris École Normale de Musique; also received private instruction in counterpoint from her. Returning to Harvard in 1922, he was made organist and choirmaster at King's College; after graduating in 1923, he went to N.Y. to study conducting with Clifton and counterpoint with Scalero at the Juilliard Graduate School. In 1925 he returned to Paris, which remained his base until 1940. He established friendly contacts with cosmopolitan groups of musicians, writers, and painters; his association with Gertrude Stein was particularly significant in the development of his aesthetic ideas. In his music, he refused to follow any set of modernistic doctrines; rather, he embraced the notion of popular universality, which allowed him to use the techniques of all ages and all degrees of simplicity or complexity, from simple triadic harmonies to dodecaphonic intricacies; in so doing he achieved an eclectic illumination of astonishing power of direct communication, expressed in his dictum "jamais de banalité, toujours le lieu commun." Beneath the characteristic Parisian persiflage in some of his music there is a profoundly earnest intent. His most famous composition is the opera *Four Saints in Three Acts,* to the libretto by Gertrude Stein, in which the deliberate confusion wrought by the author of the play (there are actually 4 acts and more than a dozen saints, some of them in duplicate) and the composer's almost solemn, hymn-like treatment, create a hilarious modern opera-buffa. It was first introduced at Hartford, Conn., on Feb. 8, 1934, characteristically announced as being under the auspices of the "Society of Friends and Enemies of Modern Music," of which Thomson was director (1934–37); the work became an American classic, with constant revivals staged in America and Europe. In 1940 Thomson was appointed music critic of the *N.Y. Herald-Tribune*; he received the Pulitzer Prize in Music in 1948 for his score to the film *Louisiana Story.* Far from being routine journalism, Thomson's music reviews are minor masterpieces of literary brilliance and critical acumen. He resigned in 1954 to devote himself to composition and conducting. He received the Légion d'honneur in 1947; was elected to membership in the National Inst. of Arts and Letters in 1948 and in the American Academy of Arts and Letters in 1959. In 1982 he received an honorary degree of D.Mus. from Harvard Univ. In 1983 he was awarded the Kennedy Center Honor for lifetime achievement. He received the Medal of Arts in 1988.

WORKS: DRAMATIC: OPERAS: *Four Saints in Three Acts* (1927–28; orchestrated 1933; Hartford, Conn., Feb. 8, 1934); *The Mother of Us All,* to a libretto by Gertrude Stein on the life of the American suffragist Susan B. Anthony (N.Y., May 7, 1947); *Lord Byron* (1961–68; N.Y., April 13, 1972). **BALLETS:** *Filling Station* (1937; N.Y., Feb. 18, 1938); *The Harvest According* (N.Y., Oct. 1, 1952; based on the *Symphony on a Hymn Tune,* the Cello Concerto, and the Suite from *The Mother of Us All*); *Parson Weems and the Cherry Tree* (Amherst, Mass., Nov. 1, 1975). **FILM SCORES:** *The Plow that Broke the Plains* (N.Y., May 25, 1936; orch. suite, Philadelphia, Jan. 2, 1943); *The River* (New Orleans, Oct. 29, 1937; orch. suite, N.Y., Jan. 12, 1943); *The Spanish Earth* (1937; in collaboration with M. Blitzstein); *Tuesday in November* (1945); *Louisiana Story* (Edinburgh, Aug. 22, 1948; orch. suite as *Acadian Songs and Dances,* Philadelphia, Jan. 11, 1951); *The Goddess* (1957; Brussels, June 1958); *Power among Men* (1958; N.Y., March 5, 1959; orch. suite as *Fugues and Cantilenas,* Ann Arbor, May 2, 1959); *Journey to America* (N.Y., July 1964; orch. suite as *Pilgrims and Pioneers,* N.Y., Feb. 27, 1971). **ORCH.:** 3 syms.: No. 1, *Symphony on a Hymn Tune* (1928; N.Y., Feb. 22, 1945), No. 2 (1931; rev. version, Seattle, Nov. 17, 1941), and No. 3 (1972; N.Y., Dec. 26, 1976); *The John Moser Waltzes* (1935; orchestrated 1937); *The Plow that Broke the Plains,* suite from the film score (1936; Philadelphia, Jan. 2, 1943); *The River,* suite from the film score (1937; N.Y., Jan. 12, 1943); *Filling Station,* suite from the ballet (1937; WNYC Radio, N.Y., Feb. 2, 1941); *Canons for Dorothy Thompson* (N.Y., July 23, 1942); *The Major LaGuardia Waltzes* (Cincinnati, May 14, 1942); *Bugles and Birds: Portrait of Pablo Picasso* (1940; orchestrated 1944; Philadelphia, Nov. 17, 1944); *Cantabile for Strings: Portrait of Nicolas de Chatelain* (1940; orchestrated 1944; Philadelphia, Nov. 17, 1944); *Fanfare for France: Portrait of Max Kahn* (1940; Cincinnati, Jan. 15, 1943); *Fugue: Portrait of Alexander Smallens* (1940; orchestrated 1944; Philadelphia, Nov. 17, 1944); *Meditation: Portrait of Jere Abbott* (1935; orchestrated 1944; Vancouver, Nov. 21, 1948); *Aaron Copland: Persistently Pastoral* (1942; orchestrated as Pastorale, 1944; N.Y., March 15, 1945); *Percussion Piece: Portrait of Jessie K. Lasell* (1941; orchestrated 1944; Philadelphia, Nov. 17, 1944); *Tango Lullaby: Portrait of Mlle Alvarex de Toledo* (1940; orchestrated 1944; Philadelphia, Nov. 17, 1944); *Fugue and Chorale on Yankee Doodle,* suite from the film score *Tuesday in November* (1945; Atlanta, April 16, 1969); *The Seine at Night* (1947; Kansas City, Mo., Feb. 24, 1948); *Acadian Songs and Dances* from the film score *Louisiana Story* (1948; Philadelphia, Jan. 11, 1951); *Louisiana Story,* suite from the film score (Philadelphia, Nov. 26, 1948); *Wheat Field at Noon* (Louisville, Dec. 7, 1948); *At the Beach,* concert waltz for Trumpet and Band (1949; N.Y., July 21, 1950; based on *Le bains-bar* for Violin and Piano, 1929); *The Mother of Us All,* suite from the opera (1949; Knoxville, Tenn., Jan. 17, 1950); *A Solemn Music* for Band (N.Y., June 17, 1949; also for orch., 1961; N.Y., Feb. 15, 1962); Cello Concerto (Philadelphia, March 24, 1950); *Sea Piece with Birds* (Dallas, Dec. 10, 1952); *Concerto: Portrait of Roger Baker* for Flute, Harp, Strings, and Percussion (Venice, Sept. 14, 1954; also for Flute and Piano); *Eleven Chorale Preludes* (1956; New Orleans, March 25, 1957; arr. from Brahms's op. 122); *The Lively Arts Fugue* (1957); *Fugues and Cantilenas* from the film score *Power among Men* (Ann Arbor, May 2, 1959); *A Joyful Fugue* (1962; N.Y., Feb. 1, 1963; also for Band); *Autum,* concertino for Harp, Strings, and Percussion (Madrid, Oct. 19, 1964; based on the *Homage to Marya Freund* and the Harp and the Piano Sonata No. 2); *Pilgrims and Pioneers* from the film score *Journey to America* (1964; N.Y., Feb. 27, 1971; also for Band); *Ode to the Wonders of Nature* for Brass and Percussion (Washington, D.C., Sept. 16, 1965); *Fantasy in Homage to an Earlier England* (Kansas City, Mo., May 27, 1966); *Edges: Portrait of Robert Indiana* (1966; also for Band, 1969); *Study Piece: Portrait of a Lady* for Band (1969; originally *Insistences: Portrait of Louise Crane,* 1941); *Metropolitan Museum Fanfare: Portrait of an American Artist* for Brass and Percussion (N.Y., Oct. 16, 1969; originally *Parades: Portrait of Florine Stettheimer,* 1941); *Thoughts for Strings* for Strings (1981); *A Love Scene* (1982; originally *Dead Pan: Mrs. Betty Freeman*); *Intensely Two: Karen Brown Waltuck* (1981; orchestrated 1982); *Loyal, Steady, and Persistent: Noah Creshevsky* (1981; orchestrated 1982); *Something of a Beauty: Ann-Marie Soullière* (1981; orchestrated 1982); *David Dubal in Flight* (1982). **CHAMBER:** *Sonata da chiesa* for Clarinet, Trumpet, Horn, Trombone, and Viola (Paris, May 5, 1926; rev. 1973); (8) *Portraits for Violin Alone* (1928–40); *Five Portraits for Four Clarinets* for 2 Clarinets, Alto Clarinet, and Bass Clarinet (1929); *Le bains-bar* for Violin and Piano (1929; arr. as *At the Beach,* concert waltz for Trumpet and Band, 1949; N.Y., July 21, 1950); *Portraits* for Violin and Piano (1930–40); Violin Sonata (1930; Paris, Jan. 24, 1931); *Serenade* for Flute and Violin (1931); 2 string quartets: No. 1 (Paris, June 15, 1931; rev. 1957) and No. 2 (1932; Hartford, Conn., April 14, 1933; rev. 1957); *Sonata for Flute Alone* (1943); *Barcarolle for Woodwinds: A Portrait of Georges Hugnet* for Flute, Oboe, English Horn, Clarinet, Bass Clarinet, and Bassoon (1944; Pittsburgh, Nov. 29, 1946; based on a piano piece); *Lamentations: Étude for Accordion* (1959); *Variations* for Koto (1961); *Étude for Cello and Piano: Portrait of Frederic James* (1966); *Family Portrait* for 2 Trumpets, Horn, and 2 Trombones (1974; N.Y., March 24, 1975); *For Lou Harrison and his Jolly Games of 16 Measures (count 'em),* theme without instrumentation (1981); *A Short Fanfare* for 2 Trumpets or 3 Trumpets or 3 Trumpets and 2 Drums (1981); *Bell Piece* for 2 or 4 Players (1983); *Cynthia Kemper: A Fanfare* (1983); *Lili*

Hasings for Violin and Piano (1983); *A Portrait of Two* (1984); *Jay Rosen: Portrait and Fugue* for Bass Tuba and Piano (1984–85); *Stockton Fanfare* for 3 Trumpets and 2 Drums (1985); also numerous solo piano pieces. **VOCAL:** Choral pieces; solo vocal works.

WRITINGS (all publ. in N.Y.): *The State Of Music* (1939; 2nd ed., rev., 1961); *The Musical Scene* (1945); *The Art of Judging Music* (1948); *Music Right and Left* (1951); *Virgil Thomson* (1966); *Music Reviewed, 1940–1954* (1967); *American Music Since 1910* (1971); *A Virgil Thomson Reader* (1981); *Music with Words: A Composer's View* (1989).

BIBL.: P. Glanville-Hicks, "V. T.," *Musical Quarterly*, XXXV (1949); M. Field, "V. T. and the Maturity of American Music," *The Chesterian*, XXVIII (1953–54); K. Hoover and J. Cage, *V. T.: His Life and Music* (N.Y., 1959); K. Ward, *An Analysis of the Relationship between Text and Musical Shape and an Investigation of the Relationship between Text and Surface Rhythmic Detail in "Four Saints in Three Acts" by V. T.* (diss., Univ. of Texas, Austin, 1978); H. Gleason and W. Becker, "V. T.," *20th-century American Composers* (Bloomington, Ind., 2nd ed., rev., 1981); M. Meckna, *The Rise of the American Composer-critic: Aaron Copland, Roger Sessions, V. T., and Elliott Carter in the Periodical Modern Music, 1924–1946* (diss., Univ. of Calif., Santa Barbara, 1984); A. Tommasini, *The Musical Portraits of V. T.* (N.Y., 1985); M. Meckna, *V. T.: A Biography* (Westport, Conn., 1986); T. and V. Page, eds., *Selected Letters of V. T.* (N.Y., 1988).

Thórarinsson, Leifur, Icelandic composer; b. Reykjavík, Aug. 13, 1934. He studied with Jón Thórarinsson at the Reykjavík College of Music; then in Vienna with Jelinek (1954); finally with Riegger and Schuller in N.Y. Returning to Iceland, he became a music critic and member of the modern group Musica Nova; later moved to Denmark.

WORKS: MUSICAL COMEDY: *Hornakórallinn* (1966). **ORCH.:** *Epitaph (Wallingford Riegger in Memoriam)* (1961); 2 syms. (1963, 1975); Violin Concerto (1969; rev. 1976); *Rent* for Strings (1976); Oboe Concerto (1982); *Autumn Play* (1983); *Styr*, concerto for Piano and Chamber Orch. (1988); *För* (Journey; 1988); *Mót* (Meeting; 1990). **CHAMBER:** Piano Sonata (1957); *Mosaic* for Violin and Piano (1960); Piano Trio (1961); *Kadensar* for Harp, Oboe, Clarinet, Bass Clarinet, and Bassoon (1962); String Quartet (1969); *A Small Trio* for Flute, Cello, and Piano (1975); *Per Voi* for Flute and Piano (1975); *The Coming of Summer* for Flute and Harpsichord (1978); *Terms* for Clarinet, Violin, and Piano (1979); *Capriccio* for Horn and Harpsichord (1982). **VOCAL:** Cantata for Soloists, Chorus, and Organ (1979); *Medeumusik* for Alto, Clarinet, Cello, and Percussion (1990); choruses; songs.

Thorborg, Kerstin, noted Swedish contralto; b. Venjan, May 19, 1896; d. Falun, Dalarna, April 12, 1970. She studied at the Royal Cons. in Stockholm. She made her operatic debut there as Ortrud at the Royal Theater in 1924, remaining on its roster until 1930; sang in Prague (1932–33), at the Berlin Städtische Oper (1933–35), at the Salzburg Festivals (1935–37), at the Vienna State Opera (1935–38), and at London's Covent Garden (1936–39). On Dec. 21, 1936, she made her Metropolitan Opera debut in N.Y. as Fricka, remaining on the company's roster until 1946; sang there again from 1947 to 1950; also appeared in concerts. In 1944 she was made a Swedish court singer; taught voice in Stockholm from 1950. She was particularly esteemed as a Wagnerian; also excelled as Gluck's Orfeo, Saint-Saëns's Delilah, and Strauss's Herodias and Clytemnestra.

Thoresen, Lasse, Norwegian composer and teacher; b. Oslo, Oct. 18, 1949. He was a student of Mortensen at the Oslo Cons. (graduated, 1972) and then of Kaegi at the Inst. of Sonology at the Univ. of Utrecht. In 1975 he joined the faculty of the Norwegian State Academy of Music in Oslo. His *Stages of the Inner Dialogue* for Piano was named the Norwegian composition of the year in 1981, an honor he received again in 1993 with his *Ab Uno* for Flute, Clarinet, String Quartet, Percussion, and Synthesizer. His music reflects the influence of French spectral music, Harry Partch's microtonal system, and Norwegian folk music. He was the first composer in Norway to incorporate the non-tempered intervals of folk music into concert music. His Bahai faith is reflected in his choice of titles for many of his scores.

WORKS: DRAMATIC: *Skapelser*, television ballet (1977); *Vidunderlampen* (The Wonder Lamp), children's operetta (1984). **ORCH.:** *Rettferdighetens Sol* (The Sun of Justice), symphonic poem (Bergen, Dec. 2, 1982); *Transition* for Strings (1983); Symphonic Concerto for Violin and Orch. (1984–86); *Illuminations*, concerto for 2 Cellos and Orch. (1986–90); *Hymnisk Dans* (1987); *Carmel Eulogies*, symphonic poem for the 75th anniversary of the Oslo Phil. (Oslo, Nov. 9, 1994). **CHAMBER:** *Etter-Kvart* for 2 Violins, Viola, and Cello (1971); *With an Open Hand or a Clenched Fist?* for Flute (1976); *Origins* for 3 Instruments (1980); *Interplay* for Flute and Piano (1981); *Bird of the Heart*, piano trio (1982); *Les Trois Régénérations* for 2 Cellos, Harp, 2 Percussion, Tape, and Electronics (Paris, Oct. 29, 1985); *Miranda's Flourish* for Recorder (1985); *Qudrat* for 3 Percussionists and 3 Synthesizers (1987); *Narrative* for 4 Saxophones (1988); *Thus* for Flute, Clarinet, 3 Percussion, and Synthesizer (1990); *Yr* for Violin (1991); *Ab Uno* for Flute, Clarinet, String Quartet, Percussion, and Synthesizer (1992). **PIANO:** *4 Inventions: To the Memory of Fartein Valen* (1967–68); *Stages of the Inner Dialogue* (1980); *Arise!* (1980); *Solspill* (1983–86). **VOCAL:** *Magnificetur nomen tuum* for 4 Voices and Chorus (1974); *Aeterne rerum conditor* for 2 Voices, Women's Voices, and 3 Percussion (1975); *The Garden* for Voice, Violin, Cello, 2 Percussion, and Piano (1976); *Helligkvad* for Voice (1979–93); *Tidings of Light* for 4 Voices and Chorus (1981); *Banners of Peace*, cantata for 2 Voices, Cello, and 2 Percussion (1986); *Say: God is the Lord* for 2 Choruses (1986); *Bicinium nuptiale* for 2 Voices (1989); *Cantio PM CL* for 4 Voices (1989). **ELECTRONIC:** *Marm* (1973); *Utstrømning* (1976).

Thorne, Francis, American composer; b. Bay Shore, Long Island, N.Y., June 23, 1922. Of a cultural heritage (his maternal grandfather was Gustav Kobbé), he absorbed musical impressions crouching under the grand piano while his father, a banker, played ragtime; received instruction in composition from Donovan and Hindemith at Yale Univ. (B.A., 1942). After working in banking and stock brokerage (1946–54), he was active as a jazz pianist in the U.S. and Italy (1955–61); also studied with Diamond in Florence. Impressed, depressed, and distressed by the inhumanly impecunious condition of middle-aged atonal composers, he established the eleemosynary Thorne Music Fund (1965–75), drawing on the hereditary wealth of his family, and disbursed munificent grants to those who qualified, among them Wolpe, Weber, Harrison, Trimble, Cage, and Diamond. He served as executive director of the Lenox Arts Center (1972–76) and of the American Composers' Alliance (1975–85); in 1976 he co-founded the American Composers' Orch. in N.Y., subsequently serving as its president. In 1988 he was elected to membership in the American Academy and Inst. of Arts and Letters. In 1994 he was composer-in-residence at the American Academy in Rome. Thorne's music shares with that of his beneficiaries the venturesome spirit of the cosmopolitan avant-garde, with a prudently dissonant technique serving the conceptual abstractions and titular paronomasia of many modern compositions.

WORKS: DRAMATIC: *Fortuna*, operetta (N.Y., Dec. 20, 1961); *Opera buffa for Opera Buffs* (1965); *After the Teacups*, ballet (N.Y., July 31, 1974); *Echoes of Spoon River*, ballet (N.Y., June 20, 1976); *Mario and the Magician*, opera (1991–93; N.Y., March 12, 1994). **ORCH.:** 5 syms. (1961, 1964, 1969, 1977, 1984); *Elegy* (1963); *Burlesque Overture* (1964); *Rhapsodic Variations* for Piano and Orch. (1964); 3 piano concertos (1965, 1974, 1990); Double Concerto for Viola, Double Bass, and Orch. (1967–68); *Sonar Plexus* for Electric Guitar and Orch. (1968); *Liebesrock* for 3 Electric Guitars and Orch. (1969); *Fanfare, Fugue and Funk* for 3 Trumpets and Orch. (1972); Violin Concerto (1976); *Pop Partita* for Piano and Chamber Orch. (1976); *Divertimento No. 1* for Flute and Strings (1979) and *No. 2* for

Bassoon and Strings (1980); *Humoresque*, overture (1985); *Concerto Concertante* for Flute, Clarinet, Violin, Cello, and Orch. (1985); *Rhapsodic Variations No. 3* for Oboe and Strings (1986). **CHAMBER:** 4 string quartets (1960, 1967, 1975, 1983); *Music for a Circus* for 7 Instruments (1963); *Lyric Variations II* for Woodwind and Percussion (1972) and *III* for Piano, Violin, and Cello (1972); Piano Sonata (1972); *Evensongs* for Flute, Harp, Guitar, Celesta, and Percussion (1972); *Prufrock Ballet Music* for 7 Instruments (1974); Chamber Concerto for Cello and 10 Instruments (1975); *5 Set Pieces* for Saxophone Quartet (1977); *Grand Duo* for Oboe and Harpsichord (1977); *Eine Kleine Meyermusik* for Clarinet and Cello (1980); *Burlesk Pit Music* for Clarinet and Cello (1983); *Divertimento No. 3* for Woodwind Quintet (1983); *Rhapsodic Variations No. 2* for Clarinet, Violin, and Cello (1985), *No. 3* for Oboe and String Quartet (1986), and *No. 5* for Viola and Piano (1988); *2 Environments* for Brass Quintet (1990); Partita No. 2 for Chamber Ensemble (1991). **VOCAL:** *De profundis* for Soprano, Chorus, and Organ (1959); *Nocturnes* for Voice and Piano or String Quartet (1962); *Song of the Carolina Low Country* for Chorus and Orch. (1968); *A Mad Wriggle*, madrigal (1970); *Cantata Sauce* for Mezzo-soprano, Baritone, and 8 Players (1973); *Love's Variations* for Flute, Soprano, and Piano (1977); *La Luce Eterna* for High Voice and Orch. (1978); *Praise and Thanksgiving* for Chorus and Orch. (1983); *The Affirming Flame* for Soprano and Small Ensemble (1987); *Money Matters* for Tenor and Ensemble (1988).

Thorpe Davie, Cedric, Scottish composer and teacher; b. London, May 30, 1913; d. Kirkcudbrightshire, Jan. 18, 1983. He began his training at the Royal Scottish Academy of Music in Glasgow; then studied in London with Craxton, Thiman, and A. Brain at the Royal Academy of Music and with R.O. Morris, Vaughan Williams, and G. Jacob at the Royal College of Music, where he won the Cobbett and Sullivan prizes in composition (1935); subsequently received instruction in piano from Petri, and also in composition from Kodály in Budapest and from Kilpinen in Helsinki. He taught theory and composition at the Royal Scottish Academy of Music (1936–45); then was master (1945–73) and prof. (1973–78) of music at St. Andrews Univ. In 1955 he was awarded the Order of the British Empire. He publ. *Musical Structure and Design* (London, 1953) and ed. the *Oxford Scottish Song Book* (London, 1968).

WORKS: DRAMATIC: *Gammer Gurton's Needle*, opera (1936); comic operas; operettas; music for theater, films, and broadcasting. **ORCH.:** *Elegy* (1932); *Concert Overture* (1934); Concerto for Piano and Strings (1943); Sym. (1945); *The Beggar's Benison* (1949); *Festival Overture* (1950); *Royal Mile*, march (1952); *Diversions on a Tune by Dr. Arne* (1964); *New Town*, suite (1966). **CHAMBER:** Piano Trio (1932); *Fantasy-Quartet* for Strings (1935); Violin Sonata (1939). **VOCAL:** *Dirge for Cuthullin* for Chorus and Orch. (1935); 3 anthems for Chorus and Organ (1937); *Ode for St. Andrew's Night* for Tenor and Orch. (1950); part songs; solo songs; arrangements.

BIBL.: *C. T.D.: Catalogue of Works* (Fife, 1988).

Thursfield, Anne (née **Reman**), English mezzo-soprano; b. N.Y., March 28, 1885; d. London, June 5, 1945. She received her training principally in Berlin, and then developed a fine concert career in England. Thursfield's interpretations of the song literature were particularly admired for their insight in and handling of both German and French texts, as well as those in her native English tongue.

Thurston, Frederick (John), English clarinetist and pedagogue; b. Lichfield, Sept. 21, 1901; d. London, Dec. 12, 1953. After initial training from his father, he was a student of Charles Draper in London. He played in several orchs. before serving as principal clarinetist in the BBC Sym. Orch. in London from 1930 to 1946. Thereafter he pursued a distinguished career as a soloist with orchs. and as a chamber music player. From 1930 he taught at the Royal College of Music in London. Among his students was **Thea King**, who became his wife. With A. Frank he publ. *The Clarinet* (London, 1939). He was also the author of *Clarinet Technique* (London, 1956). In 1952 he was made a Commander of the Order of the British Empire. Thurston gave premiere performances of works by such composers as Bax, Bliss, Howells, Finzi, Ireland, and Rawsthorne.

Thybo, Leif, Danish organist, teacher, and composer; b. Holstebro, June 12, 1922. He studied in Copenhagen at the Cons. (1940–45) and the Univ. (1945–48). He taught harmony and counterpoint at the Univ. of Copenhagen (1949–65); taught theory (from 1952) and organ (from 1960) at the Copenhagen Cons.; was also active as a church organist.

WORKS: CHAMBER OPERA: *Den odödliga berättelsen* (The Immortal Story; Vadstena, Sweden, July 8, 1971). **ORCH.:** Concerto for Chamber Orch. (1947); 2 organ concertos (1954, 1956); Concerto for Strings (1957); *Philharmonic Variations* (1958); Cello Concerto (1961); Piano Concerto (1961–63); Concerto for Flute and Chamber Orch. (1966); Violin Concerto (1969); Viola Concerto (1972). **CHAMBER:** Cello Sonata (1950); 2 violin sonatas (1953, 1960); Sonata for Violin and Organ (1955); Trio for Clarinet, Cello, and Piano (1963); 2 string quartets (1963, 1990); Flute Quintet (1965); *Concerto breve* for Piano, Flute, Violin, Viola, and Cello (1966); *Hommage à Benjamin Britten* for Flute Quartet (1968); Trio for Oboe, Horn, and Bassoon (1970); *Engels nachtegaaltje* for Recorder, Flute, and Organ (1974); Concertino for 2 Trumpets and Organ (1976); 2 piano trios (1976, 1985); also solo piano works, including 2 sonatas (1947, 1956); organ pieces. **VOCAL:** Concertino for Organ, Chamber Orch., and Mezzo-soprano (Copenhagen, Oct. 19, 1960); *Markus-passionen* (Passion According to St. Mark) for Soloists, Chorus, and Orch. (Copenhagen, March 19, 1964); *Te Deum* for Chorus and Winds (Copenhagen, Nov. 18, 1965); *Prophetia* for Soprano, Bass, Chorus, and Orch. (Copenhagen, Feb. 28, 1965); *In dieser Zeit* for Solo Voice, Vocal Quartet, and Instruments (1967); *Dialogue* for Soloists, Chorus, and Instruments (Copenhagen, May 27, 1968); *The Ecstacy* for Soprano, Narrator, Recorder, Oboe, Viola da Gamba, and Spinet (1972); songs.

Tibbett (real name, **Tibbet**), **Lawrence,** outstanding American baritone; b. Bakersfield, Calif., Nov. 16, 1896; d. N.Y., July 15, 1960. His real name was accidentally misspelled when he appeared in opera, and he retained the final extra letter. His ancestry was connected with the California Gold Rush of 1849; his great-uncle was reputed to be a pioneer in the navel orange industry; Tibbett's father was a sheriff of Bakersfield who was shot dead by one of the outlaws he had hunted. His mother ran a hotel in Long Beach. Tibbett led a typical cowboy life, but dreamed of a stage career; he played parts in Shakespearian productions. During World War I, he served in the U.S. Navy; after the Armistice, he earned a living by singing at weddings and funerals in a male quartet. He also took vocal lessons with Joseph Dupuy, Basil Ruysdael, Frank La Forge, and Ignaz Zitomirsky. He made his operatic debut in N.Y. with the Metropolitan Opera on Nov. 24, 1923, in the minor role of Lovitsky in *Boris Godunov*; then sang Valentin in *Faust* (Nov. 30, 1923); achieved a striking success as Ford in Verdi's *Falstaff* (Jan. 2, 1925), and thereafter was one of the leading members on its roster. Among his roles were Tonio in *Pagliacci*, Wolfram in *Tannhäuser*, Telramund in *Lohengrin*, Marcello in *La Bohème*, Scarpia in *Tosca*, Iago in *Otello*, and the title roles in *Rigoletto* and *Falstaff*. He also sang important parts in modern American operas, such as Colonel Ibbetson in Taylor's *Peter Ibbetson*, Brutus Jones in Gruenberg's *The Emperor Jones*, and Wrestling Bradford in Hanson's *Merry Mount*. During his first European tour in 1937, he sang the title role in the premiere of *Don Juan de Mañara* by Eugene Goossens (Covent Garden, London, June 24, 1937); he also sang in Paris, Vienna, and Stockholm. A sincere believer in musical democracy, he did not disdain the lower arts; he often appeared on the radio and in films, among them *The Rogue Song*, *The Southerner*, and *Cuban Love Song*. During World War II, he sang in army camps. He made his farewell appearance at the Metropolitan Opera as Ivan in *Khovanshchina* on March 24, 1950. His last stage appearance was in the musical comedy *Fanny* in 1956. He publ. an autobiography, *The Glory Road* (Brattleboro, Vt., 1933; reprint, 1977, with discography by W. Moran).

BIBL.: A. Farkas, ed., *L. T.: Singing Actor* (Portland, Maine, 1989).

Tibbits, George (Richard), Australian composer and architect; b. Boulder, Nov. 7, 1933. He studied architecture and urban planning at the Univ. of Melbourne; music was his avocation, which he plied off and on at leisure hours. His compositions often follow pictorial and literary images; a number of his instrumental pieces bear titles related to passages from the writings of James Joyce; their technical idiom oscillates quaquaversally from a Dorian columnar manner to lapidary dodecaphony. In 1968 he was appointed lecturer in architectural history at the Univ. of Melbourne.

WORKS: ORCH.: *Neuronis Nephronicus and His Lowly Queen* (1968); *Fanfare for the Great Hall* (1968); *I thought you were all glittering with the noblest of carriage*, after James Joyce (1969); *Serenade* (1969); *Beside the rivering waters of*, after James Joyce (1970); *Where oranges have been laid to rest upon the green*, after James Joyce (1971); *Antediluvia* for Strings (1971); *The Rose Garden of the Queen of Navarre* (1975); Violin Concerto (1975). **CHAMBER:** *Silop* for Flute and Celesta (1963); Quintet for Flute, Clarinet, Viola, Cello, and Piano (1964); String Sextet (1964); Trio for Flute, Viola, and Harpsichord (1964); *Ziz, King of Birds* for Flute, Clarinet, English Horn, French Horn, Violin, and Piano (1966); *Quashq* for Flute, Clarinet, Horn, and Piano (1966); *Pili* for 13 Instruments (1966); String Quartet (1968); *Macrame* for Flute, Bassoon, and Guitar (1974); *Gâteau* for Wind Quintet (1975). **KEYBOARD: PIANO:** *Variations* for Piano, 4-hands (1969); *Stasis*, 12 pieces (1970). **ORGAN:** *Fantasy on the ABC* (1975). **VOCAL:** *5 Songs for* Contralto and Piano (1969); *Golden Builders* for Soprano, Small Chorus, and Chamber Ensemble (1972); *5 Bells* for Soprano and String Quartet, after Kenneth Slesson (1972); *Shadows* for Soprano, Harpsichord, and Small String Orch., after Kenneth Slesson (1974); *The Ice Fisherman—Lake Erie* for Soprano and Orch. (1974).

Tiby, Ottavio, Italian musicologist; b. Palermo, May 19, 1891; d. there, Dec. 4, 1955. He studied at the Palermo Cons., graduating in composition in 1921; later studied in Rome. Returning to Palermo, he devoted himself to collecting Sicilian songs; was also an authority on Byzantine music.

WRITINGS: *Acustica musicale e organologia degli strumenti musicali* (Palermo, 1933); *Antichi musicisti siciliani* (Palermo, 1933); *La musica bizantina: Teoria e storia* (Milan, 1938); *Vincenzo Bellini* (Turin, 1938); *Carl Maria von Weber* (Turin, 1941); *Claudio Monteverdi* (Turin, 1942); *La musica in Grecia e a Roma* (Florence, 1942); *I polifonisti siciliani del XVI e XVII secolo* (Palermo, 1969).

Tiensuu, Jukka, prominent Finnish harpsichordist, pianist, conductor, teacher, and composer; b. Helsinki, Aug. 30, 1948. He was a pupil of Heininen at the Sibelius Academy in Helsinki (1967–72), where he received diplomas in piano and composition (1972); after attending the Juilliard School in N.Y. (1972–73), he pursued studies in harpsichord and Baroque chamber music at the Freiburg im Breisgau Staatliche Hochschule für Musik (diplomas, 1976). He then was active as a researcher and composer at IRCAM in Paris (1978–82); pursued computer music research at the Univ. of Calif. at San Diego and at the Mass. Inst. of Technology (1989). He toured widely as a performer in Europe, North America, and Asia; served as director of the Helsinki Biennale in 1981 and 1983; was founder-director of the International Festival and Summer Academy of Contemporary Music in Viitasaari (1982); taught at the Sibelius Academy and gave master classes on Baroque and avant-garde music. In 1988 his *Tokko* was awarded 1st prize at the UNESCO International Composers Rostrum in Paris. As a performing musician, Tiensuu has won accolades for his insightful interpretations of both contemporary and Baroque scores. His own compositions utilize various avant-garde techniques.

WORKS: ORCH.: *Largo* for Strings (1971); *Flato* for Wind Orch. (Helsinki, Nov. 22, 1974); *Mxpzkl* (1977; Helsinki, March 13, 1985); *M* for Amplified Harpsichord, Percussion, and Strings (1980; Hilversum, Sept. 13, 1981); *Puro* for Clarinet and Orch. (Helsinki, April 26, 1989); *Lume* for Orch. and Tape (Helsinki, March 14, 1991); *Halo* (Kuopio, Nov. 19, 1994); *Plus V* for Accordion and Strings (Tampere, April 8, 1994); *Alma* for Orch. and Tape (Helsinki, Aug. 23, 1995); *Vento* for Clarinet Choir (1995). **CHAMBER:** *Cadenza* for Flute (Helsinki, Oct. 1, 1972); *Concerto da camera* for Cello, Flute, English Horn, Clarinet, and Bassoon (1972; Helsinki, March 24, 1973); *Ouverture* for Flute and Harpsichord (Helsinki, Oct. 1, 1972); *4 Etudes* for Flute (1974; No. 1, Helsinki, Feb. 22, 1978; Nos. 2 and 3, Helsinki, March 5, 1979; No. 4, Viitasaari, June 22, 1982); *PreLUDI, LUDI, postLUDI* for Guitar (1974; Helsinki, Nov. 8, 1983); *Aspro* for Clarinet, Trombone, Cello, and Piano (1975; Amsterdam, Sept. 1976); *Rubato* for Any Ensemble (1975; Helsinki, May 11, 1977); *Aufschwung* for Accordion (Lahti, Nov. 3, 1977); *Dolce amoroso* for Guitar (1978); *Sinistro* for Accordion and Guitar (Helsinki, Oct. 17, 1977); *Yang I* (Helsinki, Nov. 17, 1978) and *II* (1979; Helsinki, Nov. 8, 1983) for Ensemble; *Narcissus* for Oboe and Tape (Hameenlinna, July 3, 1979); *Le Tombeau de Beethoven* for Oboe, Cello, Piano, and Tape (Helsinki, Sept. 23, 1980); *Prélude mesuré* for Harpsichord and Optional Live Electronics (Viitasaari, July 26, 1983); *Fantango* for Any Keyboard Instrument (1984; with harpsichord, Viitasaari, Aug. 11, 1985); *Tango lunaire* for Oboe or Flute, Clarinet, Violin, Cello, and Any Keyboard Instrument (1985; Tampere, Feb. 15, 1986); *, mutta* for 3 Accordions (1985–87; Helsinki, Nov. 2, 1985; rev. version, Viitasaari, July 27, 1987); *Manaus (Ghost Sonata)* for Concert Kantele (1988; Viitasaari, July 23, 1989); *Le Tombeau de Mozart* for Violin, Clarinet, and Piano (Turku, Aug. 18, 1990); *Arsenic and Old Lace* for Micro-tonally Tuned Harpsichord and String Quartet (Helsinki, Sept. 4, 1990); *Plus I* for Clarinet and Accordion (Helsinki, May 9, 1992), *II* for Clarinet and Cello (Helsinki, March 8, 1992), *III* for Cello and Accordion (Karkkila, Feb. 19, 1992), and *IV* for Clarinet, Accordion, and Cello (1992; Toronto, March 28, 1993); *oddjob* for Viola or Violin or Cello and Electronics (Helsinki, March 11, 1995). **PIANO:** *Solo* for Piano and Live Electronics (Darmstadt, July 24, 1976); *Prélude non-mesuré* (Helsinki, June 15, 1976); */L* for Amplified Piano, 4-hands (1981; Joensuu, Sept. 29, 1982); *. . . kahdenkesken* for Piano, 4-hands (Helsinki, May 14, 1983); *Ground* (Helsinki, Feb. 15, 1990). **VOCAL:** *Tanka* for High Voice and Small Orch. (1973; Helsinki, April 23, 1976); *Passage* for Soprano, Chamber Ensemble, and Live Electronics (Paris, Feb. 25, 1980); *P=Pinocchio?* for Soprano, Flute, Bass Clarinet, Harpsichord, Violin, Cello, Tapes, and Computer (Paris, Dec. 3, 1982); *Tokko* for Men's Chorus and Computer-generated Tape (1987; Helsinki, May 14, 1988). **TAPE:** *Interludes I–IV* for Tape and Optional Harpsichord (Helsinki, March 11, 1987); *Prologi* (Helsinki, March 11, 1993); *Logos I–II* (Helsinki, March 11, 1993); *Epilogi* (Helsinki, March 11, 1993); *Sound of Life* (Helsinki, Nov. 27, 1993); *Ai* (Helsinki, Nov. 11, 1994).

Tiersot, (Jean-Baptiste-Elisée-) Julien, French musicologist; b. Bourg-en-Bresse, July 5, 1857; d. Paris, Aug. 10, 1936. He was a pupil of Savard, Massenet, and Franck at the Paris Cons. In 1883 he was appointed assistant librarian at the Cons., and in 1909, chief librarian, retiring in 1921. He was also a prof. at the École des Hautes Études Sociales and president of the Société Française de Musicologie. His compositions include a Mass on the tercentenary of the death of Roland de Lassus (1894); *Danses populaires françaises* for Orch. (1900); and *Hellas* (after Shelley) for Chorus and Orch.

WRITINGS (all publ. in Paris): *Histoire de la chanson populaire en France* (1889); *Musiques pittoresques: Promenades musicales à l'Exposition de 1889* (1889); *Rouget de Lisle, Son oeuvre, sa vie* (1892); *Le messe Douce mémoire de Roland de Lassus* (1894); *Les Types mélodiques dans la chanson populaire française* (1894); *Étude sur les Maîtres-Chanteurs de Nuremberg de Richard Wagner* (1899); *Hector Berlioz et la société de son temps* (1904); *Les Fêtes et les chants de la Révolution française*

(1908); *Gluck* (1910); *Beethoven, musicien de la Révolution* (1910); *Jean-Jacques Rousseau* (1912; 2nd ed., 1920); *Histoire de la Marseillaise* (1915); *Un Demi-siècle de musique française: Entre deux guerres 1870–1917* (1918; 2nd ed., 1924); *La Musique dans la comédie de Molière* (1921); *La Damnation de Faust de Berlioz* (1924); *Les Couperin* (1926; 2nd ed., 1933); *Smetana* (1926); *La Musique aux temps romantiques* (1930); *La Chanson populaire et les écrivains romantiques* (1931); *Don Juan de Mozart* (1933); *J.-S. Bach* (1934).

FOLKSONG EDITIONS: *Mélodies populaires des provinces de France* (1888–1928); *Noëls français* (1901); *Chansons populaires recueillies dans les Alpes françaises* (1903); *Chants populaires, pour les écoles* (1896–1902); *44 French Folksongs and Variants from Canada, Normandy, and Brittany* (1910); *60 Folksongs of France* (1915); *Chansons populaires françaises* (1921); *Chansons nègres* (1933).

BIBL.: L. de La Laurencie, *Un musicien bressan: J. T.* (Bourg-en-Bresse, 1932); C. Engel, "J. T.," *Musical Quarterly*, XXIII (1937).

Tiessen, (Richard Gustav) Heinz, German conductor, music critic, teacher, and composer; b. Königsberg, April 10, 1887; d. Berlin, Nov. 29, 1971. He studied music with Rüfer and Klatte in Berlin. He was music critic of the *Allgemeine Musikzeitung* (1911–17); led Der Jungen Chor for children of workers (1922–32). In 1925 he was appointed to the faculty of the Hochschule für Musik in Berlin; from 1946 to 1949, was director of the Berlin Cons., returning in 1949 to the Hochschule. He left the Hochschule in 1955 to become director of the music division at the West Berlin Academy of the Arts. He publ. an autobiography, *Wege eines Komponisten* (Berlin, 1962). He composed in both traditional and modern idioms; birdcalls played a prominent role in a number of his works. His compositions include 2 syms. (1911, 1912); *Totentanz-Suite* for Violin and Orch. (1918; rev. as *Visionen*, 1954); *Konzertante Variationen über eine eigene Tanzmelodie* for Piano and Orch. (1962); *Amsel-Septett* for Flute, Clarinet, Horn, and String Quartet (1915; rev. 1957); String Quintet (1919–22); piano pieces, including a Sonata (1910); choruses; musical plays; songs.

Tietjen, Heinz, noted German conductor and opera producer; b. Tangier, June 24, 1881; d. Baden-Baden, Nov. 30, 1967. He studied conducting with Nikisch. He was then active as an opera producer in Trier (1904–22); later was administrator of the Berlin City Opera (1925–27); from 1931 to 1944, was artistic director of the Bayreuth Festivals, where he also conducted. He was again administrator of the Berlin City Opera (1948–55) and also of the Hamburg State Opera (1956–59); then retired in Baden-Baden.

Tigranian, Armen (Tigran), Armenian composer and teacher; b. Alexandropol, Dec. 26, 1879; d. Tbilisi, Feb. 10, 1950. He studied flute and theory in Tiflis. He returned to Alexandropol in 1902 and organized a choral society, specializing in Armenian music; in 1913 he settled in Tiflis, where he became an esteemed music pedagogue; received the Order of Lenin in 1939. He composed the operas *Anush* (1908–12; Alexandropol, Aug. 17, 1912) and *David-bek* (1949; Yerevan, Dec. 3, 1950); *Dance Suite* for Orch. (1946); *The Bloody Night*, cantata (1936); *Suite of Armenian Dances* for Piano (1938); numerous other piano pieces; songs; theater music.

BIBL.: K. Melik-Wrtanessian, *A. T.* (Moscow, 1939); R. Atanian and M. Muradian, *A. T.* (Moscow, 1966).

Tijardović, Ivo, Croatian composer; b. Split, Sept. 18, 1895; d. Zagreb, March 19, 1976. He studied in Zagreb. He began his professional career by conducting theater orchs.; wrote operettas of the Viennese type; of these, *Little Floramy* (1924) became successful in Yugoslavia. His opera *Dimnjiaci uz Jadran* (The Chimneys of the Adriatic Coast; Zagreb, Jan. 20, 1951) depicts the patriotic uprising of Yugoslav partisans during World War II; he also wrote the opera *Marco Polo* (Zagreb, Dec. 3, 1960).

BIBL.: I. Plamenac, *I. T.* (Split, 1954).

Tikka, Kari (Juhani), Finnish conductor and composer; b. Siilinjärvi, April 13, 1946. He received training in oboe (diploma, 1968), in conducting from Panula (diploma, 1979), and in composition from Englund, Kokkonen, and Rautavaara at the Sibelius Academy in Helsinki; also studied conducting with Arvid Jansons in Leningrad and with Luigi Ricci in Rome. He played oboe in the Helsinki Phil. (1965–67) and the Finnish National Opera Orch. in Helsinki (1967–68). In 1968 he made his conducting debut in Helsinki; subsequently conducted at the Finnish National Opera there (1970–72), then was a conductor of the Finnish Radio Sym. Orch. (1972–76) and director of the Ensemble for Modern Music of the Finnish Radio. From 1975 to 1977 he was a conductor of the Royal Opera in Stockholm; then again was a conductor at the Finnish National Opera (from 1979); also appeared as a guest conductor throughout Europe. His works include a Cello Concerto (1984) and other orch. pieces; *The Prodigal Son*, oratorio for 3 Soloists, Chorus, and Orch. (1985); cantatas; accompanied and unaccompanied choral works; chamber music; and solo songs.

Tikotsky, Evgeni (Karlovich), Russian composer of Polish descent; b. St. Petersburg, Dec. 25, 1893; d. Minsk, Nov. 24, 1970. He studied composition with Volkova-Bonch-Bruievich in St. Petersburg (1912–14) before pursuing the study of physics and mathematics at the Univ. there (1914–15). He taught in a music school in Bobruysk (1927–34); then settled in Minsk, where he taught at the music school (1934–41); was artistic director of the Belorussian State Phil. (1944–45; 1953–57). In 1944 he received the Order of Lenin and in 1955 was made a People's Artist of the U.S.S.R.

WORKS: DRAMATIC: OPERAS: *Mihas Podhorny* (Minsk, March 10, 1939); *Alesya* (Minsk, Dec. 24, 1944; rev. 1952–53). Also incidental music and film scores. **ORCH.:** 5 syms. (1927; 1941; 1948–59; 1958; 1963); Trombone Concerto (1934); Concerto for Piano and Belorussian Folk Orch. (1953; also for Piano and Sym. Orch., 1954); *Slava* (Glory), overture (1961). **OTHER:** Chamber works; choruses; folk song arrangements.

BIBL.: I. Gusin, *E.K. T.* (Moscow and Leningrad, 1965).

Tilles, Nurit, American pianist; b. N.Y., May 29, 1952. She studied at the preparatory division of the Juilliard School of Music in N.Y. (1961–68) and at the Oberlin (Ohio) College Cons. of Music (B.Mus., 1973); after taking courses in tabla and gamelan at the Center for World Music (1974), she attended the State Univ. of N.Y. at Stony Brook (M.Mus., 1976), where she studied piano with Gilbert Kalish and chamber music with Arthur Weisberg. She performed and recorded with Steve Reich and Musicians (from 1975), Laura Dean Dancers & Musicians (1980–82), the Mother Mallard Band, a.k.a. the David Borden Music Co. (1980–87), and the Meredith Monk Ensemble (from 1984); collaborated with Monk on Fayum Music for Voice and Hammered Dulcimer and frequently toured with her. In 1978 she formed the piano duo Double Edge with Edmund Niemann, giving premiere performances in the U.S. and Europe of works specially composed for them by Borden, John Cage, "Blue" Gene Tyranny et al. Her solo recording *Ragtime: Here and Now* received high critical praise.

Tillyard, H(enry) J(ulius) W(etenhall), English musicologist; b. Cambridge, Nov. 18, 1881; d. Saffron Walden, Jan. 2, 1968. He studied at Gonville and Caius College, Cambridge (1900–1904); then studied Greek church music with J. Sakellarides in Athens (1904–07). After teaching Greek at the Univ. of Edinburgh (1908–17), he was a prof. of classics at the Univ. of Johannesburg, South Africa (1919–21), prof. of Russian at the Univ. of Birmingham (1921–26), and prof. of Greek at the Univ. of Cardiff (1926–44); he then was a lecturer in classics at Rhodes Univ. in Grahamstown, South Africa (1946–49). Tillyard was an authority on Byzantine chant. He publ. *Byzantine Music and Hymnography* (London, 1923) and *Handbook of the Middle Byzantine Notation* in Monumenta Musicae Byzantinae, *Subsidia*, I (1935).

Tilmouth, Michael, English musicologist; b. Grimsby, Lincolnshire, Nov. 30, 1930; d. Edinburgh, Nov. 12, 1987. He was a student of Dart, John Stevens, and Orr at Christ's College, Cambridge (B.A., 1954; Ph.D., 1960, with the diss. *Chamber Music in England, 1675–1720*). He was assistant lecturer (1959–62), lecturer (1962–71), and Tovey Prof. of Music (from 1971) at the Univ. of Edinburgh. From 1968 to 1976 he was ed. of the *RMA Research Chronicle.* He also was general series ed. of Musica Britannica, for which he compiled the chamber music of Matthew Locke, XXXI–XXXII (1971–72).

Tilney, Colin, English harpsichordist; b. London, Oct. 31, 1933. He studied modern languages and music at King's College, Cambridge; then took lessons in harpsichord with Mary Potts and with Gustav Leonhardt in Amsterdam. He subsequently became engaged as a soloist and ensemble player in England and on the Continent; made his first tour of the U.S. in 1971. His extensive repertoire covers the harpsichord literature of the 16th, 17th, and 18th centuries; it is his preference to use historical instruments or modern replicas of harpsichords, clavichords, and fortepianos in his concerts.

Timmermans, Ferdinand, Dutch organist and carillonneur; b. Rotterdam, Sept. 7, 1891; d. Oostenrijk, July 8, 1967. He studied organ with J.H. Besselaar and H. de Vries. In 1924 he became the municipal carillonneur at Rotterdam, and in 1926, at Schiedam. He subsequently gave exhibitions in Belgium, France, and England; soon he won the reputation of being one of the world's greatest carillonneurs. On May 5, 1954, he gave a concert in Washington, D.C., playing on the 50-bell carillon presented to the U.S. by the people of the Netherlands. He publ. *Luidklokken en beiaarden in Nederland* (Amsterdam, 1944).

Tinayre, Yves (Jean), French singer and music scholar; b. Paris, April 25, 1891; d. N.Y., July 12, 1972. He studied voice in London and Milan. He gave recitals in France, England, Austria, etc., specializing in early songs; also revived some medieval French, German, and Italian sacred songs.

Tinsley, Pauline (Cecilia), English soprano; b. Wigan, March 27, 1928. She studied at the Northern School of Music in Manchester; then with Joan Cross at the National School of Opera in London. She made her operatic debut in London in 1951 as Desdemona in Rossini's *Otello*; sang with the Welsh National Opera in Cardiff (from 1962) and the Handel Opera Soc. She joined the Sadler's Wells Opera in London in 1963; sang at London's Covent Garden from 1965. In 1969 she made her U.S. debut as Anna Bolena at the Santa Fe Opera, and later sang with other U.S. opera companies. Among her prominent roles were Mozart's Countess and Fiordiligi, Aida, Lady Macbeth, Elektra, and Turandot.

Tintner, Georg (Bernhard), Austrian-born New Zealand conductor; b. Vienna, May 22, 1917. He sang in the Vienna Boys' Choir (1926–30), with which he gained experience as a youthful conductor. He studied composition with Marx (diploma, 1936) and conducting with Weingartner (diploma, 1937) at the Vienna Academy of Music. In 1937 he became an assistant conductor at the Vienna Volksoper, but the Anschluss in 1938 compelled him to flee the Nazis. He settled in New Zealand and became a naturalized New Zealand citizen. He conducted the Auckland Choral Soc. (1946–54) and the Auckland String Players (1947–54), and then was resident conductor of the National Opera of Australia (1954–56) and the Elizabethan Trust Opera Co. (later the Australian Opera; 1956–63; 1965–67). From 1964 to 1968 he was music director of the New Zealand Opera in Wellington. He conducted the Cape Town Municipal Orch. (1966–67) and at the Sadler's Wells Opera in London (1967–70). From 1970 to 1973 he was music director of the West Australian Opera Co. He conducted at the Australian Opera from 1973 to 1976. From 1977 to 1987 he was music director of the Queensland Theatre Orch. in Brisbane. He was music director of Sym. Nova Scotia in Canada from 1987 to 1994, thereafter serving as its conductor laureate.

Tiomkin, Dimitri, Ukrainian-born American composer of film music; b. Poltava, May 10, 1894; d. London, Nov. 11, 1979. He studied composition with Glazunov and piano with Blumenfeld and Vengerova at the St. Petersburg Cons.; in 1921 he went to Berlin, where he studied with Busoni, Petri, and Zadora. He was soloist in Liszt's 1st Piano Concerto with the Berlin Phil. (June 15, 1924), and that same year gave several concerts with Michael Khariton in Paris. He appeared in vaudeville in the U.S. in 1925. In 1937 he became a naturalized American citizen. He made his conducting debut with the Los Angeles Phil. (Aug. 16, 1938), and later conducted his music with various U.S. orchs. Tiomkin married Albertina Rasch, a ballerina, for whose troupe he wrote music. From 1930 to 1970 he wrote over 150 film scores, including several for the U.S. War Dept. Among his most notable scores were *Alice in Wonderland* (1933), *Mr. Smith Goes to Washington* (1939), *The Corsican Brothers* (1942), *The Moon and Sixpence* (1943), *The Bridge of San Luis Rey* (1944), *Duel in the Sun* (1946), *Champion* (1949), *High Noon* (1952; Academy Award), *Dial M for Murder* (1954), *The High and the Mighty* (1954; Academy Award), *Giant* (1956), *The Old Man and the Sea* (1958; Academy Award), *The Alamo* (1960), *The Guns of Navarone* (1961), *55 Days at Peking* (1963), *The Fall of the Roman Empire* (1964), and *Tchaikovsky* (1970). His film music betrayed his strong Russian Romantic background, tempered with American jazz. He received an honorary LL.D. from St. Mary's Univ., San Antonio, Texas; was made a Chevalier and an Officer of the French Légion d'honneur; also received awards of merit, scrolls of appreciation, plaques of recognition, and a Golden Globe. With P. Buranelli, he publ. the autobiography *Please Don't Hate Me* (N.Y., 1959).

BIBL.: C. Palmer, *D. T.: A Portrait* (London, 1984).

Tipo, Maria (Luisa), Italian pianist and pedagogue; b. Naples, Dec. 23, 1931. She studied in Naples before completing her training with Casella and Agosti. In 1948 she won 2nd prize (no 1st prize was given) at the Geneva International Competition, and returned in 1949 to capture its 1st prize; after winning 3rd prize at the Queen Elisabeth of Belgium Competition in Brussels in 1952, she toured in Europe and abroad; in 1955 she made her N.Y. debut; she eventually devoted much time to teaching, giving courses at the Bolzano Cons. and in Florence and Geneva. After an absence of 32 years, she returned to N.Y. in 1991 as a recitalist at the Metropolitan Musem of Art. She championed the cause of traditional Italian keyboard music, most notably the works of Scarlatti and Clementi.

Tippett, Sir Michael (Kemp), greatly renowned English composer; b. London, Jan. 2, 1905. His family was of Cornish descent, and Tippett never refrained from proclaiming his pride of Celtic ancestry. He was equally emphatic in the liberal beliefs of his family. His father was a free thinker, which did not prevent him from running a successful hotel business. His mother was a suffragette who once served a prison term. Her last name was Kemp, which Tippett eventually accepted as his own middle name. He took piano lessons as a child and sang in his school chorus but showed no exceptional merit as a performer. He studied in London at the Royal College of Music (1923–28), where his teachers in composition were Charles Wood and C.H. Kitson; took piano lessons there with Aubin Raymar and attended courses in conducting with Boult and Sargent; studied counterpoint and fugue with R.O. Morris (1930–32). He subsequently held several positions as a teacher and conductor; from 1933 to 1940 he led the South London Orch. at Morley College; then served as director of music there (1940–51). Socially Tippett had difficulties even early in life. He openly proclaimed his extremely liberal political views, his overt atheism, and his strenuous pacifism. His oratorio *A Child of Our Time* was inspired by the case of Henschel Grynsban, a Jewish boy who assassinated a member of the German embassy in Paris in 1938. As a conscientious objector during World War II, he refused to serve even in a non-combatant capacity in the British military forces; for this intransigent attitude he was sentenced to prison for 3 months; he served his term in a Surrey County gaol with the suggestive name Wormwood Scrubs (June 21–Aug. 21, 1943). He regained the respect of the community after the end of the war. In 1951 he initiated a series of broadcasts for the BBC; from 1969 to 1974 he directed the Bath Festival. He received high honors from the British government; in 1959 he was named a Commander of the Order of the British Empire; in 1966 he was knighted; in 1979 he was made a Companion of Honour; in 1983 he received the Order of Merit. He visited the U.S. in 1965, and thereafter was a frequent guest in America; his symphonic works were often performed by major American orchs. Tippett's works have a grandeur of Romantic inspiration that sets them apart from the prevalent type of contemporary music; they are infused with rhapsodic eloquence and further enhanced by a pervading lyric sentiment free from facile sentimentality. He excelled in large-scale vocal and instrumental forms; he was a consummate master of the modern idioms, attaining heights of dissonant counterpoint without losing the teleological sense of inherent tonality. Yet he did not shun special effects; 3 times in his 4th Sym. he injects episodes of heavy glottal aspiration, suggested to him by viewing a film depicting the dissection of fetuses of pigs. A man of great general culture, Tippett possesses a fine literary gift; he writes his own librettos for his operas and oratorios. He publ. *Moving into Aquarius* (London, 1958; 2nd ed., 1974). M. Bowen ed. *Music of the Angels: Essays and Sketchbooks of Michael Tippett* (London, 1980). Tippett's autobiography was publ. as *Those Twentieth-Century Blues* (London, 1991). M. Bowen ed. the vol. *Tippett on Music* (Oxford, 1995).

WORKS: DRAMATIC: *Don Juan*, incidental music to Flecker's play (Oxted, Feb. 1930); *Robin Hood*, folk song opera (1934); *Robert of Sicily*, children's opera (1938); *The Midsummer Marriage*, opera (1946–52; London, Jan. 27, 1955); *King Priam*, opera (1958–61; Coventry, May 29, 1962); *The Tempest*, incidental music to Shakespeare's play (London, May 29, 1962); *The Knot Garden*, opera (1966–69; London, Dec. 2, 1970); *The Ice Break*, opera (1973–76; London, July 7, 1977); *New Year*, opera (1986–88; Houston, Oct. 27, 1989). **ORCH.:** 1 unnumbered sym. (1933; rev. 1934); 4 numbered syms.: No. 1 (1944–45; Liverpool, Nov. 10, 1945), No. 2 (1956–57; London, Feb. 5, 1958), No. 3 for Soprano and Orch. (1970–72; London, June 22, 1972), and No. 4 (1976–77; Chicago, Oct. 6, 1977); Concerto for Double String Orch. (1938–39; London, April 21, 1940, composer conducting); *Fantasia on a Theme by Handel* for Piano and Orch. (1939–41; London, March 7, 1942); *Little Music* for Strings (London, Nov. 9, 1946); *Ritual Dances from The Midsummer Marriage* (1947–52; Basel, Feb. 13, 1953); *Suite in D for the Birthday of Prince Charles* (BBC, London, Nov. 15, 1948); *Fantasia Concertante on a Theme by Corelli* for Strings (London, Aug. 29, 1953, composer conducting); *Divertimento on Sellinger's Round* (1953–54; Zürich, Nov. 5, 1954); Piano Concerto (1953–55; Birmingham, Oct. 30, 1956); *Concerto for Orchestra* (1962–63; Edinburgh, Aug. 28, 1963); *Braint* (1966; Swansea, Jan. 11, 1967); Triple Concerto for Violin, Viola, Cello, and Orch. (1978–79; London, Aug. 22, 1980); *Water Out of Sunlight* for Strings (London, June 15, 1988; arr. from the String Quartet No. 4 by M. Bowen); *New Year Suite* (1989); *The Rose Lake* (1991–93). **BAND:** *Festal Brass with Blues* (1983; Hong Kong, Feb. 6, 1984); *Triumph* (1992). **CHAMBER:** String Trio (1932; London, Jan. 13, 1965); 5 string quartets: No. 1 (1934–35; London, Dec. 9, 1935; rev. 1943), No. 2 (1941–42; London, March 27, 1943), No. 3 (1945–46; London, March 27, 1946), No. 4 (1977–78; Bath, May 20, 1979), and No. 5 (1990–91); 5 fanfares for Brass: No. 1 (Northampton, Sept. 21, 1943), No. 2 (St. Ives, June 6, 1953), No. 3 (St. Ives, June 6, 1953), No. 4, *Wolf Trap* (Vienna, Va., June 29, 1980), and No. 5 (1987); *4 Inventions* for Descant and Treble Recorders (London, Aug. 1, 1954); Sonata for 4 Horns (London, Dec. 20, 1955); *Praeludium* for Brass, Bells, and Percussion (London, Nov. 14, 1962); *In memoriam magistri* for Flute, Clarinet, and String Quartet (1971; London, June 17, 1972); *The Blue Guitar* for Guitar (1982–83; Pasadena, Calif., Nov. 9, 1983); *Prelude: Autumn* for Oboe and Piano (1991). **KEYBOARD: PIANO:** *Jockey to the Fair* (1929–30; Oxted, April 5, 1930); 4 sonatas: No. 1 (1936–38; London, Nov. 11, 1938; rev. 1942 and 1954), No. 2 (Edinburgh, Sept. 3, 1962), No. 3 (1972–73; Bath, May 26, 1973), and No. 4 (1984; Los Angeles, Jan. 14, 1985). **ORGAN:** *Preludio al Vespro di Monteverdi* (London, July 5, 1946). **VOCAL:** *A Child of Our Time*, oratorio for Soprano, Alto, Tenor, Bass, Chorus, and Orch., to a text by the composer about a Jewish boy (Henschel Grynsban) who, in 1938, assassinated a Nazi member of the German embassy in Paris (1939–41; London, March 19, 1944); *The Source* for Chorus (1942; London, July 17, 1943); *The Windhover* for Chorus (1942; London, July 17, 1943); *Boyhood's End*, cantata for Tenor and Piano, after W.H. Hudson (London, June 5, 1943); *Plebs angelica* for Double Chorus (1943–44; Canterbury, Sept. 16, 1944); *The Weeping Babe* for Soprano and Chorus (London, Dec. 24, 1944); *The Heart's Assurance*, song cycle for Voice and Piano, after Sidney Keyes and Alun Lewis (1950–51; London, May 7, 1951; arr. for Voice and Orch. by M. Bowen, 1990); *Dance, Clarion Air*, madrigal for 5 Voices, after Christopher Fry (1952; London, June 1, 1953); *Bonny at Morn* for Unison Voices and 3 Recorders (Trogen, Switzerland, April 1956); *4 Songs from the British Isles* for Chorus (1956; Royaumont, France, July 6, 1958); *Crown of the Year*, cantata for Chorus and Chamber Ensemble, after Christopher Fry (Bristol, July 25, 1958); *Lullaby* for Alto and Chorus (1959; London, Jan. 31, 1960); *Music* for Voices, Strings, and Piano (Tunbridge Wells, April 26, 1960; also for Voices and Piano); *Music for Words, Perhaps* for Narrator and Chamber Ensemble, after W.B. Yeats (London, June 8, 1960); *Magnificat and Nunc Dimittis* for Chorus and Organ (1961; Cambridge, March 13, 1962); *Songs for Achilles* for Tenor and Guitar (Aldeburgh, July 7, 1961); *Songs for Ariel* for Voice and Piano or Harpsichord or Chamber Ensemble (1962; London, Sept. 21, 1963); *The Vision of Saint Augustine* for Baritone, Chorus, and Orch. (1963–65; London, Jan. 19, 1966, Dietrich Fischer-Dieskau soloist, composer conducting); *The Shires Suite* for Chorus and Orch. (1965–70; Cheltenham, July 8, 1970, composer conducting); *Songs for Dov* for Tenor and Small Orch. (1969–70; Cardiff, Oct. 12, 1970); *The Mask of Time* for Soprano, Mezzo-soprano, Tenor, Baritone, Chorus, and Orch. (1980–82; Boston, April 5, 1984); *Byzantium* for Soprano and Orch. (1989–90; Chicago, April 11, 1991).

BIBL.: I. Kemp, ed., *M. T.: A Symposium on His 60th Birthday* (London, 1965); A. Milner, "The Music of M. T.," *Musical Quarterly* (Oct. 1974); M. Hurd, *T.* (London, 1978); E. White, *T. and His Operas* (London, 1979); D. Matthews, *M. T.: An Introductory Study* (London, 1980); M. Bowen, *M. T.* (London, 1982); A. Whittall, *The Music of Britten and T.: Studies in Themes and Techniques* (Cambridge, 1982; 2nd ed., 1990); R. Dyer, "Sir M. T.," *Ovation* (Dec. 1984); I. Kemp, *T.: the Composer and his Music* (London, 1984); P. Dennison, "Reminisence and Recomposition in T.," *Musical Times* (Jan. 1985); P. Driver, "T. at 80: A Personal Tribute," ibid.; G. Lewis, "T.: The Breath of Life; An Approach to Formal Structure," ibid.; N. John, ed., *Operas of M. T.* (London, 1985); G. Lewis, ed., *M. T. O. M.: A Celebration* (Tunbridge Wells, 1985); idem, "Behind T.'s Mask," *Musical Times* (Feb. 1988); M. Bowen, "Sir M. T.," *Musical America* (Nov. 1989); G. Lewis, "'New Year' in the New World," *Musical Times* (Nov. 1989); G. Theil, *M. T.: a Bio-Bibliography* (Westport, Conn., 1989); M. Scheppach, *Dramatic Parallels in M. T.'s Operas: Analytical Essays on the Musico-Dramatic Techniques* (Lewiston, N.Y., 1990).

Tischhauser, Franz, Swiss composer; b. Bern, March 28, 1921. He studied counterpoint and composition with Paul Müller and piano with Walter Lang and Rudolf Wittelsbach at the Zürich Cons. In 1951 he joined the staff of the Zürich Radio, and later served as director of its music dept. (1971–83).

WORKS: ORCH.: *Der Geburtstag der Infantin* (1941); Concertino for Piano and Small Orch. (1945); *Feierabendmusik* for Strings (1946); *Landpartie* for 2 Horns and Strings (1948); *Seldwyliana* for Orch. and Percussion (1960–61); *Omaggi a Mälzel* for 12 Strings (1963); *Mattinata* for 23 Winds (1965); *Konz-*

ertänze for 2 Orchs. (1967–68); *The Beggar's Concerto*, concerto for Clarinet and Strings (1975–76); *Dr. Bircher und Rossini* for Harpsichord and Strings (1978–79). **CHAMBER:** *Kassation* for 9 Instruments (1951); Octet for Clarinet, Horn, Bassoon, 2 Violins, Viola, Cello, and Double Bass (1953); *Die Bremer Stadtmusikanten* for Bassoon, Clarinet, Oboe, Flute, and Piano (1982–83); *Das Vierklaklavier* for 4 Clarinets (1984); *Beschallung der Stadt Kalau* for Horn Quartet and Wind Octet (1989); piano music. **VOCAL:** *Klein Irmchen*, 6 songs for Soprano and Piano (1937); *Duo Catulli carmina* for Tenor and Guitar (1949); *Das Nasobem* for Chorus (1950); *Amores* for Tenor, Trumpet, Percussion, and Stringed Instrument (1955–56); *Punctus contra punctum* for Tenor, Bass, and Small Orch. (1962); *Antiphonarium profanum* for 2 Men's Choruses (1966–67); *Eve's Meditation on Love* for Soprano, Tuba, and String Orch. (1970–71); *Die Hampeloper oder Joggeli söll ga Birli schüttle!* for 11 Vocalists, 3 Choral Groups, and Small Orch. (1985–86).

Tischler, Hans, distinguished Austrian-American musicologist; b. Vienna, Jan. 18, 1915. He studied piano with Paul Wittgenstein and Bertha Jahn-Beer, composition with Richard Stohr and Franz Schmidt, and musicology with Robert Lach, Robert Haas, and Egon Wellesz at the Univ. of Vienna (Ph.D., 1937, with the diss. *Die Harmonik in den Werken Gustav Mahlers*). He left Austria in 1938, settling in the U.S.; continued his musicological studies with Leo Schrade at Yale Univ. (Ph.D., 1942, with the diss. *The Motet in 13th-Century France*). He taught music history at West Virginia Wesleyan College (1945–47) and at Roosevelt Univ. in Chicago (1947–65). In 1965 he was appointed prof. of musicology at Indiana Univ. in Bloomington, where he remained until his retirement in 1985.

WRITINGS: *The Perceptive Music Listener* (N.Y., 1955); *Practical Harmony* (Boston, 1964); *A Structural Analysis of Mozart's Piano Concertos* (Brooklyn, N.Y., 1966); the Eng. ed. of Willi Apel's *History of Keyboard Music to 1700* (Bloomington, Ind., 1973); *A Medieval Motet Book* (N.Y., 1973); *The Montpellier Codex* (3 vols., Madison, Wis., 1978); *Chanter m'estuet: Songs of the Trouvères* (with S. Rosenberg; Bloomington, 1981); *The Earliest Motets: A Complete Comparative Edition* (New Haven, Conn., 1982); *The Earliest Motets: Their Style and Evolution* (Henryville, Pa., 1985); *The Parisian Two-Part Organa: A Complete Comparative Edition* (N.Y., 1987); *The Monophonic Songs in the Roman de Fauvel* (Toronto, 1988).

Tishchenko, Boris (Ivanovich), Russian composer and teacher; b. Leningrad, March 23, 1939. He was a student of Salmanov, Voloshinov, and Evlakhov at the Leningrad Cons. (graduated, 1962), and then of Shostakovich (1962–65). In 1965 he joined the faculty of the Leningrad Cons., where he was made an assoc. prof. in 1980 and a full prof. in 1986. In 1978 he was awarded the Glinka Prize and in 1987 was made a People's Artist of the U.S.S.R. Tishchenko's music is crafted in a masterly fashion in an advanced idiom without overstepping the bounds of tonality.

WORKS: DRAMATIC: *The 12*, ballet (1963); *Fly-bee*, ballet (1968); *The Stolen Sun*, opera (1968); *A Cockroach*, musical comedy (1968); *The Eclipse*, ballet (1974); incidental music. **ORCH.:** 2 violin concertos (1958, 1961); 7 syms. (1960, 1964, 1966, 1970, 1974, 1988, 1993); Piano Concerto (1962); 2 cello concertos (1963, 1969); Concerto for Flute, Piano, and Strings (1972); Harp Concerto (1977); *Concerto allamarcia* for 16 Performers (1989). **CHAMBER:** 5 string quartets (1957, 1959, 1969, 1980, 1984); 2 sonatas for Solo Violin (1957, 1976); 2 sonatas for Solo Cello (1960, 1979); *Capriccio* for Violin and Piano (1965); Piano Quintet (1985); *Dog Hearts*, novelettes for Chamber Ensemble (1988); Concerto for Clarinet and Piano Trio (1990). **KEYBOARD: PIANO:** 2 suites (1957, 1957); 9 sonatas (1957–92). **ORGAN:** *12 Inventions* (1964); *12 Portraits* (1992). **VOCAL:** *Lenin is Alive*, cantata (1959); *Requiem* (1966); *To My Brother* for Soprano, Flute, and Harp (1986); *The Will* for Soprano, Harp, and Organ (1986); *The Garden of Music*, cantata (1987); *The Chelom Wise Men* for Soprano, Bass, Violin, and Piano (1991); choral pieces.

Tisné, Antoine, French composer; b. Lourdes, Nov. 29, 1932. He studied at the Paris Cons. with Hugon, N. Gallon, Dufourcq, Milhaud, and Rivier, taking premiers prix in harmony, counterpoint, fugue, and composition. In 1962 he won the 2nd Grand Prix de Rome and the Lili Boulanger Prize. From 1967 to 1992 he served as an inspector of music for the French Ministry of Culture. He also was a prof. of composition and orchestration at the Univ. of Paris. In 1992 he became inspector of music for the municipal conservatoires of the City of Paris. Among his honors were the Grand Prix musical of the City of Paris (1979) and the prize for composers of the Soc. of Authors, Composers, and Editors of Music (1988). In his music, Tisné has adopted various contemporary techniques.

WORKS: DRAMATIC: *La Ramasseuse de sarments*, music theater (1980); *Point fixe*, ballet (1982); *Les Enfants du Ciel*, children's musical spectacle (1984); *Instant*, ballet (1985); *Le Chemin des bulles*, children's opera (1988); *Pour l'amour d'Alban*, opera (1993). **ORCH.:** 4 piano concertos (1959, 1961, 1962, 1992); 3 syms. (1959, 1963, 1994); *Chant d'amour et de mort* (1962); *A une ombre* (1962); *Mouvements symphoniques* (1963); Cello Concerto (1965); Concerto for Flute and Strings (1965); *Étude d'après Goya* (1966); *Cosmogonies* for 3 Orchs. (1967); *Séquences pour un rituel* for Strings (1968); Violin Concerto (1969); *Arches de lumière* (1972); *Ondes flamboyantes* for Strings (1973); *Stratégies* for 4 Brass Groups (1973); *Impacts* for Ondes Martenot and 2 String Orchs. (1973); *Dolmen II* for Percussion Ensemble (1978); *Reliefs irradiants de N.Y.* (1979); *Orbes de feu* (1981); *Temps spectral* for Piano, 2 Wind Ensembles, and Percussion (1982); *Mouvement concertant* for Piano, Brass, and Strings (1985); *La Tour* for Harmony Orch. (1987); *Hymne pour notre temps* for 15 Saxophones (1989); *Les Voiles de la nuit* (1991); *De la nuit à l'aurore* for Oboe and Strings (1991); *Célébration II* for Strings (1991). **CHAMBER:** 4 string quartets (1956, 1979, 1979, 1988); Cello Sonata (1960); Wind Quintet (1961); Violin Sonata (1963); *Visions des temps immémoriaux* for Ondes Martenot, Piano, and Percussion (1964); Flute Sonata (1964); Viola Sonata (1966); *Musique en trio* for Piano, Violin, and Cello (1967); *Strates colorées* for Oboe, Trumpet, Trombone, and Viola (1970); *Profils d'ombres* for Violin and Piano (1972); *Héraldiques* for Trumpet and Piano (1975); *Les Muses inquiétantes* for Wind Septet and Percussion (1975); *Isomorphies* for String Sextet (1975); *Musique en quatuor* for Flute, Clarinet, Violin, and Cello (1976); *Profils éclatés* for Organ and 5 Brass (1976); *Reflets d'un songe* for Flute, Viola, and Harp (1977); *Cyclades* for Ondes Martenot and Piano (1978); *Espaces irradiés* for Alto Saxophone and Piano (1978); *3 Études* for String Quartet (1978); *Iles de temps* for Ondes Martenot Sextet (1980); *Épisodes new-yorkais* for Flute, Clarinet, Violin, Cello, Piano, and Reciter ad libitum (1985); *Sérénade de la nuit* for Flute, Violin, and Viola (1990); *Les Voix de l'ombre* for Flute and String Trio (1991); *3 Études d'apres des toiles de Maurice Denis* for Flute and String Trio (1994). **KEYBOARD: PIANO:** Sonata (1964); *Soleils noirs* (1967); *Solars Vortices* (1970); *Bocéphal* for 2 Pianos (1982). **ORGAN:** *Luminescenes* (1974); *Alatamira* (1975); *Préludes* (1989); *Processional* (1993). **VOCAL:** *Cantique du printemps* for Soprano, Tenor, and Orch. (1960); *Chants d'espace I* and *II* for Children's Chorus (1974); *Célébration I* for 3 Choruses and 3 Orchs. (1975); *Ragas* for Reciter and Ondes Martenot Trio (1978); *Passage* for Soprano and Strings (1985); *L'Heure des hommes*, oratorio for Soprano, Men's Chorus, and Harmony Orch. (1985); *Le Fond du temps* for 12 Voices (1986); *Le Chant des yeux*, oratorio for Soprano, Chorus, and Orch. (1986); *Antienne pour l'au-delà* for Baritone and Strings (1987); *Psaume 138* and *57* for Vocal Ensemble, Chorus, and Organ (1989); *Maryam*, oratorio for Soloists, Chorus, and Orch. (1990); *Dans la lumière d'Orcival* for Chorus (1992); *Invocation* for Baritone and Orch. (1993).

BIBL.: D. Niemann, *A. T., ou composer c'est exister* (Paris, 1991).

Titta, Ruffo Cafiero. See **Ruffo, Titta.**

Titus, Alan (Wilkowski), American baritone; b. N.Y., Oct. 28, 1945. He was a student of Aksel Schiøtz at the Univ. of Colo. and of Hans Heinz at the Juilliard School of Music in N.Y., where he sang as Rossini's Figaro. In 1969 he made his formal operatic debut as Marcello in Washington, D.C. He first gained wide recognition when he created the role of the Celebrant in Bernstein's *Mass* at the inauguration of the Kennedy Center in Washington, D.C., on Sept. 8, 1971. After appearing with the N.Y. City Opera and the San Francisco Spring Opera in 1972, he made his European debut as Pelléas in Amsterdam in 1973. On March 20, 1976, he made his Metropolitan Opera debut in N.Y. as Harlekin in *Ariadne auf Naxos*. He made his first appearance at the Glyndebourne Festival in 1979 as Guglielmo. In 1984 he sang Don Giovanni at the Deutsche Oper am Rhein in Düsseldorf. In 1985 he appeared as Storch in *Intermezzo* in Santa Fe. In 1987 he sang Oliviero in *Capriccio* at the Maggio Musicale in Florence. He appeared as Creonte in Haydn's *Orfeo ed Euridice* at the Salzburg Festival in 1990, and that same year sang Storch in the Italian premiere of *Intermezzo* in Bologna. In 1992 he sang Donizetti's Duca d'Alba at the Spoleto Festival. In 1995 he appeared in the title role of Hindemith's *Mathis der Maler* at London's Covent Garden.

Titus, Hiram, American pianist and composer; b. Minneapolis, Jan. 28, 1947. He studied with Emil Dananberg (piano) and Richard Hoffman (composition) at Oberlin (Ohio) College (B.A., 1958), with Guy Duckworth (piano) and Dominick Argento (composition) (1957–63), and with Walter Hartley in Interlochen, Mich. (summers, 1963–64). In addition to concert and stage works, he composed a number of scores for television and theater productions, winning DramaLogue awards for music (1979, 1980). Among his compositions are *Bach Abashed* for Chamber Ensemble (1968), the opera *Rosina* (Minneapolis, 1980), Guitar Concerto (1984), and *The Sand Hills*, oratorio for Soloists, Men's Chorus, Tape, and Ensemble (Los Angeles, 1987).

Tocchi, Gian Luca, Italian composer; b. Perugia, Jan. 10, 1901; d. Rome, Sept. 14, 1992. He studied with Respighi (composition) and Molinari (conducting) at the Cons. di Santa Cecilia in Rome, and in 1930 he won the composition prize of the Governatorato di Roma. After appearances as a conductor (1935–45), he was active as a composer, writer, and producer with the Italian radio (from 1952); he also taught composition at the Accademia di Santa Cecilia in Rome (1959–71).

WORKS: ORCH.: *Danza sull'aia* (1927); *Il destino*, symphonic poem (1930); *Rapsodia romantica* (1931); *Record* (1935); Concerto for 3 Saxophones, 2 Pianos, and Orch. (1935); *Film* (1936); *Luna Park* (1937); *3 Pieces* (1938); *Divertimento con antiche musiche* (1939); *Quadro sonore* (1941); *Omaggi* for Harpsichord and Strings (1961). **CHAMBER:** *Arlecchino* for 6 Instruments (1937); Quartet; *Arie e danze tedesche* for Harp, Flute, and Viola; *Canzone, notturno, e ballo* for Harp, Flute, and Viola (1945); 12 studies for Harp; piano pieces. **OTHER:** Incidental music to plays; film scores; choral works; songs.

Tocco, James, American pianist and teacher; b. Detroit, Sept. 21, 1943. He began piano lessons when he was 6 and made his debut as soloist in Beethoven's 2nd Piano Concerto at age 12. Following training at the Salzburg Mozarteum and in Paris with Tagliaferro, he completed his studies in N.Y. with Arrau. In 1973 he won 1st prize in the ARD Competition in Munich. In 1975 he won critical accolades when he played Tchaikovsky's 1st Piano Concerto at the Vienna Festival. In subsequent years, he toured internationally as a soloist with orchs., as a recitalist, and as a chamber music artist. In 1977 he joined the faculty of the Indiana Univ. School of Music in Bloomington. In 1991 he became eminent scholar and artist-in-residence at the Univ. of Cincinnati College-Cons. of Music, and he also served as prof. of piano at the Lübeck Hochschule für Musik. Tocco maintains an extraordinarily diversified repertoire, ranging from Bach and Handel to Berg and Bernstein. He also performs rarely heard scores from the past and present, including transcriptions.

Toch, Ernst, eminent Austrian-born American composer and teacher; b. Vienna, Dec. 7, 1887; d. Los Angeles, Oct. 1, 1964. His father was a Jewish dealer in unprocessed leather, and there was no musical strain in the family; Toch began playing piano without a teacher in his grandmother's pawnshop; he learned musical notation from a local violinist, and then copied Mozart's string quartets for practice; using them as a model, he began to compose string quartets and other pieces of chamber music; at the age of 17, he had one of them, his 6th String Quartet, op. 12 (1905), performed by the famous Rosé Quartet in Vienna. From 1906 to 1909 he studied medicine at the Univ. of Vienna. In 1909 he won the prestigious Mozart Prize and a scholarship to study at the Frankfurt am Main Cons., where he studied piano with Willy Rehberg and composition with Iwan Knorr. In 1910 he was awarded the Mendelssohn Prize; also won 4 times in succession the Austrian State Prize. In 1913 he was appointed instructor in piano at Zuschneid's Hochschule für Musik in Mannheim. From 1914 to 1918 he served in the Austrian army during World War I. After the Armistice he returned to Mannheim, resumed his musical career, and became active in the modern movement, soon attaining, along with Hindemith, Krenek, and others, a prominent position in the new German school of composition. He also completed his education at the Univ. of Heidelberg (Ph.D., 1921, with the diss. *Beiträge zur Stilkunde der Melodie*; publ. in Berlin, 1923, as *Melodielehre*). In 1929 he went to Berlin, where he established himself as a pianist, composer, and teacher of composition. In 1932 he made an American tour as a pianist playing his own works; he returned to Berlin, but with the advent of the Nazi regime was forced to leave Germany in 1933. He went to Paris, then to London, and in 1935 emigrated to the U.S.; gave lectures on music at the New School for Social Research in N.Y.; in 1936, moved to Hollywood, where he wrote music for films. He became a naturalized American citizen on July 26, 1940. In 1940–41 he taught composition at the Univ. of Southern Calif. in Los Angeles; subsequently taught privately; among his students were many, who, like Andre Previn, became well-known composers in their own right. From 1950 until his death, Toch traveled frequently and lived in Vienna, Zürich, the MacDowell Colony in New Hampshire, and Santa Monica, Calif.

Toch's music is rooted in the tradition of the German and Austrian Romantic movement of the 19th century, but his study of the classics made him aware of the paramount importance of formal logic in the development of thematic ideas. His early works consist mostly of chamber music and pieces for piano solo; following the zeitgeist during his German period, he wrote several pieces for the stage in the light manner of sophisticated entertainment; he also composed effective piano works of a virtuoso quality, which enjoyed considerable popularity among pianists of the time. Toch possessed a fine wit and a sense of exploration; his *Geographical Fugue* for speaking chorus, articulating in syllabic counterpoint the names of exotic places on earth, became a classic of its genre. It was not until 1950 that Toch wrote his first full-fledged sym., but from that time on, until he died of stomach cancer, he composed fully 7 syms., plus sinfoniettas for Wind and String Orch. He was greatly interested in new techniques; the theme of his last String Quartet (No. 13, 1953) is based on a 12-tone row. In the score of his 3rd Sym. he introduced an optional instrument, the Hisser, a tank of carbon dioxide that produced a hissing sound through a valve.

Among the several honors Toch received were the Pulitzer Prize in Music for his 3rd Sym. (1956), membership in the National Inst. of Arts and Letters (1957), and the Cross of Honor for Sciences and Art from the Austrian government (1963). An Ernst Toch Archive was founded at the Univ. of Calif., Los Angeles, in 1966, serving as a depository for his MSS.

WORKS: DRAMATIC: OPERAS: *Wegwende* (1925; unfinished; sketches destroyed); *Die Prinzessin auf der Erbse* (Baden-Baden, July 17, 1927); *Der Facher* (Königsberg, June 8, 1930); *The Last Tale* (1960–62). **FILM SCORES:** *Peter Ibbetson* (1935); *Outcast* (1937); *The Cat and the Canary* (1939); *Dr. Cyclops* (1940); *The Ghost Breakers* (1940); *Ladies in Retirement* (1941); *First Comes Courage* (1943); *None Shall Escape* (1944); *Address Unknown* (1944); *The Unseen* (1945). Also incidental music for stage and radio plays.

ORCH.: *Scherzo* (1904); Piano Concerto (1904; not extant); *Phantastische Nachtmusik* (1920; Mannheim, March 22, 1921); *Tanz-Suite* for Chamber Orch. (1923); *5 Pieces* for Chamber Orch. (1924); Concerto for Cello and Small Orch. (1924; Kiel, June 17, 1925); Piano Concerto (Düsseldorf, Oct. 8, 1926; Gieseking, soloist); *Spiel für Blasorchester* (Donaueschingen, July 24, 1926); *Narziss* (1927; not extant); *Gewitter* (1927; not extant); *Komödie für Orchester* (Berlin, Nov. 13, 1927); *Vorspiel zu einem Märchen* (for the opera *Die Prinzessin auf der Erbse*; 1927); *Fanal* for Organ and Orch. (1928); *Bunte Suite* (1928; Frankfurt am Main, Feb. 22, 1929); *Kleine Theater-Suite* (1930; Berlin, Feb. 9, 1931); *Tragische Musik* (1931; not extant); *2 kultische Stücke* (1931; not extant); Sym. for Piano and Orch. (Piano Concerto No. 2, 1932; London, Aug. 20, 1934); *Miniature Overture* for Winds (1932); *Variations on Mozart's Unser dummer Pöbel meint* (1933); *Big Ben*, variation fantasy on the Westminster Chimes (Cambridge, Mass., Dec. 20, 1934; rev. 1955); *Pinocchio*, "a merry overture" (1935; Los Angeles, Dec. 10, 1936); *Musical Short Story* (1936; not extant); *Orchids* (1936; not extant); *The Idle Stroller*, suite (1938); "The Covenant," 6th movement of 7-movement, collaborative *Genesis Suite* (Los Angeles, Nov. 18, 1945; not extant); *Hyperion*, dramatic prelude after Keats (1947; Cleveland, Jan. 8, 1948); 7 syms.: No. 1 (1949–50; Vienna, Dec. 20, 1950), No. 2, dedicated to Albert Schweitzer (1950–51; Vienna, Jan. 11, 1952), No. 3 (Pittsburgh, Dec. 2, 1955), No. 4 (Minneapolis, Nov. 22, 1957), No. 5, *Jephta, Rhapsodic Poem* (1961–62; Boston, March 13, 1964), No. 6 (1963; Zürich Radio, Jan. 22, 1967), and No. 7 (1964; Bavarian Radio, 1967); *Circus Overture* (1953; Chicago, July 8, 1954); *Notturno* (1953; Louisville, Jan. 2, 1954); *Peter Pan*, fairy tale (Seattle, Feb. 13, 1956); *Epilogue* (1959); *Intermezzo* (1959); *Short Story* (1961); *Capriccio* (1963); *Puppetshow* (1963); *The Enamoured Harlequin* (1963); *Sinfonietta* for Strings (1964; Philadelphia, Feb. 13, 1967); Theme with Variations "Muss i denn zum Stadle hinaus" (1964).

CHAMBER: 13 string quartets: Nos. 1–5 (1902–03; not extant), No. 6 (1905), No. 7 (1908), No. 8 (1910), No. 9 (1919), No. 10, on "BASS" (1921), No. 11 (1924), No. 12 (1946), and No. 13 (1953); *Kammersymphonie* (1906); Duos for Violins (1909; for open strings only in the pupil's part); *Serenade* for 3 Violins (1911); 2 violin sonatas (1913, 1928); *"Spitzweg" Serenade* for 2 Violins and Viola (1916): *Tanz Suite* for Flute, Clarinet, Violin, Viola, Bass, and Percussion (1923; excerpts choreographed as *Der Wald*, Mannheim, Nov. 19, 1923; Münster, Oct. 29, 1924); *2 Divertimenti* for String Duos (1926); *Studie* for Mechanical Organ (1927); Cello Sonata (1929); *2 Études* for Cello (1930); String Trio (1936); Piano Quintet (1938); *Dedication* for String Quartet or String Orch. (1948); *Adagio elegiaco* for Clarinet and Piano (1950); *5 Pieces* for Flute, Oboe, Clarinet, Bassoon, 2 Horns, and Percussion (1959); *Sonatinetta* for Flute, Clarinet, and Bassoon (1959); *3 Impromptus* for Solo Violin, Solo Viola, and Solo Cello (1963); *Sinfonietta* for Winds and Percussion (1964; Zürich Radio, Nov. 11, 1967); Quartet for Oboe, Clarinet, Bassoon, and Viola (1964). **PIANO:** *Melodische Skizzen* (1903); *3 Preludes* (1903); *Impromptu* (1904; not extant); *Capriccio* (1905; not extant); 3 sonatas (1905, not extant; 1905, not extant; 1928); *Stammbuchverse* (1905); *Begegnung* (1908); *Reminiszenzen* (1909); *4 Klavierstücke* (1914; not extant); *Canon* (1914); *3 Burlesken* (1923; includes the popular *Der Jongleur*, publ. separately); *3 Klavierstücke* (1924); *5 Capriccetti* (1925); *3 Originalstücke für das Welte-Mignon Klavier* (1926); *Tanz- und Spielstücke* (1926?); *Kleinstadtbilder* (1929); *Fünfmal Zehn Etüden*, 50 études (1931); *Profiles* (1946); *Ideas* (1946); *Diversions* (1956); *Sonatinetta* (1956); *3 Little Dances* (1961); *Reflections*, 5 pieces (1961); Sonata for Piano, 4-hands (1962).

VOCAL: *An mein Vaterland*, sym. for Soprano, Mixed and Boy's Choruses, Orch., and Organ (1913); *Die chinesische Flöte*, chamber sym. for Soprano and 14 Solo Instruments (1921; Frankfurt am Main, June 24, 1923; rev. 1949); 9 songs for Soprano and Piano (1926); *Der Tierkreis* for Chorus (1930); *Das Wasser*, cantata for Tenor, Baritone, Narrator, Flute, Trumpet, Percussion, and Strings (Berlin, June 18, 1930); *Gesprochene Musik* for Speaking Chorus (Berlin, June 17, 1930; includes the famous *Fuge aus der Geographie*, publ. separately in Eng. and Ger. eds.); *Music for Orchestra and Baritone Solo on Poems by Rilke* (1931); *Cantata of the Bitter Herbs* for Soloists, Narrator, and Chorus (1938); *Poems to Martha* for Voice and String Quintet (1942); *The Inner Circle*, 6 choruses (1947–53); *There Is a Season for Everything* for Soprano, Flute, Clarinet, Violin, and Cello, after Ecclesiastes (1953); *Vanity of Vanities, All Is Vanity* for Soprano, Tenor, Flute, Clarinet, Violin, and Cello, after Ecclesiastes (1954); *Phantoms* for Solo Voices and Chorus (1958); *Lange schon haben meine Freunde versucht* for Soprano and Baritone (1958); *Song of Myself* for Chorus, after Whitman (1961); *Valse* for Speaking Chorus (1961; in separate Eng. and German eds.); folk song arrangements.

WRITINGS: *The Shaping Forces in Music* (N.Y., 1948; new ed. by L. Weschler, 1977); M. Hood, ed., *Placed as a Link in this Chain: A Medley of Observations by Ernst Toch* (Los Angeles, 1971).

BIBL.: E. Beninger, "Pianistische Probleme, im Anschluss an die Klavierwerke von E. T.," *Melos* (1928); P. Pisk, "E. T.," *Musical Quarterly* (Oct. 1938); C. Johnson, *The Unpublished Works of E. T.* (diss., Univ. of Calif., Los Angeles, 1973); L. Weschler, *E. T., 1887–1964: A Biographical Essay Ten Years after His Passing* (Los Angeles, 1974); B. Barclay and M. Cole, "The T. and Zeisl Archives at UCLA," *Notes*, XXXV (1978–79); J. Diane, *The Musical Migration and E. T.* (Ames, Iowa, 1989).

Toczyska, Stefania, Polish mezzo-soprano; b. Gdańsk, Feb. 19, 1943. She was a pupil of Barbara Iglikovska at the Gdańsk Cons. She took prizes in competitions in Toulouse (1972), Paris (1973), and s'Hertogenbosch (1974). In 1973 she made her operatic debut as Carmen at the Gdańsk Opera, and then sang throughout Poland. In 1977 she made her Western European operatic debut as Amneris with the Basel Opera. Later that year she made her first appearance at the Vienna State Opera as Ulrica, and returned there to sing Carmen, Azucena, Eboli, and Preziosilla. In 1979 she sang Eboli at the Bavarian State Opera in Munich and at the Hamburg State Opera, and then appeared as Laura in *La Gioconda* at the San Francisco Opera. She made her Covent Garden debut in London in 1983 as Azucena and in 1986 made her first appearance at the Chicago Lyric Opera as Giovanna Seymour in *Anna Bolena*. In 1987 she sang Adalgisa at the Houston Grand Opera and Venus in *Tannhäuser* at the Barcelona Opera. She made her Metropolitan Opera debut in N.Y. as Laura in *La Gioconda* in 1989. In 1990 she sang at the Caracalla Festival in Rome. In 1992 she appeared as Massenet's Dulcinée in Toulouse. In addition to her active operatic career, she has also toured widely as a concert artist.

Toda, Kunio (actually, **Morikuni**), Japanese composer and teacher; b. Tokyo, Aug. 11, 1915. He studied at the Univ. of Heidelberg (1938–39); following diplomatic service in Moscow (1939–41), he returned to Tokyo to study with Saburo Moroi. He was sent to Indochina in 1944; when World War II ended in 1945, he was detained until 1948. Upon his return to Tokyo, he became active in contemporary-music circles; introduced 12-note serialism to his homeland. He remained active as a diplomat until 1964; taught at the Toho Gakuen School of Music (from 1955), remaining on its faculty as a prof. when it became a college in 1961; also was director and a prof. at the Senzolku Gakuen Academy of Music (from 1975); he retired in 1988 from the latter, but continued as a guest prof. until 1991.

WORKS: DRAMATIC: OPERAS: *Akemi* (Tokyo, 1956); *Kyara monogatari* (History of the City of Kyara; Tokyo, 1973). **BALLETS:** *Atorie no Salome* (Salome in Studio; Tokyo, Nov. 23, 1951); *Akai tenmaku* or *Le Cirque rouge* (Tokyo, Nov. 4, 1953); *Dokutsu* (The Cave; Tokyo, Nov. 7, 1954); *Miranda* (Tokyo, Oct. 26, 1968). **SCENIC-ORATORIO MYSTERY:** *Shito Paolo* (St. Paul; 1961–64; concert perf., Tokyo, Feb. 15, 1973). **ORCH.:** *Overture* (1943); *Densetsu* (Legend), symphonic fantasy (1944); 2 piano concertos (1944, 1955); *Passacaglia and Fugue* (1949); *Overtura buffa* (1950); Sym. (1956); *Concerto grosso* for 6 Solo Instruments and Orch. (Tokyo, Jan. 25, 1968). **CHAMBER:** Piano Trio (1947); *Amoroso* for Violin and Piano (1951); Violin

Sonata (1957; rev. 1959); *Music* for 2 Koto (1959); Bassoon Sonata (1966); *Introduzione-Movimento-Rapido* for String Quartet, Quintet, or Ensemble (1994). **PIANO:** *3 intermezzi* (1942); *Koto no ne ni yoru gensōkyoku* (Fantasy on the Sound of the Koto; 1965); Sonatina (1966); *Yottsu no yuganda kyoku* or *4 pezzi deformati* (1968). **VOCAL:** *Jochu no Anna* (Anna la Bonne), monodrama for Soprano, 2 Violas, and Tape (Tokyo, Nov. 17, 1978); *Kesa to Morito* (Kesa and Morito), dramatic cantata for Soprano, Baritone, and String Quintet (Tokyo, Nov. 16, 1979); *Toraware no O'Shichi* (O'Shichi, the Prisoner), monocantata for Soprano, Flute, and Marimba (Tokyo, Sept. 16, 1981); *Ô-kawa no Uta* (Song of River) for Mezzo-soprano, Baritone, and Orch. (Tokyo, March 6, 1989); choruses; songs. **ELECTRONIC:** *Passacaglia and Fugue* (Tokyo, Aug. 5, 1994).

Toduţă, Sigismund, Romanian composer and teacher; b. Simeria, May 30, 1908; d. Cluj, July 3, 1991. He studied with Negrea at the Cluj Cons. (1931–33), and later at the Accademia di Santa Cecilia in Rome (1936–38) with Pizzetti (composition) and Casella (piano); also took courses in musicology at the Pontificio Istituto di Musica Sacra in Rome (Ph.D., 1938, with a diss. on G.F. Anerio). In 1946 he was appointed to the faculty of the Cluj Cons. (he was its director from 1962 to 1964); in 1971 he became managing director of the Cluj State Phil. His music was distinguished by a flowing Romantic melody in large rhapsodic sonorities.

WORKS: OPERA: *Meşterul Manole* (Master-builder Manole; 1943–47; as an opera-oratorio, 1977–82; Cluj, Oct. 1, 1985). **ORCH.:** *Egloga* (1933); *Symphonic Variations* (1940); Piano Concerto (1943); 4 concertos for Strings (1951; 1972–73; 1974; 1980); *Divertisement* for Strings (1951); 5 syms.: No. 1 (1954), No. 2, "in memoria lui George Enesco" (1954–56), No. 3, *Ovidiu* (1957), No. 4 (1961), and No. 5 (1963–76; Cluj, Feb. 7, 1976); *Uvertură festivă* (1959); *Simfonieta* (1966; Cluj, Jan. 21, 1977); Concerto for Winds and Percussion (1975–76; Cluj, Sept. 4, 1976); Concerto for Flute and Strings (Sibiu, April 3, 1984); *Simfonia B—A—C—H* (1984); Concerto for Oboe and Strings (1986). **CHAMBER:** Cello Sonata (1952); Flute Sonata (1952); Violin Sonata (1953); Oboe Sonata (1956); *Ioko,* 4 pieces for Harp (1975); *6 Pieces* for Oboe (1981); piano pieces, including *Passacaglia* (1943), Sonatina (1950), *Preludiu, Coral, Toccata* (1973–75), and *3 Pieces* (1980). **VOCAL:** 3 oratorios: *Mioriţa* (1958–68; Bucharest, Oct. 7, 1968), *Balada steagului* (1961), and *Pe urmele lui Horea* (1976–78; Cluj, Dec. 2, 1978); choruses; songs.

Toebosch, Louis, Dutch organist, conductor, teacher, and composer; b. Maastricht, March 18, 1916. He studied at the School of Church Music in Utrecht, the Music Lyceum in Maastricht, and then the Royal Cons. in Liège (1934–39). He was active as a church organist in Breda (1940–65); conducted the Tilburg Sym. Orch. (1946–52); was founder-conductor of the Orlando di Lasso Choir (from 1953). He taught at the conservatories of Tilburg and Maastricht (1944–65); was director of the Brabant Cons. (1965–74). His music combines the polyphonic style of the Renaissance with modern techniques; he applies the 12-tone method of compostion in both secular and sacred music.

WORKS: ORCH.: 2 suites (1939, 1948); *Allegro* for Organ and Orch. (1941); *Tema con variazioni* (1945); *Het Lied van Hertog Jan* (1949); *Carnavalsige Ouverture* (1955); *Concertante Ouverture* (1956); *Variaties* (1957); *Feestelijke Ouverture* (1960); Sinfonietta No. 2 (1961); *Agena* (1966); *Changements* for Organ and Orch. (1968); Organ Concerto (1983). **CHAMBER:** *Sarabande en allegro* for Wind Quintet (1959); *The King's Quartet* for String Quartet (1968); *Toccata, aria e finale* for Viola (1969); *Bilingua* for Recorder and Harpsichord (1977); *Muziek voor 3 barokinstrumenten* for Recorder, Viola da Gamba, and Harpsichord (1980). **KEYBOARD: PIANO:** Sonata (1947); *Suite polyphonica* for 2 Pianos (1962); *Pasticcio di Rofena* for Piano, 4-hands (1973); *Zes speelstukken* for 3 Pianos (1983). **ORGAN:** *Tryptique* (1939; rev. 1980); *Praeludium et Fuga super Te Deum laudamus* (1954); *2 postludia* (1964); *Toccana* (1973); *Orgelspiegel* (1975); *3 Movements* (1986). **VOCAL:** *Cantatorium carnevale* for Tenor, Baritone, and Orch. (1957); *Philippica-moderata* for Solo Voices, Chorus, and Orch. (1963); *De vier seizoenen,* cantata-oratorio for Chorus and Orch. (1981); *Cantata alfabetica* for Chorus and Organ (1982).

BIBL.: W. Paap, "L. T.," *Sonorum speculum,* No. 21 (1964).

Togi, Suenobu, Japanese performer and ethnomusicologist; b. Tokyo, Jan. 1, 1932. He attended the Imperial Court Music School in Tokyo (1943–52), where he learned Japanese court music and dance as well as Western music (cello and violin); also studied Western music at the Tokyo Univ. of Fine Arts (1950–52). He taught and performed in the Imperial Court Music Dept. in both the Japanese Court Orch. (gagaku and bugaku) and the Imperial Court Orch. (Western music) from 1952 to 1961; then went to the U.S., where he taught Japanese court music and dance at the Univ. of Calif., Los Angeles (1961). He returned to Tokyo in 1964; in 1968, joined the faculty at the Univ. of Calif., Los Angeles; also gave concerts and lectures throughout the U.S. Togi is the only former court musician teaching gagaku outside of Japan. He employs the strictest court tradition (which determines gagaku practice throughout Japan); revisited Tokyo in 1973 and 1985 to remain current with changes in Imperial practice.

Togni, Camillo, Italian composer; b. Brescia, Oct. 18, 1922; d. there, Nov. 27, 1993. He received training from Casella in Siena and Rome (1939–42), attended the Parma Cons. (diploma, 1946), and studied philosophy at the Univ. of Padua (graduated, 1948). After composing in a neo-Classical vein, Togni embraced the 12-tone method.

WORKS: ORCH.: *Variations* for Piano and Orch. (1946); *Fantasia concertante* for Flute and Strings (1957; Cologne Radio, March 25, 1958); *Some Other Where* (RAI, Naples, June 16, 1977). **CHAMBER:** *Aubade* for 6 Instruments (Rome, April 22, 1965); *Cinque pezzi* for Flute and Guitar (1975–76; RAI, Naples, June 16, 1976); *Für Herbert* for 2 Violins, Viola, and Harpsichord (Milan, Nov. 21, 1976); Trio for Violin, Viola, and Cello (Naples, June 15, 1978); *Quasi una serenata* for Guitar (Spoleto, July 8, 1979); *Due preludi* for Piccolo (Perugia, Aug. 20, 1980); *Du bleicher Geselle* for Chamber Group (1989); *Per Maila* for Piano or Flute and Piano (1992); *Fantasia* for Harp (1993); many piano pieces. **VOCAL:** *Psalmus CXXVII* for Solo Voices, Violin, Viola, and Cello (Brussels, June 24, 1950); *Ricercar* for Baritone and 5 Instruments (1953); *Helian di Trakl* for Voice and Piano (1955; also for Soprano and Chamber Orch., Palermo, May 24, 1961); *Gesang zur Nacht* for Soprano and Chamber Orch. (Venice, April 11, 1962); *Rondeaux per 10* for Soprano and 9 Instruments (1963; Madrid, June 24, 1965); *Preludes et rondeaux* for Soprano and Harpsichord (1963–64; Florence, April 17, 1964); *Sei notturni* for Contralto, Clarinet, Violin, and 2 Pianos (1965; Rome, March 4, 1966); *Tre pezzi* for Chorus and Orch. (Venice, Sept. 17, 1972); *Tre duetti* for Soprano and Flute (1977–80); *La Guirlande de Blois* for Soprano and Piano (Naples, June 15, 1978); *Les Feuilles Amères* for Soprano (RAI, Milan, Sept. 30, 1989). **ELECTRONIC:** *Recitativo* (Venice, April 15, 1962).

Tokatyan, Armand, Bulgarian tenor of Armenian descent; b. Plovdiv, Feb. 12, 1896; d. Pasadena, Calif., June 12, 1960. He was educated in Alexandria, Egypt; then studied voice with Cairone in Milan and Wolf in Vienna. He made his operatic debut in Milan in 1921; then went to the U.S., where he toured with the Scotti Opera Co. He made his debut at the Metropolitan Opera in N.Y. on Nov. 19, 1922, as Turiddu in a concert performance of *Cavalleria rusticana,* and remained a member of the company, with interruptions, until 1946. He also made appearances in London, Berlin, and Vienna.

Toldrá, Eduardo, Catalan violinist, conductor, and composer; b. Villanueva y Geltru, Catalonia, April 7, 1895; d. Barcelona, May 31, 1962. He studied violin and composition at Barcelona's municipal music school. He made his debut as a soloist at the Barcelona Ateneo (1912), then was founder-1st violinist of the Quartet Renaixement (1912–21). In 1921 he became a prof. of violin at Barcelona's municipal music school; in 1944, was appointed conductor of the Municipal Orch. He composed the comic opera *El giravolt de Maig* (Barcelona, 1928), orch. pieces, chamber music, and songs.

BIBL.: M. Capdevila Massana, *E. T.* (Barcelona, 1964; 2nd ed., rev., 1972).

Tollefsen, Carl H(enry), English-American violinist and teacher; b. Hull, Aug. 15, 1882; d. N.Y., Dec. 10, 1963. He went to N.Y. as a youth, and studied at the National Cons. (1898–1902) and at the Inst. of Musical Art (1906–08), where his teachers were Franz Kneisel (violin), and Goetschius and Rubin Goldmark (composition). He was a violinist in various orchs. in N.Y. On Aug. 7, 1907, he married the pianist Augusta Schnabel (b. Boise, Idaho, Jan. 5, 1885; d. N.Y., April 9, 1955), and formed the Tollefsen Trio with her and with Paul Kefer in 1909; this trio toured the U.S. for more than 30 years (succeeding cellists were M. Penha, P. Gruppe, R. Thrane, and W. Durieux). In 1939 he founded the Brooklyn Chamber Music Soc. He formed a large collection of autographs of famous musicians and MS biographies (including the biographical archives gathered by Alfred Remy, editor of the 3rd ed. of *Baker's Biographical Dictionary of Musicians*). In 1947 the cellist Yuri Bilstin bequeathed to him a collection of old instruments. His entire collection was turned over to the Southern Illinois Univ. Lovejoy Library at Edwardsville in 1969.

Tolonen, Jouko (Paavo Kalervo), Finnish musicologist and composer; b. Porvoo, Nov. 2, 1912; d. Turku, July 23, 1986. He studied piano with Linko, composition with Krohn, Madetoja, and Fougestedt, and conducting in Helsinki; pursued training in musicology at the Univ. there (Ph.D., 1969). He was director of the music dept. of the Finnish Broadcasting Co. (1946–55) and general director of the Finnish National Opera (1956–60); taught at the Sibelius Academy in Helsinki (1960–66) and at the Univ. of Turku (from 1965), where he was prof. of musicology (1972–77). He composed *Andante and Rondo alla burla* for Orch. (1948); *Andante* for Piano and Strings (1950); Sym. (1952); *3 Arabesques* for Orch. (1953); *Les Fanfares* for Brass (1970); incidental music for plays and films; vocal pieces.

Tolstoy, Dmitri, Russian composer, son of the writer Alexei Tolstoy; b. Berlin, Jan. 20, 1923. He went to Russia with his father after the latter's temporary emigration; studied at the Leningrad Cons., graduating in 1947; took courses in composition with Shebalin in Moscow and Shostakovich in Leningrad.

WORKS: 2 operas: *Masquerade* (1955; Moscow, Jan. 17, 1956) and *Mariuta* (Perm, Dec. 30, 1960); *Poem about Leningrad* for Orch. (1953); piano pieces; cantatas; songs.

Tomášek, Jaroslav, Czech composer; b. Koryčany, Moravia, April 10, 1896; d. Prague, Nov. 26, 1970. He studied music with Novák; also attended a course in musicology at the Univ. of Prague. He composed mostly in small forms; wrote 2 song cycles: *To Woman* for High Voice (1919–20; with Orch., 1944–46) and *Grief* for Tenor, Soprano, Bass, and Orch. (1958–59); *Rondo* for Piano, left hand (1924); Piano Sonata for left hand (1925); 2 string quartets; *Symphonic Rondo* for Piano and Orch. (1962); songs. His wife, Jaromíra Tomášková-Nováková (b. Jaroměř, May 23, 1892; d. Prague, April 25, 1957), was a soprano; she taught singing at the Prague Cons. (from 1920).

Tomasi, Henri (Frédien), French composer; b. Marseilles, Aug. 17, 1901; d. Paris, Jan. 13, 1971. He studied with Paul Vidal at the Paris Cons.; won the 2nd Grand Prix de Rome for his cantata *Coriolan* (1927). He served in the French army (1939–40). Tomasi was awarded the Grand Prix de Musique Française in 1952. His music is marked by impressionistic colors; he was particularly attracted to exotic subjects, depicting in fine instrumental colors scenes in Corsica, Cambodia, Laos, Sahara, Tahiti, etc. He also wrote music inspired by Gregorian chant and medieval religious songs. During his last period he was motivated in his music by political events, and wrote pieces in homage to the Third World and Vietnam.

WORKS: DRAMATIC: OPERAS: *Miguel de Manâra* (1942; Munich, March 29, 1956); *L'Altantide* (1952; Mulhouse, Feb. 26, 1954); *La triomphe de Jeanne* (1955; Rouen, 1956); *Sampiero Corso* (Bordeaux, May 1956); *Il Poverello* (1957); *Le silence de la mer* (1959); *Ulysse* (1961); *L'élixir du révérend père Gaucher* (1962). **BALLETS:** *La Grisi* (Paris, Oct. 7, 1935); *La Rosière de village* (Paris, May 26, 1936); *Les Santons* (Paris, Nov. 18, 1938); *La Féerie cambodgienne* (Marseilles, Jan. 31, 1952); *Les Folies mazarguaises* (Marseilles, Oct. 5, 1953); *Noces de cendre* (Strasbourg, Jan. 19, 1954); *Les Barbaresques* (Nice, 1960); *Nana*, after Émile Zola (1962). **CHOREOGRAPHIC POEM:** *Dassine, sultane du Hoggar* for 2 Speakers, Chorus, and Orch. (1959). **ORCH.:** *Chants de Cyrnos*, symphonic poem (Paris, Nov. 30, 1929); *Mélodies corses* (1931); *Vocero*, symphonic poem (Paris, Feb. 5, 1933); *Scènes municipales* (1933); *Tam-Tam*, symphonic poem (Paris, June 13, 1933); *Chants laotiens* (1934); *2 danses cambodgiennes* (1934); *Chant des geishas* (1936); *Impressions sahariennes* (1938); Sym. (Paris, May 4, 1943); *Concert asiatique* for Percussion and Orch. (1939); Flute Concerto (1947); Trumpet Concerto (1949); Viola Concerto (1951); Saxophone Concerto (1951); Horn Concerto (1955); Clarinet Concerto (1956); Trombone Concerto (1956); Bassoon Concerto (1958); Oboe Concerto (1958); *Jabadao*, symphonic poem (Paris, Jan. 10, 1960); Violin Concerto (1962); *Taïtienne de Gauguin* (1963); *Symphonie du tiers monde* (Paris, Feb. 18, 1968); *Chant pour le Vietnam*, symphonic poem for Wind Band and Percussion (Paris, Dec. 7, 1969); Cello Concerto (1970). **CHAMBER:** *Concerto champêtre* for Oboe, Clarinet, and Bassoon (1939); String Trio (1943); *Divertimento Corsica* for Woodwind Trio (1952); Wind Quintet (1952); *Danseuses de Degas* for Harp and String Quartet (1964); *Concerto de printemps* for Flute, Strings, and Percussion (1965); *La Moresca* for 8 Wind Instruments (1965); *Sonatine attique* for Clarinet (1966); many piano pieces. **VOCAL:** Song cycles.

Tómasson, Jónas, Icelandic composer, teacher, and conductor; b. Ísafjördur, Nov. 21, 1946. He studied theory with Jón Thorárinsson and counterpoint and composition with Thorkell Sigurbjörnsson at the Reykjavík College of Music (graduated, 1967); received training in flute from Simon Hunt, David Evans, and Josef Magnusson; studied composition with Ton de Leeuw and Jos Kunst, orchestration with Leon Ortel, and flute with Pieter Ode in Amsterdam (1969–72); then took courses in musicology at the Univ. of Munich (1976). He was a conductor of the Ísafjördur Chamber Orch. (1973–76); in 1978 he became a teacher at the Ísafjördur School of Music, where he also conducted its choir and orch.

WORKS: ORCH.: 2 syms. (1969, 1973); *1,41* (1970); *Play, Play* (1971–72); *11 Meditations on the Settlement* (1974); Concerto for Violin and Small Orch. (1974–75); *Orgia* (1975); *Notturno IV* (1981–82); *Skerpla II* (1983); *Concerto trittico* (1985); *Midi* for 2 Pianos and Orch. (1985). **OTHER:** Chamber works, including 17 pieces entitled Sonata for various instruments; piano pieces; vocal music.

Tomilin, Victor, Russian composer; b. Berdichev, May 15, 1908; d. in combat near Leningrad, Dec. 9, 1941. He was a pupil of Vladimir Shcherbachev at the Leningrad Cons., graduating in 1932. He wrote 2 symphonic suites, *Episodes of Civil War* (1936) and *Crimean Suite* (1939), as well as a number of songs and piano pieces.

Tomlinson, John (Rowland), distinguished English bass; b. Oswaldtwistle, Lancashire, Sept. 22, 1946. He took a B.Sc. degree in civil engineering at the Univ. of Manchester, and also received vocal training at the Royal Northern College of Music in Manchester and from Otakar Kraus in London. In 1970 he became a member of the Glyndebourne Festival Chorus; his first operatic role of consequence was as the 2nd Armed Man in *Die Zauberflöte* with the Glyndebourne Touring Opera Co. in 1970, which led to his first major role with the company in 1972 as Colline; he also appeared as Leporello that year with the Kent Opera. After an engagement with the New Opera Co.

in London (1972–74), he sang regularly with the English National Opera in London (1975–80), where he distinguished himself as Masetto, King Marke, Rossini's Moses, Méphistophélès, Baron Ochs, and Bartók's Bluebeard. He made his debut at London's Covent Garden in 1979 as Colline, and returned there successfully in such roles as Mozart's Figaro, Leporello, the Commendatore, and Don Basilio. In 1988 he made his first appearance at the Bayreuth Festival as Wotan, a role he sang there regularly for 5 seasons; he also appeared as the Wanderer there (from 1989). In 1992 he sang Gurnemanz at the Berlin State Opera, and in 1993 returned to Covent Garden as Hans Sachs. In 1994 he again appeared as Wotan at the Bayreuth Festival. Tomlinson's commanding vocal technique and histrionic abilities have rendered him as one of the leading bassos of his generation. Among his other notable roles are Hunding, Philip II, Boris Godunov, Attila, and John Claggart.

Tommasini, Vincenzo, Italian composer; b. Rome, Sept. 17, 1878; d. there, Dec. 23, 1950. He studied violin with Pinelli, and later theory with Falchi at the Liceo di Santa Cecilia in Rome; then went to Berlin, where he took lessons with Bruch; after sojourns in Paris, London, and N.Y., he returned to Rome. He wrote music in the poetic tradition of Italian Romanticism; his operas, symphonic works, and chamber music obtained immediate performances and favorable receptions; however, his most successful piece, *Le Donne di buon umore,* was not an original work but a comedy-ballet written on music from sonatas by Domenico Scarlatti, arranged in a series of tableaux and brilliantly orchestrated; this was a commission for the Ballets Russes of Diaghilev, who staged it at Rome in April 1917, and kept it in the repertoire during his tours all over the world. He publ. *La luce invisible* (1929) and *Saggio d'estetica sperimentale* (1942).

WORKS: DRAMATIC: OPERAS: *Medea* (1902–04; Trieste, April 8, 1906); *Amore di terra lontana* (1907–08); *Uguale fortuna* (1911; Rome, 1913); *Dielja* (c.1935); *Il tenore sconfitto, ovvero La presunzione punita* (Rome, 1950). **BALLETS:** *Le donne di buon umore* (1916; Rome, April 1917; suite, 1920; based on sonatas by D. Scarlatti); *Le diable s'amuse* (1936; N.Y., 1937); *Tiepolesco* (Naples, 1945). **ORCH.:** *La vita e un sogno* (1901); *Poema erotico* (1908–09); *Inno alla belta* (1911); *Ciari di luna* (1914–15; Rome, 1916); *Il beato regno* (1919–20; Rome, 1922); *Paesaggi toscani* (1922; Rome, 1923); *Il carnevale di Venezia* (1928; N.Y., Oct. 10, 1929); *Napule* (1929–30; Freiburg im Breisgau, Dec. 7, 1931); Concerto for Violin and Small Orch. (1932); *4 pezzi* (1931–34); Concerto for String Quartet and Orch. (1939); *La tempesta* (1941); Concerto for Orch. and Cello Obbligato (1943); *Duo concertante* for Piano and Orch. (1948). **CHAMBER:** 4 string quartets (1898; 1908–09; 1926; 1943); Violin Sonata (1916–17); 2 piano trios (1929, 1946); Harp Sonata (1938); piano pieces. **VOCAL:** *Messa da requiem* for Chorus and Organ (1944); choruses; songs.

BIBL.: A. Casella, "V. T.," *Revue Musicale,* VIII/2 (1927); M. Rinaldi, "V. T.," *Rivista Musicale Italiana,* LIII (1951).

Tomotani, Kōji, Japanese composer; b. Hiroshima, Sept. 26, 1947. He studied at the Kunitachi Music College in 1974; then went to France, where he had lessons with M. Bitsch and Messiaen (1974–76) and also studied at the École Normale de Musique de Paris (degree, 1975). His *Cosmic Landscape* trilogy is rooted in the concept of "eternal return," the "wheel of time symbolizing an intimate link between boundless space (the cosmos) and boundless time (eternity); each of the three works variously contrasts the elements of 'sound-space,' represented by tone-clusters and time relationships, and 'spaces,' which punctuate the elements comprising the 'sound-space.'"

WORKS: Concerto for Biwa and Orch. (1977); *Gyō* for Fué and Biwa (1978); *Livre de Shura* for Percussion Ensemble (1980); *Kâla-Cakra I* for Flute and Piano (1981) and *II* for Shakuhachi and Percussion (1983); *Torana* for Soprano, Oboe d'Amore, and Piano (1982); *Cosmic Landscape I* for Flute and Harpsichord (1985), *II* for Orch. (1987), and *III* for Clarinet (1990); *Spectrum I* for Flute and Piano (1988) and *II* for Piano (1989).

Tomowa-Sintow, Anna, admired Bulgarian soprano; b. Stara Zagora, Sept. 22, 1941. She studied at the Bulgarian State Cons. in Sofia with Zlatew-Tscherkin and Zpiridonowa. In 1965 she made her operatic debut as Tatiana in Stara Zagora. She made her first appearance at the Leipzig Opera as Abigaille in 1967, and subsequently sang Arabella, Cio-Cio San, Desdemona, and Violetta there. After winning the Sofia (1970) and Rio de Janeiro (1971) competitions, she made her debut at the Berlin State Opera as Mozart's Countess in 1972. Her career was assured when Karajan chose her to create the role of Sibyl in the premiere of Orff's *De temporum fine comoedia* at the Salzburg Festival in 1973. She continued to sing there with much success in subsequent years, and also appeared at Karajan's Salzburg Easter Festivals. In 1974 she sang Donna Anna at the Bavarian State Opera in Munich, and made her U.S. debut that same year at the San Francisco Opera in the same role. In 1975 she appeared for the first time at London's Covent Garden as Fiordiligi. She made her debut at the Vienna State Opera in 1977 as Mozart's Countess. Her subsequent successes there led to her being made an Austrian Kammersängerin in 1988. On April 3, 1978, she made her Metropolitan Opera debut in N.Y. as Donna Anna. She appeared as Wagner's Elisabeth at the Paris Opéra in 1984. In 1990 she sang Yaroslavna in *Prince Igor* at Covent Garden. In 1992 she appeared as Tosca in Helsinki. She also sang extensively as a concert artist. Among her other notable roles are Verdi's Amelia and Aida, Wagner's Elsa, and Strauss' Marschallin.

Tone, Yasunao, Japanese multimedia artist and experimental composer; b. Tokyo, March 31, 1935. He graduated with a degree in literature from the Japanese National Univ. in Chiba (1957); then studied at the Tokyo Univ. of Arts, where he cofounded the group Ongaku, dedicated to "event music." In 1962 he joined the American modern movement FLUXUS, which presented his first works in a Tokyo program under the title "One Man Show by a Composer"; also joined other modernistic groups that encompassed experimental happenings. His tape pieces *Days, Number,* and *Clapping Piece* won special prizes in the 1964 Nova Consonanza Festival in Rome. He further wrote works for theater and dance scenarios, among them 4 for the Merce Cunningham Dance Co., of which *Geography* and *Music* became one of the company's most popular productions under the title *Roadrunners* (1979). He publ. a book of collected essays, *Gendai Bijutsu no Iso* (Can Art Be Thought; 1970), and pursued his multiplicity of artistic interests as an ed. for the leading Japanese art magazine, the *Bijutsu Shihyo.* In 1972 he settled in N.Y. while continuing to travel widely as a guest of several New Wave music events. Beginning in 1976, Tone produced musical compositions as compounds of cultural studies, using visual materials compiled in combination with ancient oriental texts and electronic sounds. He contributed numerous works to ultramodern media groups, among them *Dinner Happening* (1962), *Miniature Restaurant* (1963), *Metropolitan Scavening Movement* (1964), *Dance Concert with 2 Titles* (1966), *Intermedia Art Festival* (1969), *Multi Performance* (1972), *Voice and Phenomenon* (1976), *The Wall and the Books* (1982), and *Word of Mouth* (1988). From 1979 he received a steady stream of commissions for multimedia works; received a N.Y. Foundation for the Arts Fellowship (1987; performance art/emergent forms). He has been a regular participant in festivals of avant-garde art, including the Annual Avant-Garde Festival (1973–77; 1980), FLUXUS festivals (1975, 1979, 1984, 1987), Dharma Music Festival (1985), Pioneer Performance Artists (1985), Japon des Avantgardes (1986), Miami New Wave Media Festival (1988), Venice Biennale (1990), and the 2nd Acoustic International Festival (1990).

WORKS: DRAMATIC: *Anti-Dance and Anti-Music* (1961); *Ki* and *Waranin* (for Kaoru Kawana; 1962); *Kimigayo Electronic* and *Dictionary Music* (for Yoshie Aotsu and Mika Suzuki; 1963); *Theater Piece for Computer* (1966); *Kin no Sai Sarushima Dairi,* electronic music for a Kabuki play (1968); *Clockwork Video* (for the Merce Cunningham Dance Co. as

Events #82 and #83; 1973); *Theatrum Philosophicum* (for the Merce Cunningham Dance Co. as Events #151 and #152; 1975); *Genealogy, Music* (for the Merce Cunningham Dance Co. as Event #201; 1978); *Geography and Music* (for the Merce Cunningham Dance Co. as *Roadrunners*; 1979); *Blind Dates* (for Blondel Cummings and Senga Nengudi; 1982); *Personal Documents* (for Susana Heyman-Chaffey; 1984); *Caught in the Fringe* (for Nancy Zendora; 1985); *Econologos* (with Nancy Zendora and Barbara Held; 1986); *Techno Eden* (for Kay Nishikawa; 1986); *Setsubun, Day of Chance* (1990; in collaboration with A. Knowles); *Spectaclum Lyrictronica*, "anarchic flight in paramedia space" (1990; in collaboration with B. Held). **INSTRUMENTAL:** *Improvisation and Object Sonore* (Ongaku collaboration; 1961); *Piano sound with magnetic tape* (1962); *Tone Work* (1963); *Mono Tone* (1963); *Ready-made Prohibition* (1965); *Kinegraphia* (1967); *815 Catch passage* (1968); *A 2nd Music* (1972); *One day Wittgenstein . . .* (1973); *Communication with Mr.* (1974); *Geodesy* for Harpsichord (1975); *Harpsichord* for 50 Fingers (1975); *Voice and phenomenon* (1976); *Fruits for towers* (1977); *Trio for a flute player* (1985); *Piano for Taoists* (1985); *Aletheia* (1987); *Lyrictron* for Flute (1988); *What is left from a Rembrandt . . .* (1989), **OTHER:** Tape pieces, including *T.V. is a chewing gum for eyes* (1969), *This is not a condom* (for Vernita Nemec; 1984), and *Music for 2 C.D. Players* (1986; rev. 1989); graphic scores, including *Music for Reed Organ* (1962); film scores, including *An event for film projector* (for Taka Imura; 1962) and *Gingakei . . . Galaxy* (for Masao Adachi; 1967).

Toni, Alceo, Italian musicologist and composer; b. Lugo, May 22, 1884; d. Milan, Dec. 4, 1969. He was a pupil of L. Torchi and E. Bossi in Bologna. He was director of the Rovereto Cons. (1908–10), technical director of D'Annunzio's Raccolta Nazionale delle Musiche Italiane (1918–21), a critic for the *Popola d'Italia* (1922–43), and president of the Milan Cons. (1936–40). He ed. numerous works by Corelli, Locatelli, Torelli, Monteverdi, Carissimi, and other early Italian composers. His own compositions include the opera *Su un cavallin di legno* (1914), the ballet *I Fantocci ribelli* (1930), a Sym., choral works, chamber music, and songs. Some of his many articles were collected in a book, *Studi critici di interpretazione* (Milan, 1923; 2nd ed., 1955). With Tullio Serafin, he publ. *Stile, tradizioni e convenzioni del melo dramma italiano del Settecento e dell'Ottocento* (2 vols., Milan, 1958–64).

Töpper, Hertha, Austrian mezzo-soprano; b. Graz, April 19, 1924. She received her musical training in Graz, studying violin with her father at the Cons. and voice with Franz Mixa at the opera school. She made her operatic debut in 1945 as Ulrica at the Graz Landestheater, where she sang until 1952. In 1951 she appeared at the Bayreuth Festival; after singing as a guest artist at the Bavarian State Opera in Munich in 1951–52, she joined its roster; was made a Bavarian Kammersängerin in 1955. In 1953 she made her first appearance at London's Covent Garden as Clairon with the visiting Bavarian State Opera, and later returned for guest appearances. She made her U.S. debut at the San Francisco Opera in 1960 as Octavian, a role she repeated for her Metropolitan Opera debut in N.Y. on Nov. 19, 1962. From 1971 to 1981 she was a prof. at the Munich Hochschule für Musik. In 1980 she retired from the operatic stage. Her operatic repertoire included many roles by Wagner, Verdi, and Strauss; as a concert artist, she was particularly noted for her performances of the music of Bach.

Toradze, Alexander (David), Russian-American pianist and teacher, son of **David (Alexandrovich) Toradze**; b. Tbilisi, May 30, 1952. He was a pupil at the Central Music School (1958–69) and Cons. (1969–71) in Tbilisi; later studied at the Moscow Cons. with Yakov Zak, Boris Zemlyansky, and Lev Naumov. He began his career at the age of 9 with an appearance with the Tbilisi Sym. Orch., and subsequently toured widely in his homeland; he attracted wide notice in the West when he won the Silver Medal at the Van Cliburn Competition in 1977, which led to engagements in the U.S. In 1983 he settled in the U.S. but continued to pursue an international career in his many tours. In 1992 he became prof. of piano at Indiana Univ. in South Bend.

Toradze, David (Alexandrovich), noted Russian composer, father of **Alexander (David) Toradze**; b. Tiflis, April 14, 1922; d. there (Tbilisi), Nov. 7, 1983. He studied composition with Barkhudarian and piano with Virsaladze at the Tbilisi Cons.; after pursuing composition studies with Glière at the Moscow Cons., he completed postgraduate work at the Tbilisi Cons. (1948–51); then in 1952 joined its faculty; was made a reader in 1966 and a prof. in 1973. He received various honors, including the State Prize (1951), People's Artist of the Georgian S.S.R. (1961), and the Order of Lenin.

WORKS: DRAMATIC: OPERAS: *The Sumarmi Fortress* (1942); *The Call of the Mountains* (Tbilisi, Nov. 20, 1947); *The Bride of the North* (Tbilisi, 1958). **BALLETS:** *Gorda* (Tbilisi, 1949); *For Peace* (Tbilisi, June 17, 1953; rev. as *The Unsubdued*, 1970). **MUSICAL COMEDIES:** *Natel* (1948); *The Avengers* (1952). Also film scores. **ORCH.:** *Festival*, overture (1944); 2 syms. (1946, 1968); *Afrikanskiye eskizi*, symphonic poem for Soloists, Chorus, and Orch. (1962); *Georgian Folk Refrains*, choral sym. (1972). **OTHER:** Chamber music; songs.

Torjussen, Trygve, Norwegian composer and teacher; b. Drammen, Nov. 14, 1885; d. Oslo, Feb. 12, 1977. He studied in Christiania, Rome, and Stuttgart. He was on the staff of the Christiania Cons. (1911–17) and the Barratt-Due Music Inst. (1931–41). Among his works are various suites for small orch.; *Kark* for Tenor, Bass, Women's Chorus, and Orch. (Oslo, 1939); *A Musical Bridge-Evening* for String Quartet (Oslo, 1935); over 70 piano pieces, including a sonata; 30 songs.

Torkanowsky, Werner, German-born American conductor, violinist, and composer; b. Berlin, March 30, 1926; d. Bar Harbor, Maine, Oct. 20, 1992. He was taken to Palestine in 1933; after obtaining a violin diploma at the Palestine Cons. in Tel Aviv (1947), he emigrated to the U.S. in 1948 and pursued his studies with Rafael Bronstein. In 1952 he became a naturalized American citizen and a violinist in the Pittsburgh Sym. Orch. Following studies in conducting with Pierre Monteux (1954–59), he won the Naumburg Award for conducting in N.Y. in 1961. From 1963 to 1977 he was music director of the New Orleans Phil., and then of the Bangor Sym. Orch. from 1981. He also was active as a violinist, mainly as a chamber musician. Among his works were orch. pieces, chamber music, and songs.

Torke, Michael, American composer and pianist; b. Milwaukee, Sept. 21, 1961. He began piano lessons at 5 and commenced composing while still a youth. After studying composition with Rouse and Schwantner and piano with Burge at the Eastman School of Music in Rochester, N.Y. (graduated, 1984), he pursued graduate studies with Druckman and Bresnick at Yale Univ. (1984–85). He won the Prix de Rome and held a residency at the American Academy in Rome in 1986. His output reveals an effective blend of serious and pop music genres.

WORKS: DRAMATIC: *Estatic Orange*, ballet (N.Y., May 10, 1985; includes *Verdant*, later renamed *Green*, for Orch., Milwaukee, Nov. 20, 1986, and the ballet *Purple*, N.Y., June 11, 1987); *The Directions*, chamber opera (Iraklion, Crete, Aug. 6, 1986); *Black and White*, ballet (N.Y., May 7, 1988); *Slate*, ballet (N.Y., June 15, 1989); *King of Hearts*, television opera (1993; Channel 4, England, Jan. 1995). **ORCH.:** *Vanada* for Chamber Ensemble (1984; Amsterdam, Oct. 11, 1985); *Bright Blue Music* (N.Y., Nov. 23, 1985; also as *The Harlequins Are Looking at You* for Piano Trio); *Adjustable Wrench* for Chamber Ensemble (Huddersfield, Nov. 24, 1987); *Copper* for Brass Quintet and Orch. (Midland, Mich., June 3, 1988); *Ash* for Chamber Orch. (St. Paul, Minn., Feb. 3, 1989; also for Orch.); *Rust* for Piano and Wind Ensemble (Huddersfield, Nov. 21, 1989); *Bronze* for Piano and Orch. (1990; N.Y., Jan. 6, 1991, composer soloist); *Red* (1991); *Music on the Floor* for Chamber Ensemble (Milwaukee, April 10, 1992); *Monday and Tuesday* for Chamber Ensemble (London, Dec. 8, 1992); *Run* (1992); Piano Concerto (1993; Troy, N.Y., Jan. 14,

1994, composer soloist); Saxophone Concerto (1993; Troy, N.Y., Jan. 14, 1994); *Bone* for Chamber Ensemble and Wordless Woman's Voice (Rensselaer, N.Y., April 15, 1994); *Javelin* (Atlanta, Sept. 8, 1994); *Nylon* for Guitar and Chamber Orch. (Derby, England, Nov. 9, 1994). **CHAMBER:** *Ceremony of Innocence* for Flute, Clarinet, Violin, Cello, and Piano (Tanglewood, July 30, 1983); *The Yellow Pages* for Flute, Clarinet, Violin, Cello, and Piano (New Haven, Conn., April 8, 1985); *The Harlequins Are Looking at You* for Piano Trio (N.Y., Nov. 22, 1985; also for Orch.); *Chalk* for String Quartet (Manchester, England, Oct. 1, 1992); *Chroma* for Flute and Piano (1993). **PIANO:** *Laetus* (1981). **VOCAL:** *Mass* for Baritone, Chorus, and Chamber Orch. (N.Y., June 27, 1990); *4 Proverbs* for Woman's Voice and Chamber Ensemble (Milwaukee, May 28, 1993).

Törne, Bengt (Axel) von, Finnish composer; b. Helsinki, Nov. 22, 1891; d. Turku, May 4, 1967. He studied composition with Furuhjelm at the Helsinki Inst. of Music (1910–16) and orchestration with Sibelius (1916–17). He wrote 6 syms. (1935–66); 3 sinfoniettas; *Sinfonia da camera* for Strings (1951); Piano Concerto; Piano Quintet; 2 string quartets; 2 violin sonatas; Piano Trio. He publ. a monograph on Sibelius (London, 1937; in Italian, Florence, 1943; in Finnish, Helsinki, 1945; in Swedish, Stockholm, 1945) and an autobiography (Borga, 1945).

Torner, Eduardo Martínez, Spanish writer on music and literature; b. Oviedo, April 8, 1888; d. London, Feb. 17, 1955. He was a pupil of d'Indy at the Schola Cantorum in Paris; returned to Spain in 1914 and settled in Madrid. He was director of research of Spanish folk song at the Centro de Estudios Historicos (from 1916); also taught at the Cons.; at the close of the Civil War (1939), he went to London. He publ., in Madrid, the folk song collections *Cancionero musical de la lírica popular asturiana* (1920), *Cuarenta canciones españolas* (1924), and *Cancionero musical* (1928); also the book *Temas folklóricos: Música y poesía* (Madrid, 1935); ed. and arr. for piano selected pieces from tablature books of the 16th century, and publ. them under the title *Colección de vihuelistas españoles del siglo XVI* (Madrid, 1923).

BIBL.: A. Muñiz Tocas, *Vida y obra de E.M. T.* (Oviedo, 1961).

Torrefranca, Fausto (Acanfora Sansone dei duchi di Porta e), eminent Italian musicologist; b. Monteleone Calabro, Feb. 1, 1883; d. Rome, Nov. 26, 1955. Trained as an engineer, he took up music under E. Lena in Turin (harmony and counterpoint) and also studied by himself. It was through his initiative that the first chair of musicology was established in Italy. In 1913 he became a lecturer at the Univ. of Rome; from 1914 to 1924, was a prof. of music history at the Cons. di S. Pietro in Naples, and from 1915, also librarian there; from 1924 to 1938, was librarian of the Milan Cons. From 1907 he was ed. of the *Rivista Musicale Italiana.* In 1941 he was appointed a prof. of music history at the Univ. of Florence.

WRITINGS: *La vita musicale dello spirito: La musica, le arti, il dramma* (Turin, 1910); *Giacomo Puccini e l'opera internazionale* (Turin, 1912); *Le origine italiane del romanticismo musicale: I primitivi della sonata moderna* (Turin, 1930); *Il segreto del quattrocento: Musiche ariose e poesia popularesca* (Milan, 1939).

Torres-Santos, Raymond, Puerto Rican composer, conductor, keyboardist, and music educator; b. San Juan, June 19, 1958. He grew up in a musical family; one of his grandfathers was a violinist, and the other played the German accordion. He was educated in Puerto Rico at the Univ. (B.A. in humanities, 1980) and the Cons. of Music (B.A. in music, 1980); also had lessons with Ginastera (summers, 1977–78); continued his studies at the Univ. of Calif. at Los Angeles (M.A., 1982; Ph.D., 1986), where his mentors were Henri Lazarof, Paule Reale, and David Raksin; also attended new music courses in Darmstadt (1982). He was a visiting composer at the Center for Computer Research in Music and Acoustics at Stanford Univ. (1984) and the Centro di Sonologia Computazionale at the Univ. of Padua (1988). From 1986 to 1991 he was a prof. at Calif. State Univ. in San Bernardino, where he also was director of the electronic and commercial music programs. After serving as chairman of the music dept. at the Univ. of Puerto Rico (1991–93), he was chancellor of the Puerto Rico Cons. of Music (from 1994). His compositional style is eclectic and inclusive, and his craftsmanship applicable to virtually any genre; in some of his works, he makes effective use of indigenous Puerto Rican instruments. His more than 60 popular songs and over 300 arrangements have been performed by singers and orchs. throughout Latin America and in Los Angeles.

WORKS: ORCH.: *Sinfonia Concertante* (1980); *Exploraciones* for Strings (1980); *Areytos: a Symphonic Picture* (1985); *El pais de los cuatro pisos* (1988); *La cancion de las Antillas* (San Juan, Sept. 8, 1990). **CHAMBER:** Flute Sonata (1975); Violin Sonata (1977); *Un jibarito en N.Y.* for String Quartet (1977); *Music* for Brass and Percussion (1977); String Quartet (1978); *Cordillera central* for Clarinet and Cuatro (Puerto Rican stringed instrument; 1980); *La guaracha del macho camacho* for Acoustic Piano and Electronically Modified Electric Piano (1983); Brass Quintet (1985); *Epitafio* for 6 Horns (1988); *Descarga* for Percussion Ensemble (1988); *Danzas tropicales* for Chamber Ensemble (1988). **VOCAL:** *Esta es mi vida: A Cantata* for Chorus and Orch. (1979); *Elegia de Reyes: A Christmas Cantata* for Narrator, Soprano, Chorus, Symphonic Band, and "Rondalla" (an ensemble of Spanish Guitars, Mandolins, Cuatros, etc.; 1981); *Gwakia Baba* for Chorus (1988). **OTHER:** Numerous solo pieces; electronic and computer music; dance pieces; film scores; commercials; arrangements and orchestrations; popular songs; stage works.

Tortelier, Paul, noted French cellist, pedagogue, composer, and political idealist, father of **Yan Pascal Tortelier**; b. Paris, March 21, 1914; d. Villarceaux, Yvelines, Dec. 18, 1990. He studied cello with Gérard Hekking at the Paris Cons., winning 1st prize at the age of 16. He made his debut with the Lamoureux Orch. at the age of 17; from 1935 to 1937 he was 1st cellist of the orch. in Monte Carlo; from 1937 to 1939 he was a member of the Boston Sym. Orch. He was subsequently 1st cellist of the Paris Cons. Orch. in Paris (1946–47). In 1947 he was a soloist at the Festival of Richard Strauss in London. Tortelier inherited his progressive ideals from his father, a cabinetmaker by profession and a Marxist by political persuasion. He participated in a number of organizations destined to create a better world-at-large; he was quite serious in his work to prevent aggression or injustices to countries governed by repressive rules. Although not a Jew, he saw great hope in the formation of individual communes in Israel and spent a year there working in a kibbutz (1955–56). He then resumed his career as a professional musician; also was a prof. at the Paris Cons. (1957–59) and at the Nice Cons. (1978–80). He made some appearances as a conductor. His wife, Maud Martin Tortelier, was also a cellist, and his daughter, Maria de la Pau, was a pianist; both appeared in performances of Tortelier's works, which included *Israel Symphony*, several cello concertos, a Cello Sonata, and a *Suite* for Solo Cello. He publ. *How I Play, How I Teach* (London, 1975) and *Paul Tortelier, Self-Portrait* (with D. Blum; London, 1984).

Tortelier, Yan Pascal, French conductor, son of **Paul Tortelier**; b. Paris, April 19, 1947. At the age of 12, he began studying harmony and counterpoint with Boulanger; after winning the premier prix for violin at the Paris Cons. when he was 14, he made his debut as a soloist in the Brahms Double Concerto in London (1962). Following conducting studies with Ferrara at the Accademia Musicale Chigiana in Siena (1973), he served as assoc. conductor of the Orchestre du Capitole in Toulouse (1974–83); also conducted opera there and appeared as a guest conductor in other French cities. In 1978 he made his British debut as a guest conductor with the Royal Phil. of London. In 1985 he made his U.S. debut as a guest conductor with the Seattle Sym. Orch., and subsequently appeared with other North American orchs. In 1989 he became principal conductor and artistic director of the Ulster Orch. in Belfast. In 1992 he became principal conductor of the BBC Phil. in Manchester.

Tosar Errecart, Héctor, Uruguayan composer; b. Montevideo, July 18, 1923. He studied piano and composition in Montevideo; after receiving a Guggenheim fellowship (1946), he went to the U.S. to study composition with Copland and Honegger and conducting with Koussevitzky; also took courses at Columbia Univ.; subsequently went to Paris on a French government fellowship, where he studied composition with Rivier and Milhaud at the Cons. and composition with Honegger and conducting with Bigot and Fournet at the École Normale de Musique. He was a prof. at the Montevideo Cons. (1951–54); served as prof. of the history of instruments at the Univ. of Montevideo before becoming chairman of the composition dept. of the Puerto Rico Cons. in 1974. His music is neo-Classical in facture, with a considerable influx of Latin American melorhythms.

WORKS: ORCH.: Piano Concertino (1941); 3 syms. (1945, 1950, 1973); *Oda a amigas* (1951); *Sinfonia concertante* (1957); *Naves Errantes* (1964); *Recitativo y variaciones* (1967); *A 13* (1970); choral works; chamber music; songs; piano pieces.

Tosatti, Vieri, Italian composer; b. Rome, Nov. 2, 1920. He studied piano on his own; also composition with Dobici, Ferdinandini, Jachino, and Petrassi at the Rome Cons. (diploma, 1942) and with Pizzetti. In his compositions he often exploits sensational or morbid subjects, setting them to pungent music, with a liberal application of special effects.

WORKS: OPERAS: *Dionisio* (1947); *Il sistema della dolcezza* (1949); *La partita a pugni* (Venice, Sept. 8, 1953); *Il giudizio universale* (1955); *L'isola del tesoro* (1958); *La fiera della Meraviglie* (1963); *Il paradiso e il poeta* (1971). **ORCH.:** Piano Concerto (1945); Viola Concerto (1966); Concerto iperciclico for Clarinet and Orch. (1970). **CHAMBER:** Concerto for Wind Quintet and Piano (1945); *Introduzione fiabesca* for Piano Trio (1943); *Piccola sonata* for Violin and Piano (1945); a variety of whimsical piano pieces. **VOCAL:** *Sinfonia corale* for Chorus and Orch. (1944); *Il concerto della demenza* for Narrator, 2 Pianos, and Chamber Orch. (1946); *Requiem* (1963); *2 coretti* for 3 Women's Voices (1970); songs.

Toscanini, Arturo, great Italian conductor; b. Parma, March 25, 1867; d. N.Y., Jan. 16, 1957. He entered the Parma Cons. at the age of 9, studying the cello with Carini and composition with Dacci; graduated in 1885 as winner of the 1st prize for cello; received the Barbacini Prize as the outstanding graduate of his class. In 1886 he was engaged as cellist for the Italian opera in Rio de Janeiro; on the evening of June 30, 1886, he was unexpectedly called upon to substitute for the regular conductor, when the latter left the podium at the end of the introduction after the public hissed him; the opera was *Aida*, and Toscanini led it without difficulty; he was rewarded by an ovation and was engaged to lead the rest of the season. Returning to Italy, he was engaged to conduct the opera at the Teatro Carignano in Turin, making his debut there on Nov. 4, 1886, and later conducted the Municipal Orch. there. Although still very young, he quickly established a fine reputation. From 1887 to 1896 he conducted opera in the major Italian theaters. On May 21, 1892, he led the premiere of *Pagliacci* in Milan, and on Feb. 1, 1896, the premiere of *La Bohème* in Turin. He also conducted the first performance by an Italian opera company, sung in Italian, of *Götterdämmerung* (Turin, Dec. 22, 1895) and *Siegfried* (Milan, 1899); he made his debut as a sym. conductor on March 20, 1896, with the orch. of the Teatro Regio in Turin. In 1898 the impresario Gatti-Casazza engaged him as chief conductor for La Scala, Milan, where he remained until 1903, and again from 1906 to 1908. In the interim, he conducted opera in Buenos Aires (1903–4; 1906). When Gatti-Casazza became general manager of the Metropolitan Opera (1908), he invited Toscanini to be principal conductor; Toscanini's debut in N.Y. was in *Aida* (Nov. 16, 1908). While at the Metropolitan, Toscanini conducted Verdi's *Requiem* (Feb. 21, 1909), as well as 2 world premieres, Puccini's *The Girl of the Golden West* (Dec. 10, 1910) and Giordano's *Madame Sans-Gêne* (Jan. 25, 1915); he also brought out for the first time in America Gluck's *Armide* (Nov. 14, 1910), Wolf-Ferrari's *Le Donne curiose* (Jan. 3, 1912), and Mussorgsky's *Boris Godunov* (March 19, 1913). On April 13, 1913, he gave his first concert in N.Y. as a sym. conductor, leading Beethoven's 9th Sym. In 1915 he returned to Italy; during the season of 1920–21, he took the La Scala Orch. on a tour of the U.S. and Canada. From 1921 to 1929 he was artistic director of La Scala; there he conducted the posthumous premiere of Boito's opera *Nerone*, which he completed for performance (May 1, 1924). In 1926–27 he was a guest conductor of the N.Y. Phil., returning in this capacity through the 1928–29 season; then was its assoc. conductor with Mengelberg in 1929–30; subsequently was its conductor from 1930 to 1936; took it on a tour of Europe in the spring of 1930. He conducted in Bayreuth in 1930 and 1931. Deeply touched by the plight of the Jews in Germany, he acceded to the request of the violinist Huberman, founder of the Palestine Sym. Orch., to conduct the inaugural concert of that orch. at Tel Aviv (Dec. 26, 1936). During this period, he also filled summer engagements at the Salzburg Festivals (1934–37), and conducted in London (1935; 1937–39). He became music director of the NBC Sym. Orch. in N.Y. in 1937, a radio orch. that had been organized especially for him; he conducted his first broadcast on Dec. 25, 1937, in N.Y. He took it on a tour of South America in 1940, and on a major tour of the U.S. in 1950. He continued to lead the NBC Sym. Orch. until the end of his active career; he conducted his last concert from Carnegie Hall, N.Y., on April 4, 1954 (10 days after his 87th birthday).

Toscanini was one of the most celebrated masters of the baton in the history of conducting; undemonstrative in his handling of the orch., he possessed an amazing energy and power of command. He demanded absolute perfection, and he erupted in violence when he could not obtain from the orch. what he wanted (a lawsuit was brought against him in Milan when he accidentally injured the concertmaster with a broken violin bow). Despite the vituperation he at times poured on his musicians, he was affectionately known to them as "The Maestro" who could do no wrong. His ability to communicate his desires to singers and players was extraordinary, and even the most celebrated opera stars or instrumental soloists never dared to question his authority. Owing to extreme nearsightedness, Toscanini committed all scores to memory; his repertoire embraced virtually the entire field of Classical and Romantic music; his performances of Italian operas, of Wagner's music dramas, of Beethoven's syms., and of modern Italian works were especially inspiring. Among the moderns, he conducted works by Richard Strauss, Debussy, Ravel, Prokofiev, and Stravinsky, and among Americans, Samuel Barber, whose *Adagio for Strings* he made famous; he also had his favorite Italian composers (Catalani, Martucci), whose music he fondly fostered. In his social philosophy, he was intransigently democratic; he refused to conduct in Germany under the Nazi regime. He militantly opposed Fascism in Italy, but never abandoned his Italian citizenship, despite his long years of residence in America. In 1987 his family presented his valuable private archive to the N.Y. Public Library.

BIBL.: G. Ciampelli, *A. T.* (Milan, 1923); E. Cozzani, *A. T.* (Milan, 1927); T. Nicotra, *A. T.* (tr. from the Italian, N.Y., 1929); D. Bonardi, *T.* (Milan, 1929); P. Stefan, *A. T.* (Vienna, 1936; Eng. tr., N.Y., 1936); L. Gilman, *T. and Great Music* (N.Y., 1938); S. Hoeller, *A. T.* (N.Y., 1943); G. Ciampelli, *T.* (Milan, 1946); A. Della Corte, *T.* (Vicenza, 1946); D. Nives, *A. T.* (Milan, 1946); A. Segre, "T.: The First Forty Years," and H. Taubman, "T. in America," *Musical Quarterly* (April 1947); F. Sacchi, *T.* (Milan, 1951; Eng. tr. as *The Magic Baton: T.'s Life for Music*, N.Y., 1957); H. Taubman, *The Maestro: The Life of A. T.* (N.Y., 1951); S. Chotzinoff, *T.: An Intimate Portrait* (N.Y., 1956); R. Marsh, *T. and the Art of Orchestral Performance* (Philadelphia, 1956); B. Haggin, *Conversations with T.* (N.Y., 1959; 2nd ed., enl., 1979); S. Hughes, *The T. Legacy: A Critical Study of A. T.'s Performances* *of Beethoven, Verdi, and Other Composers* (London, 1959); L. Frassati, *Il Maestro A. T. e il suo mondo* (Turin, 1967); H. Schonberg, *The Great Conductors* (N.Y., 1967); A. Armani, ed., *T. e La Scala* (Milan, 1972); G. Marek, *T.* (N.Y., 1975); H. Sachs, *T.* (Philadelphia, 1978); D. Matthews, *A. T.* (Tunbridge Wells and N.Y., 1982); J. Freeman and W. Toscanini, *T.* (N.Y., 1987); J. Horowitz, *Understanding T.: How He Became an American Culture-God and Helped to Create a New Audience for Old Music* (N.Y., 1987); H. Sachs, *A. T. dal 1915 al 1946: l'arte all'ombra della politica: omaggio al maestro nel 30° anniversario della scomparsa* (Turin, 1987); idem, *Reflections on T.* (N.Y., 1991); G. Marchesi, *A. T.* (Turin, 1993).

Toselli, Enrico, Italian pianist, teacher, and composer; b. Florence, March 13, 1883; d. there, Jan. 15, 1926. He studied with Sgambati and Martucci. He gave concerts in Italy as a pianist. He wrote the operettas *La cattiva Francesca* (1912) and *La principessa bizzarra* (1913), the symphonic poem *Il fuoco*, and various salon pieces for Voice and Piano, the most celebrated being *Serenata* (1900). In 1907 he married the former Crown Princess Luise of Saxony, creating an international furor; following their separation in 1912, he recounted this affair in his book *Mari d'altessee: 4 ans de mariage avec Louise de Toscane, ex-princesse de Saxe* (Paris, 1913; Eng. tr., 1913).

Totenberg, Roman, Polish-born American violinist and pedagogue; b. Łódž, Jan. 1, 1911. He studied violin with Mieczyslaw Michalowicz in Warsaw, Flesch in Berlin, and Enesco in Paris. In 1932 he won the Mendelssohn Prize in Berlin. In 1935–36 he toured Europe with Karol Szymanowski, giving violin-piano recitals; then emigrated to the U.S.; became a naturalized American citizen in 1943. In 1943–44 he taught at the Peabody Cons. of Music in Baltimore. In 1947 he was made chairman of the string dept. at the Music Academy of the West in Santa Barbara. He was head of the violin dept. at the Aspen (Colo.) School of Music (1950–60) and a teacher at the Mannes College of Music in N.Y. (1951–57) before serving as prof. of music and chairman of the string dept. at Boston Univ. (1961–78); then was director of the Longy School of Music (1978–85).

Tóth, Aladár, eminent Hungarian writer on music and opera administrator; b. Székesfehérvár, Feb. 4, 1898; d. Budapest, Oct. 18, 1968. He received training in piano and composition in his native city; then studied at the Scientific Univ. of Budapest (Ph.D., 1925, with the diss. *Adatok Mozart zenedrámáinak esztétikájához*; Contribution to the Aesthetics of Mozart's Dramatic Music). He was a music critic for the newspapers *Új nemzedék* (1920–23) and *Pesti napló* (1923–39), and also for the literary journal *Nyugat* (1923–40). After living in Switzerland during World War II, he returned to Budapest to serve as director of the Hungarian State Opera (1946–56). In 1952 he was awarded the Kossuth Prize. He married **Annie Fischer** in 1937.

WRITINGS (all publ. in Budapest unless otherwise given): *Mozart: Figaro lakodalma* (Mozart: Marriage of Figaro; 1928); ed. with B. Szabolcsi, *Zenei lexikon* (1930–31; 2nd ed., rev., 1965); *Zoltán Kodály* (Vienna, 1932); *Liszt Ferenc a magyar zene útján* (Franz Liszt on the Trail of Hungarian Music; 1940); with B. Szabolcsi, *Mozart* (1941); *Verdi művészi hitvallása* (Verdi's Artistic Confession; 1941); F. Bónis, ed., *Tóth Aladár válogatott zenekritikái* (Aladár Tóth's Selected Criticisms of Music; 1968).

Touma, Habib Hassan, Arab composer and ethnomusicologist; b. Nazareth, Dec. 12, 1934. He studied at the Haifa Cons. and the Rubin Academy of Music in Tel Aviv (1956–62); then went to the Free Univ. of Berlin, where he received a Ph.D. with a diss. on Arab music theory (1968). He went on to teach there, and to work at the Internationale Institut für Vergleichende Musikstudien und Dokumentation. His studies of Arab music theory and history greatly influenced his compositions, which include *Oriental Rhapsody* for 2 Flutes and Percussion (1958), *Reflexus I* for 23 Strings (1965), and *Maqam for Natalie* for Piano (1974). He publ. *Die Musik der Araber* (Wilhelmshaven, 1975).

Tourangeau, (Marie Jeannine) Huguette, Canadian mezzo-soprano; b. Montreal, Aug. 12, 1940. She studied voice at the Montreal Cons. with Ruzena Herlinger, repertoire with Otto-Werner Mueller, and declamation with Roy Royal. In 1962 she made her debut in Monteverdi's *Vespro della Beata Virgine* at the Montreal Festival; her operatic debut followed as Mercedes in *Carmen* in Montreal in 1964. She toured in the U.S. as a member of the Metropolitan Opera National Co. (1964–65); then appeared in Seattle, London, San Francisco, and Hamburg. On Nov. 28, 1973, she made her formal Metropolitan Opera debut in N.Y. as Nicklausse in *Les Contes d'Hoffmann*, and returned in later seasons as a guest artist. In 1974 she sang at the Sydney Opera and made her debut at London's Covent Garden as Elisabetta in *Maria Stuarda* in 1977. Her repertory included roles from French, German, and Italian operas.

Tourel (real name, **Davidovich**), **Jennie,** prominent Russian-born American mezzo-soprano; b. Vitebsk, June 22, 1900; d. N.Y., Nov. 23, 1973. She played flute; then studied piano. After the Revolution, her family left Russia and settled temporarily near Danzig; they later moved to Paris, where she continued to study piano and contemplated a concert career; she then began to take voice lessons with Anna El-Tour, and decided to devote herself to professional singing; she changed her last name to Tourel by transposing the syllables of her teacher's name. She made her operatic debut at the Opéra Russe in Paris in 1931; then her debut at the Metropolitan Opera in N.Y. on May 15, 1937, as Mignon. In 1940, just before the occupation of Paris by Nazi troops, she went to Lisbon, and eventually emigrated to the U.S.; appeared on the Metropolitan Opera roster in 1943–45 and 1946–47. She became a naturalized American citizen in 1946. In 1951 she created the role of Baba the Turk in Stravinsky's *The Rake's Progress* in Venice. In later years, she devoted herself to recitals and orch. engagements, excelling particularly in the French repertoire. She also taught at the Juilliard School of Music in N.Y. and at the Aspen (Colo.) School of Music.

Tournemire, Charles (Arnould), distinguished French organist and composer; b. Bordeaux, Jan. 22, 1870; d. Arachon, Nov. 3, 1939. He began his training as a child in Bordeaux; was only 11 when he became organist at St. Pierre, and later was organist at St. Seurin; then went to Paris, where he studied piano with Bériot, harmony with Taudou, and organ (premier prix, 1891) with Widor and Franck at the Cons.; also studied composition with d'Indy at the Schola Cantorum. He was organist at Ste. Clotilde (from 1898) and a prof. at the Cons. (from 1919); also toured Europe. His major achievement as a composer was *L'Orgue mystique*, comprising 51 Offices for the Roman Catholic liturgy.

WORKS: OPERAS: *Nittetis* (1905–07); *Les Dieux sont morts* (1910–12; Paris, March 19, 1924); *La Légende de Tristan* (1925–26); *Il Poverello di Assisi* (1936–38). **ORCH.:** 8 syms.: No. 1, *Romantique* (1900), No. 2, *Ouessant* (Paris, April 4, 1909), No. 3, *Moscou* (Amsterdam, Oct. 19, 1913), No. 4, *Pages symphoniques* (1912–13; Paris, 1914), No. 5, *Dans les Alpes* (1913–14; The Hague, March 10, 1920), No. 6 for Soloist, Chorus, Organ, and Orch. (1915–18), No. 7, *Les Danses de la vie* (1918–22), and No. 8, *La Symphonie du triomphe de la mort* (1920–24); *Poème* for Organ and Orch. (1909–10). **CHAMBER:** Violin Sonata (1892–93); 3 pièces for Oboe and Piano (1894); Cello Sonata (1895); *Andante* for Horn and Piano (1896); Suite for Viola and Piano (1897); Piano Quartet (1897–98); Piano Trio (1901); *Poème* for Cello and Piano (1908); *Pour une épigramme de Théocrite* for 3 Flutes, 2 Clarinets, and Harp (1910); *Musique orante* for String Quartet (1933); *Sonate-poème* for Violin and Piano (1935). **KEYBOARD: PIANO:** *Sérénade* (1896); Sonata (1899); *Sarabande* (1901); *Rhapsodie* (1904); *Poème mystique* (1908); (12) *Préludes-poèmes* (1932); *Cloches de Châteauneuf-du-Faou* (1933); *Études de chaque jour* (1936). **ORGAN:** *Andantino* (1894); *Sortie* (1894); *Offertoire* (1894–95); *Pièce symphonique* (1899); *Suite de morceaux I* (1901) and *II* (1902); *Triple choral* (1901); *L'Orgue mystique* (1927–32); *3 poèmes* (1932); *6 Fioretti* (1932); *Fantaisie symphonique* (1933–34);

Petites fleurs musicales (1933–34); *7 chorals-poèmes* (1935); *Postludes libres* (1935); *Symphonie-choral* (1935); *Symphonie sacrée* (1936); *Suite évocatrice* (1938); *2 fresques symphoniques sacrées* (1938–39). **VOCAL:** *Le Sang de la sirène* for Soloists, Chorus, and Orch. (1902–03; Paris, Nov. 17, 1904); *Psalm LVII* for Chorus and Orch. (1908–09); *Psalm XLVI* for Chorus and Orch. (1913); *Trilogie: Faust-Don Quichotte-St. François d'Assise* for Soloists, Chorus, and Orch. (1916–29); *La Queste du Saint-Graal* for Soloists, Chorus, and Orch. (1926–27; Lyons, Jan. 1930); *Apocalypse de St. Jean* for Soloists, Chorus, Organ, and Orch. (1932–35); *La Douloureuse Passion du Christ* for Soloists, Chorus, and Organ (1936–37); songs.

WRITINGS: *César Franck* (Paris, 1931); *Précis d'exécution, de registration et d'improvisation à l'orgue* (Paris, 1936); *Petite méthode d'orgue* (Paris, 1949).

BIBL.: F. Peeters, "L'Oeuvre d'orgue de C. T.," *Musica Sacra* (Bruges, 1940); idem, "In memoriam C. T.," *Orgue*, No. 113 (1965); G. Beechey, "C. T., 1870–1939," *Musical Times*, CXI (1970); B. Lespinard, "'L'Orgue mystique' de C. T.: 'Impressions plain-chantesques'," *Orgue*, No. 139b (1971); J.-M. Fauquet, *Catalogue de l'oeuvre de C. T.* (Geneva, 1979).

Tours, Frank E(dward), English-American composer; b. London, Sept. 1, 1877; d. Santa Monica, Calif., Feb. 2, 1963. His father was the Dutch-born English organist, violinist, and composer Berthold Tours (b. Rotterdam, Dec. 17, 1838; d. London, March 11, 1897). He studied with Stanford, Parratt, and Bridge at the Royal College of Music in London. He went to N.Y. in 1904 and conducted light opera productions. Later he entered the motion picture field. He wrote many successful songs, among them *Mother o' Mine, Beyond the Sunset, Red Rose,* and *In Flanders Fields.*

Tovey, Sir Donald (Francis), eminent English music scholar, pianist, and composer; b. Eton, July 17, 1875; d. Edinburgh, July 10, 1940. He studied privately with Sophie Weisse (piano), Parratt (counterpoint), and James Higgs and Parry (composition) until 1894, when he won the Nettleship scholarship at Balliol College, Oxford; graduated with Classical Honors (B.A., 1898). In 1894 he appeared as a pianist with Joachim, and subsequently performed regularly with his quartet; in 1900–1901 he gave a series of chamber music concerts in London, at which he performed several of his own works; in 1901–02 he gave similar concerts in Berlin and Vienna; played his Piano Concerto in 1903 under Henry Wood and in 1906 under Hans Richter; then was an active participant in the concerts of the Chelsea Town Hall and of the Classical Concert Society. In 1914 he succeeded Niecks as Reid Prof. of music at the Univ. of Edinburgh; founded the Reid Orch. in 1917. He made his U.S. debut as a pianist in 1925; presented a series of concerts with renowned guest artists in Edinburgh in 1927–28. In 1935 he was knighted. Though highly esteemed as a composer, he was most widely known as a writer and lecturer on music, his analytical essays being models of their kind. Besides much chamber music and several piano pieces (a sonata, *Balliol Dances* for 4-hands, etc.), he composed an opera, *The Bride of Dionysus* (Edinburgh, April 23, 1929); Sym. (1913); Cello Concerto (Edinburgh, Nov. 22, 1934, Casals soloist, composer conducting).

WRITINGS (all publ. in London): *A Companion to the Art of the Fugue* (1931); *Essays in Musical Analysis* (6 vols., 1935–39); with G. Parratt, *Walter Parratt: Master of Music* (1941); *A Musician Talks* (1941); H. Foss, ed., *Essays in Musical Analysis: Chamber Music* (1944); idem, ed., *Musical Articles from the Encyclopaedia Britannica* (1944); idem, ed., *Beethoven* (1944); *A Companion to Beethoven's Piano Sonatas* (1948); H. Foss, ed., *Essays and Lectures on Music* (1949).

BIBL.: M. Grierson, *D.F. T.* (London, 1952).

Tower, Joan (Peabody), American composer, pianist, and teacher; b. New Rochelle, N.Y., Sept. 6, 1938. She took courses in composition with Brant and Calabro and studied piano at Bennington (Vt.) College (B.A., 1961); completed her training with Luening, Beeson, Ussachevsky, and others at Columbia Univ. (M.A., 1964; D.M.A., 1978). In N.Y. in 1969 she co-founded the Da Capo Chamber Players, which became known for its promotion of contemporary music; she served as its pianist until 1984. She taught at Bard College in Annandale-on-Hudson (from 1972) and was composer-in-residence of the St. Louis Sym. Orch. (1985–87). In 1976 she held a Guggenheim fellowship; held NEA fellowships in 1974, 1975, 1980, and 1984; received a Koussevitzky Foundation grant in 1982, and an American Academy and Inst. of Arts and Letters award in 1983. In 1990 she received the Grawemeyer Award of the Univ. of Louisville for her *Silver Ladders* for Orch. Her music is marked by an innovative handling of structural forms, sweeping energy, and a deft handling of coloristic writing.

WORKS: BALLET: *Stepping Stones* (1993). **ORCH.:** *Composition* (1967); *Amazon II* (Poughkeepsie, N.Y., Nov. 10, 1979; orchestrated from the work for Flute, Clarinet, Viola, Cello, and Piano, 1977) and *III* for Chamber Orch. (1982); *Sequoia* (N.Y., May 18, 1981); *Music* for Cello and Orch. (N.Y., Sept. 29, 1984); *Island Rhythms* (Tampa, June 29, 1985); Piano Concerto, *Homage to Beethoven* (1985; Annandale-on-Hudson, Jan. 31, 1986); *Silver Ladders* (1986; St. Louis, Jan. 9, 1987); Clarinet Concerto (N.Y., April 10, 1988); *Island Prelude* for Oboe and Strings (St. Louis, May 4, 1989; also for Chamber Ensemble); Flute Concerto (1989; N.Y., Jan. 28, 1990); *Concerto for Orchestra* (St. Louis, May 16, 1991); Violin Concerto (Salt Lake City, April 24, 1992); Concerto for Chamber Orch. (1994; Los Angeles, Jan. 23, 1995). **CHAMBER:** *Pillars* for 2 Pianos and Percussion (1961); *Study* for 2 Strings and 2 Winds (1963); Percussion Quartet (Bennington, Vt., Aug. 17, 1963; rev. 1969); *Brimset* for 2 Flutes and Percussion (1965); *Opa eboni* for Oboe and Piano (1968); *Movements* for Flute and Piano (1968); *Prelude* for 5 Players (1970); *Hexachords* for Flute (1972); *Breakfast Rhythms I* and *II* for Clarinet, Flute, Violin, Cello, Piano, and Percussion (1974–75); *Black Topaz* for Piano, Flute, Clarinet, Trumpet, Trombone, and 2 Percussion (1976); *Platinum Spirals* for Violin (1976); *Amazon I* for Flute, Clarinet, Violin, Cello, and Piano (1977; orchestrated as *Amazon II*, 1979); *Petroushskates* for Flute, Clarinet, Violin, Cello, and Piano (1980); *Wings* for Flute (1981); *Noon Dance* for Flute, Clarinet, Violin, Cello, Piano, and Percussion (1982); *Fantasy . . . Harbor Lights* for Clarinet and Piano (1983); *Snow Dreams* for Flute and Guitar (1983); *Clocks* for Guitar (1985); *Fanfare for the Uncommon Woman Nos. 1–5* for Instrumental Ensemble (1986–93); *Island Premiere* for Wind Quintet (1989; also for Oboe and String Quintet and for Oboe and String Orch.); *Elegy* for Trombone and String Quartet (1993); *Night Fields* for String Quartet (1994); *Très Lent* for Cello and Piano (1994); Clarinet Quintet (1995); piano pieces.

Townsend, Douglas, American composer and musicologist; b. N.Y., Nov. 8, 1921. He studied at the High School of Music and Art in N.Y.; then received lessons in composition from Serly, Wolpe, Copland, Luening, Greissle et al. He taught at Brooklyn College of the City Univ. of N.Y. (1958–69), Lehman College of the City Univ. of N.Y. (1970–71), the Univ. of Bridgeport, Conn. (1973–75), and the State Univ. of N.Y. in Purchase (1973–76); served as ed. of the *Musical Heritage Review* (1977–80).

WORKS: DRAMATIC: 3 4-minute operas (1947); 3 folk operettas (1947); *Lima Beans*, chamber opera (1954; N.Y., Jan. 7, 1956); *The Infinite*, ballet (1951; N.Y., Feb. 13, 1952); film and television scores. **ORCH.:** *Divertimento* for Strings and Winds (1949); *Fantasy* for Chamber Orch. (1951); *Adagio* for Strings (1956); 2 chamber syms. (1958, 1961); 2 syms. for Strings: No. 1 (N.Y., Nov. 29, 1958) and No. 2 (1984); 3 chamber concertos: No. 1 for Violin and Strings (1959), No. 2 for Trombone and Strings (1962), and No. 3 for Flute, Horns, Piano, and Strings (1971); 2 suites for Strings (1970, 1974); *Fantasy on Motives of Burt Bacharach* (1979); *Gentlewoman's Polka* for Band (1985); *Ridgefield Rag* for Band (1985). **CHAMBER:** Septet for Brass (1945); *Ballet Suite* for 3 Clarinets (1953); Duo for 2 Violas (1957); *Tower Music* for Brass Quintet (1959); *Dr. Jolly's Quickstep* for Brass Quintet (1974); piano pieces. **VOCAL:** Choral works; folk song arrangements.

Toyama, Yuzo, Japanese composer; b. Tokyo, May 10, 1931. He received his training at the Tokyo Academy of Music (graduated, 1951) and in Vienna (1958–60).

WORKS: DRAMATIC: *Yugen*, ballet (1965); *Gion Festival*, musical (1966); *Such a Long Absence*, opera (Osaka, April 3, 1972). **ORCH.:** 5 syms.: *Little Symphony* (1953), *Homeward* (1966), *Song of Flame* for Chorus and Orch. (1970), *Nagoya* for 2 Percussionists and Strings (1984), and *Sinfonia per Archi* (1990); *Rhapsody on an Okinawan Melody* (1961); *Divertimento* (1961); 2 piano concertos (1962, 1963); 2 violin concertos (1963, 1966); *Fantasy* for Clarinet and Strings (1963); *War Cry 1* (1965) and *2* (1966); Cello Concerto (1967); *Kaleidoscope* (1968); *Fantasy* for Violin and Orch. (1983); *Kyoto*, fantasia for Percussion and Strings (1983); Concerto for Piano, Percussion, and Strings (1984); *Midorino Honō* (1985); Concerto for Flute, Glockenspiel, Fūrin, and Strings (1986); *Fantasy* for Flute and Orch. (1989); *Maruyama-gawa*, symphonic poem (1990); *Ishikawa* (1992); Harp Concerto (1992). **CHAMBER:** Trio for Flute, Cello, and Piano (1958); Chamber Concerto for Wind Quintet, Piano, Double Bass, Vibraphone, and Percussion (1958); Violin Sonata (1964); *Guzai* for String Quartet (1965); Sonata for Solo Flute (1983); *Quartettuba* for 4 Tubas (1987); Bassoon Sonata (1987); *Passa Tempo* for 6 Horns (1989); Sonata for Solo Violin (1991). **VOCAL:** *Ofukuro* for Chorus and Strings (1968); *Response* for Chorus and Strings (1968–69); *Kyoto*, cantata for Soprano, Chorus, Harp, and Orch. (1970); *If We Shall . . .*, cantata for Chorus, Percussion, and String Ensemble (1984); *Kono Hachigatsu ni* for Chorus and Orch. (1988); *Dream Time* for Chorus and Orch. (1992).

Toye, (John) Francis, English writer on music, brother of **(Edward) Geoffrey Toye**; b. Winchester, Jan. 27, 1883; d. Florence, Oct. 31, 1964. He was a pupil of S.P. Waddington and E.J. Dent. He became a critic for various newspapers in London; in 1923 he lectured on modern music in the U.S.; from 1939 to 1946, lived in Rio de Janeiro; from 1946, in Florence.

WRITINGS (all publ. in London unless otherwise given): *The Well-Tempered Musician* (1925); *Giuseppe Verdi: His Life and Works* (1931; 2nd ed., 1962); *Rossini: A Study in Tragicomedy* (1934; 2nd ed., 1954); *For What We Have Received: An Autobiography* (Melbourne, 1950); *Italian Opera* (1952); *Truly Thankful? A Sequel to an Autobiography* (1957).

Toye, (Edward) Geoffrey, English conductor and composer, brother of **(John) Francis Toye**; b. Winchester, Feb. 17, 1889; d. London, June 11, 1942. He studied at the Royal College of Music in London. He became a conductor at various theaters there. He wrote an opera, *The Red Pen* (London, Feb. 7, 1927); a ballet; and some other works.

Tozzi, Giorgio (actually, **George**), gifted American bass; b. Chicago, Jan. 8, 1923. He commenced vocal training when he was 13, and later studied biology at De Paul Univ. while pursuing his vocal studies with Rosa Raisa, Giacomo Rimini, and John Daggett Howell in Chicago. On Dec. 29, 1948, he made his professional debut under the name George Tozzi as Tarquinius in Britten's *The Rape of Lucretia* in N.Y. After singing in the musical comedy *Tough at the Top* in London in 1949, he received further vocal instruction from Giulio Lorandi in Milan. In 1950 he made his debut as Rodolfo in *La sonnambula* at Milan's Teatro Nuovo. He sang for the first time at Milan's La Scala in 1953 as Stromminger in *La Wally*. On March 9, 1955, he made his Metropolitan Opera debut in N.Y. as Alvise. He remained on its roster until 1975, becoming well known for such roles as Rossini's Basilio, Mozart's Figaro, Pimen, Boris Godunov, Sparafucile, Ramfis, Hans Sachs, and Pogner; he also created the role of the Doctor in Barber's *Vanessa* there in 1958. His career took him to such operatic centers as San Francisco, Hamburg, Salzburg, Florence, and Munich. In 1977 he appeared in the U.S. premiere of Glinka's *Ruslan and Ludmilla* in Boston. A remarkably versatile artist, he was successful not only in opera and concert settings but also in films, television, and musical comedy. His fine vocal technique was complemented by his assured dramatic gifts. From 1991 he taught at the Indiana Univ. School of Music in Bloomington.

Tracy, Hugh (Travers), South African ethnomusicologist; b. Willand, Devon, Jan. 29, 1903; d. Krugersdorp, Transvaal, Oct. 23, 1977. He emigrated to Southern Rhodesia in 1921; in 1929 he began to record indigenous songs; from 1930, on advice from Holst and Vaughan Williams, he devoted himself to recording folk music from sub-Saharan Africa; also began a career as a broadcaster. He was regional director for Natal of the South African Broadcasting Corp. (1935–47); was co-founder of the African Music Soc. (1947), serving as its secretary and ed. of its newsletter (1948–53); also ed. the journal *African Music* (1955–71). He established the International Library of African Music in Roodepoort (1953); under his direction, it acquired an important collection of instruments and recordings, largely through his own fieldwork; he also ed. a series of more than 200 commercial recordings from its holdings. Tracey lectured at more than 50 univs. in Africa, Britain, and the U.S., and was awarded an honorary doctorate by the Univ. of Cape Town (1965). His publications and broadcasts were largely concerned with the role of African music in African education, and in the growth and understanding of modern African society.

WRITINGS: *Nyoma: An Introduction to Music for Southern Africans* (London, 1941); *Chopi Musicians: Their Music, Poetry, and Instruments* (London, 1948; 2nd ed., 1970); *African Dances of the Witwatersrand Gold Mines* (Johannesburg, 1952); *The Lion on the Path* (London, 1967).

Trambitsky, Victor (Nikolaievich), Russian pianist, conductor, teacher, and composer; b. Brest-Litovsk, Feb. 12, 1895; d. Leningrad, Aug. 13, 1970. He went to Petrograd, where he began training with Kalafati in 1915, and then became his pupil at the Cons. in 1917. In 1930 he moved to Sverdlovsk; he taught at the Cons. from 1933. He composed the operas *Gadfly* (Sverdlovsk, 1929), *Orlena* (1934; rev. as *For Life*, 1937), *The Storm* (1941; rev. 1957), *Days and Nights* (1950), and *The Laceworker Nastia* (Leningrad, 1963); also Violin Concerto (1921); Sym. (1945); *Symphonic Pictures* (1955); piano pieces; songs; folk-song arrangements.

Trampler, Walter, eminent German-American violist and pedagogue; b. Munich, Aug. 25, 1915. He received his early musical training from his father; later enrolled at the Munich Academy of Music. He made his debut in Munich as a violinist in 1933 and in Berlin as a violist in 1935; from 1935 to 1938, served as 1st violist in the Deutschlandsender orch.; then emigrated to America. From 1947 to 1955 he was a member of the New Music String Quartet; also made appearances with the Budapest, Juilliard, and Guarneri quartets and with the Beaux Arts Trio; was a member of the Chamber Music Soc. of Lincoln Center (1969–94). He taught at the Juilliard School of Music in N.Y (1962–72), the Peabody Cons. of Music in Baltimore (1968–70), the Yale School of Music (1970–72), Boston Univ. (1972–82), the New England Cons. of Music in Boston (1982–95), and the Mannes College of Music in N.Y. (from 1993). One of the foremost masters of the viola, he appeared as a solist with leading orchs. of North America and Europe. He premiered works by several composers, including Henze, Berio, and Persichetti.

Trân, Van Khê, Vietnamese ethnomusicologist; b. Binh Hoa Dong, July 24, 1921. He studied medicine in Hanoi (1941–43), then went to Paris to attend the Institut d'Études Politiques (1949–51). He studied organology with Schaeffner and musicology with Chailley of the Faculté des Lettres (1952–58), and historical research with Gaspardone at the Collège de France (1954–57); received his doctorate with the diss. *La Musique vietnamienne traditionelle* (1958; publ. in Paris, 1962). In 1960 he joined the CNRS, where he became director of research in 1973. In 1964 he became director of the Centre d'Études de Musique Orientale, where he taught Vietnamese instrumental performance. He began teaching at the Institut de Musicologie of the Univ. of Paris in 1968. His research focuses on the systematic and comparative study of Asian musical languages. He publ. *Việt-Nam: Les Traditions musicales* (Paris, 1967).

Tranchell, Peter (Andrew), English composer and teacher; b. Cuddalore, India, July 14, 1922. He studied at King's College, Univ. of Cambridge (B.A., 1946; Mus.B., 1949; M.A., 1950); taught at the Univ. from 1950 to 1989; was made a Fellow and director of music at Gonville and Caius College, Cambridge, in 1960.

WORKS: DRAMATIC: OPERAS: *The Mayor of Casterbridge* (Cambridge, July 30, 1951); *Zuleika* (1954); *Bacchae* (1956); *Troades* (1957); *Antigone* (1959). **BALLETS:** *Falstaff* (1950); *Fate's Revenge* (1951); *Euridice* (1952); *Spring Legend* (1957); *Images of Love* (1964). **CONCERT ENTERTAINMENTS:** *Daisy Simpkins* for Solo Voices, Chorus, and 2 Pianos (1954); *Murder at the Towers* for Solo Voices, Chorus, and 2 Pianos (1955; rev. 1986); *Aye, aye, Lucian!* for Men's Voices, Men's Chorus, and Piano (1960); *The Mating Season* for Solo Voices, Men's Chorus, and Piano (1962; rev. 1969); *His 1st Mayweek* for Solo Voices, Men's Chorus, and 2 Pianos (1963); *The Robot Emperor* for Men's Voices, Men's Chorus, and Orch. (1965). **ORCH.:** *Decalogue* for Brass, Percussion, and Organ (1956); *Scherzetto* (1960); *Eclogue* (1962); *Festive Overture* (1966); Concerto Grosso (1972). **CHAMBER:** Organ Sonata (1958); Organ Sonatina (1968); *Movements* for Flute, Viola, Bassoon, Harpsichord, and Piano (1987); piano pieces. **VOCAL:** *The Joyous Year* for Chorus and Orch. (1961); *3 Poems of Po Chü-i* for Baritone, Men's Chorus, and Orch. (1964); *Saul's Successor*, cantata for Soloists, Men's Voices, Organ, Percussion, and Timpani (1969); *Te Deum* for Chorus, 2 Violins, Piano, and Organ (1975); choral songs; anthems and carols; Psalms.

Trapp, (Hermann Emil Alfred) Max, German composer and teacher; b. Berlin, Nov. 1, 1887; d. there, May 29, 1971. He studied piano with Dohnányi and composition with Juon at the Berlin Hochschule für Musik (1905–11), where he later was on its piano faculty (1920–34); also gave a master class in composition at the Dortmund Cons. (1924–30); in 1929, became a member of the Prussian Academy of Arts in Berlin, where he taught a master class in composition (1934–45); from 1951 to 1953 he taught at the Berlin Cons. In 1955 he was elected to membership in the Berlin Academy of Arts. His style was neo-Classical with a strong polyphonic texture, in the tradition of Max Reger. He was also active as a landscape painter.

WORKS: ORCH.: 7 syms., including No. 1, *Sinfonia giocosa* (1915), No. 2 (1918), No. 3 (1924), No. 4 (1931), No. 5 (1936), and No. 6 (1946); Violin Concerto (1922); Piano Concerto (1930); 3 concertos for Orch. (1934, 1940, 1946); Cello Concerto (1935); *Allegro deciso* (1942); *Kleine Spielmusik* for Chamber Orch. (1944); *Symphonischer Prolog* (1944). **CHAMBER:** 2 piano quintets; 3 piano quartets; String Quartet (1935); Violin Sonata; piano pieces. **VOCAL:** Choral works, including *Vom ewigen Licht* for Soprano, Baritone, Chorus, and Orch. (1942); songs.

Traubel, Helen (Francesca), noted American soprano; b. St. Louis, June 20, 1899; d. Santa Monica, Calif., July 28, 1972. She studied with Vetta Karst. She made her concert debut as soloist in Mahler's 4th Sym. with the St. Louis Sym. Orch. on Dec. 13, 1923. On May 12, 1937, she made her Metropolitan Opera debut in N.Y. as Mary Rutledge in Damrosch's *The Man without a Country*; her first major role there was Sieglinde on Dec. 28, 1939; subsequently became the leading American Wagnerian soprano on its roster, excelling especially as Isolde, Elisabeth, Brünnhilde, Elsa, and Kundry. In 1953 she made appearances in N.Y. nightclubs; this prompted objections from the Metropolitan Opera management, and as a result she resigned from the Metropolitan. She also appeared on Broadway in *Pipe Dream* (1955), in films, and on television. She publ. the mystery novels *The Ptomaine Canary* and *The Metropolitan Opera Murders* (N.Y., 1951), and an autobiography, *St. Louis Woman* (N.Y., 1959).

Traugott, Rohner, Swiss-born American music magazine publisher and music educator; b. St. Gallen, Dec. 23, 1906. His family moved to the U.S. in 1914. He was educated at Central Wesleyan College (degree, 1928) and Northwestern Univ. (M.A., 1932). He held teaching positions in Marshall, Minn., and Asheville, N.C., then joined the faculty at Northwestern Univ. (1933–60). He was the founding ed. of 2 important music publications, *The Instrumentalist* (1946) and *Clavier* (1962); also was founding president of the National School Orch. Assn. at Interlochen, Mich. (1958), and in 1960 organized the National Band Assn.

Trautwein, Friedrich (Adolf), German electrical engineer; b. Würzburg, Aug. 11, 1888; d. Düsseldorf, Dec. 20, 1956. He was trained in electrical engineering; then was active in radio work. He became a lecturer (1930) and a prof. of musical acoustics (1935) at the Berlin Hochschule für Musik; founded his own composition school in Düsseldorf after World War II, which was made part of the Robert Schumann Cons. in 1950. In 1930 he constructed an electronic musical instrument which became known, after the first syllable of his name, as the Trautonium. Hindemith wrote a concerto for it. Trautwein publ. a Trautonium method as *Trautoniumlehre* (1936); also wrote numerous articles on acoustics and electronic music.

BIBL.: F. Winckel, "F. T.," *Musica*, XI (1957).

Travis, Roy (Elihu), American composer and teacher; b. N.Y., June 24, 1922. He studied with William J. Mitchell and Luening at Columbia Univ. (B.A., 1947; M.A., 1951); also studied privately with Salzer (1947–50), with Wagenaar at the Juilliard School of Music in N.Y. (B.S., 1949; M.S., 1950), and with Milhaud on a Fulbright scholarship in Paris (1951–52). He taught at Columbia Univ. (1952–53), the Mannes College of Music (1952–57), and at the Univ. of Calif. at Los Angeles (from 1957), where he was a prof. (from 1968). In 1972–73 he held a Guggenheim fellowship.

WORKS: OPERAS: *The Passion of Oedipus* (1965; Los Angeles, Nov. 8, 1968); *The Black Bacchants* (1982). **ORCH.:** *Symphonic Allegro* (1951); *Collage* (1967–68); Piano Concerto (1969). **CHAMBER:** String Quartet (1958); *Duo concertante* for Violin and Piano (1967); *Barma*, septet for Flute or Piccolo, Piano, Clarinet, Violin, Cello, Double Bass, and Percussion (1968); *Switched-on Ashanti* for Flute or Piccolo and Tape (1973); piano pieces, including 2 sonatas (1954; *African*, 1966). **VOCAL:** Songs.

Traxel, Josef, German tenor; b. Mainz, Sept. 29, 1916; d. Stuttgart, Oct. 8, 1975. He studied at the Hochschule für Musik in Darmstadt. He made his operatic debut as Don Ottavio in Mainz in 1942; in 1946 he joined the Nuremberg Opera; from 1952 he was a member of the Württemberg State Theater in Stuttgart; later taught at the Hochschule für Musik there. He also sang at Salzburg, Bayreuth, Berlin, Vienna, and Munich; toured North America as well. His operatic repertoire ranged from Mozart to Wagner; he was also a concert singer.

Treger, Charles, American violinist, teacher, and administrator; b. Detroit, May 13, 1935. He studied with William Engels (1944–52), Szymon Goldberg, Ivan Galamian, and William Kroll. He made his debut as a soloist in the Wieniawski 2nd Violin Concerto when he was 11. After winning the Wieniawski Competition in Warsaw in 1962, he toured Europe as soloist with the Pittsburgh Sym. Orch. (1964); in 1969 he was a founding member of the Chamber Music Soc. of Lincoln Center, with which he remained active until 1973; from 1978 he toured widely with Andre Watts. He became a visiting prof. at the Hartt School of Music in Hartford, Conn., in 1972, and also gave master classes; in 1984 he was named president and director of the Meadowmount School in Westport, Conn. Treger has won accolades for his championship of neglected works from the violin repertoire.

Treharne, Bryceson, English-American music editor and composer; b. Merthyr Tydfil, Wales, May 30, 1879; d. N.Y., Feb. 4, 1948. He studied at the Royal College of Music in London, under Parry, Stanford, and Davies. In 1901 he went to Australia; was a prof. at the Univ. of Adelaide; returning to Europe in 1911, he lived in Paris, Milan, Vienna, and Munich; at the outbreak of World War I, he was interned in Ruhleben. There he wrote nearly 200 songs and other works; an exchange of prisoners of war enabled him to return to England. In 1917 he settled in America; was music ed. for the Boston Music Co. and Willis Music Co. (1928–47). Among his songs are *Ozymandias, The Fair Circassian, A Lover's Prayer, The Night, Dreams, Love's Tribute,* and *Renunciation.*

Treigle, Norman, remarkable American bass-baritone; b. New Orleans, March 6, 1927; d. there, Feb. 16, 1975. He sang in a church choir as a child; upon graduation from high school in 1943, he served in the navy. After two years in service, he returned to New Orleans and studied voice with Elizabeth Wood. He made his operatic debut in 1947 with the New Orleans Opera as Lodovico in Verdi's *Otello.* He then joined the N.Y. City Opera, making his debut there on March 28, 1953, as Colline in *La Bohème*; he remained with the company for 20 years, establishing himself as a favorite with the public. Among his most successful roles were Figaro in Mozart's *Le nozze di Figaro,* Don Giovanni, Méphistophélès, and Boris Godunov; he also sang in modern operas, including leading roles in the premieres of 3 operas by Carlisle Floyd: *The Passion of Jonathan Wade* (N.Y., Oct. 11, 1962), *The Sojourner and Mollie Sinclair* (Raleigh, N.C., Dec. 2, 1963), and *Markheim* (New Orleans, March 31, 1966). Treigle's other parts in contemporary operas were the title role in Dallapiccola's *The Prisoner* and that of the grandfather in Copland's *The Tender Land.* His untimely death, from an overdose of sleeping pills, deprived the American musical theater of one of its finest talents.

Treitler, Leo, German-born American musicologist; b. Dortmund, Jan. 26, 1931. He emigrated to the U.S. and became a naturalized citizen in 1946; studied at the Univ. of Chicago (B.A., 1950; M.A., 1957); after training in composition from Blacher at the Berlin Hochschule für Musik (1957–58), he pursued studies in musicology at Princeton Univ. (M.F.A., 1960; Ph.D., 1966, with the diss. *The Aquitanian Repertories of Sacred Monody in the 11th and 12th Centuries*). He taught briefly at Princeton Univ. (1960–61) and more extensively at the Univ. of Chicago (1962–66) and Brandeis Univ. (1966–75). In 1974 he became a prof. at the State Univ. of N.Y. at Stony Brook, and in 1987 a Distinguished Prof. at the City Univ. of N.Y. Graduate Center. His valuable articles on the music of the Middle Ages and early Renaissance have appeared in many scholarly journals. He publ. *Music and the Historical Imagination* (1989).

Tremblay, George (Amedée), Canadian-born American pianist, teacher, and composer; b. Ottawa, Jan. 14, 1911; d. Tijuana, Mexico, July 14, 1982. He studied music with his father, a church organist; in 1919 he was taken to the U.S.; eventually settled in Los Angeles; there he met Schoenberg (1936) and became his ardent disciple and friend. In 1939 he became a naturalized American citizen. He adopted the method of composition with 12-tones, which he diversified considerably, expounding his theoretical ideas in a book, *The Definitive Cycle of the 12-Tone Row and its Application in all Fields of Composition, including the Computer* (1974). He became an esteemed teacher; among his students were André Previn, Quincy Jones, and Johnny Mandel, as well as numerous successful composers for television and films.

WORKS: ORCH.: 2 unnumbered syms.: *Chaparral Symphony* (1938) and *The Phoenix: A Dance Symphony* (1982); 3 numbered syms. (1949, 1952, 1973); *Prelude, Aria, Fugue and Postlude* for Symphonic Band (1967). **CHAMBER:** 4 string quartets (1936–63); 2 wind quintets (1940, 1950); Piano Trio (1959); Quartet for Oboe, Clarinet, Bassoon, and Viola (1964); String Trio (1964); Duo for Viola and Piano (1966); Double Bass Sonata (1967); Wind Sextet (1968); piano pieces, including 3 sonatas.

Tremblay, Gilles (Léonce), Canadian composer, teacher, pianist, and ondist; b. Arvida, Quebec, Sept. 6, 1932. He studied privately with Jocelyne Binet (counterpoint), Isabelle Delorme (solfège), Papineau-Couture (acoustics), and Edmond Trudel (piano) before pursuing his training at the Montreal Cons. (1949–54), where he was a student of Champagne (composition and theory) and Germaine Malépart (piano; premier prix, 1953). After attending the Marlboro (Vt.) Music School (summers, 1950–51; 1953) and studying music history with Vallerand at the Univ. of Montreal (1952–53), he went to Paris and pursued his training at the Cons. with Loriod (theory and piano, 1954–57), Messiaen (analysis, 1954–57; premier prix, 1957), and Martenot (Ondes Martenot, 1956–58; première médaille, 1958). He also studied electroacoustic music with Stockhausen at the summer courses in new music in Darmstadt and was a student of Vaurabourg-Honegger at the École Normale Superieure de Musique in Paris (counterpoint; licence en musique, 1958). From 1959 to 1961 he worked with the Groupe de recherches musicales at the ORTF in Paris, and he returned to Darmstadt to attend the courses given by Boulez and Pousseur in 1960. Returning to Canada, he taught at the Quebec Cons. (1961–66). From 1982 to 1988 he was president of the Société de musique contemporaine du Quèbec in Montreal, serving also as its artistic director from 1986 to 1988. In 1968 he was awarded the Prix de musique Calixa-Lavallée. He was made an Officer of the Ordre national du Quèbec in 1991. In his music, Tremblay is ever cognizant of the many-faceted elements of sonority. His compositions are particularly notable for their pointillistic writing.

WORKS: DRAMATIC: *Un 9* for Mime, 2 Trumpets, and 2 Percussion (Montreal, April 9, 1987). **ORCH.:** *Cantique de durées* (1960; Paris, March 24, 1963); *Jeux de solstices* (Ottawa, April 23, 1974); *Fleuves* (1976; Montreal, May 3, 1977); *Vers le soleil* (Paris, March 11, 1978); *Katadrone (Contrecri)* (Montreal, Oct. 19, 1988); *Musique du feu* for Piano and Orch. (1991). **CHAMBER:** *Mobile* for Violin and Piano (1962); *Champs I* for Piano and 2 Percussion (1965; rev. 1969), *II: Souffles* for 2 Flutes, Oboe, Clarinet, Horn, 2 Trumpets, 2 Trombones, 2 Percussion, Double Bass, and Piano (Montreal, March 21, 1968), and *III: Vers* for 2 Flutes, Clarinet, Trumpet, Horn, 3 Violins, Double Bass, and 3 Percussion (Stratford, Ontario, Aug. 2, 1969); *. . . le sifflement des vents porteurs de l'amour . . .* for Flute, Percussion, and Microphones (Ottawa, March 1, 1971); *Solstices (ou Les Jours et les saisons tournent)* for 1, 2, 3, or 4 Groups of 6 Instruments (1971; Montreal, May 17, 1972); *Compostelle I* for 18 Instruments (Paris, Nov. 30, 1978); *Le Signe du lion* for Horn and Tam-tam (Montreal, Oct. 8, 1981); *Envoi* for Piano and 15 Instruments (Montreal, Feb. 17, 1983); *Envol* for Flute (1984); *Triojubilus* for Flute, Harp, and Cowbells (1985); *Cedres en voiles* for Cello (1989). **PIANO:** *Deux Pièces pour piano: Phases* and *Réseaux* (1956–58); *Traçantes* (1976). **VOCAL:** *Kèkoba* for Soprano, Mezzo-soprano, Tenor, Percussion, and Ondes Martenot (1965; Montreal, Feb. 25, 1966; rev. 1967); *Oralléluiants* for Soprano, Flute, Bass Clarinet, Horn, 3 Double Basses, 2 Percussion, and Microphones (Toronto, Feb. 8, 1975); *DZEI (Voies de feu)* for Soprano, Flute, Bass Clarinet, Piano, and Percussion (Vancouver, April 12, 1981); *Les Vêpres de la Vierge* for Soprano, Chorus, and 13 Instruments (Abbey of Notre-Dame de Sylvanès, France, July 20, 1986). **ELECTROACOUSTIC:** *Exercise I* (1959) and *II* (1960); *Centre-elan* (1967); *Sonorisation de Pavillion du Québec* (1967).

Treptow, Günther (Otto Walther), German tenor; b. Berlin, Oct. 22, 1907; d. there, March 28, 1981. He studied at the Berlin Hochschule für Musik. He made his operatic debut in 1936 at the Deutsches Opernhaus in Berlin as the Italian Tenor in *Der Rosenkavalier.* Although placed on the forbidden list of non-Aryans by the Nazis, he continued to sing in Berlin until 1942, when he joined the Bavarian State Opera in Munich. After the Nazi collapse, he again sang in Berlin at the Städtische Oper (1945–50) and at the Vienna State Opera (1947–55); appeared as Siegmund in 1951 and 1952 at the Bayreuth Festival and as Siegfried at London's Covent Garden in 1953. He made his Metropolitan Opera debut in N.Y. as Siegmund in *Die Walküre* on

Feb. 1, 1951; remained on its roster until the close of that season; continued to sing in Europe until his retirement in 1961. In 1971 he was made a Kammersänger.

Tretyakov, Viktor (Viktorovich), noted Russian violinist; b. Krasnoyarsk, Oct. 17, 1946. He studied at the Irkutsk Music School as a child, stoutly braving the Siberian cold; then moved to a more temperate climate in Moscow, where he studied at the Central Music School with Yury Yankelevich (from 1959), continuing with him at the Cons. (graduated, 1970) and as a postgraduate student. In 1966 he won the Tchaikovsky Competition, which automatically lifted him to the upper layers of the violinistic firmament, with applause-rich tours in Russia and later the enviable European and American engagements. A typical product of the Russian school of violin playing, Tretyakov combines the expected virtuosity in technical resources with a diffuse lyricism touched with melancholy in the Romantic repertoire.

Tréville, Yvonne de (real name, **Edyth La Gierse**), American soprano; b. Galveston, Texas (of a French father and an American mother), Aug. 25, 1881; d. N.Y., Jan. 25, 1954. She made her debut in N.Y. as Marguerite (1898); then went to Paris, where she studied with Madame Marchesi. She appeared at the Opéra-Comique as Lakme (June 20, 1902); sang in Madrid, Brussels, Vienna, Budapest, Cairo, and in Russia; from 1913, gave concert tours in the U.S. and sang in light operas. Her voice had a compass of 3 full octaves, reaching high G.

Trifunović, Vitomir, Serbian composer; b. Bukovica, Nov. 4, 1916. He studied composition with Slavenski and Živković at the Belgrade Academy of Music. He became an ed. for new music at Radio Belgrade in 1959. His early music is Romantic, but later he acquired a thoroughly modern sound.

WORKS: ORCH.: *Šumadija,* suite for Chamber Orch. (1960); *Lamentoso* for Strings (1961); *Heroic Overture* (1962); *Toccata* (1963); *Simfonijska slika* (Symphonic Picture; 1964); *Folklorni triptih* (Folklore Triptychon; 1961); *Symphonic Dance* (1968); *Synthesen 4* (1969); *Antinomije* (1972); *Asocijacije* (Associations; 1973). **CHAMBER:** Piano Sonatina (1956); Violin Sonata (1958); 2 string quartets (1959, 1973). **VOCAL:** *Vidici* (The Horizons), cantata (1971); arrangements of folk music.

Trimble, Lester (Albert), American music critic, teacher, and composer; b. Bangor, Wis., Aug. 29, 1920; d. N.Y., Dec. 31, 1986. He began violin studies in Milwaukee when he was 9; later studied with Lopatnikoff and Dorian at the Carnegie Inst. of Technology in Pittsburgh (B.F.A., 1948; M.F.A.); also studied with Milhaud and Copland at the Berkshire Music Center at Tanglewood, and then with Boulanger, Milhaud, and Honegger in Paris (1950–52). He began writing music criticism for the *Pittsburgh Post-Gazette* while in school; then was a music critic for the *N.Y. Herald-Tribune* (1952–62), the *Nation* (1957–62), the *Washington Evening Star* (1963–68), and *Stereo Review* (1968–74); also was managing ed. of *Musical America* (1960–61). He was composer-in-residence of the N.Y. Phil. (1967–68) and at the Wolf Trap Farm Park (1973). He was prof. of composition at the Univ. of Maryland (1963–68) and taught at N.Y.'s Juilliard School (from 1971).

WORKS: DRAMATIC: *Little Clay Cart,* incidental music (1953); *The Tragical History of Dr. Faustus,* incidental music (1954); *Boccaccio's Nightingale,* opera (1958–62; rev. 1983); film scores. **ORCH.:** 3 syms.: No. 1 (1951), No. 2 (1968), and No. 3, *The Tricentennial* (1984–85; Troy, N.Y., Sept. 26, 1986); Concerto for Wind and Strings (1954); *Closing Piece* (1957; rev. as *Sonic Landscape,* 1967); *5 Episodes* (1961–62; also for Piano); *Notturno* for Strings (1967; arranged from the String Quartet No. 2); *Duo Concertante* for 2 Violins and Orch. (1968); *Panels I* for 11 Instruments (1969–70), *II* for 13 Instruments (1971–72), and *IV* for 16 Instruments (1973–74; orig. a ballet); *Panels for Orchestra* (1976; rev. 1983); Violin Concerto (1976–81); band music. **CHAMBER:** 2 string quartets (1949, 1955); *Woodwind Serenade* (1952); Double Concerto for Instrumental Ensemble (1964); *Panels V* for String Quartet (1974–75), *VI: Quadraphonics* for Percussion Quartet (1974–75), and *VII: Serenade* for Oboe, Clarinet, Horn, Harpsichord, Violin, Viola, Cello, and Percussion (1975). **OTHER:** Choruses; song cycles; solo songs; electronic pieces.

Trimpin, (Gerhard), German-born inventor, practitioner, and builder of soundsculpture and computerized acoustical instruments; b. Istein bei Lörrach, Basel, Nov. 26, 1951. Professionally he is known by only his surname. He had an ordinary musical training, with an emphasis on playing wind instruments, but recurrent lip infections forced him to abandon such labial practices; he then studied electro-mechanic engineering (1966–73). In 1979 he received a degree from the Univ. of Berlin in social pedagogy; later was an instructor at the Sweelinck Cons. in Amsterdam (1985–87), where he also conducted research in music and acoustic sound technologies. From 1976 to 1979 he also was active with Berlin;s Theater Zentrifuge; also produced set designs for San Quentin Drama Workshop. Trimpin designed 4 Bowed Cymbals for Ton de Leeuw's *Resonances* (1987). He also designed a percussive installation of 96 suspended Dutch wooden shoes for the 1986 New Music Festival in Middelburg; in 1987 he designed a similar installation, *Floating Klompen,* at the Jan van Eyck Art Academy in Maastricht, which was subsequently seen at the San Francisco Exploratorium in 1990. From 1988 he collaborated with Conlon Nancarrow in Mexico City. Trimpin originated his own composition entitled *Circumference* for specially adapted instruments, first seen at the New Music America Festival in N.Y. in 1989, and subsequently in Seattle, Minneapolis, and Vancouver. Other works include *Three Ply* (Seattle, 1984), *The Cocktail Party Effect* (Banff, 1990), *Messing Around* (Seattle, 1990; Valencia, Calif., 1992; Mexico City, 1993), *Contraption 1PP71512* (San Francisco, 1991; Newfoundland, 1992; Los Angeles, 1992; Seattle, 1993; Montreal, 1994), *D.R.A.M.A.ohno* (Seattle, 1993; Minneapolis, 1993; Iowa City, 1993), *Ringo* (Amsterdam, 1985; Madrid, 1994), *Liquid Percussion* (N.Y. and San Francisco, 1991), and *PHFFFT* (N.Y., 1991; Portland, Oreg., 1992; Tacoma, 1993; Ghent and Donaueschingen, 1994). In 1979 he settled in Seattle, where he resides in a Faustian workshop-laboratory, filled with synchronously and anachronously activated sound objects. In 1989 he participated in the "Composer-to-Composer" symposium in Telluride, Colo., and in 1990 was artist-in-residence at the Banff Art Center. Among his awards are grants from the Seattle Arts Commission (1990), the NEA (1992), Meet the Composer (1993), the Foundation for Contemporary Performance Arts (1994), and the Lila Wallace-Reader's Digent "Artist in Giverny, France" program. In 1995 he received a commission from the Merce Cunningham Dance Foundation. In 1995 he also designed a lavish installation of sounding fabrics, entitled *Singing Textiles,* for Switzerland's Museum Technorama. When not engaged in musical endeavors, Trimpin periodically engages in one of his other specialties, salmon fishing.

Trojahn, Manfred, German composer and teacher; b. Cremlingen, near Braunschweig, Oct. 22, 1949. He received training in orch. music at the Niedersächsische Musikschule in Braunschweig (1966–70; diploma, 1970) and composition with Diether de la Motte at the Staatlichen Hochschule für Musik in Hamburg. In 1975 he won the Bach Prize in Hamburg. In 1979–80 he was in residence at the Villa Massimo in Rome. He was awarded the Niedersächsisches Künstlerstipendium in 1984. In 1991 he became a teacher of composition at the Robert-Schumann-Hochschule in Düsseldorf. Trojahn utilizes various contemporary modes of expression with a subsuming individuality.

WORKS: DRAMATIC: *Enrico,* dramatic comedy (1989–91; Schwetzingen, April 11, 1991); *Das wüste Land,* opera (1994). **ORCH.:** 4 syms.: No. 1 (1973), No. 2 (Donaueschingen, Oct. 22, 1978), No. 3 (1984; Berlin, April 19, 1985), and No. 4 for Tenor and Orch. (Hamburg, Aug. 16, 1992); *Notturni trasognati* for Alto Flute and Chamber Orch. (London, June 13, 1977); *Abschied . . .* (Düsseldorf, Oct. 18, 1978); *Conduct* for Strings and Percussion (1978; Gelsenkirchen, May 14, 1979; also for

Organ); *Erstes See-Bild* (1979–80; Berlin, Nov. 9, 1980; 1st part of *Fünf See-Bilder* for Mezzo-soprano and Orch., 1981–83); *Berceuse* (Stuttgart, Oct. 4, 1980); Flute Concerto (1981–83; Berlin, Sept. 14, 1983); *L'Autunno* (1986–90; Berlin, June 23, 1990); *Cinq Epigraphes* (Berlin, Sept. 12, 1987); *Variationen* (Cleveland, Sept. 24, 1987); *Transir* (Freiburg im Breisgau, May 24, 1988); *Notturno* for Winds, Strings, Celesta, and Harp (Hamburg, Sept. 3, 1989); Oboe Concerto (1990–91; Munich, June 7, 1991); *Quattro pezzi* (1992; Kiel, Sept. 1993); *Divertissement* for Oboe and Chamber Orch. (1992–93; Munich, May 7, 1993); *Cornisches Nachtlied* (1994). **CHAMBER:** *Deux pièces brèves* for String Quartet (Aurillac, France, Aug. 29, 1973); 3 string quartets: No. 1 (1976), No. 2 with Clarinet and Mezzo-soprano (1979–80; Frankfurt am Main, Sept. 9, 1981), and No. 3 (Hamburg, Nov. 4, 1983); *Fantasia* for Guitar (Stuttgart, Oct. 10, 1979); *. . . une campaagne noire de soleil*, 7 ballet scenes for Chamber Ensemble: *I: Déplorations* (Berlin, Dec. 14, 1982), *II: Silences* (1982; Cambridge, Mass., April 2, 1983), *III: Chimèrès* (Nuremberg, Nov. 19, 1983), *IV: Cigales* (1992), *V: Chants noirs* (Cologne, Oct. 10, 1986), *VI: Exaltations* (1992–92), and *VII: Processions* (1986; Ludwigshafen, Jan. 12, 1987); *Berceuse* for 5 Strings (1983; Bavarian Radio, Munich, May 26, 1984); Violin Sonata (Mannheim, Oct. 11, 1983); Cello Sonata (1983; Hamburg, Feb. 11, 1984); *Soleares*, 2 pieces for Piano and String Quartet (1st piece, Braunschweig, Oct. 20, 1985; 2nd piece, 1988; Cologne, Nov. 14, 1990); *Épitaphe* for 4 Flutes (Berlin, Aug. 27, 1986); *Fragmente für Antigone*, 6 pieces for String Quartet (Barcelona, Oct. 11, 1988); *Fünf Intermezzi* for Guitar and Chamber Ensemble (1988–89); *Poème abandonné* for Saxophone Quartet, Viola, Cello, and Double Bass (1989; Łwów, April 17, 1990). **KEYBOARD: PIANO:** *Berceuse* (1980; Hannover, Jan. 26, 1981); *La folia* for 2 Pianos (Berlin, Sept. 16, 1982). **ORGAN:** *Conduct* for 2 Organists (Kassel, Sept. 22, 1977; also for Strings and Percussion). **VOCAL:** *Madrigal* for Chorus (1975); *. . . stiller Gefährt der Nacht* for Soprano, Flute, Cello, Percussionist, and Celesta (Karlsruhe, June 6, 1978); *Fünf See-Bilder* for Mezzo-soprano and Orch. (1979–83; 1st complete perf., Hamburg, Feb. 12, 1984); *Elegía del tiempo final* for Tenor and 7 Instruments (1981–82); *Quattro Madrigali* for Chorus, 4 Violins, and 4 Cellos (1983; Stuttgart, Feb. 28, 1984); *Trakl-Fragmente* for Mezzo-soprano and Piano (1983–84; Hamburg, Feb. 10, 1984); *Nachtwandlung* for Mezzo-soprano and 14 Instruments (1983–84; Paris, Feb. 17, 1986); *Requiem* for Soprano, Mezzo-soprano, Baritone, Chorus, and Chamber Orch. (1983–85; Braunschweig, Nov. 10, 1985); *Die Nachtigall* for 2 Sopranos, Mezzo-soprano, and 3 Clarinets (Hannover, Nov. 17, 1984); *Zwei Motetten* for Chorus (1984; Hannover, May 23, 1985); *Aubade* for 2 Sopranos (1987; Leningrad, April 18, 1990); *Spätrot* for Mezzo-soprano and Piano (1987); *Lieder auf der Flucht* for Baritone, Guitar, and 13 Instruments (1988–89; Frankfurt am Main, Sept. 2, 1989); *Ave Maria* for Chorus (1991; Braunschweig, May 27, 1992); *Grodek* for Baritone and 8 Instruments (Berlin, Sept. 29, 1991).

Trojan, Václav, Czech composer and teacher; b. Pilsen, April 24, 1907; d. Prague, July 5, 1983. He was a student of Wiedermann (organ) and of Ostrčil and Dědeček (conducting) at the Prague Cons. (1923–27) He also attended the master classes in composition given by Suk and Novák (1927–29), and received instruction in quarter tone and 6th tone music in A. Hába's class there. From 1937 to 1945 he was music manager of the Prague Radio, and then lectured on theater and film music at the Prague Academy of Music from 1949. In 1982 he was made a National Artist by the Czech government.

WORKS: DRAMATIC: *Kolotoč* (The Merry-Go-Round), children's opera (1936–39); *Zlatá brána* (Golden Gate), scenic poem (1971–73); *Sen noci svatojánské* (A Midsummer Night's Dream), ballet-pantomime (1982); music for puppet films. **ORCH.:** *Tarantella* (1940); *Pohádka* (Fairy Tale; 1946); *Průvod starobylou Prahou* (Procession Through Old Prague; 1956–57); *Tarantella di Taranto* (1957); *Pohádky* (Fairy Tales) for Accordion and Orch. (1959); *Sinfonietta armoniosa* for Chamber Orch. (1970); *Čtyři karikatury (s jednou navíc)* [4 Caricatures (and 1 Extra)] for Wind Orch., Percussion Instruments, and Piano (1974); Concertino for Trumpet and Small Orch. (1977). **CHAMBER:** String Quartet (1927); 2 string quartets (1929, 1945); 2 wind quintets (1937, 1953); *Princ Bajaja* (Bajaja the Prince), fairy suite for Violin, Guitar, and Accordion (1967); *Divertimento* for Wind Quintet (1977); *Noneto Favoloso* for Flute, Oboe, Clarinet, Horn, Violin, Viola, Cello, and Double Bass (1977). **VOCAL:** Cantatas; choruses; songs.

Trombly, Preston (Andrew), American composer; b. Hartford, Conn., Dec. 30, 1945. He studied composition with Whittenberg at the Univ. of Conn. (B.M., 1968), with Arel and Davidovsky at Yale Univ. (M.M.A., 1972), and with Crumb at the Berkshire Music Center at Tanglewood; also had some instruction in conducting from Bernstein and Barzin; then devoted himself to teaching and composing.

WORKS: ORCH.: *Set* for Jazz Orch. (1968); *Doubles* (1970); *Music for the Theatre* (1972); Chamber Concerto for Piano and 11 Instruments (1975). **CHAMBER:** Woodwind Quintet (1968); *Opera/Septima* for Flute, Oboe, Bass Clarinet, Trumpet, Violin, Viola, and Cello (1969–70); *Music* for Violin, Viola, and Cello (1970); *In memoriam: Igor Stravinsky* for Woodwind Quartet, Viola, and Double Bass (1972); Trio in 3 Movements for Flute, Double Bass, and Percussion (1973); *Trio da camera* for Flute, Cello, and Piano (1975); *The Windmills of Paris* for Flute, Clarinet, Violin, Cello, and Piano (1976); *The Bridge: 3 Pieces after Hart Crane* for Clarinet, Saxophone, Cello, and Piano (1979); String Quartet (1979); *Time of the Supple Iris* for Viola, Double Bass, Oboe or English Horn, Bass Clarinet, and Percussion (1980); *Aurora Quartet* for Oboe, Violin, Cello, and Harpsichord (1983–84). **WITH TAPE:** *Kinetics III* for Flute (1971); *G.H.M.T.S.* for Flute, Clarinet, Double Bass, and Vibraphone (1971–72); *Fantasy* for Cello (1974); *Toccata* for Trombone (1974); *The Trumpets of Solitude* for Flute, Clarinet, Violin, Cello, and Piano (1982).

Trowell, Brian (Lewis), English musicologist; b. Wokingham, Berkshire, Feb. 21, 1931. He was educated at Christ's Hospital and Gonville and Caius College, Cambridge (B.A., 1953; Mus.B., 1956; Ph.D., 1960, with the diss. *Music Under the Later Plantagenets*). He taught at the Univ. of Birmingham (1957–62) and at King's College, London (1964–65). From 1967 to 1970 he was head of radio opera for the BBC in London. In 1970 he was Regents' Prof. at the Univ. of Calif. at Berkeley. He rejoined the faculty of King's College as a reader in music in 1970, and then was King Edward VII Prof. of Music there from 1974 to 1988. In 1988 he became Heather Prof. of Music at the Univ. of Oxford. He was president of the Royal Musical Assn. from 1983 to 1988. From 1983 to 1993 he was chairman of the editorial committee of Musica Britannica. Trowell is an authority on English music of the 15th century and on opera in all eras. He has contributed valuable articles to various journals, reference works, and other publications. With M. and I. Bent, he edited the 2nd edition, rev., of Dunstable's complete works in Musica Britannica, VIII (1970).

Troyanos, Tatiana, brilliant American mezzo-soprano; b. N.Y., Sept. 12, 1938; d. there, Aug. 21, 1993. She studied at the Juilliard School of Music in N.Y. (graduated, 1963) and with Hans Heinz. On April 25, 1963, she made her operatic debut as Hippolyta in *A Midsummer Night's Dream* at the N.Y. City Opera, where she then appeared as Marina, Cherubino, and Jocasta. In 1965 she made her first appearance at the Hamburg State Opera as Preziosilla. She remained on its roster until 1975, winning distinction for such roles as Elisetta, Dorabella, and Baba. She also created the role of Jeanne in *The Devil's of Loudun* there in 1969. In 1966 she sang for the first time at the Aix-en-Provence Festival as Strauss' Composer. In 1969 she made her debut at London's Covent Garden and at the Salzburg Festival as Octavian. In 1971 she sang Ariodante in the first operatic production given at the Kennedy Center in Washington, D.C.; that same year she also made her debut at the Chicago Lyric Opera as Charlotte. In 1975 she sang Bellini's Romeo in Boston. On March 8, 1976, she made a memorable debut at the Metropolitan Opera in N.Y. as Octavian. In subsequent years, Troyanos was one of the leading members of the Metropolitan Opera, excelling in such roles as Amneris, Brangäne, Eboli, the Composer, Kundry, Didon, Santuzza, Orlovsky, Adalgisa, and Geschwitz. In 1992 she created the role of Queen Isabella in Glass's *The Voyage* there. Her death from cancer deprived the Metropolitan Opera of the extraordinary gifts of one of America's finest singers.

Truax, Barry (Douglas), Canadian composer; b. Chatham, Ontario, May 10, 1947. He studied physics and mathematics at Queen's Univ., Kingston (B.S., 1969); became interested in electronic sounds and pursued training with Cortland Hultberg at the Univ. of British Columbia (M.M., 1971); completed his studies with Laske and Koenig at the Inst. of Sonology at the Univ. of Utrecht (1971–73). In 1973 he became associated with R. Murray Schafer through the World Soundscape Project in Vancouver; was director of the Sonic Research Studio and assistant prof. in the dept. of communication at Simon Fraser Univ. (1976–83), where he subsequently was assoc. prof.; also was assoc. prof. in the Centre for the Arts. He publ. *Handbook for Acoustic Ecology* (1978) and *Acoustic Communication* (1985). Truax devoted most of his compositional efforts to producing electronic and computer works.

WORKS: DRAMATIC: *The Little Prince* for Narrator, Vocal Soloists, and Tape, after Saint-Exupéry (1971); *Gilgamesh* for Voices, Narrator, Chorus, Sopranino Recorder, Oboe, Dancers, and Tape (1972–74). **WITH TAPE:** *Hexameron* for Flute, Clarinet, Horn, Viola, and Piano (1970); *Children* for Soprano (1970); *From the Steppenwolf* for 12 Singers (1970); *Sonic Landscape No. 1* for Horn (1970), *No. 2* for Flute and Piano (1971), and *No. 4* for Organ (1977); *Nautilus* for Percussion (1976); *Aerial* for Horn (1979); *East Wind* for Amplified Recorder (1981); *Letter to My Grandmother* for Voice (1981); *Nightwatch* for Marimba (1982); *Etude* for Cello (1983–84); *Tongues of Angels* for Oboe d'Amore and English Horn (1988). **OTHER:** Works for computer graphic slides and tape, including *Divan* (1985) and *Wings of Nike* (1987); *Dominion* for Chamber Ensemble and 2 Digital Soundtracks (Toronto, Nov. 30, 1991); *Song of Songs* for Oboe d'Amore, English Horn, 2 Digital Soundtracks, and Computer Images (1993); solo tape pieces; vocal works; piano pieces.

Trunk, Richard, German pianist, conductor, music critic, and composer; b. Tauberbischofsheim, Baden, Feb. 10, 1879; d. Herrsching-am-Ammersee, June 2, 1968. He studied with Iwan Knorr at the Hoch Cons. in Frankfurt am Main (1894–95) and with Rheinberger at the Munich Academy of Music (1896–99). He was then active as a choral conductor and music critic in Munich; went to Cologne in 1925 as director of the Rheinische Hochschule für Musik and as a prof. at the Staatliche Hochschule für Musik; also was active as a choral conductor; from 1934 to 1945, was president of the Munich Academy of Music and also director of the Lehrergesangverein (1934–39). He was a prolific composer of choral music; also wrote a Singspiel, *Herzdame* (Munich, 1917), as well as orch. pieces and chamber music; also over 200 lieder.

BIBL.: A. Ott, *R. T.: Leben und Werk* (Munich, 1964).

Trythall, (Harry) Gil(bert), American composer and teacher, brother of **Richard Trythall**; b. Knoxville, Tenn., Oct. 28, 1930. He studied theory and composition with David Van Vactor at the Univ. of Tenn. (B.A., 1951), composition with Riegger at Northwestern Univ. (M.Mus., 1952), and composition with Palmer and musicology with Grout at Cornell Univ. (D.M.A., 1960). He was assistant prof. at Knox College in Galesburg, Ill. (1960–64); after serving as prof. of theory and composition (1964–75) and chairman of the music school (1973–75) at George Peabody College for Teachers in Nashville, he was prof. of music (from 1975) and dean of the creative arts center (1975–81) at West Virginia Univ. in Morgantown. He publ. *Principles and Practices of Electronic Music* (N.Y., 1974), *Eighteenth Century Counterpoint* (Dubuque, Iowa, 1993), and *Sixteenth Century Counterpoint* (Dubuque, Iowa, 1994).

WORKS: OPERAS: *The Music Lesson*, opera buffa (1960); *The Terminal Opera* (1982; rev. 1987). **ORCH.:** *A Solemn Chant* for Strings (1955); Sym. No. 1 (1958; rev. 1963); Harp Concerto (1963); *Dionysia* (1964); *Chroma I* (1970); *Cindy the Synthe (Minnie the Moog)* for Synthesizer and Strings (1975); Sinfonia Concertante 1989). **CHAMBER:** Flute Sonata (1964); *A Vacuum Soprano* for Brass Quintet and Tape (1966); *Entropy* for Brass, Harp, Celesta, Piano, and Tape (1967); *Parallax* for 4 to 40 Brass, Tape, Audience, and Slide Projection (1968); *Echospace* for Brass and Tape (1973); piano pieces; organ works. **VOCAL:** *In the Presence* for Chorus and Tape (1969); *Spanish Songs* for Soprano and Synthesizer (1986–87); Mass in English and Spanish for Congregation, Organ, and Descant (1988); *From the Egyptian Book of the Dead* for Soprano, Saxophone or Wind Controller, and Synthesizer (1990); *9:01 Hard Start Variations* for Jazz Soprano, Wind Controller, Synthesizer, and Sequencer (1991); *The Pastimes of Lord Chaitanya* for Jazz Soprano and Synthesizer (1993); *Intermission* for Soprano and Synthesizer (1994). **OTHER:** Electronic pieces; mixed media works; film scores.

Trythall, Richard, American pianist and composer, brother of **(Harry) Gil(bert) Trythall**; b. Knoxville, Tenn., July 25, 1939. He studied with David Van Vactor at the Univ. of Tenn. (B.M., 1961) and with Sessions, Kim, and Cone at Princeton Univ. (M.F.A., 1963); then continued his training at the Berlin Hochschule für Musik on a Fulbright fellowship (1963–64); held a Guggenheim fellowship (1967–68). He settled in Rome, where he became a teacher at St. Stephen's School in 1966 and music liaison at the American Academy in 1975. As a pianist, Trythall is a determined champion of modern music and has performed scores ranging from Ives to Stockhausen.

WORKS: ORCH.: Sym. (1961); *Composition* for Piano and Orch. (1965); *Penelope's Monologue* for Soprano and Orch. (1966); *Costruzione* (1967); *Continuums* (1968). **CHAMBER:** Duets for Treble Instruments (1958); Suite for Harpsichord and Tape (1973); *Variations on a Theme by Haydn* for Woodwind Quintet and Tape (1976); *Salute to the '50s* for Percussionist and Tape (1977); *Bolero* for 4 Percussion (1979); piano pieces. **OTHER:** Vocal works, including *4 Songs* for Soprano and Piano (1962); tape pieces, including *Study No. 1* (1967) and *Omaggio a Jerry Lee Lewis* (1975).

Tseitlin, Lev (Moiseievich), Russian violinist and pedagogue; Tiflis, March 15, 1881; d. Moscow, Jan. 9, 1952. He was a pupil of Auer at the St. Petersburg Cons. (graduated, 1901). After touring as a soloist in Europe, he was concertmaster of Koussevitzky's orch. in Moscow (1908–17). From 1918 to 1920 he was a prof. at the Moscow Inst. of Musical Drama, and then was a prof. of violin at the Moscow Cons. from 1920 until his death.

Tsintsadze, Sulkhan, Georgian composer, teacher, and cellist; b. Gori, Aug. 23, 1925; d. 1991. He studied cello and composition at the Moscow Cons. In 1963 he joined the faculty of the Tbilisi Cons. In his music, he emphasized ethnic elements, presenting them in congenial modal harmonies.

WORKS: DRAMATIC: OPERAS: *The Golden Fleece* (1953); *The Hermit* (1972). **BALLETS:** *The Treasure of the Blue Mountain* (1956); *The Demon*, after Lermontov (1961). **ORCH.:** 2 violin concertos (1947, 1968); 2 cello concertos (1947, 1964); 3 suites for Strings (1948, 1950, 1955); 2 piano concertos (1949, 1968); 4 syms. (1952, 1963, 1969, 1979); *Georgian Rhapsody* for Violin and Orch. (1955). **CHAMBER:** 9 string quartets (1947–78). **PIANO:** *24 Preludes* (1980). **VOCAL:** *Immortality*, oratorio for the centenary of Lenin's birth (1970).

Tsontakis, George, American composer; b. N.Y., Oct. 24, 1951. He studied with Sessions (1974–79), at the Juilliard School in N.Y. (1978–86), and with Stockhausen in Rome (1981). He was an assistant to the electronic faculty at the Juilliard School (1978) and an assistant prof. at the Brooklyn College Cons. of Music (1986–87). In 1987 he received the Koussevitzky Foundation orchestral commission.

WORKS: ORCH.: *5 Sighs and a Fantasy* (N.Y., Oct. 20, 1984); *Fantasia Habanera* (Baltimore, May 28, 1986); *Overture Vera* (1988); *To the Sowers of the Seed* (Aspen, Colo., Aug. 18, 1989). **CHAMBER:** 4 string quartets: No. 1, *The Mother's Hymn*, with Mezzo-soprano (1980), No. 2, *Emerson* (N.Y., April 29, 1984), No. 3, *Coraggio* (Aspen, Colo., July 26, 1986), and No. 4, *Beneath the Tenderness of Thy Heart* (N.Y., Jan. 17, 1989); *3 Sighs*, 3 variations for Violin (Haywood, Calif., Sept. 25, 1981); *Preludio ed Fantasia* for Cello, Brass Quintet, Piano, and Timpani (N.Y., May 22, 1983); *Birdwind Quintet* for Wind Quintet (Aspen, Colo., July 10, 1983); Brass Quintet (N.Y., April 18, 1984); *The Past, The Passion* for 14 to 15 Players (N.Y., March 4, 1987); *Mercurial Etudes* for Flute (N.Y., Dec. 7, 1988); *3 Mood Sketches* for Wind Quintet (Leningrad, Nov. 22, 1989); *Heartsounds*, quintet for Piano and Strings (Cambridge, Mass., April 20, 1990). **VOCAL: SACRED:** *Scenes from the Apocalypse* for Vocal Soloists, Actor, Chorus, and Orch. (1978); *The Epistle of James, Chapter 1* for Reader, Chorus, and Orch. (1980); *5 Choral Sketches on "Is Aghios" (One, Holy)* for Chorus and Clarinet obbligato (N.Y., May 22, 1984); *Saviors* for Soprano, Chorus, and Orch. (N.Y., May 11, 1985); *Byzantium Kanon* for Chorus and Brass Quintet (N.Y., June 1, 1986); *3 Byzantine Hymns* for Chorus and Brass Quintet (1988); *Stabat Mater* for Soprano, Chorus, and Orch. (N.Y., May 19, 1990). **SECULAR:** *Erotokritos*, oratorio for Chorus and Orch. (N.Y., May 15, 1982); *Galway Kinnell Songs* for Mezzo-soprano, Piano, and String Quartet (N.Y., Feb. 4, 1987).

Tsoupaki, Calliope, Greek pianist and composer; b. Piraeus, May 27, 1963. She studied piano and theory at the Hellinicon Cons. in Athens; then entered the composition class of Yannis Ionnithis at the Nikos Skalkottas Cons. (1985); in 1988 she settled in The Hague, where she continued her studies with Louis Andriessen and with Gilus van Bergeyk and Dick Raaijmakers (electronic composition) at the Royal Cons. of Music; also attended summer courses with Xenakis (1985), Messiaen (1987), and Boulez (1988) at Darmstadt. In 1991 and 1993 her music was performed at the Gaudeamus International Music Week in Amsterdm; in 1993 she was a composer-in-residence at Budapest's Pepiniéres for Young Artists Foundation. In 1995 she was a featured composer at the "Other Minds" Festival in San Francisco.

WORKS: MUSIC THEATER: *Nadere kenmismaking* (1995). **ORCH.:** *Eclipse* (1986). **CHAMBER:** *Earinon* for 8 Horns and Percussion (1986); *Krystallina Ymenea* for Chamber Ensemble (1986); *Orfikon* for Viola (1986); *Revealing Moment* for Alto Flute (1987); *Touch of a Silent Echo* for Oboe, Viola, Cello, Percussion, and Piano (1987); *Silver Moments* for 2 Pianos and 2 Percussion Players (1987); *Mania* for Amplified Violin (1988); *Nocturnal Sounds . . . and the Ivy Leafs Are Trembling* for Cello and Piano (1988); *Music for Saxophones* for Saxophone Quartet (1989); *Visions of the Night* for Amplified Chamber Ensemble (1989); *When I Was 27* for Amplified Viola and Double Bass (1990); *Kentavros* for Wind Ensemble, Double Bass, and Piano (1991); *Episode* for Chamber Ensemble (1991); *Song for Four* for String Quartet (1991); *Dance* for 16 Oboes (1991); *Echoing Purple* for Violin and Chamber Ensemble (1992); *Eros and Psyche* for Wind Octet and Double Bass (1992); *Orphic Fields* for Flute, 2 Harps, and 2 Pianos (1993); *Compulsive Caress* for Guitar (1993); *Phantom* for Tuba (1994); *Her Voice* for Harp (1994); *Sweet if you Like* for Electric Guitar, Tuba, Double Bass, and Percussion (1994); *Charavgi* for Alto ("Ganassi") Recorder (1994); *Ethra* for Flute, Violin, Viola, Cello, and Harp (1995); *Blue* for Oboe (1995); *Pas de deux* for Harp (1995); *Ketting* for 3 Ensembles (1995; in collaboration with others). **KEYBOARD: PIANO:** *Echoes of a Deep Sea*, children's piece (1988); *Moments I* and *II* (1988); *Greek Dance* (1990); *Ananda* (1991). **HARPSICHORD:** *Common Passion* (1993). **VOCAL:** *For Always* for Women's Voice, Tape, and Lights (1989); *Your Thought* for Voice, Tape, and Lighting (1989); *Paraklitikon* for Vocal Ensemble (1990); *Sappho's Tears* for Violin, Tenor Recorder, and Woman's Voice (1990); *Melos Hidiston* for Woman's Voice, Tenor Recorder, Viola, Cello, Double Bass, and Piano (1991); *Offerande* and *Untitled Love* for Woman's Voice and Fortepiano (1993); *Epigramma* for Chorus and Orch. (1995); *Lineos* for Chorus and Ensemble (1995).

Tsuji, Shōichi, Japanese musicologist; b. Gifu, Dec. 20, 1895; d. Tokyo, April 21, 1987. He took a degree in psychology at the Univ. of Tokyo (1920); also studied composition and conducting with Ryūtarō Hirota, violin with Shin Kusakawa, and gagaku with Yoshiisa Oku. He taught at St. Paul's Univ., Tokyo (1922–65); lectured at the Univ. of Tokyo, the Tokyo National Univ. of Fine Arts and Music, and Kyūshū Univ. In 1968 he became a prof. at Kunitachi Music College. Tsuji, the first important Japanese scholar to specialize in Western music, introduced musicology to Japan. He specialized in J.S. Bach and Protestant church music, and wrote biographies of Bach, Mozart, and Schubert. He was one of the founders of the Japanese Musicological Soc.; served as its president (1964–70). After his death, St. Paul's Univ. instituted the annual Shōichi Tsuji Award for achievement in the enhancement of Christian music studies and/or performance.

Tsukatani, Akihirô, Japanese composer and pedagogue; b. Tokyo, March 16, 1919. He studied law at the Univ. of Tokyo (graduated, 1941) and received training in theory from Saburo Moroi. He taught economic history at the Univ. of Tokyo before serving on its music faculty.

WORKS: DRAMATIC: OPERAS: *Pongo* (1965); *Ajatasatru* (1966); *Kakitsubata* (Tokyo, May 24, 1967). **MUSICAL:** *Fairy's Cap* (Tokyo, Dec. 9, 1968). **BALLET:** *Mythology of Today* (1956). **ORCH.:** *Festival*, symphonic suite (1950); Suite for Percussion and Strings (1960); Piano Concerto (1961); *Japan Festival Dance Music* for Chamber Orch. (1969); *Musashino*, symphonic poem (1989); *Music* for Violin and Chamber Orch. (1991). **CHAMBER:** Sonata for Flute, Cello, and Piano (1949); Clarinet Sonata (1952); Suite for Horn, Trumpet, Trombone, and Timpani (1959); *Fu 1* and *2* for Flute (1970); *3 Worlds* for Flute (1971–72); *2 Movements* for Cello (1972); *Fantasia* for Violin, Piano, and Tam-tam (1973); *Oracle* for Nonet (1983); *Composition* for Oboe and Piano (1984); *Images* for Ondes Martenot, Flute, Oboe, and String Quartet (1987); *2 Compositions* for Oboe (1988); *3 Movements* for Guitar (1990). **VOCAL:** Choruses; songs.

Tsvetanov, Tsvetan, Bulgarian composer and teacher; b. Sofia, Nov. 6, 1931; d. Paris, April 4, 1982. He studied composition with Hadzhiev and Vladigerov at the Bulgarian State Cons. in Sofia (graduated, 1956); in 1958 he joined its faculty, becoming a prof. in composition and harmony in 1976; also was its rector (1976–80). He served as secretary of the Union of Bulgarian Composers (1969–75; 1976–80).

WORKS: DRAMATIC: *Orpheus and Rodopa*, ballet (1960; also an orch. suite); incidental music for plays; film scores. **ORCH.:** Sinfonietta (1956); 4 syms.: No. 1 (1965), No. 2 (1968), No. 3, *1923* (1972), and No. 4 for Chamber Orch. (1975); *Overture* (1968); Concertino for Piano and Chamber Orch. (1970); *Overture of Joy* (1971); *Festive Concerto* (1974); *Symphonic Variations* (1976). **CHAMBER:** *Variations* for String Quartet (1953); Violin Sonata (1955); Piano Sonata (1961); Cello Sonata (1973). **VOCAL:** *The Great Beginning*, symphonic poem for Narrator and Orch. (1961–63); *The Staircase*, ballad for Alto, Men's Chorus, and Orch. (1966); *Ballad of Botev's Kiss*, poem for Chorus and Orch. (1973); *Back to the Feat*, symphonic poem for Narrator and String Orch. (1977); *Immortality*, oratorio (1981); songs; vocal pieces for amateurs; folk song transcriptions.

Tua, Teresina (actually, **Maria Felicità**), Italian violinist; b. Turin, May 22, 1867; d. Rome, Oct. 29, 1955. She studied with Massart at the Paris Cons., where she took the 1st prize in 1880. She toured the Continent with brilliant success; made her English debut at the Crystal Palace in London, May 5, 1883; appeared in America (1887). In 1889 she married Count Franchi-Verney della Valetta, and withdrew from the concert stage until the autumn of 1895, when she set out on a successful European tour, including Russia, where her accompanist and joint artist was Rachmaninoff. Franchi died in 1911; in 1913 she married Emilio Quadrio. She taught at the Milan Cons. from 1915 to 1924, and then at the Accademia di Santa Cecilia in Rome; subsequently abandoned her career, and entered the Convento dell'Adorazione in Rome as Sister Maria di Ges.

Tubb, Carrie (actually, **Caroline Elizabeth**), English soprano; b. London, May 17, 1876; d. there, Sept. 20, 1976. She studied at the Guildhall School of Music in London. She began her career singing in a vocal quartet during her student days; after winning notice as an oratorio singer, she appeared at Covent Garden and at His Majesty's Theatre in London (1910); however, she soon abandoned opera and pursued a career as a concert artist until her retirement in 1930; in the latter year, she became a prof. at the Guildhall School of Music, where she taught for almost 30 years. She excelled both in Mozart arias and in concert excerpts from Wagner and Verdi.

Tubin, Eduard, Estonian-born Swedish composer and conductor; b. Kallaste, near Tartu, June 18, 1905; d. Stockholm, Nov. 17, 1982. He studied with A. Kapp at the Tartu Cons. and later with Kodály in Budapest. From 1931 to 1944 he conducted the Vanemuine Theater Orch. in Tartu. In 1944 he settled in Stockholm and in 1961 became a naturalized Swedish citizen. In 1982 he was elected to the Royal Swedish Academy of Music. He was at work on his 11th Sym. at the time of his death.

WORKS: DRAMATIC: OPERAS: *Barbara von Tisenhusen* (Tallinn, Dec. 4, 1969); *Prosten fran Reigi* (The Priest from Reigi; 1971). **BALLET:** *Skratten* (Laughter; 1939–41). **ORCH.:** 10 syms.: No. 1 (1934), No. 2, *Legendary* (1937), No. 3 (1942; Tallinn, Feb. 26, 1943), No. 4, *Lyrical* (1943; Tallinn, April 16, 1944; rev. 1978; Bergen, Nov. 5, 1981), No. 5 (1946), No. 6 (1954), No. 7 (1958), No. 8 (1966), No. 9, *Sinfonia semplice* (1969; Stockholm, Nov. 20, 1971), and No. 10 (1973); *Estonian Dance Suite* (1938); 2 violin concertos (1942, 1945); Piano Concertino (1944–46); Double Bass Concerto (1948); Balalaika Concerto (1964). **CHAMBER:** 2 violin sonatas (1936, 1949); Saxophone Sonata (1951); Sonata for Solo Violin (1962); Viola Sonata (1965); *Capriccio* for Violin and Piano (1971); Flute Sonata (1979); *Suite on Estonian Dance Tunes* for Violin (1979); *Quartet on Estonian Motifs* for String Quartet (1979). **PIANO:** *10 preludes* (1928–76). **VOCAL:** *Ylermi*, ballad for Baritone and Orch. (1935; rev. 1977); *5 Kosjalaulud* for Baritone and Orch. (1975); *Requiem for Fallen Soldiers* for Alto, Men's Chorus, Trumpet, Percussion, and Organ (1979).

Tucci, Gabriella, Italian soprano; b. Rome, Aug. 4, 1929. She studied at the Accademia di Santa Cecilia in Rome, and then with Leonardo Filoni, who became her husband. In 1951 she made her operatic debut in Lucca. After winning the Spoleto competition that year, she sang Leonora in *La Forza del Destino* at the Spoleto Festival. In 1953 she appeared as Cherubini's Médée in Florence. She made a tour of Australia in 1955. In 1959 she made her first appearance at Milan's La Scala as Mimi. On Sept. 25, 1959, she made her U.S. debut as Giordano's Madeleine at the San Francisco Opera. From 1959 to 1969 she sang regularly at the Verona Arena. She made her Metropolitan Opera debut in N.Y. as Cio-Cio-San on Oct. 29, 1960, and remained on its roster until 1973. Among her most successful roles there were Euridice, Marguerite, both Verdi Leonoras, Aida, Violetta, Alice Ford, and Mimi. She also sang Tosca at her Covent Garden debut in London in 1960. As a guest artist, she sang at the Vienna State Opera, the Deutsche Oper in Berlin, the Bavarian State Opera in Munich, the Bolshoi Theater in Moscow, and the Teatro Colón in Buenos Aires. She later taught at the Indiana Univ. School of Music in Bloomington (1983–86).

Tucker, Richard (real name, **Reuben Ticker**), brilliant American tenor; b. N.Y., Aug. 28, 1913; d. Kalamazoo, Mich., Jan. 8, 1975. He sang in a synagogue choir in N.Y. as a child; studied voice with Paul Althouse; subsequently sang on the radio. His first public appearance in opera was as Alfredo in *La Traviata* in 1943 with the Salmaggi Co. in N.Y. On Jan. 25, 1945, he made his Metropolitan Opera debut in N.Y. as Enzo in *La Gioconda*; he remained on its roster until his death, specializing in the Italian repertoire. In 1947 he made his European debut at the Verona Arena as Enzo (Maria Callas made her Italian debut as Gioconda in the same performance); he also sang at Covent Garden in London (debut as Cavaradossi, 1958), at La Scala in Milan (1969), in Vienna, and in other major music centers abroad. He died while on a concert tour. He was the brother-in-law of **Jan Peerce**.

BIBL.: J. Drake, *R. T.: a Biography* (N.Y., 1984).

Tuckwell, Barry (Emmanuel), noted Australian-born American horn player and conductor; b. Melbourne, March 5, 1931. He was taught piano by his father and violin by his older brother; was a chorister at St. Andrew's Cathedral in Sydney, and also acted as an organist there. At age 13, he began studying the horn with Alan Mann at the Sydney Cons.; making rapid progress, he played in the Sydney Sym. Orch. (1947–50). He then went to England, where he received valuable advice on horn technique from Dennis Brain; he also gathered some ideas about horn sound from listening to recordings by Tommy Dorsey. He filled positions as assistant 1st horn with the Halle Orch. in Manchester (1951–53), with the Scottish National Orch. in Glasgow (1953–54), and, as 1st horn, with the Bournemouth Sym. Orch. (1954–55); then served as 1st horn player in the London Sym. Orch. (1955–68). He subsequently launched a solo career, achieving recognition as one of the foremost virtuosos on the instrument. In the academic field, he compiled a horn method and ed. horn literature. Several composers wrote special works for him: Thea Musgrave (a Concerto that requires the horn to play quarter-tones); Richard Rodney Bennett (*Actaeon* for Horn and Orch.); Iain Hamilton (*Voyage* for Horn and Orch.); Alun Hoddinott (Concerto); and Don Banks (Concerto). He also pursued a career as a conductor, making guest appearances in Australia, Europe, and the U.S. He was conductor of the Tasmanian Sym. Orch. (1980–83); was music director of the newly-founded Maryland Sym. Orch. in Hagerstown (from 1982). In 1965 he was made an Officer of the Order of the British Empire. In 1996 he became a naturalized American citizen.

BIBL.: W. Sargeant, "Profiles: Something I Could Do," *New Yorker* (March 14, 1977).

Tudor, David (Eugene), significant American pianist and composer; b. Philadelphia, Jan. 20, 1926; d. Tomkins Cove, N.Y., Aug. 13, 1996. He studied piano with Josef Martin and Irma Wolpe, organ and theory with H. William Hawke, and composition and analysis with Stepan Wolpe. At the age of 11, he encountered one of Messiaen's organ compositions, an occasion marking the beginning of his devotion to the music of his time. Although for many years he performed a wide variety of earlier music in his capacity as accompanist for such dancers as Katherine Litz and Jean Erdman and the saxophonist Sigurd Rascher, Tudor's role as a pioneer in the performance of new music was established as early as 1950, when he gave the U.S. premiere of Boulez's 2nd Piano Sonata (N.Y., Dec. 17, 1950). At that time, he also began a close association with John Cage, whose works he propagated with eloquence in the U.S., Europe, and Japan. From 1950 to 1965 he was a touchstone and at times even a catalyst for the composition of a body of music of often extreme radicalism, giving first or early performances of works by Brown, Bussotti, Feldman, Stockhausen, Wolff, Wolpe, and Young, many written expressly for him. A number of these composers have stated unequivocably that Tudor's unerring ability to find his own imaginative and virtuosic solutions to the often puzzingly and sometimes deliberately difficult problems of notation and performance was essential to the actual composition of their music.

Tudor was affiliated with the Merce Cunningham Dance Co. from its inception in 1953. Works created for the Company include *RainForest I* (1968), *Toneburst* (1974), *Forest Speech* (1976), *Weatherings* (1978), *Phonemes* (1981), *Sextet for Seven* (1982), *Fragments* (1984), *Webwork* (1987), *Five Stone Wind*

(1988; with J. Cage and T. Kosugi), *Virtual Focus* (1990), and *Neural Network Plus* (1992). In 1993 he composed the electronic portion of the score created for the Cage-Cunningham collaboration, *Ocean*. Tudor was a member of the summer faculty of Black Mountain College from 1951 to 1953. He also taught courses in piano and the performance of new music in Darmstadt (1956, 1958, 1959, and 1961). He gave seminars in live electronic music at the State Univ. of N.Y. at Buffalo (1965–66), the Univ. of Calif. at Davis (1967), Mills College in Oakland, Calif. (1967–68), and the National Inst. of Design in Ahmedabad, India (1969). In 1968 he was selected as one of the four Core Artists for the design and construction of the Pepsico Pavilion at Expo 70 in Osaka.

Recent research into Tudor's work as a performer during the critical period of 1950 to 1965, in particular by John Holzaepfel, has shown 2 common assumptions to be false. First, Tudor did not work under the supervision of the American avant-garde composers whose music he played but rather prepared his performances of their works privately and independently. Second, in music in which some degree of indeterminacy is a compositional principle, Tudor did not limit himself to improvising from the score. Rather, it was his practice in numerous cases to undertake a rigorous series of preparatory steps, including measurements, calculations, computations, and conversation tables, translating the results into a more conventional notation for use in performance. Nevertheless, it may have been inevitable that the freedoms entrusted him by composers, combined with Tudor's own extensions of the use of sonic materials in his realizations and his sense of a decrease in the challenge he saw as essential to the composer-performer relationship, gradually led him away from piano playing and into the performance of live electronic music, an area in which he was also a pioneer, with a series of works to which he signed his own name. As a composer, Tudor drew upon technological resources that were both flexible and complex, including custom-built modular electronic devices, many of his own manufacture. His method employed choices of specific electronic components and transducers, and their interconnections, that defined both composition and performance. His sound materials unfolded through large gestures, and were often heard in association with a variety of visual forces, including lighting systems, dance, television, theater, and film.

WORKS: *Fluorescent Sound* (Stockholm, Sept. 13, 1964); *Bandoneon!* for Factorial Bandoneon (1966); *Reunion* (1968; in collaboration with J. Cage, L. Cross, M. and T. Duchamp, and G. Mumma); *Pepsi Bird, Pepscillator*, and *Anima Pepsi* (1970); *Untitled* (1972); *Melodics* (1972); *RainForest III* (1972) and *IV* (1973); *Microphone (1–9)* (1973); *Laser Bird* and *Laser Rock* (1973); *Photocell Action* (1974; in collaboration [light composition] with A. Martin); *Island Eye Island Ear*, sound and fog environment (1974–78; in collaboration with F. Nakaya); *Pulsars* (1976); *Pulsars 2* (1978); *Likeness to Voices/Dialects* (1982); *Sea Tails* (1983; in collaboration [film] with M. Davies and [underwater kites] J. Monnier); *Hedgehog* (1985); *Tailing Dream* (1985; in collaboration [video] with J. Monnier); *Electronics With Talking Shrimp* (1986); *9 Lines, Reflected* (1986); *For "Bye, Bye, Kipling"* (1986; in collaboration with J. Monnier); *Line & Cluster* (1986); *Web for J.C., Web for J.C. II*, and *Electronic Web* (1987); *Lines and Reflections*, installation (1987; in collaboration with J. Monnier); *Volatils with Sonic Reflections* (1988; in collaboration [aluminum kite installation] with J. Monnier); *Neural Synthesis (No. 2)* (1993).

BIBL.: J. Holzaepfel, *D. T. and the Performance of American Experimental Music 1950–1959* (diss., City Univ. of N.Y., 1993).

Tudoran, Ionel, Romanian tenor; b. Baragtii de Vede, June 24, 1913. He studied at the Iaşi Cons. He made his operatic debut as Roland in Ziehrer's *Landstreicher* in 1936 in Iaşi; then sang with the Cluj Opera (1937–48) and the Bucharest Opera (1948–63); also made guest appearances in Prague, Leipzig, Berlin, Dresden, Moscow, and other music centers. He retired in 1963 and taught voice at the Bucharest Cons. until 1972. His finest roles were Don José, Faust, and Cavaradossi.

Tuksar, Stanislav, Croatian musicologist; b. Gornji Kraljevec, July 27, 1945. He studied philosophy and English at the Univ. of Zagreb; then cello with R. Matz and musicology with I. Supičić at the Zagreb Cons.; subsequently studied with E. Weber in Paris (1974–76). He was a researcher at the Zagreb Inst. of Musicology and taught at the Cons.; received the Humboldt scholarship from the Institut für Musikforschung in Berlin (1986). He wrote numerous articles about aesthetics, philosophy, and terminology of music of the 16th to 18th centuries and about the musical archives in Croatia. He publ. a book on Croatian music theorists of the Renaissance, *Hrvatski renesansni teoreticari glazbe* (Zagreb, 1978; Eng. tr., 1980). Among the books he ed. were *Glazba, ideje i društvo: Svečani zbornik za Evana Supičića/Music, Ideas, and Society: Essays in Honor of Ivan Supičić* (Zagreb, 1993) and *The Musical Baroque, Western Slavs, and the Spirit of the European Cultural Communion/Glazbeni barok i zapadni Slaveni u kontekstu europskog kulturnog zajedništva* (Zagreb, 1993). He also wrote music criticism and tr. several books by Zofia Lissa and Erich Fromm into Croatian.

Tully, Alice, American mezzo-soprano, soprano, and music patroness; b. Corning, N.Y., Sept. 11, 1902; d. N.Y., Dec. 10, 1993. A scion of a family of wealth, she studied voice in Paris with Jean Périer and Miguel Fontecha, where she made her concert debut with the Pasdeloup Orch. in 1927. Returning to the U.S., she gave a song recital in N.Y. in 1936, and received critical praise for her interpretation of French songs. She eventually gave up her artistic ambition and devoted herself to various philanthropic endeavors. Her major gift was to Lincoln Center in N.Y. for the construction of a chamber music hall; it was dedicated as Alice Tully Hall in 1969. She also helped to organize the Chamber Music Soc. of Lincoln Center. She received the National Medal of Arts in 1985. Her 90th birthday was celebrated in a N.Y. gala on Sept. 14, 1992, at Lincoln Center.

Tunley, David (Evatt), respected Australian musicologist and composer; b. Sydney, May 3, 1930. He studied at the New South Wales State Conservatorium of Music in Sydney (diploma, 1950), at Trinity College, London (diploma, 1950), at the Univ. of Durham (B.Mus., 1958; M.Mus., 1963), with Boulanger in Paris (1964–65), and at the Univ. of Western Australia (D.Litt., 1970, with the diss. *The Eighteenth Century Secular French Cantata*; publ. in London, 1974). In 1958 he joined the faculty of the Univ. of Western Australia, where he served as a prof. (from 1979) and as head of the music dept. (from 1985). In 1980–81 he was national president of the Musicological Soc. of Australia. In 1987 he was made a member of the Order of Australia. He contributed articles to various learned journals, and also to *The New Grove Dictionary of Music and Musicians* (1980). Among his compositions are *Wedding Masque* for Soloists, Women's Chorus, and Orch. (1961; rev. 1970), Concerto for Clarinet and Strings (1966), *Inflorescence* for Chorus, Clarinet, and Timpani (1978), and *Elegy—in memoriam Salek Minc* for Chamber Ensemble (1986). His books include *Australian Composition in the 20th Century* (ed., with F. Callaway; Melbourne, 1980), *Couperin* (London, 1982), and *Harmony in Action* (London, 1984). He also ed. *The French Cantata Facsimile* (17 vols., N.Y., 1990–91) and *Romantic French Song, 1830–1870* (6 vols., 1994–95).

Tupkov, Dimiter, Bulgarian composer; b. Sofia, July 12, 1929. He studied with Goleminov at the Bulgarian State Cons. in Sofia, graduating in 1956; then joined its faculty.

WORKS: ORCH.: Flute Concerto (1955); *The Story of Belassitsa Mountain*, overture (1956); *3 Children's Sinfoniettas* (1961, 1968, 1975); *Concerto for Orchestra* (1969); *Rhapsodic Divertimento* (1970); Harp Concerto (1971); *6 Bagatelles* (1972); *September Overture* (1974). **CHAMBER:** 2 string quartets (1956, 1958). **VOCAL:** *Peace Cantata* (1975); choral songs; folk song arrangements.

Turchi, Guido, Italian composer and teacher; b. Rome, Nov. 10, 1916. He studied piano and composition with Dobici, Ferdinandi, and Bustini at the Rome Cons. (diplomas, 1940) and pursued graduate training with Pizzetti at the Accademia di Santa Cecilia in Rome (diploma, 1945). He taught at the Rome Cons. (1941–67; again from 1972); was artistic director of the Accademia Filarmonica in Rome (1963–66); served as director of the Parma and Florence cons. (1967–72); was artistic director of the Teatro Comunale in Bologna (1968–70) and at the Accademia di Santa Cecilia in Rome (from 1970). In his early music, Turchi followed Pizzetti's style of Italian Baroque, with Romantic and impressionistic extensions; he then changed his idiom toward a more robust and accentuated type of music-making, influenced mainly by a study of the works of Béla Bartók. Turchi's Concerto for String Orch. is dedicated to Bartók's memory.

WORKS: DRAMATIC: *Il buon soldato Svejk*, opera (Milan, April 6, 1962); *Dedalo*, ballet (Florence, 1972); incidental music to plays; film scores. **ORCH.:** Concerto for Strings (Venice, Sept. 8, 1948); *Piccolo concerto notturno* (1950); *3 metamorfosi* (1970); *Adagio* (1983); *Parabola* (1993). **CHAMBER:** Trio for Flute, Clarinet, and Viola (1945); *Dedica* for Flute (1972). **VOCAL:** *Invettiva* for Small Chorus and 2 Pianos (1946); choral works; songs.

Tureck, Rosalyn, eminent American pianist, harpsichordist, and clavichordist; b. Chicago, Dec. 14, 1914. She studied piano in Chicago with Sophia Brilliant-Liven (1925–29), Jan Chiapusso (1929–31), and Gavin Williamson (1931–32); then went to N.Y., where she studied with Olga Samaroff at the Juilliard School of Music, graduating in 1935. In her concert career she dedicated herself mainly to Bach. In 1947 she made her first European tour; subsequently gave concerts in South America, South Africa, and Israel. She made some appearances as a conductor from 1956; however, she concentrated her activities on the keyboard, making appearances as a harpsichordist and a clavichordist (from 1960) as well as a pianist. In 1971 she made a world tour. She held teaching posts at the Philadelphia Cons. of Music (1935–42), Juilliard School of Music (1943–55), and Univ. of Calif., San Diego (1966–72). In 1966 she founded the International Bach Inst. and in 1981 the Tureck Bach Inst. She received honorary doctorates from Roosevelt Univ. in 1968 and the Univ. of Oxford in 1977. In order to demonstrate the universal applicability of Bach's keyboard techniques, she played Bach on the Moog synthesizer; in 1971 she gave a concert announced as "Bach and Rock." She publ. *An Introduction to the Performance of Bach* (3 vols., London, 1959–60; also publ. in Japanese, 1966, and Spanish, 1972).

Turetzky, Bertram (Jay), American double bass player and composer; b. Norwich, Conn., Feb. 14, 1933. He was a pupil of Joseph Iadone and Josef Marx at the Hartt School of Music in Hartford, Conn. (graduated, 1955), and also studied privately with David Walter. He studied musicology with Sachs at N.Y. Univ. and took courses in music history at the Univ. of Hartford (M.M., 1965). On Oct. 19, 1964, he made his N.Y. recital debut in a program featuring specially commissioned works for the double bass. In subsequent years, he toured widely as a virtuoso double bass player in programs largely devoted to avant-garde scores. He publ. *The Contemporary Contrabass* (1974). Among his compositions were pieces for double bass.

Turina (y Perez), Joaquín, prominent Spanish composer and teacher; b. Seville, Dec. 9, 1882; d. Madrid, Jan. 14, 1949. He studied with local teachers; then entered the Madrid Cons. as a pupil of Tragó (piano). In 1905 he went to Paris, where he studied composition with d'Indy at the Schola Cantorum and piano with Moszkowski. At the urging of Albéniz, he turned to Spanish folk music for inspiration. Returning to Madrid in 1914, he produced 2 symphonic works in a characteristic Spanish style: *La procesión del rocío* and *Sinfonía sevillana*, combining Romantic and impressionist elements in an individual manner; the same effective combination is found in his chamber music of Spanish inspiration (*Escena andaluza, La oración del torero* et al.) and his piano music (*Sonata romántica, Mujeres españolas* et al.); he also wrote operas and incidental music for the theater. In 1930 he was appointed a prof. of composition at the Madrid Cons.; also founded the general music commission of the Ministry of Education, serving as its commissioner in 1941.

WORKS: DRAMATIC: *La sulamita*, opera (c.1900); *Fea y con gracia*, zarzuela (1904); *Margot*, lyric comedy (Madrid, Oct. 10, 1914); *Navidad*, incidental music (1916); *La adúltera penitente*, incidental music (1917); *Jardín de oriente*, opera (Madrid, March 6, 1923); *La anunciación*, comedia (1924). **ORCH.:** *La procesión del rocío*, symphonic poem (Madrid, March 30, 1913); *Evangelio*, symphonic poem (Madrid, April 8, 1915); *3 danzas fantásticas* (1920); *Sinfonía sevillana* (San Sebastian, Sept. 11, 1920); *Rítmos*, choreographic fantasy (Barcelona, Oct. 25, 1928); *Rapsodia sinfónica* for Piano and Strings (Madrid, March 11, 1933). **CHAMBER:** Piano Quintet (1907); String Quartet (1911); *Escena andaluza* for Viola, String Quartet, and Piano (1912); *La oración del torero* for String Quartet (1925); 2 piano trios (1926, 1933); 2 violin sonatas (1929, 1934); Piano Quartet (1931); *Serenata* for String Quartet (1935); *Círculo* for Violin, Cello, and Piano (1936); *Las nueve Musas* (9 pieces for Various Instruments; 1945). **KEYBOARD: PIANO:** *Sevilla, suite pintoresca* (1909); *Sonata romántica* (1909); *Coins de Séville*, suite (1911); *3 danzas andaluzas* (1912); *Album de viaje* (1916); *Mujeres españolas* (2 sets; 1917, 1932); *Cuentos de España*, 2 sets of 7 pieces each (1918, 1928); *Niñerías*, 2 sets of children's pieces (1919, 1931); *Sanlúcar de Barrameda* (1922); *El Cristo de la Calavera* (1924); *Jardines de Andalucía*, suite (1924); *La venta de los gatos* (1925); *El Barrio de Santa Cruz* (1925); *La leyenda de la Giralda*, suite (1927); *2 danzas sobre temas populares españoles* (1927); *Verbena madrileña*, 5 pieces (1927); *Mallorca*, suite (1928); *Evocaciones*, 3 pieces (1929); *Recuerdos de la antigua España*, 4 pieces (1929); *Viaje marítimo*, suite (1930); *Miniaturas*, 8 pieces (1930); *Sonata fantasía* (1930); *Ciclo pianistico: Tocata y fuga, Partita, Pieza romántica, El castillo de Almodóvar* (1930–31); *Danzas gitanas*, 2 sets of 5 pieces each (1930, 1934); *Tarjetas postales* (1931); *Radio Madrid*, suite (1931); *Jardín de niños*, 8 pieces (1931); *El circo*, 6 pieces (1932); *Silhuetas*, 5 pieces (1932); *En la zapateria*, 7 pieces (1933); *Fantasia italiana* (1933); *Trilogia: El poema infinito* (1933); *Rincones de Sanlúcar* (1933); *Bailete, suite de danzas del siglo XIX* (1933); *Preludios* (1933); *Ofrenda* (1934); *Hipócrates* (1934); *Fantasía sobre cinco notas* (1934); *Concierto sin orquesta* (1935); *En el cortijo*, 4 pieces (1936–40). **ORGAN:** *Prelude* (1914); *Musette* (1915). **GUITAR:** *Sevillana* (1923); *Fandanguillo* (1926); *Ráfaga* (1930); Sonata (1932); *Homenaje a Tárrega*, 2 pieces (1935). **SONGS:** *Rima* (1911); *Poema en forma de canciones* (1918); 3 arias (1923); *Canto a Sevilla*, song cycle (1927); *2 canciones* (1927); *Corazón de mujer* (1927); *Tríptico* (1929); *3 sonetos* (1930); *3 poemas* (1933); *Homenaje a Lope de Vega* (1935).

WRITINGS: *Enciclopedia abreviada de la música* (Madrid, 1917); *Tratado de composición* (Madrid, 1946); A. Iglesias, ed., *Escritos de Joaquín Turina* (1982).

BIBL.: F. Sopeña, *J. T.* (Madrid, 1943; 2nd ed., rev., 1956); W. Dean, "J. T.," *Chesterian* (April 1949); L. Powell, *The Piano Music of J. T.* (diss., Univ. of N.C., 1974); idem, "The Influence of Dance Rhythms on the Piano Music of J. T.," *Music Review*, XXXVII (1976); J. Benavente, ed., *Aproximación al Lenguaje Musical de T.* (1982).

Turini, Ronald, Canadian pianist and teacher; b. Montreal, Sept. 30, 1934. He received piano lessons as a child and was a student of Frank Hanson at the McGill Cons. in Montreal. At 9, he entered the Montreal Cons., where he continued his training with Yvonne Hubert, Germaine Malépart, and Isidor Philipp. In 1950 he received the premier prix there, and also won the Prix Archambault. In 1953 he became a student of Isabelle Vengerova and Olga Stroumillo at the Mannes College of Music in N.Y., and then studied for 5 years with Vladimir Horowitz. From 1956 he made regular tours. In 1958 he captured 2nd prize in the Busoni competition in Bolzano and in the Geneva competition, and in 1960 won 2nd prize in the Queen of Elisabeth of Belgium competition in Brussels. In 1961 he made his Carnegie Hall debut in N.Y., and played there again in 1964 and 1967. He was a soloist with the Montreal Sym. Orch. on its tour of Europe in 1962, and again in 1976. In 1971 he was soloist with the Melbourne Sym. Orch. on its North American tour. In 1975 he became a founding member of Quartet Canada. From 1977 he also taught at the Univ. of Western Ontario.

Turnage, Mark-Anthony, English composer; b. Grays, Essex, June 10, 1960. He was a student of Knussen in the junior dept. of the Royal College of Music in London (1974–78), where he continued his training as a senior student of John Lambert (diploma, 1982); he then studied with Schuller and Henze at the Berkshire Music Center in Tanglewood (summer, 1983). From 1989 to 1993 he served as composer-in-association with the City of Birmingham Sym. Orch. In his music, Turnage has pursued an eclectic course in an accessible style which has found inspiration in various contemporary modes of expression, including rock and jazz.

WORKS: OPERAS: *Greek* (1986–88; Munich, June 17, 1988); *Killing Time*, television opera (1991). **ORCH.:** *Let Us Sleep Now* for Chamber Orch. (1979–82; Shape, June 14, 1983); *Night Dances* (1981–82; London, Feb. 1, 1982); *Kind of Blue: In Memoriam, Thelonious Monk* (1981–82; London, March 21, 1982); *Ekaya: Elegy in Memory of Marvin Gaye* (1984; Greenwich, March 29, 1985); *Gross Intrusion* for Amplified String Quartet and String Orch. (Glasgow, Sept. 19, 1987); *3 Screaming Popes* (Birmingham, Oct. 5, 1989); *Momentum* (1990–91; Birmingham, June 12, 1991); *Drowned Out* (1992–93); *Your Rockaby*, saxophone concerto (1993). **CHAMBER:** *And Still a Softer Morning* for Flute, Vibraphone, Harp, and Cello (1978; rev. 1983; Montepulciano, July 31, 1984); *After Dark* for Wind Quintet and String Quintet (1982–83; London, April 13, 1983); *On All Fours* for Chamber Ensemble (1985; London, Feb. 4, 1986); *Sarabande* for Soprano Saxophone and Piano (1985; London, Jan. 10, 1986); *Release* for 8 Players (1987; BBC Radio, Dec. 4, 1988); *Kai* for Cello and Ensemble (1989–90; Birmingham, Dec. 18, 1990); *3 Farewells* for Flute, Clarinet, Harp, and String Quartet (London, July 8, 1990); *Are You Sure?* for String Quartet (1990; rev. 1991); *3 Lullabies* for Cello and Piano (1992); *This Silence* for Clarinet, Horn, Bassoon, and String Quartet (1992–93); *Set To* for Brass Ensemble (1992–93); *Blood on the Floor* for Chamber Ensemble (1993–94). **PIANO:** *Entranced* (Huddersfield, Nov. 25, 1982). **VOCAL:** *Lament for a Hanging Man* for Soprano and Ensemble (1983; Durham, Feb. 4, 1984); *1 Hand in Brooklyn Heights* for 16 Voices and Percussion (Bath, June 3, 1986); *Beating About the Bush* for Mezzo-soprano and 6 Instruments (London, June 14, 1987); *Greek Suite* for Mezzo-soprano, Tenor, and Chamber Ensemble (Frankfurt am Main, March 20, 1989); *Some Days* for Mezzo-soprano and Orch. (1989; London, July 21, 1991); *Leaving* for Soprano, Tenor, Chorus, and Ensemble (1990; rev. 1992); *Her Anxiety* for Soprano and Ensemble (1991).

Turner, Dame Eva, distinguished English soprano; b. Oldham, March 10, 1892; d. London, June 16, 1990. She was a pupil of Dan Roothan in Bristol; Giglia Levy, Edgardo Levy, and Mary Wilson at the Royal Academy of Music in London; and Albert Richards Broad. In 1916 she made her operatic debut as a Page in *Tannhäuser* with the Carl Rosa Opera Co., with which she sang until 1924; sang with the company at London's Covent Garden in 1920. In 1924 she made her first appearance at Milan's La Scala as Freia in *Das Rheingold*; then toured Germany with an Italian opera company in 1925. She sang Turandot in Brescia in 1926; appeared at Covent Garden (1928–30; 1933; 1935–39; 1947–48); was a guest artist in other European music centers, in Chicago, and in South America. She taught at the Univ. of Okla. (1950–59) and then at the Royal Academy of Music. In 1962 she was made a Dame Commander of the Order of the British Empire. Her other esteemed roles included Agatha, Amelia, Santuzza, Aida, Isolde, Sieglinde, and Cio-Cio-San.

Turner, Godfrey, English composer; b. Manchester, March 27, 1913; d. (suicide) N.Y., Dec. 7, 1948. He studied with E.J. Dent at the Univ. of Cambridge (musicology) and with Boulanger (composition) in Paris. He went to the U.S. in 1936; taught at the San Francisco Cons. (1938–43); was music ed. for Boosey & Hawkes, N.Y. (1944–46); then secretary of the American Music Center, N.Y. (1946–48). His compositions include *Trinity Concerto* for Chamber Orch.; Viola Concerto; *Sonata concertante* for Piano and String Orch.; *Fanfare, Chorale and Finale* for Brass; *Saraband and Tango; Gregorian Overture* (Columbus, Ohio, Dec. 2, 1947).

Turner, Robert (Comrie), Canadian composer and teacher; b. Montreal, June 6, 1920. He was a student of Douglas Clarke and Claude Champagne at McGill Univ. in Montreal (B.Mus., 1943; D.Mus., 1953), of Howells and Jacob at the Royal College of Music in London (1947–48), of Roy Harris at the George Peabody College for Teachers in Nashville, Tenn. (1947–50), and of Messiaen at the Berkshire Music Center in Tanglewood (summer, 1949). From 1952 to 1968 he was a music producer for the CBC in Vancouver. He taught at the Univ. of British Columbia in Vancouver (1955–57), Acadia Univ. in Wolfville, Nova Scotia (1968–69), and the Univ. of Manitoba (1969–85). In 1982 he held a Manitoba Arts Council grant. In 1987 he was a fellow at the MacDowell Colony. In 1990–91 he held a Canada Council Artists grant. He was awarded a commemorative medal marking the 125th anniversary of Canadian confederation in 1992. His compositions are couched in an eclectic style which generally adheres to tonal parameters.

WORKS: DRAMATIC: *The Brideship*, lyric drama (1966–67; Vancouver, Dec. 12, 1967); *Vile Shadows*, opera (1982–83; rev. 1986); music for radio and television. **ORCH.:** *Opening Night*, theater overture (1955); *Lyric Interlude* (1956); *Nocturne* (1956–65); *A Children's Overture* (1958); *The Pemberton Valley*, suite (1958; rev. 1988; Winnipeg, Jan. 18, 1991); *Robbins' Round*, concertino for Jazz Band (1959); 3 syms.: Sym. for Strings (1960; Montreal, March 27, 1961), *Symphony in 1 Movement: Gift from the Sea* (1983; Winnipeg, Dec. 5, 1986), and Sym. No. 3 (Winnipeg, Sept. 21, 1990); *3 Episodes* (1963; Toronto, Feb. 27, 1966); Concerto for 2 Pianos and Orch. (1971); *Eidolons*, 12 images for Chamber Orch. (Vancouver, Sept. 12, 1972); Chamber Concerto for Bassoon and 17 Instruments (1973); *Variations on the Prairie Settler's Song* (1974); *Capriccio Concertante* for Cello, Piano, and Orch. (1975); *From a Different Country: Homage to Gabrieli* (1976); *Encounters I-IX* for Various Soloists and Orch. (1985); *Playhouse Music* (1986); Viola Concerto (1987; Montreal, May 24, 1988); *Shades of Autumn* (1987; Edmonton, Sept. 21, 1990); *Manitoba Memoir* for Strings (1989; Manitoba, Feb. 26, 1991); *House of Shadows* (1994). **CHAMBER:** 3 string quartets (1949, 1954, 1975); *Lament* for Flute, Oboe, Clarinet, Bassoon, and Piano (1951); Violin Sonata (1956); *Little Suite* for Harp (1957); *Vignette* for Clarinet and String Quartet (1958; rev. 1988); *Variations and Toccata* for Woodwind Quintet and String Quintet (1959); *Serenade* for Woodwind Quintet (1960); *4 Fragments* for Brass Quintet (1961); *Fantasia* for Organ, Brass Quintet, and Timpani (1962); *Diversities* for Violin, Piano, and Bassoon (1967); Trio for Violin, Cello, and Piano (1969); *Fantasy and Festivity* for Harp (1970); *Nostalgia* for Soprano Saxophone and Piano (1972); *Shadow Pieces I* for Flute, Bassoon, Violin, Cello, and Piano (1981). **KEYBOARD: PIANO:** *Sonata Lyrica* (1955; rev. 1963); *Dance of the Disenchanted* (1959; rev. 1988); *Vestiges* (1987). **ORGAN:** *6 Voluntaries* (1959). **VOCAL:** *Mobile* for Chorus and 7 Percussion (1960); *Prophetic Song* for Women's Chorus (1961); *The 3rd Day* for Soloists, Chorus, and Orch. (1962); *The House of Christmas* for Chorus (1963); *The Phoenix and the Turtle* for Mezzo-soprano and 8 Instruments (1964); *Suite: In Homage to Melville* for Soprano, Contralto, Viola, and Piano (1966); *Johann's Gift to Christmas* for Narrator and Orch. (1972); *10 Canadian Folksongs* for High and Medium Voice and Piano (1973; orchestrated 1980; Vancouver, March 25, 1987); *Amoroso Canto* for Chorus (1978); *Lament for Linos* for Reciter, Flute, Clarinet, and Piano (1978); *Time for 3* for Mezzo-soprano, Viola, and Piano (1985); *A Group of 7* for Reciter, Viola, and Orch. (1991; Ottawa, Oct. 28, 1992); *The River of Time* for Chorus and Orch. (1994; Winnipeg, Sept. 15, 1995).

Turner, W(alter) J(ames Redfern), Australian poet and writer on music; b. Shanghai, Oct. 13, 1889; d. London, Nov. 18, 1946. He studied with his father (who was organist of St. Paul's Cathedral, Melbourne, Australia) and privately in Dresden, Munich, and Vienna. He settled in London, where he was music critic for the *New Statesman* (1916–40); also was drama critic of the *London Mercury* (1919–23) and literary ed. of the *Daily Herald* (1920–23) and *The Spectator* (from 1942).

WRITINGS (all publ. in London): *Music and Life* (1922); *Variations on the Theme of Music* (1924); *Orpheus, or The Music of the Future* (1926); *Beethoven: The Search for Reality* (1927; new ed., 1933); *Musical Meanderings* (1928); *Music: A Short History* (1932; 2nd ed., 1949); *Facing the Music: Reflections of a Music Critic* (1933); *Wagner* (1933); *Berlioz: The Man and His Work* (1934; 2nd ed., rev., 1939); *Music: An Introduction to Its Nature and Appreciation* (1936); *Mozart: The Man and His Works* (1938; 2nd ed., rev., 1965, by C. Raeburn); *English Music* (1941); *English Ballet* (1944).

Turnovský, Martin, Czech conductor; b. Prague, Sept. 29, 1928. He studied at the Prague Academy of Music (1948–52), his principal mentors being Robert Brock (piano) and Ančerl (conducting); later he pursued private instruction in conducting with Szell (1956). In 1952 he made his debut as a conductor with the Prague Sym. Orch. From 1955 to 1960 he conducted the Czech Army Sym. Orch. In 1958 he captured 1st prize in the Besançon competition. He was music director of the Brno State Phil. (1959–63) and the Plzeň Radio Sym. Orch. (1963–66). In 1966 he became Generalmusikdirektor of the Dresden State Opera and Orch. However, he resigned his position in 1968 when East German troops participated in the Soviet invasion of his homeland. After making his U.S. debut as a guest conductor with the Cleveland Orch. in 1968, Turnovsky appeared as a conductor with various orchs. and opera houses. From 1975 to 1980 he was music director of the Norwegian Opera in Oslo. He was music director of the Bonn City Theater from 1979 to 1983. During this time, he also served as co-chief conductor (with Jan Krenz) of the Beethovenhalle Orch. in Bonn. In 1992 he became music director of the Prague Sym. Orch.

Turok, Paul (Harris), American composer and music critic; b. N.Y., Dec. 3, 1929. He studied composition at Queens College with Rathaus (B.A., 1950); then at the Univ. of Calif., Berkeley, with Sessions (M.A., 1951) and at the Juilliard School of Music with Wagenaar (1951–53); later studied at Baruch College (M.S., 1986). He was a lecturer on music at the City College of N.Y. (1960–63) and was a visiting prof. at Williams College in Williamstown, Mass. (1963–64); then wrote music criticism for the *N.Y. Herald-Tribune* (1964–65), the *Music Journal* (1964–80), *Ovation* (1980–89), and *Fanfare* (from 1980). As a composer, Turok follows the principle of stylistic freedom and technical precision, without doctrinaire adherence to any circumscribed modernistic modus operandi.

WORKS: DRAMATIC: OPERAS: *Scene: Domestic*, chamber opera (1955; Aspen, Colo., Aug. 2, 1973); *Richard III* (1975); *A Secular Masque* (1979). **BALLET:** *Youngest Brother* (N.Y., Jan. 23, 1953). **ORCH.:** Violin Concerto (1953); *Symphony in 2 Movements* (1955); *Lyric Variations* for Oboe and Strings (1971; Louisville, March 9, 1973); *A Scott Joplin Overture* (Cleveland, June 19, 1973); *A Sousa Overture* (1975; Philadelphia, May 13, 1976); *Ragtime Caprice* for Piano and Orch. (1976); *Threnody* for Strings (1979); *Canzona concertante No. 1* for English Horn and Orch. (1980) and *No. 2* for Trombone and Orch. (1982); *Ultima Thule* (1981). **CHAMBER:** *Variations on a Theme by Schoenberg* for String Quartet (1952); String Trio (1954); 3 string quartets (1955, 1969, 1980); Wind Quintet (1960); Brass Quintet (1971); Clarinet Trio (1974); Quintet for English Horn and String Quartet (1981); piano pieces. **VOCAL:** Choruses; songs.

Turovsky, Yuli, Russian-born Canadian cellist, conductor, and teacher; b. Moscow, June 7, 1939. He began training in cello at the age of 7; after studies at the Moscow Central Music School (1946–57), he pursued training with Galina Kozolupova at the Moscow Cons. (diploma, 1962; Ph.D., 1969). He was principal cellist in the Moscow Chamber Orch., conductor of a chamber orch. at the Gnesin College of Music in Moscow, and a teacher at the Moscow Central Music School. In 1969 he won the U.S.S.R. Cello Competition and in 1970 took 2nd prize in the Prague Spring Competition. In 1976 he organized the Borodin Trio, with which he toured widely. In 1977 he settled in Canada and in 1980 became a naturalized Canadian citizen. In 1983 he became founder and artistic director of I Musici de Montréal, a string orch. he conducted in a vast repertoire at home and abroad. He also taught at the Montreal Cons. (1977–85) and the Univ. of Montreal (from 1981). His wife, Eleonora Turovsky (b. Moscow, Sept. 23, 1939), is a violinist and teacher. She was educated at the Moscow Central Music School (1956–58) and the Moscow Cons. (diploma, 1963; Ph.D., 1966). In 1977 she went to Canada with her husband and became a naturalized Canadian citizen in 1980. From 1978 to 1990 she played in the Montreal Sym. Orch. She was also founding concertmaster of I Musici de Montréal from 1983.

Turski, Zbigniew, Polish composer; b. Konstancin, near Warsaw, July 28, 1908; d. Warsaw, Jan. 7, 1979. He was a student of Rytel (composition) and Bierdiajew (conducting) at the Warsaw Cons. From 1936 to 1939 he was music producer of the Polish Radio in Warsaw. In 1945–46 he was conductor of the Baltic Phil. in Gdańsk. His compositions were in an advanced harmonic idiom.

WORKS: DRAMATIC: *Rozmowki* (Chats), micro-opera (1966); *Tytania i osiol* (Titania and the Donkey), ballet (1966); incidental music for the theater, films, and radio. **ORCH.:** 3 syms. (*Sinfonia da camera*, 1947; *Sinfonia Olimpica*, 1948; 1953); 2 violin concertos (1951, 1959); *Little Overture* (1955). **CHAMBER:** 2 string quartets (n.d., 1951); piano pieces. **VOCAL:** *L'Ombre* for Tenor, Chorus, and Percussion (1967); *Canti de nativitate patriae* for Tenor, Bass, Chorus, and Orch. (1969); *Regno Ejukori* for Bass and Orch. (Wroclaw, Sept. 2, 1974); cantatas; songs.

Tusler, Robert Leon, American musicologist; b. Stoughton, Wis., April 1, 1920. He studied piano and organ at Friends' Univ., Wichita, Kans. (B.M., 1947); musicology at the Univ. of Calif., Los Angeles (M.A., 1952); then at the Univ. of Utrecht, the Netherlands (1956–58). In 1958 he joined the music faculty of the Univ. of Calif., Los Angeles; retired in 1983. He publ. *The Style of J.S. Bach's Chorale Preludes* (1956), *The Organ Music of Jan Pieterszoon Sweelinck* (2 vols., 1958), *Music: Catalyst for Healing* (1991), *Willem de Fesch: An Excellent Musician and a Worthy Man* (1995), *and Willem de Fesch: The Collected Works* (1995).

Tuthill, Burnet Corwin, American composer and conductor; b. N.Y., Nov. 16, 1888; d. Knoxville, Tenn., Jan. 18, 1982. His father, William Burnet Tuthill, was the architect of Carnegie Hall in N.Y. He studied at Columbia Univ. (B.A., 1909; M.A., 1910) and the Cincinnati College of Music (M.M., 1935). He conducted the Columbia Univ. Orch. (1909–13). In 1919 he organized the Soc. for Publication of American Music, which continued to function for nearly half a century, and which publ. about 85 works by American composers; also was executive secretary of the National Assn. of Schools of Music in Cincinnati (1924–59). After serving as general manager of the Cincinnati College of Music (1922–30), he was head of the music dept. at Southwestern Univ. in Memphis (1935–59); also was conductor of the Memphis Sym. Orch. (1938–46) and head of the fine arts dept. of Shrivenham American Univ. in England (1945). He began to compose rather late in life, but compensated for this delay by increasing productivity in subsequent years. His autobiography was publ. as *Recollections of a Musical Life, 1900–74* (Memphis, 1974).

WORKS: ORCH.: *Bethlehem*, pastorale (Interlochen, Mich., July 22, 1934); *Laurentia*, symphonic poem (Rochester, N.Y., Oct. 30, 1936); *Come 7*, rhapsody (1935; St. Louis, Feb. 19, 1944); Sym. (1940); Concertos for clarinet (1949), double bass (1962), saxophone (1965), trombone (1967), and tuba (1975).

OTHER: Numerous pieces with a multiplicity of clarinets; Flute Sonata; Oboe Sonata; Trumpet Sonata; Saxophone Sonata; a plethora of sacred choruses.

BIBL.: J. Raines, *B.C. T.: His Life and Music* (diss., Michigan State Univ., 1979).

Tuukkanen, Kalervo, Finnish conductor and composer; b. Mikkeli, Oct. 14, 1909; d. Helsinki, July 12, 1979. He studied composition with Leevi Madetoja and theory with Krohn in Helsinki. He subsequently conducted local orchs. and choirs; from 1967 to 1969 he was a visiting prof. of music at the Chinese Univ. of Hong Kong. He wrote 2 violin concertos (1943, 1956); 6 syms. (1944, 1949, 1952, 1958, 1961, 1978); Cello Concerto (1946); Sinfonietta (1948); *Man and the Elements* for Soprano, Chorus, and Orch. (1949); *Indumati,* opera (1962); *Youth Cantata* (1963); *A Chorale Echo* for Flute and Piano (1967). He also publ. a monograph on the life and works of Leevi Madetoja (Helsinki, 1947).

Tuxen, Erik (Oluf), Danish conductor; b. Mannheim (of Danish parents), July 4, 1902; d. Copenhagen, Aug. 28, 1957. After training in architecture, medicine, and philosophy, he pursued studies in music in Copenhagen, Paris, Vienna, and Berlin. He conducted at the Lübeck Opera (1927–29), and then at the Royal Theater in Copenhagen. In 1936 he became conductor of the Danish Radio Sym. Orch. in Copenhagen. During World War II (1939–45), he lived in Sweden. Returning to Copenhagen in 1945, he was again conductor of the Danish Radio Sym. Orch. until his death. He conducted it at the Edinburgh Festival in 1950 in an acclaimed performance of Nielsen's 5th Sym. In 1950–51 he conducted in the U.S. and in 1954 in South America. Tuxen was a particularly persuasive interpreter of Nielsen.

Tveitt, (Nils) Geirr, Norwegian composer, teacher, and pianist; b. Kvam, Oct. 19, 1908; d. Oslo, Feb. 1, 1981. He learned to play the piano and violin in childhood. Following studies with Grabner and Weninger in Leipzig (1928–32), he pursued his training in Vienna with Wellesz and in Paris with Honegger and Villa-Lobos (1932–35). Returning to Norway, he devoted himself mainly to composition, producing over 300 works. He also made some tours abroad as a pianist. In 1941 the Norwegian government granted him an annual income. However, his activities during the German occupation of Norway led to his loss of the Norwegian government grant after the liberation in 1945. It was finally restored in 1958. In his study *Tonalitätstheorie des parallelen Leittonssystems* (Oslo, 1937), Tveitt attempted to formulate the foundation of his own compositional style by claiming that the modal scales are in actuality old Norse keys. Many of his works employ modal scales.

WORKS: DRAMATIC: OPERAS: *Nordvest—Sud—Nordaust—Nord* (1939); *Dragaredokko* (1940); *Roald Amundsen* (n.d.); *Stevleik,* chamber opera (n.d.); *Jeppe* (1964; Bergen, June 10, 1966; rev. 1968). **BALLETS:** *Baldurs draumar* (1935); *Birgingu* (1939); *Husguden* (1956). **INCIDENTAL MUSIC:** *Jonsoknatt* (1936). **ORCH.:** 6 piano concertos (1930, 1933, 1947, 1947, 1954, 1960); Concerto for String Quartet and Orch. (1933); *Variations* for 2 Pianos and Orch. (1937); Violin Concerto (1939); 2 Hardanger fiddle concertos (1956); 3 syms.; 5 Hardanger suites (based on a set of piano pieces). **CHAMBER:** Quartet for 4 Violins; 2 string quartets; 3 string sextets. **PIANO:** 29 sonatas; *100 Folk Tunes from Hardanger.* **OTHER:** Vocal pieces.

BIBL.: R. Storass, *Tonediktaren G. T.: Songjen i fossaduren* (Oslo, 1990).

Twardowski, Romuald, Polish composer and teacher; b. Vilnius, June 17, 1930. He studied composition and piano with Juzeliunas at the Vilnius Cons. (1952–57); after further training with Woytowicz at the Warsaw Cons. (1957–60), he studied medieval polyphony and Gregorian chant with Boulanger in Paris (1963). He later taught at the Warsaw Academy of Music.

WORKS: DRAMATIC: OPERAS: *Cyrano de Bergerac* (1962; Bytom, July 6, 1963); *Tragedyja albo rzecz o Janie i Herodzie* (Tragedy, or Story of John and Herod; 1965; Łódź, April 24, 1969); *Lord Jim* (1972–73); *Upadek ojca Suryna* (The Fall of Father Surin), radio opera (1968; scenic version, Kraków, 1969); *Maria Stuart* (1978); *Story of St. Katherine* (1981; Warsaw, Dec. 14, 1985). **BALLETS:** *The Naked Prince* (1960); *The Magician's Statues* (1963). **ORCH.:** *3 Sketches* for Strings (1955); Piano Concerto (1956); *Concerto for Orchestra* (1957); *Suita w dawnym stylu* (Suite in Old Style; 1957); *Mala symfonia konzertujaca* (Little Symphony Concertante) for Piano, Strings, and Percussion (1958); *Antifone* for 3 Orch. Groups (1961); *Nomopedia,* 5 movements (1962); *Ode 64* (1964); *The St. Mary Triptych,* 3 scenes and dances for Strings (1973); *Prelude, Toccata and Chorale* (1973); *Study in A* (1974; Warsaw, Sept. 21, 1976); *2 Landscapes* (1975); *Capriccio in Blue (George Gershwin in memoriam)* for Violin and Orch. (1979); *Little Concerto* for Piano and Instrumental Group (1980); Piano Concerto (1984); *Spanish Fantasia* for Violin and Orch. (1985); *3 Frescoes* (1986); *Symphonic Variations on a Theme by Gershwin* for Solo Percussion and Orch. (1986). **CHAMBER:** *Burlesque* for Wind Quintet (1984); *Allegro rustico* for Oboe and Piano (1986); Trio for Violin, Cello, and Piano (1987); *Lithuanian Variations* for Wind Quintet (1988); *Espressioni* for Violin and Piano (1990). **PIANO:** *Little Sonata* (1958); *Toccata* for 2 Pianos (1974); *Improvisations and Toccata* for 2 Pianos (1974). **VOCAL:** *Pieśń o Bialym Domu* (Song about the White House), cantata for Tenor, Chorus, 2 Pianos, and Percussion (1959); *Cantus antiqui* for Soprano, Harpsichord, Piano, and Percussion (1962); *Trittico fiorentino: I, 3 studi secondo Giotto* for Chamber Orch. (1966), *II, Sonetti di Petrarca* for Tenor Solo and 2 Choruses (1965), and *III, Impressioni fiorentini* for 4 Instrumental Choruses (1967); *Mala liturgia prawoslawna* (Little Orthodox Liturgy) for Vocal Ensemble and 3 Instrumental Groups (1969); *Oda do mlodości* (Ode to Youth) for Narrator, Chorus, and Orch. (1969); *3 sonnets d'adieux* for Bass-baritone, Piano, Strings, and Percussion (1971); *Polish Landscape,* 3 songs for Bass-baritone and Orch. (1975); *Michelangelo Sonnets* for Baritone and Piano (1988); *Alleluia* for Chorus (1990).

Tweedy, Donald (Nichols), American composer and teacher; b. Danbury, Conn., April 23, 1890; d. there, July 21, 1948. He was educated at Harvard Univ. (B.A., 1912; M.A., 1917), where his teachers were William Heilman, E.B. Hill, and Walter Spalding; later studied in Europe and with Goetschius in N.Y. He taught at Vassar College (1914–16), the Eastman School of Music (1923–27), Hamilton College (1937–38), and Texas Christian Univ. (1945–46). He publ. a *Manual of Harmonic Technic Based on the Practice of J.S. Bach* (1928).

WORKS: BALLET: *Alice in Wonderland* (1935). **ORCH.:** *L'Allegro,* symphonic study (Rochester, N.Y., May 1, 1925); *3 Dances* (1925); *Williamsburg,* suite (1941). **CHAMBER:** Viola Sonata (1916); Violin Sonata (1920); Cello Sonata (1930); piano pieces.

Tyler, James (Henry), American lutenist and cittern and viol player; b. Hartford, Conn., Aug. 3, 1940. He studied at the Hartt School of Music in Hartford; also took lessons with Joseph Iadone. He made his debut in 1962 with the N.Y. Pro Musica; later went to Germany, where he specialized in performances on early Renaissance instruments; was a member of the Studio der frühen Musik in Munich. He went to England in 1969, where he joined the Early Music Consort of London and Musica Reservata; also served as co-director of the Consort of Musicke with Anthony Rooley. In 1974 he became a member of the Julian Bream Consort. In 1976 he organized the London Early Music Group, devoted principally to performing works of the 16th and 17th centuries. A versatile musician, he also gave concerts of ragtime music with his own quintet, the New Excelsior Talking Machine. In 1986 he became prof. of music and director of the early music program at the Univ. of Southern Calif. in Los Angeles. He wrote *The Early Guitar* (London, 1980) and *The Early Mandolin* (with P. Sparks; Oxford, 1989).

Tyranny, Blue Gene (real name, **Robert Nathan Sheff**), American keyboardist and composer; b. San Antonio, Jan. 1, 1945. He studied piano and composition privately (1957–62), winning a BMI Student Composers award for his *Piano Sonata on Expanding Thoughts* (1961). He was active in the ONCE Group in Ann Arbor (1962–68), helping to establish its reputation for mixed media and cross-cultural performance; also taught keyboard and jazz composition at Mills College in Oakland, California (1971–81). He made numerous recordings, and performed with Laurie Anderson and Peter Gordon; collaborated on Robert Ashley's *Perfect Lives (Private Parts)* (1976–83); also wrote scores for dance, theater, film, and video. A 1975 fire destroyed about half of his early scores, many of which he is reconstructing. Tyranny is an important proponent of integrating jazz and rock elements into concert music; the range of imagination and genre evidenced by his catalog is remarkable.

WORKS: PROCEDURAL SCORES: *The Interior Distance* (1960; realized for 7 Instruments or Voices, 1990); *How to Make Music from the Sounds of Your Daily Life* (1967; realized on Tape as *Country Boy Country Dog*); *How to Do It* (1973; intentionally incomplete); *Archaeo-Acoustics (The Shining Net)* (1977); *PALS/Action at a Distance* (1977); *The Telekinesis Tape* (1977); *Taking Out the Garbage* (1977); *The Intermediary* (1981; realized for Piano, Tape, and Computer); *The More He Sings, The More He Cries, The Better He Feels . . . Tango* (1984; realized for Tape and Piano; orchestrated, 1985); *A Letter from Home* (1986; orig. for Voice and Electronics, 1976); *Somewhere in Arizona, 1970* (1987); *Extreme Realizations Just Before Sunset (Mobile)* (1987; realized for Tape and Piano). **OTHER:** *Music for 3 Begins* for Tapes and Audio Engineer (1958); *4 Chorales* for Keyboard and Electronic Sampling (1958); *How Things That Can't Exist May Exist*, 20-odd theater and street pieces (1958–76); *Ballad/The Road and Other Lines* for 1 to 40 Instruments or Voices (1960); *Meditation/The Reference Moves, The Form Remains*, graphic score (1962; orchestrated, 1963); *Diotima*, graphic score with Tape (1963); *Home Movie* for Film, Tape, and Rock Band (1963); *Just Walk On In*, theater work (1965); *Closed Transmission* for Tape (1966); *The Bust* for Any Kind of Band (1967); *The CBCD Transforms*, electronic codes for acoustic performance (1968–71); *Live and Let Live* for Video and Live Electronics (1972); *Remembering* for Voice and Electronics (1974); *A Letter from Home* for Voice and Electronics (1976; recomposed as procedural score, 1986); *No Job, No Warm, No Nothing*, songs with Electronics (1976); *David Kopay (Portrait)* for Instruments (1976); *Harvey Milk (Portrait)* for Tape (1978); *The White Night Riot* for Tape and Movement (1979); *The Country Boy Country Dog Concert* for Improvisors and Electronics (1980; arranged as *The Country Boy Country Dog Variations* for Soloist[s] and Orch.); *The World's Greatest Piano Player* for Electric Keyboard (1981); *The Song of the Street of the Singing Chicken* for Keyboard (1981); *A Rendition of Stardust* for Tape (1982); *Choral Ode 3* for Voice and Electronics (1987); *The Forecaster* for Orch. and Electronics (1988–89); *Nocturne with and without Memory* for 1 to 3 Pianos (1988–89); *The Great Seal (Transmigration)* for Piano Duo (1990); *My Language Is Me (Millennium)* for Voice and Electronics (1990); *Vocal Responses during Transformation* for Voices and Live Electronics (1990); songs.

Tyrwhitt-Wilson, Sir Gerald Hugh, Baronet. See **Berners, Lord.**

Tyson, Alan (Walker), esteemed Scottish musicologist; b. Glasgow, Oct. 27, 1926. He was educated at Magdalen College, Oxford; studied litterae humaniores there (1947–51); in 1952 he was elected a fellow of All Souls College, Oxford; later pursued training in psychoanalysis and medicine (qualified, 1965). In 1971 he became a senior research fellow at All Souls College, a position he retained until 1994. He also was a visiting prof. of music at Columbia Univ. (1969), the Lyell Reader in Bibliography at the Univ. of Oxford (1973–74), the Ernest Bloch Prof. of Music at the Univ. of Calif., Berkeley (1977–78), a member of the Inst. for Advanced Study at Princeton Univ. (1983–84), and a visiting prof. at the Graduate Center of the City Univ. of N.Y. (1985). In 1989 he was made a Commander of the Order of the British Empire. In 1991 he was made a corresponding member of the American Musicological Soc. He has made extensive textual and bibliographical studies of the period 1770–1850; particularly noteworthy are his contributions to the study of Beethoven.

WRITINGS: *The Authentic English Editions of Beethoven* (London, 1963); with O. Neighbour, *English Music Publishers' Plate Numbers in the First Half of the Nineteenth Century* (London, 1965); *Thematic Catalogue of the Works of Muzio Clementi* (Tutzing, 1967); ed., *Beethoven Studies* (N.Y., 1974), *Beethoven Studies 2* (London, 1977), *Beethoven Studies 3* (London, 1982); *Mozart: Studies of the Autograph Scores* (Cambridge, Mass., 1987); ed. with A. Rosenthal, *Mozart's Thematic Catalogue: A Facsimile* (1990); *Watermarks in Mozart's Autographs* in the *Neue Mozart-Ausgabe* (X/33/Abteilung, 2, 1992).

BIBL.: S. Brandenburg, ed., *Haydn, Mozart, and Beethoven: Studies in the Music of the Classical Period: Essays in Honour of A. T.* (Oxford, 1995).

Tzipine, Georges, French conductor; b. Paris, June 22, 1907; d. there, Dec. 8, 1987. He studied violin at the Paris Cons., winning a premier prix. He made his debut as a violinist with the Paris Radio (1926); then pursued training in harmony, counterpoint, and conducting. In 1931 he began his career as a conductor with the Paris Radio; after further studies with Marc de Rance and Reynaldo Hahn, he appeared as a guest conductor with various Paris orchs. and toured France as a ballet conductor. He was music director of the Cannes Casino (1945–49); then toured Europe and North and South America as a guest conductor. After serving as music director of the Melbourne Sym. Orch. (1961–65), he taught conducting at the Paris Cons. (from 1966).

Tzybin, Vladimir, Russian flutist, teacher, and composer; b. Ivanovo-Voznesensk, 1877; d. Moscow, May 31, 1949. He played the flute in the orch. of the Bolshoi Theater in Moscow from 1896 to 1907 and from 1921 to 1929. From 1907 to 1920 he was 1st flutist at the Imperial Opera of St. Petersburg. He composed 2 operas: *Flengo* (1918) and *Tale of the Dead Princess and 7 Heroes* (1947); publ. several collections of flute pieces. He was esteemed as a pedagogue.

Uchida, Mitsuko, talented Japanese pianist; b. Tokyo, Dec. 20, 1948. She began training in childhood in her native city, and at the age of 12 became a pupil of Richard Hauser at the Vienna Academy of Music. In 1968 she won the Beethoven Competition, and in 1970 received 2nd prize at the Chopin Competition in Warsaw. In 1982 she won particular notice in London and Tokyo for her performances of the complete piano sonatas of Mozart. During the 1985–86 season, she appeared as soloist-conductor in all the piano concertos of Mozart with the English Chamber Orch. in London. On Feb. 15, 1987, she made her N.Y. recital debut. In 1989 she was soloist in Mozart's Piano Concerto, K.271, in Salzburg. In subsequent years, she toured all over the world, appearing as a soloist with leading orchs. and as a recitalist. Her repertoire includes, in addition to the classics, works by Debussy, Schoenberg, and Bartók.

Ugarte, Floro M(anuel), Argentine composer and teacher; b. Buenos Aires, Sept. 15, 1884; d. there, June 11, 1975. He studied in Buenos Aires, and at the Paris Cons. under Pessard, Lavignac, and Fourdrain, with whom he collaborated in writing the ballet *Sigolene.* He returned to Argentina in 1913; in 1924, became a prof. at the National Cons. in Buenos Aires; was general director of the Teatro Colón, founder-president of the National Music Soc., prof. at the Escuela Superior de Bellas Artes at La Plata Univ., and director of the Buenos Aires Municipal Cons.

WORKS: OPERATIC FAIRY TALE: *Saika* (1918; Buenos Aires, July 21, 1920). **ORCH.:** *Entre las montañas,* symphonic suite (1922); *De mi tierra,* 2 symphonic suites (1923, 1934); *La rebelión del agua,* symphonic poem (1931; Buenos Aires, Oct. 16, 1935); *Piri,* choreographic poem (1944); Sym. (1946; Buenos Aires, May 13, 1952); *Vidala* (1948); *Preludio* (1949); *Tango* (Buenos Aires, Sept. 5, 1951); Violin Concerto (1963). **CHAMBER:** Piano Quartet (1921); Sonata for Violin or Cello and Piano (1928); String Quartet (1935); piano pieces. **VOCAL:** Songs.

Ughi, Uto, talented Italian violinist; b. Busto Arsizio, near Milan, Jan. 21, 1944. A child prodigy, he commenced musical training when he was 4 and made his formal debut at 7 in a recital at Milan's Teatro Lirico; pursued studies at the Conservatorio di Santa Cecilia in Rome; also received lessons from Enesco (1954). In 1959 he made an extensive tour of Europe; after performing in Australia (1963), he made his U.S. debut in N.Y. on Feb. 27, 1967; subsequently toured worldwide. In 1977 he was made a member of the Accademia di Santa Cecilia in Rome. In 1979 he organized the "Hommage to Venice" festival to raise funds for restoring the city's art treasures. His instrument is the "Van Houten-Kreutzer" Stradivarius, which dates from 1701. His repertoire includes, besides the classics, a wide selection of modern concertos for the violin.

Uhde, Hermann, noted German bass-baritone; b. Bremen, July 20, 1914; d. during a performance in Copenhagen, Oct. 10, 1965. He studied at Philipp Kraus's opera school in Bremen, making his operatic debut there as Titurel in *Parsifal* in 1936; appeared in Freiburg im Breisgau and then sang with the Bavarian State Opera in Munich (1940–43) and with the German Opera at The Hague (1943–44). He subsequently was engaged at Hannover (1947–48), Hamburg (1948–50), Vienna (1950–51), Munich (1951–56), Stuttgart (1956–57), and again in Vienna (1957–61). He made his American debut at the Metropolitan Opera in N.Y. as Telramund in *Lohengrin* on Nov. 18, 1955; was on its roster until 1957, then again from 1958 to 1961 and in 1963–64. He was particularly acclaimed for his performances in Wagnerian roles.

Uhl, Alfred, Austrian composer and pedagogue; b. Vienna, June 5, 1909; d. there, June 8, 1992. He studied composition with Franz Schmidt at the Vienna Academy of Music (diploma, 1932); then in 1940–41, during World War II, was in the Austrian army, where he was severely wounded. In 1943 he became a composition teacher at the Vienna Academy of

Music; also served as president of the Austrian copyright society (1970–75). In 1980 he was awarded the Austrian Badge of Honor for Science and Arts. His music was patterned after Classical forms, with emphasis on contrapuntal clarity.

WORKS: DRAMATIC: *Katzenmusik*, ballet-opera (1957); *Der Mysteriöse Herr X*, opera (1962–65; Vienna, June 8, 1966). **ORCH.:** *Wiener Waltz* (1938); *Sinfonischer Marsch* (1942); *Konzertante Sinfonie* for Clarinet and Orch. (1943; Vienna, Nov. 5, 1944); *4 Capricen* (1944–45); *Introduktion und Variationen über eine Melodie aus dem 16. Jahrhundert* for Strings (1947); *Sonata graziosa* (1947); *Rondeau* (1948); Concertino for Violin and 22 Winds (1949; also for Violin and Orch., 1964); *Concerto a ballo* (1966; N.Y., Oct. 9, 1967); Sinfonietta (1978; Vienna, May 31, 1979); *3 Sketches* (1980); Concerto for 2 Oboes, 2 Horns, and Strings (Murcia, Spain, April 21, 1984). **CHAMBER:** Trio for Violin, Viola, and Guitar (1928; rev. 1981); *Kleines Konzert* for Clarinet, Viola, and Piano (1936; rev. for Violin, Cello, and Piano, 1972); *Divertimento* for 3 Clarinets and Bass Clarinet (1943); *Eine vergnügliche Musik* for 8 Winds (1944); 2 string quartets (1945–46, rev. 1969; *Jubiläumsquartett*, 1961); 15 études for Bassoon (1972); 20 études for Viola (1974); *Commedia Musicale* for Clarinet, Viola, and Piano (1982); *3 Stücke* for Flute and Guitar (1982). **VOCAL:** *Gilgamesh*, oratorio (1954–56; rev. 1967–68; Vienna, June 13, 1969); *Wer einsam ist, der hat es gut*, cantata (1960; rev. 1963; Linz, Jan. 27, 1964); *Festlicher Auftrakt* for Chorus, Organ, and Orch. (1970); choruses; songs.

BIBL.: A. Witeschnik, *A. U.: Eine biographische Studie* (Vienna, 1966).

Uhl, Fritz, Austrian tenor; b. Matzleinsdorf, near Vienna, April 2, 1928. He studied at the Vienna Academy of Music (1947–52). In 1952 he made his operatic debut in Graz. In 1957 he made his first appearance at the Bayreuth Festival as Vogelsang, and continued to sing there until 1964. In 1958 he became a member of the Bavarian State Opera in Munich, where he was made a Kammersänger in 1962. From 1961 he also sang at the Vienna State Opera. He made his debut at London's Covent Garden as Walther von Stolzing in 1963. In 1968 he sang for the first time at the Salzburg Festival as Florestan, and continued to appear there until 1972. In 1981 he became a prof. at the Vienna Cons. Uhl was particularly known for his Wagnerian portrayals.

Ujfalussy, József, eminent Hungarian musicologist; b. Debrecen, Feb. 13, 1920. He received training in piano and composition at the Debrecen Music School, and in the classics at the Univ. of Debrecen (Ph.D., 1944, with a diss. on Homer's epics); then studied composition with Veress, conducting with Ferencsik, musicology with Szabolcsi and Bartha, and folk music with Kodály at the Budapest Academy of Music (1946–49). He became a member (1948) and served as head of the music dept. (1951–55) of the Ministry of Culture; then was prof. of aesthetics and theory at the Budapest Academy of Music (from 1955). In 1961 he became associated with the Bartók Archives (the Inst. of Musicology from 1969) of the Hungarian Academy of Sciences; in 1973 he was made a corresponding member of the latter, where he was president of the musicological commission and director of the Inst. of Musicology (from 1973). In 1961 he received the Erkel Prize and in 1966 the Kossuth Prize.

WRITINGS: Ed. *Bartók-breviárium* (Bartók Breviary; Budapest, 1958; 2nd ed., rev., 1974; letters, writings, and documents); *Achille-Claude Debussy* (Budapest, 1959); *A valóság zenei képe* (The Musical Image of Reality; Budapest, 1962); *Bartók Béla* (Budapest, 1965; 2nd ed., enl., 1970; Eng. tr., 1971); *Az esztétika alapjai és a zene* (The Bases of Aesthetics and Music; Budapest, 1968); *Farkas Ferenc* (Budapest, 1969); ed. *A Liszt Ferenc zeneművészeti föiskola 100 eve* (100 Years of the Franz Liszt Academy of Music; Budapest, 1977).

Ujj, Béla, Hungarian composer of operettas; b. Vienna, July 2, 1873; d. there, Feb. 1, 1942. He lost his sight in childhood, but studied music and composed a number of successful operettas which were premiered in Vienna: *Der Herr Professor* (Dec. 4, 1903); *Kaisermanöver* (March 4, 1905); *Die kleine Prinzessin* (May 5, 1907); *Drei Stunden Leben* (Nov. 1, 1909); *Chanteclee* (Oct. 25, 1910); *Der Turmer von St. Stephan* (Sept. 13, 1912); *Teresita* (June 27, 1914); *Der Müller und sein Kind* (Oct. 30, 1917).

Ulanowsky, Paul, Austrian-born American pianist and teacher; b. Vienna, March 4, 1908; d. N.Y., Aug. 4, 1968. He studied theory and composition with Marx and piano with Eisenberger at the Vienna Academy of Music, taking diplomas in conducting and composition (1930). He also received private instruction in violin and viola, and took courses in musicology at the Univ. of Vienna (1926–30) with Adler, Fischer, and Ficker. After performing in Vienna, he went to the U.S. as accompanist to Enid Szantho in 1935. He decided to settle there and became a naturalized American citizen in 1943. From 1937 to 1951 he toured as accompanist to Lotte Lehmann and other celebrated artists. From 1960 he served as the pianist of the Bach Aria Group. He taught at the Berkshire Music Center in Tanglewood (summers, 1950–56) and at Boston Univ. (1951–55). In 1952–53 he was a visting artist at the Univ. of Ill., where he became a prof. in 1960.

Ulfrstad, Marius Moaritz, Norwegian composer; b. Borgund, Sept. 11, 1890; d. Oslo, Oct. 29, 1968. He studied piano and composition at the Christiania Cons. (graduated, 1910); continued his training in Berlin, with Pizzetti in Florence, Respighi in Rome, and Ravel in Paris. He settled in Christiania, where he founded his own music school (1921); was music critic of the *Morgenposten* (1922–40) and the *Aftenposten* (1945–47).

WORKS: DRAMATIC: Incidental music. **ORCH.:** 5 syms. (1921–44); 2 violin concertos (1923, 1935); Piano Concerto (1935); several suites, most inspired by the geography of Norway, Iceland, and Greenland (Stavern og Sörlands, Islandia, Arctic, Norvegia, Grönlandia, Svalbardia, Möre og Romsdal, Oslo, Norwegian Middleage, etc.). **OTHER:** Chamber music; cantatas; about 250 choral pieces; nearly 1,000 songs, including folk song arrangements.

Ulfung, Ragnar (Sigurd), Norwegian tenor and opera director; b. Oslo, Feb. 28, 1927. He studied at the Oslo Cons. and in Milan. In 1949 he launched his career singing in concerts. In 1952 he made his stage debut as Magadoff in Menotti's *The Consul* in Stockholm, and then sang in Bergen and Göteborg. In 1958 he became a member of the Royal Opera in Stockholm, where he created the role of the Deaf Mute in Blomdahl's *Aniara* in 1959. In 1959 he also made his British debut as Verdi's Gustavus III with the visiting Royal Opera of Stockholm at the Edinburgh Festival, and returned with it in 1960 in the same role at London's Covent Garden. In 1963 he returned to Covent Garden as Don Carlos. He made his U.S. debut in Santa Fe in 1966, and then appeared at the San Francisco Opera in 1967. In 1969 he sang at the Hamburg State Opera. In 1971 he appeared at the Chicago Lyric Opera. He created the title role in Maxwell Davies's *Taverner* at Covent Garden in 1972, and also made his first appearance at Milan's La Scala. On Dec. 12, 1972, he made his Metropolitan Opera debut in N.Y. as Mime in *Siegfried*, and then returned there for occasional appearances in subsequent years in such roles as Mime, Loge, Herod, Berg's Captain, and Weill's Fatty. In 1973 he made his bow as an opera director with *La Bohême* in Santa Fe, and thereafter directed works there and in Stockholm and Seattle. During the 1974–76 seasons, he sang Mime in the *Ring* cycle at Covent Garden. In 1986 he appeared as Herod in San Francisco. He created the role of Jadidja in *Die schwarze Maske* at its U.S. premiere in Santa Fe in 1988. In 1989 he sang Strauss's Aegisthus in London. In 1990 he appeared as Puccini's Goro in Lyons.

Ullmann, Viktor, Austrian composer, pianist, conductor, and music critic; b. Teschen, Jan. 1, 1898; d. in the concentration camp in Auschwitz, on or about Oct. 15, 1944. After initial training in Teschen, he went to Vienna in 1914, where he later was a student of Schoenberg (1918–19). From 1920 to 1927 he was an assistant to Zemlinsky at the New German Theater in Prague. In 1927–28 he served as director of the Ústí nad Labem

Opera. He was active in Germany until the Nazi takeover of 1933 compelled him to return to Prague. He was associated with the Czech Radio, wrote music and book reviews, and taught privately. From 1935 to 1937 he attended A. Hába's classes in quarter tone music at the Cons. With the Nazi dismemberment of Czechoslovakia in 1939, Ullmann's life became precarious. In 1942 the Nazis deported him to the Theresienstadt ghetto. In spite of the hardships there, he played an active role in the artistic endeavors of the ghetto. He composed the opera *Der Kaiser von Atlantis* during this time, a work depicting a tyrannical monarch who outlaws death only to beg for its return in order to relieve humanity from the horrors of life. The opera reached its dress rehearsal in 1944, but when the Nazi guards realized that the monarch was a satirical characterization of Hitler, Ullmann was sent to the Auschwitz concentration camp and put to death in the gas chamber. While a number of his works have been lost, several of his surviving scores have been revived. In his early music, Ullmann was influenced by Schoenberg. His later works were classical in form with polytonal textures. His fine songs reveal the influence of Mahler.

WORKS: OPERAS: *Peer Gynt* (1928); *Der Sturz des Antichrist* (1935; Bielefeld, Jan. 7, 1995); *Der zerbrochene Krug* (1941); *Der Kaiser von Atlantis oder der Tod dankt ab* (1943; Amsterdam, Dec. 16, 1975). **ORCH.:** *Variations and Double Fugue on a Theme of Arnold Schoenberg* (1929–34; based on the piano piece, 1925–29); Piano Concerto (1939); *Slavonic Rhapsody* for Alto Saxophone and Orch. (1940); 2 syms.: No. 1, *Vom meiner Jugen* (1943; partial reconstruction by B. Wulff; Philadelphia, Jan. 26, 1995) and No. 2 (1944; partial reconstruction by B. Wulff; Stuttgart, Oct. 18, 1989); *Don Quixote tanzt Fandango*, overture (1944; partial reconstruction by B. Wulff; Lucerne, Sept. 2, 1995). **CHAMBER:** 3 string quartets (n.d., n.d., 1943); Octet for Piano, Winds, and Strings; Sonata for Quarter Tone Clarinet and Piano; Violin Sonata. **PIANO:** *Variations and Double Fugue on a Theme of Arnold Schoenberg* (1925–29; also for Orch., 1929–34); 7 sonatas (1936; 1938–39; 1940; 1941; n.d.; n.d.; 1944). **VOCAL:** *Sechs Lieder nach Gedichten von Albert Steffen* for Soprano and Piano (1937); *Fünf Liebeslieder von Ricarda Huch* for Soprano and Piano (1938–39); *Drei Sonette aus dem Portugiesischen* by Elizabeth Barrett Browning for Voice and Piano (1939–40); *Geistliche Lieder* for High Voice and Piano (1940); *Liederbuch des Hafis* for Bass and Piano (1940); *Six Sonnets de Louize Labé* for Voice and Piano (1941); *Die Weise von Liebe und Tod des Cornets Christoph Rilke* for Speaker and Orch. (1944; partial reconstruction by H. Brauel; Prague, May 27, 1995).

BIBL.: H.-G. Klein, ed., *V. U., Materialien* (Hamburg, 1992).

Ulrich, Homer, American musicologist; b. Chicago, March 27, 1906; d. Silver Spring, Md., Nov. 28, 1987. He studied bassoon and cello at the Chicago Musical College, and played these instruments in various orchs.; was bassoonist with the Chicago Sym. Orch. (1929–35); received his M.A. at the Univ. of Chicago with the thesis *The Penitential Psalms of Lasso* (1939). He was head of the music dept. of Monticello College (1935–38); then taught at the Univ. of Texas (assoc. prof., 1939; prof., 1951); also played bassoon with the San Antonio Sym. Orch. In 1953 he was appointed head of the music dept. of the Univ. of Maryland; retired in 1972. He publ. *Chamber Music* (N.Y., 1948; 2nd ed., 1966); *Education of a Concert-Goer* (N.Y., 1949); *Symphonic Music* (N.Y., 1952); *Famous Women Singers* (N.Y., 1953); *Music: A Design for Listening* (N.Y., 1957; 3rd ed., 1970); with P. Pisk, *A History of Music and Musical Style* (N.Y., 1963); *A Survey of Choral Music* (N.Y., 1973).

Underwood, James, American composer; b. Richmond, Calif., March 4, 1951. He played the trumpet as a youth; then studied composition with Robert Basart at Calif. State Univ. in Hayward (1969–75; M.A., 1975) and with Frederick Fox at Indiana Univ. (1978–82; D.A., 1982). His music is prudently modernistic, with atonal and polytonal divagations from modal harmonic structures within a general Baroque framework; there is an element of neo-Handelian humor in some of his compositions.

WORKS: ORCH.: *Variations on B-A-C-H* (Hayward, Calif., June 8, 1973); *The Orchestral Noises of October Nights* (1980–81; Bloomington, Ind., March 31, 1982); *Joyyoku* (1984; Indianapolis, Sept. 24, 1985); *Sonorous Regions* for Chamber Orch. (1986); *Bachanlia for a Lot of Cellos* (1986; perf. by 40 cellos, Bloomington, Ind., Feb. 3, 1987); *Glider* (Bloomington, Ind., April 24, 1990); *Kyrie* (1991); *Grendel* (Bloomington, Ind., Oct. 25, 1992); *Grendel's Mother* (Bloomington, Ind., Oct. 24, 1993); *Back Home? Again??* (1995). **CHAMBER:** *Lament* for Clarinet (1970); *Textures I* for 5 Instruments (1971), *II* for Flute (1979), and *III* for 2 Cellos (1972); *Loomings* for Double String Quartet and Bass (1979); *4 Jurassic Scenes* for Trombone, Bass Trombone, and 3 Percussionists (1980); *Nightwork* for 8 Instruments (1981); *Brave New Zoos* for String Quartet (1982); *Reactions* for Piccolo (1982); *Green County Purple* for Bassoon (1983); *Cadenzas* for Alto Trombone, String Quartet, Piano, and Percussion (1983); *Deluge* for Brass Quintet (1983); *3 Phantasms* for Violin and Piano (1987); *Intro and Weird Boogaloo* for 4 Horns (1994). **VOCAL:** *The Road* for Chorus and Orch. (Richmond, Calif., June 11, 1969); *Requiem* for Man's Voice and Orch. (1970); *Dynamisms* for Soprano and Orch. (Hayward, Calif., May 2, 1975); *Arms and the Boy* for Soprano, Narrator, Flute, Bass Clarinet, Trumpet, 2 Violins, Viola, Piano, and 5 Percussionists (1979); *To Eros* for Soprano, Violin, Viola, Piano, and Percussion (1980); *After Dinner with Al Capone* for Soprano and Trumpet (1981); *Remembrance* for Soprano and 6 Instruments (1982); *Dulce et Decorum est* for Soprano and Chamber Orch. (1987; Bloomington, Ind., Dec. 1, 1988); *Friends* for Soprano and 5 Instruments (1991).

Ung, Chinary, Cambodian-born American composer; b. Prey Lovea, Nov. 24, 1942. He left his homeland in 1964 and settled in the U.S. He studied clarinet at the Manhattan School of Music in N.Y.; then composition with Chou Wen-Chung at Columbia Univ. in N.Y. (D.M.A., 1974). He then devoted himself to composing and teaching; from 1987 to 1995 he was Regents Prof. at Arizona State Univ. in Tempe, and in 1995 he assumed the position of prof. of music at the Univ. of Calif. at San Diego. He received awards from the American Academy of Arts and Letters, NEA grants, and a Guggenheim fellowship; also a Kennedy Center Friedheim Award (1992) and a Koussevitsky Foundation commission (1993). In 1990 he was awarded the Cultural Preservation Award for commitment to traditional music from the United Cambodian Community Circle of Friends in Long Beach, California, and in 1989 he became the first and youngest American composer to receive the prestigious Grawemeyer Award for his *Inner Voices* for Chamber Orch. (1986). Ung's compositions reveal a strong sense of commitment to tradition, as well as to ingenuity, technique, and imagination.

WORKS: ORCH.: *Anicca* for Chamber Orch. (1970); *Inner Voices* for Chamber Orch. (1986); *Grand Spiral ("Desert Flowers Bloom")* (1990; Sendai, Japan, June 1, 1992; also for Band); *Triple Concerto: A Sonorous Path* for Solo Cello, Percussion, Piano, and Orch. (1993); *Water Rings* for Chamber Orch. (1993); *Antiphonal Spirals* (1995). **BAND:** *Grand Spiral ("Desert Flowers Bloom")* (1990; also for Orch.). **CHAMBER:** *Khse Buon* for Cello (1979); *Child Song I* for Flute, Violin, Cello, and Piano, and *II* for Alto Flute, Viola, Cello, and Piano (both 1985); *Spiral I* for Cello, Piano, and Percussion (1986), *II* for High Voice, Tuba, and Piano (1987), *III* for String Quartet (1988), *VI* for Clarinet, Violin, Cello, and Piano (1988), and *VII* for Alto Flute, English Horn, Bass Clarinet, Horn, and Bassoon (1989); *". . . Still Life after Death"* for High Voice, Flute, Clarinet, Violin, Cello, Piano, and Percussion (1995). **VOCAL:** *Tall Wind* for Soprano, Flute, Oboe, Guitar, and Cello, after e.e. cummings (1969; requiring 5 scores for performance); *Mohori* for Mezzo-soprano, Flute, Oboe, 2 Percussion, Piano, Guitar, Harp, Cello, and Strings (1974).

Unger, Gerhard, German tenor; b. Bad Salzungen, Nov. 26, 1916. He received training in Eisenach and at the Berlin Hochschule für Musik. After beginning his career as a concert artist, he joined the Weimar Opera in 1947. From 1949 to 1961 he was a member of the (East) Berlin State Opera. He also appered as David at the Bayreuth Festivals (1951–52). From 1961 to 1963 he sang in Stuttgart, and in 1962 appeared as Pedrillo at the Salzburg Festival. He then was a member of the Hamburg State Opera (1963–66) and the Vienna State Opera (1966–70). In later years, he became particularly esteemed for his character roles. His last major appearance was as Mime in Stuttgart in 1987. As a concert artist, his repertoire ranged from the Baroque era to contemporary scores.

Unger, Heinz, German-Canadian conductor; b. Berlin, Dec. 14, 1895; d. Toronto, Feb. 25, 1965. He studied in Berlin and Munich; was active as a choral conductor in Berlin until the advent of the Nazi regime in 1933; then was conductor of the Leningrad Radio Orch. (1934–36). After a sojourn in England, he settled in Toronto in 1948; that same year, he founded the York Concert Soc., which he conducted in many works by Mahler. He publ. an account of his conducting experiences in Russia under the title *Hammer, Sickle and Baton* (London, 1939).

Unger, (Gustav) Hermann, German composer and writer on music; b. Kamenz, Oct. 26, 1886; d. Cologne, Dec. 31, 1958. He studied classical philology in Freiburg im Breisgau, Leipzig, and Munich (graduated, 1910, with a work on Greek poetry); also took a course in musicology in Munich with Edgar Istel and Joseph Haas; subsequently went to Meiningen, where he took lessons with Max Reger (1910–13). He settled in Cologne, where he taught at the Cons. (1919–25) and Univ. (1922–45); also was prof. at the Staatliche Hochschule für Musik (1925–47) and director of the Rheinische Musikschule (from 1934). Among his compositions were 2 operas: *Der Zauberhandschuh* (1927) and *Richmodis von Aducht* (1928); *Die Geschichten vom Weihnachtsbaum*, Christmas fairy tale (1943); 2 syms.; several symphonic poems; much chamber music; choral works; song cycles; piano suites.

WRITINGS: *Max Reger* (Munich, 1921; 2nd ed., 1924); *Musikalisches Laienbrevier* (Munich, 1921); *Das Volk und seine Musik* (Hamburg, 1922); *Musikgeschichte in Selbstzeugnissen* (Munich, 1928); *Musikanten gestern und heute* (Siegen, 1935); *Anton Bruckner und seine 7. Sinfonie* (Bonn, 1944); *Harmonielehre* (Frankfurt am Main, 1946); *Die musikalische Widmung* (Munich, 1958).

Unger, (Ernst) Max, German musicologist, conductor, and painter; b. Taura, Saxony, May 28, 1883; d. Zürich, Dec. 1, 1959. He studied at the Leipzig Cons., and also attended Riemann's lectures at the Univ. of Leipzig (Ph.D., 1911, with the diss. *Muzio Clementis Leben*; publ. in Langensalza, 1914). He was conductor of the Vereinigte Leipziger Schauspielhauser in 1906; then was conductor of the Leipzig Madrigal Soc. (1912–14) and ed. of the *Neue Zeitschrift für Musik* (1919–20); after living in Zürich (1932–40), he went to Italy; returned to Germany after World War II. He devoted his research mainly to Beethoven; publ. about 150 papers dealing with various aspects of Beethoven's life and works; among his books are *Mendelssohn-Bartholdys Beziehungen zu England* (Langensalza, 1909); *Auf Spuren von Beethovens unsterblicher Geliebten* (Langensalza, 1911); *Beethoven über eine Gesamtausgabe seiner Werke* (Bonn, 1920); *Ludwig van Beethoven und seine Verleger S.A. Steiner und Tobias Haslinger in Wien, Ad. Mart. Schlesinger in Berlin* (Berlin and Vienna, 1921); *Beethovens Handschrift* (Bonn, 1926); *Ein Faustopernplan Beethovens und Goethes* (Regensburg, 1952); he also ed. the catalogue of the Bodmer Beethoven collection in Zürich, under the title *Eine schweizer Beethovensammlung: Katalog* (Zürich, 1939).

Uninsky, Alexander, Russian-American pianist and teacher; b. Kiev, Feb. 2, 1910; d. Dallas, Dec. 19, 1972. He was trained at the Kiev Cons. and the Paris Cons. (premier prix). In 1927 he made his debut. After winning 1st prize in the Chopin Competition in Warsaw in 1932, he made tours of Europe until the outbreak of World War II in 1939 prompted him to go to South America. In 1943 he settled in the U.S. He later taught at the Royal Cons. of Music of Toronto and at Southern Methodist Univ. in Dallas. Uninsky excelled as an interpreter of Chopin.

Uppman, Theodor, American baritone and teacher; b. San Jose, Calif., Jan. 12, 1920. He received training at the Curtis Inst. of Music in Philadelphia (1939–41) before attending opera workshops at Stanford Univ. (1941–42) and the Univ. of Southern Calif. in Los Angeles (1948–50). In 1941 he made his professional debut with the Northern Calif. Sym. Orch. He first gained notice when he sang Debussy's Pelléas in a concert version with the San Francisco Sym. Orch. in 1947. In 1948 he chose that same role for his debut with the N.Y. City Opera. On Dec. 1, 1951, he created the title role in Britten's *Billy Budd* at London's Covent Garden. He made his Metropolitan Opera debut in N.Y. as Pelléas on Nov. 27, 1953, and then was on its roster from 1955 to 1978, appearing in such roles as Papageno, Marcello, Eisenstein, Guglielmo, Paquillo, Sharpless et al. He also was a guest artist with other U.S. opera companies and toured as a concert artist. In 1962 he created Floyd's Jonathan Wade at the N.Y. City Opera and in 1983 Bernstein's Bill in *A Quiet Place* at the Houston Grand Opera. He taught at the Manhattan School of Music, the Mannes College of Music in N.Y., and the Britten-Pears School for Advanced Musical Studies in Aldeburgh.

Upshaw, Dawn, American soprano; b. Nashville, Tenn., July 17, 1960. She studied at Illinois Wesleyan Univ. (B.A., 1982) and then pursued vocal training with Ellen Faull at the Manhattan School of Music in N.Y. (M.A., 1984); she also attended courses given by Jan DeGaetani at the Aspen (Colo.) Music School. In 1984 she won the Young Concert Artists auditions and entered the Metropolitan Opera's young artists development program. She was co-winner of the Naumburg Competition in N.Y. (1985). After appearing in minor roles at the Metropolitan Opera in N.Y., she displayed her vocal gifts in such major roles as Donizetti's Adina and Mozart's Despina in 1988. In 1990 she sang Pamina in a concert performance of *Die Zauberflöte* at the London Promenade Concerts. In 1992 she appeared as the Angel in Messiaen's *St. François d'Assise* at the Salzburg Festival. She also pursued a notably successful career as a soloist with major orchs. and as a recitalist. Her remarkable concert repertoire ranges from early music to the most intimidating of avant-garde scores.

Upton, William Treat, American pianist, organist, teacher, and musicologist; b. Tallmadge, Ohio, Dec. 17, 1870; d. Adelphi, Md., Jan. 19, 1961. He was educated at the Oberlin (Ohio) Cons. of Music (B.A., 1896; Mus.B., 1904; M.A., 1924); also studied piano with Leschetizky in Vienna (1896–98) and with Josef Lhévinne in Berlin (1913–14). He taught piano at the Oberlin Cons. of Music (1894–1936); also was organist at the Calvary Presbyterian Church in Oberlin (until 1918).

WRITINGS: *Art-Song in America* (Boston, 1930; supplement, 1938); *Anthony Philip Heinrich: A 19th-Century Composer in America* (N.Y., 1939); ed. O. Sonneck's *Bibliography of Early Secular American Music* (2nd ed., rev., 1945); *The Musical Works of William Henry Fry in the Collection of the Library Company of Philadelphia* (Philadelphia, 1946); *William Henry Fry, American Journalist and Composer-Critic* (N.Y., 1954).

Urbanner, Erich, Austrian composer, teacher, and conductor; b. Innsbruck, March 26, 1936. He was a student of Schiske and Jelinek (composition), Grete Hinterhofer (piano), and Swarowsky (conducting) at the Vienna Academy of Music (1955–61). He also attended the composition courses of Fortner, Stockhausen, and Maderna in Darmstadt. In 1961 he became an instructor at the Vienna Academy of Music. From 1968 he was also active as a conductor. In 1969 he was named a prof. of composition and harmony at the Vienna Hochschule für Musik. Among his honors were Vienna's Förderungspreis (1962), the City of Innsbruck prize (1980), the Würdigungspreis of the Austrian Ministry of Education and Art (1982), the City of Vienna prize (1984), and the Tiroler Landespreis for the arts (1993). Urbanner's music is strikingly modern without adhering to any particular school.

WORKS: DRAMATIC: *Der Gluckerich, oder Tugend und*

Tadel der Nützlichkeit, musical burlesque (1963; Vienna, May 26, 1965); *Ninive, oder Das leben geht weiter,* opera (1987; Innsbruck, Sept. 24, 1988); *Johannes Stein, oder Der Rock des Kaisers,* monodrama (1990–91; Vienna, March 31, 1992); *Die Tochter des Kerensteiners,* musical scenes (1994). **ORCH.:** *Prolog* (1957; Innsbruck, May 11, 1958); *Intrada* for Chamber Orch. (1957; Vienna, June 1958); 2 piano concertos: No. 1 (1958; Innsbruck, June 1959) and No. 2 (1976; Innsbruck, May 11, 1977); Flute Concerto (1959; Innsbruck, June 4, 1964); Concertino for Organ and Strings (Innsbruck, May 1961); *Symphony in 1 Movement* (1963; Vienna, April 5, 1964); *Dialoge* for Piano and Orch. (1965; Vienna, April 2, 1967); Concerto for Oboe and Chamber Orch. (1966; Innsbruck, June 9, 1968); *Rondeau* (1967; Vienna, Jan. 15, 1971); *Thema, 19 Variationen und ein Nachspiel* (1968); *Kontraste II* (1970; Innsbruck, April 27, 1971); Violin Concerto (1971; Innsbruck, Oct. 19, 1972); *Concerto "Wolfgang Amadeus"* for 3 Trombones, Celesta, and 2 Orchs. (1972; Salzburg, Jan. 20, 1973); Double Bass Concerto (1973; Innsbruck, Nov. 26, 1974); *Retrospektiven* (1974–75; rev. version, Graz, Oct. 13, 1979); Concerto for Alto Saxophone and 12 Players (1978–79; Graz, Nov. 4, 1982); *Sinfonietta 79* for Chamber Orch. (1979; Innsbruck, April 30, 1980); *Sonata brevis* for Chamber Orch. (1980; Vienna, March 7, 1981); Cello Concerto (1981; Innsbruck, May 2, 1982); *Sinfonia Concertante* for Chamber Orch. (1982; Vienna, March 12, 1983); Double Concerto for Flute, Clarinet, and Orch. (Salzburg, Aug. 8, 1984). **CHAMBER:** 4 string quartets: No. 1 (1956; Vienna, March 1958), No. 2 (1957), No. 3 (1972; Vienna, May 8, 1973), and No. 4 (1991–92; Vevey, Jan. 31, 1993); *5 Pieces* for Violin and Piano (1961); *Étude* for Wind Quintet (1965; Vienna, Feb. 16, 1966); *Acht Aphorismen* for Flute, Clarinet, and Bassoon (Vienna, May 26, 1966); *4 Pieces* for Viola (1967); *5 Pieces* for Flute (1967); *Improvisation III* for Chamber Ensemble (1969; Vienna, Jan. 23, 1970) and *IV* for Wind Quintet (1969; Vienna, March 30, 1979); *Lyrica* for Chamber Ensemble (1971; Vienna, Jan. 13, 1974); *Solo* for Violin (Solbad Hall, April 2, 1971); *Burleske* for Flute and Organ (1973; Düsseldorf, Sept. 18, 1974); *Pastorale* for Chamber Ensemble (1975; Innsbruck, March 24, 1976); *Takes* for Piano Trio (1977; Vienna, May 2, 1978); *Quartetto Concertato* for String Quartet and 6 String Duos (Innsbruck, April 5, 1978); *Nachtstück* for Recorder Ensemble (1978; Ossiach, Aug. 9, 1980); *Arioso-Furioso* for Cello and Piano (Vienna, Oct. 21, 1980); *Sechs Phan-Tasten und zwei Schlagzeuger* for 7 Instrumentalists (1980; Innsbruck, Feb. 24, 1981); *Nonett 1981* (Utrecht, Sept. 7, 1981); *Ballade* for Guitar (1982; Alpbach, Aug. 28, 1983); *Emotionen* for Saxophone Quartet (1984; Washington, D.C., Feb. 10, 1985); *Trio Mobile* for Flute, Viola, and Cello (Brussels, Dec. 8, 1987); *. . . In Bewegung . . .*, trio for Violin, Cello, and Piano (1990; Vienna, April 9, 1991); Duo for Accordion and Double Bass (1992; Linz, March 16, 1993); *quasi una fantasia,* 6 concertante pieces for 15 Instruments (1993). **KEYBOARD: PIANO:** 2 sonatinas (1956, 1957); *Variation* (1958); *5 Pieces* (1959); *Adagio* (1966); *Variation* (1981); *13 Charakterstücke* (1988–89; Innsbruck, June 20, 1989). **ORGAN:** *Improvisation I* (1961; Innsbruck, Aug. 30, 1974); *Zyklus* (1992; Vienna, March 5, 1993). **VOCAL:** *Missa benedicite gentes* for Chorus and Organ (Innsbruck, May 15, 1958); 5 Songs for Mezzo-soprano and Small Ensemble (1961); *Das Ahnenbild* for Soprano and Piano (1961); *Requiem* for Soli, Chorus, and Orch. (1982–83; Innsbruck, Feb. 20, 1985); *Acht Ächte Tyroller Lieder* for Soprano, Tenor, and Chamber Ensemble (1985; Innsbruck, April 5, 1986).

Uribe-Holguín, Guillermo, eminent Colombian composer and pedagogue; b. Bogotá, March 17, 1880; d. there, June 26, 1971. He studied violin with Figueroa at the Bogotá Academy of Music (1890) and with Narciso Garay; taught at the Academy (1905–07). In 1907 he went to Paris, where he studied with d'Indy at the Schola Cantorum; then took violin lessons with César Thomson and Emile Chaumont in Brussels. He returned to Colombia in 1910 and became director of the newly reorganized National Cons. in Bogotá; resigned in 1935 and devoted his time to the family coffee plantation. He continued to compose and was active as a conductor; was again director of the Cons. from 1942 to 1947. In 1910 he married the pianist Lucia Gutiérrez. His music bears the imprint of the modern French style, but his thematic material is related to native musical resources; particularly remarkable are his *Trozos en el sentimiento popular* for Piano, of which he wrote about 350; they are stylizations of Colombian melorhythms in a brilliant pianistic setting. He publ. an autobiography, *Vida de un músico colombiano* (Bogotá, 1941).

WORKS: OPERA: *Furatena.* **ORCH.** (all 1st perf. in Bogotá): 11 syms. (1910–50); *Sinfonia del terruño* (Oct. 20, 1924); *3 danzas* (May 27, 1927); *Marcha festiva* (Aug. 20, 1928); *Serenata* (Oct. 29, 1928); *Carnavalesca* (July 8, 1929); *Cantares* (Sept. 2, 1929); *Villanesca* (Sept. 1, 1930); *Bajo su ventana* (Oct. 20, 1930); *Suite típica* (Nov. 21, 1932); *Concierto a la manera antigua* for Piano and Orch. (Oct. 15, 1939); *Bochica* (April 12, 1940); *Conquistadores* (April 3, 1959); 2 violin concertos; Viola Concerto. **CHAMBER:** 10 string quartets; 2 piano trios; 7 violin sonatas; Cello Sonata; Viola Sonata; Piano Quartet; 2 piano quintets. **VOCAL:** Choruses; song cycles.

Urner, Catherine Murphy, American singer, teacher, and composer; b. Mitchell, Ind., March 23, 1891; d. San Diego, April 30, 1942. She studied at the Univ. of Calif. at Berkeley and with Koechlin in Paris (1920–21). After serving as director of vocal music at Mills College in Oakland, California (1921–24), she devoted much time to performing, teaching and composing. She made tours of the U.S., France, and Italy. Urner studied Amerian Indian tribal melodies, which she utilized in a number of compositions. She also collaborated with Koechlin on several scores.

WORKS: ORCH.: *Esquisses normandes,* suite (1929; rev. and orchestrated by Koechlin, 1945); *3 Movements* for Chamber Orch. (1938); Flute Concerto (1940). **CHAMBER:** *Petite Suite* for Flute, Violin, Viola, and Cello (1930); *Jubilee Suite* for Flute and Piano (1931); Violin Sonata (1942); piano pieces; organ works. **VOCAL:** Over 100 songs.

Urreta, Alicia, Mexican pianist, teacher, and composer; b. Veracruz, Oct. 12, 1935; d. Mexico City, Dec. 20, 1986. She studied piano with Joaquin Amparán and harmony with Rodolfo Halffter in Mexico City (1948–54); then engaged in teaching. Among her works were a radio opera, *Romance de Doña Balada* (Mexico City, 1972); *De natura mortis* for Voice, Instruments, and Tape (1972); several scores of *musique concrète.*

Urrutia-Blondel, Jorge, Chilean composer, teacher, and writer on music; b. La Serena, Sept. 17, 1903; d. Santiago, July 5, 1981. He studied with Pedro Humberto Allende and Domingo Santa Cruz; in 1928, traveled to Europe, where he took lessons with Koechlin, Dukas, and Boulanger in Paris, and with Hindemith and Mersmann in Berlin. Returning to Chile, he was appointed prof. of harmony at the Cons. in Santiago (1931). His early works followed along nationalist lines but he later turned to post-impressionism and neo-classicism. He wrote many articles on contemporary music and folk music in his homeland; with S. Claro, he publ. the study *Historia de la música en Chile* (Santiago, 1973).

WORKS: BALLET: *La guitarra del diablo* (Santiago, Nov. 27, 1942; 2 sym. suites., 1942). **ORCH.:** *Música para un Cuento de Antaño* (1948); Piano Concerto (1950). **CHAMBER:** Piano Trio (1933); Concertino for Harp and Guitar (1943); String Quartet (1944); Violin Sonata (1954); piano pieces. **VOCAL:** Choruses; song cycles on Chilean motifs.

Ursprung, Otto, learned German musicologist; b. Günzlhofen, Jan. 16, 1879; d. Schöndorf-am-Ammersee, Sept. 14, 1960. He studied philosophy and theology at the Univ. of Munich (1899–1904) and was ordained as a Catholic priest; returned to the Univ. of Munich (Ph.D., 1911, with the diss. *Jacobus de Kerle: sein Leben und seine Werke (1531/32–91)*; publ. in Munich, 1913); held the title of honorary prof. of music history there (1932–49). He was an authority on Catholic church music and the musical history of Munich.

WRITINGS: *Restauration und Palestrina-Renaissance in der katholischen Kirchenmusik der letzten zwei Jahrhunderte* (Augsburg, 1924); *Münchens musikalische Vergangenheit* (Munich, 1927); *Die katholische Kirchenmusik* (Potsdam, 1931).

Ursuleac, Viorica, noted Romanian soprano; b. Cernăuţi, March 26, 1894; d. Ehrwald, Tirol, Oct. 22, 1985. She studied in Vienna with Franz Steiner and Philip Forstén and in Berlin with Lilli Lehmann. She made her operatic debut as Charlotte in Massenet's *Werther* in Agram in 1922; then sang in Cernăuţi (1923–24) and with the Vienna Volksoper (1924–26). In 1926 she joined the Frankfurt am Main Opera, and then pursued a distinguished career as a member of the Vienna State Opera (1930–34), the Berlin State Opera (1935–37), and the Bavarian State Opera in Munich (1937–44). Richard Strauss held her in the highest esteem; in his operas she created the roles of Arabella (1933), Maria in *Der Friedenstag* (1938), the Countess in *Capriccio* (1942), and Danae in *Die Liebe der Danae* (public dress rehearsal, 1944). She was also highly successful in the operas of Mozart, Wagner, and Verdi. She was married to **Clemens Krauss**, with whom she often appeared in concert. After his death in 1954, she settled in Ehrwald. With R. Schlötterer, she wrote *Singen für Richard Strauss: Erinnerungen und Dokumente* (Vienna, 1986).

Usmanbaş, Ilhan, Turkish composer and teacher; b. Constantinople, Sept. 28, 1921. He was a student of Cemal Reşit Rey at the Constantinople Cons. (1941–42), and then studied with Hasan Ferit Alnar (piano) and Ulvi Cemal Erkin (composition) at the Ankara State Cons. (1942–48); he subsequently received additional training from Dallapiccola at the Berkshire Music Center in Tanglewood (summer, 1952). From 1948 he taught at the Ankara State Cons. His early works followed the ethnic patterns of Turkish folk songs, but he later adopted serial techniques, with occasional aleatory episodes.

WORKS: ORCH.: Violin Concerto (1946); 2 syms.: No. 1 (1948) and No. 2 for Strings (Ankara, April 20, 1950); *On 3 Paintings of Salvador Dali* for Strings (1953); *Gölgeler* (Shadows; 1964); *Bursting Sinfonietta* (1968); *Music for a Ballet* (1969); *Symphonic Movement* (1972); *Little Night Music* (1972). **CHAMBER:** 2 string quartets (1947, 1970); Clarinet Quintet (1949); Oboe Sonata (1949); Trumpet Sonata (1949); *A Jump into Space* for Violin and 4 Instruments (1966); piano pieces. **VOCAL:** *Music* for Strings, Percussion, Piano, and Narrator (1950); *Mortuary* for Narrator, Chorus, and Orch. (1952–53); *Japanese Music* for Women's Chorus and Orch. (1956); *Music with a Poem* for Mezzo-soprano, Flute, Clarinet, Bassoon, and 2 Violins (1958); *Un coup de des* for Chorus and Orch. (1959).

Uspensky, Victor Alexandrovich, Russian composer and ethnomusicologist; b. Kaluga, Aug. 31, 1879; d. Tashkent, Oct. 9, 1949. He was brought up in Central Asia, where his father held a government post; attended the composition classes of Liadov at the St. Petersburg Cons.; graduated in 1913. In 1918 he went to Tashkent. From 1932 to 1948 he was active with the Musical Folklore Division of Uzbekistan, and did valuable research work in native folklore. He also worked on the restoration of Uzbek musical instruments; from these authentic materials he fashioned an Uzbek opera, *Farhad and Shirin*, premiered in Tashkent on Feb. 26, 1936. Other works include *Turkmenian Capriccio* for Orch. (1945); *Uzbek Rhapsody* for Orch. (1946); several choral works; piano pieces; songs. With V. Belaiev, he publ. a treatise on Turkmenian music (Moscow, 1928).

BIBL.: J. Pekker, *V.A. U.* (Moscow, 1953; 2nd ed., 1958).

Ussachevsky, Vladimir (Alexis), innovative Russian-born American composer; b. Hailar, Manchuria, Nov. 3, 1911; d. N.Y., Jan. 2, 1990. His parents settled in Manchuria shortly after the Russo-Japanese War of 1905, at the time when Russian culture was still a powerful social factor there. His father was an officer of the Russian army, and his mother was a professional pianist. In 1930 he went to California, where he took private piano lessons with Clarence Mader; from 1931 to 1933 he attended Pasadena Junior College; in 1933 he received a scholarship to study at Pomona College (B.A., 1935). He then enrolled in the Eastman School of Music in Rochester in N.Y. in the classes of Hanson, Rogers, and Royce in composition (M.M., 1936; Ph.D., 1939); he also had some instruction with Burrill Phillips. In 1942, as a naturalized American citizen, Ussachevsky was drafted into the U.S. Army; thanks to his fluency in Russian, his knowledge of English and French, and a certain ability to communicate in rudimentary Chinese, he was engaged in the Intelligence Division; subsequently he served as a research analyst at the War Dept. in Washington, D.C. He then pursued postdoctoral work with Luening at Columbia Univ., joining its faculty in 1947; was prof. of music (1964–80). At various times he taught at other institutions, including several years as composer-in-residence at the Univ. of Utah (from 1970) and was a faculty member there (1980–85). His early works were influenced by Russian church music, in the tradition of Tchaikovsky and Rachmaninoff. A distinct change in his career as a composer came in 1951, when he became interested in the resources of electronic music; to this period belong his works *Transposition, Reverberation, Experiment, Composition* and *Underwater Valse*, which make use of electronic sound. On Oct. 28, 1952, Stokowski conducted in N.Y. the first performance of Ussachevsky's *Sonic Contours*, in which a piano part was metamorphosed with the aid of various sonorific devices, superimposed on each other. About that time, he began a fruitful partnership with Luening; with him he composed *Incantation for Tape Recorder*, which was broadcast in 1953. Luening and Ussachevsky then conceived the idea of combining electronic tape sounds with conventional instruments played by human musicians; the result was *Rhapsodic Variations*, first performed in N.Y. on March 20, 1954. The work anticipated by a few months the composition of the important score *Déserts* by Varèse, which effectively combined electronic sound with other instruments. The next work by Ussachevsky and Luening was *A Poem in Cycles and Bells* for Tape Recorder and Orch., first performed by the Los Angeles Phil. on Nov. 22, 1954. On March 31, 1960, Leonard Bernstein conducted the N.Y. Phil. in the commissioned work by Ussachevsky and Luening entitled *Concerted Piece for Tape Recorder and Orchestra*. On Jan. 12, 1956, Ussachevsky and Luening provided taped background for Shakespeare's *King Lear*, produced by Orson Welles, at the N.Y. City Center, and for Margaret Webster's production of *Back to Methuselah* for the N.Y. Theater Guild in 1958. They also provided the electronic score for the documentary *The Incredible Voyage*, broadcast over the CBS-TV network on Oct. 13, 1965. Among works that Ussachevsky wrote for electronic sound without partnership were *A Piece for Tape Recorder* (1956), *Studies in Sound, Plus* (1959), and *The Creation* (1960). In 1968 Ussachevsky began experimenting with the synthesizer, with the aid of a computer. One of the works resulting from these experiments was *Conflict* (1971), intended to represent the mystical struggle between 2 ancient deities. In 1959 Ussachevsky was one of the founders of the Columbia-Princeton Electronic Music Center; was active as a lecturer at various exhibitions of electronic sounds; traveled also to Russia and to China to present his music. He held 2 Guggenheim fellowships (1957, 1960). In 1973 Ussachevsky was elected to membership in the National Inst. of Arts and Letters.

WORKS: TAPE: *Transposition, Reverberation, Experiment, Composition* (1951–52); *Sonic Contours* (N.Y., Oct. 28, 1952); *Underwater Valse* (1952); *Piece for Tape Recorder* (1956); *Metamorphoses* (1957); *Improvisation on 4711* (1958); *Linear Contrasts* (1958); *Studies in Sound, Plus* (1959); *Wireless Fantasy: De Forrest Murmurs* (1960); *Of Wood and Brass* (1964–65); *Suite from Music for Films* (1967); *Piece for Computer* (1968); *2 Sketches for Computer Piece No. 2* (1971); *Conflict*, electronic scene from *Creation* (1973–75). **WITH TAPE:** *3 Scenes from Creation: Prologue "Enumu Elish"* for 2 Choruses and Tape, *Interlude* for Soprano, Mezzo-soprano, and Tape (1960; rev. 1973), and *Epilogue: "Spell of Creation"* for Soprano and Chorus (1971); *Creation Prologue* for 4 Choruses and Tape (1960–61); *Scenes from No Exit* for Speaker and Tape (1963); *Colloquy* for Solo Instruments, Orch. and Tape (Salt Lake City, Feb. 20, 1976); *Two*

Experiments for Electronic Valve Instrument and Tape (1979; in collaboration with N. Steiner); *Celebration 1980* for Electronic Valve Instrument, String Orch., and Tape (N.Y., April 1980); *Pentagram* for Oboe and Tape (BBC, London, Nov. 1980); *Celebration 1981* for Electronic Valve Instrument, 6 Winds, Strings, and Tape (N.Y., Oct. 30, 1981; rev. as *Divertimento* for Electronic Valve Instrument, 3 Winds, 3 Brass, Strings, Percussion, and Tape, 1980–81); *Dialogues and Contrasts* for Brass Quintet and Tape (N.Y., Feb. 12, 1984). **INCIDENTAL MUSIC FOR TAPE:** *To Catch a Thief* (sound effects for the film; 1954); *Mathematics* (television score; 1957); *The Boy who Saw Through* (film; 1959); *No Exit* (film; 1962); *Line of Apogee* (film; 1967); *Mourning Becomes Electra* (sound effects for the opera by M. Levy; 1967); *The Cannibals* (play; 1969); *2 Images for the Computer Piece* (film; 1969); *Duck, Duck* (film; 1970); *We* (radio play; 1970). **FILM SCORE:** *Circle of Fire* (1940). **ORCH.:** *Theme and Variations* (1936); *Piece* for Flute and Chamber Orch. (1947); *Miniatures for a Curious Child* (1950); *Intermezzo* for Piano and Orch. (1952); *Dances and Fanfares for a Festive Occasion* (1980). **CHAMBER:** *2 Dances* for Flute and Piano (1948); *4 Studies* for Clarinet and Electronic Valve Instrument (1979); *Suite* for Trombone Choir (1980); *Triskelion* for Oboe and Piano (1982); *Nouvelette pour Bourges* for Electronic Valve Instrument and Piano (1983); piano pieces. **VOCAL:** *Jubilee Cantata* for Baritone, Reader, Chorus, and Orch. (1937–38); *Psalm XXIV* for Chorus and Organ, or for Organ and 5 Brass, or for 7 Brass (1948); *2 Autumn Songs on Rilke's Text* for Soprano and Piano (1952); *Missa Brevis* for Soprano, Chorus, and Brass (1972). **WITH OTTO LUENING:** *Incantation* for Tape (1953); *Rhapsodic Variations* for Orch. and Tape (1953–54; N.Y., March 20, 1954); *A Poem in Cycles and Bells* for Orch. and Tape (Los Angeles, Nov. 22, 1954); *Of Identity*, ballet for Tape (1954); *Carlsbad Caverns*, television score for Tape (1955); *King Lear*, incidental music (3 versions, 1956); *Back to Methuselah*, incidental music for Tape (1958); *Concerted Piece* for Orch. and Tape (N.Y., March 31, 1960); *Incredible Voyage*, television score for Tape (1968; also with Shields and Smiley).

Ustvolskaya, Galina (Ivanovna), significant Russian composer and pedagogue; b. Petrograd, June 17, 1919. She studied at the arts college affiliated with the Leningrad Cons. (1937–39) and composition with Shostakovich and Steinberg at the Leningrad Cons. (1940–41; 1945–47), where she pursued postgraduate training with G. Rimsky-Korsakov (1947–50). From 1948 to 1977 she taught composition there. In 1992 she was awarded the Artist's Prize of Heidelberg. During the Stalin era, her music was rarely performed; although never officially condemned by the Soviet state, her compositions were accused of being difficult to understand, "narrow-minded," and "obstinate." Shostakovich defended her against such accusations and held her in such esteem that he sent MSS of his own scores to her for comment. He quoted from the finale of her Clarinet Trio (1949) in his String Quartet No. 5 and in his *Suite on Verses of Michelangelo.* Ustvolskaya's early music was marked by a Romantic Russian manner, but she later developed greater melodic diversity and harmonic complexity, with occasional usages of serial techniques. Some of her works are of vast dimensions. The spiritual qualities of many of her scores are a welcome complement to their startling dissonances and rhythmic drive.

WORKS (all 1st perf. in Leningrad unless otherwise given): **ORCH.:** Concerto for Piano, Strings, and Timpani (1946); 5 syms.: No. 1 for 2 Boy's Voices and Orch. (1955), No. 2, *True and Eternal Bliss*, for Voice and Orch. (1979; Oct. 8, 1980), No. 3, *Jesus, Messiah, Save Us!* (1983; Amsterdam, Jan. 18, 1995), and Nos. 4 and 5 (See **CHAMBER**). **CHAMBER:** String Quartet (1945); Trio for Clarinet, Violin, and Piano (1949; Jan. 11, 1968); Octet for 2 Oboes, 4 Violins, Timpani, and Piano (1949–50; Nov. 17, 1970); Violin Sonata (1953; March 5, 1961); *Grand Duet* for Cello and Piano (1959; Dec. 14, 1977); Duet for Violin and Piano (1964; May 23, 1968); *Composition No. 1: Dona nobis pacem* for Piccolo, Tuba, and Piano (1970–71; Feb. 19, 1975), *No. 2: Dies irae* for 8 Double Basses, Percussion, and Piano (1972–73; Feb. 14, 1977), and *No. 3: Benedictus, Qui Venit* for 4 Flutes, 4 Bassoons, and Piano (1974–75; Dec. 14, 1977); Sym. No. 4, *Prayer*, for Contralto, Trumpet, Tam-tam, and Piano (1985–87; Heidelberg, June 24, 1988); Sym. No. 5, *Amen*, for Male Speaker, Oboe, Trumpet, Tuba, Violin, and Percussion (1989–90). **PIANO:** 6 sonatas: No. 1 (1947; Feb. 20, 1974), No. 2 (1949; Dec. 14, 1977), No. 3 (1952; Feb. 16, 1972), No. 4 (1957; April 4, 1973), No. 5 (1986), and No. 6 (1988); *12 Preludes* (1953; March 20, 1968).

Vacek, Miloš, Czech composer; b. Horní Roveň, June 20, 1928. He studied organ at the Prague Cons. (1943–47); then took a course in composition with Řídký and Pícha at the Prague Academy of Arts and Music (1947–51). From 1954 he devoted himself totally to composition.

WORKS: DRAMATIC: OPERAS: *Jan Želivský* (1953–56; rev. 1974; Olomouc, April 15, 1984); *Bratr Žak* (Brother Jacques; 1976–78; Ostrava, June 12, 1982); *Romance pro křídlovku* (Romance for Bugle Horn; 1980–81; Czech Radio, Plzeň, Oct. 26, 1983; 1st stage perf., České Budějovice, Dec. 12, 1987); *Kocour Mikeš* (Mikeš the Tom Cat; 1981–82; Brno, March 28, 1986). **BALLETS:** *Komediantská pohádka* (The Comedian's Fairytale; 1957–58); *Vitr ve vlasech* (Wind in the Hair; 1960–61); *Posledni pampeliška* (The Last Dandelion; 1963–64); *Milá sedmi loupežníků* (The Mistress of Seven Robbers; 1966); *Meteor* (1966); *Štastná sedma* (Lucky Sevens; 1966). **MUSICALS:** *Noc je můj den* (The Night Is My Day), blues drama about the life of Bessie Smith (1962; Frankfurt am Main, March 15, 1964); *Císařovy nové šaty* (The Emperor's New Clothes; 1962); *Madame Sans Gêne* (1968); *Vitr z Alabamy* (Wind from Alabama; 1970). **ORCH.:** *Sinfonietta* (1951); *Jarní suita* (Spring Suite) for Flute, Clarinet, Horn or English Horn, and Strings (1963); *Serenáda* for Strings (1965); *Symfonie Májová* (May Sym.; 1974); *Olympijský oheň* (Olympic Flame), symphonic poem (1975); *Mé Kamenici nad Lipou* (To My Kamenici nad Lipou), suite (1979); *Svědomí světa* (World's Conscience), symphonic poem to commemorate the 40th anniversary of the razing of Lidice and Ležáky (1981). **CHAMBER:** Suite for Cello and Piano (1947); Violin Sonatina (1949); String Quartet (1949); *Divertimento* for Violin, Cello, Guitar, and Bass Clarinet (1965); *Šumavské metamorfózy* (Šumava Metamorphoses), quintet for Flute, Oboe, Violin, Viola, and Cello (1971); *Lovecká suita* (Hunting Suite) for 4 Horns (1973); *Bukolická suita* (Bucolic Suite) for 4 Trombones (1977); *Dialogue* for Oboe and Piano (1977); also works for Piano, including *Sonata drammatica* (1972) and *Zatoulané listy z milostného deníčku* (Sheets from a Love Diary Gone Astray; 1972; also for Chamber Orch.). **VOCAL:** *Poéma o padlých hrdinech* (Poem of Fallen Heroes) for Alto and Orch. (1974); cantatas; choruses; songs.

Vačkář, family of Czech composers:

(1) Václav Vačkář; b. Prague, Aug. 12, 1881; d. there, Feb. 4, 1954. He received training in military music in Przemyśl, Poland (1895–98), then was active as a conductor and orch. player in various locales before playing in the Czech Phil. (1913–19), the Vinohrad Opera Orch. (1919–20), and the Šak Phil. (1920–21); after composition studies with Říhovský and Křička (1920–22), he devoted himself to composing, writing on music, and administrative work. He was awarded the Smetana Prize of Prague in 1952. He wrote *Lidová nauka o harmonii* (Popular Treatise on Harmony; Prague, 1942) and with D. Vačkář, *Instrumentace symfonického orchestru a hudby dechové* (Instrumentation for the Symphony Orchestra and Wind Music; Prague, 1954). Of his more than 300 works, about half are in a popular or light vein, including numerous marches and waltzes. He also wrote several symphonic poems, a Clarinet Concertino, 4 string quartets, choral pieces, and songs.

(2) Dalibor Cyril Vačkář, son of the preceding; b. Korčula, Sept. 19, 1906; d. Prague, Oct. 21, 1984. He studied violin with Reissig and composition with Šín at the Prague Cons. (1923–29); also attended master classes of Hoffmann and Suk (1929–31). From 1934 to 1945 he played violin in the Prague Radio Orch.; after working as a film dramatist (1945–47), he devoted himself mainly to composition; also wrote music criticism, poetry, and plays. He used the pseudonyms Pip Faltys, Peter Filip, Tomáš Martin, and Karel Raymond for his light music. With his father, he wrote *Instrumentace symfonického orchestru a hudby dechové* (Instrumentation for the Symphony Orchestra and Wind Music; Prague, 1954).

WORKS: BALLETS: *Švanda dudák* (Svanda the Bagpiper; 1950–53; Prague Radio, April 7, 1954); *Sen noci svatojanské* (A

Midsummer Night's Dream), after Shakespeare (1955–57). **ORCH.:** *Overture* (1929); 2 violin concertos (1931, 1958); 5 syms.: No. 1, *Optimistická* (Optimistic; 1941), No. 2, *Země vyvolená* (The Chosen Land), for Contralto, Chorus, and Orch. (1947), No. 3, *Smoking Symphony* (1947–48; orchestration of his *Smoking Sonata* for Piano; the curious subtitle, symbolizing fire and smoke in the life of men from antiquity to the present day, is in Eng. only), No. 4, *O míru* (Of Peace; 1949–50), and No. 5, *Pro juventute* (1978–82); *Symphonic Scherzo* (1945); 2 sinfoniettas (1947; *Jubilee*, 1984); *Czech Concerto* for Piano and Orch. (1952); *Prelude and Metamorphoses* (1953); *Furiant-Fantasie* for Chamber Orch. (1960); *Concerto da camera* for Bassoon and Chamber String Orch. (1962); *Charakteristikon*, trombone concerto (1965); *Legenda o člověku* (Legend of Men), concerto for Harpsichord, Winds, and Percussion (1966); Clarinet Concerto (1966); *Prelude* for Chamber String Orch. (1966); *Concerto grosso* for Soprano Saxophone, Accordion, Guitar, and Orch. (1967); *In fide, spe et caritate*, concerto for Organ, Winds, and Percussion (1969); *Appellatio* for Women's Chorus and Orch. (1970; Prague, Oct. 20, 1977); *Příběh o pěti kapitolách* (5-Chapter Story) for Clarinet, Strings, and Percussion (1971); *Musica concertante* (1973). **CHAMBER:** *Trio giocoso* for Piano Trio (1929); 2 violin sonatas (1930; *Dedication*, 1961, with each movement dedicated to Vačkář's teachers: Reissig, Šín, Hoffmann, and Suk); String Quartet (1931–32); *Jaro 38*, piano trio (1938); *Monolog* for Violin (1940); Quartet for Piano, Oboe, Clarinet, and Bassoon (1948); *Quintetto giocoso* for Wind Instruments (1950; music from the ballet *Švanda dudák*); *Suite giocoso* for Piano Trio (1960); *Dialogue* for Violin (1961); *3 Studies* for Harpsichord (1961); Concerto for String Quartet (1962); Concerto for Trumpet, Piano, and Percussion (1963); *Pianoforte cantante*, 5 lyric reminiscences for Piano, Double Bass, and Percussion (1968); *Partita* for Trumpet (1968); *Milieu d'enfant* for 5 Percussion Groups (1970); *Intimní hudba* (Private Music) for Violin and Piano (1972); *Furiant-fantasie* for Piano Trio (1974); *Verses* for Flute and Guitar (1975); *Symposium* for Brass Quintet (1976); *Oboe concertante* for Oboe, Clarinet, Bass Clarinet, Horn, String Quartet, Percussion, and Piano (1977); *Monograms*, 4 poems for String Quartet (1979; transcribed from the piano work); *Portraits* for Wind Quintet (1980; transcribed from the piano work); *Juniores*, 4 movements for String Quartet (1981; transcribed from the piano work); *Extempore*, piano quartet (1983). **PIANO:** *Smoking Sonata* (1936); *Extempore*, 6 pieces (1937); *Piano Fantasy*, on a theme from Schubert's *The Arch* (1962); *Perspektivy* (1971); *3 Etudes* (1977); *Monograms* (1978); *Portraits* (1980); *Juniores* (1981).

(3) Tomas Vačkář, son of the preceding; b. Prague, July 31, 1945; d. (suicide) there, May 2, 1963. He was a gifted composer, but chose to end his life shortly after his graduation from the Prague Cons. at the age of 18. His works, all written between July 1960 and April 1963, include *Sonatina furore* for Piano; *Concerto recitativo* for Flute, String Orch., and Piano; *Tři dopisy divkam* (3 Letters to a Girl), after a poem by an anonymous Czech student, for Voice and Piano or Winds and Percussion; *Teen-agers*, piano sonata; *Metamorfózy na tema japonske ukolebavky* (Metamorphoses on the Theme of a Japanese Lullaby) for Orch.; *Scherzo melancolico* for Orch.; *Skicář Tomáše Vačkáře* (Tomáš Vačkář's Sketchbook), 10 pieces for Piano; a *Requiem* remained unfinished.

Vainberg, Moisei, Polish-born Russian composer; b. Warsaw, Dec. 8, 1919; d. Moscow, Feb. 1996. He studied piano with Turczynski at the Warsaw Cons., graduating in 1939; then studied composition with Zolotarev at the Minsk Cons.; in 1943 he settled in Moscow. In his music he followed the precepts of socialist realism in its ethnic aspects; according to the subject, he made use of Jewish, Polish, Moldavian, or Armenian folk melos, in tasteful harmonic arrangements devoid of abrasive dissonances.

WORKS: DRAMATIC: OPERAS: *The Sword of Uzbekistan* (1942); *The Woman Passenger* (1968); *Love of D'Artagnan*, after Alexandre Dumas (1972). **BALLETS:** *Battle for the Fatherland* (1942); *The Golden Key* (1955); *The White Chrysanthemum* (1958); *Requiem* (1967). **ORCH.:** 16 syms.: No. 1 (1942), No. 2 for Strings (1946), No. 3 (1949), No. 4 (1957), No. 5 (1962), No. 6 for Boy's Chorus and Orch. (1963), No. 7 for Strings and Harpsichord (1964), No. 8, *The Flowers of Poland*, for Tenor, Chorus, and Orch. (1964), No. 9, *Surviving Pages*, for Reader, Chorus, and Orch. (1967), No. 10 for Strings (1968), No. 11, *Triumphant Symphony*, for Chorus and Orch., dedicated to Lenin's centennial (1969), No. 12 (1976; Moscow, Oct. 13, 1979), No. 13 (1976), No. 14 (1977; Moscow, Oct. 8, 1980), No. 15, "I have faith in this earth," for Chorus and Orch. (1977; Moscow, April 12, 1979), and No. 16 (1981; Moscow, Oct. 19, 1982); 2 sinfoniettas (1948, 1960); *Moldavian Rhapsody* (Moscow, Nov. 30, 1949); *Slavic Rhapsody* (1950); Cello Concerto (1956); Violin Concerto (1960); Flute Concerto (1961); Trumpet Concerto (1967); Clarinet Concerto (1970). **CHAMBER:** 12 string quartets (1937–70); Piano Quintet (1944); Piano Trio (1945); String Trio (1951); 20 sonatas and 2 sonatinas for Various Instruments, with Piano; 24 preludes for Cello Solo; 23 preludes for Piano. **VOCAL:** 3 cantatas: *The Diary of Love* (1965), *Hiroshima Haikus* (1966), *On This Day Lenin Was Born* for Chorus and Orch. (1970); songs.

Vajda, János, Hungarian composer; b. Miskolc, Oct. 8, 1949. He received training in choral conducting from István Párkai and in composition from Emil Petrovics at the Budapest Academy of Music (graduated, 1975); after serving as répétiteur with the Hungarian Radio and Television Choir (1974–79), he completed his composition studies at the Sweelinck Cons. in Amsterdam (1979–80). From 1981 he taught at the Budapest Academy of Music. He won the Erkel Prize in 1981.

WORKS: DRAMATIC: OPERAS: *Barabbás* (1976–77); *Mario és a varázsló* (Mario and the Magician; 1983–85). **BALLETS:** *Az igazság pillanata* (The Moment of Truth; 1981); *Don Juan árnyéka rajtunk* (Don Juan's Shadow Is Cast on Us; 1981); *Izzó planéták* (Glowing Planets; 1983); *Jön a cirkusz* (Circus Is Coming; 1984). **ORCH.:** *Holland anziksz* (Picture Postcard from Holland) for Chamber Ensemble (1979); *Búcsú* (Farewell; 1978–80); *Pentaton, in memoriam R.M.* for Chamber Ensemble (1983). **CHAMBER:** *Gregorián ének* (Gregorian Chant) for Cimbalom (1974); *De angelis* for Wind Quintet and Tape (1978); *All That Music* for 2 Cimbaloms (1981); *Just for You No. 1* for Cello (1984) and *No. 2* for Violin (1987); *Mozi-zene* (Movie Music) for Piano and String Trio (1986); *Változatok* (Variations) for Piano (1987). **VOCAL:** *Tenebrae factae sunt* for Chorus (1972); *Két teszt* (2 Tests) for Mezzo-soprano, Flute, Clarinet, and Bassoon (1975); *Fekete gloria* (Black Halo) for Chorus (1977); *Stabat Mater* for 2 Women's Voices, Women's Chorus, and Chamber Ensemble (1978); *Ave Maris Stella* for Chorus (1979); Cantata for Chamber Chorus, Wind Quintet, String Quintet, and Celesta (1981); *Tristis est anima mea* for Chorus (1982); *Via crucis* for Chorus, 8 Winds, and Organ (1983); *Alleluja* for Chorus (1983); *Kolinda* for Chorus (1984); *Karácsonyi kantáta* (Christmas Cantata) for 2 Child Soloists, Chorus, Children's Chorus, and Orch. (1984–86); *Rapszódia* for Chorus (1987–88).

Valcárcel, Edgar, Peruvian composer and teacher, nephew of **Teodoro Valcárcel**; b. Puno, Dec. 4, 1932. He studied composition with Andrés Sas at the Lima Cons.; then went to N.Y., where he studied with Donald Lybbert at Hunter College; subsequently traveled to Buenos Aires, where he took composition lessons with Ginastera; also had sessions with Messiaen in Paris, and with Malipiero, Maderna, and Dallapiccola in Italy; furthermore, he joined the Columbia-Princeton Electronic Music Center and worked with Ussachevsky. He held 2 Guggenheim fellowships (1966, 1968). He was prof. of composition at the Lima Cons. (from 1965). In his compositions, he adopted an extremely advanced idiom that combined serial and aleatory principles, leaving to the performer the choice to use or not to use given thematic materials.

WORKS: ORCH.: Concerto for Clarinet and Strings (1965; Lima, March 6, 1966); *Quenua* (Lima, Aug. 18, 1965); *Aleaciones* (Lima, May 5, 1967); Piano Concerto (Lima, Aug. 8,

1968); *Checán II* (Lima, June 5, 1970); *Ma'karabotasaq hachana* (1971); *Sajra* (1974); *Anti Memoria II* (Washington, D.C., April 25, 1980). **CHAMBER:** 2 string quartets (1962, 1963); *Espectros I* for Flute, Viola, and Piano (1964), *II* for Horn, Cello, and Piano (1968), and *III* for Oboe, Violin, and Piano (1974); *Dicotomías III* for 12 Instruments (Mexico City, Nov. 20, 1966); *Fisiones* for 10 Instruments (1967); *Hiwana uru* for 11 Instruments (1967); Trio for Amplified Violin, Trombone, and Clarinet (1968); *Poema* for Amplified Violin, Voice, Piano, and Percussion (1969); *Checán I* for 6 Instruments (1969), *III* for 19 Instruments (1971), and *V* for Strings (1974); *Montage 59* for String Quartet, Clarinet, Piano, and Lights (1971). **PIANO:** 2 sonatas (1963, 1972); *Dicotomías I* and *II* (1966). **OTHER:** Choral pieces; multimedia works; electronic music, including *Antaras* for Flute, Percussion, and Electronics (1968).

Valcárcel, Teodoro, Peruvian composer, uncle of **Edgar Valcárcel**; b. Puno, Oct. 17, 1900; d. Lima, March 20, 1942. He studied at the Milan Cons. (1914–16) and with Felipe Pedrell in Barcelona. In 1928 he won the National Prize for Peruvian composers, and was awarded a gold medal from the municipality of Lima for his studies in Peruvian folk music. In 1929 he went to Europe once more; presented a concert of his works in Paris (April 12, 1930). In 1931 he settled in Lima. He was of pure Indian origin; as a native of the highlands, he was able to collect Indian songs unpolluted by urban influences. He publ. *30 cantos de alma vernacular; 4 canciones incaicas; 25 romances de costa y sierra peruana; 180 melodias del folklore.* Among his original works are the ballets (with singing) *Suray-Surita* and *Ckori Kancha*; 2 symphonic suites (both 1939); *En las ruinas del Templo del Sol,* tone poem (1940); *Concierto indio* for Violin and Orch. (1940); *3 ensayos* for an ensemble of Native Instruments; *Fiestas andinas* for Piano; *Suite autóctona* for Violin and Piano; songs. A catalogue of his works was publ. by R. Holzmann in *Boletín Bibliográfico de la Universidad nacional mayor de San Marcos,* XII (1942).

Valdengo, Giuseppe, Italian baritone; b. Turin, May 24, 1914. He studied cello at the Turin Cons., and also played the oboe; then decided to cultivate his voice, and took singing lessons with Michele Accoriutti. In 1936 he made his operatic debut as Figaro in *Il Barbiere di Siviglia* in Parma; in 1939, was engaged to sing at La Scala in Milan. On Sept. 19, 1946, he made his N.Y. City Opera debut as Sharpless, remaining on its roster until 1948. On Dec. 19, 1947, he made his Metropolitan Opera debut in N.Y. as Tonio; continued on the company's roster until 1954; was also chosen by Toscanini to sing the roles of Amonasro, Renato, Iago, and Falstaff with the NBC Sym. Orch. He made guest appearances in London, Paris, Vienna, and South America. He also acted the part of Antonio Scotti in the film *The Great Caruso.* His association with Toscanini is related in his *Ho cantato con Toscanini* (Como, 1962).

Valderrama, Carlos, Peruvian composer; b. Trujillo, Sept. 4, 1887; d. Lima, Aug. 1, 1950. He studied engineering at Cornell Univ., then decided to devote himself to music. He made his debut as a pianist at Carnegie Hall in N.Y. (Feb. 22, 1920). He wrote many piano pieces on old Inca themes in a salon style and some ballet music.

Valdes, Maximiano, Chilean conductor; b. Santiago, June 17, 1949. He studied piano, violin, and music history at the Santaigo Cons. After taking courses in composition and conducting at the Santa Cecilia Cons. in Rome, he continued conducting studies with Ferrara in Bologna, Siena, and Venice; also attended conducting courses given by Bernstein and Ozawa at the Berkshire Music Center in Tanglewood (summer, 1977). From 1976 to 1980 he was an assistant conductor at the Teatro La Fenice in Venice. After winning 1st prize in the Malko conducting competition in Copenhagen in 1980, he appeared as a guest conductor throughout Europe. In 1984 he became principal guest conductor of the Orquesta Nacional de España in Madrid. In 1986–87 he conducted the Orquesta Sinfónica de Euskadi in San Sebastian. He was music director of the Buffalo Phil. from 1989.

Válek, Jiří, notable Czech composer, writer, and teacher; b. Prague, May 28, 1923. He was a composition student of Řídký at the Prague Cons., graduating from its master school in 1947. He also received private training in philosophy, aesthetics, music history, and theory. After graduating from the Prague College of Higher Education in 1950, he took his Ph.D. at the Charles Univ. in Prague in 1952. From 1949 to 1952 he held the position of creative secretary of the Union of Czech Composers. He was a senior staff member of the state publishing firm Panton from 1959 to 1973. In 1966 he became a prof. at the Prague Cons. He also was artistic director of the state recording firm Supraphon (1974–79) and an assoc. prof. of composition at the Prague Academy of Musical Arts (from 1979). Among his writings are literary works and monographs. In his 17 syms., Válek has traversed an extensive ideological and artistic landscape, embracing both historical and contemporary events. Several of his stage pieces are rich in topical and satirical expression.

WORKS: DRAMATIC: *Shakespearean Variations,* music drama for 9 Actors, Commentator, and Nonet (1967); *Hour of Truth,* opera (1980); *Sonata on Auxiliary Life* for Moderator, Violin, Piano, and Percussion (1983); *Hamlet, our Contemporary,* satirical opera (1985); *Don't let us stone pygmies,* satirical opera (1991). **ORCH.:** *Sinfonietta* (1945); 17 syms.: No. 1, *Year 1948,* for Trumpet, Piano, and Orch. (1948), No. 2, *Classical,* for Chamber Orch. (1957; also for 2 Flutes, 2 Oboes, and Chamber String Orch.), No. 3, *Romantic,* for Soprano Saxophone, Tenor Saxophone, and Orch. (1957–63), No. 4, *Dialogues with an Inner Voice,* for Mezzo-soprano, Baritone, Wind Orch., Piano, and Percussion, after Shakespeare (1964–65), No. 5, *Guernica,* after the Picasso painting (1968), No. 6, *Ekpyrosis,* for Flute, Piano, Percussion Ensemble, and Chamber Orch. (1969), No. 7, *Pompeian Frescoes,* for Chamber Orch., Piano, and Percussion Ensemble (1970), No. 8, *Hic sunt homines,* for Soprano and Orch., after a novella by Stefan Zweig (1971), No. 9, *Renaissance,* sym.-triple concerto for Violin, Viola, Cello, and Orch. (1971), No. 10, *Baroque,* for Violin, Piano, and Orch. (1973), No. 11, *Revolutionary,* for Violin, Viola, Piano, Wind Quintet, and Orch. (1974), No. 12, *Shakespearean,* sym.-concerto for Violin, Viola, and Orch. (1975; also for Violin, Viola, String Orch., Piano, and Percussion), No. 13, *Gothic,* for Chorus and Orch., to commemorate the 600th anniversary of the death of the Czech King Charles IV (1978), No. 14, *Trionfale,* for 2 Pianos and Orch. (1983), No. 14, *Sarcastic,* sym.-oratorio for Baritone, Bass, Women's Chorus, and Orch., after Karel Borovský (1986), No. 16, *Neter,* for Bass-baritone and Orch. (1987), and No. 17, *Station of Hradčany,* sym.-opera for Soprano, Mezzo-soprano, Tenor, Baritone, Bass-baritone, Chorus, and Orch. (1992); *The Dam,* symphonic poem (1959); *3 Nocturnes* for Viola and Chamber String Orch. (1960); *Beyond the Bounds of Tomorrow,* ceremonial march (1972); *Concerto drammatico* for Double Bass, Chamber Orch., and Percussion (1974); Violin Concerto, *Hymn of the Sun* (1975); Concerto for 2 Flutes and Chamber Orch. (1975); Marimba Concerto, *Festivo* (1975); *Ceremonial Overture* (1976); Piano Concerto, *Eroico* (1977); Viola Concerto, *Lirico* (1977); Concerto for Flute, Marimba, Harp, and Orch., *Giocoso* (1978); *Ceremonial fresco* (1979); *Cathedral* for Viola and Chamber String Orch. (1979); Cello Concerto, *Maestoso* (1981); *Concerto burlesco* for Horn and Chamber Orch. (1986). **CHAMBER:** 4 string quartets (1943; 1945; 1960; *Quattrocento,* 1972–73); 2 violin sonatas (1944, 1960); Suite for Flute, Clarinet, and Piano (1946); 2 viola sonatas (1948; *Tragic,* 1961); Concertino for 9 Winds and Piano (1960); Trumpet Sonata, *Eroica* (1960; also for Clarinet and Piano or String Orch.); *Concerto notturno* for Violin, Viola, and Cello (1967); *Suite drammatica* for Double Bass and Piano (1967); Flute Sonata (1969); 2 concertos for Flute, Oboe, Violin, Viola, Cello, and Harpsichord (1970; *Discovering the Day,* 1979); *Villa dei Misteri* for Violin and Piano (1971); *3 Sentences in Memory of A. Einstein* for Violin, Cello, and Piano (1973); *Cinque canzoni da sonar* for Oboe, Flute, Clarinet, and Bassoon (1974); *Revolutionary Quartet* for Violin, Viola, Clarinet, and Piano (1974); *5 Meditations on Themes from Czech Folk*

Songs for Bass Clarinet and Piano (1974); *Tre sorrisi in onore W. A. Mozart* for Flute, Oboe, Violin, Viola, Cello, and Harpsichord (1975); *Fireworks and Fountains* for Marimba and Piano (1976); *4 Sculptures* for Renaissance Instruments (1977); Wind Quintet, *Gaiaemente e degnamente* (1977); Trio for Flute, Violin, and Piano (1978); *Clouds* for Violin and Piano (1979); *Dramas* for Cello and Guitar (1979); *4 Profiles after Shakespeare* for Oboe and Bassoon (1979); *Rectangular Circle*, grotesque for 5 Flutes (1979); *Concertant meditation* for Clarinet, Violin, Viola, and Cello (1980); *Dramatic Fresco* for Viola (1980); *5 capricci concerti* for Flute, Guitar, and Marimbaphone (1981); *Burlesque* for Flute and Piano (1986); *To be or not to be* for 8 Winds and 3 Timpani (1990). **PIANO:** 3 sonatas (*The Year 1942*, 1942; 1965; 1970); *To have or to be*, concerto drammatico "in memory of Alexander Dubček" (1993). **VOCAL:** *The Glory of Nameless People*, cantata for Solo Voices, Chorus, and Piano (1958); 7 *Monologues about Love* for Soprano and Piano (1959); *5 Variations on the Theme VERITAS* for Soprano and Piano (1970–76; also for Soprano, Men's Chorus, Wind Quintet, and Percussion, or Soprano, Men's Chorus, and Chamber Orch.); *La partenza della primavera* for Soprano and Orch. (1971; also for Soprano and Piano); 7 *Musical Fables* for Low Voice and Piano (1972; also for Children's Chorus, Reciter, Children's Games, Flute, 2 Clarinets, Bassoon, and Percussion); *Life*, 5 sonnets for Men's Chorus (1975); *Sonatine of the Universe* for Children's Chorus, Vibraphone, and Piano (1976); *Virelais festivo in onore G. de Machaut et imperatore Bohemiae Carolus IV* for Soprano and Gothic Instruments (1978); *5 Shadows and Epilogue* for Bass Baritone, Piano, and Percussion (1978); *Song of Praise* for Soprano, Alto, Tenor, Bass, and Piano (1981); *Satirikon* for 1 or 2 Low Voices and Piano (1989).

Valen, (Olav) Fartein, noted Norwegian composer; b. Stavanger, Aug. 25, 1887; d. Haugesund, Dec. 14, 1952. His father was a missionary in Madagascar, and Valen spent his early childhood there; when he was 6 the family returned to Stavanger, and he received piano lessons from Jeannette Mohr and others; taught himself theory. In 1906 he entered the Univ. of Christiania as a student of language and literature; he soon devoted himself entirely to music, pursuing his training in theory with Elling at the Christiania Cons., graduating as an organist in 1909; then received instruction in composition from Bruch, in theory and composition from Karl Leopold Wolf, and in piano from Heschberg at the Berlin Hochschule für Musik (1909–11). From 1916 to 1924 he lived on his family's farm in Valevåg; he then was active in Oslo, where he held the post of inspector of the Norwegian Music Collection at the library of the Univ. (1927–36). In 1935 he received the Norwegian State Salary of Art (a government life pension). His early music reflects the influence of Brahms, but later he developed a sui generis method of composition that he termed "atonal polyphony," completely free from traditional tonal relationships but strongly cohesive in contrapuntal fabric and greatly varied in rhythm; his first work in which he made use of this technique was a Piano Trio written in 1924. He never adopted an explicit 12-tone method of composition, but a parallelism with Schoenberg's music is observable. Valen stood apart from all nationalist developments in Oslo, yet his music attracted attention in modern circles; a Valen Soc. was formed in Norway in 1949, and in England in 1952, shortly before his death.

WORKS: ORCH.: *Pastorale* (1929–30); *Sonetto di Michelangelo* (1932); *Nenia* (1932); *Cantico di ringraziamento* (1932–33); *An die Hoffnung* (1933); *Epithalamion* (1933); *Le Cimetière marin* (1933–34); *La isla de las calmas* (1934); 5 syms.: No. 1 (1937–39; Bergen, Feb. 2, 1956), No. 2 (1941–44; Oslo, March 28, 1957), No. 3 (1944–46; Oslo, April 13, 1951), No. 4 (1947–49; Malmö, Oct. 16, 1956), and No. 5 (1951–52; unfinished); *Ode til Ensombeten* (Ode to Silence; 1939); Violin Concerto (1940; Oslo, Oct. 24, 1947); Concerto for Piano and Chamber Orch. (1949–51; Oslo, Jan. 15, 1953). **CHAMBER:** Violin Sonata (1916); Piano Trio (1917–24); 2 string quartets (1928–29; 1930–31); *Serenade* for Wind Quintet (1946–47). **KEYBOARD: PIANO:** *Legend* (1907); 2 sonatas (1912; *The Hound of Heaven*, 1940–41); *4 Pieces* (1934–35); *Variations* (1935–36); *Gavotte and Musette* (1936); *Prelude and Fugue* (1937); *2 Preludes* (1937); *Intermezzo* (1939–40). **ORGAN:** *Prelude and Fugue* (1939); *Pastoral* (1939). **VOCAL:** *Ave Maria* for Soprano and Orch. (1917–21); *Mignon*, 2 songs for Soprano and Orch., after Goethe (1920–27); *Dearest Thou Now, O Soul* for Soprano and Orch., after Whitman (1920–28); *3 Gedichte von Goethe* for Soprano and Orch. (1925–27); *2 chinesische Gedichte* for Soprano and Orch. (1925–27); *La noche oscura del alma* for Soprano and Orch., after St. John of the Cross (1939); motets.

BIBL.: O. Gurvin, *F. V., En banebryter i nyere norsk musikk* (F. V., a Pioneer in Norwegian Music; Oslo, 1962); B. Kortsen, *Studies of Form in F. V.'s Music* (Oslo, 1962); idem, *Melodic Structure and Thematic Unity in F. V.'s Music* (2 vols., Glasgow, 1963); idem, *F. V., Life and Music* (3 vols., Oslo, 1965); Anonymous, *Komponisten F. V. 1887–1952* (Oslo, 1976); P. Rapoport, *Opus Est: Six Composers from Northern Europe* (London, 1978).

Valencia, Antonio María, Colombian pianist and composer; b. Cali, Nov. 10, 1902; d. there, July 22, 1952. He studied at the Schola Cantorum in Paris (from 1923) with d'Indy, Pierné, Le Flem, and others; returning to Colombia in 1930, he was founder-director of the Cali Conservatorio y Escuela de Bellas Artes (1933–37; 1938–52); also was director of the Bogotá Cons. (1937–38).

WORKS: *Chirimía y bambuco sotareño* for Orch. (1942); *Egloga incaica* for Flute, Oboe, Clarinet, and Bassoon (1935); *Emociones caucanas* for Piano, Violin, and Cello (1938); numerous piano pieces inspired by native melorhythms, including *8 ritmos y cantos suramericanos* and *Sonatina boyacense*; *Requiem* (1943); other church music; choruses and songs.

BIBL.: A. Tovar, *A.M. V., artista integral* (Cali, 1958).

Valente, Benita, distinguished American soprano; b. Delano, Calif., Oct. 19, 1934. She began serious musical training with Chester Hayden at Delano High School; at 16, she became a private pupil of Lotte Lehmann, and at 17 received a scholarship to continue her studies with Lehmann at the Music Academy of the West in Santa Barbara; in 1955 she won a scholarship to the Curtis Inst. of Music in Philadelphia, where she studied with Singher. Upon graduation in 1960, she made her formal debut in a Marlboro (Vt.) Festival concert. On Oct. 8, 1960, she made her N.Y. concert debut at the New School for Social Research. After winning the Metropolitan Opera Auditions in 1960, she pursued further studies with Margaret Harshaw. She then sang with the Freiburg im Breisgau Opera, making her debut there as Pamina in 1962; after appearances with the Nuremberg Opera (1966), she returned to the U.S. and established herself as a versatile recitalist, soloist with orchs., and opera singer. Her interpretation of Pamina was especially well received, and it was in that role that she made her long-awaited Metropolitan Opera debut in N.Y. on Sept. 22, 1973. She won praise for her performances in operas by Monteverdi, Handel, Verdi, Puccini, and Britten. Her extensive recital and concert repertoire ranges from Schubert to Ginastera.

Valente, Giorgio. See **Vitalis, George.**

Valenti, Fernando, noted American harpsichordist and teacher; b. N.Y., Dec. 4, 1926; d. Red Bank, N.J., Sept. 6, 1990. He studied piano with José Iturbi; then attended Yale Univ., where he took instruction in harpsichord with Ralph Kirkpatrick. He made his N.Y. recital debut in 1950. In 1951 he was appointed prof. of harpsichord at the Juilliard School of Music in N.Y.; also taught at various other academic institutions. He publ. the book *The Harpsichord: A Dialogue for Beginners* (1982). His performances of the music of Domenico Scarlatti were highly praised.

Valentin, Erich, distinguished German musicologist; b. Strasbourg, Nov. 27, 1906; d. Bad Aibling, March 16, 1993. He studied music with Courvoisier and Rohr in Munich; took courses in musicology with Sandberger at the Univ. of Munich, where he received his Ph.D. in 1928 with the diss. *Die Entwicklung der Tokkata im 17. und 18. Jahrhundert* (publ. in Munich, 1930). From 1929 to 1935 he taught at the Staatliches Privatmusiklehrer-Seminar in Magdeburg; from 1939 to 1945 he was director of the Zentralinstitut für Mozartforschung. He taught at the Hochschule für Musik in Munich from 1953, where he was a prof. from 1955 and its director (1964–72). From 1950 to 1955 he was ed.-in-chief of the *Zeitschrift für Musik*, and from 1955 to 1959 he was co-ed. of the *Neue Zeitschrift für Musik*. He became ed.-in-chief of *Acta Mozartiana* in 1954. In addition to his many articles for music journals, he also prepared eds. of works by Mozart, Telemann, and others.

WRITINGS: *Georg Philipp Telemann* (Burg, 1931; 3rd ed., 1952); *Richard Wagner* (Regensburg, 1937); *Dichtung und Oper: Eine Untersuchung zum Stilproblem der Oper* (Leipzig, 1938); *Hans Pfitzner* (Regensburg, 1939); *Wege zu Mozart* (Regensburg, 1941; 4th ed., 1950); *Beethoven* (Salzburg, 1942; Eng. ed., N.Y., 1958); *W.A. Mozart: Wesen und Wandlung* (Hamelin, 1948); *Kleine Bilder grosser Meister* (Mainz, 1952); *Handbuch der Chormusik* (Regensburg, 1953–74); *Handbuch der Instrumentenkunde* (Regensburg, 1954; 6th ed., 1974); *Der früheste Mozart* (Munich, 1956); *Beethoven* (pictorial bibliography; Munich, 1957); *Die Tokkata*, in *Das Musikwerk*, XVII (1958); *Mozart* (pictorial bibliography; Munich, 1959); *Musica domestica: Über Wesen und Geschichte der Hausmusik* (Trossingen, 1959); *Telemann in seiner Zeit* (Hamburg, 1960); *Handbuch der Schulmusik* (Regensburg, 1962); *Die goldene Spur: Mozart in der Dichtung Hermann Hesses* (Augsburg, 1965); with F. Hofmann, *Die evangelische Kirchenmusik* (Regensburg, 1967); with W. Gebhardt and W. Vetter, *Handbuch des Musikunterrichts* (Regensburg, 1970); *Die schönsten Beethoven-Briefe* (Munich, 1973); *Lübbes Mozart-Lexikon* (Bergisch-Gladbach, 1983); *Don-Juan-Reflexionen: Eine Auswahl literarischer Zeugnisse* (Augsburg, 1988).

BIBL.: G. Weiss, ed., *E. V. zum 70. Geburtstag* (Regensburg, 1976).

Valentini-Terrani, Lucia, Italian mezzo-soprano; b. Padua, Aug. 28, 1948. She received training in Padua. In 1969 she made her operatic debut in the title role of Rossini's *La Cenerentola* in Brescia, and then appeared in various Italian operatic centers. From 1973 she sang at Milan's La Scala. On Nov. 16, 1974, she made her Metropolitan Opera debut in N.Y. as Rossini's Isabella. In 1979 she appeared as a soloist in the Verdi *Requiem* with Giulini and the Los Angeles Phil., returning to Los Angeles in 1982 to sing Mistress Quickly under Giulini's direction. From 1984 she sang at the Pesaro Festivals. In 1987 she appeared as Rossini's Rosina at London's Covent Garden. She sang Gluck's Orféo in Naples in 1990. In 1992 she appeared as Rossini's Isabella in Turin. Her guest engagements also took her to the Vienna State Opera, the Paris Opéra, the Bolshoi Theater in Moscow, and the Lyric Opera in Chicago. She was particularly known for her roles in operas by Rossini and Verdi.

Valkare, Gunnar, Swedish organist, teacher, and composer; b. Norrköping, April 25, 1943. He studied piano with Stina Sundell, organ with Alf Linder, and composition with Ingvar Lidholm at the Stockholm Musikhögskolan (1963–69). He was active as an organist and teacher (1964–79); served as resident composer in Gislaved (1973) and Kalmar (1977–78). His music is militantly aggressive in its tonal, atonal, and polytonal assault on the most cherished notions of harmonious sweetness.

WORKS: *4 Cardiograms* for Solo Singers, Chorus, and Instruments in varying combinations (1965–66); *A Study in the Story of Human Stupidity* for Orch. (Århus, Feb. 5, 1968); *Nomo* for 7 Narrators, 6 Winds, and Tape (1967); *Eld för ett altare* (Fire from an Altar), church drama (1968); *Kanske en pastoral om det får tina upp* (Perhaps a Pastorale If It Will Thaw) for Percussion, Piano, and Strings (1968); *A Play about the Medieval Värend and the Dacke Feud*, musical-dramatic dance for Winds, Violin, Nickelharp, and Xylophone (1971); *Från mitt rosa badkar* (From My Rosy Bathtub) for Orch., Pop Group, and Chorus (1971); *Det ringer i mitt öra* (There Is a Ringing in My Ears) for Voices and Instruments (1972); *Tahuantisuyos ekonomi* for Chorus, Winds, and Strings (1974); *Mellan berg och hav, mellan himmel och jard* (Between the Mountains and the Ocean, Between the Sky and the Earth), play on Chinese history, for Singer, Actor, and Instrumental Ensemble (1975); *Stages* for 6 Musicians (1976); *Variationer och tema* for 4 Clarinets (1978); *Gesellen* for Chorus and Organ (1979); *Blöpark* for Wind Orch. and Percussion (1982); Concerto for Treble Recorder and Chamber Orch. (1983); *Flight of the Mechanical Heart* for Flute, Guitar, and Harpsichord (1984); Sym. (1986; Norrköping, Nov. 12, 1987); *Kinema* for Orch. (1988); *Örnen och ugglan: En inidansk saga* for Voices and Instrumental Accompaniment (1988); *Second Flight of the Mechanical Heart* for Chamber Orch. (1990); *Intermedium I* for Chamber Orch. and Tape (1991) and *II* for Chamber Orch. (1991); *Concerto d'incontro*, theater piece (1992); *Passage I–V* for Solo Instrument (1993); *Refrains* for 6 Instruments (1994).

Vallas, Léon, distinguished French musicologist; b. Roanne, Loire, May 17, 1879; d. Lyons, May 9, 1956. After studying medicine in Lyons, he pursued his musicological training at the Univ. there (Ph.D., 1908). In 1902 he became music critic of *Tout Lyon*; in 1903, founded the *Revue Musicale de Lyon*, which became the *Revue Française de Musique* in 1912 and the *Nouvelle Revue Musicale* in 1920; also wrote for the *Progrès de Lyon* (1919–54). With G. Witkowski, he founded a schola cantorum in Lyons in 1902; taught theory at the Univ. (1908–11) and the Cons. (1912) there, and later at the Sorbonne in Paris (1928–30). He was president of the Société Française de Musicologie (1937–43) and artistic director of Radiodiffusion de Lyon (1938–41).

WRITINGS: *Georges Migot* (Paris, n.d.); *Debussy, 1862–1918* (Paris, 1926); *Les Idées de Claude Debussy, musicien français* (Paris, 1927; 2nd ed., 1932; Eng. tr., 1929, as *The Theories of Claude Debussy*); *Claude Debussy et son temps* (Paris, 1932; 2nd ed., 1958; Eng. tr., 1933, as *Claude Debussy: His Life and Works*); *Achille-Claude Debussy* (Paris, 1944); *Vincent d'Indy* (2 vols., Paris, 1946, 1949); *César Franck* (London, 1951; in French, 1955, as *La Véritable Histoire de César Franck*).

Vallerand, Jean (d'Auray), Canadian composer, music critic, teacher, and administrator; b. Montreal, Dec. 24, 1915. He received violin lessons from Lucien Sicotte (1921–36); also studied at the Collège Ste.-Marie de Montréal (B.A., 1935), and was a composition pupil of Claude Champagne (1935–42); also obtained a diploma in journalism (1938) and a licence ès lettres (1939) from the Univ. of Montreal. He ed. *Quartier Latin* (1937–39); then wrote music criticism for *Le Canada* (1941–46), *Montréal-Matin* (1948–49), *Le Devoir* (1952–61), *Nouveau Journal* (1961–62), and *La Presse* (1962–66). From 1942 to 1963 he was secretary general of the Montreal Cons., where he also taught orchestration. He also taught orchestration and music history at the Univ. of Montreal from 1950 to 1966. After serving as head of radio music for the CBC in Montreal (1963–66), he was cultural attaché for the Quebec government in Paris (1966–70). In 1971 he was named director of music education for the Ministry of Cultural Affairs of Quebec. Following its reorganization that year, he was its director of performing arts until 1975. From 1971 to 1978 he also was director of the Cons. de musique et d'art dramatique du Québec. In 1967 he was awarded the Centenary Medal of Canada, and in 1975 received an honorary doctorate from the Univ. of Ottawa. In 1991 he was made a Chevalier of the Ordre national du Québec. In addition to his many reviews and articles in journals, he publ. the books *Introduction a la musique* (Montreal, 1949) and *La Musique et les tout-petits* (Montreal, 1950). He wrote music in a neo-Romantic manner; in his later compositions he experimented with serial techniques.

WORKS: OPERA: *Le Magicien* (Orford, Quebec, Sept. 2, 1961, with piano; Montreal, May 30, 1962, with orch.). **ORCH.:** *Le Diable dans le beffroi*, symphonic poem (1939; Montreal,

April 24, 1942); *Nocturne* (1944); *Prélude* (1946); *Réverbérations contradictoires* (1960; Montreal, Feb. 26, 1961); *Cordes en mouvement* for Strings (Montreal, March 27, 1961); *Étude concertante* for Violin and Orch. (1968; Montreal, June 1969). **CHAMBER:** Violin Sonata (Montreal, Nov. 9, 1950; also for Violin and Orch., 1951); String Quartet (Radio Canada, Feb. 28, 1955). **VOCAL:** *Les Roses a la mer* for Voice and Piano (1939; also for Voice and String Orch.); *Notre-Dame de la Couronne* and *Notre-Dame du Pain,* cantatas for Tenor, Chorus, and Orch. (1946); *Quatre mélodies sur des poèmes de St. Denys Garneau* for Voice and Piano (1954).

Valletti, Cesare, notable Italian tenor; b. Rome, Dec. 18, 1922. He was a student of Tito Schipa. In 1947 he made his operatic debut as Alfredo in Bari. After singing in Rome (1947–48), he appeared as Count Almaviva in Palermo and as Elvino in *La Sonnambula* in Naples in 1949. In 1950 he sang Don Narciso in *Il Turco in Italia* at the Eliseo in Rome. Following his London debut as Fenton with the visiting La Scala company of Milan in 1950, he appeared with the company in Milan in such roles as Lindoro in *L'Italiana in Algeri,* Nemorino, and Vladimir in *Prince Igor.* In 1951 he sang Alfredo in Mexico City opposite Callas. He made his U.S. debut as Werther at the San Francisco Opera in 1953. On Dec. 10, 1953, he made his Metropolitan Opera debut in N.Y. as Don Ottavio, where he remained on the roster until 1960 singing such admired roles as Tamino, Ferrando, Count Almaviva, Alfredo, Massenet's Des Grieux, and Alfred in *Die Fledermaus.* In 1958 he sang Alfredo opposite Callas at London's Covent Garden, and appeared as Giacomo in *Donna del lago* at the Florence Maggio Musicale Fiorentino. In 1960 he sang Don Ottavio at the Salzburg Festival. In 1968 he appeared as Nero in *L'Incoronazione di Poppea* at the Caramoor Festival in Katonah, N.Y. He retired from the operatic stage that same year. Valletti's admired vocal gifts placed him in the forefront of the bel canto revival of his day.

Vallin, Ninon, French soprano; b. Montalieu-Vercieu, Sept. 8, 1886; d. Lyons, Nov. 22, 1961. She studied at the Lyons Cons. and with Meyriane Heglon in Paris. After appearing in concerts, she attracted the notice of Debussy who chose her to sing in the premiere of his *Le martyre de Saint Sébastien* in 1911. He later accompanied her in recitals. In 1912 she made her operatic debut as Micaëla at the Paris Opéra-Comique, where she sang until 1916. In 1916 she made her first appearance at the Teatro Colón in Buenos Aires, continuing to sing there until 1936. She appeared at Milan's La Scala in 1916 and in Rome in 1917. In 1920 she made her debut at the Paris Opéra as Thaïs. In 1934 she sang at the San Francisco Opera. Thereafter she toured as a concert artist. After teaching at the Montevideo Cons. (1953–59), she settled in Lyons. Among her finest roles were Zerlina, Alceste, Charlotte, Mignon, Juliette, and Mélisande. As a concert singer, she excelled in works by French and Spanish composers.

BIBL.: R. de Fragny, *N. V.: Princesse du chant* (Lyons, 1963).

Van Allan, Richard (real name, **Alan Philip Jones**), English bass; b. Clipstone, Nottinghamshire, May 28, 1935. He studied at the Worcester College of Education and received vocal training from David Franklin at the Birmingham School of Music; he also had private vocal lessons with J. Strasser. In 1964 he became a member of the Glyndebourne Festival Chorus. In 1966 he made his operatic debut at the Glyndebourne Opera in a minor role in *Die Zauberflöte.* In 1969 he joined the Sadler's Wells Opera in London, and later sang there after it became the English National Opera in 1974. In 1970 he created the role of Jowler in Maw's *The Ring of the Moon* at Glyndebourne. He made his debut at London's Covent Garden as the Mandarin in *Turandot* in 1971. In 1976 he sang Baron Ochs at the San Diego Opera. In 1986 he became director of the National Opera Studio. However, he continued to pursue his stage career. In 1990 he sang Don Alfonso at the Metropolitan Opera in N.Y. In 1992 he created the role of Jerome in the stage premiere of Gerhard's *The Duenna* in Madrid. He appeared as Massenet's Don Quichotte at the Victoria State Opera in Melbourne in 1995. Among his other roles are Osmin, Don Giovanni, Leporello, Mozart's Figaro, the Grand Inquisitor, Philip II, and Verdi's Banquo.

van Appledorn, Mary Jeanne, American composer, pianist, and teacher; b. Holland, Mich., Oct. 2, 1927. She studied piano with Cecile Staub Genhart (B.Mus., 1948), theory (M.Mus., 1950), and composition with Rogers and Hovhaness at the Eastman School of Music in Rochester, N.Y., where she received her Ph.D. in 1966 with the diss. *A Stylistic Study of Claude Debussy's Opera, Pelléas et Mélisande*; pursued postdoctoral studies at the Mass. Inst. of Technology (1982). She served as prof. and as chairman of the theory and composition dept. in the music school at Texas Technical Univ. in Lubbock (1950–87); also made appearances as a pianist.

WORKS: BALLET: *Set of 7* (N.Y., May 10, 1988). **ORCH.:** *Concerto brevis* for Piano and Orch. (1954); *A Choreographic Overture* for Concert Band (1957); Concerto for Trumpet and Band (1960); *Passacaglia and Chorale* (1973); *Cacophony* for Wind Ensemble, Percussion, and Toys (1980); *Lux: Legend of Sankta Lucia* for Symphonic Band, Harp, Percussion Ensemble, and Handbells (1981); *Ayre* for Strings, Viola da Gamba Consort, and Clarinet or Saxophone Choir (1989); *Terrestial Music,* double concerto for Violin, Piano, and Strings (Nagano, Japan, Aug. 8, 1992); *Cycles of Moons and Tides* for Symphonic Band (1995). **CHAMBER:** *Cellano Rhapsody* for Cello and Piano (1948); *Burlesca* for Piano, Brass, and Percussion (1951); *Matrices* for Saxophone and Piano (1979); *Liquid Gold* for Saxophone and Piano (1982); *4 Duos* for Alto Saxophones (1985); *4 Duos* for Viola and Cello (1986); *Sonic Mutation* for Harp (1986); Clarinet Sonatine (N.Y., Oct. 17, 1988); *Cornucopia* for Trumpet (1988); *Windsongs* for Brass Quintet (1991); *Incantations* for Trumpet and Piano (1992); *Atmospheres* for Trombone Ensemble (1993); *Reeds Afire,* duos for Clarinet and Bassoon (1994); various piano pieces. **VOCAL:** *Peter Quince at the Clavier* for Women's Chorus, Narrator, Flute, Oboe, Horn, and Piano (1958); *Darest Thou Now, O Soul* for Women's Chorus and Organ (1975); *West Texas Suite* for Chorus, Symphonic Band, and Percussion Ensemble (1976); *Rising Night After Night,* cantata for 3 Soloists, Narrator, Choruses, and Orch. (1978; Lubbock, Texas, Jan. 27, 1979); *Danza Impresión de España* for Vocal Octet and Ballet (1979); *Missa Brevis* for Voice and Organ (1988); *Les Hommes Vidés* for Chorus (1994).

Van Beinum, Eduard (Alexander), eminent Dutch conductor; b. Arnhem, Sept. 3, 1900; d. while rehearsing the Concertgebouw Orch. in Amsterdam, April 13, 1959. He studied at the Amsterdam Cons.; received lessons in violin from his brother, in piano from J.B. de Pauw, and in composition from Sem Dresden. He conducted the Toonkunst Choir in Schiedam (1921–30), the Toonkunst Choir and Orchestral Soc. in Zutphen (1923–31), and the Haarlem Sym. Orch. (1927–31). In 1931 he was named to the position of 2nd conductor of the Concertgebouw Orch. in Amsterdam under Mengelberg; after serving as its assoc. conductor from 1938 to 1945, he succeeded Mengelberg as its chief conductor in 1945, a position he held with great distinction until his death. From 1949 to 1951 he also served as principal conductor of the London Phil. On Jan. 8, 1954, he made his U.S. debut as a guest conductor with the Philadelphia Orch., and later that year toured the U.S. with the Concertgebouw Orch. to notable critical acclaim. From 1956 until his death he was also music director of the Los Angeles Phil. Van Beinum's interpretations of the Classical and Romantic repertory were particularly distinguished by their lucidity, precision, and balance.

BIBL.: W. Paap, *E. v. B.* (Baarn, 1957); K. Bernet Kempers and M. Flothius, eds., *E. v. B.* (Haarlem, 1959).

Vancea, Zeno (Octavian), outstanding Romanian composer and musicologist; b. Bocşa-Vasiova, Oct. 21, 1900. He studied at the Cluj Cons. (1919–21) and with Kanitz (composition) at the Vienna Cons. (1921–26; 1930–31). He taught at conservatories in

Tîrgu-Mureş (1926–40; director, 1946–48), Timişoara (1940–45), and Bucharest (1949–73). He was the ed. of the important Romanian monthly *Muzica* (1953–64). Vancea belongs to the national school of Romanian composers; in his music he makes use of folk-song patterns without direct quotations. Harmonically, he adopts many procedures of cosmopolitan modern music while cautiously avoiding abrasive sonorities.

WRITINGS: *Istoria muzicii româneşti* (Bucharest, 1953); *Creaţia muzicală românească, secolele XIX–XX* (Romanian Musical Compositions of the XIX–XX Centuries; Bucharest, 1968); *Studii şi eseuri muzicale* (Musical Studies and Essays; Bucharest, 1974).

WORKS: BALLET-PANTOMIME: *Priculiciul* (The Werewolf; 1933; Bucharest, April 30, 1943; rev. 1957). **ORCH.:** *Rapsodia bănăteană No. 1* (1926); *Scoarte*, suite for Chamber Orch. (1928); *2 Grotesque Dances* (1937); *Simfonieta I* (1948); *O zi de vară* (On a Summer Day), suite (Bucharest, Sept. 23, 1951); *Triptic simfonic: Preambul, Intermezzo, Marş* (1958; Bucharest, May 10, 1959); *Burlesca* (1959); *Concerto for Orchestra* (1961; Bucharest, May 10, 1962); *5 Piese* (Pieces) for Strings (1964; Romanian TV, Feb. 4, 1965); *Prolog simfonic* (Bucharest, March 9, 1974); *Elegie* for Strings (Tîrgu-Mureş, June 10, 1977). **CHAMBER:** *Cvartet bizantin* (Byzantine Quartet; 1931); 8 string quartets (1934, 1953, 1957, 1965, 1970, 1970, 1978, 1980); String Trio (1981). **VOCAL:** *Requiem* for Soprano, Alto, Tenor, Bass, Chorus, and Orch. (1941); *Cîntecul păcii* (Song of Peace) for Soprano, Chorus, and Orch. (1961); 5 songs for Tenor and Orch. (Tîrgu-Mureş, Sept. 25, 1977); choruses; solo songs with piano.

Van Dam, José (real name, **Joseph Van Damme**), outstanding Belgian bass-baritone; b. Brussels, Aug. 25, 1940. He began to study piano and solfège at 11; commenced vocal studies at 13, and then entered the Brussels Cons. at 17, graduating with 1st prizes in voice and opera performance at 18; subsequently captured 1st prizes in vocal competitions in Liège, Paris, Toulouse, and Geneva. After making his operatic debut as Don Basilio in *Il Barbiere di Siviglia* in Liège, he gained experience as a member of the Opéra and the Opéra-Comique in Paris (1961–65) and of the Geneva Opera (1965–67). In 1967 he joined the Berlin Deutsche Oper, where he established himself as one of its principal artists via such roles as Figaro, Leporello, Don Alfonso, Caspar, and Escamillo. While continuing to sing in Berlin, he pursued a notable international career. In 1973 he made his first appearance at London's Covent Garden as Escamillo, a role he also chose for his Metropolitan Opera debut in N.Y. on Nov. 21, 1975. He was chosen to create the title role in Messiaen's opera *Saint François d'Assise* at the Paris Opéra on Nov. 28, 1983, thereby adding further luster to his reputation. During the 1985–86 season, he appeared as Hans Sachs at the Chicago Lyric Opera. He sang Saint François at the Salzburg Festival in 1992. On Feb. 25, 1994, he made his Carnegie Hall recital debut in N.Y. Among his other esteemed roles are Don Giovanni, Verdi's Attila, the Dutchman, Golaud, and Wozzeck. He has also won renown as a concert artist, making appearances with the foremost orchs. of Europe and the U.S.

Van Delden, Lex. See **Delden, Lex van.**

Van den Borren, Charles (-Jean-Eugène), eminent Belgian musicologist; b. Ixelles, near Brussels, Nov. 17, 1874; d. Brussels, Jan. 14, 1966. He received training in music history from Kufferath and in harmony, counterpoint, and fugue from E. Closson. He was a barrister in the court of appeals until 1905; was music critic of *L'Indépendance Belge* (1909–14); then taught at the Brussels Institut des Hautes Études Musicales et Dramatiques and at the Free Univ., where he later was prof. of music history (1926–45); also was librarian at the Royal Cons. in Brussels (1919–40) and a lecturer in musicology at the Univ. of Liège (1927–44). He served as first chairman of the Société de Musicologie Belge (1946); in 1939, was elected a member of the Academie Royale de Belgique, Classe des Beaux-Arts, serving as its president in 1953. **Safford Cape** was his son-in-law.

WRITINGS: *L'Oeuvre dramatique de César Franck, Hulda et Ghiselle* (Brussels, 1907); *Les Origines de la musique de clavecin en Angleterre* (Brussels, 1912; Eng. tr., 1914, as *The Sources of Keyboard Music in England*); *Les Musiciens belges en Angleterre à l'époque de la Renaissance* (Brussels, 1913); *Les Débuts de la musique à Venise* (Brussels, 1914); *Origine et développement de l'art polyphonique vocal du XVIe siècle* (Brussels, 1920); *Orlando de Lassus* (Paris, 1920); *Le Manuscrit musical M.222 C.22 de la Bibliothèque de Strasbourg* (Antwerp, 1924); *Guillaume Dufay: Son importance dans l'évolution de la musique au XVe siècle* (Brussels, 1926); *Études sur le quinzième siècle musical* (Antwerp, 1941); *Peter Benoît* (Brussels, 1942); *Roland de Lassus* (Brussels, 1943); *Geschiedenis van de muziek in de Nederlanden* (2 vols., Amsterdam, 1948, 1951); *César Franck* (Brussels, 1949); with E. Closson, *La musique en Belgique du Moyen-Âge à nos jours* (Brussels, 1950). **EDITIONS:** With G. van Doorslaer, *Philippe de Monte: Opera omnia* (Bruges and Düsseldorf, 1927–39); *Polyphonia sacra: A Continental Miscellany of the Fifteenth Century* (Burnham, Buckinghamshire, 1932; 2nd ed., rev., 1962).

BIBL.: *Hommage à C. V.d. B. à l'occasion du centenaire de sa naissance* (Brussels, 1974).

Van der Horst, Anthon. See **Horst, Anthon van der.**

Vandermaesbrugge, Max, Belgian composer; b. Couillet, June 14, 1933. He studied with Moulaert, Souris, Stehman, Louel, and Absil at the Royal Cons. of Music in Brussels (1951–60). He taught piano and solfeggio at the music academies in Anderlecht (1955–62), Josse-ten-Noode (1958–62), and de Forest (1959–62), and at Etterbeck (1963–66). In 1966 he was appointed to the faculty of the Royal Cons. of Music in Brussels and in 1972 he succeeded Defossez as inspector of Belgian music schools.

WORKS: *Drum Follies*, variations for 10 Percussionists (1961); *Caprice* for Violin and Piano (1961); *4 fables de Florian* for Soprano, Contralto, and Baritone (1961); *Miniature Variations* for Guitar (1962); *Duo* for Flute and Viola (1962); *En petits caractères* for 2 Trumpets and Piano obbligato (1963); Quartet for 4 Clarinets (1965); *Tema e Variazioni* for Carillon (1967); *Divertimento* for Flute and Strings (1969); *Hiver*, symphonic poem (1970); *4 instantanés* for Flute and Guitar (1972); *Sinfonia* for Strings (1972); *Saxofolies* for Saxophone Septet (1974); *Intrada e Scherzando* for Trumpet and Piano (1978).

Vandernoot, André, Belgian conductor; b. Brussels, June 2, 1927; d. there, Nov. 6, 1991. He received training at the Royal Cons. of Music in Brussels and at the Vienna Academy of Music. In 1951 he was a laureate in the Besançon conducting competition. From 1954 he appeared regularly as a conductor with the Orchestre National de Belgique in Brussels. In 1958 he was named to the post of 1st conductor of the Royal Flemish Opera in Antwerp. He was music director of the Théâtre Royal de la Monnaie in Brussels from 1959 to 1973. In 1974–75 he was music director of the Orchestre National de Belgique. From 1976 to 1983 he held the title of 1st guest conductor of the Antwerp Phil. He also was music director of the Noordhollands Phil. in Haarlem in 1978–79. From 1979 to 1989 he was music director of the Brabants Orch. From 1987 he also was chief conductor of the Orchestre Symphonique de la RTBF in Brussels.

Van der Slice, John, American composer, ethnomusicologist, and teacher; b. Ann Arbor, Feb. 19, 1940. He studied at the Univ. of Calif., Berkeley (B.A., 1964), with Russell, McKay, and Dahl at the Univ. of Hawaii (M.A. in ethnomusicology; M.M., 1973), and at the Univ. of Ill., Urbana (Ph.D., 1980, with a diss. on Ligeti's *Atmosphères*). He taught at the Univ. of Hawaii at Hilo and served in an administrative position at the Univ. of Hawaii at Honolulu; then joined the faculty of the Univ. of Miami. His musical tastes range from the medieval period to the contemporary era, and also include jazz and non-Western musics; he studied performance traditions of the Japanese koto, the Korean kayakeum, and the bonang panerus member of the Javanese gamelan. His compositional language involves both pitch set permutation and a subtle implication of tonal hierarchy.

WORKS: ORCH.: *Jo-ha-kyu* (1977–79); *Fantasia* (1988). **CHAMBER:** *Pulse/Impulse* for Percussion (1983); Trio for Clarinet, Viola, and Marimba (1984); *Doodle Music* for Piccolo and Percussion (1985); Piano Trio (1986); *Animistic Study* for Double Bass (1986); *Time Shadows* for 11 Instruments (1987).

Van der Velden, Renier, Belgian composer; b. Antwerp, Jan. 14, 1910; d. there, Jan. 19, 1993. He received training from Jan Broeckx, Karel Candael, and Joseph Jongen in Brussels. In 1945 he was became program director of the French services of the Belgian Radio in Antwerp. In 1970 he was made a member of the Royal Flemish Academy of Arts, Letters, and Sciences.

WORKS: BALLETS: *Indruk aan Zee* (1930); *Provinciestad 1900* (1937); *L'Enlèvement de Proserpine* (1947); *De zakdoekjes* (1947); *Les Amours de torero* (1948); *Dulle Griet* (1949; rev. 1967); *Les Ancêtres* (1949); *Arlequinade* (1950); *Judith* (1951); *De Triomf van de dood* (1963); *Oostendse maskers* (1965); *Ballet Music* (1972). **ORCH.:** *Impression maritime* for Small Orch. (1930); *Divertimento* for Strings (1938); *Hommage à Ravel* (1938); Trumpet Concerto (1940); Oboe Concerto (1941); 2 sinfoniettas (1942, 1969); 2 suites (1945, 1955); 4 concertinos: No. 1 for Clarinet, Bassoon, Piano, and Strings (1949), No. 2 for Viola and Chamber Orch. (1964), No. 3 for Flute and Strings (1965), and No. 4 for Piano and Strings (1971); *Beweging* (Movement; 1968); *Hulde aan Janáček* for Flute, Oboe, and Strings (1973); *Landschappen* for Chamber Orch. (1976); *Nocturne voor beeldhouwer Mark Macken* for Strings (1979). **CHAMBER:** 2 concertos for Wind Quintet (1939, 1955); *Adagio and Finale* for String Trio (1940); Trio for Oboe, Clarinet, and Bassoon (1943); Sextet for Wind Quintet and Piano (1948); *Divertimento* for Oboe, Clarinet, and Bassoon (1957); Concertino for Brass Quintet and 2 Pianos (1965); *Fantaisie* for 4 Clarinets (1967); *2 Dialogues* for Clarinet and Piano (1971); *Nocturne* for Flute, Guitar, and Cello (1980). **PIANO:** 2 suites (1937, 1944); *Beweging* (Movement) for 2 Pianos (1965). **VOCAL:** Songs, including *8 poèmes de Karel van de Woestijne* for High Voice and Piano (1946; orchestrated 1951).

Van de Vate, Nancy, American composer; b. Plainfield, N.J., Dec. 30, 1930. She studied piano at the Eastman School of Music in Rochester, N.Y., Wellesley College (A.B., 1952), and with Bruce Simonds at Yale Univ.; then concentrated on composition at the Univ. of Mississippi (M.M., 1958) and later at Florida State Univ. (D.M., 1968). She taught at Memphis State Univ. (1964–66), the Univ. of Tenn. (1967), Knoxville College (1968–69; 1971–72), Maryville College (1973–74), the Univ. of Hawaii (1975–76), and Hawaii Loa College (1977–80). She was secretary and then president of the Southeast Composers League (1965–73; 1973–75); in 1975 she founded the International League of Women Composers, and served as chairperson until 1982, when she moved to Indonesia; from 1985 she lived in Vienna. Her music—highly charged and dissonantly colored by way of influences as varied as Prokofiev, Shostakovich, Penderecki, Crumb, and Varèse—has won international awards.

WORKS: DRAMATIC: *A Night in the Royal Ontario Museum,* theater piece for Soprano and Tape (1983; Washington, D.C., April 13, 1984); *The Saga of Cocaine Lil,* theater piece for Mezzo-soprano, 4 Singers, and Percussion (1986; Frankfurt am Main, April 20, 1988). **ORCH.:** *Adagio* (1957); *Variations* for Chamber Orch. (1958); Piano Concerto (1968); *Concertpiece* for Cello and Small Orch. (1975–76; rev. 1978); *Dark Nebulae* (1981; Columbus, Ohio, Jan. 29, 1983); *Gema Jawa* for Strings (1984); *Journeys* (1981–84); *Distant Worlds* for Violin and Orch. (1985; Kraków, June 20, 1987); Violin Concerto No. 1 (1985–86; Pittsburgh, Kansas, Nov. 15, 1987); *Chernobyl* (1987); Pura Besakih (1987); *Kraków Concerto* for Percussion and Orch. (1988; Kraków, Nov. 28, 1989); Viola Concerto (1990; Kraków, Sept. 14, 1993); *Adagio and Rondo* for Violin and String Orch. (1994). **CHAMBER:** *Short Suite* for Brass Quintet (1960); Wind Quartet (1964); String Quartet No. 1 (1969); Clarinet Sonata (1970); *3 Sound Pieces* for Brass and Percussion (1973); String Trio (1974); Quintet for Flute, Violin, Clarinet, Cello, and Piano (1975); Trio for Bassoon, Percussion, and Piano (1980); Piano Trio (1983); *Music for MW2* for Flute, Cello, Piano, 4-hands, and Percussion (1985); *Teufelstanz* for 6 Percussionists (1988); *7 Fantasy Pieces* for Violin and Piano (1989). **KEYBOARD: PIANO:** 2 sonatas (1978, 1983); *9 Preludes* (1978); *Contrasts* for 2 Pianos, 6-hands (1984); *12 Pieces on 1 to 12 Notes* (1986). **HARPSICHORD:** Sonata (1982); *Fantasy* (1982). **VOCAL:** *An American Essay* for Chorus, Piano, and Percussion, after Whitman (Knoxville, May 16, 1972); *Letter to a Friend's Loneliness* for Soprano and String Quartet (1976); *Cantata* for Women's Voices for Women's Chorus and 7 Instrumentalists (1979; expanded version as *Voices of Women* for Soprano, Mezzo-soprano, Women's Chorus, and Orch., 1993); *Katyn* for Chorus and Orch., dedicated to the victims of the Katyn Forest massacre (Kraków, Nov. 28, 1989); choruses; songs.

Van de Woestijne, David, Belgian composer; b. Llanidloes, Wales, Feb. 18, 1915; d. Brussels, May 18, 1979. He was the son of the painter Gustav van de Woestijne and the nephew of the Flemish poet Karel van de Woestijne. After studies in harmony and counterpoint with Defauw and Gilson, he took lessons with Espla. Van de Woestijne's music reflects the trends of cosmopolitan modernism.

WORKS: OPERAS: *Le Débat de la folie et de l'amour,* opera-ballet (1959); *De zoemende musikant,* television opera (1967); *Graal 68 ou L'Impromptu de Gand* (Ghent, 1968). **ORCH.:** Double Concerto for Piano, Cello, and Orch. (1935); *Fantasia* for Oboe and Orch. (1936); Piano Concerto (1938); *Ballade* for Piano and Orch. (1940); Concerto for Violin and 12 Solo Instruments (1945); *Sérénades* for Piano, 12 Wind Instruments, Double Bass, and Percussion (1946; Copenhagen, June 2, 1947); Sym. (1958); Sym. in 1 Movement (1965); *Concertino da camera* for Flute, Oboe, and Strings (1967); Concerto for 2 Pianos and Orch. (1972); Concerto for String Quartet, 14 Wind Instruments, and Double Bass (1974); *Hommage à Purcell* for Harpsichord and Strings (1974); *Eénentwintig* for Piano, 19 Winds, and Double Bass (1976). **CHAMBER:** *Divertimento* for Oboe, Clarinet, and Bassoon (1942); Quintet for Flute, Oboe, Violin, Viola, and Cello (1953); Violin Sonata (1956); *Variations* for 7 Instruments (1965); *Sarabande* for 2 Guitars (1965); *Devant une sculpture* for 12 Instruments (1969); String Quartet (1970); *Notturno* for Flute and Piano (1976); *Music* for Tuba or Saxhorn and Piano (1976); *Minuetto capriccioso* for Trumpet and Piano (1976). **PIANO:** *Toccata* (1935); Sonatina (1945); Sonata for 2 Pianos (1955). **VOCAL:** 2 cantatas: La *Belle Cordière* for Soprano and Orch. (1954) and *Les Aéronautes* for Soli, Chorus, Speaking Chorus, and Orch. (1963); *Aswoendag* (Ash Wednesday) for Narrator, Soli, Chorus, and Orch. (1971); songs.

Van Dieren, Bernard. See **Dieren, Bernard van.**

Van Durme, Jef, Belgian composer; b. Kemzeke-Waas, May 7, 1907; d. Brussels, Jan. 28, 1965. He was a pupil of Alpaerts at the Royal Flemish Cons. of Music in Antwerp and of Berg in Vienna (1931).

WORKS: DRAMATIC: OPERAS: *Remous,* after Weterings (1936); *The Death of a Salesman,* after Arthur Miller (1954–55); *King Lear* (1955–57); *Anthony and Cleopatra* (1957–59); *Richard III* (1960–61). **BALLETS:** *De dageraad* (1932–33); *Orestes* (1934–35; orch. suite, 1936–40). **ORCH.:** 2 symphonic poems (*Hamlet,* 1929; *Beatrice,* 1930); *2 Elegies* (1933, 1938); 6 numbered syms.: (1934; 1938–39; 1945–46; 1950–51; 1952; 1953); 1 unnumbered sym.: *Breughel* (1935–42); *Poème héroïque* (1935); *2 Sinfonie da camera* (1937, 1949); *3 Ballads* (*In memoriam Alban Berg,* 1938; 1947–48; 1961); 2 piano concertos (1943, 1946); *Symphonic Prologue* (1944–45); Violin Concerto (1946–47); 4 suites (1947; 1948–60; *Van Gogh,* 1954; 1962); Sinfonietta for Strings (1962). **CHAMBER:** 3 violin sonatas (1928, 1938, 1947); 4 piano trios (1928, 1929, 1942, 1949); Sextet for Piano and Wind Quintet (1930); 5 string quartets (1932–33; 1937; 1945–48; 1948–53; 1953); Piano Quartet (1934); Wind Quintet (1951–52); Cello Sonata (1952). **PIANO:** 2 sonatas (1946; 1952–53). **VOCAL:** *De 14 stonden,* oratorio (1931); songs.

Vaness, Carol (Theresa), talented American soprano; b. San Diego, July 27, 1952. She grew up in Pomona, where she took piano lessons; while attending a parochial girls' school, she sang in its choir, then studied English and piano at Calif. State Polytechnic College before concentrating on music at Calif. State Univ. in Northridge (M.A., 1976), where her vocal instructor was David Scott. After serving an apprenticeship at the San Francisco Opera, she made her N.Y. City Opera debut as Vitellia in *La clemenza di Tito* on Oct. 25, 1979, and continued to appear there until 1983, when she scored a major success as Handel's Alcina. On Jan. 9, 1981, she made her European debut as Vitellia in Bordeaux. She made her first appearance at the Glyndebourne Festival in 1982 as Donna Anna in *Don Giovanni,* a role she subsequently sang to much acclaim throughout Europe. In 1982 she also made her debut at London's Covent Garden as Mimi. On Feb. 14, 1984, she made her Metropolitan Opera debut in N.Y. as Armida in Handel's *Rinaldo,* and continued to sing there in later seasons; also appeared with other U.S. opera houses and toured as a concert artist. In 1988 she made her first appearance at the Salzburg Festival as Vitellia. In 1990 she sang Mozart's Elettra at Milan's La Scala. On Dec. 19, 1991, she made her N.Y. Phil. debut singing excerpts from Strauss's *Daphne* under Leinsdorf's direction. In 1992 she appeared as Rossini's Mathilde in San Francisco. In 1994 she appeared as Desdemona at the Metropolitan Opera. Her other roles include Dalila in Handel's *Samson,* Electra in *Idomeneo,* Fiordiligi, the Countess in *Le nozze di Figaro,* Rosina, Violetta, Gilda, Nedda, and Mimi.

Van Gilse, Jan. See **Gilse, Jan van.**

Van Hoogstraten, Willem. See **Hoogstraten, Willem van.**

Van Katwijk, Paul. See **Katwijk, Paul van.**

Van Lier, Bertus, Dutch composer, conductor, music critic, and teacher; b. Utrecht, Sept. 10, 1906; d. Roden, Feb. 14, 1972. He was a student of Pijper (composition) in Amsterdam and of Scherchen (conducting) in Strasbourg. After a period as a conductor, music critic, and composer in Utrecht, he taught at the Rotterdam Cons. (1945–60) and then was active in the art history dept. at the Univ. of Groningen. He publ. the vols. *Buiten de maastreep* (Beyond the Bar Line; Amsterdam, 1948) and *Rhythme en metrum* (Groningen, 1967). Van Lier's early compositions were modeled on Pijper's "germ-cell" theory, to which he imparted a literary symbolism.

WORKS: DRAMATIC: BALLET: *Katharsis* (1945; concert version, Utrecht, Nov. 29, 1950). **INCIDENTAL MUSIC TO:** Sophocles's *Ajax* (1932) and *Antigone* (1952). **ORCH.:** 3 syms. (1928; 1930–31, rev. 1946; 1938–39); Concertino for Cello and Chamber Orch. (1933); Bassoon Concerto (1950); *Symfonia* for 2 String Orchs., Double Wind Quintet, and Timpani (1954); *Divertimento facile* (1957); *Concertante Music* for Violin, Oboe, and Orch. (1959); *Intrada reale e Sinfonia festiva* (1964); *Variaties en thema* (1967; Bergen, Jan. 17, 1968). **CHAMBER:** String Quartet (1929); Sonata for Solo Violin (1931); *Small Suite* for Violin and Piano (1935); piano pieces. **VOCAL:** *De dijk* (The Dike) for Narrator and Chamber Orch. (1937); *Canticum* for Women's Chorus, 2 Flutes, Piano, 4-hands, and Strings (1939); *O Netherlands, Pay Attention,* cantata for Chorus, Timpani, and Strings (1945); *Het Hooglied* (The Song of Songs) for Soloists, Chorus, and Small Orch. (1949); *Cantate voor Kerstmis* (Christmas Cantata) for Chorus and Orch. (1955); *3 Old Persian Quatrains* for Soprano, Bass Flute, Oboe d'Amore, and Piano (1956); *5 Mei: Zij* (5th of May: They), oratorio (Radio Hilversum, May 5, 1963); choruses.

Van Lier, Jacques, Dutch cellist; b. The Hague, April 24, 1875; d. Worthing, England, Feb. 25, 1951. He studied cello with Hartog in The Hague and with Eberle in Rotterdam. He joined the Berlin Phil. in 1897; from 1899 to 1915 he was a cello instructor at the Klindworth-Scharwenka Cons. in Berlin. He was cellist in the Hollandisches Trio with J. van Veen (violin) and Coenraad Bos (piano); the trio enjoyed a European reputation (1900–07); in 1915 he settled in The Hague; went to England in 1939. He publ. *Violoncellbogentechnik and Moderne Violoncelltechnik der linken und der rechten Hand;* also ed. about 400 classical pieces for cello.

Van Nes, Jard, Dutch mezzo-soprano; b. Zwollerkarspel, June 15, 1948. Following vocal studies in her homeland, she was active mainly as a concert artist, winning critical acclaim as a soloist in Mahler's 2nd Sym. in 1983 with Haitink and the Concertgebouw Orch. in Amsterdam; in subsequent years, became a great favorite with the orch. and toured with it abroad. She made her operatic stage debut also in 1983 as Bertarido in Handel's *Rodelinda* with the Netherlands Opera in Amsterdam, where she returned to sing such successful roles as Handel's Orlando and Wagner's Magdalena; also sang at the Holland Festivals. During the 1987–88 season, she toured North America as soloist with Edo de Waart and the Minnesota Orch. She made her N.Y. recital debut at the Frick Collection during the 1994–95 season. Her concert repertoire ranges from Bach to Berio, but she has won greatest acclaim as an interpreter of Mahler.

Vanni-Marcoux. See **Marcoux, Vanni.**

Van Otterloo, (Jan) Willem. See **Otterloo, (Jan) Willem van.**

Van Raalte, Albert. See **Raalte, Albert van.**

Van Slyck, Nicholas, American pianist, conductor, music educator, and composer; b. Philadelphia, Oct. 25, 1922; d. Boston, July 3, 1983. He studied piano with George Reeves, conducting with Henry Swoboda, and composition with Piston at Harvard Univ., where he obtained his M.A. He was founder and conductor of the Dedham (Mass.) Chorus in 1954 and also led the Quincy (Mass.) Orch. (1962–67); served as director of the South End Music Center of Boston (1950–62) and of the Longy School of Music (1962–76). In 1976 he organized the New School of Music in Cambridge, Mass. His music is pragmatic in its form and destination, while the technical structure is catholic, ranging from triadic to dodecaphonic. He compiled a piano anthology, *Looking Forward* (1981).

WORKS: ORCH.: *Variations* for Piano and Orch. (1947); 2 divertimenti for Chamber Orch. (1947, 1948); Sonatina for Clarinet and Strings (1948); *Concert Music* for Piano and Orch. (1954); Piano Concerto No. 2 (1957); *2 Symphonic Paraphrases* (1960, 1966); *Legend of Sleepy Hollow* for Chamber Orch. (1963). **CHAMBER:** 2 clarinet sonatas (1947, 1958); 2 cello sonatas (1954, 1968); 4 violin sonatas (1956–65); Flute Sonata (1957); Quartet for Clarinet, Violin, Cello, and Piano (1959); Octet for Flute, Clarinet, Horn, Violin, Viola, Cello, Timpani, and Piano (1962). **PIANO:** 6 sonatas (1947–59); 6 sonatinas (1956–68). **VOCAL:** Songs.

Van Tieghem, David, American composer and percussionist; b. Washington, D.C., April 21, 1955. He studied in N.Y. with Justin DiCioccio at the High School of Music and Art, and also attended the Manhattan School of Music (1973–76), where he studied with Paul Price. In 1977 he created a solo percussion theater piece using found objects and sophisticated technology; he then performed variations on this work throughout the U.S. and Europe as *Message Received . . . Proceed Accordingly* or *A Man and His Toys.* He performed with Steve Reich and Musicians (1975–80), and recorded with Laurie Anderson, Robert Ashley, and Brian Eno; also created scores for films, performance works, and dance pieces. In 1989 he wrote the music for and performed the lead role in the theater piece *The Ghost Writer.* His interesting variations on dance and percussion textures have led to his widespread popularity in the N.Y. commercial and avant-garde music communities. Other works include *These Things Happen* (1984), *Safety in Numbers* (1987), and *Strange Cargo* (1989).

Van Vactor, David, American flutist, conductor, teacher, and composer; b. Plymouth, Ind., May 8, 1906; d. Los Angeles, March 24, 1994. He enrolled in the premedical classes at Northwestern Univ. (1924–27); then changed to the music school there, studying flute with Arthur Kitti and theory with Arne Oldberg, Felix Borowski, and Albert Noelte (B.M., 1928; M.M., 1935); also studied flute with Josef Niedermayr and composition with Franz Schmidt at the Vienna Academy of Music (1928–29), and then flute with Marcel Moyse at the Paris Cons. and composition with Dukas at the École Normale de Musique in Paris. Returning to the U.S., he was engaged as a flutist in the Chicago Sym. Orch. (1931–43); also was an assistant conductor of the Chicago Civic Orch. (1933–34) and a teacher of theory at Northwestern Univ., where he was conductor of its sym. and chamber orchs. (1935–39). From 1943 to 1945 he was assistant conductor of the Kansas City Phil., where he also was a flutist; was founder-conductor of the Kansas City Allied Arts Orch. (1945–47); concurrently was head of the theory and composition dept. at the Kansas City Cons. From 1947 to 1972 he was conductor of the Knoxville Sym. Orch.; in 1947 he organized the fine arts dept. at the Univ. of Tenn., where he was a prof. until 1976. In 1941 he toured as a flutist with the North American Woodwind Quintet and in 1945, 1946, and 1964 as a conductor in South America under the auspices of the U.S. State Dept. He held Fulbright and Guggenheim fellowships in 1957–58. In 1976 he was honored with the title of Composer Laureate of the State of Tennessee. He publ. *Every Child May Hear* (1960). As a composer, Van Vactor adhered mainly to basic tonalities, but he enhanced them with ingeniously contrived melodic gargoyles, creating a simulation of atonality. The rhythmic vivacity of his inventive writing created a cheerful, hedonistic atmosphere.

WORKS: ORCH.: *Chaconne* for Strings (Rochester, N.Y., May 17, 1928); *5 Small Pieces for Large Orchestra* (Ravinia Park, Ill., July 5, 1931); *The Masque of the Red Death*, after Edgar Allan Poe (1932); Flute Concerto (Chicago, Feb. 26, 1933); *Passacaglia and Fugue* (Chicago, Jan. 28, 1934); *Concerto grosso* for 3 Flutes, Harp, and Orch. (Chicago, April 4, 1935); 8 syms.: No. 1 (1936–37; N.Y., Jan. 19, 1939, composer conducting), No. 2, *Music for the Marines* (Indianapolis, March 27, 1943; programmed as a suite, not a sym.), No. 3 (1958; Pittsburgh, April 3, 1959; perf. and recorded as No. 2), No. 4, *Walden*, for Chorus and Orch., after Thoreau (1970–71; 1st complete perf., Maryville, Tenn., May 9, 1971; listed as Sym. No. 3 at its premiere), No. 5 (Knoxville, Tenn., March 11, 1976), No. 6 for Orch. or Band (1980; for Orch., Knoxville, Nov. 19, 1981; for Band, Muncie, Ind., April 13, 1983), No. 7 (1983), and No. 8 (1984); *Overture to a Comedy No. 1* (Chicago, June 20, 1937) and *No. 2* (Indianapolis, March 14, 1941); *5 Bagatelles* for Strings (Chicago, Feb. 7, 1938); *Symphonic Suite* (Ravinia Park, Ill., July 21, 1938); Viola Concerto (Ravinia Park, July 13, 1940); *Variazioni Solenne* (1941; 1st perf. as *Gothic Impressions*, Chicago, Feb. 26, 1942); *Pastorale and Dance* for Flute and Strings (1947); Violin Concerto (Knoxville, April 10, 1951); *Fantasia, Chaconne and Allegro* (Louisville, Feb. 20, 1957); Suite for Trumpet and Small Orch. (1962); *Suite on Chilean Folk Tunes* (1963); *Passacaglia, Chorale and Scamper* for Band (1964); *Sinfonia breve* (1964; Santiago, Chile, Sept. 3, 1965); *Sarabande and Variations* for Brass Quintet and Strings (1968; Knoxville, May 4, 1969); *Requiescat* for Strings (Knoxville, Oct. 17, 1970); *Andante and Allegro* for Saxophone and Strings (1972); *Set of 5* for Winds and Percussion (1973); *Nostalgia* for Band (1975); *Prelude and Fugue* for Strings (1975); *Fanfare and Chorale* for Band (1977); *The Elements* for Band (Knoxville, May 22, 1979). **CHAMBER:** Quintet for 2 Violins, Viola, Cello, and Flute (1932); *Suite* for 2 Flutes (1934); *Divertimento* for Wind Quintet (1936); 2 string quartets (1940, 1949); Piano Trio (1942); Flute Sonatina (1949); *Duettino* for Violin and Cello (1952); Wind Quintet (1959); *Children of the Stars*, 6 pieces for Violin and Piano (1960); *5 Etudes* for Trumpet (1963); Octet for Brass (1963); *Economy Band No. 1* for Trumpet, Trombone, and Percussion (1966) and *No. 2* for Horn, Tuba, and Percussion (1969); *Music* for Woodwinds (1966–67); *4 Etudes* for Wind Instruments and Percussion (1968); Tuba Quartet (1971); Suite for 12 Solo Trombones (1972); *5 Songs* for Flute and Guitar (1974). **VOCAL:** *Credo* for Chorus and Orch (1941); Cantata for 3 Treble Voices and Orch. (1947); *The New Light*, Christmas cantata (1954); *Christmas Songs for Young People* for Chorus and Orch. (1961); *A Song of Mankind*, 1st part of a 7-part cantata (Indianapolis, Sept. 26, 1971); *Processional "Veni Immanuel"* for Chorus and Orch. (1974); *Brethren We Have Met to Worship* for Chorus and Orch. (1975); *Episodes—Jesus Christ* for Chorus and Orch. (Knoxville, May 2, 1977); *Processional* for Chorus, Wind Instruments, and Percussion (Knoxville, Dec. 1, 1979).

Van Vechten, Carl, American novelist and writer on music; b. Cedar Rapids, Iowa, June 17, 1880; d. N.Y., Dec. 21, 1964. He graduated from the Univ. of Chicago (1903). He was music critic of the *N.Y. Times* (1906–07; 1910–13); was its Paris correspondent in 1908–09. From 1931 he occupied himself with photography, and took a great number of pictures of musicians; his collection of photographs is at Fiske Univ. in Nashville. He publ. *5 Old English Ditties* (1904). His books on music are *Music after the Great War* (1915); *Music and Bad Manners* (1916); *Interpreters and Interpretations* (1917); *The Music of Spain* (1918); *Red: Papers on Musical Subjects* (1925).

BIBL.: E. Lueders, *C. V.V. and the Twenties* (Albuquerque, 1955).

Van Wyk, Arnold. See **Wyk, Arnold(us Christian Vlok) van.**

Varady, Julia, Hungarian-born German soprano; b. Nagyvárad, Sept. 1, 1941. She received training at the Cluj Cons. and the Bucharest Cons. In 1962 she made her operatic debut as Fiordiligi at the Cluj Opera, where she sang until 1970. From 1970 to 1972 she was a member of the Frankfurt am Main Opera. In 1972 she joined the Bavarian State Opera in Munich. In 1974 she made her British debut as Gluck's Alcestis with Glasgow's Scottis Opera during its visits to the Edinburgh Festival. She made her first appearance at the Salzburg Festival in 1976 as Mozart's Elettra. On March 10, 1978, she made her Metropolitan Opera debut in N.Y. as Mozart's Donna Elvira. On July 9, 1978, she created the role of Cordelia in Reimann's *Lear* in Munich. While continuing to sing in Munich, she also appeared as a guest artist in Hamburg, Vienna, Berlin, Paris, and other operatic centers. Among her other roles are Countess Almaviva, Elisabeth de Valois, Tatiana, Desdemona, and Lady Macbeth. Her concert repertoire embraces works from Mozart to Reimann. In 1974 she married **Dietrich Fischer-Dieskau**.

Vardi, Emanuel, outstanding Israeli-American violist; b. Jerusalem, April 21, 1917. He began to study the viola in his youth; also studied painting at the Florence Academy of Fine Arts. In 1940 he went to the U.S., and soon established himself as an outstanding virtuoso in the limited field of viola literature. He arranged works by Bach, Frescobaldi, Tartini, Paganini, and Chopin for viola; also commissioned works for the viola from Michael Colgrass, Alan Hovhaness, Alan Shulman, and others. For variety's sake, he made an incursion into the conducting arena; was music director of the South Dakota Sym. Orch. (1978–82). In his leisure time, he painted. In 1951 he won the International Prize of Rapallo, and had one-man exhibits in N.Y., South Dakota, and Italy.

Varèse, Edgard (Victor Achille Charles), remarkable French-born American composer, who introduced a totally original principle of organizing the materials and forms of sound, profoundly influencing the direction of new music; b. Paris, Dec. 22, 1883; d. N.Y., Nov. 6, 1965. The original spelling of his first Christian name was Edgard, but most of his works were first publ. under the name **Edgar**; about 1940 he chose to return to the legal spelling. He spent his early childhood in Paris and in Burgundy, and began to compose early in life. In 1892 his parents went to Turin; his paternal grandfather was Italian; his other grandparents were French. He took private lessons in composition with Giovanni Bolzoni, who taught him gratis. Varèse gained some performing experience by playing percussion in the school orch. He stayed there until 1903; then went to Paris. In 1904 he entered the Schola Cantorum, where he studied composition, counterpoint, and fugue with Roussel, preclassical music with Bordes, and conducting with d'Indy; then entered the composition class of Widor at the Cons. in 1905. In 1907 he received the "bourse artistique" offered by the City of Paris; at that time, he founded and conducted the chorus of the Université Populaire and organized concerts at the Château du Peuple. He became associated with musicians and artists of the avant-garde; also met Debussy, who showed interest in his career. In 1907 he married a young actress, Suzanne Bing; they had a daughter. Together they went to Berlin, at that time the center of new music that offered opportunities to Varèse. The marriage was not successful, and they separated in 1913. Romain Rolland gave Varèse a letter of recommendation for Richard Strauss, who in turn showed interest in Varèse's music. He was also instrumental in arranging a performance of Varèse's symphonic poem *Bourgogne*, which was performed in Berlin on Dec. 15, 1910. But the greatest experience for Varèse in Berlin was his meeting and friendship with Busoni. Varèse greatly admired Busoni's book on new music aesthetics, and was profoundly influenced by Busoni's views. He composed industriously, mostly for orch.; the most ambitious of these works was a symphonic poem, *Gargantua*, but it was never completed. Other works were *Souvenirs, Prélude à la fin d'un jour, Cycles du Nord*, and an incomplete opera, *Oedipus und die Sphinx*, to a text by Hofmannsthal. All these works, in manuscript, were lost under somewhat mysterious circumstances, and Varèse himself destroyed the score of *Bourgogne* later in life. A hostile reception that he encountered from Berlin critics for *Bourgogne* upset Varèse, who expressed his unhappiness in a letter to Debussy. However, Debussy responded with a friendly letter of encouragement, advising Varèse not to pay too much attention to critics. As early as 1913, Varèse began an earnest quest for new musical resources; upon his return to Paris, he worked on related problems with the Italian musical futurist Luigi Russolo, although he disapproved of the attempt to find a way to new music through the medium of instrumental noises. He was briefly called to the French army at the outbreak of the First World War, but was discharged because of a chronic lung ailment. In 1915 he went to N.Y. There he met the young American writer Louise Norton, with whom he set up household; in 1921, when she obtained her own divorce from a previous marriage, they were married. As in Paris and Berlin, Varèse had chronic financial difficulties in America; the royalties from his few publ. works were minimal; in order to supplement his earnings he accepted a job as a piano salesman, which was repulsive to him. He also appeared in a minor role in a John Barrymore silent film in 1918. Some welcome aid came from the wealthy artist Gertrude Vanderbilt, who sent him monthly allowances for a certain length of time. Varèse also had an opportunity to appear as a conductor. As the U.S. neared the entrance into war against Germany, there was a demand for French conductors to replace the German music directors who had held the monopoly on American orchs. On April 1, 1917, Varèse conducted in N.Y. the *Requiem Mass* of Berlioz. On March 17, 1918, he conducted a concert of the Cincinnati Sym. Orch. in a program of French and Russian music; he also included an excerpt from *Lohengrin*, thus defying the general ban on German music. However, he apparently lacked that indefinable quality that makes a conductor, and he was forced to cancel further concerts with the Cincinnati Sym. Orch. Eager to promote the cause of modern music, he organized a sym. orch. in N.Y. with the specific purpose of giving performances of new and unusual music; it presented its first concert on April 11, 1919. In 1922 he organized with Carlos Salzedo the International Composers' Guild, which gave its inaugural concert in N.Y. on Dec. 17, 1922. In 1926 he founded, in association with a few progressive musicians, the Pan American Soc., dedicated to the promotion of music of the Americas. He intensified his study of the nature of sound, working with the acoustician Harvey Fletcher (1926–36), and with the Russian electrical engineer Leon Theremin, then resident in the U.S. These studies led him to the formulation of the concept of "organized sound," in which the sonorous elements in themselves determined the progress of composition; this process eliminated conventional thematic development; yet the firm cohesion of musical ideas made Varese's music all the more solid, while the distinction between consonances and dissonances became no longer of basic validity. The resulting product was unique in modern music; characteristically, Varèse attached to his works titles from the field of mathematics or physics, such as *Intégrales, Hyperprism* (a projection of a prism into the 4th dimension), *Ionisation, Density 21.5* (the specific weight of platinum), etc., while the score of his large orch. work *Arcana* derived its inspiration from the cosmology of Paracelsus. An important development was Varèse's application of electronic music in his *Deserts* and, much more extensively, in his *Poème électronique*, commissioned for the Brussels World Exposition in 1958. He wrote relatively few works in small forms, and none for piano solo. The unfamiliarity of Varèse's idiom and the tremendous difficulty of his orch. works militated against frequent performances. Among conductors, only Leopold Stokowski was bold enough to put Varèse's formidable scores *Amériques* and *Arcana* on his programs with the Philadelphia Orch.; they evoked yelps of derision and outbursts of righteous indignation from the public and the press. Ironically, it was left to a mere beginner, Nicolas Slonimsky, to be the first to perform and record Varèse's unique masterpiece, *Ionisation*. An extraordinary reversal of attitudes toward Varèse's music, owing perhaps to the general advance of musical intelligence and the emergence of young music critics, took place within Varèse's lifetime, resulting in a spectacular increase of interest in his works and the number of their performances; also, musicians themselves learned to overcome the rhythmic difficulties presented in Varèse's scores. Thus Varèse lived to witness this long-delayed recognition of his music as a major stimulus of modern art; his name joined those of Stravinsky, Ives, Schoenberg, and Webern among the great masters of 20th-century music. Recognition came also from an unexpected field when scientists working on the atom bomb at Oak Ridge in 1940 played Slonimsky's recording of *Ionisation* for relaxation and stimulation in their work. In 1955 he was elected to membership in the National Inst. of Arts and Letters and in 1962 in the Royal Swedish Academy. He became a naturalized American citizen in 1926. Like Schoenberg, Varèse refused to regard himself as a revolutionary in music; indeed, he professed great admiration for his remote predecessors, particularly those of the Notre Dame school, representing the flowering of the Ars Antiqua. On the centennial of his birth in 1983, festivals of his music were staged in Strasbourg, Paris, Rome, Washington, D.C., N.Y., and Los Angeles. In 1981, Frank Zappa, the leader of the modern school of rock music and a sincere admirer of Varèse's music, staged in N.Y. at his own expense a concert of Varèse's works; he presented a similar concert in San Francisco in 1982.

WORKS: *Un Grand Sommeil noir* for Voice and Piano (1906); *Amériques* for Orch. (1918–21; Philadelphia, April 9, 1926, Stokowski conducting; rev. 1927; Paris, May 30, 1929, Poulet conducting); *Dedications*, later renamed *Offrandes*, for Soprano and Chamber Orch. (1921; N.Y., April 23, 1922, Koshetz soloist, Salzedo conducting); *Hyperprism* for 9 Wind Instruments and 18 Percussion Devices (N.Y., March 4, 1923, composer conducting); *Octandre* for Flute, Oboe, Clarinet, Bassoon, Horn, Trombone, and Double Bass (1923; N.Y., Jan. 13, 1924, Schmitz conducting); *Intégrales* for 11 Instruments and 4 Percussion (N.Y., March 1, 1925, Stokowski conducting); *Arcana* for Orch. (1925–27; Philadelphia, April 8, 1927, Stokowski conducting; rev. 1960); *Ionisation* for 13 Percussionists (using instruments of indefinite pitch), Piano, and 2 Sirens (1929–31; N.Y., March 6, 1933, Slonimsky conducting); *Ecuatorial* for Bass, 4 Trumpets, 4 Trombones, Piano, Organ, Percussion, and Thereminovox (1932–34; N.Y., April 15, 1934, Baromeo soloist, Slonimsky conducting; also for Men's Chorus, 2 Ondes Martenot, and Orch.); *Density 21.5* for Flute (N.Y., Feb. 16, 1936; Barrère, soloist, on his platinum flute of specific gravity 21.5); *Étude pour Espace* for Chorus, 2 Pianos, and Percussion (N.Y., Feb. 23, 1947, composer conducting); *Dance for Burgess* for Chamber Ensemble (1949); *Déserts* for Wind Instruments, Percussion, and 3 Interpolations of Electronic Sound (1950–54; Paris, Dec. 2, 1954, Scherchen conducting); *La Procession de Vergès*, tape for the film *Around and About Joan Mirò* (1955); *Poème électronique* for More Than 400 Spatially Distributed Loudspeakers (1957–58; Brussels Exposition, May 2, 1958); *Nocturnal* for Soprano, Bass Chorus, and Chamber Orch. (N.Y., May 1, 1961, R. Craft conducting; unfinished; completed from notes and sketches by Chou Wen-Chung).

WRITINGS: L. Hirbour, ed., *Écrits* (Paris, 1983).

BIBL.: H. Cowell, "The Music of E. V.," *Modern Music*, V/2 (1928; reprint in H. Cowell, ed., *American Composers on American Music*, Stanford, Calif., 1933); J. Klaren, *E. V., Pioneer of New Music in America* (Boston, 1928); M. Wilkinson, "An Introduction to the Music of E. V.," *The Score*, No. 19 (1957); G. Schuller, "Conversation with V.," *Perspectives of New Music*, III/2 (1965); Chou Wen-Chung, "V: A Sketch of the Man and His Music," *Musical Quarterly*, LII (1966); F. Ouellette, *E. V.* (Paris, 1966; rev. and aug. ed., 1989; Eng. tr., 1968); L. Varèse, *V.: A Looking Glass Diary* (N.Y., 1972); O. Vivier, *V.* (Paris, 1973); J.-J. Nattiez, *Essai d'analyse distributionelle de 'Densité 21.5' de V.* (Montreal, 1975; Eng. tr. by A. Barry in *Music Analysis*, I, 1982); G. Wehmeyer, *E. V.* (Regensburg, 1977); S. Van Solkema, ed., *The New Worlds of E. V.: Symposium* (Brooklyn, 1979); A. Carpentier, *V. vivant* (Paris, 1982); M. Bredel, *E. V.* (Paris, 1984); J. Bernard, *The Music of E. V.* (New Haven, Conn., 1987); P. Griffiths, "The Mystery of E. V.," *Musical Times* (Sept. 1987); H. de la Motte-Haber and K. Angermann, eds., *E. V., 1883–1965: Dokumente zu leben und Werk* (Frankfurt am Main, 1990); H. de la Motte-Haber, ed., *Die Befreiung des Klangs: Symposium E. V. Hamburg 1991* (Hofheim, 1992).

Varga, Gilbert (Anthony), English conductor of Hungarian descent, son of **Tibor Varga**; b. London, Jan. 17, 1952. He received training from Ferrara, Celibidache, and Bruck. In 1974 he commenced his conducting career; after serving as music director of the Hofer Sym. Orch. (1980–85) and the Philharmonia Hungarica in Marl Kreis Recklinghausen (1985–90), he was principal guest conductor of the Stuttgart Chamber Orch. (from 1992).

Varga, Ovidiu, Romanian composer and teacher; b. Pascani, Oct. 5, 1913; d. Bucharest, July 15, 1993. He received training in violin and composition in Iaşi, and later taught at the Bucharest Cons. He composed much vocal music, including *Scînteia Eliberării*, oratorio for Soloists, Chorus, and Orch. (1954), the *Cantata bucuriei* for Soloists, Chorus, and Orch. (Bucharest, July 1960), mass songs, and solo songs. Among his other works were a String Quartet, *Primăvara vieţii* (1953), and a Concerto for Strings and Percussion (1957).

Varga, Tibor, respected Hungarian-born English violinist, conductor, and pedagogue, father of **Gilbert (Anthony) Varga**; b. Györ, July 4, 1921. He was a pupil of Hubay at the Budapest Academy of Music and of Flesch at the Berlin Hochschule für Musik; he also studied philosophy at the Univ. of Budapest. He made his debut at 10 and, following World War II, pursued an international career as a violin virtuoso. In 1949 he became a prof. of violin at the North West German Music Academy in Detmold, where he founded the Tibor Varga Chamber Orch. in 1954. In 1955 he settled in Switzerland and in 1964 he organized the Tibor Varga Festival in Sion, where he oversaw his own music academy and international violin competition; he also taught master classes at the Salzburg Mozarteum. He continued to conduct his chamber orch. until 1988, and then was music director of l'Orchestre des Pays de Savoie à Annecy from 1989. While he was admired for his performances of the standard violin repertoire, he won special distinction for his championship of such modern masters as Nielsen, Schoenberg, Stravinsky, Berg, Bartók, and Blacher.

Varkonyi, Béla, Hungarian-American composer and teacher; b. Budapest, July 5, 1878; d. N.Y., Jan. 25, 1947. He studied with Koessler and Thomán at the Royal Academy of Music in Budapest (Ph.D. in law and M.M. in music, 1902). After winning the Robert Volkmann Competition twice and receiving the Hungarian national scholarship, he studied in London and Paris. He returned in 1907 to Budapest, where he taught at the Royal Academy of Music. At the outbreak of World War I in 1914, he joined the Hungarian army; was captured by the Russians, and spent 3 years as a prisoner of war; he continued to compose, but his MSS were destroyed when the Danish Consulate was burned. After the war, he emigrated to the U.S. (1923); taught at Breneau College, Georgia (until 1928), and Centenary College in Tennessee (1928–30); then settled in N.Y., where he was active as a teacher and composer. Varkonyi is reported to have had a fantastic memory; he was able to recount more than 40 years of his life by day and date; S. Rath devotes a chapter to it in his book *Hungarian Curiosities* (1955).

WORKS: MELODRAMAS: *Captive Woman* (1911); *Spring Night* (1912). **ORCH.:** Piano Concerto (1902); Overture (1902); *Dobozy*, symphonic poem (1903); *Symphonic Ballad* (1907); Sym. (1913); *Fantastic Scenes* (n.d.). **CHAMBER:** Piano Trio (N.Y., Nov. 24, 1918); Scherzo for String Quartet (N.Y., Nov. 24, 1918); many piano pieces. **VOCAL:** *Hungarian Chorus Rhapsody*; about 100 songs.

Várnai, Péter P(ál), Hungarian writer on music; b. Budapest, July 10, 1922; d. there, Jan. 31, 1992. He studied composition with Szervánszky and conducting with Ferencsik at the Budapest Cons. He worked for the Hungarian Radio (1945–50) and was active as a conductor (1951–54). He then devoted himself to music research and criticism; was an ed. of Editio Musica in Budapest (1956–82). In addition to his writings on contemporary Hungarian music and musicians, he also wrote authoritatively on Verdi.

WRITINGS (all publ. in Budapest): *Goldmark Károly* (1956); *A lengyel zene története* (History of Polish Music; 1959); *Heinrich Schütz* (1959); *Tardos Béla* (1966); *Maros Rudolf* (1967); *Székely Mihály* (1967); *Rösler Endre* (1969); *Oratóriumok könyve* (Book of Oratorios; 1972); *Operalexikon* (1975); *Verdi Magyarországon* (Verdi in Hungary; 1975); *Verdi-operakalauz* (Verdi's Operas; 1978); *Beszélgetések Ligeti György-gyel* (In Conversation with György Ligeti; 1979; Eng. tr., 1983).

Varnay, Astrid (Ibolyka Maria), noted Swedish-born American soprano and mezzo-soprano; b. Stockholm (of Austro-Hungarian parents), April 25, 1918. Her parents were professional singers; she was taken to the U.S. in 1920, and began vocal studies with her mother; then studied with Paul Althouse, and with the conductor Hermann Weigert (1890–1955), whom she married in 1944. She made her debut as Sieglinde at the Metropolitan Opera in N.Y. (Dec. 6, 1941), substituting for Lotte Lehmann without rehearsal; appeared at the Metropolitan until 1956, and again from 1974 to 1976; her last performance there was in 1979. From 1962 she sang mezzo-soprano roles, appearing as Strauss's Herodias and Clytemnestra and as Begbick in Weill's *Aufstieg und Fall der Stadt Mahagonny*; however, she was best known for such Wagnerian roles as Isolde, Kundry, Senta, and Brünnhilde.

BIBL.: B. Wessling, *A. V.* (Bremen, 1965).

Varro, Marie-Aimée, French pianist; b. Brunoy, Feb. 18, 1915; d. Neuchâtel, Sept. 14, 1971. She studied piano at the Paris Cons., obtaining the premier prix; subsequently worked with Robert Casadesus and Cortot; she completed her advanced studies with Sauer in Vienna, who gave her indications for authentic interpretation of Liszt's piano works, which he had received from Liszt himself. She specialized in the works of the great Romantic composers, particularly Schumann, Chopin, Liszt, and Brahms. She gave recitals in Europe and America; also appeared as a soloist with major orchs.

Varviso, Silvio, Swiss conductor; b. Zürich, Feb. 26, 1924. He studied piano at the Zürich Cons. and conducting in Vienna with Clemens Krauss. In 1944 he made his debut at St. Gallen, conducting *Die Zauberflöte*, and remained at the theater there until 1950; then conducted at the Basel Stadttheater, where he later served as its music director (1956–62); also made guest appearances in Berlin and Paris in 1958, and then made his U.S. debut with the San Francisco Opera in 1959. On Nov. 26, 1961, he made his Metropolitan Opera debut in N.Y., conducting *Lucia di Lammermoor*; remained on its roster until 1966, and returned there in 1968–69 and in 1982–83. In 1962 he made his British debut at the Glyndebourne Festival; later that year he made his first appearance at London's Covent Garden; in 1969 he made his Bayreuth Festival debut with *Der fliegende Holländer*. From 1965 to 1972 he was chief conductor of the Royal Theater in Stockholm; after serving as Generalmusikdirektor at the Württemberg State Theater in Stuttgart (1972–80), he was chief conductor of the Paris Opéra (1980–86).

Varvoglis, Mario, Greek composer and teacher; b. Brussels, Dec. 22, 1885; d. Athens, July 30, 1967. He studied in Paris at the Cons. with Leroux and G. Caussade and at the Schola Cantorum with d'Indy. Returning to Athens, he taught at the Cons. (1920–24) and at the Hellenic Cons. (from 1924), where he was co-director in 1947; served as president of the League of Greek Composers (from 1957). His output was strongly influenced by d'Indy, Fauré, and Ravel.

WORKS: DRAMATIC: OPERAS: *Aya Varvara* (1912; only fragments extant); *Tó apóyeme tís agápis* (The Afternoon of Love; 1935; Athens, June 10, 1944). Also incidental music to 6 Greek dramas. **ORCH.:** *Tó panigyri*, tone poem (1906–09); *Suite pastorale* for Strings (1912; also for String Quartet); *Sainte-Barbara*, symphonic prelude (1912); *Caprice grec* for Cello and Orch. (1914; also for Cello and Piano); Sym. (c.1919; destroyed); *Dáphnes ke kyparíssia* (Laurels and Cypresses), symphonic study (1950). **CHAMBER:** *Hommage à César Franck* for Violin and Piano (1922); *Meditation of Areti* for String Quartet (1929); *Stochasmós* (Meditation) for String Quartet (1932; rev. for String Orch., 1936); *Laikó poíma* (Folk Poem) for Piano Trio (1943); piano pieces, including 14 for children. **VOCAL:** Choruses; songs.

Vásáry, Tamás, noted Hungarian-born Swiss pianist and conductor; b. Debrecen, Aug. 11, 1933. He studied piano at the Franz Liszt Academy of Music in Budapest. In 1947 he won 1st prize in the Liszt Competition, and later garnered several more prizes. He made his London debut in 1961, and played in N.Y. in 1962. In 1971 he became a naturalized Swiss citizen. He made his conducting debut at the Merton Festival in 1971, and subsequently appeared as a guest conductor throughout Europe and the U.S. With Iván Fischer, he served as co-conductor of the Northern Sinfonia in Newcastle upon Tyne (1979–82). From 1989 to 1991 he was principal conductor of the Bournemouth Sinfonietta. In 1993 he became music director of the Budapest Sym. Orch.

Vasconcelos, Jorge Croner de, Portuguese composer and teacher; b. Lisbon, April 11, 1910; d. there, Dec. 9, 1974. He studied in Lisbon with Aroldo Silva (piano; 1927–31) and at the Cons. with Freitas Branco (composition; 1927–34); then completed his training with Dukas, Boulanger, and Roger-Ducasse in Paris (1934–37). From 1939 he taught composition at the Lisbon Cons.

WORKS: *Melodias sobre antigos textos portugueses* for Voice, Flute, and String Quartet (1937); Piano Quartet (1938); 2 ballets: *A Faina do mar* (1940) and *Coimbra* (1959); *Partita* for Piano (1961); *A vela vermelha* for Orch. (1962); *Vilancico para a Festa de Santa Cecilia* for Chorus and Orch. (1967).

BIBL.: G. Miranda, *J.C.d. V., 1910–1974: Vida e obra musical* (Lisbon, 1992).

Vasilenko, Sergei (Nikiforovich), noted Russian conductor, pedagogue, and composer; b. Moscow, March 30, 1872; d. there, March 11, 1956. He studied jurisprudence at the Univ. of Moscow, graduating in 1895; took private music lessons with Gretchaninoff and G. Conus; in 1895, entered the Moscow Cons. in the classes of Taneyev, Ippolitov-Ivanov, and Safonov, graduating in 1901. He also studied ancient Russian chants under the direction of Smolensky. In 1906 he joined the faculty of the Moscow Cons.; subsequently was prof. there (1907–41; 1943–56). From 1907 to 1917 he conducted in Moscow a series of popular sym. concerts in programs of music arranged in a historical sequence. In 1938 he went to Tashkent to help native musicians develop a national school of composition. His music is inspired primarily by the pattern of Russian folk song, but he was also attracted by exotic subjects, particularly those of the East; in his harmonic settings, there is a distinct influence of French Impressionism.

WORKS: DRAMATIC: OPERAS: *Skazaniye o grade velikom Kitezhe i tikhom ozere Svetoyare* (The Legend of the Great City of Kitezh and the Calm Lake Svetoyar), dramatic cantata (Moscow, March 1, 1902; operatic version, Moscow, March 3, 1903); *Sin solntsa* (Son of the Sun; Moscow, May 23, 1929); *Khristofor Kolumb* (Christopher Columbus; 1933); *Buran* (The Snowstorm; 1938; Tashkent, June 12, 1939; in collaboration with M. Ashrafi); *Suvorov* (1941; Moscow, Feb. 23, 1942). **BALLETS:** *Noyya*, ballet-pantomime (1923); *Iosif prekrasniy* (Joseph the Handsome; Moscow, March 3, 1925); *V solnechnikh luchakh* (In the Rays of the Sun; 1926); *Lola* (1926; rev. version, Moscow, June 25, 1943); *Treugolka* (The Tricorn; 1935); *Tsigani* (The Gypsies; 1936; Leningrad, Nov. 18, 1937); *Akbilyak* (1942; Tashkent, Nov. 7, 1943); *Mirandolina* (1946; Moscow, Jan. 16, 1949). **ORCH.:** *3 Combats*, symphonic poem (1900); *Poème épique*, symphonic poem (Moscow, March 14, 1903); 5 syms.: No. 1 (1904; Moscow, Feb. 17, 1907), No. 2 (Moscow, Jan. 7, 1913), No. 3, *Italian*, for Wind Instruments and Russian Folk Instruments (1925), No. 4, *Arctic* (Moscow, April 5, 1933), and No. 5 (1938); *Sad smerti* (The Garden of Death; Moscow, May 4, 1908); *Hircus nocturnus* (Moscow, Feb. 3, 1909); Violin Concerto (1910–13); *Au Soleil*, suite (Moscow, 1911); *Valse fantastique* (Moscow, Jan. 16, 1915); *Zodiac*, suite on old French melodies (1914); *Chinese Suite* (Leningrad, Oct. 30, 1927); *Hindu Suite* (Moscow, 1927); *Turkmenian Suite* (Moscow, 1931); Balalaika Concerto (1931); *Soviet East* (1932); *Uzbek Suite* (1942); Cello Concerto (1944); *Ukraine* (1945); Trumpet Concerto (1945). **CHAMBER:** 3 string quartets; Piano Trio; Viola Sonata; *Serenade* for Cello and Piano; Oriental Dance for Clarinet and Piano (1923); *Japanese Suite* for Wind Instruments, Xylophone, and Piano (1938); *Chinese Sketches* for Woodwind Instruments (1938); Woodwind Quartet on American themes (1938); Suite for Balalaika and Accordion (1945). **VOCAL:** *Vir* for Bass and Orch. (Kislovodsk, July 6, 1896); *A Maiden Sang in a Church Choir*, song (1908); *Incantation* for Voice and Orch. (1910); *Exotic Suite* for Tenor and 12 Instruments (1916); *10 Russian Folk Songs* for Voice, Oboe, Balalaika, Accordion, and Piano (1929).

WRITINGS: *Stranitsi vospominaniy* (Pages of Reminiscences; Moscow and Leningrad, 1948); *Instrumentovka dlya simfonicheskovo orkestra* (Vol. I, Moscow, 1952; ed. with a supplement by Y. Fortunatov, Moscow, 1959); T. Livanova, ed., *Vospominaniya* (Memoirs; Moscow, 1979).

BIBL.: V. Belaiev, *S.N. V.* (Moscow, 1927); G. Polianovsky, *S.N. V.* (Moscow, 1947); idem, *S.N. V.: Zhizn i tvorchestvo* (S.N.V.: Life and Work; Moscow, 1964).

Vasiliev-Buglay, Dmitri, Russian composer; b. Moscow, Aug. 9, 1888; d. there, Oct. 15, 1956. He studied with Kastalsky at the Moscow Synod Seminary (1898–1906). After the Revolution, he became an active member of RAPM (Russian Assn. of Proletarian Musicians), postulating the necessity of creating music for the needs of the class-conscious, socialist proletariat, and also joined the Union of Revolutionary Composers and Musical Workers. He was one of the pioneers of mass Soviet songs; wrote patriotic ballads and many choruses to revolutionary texts. He also composed the opera *Fatherland's Call*, to promote self-discipline on collective farms.

BIBL.: D. Lokshin, *D. V.-B.* (Moscow, 1958).

Vatielli, Francesco, Italian musicologist and composer; b. Pesaro, Dec. 31, 1876; d. Portogruaro, Dec. 12, 1946. He studied in Bologna at the Univ. (arts degree, 1895) and with Mascagni and Antonio Cicognani at the Liceo Musicale. From 1905 to 1906 he was an instructor of music history at the Liceo Musicale in Bologna; then was director of its library until 1945; he also was prof. of music history at the Univ. (from 1908). He was co-founder of the Associazione dei Musicologisti Italiani; also ed. various music journals. He wrote incidental music for several plays; also piano pieces and songs. Among his important writings were *La civilta musicale di moda: ragionamenti di Petronio Isaurico* (Turin, 1913; 2nd ed., 1924, as *Ragionamenti e fantasie musicali di Petronio Isaurico*), *Arte e vita musicale a Bologna* (Bologna, 1927), and *Il Principe di Venosa e Leonora d'Este* (Milan, 1941).; also ed. *Antiche cantate d'amore* (Bologna, 1907–20); *A. Banchieri: Musiche corali*, CMI, I–III (1919); *Antiche cantate bolognesi* (Bologna, 1919); *F. Azzaiolo: Villote del fiore* (Bologna, 1921), and *Madrigali di Carlo Gesualdo, principe de Venosa*, PIISM, Monumenta, II (1942).

Vaughan, Denis (Edward), Australian conductor and music scholar; b. Melbourne, June 6, 1926. He studied at Wesley College, Melbourne (1939–42), and at the Univ. of Melbourne (Mus.B., 1947), then went to London, where he studied organ with G. Thalben-Ball and double bass with E. Cruft at the Royal College of Music (1947–50); also studied organ with A. Marchal in Paris. He played double bass in the Royal Phil. in London (1950–54); in 1953 he made his debut as a conductor in London; served as Beecham's assistant (1954–57), and was founder-conductor of the Beecham Choral Soc.; also toured in Europe as an organist, harpsichordist, and clavichordist. He made a special study of the autograph scores versus the printed eds. of the operas of Verdi and Puccini, discovering myriad discrepancies in the latter; proceeded to agitate for published corrected eds. of these works. From 1981 to 1984 he was music director of the State Opera of South Australia.

Vaughan, Elizabeth, Welsh soprano, later mezzo-soprano; b. Llanfyellin, Montgomeryshire, March 12, 1937. She studied with Olive Groves at the Royal Academy of Music in London (1955–58), where she took the gold and silver medals, and also won the Kathleen Ferrier Scholarship (1959); she also studied privately with Eva Turner. In 1960 she sang Abigail in *Nabucco* with the Welsh National Opera in Cardiff. In 1962 she made her debut at London's Covent Garden as Gilda. She made her Metropolitan Opera debut in N.Y. as Donna Elvira on Sept. 23, 1972. She also appeared with other English opera companies and was a guest artist in Vienna, Berlin, Paris, Hamburg, Munich, Prague, and other European opera centers. In 1984 she toured the U.S. with the English National Opera of London. After singing such roles as Violetta, Li, Mimi, Tatiana, Tosca, and Cio-Cio-San, she turned to mezzo-soprano roles. In 1990 she appeared as Herodias at Glasgow's Scottish Opera, returning there as Kabanicha in 1993. She also was a prof. of voice at the Guildhall School of Music and Drama in London.

Vaughan Thomas, David, Welsh organist, teacher, and composer; b. Ystelyfera, March 15, 1873; d. Johannesburg, Sept. 15, 1934. He won the solo harmonium competition at the National Eisteddfod in 1883. After training from Joseph Parry in Swansea, he attended Llandovery College and then took courses in music and mathematics at Exeter College, Oxford (B.A., 1895; B.Mus., 1907; D.Mus., 1909). He pursued a career as a church organist, recitalist, and teacher. He was an accomplished composer of choral music and songs. Among his other works were orch. pieces, chamber music, and piano pieces.

BIBL.: E. Cleaver, *D. V.T.* (Llandybie, 1964).

Vaughan Williams, Ralph, great English composer who created the gloriously self-consistent English style of composition, deeply rooted in native folk songs, yet unmistakably participant of modern ways in harmony, counterpoint, and instrumentation; b. Down Ampney, Gloucestershire, Oct. 12, 1872; d. London, Aug. 26, 1958. His father, a clergyman, died when Vaughan Williams was a child; the family then moved to the residence of his maternal grandfather at Leith Hill Place, Surrey. There he began to study piano and violin; in 1887 he entered Charterhouse School in London and played violin and viola in the school orch. From 1890 to 1892 he studied harmony with F.E. Gladstone, theory of composition with Parry, and organ with Parratt at the Royal College of Music in London; then enrolled at Trinity College, Cambridge, where he took courses in composition with Charles Wood and in organ with Alan Gray, obtaining his Mus.B. in 1894 and his B.A. in 1895; he subsequently returned to the Royal College of Music, studying with Stanford. In 1897 he went to Berlin for further instruction with Max Bruch; in 1901 he took his Mus.D. at Cambridge. Dissatisfied with his academic studies, he decided, in 1908, to seek advice in Paris from Ravel in order to acquire the technique of modern orchestration that emphasized color. In the meantime, he became active as a collector of English folk songs; in 1904 he joined the Folk Song Soc.; in 1905 he became conductor of the Leith Hill Festival in Dorking, a position that he held, off and on, until his old age. In 1906 he composed his *3 Norfolk Rhapsodies*, which reveal the ultimate techniques and manners of his national style; he discarded the 2nd and 3rd of the set as not satisfactory in reflecting the subject. In 1903 he began work on a choral sym. inspired by Walt Whitman's poetry and entitled *A Sea Symphony*; he completed it in 1909; there followed in 1910 *Fantasia on a Theme of Thomas Tallis*, scored for string quartet and double string orch.; in it Vaughan Williams evoked the song style of an early English composer. After this brief work, he engaged in a grandiose score, entitled *A London Symphony* and intended as a musical glorification of the great capital city. However, he emphatically denied that the score was to be a representation of London life. He even suggested that it might be more aptly entitled *Symphony by a Londoner*, which would explain the immediately recognizable quotations of the street song *Sweet Lavender* and of the Westminster chimes in the score; indeed, Vaughan Williams declared that the work must be judged as a piece of absolute or abstract music. Yet prosaically minded commentators insisted that *A London Symphony* realistically depicted in its 4 movements the scenes of London at twilight, the hubbub of Bloomsbury, a Saturday-evening reverie, and, in conclusion, the serene flow of the Thames River. Concurrently with *A London Symphony*, he wrote the ballad opera *Hugh the Drover*, set in England in the year 1812, and reflecting the solitary struggle of the English against Napoleon.

At the outbreak of World War I in 1914, Vaughan Williams enlisted in the British army, and served in Salonika and in France as an officer in the artillery. After the Armistice, he was from 1919 to 1939 a prof. of composition at the Royal College of Music in London; from 1920 to 1928 he also conducted the London Bach Choir. In 1921 he completed *A Pastoral Symphony*, the music of which reflects the contemplative aspect of his inspiration; an interesting innovation in this score is the use of a wordless vocal solo in the last movement. In 1922 he visited the U.S. and conducted *A Pastoral Symphony* at the Norfolk (Conn.) Festival; in 1932 he returned to the U.S. to lecture at Bryn Mawr College. In 1930 he was awarded the Gold Medal of the Royal Phil. Soc. of London; in 1935 he received the Order of Merit from King George V. In 1930 he wrote a masque, *Job*, based on Blake's *Illustrations of the Book of Job*, which was first performed in a concert version in 1930 and was then presented on the stage in London on July 5, 1931. His 4th Sym., in F minor, written between 1931 and 1935 and first performed by the BBC Sym. Orch. in London on April 10, 1935, presents an extraordinary deviation from his accustomed solid style of composition. Here he experimented with dissonant harmonies in conflicting tonalities, bristling with angular rhythms. A peripheral work was *Fantasia on Greensleeves*, arranged for harp, strings, and optional flutes; this was the composer's tribute to his fascination with English folk songs; he had used it in his opera *Sir John in Love*, after Shakespeare's *The Merry Wives of Windsor*, performed in London in 1929. He always professed great admiration for Sibelius; indeed, there was a harmonious kinship between the 2 great contemporary nationalist composers; there was also the peculiar circumstance that in his 4th Sym. Sibelius ventured into the domain of modernism, as did Vaughan Williams in his own 4th Sym., and both were taken to task by astounded critics for such musical philandering. Vaughan Williams dedicated his 5th Sym., in D major, composed between 1938 and 1943, to Sibelius as a token of his admiration. In the 6th Sym., in E minor, written during the years 1944 to 1947, Vaughan Williams returned to the erstwhile serenity of his inspiration, but the sym. has its turbulent moments and an episode of folksy dancing exhilaration. Vaughan Williams was 80 years old when he completed his challenging *Sinfonia antartica,* scored for soprano, women's chorus, and orch.; the music was an expansion of the background score he wrote for a film on the expedition of Sir Robert Scott to the South Pole in 1912. Here the music is almost geographic in its literal representation of the regions that Scott had explored; it may well be compared in its realism with the *Alpine Symphony* of Richard Strauss. In *Sinfonia antartica* Vaughan Williams inserted, in addition to a large orch., several keyboard instruments and a wind machine. To make the reference clear, he used in the epilogue of the work the actual quotations from Scott's journal. Numerically, *Sinfonia antartica* was his 7th; it was first performed in Manchester on Jan. 14, 1953. In the 8th Sym. he once more returned to the ideal of absolute music; the work is conceived in the form of a neo-Classical suite, but, faithful to the spirit of the times, he included in the score the modern instruments, such as vibraphone and xylophone, as well as the sempiternal gongs and bells. His last sym. bore the fateful number 9, which had for many composers the sense of the ultimate, since it was the numeral of Beethoven's last sym. In this work Vaughan Williams, at the age of 85, still asserted himself as a composer of the modern age; for the first time, he used a trio of saxophones, with a pointed caveat that they should not behave "like demented cats," but rather remain their romantic selves. Anticipating the inevitable, he added after the last bar of the score the Italian word "niente." The 9th Sym. was first performed in London on April 2, 1958; Vaughan Williams died later in the same year. It should be mentioned as a testimony to his extraordinary vitality that after the death of his first wife, he married, on Feb. 7, 1953 (at the age of 80), the poet and writer Ursula Wood, and in the following year he once more paid a visit to the U.S. on a lecture tour to several American univs.

Summarizing the aesthetic and technical aspects of the style of composition of Vaughan Williams, there is a distinctly modern treatment of harmonic writing, with massive agglomeration of chordal sonorities; parallel triadic progressions are especially favored. There seems to be no intention of adopting any particular method of composition; rather, there is a great variety of procedures integrated into a distinctively personal and thoroughly English style, nationalistic but not isolationist. Vaughan Williams was particularly adept at exploring the modern ways of modal counterpoint, with tonality freely shifting between major and minor triadic entities; this procedure astutely evokes sweetly archaic usages in modern applications; thus Vaughan Williams combines the modalities of the Tudor era with the sparkling polytonalities of the modern age.

WORKS: DRAMATIC: OPERAS: *Hugh the Drover,* ballad opera (1911–14; London, July 14, 1924); *The Shepherds of the Delectable Mountains,* "pastoral episode" after Bunyan's *The Pilgrim's Progress* (1921–22; London, July 11, 1922); *Sir John in Love,* after Shakespeare's *The Merry Wives of Windsor* (1925–29; London, March 21, 1929); *Riders to the Sea,* after the drama by John Millington Synge (1925–32; London, Dec. 1, 1937); *The Poisoned Kiss,* "romantic extravaganza" (1927–29; Cambridge, May 12, 1936; rev. 1934–37 and 1956–57); *The Pilgrim's Progress,* "morality" (includes material from the earlier opera *The Shepherds of the Delectable Mountains;* 1925–36, 1944–51; London, April 26, 1951). **BALLETS:** *Old King Cole* (Cambridge, June 5, 1923); *On Christmas Night,* masque (1925–26; Chicago, Dec. 26, 1926); *Job, a Masque for Dancing* (1927–30; concert perf., Norwich, Oct. 23, 1930; stage perf., London, July 5, 1931). **INCIDENTAL MUSIC TO:** Ben Jonson's *Pan's Anniversary* (Stratford-upon-Avon, April 24, 1905); Aristophanes's *The Wasps* (Cambridge, Nov. 26, 1909). **FILM MUSIC:** *49th Parallel* (1940–41); *The People's Land* (1941–42); *Coastal Command* (1942); *The Story of a Flemish Farm* (1943; suite for Orch., London, July 31, 1945); *Stricken Peninsula* (1944); *The Loves of Joanna Godden* (1946); *Scott of the Antarctic* (1947–48; material taken from it incorporated in the *Sinfonia antartica*); *Dim Little Island* (1949); *Bitter Springs* (1950); *The England of Elizabeth* (1955); *The Vision of William Blake* (1957). **OTHER:** *The Mayor of Casterbridge,* music for a radio serial after Thomas Hardy (1950).

ORCH.: *Serenade* for Small Orch. (1898); *Bucolic Suite* (Bournemouth, March 10, 1902); *2 Impressions: Harnham Down* and *Boldrewood* (1902; London, Nov. 12, 1907); 9 syms.: No. 1, *A Sea Symphony,* for Soprano, Baritone, Chorus, and Orch., after Walt Whitman (1906–09; Leeds Festival, Oct. 12, 1910, composer conducting), No. 2, *A London Symphony* (1911–14; London, March 27, 1914; rev. version, London, May 4, 1920), No. 3, *A Pastoral Symphony* (1916–21; London, Jan. 26, 1922), No. 4, in F minor (1931–35; London, April 10, 1935, Boult conducting), No. 5, in D major (1938–43; London, June 24, 1943, composer conducting), No. 6, in E minor (1944–47; London, April 21, 1948, Boult conducting), No. 7, *Sinfonia antartica* (1949–52; Manchester, Jan. 14, 1953, Barbirolli conducting), No. 8, in D minor (1953–55; Manchester, May 2, 1956, Barbirolli conducting), and No. 9, in E minor (1956–58; London, April 2, 1958, Sargent conducting); *3 Norfolk Rhapsodies* (1906; No. 1, in E minor, London, Aug. 23, 1906, No. 2, Cardiff Festival, Sept. 27, 1907, and No. 3, not perf.; Nos. 2 and 3 withdrawn by the composer); *In the Fen Country,* symphonic impression (1904 and subsequent revs.; London, Feb. 22, 1909, Beecham conducting); *The Wasps,* Aristophanic suite (1909; London, July 23, 1912, composer conducting); *Fantasia on a Theme by Thomas Tallis* for String Quartet and Double String Orch. (Gloucester Festival, Sept. 6, 1910, composer conducting; rev. 1923); *The Lark Ascending,* romance for Violin and Orch. (1914–20; London, June 14, 1921); Concerto in D minor for Violin and Strings, *Concerto accademico* (1924–25; London, Nov. 6, 1925); Piano Concerto in C major (1926–31; London, Feb. 1, 1933; also rev. for 2 Pianos and Orch., 1946); *Fantasia on Sussex Folk-Tunes* for Cello and Orch. (London, March 13, 1930, Casals, soloist, Barbirolli conducting); Prelude and Fugue in C minor (Hereford, Sept. 12, 1930); Suite for Viola and Small Orch. (London, Nov. 12, 1934); *Fantasia on Greensleeves* (arr. from the opera *Sir John in Love* by Greaves, 1934); *5 Variants of "Dives and Lazarus"* for String Orch. and Harp, commissioned by the British Council for the N.Y. World's Fair (1939; N.Y., June 10, 1939); *Serenade to Music* (orch. version of 1938 original, 1940; London, Feb. 10, 1940); Concerto in A minor for Oboe and Strings (1943–44; Liverpool, Sept. 30, 1944); *Partita* for Double String Orch. (orch. version of Double Trio for String Sextet, 1946–48; BBC, London, March 20, 1948); Concerto Grosso for Strings (London, Nov. 18, 1950, Boult conducting); *Romance* in D-flat major for Harmonica, Strings, and Piano (1951; N.Y., May 3, 1952); Concerto in F minor for Tuba and Orch. (London, June 14, 1954); *Flourish for Glorious John* (for Barbirolli; Manchester, Oct. 16, 1957, Barbirolli conducting).

CHAMBER: 1 unnumbered string quartet, in C minor (1898; June 30, 1904); 2 numbered string quartets: No. 1, in G minor (London, Nov. 8, 1909) and No. 2, in A minor (1942–44; London, Oct. 12, 1944); Quintet in D major for Clarinet, Horn, Violin, Cello, and Piano (June 5, 1900); Piano Quintet in C minor for Piano, Violin, Viola, Cello, and Double Bass (London, Dec. 14, 1905); *Phantasy Quintet* for 2 Violins, 2 Violas, and Cello (1912; London, March 23, 1914); 6 studies in English folk song for Cello and Piano (London, June 4, 1926); Double Trio for String Sextet (London, Jan. 21, 1939); Violin Sonata in A minor (BBC, London, Oct. 12, 1954); also some short piano pieces; Introduction and Fugue for 2 Pianos (1946); organ pieces.

VOCAL: *Willow Wood* for Baritone, Women's Chorus, and Orch., after Dante Gabriel Rossetti (1903; Liverpool Festival,

Sept. 25, 1909); *Songs of Travel* for Voice and Piano, after Robert Louis Stevenson (London, Dec. 2, 1904); *Toward the Unknown Region* for Chorus and Orch., after Walt Whitman (1905–07; Leeds Festival, Oct. 10, 1907; rev. 1918); *On Wenlock Edge*, song cycle for Tenor, Piano, and String Quartet ad libitum, after A.E. Housman's *A Shropshire Lad* (London, Nov. 15, 1909); *5 Mystical Songs* for Baritone, Optional Chorus, and Orch. (Worcester Cathedral, Sept. 14, 1911); *Fantasia on Christmas Carols* for Baritone, Chorus, and Orch. (Hereford Festival, Sept. 12, 1912); *4 Hymns* for Tenor and Piano, with Viola obbligato (1914; Cardiff, May 26, 1920); *Mass* in G minor (1920–21; Birmingham, Dec. 6, 1922); *Sancta civitas* for Tenor, Baritone, Chorus, and Orch. (1923–25; Oxford, May 7, 1926); *Flos Campi*, suite for Viola, Wordless Mixed Chorus, and Small Orch. (London, Oct. 19, 1925); *Te Deum* for Chorus and Organ (Canterbury Cathedral, Dec. 4, 1928); *Benedicite* for Soprano, Chorus, and Orch. (1929; Dorking, May 2, 1930); *The Hundredth Psalm* for Chorus and Orch. (1929; Dorking, April 29, 1930); *3 Choral Hymns* for Baritone, Chorus, and Orch. (Dorking, April 30, 1930); *In Windsor Forest*, cantata for Chorus and Orch., adapted from the opera *Sir John in Love* (Windsor, Nov. 9, 1931); *Magnificat* for Contralto, Women's Chorus, and Orch. (Worcester Cathedral, Sept. 8, 1932); *5 Tudor Portraits* for Mezzo-soprano, Baritone, Chorus, and Orch. (1935; Norwich Festival, Sept. 25, 1936); *Dona nobis pacem* for Soprano, Baritone, Chorus, and Orch. (Huddersfield, Oct. 2, 1936); *Festival Te Deum* (1937); *Flourish for a Coronation* (London, April 1, 1937); *Serenade to Music* for 16 Solo Voices and Orch. (London, Oct. 5, 1938); *The Bridal Day*, masque after Edmund Spenser's *Epithalamion* (1938–39; rev. 1952–53; BBC television, London, June 5, 1953, in celebration of the coronation of Elizabeth II; rev. as the cantata *Epithalamion*, London, Sept. 30, 1957); *Thanksgiving for Victory* for Soprano, Speaker, Chorus, and Orch. (1944; BBC broadcast, London, May 13, 1945); *An Oxford Elegy* for Speaker, Chorus, and Orch., after Matthew Arnold (Dorking, Nov. 20, 1949); *Folk Songs of the 4 Seasons*, cantata on traditional folk songs, for Women's Voices and Orch. (1949; London, June 15, 1950); *The Sons of Light* for Children's Chorus (London, May 6, 1951); *Hodie (This Day)*, Christmas cantata for Soprano, Tenor, Baritone, Chorus, and Orch. (1953–54; Worcester, Sept. 8, 1954); *A Vision of Aeroplanes*, motet for Chorus and Organ, after Ezekiel, Chapter 1 (1955; St. Michael's, Cornhill, London, June 4, 1956); *10 Blake Songs* for Tenor and Oboe (BBC, London, Oct. 8, 1958); other songs to words by English poets; arrangements of English folk songs; hymn tunes; carols.

WRITINGS: *The English Hymnal* (1906; 2nd ed., 1933); *Songs of Praise* (with M. Shaw; 1925; 2nd ed., 1931); *The Oxford Book of Carols* (with P. Dearmer and M. Shaw; 1928); lectures and articles, reprinted in *National Music and Other Essays* (London, 1963); R. Palmer ed. *Folk Songs Collected by Ralph Vaughan Williams* (London, 1983).

BIBL.: A.H. Fox Strangways, "R. V.W.," *Music & Letters*, I (1920); H. Colles, "The Music of V.W.," *Chesterian*, XXI (1922); H. Howells, "V.W.'s 'Pastoral Symphony'," *Music & Letters*, III (1922); A. Dickinson, *An Introduction to the Music of R. V.W.* (London, 1928); H. Ould, "The Songs of R. V.W.," *English Review*, XLVI (1928); F. Toye, "Studies in English Music: V.W. and the Folk Music Movement," *Listener*, V (1931); E. Rubbra, "V.W., Some Technical Characteristics," *Monthly Musical Record*, LXIV (1934); idem, "The Later V.W.," *Music & Letters*, XVIII (1937); S. Goddard, "The Operas of V.W.," *Listener*, XX (1938); W. Kimmel, "V.W.'s Choice of Words," *Music & Letters*, XIX (1938); idem, "V.W.'s Melodic Style," *Musical Quarterly* (Oct. 1941); H. Foss, *R. V.W.* (London, 1950); A. Hutchings, "V.W. and the Tudor Tradition," *Listener*, XLV (1951); E. Payne, *The Folksong Element in the Music of V.W.* (diss., Univ. of Liverpool, 1953); R. Taylor, "V.W. and English National Music," *Cambridge Journal*, VI (1953); P. Young, *V.W.* (London, 1953); F. Howes, *The Music of R. V.W.* (London, 1954); E. Payne, "V.W. and Folksong," *Music Review*, XV (1954); J. Bergsagel, *The National Aspects of the Music of R. V.W.* (diss., Cornell Univ., 1957); S. Pakenham, *R. V.W.: A Discovery of His Music* (London, 1957); J. Warrack, "V.W. and Opera," *Opera*, IX (1958); D. Brown, "V.W.'s Symphonies: Some Judgments Reviewed," *Monthly Musical Record*, XC (1960); J. Day, *V.W.* (London, 1961; 2nd ed., rev., 1975); P. Willetts, "The R. V.W. Collection," *British Museum Quarterly*, XXIV (1961); A. Dickinson, "The V.W. Manuscripts," *Music Review*, XXIII (1962); idem, *V.W.* (London, 1963); M. Kennedy, *The Works of R. V.W.* (London, 1964; 2nd ed., rev., 1980); E. Schwartz, *The Symphonies of R. V.W.* (Amherst, 1964); U. Vaughan Williams, *R. V.W.: A Biography* (London, 1964); H. Ottaway, *V.W.* (London, 1966); P. Starbuck, *R. V.W., O.M., 1872–1958: A Bibliography of His Literary Writings and Criticism of His Musical Works* (diss., Library Assn., 1967); M. Hurd, *V.W.* (London, 1970); J. Lunn and U. Vaughan Williams, *R. V.W.: A Pictorial Biography* (London, 1971); U. Vaughan Williams, "V.W. and Opera," *Composer*, XLI (1971); R. Douglas, *Working with R. V.W.* (London, 1972); H. Ottaway, *V.W. Symphonies* (London, 1972; rev. ed., 1988); U. Vaughan Williams, "The VW Centenary," *Musical Times*, CXIII (1972); M. Kennedy, "The Unknown V.W.," *Proceedings of the Royal Musical Association*, XCIX (1972–73); A. Frogley, "V.W. and Thomas Hardy: 'Tess' and the Slow Movement of the Ninth Symphony," *Music & Letters* (Jan. 1987); U. Vaughan Williams, *R. V.W.: A Biography of R. V.W.* (Oxford, 1988); N. Butterworth, *R. V.W.: A Guide to Research* (N.Y., 1989); W. Mellers, *V.W. and the Vision of Albion* (1989); J. Northrop Moore, *V. W.: A Life in Photographs* (Oxford, 1992).

Vázsonyi, Bálint, distinguished Hungarian-born American pianist; b. Budapest, March 7, 1936. He entered the Franz Liszt Academy of Music in Budapest as a youth; made his debut as a pianist at 12. He left Hungary in the midst of political turmoil in 1956; then continued his training at the Vienna Academy of Music (1957–58); eventually went to America, where he continued his studies with Ernst von Dohnányi at Florida State Univ. (1960). In 1964 he became a naturalized American citizen. In 1977 he made a transcontinental tour of the U.S. He served on the faculty of the Indiana Univ. School of Music in Bloomington (1978–84). In 1983 he founded Telemusic, a film and video music production company. One of his notable feats of pianofortitude was his performance, on 2 consecutive days, of all 32 piano sonatas of Beethoven in chronological order (N.Y., Oct. 31 and Nov. 1, 1976); he repeated this cycle in Boston and London shortly afterward. He is the author of the standard biography of Dohnányi (Budapest, 1971). His pianism is marked by a transcendental virtuosity of technique coupled with the mellow lyricism typical of traditional Hungarian pianism, and particularly effective in the music of Liszt. In 1991 he embarked on a new venture as the Republican candidate for mayor of Bloomington, Ind., but was defeated by his Democratic opponent.

Vazzana, Anthony, American composer and educator; b. Troy, N.Y., Nov. 4, 1922. He was of a musical family; his father played the mandolin. He studied piano with George H. Pickering; attended the State Univ. of N.Y. College at Potsdam; in 1943 he was inducted into the U.S. Air Force, where he arranged and conducted suitable music in concert bands. He resumed his musical studies after his discharge, and in 1946 enrolled at the Berkshire Music Center at Tanglewood, where his instructors were Fine, Shaw, Chapple, Bernstein, and Ross. In 1948 he enrolled at the Univ. of Southern Calif. in Los Angeles in the classes of Stevens, Dahl, and Kanitz; received his M.M. in 1948. Subsequently he divided his time between composing and teaching; was successively on the faculty of Calif. State Univ. at Long Beach and at Los Angeles, Champlain College, and Danbury (Conn.) State College. In 1959 he received the degree of doctor in composition at the Univ. of Southern Calif., and in 1959 joined the faculty of its School of Music. In his teaching, he resolutely promoted advanced techniques in composition; wrote a set of books on theory, *Projects in Musicianship* (4 vols., 1965–68). In his compositions, he pursued a logical evolutionary line, beginning with neo-Classical formations and continuing with progressive harmonic and contrapuntal complications, in which dissonances are ultimately emancipated and rhythms become increasingly asymmetrical, all this aided and abetted by eloquent pregnant pauses separating brief melodic ejaculations. Special effects, such as whipping and scourging the bodies of musical instruments with taps and kicks, soundlessly blowing through the embouchure of a wind instrument, such as a horn, and the like, add to the quaquaversal quality of sonorism in his works.

WORKS: ORCH.: *Andante and Allegro* (1949); *Symphonic Allegro* (1958); *Harlequin Suite* (1959); *Suite* for Strings (1963); Sym. No. 1 (1963); *Spectra* for Band (1965); *Partite sopra victimae paschali laudes* for Wind Orch. (1976); *Trinakie* (1977); *Varianti* (1982); *Odissea* (1989); *Metamorphoses* for Wind Orch. (1989); *Concerto Sapporo* for Euphonium and Orch. (Sapporo, Aug. 10, 1990); *Sinfonia Tejana* for Symphonic Band (1992). **CHAMBER:** Sonata for Clarinet, Horn, and Piano (1947); String Quartet (1948); Woodwind Quintet (1948); Suite for Viola and Piano (1948); Quartet for Violin, Viola, Cello, and Piano (1949); Violin Sonata (1958); *Music* for 2 Flutes (1962); *Fantasia concertante* for Cello and Piano (1970); *Incontri* for Violin and Piano (1971); *Tre monodie* for Trombone (1976); *Cambi* for Tuba and Percussion (1977); *Montaggi* for 4 Tubas (1978); *Studi* for Saxophone (1979); *Buccina* for Horn and Piano (1979); *Partita* for Euphonium, Piano, and Percussion (1980); *Concerto a tre* for Clarinet, Double Bass, and Instrumental Ensemble (1981); *Corivolano* for Viola and Horn (1982); *Lamentazione* for Viola (1985); *Fantasia Concertante* for Cello and Piano (1985); *Introduzione e Danza* for Bass Clarinet and Piano (1986); *Capriccio* for Clarinet and Piano (1987); *Saggi Musicali* for Soprano Saxophone and Piano (1988); *Disegni II* for Cello, Piano, and Percussion (1989); *Linea* for Horn (1990); *Chamber Concertino* for Piano and Chamber Ensemble (1991–93); *Gesti* for Bassoon (1992). **KEYBOARD: PIANO:** Sonata (1962); *Disegni I* (1978). **ORGAN:** *Meditation* (1994). **VOCAL:** *Songs of Life and Nature* for Voice and Piano (1962).

Veasey, Josephine, English mezzo-soprano and teacher; b. Peckham, July 10, 1930. She studied with Audrey Langford in London. In 1949 she joined the chorus at London's Covent Garden; made her Covent Garden debut as the Shepherd Boy in *Tannhäuser* in 1955, and later appeared as Waltraute, Fricka, Brangäne, Berlioz's Dido, Dorabella et al. there; she created the role of the Emperor in Henze's *We Come to the River* there (1976). From 1957 to 1969 she appeared at the Glynebourne Festivals. On Nov. 22, 1968, she made her Metropolitan Opera debut in N.Y. as Fricka, remaining on the roster until 1969; also made guest appearances throughout Europe and in South America; likewise sang in concerts. In 1982 she retired from the operatic stage and became active as a teacher; taught at the Royal Academy of Music (1983–84), and was a voice consultant to the English National Opera (from 1985) in London. In 1970 she was made a Commander of the Order of the British Empire.

Vécsey, Jenö, Hungarian musicologist and composer; b. Felsöcéce, July 19, 1909; d. Budapest, Sept. 18, 1966. He studied composition with Kodály at the Budapest Academy of Music (diploma, 1935); took courses in chemistry and biology at the Univ. of Budapest (graduated, 1941), and completed his musical training in Vienna (1941–42). He joined the staff of the National Széchényi Library in Budapest in 1942, where he was head of its music dept. from 1945 until his death. He made valuable contributions to the historical and bibliographical music literature preserved there; initiated and directed editorial work on the Musica Rinata series (1963–66); did preparatory work on the new Haydn Collected Edition. He publ. *Joseph Haydn művei az Országos Széchényi könyvtár zenei gyűjteményében* (Joseph Haydn's Compositions in the Music Collection of the National Széchényi Library; Budapest, 1959; Eng. tr., 1960).

WORKS: BALLET: *Kele diák* (Scholar Kele; 1943). **ORCH.:** *Divertimento* (1939–40); *Rhapsody* (1940–41); *Intermezzi* for Strings (1942); *2 Symphonic Dances* (1945; from *Kele diák*); *Boldogkő vara* (Boldogkő Castle), symphonic poem (1951; rev. as *Praeludium, notturno és scherzo*, 1958); Piano Concertino (1953); Double Bass Concertino (1954); *Szimfonikus concerto Krúdy Gyula emlékeré* (Symphonic Concerto in Memory of Gyula Krúdy; 1958). **CHAMBER:** String Quartet (1942); String Sextet (1956); *Bagatelles* for 2 Pianos (1962). **VOCAL:** Songs.

Vedernikov, Alexander, Russian bass; b. Mokino, Dec. 23, 1927. He studied voice at the Moscow Cons., graduating in 1955. He won 1st prize at the International Schumann Competition in Berlin in 1956 and, in the same year, 1st prize at the Soviet competition for his performance of songs by Soviet composers. In 1957 he made his debut at the Bolshoi Theater in Moscow as Susanin. In 1961 he entered the La Scala Opera School of Milan as an aspirant; subsequently toured as a concert singer in France, Italy, England, Austria, and Canada; also sang with the Bolshoi Theater, with which he made tours abroad. He was particularly noted for his performances of the Russian repertoire; his portrayal of Boris Godunov in Mussorgsky's opera approached Chaliapin's in its grandeur. He also distinguished himself in Italian buffo roles.

Veerhoff, Carlos, Argentine-German composer; b. Buenos Aires, June 3, 1926. He was a student of Grabner at the Berlin Hochschule für Musik (1943–44). After teaching at the National Univ. in Tucuman (1948–51), he returned to Berlin as an assistant to Fricsay (1951–52). After completing his training with Blacher at the Hochschule für Musik (1952) and privately with Thomas and Scherchen, he chose to remain in Germany.

WORKS: DRAMATIC: *Pavane royale*, ballet (1953); *Targusis*, chamber opera (1958); *El porquerizo del ray*, ballet (1963); *Die goldene Maske*, opera (1968; rev. 1978); *Es gibt doch Zebrastreifen*, mini–opera (1971; Ulm, Jan. 20, 1972); *Der Grüne*, chamber opera (1972); *Dualis*, ballet (1978). **ORCH.:** *Prólogo sinfónico* (1951); *Symphonic Movement* (1952); 5 syms.: No. 1, *Panta rhei* (Everything Flows; 1953), No. 2 (1956), No. 3, *Spirales* (1966; rev. 1969), No. 4 (1974), and No. 5 for Strings (1977); *Mirages* (1961); *Akroasis* for 24 Winds and Percussion (1966); *Textur* for Strings (1969; rev. 1971); *Sinotrauc* (1972; Munich, Jan. 19, 1973); *Torso* (1973; Lübeck, Jan. 14, 1974); *Dorefamie* (1975); Violin Concerto (1975–76); 2 piano concertos (1978–79; 1990); *Concertino da camera* (1979); Concerto for 2 Violins and Orch. (1985); Concerto for Cello, Double Bass, and Orch. (1989); Percussion Concerto (1993–94; Munich, Oct. 28, 1994). **CHAMBER:** 2 string quartets (1951, 1974); Sonata for Solo Violin (1954); 2 wind quintets (1958, 1969); *Dialogue I* for Saxophone and Piano (1967) and *II* for Viola and Percussion (1987); String Trio (1986); Horn Trio (1994). **VOCAL:** *Gesänge auf dem Wege* for Baritone and Orch. (1964); *Ut omnes unum sint*, chamber cantata (1967); *Gesänge für Sangsâra* for Mezzo-soprano, Voices, Orch., and Tape (1976); *Pater noster in Form einer Messe "en miniature"* for Chorus and Orch. (1988).

Vega, Aurelio de la, Cuban-born American composer, teacher, and writer on music; b. Havana, Nov. 28, 1925. He studied in Havana at De La Salle College (B.A. in humanities, 1944), with Fritz Kramer (1943–46), at the Univ. (M.A. in diplomacy, 1946), and at the Ada Iglesias Music Inst. (M.A. in musicology, 1956); he also studied with Toch in Calif. (1947–48). During the Cuban years of his career, he was president of the Cuban section of the ISCM (1952–54), worked as a music critic (1952–57), and served as prof. of music and chairman of the music dept. at the Univ. of Oriente in Santiago de Cuba (1953–59). In 1959 he settled in Los Angeles and in 1966 became a naturalized American citizen. In the summer of 1959 he was a visiting prof. of music at the Univ. of Southern Calif. In 1959 he joined the faculty of San Fernando Valley State College (later Calif. State Univ. at Northridge), where he subsequently was a distinguished prof. of music, director of the electronic music studio, and composer-in-residence. In 1992 he retired as distinguished prof. emeritus. In 1978 and 1984 he received Kennedy Center Friedheim awards. He held a Fulbright Research Award in 1985. His numerous articles and essays, as well as paintings, have appeared in various publications. In his compositions, he experimented with various avant-garde means of expression without proscribing the use of Cuban nationalist elements.

WORKS: ORCH.: *Obertura a una Farsa Seria* (1950; Havana, April 28, 1951); *Introducción y Episodio* (1952; Havana, April 3, 1953); *Elegía* for Strings (London, Nov. 16, 1954); *Divertimento* for Piano, Violin, Cello, and Strings (1956; Redlands, Calif., Jan. 28, 1958); *Symphony in 4 Parts* (1960; Washington, D.C., April 30, 1961); *Intrata* (Los Angeles, May 12, 1972); *Adiós* (1977; Los Angeles, April 20, 1978, Mehta conducting). **CHAMBER:** *La Muerte de Pan* for Violin and Piano (Redlands, Calif., March 16, 1948); Trio for Violin, Cello, and Piano (1949; Havana, April 27, 1952); *Soliloquio* for Viola and Piano (1950; Havana, April 1, 1951); *Levenda del Ariel Criollo* for Cello and Piano (1953; Havana, March 25, 1954); String Quartet, "In Memoriam Alban Berg" (1957; Washington, D.C., April 20, 1958); Woodwind Quintet (1959; Los Angeles, Jan. 30, 1961); Trio for Flute, Oboe, and Clarinet (1960; Northridge, Calif., March 19, 1961); *Structures* for Piano and String Quartet (1962; Washington, D.C., May 8, 1964); *Segmentos* for Violin and Piano (Berkeley, Calif., Oct. 2, 1964); *Exametron* for Flute, Cello, and 4 Percussionists (Los Angeles, Oct. 11, 1965); *Interpolation* for Clarinet with or without Pre-recorded Sounds (1965; Los Angeles, April 23, 1966); *Exospheres* for Oboe and Piano (1966; Los Angeles, Nov. 25, 1968); *Labdanum* for Flute, Vibraphone, and Viola (Los Angeles, Nov. 30, 1970); *Tangents* for Violin and Pre-recorded Sounds (1973; Los Angeles, Oct. 21, 1974); *Para-Tangents* for Trumpet and Pre-recorded Sounds (1973; Los Angeles, Dec. 14, 1974); *Septicilium* for Clarinet and 6 Instrumentalists (1974; Los Angeles, April 12, 1975); *Olep ed Arudamot* for Any Number of Instruments and/or Voices (1974; Tujunga, Calif., March 14, 1976); *The Infinite Square* for Any Number of Instruments and/or Voices (1975; Northridge, Calif., Nov. 12, 1976); *Andamar-Ramadna* for Any Number of Instruments and/or Voices (1975; Mexico City, May 22, 1977); *Sound Clouds* for Guitar (1975; Los Angeles, Feb. 11, 1978); *Astralis* for Any Number of Instruments and/or Voices (1977; Buenos Aires, July 27, 1979); *Nones* for Any Number of Instruments and/or Voices (1977; San Francisco, Feb. 20, 1979); *Undici Colori* for Bassoon with or without Projected Color Transparencies (1981; Los Angeles, Jan. 25, 1982); *Galandiacoa* for Clarinet and Guitar (1982; Los Angeles, Jan. 10, 1983); *Tropimapal* for 9 Instruments (Los Angeles, April 18, 1983); piano pieces. **VOCAL:** *La Fuente Infinata*, song cycle for Soprano and Piano (1944; Havana, Dec. 18, 1945); Cantata for 2 Sopranos, Contralto, and 21 Instruments (1958; Washington, D.C., Nov. 1, 1964); *Inflorescenia* for Soprano, Bass Clarinet, and Pre-recorded Sounds (Los Angeles, Oct. 25, 1976); *Asonante* for Soprano, Female Dancer, 7 Instruments, and Tape (1985; Los Angeles, March 4, 1987); *Adramante* for Soprano and Piano (La Jolla, Calif., Dec. 7, 1985); *Magias e Invenciones*, song cycle for Soprano and Piano (1986; Mexico City, April 27, 1988); *Testimonial* for Mezzo-soprano and 5 Instruments (Buenos Aires, July 5, 1990); *Madrigales de Entonces* for Chorus (1991; Mexico City, May 28, 1993). **ELECTRONIC:** *Vectors* (1963; Ojai, Calif., May 30, 1964); *Extrapolation* (Los Angeles, Dec. 5, 1981).

Vega, Carlos, Argentine writer on music; b. Cañuelas, near Buenos Aires, April 14, 1898; d. Buenos Aires, Feb. 10, 1966. He studied at the Univ. of Buenos Aires (philosophy and literature); subsequently devoted himself mainly to folklore research in music. In 1926 he became head of musicology at the Argentine Museum of Natural Sciences and in 1933 he was placed in charge of the folklore division of the literature faculty at the Univ. of Buenos Aires; also was founder-director of the Inst. of Musicology of the Ministry of Education (from 1931). He traveled throughout the rural regions of Argentina and other South American countries to collect materials on folk songs and folk dances, using a phonograph to record them; devised a special choreographic notation. His many books are basic sources for the study of Argentine folk music.

WRITINGS (all publ. in Buenos Aires): *La música de un códice colonial del siglo XVII* (1931); *Danzas y canciones argentinas* (1936); *La música popular argentina: Canciones y danzas criollas* (1941); *Panorama de la música popular argentina* (1944); *Los instrumentos musicales de la Argentina* (1946); *Danzas argentinas* (1962); *Las canciones folklóricas argentinas* (1964); *Lectura y notación de la música* (1965).

Végh, Sándor (Alexandre), Hungarian-born French violinist, conductor, and pedagogue; b. Klausenburg, May 17, 1912. He was a pupil of Zsolt, Waldbauer, and Weiner at the Budapest Academy of Music; then studied violin with Hubay and composition with Kodály. He was a member of the Hungarian Trio (1931–33) and the Hungarian Quartet (1934–40); also made appearances as a soloist (from 1934). In 1940 he founded the Végh Quartet, which remained active until 1980. From 1941 to 1946 he was a prof. at the Budapest Academy of Music; he subsequently emigrated to France, becoming a naturalized French citizen in 1953. From 1953 to 1969 he was active at the Prades Festivals; also taught master classes in various European locales. From 1968 to 1971 he conducted the Orchestre du Chambre Sándor Végh; he taught at the Salzburg Mozarteum (from 1971), where he was conductor of its Camerata Academica (from 1978).

Veinus, Abraham, American musicologist; b. N.Y., Feb. 12, 1916. He studied at the City College of N.Y. (B.A., 1936), Cornell Univ. (M.A., 1937), and Columbia Univ. (1946–48). He was prof. of musicology and fine arts at Syracuse Univ. (from 1948). He wrote *The Concerto* (1944; 2nd ed., rev. 1964); *The Victor Book of Concertos* (1948); *The Pocket Book of Great Operas* (with H. Simon, 1949); *Understanding Music: Style, Structure and History* (with W. Fleming, 1958).

Velázquez, Higinio, Mexican violinist and composer; b. Guadalajara, Jan. 11, 1926. He studied composition with Bernal Jiménez and Rodolfo Halffter. He was a violinist in the National Sym. Orch.; in 1969, became violinist in the string quartet of the National Inst. of Fine Arts.

WORKS: ORCH.: *Vivencias* (1958); *Cacique*, overture (1958); *Juárez*, "sinfonia breve" (1961); *Revolución*, symphonic poem (1963); *Andante atonal* for Strings (1971). **CHAMBER:** *Elegía* for Oboe and Piano (1969); *Estructuas* for Piano (1969); Sonatina for Solo Cello (1970); String Quartet (1970).

Velimirović, Miloš, eminent Serbian-American music scholar; b. Belgrade, Dec. 10, 1922. He studied violin and piano at the Belgrade Academy of Music with Stojanović. In 1943 he was sent to a forced labor camp by the German occupation authorities. After the liberation, he studied Byzantine art at the Univ. of Belgrade, graduating in 1951; simultaneously took composition lessons with Mihovil Logar at the Belgrade Academy of Music. In 1952 he emigrated to the U.S.; studied at Harvard Univ., obtaining his M.A. in 1953 and his Ph.D. in 1957 with the diss. *Byzantine Elements in Early Slavic Chant* (publ. in an enl. ed., 1960, in Monumenta Musicae Byzantinae, *Subsidiae*, IV, 1960); also took a course in Byzantine music with Wellesz at Dumbarton Oaks in Washington, D.C. (1954). He was on the faculty of Yale Univ. (1957–69) and the Univ. of Wisc. (1969–73); in 1973, was appointed a prof. of music at the Univ. of Virginia in Charlottesville; served as chairman of the music dept. there (1974–77). A linguist, he has contributed a number of scholarly articles to various publications, mainly on subjects connected with liturgical music in Byzantium and in the Slavic countries. He was general ed. of Collegium Musicum (1958–73) and assoc. ed. (jointly with E. Wellesz) of *Studies in Eastern Chant* (4 vols., London, 1966–78); wrote articles on Russian and Slavic church music for *The New Grove Dictionary of Music and Musicians* (1980).

Veltri, Michelangelo, Argentine conductor; b. Buenos Aires, Aug. 16, 1940. After training in Buenos Aires, he completed his studies with Panizza in Milan. He began his career conducting at the Teatro Colón in Buenos Aires; then went to Barcelona in 1966 as music director of the Teatro Liceo. In 1970 he made his first appearance at Milan's La Scala conducting *Don Carlos,* which he also conducted at the Vienna State Opera. On Nov. 10, 1971, he made his Metropolitan Opera debut in N.Y. conducting *Rigoletto*, where he returned in subsequent years to conduct the Italian repertoire. From 1972 to 1977 he was artistic director of the Caracas International Festival, and then of the Opéra d'Avignon from 1984 to 1987; subsequently served as music director of the Opera and Phil. in Santiago, Chile. His appearance at London's Covent Garden in 1986 conducting *Lucia di Lammermoor* was highly successful.

Vengerov, Maxim, accomplished Russian violinist; b. Novosibirsk, Aug. 15, 1974. He was a student of Zakhar Bron. After making his formal debut in a recital in Moscow in 1985, he played throughout Russia; soon began to tour abroad in Western Europe. After winning the Flesch competition in London in 1990, he made his U.S. debut as soloist with the N.Y. Phil.; in subsequent years, appeared as a soloist with the principal orchs. of the globe and as a recitalist in the leading music centers. His playing is marked by an extraordinary virtuoso technique.

Vengerova, Isabelle (actually, **Isabella Afanasievna**), distinguished Russian-born American pianist and pedagogue; b. Minsk, March 1, 1877; d. N.Y., Feb. 7, 1956. She studied at the Vienna Cons. with Joseph Dachs, and privately with Leschetizky; then with Essipova in St. Petersburg. In 1906 she was appointed an instructor at the St. Petersburg Cons.; in 1910 she became a prof. there, remaining on its faculty until 1920. She made tours in Russia and Europe (1920–23); then went to the U.S. in 1923; made her American debut with the Detroit Sym. Orch. (Feb. 8, 1925) in Schumann's Piano Concerto. She became a prof. at the Curtis Inst. of Music in Philadelphia when it was founded in 1924; in 1950 she received an honorary doctor's degree there. Among her piano pupils at the Curtis Inst. were Bernstein, Barber, and Foss. She also taught privately in N.Y. Her nephew was **Nicolas Slonimsky**.

BIBL.: N. Slonimsky, "'Musique': Reminiscences of a Vanished World and a Great Teacher," *Piano Teacher*, VI/1 (1963); E. Flissler, "The Venerable V.: Magician of Pianoforte," *Music Journal*, XXIII/3 (1965); R. Schick, *The V. System of Piano Playing* (University Park, Pa., 1982); N. Slonimsky, *Perfect Pitch: A Life Story* (Oxford and N.Y., 1988).

Veprik, Alexander (Moiseievich), Russian composer and musicologist; b. Balta, near Odessa, June 23, 1899; d. Moscow, Oct. 13, 1958. While still a young boy he went to Leipzig, where he took piano lessons with Karl Wendling; then pursued training in composition with Zhitomirsky at the Petrograd Cons. (1918–21) and with Miaskovsky at the Moscow Cons. (1921–23), where he subsequently taught orchestration (1923–43). He was associated with the Jewish cultural movement in Russia, and composed several works in the traditional ethnic manner of Jewish cantillations. In his harmonic and formal treatment, he followed the "orientalistic" tradition of the Russian national school.

WORKS: DRAMATIC: OPERAS: *Toktogul*, on Kirghiz motifs (1938–39; Frunze, 1940); *Toktogul* (1949; in collaboration with A. Maldibaiev). Also film music. **ORCH.:** 2 syms. (1931, 1938); *Traurnaya pesnya* (Sad Song; 1932); *Pesnya likovaniya* (Peace Song; 1935); *Pastorale* (1946; rev. 1958); *2 poems* (1957); *Improvizatsiya* (1958). **CHAMBER:** *Rhapsody* for Viola and Piano (1926); piano pieces, including 3 sonatas (1922, 1924, 1928). **VOCAL:** 2 cantatas: *Proklyatiye fashizmu* (Fascism Be Cursed; 1944) and *Narod-geroy* (The People-The Hero; 1955); songs.

WRITINGS: *O metodakh prepodavaniya instrumentovki: K voprosu o klassovoy obuslovlennosti orkestrovovo pisma* (Methods of Instrument Teaching: On the Question of the Classification of Orchestral Writing; Moscow, 1931); *Traktovka instrumenov orkestra* (The Treatment of Orchestral Instruments; Moscow, 1948; 2nd ed., 1961).

BIBL.: V. Bogdanov-Berezovsky, *A.M. V.* (Moscow and Leningrad, 1964).

Verbesselt, August, Belgian flutist and composer; b. Klein-Willebroek, Oct. 22, 1919. He studied at the Antwerp Cons. From 1942 he was flutist in the orch. of the Antwerp Royal Flemish Opera.

WORKS: ORCH.: Flute Concerto (1952); *Diagrams* for Chamber Orch. (1972); *Universum* for 2 Orchs. and Tape (1975); *Strukturen* (1981); Clarinet Concerto (1983); Piano Concerto (1986); Oboe Concerto (1986); Concerto for Clarinet Quartet and Chamber Orch. (1986); *Pax* for Chamber Orch. (1986); *Sluierdans* for Harmony Orch. (1988); *Oase* for Chamber Orch. (1988); Chamber Concerto for Bass Clarinet and Strings (1988); ballet music. **CHAMBER:** *Hexatone-Synthèse* for Flute, Oboe, Clarinet, Cello, and Harp (1964); *3 Monologhi* for Flute (1981); *Tre movimenti* for Clarinet (1982); *Conversazione* for Oboe and Piano (1982); *Introduzione ed Allegro* for Saxophone and Piano (1982); *Iberia* for Flute and Guitar (1982); *12 Concert Studies* for Flute (1984); *Due dialoghi* for Bassoon and Piano (1984); *Iskato*, trio for Oboe, Clarinet, and Bassoon (1985); 2 clarinet quartets (both 1985); *Per flauto* for Flute (1986); *Per violino* for Violin (1987); *Metropolis* for Flute and Piano (1987). **OTHER:** Vocal pieces.

Verbrugghen, Henri, Belgian violinist and conductor; b. Brussels, Aug. 1, 1873; d. Northfield, Minn., Nov. 12, 1934. He studied with Hubay and Ysaÿe at the Brussels Cons.; in 1893, was engaged as a violinst in the Scottish Orch. in Glasgow; then was concertmaster in various orchs. in Wales; also conducted summer concerts there while retaining his position in Glasgow. In 1915 he went to Australia, where he was director of the State Conservatorium and conductor of its orch. in Sydney; also was conductor of the New South Wales State Orch.; then was conductor of the Minneapolis Sym. Orch. (1923–31).

Vercoe, Barry, New Zealand-born American composer and computer-music specialist; b. Wellington, July 24, 1937. He was educated at the Univ. of Auckland (Mus.B. in composition, 1959; B.A. in mathematics, 1962) and the Univ. of Mich. (A.Mus.D., 1968). After completing postdoctoral research at Princeton Univ. (1968–70), he served as U.S. adviser to the UNESCO Joint European Studies Committee on Technology and Arts (1977–78); also was resident composer/researcher at IRCAM (1983–84), where he developed "cpmusic," a system for synchronizing computer-processed sound with live instruments by computer tracking of performers in real time. He was a visiting lecturer at the Yale Univ. School of Music (1970–71); then joined the faculty at the Mass. Inst. of Technology, first as an assoc. prof. in its dept. of humanities (1971–85) and then as a prof. in its dept. of media arts and sciences (from 1985). His work in psychoacoustic and computer music research has been supported by sizable grants from the National Science Foundation (1976; 1987–89), the NEA (1978–82), and the John D. and Catherine T. MacArthur Foundation (1981), among others. He held a Guggenheim fellowship (1982–83). His developments in the field of computer audio systems include "Music-11" (1976; in 1984, rewritten to "Csound"), for fast digital processing of audio on PDP-11 minicomputers, and "MUSIC 360" (1969), a programming language used for processing sound on large IBM machines. He is married to **Elizabeth Vercoe**.

WORKS: *Digressions* for Band, 2 Choruses, Computer, and Orch. (1968); *Synthesism* for Computer (1970); *Synapse I* for Viola and Computer (1976) and *II* for Flute and 4X Processor (1984).

Vercoe, Elizabeth, American composer; b. Washington, D.C., April 23, 1941. She was educated at Wellesley College (B.A., 1962), the Univ. of Mich. (M.M., 1963), and Boston Univ. (D.M.A., 1978). She taught at Westminster Choir College in Princeton, N.J. (1969–71), and Framingham (Mass.) State College (1973–74). She was composer-in-residence at the Cité Internationale des Arts in Paris and the Charles Ives Center for American Music; in 1988, participated in the U.S./U.S.S.R. Young Composers' Exchange. She wrote a variety of articles actively promoting the cause of women's music; was a founding member of the Mass. Chapter of American Women Composers (1984) and a board member of the International League of Women Composers; co-directed the Women's Music Festival/85 in Boston. She is married to **Barry Vercoe**.

WORKS: *Children's Caprice* for Orch. (1963); *Herstory I* for Soprano, Piano, and Vibraphone, after American women poets (1975), *II: 13 Japanese Lyrics* for Soprano, Piano, and Percussion, after medieval Japanese women poets (1979), and *III: Jehanne de Lorraine*, staged monodrama for Voice and Piano, after Villon, Shaw, Twain et al. (1986); Violin Concerto (1977); *Irreveries from Sappho* for Women's Chorus and Piano (1981); *Fantavia* for Flute and Percussion (1982); *Suite française* for Violin (1983); *Despite our Differences No. 1* for Violin, Cello, and Piano (1984) and *No. 2* for Piano and Chamber Orch. (1988); *9 Epigrams from Poor Richard* for Voice and Tape (1986).

Vered, Ilana, Israeli pianist; b. Tel Aviv, Dec. 6, 1939. Her mother was a concert pianist and her father was a violinist; she took piano lessons as a child with her mother; at 13, won an Israeli government grant to continue her studies at the Paris Cons.; subsequently took lessons with Rosina Lhévinne and Nadia Reisenberg at the Juilliard School of Music in N.Y. In 1969 she received a grant from the Martha Baird Rockefeller Foundation for a major tour of Europe; subsequently made regular tours there and in the U.S.

Veremans, Renaat, Belgian composer, opera administrator, and teacher; b. Lierre, March 2, 1894; d. Antwerp, June 5, 1969. He received training at the Lemmens Inst. in Mechelen and from De Boeck at the Antwerp Cons., winning the premier prix in organ and piano (1914). From 1921 to 1944 he was director of the Flemish Opera in Antwerp. He also taught at the Antwerp Cons. As a composer, Veremans remained faithful to the Romantic tradition.

WORKS: DRAMATIC: OPERAS: *Beatrijs* (1928); *Anna-Marie* (Antwerp, Feb. 22, 1938); *Bietje* (1954); *Lanceloot en Sanderien* (Antwerp, Sept. 13, 1968). Also operettas. **ORCH.:** 3 syms. (1959, 1961, 1968); Trumpet Concerto (1960); Concerto for Flute and Chamber Orch. (1962); Concerto for Oboe and Small Orch. (1964); Horn Concerto (1965); symphonic poems. **OTHER:** Chamber music; choruses; many songs.

Veress, Sándor, eminent Hungarian-born Swiss composer and pedagogue; b. Kolozsvár, Feb. 1, 1907; d. Bern, March 6, 1992. He studied piano with his mother; also received instruction in piano from Bartók and in composition from Kodály at the Royal Academy of Music in Budapest (1923–27); obtained his teacher's diploma (1932); also took lessons with Lajtha at the Hungarian Ethnographical Museum (1929–33). He worked with Bartók on the folklore collection at the Academy of Sciences in Budapest (1937–40); subsequently taught at the Academy of Music in Budapest (1943–48). In 1949 he went to Switzerland, where he received an appointment as guest prof. on folk music at the Univ. of Bern; then taught at the Bern Cons. from 1950 to 1977; also was active as a guest lecturer in the U.S. and elsewhere; taught musicology at the Univ. of Bern (1968–77). In 1975 he became a naturalized Swiss citizen.

WORKS: DRAMATIC: CHILDREN'S OPERA: *Hangjegyek lázadása* (Revolt of the Musical Notes; 1931). **BALLETS:** *Csodafurulya* (The Miraculous Pipe; 1937; Rome, 1941); *Térszili Katicza* (Katica from Térszil; 1942–43; Stockholm, Feb. 16, 1949). **ORCH.:** *Divertimento* for Small Orch. (1935); *Partita* for Small Orch. (1936); Violin Concerto (1937–39; Zürich, Jan. 9, 1951); *Csürdöngölő* (Hungarian Barn Dance; 1938); 2 syms: No. 1 (1940) and No. 2, *Sinfonia minneapolitana* (1952; Minneapolis, March 12, 1954); *4 danze transilvane* for Strings (1944–49); *Sirató ének* [Threnody] *in memoriam Béla Bartók* (1945); *Előjáték egy tragédiahoz* (Prelude to a Tragedy; 1947); *Drámai változatok* (Dramatic Variations; 1947); *Respublica*, overture (1948); *Hommage à Paul Klee*, fantasia for 2 Pianos and Strings (1951; Bern, Jan. 22, 1952); Concerto for Piano, Strings, and Percussion (1952; Baden-Baden, Jan. 19, 1954); Sonata (Brussels, July 8, 1952); Concerto for String Quartet and Orch. (1960–61; Basel, Jan. 25, 1962); *Passacaglia concertante* for Oboe and Strings (Lucerne, Aug. 31, 1961); *Variations on a Theme by Zoltán Kodály* (1962); *Expovare* for Flute, Oboe, and Strings (1964); *Musica concertante* for 12 Strings (1965–66); Clarinet Concerto (1981–82); *Orbis tonorum* for Chamber Orch. (1986); *Concerto Tilinko* for Flute and Orch. (1988–89); Concerto for 2 Trombones and Orch. (1989). **CHAMBER:** 2 string quartets (1931; 1936–37); Sonata for Solo Violin (1935); 2nd Violin Sonata (1939); Trio for Violin, Viola, and Cello (1954); Trio for Piano, Violin, and Cello (1963); Sonata for Solo Cello (1967); Wind Quintet (1968); *Introduzione e Coda* for Clarinet, Violin, and Cello (1972); Trio for Baryton, Viola, and Cello (1985); *Stories and Fairy Tales* for 2 Percussionists (1987); piano pieces, including *Fingerlarks*, 88 pieces (1946). **VOCAL:** *Elegie* for Baritone, String Orch., and Harp (1964); choral works; songs.

WRITINGS: With L. Lajtha, *Népdal, népzenegyűtjés* (Folk Song, Folk Music Collecting; Budapest, 1936); *Béla Bartók, the Man and the Artist* (London, 1948); *La raccolta della musica popolare ungherese* (Rome, 1949).

BIBL.: A. Traub, *S. V.: Festschrift zum 80. Geburtstag* (Berlin, 1986).

Veretti, Antonio, Italian composer and music educator; b. Verona, Feb. 20, 1900; d. Rome, July 13, 1978. After initial training in Verona, he studied with Mattioli and Alfano at the Bologna Liceo Musicale (graduated, 1921). He then founded his own Cons. Musicale della Giovent Italiana in Rome, which he directed until 1943; subsequently was director of the Pesaro Cons. (1950–52), the Cagliari Cons. (1953–55), and the Florence Cons. (1956–70). While his music generally followed Italian modernist traditions, he later experimented with serial techniques.

WORKS: DRAMATIC: *Il Medico volante*, opera (1928); *Il Favorito del re*, opera (1931; Milan, March 17, 1932; rev. as the opera-ballet, *Burlesca*, Rome, Jan. 29, 1955); *Il galante tiratore*, ballet (1932; San Remo, Feb. 11, 1933); *Un favola di Andersen*, ballet (Venice, Sept. 15, 1934); *I sette peccati*, choreographic musical mystery (Milan, April 24, 1956); film music. **ORCH.:** *Sinfonia italiana* (Liège, Sept. 4, 1930); Suite (1934); *Sinfonia epica* (1938); Piano Concerto (Venice, Sept. 9, 1950); *Ouverture della campana* (RAI, Nov. 10, 1951); *Fantasie* for Clarinet and Orch. or Piano (1959); Concertino for Flute and Chamber Orch. or Piano (1959). **CHAMBER:** *Duo strumentale* for Violin and Piano (1925); Cello Sonata (1926); Piano Trio (1927); *Divertimento* for Harpsichord and 6 Instruments (1939); Violin Sonata (1952). **VOCAL:** *Il Cantico dei Cantici*, oratorio (1922); *Morte e deificazione di Dafni* for Voice and 11 Instruments (Venice, Sept. 8, 1937); *Il Figliuol prodigo*, oratorio (Rome, Nov. 21, 1942); *Sinfonia sacra* for Men's Voices and Orch. (1946; Rome, April 1947); *4 poesie di Giorgio Vigolo* for Voice and Orch. (1950; Turin, Feb. 17, 1956; also for Voice and Piano); *Elegie in Friulano* for Voice, Violin, Clarinet, and Guitar (1963).

Verevka, Grigori, Ukrainian composer; b. Bereznia, Chernigov district, Dec. 25, 1895; d. Kiev, Oct. 21, 1964. He was a boy chorister in Chernigov; then studied at the Kiev Inst. of Music and Drama; became engaged in choral conducting. He wrote a number of choruses that entered the general repertoire; made choral arrangements of nearly 100 revolutionary songs.

Verikovsky, Mikhail (Ivanovich), Ukrainian conductor, teacher, and composer; b. Kremenetz, Nov. 20, 1896; d. Kiev, June 14, 1962. He was a pupil of Yavorsky at the Kiev Cons. He was conductor of the operas in Kiev (1926–28) and Kharkov (1928–35), and also director of the opera studio of the Kharkov Inst. of Music and Drama (1934–35). In 1946 he became a prof. at the Kiev Cons. He composed the first Ukrainian ballet, *Pan Kanyovsky* (1930).

WORKS: DRAMATIC: OPERAS: *Dela nebesniye* (Heavenly Things; 1932); *Sotnik* (The Ensign; 1938); *Naymichka* (For Purchase; 1943); *Batrachka* (The Maid; 1946); *Basnya o chertopolokhe i roze* (The Fable of the Thistle and the Rose; 1948); *Begletsi* (Fugitives; 1948); *Slava* (Glory; 1961). **MUSICAL COMEDY:** *Viy* (1946). **BALLET:** *Pan Kanyovsky* (1930). **OTHER:**

Orch. music; chamber music; piano pieces; oratorios and cantatas on political themes; choruses; songs.

BIBL.: N. Herasimova-Persidska, *M.I. V.* (Kiev, 1959); N. Shurova, *M. V.* (Kiev, 1972).

Vermeulen, Matthijs, remarkable Dutch composer and music critic; b. Helmond, Feb. 8, 1888; d. Laren, July 26, 1967. Principally self-taught, he traveled in 1905 to Amsterdam, where he received musical guidance from Daniël le Lange and Alphons Diepenbrock. In 1907 he began to write music criticism for Dutch and French publications, and continued his journalistic activities until 1956. In 1921 Vermeulen went to France; returned to the Netherlands in 1947, when he became music ed. of *De Groene Amsterdammer.* He entertained a strong belief in the mystical powers of music; in order to enhance the universality of melodic, rhythmic, and contrapuntal elements, he introduced in his compositions a unifying set of cantus firmi against a diversified network of interdependent melodies of an atonal character; it was not until the last years of his life that his works began to attract serious attention for their originality and purely musical qualities.

WORKS: ORCH.: 7 syms.: No. 1, *Symphonia Carminum* (1912–14; Arnhem, March 12, 1919; 1st professional perf., Amsterdam, May 5, 1964), No. 2, *Prélude à la nouvelle journée* (1919–20; 1st perf. as an identified work, Amsterdam, July 5, 1956; had won 5th prize at the Queen Elisabeth Composition Competition in Brussels in 1953, and was performed anonymously on Dec. 9), No. 3, *Thrène et Péan* (1921–22; Amsterdam, May 24, 1939), No. 4, *Les Victoires* (1940–41; Rotterdam, Sept. 30, 1949), No. 5, *Les Lendemains Chantants* (1941–45; Amsterdam, Oct. 12, 1949), No. 6, *Les Minutes heureuses* (1956–58; Utrecht, Nov. 25, 1959), and No. 7, *Dithyrambes pour les temps à venir* (1963–65; Amsterdam, April 2, 1967); *Passacaille et Cortège* (1930; concert fragments from his music for the open-air play *The Flying Dutchman*); *Symphonic Prolog* (1930). **CHAMBER:** 2 cellos sonatas (1918; 1938); String Trio (1924); Violin Sonata (1925); String Quartet (1960–61). **VOCAL:** Songs.

WRITINGS: *De twee muzieken* (The Two Musics; 2 vols., Leyden, 1918); "Klankbord" (Sound Board) and "De eene grondtoon" (The One Key Note) in *De vrije bladen* (Amsterdam, 1929 and 1932); *Het avontuur van den geest* (The Adventure of the Spirit; Amsterdam, 1947); *Principen der Europese Muziek* (Principles of European Music; Amsterdam, 1948); *De Muziek, Dat Wonder* (Music, A Miracle; The Hague, 1958).

BIBL.: W. Paap, "De Componist M. V.," *Mens en Melodie* (Nov. 1949); E. Vermeulen, "M. V.," *Sonorum Speculum,* 28 (1966); W. Paap, "In Memoriam M. V.," *Mens en Melodie* (Sept. 1967); R. de Leeuw, "M. V.," *Sonorum Speculum,* 52 (1973); J. Bernlef, "'I've Never Felt the Need of a System'," and O. Ketting, "Prelude as Postlude," *Key Notes,* 3 (1976); P. Rapoport, *Opus Est: Six Composers from Northern Europe* (London, 1978).

Verne (real name, **Wurm**), family of English pianists, all sisters. They adopted the name Verne in 1893. **Mathilde Verne** (b. Southampton, May 25, 1865; d. London, June 4, 1936) studied with her parents, and then became a pupil of Clara Schumann in Frankfurt am Main; was very successful in England; from 1907 to 1936, gave concerts of chamber music in London; was a renowned teacher. **Alice Verne Bredt** (b. Southampton, Aug. 9, 1868; d. London, April 12, 1958) was best known as a piano teacher; she also composed pedagogical works. **Adela Verne** (b. Southampton, Feb. 27, 1877; d. London, Feb. 5, 1952) studied with her sisters, and later took lessons from Paderewski in Switzerland; returning to London, she developed a successful career, and became extremely popular as a concert player in England; also made tours in the U.S.

BIBL.: M. Verne, *Chords of Remembrance* (London, 1936).

Vernon, Ashley. See **Manschinger, Kurt.**

Verrall, John (Weedon), American composer and teacher; b. Britt, Iowa, June 17, 1908. He studied piano and composition with Donald Ferguson; then attended classes at the Royal College of Music in London with R.O. Morris, and took lessons with Kodály in Budapest. Returning to the U.S., he studied at the Minneapolis College of Music and Hamline Univ. (B.A., 1932); received further training at the Berkshire Music Center at Tanglewood, with Roy Harris, and with Frederick Jacobi; held a Guggenheim fellowship (1947). He held teaching positions at Hamline Univ. (1934–42), at Mount Holyoke College (1942–46), and at the Univ. of Wash. in Seattle (1948–73).

WORKS: OPERAS: *The Cowherd and the Sky Maiden,* after a Chinese legend (1951; Seattle, Jan. 17, 1952); *The Wedding Knell,* after Hawthorne (Seattle, Dec. 5, 1952); *3 Blind Mice* (Seattle, May 22, 1955). **ORCH.:** 3 syms: No. 1 (1939; Minneapolis, Jan. 16, 1940), No. 2 (1948), and No. 3 (1968); Violin Concerto (1946); *Symphony for Young Orchestras* (1948); *The Dark Night of St. John* for Chamber Orch. (1949); *Sinfonia festiva* for Band (1954); Piano Concerto (1960); Viola Concerto (1968); *Radiant Bridge* (1976); *Rhapsody* for Horn and Strings (1979). **CHAMBER:** 2 viola sonatas (1939, 1963); 7 string quartets (1941, 1942, 1948, 1949, 1952, 1956, 1961); 2 serenades for Wind Quintet (1944, 1950); Piano Quintet (1953); *Nocturne* for Bass Clarinet and Piano (1956); Septet for Winds (1966); Nonet for Wind Quintet and String Quartet (1966); Flute Sonata (1972); *Eusebius Remembered* for Horn and Piano (1976); *Invocation to Eos* for Horn and Piano (1983); Sonata for 2 Pianos (1984). **VOCAL:** Choruses; songs.

WRITINGS: *Elements of Harmony* (n.p., 1937); with S. Moseley, *Form and Meaning in the Arts* (N.Y., 1958); *Fugue and Invention in Theory and Practice* (Palo Alto, Calif., 1966); *Basic Theory of Scales, Modes and Intervals* (Palo Alto, Calif., 1969).

Verrett, Shirley, noted black American mezzo-soprano, later soprano; b. New Orleans, May 31, 1931. Her father, a choirmaster at the Seventh-Day Adventist church in New Orleans, gave her rudimentary instruction in singing. Later she moved to California and took voice lessons with John Charles Thomas and Lotte Lehmann. In 1955 she won the Marian Anderson Award and a scholarship at the Juilliard School of Music in N.Y., where she became a student of Marion Székely-Freschl; while still a student, she appeared as soloist in Falla's *El amor brujo* under Stokowski, and made her operatic debut as Britten's Lucretia in Yellow Springs, Ohio (1957). In 1962 she scored a major success as Carmen at the Festival of Two Worlds at Spoleto, Italy. In 1963 she made a tour of the Soviet Union, and sang Carmen at the Bolshoi Theater in Moscow. In 1966 she made her debut at Milan's La Scala and at London's Covent Garden. On Sept. 21, 1968, she made her debut at the Metropolitan Opera in N.Y., again as Carmen. On Oct. 22, 1973, she undertook 2 parts, those of Dido and Cassandra, in *Les Troyens* of Berlioz, produced at the Metropolitan. As a guest artist, she also appeared in San Francisco, Boston, Paris, Vienna, and other operatic centers. In 1990 she sang Dido at the opening performance of the new Opéra de la Bastille in Paris. She won distinction in mezzo-soprano roles, and later as a soprano; thus she sang the title role in Bellini's *Norma,* a soprano, and also the role of mezzo-soprano Adalgisa in the same opera. Her other roles included Tosca, Azucena, Amneris, and Dalila. She also showed her ability to cope with the difficult parts in modern operas, such as Bartók's *Bluebeard's Castle.* Her voice is of a remarkably flexible quality, encompassing lyric and dramatic parts with equal expressiveness and technical proficiency. Her concert repertory ranges from Schubert to Rorem, and also includes spirituals.

BIBL.: W. Sargeant, "Profiles: S. V.," *New Yorker* (April 14, 1975).

Vetter, Michael, German composer and performer; b. Obertsdorf, Allgau, Sept. 18, 1943. He studied philosophy and theology (1964–69), then became known as a recorder player, specializing in early and contemporary works. He was associated with Stockhausen's circle, and performed in *Alphabet pour Liège* (1972). His notated compositions are almost exclusively graphic. His recordings of the 1980s include *Overtones, Tam-*

bura Preludes, and *Pro-Vocationes*, all scored for voice and tambura; the voice uses a multiphonic technique similar to Buddhist chant, supported by the dense overtones of the tambura in an improvisational structure. He publ. a textbook, *Il flauto dolce e acerbo* (Celle, 1964–69).

WORKS: *Figurationen III* for Any Instrument (1965); *Orzismus* for Audience, Players, and Projections (1969); *Sonnenuntergang* for Electric Guitar, Electric Recorder, Trumpet, and Percussion (1971).

Vetter, Walther, distinguished German musicologist; b. Berlin, May 10, 1891; d. there, April 1, 1967. He studied at the Leipzig Cons.; subsequently took a course in musicology with Hermann Abert at the Univ. of Halle, where he received his Ph.D. in 1920 with the diss. *Die Arie bei Gluck*; he completed his Habilitation at the Univ. of Breslau with his *Das frühdeutsche Lied* in 1927 (publ. in Munster, 1928). He taught at the Univs. of Halle, Hamburg, Breslau, and Greifswald before joining the Univ. of Poznań in 1941; from 1946 to 1958 he was a prof. at Humboldt Univ. in Berlin, and also served as director of its Inst. of Musicology. From 1948 to 1961 he was co-ed. of *Die Musikforschung*; from 1956 to 1966 he was ed. of the *Deutsches Jahrbuch für Musikwissenschaft*.

WRITINGS: *Der humanistische Bildungsgedanke in Musik und Musikwissenschaft* (Langensalza, 1928); *Franz Schubert* (Potsdam, 1934); *Antike Musik* (Munich, 1935); *J.S. Bach: Leben und Werk* (Leipzig, 1938); *Beethoven und die militär-politischen Ereignisse seiner Zeit* (Poznań, 1943); *Der Kapellmeister Bach: Versuch einer Deutung Bachs auf Grund seines Wirkens als Kapellmeister in Köthen* (Potsdam, 1950); *Der Klassiker Schubert* (2 vols., Leipzig, 1953); *Mythos—Melos—Musica: Ausgewählte Aufsätze zur Musikgeschichte* (a collection of articles; 2 vols., Leipzig, 1957 and 1961); *Christoph Willibald Gluck* (Leipzig, 1964).

BIBL.: *Musa—mens—musici: Im Gedenken an W. V.* (Leipzig, 1969).

Veyron-Lacroix, Robert, noted French harpsichordist, pianist, and teacher; b. Paris, Dec. 13, 1922; d. Garches, Hauts-de-Seine, April 3, 1991. He studied with Samuel-Rousseau and Nat at the Paris Cons., where he won premier prix in piano, harpsichord, and theory. After making his formal debut in a concert broadcast on the French Radio in 1949, he pursued a career as a soloist and chamber music artist. He became closely associated with Jean-Pierre Rampal, with whom he gave numerous concerts. He taught at the Schola Cantorum in Paris (1956) and at the Nice International Academy (1959) before becoming a prof. at the Paris Cons. (1967). He was the author of *Recherches de musique ancienne* (Paris, 1955). While he was particularly known for his interpretations of early music, he frequently programmed modern pieces, including those by Falla, Poulenc, Milhaud, Jolivet, Ohana, and Françaix.

Vianna, Fructuoso (de Lima), Brazilian pianist, teacher, and composer; b. Itajubá, Oct. 6, 1896; d. Rio de Janeiro, April 22, 1976. He studied music with his father, a municipal judge, who composed polkas and waltzes. In 1917 he entered the Rio de Janeiro Cons., and studied piano with Oswald and harmony with Gouveia and França; in 1923 he went to Europe, where he pursued piano training with Hanschild in Berlin, De Greef in Brussels, and Selva in Paris, where he also studied the Dalcroze method of eurhythmics. Returning to Brazil, he was active as a teacher; was prof. of piano at the Belo Horizonte Cons. (1929–30) and the São Paulo Cons. (1930–38), and prof. of choral singing at the National Technical School in Rio de Janeiro (from 1942); also was prof. of piano at Bennet College. His works are based on native Brazilian melorhythms pleasurably seasoned with acrid dissonances, achieving a certain *trompe-l'oreille* euphony. His musical output consists mainly of piano pieces and songs of such nature; among them are numerous "valsas" (European waltzes in a Brazilian dressing), "toadas" (melodious romances), and "tanguinhos" (little tangos à la *brésilienne*). They are all perfumed with impressionistic overtones.

Vianna da Motta, José, esteemed Portuguese pianist and pedagogue; b. Isle St. Thomas, Portuguese Africa, April 22, 1868; d. Lisbon, May 31, 1948. His family returned to Lisbon when he was a year old; he studied with local teachers; gave his first concert at the age of 13; then studied piano in Berlin with X. Scharwenka and composition with P. Scharwenka. In 1885 he went to Weimar, where he became a pupil of Liszt; also took lessons with Hans von Bülow in Frankfurt am Main (1887). He then undertook a series of concert tours throughout Europe (1887–88), the U.S. (1892–93; 1899), and South America (1902). He was in Berlin until 1915; then became director of the Geneva Cons. In 1919 he was appointed director of the Lisbon Cons., retiring in 1938. At the height of his career, he was greatly esteemed as a fine interpreter of Bach and Beethoven. He was also the author of many articles in German, French, and Portuguese; wrote *Studien bei Bülow* (1896); *Betrachtungen über Franz Liszt* (1898); *Die Entwicklung des Klavierkonzerts* (as a program book to Busoni's concerts); essays on Alkan; critical articles in the *Kunstwart, Klavierlehrer, Bayreuther Blätter*, etc. He was a prolific composer; among his works were *Die Lusiaden* for Orch. and Chorus; Sym.; String Quartet; many piano pieces, in some of which (e.g., the *5 Portuguese Rhapsodies* and the Portuguese dance *Vito*) he employs folk themes with striking effect. In 1951 the Vianna da Motta International Piano Competition was founded in Lisbon in his memory.

BIBL.: F. Lopes Graça, *V. d.M.: Subsidios para una biographia* (Lisbon, 1949).

Vickers, Jon(athan Stewart), renowned Canadian tenor; b. Prince Albert, Saskatchewan, Oct. 29, 1926. He began singing as a child. After his voice developed into the tenor range, he acquired experience singing in Baptist church choirs in Prince Albert and Flin Flon. While accepting various singing engagements, he worked in chain stores to make ends meet. After singing major roles in Gilbert & Sullivan and Victor Herbert operettas, he won a scholarship to the Royal Cons. of Music of Toronto in 1950 to study with George Lambert. During this time, he continued to sing in concerts. In 1954 he sang the Duke of Mantua with the Canadian Opera Co. in Toronto, and returned there in such roles as Alfredo in *La Traviata* (1955) and Don José (1956); in the latter year, he appeared in a concert performance of *Medea* in N.Y. In Jan. 1957 he made his first appearance with the Royal Opera of Covent Garden, London, on tour. It was as Siegmund in *Die Walküre* at the Bayreuth Festival in 1958 that Vickers first won notable acclaim. In 1959 he sang Jason in *Medea* in Dallas and Radames in San Francisco. On Jan. 17, 1960, he made his Metropolitan Opera debut in N.Y. as Canio, where he continued to sing with success in subsequent years. He sang Florestan at Milan's La Scala and Siegmund at the Chicago Lyric Opera in 1961. In 1966, 1967, and 1968 he appeared at Karajan's Easter Festivals. He sang Otello at Expo 67 in Montreal in 1967. In 1975 he appeared as Tristan with the Opéra du Québec. In 1985 Vickers sang Handel's Samson at Covent Garden in a production marking the 300th anniversary of the composer's birth. Throughout the years, he continued to make occasional appearances as a soloist with orchs. and as a recitalist. His remarkable career came to a close with his retirement in 1988. In 1968 Vickers was made a Companion of the Order of Canada. Vickers was acknowledged as one of the principal dramatic and Heldentenors of his era. In addition to roles already noted, he also excelled as Berlioz's Aneas, Don Alvaro, Don Carlos, Parsifal, and Peter Grimes.

Victory, Gerard (real name, **Alan Loraine**), Irish composer, conductor, and broadcasting administrator; b. Dublin, Dec. 24, 1921; d. there, March 14, 1995. He was educated at Belvedere College, Dublin, the Univ. of Ireland (B.A.), and Trinity College, Univ. of Dublin (B.Mus.). From 1948 to 1953 he was active with the Irish Radio Service. He was a radio (1953–61) and television (1961–62) producer with Radio Telefis Eireann. After serving as its deputy director of music (1962–67), he was its director of music (1967–82). From 1981 to 1983 he was president of UNESCO's International Rostrum of Composers. In 1972 he was awarded an honorary Mus.D. degree from Trinity College. In 1975 he received the Chevalier de l'Ordre des Arts et des Lettres of France and the Order of Merit of the Federal Republic of Germany. Victory created an extensive body of music in various genres and styles. His works were always handsomely crafted and couched in a generally accessible idiom.

WORKS: DRAMATIC: OPERAS: *An Fear a phós Balbhán* (The Silent Wife; 1952; Dublin, April 6, 1953); *Iomrall Aithne* (1955–56); *The Stranger* (1958); *The Music Hath Mischief* (1960); *Chatterton* (1967); *Eloise and Abelard* (1970–72); *Circe 1991,* radio opera (1971); *An Evening for Three* (1975); *The Rendezvous* (1988–89; Dublin, Nov. 2, 1989); *The Wooing of Etain,* children's opera (1994). **OPERETTAS:** *Nita* (1944); *Once upon a Moon* (1949); *The 2 Violins* (1955). **MUSICAL PLAYS:** *Eldorado* (1953); *The Martinique Story* (1960–61). Also incidental music for plays; film music. **ORCH.:** *The Enchanted Garden* (1950–51); *Elegy* (1951); *Marche Pittoresque* (1951); 2 piano concertos (1954, 1972); *Charade,* overture (1955); *Patrician Theme* (1956); *The Rapparee,* overture (1959); 4 syms.: No. 1, *Short Symphony* (1961), No. 2, *Il Ricorso* (1977), No. 3, *Refrains* (1984; Dublin, July 19, 1985), and No. 4 (1990; Dublin, Dec. 7, 1991); *Ballade* (1963); *5 Mantras* for Strings (1963); *Pariah Music* (1965); *La Montana* (1965); *Treasure Island,* overture (1966); *Favola di Notte* (1966; Dublin, Feb. 26, 1967); *Spook Galop* (1966); *Homage to Petrarch* for Strings (1967); *4 Tableaux* (1968); Accordion Concerto (1968; RTE, Dublin, May 22, 1970); *Miroirs* (1969); *Jonathan Swift-A Symphonic Portrait* (1970); *Praeludium* (1970); *Cyrano de Bergerac Overture* (1970; Dublin, March 14, 1972); *The Spirit of Molière,* suite (1971); Harp Concerto (1971); *Tetragon* for Oboe and Orch. (1971); *From Renoir's Workshop* (1973; RTE, Dublin, Aug. 20, 1974); *Canto* (1973); *Capriccio* for Violin and Orch. (1975); *Olympic Festival Overture* (RTE, Dublin, Sept. 1, 1975); *Barocco Suite* (1978); Cello Concerto (1978); *9 Variations on the Cravate* (1978); *Fabula Mystica Graeca* for Strings (1980); *3 Irish Pictures* (1979–80); *6 Epiphanies on the Author (In Memory of James Joyce)* (1981; Dublin, Feb. 5, 1982); *5 Inventions* for Violins and Strings (Galway, May 1, 1982); *The Broad and the Narrow Ways,* suite (1984; Dublin, June 1985); *Tableaux Sportifs* (1984; Radio France, June 1985; also for Chamber Ensemble); *Monte Cristo,* concert overture (1987; also for Concert Band); *Concertino à la Grecque* for Trombone and Orch. (1987; Dublin, Feb. 23, 1995); *Salute to the President* or *Ómós don Uachtarán,* concert overture (Dublin, Oct. 10, 1990); *Eblana: A Symphonic Portrait of Dublin* (1990–91; Belfast, June 20, 1993); *Ave Scientia,* concert overture (1994; Galway, Oct. 1995); also pieces for Brass and Concert Bands. **CHAMBER:** Wind Quintet (1957); *Esquisse* for Oboe and Piano (1960); *Canzona* for Violin and Piano (1962); String Quartet (1963); *Rodomontade* for Woodwind Quintet (1964); *Semantiques* for Flute and Piano (1967); *3 Legends* for Piano, Violin, Clarinet, and Cello (1969); Piano Quintet (1970); *Trois contes de fee* for Clarinet and Piano (1970); Trio for Accordion, Guitar, and Percussion (1970); Alto Saxophone Sonatine (1975); *Adest Hora* for Violin, Clarinet, Cello, Piano, and Percussion (1977); *5 Exotic Dances* for Brass Sextet (1979); String Trio (1982; Dublin, Jan. 30, 1984); *Commedia* for Brass Quintet (1985; Dublin, Jan. 1986); Trio for Violin, Horn, and Piano (1986); *Runic Variations* for Flute and Clarinet (1988); *Moresca* for Violin, Cello, and Harp (1989; Dublin, Feb. 6, 1990); *Denkmal* for String Trio (1993). **PIANO:** Sonata (1958); *Prélude and Toccata* (1962); *3 Masks* (1965); *Cinque Correlazioni* (1966; Dublin, Jan. 10, 1971); *Verona Préludes* (1979; Dublin, Jan. 5, 1980). **VOCAL:** *Quartetto* for Soli, Narrator, and Chorus (1965); *The Island People,* cantata for Children's Chorus, Narrator, and Instruments (1967); *Civitas Nova* for Soli, Chorus, and Organ (1968); *The Magic Trumpet* for Speaker, Chorus, and Orch. (1970; rev. 1983); *Mass for Christmas Day* for Baritone, Chorus, and Organ (1973); *Processus,* cantata for Chorus, Instruments, and Tape (1973–75; RTE, Dublin, June 28, 1976); *Sailing to Byzantium* for Alto and Orch. (1975); *Mass of the Resurrection* for Chorus and Organ (1977); *7 Songs of Experience* for Soli and Chorus (1977–78); *Ultima Rerum,* symphonic Requiem for Soli, Chorus, and Orch. (1979–81; Dublin, March 3, 1984); *King Sweeney,* cantata for Speaker, Tenor, Chorus, and Chamber Ensemble (1983); *Songs from Lyonnesse,* cantata for Chorus and Piano (1983); *Children of the Last Music,* dramatic cantata for Narrator, Soli, Chorus, Piano, and 2 Percussion (1990); *Seasons of Eros* for Baritone and Piano or Orch. (1990); *Responsibilities* for Chorus (1991); *The Everlasting Voices,* cantata for Chorus and Organ (Belfast, Aug. 27, 1993); *A Musical Instrument* for Soprano and Chorus (1993); many other choral works, song cycles, and solo songs.

Vidal, Paul (Antonin), noted French conductor, pedagogue, and composer; b. Toulouse, June 16, 1863; d. Paris, April 9, 1931. He studied at the Paris Cons., and in 1883 won the Prix de Rome with his cantata *Le Gladiateur.* In 1889 he joined the staff of the Paris Opéra as assistant choral director; later became chief conductor there (1906). He taught elementary courses at the Paris Cons. from 1894 until 1909, when he was appointed a prof. of composition. He was music director of the Opéra-Comique from 1914 to 1919. His brother, Joseph Bernard Vidal (b. Toulouse, Nov. 15, 1859; d. Paris, Dec. 18, 1924), was a conductor and composer; made a name for himself as a composer of operettas.

WORKS: DRAMATIC: *Eros,* fantaisie lyrique (Paris, April 22, 1892); *L'Amour dans les enfers* (1892); *La Maladetta,* ballet (Paris, Feb. 24, 1893); *Fête russe,* ballet (Paris, Oct. 24, 1893); *Guernica,* drame lyrique (Paris, June 7, 1895); *La Burgonde,* opera (Paris, Dec. 23, 1898); *Ramsès,* drame (Paris, June 27, 1900); *L'Impératrice,* ballet (1903); *Zino-Zina* (1908); *Ballet de Terpsichore* (1909); also pantomimes, incidental music to plays. **OTHER:** Orch. pieces; choral works; chamber music; songs; piano pieces.

BIBL.: A. Hoérée, "Nécrologie: Hommage à P. V.," *Revue Musicale,* XII (1931).

Viderø, Finn, noted Danish organist, pedagogue, and composer; b. Fuglebjerg, Aug. 15, 1906; d. Copenhagen, March 13, 1987. He went to Copenhagen and studied at the Cons. (graduated, 1926), then pursued musicological training at the Univ. (M.A., 1929); was active as a church organist there, holding appointments at the German-French Reformed (1928), Jaegersborg (1940), Trinitas (1947), and St. Andreas (1971) churches; also toured as a recitalist. He taught theory (1935–45) and organ and harpsichord (1949–74) at the Univ. of Copenhagen; was a visiting prof. at Yale Univ. (1959–60) and North Texas State Univ. (1967–68); also gave master classes. He wrote valuable articles on 16th- and 17th-century performance practice and ed. vols. of organ music, hymn tunes, choral pieces, and folk songs; also publ. *Orgelskole* (with O. Ring; 1933; 2nd ed., 1963). He composed choral works, organ music, piano pieces, and songs.

Vidu, Ion, Romanian choral conductor and composer; b. Mînerău, Dec. 14, 1863; d. Lugoj, Feb. 7, 1931. He studied in Iaşi. He became a choral conductor in Lugoj. He wrote a great number of choruses in a distinct native style, but harmonized his melodies according to German models; many of his arrangements have become repertoire pieces in Romania.

BIBL.: V. Cosma, *Un maestru al muzicii corale: I. V.* (Bucharest, 1965).

Vierk, Lois V, American composer; b. Hammond, Ind., Aug. 4, 1951. (The middle V is without punctuation; it is derived from Von Viereck, the old version of her family name, traditionally abbreviated without a period.) She studied composition privately with Stein and at the Calif. Inst. of the Arts with Powell and Subotnick (M.F.A., 1978); also studied gagaku with Suenobu Togi in Los Angeles (1971–78), and ryuteki (a transverse flute) in Tokyo with Sukeyasu Shiba (1982–84). She produced radio programs of world music for KPFK-FM in Los Angeles; collaborated with choreographer Anita Feldman to create a unified approach to tap dance and sound. In 1989 she formed LVV, an ensemble devoted to the performance of her music, which was featured on the "Lois V Vierk Special" on

WNYC-FM in N.Y. Her minimalistic music is often microtonal and monochromatic, involving numerous similar instruments live or on tape; they typically reach an intense, gradual climax consisting of sensually overlapping textures. Her most frequently played work, *Go Guitars* for 5 Electric Guitars (1981), makes use in its title of the Japanese character for "5," transcribed as "go." Other works include *Dark Bourn* for 4 Bassoons and 4 Cellos (1985), *Manhattan Cascade* for 4 Accordions (1985), *Hexie Mountain Torrent* for Flute, Clarinet, Bassoon, Saxophones, Synthesizer, and Percussion (1987, and *Simoom* for 8 Cellos (1988).

Vierne, Louis, eminent French organist, pedagogue, and composer; b. Poitiers, Oct. 8, 1870; d. while playing his 1,750th recital at Notre-Dame Paris, June 2, 1937. He was born blind but gained limited sight through an operation in 1877. He showed musical talent at an early age, and studied at the Institution Nationale des Jeunes Aveugles in Paris (1881–88); received organ lessons from Franck, then was a pupil of Widor at the Paris Cons. (1890–93), winning a premier prix in organ (1894). In 1892 he became Widor's assistant at St.-Sulpice in Paris, and in 1900 was appointed organist at Notre-Dame in Paris, where he remained until his death. He taught organ in Paris at the Cons. (1894–1911) and at the Schola Cantorum (from 1911); among his pupils were Nadia Boulanger and Marcel Dupré. In 1927 he made a 4-month North American concert tour. His 6 organ syms. are principal works of the genre.

WORKS: ORCH.: Sym. (1907–08; Paris, Jan. 26, 1919); *Les djinns*, symphonic poem (1919); *Marche triomphale pour le centenaire de Napoléon* for Brass, Timpani, and Organ (1921); *Poème* for Piano and Orch. (1926); *Symphonic Piece* for Organ and Orch. (1926; arranged from the 1st 3 organ syms.). **CHAMBER:** String Quartet (n.d.); Violin Sonata (1906); Cello Sonata (1910); Piano Quintet (1917); *Soirs étrangers* for Cello and Piano (1928). **KEYBOARD: ORGAN:** *Allegretto* (1894); 6 syms. (1898–99; 1902–3; 1911; 1914; 1923–24; 1930); *Messe basse* (1912); *24 pièces en style libre* (1913–14); *Pièces de fantaisie* (4 books, 1926–27); *Triptyche* (1929–31); *Messe basse pour les défunts* (1934); also several piano pieces. **VOCAL:** *Messe solonnelle* for 4 Voices and 2 Organs (1900); *Praxinoé*, symphonic legend for Soloists, Chorus, and Orch. (1903–06); *Psyché* for Voice and Orch. (1914); *Les Angélus* for Voice and Organ or Orch. (1930); *Ballade du désespéré* for Tenor and Piano or Orch. (1931); songs.

BIBL.: *In Memoriam L. V.* (Paris, 1939); B. Gavoty, *L. V., La Vie et l'oeuvre* (Paris, 1943).

Vieru, Anatol, distinguished Romanian composer and musicologist; b. Iaşi, June 8, 1926. He was a student of Klepper (composition), Constantinescu (harmony), and Silvestri (conducting) at the Bucharest Cons. (1946–51) before pursuing training with Khachaturian (composition) at the Moscow Cons. (1951–54); later he attended the summer courses in new music at Darmstadt (1967) and subsequently took his Ph.D. in musicology at the Cluj Cons. (1978) with the diss. *De la moduri, spre un model al gîndirii muzicale intervalice* (From Modes Towards a Model of Intervallic Musical Thought; publ. as *Cartea Modurilor* [Book of Modes], Bucharest, 1980; 2nd ed., 1993). From 1955 he taught composition at the Bucharest Cons. He was founder-director of the Musiques parallèles concerts (1970–84), at which he presented the first Romanian performances of works by such modern masters as Schoenberg, Varèse, and Ives. In 1973 he was in Berlin under the auspices of the Deutscher Akademischer Austauschdienst. In 1984, 1992, and 1994 he gave courses in Darmstadt and in 1992–93 he was composer-in-residence at N.Y. Univ. Among his honors were the Reine Marie José prize of Geneva (1962), a Koussevitzky Foundation grant (1966), the prize of the Romanian Academy (1967), and the Gottfried von Herder Prize of the Univ. of Vienna (1986). He contributed articles to various journals and publ. the vol. *Cuvinte despre sunete* (Words About Sounds; Bucharest, 1993). Beginning with neomodal models, Vieru has developed a highly personal compositional style in which microstructures serve as the foundation upon which to build scores notable for their inventive handling of modal, tonal, and serial elements.

WORKS (all 1st perf. in Bucharest unless otherwise given): **DRAMATIC: OPERAS:** *Jonah* (1972–75; concert perf., Oct. 30, 1976); *The Feast of the Cadgers* (1978–81; concert perf., June 24, 1984; 1st stage perf., Berlin, Nov. 10, 1990); 3 "pocket" operas (1982–83): *Telegrams* (Nov. 8, 1983), *Theme and Variations* (Nov. 8, 1983), and *A Pedagogue of the New School* (April 7, 1987); *The Last Days, the Last Hours* (1990–95); film and television scores. **ORCH.:** *Suite in Ancient Style* for Strings (1945; May 21, 1966); *Concerto for Orchestra* (1954–55; Feb. 2, 1956); Concerto for Strings (1958; transcription of String Quartet No. 1, 1955); Flute Concerto (1958–59; Dec. 7, 1961); 2 cello concertos: No. 1 (1962; Geneva, March 27, 1963) and No. 2 (1992)); *Jeux* for Piano and Orch. (1963; Iaşi, March 18, 1966); Violin Concerto (1964; Cluj, Oct. 14, 1967); 6 syms.: No. 1, *Ode to Silence* (1966–67; March 28, 1968), No. 2 (1973; Berlin, Jan. 26, 1974), No. 3, *An Earthquake Symphony* (1977–78; March 1, 1979), No. 4 (1979–83; Cluj, May 5, 1983), No. 5 for Chorus and Orch. (1984; Jan. 30, 1986), and No. 6, *Exodus* (1988–89); *Museum Music* for Harpsichord and 12 Strings (1968; Paris, July 2, 1970); *Clepsydra I* (1968–69; Donaueschingen, Oct. 10, 1969); *Screen* (1970; Royan, April 4, 1971); Clarinet Concerto (1974–75; Iaşi, Feb. 3, 1978); Concerto for Violin, Cello, and Orch. (June 3, 1980); *Shell* for 15 Strings (1981; Timişoara, Nov. 6, 1982); *Narration II* for Saxophone(s) and Orch. (1985; Nice, Feb. 9, 1986); Sinfonia Concertante for Cello and Orch. (Feb. 2, 1989); *Taragot* for 2 Instrumentalists and Orch. (May 24, 1992); *Kaleidoscope* for Piano and Orch. (1993). **CHAMBER:** 2 Pieces for Trumpet and Piano (1953); 8 string quartets: No. 1 (1955; Moscow, Dec. 12, 1957), No. 2 (1956; June 7, 1957), No. 3, with Woman's Voice (1973; Sept. 8, 1977), No. 4 (1980; Nov. 6, 1981), No. 5 (1981–82; June 16, 1984), No. 6 (1986; April 7, 1987), No. 7 (1987; Turin, Sept. 29, 1988), and No. 8 (1991); Clarinet Quintet (1957); Sonata for Solo Cello (1962; May 16, 1968; also with Percussion, 1975); *Steps of Silence* for String Quartet and Percussionist (1967; Washington, D.C., Jan. 12, 1968); *The Eratosthenes Sieve* for Clarinet, Violin, Viola, Cello, and Piano (Mainz, Oct. 8, 1969); *Mosaics* for 3 Percussionists (1972; Zagreb, May 13, 1977); *Inscriptio* for 2 Flutes, 2 Trombones, Electric Guitar, and Bass Guitar (June 20, 1978); *Over the Treetops* for 8 Instrumentalists (1979); *Joseph and His Brothers* for 11 Instrumentalists and Tape (Metz, Nov. 16, 1979); *Double Duos* for Alto Saxophone, Vibraphone, and Piano (1983; Darmstadt, July 15, 1990; also for Alto Saxophone and Vibraphone, Sept. 15, 1986); *Soroc I* for 6 or 7 Instrumentalists (July 16, 1984) and *II* for Wind Quintet, Viola, and 2 Percussionists (Darmstadt, July 29, 1984); Sonata for Violin and Cello (1985; April 7, 1987); *Millefolium* for 4 Flutists Playing 12 Flutes (1986; Amsterdam, Nov. 11, 1987); *Trinta* for Saxophone(s) and Percussion (1987); *Diaphonie* for Cello and Double Bass (1987; Cologne, June 28, 1988); *Dar I* for Flute (1988) and *II* for Cello (1989); *Multigen* for Alto Flute, Oboe, Alto Saxophone, Percussion, and Piano (1988); *Giusto* for Alto Saxophone, Synthesizer, Electric Guitar, and Bass Guitar (1988; Berlin, Jan. 29, 1990); *Versete* for Violin and Piano (1989); *4 Sax* for Saxophone Quartet (1990; Berlin, Nov. 17, 1991); Cello Sonata (Radio classique, Paris, Dec. 15, 1992); *Eclisse* for Violin, Viola, Cello, Double Bass, and Piano (May 30, 1992); *Ricercar for NYU* for Chamber Ensemble (N.Y., Dec. 7, 1992); *Tabor* for 7 Instrumentalists (1992; Feb. 2, 1993); Trio for Bassoon, Guitar, and Double Bass (1992; N.Y., May 13, 1994); *Cracium*, violin sonata (1994); *Couple* for Clarinet and Viola (1995); *Leggero* for Flute(s) and Percussion (1995). **KEYBOARD: PIANO:** *Die Kinderwelt*, 20 miniatures (1958); *Nautilos* for Piano and Tape (Dec. 10, 1968); 2 sonatas: No. 1 (Oct. 30, 1976) and No. 2 (1994). **ORGAN:** *Narration* (1975; Berlin, March 6, 1977). **VOCAL:** *Mioritsa*, oratorio for Tenor, Baritone, Chorus, Children's Chorus, and Orch. (1956–57; Feb. 27, 1958); *Music for Bacovia and Labis* for Voices and Instruments (1959–63; Oct. 4, 1982); *Cantata of the Light Years* for Chorus and Orch. (June 18, 1960); Sym. for Mezzo-soprano and 15

Instrumentalists (1963; Cluj, Dec. 11, 1965); *Clepsydra II* for Chorus and Orch. (1971; Nov. 20, 1972); *Quatre angles pour regarder Florence* for Soprano, Piano or Harpsichord, and Percussion (1973; Champigny, April 19, 1974); *The Treasure in the Current* for Children's Chorus and Orch. (Braşov, July 3, 1982); *Psalm 91* for Baritone, Organ, Cello, and Double Bass (1983; Berlin, Jan. 15, 1984); *Archaic Love Songs* for Various Vocalists and Instrumental Combinations (1985–89); *Life Sentence* for Mezzo-soprano, Clarinet, and Percussionist (1992; Nov. 25, 1993); *Archipelagus* for Baritone and Percussion (1994). **MULTIMEDIA AND TAPE:** Quartet for Dancer, Clarinet, Horn, and Percussion (1967; April 20, 1970); *Clocks* for Tape, Instruments, Dancer, and Reciter (April 20, 1970); *Stone Land* for Tape (1972); *Antiphony to Stone Land* for Trombone, Organ, and Tape (1984); *Die Waage* for Tape, Violin, Cello, Clarinet, Bassoon, Guitar, Piano, and Reciter (Nov. 25, 1986); *Pelinarium* for Synthesizer and Tape (1986).

Viglione-Borghese, Domenico, Italian baritone; b. Mondovi, July 3, 1877; d. Milan, Oct. 26, 1957. He studied in Milan and Pesaro. He made his operatic debut as the Herald in *Lohengrin* in Lodi in 1899, and continued to sing in provincial Italian opera companies; then gave up singing in 1901, and went to the U.S., where he earned his living as a railroad worker in San Francisco. There he met Caruso, who recommended him to the impresario Scognamillo, who engaged him for a South American tour (1905–06); subsequently pursued his career in Italy, retiring in 1940. He sang some 40 roles, the best known being Jack Rance in Puccini's *La Fanciulla del West,* which he first sang in Brescia in 1911 and for the last time in Rome in 1940.

Vignas, Francisco, noted Spanish tenor; b. Moya, near Barcelona, March 27, 1863; d. Barcelona, July 14, 1933. He studied at the Barcelona Cons., and later in Paris. He made his debut in Barcelona in 1888 as Lohengrin; then sang in Italian opera houses; made his first appearance in London in 1893 at the Shaftesbury Theatre. On Nov. 29, 1893, he made his Metropolitan Opera debut in N.Y. as Turiddu; after only one season there, he returned to Europe.

Villa, Ricardo, Spanish composer and conductor; b. Madrid, Oct. 23, 1873; d. there, April 10, 1935. He studied at the Madrid Cons. He was founder-conductor of the Madrid municipal band (from 1909). He wrote the operas *El Cristo de la Vega* and *Raimundo Lulio*; a number of pieces for band in the Spanish vein: *La visión de Fray Martin, Impresiones sinfónicas,* and *Cantos regionales asturianos; Rapsodía asturiana* for Violin and Orch.; *Fantasía española* for Piano and Orch.; light music.

Villa-Lobos, Heitor, remarkable Brazilian composer of great originality and unique ability to recreate native melodic and rhythmic elements in large instrumental and choral forms; b. Rio de Janeiro, March 5, 1887; d. there, Nov. 17, 1959. He studied music with his father, a writer and amateur cello player; after his father's death in 1899, Villa-Lobos earned a living by playing the cello in cafés and restaurants; also studied cello with Benno Niederberger. From 1905 to 1912 he traveled in Brazil in order to collect authentic folk songs. In 1907 he entered the National Inst. of Music in Rio de Janeiro, where he studied with Frederico Nascimento, Angelo França, and Francisco Braga. In 1912 he undertook an expedition into the interior of Brazil, where he gathered a rich collection of Indian songs. On Nov. 13, 1915, he presented in Rio de Janeiro a concert of his compositions, creating a sensation by the exuberance of his music and the radical character of his technical idiom. He met Artur Rubinstein, who became his ardent admirer; for him Villa-Lobos composed the transcendentally difficult *Rudepoema.* In 1923 Villa-Lobos went to Paris on a Brazilian government grant; upon returning to Brazil in 1930, he was active in São Paulo and then in Rio de Janeiro in music education; founded a Cons. under the sponsorship of the Ministry of Education in 1942. He introduced bold innovations into the national program of music education, with an emphasis on the cultural resources of Brazil; compiled a *Guia pratico,* containing choral arrangements of folk songs of Brazil and other nations; organized the "orpheonic concentrations" of schoolchildren, whom he trained to sing according to his own cheironomic method of solfeggio. In 1944 he made his first tour of the U.S., and conducted his works in Los Angeles, Boston, and N.Y. in 1945. In 1945 he established in Rio de Janeiro the Brazilian Academy of Music, serving as its president from 1947 until his death. He made frequent visits to the U.S. and France during the last 15 years of his life.

Villa-Lobos was one of the most original composers of the 20th century. He lacked formal academic training, but far from hampering his development, this deficiency liberated him from pedantic restrictions, so that he evolved an idiosyncratic technique of composition, curiously eclectic, but all the better suited to his musical aesthetics. An ardent Brazilian nationalist, he resolved from his earliest attempts in composition to use authentic Brazilian song materials as the source of his inspiration; yet he avoided using actual quotations from popular songs; rather, he wrote melodies which are authentic in their melodic and rhythmic content. In his desire to relate Brazilian folk resources to universal values, he composed a series of extraordinary works, *Bachianas brasileiras,* in which Brazilian melorhythms are treated in Bachian counterpoint. He also composed a number of works under the generic title *Chôros,* a popular Brazilian dance form, marked by incisive rhythm and a ballad-like melody. An experimenter by nature, Villa-Lobos devised a graphic method of composition, using geometrical contours of drawings and photographs as outlines for the melody; in this manner he wrote *The New York Skyline,* using a photograph for guidance. Villa-Lobos wrote operas, ballets, syms., chamber music, choruses, piano pieces, songs; the total number of his compositions is in excess of 2,000.

WORKS: DRAMATIC: OPERAS: *Izaht* (1912–14; rev. 1932; concert premiere, Rio de Janeiro, April 6, 1940; stage premiere, Rio de Janeiro, Dec. 13, 1958); *Magdalena* (1947; Los Angeles, July 26, 1948); *Yerma* (1953–56; Santa Fe, Aug. 12, 1971); *A menina das nuvens* (1957–58; Rio de Janeiro, Nov. 29, 1960); others left unfinished. **BALLETS** (many converted from symphonic poems): *Uirapuru* (1917; Buenos Aires, May 25, 1935; rev. 1948); *Possessão* (1929); *Pedra Bonita* (1933); *Dança da terra* (1939; Rio de Janeiro, Sept. 7, 1943); *Rudá* (1951); *Gênesis* (1954; as a symphonic poem, 1969); *Emperor Jones* (1955; Ellenville, N.Y., July 12, 1956).

9 BACHIANAS BRASILEIRAS: No. 1 for 8 Cellos (Rio de Janeiro, Sept. 12, 1932), No. 2 for Chamber Orch. (1933), No. 3 for Piano and Orch. (1934), No. 4 for Piano (1930–40; orchestrated, N.Y., June 6, 1942), No. 5 for Voice and 8 Cellos (1938; Rio de Janeiro, March 25, 1939), No. 6 for Flute and Bassoon (1938), No. 7 for Orch. (1942; Rio de Janeiro, March 13, 1944), No. 8 for Orch. (1944; Rome, Aug. 6, 1947), and No. 9 for Chorus or String Orch. (1944).

15 CHÔROS: No. 1 for Guitar (1920), No. 2 for Flute and Clarinet (1921), No. 3 for Men's Chorus and 7 Wind Instruments (1925), No. 4 for 3 Horns and Trombone (1926), No. 5, *Alma brasileira,* for Piano (1926), No. 6 for Orch. (1926; Rio de Janeiro, July 15, 1942), No. 7 for Flute, Oboe, Clarinet, Saxophone, Bassoon, Violin, and Cello (1924), No. 8 for Large Orch. and 2 Pianos (1925; Paris, Oct. 24, 1927), No. 9 for Orch. (1929; Rio de Janeiro, July 15, 1942), No. 10, *Rasga o Coração,* for Chorus and Orch. (1925; Rio de Janeiro, Dec. 15, 1926), No. 11 for Piano and Orch. (1928; Rio de Janeiro, July 15, 1942), No. 12 for Orch. (1929; Cambridge, Mass., Feb. 21, 1945), No. 13 for 2 Orchs. and Band (1929), No. 14 for Orch., Band, and Chorus (1928), and No. 15, a supernumerary *Chôros bis* for Violin and Cello (1928).

OTHER ORCH.: *Dansas africanas* (1914; Paris, April 5, 1928); 2 cello concertos: No. 1, *Grand Concerto* (1915), and No. 2 (1953; N.Y., Feb. 5, 1955); 12 syms.: No. 1, *Imprevisto* (1916; Rio de Janeiro, Aug. 30, 1920), No. 2, *Ascenção* (1917), No. 3, *Guerra* (Rio de Janeiro, July 30, 1919), No. 4, *Vitória* (1920), No. 5, *Paz* (1921), No. 6, *Montanhas do Brasil* (1944), No. 7, *Odisséia da paz* (1945; London, March 27, 1949), No. 8

(1950; Philadelphia, Jan. 14, 1955), No. 9 (1951; Caracas, May 16, 1966), No. 10, *Sume Pater Patrium*, for Soloists, Chorus, and Orch. (1952; Paris, April 4, 1957), No. 11 (1955; Boston, March 2, 1956), and No. 12 (1957; Washington, D.C., April 20, 1958); 2 sinfoniettas (1916, 1947); *Amazonas* (1917; Paris, May 30, 1929); *Fantasy of Mixed Movements* for Violin and Orch. (Rio de Janeiro, Dec. 15, 1922); *Momoprecoce* for Piano and Orch. (Amsterdam, 1929); *Caixinha de Boãs Festas* (Rio de Janeiro, Dec. 8, 1932); *Ciranda das sete notes* for Bassoon and Strings (1933); 3 of 4 suites titled *Descobrimento do Brasil* (1937; No. 4 is an oratorio); *The New York Skyline* (1939); *Rudepoema* (orch. version of the piano work of that name; Rio de Janeiro, July 15, 1942); *Madona*, tone poem (1945; Rio de Janeiro, Oct. 8, 1946); 5 piano concertos (1945; 1948; 1952–57; 1952; 1954); *Fantasia* for Cello and Orch. (1945); *Fantasia* for Soprano Saxophone, Strings, and 2 Horns (1948); *Erosion, or The Origin of the Amazon River* (Louisville, Nov. 7, 1951); Guitar Concerto (1951); Harp Concerto (1953; Philadelphia, Jan. 14, 1955); *Odyssey of a Race*, symphonic poem written for Israel (1953; Haifa, May 30, 1954); *Dawn in a Tropical Forest* (1953; Louisville, Jan. 23, 1954); Harmonica Concerto (1955; Jerusalem, Oct. 27, 1959); *Izi*, symphonic poem (1957).

OTHER CHAMBER: 3 piano trios (1911, 1916, 1918); *Quinteto duplo de cordas* (1912); 4 *Sonatas-Fantasia* for Violin and Piano (1912, 1914, 1915, 1918); 17 string quartets (1915, 1915, 1916, 1917, 1931, 1938, 1942, 1944, 1945, 1946, 1948, 1950, 1952, 1953, 1954, 1955, 1958); 2 cello sonatas (1915, 1916); Piano Quintet (1916); *Mystic Sextet* for Flute, Clarinet, Saxophone, Celesta, Harp, and Guitar (1917); Trio for Oboe, Clarinet, and Bassoon (1921); Woodwind Quartet (1928); *Quintet in the Form of a Chôros* for Flute, Oboe, Clarinet, Bassoon, and English Horn (1928; rev. 1953, replacing English Horn with French Horn); String Trio (1946); *Duo* for Violin and Viola (1946); *Fantasia concertante* for Piano, Clarinet, and Bassoon (1953); *Duo* for Oboe and Bassoon (1957); Quintet for Flute, Harp, Violin, Viola, and Cello (1957); *Fantasia concertante* for Cello Ensemble (N.Y., Dec. 10, 1958).

OTHER VOCAL: *Crianças* for Chorus (1908); *Vidapura*, oratorio for Chorus, Orch., and Organ (1918; Rio de Janeiro, Nov. 11, 1922); *Hinos aos artistas* for Chorus and Orch. (1919); Quartet for Harp, Celesta, Flute, Saxophone, and Women's Voices (1921); Nonetto for Flute, Oboe, Clarinet, Saxophone, Bassoon, Harp, Celesta, Percussion, and Chorus (1923); *Cantiga da Roda* for Women's Chorus and Orch. (1925); *Na Bah a tem* for Chorus (1925); *Canção da Terra* for Chorus (1925); *Missa São Sebastião* for Chorus (1937); Suite No. 4 of *Descobrimento do Brasil* for Orch. and Chorus (1937); *Mandu-Carará*, cantata profana for Chorus and Orch. (1940; N.Y., Jan. 23, 1948; also a ballet); *Bendita sabedoria* (Blessed Wisdom) for Chorus (1958); *Magnificat-Alleluia* for Boy Contralto, Chorus, Organ, and Orch. (Rio de Janeiro, Nov. 8, 1958; by request of Pope Pius XII); etc. **SONGS:** *Confidencia* (1908); *Noite de Luar* (1912); *Mal secreto* (1913); *Fleur fanée* (1913); *Il nome di Maria* (1915); *Sertão no Estio* (1919); *Canções típicas brasileiras* (10 numbers; 1919); *Historiettes* (6 numbers; 1920); *Epigrammes ironiques et sentimentales* (8 numbers; 1921); *Suite* for Voice and Violin (1923); *Poème de l'Enfant et de sa Mère* for Voice, Flute, Clarinet, and Cello (1923); *Serestas* (suite of 14 numbers; 1925); *3 poemas indígenas* (1926); *Suite sugestiva* for Voice and Orch. (1929); *Modinhas e canções* (2 albums; 1933, 1943); *Poem of Itabira* for Alto and Orch. (1941; Rio de Janeiro, Dec. 30, 1946); *Canção das aguas claras* for Voice and Orch. (1956).

OTHER PIANO: *Valsa romantica* (1908); *Brinquedo de Roda* (6 pieces; 1912); *Primeira suite infantil* (5 pieces; 1912); *Segunda suite infantil* (4 pieces; 1913); *Fábulas características* (3 pieces; 1914–18); *Danças africanas* (1915); *Prole do Bebé*, Suite No. 1 (8 pieces, including the popular *Polichinello*; 1918), No. 2 (9 pieces; 1921), and No. 3 (9 pieces; 1929); *Historia da Carochinha* (4 pieces; 1919); *Carnaval das crianças brasileiras* (8 pieces; 1919); *Lenda do Caboclo* (1920); *Dança infernal* (1920); *Sul América* (1925); *Cirandinhas* (12 pieces; 1925); *Rudepoema* (1921–26); *Cirandas* (16 pieces; 1926); *Alma brasileira* (*Chôros* No. 5; 1926); *Lembrança do Sertão* (1930); *Caixinha de música quebrada* (1931); *Ciclo brasileiro* (4 pieces; 1936); *As Três Marías* (3 pieces; 1939); *Poema singelo* (1942); *Homenagem a Chopin* (1949).

BIBL.: F. Lange, "V.-L., un pedagogo creador," *Boletín Latino-Americano de Música*, I (Montevideo, 1935); special issue of *Musica Viva*, I (Rio de Janeiro, 1940–41); N. Slonimsky, *Music of Latin America* (N.Y., 1945); O. Fernández, "A Contribuição Harmonica de V.-L. para a Música Brasiliera," *Boletín Latino-Americano de Música* (Rio de Janeiro, 1946); V. Mariz, *H. V.-L.* (Rio de Janeiro, 1949; 11th ed., 1990); C. de Paula Barros, *O Romance de V.-L.* (Rio de Janeiro, 1951); *Homenagem a V.-L.* (Rio de Janeiro, 1960); M. Beaufils, *V.-L., Musicien et poete du Brésil* (Rio de Janeiro, 1967); E. Nogueria França, *V.-L.: Síntese critica e biográfica* (Rio de Janeiro, 1970; 2nd ed., 1973); L. Guimarães, *V.-L. visto da plateia e na intimidade (1912–1935)* (Rio de Janeiro, 1972); L. Peppercorn, *H. V.-L.: Leben und Werk des Brasilianischen Komponisten* (Zürich, 1972); F. Pereira da Silva, *V.-L.* (Rio de Janeiro, 1974); T. Santos, *H. V.-L. and the Guitar* (Bank, County Cork, 1985); P. Carvalho, *V.-L.: Do crépusculo à alvorada* (Rio de Janeiro, 1987); M. Claret, ed., *O Pensamento vivo de H. V.-L.* (São Paulo, 1987); M. Machado, *H. V.-L.: Tradição e renovacão na música brasileira* (Rio de Janeiro, 1987); A. Schic, *V.-L.: Souvenirs de l'indien blanc* (Arles and Paris, 1987); E. Stornio, *V.-L.* (Madrid, 1987); D. Appleby, *H. V.-L.: A Bio-bibliography* (N.Y., 1988); L. Peppercorn, *V.-L.: Collected Studies* (Aldershot, 1992); S. Wright, *V.-L.* (Oxford, 1992); G. Behague, *H. V.-L.: The Search for Brazil's Musical Soul* (Austin, Texas, 1994).

Villar, Rogelio del, Spanish musicologist, teacher, and composer; b. Leon, Nov. 13, 1875; d. Madrid, Nov. 4, 1937. He studied at the Madrid Cons., where he later taught (1919–36); was ed. of the *Revista Musical Hispano-Americana* (ceased publication in 1917).

WORKS: ORCH.: *Suite romantica* (1907); *Las hilanderas* (1915); *Escenas populares* (1917); *Egloga* (1919). **CHAMBER:** 3 string quartets; piano pieces. **VOCAL:** Songs.

WRITINGS (all publ. in Madrid): *"El anillo de los Nibelungos" de Wagner* (1914); *El sentimiento nacional en la música española* (1917); *Músicos españoles* (1918); *Téoricos y músicos* (1920); *Soliloquios de un músico español* (1923); *La armonia en la música contemporánea* (1927); *Falla y su concierto de cámara* (1932).

Vinay, Ramón, Chilean baritone, later tenor; b. Chillán (of French and Italian parents), Aug. 31, 1912. He was a pupil of José Pierson in Mexico City, where he made his operatic debut as Alfonso in *La Favorite* (1931); after appearances in baritone roles, he pursued further training and turned to the tenor repertory, making his 2nd debut as Don José in Mexico City in 1943; chose that same role for his N.Y. debut in 1945. On Feb. 22, 1946, he made his Metropolitan Opera debut in N.Y. as Don José; remained on its roster until 1958, and sang there again from 1959 to 1962 and in 1965–66. He also appeared in Europe, opening the 1947–48 season at Milan's La Scala in his most famous role, Othello; sang at the Bayreuth Festivals (1952–57) and regularly at London's Covent Garden (1953–60). From 1969 to 1971 he was artistic director of the Santiago Opera. Among his other roles were Bartolo, Iago, Falstaff, Scarpia, Telramund, Parsifal, Tristan, Siegfried, and Tannhäuser.

Vincent, John, American composer and teacher; b. Birmingham, Ala., May 17, 1902; d. Santa Monica, Calif., Jan. 21, 1977. He studied flute with Georges Laurent at the New England Cons. of Music in Boston (1922–26), and composition there with Converse and Chadwick (1926–27); then took courses at the George Peabody College in Nashville, Tenn. (M.A., 1933) and at Harvard Univ., where his principal teacher was Piston (1933–35); then went to Paris, where he studied at the École Normale de Musique (1935–37), and took private lessons with Boulanger; received his Ph.D. from Cornell Univ. in 1942. He was in charge of music in the El Paso (Texas) public schools

(1927–30); taught at George Peabody College in Nashville (1930–33), at Western Kentucky Teachers College (1937–46), and at the Univ. of Calif., Los Angeles (1946–69). After his death, the John Vincent Archive was established at UCLA. In his music, he evolved a tonal idiom which he termed "paratonality"; fugal elements are particularly strong in his instrumental compositions. He publ. the books *Music for Sight Reading* (N.Y., 1940); *More Music for Sight Reading* (N.Y., 1941); *The Diatonic Modes in Modern Music* (N.Y., 1951; 2nd ed., rev., 1974).

WORKS: DRAMATIC: *3 Jacks*, ballet (1942; rev. 1954; rev. as an orch. suite, 1954; rev. as *The House That Jack Built* for Narrator and Orch., 1957); *The Hallow'd Time*, incidental music (1954); *Primeval Void*, opera (1969). **ORCH.:** Suite (1929); *A Folk Symphony* (1931; not extant); *Nude Descending a Staircase* for Strings (1948; also for Xylophone and Piano or Strings, 1974); *Symphonic Poem after Descartes*, with the motto of Descartes, "Cogito ergo sum," suggested by the thematic rhythm on the kettledrums (1958; Philadelphia, March 20, 1959); *La Jolla Concerto* for Chamber Orch. (La Jolla, Calif., July 19, 1959; rev. 1966 and 1973); *Overture to Lord Arling* (1959); *Benjamin Franklin Suite* for Glass Harmonica and Orch. (Philadelphia, March 24, 1963); *Rondo Rhapsody* (Washington, D.C., May 9, 1965); *The Phoenix, Fabulous Bird*, symphonic poem (Phoenix, Ariz., Feb. 21, 1966). **CHAMBER:** *Nacre, Mother of Pearl* for Flute and Piano (1925; rev. 1973; also for Band, 1973); *Suite: Prelude, Canon, and Fugue* for Flute, Oboe, and Bassoon (1936); 2 string quartets (1936, rev. as *Recitative and Dance* for Cello Obbligato and Strings, 1948; 1967, rev. 1969); *Consort* for Piano and String Quartet (1960; also for Piano and String Orch.; also as Sym. No. 2 for Strings, 1976); *Victory Salute* for 12 Brass (1968); Suite for 6 Percussion (1973); piano pieces. **VOCAL:** *3 Grecian Songs* for Chorus (1935); *How Shall we Sing* for Voices and Piano (1944; rev. 1951); *Sing Hollyloo* for Mezzo-soprano or Baritone and Piano (1951; also for Men's Voices and Piano); *Stabat Mater* for Soprano, Men's Voices, and Piano or Organ (1969; also for Soprano, Men's Voices, and Orch., 1970); *A Christmas Psalm* for Voice and Piano (1969; rev. as *Prayer for Peace* for Soprano, Alto, Chorus, and Organ or Piano, 1971).

Vinco, Ivo, Italian bass; b. Verona, Nov. 8, 1927. He studied at the Verona Liceo Musicale and with Ettore Campogalliani in Milan. After making his operatic debut as Ramfis in Verona in 1954, he sang there regularly in succeeding years; also appeared in virtually all Italian opera centers. On March 19, 1970, he made his Metropolitan Opera debut in N.Y. as Oroveso, remaining on its roster until 1973, and returning for the 1976–78 seasons. Among his prominent roles were the Grand Inquisitor, Mozart's Dr. Bartolo, Alvise, Ferrando, Donizetti's Raimondo, and Sparafucile. In 1958 he married **Fiorenza Cossotto**.

Vincze, Imre, Hungarian composer and teacher; b. Kocs, Sept. 26, 1926; d. Budapest, May 3, 1969. He studied with Szabó at the Budapest Academy of Music (graduated, 1951); after serving as Szabó's assistant there, he was a prof. until 1968. In 1952 and 1956 he won the Erkel Prize.

WORKS: DRAMATIC: Film music. **ORCH.:** 3 syms. (1951, 1953, 1967); *Greeting*, overture (1954); *Movimento sinfonico* (1957); *Aforismo* for Strings (1959); *Cantata senza parole* (1960); Concertino (1961); *Rapsodia concertante* for Piano and Orch. (1966). **CHAMBER:** 4 string quartets (1954, 1958, 1961, 1965); Violin Sonata (1956); *Divertimento* for Wind Quintet (1962); Bassoon Sonata (1964). **ORGAN:** *Fantasy and Fugue* (1960). **VOCAL:** *Szerelem, szerelem* (Love, Love) for Chorus (1955); *Perzsa dalok* (Persian Songs) for Voice and Piano (1967).

Vine, Carl, Australian composer and pianist; b. Perth, Oct. 8, 1954. He was a student at the Univ. of Western Australia in Nedlands of Stephen Dornan (piano) and John Exton (composition). After serving as pianist of the West Australian Sym. Orch. in Perth (1973–75), he was a pianist with various organizations, including the Sydney Dance Co. (1975–78), where he was also resident composer (1978). In 1979 he was guest resident composer of the London Contemporary Dance Theatre. From 1979 to 1989 he was co-director, pianist, and conductor of the contemporary music ensemble Flederman. He lectured on electronic music at the Queensland Conservatorium of Music in Brisbane (1980–82), and then was resident composer of the New South Wales State Conservatorium of Music in Sydney (1985), the Australian Chamber Orch. (1987), and Western Australian Univ. (1989). From 1992 to 1995 he was deputy chairman of the Australia Council. In 1993 he was honored with the Australian Screen Composers Guild Award for his music to the film *Bedevil.* Vine has composed in various genres, ranging from dance, film, and theater scores to orch., chamber, and electronic pieces. He has demonstrated a deft handling of tonal writing, notable for its harmonic refinement and lyricism.

WORKS: DRAMATIC: THEATER: Music for: Shakespeare's *The Tempest* (1975); Andrew Simon's *The Dreamers* (1975); Judith Anderson's *New Sky* (1981); Patrick White's *Singal Driver* (1982), *Shepherd on the Rocks* (1987), and *Ham Funeral* (1989); Ibsen's *Master Builder* (1991). **DANCE:** *961 Ways to Nirvana* (1977); *Incident at Bull Creek* (1977); *Everymans Troth* (1978); *Poppy* (1978); *Knips Suite* (1979); *Kisses Remembered* (1979); *Scene Shift* (1979); *Return* (1980); *Missing Film* (1980); *Colonial Sketches* (1981); *Donna Maria Blues* (1981); *Hate* (1982); *Daisy Bates* (1982); *A Christmas Carol* (1983); *Porologue+Canzona* (1986); *Legend* (1988); *On the Edge* (1988); Piano Sonata (1990); *The Tempest* (1991); *Beauty and the Beast* (1993). **FILM:** *You Can't Push the River* (1992); *Bedevil* (1993). **ORCH.:** *Curios* (Sydney, Feb. 5, 1980); *Canzona* for Strings (1985); 6 syms.: No. 1, *MicroSymphony* (Sydney, Aug. 17, 1986), No. 2 (Melbourne, April 23, 1987), No. 3 (Adelaide, March 5, 1990), No. 4 (Sydney, May 23, 1993), No. 5, *Percussion Symphony* (1994; Sydney, March 17, 1995), and No. 6, *Choral Symphony* (1995); Concerto for Percussion and Orch. or Tape (1987); *Legend Suite* (Perth, July 8, 1988); Concerto grosso for Chamber Orch. (1989; Sydney, June 16, 1991); *Celebrare Celeberrime* (1993; Dayton, Ohio, Jan. 10, 1994); *Gaijin* for Koto, Strings, and Tape (Adelaide, March 11, 1994). **CHAMBER:** *Miniature I* for Viola (1973), *II* for 2 Violas (1974), *III* for Flute, Trombone or Cello, Piano, and Percussion (1983), and *IV* for Flute, Clarinet, Violin, Viola, Cello, and Piano (1988); *Tergiversative Blues* for Lute (1977); *Free Game* for Trombone and Electronics (1979); *Occasional Poetry* for Trombone and Piano (1979); *Images* for Flute, Trombone, Cello, Piano, Harpsichord, and Percussion (1981); Sinfonia for Flute, Clarinet, Violin, Cello, Piano, and Percussion (1982); 3 string quartets, including No. 2 (1984) and No. 3 (1994); *Cafe Concertino* for Flute, Clarinet, Violin, Viola, Cello, and Piano (1984); *Elegy* for Flute, Cello, Trombone, Piano 4-hands, and Percussion (1985); *Love Song* for Trombone and Tape (1986); *Defying Gravity* for Percussion Quartet (1987); Flute Sonata (1992); *Harmony in Concord* for Trombone, Marimba or Vibraphone, Percussion, and Tape (1992); *Inner World* for Cello and Tape (1994). **VOCAL:** *Aria* for Soprano, Flute, Cello, Piano, Celesta, and Percussion (1984); *After Campion* for Chorus and 2 Pianos (1989). **OTHER:** *Tape Piano Piece* for Tape (1976); *Heavy Metal* for Tape and Improvisation (1980); *Kondallila Mix* for Tape and Improvisation (1980); *Intimations of Mortality* for Computer Tape (1985).

Viñes, Ricardo, Spanish pianist; b. Lérida, Feb. 5, 1875; d. Barcelona, April 29, 1943. He studied in Barcelona with Juan Pujol; settled in Paris in 1887, where he studied piano with Beriot (premier prix, 1894), composition with Godard, and harmony with Lavignac at the Cons. In 1895 he gave his first concert in Paris. He established himself in later years as an ardent propagandist of new French and Spanish music; he possessed particular affinity with the composers of the modern French school, and performed their works in a colorful and imaginative manner. He gave concerts in London, Berlin, and other music centers, but lived most of his life in Paris. He contributed articles on Spanish music to publications in France and Spain.

BIBL.: E. Brody, "V. in Paris: New Light on Twentieth-Century Performance Practice," *A Musical Offering: Essays in Honor of Martin Bernstein* (N.Y., 1977).

Viotti, Marcello, Italian conductor; b. Vallorbe, June 29, 1954. He received training at the Lausanne Cons. In 1981 he took 1st prize in the Gino Martinuzzi Competition in San Remo. He was permanent guest conductor of the Teatro Regio in Turin from 1985 to 1987. From 1987 to 1990 he was artistic director of the Lucerne Opera. He was Generalmusikdirektor in Bremen from 1990 to 1993. In 1991 he became chief conductor of the Saarland Radio Sym. Orch. in Saarbrücken and was named to the post of 1st guest conductor of the Vienna State Opera. He concurrently served as 1st guest conductor of the Deutsche Oper in Berlin and permanent guest conductor of the Bavarian State Opera in Munich from 1993.

Virizlay, Mihály, Hungarian-born American cellist, teacher, and composer; b. Budapest, Nov. 2, 1931. He began violin studies at an early age with his father; after receiving instruction in cello from Janos Starker, he studied with Miklós Zsambolski and Edi Banda (cello) and Pál Járdanyi and Kodály (composition) at the Budapest Academy of Music (graduated, 1955). In 1957 he emigrated to the U.S., and became a naturalized American citizen (1962). After playing in the Dallas Sym. Orch., he was assistant principal cellist of the Pittsburgh Sym. Orch. (1960–62) and then principal cellist of the Baltimore Sym. Orch. (from 1962); also pursued a career as an orch. soloist, recitalist, and chamber music artist, making appearances on both sides of the Atlantic. He taught at the Peabody Cons. of Music in Baltimore (from 1963), and also held master classes throughout the U.S. He was distinguished for his performances of contemporary music.

WORKS: ORCH.: *The Emperor's New Clothes*, suite (1964); Trombone Concerto (Baltimore, Nov. 2, 1985); Cello Concerto (1985; Baltimore, Feb. 12, 1987). **CHAMBER:** *Ének* (Song) for Cello and Piano (1955); Sonata for Solo Cello (1972); *Rhapsody* for Cello and Piano (1973); Piano Sonata (1981); *Grand Duo* for 2 Flutes (1985).

Viscarra Monje, Humberto, Bolivian composer; b. Sorata, March 30, 1898; d. La Paz, Sept. 2, 1971. He studied at the National Cons. of Bolivia in La Paz; then went to Europe, and studied piano and composition in Italy and France. Returning to La Paz, he served as director of the Cons. (1930–32; 1950–68). He composed some attractive piano pieces based on Bolivian motifs.

Visconti (di Modrone), Count Luchino, prominent Italian film, theater, and opera director; b. Milan, Nov. 2, 1906; d. Rome, March 17, 1976. After World War II, he assumed a leading position among film directors, producing films notable for their realism. In 1954 he enlarged the scope of his work to include opera, his first production being Spontini's *Le vestale* at Milan's La Scala with Maria Callas; his first production outside his homeland was *Don Carlos* at London's Covent Garden in 1958; that same year, his *Macbeth* opened the Spoleto Festival, where he maintained a close association in subsequent seasons. His opera productions were impressive, particularly for his ability to complement the dramatic qualities of the music with the action on stage to effect a total theatrical experience.

BIBL.: M. Estève, ed., *L. V.: L'Histoire et l'esthétique* (Paris, 1963); G. Smith, *L. V.* (London, 1967).

Vishnevskaya, Galina (Pavlovna), prominent Russian soprano; b. Leningrad, Oct. 25, 1926. After vocal studies with Vera Garina in Leningrad, she sang in operetta; in 1952 she joined the operatic staff of the Bolshoi Theater in Moscow; there her roles were Violetta, Tosca, Madama Butterfly, and an entire repertoire of soprano parts in Russian operas. In 1955 she married **Mstislav Rostropovich**, with whom she frequently appeared in concert. She made her debut at the Metropolitan Opera in N.Y. on Nov. 6, 1961, as Aida. Owing to the recurrent differences that developed between Rostropovich and the cultural authorities of the Soviet Union (Rostropovich had sheltered the dissident writer Solzhenitsyn in his summer house), they left Russia in 1974; settled in the U.S., when Rostropovich was appointed music director of the National Sym. Orch. in Washington, D.C., in 1977. In March 1978, both he and Vishnevskaya, as "ideological renegades," were stripped of their Soviet citizenship by a decree of the Soviet government. Her autobiography was publ. as *Galina: A Russian Story* (N.Y., 1984). After Gorbachev's rise to power in her homeland, her Soviet citizenship was restored in 1990.

BIBL.: C. Samuel, *Mstislav Rostropovich and G. V.: Russia, Music, and Liberty: Conversations with Claude Samuel* (Portland, Oreg., 1995).

Viski, János, Hungarian composer and teacher; b. Kolozsvár, June 10, 1906; d. Budapest, Jan. 16, 1961. He was a student of Kodály at the Budapest Academy of Music (1927–32). In 1940 he became a prof. at the Budapest National Cons. After serving as director of the Cluj Cons. (1941–42), he was a prof. of composition at the Budapest Academy of Music from 1942 until his death. In 1954 he won the Erkel Prize, in 1955 he was made a Merited Artist by the Hungarian government, and in 1956 he received the Kossuth Prize. His music was permeated by Hungarian melorhythms set in classical forms.

WORKS: ORCH.: *Symphonic Suite* (1935); *2 Hungarian Dances* (1938); *Enigma* (1939); Violin Concerto (1947); Piano Concerto (1953); Cello Concerto (1955). **CHAMBER:** String Trio (1930; not extant); *5 Little Piano Pieces* (1948); *Epitaph for Anton Webern* for Piano (1960). **VOCAL:** *Az irisórai szarvas* (The Heart of Irisóra), ballad for Baritone and Orch. (1958); choruses; solo songs.

Vitale, Edoardo, Italian conductor; b. Naples, Nov. 29, 1872; d. Rome, Dec. 12, 1937. He studied composition with Terziani at the Accademia di Santa Cecilia in Rome, where he then taught harmony (1893–97). He was only 14 when he began conducting operettas at Rome's Teatro Metastasio. From 1897 he conducted throughout Italy. After conducting at Milan's La Scala (1908–10), he was chief conductor of the Rome Opera (1913–26). He conducted the first Italian performances of *Elektra* (1904) and *Boris Godunov* (1909). He also led many premieres, including Mascagni's *Parisina* and Zandonai's *Francesca da Rimini*, and revived many works. In 1897 he married the soprano Lina Pasini.

Vitalini, Alberico, Italian conductor and composer; b. Rome, July 18, 1921. He studied at the Santa Cecilia Cons. in Rome, obtaining diplomas in violin (1940), viola (1942), composition (1944), and conducting (1945). He subsequently became active mainly as a conductor; in 1950, was appointed director of musical programs of Radio Vaticana; in 1973, was nominated a member of the Accademia Internazionale de Propaganda Culturale. He specialized in sacred choral music.

WORKS: *Fantasia* for Piano and Orch. (1949); *Assisi* for Chorus and Orch. (1949); *Le sette parole di Cristo* for Baritone and String Orch. (1952); *Magnificat* for Soprano, Chorus, and Orch. (1954); *Tiberiade* for Small Orch. (1955); *Canti in italiano*, for a new liturgy in the Italian language (1965–71).

Vitalis, George, Greek composer and conductor; b. Athens, Jan. 9, 1895; d. there, April 27, 1959. He studied with Armani in Milan. He conducted light opera in Athens (1923–36); went to the U.S. in 1945; settled in N.Y. He composed the operas *Perseus and Andromeda, The Return of the Gods*, and *Golfo* (concert perf., N.Y., Jan. 1, 1949); also *Greek Fantasy* for Orch. (Athens, Nov. 11, 1945); light orch. pieces under the pseudonym Giorgio Valente.

Vitoliņš, Jēkab, Latvian musicologist; b. Bākšani, Aug. 5, 1898. He studied composition with Jāzeps Vītols at the Latvian Cons. in Riga (1920–24); later took lessons in conducting with Emil Cooper, and took courses in music history at the Univ. of Vienna (1929, 1931); then attended the Sorbonne in Paris (1936–37). He received a *kandidat* degree from the Univ. of

Leningrad (1956) and a doctorate there for his work on Latvian folk music (1961). He was a dramaturge at the Latvian National Opera (1925–29), ed. of the journal *Mūzikas apskats* (1932–39), and senior research fellow at the Inst. of Ethnography and Folklore of the Latvian Academy of Sciences. He taught at the College of Education in Riga (1922–38) and at the Latvian Cons. (1938–44; 1946–61), becoming a prof. in 1941. He was dismissed from his post at the Cons. in 1961 for publishing a collection of reviews by Jānis Zālītis (1884–1943), the anti-Soviet Latvian composer and music critic. His numerous books and articles, mostly in Latvian or Russian, are concerned principally with Latvian folk music.

Vittadini, Franco, Italian composer; b. Pavia, April 9, 1884; d. there, Nov. 30, 1948. He studied at the Milan Cons. After serving as organist and maestro di cappella in Varese, he returned to Pavia, where he was founder-director of the Istituto Musicale (1924–48).

WORKS: DRAMATIC: OPERAS: *Il mare di Tiberiade* (c.1912–14); *Anima allegra* (1918–19; Rome, April 15, 1921); *Nazareth* (Pavia, May 28, 1925); *La Sagredo* (Milan, April 26, 1930); *Caracciolo* (Rome, Feb. 7, 1938); *Fiammetta e l'avvaro* (1942). **PASTORAL TRIPTYCH:** *Il natale di Ges* (Bari, Dec. 20, 1933). **BALLETS:** *Vecchia Milano* (1928); *Fiordisole* (Milan, Feb. 14, 1935); *La Taglioni* (1945). Also film music. **ORCH.:** *Armonie della notte* (1923); *Scherzo* (1931); *Poemetto romantico* for Strings (1938). **OTHER:** Chamber music; piano pieces; organ music; masses; motets; songs.

BIBL.: A. Baratti, *Vita del musicista F. V.* (Milan, 1955).

Vives, Amadeo, Spanish composer; b. Collbató, near Barcelona, Nov. 18, 1871; d. Madrid, Dec. 1, 1932. He was a pupil of Ribera and then of Felipe Pedrell in Barcelona. With L. Millet, he founded the famous choral society Orfeó Català (1891). In his first opera, *Artus* (Barcelona, 1895), he made use of Catalonian folk songs. Subsequently he moved to Madrid, where he produced his comic opera *Don Lucas del Cigarral* (Feb. 18, 1899); his opera *Euda d'Uriach*, originally to a Catalan libretto, was brought out in Italian at Barcelona (Oct. 24, 1900). Then followed his most popular opera, *Maruxa* (Madrid, May 28, 1914); other operas are *Balada de Carnaval* (Madrid, July 5, 1919) and *Doña Francisquita* (Madrid, Oct. 17, 1923). The style of his stage productions shared qualities of the French light opera and the Spanish zarzuela; he wrote nearly 100 of these; also composed songs and piano pieces; publ. a book of essays, *Sofia* (Madrid, 1923).

BIBL.: A. Sagardía, *A. V.: Vida y obra* (Madrid, 1971).

Vivier, Claude, Canadian composer; b. Montreal, April 14, 1948; d. (murdered) Paris, March 7, 1983. He studied with Tremblay (composition) and Heller (piano) at the Montreal Cons. (1967–71). From 1971 he lived in Europe on a Canada Council grant, where he studied with Koenig at the Inst. of Sonology at the Univ. of Utrecht, with Stockhausen and Humpert in Germany, and with Méfano in France. His love for the music of the Orient prompted him to tour that region in 1977, where he spent much time on the island of Bali. In 1981 the Canada Music Council named him its composer of the year. In 1982 he went to Paris on another Council grant, where he was brutally murdered by a chance acquaintance. In 1983 Les Amis de Claude Vivier was organized in Montreal to champion his compositions and writings. Vivier developed a thoroughly individual compositional style in which simplicity became its hallmark. In some of his vocal works, he created texts based on his own invented language.

WORKS: DRAMATIC: *Love Songs*, ballet (1977); *Nanti malam*, ballet (1977); *Kopernicus*, opera (Montreal, May 8, 1980). **ORCH.:** *Siddhartha* (1976); *Orion* (1979); *Zipangu* for Strings (1980). **CHAMBER:** String Quartet (1968); *Prolifération* for Ondes Martenot, Piano, and Percussion (1968; rev. 1976); *Deva et Asura* for Chamber Ensemble (1972); *Désintégration* for 2 Pianos, 4 Violins, and 2 Violas (1972); *Improvisation* for Bassoon and Piano (1975); *Pièce* for Flute and Piano (1975); *Pièce* for Cello and Piano (1975); *Pièce* for Violin and Piano (1975); *Pour guitare* (1975); *Pour Violin et Clarinet* (1975); *Learning* for 4 Violins and Percussion (1976); *Pulau Dewata* for Percussion Ensemble or Instrumental Ensemble (1977); *Paramirabo* for Flute, Violin, Cello, and Piano (1978); *Cinq Chansons* for Percussion (1980); *Et je reverrai cette ville étrange* for Trumpet, Viola, Cello, Doubla Bass, Piano, and Percussion (1981); *Samarkind* for Wind Quintet (1981). **KEYBOARD: PIANO:** *Pianoforte* (1975); *Shiraz* (1977). **ORGAN:** *Les Communiantes* (1977). **VOCAL:** *Ojikawa* for Soprano, Clarinet, and Percussion (1968); *Hiérophanie* for Soprano, 2 Percussion, and Winds (1971); *Musik für das Ende* for 20 Voices and Percussion (1971); *Chants* for 7 Women's Voices (1973); *O! Kosmos* for Chorus (1974); *Jesus erbarme Dich* for Chorus (1974); *Lettura di Dante* for Soprano, Oboe, Clarinet, Bassoon, Trumpet, Trombone, Viola, and Percussion (1974); *Hymnen an die Nacht* for Soprano and Piano (1975); *Liebesgedichte* for Vocal Quartet and Winds (1976); *Journal* for 4 Voices, Chorus, and Percussion (1977); *Lonely Child* for Soprano and Orch. (1980); *Prologue pour un Marco Polo* for 5 Voices, Speaker, Percussion, 6 Clarinets, and Strings (1981); *Bouchara* for Soprano, Wind Quintet, String Quintet, and Percussion (1981); *Wo bist du Licht!* for Mezzo-soprano, Percussion, 20 Strings, and Tape (1981); *Trois airs pour un opéra imaginaire* for Soprano, Bass, Piccolo, 2 Clarinets, Horn, Strings, and Percussion (1982); *Crois-tu en l'immortalité de l'âme* for Chorus, 3 Synthesizers, and 2 Percussion (1983).

Vix, Geneviève, French soprano; b. Nantes, Dec. 31, 1879; d. Paris, Aug. 25, 1939. She studied at the Paris Cons.; won 1st prize for opera (1908). She sang at the Paris Opéra, in Madrid, and in Buenos Aires; made her American debut with the Chicago Opera Co. as Manon in Massenet's opera (Dec. 1, 1917); married Prince Cyril Naryshkin in N.Y. (Feb. 9, 1918). She possessed a fine lyric voice, and was also adept as an actress.

Vlad, Roman, prominent Romanian-born Italian composer, administrator, teacher, pianist, and writer on music; b. Cernăuți, Dec. 29, 1919. After training at the Cernăuți Cons., he went to Rome and studied engineering at the Univ. and attended Casella's master classes at the Accademia di Santa Cecilia (graduated, 1942). He began his career as a pianist and lecturer. In 1951 he became a naturalized Italian citizen. From 1955 to 1958 he was artistic director of the Accademia Filarmonica in Rome. He was president of the Italian section of the ISCM from 1960 to 1963. In 1964 he was artistic director of the Maggio Musicale Fiorentino in Florence, and returned to that city in that capacity with the Teatro Comunale from 1968 to 1973. He also was prof. of composition at the Turin Cons. from 1968. From 1976 to 1980 he was artistic director of the RAI orch. in Turin. From 1982 to 1984 he was president of the International Confederation of the Soc. of Authors and Composers. In 1987 he became president of the Società Italiana Autori ed Composers. In 1995 he was made artistic director of Milan's La Scala. He was ed. of the journals *Musica e Dossier* and *Lo Spettatore*, and co-ed. of the journal *Nuova Rivista Musicale*. His scholarly articles appeared in various Italian and foreign publications. He also publ. several books. In his music, Vlad developed a non-dogmatic serial technique which respected the role of tradition in the compositional process. In some of his works, he utilized quarter tones and electronics.

WORKS: DRAMATIC: OPERAS: *Storia di una mamma* (Venice, Oct. 5, 1951); *Il dottore di vetro*, radio opera (RAI, Turin, Feb. 23, 1959); *La fantarca*, television opera (1967); *Il Sogno* (Bergamo, Oct. 3, 1973). **BALLETS:** *La strada sul caffè* (1942–43); *La dama delle camelie* (Rome, Nov. 20, 1945; rev. 1956); *Masques ostendais* (Spoleto, June 12, 1959; rev. 1960); *Die Wiederkehr* (1962; rev. 1968 as *Ricercare*); *Il Gabbiano* (Siena, Sept. 5, 1968). Also incidental music for plays and film scores. **ORCH.:** Sinfonietta (1941); Suite (1941); *Sinfonia all'antica* (1947–48; Venice, Sept. 8, 1948); *Variazioni concertanti su una serie di 12 note dal Don Giovanni di Mozart* for Piano and Orch. (Venice, Sept. 18, 1955); *Musica per archi* (1955–57); *Musica concertata* for Harp and Orch. (Turin, April 24, 1958);

Ode super Chrysaea Phorminx for Guitar and Orch. (1964); *Divertimento sinfonico* (1965–67; RAI, Naples, March 29, 1968). **CHAMBER:** Flute Sonatina (1945); *Divertimento* for 11 Instruments (1948); String Quartet (1955–57); *Serenata* for 12 Instruments (1959); *Improvvisazione su di una melodia* for Clarinet and Piano (Spoleto, July 8, 1970); *Il magico flauto di Severino* for Flute and Piano (1971); *Meditazioni sopra un antico canto russo, ricordando Igor Strawinsky* for Clarinet and 7 Instrumentalists (L'Aquila, Oct. 30, 1982); *Musica per archi N. 2 sempre di nuovo "Immer Wieder"* for 11 Strings (1987–88; L'Aquila, July 28, 1988). **KEYBOARD: PIANO:** *Studi dodecafonici* (1943; rev. 1957); *Variazioni intorno all'ultima mazurka di Chopin* (1964); *Sognando il sogno* (1971; Rome, March 10, 1974). **HARPSICHORD:** *Giochi con Bach sul clavicembalo* (Rome, March 23, 1979). **VOCAL:** *Poemi della luce* for Voice and Piano (1939); 3 cantatas: No. 1, *Dove sei, Elohim?*, for Chorus and Orch. (1940–42), No. 2, *De profundis*, for Chorus and Orch. (1942–46), and No. 3, *Le ciel est vide*, for Chorus and Orch. (1952–53); *3 invocazioni* for Voice and Orch. or Piano (1948–49); *5 elegie* for Voice and Strings or Piano (1952); *Colinde trasilvane* for Chorus (1957); *Lettura di Michelangelo* for Chorus (1964; Cork, Ireland, May 6, 1966; rev. version as *Cadenze michelangiolesche* for Soprano or Tenor and Orch., Venice, Sept. 13, 1967); *Immer wieder* for Soprano and 8 Instruments (1965); *Piccolo divertimento corale* for Chorus (1968); *"Ego autem" in memoria di Alfredo Casella* for Baritone and Organ (Rome, March 12, 1972); *Lettura di Lorenzo il Magnifico* for Chorus (Cork, Ireland, April 26, 1974); *Due letture* for Chorus and 13 Instruments (Rome, Oct. 25, 1976); *3 Poesie di Montale* for Baritone and Piano (Siena, Aug. 28, 1978; rev. version for Baritone and Orch., 1980); *Preludio, recitativo e rilettura di Michelangelo* for Bass and Piano (Lille, Oct. 24, 1981); *3 Poesie di Alberto Bevilacqua* for Soprano and Piano (L'Aquila, May 26, 1984); *1 Poesia di Valerio Magrelli* for Baritone and Piano (1987; Turin, March 5, 1990); *Temura* for Baritone and Piano (Turin, March 5, 1990). **OTHER:** Tape music; transcriptions.

WRITINGS: *Modernita e tradizione nella musica contemporanea* (Turin, 1955); with A. Piovesan and R. Craft, *Le musiche religiose di Igor Strawinsky* (Venice, 1956); *Luigi Dallapiccola* (Milan, 1957); *Storia della dodecafonia* (Milan, 1958); *Strawinsky* (Turin, 1958; Eng. tr., 1960; 3rd ed., rev., 1979); co-ed., *Enciclopedia dello spettacolo* (1958–62).

Vladigerov, Pantcho, prominent Bulgarian composer; b. Zürich, March 13, 1899, in a geminal parturition; d. Sofia, Sept. 8, 1978. Distrustful of Bulgarian puerperal skill, his mother sped from Shumen to Zürich as soon as she learned that she was going to have a plural birth. Pantcho's non-identical twin brother, Luben, a violinist, was born 16 hours earlier than Pantcho, on the previous day, March 12, 1899. Vladigerov studied piano and theory with local teachers in Sofia (1910–12); then went to Berlin, where he took lessons in composition with Paul Juon and Georg Schumann, and piano with Leonid Kreutzer at the Akademie der Künste. He then served as conductor and composer of the Max Reinhardt Theater (1921–32); subsequently was a reader (1932–38) and a prof. of piano and composition (1938–72) at the Bulgarian State Cons. of Music in Sofia. His music was rooted in Bulgarian folk songs, artfully combining the peculiar melodic and rhythmic patterns of native material with stark modern harmonies; the method was similar to that of Bartók. His son, Alexander Vladigerov (b. Sofia, Aug. 4, 1933), was a conductor and composer.

WORKS: DRAMATIC: *Tsar Kaloyan*, opera (1935–36; Sofia, April 20, 1936); *Legenda za ezeroto* (Legend of the Lake), ballet (1946; Sofia, Nov. 11, 1962). **ORCH.:** 5 piano concertos (1918, 1930, 1937, 1953, 1963); *Legend* (1919); *3 Impressions* (1920; orchestration of 3 of his *10 Impressions* for Piano); 2 violin concertos (1921, 1968); *Burlesk Suite* for Violin and Orch. (1922); *Scandinavian Suite* (1924); *Bulgarian Suite* (1927); *Vardar*, Bulgarian rhapsody (1927; orchestration of his earlier violin and piano piece); *7 Bulgarian Symphonic Dances* (1931); 2 overtures: *Zemja* (1933) and *The 9th of September* (1949); 2 syms.: No. 1 (1939) and No. 2, *Majska* (May) for Strings (1949); *Concert Fantasy* for Cello and Orch. (1941); *4 Rumanian Symphonic Dances* (1942); *Improvisation and Toccata* (1942; orchestration of the final 2 pieces of his piano cycle *Episodes*); *2 Rumanian Symphonic Sketches* (1943); 2 suites (1947, 1953); *Prelude and Balkan Dance* (1950); *Evreyska poema* (Jewish Poem) (1951); *Song of Peace*, dramatic poem (1956); *7 Pieces* for Strings (1969–70; orchestration of pieces taken from 3 different piano cycles). **CHAMBER:** Violin Sonata (1914); Piano Trio (1916); 5 works for Violin and Piano: *2 Improvisations* (1919), *4 Pieces* (1920), *Vardar* (1922), *2 Bulgarian Paraphrases* (1925), and *2 Pieces* (1926); String Quartet (1940); several piano cycles, many of which are also scored for chamber orch.: *4 Pieces* (1915); *11 Variations* (1916); *10 Impressions* (1920); *4 Pieces* (1920); *3 Pieces* (1922); *6 Exotic Preludes* (1924); *Classical and Romantic*, 7 pieces (1931); *Bulgarian Songs and Dances* (1932); *Sonatina concertante* (1934); *Shumen*, 6 miniatures (1934); *5 Episodes* (1941); *Aquarelles* (1942); *3 Pictures* (1950); *Suite*, 5 pieces (1954); *3 Pieces* (1957); *3 Concert Pieces* (1959); *5 Novelettes* (1965); *5 Pieces* (1965). **OTHER:** Orchestration of Dinicu's *Hora staccato*.

BIBL.: E. Pavlov, *P. V.: A Monograph* (Sofia, 1961); S. Dimitrov, *Slovoto na P. V.* (Sofia, 1988).

Vlasov, Vladimir (Alexandrovich), Russian conductor, ethnomusicologist, and composer; b. Moscow, Jan. 7, 1903; d. there, Sept. 7, 1986. He studied violin at the Moscow Cons., then was active as a teacher. In 1936 he traveled to Frunze, Kirghizia, where he diligently went about collecting authentic songs of the natives. In collaboration with Vladimir Fere, similarly intentioned, he wrote a number of operas based on Kirghiz national melorhythms supplied by local musicians. These included: *Altin kiz* (The Golden Girl; Frunze, May 1, 1937); *Aychurek* (Moon Beauty; Frunze, May 1, 1942); *Za schastye naroda* (For the People's Happiness; Frunze, May 1, 1941); *Sin naroda* (A Son of His People; Frunze, Nov. 8, 1947); *Na beregakh Issikh-kulya* (On the Shores of Lake Issik; Frunze, Feb. 1, 1951); *Vedma* (The Witch; 1961); etc. He also composed 2 operettas and several ballets. Among his other works were 2 cello concertos, 3 string quartets, a Suite for Folk Instruments (1955), and more than 1,000 songs.

BIBL.: V. Vinogradov, *A. Maldibayev, V. V., Vladimir Fere* (Moscow, 1958).

Vlijmen, Jan van, Dutch composer, music educator, and administrator; b. Rotterdam, Oct. 11, 1935. He received training in piano and organ at the Utrecht Cons., where he later studied composition with Kees van Baaren. From 1961 to 1965 he was director of the Amersfoort Music School, and then was a lecturer in theory at the Utrecht Cons. from 1965 to 1967. In 1967 he became deputy director and in 1971 director of the Royal Cons. of Music at The Hague. From 1985 to 1988 he was general manager of the Netherlands Opera in Amsterdam. In 1991 he was director of the Holland Festival.

WORKS: OPERAS: *Reconstructie* (Amsterdam, June 29, 1969; in collaboration with L. Andriessen, R. de Leeuw, M. Mengelberg, and P. Schat); *Axel* (1975–77; Scheveningen, June 10, 1977; in collaboration with R. de Leeuw); *A Wretch Clad in Black* (Amsterdam, Nov. 16, 1990). **ORCH.:** *Gruppi* (1961–62; rev. 1980); *Spostamenti* (1963); *Serenata II* for Flute and 4 Instrumental Groups (Amsterdam, Sept. 10, 1965); *Sonata* for Piano and 3 Instrumental Groups (1966); *Per diciasette* for Wind Orch. (1967); *Interpolations* for Orch. and Electronics (Rotterdam, Nov. 24, 1968; rev. 1981); *Ommagio a Gesualdo* for Violin and 6 Instrumental Groups (Amsterdam, April 9, 1971); *Quaterni* (1979); Piano Concerto (1991). **CHAMBER:** String Quartet (1955); 2 wind quintets (1958, 1972); *Construzione* for 2 Pianos (1959); *Serie* for 6 Instruments (1960); *Serenata I* for 12 Instruments and Percussion (1963–64; rev. 1967); *Dialogue* for Clarinet and Piano (1966); *Trimurti, trittico* for String Quartet (1980); *Faithful* for Viola (1984); Nonet (1985); *Solo II* for Clarinet (1986). **VOCAL:** *Morgensternlieder* for Mezzo-soprano and Piano (1958); *Mythos* for Mezzo-soprano and 9 Instruments

(1962); *4 Songs* for Mezzo-soprano and Orch. (1975); *Inferno*, cantata for Chorus and Instrumental Ensemble (1991–93).

Vodušek, Valens, Slovenian ethnomusicologist and conductor; b. Ljubljana, Jan. 29, 1912. He studied at the Univ. of Ljubljana (L.L.D., 1938) and took courses in piano and conducting at the Ljubljana State Cons. (1930–36); was self-taught in musicology and ethnomusicology. He was head of the music section at the Ministry of Culture in Slovenia (1946–51), then joined the Inst. for Ethnomusicology in Ljubljana. He was director of the Ljubljana Opera (1951–55), returning to the Inst. as director until 1972, when it combined with the Inst. of Ethnology of the Slovene Academy of Sciences and Arts; at that time he became head of its ethnomusicology dept. He conducted the Ljubljana Radio Choir (1946–51; renamed the Slovene Phil. Choir in 1948), and was artistic director of the Slovene Octet (1956–72). Vodušek instigated systematic fieldwork and classification in Slovene ethnic music.

Vogel, Adolf, German bass-baritone; b. Munich, Aug. 18, 1897; d. Vienna, Dec. 20, 1969. He studied voice with Anna Bahr-Mildenburg and J. Kiechle. He made his operatic debut as Daland in Klagenfurt (1923), then sang at the Leipzig Opera (1928–30); was a member of the Bavarian State Opera in Munich from 1930 to 1937; made his U.S. debut at the Metropolitan Opera in N.Y. as Alberich (Dec. 3, 1937); remained on its roster until 1939; then taught voice at the Vienna Academy of Music (from 1940). He became best known for his buffo roles.

Vogel, Jaroslav, Czech conductor and composer; b. Pilsen, Jan. 11, 1894; d. Prague, Feb. 2, 1970. He studied violin with Ševčik and composition with Novák in Prague; after taking courses in Munich (1910–12) and at the Paris Schola Cantorum with d'Indy (1912–13), he completed his training with Novák at the Prague Cons. (graduated, 1919). He was a conductor at the Pilsen Opera (1914–15) and in Ostrava (1919–23); after conducting in Prague (1923–27), he was chief conductor of the Ostrava Opera (1927–43); then conducted at the Prague National Theater (1949–58), and was chief conductor of the Brno State Phil. (1959–62). In 1964 he was made an Artist of Merit by the Czech government. As a conductor, he championed the music of Smetana, Janáček, and Novák. He publ. (in German) the useful study *Leoš Janáček: Sein Leben und Werk* (Prague, 1958; abr. Eng. tr., 1962; Czech original, 1963). He composed the operas *Maréja* (Olomouc, 1923), *Meister Georg or Mistr Jíra* (Prague, 1926), *Jovana* (Ostrava, 1939), and *Hiawatha* (Ostrava, 1974), orch. pieces, and chamber music.

Vogel, Wladimir (Rudolfovich), significant German-Russian-born Swiss composer; b. Moscow (of a German father and a Russian mother), Feb. 29, 1896; d. Zürich, June 19, 1984. He began composing in his youth. At the outbreak of World War I (1914), he was interned in Russia as an enemy alien; after the Armistice in 1918, he went to Berlin, where he studied with Tiessen (1919–21) and Busoni (1921–24). He was greatly influenced by both Busoni and Schoenberg. From 1929 to 1933 Vogel taught at the Klindworth-Scharwenka Cons. in Berlin; with the advent to power of the Nazi government, Vogel, although not a Jew, chose to leave Germany. He worked in Strasbourg and Brussels with Scherchen on various problems of musical techniques; then went to Switzerland, and in 1954 became a naturalized Swiss citizen. Vogel's idiom of composition underwent several changes throughout the years. A convinced believer in the mystical power of music, he felt great affinity with Scriabin's mystical ideas and techniques; he built his melodies along the upper overtones of the harmonic series, and his harmonies on a massive superimposition of perfect fourths and tritones. Gradually he approached the method of composition in 12 tones as promulgated by Schoenberg, while Busoni's precepts of neo-Classical structures governed Vogel's own works as far as formal design was concerned; many of his polyphonic compositions adhered to the Classical harmonic structures in 4 parts, which he maintained even in choral pieces using the Sprechstimme. Serialist procedures were adumbrated in Vogel's music through the astute organization of melodic and rhythmic elements.

WORKS: ORCH.: *Sinfonia fugata* (1924); *4 Studies: Ritmica funèbre, Ritmica scherzosa, Ostinato perpetuo,* and *Ritmica ostinata* (1930–32); *Rallye* (1932); *Tripartita* (1934; Geneva, Nov. 21, 1935); Violin Concerto (1937); *Passacaglia* (1946); *Sept aspects d'une série de douze sons* (1949–50); *Spiegelungen* (1952; Frankfurt am Main, June 26, 1953); Cello Concerto (1954; Zürich, Nov. 27, 1956); *Interludio lirico* (1954); *Preludio, Interludio lirico, Postludio* (1954); *Hörformen I* (1967) and *II* (1967–69); *Cantique en forme d'un canon à quatre voix* (1969); *Abschied* for Strings (1973); *Meloformen* for Strings (1974); *Hommage* for Strings (1974). **CHAMBER:** *La Ticinella* for Flute, Oboe, Clarinet, Saxophone, and Bassoon (1941); *12 variétudes* for Flute, Clarinet, Violin, and Cello (1942); *Inspiré par Jean Arp* for Violin, Flute, Clarinet, and Cello (1965); *Analogien*, "Hörformen" for String Quartet (1973); *Monophonie* for Violin (1974); *Für Flöte, Oboe, Klarinette, und Fagott* (1974); *Poème* for Cello (1974); *Terzett* for Flute, Clarinet, and Bassoon (1975). **PIANO:** *Nature vivante*, 6 expressionistic pieces (1917–21); *Einsames Getröpfel und Gewuchsel* (1921; rev. 1968); *Dai tempi pi remoti*, 3 pieces (1922–31; rev. 1968); *Etude-Toccata* (1926); *Epitaffio per Alban Berg* (1936); *Klavier-eigene Interpretationsstudie einer varierten Zwölftonfolge* (1972); *4 Versionen einer Zwölftonfolge* (1972); *Musik* for Wind Quartet and Strings (1975). **VOCAL:** *Wagadus Untergang durch die Eitelkeit*, cantata for 3 Soloists, Mixed Chorus, Speaking Chorus, and 5 Saxophones (1930); *Thyl Claes* (Till Eulenspiegel), oratorio in 2 parts: *Oppression* (1938) and *Liberation* (1943–45; orch. suite, Palermo, April 26, 1949); *An die Jugend der Welt* for Chorus and Chamber Orch. (1954); *Goethe-Aphorismen* for Soprano and Strings (Venice, Sept. 1955); *Eine Gotthardkantate* for Baritone and Strings (1956); *Jona ging doch nach Ninive* for Baritone, Speaking Soloists and Chorus, Mixed Chorus, and Orch. (1958); *Meditazione su Amadeo Modigliani* for 4 Soloists, Narrator, Chorus, and Orch. (Lugano, March 31, 1962); *Die Flucht*, dramatic oratorio (1963–64; Zürich, Nov. 8, 1966); *Schritte* for Alto and Orch. (1968); *Gli Spaziali* for Speakers, Vocalists, and Orch., after the writings of Leonardo da Vinci, *Autour de la lune* by Jules Verne, and utterances of the American astronauts (1969–71).

BIBL.: H. Oesch, *W. V.: Sein Weg zu einer neuen musikalischen Wirklichkeit* (Bern, 1967); W. Labhart, *W. V.: Konturen eines Mitbegrundes der Neuen Musik* (Zürich, 1982).

Vogl, Adolf, German writer on music and composer; b. Munich, Dec. 18, 1873; d. there, Feb. 2, 1961. He was a pupil of Hermann Levi. After a brief career as a conductor in Trier, Saarbrücken, St. Gallen, and Bern, he returned to Munich and devoted his energies to writing and composing. During the Nazi era, he was imprisoned but resumed his activities after the demise of the Third Reich. Among his insightful books were *Tristan und Isolde: Briefe an eine deutsche Künstlerin* (Munich, 1913; 3rd ed., 1922) and *Parsifal: Tiefe Schau in die Mysterien des Bühnenweihfestspiels* (Munich, 1914). He composed the operas *Maja* (1908) and *Die Verdammten* (1934), various choral pieces, and songs.

Vogler, Carl, Swiss organist, conductor, pedagogue, and composer; b. Oberrohrdorf, Feb. 26, 1874; d. Zürich, June 17, 1951. He was a pupil of Breitenbach at the Lucern Organistenschule (1891–93), of Hegar and Kempter at the Zürich Music School (1893–95), and of Rheinberger at the Munich Cons. (1895–97). From 1897 to 1919 he was an organist and music teacher in Baden in Aargau, and also was founder-director of the Gemischter Chor and the Musikkollegium. He taught counterpoint at the Zürich Cons. from 1915, where he was co-director (1919–39) and director (1939–45). From 1907 to 1932 he was president of the Musikpädagogischer Verband, and also of the Schweizerischer Tonkünstlerverein from 1931 to 1941. In 1924 he founded the Gesellschaft für Aufführungsrechte, serving as its president until his death. He ed. the book *Der Schweizerische Tonkünstlerverein* (Zürich, 1925) and publ. the study

Der Schweizer Musiker und seine Berufsbildung (Zürich, 1942). His music, which included *Mutter Sybille*, Singspiel (1906), *Rübezsahl*, Märchenspiel (1917), *Friedelhänschen*, Märchenspiel (1924), choral music, songs, and organ pieces, followed mainly the precepts of late Romanticism.

BIBL.: "C. V. zum 70. Geburtstag," *Schweizerische Musikzeitung/Revue musicale suisse*, LXXXIV (1944).

Vogt, Hans, German composer and pedagogue; b. Danzig, May 14, 1911; d. Metternich, May 19, 1992. He studied with Georg Schumann (master class in composition, 1929–34) at the Prussian Academy of Arts and received training in piano, cello, conducting, and music education at the Akademie für Kirchen- und Schulmusik (1930–34) in Berlin. In 1933 he won the Mendelssohn Prize in Berlin. From 1935 to 1938 he was chief conductor of the Detmold Opera, and then was music director in Stralsund from 1938 to 1944. In 1951 he became a teacher of composition at the Mannheim Hochschule für Musik, where he was a prof. from 1971 to 1978. From 1963 to 1984 he was also chairman of the Gesellschaft für Neue Musik in Mannheim. In 1961 and 1969 he won the Prix Reine Elisabeth of Belgium. He won the Prix Rainer III Prince de Monaco in 1961. He received the Premio Città di Trieste in 1968. In 1978–79 he was in residence at the Villa Massimo in Rome. He was a contributor to *Neue Musik seit 1945* (Stuttgart, 1972; 3rd ed., 1982) and author of *Johann Sebastien Bachs Kammermusik* (Stuttgart, 1981).

WORKS: DRAMATIC: *Die Stadt hinter dem Strom*, oratorio-opera (1953); *Athenerkomödie (The Metropolitans)*, comic opera (1962; rev. 1987). **ORCH.:** 2 concertos for Orch. (1950, 1960); *Rhythmische Suite* for Strings (1952); Piano Concerto (1955); *Monologue*, 4 pieces (1964); Cello Concerto (1968); *Konzertante Divertimenti* for Piano and Small Orch. (1968; rev. 1982); *Azioni sinfoniche* (1971); *Arco trionfale* (1979); Violin Concerto (1981); *Symphony in 1 Movement, Dona nobis pacem* (1984); *Tim Finnigan's Wake* for Oboe and Strings (1987); *Aprèslude* for Orch. and Mezzo-soprano ad libitum (1988); *Gestalten-Szenen-Schatten* for Strings (1988). **CHAMBER:** Trio for Flute, Viola, and Harp (1951; rev. 1989); Quintet for Flute, Oboe, Violin, Bassoon, and Harpsichord (1958); Flute Sonata (1958); *Konzertante Sonata* for Chamber Ensemble (1959); 4 string quartets (1960; 1975; 1977; 1984, rev. 1991); *Dialog* for Piano, Violin, and Cello (1960); String Quintet (1967); String Trio (1969); *Elemente zu einer Sonate* for Cello and Piano (1973); *Giuoco degli flauti* for 5 Flutes and Percussionist (1974); *Antiphonen* for Oboe and Organ (1976); Sonatina for Violin and Double Bass (1976); *Preludio, Presto 3 Pezzo variato* for Cello (1977); *Rondo sereno* for Cello and Contrabass (1980; also for Violin and Viola, 1987); *Sonata lirica* for Violin and Piano (1983); *Movimenti*, duo for Violin and Cello (1985); String Octet (1988); *Sonata per quattro archi* for Violin, Viola, Cello, and Double Bass (1989); String Sextet, *Ballata Notturna* (1990); *Fantasie über das Magnificat* for Violin (1990); *La Danza* for Contrabass (1991). **PIANO:** *Sonata alla toccata* (1957); Sonata for Piano, 4-hands (1959); *Musik* for 2 Pianos (1967). **VOCAL:** *De profundis clamavi ad te, Domine* for Chorus (1951); *Historie der Verkündigung*, chamber oratorio for 3 Women Soloists, Chorus, and 13 Instruments (1955); *Masken* for Soprano, String Orch., and 3 Percussionists (1956); *Vier englische Lieder* for Soprano, Oboe, Clarinet, Violin, Cello, and Harp (1957); *Fabeln des Äsop* for Chorus, Clarinet, Double Bass, and Percussionist (1959); *Poems from Herman Moon's London Hourbook* for Vocal Quartet and Piano (1960); *Ihr Töchter von Jerusalem, weinet nicht über mich* for Tenor, Chorus, and 2 Percussionists (1963); *Sine nomine* for Tenor, Chorus, and Orch. (1964); *Magnificat* for Soprano, Chorus, and Orch. (1966); *Requiem* for Soprano, Bass, Chorus, and 2 Percussionists (1969); *Drei Madrigale nach Gedichten von W.H. Auden* for Chorus (1973); *Strophen* for Baritone and Orch. (1975); *Canticum Simeonis* for Chorus and Flute (1976); *Historie vom Propheten Jona*, chamber oratorio for Alto, Tenor, Chorus, and 6 Instruments (1979); *Drei geistliche Gesänge nach barocken Dichtungen* for Baritone and Organ (1981–83); *Drei deutsche Madrigale* for Chorus and Percussionist (1983–89).

Voicu, Ion, Romanian violinist and conductor; b. Bucharest, Oct. 8, 1925. He enrolled at the Bucharest Cons. at 13 as a violin pupil of George Enacovici; after making his debut on the Bucharest Radio in 1940, he continued his training with Enesco (1945); then studied with Yampolsky and Oistrakh at the Moscow Cons. (1955–57). In 1969 he founded a chamber orch. in Bucharest; toured widely with this ensemble in succeeding years. From 1971 to 1982 he was music director of the Georges Enesco Phil. in Bucharest.

Voisin, Roger (Louis), distinguished French-born American trumpeter and teacher; b. Angers, June 26, 1918. He was taken to Boston as a child by his family; became a naturalized American citizen in 1932; studied initially with his father, a member of the Boston Sym. Orch., then with Georges Mager (1933) and Marcel LaFosse (1934). In 1935 he became 3rd trumpeter in the Boston Sym. Orch.; after serving as its 1st trumpeter (1949–67), he was again 3rd trumpeter from 1967 until his retirement in 1973. He taught at the Berkshire Music Center in Tanglewood, the New England Cons. of Music in Boston, and Boston Univ.

Volans, Kevin, South African-born Irish composer; b. Pietermaritzburg, July 26, 1949. Following training in South Africa, he studied with Stockhausen and Kagel in Cologne (1973–81). He taught at the Univ. of Natal, Durban (1982–84), and then was composer-in-residence at Queen's Univ. in Belfast (1986–89). In 1989 he settled in Ireland. In 1992 he was composer-in-residence at Princeton Univ. in Princeton, N.J.

WORKS: *9 Beginnings* for 2 Pianos (1976; rev. 1979); *Monkey Solo* for Piano (1977); *Mbira* for 2 Harpsichords and Rattles (1980); *Matepe* for 2 Harpsichords and Rattles (1980); *Renewed Music* for 8 Percussionists (1981); 5 string quartets: No. 1, *White Man Sleeps* (1986; original version for 2 Harpsichords, Viola da Gamba, and Percussion, 1982), No. 2, *Hunting: Gathering* (1987), No. 3, *The Songlines* (1988), No. 4, *The Ramanujan Notebooks* (1990), and No. 5, *Dancers on a Plane* with taped natural sounds (1993); *Walking Song* for Flute, Harpsichord, and 2 Hand-Clappers (1984); *Leaping Dance* for 2 Pianos (1984); *Kneeling Dance* for 2 Pianos (1985; rev. 1987); *She Who Sleeps with a Small Blanket* for Percussion (1985–86); *Notes d'un peintre* for String Quartet (1987); *Into Darkness* for Piano, Clarinet, Trumpet, Violin, Cello, and Marimba (1987; rev. 1989); *The Man Who Strides the Wind*, chamber opera (1988–93; London, July 2, 1993); *Chevron* for 14 Instruments (1989); *Correspondences*, dance opera for Baritone and String Quartet (1990); *One Hundred Frames* for Orch. (Belfast, Dec. 6, 1991); *Wanting to Tell Stories*, choreographed music for Piano, Clarinet, Viola, and Double Bass (1993); *Cicada* for 2 Pianos (1994).

Volbach, Fritz, German choral conductor, music scholar, and composer; b. Wipperfürth, near Cologne, Dec. 17, 1861; d. Wiesbaden, Nov. 30, 1940. He studied at the Cologne Cons. with Hiller, Jensen, and Seiss, and in Berlin with Taubert and Löschhorn; completed his education at the Univ. of Bonn (Ph.D., 1899, with the diss. *Die Praxis der Händel-Aufführung*). In 1892 he was appointed conductor of the Liedertafel and the Damengesangverein in Mainz; after serving as music director at the Univ. of Tübingen (1907–18), he went to Münster as prof. at the Univ. and as conductor of the city orch.; retired to Wiesbaden in 1930. A versatile musician, he had command of almost every orch. instrument.

WORKS: OPERA: *Die Kunst zu lieben* (1910). **ORCH.:** 3 symphonic poems: *Ostern* (1895), *Es waren zwei Königskinder* (1901), and *Alt-Heidelberg, du feine* (1904); Sym. (1909). **OTHER:** Chamber music, including a Piano Quitet (1912) and piano pieces; numerous choral works; lieder.

WRITINGS: *Lehrbuch der Begleitung des gregorianischen Gesangs* (Berlin, 1888); *G.F. Händel* (Berlin, 1898; 2nd ed., 1907); *Beethoven: Die Zeit des Klassizismus* (Munich, 1905; 2nd ed., 1929); *Die deutsche Musik im 19. Jahrhundert* (Kempten, 1909); *Das moderne Orchester in seiner Entwicklung* (Leipzig, 1910; 2nd ed., 1919); *Die Instrumente des Orchesters* (Leipzig,

1913; 2nd ed., 1921); *Erläuterwungen zu den Klavier-Sonaten Beethovens* (Cologne, 1919; 3rd ed., 1924); *Handbuch der Musikwissenschaften* (2 vols., Münster, 1926, 1930); *Die Kunst der Sprache* (Mainz, 1929); *Der Chormeister* (Mainz, 1931); *Erlebtes und Erstrebtes* (autobiography; Mainz, 1956).

BIBL.: J. Hagemann, *F. V., Monographien Moderner Musiker,* III (Leipzig, 1909); G. Schwake, *F. V.s Werke* (Münster, 1921); K. Hortschansky, ed., *F. V., 1861–1940: Komponist, Dirigent und Musikwissenschaftler* (Hagen, 1987).

Volek, Jaroslav, prominent Czech musicologist and aesthetician; b. Trenčín, July 15, 1923; d. Prague, Feb. 22, 1989. He studied composition at the Prague Cons. (1941–46) and then attended the master classes of Šín, Hába, and Řídký there (1946–48); took courses in musicology and aesthetics at the Univ. of Bratislava (Ph.D., 1952, with the diss. *Teoretické základy harmonie z hladiska vedeckej filozófie* [The Theoretical Bases of Harmony from the Viewpoint of Scientific Philosophy]; publ. in Bratislava, 1954) and at the Univ. of Prague (C.Sc., 1958, with the diss. *O specifičnosti předmětu uměleckého odrazu skutečnosti* [Specific Quality in the Artistic Reflection of Reality]; publ. in L. Tondl et al., *Otázky teorie poznáni,* Prague, 1957; D.Sc., 1968, with the diss. *Základy obecné teorie umění* [The Bases of General Art Theory]; publ. in Prague, 1968). He was a lecturer (1952–57), reader (1957–68), and prof. (from 1968) at the Univ. of Prague; also was active as a music critic and served as ed. of the journal *Estetika* (1969–71). He played a significant role in the development of Marxist music criticism.

WRITINGS (all publ. in Prague): *Novodobé harmonické systémy* (Contemporary Harmonic Systems; 1961); *Kotázkám předmětu a metod estetiky a obecné teori uměni* (The Subject and Methods of Aesthetics and the General Theory of Art; 1963); *Die Frage der Zahl der Funktion in der traditionellen Harmonik* (1968); *Kapitoly z dějin estetiky* (Chapters from the History of Aesthetics; 1969); *K antropologické problematice estetiky a obecné teorie uměni* (Anthropological Problems in the Aesthetics and General History of Art; 1970).

Völker, Franz, gifted German tenor; b. Neu-Isenburg, March 31, 1899; d. Darmstadt, Dec. 5, 1965. He studied in Frankfurt am Main. He made his operatic debut at the Frankfurt am Main Opera as Florestan in 1926; continued on its roster until 1935; also sang at the Vienna State Opera (1931–36; 1939–40; 1949–50), the Berlin State Opera (1933–43), and the Bavarian State Opera in Munich (1936–37; 1945–52); he made guest appearances at Covent Garden in London, and in Salzburg and Bayreuth. After his retirement in 1952, he taught voice in Neu-Isenburg; was a prof. at the Stuttgart Hochschule für Musik from 1958. Among his finest roles were Parsifal, Lohengrin, Siegmund, Florestan, the Emperor in *Die Frau ohne Schatten,* Othello, and Max in *Der Freischütz.*

Volkonsky, Andrei (Mikhailovich), Russian harpsichordist, conductor, and composer; b. Geneva (of Russian parents of princely nobility), Feb. 14, 1933. He was 11 when he began piano studies with Auber at the Geneva Cons.; received training in composition from Boulanger in Paris (1945–47), and also continued his piano study with Lipatti; then went to Russia and pursued training at the Tambov Music School; completed his training in composition with Shaporin at the Moscow Cons. (1950–54). In 1955 he was a co-founder, with Barshai, of the Moscow Chamber Orch.; then devoted himself to harpsichord playing; in 1964 he organized in Moscow the concert group Madrigal, with which he gave annual series of highly successful concerts in the Soviet Union, East Germany, and Czechoslovakia. His early works were set in evocative impressionistic colors, in the manner of the French modern school, but soon he deployed a serial technique of composition analogous to Schoenberg's method of composition with 12 tones outside traditional tonality. He was outspoken in his criticism of the direction that Soviet music was taking, and he entirely rejected the official tenets of socialist realism. This attitude, and the nature of his own music, resulted in the cancellation of performances of his works; he was expelled from the Union of Soviet Composers, and could no longer give concerts. In 1973 he returned to Switzerland.

WORKS: DRAMATIC: Music for plays. **ORCH.:** *Concerto for Orchestra* (Moscow, June 10, 1954); *Capriccio*; *Serenade to an Insect* for Chamber Orch. (1959); *Réplique* for Small Orch. (1969). **CHAMBER:** Piano Quintet (1954); String Quartet (1955); Piano Sonata (1956); *Musica stricta* for Piano (1956); *Music* for 12 Instruments (1957); Viola Sonata (1960); *Jeux à trois* for Flute, Violin, and Harpsichord (1962); *Les Mailles du temps* for 3 Instrumental Groups (1969). **VOCAL:** 2 cantatas: *Rus* (Russia), after Gogol (1952) and *The Image of the World* (Moscow, May 8, 1953); *2 Japanese Songs* for Chorus, Electronic Sound, and Percussion (1957); *Suite des miroirs* for Soprano, Organ, Guitar, Violin, Flute, and Percussion (1960); *The Lament of Shaza* for Soprano and Small Orch. (1961; Moscow, May 12, 1965); *Concerto itinerant* for Soprano, Violin, Percussion, and 26 Instruments (1967).

Vollenweider, Andreas, popular Swiss composer and instrumentalist; b. Zürich, Oct. 4, 1953. His father was the organist Hans Vollenweider; the family home was frequented by artists and musicians. He studied guitar, flute, and other instruments before settling on the harp, which he modified and amplified in developing his own technique; played concerts and made recordings with the ensemble Poetry and Music. His first solo recording was *Eine art Suite* (1979); it was followed by the debut concert of Andreas Vollenweider and Friends at the 1981 Montreux Jazz Festival. His ensuing recordings were highly successful, marketed under jazz, pop, and classical categories, and considered among the most engaging of New Age recordings. His first U.S. tour was in 1984; that same year he directed the video *Pace verde.* In 1989 he produced another video, *Pearls and Tears.* His titles reflect his mystical roots; the music itself involves a delicate mix of electric and acoustic timbres in lively, syncopated textures. Other noteworthy recordings include . . . *Behind the Gardens—Behind the Wall—Under the Tree . . .* (1981), *Caverna Magica (. . . Under the Tree—In the Cave . . .)* (1983), *White Winds* (1985), *Down to the Moon* (1986), and *Dancing with the Lion* (1989).

Vollerthun, Georg, German composer; b. Fürstenau, Sept. 29, 1876; d. Strausberg, near Berlin, Sept. 15, 1945. He studied with Tappert, Radecke, and Gernsheim. He was a theater conductor in Prague, Berlin, Barmen, and Mainz (1899–1905); went to Berlin as a music critic and teacher in 1910; from 1922, lived mostly in Strausberg.

WORKS: OPERAS: *Veeda* (Kassel, 1916); *Island-Saga* (Munich, Jan. 17, 1925); *Der Freikorporal* (Hannover, Nov. 10, 1931); *Das königliche Opfer* (1942). **OTHER:** *Alt-Danzig Suite* for Orch. (1938); cantatas and other vocal works, including many German songs.

BIBL.: E. Krieger, *G. V.* (Berlin, 1942).

Voloshinov, Victor, Russian composer and teacher; b. Kiev, Oct. 17, 1905; d. Leningrad, Oct. 22, 1960. He studied composition with Scherbatchev at the Leningrad Cons.; later became a prof. there. He wrote the operas *Glory* (1939) and *Stronger Than Death* (1942); several symphonic suites on Central Asian themes; chamber music; songs; incidental music for the theater. He enjoyed great renown as a pedagogue.

Volpe, Arnold (David), Russian-born American conductor and composer; b. Kovno, Lithuania, July 9, 1869; d. Miami, Fla., Feb. 2, 1940. He studied violin with Auer (1887–91) and composition with Soloviev (1893–97) at the St. Petersburg Cons. In 1898 he emigrated to America, settling in N.Y.; in 1902, founded the Young Men's Sym. Orch. of N.Y., which he conducted until 1919; also conducted the Volpe Sym. Orch. (1904–14). In 1918–19 he conducted the summer concerts at the Lewisohn Stadium in N.Y.; then moved to Washington, D.C., where he was music director of the Washington, D.C., Community Opera (1919–22); subsequently was director of the Kansas City Cons. (1922–25); in 1926 he went to Florida, where he organized the

Univ. of Miami Sym. Orch. He composed orch. works, chamber music, solo instrumental pieces, and songs.

BIBL.: M. Volpe (his widow), *A. V.: Bridge between Two Musical Worlds* (Coral Gables, Fla., 1950).

Vomáčka, Boleslav, Czech composer; b. Mladá Boleslav, June 28, 1887; d. Prague, March 1, 1965. He studied law at the Charles Univ. in Prague (LL.D., 1913); studied organ (1906–09), composition (with Novák; 1909–10), and singing (with Krummer) at the Prague Cons. He was in the service of the Labor Ministry in Prague (1919–50); wrote music criticism in several newspapers there; was ed. of *Listy Hudební Matice* (1922–35). In 1955 he was made an Artist of Merit by the Czech government. He publ. *Josef Suk* (Prague, 1922), *Stanislav Suda* (Prague, 1933), and *Sukova sborová tvorba* (Suk's Choral Works; Prague, 1935). He began to compose early in life, developing a strong national style.

WORKS: OPERAS: *Vodník* (The Water Spirit; 1934–37; Prague, Dec. 17, 1937); *Čekanky* (Waiting for a Husband; 1939; 1956–57); *Boleslav I* (1953–55; Prague, March 8, 1957). **ORCH.:** *Ciaconna* (1910); Sym. (1945); *Dukla*, overture (1948); *Fanfary miru* (Fanfares of Peace) for Trumpet and Orch. (1960). **CHAMBER:** Violin Sonata (1912); Duo for Violin and Cello (1925–27); Sonatina for 2 Violins (1936; also for Violin and Viola and as *Kvartetino* for String Quartet, 1941); Nonet for Wind Instruments (1957); String Quartet (1959); 2 piano sonatas (1917; *Sonata quasi fantasia*, 1942); other piano pieces. **VOCAL: CANTATAS:** *Romance Svatojiršká* (Romance of St. George; 1920, 1943); *Živí mrtvým* (To the Dead; 1927–28; Prague, Feb. 24, 1929); *Strážce majáku* (The Keeper of the Lighthouse; 1931–33); *Prapor míru nad Duklou* (The Banner of Peace Over Duklou; 1951); *Bojka partyzánka* (The Partisan Struggle; 1952); many choral works; sets of songs.

BIBL.: H. Doležil, *B. V.* (Prague, 1941).

Von Blon, Franz, German composer and conductor; b. Berlin, July 16, 1861; d. there, Oct. 21, 1945. He studied in Berlin at the Stern Cons. He was active as a conductor in Warsaw and Berlin; wrote several operettas (*Sub rosa, Die Amazone, Die tolle Prinzess* et al.) and much light music for piano; also a number of military marches, of which one, *Unter dem Siegesbanner*, became extremely popular.

Vonk, Hans, prominent Dutch conductor; b. Amsterdam, June 18, 1942. He studied law at the Univ. of Amsterdam; took courses in piano, conducting, and composition at the Amsterdam Cons., then studied conducting with Scherchen and Ferrara. From 1966 to 1973 he was conductor of the Netherlands National Ballet; also was assistant conductor of the Concertgebouw Orch. in Amsterdam. In 1974 he made his U.S. debut as a guest conductor with the San Francisco Sym. Orch. He was conductor of the Netherlands Radio Phil. in Hilversum (1973–79); also was assoc. conductor of the Royal Phil. in London (1976–79). He served as chief conductor of the Netherlands Opera in Amsterdam (1976–85) and of the Residentie Orch. in The Hague (1980–85). He appeared regularly as a guest conductor with the Dresden State Orch. and Opera from 1980; was permanent conductor (1984–85) and chief conductor (1985–91) of the Dresden State Opera, and also chief conductor of the Dresden State Orch. (1985–91). In 1991 he became chief conductor of the Cologne Radio Sym. Orch. In 1996 he became music director of the St. Louis Sym. Orch.

Von Stade, Frederica, remarkable American mezzo-soprano; b. Somerville, N.J., June 1, 1945. She was educated at the Norton Academy in Conn.; after an apprenticeship at the Long Wharf Theater in New Haven, she studied with Sebastian Engelberg, Paul Berl, and Otto Guth at the Mannes College of Music in N.Y. Although she reached only the semi-finals of the Metropolitan Opera Auditions in 1969, she attracted the attention of Rudolf Bing, its general manager, who arranged for her debut with the company in N.Y. as the 3rd boy in *Die Zauberflöte* on Jan. 11, 1970; she gradually took on more important roles there before going to Europe, where she gave an arresting portrayal of Cherubino at the opera house at the palace of Versailles in 1973. In 1974 she sang Nina in the premiere of Pasatieri's *The Seagull* at the Houston Grand Opera. In 1975 she made her debut at London's Covent Garden as Rosina; subsequently attained extraordinary success in lyric mezzo-soprano roles with the world's major opera houses and also pursued an extensive concert career, appearing regularly with the Chamber Music Soc. of Lincoln Center in N.Y. In 1988 she sang the role of Tina in the premiere of Argento's *The Aspern Papers* at the Dallas Opera, and in 1990 appeared in recital in N.Y.'s Carnegie Hall. Her memorable roles include Dorabella, Idamante, Adalgisa in *Norma*, Charlotte in *Werther*, Mélisande, Octavian, and Malcolm in *La Donna del lago*. She has also proved successful as a crossover artist, especially in Broadway musical recordings.

BIBL.: H. Saal, "'The Prima Donna Next Door': F. v.S.," *Ovation* (May 1983); S. Shirakawa, "F. v.S.," ibid. (Nov. 1988).

Voorhees, Donald, American conductor; b. Guthville, Pa., July 26, 1903; d. Cape May Court House, N.J., Jan. 10, 1989. He joined the Lyric Theatre orch. in Allentown, Pa., as a pianist at age 12, becoming its conductor when he was 15; at 17, he made his first appearance as a conductor on Broadway with the musical revue *Broadway Brevities* of 1920; subsequently conducted various Broadway shows. He also was active as a conductor on radio from 1925; in 1940 he became music director of the highly successful network radio show the "Bell Telephone Hour," for which he composed its signature theme, the *Bell Waltz*; after the show moved to television in 1959, he remained as its music director until its last telecast in 1968.

Voormolen, Alexander (Nicolas), Dutch composer; b. Rotterdam, March 3, 1895; d. The Hague, Nov. 12, 1980. He was a scion of a family of municipal functionaries in the Netherlands, and on his mother's side was a descendant of Claude Rameau, a brother of Jean-Philippe Rameau. He entered the Utrecht School of Music, where he studied with Johan Wagenaar and Willam Petri; he began to compose as a very young man; from his earliest steps he experienced a strong influence of French Impressionism; he went to Paris in 1916, where he was befriended by Ravel, whose influence became decisive. In 1923 he settled in The Hague; after serving as a music critic of the *Nieuwe Rotterdamsche Courant*, he was librarian of the Royal Cons. of Music of The Hague (1938–55). In his early idiom, Voormolen affected richly extended harmonies, and followed Ravel's example in writing works in neo-Baroque forms, marked by gentle symmetric melodies. His compositions later followed along neo-Classical lines. His works were initially successful in his homeland, but eventually fell into desuetude.

WORKS: BALLETS: *Le Roi Grenouille* (1916; withdrawn); *Baron Hop* (2 suites, 1923–24; 1931); *Diana* (1935–36); *Spiegel-Suite*, after Langendijk's play (1943). **ORCH.:** *De drei ruitertjes* (The 3 Little Horsemen), variations on a Dutch song (1927); *Een Zomerlied* (1928); Oboe Concerto (1938); *Sinfonia* (1939); *Kleine Haagsche Suite* for Small Orch. (1939); *Pastorale* for Oboe and Strings (1940); Cello Concerto (1941); *Arethuza*, symphonic myth, after L. Couperus (1947; Amsterdam, Nov. 11, 1948); *La Sirène* for Saxophone and Orch. (1949); Concerto for 2 Harpsichords or Pianos and Orch. (1950); *Sinfonia concertante* for Clarinet, Horn, and Strings (1951); *Eline*, nocturne (1957; orchestrated and enlarged version of the 1951 piano piece); *Chaconne en Fuga* (1958). **CHAMBER:** 2 violin sonatas (1917, 1934); Suite for Cello and Piano (1917); Piano Trio (1918); Suite for Harpsichord (1921); *Divertissement* for Cello and Piano (1922); 2 string quartets (1939, 1942); Viola Sonata (1935). **PIANO:** *Valse triste* (1914); Suite No. 1 (1914–16); *Falbalas* (1915); *Elephants* (1919); *Tableaux des Pays Bas*, in 2 series (1919–20, 1924); *Scène et danse érotique* (1920); *Le Souper clandestin* (1921); *Sonnet* (1922); *Livre des enfants* (2 series, 1923, 1925); *Berceuse* (1924); Sonata (1944); *Eline*, nocturne (1951). **VOCAL:** *Beatrijs*, melodrama for Narrator and Piano (1921); *3 Gedichten* for Voice and Orch. (1932); *Een nieuwe Lente op Holland's erf* for Voice and Orch. (1936); *Herinneringen aan Holland* (Memories of Holland) for Baritone, Bass Clarinet, and Strings (1966); *Stanzas of Charles II* for Baritone, Flute, English Horn, Celesta, Percussion, and Strings (1966); *Amsterdam*, cantata (1967); *From: The Recollection* for Medium Voice, String Orch., and Celesta (1970); *Ex minimis patet ipse Deus*, hymn for Middle Voice, Strings, and Celesta (1971; many alternate versions); *Ave Maria* for Chorus, Harp, and String Orch. (1973; many alternate versions); choruses.

Voorn, Joop, Dutch composer and teacher; b. The Hague, Oct. 16, 1932. He received training at the Brabant Cons., where he subsequently taught (from 1969).

WORKS: ORCH.: *Immobile: Music for Tutankhamun* (1973; Brabant, Dec. 2, 1975); *Petit concert* for Flute and Chamber Orch. (1975; Brabant, April 25, 1976); Sym. (1981); *Symphony for Gemet* for Winds (1981); *Petit concert d'automne* for Alto Saxophone and Orch. (1989); *The Sun Dances* (1990). **CHAMBER:** 2 string quartets (n.d.; 1970, rev. 1980); *Nakupenda*, trio for Flute, Violin, and Viola (1971); *Sucevita chorals* for 2 Oboes, 2 Clarinets, Bass Clarinet, and Bassoon (1972; rev. 1974); *Soft Music for Angela* for Flute (1973); Trio for Oboe, Clarinet, and Bassoon (1975); *Preludium en fuga*, quintet for Oboe, Clarinet, Bassoon, Horn, and Piano (1976); *Divertimento* for 3 Flutes (1978); *3 Pieces* for English Horn (1979); Clarinet Quintet (1983); Saxophone Sonata (1984); *Vjif schetsen* for 2 Guitars (1984); Piano Trio (1985); *Schrijdende* for Oboe, Clarinet, Bassoon, Horn, and Organ (1985); *Serenade* for Bassoon and Piano (1986); piano pieces; organ music. **VOCAL:** *Psalm CXIV—In Exitu* for Soprano, Children's Chorus, and Orch. (1968); *Speaking of Siva* for Chorus and Chamber Orch. (1977); *Song of Enitharmon* for Chorus and Orch. (1980); *Perceval et Blanchefleur* for Tenor and Orch. (1982).

Vorlová, Sláva (actually, **Miroslava Johnova**), Czech composer; b. Náchod, March 15, 1894; d. Prague, Aug. 24, 1973. She studied piano with her mother, then received training in voice at the Vienna Academy of Music; took private lessons in composition with Novák and in piano with Štěpán in Prague. After passing her state examinations in piano and singing (1918), she continued her piano studies with Maxián and her composition studies with Řídký, completing her training with the latter at the Prague Cons. master classes (graduated, 1948). She became interested in writing music for instruments rarely used for solo performances; wrote one of the few concertos for bass clarinet. Her music is tinted with impressionistic colors.

WORKS: OPERAS: *Zlaté ptáče* (The Golden Birds; 1949–50); *Rozmarýnka* (Rosemary; 1952; Kladno, 1955); *Náchodská kasace* (The Náchod Cassation; 1955); *Dva světy* (2 Worlds; 1958). **ORCH.:** *Fantasy* for Cello and Orch. (1940); *Symphony JM*, dedicated to Jan Masaryk (1947–48); *Božena Němcová*, suite (1950–51); Oboe Concerto (1952); *3 Bohemian Dances* (1952–53); Trumpet Concerto (1953); Viola Concerto (1954); Clarinet Concerto (1957); *Memento* (1957); *Thuringian Dances* (1957); Flute Concerto (1959); Concerto for Bass Clarinet and Strings (1961); *Kybernetic Studies* (1962); Concerto for Oboe, Harp, and Orch. (1963); *Dedications* (1965); *Bhukhar* (Fever Birds; 1965); Concerto for Double Bass and Strings (1968); *Correlations* for Bass Clarinet, Piano, and Strings (1968); *Polarization* for Harp, Wind Orch., and Percussion (1970); *Emergence* for Violin and Orch. (1973; Prague, March 24, 1974). **CHAMBER:** String Quartet (1939); Nonet (1944); *Melodious Variations* for String Quartet (1950); *Puzzles* for 2 Pianos (1953); *Miniatures* for Bass Clarinet and Piano (1962); *Dessins tetraharpes* for 4 Harps (1963); *Variations on a Theme by Handel* for Bass Clarinet and Piano (1965); *6 pro 5* for Brass Quintet (1967); *Immanence* for Bass Clarinet, Piano, and Percussion (1970). **VOCAL:** *Songs of Gondwana*, symphonic epos for Soloists, Chorus, and Orch. (1948–49); *2 African Fables* for Narrator, Alto Flute, and Percussion (1964); *Brief Considerations* for Soprano, Alto, and Piano (1971); songs.

Voss, Friedrich, German composer, b. Halberstadt, Dec. 12, 1930. He studied composition and piano at the (West) Berlin Hochschule für Musik (1949–54), then devoted himself to composition, winning the Munich Chamber Orch. competition (1955), the Stuttgart Music Prize (1960), the (West) Berlin Art Prize (1961), the Düsseldorf Robert Schumann Prize (1962), the Villa Massimo Award (1964, 1977), and the Mannheim Johann Wenzel Stamitz Prize (1985).

WORKS: BALLET: *Die Nachtigall und die Rose*, after Oscar Wilde (1961; Oberhausen, Jan. 5, 1962). **ORCH.:** *Concerto da camera* for Strings (1953); Symphonic Suite (1954; Berlin, July 9, 1958); 4 syms.: No. 1 (1958–59; Berlin, March 23, 1960), No. 2 (1962–63; Bonn, March 7, 1966), No. 3 (1966–67; Berlin, Nov. 12, 1969), and No. 4 (1972–76); 2 violin concertos: No. 1 (1962; Brussels, May 28, 1966) and No. 2 (1985–87); *Hamlet Overture* (1968–69); *Dithyrambus über ein Motiv von Beethoven* (1969); *Metamorphosis* (1978–79; Tokyo, June 10, 1980). **OTHER:** Chamber music, including 3 string quartets; choral pieces.

Vostřák, Zbyněk, Czech composer and conductor; b. Prague, June 10, 1920; d. Strakonice, Aug. 4, 1985. He studied composition privately with Rudolf Karel (1938–43) and attended the conducting classes of Pavel Dědeček at the Prague Cons. In 1963 he became conductor of the Prague chamber ensemble Musica Viva Pragensis. He also worked in an electronic music studio in Prague. His music evolved from the Central European type of modernism; later he annexed serial techniques, electronic sound, and aleatory practices.

WORKS: DRAMATIC: OPERAS: *Rohovín čtverrohý* (The 4-horned Rohovin; 1947–48; Olomouc, 1949); *Kutnohorští havíři* (The King's Master of the Mint; 1951–53; Prague, 1955); *Pražské nokturno* (A Prague Nocturne; 1957–58; Ustí-on-the-Elbe, 1960); *Rozbitý džbán* (The Broken Jug; 1960–61; Prague, 1963). **BALLETS:** *The Primrose* (1944–45); *Filosofská historie* (A Story of Students of Philosophy; 1949); *Viktorka* (Little Victoria; 1950); *Sněhurka* (Snow White; 1955); *Veselí vodníci* (Jolly Water Sprites; 1978–79). **ORCH.:** *Prague Overture* (1941); *Zrození měsíce* (The Birth of the Moon) for Chamber Orch. (1966; Prague, March 8, 1967); *Kyvadlo času* (The Pendulum of Time) for Cello, 4 Instrumental Groups, and Electric Organ (1966–67; Donaueschingen, Oct. 19, 1968); *Metahudba* (Metamusic) (1968; Prague, March 2, 1970); *Tajemství elipsy* (The Secret of Ellipsis) (1970; Prague, March 5, 1971); *Parable* for Orch. and Tape (1976–77); *Kapesní vesmír* (The Pocket Universe) for Flute, Dulcimer, and Strings (1980–81); *The Cathedral* (1982); *The Crystals* for English Horn, Strings, and Percussion (1983); Piano Concerto (1984). **CHAMBER:** *Elements* for String Quartet (1964); *Synchronia* for 6 Instruments (1965); *Trigonum* for Violin, Oboe, and Piano (1965); *Kosmogonia* for String Quartet (1968); *Sextant* for Wind Quintet (1969); *Fair Play* for Harpsichord and 6 Instruments (1978); String Quartet No. 4 (1979); *The Secret of the Rose* for Organ, Brass Quintet, and Percussion (1985); piano works. **OTHER:** Tape pieces.

Votapek, Ralph, American pianist and teacher; b. Milwaukee, March 20, 1939. He studied at Northwestern Univ. (B.A., 1960), with Gui Mombaerts and Robert Goldsand at the Manhattan School of Music in N.Y. (M.M., 1961), and with Rosina Lhévinne at the Juilliard School of Music in N.Y. (1961–62). He won the Van Cliburn Competition in 1962, and then embarked on a concert career. He taught at Michigan State Univ. in East Lansing (from 1968).

Votto, Antonino, Italian conductor; b. Piacenza, Oct. 30, 1896; d. Milan, Sept. 9, 1985. He studied piano with Longo and composition with De Nardis at the Cons. di Musica S. Pietro a Majella in Naples. He made his debut as a concert pianist in Trieste in 1919. From 1919 to 1921 he taught piano at the Cons. di Musica G. Verdi in Trieste. In 1921 he became a conductor at the Teatro Colón in Buenos Aires; in 1923 he made his first appearance at Milan's La Scala conducting *Manon Lescaut*; then was a répétiteur and assistant conductor there under Toscanini until 1929. He subsequently made guest conducting appearances throughout Italy, Europe, and South America. From 1948 to 1970 he was a regular conductor at La Scala, during which period he led performances in major productions with Callas and other famous singers; also conducted at the Chicago Lyric Opera (1960–61; 1970). He was on the faculty of the Milan Cons. (1941–67).

Vranken, Jaap, Dutch organist, teacher, and composer; b. Utrecht, April 16, 1897; d. The Hague, April 20, 1956. He was the son of the organist Joseph Vranken (1870–1948), with whom he studied organ and theory. From 1916 to 1918 he was in the U.S., studying with Percy Goetschius. He returned to the Netherlands in 1920, and was appointed organist at the church of St. Anthonius in The Hague. Vranken acquired a fine reputation as a teacher. He composed mostly sacred music; also instrumental music in Classical style; publ. a manual on counterpoint (1948).

Vredenburg, Max, Dutch composer; b. Brussels (of Dutch parents), Jan. 16, 1904; d. Laren, the Netherlands, Aug. 9, 1976. He was taken to the Netherlands as a child and received an elementary musical education there. In 1926 he went to Paris and studied at the École Normale de Musique with Dukas; was a music correspondent for the *Nieuwe Rotterdamsche courant* (1936–40). He fled the Nazis and went to Java in 1941, where he was interned by the Japanese (1942–45), but was allowed to organize concerts with his fellow internee, Szymond Goldberg; after his liberation, he settled in Amsterdam; was director of the Dutch section of the Federation Internationale des Jeunesses Musicales (1953–69); also was founder-director of the National Youth Orch. (1957–76). He wrote the book *Langs de vijf Lijnen* (1947).

WORKS: *Au pays des vendanges,* wind quintet (1951); Oboe Concerto (1951); *Akiba* for Mezzo-soprano and Chamber Orch. (1951); *Du printemps* for Mezzo-soprano and Chamber Orch. (1952); *Lamento* for Viola and Piano (1953); *Suite dansante* for Youth Orch. (1956); *Horizons hollandaises* for Orch. (1959); Trio for Oboe, Clarinet, and Bassoon (1965); piano pieces; many songs.

Vretblad, Viktor Patrik, Swedish organist, musicologist, and composer; b. Svartnäs, April 5, 1876; d. Stockholm, Jan. 15, 1953. He received his training at the Stockholm Cons. (1895–1900) and in Berlin. He made his livelihood as a post office official (1900–1940); also served as organist of Stockholm's French Reformed Church (1900–1907) and of St. Oskar's (1906–43); likewise as music critic for several journals. He composed some instrumental and vocal music.

WRITINGS (all publ. in Stockholm): *Johan Helmich Roman 1694–1758: Svenska musikens fader (1914); Konsertlivet i Stockholm under 1700–talet* (1918); *Andreas Hallén* (1918); *Den tjeckiscka tonkonsten* (1930); *Polen i musikhistorien* (1938).

Vreuls, Victor (Jean Léonard), Belgian composer and music educator; b. Verviers, Feb. 4, 1876; d. Brussels, July 27, 1944. He studied at the Verviers Cons., with Dupuis (harmony) and Radoux (counterpoint) at the Liège Cons., and with d'Indy in Paris. After serving as a prof. of harmony at the Schola Cantorum in Paris (1901–06), he was director of the Luxembourg Cons. (1906–26). In 1925 he was elected a member of the Belgian Royal Academy in Brussels. His major works were written in an expansive Romantic style.

WORKS: DRAMATIC: OPERAS: *Olivier le simple* (1909–11; Brussels, March 9, 1922); *Un Songe d'une nuit d'été,* after Shakespeare (1923–24; Brussels, Dec. 17, 1925). **BALLET:** *Le Loup-garou* (1935). **ORCH.:** 3 symphonic poems: *Cortège heroïque* (1894), *Jour de fête* (1904), and *Werther* (1907); Sym. (1899); 2 *poèmes* for Cello and Orch. (1900, 1930); *Elégie* for Flute and Chamber Orch. (1917); *Morceau de concert* for Trumpet and Orch. (1917); *Fantaisie* for Horn and Orch. (1918); *Romance* for Violin and Chamber Orch. (1924); *Caprice* for Violin and Chamber Orch. (1924); *Suite de danses* (1939); *Ouverture pour un drame* (1940). **CHAMBER:** Piano Quartet (1894); Piano Trio (1896); 2 violin sonatas (1899, 1919); String Quartet (1918); Cello Sonata (1922). **VOCAL:** Choruses; songs.

Vriend, Jan, Dutch composer and conductor; b. Sijbekarspel, Nov. 10, 1938. He studied with Ton de Leeuw at the Amsterdam Cons. (1960–67), with Koenig at the Inst. of Sonology at the Univ. of Utrecht (1965–67), and with Xenakis at the Paris Schola Cantorum (1967–68). While in Paris, he also was active with the Groupe de Recherches Musicales of the ORTF. Returning to the Netherlands, he was active as a conductor and as a lecturer. He later was active in England and was conductor of the New Stroud Orch. (1989–94). Having taught himself mathematics, he became interested in its applications to music. His works reflect advanced compositional modes of expression.

WORKS: ORCH.: *Diamant,* "sym. for the Earth" (1964–67); *Mater-Muziek* for Orch. and Electronics (1966); *Huantan* for Organ and Wind Orch. (1967–68); *Bau* (1970); *Elements of Logic* for Wind Orch. (1972; Scheveningen, Feb. 25, 1973; in collaboration with J. Kunst); *Hallelujah II: Ouverture à la Nouvelle alliance* (1988) and *I: A Symphony of the North* for Bass Clarinet and Orch. (1990). **CHAMBER:** *Pour le flûte* (1961); String Quartet (1962–63); *Paroesie* for 10 Instruments (1963); *Eclipse I: Heterostase* for Flute, Bass Clarinet, and Piano (1981), *II: Athema Keramitis* for Flute and Clarinet (1985), and *III: Aura (Interlude)* for Piano (1994); *Toque por la tierra vacía* for 2 Guitars (1981; rev. 1983); *Vectorial,* "a monument for J.S. Bach" for Oboe, Clarinet, Bass Clarinet, Bassoon, 2 Trumpets, and Piano (1983; rev. 1987); *Gravity's Dance* for Piano (1984; rev. 1986); *Wu Li* for Cello (1986; rev. 1987); *Symbiosis* for 9 Instruments (1993); organ music. **VOCAL:** *Transformation (on the way to Halleluja)* for Chorus and Orch. (1965–67); *Introitus (Hommage to Ton de Leeuw)* for Chorus, 6 Clarinets, 2 Bass Clarinets, and 4 Trombones (1969); *3 Songs* for Mezzo-soprano and Orch. (1991).

Vrieslander, Otto, German composer and writer on music; b. Münster, July 18, 1880; d. Tegna, Switzerland, Dec. 16, 1950. He was a student of Stemhauer and Buths in Düsseldorf (1891–1900), of Van de Sandt and Klauwell at the Cologne Cons. (1901–02), and of Schenker in Vienna (1911–12). In 1929 he settled in Switzerland. He publ. *Carl Philipp Emanuel Bach* (Munich, 1923), and also wrote articles on and prepared eds. of C.P.E. Bach's music. Vrieslander was an accomplished lieder composer.

Vronsky, Vitya, Russian-born American pianist; b. Evpatoria, Crimea, Aug. 22, 1909; d. Cleveland, June 28, 1992. She received training at the Kiev Cons., from Petri and Schnabel in Berlin, and from Cortot in Paris. From 1930 she performed in Europe. In 1933 she married **Victor Babin**, with whom she regularly performed in a piano duo. In 1937 they emigrated to the U.S. and established themselves as the leading piano duo of the day. From 1945 their tours took them to principal music centers of the world. Their repertoire extended from Bach to Babin.

Vroons, Frans (actually, **Franciscus**), Dutch tenor; b. Amsterdam, April 28, 1911; d. 's-Hertogenbosch, June 1, 1983. He studied in Amsterdam and Paris. He made his operatic debut as Pelléas in 1937; in 1945 he became the principal tenor at the Netherlands Opera in Amsterdam, where he sang for 2 decades; also was its co-director (1956–71). In 1948 he made his first appearance at London's Covent Garden as Don José and in 1951 in San Francisco as Massenet's Des Grieux. He taught voice in Amsterdam (from 1971). His other roles included Florestan, Tamino, Hoffmann, and Peter Grimes.

Vuataz, Roger, distinguished Swiss organist, conductor, broadcasting administrator, and composer; b. Geneva, Jan. 4, 1898; d. Chêne-Bougeries, Aug. 2, 1988. He studied at the Collège Calvin and pursued musical training at the Academy of Music and at the Cons. in Geneva, his principal mentors being Delaye, Mottu, and O. Barblan. He later studied Ondes Martenot in Paris (diploma, 1931) and attended the Institut Jaques-Dalcroze in Geneva (rhythm dipoloma, 1936). Vuataz's career was centered on Geneva, where he served as an organist of the Protestant Reformed Church from 1917 to 1978. He was founder-director of the Cathedral Choir (1940–60). From 1944 to 1964 he was head of the music dept. of Radio Geneva.

From 1961 to 1971 he taught at the Geneva Cons. He was president of the International Music Competition from 1962 to 1969, and also of the Viñes singing competition in Barcelona from 1963 to 1978. In 1967 he was awarded the music prize of the City of Geneva. In 1975 the Assn. of Swiss Musicians gave him its composer's prize. Vuataz's music was well crafted and displayed the influence of the Protestant Reformed tradition in his sacred scores.

WORKS: DRAMATIC: *Le Rhône*, ballet (1929); *Poème méditerranéen pour un ballet* (1938–50); *Monsieur Jabot*, opera-buffa (1957; Geneva, Nov. 28, 1958); *Solitude*, ballet (1962); *L'Esprit du Mal*, lyric drama (1967); *Cora, Amour et Mort*, lyric tragedy (1978–80); radiophonic pieces; film music. **ORCH.:** *Triptyque* (1929–42); *Petit Concert* for Small Orch. (1932); *Deuxième Suite sur des Thèmes populaires* for Strings (1937); *Images de Grèce*, sym. (1938); *Nocturne heroïque* for Trumpet and Orch. (1940; also for Trumpet and Piano); *Impromptu* for Saxophone and Orch. (1941; also for Saxophone and Piano); *Promenade et Poursuite* for Bassoon and Orch. (1943; also for Bassoon and Piano); *Epopée antique*, 2 suites (1947, 1951); Violin Concerto (1948); *Cinq Estampes genevoises* (1959); *Ouverture pour Phèdre* (1959); Piano Concerto (1963–64); Harp Concerto, *Fantaisies I-III* (1972); *Les Tragiques*, sym. for Reciter and Orch. (1974–75); Cello Concerto, *Images poétiques et pathétiques* (1977). **CHAMBER:** Cello Sonata (1928); 2 suites for Ondes Martenot (1930); Violin Sonatina (1933–34); *Musique* for Wind Quintet (1935–65); *Nocturne et Danse* for Alto Saxophone and Piano (1940: *Nocturne heroïque* for Trumpet and Piano (1940; also for Trumpet and Orch.); *Impromptu* for Saxophone and Piano (1941; also for Saxophone and Orch.); *Promenade et poursuite* for Bassoon and Piano (1943; also for Bassoon and Orch.); *Frivolités* for Sextet (1952); *Incantation* for Alto Saxophone and Piano (1953); Flute Sonata (1954–57); *Destin* for Saxophone, Harp, and Percussion (1954–79); *Thrène* for Horn and Piano (1960); *Ballade* for Viola and Piano (1960); String Quartet (1966–70); *Quatre Conversations avec Bach* for Flute, Oboe, Bassoon, and Clarinet (1966–83); *Plaintes et Ramages* for Oboe and Piano (1971); *Nocturnes I-III* for Cello (1974); *Élégie et Danse* for Flute (1978); *Méditation sur BACH* for Violin (1985). **PIANO:** 2 sonatas (*Sonate française*, 1937; *Variations-Sonate*, 1956–59, rev. 1978); *Rhapsodie sur trois thèmes grecs* for 2 Pianos (1937–59); *Trois Sonatines* (1962–63). **VOCAL:** *Huit Poèmes d'Orient* for Soprano and Orch. or Piano (1922–66); *La Flûte de Roseau*, motet for Children's, Women's, and Men's Choruses (1937); *Genève ouverte au ciel* for Tenor, Narrator, Children's, Men's, and Women's Choruses, and Orch. (1940–41); *Grande Liturgie* for Men's Chorus (1943); *Quatre Rondeaux de Charles d'Orleans* for Soprano and Orch. or Piano (1944–61); *Le Temps de vivre* for Mezzo-soprano and Piano (1944–66);*Jésus*, oratorio for Vocal Quintet, Narrator, Double Men's Chorus, and Orch. (1949–50); *Cantate de Psaumes* for Men's Chorus and 21 Instruments (1954); *Motet poétique* for Men's Chorus (1974); *Huit Villanelles* for Soprano, Baritone, and Piano (1982); *Sechs Lieder* for Mezzo-soprano and Piano (1983).

Vučković, Vojislav, Serbian conductor, musicologist, and composer; b. Pirot, Oct. 18, 1910; d. (murdered by the German police) Belgrade, Dec. 25, 1942. He went to Prague and studied composition with Karel and conducting with Malko at the Cons., becoming a pupil in Suk's master class in composition there in 1943; he also took courses in musicology at the Univ. of Prague (Ph.D., 1934). He then returned to Belgrade, where he was active as a conductor, lecturer, broadcaster, and writer on music; also taught at the Stanković Music School. He publ. pamphlets on the materialistic interpretation of music in the light of Marxist dialectics. He was in the resistance movement during the German occupation of his homeland, but was hunted down and murdered. His collected essays were publ. as *Studije, eseji, kritike* (Belgrade, 1968). After a period of composition in the expressionistic manner (including the application of quarter-tones), he abruptly changed his style out of ideological considerations and embraced programmatic realism.

WORKS: BALLET: *Čovek koji je ukrao sunce* (The Man Who Stole the Sun; 1940). **ORCH.:** Overture for Chamber Orch. (1933); 3 syms.: No. 1 (1933), No. 2 (1942; unfinished; orchestrated by P. Osghian), and No. 3, *Heroic Oratorio* for Soloists, Chorus, and Orch. (1942; unfinished; orchestrated by A. Obradović; Cetinje, Sept. 5, 1951); *Zaveštanje Modesta Musorgskog* (Modest Mussorgsky's Legacy; 1940); *Ozareni put* (The Radiant Road), symphonic poem (1940); *Vesnik bure* (The Harbinger of the Storm), symphonic poem (1941); *Burevesnik* (Stormy Petrel), symphonic poem (1942; Belgrade, Dec. 25, 1944). **OTHER:** Chamber music; choral works; songs.

BIBL.: *V. V.: Umetnik i borac* (Belgrade, 1968).

Vuillermoz, Emile, French music critic; b. Lyons, May 23, 1878; d. Paris, March 2, 1960. He studied organ and piano in Lyons, and composition at the Paris Cons. with Fauré. He was one of the organizers of the Société Musicale Indépendante (1909), and ed. the *Revue Musicale S. I. M.* (from 1911); eventually became music critic of the daily *L'Excelsior*, and also contributed articles to *Le Temps*. Among his publications are *Musiques d'aujourd'hui* (Paris, 1923), *La Vie amoureuse de Chopin* (Paris, 1927), *Histoire de la musique* (Paris, 1949; rev. ed., 1973, by J. Lonchampt), *Claude Debussy* (Geneva, 1957; 2nd ed., 1962), and *Gabriel Fauré* (Paris, 1960).

Vuillermoz, Jean, French composer; b. Monte Carlo, Dec. 29, 1906; d. (killed while on patrol duty in the last hours before the Franco-German armistice), Lobsonn, Alsace, June 21, 1940. He studied with Büsser and Rabaud at the Paris Cons.; received the 2nd Prix de Rome for his cantata *Le Pardon* (1932).

WORKS: BALLET: *Veglione* (1937). **ORCH.:** *Triptique* (Paris, May 31, 1932); Horn Concerto (Paris, March 11, 1934); Cello Concerto; *Promenade zoologique* for Chamber Orch. **CHAMBER:** Piano Trio; String Trio.

Vukdragović, Mihailo, Serbian conductor, pedagogue, and composer; b. Okučani, Nov. 8, 1900; d. Belgrade, March 14, 1986. He was a pupil in composition of Milojević at the Belgrade School of Music; then studied composition with Jirák and Novák and conducting with Talich at the Prague Cons. (graduated, 1927). He subsequently was active as a choral, operatic, and sym. conductor in Zagreb and Belgrade. He was prof. and director of the Stanković School of Music, prof. of conducting (1940–73) and rector (1947–52) of the Belgrade Academy of Music, and also of the Belgrade Academy of the Arts (1957–59); was made a corresponding member (1950) and a full member (1961) of the Serbian Academy. He wrote several works in an impressionistic style before embracing the aesthetics of socialist realism.

WORKS: DRAMATIC: Theater music; film scores. **ORCH.:** *Simfonijska meditacija* (1938); *Put u pobedu* (Road to Victory), symphonic poem (1944; Belgrade, Oct. 19, 1945); *Besmirtna mladost* (Immortal Youth), symphonic suite (1948). **CHAMBER:** 2 string quartets (1925, 1944). **VOCAL:** *Vezilja slobode* (The Embroidress of Freedom), cantata (1947; Belgrade, Jan. 5, 1948); *Svetli groboiv* (Illustrious Tombs), cantata (1954); *Vokalna lirika* for Voice and Orch. (1955); *Srbija* (Serbia), cantata (Nis, July 6, 1961); choruses; folk song arrangements.

Vycpálek, Ladislav, eminent Czech composer; b. Prague, Feb. 23, 1882; d. there, Jan. 9, 1969. He received training in voice, violin, and piano in his youth; studied Czech and German at the Univ. of Prague (Ph.D., 1906, with a diss. on legends in Czech literature concerning the youth of Mary and Jesus); took composition lessons with Novák (1908–12). In 1907 he joined the staff of the Univ. of Prague library, where he later was founder-director of its music section (1922–42); also was active as a violinist in the amateur quartet led by Josef Pick (1909–39); in 1936 he served as artistic director of the National Theater. In 1924 he became a member of the Czech Academy; was chairman of its music section (1950–51). In 1957 he was made an Artist of Merit and in 1967 a National Artist by the Czech government. He greatly distinguished himself as a composer of vocal music;

among his finest scores is the *Kantáta o posledních věcech člověka* (Cantata on the Last Things of Man; 1920–22).

WORKS: ORCH.: *Vzůhru srdce* (Lift Up Your Hearts), 2 variation fantasias on hymns from Hus's day (1950). **CHAMBER:** String Quartet (1909); Sonata "Chvála housli" (Praise to the Violin) for Violin, Mezzo-soprano, and Piano (1927–28); Suite for Viola (1929); Suite for Violin (1930); Violin Sonatina (1947); solo piano pieces, including *Cestou* (On the Way), 5 pieces (1911–14), and *Doma* (Home), suite (1959). **VOCAL:** *Kantáta o posledních věcech člověka* (Cantata on the Last Things of Man) for Soprano, Baritone, Chorus, and Orch. (1920–22); *Blashoslavený ten člověk* (Blessed Is This Man), cantata for Soprano, Baritone, Chorus, and Orch. (1933); *České requiem "Smrt a spaseni"* (Czech Requiem "Death and Redemption") for Soprano, Alto, Baritone, Chorus, and Orch. (1940); choruses; songs; folk song arrangements.

BIBL.: J. Smolka, *L. V.: Tvůrči vývoj* (L. V.: Creative Evolution; Prague, 1960); M. Svobodova and H. Krupka, *Národní umělec L. V.* (Prague, 1973).

Vysloužil, Jiří, distinguished Czech musicologist; b. Košice, May 11, 1924. He studied musicology with Jan Racek and Bohumír Štědroň, philosophy with Arnošt Bláha and Mirko Novák, and history with Josef Macůrek at the Univ. of Brno (Ph.D, 1949, with the diss. *Problémy a metody hudebního lidopisu* [Problems and Methods of Music Ethnography]; C.Sc., 1959, with the diss. *Leoš Janáček a lidova piseň* [Leos Janáček and Folk Song]; D.Sc., 1974, with the diss. *Alois Hába*; publ. in Prague, 1974). He worked at the Dept. for Ethnography and Folklore in Brno until 1952; after serving as a lecturer and vice-dean at the Brno Academy (1952–61), in 1961 he joined the faculty of the Univ. of Brno, where he became a prof. in 1973. He served as head of the editorial board of the complete critical ed. of the works of Janáček, which commenced publication in Prague in 1978. He publ. *Hudobníci 20. storočia* (Musicians of the 20th Century; Bratislava, 1964; 2nd ed., 1981), *Leoš Janáček* (Brno, 1978), and *Leoš Janáček: Für Sie porträtiert von Jiří Vysloužil* (Leipzig, 1981).

Vyvyan, Jennifer (Brigit), English soprano; b. Broadstairs, Kent, March 13, 1925; d. London, April 5, 1974. She studied piano and voice at the Royal Academy of Music in London (1941–43), then voice with Roy Henderson. She made her operatic debut as Jenny Diver in *The Beggar's Opera* with the English Opera Group (1947). After further vocal training with Fernando Carpi in Switzerland (1950), she won 1st prize in the Geneva international competition (1951). She gained success with her portrayal of Constanze at London's Sadler's Wells Opera Co. (1952); then created the role of Penelope Rich in Britten's *Gloriana* at London's Covent Garden (1953). She made guest appearances at the Glyndebourne Festivals, and in Milan, Rome, Vienna, and Paris. She appeared in many contemporary operas, and was closely associated with those of Britten; created the Governess in his *Turn of the Screw* (1954), Tytania in *A Midsummer Night's Dream* (1960), and Miss Julian in *Owen Wingrave* (1971).

Waart, Edo (actually, **Eduard**) **de,** noted Dutch conductor; b. Amsterdam, June 1, 1941. He began piano lessons as a child and at 13 began to study the oboe. He pursued training at the Amsterdam Muzieklyceum as an oboe and cello student (1957–62; graduated, 1962), and also studied conducting with Dean Dixon in Salzburg (summer, 1960). In 1962–63 he was an oboist in the Amsterdam Phil., and then played in the Concertgebouw Orch. in Amsterdam. He also studied conducting with Franco Ferrara in Hilversum, where he made his debut as a conductor with the Netherlands Radio Phil. in 1964. That same year he was a co-winner in the Mitropoulos Competition in N.Y., and then served as an assistant conductor of the N.Y. Phil. (1965–66). In 1966 he became assistant conductor of the Concertgebouw Orch., which he accompanied on its 1967 tour of the U.S. He first attracted notice with his Netherlands Wind Ensemble, with which he toured and recorded. In 1967 he became a guest conductor of the Rotterdam Phil. In 1969 he made his British debut as a guest conductor with the Royal Phil. of London in Folkestone. In 1971 he toured the U.S. with the Rotterdam Phil. and also made his first appearance as an opera conductor in the U.S. in Santa Fe. In 1974 he was a guest conductor with the San Francisco Sym., and in 1975 he was named its principal guest conductor. He made his debut at London's Covent Garden in 1976 conducting *Ariadne auf Naxos.* In 1977 he became music director of the San Francisco Sym., which he conducted in a gala concert at the opening of its new Louise M. Davies Symphony Hall in 1980. In 1979 he made his first appearance at the Bayreuth Festival. He resigned as music director of the San Francisco Sym. in 1986 and served in that capacity with the Minnesota Orch. in Minneapolis until 1995. From 1988 he also was artistic director of the Dutch Radio Orch. in Hilversum. He likewise served as chief conductor of the Sydney Sym. Orch. from 1993. De Waart's objective approach to interpretation, combined with his regard for stylistic propriety and avoidance of ostentatious conductorial display, makes his performances of the traditional and contemporary repertoire particularly appealing.

Wachsmann, Klaus P(hilipp), noted German ethnomusicologist; b. Berlin, March 8, 1907; d. Tisbury, Wiltshire, July 17, 1984. He received training in musicology with Blume and Schering and in comparative musicology with Hornbostel and Sachs at the Univ. of Berlin (1930–32); after further studies with Fellerer at the Univ. of Fribourg in Switzerland (Ph.D., 1935, with the diss. *Untersuchungen zum vorgregorianischen Gesang*; publ. in Regensburg, 1935), he pursued linguistic studies at the London School of Oriental and African Studies. He then was active in Uganda, where he was made curator of the Uganda Museum in Kampala in 1948; after serving as scientific officer in charge of ethnological collections at the Wellcome Foundation in London (1958–63), he taught in the music dept. and Inst. of Ethnomusicology at the Univ. of Calif. at Los Angeles (1963–68); then was prof. in the school of music and dept. of linguistics at Northwestern Univ. in Evanston, Ill. (from 1968). He was an authority on African music, specializing in organology and tribal music of Uganda; his years spent outside of academic circles made him an independent and imaginative thinker about music in its relation to culture and philosophy. C. Seeger ed. *Essays for a Humanist: An Offering to Klaus Wachsmann* (N.Y., 1977).

WRITINGS: *Folk Musicians in Uganda* (Kampala, 1956); ed. *An International Catalogue of Published Records of Folk Music* (London, 1960); ed. *A Select Bibliography of Music in Africa* (London, 1965); ed. *Essays on Music and History in Africa* (Evanston, Ill., 1971).

Wachtmeister, Axel Raoul, Count, Swedish composer; b. London (son of the Swedish ambassador there), April 2, 1865; d. Paris, Dec. 12, 1947. He studied music with Gédalge and d'Indy. He lived mostly in Paris, going to Sweden in the summers; spent some time in the U.S. His cantata *Sappho* was performed in N.Y.

in 1917. He also wrote 2 syms.; a symphonic poem, *Le Récit de l'horloge; Hymne à la lune* for Baritone, Chorus, and Orch. (Cincinnati, 1933); *Suite romantique* for Piano; songs.

Wadsworth, Charles (William), American pianist and harpsichordist; b. Barnesville, Ga., May 21, 1929. He studied piano with Tureck and conducting with Morel at the Juilliard School of Music in N.Y. (B.S., 1951; M.S., 1952); also studied the French song repertoire with Bernac in Paris and German lieder with Zallinger in Munich. In 1960 Menotti invited him to organize the Chamber Music Concerts at the Festival of Two Worlds in Spoleto, Italy; he was its director and pianist for 20 years. In 1969 he helped to found the Chamber Music Society of Lincoln Center in N.Y., and was its artistic director until 1989; in 1977 he also created the chamber music series for the Charleston, S.C., Spoleto Festival U.S.A. In addition to numerous appearances as a pianist and harpsichordist with various ensembles, he also appeared in performances with many noted artists of the day, including Dietrich Fischer-Dieskau, Beverly Sills, Hermann Prey, and Shirley Verrett.

Waechter, Eberhard, Austrian baritone and operatic administrator; b. Vienna, July 9, 1929; d. there, March 29, 1992. He studied at the Univ. of Vienna, the Vienna Academy of Music (1950–53), and with Elisabeth Rado. In 1953 he made his operatic debut as Silvio at the Vienna Volksoper. From 1954 he was a member of the Vienna State Opera, and in 1963 he was named an Austrian Kammersänger. He made his debut at London's Covent Garden as Count Almaviva and his first appearance at the Salzburg Festival as Arbace in *Idomeneo* in 1956. In 1958 he made his debut at the Bayreuth Festival as Amfortas. He sang for the first time at the Paris Opéra as Wolfram in 1959. In 1960 he sang Count Almaviva at his debuts at Milan's La Scala and Chicago's Lyric Opera. On Jan. 25, 1961, he made his Metropolitan Opera debut in N.Y. as Wolfram. In subsequent years, he continued to appear regularly in Vienna, where he created the role of Joseph in Einem's *Jesu Hochzeit* in 1980. In 1987 he became director of the Vienna Volksoper. From 1991 he was also co-director of the Vienna State Opera.

Waesberghe, Jos(eph Maria Antonius Franciscus) Smits van. See **Smits van Waesberghe, Jos(eph Maria Antonius Franciscus).**

Wagemans, Peter-Jan, Dutch composer; b. The Hague, Sept. 7, 1952. He studied organ, composition (with Vlijmen), and theory.

WORKS: ORCH.: Overture for Wind Orch. (1972); Sym. (1972); *Muziek I* for Wind Orch. (1974), *II* for Orch. (1977), and *III* for Wind Orch. (1985; rev. 1987); *Alla marcia* (1977); *Romance* for Violin and Orch. (1981; rev. 1983); *Irato* (1983; rev. 1990); *Klang* (1986); *What did the last dinosaur dream of?*, 4 pieces (1991). **CHAMBER:** 2 wind quintets (1973; 1992–93); Saxophone Quartet (1975); *3 Small Pieces* for 4 Recorders and 2 Xylophones (1979); String Quartet (1980; rev. 1986); Octet for 2 Clarinets, 2 Bassoons, 2 Violins, Viola, and Cello (1980); *Great Expectations* for Violin and Piano (1986); Quartet for 4 Recorders (1993). **PIANO:** *2 Pieces* (1972); *Ira* for 2 Pianos, 8-hands (1983–84).

Wagenaar, Bernard, Dutch-born American composer and teacher, son of **Johan Wagenaar**; b. Arnhem, July 18, 1894; d. York, Maine, May 19, 1971. He was a student of Gerard Veerman (violin), Lucie Veerman-Becker (piano), and his father (composition) in Utrecht. After conducting and teaching in the Netherlands (1914–20), he settled in the U.S. and became a naturalized American citizen in 1927. He was a violinist in the N.Y. Phil. (1921–23). From 1925 to 1946 he taught fugue, orchestration, and composition at the Inst. of Musical Art in N.Y., and then at its successor, the Juilliard School of Music, from 1946 to 1968. He was made an Officer of the Order of Oranje-Nassau of the Netherlands. His output followed along neo-Classical lines.

WORKS: CHAMBER OPERA: *Pieces of Eight* (1943; N.Y., May 9, 1944). **ORCH.:** 4 syms.: No. 1 (1926; N.Y., Oct. 7, 1928), No. 2 (1930; N.Y., Nov. 10, 1932), No. 3 (1936; N.Y., Jan. 23, 1937), and No. 4 (1946; Boston, Dec. 16, 1949); 2 divertimentos: No. 1 (1927; Detroit, Nov. 28, 1929) and No. 2 (1952); *Sinfonietta* (1929; N.Y., Jan. 16, 1930); Triple Concerto for Flute, Harp, Cello, and Orch. (1935; N.Y., May 20, 1941); *Fantasietta on British-American Ballads* for Chamber Orch. (1939); Violin Concerto (1940); *Fanfare for Airmen* (1942); *Feuilleton* (1942); *Song of Mourning* (1944); Concert Overture for Small Orch. (1952); *5 Tableaux* for Cello and Orch. (1952); *Preamble* (1956). **CHAMBER:** Violin Sonata (1925); 4 string quartets (1926, 1932, 1936, 1960); Cello Sonatina (1934); Concertino for 8 Instruments (1942); *4 Vignettes* for Harp (1965). **KEYBOARD: PIANO:** Sonata (1928); *Ciacona* (1942). **ORGAN:** *Eclogue* (1940). **VOCAL:** *3 Songs from the Chinese* for Soprano, Flute, Harp, and Piano (1921); *From a Very Little Sphinx* for Voice and Piano (1925); *El trillo* for Chorus, 2 Guitars, and Percussion (1942); *No quiero tus avellanas* for Alto, Women's Chorus, Flute, English Horn, 2 Guitars, and Percussion (1942).

BIBL.: D. Fuller, "B. W.," *Modern Music* (May 1944).

Wagenaar, Johan, distinguished Dutch organist, choral conductor, pedagogue, and composer, father of **Bernard Wagenaar**; b. Utrecht, Nov. 1, 1862; d. The Hague, June 17, 1941. He studied with Richard Hol in Utrecht (1875–85) and with H. von Herzogenberg in Berlin (1889). From 1887 to 1904 he was director of the Utrecht Music School; also was organist at the Cathedral (1887–1919). From 1919 to 1936 he was director of the Royal Cons. in The Hague.

WORKS: OPERAS: *De Doge van Venetie* (1901; Utrecht, 1904); *De Cid* (1915; Utrecht, 1916); *Jupiter Amans*, burlesque opera (Scheveningen, 1925). **ORCH.:** 3 symphonic poems: *Levenszomer* (1901), *Saul en David* (1906), and *Elverhoi* (1939); 5 overtures: *Koning Jan* (1889), *Cyrano de Bergerac* (1905), *De getemde feeks* (1906), *Driekoningenavond* (1927), and *De philosofische prinses* (1931). **OTHER:** Numerous choral works; songs; organ pieces.

BIBL.: Special issue of *De Muziek* (1932).

Waghalter, Ignatz, German conductor and composer; b. Warsaw, March 15, 1882; d. N.Y., April 7, 1949. He studied in Berlin, where he later was conductor of the Komische Oper (1907–11); then conducted in Essen (1911–12), and at the Deutsches Opernhaus in Berlin-Charlottenburg. In 1925 he succeeded Stransky as conductor of the State Sym. Orch. in N.Y. (for one season only); then returned to Berlin; in 1933 he went to Prague, and in 1934 to Vienna. He settled in N.Y. in 1938.

WORKS: DRAMATIC: OPERAS: *Der Teufelsweg* (Berlin, 1911); *Mandragola* (Berlin, Jan. 23, 1914); *Jugend* (Berlin, 1917); *Der späte Gast* (Berlin, 1922); *Sataniel* (Berlin, 1923). **OPERETTAS:** *Der Weiberkrieg*; *Wem gehört Helena?*. **ORCH.:** Violin Concerto. **CHAMBER:** Violin Sonata; String Quartet; piano pieces.

BIBL.: H. Leichtentritt, *I. W.* (N.Y., 1924).

Wagner, Joseph (Frederick), American conductor, composer, and teacher; b. Springfield, Mass., Jan. 9, 1900; d. Los Angeles, Oct. 12, 1974. He was a student of Converse (composition) at the New England Cons. of Music in Boston (diploma, 1923). After further training from Casella in Boston (1927), he studied at Boston Univ. (B.M., 1932). In 1934–35 he completed his studies with Boulanger (composition) and Monteux (conducting) in Paris, and with Weingartner (conducting) in Basel. From 1923 to 1944 he was assistant director of music in the Boston public schools. He also was founder-conductor of the Boston Civic Sym. Orch. (1925–44) and a teacher at Boston Univ. (1929–40). He taught at Brooklyn College (1945–47) and at Hunter College (1945–56) in N.Y., and was conductor of the Duluth Sym. Orch. (1947–50) and the Orquesta Sinfónica Nacional de Costa Rica in San José (1950–54). In 1961 he became a prof. at Pepperdine College in Los Angeles. He publ. the useful books *Orchestration: A Practical Handbook* (N.Y., 1958) and *Band Scoring* (N.Y., 1960). His music was distinguished by excellent craftsmanship, and was set in a fairly advanced idiom, with bitonality as a frequent recourse in his later works.

WORKS: DRAMATIC: OPERA: *New England Sampler* (1964; Los Angeles, Feb. 26, 1965). **BALLETS:** *The Birthday of the Infanta* (1935); *Dance Divertissement* (1937); *Hudson River Legend* (1941; Boston, March 1, 1944). **ORCH.:** 2 violin concertos (1919–30; 1955–56); *Miniature Concerto* for Piano and Orch. (1919; Providence, R.I., June 11, 1920; rev. version, New Brunswick, N.J., Aug. 3, 1930); *Rhapsody* for Piano, Clarinet, and Strings (1925); 4 syms.: No. 1 (Rochester, N.Y., Oct. 19, 1944), No. 2 (1945; Wilmington, March 1, 1960), No. 3 (1951), and No. 4, *Tribute to America*, for Narrator, Soprano, Chorus, and Orch. (1974); *Sinfonietta* No. 1 (1931) and No. 2 for Strings (1941); *Pastoral Costarricense* (1958); *Merlin and Sir Boss* for Concert Band, after Mark Twain's *A Connecticut Yankee* (1963); Concerto for Organ, Brass, and Percussion (1963); Harp Concerto (1964). **CHAMBER:** Quintet for Flute, Clarinet, Viola, Cello, and Piano (1933); String Quartet (1940); Violin Sonata (1941); Cello Sonata (1943); *Introduction and Scherzo* for Bassoon and Piano (1951); *Patterns of Contrast* for Wind Quartet (1959); *Fantasy Sonata* for Harp (1963); *Preludes and Toccata* for Harp, Violin, and Cello (1964); *Fantasy and Fugue* for Woodwind Quartet (1968). **KEYBOARD: PIANO:** *Radio City Snapshots* (1945); Sonata (1946); Sonata for 2 Pianos (1963). **ORGAN:** *12 Concert Preludes* (1974). **VOCAL:** *David Jazz* for Men's Chorus and Piano (1934); *Under Freedom's Flag* for Chorus (1940); *Ballad of Brotherhood* for Chorus (1947); *Missa sacra* for Mezzo-soprano, Chorus, and Orch. (1952); *American Ballad* for Chorus (1963).

BIBL.: L. Bowling, ed., *J. W.: A Retrospective of a Composer-Conductor* (Lomita, Calif., 1976).

Wagner, Peter (Joseph), eminent German musicologist; b. Kurenz, near Trier, Aug. 19, 1865; d. Fribourg, Switzerland, Oct. 17, 1931. He studied at the Univ. of Strasbourg; received his Ph.D. in 1890 with the diss. *Palestrina als weltlicher Komponist* (publ. as "Das Madrigal und Palestrina," *Vierteljahrsschrift für Musikwissenschaft*, VIII, 1892); studied further in Berlin under Bellermann and Spitta. In 1893 he was appointed an instructor at the Univ. of Fribourg in Switzerland; subsequently was a prof. (1902–21) and rector (1920–21). In 1901 he established its Académie Grégorienne for theoretical and practical study of plainsong, in which field he was an eminent authority. He was a member of the Papal Commission for the Editio Vaticana of the Roman Gradual (1904), and was made a Papal Chamberlain.

WRITINGS: *Einführung in die gregorianischen Melodien: Ein Handbuch der Choralwissenschaft* (vol. I, Fribourg, 1895; 3rd ed., 1911; Eng. tr., 1907; vol. II, Leipzig, 1905; 2nd ed., 1912; vol. III, Leipzig, 1921); *Elemente des gregorianischen Gesanges zur Einführung in die vatikanische Choralausgabe* (Regensburg, 1909); *Geschichte der Messe I: bis 1600* (Leipzig, 1913); *Einführung in die katholische Kirchenmusik: Vorträge gehalten an der Universität Freiburg in der Schweiz für Theologen und andere Freunde kirchlicher Musik* (Düsseldorf, 1919).

BIBL.: K. Weinmann, ed., *Festschrift P. W. zum 60. Geburtstag* (Leipzig, 1926).

Wagner, Roger (Francis), French-born American choral conductor; b. Le Puy, Jan. 16, 1914; d. Dijon, Sept. 17, 1992. He was taken to the U.S. as a child; after studying for the priesthood in Santa Barbara, Calif., he returned to France to study organ with Dupré; he settled in Los Angeles in 1937 and became organist and choirmaster at St. Joseph's; also took courses in philosophy and French literature at the Univ. of Calif. and the Univ. of Southern Calif. He studied conducting with Klemperer and Walter, and orchestration with Caillet. In 1946 he founded the Roger Wagner Chorale, and toured extensively with it in the U.S., Canada, and Latin America. He was also founder-conductor of the Los Angeles Master Chorale and Sinfonia Orch. (1965–85). He was head of the dept. of music at Marymount College in Los Angeles (1951–66); also taught at the Univ. of Calif. from 1959 to 1981. He was knighted by Pope Paul VI in 1966.

Wagner, Siegfried (Helferich Richard), German conductor and composer; b. Triebschen, June 6, 1869; d. Bayreuth, Aug. 4, 1930. He was the son of (Wilhelm) Richard (b. Leipzig, May 22, 1813; d. Venice, Feb. 13, 1883) and Cosima Wagner (b. Bellagio, on Lake Como, Dec. 24, 1837; d. Bayreuth, April 1, 1930), who were married on Aug. 25, 1870, and thus Siegfried was legitimated. Richard Wagner named the *Siegfried Idyll* for him, and it was performed in Wagner's house in Triebschen on Christmas Day, 1870. He studied with Humperdinck in Frankfurt am Main and then pursued training as an architect in Berlin and Karlsruhe; during his tenure as an assistant in Bayreuth (1892–96), he studied with his mother, Hans Richter, and Julius Kniese. From 1896 he was a regular conductor in Bayreuth, where he was general director of the Festival productions from 1906. On Sept. 21, 1915, he married Winifred Williams, an adopted daughter of Karl Klindworth. In 1923–24 he visited the U.S. in order to raise funds for the reopening of the Bayreuth Festspielhaus, which had been closed during the course of World War I. He conducted from memory, and left-handed. In his career as a composer, he was greatly handicapped by inevitable comparisons with his father. His memoirs were publ. in Stuttgart in 1923.

WORKS: OPERAS: *Der Bärenhäuter* (1898; Munich, Jan. 22, 1899); *Herzog Wildfang* (Munich, March 14, 1901); *Der Kobold* (1903; Hamburg, Jan. 29, 1904); *Bruder Lustig* (Hamburg, Oct. 13, 1905); *Sternengebot* (1907; Hamburg, Jan. 21, 1908); *Banadietrich* (1909; Karlsruhe, Jan. 23, 1910); *Schwarzschwanenreich* (1911; Karlsruhe, Dec. 6, 1917); *Sonnenflammen* (1914; Darmstadt, Oct. 30, 1918); *Der Heidenkönig* (1914; Cologne, Dec. 16, 1933); *Der Friedensengel* (1915; Karlsruhe, March 4, 1926); *An allem ist Hütchen Schuld* (1916; Stuttgart, Dec. 6, 1917); *Der Schmied von Marienburg* (1920; Rostock, Dec. 16, 1923); *Wahnopfer* (1928; unfinished). **ORCH.:** *Sehnsucht*, symphonic poem (1895); *Konzertstück* for Flute and Orch. (1914); Violin Concerto (1915); *Und wenn die Welt voll Teufel wär!*, scherzo (1923); *Glück*, symphonic poem (1924); Sym. in C major (1925). **VOCAL:** *Das Märchen von dicken fetten Pfannkucken* for Baritone and Orch. (1913); *Der Fahnenschwur* for Men's Chorus, Orch., and Organ (1915); *Wer liebt uns* for Men's Chorus and Woodwinds (1924). **OTHER:** Chamber music.

BIBL.: L. Karpeth, *S. W. als Mensch und Künstler* (Leipzig, 1902); C. Glasenapp, *S. W.* (Berlin, 1906); idem, *S. W. und seine Kunst* (Leipzig, 1911; essays on the operas; new series, 1913, as *Schwarzschwanenreich*; 2nd new series, ed. by P. Pretzsch, 1919, as *Sonnenflammen*); P. Pretzsch, *Die Kunst S. W.s* (Leipzig, 1919); O. Daube, *S. W. und sein Werk* (Bayreuth, 1925); *Festschrift zu S. W.s 60. Geburtstag* (Bayreuth, 1929); H. Rebois, *Lettres de S. W.* (Paris, 1933); O. Daube, *S. W. und die Märchenoper* (Leipzig, 1936); F. Starsen, *Erinnerungen an S. W.* (Detmold, 1942); Z. von Kraft, *Der Sohn: S. W.s Leben und Umwelt* (Graz, 1963); P. Pachl, *S. W.s musikdramatisches Schaffen* (Tutzing, 1979).

Wagner, Sieglinde, Austrian mezzo-soprano; b. Linz, April 21, 1921. She studied at the Linz Cons. and with Luise Willer and Carl Hartmann in Munich. In 1942 she made her operatic debut as Erda in Linz. From 1947 to 1952 she sang at the Vienna Volksoper. In 1949 she made her first appearance at the Salzburg Festival as the 2nd Lady in *Die Zauberflöte*, and returned there to create the roles of Lady Capulet in Blacher's *Romeo und Julia* (1950), Leda in Strauss' *Die Liebe der Danae* (official premiere, 1952), and Frau Jensen in Wagner-Régeny's *Das Bergwerk zu Falun* (1961). In 1952 she became a member of the Berlin Städtische Oper. After it became the Deutsche Oper in 1961, she continued as a member until 1986. In 1962 she made her debut at the Bayreuth Festival as Flosshelde, where she made regular appearances until 1973. She also pursued an active career as a concert artist.

Wagner, (Adolf) Wieland (Gottfried), German opera producer and stage designer, son of **Siegfried (Helferich Richard)** and brother of **Wolfgang (Manfred Martin) Wagner**; b. Bayreuth, Jan. 5, 1917; d. Munich, Oct. 16, 1966. He received his general education in Munich, and devoted himself to the problem of modernizing the productions of Wagner's operas. With his brother, Wolfgang Wagner, he served as co-director of the Bayreuth Festivals from 1951 to 1966. Abandoning the luxuriant scenery of 19th-century opera, he emphasized the symbolic meaning of Wagner's music dramas, eschewing realistic effects, such as machinery propelling the Rhine maidens through the wavy gauze of the river, or the bright paper flames of the burning Valhalla. He even introduced Freudian sexual overtones, as in his production of *Tristan und Isolde*, where a phallic pillar was conspicuously placed on the stage.

BIBL.: W. Panofsky, *W. W.* (Bremen, 1964); C. Lust, *W. W. et la survie du théâtre lyrique* (Lausanne, 1969); W. Schafer, *W. W.: Persönlichkeit und Leistung* (Tübingen, 1970); G. Skelton, *W. W.: The Positive Sceptic* (London, 1971).

Wagner, Wolfgang (Manfred Martin), German opera producer, son of **Siegfried (Helferich Richard)** and brother of **(Adolf) Wieland (Gottfried) Wagner**; b. Bayreuth, Aug. 30, 1919. He studied music privately in Bayreuth; then worked in various capacities at the Bayreuth Festivals and the Berlin State Opera. With his brother, Wieland Wagner, he was co-director of the Bayreuth Festivals from 1951 to 1966; after his brother's death in 1966, he was its sole director. Like his brother, he departed radically from the traditional staging of the Wagner operas, and introduced a psychoanalytic and surrealist mise en scène, often with suggestive sexual symbols in the decor. His autobiography was publ. in both Ger. and Eng. in 1994.

Wagner-Régeny, Rudolf, Romanian-born German composer, pedagogue, pianist, and clavichordist; b. Szász-Régen, Transylvania, Aug. 28, 1903; d. Berlin, Sept. 18, 1969. He entered the Leipzig Cons. as a piano pupil of Robert Teichmüller in 1919; in 1920 he enrolled at the Berlin Hochschule für Musik as a student in conducting of Rudolf Krasselt and Siegfried Ochs, in orchestration of Emil Rezniček, and in theory and composition of Friedrich Koch and Franz Schreker. He first gained notice as a composer with his theater pieces for Essen; in 1930 he became a naturalized German citizen, and with the rise of the Nazis was promoted by a faction of the party as a composer of the future; however, the success of his opera *Der Günstling* (Dresden, Feb. 20, 1935) was followed by his supporters' doubts regarding his subsequent output, ending in a scandal with his opera *Johanna Balk* at the Vienna State Opera (April 4, 1941). In 1942 he was drafted into the German army; after the close of World War II, he settled in East Germany; was director of the Rostock Hochschule für Musik (1947–50); then was a prof. of composition at the (East) Berlin Hochschule für Musik and at the Academy of Arts. After composing works along traditional lines, he adopted his own 12-note serial technique in 1950.

WORKS: DRAMATIC: OPERAS: *Sganarelle oder Der Schein trügt* (1923; Essen, March 1929); *Moschopulos* (Gera, Dec. 1, 1928); *Der nackte König* (1928; Gera, Dec. 1, 1930); *Der Günstling oder Die letzten Tage des grossen Herrn Fabiano* (1932–34; Dresden, Feb. 20, 1935); *Die Bürger von Calais* (1936–38; Berlin, Jan. 28, 1939); *Johanna Balk* (1938–40; Vienna, April 4, 1941); *Das Bergwerk zu Falun* (1958–60; Salzburg, Aug. 16, 1961). **BALLETS:** *Moritat* (1928; Essen, March 1929); *Der zerbrochene Krug* (Berlin, 1937). **OTHER DRAMATIC:** *Esau und Jacob*, biblical scene for 4 Soloists, Speaker, and String Orch. (1929; Gera, 1930); *La Sainte Courtisane* for 4 Speakers and Chamber Orch. (Dessau, 1930); *Die Fabel vom seligen Schlachtermeister* (1931–32; Dresden, May 23, 1964); *Persische Episode* (1940–50; Rostock, March 27, 1963); *Prometheus*, scenic oratorio (1957–58; Kassel, Sept. 12, 1959); incidental music to 7 plays. **ORCH.:** *Orchestermusik mit Klavier* (Piano Concerto; 1935); *Mythologische Figurinen* (1951; Salzburg, June 21, 1952); *3 Orchestersätze* (1952); *Einleitung und Ode* (1967); *8 Kommentare zu einer Weise des Guillaume Machauts* for Chamber Orch. (1968). **CHAMBER:** *Kleine Gemeinschaftsmusik* for 6 Instruments (1929); *Spinettmusik* (1934); String Quartet (1948); *Introduction et communication à mon ange gardien* for String Trio (1951); *Divertimento* for 3 Winds and Percussion (1954); piano pieces. **VOCAL:** *Cantica Davidi regis* for Boy's Chorus, Bass Chorus, and Chamber Orch. (1954); *Genesis* for Alto, Chorus, and Small Orch. (1955–56); *An die Sonne*, cantata for Alto and Orch. (1967–68); *Hermann-Hesse-Gesänge* for Baritone and Small Orch. (1968–69); many songs with piano.

BIBL.: A. Burgartz, *R. W.-R.* (Berlin, 1935); T. Müller-Medek, ed., *R. W.-R.: Begegnungen, biographische Aufzeichnungen, Tagebücher und sein Briefwechsel mit Caspar Neher* (Berlin, 1968).

Wahlberg, Rune, Swedish conductor, pianist, and composer; b. Gävle, March 15, 1910. He received training in piano, conducting, and composition at the Stockholm Musikhögskolan (1928–35) and in conducting at the Leipzig Cons. (1936–37; diploma, 1937). He made tours as a pianist. After serving as music director of the Göteborg City Theater (1943–51), he was municipal music director in Kramfors (1953–57), Hofors (1957–64), Härnösand (1964–69), and Hudiksvall (1969–75). His music generally followed along romantic lines with expressionistic infusions.

WORKS: OPERA: *En Saga* (1952). **ORCH.:** Piano Concerto (1938); 7 syms.: No. 1 (1941), No. 2 (1945), No. 3 (1951; Toronto, March 6, 1961), No. 4 (1959; Hofors, March 13, 1960), No. 5, *Havet*, for Men's Chorus and Orch. (1979), No. 6, *Episoder* (1980), and No. 7, *Jordesång* (1981); *Meditation* for Violin and Orch. (1941); *Nordic Suite* (1943); *Afrodite*, suite (1944); *Preludium, Larghetto and Fugue* (1952); *Oriental Dance* (1953); Violin Concerto (1958); *Concerto barocco* for Violin and Strings (1960); Cello Concerto (1961); Bass Clarinet Concerto (1961); *Concert Suite* for Strings (1961); *Concert Fantasy* for Piano and Orch. (1967); *Lantlig Suite* for Strings (1977); *Canzone* for Violin and Orch. (1980); *Jubileumsspel* (1980); *Ett vårepos* (1981); 3 symphonic poems (1982); *Introduction and rondo giocoso* for Piano and Strings (1983); *Fantasia concertante* for 2 Violas and Orch. (1985); *Amoroso* for Chamber Orch. (1988–91). **CHAMBER:** *Preludium and Fugue* for String Trio (1937); Violin Sonata (1959); *Prisma* for String Quartet (1961); *Helgdagsvisa* for 4 Violins (1971); String Quartet (1972); *Lyric Fantasy* for Violin and Piano (1975); *Preludium and Largo* for Violin (1981); Trio for Violin, Cello, and Piano (1977); *Seriös dans* for Piano Trio (1981); *Två lyriska poem* for Piano Trio (1982); Cello Sonata (1983); *Preludium and Fugue* for String Quartet (1985); *Preludium and Finale* for String Quartet (1987); *Notturno* for Flute or Violin and Piano (1988); *Dance-Poem* for Clarinet and Piano (1992); many piano pieces. **VOCAL:** *Nordland* for Men's Chorus and Orch. (1957); *Florez och blanzeflor* for Men's Chorus and Orch. (1963); *Det signade landet* for Chorus, Men's Chorus, and Wind Band (1966); *Havsfuren* for Men's Chorus and Orch. (1971); *Ottesång* for Women's Chorus and String Orch. (1976); *En vårfantasi* for Chorus, Piano, and String Orch. (1993); many songs.

Wakasugi, Hiroshi, Japanese conductor; b. Tokyo, May 31, 1935. He studied conducting with Hideo Saito and Nobori Kaneko; in 1967 he was awarded a prize by the Japanese Ministry of Culture. In 1975 he became conductor of the Kyoto Sym. Orch. From 1977 to 1983 he was chief conductor of the Cologne Radio Sym. Orch.; also was Generalmusikdirektor of the Deutsche Oper am Rhein in Düsseldorf (1982–87). In 1981 he made his U.S. debut as a guest conductor of the Boston Sym. Orch. He was chief conductor of the Tonhalle Orch. in Zürich (1985–91) and of the Tokyo Metropolitan Sym. Orch. (1987–95). In 1995 he became permanent conductor of the NHK Sym. Orch. in Tokyo.

Walaciński, Adam, Polish composer and teacher; b. Kraków, Sept. 18, 1928. He studied violin with E. Umińska at the Kraków Cons. (1947–52); had private composition lessons with Kisielewski (1953–55) and with Schaeffer. He was a violinist in the Kraków Radio Orch. (1948–56). In 1972 he was appointed instructor at the Kraków Cons. He was a member of the avant-garde Grupa Krakówska.

WORKS: ORCH.: *Composition "Alfa"* (1958); *Horizons* for Chamber Orch. (1962); *Sekwencje* for Concertante Flute and Orch. (1963); *Concerto da camera* for Violin and String Orch.

(1964; rev. 1967); *Refrains et réflexions* (1969); *Notturno 70* for 24 Strings, 3 Flutes, and Percussion (1970); *Torso* (1971; Kraków, Jan. 21, 1972); *Drama e burla* (Warsaw, Oct. 21, 1988). **CHAMBER:** String Quartet (1959); *Modifications* for Viola and Piano (1960); *Intrada* for 7 Players (1962); *Canto tricolore* for Flute, Violin, and Vibraphone (1962); *Fogli volanti*, optically notated composition for String Trio (1965); *Canzona* for Cello, Piano, and Tape (1966); *Epigrams* for Chamber Ensemble (1967); *Dichromia* for Flute and Piano (1967); *On peut écouter* for Flute, Oboe, and Bassoon (1971); *Divertimento interrotto* for 13 Players (1974); *Ballada* for Flute and Piano (1986); *Little Autumn Music* for Oboe, Violin, Viola, and Cello (1986). **PIANO:** *Rotazioni* (1961); *Allaloa*, optically notated composition for electronically transformed Piano (1970). **VOCAL:** *Liryka sprzed zaśniecia* (A Lyric before Falling Asleep) for Soprano, Flute, and 2 Pianos (1963); *Mirophonies* for Soprano, Actor, Clarinet, Viola, Cello, Harp, and Percussion (1974).

Walcha, (Arthur Emil) Helmut, renowned German organist and pedagogue; b. Leipzig, Oct. 27, 1907; d. Frankfurt am Main, Aug. 11, 1991. Although stricken with blindness at age 16, he courageously pursued organ studies with Ramin at the Leipzig Cons. (1922–27). At 17, he made his debut in Leipzig, where he then served as assistant organist at the Thomaskirche (1926–29). In 1929 he settled in Frankfurt am Main as organist of the Friedenskirche. In 1944 he became organist at the Dreikönigskirche. In 1933 he became a teacher at the Hoch Cons. From 1938 to 1972 he was a prof. at the Hochschule für Musik. After World War II, Walcha became internationally known via his recital tours and recordings. His performances of the complete organ works of Bach were distinguished by their insightful interpretations and virtuoso execution. He also championed Bach's music on period instruments and made appearances as a harpsichordist. Walcha ed. the organ concertos of Handel and composed 25 organ chorales of his own invention.

BIBL.: W. Dehnhard and G. Ritter, eds., *Bachstunden* (Frankfurt am Main, 1978; Festschrift for W.'s 70th birthday).

Wald, Max, American composer and teacher; b. Litchfield, Ill., July 14, 1889; d. Dowagiac, Mich., Aug. 14, 1954. After studying in Chicago, he was active as a theater conductor; went to Paris in 1922 to study with d'Indy, and remained in Europe until 1936. He then became chairman of the theory dept. of the Chicago Musical College. His symphonic poem *The Dancer Dead* won 2nd prize in the NBC competition in 1932, and was broadcast from N.Y. on May 1, 1932. His other works included the operas *Mirandolina* (1936) and *Gay Little World* (1942); *Retrospectives* for Orch. (Chicago, Jan. 15, 1926); *Comedy Overture* (1937); *In Praise of Pageantry* for Orch. (Chicago, Oct. 31, 1946); *October Moonlight*, song cycle for Soprano, String Quartet, Flute, Clarinet, and Piano (1937); 2 piano sonatas; other piano music.

Waldman, Frederic, Austrian-born American conductor and teacher; b. Vienna, April 17, 1903; d. N.Y., Dec. 1, 1995. He studied piano with Richard Robert, orchestration and conducting with Szell, and composition with Weigl. After serving as music director of the Ballet Joos of the Netherlands, he was active in England from 1935 In 1941 he settled in N.Y. and was active as a piano accompanist. After teaching at the Mannes College of Music, he taught at the Juilliard School of Music (1947–67), where, as music director of its Opera Theater, he conducted the American premieres of Strauss' *Capriccio* (1954) and Kodály's *Háry János* (1960). In 1961 he founded the Musica Aeterna Orch. and Chorus, which he conducted in enterprising programs of rarely-heard music of the past and present eras, ranging from Monteverdi to Rieti.

Waldrop, Gideon W(illiam), American music educator, conductor, and composer; b. Haskell County, Texas, Sept. 2, 1919. He studied at Baylor Univ. (B.M., 1940) and took courses in composition with Rogers and Hanson at the Eastman School of Music in Rochester, N.Y. (M.M., 1941; Ph.D., 1952). He was conductor of the Waco-Baylor Sym. Orch. (1939–51); also was assoc. prof. at Baylor Univ. (1946–51). He served as ed. of the *Musical Courier* (1953–58) and as music consultant to the Ford Foundation (1958–61). He was assistant to the president (1961–63) and then dean (1963–85) of the Juilliard School in N.Y.; then was president of the Manhattan School of Music (1986–88).

WORKS: ORCH.: *From the Southwest*, suite (1948); Sym. No. 1 (1951); *Pressures* for Strings (1955); *Prelude and Fugue* (1962). **VOCAL:** *Songs of the Southwest* for Baritone and Chamber Orch. (1982); choral pieces; other songs. **OTHER:** Chamber music.

Walker, Alan, English musicologist; b. Scunthorpe, April 6, 1930. He was educated at the Guildhall School of Music in London (ARCM, 1949) and at the Univ. of Durham (B.Mus., 1956; D.Mus., 1965); also studied with Hans Keller (1958–60). He was prof. of harmony and counterpoint at the Guildhall School of Music (1958–60); after serving as a producer for the BBC music division (1961–71), he was chairman of the music dept. and a prof. at McMaster Univ. in Hamilton, Ontario (from 1971).

WRITINGS (all publ. in London unless otherwise given): *A Study in Musical Analysis* (1962); *An Anatomy of Musical Criticism* (1966); ed., *Frederic Chopin: Profiles of the Man and the Musician* (1966; 2nd ed., rev. and enl., 1978); ed., *Franz Liszt: The Man and His Music* (1970; 2nd ed., rev., 1976); Liszt (1971); ed., *Robert Schumann: The Man and His Music* (1972; 2nd ed., rev., 1976); *Schumann* (1976); *Franz Liszt: Vol. I, The Virtuoso Years, 1811–1847* (1983; rev. 1987); *Franz Liszt: Vol. II, The Weimar Years, 1848–1861* (1989); with G. Erasmi, *Liszt, Carolyne, and the Vatican: The Story of a Thwarted Marriage* (Stuyvesant, N.Y., 1991).

Walker, Edyth, American mezzo-soprano; b. Hopewell, N.Y., March 27, 1867; d. N.Y., Feb. 19, 1950. She studied singing with Aglaja Orgeni at the Dresden Cons. She made her debut as Fidès in *Le Prophète* at the Berlin Royal Opera on Nov. 11, 1894. She was a member of the Vienna Court Opera (1895–1903); made her debut at London's Covent Garden as Amneris in 1900. She made her U.S. debut at the Metropolitan Opera in N.Y. (Nov. 30, 1903), remaining on its roster until 1906, singing soprano as well as mezzo-soprano roles; also sang both mezzo-soprano and soprano roles at the Hamburg Opera (1903–12); was the first London Electra (1910). After singing at the Bayreuth and Munich Festivals (1912–17), she turned to private teaching; was on the faculty of the American Cons. in Fontainebleau (1933–36) before settling in N.Y.

Walker, Ernest, English pianist, teacher, writer on music, and composer; b. Bombay, India, July 15, 1870; d. Oxford, Feb. 21, 1949. He was educated at Balliol College, Oxford (D.Mus., 1898); was director of music there (1901–25). He publ. the valuable compendium *A History of Music in England* (Oxford, 1907; 2nd ed., 1924; 3rd ed., rev. by J. Westrup, 1952). He also publ. a monograph on Beethoven in the Music of the Masters series (1905). His collection of essays, *Free Thought and the Musician*, was publ. in 1946. Among his compositions were *Fantasia-Variations on a Norfolk Folksong* for Small Orch. (1930; also for Piano Duet), *Fantasia* for String Quartet (1905), Cello Sonata (1914), and *Variations on a Theme of Joachim* for Violin and Piano (1918).

BIBL.: M. Deneke, *E. W.* (London, 1951).

Walker, Frank, English musicologist; b. Gosport, Hampshire, June 10, 1907; d. (suicide) Tring, Feb. 25?, 1962. He studied telegraphy. In 1926 he went to Rio de Janeiro as a representative of the Western Telegraph Co. From 1931 to 1943 he was in London; in 1944–45 he was in Naples, and later in Vienna, before returning to London. He contributed valuable articles on the composers of the Neapolitan School; wrote the books *Hugo Wolf: A Biography* (London, 1951; 2nd ed., 1968) and *The Man Verdi* (London, 1962).

Walker, George (Theophilus), black American composer, pianist, and teacher; b. Washington, D.C., June 27, 1922. After piano lessons with local teachers, he pursued his musical training at the Oberlin (Ohio) College Cons. of Music (M.B., 1941). He then studied at the Curtis Inst. of Music in Philadelphia with Serkin (piano) and Scalero (composition), taking his artist diploma in both in 1945. His other mentors there included Horszowski, Primrose, Menotti, and Piatigorsky. In 1945 he won critical accolades when he made his debut as a pianist at N.Y.'s Town Hall. That same year he became the first black instrumentalist to win the Philadelphia Orch. auditions which resulted in his appearance as soloist in Rachmaninoff's 3rd Piano Concerto under Ormandy's direction. Further study with Casadesus earned him an artist diploma at the American Academy in Fontainebleau in 1947. He later studied at the Eastman School of Music in Rochester, N.Y., where he became the first black to earn the D.M.A. degree in 1956. In 1957 he went to France to study composition with Boulanger, and returned there in 1959 as the 1st John Hay Whitney composition fellow. He taught at Dillard Univ. in New Orleans (1953–54), the Dalcroze School of Music and the New School for Social Research in N.Y. (1960–61), and at Smith College (1961–68). After serving as a visiting prof. at the Univ. of Colo. in Boulder (1968–69), he joined the faculty of Rutgers Univ. in 1969, where he was a Distinguished Prof. from 1976 until his retirement in 1992. He also held the 1st Minority Distinguished Chair at the Univ. of Delaware (1975–76) and was a teacher of piano and composition at the Peabody Inst. in Baltimore (1975–78). Among his numerous honors are 2 Guggenheim fellowships (1969, 1988), NEA grants (1971, 1975, 1978, 1984), Rockefeller Foundation grants (1971, 1974), a Koussevitzky Foundation grant (1988), and various commissions. In his music, Walker has utilized several compositional techniques, including serialism. In a few of his scores he has also demonstrated a deft handling of jazz infusions.

WORKS: ORCH.: *Lyric* for Strings (1946; rev. 1990; based on String Quartet No. 1); Trombone Concerto (1957; also for Trombone and Wind Ensemble, 1995); *Address* (1959; rev. 1991 and 1995); *Antifonys* (1968; also for Strings); *Variations* (1971); *Spirituals*, later renamed *Folksongs* (1974); Piano Concerto (1975); Violin Concerto (1975; rev. as *Poème* for Violin and Orch., 1991); *Dialogus* for Cello and Orch. (1975; Cleveland, April 22, 1976); *In Praise of Folly*, overture (1980); Cello Concerto (1981; N.Y., Jan. 14, 1982); *An Eastman Overture* (1983); *Serenata* for Chamber Orch. (1983); 2 sinfonias (1984, 1990); *Orpheus* for Chamber Orch. (1994; Cleveland, March 12, 1995). **CHAMBER:** 2 string quartets (1946, 1968); 2 violin sonatas (1957, 1979); Cello Sonata (1957); *Perimeters* for Clarinet and Piano (1966); *Music for 3* for Violin, Cello, and Piano (1970); *5 Fancies* for Clarinet and Piano, 4-hands (1975); *Music for Brass, Sacred and Profane* for Brass Quintet (1975); Viola Sonata (1989). **PIANO:** *Caprice* (1940); *Prélude* (1945); 4 sonatas (1953, 1957, 1975, 1984); *Variations on a Kentucky Folksong* (1953); *Spatials* (1961); *Spektra* (1971); Sonata for 2 Pianos (1975; based on Piano Sonata No. 2). **VOCAL:** Mass for Soprano, Contralto, Tenor, Baritone, Chorus, and Orch. (1977; Baltimore, April 13, 1979); Cantata for Soprano, Tenor, Boys' Chorus, and Orch. (1982); *Poem* for Soprano and Chamber Ensemble (1986); choruses; songs; arrangements of spirituals.

Walker, Robert (Ernest), English composer; b. Northampton, March 18, 1946. He was a chorister at St. Matthew's Church in Northampton and a choral and then organ scholar at Jesus College, Cambridge (1965–68; M.A., 1968). After serving as an organist and schoolmaster in Lincolnshire, he devoted himself to composing, teaching, and broadcasting.

WORKS: ORCH.: *Pavan* for Violin and Orch. (Eltham Palace, June 26, 1975); *At Bignor Hill* (Lisbon, April 9, 1979); Chamber Sym. No. 1 (1981; Greenwich, June 15, 1982); *Variations on a Theme of Elgar* (Chichester, July 13, 1982); *Charms and Exultations of Trumpets* (1985; Salisbury, April 2, 1986); Sym. No. 1 (Exeter, May 26, 1987). **CHAMBER:** String Quartet No. 1 (1982); *Gonfalons* for 4 Trumpets, 4 Trombones, Organ, and Optional Unison Chorus (1983); Piano Quintet (1984); *Serenade* for Flute, Harp, Violin, Viola, and Cello (1987). **PIANO:** *Five Capriccios*, Set 1 (1982) and Set 2 (1985); *Passacaglia* for 2 Pianos (1984). **VOCAL:** *Requiem* for Tenor, Chorus, and Orch. (1976); *Canticle of the Rose* for Soprano, Baritone, Chorus, and Orch. (1980); *The Sun Used to Shine* for Tenor, Harp, and String Orch. (1983); *Magnificat and Nunc Dimittis* for Chorus and Organ (1985); *Missa Brevis* for Chorus and Organ (1985); *Singer by the Yellow River* for Soprano, Flute, and Harp (1985); *Jubilate* for Chorus and Brass Quintet (1987); *English Parody Mass* for Chorus and Organ (1988); *Journey into Light*, choral sym. (1992); also various unaccompanied vocal pieces.

Walker, Sarah, English mezzo-soprano; b. Cheltenham, March 11, 1943. She studied violin with A. Brosa, cello with H. Philips, and voice with R. Packer and V. Rozsa at the Royal College of Music in London (1961–65). In 1969 she made her operatic debut as Monteverdi's Ottavia with the Kent Opera, and then sang Diana and Jove in Cavalli's *Calisto* at the Glyndebourne Festival in 1970. In 1972 she became a member of the Sadler's Wells Opera in London, and continued to appear there after it became the English National Opera in 1974. She appeared as Magdalene in *Die Meistersinger von Nürnberg* in Chicago in 1977. In 1979 she made her debut at London's Covent Garden as Charlotte. In 1981 she sang Berlioz's Dido in Vienna. On Feb. 3, 1986, she made her Metropolitan Opera debut in N.Y. as Micah in Handel's *Samson*. In 1987 she created the role of Caroline in the British premiere of Sallinen's *The King Goes Forth to War* at Covent Garden. As a concert artist, she appeared throughout Europe and North America. In 1991 she was made a Commander of the Order of the British Empire.

Wallace, John, Scottish trumpeter; b. Fife, April 14, 1949. He studied at King's College, Cambridge, the Royal Academy of Music in London, and the Univ. of York. In 1976 he became principal trumpet in the Philharmonia Orch. in London, a position he held until 1995. During this period, he also garnered wide recognition via solo appearances with it and many other orchs. of the world. In 1986 he founded the Wallace Collection, an ensemble devoted to the performance of the vast brass repertoire. He toured widely with it, making his first visit to the U.S. in 1993. In addition to the standard literature for his instrument, Wallace has introduced various modern scores, including concertos by Sir Malcolm Arnold (1981), Sir Peter Maxwell Davies (1988), and Tim Souster (1988).

Wallace, Lucille, American-born English harpsichordist and pianist; b. Chicago, Feb. 22, 1898; d. London, March 21, 1977. She studied at the Bush Cons. in Chicago (B.Mus.), attended Vassar College, took courses in music history with Adler at the Univ. of Vienna (1923–24), and was a student of Boulanger and Landowska in Paris, and of Schnabel in Berlin. She became principally known as an accomplished harpsichordist, winning esteem as an interpreter of Domenico Scarlatti and Couperin. In 1931 she married **Clifford Curzon**.

Wallace, William, Scottish composer and music educator; b. Greenock, July 3, 1860; d. Malmesbury, Wiltshire, Dec. 16, 1940. The son of a surgeon, he studied medicine at Glasgow Univ. (M.D., 1888); specialized in ophthalmology in Vienna, and was employed in the Royal Army Medical Corps during World War I. He was 29 when he took up musical studies, pursuing training at the Royal Academy of Music in London. He devoted much of his energy to the protection of the rights of British composers; served on the Composers' Copyright Committee of the Soc. of British Authors; also taught at the Royal Academy of Music.

WORKS: 6 symphonic poems: *The Passing of Beatrice* (1892), *Amboss oder Hammer*, after Goethe (1896), *Sister Helen* (1899), *To the New Century* (1901), *William Wallace* (for the 6th centenary of the death of the national hero of Scotland, and namesake of the composer; 1905), and *François Villon* (1909); *The Creation*, sym. (1899); 2 suites for Orch.: *The Lady from the Sea*, after Ibsen (1892), and *Pelléas and Mélisande*, after Maeterlinck (1900); *In Praise of Scottish Poesie*, overture (1894); *The Massacre of the Macpherson*, burlesque cantata; 3 song cycles: *Freebooter Songs* (with Orch.), *Lords of the Sea*, and *Jacobite Songs*.

WRITINGS: *The Threshold of Music: An Inquiry into the Development of the Musical Sense* (1908); *The Musical Faculty: Its Origins and Processes* (1914); *Richard Wagner as He Lived* (1925); *Liszt, Wagner and the Princess* (1927).

Wallat, Hans, German conductor; b. Berlin, Oct. 18, 1929. He was educated at the Schwerin Cons. and then conducted in several provincial German music centers. He was music director in Cottbus (1956–58) and 1st conductor of the Leipzig Opera (1958–61); then conducted in Stuttgart (1961–64) and at the Deutsche Oper in West Berlin (1964–65). He was Generalmusikdirektor at the Bremen Opera (1965–70). Wallat made appearances as a guest conductor with various opera houses and orchs. in Europe. On Oct. 7, 1971, he made his Metropolitan Opera debut in N.Y. conducting *Fidelio.* He was Generalmusikdirektor in Mannheim (1970–80), Dortmund (1980–85), and of the Deutsche Oper am Rhein in Düsseldorf (from 1987).

Wallberg, Heinz, German conductor; b. Herringen-Hamm, March 16, 1923. He studied at the Dortmund Cons. and the Cologne Hochschule für Musik. After pursuing a career as a trumpeter and violinist, he turned to conducting; was Generalmusikdirektor in Wiesbaden (1961–74) and chief conductor of the Vienna Niederösterreichisches Tonkünstler-Orch. (1964–75); subsequently was music director of the Munich Radio Orch. (1975–82) and of the Essen Phil. (1975–91). In 1991 he made his U.S. debut as a guest conductor with the National Sym. Orch. in Washington, D.C.

Wallek-Walewski, Boleslaw, Polish conductor, pedagogue, and composer; b. Lemberg, Jan. 23, 1885; d. Kraków, April 9, 1944. He studied theory and composition with Soltys and Niewiadomski and piano with Maliszowa and Zelinger in Lemberg; then continued his training with Żeleński and Szopski at the Kraków Cons.; completed his studies with Riemann and Prüfer in Leipzig. He became a prof. (1910) and director (1913) of the Kraków Cons.; was founder-conductor of his own choral society, and also appeared as an operatic and sym. conductor. His compositions followed along Romantic lines.

WORKS: OPERAS: *Pan Twardowski* (1911; Kraków, 1915); *Dola* (Lot; Kraków, 1919); *Pomsta Jontkowa* (1926); *Legenda o królewnie Wandzie* (The Legend of the King's Daughter Wanda; 1936). **ORCH.:** 2 symphonic poems: *Pawel i Gawel* (1908) and *Zygmunt August i Barbara* (1912). **VOCAL:** Oratorios; cantatas; songs.

Wallenstein, Alfred, American cellist and conductor; b. Chicago, Oct. 7, 1898; d. N.Y., Feb. 8, 1983. His parents were of German and Austrian extraction; Wallenstein believed that he was a direct descendant of Albrecht von Wallenstein, the illustrious leader during the Thirty Years' War. The family moved to Los Angeles in 1905; Wallenstein took cello lessons with the mother of Ferde Grofé; as a young boy, he played in hotels and movie theaters; also gave public recitals advertised as "the wonder-boy cellist." He played with the San Francisco Sym. Orch. (1916–17); subsequently toured in South America with the troupe of Anna Pavlova, being featured as cello soloist to accompany her famous portrayal of the dying swan. In 1919 he became a member of the Los Angeles Phil. In 1920 he studied cello with Julius Klengel in Leipzig. He was a cellist in the Chicago Sym. Orch. (1922–29), and also appeared with it as a soloist; from 1927 to 1929 he was head of the cello dept. of the Chicago Musical College. In 1929 Toscanini engaged him as 1st cellist with the N.Y. Phil.; it was Toscanini who urged Wallenstein to try his hand at conducting; he began his conducting career by leading classical programs over the radio. In 1933 he formed the Wallenstein Sinfonietta, giving regular Sunday broadcasts; an important feature was a series of performances of Bach's cantatas. He also programmed numerous premieres of works by contemporary composers. After Toscanini resigned as music director of the N.Y. Phil. in 1936, Wallenstein also left his job as 1st cellist of the orch., and devoted himself exclusively to radio performances and guest conducting. In 1943 he was named conductor of the Los Angeles Phil.; was also director of the Hollywood Bowl (1952–56). In 1956 he made a tour of the Orient with the Los Angeles Phil. under the auspices of the State Dept.; after this tour he resigned as its conductor; subsequently made appearances as a guest conductor. In 1968 he joined the faculty of the Juilliard School of Music in N.Y. as instructor in conducting. In 1979, at the age of 81, he made his last public appearance as a conductor, leading the Juilliard School Orch. in N.Y. Wallenstein never pretended to be a glamorous virtuoso of the baton, but he was a master builder of orch. organizations; more in praise than in dispraise, he was described as a "vertical" conductor who offered dispassionate rather than impassionate interpretations; but no one doubted his selfless devotion to music and musicians.

Wallerstein, Lothar, Bohemian-born American pianist and conductor; b. Prague, Nov. 6, 1882; d. New Orleans, Nov. 13, 1949. He studied art and music in Prague and Munich; also attended the Geneva Cons., where he later taught piano. After serving as accompanist at the Dresden Court Opera (1909), he was conductor and stage director in Posen (1910–14), Breslau (1918–22), Duisberg (1922–24), and Frankfurt am Main (1924–26); was producer at the Vienna State Opera (1927–38); conducted at La Scala in Milan (1929). He went to the U.S. in 1941; was a producer at the Metropolitan Opera in N.Y. (1941–46). In 1945 he became a naturalized American citizen.

BIBL.: A. Berger, *Über die Spielleitung der Oper: Betrachtungen zur musikalischen Dramaturgie Dr. L. W.s* (Graz, 1928).

Wallfisch, Raphael, English cellist and teacher; b. London, June 15, 1953. He commenced cello playing at age 8; studied with Amaryllis Fleming in London (1966–69), Amadeo Baldovino in Rome (1969), Derek Simpson at the Royal Academy of Music in London (1969–72), and with Gregor Piatigorsky in Los Angeles (1972–74); won 1st prize in the Gaspar Cassadó competition in Florence in 1977. He made his formal debut as soloist in the Schumann Cello Concerto with the English Chamber Orch. in London in 1974; subsequently appeared as a soloist with major orchs. on both sides of the Atlantic, and also gave recitals and played in chamber music settings. In 1980 he became a prof. at the Guildhall School of Music in London. His repertoire includes some 60 concertos, ranging from early scores to contemporary works, as well as numerous solo and chamber music pieces.

Walter, Arnold (Maria), prominent Moravian-born Canadian music educator, administrator, musicologist, and composer; b. Hannsdorf, Aug. 30, 1902; d. Toronto, Oct. 6, 1973. He studied harmony and composition with Bruno Weigl in Brno. After taking a doctorate in jurisprudence at the Univ. of Prague (1926), he studied musicology with Abert, Sachs, and Wolf at the Univ. of Berlin. He concurrently pursued training in piano with Breithaupt and Lamond, and in composition with Schreker. When the Nazis came to power in Germany in 1933, Walter went to Majorca. In 1936 he went to England. He settled in Toronto in 1937 and taught at the Upper Canada College until 1943. In 1945 he founded the Senior School as the graduate dept. of the Toronto Cons. of Music, where he also founded its opera school. From 1952 to 1968 he was director of the music faculty of the Univ. of Toronto. Walter served as president of the International Soc. for Music Education (1953–55), the Canadian Music Centre (1959, 1970), the Canadian Music Council (1965–66), the Canadian Assn. of Univ. Schools of Music (1965–67), and the Inter-American Music Council (1969–72). From 1956 to 1962 he was chairman of the editorial board of the *Canadian Music Journal.* In 1945 Walter was awarded the Christian Culture Medal of Assumption College in Windsor, Ontario. He was made an Officer of the Order of Canada in 1972. In 1974 the concert hall of the Edward Johnson Building at the Univ. of Toronto was dedicated in his memory. He contributed articles to several journals, publ. the study *Music and the Common Understanding* (Saskatoon, 1966), and ed. the vol. *Aspects of Music in Canada* (Toronto, 1969). In his compositions, he remained faithful to traditional forms and modes of expression.

WORKS: DRAMATIC: Music for radio plays. **ORCH.:** Sym. (1942; Toronto, Feb. 1, 1944); *Concerto for Orchestra* (1958). **CHAMBER:** Cello Sonatina (1940); Trio for Violin, Cello, and Piano (1940); Violin Sonata (1940). **PIANO:** Suite (1945); *Toccata* (1947); Sonata (1950); *Legend* (1962). **VOCAL:** *Sacred Songs* for Soprano and String Trio (1941); *For the Fallen* for Soprano, Chorus, and Orch. (1949). **TAPE:** *Summer Idyll* (1960; in collaboration with M. Schaeffer and H. Olnick).

BIBL.: E. Seiffert, *A. W.: His Contribution to Music Education in Canada 1946–68* (thesis, Univ. of Western Ontario, 1980).

Walter, Bruno (full name, **Bruno Walter Schlesinger**), eminent German-born American conductor; b. Berlin, Sept. 15, 1876; d. Beverly Hills, Feb. 17, 1962. He entered the Stern Cons. in Berlin at age 8, where he studied with H. Ehrlich, L. Bussler, and R. Radecke. At age 9, he performed in public as a pianist but at 13 decided to pursue his interest in conducting. In 1893 he became a coach at the Cologne Opera, where he made his conducting debut with Lortzing's *Waffenschmied*; in the following year he was engaged as assistant conductor at the Hamburg Stadttheater, under Gustav Mahler; this contact was decisive in his career, and he became in subsequent years an ardent champion of Mahler's music; conducted the premieres of the posthumous Sym. No. 9 and *Das Lied von der Erde.* During the 1896–97 season, Walter was engaged as 2nd conductor at the Stadttheater in Breslau; then became principal conductor in Pressburg, and in 1898 at Riga, where he conducted for 2 seasons. In 1900 he received the important engagement of conductor at the Berlin Royal Opera under a 5-year contract; however, he left this post in 1901 when he received an offer from Mahler to become his assistant at the Vienna Court Opera. He established himself as an efficient opera conductor; also conducted in England (1st appearance, March 3, 1909, with the Royal Phil. Soc. in London). He remained at the Vienna Court Opera after the death of Mahler. On Jan. 1, 1913, he became Royal Bavarian Generalmusikdirektor in Munich; under his guidance, the Munich Opera enjoyed brilliant performances, particularly of Mozart's works. Seeking greater freedom for his artistic activities, he left Munich in 1922, and gave numerous performances as a guest conductor with European orchs.; conducted the series "Bruno Walter Concerts" with the Berlin Phil. from 1921 to 1933; from 1925 he also conducted summer concerts of the Salzburg Festival; his performances of Mozart's music there set a standard. He also appeared as pianist in Mozart's chamber works. On Feb. 15, 1923, he made his American debut with the N.Y. Sym. Soc., and appeared with it again in 1924 and 1925. From 1925 to 1929 he was conductor of the Städtische Oper in Berlin-Charlottenburg; in 1929 he succeeded Furtwängler as conductor of the Gewandhaus Orch. in Leipzig, but continued to give special concerts in Berlin. On Jan. 14, 1932, he was guest conductor of the N.Y. Phil., acting also as soloist in a Mozart piano concerto; was reengaged during the next 3 seasons as assoc. conductor with Toscanini. He was also a guest conductor in Philadelphia, Washington, D.C., and Baltimore. With the advent of the Nazi regime in Germany in 1933, his engagement with the Gewandhaus Orch. was canceled, and he was also prevented from continuing his orch. concerts in Berlin. He filled several engagements with the Concertgebouw Orch. in Amsterdam, and also conducted in Salzburg. In 1936 he was engaged as music director of the Vienna State Opera; this was terminated with the Nazi annexation of Austria in 1938. Walter, with his family, then went to France, where he was granted French citizenship. After the outbreak of World War II in 1939, he sailed for America, establishing his residence in California, and eventually became a naturalized American citizen. He was guest conductor with the NBC Sym. Orch. in N.Y. (1939); also conducted many performances of the Metropolitan Opera in N.Y. (debut in *Fidelio* on Feb. 14, 1941). From 1947 to 1949 he was conductor and musical adviser of the N.Y. Phil.; returned regularly as guest conductor until 1960; also conducted in Europe (1949–60), giving his farewell performance in Vienna with the Vienna Phil. in 1960.

Walter achieved the reputation of a perfect classicist among 20th-century conductors; his interpretations of the masterpieces of the Vienna School were particularly notable. He is acknowledged to have been a foremost conductor of Mahler's syms. His own compositions include 2 syms.; *Siegesfahrt* for Solo Voices, Chorus, and Orch.; String Quartet; Piano Quintet; Piano Trio; several albums of songs. He publ. the books *Von den moralischen Kräften der Musik* (Vienna, 1935); *Gustav Mahler* (Vienna, 1936; 2nd ed., 1957; Eng. tr., 1927; 2nd ed., 1941); *Theme and Variations: An Autobiography* (N.Y., 1946; Ger. original, 1947); *Von der Musik und vom Musizieren* (Frankfurt am Main, 1957; Eng. tr., 1961); L. Walter-Lindt, ed., *Briefe 1894–1962* (Frankfurt am Main, 1970).

BIBL.: M. Komorn-Rebhan, *Was wir von B. W. lernten* (Vienna, 1913); P. Stefan, *B. W.* (Vienna, 1936); B. Gavoty, *B. W.* (Geneva, 1956).

Walter, David Edgar, American bass-baritone and composer; b. Boston, Feb. 2, 1953. He studied voice with John Powell at Rutgers Univ. (1970–75), Oren Brown, Lois Bove, and Shirley Meier at Trenton (N.J.) State College (M.A., 1978), and Janet Wheeler at the New England Cons. of Music in Boston. He also studied with Diamond, Luening, and Persichetti at the Juilliard School in N.Y. (B.M. in composition, 1975), Edward Richter and Calvin Hampton (1976–78), and Del Tredici, Mekeel, and John Thow at Boston Univ. (1978–81). Walter subsequently was active as a singer in Boston and N.Y. churches. As a composer, he writes in an accessible style. Among his works are dramatic pieces, sacred scores, chamber music, piano pieces, organ music, and choruses.

Walter, Georg A., German tenor, pedagogue, and composer; b. Hoboken, N.J., Nov. 13, 1875; d. Berlin, Sept. 13, 1952. He studied singing in Milan, Dresden, Berlin, and London, and composition with Wilhelm Berger in Berlin. He made a career as a singer, particularly distinguishing himself in the works of Bach and Handel. He was a prof. at the Stuttgart Hochschule für Musik (1925–34); then settled in Berlin as a vocal teacher; his most celebrated student was Dietrich Fischer-Dieskau. He brought out new eds. of works by the sons of Bach, Schütz et al.

Waltershausen, H(ermann) W(olfgang Sartorius), Freiherr von, German composer, writer on music, and teacher; b. Göttingen, Oct. 12, 1882; d. Munich, Aug. 13, 1954. He began his music studies with M.J. Erb in Strasbourg; although he lost his right arm and leg in an accident when he was 10, he learned to play the piano and conduct with his left hand. He settled in Munich in 1901, where he studied composition with Thuille and piano with Schmid-Lindner; also studied music history with Sandberger at the Univ. of Munich. In 1917 he established there a seminar for operatic dramaturgy, the Praktisches Seminar für Fortgeschrittene Musikstudierende; was a prof. and assistant director of the Munich Akademie der Tonkunst (1920–22), then director (1922–33); later founded his own Seminar für Privatmusiklehrer, which became the Waltershausen-Seminar in 1948. In his music he adopted a neo-Romantic style, rather advanced in harmonic treatment.

WORKS: DRAMATIC: 2 operas: *Else Klapperzehen* (Dresden, May 15, 1909) and *Oberst Chabert* (Frankfurt am Main, Jan. 18, 1912); *Richardis*, dramatic mystery (Karlsruhe, Nov. 14, 1915); *Die Rauensteiner Hochzeit* (Karlsruhe, 1919); *Die Gräfin von Tolosa* (1934; Bavarian Radio, Munich, 1958). **ORCH.:** *Apokalyptische Symphonie* (1924); *Hero und Leander*, symphonic poem (1925); *Krippenmusik* for Chamber Orch. and Harpsichord Obbligato (1926); *Orchesterpartita über 3 Kirchenlieder* (1928). **CHAMBER:** String Quartet (1910); piano pieces, including studies and transcriptions for left hand alone. **VOCAL:** Songs.

WRITINGS (all publ. in Munich unless otherwise given): *Der Freischütz: Ein Versuch über die musikalische Romantik* (1920); *Das Siegfried-Idyll oder die Rückkehr zur Natur* (1920); *Die Zauberflöte: Eine operndramaturgische Studie* (1920); *Richard Strauss: Ein Versuch* (1921); *Orpheus und Euridike: Eine opern-*

dramaturgische Studie (1923); *Musik, Dramaturgie, Erziehung* (collected essays; 1926); *Dirigentenerziehung* (Leipzig, 1929); *Die Kunst des Dirigierens* (Berlin, 1942; 2nd ed., 1954); *Dramaturgie der Oper* (in manuscript).

BIBL.: K.-R. Danler and R. Mader, *H.W. v.W.* (Tutzing, 1984).

Walthew, Richard Henry, English composer, conductor, and pedagogue; b. London, Nov. 4, 1872; d. East Preston, Sussex, Nov. 14, 1951. He studied with Parry at the Royal College of Music in London (1890–94). After a directorship of the Passmore Edwards Settlement Place (1900–1904), he was appointed instructor of the opera class at the Guildhall School of Music in London; in 1907 he became a prof. of music at Queen's College; also conducted provincial orchs. His works included 2 operettas: *The Enchanted Island* (London, May 8, 1900) and *The Gardeners* (London, Feb. 12, 1906); 2 cantatas: *Ode to a Nightingale* and *The Pied Piper of Hamelin*; Piano Concerto; Piano Quintet; Piano Quartet; 2 piano trios; Violin Sonata; vocal quartets, with piano; songs. He was the author of *The Development of Chamber Music* (1909).

Walton, Sir William (Turner), eminent English composer; b. Oldham, Lancashire, March 29, 1902; d. Ischia, Italy, March 8, 1983. Both his parents were professional singers, and Walton himself had a fine singing voice as a youth; he entered the Cathedral Choir School at Christ Church, Oxford, and began to compose choral pieces for performance. Sir Hugh Allen, organist of New College, advised him to develop his interest in composition, and sponsored his admission to Christ Church at an early age; however, he never graduated, and instead began to write unconventional music in the manner that was fashionable in the 1920s. His talent manifested itself in a string quartet he wrote at the age of 17, which was accepted for performance for the first festival of the ISCM in 1923. In London he formed a congenial association with the Sitwell family of quintessential cognoscenti and literati who combined a patrician sense of artistic superiority with a benign attitude toward the social plebs; they also provided Walton with residence at their manor in Chelsea, where he lived off and on for some 15 years. Fascinated by Edith Sitwell's oxymoronic verse, Walton set it to music bristling with novel jazzy effects in brisk, irregular rhythms and modern harmonies; Walton was only 19 when he wrote it. Under the title *Facade*, it was first performed in London in 1923, with Edith Sitwell herself delivering her doggerel with a megaphone; as expected, the show provoked an outburst of feigned indignation in the press and undisguised delight among the young in spirit. But Walton did not pursue the path of facile hedonism so fashionable at the time; he soon demonstrated his ability to write music in a Classical manner in his fetching concert overture *Portsmouth Point*, first performed in Zürich in 1926, and later in the comedy-overture *Scapino*. His biblical oratorio *Belshazzar's Feast*, written in 1931, reveals a deep emotional stream and nobility of design that places Walton directly in line from Handel and Elgar among English masters. His symphonic works show him as an inheritor of the grand Romantic tradition; his concertos for violin, for viola, and for cello demonstrate an adroitness in effective instrumental writing. Walton was a modernist in his acceptance of the new musical resources, but he never deviated from fundamental tonality and formal clarity of design. Above all, his music was profoundly national, unmistakably British in its inspiration and content. Quite appropriately, he was asked to contribute to two royal occasions: he wrote *Crown Imperial March* for the coronation of King George VI in 1937 and *Orb and Sceptre* for that of Queen Elizabeth II in 1953. He received an honorary doctorate from the Univ. of Oxford in 1942. King George VI knighted him in 1951. He spent the last years of his life on the island of Ischia off Naples with his Argentine-born wife, Susana Gil Passo.

WORKS: DRAMATIC: OPERAS: *Troilus and Cressida*, after Chaucer (1947–54; London, Dec. 3, 1954; rev. 1963 and 1972–76; London, Nov. 12, 1976); *The Bear*, after Chekhov (1965–67; Aldeburgh, June 3, 1967). **BALLETS:** *The First Shoot* (1935); *The Wise Virgins*, after J.S. Bach (1939–40; London, April 24, 1940); *The Quest* (1943). **ENTERTAINMENT:** *Façade* for Reciter and Instrumental Ensemble, after Edith Sitwell (1921; 1st perf. privately at the Sitwell home in London, Jan. 24, 1922; 1st public perf., London, June 12, 1923; rev. 1926, 1928, 1942, and 1951; rev. as *Façade 2*, 1978; arranged as a ballet, 1929, with subsequent changes). **INCIDENTAL MUSIC FOR THE THEATER AND RADIO:** *A Son of Heaven* (1924–25); *The Boy David* (1935); *Macbeth* (1941–42); *Christopher Columbus* (1942). **FILM SCORES:** *Escape Me Never* (1934); *As You Like It* (1936); *Dreaming Lips* (1937); *Stolen Life* (1938); *Major Barbara* (1940); *Next of Kin* (1941); *The Foreman Went to France* (1941–42); *The First of the Few* (1942); *Went the Day Well?* (1942); *Henry V* (1943–44); *Hamlet* (1947); *Richard III* (1955); *The Battle of Britain* (1969); *Three Sisters* (1969). **ORCH.:** *Portsmouth Point*, overture (1924–25; Zürich, June 22, 1926); *Siesta* (1926); *Façade*, 2 suites after the entertainment: No. 1 (1926; Siena, Sept. 14, 1928) and No. 2 (N.Y., March 30, 1938); *Sinfonia concertante* for Piano and Orch. (1926–27; London, Jan. 5, 1928; rev. 1943); Viola Concerto (1928–29; London, Oct. 3, 1929, Paul Hindemith soloist; rev. 1936 and 1961; London, Jan. 18, 1962); 2 syms.: No. 1 (1931–35; London, Nov. 6, 1935) and No. 2 (1957–60; Edinburgh, Sept. 2, 1960); *Crown Imperial*, coronation march for King George VI (Westminster Abbey, London, May 12, 1937; rev. 1963); Violin Concerto (1938–39; Cleveland, Dec. 7, 1939, Jascha Heifetz soloist; rev. 1943); *The Wise Virgins*, suite from the ballet (1940); *Music for Children* (1940; orchestration of *Duets for Children* for Piano); *Scapino*, comedy overture (1940; Chicago, April 3, 1941; rev. 1950); *Spitfire Prelude and Fugue* (1942); *2 Pieces* for Strings from the film score to *Henry V* (1943–44); *Orb and Sceptre*, coronation march for Queen Elizabeth II (1952–53; Westminster Abbey, London, June 2, 1953); Finale for *Sellinger's Round, Variations on an Elizabethan Theme* for Strings (1953; in collaboration with others); Cello Concerto (1955–56; Boston, Jan. 25, 1957, Piatigorsky soloist); *Johannesburg Festival Overture* (Johannesburg, Sept. 25, 1956); *Partita* (1957; Cleveland, Jan. 30, 1958); *Variations on a Theme by Hindemith* (1962–63; London, March 8, 1963); *Capriccio Burlesco* (N.Y., Dec. 7, 1968); *Improvisations on an Impromptu of Benjamin Britten* (1968–69; San Francisco, Jan. 14, 1970); *Sonata* for Strings (1971; orchestration of the String Quartet, 1945–47); *Varii Capricci* (1975–76; London, May 4, 1976; orchestration of the *5 Bagatelles* for Guitar); *Prologo e Fantasia* (1981–82; London, Feb. 20, 1982). **CHAMBER:** Piano Quartet (1918–21; rev. 1974–75); 2 string quartets (1919, rev. 1921–22; London, July 5, 1923; 1945–47; orchestrated as *Sonata* for Strings, 1971); *Toccata* for Violin and Piano (1922–23); Violin Sonata (1947–48; rev. 1949–50); *2 Pieces* for Violin and Piano (1948–50); *5 Bagatelles* for Guitar (1970–71; orchestrated as *Varii Capricci*, 1975–76); *Passacaglia* for Cello (1979–80); *Duettino* for Oboe and Violin (1982). **KEYBOARD: PIANO:** *Duets for Children* (1940; orchestrated as *Music for Children*). **ORGAN:** *3 Pieces* from the film score to *Richard III* (1955). **VOCAL:** *Belshazzar's Feast*, oratorio for Baritone, Chorus, and Orch. (1930–31; Leeds, Oct. 8, 1931; rev. 1948 and 1957); *In Honour of the City of London* for Chorus and Orch. (1937); *Coronation Te Deum* for 2 Choruses, 2 Semi Choruses, Boys' Chorus, Organ, Orch., and Military Brass, for the coronation of Queen Elizabeth II (1952–53; London, June 2, 1953); *Anon in Love*, 6 songs for Tenor and Guitar (1959; also for Tenor and Small Orch., 1971); *Gloria* for Contralto, Tenor, Bass, Chorus, and Orch. (1960; Liverpool, Nov. 24, 1961); *A Song for the Lord Mayor's Table*, 6 songs for Soprano and Piano (London, July 18, 1962; also for Soprano and Orch., 1970); *The Twelve* for Chorus and Organ (1964–65; Oxford, May 16, 1965); *Missa Brevis* for Double Chorus and Organ (1965–66; Coventry, April 10, 1966); *Jubilate Deo* for Chorus and Organ (1972); *Magnificat and Nunc Dimittis* for Chorus and Organ (1974; rev. 1975); *Antiphon* for Chorus and Organ (1977); other vocal pieces, including choruses and songs.

BIBL.: H. Foss, "W. W.," *Musical Quarterly* (Oct. 1940); F. Howes, *The Music of W. W.* (2 vols.; London, 1942 and 1943; new amplified ed., 1965); E. Evans, "W. W.," *Musical Times*

(1944); K. Avery, "W. W.," *Music & Letters* (Jan. 1947); S. Craggs, *W. W.: A Thematic Catalogue of His Musical Works* (London, 1977; rev. ed., 1990); A. Poulton, *Sir W. W.: A Discography* (London, 1980); B. Northcott, "In Search of W.," *Musical Times* (March 1982); N. Tierney, *W. W.: His Life and Music* (London, 1984); S. Walton, *W. W.: Behind the Facade* (Oxford, 1988); M. Kennedy, *Portrait of W.* (Oxford, 1989); S. Craggs, *W. W.: A Source Book* (Aldershot, 1993).

Wand, Günter, distinguished German conductor; b. Elberfeld, Jan. 7, 1912. He studied in Wuppertal; attended the Univ. of Cologne and took courses in composition with Philipp Jarnach and in piano with Paul Baumgartner at the Cologne Cons. and Hochschule für Musik; received instruction in conducting from Franz von Hoesslin at the Munich Academy of Music. After working as a répétiteur and conductor in Wuppertal and other provincial music centers, he became chief conductor in Detmold. He was conductor at the Cologne Opera (1939–44), then of the Salzburg Mozarteum Orch. (1944–45). In 1946 he was appointed Generalmusikdirektor of Cologne, being responsible for both orch. and operatic performances; in 1947 he was named conductor of the Gurzenich Orch. there, a post he retained until 1974; also was prof. of conducting at the Cologne Hochschule für Musik (from 1948). He appeared as a guest conductor throughout Europe and also in Japan. After leaving Cologne, he conducted in Bern. He subsequently served as chief conductor of the North German Radio Sym. Orch. in Hamburg (1982–91); also was a principal guest conductor of the BBC Sym. Orch. in London and later of the (West) Berlin Radio Sym. Orch. (1989–90). On Jan. 19, 1989, he made his belated U.S. debut at the age of 77 as a guest conductor with the Chicago Sym. Orch. A conductor in the revered Austro-German tradition, Wand acquired a fine reputation as an interpreter of Mozart, Beethoven, Brahms, and most especially Bruckner; also did much to foster contemporary music.

BIBL.: F. Berger, *G. W.: Gürzenichkapellmeister 1947–1974* (Cologne, 1974).

Wangenheim, Volker, German conductor, teacher, and composer; b. Berlin, July 1, 1928. He studied piano, oboe, violin, composition, and conducting at the Hochschule für Musik in Berlin. He began his career as an oboist with several Berlin ensembles. He was founder-principal conductor of the Berlin Mozart Orch. (1950–59); also conducted at the Mecklenburg State Theater in Schwerin (1951–52) and with the Berlin Academic Orch. (1954–57). He was music director (1957–63) and then Generalmusikdirektor (1963–78) in Bonn, where he served as principal conductor of the Beethovenhalle Orch., the Phil. Choir, and the Bonn Beethoven Festivals; also was co-founder and artistic director of the German National Youth Orch. (1969–84). He appeared as a guest conductor in Germany and abroad from 1954. In 1972 he became a prof. at the Cologne Hochschule für Musik, which position he held until 1993.

WORKS: ORCH.: *Sinfonietta concertante* (1963); Concerto for Strings (1964); *Sinfonia notturna* (1965); *Symphony 1966* (1968); *Klangspiel I* for Strings (1971) and *II* for Chamber Ensemble (1973). **VOCAL:** *Psalm 123* for Chorus (1973); *Nicodemus Iesum nocte visitat: Canticum secundum Ioannem* for Chorus (1980); various folksongs for chorus.

Wangermée, Robert, distinguished Belgian musicologist; b. Lodelinsart, Sept. 21, 1920. He received training in music from J. Absil; pursued musicological studies at the Free Univ. of Brussels (Ph.D., 1946, with the diss. *Le Goût musical en France au XIXe siècle*); then was on its faculty as a lecturer (1948–62), reader (1962–65), and prof. (from 1975); also was active with the Belgian Radio and Television (from 1946), serving as its director of music (1953–60) and as director-general of its French-language broadcasts (1960–84).

WRITINGS (all publ. in Brussels): *Jean-Sébastien Bach* (1944); *Ludwig van Beethoven* (1945); *Les Maîtres de chant des XVIIe et XVIIIe siècles à la collégiale des SS. Michel et Gudale, à Bruxelles* (1950); *François-Joseph Fétis, musicologue et compositeur* (1951); *La Musique belge contemporaine* (1959); *La Musique flamande dans la société des XVe et XVIe siècles* (1965; Eng. tr., 1965); *La Musique en Wallonie et à Bruxelles* (2 vols., 1980–82).

BIBL.: H. Vanhulst and M. Haine, eds., *Musique et Société: Hommages à R. W.* (Brussels, 1988).

Ward, David, esteemed Scottish bass; b. Dumbarton, July 3, 1922; d. Dunedin, New Zealand, July 16, 1983. He was a student of Clive Carey at the Royal College of Music in London and of Hans Hotter in Munich. In 1952 he joined the chorus of the Sadler's Wells Opera in London, where he made his operatic debut as the Old Bard in Boughton's *The Immortal Hour* in 1953. He continued to sing there until 1958. In 1960 he made his debut at London's Covent Garden as Pogner, and returned there as Arkel and Rocco. He also created the role of Morosus in the first British staging of Strauss' *Die Schweigsame Frau* there in 1961. In 1960 he appeared as Titurel at the Bayreuth Festival, where he sang again in 1961 and 1962. In 1964 he sang Wotan at Covent Garden and in 1967 at the Teatro Colón in Buenos Aires. On Jan. 3, 1964, he made his Metropolitan Opera debut in N.Y. as Sarastro, where he remained on the roster until 1966; he was again on its roster from 1973 to 1975 and from 1978 to 1980. Ward also pursued a highly distinguished concert career. In 1972 he was made a Commander of the Order of the British Empire. Among his other roles were Hunding, Fasolt, King Marke, Philip II, and Boris Godunov.

Ward, John M(ilton), American musicologist; b. Oakland, Calif., July 6, 1917. He studied at San Francisco State College (B.A., 1941), the Univ. of Wash. (M.M., 1942), with Milhaud (composition, 1943–44), and at N.Y. Univ. (Ph.D., 1953, with the diss. *The Vihuela de Mano and Its Music (1536–1576)*. He taught at Michigan State Univ. (1947–53), the Univ. of Ill. (1953–55), and at Harvard Univ. (1955–85). He ed. *The Dublin Virginal Manuscript, Wellesley Edition*, III (1954; 2nd ed., rev. and aug., 1964; new ed., 1983) and *Music for Elizabethan Lutes* (2 vols., Oxford, 1992); also contributed numerous essays and specialized articles to various scholarly music magazines.

BIBL.: A. Shapiro, ed., *Music and Context: Essays for J.M. W.* (1985).

Ward, Robert (Eugene), American composer and teacher; b. Cleveland, Sept. 13, 1917. He studied with Rogers, Royce, and Hanson at the Eastman School of Music in Rochester, N.Y. (B.Mus., 1939) and with Jacobi at the Juilliard Graduate School in N.Y. (certificate, 1946); also studied conducting with Stoessel and Schenkman and received some training in composition from Copland. He taught at Columbia Univ. (1946–48) and at the Juilliard School of Music (1946–56); also was music director of the 3rd Street Music Settlement (1952–55); then was vice-president and managing ed. of the Galaxy Music Corp. (1956–67). After serving as president of the North Carolina School of the Arts in Winston-Salem (1967–74), where he continued as a teacher of composition until 1979, he held the chair of Mary Duke Biddle Prof. of Music at Duke Univ. (1979–87). In 1950, 1952, and 1966 he held Guggenheim fellowships; in 1962 he won the Pulitzer Prize in Music and the N.Y. Music Critics' Circle Award for his opera *The Crucible*. In 1972 he was elected a member of the National Inst. of Arts and Letters. He evolved an effective idiom, modern but not aggressively so; composed a number of dramatic and compact stage works on American subjects.

WORKS: DRAMATIC: OPERAS: *He Who Gets Slapped* (1955; N.Y., May 17, 1956; rev. 1973); *The Crucible* (N.Y., Oct. 26, 1961); *The Lady from Colorado* (Central City, Colo., July 3, 1961; rev. as *Lady Kate*, 1981; Wooster, Ohio, June 8, 1994); *Claudia Legare* (1973; Minneapolis, April 14, 1978); *Minutes till Midnight* (1978–82; Miami, June 4, 1982); *Abelard and Heloise* (1981); *Roman Fever* (1993). **BALLET:** *The Scarlet Letter* (1990). **ORCH.:** *Slow Music* (1938); *Ode* (1939); 6 syms.: No. 1 (N.Y., May 10, 1941), No. 2 (1947; Washington, D.C., Jan. 25, 1948), No. 3 (Washington, D.C., March 31, 1950), No. 4 (1958), No. 5,

Canticles of America, for Soprano, Baritone, Narrator, Chorus, and Orch., after Whitman and Longfellow (1976), and No. 6 (1989); *Jubilation Overture* (Los Angeles, Nov. 21, 1946); *Concert Piece* (1947–48); *Concert Music* (1948); *Night Music* for Small Orch. (1949); *Fantasia* for Brass Choir and Timpani (1953); *Euphony* (1954); *Divertimento* (1960); *Night Fantasy* for Band (1962); *Invocation and Toccata* (1963); *Antiphony* for Winds for Woodwinds and Percussion (1968); Piano Concerto (1968); *Sonic Structure* (1981); *Dialogues* for Violin, Cello, and Orch. (1983; arr. for Piano Trio, 1984); Tenor Saxophone Concerto (1984; rev. 1987); *Byways of Memories* (1991). **CHAMBER:** 2 violin sonatas (1950, 1990); String Quartet (1966); *Raleigh Divertimento* for Wind Quintet (1986); *Appalachian Ditties and Dances* for Violin and Piano (1989); piano pieces. **VOCAL:** *Fatal Interview* for Soprano and Orch. (1937); *Jonathan and the Gingery Snare* for Narrator, Small Orch., and Percussion (N.Y., Feb. 4, 1950); *Sacred Songs for Pantheists* for Soprano and Orch. (1951); *Earth Shall Be Fair*, cantata for Soprano, Chorus, Children's Chorus, Organ, and Orch. (1960); *Let the Word Go Forth* for Chorus and Instruments (1965); *Sweet Freedom Songs*, cantata for Bass, Narrator, Chorus, and Orch. (1965); *Images of God* for Chorus (1989); songs.

BIBL.: K. Kreitner, *R. W.: A Bio-Bibliography* (Westport, Conn., 1988).

Ward-Steinman, David, American composer, teacher, and pianist; b. Alexandria, La., Nov. 6, 1936. He studied at Florida State Univ. (B.Mus., 1957); also received training from Riegger (1954), Milhaud at the Aspen (Colo.) Music School (1956), and Babbitt and Copland at the Berkshire Music Center, Tanglewood (summer, 1957); after further studies at the Univ. of Ill. (M.M., 1958), he pursued private training with Boulanger in Paris (1958–59); then returned to the Univ. of Ill. to complete his education (D.M.A., 1961). In 1961 he became a faculty member and composer-in-residence at San Diego State Univ., where he served as prof. of music (from 1968); also was the Ford Foundation composer-in-residence of the Tampa Bay area in Florida (1970–72) and the Fulbright Senior Scholar at Victorian College of the Arts and La Trobe Univ. in Melbourne, Australia (1989–90). In 1995 he was a participant at the Académie d'été at IRCAM in Paris. With S. Ward-Steinman, he publ. *Comparative Anthology of Musical Forms* (2 vols., Belmont, Calif., 1976); also publ. *Toward a Comparative Structural Theory of the Arts* (San Diego, 1989).

WORKS: DRAMATIC: *Western Orpheus*, ballet (1964; San Diego, Feb. 26, 1965; rev. version, El Cajon, Calif., April 17, 1987); *These Three*, ballet (N.Y., Sept. 13, 1966); *Tamar*, music drama (1970–77); *Rituals* for Dancers and Musicians (Channel 13 TV, Tampa, Dec. 5, 1971). **ORCH.:** Concert Overture (1957; Urbana, Ill., May 6, 1958); Sym. (1959; San Diego, Dec. 4, 1962); Concerto Grosso for Combo and Chamber Orch. (1960; N.Y., Nov. 8, 1964); Concerto No. 2 for Chamber Orch. (1960–62; La Jolla, Calif., March 3, 1963); *Prélude and Toccata* (1962; Albuquerque, March 21, 1963); Cello Concerto (1963–65; Tokyo, June 13, 1967); *Antares* for Orch., Synthesizer or Tape, and Gospel Choir ad libitum (Tampa, April 22, 1971); *Arcturus* for Orch. and Synthesizer (Chicago, June 15, 1972); *Season's Greetings* (1981; San Diego, Dec. 15, 1983); *Olympics Overture* (San Diego, June 10, 1984); *Chroma*, concerto for Multiple Keyboards, Percussion, and Chamber Orch. (Scottsdale, Ariz., May 7, 1985); *Elegy for Astronauts* (San Diego, Dec. 7, 1986); *Winging It* for Chamber Orch. (Las Cruces, N.M., Nov. 22, 1986); *Cinnabar Concerto* for Viola and Chamber Orch. (1991–93; Tijuana, Mexico, April 2, 1993); Double Concerto for 2 Violins and Orch. (1994–95). **BAND OR WIND ENSEMBLE:** *Jazz Tangents* (Grand Forks, N.D., April 23, 1967); *Gasparilla Day* (1970); *Rāga* (Atlanta, March 10, 1972); *Scorpio* (Tucson, April 10, 1976); *Bishop's Gambit* (1979; Alexandria, Va., March 22, 1980); *Quintessence* (1985; Anaheim, April 11, 1986). **CHAMBER:** *3 Songs* for Clarinet and Piano (1957); *Quiet Dance* for Flute, Clarinet, Guitar, and Cello (1958); 2 brass quintets: No. 1 (1958–59; Urbana, Ill., April 5, 1960) and No. 2, *Brancusi's Brass Beds* (1976; Bowling Green, Ky., Jan. 22, 1978); Duo for Cello and Piano (1964–65; San Diego, April 16, 1970); *Child's Play* for Bassoon and Piano (1968); 2 woodwind quintets: No. 1, *Montage* (San Diego, June 6, 1968) and No. 2, *Night Winds* (San Diego, Nov. 4, 1993); *Putney 3* for Woodwind Quintet, Prepared Piano, and Putney Synthesizer or Tape (1970; Tampa, Nov. 9, 1971); *The Tracker* for Clarinet, Fortified Piano, and Tape (Fullerton, Calif., Nov. 13, 1976); *Toccata* for Synthesizer and Slide Projectors (Tempe, Ariz., Nov. 2, 1978); *Golden Apples* for Alto Saxophone and Piano (San Diego, Dec. 4, 1981); *Epithalamion* for Flute and Cello (1981); *Intersections I* for Fortified Piano and Tape (1982) and *II: Borobudur* for Fortified Piano and Percussion (1989; Canberra, March 5, 1990); *Moiré* for Piano and Chamber Ensemble (1983; Redlands, Calif., April 27, 1984); *Summer Suite* for Oboe and Piano (1987); *Étude on the Name of Barney Childs* for Clarinet (1990); *Cinnabar* for Viola and Piano (Ithaca, N.Y., June 15, 1991). **PIANO:** Sonata (1956–57); *Improvisations on a Theme of Darius Milhaud* (1960); *3 Lyric Preludes* (1961–65); *Latter-Day Lullabies* (1961–66); *3 Miniatures* (1964); *Improvisations on Children's Songs* (1966); *Elegy for Martin Luther King* (San Diego, April 7, 1968); Sonata for Fortified Piano (Tampa, June 23, 1972); *What's Left* for Piano, Left-Hand (1987); *Under Capricorn* (1989). **VOCAL:** *Psalms of Rejoicing* for Chorus (1960); *Fragments from Sappho* for Soprano, Flute, Clarinet, and Piano (1962–65; La Jolla, Calif., April 29, 1966); *The Song of Moses* for Narrator, Soloists, Double Chorus, and Orch. (1963–64; San Diego, May 31, 1964); *The Tale of Issoumbochi* for Narrator, Soprano, Flute, Clarinet, Percussion, Piano, and Cello (San Diego, April 18, 1968); *Grant Park* for Baritone and Chamber Ensemble (1969; Cedar Falls, Iowa, March 16, 1970); *Season* for Soprano and Fortified Piano (1970); *God's Rock* for Soprano, Chorus, Piano or Organ, and Optional Double Bass and Percussion (1973); *And in These Times*, Christmas cantata for Narrator, Soloists, Chorus, Cello, and Ensemble (1979–81; San Diego, Dec. 12, 1982); *Of Wind and Water* for Chorus, Piano, and 2 Percussion (Bloomington, Ill., March 4, 1982); *. . . And Waken Green*, 7 poems for Medium Voice or Voices and Piano (1983); *Children's Corner Revisited*, 4 songs for Medium Voice and Piano (1985); *Voices from the Gallery* for Soprano, Tenor, Baritone, and Piano (1990; San Diego, Feb. 13, 1994); *Seasons Fantastic* for Chorus and Harp (1991–92; San Diego, June 25, 1992).

Ware, Harriet, American pianist and composer; b. Waupun, Wis., Aug. 26, 1877; d. N.Y., Feb. 9, 1962. She received her musical instruction from her father, a choral conductor; then studied piano with William Mason in N.Y. and Sigismund Stojowski in Paris, and composition with Hugo Kaun in Berlin. Her *Women's Triumphal March* was made the national song of the Federation of Women's Clubs in 1927; her symphonic poem *The Artisan* was given by the N.Y. Sym. Orch. in 1929. Some of her songs (*Boat Song, Joy of the Morning, The Call of Radha, Stars*, and *Sunlight Waltz Song*) achieved considerable popularity. She also wrote the choral cycles *Trees* and *Undine;* an operetta, *Waltz for 3*; piano pieces.

Warfield, Sandra, American mezzo-soprano; b. Kansas City, Mo., Aug. 6, 1929. After training at the Kansas City Cons., she began her career singing in operettas. She then pursued her studies in N.Y. with Fritz Lehmann. In 1953 she won the Metropolitan Opera Auditions of the Air and made her debut with the company in N.Y. as a peasant girl in *Le nozze di Figaro* on Nov. 20, 1953. By 1955 she was singing major roles there, most notably Ulrica. When her husband, **James McCracken**, left the Metropolitan Opera in 1957, Warfield did likewise and made her debut at the Vienna State Opera as Ulrica. In 1961 she created the role of Katerina in Martinů's *Greek Passion* at the Zürich Opera. She sang Dalila at the San Francisco Opera in 1963. She was again on the roster of the Metropolitan Opera in 1965–66, 1967–68, and 1971–72. As a guest artist, she sang with various American and European opera houses. She also toured extensively as a concert artist, frequently appearing with her husband. Warfield was especially admired for her dramatic vocal gifts. Among her best roles were Dalila, Amneris, Carmen, Ulrica,

Marcellina, and Fricka. With her husband, she publ. the autobiographical vol. *A Star in the Family* (N.Y., 1971).

Warfield, William (Caesar), black American baritone and teacher; b. West Helena, Ark., Jan. 22, 1920. He studied at the Eastman School of Music in Rochester, N.Y. (B.Mus., 1942). Following service in the U.S. Army, he returned to Eastman in 1946 to pursue graduate training. After further studies with Otto Herz and Yves Tinayre, he completed his training with Rosa Ponselle (1958–65). From 1947 he appeared in N.Y. theaters. On March 19, 1950, he made his recital debut at N.Y.'s Town Hall. After a concert tour of Australia in 1950, he sang Joe in *Showboat* in N.Y. in 1951. In 1952–53 he toured Europe as Porgy in *Porgy and Bess.* He continued to sing in musicals and operas in the U.S. and abroad, and also made concert tours of Africa and the Middle East (1956), Europe (with the Philadelphia Orch., 1956), and Asia (1958). In 1974 he became a teacher at the Univ. of Ill. In 1984 he was elected president of the National Assn. of Negro Musicians. He married **Leontyne Price** in 1952, but they were divorced in 1974. With A. Miller, he publ. *William Warfield: My Music & My Life* (Champaign, Ill., 1991).

Waring, Fred(eric Malcolm), famous American conductor of popular music and inventor of sundry kitchen appliances; b. Tyrone, Pa., June 9, 1900; d. Danville, Pa., July 29, 1984. He learned music at his mother's knee, and a sense of moral rectitude was inculcated in him by his father, a banker who gave speeches at spiritual revivals and temperance meetings. He took up the banjo at 16, and organized a quartet that he called The Banjazzatra. He studied engineering and architecture at Pa. State Univ.; he retained his love for gadgets throughout his musical career, and in 1937 patented the Waring Blender, for whipping food or drinks to a foam; another invention was a traveling iron. He acquired fame with his own band, the Pennsylvanians, which played on national tours at concert halls, hotels, and college campuses; the group was particularly successful on radio programs sponsored by tobacco companies and the Ford Motor Co. His repertoire consisted of wholesome American songs, many composed by himself. Among his soloists on special programs were Bing Crosby, Hoagy Carmichael, Irving Berlin, and Frank Sinatra. Waring had a natural streak for publicity; he once bet that he could lead a bull into a Fifth Avenue china shop, and succeeded, without breaking a single piece of crockery. He was a friend of President Dwight Eisenhower. In 1983 President Ronald Reagan awarded him the Congressional Gold Medal. He continued to lead youth choral groups, giving a concert at Pa. State Univ. a day before he suffered a stroke, and 2 days before his death.

Warland, Dale, eminent American conductor and composer; b. Fort Dodge, Iowa, April 14, 1932. He was educated at St. Olaf College (B.A., 1954), the Univ. of Minnesota (M.A. in theory and composition, 1960), and the Univ. of Southern Calif. in Los Angeles (D.M.A. in choral conducting, 1965). After serving as director of choral music at Humboldt State College in Arcata, California, and at Keuka College in Keuka Park, N.Y., he was prof. of music and director of choral activities at Macalester College in St. Paul, Minn. (1967–85). In 1972 he established the Dale Warland Singers, a professional mixed chorus, which he led with notable distinction. While his expansive repertoire ranges from the 16th century to the present era, his primary emphasis has been on music of the 20th century, including the commissioning of new works.

Warlich, Reinhold von, German baritone; b. St. Petersburg, May 24, 1877; d. N.Y., Nov. 10, 1939. His father was an opera conductor active in St. Petersburg; studied at the Hamburg Cons., in Florence, and in Cologne. He toured in Europe as a singer of German lieder, and was especially distinguished as an interpreter of Schubert, whose song cycles he gave in their entirety. He lived for some time in Canada; later was a singing teacher in Paris and London; made concert tours in the U.S. from 1909, eventually settling in N.Y.

Warlock, Peter. See **Heseltine, Philip (Arnold).**

Warner, Harry Waldo, English violist and composer; b. Northampton, Jan. 4, 1874; d. London, June 1, 1945. He studied violin with Alfred Gibson and theory with R. Orlando Morgan at the Guildhall School of Music in London. He was engaged as violist in the London String Quartet (1907–28). In 1921 he received the Elizabeth Sprague Coolidge prize for a piano trio, and a Cobbett prize for another piano trio. He also wrote several other attractive pieces for string quartet; one of them, arr. for string orch., was performed in London on Sept. 22, 1928, under the title *Suite in the Olden Style.*

Warrack, Guy (Douglas Hamilton), Scottish conductor and composer, father of **John (Hamilton) Warrack**; b. Edinburgh, Feb. 8, 1900; d. Englefield Green, Feb. 12, 1986. He studied at the Univ. of Oxford and received training in conducting from Boult and in composition from Vaughan Williams at the Royal College of Music in London, where he subsequently taught (1925–35); in 1925 he made his conducting debut in London. After conducting the BBC Scottish Orch. in Glasgow (1936–45), he returned to London to serve as music director of the Sadler's Wells Royal Ballet (1948–51). He publ. the book *Sherlock Holmes and Music* (1947) and wrote articles for many journals. Among his compositions are a Sym. and a number of documentary film scores, including the official coronation film for Queen Elizabeth II, *A Queen Is Crowned* (1953).

Warrack, John (Hamilton), English writer on music, son of **Guy (Douglas Hamilton) Warrack**; b. London, Feb. 9, 1928. He studied at Winchester College; then took up oboe and composition at the Royal College of Music in London; subsequently played oboe in several ensembles. In 1953 he became music ed. of the Oxford Univ. Press; in 1954 he joined the staff of the *Daily Telegraph*, where he was a music critic; then was chief music critic of the *Sunday Telegraph* (1961–72). After serving as director of the Leeds Festival (1977–83), he was a lecturer in music and a fellow at St. Hughes College, Oxford (1984–93). He contributed numerous articles and reviews to *Opera* and *Gramophone.* His biography of Weber is the standard modern source.

WRITINGS: *Six Great Composers* (London, 1958); co-ed. with H. Rosenthal, *The Concise Oxford Dictionary of Opera* (London, 1964; 2nd ed., rev., 1979); *Carl Maria von Weber* (London, 1968; also in Ger., 1972; 2nd ed., rev., London, 1976); *Tchaikovsky Symphonies and Concertos* (London, 1969; 2nd ed., rev., 1974); *Tchaikovsky* (London, 1973); *Tchaikovsky Ballet Music* (London, 1978); ed. *Carl Maria von Weber: Writings on Music* (Cambridge, 1982); co.-ed. with E. West, *The Oxford Dictionary of Opera* (Oxford, 1992).

Warren, Elinor Remick, American pianist and composer; b. Los Angeles, Feb. 23, 1900; d. there, April 27, 1991. She studied piano as a small child with Kathryn Cocke, taking up composition studies at 14; her first works were publ. while she was still in high school. After attending Mills College in Oakland, California, she studied with Olga Steeb, Paolo Gallico, Frank La Forge, and Clarence Dickinson in N.Y.; much later received training from Boulanger in Paris (1959). She was mainly active as a piano accompanist to such singers as Bori and Tibbett.

WORKS: ORCH.: *The Fountain* (1942); Suite (1955; rev. 1958); *The Crystal Lake* (1958); *Along the Western Shore: Dark Hills, Nocturne, Sea Rhapsody* (1963); *Intermezzo* (1970); Sym. in 1 Movement (1971). **CHAMBER:** Woodwind Quintet; various piano pieces. **VOCAL:** Sacred and secular choral pieces; numerous songs.

BIBL.: V. Bortin, *E.R. W.: Her Life and her Music* (Metuchen, N.J., 1987); idem, *E.R. W.: A Bio-Bibliography* (Westport, Conn., 1993).

Warren, Leonard, outstanding American baritone; b. N.Y., April 21, 1911; d. there, March 4, 1960, on the stage of the Metropolitan Opera House while singing the role of Don Carlo during a performance of *La forza del destino.* The original family name was Warenoff; it was Americanized as Warren when his Russian father settled in the U.S. He was first employed in his father's fur business in N.Y.; in 1935 he joined the chorus of Radio City Music Hall; he also studied voice with Sidney Dietch and Giuseppe De Luca. In 1938 he won the Metropolitan Opera Auditions of the Air and was granted a stipend to study in Italy, where he took voice lessons with Pais and Piccozi. Returning to America, he made his debut at the Metropolitan Opera in excerpts from *La Traviata* and *Pagliacci* during a concert in N.Y. on Nov. 27, 1938; his formal operatic debut took place there on Jan. 13, 1939, when he sang Paolo in *Simon Boccanegra.* He quickly advanced in public favor, eventually assuming a leading place among the noted baritones of his time. He also sang in San Francisco, Chicago, Canada, and South America. He appeared at La Scala in Milan in 1953; in 1958 he made a highly successful tour of the Soviet Union. His last complete performance at the Metropolitan Opera was as Simon Boccanegra on March 1, 1960, 3 days before his tragic death. He was particularly acclaimed as one of the foremost interpreters of the great Verdi baritone roles; he also sang the parts of Tonio in *Pagliacci*, Escamillo in *Carmen*, and Scarpia in *Tosca.* He collapsed while singing the aria "Urna fatale dal mio destino," underlining the tragic irony of the words, and died of a cerebral hemorrhage backstage. He was reputed to be a person of an intractable character, who always tried to impose his will on stage designers, managers, and even conductors, in matters of production, direction, and tempi. He caused pain, a colleague said, but he had a great voice.

Warren, Raymond (Henry Charles), English composer and teacher; b. Weston-super-Mare, Dec. 7, 1928. He studied with Robin Orr at Corpus Christi College, Cambridge (1949–52; M.A., 1952), continuing his education at the Univ. of Cambridge (M.A., 1955; Mus.D., 1967); he also was a student of Tippett (1952–54) and Berkeley (1958). In 1955 he became a teacher at Queen's Univ. in Belfast, where he was a prof. from 1966 to 1972. From 1972 he was a prof. at the Univ. of Bristol. He publ. *Opera Workshops: Studies in Understanding and Interpretation* (Brookfield, 1995).

WORKS: DRAMATIC: *The Lady of Ephesus*, chamber opera (1958; Belfast, Feb. 16, 1959); *Finn and the Black Hag*, children's opera (Belfast, Dec. 11, 1959); *Graduation Ode*, comic opera (Belfast, Nov. 20, 1963); 3 children's church operas: *Let My People Go* (Liverpool, March 22, 1972), *St. Patrick* (Liverpool, May 3, 1979), and *In the Beginning* (Clifton, July 22, 1982); incidental music for plays. **ORCH.:** *Nocturne* (1964); 3 syms. (1965, 1969, 1996); Violin Concerto (1966); *Seaside Sketches* (1968); *Wexford Bells* (1970). **CHAMBER:** 3 string quartets (1965, 1975, 1977); Duo Concertante for Cello and Piano (1972); *Burnt Norton Sketches* for Piano Trio (1985); *Exchanges* for Oboe and Piano (1986); Violin Sonata (1993). **PIANO:** 2 sonatas (1952, 1977). **VOCAL:** 2 oratorios: *The Passion* (Belfast, Dec. 11, 1959) and *Continuing Cities* (Bristol, April 22, 1989); choral pieces; song cycles; solo songs.

Washburn, Robert, American composer and music educator; b. Bouckville, N.Y., July 11, 1928. He received training in music education at the Crane School of Music at the State Univ. of N.Y. at Potsdam (B.S., 1949; M.S., 1955) and in composition at the Eastman School of Music in Rochester, N.Y. (Ph.D., 1960), with Milhaud at the Aspen (Colo.) Music School (summer, 1963), and with Boulanger in Paris (1964). From 1954 to 1985 he taught at the Crane School of Music, where he also was its dean (1982–85). Thereafter he held the titles of dean emeritus and senior fellow in music. He made tours throughout North America and overseas as a guest composer-conductor. His articles on music education appeared in various journals. Among his honors were a Ford Foundation fellowship (1959–60), a MacDowell Colony fellowship (1963), an NEA grant (1981), a Fulbright fellowship (1986), and Meet the Composer grants (1991, 1993). Washburn has been especially effective in composing works for college and high school groups. He favors a tonal mode of expression along neo-Classical lines. He has also utilized non-Western elements in some of his scores.

WORKS: ORCH.: 3 Pieces (1959); Suite for Strings (1959); Sym. No. 1 (1959; 1st movement publ. as *Festive Overture*); *Synthesis* (1959); *St. Lawrence Overture* (1962); *Passacaglia and Fugue* for Strings (1963); *Sinfonietta* for Strings (1963); *Serenade* for Strings (1966); *Song and Dance* for Strings (1967); *North Country Sketch* (1969); *Prologue and Dance* (1970); *Excursion* (1970); *Elegy* (1974); *Mid-America*, overture (1976); *5 Adirondack Sketches* for Small Orch. (1989); *Saraswati Suite* for Strings and Tabla (1990); *New England Holiday* (1992); *Queen Noor Suite* for Strings (1992); *Scottish Fantasy* (1993); *Knightsbridge Suite* for Strings (1993); *Caravelle Overture* (1994); *It's the Pizz.!* for Strings (1994). **BAND:** *March and Chorale* (1955); *Ode* (1955); *Burlesk* (1956); *Pageantry* (1962); Sym. (1963); *Partita* (1964); Suite (1967); *Ceremonial Music* (1968); *Intrada, Chorale, and Toccata* (1970); *Prelude and Paragrams* (1972); *Epigon IV* (1974); *Trigon* (1975); *3 Diversions* (1978); *Impressions of Cairo* (1978); *Olympic March* (1979); *Kilimanjaro* (1981); *Equinox* (1983); *Pageant Royale* (1988); *Tower Bridge* (1992); *Temple on the Nile* (1992); *Hoosier Holiday* (1994); *Tidewater Festival Overture* (1994); *Far East Fantasy* (1995); *Song of Krishna* (1995). **CHAMBER:** Suite for Wind Quintet (1960); String Quartet (1963); Concertino for Brass and Wind Quintets (1964); Woodwind Quintet (1967); Brass Quintet (1970); *Prayer and Alleluia* for Organ, 2 Trumpets, Trombone, and Timpani (1972); *Pent-agons* for Percussion (1973); *Festive Fanfare* for Brass and Percussion (1975); *French Suite* for Oboe, Clarinet, and Bassoon (1980); Trio for Piano and Strings (1984); *Hornography* for Horn Quartet (1990). **VOCAL:** *3 Shakespearean Love Songs* for Men's Chorus, Piano, and Optional Horn (1963); *Spring Cantata* for Chorus (1973); *We Hold These Truths* for Narrator, Chorus, and Band or Orch. (1974); *3 Thoughts from Thoreau* for Voices and Piano (1976).

Wasitodiningrat, K.R.T. (Kanjeng Raden Tumengung, a title of honorary royal status), important Indonesian composer and performer; b. Yogyakarta, Java, March 17, 1909. (His former names are Wasitolodoro, Tjokrowasito, and Wasitodipuro; he is frequently known as Ki Wasitodiningrat, Ki being an honorific for artistic achievement.) He was born in the Pakualaman Palace, one of 3 principal courts of central Java, where his father was director of musical activities. Wasitodiningrat studied dance from the age of 6, graduating from the SMA National High School in 1922. He became music director of the Yogyakarta radio station MAVRO in 1934, and remained there through the Japanese occupation, when the station was called Jogja Hosokjoku. In 1945 the station became RRI (Radio Republic Indonesia); he served as director there again in 1951. Between 1951 and 1970 he taught dance at the Konservatori Tari and the Academy Tari, both in Yogyakarta, and music at the Academy Karawitan in Surakarta; he also founded and directed the Wasitodipuro Center for Vocal Studies in Yogyakarta. In 1953 he toured Asia, North America, and Europe. In 1961 he became associated with the new dance/theater form *sendratari*, later becoming music director for P.L.T. Bagong Kussudiardjo's troupe. He succeeded his father as director of the Pakualaman gamelan in 1962. In 1971 he joined the faculty of the Calif. Inst. of the Arts as master of Javanese gamelan; taught workshops at both the Los Angeles and Berkeley campuses of the Univ. of Calif. Wasitodiningrat is a leading performer and composer of central Javanese music; the Pakualaman gamelan's recordings are considered exemplary; one is included in the 40 minutes of music installed in the spacecraft *Voyager*, intended to represent our planet's music to outsiders. His numerous awards include a gold medal from the Indonesian government honoring his devotion to Javanese music. He frequently performs with his daughter, Nanik, and her Balinese husband, **Nyoman Wenten**.

Watanabe, Akeo, Japanese conductor; b. Tokyo, June 5, 1919; d. there, June 22, 1990. He studied piano and violin as a youth; received training in conducting from Joseph Rosenstock at the Tokyo Academy of Music and from Jean Morel at the Juilliard School of Music in N.Y. In 1945 he made his conducting debut with the Tokyo Sym. Orch. He was conductor of the Tokyo Phil. (1948–54); served as founder-conductor of the Japan Phil. in Tokyo (1956–68); was conductor of the Tokyo Metropolitan Sym. Orch. (1972–78); also appeared as guest conductor in the U.S. and Europe. He served again as conductor of the Japan Phil. (1978–83), then was music director of the Hiroshima Sym. Orch. (from 1988).

Waters, Edward N(eighbor), American musicologist; b. Leavenworth, Kansas, July 23, 1906; d. Mitchellville, Md., July 27, 1991. He studied piano and theory at the Eastman School of Music in Rochester, N.Y. (B.M., 1927; M.M. in musicology, 1928). In 1931 he joined the staff of the Music Division of the Library of Congress in Washington, D.C.; from 1972 to 1976 he served as chief of the Music Division. He was the program annotator of the National Sym. Orch. in Washington, D.C. (1934–43) and president of the Music Library Assn. (1941–46), later serving as ed. of the latter's journal *Notes* (1963–66); also wrote many articles and book reviews for professional journals. The Cleveland Inst. of Music conferred upon him the honorary degree of D.Mus. (1973). He wrote a definitive biography of Victor Herbert (N.Y., 1955).

Watkinson, Carolyn, English mezzo-soprano; b. Preston, March 19, 1949. She received her training at the Royal Manchester College of Music and in The Hague. She first established herself as a fine concert singer, especially excelling in Baroque music. In 1978 she sang Rameau's Phèdre at the English Bach Festival at London's Covent Garden. In 1979 she appeared as Monteverdi's Nero with the Netherlands Opera in Amsterdam. In 1981 she made her debut at Milan's La Scala as Ariodante and sang Rossini's Rosina in Stuttgart. She appeared as Gluck's Orfeo with the Glyndebourne Touring Opera in 1982, and then made her formal debut at the Glyndebourne Opera as Cherubino in 1984. In 1987 she made a tour of Australia. She was a soloist in Bach's *St. John Passion* at Gloucester Cathedral in a performance shown on BBC-TV on Good Friday in 1989. In 1990 she appeared as Purcell's Dido at the Salerno Cathedral and sang Nero at the Innsbruck Festival. She also continued to sing regularly as a concert artist in a repertoire ranging from early music to the contemporary period.

Watson (real name, **McLamore**), **Claire,** American soprano; b. N.Y., Feb. 3, 1924; d. Utting, Germany, July 16, 1986. She studied voice in N.Y. with Elisabeth Schumann and Sergius Kagen; received further training in Vienna. She made her operatic debut as Desdemona in Graz in 1951; was a member of the Frankfurt am Main Opera (1956–58) and the Bavarian State Opera in Munich from 1958 until her farewell as the Marschallin in 1976. As a guest artist, she appeared at London's Covent Garden (1958–63; 1964; 1970; 1972), the Glyndebourne Festival (1959), and the Salzburg Festival (1966–68). She also sang in Vienna, Milan, Rome, Chicago, Buenos Aires, and San Francisco. Among her other roles were Donna Elvira, Elisabeth de Valois, Eva, Sieglinde, Ariadne, and Tatiana.

Watts, André, brilliant American pianist; b. Nuremberg, June 20, 1946. He was born in a U.S. Army camp to a black American soldier and a Hungarian woman. His mother gave him his earliest piano lessons. After the family moved to the U.S., he studied with Genia Robiner, Doris Bawden, and Clement Petrillo at the Philadelphia Musical Academy. At the age of 9, he made his first public appearance playing the Haydn Concerto in D major at a children's concert of the Philadelphia Orch. His parents were divorced in 1962, but his mother continued to guide his studies. At 14, he played César Franck's *Symphonic Variations* with the Philadelphia Orch.; at 16, he became an instant celebrity when he played Liszt's 1st Piano Concerto at one of the televised Young People's Concerts with the N.Y. Phil., conducted by Leonard Bernstein, on Jan. 15, 1963. His youth and the fact that he was partly black contributed to his success, but it was the grand and poetic manner of his virtuosity that conquered the usually skeptical press. Still, he insisted on completing his academic education. In 1969 he joined the class of Leon Fleisher at the Peabody Cons. of Music in Baltimore, obtaining his Artist's Diploma in 1972. In the meantime, he developed an international career. He made his European debut as soloist with the London Sym. Orch. on June 12, 1966; then played with the Concertgebouw Orch. in Amsterdam. On Oct. 26, 1966, he played his first solo recital in N.Y., inviting comparisons in the press with the great piano virtuosos of the past. In 1967 he was soloist with the Los Angeles Phil. under Zubin Mehta on a tour of Europe and Asia. On his 21st birthday he played the 2nd Piano Concerto of Brahms with the Berlin Phil. In 1970 he revisited his place of birth and played a solo recital with a success that was made all the more sensational because he was a native son, albeit not of the native race. He also became a favorite at important political occasions; he played at President Richard Nixon's inaugural concert at Constitution Hall in Washington, D.C., in 1969, at the coronation of the Shah of Iran, and at a festive celebration of the President of the Congo. In 1973 he toured Russia. On Nov. 28, 1976, he played a solo recital on live network television. He was also the subject of a film documentary. In 1973 he received an honorary doctorate from Yale Univ.; in 1975 he was given another honorary doctorate by Albright College. He celebrated the 25th anniversary of his debut with the N.Y. Phil. as soloist under Zubin Mehta in the Liszt 1st Concerto, the Beethoven 2nd Concerto, and the Rachmaninoff 2nd Concerto in a concert telecast live on PBS (Jan. 13, 1988). In 1988 he received the Avery Fisher Prize. In 1995 he marked the 40th anniversary of his debut.

Watts, Helen (Josephine), admired Welsh contralto; b. Milford Haven, Dec. 7, 1927. She was a student of Caroline Hatchard and Frederick Jackson at the Royal Academy of Music in London. She began her career singing in the Glyndebourne Festival Chorus and the BBC Chorus in London. Her first appearance as a soloist was in 1953. In 1955 she made her first appearance at the London Promenade Concerts singing Bach arias under Sargent's direction. Thereafter she distinguished herself as a concert artist, appearing in principal European and North American music centers. She also pursued an operatic career. In 1958 she made her operatic debut as Didymus in *Theodora* with the Handel Opera Soc. at the Camden Festival, and continued to appear with the Soc. until 1964. In 1964 she made her debut at the Salzburg Festival as the 1st Maid in *Elektra* and toured Russia with the English Opera Group as Britten's Lucretia. She made her first appearance at London's Covent Garden as the 1st Norn in *Götterdammerung* in 1965, and continued to sing there until 1971. In 1966 she made her U.S. debut in Delius' *A Mass of Life* in N.Y. She sang Mistress Quickly at her first appearance with the Welsh National Opera in Cardiff in 1969, where she was a leading member of the company until 1983. In 1978 she was made a Commander of the Order of the British Empire. While she had success in opera, she particularly excelled as a concert artist. Her concert repertoire extended from Bach to the masters of the 20th century.

Watts, John (Everett), American composer and synthesizer player; b. Cleveland, Tenn., July 16, 1930; d. N.Y., July 1, 1982. He was educated at the Univ. of Tenn. (B.A., 1949), the Univ. of Colo. (M.M., 1953), the Univ. of Ill. (1955–56), Cornell Univ. (1958–60), and the Univ. of Calif. at Los Angeles (1961–62); among his mentors were David Van Vactor, Cecil Effinger, Burrill Phillips, Robert Palmer, and Roy Harris. He was founder-director of the Composers Theatre in N.Y. (1964–82), which presented a vast number of works by American composers; taught at the New School for Social Research in N.Y. (from 1967), where he was founder-director of its electronic music program (from 1969); made many appearances as a virtuoso on the ARP synthesizer.

WORKS: INSTRUMENTAL AND/OR VOCAL: Piano Sonata (1958; rev. 1960); *Signals* for Soprano and Orch. (1970); *Piano for Te* for Piano, 13 Players, and Tape (1973); *Laugharne* for Soprano, Tape, and Orch. (1974); *Mots d'heures: Gousses, Rames* for Voices and Tape (1974); *Piano for Te Tutti* for Piano and Tape (1975); *Maxi-concerto* (1976); *Canonades* for Strings

(1978); *Keepsakes* for Tape and Orch. (1978); *Le Match de Boxe* (1978); *Barbro Variations* for Piano, 4-Hands (1979); *Easy Songs for Lazy Singers* (1981). **ELECTRONIC:** *WARP* for Brass Quintet, Synthesizer, and Tape (1971); *Elegy to Chimney: in memoriam* for Trumpet, Synthesizer, and Tape (1972); *MAS* (1976); *Entectics* for Tape and Synthesizer (1978); *Processional* for Tape and 10 Trumpets (1978); *A Little Night Music* (1979); *Timespace* for Tape (1979); *Ach!* for Tape and Optional Synthesizer (1980). **DANCE SCORES:** *Study for Solo Figure/Film* (1968); *Perimeters* (1969); *Glass and Shadows* (1971); *Laura's Dance* (1971); *Margins* (1972); *Still Life* (1972); *Locrian* (1973); *Songandance* (1973); *BUD (1975)* (1975); *Heirlooms* (1977); *#SS* (1977); *UPS* (1977); *Entries* (1978); *GO* (1978); *Night Remembrance* (1979). **OTHER:** Film scores; conceptual art.

Watts, Wintter (Haynes), American composer; b. Cincinnati, March 14, 1884; d. N.Y., Nov. 1, 1962. He studied at the Inst. of Musical Art in N.Y. He received the American Prix de Rome, which enabled him to study at the American Academy in Rome (1923–25). He lived for some time in Europe, returning to N.Y. in 1931. Among his larger works are a *Bridal Overture* (1916) and an orch. suite, *Etchings* (1922), but he was chiefly known as a composer of fine songs.

Watzke, Rudolf, German bass and pedagogue; b. Niemes, April 5, 1892; d. Wuppertal, Dec. 18, 1972. He studied with Kreisel-Hauptfeld in Reichenberg, Kittel in Bayreuth, and Armin in Berlin. After singing at the Karlsruhe Opera (1923–24), the Bayreuth Festivals (1924, 1925, 1927), and the Berlin State Opera (1924–28), he devoted himself principally to a career as a concert artist. He was especially noted for his oratorio and lieder appearances. From 1956 to 1969 he taught at the Dortmund Cons.

Waxman (real name, **Wachsmann**), **Franz,** German-American composer and conductor; b. Königshütte, Dec. 24, 1906; d. Los Angeles, Feb. 24, 1967. He studied in Dresden and Berlin. He went to the U.S. in 1934 and settled in Hollywood, where he took lessons with Schoenberg. Waxman became a successful composer for films; his musical score for *Sunset Boulevard* won the Academy Award for 1950; also was active as a conductor; was founder-conducter of the Los Angeles Music Festival (1947–67). His other film scores included *Magnificent Obsession* (1935), *Captains Courageous* (1937), *The Philadelphia Story* (1940), *Sunset Boulevard* (1950), *Stalag 17* (1953), *Sayonara* (1957), and *Sunrise at Campobello* (1960); he also composed the orch. works *Athaneal the Trumpeter*, overture (1945), a Trumpet Concerto (1946), *Carmen Fantasy* for Violin and Orch., after Bizet (1947), *Sinfonietta* for Strings and Timpani (1955), *Goyana* for Piano and Strings (1960), and a Cello Concerto; also some vocal pieces, including *Joshua*, oratorio for Narrator, Solo Voices, Chorus, and Orch. (Dallas, May 23, 1959).

Wayditch, Gabriel (real name, **Baron Gabriel Wajditsch Verbovac von Dönhoff**), Hungarian-American composer; b. Budapest, Dec. 28, 1888; d. N.Y., July 28, 1969. He studied piano with Emil von Sauer and composition with Hans Koessler at the Budapest Academy of Music. In 1907 he emigrated to the U.S. He wrote 14 lengthy operas to his own libretti in Hungarian, dealing mostly with oriental or religious subjects; of these only one, *Horus*, was performed in his lifetime, at his own expense (Philadelphia, Jan. 5, 1939). His longest opera, *The Heretics*, takes 8 hours to perform; the shortest, *The Caliph's Magician*, in one act, takes 2 hours. The other operas are *Opium Dreams, Buddha, Jesus before Herod, Maria Magdalena, Maria Tesztver, Nereida, Sahara, The Catacombs, Anthony of Padua, The Venus Dwellers*, and *Neptune's Daughter*.

Weathers, Felicia, black American soprano; b. St. Louis, Aug. 13, 1937. She took vocal lessons at the Indiana Univ. School of Music in Bloomington with St. Leger, Kullman, and Manski. She made her operatic debut in Zürich in 1961. In 1963 she sang at the Hamburg State Opera and subsequently was a regular member there (1966–70). In 1965 she made her Metropolitan Opera debut in N.Y.; also sang at Covent Garden in London in 1970.

Weaver, James (Merle), American harpsichordist, pianist, fortepianist, and teacher; b. Champaign, Ill., Sept. 25, 1937. He was educated at the Univ. of Ill. (B.A., 1961; M.M., 1963), where he received instruction in harpsichord from George Hunter. He also was a student of Leonhardt at the Sweelinck Cons. in Amsterdam (1957–59). In 1967 he became curator of historic instruments at the Smithsonian Institution in Washington, D.C., where he co-founded the period instrument group the Smithsonian Chamber Players in 1976. He also pursued a solo career as a keyboard artist, taught at Cornell Univ. and the American Univ., and gave master classes in 18th-century performance practice.

Weaver, Powell, American pianist, organist, and composer; b. Clearfield, Pa., June 10, 1890; d. Oakland, Calif., Dec. 22, 1951. He studied organ with Dethier, piano with Caroline Beebe, and composition with Goetschius at the Inst. of Musical Art in N.Y. (1909–12); after further organ studies with Pietro Yon in N.Y., he went to Rome to study organ with Remigio Renzi and later received training in composition with Respighi (1924–25). He was active as an organist at Kansas City's Grand Ave. Temple (1912–37) and the First Baptist Church (1937–51); was engaged as accompanist to prominent singers; also gave organ recitals. From 1937 to 1945 he was head of the music dept. at Ottawa Univ. in Kansas City.

WORKS: COMIC OPERA PASTICHE: *As We Like It* (1922). **ORCH.:** *Plantation Overture* (1925); *The Little Faun* (1925; Boston, April 14, 1929); *The Vagabond*, symphonic poem (Minneapolis, March 6, 1931); *Dance of the Sand-Dune Cranes* for Piano and Orch. (1941). **CHAMBER:** Piano Quintet (1936); String Quartet (1937); Violin Sonata (1945); piano pieces; organ music. **OTHER:** Much vocal music.

BIBL.: M. Schwartz, *P. W.: His Life and Contributions to Organ Music in Kansas City* (diss., Univ. of Missouri, 1976).

Webb, Charles H(aizlip, Jr.), American pianist, organist, conductor, and music educator; b. Dallas, Feb. 14, 1933. He was educated at Southern Methodist Univ. (A.B. and M.Mus., 1955) and Indiana Univ. (D.Mus., 1964). He joined the faculty of Indiana Univ. as an instructor in piano (1958); became an assistant prof. of music in 1964 and an assoc. prof. in 1967. He was named assistant dean of the School of Music in 1964, assoc. dean in 1969, and dean in 1973; retired in 1997. He toured the U.S. with the pianist Wallace Hornibrook in duo-recitals; also toured as a concert organist; served as organist at the 1st Methodist Church in Bloomington, Ind. (from 1961) and as conductor of the Indianapolis Symphonic Choir (1967–81). In 1967 he was appointed commissioner of the Indiana Arts Commission. In 1983 he was named a member of the Indiana Academy.

Webber, Andrew Lloyd. See **Lloyd Webber, Andrew.**

Webber, Julian Lloyd. See **Lloyd Webber, Julian.**

Weber, Alain, French composer and teacher; b. Château-Thierry, Dec. 8, 1930. He studied at the Paris Cons. with Robert Dussault (theory), Jules Gentil (piano), Jean Gallon and Henri Challan (harmony), Tony Aubin (composition), and Olivier Messiaen (analysis). In 1952 he won the Premier Grand Prix de Rome and worked at the Villa Medici there. Upon returning to Paris, he taught at the Cons. He was the author of various pedagogical tomes. His opera *La Rivière Perdue* was awarded the Grand Prix Audiovisuel de l'Europe by the Académie du Disque Français in 1982. He also was made an Officier de l'Ordre National du Merite.

WORKS: DRAMATIC: OPERAS: *La Voie Unique* (1957); *La Rivière Perdue* (1981–82); *Le Rusé Petit Jean* (1984). **BALLETS:** *Le Petit Jeu* (1951); *Épitomé* (1972). **ORCH.:** *Suite Pour une Pièce Vue* (1954); Sym. (1954–55); *Scherzo Burlesque* (1957); *Croquis de Table* for Chamber Orch. (1957); Concerto for Horn and Strings (1958); *Exergues* for Strings (1959); Piano Concertino (1961); *Midjaay*, symphonic poem (1964); Trombone Concerto (1964); *Variantes* for 2 Percussion and Orch. (1964); *Variations* (1965); *Strophes* for Trumpet, Strings, and Percussion

(1966); *Commentaires Concertants* for Flute and Orch. (1967); *Gravitations* for Piano, Strings, and Percussion (1968); *Solipsisme* for String Quartet, String Orch., Piano, and Percussion (1968); *D'Après Wols* for Cello and Orch. (1969); *Cercles* for Violin and Orch. (1970); *Linéaire I* for Alto Saxophone and Orch. (1973); *Paraphrases Dialoguées* for Ondes Martenot and Orch. (1975); *Ricordarsi* for Strings (1975); *Cantus* for Harp or Celtic Harp and Strings (1976); *Traces* for 2 Violins and Strings (1978); *Haltia* (1980); *Lied* for Strings (1980); *Concert* for Winds (1983). **CHAMBER:** Wind Quintet (1955); Clarinet Sextet (1956); Sonata for Oboe and Harp or Piano (1961; also for Clarinet and Harp or Piano, 1992); *Sonate da tre* for Piano, Violin, and Cello (1968); Viola Sonata (1968); *Liminaire* for Wind Quintet (1973); *Epodes* for Saxophone, Oboe, Clarinet, and Bassoon (1974); *Projections* for 5 or More Percussionists (1974); *Linéaire II* for 8 Instruments (1977) and *III* for Ondes Martenot Sextet (1977); *Syllepse* for Piano, Percussion, and Ondes Martenot (1977); *Oracles* for 4 Trumpets, 3 Trombones, and Tuba (1978); *Huaco* for Flute, Viola, and Harp (1979); *Assonances* for Oboe, Alto Saxophone, and Cello (1980); *Improvisations Enchaînées* for Celtic or Grand Harp and Flute (1980); *Octuor* for 8 Instruments (1981); Saxophone Quartet (1984); *Alternances* for Piano and Violin (1988); *Anamorphoses* for Trombone and Harp Soloists and 3 Trombones (1991); *Versets* for Organ and Trombone Quartet (1992); *Neumes* for Organ and Trombone Quartet (1992); *Constellaire* for Mandolin, Guitar, and Celtic Harp (1994); *Et L'On Vit des Fées Débarquer sur la Plage* for Harp (1994); many pieces for solo instrument. **VOCAL:** Choral music; songs.

Weber, Ben (actually, **William Jennings Bryan**), American composer; b. St. Louis, July 23, 1916; d. N.Y., May 9, 1979. He received lessons in piano and singing but was autodidact in composition. He also studied medicine briefly at DePaul Univ. in Chicago. In 1945 he settled in N.Y., where he was active as a copyist. He was associated with the ISCM and the American Composers Alliance, becoming president of the latter in 1959. In 1950 and 1953 he held Guggenheim fellowships, in 1960 he received an award and citation from the National Inst. of Arts and Letters, and from 1965 to 1968 he held the 1st Phoebe Ketchum Thorne Music Fund Award. In 1971 he was elected to membership in the National Inst. of Arts and Letters. He left the memoir, *How I Took 63 Years to Commit Suicide* (1979; excerpts in the *Brooklyn Literary Review*, II, 1981). In 1938 Weber embraced 12-tone writing but he retained the firm tonal foundation of his melodic and contrapuntal structures. His chamber and vocal works were particularly notable.

WORKS: ORCH.: *Piece* for Oboe and Orch. (1943–44); 2 sinfonias: No. 1 for Cello and Orch. (1945–46; also for Cello and Piano) and No. 2, *Sinfonia Clarion*, for Small Orch. (1973; N.Y., Feb. 26, 1974); *Symphony on Poems of William Blake* for Baritone and Chamber Orch. (1950; N.Y., Oct. 28, 1952); *2 Pieces* for Strings (1950); Violin Concerto (1954); *Prelude and Passacaglia* (1954; Louisville, Jan. 1, 1955); *Rapsodie concertante* for Viola and Small Orch. (1957); Piano Concerto (N.Y., March 21, 1961); *Dolmen: An Elegy* for Winds and Strings (1964); *Dramatic Piece* for Violin and Orch. (1970). **CHAMBER:** *Intermezzo* for Clarinet and Piano (1935–36); *The Pool of Darkness* for Flute, Trumpet, Bassoon, Violin, Cello, and Piano (1939); 2 pieces for Clarinet and Piano (1939); *Pastorale* for Wind Quintet (1939); *Scherzino* for Wind Quintet (1939); 2 violin sonatas (1939; 1942, rev. 1943); *Fantasie* for Violin and Piano (1939–40); *Lyric Piece* for String Quartet (1940); *Variations* for Clarinet, Violin, Cello, and Piano (1941); 2 concertinos: No. 1 for Clarinet, Violin, and Cello (1941) and No. 2 for Flute, Oboe, Clarinet, and String Quartet (1956); *5 Pieces* for Cello and Piano (1941); *Divertimento* for 2 Cellos (1941); 3 string quartets (1941; 1951; 1959, unfinished); *Rhapsodie* for Cello and Wind Quintet (1942); *Ballade* for Cello and Piano (1943; also for Orch., 1945); Piano Trio (n.d.; unfinished); Oboe Quintet (n.d.; destroyed); *Dance No. 1* (1948) and *No. 2* (1949) for Cello; *Sonata da camera* for Violin and Piano (1950); Concerto for Piano, Cello, and Wind Quintet (1950); 2 serenades: No. 1 for Harpsichord, Flute, Oboe, and Cello (1953) and No. 2 for String Quartet and Double Bass (1956); *Colloquy* for 2 Trumpets, 2 Horns, 2 Trombones, and Tuba (1955); *Chamber Fantasie* for 2 Clarinets, Bass Clarinet, Harp, Violin, 2 Cellos, and Double Bass (1959); Duo for Clarinet and Cello (1960); *Prelude and Nocturne* for Flute, Celesta, and Cello (1965); *Consort of Winds* for Wind Quintet (1974); *Capriccio* for Cello and Piano (1977). **PIANO:** *5 Bagatelles* (1939); 3 suites (1940–41; 1948; for 4-hands, 1964); *Fantasy (Variations)* (1946); *New Adventures* (1956); Sonata (1970; unfinished); *Intermezzo* (1972); *Ciaconna, Capriccio* (1979; unfinished). **VOCAL:** *Song of the Idiot* for Soprano and Orch. (1941); *Concert Aria after Solomon* for Soprano and 8 Instruments (1949); *3 Songs* for Soprano and String Quartet or String Orch. (1958); *The Ways*, song cycle for Soprano or Tenor and Piano (1961); *Fugue and Finale* for Soprano and 7 Instruments (1969); choral pieces; other songs.

Weber, Ludwig, German composer and teacher; b. Nuremberg, Oct. 13, 1891; d. Essen-Werden, June 30, 1947. He was mainly autodidact in composition. After teaching school in Nuremberg (1912–25), he taught at the Essen Folkwangschule (from 1927). Among his compositions were *Christgeburt*, chamber play (1925); Sym. (1915–16); *Streichermusik* for Strings (1920); *Musik* for Organ and Brass (1928); 2 string quartets (1913, 1921); Wind Quintet (1923); and piano pieces.

Weber, Ludwig, eminent Austrian bass; b. Vienna, July 29, 1899; d. there, Dec. 9, 1974. He studied with Alfred Boruttau in Vienna. He made his operatic debut there at the Volksoper as Fiorello in 1920; then sang in Barmen-Elberfeld (1925–27), Düsseldorf (1927–30), and Cologne (1930–33). After singing at the Bavarian State Opera in Munich (1933–45), he was one of the principal members of the Vienna State Opera (1945–60); also appeared at London's Covent Garden (1936–39; 1947; 1950–51) and at the Bayreuth Festivals (1951–60). He was a prof. at the Salzburg Mozarteum (from 1961). He was one of the foremost Wagnerian bass singers of his time, excelling particularly as Daland, Gurnemanz, and Hagen; he also distinguished himself in such roles as Rocco, Kaspar, Baron Ochs, Méphistophélès, and Wozzeck.

Weber, Margrit, Swiss pianist; b. Ebnat-Kappel, Feb. 24, 1924. She studied organ with Heinrich Funk in Zürich; then received training in piano from Max Egger and Walter Lang at the Cons. there. She was employed as an organist at the age of 15; then devoted herself chiefly to the piano. She toured Europe, presenting many new works; also played in the U.S. and Canada. She was the soloist in the first performances of piano concertos by Martinů and Alexander Tcherepnin, and of Stravinsky's *Movements* for Piano and Orch., which she performed under Stravinsky's direction in N.Y. on Jan. 10, 1960.

Webern, Anton (Friedrich Wilhelm) von, remarkable Austrian composer (he removed the nobiliary particle "von" in 1918 when such distinctions were outlawed in Austria); b. Vienna, Dec. 3, 1883; d. (accidentally shot and killed by an American soldier) Mittersill, Sept. 15, 1945. He received his first instruction in music from his mother, an amateur pianist; then studied piano, cello, and theory with Edwin Komauer in Klagenfurt; also played cello in the orch. there. In 1902 he entered the Univ. of Vienna, where he studied harmony with Graedener and counterpoint with Navratil; also attended classes in musicology with Adler; received his Ph.D. in 1906 with a diss. on *Heinrich Isaac's Choralis Constantinus II.* In 1904 he began private studies in composition with Schoenberg, whose ardent disciple he became; Berg also studied with Schoenberg; together, Schoenberg, Berg, and Webern laid the foundations of what became known as the 2nd Viennese School of composition. The unifying element was the adoption of Schoenberg's method of composition with 12 tones related only to one another. Malevolent opponents referred to Schoenberg, Berg, and Webern as a Vienna Trinity, with Schoenberg as God the Father, Berg as the Son, and Webern as the Holy Ghost; the last appellation was supposed to describe the phantomlike substance of some of Webern's works. From 1908 to 1914 Webern was active as a conductor in Vienna and in Germany; in 1915–16 he served in the army; in 1917–18, was conductor at the Deutsches Theater in Prague. In 1918 he settled in Mödling, near Vienna, where he taught composition privately; from 1918 to 1922 he supervised the programs of the Verein für Musikalische Privataufführungen (Society for Private Musical Performances), organized in Vienna by Schoenberg with the intention of promoting modern music without being exposed to reactionary opposition (music critics were not admitted to these performances). Webern was conductor of the Schubertbund (1921–22) and the Mödling Male Chorus (1921–26); he also led the Vienna Workers' Sym. concerts (1922–34) and the Vienna Workers' Chorus (1923–34), both sponsored by the Social Democratic Party. From 1927 to 1938 he was a conductor on the Austrian Radio; furthermore, he conducted guest engagements in Germany, Switzerland, and Spain; from 1929, made several visits to England, where he was a guest conductor with the BBC Sym. Orch. For the most part, however, he devoted himself to composition, private teaching, and lecturing. After Hitler came to power in Germany in 1933, Webern's music was banned as a manifestation of "cultural Bolshevism" and "degenerate art." His position became more difficult after the Anschluss in 1938, for his works could no longer be publ.; he eked out an existence by teaching a few private pupils and making piano arrangements of musical scores by others for Universal Edition. After his son was killed in an air bombardment of a train in Feb. 1945, he and his wife fled from Vienna to Mittersill, near Salzburg, to stay with his married daughters and grandchildren. His life ended tragically on the evening of Sept. 15, 1945, when he was shot and killed by an American soldier after stepping outside his son-in-law's residence (for a full account, see H. Moldenhauer, *The Death of Anton Webern: A Drama in Documents*, N.Y., 1961).

Webern left relatively few works, and most of them are of short duration (the 4th of his 5 Pieces for Orch., op. 10, scored for clarinet, trumpet, trombone, mandolin, celesta, harp, drum, violin, and viola, takes only 19 seconds to play), but in his music he achieves the utmost subtilization of expressive means. He adopted the 12-tone method of composition almost immediately after its definitive formulation by Schoenberg (1924), and extended the principle of nonrepetition of notes to tone colors, so that in some of his works (e.g., Sym., op. 21) solo instruments are rarely allowed to play 2 successive thematic notes. Dynamic marks are similarly diversified. Typically, each 12-tone row is divided into symmetric sections of 2, 4, or 6 members, which enter mutually into intricate but invariably logical canonic imitations. Inversions and augmentations are inherent features; melodically and harmonically, the intervals of the major seventh and minor ninth are stressed; single motifs are brief, and stand out as individual particles or lyric ejaculations. The impact of these works on the general public and on the critics was disconcerting, and upon occasion led to violent demonstrations; however, the extraordinary skill and novelty of technique made this music endure beyond the fashions of the times; performances of Webern's works multiplied after his death, and began to influence increasingly larger groups of modern musicians; Stravinsky acknowledged the use of Webern's methods in his latest works; jazz composers have professed to follow Webern's ideas of tone color; analytical treatises have been publ. in several languages. The International Webern Festival celebrated the centennial of his birth in Dec. 1983 in Vienna.

WORKS: ORCH.: *Im Sommerwind*, idyll for Large Orch. (1904; Seattle, May 25, 1962, Ormandy conducting); *Passacaglia*, op. 1 (1908; Vienna, Nov. 4, 1908, composer conducting); *6 Orchestral Pieces*, op. 6 (1909; Vienna, March 31, 1913, Schoenberg conducting; rev. 1928; Berlin, Jan. 27, 1929); *5 Orchestral Pieces*, op. 10 (1911–13; Zürich, June 22, 1926, composer conducting); *5 Orchestral Pieces*, op. posthumous (1913; Cologne, Jan. 13, 1969); Sym. for Chamber Ensemble, op. 21 (1928; N.Y., Dec. 18, 1929); *5 Movements* for String Quartet, op. 5, arr. for String Orch. (1928–29; Philadelphia, March 26, 1930); *Variations*, op. 30 (1940; Winterthur, March 3, 1943). **CHAMBER:** String Quartet, in one movement (1905; Seattle, May 26, 1962); Piano Quintet, in one movement (Vienna, Nov. 7, 1907); 5 Movements for String Quartet (1909; Vienna, Feb. 8, 1910); 4 pieces for Violin and Piano, op. 7 (1910; rev. 1914); 6 bagatelles for String Quartet, op. 9 (1911–13; Donaueschingen, July 19, 1924); *3 Little Pieces* for Cello and Piano, op. 11 (1914; Mainz, Dec. 2, 1924); String Trio, op. 20 (1926–27; Vienna, Jan. 16, 1928); Quartet for Violin, Clarinet, Tenor Saxophone, and Piano, op. 22 (1930; Vienna, April 13, 1931); Concerto for 9 Instruments, op. 24 (1934; Prague, Sept. 4, 1935); String Quartet, op. 28 (1936–38; Pittsfield, Mass., Sept. 22, 1938). **PIANO:** *Variations* (1936; Vienna, Oct. 26, 1937). **VOCAL:** *Entflieht auf leichten Kähnen* for Chorus, op. 2 (1908; Furstenfeld, April 10, 1927); 2 songs for Chorus, Celesta, Guitar, Violin, Clarinet, and Bass Clarinet, after Goethe, op. 19 (1926); *Das Augenlicht* for Chorus and Orch., op. 26 (1935; London, June 17, 1938); *1st Cantata* for Soprano, Chorus, and Orch. (1938–39; London, July 12, 1946); *2nd Cantata* for Soprano, Bass, Chorus, and Orch. (1941–43; Brussels, June 23, 1950); 2 sets of 5 songs for Voice and Piano, after Stefan George, opp. 3 and 4 (1908–09); 2 songs for Voice and Instrumental Ensemble, after Rilke, op. 8 (1910; rev. 1921 and 1925); 4 songs for Voice and Piano, op. 12 (1915–17); 4 songs for Voice and Orch., op. 13 (1914–18); 6 songs for Voice and Instruments, after Georg Trakl, op. 14 (1919–21; Donaueschingen, July 20, 1924); *5 Sacred Songs* for Voice and Instruments, op. 15 (1917–22; Vienna, Oct. 9, 1924, composer conducting); *5 Canons* on Latin texts for Voice, Clarinet, and Bass Clarinet, op. 16 (1923–24; N.Y., May 8, 1951); *3 Traditional Rhymes* for Voice and Instruments, op. 17 (1924–25; N.Y., March 16, 1952); 3 songs for Voice, Clarinet, and Guitar, op. 18 (1925; Los Angeles, Feb. 8, 1954); 3 songs for Voice and Piano, op. 23 (1933–34); 3 songs for Voice and Piano, op. 25 (1934). **OTHER:** Arrangements for Chamber Orch. of Schoenberg's Chamber Sym., op. 9 (1923), Schubert's *Deutsche Tanze* (1931), and Bach's *Ricercare a 6* from *Das musikalische Opfer* (London, April 25, 1935, composer conducting).

WRITINGS: W. Reich ed. *Der Weg zur neuen Musik* (Vienna, 1933; new ed., 1960; Eng. tr., 1963) and *Anton Webern: Weg und Gestalt: Selbstzeugnisse und Worte der Freunde* (Zürich, 1961).

BIBL.: "W. zum 50. Geburtstag," special issue of the magazine *23*, no. 14 (Vienna, 1934); R. Leibowitz, *Schoenberg et son école* (Paris, 1947; Eng. tr., 1949); L. Rognoni, *Espressionismo e dodecafonia* (Turin, 1954; 2nd ed., rev., 1966, as *La scuola musicale di Vienna*); "A. W.: Dokumente, Bekenntnis, Erkenntnisse, Analysen," *Die Reihe*, no. 2 (1955; Eng. tr. in *Die Reihe*, 1958); W. Kolneder, *A. W.: Einführung in Werk und Stil* (Rodenkirchen, 1961; Eng. tr., 1968); H. Moldenhauer, *The Death of A. W.: A Drama in Documents* (N.Y., 1961); G. Perle, *Serial Composition and Atonality: An Introduction to the Music of Schoenberg, Berg and W.* (Berkeley, 1962; 5th ed., rev., 1982); H. Moldenhauer and D. Irvine, eds., *A. v. W.: Perspectives* (Seattle, 1966); F. Wildgans, *A. W.* (London, 1966); *A. v.W.: Sketches (1926–1945)* (facsimile reproductions from W.'s sketchbooks, with commentary by E. Krenek and foreword by H. Moldenhauer; N.Y., 1968); R. Ringger, *A. W.s Klavierlieder* (Zürich, 1968); L. Somfai, *A. W.* (Budapest, 1968); C. Rostand, *A. W.: L'Homme et son oeuvre* (Paris, 1969); H. Deppert, *Studien zur Kompositionstechnik im instrumentalen Spätwerk A. W.s* (Darmstadt, 1972); W. Stroh, *A. v.W.; Historische Legitimation* (Göppingen, 1973); F. Döhl, *W.s Beitrag zur Stilwende der neuen Musik* (Munich, 1976); H. and R. Moldenhauer, *A. v.W.: Chronicle of His Life and Work* (N.Y., 1978); R. Schulz, *Über das Verhältnis von Konstruktion und Ausdruck in den Werken A. W.s* (Munich, 1982); E. Hilmar, ed., *A. W. 1883–1983: Eine Festschrift zum hundertsten Geburtstag* (Vienna, 1983); A. Whittall, "W. and Atonality: The Path from the Old Aesthetic," *Musical Times* (Dec. 1983); Z. Roman, *A. v.W.: An Annotated Bibliography* (Detroit, 1983); J. Straus, "Recompositions by

Schoenberg, Stravinsky, and W.," *Musical Quarterly*, no. 3 (1986); E. Jensen, "W. and Giovanni Segantini's Trittico della natura," *Musical Times* (Jan. 1989); K. Bailey, *The Twelve-Note Music of A. W.: Old Forms in a New Language* (Cambridge, 1991); K. Essl, *Das Synthses-Denken bei A. W.: Studien zur Musikauffassung des späten W. unter besonderer Berücksichtigung seiner eigenen Analysen zu op. 28 und 30* (Tutzing, 1991); G. Cox, *A. W.s Studienzeit: Seine Entwicklung im Lichte der Sätze und Fragmente für Klavier* (Frankfurt am Main, 1992); A. Schreffler, *W. and the Lyric Impulse: Songs and Fragments on Poems of George Trakl* (Oxford, 1995).

Webster, Beveridge, respected American pianist and teacher; b. Pittsburgh, May 13, 1908. He studied music with his father, who was director of the Pittsburgh Cons. of Music; at the age of 13, he was sent to Paris to study with Isidor Philipp at the Cons.; graduated in 1926, winning the premier prix for piano. He gave concerts in Europe; returned to the U.S. in 1934, and developed a successful concert career, appearing with major orchs.; also continued to give concerts in Europe. In 1946 he was appointed prof. of piano at the Juilliard School of Music in N.Y.; gave a piano recital at the Juilliard Theater on his 70th birthday, in May 1978; on Nov. 11, 1984, he celebrated the 50th anniversary of his U.S. debut with a recital in N.Y. In addition to works from the 18th and 19th centuries, he won particular distinction for his insightful performances of Debussy, Ravel, and contemporary American composers.

Webster, Sir David (Lumsden), Scottish operatic administrator; b. Dundee, July 3, 1903; d. London, May 11, 1971. He was educated at the Univ. of Liverpool; then commenced a commercial career while pursuing his various interests in the arts. From 1940 to 1945 he was chairman of the Liverpool Phil. Soc. In 1945 he became general administrator of the Covent Garden Opera Trust; in this capacity he helped to launch the careers of many famous singers, among them Jon Vickers and Joan Sutherland. He was knighted in 1961 and was made a Knight Commander of the Royal Victorian Order in 1970. An account of his career by M. Haltrecht, under the title *The Reluctant Showman*, was publ. in 1975.

Weede (real name, **Wiedefeld**), **Robert,** American baritone; b. Baltimore, Feb. 11, 1903; d. Walnut Creek, Calif., June 9, 1972. After winning the National Federation of Music Clubs award (1927), he studied at the Eastman School of Music in Rochester, N.Y., and in Milan. In 1933 he became a soloist at N.Y.'s Radio City Music Hall. On May 15, 1937, he made his Metropolitan Opera debut in N.Y. as Tonio, where he was on the roster until 1942, and then again in 1944–45, 1948–50, and 1952–53. He also sang Rigoletto in Chicago (1939), San Francisco (1940), and at the N.Y. City Opera (1948). In later years he made appearances on Broadway and toured in the musicals *The Most Happy Fella* and *Milk and Honey.* During his operatic career, he sang mainly in operas by Verdi and Puccini.

Wehle, Gerhard Fürchtegott, German musicologist and composer; b. Paramaribo, Dutch Guiana, Oct. 11, 1884; d. Berlin, Oct. 15, 1973. He studied in Germany, and settled in Berlin (1907); he was active primarily as a music critic and pedagogue; taught improvisation and other subjects. He publ. *Die Kunst der Improvisation* (2 vols., Münster, 1925–26) and *Die Orgel-Improvisation* (Leipzig, 1932; both titles reissued in 3 vols., Hamburg, 1950–53); also *Neue Wege im Kompositions-Unterricht* (2 vols., Hamburg, 1955); *Die höhere Kompositionstechnik* (2 vols., Hamburg, n.d.). Among his musical works are 26 symphonic cantatas; 3 syms.; much chamber music. He was also a successful novelist.

Wehrli, Werner, Swiss composer and teacher; b. Aarau, Jan. 8, 1892; d. Lucerne, June 27, 1944. He was a student of Hegar and Kempter at the Zürich Cons. and of Knorr at the Frankfurt am Main Cons. He also took courses in musicology and art history at the univs. of Munich, Basel, and Berlin. From 1918 he taught music at the Aarau Lehrerseminar. He also was conductor of the Aarau Cäcilien-Verein (1920–29). His compositions generally followed the precepts of late Romanticism.

WORKS: DRAMATIC: *Das heisse Eisen*, comic opera (Bern, Dec. 11, 1918); *Der Märchenspiegle*, Singspiel (1922); *Das Vermächtnis*, opera (1931); *Auf dem Mond*, school opera (1933); 5 festival plays. **ORCH.:** 2 sinfoniettas (1915, 1920); *Chilbizite*, overture (1917); *Variationen und Fuge über einem lustigen Sang* (1927); *Romanze* for Cello and Orch. (1932); *Serenade* (1933); *Pantomime* for Chamber Orch. (1937); *Introitus zu König Oedipus* (1943). **CHAMBER:** 2 string quartets (1912, 1933); 2 cello sonatas (1913, 1938); Trio for Flute, Violin, and Viola (1920); Trio for Violin, Horn, and Piano (1921); Suite for Flute and Piano (n.d.); *Tafelmusik* for 3 Recorders (1933); *Christgeburt* for Flute and Violin (1935); Flute Sonata (n.d.); piano pieces; organ music. **VOCAL:** Choral music; solo vocal pieces.

Weidt, Lucie, German-born Austrian soprano; b. Troppau, Silesia, c.1876; d. Vienna, July 28, 1940. She studied with her father, and then with Rosa Papier in Vienna. She made her operatic debut in Leipzig in 1900; in 1902 she made her first appearance at the Vienna Opera as Elisabeth, remaining on its roster until 1927. She sang in Munich from 1908 to 1910. On Nov. 18, 1910, she made her first American appearance, as Brünnhilde in *Die Walküre*, at the Metropolitan Opera in N.Y.; after a season there, she sang in Italy. In 1909 she married Baron Joseph von Urmenyi. Her voice was of unusual attractiveness and power, enabling her to perform Wagnerian parts with distinction.

Weigel, Eugene (Herbert), American composer, violist, organist, and teacher; b. Cleveland, Oct. 11, 1910. He studied composition with Arthur Shepherd at Western Reserve Univ. and violin with Maurice Hewitt at the Cleveland Inst. of Music (1930–32); later had composition lessons with Hindemith at Yale Univ. (B.M., 1946) and viola lessons with Hugo Kortschak. He was active as an organist and choirmaster (1929–41); also was a founding member of the Walden String Quartet (1930–35). While at Yale Univ., he served as music director of its Thomas More Chapel and played viola in the New Haven (Conn.) Sym. Orch.; appeared in various ensembles, including one in N.Y. with Hindemith on the viola d'amore in a performance of Bach's *St. John Passion.* In 1946–47 he was again a member of the Walden String Quartet during its residency at Cornell Univ.; played in the first performances of Schoenberg's String Trio and Ives's 2nd String Quartet; continued to play with the quartet at the Univ. of Ill. (1947–57), where he also taught composition and experimental theory. In 1954–55 he held a Guggenheim fellowship. In 1955 he became composer-in-residence at Montana State Univ. in Missoula, which was renamed the Univ. of Montana that same year; remained there until 1972. He also was a founder-member of the Montana String Quartet (1957–72). In 1972 he retired to Vancouver Island, Canada; conducted the Malespina Chorus and was prof. emeritus at Malespina College (1974–76). In later years, he devoted much time to writing poetry, preparing his memoirs, and pursuing an avid interest in architecture.

WORKS: OPERAS: *The Lion Makers* (1953); *The Mountain Child* (1959). **ORCH.:** *Sonata* for Strings (1948); *Festival Fanfare* (1948); *Prairie Symphony* (1952); *Concerto festivo* for Flute, Harpsichord, and Strings (Berlin Festival, 1959); *Fantasy and Fugue* for Concert Band (1967). **CHAMBER:** Clarinet Quintet (1946); Woodwind Quintet (1949); Trombone Quartet (1953); *Maine Sketches* for Horn and Piano (1954); Duo for Clarinet and Bassoon (1955); piano pieces. **VOCAL:** *Fall of the Leaf* for Baritone and String Quartet (1938); *Prayer for Peace* for Chorus, Brass, and Percussion (1961); songs.

Weigl, Karl, Austrian-born American composer; b. Vienna, Feb. 6, 1881; d. N.Y., Aug. 11, 1949. He studied piano with Door and theory with Fuchs at the Cons. of the Gesellschaft der Musikfreunde in Vienna (graduated, 1902); then took composition lessons with Zemlinsky; attended courses in musicology at the Univ. of Vienna with Adler (Ph.D., 1903). From 1918 to

1928 he was on the faculty of the New Vienna Cons.; from 1930 to 1938, taught theory at the Univ. of Vienna. After the Anschluss in 1938, he emigrated to N.Y.; became a naturalized American citizen in 1943. He was respected both in Austria and in America as a composer, and a concerted effort was made to promote his music, but with little success. His 5th Sym., *Apocalyptic* (1945), was performed posthumously by Leopold Stokowski with the American Sym. Orch. (N.Y., Oct. 27, 1968). He wrote 6 syms. (1908, 1922, 1931, 1936, 1945, 1947); several overtures; Violin Concerto (1928); 8 string quartets; String Sextet; 2 violin sonatas; numerous choruses; piano pieces; songs. He was married to **Valery (Vally) Weigl**.

Weigl, Valery (Vally), Austrian-born American composer and music therapist; b. Vienna, Sept. 11, 1894; d. N.Y., Dec. 25, 1982. She studied music in Vienna with her husband, **Karl Weigl**. She taught music in Vienna and Salzburg (1921–38). After the Anschluss in 1938, she and her husband went to the U.S., where she obtained employment as music adviser with the American Theater Wing in N.Y. (1947–58); from 1954 to 1964 she gave courses in music therapy at the N.Y. Medical College and wrote therapy programs for UNESCO. She was an energetic peace activist, and served as a co-founder of the Friends' Arts for World Unity Committee. With equal energy, she promoted her husband's compositions, which were little appreciated and seldom played.

WORKS: *New England Suite* for Clarinet, Cello, and Piano (1955); *Nature Moods* for Soprano, Clarinet, and Violin (1960); *Mood Sketches* for Wind Quintet (1964); *Peace Is a Shelter* for Chorus, Soloist, and Piano (1970); *The People Yes*, cantata (1976).

Weikert, Ralf, Austrian conductor; b. St. Florian, Nov. 10, 1940. He studied at the Bruckner Cons. in Linz; then took a course in conducting with Swarowsky at the Vienna Academy of Music. In 1965 he won 1st prize in the Nicolai Malko Conducting Competition in Copenhagen. In 1966 he became conductor of the City Theater in Bonn; then was chief conductor there (1968–77). In 1977 he was appointed deputy Generalmusikdirektor of the Frankfurt am Main Opera; also conducted at the Hamburg State Opera, the Deutsche Oper in Berlin, the Vienna State Opera, and the Zürich Opera. In 1981 he was named chief conductor of the Salzburg Mozarteum Orch. and music director of the Landestheater in Salzburg. He was music director of the Zürich Opera from 1983 to 1992.

Weikl, Bernd, esteemed Austrian baritone; b. Vienna, July 29, 1942. He received his training at the Mainz Cons. (1962–65) and the Hannover Hochschule für Musik (1965–67). In 1968 he made his operatic debut as Ottakar in *Der Freischütz* at the Hannover Opera, where he sang until 1970. From 1970 to 1973 he was a member of the Deutsche Oper am Rhein in Düsseldorf. In 1971 he made his first appearance at the Salzburg Easter Festival as Melot in *Tristan und Isolde*. In 1972 he sang for the first time at the Bayreuth Festival as Wolfram. He appeared at the Hamburg State Opera (from 1973) and at the Berlin Deutsche Opera (from 1974). In 1975 he made his debut at London's Covent Garden as Rossini's Figaro. In 1976 he created the role of Ferdinand in Einem's *Kabale und Liebe* in Vienna. On Dec. 22, 1977, he made his Metropolitan Opera debut in N.Y. as Wolfram, where he returned in such roles as Amfortas, Jochanaan, Beethoven's Don Fernando, and Mandryka. He was a soloist in Bach's *St. Matthew Passion* at his Salzburg Festival debut in 1984. His portrayal of Hans Sachs was greatly admired, and he sang that role at Milan's La Scala and at Covent Garden in 1990 and at the Metropolitan Opera and the San Francisco Opera in 1993. As a concert artist, he appeared widely in oratorio and lieder performances.

Weil, Bruno, German conductor; b. Hahnstätten, Nov. 24, 1949. He studied with Swarowsky in Vienna and Ferrara in Italy. He conducted opera in Wiesbaden (1975–77) and Braunschweig (1977–81). After winning 2nd prize in the Karajan conducting competition in 1979, he appeared with the Berlin Phil. In 1980 he conducted at the Deutsche Oper in Berlin. He became Generalmusikdirektor in Augsburg in 1981. In 1984 he was a guest conductor of the Yomiuri Nippon Sym. Orch. in Tokyo. In 1985 he made his debut at the Vienna State Opera conducting *Aida*. He conducted *Don Giovanni* at the Salzburg Festival in 1988, the year he also made his U.S. debut at a N.Y. Schubertiade. During the 1990–91 season, he toured Germany with the English Chamber Orch. In 1991 he became music director of the Carmel (Calif.) Bach Festival. He made his Glyndebourne Festival debut conducting *Così fan tutte* in 1992. In 1994 he became Generalmusikdirektor of the Duisburg Sym. Orch.

Weil, Hermann, German baritone; b. Karlsruhe, May 29, 1876; d. (of a heart attack, while fishing in Blue Mountain Lake, N.Y.) July 6, 1949. He studied voice with Adolf Dippel in Frankfurt am Main. He made his operatic debut as Wolfram in *Tannhäuser* at Freiburg, Baden, on Sept. 6, 1901; then sang in Vienna, Brussels, Amsterdam, Milan, and London; participated in the Bayreuth Festivals (1909–12). On Nov. 17, 1911, he made a successful debut as Kurvenal in *Tristan und Isolde* at the Metropolitan Opera in N.Y. In 1917 he returned to Germany. He sang at the Vienna State Opera (1920–23), toured the U.S. with the German Opera Co. (1923–24), and appeared at the Bayreuth Festival (1924–25); in 1939 he settled in N.Y. as a vocal teacher. The extensive range of his voice, spanning 3 full octaves, enabled him to undertake bass parts as well as those in the baritone compass. He had about 100 roles in his repertoire, excelling in Wagnerian operas.

Weill, Kurt (Julian), remarkable German-born American composer; b. Dessau, March 2, 1900; d. N.Y., April 3, 1950. He was a private pupil of Albert Bing in Dessau (1915–18); in 1918–19 he studied at the Berlin Hochschule für Musik with Humperdinck (composition), Friedrich Koch (counterpoint), and Krasselt (conducting). He was then engaged as an opera coach in Dessau and was also theater conductor at Ludenscheid. In 1920 he moved to Berlin and was a student of Busoni at the Prussian Academy of Arts until 1923; also studied with Jarnach there (1921–23). His first major work, the Sym. No. 1, *Berliner Sinfonie*, was composed in 1921. However, it was not performed in his lifetime; indeed, its MS was not recovered until 1955, and it was finally premiered by the North German Radio Sym. Orch. in Hamburg in 1958. Under the impact of new trends in the musical theater, Weill proceeded to write short satirical operas in a sharp modernistic manner: *Der Protagonist* (1924–25) and *Royal Palace* (1925–26). There followed a striking "songspiel" (a hybrid term of English and German words), *Mahagonny*, to a libretto by Bertolt Brecht, savagely satirizing the American primacy of money (1927); it was remodeled and was presented as the 3-act opera *Aufstieg und Fall der Stadt Mahagonny* (1929). Weill's greatest hit in this genre came with a modernistic version of Gay's *The Beggar's Opera*, to a pungent libretto by Brecht; under the title *Die Dreigroschenoper* (1928), it was staged all over Germany, and was also produced in translation throughout Europe. Marc Blitzstein later made a new libretto for the opera, versified in a modern American style, which was produced as *The Threepenny Opera*, the exact translation of the German title. Its hit number, *Mack the Knife*, became tremendously successful.

After the Nazi ascent to power in Germany, Weill and his wife, **Lotte Lenya**, who appeared in many of his musical plays, went to Paris in 1934. They settled in the U.S. in 1935; Weill became a naturalized American citizen in 1943. Quickly absorbing the modes and fashions of American popular music, he recreated, with astonishing facility, and felicity, the typical form and content of American musicals; this stylistic transition was facilitated by the fact that in his European productions he had already absorbed elements of American popular songs and jazz rhythms. His highly developed assimilative faculty enabled him to combine this Americanized idiom with the advanced techniques of modern music (atonality, polytonality, polyrhythms) and present the product in a pleasing, and yet sophisticated and challenging, manner. But for all his success in American-produced scores, the great majority of his European works remained to be produced in America only posthumously.

WORKS: DRAMATIC: *Zaubernacht*, ballet (Berlin, Nov. 18, 1922); *Der Protagonist*, opera (1924–25; Dresden, March 27, 1926); *Royal Palace*, ballet-opera (1925–26; Berlin, March 2, 1927; original orchestration not extant; reconstructed as a ballet by Gunther Schuller and Noam Sheriff, San Francisco, Oct. 5, 1968); *Na und?*, opera (1926–27; not perf.; not extant); *Der Zar lässt sich photographieren*, opera (1927; Leipzig, Feb. 18, 1928; U.S. premiere as *The Shah Has Himself Photographed*, N.Y., Oct. 27, 1949); *Mahagonny*, "songspiel" (Baden-Baden, July 17, 1927; remodeled as a 3-act opera, *Aufstieg und Fall der Stadt Mahagonny*, 1927–29; Leipzig, March 9, 1930; U.S. premiere, N.Y., April 28, 1970); *Happy End*, comedy (Berlin, Sept. 2, 1929; professional U.S. premiere, New Haven, Conn., April 6, 1972); *Der Jasager*, school opera (Berlin radio, June 23, 1930; U.S. premiere as *The One Who Sang Yes*, N.Y., April 25, 1933); *Die Burgschaft*, opera (1930–31; Berlin, March 10, 1932); *Der Silbersee*, musical play (1932–33; simultaneous premiere in Leipzig, Erfurt, and Magdeburg, Feb. 18, 1933; U.S. premiere as *Silverlake*, slightly abr. and with the addition of his 1927 incidental music to Strindberg's play *Gustav III*, N.Y., March 20, 1980); *Die sieben Todsünden der Kleinbürger*, ballet (Paris, June 7, 1933; U.S. premiere, N.Y., Dec. 4, 1958); *Der Kuhnhandel*, operetta (1934; Düsseldorf, March 22, 1990; rev. as a musical comedy, *A Kingdom for a Cow*, London, June 28, 1935); *Der Weg der Verheissung*, biblical drama (1934–35; not perf.; rev. by L. Lewisohn as *The Eternal Road*, 1935–36; N.Y., Jan. 7, 1937); *Johnny Johnson*, musical fable (N.Y., Nov. 19, 1936); *Davy Crockett*, musical play (1938; unfinished); *Knickerbocker Holiday*, operetta (Hartford, Conn., Sept. 26, 1938; contains the popular *September Song*); *Railroads on Parade*, historical pageant (1938–39; N.Y. World's Fair, April 30, 1939); *The Ballad of Magna Carta*, scenic cantata (1939; CBS, Feb. 4, 1940); *Ulysses Africanus*, musical play (1939; unfinished); *Lady in the Dark*, musical play (1940; N.Y., Jan. 23, 1941); *One Touch of Venus*, musical comedy (N.Y., Oct. 7, 1943); *The Firebrand of Florence*, operetta (1944; N.Y., March 22, 1945); *Down in the Valley*, folk opera (1945–48; Bloomington, Ind., July 15, 1948); *Street Scene*, opera (1946; N.Y., Jan. 9, 1947); *Love Life*, vaudeville (1947; N.Y., Oct. 7, 1948); *Lost in the Stars*, musical tragedy, after Alan Paton's *Cry, the Beloved Country* (N.Y., Oct. 30, 1949); *Huckleberry Finn*, musical (1950; unfinished). **FILM SCORES:** *You and Me* (1937–38); *The River Is Blue* (1937–38; discarded); *Where Do We Go from Here?* (1943–44); *Salute to France* (1944). **ORCH.:** Symphonic Poem (1920?; not extant); 1 unnumbered sym. (1920; not extant); 2 numbered syms.: No. 1, *Berliner Sinfonie* (1921; Hamburg, Jan. 17, 1958) and No. 2, *Pariser Symphonie* (1933; Amsterdam, Oct. 11, 1934; U.S. premiere as *3 Night Scenes*, N.Y., Dec. 13, 1934); Divertimento (1922); *Sinfonia sacra* or *Fantasia, Passacaglia, und Hymnus* (1922); *Quodlibet*, suite from *Zaubernacht* (1923; Coburg, Feb. 6, 1926); Concerto for Violin, Woodwinds, Double Bass, and Percussion (1924; Paris, June 11, 1925); *Berlin im Licht* for Military Band (1928); *Kleine Dreigroschenmusik* for Winds, concert suite from *Die Dreigroschenoper* (1929). **CHAMBER:** 2 movements for String Quartet: *Allegro deciso* and *Andantino* (n.d.; N.Y., March 7, 1977); 1 unnumbered string quartet (1919); 1 numbered string quartet (1923); Cello Sonata (1920). **VOCAL:** *Sulamith*, cantata for Soprano, Women's Chorus, and Orch. (1920; not extant); *Psalm VIII* for 8 Voices (1921; partly lost); *Recordare* for Chorus and Children's Chorus (1923); *Das Studenbuch*, 6 songs for Tenor or Soprano and Orch. (1924; partly lost); *Der neue Orpheus*, cantata for Soprano, Violin, and Orch. (1925; Berlin, March 2, 1927); *Vom Tod im Wald*, ballad for Bass and 10 Wind Instruments (Berlin, Nov. 23, 1927); *Das Berliner Requiem*, cantata for Tenor, Baritone, Bass, Chorus, and 15 Instruments (1928; Frankfurt am Main Radio, May 22, 1929); *Der Lindberghflug*, cantata after a radio score for Tenor, Baritone, Chorus, and Orch. (with Hindemith; Baden-Baden, July 28, 1929; rescored by Weill as totally his own work, Berlin, Dec. 5, 1929; rev. 1930 as *Der Flug des Lindberghs* and then later retitled *Der Ozeanflug*, without Lindbergh's name, as a gesture of protest against Lindbergh's militant neutrality toward Nazi Germany); *Zu Potsdam unter den Eichen* for Men's Voices (1929); *Song of the Railroads* (1938); *4 American Songs* (1939); *Kiddush* for Tenor, Chorus, and Organ (1946); many songs.

WRITINGS: S. Hinton and J. Schebera, eds., *Musik und Theater: Gesammelte Schriften* (Leipzig, 1990).

BIBL.: V. Thomson, "Most Melodious Tears," *Modern Music*, XI (1933); H. Heinsheimer, "K. W.," *Tomorrow* (March 1948); H. Strobel, "Erinnerung an K. W.," *Melos* (May 1950); D. Drew, "Topicality and the Universal: The Strange Case of W.'s Die Burgschaft," *Music & Letters* (July 1958); H. Kotschenreuther, *K. W.* (Berlin, 1962); J. Waterhouse, "W.'s Debt to Busoni," *Musical Times*, CV (1964); K. Kowalke, *K. W. in Europe* (Ann Arbor, 1979); R. Sanders, *The Days Grow Short: The Life and Music of K. W.* (N.Y., 1980); D. Jarman, *K. W.: an Illustrated Biography* (Bloomington, Ind., 1982); J. Schebera, *K. W.: Leben und Werk* (Leipzig, 1983); K. Kowalke, ed., *A New Orpheus: Essays on K. W.* (New Haven, 1986); S. Cook, *Opera During the Weimar Republic: The Zeitopern of Ernst Krenek, K. W., and Paul Hindemith* (Ann Arbor, 1987); D. Drew, *K. W.: A Handbook* (Berkeley, 1987); idem, "K. W.: Doubtful and Chimerical Works," *Musical Times* (Oct. 1987); S. Hinton, ed., *K. W.: The Threepenny Opera* (Cambridge, 1990); J. Schebera, *K. W. 1900–1950. Eine Biographie in Texten, Bildern und Dokumenten* (Leipzig, 1990); R. Taylor, *K. W.: Composer in a Divided World* (London, 1991); K. Kowalke and H. Edler, eds., *A Stranger Here Myself: K. W.-Studien* (Hildesheim, 1993).

Weinberg, Jacob, Russian-American pianist, teacher, and composer; b. Odessa, July 7, 1879; d. N.Y., Nov. 2, 1956. He studied at the Moscow Cons. with Igumnov (piano) and with Taneyev and Ippolitov-Ivanov (composition); was a private pupil of Leschetizky in Vienna (1910–11). He taught piano at the Odessa Cons. (1915–21); after living in Palestine (1921–26), he emigrated to the U.S.; taught piano at Hunter College and the N.Y. College of Music. He composed an opera on a modern Hebrew subject, *Hechalutz* (The Pioneers), fragments of which were performed in Jerusalem, in Hebrew, on April 4, 1925; the complete opera was performed in N.Y. on Nov. 25, 1934, under the title *The Pioneers of Israel*, in English; he also wrote the oratorios *Isaiah* (1948) and *The Life of Moses* (1952); *The Gettysburg Address*, ode for Chorus and Orch. (N.Y., 1936); *Sabbath Liturgy* for Baritone, Chorus, and Organ; Piano Concerto; Piano Trio; String Quartet; Violin Sonata. He contributed essays on Russian music to the Musical Quarterly and other periodicals.

Weinberger, Jaromir, Czech-born American composer; b. Prague, Jan. 8, 1896; d. (suicide) St. Petersburg, Fla., Aug. 8, 1967. He was a student of Křička and Hoffmeister in Prague and of Reger in Leipzig. In 1922 he became a teacher of composition at Ithaca (N.Y.) College. Returning to his homeland, he scored a remarkable success with his opera *Švanda dudák* (Schwanda the Bagpiper; Prague, April 27, 1927). It subsequently was performed throughout Europe to critical acclaim. With the dismemberment of his homeland by the Nazis in 1939, Weinberger fled to the U.S. and later became a naturalized citizen. Weinberger's success with *Švanda dudák* was a signal one. Even though the opera eventually went unperformed, its *Polka and Fugue* became a popular concert piece. He committed suicide, despondent over the lack of interest in his works.

WORKS: DRAMATIC: OPERAS: *Kocourkov* (c. 1926); *Švanda dudák* (Schwanda the Bagpiper; Prague, April 27, 1927); *Die geliebte Stimme* (Munich, Feb. 28, 1931); *Lidé z Polkerflatu* (The Outcasts of Polker Flat; Brno, Nov. 19, 1932); *Valdstejn* (Vienna, Nov. 18, 1937). **OPERETTAS:** *Frühlingssturme* (1933); *Apropo co dela Andula* (n.d.); *Na ruzich ustlano* (Bed of Roses; 1934); *Cisar pan na tresnich* (n.d.). **ORCH.:** *Overture to a Marionette Play* (1916); *Christmas* for Organ and Orch. (1929); *Liebesplauder, Neckerei* for Small Orch. (1929); *Passacaglia* for Organ and Orch. (1931); *Overture to a Knightly Play* (1931); *Neima Ivrit* (Hebrew Song; 1936); Concerto for Timpani, 4 Trumpets, and 4 Trombones (1939); *Under the Spreading Chestnut Tree* for

Piano and Orch. (N.Y., Oct. 12, 1939; rev. 1941); *The Legend of Sleepy Hollow* (1940); *Prelude and Fugue on Dixie* (1940); *The Bird's Opera*, overture (1940; Detroit, Nov. 13, 1941); *Song of the High Seas* (N.Y., Nov. 9, 1940); *Mississippi Rhapsody* for Band (1940); Alto Saxophone Concerto (1940); *Czech Rhapsody* (Washington, D.C., Nov. 5, 1941); *The Lincoln Symphony* (Cincinnati, Oct. 17, 1941); *Prelude to the Festival* for Band (1941); *Afternoon in the Village* for Band (1951); *Préludes religieux et profanes* (1953); *Aus Tirol* (1959); *A Waltz Overture* (1960). **CHAMBER:** *Colloque sentimental* for Violin and Piano (1920); *Cowboy's Christmas* for Violin and Piano (1924); *Banjos* for Violin and Piano (1924); *Czech Songs and Dances* for Violin and Piano (1929); sonatinas for Clarinet or Oboe or Bassoon or Piano (1940); *10 Characteristic Solos* for Snare Drum and Piano (1940). **KEYBOARD: PIANO:** 2 sonatas (1915; *Spinet Sonata*, 1915); *Gravures* (1924); *Etude on a Polish Chorale* (1924). **ORGAN:** *Bible Poems* (1939); Sonata (1941); *6 Religious Preludes* (1946); *Dedications* (1954); *Meditations* (1956). **VOCAL:** *Psalm CL* for Soprano or Tenor and Organ (1940); *The Way to Emmaus* for Soprano or Tenor and Organ (1940); *Ecclesiastes* for Soprano, Baritone, Chorus, Organ, and Bells (1945); *Ave* for Chorus and Orch. (1962); *5 Songs from Des Knaben Wunderhorn* (1962); many Czech songs.

Weiner, Lazar, Russian-American pianist, conductor, and composer, father of **Yehudi Wyner**; b. Cherkassy, near Kiev, Oct. 27, 1897; d. N.Y., Jan. 10, 1982. He emigrated to America in 1914, and became associated with numerous Jewish artistic activities in N.Y.; also took private lessons in composition with Robert Russell Bennett, Frederick Jacobi, and Joseph Schillinger. From 1929 to 1975 he was music director of the Central Synagogue in N.Y.; conducted classes in the Yiddish art song at Hebrew Union College, the Jewish Theological Seminary, and the 92nd Street Y; served as music director of the WABC weekly radio program "The Message of Israel" (1934–69). His compositions include an opera, *The Golem* (1956; White Plains, N.Y., Jan. 13, 1957); 5 ballets; 7 cantatas, including *Man of the World* (1939), *To Thee, America* (1943), *The Legend of Toil* (1945), *The Last Judgement* (1966), and *Amos* (1970); over 100 liturgical works; more than 150 songs, many to Yiddish texts; some orch. and chamber music.

BIBL.: M. Edelman, "In memoriam: L. W. (1897–1982)," *Musica judaica*, IV (1981–82).

Weiner, Leó, eminent Hungarian composer and pedagogue; b. Budapest, April 16, 1885; d. there, Sept. 13, 1960. He was a student of Koessler at the Budapest Academy of Music (1901–06). In 1908 he joined its faculty as a teacher of theory, becoming a prof. of composition in 1912 and of chamber music in 1920. He retired in 1957 but continued to teach there as prof. emeritus until his death. In 1907 he won the Franz-Josef-Jubiläumspreis, and in 1950 and 1960 the Kossuth Prize. In 1953 he was made an Eminent Artist by the Hungarian government. Weiner was particularly influential as a pedagogue. Many outstanding Hungarian composers and performers studied with him, among them Doráti, Foldes, Solti, Starker, and Varga. In his compositions, he generally remained faithful to the precepts of the Austro-German Romantic tradition.

WORKS: DRAMATIC: *A gondolás* (The Gondolier), opera (n.d.; in collaboration with A. Szirmai; not extant); *Csongor és Tünde*, incidental music to M. Vörösmarty's play (1913; Budapest, Dec. 6, 1916; as a ballet, Budapest, Nov. 8, 1930; orch. suite, 1937). **ORCH.:** *Scherzo* (1905); *Serenade* for Small Orch. (Budapest, Oct. 22, 1906); *Farsang* (Carnival) for Small Orch. (1907); Piano Concertino (1923); *Katonásdi* (Toy Soldiers; 1924); Suite (1931); *Divertimento No. 1* for Strings (1934), *No. 2* for Strings (1938), *No. 3: Impressioni ungheresi* (1949), *No. 4* (1951), and *No. 5* (1951); *Pastorale, phantaisie et fugue* for Strings (1934); *Ballata* for Clarinet and Orch. (1949); *Romanze* for Cello, Harp, and Strings (1949); *Változatok egy magyar népdal fölött* (Variations on a Hungarian Folk Song; 1949); *Preludio, notturno e scherzo diabolico* (1950); *Három magyar népi tánc* (3 Hungarian Folk Dances) for Salon Orch. (1951); *Ünnepi hangok* (Festal Sounds; 1951); 2 violin concertos (1950, 1957; both arranged from the 2 violin sonatas, 1911, 1918); *Toldi*, symphonic poem (1952); *Passacaglia* (1955); *Magyar gyermek- és népdalok* (Hungarian Children's Songs and Folk Songs) for Small Orch. (1955). **CHAMBER:** *Scherzo* for String Quintet (1905); *Magyar ábránd* (Hungarian Fantasy) for Tárogató and Cimbalom (1905–06); 3 string quartets (1906; 1921; *Pastorale, phantaisie et fugue*, 1938); String Trio (1908); *Ballade* for Clarinet or Viola and Piano (1911); 2 violin sonatas (1911, 1918; both arranged as violin concertos, 1950, 1957); *Romanze* for Cello and Piano (1921); *Peregi verbunk* (Pereg Recruiting Dance) for Violin or Viola or Clarinet and Piano (1951; also for Wind Quintet and String Quintet, 1957); *Bevezetés és csürdöngölö* (Introduction and Stamping Dance) for Wind Quintet and String Quintet (1957). **PIANO:** *Tarantella* for 2 Pianos, 8-hands (1905); *Változatok* (Variations; 1905); *Caprice* (1908); 2 passacaglias (n.d., 1936); *Präludieum, Nocturne und Scherzo* (1911); *Miniatür-Bilder* (1918); *Magyar parasztdalok* (Hungarian Peasant Songs; 5 sets, 1932–50); *Lakodalmas* (Wedding Dance; 1936); *Három magyar népi tánc* (3 Hungarian Folk Dances; 1941); *Változatok egy magyar népdal fölött* (Variations on a Hungarian Folk Song; 1950); Suite for 2 Pianos (1950); *Farsang* (Carnival) for 2 Pianos (1950); *Magyar népi muzsika* (Hungarian Folk Music; 1953); pieces for young people. **VOCAL:** *Agnus Dei* for Chorus (1906); *Gloria* for Chorus (1906). **OTHER:** Transcriptions for orch. of works by Bach, Schubert, Berlioz, Liszt, Tchaikovsky, and Bartók; cadenzas for Beethoven's piano concertos Nos. 1–4 (Milan, 1950).

WRITINGS (all publ. in Budapest): *Összhangzattanra előkeszitő jegyzetek* (Notes inn Preparation for a Harmony Treatise; 1910; 3rd ed., 1917, as *Az összhangzattan előkészitő iskolája* [Preparatory School in Harmony]; 6th ed., 1955); *A zenei formák vázlatos ismertetése* (A General Sketch of Musical Forms; 1911); *Elemző összhanszattan: Funkciótan* (Analytic Harmony: Function; 1944); *A hangszeres zene formái* (The Forms of instrumental Music; 1955).

BIBL.: G. Gál, *W. L. Életműve* (L. W.'s Lifework; Budapest, 1959).

Weingartner, (Paul) Felix, Edler von Münzberg, illustrious Austrian conductor; b. Zara, Dalmatia, June 2, 1863; d. Winterthur, May 7, 1942. After his father's death in 1868, his mother took him to Graz, where he studied music with W.A. Rémy. He publ. some piano pieces when he was 16 years old; Brahms recommended him for a stipend that enabled him to take music courses with Reinecke, Jadassohn, and Paul at the Leipzig Cons. (1881–83). He received the Mozart Prize at his graduation. He was introduced to Liszt, who recommended Weingartner's opera *Sakuntala* for production in Weimar (March 23, 1884), a signal honor for a young man not yet 21 years old. While progressing rapidly as a composer, Weingartner launched a brilliant career as a conductor, which was to become his prime vocation. He conducted in Königsberg (1884–85), Danzig (1885–87), Hamburg (1887–89), and Mannheim (1889–91). In 1891 he was engaged as court conductor in Berlin, where he led the Royal Opera until 1898 and the royal orch. concerts until 1907; also conducted the Kaim Orch. in Munich (1898–1905). His reputation as a fine musician was enhanced by his appearances as an ensemble player in the Weingartner Trio, with himself as pianist, Rettich as violinist, and Warnke as cellist. In 1908 he succeeded Mahler as music director of the Vienna Court Opera, and conducted there until 1911. He also was Mahler's successor as conductor of the Vienna Phil. (1908–27), with which he won great renown. He likewise served as Generalmusikdirektor in Darmstadt (1914–19) and as director of the Vienna Volksoper (1919–24). In 1927 he became director of the Basel Cons. He also conducted sym. concerts in Basel. After serving as a guest conductor of the Vienna State Opera (1934–35), he again was its director (1935–36); then once more was a guest conductor there (1936–38). Throughout the years he had engagements as guest conductor with major European orchs. He made his American debut with the N.Y.

Phil. on Feb. 12, 1904, and later conducted the N.Y. Sym. Soc. (Jan.–March 1906). He appeared with the Boston Opera Co. on Feb. 12, 1912, conducting *Tristan und Isolde*; he and his 3rd wife, **Lucille Marcel**, were engaged for a season with the Boston Opera Co. in 1913. (His 1st wife was Marie Juillerat, whom he married in 1891; his 2nd wife was the Baroness Feodora von Dreifus, whom he married in 1903). He made his debut at Covent Garden in London in 1939 conducting *Parsifal*. He eventually settled in Interlaken, where he established a summer conducting school. Although Weingartner was trained in the Austro-German Romantic tradition, his approach to conducting was notable for its eschewing of Romantic excess. Indeed, he acquired a remarkable reputation for his devotion to the composer's intentions, which he conveyed to his musicians via an unostentatious baton technique. His interpretations of the Austro-German repertoire were acclaimed for their authority and integrity. He was the first conductor to record all the Beethoven syms. Weingartner was also a competent music editor; he was on the editorial board for the complete works of Berlioz (1899) and of Haydn (1907). Despite the pressure of his activities as a conductor, he found time for composition. In addition to his first opera, *Sakuntala*, he wrote the operas *Malawika* (Munich, 1886), *Genesius* (Berlin, Nov. 15, 1892), *Orestes*, a trilogy (Leipzig, Feb. 15, 1902), *Kain und Abel* (Darmstadt, May 17, 1914), *Dame Kobold* (Darmstadt, Feb. 23, 1916), *Die Dorfschule* (Vienna, May 13, 1920), *Meister Andrea* (Vienna, May 13, 1920), and *Der Apostat* (not perf.). He also composed 7 syms. (1899–1937); various other orch. works, including pieces for Voice and Orch. and Chorus and Orch.; songs; much chamber music, including 5 string quartets, 2 violin sonatas, and piano pieces. He made arrangements of Beethoven's "Hammerklavier" Sonata, op. 106, and of Weber's *Aufforderung zum Tanz*. He was an excellent writer on musical subjects. Among his publs. were: *Die Lehre von der Wiedergeburt und das musikalische Drama* (1895); *Über das Dirigieren* (1896; 5th ed., 1913; a fundamental essay on conducting); *Bayreuth 1876–1896* (1897; 2nd ed., 1904); *Die Symphonie nach Beethoven* (1897; 4th ed., 1901; Eng. tr., 1904; new tr. as *The Symphony since Beethoven*, 1926); *Ratschläge für Aufführung der Sinfonien Beethovens* (1906; 3rd ed., 1928; Eng. tr., London, 1907); *Akkorde: Gesammelte Aufsätze von Felix Weingartner* (1912); a polemical pamphlet, *Erlebnisse eines kgl. Kapellmeisters in Berlin* (1912; an attack upon the Berlin intendancy; a rebuttal was publ. by A. Wolff in *Der Fall Weingartner*, 1912); *Ratschläge für Aufführung der Sinfonien Schuberts und Schumanns* (1918); *Ratschläge für Aufführung der Sinfonien Mozarts* (1923); *Lebenserinnerungen* (vol. I, 1923; vol. II, 1929; Eng. version, London, 1937, as *Buffets and Rewards: A Musician's Reminiscences*); *Unwirkliches und Wirkliches* (1936).

BIBL.: E. Krause, *F. W. als schaffender Künstler* (Berlin, 1904); P. Riesenfeld, *F. W. Ein kritischer Versuch* (Breslau, 1906); W. Hutschenruyter, *Levensschets en portret van F. W.* (Haarlem, 1906); J. Lustig, *F. W. Persönlichkeiten* (Berlin, 1908); W. Jacob, *F. W.* (Wiesbaden, 1933); *Festschrift für Dr. F. W. zu seinem siebzigsten Geburtstag* (Basel, 1933); C. Dyment, *F. W.: Recollections and Recordings* (Rickmansworth, 1975).

Weinmann, Karl, eminent German musicologist; b. Vohenstrauss, Upper Palatinate, Dec. 22, 1873; d. Pielenhofen, near Regensburg, Sept. 26, 1929. He was a pupil of Haberl and Haller at the Kirchenmusikschule in Regensburg, in Berlin, and in Innsbruck; after further study with Peter Wagner at the Univ. of Freiburg im Breisgau, he obtained the degree of Ph.D. there (1905) with the diss. *Das Hymnarium Parisiense*; later obtained a doctorate in theology at the Kirchenmusikschule in Regensburg (1917). After his ordination to the priesthood, he became a prof. at the Kirchenmusikschule in Regensburg; in 1910, succeeded Haberl as its director. He was ed. of the *Kirchenmusikalisches Jahrbuch* (1909–11), *Musica Sacra* (from 1911), and *Cäcilienvereinsorgan* (from 1926). He ed. for Pustet (after the *Editio vaticana*) *Römisches Gradualbuch* (1909; 4th ed., 1928); *Graduale* (1910); *Kyriale* (1911); *Totenoffizium* (1912; 2nd ed., 1928); *Graduale parvum* (1913); *Römisches Vesperbuch mit Psalmenbuch* (1915); *Karwochenbuch* (1924); *Feier der heiligen Karwoche* (1925); *Sonntagsvesper und Komplet* (2nd ed., 1928). He was also ed. of the collection *Kirchenmusik*, for which he wrote *Geschichte der Kirchenmusik* (1906; 4th ed., 1925; Eng. tr., 1910; also tr. into French, Italian, Polish, and Hungarian), and monographs on Leonhard Paminger (1907) and Carl Proske (1909). Other writings included *Palestrinas Geburtsjahr* (Regensburg, 1915); *Stille Nacht, heilige Nacht: Die Geschichte des Liedes zu seinem 100. Geburtstag* (1918; 2nd ed., 1920); *Das Konzil von Trent und die Kirchenmusik* (1919).

Weinrich, Carl, eminent American organist and teacher; b. Paterson, N.J., July 2, 1904; d. Princeton, N.J., May 13, 1991. After graduation from N.Y. Univ. (B.A., 1927), he studied at the Curtis Inst. of Music in Philadelphia (1927–30); also studied organ privately with Farnam and Dupré, and piano with Chasins. In 1930 he became the successor of Farnam as organist at the Holy Communion Church in N.Y. He taught at Westminster Choir College in Princeton, N.J. (1934–40), Wellesley College (1936–46), and at Columbia Univ. (1942–52); also was director of music at Princeton Univ. Chapel (1943–73). Weinrich toured extensively as a recitalist.

Weinstock, Herbert, American writer on music; b. Milwaukee, Nov. 16, 1905; d. N.Y., Oct. 21, 1971. He was educated in his native town; later took courses at the Univ. of Chicago. He was active in N.Y. as a music ed. for the publisher Alfred A. Knopf.

WRITINGS (all publ. in N.Y.): With W. Brockway, *Men of Music* (1939; 2nd ed., rev. and enl., 1950); with W. Brockway, *The Opera: A History of its Creation and Performance* (1941; 2nd ed., 1962, as *The World of Opera*); *Tchaikovsky* (1943); *Handel* (1946; 2nd ed., 1959; also in Ger.); *Chopin: The Man and His Music* (1949; 2nd ed., 1959); *Music As an Art* (1953; 2nd ed., 1966, as *What Music Is*); *Donizetti and the World of Opera in Italy, Paris and Vienna in the First Half of the Nineteenth Century* (1963); *Rossini: a Biography* (1968); *Vincenzo Bellini: His Life and Operas* (1971).

Weinzweig, John (Jacob), Canadian composer, teacher, and administrator; b. Toronto, March 11, 1913. He learned to play the mandolin, piano, tuba, tenor saxophone, and double bass. He was a student of Willan (counterpoint and fugue), Leo Smith (harmony), and MacMillan (orchestration) at the Univ. of Toronto (B.Mus., 1937), of Reginald Stewart (conducting) at the Toronto Cons. of Music, and of Rogers (orchestration and composition) at the Eastman School of Music in Rochester, N.Y. (M.Mus., 1938). After serving as founder-conductor of the Univ. of Toronto Sym. Orch. (1934–37), he taught at the Toronto Cons. of Music (1939–43; 1945–60) and at the Univ. of Toronto (1952–78). Inn 1951 he founded the Canadian League of Composers and was its first president until 1957, and then again from 1959 to 1963. He was the author of *John Weinzweig: His Words and His Music* (Grimsby, Ontario, 1986) and *Sounds and Reflections* (Grimsby, 1990). In 1974 he was made an Officer of the Order of Canada and in 1988 he received the Order of Ontario. In his music, Weinzweig began using serial procedures in 1939. His output continued to reflect his interest in advanced compositional means of expression throughout his career.

WORKS: DRAMATIC: 2 ballets: *The Whirling Dwarf* (1939) and *Red Ear of Corn* (Toronto, March 2, 1949); 4 film scores; more than 100 radio scores. **ORCH.:** *Legend* (1937); *The Enchanted Hill* (1938); Suite (1938); *Spectre* for Timpani and Strings (1938); *A Tale of Tuamotu* for Bassoon and Orch. (1939); Sym. (1940); *Rhapsody* (1941); *Interlude in an Artist's Life* for Strings (1943); *Our Canada* (1943); *Band-Hut Sketches* for Band (1944); *Edge of the World* (1946); 11 divertimentos: No. 1 for Flute and Strings (1946), No. 2 for Oboe and Strings (1948), No. 3 for Bassoon and Strings (1960), No. 4 for Clarinet and Strings (1968; out of chronological order), No. 5 for Trumpet, Trombone, and Winds (1961), No. 6 for Alto Saxophone and Strings (1972), No. 7 for Horn and Strings (1979), No. 8 for

Tuba and Orch. (1980), No. 9 for Full Orch. (1982), No. 10 for Piano and Strings (1988), and No. 11 for English Horn and Strings (1990); *Round Dance* (1950); Violin Concerto (1951–54; Toronto, May 30, 1955); *Symphonic Ode* (1958); Piano Concerto (Toronto, Dec. 15, 1966); Concerto for Harp and Chamber Orch. (Toronto, April 30, 1967); *Dummiyah* (Silence; Toronto, July 4, 1969); *Out of the Blues* for Concert Band (1981). **CHAMBER:** 3 string quartets (1937, 1946, 1962); Violin Sonata (1943); *Fanfare* for 3 Trumpets, 3 Trombones, and Percussion (1943); *Intermissions* for Flute and Oboe (1943); Cello Sonata, *Israel* (1949); Woodwind Quintet (1964); Clarinet Quintet (1965); *Around the Stage in 25 Minutes During Which a Variety of Instruments Are Struck* for Percussionist (1970); *Riffs* for Flute (1974); *Contrasts* for Guitar (1976); *Pieces of 5* for Brass Quintet (1976); *Refrains* for Double Bass and Piano (1977); *18 Pieces* for Guitar (1980); *15 Pieces* for Harp (1983); *Music Centre Serenade* for Flute, Horn, Viola, and Cello (1984); *Conversations* for 3 Guitars (1984); *Cadenza* for Clarinet (1986); *Birthday Notes* for Flute and Piano (1987); *Tremologue* for Viola (1987). **KEYBOARD: PIANO:** 2 suites (1939, 1950); *Swing a Fugue* (1949); *Melos* (1949); Sonata (1950); *Impromptus* (1973); *CanOn Stride* (1986); *Tango for 2* (1986; rev. 1987); *Micromotions* (1988); *3 Pieces* (1989); *Duologue* for 2 Pianos (1990). **ORGAN:** *Improvisations on an Indian Tune* (1942). **VOCAL:** *Wine of Peace* for Soprano and Orch. (1957); *Trialogue* for Soprano, Flute, and Piano (1971); *Private Collection* for Soprano and Piano (1975); *Choral Pieces* (1985–86).

BIBL.: E. Keillor, *J. W. and His Music: The Radical Romantic of Canada* (Metuchen, N.J., 1994).

Weir, Dame Gillian (Constance), outstanding New Zealand organist and harpsichordist; b. Martinsborough, Jan. 17, 1941. She studied with Ralph Downes at the Royal College of Music in London (1962–65), then privately with Anton Heiller, Marie-Claire Alain, and Boulanger (1965–66); won the St. Albans International Organ Competition in 1964. In 1965 she made her debut at London's Royal Festival Hall; she appeared throughout the world as a recitalist on both the organ and the harpsichord. In 1982 she was featured in the television film "Toccata: Two Weeks in the Life of Gillian Weir." In 1984 she gave a recital at N.Y.'s Alice Tully Hall on an organ designed by her husband. She served as president of the Incorporated Assn. of Organists (1982–83) and of the Incorporated Soc. of Musicians (1992–93). In 1989 she was made a Commander of the Order of the British Empire. In 1996 she was made a Dame Commander of the Order of the British Empire. Weir maintains a catholic repertory; has given the premiere performances of many works written for her, including William Mathias's Organ Concerto (London, Sept. 12, 1984).

Weir, Judith, English composer; b. Cambridge, May 11, 1954. After studies with Tavener in London, she received training in computer music from Vercoe at the Mass. Inst. of Technology (1973). From 1973 to 1976 she was a student of Holloway at King's College, Cambridge. She also studied with Schuller and Messiaen at the Berkshire Music Center in Tanglewood (summer, 1975). From 1979 to 1982 she taught at the Univ. of Glasgow, and then held a creative arts fellowship at Trinity College, Cambridge, from 1983 to 1985. She was composer-in-residence of the Royal Scottish Academy of Music and Drama in Glasgow from 1988 to 1991. In her diverse output, Weir has effectively utilized both traditional and contemporary techniques in creating a highly individual means of expression.

WORKS: OPERAS: *The Black Spider* (1984; Canterbury, March 6, 1985); *A Night at the Chinese Opera* (1986–87; Cheltenham, July 8, 1987); *Heaven Ablaze in His Breast*, opera-ballet (Basildon, Oct. 5, 1989); *The Vanishing Bridegroom* (Glasgow, Oct. 17, 1990); *Supio's Dream* (BBC-TV, Nov. 2, 1991; recomposition of Mozart's *Il Sogno di Scipione*); *Blond Eckbert* (1993–94; London, April 20, 1994). **ORCH.:** *Wunderhorn* (1978); *Isti Mirant Stella* (Orkney, June 23, 1981); *The Ride Over Lake Constance* (1983–84; London, March 12, 1984); *Variations on "Sumer is icumen in"* (Snape, June 13, 1987; in collaboration with others); *Sederunt principes* (1987); *Music Untangled*, overture (Tanglewood, Aug. 3, 1991; rev. 1992); *Heroische Bogenstricke* (Leverkusen, Oct. 26, 1992). **CHAMBER:** *Out of the Air* for Flute, Oboe, Clarinet, Horn, and Bassoon (London, Feb. 8, 1975); *Harmony and Invention* for Harp (1978; rev. 1980); *King Harald Sails to Byzantium* for Flute, Clarinet, Violin, Cello, Piano, and Marimba (Orkney, June 18, 1979); *Pas de Deux* for Violin and Oboe (1980); *Several Concertos* for Flute, Cello, and Piano (1980; Dundee, Jan. 21, 1981); Cello Sonata (1980); *Music for 247 Strings* for Violin and Piano (London, Oct. 5, 1981); *Spij Dobrze* (Pleasant Dreams) for Double Bass and Tape (Kazimierz Dolny, Poland, Sept. 8, 1983); *A Serbian Cabaret* for Piano Quartet (1983–84); *Sketches from a Bagpiper's Album* for Clarinet and Piano (Huddersfield, June 8, 1984); *The Bagpiper's String Trio* for Violin, Viola, and Cello (Cambridge, May 19, 1985); *Airs from Another Planet* for Flute, Oboe, Clarinet, Bassoon, Horn, and Piano (St. Andrews, Fife, Oct. 14, 1986); *Gentle Violence* for Piccolo and Guitar (London, April 10, 1987); *Mountain Airs* for Flute, Oboe, and Clarinet (Tunbridge Wells, Feb. 25, 1988); *Distance and Enchantment* for Piano, Violin, Viola, and Cello (London, Sept. 26, 1989); String Quartet (London, Oct. 2, 1990); *I broke off a golden branch* for Violin, Viola, Cello, Double Bass, and Piano (1991); *El Rey de Francia* for Violin, Viola, Cello, and Piano (1993); *Musicians Wrestle Everywhere* for 10 Instruments (1994). **KEYBOARD: PIANO:** *An mein Klavier* (1980); *The Art of Touching the Keyboard* (1983); *Michael's Strathspey* (1985; also for Organ); *Ardnamurchan Point* for 2 Pianos (1990); *Roll Off the Ragged Rocks of Sin* (1992). **ORGAN:** *Wild Mossy Mountains* (1982); *Ettrick Banks* (1983); *Michael's Strathspey* (1985; also for Piano). **VOCAL:** *25 Variations* for Soprano and 6 Players (1976); *Black Birdsong* for Baritone, Flute, Oboe, Violin, and Cello (1977); *Hans the Hedgehog* for Speaker, 2 Oboes, Bassoon, and Harpsichord (1978); *King Harald's Saga* for Soprano (1979); *Ballad* for Baritone and Orch. (Glasgow, Sept. 17, 1981); *Thread!* for Narrator and 8 Players (1981); *Scotch Minstrels* for Tenor or Soprano and Piano (1982); *Ascending into Heaven* for Chorus and Organ (1983); *Illuminare, Jerusalem* for Chorus and Organ (1985); *The Consolations of Scholarship* for Soprano and 9 Players (1985); *Lovers, Learners and Libations* for Early Music Consort (1987); *Songs from the Exotic* for Low Voice and Piano (1987); *Missa del Cid* for Speaker and Chorus (1988); *A Spanish Liederbooklet* for Soprano and Piano (1988); *The Romance of Count Arnaldos* for Soprano, 2 Clarinets, Viola, Cello, and Double Bass (1989); *Ox Mountain Was Covered by Trees* for Soprano, Countertenor, Baritone, and Orch. (Canterbury, Sept. 30, 1990); *Don't Let That Horse* for Soprano and Horn (1990); *On Buying a Horse* for Medium Voice and Piano (1991); *The Alps* for Soprano, Clarinet, and Viola (1992); *Broken Branches* for Soprano, Piano, and Double Bass (1992); *2 Human Hymns* for Chorus and Organ (1995).

Weis, (Carl) Flemming, Danish composer and organist; b. Copenhagen, April 15, 1898; d. there, Sept. 30, 1981. He studied organ and theory with Gustav Helsted at the Copenhagen Cons. (1916–20); then took courses in organ with Karl Straube and in theory and composition with Paul Graener at the Leipzig Hochschule für Musik (graduated, 1923). He served as organist of the St. Anna Church in Copenhagen (1929–68); was a member of the board of the Soc. for Contemporary Music (1926–56; president, 1942–56) and a member of the board of the Danish Soc. of Composers (president, 1963–75). His music follows the traditions of the Danish School; under the influence of Carl Nielsen, he wrote a number of symphonic pieces imbued with Romantic fervor and gentle humor.

WORKS: ORCH.: *Praeludium og Intermezzo* for Oboe and Strings (1933); Concertino for Clarinet and Strings (1935); *Symphonic Overture* (1938); *Introduction grave* for Piano and Orch. (1941); 2 syms. (1942, 1948); *In temporis vernalis* (1945; Copenhagen, Jan. 14, 1948); *Musikantiski ouverture* (1949); Concertino for Strings (1960); *Femdelt form III* (Quintuple Form III; Randers, Feb. 5, 1963); *Sine nomine* (Copenhagen, March 18, 1973); *Chaconne* (1974). **CHAMBER:** 4 string quartets (1922,

1925, 1937, 1977); *Music* for 3 Woodwinds (1928); Clarinet Sonata (1931); Violin Sonata (1932–41); *Serenade uden reelle hensigter* (Serenade without Serious Intentions) for Wind Quintet (1938); Sonatina for Flute, Violin, and Cello (1942); *Diverterende musik* (Diverting Music) for Flute, Violin, Viola, and Cello (1943); Oboe Sonata (1946); *Variations* for Wind Quintet (1946); Flute Sonata (1956); *Fantasia seria* for String Quartet (1956); *5 Epigrams* for String Quartet (1960); *Femdelt form II* (Quintuple Form II) for String Quintet (1962); *Rhapsodic Suite* for Violin (1966); *Static Situations* for String Quartet (1970); *3 søstre* (3 Sisters) for Cello (1973); *3 Mobiles* for Flute, Violin, Viola, and Cello (1974); *3 Aspects* for Guitar (1975); *Dialogues* for Flute and Guitar (1977). **KEYBOARD: PIANO:** Suite (1945–46); Sonatina (1949); *12 Monologues* (1958); *Femdelt form I* (Quintuple Form I; 1961); *Limitations I* (1965) and *II* (1968). **ORGAN:** Concertino (1957). **VOCAL:** *Det forjoettede land* (The Promised Land) for Chorus and Orch. (Copenhagen, Nov. 8, 1949); *Coeli enarrant* for Soprano and Organ (1955–56); *Sinfonia proverbiorum* for Chorus and Orch. (Copenhagen, June 21, 1959); *3 Japanese Bird Cries* for Soprano, Viola, and Guitar (1976); choruses; anthems; songs.

Weis, Karel, Czech writer on music, ethnomusicologist, and composer; b. Prague, Feb. 13, 1862; d. there, April 4, 1944. He studied violin at the Prague Cons.; also organ with Skuherský and composition with Fibich at the Organ School in Prague. He subsequently filled various posts as organist and conductor in Prague and other cities. He devoted much of his time to collecting Bohemian folk songs, and publ. them in 15 vols. (1928–41).

WORKS: OPERAS: *Viola*, after Shakespeare's *Twelfth Night* (Prague, Jan. 17, 1892; rev. version as *Blíženci* [The Twins], Prague, Feb. 28, 1917); *Der polnische Jude* (Prague, March 3, 1901); *Die Dorfmusikanten* (Prague, Jan. 1, 1905); *Der Revisor*, after Gogol (1907); *Utok na mlýn*, after Zola's *L'Attaque du moulin* (Prague, March 29, 1912); *Lešetínský kovář* (The Blacksmith of Lesetin; Prague, June 6, 1920); *Bojarská nevěsta* (The Boyar's Bride; Prague, Feb. 18, 1943). **OTHER:** *Helios a Selene*, symphonic poem; Sym.; choral pieces; songs; piano works.

BIBL.: L. Firkušný, *K. W.* (Prague, 1949).

Weisberg, Arthur, American bassoonist and conductor; b. N.Y., April 4, 1931. He attended the Juilliard School of Music in N.Y., where he studied bassoon with Simon Kovar and conducting with Jean Morel. He played bassoon with the Houston, Baltimore, and Cleveland orchs.; from 1956 to 1970, was bassoonist with the N.Y. Woodwind Quintet. In 1960 he formed the Contemporary Chamber Ensemble, with which he travels widely in Europe and America. He held teaching posts at the Juilliard School of Music (1960–68), at the State Univ. of N.Y. at Stony Brook (1971–89), and at Yale Univ. (1975–89). In 1987–88 he was chief conductor of the Iceland Sym. Orch. in Reykjavík. He publ. *The Art of Wind Playing* (1973) and *Performing Twentieth-Century Music: A Handbook for Conductors and Instrumentalists* (1993).

Weisgall, Hugo (David), distinguished Moravian-born American composer and pedagogue; b. Eibenschütz, Oct. 13, 1912. He emigrated with his family to the U.S. and became a naturalized American citizen in 1926. He studied at the Peabody Cons. of Music in Baltimore (1927–32); subsequently had composition lessons with Sessions at various times between 1932 and 1941; also was a pupil of Reiner (conducting diploma, 1938) and Scalero (composition diploma, 1939) at the Curtis Inst. of Music in Philadelphia, and pursued academic studies at Johns Hopkins Univ. (Ph.D., 1940, with a diss. on primitivism in 17th-century German poetry). After military service in World War II, he was active as a conductor, singer, teacher, and composer. He was founder-conductor of the Chamber Soc. of Baltimore (1948) and the Hilltop Opera Co. (1952), and was director of the Baltimore Inst. of Musical Arts (1949–51). He taught at Johns Hopkins Univ. (1951–57); also was made chairman of the faculty of the Cantors' Inst. at the Jewish Theological Center in N.Y. in 1952. He taught at the Juilliard School of Music (1957–70) and at Queens College of the City Univ. of N.Y. (from 1961). He served as president of the American Music Center (1963–73). In 1966 he was composer-in-residence at the American Academy in Rome. He held 3 Guggenheim fellowships and received many prizes and commissions; in 1975 he was elected to membership in the National Inst. of Arts and Letters, and in 1990 became president of the American Academy and Inst. of Arts and Letters, which, in 1994, awarded him its Gold Medal for Music. Weisgall's music constitutes the paragon of enlightened but inoffensive modernism; he is a master of all musical idioms, and bungler of none. His intentions in each of his works never fail in the execution; for this reason his music enjoys numerous performances, which are usually accepted with pleasure by the audiences, if not by the majority of important music critics.

WORKS: DRAMATIC: OPERAS: *Night* (1932); *Lillith* (1934); *The Tenor* (1948–50; Baltimore, Feb. 1, 1952); *The Stronger* (Lutherville, Md., Aug. 9, 1952); *6 Characters in Search of an Author* (1953–56; N.Y., April 26, 1959); *Purgatory* (1958; Washington, D.C., Feb. 17, 1961); *The Gardens of Adonis* (1959; rev. 1977–81; Omaha, Sept. 12, 1992); *Athaliah* (1960–63; N.Y., Feb. 17, 1964); *9 Rivers from Jordan* (1964–68; N.Y., Oct. 9, 1968); *Jennie, or The Hundred Nights* (1975–76; N.Y., April 22, 1976); *Esther* (N.Y., Oct. 6, 1993). **BALLETS:** *Quest* (Baltimore, May 17, 1938; suite, N.Y., March 21, 1942); *Art Appreciation* (Baltimore, 1938); *One Thing Is Certain* (Baltimore, Feb. 25, 1939); Outpost (1947). **ORCH.:** *Overture in F* (London, July 29, 1943); *Appearances and Entrances* (1960); *Proclamation* (1960); *Prospect* (1983); *Tekiator* (1985). **CHAMBER:** *Graven Images*, chamber pieces for Various Instruments (1964 et seq.); *Arioso and Burlesca* for Cello and Piano (1984); *Tangents* for Flute and Marimba (1985). **KEYBOARD: PIANO:** 2 sonatas (1931, 1982); *Variations* (1939). **ORGAN:** *Chorale Prelude* (1938). **VOCAL:** *Hymn* for Chorus and Orch. (1941); *Soldier Songs* for Baritone and Orch. (1944–46; N.Y., April 26, 1954; rev. 1965; Baltimore, March 30, 1966); *A Garden Eastward*, cantata for High Voice and Orch. (1952; Baltimore, Jan. 31, 1953); solo songs.

Weisgarber, Elliot, American-born Canadian composer, clarinetist, and teacher; b. Pittsfield, Mass., Dec. 5, 1919. He received training in clarinet from Rosario Mazzeo, from Gustave Lanzenus in N.Y., and from R. Mont Arey at the Eastman School of Music in Rochester, N.Y., where he also studied composition (B.Mus., 1942; M.Mus., 1943). He later pursued his studies in composition with Boulanger in Paris (1952–53) and with Halsey Stevens in Los Angeles (1958–59). From 1944 to 1958 he taught at the Women's College of the Univ. of North Carolina. He also played clarinet in orchs. and chamber music groups. After teaching at the Univ. of Calif. at Los Angeles (1958–59), he was on the faculty of the Univ. of British Columbia in Vancouver (1960–84). In 1973 he became a naturalized Canadian citizen. He received Canada Council grants to study music in Japan (1966; 1967; 1968–69), where he learned to play the shakuhachi. In his music, Weisgarber has composed not only scores along traditional Western lines but also pieces utilizing Japanese folk melos and instruments.

WORKS: DRAMATIC: Television and radio scores. **ORCH.:** 3 syms. (1961–83); *Sinfonia Concertante* for Oboe, 2 Horns, and Strings (1962); *Kyoto Landscapes: Lyrical Evocations* (1970; rev. 1972); *Illahee Chanties* for Chamber Orch. (1971); *Autumnal Music* for English Horn and Strings (1973); *Musica serena* for Small Orch. (1974); *Netori: A Fantasie* for Alto Saxophone and Orch. (1974); Violin Concerto (1974; rev. 1987); *A Pacific Trilogy* (1974); *A Northumbrian Elegy* (1977). **CHAMBER:** Sonata for Flute, Clarinet, and Piano (1953); *Divertimento* for String Trio (1956) and for Horn, Viola, and Piano (1959); Flute Sonata (1963); Suite for Viola and Piano (1964); Sonata for Solo Cello (1965); *Epigrams* for Flute and Koto or Piano (1970; rev. 1973); *Rokudan Henko-no-shirabe* for 2 Kotos and 2 Shamisen (1971); *6 Miniatures After Hokusai* for Violin and Piano (1972); *Fantasia a Tre* for Violin, Horn, and Piano (1975); Cello Sonata (1980); String Quartet No. 6 (1980); *32 Concert Études* for Clarinet (1986); Clarinet Quintet (1988); *Sonata Piacevole* for Clarinet and Piano (1990); *Music in Memory of Andrei Sakharov* for Flute, Violin, Viola, Cello, and Piano (1990); Trio for Violin, Cello, and Piano (1993); *Amadablam: A Soliloquy* for Piano (1994). **VOCAL:** *Num mortuis resurgent?*, cantata for Chorus (1963; rev. 1973); *Ren-ai-to toki ni tsuite* (Of Love and Time) for Soprano, Flute, Oboe, String Trio, and Harpsichord (1971); *Night* for Baritone, Chorus, and String Quartet or String Orch. (1973; rev. 1982); *As We Stood Then*, song cycle for Mezzo-soprano or Baritone, Viola, and Piano (1975); *Illusions of Mortality*, song cycle for Voice and Piano (1975); *Canticle* for Chorus, Horn, and Strings (1978); *10 Japanese Folk Songs* for Soprano and Piano (1981); *Omnia Exeunt in Misterium*, song cycle for Soprano and Orch. (1994).

Weismann, Julius, German pianist, conductor, and composer; b. Freiburg im Breisgau, Dec. 26, 1879; d. Singen am Hohentweil, Dec. 22, 1950. He began piano lessons at 9 with Seyffart; later studied composition with Rheinberger in Munich (1892); received advanced piano training from Dimmler in Freiburg im Breisgau (1893), and took courses at the Univ. of Lausanne; also studied composition with Bussmeyer, von Herzogenberg in Berlin (1898–99), and Thuille in Munich (1899–1902). He was active as a pianist and conductor in Freiburg im Breisgau from 1906, where he founded (with E. Doflein) the Musikseminar in 1930, subsequently serving as a teacher of harmony and as director of the piano master class; after retiring in 1939, he devoted himself fully to composition. He received the Beethoven Prize (1930), the Bach Prize of Leipzig (1939), and the Ehrenbürgerrecht of Freiburg im Breisgau (1939); was made an honorary prof. by the government (1936) and by the state of Baden (1950). The Julius Weismann Archive was founded in his memory in Duisburg in 1954.

WORKS: DRAMATIC: OPERAS: *Schwanenweiss* (1919–20; Duisburg, Sept. 29, 1923); *Ein Traumspiel* (1922–24; Duisburg, 1925); *Leonce und Lena* (Mannheim, 1924); *Regina del lago* (Karlsruhe, 1928); *Die Gespenstersonate* (1929–30; Munich, Dec. 19, 1930); *Die pfiffige Magd* (1937–38; Leipzig, Feb. 11, 1939). **BALLETS:** *Tanzphantasie* (1910; orchestrated from the piano piece); *Die Landsknechte: Totentanz* (1936); *Sinfonisches Spiel* (1937). **ORCH.:** 3 piano concertos (1909–10, rev. 1936; 1941–42; 1942–48); 4 violin concertos (1910–11; 1929; 1942; 1943); *Suite* for Piano and Orch. (1927); Concerto for Flute, Clarinet, Bassoon, Trumpet, Timpani, and Strings (1930); Horn Concerto (1935); Cello Concerto (1941–43); 2 syms. (1940, 1940); *Theme, Variations and Fugue* for Trautonium and Orch. (1943; also for Violin and Piano); *Musik* for Bassoon and Orch. (1947). **CHAMBER:** Piano Quintet (1902); 13 string quartets (1905; 1907; 1910; *Fantastischer Reigen*, 1913; 1914; 1918–22; 1922; 1929; *Fugue*, 1931; 1932; 1940; 1943–45; 1947); 3 piano trios (1908–09; 1916; 1921); 4 violin sonatas (1909; 1917; 1917, arranged for Clarinet and Piano, 1941; 1921); Flute Sonata (1941); *Sonatina concertante* for Cello and Piano (1941; also for Cello and Chamber Orch.); Trio for Flute, Clarinet, and Bassoon (1942); *Theme, Variations and Fugue* for Violin and Piano (1943; also for Trautonium and Orch.); Viola Sonata (1945); various other chamber works; piano pieces. **VOCAL:** *Macht hoch die Tür*, Christmas cantata for Soprano, Chorus, and Orch. (1912); *Psalm XC* for Baritone, Chorus, and Orch. (1912); *Der Wächterruf* for Soprano, Baritone, Chorus, and Orch. (1947–50); various men's and women's choruses; solo songs.

BIBL.: F. Herzfeld, *J. W. und seine Generation* (Duisburg, 1965).

Weiss, Adolph, American composer and bassoonist; b. Baltimore, Sept. 12, 1891; d. Van Nuys, Calif., Feb. 21, 1971. He studied piano, violin, and bassoon; at the age of 16, was engaged as 1st bassoonist of the Russian Sym. Orch. of N.Y.; then joined the N.Y. Phil. (1909) and the N.Y. Sym. Orch. (1910); he also studied composition with Cornelius Rybner at Columbia Univ. In 1916 he joined the Chicago Sym. Orch. as bassoonist; he also studied theory with Adolf Weidig and Theodore Otterstrom in Chicago; then was bassoonist with the Eastman Theatre Orch. in Rochester, N.Y. (from 1921). In 1926 he went to Berlin and became the first American student of Schoenberg, whose influence was decisive in the formation of his musical style. Returning to the U.S., he played in the San Francisco Sym. Orch. (from 1936), the MGM Studios Orch. (from 1938), and the Los Angeles Phil. (from 1951). He held a Guggenheim fellowship (1931); received a National Inst. of Arts and Letters award in 1955.

WORKS: ORCH.: *I segreti* (1922; Rochester, N.Y., May 1, 1925); Chamber Sym. (1927); *American Life*, "scherzoso jazzoso" (1929; N.Y., Feb. 21, 1930); *Theme and Variations* (1933); Suite (1938); *10 Pieces* for Low Instrument and Orch. (1943); Trumpet Concerto (1952). **CHAMBER:** 3 string quartets (1925, 1926, 1932); *Sonata da camera* for Flute and Viola (1929); Quintet for Flute, Oboe, Clarinet, Bassoon, and Horn (1931); *Petite suite* for Flute, Clarinet, and Bassoon (1939); Violin Sonata (1941); *Passacaglia* for Horn and Viola (1942); Sextet for Flute, Oboe, Clarinet, Bassoon, Horn, and Piano (1947); Trio for Clarinet, Viola, and Cello (1948); Concerto for Bassoon and String Quartet (1949); Trio for Flute, Violin, and Piano (1955); *5 Fantasies* for Violin and Piano (1956); *Tone Poem* for Brass and Percussion (1957); *Rhapsody* for 4 Horns (1957); *Vade mecum* for Wind Instruments (1958). **PIANO:** *Fantasie* (1918); *12 Preludes* (1927); Sonata (1932); *Protest* for 2 Pianos (1945); *Pulse of the Sea* (1950). **VOCAL:** *7 Songs* for Soprano and String Quartet (1928); *The Libation Bearers*, choreographic cantata for Soloists, Chorus, and Orch. (1930); *Ode to the West Wind* for Baritone, Viola, and Piano (1945).

BIBL.: W. Riegger, "A. W. and Colin McPhee," in H. Cowell, ed., *American Composers on American Music* (Stanford, Calif., 1933); W. George, *A. W.* (diss., Univ. of Iowa, 1971); B. Kopp, *The Twelve-tone Techniques of A. W.* (diss., Northwestern Univ., 1981).

Weissberg, Yulia (Lazarevna), Russian composer; b. Orenburg, Jan. 6, 1880; d. Leningrad, March 1, 1942. She studied piano with Rimsky-Korsakov and instrumentation with Glazunov at the St. Petersburg Cons. (1903–05) and continued her musical training with Humperdinck and Reger in Germany (1907–12). She was a co-ed. of the journal *Muzykalny Sovremennik* (1915–17) and choral director of the Young Workers' Cons. (1921–23). She married **Andrei Rimsky-Korsakov**.

WORKS: OPERAS: *Rusalochka* (1923); *Gulnara* (1935); *Gusi-lebedi* (Geese Swans; 1937); *Myortvaya tsarevna* (The Dead Princess; 1937). **ORCH.:** *Skazochka* (Tale; 1928); *Nochyu* (At Night), symphonic poem (1929); *Ballade* (1930); *Sailor's Dance* (1936). **VOCAL:** *Rautendelein* for Voice and Orch. (1912); *Poyot pechalniy golos* (A Sad Voice Sings) for Voice and Orch. (1924); *Dvenadsat* (The 12) for Chorus and Orch. (Leningrad, May 12, 1926); *5 Children's Songs* for Voice and Orch. (1929); *Lunnaya skazka* (The Story of the Moon) for Voice, Flute, and String Quartet (1929); *Garafitsa* for Voice, Cello, and Harp or Piano (1938); numerous solo songs; children's choruses; folk song arrangements.

Weisse, Hans, Austrian music theorist and composer; b. Vienna, March 31, 1892; d. N.Y., Feb. 10, 1940. He studied with Schenker and became an exponent of his theory. In 1931 he went to the U.S. and gave courses in theory at the Mannes Music School in N.Y. He wrote mostly chamber music: 3 string quartets (1920–36); String Sextet (1924); Quintet for Clarinet and Strings (1928); Octet for Strings and Winds (1929); Concerto for Flute, Oboe, and Harpsichord (1937); *Choral Partita* for Strings and Winds (1938).

Weissenbäck, (Franz) Andreas, Austrian choral conductor and composer; b. St. Lorenzen, Styria, Nov. 26, 1880; d. Vienna, March 14, 1960. He studied in Graz; in 1899, entered the monastery at Klosterneuburg, near Vienna; became a Catholic priest in 1904; then took up musicology under Adler at the Univ. of Vienna (Ph.D., 1912). He was for many years choirmaster at Klosterneuburg. He publ. *Sacra musica*, a lexicon of Catholic church music (1937); contributed valuable papers to various publs., particularly on Gregorian chant; also was an expert on church bells. He composed a German Mass for Men's Chorus, a Mass for Chorus and 17 Winds, and many other sacred works.

Weissenberg, Alexis (Sigismond), noted Bulgarian-born French pianist; b. Sofia, July 26, 1929. He studied piano at a very early age with his mother, and then pursued training with Pantcho Vladigerov. During the German occupation of his homeland, he and his mother were briefly confined in a concentration camp but then were allowed to emigrate to Palestine; in 1945 he made his first appearance as a soloist with an orch. there. In 1946 he went to N.Y. to study at the Juilliard School of Music; his principal mentor was Olga Samaroff, but he also received instruction from Artur Schnabel and Wanda Landowska. In 1947 he won the Leventritt Competition, which led to his U.S. debut that same year with George Szell and the N.Y. Phil.; after touring extensively, he settled in France in 1956, became a naturalized citizen, and withdrew from public appearances for a decade in which he devoted himself to further study and teaching. In 1966 he resumed his career and subsequently toured all over the world.

Weissenborn, Günther (Albert Friedrich), German pianist and conductor; b. Coburg, June 2, 1911. He studied at the Hochschule für Musik in Berlin. He was an organist and choir director in Berlin (1934–37). He was then a conductor in Halle (1937–42), Hannover (1944), and Göttingen (1945–47) before returning to Hannover as conductor of the Hausegger Chamber Orch. Apart from his activities as a conductor, Weissenborn earned a fine reputation as a piano accompanist in lieder recitals.

Welcher, Dan, American composer, conductor, and teacher; b. Rochester, N.Y., March 2, 1948. He studied bassoon and composition (with Adler and Benson) at the Eastman School of Music in Rochester (B.Mus., 1969). Following further training in composition with Ulehla and Flagello at the Manhattan School of Music in N.Y. (M.M., 1972), he pursued postgraduate studies in electronic music at the Aspen (Colo.) Music School (summer, 1972). He was a bassoonist in the Rochester Phil. (1968–69) and the U.S. Military Academy Band at West Point, N.Y. (1969–72), and then was 1st bassoonist in the Louisville Orch. (1972–78). From 1972 to 1978 he also taught at the Univ. of Louisville. In 1976 he became a member of the artist faculty at the Aspen Music Festival, where he served each summer until 1993. In 1978 he joined the faculty of the Univ. of Texas at Austin, where he was a prof. from 1989. In 1985–86 he was a visiting assoc. prof. at the Eastman School of Music. From 1980 to 1990 he was assistant conductor of the Austin Sym. Orch. He served as composer-in-residence of the Honolulu Sym. Orch. from 1990 to 1993.

WORKS: OPERA: *Della's Delight* (1986; Austin, Texas, Feb. 1987). **ORCH.:** *Walls and Fences* (1970); *Episode* (1970; Buffalo, Jan. 1971); Flute Concerto (Louisville, April 1974); *Concerto da camera* for Bassoon and Small Orch. (1975); *Dervishes: Ritual Dance-Scene* (1976; Louisville, April 1977); *The Visions of Merlin* (1980); *Prairie Light: 3 Texas Watercolors of Georgia O'Keefe* (1985; Sherman, Texas, March 1, 1986); *Arches: An Impression* for Concert Band (1985); *The Yellowstone Fires* for Wind Ensemble (1988); *Castle Creek*, fanfare-overture (Aspen, Colo., July 7, 1989); Clarinet Concerto (Honolulu, Oct. 15, 1989); *Haleakala: How Maui Snared the Sun* for Narrator and Orch. (Honolulu, Sept. 15, 1991); *Bridges*, 5 pieces for Strings (1991); 2 syms.: No. 1 (1992; Honolulu, April 4, 1993) and No. 2, *Night Watchers* (Flagstaff, Ariz., Nov. 9, 1994); Violin Concerto (Aspen, Colo., July 2, 1993); Piano Concerto, *Shiva's Dream* (1993–94; Round Top Festival, Texas, June 11, 1994); *Zion* for Wind Ensemble (1994; Boulder, Colo., Feb. 24, 1995). **CHAMBER:** *Nocturne and Dance* for Trumpet and Piano (1966); *Elizabethan Variations* for 4 Recorders (1968); 2 wind quintets (1972, 1977); Violin Sonata (1974); Trio for Violin, Cello, and Piano (1976); *Partita* for Horn, Violin, and Piano (1980); *Fantasy: In Memoriam Anwar Sadat* for Carillon (1982); Brass Quintet (1983; N.Y., Feb. 1984); Quintet for Clarinet and Strings (N.Y., April 1984); *Hauntings* for Tuba Ensemble (1986); *Listen Up!* for Wind Quintet (1986); *White Mares of the Moon* for Flute and Harp (1986); 2 string quartets: No. 1 (1987; N.Y., May 11, 1988) and No. 2, *Harbor Music* (Cleveland, Oct. 28, 1992); *Firewing: The Flame and the Moth* for Oboe and Percussion (1987); *Chameleon Music* for 10 Percussionists (San Antonio, Nov. 1988); *Stigma* for Contrabass and Piano (N.Y., June 1989); *Zephyrus* for Flute, Violin, Viola, and Cello (1990); *Tsunami* for Cello, Percussion, and Piano (1991); piano pieces. **VOCAL:** *Black Riders* for High Voice and Chamber Ensemble (1971); *Abeja Blanca* for Mezzo-soprano, English Horn, and Piano (1978); *Vox Femina* for Soprano and Ensemble (1984); *Evening Scenes: 3 Poems of James Agee* for Tenor and Ensemble (1985; Dallas, Jan. 1986).

Weldon, George, English conductor; b. Chichester, June 5, 1906; d. Cape Town, South Africa, Aug. 16, 1963. He studied at the Royal College of Music in London with Sargent. He conducted various provincial orchs.; traveled as a guest conductor in North Africa, Turkey, and Yugoslavia. He was conductor of the City of Birmingham Sym. Orch. (1943–51); was 2nd conductor of the Halle Orch. in Manchester under Barbirolli (from 1952); also conducted the Sadler's Wells Royal Ballet in London (1955–56).

Welin, Karl-Erik (Vilhelm), Swedish organist, pianist, and composer; b. Genarp, May 31, 1934; d. Mallorca, May 30, 1992. He studied organ with Alf Linden at the Stockholm Musikhögskolan (graduated, 1961). He also received training in composition from Bucht (1958–60) and Lidholm (1960–64), in piano from Sven Brandel, and at the summer courses in new music in Darmstadt with David Tudor (1960–62). As a performer, he was a proponent of the extreme avant-garde in Sweden. He became well known via many appearances on Swedish TV. In contrast, his compositions followed a more mellow path. While he embraced serial techniques, he did so with Romantic elan.

WORKS: DRAMATIC: *Dummerjöns* (Tom Fool), children's television opera (1966–67); *Copelius*, ballet (1968); *Ondine*, theater music (1968); *Vindarnas grotta* (Cave of the Winds), television ballet (Stockholm TV, March 30, 1969); *Drottning Jag* (Queen Ego), opera (1972; Stockholm, Feb. 17, 1973); *Don Quijote*, scenic oratorio (1990–91). **ORCH.:** *Pereo* for 36 Strings (1964); Sym. (1985–86; Malmö, Oct. 22, 1987); Concertino for Clarinet, Viola, Piano, and Orch. (1987). **CHAMBER:** *Sermo modulatus* for Flute and Clarinet (1959); *Manzit* for Clarinet, Trombone, Violin, Piano, and Percussion (1962); *Esservecchia* for Electric Guitar, Horn, Trombone, and Piano (1963); *Warum nicht?* for Flute, Violin, Cello, Xylophone, Vibraphone, and Tam-tam (1964); 9 string quartets (c.1964–90); *Etwas für . . .* for Wind Quintet (1966); *Ben fatto* for Instrument or an infinite number of Instruments (1968); *PC-132* for String Quartet (1970); *Harmonies* for Clarinet, Trombone, Cello, and Piano (1972); *Pagabile* for Chamber Ensemble (1972); *Eurytmi* for Piano Quartet (1979); *Denby-Richard* for Flute and Cello (1981); *Solo* for Bassoon (1983); *EssAEG* for 2 Pianos and Electronics (1988); *Viriditas per Omnibus* for 12 Instruments (1988). **VOCAL:** *4 Chinese Poems* for Chorus (1956); *Renovations* for Soprano, Flute, Violin, Mandolin, Celesta, and Percussion (1960); Cantata for Children's Chorus, Violin, Flute, and Harpsichord (1960); *Glazba* for Soprano, 3 Flutes, and Bassoon (1968); *A New Map of Hell* for Chorus (1971); *Aver la forza di . . .* for Chorus and String Orch. (1972); *Ett svenskt rekviem* for Soloists, Chorus, and Orch. (1976); *Flying Safe* for Soprano, Flute, and Chorus (1980); *L'aveu* for Soloists, Chorus, and Orch. (1982–83); *Crepusculo* for Chorus (1992).

Welitsch (real name, **Veličkova**), **Ljuba,** remarkable Bulgarian-born Austrian soprano; b. Borissovo, July 10, 1913; d. Vienna, Sept. 2, 1996. She studied violin as a child; after attending the Sofia Cons. and the Univ. of Sofia, she studied voice with Lierhammer in Vienna. In 1936 she made her operatic debut at the

Sofia Opera; after singing in Graz (1937–40), Hamburg (1942–43), and Munich (1943–46), she joined the Vienna State Opera, having sung there previously at the 80th birthday celebration for Richard Strauss on June 11, 1944, as Salome, which became her most celebrated role. She made her London debut with the visiting Vienna State Opera as Donna Anna in Don Giovanni on Sept. 20, 1947, a role she repeated in 1948 at the Glyndebourne Festival. On Feb. 4, 1949, she made her Metropolitan Opera debut in N.Y. as Salome, remaining on the company's roster until 1952; she sang at London's Covent Garden in 1953. In subsequent years, she appeared in character roles in Vienna; returned to the Metropolitan Opera in 1972 in a speaking role in *La Fille du régiment.* Among her other notable roles were Aida, Musetta, Minnie, Rosalinde, Jenůfa, and Tosca.

Wellek, Albert, eminent Austrian musicologist and psychologist; b. Vienna, Oct. 16, 1904; d. Mainz, Aug. 27, 1972. He studied composition and conducting at the Prague Cons. (graduated, 1926) and music history, literature, and philosophy at the Univ. of Prague; was a student of Adler, Lach, Ficker, and Wellesz at the Univ. of Vienna (Ph.D., 1928, with the diss. *Doppelempfinden und Programmusik*); then studied psychology in Vienna and at the Univ. of Leipzig; in 1938 he completed his Habilitation at the Univ. of Munich with his *Typologie der Musikbegabung im deutschen Volke: Grundlegung einer psychologischen Theorie der Musik und Musikgeschichte* (publ. in Munich, 1939; 2nd ed., 1970). He became an assistant lecturer and then lecturer at the Univ. of Leipzig Inst. of Psychology in 1938; in 1942 he was made acting prof. of psychology at the Univ. of Halle; after serving as prof. of psychology and educational science at the Univ. of Breslau (1943–46), he founded the Univ. of Mainz Inst. of Psychology in 1946, remaining there until his death. Wellek was the foremost music psychologist of his time, being an authority on the theory of hearing.

WRITINGS: *Das absolute Gehör und seine Typen* (Leipzig, 1938; 2nd ed., 1970); *Das Problem des seelischen Seins: Die Strukturtheorie Felix Kruegers: Deutung und Kritik* (Leipzig, 1941; 2nd ed., 1953); *Die Polarität im Aufbau des Charakters: System der konkreten Charakterkunde* (Bern and Munich, 1950; 3rd ed., 1966); *Die Wiederherstellung der Seelenwissenschaft im Lebenswerk Felix Kruegers: Längsschnitt durch ein halbes Jahrhundert der Psychologie* (Hamburg, 1950; 2nd ed., 1968); *Ganzheitpsychologie und Strukturtheorie* (Bern, 1955; 2nd ed., 1969); ed. *20. Kongress der Deutschen Gesellschaft für Psychologie: Berlin 1955* (Berlin, 1955); *Der Rückfall in die Methodenkrise der Psychologie und ihre Überwindung* (Göttingen, 1959; 2nd ed., 1970); *Musikpsychologie und Musikästhetik: Grundriss der systematischen Musikwissenschaft* (Frankfurt am Main, 1963); *Psychologie* (Berlin and Munich, 1963; 3rd ed., 1971); *Melancholie in der Musik* (Hamburg, 1969); *Witz-Lyrik-Sprache* (Bern and Munich, 1970).

BIBL.: *Archiv für die Gesamt Psychologie*, CXVI (1964; includes Festschrift for Wellek's 60th birthday).

Weller, Walter, distinguished Austrian conductor; b. Vienna, Nov. 30, 1939. He received training in violin from Moravec and Samohyl at the Vienna Academy of Music. He also studied conducting with Böhm and Stein, and later received guidance from Krips and Szell. In 1956 he became a violinist in the Vienna Phil., subsequently serving as one of its concertmasters (1964–69). He also was 2nd violin in the Wiener Kozerthaus Quartet until founding his own Weller Quartet in 1958, with which he toured with notable success throughout Europe, North America, and Asia. In 1966 he began conducting but it was not until 1968 that he made his professional debut as a conductor of the Vienna Phil. From 1969 he conducted at the Volksoper and State Opera in Vienna. After serving as Generalmusikdirektor in Duisburg (1971–72), he was music director of the Niederösterreichesche Tonkünster-Orch. in Vienna (1975–78). He also began to appear as a guest conductor with major European orchs. and opera houses. From 1977 to 1980 he was principal conductor and musical adviser of the Royal Liverpool Phil., and then was principal conductor of the Royal Phil. in London from 1980 to 1985. In 1991 he was named music director of the Royal Scottish National Orch. in Glasgow, and he concurrently served as music director of the Theater and Sym. Orch. in Basel from 1994. While Weller is esteemed for his unmannered interpretations of the great Austro-German masterworks, he has also demonstrated a capacity to project modern scores with fine results.

Wellesz, Egon (Joseph), eminent Austrian-born English composer, musicologist, and pedagogue; b. Vienna, Oct. 21, 1885; d. Oxford, Nov. 9, 1974. He studied harmony with Carl Frühling in Vienna and then was a pupil in musicology with Adler at the Univ. of Vienna (graduated, 1908); also received private instruction from Schoenberg. From 1911 to 1915 he taught music history at the Neues Cons. in Vienna; in 1913 he was engaged as a lecturer on musicology at the Univ. of Vienna, and was a prof. there from 1930 to 1938, when the annexation of Austria by Nazi Germany compelled him to leave. He went to England in 1938; joined the music dept. of the Univ. of Oxford, which in 1932 had conferred upon him the degree of Mus.Doc. (*honoris causa*). In 1943 he became a lecturer in music history at the Univ. of Oxford; in 1946 he was appointed to the editorial board of the *New Oxford History of Music*, to which he then contributed, and was Univ. Reader in Byzantine music at Oxford (1948–56). Wellesz received the Prize of the City of Vienna in 1953. He was president of the Univ. of Oxford Byzantine Soc. (1955–66). In 1957 he was made a Commander of the Order of the British Empire and was awarded the Grande Médaille d'Argent of the City of Paris. In 1961 he was awarded the Austrian Great State prize. A scholar and a musician of extraordinary capacities, Wellesz distinguished himself as a composer of highly complex musical scores, and as an authority on Byzantine music.

WORKS: DRAMATIC: OPERAS: *Die Prinzessin Girnara* (1919–20; Hannover, May 15, 1921; rev. version, Mannheim, Sept. 2, 1928); *Alkestis* (1922–23; Mannheim, March 20, 1924); *Opferung des Gefangenen* (1924–25; Cologne, April 10, 1926); *Scherz, List und Rache* (1926–27; Stuttgart, March 1, 1928); *Die Bakchantinnen* (1929–30; Vienna, June 20, 1931); *Incognita* (Oxford, Dec. 5, 1951). **BALLETS:** *Das Wunder der Diana* (1915; Mannheim, March 20, 1924); *Persisches Ballett* (1920; Donaueschingen, 1924); *Achilles auf Skyros* (1921; Stuttgart, March 4, 1926); *Die Nächtlichen* (1923; Berlin, Nov. 20, 1924). **ORCH.:** *Vorfrühling*, symphonic poem (1912); *Suite* for Violin and Chamber Orch. (1924); Piano Concerto (1934); *Prosperos Beschwörungen*, after Shakespeare's *The Tempest* (1936–38; Vienna, Feb. 19, 1938); 9 syms.: No. 1, in C (1945), No. 2, in E-flat (1948), No. 3, in A (1951), No. 4, *Symphonia Austriaca*, in G (1953), No. 5 (1956; Düsseldorf, Feb. 20, 1958), No. 6 (1965; Nuremberg, June 1, 1966), No. 7 (1968), No. 8 (1971), and No. 9 (1971; Vienna, Nov. 22, 1972); Violin Concerto (1961; Vienna, Jan. 19, 1962); *Music* for Strings (1964); *Divertimento* for Chamber Orch. (1969); *Symphonischer Epilog* (1969). **CHAMBER:** 9 string quartets (1912, 1917, 1918, 1920, 1944, 1947, 1948, 1957, 1966); *Geistiges Lied* for Piano Trio (1918); Sonata for Solo Cello (1921); *2 Pieces* for Clarinet and Piano (1922); Sonata for Solo Violin (1924); Suite for Violin and Piano (1937); *Little Suite* for Flute (1937); Octet for Clarinet, Horn, Bassoon, and String Quintet (1948–49); Suite for Wind Quintet (1954); Suite in 3 movements for Bassoon (1956); Clarinet Quintet (1959); 2 string trios (1962, 1969); *5 Miniatures* for Violin and Piano (1965); *Music* for String Quartet (1968); String Quintet (1970). **KEYBOARD: PIANO:** *3 Piano Pieces* (1912); *Epigramme* (1913); *5 Dance Pieces* (1927); *Triptych* (1966); *Studies in Grey* (1969). **ORGAN:** *Partita* (1966). **VOCAL:** *Gebete der Mädchen zur Maria* for Soprano, Chorus, and Orch. (1909); *Mitte des Lebens*, cantata (1932); *Amor timido*, cantata for Soprano and Orch. (1935); *5 Sonnets by Elizabeth Barrett Browning* for Soprano and String Quartet (1935); *Lied der Welt* for Soprano and Orch. (1937); *Leben, Traum und Tod* for Contralto and Orch. (1937); *Short Mass* for Chorus and Small Orch. (1937); *The Leaden Echo and the Golden Echo* for Soprano, Violin, Clarinet, Cello, and

Piano, after Hopkins (1944); *4 Songs of Return* for Soprano and Small Orch. (1961); *Duineser Elegie* for Soprano, Chorus, and Chamber Ensemble (1963); *Ode to Music* for Baritone and Chamber Orch. (1964); *Vision* for Soprano and Orch. (1966); *Mirabile Mysterium*, Christmas cantata (1967); *Canticum Sapientiae* for Baritone, Chorus, and Orch. (1968; Graz, Oct. 25, 1969).

WRITINGS: *Arnold Schönberg* (Vienna, 1921; Eng. tr., 1924); *Byzantinische Kirchenmusik* (Breslau, 1927); *Eastern Elements in Western Chant: Studies in the Early History of Ecclesiastical Music*, Monumenta Musicae Byzantinae, subsidia, II (1947; 2nd ed., 1967); *A History of Byzantine Music and Hymnography* (Oxford, 1949; 3rd ed., rev., 1963); *Essays on Opera* (London, 1950); *The Origin of Schoenberg's 12-tone System* (Washington, D.C., 1958); *Byzantinische Musik, Das Musikwerk*, I (1959; Eng. tr., 1959); *Die Hymnen der Ostkirche*, Basiliensis de musica orationes, I (Kassel, 1962); *J.J. Fux* (London, 1965); also ed. *Ancient and Oriental Music*, Vol. I, *The New Oxford History of Music* (Oxford, 1957); ed. with M. Velimirović, *Studies in Eastern Chant*, I–III (London, 1966–71); ed. with F. Sternfeld, *The Age of Enlightenment (1745–1790)*, Vol. VII, *The New Oxford History of Music* (Oxford, 1973).

BIBL.: R. Schollum, *E. W.* (Vienna, 1964); C. Benser, *E. W. (1885–1974): Chronicle of a Twentieth-Century Musician* (N.Y., 1985); L. Wedl, *Die Bakchantinnen von E. W.: Oder Das göttliche Wunder* (Vienna, 1992).

Welser-Möst (real name, **Möst**), **Franz,** Austrian conductor; b. Linz, Aug. 16, 1960. He studied at the Munich Hochschule für Musik. After becoming a finalist in the Karajan conducting competition in 1979, he served as principal conductor of the Austrian Youth Orch. In 1985 he was named music director of the Winterthur and Norrköping sym. orchs. He made a successful British debut as a guest conductor with the London Phil. in 1986, and subsequently led it on a tour of Europe. In 1987 he made his debut as an opera conductor in Vienna with *L'Italiana in Algeri*. In 1989 he made his U.S. debut as a guest conductor with the St. Louis Sym. Orch. From 1990 to 1996 he was principal conductor of the London Phil. In 1995 he became music director of the Zürch Opera.

Welting, Ruth, American soprano; b. Memphis, Tenn., May 11, 1949. She received her training from Daniel Ferro in N.Y., Luigi Ricci in Rome, and Jeanne Reiss in Paris. In 1970 she made her operatic debut as Blondchen at the N.Y. City Opera. As a guest artist, she sang in Houston, San Antonio, Dallas, Sante Fe, and San Francisco. In 1975 she made her first appearance at London's Covent Garden as Zerbinetta, which role she also sang at her Metropolitan Opera debut in N.Y. on March 20, 1976. She continued to make occasional appearances at the Metropolitan Opera until 1982. In 1979 she sang the Fairy Godmother in *Cendrillon* in Ottawa and in 1980 in Washington, D.C. In 1982 she made her first appearance at the Salzburg Festival as Zerbinetta. She sang Marie in *La Fille du Régiment* in Barcelona in 1984. In 1990 she appeared as Ophelia in Thomas' *Hamlet* at the Chicago Lyric Opera. Among her other roles are Zerlina, Gilda, Norina, Adele, Sophie, and the Princess in *L'Enfant et les Sortilèges*. She has also appeared frequently as a lieder artist.

Wendt, Larry (Lawrence Frederick), American composer and writer on music; b. Napa, Calif., April 5, 1946. After training in chemistry at San Jose State College (1964–67) and the Univ. of Montana (1967–68), he studied with Strang (composition) and took courses in comparative literature at San Jose State Univ. (B.A., 1975). He was active as an electronics technician in the music dept. and recording studios at San Jose State Univ. From 1978 he utilized his own electronic and computer equipment to produce various works, a number of which he recorded on his own Frog Hollow label. With S. Ruppenthal, he publ. the books *Vocable Gestures: A Historical Survey of Sound Poetry* (1977) and *A Sketch of American Text-Sound Composition and the Works of Charles Amirkhanian* (1979). Most of his music is for tape.

Wenkel, Ortrun, German mezzo-soprano; b. Buttstadt, Oct. 25, 1942. After training at the Franz Liszt Hochschule für Music in Weimar, she attended the master classes of Paul Lohmann at the Frankfurt am Main Hochschule für Musik; she also studied with Elsa Cavelti. While still a student, she made her concert debut in London in 1964. In 1971 she made her operatic debut as Gluck's Orfeo in Heidelberg, and subsequently appeared in opera at Milan's La Scala, London's Covent Garden, Munich, Hamburg, Salzburg, Berlin, Vienna, and Zürich. She also pursued a highly active career as a concert artist, singing with major orchs. and as a recitalist. Her expansive repertoire ranges from the Baroque era to the contemporary period.

Wenkoff, Spas, Bulgarian tenor; b. Tirnovo, Sept. 23, 1928. He received his training from Jossifow in Sofia, Safirowa in Russe, and Kemter in Dresden. In 1954 he made his operatic debut as Kote in Dolidse's *Keto und Kote* in Tirnovo. After singing in Russe (1962–65), Döbeln (1965–68), Magdeburg (1968–71), and Halle (1971–75), he appeared as Tristan at the Dresden State Opera in 1975. From 1976 he sang at the Berlin State Opera. In 1976 he made his debut at the Bayreuth Festival as Tristan, and continued to appear there until 1983. He made his Metropolitan Opera debut in N.Y. as Tristan on Jan. 9, 1981. In 1982 he sang Tannhäuser at the Vienna State Opera. In 1984 he appeared at the Deutsche Oper in Berlin. He sang Tannhäuser in Bern in 1987. In addition to his Heldentenor roles, he also sang roles in operas by Verdi and Puccini.

Wennerberg-Reuter, Sara (Margareta Eugenia Euphrosyne), Swedish composer; b. Otterstad, Feb. 11, 1875; d. Stockholm, March 29, 1959. She was a niece of the writer, politician, and composer Gunnar Wennerberg (b. Lidköping, Oct. 2, 1817; d. Läckö, Aug. 22, 1901). She studied organ and harmony in Göteborg with Andrée. After training in organ and choral music at the Stockholm Cons. (1893–95), she was a student of Jadassohn and Reinecke at the Leipzig Cons. (1896–98) and of Bruch at the Berlin Hochschule für Musik (1901–02). She composed instrumental pieces, cantatas, and songs.

Wenten, Nyoman, Indonesian musician and dancer; b. Sading, near Denpasar, Bali, June 15, 1945. He studied dance and music from an early age with his grandfather; continued studies at the National Cons. of Music and Dance in Bali, the Traditional Music Cons. in Surakarta (1962–65), and the National Music and Dance Academy in Yogyakarta (B.F.A., 1970); taught at the latter institutions as well as the Dance Cons. in Yogyakarta (1964–70). He received an M.F.A. from the Calif. Inst. of the Arts (1974); taught there (from 1971) and also gave workshops at both the Los Angeles and Berkeley campuses of the Univ. of Calif. He was director of the Music, Dance, and Language Program for the Indonesian consulate in Los Angeles. He toured in Asia, North America, and Europe (from 1964); appeared at the Los Angeles Olympic Arts Festival (1984) and the International Festival of Arts in Mexico (1985). He is a remarkable performer in both Balinese and Javanese dance and music; he frequently performs with his wife, Nanik, and her father, **K.R.T. Wasitodiningrat**.

Wenzinger, August, prominent Swiss cellist, viola da gambist, conductor, teacher, and music editor; b. Basel, Nov. 14, 1905. He received his basic training at the Basel Cons.; then studied cello with Paul Grümmer and theory with Jarnach at the Hochschule für Musik in Cologne; also took private cello lessons with Feuermann in Berlin. He subsequently served as 1st cellist in the Bremen City Orch. (1929–34) and the Basel Allgemeine Musikgesellschaft (1936–70). He became interested in reviving the classical Baroque repertoire on original instruments, and acquired facility on the viola da gamba; conducted early music with the Capella Coloniensis of the West German Radio in Cologne (1954–58) and later led performances of Baroque operas in Hannover (1958–66). He taught at the Schola Cantorum Basiliensis (from 1933); founded its viola da gamba trio in 1968. He ed. Bach's unaccompanied cello suites and several Baroque operas; publ. exercises for the viola da gamba, *Gambenübung* (2 vols., 1935, 1938) and *Gambenfibel* (with M. Majer; 1943).

Werba, Erik, eminent Austrian pianist, teacher, composer, and writer on music; b. Baden, near Vienna, May 23, 1918; d. Hinterbrühl, April 9, 1992. He studied piano with Oskar Dachs and composition with Joseph Marx at the Vienna Academy of Music and musicology with Lach, Wellesz, and Schenk at the Univ. of Vienna (1936–40). He was active as a music critic for various newspapers (1945–65); also was on the staff of the *Österreichische Musikzeitschrift* (from 1952). In 1949 he commenced touring throughout Europe as an accompanist to leading singers of the day; also was a prof. of song and oratorio at the Vienna Academy of Music (from 1949). In addition to numerous articles, he publ. *Joseph Marx* (Vienna, 1964), *Hugo Wolf oder der zornige Romantiker* (Vienna, 1971), *Erich Marckhl* (Vienna, 1972), and *Hugo Wolf und seine Lieder* (Vienna, 1984). He composed a Singspiel, *Trauben für die Kaiserin* (Vienna, 1949), several song cycles, and chamber music pieces, among them *Sonata notturna* for Bassoon and Piano (1972).

Werder, Felix, German-born Australian composer and music critic; b. Berlin, Feb. 22, 1922. He acquired early music training from his father, a cantor and composer of liturgical music. He also learned to play piano, viola, and clarinet. Among his teachers were Boas Bischofswerder and Arno Nadel. His family went to England in 1934 to escape Nazi persecution, and then settled in Australia in 1941. He taught music in Melbourne high schools, and was a music critic for the Melbourne newspaper *Age* (1960–77). He was a prolific composer but discarded many of his scores. Werder's musical idiom was determined by the cross-currents of European modernism, with a gradual increase in the forcefulness of his resources, among them electronics.

WORKS: DRAMATIC: *Kisses for a Quid*, opera (1960); *En passant*, ballet (1964); *The General*, opera (1966); *Agamemnon*, opera (1967); *The Affair*, opera (1969); *Private*, television opera (1969); *The Vicious Square*, opera (1971); *The Conversion*, opera (1973); *Banker*, music theater (1973); *La belle dame sans merci*, ballet (1973); *Quantum*, ballet (1973); *Bellifull*, music theater (1976); *The Director*, music theater (1980); *The Medea*, opera (1984–85; Melbourne, Sept. 17, 1985); *Business Day*, music theater (1988). **ORCH.:** 6 syms.: No. 1 (1948–51; withdrawn), No. 2 (1959), No. 3, *Laocoön* (1965), No. 4 (1970), No. 5 (1971), and No. 6 (1979); Flute Concerto (1954); Piano Concerto (1955); 2 violin concertos (1956, 1966); *Brand*, symphonic poem (1956); *Sinfonia in Italian Style* (1957); *La Primavera*, symphonic poem (1957); *Abstraction* (1958); *Hexastrophe* (1961); *Monostrophe* (1961); Clarinet Concerto (1962); Viola Concerto (1963); *Konzert Musik* for 10 Solo Instruments and Orch. (1964); *Dramaturgie* (1966); *Morgen Rot* for Violin and Chamber Orch. (1968); *Strettophone* (1968); *Tower Concerto* (1968); *After Watteau* for Violin and Orch. (1968); *Sound Canvas* (1969); *Klang Bilder* (1969); *Triple Measure* (1970); *Don Giovanni Retired* (1971); *Prom Gothic* for Organ and Orch. (1972); *Sans souci*, flute concerto (1974); *Brandenburgisches Konzert I* for Strings (1974) and *II* for Saxophone and Orch. (1988); Concerto No. 2 for Piano, Winds, and Percussion (1975); *Cranach's Hunt*, horn concerto (1975); *Strettone* (1978); *Concerto for Orchestra* (1986); *Concert Music* for Bass Clarinet and Orch. (1987); *Renunciation* for Viola and Orch. (1987); *The Wenzel Connection*, clarinet concertino (1990); *Music a While* for Chamber Orch. (1991). **CHAMBER:** 4 violin sonatas: No. 1 (1958; old No. 2; former No. 1 of 1947 withdrawn), No. 2 (1963; old No. 3), No. 3 (1986), and No. 4, *Music Today* (1988); 12 string quartets, including Nos. 1–3 (withdrawn) and Nos. 4–12 (1955, 1956, 1962, 1965, 1966, 1968, 1970, 1972, 1974); 3 violin sonatas (1947, 1958, 1963); 2 piano quartets (1954, 1978); Cello Sonata (1956); 3 piano trios (1958, 1963, 1969); Quintet for Clarinet, Horn, and String Trio (1959); Flute Sonata (1960); Clarinet Sonata (1960); Horn Sonata (1960); Sonata for Wind Quintet (1961); Septet for Flute, Clarinet, Horn, and Strings (1963); Piano Quintet (1963); Sonata for Solo Violin (1965); *Apostrophe* for Wind Quintet (1965); Clarinet Quintet (1965); *Satyricon* for 6 Horns (1967); Sonata for Solo Cello (1968); Trio for Harp, Bass Clarinet, and Percussion (1969); *Activity* for Piano and Percussion (1969); *Triphony* for Flute, Guitar, and Bongos (1969); *Faggotiana* for Bassoon and String Trio (1970); *Tetract* for Viola, Oboe, and 2 Percussion (1970); *Divertimento* for Guitar and String Quartet (1970); Wind Quartet (1971); *Percussion Play* for Percussion (1971); *Index* for Chamber Ensemble (1976); *3* for Piano Trio (1976); *Night Out*, flute quartet (1982); *Aurora Australis* for Chamber Ensemble (1984); *Interconnections* for 2 Violins (1986); *Music at Night*, flute quartet (1986); *Off Beat* for Cello and Piano (1990); *Quadrella*, saxophone quartet (1990); *Taffelmusik* for Clarinet, Cello, and Piano (1991). **KEYBOARD: PIANO:** 5 sonatas (1942, 1953, 1968, 1970, 1973); Sonata for 2 Pianos (1960). **ORGAN:** *Toccata* (1971); *Holy Thursday* (1975); *Epiphanien Weg* (1987). **HARPSICHORD:** Sonata (1963). **VOCAL:** *Radica Piece*, anti-Vietnam War cantata (1967); *Francis Bacon Essays*, choral oratorio (1971); *Terror Australis*, cantata for Soprano, Percussion, and Strings (1980); *Requiem* for Soprano, Flute, Oboe, Clarinet, Percussion, Organ, and Strings (1980); *Belsazar* for Chorus and Instrumental Ensemble (1988); *Lost Dramas* for Soprano and Chamber Ensemble (1990).

Werle, Lars Johan, Swedish composer; b. Gavle, June 23, 1926. He studied with Back (composition) and Moberg (musicology) at the Univ. of Uppsala (1948–51). He held positions at the Swedish Radio (1958–70) and as an instructor at the National School of Music Drama in Stockholm (1970–76); then was resident composer of Göteborg (1976–79). In his music, he employs an amiably modern idiom, stimulating to the untutored ear while retaining the specific gravity of triadic tonal constructions. His theater operas have been received with smiling approbation.

WORKS: DRAMATIC: *Drömmen om Thérèse* (The Dream of Thérèse), opera, after Zola's *Pour une nuit d'amour* (Stockholm, May 26, 1964); *Zodiak*, ballet (1966; Stockholm, Feb. 12, 1967); *Resan* (The Voyage), opera, after J.P. Jersild (Hamburg, March 2, 1969); *En saga om sinnen*, television opera (Swedish TV, June 21, 1971); *Tintomara*, opera, after C.J.L. Almquist's *The Queen's Jewels* (1972; Stockholm, Jan. 18, 1973); *Medusan och djävulen* (Medusa and the Devil), lyrical mystery play (1973); *Animalen*, musical (Göteborg, May 19, 1979); *Är gryningen redan här*, ballet (Göteborg, Sept. 5, 1980); *En midsommarnattsdröm* (A Midsummer Night's Dream), opera, after Shakespeare (1984; Malmö, Feb. 8, 1985); *Gudars skymning eller När kärleken blev blind . . .* , cabaret (1985); *Lionardo*, opera (1985–88; Stockholm, March 31, 1988); *Kvinnogräl*, opera (Göteborg, Oct. 18, 1986); *Tavlan eller En eftermiddag på Prado*, chamber opera (1991–93); *Hercules*, opera (1993). **ORCH.:** *Sinfonia da camera* (1960); *Summer Music 1965* for Strings and Piano (1965); *Vaggsång för jorden* (1977); *Animalen* (1986); *Födelse* for Band (1992). **CHAMBER:** *Pentagram* for String Quartet (1959–60); *Attitudes* for Piano (1965); *Variété* for String Quartet (1971); *Tva miniatyrer* for Flute and Marimba (1988–89). **VOCAL:** *Canzone 126 di Francesco Petrarca* for Chorus (1967); *Nautical Preludes* for Chorus (1970); *Chants for Dark Hours* for Mezzo-soprano, Flute, Guitar, and Percussion (1972); *Flower Power* for 6 or More Voices and Instruments (1974); *Trees*, 4 poems for Baritone and Chorus, after e.e. cummings (1979); *Sweet sixties: Dialog* for Solo Voices and Keyboard (1990); *Ännu sjunger valarna*, cantata for Soloists and Chamber Ensemble (1992); *Sonetto 292* for Soprano and Chorus (1993).

Werner, Arno, German organist and musicologist; b. Prittitz, Weissenfels, Nov. 22, 1865; d. Bitterfeld, Feb. 15, 1955. He studied at the Royal Inst. for Church-Music in Berlin (1889–90). In 1890 he became municipal organist at Bitterfeld; in 1894 was appointed music teacher at the Gymnasium there, retiring in 1931; he continued his activities as a musicologist until his death; contributed articles to *Die Musik in Geschichte und Gegenwart* (1953).

WRITINGS: *Samuel und Gottfried Scheidt* (1900); *Geschichte der Kantorei-Gesellschaften im Gebiete des Kurfürstentums*

Sachsen (1902); *Die Kantorei zu Bitterfeld* (1903); *Städtische und fürstliche Musikpflege in Weissenfels* (1911); *Städtische und fürstliche Musikpflege in Zeitz* (1922); *Zur Geschichte der Kantorei in Zörbig* (1927); *Musikpflege in Stadt und Kreis Bitterfeld* (1931); *Vier Jahrhunderte im Dienste der Kirchenmusik. Geschichte der Kantoren, Organisten und Stadtpfeifer seit der Reformation* (1932); *Der deutsche Kantor* (1933); *Freie Musikgemeinschaften im mitteldeutschen Raum* (1940).

Werner, Eric, Austrian-American musicologist; b. Lundenberg, near Vienna, Aug. 1, 1901; d. N.Y., July 28, 1988. He studied composition with Kornauth in Vienna, and with Schrecker and Busoni in Berlin; also took courses at the univs. of Graz, Vienna, Prague, Berlin, Göttingen, and Strasbourg; received his Ph.D. in 1928 from the Univ. of Strasbourg. He held teaching positions at the Saarbrücken Cons. (1926–33) and the Breslau Jewish Theological Seminary (1935–38). In 1938 he went to the U.S.; was a prof. at the Hebrew Union College (later merged with the Jewish Inst. of Religion in N.Y.) in Cincinnati (1939–67); then was chairman of the musicology dept. at the Univ. of Tel Aviv (1967–72). He was an authority on Jewish and early Christian music.

WRITINGS: *In the Choir Loft: A Manual for Organists and Choir Directors in American Synagogues* (N.Y., 1957); *The Sacred Bridge: Liturgical Parallels in Synagogue and Early Church* (2 vols., N.Y., 1959, 1984); *Hebrew Music* (Cologne, 1961); *From Generation to Generation: Studies on Jewish Musical Tradition* (N.Y., 1962); *Mendelssohn: A New Image of the Composer and His Age* (N.Y., 1963); *A Voice Still Heard: The Sacred Songs of the Ashkenazic Jews* (Philadelphia, 1976).

BIBL.: J. Cohen, *Bibliography of the Publications of E. W.* (Tel Aviv, 1968).

Wernick, Richard, American composer, teacher, and conductor; b. Boston, Jan. 16, 1934. He was a student in theory and composition of Fine, Shapero, and Berger at Brandeis Univ. (B.A., 1955), in composition of Toch, Blacher, and Copland and in conducting of Bernstein and Lipkin at the Berkshire Music Center at Tanglewood (summers, 1954–55), and in composition of Kirchner at Mills College in Oakland, Calif. (M.A., 1957). In 1957–58 he was music director and composer-in-residence of the Royal Winnipeg Ballet in Canada. In 1964–65 he taught at the State Univ. of N.Y. at Buffalo, and in 1965–66 at the Univ. of Chicago, where he conducted its sym. orch. (1965–68). In 1968 he joined the faculty of the Univ. of Pa., where he conducted its sym. orch. (until 1970); he was also chairman of its music dept. (1969–74), served as prof. of music (1977–86), the Irving Fine Prof. of Music (1986–92), and the Magnin Prof. of Humanities (from 1992). From 1968 he also was music director of the Penn Contemporary Players. He held grants from the Ford Founation (1962–64) and the NEA (1975, 1979, 1982). In 1976 he received a Guggenheim fellowship and an award from the National Inst. of Arts and Letters. He won the Pulitzer Prize in Music in 1977 for his *Visions of Terror and Wonder* for Mezzo-soprano and Orch. In 1986 he received a Kennedy Center Friedheim Award for his Violin Concerto. As a composer, Wernick has followed an eclectic course in which he utilizes the most advantageous traditional and modern means of expression.

WORKS: DRAMATIC: OPERA: *Maggie* (1959; unfinished; in collaboration with I. Fine). **BALLETS:** *The Twisted Heart* (Winnipeg, Nov. 27, 1957); *Fête Brilliante* (Winnipeg, Jan. 13, 1958); *The Emperor's Nightingale* (1958); *The Queen of Ice* (1958); *The Nativity* (1960; CBS-TV, Jan. 1, 1961). Also incidental music to plays and film scores. **ORCH.:** *Aeva* (Chicago, Dec. 1966); Concerto for Cello and 10 Players (Washington, D.C., Feb. 1980); *Fanfare for a Festive Occasion* (Pittsburg, Oct. 23, 1981); Violin Concerto (1984; Philadelphia, Jan. 17, 1986); Viola Concerto, *Do not go gentle . . .* (1986; Annandale-on-Hudson, N.Y., May 8, 1987); 2 syms.: No. 1 (1988; Wilkes-Barre, Pa., Jan. 1989) and No. 2 (1993; Philadelphia, Jan. 19, 1995); Piano Concerto (1989–90; Washington, D.C., Feb. 1991); Saxophone Quartet Concerto (1991); Cello Concerto (1992). **CHAMBER:** *4 Pieces* for String Quartet (1955); *Divertimento* for Viola, Cello, Clarinet, and Bassoon (Oakland, Calif., May 1956); Duo Concertante for Cello and Piano (1960); Trio for Violin, Clarinet, and Cello (1961; Waltham, Mass., Dec. 7, 1962); 5 string quartets: No. 1 (Rochester, N.Y., Dec. 5, 1963), No. 2 (1972–73), No. 3 (1988; N.Y., Jan. 1990), No. 4 (1990; Philadelphia, April 29, 1991), and No. 5, with soprano (1995); *Music* for Viola d'Amore (1964; Buffalo, April 1965); *Stretti* for Clarinet, Violin, Viola, and Guitar (1965); *Cadenzas and Variations II* for Violin (1970) and *III* for Cello (1972); *Introits and Canons* for Chamber Ensemble (1977; N.Y., Jan. 1978); *Partita* for Violin (N.Y., Sept. 1978); *In Praise of Zephyrus* for Oboe and String Trio (1981); *Formula: P—-——m* for Violin and Cello (1981; Chicago, Jan. 22, 1982); Piano Sonata (1982; Washington, D.C., Jan. 15, 1983); Cello Sonata (1982; N.Y., Dec. 5, 1983); Brass Quintet, *Musica Ptolemeica* (1987); *Cassation* for Horn, Oboe, and Piano (1995). **VOCAL:** *From Tulips and Chimneys* for Baritone and Orch. (Salt Lake City, June 1956); *Full Fadom 5* for Chorus and Chamber Ensemble (Bay Shore, N.Y., May 1964); *what if a much of a which of a wind* for Chorus and Prepared Piano, 4-hands (1964); *Lyrics from IXI* for Soprano, Vibraphone-Marimba, and Contrabass (1966); *Haiku of Bashō* for Soprano, Flute, Clarinet, Violin, Contrabass, 2 Percussion, Piano, and Tape (Chicago, March 1, 1968); *Moonsongs from the Japanese* for Soprano and Tape (1969); *Beginnings* for Chorus (1970); *A Prayer for Jerusalem* for Mezzo-soprano and Percussion (1971); *Kaddish-Requiem* for Cantor, Mezzo-soprano, and Chamber Ensemble (1971); *Kee el Asher* for Chorus (1972); *Songs of Remembrance* for Mezzo-soprano, Shawm, English Horn, and Oboe (1973); *Visions of Terror and Wonder* for Mezzo-soprano and Orch. (Aspen, Colo., July 19, 1976); *Contemplations of the 10th Muse* for Soprano (2 books, 1977, 1979); *And on the 7th Day . . .* for Cantor and Percussionists (Bridgeport, Conn., April 1979); *A Poison Tree* for Soprano, Flute, Clarinet, Violin, Cello, and Piano (1979; Syracuse, N.Y., Jan. 1980); *The Oracle of Shimon bar Yochai* for Soprano, Cello, and Piano (N.Y., Dec. 8, 1983); *Oracle II* for Soprano, Oboe, and Piano (1985; Baltimore, Feb. 1987); *Fragments of Prophecy* for Boys' Chorus and Mixed Chorale (1991); *. . . and a time for peace* for Soprano and Orch. (1994).

Werrenrath, Reinald, American baritone; b. Brooklyn, Aug. 7, 1883; d. Plattsburg, N.Y., Sept. 12, 1953. He was a pupil of his father, a tenor, then of David Bispham and Herbert Witherspoon. He began his career as a concert singer; also in oratorio; made his operatic debut on Feb. 19, 1919, at the Metropolitan Opera in N.Y., as Silvio in Pagliacci, and remained with the company until 1921; then devoted himself to teaching and concert singing; appeared in public for the last time at Carnegie Hall in N.Y. on Oct. 23, 1952. He ed. *Modern Scandinavian Songs* (2 vols., Boston, 1925–26).

Wesley-Smith, Martin, Australian composer and teacher; b. Adelaide, June 10, 1945. He was educated at the univs. of Adelaide (B.M., 1969; M.M., 1971) and of York in England (Ph.D., 1974), his mentors in composition being Peter Tahourdin, Peter Maxwell Davies, Sandor Veress, and Jindrich Feld. In 1974 he became a lecturer in electronic music at the New South Wales State Conservatorium of Music in Sydney, where he was senior lecturer in composition and electronic music from 1980; also was a reader in composition at the Univ. of Hong Kong (1994–95). He was founder-director of watt, an electronic music and audio-visual performing group, with which he toured internationally; also was founder-musical director of T.R.E.E. (Theatre Reaching Environments Everywhere). With Ian Fredericks, he organized the first computer music studio in mainland China in 1986. In 1987 he was the Australia Council's Don Banks Composer Fellow. In his extensive output, Wesley-Smith follows an imaginative, eclectic course. While he has composed in most genres, he has gained particular notice for his effective computer and audio-visual works, finding particular inspiration in the writings of Lewis Carroll. Some of his works are overtly political.

WORKS: DRAMATIC: *Pi in the Sky,* children's opera (1971); *The Wild West Show,* children's music theater (1971); *Machine,* children's music theater (1972); *Boojum!*, music theater (1985–86); *Quito*, audio-visual music theater (1994); *Encountering Sorro (Ch'ü Yüan Laments)*, radiophonic piece (1994). **ORCH.:** *Interval Piece* (1970); *Hansard Music* (1970); *Sh . . .* for Audience and Orch. (1973); *Beta-Globin DNA 3* (1990). **CHAMBER:** *Improvistions* for Trumpet and Piano (1966); *Tiger, Tiger* for Violin Duet (1970); *Doublets 2(a)* for Saxophone, Tape, and Delay (1974), *2(d)* for Trombone, Tape, and Delay (1987), and *2(e)* for Clarinet, Tape, and Delay (1987); *Dodgson's Dream* for Clarinet, Tape, and Transparencies (1979); *Pat-a-Cake* for Trombone and Tape (1980); *For Marimba and Tape* (1982); *Doodles* for Soloist and Tape (1983); *For (Bass) Clarinet and Tape* (1983); *Snark-Hunting* for Flute, Piano, Percussion, Cello, and Tape (1984); *White Knight* for Trombone, Marimba, and Tape (1984; also various other versions); *Smudge (Malin 2)* for MIDI Keyboard and Apple Macintosh Computer (1989); *hex D2* for Percussion Quartet (1990); *db* for Flute, Clarinet, Piano, and Cello (1991); *Visiting the Queen* for Marimba and Yamaha Disklavier (1992); *Balibo* for Flute and Tape (1992). **VOCAL:** *Gum Tears of an Arabian Tree* for Tenor and Quintet (1966); *2 Shakespearean Songs* for Chorus (1967); *To Noddy-Man* for High Voice and Piano Duet (1969); *Doublets 2(b)* for Countertenor, Tape, and Tape Delay (1974); *Who Killed Cock Robin?* for Chorus (1979); *Lost in Space* for Children's Chorus and Orch. (1982); *Songs for Snark-Hunter* for Chorus and Piano (1985); *Songs of Australia* for Chorus, Piano, Percussion, and Tape (1988); *Tianamen Square* for Chorus (1989); *Timor et Tremor*, song cycle for Tenor, Flute, Clarinet, Piano, Cello, and Tape (1991); *Flora, Fauna, and LORNA!* for Vocal Sextet (1992). **TAPE:** *Vietnam Image* (1970); *Media Music 1* (1972) and *2* (1973); *Kdadalak (For the Children of Timor)* for Tape and Transparencies (1977); *Japanese Pictures* for Tape and Transparencies (1981); *Echoes and Star Tides* for Tape and Transparencies (1981; in collaboration with I. Fredericks); *Electronic Study 37(b)* (1982); *Dah Dit Dah Dah* (1983; in collaboration with J. Piché and O. Shoji); *Wattamolla Red* for Tape and Transparencies (1983); *VENCEREMOS!* for Tape and Transparencies (1984); *Snark-Hunting 2* for Tape and Transparencies (1986); *Chi'il Yüan, By the Burning River* (1988); *Rabbit-Hole Music 1 and 2* (1990).

Wessely, Othmar, Austrian musicologist; b. Linz, Oct. 31, 1922. He was educated at the Bruckner Cons. in Linz, the Vienna Academy of Music, and the Univ. of Vienna (Ph.D., 1947, with the diss. *Anton Bruckner in Linz*; Habilitationsschrift, 1959, with his *Arnold von Bruck: Leben und Umwelt*). From 1950 to 1963 he was a member of the faculty of the Univ. of Vienna; after teaching at the Univ. of Graz (1963–71), he returned to the Univ. of Vienna in 1971 as prof. of musicology, retiring in 1993. From 1974 to 1991 he also was president of the Publishing Soc. for Monuments of Music in Austria.

WRITINGS: *Musik in Oberösterreich* (Linz, 1951); *Die Musikinstrumentsammlung des Oberösterreichischen Landesmuseums* (Linz, 1952); *Johann Joseph Fux und Johann Mattheson* (Graz, 1966); ed. *Ernst Ludwig Gerber: Historisch-biographisches Lexikon der Tonkünstler (1790–1792) und Neues historisch-biographisches Lexikon der Tonkünstler (1812–1814)* (4 vols., Graz, 1966–77); *Johann Joseph Fux und Francesco Antonio Vallotti* (Graz, 1967); *Pietro Pariatis Libretto zu Johann Joseph Fuxens "Costanza e fortezza"* (Graz, 1969); *Johann Joseph Fux: Persönlichkeit, Umwelt, Nachwelt* (Graz, 1979).

Wessman, Harri (Kristian), Finnish composer; b. Helsinki, March 29, 1949. He learned to play the cello and double bass in his youth; took courses in musicology and languages at the Univ. of Helsinki (1967–73) and also studied composition privately with Kokkonen, continuing under his tutelage at the Sibelius Academy in Helsinki (1973–78). His works are lyrical and melodic.

WORKS: DRAMATIC: *Onnen arvoitus* (The Riddle of Happiness), play for Children's Chorus, Recorder, and Percussion (1986); *Päivikki*, ballet (1987). **ORCH.:** *Serenade* for Trumpet and Strings (1976); *Sarja jousiorkesterille musiikista Eha Lättemäen runoihin* (Suite for String Orch. from the Music to Poems by Eha Lättemäe; 1978); *Prinsessa joka nukkui sata vuotta* (The Princess Who Slept a Hundred Years) for Trumpet or Soprano and String Orch. (1981); 2 piano concertinos (1982, 1987); *Loitsunpuhallus* for Wind Orch. (1984); *Koraalialkusoitto* (Choral Overture; 1984); *Serenade* for Piano and Strings (1985); *Tango tan-tan-tan* (1985); *Väinämöinen* (1985); Trumpet Concerto (1987); *Adagio and Andante* for Strings (1988); *Parodioita Parodies* for Strings (1988); *Larghetto Espressivo* for Strings (1990). **CHAMBER:** *Musiikkia uruille* (Music for Organ; 1977); Violin Sonata (1978); 2nd Cello Sonata (1979); *Syksyn sävyinen fantasia* (Autumnal Fantasia) for Cello and Piano (1980); *2 intermezzi* for Piano (1980, 1981); Trio for Accordion, Flute, and Guitar (1981); *Je chante la beauté de la solitude* for Accordion (1982); *Prelude and Sicilienne* for Violin, Cello, and Piano (1983); Piano Quartet (1985); *Es sangen drei Engel* for Oboe and Organ (1986); Accordion Sonata (1986); 2 suites for 2 Violins (1986, 1988); *Teema ja muunnelmia vaskiyhtyeelle* (Theme and Variations for Brass Ensemble; 1986–87); *Dialogos*, 25 pieces for Flute and Piano (1988); Sonata for Solo Violin (1988); Horn Sonata (1989); *Capriccio* for Wind Nonet (1990). **VOCAL:** *Lauluja tuimista linnuista* for Chorus and Piano (1977); *Kolme laulua V.A. Koskenniemen runoihin* (3 Songs to Poems by V.A. Koskenniemi) for Chorus (1979); *Kaksi laulua sekakuorolle Marianna Kalliolan runoihin* (2 Songs for Mixed Chorus to Poems by Marianna Kalliola; 1980); *Vaggvisa, Det viner på fjällen* for Children's Chorus (1982); *Nelja laulua Lauri Pohjanpään runoihin* (4 Songs to Poems by Lauri Pohjanpää) for Children's Chorus (1983); *Ligg ej och dra dig!* for Men's Chorus (1984); *Det blir kyligt* for Men's Chorus (1985); *Ljusa vindar* (Light Winds), cantata for Children's Chorus and Instrumental Ensemble (1989).

Westenburg, Richard, American conductor; b. Minneapolis, April 26, 1932. He studied at Lawrence Univ. (B.Mus., 1954) and at the Univ. of Minnesota (M.A., 1956); then went to Paris, where he studied with Boulanger and Cochereau (1959–60); subsequently did postgraduate work at the Theological Seminary School of Sacred Music in N.Y. (1960–66). From 1956 to 1960 he taught music at the Univ. of Montana; then served as director of music at the First Unitarian Church in Worcester, Mass. (1960–62). In 1964 he went to N.Y., where he was engaged as organist and choirmaster of the Central Presbyterian Church, holding this position until 1974. In 1968 he founded Musica Sacra and became its music director; also served as music director of the Collegiate Chorale (1973–79). He was conductor-in-residence at the Cathedral Church of St. John the Divine (1974–86) and music director there (1976–83). He served as head of the choral dept. of the Juilliard School in N.Y. from 1977 to 1989; was appointed visiting prof. at Rutgers, the State Univ. of N.J., in 1986; became music director at the Fifth Avenue Presbyterian Church in N.Y. in 1990.

Westerberg, Stig (Evald Börje), Swedish conductor; b. Malmö, Nov. 26, 1918. He studied at the Stockholm Musikhögskolan (1937–42) and with Kletzki in Paris. He was a répétiteur at Stockholm's Royal Theater (1943–46), and then conducted at the Oscarsteatern; after conducting the Gävleborg Sym. Orch. (1949–53), he returned to Stockholm as a conductor at the Royal Theater; in 1957 he became chief conductor of the Swedish Radio Sym. Orch.; taught conducting at the Musikhögskolan from 1969, becoming a prof. there in 1971. From 1978 to 1985 he was chief conductor of the Malmö Sym. Orch. He became well known for his performances of both traditional and contemporary Swedish scores.

Westergaard, Peter (Talbot), American composer, music theorist, and teacher; b. Champaign, Ill., May 28, 1931. He was a student of Piston at Harvard College (A.B., 1953), of Milhaud at the Aspen (Colo.) Music School (summers, 1951–52) and at the Paris Cons. (1953), of Sessions at Princeton Univ. (M.F.A., 1956), and of Fortner in Detmold (1956) and in Freiburg im

Breisgau (1957) on a Fulbright fellowship. After serving as a guest lecturer at the Staatliche Hochschule für Musik in Freiburg im Breisgau (1958), he taught at Columbia Univ. (1958–66). In 1966–67 he was a vistiting lecturer at Princeton Univ. In 1967–68 he taught at Amherst College. He became an assoc. prof. at Princeton Univ. in 1968, and a full prof. in 1971. He served as chairman of its music dept. (1974–78; 1983–86). In 1995 he was named the William Shubael Conant Prof. of Music there. He also held the endowed chair at the Univ. of Alabama School of Music in 1995. In addition to various commissions, he held a Guggenheim fellowship (1964–65) and an NEA grant (1990–91). He wrote various articles for journals and publ. the study *An Introduction to Tonal Theory* (N.Y., 1975). In his compositions, Westergaard explored the potentialities of total organization of tones, rhythms, and other compositional elements.

WORKS: DRAMATIC: *Charivari*, chamber opera (1953); *Mr. and Mrs. Discobbolos*, chamber opera (1966); *The Tempest*, opera (1988–90; Lawrenceville, N.J., July 8, 1994). **ORCH.:** *Symphonic Movement* (1954); *5 Movements* for Small Orch. (1958); *Noises, Sounds, and Sweet Airs* for Chamber Orch. (1968); *Tuckets and Sennets* for Band (1969). **CHAMBER:** *Partita* for Flute, Violin, and Harpsichord (1953; rev. 1956); *Invention* for Flute and Piano (1955); String Quartet (1957); Quartet for Violin, Vibraphone, Clarinet, and Cello (1960); Trio for Flute, Cello, and Piano (1962); *Variations for 6 Players* for Flute, Clarinet, Percussion, Piano, Violin, and Cello (1963); *Divertimento on Discobbolic Fragments* for Flute and Piano (1967); *Moto perpetuo* for Flute, Oboe, Clarinet, Bassoon, Trumpet, and Horn (1976); *Alonzo's Grief* for Piano (1977); *2 Fanfares* for 3 Trumpets and 3 Trombones (1988). **VOCAL:** *Cantata I: The Plot Against the Giant* for Women's Chorus, Clarinet, Cello, and Harp (1956), *II: A Refusal to Mourn the Death, by Fire, of a Child in London* for Bass and 10 Instruments (1958), and *III: Leda and the Swan* for Mezzo-soprano, Vibraphone, Marimba, and Viola (1961); *Spring and Fall: To a Young Child* for Voice and Piano (1960; also for Voice and 5 Instruments, 1964); *There Was a Little Man* for Soprano and Violin (1982); *Ariel Music* for High Soprano and Chamber Ensemble (1987); *Ode* for Soprano, Flute, Clarinet, Violin, Viola, and Harp (1989).

Westergaard, Svend, Danish composer and pedagogue; b. Copenhagen, Oct. 8, 1922; d. Hillerød, near Copenhagen, June 22, 1988. He studied composition with Høffding, Hjelmborg, and Jersild at the Copenhagen Cons.; began teaching there in 1951; was a prof. of theory from 1967; also its director (1967–71). He publ. the study *Harmonilaere* (Copenhagen, 1961).

WORKS: ORCH.: *Elegy* for Strings (1949); *Pezzo sinfonico* (1950); Oboe Concerto (1950); 2 syms.: No. 1, *Sinfonia* (1955) and No. 2, *Sinfonia da camera* (1968); *L'Homme arme*, canzona for 16 Instruments (1959; rev. for Orch., 1970); *Capriccio* for Violin and String Orch. (1960); *Variazioni sinfoniche* (Danish Radio, June 12, 1960); Cello Concerto (1961; Århus, Oct. 22, 1962; rev. 1973); *Pezzo concertante* (Danish Radio, Aug. 19, 1965); *Sinfonia da camera* (Copenhagen, March 24, 1969); *Varianti sinfoniche* for Winds and Percussion (1972); *Transformazioni sinfonische* for Piano and Orch. (1976; Danish Radio, Oct. 27, 1977). **CHAMBER:** 2 wind quintets (1948, 1949); *Tema con variazioni* for Clarinet Quintet (1949); String Quartet (1968); Sonata for Solo Flute (1971); Sonata for Solo Cello (1979).

Westerlinck, Wilfried, Belgian composer and teacher; b. Louvain, Oct. 3, 1945. He was a student of Legley (harmony) at the Brussels Cons. and of Verbesselt (analysis) and Sternefeld (conducting) at the Royal Flemish Cons. of Music in Antwerp. From 1971 to 1983 he taught at the latter. In 1977 he won the Antwerp composition prize and in 1985 his total output was awarded the Baie Prize.

WORKS: ORCH.: *Metamorfose* (1971); *Elegie van de zee en van de liefde* (1975); *Landschappen II* for Strings (1979). **CHAMBER:** Clarinet Quintet (1966); *Epigrammen* for String Trio (1968); *"S"* for Trumpet and Tape (1972–80); *Maclou* for Horn (1975); *Canto I* for Guitar (1976), *II* for Cello (1982), and *III* for Harp (1982); *Aquarel* for Flute (1977); *Landschappen I* for Wind Quintet (1977) and *IV* for Flute, Harp, and String Trio (1981); String Quartet (1978); *Epitaphe* for String Quartet (1983); Sinfonietta for Chamber Ensemble (1986). **PIANO:** 3 sonatas (1983, 1985, 1986); *Variations on a Theme by Paganini* (1985).

Westlake, Nigel, Australian clarinetist and composer; b. Perth, Sept. 6, 1958. He received training in clarinet from his father, Donald Westlake (1970–78), principal clarinetist in the Sydney Sym. Orch. After studying film music at the Australian Film and TV School (1982), he studied clarinet and contemporary music with Harry Sparnaay in Amsterdam (1983). In 1993 he received an Australia Council grant which enabled him to study composition with Richard Meale and composition and conducting with Richard Mills. From 1975 he was active as a freelance clarinetist. In 1987 he served as composer-in-residence for the ABC Radio. From 1987 to 1992 he was a principal member of the Australia Ensemble, a chamber music septet which toured extensively in Australia and abroad. In 1992 he toured Australia and England with John Williams's septet Attacca. Westlake has pursued a highly successful dual career as a clarinetist and composer. As a performer, he has demonstrated his mastery of the clarinet in an expansive repertoire ranging from the classics to popular music. As a composer, he has written both serious and lighter scores, proving himself especially adept at film, radio, and television scores.

WORKS: DRAMATIC: Theater music; film scores, including *Antarctica* (1991) and *Breaking Through* (1993); radio and television music. **ORCH.:** *Cudmirrah Fanfare* (1985); *Antarctica*, suite from the film score for Guitar and Orch. (1992); *Out of the Blue* for Strings (1994). **CHAMBER:** *Omphalo Centric Liecture* for 4 Percussion (1984); *Onomatopoeia* for Bass Clarinet and Digital Delay (1984); *Our Mum Was a Waterfall* for Soprano Saxophone, Percussion, and Electronics (1984); *Fabian Theory* for Percussion and Digital Delay (1987); *Moving Air* for 4 Percussion (1989); *Refractions at Summercloud Bay* for Bass Clarinet, Alto Flute, Violin, Viola, and Cello (1989); *Entomology* for Chamber Group and Tape (1990); *Malachite Glass* for Bass Clarinet and 4 Percussion (1990); *Call of the Wild* for Bass Clarinet, Percussion, and Tape (1992); *Tall Tales But True* for Violin, Double Bass, 2 Guitars, Piano, Clarinet, and Percussion (1992); *Touching Wood* for Violin, Double Bass, 2 Guitars, Piano, Clarinet, and Percussion (1992); *The Devil's Marbles* for Guitar and Digital Delay (1994); *High Tension Wires* for String Quartet (1994); *Songs from the Forest* for 2 Guitars (1994).

Westrup, Sir Jack (Allan), eminent English musicologist; b. London, July 26, 1904; d. Headley, Hampshire, April 21, 1975. He received his education at Dulwich College, London (1917–22), and at Balliol College, Oxford (B.A. and B.Mus., 1926; M.A., 1929). He was an assistant classics master at Dulwich College (1928–34); then was a music critic for the *Daily Telegraph* (1934–39); also was ed. of the *Monthly Musical Record* (1933–45). He gave classes at the Royal Academy of Music in London (1938–40); then was lecturer in music at King's College, Newcastle upon Tyne (1941–44), the Univ. of Birmingham (1944–47), and Wadham College, Oxford (1947–71). In 1946 he received an honorary degree of D.Mus. at the Univ. of Oxford. In 1947 he was named chairman of the editorial board of *The New Oxford History of Music.* In 1959 he succeeded Eric Blom as ed. of *Music & Letters.* From 1958 to 1963 he was president of the Royal Musical Assn. He was also active as a conductor; he conducted the Oxford Opera Club (1947–62), the Oxford Univ. Orch. (1954–63), and the Oxford Bach Choir and Oxford Orch. Soc. (1970–71). He was knighted in 1961. Westrup prepared major revisions of Walker's *A History of Music in England* (Oxford, 3rd ed., 1952) and of Fellowes's *English Cathedral Music* (London, 5th ed., 1969); he also supervised rev. eds. of Blom's *Everyman's Dictionary of Music* (4th ed., 1962; 5th ed., 1971). He was co-ed., with F. Harrison, of the *Collins Music*

Encyclopedia (London, 1959; American ed. as *The New College Encyclopedia of Music*, N.Y., 1960).

WRITINGS (all publ. in London unless otherwise given): *Purcell* (1937; 4th ed., rev., 1980); *Handel* (1938); *Liszt* (1940); *Sharps and Flats* (1940); *British Music* (1943; 3rd ed., 1949); *The Meaning of Musical History* (1946); *An Introduction to Musical History* (1955); *Music: Its Past and Its Present* (Washington, D.C., 1964); *Bach Cantatas* (1966); *Schubert Chamber Music* (1969); *Musical Interpretation* (1971).

BIBL.: F. Sternfeld et al., eds., *Essays on Opera and English Music in Honour of Sir J. W.* (Oxford, 1975).

Wettergren, Gertrud (née **Pålson**), Swedish contralto; b. Eslöv, Feb. 17, 1897; d. Stockholm, June 1991. She studied at the Stockholm Cons., and later in London. She made her operatic debut as Cherubino at the Royal Opera in Stockholm in 1922, and remained on its roster for 30 years. On Dec. 20, 1935, she appeared at the Metropolitan Opera in N.Y. as Amneris in *Aida*; sang there until 1938; also sang with the Chicago Opera (1936–38) and at London's Covent Garden (1936, 1939). In 1925 she married Erik Wettergren, director of the National Museum of Stockholm. Among her most esteemed roles were Venus, Fricka, Brangäne, Dalila, Carmen, Mignon, Marfa, and Herodias; she also sang in many Swedish operas.

Wetz, Richard, German composer, conductor, and teacher; b. Gleiwitz, Feb. 26, 1875; d. Erfurt, Jan. 16, 1935. He studied with R. Hofmann in Leipzig and Thuille in Munich (1899–1900); also attended the Univ. of Munich. He was a theater conductor in Straslund and Barmen; in 1906 he settled in Erfurt as conductor of the Musikverein and the Singakademie; also taught at the Weimar Hochschule für Musik (from 1916). His output was greatly influenced by Bruckner. A Richard Wetz-Gesellschaft was founded in Gleiwitz in 1943 to promote his music, which included an opera, *Das ewige Feuer* (Düsseldorf, March 19, 1907); *Kleistouvertüre* for Orch.; 2 violin concertos; 3 syms.; also various choral works, including a *Requiem* for Baritone, Chorus, and Orch. and the *Weihnachtsoratorio* for Soprano, Baritone, Chorus, and Orch.; lieder; some chamber music, including 2 string quartets.

WRITINGS: *Anton Bruckner* (Leipzig, 1922); *Franz Liszt* (Leipzig, 1925); *Beethoven* (Erfurt, 1927; 2nd ed., 1933).

BIBL.: G. Armin, *Die Lieder von R. W.* (Leipzig, 1911); E. Schellenberg, *R. W.* (Leipzig, 1911; 2nd ed., 1914); H. Polack, *R. W. Sein Werk* (Leipzig, 1935).

Wetzel, Justus Hermann, German composer and musicologist; b. Kyritz, March 11, 1879; d. Überlingen (Bodensee), Dec. 6, 1973. He studied natural sciences, philosophy, and art history in Berlin, Munich, and Marburg (Ph.D., 1901); then studied composition with Schrader and Taubert. He taught at the Riemann Cons. in Stettin (1905–07); settled in Berlin in 1910; taught at the Academy for Church and School Music (from 1926; became a prof. in 1935). He composed about 400 songs; choral works; chamber music; piano pieces; ed. and arr. several collections of German songs.

BIBL.: F. Welter, *J.H. W.* (Berlin, 1931; with list of works).

Wetzler, Hermann (Hans), American organist, conductor, and composer; b. Frankfurt am Main (of American parents), Sept. 8, 1870; d. N.Y., May 29, 1943. He was taken to the U.S. as a child, but in 1882 returned to Germany, where he studied at the Hoch Cons. in Frankfurt am Main and studied with Clara Schumann (piano), Iwan Knorr (counterpoint), and Humperdinck (instrumentation). In 1892 he went to N.Y., where he was organist at Old Trinity Church (1897–1901); in 1903 he established the Wetzler Sym. Concerts, which had considerable success; Richard Strauss conducted a series of 4 concerts of his own works with the Wetzler group (Feb.–March, 1904), including the premiere of the *Sinfonia domestica*. In 1905 he returned to Germany and conducted in various German cities and throughout Europe. In 1940 he returned to the U.S. He publ. *Wege zur Musik* (Leipzig, 1938).

WORKS: DRAMATIC: OPERA: *Die baskische Venus* (Leipzig, Nov. 18, 1928; the *Symphonic Dance in the Basque Style* was extracted from this score as a concert piece). **INCIDENTAL MUSIC TO:** Shakespeare's *As You Like It* (1917). **ORCH.:** *Symphonic Fantasy* (1922); *Visionen* (1923); *Assisi*, legend (1924); *Symphonie concertante* for Violin and Orch. (1932). **OTHER:** Chamber music, including a String Quartet (1937); much vocal music, including a *Magnificat* for Soprano, Boys' or Women's Chorus, and Organ (1936), choruses, and songs.

Whear, Paul William, American composer; b. Auburn, Ind., Nov. 13, 1925. He studied engineering at Marquette Univ. (B.N.S.), DePauw Univ. (B.A.), and Case Western Reserve Univ. (Ph.D.); then made a 180° turn toward the art of music; attended classes of Gardner Read at Boston Univ. and of Wayne Barlow at the Eastman School of Music in Rochester, N.Y. From 1960 to 1969 Whear served as chairman of the music dept. at Doane College; in 1969 he was appointed a prof. of music and chairman of the theory and composition dept. at Marshall Univ. He wrote 4 syms., including No. 2, *The Bridge* (1971), No. 3, *The Galleries* (1975), and No. 4 for Band (1979); overtures, chamber music, and choral works.

Whettam, Graham (Dudley), English composer; b. Swindon, Sept. 7, 1927. He received guidance from Eric Fenby but otherwise was an autodidact as a musician; devoted himself principally to composition and the cause of copyright protection. He served as chairman of the Composers' Guild of Great Britain (1971; 1983–86), and subsequently was its copyright consultant. He withdrew most of his compositions written prior to 1959. Whettam has revealed a fine command of orch. writing. His works have been widely performed in England and on the Continent.

WORKS: ORCH.: 2 clarinet concertos: No. 1 (Bournemouth, Nov. 5, 1959) and No. 2 (1982; Warwick, Jan. 8, 1983); *Introduction and Scherzo impetuoso* (1960); *Variations* for Oboe, Bassoon, and Strings (1961); *Sinfonia contra timore* (1962; Birmingham, Feb. 25, 1965); Cello Concerto (1962; Manchester, Dec. 1981); *Sinfonietta stravagante* (1964); *Sinfonia concertante* (Newcastle upon Tyne, Oct. 1966); *The Masque of the Red Death*, 2 dance scenes (1968); *Sinfonia intrepida* (1976; Liverpool, Jan. 18, 1977); *Sinfonia drammatica* (Jena, March 15, 1978); *Hymnos* for Strings (1978; adapted from the String Quartet No. 2); *Concerto conciso* for Strings (Stratford-upon-Avon, Aug. 21, 1981); *An English Suite* (1984); *Symphonic Prelude* (1985); *Ballade* for Violin and Orch. (1988); *Concerto Ardente* for Horn and Strings (1992; Malvern, June 1993); *Les Roseaux au Vent* for 2 Oboes, English Horn, and Strings (Utrecht, Oct. 1993). **BRASS BAND:** *Partita* (1975); *Invocation* (1977). **CHAMBER:** *Prelude, Allegro and Postlude* for Flute, Oboe, and Piano (1955); 3 sonatas for Solo Violin (1957, rev. 1987; 1972; 1989); *Fantasy* for 10 Winds (1960; rev. 1979); 2 oboe quartets (1960, 1973); *Music* for Brass for 3 Trumpets and 3 Trombones (1964); 3 string quartets: No. 1 (1967), No. 2, *Hymnos* (1978), and No. 3 (1980); Sextet for Flute, Oboe, Clarinet, Bassoon, Horn, and Piano (1970); *Duo declamando* for Horn and Piano (1972); Trio for Oboe, Clarinet, and Bassoon (1975); Trio for Horn, Violin, and Piano (1976); Concerto for 10 Winds (1979); *Quintetto concertato* for Flute, Oboe, Clarinet, Bassoon, and Horn (1979); *Serenade* for Viola or Clarinet and Guitar (1981); *Suite* for Timpani (1982); *Percussion Partita* for 6 Players (1985); Quartet for 4 Horns (1986); *Canticles* for Horn Quartet and Organ (1987); Clarinet Sonata (1988); Sonata for Solo Cello (1990); *Andromeda* for Percussion Quartet (1990); *Idyll* for Horn and Organ (1992); Concerto for Brass Quintet (1993). **KEYBOARD: PIANO:** *Prelude, Scherzo, and Elegy* (1964; rev. 1986); *Prelude and Scherzo impetuoso* (1967); *Night Music* (1969). **ORGAN:** *Partita* (1962); *Triptych* (1966). **VOCAL:** *The Wounded Surgeon Plies the Steel* for Chorus (1959); *Magnificat and Nunc dimittis* for Chorus and Organ (1961); *Missa brevis* for Chorus and Organ (1963); *Mary Modyr Cum and Se* for Chorus and Organ (1963); *Do Not Go Gentle into That Good Night* for 5 Solo Voices or 5-part Chorus (1965); *Celebration* for Contralto, Chorus, Organ, Orch., Brass Band, and Audience Unisono (1975); *On* *the Beach at Night* for Chorus (1979); *Consecration* for Chorus, Organ, Brass, and Percussion (1982); *A Mass for Canterbury* for Chorus (1986; Utrecht, June 25, 1988); songs.

White, Clarence Cameron, black American violinist and composer; b. Clarksville, Tenn., Aug. 10, 1880; d. N.Y., June 30, 1960. He studied at the Oberlin (Ohio) Cons. (1896–1901), with Samuel Coleridge-Taylor in London (1906; 1908–10), and with Raoul Laparra in Paris (1930–32). He taught at various institutions while pursuing a concert career; was director of music at the Hampton (Va.) Inst. (1932–35). In 1919 he helped to organize the National Assn. of Negro Musicians. He won the Bispham Medal for his opera *Ouanga* (1932) and the Benjamin Award for his *Elegy* for Orch. (1954). His major works were written in a neo-Romantic style with occasional infusions of Negro folk melos.

WORKS: DRAMATIC: OPERAS: *Ouanga* (concert perf., Chicago, Nov. 1932; stage perf., South Bend, Ind., June 10, 1949); *Carnival Romance* (1952). **BALLET:** *A Night in Sans Souci* (1929). **INCIDENTAL MUSIC TO:** J. Matheus's *Tambour* (1929). **ORCH.:** Sym.; *Kutamba Rhapsody* (1942); *Elegy* (1954); *Dance Rhapsody* (1955); *Poeme* (1955). **CHAMBER:** *Bandana Sketches*, violin suite (1918); *From the Cotton Fields*, violin suite (1920); 2 string quartets (1931, 1931); *Legende d'Afrique* for Cello and Piano (1955); keyboard pieces. **VOCAL:** *Heritage* for Soprano, Tenor, Chorus, and Orch. (1959); songs; numerous arrangements of spirituals, including *40 Negro Spirituals* (1927) and *Traditional Negro Spirituals* (1940).

BIBL.: V. Edwards and M. Mark, "In Retrospect: C.C. W.," *Black Perspective in Music*, IX (1981).

White, Donald H(oward), American composer and pedagogue; b. Narberth, Pa., Feb. 28, 1921. He studied music education at Temple Univ. in Philadelphia (B.S., 1942) and composition with Persichetti at the Philadelphia Cons. (1946) and with Rogers and Hanson at the Eastman School of Music in Rochester, N.Y. (M.M., 1947; Ph.D., 1952). In 1947 he joined the faculty of DePauw Univ. in Greencastle, Ind., where he was chairman of composition and theory studies (1948–81), a prof. (1959–81), and director of the school of music (1974–78); was chairman of the music dept. at Central Washington Univ. in Ellensburg, Wash. (1981–90).

WORKS: ORCH.: *Sagan*, overture (1946); *Kennebec Suite* (1947); Overture (1951); Cello Concerto (1952); *Divertimento No. 2* for Strings (1968). **BAND:** *Ambrosian Hymn Variants* (1963); *Terpsimetrics* (1968); Concertino for Timpani, Winds, and Percussion (1973); *Lyric Suite* for Euphonium and Wind Ensemble (1978); *4 Bagatelles* (1989). **CHAMBER:** Trumpet Sonata (1946); *3 to 5* for Woodwind Quintet (1964); *Serenade No. 3* for Brass Quintet (1965); Trombone Sonata (1966); Tuba Sonata (1978); Quintet for Brass (1980). **VOCAL:** *Song of Mankind* for Soloists, Chorus, and Orch. (1970); *From the Navajo Children* for Chorus and Wind Ensemble (1978); choruses.

White, Eric Walter, English writer on music and administrator; b. Bristol, Sept. 10, 1905; d. London, Sept. 13, 1985. He attended Clifton College, Bristol, and studied English at Balliol College, Oxford (1924–27). After working as a translator for the League of Nations in Geneva (1929–33), he was employed by the National Council for Social Service in London (1935–42); in 1942 he became assistant secretary of the Council for the Encouragement of Music and the Arts, which became the Arts Council of Great Britain in 1946; he retired in 1971. He publ. valuable studies on Stravinsky and an invaluable register of English opera premieres.

WRITINGS (all publ. in London): *Stravinsky's Sacrifice to Apollo* (1930); *Stravinsky: A Critical Survey* (1947); *Benjamin Britten: A Sketch of His Life and Works* (1948; 3rd ed., enl., 1970 as *Benjamin Britten: His Life and Operas*); *The Rise of English Opera* (1951); *Stravinsky: The Composer and His Works* (1966; 2nd ed., rev., 1979); *A History of English Opera* (1983); *A Register of First Performances of English Operas and Semi-Operas from the 16th Century to 1980* (1983).

White, Felix Harold, English composer; b. London, April 27, 1884; d. there, Jan. 31, 1945. He studied piano with his mother but otherwise was self-taught in music. He devoted himself mainly to composition but also publ. a *Dictionary of Musical Terms* and some short monographs on musicians.

WORKS: ORCH.: *Shylock*, overture (London, Sept. 1907); *Polonaise* (1908); *Astarte Syriaca*, tone poem (1909; London, Jan. 1911); *Meditation* (1911); Suite (1913); *Impressions of England*, suite (1918); *The Deserted Village*, tone poem (1923); *Nocturne* (1936); Overture (1937). **CHAMBER:** *Romance* for Cello and Piano (1907); Cello Sonata (1910); *Dawn* for 12 Cellos (1922); Trio for Oboe or Violin, Viola, and Piano (1922); *4 Proverbs* for Flute, Oboe, Violin, Viola, and Cello (1925); *Orison* for 4 Cellos (1937); many piano pieces. **VOCAL:** Choral pieces; part songs; numerous solo songs.

White, Frances, American composer; b. Philadelphia, Aug. 30, 1960. She studied at the Univ. of Maryland (B.Mus., 1981), Brooklyn College (M.A., 1982), and Princeton Univ. (M.A., 1990), where she subsequently began a Ph.D. program in composition. In 1980–81 she was a member of the Univ. of Maryland's 20th-Century Music Ensemble; in 1993 she was composer-in-residence at the Univ. of Missouri in Kansas City. From 1985 to 1987 she served as technical assistant to John Cage in the creation of his works for computer-generated tape, *Essay*, *Stratified Essay*, and *Voiceless Essay*. In 1990 she won 1st prize in the program music category and 2nd prize in the mixed category in the 18th Bourges International Electro-Acoustic Music Competition; she also received ASCAP awards (1990, 1993, 1994). White's compositions, often of exquisite beauty, have been almost exclusively for instruments and tape, with particular emphasis on the creation of interactive sonic landscapes; her *Winter Aconites* (a species of flowering bulb, *Eranthis hyemalis*) for 6 Instruments and Tape (1993), a commission from ASCAP in memory of John Cage, was created at the Winham Laboratory at Princeton Univ. on a NeXT workstation using Cmix and Csound software. White currently lives in Princeton, N.J., with her husband, the writer James Pritchett, 2 cats, and an ever-expanding collection of species and hybrid orchids.

WORKS: *Ogni pensiero vola* for Tape (1985); *Chiaroscura* for Percussion and Tape (1986); *Design for an Invisible City* for Tape (1987); *Valdrada* for Tape (1988); *Still Life With Piano* for Piano and Tape (1989); *Resonant Landscape*, interactive computer-music installation (1990); *Trees* for 2 Violins, Viola, and Tape (1992); *Nocturne* for Tape (1992); *Walks Through Resonant Landscape 1–5* for Tape (1992; derived from the interactive computer-music installation *Resonant Landscape*, 1990); *Winter Aconites* for Clarinet, Electric Guitar, Cello, Double Bass, Piano, Vibraphone, and Tape (1993).

White, John (Reeves), American musicologist and conductor; b. Houston, Miss., May 2, 1924; d. N.Y., July 12, 1984. He studied at the Cincinnati Cons. (1941–43); also took courses at the Paris Cons. (1945); obtained his M.A. at Colorado College in 1948, and his Ph.D. at Indiana Univ. in 1952; also received the degree of Dr. of Natural Philosophy at the Inst. of Neurophenomenology in Amherst, Mass. (1975). He held teaching posts at Colorado College (1947–52), the Univ. of Richmond (1953–61), Indiana Univ. (1961–66; 1970–71), and Hunter College of the City Univ. of N.Y. (from 1971). From 1966 to 1970 he conducted the N.Y. Pro Musica. White produced reconstructions of several medieval and Renaissance dramatic works. He ed. *The Keyboard Tablature of Johannes of Lublin* (6 vols., 1964–67), *François Dandrieu: Harpsichord Music* (1965), and *Michelangelo Rossi: Complete Keyboard Works* (1967). With J. Dos Passos and H. Fitzgerald, he ed. *The Arts between the Wars: A Symposium* (1964).

White, Michael, American composer and teacher; b. Chicago, March 6, 1931. He studied at the Chicago Musical College and at the Juilliard School of Music in N.Y. with Peter Mennin. In 1963 he received a Guggenheim fellowship. He taught at the Oberlin (Ohio) College Cons. of Music (1964–66), the Philadelphia College of Performing Arts (1966–79), and the Juilliard School in N.Y. (from 1979). Among his works are several operas, including *Metamorphosis* (1968); *Opposites* for Wind Ensemble (1970); *Passion According to a Cynic* (1971); Violin Concerto (1979); Double Concerto for Violin, Viola, and Orch. (1981); *The 3 Muses* for Harpsichord (1984); *Museum Pieces* for Flute and Guitar (1987); Sonata for Solo Viola (1988); other chamber pieces; guitar music; choruses; song cycles.

White, Robert, American tenor; b. N.Y., Oct. 27, 1936. He was the son of Joseph White, the "Silver Masked Tenor" of the early radio era in N.Y. He began his career with appearances on Fred Allen's radio program when he was 9; after studying music at Hunter College, he continued his training with Boulanger and Souzay in France; then completed his studies at the Juilliard School of Music in N.Y. (M.S., 1968), where he found a mentor in Beverley Peck Johnson. He sang with the N.Y. Pro Musica and appeared with various American opera companies before becoming successful as a concert singer. His repertoire ranges from the Baroque to Irish ballads. He sang in a "Homage to John McCormack" at N.Y.'s Alice Tully Hall during the 1985–86 season.

White, Ruth, American composer; b. Pittsburgh, Sept. 1, 1925. She studied composition with Lopatnikoff (B.F.A., 1948; M.F.A., 1949) and received training in piano at the Mellon Inst. in Pittsburgh; then studied at the Univ. of Calif. at Los Angeles (1951–54) and had private composition lessons with Antheil (1952–54). She specialized in teaching music to children and wrote much didactic music. Her other music followed along conventional lines until she took up electronic composition in 1964.

WORKS: DRAMATIC: *Pinions*, opera (1967); film and television music. **ORCH.:** Suite (1949); *Shofar Symphony* (1965). **CHAMBER:** Various works; piano pieces. **VOCAL:** *Palestinean Song Cycle* for Voice, Bassoon, Piano, and Percussion (1949); *Songs from the Japanese Poets* for Voice and Piano (1949); *Settings for Lullabies from 'round the World* for Tenor, Soprano, Piano, Cello, and Horn (1955); *Garden of Delights* for Soprano and Electronics (1971); about 150 songs for children. **ELECTRONIC:** *7 Trumps from the Tarot Cards* (1967); *Flowers of Evil* (1969); *Short Circuits* (1970). **OTHER:** Pedagogical pieces.

White, William C., American bandmaster and march composer; b. Centerville, Utah, Sept. 29, 1881; d. Tenafly, N.J., Sept. 30, 1964. He studied violin at the New England Cons. of Music in Boston and at the Inst. of Musical Art in N.Y., graduating in 1914. He was a member of the 10th U.S. Coast Artillery Band (1907–12) and led the Mecca Temple Band (1919–20) and the Almes Temple Band in Washington, D.C. (1921–28); then served as principal of the Army Music School on Governors Island. He composed several marches, among them the popular *American Doughboy.* White publ. *A History of Military Music in America* (1943) and *Military Band Arranging; Tone Building and Intonation Studies for Military Bands.*

Whitehead, Alfred (Ernest), English-born Canadian organist, choirmaster, teacher, and composer; b. Peterborough, July 10, 1887; d. Amherst, Nova Scotia, April 1, 1974. He was a pupil of Haydn Keeton and C.C. Francis of Peterborough Cathedral, and then of A. Eaglefield Hull. In 1912 he emigrated to Canada, and in 1913 became the 1st fellow by examination of the Canadian Guild (later College) of Organists; in 1916 he obtained his B.Mus. at the Univ. of Toronto and in 1922 his D.Mus. at McGill Univ. in Montreal; in 1924 he became a fellow of the Royal College of Organists and winner of the Lafontaine Prize. He was organist and choirmaster at St. Andrew's Presbyterian Church in Truro, Nova Scotia (1912–15); then was organist and choirmaster at St. Peter's Anglican Church in Sherbrooke, Quebec (1915–22), and at Christ Church Cathedral in Montreal (1922–47); also taught organ, theory, and composition at the McGill Cons. (1922–30). After serving as head of the music dept. at Mt. Allison Univ. (1947–53), he was organist and choirmaster at Trinity United Church in Amherst (1953–71). He was president of the Canadian College of Organists (1930–31; 1935–37); was honorary vice-president (1971–73) and honorary president (1973–74) of the Royal Canadian College of Organists. He wrote a number of distinguished sacred works, excelling as a composer of motets and anthems. He was also a painter and philatelist.

Whitehill, Clarence (Eugene), American baritone, later bass-baritone; b. Parnell, Iowa, Nov. 5, 1871; d. N.Y., Dec. 18, 1932. He studied with L.A. Phelps in Chicago; earned his living as a clerk in an express office, and also sang in churches; then went to Paris in 1896, where he studied with Giraudet and Sbriglia. He made his operatic debut on Oct. 31, 1898, at the Théâtre de la Monnaie in Brussels; was the first American male singer to be engaged at the Opéra-Comique in Paris (1899); then was a member of Henry Savage's Grand English Opera Co. at the Metropolitan Opera in N.Y. in 1900; went for further study to Stockhausen in Frankfurt am Main, and from there to Bayreuth, where he studied the entire Wagnerian repertoire with Cosima Wagner; after engagements in Germany, he was a member of the Cologne Opera (1903–08). On Nov. 25, 1909, he made his Metropolitan Opera debut in N.Y. as Amneris with notable success, where he sang for a season. He then was again on its roster from 1914 until his death. He also sang with the Chicago Opera (1911–14; 1915–17). Among his finest roles were Hans Sachs, Gounod's Méphistophélès, and Golaud.

Whiteman, Paul, celebrated American conductor of popular music; b. Denver, Colo., March 28, 1890; d. Doylestown, Pa., Dec. 29, 1967. He played viola in the Denver Sym. Orch. and later in the San Francisco People's Orch. In 1917–18 he was conductor of a 40-piece band in the U.S. Navy. He then formed a hotel orch. in Santa Barbara, Calif., and began to develop a style of playing known as "symphonic jazz," which soon made him famous. On Feb. 12, 1924, he gave a concert in Aeolian Hall in N.Y., at which he introduced Gershwin's *Rhapsody in Blue*, written for his orch., with Gershwin himself as soloist. In 1926 he made a tour in Europe. While not himself a jazz musician, Whiteman was popularly known as the "King of Jazz," and frequently featured at his concerts such notables of the jazz world as Bix Beiderbecke, Frank Trumbauer, and Benny Goodman; Bing Crosby achieved his early fame as a member of Paul Whiteman's Rhythm Boys. Whiteman established the Whiteman Awards, made annually for "symphonic jazz" compositions written by Americans. He publ. the books *Jazz* (with M. McBride; N.Y., 1926), *How to Be a Bandleader* (with L. Lieber; N.Y., 1941), and *Records for the Millions* (N.Y., 1948).

BIBL.: C. Johnson, *P. W.: A Chronology* (Williamstown, N.J., 1977); T. DeLong, *Pops: P. W., the King of Jazz* (Piscataway, N.J., 1983).

Whithorne (real name, **Whittern**), **Emerson,** American composer; b. Cleveland, Sept. 6, 1884; d. Lyme, Conn., March 25, 1958. He had his name legally changed in 1918 to Whithorne (the original family name of his paternal grandfather). He studied in Cleveland with J.H. Rogers; embarked on a musical career at the age of 15, and appeared as a pianist on the Chautauqua circuit for 2 seasons. In 1904 he went to Vienna and took piano lessons with Leschetizky and theory and composition lessons with Robert Fuchs; from 1905 to 1907 he was a piano pupil of Artur Schnabel. In 1907 he married Ethel Leginska, acting as her impresario in Germany until 1909; they were separated in 1912, and divorced in 1916. Between 1907 and 1915, Whithorne lived mainly in London; he studied Chinese and Japanese music from materials in the British Museum, and wrote several pieces based on oriental tunes (*Adventures of a Samurai*; settings for *The Yellow Jacket*; *The Typhoon*). Returning to America, he became ed. for the Art Publication Society of St. Louis (1915–20); then settled in N.Y. and devoted himself entirely to composition; was an active member of the League of Composers in N.Y. In his music, he assumed a militantly modernistic attitude; wrote several pieces in the fashionable "machine music" style.

WORKS: DRAMATIC: Incidental music. **ORCH.:** *The Rain* (Detroit, Feb. 22, 1913); *La nuit* (1917); *Adventures of a Samurai*, suite (1919); *Ranga*, symphonic suite (1920); *The Aeroplane* (1920; Birmingham, England, Jan. 30, 1926; arranged from the piano piece); *N.Y. Days and Nights* (1923; Philadelphia, July 30, 1926; arranged from the piano piece); *Poem* for Piano and Orch. (Chicago, Feb. 4, 1927); *Fata Morgana*, symphonic poem (1927; N.Y., Oct. 11, 1928); Violin Concerto (1928–31; Chicago, Nov. 12, 1931); 2 syms.: No. 1 (1929; Cincinnati, Jan. 12, 1934) and No. 2 (1935; Cincinnati, March 19, 1937); *The Dream Pedlar*, symphonic poem (1930; Los Angeles, Jan. 15, 1931); *Fandango* (1931; N.Y., April 19, 1932); *Moon Trail*, symphonic poem (Boston, Dec. 15, 1933); *Sierra Morena* (N.Y., May 7, 1938); *Serenade* for Strings (1943). **CHAMBER:** 2 string quartets (n.d., 1930); *Quartettino orientale* (1916?); *Greek Impressions* for String Quartet (1917); Piano Quintet (1928); Violin Sonata (1932). **PIANO:** *The Aeroplane* (1920?; also arranged for Orch.); *N.Y. Days and Nights* (1922; also arranged for Orch.); *El camino real*, suite (1937). **VOCAL:** *2 Chinese Poems* for Voice and Piano (1921); *2 Chinese Nocturnes* for Voice and Piano (1921); *Saturday's Child* for Mezzo-soprano, Tenor, and Chamber Orch. (N.Y., March 13, 1926); *The Grim Troubador* for Medium Voice and String Quartet (1927; also for Medium Voice and Piano).

BIBL.: J. Howard, *E. W.* (N.Y., 1929).

Whitlock, Percy (William), English organist and composer; b. Chatham, June 1, 1903; d. Bournemouth, May 1, 1946. He received musical instruction as a choirboy at Rochester Cathedral, and then studied in London at the Guildhall School of Music and the Royal College of Music. After serving as assistant organist at Rochester Cathedral (1921–30), he settled in Bournemouth and was director of music at St. Stephen's (1930–35) and borough organist (1932–46). He became well known as a recitalist. He composed a Sym. for Organ and Orch.; much organ music, including a Sonata, *Plymouth Suite*, and *5 Short Pieces in Various Styles*; many vocal works, among them services, anthems, hymn tunes, and motets.

Whitmer, T(homas) Carl, American organist, teacher, and composer; b. Altoona, Pa., June 24, 1873; d. Poughkeepsie, N.Y., May 30, 1959. He studied piano with C. Jarvis, organ with S.P. Warren, and composition with W.W. Gilchrist. He was director of the School of Music, Stephens College, Columbia, Mo. (1899–1909); director of music at the Pa. College for Women in Pittsburgh (1909–16); organist and choirmaster of the Sixth Presbyterian Church in Pittsburgh (1916–32); then taught privately at Dramamount, his farm near Newburgh, N.Y. He publ. *The Way of My Heart and Mind* (Pittsburgh, 1920) and *The Art of Improvisation: A Handbook of Principles and Methods* (N.Y., 1934; rev. ed., 1941).

WORKS: DRAMATIC: *Oh, Isabel*, opera (1951); sacred music dramas. **ORCH.:** *Poem of Life* for Piano and Orch. (1914); *A Syrian Night*, ballet suite (Pittsburgh, Feb. 17, 1919); *Radiations over a 13th Century Theme* for Strings (1935). **CHAMBER:** Several works, including piano pieces and organ music. **VOCAL:** *Supper at Emmaus*, choral suite (Pittsbirgh, Feb. 21, 1939); *Chant Me the Poem That Comes from the Soul*, cantata, after Walt Whitman (Pittsburgh, Feb. 19, 1942); anthems; songs.

Whitney, John, American experimental filmmaker, computer-graphics artist, and Pythagorean-inspired speculative theorist of the analogies between music and the visual arts; b. Pasadena, Calif., April 8, 1917; d. Santa Monica, Calif., Sept. 22, 1995. He is a pioneer in 20th-century motion graphics, having invented cinema techniques in the 1940s that became an established part of the repertoire of special effects later used in film titles and television. His interest in the complementarity of visual and aural arts began with a series of experimental films made with his brother James, including the silent *24 Variations* (1939–40) and the series of *5 Film Exercises* (1943–44), which made use of synthesized pendulum music. With the development of computer graphics, he produced a number of what are now classic pieces, utilizing the music of a variety of composers; these include *Permutations* (1968; re-ed., 1979; with Indian tabla music by Balachandra), *Matrix I* (1971; with music adapted from sonatas by Antonio Soler) and *III* (1972; with music from Terry Riley's *Rainbow in Curved Air*), and Arabesque (1975; with improvised music by Manoocheher Sadeghi). His *Moondrum: Twelve Works for Videodisc* (1989–95) is a poetic response to the arts of Native Americans and was produced using a real-time composing program developed by Whitney and Jerry Reed; the series comprises *Moondrum: Dream Songs* (Memories of prehistory), *Navajo: Weaver's Art, Hopi: Dance Ceremonies, Kwakiutl* (The Northern Pacific tootem sculptors and Dance of the Dream Catcher), *Qxaquitl (Quetzalcoatl): About Time and Deity* (*Introduction, Blood Sacrifice at Pyramids of Copan, Stone Bells: Quetzacotl, Stone Bells: A Marching Procession*, and *A Noisy Festival at the Great Calendar Stone*), *Black Elk Requiem* (a memorial to the exiled Oglala Sioux people), *Chaco* (Fajada Buttle spiral petroglyph wedge of solstice sunlight), *Mimbres Star* (a pottery design marks the supernova event of 1054 A.D.), *Chumash* (rock paintings of the Southern Calif. coastline), *Kachina: A Memory of Bird and Snake Deities-Sand Paintings* (*Introduction to all symbols, Sand paintings*, and *Beatification of the Kachina Deity*), *Chapala* (Snapshots: dream symbols on warrior shields), and *Acoma: For The Infanta. The God King.* (3 cradle songs in 3 colors, With earthquake and Official Royal Seal, and "When the wind blow the cradle will rock"). These and many other computer-generated aural/visual compositions exemplify his ideas about the inherent complementarity of music and visual art, with the harmonic motion evident in tonal music made visible in the charge and release of tensional visual forces. His work was supported by IBM; he also received NEA grants, a Guggenheim fellowship (1947–48), and a bronze medal from the Academy of Motion Picture Arts and Science for pioneering achievements in film. After retiring from his teaching position in the art dept. of the Univ. of Calif. at Los Angeles in 1986, he devoted himself to composition in his studio in Pacific Palisades, Calif. He publ. *Digital Harmony: On the Complementarity of Music and Visual Art* (Peterborough, N.H., 1980); also the articles "Writing on Water—Action Painting with Music," *Media Arts Journal* (Spring–Summer 1990) and "To Paint on Water: The Audiovisual Duet of Complementarity," *Computer Music Journal* (Fall 1994), and the video documentary, *A Personal Search: For the Complementarity of Music and Visual Art* (Santa Monica, Calif., 1992).

Whitney, Robert (Sutton), American conductor; b. Newcastle upon Tyne, England (of an American father and an English mother), July 9, 1904; d. Louisville, Ky., Nov. 22, 1986. He studied with Sowerby in Chicago; took lessons in conducting with Eric De Lamarter there. In 1937 he was engaged as conductor of the Louisville Phil. (later renamed the Louisville Orch.), a post he held until 1967. A munificent grant from the Rockefeller Foundation enabled the Louisville Orch. to commission works from American and foreign composers, each to be paid a set fee of $1,000; the project proved highly successful, and the orch. was able to give first performances of works by Honegger, Milhaud, Malipiero, Petrassi, Krenek, Dallapiccola, Toch, Chávez, Villa-Lobos, Ginastera, Schuman, Virgil Thomson, Cowell, Piston, Sessions, Antheil, Creston, Mennin, and others; it recorded some 200 contemporary symphonic works on Louisville Orch. Records. From 1956 to 1972 he was dean of the Univ. of Louisville School of Music; also taught conducting at the Univ. of Cincinnati College-Cons. of Music (1967–70). He composed a *Concerto Grosso* (1934); Sym. in E minor (1936); *Sospiri di Roma* for Chorus and Orch. (1941); Concertino (1960).

Whittaker, W(illiam) G(illies), respected English choral conductor, pedagogue, and composer; b. Newcastle upon Tyne, July 23, 1876; d. Orkney Islands, July 5, 1944. He studied science at Armstrong College, Univ. of Durham, and also received training in organ and singing before joining its faculty in 1898; was the 1st Gardiner Prof. of Music at the Univ. of Glasgow (1929–38) and was principal of the Royal Scottish Academy of Music in Glasgow (1929–41); also was active as a choral conductor; conducted various choral societies in Newcastle and

London. He became well known as a Bach conductor and scholar; ed. various instrumental works of the 17th and 18th centuries. He composed *A Lykewake Dirge* and *The Celestial Sphere* for Chorus and Orch.; *Psalm CXXXIX; Among the Northumbrian Hills*, piano quintet; piano pieces; songs; prepared folk-song arrangements.

WRITINGS: *Fugitive Notes on Certain Cantatas and the Motets of J.S. Bach* (London, 1924); *Class Singing* (London, 1925; 2nd ed., 1930); *Collected Essays* (Oxford, 1940); *The Cantatas of J.S. Bach, Sacred and Secular* (London, 1959).

Whittal, Arnold (Morgan), English musicologist; b. Shrewsbury, Nov. 11, 1935. He took courses at Emmanuel College, Cambridge (B.A., 1959), completing his training at the Univ. there (Ph.D., 1964, with the diss. *La Querelle des Bouffons*). He then taught at the Univ. of Nottingham (1964–69), Univ. College, Cardiff (1969–75), and King's College, London (from 1976).

WRITINGS: *Schoenberg Chamber Music* (London, 1972); *Music since the First World War* (London, 1977; 3rd ed., 1988); *Britten and Tippett: Studies in Themes and Techniques* (Cambridge, 1982); *Romantic Music: A Concise History from Schubert to Sibelius* (London, 1987); with J. Dunsby, *Music Analysis in Theory and Practice* (New Haven, Conn., 1988).

Whittall, Gertrude Clarke, American patroness of music and literature; b. Bellevue, Nebr., Oct. 7, 1867; d. Washington, D.C., June 29, 1965. Her maiden name was Clarke; she married Matthew John Whittall on June 4, 1906. In 1935 she donated to the Library of Congress in Washington, D.C., a quartet of Stradivari instruments—2 violins (including the famous "Betts"), a viola, and a cello—together with 4 Tourte bows; she added another Stradivari violin (the "Ward") and another Tourte bow in 1937. In 1936 she established an endowment fund in the Library of Congress to provide public concerts at which these instruments would be used, and in 1938 the Whittall Pavilion was built in the library to house them and to serve other purposes in the musical life of the library. In subsequent years, she continued to add to her gifts to the library on behalf of both music and literature; one series enabled the Whittall Foundation to acquire many valuable autograph MSS of composers from Bach to Schoenberg, and in particular the finest single group of Brahms MSS gathered anywhere in the world.

BIBL.: W. Orcutt, *The Stradivari Memorial at Washington* (Washington, D.C., 1938); E. Waters, *Autograph Musical Scores in the W. Foundation Collection* (Washington, D.C., 1951).

Whittenberg, Charles, American composer and teacher; b. St. Louis, July 6, 1927; d. Hartford, Conn., Aug. 22, 1984. He was a student of Phillips and Rogers at the Eastman School of Music in Rochester, N.Y. (B.A., 1948). From 1961 to 1963 he was ed. of the *American Composers Alliance Bulletin*. In 1962 he became associated with the Columbia-Princeton Electronic Music Center and became a teacher at Bennington (Vt.) College. After teaching at the Center of Liberal Studies in Washington, D.C. (1965), he served as an assoc. prof. at the Univ. of Conn. in Storrs (1967–77), where he was director of its Contemporary Music Projects. In 1963 and 1964 he held Guggenheim fellowships, and in 1965–66 the prize of the American Academy in Rome. Whittenberg was especially adept at writing brass music.

WORKS: ORCH.: *Event* for Chamber Orch. and Tape (1963; N.Y., April 28, 1964); *Correlatives* (1969); *Serenade* for Strings (1971–73). **CHAMBER:** *Dialogue and Aria* for Flute and Piano (1956); *Fantasy* for Wind Quintet (1961); *Concert Piece* for Bassoon and Piano (1961; rev. 1971); *Structures* for 2 Pianos (1961); *Triptych* for Brass Quintet (1962); Chamber Concerto for Violin and 7 Instruments (1963); Cello Sonata (1963); *Duo-Divertimento* for Flute and Double Bass (1963); *3 Pieces* for Clarinet (1963; rev. 1969); *Variations* for 9 Players (1964; rev. 1970); 2 string quartets (1965; 1974–75); *4 Forms and an Epilogue* for Harpsichord (1965); *Polyphony* for Trumpet (1965); Sextet for Flute, Clarinet, Bassoon, Violin, Cello, and Double Bass (1967); *Conversations* for Double Bass (1967); *3 Compositions* for Piano (1967; rev. 1969); *Games of 5* for Wind Quintet (1968); *Iambi* for 2 Oboes (1968; rev. 1972); Concerto for Brass Quintet (1968–69); *Winter Music* for Violin (1971); *Sonata-fantasia* for Cello (1973); *5 Feuilletons* for Clarinet (1976); *In Memoriam Benjamin Britten* for Percussion (1977). **VOCAL:** *3 Songs on Texts of Rilke* for Soprano and 9 Instruments (1957–62); *Concertante* for Baritone, Viola, Flute, and Vibraphone (1961); *From the Sonnets to Orpheus* for Narrator and Soprano (1962); *Vocalise* for Soprano and Viola (1963); *A Sacred Triptych* for Chorus (1971). **TAPE:** *Study I* for Cello and Tape (1961); *Electronic Study II* for Double Bass and Tape (1961); *Study* for Clarinet and Electronic Extensions (1961); *Event II* for Double Bass, Flute, Strings, and Tape (1963).

Whyte, Ian, Scottish conductor, broadcasting administrator, and composer; b. Dunfermline, Aug. 13, 1901; d. Glasgow, March 27, 1960. He was a pupil of David Stephen (composition) and Philip Halstead (piano) at the Carnegie Dunfermline Trust Music School, and later was a student of Stanford and Vaughan Williams at the Royal College of Music in London. Upon his return to Scotland, he was made music director to Lord Glentanar in 1923. From 1931 to 1945 he was head of music for the BBC in Glasgow, and then conductor of its orch. from 1945 until his death. His extensive output, which includes operas, operettas, ballets, 2 syms., symphonic poems, overtures, concertos, chamber music, piano pieces, choruses, hymns, carols, and many songs, reflects his Scottish heritage.

Wich, Günther, German conductor; b. Bamberg, May 23, 1928. He studied flute with Gustav Scheck in Freiburg im Breisgau (1948–52). In 1952 he made his conducting debut there, serving as chief conductor of its Opera until 1959; then was conductor of the Graz Opera (1959–61); later was Generalmusikdirektor in Hannover (1961–65) and at the Deutsche Oper am Rhein in Düsseldorf (1965–80). From 1982 to 1994 he was prof. of conducting at the Würzburg Hochschule für Musik.

Wickham, Florence, American contralto and composer; b. Beaver, Pa., 1880; d. N.Y., Oct. 20, 1962. She studied in Philadelphia; then was a pupil of Franz Emerich in Berlin; also studied with Mathilde Mallinger. In 1902 she made her operatic debut as Meyerbeer's Fidès in Wiesbaden; after appearances in Schwerin and Munich, she sang the role of Kundry in *Parsifal* in Henry W. Savage's touring opera troupe in America (1904–05). In 1908 she appeared in Wagnerian roles at London's Covent Garden. On Nov. 17, 1909, she made her Metropolitan Opera debut in N.Y. as Verdi's Emilia; remained on its roster until 1912, then sang in concerts and devoted herself to composition. She wrote the operettas *Rosalynd* (1938) and *The Legend of Hex Mountain* (1957), as well as a number of songs.

Wicks, (Edward) Allan, English organist and choirmaster; b. Harden, Yorkshire, June 6, 1923. He studied organ with Thomas Armstrong at Christ Church, Oxford; also was made a Fellow of the Royal College of Organists. He was assistant organist at York Minster (1947–54); after serving as organist and choirmaster at Manchester Cathedral (1954–61), he distinguished himself in those capacities at Canterbury Cathedral (1961–88); also toured as a recitalist in England, Europe, and the U.S. In 1974 he was awarded a D.Mus. by the Archbishop of Canterbury and in 1985 was given an honorary D.Mus. by the Univ. of Kent; in 1988 he was made a Commander of the Order of the British Empire. His repertoire is exhaustive, ranging from early music to modern English compositions.

Widdop, Walter, English tenor; b. Norland, April 19, 1892; d. London, Sept. 6, 1949. He was a student of Dinh Gilly. In 1923 he made his operatic debut as Radames with the British National Opera Co. in Leeds. In 1924 he sang in *Siegfried* at London's Covent Garden, returning there as Siegmund (1932) and Tristan (1933; 1937–38). He was also a guest artist in Spain, Holland, and Germany. In addition to his operatic roles, he also was admired as an oratorio singer. The night before he died he sang Lohengrin's Farewell at a London Promenade concert.

Wiechowicz, Stanislaw, Polish composer, pedagogue, choral conductor, and writer on music; b. Kroszyce, Nov. 27, 1893; d. Kraków, May 12, 1963. He received his training at the Kraków Cons., the Dalcroze Inst. in Dresden, the St. Petersburg Cons., and the Schola Cantorum in Paris. After teaching theory (1921–30) and composition (1930–39) at the Poznań Cons., he was a prof. of composition at the Kraków Cons. from 1945 until his death. In 1950 he was awarded the Polish State Prize for composition. Wiechowicz excelled as a composer of vocal music.

WORKS: ORCH.: *Babie lato* (Martinmas Summer), symphonic poem (1922); *Chmiel* (The Hopvine), symphonic scherzo (1926); *Ruta* (Rue), sumphonic poem (1930); *Ulegalki* (The Wild Pears), symphonic portraits (1944); *Kasia* (Kate), folk suite for 2 Clarinets and Strings (1946); *Suita pastoralna* (1952); *Serenade polska* (1953); *Koncert staromiejski* (Old Town Concerto) for Strings (1954). **VOCAL:** *Pastoralki*, Christmas cantata for Voice, Chorus, and Percussion (1929); *Dzień slowiański* (Slav Day), cantata for Chorus and Brass Band (1929); *Kantata romantyczna* for Soprano, Chorus, and Orch. (1930); *3 suity ludowe* (3 Folk Suites) for Solo Voices, Chorus, and Orch. (1942); *Psalmodia* for Chorus and Orch. (1944); *Z Wojtusiowej izbyi* (From Wojtek's Room), children's cantata for Solo Voices, Chorus, and Orch. (1944); *A czemużeś nie przyjechal* (Why Did You Not Come?), rustic scene for Chorus and Orch. (1948); *Na glinianym wazoniku* (On a Little Clay Pot) for Chorus and Orch. (1948); *Kantata żniwna* (Harvest Cantata) for Chorus (1948); *Kantata Mickiewiczowska* for Chorus and Orch. (1950); *List do March Chagalla* (Letter to Marc Chagall), dramatic rhapsody for 2 Solo Voices, Male and Female Speakers, Chorus, and Orch. (1961); *Zstąp, gołębico* (O Dove, Descend), cantata for Soprano, Chorus, and Orch. (1962–63); many other pieces; numerous folk song arrangements.

Wiedemann, Hermann, German baritone; b. 1879; d. Berlin, July 2, 1944. He made his operatic debut in Elberfeld in 1905. After singing in Brünn (1906–10), he was a member of the Hamburg Opera (1910–14), the Berlin Royal Opera (1914–16), and the Vienna Court (later State) Opera (1916–44). He also sang at the Salzburg Festivals (1922–41) and at London's Covent Garden (1933, 1938). Among his best roles were Guglielmo, Beckmesser, Alberich, and Donner.

Wiedermann, Bedřich Antonín, Czech organist, pedagogue, and composer; b. Ivanovice na Hané, Nov. 10, 1883; d. Prague, Nov. 5, 1951. He studied theology in Olmütz (1904–08), during which period he deputized as organist and choirmaster at the Cathedral. He then studied with Klička (organ, 1908–09) and Novák (composition, 1909–10) at the Prague Cons. After serving as organist in Brünn (1910–11) and Prague (1911–17), he was choirmaster in Karlín (1917–19) and a violist in the Czech Phil. in Prague. From 1920 to 1932 he gave a series of organ recitals at Prague's Smetana Hall, which featured works of Bach, Handel, Franck, and Czech composers of the Baroque era. He also toured England and the U.S. (1924), Germany (1925), Sweden (1926), and Belgium (1935). In 1917 he became a teacher at the Prague Cons., where he led a master class from 1944. In 1946 he was made a prof. at the Prague Academy of Arts. Among his compositions were various organ pieces.

Wiemann, Ernst, German bass; b. Stapelberg, Dec. 21, 1919; d. Hamburg, May 17, 1980. He studied in Hamburg and Munich. After making his operatic debut in Kiel (1938), he sang in provincial German opera houses until joining the Hamburg State Opera in 1955. On Nov. 17, 1961, he made his Metropolitan Opera debut in N.Y. as Heinrich in *Lohengrin*, and remained on its roster until 1969. In 1971 he sang Gurnemanz at London's Covent Garden. He also appeared as a guest artist with opera companies on both sides of the Atlantic. He was best known for his Mozart, Wagner, and Verdi roles.

Wiéner, Jean, French pianist and composer of Austrian descent; b. Paris, March 19, 1896; d. there, June 8, 1982. He studied with Gédalge at the Paris Cons. From 1920 to 1924 he presented the Concerts Jean Wiéner, devoted to the energetic propaganda of new music; he presented several premieres of works by modern French composers; also performed pieces by Schoenberg, Berg, and Webern. He was the first Frenchman to proclaim jazz as a legitimate art form; also teamed with Clément Doucet in duo-piano recitals, in programs stretching from Mozart to jazz. His compositions reflect his ecumenical convictions, as exemplified in such works as *Concerto franco-americain* for Clarinet and Strings (1923) and a desegregationist operetta, *Olive chez les nègres* (1926). He also wrote an Accordion Concerto (1957) and a Concerto for 2 Guitars (1966), but he became famous mainly for his idiosyncratic film music.

Wiener, Otto, Austrian baritone; b. Vienna, Feb. 13, 1913. He was a student in Vienna of Küper and Duhan. In 1939 he began his career as a concert singer. In 1952 he appeared for the first time at the Salzburg Festival, and in 1953 made his operatic stage debut as Simon Boccanegra in Graz. He was a member of the Deutsche Oper am Rhein in Düsseldorf (1956–59). From 1957 to 1963 he sang at the Bayreuth Festivals. From 1957 he also sang at the Vienna State Opera and from 1960 to 1970 at the Bavarian State Opera in Munich. On Oct. 18, 1962, he made his Metropolitan Opera debut in N.Y. as Hans Sachs, remaining on its roster for a season. As a guest artist, he appeared in London, Rome, Milan, and other operatic centers. Throughout the years he continued his concert career as well. Following his retirement in 1976, he served as director of the opera school at the Vienna State Opera. Among his other roles were the Dutchman, Gunther, Wotan, La Roche in *Capriccio*, and Pfitzner's Palestrina.

Wieniawski, Adam Tadeusz, Polish composer and music educator; b. Warsaw, Nov. 27, 1879; d. Bydgoszcz, April 21, 1950. He was the nephew of the famous Polish violinist, teacher and composer Henryk Wieniawski (b. Lublin, July 10, 1835; d. Moscow, March 31, 1880) and of the distinguished Polish pianist, pedagogue, and composer Jozef Wieniawski (b. Lublin, May 23, 1837; d. Brussels, Nov. 11, 1912). He studied in Warsaw with Melcer-Szczawiński and Noskowski; then in Berlin with Bargiel, and in Paris with d'Indy, Fauré, and Gédalge. He fought in the French army during World War I; returned to Warsaw in 1918 as a teacher at the Chopin School of Music; was appointed its director in 1928.

WORKS: DRAMATIC: OPERAS: *Megaië* (1910; Warsaw, Dec. 28, 1912); *Zofka*, comic opera (1923); *Wyzwolony* (The Freed Man; Warsaw, July 5, 1928); *Król Kochanek* (The King as Paramour), musical comedy (Warsaw, March 19, 1931). **BALLETS:** *Lalita* (1922); *Aktea w Jerozolimie* (Actea in Jerusalem; Warsaw, June 4, 1927). **OTHER:** Orch. pieces, including *Bajeczki* (Tittle-tattle), sinfonietta, and 8 symphonic poems; chamber music; piano pieces; folk song arrangements.

Wiens, Edith, Canadian soprano; b. Saskatoon, Saskatchewan, June 9, 1950. She studied on scholarship at the Hannover Hochschule für Musik (concert performance dipiloma, 1974); continued her training at the Oberlin (Ohio) College Cons. of Music (M.A. in music theater, 1976). In 1979 she went to Munich to complete her vocal training with Ernst Haefliger and Erik Werba, taking the gold medal at the Schumann Competition in Zwickau that same year. In 1981 she made her first appearance as a soloist with the Berlin Phil., and thereafter was engaged to sing with principal orchs. of Europe and North America. As a recitalist, she sang in various Canadian cities as well as in N.Y., Paris, Berlin, Leipzig, Munich, and Vienna. In 1986 she made her operatic debut as Donna Anna with the Glyndebourne Opera; subsequently sang at the Amsterdam Opera, Milan's La Scala, Buenos Aires's Teatro Colón, and the National Arts Centre in Ottawa. Her concert repertoire extends from Bach to Richard Strauss.

Wier, Albert Ernest, American music editor; b. Chelsea, Mass., July 22, 1879; d. N.Y., Sept. 8, 1945. He was educated at the New England Cons. of Music in Boston and at Harvard Univ. (graduated, 1910). He was a music ed. for N.Y. publ. firms.

Wier devised the "arrow signal" system, in which arrows and other markings are added to orch. scores to identify the main themes. He also ed. *The Macmillan Encyclopedia of Music and Musicians* (N.Y., 1938), which was withdrawn from circulation owing to an excessive number of errors, and other reference works of questionable scholarship.

Wiesengrund-Adorno, Theodor. See **Adorno, Theodor.**

Wieslander, (Axel Otto) Ingvar, Swedish composer and conductor; b. Jönköping, May 19, 1917; d. Malmö, April 29, 1963. He received training in theory from Sven Svensson at the Univ. of Uppsala. He also took some lessons in composition with Lars-Erik Larsson. After training at the Stockholm Musikhögskolan (conducting with Tor Mann; music teacher's diploma, 1945), he completed his studies in Paris on a French scholarship (1947–48) with Tony Aubin (composition) and Eugène Bigot (conducting). From 1949 to 1960 he was director of music at the Malmö City Theater, and then was its chorus master from 1960 to 1963. He was co-founder of the Ars Nova Concert Soc., of which he was chairman (1960–63). In his music, his erstwhile neo-Classical style with infusions of 12-tone writing eventually evolved into a highly personal 12-tone style.

WORKS: DRAMATIC: *Nordisk saga*, ballet (1950); *Frökarna i parken*, radio opera (1953); *Skymningslekar*, ballet (1954); *Skalknallen*, chamber opera (1958; Malmö, Feb. 7, 1959); incidental music. **ORCH.:** 6 syms. (1951; *Sinfonia piccola*, 1953; *Sinfonia notturna*, 1954; *Sinfonia seria*, 1956; *Sinfonia da camera*, 1962; *Sinfonia ecloga*, 1962); *Overtura giocosa* (1957); Concerto for Strings (1961); *Forspel (Intrada seria)* (1961); *Mutazioni* for 2 Pianos and Orch. (Malmö, Nov. 27, 1962). **CHAMBER:** 5 string quartets (1948; 1949, rev. 1954; 1957; 1958; 1961). **VOCAL:** Choruses; songs.

Wigglesworth, Frank, American composer and teacher; b. Boston, March 3, 1918. He was educated at Columbia Univ. (B.S., 1940) and Converse College, Spartanburg, S.C. (M.Mus., 1942), his principal mentors being Ernest White, Luening, and Cowell; also studied with Varèse (1948–51). He taught at Converse College (1941–42), Greenwich House, N.Y. (1946–47), Columbia Univ. and Barnard College (1947–51), and Queens College of the City Univ. of N.Y. (1955–56); in 1954 he joined the faculty of the New School for Social Research in N.Y., where he was chairman of the music dept. (from 1965); also taught at the Dalcroze School in N.Y. (from 1959) and at the City Univ. of N.Y. (1970–76). From 1951 to 1954 he was a fellow and in 1969–70 composer-in-residence at the American Academy in Rome; held MacDowell Colony fellowships in 1965 and 1972; in 1985 he was composer-in-residence at Bennington College's Chamber Music Conference and Composers' Forum of the East. He is a great-nephew of **Elizabeth Sprague Coolidge**. His output reflects a fine command of orch., instrumental, and vocal writing; he makes use of both tonal and atonal techniques.

WORKS: DRAMATIC: *Young Goodman Brown*, ballet (1951); *Between the Atoms and the Stars*, musical play (1959); *Hamlet*, incidental music to Shakespeare's play (1960); *Ballet for Esther Brooks*, ballet (1961); *The Willowdale Handcar*, opera (1969). **ORCH.:** *New England Concerto* for Violin and Strings (1941); *Music* for Strings (1946); *Fantasia* for Strings (1947); *3 Movements* for Strings (1949); *Summer Scenes* (1951); *Telesis* (1951); Concertino for Piano and Strings (1953); 3 syms. (1953, 1958, 1960); *Concert Piece* (1954); Viola Concertino (1965); *3 Portraits* for Strings (1970); *Music* for Strings (1981); *Aurora* (1983); *Sea Winds* (1984). **CHAMBER:** Trio for Flute, Banjo, and Harp (1942); *Serenade* for Flute, Viola, and Guitar (1954); Brass Quintet (1958); Harpsichord Sonata (1960); Viola Sonata (1965); String Trio (1972); Woodwind Quintet (1975); *4 Winds* for Horn, 2 Trumpets, and Trombone (1978); Brass Quintet (1980); Viola Sonata (1980); *After Summer Music* for Flute, Viola, and Guitar (1983); *Honeysuckle* for Viola (1984); piano pieces. **VOCAL:** *Isaiah* for Chorus and Orch. (1942); *Sleep Becalmed* for Chorus and Orch. (1950); *Super flumina Babilonis* for Chorus (1965); *Psalm CXLVIII* for Chorus, 3 Flutes, and 3 Trombones (1973); *Duets*, song cycle for Mezzo-soprano and Clarinet (1977–78); various masses; anthems; solo songs.

Wigglesworth, Mark, English conductor; b. Sussex, July 19, 1964. He was a student of George Hurst at the Royal Academy of Music in London. In 1989 he captured 1st prize in the Kondrashin competition in the Netherlands; that same year, became music director of the Premiere Ensemble of London. In 1990 he conducted *Don Giovanni* with the Opera Factory in London; subsequently served as its music director (1991–94) and appeared as a guest conductor with principal British orchs. as well as those on the Continent. From 1991 to 1993 he was assoc. conductor of the BBC Sym. Orch. in London. In 1992 he made his U.S. debut as a guest conductor with the Dallas Sym. Orch., and subsequently appeared with the Philadelphia Orch., the Chicago Sym. Orch., the Minnesota Orch. in Minneapolis, the St. Louis Sym. Orch., the Los Angeles Phil., and the N.Y. Phil. In 1996 he became music director of the BBC National Orch. of Wales in Cardiff, while retaining his post with the Premiere Ensemble.

Wihtol (Vitols), Joseph (actually, **Jāzeps**), eminent Latvian composer and pedagogue; b. Volmar, July 26, 1863; d. Lübeck, April 24, 1948. He studied at the St. Petersburg Cons. (1880–86) with Rimsky-Korsakov; after graduation, was engaged as an instructor there; succeeded Rimsky-Korsakov in 1908 as prof. of composition; among his students were Prokofiev and Miaskovsky. He was also music critic for the German daily *St. Petersburger Zeitung* (1897–1914). In 1918 he left St. Petersburg; was director of the Latvian Opera in Riga (from 1918); in 1919, founded the National Cons. there, serving as its rector from 1919 to 1935 and again from 1937 to 1944; many Latvian composers were his students. As the Soviet armies approached Riga (1944), Wihtol went to Germany, remaining there until his death. His autobiography and collection of writings appeared in 1944. He composed the first Latvian sym. In his music, he followed the harmonic practices of the Russian school, but often employed Latvian folk-song patterns.

WORKS: ORCH.: Sym. (St. Petersburg, Dec. 17, 1887); *La Fête Ligho*, symphonic tableau (1890); *Spriditis*, Latvian fairy tale (1908). **CHAMBER:** String Quartet (1899); *10 chants populaires lettons*, "miniature paraphrases" for Piano. **VOCAL:** *Beverinas dziedonis* (The Bard of Beverin) for Chorus and Orch. (1891); *Ouverture dramatique* (1895); *Gaismas pils* (The Castle of Light) for Chorus and Orch. (1899); *Upe un cilvēka dzive* (River and Human Life) for Chorus (1903); 2 cantatas: *Song* (1908) and *Aurora Borealis* (1914); arrangements of 200 Latvian songs for voice and piano and for piano solo (2 books; 1906, 1919); many Latvian choral ballads; songs.

BIBL.: O. Gravitis, *Jāzeps Vitols un latviešu tautas dziesma* (Jāzeps Vitols and Latvian Folk Song; Riga, 1958).

Wijdeveld, Wolfgang, Dutch composer, pianist, music educator, and music critic; b. The Hague, May 9, 1910; d. Laren, Dec. 12, 1985. He was the son of the noted Dutch architect Hendricus Wijdeveld. He studied piano with Willem Andriessen, theory with Sem Dresden, and violin with Kint at the Amsterdam Cons.; also took private lessons in composition with Pijper. After serving as director of the Zwolle Cons. (1940–46), he taught piano at the Utrecht Cons. (1946–76). From 1956 to 1968 he also was music critic of the Amsterdam newspaper *Het Vrije Volk*. He made tours as a pianist at home and abroad.

WORKS: ORCH.: *Concertstuk* (1952); *Intro in Hollandse trant* (1981). **CHAMBER:** Piano Trio (1933); Wind Quintet (1934); *Litanie* for Cello and Piano (1945; rev. 1978); Violin Sonata (1948); Flute Sonatina (1948); *Sarabande du roi* for Oboe and Piano (1950; also for Piano); *Sonatine Simple* for Violin and Piano (1952); *Little Suite* for Violin and Piano (1953); Sonata for 2 Violins and Piano (1954); *Introduction and Caprice* for Violin and Piano (1954); Trio for Flute, Oboe, and Bassoon (1958); *Snarenspel* for Guitar and Piano (1958); Concerto for Guitar and String Trio (1960); Sonatina for Solo Accordion (1963); *Notebook V* for Harpsichord (1968); Trio for Flute, English Horn, and Bassoon (1978). **KEYBOARD: PIANO:** *Kermesse* for 2 Pianos (1935); 3 sonatas (1940; 1956; *For Americans,* 1963); *Escapades* (1945); 2 sonatinas (1946, 1953); *Sarabande du roi* (1950; rev. 1979; also for Oboe and Piano); *Notebooks I–IV* (1968–69); *Gregorius in Eden* for Piano, 4-hands (1977). **ORGAN:** *Introduction and Gigue* (1949); *12 pezzi diversi* for Organ, 4-hands (1977). **VOCAL:** *Psalm 150* for Chorus and Orch. (1950); *Matrooslied* for Chorus and Small Orch. (1966); songs.

Wijk, Arnold(us Christian Vlok) van. See **Wyk, Arnold(us Christian Vlok) van.**

Wiklund, Adolf, Swedish conductor, pianist, and composer; b. Långserud, June 5, 1879; d. Stockholm, April 3, 1950. He was the son of an organist. He entered the Stockholm Cons. in 1896, and graduated in 1901 as an organist and music teacher. After studies with Richard Andersson (piano) and Johan Lindegren (composition and counterpoint), he held a state composer's fellowship (1902–04) and the Jenny Lind fellowship (1905–06). During this period, he studied in Paris, where he was organist of the Swedish Church (1903–04), and in Berlin with Kwast (piano). In 1902 he made his formal debut as a piano soloist in his own *Konsertstycke* for Piano and Orch. From 1906 he was principally active as a conductor and composer. After working at the Karlsruhe Opera and then the Berlin Royal Opera (1908–11), he returned to Stockholm as a conductor at the Royal Theater (from 1911), serving as music director (1923–24). From 1924 to 1938 he held the post of 2nd conductor of the Concert Soc. He also appeared frequently as a guest conductor throughout Europe. In 1915 he became a member of the Royal Academy of Music in Stockholm. His music, marked by fine workmanship, remained faithful to Nordic Romanticism. He composed 2 fine piano concertos, and the popular *Tre stycken* for Harp and Strings.

WORKS: ORCH.: *Konsertstycke* for Piano and Orch. (1902); Concerto Overture (1903); 2 piano concertos (1906, rev. 1935; 1917); *Sommarnatt och soluppgång,* sumphonic poem (1918); Sym. (1922); *Tre stycken* (3 Pieces) for Harp and Strings (1924); *Little Suite* (1928); *Sång till våren,* symphonic poem (1934); *Symfonisk prolog* (1934); suites. **CHAMBER:** Violin Sonata (1906); piano pieces. **VOCAL:** Songs.

Wild, Earl, greatly talented American pianist; b. Pittsburgh, Nov. 26, 1915. He was a child prodigy; blessed with absolute pitch, he could read music and play piano by age 6; when he was 12, he became a student of Selmar Jansen; also pursued training at the Carnegie Inst. of Technology (graduated, 1934). While still a teenager, he played on KDKA Radio in Pittsburgh and in the Pittsburgh Sym. Orch. After appearing as a soloist with the NBC Orch. in N.Y. in 1934, he settled there; pursued further training with Egon Petri, and later with Paul Doguereau and Volya Lincoln. In 1937 he became the staff pianist of Toscanini's NBC Sym. Orch. in N.Y. He was the first American pianist to give a recital on U.S. television in 1939. In 1942 he appeared as soloist in Gershwin's *Rhapsody in Blue* with Toscanini and the NBC Sym. Orch. He made his N.Y. recital debut at Town Hall on Oct. 30, 1944. From 1944 to 1968 he worked as a staff pianist, conductor, and composer for ABC while continuing to make occasional appearances as a soloist with orchs. and as a recitalist. After leaving ABC, he pursued a brilliant international career as a virtuoso par excellence; also served as artistic director of the Concert Soloists of Wolf Trap, a chamber ensemble (1978–81). He devoted part of his time to teaching; was on the faculties of Pennsylvania State Univ. (1965–68), the Juilliard School in N.Y. (1977–87), the Manhattan School of Music (1982–84), and Ohio State Univ. (from 1987). Among his compositions are the Easter oratorio *Revelations* (1962), a ballet, incidental music, orch. pieces, including *Variations on an American Theme,* after Stephen Foster's *Camptown Races,* for Piano and Orch. (Des Moines, Sept. 26, 1992, composer soloist), and a number of transcendentally resonant piano transcriptions of vocal and orch. works. A phenomenal technician of the keyboard, he won particular renown for his brilliant performances of the Romantic repertoire. In addition to works by such masters as Liszt and Chopin, he sought out and performed rarely heard works of the past. He also performed contemporary music, becoming especially esteemed for his idiomatic interpretations of Gershwin. Among the scores he commissioned and introduced to the public were concertos by Paul Creston (1949) and Marvin David Levy (1970).

Wildberger, Jacques, Swiss composer and teacher; b. Basel, Jan. 3, 1922. He received training in piano from Eduard Ehrsam, Eduard Henneberger, and Paul Baumgartner and in theory from Gustav Güldenstein at the Basel Cons., and later pursued studies in composition with Vogel in Ascona (1948–52). From 1959 to 1966 he taught composition, analysis, and instrumentation at the Karlsruhe Hochschule für Musik. After living in Berlin on a Deutscher Akademischer Austauschdienst scholarship (1967), he taught composition, analysis, and counterpoint at the Basel Academy of Music until 1987. In 1981 he was awarded the composition prize of the Swiss Musicians Assn. In his music, he developed a sui generis serial system, with a total emancipation of dissonances.

WORKS: DRAMATIC: *Épitaphe pour Évariste Galois,* "documented action" for Narrator, Soprano, Baritone, Speaking Chorus, Tape, and Orch. (1962; Basel, May 20, 1964). **ORCH.:** *Tre mutazioni* for Chamber Orch. (1953); *Intensio-Centrum-Remissio* (1958); *Musik* for 22 Solo Strings (1960); Oboe Concerto (1963); *Mouvements* (1964); *Contratempi* for Flute and 4 Orch. Groups (1970); *Konzertante Szenen* for Saxophone and Orch. (1981); *Canto* (1982); *. . . und füllet die Erde und machet sie euch untertan . . .* (1988–89); *Concerto for Orchestra* (1991–92). **CHAMBER:** Quartet for Flute, Clarinet, Violin, and Cello (1952); Trio for Oboe, Clarinet, and Bassoon (1952); *Concentrum* for Harpsichord (1956); *Zeitebenen* for 8 Players (1958); *Musik* for Cello and Piano (1959); *Rondeau* for Oboe (1962); Quartet for Flute, Oboe, Harp, and Piano (1967); *Recontres* for Flute and Piano (1967); *Diario* for Clarinet (1971–75); *Retrospective I* and *II* for Flute (both 1972); *Prismes* for Alto Saxophone (1975); *Portrait* for Alto Saxophone (1983); *Kanons und Interludien* for 4 Clarinets (1984); *Diaphonie* for Viola (1986); *Los pajarillos no cantan* for Guitar (1987); *Notturno* for Viola and Piano (1990); *Tantôt libre, tantôt recherchée* for Cello (1992–93); piano pieces; organ music. **VOCAL:** *Vom Kommen und Gehen des Menschen,* cantata for Soprano, Baritone, Chorus, and Orch. (1954); *Ihr meint, das Leben sei kurz . . . ,* cantata for Chorus and 10 Instruments (1957); *In My End Is My Beginning,* cantata for Soprano, Tenor, and Small Orch. (1964); *La Notte* for Mezzo-soprano, 5 Instruments, and Tape (1967); *Double Refrain* for Flute, English Horn, Guitar, and Tape (1972); *. . . die Stimme, die alte schwächer werdende Stimme . . .* for Soprano, Cello, Orch., and Tape (1973–74); *Tod und Verklärung* for Baritone and Chamber Orch. (1977); *An die Hoffnung* for Soprano, Narrator, and Orch. (1979); *Du holde Kunst* for Narrator, Soprano, and Orch. (1987–88).

Wildbrunn (real name, **Wehrenpfennig**), **Helene,** Austrian soprano; b. Vienna, April 8, 1882; d. there, April 10, 1972. She studied with Rosa Papier in Vienna. She made her operatic debut as a contralto at the Vienna Volksoper in 1906; then sang in Dortmund (1907–14). She began singing soprano roles in 1914, when she joined the Stuttgart Opera, where she remained until 1918; sang in Berlin at the State Opera (1916–25) and the Deutsche Oper (1926–29); was a principal member of the Vienna State Opera (1919–32); made guest appearances at Covent Garden in London, La Scala in Milan, and the Teatro Colón in Buenos Aires. After her retirement in 1932, she taught voice at the Vienna Academy of Music (until 1950). Among her finest roles were Kundry, Brünnhilde, Fricka, Isolde, Donna Anna, and Leonore.

Wilder, Alec (actually, **Alexander Lafayette Chew**), remarkably gifted American composer, distinguished in both popular and serious music; b. Rochester, N.Y., Feb. 16, 1907; d. Gainesville, Fla., Dec. 22, 1980. He studied composition at the Eastman School of Music in Rochester with Herbert Inch and Edward Royce; then moved to N.Y., where he entered the world of popular music; he also wrote excellent prose. His popular songs were performed by Frank Sinatra, Judy Garland, and other celebrated singers; his band pieces were in the repertoire of Benny Goodman and Jimmy Dorsey. He excelled in the genre of short operas scored for a limited ensemble of singers and instruments and suitable for performance in schools, while most of his serious compositions, especially his chamber music, are set in an affably melodious, hedonistic, and altogether ingratiating manner. He publ. a useful critical compilation, *American Popular Song: The Great Innovators* (N.Y., 1972), which included analyses of the songs of Jerome Kern, Vincent Youmans, George Gershwin, Cole Porter, and others. He also publ. the vol. *Letters I Never Mailed* (1975).

WORKS: DRAMATIC: *Juke Box*, ballet (1942); *The Lowland Sea*, folk drama (Montclair, N.J., May 8, 1952); *Cumberland Fair*, a jamboree (Montclair, May 22, 1953); *Sunday Excursion*, musical comedy (Interlochen, Mich., July 18, 1953); *Miss Chicken Little* (CBS-TV, Dec. 27, 1953; stage production, Piermont, N.Y., Aug. 29, 1958); 3 operas: *Kittiwake Island* (Interlochen, Aug. 7, 1954), *The Long Way* (Nyack, N.Y., June 3, 1955), and *The Impossible Forest* (Westport, Conn., July 13, 1958); *The Truth about Windmills*, chamber opera (Rochester, N.Y., Oct. 14, 1973); *The Tattooed Countess*, chamber opera (1974); *The Opening*, comic opera (1975); 3 children's operas: *The Churkendoose, Rachetty Pachetty House*, and *Herman Ermine in Rabbit Town*. **ORCH.:** *Symphonic Piece* (Rochester, N.Y., June 3, 1929); Suite for Clarinet and Strings (1947); Concerto for Oboe and Strings (1950); *Beginner's Luck* for Wind Ensemble (1953); 2 concertos for Horn and Chamber Orch. (1954, 1960); 4 works entitled *An Entertainment* (1961–71): No. 1 for Wind Ensemble, No. 2 for Orch., No. 3 for Wind Ensemble, and No. 4 for Horn and Chamber Orch.; 2 concertos for Trumpet and Wind Ensemble; Concerto for Tuba and Wind Ensemble; Suite for Horn and Strings (1965); Suite for Saxophone and Strings (1965); Concerto for Saxophone and Chamber Orch. (1967); *Air* for Horn and Wind Ensemble (1968); Concerto for Euphonium and Wind Ensemble (1971). **CHAMBER:** 10 wind quintets (1953–72); 3 horn sonatas (1954, 1957, 1965); 2 flute sonatas (1958, 1962); Saxophone Sonata (1960); Clarinet Sonata (1963); 3 bassoon sonatas (1964, 1968, 1973); Nonet for Brass (1969); many other sonatas; numerous pieces for wind and brass instruments; piano music, including a sonata. **VOCAL:** *8 Songs* for Voice and Orch. (Rochester, N.Y., June 8, 1928); *Children's Plea for Peace* for Narrator, Chorus, and Orch. (1969); many other songs.

BIBL.: *A. W. and His Friends* (Boston, 1974); *A. W. (1907–1980): An Introduction to the Man and His Music* (Newton Centre, Mass., 1991); D. Demsey and R. Prather, *A. W.: A Bio-Bibliography* (Westport, Conn., 1993).

Wildgans, Friedrich, Austrian composer and teacher; b. Vienna, June 5, 1913; d. Mödling, near Vienna, Nov. 7, 1965. He studied with J. Marx. He taught at the Salzburg Mozarteum (1934–36). In 1936 he became a clarinetist in the Vienna State Opera orch.; owing to his opposition to the Nazis, he lost his position in 1939 and remained suspect until the destruction of the Third Reich. He then was a teacher (1945–47; 1950–57) and a prof. (1957–65) at the Vienna Academy of Music. In 1946 he married **Ilona Steingruber**. He publ. *Entwicklung der Musik in Österreich im 20. Jahrhundert* (Vienna, 1950) and *Anton Webern* (London, 1966). He wrote in all genres, in an ultramodern style, eventually adopting the 12-tone technique.

WORKS: DRAMATIC: *Der Baum der Erkenntniss*, opera (1932); *Der Diktator*, operetta (1933); theater, film, and radio scores. **ORCH.:** *Griechischer Frühling* (1926–27); *Little Symphony* for Chamber Orch. (1929); *Mondnächte* (1932); Concerto for Trumpet, Strings, and Percussion (1933); 2 concertos for Clarinet and Small Orch. (1933, 1948); Concerto for Horn and Chamber Orch. (1934); Concerto for Organ, Brass, and Percussion (1934); *Sinfonia austriaca* (1934); *Laienmusik* (1941). **CHAMBER:** Flute Sonata (1926); Horn Sonatine (1927); *Little Trio* for Strings (1929); *Little Trio* for Flute, Clarinet, and Bassoon (1930); *Little Duo* for 2 Violins (1930); Sonatine for Clarinet and Bassoon (1930); Sonatine for 2 Clarinets (1931); *Little Trio* for Oboe, English Horn, and Bassoon (1932); *Capriccio* for 2 Clarinets and Bass Clarinet (1932); *Little Sonatine* for Trumpet and Piano (1933); *3 Inventions* for Clarinet and Horn (1935); *Spielmusik* for Recorders (1935); *Salzburger Hornmusik* (1935); *Kleine Trompetenmusik* (1935); *Kleine Haus- und Spielmusik* for Flute, Violin, and Viola (1935); Duo-Sonatine for Violin and Cello (1942); Clarinet Sonatine (1950). **KEYBOARD: PIANO:** 2 sonatas (1926, 1929). **ORGAN:** Concerto (1930). **VOCAL:** Choral pieces; lieder.

Wilding-White, Raymond, American composer, teacher, and photographer; b. Caterham, Surrey, England, Oct. 9, 1922. He was a student at the Juilliard School of Music in N.Y. (1947–49), the New England Cons. of Music in Boston (B.M., 1951; M.M., 1953), of Copland and Dallapiccola at the Berkshire Music Center in Tanglewood (summers, 1949–51), and of Read at Boston Univ. (D.M.A., 1962). He taught at the Case Inst. of Technology in Cleveland (1961–67) and at De Paul Univ. in Chicago (1967–88). In 1969 he founded the Loop Group for the performance of 20th-century music, which continued to be active through various transformations until its demise in 1989. He also was active on the radio and prepared numerous programs for WFMT-FM in Chicago, including 366 broadcasts of "Our American Music" for the American bicentennial (1976), "Music Chicago Style" for the Chicago sesquicentennial (1987), and a memorial tribute to John Cage (1992). As a photographer, he has had his work exhibited in many settings.

WORKS: DRAMATIC: *The Trees*, ballet (1949); *The Tub*, chamber opera (1952); *The Selfish Giant*, television fable (1952); *The Lonesome Valley*, ballet (1960); *Yerma*, opera (1962); *Encounters*, ballet (1967); *Beth*, musical (1989–90; renamed *Trio* in 1994); *Gifts*, liturgical drama (1993); "action pieces" entitled *MY aLBUM*. **ORCH.:** Sym. for Swing Orch. (1947); Piano Concerto (1949); Concertante for Violin, Horns, and Strings (1963); *Bandmusic* for Concert Band (1966); *Whatzit* No. 4 for Orch. and Tape (1969); Violin Concerto (1978); 3 *Symphony of Symphonies* (1995, et seq.). **CHAMBER:** 6 string quartets: No. 1 (1948), No. 2 (1966), No. 3, *The Forrest*, for Tenor and String Quartet (1970), No. 4 (1981), No. 5 (1987–88), and No. 6, *The Song Quartet* (1987–88); Violin Sonata (1956); *Variations* for Chamber Organ and String Trio (1959); *5 Fragments* for Jazz Ensemble (1966); pieces entitled *Whatzit* mostly for Solo Instrument and Tape (1967–75); piano music. **VOCAL:** *Even Now* for Baritone and Orch. (1954); *Paraphernalia* for Chorus and 5 Instruments (1959); *Haiku* for Soprano, Tenor, and Instruments (1967); *The Southern Harmony* for Amateur Chorus and Orch; *De Profundis* for Solo Voices, Chorus, and Orch.; various Psalm settings, etc.

Wilkes, Josué Teófilo, Argentine composer and teacher; b. Buenos Aires, Jan. 8, 1883; d. there, Jan. 10, 1968. He was a pupil of Williams (harmony and composition), Marchal (cello), and Rinaldi (singing) at the National Cons. in Buenos Aires. After further training with Liapunov in St. Petersburg and studies at the Schola Cantorum in Paris, he taught music in primary schools in Buenos Aires. From 1948 to 1956 he taught music history at the Universidad del Litoral in Santa Fé. With I. Guerrero Cárpena, he publ. *Formas musicales rioplatenses: Cifras, estilas y milongas-su génesis hispánica* (Buenos Aires, 1946).

WORKS: 3 operas: *Nuite persane* (1916–20), *Por el cetro y la corona* (1924), and *El horoscopo* (1926–27); *Humahuaca*, symphonic trilogy (1911–14); chamber music; *La cautiva*, secular oratorio (1930); songs; transcriptions and harmonizations of various vocal pieces.

Wilkins, Christopher, American conductor; b. Boston, May 28, 1957. After taking his bachelor's degree from Harvard College (1978), he studied conducting with Otto-Werner Mueller at Yale Univ. (M.M., 1981); also held the John Knowles Paine Traveling Fellowship for study at the (West) Berlin Hochschule für Musik. In 1981–82 he was conductor-in-residence at the State Univ. of N.Y. at Purchase. In 1982–83 he was the Exxon Conducting Assistant with the Oregon Sym. Orch. in Portland and a conducting fellow at the Berkshire Music Center at Tanglewood. He was assistant conductor of the Cleveland Orch. (1983–85) and assoc. conductor of the Utah Sym. Orch. in Salt Lake City (1986–89). In 1989 he became music director of the Colorado Springs Sym. Orch.; concurrently held that title with the San Antonio Sym. Orch. from 1991. In 1992 he received the Seaver/NEA award.

Wilkomirska, Maria, Polish pianist, daughter of **Alfred Wilkomirski**; b. Moscow, April 3, 1904. She studied at the Moscow Cons. with Briusova and Yavorsky; in 1920 she went to Warsaw and continued her studies with Turczyński. She subsequently taught piano in Kalisz, Gdańsk, and Łódź; in 1951 she became a prof. at the Warsaw Music School. With her brother, **Kazimierz Wilkomirski**, and her sister, **Wanda Wilkomirska**, she organized a trio that toured widely.

Wilkomirska, Wanda, Polish violinist, daughter of **Alfred Wilkomirski**; b. Warsaw, Jan. 11, 1929. She studied violin with her father, and later with Irene Dubiska in Warsaw and with Zathureczky in Budapest. She won a prize at the international violin competition in Geneva in 1946 and similar prizes in Budapest in 1948 and in Poznań in 1953. In 1960 she went to Paris and took lessons with Henryk Szeryng. With her brother, **Kazimierz Wilkomirski**, and her sister, **Maria Wilkomirska**, she formed a trio that toured widely.

Wilkomirski, Alfred, Polish violinist and pedagogue, father of **Kazimierz Wilkomirski** and of **Maria** and **Wanda Wilkomirska**; b. Asov, Russia, Jan. 3, 1873; d. Łódź, July 31, 1950. He studied with Hřimaly at the Moscow Cons. He taught violin in Kalisz (1920–26) and in Łódź (1929–39; 1945–50).

Wilkomirski, Kazimierz, Polish cellist, conductor, composer, and pedagogue, son of **Alfred Wilkomirski**; b. Moscow, Sept. 1, 1900. He studied cello and conducting at the Moscow Cons.; then took courses in composition with Statkowski and in conducting with Mlynarski at the Warsaw Cons. (diploma, 1929); later studied conducting with Scherchen in Switzerland (1932–34). From 1934 to 1939 he served as director of the Gdańsk Cons. and also conducted the Gdańsk Opera. The Nazi assault on Poland forced Wilkomirski to interrupt his musical activities. After the liberation, he was rector of the Łódź Cons. (1945–47), and later served as a pedagogue at the conservatories of Zopport (1952–57), Wroclaw (1958–65), and Warsaw (from 1963); also was chief conductor of the Wroclaw Opera (1957–62). His works are attractively eclectic and Romantically imitative; the best of them are his cello pieces, including several concertos, a method of cello playing, and 12 études. His autobiography, *Wospomnenia,* was publ. in 1971. With his sisters, **Maria** and **Wanda Wilkomirska**, he formed a trio that achieved notable success in tours in Europe and the Orient.

Willan, (James) Healey, eminent English-born Canadian composer, organist, choral conductor, and teacher; b. Balham, Oct. 12, 1880; d. Toronto, Feb. 16, 1968. He received training in piano, organ, harmony, and counterpoint at the St. Saviour's Choir School in Eastbourne (1888–95), where he found a mentor in its headmaster and organist-choirmaster Walter Hay Sangster. He then studied organ with William Stevenson Hoyte and piano with Evlyn Howard-Jones in London. Willan began his career as organist of the St. Cecilia Soc. (1895–1900), and then was conductor of the Wanstead Choral Soc. (1904–05) and of the Thalian Operatic Soc. (1906). He also served as organist-choirmaster at St. Saviour's Church, St. Alban's, Herts (1898–1900), Christ Church, Wanstead (1900–1903), and St. John the Baptist, Holland Rd., Kensington (1903–13). In 1913 he settled in Toronto as head of theory at the Cons. of Music and as organist at St. Paul's Anglican Church, Bloor Street. In 1914 he also became a lecturer and examiner at the Univ. of Toronto, where he served as music director of its Hart House Theatre (1919–25). From 1920 to 1936 he was vice-principal of the Toronto Cons. of Music. In 1921 he became organist-choirmaster at the Anglican Church of St. Mary Magdalene, a position he retained until his death. From 1932 to 1964 he was the organist of the Univ. of Toronto, where he also taught counterpoint and composition from 1937 to 1950. In 1933 he founded the Tudor Singers, conducting them until 1939. In 1953 he founded the Toronto Diocesan Choir School, which he served as music director. In 1956 the Archbishop of Canterbury conferred upon him the Lambeth Doctorate, the highest honor that can be bestowed upon a musician by the Anglican church. He received the Canada Council Medal in 1961. In 1967 he was made a Companion of the Order of Canada. On July 4, 1980, the Canadian Post Office issued a commemorative stamp bearing his likeness, making Willan the first composer to receive that distinction. As a composer, Willan excelled in music for liturgical use. He was a determined proponent of the Oxford Movement in the Anglican Church, and thus championed the cause of Anglo-Catholicism. Particularly notable in this regard were his 14 settings of the *Missa brevis* (1928–63), the set of 11 *Liturgical Motets* (1928–37), the plainsong-with-fauxbourdons settings of the Canticles, and the *Responsaries for the Offices of Tenebrae* (1956). In 1953 Willan's commissioned homage anthem, *O Lord, Our Governour,* was performed at the coronation of Queen Elizabeth II in London. Willan was thus the first non-resident of Great Britain to receive such an honor. His organ music is also of great distinction. His *Introduction, Passacaglia, and Fugue* (1916) is his masterpiece in that genre. Of his other works, the opera *Deirdre*, the 2 syms., and the Piano Concerto are worthy achievements.

WORKS: DRAMATIC: *The Beggar's Opera,* ballad opera (1927); *The Order of Good Cheer,* ballad opera (1928); *Transit Through Fire: An Odyssey of 1942,* radio opera (1941–42; CBC, March 8, 1942); *Hymn for Those in the Air,* incidental music (1942); *Dierdre,* radio opera (1943–45; CBC, April 20, 1946; rev. version for the stage, Toronto, April 2, 1965); *Brebeuf,* pageant (CBC, Sept. 26, 1943); 4 other ballad operas; 14 sets of incidental music, etc. **ORCH.:** 2 syms.: No. 1 (Toronto, Oct. 8, 1936) and No. 2 (1941; rev. 1948; Toronto, May 18, 1950); Piano Concerto (Montreal, Aug. 24, 1944; rev. 1949); *Royce Hall Suite* for Concert Band (1949); *Overture to an Unwritten Comedy* (1951); *3 Fanfares* (1959); *Poem* for Strings (1959); 5 marches and other pieces. **CHAMBER:** Trio for Violin, Cello, and Piano (1907); 2 violin sonatas (1916, 1921). **KEYBOARD: PIANO:** *Variations and Epilogue on an Original Theme* (1913–15). **ORGAN:** 2 preludes and fugues (1908, 1909); *Introduction, Passacaglia and Fugue* (1916); *Rondino, Elegy and Chaconne* (1956); *Fugal Trilogy* (1958); *5 Pieces* (1958); *Passacaglia and Fugue* (1959); 97 chorale preludes; many other pieces, including arrangements. **VOCAL:** *An Apostrophe to the Heavenly Hosts* for Chorus (1921); *The Mystery of Bethlehem,* cantata for Soprano, Bass, Chorus, and Organ (1923); *6 Motets* for Chorus (1924); *The 3 Kings* for Chorus (1928); *Rise Up, My Love, My Fair One* for Chorus (1929); *Behold the Tabernacle of God* for Chorus (1933); *Gloria Deo per immensa saecula* for Chorus (1950); *O Lord, Our Governour* for Chorus and Orch. (1952); *Coronation Suite* for Chorus and Orch. (1952); *The Story of Bethlehem* for Chorus and Organ (1955); other choral works include 14 settings of the *Missa brevis* (1928–63), 11 *Liturgical Motets* (1928–37), other motets, 39 fauxbourdons and 15 full settings of the Canticles, more than 40 anthems, over 30 hymn-anthems, 31 hymn tunes, more than 40 fauxbourdons to hymn tunes, many plainsong adaptions, carols, secular vocal pieces, etc.

BIBL.: F. Clarke, *H. W.: Life and Music* (Toronto, 1983).

Willcocks, Sir David (Valentine), English organist, conductor, and music educator; b. Newquay, Dec. 30, 1919. He was educated at Clifton College, the Royal College of Music, and King's College, Cambridge. During World War II, he served in the British army. He was organist at Salisbury Cathedral (1947–50) and Worcester Cathedral (1950–57); then at King's College,

Cambridge (1957–73); also held the posts of univ. lecturer (1957–74) and univ. organist (1958–74) at Cambridge; concurrently he led the City of Birmingham Choir (1950–57) and was conductor of the Cambridge Univ. Musical Soc. (1958–73). In 1960 he became music director of the Bach Choir; in 1974 he also assumed the post of director of the Royal College of Music in London, remaining there until 1984. He was made a Commander of the Order of the British Empire in 1971; was knighted in 1977. He served as general ed. of the Church Music series of the Oxford Univ. Press.

Williams, Alberto, important Argentine composer and music educator; b. Buenos Aires, Nov. 23, 1862; d. there, June 17, 1952. He was the grandson of an Englishman; his maternal grandfather, Amancio Alcorta, was one of Argentina's early composers. Williams studied piano with Mathías, harmony with Durand, counterpoint with Godard, and composition with Franck and Bériot on a scholarship at the Paris Cons. He returned to Argentina in 1889; founded the Alberto Williams Cons. in 1893; also organized branches of the Cons. in provincial towns of Argentina, numbering more than 100; founded a music publ. firm, La Quena (also a music magazine of that name). The greatest influence in his music was that of Franck, but modernistic usages are found in Williams's application of whole-tone scales, parallel chord progressions, etc. In many of his works he used characteristic melorhythms of Argentina. He composed a number of piano pieces in Argentine song and dance forms (milongas, gatos, cielitos, etc.). Williams also publ. numerous didactic works and several books of poetry.

WORKS: 9 syms. (all 1st perf. in Buenos Aires): No. 1 (Nov. 25, 1907), No. 2, *La bruja de las montañas* (Sept. 9, 1910), No. 3, *La Selva sagrada* (Dec. 8, 1934), No. 4, *El Ataja-Caminos* (Dec. 15, 1935), No. 5, *El corazón de la muñeca* (Nov. 29, 1936), No. 6, *La muerte del cometa* (Nov. 26, 1937), No. 7, *Eterno reposo* (Nov. 26, 1937), No. 8 (1938), and No. 9 (1939); several suites of Argentine dances; 3 violin sonatas (1905, 1906, 1907); Cello Sonata (1906); Piano Trio (1907); a great number of piano albums, the last of which was *En el parque* (1952).

BIBL.: Z. Lacoigne, *A. W.: Músico argentino* (Buenos Aires, 1942); *Homenajes a A. W.* (Buenos Aires, 1942); V. Risolía, *A. W., Curriculum vitae* (Buenos Aires, 1944).

Williams, Camilla, black American soprano and teacher; b. Danville, Va., Oct. 18, 1922. She studied at Virginia State College (B.S., 1941) and with Marion Szekely-Freschl, Hubert Giesen, Sergius Kagen, and Leo Taubman in Philadelphia; won the Marian Anderson Award twice (1943, 1944), as well as the Philadelphia Orch. Youth Award (1944). On May 15, 1946, she made her operatic debut at the N.Y. City Opera as Cio-Cio-San, remaining on its roster until 1954; also toured widely as a concert artist. She taught at Brooklyn College of the City Univ. of N.Y. (1970–73) and at the Indiana Univ. School of Music in Bloomington (from 1977).

Williams, Clifton, American bandmaster and composer; b. Traskwood, Ark., March 26, 1923; d. South Miami, Fla., Feb. 12, 1976. He studied at Louisiana State Univ. (B.M., 1947) and with Rogers and Hanson at the Eastman School of Music in Rochester, N.Y. (M.M., 1948). He played horn with the sym. orchs. of San Antonio and New Orleans; was on the staff of the music dept. at the Univ. of Texas in Austin (1949–66); then at the Univ. of Miami (1966–76). He composed band music, including the phenomenally popular *Sinfonians*. His other band pieces include *Trail Scenes; Trilogy Suite*; Concertino for Percussion and Band; 3 symphonic dances; *Fanfare and Allegro; Dedicatory Overture; Dramatic Essay: The Ramparts; The Patriots* (commissioned by NORAD); *Songs of Heritage; Academic Procession; Castle Gap March; Strategic Air Command.*

Williams, Grace (Mary), Welsh composer; b. Barry, Glamorganshire, Feb. 19, 1906; d. there, Feb. 10, 1977. Her father led the local boys' chorus and played the piano in a home trio, with Grace on the violin and her brother on the cello. In 1923 she entered the music dept. of the Univ. of Wales in Cardiff, in the composition class of David Evans. Upon graduation in 1926, she enrolled at the Royal College of Music in London. There she was accepted as a student of Vaughan Williams, who had the greatest influence on her career as a composer, both in idiom and form; she also took classes with Gordon Jacob. She subsequently received the Octavia Traveling Scholarship and went to Vienna to take lessons with Wellesz (1930–31). She did not espouse the atonal technique of the 2nd Viennese School, but her distinctly diatonic harmony with strong tertian underpinning was artfully embroidered with nicely hung deciduous chromatics of a decidedly nontonal origin. She marked May 10, 1951, in her diary as a "day of destruction," when she burned all her MSS unworthy of preservation. Among her practical occupations were teaching school and writing educational scripts for the BBC. She was particularly active in her advancement of Welsh music.

WORKS: DRAMATIC: *Theseus and Ariadne*, ballet (1935); *The Parlour*, opera (1961). **ORCH.:** *Sinfonia concertante* for Piano and Orch. (1941); 2 syms. (1943; 1956, rev. 1975); *Sea Sketches* for Strings (1944); Violin Concerto (1950); Trumpet Concerto (1963); *Castell Caernarfon*, for the investiture of the Prince of Wales (1969). **CHAMBER:** Sextet for Oboe, Trumpet, Violin, Viola, Cello, and Piano (1931); Suite for 9 Instruments (1934). **VOCAL:** Numerous choruses; songs.

BIBL.: M. Boyd, *G. W.* (Cardiff, 1980).

Williams, John (Christopher), remarkable Australian guitarist; b. Melbourne, April 24, 1941. He began his training with his father, the guitarist Leonard Williams. In 1952 he settled in London, where he made his first appearance in 1955. He continued his studies with Segovia at the Accademia Musicale Chigiana in Siena (1957–59). In 1958 he made his formal debut at London's Wigmore Hall. From 1960 to 1973 he was prof. of guitar at the Royal College of Music in London. Following successful tours to the Soviet Union in 1962 and the U.S. and Japan in 1963, he performed with outstanding success on regular tours of Europe, North and South America, Australia, and the Far East. In 1980 he was made an Office of the Order of the British Empire. Williams' repertoire is truly egalitarian in its scope. While he is admired for his performances of the standard works for the guitar, he has done much to expand the repertoire by giving the premieres of scores by Brouwer, Dodgson, Previn, Schulthorpe, Takemitsu, and Westlake. In addition, he has found success in jazz and pop genres.

Williams, John (Towner), enormously successful American composer and conductor; b. N.Y., Feb. 8, 1932. He grew up in a musical atmosphere; his father was a film studio musician. He began to take piano lessons; later he learned to play trombone, trumpet, and clarinet. In 1948 the family moved to Los Angeles, where he studied orchestration with Robert van Epps at Los Angeles City College and composition privately with Mario Castelnuovo-Tedesco; he also took piano lessons with Rosina Lhévinne at the Juilliard School of Music in N.Y. He began his career as a composer, arranger, and conductor for films and television; wrote the film scores, rich in sounding brass and tinkling cymbals, for *Close Encounters of the Third Kind, Superman, The Empire Strikes Back, Raiders of the Lost Ark, E.T., The Extraterrestrial*, and *Return of the Jedi.* He won Academy Awards for *Fiddler on the Roof* (1971), *Jaws* (1975), and *Star Wars* (1977). The record albums for these background scores sold into the millions. In 1980 Williams became conductor of the Boston Pops Orchs., a position he retained until 1993. During his generally successful tenure, he diversified his appeal to Boston Pops audiences by conducting selections from his own extraordinarily popular film scores. Among his other compositional efforts were *Essay* for Strings (1966); Sym. (1966); *Sinfonietta* for Wind Ensemble (1968); Concerto for Flute, Strings, and Percussion (1969); Violin Concerto (1974–76; St. Louis, Jan. 29, 1981); Tuba Concerto (1985); *Celebration Fanfare* for Orch. (1986); *The 5 Sacred Trees*, concerto for Bassoon and Strings (1992–94; N.Y., April 12, 1995); Cello Concerto (Tanglewood, July 7, 1994).

Williams, Peter (Fredric), eminent English musicologist, organist, and harpsichordist; b. Wolverhampton, May 14, 1937. He was educated at St. John's College, Cambridge (B.A., 1958; Mus.B., 1959; M.A., 1962; Ph.D., 1963). In 1962 he joined the faculty of the Univ. of Edinburgh as a lecturer, subsequently becoming a reader (1972) and a prof. (1982), where he held the first chair in performance practice in the United Kingdon. In 1985 he was made Arts and Sciences Distinguished Prof. at Duke Univ. in Durham, N.C., where he was chairman of the music dept. (1985–88), univ. organist (1985–90), and director of the graduate center for performance practice studies (from 1990). As a performing artist, Williams made appearances as a recitalist from 1965. As a scholar, he ranks among the foremost authorities on the organ. In addition to his learned books and articles, he has served as general ed. of the series Biblioteca Organologica (80 vols., 1966 et seq.) and as founding ed. of *The Organ Yearbook* (from 1969). He is also founder-general ed. of the series Cambridge Studies in Performance Practice and of the Duke Univ. series Sources and Interpretation of Music. He is also general ed. of the New Oxford J.S. Bach Edition.

WRITINGS: *The European Organ 1450–1850* (London, 1966; 2nd ed., 1968); *Figured Bass Accompaniment* (2 vols., Edinburgh, 1970; 2nd ed., 1972); *Bach Organ Music* (London, 1972; 2nd ed., 1974); *A New History of the Organ From the Greeks to the Present Day* (London, 1980); *The Organ Music of J.S. Bach* (3 vols., Cambridge, 1980–84); ed., *Bach, Handel and Scarlatti: Tercentenary Essays* (Cambridge, 1985); *Playing the Works of Bach* (N.Y., 1986); *The Organ* (London and N.Y., 1988); with L. Todd, ed., *Mozart: Perspectives in Performance* (Cambridge, 1991); *The Organ in Western Culture 750–1250* (Cambridge, 1993); *The King of Instruments or, How Do Churches Come to Have Organs?* (London, 1993).

Williams, Ralph Vaughan. See **Vaughan Williams, Ralph.**

Williamson, John Finley, distinguished American choral conductor and music educator; b. Canton, Ohio, June 23, 1887; d. Toledo, Ohio, May 28, 1964. He studied at Otterbein College in Westerville, Ohio (graduated, 1911); then studied singing with Herbert Wilbur Greene, Herbert Witherspoon, and David Bispham in N.Y. and organ with Karl Straube in Leipzig. He became minister of music at the Westminster Presbyterian Church in Dayton, Ohio, where he founded a choir in 1920; in 1926 he founded the Westminster Choir School there; in 1929 he moved it to Ithaca, N.Y., and in 1932 to Princeton, N.J., where it later became Westminster Choir College; was its president until 1958. He led its choir on many tours of the U.S. and took it on 4 world tours; ed. the Westminster Series of choral music.

BIBL.: D. Wehr, *J.F. W. (1887–1964): His Life and Contribution to Choral Music* (diss., Miami Univ., Oxford, Ohio, 1971).

Williamson, Malcolm (Benjamin Graham Christopher), prominent Australian composer, pianist, organist, and conductor; b. Sydney, Nov. 21, 1931. He attended the New South Wales State Conservatorium of Music in Sydney (1944–50), where he received training from Goossens (composition) and Sverjensky (piano). He also studied horn and violin. Settling in London, he pursued his training in composition with Lutyens and Erwin Stein (1953–57). He also studied the organ. As a performing artist, he appeared in his own organ and piano concertos. In 1963 he was awarded the Bax Memorial Prize. In 1970–71 he served as composer-in-residence at Westminster Choir College in Princeton, N.J. Williamson was made Master of the Queen's Musick in 1975. He was named a Commander of the Order of the British Empire in 1976. From 1983 to 1986 he was a visiting prof. at Strathclyde Univ. In his output, Williamson has been influenced by Stravinsky, Britten, and Messiaen along with jazz and popular music. The general accessibility of his works is complemented by fine craftsmanship.

WORKS: OPERAS: *Our Man in Havana* (1962–63; London, July 2, 1963); *The English Eccentrics,* chamber opera (1963–64; Aldeburgh, June 11, 1964); *The Happy Prince,* children's opera (1964–65; Farnham, May 22, 1965); *Julius Caesar Jones,* children's opera (1965; London, Jan. 4, 1966); *The Violins of St. Jacques* (London, Nov. 29, 1966); *Dunstan and the Devil* (Cookham, May 19, 1967); *The Growing Castle,* chamber opera (Dynevor, Aug. 13, 1968); *Lucky Peter's Journey* (London, Dec. 18, 1969); *The Red Sea* (1971–72; Dartington, April 14, 1972). **CASSATIONS:** *The Moonrakers* (Brighton, April 22, 1967); *Knights in Shining Armour* (Brighton, April 29, 1968); *The Snow Wolf* (Brighton, April 29, 1968); *Genesis* (Black Mountain, N.C., June 1971); *The Stone Wall* (London, Sept. 18, 1971); *The Winter Star* (Holm Cutram, June 19, 1973); *The Glitter Gang* (1973–74; Sydney, Feb. 23, 1974); *La Terre des Rois* (1974); *The Valley and the Hill* (Liverpool, June 21, 1977); *Le Pont du diable* or *The Devil's Bridge* (Angouleme, March 1982). **BALLETS:** *The Display* (Adelaide, March 14, 1964); *Spectrum* (1964; Bury St. Edmunds, Sept. 21, 1967); *Sun into Darkness* (1965–66; London, April 13, 1966); *Bigfella Toots Squoodge and Nora* (1967; Manchester, Sept. 25, 1976); *Perisynthyon* (1974); *Heritage* (1985). Also incidental music and film, radio, and television scores. **ORCH.:** 7 syms.: No. 1, *Elevamini* (1956–57; private perf., London, June 1957; public perf., Melbourne, Nov. 13, 1963), No. 2, *Pilgrim på havet* (1968–69; Bristol, Oct. 29, 1969), No. 3, *The Icy Mirror,* for Soprano, Mezzo-soprano, 2 Baritones, Chorus, and Orch. (Cheltenham, July 9, 1972), No. 4 (1977), No. 5, *Aquerò* (1979–80; London, April 23, 1980), No. 6 (1982; Australian Broadcasting Corp. FM, Sept. 29, 1986), and No. 7 for Strings (1984); *Santiago de Espada,* overture (private perf., London, June 1957; public perf., BBC, Feb. 8, 1958); 4 piano concertos: No. 1 (1957–58; Cheltenham, July 15, 1958), No. 2 for Piano and Strings (1960), No. 3 (1962; Sydney, June 1964), and No. 4 (1993–94); *Sinfonia concertante* for 3 Trumpets, Piano, and Strings (1958–62; Glasgow, May 21, 1964); Organ Concerto (London, Sept. 8, 1961); *Our Man in Havana,* suite from the opera (1963; Glasgow, Jan. 6, 1966); *The Display,* suite from the ballet (1963–64; Adelaide, March 14, 1964); Violin Concerto (1964–65; Bath, June 12, 1965); *Concerto Grosso* (1964–65; London, Aug. 28, 1965); *Symphonic Variations* (Edinburgh, Sept. 9, 1965); *Sinfonietta* (1965–67; *Toccata, Elegy,* and *Tarantella,* BBC, March 21, 1965; *Prelude,* Stratford upon Avon, Feb. 10, 1967); *Epitaphs for Edith Sitwell* for Strings (1966; London, April 1972; arranged from the organ piece); *A Word from Our Founder* (1969); Concerto for 2 Pianos and Strings (1972); Concerto for Harp and Strings, *Au Tombeau du Martyr Juif Inconnu* (1973–76; London, Nov. 17, 1976); *2 Pieces* for Strings (1975; from the piano pieces *The Bridge That Van Gogh Painted*); *The Bridge That Van Gogh Painted* for Strings (1975; arranged from the piano pieces); *The House of Windsor,* suite (1977); *Fiesta* (Geneva, March 14, 1978); *Ochre* (London, Sept. 2, 1978; also for Organ and Strings); *Fanfarade* (London, May 10, 1979); *Lament (in Memory of Lord Mountbatten of Burma)* for Violin and Strings (1979–80; Edinburgh, May 5, 1980); *Ode for Queen Elizabeth* for Strings (private perf., Edinburgh, July 3, 1980; public perf., Edinburgh, Aug. 25, 1980); *In Thanksgiving—Sir Bernard Heinze* (Sydney, July 1, 1982); *Cortège for a Warrior* (1984); *Lento* for Strings (1985); *Bicentennial Anthem* (1988). **CHAMBER:** 3 string quartets (*Winterset,* 1947–48; 1954; 1993); Nonet for Strings, Wind, and Harp (1949); *Piece* for 7 Winds and Piano (1953); *Variations* for Cello and Piano (London, Nov. 21, 1964); Concerto for Wind Quintet and 2 Pianos, 8-hands (1964–65; London, April 9, 1965); *Serenade* for Flute, Piano, and String Trio (London, March 8, 1967); *Pas de Quatre* for Flute, Oboe, Clarinet, Bassoon, and Piano (Newport, R.I., Aug. 21, 1967); Piano Quintet (1967–68; Birmingham, March 23, 1968); *Partita on Themes of Walton* for Viola (BBC-TV, March 29, 1972); *Canberra Fanfare* for Brass and Percussion (1973); *Adelaide Fanfare* for Brass and Organ (1973); Piano Trio (1976); *Konstanz Fanfare* for Brass, Percussion, and Organ (1980); *Richmond Fanfare* for Brass, Percussion, and Organ (1980); *Fontainebleu Fanfare* for Brass, Percussion, and Organ (1981); *Ceremony for Oodgeroo* for Brass Quintet (1988); *Fanfares and Chorales* for Brass Quintet (1991); *Day That I Have Loved* for Harp (1993–94). **KEYBOARD: PIANO:** 4 sonatas (1955–56; 1957, rev. 1970–71; 1958; 1963); *Travel Diaries*

(1960–61); *5 Preludes* (1966); Sonata for 2 Pianos (1967); *Haifa Watercolours* (1974); *The Bridge That Van Gogh Painted and the French Camargue* (1975); *Ritual of Admiration* (1976); *Himna Titu* (1984); *Springtime on the River Moskva* (1987). **ORGAN:** *Fons Amoris* (1955–56); *Résurgence du Feu (Paques 1959)* (1959); Sym. (1960); *Vision of Christ Phoenix* (1961; rev. 1978); *Elegy-J.F.K.* (1964); *Epitaphs for Edith Sitwell* (Aldeburgh, June 17, 1966; arranged for String Orch.); *Peace Pieces* (2 vol., 1970–71); *Little Carols of the Saints* (1971–72); *Mass of a Medieval Saint* (1973); *Fantasy on This Is May Father's World* (1975); *Fantasy on O Paradise!* (1976); *The Lion of Suffolk (for Benjamin Britten)* (1977). **VOCAL:** *Mass* for Chorus (1957); Concerto for Soprano, Oboe, English Horn, Cello, and Organ (1957); *Adoremus*, Christmas cantata for Alto, Tenor, Chorus, and Organ (1959); *Tu es Petrus*, cantata for Speaker, Chorus, and Organ (1961); *Agnus Dei* for Soprano, Chorus, and Organ (1961); *Dignus est Agnus* for Soprano, Chorus, and Organ (1961); *Procession of Psalms* for Chorus and Organ or Piano (1961); *Symphony for Voices* for Contralto and Chorus (London, May 2, 1962); *The Morning of the Day of Days*, Easter cantata for Soprano, Tenor, Chorus, and Organ (1962); *Te Deum* for Unison Voices and Piano or Organ (1963); *Celebration of Divine Love*, cantata for Soprano or Tenor and Piano (London, April 8, 1963); *Mass of St. Andrew* for Unison Voices and Piano or Organ (1964); *A Psalm of Praise* for Unison Voices and Organ (1965); *The Brilliant and the Dark* for Women's Voices and Orch. (1966; London, June 3, 1969); *6 English Lyrics* for Alto or Baritone and Piano or String Orch. (1966); *Mowing the Barley* for Chorus and Orch. (London, March 1, 1967); *I Will Lite up Mine Eyes*, anthem for Chorus, Echo Chorus, and Organ (Syndey, May 3, 1970); *Cantate domino* for Chorus and Organ (Princeton, N.J., Oct. 21, 1970); *Te Deum* for Chorus, Organ, and Optional Brass (1971); *The Death of Cuchulain* for 5 Men's Voices and Percussion (London, Nov. 6, 1971); *The Musicians of Bremen* for 6 Men's Voices (1972); *Ode to Music* for Chorus, Echo Chorus, and Orch. (1972–73; London, Feb. 3, 1973); *Pietà* for Soprano, Oboe, Bassoon, and Piano (London, Oct. 31, 1973); *Canticle of Fire* for Chorus and Organ (N.Y., May 20, 1973); *The World at the Manger*, Christmas cantata for Soprano, Baritone, Chorus, and Organ or Piano Duet (Leicester, Dec. 6, 1973); *Hammarskjöld Portrait* for Soprano and String Orch. (London, July 30, 1974); *Mass of St. James* for Unison Voices and Piano or Organ (1975); *Les Olympiques* for Mezzo-soprano and String Orch. (1976; Meyer, Germany, June 19, 1977); *Jubilee Hymn* for Chorus and Orch. or Piano (London, Feb. 6, 1977); *Mass of Christ the King* for 2 Sopranos, Baritone, Echo Chorus, Chorus, and Orch. (1977–78; London, Nov. 3, 1978); *Kerygma*, anthem for Chorus and Organ (London, March 11, 1979); *Little Mass of St. Bernadette* for Unbroken Voices and Organ or Instruments (London, Nov. 26, 1980); *Mass of St. Margaret of Scotland* for Congregation, Optional Chorus, and Organ (1980); *Josip Broz Tito* for Baritone and Orch. (1980–81; Skopje, March 9, 1981; also for Baritone and Piano); *Mass of the People of God* for Voices and Organ (1980–81; Bromsgrove, April 29, 1981); *The Feast of Eurydice* for Mezzo-soprano, Piano, Flute, and Percussion (1983); *A Pilgrim Liturgy*, cantata for Mezzo-soprano, Baritone, Chorus, and Orch. (1984–85); *The True Endeavour* for Speaker, Chorus, and Orch. (1988); *The Dawn Is at Hand*, choral sym. (1989); *Mass of St. Ethelreda (on Themes of Lennox Berkeley)* for Chorus and Organ (1990); *Requiem for a Tribe Brother* for Chorus (1992); *A Year of Birds* for Soprano and Orch. (1995); numerous other vocal works.

Willis Music Co., American music publishers. The business was founded by Charles H. Willis at Cincinnati in 1899, in association with his son William H. Willis. The firm became known as W.H. Willis & Co.; after the absorption of G.B. Jennings & Co. in 1910 it was incorporated as the Willis Music Co. On July 1, 1919, the business was acquired by Gustave Schirmer of N.Y. The company specialized in educational publications.

Wills, Arthur, English organist, teacher, and composer; b. Coventry, Sept. 19, 1926. He was educated at the College of St. Nicholas, Canterbury, and at the Univ. of Durham (D.Mus.). In 1949 he became assistant organist at Ely Cathedral, and then was organist and director of music there from 1958 to 1990. From 1964 to 1992 he was also a prof. at the Royal Academy of Music in London. As a recitalist, he toured throughout Europe, the U.S., and the Far East. He was the author of the vol. *Organ* (1984; 2nd ed., 1992). In 1990 he was made an Officer of the Order of the British Empire.

WORKS: OPERA: *1984* (1988). **ORCH.:** Sym. (1957); Concerto for Organ, Timpani, and Strings (1971); *The Fenlands*, symphonic suite for Organ and Brass Band (1981); *A Muse of Fire*, overture for Brass Band (1983). **CHAMBER:** Guitar Sonata (1972); *Moods and Diversions* for Guitar (1975); *Sonata 1984* for Piano (1984); *Sacrae symphoniae: Venice Creator Spiritus* for Double Wind Quintet (1987); *Concerto lirico* for Guitar Quartet (1987); Concerto for Guitar and Organ (1988); *Oration* for Trombone and Piano (1993); numerous organ pieces, including a Sonata (n.d.); *Sinfonia eliensis* (1976); *Remembrance of Things Past: Nov. 14th*, suite (1991); *Oriental* (1993); *Scherzo-Fantasy* (1994); *Celebration of Life* (1995); transcription of Mussorgsky's *Pictures at an Exhibition*. **VOCAL:** *Missa eliensis* for Chorus (1959); *Jubilate Deo* for Chorus (1965); *Te Deum* for Chorus (1967); *An English Requiem* for Soprano, Baritone, Chorus, and Orch. (1971); *The Gods of Music*, choral concerto for Chorus, Brass, Percussion, and Organ (1992); *A Toccata of Galuppi's*, scena for Countertenor and String Quartet (1993); *The Shining Sea* for Tenor, Chorus, Strings, Organ, Piano, and Percussion (1995); 7 song cycles; services; anthems; motets.

Willson, (Robert Reiniger) Meredith, American composer of coruscating Americanistic musicals, and a fine flutist; b. Mason City, Iowa, May 18, 1902; d. Santa Monica, Calif., June 15, 1984. He learned to play the flute as a child, then went to N.Y. and studied at the Damrosch Inst. (1919–22) and received instruction in flute from Georges Barrère (1920–29); also studied with H. Hadley (1923–24) and Julius Gold (1921–23). He was 1st flutist in Sousa's band (1921–23) and a member of the N.Y. Phil. (1924–29); then became a musical director for various radio shows. For the 30th anniversary of the San Francisco earthquake he wrote a Sym., which he conducted in its first performance (San Francisco, April 19, 1936). His 2nd Sym. was first played by the Los Angeles Phil. on April 4, 1940. His other symphonic works include *The Jervis Bay; Symphonic Variations on an American Theme*; and *O.O. McIntyre Suite*. He also wrote many band pieces and a choral work, *Anthem of the Atomic Age*. However, he devoted himself mainly to the composition of popular music, in which he revealed a triple talent as a performer, writer, and composer. He appeared as a comedian on a radio program, "The Big Show," in which he engaged in a comic colloquy with Tallulah Bankhead, closing with an inspirational hymn, *May the Good Lord Bless and Keep You*, which became very popular as an anthem. Willson achieved his triumph with his musical revue *The Music Man*, for which he wrote the book, the lyrics, and the music. It opened on Broadway on Dec. 19, 1957, and became an immediate success, thanks to the satirical and yet somehow patriotic subject, dealing with a traveling salesman of band uniforms and instruments who sells them to hick-town suckers; and to the sparkling score, containing the hit chorus *76 Trombones*. His subsequent musicals were *The Unsinkable Molly Brown*, produced on Broadway on Nov. 3, 1960, for which he wrote the musical score, and *Here's Love*, produced on Broadway on Oct. 3, 1963, an adaptation of the film *Miracle on 34th Street*. *The Music Man* and *The Unsinkable Molly Brown* were made into films. Willson was also active as an arranger and orchestrator in Hollywood; he helped Charlie Chaplin in arranging the score for his anti-Hitler, anti-Mussolini film, *The Great Dictator* (1940). He publ. the autobiographical books *And There I Stood with My Piccolo* (N.Y., 1948), *Eggs I Have Laid* (N.Y., 1955), and *But He Doesn't Know the Territory* (descriptive of the origin of *The Music Man*; N.Y., 1959).

Wilson, Charles (Mills), Canadian composer, conductor, and teacher; b. Toronto, May 8, 1931. He studied composition with

Ridout at the Royal Cons. of Music of Toronto, and also with Foss (summer, 1950) and Chávez (summer, 1951) at the Berkshire Music Center in Tanglewood. Returning to Toronto, he received his B.Mus. (1952) and later was awarded his D.Mus. (1956). From 1954 to 1964 he was organist-choirmaster at Chalmers United Church in Guelph. He also was founder-conductor of the Guelph Light Opera and Oratorio Co. (1955–74) and conductor of the Bach-Elgar Choir of Hamilton (1962–74). In 1979 he became a teacher at the Univ. of Guelph. In his music, Wilson has adopted many of the prevailing stylistic elements of his era.

WORKS: DRAMATIC: *The Strolling Clerk from Paradise*, chamber opera (1952); *Ballet Score* (1969); *Phrases from Orpheus*, piece for Chorus and Dancers (1970; Guelph, May 10, 1971); *Heloise and Abelard*, opera (1972; Toronto, Sept. 8, 1973); *The Selfish Giant*, children's opera (1972; Toronto, Dec. 20, 1973); *The Summoning of Everyman*, church opera (1972; Halifax, April 6, 1973); *Kamouraska*, opera (1975); *Psycho Red*, opera (1977); *Tim*, radio opera (1990). **ORCH.:** Sym. (1953); *Sonata da chiesa* for Oboe and Strings (1960); *Theme and Evolutions* (1966); Sinfonia for Double Orch. (1972; Toronto, March 3, 1973); *Symphonic Perspectives: Kingsmere* (Ottawa, Oct. 4, 1974); *Conductus* for Piano and Orch. (1979). **CHAMBER:** 4 string quartets (1950, 1968, 1975, 1983); String Trio (1963); *Concerto 5x4x3* for String Quintet or Woodwind Quartet or Brass Trio (1970). **VOCAL:** *On the Morning of Christ's Nativity*, cantata for Soprano, Tenor, Baritone, Chorus, and Orch. (1963); *The Angels of the Earth*, oratorio for Soprano, Baritone, Narrators, Chorus, and Orch. (1966; Guelph, June 19, 1967); *En Guise d'Orphée* for Baritone and String Orch. (1968); *Christo paremus canticam* for Chorus and Orch. (Hamilton, Dec. 2, 1973); *Image out of Season* for Chorus and Brass Quintet (1973); *Missa brevis* for Chorus and Brass (1975); *Song for St. Cecilia's Day* for Soprano, Tenor, Chorus, and Orch. (1976); *First Book of Madrigals* for Soprano and Instrumental Ensemble (1980); *Un Canadien errant* for Mezzo-soprano, Tenor, Chorus, and Instrumental Ensemble (1981); *Invocation* for 8 Solo Voices and Tape (1982); *2 Voices* for Mezzo-soprano, Clarinet, Cello, Piano, 2 Percussion, and Tape (1983); *The Revelation to St. John* for 3 Choruses, 3 Conductors, and Organ (1984); solo songs. **OTHER:** Tape pieces.

Wilson, Olly (Woodrow), black American composer, conductor, and teacher; b. St. Louis, Sept. 7, 1937. He taught himself to play the piano and double bass, and gained valuable experience performing in both jazz and classical settings. He studied at Washington Univ. in St. Louis (B.M., 1959), the Univ. of Ill. (M.M., 1960), with Wykes, Kelley, and Bezanson at the Univ. of Iowa (Ph.D., 1964), and at the Illinois Studio for Experimental Music (1967). In 1971–72 he pursued research in indigenous music in West Africa. After teaching at Florida A.&M. Univ. (1960–62) and the Oberlin (Ohio) College Cons. of Music (1965–70), he was prof. of music at the Univ. of Calif. at Berkeley (from 1970). In 1977–78 he also was a visiting artist at the American Academy in Rome. He conducted much contemporary music and contributed important articles on African and Afro-American music to scholarly journals. In 1968 he won the Dartmouth Arts Council Prize for his electronic piece *Cetus*. In 1971 and 1977 he held Guggenheim fellowships. Wilson found inspiration in jazz and West African music to develop his own highly diverse and often complex style of composition. He has also used electronic elements to great effect.

WORKS: DRAMATIC: *Dance Music I* (1963) and *II* (1965), ballets; *The 18 Hands of Jerome Harris*, ballet (1971); incidental music. **ORCH.:** *Structure* (1960); *3 Movements* (1964); *Voices* (1970); *Akwan* for Piano, Electric Piano, and Orch. (1972); *Reflections* (1978); *Trilogy* (1979–80); *Lumina* (1981); Sinfonia (1984); *Houston Fanfare* (1986); *Expansions II* (1990) and *III* (1993); Viola Concerto (1994). **CHAMBER:** *Prelude and Line Study* for Wind Quintet (1959); Trio for Flute, Cello, and Piano (1959); String Quartet (1961); Violin Sonata (1961); *Dance Suite* for Winds (1962); *Soliloquy* for Double Bass (1962); Sextet for Flute, Clarinet, Bassoon, Horn, Trumpet, and Trombone (1963); *Piece for 4* for Flute, Trumpet, Double Bass, and Piano (1966); *Piano Piece* for Piano and Tape (1969); *Echoes* for Clarinet and Tape (1974–75); Trio for Violin, Cello, and Piano (1977); *A City Called Heaven* for Flute, Clarinet, Violin, Cello, Piano, and Percussion (1989). **VOCAL:** *2 Dutch Poems* for Voice and Piano (1960); *Gloria* for Voice (1961); *Wry Fragments* for Tenor and Percussion (1961); *And Death Shall Have No Dominion* for Tenor and Percussion (1963); *Chanson Innocent* for Alto and 2 Bassoons (1965); *Biography* for Soprano and Ensemble (1966); *In Memoriam Martin Luther King, Jr.* for Chorus and Tape (1968); *Spirit Song* for Soprano, Chorus, and Orch. (1973); *Sometimes* for Tenor and Tape (1976); *No More* for Tenor and Chamber Ensemble (1985); *I Shall Not Be Moved* for Soprano and Chamber Ensemble (1992–93). **ELECTRONIC:** *Cetus* (1967); *Black Martyrs* (1972).

Wilson, Philip, English singer and music editor; b. Hove, Sussex, Nov. 29, 1886; d. London, July 26, 1924. After studying singing in London, he went to Australia in 1913 as a vocal teacher at the Sydney Cons.; returning to England in 1920, he gave historical recitals, especially of Elizabethan songs. With Peter Warlock (Philip Heseltine), he ed. *English Ayres, Elizabethan and Jacobean* and *Chromatic Tunes of 1606*; also ed. *The Musical Proverbs* (London, 1924), from the "Lekingfelde" MS.

Wilson, Ransom, American flutist and conductor; b. Tuscaloosa, Ala., Oct. 25, 1951. He studied with Philip Dunigan at the North Carolina School of the Arts; also profited from advice given by Rampal. He made a European tour with the Juilliard Chamber Orch. under Maag, and soon established himself as a brilliant virtuoso. In 1980 he founded and served as conductor-soloist with his own ensemble, Solisti New York; also appeared as guest conductor with other ensembles; served as music director of Opera Omaha and the San Francisco Chamber Sym. His repertoire as a flutist is catholic, covering all periods and styles; he also commissioned special works for the flute, and arranged music for use in his concerts.

Wilson, Richard (Edward), American composer, pianist, and teacher; b. Cleveland, May 15, 1941. Following lessons in piano, theory, and composition at the Cleveland Music School Settlement (1954–59), he pursued his studies with Moevs (composition) at Harvard Univ. (A.B., 1963), at the American Academy in Rome, and at Rutgers Univ. (M.A. in theory, 1966). He also studied piano with Shure in Aspen, Colo., and N.Y. (1960), and with Wührer in Munich (1963). In 1966 he joined the faculty of Vassar College, where he was made a prof. of music in 1976. He also served as chairman of its music dept. (1979–82; 1985–88; from 1995). In 1992 he became composer-in-residence of the American Sym. Orch. in N.Y. He received annual ASCAP awards from 1970. In 1986 he received the Walter Hinrichsen Award of the American Academy and Inst. of Arts and Letters. In 1992–93 he held a Guggenheim fellowship. He received the Stoeger Prize of the Chamber Music Soc. of Lincoln Center in 1994. In his output, Wilson has followed a freely atonal course with special attention paid to lyrical expressivity.

WORKS: OPERA: *Æthelred the Unready* (1993–94). **ORCH.:** *Initiation* (1970); Concerto for Voice and Chamber Orch. (1979; Poughkeepsie, N.Y., Jan. 13, 1980); *11 Sumner Place* for Symphonic Band (1981; N.Y., June 23, 1982); Concerto for Bassoon and Chamber Orch. (1983); 2 syms.: No. 1 (Kingston, N.Y., Oct. 19, 1984) and No. 2 (1986; Annandale-on-Hudson, N.Y., Jan. 30, 1987); *Jubilation* for Wind Ensemble (Poughkeepsie, N.Y., June 7, 1987); *Silhouette* (London, Nov. 12, 1988); Suite for Small Orch. (Great Barrington, Mass., Sept. 10, 1988); *Articulations* (San Francisco, May 11, 1989); Piano Concerto (N.Y., May 5, 1991); *Agitations* (1994). **CHAMBER:** Trio for Oboe, Violin, and Piano (1964); *Fantasy and Variations* for Chamber Ensemble (1965; N.Y., April 27, 1967); *Concert Piece* for Violin and Piano (1967); 3 string quartets (1969, 1977, 1982); Quartet for 2 Flutes, String Bass, and Harpsichord (1969); *Music* for Cello (1971; N.Y., Jan. 24, 1972); *Music* for Flute (1972); Wind Quintet (1974); *Ser-*

enade: Variations on a Simple March for Clarinet, Viola, and Brass (1978); *Deux pas de trois: Pavane and Tango* for Flute, Oboe, and Harpsichord (1979); *Profound Utterances: Music* for Bassoon (1980); *Figuration: Music* for Clarinet, Cello, and Piano (1980); *Short Notice* for Clarinet and Cello (1981); *Gnomics* for Flute, Oboe, and Clarinet (1981); *Character Studies* for Oboe and Piano (1982); *Dithyramb* for Oboe and Clarinet (1982); Suite for Winds (1983); *Line Drawings* for 2 Clarinets (1984); *Flutations* for Flute (1985); *Lord Chesterfield to His Son* for Cello (1987); *Music* for Viola (1988); *Contentions* for Chamber Ensemble (1988); Viola Sonata (1989); *Intonations,* 5 pieces for Horn (1989); *Affirmations* for Flute, Clarinet, Violin, Cello, and Piano (1990; N.Y., March 7, 1991); *Touchstone* for Flute (1991; rev. 1995); *Civilization and Its Discontents* for Tuba (1992). **PIANO:** *Eclogue* (Poughkeepsie, N.Y., Dec. 5, 1974); *Sour Flowers: 8 Piano Pieces in the Form of an Herbal* (Poughkeepsie, N.Y., Sept. 19, 1979); *A Child's London,* 6 pieces (1984); *Fixations* (1985; Poughkeepsie, N.Y., Jan. 28, 1986); *Intercalations* (N.Y., Nov. 9, 1986). **VOCAL:** *In Schrafft's* for Men's Chorus and Piano, 4-hands (1966; also for Chorus, Clarinet, Harpsichord, and Marimba, 1979); *A Dissolve* for Women's Chorus (1968); *Can* for Chorus (1968); *Light in Spring Poplars* for Chorus (1968); *Soaking* for Chorus (1969); *Home from the Range* for Chorus (1970); *Elegy* for Chorus (1971); *Hunter's Moon* for Chorus (1972); *The Ballad of Longwood Glen* for Tenor and Harp (1975); *August 22* for Chorus, Piano, and Percussion (1976); *A Theory* for Soprano and Vibraphone (1980); *3 Painters* for High Voice and Piano (1984); *Tribulations,* 5 songs for Voice and Piano (1988); *Persuasions* for Soprano, Flute, Oboe, Bassoon, and Harpsichord (Washington, D.C., Nov. 30, 1990); *The 2nd Law* for Baritone and Piano (1991); *On the Street* for Baritone and Piano or Strings (1992); *Poor Warren* for Chorus and Piano (Poughkeepsie, N.Y., March 28, 1995).

Wimberger, Gerhard, Austrian composer, conductor, and pedagogue; b. Vienna, Aug. 30, 1923. He was educated at the Salzburg Mozarteum (1940–41; 1945–47), where he received training in composition from Bresgen and J.N. David and in conducting from Krauss and Paumgartner. From 1948 to 1951 he conducted at the Salzburg Landestheater. In 1953 he joined the faculty of the Salzburg Mozarteum, where he taught conducting until 1968 and composition from 1968 until his retirement in 1991. In 1990 he served as president of the AKM (Staatlich genehmigte Gesellschaft der Autoren, Komponisten, und Musikverleger) of Austria. In 1967 he was awarded the Austrian State Prize for composition. He won the Würdigungspreis for music in 1977, the same year that he was made a corresponding member of the Akademie der Schönen Künste in Munich. In his works, Wimberger makes use of various styles and techniques, including jazz and other popular genres. His dramatic works reveal a penchant for the use of wit and irony.

WORKS: DRAMATIC: *König für einem Tag,* ballet (1951); *Schaubudengeschichte,* opera (1952–53; Mannheim, Nov. 25, 1954); *Der Handschuh,* chamber ballet (1955); *La Battaglia oder Der rote Federbusch,* comic opera (1959–60; Schwetzingen, May 12, 1960); *Hero und Leander,* dance drama (1962–63); *Dame Kobold,* musical comedy (1963–64; Frankfurt am Main, Sept. 24, 1964); *Das Opfer Helena,* chamber musical (1967); *Lebensregeln,* catechism with music (1970–72; Munich, Aug. 27, 1972); *Paradou,* opera (1985); *Fürst von Salzburg—Wolf Dietrich,* scenic chronicle (Salzburg, June 11, 1987); other works for the theater, radio, and television. **ORCH.:** *Musica brevis* (1950); Chamber Concerto for 4 Winds, Percussion, and Strings (1952); *Divertimento* for Strings (1954); 2 piano concertos: No. 1 for Piano and Chamber Orch. (1955) and No. 2 (1980–81; Munich, June 4, 1984); *Augustin-Variationen* (1956); *Figuren und Phantasien* (1956); *Partita giocosa* for Small Orch. (1960); *Étude dramatique* (1961); *Risonanze* for 3 Orch. Groups (1965–66; Berlin, Jan. 31, 1968); *Chronique* (1968–69); *Multiplay* for 23 Players (1972–73; Salzburg, April 9, 1974); *Motus* (1976; Wuppertal, May 5, 1978); *Programm* (1977–78; Bonn, May 10, 1978); *Ausstrahlungen W.A. Mozart'scher Themen* (1978; Munich, Nov. 25, 1979); Concertino (1981; Lugano, March 25, 1982); *Nachtmusik Trauermusik Finalmusik* (1988); *Vagabondage* for Big Band (1988; Salzburg, Oct. 19, 1989); Synthesizer Concerto (1989); *Tanzkonzert* for Chamber Orch. (1992; Vienna, Feb. 11, 1993); *Ahnungen* (1994). **CHAMBER:** Trio for Flute, Violin, and Piano (1951); *4 Stücke* for Flute and Piano (1952); *Stories* for Winds and Percussion (1962); *Short Stories* for 11 Winds (1974–75; Frankfurt am Main, Feb. 6, 1977); *Plays* for 12 Cellos, Winds, and Percussion (1975; Salzburg, Aug. 27, 1976); *Concerto a dodici (Viaggi)* for 12 Instruments (1977; Vienna, Feb. 20, 1978); String Quartet (1978; Salzburg, Aug. 23, 1980); *Rufe* for 12 Brass Instruments (1979); *Phantasie* for 6 Players (1982; Salzburg, Aug. 4, 1983); 3 synthesizer sonatas (1990); Quintet for Flute, Oboe, Clarinet, Bassoon, and Horn (1990); *Szenerie* for Violin and Piano (1993; Hannover, Dec. 9, 1994); *Burletta* for Violin and Piano (1993). **KEYBOARD: PIANO:** Sonata for 2 Pianos (1950); *5 Studien* (1952); *Konturen* (1977); *Disegni* (1991; Vienna, April 29, 1992). **ORGAN:** *Signum* (1969; Salzburg, Jan. 10, 1970). **VOCAL:** *Kantate vom Sport* (1952); *Drei lyrische Chanons nach Gedichten von Jacques Prévert* for Voice and Chamber Orch. (1957); *Heiratspostkantate* for Chorus, Harpsichord, and Double Bass (1957); *4 Sätze nach deutschen Volksliedern* for Soprano, Chorus, and Jazz Combo (1966); *Ars amatoria,* cantata for Soprano, Baritone, Chorus, Combo, and Chamber Orch. (1967); *4 Songs* for Voice and 16 Instruments (1969; Gelsenkirchen, Feb. 26, 1975); *Singsang* for Voice and Beat Combo (1970); *Memento Vivere* for Mezzo-soprano, Baritone, 3 Speakers, Chorus, Orch., and Tape (1973–74; Salzburg, Aug. 7, 1975); *Mein Leben mein Tod* for Baritone, Instruments, and Tape (1976; Salzburg, March 30, 1977); *Sonetti in vita e in morte di Madonna Laura* for Chorus (1979; Vienna, May 10, 1983); *Sechs Liebeslieder* for Baritone and Harpsichord (1980); *Wir hören zu atmen nicht auf,* song cycle for Woman's Voice and Piano (1988); *Tagebuch 1942—Jochen Klepper* for Baritone, Chorus, and Orch. (1990–91); *Die Eitelkeit im Leben des Managers* for Soprano, Mezzo-soprano, and Orch. (Gutersloh, July 1, 1991); *Im Namen der Liebe,* song cycle for Man's Voice and Piano (Salzburg, Nov. 16, 1992). **ELECTRONIC:** *Versuch I: Klänge* (1975) and *II: Natur Musik* (1975).

BIBL.: H. Goertz, *G. W.* (Vienna, 1991).

Winant, William, American percussionist; b. N.Y., Feb. 11, 1953. His mother was the well-known casting director Ethel Winant; his father, H.M. Wynant, was an actor. He was educated at York Univ. in Toronto (B.F.A., 1977) and Mills College in Oakland, Calif. (M.F.A., 1982). He toured with Steve Reich and Musicians (1973) and the Kronos Quartet (1984). In 1983 he became a visiting lecturer at the Univ. of Calif. at Santa Cruz, and in 1984 joined the percussion faculty at the Univ. of Calif. at Berkeley; also was principal percussionist of the Cabrillo Music Festival (1984–93) and of the San Francisco Contemporary Music Players (from 1988). A leading avant-garde percussionist, Winant has given first performances of works by such composers as John Cage, Frederic Rzewski, Daniel Lentz, John Zorn, Somei Satoh, and Morton Feldman. He appeared as a soloist with the Los Angeles Phil. and Cabrillo Festival Orch., and at the Ravinia Music Festival. In 1984 he formed (with David Abel, violin, and Julie Steinberg, piano) the Abel-Steinberg-Winant Trio, with which he toured widely and recorded; he also performed with Room (with Larry Ochs and Chris Brown) and with the live electroacoustic ensemble Challenge (with Anthony Braxton and David Rosenboom). From 1993 he became active with the rock bands Oingo Boingo and Mr. Bungle.

Winbeck, Heinz, German composer and teacher; b. Piflas, near Landshut, Feb. 11, 1946. He received his training in Munich, where he took courses with Magda Rusy (piano) and Fritz Rieger (conducting) at the Richard Strauss Cons. (1964–67), and with Genzmer and Bialas (composition) and Koetsier (conducting) at the Hochschule für Musik (1967–73). From 1974 to 1978 he was active as a conductor and composer in Ingolstadt and Wunsiedel. After teaching at the Munich Hochschule für Musik (1980–88), he was prof. of composition at the Würzburg Hochschule für Musik (from 1988). In 1985 he received the music prize of the Akademie der Schönen Künste in Berlin. In 1988 he was composer-in-residence at the Cabrillo (Calif.) Music Festival. Winbeck's compositions are personal reflections in a modern, expansive style.

WORKS: ORCH.: *Sonosoillent* for Cello and Strings (1971); *Entgegengesang* (1973; Stuttgart, June 16, 1974); *Lenau-Fantasien* for Cello and Chamber Orch. (1979; Munich, Oct. 7, 1980); *Denk ich an Haydn*, 3 fragments (Remscheid, March 31, 1982); 4 syms.: No. 1, *Tu Solus* (1983; Donaueschingen, Oct. 19, 1984; rev. version, Munich, April 19, 1985), No. 2 (1986–87; Saarbrücken, May 31, 1987), No. 3, *Grodek*, for Alto, Speaker, and Orch. (1987–88; Munich, Nov. 25, 1988), and No. 4, *De Profundis*, for Speaker, Alto, Baritone, Chorus, Orch., Electronics, and Tape (1991–93; Bonn, Sept. 13, 1993). **CHAMBER:** *Musik* for Wind Quintet (1971); *Espaces* for 4 Percussionists, Piano, and Flute (1971–72); *Nocturne I* for Chamber Ensemble (1972); *Poco a poco . . .* for Piano and String Trio (Hitzacker, July 21, 1974); 3 string quartets: No. 1 (1979), No. 2, *Tempi notturni* (1979; Hitzacker, July 27, 1980), and No. 3, *Jagdquartett* (1983–84; Hamburg, Oct. 12, 1984); *Blick in den Strom* for String Quintet (1981; N.Y., Jan. 26, 1993). **VOCAL:** *In Memoriam Paul Celan* for Soprano, Flute, Piano, and Percussion (1970); *Sie Tanzt* for Baritone and Chamber Ensemble (1971); *Nocturne II, Nacht mein Augentrost*, for Chorus, 5 Flutes, 2 Guitars, Bandolon, Organ, and 5 Percussionists (1973); *Chansons à temps* for Women's Voices and 13 Instruments (1976).

Winbergh, Gösta, Swedish tenor; b. Stockholm, Dec. 30, 1943. He studied in Stockholm with Erik Saedén at the Musikhögskolan and pursued training at the Royal Opera School. In 1971 he made his operatic debut as Rodolfo in Göteborg; after singing with the Royal Opera in Stockholm (1973–80), he was a member of the Zürich Opera (from 1981). In 1982 he sang for the first time at London's Covent Garden as Titus. He made his debut at the Metropolitan Opera in N.Y. on Nov. 22, 1983, as Don Ottavio. In 1985 he sang at Milan's La Scala for the first time as Tamino; also had guest engagements in Berlin, Hamburg, Munich, Paris, Vienna, Chicago, Houston, and San Francisco. As a concert artist, Winbergh sang widely in Europe and abroad. His other roles include Count Almaviva, Ferrando, Mithridates, Nemorino, Lensky, Massenet's Des Grieux, Alfredo, Faust, and Lohengrin.

Wincenc, Carol, talented American flutist and teacher; b. Buffalo, June 29, 1949. She studied in Italy with Severino Gazzelloni, taking courses at the Accademia Musicale Chigiana in Siena (1966–67) and at the Accademia di Santa Cecilia in Rome (1967–68); was a pupil of Robert Willoughby at the Oberlin (Ohio) College Cons. of Music (1967–69), of Harold Bennett at the Manhattan School of Music in N.Y. (B.Mus., 1971), and of Arthur Lora at the Juilliard School in N.Y. (M.M., 1972). She was 1st flutist in the National Orchestral Assn. in N.Y. (1970–71), the Aspen (Colo.) Festival Chamber Orch. (1970–72), and the St. Paul (Minn.) Chamber Orch. (1972–77). After winning the Concert Artist's Guild Award, she made her recital debut at N.Y.'s Carnegie Recital Hall in 1972. She won 1st prize at the Naumburg Competition in 1978. In subsequent years, she appeared as a soloist with major world orchs., as a recitalist and as a chamber music player. She was founder-artistic director of the International Flute Festival in St. Paul, Minn. (1985–87). She taught at the Manhattan School of Music (1980–86), the Indiana Univ. School of Music in Bloomington (1986–88), and the Juilliard School (from 1988). She won particular distinction for her promotion of contemporary music; commissioned and premiered various works for flute, including pieces by Lukas Foss, Joan Tower, Giya Kancheli, and Henryk Gorecki.

Windgassen, Wolfgang (Fritz Hermann), distinguished German tenor; b. Annemasse, Haute Savoie, June 26, 1914; d. Stuttgart, Sept. 8, 1974. He received his early vocal training from his father, Fritz Windgassen (b. Hamburg, Feb. 9, 1883; d. Murnau, April 17, 1963), who was a leading tenor at the Stuttgart Opera; then continued his studies at the Stuttgart Cons. with Maria Ranzow and Alfons Fischer. He made his operatic debut in Pforzheim in 1941 as Alvaro in *La forza del destino;* after military service in the German army, he joined the Stuttgart Opera in 1945, remaining on its roster until 1972. From 1951 to 1970 he appeared at the Bayreuth Festivals, where he was a leading Heldentenor. He made his Metropolitan Opera debut in N.Y. on Jan. 22, 1957, as Siegmund, but sang there only that season. He sang regularly at Convent Garden in London from 1955 to 1966. He was especially successful in Wagnerian roles, as Tannhäuser, Tristan, Parsifal, Siegfried, and Lohengrin; he also appeared as Radames and Don José.

BIBL.: B. Wessling, *W. W.* (Bremen, 1967).

Windingstad, Ole, Norwegian-American conductor and composer; b. Sandefjord, May 18, 1886; d. Kingston, N.Y., June 3, 1959. He graduated from the Oslo Cons. in 1902; then studied at the Leipzig Cons. He went to N.Y. in 1913, and established the Scandinavian Sym. Orch., which he conducted until 1929; also conducted the Brooklyn Sym. Orch. (1930–32), the Knickerbocker Sym. Orch. in Albany, N.Y. (1937–39), the New Orleans Sym. Orch. (1940–44), the Albany Sym. Orch. (1945–48), and the Dutchess County (N.Y.) Phil. (1945–59). In 1929 he was decorated with the Norwegian Order of Saint Olaf. He composed a Sym. (1913); a cantata, *The Skald of Norway* (1929); *The Tides* for Orch. (Albany, Feb. 13, 1938, composer conducting); many minor pieces.

Winham, Godfrey, English-American composer and computer specialist; b. London, Dec. 11, 1934; d. Princeton, N.J., April 26, 1975. He studied composition and piano at the Royal Academy of Music in London. In 1954 went to the U.S., where he took courses at Princeton Univ. (A.B., 1956; M.F.A., 1958); received his Ph.D. degree there with the diss. *Composition with Arrays* (1965); then joined the staff as a lecturer on electronic music and computer composition. In 1969 he worked on the computerized synthesis of music and speech. Apart from his programmed compositions on a computer, he wrote 2 string quartets, *The Habit of Perfection* for Voice and String Quartet, and several piano pieces. He married **Bethany Beardslee** in 1956.

Winkler, Peter (Kenton), American composer, teacher, and editor; b. Los Angeles, Jan. 26, 1943. He was a student of Schifrin, Lewin, and Imbrie at the Univ. of Calif. at Berkeley (B.A., 1964) and of Kim, Babbitt, and Cone at Princeton Univ. (M.F.A., 1967). He taught at the State Univ. of N.Y. at Stony Brook (from 1971) and was ed. of the *Journal of Popular Music Studies* (from 1992). In 1978 he held a MacDowell Colony fellowship.

WORKS: DRAMATIC: *Tingle-Tangle: A Wedekind Cabaret* (N.Y., July 1994; in collaboration with W. Bolcom and A. Black); other theater pieces; incidental music for plays, radio, and television. **ORCH.:** Sym. (1971–78). **CHAMBER:** String Quartet (1965–67); *Clarinet Bouquet: 4 Concert Rags* for Clarinet, Piano, and Bassoon (1976–80); *Recitativo e Terzetto* for Oboe, Clarinet, and Bassoon (1980); *No Condition is Permanent* for Flute, Clarinet, Violin, Cello, Piano, and Percussion (1980–89); *Solitaire* for Clarinet (1989); *Gospel Hymn* for Violin and Piano (1990); *Waterborne* for Violin and Tape (1991); *Saboreando el Gusto Cubano* for Violin, Piano, and Percussion (Havana, Oct. 6, 1994); *Fanfare for Stony Brook* for Trumpet (Stony Brook, N.Y., April 15, 1995). **VOCAL:** *Praise of Silence* for Soprano, Chorus, Renaissance Ensemble, and Tape (1969); *Sing Out the Old, Sing in the New* for Men's Chorus, Tuba, and Violin Obbligato (1992); *One Light* for Men's Chorus, Piano, and Percussion (1994); songs.

Winograd, Arthur, American cellist and conductor; b. N.Y., April 22, 1920. He studied at the New England Cons. of Music in Boston (1937–40) and at the Curtis Inst. of Music in Philadelphia (1940–41). He played the cello in the Boston Sym. Orch. (1940–41) and in the NBC Sym. Orch. in N.Y. (1942–43); then was a member of the Juilliard String Quartet and the faculty of the Juilliard School of Music in N.Y. (1946–55). He was active as a conductor for MGM Records (1954–58) and Audio Fidelity Records (1958–60); then was music director of the Birmingham (Ala.) Sym. Orch. (1960–64) and the Hartford (Conn.) Sym. Orch. (1964–85).

Winter, Paul, American composer and instrumentalist; b. Altoona, Pa., Aug. 31, 1939. He was in the 3rd generation of a family of professional musicians; his great-aunts and -uncles belonged to the vaudeville troupe that introduced the saxophone to the U.S. He began playing drums at the age of 5, piano at 6, and clarinet at 8; by the time he was 12, he had discovered bebop, chosen the saxophone as his primary instrument, and formed his first band. He studied English composition at Northwestern Univ. (B.A., 1961) while frequenting jazz clubs in Chicago. In 1961 he formed with fellow students the Paul Winter Sextet, which was subsequently sent abroad on a State Dept. cultural exchange program (1962); before disbanding in 1965, the group had released 7 recordings. Winter moved to Connecticut and in 1967 formed the stylistically eclectic Paul Winter Consort, which released 4 highly successful recordings before disbanding in 1972; the group was re-formed in 1977 with a more consistent style that integrated natural sounds with gentle, improvisatory music. In 1980 Winter founded Living Music Records, whose name suggests his strong environmental and humanistic concerns. Many of his concerts and recordings take place in unusual locations or for the benefit of social causes; he was an artist-in-residence at the Cathedral of St. John the Divine in N.Y. His compositions combine jazz, folk, ethnic, and classical elements in a style that has been a prototype for New Age music. Among his noteworthy recordings are *Icarus* (1972), *Common Ground* (1977), and *Earth: Voices of a Planet* (1990).

Winternitz, Emanuel, Austrian-American musicologist and museum curator; b. Vienna, Aug. 4, 1898; d. N.Y., Aug. 22, 1983. He served in the Austrian army in World War I; after the Armistice, he studied jurisprudence at the Univ. of Vienna (LL.D., 1922). He was engaged as a corporate lawyer in Vienna (1929–38). After the Anschluss in 1938, he emigrated to the U.S., where he devoted himself mainly to lecturing on art; served as Peripatetic Professor for the Carnegie Foundation. In 1942 he was appointed keeper of musical instruments at the Metropolitan Museum in N.Y.; in 1949, was named curator of the Crosby Brown Collection of Musical Instruments of All Nations at the Metropolitan. He also administered the André Mertens Galleries for Musical Instruments (1971–73). In 1973 he became curator emeritus of the Metropolitan. Among his principal endeavors was musical iconography; he publ. a valuable reference work, *Musical Autographs from Monteverdi to Hindemith* (2 vols., Princeton, N.J., 1955); other books were *Keyboard Instruments in the Metropolitan Museum of Art* (N.Y., 1961); *Die schönsten Musikinstrumente des Abendlandes* (Munich, 1966; Eng. tr., 1967, as *Musical Instruments of the Western World*); *Gaudenzio Ferrari, his School, and the Early History of the Violin* (Milan, 1967); *Musical Instruments and their Symbolism in Western Art* (N.Y., 1967; 2nd ed., 1979); *Leonardo da Vinci as a Musician* (New Haven, Conn., 1982).

Wintzer, Richard, German composer; b. Nauendorf, near Halle, March 9, 1866; d. Berlin, Aug. 14, 1952. He studied painting, and also music (with Bargiel). He lived mostly in Berlin, where he was active as a painter, composer, and music critic. He wrote 2 operas, *Die Willis* (1895) and *Marienkind* (1905); *Auf hohen Bergen* for Baritone, Chorus, and Orch.; some fine songs (*Ernste Gesänge, Kinderlieder*, and *Sturmlieder*); piano pieces. He also publ. *Menschen von anderem Schlage* (1912) and an autobiography.

BIBL.: H. Killer, "R. W., Ein Leben zwischen den Künsten," *Musik* (March 1941).

Wiora, Walter, renowned German musicologist; b. Kattowitz, Dec. 30, 1906. He studied in Berlin at the Hochschule für Musik (1925–27) and received training in musicology from Abert, Blume, Hornbostel, Sachs, Schering, and Schünemann; continued his studies with Gurlitt at the Univ. of Freiburg im Breisgau (Ph.D., 1937, with the diss. *Die Variantenbildung im Volkslied: Ein Beitrag zur systematischen Musikwissenschaft*); completed his Habilitation there in 1941 with his *Die Herkunft der Melodien in Kretschmers und Zuccalmaglios Sammlung* (publ. in an enl. ed. as *Die rheinisch-bergischen Melodien bei Zuccalmaglio und Brahms*, Bad Godesberg, 1953). He was an assistant at the Deutsches Volksliedarchiv in Freiburg im Breisgau (1936–41); after serving as a reader in musicology at the Univ. of Posen, he returned to Freiburg im Breisgau and was archivist at the Deutsches Volksliedarchiv (1946–58); then was prof. of musicology at the Univ. of Kiel (1958–64) and at the Univ. of Saarbrücken (1964–72). His principal achievement was his advocacy of a system of "essential research" in musicology that utilizes both traditional and contemporary principles.

WRITINGS: *Die deutsche Volksliedweise und der Osten* (Wolfenbüttel and Berlin, 1940); *Zur Frühgeschichte der Musik in den Alpenlandern* (Basel, 1949); *Das echte Volkslied* (Heidelberg, 1950); *Europäische Volksmusik und abendländische Tonkunst* (Kassel, 1957); *Die geschichtliche Sonderstellung der abendländischen Musik* (Mainz, 1959); *Die vier Weltalter der Musik* (Stuttgart, 1961; Eng. tr., 1965, as *The Four Ages of Music*); *Komponist und Mitwelt* (Kassel, 1964); ed. *Die Ausbreitung des Historismus über die Musik* (Regensburg, 1969); *Das deutsche Lied: Zur Geschichte und Ästhetik einer musikalischen Gattung* (Wolfenbüttel and Zürich, 1971); *Historische und systematische Musikwissenschaft* (Tutzing, 1972); *Ergebnisse und Aufgaben vergleichender Musikforschung* (Darmstadt, 1975); *Das musikalische Kunstwerk* (Tutzing, 1983).

BIBL.: L. Finscher and C.-H. Mahling, eds., *Festschrift für W. W.* (Kassel, 1967); C.-H. Mahling, ed., *Beiträge zu einer musikalischen Gattung: W. W. zum 70. Geburtstag* (Tutzing, 1979).

Wirén, Dag (Ivar), prominent Swedish composer; b. Striberg, Oct. 15, 1905; d. Danderyd, April 19, 1986. He studied at the Stockholm Cons. with Oskar Lindberg and Ernest Ellberg (1926–31); then in Paris with Leonid Sabaneyev (1932–34). He returned to Sweden in 1934, and was music critic for the *Svenska Morgonbladet* (1938–46); was vice-president of the Soc. of Swedish Composers (1947–63). His early music was influenced by Scandinavian Romanticism; later he adopted a more sober and more cosmopolitan neo-Classicism, stressing the symmetry of formal structure; in his thematic procedures he adopted the method of systematic intervallic metamorphosis rather than development and variation. He ceased composing in 1972.

WORKS: DRAMATIC: *Blått, gult, rott* (Blood, Sweat, Tears), radio operetta (1940); *Den glada patiensen*, radio operetta (1941); *Oscarbalen* (Oscarian Ball), ballet (1949); *Den elaka drottningen* (The Wicked Queen), television ballet (1960; Swedish TV, Nov. 22, 1961); incidental music for plays and films. **ORCH.:** 2 overtures (1931, 1940); 5 syms. (1932; 1939; 1943–44; 1951–52; Stockholm, Dec. 5, 1964); *Sinfonietta* (1933–34); Cello Concerto (1936); *Serenade* for Strings (1937); *Little Suite* (1941); *Romantic Suite* (1945); Violin Concerto (1945–46); Piano Concerto (1947–50); *Divertimento* (1954–57); *Triptyk* (1958); *Music* for Strings (1966–67; Stockholm, Jan. 12, 1968); Flute Concertino (1972). **CHAMBER:** 5 string quartets (1930; 1935; 1941–45; 1952–53; 1969–70); 2 piano trios (1933, 1961); Violin Sonatina (1939); Quartet for Flute, Oboe, Clarinet, and Cello (1956); *Little Serenade* for Guitar (1964); Wind Quintet (1971). **PIANO:** *Theme and Variations* (1933); *5 Ironic Miniatures* (1942–45); Sonatina (1950); *5 Improvisations* (1959); *Little Piano Suite* (1971). **VOCAL:** Songs.

BIBL.: L. Hedwall, "D. W.," *Musikrevy*, IX (1954; Eng. tr. in *Music in Sweden: Musikrevy International*, 1954).

Wirth, Helmut (Richard Adolf Friedrich Karl), German musicologist and composer; b. Kiel, Oct. 10, 1912. He studied composition with R. Oppel; then took courses in musicology with Fritz Stein and Blume at the Univ. of Kiel (Ph.D., 1937, with the diss. *Joseph Haydn als Dramatiker*, publ. in Wolfenbüttel and Berlin, 1940). From 1936 he was active with the Hamburg Radio; also was lecturer at the Schleswig-Holstein Academy of Music in Lübeck (1952–72). He was a founder-member of the Haydn Inst. of Cologne, and edited works for the complete ed. of Haydn's works. He publ. the study *Max Reger* (Hamburg, 1973). Among his compositions are orch. pieces, chamber music, piano pieces, and songs.

Wishart, Peter (Charles Arthur), English composer and teacher; b. Crowborough, June 25, 1921; d. Frome, Aug. 14, 1984. He received training in composition from Hely-Hutchinson at the Univ. of Birmingham (1938–41) and from Boulanger in Paris (1947–48). He taught at the Univ. of Birmingham (1950–59), the Guildhall School of Music in London (from 1961), King's College, London (1972–77), and the Univ. of Reading (1977–84). He publ. the books *Harmony* (London, 1956) and *Key to Music* (London, 1971).

WORKS: DRAMATIC: OPERAS: *2 in the Bush* (1956); *The Captive* (1960); *The Clandestine Marriage* (1971); *Clytemnestra* (1973). Also ballets; incidental music. **ORCH.:** 2 violin concertos (1951, 1968); 2 syms. (1953, 1973); *Aubade* for Flute and Strings (1955); *Concerto piccolo* (1955); *Concerto for Orchestra* (1957); Concerto for Piano and Small Orch. (1958); *Divisions* (1965); *5 Pieces* for Strings (1967). **CHAMBER:** 2 cassations for Violin and Viola (1948, 1950); Sonata for Piano Duet (1949); 2 string quartets (1951, 1954); *Cantilena* for 4 Cellos (1957); *Profane Concerto* for Flute, Oboe, and Harpsichord (1962); organ music. **VOCAL:** Sacred and secular pieces.

Wislocki, Stanislaw, Polish conductor and composer; b. Rzeszów, July 7, 1921. He studied in Lwów and Timişoara. He conducted the Poznań Phil. (1947–58); served as chief conductor of the Polish Radio National Sym. Orch. in Katowice (1977–81) and of the Buenos Aires Phil. (1981). He composed a Sym. (1944); *4 Poems* for Tenor and Chamber Orch. (1944); *Symphonic Nocturne* (1947); Piano Concerto (1948–49); *Symphonic Ballad* (1950); *Symfonia tańcu* (Symphony on Dancing; 1952); Violin Sonata (1942); Piano Quartet (1943); piano pieces.

Wissmer, Pierre, Swiss-born French composer and pedagogue; b. Geneva, Oct. 30, 1915; d. Valcros, France, Nov. 4, 1992. He went to Paris to study with Roger-Ducasse (composition) at the Cons., Daniel-Lesur (counterpoint) at the Schola Cantorum, and Munch (conducting) at the École Normale de Musique. Returning to Geneva, he taught composition at the Cons. (1944–48). He was active as a music critic, and also served as head of the chamber-music dept. of the Geneva Radio. After serving as assistant director of programming of Radio Luxembourg (1951–57), he was director of programming of Luxembourg Television (1957–63). In 1958 he became a naturalized French citizen. He was director of the Schola Cantorum in Paris (1957–63) and of the École Nationale de Musique in Le Mans (1969–81), and also was prof. of composition and orchestration at the Geneva Cons. (1973–86). In 1983 he was awarded the Grand Prix Musical of Geneva for his creative efforts. His output reveals an adept handling of traditional and contemporary styles.

WORKS: DRAMATIC: *Le Beau dimanche*, ballet (1939; Geneva, March 20, 1944); *Marion ou la belle au tricorne*, comic opera (1945; Radio Suisse Romande, Geneva, April 16, 1947); *Capitaine Bruno*, opera (Geneva, Nov. 9, 1952); *Léonidas ou la cruauté mentale*, opéra bouffe (Paris, Sept. 12, 1958); *Alerte, puits 21*, ballet (1963); *Christina et les Chimères*, ballet (1964). **ORCH.:** *Mouvement* for Strings (1937); 3 piano concertos (1937, 1948, 1971); 9 syms. (1938; 1951; 1955; 1962; 1969; 1975–77; 1983; 1985–86; 1988–89); *Antoine et Cléopâtre*, symphonic suite (1943); 3 violin concertos (1944, 1954, 1987); *La Mandrellina*, overture (1952); *Divertimento* (1953); *L'Enfant et la rose*, symphonic variations (1957); *Clamavi*, triptych (1957); Clarinet Concerto (1960); Oboe Concerto (1963); *Concerto valcrosiano* (1966); *Concertino-croisière* for Flute, Piano, and Strings (1966); *Stèle* for Strings (1969); *Triptyque romand* (1972); *Dialogue* for Bassoon or Cello and Orch. (1974); *Variations sur un Noël imaginaire* (1975); *Symphonietta concertante* for Flute, Harp, and Orch. (1982); *Musique à divers temps* for Strings (1988–89). **CHAMBER:** 3 string quartets (1937, 1949, 1972); *Sérénade* for Oboe, Clarinet, and Horn (1938); *Divertissement sur un choral* for 11 Instruments (1939); Clarinet Sonatina (1941); Violin Sonatina (1946); *Prestilagoyana* for 2 Guitars (1959); *Quadrige* for Flute, Violin, Cello, and Piano (1961); Sonatina for Flute and Guitar (1962); Wind Quintet (1964); *Partita* for Guitar (1971); *Trio Adelfiano* for Flute, Cello, and Piano (1978); *Quattro piccoli quadri Veneziano* for Violin, Viola, and Cello (1984); *Askok* for Flute and Guitar (1984); *Ritratto* for 2 Guitars (1984); *Propos* for Oboe, Clarinet, and Bassoon (1986); *Tre pezzi valcorsiani* for 2 Guitars (1987); *Automne* for Guitar (1988–89); *Primavera* for Guitar (1988–89). **KEYBOARD: PIANO:** Sonata (1949); *Trois Études* (1967); *Trois Silhouettes* (1968); *Bea, Sandrine et Monsieur Pompon (le chat)* (1986); *Cavaliere e cavallo* (1986); *3 Romances* for Piano, 4-hands (1988–89); *Épisodes* (1988–89); *Musique pour jeunes virtuoses* (1988–89). **ORGAN:** *Réflexions* (1973); *Apôtre Paul* (1985). **VOCAL:** *Naïdes* for Narrator, Soli, Chorus, and Orch. (1941); *Hérétique et Relapse* for Tenor, Chorus, and Orch. (1962); *Un Banquier sans visage* for Soli, Dancers, and Orch. (1964); *Le Quatrième Mage*, oratorio for Soli, Chorus, and Orch. (1965); *I Cadieni* for Voices and Orch. (1980); choruses; songs.

Wiszniewski, Zbigniew, Polish composer and teacher; b. Lwów, July 30, 1922. He received training in classical philology (1946–49) and in composition, theory, and viola (1946–51) in Łódź. From 1948 to 1957 he was active as a violist. He was an ed. with the Polish Radio in Warsaw from 1957 to 1966, and again from 1968 to 1985. He taught at the Warsaw Academy of Music from 1977 to 1988, and again from 1993. He also served as chief ed. of the music journal *Poradnik Muzyczny* (Music Adviser; 1982–84).

WORKS: DRAMATIC: *Neffru*, radio opera (1958); *Ad If*, radio opera (1973); *Pater Noster*, radio opera (1973); other film, radio, and theater scores. **ORCH.:** *Tre pezzi della tradizion* (1964); *Triptychon* (1967); Concerto for Clarinet and Strings (1970); Violin Concerto (1986); Concertante for Oboe, Harpsichord, and Strings (1987); *Sinfonia da camera* for Strings (1987); Double Concerto for Trumpet, Accordion, and Orch. (1989). **CHAMBER:** 2 string quartets (1952, 1990); Trio for Oboe, Harp, and Viola (1963); *Tristia* for Chamber Ensemble (1965); *Chamber Music No. 2* for 10 Instruments (1966) and *No. 4* for 10 Instruments (1972); Sonata for Solo Cello (1976); Duo for Bass Tuba and Percussion (1981); Quartet for 4 Violins (1981); Duo for Accordion and Guitar (1984); Trio for Alto Saxophone, Percussion, and Accordion (1985); *Ballade* for Mandolin and Celtic Harp (1985); *Trigones* for 2 Accordions and Organ (1987); Trio for Accordion, Viola d'Amore, and Organ (1987); Trio for Flute, Harpsichord, and Cello (1988); Sonata for Solo Oboe (1989); Duo for Accordion and Trombone (1990); Sonata for Solo Viola d'Amore (1992). **VOCAL:** *Ad Hominem* for Chorus and Orch. (1963); *Genesis*, television oratorio for Baritone, Actor, Chorus, and Orch. (1967); *The Brothers*, television oratorio for Actor, Men's Chorus, and Orch. (1970); *Sichel versäumter Stunden*, cantata for Chorus and Orch. (1971); *Ballade de Villon de la Grosse Margot* for Baritone, Chorus, and 5 Instruments (1988); Canon for Chorus and Instruments (1992); songs.

Wit, Antoni, Polish conductor; b. Kraków, Feb. 7, 1944. He was educated in his native city, taking courses in conducting at the State College of Music (graduated, 1967) and in law at the Jagiellonian Univ. (graduated, 1969); won 2nd prize in the Karajan Competition in Berlin (1971) and completed his conducting studies at the Berkshire Music Center, Tanglewood (summer, 1973). He was assistant conductor of the National Phil. in Warsaw (1967–70); then conducted the Poznań State Phil. (1970–72) and the Pomeranian Phil. in Bydgoszcz (1974–77). After serving as artistic director of the Polish Radio and Television Sym. Orch. in Kraków (1977–83), he held that title with the Polish Radio and Television National Sym. Orch. in Katowice (from 1983); also toured widely as a guest conductor.

Witherspoon, Herbert, American bass; b. Buffalo, N.Y., July 21, 1873; d. N.Y., May 10, 1935. He studied composition with Horatio Parker and voice with Gustav Stoeckel at Yale Univ. (graduated, 1895); then was a pupil of MacDowell in N.Y. He then studied singing with Bouhy in Paris, Henry Wood in London, and G.B. Lamperti in Berlin. Returning to America, he made his operatic debut as Ramfis in *Aida* with Savage's Castle Square Opera Co. in N.Y. in 1898. On Nov. 26, 1908, he made his Metropolitan Opera debut in N.Y. as Titurel in *Parsifal*; remained on its roster until 1916, where he distinguished himself in such roles as Sarastro, King Marke, Pogner, the Landgrave, and Gurnemanz. In 1922 he founded the American Academy of Teachers of Singing, subsequently serving as its first president. In 1925 he became president of the Chicago Musical College, and in 1931, president of the Cincinnati Cons. of Music; in 1933 he returned to N.Y., and in May 1935, was chosen to succeed Gatti-Casazza as general manager of the Metropolitan Opera, but he died of a heart attack after only a month in his post. He publ. *Singing: A Treatise for Teachers and Students* (N.Y., 1925) and *36 Lessons in Singing for Teacher and Student* (Chicago, 1930).

Witkowski, Georges-Martin, French conductor, pedagogue, and composer; b. Mostaganem, Algeria (of a French father and a Polish mother), Jan. 6, 1867; d. Lyons, Aug. 12, 1943. He was educated at the military school of St.-Cyr; studied composition with d'Indy at the Paris Schola Cantorum (1894–97); later left for the army and settled in Lyons, where he founded the Société des Grands Concerts in 1905 for the production of oratorios. In 1924 he was appointed director of the Lyons Cons., retiring in 1941.

WORKS: OPERA: *La Princesse lointaine*, after Rostand (1928–32; Paris, March 26, 1934). **ORCH.:** 2 syms. (1900, 1910); *Mon lac* for Piano and Orch. (Lyons, Nov. 20, 1921); *Introduction et Danse* for Violin and Orch. (Paris, Oct. 10, 1937). **CHAMBER:** Piano Quintet (1897); String Quartet (1902); Violin Sonata (1907). **VOCAL:** *Poème de la maison* for Solo Voices, Chorus, and Orch. (Lyons, Jan. 25, 1919); *4 poèmes du coeur innombrable* for Voices and Orch. (1925); *3 poèmes de Ronsard* for Voices and Orch. (1935); *Paysage rêve* for Voices and Orch. (1937);

BIBL.: M. Boucher, "G.-M. W.," *Revue Musicale* (March 1926).

Wittgenstein, Paul, noted Austrian-born American pianist and teacher; b. Vienna, Nov. 5, 1887; d. Manhasset, N.Y., March 3, 1961. He was of a musical family; studied piano with Malvine Brée and Theodor Leschetizky and theory with Josef Labor. He made his first public appearance as a pianist in 1913 in Vienna. He lost his right arm in World War I, at the Russian front; was a prisoner of war in Omsk, Siberia; was repatriated in 1916. He then developed an extraordinary technique for left hand alone, and performed a concerto specially composed for him by his teacher, Labor. Wittgenstein subsequently commissioned left-hand piano concertos from Richard Strauss, Ravel, Prokofiev, Korngold, Benjamin Britten, and other composers, of which he gave the premieres (except the Prokofiev concerto, which he found unsuitable). He appeared in the major musical centers in Europe; toured America in 1934; in 1938, settled in N.Y.; became a naturalized American citizen in 1946. He taught privately in N.Y. (1938–60); also at the Ralph Wolfe Cons. in New Rochelle (1938–43), and at Manhattanville College of the Sacred Heart (1940–45). John Barchilon's novel *The Crown Prince* (1984) is based on his career. He was a brother of the famous philosopher Ludwig Wittgenstein.

Wittinger, Robert, Austrian-born German composer; b. Knittelfeld, April 10, 1945. He grew up in Budapest, where he studied with Zsolt Durkó; then studied in Warsaw (1964), received training in electronic music in Munich (1965), and attended the summer courses in new music in Darmstadt (1965–68); subsequently was active at the Villa Massimo in Rome on a scholarship (1972–73). His technique of composition is sonoristic, with sound blocks forming thematic groups, while the continuity is achieved by Baroque formulas; the titles of his pieces are often indicative of their construction.

WORKS: ORCH.: 3 syms.: No. 1 (1962–63; rev. 1976), No. 2 for Women's Chorus and Orch. (1978–80), and No. 3, *Funèbre* (1982); *Dissoziazioni* (1964); *Consonante* for English Horn and Orch. (1965); *Espressioni*, ballet music (1966); *Concentrazione* (1966); *Compensazioni* for Small Orch. (1967); *Irreversibilitazione* for Cello and Orch. (1967); *Om* (1968); *Divergenti* (West Berlin, Oct. 4, 1970); *Sinfonia* for Strings (1970); *Costellazioni* (Stuttgart, Sept. 25, 1971); *Montaggio*, concerto No. 1 for Small Orch. (1972); *Relazioni* for 7 Soloists and Orch. (West Berlin, April 11, 1972); Concerto for Oboe, Harp, and Strings (1972); *Concerto Polemica* (1975); *Concerto Lirico* (1977); *Concerto Entusiastico* (1977); Concerto for 2 Pianos and Orch. (1981); *Concerto Grosso* (1983); *Intreccio*, sinfonietta (1985); Violin Concerto (1988); *Cronogramme I* for Strings, Harp, Piano, and Percussion (1992–93; Graz, Oct. 8, 1993). **CHAMBER:** 4 string quartets (1964, 1966, 1970, 1977); *Concentrazioni*, wind quintet (1965); *Itrospezioni* for Bassoon (1967); *Tendenze* for Piano, Cello, and Percussion (1970); *Tensioni*, wind quintet (1970); *Tolleranza* for Oboe, Celesta, and Percussion (1970); *6 Strutture simmetriche*, each for a different Solo Instrument (1970); *Sillogismo* for Violin and Percussion (1974); *Dialoghi e scherzino* for 2 Pianos (1985). **VOCAL:** *Catalizzazioni* for 24 Vocalists and 7 Instrumentalists (1972); *Maldoror-Requiem* for Chorus and Orch. (1984–86).

Wittrisch, Marcel, German tenor; b. Antwerp, Oct. 1, 1901; d. Stuttgart, June 3, 1955. He studied at the Munich and Leipzig conservatories. He made his operatic debut as Konrad in *Hans Heiling* in Halle in 1925; then sang in Braunschweig (1927–29); in 1929 he became a member of the Berlin State Opera, where he sang leading roles until 1943; also made guest appearances at Covent Garden in London (1931) and at Bayreuth (1937); in 1950 he joined the Stuttgart Opera, where he remained until his death. In addition to his operatic career, he gained wide renown as a concert singer.

Wixell, Ingvar, Swedish baritone; b. Luleå, May 7, 1931. He received his training at the Stockholm Musikhögskolan. In 1952 he made his concert debut in Gavle and in 1955 his operatic debut as Papageno at the Royal Theater in Stockholm, where he sang regularly from 1956. In 1960 he sang with the Royal Opera on its visit to London's Covent Garden. He made his first appearance at the Glyndebourne Festival in 1962 as Cuglielmo. In 1966 he made his debut at the Salzburg Festival as Count Almaviva, and continued to sing there until 1969. From 1967 he sang at the Deutsche Oper in Berlin, and made his U.S. debut as Belcore in Chicago that same year. In 1971 he made his first appearance at the Bayreuth Festival as the Herald in *Lohengrin*. In 1972 he made his debut at Covent Garden as Simon Boccanegra, and continued to sing there regularly until 1977. On Jan. 29, 1973, he made his Metropolitan Opera debut in N.Y. as Rigoletto, where he made occasional appearances until 1980. He sang Amonasro in Houston in 1987. From 1987 to 1990 he sang once more at Covent Garden. In 1990 he appeared as Scarpia in Stuttgart, which role he then sang at Earl's Court in London in 1991. Among his other roles were Don Giovanni, Marcello, Germont, and Mandryka.

Wlaschiha, Ekkehard, German baritone; b. Pirna, May 28, 1938. He was trained in Leipzig. In 1961 he made his operatic debut as Don Fernando in *Fidelio* in Gera. After singing in Dresden and Weimar (1964–70), he was a member of the Leipzig Opera from 1970. From 1983 he sang at the Berlin State Opera. In 1985 he appeared as Kaspar in *Der Freischütz* in the reopening of the Semper Opera House in Dresden. He made his debut at the Bayreuth Festival as Kurwenal in 1986. For his first appearance at London's Covent Garden in 1990, he sang Alberich in *Siegfried*. Among his other roles are Pizzaro, Tonio, Telramund, Scarpia, and Jochanaan.

Wohl, Yehuda, German-born Israeli composer; b. Berlin, March 5, 1904; d. Tel Aviv, July 12, 1988. He went to Palestine in 1933 and had private studies with Ben-Haim in Tel Aviv; taught until 1972. Under the pseudonym Yehuda Bentow, he wrote popular songs in the ethnic style.

WORKS: RADIO OPERAS: *Hagadér* (1947); *The Circle* (1976). **ORCH.:** 3 syms. (1944, 1946, 1954); *Rondo patetico* for Strings (1950); *Miriam-Danze* (1955); *Discussione* for Piano and Orch. (1956); *Fata morgana* (1960); *Canto capricioso* (1967); *With Mixed Feelings* for Piano, Percussion, and Strings (1970); *Light and Shadow* (1972); *Those Were the Days* (1973); *Festival Overture* (1979). **CHAMBER:** *Quartetto appassionato* for String Quartet (1949); *Duo sensible* for Violin and Piano (1951); *Diary* for Flute, Oboe, Clarinet, and Bassoon (1961); *Associations* for Chamber Ensemble (1966); *Hagashot* (Encounters) for Chamber Ensemble (1968); *Atmosphere* for Organ and Tape (1970); *Trigon* for Piano Trio (1971); *Faces* for Brass Ensemble and Percussion (1973); many piano pieces. **VOCAL:** *Tagore-Songs* for 2 Voices, Piano, and Flute (1955); *An Arch Smile* for Narrator and Orch. (1959).

Woikowski-Biedau, Viktor Hugo von, German composer; b. Nieder-Arnsdorf, near Schweidnitz, Sept. 2, 1866; d. Berlin, Jan. 1, 1935. He studied music with Wilhelm Berger in Berlin; was employed in the government statistics bureau.

WORKS: 3 operas: *Helga* (Wiesbaden, 1904), *Der lange Kerl* (Berlin, 1906), and *Das Nothemd* (Dessau, 1913); 3 melodramas: *Jung Olaf, Der Todspieler,* and *Die Mette von Marienburg*; 4 ballads for Baritone and Orch.: *Die Jüdin von Worms, Der Triumph des Lebens, Rahab, die Jerichonitin,* and *Jan van Jühren*; *Aus einem Menschenleben* for Violin and Piano; song cycles (*Frühlingslieder; Lebensträume; Schiffslieder; Königslieder; Pagen-Balladen; Osterzauber; Des Sultans Gesetz*; etc.).

Wöldike, Mogens, Danish organist, conductor, and composer; b. Copenhagen, July 5, 1897; d. there, Oct. 20, 1988. He studied with Thomas Laube and Carl Nielsen in Copenhagen, where he also attended the Univ. (1920). From 1919 he was active as an organist and choirmaster in Copenhagen churches; in 1931 he became organist at the Christiansborg Palace Church, which post he held at the Copenhagen Cathedral (1959–72); from 1937 to 1977 he also appeared as a conductor with the Danish Radio. With his son-in-law, **Jens Peter Larsen**, he ed. the hymnbook of the Danish Church (1954, 1973); he also publ. 3 vols. of organ music (Copenhagen, 1943, 1960, 1982).

Wolf, Johannes, eminent German musicologist; b. Berlin, April 17, 1869; d. Munich, May 25, 1947. He studied at the Hochschule für Musik in Berlin; took courses in musicology at the Univ. of Berlin with Philipp Spitta and Heinrich Bellermann, and then with Riemann at the Univ. of Leipzig, where he received his Ph.D. in 1893 with the diss. *Ein anonymer Musiktraktat des 11. bis 12. Jahrhunderts*; he completed his Habilitation at the Univ. of Berlin with his *Florenz in der Musikgeschichte des 14. Jahrhunderts* in 1902, and then taught the history of early music and church music there; also was on the faculty of the Berlin Akademie für Kirchen- und Schulmusik from 1908 to 1927. He was appointed director of the early music collection of the Prussian Library in Berlin in 1915; from 1927 to 1934 he was director of its entire music collection. He was a leading authority on medieval and Renaissance music; his writings on the history of notation are especially important. He ed. a complete edition of the works of Obrecht (Leipzig, 1908–21); for Denkmäler Deutscher Tonkunst, he selected vocal works of J.R. Ahle (vol. V, 1901) and G. Rhau's *Newe deudsche geistliche Gesenge für die gemeinen Schulen* (vol. XXXIV, 1908); for Denkmäler der Tonkunst in Österreich, he ed. H. Isaac's secular works (vols. XXVIII, Jg.XIV/1, 1907, and XXXIII, Jg.XVI/1, 1909); also ed. *Der Squarcialupi-Codex aus dem Nachlass herausgegeben von H. Albrecht* (Lippstadt, 1955).

WRITINGS: *Geschichte der Mensuralnotation von 1250 bis 1460 nach den theoretischen und praktischen Quellen* (Leipzig, 1904); *Handbuch der Notationskunde* (2 parts, Leipzig, 1913, 1919); *Musikalische Schrifttafeln* (Leipzig, 1922–23; 2nd ed., 1927); *Die Tonschriften* (Breslau, 1924); *Geschichte der Musik in allgemeinverständlicher Form* (3 vols., Leipzig, 1925–29).

BIBL.: W. Lott, H. Osthoff, and W. Wolffheim, eds., *Musikwissenschaftliche Beiträge: Festschrift für J. W. zu seinem 60. Geburtstag* (Berlin, 1929); O. Gombosi, "J. W.," *Musical Quarterly* (April 1948); O. Kinkeldey, "J. W.," *Journal of the American Musicological Society* (Spring 1948).

Wolfe, Jacques (Leon), Romanian-American pianist, teacher, composer, and photographer, father of **Paul (Cecil) Wolfe;** b. Botoshan, April 29, 1896; d. Bradenton, Fla., June 22, 1973. He was taken to the U.S. in 1898 and studied with Friskin (piano) and Goetschius (composition) at the Inst. of Musical Art in N.Y. (graduated, 1915). After serving as a clarinetist in the 50th Infantry Band during World War I, he taught music in N.Y. public schools and made appearances as a pianist. In 1947 he settled in Miami, where he became well known as a photographer. Wolfe was especially adept at composing songs and making arrangements in the manner of spirituals. Among his most famous songs were *De Glory Road, Gwine to Hebb'n,* and *Shortnin' Bread.* He also composed 3 operas, including *John Henry* (1939) and *Mississippi Legend* (1951), chamber music, piano pieces, and choral works.

Wolfe, Paul (Cecil), American conductor, violinist, harpsichordist, and oboist, son of **Jacques (Leon) Wolfe**; b. N.Y., May 8, 1926. He commenced musical training as a child and made his debut as a violinist at N.Y.'s Barbison Hall in 1938. He studied at Queen's College in N.Y. (1942–45) and received training in violin from Mischakoff, Shumsky, Totenberg, and Varid, in oboe from Anton Maly, and in conducting from Barzin and Fritz Mahler. From 1946 to 1949 he was concertmaster and assistant conductor of the U.S. Air Force Orch. in Washington, D.C. He was assistant conductor of the National Orchestral Assn. (1950–61) and conductor of the Florida West Coast Sym. Orch. in Sarasota, a position he held for 35 years. He also remained active as an instrumentalist.

Wolfe, Stanley, American composer and music educator; b. N.Y., Feb. 7, 1924. He was a student of Bergsma, Persichetti, and Mennin at the Juilliard School of Music in N.Y. (B.S., 1952; M.S., 1955). In 1955 he joined its faculty and taught theory, contemporary music, and composition. From 1956 until his retirement in 1989 he served as director of the Juilliard Extension Division. In 1957 he held a Guggenheim fellowship. He received the Alice M. Ditson/American Sym. Orch. prize in 1961. In 1969, 1970, and 1977 he held NEA grants. In 1990 he received a citation and recording award from the American Academy and Inst. of Arts and Letters. In his music, Wolfe has eschewed avant-garde experimentation and has opted to infuse his well-crafted scores with welcome lyricism and melody.

WORKS: DRAMATIC: *King's Heart,* dance piece (1956). **ORCH.:** 7 syms.: No. 1 (1952), No. 2 (1955), No. 3 (Albuquerque, Nov. 18, 1959), No. 4 (1965; Albuquerque, Dec. 7, 1966), No. 5 (N.Y., April 2, 1971), No. 6 (1981), and No. 7 (1995); *Canticle* for Strings (1957); *Lincoln Square Overture* (1958); *Variations* (1967); Violin Concerto (1989). **CHAMBER:** *Adagio* for Woodwind Quintet (1948); String Quartet (1961).

Wolfes, Felix, German-American pianist, conductor, teacher, and composer; b. Hannover, Sept. 2, 1892; d. Boston, March 28, 1971. He was a pupil of Reger (theory) and Teichmüller (piano) at the Leipzig Cons., and of Pfitzner (composition) in Strasbourg. In 1923 he made his debut as a conductor at the Breslau Opera. From 1924 to 1931 he conducted in Essen. In 1931 he became music director of the Dortmund Opera, but when the Nazis came to power in 1933 Wolfes went to Paris. In 1936–37 he conducted the Monte Carlo Opera. In 1938 he emigrated to the U.S. He taught at the New England Cons. of Music in Boston, and also made some appearances as a pianist. As a teacher, he was especially admired for his knowledge of the vocal repertoire. He publ. a collection of songs (5 vols., 1962) which reveal him as a gifted composer in the late Romantic lieder tradition.

Wolff, Albert (Louis), noted French conductor and composer; b. Paris (of Dutch parents), Jan. 19, 1884; d. there, Feb. 20, 1970. He studied with Leroux, Gédalge, and Vidal at the Paris Cons. From 1906 to 1910 he was organist of St. Thomas Aquinas in Paris. In 1908 he became a member of the staff of the Paris Opéra-Comique; after serving as its chorus master, he made his conducting debut there, leading the premiere of Laparra's *La Jota*, on April 26, 1911. From 1919 to 1921 he was conductor of the French repertoire at the Metropolitan Opera in N.Y.; conducted the premiere of his opera *L'Oiseau bleu* there on Dec. 27, 1919. Upon his return to Paris in 1921, he was music director of the Opéra-Comique until 1924; in 1925 he became 2nd conductor of the Concerts Pasdeloup, and then was principal conductor from 1934 to 1940; also was conductor of the Concerts Lamoureux from 1928 to 1934. He toured South America from 1940 to 1945; then returned to Paris, where he was director-general of the Opéra-Comique in 1945–46; thereafter he continued to conduct occasionally there; also at the Paris Opéra from 1949; in addition, he made appearances as a sym. conductor. He particularly distinguished himself as a champion of French music of his era; he conducted the premieres of Debussy's *La Boîte à joujoux*, Ravel's *L'Enfant et les sortilèges*, Roussel's Sym. No. 4, and Poulenc's *Les Mamelles de Tirésias*.

WORKS: OPERAS: *Soeur Beatrice* (1911; Nice, 1948); *Le marchand de masques* (Nice, 1914); *L'Oiseau bleu* (N.Y., Dec. 27, 1919). **ORCH.:** *La randonnée de l'âme défunte*, symphonic poem (1926); Flute Concerto (1943); Sym. (1951). **OTHER:** *Requiem* for Soloists, Chorus, and Orch. (1939); other vocal music; chamber pieces; film music.

Wolff, Beverly, American mezzo-soprano; b. Atlanta, Nov. 6, 1928. She learned to play the trumpet and then played in the Atlanta Sym. Orch.; subsequently received vocal training from Sidney Dietch and Vera McIntyre at the Academy of Vocal Arts in Philadelphia. In 1952 she won the Philadelphia Youth Auditions and made her formal debut with Ormandy and the Philadelphia Orch.; also appeared as Dinah in the television premiere of Bernstein's *Trouble in Tahiti*. On April 6, 1958, she made her N.Y. City Opera debut as Dinah, and subsequently sang there regularly until 1971; also was a guest artist with various other opera companies in the U.S. and abroad.

Wolff, Christian, French-born American composer and teacher; b. Nice, March 8, 1934. He went to the U.S. in 1941 and became a naturalized citizen in 1946. He studied piano with Grete Sultan (1949–51) and composition with John Cage (1950–51); then pursued training in classical languages at Harvard Univ. (B.A., 1955); after studying Italian literature and classics at the Univ. of Florence (1955–56), he returned to Harvard (Ph.D. in comparative literature, 1963). From 1962 to 1970 he taught classics at Harvard; in 1971 he joined the faculty of Dartmouth College to teach classics, comparative literature, and music; was made prof. of music and of classics in 1978; also was a guest lecturer at various institutions of higher learning; contributed articles on literature and music to many publications. He evolved a curiously static method of composition, using drastically restricted numbers of pitches. His only structural resources became arithmetical progressions of rhythmic values and the expressive use of rests. He used 3 different pitches in his Duo for Violin and Piano; 4 different pitches in the Trio for Flute, Cello, and Trumpet (1951); 9 in a piano piece called *For Piano I*. Beginning in 1957 he introduced into his works various degrees of free choice; sometimes the players are required to react to the musical activities of their partners according to spontaneous and unanticipated cues.

WORKS: Trio for Flute, Trumpet, and Cello (1951); *Summer* for String Quartet (1961); *For 5 or 10 Players* for Any Instruments (1962); *In Between Pieces* for 3 Players Using Any Sound Sources (1963); *For 1, 2 or 3 People* for Any Sound-producing Means (1964); Septet for Any 7 Players and Conductor (1964); *Pairs* for Any 2, 4, 6, or 8 Players (1968); *Prose Collection* for Variable Numbers of Players, Found and Constructed Materials, Instruments, and Voices (1968–71); *Lines* for String Quartet (1972); *Changing the System* for 8 or More Instruments, Voices, and Percussion (1972–73); *Wobbly Music* for Chorus, Keyboard, Guitars, and at Least 2 Melody Instruments (1975–76); *Braverman Music* for Chamber Ensemble (1978); *Rock About, Instrumental, Starving to Death on a Government Claim* for Violin and Viola (1979–80); *Isn't This a Time* for Any Saxophone or Multiple Reeds (1982); *Peace March 1* for Flute (1983–84), *2* for Flute, Clarinet, Cello, Percussion, and Piano (1984), and *3* for Flute, Cello, and Percussion (1984); *Leaning Forward* for Soprano, Baritone, Clarinet, and Cello (1988); *Emma* for Viola, Cello, and Piano (1989); *Rosas* for Piano and Percussion (1990).

Wolff, Christoph (Johannes), eminent German musicologist; b. Solingen, May 24, 1940. He studied church music at the Berlin Hochschule für Musik and in Freiburg im Breisgau; took courses in musicology at the univs. of Berlin and Erlangen; obtained his Ph.D. in 1966 from the latter (diss., *Der stile antico in der Musik Johann Sebastian Bachs: Studien zu Bachs Spätwerk*, publ. in Wiesbaden, 1968). He taught at the Univ. of Erlangen (1965–69); also at the Univ. of Toronto (1968–70); then at Columbia Univ. (1970–76). In 1976 he became a prof. of music at Harvard Univ. He has written extensively on the history of music from the 15th to the 20th century, particularly on Bach and Mozart. He has distinguished himself by innovative research into formative elements in Bach's works. He became ed. of the *Bach-Jahrbuch* in 1974; ed. vols. of the *Neue Bach-Ausgabe* (V/2, *Goldberg Variations*; 14 Canons; VIII/1, *Musical Offering*; Canons); the *Neue Mozart-Ausgabe* (V/15, 2–3, Piano Concertos), and the *Hindemith-Gesamtausgabe* (opera *Cardillac*, op. 39). He wrote the major portion of the article on the Bach family for *The New Grove Dictionary of Music and Musicians* (1980); also ed. *The String Quartets of Haydn, Mozart, and Beethoven: Studies of the Autograph Manuscripts* (Cambridge, Mass., 1980) and with H.-J. Schulze, *Bach Compendium: Analytisch-bibliographisches Repertorium der Werke Johann Sebastian Bachs* (5 vols., Leipzig and Dresden, 1985 et seq.). Wolff publ. *Bach: Essays on His Life and Music* (Cambridge, Mass., 1991) and *Mozart's Requiem: Historical and Analytical Studies, Documents, Score* (Berkeley, 1993). In 1984 he discovered 31 unknown organ chorales by Bach in the Neumeister Collection of the music library at Yale Univ.; they were publ. in 1985. In 1978 he was awarded the Dent Medal of the Royal Musical Assn. of London and in 1982 he was elected a Fellow of the American Academy of Arts and Sciences.

Wolff, Fritz, German tenor; b. Munich, Oct. 28, 1894; d. there, Jan. 18, 1957. He studied with Heinrich König in Würzburg. He made his operatic debut as Loge in 1925 at the Bayreuth Festival, where he continued to make appearances until 1941; also sang in Hagen and Chemnitz. In 1930 he joined the Berlin State Opera, remaining on its roster until 1943; also made guest appearances at Covent Garden in London (1929–33; 1937–38), and in Vienna, Paris, Chicago, and Cleveland. From 1950 he was a prof. at the Hochschule für Musik in Munich. His finest roles included Parsifal and Lohengrin.

Wolff, Hellmuth Christian, German musicologist and composer; b. Zürich, May 23, 1906; d. Leipzig, July 1, 1988. He studied musicology at the Univ. of Berlin with Abert, Schering, Blume, and Sachs (Ph.D., 1932, with the diss. *Die Venezianische Oper in der zweiten Hälfte des 17. Jahrhunderts*; publ. in Berlin, 1937; 2nd ed., 1975). He completed his Habilitation at the Univ. of Kiel in 1942 with his *Die Barockoper in Hamburg 1678–1738* (publ. in Wolfenbüttel, 1957). From 1954 to 1971 he was a prof. of musicology at the Univ. of Leipzig. Beginning in 1956 he devoted a great deal of his time to painting, and exhibited in Leipzig and other German cities.

WORKS: DRAMATIC: OPERAS: *Der kleine und der grosse Klaus* (1931; rev. 1940); *Die törichten Wünsche* (1942–43); *Der Tod des Orpheus* (1947); *Ich lass' mich scheiden* (1950). **BALLET:** *Moresca* (1969). **SCENIC ORATORIO:** *Esther* (1945). Also incidental music. **ORCH.:** *3 Werke* for Chamber Orch. (1932); *Concerto for Orchestra* (1933); Concerto for Oboe and Chamber

Orch. (1933); *Heitere Musik über ostinate Rhythmen* (1938); Suite (1940); *Inferno 1944* (1946); *Serenade* for Strings (1946); Concerto for Piano and Strings (1947); Violin Concerto (1948); *Sinfonia da missa* (1949); Double Bass Concerto (1968); *Handel Suite* (1970); *Paul Klee Suite* (1973). **OTHER:** Chamber music; piano pieces; songs.

WRITINGS: *Agrippina, eine italienische Jugendoper von G. Fr. Händel* (Wolfenbüttel and Berlin, 1943); *Die Musik der alten Niederländer (15. und 16. Jahrhundert)* (Leipzig, 1956); *Die Händel-Oper auf der modernen Bühne* (Leipzig, 1957); *Oper: Szene und Darstellung von 1600 bis 1900* (Leipzig, 1968); *Die Oper* (3 vols., Cologne, 1971–72; also in Eng.); *Ordnung und Gestalt: die Musik von 1900 bis 1950* (Bonn, 1977).

Wolff, Hugh (MacPherson), American conductor; b. Paris (of American parents), Oct. 21, 1953. He was taken to the U.S. by his family when he was 10; studied piano with Fleisher and Shure and composition with Crumb; then received instruction in composition from Kirchner at Harvard Univ. (B.A., 1975). After studying composition with Messiaen, piano with Sancan, and conducting with Bruck at the Paris Cons., he completed his training with Fleisher at the Peabody Inst. in Baltimore (M.M. in piano, 1977; M.M. in conducting, 1978). He was Exxon/Arts Endowment Conductor (1979–82) and assoc. conductor (1982–85) of the National Sym. Orch. in Washington, D.C.; also was music director of the Northeastern Pennsylvania Phil. (1981–86); likewise appeared as a guest conductor throughout the U.S.; made his European debut with the London Phil. (1983). In 1985 he became the first co-recipient (with Kent Nagano) of the Affiliated Artists' Seaver Conducting Award. He was music director of the New Jersey Sym. Orch. (1985–92), and then its principal guest conductor (1992–93). In 1986 he made his N.Y. City Opera debut conducting *Le nozze di Figaro*. From 1988 to 1991 he was principal conductor of the St. Paul (Minn.) Chamber Orch., then became its music director in 1991. He also was principal conductor of the Grant Park Sym. Orch. in Chicago from 1994 and chief conductor of the Frankfurt am Main Radio Sym. Orch. from 1995.

Wolf-Ferrari (real name, **Wolf**), **Ermanno,** famous Italian opera composer; b. Venice, Jan. 12, 1876; d. there, Jan. 21, 1948. His father was a well-known painter of German descent and his mother was Italian; about 1895 he added his mother's maiden name to his surname. He began piano study as a small child but also evinced a talent for art; after studying at the Accademia di Belle Arti in Rome (1891–92), he went to Munich to continue his training but then turned to music and studied counterpoint with Rheinberger at the Akademie der Tonkunst (1892–95). In 1899 he returned to Venice, where his oratorio *La Sulamite* was successfully performed. This was followed by the production of his first major opera, *Cenerentola* (1900), which initially proved a failure; however, its revised version for Bremen (1902) was well received and established his reputation as a composer for the theater. From 1903 to 1909 he was director of the Liceo Benedetto Marcello in Venice; then devoted himself mainly to composition; later was prof. of composition at the Salzburg Mozarteum (1939–45). He obtained his first unqualified success with the production of the comic opera *Le donne curiose* (Munich, 1903); the next opera, *I quattro rusteghi* (Munich, 1906), was also well received; there followed his little masterpiece, *Il segreto di Susanna* (Munich, 1909), a one-act opera buffa in the style of the Italian verismo (Susanna's secret being not infidelity, as her husband suspected, but indulgence in surreptitious smoking). Turning toward grand opera, he wrote *I gioielli della Madonna*; it was brought out at Berlin in 1911, and soon became a repertoire piece everywhere; he continued to compose, but his later operas failed to match the appeal of his early creations.

WORKS: OPERAS: *Cenerentola* (Venice, Feb. 22, 1900; rev. version as *Aschenbrödel*, Bremen, Jan. 31, 1902); *Le Donne curiose* (1902–03; in Ger. as *Die neugierigen Frauen*, Munich, Nov. 27, 1903; in Italian, N.Y., Jan. 3, 1912); *I quattro rusteghi* (in Ger. as *Die vier Grobiane*, Munich, March 19, 1906); *Il segreto di Susanna* (in Ger. as *Susannens Geheimnis*, Munich, Dec. 4, 1909; in Italian, N.Y., March 14, 1911); *I gioielli della Madonna* (in Ger. as *Der Schmuck der Madonna*, Berlin, Dec. 23, 1911; in Italian, Chicago, Jan. 16, 1912; in Eng. as *The Jewels of the Madonna*, N.Y., Oct. 14, 1913); *L'amore medico* (in Ger. as *Der Liebhaber als Arzt*, Dresden, Dec. 4, 1913; in Italian, N.Y., March 25, 1914); *Gli Amanti sposi* (c.1916; Venice, Feb. 19, 1925); *Das Himmelskleid* (c.1917–25; Munich, April 21, 1927; in Italian as *La veste di cielo*); *Sly, ovvero La leggenda del dormiente risvegliato* (Milan, Dec. 29, 1927); *La vedova scaltra* (Rome, March 5, 1931); *Il campiello* (Milan, Feb. 11, 1936); *La dama boba* (Milan, Feb. 1, 1939); *Gli dei a Tebe* (in Ger. as *Der Kuckuck in Theben*, Hannover, June 5, 1943); also an ed. of Mozart's *Idomeneo* (Munich, June 15, 1931). **ORCH.:** *Serenade* for Strings (c.1893); *Kammersymphonie* (1901); *Idillio-concertino* for Oboe, 2 Horns, and Strings (1933); *Suite-concertino* for Bassoon, 2 Horns, and Strings (Rome, March 26, 1933); *Suite veneziano* for Small Orch. (1936); *Divertimento* (1937); *Arabeschi* (1940); Violin Concerto (1946); *Symphonia brevis* (1947); Cello Concerto (c.1947). **CHAMBER:** String Quintet (1894); 3 violin sonatas (1895, 1901, c.1940); 2 piano trios (c.1897, 1900); Piano Quintet (1900); String Quartet (1940); String Quintet (1942); String Trio (1946); *Introduzione e balletto* for Violin and Cello (1946); piano pieces. **VOCAL:** *La Sulamite*, canto biblico (1889); *Talitha kumi*, oratorio (1900); *La vita nuova*, cantata (1901; Munich, Feb. 21, 1903); *La passione* for Chorus (1939; also for Voice and Piano, 1940); other large and small choral works.

BIBL.: H. Teibler, *E. W.-F.* (Leipzig, 1906); E. Stahl, ed., *E. W.-F.* (Salzburg, 1936); R. de Rensis, *E. W.-F., La sua vita d'artista* (Milan, 1937); A. Grisson, *E. W.-F.: autorisierte Lebensbeschreibung* (Regensburg, 1941; 2nd ed., enl., 1958); R. de Rensis and G. Vannini, *In memoria di E. W.-F.* (Siena, 1948); W. Pfannkuch, *Das Opernschaffen E. W.-F.s* (diss., Univ. of Kiel, 1952); A. Suder, ed., *E. W.-F.* (Tutzing, 1986).

Wolfurt, Kurt von, German composer; b. Lettin, Sept. 7, 1880; d. Munich, Feb. 25, 1957. He studied science at the univs. of Dorpat, Leipzig, and Munich; then took lessons in composition with Reger and in piano with Krause in Munich. He eventually went to Berlin as a teacher at the municipal cons. (1936–45); later taught in Göttingen (1945–49) and in Johannesburg (1949–52). He publ. monographs on Mussorgsky (Stuttgart, 1927) and Tchaikovsky (Zürich, 1951). Among his works is the opera *Dame Kobold* (Kassel, March 14, 1940); *Gesang des Meeres*, symphonic poem; Concerto grosso for Chamber Orch. (1931); Piano Concerto (1933); *Serenade* for Orch. (1936); *Sinfonia classica* (c.1947); Cello Concerto (c.1948); chamber music; vocal works; etc.

Wolpe, Stefan, significant German-American composer and pedagogue; b. Berlin, Aug. 25, 1902; d. N.Y., April 4, 1972. He studied theory with Juon and Schreker at the Berlin Hochschule für Musik (1919–24). After graduation, he became associated with choral and theatrical groups in Berlin, promoting social causes; composed songs on revolutionary themes. With the advent of the anti-Semitic Nazi regime in 1933, he went to Vienna, where he took lessons with Webern; then traveled to Palestine in 1934; taught at the Jerusalem Cons. In 1938 he emigrated to the U.S., where he devoted himself mainly to teaching; was on the faculty of the Settlement Music School in Philadelphia (1939–42); at the Philadelphia Academy of Music (1949–52); at Black Mountain College, N.C. (1952–56); and at Long Island Univ. (1957–68). He also taught privately. Among his students were Elmer Bernstein, Ezra Laderman, Ralph Shapey, David Tudor, and Morton Feldman. He was married successively to Ola Okuniewska, a painter, in 1927, to Irma Schoenberg (1902–84), a Romanian pianist, in 1934, and to Hilda Morley, a poet, in 1948. In 1966 he was elected a member of the National Inst. of Arts and Letters. He contributed numerous articles to German and American music magazines. In his style of composition, he attempted to reconcile the contradictions of triadic tonality (which he cultivated during his early period of writing "proletarian" music), atonality without procrustean dodecaphony, and serialism of contrasts obtained by intervallic contraction and expansion, metrical alteration, and dynamic variegation; superadded to these were explorations of Jewish cantillation and infatuation with jazz. Remarkably enough, the very copiousness of these resources contributed to a clearly identifiable idiom.

WORKS: DRAMATIC: OPERAS: *Schöne Geschichten* (1927–29); *Zeus und Elida* (1928). **BALLET:** *The Man from Midian* (1942). **INCIDENTAL MUSIC TO:** *De liegt Hund begraben* (1932); Bertolt Brecht's *The Good Woman of Setzuan* (1953) and *The Exception and the Rule* (1961); *Peer Gynt* (1954); *The Tempest* (1960). **ORCH.:** *Passacaglia* (1937); *The Man from Midian*, suite from the ballet (1942); Sym. (1955–56; rev. 1964); Piece for Piano and 16 Players (1961); *Chamber Piece No. 1* for 14 Players (1964) and *No. 2* for 13 Players (1965–66). **CHAMBER:** *Duo in Hexachord* for Oboe and Clarinet (1936); *Lied, Anrede, Hymnus* for Oboe and Piano (1939); Oboe Sonata (1941); Violin Sonata (1949); Quartet for Tenor Saxophone, Trumpet, Percussion, and Piano (1950; rev. 1954); *12 Pieces* for String Quartet (1950); *Piece* for Oboe, Cello, Percussion, and Piano (1955); Quintet for Clarinet, Horn, Cello, Harp, and Piano with Baritone (1957); *Piece in 2 Parts* for Flute and Piano (1960); *In 2 Parts* for Clarinet, Trumpet, Violin, Cello, Harp, and Piano (1962); *Piece for 2 Instrumental Units* for Flute, Oboe, Violin, Cello, Double Bass, Percussion, and Piano (1963); *Trio in 2 Parts* for Flute, Cello, and Piano (1964); *Piece in 2 Parts for Violin Alone* (1964); *Solo Piece* for Trumpet (1966); *Piece for Violin Alone* (1966); *From Here on Farther* for Clarinet, Bass Clarinet, Violin, and Piano (1969); String Quartet (1969); *Piece for Trumpet and 7 Instruments* for Trumpet, Clarinet, Bassoon, Horn, Violin, Viola, Cello, and Double Bass (1971). **PIANO:** *March and Variations* for 2 Pianos (1933); *4 Studies on Basic Rows* (1935–36); *Zemach Suite* (1939–41); *Pastorale* (1941); *Toccata* (1941); *Music for Any Instruments: Interval Studies* (1944–49); *Battle Piece* (1947); *2 Studies* (part 2, 1948); *Music for a Dancer* (1950); *7 Pieces* for 3 Pianos (1951); *Waltz for Merle* (1952); *Enactments* for 3 Pianos (1953); *Form* (1959); *Form IV: Broken Sequences* (1969). **VOCAL:** 4 cantatas: *Yigdal* for Baritone, Chorus, and Organ (1945), *Lazy Andy Ant* for Voice and 2 Pianos (1947), *Street Music* for Baritone, Speaker, Flute, Oboe, Clarinet, Cello, and Piano (1962), and Cantata for Mezzo-soprano, 3 Women's Voices, and 9 Instruments (1963); choral songs; solo songs.

BIBL.: H. Sucoff, *Catalogue and Evaluation of the Work of S. W.* (N.Y., 1969); M. Babbitt, E. Carter, L. Stempel, and C. Wuorinen, "In Memoriam S. W.," *Perspectives of New Music*, XI/1 (1972).

Wolpert, Franz Alfons, German composer and music theorist; b. Wiesentheid, Oct. 11, 1917; d. there, Aug. 7, 1978. He sang in the Cathedral choir in Regensburg, and studied there at a Catholic church music school; took lessons in composition with Wolf-Ferrari at the Salzburg Mozarteum (1939–41), where he subsequently taught (1941–44); was a teacher in Salem, Lake Constance (from 1950). He publ. the useful vol. *Neue Harmonik: die Lehre von den Akkordtypen* (Regensburg, 1952; 2nd ed., rev. and enl., 1972). His compositions include a comic opera, *Der eingebildete Kranke* (1975), a ballet, *Der goldene Schuh* (1956), *Banchetto musicale No. 1* for Violin and Chamber Orch. (1952) and *No. 2* for Piano and Orch. (1953), chamber music, organ and piano pieces, choral works, and over 50 lieder.

Wood, Charles, Irish pedagogue and composer; b. Armagh, June 15, 1866; d. Cambridge, England, July 12, 1926. He studied at the Royal College of Music in London, and subsequently taught harmony there; received his Mus.Doc. degree from Cambridge in 1894. He was a univ. lecturer in harmony and counterpoint there from 1897, succeeding Stanford as prof. of music in 1924. He wrote 6 string quartets (mostly in an Irish manner); vocal works with Orch.: *Ode on Time* (1898), *Dirge for 2 Veterans* (1901), *Song of the Tempest* (1902), and *Ballad of Dundee* (1904); a comic opera, *Pickwick Papers* (London, 1922); church music. He also ed. a collection of Irish folk songs (1897). He was the brother of the Irish organist and composer William G. Wood (b. Armagh, Jan. 16, 1859; d. London, Sept. 25, 1895).

Wood, Haydn, English violinist and composer; b. Slaithwaite, March 25, 1882; d. London, March 11, 1959. He entered the Royal College of Music in London at 15; studied there with Fernández Arbós (violin) and Stanford (composition); later studied with César Thomson in Brussels. His works include a Piano Concerto, a Violin Concerto, 8 overtures, 8 rhapsodies for band, 18 orch. studies, 31 entr'actes for orch., 12 violin solos, 2 flute pieces, 3 accordion solos, and about 200 songs.

Wood, Sir Henry J(oseph), eminent English conductor; b. London, March 3, 1869; d. Hitchin, Hertfordshire, Aug. 19, 1944. Of musical parentage, he was taught to play the piano by his mother; he participated in family musicales from the age of 6; was equally precocious on the organ; at the age of 10 he often acted as a deputy organist, and gave organ recitals at the Fisheries Exhibition (1883) and at the Inventions Exhibition (1885). In 1886 he entered the Royal Academy of Music in London, where his teachers were Prout, Steggall, Macfarren, and Garcia; he won 4 medals. In 1888 he brought out some of his songs; then composed light operas and cantatas. But soon his ambition crystallized in the direction of conducting; after making his debut in 1888, he was active with various theater companies. On Aug. 10, 1895, he began his first series of Promenade Concerts (the famous "Proms") in Queen's Hall, London, with an orch. of about 80 members. Their success was so conspicuous that a new series of concerts was inaugurated on Jan. 30, 1897, under Wood's direction, and flourished from the beginning. In 1899 he founded the Nottingham Orch.; also was conductor of the Wolverhampton Festival Choral Soc. (1900), the Sheffield Festival (1902–11), and the Norwich Festival (1908). In 1904 he was a guest conductor of the N.Y. Phil. He was married to Olga Urusova, a Russian noblewoman, and became greatly interested in Russian music, which he performed frequently at his concerts. He adopted a Russian pseudonym, Paul Klenovsky, for his compositions and arrangements, and supplied an imaginary biography of his alter ego for use in program notes. His wife died in 1909, and Wood married Muriel Greatorex in 1911. In 1921 he received the Gold Medal of the Royal Phil. Soc. He was made a Companion of Honour in 1944. In 1918 he was offered the conductorship of the Boston Sym. Orch. as successor to Muck, but declined. In 1923 he was appointed prof. of conducting and orch. playing at the Royal Academy of Music. Wood continued to conduct the Promenade Concerts almost to the end of his life, presenting the last concert on July 28, 1944. Among his popular arrangements were Chopin's *Marche Funèbre*, some works by Bach, and the *Trumpet Voluntary* (mistakenly attributed to Purcell, but actually by Jeremiah Clarke). He publ. *The Gentle Art of Singing* (4 vols.; 1927–28) and *About Conducting* (London, 1945), and ed. the *Handbook of Miniature Orchestral and Chamber Music Scores* (1937); wrote an autobiography, *My Life and Music* (London, 1938). A commemorative postage stamp with his portrait was issued by the Post Office of Great Britain on Sept. 1, 1980.

BIBL.: R. Newmarch, *H.J. W.* (London, 1904); T. Russell et al., eds., *Homage to Sir H. W.: A World Symposium* (London, 1944); W. Thompson et al., *Sir H. W.: Fifty Years of the Proms* (London, 1944); J. Wood, *The Last Years of H.J. W.* (London, 1954); R. Pound, *Sir H. W.: A Biography* (London, 1969); A. Orga, *The Proms* (London, 1974); D. Cox, *The H. W. Proms* (London, 1980); D. Lambourn, "H. W. and Schoenberg," *Musical Times* (Aug. 1987); A. Jacobs, *H.J. W.: Maker of the Proms* (London, 1994).

Wood, Hugh (Bradshaw), English composer and teacher; b. Parbold, Lancashire, June 27, 1932. After attending the Univ. of Oxford, he studied in London with W.S. Lloyd Webber, Anthony Milner, Iain Hamilton, and Mátyás Seiber. From 1958 to 1967 he taught at Morley College, London. He also was a prof. of harmony at the Royal Academy of Music in London from 1962 to 1965. After serving as a research fellow in composition at the Univ. of Glasgow (1966–70), he lectured on music at the univs. of Liverpool (1971–73) and Cambridge (from 1977). His output is reflective of contemporary compositional trends but not without a welcome infusion of lyricism undergirded by fine craftsmanship.

WORKS: ORCH.: Cello Concerto (1965–69); Violin Concerto (1970–72); Chamber Concerto (1971; rev. 1978); Sym. (1979–82); *Comus Quadrilles* for Small Orch. (1989); Piano Concerto (1990–91). **CHAMBER:** *Variations* for Viola and Piano (1958); 1 unnumbered string quartet (1959); 4 numbered string quartets (1960–62; 1969–70; 1976–78; 1992–93); Trio for Flute, Viola, and Piano (1961); Quintet for Clarinet, Horn, Violin, Cello, and Piano (1967); Piano Trio (1984); *Paraphrase on Bird of Paradise* for Clarinet and Piano (1985); Horn Trio (1987–89). **KEYBOARD: PIANO:** *3 Pieces* (1961). **ORGAN:** *Capriccio* (1968). **VOCAL:** *Laurie Lee Songs* for High Voice and Piano (1959; also for High Voice and Orch., 1986–87); *Scenes from Comus* for Soprano, Tenor, and Orch. (1962–65); *3 Choruses* (1965–66); *Song-Cycle to Poems of Neruda* for High Voice and Chamber Ensemble (1973–74); *To a friend whose work has come to nothing* for Chorus (1973–89); *A Christmas Poem* for Chorus (1984); *Marina* for High Voice, Violin, Alto Flute, Horn, Harp, and Viola (1988–89); many other songs.

Wood, Joseph, American composer and teacher; b. Pittsburgh, May 12, 1915. He was a student of Wagenaar at the Juilliard School of Music (graduated, 1949) and of Luening at Columbia Univ. (M.A., 1950) in N.Y. From 1950 to 1985 he was a prof. of composition at the Oberlin (Ohio) College Cons. of Music. He composed in a generally accessible vein with some excursions into serialism.

WORKS: DRAMATIC: *The Mother,* opera (1945); *The Progression,* ballet-cantata (1968); incidental music. **ORCH.:** 4 syms. (1939, 1952, 1958, 1983); *Divertimento* for Piano and Chamber Orch. (1959); Violin Concerto (1961); Concerto for Chamber Orch. (1973–74). **CHAMBER:** Piano Trio (1937); Viola Sonata (1938); 3 string quartets (1942, 1965, 1975); Violin Sonata (1947); Piano Quintet (1956); piano pieces. **VOCAL:** *Te Deum* for Chorus and Orch. (1982); choruses; songs.

Wood, Thomas, English composer and author; b. Chorley, Lancashire, Nov. 28, 1892; d. Bures, Essex, Nov. 19, 1950. He was educated at Exeter College, Oxford; then studied at the Royal Academy of Music in London with Stanford (composition) and Herbert Fryer (piano); subsequently took his D.Mus. at the Univ. of Oxford (1920). He was music director at Tonbridge School (1920–24); lecturer and precentor at Exeter College (1924–28). His extensive travels took him to the Far East and the Arctic; his familiarity with the sea was reflected in many of his compositions for Chorus and Orch., such as *40 Singing Seamen* (1925), *Master Mariners* (1927), and *Merchantmen* (1934), and in *A Seaman's Overture* for Orch. (1927). He ed. vol. II of the *Oxford Song Book* (1928; 3rd ed., 1937). His books include *Music and Boyhood* (1925) and the autobiographical *True Thomas* (1936); he also publ. *Cobbers* (on his Australian tour of 1930–32), which became highly popular in England, and a sequel to it, *Cobbers Campaigning* (1940).

BIBL.: N. Coghill, "T. W.," *Music & Letters* (April 1951).

Woodbury, Arthur N(eum), American composer, bassoonist, saxophonist, and teacher; b. Kimball, Nebr., June 20, 1930. He studied composition with William Billingsley at the Univ. of Idaho (B.S., 1951; M.M., 1955); after private composition lessons with Robert Morton in San Francisco (1956–57), he pursued postgraduate composition studies with Imbrie at the Univ. of Calif. at Berkeley (1957–58); later studied computer music at Stanford Univ. (1970). He pursued a vigorous career as a performer, both as a member of various orchs. and as a soloist; from 1963 to 1972 he taught at the Univ. of Calif. at Davis. From 1967 to 1972 he served as ed. of the avant-garde journal *Source.* In 1972 he joined the faculty of the Univ. of South Florida in Tampa, where he was a prof. from 1987. His early works were written in a traditional modern idiom; later he branched out as a composer of experimental music, making use of electronics and aleatory techniques.

WORKS: Woodwind Quartet (1955); Sym. (1958); *Introduction and Allegro* for Band (1965); *Autobiography: Patricia Belle* for Soprano, Live Electronics, and Amplified Instruments (1968); *Recall,* theater piece for Actor, Tape, and Live Electronics (1969); *Remembrances,* trio for Violin, Alto Saxophone, and Vibraphone (1969); *Velox,* computer piece (1970); *WernerVon-Braunasaurus Rex* for Electronic Piano, Guitar, and Moog Synthesizer (1979); *Jazz Fugue* for Saxophone Quartet and Accompaniment (1980); *Diversions* for Piano (1980–83); *Passacaglia, Interlude, and Canon* for Organ (1981; also for Concert Band, 1984); *Tocata española* for Marimba or Percussion and Cello (1983); *No More Jim Beam, Please* for Jazz Quartet (1985); *Learnin' the Blues* for Jazz Quintet (1986); *Wild Nights* for Voice and Piano (1988); *Variations on a Cadenza* for Flute and Percussion (1989); *3 Brief Pieces* for Clarinet and Bassoon (1990); *Homage to Erik* for Trumpet and Piano (1993); *When Nod Dreams* for 2 Oboes and English Horn (1994); *Little Serenade* for Guitar (1995).

Woodward, Roger (Robert), Australian pianist; b. Sydney, Dec. 20, 1942. He studied piano with Alexander Sverjensky in Sydney; then obtained a Polish government scholarship and went to Warsaw, where he took lessons with Zbigniew Drzwiecki. He won 1st prize in the Chopin Competition in 1968, an auspicious award that propelled him on an international career. In 1971 he settled in London, where he gained renown among international avant-garde composers by repeatedly performing works by such uncompromising celebrants of quaquaversal modern idioms as Takemitsu, Barraqué, Stockhausen, and Birtwistle; faithful to his antecedents, he also placed on his programs works of Australian composers such as Boyd, Meale, and Sculthorpe. He participated in several American concerts of contemporary music, including a marathon series presented in Los Angeles. In 1985 he played the complete works of Chopin in a series of 16 concerts. In 1986 he was soloist in the first performance of Xenakis's *Keqrops* with Zubin Mehta and the N.Y. Phil. In 1980 he was made an Officer of the Order of the British Empire.

Woodworth, G(eorge) Wallace, American choral conductor, organist, and music educator; b. Boston, Nov. 6, 1902; d. Cambridge, Mass., July 18, 1969. He was educated at Harvard Univ. (B.A., 1924; M.A., 1926); then studied conducting with Malcolm Sargent at the Royal College of Music in London (1927–28). In 1924 he joined the staff of the music dept. at Harvard, and was engaged as conductor of the Radcliffe Choral Soc.; also led the Pierian Sodality Orch. of Harvard Univ. (1928–32) and the Harvard Glee Club (1933–38). In 1940 he was appointed organist and choirmaster for the Harvard Univ. Chapel. He was made James Edward Ditson Professor of Music at Harvard in 1954. He conducted the Harvard-Radcliffe Chorus on its transcontinental U.S. tour in 1954, and took the Harvard Glee Club on its European tour in 1956. He retired in 1969. Woodworth publ. *The World of Music* (Cambridge, Mass., 1964).

BIBL.: L. Berman, ed., *Words and Music: The Composer's View: A Medley of Problems and Solutions in Honor of G.W. W.* (Cambridge, 1972).

Wooldridge, David (Humphry Michael), English conductor, writer on music, and composer; b. Deal, Aug. 24, 1927. He was the grandson of H.E. Wooldridge and godson of Rachmaninoff. He began violin lessons at 6 and made his conducting debut at 16. After graduating from the Univ. of London (1952), he was apprenticed to Krauss at the Vienna State Opera. In 1954–55 he was at the Bavarian State Opera in Munich. After guest conducting in the U.S., he was music director of the Lebanese National Orch. in Beirut (1961–65) and conductor of the Cape Town Sym. Orch. (1965–67). He was the author of *Conductor's*

World (N.Y., 1970) and *From the Steeples and Mountains: A Study of Charles Ives* (N.Y., 1974).

WORKS: DRAMATIC: 3 ballets: *Les Parapluies* (1956), *Octet* (1958), and *Movements* (1970); *The Duchess of Amalfi*, opera (1978); incidental music; film scores. **ORCH.:** Viola Concerto (1949); Cello Concerto (1957); *Suite Libanaise* (1962); *4 Armenian Dances* (1964); *Partita* (1968); *The Legend of Lillanonah*, symphonic poem (1975).

Woollen, (Charles) Russell, American composer, pianist, and organist; b. Harford, Conn., Jan. 7, 1923; d. Charlottesville, Va., March 16, 1994. He was educated at St. Mary's Univ. in Baltimore (B.A., 1944) and at the Catholic Univ. of America in Washington, D.C. (M.A., in Romance languages, 1948). He also studied for the priesthood and attended the Pius X School of Liturgical Music in N.Y. After being ordained a priest in the Hartford Diocese in 1947, he studied Gregorian chant at the Benedictine Abbey in Solesmes in 1948. He also received private training in piano and organ, and also in composition from Franz Wasner. His other mentors in composition were Nabakov at the Peabody Cons. of Music in Baltimore (1949–51), Boulanger in Paris (1951), and Piston at Harvard Univ. (1953–55). From 1948 to 1962 he taught at the Catholic Univ. of America. He was staff keyboard player with the National Sym. Orch. in Washington, D.C., from 1956 to 1980. After leaving the priesthood in 1964, he taught at Howard Univ. in Washington, D.C. (1969–74). In 1982 he became organist at the Arlington (Va.) Unitarian Church. Although considered a minor composer, with the bulk of his manuscripts remaining unpublished at the time of his death, with Robert Evett and Robert Parris, Wollen contributed to the development of the so-called Washington School of Composers that flourished in the 1960s and 1970s.

WORKS: DRAMATIC: *The Decorator*, television opera (N.Y., May 24, 1959). **ORCH.:** *Toccata* (1955); 2 syms.: No. 1 (1957–61) and No. 2 (1977–78; Washington, D.C., April 8, 1979); *Summer Jubilee Overture* (1958); *Modal Offerings* (1960); 2 Pieces for Piano and Orch. (1962–76); *Miranda's Supper* (1964–65); Suite for Flute and Strings (1966; rev. 1979); Suite for Bassoon and Orch. (1988–91); *Prayer and Celebration* (1990). **CHAMBER:** Piano Quartet (1952); Flute Quartet (1953); Wind Quintet (1955); Piano Trio (1957); *Triptych* for 10 Brasses (1960); Trio for Flute, Oboe, and Harpsichord (1967); Trombone Sonata (1972); Wind Quartet (1975). **PIANO:** 2 sonatinas (1954, 1962); Sonata for Piano, 4-hands (1955). **VOCAL:** *Hymn on the Morning of Christ's Nativity* for Soprano, Alto, Chorus, and Orch. (1958); *In martyrum memoriam*, cantata in memory of President John F. Kennedy, Robert F. Kennedy, and Martin Luther King, Jr., for Soprano, Baritone, Chorus, and Orch. (1968–69; Washington, D.C., Nov. 16, 1969); *The Pasch*, cantata for Soprano, Bass, Chorus, and Orch. (1974; rev. 1984); *Mass for a Great Space* for Chorus and Orch. (1986); *Alexandria Suite* for Chorus and Small Orch. (1987); other masses; choruses; songs.

Woollett, Henri (Henry) Edouard, French composer; b. Le Havre (of English parents), Aug. 13, 1864; d. there, Oct. 9, 1936. He studied in Paris with Pugno (piano) and Massenet (composition). Returning to Le Havre, he established himself as a teacher; among his students were Caplet and Honegger. His music was of a lyrical nature, in the manner of Massenet. He publ. *Petit traité de prosodie* (Paris, 1903) and *Histoire de la musique depuis l'antiquité jusqu'à nos jours* (4 vols., Paris, 1909–25).

WORKS: *La Rose de Sharon*, "poème lyrique" for Orch. (1895); *Konzertstück* for Cello and Orch. (1911); 2 violin sonatas (1908, 1922); String Quartet (1929); Viola Sonata; Flute Sonata; Cello Sonata; many piano pieces in a Romantic vein (*Nocturnes et pastorales, Pièces intimes, A travers la vie, Au jardin de France*, and *Préludes et valses*); many attractive songs.

Worbs, Hans Christoph, German music scholar; b. Guben, Jan. 13, 1927. He studied at the Humboldt Univ. in Berlin (degrees, 1952 and 1958). He subsequently settled in Hamburg, where he was active as a music critic and writer.

WRITINGS: *Der Schlager: Bestandsaufnahme, Analyse, Dokumentation* (Bremen, 1963); *Welterfolge der modernen Oper* (Berlin, 1967); *Felix Mendelssohn-Bartholdy* (Reinbek, 1974); *Modest Mussorgsky* (Reinbek, 1976); *Albert Lortzing* (Reinbek, 1980); *Das Dampkonzert: Musik und Musikleben des 19. Jahrhunderts in der Karikatur* (Wilhelmshaven, 1981).

Wordsworth, Barry, English conductor; b. Worcester Park, Surrey, Feb. 20, 1948. He studied conducting with Boult, winning the Tagore Gold Medal at the Royal College of Music in London in 1970. That same year he was co-winner of the Sargent Conductors' Prize. He received training in harpsichord from Leonhardt in Amsterdam. He appeared as a conductor with the Royal Ballet of London (1974–84), and with the Australian Ballet and the Ballet of Canada. From 1982 to 1984 he was music director of the New Sadler's Wells Opera in London. In 1989 he became principal conductor of the Brighton Phil. and the BBC Concert Orch. in London. He also was music director of the Royal Ballet in London and of the Birmingham Royal Ballet from 1990. In 1991 he made his debut at London's Covent Garden conducting *Carmen*. In 1993 he was conductor of the Last Night of the Proms gala with the BBC Sym. Orch. in London.

Wordsworth, William (Brocklesby), English composer; b. London, Dec. 17, 1908; d. Kingussie, Scotland, March 10, 1988. He was descended from the brother of the poet William Wordsworth. He studied with his father; then with George Oldroyd (1921–31), and later with Tovey at the Univ. of Edinburgh (1934–36). In 1950 he won 1st prize in the Edinburgh International Festival Soc. competition with his 2nd Sym. In 1959 he served as president of the Composers' Guild of Great Britain. His music is marked by a certain austerity in the deployment of thematic materials.

WORKS: ORCH.: *Sinfonia* for Strings (1936); *3 Pastoral Sketches* (1937); *Theme and Variations* (1941); 8 syms. (1944; 1947–48; 1951; 1953; 1959–60; 1976–77; 1981; 1986); Piano Concerto (1946); *Divertimento* (1954); Violin Concerto (1955); *Sinfonietta* for Small Orch. (1957); *Variations on a Scottish Theme* for Small Orch. (1962); Cello Concerto (1963); *A Highland Overture* (1964); *Jubilation* (1965); *Conflict*, overture (1968); *Sinfonia semplice* for Amateur String Orch. (1969); *Valediction* (1969); *Spring Festival Overture* (1970); *Confluence*, symphonic variations (1975); *Elegy for Frieda* for Strings (1982). **CHAMBER:** 2 cello sonatas (1937, 1959); 6 string quartets (1941, 1944, 1947, 1950, 1957, 1964); 2 violin sonatas (1944, 1967); String Trio (1945); Piano Quartet (1948); Piano Trio (1949); Oboe Quartet (1949); Clarinet Quintet (1952); Wind Trio (1953); Piano Quintet (1959); Sonata for Solo Cello (1961); *Symposium* for Violin, Strings, Piano, and Percussion (1972); *Conversation Piece* for Violin and Guitar (1983); solo piano pieces, including a Sonata (1939). **VOCAL:** *The Houseless Dead* for Baritone, Chorus, and Orch., after D.H. Lawrence (1939); *Dies Domini*, oratorio (1942–44); *Lucifer Yields* for Soloists, Chorus, and Orch. (1949); *A Vision* for Women's Chorus and String Orch. (1950); *A Song of Praise* for Chorus and Orch. (1956); *A Pattern of Love* for Low Voice and String Orch. (1969–70); *The 2 Brigs*, dramatic cantata (1971); *The Solitary Reaper* for Soprano, Piano, and Clarinet (1973); solo songs.

Workman, William, American baritone; b. Valdosta, Ga., Feb. 4, 1940. He studied with Martial Singher at the Curtis Inst. of Music in Philadelphia and at the Music Academy of the West in Santa Barbara, Calif.; then went to Europe and took voice lessons with Hedwig Schilling in Hamburg. He made his operatic debut with the Hamburg State Opera in 1965. In 1972 he became a member of the Frankfurt am Main Opera; also made guest appearances in Stuttgart, Strasbourg, Paris, and Vienna. In 1984 he appeared at London's Covent Garden.

Wörner, Karl(heinz) H(einrich), German musicologist; b. Waldorf, near Heidelberg, Jan. 6, 1910; d. Heiligenkirchen, near Detmold, Aug. 11, 1969. He studied at the Berlin Hochschule für Musik and took courses in musicology with Schünemann,

Schering, Blume, Hornbostel, and Sachs at the Univ. of Berlin (Ph.D., 1931, with the diss. *Beiträge zur Geschichte des Leitmotivs in der Oper*). He was music critic of the *Berliner Zeitung am Mittag* (1933–34); then (1935–40) opera conductor at Stettin, Magdeburg, and Frankfurt am Main. He was in the German army during World War II; in 1944, was taken prisoner of war by the U.S. Army and spent 2 years in an American internment camp. After his release, he taught at the Heidelberg Hochschule für Musik (1946–54). From 1954 to 1958 he was on the staff of B. Schotts Söhne (Mainz); in 1958, joined the faculty of the Folkwangschule in Essen; from 1961, taught at the North-West Germany Academy of Music in Detmold.

WRITINGS: *Mendelssohn-Bartholdy* (Wiesbaden, 1947); *Musik der Gegenwart: Geschichte des neuen Musik* (Mainz, 1949); *Robert Schumann* (Zürich, 1949); *Musiker-Worte* (Baden-Baden, 1949); *Geschichte der Musik* (Göttingen, 1954; 6th ed., aug., 1975; Eng. tr., 1973); *Neue Musik in der Entscheidung* (Mainz, 1954); *Gotteswort und Magie: Die Oper "Moses und Aron" von Arnold Schönberg* (Heidelberg, 1959; Eng. tr., aug., 1963); *Karlheinz Stockhausen: Werk und Wollen 1950–1962* (Rodenkirchen, 1963; Eng. tr., aug., 1973); *Das Zeitalter der thematischen Prozesse in der Geschichte der Musik* (Regensburg, 1969); *Die Musik in der Geistesgeschichte: Studien zur Situation der Jahre um 1910* (Bonn, 1970).

Woronoff, Wladimir, Russian-born Belgian composer; b. St. Petersburg, Jan. 5, 1903; d. Brussels, April 21, 1980. He studied violin as a child; left Russia after the Revolution and settled in Belgium in 1922; took lessons in composition with Souris in Brussels. In 1954 he destroyed most of his early works, including the ballet *Le Masque de la mort rouge, Suite de Bruxelles* for Orch., and *Concert lyrique* for Piano and Orch.; he revised most of his remaining scores. His catalogue of extant works after this self-auto-da-fé includes *La Foule* for Bass, Chorus, and Orch. (1934; rev. 1965); *Annas et le Lépreux* for Low Voice and Piano (1946); *Les 12*, 3 fragments from the poem by Alexander Blok, for Low Voice and Orch. or Piano (1921–63); *Strophes concertantes* for Piano and Orch. (1964); *Lueur tournante* for Narrator and Orch. (1967); *Tripartita* for Viola and Chamber Orch. (1970); *Vallées* for 2 Pianos (1971).

Wöss, Josef Venantius von, Austrian editor and composer; b. Cattaro, Dalmatia, June 13, 1863; d. Vienna, Oct. 22, 1943. He received his first musical instruction from his mother and an uncle; studied theory at the Vienna Cons. with Franz Krenn. He was an ed. for Universal Edition (1908–31) and also ed. the journal *Musica Divina* (1913–34).

WRITINGS: *Deutsche Meister des Liedes* (Vienna, 1910); *Gustav Mahler, Das Lied von der Erde: thematische Analyse* (Leipzig, 1912); *Die Modulation* (Vienna, 1921).

WORKS: 3 operas: *Lenzlüge* (Elberfeld, 1905), *Flaviennes Abenteuer* (Breslau, 1910), and *Carmilhan* (n.d.); *Serenade* for Orch.; *Sakuntala*, overture; sacred music; various secular vocal works, including choruses and about 150 lieder; chamber works, including a Violin Sonata, String Quartet, Piano Sextet, and organ music.

Wöss, Kurt, Austrian conductor; b. Linz, May 2, 1914; d. Dresden (while rehearsing the Dresden Phil.), Dec. 4, 1987. He studied conducting with Weingartner in Vienna, and also pursued musicological studies at the Univ. of Vienna with Haas, Lach, Orel, and Wellesz; taught an orch. class at the Vienna Academy of Music (1938–40). He conducted the Niederösterreichisches Tonkünstler-Orch. in Vienna (1948–51) and the Nippon Phil. in Tokyo (1951–54). From 1956 to 1959 he was principal conductor of the Victoria Sym. Orch. in Melbourne and of the Australian National Opera; in 1961 he returned to Linz, where he was chief conductor of the Bruckner Orch. until 1976; also conducted again in Tokyo. He publ. *Ratschläge zur Aufführung der Symphonien Anton Bruckners* (Linz, 1974).

Wotquenne (-Plattel), Alfred (Camille), Belgian musicologist; b. Lobbes, Jan. 25, 1867; d. Antibes, France, Sept. 25, 1939. He studied at the Royal Cons. in Brussels with Brassin (piano), Mailly (organ; premier prix, 1888), and Dupont and Gevaert (theory); from 1894 to 1896 he was deputy secretary and librarian and from 1896 to 1918 secretary and librarian there. He settled in Antibes as a singing teacher and organist, and subsequently was made maître de chapelle at its cathedral (1921). He prepared a card catalogue of 18,000 Italian "cantate da camera" of the 18th century; ed. *Chansons italiennes de la fin du XVI*e *siècle* (canzonette *a* 4); continued the collections begun by Gevaert, *Répertoire classique du chant français and Répertoire français de l'ancien chant classique*; and ed. a new collection, *Répertoire Wotquenne* (4 vols. publ.); also ed. violin sonatas of Tartini, Veracini, and others; composed much sacred music. The MSS of several important bibliographies in his collection were bought by the Library of Congress in Washington, D.C., in 1929; these comprise *Répertoire des textes publiés par les éditeurs parisiens Ballard; Histoire musicale et chronologique du Théâtre de la Foire depuis 1680 jusqu'à 1762; Histoire du nouveau Théâtre-Italien à Paris (1718–1762)*; etc. A large part of his private music library was also bought by the Library of Congress.

WRITINGS: *Catalogue de la bibliothèque du Conservatoire Royal de Musique de Bruxelles* (vol. I, 1894; with a supplement, *Libretti d'opéras et d'oratorios italiens du XVII*e *siècle*, 1901; II, 1902; III, 1908; IV, 1912; V, 1914); *Étude bibliographique sur les oeuvres de Baldassare Galuppi* (1899; 2nd ed., aug., 1902 as *Baldassare Galuppi: Étude bibliographique sur ses oeuvres dramatiques*); *Thematisches Verzeichnis der Werke von Christoph Willibald von Gluck* (1904); *Alphabetisches Verzeichnis der Stücke in Versen aus den dramatischer Werken von Zeno, Metastasio und Goldoni* (1905); *Thematisches Verzeichnis der Werke von Carl Philipp Emanuel Bach* (1905); *Étude bibliographique sur le compositeur napolitain Luigi Rossi* (1909; with thematic catalogue).

Woytowicz, Boleslaw, Polish pianist, pedagogue, and composer; b. Dunajowce, Dec. 5, 1899; d. Katowice, July 11, 1980. He began musical training with his grandfather, the organist and composer Mikolaj Woytowicz. After piano lessons with Nowacki and Hanicki (1913–15) and Wielhorski (1916–17), he took his Ph.D. in philology at the Univ. of Kiev and studied mathematics and law at the Univ. of Warsaw. He pursued further piano instruction with Michalowski at the Chopin Music College in Warsaw (1920–24) and received composition training with Wielhorski, Szopski, and Maliszewski, and later with Boulanger in Paris (1929–32). In 1924 he launched his career as a pianist. He also was a prof. of piano and theory at the Chopin Music College (1924–39), a teacher of piano and composition at the Katowice Cons. (from 1945), and a prof. of composition at the Kraków Cons. (from 1963). In 1937 he received the Polish State Prize for music.

WORKS: BALLET: *Powrót* (1937). **ORCH.:** Piano Concerto (1932); *Zalobny poema* (Funeral Poem; 1935); 3 syms.: No. 1 (1938), No. 2 (1945; Kraków, Sept. 27, 1946), and No. 3, *Concertante*, for Piano and Orch. (1963); *Symphonic Sketches* (1949). **CHAMBER:** 2 string quartets (1932, 1953); Flute Sonata (1952). **PIANO:** *12 Études* (1948); *10 Études* (1960); *Little Piano Sonata* (1974). **VOCAL:** *Kolysanka* (Cradle Song) for Soprano, Flute, Clarinet, Bassoon, and Harp (1931); *Kantata na pochwale pracy* (Cantata in Praise of Labor; 1948); *Prorok* (The Prophet), cantata (1950); *Lamento* for Soprano, Piano, and Clarinet (1960).

Wright, Maurice, American composer and teacher; b. Front Royal, Va., Oct. 17, 1949. He studied with Iain Hamilton at Duke Univ. (B.A., 1972) and Beeson, Davidovsky, Ussachevsky, and Dodge at Columbia Univ. (M.A., 1974). He taught at Columbia Univ. (1975–77), Boston Univ. (1978–79), and Temple Univ. (from 1980).

WORKS: OPERA: *The 5th String* (1978–80; also an orch. piece, *Music from The 5th String*). **ORCH.:** *Progression* (1971); *Aulos* for Oboe and Strings (1972); *Orchestral Composition* (1974); *Stellae* for Orch. and Tape (Tanglewood, Aug. 10, 1978); *Wellington's Defeat* (1978); *The Times Will Change* (1981); *Night Scenes* (1988–89); Marimba Concerto (1993; Boston, April 15,

1994). **CHAMBER:** *Sonata Exotica* for Trombone and Piano (1973); 3 chamber syms. (1973, 1974, 1977); *The Constant Flow* for 4 Clarinets (1974); 5 Pieces for Viola (1974); *Music* for 4 Trombones (1975); *A Noise Did Rise Like Thunder in My Hearing* for Trombone and Chamber Group (1976); *Wind of Change* for Wind Quintet (1980); *Music* for 10 Instruments and Tape (1981); Trio for Flute, Violin, and Viola (1983); Brass Quintet (1986). **PIANO:** Chamber Sym. for Piano and Tape (1976); 2 sonatas (1982, 1983); Suite (1983). **VOCAL:** *Mozartian Constraint* for Soprano, Flute, Violin, Bassoon, and Guitar (1974); Cantata for Tenor, Percussion, and Tape (1975); *The Fat Man* for Chorus, Bassoon, Trombone, and Cello (1977); *Loneliness* for 3 Sopranos, Trumpet, Cello, and Piano (1980); *Like an Autumn Sky* for Chorus, Piano, and 2 Percussionists (1980); choruses; songs.

Wuensch, Gerhard (Joseph), Austrian-Canadian composer and teacher; b. Vienna, Dec. 23, 1925. He received training in musicology at the Univ. (Ph.D., 1950) and in piano and composition at the Academy of Music (diplomas in both, 1952) in Vienna. As a Fulbright fellow, he pursued studies in theory with Pisk and Kennan at the Univ. of Texas (1954–56). After teaching at Butler Univ. in Indianapolis (1956–63), he settled in Canada and taught at the univs. of Toronto (1964–69) and Calgary (1969–73). In 1973 he joined the faculty of the Univ. of Western Ontario in London, where he was chairman of the theory and composition dept. (1973–76) and a prof. (1978–91). In 1991 he was made prof. emeritus. As a composer, his works reveal a familiarity with a wide spectrum of styles and genres.

WORKS: DRAMATIC: *Labyrinth*, ballet (1957); *Il Pomo d'Oro*, comedy-ballet (1958); *Nice People: 3 Scenes from Contemporary Life*, chamber opera (1990; London, Ontario, Nov. 28, 1991). **ORCH.:** *Nocturne* (1956); *Variations on a Dorian Hexachord* (1959); 3 syms.: No. 1 (1959), No. 2 for Band (1960), and No. 3 for Brass and Percussion (1967); *Ballad* for Trumpet and Orch. (1962); Concerto for Piano and Chamber Orch. (1971); *Scherzo* for Piano and Winds (1971); Concerto for Bassoon and Chamber Orch. (1976); Concerto for Organ, 3 Trumpets, Timpani, and Strings (1976); *Ad Usum Ligorum*, concerto for 2 Pianos and Orch. (1981); *Serenade for a Summer Evening* (1986); *Variations and Fugue on a Mozartian Theme* (1986). **CHAMBER:** Trio for Clarinet, Bassoon, and Piano (1948); 2 string quartets (1953, 1963); 2 woodwind quintets (1963, 1967); *Music* for 7 Brass Instruments (1966); *4 Mini-Suites* for Accordion (1968); *Polysonics* for Variable Instrumentation (1969); *Cameos* for Fluteand Piano (1969); *Music Without Pretensions* for Accordion and String Quartet (1969); Suite for Trumpet and Organ (1970); *Variations* for Clarinet and Piano (1971); 6 Duets for Flute and Clarinet (1971); *Prélude, Aria, and Fugue* for Accordion and Brass Quartet (1971); *Musica Giocosa* for Flute and Piano (1976); *Ménage à Trois* for Violin, Clarinet, and Piano (1987); *Recycling* for Tuba, Horn, and Piano (1989). **PIANO:** *Esquisse* (1950; rev. 1970); 2 mini suites (1969, 1976); *12 Glimpses into 20th Century Idioms* (1969); *Valses nostalgiques* for Piano, 4-hands (1972); Sonata for Piano, 4-hands (1977); *Ping Pong Anyone?* (1986). **VOCAL:** *Symphonia sacra* for Soprano, Baritone, Chorus, Brass, Percussion, and Organ (1961); *Vexilla regis prodeunt* for Soli, Chorus, and Organ (1968); 6 Songs for Voice, Flute, and Accordion (1970); *Laus sapientiae* for Soprano, Tenor, Baritone, Chorus, Organ, Brass, and Orch. (1977); *Songs, Lieder, and Melodies* for Voice, Clarinet, and Piano (1982); *4 Episodes from the Gospel of St. John* for Soli, Chorus, Congregation, and Organ (1988); *Pygmalion* for Baritone and String Quartet (1989; London, Ontario, Jan. 29, 1995).

Führer, Friedrich (Anton Franz), distinguished Austrian pianist and pedagogue; b. Vienna, June 29, 1900; d. Mannheim, Dec. 27, 1975. He studied piano with Franz Schmidt, theory and composition with Joseph Marx, and conducting with Ferdinand Löwe at the Vienna Academy of Music (1915–20); also studied law and musicology at the Univ. of Vienna. From 1923 he made regular tours of Europe. He taught at the Vienna Academy of Music (1922–32), at the Hochschule für Musik in Mannheim (1934–36), in Kiel (1936–39), in Vienna (1939–45), at the Salzburg Mozarteum (1948–51), in Mannheim (1952–57), and in Munich (1957–68). He publ. *Meisterwerke der Klaviermusik* (Wilhelmshaven, 1966). His performances of the Classical and Romantic repertoires were highly regarded. He also championed the cause of 20th-century composers, ranging from Schoenberg to Prokofiev.

Wunderer, Alexander, Austrian oboist, composer, and teacher; b. Vienna, April 11, 1877; d. Zinkenbach, near St. Gilgen (Salzkammergut), Dec. 29, 1955. He taught oboe and other wind instruments at the Vienna Academy of Music (1919–37) and oboe at the Salzburg Mozarteum (from 1945). He composed chamber music and was co-author of a book on orchestration.

Wunderlich, Fritz (actually, **Friedrich Karl Otto**), outstanding German tenor; b. Kusel, Sept. 26, 1930; d. Heidelberg, Sept. 17, 1966. He was a student of Margarete von Wintenfeld at the Freiburg im Breisgau Hochschule für Musik (1950–55). While still a student, he appeared as a soloist with the Freiburg im Breisgau Choir, and then sang Tamino in a school performance of *Die Zauberflöte* (1954). In 1955 he made his professional operatic debut in Stuttgart as Eislinger in *Die Meistersinger von Nürnberg*, where he sang until 1958. From 1958 to 1960 he was a member of the Frankfurt am Main Opera. In 1958 he sang at the Aix-en-Provence Festival, and then appeared as Henry in *Die schweigsame Frau* at the Salzburg Festival in 1959. In 1960 he became a member of the Bavarian State Opera in Munich and in 1962 was made a Kammersänger. He also was a member of the Vienna State Opera from 1962. In 1965 he made his debut as Don Ottavio at London's Covent Garden. He appeared at the Edinburgh Festival in 1966. Wunderlich was scheduled to make his Metropolitan Opera debut in N.Y. as Don Ottavio on Oct. 8, 1966, but his career of great promise was tragically cut short by his death in a fall at his home. He was acclaimed for the extraordinary beauty of his lyric tenor voice. In addition to his remarkable Mozartian roles, he also was admired for such roles as Alfredo, Lenski, Jeník, Palestrina, and Leukippos. He likewise was noted for his operetta and lieder performances.

BIBL.: W. Pfister, *F. W.: Biographie* (Zürich, 1990).

Wunderlich, Heinz, noted German organist, choral conductor, and pedagogue; b. Leipzig, April 25, 1919. He studied organ with Straube in Leipzig (1935–41); then composition and conducting with J.N. David. He held several organ and choral conducting posts (1943–58); taught at the Halle Staatliche Hochschule für Musik (1947–58); was Kirchenmusikdirektor at St. Jacobi in Hamburg (1958–82), where his concerts of choral music by the German masters and of the organ works of Reger, as well as his restoration of the famous Arp Schnitger organ, received great acclaim; he toured the U.S. with his choir (1978). As prof. of organ at the Hamburg Hochschule für Musik (from 1974), he attracted students from many countries.

Wunsch, Hermann, German composer and teacher; b. Neuss, Aug. 9, 1884; d. Berlin, Dec. 21, 1954. He studied in Düsseldorf and Cologne, and later at the Hochschule für Musik in Berlin, where he subsequently taught, becoming a prof. in 1945. He composed 6 syms., of which the 5th won the Schubert Memorial Prize (German section) of the Columbia Phonograph Co. contest (Schubert Centennial, 1928). Other works included the chamber operas *Bianca* (Weimar, May 22, 1927), *Don Juans Sohn* (Weimar, 1928), and *Franzosenzeit* (Schwerin, 1933); 2 masses; *Südpolkantate* for Chorus and Orch.; *Helden* for Chorus and Orch. (Berlin, 1941); 3 violin concertos; Concerto for Piano and Small Orch.; *Kleine Lustspielsuite* for Orch.; *Fest auf Monbijou*, suite for Chamber Orch.; *Erntelied*, sym. with a concluding chorus.

Wünsch, Walther, Austrian ethnomusicologist; b. Gablonz an der Niesse, July 23, 1908; d. Vienna, Feb. 24, 1991. He studied with Becking at the German Univ. in Prague (Ph.D., 1932, with the diss. *Die Geigentechnik der jugoslawischen Guslaren*; publ.

in Brno, 1934); completed his Habilitation in 1960 at the Univ. of Graz. After working at the musicological inst. of the Pestalozzi Academy in Prague (1932–35), he was active at the Inst. for Acoustics in Berlin (1935–38); from 1945 he was active as a chamber music player and taught at the Steiermarkischen Landeskonservatorium; in 1960 he joined the faculty of the Inst. for Music Ethnology at the Graz Hochschule für Musik, where he became a prof. in 1968. He publ. several important studies on ethnomusicology, including *Heldensänger in Südosteuropa* (Leipzig, 1937).

Wuorinen, Charles (Peter), prominent American composer, pedagogue, pianist, and conductor; b. N.Y., June 9, 1938. He was a student of Beeson, Ussachevsky, and Luening at Columbia Univ. (B.A., 1961; M.A., 1963), where he then taught (1964–71). With Harvey Sollberger, he founded the Group for Contemporary Music in 1962, which became a vital force in the propagation of modern music via concerts and recordings. He was a visiting lecturer at Princeton Univ. (1967–68) and the New England Cons. of Music in Boston (1968–71). After serving as adjunct lecturer at the Univ. of South Florida (1971–72), he was on the faculty of the Manhattan School of Music in N.Y. (1972–79). From 1973 to 1987 to was artistic director and chairman of the American Composers Orch. in N.Y. In 1984 he became a prof. at Rutgers, the State Univ. of N.J. From 1985 to 1989 he served as composer-in-residence of the San Francisco Sym. He was a visiting prof. at the State Univ. of N.Y. at Buffalo from 1989 to 1994. Wuorinen has received numerous prizes, grants, and commissions, among them the Joseph Bearns Prize (1958, 1959, 1961), a National Inst. of Arts and Letters Award (1967), 2 Guggenheim fellowships (1968, 1972), the Pulitzer Prize in Music for his *Times Encomium* (1970), the Brandeis Univ. Creative Arts Award (1970), NEA grants (1974, 1976), Rockefeller Foundation fellowships (1979, 1980, 1981), and a MacArthur Foundation fellowship (1986–91). He also was elected to membership in the American Academy and Inst. of Arts and Letters. Wuorinen publ. the book *Simple Composition* (N.Y., 1979), which gives insight into his use of 12-tone composition. Wuorinen is one of the most representative of contemporary composers of his generation. His techniques derive from Stravinsky's early period, when stark primitivism gave way to austere linear counterpoint. An even greater affinity in Wuorinen's music is with the agglutinative formations of unrelated thematic statements as practiced by Varèse. A more literal dependence connects Wuorinen's works with the dodecaphonic method of composition as promulgated by Schoenberg. These modalities and relationships coalesce in Wuorinen's writing into a sui generis complex subdivided into melodic, harmonic, and contrapuntal units that build a definitive formal structure. The foundation of his method of composition is serialism, in which pitch, time, and rhythmic divisions relate to one another in a "time point system," which lends itself to unlimited tonal and temporal arrangements, combinations, and permutations. In his prolific output, Wuorinen has explored the entire vocabulary of serial composition.

WORKS: DRAMATIC: *The Politics of Harmony*, masque (1966–67; N.Y., Oct. 28, 1968); *The W. of Babylon (or The Triumph of Love Over Moral Depravity)*, Baroque burlesque (partial perf., N.Y., Dec. 15, 1975; 1st complete perf., San Francisco, Jan 20, 1989); *Delight of the Muses*, ballet (1991; N.Y., Jan. 29, 1992; based on the orch piece). **ORCH.:** Concert-Piece for Piano and Strings (Bennington, Vt., Aug. 18, 1956); *Music* (N.Y., Dec. 1, 1956); *Alternating Currents* for Chamber Orch. (1957); *Concertante I* for Violin and Strings (Middlebury, Vt., July 7, 1957) and *IV* for Violin, Piano, and Chamber Orch. (Bennington, Vt., Aug. 29, 1959); 3 numbered syms.: No. 1 (1957–58; N.Y., March 7, 1958), No. 2 (1958; N.Y., Feb. 27, 1959), and No. 3 (N.Y., Nov. 11, 1959); 2 violin concertos: No. 1 (1958) and No. 2 for Amplified Violin and Orch. (1971–72; Tanglewood, Aug. 4, 1972); *Concertone* for Brass Quintet and Orch. (1960; Iowa City, Feb. 19, 1964); *An Educator's "Wachet Auf"* for Chamber Orch. (1961); *Evolutio Transcripta* for Chamber Orch. (Bennington, Vt., Aug. 19, 1961; transcription of the organ piece); *Orchestral and Electronic Exchanges* for Orch. and Tape (1964–65; N.Y., July 30, 1965); 3 piano concertos: No. 1 (1965–66; Iowa City, May 4, 1966), No. 2 for Amplified Piano and Orch. (1973–74; N.Y., Dec. 6, 1974), and No. 3 (1982–83; Troy, N.Y., May 4, 1984); *Contrafactum* (Iowa City, Nov. 19, 1969); *Grand Bamboula* for Strings (1971; Iowa City, Sept. 30, 1972); *A Reliquary for Igor Stravinsky* (1974–75; Ojai, Calif., June 1, 1975); Percussion Sym. (1976; Somerville, N.J., Jan. 26, 1978); *Tashi* for Clarinet, Violin, Cello, Piano, and Orch. (1975–76; Cleveland, Oct. 13, 1976); *Two-Part Symphony* (1977–78; N.Y., Dec. 11, 1978); *The Magic Art*, instrumental masque, after Purcell (1977–79; St. Paul, Minn., Sept. 26, 1979); *Ancestors* for Chamber Orch. (Portland, Oreg., Aug. 10, 1978); *Short Suite* (1981; Purchase, N.Y., Feb. 13, 1983); *Rhapsody* for Violin and Orch. (1983; San Francisco, Jan. 16, 1985); *Bamboula Squared* for Orch. and Tape (1983–84; N.Y., June 4, 1984); Concertino (1984; also for 15 Solo Instruments, N.Y., Feb. 5, 1985); *Movers and Shakers* (Cleveland, Dec. 13, 1984); *Crossfire* (1984; Baltimore, May 9, 1985); *Prelude to Kullervo* for Tuba and Orch. (N.Y., Nov. 21, 1985); *The Golden Dance* (1985–86; San Francisco, Sept. 10, 1986); *Fanfare for the Houston Symphony* (Houston, March 15, 1986); *Galliard* for Chamber Orch. (Cleveland, Sept. 27, 1987); *Five*, concerto for Amplied Cello and Orch. (1987; N.Y., April 28, 1988); *Bamboula Beach*, overture (1987; Miami, Feb. 4, 1988); *Another Happy Birthday* (San Francisco, Sept. 14, 1988); *Machault Mon Chou* (1988; San Francisco, May 24, 1989); *Astra* (1989–90; Copenhagen, Aug. 11, 1990); *Delight of the Muses* (Stony Brook, N.Y., Nov. 9, 1991; as a ballet, N.Y., Jan. 29, 1992); *Microsymphony* (1992); Saxophone Quartet Concerto (1992); *The Mission of Virgil* (1993); *Windfall* (1994). **CHAMBER:** *Prelude and Fugue* for 4 Percussionists (1955; Urbana, Ill., March 1, 1956); Sonatina for Woodwind Quartet (Bennington, Vt., Aug. 15, 1956); *Into the Organ Pipes and Steeples* for 11 Instruments (1956); *Subversion* for String Septet (1956; Bennington, Vt., Aug. 1957); 3 wind quintets: No. 1 (1956; N.Y., Jan. 16, 1957), No. 2 (1958), and No. 3 (1977; N.Y., Feb. 24, 1978); 1 unnumbered string quartet (Bennington, Vt., Aug. 1957); 3 numbered string quartets: No. 1 (1970–71; Chicago, Oct. 11, 1971), No. 2 (1978–79; Jackson, Wy., Aug. 1, 1979), and No. 3 (1986–86; Hanover, N.H., Nov. 6, 1987); *3 Mass Movements* for Violin (East Hampton, N.Y., July 28, 1957); *Triptych* for Violin, Viola, and Percussion (1957; N.Y., Jan. 19, 1958); *Spectrum* for Violin and Brass Quintet (Philadelphia, April 10, 1958); *Movement* for Wind Quintet (1958; 1st movement of his 2nd Wind Quintet); *Concertante II* for Violin and Chamber Ensemble (Middlebury, Vt., July 6, 1958) and *III* for Harpsichord, Oboe, Violin, Viola, and Cello (1959; N.Y., Aug. 2, 1961); *3 Pieces* for String Quartet (Bennington, Vt., Aug. 9, 1958); *Trio Concertante* for Oboe, Violin, and Piano (Troy, N.Y., Oct. 31, 1958); *Musica duarum partium ecclesiastica* for Brass Quartet, Timpani, Piano, and Organ (1959); Flute Sonata (1960; WNYC Radio, N.Y., Nov. 17, 1962); *Consort of 4 Trombones* (N.Y., April 4, 1960); *Turetzky Pieces* for Flute, Clarinet, and Double Bass (Westbrook, Conn., Aug. 7, 1960); *8 Variations* for Violin and Harpsichord (1960; N.Y., June 21, 1961); *Consort from Instruments and Voices* (1960–61; N.Y., Jan. 15, 1961); *Tiento Sobre Cabezón* for Flute, Oboe, Violin, Viola, Cello, Harpsichord, and Piano (N.Y., Aug. 2, 1961); Concert for Double Bass (1961; Southport, Conn., May 11, 1962); 3 trios for Flute, Cello, and Piano: No. 1 (N.Y., Dec. 14, 1961), No. 2 (1962; N.Y., May 6, 1963), and No. 3 (1972–73; N.Y., May 28, 1973); Octet for Oboe, Clarinet, Horn, Trombone, Violin, Cello, Double Bass, and Piano (1961–62; N.Y., Sept. 27, 1962); *Invention* for Percussion Quintet (N.Y., March 6, 1962); *Duuiensela* for Cello and Piano (New Haven, Conn., April 30, 1962); *Bearbeitungen über das Glogauer Liederbuch* for Flute, Clarinet, Violin, and Double Bass (Hartford, Conn., July 17, 1962); chamber concertos for Cello and 10 Players (1963; N.Y., Feb. 17, 1964), for Flute and 10 Players (Tanglewood, Aug. 9, 1964), for Oboe and 10 Players (N.Y., Nov. 8, 1965), and for Tuba, 12 Winds, and 12 Drums (1969–70; N.Y., March 7, 1971);

Flute Variations I (N.Y., Dec. 18, 1963) and *II* (1968; Jersey City, N.J., April 17, 1969); *Variations à 2* for Flute and Piano (1963–64); Composition for Violin and 10 Instruments (1963–64; N.Y., April 26, 1964); Composition for Oboe and Piano (1964–65; Boston, April 3, 1966); *The Bells* for Percussion (1965–66); *Bicinium* for 2 Oboes (1966; N.Y., May 10, 1967); *Janissary Music* for Percussionist (part 1, Swarthmore, Pa., Oct. 26, 1966; part 2, N.Y., March 12, 1967); *Salve Regina: John Bull* for 14 Instruments (N.Y., Oct. 31, 1966); Duo for Violin and Piano (1966–67; N.Y., April 17, 1968); String Trio (1967–68; Washington, D.C., Oct. 27, 1968); *Adapting to the Times* for Cello and Piano (1968–69; Amherst, Mass., Feb. 25, 1970); *Nature's Concord* for Trumpet and Piano (1969); *The Long and the Short* for Violin (Berkeley, Calif., Aug. 4, 1969); *Ringing Changes* for Percussion Ensemble (1969–70; Wayne, N.J., April 28, 1970); *Cello Variations I* (Philadelphia, Dec. 8, 1970) and *II* (1975; WQXR Radio, N.Y., Dec. 1976); *Canzona* for 12 Instruments (1971; N.Y., Jan. 31, 1972); *Bassoon Variations* for Bassoon, Harp, and Timpani (1971–72; Cambridge, Mass., Oct. 28, 1973); *Harp Variations* for Harp, Violin, Viola, and Cello (1971–72; N.Y., April 17, 1973); *Violin Variations* (N.Y., May 14, 1972); *On Alligators* for 8 Instruments (1972); *Speculum speculi* for 6 Players (1972; Grand Forks, N.D., Jan. 14, 1973); *Arabia Felix* for 6 Instruments (1973; N.Y., Feb. 23, 1974); *Grand Union* for Cello and Drums (Chicago, Nov. 5, 1973); *Fantasia* for Violin and Piano (1974; Baltimore, Dec. 14, 1975); *Tashi* for Clarinet, Violin, Cello, and Piano (1975; Colorado Springs, Jan. 15, 1976); *Hyperion* for Chamber Ensemble (1975; Adelaide, March 21, 1976); *Album Leaf* for Violin and Cello (1976); *The Winds* for 8 Winds and Piano (1976–77; N.Y., May 19, 1977); *6 Pieces* for Violin and Piano (1977; N.Y., April 18, 1978); *Fast Fantasy* for Cello and Piano (1977); *Archangel* for Bass Trombone and String Quartet (1977; N.Y., Dec. 18, 1978); *Archaeopteryx* for Bass Trombone and 10 Players (1978; Caramoor, N.Y., July 1, 1982); Percussion Duo for Mallet Instruments and Piano (Iowa City, Oct. 29, 1979); *Fortune* for Clarinet, Violin, Cello, and Piano (1979); *Joan's* for Flute, Clarinet, Violin, Cello, and Piano (1979; N.Y., March 23, 1980); *Beast 708* for Computer-generated Tape or 10 Instruments (1980); Horn Trio (1981; N.Y., April 18, 1983); Trio for Bass Trombone, Tuba, and Contrabass (1981; N.Y., April 14, 1983); *N.Y. Notes* for 6 Instruments (1981–82; Sacramento, Nov. 8, 1982); *Divertimento* for Alto Saxophone and Piano (1982; N.Y., March 6, 1983); *Divertimento* for String Quartet (1982; Glen Falls, N.Y., May 9, 1983); *Spinoff* for Violin, Contrabass, and Conga Drums (N.Y., May 18, 1983); Trio for Violin, Cello, and Piano (Union, N.J., Oct. 1, 1983); Concertino for 15 Instruments (1984); *Horn Trio Continued* (1985; Los Angeles, May 24, 1988); Trombone Trio (1985; N.Y., Nov. 6, 1986); Double Solo for Horn Trio (1985; N.Y., March 16, 1986); *Fanfare for Rutgers University* for 2 Horns, 2 Trumpets, and 2 Trombones (1986); *A Doleful Dompe on Deborah's Departure as well as Borda's Bawdy Badinage* for English Horn, Violin, and Cello (1986); Violin Sonata (Washington, D.C., Nov. 25, 1988); String Sextet (1988–89; Covington, Ga., Nov. 4, 1989); Saxophone Quartet (1992); Percussion Quartet (1994); Piano Quintet (1994; Chicago, Feb. 19, 1995); *Guitar Variations* (1994). **KEYBOARD: PIANO:** *Scherzo* (1953; N.Y., May 13, 1956); *Song and Dance* (1955; N.Y., May 13, 1956); *2 Tranquil Pieces* (1956); 1 unnumbered sonata (N.Y., Dec. 16, 1958); 3 numbered sonatas: No. 1 (1969; Washington, D.C., Dec. 14, 1970), No. 2 (Washington, D.C., Oct. 2, 1976), and No. 3 (1986; N.Y., March 29, 1989); *3 Prepositions* (1958); *Piano Variations* (1963; N.Y., Jan. 13, 1964); *Making Ends Meet* for Piano, 4-hands (1966; Washington, D.C., May 19, 1968); *12 Short Pieces* (1973); *Self-Similar Waltz* (1977; Evanston, Ill., May 11, 1978); *The Blue Bamboula* (1980; Tokyo, May 29, 1981); *Capriccio* (1980–81; N.Y., April 14, 1982); *Album Leaf* (N.Y., May 30, 1984); *Bagatelle* (1987–88; Buffalo, June 12, 1989). **ORGAN:** *Homage à Bach* (1955; Gardner, Mass., June 30, 1956); *Evolutio: Organ* (1961; Boston, April 8, 1962; also transcribed for Orch.); *Natural Fantasy* (1985; N.Y., Jan. 31, 1988). **HARPSICHORD:** *Harpsichord Diversions* (1966). **VOCAL:** *O Filii et Filiae* for Chorus (1953; N.Y., May 2, 1954); *Te decet hymnus* for Soli, Chorus, Timpani, Organ, and Piano (1954; N.Y., May 13, 1956); *Faire, If You Expect Admiring, and Turne Backe, You Wanton Flyer* for Men's Chorus (N.Y., May 13, 1956); *Dr. Faustus Lights the Lights* for Narrator and 7 Players (1956–57; N.Y., April 8, 1957); *Wandering in This Place* for Mezzo-soprano (1957); *Be Merry All That Be Present* for Chorus and Organ (1957; N.Y., Jan. 26, 1958); *The Door in the Wall* for 2 Mezzo-sopranos and Piano (N.Y., April 22, 1960; also for Mezzo-soprano, Soprano, and Piano); *On the Raft* for 2 Mezzo-sopranos and Piano (N.Y., April 22, 1960; also for Mezzo-soprano, Soprano, and Piano); *Madrigale spirituale sopra Salmo Secundo* for Tenor, Bass, and 6 Instruments (Bennington, Vt., Aug. 27, 1960); *Symphonia sacra* for Tenor, Baritone, Bass, and 6 Instruments (N.Y., March 27, 1961); *The Prayer of Jonah* for Chorus and String Quintet (1962; N.Y., March 21, 1963); *Super salutem* for Men's Voices and Instruments (1964); *A Song to the Lute in Musicke* for Soprano and Piano (1969–70; N.Y., Jan. 11, 1971); *A Message to Denmark Hill* for Baritone, Flute, Cello, and Piano (1970); *Mannheim 87.87.87.* for Chorus and Organ (N.Y., May 1, 1973); *An Anthem for Epiphany* for Chorus, Trumpet, and Organ (1974); 6 Songs for Countertenor or Alto, Tenor, and 6 Instruments (1977; Wayne, N.J., Jan. 26, 1978); 3 Songs for Tenor and Piano (1978–79); *Psalm 39* for Baritone and Guitar (1979); *The Celestial Sphere,* oratorio for Chorus and Orch. (1980; Rock Island, Ill., April 25, 1981); Mass for Soprano, Chamber Chorus, Violin, 3 Trombones, and Organ (1982; N.Y., Nov. 23, 1983); *A Solis Ortu* for Chorus (1988–89; N.Y., Dec. 30, 1990); *Twang* for Mezzo-soprano or Soprano and Piano (1988–89); *Genesis* for Chorus and Orch. (1989; San Francisco, Sept. 26, 1991); *Missa Brevis* for Chorus and Organ (1991; N.Y., Feb. 23, 1992); *A Winter's Tale* for Soprano and Piano (Atlanta, Oct. 12, 1992; also for Soprano, Clarinet, Horn, String Trio, and Piano, Houston, Jan. 10, 1995). **ELECTRONIC:** *Time's Encomium* (1968–69).

BIBL.: R. Burbank, *C. W.: A Bio-Bibliography* (Westport, Conn., 1994).

Wurlitzer, family of German-American instrument dealers and makers: (Franz) Rudolph Wurlitzer (b. Schoneck, Saxony, Jan. 31, 1831; d. Cincinnati, Jan. 14, 1914) emigrated to the U.S. in 1853; after settling in Cincinnati, he became active as an instrument dealer; with his brother Anton, he organized Rudolph Wurlitzer & Bro. in 1872; the business became the Rudolph Wurlitzer Co. in 1890, with Rudolph serving as president (1890–1912) and as chairman (1912–14). In 1889 his eldest son, Howard Eugene Wurlitzer (b. Cincinnati, Sept. 5, 1871; d. N.Y., Oct. 30, 1928), joined the firm; through his efforts, the company became highly successful; he served as its president (1912–27) and chairman (1927–28). Rudolph's 2nd son, Rudolph Henry Wurlitzer (b. Cincinnati, Dec. 30, 1873; d. there, May 27, 1948), studied in Cincinnati and then went to Berlin in 1891 to study violin with Emanuel Wirth, the history of musical instruments with Oskar Fleischer, and acoustics with Hermann von Helmholtz; he also studied with the violin authority August Riechers; upon his return to Cincinnati in 1894, he joined the firm as a director, and then held the posts of secretary and treasurer (1899–1912), vice-president (1912–27), president (1927–32), and chairman (1932–42). Rudolph's 3rd son, Farny Reginald Wurlitzer (b. Cincinnati, Dec. 7, 1883; d. North Tonawanda, N.Y., May 6, 1972), studied at the Cincinnati Technical School before pursuing his education in Germany as an apprentice to various instrument makers (1901–4); he then returned to Cincinnati to join the firm and became head of the automatic musical instrument dept. in 1907; in 1909 he became head of the Rudolph Wurlitzer Manufacturing Co. in North Tonawanda, which commenced making coin-operated phonographs in 1933; he was president (1932–41) and chairman (1941–66) of the firm. Rudolph Henry's son, Rembert Wurlitzer (b. Cincinnati, March 27, 1904; d. N.Y., Oct. 21, 1963), studied at Princeton Univ.; he then received training in violin making from Amédée Dieudonné in Mirecourt and worked with Alfred Hill in

London; after returning to Cincinnati, he was made a vice-president of the company; in 1937 he became head of the company's violin dept. in N.Y., which he made an independent firm in 1949; the company won great distinction and remained active until 1974. The Wurlitzer firm brought out the Wurlitzer Hope-Jones Unit Orch., better known as "the Mighty Wurlitzer," a theater organ, in 1910; their jukeboxes were manufactured between 1933 and 1974; in 1935 they began making a console upright spinet piano; from 1947 they manufactured electronic organs.

BIBL.: J. Fairfield, *W. World of Music: 100 Years of Musical Achievement* (Chicago, 1956); J. Landon, *Behold the Mighty W.* (Westport, Conn., 1983).

Würtzler, Aristid von, Hungarian-born American harpist and composer; b. Budapest, Sept. 20, 1930. He attended the Franz Liszt Academy of Music in Budapest (1951–56), where he studied harp with Miklós Rékai and composition with Kodály. He left Hungary during the 1956 uprising and emigrated to the U.S., where he was 1st harpist with the Detroit Sym. Orch. (1957) and the N.Y. Phil. (1958–62). He subsequently served as head of the harp dept. of the Hartt College of Music in Hartford, Conn. (1963–70). In 1970 he accepted teaching positions at N.Y. Univ. and Hofstra Univ. He founded the N.Y. Harp Ensemble, for which he commissioned works from contemporary composers, including Ligeti, Stockhausen, Hovhaness, Bernstein, Serly, Saygun, and Takemitsu. In 1981 he gave master classes in China, the first of their kind.

Wyk, Arnold(us Christian Vlok) van, South African composer, pianist, and teacher; b. Calvinia, Cape Province, April 26, 1916; d. Cape Town, May 27, 1983. He studied at Stellenbosch Univ., near Cape Town (1936–38); then went to London, where he studied with Theodore Holland (composition) and Harold Craxton (piano) at the Royal Academy of Music (1938–43). From 1939 to 1944 he worked for the BBC. In 1946 he returned to South Africa and taught at the Univ. of Cape Town (1949–61) and the Stellenbosch Univ. (1961–78). He also was active as a pianist.

WORKS: ORCH.: 2 syms.: No. 1 (1941–43) and No. 2, *Sinfonia ricercata* (Cape Town, March 13, 1952); *Southern Cross* (1943); *Rhapsody* (Cape Town, March 4, 1952); *Aubade* for Small Orch. (1955); *Primavera* (1960); *Maskerade* (1962–64); *Gebede by jaargetye in die Boland* (1966). **CHAMBER:** *5 Elegies* for String Quartet (1940–41); String Quartet No. 1 (1946); *Duo concertante* for Viola and Piano (1962); *Music for 13 Players* (1969); various piano pieces. **VOCAL:** Choral pieces; songs.

Wykes, Robert (Arthur), American flutist, teacher, and composer; b. Aliquippa, Pa., May 19, 1926. He studied composition with Phillips and Barlow at the Eastman School of Music in Rochester, N.Y. (B.M. and M.M., 1949). He played flute in the Toledo Sym. Orch. while teaching at Bowling Green State Univ. (1950–52); then taught at the Univ. of Ill. (1952–55). In 1955 he joined the faculty of Washington Univ. in St. Louis, where he was a prof. (1965–88); also was a flutist with the St. Louis Sym. Orch. (1963–67) and the Studio for New Music in St. Louis (1966–69). In 1990–91 he was a visiting scholar at Stanford Univ.

WORKS: DRAMATIC: CHAMBER OPERA: *The Prankster* (1951; Bowling Green, Ohio, Jan. 12, 1952). Also scores for documentary films, including *Robert Kennedy Remembered* (Academy Award, 1969), *Monument to the Dream, John F. Kennedy 1917–1963*, and *The Eye of Jefferson*. **ORCH.:** *Divertimento* for Small Orch. (1949); *Density III* (1959; St. Louis, Jan. 8, 1960); Concertino for Flute, Oboe, Piano, and Strings (1963); *Wave Forms and Pulses* (University City, Mo., May 2, 1964); *Horizons* (1964); *The Shape of Time* (St. Louis, April 1, 1965); *In Common Cause* for Strings, Trumpet, English Horn, and Percussion (1966); *Toward Time's Receding* (St. Louis, April 7, 1972); *A Shadow of Silence I* (1972); *Western Wyndes* for Symphonic Band (Barrington, Ill., May 21, 1974); *A Lyric Symphony* (St. Louis, May 10, 1980); *Paris: 2nd Symphony* (St. Louis, Sept. 27, 1981). **CHAMBER:** Flute Sonata (1955); String Sextet (1958); Piano Quintet (1959); *Points and Excursions* for Brass Quintet (1962); *Man against Machine* for Chamber Group (1966); *Cheirality* for String Quartet (1970); *3 Concert Etudes* for Flute (1989); *For Cello* (1989); *3 Facets of Friendship* for Flute and Clarinet (1990); *9 Miniatures: 3 Sets of 3* for Violin, Cello, and Piano (1993); piano and organ pieces. **VOCAL:** *Letter to an Alto Man* for Chorus, Harp, Piano, Percussion, Soloist, and Orch. (1966–67; St. Louis, May 19, 1967); *The Adequate Earth* for 2 Male Narrators, Baritone, 3 Choruses, and Orch., after Donald Finkel's poems about Antarctica (1975–76; St. Louis, Feb. 5, 1976); *For You Shall Go Out With Joy*, anthem for Chorus, 2 Trumpets, Harp, and Organ (1992).

Wyner, Susan Davenny, American soprano; b. New Haven, Conn., Oct. 17, 1943. She was educated at Cornell Univ., graduating summa cum laude in music and English literature in 1965; then pursued vocal studies with Herta Glaz (1969–75). She received a Fulbright scholarship and a grant from the Ford Foundation; also won the Walter W. Naumberg Prize. In 1972 she made her Carnegie Recital Hall debut in N.Y.; in 1974 she made her orch. debut as a soloist with the Boston Sym. Orch. On Oct. 23, 1977, she made her first appearance at the N.Y. City Opera as Monteverdi's Poppaea. On Oct. 8, 1981, she made her Metropolitan Opera debut in N.Y. as Woglinde in *Das Rheingold.* An exceptionally intelligent singer, she became equally successful as a performer of music in all historic idioms, from early Renaissance works to the most intransigent ultramodern scores. She married **Yehudi Wyner** in 1967.

Wyner (real name, **Weiner**), **Yehudi,** Canadian-born American composer, pianist, conductor, and teacher, son of **Lazar Weiner**; b. Calgary, June 1, 1929. He studied at the Juilliard School of Music in N.Y. (graduated, 1946), with Donovan and Hindemith at Yale Univ. (A.B., 1950; B.Mus., 1951; M.Mus., 1953), and with Piston at Harvard Univ. (M.A., 1952). After working at the American Academy in Rome (1953–56), he was active in N.Y. as a pianist and conductor. He served as music director of the Turnau Opera, a repertory company. From 1968 he appeared as a keyboard artist with the Bach Aria Group. He taught at Yale Univ. (1963–77), where he was head of the music dept. (1969–73). From 1975 he was on the piano and chamber music faculty of the Berkshire Music Center in Tanglewood. He also was prof. of music at the State Univ. of N.Y. at Purchase from 1978 to 1989, where he was dean of its music division (1978–82). In 1982 he was composer-in-residence at the Santa Fe Chamber Music Festival. In 1987 he was a visiting prof. of composition at Cornell Univ. In 1987–88 he was a visiting prof. at Brandeis Univ., and then served as the Walter W. Naumburg Prof. of Composition there from 1989. He also was director of the Brandeis Contemporary Chamber Players. In 1991 he was composer-in-residence at the American Academy in Rome. In 1958–59 and 1977–78 he held Guggenheim fellowships. He married **Susan Davenny Wyner** in 1967. In his music, Wyner often seeks to reconcile disparate elements of past and present, of high and low art. Classical, chromatic, and serial elements coexist, together with notable ingredients of popular and melodic and gestural inflections from his Jewish heritage. The result is an eclectic but personal style, poetic and lyrical in its essence.

WORKS: DRAMATIC: INCIDENTAL MUSIC: *The Old Glory* (1964); *The Mirror* (1972–73). **ORCH.:** *Da camera* for Piano and Orch. (1967); *Prologue and Narrative* for Cello and Orch. (BBC, Manchester, April 29, 1994); *Lyric Harmony* (1995). **CHAMBER:** *Short Sonata* for Clarinet and Piano (1950); *Dance Variations* for Wind Quintet, Trumpet, Trombone, and Cello (1953; rev. 1959); Concert Duo for Violin and Piano (1955–57); *Serenade* for Flute, Trumpet, Horn, Trombone, Viola, Cello, and Piano (1958); *Passover Offering* for Flute, Clarinet, Trombone, and Cello (1959); *3 Informal Pieces* for Violin and Piano (1961; rev. 1969); *Cadenza!* for Clarinet and Piano or Harpsichord (1969); *De novo* for Cello and Ensemble (1971); *Dances of Atonement* for Violin and Piano (1976); *All the Rage* for Flute and Piano (1980); *Romances* for Piano Quartet (1980); *Tanz and Maissele* for Clarinet, Violin, Cello, and Piano (1981); *Pas-*

sage I for 7 Instruments (1983); Wind Quintet (1984); String Quartet (1985); *Verzagen* for Violin and Piano (1986); *Sweet Corners* for Flute and Piano (1988); *Sweet is the Work* for Winds, Brass, and Piano (1990); *Trapunto Junction* for Horn, Trumpet, Trombone, and Percussion (1991); *Changing Time* for Violin, Clarinet, Cello, and Piano (1991); *Amadeus' Billiard* for Violin, Viola, Double Bass, Bassoon, and 2 Horns, after Mozart, K.205 (1991); *Il Cane Minore* for 2 Clarinets and Bassoon (1992). **KEYBOARD: PIANO:** *Easy Suite* (1949); *Partita* (1952); Sonata (1954); *3 Short Fantasies* (1963–71); *Wedding Dances from the Notebook of Suzanne da Venné* (1964–94); *New Fantasies* (1991); *Post-Fantasies* (1993–94). **ORGAN:** *2 Chorale Preludes* (1951). **VOCAL:** *Psalm CXLIII* for Chorus (1952); *Dedication Anthem* for Chorus and Organ (1957); *Friday Evening Service* for Cantor, Chorus, and Organ (1963); *Torah Service* for Chorus and Instruments (1966); *Liturgical Fragments for the High Holidays* for Chorus (1970); *Memorial Music* for Soprano and 3 Flutes (1971–73); *Canto cantabile* for Soprano and Band (1972); *Intermedio* for Soprano and Strings (1974); *Fragments from Antiquity* for Soprano and Orch. (1978–81); *On This Most Voluptuous Night* for Soprano and 7 Instruments (1982); *Leonardo Vincitore* for 2 Sopranos, Double Bass, and Piano (1988); *O to be a Dragon* for Women's Voices and Piano (1989); *Restaurants, Wines, Bistros, Shrines*, song cycle for Soprano, Baritone, and Piano (1994); *Torah Service Responses* for Chorus and Mixed Ensemble (1994).

Wyschnegradsky, Ivan (Alexandrovich), Russian composer, master of microtonal music; b. St. Petersburg, May 16, 1893; d. Paris, Sept. 29, 1979. He studied composition with Nikolai Sokoloff at the St. Petersburg Cons.; in 1920 he settled in Paris. He devoted virtually his entire musical career to the exploration and creative realization of music in quarter tones and other microtonal intervals; had a quarter tone piano constructed for him; also publ. a guide, *Manuel d'harmonie à quarts de ton* (Paris, 1932). On Nov. 10, 1945, he presented in Paris a concert of his music, at which he conducted the first performance of his *Cosmos* for 4 Pianos, with each pair tuned at quarter tones. Bruce Mather took interest in Wyschnegradsky's music and gave a concert of his works at McGill Univ. in Montreal that included 3 premieres (Feb. 10, 1977). But with the exception of these rare concerts, Wyschnegradsky remains a figure of legend; few performances of his music are ever given in Europe or North America. He regarded his *La Journée de l'existence* for Narrator, Orch., and Chorus ad libitum (to his own text; 1916–17; rev. 1927 and 1940) as his germinal work, opening the path to microtonal harmony; he dated this "awakening to ultrachromaticism" as having occurred on Nov. 7, 1918. At his death, he left sketches for a short opera in 5 scenes, *L'Éternel Étranger*, begun in 1939 but never completed. Also unfinished was the ambitious *Polyphonie spatiale*.

WORKS (all in quarter tones unless otherwise given): *La Journée de l'existence* for Narrator, Orch., and Chorus ad libitum (1916–17; rev. 1927 and 1940); *Chant douloureux et étude* for Violin and Piano (1918); *7 Variations on the Note C* for 2 Pianos (1918–20; perf. in 1945 as *5 Variations*; then 2 more were added); *Chant funèbre* for Strings and 2 Harps (1922); *Chant nocturne* for Violin and 2 Pianos (1923; rev. 1972); 2 string quartets (1924; 1931–32); *2 Choruses* for Voices and 4 Pianos (1926); *Prélude et fugue sur un chant de l'Évangile rouge* for String Quartet (1927); *Prélude et Danse* for 2 Pianos (1928); *Ainsi parlait Zarathoustra* for Orch. (1929–30; arr. for 4 Pianos, 1936); *2 études de concert* for Piano (1931; arr. for 2 Pianos, 1936); *Étude en forme de scherzo* for 2 Pianos (1932); *Prélude et Fugue* for 2 Pianos (1933); *24 préludes* for 2 Pianos (1934; rev. 1958–60); *4 Fragments symphoniques* for 4 Pianos (1934, final version, 1968; 1937; 1946; 1956); *Le Mot* for Soprano and Piano (1935; half-tones); *Linnite*, pantomime for 3 Women's Voices and 4 Pianos (1937); *Acte chorégraphique* for Bass-baritone, Chorus, and 4 Pianos (1938–40; rev. 1958–59); *Cosmos* for 4 Pianos (1940; suppressed); *Prélude et Fugue* for 3 Pianos (1945); *2 Fugues* for 2 Pianos (1951); *5 variations sans thème et conclusion* for Orch. (1951–52); *Sonate en un mouvement* for Viola and 2 Pianos (1956; suppressed); *Transparences I* and *II* for Ondes Martenot and 2 Pianos (1956, 1963); *Arc-en-ciel* for 6 Pianos (1956); *Étude sur le carré magique sonore* for Piano (1956; based on the "magic square" principle of cyclical structure, written in a tempered scale without quarter tones); *Étude tricesimoprimal* for Fokker-organ (1959; for the Dutch physicist Adriaan Fokker's 31-tone organ); *Composition* for String Quartet (1960); *2 pièces* for Microtonal Piano (1960); *Étude sur les mouvements rotatoires* for 4 Pianos (1961; orchestrated 1964); *2 Compositions*: No. 1 for 3 Pianos and No. 2 for 2 Pianos (1962); *Prélude et étude* for Microtonal Piano (1966); *Intégrations* for 2 Pianos (1967); *Symphonie en un mouvement* for Orch. (1969); *Dialogues à trois* for 3 Pianos (1973–74; sixth tones).

Wyttenbach, Jürg, Swiss pianist, conductor, teacher, and composer; b. Bern, Dec. 2, 1935. He studied piano and theory with Fischer and Veress at the Bern Cons. After further studies with Lefébure and Calvet at the Paris Cons. (1955–57), he completed his training in piano with Karl Engel (1958–59). In 1959 he became a teacher at the Biel Music School. In 1962 he became a teacher at the Bern Cons. From 1967 he taught at the Basel Academy of Music. He also appeared frequently as a pianist and conductor, championing particularly the cause of contemporary music. His own music utilizes both aleatory and serialism.

WORKS: DRAMATIC: *Beethoven: Sacré? Sacré Beethoven!* for Singer, Speaker, Musician, and Projection (1977); *Patchwork an der Wäscheleine*, scenic collage (1979); *Chansons ricochets*, madrigal comedy for 5 Singers (1980); *Hors jeux*, "sport-opera" (1981–82). **ORCH.:** Piano Concerto (1959; rev. 1973); *Conteste* for Chamber Orch. (1969). **CHAMBER:** *Serenade* for Flute and Piano (1959–79); Oboe Sonata (1962–72); *3 Movements* for Oboe, Harp, and Piano (1963); *Divisions* for Piano and 9 Solo Strings (1964); *Anrufungen und Ausbruch* for Woodwinds and Brass (1966); *Ad libitum* for 1 or 2 Flutes (1969); *Exécution ajournée* for 13 Players (1969–70) and for String Quartet (1970); *Kunststücke, die Zeit totzuschlagen* for Player (1972); *Noch weisst du nicht, wess Kind du bist* for Piano, Violin, and Singer ad libitum (1977); *Claustrophonie* for Violin (1979); *Tarantella* for Violin (1983); piano pieces. **VOCAL:** *Sutil und Laar* for Chorus and Piano, 4-hands (1964); *Vier Kanzonen* for Soprano and Cello (1964); *2 Nonsense Verses, and Epigram and a Madrigal* for Soprano and Cello or Bassoon (1964); *De Matalli* for Baritone and Orch. (1964–65).

Xanrof (real name, **Fourneaux**), **Léon,** French composer; b. Paris, Dec. 9, 1867; d. there, May 17, 1953. Xanrof is an anagram of *fornax*, the Latin equivalent of *fourneau.* He was a lawyer by profession; from 1890, he produced light stage pieces in the Paris theaters. His chansonnette *Le Fiacre*, composed for Yvette Guilbert, achieved great popularity. He also contributed music criticism to various Paris newspapers.

Xenakis, Iannis, eminent Greek-born French composer, music theorist, and teacher; b. Brăila, Rumania (of Greek parents), May 29, 1922. At the age of 10, he was taken to Greece by his parents, where he began his music studies at 12 with Aristotle Koundourov. In 1938 he enrolled in a preparatory course in engineering at the Athens Polytechnic but then abandoned his studies when he became active in the Greek resistance movement against the Nazi occupation forces. He was severely wounded in a skirmish, and lost an eye. Shortly after, he was captured but managed to escape a death sentence by fleeing the country. He settled in France in 1947 and in 1965 became a naturalized French citizen. From 1947 to 1960 he worked as an architect in collaboration with Le Corbusier. In the meantime, he studied composition in Paris with Honegger and Milhaud at the École Normale de Musique, and with Messiaen at the Cons. (1950–52); then pursued studies with Scherchen in Gravesano, Switzerland. While working with Le Corbusier on the Philips Pavillion at the 1958 World's Fair in Brussels, he met Varèse, who was then working on his *Poème electronique* for the exhibit; Xenakis received from him some stimulating advice on the creative potentialities of the electronic medium. In 1966 he founded and became director of the Centre d'Études Mathématics et Automatiques Musicales in Paris. He also was founder-director of the Center for Mathematical and Automated Music at Indiana Univ. in Bloomington, where he served on its faculty from 1967 to 1972. From 1972 to 1974 he was associated with the Centre National de la Recherche Scientifique in Paris. He was a prof. at the Univ. of Paris from 1972 to 1989. He publ. the book *Musiques formelles* (Paris, 1963; Eng. tr., 1971, as *Formalized Music*; 2nd ed., rev. 1992). For his doctorat des lettres from the Sorbonne in Paris in 1976, he wrote the thesis *Art/Sciences: Alliages* (Paris, 1979; Eng. tr., N.Y., 1985). In 1974 he received the Ravel Medal of France. In 1975 he was elected an honorary member of the American Academy of Arts and Letters. He received the Grand Prix National de la Musique of France in 1976. Xenakis was made a member of the Académie des Beaux-arts of France in 1983. In 1987 he received the Grand Prix for music of Paris. Xenakis's hardships and sufferings during his participation in the Greek resistance movement, and his pursuit of a career in engineering and architecture, profoundly influenced him as a composer. Early in his career he moved beyond dogmatic serialism by connecting mathematical concepts to the organization of a musical composition, particularly set theory, symbolic logic, and probabalistic calculus. He promulgated the stochastic method, which is teleologically directed and deterministic. His use of the computer led him to develop the computer drawing board, UPIC, which he used for both compositional and educational purposes.

WORKS: DRAMATIC: *Oresteia*, incidental music (1965–66); *Medea*, theater music (1967); *Kraanerg*, ballet (1968–69; Ottawa, June 2, 1969); *Antikhthon*, ballet (1971; Bonn, Sept. 21, 1974); *Les Bacchantes*, theater music (1992–93). **ORCH.:** *Metastasis* (1953–54; Donaueschingen, Oct. 15, 1955); *Pithoprakta* (1955–56; Munich, March 8, 1957); *Achorripsis* (1956–57; Brussels, July 20, 1958); *Syrmos* for 18 or 36 Strings (1959); *Duel*, game for 2 "antagonistic" Orchs., mathematically based on game theory, with the audience determining the winning orch. (1959; Radio Hilversum, Oct. 1971); *ST/48–1,240162* (ST = stochastic; 48 = number of players; 1 = 1st work for this contingent; 240162 = 24 January 1962, date on which the work, derived from earlier sketches, was finally calculated by the IBM 7090 electronic computer in Paris as programmed probabilistically by Xenakis) (1959–62); *Stratégie*, game for 2 Orchs. (1959–62; Venice, April 23, 1963); *Akrata* (Pure) for 16 Winds (1964–65; Oxford, June 28, 1966); *Terrêtektorh* for 88 Players scattered among the audience (1965–66; Royan, April 3, 1966);

Polytope de Montréal, light-and-sound spectacle for 4 Small (identical) Orchs. (1967); *Nomos gamma* for 98 Players scattered among the audience (1967–68; Royan, April 3, 1969); *Synaphaï* for Piano and Orch. (1969); *Eriadnos* for 8 Brasses and 10 String Instruments or their multiples (1973); *Erikhthon* for Piano and Orch. (Paris, May 1974); *Noomena* (Paris, Oct. 16, 1974); *Empreintes* (La Rochelle, June 29, 1975); *Ionchaies* (1977); *Pour les Baleines* for Strings (1982); *Shaar* for Strings (1983); *Lichens* (1983; London, May 30, 1986); *Alax* (Cologne, Sept. 14, 1985); *Horos* (Tokyo, Oct. 24, 1986); *Kegrops* for Piano and Orch. (N.Y., Nov. 13, 1986); *Tracées* (Paris, Sept. 17, 1987); *Ata* (1987; Lisbon, May 3, 1988); *Tuorakemsu* (1990); *Kyania* (1990); *Krinoïdi* (1991); *Dok-Orkh* for Violin and Orch. (1991); *Roáï* (1991); *Trookh* for Trombone and Orch. (1991); *Dämmerschein* (1993–94). **CHAMBER:** *ST/4* for String Quartet (1956–62); *ST/10–1,080262* (ST = stochastic; 10 = number of players; 1 = 1st work of this contingent; 080262 = 8 February 1962, date on which this work was finally electronically calculated) for Clarinet, Bass Clarinet, 2 Horns, Harp, Percussion, and String Quartet (1956–62); *Morsima-Amorsima* (Morsima = that which comes by Fate; Amorsima = that which does not come by Fate) for Piano, Violin, Cello, and Double Bass (1956–62); *Analogiques* for 9 Strings and Tape (1959); *Amorisma-Morsiama* for Clarinet, Bass Clarinet, 2 Horns, Trumpet, Harps, Trombone, 2 Percussion, Violin, and Cello (1962); *Eonta* (neuter plural of the present participle of the verb "to be" in the Ionian dialect, the title being in Cypriot syllabic characters of Creto-Mycenean origin) for 2 Trumpets, 3 Trombones, and Piano (1963–64); *Nomos Alpha* (Law Alpha) for Cello (1966); *Anaktoria* for Clarinet, Bassoon, Horn, String Quintet, and Double Bass (1969); *Persephassa* for 6 Percussionists (1969); *Charisma* for Clarinet and Cello (1971); *Aroura* for 12 Strings (1971); *Mikka* for Violin (1972); *Linaia-Agon* for Horn, Trombone, and Tuba (1972); *Phlegra* for 11 Instruments (1975); *Psappha* for Percussion (1975); *Theraps* for Double Bass (1975–76); *Retours-Windungen* for 12 Cellos (1976); *Epeï* for English Horn, Clarinet, Trumpet, 2 Trombones, and Double Bass (1976); *Mikka "S"* for Violin (1976); *Dmaathen* for Oboe and Percussion (1976); *Kottos* for Cello (1977); *Ikhoor* for String Trio (1978); *Pleiades* for 6 Percussion (1978); *Palimpsest* for Piano and Percussion (1979); *Dikhthas* for Violin and Piano (1979); *Embellie* for Viola (1980); *Khal Perr* for 5 Horns and Percussion (1983); *Tetras* for String Quartet (1983); *Thalleïn* for 14 Players (1984); *A l'ile de Gorée* for Amplified Harpsichord and 12 Players (Amsterdam, July 4, 1986); *Akea* for Piano and String Quartet (Paris, Dec. 14, 1986); *Keren* for Trombone (1986); *Jalons* for Chamber Ensemble (1986; Paris, Jan. 26, 1987); *XAS* for Saxophone Quartet (Lille, Nov. 17, 1987); *Rebonds A* (1987–88; Rome, July 1, 1988) and *B* (Avignon, July 24, 1989) for Percussion; *Echange* for 13 Players (Amsterdam, April 26, 1989); *Waarg* for 13 Players (London, May 6, 1988); *Oophaa* for Amplified Harpsichord and Percussion (Warsaw, Sept. 17, 1989); *Okho* for 3 Djembes (Paris, Oct. 20, 1989); *Epicycle* for Cello and 12 Players (London, May 18, 1989); *Paille in the Wind* for Cello and Piano (1992). **VOCAL:** *Polla ta dhina* (Many Are the Wonders) for Children's Chorus, Winds, and Percussion (1962); *Hiketides* for Women's Chorus and 10 Instruments or Orch. (1964); *Nuits* for 12 Voices (1967); *Cendrées* for Chorus and Orch. (1973–74); *N'Shima* for 2 Mezzo-sopranos, Horns, 2 Trombones, and Cello (1975); *Akanthos* for 2 Sopranos, Flute, Clarinet, 2 Violins, Viola, Cello, Double Bass, and Piano (1977); *À Colone* for Men's Chorus, Horn, Trombone, and Double Bass (1977; also for Men's or Women's Chorus, 3 Horns, 3 Trombones, 3 Cellos, and 3 Double Basses); *À Hélène* for Mezzo-soprano, Women's Chorus, and 2 Clarinets (1977); *Andemoessa* for Chorus and Orch. (1979); *Aïs* for Baritone and Orch. (1980); *Nekuïa* for Chorus and Orch. (1981); *Serment-Orkos* for Chorus (1981); *Pour la Paix* for Chorus and Tape (1981); *Chant des Soleils* for Chorus, Children's Chorus, Brass, and Percussion (1983); *Idmen A* for Chorus and 4 Percussion (1985) and *B* for Chorus and 6 Percussion (1985); *Nyuyo* for Voice, Skakuhachi, and 2 Kotos (1985); *Kassandra: Oresteia II* for Amplified Baritone and Percussion (1987); *Knephas* for Chorus (London, June 24, 1990); *La Deesse Athena* for Baritone and Instruments (1992); *Pu Wijnuej We Fyp* for Children's Chorus (1992); *Sea Nymphs* for Chorus (London, Oct. 23, 1994). **TAPE:** *Diamorphoses* (1957–58); *Concret PH* (1957); *Analogique B* (1958–59); *Orient-Occident* (1960); *The Thessaloniki World Fair* (1961); *Bohor I* (1962) and *II* (1975); *Hibiki-hana-ma*, 12-channel electroacoustic music distributed kinematically over 800 loudspeakers (1969–70; also a 4-channel version); *Persepolis* (1971); *Polytope de Cluny* (1972); *Polytope II* (1974); *Diatope* (1977);*Mycènes Alpha* (1978); *Taurtriphanie* (1987); *Voyage absolu des Unari vers Andromède* (1989).

BIBL.: M. Bois, *I. X.: The Man and His Music: A Conversation with the Composer and a Description of His Works* (Westport, Conn., 1980); *Regards sur I. X.* (Paris, 1981); N. Matossian, *I. X.* (Paris, 1981; Eng. tr., 1986; 2nd ed., 1990); E. Restagno, ed., *X.* (Turin, 1988).

Y

Yamada, Kōsaku (Kōsçak), eminent Japanese conductor and composer; b. Tokyo, June 9, 1886; d. there, Dec. 29, 1965. He studied vocal music with Tamaki Shibata and cello and theory with Werkmeister at the Tokyo Imperial Academy of Music (1904–08); then composition with Bruch and Karl Leopold Wolf at the Berlin Hochschule für Musik (1908–13). He founded the Tokyo Phil. in 1915; appeared as a guest conductor with the N.Y. Phil. in 1918 in a program of Japanese music, including some of his own works; conducted in Russia in 1930 and 1933, and then throughout Europe in 1937. His compositions follow in the German Romantic tradition of Wagner and Strauss, with impressionistic overtones. Although most of his MSS were destroyed during the Allied air raid on Tokyo on May 25, 1945, several works have been restored from extant orch. parts.

WORKS; OPERAS: *Ochitaru tennyo* (The Depraved Heavenly Maiden; 1912; Tokyo, Dec. 3, 1929); *Alladine et Palomides* (1913); *Ayame* (The Sweet Flag; Paris, 1931); *Kurofune* (The Black Ships; 1939); *Yoake* (The Dawn; 1939; Tokyo, Nov. 28, 1940); *Hsiang Fei* (1946–47; Tokyo, May 1954). **ORCH.:** Sym., *Kachidoki to heiwa* (The Shout of Victory and Peace; 1912; Tokyo, Dec. 6, 1914); *Shōwa sanka* (Homage to Shōwa), symphonic poem (1938; Tokyo, May 13, 1939); *Kamikaze*, symphonic poem (1944). **CHAMBER:** Several pieces. **VOCAL:** *Meiji shōka* (Ode to the Meiji) for Chorus and Orch. (1921; Tokyo, April 26, 1925); 2 cantatas: *Bonno-Koru* (Tokyo, Oct. 9, 1932) and *Tairiku no reimei* (The Dawn of the Orient; Tokyo, July 7, 1941); nearly 1,000 choral pieces and songs.

Yamaguchi, Motohumi, Japanese instrumentalist and composer; b. Tokyo, Nov. 7, 1954. After cello studies at Masashino Music Univ., he became the main flute and shamisen player for Kodo in 1980, a highly disciplined performing ensemble founded in 1971 by Tagayasu Den, a scholar of traditional Japanese arts, under the name Ondekoza ("demon drummers"); under the direction of a new leader, Kawauchi, the group was renamed Kodo (translating to both "heartbeat" and "children of the drum," referring to the taiko that is so central to its performances). Kodo has given choreographed performances throughout Asia, the Americas, and Europe; in 1988 the ensemble held its first annual Earth Celebration on Sado Island, attracting performers from all over the world. Among his compositions for the group are *Hae* for Koto, Japanese Drum, and Caribbean Drum (1982), *Tjanang Sari* for Percussion, after Balinese gamelan (1987), and *Kariuta* for 2 Shinobue (Japanese flutes) (1989). Other members of the ensemble include Leonard Eto (b. N.Y., March 5, 1963) and Yoshiaki Oi (b. Tokyo, March 28, 1951). Among Kodo's many celebrated recordings are *Kodo* (1981), *Kodo, Heartbeat Drummers of Japan* (1985), and *Blessing of the Earth* (1989).

Yamash'ta, Stomu (real name, **Tsutomu Yamashita**), Japanese percussionist and composer; b. Kyoto, March 10, 1947. He was trained in music by his father; played piano in his infancy, and drums at puberty; in early adolescence he became a timpanist for the Kyoto Phil. and Osaka Phil.; also worked in several film studios in Tokyo. At 16, he went to London for further study; later went to the U.S. as a scholarship student at the Interlochen (Mich.) Arts Academy; continued his musical education in Boston, N.Y., and Chicago. Returning to Japan, he gave solo performances as a percussionist; developed a phenomenal degree of equilibristic prestidigitation, synchronously manipulating a plethora of drums and a congregation of oriental bells and gongs while rotating 360° from the center of a circle to reach the prescribed percussionable objects. As a composer, he cultivates a manner of controlled improvisation marked by constantly shifting meters. In 1970 he formed the Red Buddha Theater (an ensemble of actors, musicians, and dancers), for which he composed 2 musical pageants, *Man from the East* (1971) and *Rain Mountain* (1973). Other works include a ballet, *Fox* (1968); *Hito* for any 3 Instruments (1970); *Prisms* for Percussion (1970); *Red Buddha* for Chamber Ensemble (1971); percussion scores for many Japanese films, as well as for Ken Russell's *The Devils* (with Peter Maxwell Davies, 1971) and Robert Altman's *Images* (1972).

Yampolsky, Abram (Ilyich), distinguished Russian violin pedagogue, uncle of **Izrail (Markovich) Yampolsky**; b. Ekaterinoslav, Oct. 11, 1890; d. Moscow, Aug. 17, 1956. He studied violin with Korguyev at the St. Petersburg Cons. (graduated, 1913); also received instruction in composition from Sokolov, Wihtol, and Steinberg. After teaching at the Ekaterinoslav music school (1913–20), he settled in Moscow, where he was concertmaster of the conductorless ensemble Persymfans (1922–32); was also prof. (1926–56) and chairman of the violin dept. (1936–56) at the Cons. Yampolsky was made a Doctor of Arts (1940). He was teacher and adviser to a number of prominent Soviet violinists, among them Kogan, Elizaveta Gilels, Grach, Zhuk, and Sitkovetsky.

Yampolsky, Izrail (Markovich), Russian musicologist and lexicographer, nephew of **Abram (Ilyich) Yampolsky**; b. Kiev, Nov. 21, 1905; d. Moscow, Sept. 20, 1976. He studied violin with his uncle, then entered the Moscow Cons., where he took courses in advanced theory with Miaskovsky and Gliere; he subsequently taught violin at the Music Academy in Moscow (1931–58); gave lectures in music history there; also taught at the Cons. (1934–49). A fine and diligent research scholar, he publ. a number of excellent monographs dealing mainly with violin and violinists: on the foundations of violin fingering (Moscow, 1933; 3rd expanded ed., 1955; Eng. tr., London, 1967); *Henryk Wieniawski* (Moscow, 1955); *Enescu* (Moscow, 1956; also in Romanian, Bucharest, 1959); on the music of Yugoslavia (Moscow, 1958); *Paganini* (Moscow, 1961; 2nd ed., 1968); *David Oistrakh* (Moscow, 1964); *Fritz Kreisler* (1975). He was co-editor, with Boris Steinpress, of a 1-vol. encyclopedic music dictionary (Moscow, 1959; rev. 1966). He was acting ed.-in-chief of the 1st 3 vols. of the 5-vol. Soviet musical encyclopedia (Moscow, 1973, 1974, 1976).

Yang, Liqing, Chinese composer and writer on music; b. Sichuan, April 30, 1942. After taking degrees at the Shenyang Cons. of Music (B.A., 1970) and Shanghai Cons. of Music (M.A., 1980), he pursued postgraduate studies with Kurt Bauer (piano diploma, 1983) and Alfredo Koerppen (Ph.D. in composition, 1983) at the Hannover Hochschule für Musik. He was an assistant prof. of composition at Shenyang Cons. (1970–78); then was a lecturer (1983–86), assoc. prof. (1986–90), and prof. (from 1991) at the Shanghai Cons., where he also served as dean of its composition and conducting dept. (from 1991). In 1990 he was a guest prof. at the Salzburg Mozarteum. Yang has spoken throughout Germany, Austria, and in Switzerland on new music in China; in 1995 he conducted research in the U.S. on a grant from the Asian Cultural Council. His articles on such wide-ranging topics as new notation, neoromanticism, Charles Ives, and postmodernism have appeared in various Chinese publications; he also publ. *The Compositional Techniques of Olivier Messiaen* (1989).

WORKS: DRAMATIC: *The Night of a Festival* for Dancer and Small Orch. (1973); *The Seedling* for Dancer and Small Orch. (1973); *Mister O*, incidental music (1977); *The Monument without Inscription*, dance/drama for Chorus and Orch. (1989; in collaboration with Lu Pei); *Red Cherry*, film music for Soprano, Liu Qin, Zhong Ran, and Orch. (1995). **ORCH.:** *Set Sail*, concerto for Piano and Chinese Orch. (1975); *Festival by Hailan River*, rondo (1978); *Yi* (1982–83); *Suicide by the Wujiang River* for Pipa and Orch. (1986); *Festival Overture* (1987); *Ode to Apollo* (1991); *Elegy—Jian He Shui* for Erhu and Chinese Orch. (1991; also for Erhu and Traditional Orch., 1995); *Two Folksongs* for Piano and Orch. (1993; also for Violin and Orch.); *The Chess Game* for Shun, Pipa, and Orch. (1994); *Concerto for Zheng* for Zheng and Orch. (1995); *Costs of Peace* (1995). **CHAMBER:** *Violin Concerto* for Violin and Piano (1970); *Chamber Music for Ten* for Flute, Oboe, Clarinet, Bassoon, Horn, and Strings (1982–83). **PIANO:** *Two Preludes* (1962); *Nine Pieces on the Shanxi Folksongs* (1962–63); *Sonatina* (1964); *Mountain Song & Work Song* for Piano, 4-hands (1980). **VOCAL:** *Dujuan Mountain Suite* for Soprano, Baritone, Piano, Jinghu, Erhu, and Percussion (1974); *The Sun*, ballet music for Soprano, Chorus, and Orch. (1976); *Four Poems from Tang-Dynasty* for Mezzo-soprano, Piano, and 2 Percussion (1981); *Three F.G. Lorca Songs* for Mezzo-soprano, Flute, Cello, and Piano (1982); *The Story About the Birth of Tao* for Chorus, after Brecht (1982); *Prelude, Interludes, and Postlude* for Chorus and Orch. (1990).

BIBL.: F. Kouwenhoven, "Out of the Desert: Mainland China's New Music," *Chime Journal*, vol. II (part I; 1990); idem, "The Age of Pluralism: Mainland China's New Music," ibid., vol. V (part II; 1992); Z. Li, "An Interview with Composer Y. L.," *Chinese Music Yearbook* (1993; includes a list of recent works).

Yankelevich, Yuri, Russian violinist and pedagogue; b. Basel, March 7, 1909; d. Moscow, Sept. 12, 1973. He studied with Anisim Berlin in Omsk, Johannes Nalbandian at the Petrograd Cons., and A. Yampolsky at the Moscow Cons. (graduated, 1932); then taught there, becoming a prof. in 1961. Among his outstanding students were Spivakov and Tretyakov.

Yannatos, James, American composer, conductor, and teacher; b. N.Y., March 13, 1929. He was a student of Hindemith and Porter at Yale Univ. (B.M., 1951; M.M., 1952) and of Bezanson at the Univ. of Iowa (Ph.D., 1960). He also studied with Bernstein, Steinberg, Boulanger, Milhaud, and Dallapiccola. From 1964 he taught at Yale Univ. He also was active as a conductor of youth orchs. and choral groups, and conducted various chamber orchs. He was the author of *Explorations in Musical Materials* (1978). Among his works were the opera *The Rocket's Red Glare* (1971); the ballets *Oedipus* (1960) and *A Suite for Orpheus and Eurydice* (1980); pieces for chamber orch.; many choral works; didactic pieces for children.

Yannay, Yehuda, Romanian-born Israeli-American composer, conductor, and teacher; b. Timişoara, May 26, 1937. He went with his family to Israel in 1951 and studied composition with Boscovich. After graduating from the Rubin Academy of Music in Tel Aviv (1964), he went to the U.S. on a Fulbright grant and pursued training with Berger, Shapero, and Krenek at Brandeis Univ. (M.F.A., 1966). He also studied with Schuller at the Berkshire Music Center at Tanglewood (summer, 1965) before completing his training at the Univ. of Ill. in Urbana (1968–70; D.M.A., 1974). From 1970 he taught theory and composition at the Univ. of Wisc. in Milwaukee. In 1971 he organized the "Music from Almost Yesterday" concert series, with which he programmed numerous contemporary scores. In his own extensive and varied output, Yannay has experimented with live electronics, synthesizers, and environmental resources. His experimentation with the synthesizer led to his creation of the genre he described as "synthesizer theater."

WORKS: *The Chain of Proverbs*, youth cantata (1962); *Spheres* for Soprano and 10 Instruments (1963); *Incantations* for Voice, Keyboard, and Interior Piano (1964); *2 Fragments* for Violin and Piano (1966); *Wraphap*, theater piece for Actress, Amplified Aluminum Sheet, and Yannaychord (1969); *Coloring Book for the Harpist* (1969); Concerto for Audience and Orch. (1971); *The Hidden Melody* for Cello and Horn (1977); Concertino for Violin and Chamber Orch. (1980); *Celan Ensembles: Augentanz* and *Galgenlied* for Tenor and Instruments (1986–), *In Madness There is Order* for Voice, Projections, and Synthesizers (1988), and *Spiegeltanz* for Voice, Horn, and 2 Marimbas (1989); Duo for Flute and Cello (1991); *The Oranur Experiment*, music video (part 1, *Journey to Orgonon*, 1991; in collaboration with J. Fortier); *Tableau One: ". . . in sleep one often finds solutions . . ."* (from *Journey to Orgonon*) for Actor, Projections, and Synthesizers (1992; in collaboration with J. Fortier and M. Mellott); *In Madness There is Order*, music video (1992); *Cello Solo for "I can't fathom it"* for Projection Theater (1993); *5 Pieces for 3 Players* for Soprano Saxophone, Clarinet, and Marimba (1994).

Yansons, Arvid, Latvian conductor, father of **Mariss Jansons**; b. Leipaja, Oct. 24, 1914; d. Manchester, England, Nov. 21, 1984. He studied violin at the Leipaja Cons. (1929–35), then took courses in violin, conducting, and composition at the Riga Cons. (1940–44). In 1944 he made his conducting debut in

Riga; in 1948 he was made assoc. conductor of the Leningrad Phil.; also appeared as a guest conductor throughout the Soviet Union, Europe, Australia, and Japan. From 1965 he made regular guest conducting appearances with the Hallé Orch. in Manchester; also served as head of the conducting class at the Leningrad Cons. (from 1972).

Yardumian, Richard, American composer; b. Philadelphia (of Armenian parents), April 5, 1917; d. Bryn Athyn, Pa., Aug. 15, 1985. He studied harmony with William Happich, counterpoint with H. Alexander Matthews, and piano with George Boyle (1939–41); later attended Monteux's conducting school in Hancock, Maine (summer, 1947), and received additional musical training from Thomson in N.Y. (1953). His compositions reflect the spirit of Armenian folk songs and religious melodies. A number of his works were first performed by the Philadelphia Orch.

WORKS: ORCH.: *Armenian Suite* (1937–54; Philadelphia, March 5, 1954); *Symphonic Suite* (1939); *3 Pictographs of an Ancient Kingdom* (1941); *Desolate City* (1943–44; Philadelphia, April 6, 1945); Violin Concerto (1949; Philadelphia, March 30, 1950; rev. 1960); 2 syms.: No. 1 (1950; rev., Philadelphia, Dec. 1, 1961) and No. 2, *Psalms*, for Mezzo-soprano or Baritone and Orch. (1947–64; Philadelphia, Nov. 13, 1964); *Epigram: William M. Kincaid* for Flute and Strings (1951; also for Flute and String Quartet); *Passacaglia, Recitatives and Fugue*, piano concerto (1957; Philadelphia, Jan. 3, 1958); *Veni sancte Spiritus*, chorale prelude for Chamber Orch. (1958); *Num komm der heiden Heiland*, chorale prelude (1978; arranged from an organ piece). **CHAMBER:** Flute Quintet (1951; arranged for Flute and Strings); *Cantus animae et cordis* for String Quartet (1955; arranged for Strings, 1955). **KEYBOARD: PIANO:** *3 Preludes: Wind* (1938), *Sea* (1936), and *Sky* (1944; orchestrated 1945); *Dance* (1942); *Chromatic Sonata* (1946); *Prelude and Chorale* (1946); various organ pieces. **VOCAL:** *Create in Me a Clean Heart* for Mezzo-soprano or Baritone and Chorus (1962); *Magnificat* for Women's Voices (1965); *Come Creator Spirit*, mass for Mezzo-soprano or Baritone, Chorus, Congregation, and Orch. or Organ (1965–66; N.Y., March 31, 1967); *The Story of Abraham*, oratorio for Soloists, Chorus, Orch., and Film (1968–71; rev. 1973); *Narek: Der Asdvadz* for Mezzo-soprano, Horn, and Harp (1983); *Hrashapar* for Chorus, Organ, and Orch. (1984); about 100 chorales for Chorus (1944–85).

Yashirō, Akio, Japanese composer and teacher; b. Tokyo, Sept. 10, 1929; d. Yokohama, April 9, 1976. He studied piano with Leonid Kreutzer and composition with Hashimoto, Ifukube, and Ikenouchi at the Tokyo Geijutsu Daigaku, graduating in 1949; then went to Paris, where he studied composition with Noël Gallon at the Cons. (1951–54), and took private lessons with Boulanger and Messiaen. Returning to Japan, he joined the faculty of the Tokyo Geijutsu Daigaku (1956) and the Toho Gakuen School of Music (1958).

WORKS: String Quartet (1954–55); Sonata for 2 Flutes and Piano (1957–58); Sym. (Tokyo, June 9, 1958); Cello Concerto (Tokyo, June 24, 1960); Piano Sonata (1960); Piano Concerto (Tokyo, Nov. 5, 1967); *Ouverture de fête* for Brass Ensemble (Sapporo, Feb. 3, 1972).

Yasser, Joseph, Polish-born Russian-American organist, conductor, and musicologist; b. Łódź, April 16, 1893; d. N.Y., Sept. 6, 1981. He studied at the Moscow Cons., graduating in 1917 as an organist. After several years of teaching organ in Moscow and Siberia, he reached Shanghai in 1921, and conducted a choral society there; subsequently emigrated to the U.S. (1923); served as organist at Temple Rodeph Sholom in N.Y. (1929–60); held various positions in American musicological groups. His most important contribution to music theory was *A Theory of Evolving Tonality* (N.Y., 1932), in which he proffered an ingenious hypothesis as to the origin of the pentatonic and heptatonic scales, and, operating by inductive reasoning, suggested that the ultimate Western scale would contain 19 degrees. He contributed several articles to *Musical Quarterly* (April and July 1937 and July 1938) dealing with quartal harmony, which were publ. in a separate ed. (N.Y., 1938).

Yates, Peter B., Canadian-American writer on music; b. Toronto, Nov. 30, 1909; d. N.Y., Feb. 25, 1976. He studied at Princeton Univ. (B.A., 1931). He married the pianist Frances Mullen in 1933. From 1937 to 1962 he was a functionary at the Calif. Dept. of Employment in Los Angeles, but this bureaucratic occupation did not preclude his activities as a musical catalyst. In 1939 he inaugurated on the rooftop of his house in the Silver Lake district of Los Angeles a chamber concert series which was to become an important cultural enterprise in subcultural California, under the name "Evenings on the Roof"; he served as coordinator of these concerts from 1939 to 1954, when they were moved to a larger auditorium in downtown Los Angeles and became known as the "Monday Evening Concerts". In 1968 he was appointed chairman of the music dept. at the State Univ. of N.Y. at Buffalo. He publ. *An Amateur at the Keyboard* (N.Y., 1964), *Twentieth-Century Music* (N.Y., 1967), and a collection of poems.

Yavorsky, Boleslav (Leopoldovich), Russian pianist and music theorist; b. Kharkov, June 22, 1877; d. Saratov, Nov. 26, 1942. He studied piano and composition with Taneyev in Moscow. In 1906 he founded a People's Cons. there. From 1915 to 1919 he taught at the Kiev Cons.; then went to Moscow. His theory of aural gravitation as the determining factor of the formation of modes is embodied in his publications on the structure of musical speech (Moscow, 1908) and exercises in schematic formation of modal rhythm (Moscow, 1915), and in several monographs. He was also active in the field of general musical education, and his methods influenced Soviet practice in pedagogy.

Yepes, Narciso, noted Spanish guitarist and lutenist; b. Lorca, Nov. 14, 1927. He took up the guitar at the age of 6. At 12, he entered the Valencia Cons. He was 15 when he became a student of the pianist Vicente Ascencio. In 1947 he made his formal debut as a soloist in Rodrigo's *Concierto de Aranjuez* with Argenta and the Orquesta Nacional de España in Madrid. In 1950 he went to Paris for further training with Enesco and Gieseking. He subsequently pursued an international career as a virtuoso. From 1964 he played a 10-string guitar of his own design. Yepes's repertoire is remarkably expansive, extending from the 15th century to the present day. He has won particular distinction for his performances of the lute music of Bach on both lute and guitar. Among composers who have written works for him are Bacarisse, Balada, Ernesto Halffter, Moreno-Torroba, Ohana, and Françaix. He also has written film music and prepared transcriptions for the guitar.

Yeston, Maury, American composer and music theorist; b. Jersey City, N.J., Oct. 23, 1945. He studied at Yale Univ. with Waite and Forte (B.A., 1967; Ph.D., 1974), subsequently joining the composition faculty there and becoming director of the BMI Musical Theater Workshop in N.Y. His first major stage work was the Broadway musical *Nine* (1982), based on Fellini's movie *8 1/2*, which won Tony and Drama Desk awards; it includes opulent recollections of Baroque and Romantic styles, continuing the operatic trend in musical theater established by Stephen Sondheim and Andrew Lloyd Webber. He also wrote incidental music for Caryl Churchill's play *Cloud Nine* and for *Nukata*, a musical written in Japanese and premiered in Tokyo. His theoretical writings are sophisticated; his *Stratification of Musical Rhythm* (New Haven, 1975), elucidates one of the only plausible theories on rhythmic structure yet proposed. He also ed. *Readings in Schenker Analysis* (New Haven, 1977). Among his compositions are a Cello Concerto (1977), *Goya, a Life in Song* (1987), and another musical, *Grand Hotel* (1989).

Yo-Yo Ma. See **Ma, Yo-Yo.**

Yoffe, Shlomo, Polish-born Israeli composer and teacher; b. Warsaw, May 19, 1909. After training in Poland and Czechoslovakia, he emigrated to Palestine and pursued studies with Partos and Boscovich in Jerusalem and Tel Aviv. From 1953 to 1973 he was director of the Studio for Music Education for Gilboa and Bet-Shean.

WORKS: ORCH.: *Ruth*, symphonic suite (1954); 3 syms. (1955, 1957, 1958); Violin Concerto (1956); *Views of the Emek*, symphonic suite (1958); *Symphonic Poem on Jewish Themes* (1959); *Divertimento* (1959); Cello Concertino (1959); Oboe Concerto (1960); Concerto for Strings (1961); *3 Pieces* for Horn and Strings (1966); *Fantasia concertante* for Brass Quartet and Orch. (1968); *Beit-Alfa*, symphonic poem (1972); *Introduction, Dance and Finale* for Chamber Orch. (1972); *Sobu Zion*, overture (1973); *5 Sketches of Old Jerusalem* for Chamber Orch. (1973); *Fantasy* for Oboe and Chamber Orch. (1975); Sinfonietta (1977); *The Beautiful City* (1978); Concerto for Vibraphone and Strings (1979); *Variations on "Eshkolit"* for Chamber Orch. (1979); *Landscapes* (1981); *Israel Sketches* (1984). **CHAMBER:** Quartet for 2 Flutes, Cello, and Piano (1957); 2 string quartets (1961, 1969); *Fantasy* for String Quartet (1966); Chamber Concerto for Violin and 10 Players (1966); *Affettuoso* for 2 Flutes (1966); Brass Quartet (1967); *Musica concertante* for Clarinet and 3 Percussionists (1973); *Etude* for 13 Players (1974); *Serenata* for Wind Quintet (1975); *Nonetto* for Strings (1976); *Depressed Story* for Clarinet and String Quartet (1983); Quintet for Horn and String Quartet (1986); *Monologue* for Violin (1987). **VOCAL:** *What Name Shall I Call?* for Soprano and Chamber Orch. (1975); *Psalm 125* for Narrator and Orch. (1978); *Shake Thyself from the Dust* for Voice, Clarinet, and Strings (1988); various cantatas; songs.

Yon, Pietro Alessandro, Italian-born American organist, composer, and teacher; b. Settimo Vittone, Aug. 8, 1886; d. Huntington, N.Y., Nov. 22, 1943. He studied with Fumagalli at the Milan Cons.; then at the Turin Cons. (1901–04), and at the Accademia di Santa Cecilia in Rome with Remigio Renzi (organ) and Sgambati (piano), graduating in 1905. He subsequently served as organist at St. Peter's in Rome (1905–07). In 1907 he emigrated to the U.S.; from 1907 to 1919, and again from 1921 to 1926, was organist at St. Francis-Xavier's in N.Y.; then was appointed organist of St. Patrick's Cathedral in N.Y., a post he held until his death. He became a naturalized American citizen in 1921. He was greatly esteemed as an organist and teacher; composed numerous organ pieces, of which *Gesu Bambino* (1917) became popular and was publ. in various instrumental and vocal arrangements; he also wrote an oratorio, *The Triumph of St. Patrick* (N.Y., April 29, 1934); several masses and other religious services. A novel based on his life, *The Heavens Heard Him*, written by V.B. Hammann and M.C. Yon, was publ. in N.Y. in 1963.

Yoshida, Tsunezō, Japanese ethnomusicologist; b. Kohama, Fukui prefecture, Feb. 3, 1872; d. Kyoto, May 16, 1957. After graduating from the Tokyo School of Music (1897), he taught at training colleges in Fukui (1897–1903) and Kyoto (1903–35). In 1920 he began studying Buddhist music in collaboration with Dōnin Taki (1890–1943), a priest of the Tendai sect and a performer of Buddhist chant, with whom he produced several books and transcription anthologies on Buddhist chant, beginning with *Kada ongaku ron* (On the Music of Gāthā; 1934). Yoshida founded a research inst. on Buddhist music at Enryaku-ji (the headquarters of the Tendai sect) in 1950. He received a number of honors during his lifetime, including the Medal of Honor with Purple Ribbon (1955).

Youdin, Mikhail, Russian composer and teacher; b. St. Petersburg, Sept. 29, 1893; d. Kazan, Feb. 8, 1948. He studied at the St. Petersburg Cons. (graduated, 1923), and then was a teacher there (1926–42); subsequently taught at the Kazan Cons. (1942–48).

WORKS: *Farida*, opera (1943); *Poem 1926* (1926; Leningrad, March 30, 1927) and other orch. pieces; 2 string quartets; Piano Sonata; Organ Toccata; *Song of Spring and Joy*, cantata (Leningrad, Nov. 25, 1936); *Heroic Oratorio* (1937); choruses; songs; folk song arrangements.

Young-Uck Kim. See **Kim, Young-Uck.**

Young (real name, **Youngs**), **(Basil) Alexander,** English tenor; b. London, Oct. 18, 1920. He was a pupil of Steffan Pollmann at the Royal College of Music in London. He sang with the BBC and Glyndebourne choruses (1948–49); in 1950 he made his operatic debut as Scaramuccio in *Ariadne auf Naxos* at the Edinburgh Festival; sang regularly at London's Covent Garden (1955–70); also appeared with other English opera companies and in the U.S., and toured widely as a concert artist. From 1973 to 1986 he was head of the school of vocal studies at the Royal Northern College of Music in Manchester; was also founder-conductor of the Jubilate Choir of Manchester (1977). His operatic repertory ranged from Monteverdi to Stravinsky; he was particularly admired for his performances of Handel's music.

Young, Douglas, English composer and pianist; b. London, July 18, 1947. He studied at the Royal College of Music in London with Anthony Milner (composition) and Anthony Hopkins (piano), obtaining his B.Mus. in 1969. In 1970 he made his debut as a pianist at the Royal Festival Hall in London. He was founder-director of the Dreamtiger ensemble (from 1975).

WORKS: BALLETS: *Pasiphae* (1969); *Charlotte Bronte-Portrait* (1973–74); *Ludwig, Fragmente eines Ratsels* (Munich, June 14, 1986). **ORCH.:** Sinfonietta (1968–70); Piano Concertino (1972–74); *3 Regions from Terrain* (1974); *Sea Change* (1976); *Circus Band Et al (after Ives)* (1977); *Virages-Region I*, cello concerto (1978); *William Booth Enters Heaven (after Ives)* (1980); *Rain, Steam, and Speed* (1981); *Lament on the Destruction of Forests* (1986). **CHAMBER:** *Essay* for String Quartet (1971); *Compasses* for Clarinet and String Trio (1972–77); *Croquis et Agaceries (after Satie)* for Flute, Cello, and Piano (1976); *10 préludes de la porte heroïque du Ciel* for Cello and Piano (1977); *Trajet/inter/lignes* for Flute (1978–80); *Fantômes* for String Trio (1980–81); *Arabesque brève* for Cello (1982); String Trio 1985 for Violin, Viola, and Cello (1983–85); piano pieces. **VOCAL:** *The Listeners*, cantata for Narrator, Soprano, Women's Voices, and Chamber Orch. (1967); *Vers d'un voyage vers l'hiver* for 12 Solo Voices (1975–77); *Journey between 2 Worlds* for Chorus, Rock Group, Steel Band, and Orch. (1979); *Sports et Divertissement (after Satie)* for Narrator, Clarinet, String Trio, and Piano (1981); *Songs of Exile* for Countertenor or Contralto and Lute (1984).

Young, La Monte (Thornton), American composer of the extreme avant-garde; b. Bern, Idaho, Oct. 14, 1935. He studied clarinet and saxophone with William Green in Los Angeles (1951–54); also attended Los Angeles City College (1953–56) and studied counterpoint and composition privately with Leonard Stein (1955–56); was a pupil of Robert Stevenson at the Univ. of Calif. at Los Angeles (B.A., 1958); pursued further training with Seymour Shifrin and Andrew Imbrie at the Univ. of Calif. at Berkeley (1958–60) and attended the summer courses in new music in Darmstadt; subsequently studied electronic music with Richard Maxfield at the New School for Social Research in N.Y. (1960–61). In 1963 he married the artist and illustrator Marian Zazeela with whom he subsequently gave audio-visual performances in a series of "Sound/Light Environments" in Europe and America. In 1970 he visited India to study Eastern philosophy and train himself physically, mentally, and vocally for cosmic awareness, gradually arriving at the realization that any human, subhuman, or inhuman activity constitutes art; in his *Composition 1990* he starts a fire on the stage while releasing captive butterflies in the hall. In his attempt to overcome terrestrial limitations, he has decreed for himself a circadian period of 26 hours. He achieves timelessness by declaring, "This piece of music may play without stopping for thousands of years." Several of his works consist solely of imperious commands: "Push the piano to the wall; push it through the wall; keep pushing," or, more succinctly, "Urinate." He ed. *An Anthology of Chance Operations, Concept Art, Anti-Art*, etc. (N.Y., 1963; 2nd ed., rev., 1970), which, with his own *Compositions 1960*, had primary influence on concept art and the Fluxus movement; his own contribution to it was a line drawn in India ink on a 3 × 5 filing card. He has contributed extensively to the study of just intonation and to the development of tuning systems based on the set of rational numbers which make up the components of his periodic composite sound waveform environments. He received a Guggenheim fellowship and a grant from the NEA. Among his ascertainable works are *5 Little Pieces* for String Quartet (1956); *For Brass* (1957); *For Guitar* (1958); Trio for Strings (1958); *Poem* for Tables, Chairs, and Benches (moving furniture about; Univ. of Calif., Berkeley, Jan. 5, 1960); *Arabic Numeral* (any Integer) for Gong or Piano (1960); *Studies in the Bowed Disc* for Gong (1963); *The Well-Tuned Piano* (1964); *The Tortoise Droning Selected Pitches from the Holy Numbers of the 2 Black Tigers, the Green Tiger, and the Hermit* (N.Y., Oct. 30, 1964); *The Tortoise Recalling the Drone of the Holy Numbers as They Were Revealed in the Dreams of the Whirlwind and the Obsidian Gong, Illuminated by the Sawmill, the Green Sawtooth Ocelot, and the High-Tension Line Stepdown Transformer* (N.Y., Dec. 12, 1964); *Map of 49's Dream of Two Systems of 11 Sets of Galactic Intervals Ornamental Lightyears Tracery* for Voices, Various Instruments, and Sine Wave Drones (Pasadena, Calif., Jan. 28, 1968); and *The Subsequent Dreams of China* (1980). Also an arbitrary number of pieces of "conceptual" music and tape recordings of his own monophonous vocalizing achieved by both inspiration and expiration so that the vocal line is maintained indefinitely; various physical exercises with or without audible sounds. His *Selected Writings* were publ. in Munich in 1969.

BIBL.: W. Mertens, *American Minimal Music: L. Y., Terry Riley, Steve Reich, Philip Glass* (London, 1991).

Young, Percy M(arshall), English writer on music; b. Northwich, Cheshire, May 17, 1912. He studied English, music, and history as an organ scholar at Selwyn College, Cambridge (B.A., 1933; Mus.B., 1934), then went to Dublin, where he graduated from Trinity College (Mus.D., 1937); upon his return to England, he took courses with C.B. Rootham and E.J. Dent in Cambridge. He subsequently occupied various teaching posts; from 1944 to 1966, was director of music at the College of Technology in Wolverhampton. He publ. a number of arrangements of early English songs, and also composed some vocal pieces and a *Fugal Concerto* for 2 Pianos and Strings (1954); he is known principally for his scholarly biographical studies and essays.

WRITINGS (all publ. in London unless otherwise given): *Samuel Pepys' Music Book* (1942); *Handel* (1947; 3rd ed., rev., 1979); *The Oratorios of Handel* (1953); *Messiah: A Study in Interpretation* (1951); *A Critical Dictionary of Composers and Their Music* (1954; U.S. ed. as *Biographical Dictionary of Composers*); Elgar, *O.M.: A Study of a Musician* (1955; 2nd ed., 1973); ed. *Letters of Edward Elgar and Other Writings* (1956); *Tragic Muse: The Life and Works of Robert Schumann* (1957; 2nd ed., rev., 1961); *The Choral Tradition: An Historical and Analytical Survey from the 16th Century to the Present Day* (1962; 2nd ed., rev., 1982); *Zoltán Kodály* (1964); ed. *Letters to Nimrod from Edward Elgar* (1965); *A History of British Music* (1967); *Keyboard Musicians of the World* (1967); ed. *Elgar: A Future for English Music and Other Lectures* (1968); *Debussy* (1969); *The Bachs, 1500–1850* (1970); *Sir Arthur Sullivan* (1971); *A Concise History of Music* (1974); *Beethoven: A Victorian Tribute* (1976); *Alice Elgar: Enigma of a Victorian Lady* (1977); *George Grove* (1980); *Mozart* (1987); *Elgar, Newman and the Dream of Gerontius: In the Tradition of English Catholicism* (Brookfield, Vt., 1995).

Young, Victor, American pianist and composer; b. Bristol, Tenn., April 9, 1889; d. Ossining, N.Y., Sept. 2, 1968. He studied piano with Isidor Philipp in Paris. He toured in England and the U.S. as accompanist to prominent singers; held various teaching positions; was music director in Thomas A. Edison's Experimental Laboratory in West Orange, N.J., conducting tonal tests and making piano recordings under Edison's personal supervision (1919–27). He wrote the musical score for one of the earliest sound films, *In Old California*; composed some 300 film scores altogether; also wrote, for orch., *Scherzetto, Jeep, In the Great Smokies, Charm Assembly Line Ballet*, etc.; piano pieces.

Ysaÿe, Eugène (-Auguste), famous Belgian violinist, conductor, and composer, brother of **Théophile Ysaÿe**; b. Liège, July 16, 1858; d. Brussels, May 12, 1931. At the age of 4, he began to study violin with his father, a theater conductor; at the age of 7, he was enrolled at the Liège Cons. as a pupil of Désiré Heynberg, winning 2nd prize in 1867; in 1869 he left the Cons. in a dispute with his mentor, but was readmitted in 1872 as a pupil of Rodolphe Massart, winning 1st prize in 1873 and the silver medal in 1874; then continued his training on a scholarship at the Brussels Cons. with Wieniawski; later completed his studies with Vieuxtemps in Paris (1876–79). In 1879 he became concertmaster of Bilse's orch. in Berlin; appeared as a soloist at Pauline Lucca's concerts in Cologne and Aachen; in Germany he met Anton Rubinstein, who took him to Russia, where he spent 2 winters; he also toured in Norway. In 1883 he settled in Paris, where he met Franck, d'Indy et al., and gave successful concerts; he formed a duo with the pianist Raoul Pugno, and started a long series of concerts with him, establishing a new standard of excellence. On Sept. 26, 1886, he married Louise Bourdeau; Franck dedicated his Violin Sonata to them as a wedding present; Ysaÿe's interpretation of this work made it famous. In 1886 he was named prof. at the Brussels Cons. (resigned in 1898); in 1886 he also organized the Ysaÿe Quartet (with Crickboom, Léon Van Hout, and Joseph Jacob); Debussy dedicated his String Quartet to Ysaÿe's group, which gave its first performance at the Société Nationale in Paris on Dec. 29, 1893. In 1889 Ysaÿe made successful appearances in England. On Nov. 16, 1894, he made his American debut playing the Beethoven Violin Concerto with the N.Y. Phil., and creating a sensation by his virtuosity. He revisited America many times, with undiminished acclaim. He began his career as a conductor in 1894, and established in Brussels his own orch., the Société des Concerts Ysaÿe. When the Germans invaded Belgium in 1914, he fled to London, where he remained during World War I. On April 5, 1918, he made his American debut as a conductor with the Cincinnati Sym. Orch., and also led the Cincinnati May Festival in that year. His success was so great that he was offered a permanent position as conductor of the Cincinnati Sym. Orch., which he held from 1918 to 1922. He then returned to Belgium and resumed leadership of the Société des Concerts Ysaÿe. After the death of his first wife, he married, on July 9, 1927, an American pupil, Jeannette Dincin.

Ysaÿe's style of playing is best described as heroic, but his art was equally convincing in the expression of moods of exquisite delicacy and tenderness; his frequent employment of "tempo rubato" produced an effect of elasticity without distorting the melodic line. His works include 8 violin concertos; 6 sonatas for Solo Violin; *Poème nocturne* for Violin, Cello, and Strings; *Les Harmonies du soir* for String Quartet and String Orch.; *Divertimento* for Violin and Orch.; *Méditation* for Cello and String Orch.; *Chant d'hiver* for Violin and Chamber Orch.; *Trio de concert* for 2 Violins, Viola, and Orch.; *Amitié* for 2 Violins and Orch. At the age of 70, he began the composition of an opera in the Walloon language, *Piér li Houïeu* (Peter the Miner), which was premiered in Liège on March 4, 1931, in the presence of the composer, who was brought to the theater in an invalid's chair, suffering from the extreme ravages of diabetes, which had necessitated the amputation of his left foot. He began the composition of a 2nd Walloon opera, *L'Avierge di Piér* (La Vierge de Pierre), but had no time to complete it. In 1937 Queen Elisabeth of Belgium inaugurated the annual Prix International Eugène Ysaÿe in Brussels; the first winner was David Oistrakh.

BIBL.: M. Pincherle, *Feuillets d'histoire du violon* (Paris, 1927); J. Quitin, *E. Y.: Étude biographique et critique* (Brussels, 1938); E. Christen, *Y.* (Geneva, 1946; 2nd ed., 1947); A. Ysaÿe and B. Ratcliffe, *Y.: His Life, Work and Influence* (London, 1947); A. Ysaÿe, *E. Y.: Sa vie d'après les documents receuillis par son fils* (Brussels, 1948; a considerably altered version of the preceding; Eng. tr., 1980, as *Y., By His Son Antoine*); A. Ysaÿe, *E. Y., 1858–1931* (Brussels, 1972); M. Benoît-Jeannin, *E. Y.: Le dernier romantique ou le sacre du violon* (Brussels, 1989); M. Stockhem, *E. Y. et la musique de chambre* (Liège, 1990).

Ysaÿe, Théophile, Belgian pianist and composer, brother of **Eugène (-Auguste) Ysaÿe**; b. Verviers, March 22, 1865; d. Nice, March 24, 1918. He was a pupil at the Liège Cons. (1876–80); then studied at the Kullak Academy in Berlin (from 1881), and took lessons from Franck in Paris (1885). Returning to Belgium, he became director of the Académie de Musique in Brussels; was noted as a fine ensemble player, and gave sonata recitals with his brother; during the latter's absence on tours, he also conducted the Société des Concerts Ysaÿe in Brussels. After the invasion of Belgium in 1914, he went with his brother to London; fearful of the Zeppelin air raids on London, he went to Nice, where he remained until his death. He was a prolific composer; his brother conducted a concert of Théophile's works in Brussels, on Nov. 6, 1904, including the premieres of his Sym. in F major and the symphonic poem *Le Cygne*. Other works were: Piano Concerto; symphonic poems; *Fantaisie sur un thème populaire wallon* for Orch.; Piano Quintet; piano pieces; Requiem.

Yttrehus, Rolv (Berger), American composer and teacher; b. Duluth, March 12, 1926. He studied at the Univ. of Minnesota in Duluth (B.S. in music, 1950), and then was a student of Finney at the Univ. of Mich. (M.M., 1953). After training with Brustad in Oslo (1953–54) and Boulanger in Paris (1954–55), he studied with Sessions at Princeton Univ. (1957–60) before pursuing advanced studies with Petrassi at the Accademia di Santa Cecilia in Rome (1960–62). He taught at the Univ. of Missouri (1963–68), Purdue Univ. (1968–69), the Univ. of Wisc. in Oshkosh (1969–77), and Rutgers, the State Univ. of New Jersey (from 1977). He ditched the scores written in the first 35 years of his life as deciduous juvenilia; in his later works, he cultivated distributive serialism, in which each note, each interval, and each rhythmic unit stands in an esoteric but surmisable relationship with other individual note groups.

WORKS: *6 Haiku* for Soprano, Flute, Cello, and Harp (1959); *Music* for Winds, Percussion, and Viola (1961); *Espressioni* for Orch. (1962); Sextet for Horn, Trumpet, Violin, Double Bass, Piano, and Percussion (1964–70; rev. 1974); *Music* for Winds, Percussion, Cello, and Voices (1969); *Angstwagen* for Soprano and Percussion (1971; rev. 1981); Quintet for Flute, Violin, Clarinet, Cello, and Piano (1973); *Gradus ad Parnassum* for Soprano and Chamber Orch., after Nietzsche and Fux (1974–79); Percussion Sonata (1983; rev. 1988); *Explorations* for Piano (1985); Cello Sonata (1988); *Raritan Variation* for Piano (1989); Sym. No. 1 (1995).

Yuasa, Jōji, Japanese composer and teacher; b. Koriyama, Aug. 12, 1929. He was mainly autodidact in composition, but profited by his association with Kuniharu Akiyama. In 1951 he became active with the Jikkenkōbō (Experimental Workshop) in Tokyo, where he pursued his interest in avant-garde music. With Akiyama and Roger Reynolds, he organized the Crosstalk concerts in 1967. In 1972 he became a member of the new music group Transonic. After receiving a Koussevitzky Foundation grant in 1976, he worked at the electronic music studio at the Univ. of Southern Calif. in Los Angeles. In 1980–81 he was active in Sydney and Toronto. In 1981 he became a teacher of composition at the Univ. of Calif. at San Diego. In 1983 he won the Tokyo Arts Festival Prize for his *A Perspective* for Orch. and in 1986 the Osaka Prize for his *Revealed Time* for Viola and Orch. In 1988 he realized his *9 Levels by Zeami* at IRCAM in Paris. In his music, Yuasa explores various avenues of advanced composition available to the contemporary composer.

WORKS: DRAMATIC: Theater music; ballets; film scores; music for radio and television. **ORCH.:** *Projection VI* for 8 Kotos and Orch. (1967); *Chronoplastic: Between Stasis and Kinesis* (1972); *Time of Orchestral Time* (1976); *Bashō* for Small Orch. (1980); *Requiem* (1980); *A Dirge by Bach—for the sick soul* (1983); *A Perspective* (1983); *Revealed Time* for Viola and Orch. (1986); *9 Levels by Zeami* for Chamber Orch. and Computer-generated Tape (1988); *Scenes from Bashō II* (1989); *Suite Scenes from Bashō* (1990); *The Midnight Sun*, homage to Sibelius (1991); *Eye on Genesis II* (1992). **CHAMBER:** *Projection I* for 7 Players (1955), *V* for Cello and Piano (1967), *VII: Arrogance of the Dead* for Electric Guitar (1968), and *VIII* for String Quartet (1970); *Interpenetration I* for 2 Flutes (1963) and *II* for 2 Percussion (1983); *Triplicity* for 3 Double Basses (1970); *Inter-posi-play-tion I* for Flute, Piano, and 2 Percussion (1971) and *II* for Flute, Harp, and Percussion (1973); *Territory* for Marimba, Flute, Clarinet, Percussion, and Double Bass (1974); *My blue Sky III* for Violin (1977); *Clarinet Solitude* for Clarinet (1980); *A Winter Day: Homage to Bashō* for Flute, Clarinet, Harp, Piano, and Percussion (1981); *Ishibutai Kō* for Gagaku Flute, 3 Shakuhachis, 17 String Koto, and 2 Percussion (1981); *Maibarataki II* for Nō Flute (1987); *To the Genesis* for Shō (1988); *Fūshi-Gyoun* for Japanese Instrument (1988); *Terms of Temporal Detailing* for Bass Flute (1989); *Cosmos Haptic III: Empty Sky* for Koto and Shakuhachi (1990). **PIANO:** *Cosmos Haptic I* (1957) and *II: Transfiguration* (1986); *Projection II: Topologic* (1959) and *III: Esemplastic* (1961); *On the Keyboard* (1971). **VOCAL:** *Yurei no Uta*, cantata for Baritone, Soprano, Chorus, Piano, and Organ (1957); *Questions* for Chorus (1971); *Utterance* for Chorus (1971); *Calling Together* for Voices (1972); *Projection IX: On Bashō's Haiku* for Chorus and Vibraphone (1974); *Koto Song: Bashō's 5 Haiku* for Voice, Koto, and 17 String Koto (1978); *Projection X: Onomatopoetic* for Chorus (1979); *Observations on weather forecasts* for Baritone and Trumpet (1983); *Composition on Zeami's 9 Grades* for Men's Chorus (1984); *Mutterings* for Mezzo-soprano and 7 Instruments (1988). **OTHER:** Musique concrète; tape pieces; electronic scores; computer-generated pieces.

Yudina, Maria, eminent Russian pianist and pedagogue; b. Nevel, near Vitebsk, Sept. 9, 1899; d. Moscow, Nov. 19, 1970. She took piano lessons in Vitebsk with Frieda Teitelbaum-Levinson; then enrolled at the Petrograd Cons., where she studied piano with Anna Essipova, Vladimir Drozdov, and Leonid Nikolayev, theory with Maximilian Steinberg and J. Wihtol, and score reading with N. Tcherepnin and Emil Cooper. In 1921 she joined the piano faculty of the Petrograd Cons., holding this position until 1930. From 1932 to 1934 she taught at the Tiflis Cons. From 1936 to 1951 she was a prof. at the Moscow Cons., and from 1944 to 1960 taught piano and chamber music performance at the Gnessin Inst. in Moscow. Among her students was Andrei Balanchivadze. Yudina began her career as a pianist in 1921, and gave her last concert in Moscow on May 18, 1969. She also was a guest artist in East Germany (1950) and in Poland (1954). She publ. memoirs and reminiscences of famous composers she had met in Russia. Yudina enjoyed great renown as an intellectual musician capable of presenting the works she performed with a grand line, both didactic and inspired. But rather than accepting the traditional interpretation of classical music, she introduced a strong personal element differing from accepted norms, so that her performances of works by Bach, Mozart, Beethoven, and Brahms were revelations to some listeners, and abominations to the old school of pianism. Yudina was also an ardent champion of modern music, placing on her programs compositions by such masters of new techniques as Stravinsky, Schoenberg, Berg, Webern, and Bartók at a time when their works were not acceptable in Russia. She also played piano pieces by Soviet composers, particularly Prokofiev and Shostakovich. She gave numerous concerts of chamber music. A vol. of her articles, reminiscences, and materials was publ. in Moscow in 1978.

Yun, Isang, important Korean-born German composer and teacher; b. Tongyong, Sept. 17, 1917; d. Berlin, Nov. 3, 1995. He studied Western music in Korea (1935–37) and in Japan (1941–43). During World War II, he was active in the anti-Japanese underground; in 1943 he was imprisoned, and then spent the rest of the war in hiding until the liberation in 1945.

He became a music teacher in Tongyong in 1946, and later taught in Pusan; in 1953 he became a prof. of composition at the Univ. of Seoul; then studied with Revel at the Paris Cons. (1956–57) and with Blacher, Rufer, and Schwarz-Schilling at the Berlin Hochschule für Musik (1958–59); also attended the summer courses in new music in Darmstadt. He settled permanently in Berlin, where he produced several successful theatrical works, marked by a fine expressionistic and coloristic quality, and written in an idiom of euphonious dissonance. His career was dramatically interrupted when, on June 17, 1967, he and his wife were brutally abducted from West Berlin by secret police agents of South Korea, and forced to board a plane for Seoul, where they were brought to trial for sedition; he was sentenced to life imprisonment; his wife was given 3 years in jail. This act of lawlessness perpetrated on the territory of another country prompted an indignant protest by the government of West Germany, which threatened to cut off its substantial economic aid to South Korea; 23 celebrated musicians, including Stravinsky, issued a vigorous letter of protest. As a result of this moral and material pressure, South Korea released Yun and his wife after nearly 2 years of detention, and they returned to Germany. In 1969–70 he taught at the Hannover Hochschule für Musik. In 1970 he was appointed lecturer in composition at the Berlin Hochschule für Musik, where he was a prof. from 1973 to 1985. In 1971 he became a naturalized German citizen.

WORKS: OPERAS: *Der Traum des Liu-Tung* (Berlin, Sept. 25, 1965); *Träume* (1965–68; Nuremberg, Feb. 23, 1969; an amalgam of the preceding opera and the following one); *Die Witwe des Schmetterlings* (Bonn, Dec. 9, 1967; Eng. version as *Butterfly Widow*, Evanston, Ill., Feb. 27, 1970); *Geisterliebe* (1969–70; Kiel, June 20, 1971); *Sim Tjong* (1971–72; Munich, Aug. 1, 1972). **ORCH.:** *Symphonische Szenen* (1960; Darmstadt, Sept. 7, 1961); *Bara* (1960; Berlin, Jan. 19, 1962); *Colloides sonores* for Strings (Hamburg, Dec. 12, 1961); *Fluktuationen* (1964; Berlin, Feb. 10, 1965); *Réak* (Donaueschingen, Oct. 23, 1966); *Dimension* (Nuremberg, Oct. 22, 1971); *Konzertante Figuren* for Small Orch. (1972; Hamburg, Nov. 30, 1973); *Ouvertüre* (Berlin, Oct. 4, 1973; rev. 1974); *Harmonia* for Winds, Harp, and Percussion (1974; Herford, Jan. 22, 1975); Cello Concerto (Royan, March 25, 1976); Concerto for Flute and Small Orch. (Hitzacker, July 30, 1977); Double Concerto for Oboe, Harp, and Small Orch. (Berlin, Sept. 26, 1977); *Muak* (Mönchengladbach, Nov. 9, 1978); *Fanfare and Memorial* (Münster, Sept. 18, 1979); *Exemplum: im memoriam Kwangju* (Cologne, May 8, 1981); Clarinet Concerto (1981; Munich, Jan. 29, 1982); 3 violin concertos: No. 1 (1981), No. 2 (1983–86; Stuttgart, Jan. 20, 1987), and No. 3 (1992); 5 syms.: No. 1 (1983; Berlin, May 14, 1984), No. 2 (Berlin, Dec. 9, 1984), No. 3 (Saarbrücken, Sept. 22, 1985), No. 4 (Tokyo, Nov. 13, 1986), and No. 5 for Baritone and Orch. (Berlin, Sept. 17, 1987); *Gong-Hu* for Harp and Strings (1984; Lucerne, Aug. 22, 1985); *Mugung-Dong* for Winds, Percussion, and Double Bass (Hamburg, June 22, 1986); *Impression* for Small Orch. (1986; Frankfurt am Main, Feb. 9, 1987); *Duetto concertante* for Oboe or English Horn, Cello, and Strings (Rottweil, Nov. 8, 1987); 2 chamber syms. (1987, 1989); Oboe Concerto (1990); *Silia* (1992). **CHAMBER:** 6 string quartets (Nos. 1 and 2 withdrawn; 1959; 1988; 1990; 1992); *Musik* for 7 Instruments (Darmstadt, Sept. 4, 1959); *Loyang* for Chamber Ensemble (1962; Hannover, Jan. 23, 1964); *Gasa* for Violin and Piano (Prague, Oct. 2, 1963); *Garak* for Flute and Piano (1963; Berlin, Sept. 11, 1964); *Nore* for Cello and Piano (1964; Bremen, May 3, 1968); *Riul* for Clarinet and Piano (Erlangen, July 26, 1968); *Images* for Flute, Oboe, Piano, and Cello (1968; Oakland, Calif., March 24, 1969); *Glissés* for Cello (1970; Zagreb, May 8, 1971); *Piri* for Oboe or Clarinet (Bamberg, Oct. 25, 1971); Trio for Flute, Oboe, and Violin (1972–73; Mannheim, Oct. 18, 1973); Trio for Violin or Viola, Cello, and Piano (1972–73; Berlin, Feb. 23, 1973); *Etüden* for 1 or More Flutes (Kyoto, July 16, 1974); *Rondell* for Oboe, Clarinet, and Bassoon (Bayreuth, Sept. 30, 1975); *Pièce concertante* for Chamber Ensemble (Hamburg, June 15, 1976); Duo for Viola and Piano (1976; Rome, May 3, 1977); *Königliches Thema* for Violin (1976; Düsseldorf, April 1, 1977); Octet for Clarinet, Bassoon, Horn, and String Quintet (Paris, April 10, 1978); Sonata for Oboe, Harp, and Viola or Cello (Saarbrücken, July 6, 1979); *Novellette* for Flute, Violin, and Cello or Viola (1980; Bremen, Feb. 5, 1981); Concertino for Accordion and String Quartet (Trossingen, Nov. 6, 1983); Sonatina for 2 Violins (Tokyo, Dec. 15, 1983); *Monolog* for Bass Clarinet (Melbourne, April 9, 1983); *Inventionen* for 2 Oboes or 2 Flutes (1983; Witten, April 29, 1984); *Monolog* for Bassoon (1983–84; Nice, Feb. 3, 1985); Duo for Cello and Harp or Piano (Ingleheim, May 27, 1984); Quintet for Clarinet and String Quartet (Kusatsu, Japan, Aug. 24, 1984); *Li-Na im Garten* for Violin (1984–85; Berlin, Nov. 28, 1985); *Recontre* for Clarinet, Harp or Piano, and Cello (Hitzacker, Aug. 2, 1986); Quartet for 2 Piccolos, 4 Flutes, 2 Alto Flutes, and 2 Bass Flutes (Berlin, Aug. 27, 1986); Quintet for Flute and String Quartet (1986; Paris, Jan. 17, 1987); *Tapis* for String Quintet (Mannheim, Nov. 20, 1987); *In Balance* for Harp (Hamburg, April 8, 1987); *Kontraste* for Violin (Hamburg, April 10, 1987); *Pezzo fantasioso* for Chamber Ensemble (Chiusi, July 10, 1988); Quartet for Flute, Violin, Cello, and Piano (1988); *Distanzen* for Flute, Oboe, Clarinet, Bassoon, Horn, and String Quintet (Berlin, Oct. 9, 1988); *Intermezzo* for Cello and Accordion (1988); *Contemplation* for 2 Violas (Berlin, Oct. 9, 1988); *Sori* for Flute (N.Y., Nov. 7, 1988); *Together* for Violin and Double Bass (1989; Århus, April 28, 1990); *Rufe* for Oboe and Harp (Ravensburg, Nov. 10, 1989); *Kammerkonzert I* (Amsterdam, June 16, 1990) and *II* (Berlin, Oct. 21, 1990); Wind Quintet (1991); Violin Sonata (1991); Trio for Clarinet, Bassoon, and Horn (1992); Quartet for Trumpet, Horn, Trombone, and Piano (1992); *Espace I* for Cello and Piano (1992) and *II* for Cello, Harp, and Oboe ad libitum (1992); *7 Études* for Cello (1993); Wind Octet (1994); *Ostwestiche Miniaturen* for Oboe and Cello (1994). **KEYBOARD: PIANO:** *Fünf Klavierstücke* (1958; Bilthoven, Sept. 6, 1959); *Interludium A* (Tokyo, May 6, 1982). **HARPSICHORD:** *Shao Yang Yin* (1966; Freiburg im Breisgau, Jan. 12, 1968). **ORGAN:** *Tuyaux sonores* (Hamburg, March 11, 1967); *Fragment* (Hamburg, May 17, 1975). **VOCAL:** *Om mani padme hum* for Soprano, Baritone, Chorus, and Orch. (1964; Hannover, Jan. 30, 1965); *Ein Schmetterlingstraum* for Chorus and Percussion ad libitum (1968; Hamburg, May 8, 1969); *Schamanengesange aus Geisterliebe* for Alto and Chamber Orch. (1969–70; orchestrated by E. Koch-Raphael; Berlin, Dec. 16, 1977); *Namo* for 3 Sopranos and Orch. (Berlin, May 4, 1971; also for Soprano and Orch., 1975; Münster, May 10, 1976); *Gagok* for Voice, Guitar, and Percussion (Barcelona, Oct. 25, 1972; also for Voice and Harp, 1985); *Vom Tao* for Chorus, Organ, and Percussion (1972; Hamburg, May 21, 1976; rev. 1982; Vienna, Nov. 6, 1986); *Memory* for 3 Voices and Percussion (Rome, May 3, 1974); *An der Schwelle* for Baritone, Women's Chorus, Organ, Flute, Oboe, Trumpet, Trombone, and 2 Percussion (Kassel, April 5, 1975); *Der weise Mann*, cantata for Baritone, Chorus, and Orch. (Berlin, June 9, 1977); *Teile dich Nacht* for Soprano and Chamber Ensemble (1980; Witten, April 26, 1981); *O Licht . . .* for Chorus, Violin, and Percussion (Nuremberg, June 21, 1981); *Der Herr ist mein Hirte* for Chorus and Trombone (1981; Stuttgart, Nov. 14, 1982).

BIBL.: H.-W. Heister and W.-W. Sparrer, eds., *Der Komponist I. Y.* (Munich, 1987); H. Bergmeier, ed., *I. Y.: Festschrift zum 75. Geburtstag 1992* (Berlin, 1992).

Yuon, Paul. See **Juon, Paul.**

Z

Zabaleta (Zala), Nicanor, eminent Spanish harpist; b. San Sebastián, Jan. 7, 1907; d. San Juan, Puerto Rico, March 31, 1993. He studied harp with Vicenta Tormo de Calvo at the Madrid Cons. (graduated, 1920) and with Luisa Menárguez; he then went to Paris and studied harp with Marcel Tournier and harmony, counterpoint, and fugue with Marcel Rousseau and Eugène Cools. In 1926 he made his Paris debut. On July 5, 1934, he made his N.Y. debut at the Lewisohn Stadium. In subsequent years, Zabaleta pursued a far-ranging concert career, appearing as a soloist with the world's principal orchs., giving numerous recitals, and being active as a chamber music player. In 1956 he was awarded the Henriette Cohen Prize of England, in 1982 he received the Premio Nacional de Música of Spain, and in 1988 he became a member of the Real Academia de Bellas Artes de San Fernando in Madrid. Zabaleta was one of the foremost harpists of the 20th century. His repertoire embraced works from the Baroque era to his own day. He brought to light various early MSS and ed. the vol. *Spanische Meister des 16. und 17. Jahrhunderts* (Mainz, 1985). His virtuoso performances of the harp literature of the 18th and 19th centuries were highly esteemed. He also did much to further the cause of contemporary harp music by commissioning works from many notable composers, among them Villa-Lobos, Rodrigo, Montsalvatge, Milhaud, Krenek, Piston, Hovhaness, and Farkas.

Zabrack, Harold (Allen), American pianist, teacher, and composer; b. St. Louis, June 30, 1928; d. Creve Coeur, Mo., Feb. 2, 1995. He was a student of Ganz (piano) at the Chicago Musical College (M.M., 1951) and of Boulanger (composition) in Fontainebleau. After traveling in Europe on a Fulbright grant (1955–57), he was active as a pianist and teacher in St. Louis. From 1974 to 1993 he taught at Westminster Choir College in Princeton, N.J. He was the author of *Creative Musical Encounters* (N.Y., 1978).

WORKS: *Piano Variations* (1959); 2 duets for Viola and Oboe (1961); 2 piano concertos: No. 1 (St. Louis, April 5, 1964, composer soloist) and No. 2 (1965); Piano Sonata (1964); *Symphonic Variations* for Piano and Orch.

Zaccaria, Nicola (Angelo), Greek bass; b. Piraeus, March 9, 1923. He received training at the Royal Cons. in Athens. In 1949 he made his operatic debut as Raimondo in *Lucia di Lammermoor* at the Athens Opera. In 1953 he won the La Scala singing competition in Milan, where he made his first appearance as Sparafucile that same year; from then until 1974 he was a member of the company, singing many leading bass roles. He made his first appearance at the Vienna State Opera in 1956. In 1957 he made his debut at the Salzburg Festival as Don Fernando and at London's Covent Garden as Oroveso, where he sang again in 1959. In 1976 he appeared as King Marke in Dallas. He sang Colline in Macerata in 1982. His guest engagements also took him to such operatic centers as Cologne, Geneva, Moscow, Berlin, Edinburgh, Brussels, and Monte Carlo. In addition, he also appeared as a concert artist. Among his other roles were Sarastro, the Commendatore, Creon, Silva, Zaccaria, and Bellini's Rodolfo.

Zacharewitsch, Michael, Russian-born English violinist and composer; b. Ostrov, Aug. 26, 1879; d. London, Dec. 20, 1953. He studied with Ševčik in Prague, and later with Ysaÿe in Brussels. He went to London in 1903, and became a naturalized British subject in 1915; toured Australia, New Zealand, and South Africa. He wrote *The New Art of Violin Playing* (1934). Among his compositions were *Dunkirk* (1945) for Violin and Orch. and violin exercises.

Zacharias, Christian, German pianist; b. Tamshedpur, India (of German parents), April 27, 1950. He was taken to Germany as an infant and began piano lessons at an early age. He was a student of Irène Slavin at the Karlsruhe Hochschule für Musik (1960–69), and then of Perlemuter in Paris. In 1969 he took 2nd prize in the Geneva Competition, in 1973 2nd prize in the Van Cliburn Competition, and in 1975 the Ravel Prize in the European Broadcasting Union Competition. In 1976 he made his London debut. He made his U.S. debut as a soloist with the Boston Sym. Orch. in 1979. In 1981 he made his Salzburg Festival debut as soloist in the Mozart Concerto, K.453. In subsequent years, he toured throughout the world in a repertoire extending from Mozart to Ravel.

Zador, Dezsö, Hungarian baritone; b. Horna Krupa, March 8, 1873; d. Berlin, April 24, 1931. He studied in Budapest and Vienna. He made his debut as Almaviva in 1898 in Czernowitz; then sang in Elberfeld (1898–1901); was subsequently a member of the Komische Oper in Berlin (1906–11). In 1911 he joined the Dresden Court Opera, singing there until 1916; then went to the Budapest Opera (1916–19); was later a member of the Berlin Städtische Oper (1920–24). He made guest appearances at Covent Garden in London and in Paris, Milan, and Chicago. During the last years of his career, he sang bass roles.

Zador, Eugene (real name, **Jenő Zádor**), Hungarian-American composer; b. Bátaszék, Nov. 5, 1894; d. Los Angeles, April 4, 1977. He studied music with a local teacher. In 1911 he enrolled in the Vienna Cons., and studied composition with Heuberger. From 1912 to 1914 he was in Leipzig, where he took a course with Reger; also attended classes in musicology with Abert and Schering; continued musicological studies with Volbach at the Univ. of Münster (Ph.D., 1921, with the diss. *Wesen und Form der symphonischen Dichtung von Liszt bis Strauss*). He settled in Vienna, and taught at the Neues Konservatorium there. Following the Anschluss of Austria by the Nazi regime in 1938, Zador emigrated to the U.S.; he settled in Hollywood, where he became successful and prosperous as an orchestrator of film scores; made some 120 orchestrations in all; at the same time, he continued to compose music in every conceivable genre. Zador was a master of musical sciences, excelling in euphonious modern harmonies, and an expert weaver of contrapuntal voices; his colorful writing for instruments was exemplary. He possessed a special skill in handling Hungarian folk motifs in variation form; in this, he followed the tradition of Liszt. During his European period, he composed some fashionable "machine music," as demonstrated with particular effect in his *Sinfonia tecnica*.

WORKS: DRAMATIC: OPERAS: *Diana* (Budapest, Dec. 22, 1923); *A holtak szigete* (The Island of the Dead; Budapest, March 29, 1928); *Revisor* (The Inspector General; 1928; rev. and reorchestrated, Los Angeles, June 11, 1971); *X-mal Rembrandt* (referring to the multiple copies of Rembrandt's self-portraits; Gera, May 24, 1930); *Asra* (Budapest, Feb. 15, 1936); *Christoph Columbus* (N.Y., Oct. 8, 1939); *The Virgin and the Fawn* (Los Angeles, Oct. 24, 1964); *The Magic Chair* (Baton Rouge, La., May 14, 1966); *The Scarlet Mill* (N.Y., Oct. 26, 1968); *Yehu, a Christmas Legend* (1974). **BALLET:** *Maschinenmensch* (1934). **ORCH.:** *Bánk bán*, symphonic poem (1918); 4 syms.: No. 1, *Romantische Symphonie* (1922), No. 2, *Sinfonia tecnica* (Paris, May 26, 1932), No. 3, *Tanzsymphonie* (Budapest, Feb. 8, 1937), and No. 4, *Children's Symphony* (1941); *Variations on a Hungarian Folk Song* (Vienna, Feb. 9, 1927); *Rondo* (1934); *Hungarian Caprice* (Budapest, Feb. 1, 1935); *Pastorale and Tarantella* (Chicago, Feb. 5, 1942); *Biblical Triptych* (Chicago, Dec. 9, 1943); *Elegie and Dance* (Philadelphia, March 12, 1954); *Divertimento* for Strings (1955); *Fugue-Fantasia* (1958); *Rhapsody* (Los Angeles, Feb. 5, 1961); *Christmas Overture* (1961); *Variations on a Merry Theme* (1963; Birmingham, Ala., Jan. 12, 1965); *5 Contrasts* (Philadelphia, Jan. 8, 1965); Trombone Concerto (Rochester, Mich., July 20, 1967); *Rhapsody* for Cimbalom and Orch. (Los Angeles, Nov. 2, 1969); *Studies* (Detroit, Nov. 12, 1970); *Fantasia hungarica* for Double Bass and Orch. (1970); Accordion Concerto (1971); *Hungarian Scherzo* (1975); Concerto for Oboe and Strings (1975). **CHAMBER:** Chamber Concerto for Strings, 2 Horns, and Piano (1930); Piano Quintet (1933); Suite for Brass (1961); Suite for 8 Cellos (1966); Suite for Woodwind Quintet (1972); Brass Quintet (1973); piano pieces. **VOCAL:** *Cantata tecnica* (1961); *Scherzo domestico* for Chorus (1961); *The Remarkable Adventure of Henry Bold* for Narrator and Orch. (Beverly Hills, Calif., Oct. 24, 1963); *The Judgement*, oratorio (1974); *Cain*, melodrama for Baritone, Chorus, and Orch. (1976); songs.

BIBL.: L. Zador, *E. Z.: A Catalogue of His Works* (San Diego, Calif., 1978).

Zadora, Michael (actually, **Michal**), American pianist and composer; b. N.Y., June 14, 1882; d. there, June 30, 1946. He studied with his father; then at the Paris Cons. (1899), and later with Leschetizky and Busoni. He taught a master class at the Lemberg Cons. (1911–12); then at the Inst. of Musical Art in N.Y. (1913–14). He transcribed for piano several organ and violin works by Buxtehude and Bach; also composed piano pieces, songs, etc.

Zafred, Mario, Italian conductor, music critic, and composer; b. Trieste, Feb. 21, 1922; d. Rome, May 22, 1987. He was a pupil of Pizzetti at the Accademia di Santa Cecilia in Rome. After serving as music critic of *Unità* (1949–56) and *Giustizia* (1956–63), he was active as a conductor. From 1968 to 1974 he was artistic director of the Rome Opera. In conformity with his Communist convictions, he composed in an accessible style.

WORKS: OPERAS: *Amleto* (1961); *Wallenstein* (1965). **ORCH.:** 7 syms. (1943, 1944, 1949, 1950, 1954, 1958, 1970); Flute Concerto (1951); Violin Concerto (1953); Triple Concerto for Violin, Cello, Piano, and Orch. (1954); *Sinfonia breve* for Strings (1955); Harp Concerto (1956); Viola Concerto (1957); Cello Concerto (1958); Piano Concerto (1960); Concerto for 2 Pianos and Orch. (1961); *Metamorfosi* (1964); Concerto for Strings (1969). **CHAMBER:** 4 string quartets (1941, 1947, 1948, 1953); 3 piano trios (1942, 1945, 1954); Wind Quintet (1952); String Sextet (1967). **PIANO:** 4 sonatas (1941, 1943, 1950, 1960). **VOCAL:** Numerous choruses and solo songs.

Zagiba, Franz, eminent Austrian musicologist; b. Rosenau, Oct. 20, 1912; d. Vienna, Aug. 12,1977. He studied musicology with Dobroslav Orel and received training in Hungarian and Slavonic studies at the Univ. of Bratislava (Ph.D., 1937, with the diss. *Denkmäler der Musik in den Franziskanerklöstern in der Ostslovakei*; publ. in Prague, 1940, as *Hudobné pamiatky františkánskych kláštorov na východnom Slovensku*); completed his Habilitation in 1944 at the Univ. of Vienna with his *Geschichte der slowakischen Musik* (publ. in Bratislava, 1943, as *Dejiny slovenskj hudby od najstarších čias až do reformácie*). After serving as director of the musicological inst. of the Bratislava Academy of Sciences, he joined the faculty of the Univ. of Vienna in 1944, where he became a full prof. in 1972. In 1952 he founded the International Chopin Soc. His learned writings ranged from pre-medieval to 20th-century music.

WRITINGS: *Literárny a hudobný život v Rožňave v 18. a 19. storoči* (Literary and Musical Life in Roznava in the 18th and 19th Centuries; Košice, 1947); *Tvorba sovietskych komponistov* (The Music of Soviet Composers; Bratislava, 1947); *Chopin und Wien* (Vienna, 1951); *Tschaikowskij: Leben und Werk* (Vienna, 1953); *Die ältesten musikalischen Denkmäler zu Ehren des hl. Leopold: Ein Beitrag zur Choralpflege in Österreich am Ausgang des Mittelalters* (Vienna, 1954); *Johann L. Bella (1843–1936) und das Wiener Musikleben* (Vienna, 1955); *Das Geistesleben der Slaven im frühen Mittelalter: Die Anfänge des slavischen Schrifttums aus dem Gebiete des östlichen Mitteleuropa vom 8. bis 10. Jahrhundert* (Vienna, 1971); *Musikgeschichte Mitteleuropas von den Anfängen bis zum Ende des 10. Jahrhunderts* (Vienna, 1976).

Zagortsev, Vladimir, Russian composer; b. Kiev, Oct. 27, 1944. He studied composition with Liatoshinsky and Shtogarenko at the Kiev Cons. Upon graduation, he joined a group of Soviet avant-garde composers who were active in Kiev and who followed the Western techniques. Zagortsev set for himself the task of organizing the elements of pitch, rhythm, dynamics, and tone color in a total serial procedure, but he never abandoned the ethnic resources of Ukrainian folk songs, which remain the thematic source of many of his works, even those written in an extreme modern style.

WORKS: *Priskazki*, vocal cycle (1963); Violin Sonata (1964);

String Quartet (1964); *Obyomi* (Sizes) for 5 Instruments (1965); *Gradations* for Chamber Group (1966); *Games* for Chamber Orch. (1967–68); 2 syms.: No. 1 (1968) and No. 2 for Soprano, Tenor, and Orch. (1976–78); *Music I* (1968) and *II* (1978) for 4 Strings; Sonata for Strings, Piano, and Percussion (1969); *Rhythms* for Piano (1969–70); Oboe Sonata (1978); *A Day in Pereyaslavl* for Soloists, Chorus, and Orch. (1978–79); *In the Children's Room,* cantata texts (1978–79); *Mother,* opera (1985).

Zagrosek, Lothar, German conductor; b. Waging, Nov. 13, 1942. After training in Munich and at the Essen Folkwangschule, he studied conducting with Swarowsky in Vienna; also received guidance from Karajan, Kertesz, and Maderna. In 1967 he began his career, conducting opera in Salzburg, Kiel, and Darmstadt. In 1972 he became conductor in Solingen. He made his first appearance at the Salzburg Festival in 1973 conducting the Mozarteum Orch. In 1977 he became Generalmusikdirektor in Mönchengladbach. From 1978 he made frequent guest conducting appearances with the London Sinfonietta, establishing a fine reputation as an interpretor of contemporary music. From 1982 to 1987 he was chief conductor of the Austrian Radio Sym. Orch. in Vienna. He made appearances as a guest conductor in the U.S. from 1984. From 1986 to 1989 he was music director of the Paris Opéra. In 1987 he conducted *Così fan tutti* at the Glyndebourne Festival. He appeared with the English National Opera in London in 1989 conducting *Die Zauberflöte.* From 1990 to 1993 he was Generalmusikdirektor of the Leipzig Opera.

Zagwijn, Henri, Dutch composer and teacher; b. Nieuwer-Amstel, July 17, 1878; d. The Hague, Oct. 23, 1954. He was basically autodidact as a composer. In 1916 he became a teacher at the Rotterdam School of Music. With Sem Dresden, he founded the Soc. of Modern Composers of the Netherlands in 1918. From 1931 he taught at the Rotterdam Cons. He was a follower of Rudolf Steiner's anthroposophic movement and publ. *De muziek in het licht der anthroposophie* (Rotterdam, 1925). He also publ. a biography of Debussy (The Hague, 1940). In his music, Zagwijn was particularly influenced by the French school.

WORKS: ORCH.: *Auferstehung,* prelude (1918); *Weihe-Nacht,* prelude (1918); 2 piano concertantes (1939, 1941); Flute Concertante (1940); Harp Concerto (1948); *Concertstuk* (1950); *Elegia e capriccio* for Harp and Orch. (1950); *Tema con variazione* for Strings (1951); *Entrata* for Band (1951); *Marcia* for Band (1951); *Pastorale et hymne* (1952); *Scènes de ballet* (1952); *Suite symphonique* (1953). **CHAMBER:** Suite for Wind Sextet (1915); Piano Trio (1915); 2 string quartets (1918, 1949); *Nocturne* for Flute, English Horn, Clarinet, Bassoon, Horn, Harp, and Celesta (1918); String Sextet (1932); Quintet for Flute, Violin, Viola, Cello, and Harp (1937); *Pastorale* for Flute, Oboe, and Piano (1937); *Introduzione e scherzetto* for Flute, Viola, and Harp (1940); *Mystère* for Harp and Piano (1941); 2 trios for Flute, Oboe, and Clarinet (1944, 1949); *Scherzo* for Wind Sextet (1946); String Trio (1946); *Andante* for Flute and Organ (1946); *Esquisse* for Trombone and Piano (1947); Wind Quintet (1948); *Cortège* for Brass Ensemble (1948); Sonata for Flute and Harpsichord (1949); *Entrata e fuga* for Flute, Oboe, Violin, Viola, Cello, and Harpsichord (1950); Sonata for Flute, Clarinet, and Harpsichord (1950); *Elegia e ditirambo* for 2 Violins and Piano (1951); *Preludio* for 2 Violins (1951); Suite for 2 Oboes (1951); *Entrata giocosa* for Horn, 2 Trumpets, and Trombone (1952); Trio for Oboe, Clarinet, and Piano (1952); *Canzone e riddone* for Flute and Piano (1952); *Capriccio* for Violin and Harpsichord or Piano (1953); *Elegia e visione* for Cello and Piano (1953); *Suite lyrique* for 4 Recorders (1954); *Sarabande e fandango* for Guitar and Harpsichord or Piano (1954). **KEYBOARD: PIANO:** *Suite sinfonica* (1943); *Petite suite (in stile antico)* for 2 Pianos (1944); Suite (1945); *Triade* (1954). **ORGAN:** *Fantasia e fuga* (1952).

Zaidel-Rudolph, Jeanne, prominent South African composer; b. Pretoria, July 9, 1948. She began piano instruction at the age of 5 with her aunt, and in her youth began to appear publicly. In 1966 she entered the Univ. of Pretoria, where she studied composition with Johann Potgieter and Arthur Wegelin (B.Mus., 1969; M.Mus., 1972); in 1973 she studied in London with John Lambert (composition), John Lill (piano), and Tristam Carey (electronic music) at the Royal College of Music, where she won the R.O. Morris and Cobbett composition prizes. After further training in composition with Ligeti at the Hamburg Hochschule für Musik (1974), she returned to South Africa and was a lecturer in the music dept. at the Univ. of the Witwatersand in Johannesburg from 1975 to 1977. She then studied for her D.Mus. degree under Stefans Grove at the Univ. of Pretoria, becoming the first woman in South African history to receive such a degree in composition in 1979. From 1978 to 1982 she again was a lecturer at the Univ. of the Witwatersand; after serving as head of music for the Performing Arts Workshop in Johannesburg (1983–84), she was senior lecturer at the Univ. of the Witwatersand (from 1985). She was also active as a pianist and organist, serving in the latter capacity at the Sydenham/Highlands North Synagogue in Johannesburg. While her compositions utilize various contemporary techniques, she has succeeded in finding a highly personal style, frequently melding Western and African elements. Her Jewish heritage is affirmed in many of her works as well, most notably in the inspiration she has found in the Bible and Jewish mysticism.

WORKS: DRAMATIC: *Animal Farm,* opera (1978); *A Rage in a Cage,* rock opera (1983); *The River People—Abantubomlambo,* ballet (Durban, July 1987); *African Dream,* film score (1988). **ORCH.:** Concert Overture (1979); *5 Chassidic Melodies* for Small Orch. (1981); 2 syms.: No. 1, *Construction Symphony* (1985) and No. 2, *Sefirot Symphony,* for Wind, Brass, Percussion, and Harp (1990); *Fanfare Festival Overture* (1985; Johannesburg, Aug. 1986); *Tempus fugit* (Johannesburg, Oct. 1986); *At the End of the Rainbow,* symphonic poem (Johannesburg, Aug. 1988); Piano Concerto (1995). **CHAMBER:** *Kaleidoscope* for Winds and Percussion (1971); *Canonetta for 4* for Trumpet, Bassoon, Viola, and Vibraphone (1973); *Reaction* for Piano, Cello, and Percussion (1973); *Tango for Tim* for Guitar (1973); Chamber Concertino for 11 Instruments (1979); *The Fugue That Flew Away* for Flute and Piano (1979); *3 Chassidic Pieces* for Flute, Violin, and Cello (1982); *4 "Minim"* for Cello and Piano (1982); *Brass Quintet—and All That Jazz* for 2 Trumpets, Horn, Trombone, and Tuba (1983); *Margana* for Flute, Violin, Cello, and 2 Percussionists (1985); *Masada* for String Quartet and Bassoon (1989); Sextet (1990); *5 African Sketches* for Guitar (1991); *Suite Afrique* for Cello and Piano (1993). **PIANO:** Sonata (1969); *7 Variations on an Original Theme* (1971); *3 Dimensions* (1974); *Virtuoso I* (1987); *Mixed Feelings: For Sara* (1988); *Mosaic* (1989); *Awaiting Game* (1993). **VOCAL:** *Settings of a Selection of Afrikaans Poems* for Soprano and Piano (1968); *Dialogue of Self and Soul* for 8 Soloists and Speaking Chorus (1971); *Setting of the Swaziland National Anthem* for Chorus and Piano (1974); *5 Pieces* for Soprano and Wind Quartet (1976); *Boy on a Swing* for Women's Chorus, Piano, and Percussion (1983; also for Soprano and Piano, 1992); *Back to Basics* for Narrator, Piano, and Prepared Piano (1983); *It's a Woman's World* for Chorus and Piano (1985); *Peace* for Chorus and Guitar (1991); *Hell, Well Heavens* for Soprano and Piano (1993); *Ukuthula* for Soprano, Mezzo-soprano, and Orch. (1993; Johannesburg, Feb. 25, 1994).

Zajiček, Jeronym, Czech-born American composer; b. Krásné Březno, Nov. 10, 1926. He studied musicology at the Charles Univ. in Prague (1946–49); then served as program director of the Czech section of Radio Free Europe in Munich (1950–52). He emigrated to the U.S. in 1952; studied composition with Jirák at Roosevelt Univ. in Chicago (1955–58) and later with Paul Pisk (1959–60). In 1964 he was appointed an instructor in composition and conducting at the Chicago City College. He became a naturalized American citizen in 1957. His music mirrors the lyrical traditions of his Czech heritage.

WORKS: *Variations* for Piano (1956–57); Piano Trio (1957);

Clarinet Sonata (1957); Sinfonietta (1958); Violin Sonata (1961); String Quartet (1962–63); Concertino for Flute and Strings (1963–64; Chicago, Feb. 26, 1967); *Intrada and Processionale* for Brass, Timpani, and Organ (1970); Cello Sonata (1975); songs.

Zak, Yakov (Izrailevich), Russian pianist and teacher; b. Odessa, Nov. 20, 1913; d. Moscow, June 28, 1976. He studied with Starkova at the Odessa Cons., graduating in 1932; then was a student of Neuhaus at the Moscow Cons., graduating in 1935. At the International Competition for pianists in Warsaw in 1937, he received 1st prize and a special award of a posthumous mask of Chopin for his performance of a Chopin mazurka. He joined the faculty of the Moscow Cons. in 1935; became head of the piano dept. there in 1965. As a concert pianist, Zak toured all over Europe. He played in the U.S. in 1965 and 1967, and was acclaimed for his Soviet-like virtuosity. In 1966 he was made a People's Artist of the U.S.S.R.

Zallinger, Meinhard von, Austrian conductor; b. Vienna, Feb. 25, 1897; d. Salzburg, Sept. 24, 1990. He studied piano and conducting at the Salzburg Mozarteum; also took music courses at the Univ. of Innsbruck. He conducted at the Mozarteum (1920–22); then was on the staff of the Bavarian State Opera in Munich (1926–29) and the Cologne Opera (1929–35). He returned to the Bavarian State Opera in 1935, conducting there until 1944; was then made Generalmusikdirektor in Duisburg. In 1947 he became director of the Mozarteum Orch.; also held the same office at the Salzburg Landestheater. He was music director in Graz (1949–50), of the Vienna Volksoper (1950–53), and the Komische Oper in East Berlin (1953–56). He served again as a conductor at the Bavarian State Opera (1956–73); was concurrently director of the summer academy at the Mozarteum (1956–68).

Zandonai, Riccardo, Italian composer; b. Sacco di Rovereto, Trentino, May 30, 1883; d. Pesaro, June 5, 1944. He was a pupil of Gianferrari at Rovereto (1893–98); then studied with Mascagni at the Liceo Rossini in Pesaro. He graduated in 1902; for his final examination he composed a symphonic poem for Solo Voices, Chorus, and Orch., *Il ritorno di Odisseo.* He then turned to opera, which remained his favored genre throughout his career. His first opera was *La coppa del re* (c.1906), which was never performed. After writing the children's opera *L'uccelino d'oro* (Sacco di Rovereto, 1907), he won notable success with his third opera, *Il grillo del focolare,* after Dickens's *The Cricket on the Hearth* (Turin, Nov. 28, 1908). With his next opera, *Conchita,* after the novel *La Femme et le pantin* by Pierre Louÿs (Milan, Oct. 14, 1911), he established himself as an important Italian composer; the title role was created by the soprano Tarquinia Tarquini, whom Zandonai married in 1917. *Conchita* received its American premiere in San Francisco on Sept. 28, 1912; as *La Femme et le pantin* it was given at the Opéra-Comique in Paris on March 11, 1929. Zandonai's reputation was enhanced by subsequent works, notably *Francesca da Rimini,* after Gabriele d'Annunzio (Turin, Feb. 19, 1914; Metropolitan Opera, N.Y., Dec. 22, 1916), but a previous opera, *Melenis* (Milan, Nov. 13, 1912), was unsuccessful. During World War I, Zandonai participated in the political agitation for the return of former Italian provinces; he wrote a student hymn calling for the redemption of Trieste (1915). His other operas were: *La via della finestra* (Pesaro, July 27, 1919; rev. version, Trieste, Jan. 18, 1923); *Giulietta e Romeo* (Rome, Feb. 14, 1922); *I Cavalieri di Ekeb* (Milan, March 7, 1925); *Giuliano* (Naples, Feb. 4, 1928); *Una partita* (Milan, Jan. 19, 1933); *La farsa amorosa,* after Alarcón's *El sombrero de tres picos* (Rome, Feb. 22, 1933); *Il bacio* (1940–44; unfinished). Among his orch. works were *Serenata medioevale* for Cello, Harp, 2 Horns, and Strings (1909); *Terra nativa,* 2 suites: *Primavera in Val di Sole* (1914–15) and *Autonno fra i monti* (Patria lontana) (1917–18); *Concerto romantico* for Violin and Orch. (1919); *Ballata eroica* (1929); *Fra gli alberghi delle Dolomiti* (1929); *Quadri di Segantini* (1930–31); *Il flauto notturno* for Flute and Small Orch. (1934); *Concerto andaluso* for Cello and Small Orch. (1934); *Colombina overture* (1935); *Rapsodia trentina* (1936); *Biancaneve* (1940); works for band; *Messa da Requiem* for Chorus (1915) and various other choral works; several vocal works with orch.; some chamber music. In 1939 he was appointed director of the Liceo Rossini in Pesaro, remaining there for the rest of his life.

BIBL.: V. Bonajuti Tarquini, *R. Z. nel ricordo dei suoi intimi* (Milan, 1951); G. Barblan, *R. Mariani, et al., A R. Z.* (Trento, 1952); B. Cagnoli, *R. Z.* (Trento, 1978); R. Chiesa, ed., *R. Z.* (Milan, 1984); A. Bassi, *R. Z.* (Milan, 1989).

Zanella, Amilcare, Italian composer, pianist, conductor, and pedagogue; b. Monticelli d'Ongina, Piacenza, Sept. 26, 1873; d. Pesaro, Jan. 9, 1949. He studied with Andreotti in Cremona, then with Bottesini at the Parma Cons., graduating in 1891. In 1892 he went to South America as a pianist and opera conductor; returning to Italy in 1901, he organized his own orch., giving sym. concerts in the principal Italian cities and introducing his own works. He then was director of the Parma Cons. (1903–5) and the Liceo Rossini in Pesaro (1905–39); also served as pianist of the Trio di Pesaro (1927–49).

WORKS: OPERAS: *Aura* (Pesaro, Aug. 27, 1910); *La Sulamita* (Piacenza, Feb. 11, 1926); *Il Revisore,* after Gogol (1938; Trieste, Feb. 20, 1940). **ORCH.:** *Concerto sinfonico* for Piano and Orch. (1897–98); *Fede,* symphonic poem (1901); 2 syms.: No. 1 (1901) and No. 2, *Sinfonia fantastica* (1919); *Fantasia e grande fugato sinfonico* for Piano and Orch. (1902); *Vita,* symphonic poem (1907); *Fantasia sinfonica* (1918); *Edgar Poe,* symphonic impression (c.1921); *Poemetto* for Violin and Orch. (1922); *Elegia e momento frenetico* for Keyed Xylophone and Strings (1923). **CHAMBER:** 2 piano trios (1899, 1928); Brass Quintet (n.d.); Nonet (1906); 2 string quartets (1918, 1924); Piano Quintet (1917); Violin Sonata (1917); Cello Sonata (1917); various piano pieces. **VOCAL:** *Messa di Requiem* for 3 Men's Voices and Organ (1915); pieces for Solo Voice and Orch.; many choral works.

BIBL.: *A. Z., artista, uomo, educatore* (Ferrara, 1932); A. Dioli and M. Nobili, *La vita e l'arte di A. Z.* (Bergamo, 1941).

Zanelli (Morales), Renato, esteemed Chilean baritone, later tenor; b. Valparaiso, April 1, 1892; d. Santiago, March 25, 1935. After studies in Neuchâtel and Turin, he pursued a business career in his homeland; his voice was discovered by Angelo Querez, who became his mentor in Santiago; made his debut as a baritone there as Valentine in 1916. On Nov. 19, 1919, he appeared for the first time with the Metropolitan Opera in N.Y. as Amonasro; he remained on its roster until 1923; then went to Milan, where he resumed vocal studies; made his debut as a tenor in the role of Raoul at the Teatro San Carlo in Naples in 1924; subsequently appeared in Rome, in London (Covent Garden, 1928–30), at La Scala in Milan (1920–32), and at the Teatro Colón in Buenos Aires. He won great distinction with his portrayals of Othello, Lohengrin, and Tristan.

Zanten, Cornelie Van. See **Van Zanten, Cornelie.**

Zappa, Frank (actually, **Francis Vincent**), seeded American rock artist; b. Baltimore, Dec. 21, 1940; d. Los Angeles, Dec. 4, 1993. The family moved to California. From his school days, he played guitar and organized groups with weird names such as The Omens and Captain Glasspack and His Magic Mufflers. In 1960 he composed the sound track for the film *The World's Greatest Sinner,* and in 1963 he wrote another sound track, *Run Home Slow.* In 1965 he joined the rhythm-and-blues band The Soul Giants; he soon took it under his own aegis and thought up for it the surrealist logo The Mothers of Invention. His recording of it, and another album, *Freak Out!,* became underground hits; along with *We're Only in It for the Money* and *Cruising with Ruben and The Jets,* these works constituted the earliest "concept" albums, touching every nerve in a gradually decivilized California life-style—rebellious, anarchistic, incomprehensible, and yet tantalizing. The band became a mixed-media celebration of total artistic, political, and social opposition to the Establishment, the ingredients of their final album, *Mothermania.* Moving farther afield, Zappa produced a video-movie, *200 Motels*, glorifying itinerant sex activities. He became a cult figure, and as such suffered the penalty of violent adulation. Playing in London in 1971, he was painfully injured when a besotted fan pushed him off the stage. Similar assaults forced Zappa to hire an athletic bodyguard for protection. In 1982 his planned appearance in Palermo, Sicily, the birthplace of his parents, had to be cancelled because the mob rioted in anticipation of the event. He deliberately confronted the most cherished social and emotional sentiments by putting on such songs as *Broken Hearts Are for Assholes*, and his release *Jewish Princess* offended, mistakenly, the sensitivity of American Jews. His production *Joe's Garage* contained Zappa's favorite scatological materials, and he went on analyzing and ridiculing urinary functions in such numbers as *Why Does It Hurt When I Pee.* He managed to upset the members of his own faith in the number titled *Catholic Girls.* His *Hot Rats*, a jazz-rock release, included the famous *Willie the Pimp*, and exploited the natural revulsion to unclean animals. In 1980 he produced the film *Baby Snakes*, which shocked even the most impervious senses. He declared in an interview that classical music is only "for old ladies and faggots," but he astounded the musical community when he proclaimed his total adoration of the music of Edgar Varèse and gave a lecture on Varèse in N.Y. Somehow, without formal study, he managed to absorb the essence of Varèse's difficult music. This process led Zappa to produce truly astonishing full orch. scores reveling in artful dissonant counterpoint, *Bob in Dacron and Sad Jane* and *Mo' 'n Herb's Vacation*, and the cataclysmic *Penis Dimension* for chorus, soloists, and orch., with a text so anatomically precise that it could not be performed for any English-speaking audience.

An accounting of Zappa's scatological and sexological proclivities stands in remarkable contrast to his unimpeachable private life and total abstention from alcohol and narcotic drugs. An unexpected reflection of Zappa's own popularity was the emergence of his adolescent daughter, curiously named Moon Unit, as a voice-over speaker on his hit *Valley Girls*, in which she used the vocabulary of growing womanhood of the San Fernando Valley near Los Angeles, with such locutions as "grody to the max" (repellent) and "barfs me out" (disgusting). His son, Dweezil Zappa, is also a musician; his first album, *Havin' a Bad Day*, was modestly successful. In 1985 Zappa became an outspoken opponent of the activities of the PMRC (Parents Music Resource Center), an organization composed largely of wives of U.S. Senators who accused the recording industry of exposing the youth of America to "sex, violence, and the glorification of drugs and alcohol." Their demands to the RIAA (Recording Industry Assn. of America) included the labeling of record albums to indicate lyric content. Zappa voiced his opinions in no uncertain terms, first in an open letter published in Cashbox, and then in one direct to President Reagan; finally, on Sept. 19, 1985, he appeared at the first of a series of highly publicized hearings involving the Senate Commerce, Technology and Transporation Committee, the PMRC, and the RIAA, where he delivered a statement to Congress which began "The PMRC proposal is an ill-conceived piece of nonsense which fails to deliver any real benefits to children, infringes the civil liberties of people who are not children and promises to keep the courts busy for years, dealing with the interpretational and enforcemental problems inherent in the proposal's design." Audio excerpts from these hearings can be heard, in original and Synclavier-manipulated forms, on his album *Zappa Meets the Mothers of Prevention.* Later recordings which made extensive use of the Synclavier included *Francesco Zappa* and *Jazz From Hell.* With P. Occhiogrosso, he publ. an unrestrained autobiographical vol., *The Real Frank Zappa Book* (N.Y., London, Toronto, Sydney, and Tokyo, 1988), rich in undeleted scatological expletives.

BIBL.: N. Obermanns, *Z.log* (Los Angeles, 1981); J. Aikin and B. Doerschuk, "F. Z.: Sample This!," *Keyboard* (Feb. 1987); B. Watson, *Z.: The Dialectics of Negative Poodle Play* (N.Y., 1994).

Zarinš, Margeris, Latvian composer; b. Jaunpiebalga, May 24, 1910. He studied composition in Riga with Wihtol at the Latvian Cons. (1929–33); also took lessons in piano and organ. From 1940 to 1950 he was director of music of the Latvian Art Theater. From 1956 to 1968 he was secretary-general of the Union of Latvian Composers. In his works, he stylized the elements of Latvian folk songs. He was particularly successful in his operas on contemporary subjects, often with a satirical tilt. In his *Opera uz lankuma* (Opera in the Town Square; 1970), he attempted to revive the early Soviet attempts to bring theatrical spectacles into the streets.

WORKS: OPERAS: *Kungs un spēlmanitis* (The King and the Little Musician; 1939); *Uz jauno krastu* (To New Shores; 1955); *Zalās dzirnavas* (The Green Mill; 1958); *Nabaqu opera* (Beggar's Opera; 1964); *Sveta Mauricija brinumdarbs* (Miracle of St. Mauritius; 1964); *Opera uz lankuma* (Opera in the Town Square; 1970). **ORCH.:** Piano Concerto (1937); *Greek Vases* for Piano and Orch. (1946; rev. 1960). **VOCAL:** Oratorios, including *Valmieras varoni* (The Heroes of Valmiera; 1950) and *Mahagoni* (Mahagonny), a propaganda work denouncing the Western colonial policies in Africa (1965); numerous choruses based on Latvian folk songs.

BIBL.: L. Krasinska, *M. Z.* (Riga, 1960).

Zaslaw, Neal (Alexander), American musicologist; b. N.Y., June 28, 1939. He studied at Harvard Univ. (B.A., 1961); then took flute lessons at the Juilliard School of Music (M.S., 1963); subsequently studied musicology with Paul Henry Lang at Columbia Univ. (M.A., 1965; Ph.D., 1970, with the diss. *Materials for the Life and Works of Jean-Marie Leclair l'Aîné*). He taught at City College of the City Univ. of N.Y. (1968–70); in 1970 he joined the faculty of Cornell Univ. He was ed.-in-chief of *Current Musicology* (1967–70). Zaslaw publ. the vols. *Edward A. MacDowell* (N.Y., 1964) and *Mozart's Symphonies: Context, Performance Practice, Reception* (Oxford, 1990). With W. Cowdery, he ed. *The Complete Mozart: A Guide to the Musical Works of Wolfgang Amadeus Mozart* (N.Y., 1991). In 1995 he became editor of the 7th ed. of the Mozart Köchel catalog.

Zbinden, Julien-François, Swiss composer, pianist, and administrator; b. Rolle, Nov. 11, 1917. He began piano lessons at the age of 8 and later attended the Lausanne Cons. He also studied at the teacher's training college in the canton of Vaud (1934–38; graduated, 1938), and then was active as a pianist. After teaching himself harmony, form, and composition, he pursued training in counterpoint and orchestration with Gerber. In 1947 he joined Radio Lausanne as a pianist and music producer, becoming head of the music dept. in 1956. From 1965 to 1982 he was deputy director of musical broadcasts of the Radio-Télévision Suisse Romande. He served as president of the Swiss Musicians Assn. (1973–79) and of SUISA (the Swiss music copyright society; 1987–91). In 1978 the French government made him an Officier de l'ordre des Arts et des Lettres. His early love of jazz, as well as the influence of Ravel, Stravinsky, and Honegger, were important factors in the development of his own musical style. Among his works were *La Pantoufle*, farce-ballet (1958); *Fait divers*, opera (1960); radiophonic scores; Piano Concerto (1944); *Concerto da camera* for Piano and Strings (1950–51); 4 syms.; *Suite française* for Strings (1954); *Rhapsodie* for Violin and Orch. (1956); *Jazzific 59–16* for Jazz Group and Strings (1958); *Concerto breve* for Cello and Orch. (1962); Violin Concerto (1962–64); *Concerto for Orchestra* (1977); much chamber music; *Terra Dei*, oratorio for Soloists, Chorus, and Orch. (1966–67), and other vocal works.

BIBL.: C. Tappolet, *J.-F. Z., compositeur* (1994).

Zeani (real name, **Zahan**), **Virginia,** Romanian soprano; b. Solovastru, Oct. 21, 1928. She studied in Bucharest with Lipkowska and with Pertile in Milan. She made her operatic debut as Violetta in Bologna in 1948; then sang in London (1953), in Rome, at La Scala in Milan (1956), and at Covent Garden in London (1959). She made her Metropolitan Opera debut in N.Y. as Violetta on Nov. 12, 1966, where she sang for only one season. In 1980 she joined the faculty of the Indiana Univ. School of Music in Bloomington. She married **Nicola Rossi-**

Lemeni in 1958. Among her finest roles were Lucia, Elvira, Maria di Rohan, Desdemona, Aida, Leonora, and Tosca.

Zecchi, Adone, Italian composer and conductor; b. Bologna, July 23, 1904. He studied composition with Franco Alfano at the Liceo Musicale in Bologna, graduating in 1926. In 1927 he founded the choral group Corale Euridice, which he led until 1943. In 1930 he founded the Orch. Bolognese de Camera. In 1942 he was appointed to the faculty of the Bologna Cons.; he became its director in 1961. In his compositions he follows the path of Italian neo-Classicism, but applies dodecaphonic formulas in some of his music. He publ. a number of manuals on choral conducting, including the reference work *Il coro nella storia e dizionario dei nomi e dei termini* (Bologna, 1960) and *Il direttore di coro* (Milan, 1965). In collaboration with R. Allorto, he brought out *Educazione musicale* (Milan, 1962); *Canti natalizi di altri paesi* (Milan, 1965); *Canti natalizi italiani* (Milan, 1965); *Canti della vecchia America* (Milan, 1966); and *Il mondo della musica* (Milan, 1969).

WORKS: *Partita* for Orch. (1933); *Toccata, Ricercare e Finale* for Orch. (1941); *2 astrazioni in forma di fuga* for Small Ensemble (Copenhagen, June 2, 1947); *Requiem* for Chorus and Orch. (1946); *Caleidofonia* for Violin, Piano, and Orch. (1963); *Trattenimento musicale* for 11 groups of String Instruments (1969).

Zecchi, Carlo, Italian pianist and conductor; b. Rome, July 8, 1903; d. Salzburg, Aug. 31, 1984. He studied at the Liceo and Cons. in Rome, where he received instruction in piano from Bajardi and in composition from Bustini, Refice, and Setaccioli; continued his training with Schnabel and Busoni in Berlin, where he made his debut as a pianist at the age of 17. He subsequently toured throughout Europe and the U.S. until giving up his solo career in 1939 to tour in duo recitals with the cellist Enrico Mainardi; also studied conducting with H. Munch and Guarnieri; from 1947 he pursued a successful career as a guest conductor; taught at the Accademia di Santa Cecilia in Rome and also gave summer master classes in Salzburg.

Zechberger, Günther, Austrian conductor, teacher, and composer; b. Zams, Tirol, April 24, 1951. He studied composition and guitar at the Cons. (1968–74) and musicology at the Univ. (1974–80) in Innsbruck. He received training in conducting from Eric Ericson and Witold Rowicki, and in composition from Boguslaw Schaeffer. From 1970 to 1991 he taught guitar in Tirolean schools. In 1984 he founded the Tiroler Ensemble für Neue Musik, which he conducted in many performances of contemporary scores. He also taught at the Univ. of Innsbruck. In his music, structural complexities predominate but not without special regard for sonoristic effects.

WORKS: Septet for Flute, Oboe, Clarinet, and String Quartet (1972–73); Trio for Clarinet, Horn, and Bassoon (1972–73); Trio for Violins (1975); *o crux ave*, 7 pieces for Good Friday for Chorus (1978); *Schlusstück* for Chorus and Orch. (1979); *Mass* for Chorus and Orch. (1979); Trombone Quartet (1980); *stabat mater I* for Speaker's Chorus (1981) and *II* for Vocal Ensemble and 8 Players (1985–94); *Im Nebel* for Mezzo-soprano and Orch., after Hermann Hesse (1982); *Studie* for 14 Instruments (1982–83); Sextet for 3 Guitars and 3 Metronomes (1982–83); *Neunzehn* for 8 Instruments (1983); *Kanon* for 2 Tape Recorders and Audience (1983); *Hendekagon* for 26 Instruments (1983–84); *Tieferschüttert* for Mezzo-soprano, Alto Trombone, and Guitar (1984); String Quartet (1984–85); *Choros* for 5 Players (1985); *Kammermusik* for Conductor and 5 Players (1986); *Dear Mr. J.*, action music (1987); *Interview* for Tape (1987); *Stiegenhausmusik*, installation for Voice and 8 Instruments (1986); *Asambari* for 2 Guitars (1988–89); Concerto for Guitar, Live Electronics, and Orch. (1988); *Sakralcollage* for Flute, Bass Flute, Zither, Guitar, and Synthesizer (1989); *. . . with one limit . . .* for Cello, Computer, and Live Electronics (1990); *toucher* for Guitar and Live Electronics (1990); String Sextet (1990); *Partita* for Mezzo-soprano and 5 Instruments (1990); *upstairs* for Voice and 7 Instruments (1991); *Scopello* for Baritone Saxophone, Trombone, Live Electronics, and Computer (1991); *Bacchacaglia* for Soprano, Instruments, Computer, Live Electronics, and Broadcasting Equipment (1992); *stills* for Saxophone, Bass Flute, and Trombone (1992); *R.E.P.04* for Bass Flute, Trombone, Computer, and Live Electronics (1992–93); *. . . und teilen die grune Insel mit ihren Blicken . . .* for Trombone (1993); *die farbe der nacht* for Alto Saxophone, Trombone, Percussion, and UPIC (1993); *Tangenten* for Voice and Instrumental Ensemble (Turkish Radio, Istanbul, Oct. 22, 1994); *horizontal radio*, collage in collaboration with composers from all over the world (broadcast, June 22–23, 1995).

Zechlin, Ruth, German composer, pedagogue, and harpsichordist; b. Grosshartmannsdorf, near Freiberg im Breisgau, June 22, 1926. She studied at the Leipzig Hochschule für Musik (1943–45; 1946–49), where her mentors included J.N. David and Wilhelm Weismann (composition), Anton Rohden and Rudolf Fischer (piano), and Karl Straube and Günther Ramin (organ). In 1950 she went to East Berlin as a teacher at the Hochschule für Musik, and then was a prof. of composition at that city's Hanns Eisler Hochschule für Musik from 1969 to 1986. In 1970 she was made a member of the Akademie der Künste of the German Democratic Republic. From 1990 to 1993 she was vice-president of the Akademie der Künste in Berlin. Among her honors were the Goethe Prize of the City of Berlin (1962), as well as the Arts Prize (1965) and 2 National Prizes (1975, 1982) of the German Democratic Republic.

WORKS: DRAMATIC: *Reineke Fuchs*, opera (1967; Berlin, April 1968); *La Vita*, ballet (1983; Berlin, Feb. 2, 1985); *Sommernachtsträume* or *Die Salamandrin und die Bildsäule* (1990); *Die Reise*, chamber opera (1992; Leipzig, Dec. 1994); *Un baiser pour le Roi*, dance piece (Passau, June 16, 1995). **ORCH.:** *Violin Concerto 1963* (1963; Gera, Feb. 28, 1964); 3 syms.: No. 1 (Leipzig, Sept. 12, 1965), No. 2 (Potsdam, Nov. 16, 1966), and No. 3 (1971; Berlin, Jan. 7, 1972); 2 chamber syms.: No. 1 (1967; Leoben, Nov. 18, 1968) and No. 2 (1973; Stralsund, Feb. 25, 1974); Piano Concerto (1974; Berlin, Feb. 17, 1975); 2 organ concertos: No. 1 (1974; Leipzig, Sept. 20, 1975) and No. 2 (Frankfurt an der Oder, Oct. 2, 1975); *Kristalle* for Harpsichord and Strings (1975; Freiburg im Breisgau, Nov. 2, 1976); *Briefe* (1978; Halle, Jan. 28, 1980); *Situationen* (1980; Berlin, Feb. 19, 1981); *Musik* (1980; Berlin, Oct. 2, 1981); *Metamorphosen* (1982; Berlin, Feb. 24, 1983); *Musik zu Bach* (1983; Berlin, Feb. 28, 1985); *Linien* for Harpsichord and Orch. (1986; Schwerin, June 22, 1988); *Kristallisation* (1987; Cologne, Jan. 27, 1989); Violin Concerto: *Hommage à György Kurtág* (1990; Chemnitz, June 6, 1994); *Stufen* (Hamburg, Dec. 12, 1993); *Venezianisches*, concerto for Harpsichord and Strings (1994; Flensburg, Nov. 7, 1995). **CHAMBER:** 7 string quartets: No. 1 (Leipzig, Oct. 4, 1959), No. 2 (Berlin, July 5, 1965), No. 3 (1970; Berlin, Nov. 22, 1971), No. 4 (Berlin, Oct. 27, 1971), No. 5 (1971; Frankfurt an der Oder, March 9, 1972), No. 6 (1977; Berlin, Jan. 28, 1978), and No. 7 (1995); *Amor und Psyché*, chamber music with Harpsichord (1966; Berlin, Feb. 4, 1967); *Hommage à PHL* for String Quintet and Percussion (Berlin, Dec. 6, 1973); *pour la flûte* (1973; Berlin, Sept. 22, 1975); *Begegnungen*, chamber music (1977; Berlin, Feb. 4, 1978); *Hommage à Shakespeare*, scene for Chamber Ensemble (1978; Schwerin, March 9, 1980); *Reflexionen* for 14 Strings (Berlin, Nov. 5, 1979); *Beschwörungen* for Percussionist (1980; Dresden, May 25, 1981); *Katharsis* for Oboe, Cello, and Percussion (1981; Leipzig, Feb. 5, 1982); *da capo* for Violin (1982; Berlin, Nov. 3, 1986); *Musik* for Cello (1983; Berlin, March 22, 1986); *Konstellationen* for 10 Brass Instruments (1985; Eisenach, June 14, 1986); *Synthese* for Organ and Percussion (1986; Vienna, July 24, 1987); *7 Versuche und 1 Ergebnis* for Saxophone Quartet (1988; Berlin, Feb. 20, 1989); *5 Mobiles* for Harp (1988); *Szenische Kammermusik nach Heiner Müllers Hamletmaschine* for 5 Instrumentalists (Berlin, Dec. 1, 1991); *Musik zu Kafka II* for Percussionist (Heidelberg, Sept. 25, 1992); *3 Briefe an HWH* for Oboe (1992; Stuttgart, Nov. 24, 1993); *Alternativer Baukasten* for Chamber Ensemble (Nuremberg, Nov. 12, 1993); *Akzente und Flächen* for 5 Percussionists

(1993; Berlin, Feb. 22, 1994); *Circulation* for 8 Percussion (1994). **KEYBOARD: HARPSICHORD:** 11 pieces (1957–94). **ORGAN:** 12 pieces (1969–93). **VOCAL:** *Keunergeschichten* for Speaker and Chamber Ensemble, after Bertolt Brecht (Berlin, Nov. 16, 1966); *Ode an die Luft* for Mezzo-soprano and Orch., after Pablo Neruda (1974); *Canzoni alla notte* for Baritone and Orch., after Quasimodo (1974; Leipzig, Oct. 15, 1976); *An Aphrodite* for Alto, Baritone, Pantomime, and 7 Musicians (Berlin, Feb. 25, 1977); *Das Hohelied* for Tenor and Orch. (1979; Leipzig, Nov. 5, 1980); *Angelus-Silesius-Sprüche* for Chorus (1983); *Hommage à Bach* for Chorus (1985); *Prometheus* for Speaker, Piano, and Percussion (1986; Berlin, May 8, 1987).

Zedda, Alberto, Italian conductor and musicologist; b. Milan, Jan. 2, 1928. He studied organ with Galliera, conducting with Votto and Giulini, and composition with Fait at the Milan Cons. In 1956 he made his debut as a conductor in Milan. He subsequently went to the U.S., where he taught at the Cincinnati College of Music (1957–59). Returning to Europe, he conducted at the Deutsche Oper in West Berlin (1961–63); then conducted at the N.Y. City Opera. With Philip Gossett, he served as co-ed. of the complete works of Rossini. Zedda was artistic director of the Teatro Comunale in Genoa in 1992 and of Milan's La Scala in 1992–93.

Zednik, Heinz, Austrian tenor; b. Vienna, Feb. 21, 1940. He was a student of Marga Wissmann at the Vienna Cons. In 1963 he made his operatic debut as Trabuco in *La forza del destino* in Graz. In 1965 he became a member of the Vienna State Opera, where he created the role of Kalb in Einem's *Kabale und Liebe* in 1976. His guest engagements took him to such operatic centers as Munich, Paris, Nice, Moscow, and Montreal. In 1970 he made his first appearance at the Bayreuth Festival as David in *Die Meistersinger von Nürnberg*, and he returned there to sing Loge and Mime in the centenary *Ring* cycle in 1976. In 1980 he was made an Austrian Kammersänger. For his first appearance at the Salzburg Festival (1981), he sang Bardolfo in *Falstaff*. On Sept. 22, 1981, he made his Metropolitan Opera debut in N.Y. as Mime in *Das Rheingold*. He returned to Salzburg to create the roles of the Regisseur in Berio's *Un re in ascolto* (1984) and Hadank in Penderecki's *Die schwarze Maske* (1986). In 1987 he appeared as Pedrillo at the Metropolitan Opera, and returned there during the 1989–90 season as Mime.

Zeffirelli, Franco (real name, **Gian Franco Corsi**), prominent Italian opera director and designer; b. Florence, Feb. 12, 1923. He began his career as an actor, and then became an assistant to Visconti. His first operatic production was *La Cenerentola* at Milan's La Scala (1953). In 1958 he mounted *La Traviata* in Dallas, and in 1959 *Lucia di Lammermoor* at London's Covent Garden, where he later produced *Falstaff* (1961), *Alcina* and *Don Giovanni* (1962), and *Tosca*. He also worked at the Metropolitan Opera in N.Y., where he was chosen to produce Barber's *Antony and Cleopatra* as the opening work at the new house at Lincoln Center in 1966. In later years, he devoted himself to operatic film productions, winning particular acclaim for his filming of *La Traviata* (1983) and *Otello* (1986); he also brought out the film biography *The Young Toscanini* (1988).

Zehetmair, Thomas, Austrian violinist; b. Salzburg, Nov. 23, 1961. His parents were violinists. After demonstrating prodigious talent, he studied with his father, Helmut Zehetmair, and with Franz Samohyl at the Salzburg Mozarteum. He was still a small child when he began to appear in public; later pursued advanced training with Max Rostal and Nathan Milstein. After winning 1st prize in the Mozart competition in 1978, he scored a major success with his first appearance at Vienna's Musikverein. He subsequently was engaged as a soloist with leading European and U.S. orchs.; also appeared as a recitalist and chamber music player in a catholic repertoire ranging from early music to contemporary scores.

Zehnder, Max, Swiss composer; b. Turgi, Nov. 17, 1901; d. St. Gallen, July 16, 1972. He studied with Wenz, Lang, Andreae, Vogler, and Laquai at the Zürich Cons. (1923–26). He was on the faculty of the Rorschach Training College in Canton St. Gallen (1931–68), where he also conducted its orch. His compositions developed from a late-Romantic to a neo-Classical style; among them are String Quartet (1928); *Praludium und Chaconne* for Strings (1941); 2 cantatas (1947, 1960); *In memoriam* for Strings and Organ (1965); *Mouvements* for Strings (1970); various choruses; songs.

Zeidman, Boris, Russian composer and pedagogue; b. St. Petersburg, Feb. 10, 1908; d. Tashkent, Dec. 30, 1981. He studied composition at the Leningrad Cons. with Maximilian Steinberg, graduating in 1931; then taught music in various schools in Russia, Azerbaijan, and Uzbekistan.

WORKS: DRAMATIC: OPERAS: *The People's Wrath* (Baku, Dec. 28, 1941); *Son of the Regiment* (Baku, Feb. 23, 1955); *Zainab and Omon* (1958); *The Russians* (1970). **BALLETS:** *The Gold Key* (1955); *The Dragon and the Sun* (1964). **ORCH.:** 2 piano concertos (1931, 1935); Viola Concerto (1938); Bassoon Concerto (1938); Cello Concerto (1948); *Songs of Struggle* (1966); Violin Concerto (1968); *Days of Spring* (1971). **OTHER:** Chamber music; songs; teaching collections.

Zeinally, Assaf, Azerbaijani composer; b. Derbent, April 5, 1909; d. Baku, Oct. 27, 1932. He studied cello and trumpet at the Baku Cons., graduating in 1931, but died a year later, at the age of 23. He was a highly promising musician; his particular merit was the attempt to compose music in classical forms on folk themes; in this manner he wrote several violin pieces, a *Children's Suite* for Piano, and many songs to words by native poets.

BIBL.: Kh. Melikov, *A. Z.* (Baku, 1956; 2nd ed., 1969).

Zeisl, Eric(h), Austrian-born American composer; b. Vienna, May 18, 1905; d. Los Angeles, Feb. 18, 1959. A son of prosperous parents who owned a coffeehouse, he entered the Vienna Academy of Music at 14; was a pupil of Richard Stöhr, Joseph Marx, and Hugo Kauder; publ. his first songs at 16. In 1934 he won the Austrian State Prize for his *Requiem concertante*. After the seizure of Austria by the Nazis in 1938, he fled to Paris, and at the outbreak of World War II in 1939, went to the U.S.: in 1941 he settled in Los Angeles; in 1945 he became a naturalized American citizen. He taught at the Southern Calif. School of Music; from 1949 until his death he was on the staff at Los Angeles City College. Increasingly conscious in exile of his Jewish heritage, he selected biblical themes for his stage works; death interrupted the composition of his major work, the music drama *Job*; Hebraic cantillation is basic to this period. His style of composition reflects the late Romantic school of Vienna, imbued with poetic melancholy, with relief provided by eruptions of dancing optimism. He was at his best in his song cycles.

WORKS: DRAMATIC: *Die Fahrt ins Wunderland*, children's opera (Vienna, 1934); *Leonce und Lena*, Singspiel (1937; Los Angeles, 1952); *Job*, opera (1939–41; 1957–59; unfinished); *Pierrot in der Flasche*, ballet (Vienna Radio, 1935); *Uranium 235*, ballet (1946); *Naboth's Vineyard*, ballet (1953); *Jacob und Rachel*, ballet (1954). **ORCH.:** *Kleine Symphonie* (Vienna Radio, May 30, 1937); *Passacaglia-Fantasie* (Vienna, Nov. 4, 1937); *November*, suite for Chamber Orch. (N.Y., Jan. 25, 1941); *Cossack Dance* (from the unfinished opera *Job*, Los Angeles, Aug. 18, 1946); *Return of Ulysses*, suite for Chamber Orch. (Chicago, Nov. 17, 1948); *Variations and Fugue on Christmas Carols* (1950); Piano Concerto (1951); *Concerto grosso* for Cello and Orch. (1956). **CHAMBER:** Violin Sonata (1950); Viola Sonata (1950); Cello Sonata (1951); Trio for Flute, Viola, and Harp (1956). **VOCAL:** *Mondbilder* for Baritone and Orch. (1928); *Requiem ebraico* (1945); *Kinderlieder* for Soprano; *6 Lieder* for Baritone.

BIBL.: M. Cole and B. Barclay, *Armseelchen: The Life and Music of E. Z.* (Westport, Conn., 1984).

Zeitlin, Zvi, Yugoslav-American violinist and pedagogue; b. Dubrovnik, Feb. 21, 1923. He studied at the Hebrew Univ. in Jerusalem; then was a violin student of Sascha Jacobson, Louis

Persinger, and Ivan Galamian at the Juilliard School of Music in N.Y. In 1940 he made his professional debut as soloist with the Palestine Orch.; in 1951 he made his N.Y. debut. He subsequently appeared as a soloist with many orchs., and also gave recitals. In 1967 he joined the faculty of the Eastman School of Music in Rochester, N.Y. He was noted for his intelligent performances of modern violin works.

Zelenka, István, Hungarian-born Austrian, later Swiss composer; b. Budapest, July 30, 1936. After training in Budapest, he pursued studies at the Vienna Academy of Music, where he received 1st prize in composition in 1962. In 1960 he became a naturalized Austrian citizen. He later settled in Switzerland and became a naturalized Swiss citizen in 1976. In addition to working as a producer and programmer of music for the Radio Suisse Romande (from 1978), he lectured on contemporary music at the Geneva Cons. (from 1980). In 1982 he was a cofounder of the group DIGITALISMUS, and in 1983 of the collective private publishing venture EDITION ZWACHEN. In his music, Zelenka has followed an experimental course, utilizing various contemporary techniques.

WORKS: MUSIC THEATER: *Dove, dove, Signore, Signori?* (1971); *Un Faust-digest agréménte* (1979); *C'est avec reconnaissance et émotion qud j'ai appris très sincèrement dévoué à tous!* (1980); *Estouffade de volailles* (1984). **ORCH.:** *A propos FAFNER* (1971); *Le très Saint Empire de Rome, comment tient-il encore debout?* for Viola d'Amore and Orch. (1981); *Credo* for Orch. and Video (1983); *Médaille, pile ET face* (1984); *La Traque* for Cello and Orch. (1985); *État de siège(s)* (1989). **CHAMBER:** *Ritournelles* for Flute, Oboe, Bassoon, and 2 Harpsichords (1975); *Vivat Nucleus'* for Wind Quintet and Tape (1978); *Progression/Regression?* for Violin and Piano (1979); *Deus ex laminae* for 2 Pianos and 2 Cymbals (1979); *. . . The permanent variations produced by confined breeding and changing circumstances are continued and . . .* for Alto Flute and String Trio (1979); *Fünf Analysen eines Farbbildes* for Violin and Piano (1981); *Due(tt) (ll) o* for Clarinet, Violin, Cello, and Piano (1983); *Souvenir d'enfance/mémoire d'adulte* for Cello and Synthesizer (1984); *Gebeetstunde* for 2 Cellists, 3 Pianists, and 8 Cymbalists (1986); *Musique des sphères* for Clarinet, Violin, Horn, Bassoon, Viola, Cello, Double Bass, and 2 Cassettophones (1990). **OTHER:** Vocal works; electroacoustic scores.

Železný, Lubomír, Czech composer; b. Ostrava, March 16, 1925; d. Prague, Sept. 27, 1979. He studied composition with Karel Janeček at the Prague Cons. (1945–48) and with Bořkovec at the Prague Academy of Musical Arts (1948–50). He worked in the music dept. of Prague Radio; was chairman of the Union of Czech Composers and Concert Artists (1972–79).

WORKS: ORCH.: *2 Gavottes* (1954); 2 violin concertos (1958–59; 1974–75); 2 syms. (1961–62; 1970); Concerto for Flute, Strings, and Piano (1966); Cello Concerto (1968); *Concertant Music* for Viola, Strings, and Piano (1969); *Festive March* (1971). **CHAMBER:** Flute Sonata (1943); Trio for Flute, Viola, and Cello (1946); 2 violin sonatas (1948, 1971); Quartet for Flute, Violin, Viola, and Cello (1948); 2 string quartets (1959–60; 1968); Piano Trio (1966); Quintet for 2 Violins, Clarinet, Viola, and Cello (1969); Wind Quintet (1970). **VOCAL:** *Brigand Songs* for Tenor and Orch. (1958); choruses; solo songs.

Zelinka, Jan Evangelista, Czech composer; b. Prague, Jan. 13, 1893; d. there, June 30, 1969. He studied music with his father, the organist and composer, Jan Evangelista Zelinka (1856–1935), and later with J.B. Foerster, Suk, Novák, and Ostrčil.

WORKS: DRAMATIC: OPERAS: *Dceruška hostinského* (The Tavernkeeper's Little Daughter; 1921; Prague, Feb. 24, 1925); *Devátá louka* (The 9th Meadow; 1929; Prague, Sept. 19, 1931); *Odchod dona Quijota* (Departure of Don Quixote; 1936); *Paličatý švec* (The Stubborn Cobbler; 1940; Prague, March 28, 1944); *Meluzína* (The Wailing Wind; 1947; Plzeň, April 15, 1950); *Námluvy bez konce* (Endless Wooing), radio opera (Czech Radio, Jan. 27, 1950); *Masopustní noc* (Shrovetide Night; 1956); *Lásky žal i smích* (Love's Woe and Laughter), after Goldoni (1958); *Škola pro ženy* (School for Wives), after Molière (1959); *Blouznivé jaro* (A Fanciful Spring; 1960); *Dřevěný kůň* (The Wooden Horse; 1962–63). **BALLET-PANTOMIME:** *Skleněná panna* (The Glass Doll; 1927; Prague, July 2, 1928). **SCENIC MELODRAMA:** *Srdce na prázdninách* (Heart on a Fishhook; 1932; Brno, Jan. 28, 1938). Also incidental music. **ORCH.:** *Overture to a Renaissance Comedy* (1919); *Pariz—Glotton*, overture burlesque (1931); *Weekend*, suite (1939); *Sinfonia rustica* (1956); *A Slovak Summer* (1959); *Musichetta primaverale* for Chamber Orch. (1962); *Satiricon*, suite (1964). **CHAMBER:** 2 nonets: *Capriccio* (1937) and *Cassation* (1943); *Late Summer*, piano trio (1949); *Sonata leggera* for Saxophone and Piano (1962); Piano Sonata (1926); organ pieces. **VOCAL:** Cantatas; songs.

Zeljenka, Ilja, Slovak composer; b. Bratislava, Dec. 21, 1932. Following private training with Zimmer (harmony and counterpoint) and Macudzinski (piano), he studied with Cikker (composition) at the Bratislava Academy of Music and Drama (1951–56). He was a dramaturg with the Slovak Phil. (1957–61) and the Czechoslovak Radio (1961–68) in Bratislava, and later served as chairman of the Slovak Music Union (1990–91). Zeljenka has followed a varied course as a composer and has utilized various contemporary means of expression, ranging from post-Webern serialism to electronics.

WORKS: ORCH.: 5 syms.: No. 1 (1954–55), No. 2 for Strings (1961), No. 3 (1972), No. 4, *Ballet Symphony* (1978), and No. 5 (1984); *Dramatic Overture* (1955); *Revolution Overture* (1962); *Structures* (1964); 2 piano concertos (1966, n.d.); *Meditation* (1969); *Variations* (1971); Concerto for Violin and Strings (1974); *Music* for Piano and Strings (1976); *Epilogue to the Memory of E. Spitz* (1979); *Ouvertura giocosa* (1982); Concerto for Clarinet, Strings, Xylophone, and Kettledrum (1984); *Dialogues* for Cello and Chamber String Orch. (1984); *Music* (1987); Concertino for Chamber String Orch., Clarinet, Piano, and Percussion (1988); *Enchanted Movement* (1989); Violin Concerto (1989). **CHAMBER:** 2 piano quintets (1953, 1959); 5 string quartets (1965, 1976, 1979, 1986, 1988); *Polymetric Music* for 4 String Quintets (1969); *Elegy* for Strings (1973); *Musica slovaca* for Strings (1975; also for String Quartet, 1986); Piano Trio (1975); Quintet for Winds and Percussion (1977); *Monologues* for Cello (1982); *3 Pieces* for Flute (1984); Trio for Flute, Oboe, and Bassoon (1985); *Music* for Cello and Piano (1986); *Sonata-Ballad* for Viola and Piano (1988). **KEYBOARD: PIANO:** *Bagatelles* (1955); 4 sonatas (1958, 1974, 1985, 1989); *Capriccio* (1982); *Little Suite* (1987); *5 Etudes* (1988); *3 Preludes and Fugues* (1988). **ORGAN:** *Ligatures* (1972); *6 Studies* (1976); *Reliefs* (1979); *Letters to Friends* (1984). **VOCAL:** *Plays* for 13 Singers and Percussion (1968); *Metamorphoses XV* for Narrator and Chamber Ensemble (1969); *Caela Hebe* for Chorus and 13 Instruments (1970); *Galgenlieder* for Soprano, String Quartet, Clarinet, Flute, and Piano (1975); *Mutations* for Soprano, Bass, Wind Quintet, and Percussion (1979); *Music* for Voices, Wind Quintet, and Percussion (1980); *Musik für Morgenstern* for Bass, Clarinet, and Chamber String Orch. (1983); *Songs of Youth* for Chorus, Trumpet, and Kettledrums (1985); *Aztecian Songs* for Soprano, Piano, and Percussion (1986); *Magic Formulas* for Alto and String Quartet (1988).

Zeltser, Mark, Russian-born American pianist; b. Kishinev, April 8, 1947. He began piano lessons as a child under his mother's tutelage and made his debut as a soloist with the Kishinev Phil. when he was 9. He pursued training with Flier at the Moscow Cons., graduating in 1971. In the meantime, he captured 3rd prize in the Long-Thibaud Competition in Paris in 1967 and 2nd prize in the Busoni Competition in Bolzano in 1968. In 1976 he played at the Spoleto Festival. He made his first appearance at the Salzburg Festival in 1977. In 1978 he made his N.Y. debut. In subsequent seasons, he appeared as a soloist with many of the world's major orchs. and as a recitalist.

Zemlinsky, Alexander von, important Austrian composer and conductor of partly Jewish descent (he removed the nobiliary particle "von" in 1918 when such distinctions were outlawed in

Austria); b. Vienna, Oct. 14, 1871; d. Larchmont, N.Y., March 15, 1942. At the Vienna Cons. he studied piano with Door (1887–90) and composition with Krenn, Robert Fuchs, and J.N. Fuchs (1890–92). In 1893 he joined the Vienna Tonkünstlerverein. In 1895 he became connected with the orch. society Polyhymnia, and met Schoenberg, whom he advised on the technical aspects of chamber music; Schoenberg always had the highest regard for Zemlinsky as a composer and lamented the lack of appreciation for Zemlinsky's music. There was also a personal bond between them; in 1901 Schoenberg married Zemlinsky's sister Mathilde. Zemlinsky's first opera, *Sarema*, to a libretto by his own father, was premiered in Munich on Oct. 10, 1897; Schoenberg made a Klavierauszug of it. Zemlinsky also entered into contact with Mahler, music director of the Vienna Court Opera, who accepted Zemlinsky's opera *Es war einmal* for performance; Mahler conducted its premiere at the Court Opera on Jan. 22, 1900, and it became Zemlinsky's most popular production. From 1900 to 1906 Zemlinsky served as conductor of the Karlstheater in Vienna; in 1903 he conducted at the Theater an der Wien; in 1904 he was named chief conductor of the Volksoper; in 1910 he orchestrated and conducted the ballet *Der Schneemann* by the greatly talented 11-year-old wunderkind Erich Korngold. About that time, he and Schoenberg organized in Vienna the Union of Creative Musicians, which performed his tone poem *Die Seejungfrau*. In 1911 Zemlinsky moved to Prague, where he became conductor at the German Opera, and also taught conducting and composition at the German Academy of Music (from 1920). In 1927 he moved to Berlin, where he obtained the appointment of assistant conductor at the Kroll Opera, with Otto Klemperer as chief conductor and music director. When the Nazis came to power in Germany in 1933, he returned to Vienna, and also filled engagements as a guest conductor in Russia and elsewhere. After the Anschluss of 1938, he emigrated to America. As a composer, Zemlinsky followed the post-Romantic trends of Mahler and Richard Strauss. He was greatly admired but his works were seldom performed, despite the efforts of Schoenberg and his associates to revive his music. How strongly he influenced his younger contemporaries is illustrated by the fact that Alban Berg quoted some of Zemlinsky's music from the *Lyric Symphony* in his own *Lyrische Suite*.

WORKS: DRAMATIC: OPERAS: *Sarema* (1894–95; Munich, Oct. 10, 1897); *Es war einmal* (1897–99; Vienna, Jan. 22, 1900); *Der Traumgörge* (1903–06; Nuremberg, Oct. 11, 1980); *Kleider machen Leute* (1907–10; Vienna, Dec. 2, 1910; rev. 1921); *Eine florentinische Tragödie* (1915–16; Stuttgart, Jan. 30, 1917); *Der Zwerg*, after Oscar Wilde's *The Birthday of the Infanta* (1920–21; Cologne, May 28, 1922); *Der Kreidekreis* (1930–32; Zürich, Oct. 14, 1933); *Der König Kandaules* (1935–36; left in short score; completed by A. Beaumont, 1989); also 5 unfinished operas: *Malwa* (1902; 1912–13), *Herrn Arnes Schatz* (1917), *Raphael* (1918), *Vitalis* (1926), and *Circe* (1939–41). **MIMODRAMA:** Ein Lichtstrahl (1903). **BALLET:** *Das gläsende Herz*, after Hofmannsthal (1901). **INCIDENTAL MUSIC TO:** Shakespeare's *Cymbeline* (1914). **ORCH.:** 3 syms.: No. 1 (1892), No. 2 (1897; Vienna, March 5, 1899), and No. 3, *Lyrische Symphonie*, for Soprano, Baritone, and Orch., after Rabindranath Tagore (1922–23; Prague, June 4, 1924); Suite (c.1894); *Der Ring des Ofterdingen*, overture (1894–95); *Die Seejungfrau*, tone poem after Andersen (1902–03); Sinfonietta (1934). **CHAMBER:** *Serenade* for Violin and Piano (1892); Suite for Violin and Piano (c.1893); String Quintet (c.1895); Trio for Clarinet or Viola, Cello, and Piano (1895); 4 string quartets: No. 1 (c.1895; Vienna, Dec. 2, 1896), No. 2 (1913–15), No. 3 (1924), and No. 4, Suite (1936). **PIANO:** *Ländliche Tanze* (1891); *Fantasien über Gedichte von Richard Dehmel* (1898). **VOCAL:** *Lieder* for Voice and Piano (2 books, 1894–96); *Der alte Garten* for Voice and Orch. (1895); *Die Reisen* for Voice and Orch., after Eichendorff (1895); *Orientalisches Sonett* for Voice and Piano (1895); *Waldgespräch* for Soprano, 2 Horns, Harp, and Strings (1895–96); *Nun schwillt der See so bang* for Voice and Piano (1896); *Süsse Sommernacht* for Voice and Piano (1896); *Frühlingsglaube* for Voices and Strings (1896); *Frühlingsbegräbnis* for Soprano, Alto, Tenor, Bass, Chorus, and Orch. (1896; Vienna, Feb. 11, 1900); *Gesänge* for Voice and Piano (2 books, c.1896); *Walzer-Gesänge nach toskanischen Volksliedern* for Voice and Piano (1898); *Irmelin Rose und andere Gesänge* for Voice and Piano (1898); *Turmwächterlied und andere Gesänge* for Voice and Piano (1898–99); *Ehetanzlied und andere Gesänge* for Voice and Piano (c.1900); *Psalm No. 83* for Chorus and Orch. (1900); *Es war ein alter König* for Voice and Piano (1903); *Schmetterlinge* for Voice and Piano (1904); *Ansturm* for Voice and Piano (1907); *Auf See* for Voice and Piano (1907); *Jane Grey* for Voice and Piano (1907); *Psalm No. 23* for Voices and Orch. (1910); *6 Gesänge* for Mezzo-soprano or Baritone and Piano or Orch. (1910–13); *Symphonische Gesänge* for Voice and Orch. (1929); *6 Lieder* for Voice and Piano (1934); *Psalm No. 13* for Voices and Orch. (1935); *12 Lieder* for Voice and Piano (1937).

BIBL.: H. Weber, *A. Z.: Eine Studie* (Vienna, 1977); W. Loll, *Zwischen Tradition und Avantgarde: Die Kammermusik A. Z.s* (Kassel, 1990); O. Biba, *A. Z.: Bin ich ein Wiener? Ausstellung im Archiv der Gesellschaft der Musikfreunde in Wien: Katalog* (Vienna, 1992).

Zenatello, Giovanni, Italian tenor; b. Verona, Feb. 22, 1876; d. N.Y., Feb. 11, 1949. He was originally trained as a baritone by Zannoni and Moretti in Verona. He made his official operatic debut as such in Belluno in 1898 as Silvio in Pagliacci; sang in minor opera companies in Italy; then went to Naples, where he sang the tenor role of Canio in 1899. He sang the role of Pinkerton in the first performance of Puccini's *Madama Butterfly* (La Scala, Milan, Feb. 17, 1904). In 1905 he sang at Covent Garden, London. On Nov. 4, 1907, he made his American debut in N.Y. as Enzo Grimaldo in Ponchielli's *La Gioconda*. From 1909 to 1912, and again in 1913–14, he was the leading tenor of the Boston Opera Co.; during the season of 1912–13, he sang with the Chicago Opera Co; also traveled with various touring opera companies in South America, Spain, and Russia. He eventually settled in N.Y. as a singing teacher, maintaining a studio with his wife, **Maria Gay**, whom he married in 1913. Together, they trained many famous singers, among them Lily Pons and Nino Martini. He retired from the stage in 1928.

Zenck, Hermann, German musicologist; b. Karlsruhe, March 19, 1898; d. Freiburg im Breisgau, Dec. 2, 1950. He studied with Ordenstein at the Karlsruhe Cons.; pursued training in musicology with Sandberger at the Univ. of Munich and with Kroyer at the Univs. of Heidelberg and Leipzig (Ph.D., 1924, with the diss. *Sixtus Dietrich (ca.1492–1548)*; publ. in Leipzig, 1928, as *Sixtus Dietrich: Ein Beitrag zur Musik und Musikgeschichte im Zeitalter der Reformation*); then completed his Habilitation there in 1929 with his *Studien zu Adrian Willaert*. He became assistant at the Inst. for Musicology in Leipzig, where he also taught at the Cons. In 1932 he joined the faculty of the Univ. of Göttingen; in 1942, went to Freiburg im Breisgau as a prof. at the Univ. there. He ed. the periodical *Musik und Volk*; was ed. of works by Willaert (2 vols., 1937; vol. 3, 1950) and Sixtus Dietrich (1942); also ed. the *Megalynodia* of Praetorius (1934); Johann Schultz's *Musikalischer Lustgarten* (1937); Handel's Italian cantatas, etc. He publ. *Marienklage und Osterspiel des Wolfenbüttler* Codex (Hamburg, 1927).

Zender, (Johannes Wolfgang) Hans, German conductor, teacher, and composer; b. Wiesbaden, Nov. 22, 1936. He studied at the Frankfurt am Main Hochschule für Musik (1956–59), and then was a student of Fortner and Picht-Axenfeld at the Freiburg im Breisgau Hochschule für Musik. From 1959 to 1963 he was a conductor at the Freiburg im Breisgau City Theater. After further training with Zimmermann in Rome (1963), he was chief conductor of the Bonn City Theater (1964–68). From 1969 to 1972 he was Generalmusikdirektor of Kiel. He was chief conductor of the Saarland Radio Sym. Orch. in Saarbrücken from 1972 to 1984. From 1984 to 1987 he was Generalmusikdirektor of the Hamburg State Opera and Phil. In 1987 he was chief conductor of Radio Hilversum in the Netherlands. From 1988 he was prof. of composition at the Frankfurt am Main Hochschule für Musik. He publ. the vol. *Happy New Ears: Das Abenteuer, Musik zu hören* (Freiburg im Breisgau, 1991). In his compositions, he pursued advanced avenues of expression.

WORKS: DRAMATIC: *Stephen Climax*, opera (1979–84; Frankfurt am Main, June 15, 1986; concert version as *Dubliner Nachtszenen*, 1987–89); *Don Quijote*, theatrical adventure (1993). **ORCH.:** Saxophone Concerto (1952); Piano Concerto (1956); *Schachspiel* for 2 Orch. Groups (1970); *Zeitströme* (1974); *Happy Band*, 4 études (1976); *Dialog mit Haydn* for 2 Pianos and 3 Orch. Groups (1982). **CHAMBER:** Concerto for Flute and Solo Instrument (1959); *3 Pieces* for Oboe (1963); Quartet for Flute, Cello, Piano, and Percussion (1964); *Canto I* for Various Players (1965); *Trifolium* for Flute, Cello, and Piano (1966); *Modelle* for Various Players (1971–73); *Muji no kyō* for Various Players and Women's or Men's Voices ad libitum (1975); *Litanei* for 3 Cellos (1976); *Lo-Shu I* for 3 to 9 Players (1977), *II* for Flute (1979), *III* for Flute and 24 Instruments (1979; rev. 1983), and *IV: 5 Haiku* for Flute and Strings (1982); *Hölderlin lesen I* for String Quartet and Speaking Voice (1980), *II* for Speaking Voice, Viola, and Live Electronics (1987), and *III: Denn wiederkommen* for String Quartet and Speaker (1992); piano pieces. **VOCAL:** *3 Lieder* for Soprano and Orch. (1964); *Les sirènes chantent quand la raison s'endort* for Soprano and 5 Instruments (1966); *Canto I* for Soprano and Chamber Orch. (1965), *II* for Soprano, Chorus, and Orch. (1967), *III: Der mann von La Mancha* for Soprano, Tenor, Baritone, Instruments, and Moog Synthesizer (1969), *IV: 4 Aspekte* for Chorus and 16 Instruments (1971; rev. for 16 Voices and 16 Instruments, 1973), *V: Kontinuum und Fragmente* for Voices (1973), *VI* for Bass-baritone, Chorus, and Tape (1988), and *VII: Nanzens Kyō* (Canto Nonsense) for 16 Voices and Instruments (1993); Cantata for Alto, Flute, Cello, and Harpsichord (1980); *Die Wüste hat zwölf Ding* for Voices and Orch. (1985); *Jours de silence* for Baritone and Orch. (1988); *Furin No Kyō* for Soprano and Ensemble (1989); *Winterreise*, "composed interpretation" of Schubert's song cycle for Tenor and Chamber Ensemble (Frankfurt am Main, Sept. 21, 1993). **OTHER:** Tape pieces, including *Bremen Wodu*, electronic study (1967).

Žganec, Vinko, Croatian ethnomusicologist; b. Vratišinci, Jan. 22, 1890; d. Zagreb, Dec. 12, 1976. He studied law at the Univ. of Zagreb (doctorate, 1919). He then became interested in song collecting; traveled in the countryside gathering native melodies; publ. several albums of harmonizations of these songs and numerous articles in Croatian, German, and American music journals dealing with specific aspects of Croatian songs; in his analyses of their structure, he applied modern methods of ethnomusicology. He was a lecturer on folk music at the Zagreb Academy of Music (1949–68).

Zhelobinsky, Valeri (Viktorovich), Russian composer, pianist, and teacher; b. Tambov, Jan. 27, 1913; d. Leningrad, Aug. 13, 1946. He studied in Tambov and with Shcherbachev at the Leningrad Cons. (1928–32). He taught at the Tambov Music School. As a pianist, he performed mainly his own compositions. His operas were written in a fine Romantic manner.

WORKS: DRAMATIC: *Kamarinsky muzhik*, opera (Leningrad, Sept. 15, 1933); *Her Saint's Day*, opera (1934; Leningrad, Feb. 22, 1935); *Mother*, opera, after Maxim Gorky (Leningrad, Dec. 30, 1938); *The Last Ball*, operetta (Leningrad, March 30, 1939); film scores. **ORCH.:** 6 syms.: No. 1 (1930), No. 2, *To the Memory of Revolutionary Victims* (1932), No. 3, *Dramatic* (Moscow, Dec. 17, 1939), No. 4 (Moscow, May 30, 1943), No. 5 (1944), and No. 6 (1946); 3 piano concertos (1933, 1934, 1939); Violin Concerto (1934); *Romantic Poem* for Violin and Orch. (1939). **PIANO:** *24 Preludes*; 2 children's albums.

Zhiganov, Nazib, Russian composer and music educator of Tatar heritage; b. Uralsk, Jan. 15, 1911; d. Kazan, June 2, 1988. He was reared in an orphan asylum and first studied music in Kazan. He went to Moscow, where he studied at a technological school and then pursued musical training with Litinsky at the Cons. (graduated, 1938). In 1945 he became director and a prof. of the newly founded Kazan Cons. In his music, he attempted to create a new national Tatar school of composition, following the harmonic and instrumental precepts of the Russian national school.

WORKS: DRAMATIC: OPERAS (all 1st perf. in Kazan): *Katchkyn* (June 17, 1939); *Irek* (Liberty; Feb. 24, 1940); *Altyntchetch* (The Golden Haired; July 12, 1941); *Ildar* (Nov. 7, 1942); *Tulyak* (July 27, 1945); *Namus* (Honor; June 25, 1950); *Dzhalil*, operatic monologue (1950). **BALLET:** *Zugra* (Kazan, May 17, 1946). Also film music. **ORCH.:** 4 syms. (1937, 1968, 1971, 1973); overtures; suites; marches. **OTHER:** Chamber music; piano pieces; vocal music.

BIBL.: Y. Girshman, *N. Z.* (Moscow, 1957).

Zhitomirsky, Alexander, Russian composer and pedagogue; b. Kherson, May 23, 1881; d. Leningrad, Dec. 16, 1937. He took violin lessons in Odessa and in Vienna; also studied piano. Returning to Russia, he entered the St. Petersburg Cons. as a student of Rimsky-Korsakov, Liadov, and Glazunov, graduating in 1910; from 1915 to 1937 he was on its faculty, as an instructor in composition and orchestration. In his compositions, he followed the style and manner of the Russian national school; he wrote a Violin Concerto (1937); String Quartet (1923); a number of songs and choruses.

Zhivotov, Alexei, Russian composer; b. Kazan, Nov. 14, 1904; d. Leningrad, Aug. 27, 1964. He studied at the Leningrad Cons. with Shcherbachev, graduating in 1930. During the siege of Leningrad by the Nazis (1941–42), he remained in the city and was awarded a medal for valor. Among his works were film music, several orch. pieces, and much vocal music, including patriotic choruses and songs.

Zhuk, Isaak, Russian violinist; b. Poltava, Dec. 16, 1902; d. Moscow, April 4, 1973. He studied with I. Goldberg in Poltava, where he made his debut (1917); then with S. Korguyev at the Leningrad Cons. (1924) and A. Yampolsky at the Moscow Cons. (1925–30). He organized the Bolshoi Quartet and was one of its members (1931–68); was concertmaster of the U.S.S.R. Sym. Orch. (1952–69). His son, Valentin Zhuk (b. Moscow, June 28, 1934), is a talented violinist; he studied with Yampolsky, and received prizes in various international competitions, including the Tchaikovsky (Moscow, 6th, 1958), Paganini (Genoa, 2nd, 1963), and Long-Thibaud (Paris, 2nd, 1960); he was concertmaster of the Moscow Phil. (from 1970).

Zhukovsky, Herman, Ukrainian composer; b. Radzivilovo, Volynya, Nov. 13, 1913; d. Kiev, March 15, 1976. He studied piano and composition at the Kiev Cons., graduating in 1941; from 1951 to 1958 he taught theory there. He wrote operas, ballets, symphonic music, and other works in the approved style of socialist realism, using authentic Ukrainian song patterns for his materials, but a crisis supervened in his steady progress when his opera *From the Bottom of My Heart* (Moscow, Jan. 16, 1951) was viciously attacked by the cultural authorities of the Soviet government for alleged ideological and musical aberrations; he revised the score, and the new version was approved. His other operas were *Marina* (Kiev, March 12, 1939); *The First Spring* (1960); *Contrasts of Centuries*, operatic trilogy (1967); *A Soldier's Wife*, monodrama for Baritone (1968); 2 ballets: *Rostislava* (1955) and *Forest Song* (Moscow, May 1, 1961); political cantatas; several orch. suites; chamber music; film scores.

Zich, Jaroslav, Czech composer and teacher, son of **Otakar Zich**; b. Prague, Jan. 17, 1912. He studied with his father, at the Prague Cons. (1928–31) with Foerster, and at the Charles Univ. in Prague. From 1952 to 1977 he taught at the Prague Academy of Music.

WORKS: MELODRAMA: *Romance helgolandská* (1934). **ORCH.:** *Rhapsody* for Cello and Orch. (1956). **CHAMBER:** Duo for Violin and Cello (1930); String Quartet (1931); *Ekloga, nokturno a pastorale* for Piano (1932); *Matenik* for Cello and Piano

(1935); *U muziky* for Octet (1940); *Malá serenáda* for Wind Quintet (1974). **VOCAL:** *Letmý host* for Voice and Orch. (1932); solo songs.

Zich, Otakar, Czech composer and musicologist, father of **Jaroslav Zich**; b: Králové Městec, March 25, 1879; d. Ouběnice, near Benešov, July 9, 1934. He studied mathematics at the Univ. of Prague (Ph.D., 1901); also received training in musicology from Hostinský and in composition from Stecker (1897–1901); completed his Habilitation at the Univ. of Prague in 1911. After teaching in a secondary school in Domažlice (from 1901), he was made prof. of philosophy at the Univ. of Brno in 1919; from 1924 he was prof. of aesthetics at the Univ. of Prague.

WRITINGS (all publ. in Prague): *Smetanova Hubička* (Smetana's The Kiss; 1911); *Hector Berlioz a jeho Episoda ze života umělcova* (Hector Berlioz and His Episode from the Life of an Artist; 1914); *Česke lidové tance s proměnlivým taktem* (Czech Folkdances with a Changing Beat; 1917); *Symfonické básně Smetanovy* (Smetana's Symphonic Poems; 1924; 2nd ed., 1949); *Estetika dramatického uměni* (Aesthetics of Dramatic Art; 1931).

WORKS: OPERAS: *Malířský nápad* (Painter's Whim; 1908; Prague, March 11, 1910); *Vina* (Guilt; 1911–15; Prague, March 14, 1922); *Preciézky*, after Molière's *Les Précieuses ridicules* (1924; Prague, May 11, 1926); also cantatas, song cycles, part-songs, etc.

BIBL.: J. Hutter, *O. Z. a jeho "Vina"* (Prague, 1922); J. Burjanek, *O. Z.: Studie k vývoji českého muzikologického myšleni v prvni třetine našeho stoleti* (O.Z.: A Study of the Development of Czech Musicological Thought in the First Third of This Century; Prague, 1966).

Ziegler, Delores, American mezzo-soprano; b. Atlanta, Sept. 4, 1951. She studied at the Univ. of Tenn. After beginning her career with concert engagements, she made her operatic stage debut in Knoxville in 1978 as Verdi's Flora. In 1978–79 she was a member of the Santa Fe Opera apprenticeship program; in 1979, appeared as Verdi's Maddalena in St. Louis. She made her European operatic debut in Bonn in 1981 as Dorabella. In 1982 she sang for the first time at the Cologne Opera. In 1984 she appeared as Dorabella at her Glyndebourne debut and as Bellini's Romeo at her La Scala debut in Milan. She sang for the first time at the Salzburg Festival in 1985 as Minerva in Henze's setting of *Il Ritorno d'Ulisse*. In 1990 she made her Metropolitan Opera debut as Gounod's Siebel. As a guest artist, she also sang in Munich, Florence, Hamburg, San Diego, Toronto, and elsewhere; also was widely engaged as a concert artist.

Zilcher, (Karl) Hermann (Josef), German composer, pianist, and pedagogue; b. Frankfurt am Main, Aug. 18, 1881; d. Würzburg, Jan. 1, 1948. He studied piano with his father, Paul Zilcher, and then continued his training at the Hoch Cons. in Frankfurt am Main (1897–1901) with Kwast (piano) and Knorr and Scholz (composition). After serving on its faculty (1905–08), he was a prof. at the Akademie der Tonkunst in Munich (1908–20). From 1920 to 1944 he was director of the Würzburg Cons. He also made tours as a pianist. His music represents an amalgam of late Romantic and Impressionist elements.

WORKS: DRAMATIC: *Fitzebutze*, Traumspiel (1903); *Doktor Eisenbart* (1922); incidental music. **ORCH.:** 4 syms.; 2 violin concertos; *Bayerische Suite* for Accordion Orch.; Accordion Concerto. **OTHER:** Many piano pieces, including a Sym. for 2 Pianos; numerous songs.

BIBL.: W. Altmann, *H. Z.* (Leipzig, 1907); H. Oppenheim, *H. Z.* (Munich, 1921).

Zillig, Winfried (Petrus Ignatius), German conductor and composer; b. Würzburg, April 1, 1905; d. Hamburg, Dec. 17, 1963. He studied at the Würzburg Cons. and with Schoenberg in Vienna (1925–26) and in his master classes at the Prussian Academy of Arts in Berlin (1926–28). After working as répétiteur in Oldenburg (1928–32), he conducted in Düsseldorf (1932–37); was music director of the Essen Opera (1937–40), the Poznań Opera (1940–43), and the Düsseldorf Opera (1946–47); then was chief conductor of the Hesse Radio in Frankfurt am Main (1947–51). He was director of the music division of the North German Radio in Hamburg from 1959 to 1963.

WORKS: DRAMATIC: OPERAS: *Rosse* (Düsseldorf, Feb. 11, 1933); *Das Opfer* (Hamburg, Nov. 12, 1937); *Die Windsbraut* (Leipzig, May 12, 1941); *Troilus und Cressida* (1949; rev. 1963); *Bauernpassion*, television opera (1955); *Die Verlobung in St. Domingo*, radio opera (1956); *Das Verlöbnis* (1962; Linz, Nov. 23, 1963); incidental music. **ORCH.:** *Choralkonzert* (1924); Overture (1928); *Concerto for Orchestra* (1930); Concerto for Cello and Wind Orch. (1934; rev. 1952); *Tansymphonie* (1938); Concerto in One Movement (1948); Violin Concerto (1955); *Fantasia, Passacaglia, and Fugue on the Meistersinger Chorale* (1963). **OTHER:** Chamber music; choral pieces; solo vocal works.

WRITINGS: *Variationen über neue Musik* (Munich, 1959; 2nd ed., 1963, as *Die neue Musik: Linien und Porträts; Von Wagner bis Strauss* (Munich, 1966).

Ziloti, Alexander. See **Siloti, Alexander.**

Zimbalist, Efrem (Alexandrovich), eminent Russian-born American violinist and pedagogue; b. Rostov-na-Donu, April 21, 1889; d. Reno, Nev., Feb. 22, 1985. He studied violin with his father, an orch. musician; from 1901 to 1907 he was a pupil of Leopold Auer at the St. Petersburg Cons., graduating with the gold medal. He made a highly successful European appearance as a soloist in the Brahms Concerto in Berlin, Nov. 7, 1907. In 1911 he emigrated to the U.S.; made his American debut with the Boston Sym. Orch. on Oct. 27, 1911, playing the first American performance of Glazunov's Violin Concerto. In 1914 he married **Alma Gluck**, who died in 1938; his 2nd wife, whom he married in 1943, was **Mary Louise Curtis Bok**; in 1928 he joined its faculty; was its director from 1941 to 1968. After Mrs. Zimbalist's death in 1970, he moved to Reno, Nev., to live with his daughter. His son, Efrem Zimbalist, Jr., was a well-known actor. Zimbalist was also a composer. He wrote the opera *Landara* (Philadelphia, April 6, 1956); a musical comedy, *Honeydew* (N.Y., 1920); *Slavonic Dances* for Violin and Orch. (1911); *American Rhapsody* for Orch. (Chicago, March 3, 1936; rev. version, Philadelphia, Feb. 5, 1943); *Portrait of an Artist*, symphonic poem (Philadelphia, Dec. 7, 1945); Violin Concerto (1947); Cello Concerto (1969); String Quartet; Violin Sonata; *Concert Phantasy on Le Coq d'or* for Violin and Piano; *Sarasateana* for Violin and Piano; songs; etc. He publ. *One Hour's Daily Exercise* for the violin.

Zimerman, Krystian, outstanding Polish pianist; b. Zabrze, Dec. 5, 1956. He commenced piano lessons at age 5 with his father; when he was 7 he became a pupil of Andrzej Jasińki, with whom he later studied at the Katowice Cons. In 1975 he won 1st prize in the Chopin Competition in Warsaw; then played with great success in Munich, Paris, London, and Vienna. In 1976 he was a soloist with the Berlin Phil. He made his first American appearance in 1978, and subsequently toured throughout the world to great critical acclaim. His performances of the Romantic repertory are remarkable for their discerning spontaneity. He has also played contemporary works, including Lutosławski's Piano Concerto (1988), which is dedicated to him.

Zimmer, Ján, significant Slovak composer and pianist; b. Ružomberok, May 16, 1926. He studied with Suchoň at the Bratislava Cons. (graduated, 1948), with Farkas at the Budapest Academy of Music (1948–49), and in Salzburg (1949). After working for the Czech Radio in Bratislava (1945–48), he taught at the Bratislava Cons. from 1948 until losing his post in 1952 under the Communist regime. In subsequent years, Zimmer devoted himself to composition and made occasional appearances as a pianist, principally in programs of his own works. His music is marked by a mastery of form, technique, and expression. While he has sometimes utilized 12-tone and other modern techniques, he has generally forged his own course as a worthy representative of the Slovak tradition.

WORKS (all 1st perf. in Bratislava unless otherwise given): **DRAMATIC:** *Oedipus Rex*, opera (1963–64); *Héraklés*, opera-ballet (1972); *The Broken Line*, opera (1974); film music. **ORCH.:** 7 piano concertos: No. 1 (1949; March 14, 1950), No. 2 (1952), No. 3 (1958; Jan. 14, 1960), No. 4 (1960; Oct. 11, 1962), No. 5 for Piano, Left-hand, and Orch. (1964; June 3, 1965), No. 6 (1972), and No. 7 (1985); Concerto grosso for 2 Pianos, 2 String Orchs., and Percussion (1950–51); *The Tratas*, 2 suites (1952, 1956; also for Piano); Violin Concerto (1953; May 4, 1957); *Rhapsody* for Piano and Orch. (1954); Concertino for Piano and Strings (1955; Prague, Feb. 17, 1957); 12 syms.: No. 1 (1955; Dec. 2, 1956), No. 2 (1957–58), No. 3 (1959), No. 4 for Soprano, Tenor, Chorus, and Orch. (1959; Feb. 2, 1961), No. 5 (1961; March 3, 1963), No. 6, *Improvisata* (1964–65), No. 7 (1966; March 4, 1967), No. 8 (1971), No. 9 (1973), No. 10 for Chamber Orch. (1976), No. 11 (1981), and No. 12 for Orch. and Tape (1986); Concerto for Organ, Strings, and Percussion (Dec. 5, 1957); *Strečno*, symphonic poem (1959); *Small Fantasy* for Piano and Orch. (1960); *Concerto da camera* for Oboe and Strings (1961); Concerto for 2 Pianos and Orch. (1967; Nov. 3, 1968); *French Suite* for Chamber Orch. (1968); *Songs Without Words* for Strings (1970); *Music from Old Bratislava* (1975); *Concerto Prelude* (1981); Chamber Concerto for Organ and Strings (1984); *Concerto Poliphonico* (1987); *3 Dancing Pieces* for Piano and Orch. (1988); Concertino for Viola and Chamber Orch. (1989). **CHAMBER:** Suite for Violin and Piano (1958); Viola Sonata (1958); *2 Slovak Dances* for Violin and Piano (1959); 3 string quartets (1960, 1982, 1987); Wind Quintet (1968); *Ballade and Burlesque* for Viola (1976); *Poetical Sonata* for Violin and Piano (1976); *Variations* for 2 Violins and Viola (1977); Flute Sonata (1978); Trio for Flute, Violin, and Piano (1979). **KEYBOARD: PIANO:** 7 sonatas (1948, 1961, 1966, 1971, 1978, 1979, 1987); 4 sonatas for 2 Pianos (1954, 1958, 1965, 1972); *Concerto for Piano Without Orchestra* (1956); *2 Romantic Pieces* (1975); *Bagatelles* (1983); *Introduction and Toccata* (1986); *4 Pieces* for Piano, 4 hands (1988). **ORGAN:** *Prelude and Fugue* (1952); *Phantasy and Toccata* (1958); Concerto (1960); 2 sonatas (1970, 1981); *3 Small Preludes* (1977). **VOCAL:** *Magnificat* for Chorus and Orch. (1952); *Peace* for Chorus and Orch. (1954); *Death Shall Have No Dominion*, oratorio for Soloists, Chorus, and Orch. (1968); *Phantasy* for Men's Chorus, Piano, and Orch. (1975); choral pieces; song cycles.

Zimmerman, Franklin B(ershir), American musicologist; b. Wauneta, Kansas, June 20, 1923. He was educated at the Univ. of Southern Calif. in Los Angeles (B.A., 1949; M.A., 1952; Ph.D., 1958, with the diss. *Purcell's Musical Heritage: A Study of Musical Styles in 17th-century England*) and at Oxford Univ. (B.Litt., 1956). He taught at the State Univ. of N.Y. in Potsdam (1958–59) and at the Univ. of Southern Calif. (1959–64); then was prof. of music at Dartmouth College (1964–67), the Univ. of Kentucky (1967–68), and the Univ. of Pa. (from 1968). He devoted much time to the study of English Baroque music, particularly the life and works of Purcell.

WRITINGS: *Henry Purcell, 1659–1695: An Analytical Catalogue of His Music* (London, 1963); *Henry Purcell, 1659–1695: His Life and Times* (London, 1967; 2nd ed., rev., 1983); *Henry Purcell, 1659–1694: Melodic and Intervallic Indexes to His Complete Works* (Philadelphia, 1975); *Henry Purcell: A Guide to Research* (N.Y., 1988).

Zimmermann, Bernd (actually, **Bernhard**) **Alois,** important German composer and teacher; b. Bliesheim, near Cologne, March 20, 1918; d. (suicide) Königsdorf, near Cologne, Aug. 10, 1970. He studied at the Cologne Hochschule für Musik and at the Univs. of Cologne and Bonn until being drafted for military service. Following his discharge, he pursued training with Lemacher and Jarnach in 1942. Later he attended the summer courses in new music given by Fortner and Leibowitz in Darmstadt (1948–50). He taught at the Univ. (1950–52) and Hochschule für Musik (1957–57) in Cologne. In 1956–57 he served as president of the German section of the ISCM. In 1957 he held a stipend for residence at the Villa Massimo in Rome. In 1958 he was appointed prof. of composition at the Cologne Hochschule für Musik, which position he retained for the rest of his life. In 1966 he was awarded the arts prize of Cologne. Plagued by failing eyesight and obsessed with notions of death, he set his *Requiem für einen jungen Dichter* to texts of poets who had committed suicide. Shortly thereafter, he took his own life. C. Bitter ed. a vol. of Zimmermann's writings as *Intervall und Zeit: Aufsätze und Schriften* (Mainz, 1974). While he made use of serialism and electronics, Zimmermann's works were notable for their distinct individuality. In his later works, he made use of musical quotations, which he called collage, which he borrowed from both Western and non-Western traditions. The result was, in effect, a remarkable musical pluralism.

WORKS: DRAMATIC: *Alagoana (Caprichos brasileiros)*, ballet (1940–43; 1947–50; suite, Hamburg, Nov. 21, 1953; ballet, Essen, Dec. 17, 1955); *Kontraste*, ballet (1953; Bielefeld, April 24, 1954); *Perspektiven*, ballet (1955; Düsseldorf, June 2, 1957); *Die Soldaten*, opera, after J.M.R. Lenz (1958–60; rev. 1963–64; Cologne, Feb. 15, 1965; also used in the Vocal Sym., 1959); *Musique pour les soupers du Roi Ubu*, ballet noir (1966); other theater scores and much radio music. **ORCH.:** *Symphonic Variations and Fugue on In dulci jubilo* (1940); Sym. (1947–52; rev. version, Brussels, Nov. 20, 1953); Concerto for Strings (1948; based on the String Trio, 1942–43); Violin Concerto (1949–50; Baden-Baden, Dec. 10, 1950; based on the Violin Sonata, 1949); Concerto for Oboe and Small Orch. (Donaueschingen, Oct. 1952); *Canto di speranza*, "cantata" for Cello and Small Orch. (1952–57; Baden-Baden, July 28, 1958); *Nobody Knows de Trouble I Seen*, trumpet concerto (1954; Hamburg, Oct. 11, 1955); *Impromptu* (1958); *Dialoge*, concerto for 2 Pianos and Orch. (Cologne Radio, Dec. 5, 1960; rev. 1965; based on the opera *Die Soldaten*; also as *Monologe* for 2 Pianos, 1960–64); *Antophonen* for Viola and 25 Instrumentalists, some of whom speak a text drawn from Joyce, Dante, Dostoyevsky, Camus, and Novalis (1961); Cello Concerto, in the form of a "pas de trois" (1965–66; Strasbourg, April 8, 1968; as a ballet, Wuppertal, May 12, 1968); *Photoptosis*, prelude (1968; Gelsenkirchen, Feb. 19, 1969); *Stille und Umkehr*, sketch (1970; Nuremberg, March 19, 1971). **CHAMBER:** String Trio (1942–43; also as the Concerto for String Orch., 1948); Violin Sonata (1949; also as the Violin Concerto, 1949–50); *Rheinische Kirmestänze* for 13 Winds (1950; rev. 1962); Sonata for Solo Violin (1951); Sonata for Solo Viola (1955); Sonata for Solo Cello (1959–60); *Présence*, "ballet blanc" for Piano Trio (Darmstadt, Sept. 8, 1961); *5 capricci di G. Frescobaldi, "La Frescobalda,"* for 3 Recorders, Oboe d'Amore, 3 Viole da Gamba, Lute, 3 Trumpets, and 3 Trombones (1962); *Tempus loquendi*, "pezzi ellittici" for Flauto Grande, Flute in G, and Bass Flute, for 1 Performer (1963); *Ode to Eleutheria* for Jazz Quintet (1967; based on music from the radio play *Die Befristeten*); *Intercomunicazione* for Cello and Piano (1967); *4 Studies* for Cello (1970). **PIANO:** *Extemporale* (1939–46); *Capriccio* (1946); *Enchiridion* (1949–52); *Konfigurationen*, 8 pieces (1954–56); *Monologe* for 2 Pianos (1960–64; also as the Concerto for 2 Pianos and Orch., 1960). **VOCAL:** *Lob der Torheit*, burlesque cantata for Soprano, Tenor, Bass, Chorus, and Orch., after Goethe (Cologne, May 25, 1948); *Omnia tempus habent*, cantata for Soprano and 17 Instruments (1957); Vocal Sym. for Soprano, Mezzo-soprano, 2 Tenors, Bass, and Orch. (1959; based on the opera *Die Soldaten*); *Requiem für einen jungen Dichter*, "lingual" for Narrator, Soprano, Baritone, 3 Choruses, Tape, Orch., Jazz Combo, and Organ (1967–69; Düsseldorf, Dec. 11, 1969); *Ich wandte mich und sah an alles Unrecht das geschah unter der Sonne*, "ecclesiastical action" for 2 Narrators, Bass, and Orch. (1970; Kiel, Sept. 2, 1972). **TAPE:** *Tratto I* (1966) and *II* (1968).

BIBL.: W. Konold, ed., *B.A. Z.: Dokumente und Interpretationen* (Cologne, 1986); idem, *B.A. Z.:Der Komponist und sein Werk* (Cologne, 1986).

Zimmermann, Frank Peter, German violinist; b. Duisburg, Feb. 27, 1965. As a child he took violin lessons with his mother, making his public debut with the Duisburg Sym. Orch. at 10; then studied with W. Gradow at the Essen Folkwang-Musikhochschule and with H. Krebbers at the Robert-Schumann-Institut of the Düsseldorf Hochschule für Musik. In 1979 he appeared at the Lucerne Festival; made his British debut as soloist with the Royal Phil. at the Portsmouth Festival in 1981 and his U.S. debut as soloist with the Pittsburgh Sym. Orch. in 1984; also toured the Soviet Union in 1984. In subsequent years, he appeared as a soloist with principal orchs. and toured widely as a recitalist. His repertoire ranges from Bach to Prokofiev.

Zimmermann, Udo, noted German composer, conductor, pedagogue, and Intendant; b. Dresden, Oct. 6, 1943. He was a student of Johannes Thilman (composition) and took courses in conducting and voice at the Dresden Hochschule für Musik (1962–68). In 1967 and 1968 he held the Felix-Mendelssohn-Bartholdy-Stipendium. From 1968 to 1970 he attended Kochan's master classes in composition at the Akademie der Künste in East Berlin. In 1970 he became a dramaturg for contemporary music theater at the Dresden State Opera, where he was active until 1984. He became founder-director of Dresden's Studio Neue Musik in 1974. In 1976 he began teaching at the Dresden Hochschule für Musik, where he was made a prof. of composition in 1978 and a prof. of experimental music theater and composition in 1982. He was active as a conductor from 1984, making guest appearances in Europe and abroad. In 1986 he became director of Dresden's Center for Contemporary Music. He became artistic director of Dresden's musica-viva-ensemble in 1988. In 1990 he was made Intendant of the Leipzig Opera. In 1983 he was made a member of the Akademie der Künste in Berlin and of the Freien Akademie der Künste in Hamburg. He served as president of the Freien Akademie der Künste in Leipzig from 1992. Zimmermann's music owes much to the so-called "new simplicity" style. In his operatic scores, he has brought new life to the genre of Literaturoper.

WORKS: OPERAS: *Die weisse Rose* (1966; Dresden, June 17, 1967); *Die zweite Entscheidung* (1969; Magdeburg, March 10, 1970); *Levins Mühle* (Dresden, March 27, 1973); *Der Schuhu und die fliegende Prinzessin* (Dresden, Dec. 30, 1976); *Die wundersame Schustersfrau* (1981; Schwetzingen, April 25, 1982); *Weisse Rose* (Hamburg, Feb. 27, 1986); *Die Sündflut* (1991). **ORCH.:** Violin Concerto (1964); *Dramatische Impression* (1966; also for Cello and Piano, 1963); Kettledrum Concerto (1966); *Musik* for Strings (1968); *Mutazioni* (1969; Dresden, Oct. 26, 1973); *L'homme: Meditationen* (1970); *Sieh, meine Augen: Reflexionen* for Chamber Orch. (1970); *Sinfonia come un grande lamento*, in memory of García Lorca (1978); *Songerie* for Chamber Orch., in memory of Karl Böhm (1982); *Mein Gott, wer trommelt denn da: Reflexionen* (1985); Viola Concerto (1986); *Nouveaux divertissements—d'après Rameau* for Horn and Chamber Orch. (1987); *Dans la marche: Hommage à Witold Lutosławski* (1994). **CHAMBER:** *Dramatische Impression* for Cello and Piano (1963; also for Orch., 1966); Violin Sonatina (1964); *Movimenti caratteristici* for Cello (1965); *Episoden* for Wind Quintet (1971); *Tänzerinnen* for Chamber Ensemble (1973); *Canticum Marianum* for 12 Cellos (1983). **KEYBOARD: PIANO:** Sonata (1967). **HARPSICHORD:** *Die Spieldose*, étude (1981). **VOCAL:** *Vaterunserlied*, motet for 4 Voices (1959); *Wort ward Fleisch*, motet for 8 Voices (1961); *Grab und Kreuz*, motet for 8 Voices (1962); 5 Songs for Baritone and Chamber Orch., after Borchert (1964); *Neruda-Lieder* for Voice, Clarinet, and Piano (1965); *Der Mensch*, cantata for Soprano and 13 Players (1970); *Ein Zeuge der Liebe, die besiegt den Tod* for Soprano and Chamber Orch. (Frankfurt am Main, March 11, 1973); *Ode an das Leben* for Mezzo-soprano, 3 Choruses, and Orch., after Neruda and Carus (1974); *Psalm der Nacht* for Women's Chorus, Men's Voices, Percussion, and Organ, after Sachs (1976); *Hymnus an die Sonne* for Soprano, Flute, and Harpsichord, after Kleist (1977); *Pax questuosa* for 5 Solo Voices, 3 Choruses, and Orch. (1981); *Wenn ich an Hiroshima denke* for Soprano, Flute, and Piano (1982; also for Soprano and Chamber Orch.); *Gib Licht meinen Augen, oder ich entschlafe des Todes* for Soprano, Baritone, and Chamber Orch. (1985); *Wenn ein Wintervogel das Herz . . .*, song cycle for Baritone and Piano (1990–91).

BIBL.: F. Hennenberg, *U. Z., für Sie portratiert* (Leipzig, 1983).

Zimmermann, Walter, German composer; b. Schwabach, April 15, 1949. He studied piano, violin, and oboe. While serving as pianist in the "ars-nova-ensemble" of Nuremberg (1968–70), he pursued training in composition with Werner Heider. He then studied with Otto Laske at the Institut voor Sonologie at the Univ. of Utrecht and at the Jaap Kunst Ethnological Center at the Univ. of Amsterdam (1970–73). In 1974 he studied computer music in Hamilton, N.J. In 1977 he founded the Beginner Studio in Cologne, which specialized in concerts of novel music. In 1988 he lectured at the Univ. of The Hague. In 1993 he became a teacher of composition at the Berlin Hochschule für Musik. He publ. the books *Desert Plants* (Vancouver, 1976) and *Insel Musik* (Cologne, 1977), and ed. a vol. of Morton Feldman's essays (Kerpen, 1985). Among his compositions are a number of short works of varied ensembles.

WORKS: *Akkordarbeit* for Orch. (1971); *Lokale Musik*, a series of pieces for Various Forces (1977–81); *Die Blinden*, static drama for 12 Singers and 9 Instruments (1984); *Über die Dörfer*, music theater for Soloists, 3 Choruses, and Organ (1986); *Ataraxia* for Piano and Orch. (1988); *Hyperion*, short opera (1989–90); *Diastasis/Diastema* for 2 Orchs. and 1 Conductor (1991–92); *Oedipus Coloneus*, music theater (1995).

Zinman, David (Joel), talented American conductor; b. N.Y., July 9, 1936. He studied violin at the Oberlin (Ohio) College Cons. of Music (B.M., 1958), and composition at the Univ. of Minnesota (M.A., 1963); took lessons in conducting at the Berkshire Music Center at Tanglewood, and with Monteux at his summer school in Maine; from 1961 to 1964 he was Monteux's assistant. After a successful engagement as guest conductor with the Nederlands Kamerorkest, he served as its conductor from 1965 to 1977. In 1972 he was appointed music adviser to the Rochester (N.Y.) Phil.; then was its music director (1974–85); also served as chief conductor of the Rotterdam Phil. (1979–82). He was principal guest conductor (1983–85) and then music director (1985–98) of the Baltimore Sym. Orch. While retaining his latter post, he also served as artistic director of the Minnesota Orch.'s Viennese Sommerfest (1994–96) and as music director of the Zürich Tonhalle Orch. (from 1995). From 1998 he was music director of the Aspen Music Festival. He appeared as a guest conductor with various orchs. in North America and Europe.

Zipp, Friedrich, German composer, organist, and pedagogue; b. Frankfurt am Main, June 20, 1914. He studied at the Hoch Cons. in Frankfurt am Main (1933–34) and in Berlin at the Univ. and at the Staatliche Hochschule für Musik, where his composition teacher was Knab. In 1947 he became a teacher and in 1962 a prof. at the Staatliche Hochschule für Musik in Frankfurt am Main; also was active as an organist. He composed *Musik* for Orch. (1936); *Sinfonietta* for Youth Orch. (1958); *Kirchensuite* for String Orch. (1962); String Quartet (1943); *Au clair de la lune* for Oboe and Piano (1963); numerous choral pieces and songs. He publ. *Vom Wesen der Musik* (Heidelberg, 1974).

Zítek, Otakar, Czech music critic and composer; b. Prague, Nov. 5, 1892; d. Bratislava, April 28, 1955. He studied composition with Novák at the Prague Cons. and musicology with Guido Adler and Grädener at the Univ. of Vienna. Upon graduation, he wrote music criticism for the *Hudební Revue* and the *Lidové Noviny* in Prague; gave lectures on opera at the Prague Cons.; then was administrator at the National Theater in Brno (1921–29); taught at the Brno Cons. (1931–39). From 1939 to 1941 he was in the Buchenwald concentration camp, but was released, and worked as a theater director in Plzeň (1941–43); supervised opera theaters in Prague and Brno (1946–49). He composed the operas *Vznesene srdce* (The Exalted Heart; 1918) and *Pád Petra Králence* (The Downfall of Peter Kralence; Brno,

March 23, 1923); a ballet after Wilde's *Birthday of the Infanta* (Plzeň [Pilsen], 1942); *Město*, symphonic poem (1925); songs; etc. He publ. *O novou zpevohru* (On New Opera; Prague, 1920).

Ziv, Mikhail, Russian composer; b. Moscow, May 25, 1921. He studied at the Moscow Cons. with Kabalevsky; graduated in 1947. As a composer, Ziv devoted himself mainly to the musical theater; wrote the comic operas *Son of a King's Minister* (1973) and *Gentlemen Artists* (1980); several fairy tales for children; 3 syms. (1946, 1960, 1968); 2 sinfoniettas (1958, 1962); 2 string quartets (1945, 1955); Piano Quintet (1947); many choruses, piano pieces, and songs; film music.

Živković, Milenko, Serbian composer and pedagogue; b. Belgrade, May 25, 1901; d. there, June 29, 1964. He studied at the Stanković Music School in Belgrade and graduated in law from the Univ. of Belgrade (1924); then studied composition with Grabner at the Leipzig Cons. (1925–29) and d'Indy at the Paris Schola Cantorum (1929–31). Returning to Belgrade, he was director of the Stanković Music School (1937–47); taught at the Academy of Music (1945–64); was rector and prof. of composition there (1952–60). A follower of the national school of composition, he wrote music permeated with ethnic Balkan melorhythms. His works include: *Symphonic Prologue* (Belgrade, April 16, 1935); *Zelena godina* (Green Year), folk ballet scenes for Orch. (Belgrade, April 27, 1937); several suites of Serbian dances for piano, and numerous choruses.

Znosko-Borovsky, Alexander, Russian composer; b. Kiev, Feb. 27, 1908; d. there, March 8, 1983. He studied violin and composition at the Kiev Cons.; then was active as a composer for films (1931–41). In 1941 he left Kiev, threatened by the Nazi invasion, and went to Ashkhabad, Turkmenia; was instrumental in promoting indigenous music culture there; several of his works are based on Turkmenian themes.

WORKS: BALLET: *Akpamyk* (Ashkhabad, April 14, 1945). **ORCH.:** 2 symphonic poems: *Kiev* (Kiev, March 9, 1949) and *At the Mausoleum* (1960); Violin Concerto (Kiev, Dec. 17, 1955); 3 syms. (1958, 1960, 1967). **CHAMBER:** 2 string quartets (1937, 1942); *Scherzo* for 3 Trombones (1938); Sonata for Solo Violin (1950). **VOCAL:** *Our Victory*, cantata (Kiev, May 8, 1946).

Zoghby, Linda, American soprano; b. Mobile, Ala., Aug. 17, 1949. She studied voice with Elena Nikolaidi at Florida State Univ. She made her professional debut at the Grant Park Festival in Chicago in 1973; subsequently sang opera in N.Y., Washington, D.C., Dallas, Santa Fe, Houston, and New Orleans. She received a critical accolade on Jan. 19, 1982, when she substituted on short notice for Teresa Stratas and sang the role of Mimi in the Zeffirelli production of *La Bohème* at the Metropolitan Opera in N.Y. Her other roles include Pamina, Donna Elvira, and Marguerite in *Faust.*

Zöller, Karlheinz, German flutist; b. Höhr-Grenzhausen, Aug. 24, 1928. He was educated at the Frankfurt am Main Hochschule für Musik and the Northwest German Music Academy in Detmold. In 1947 he won 1st prize in the German radio competition in Frankfurt am Main; then was active as a recitalist and chamber player. Zöller was 1st flutist with the Berlin Phil. (1960–69). After a series of concert appearances in Europe and America, he rejoined the Berlin Phil. in 1977.

Zolotarev, Vasili (Andreievich), eminent Russian composer and pedagogue; b. Taganrog, March 7, 1872; d. Moscow, May 25, 1964. He studied violin and theory at the Imperial Court Chapel in St. Petersburg; from 1893 to 1897 he took composition lessons with Balakirev; then entered the St. Petersburg Cons. in the class of Rimsky-Korsakov, graduating in 1900, then received the Rubinstein Prize for his cantata *Paradise and Peri.* He was instructor of violin at the Court Chapel (1897–1900); teacher of composition at the Rostov Music School (1906–08), the Moscow Cons. (1908–18), the Ekaterinodar Cons. (1918–24), the Odessa Cons. (1924–26), the Kiev Musico-Dramatic Inst. (1926–31), the Sverdlovsk Music School (1931–33), and the Minsk Cons. (1933–41). In 1955 he was awarded the Order of Lenin. Several well-known Soviet composers were his pupils, among them Polovinkin, Dankevich, and Vainberg. In his music, Zolotarev continued the line of the Russian national school of composition, based on broad diatonic melos, mellifluous euphonious harmonies, and, in his operas, a resonant flow of choral singing. He publ. a manual on the fugue (Moscow, 1932; 3rd ed., 1965) and a vol. of reminiscences (Moscow, 1957).

WORKS: DRAMATIC: OPERAS: *The Decembrists* (Moscow, Dec. 27, 1925); *Ak-Gul* (1942). **BALLET:** *Lake Prince* (1948; Minsk, Jan. 15, 1949). **ORCH.:** 7 syms. (1902, 1905, 1935, 1936, 1942, 1943, 1962); *Moldavian Suite* (1926); *Uzbek Suite* (1931); *Tadzhik Suite* (1932); *Belorussian Suite* (1936); Cello Concerto (1943); *Rhapsodie hébraïque* (n.d.). **CHAMBER:** 6 string quartets (1899, 1902, 1907, 1912, 1916, 1945); 2 piano sonatas (1903, 1919); Piano Quintet (1904); String Quintet (1904); Piano Trio (1905); Violin Sonata (1922). **VOCAL:** Many songs.

BIBL.: S. Nisievich, *V.A. Z.* (Moscow, 1964).

Zoltán, Aladár, Romanian composer and administrator; b. Mărtinis-Harghita, May 31, 1929; d. Tîrgu-Mureş, July 9, 1978. He was a student of Jodal and Demian at the Cluj Cons. (1946–53). In 1965 he became director of the Tîrgu-Mureş Phil.

WORKS: DRAMATIC: *Poarta de sur* (The Marriage; 1962). **ORCH.:** *Divertisment* for 2 Clarinets and Strings (1952); *Dansuri din Corund*, suite (Tîrgu-Mureş, June 15, 1960); 2 syms.: No. 1 (Tîrgu-Mureş, May 5, 1961; rev. 1963) and No. 2 (Tîrgu-Mureş, June 24, 1972); *Dansuri de pe Mures*, suite (1968); *Suita piccola* (1970); *Introduction and Allegro* (1974–77; Tîrgu-Mureş, Oct. 30, 1977). **CHAMBER:** Nonet (1952–53); Bassoon Sonata (1954–55); String Quartet (1965); piano music. **VOCAL:** 4 cantatas (1953–65); songs.

Zoras, Leonidas, Greek composer and conductor; b. Sparta, March 8, 1905; d. Athens, Dec. 22, 1987. He studied law at the Univ. of Athens; at the same time, he took conducting lessons with Mitropoulos, and studied composition with Kalomiris, Lavrangas, and Riadis. From 1926 to 1938 he taught theory at the Odeon Music School in Athens; then studied conducting with Gmeindl, Schmalstich, and F. Stein and composition with Blacher, Grabner, and Hoffer at the Berlin Hochschule für Musik (1938–40). After conducting at the Greek National Opera in Athens (1948–58), he returned to Berlin as a conductor at the Deutsche Opera and RIAS (1958–68). He was director of the Athens National Cons. from 1968. He wrote an opera, *Elektra* (1969); the ballet *Violanto* (1931); *Night Song* for Cello and Chamber Orch. (1927); *Legend* for Orch. (1936); Sym. (1947); *Concertino* for Violin and 11 Woodwind Instruments (1950); Violin Sonata (1950); String Quartet (1969); numerous piano pieces, choruses, and songs.

Zorn, John, innovative American composer and instrumentalist; b. N.Y., Sept. 2, 1953. After a brief college "stint" in St. Louis and world travels, he became an active contributor to the downtown music scene in N.Y.; performed with various avant-garde and rock musicians, including pianist Wayne Horvitz, drummer David Moss, and the Kronos Quartet. His *The Big Gundown* (1986) uses the music of film composer Ennio Morricone (b. 1928) as material to be freely distorted and reworked. His major works include *Archery* (1981), *Cobra* (group improvisation; 1986), *A Classic Guide to Strategy*, Vol. I (solo with tape), *News for Lulu* for Trio (1987), and *Spillane* (1988). He also composed *Roadrunner* for Accordion (1986), *Cat O'Nine Tails* for String Quartet (1988), and, *For Your Eyes Only* for Orch. (1989; rev. version, N.Y., Oct. 14, 1994), and *The Deadman* for String Quartet (1990). He plays saxophone, keyboards, duck calls, and other semi-demi-musical instruments in dense, loud aural canvases that have been compared to the works of Jackson Pollock (and also to an elephant trapped in barbed wire).

Zorzor, Ştefan, Romanian composer; b. Oradea, April 4, 1932. After training at the Bucharest Cons. (1951–52; 1956–61), he was active as a composer and teacher.

WORKS: ORCH.: *Concerto for Orchestra* (1965; Bucharest,

June 1967); *Nocturne* (Cluj-Napoca, Feb. 12, 1966); *Musică festivă* (1967; Cluj-Napoca, Feb. 12, 1968). **CHAMBER:** 4 string quartets (1960; 1962; 1967–68; *Il ritorno,* 1977); Violin Sonata (1963); Wind Quintet (1967); *Heteroquintet* for Flute, Violin, Cello, Piano, and Percussion (1968); *Circulara,* quintet for 5 Different Instruments (1969); *Reprize* for Cello and Piano (1975); *Deformanţi,* concertino for Violin, Viola, Cello, Piano, and Harpsichord (1978). **PIANO:** *5 Pieces* (1965–74); *4 Pieces* (1970); *Acuta* (1970). **VOCAL:** *Ţara mea* (My Country), cantata for Women's Chorus and Small Orch. (1956); choruses.

Zouhar, Zdeněk, Czech composer and teacher; b. Kotvrdovice, Feb. 8, 1927. He was a pupil in Bratislava (1946–51) of Blažek and Kunz before settling in Brno, where he studied with Schaefer at the Janáček Academy of Music (1965–67) and pursued his education at the Univ. (Ph.D., 1962). After serving as head of the music dept. of the Univ. library (1953–61), he taught at the Janáček Academy of Music (from 1962). His music makes multifarious use of modern techniques, including a fairly orthodox dodecaphony.

WORKS: DRAMATIC: *Metamorphosis,* chamber radio opera (1971); *A Great Love,* comic opera (1986); ballets. **ORCH.:** *Sports Pages,* suite (1959); *Music* for Strings (1966); *Symphonic Triptych* (Brno Radio, Nov. 29, 1967); Triple Concerto for Clarinet, Trumpet, Trombone, and Orch. (1970); *Variations on a Theme by Bohuslav Martinů* (1979); *Musica giocosa* (1981); *Blanenská,* suite (1981); *Divertimento No. 3* for Brass Band (1993). **CHAMBER:** *Epilogue* for Cello (1949); *Spring Suite* for 3 Violins (1949); *Aulularia* for Chamber Ensemble (1956); *151* for Wind Quintet (1958); Trio for Flute, Clarinet, and Bass Clarinet (1962); *Études* for 4 Horns (1963); *Divertimento No. 1* for 4 Winds and Percussion (1965); *Variations* for Oboe and Piano (1965); 2 string quartets (1966, 1983); Brass Quintet (1985); piano pieces; organ music. **VOCAL:** *Midnight Mass* for Soloists, Chorus, Orch., and Organ (1957); *The Flames of Constance,* oratorio (1988); choral works; songs.

Zschau, Marilyn, American soprano; b. Chicago, Feb. 9, 1944. She studied at the Juilliard School of Music in N.Y. (1961–65) and in Montana with John Lester. In 1965–66 she toured as a member of the Met National Co. In 1967 she made her debut as Marietta in *Die Tote Stadt* at the Vienna Volksoper, and in 1971 appeared for the first time at the Vienna State Opera as the Composer in *Ariadne auf Naxos.* She made her N.Y. City Opera debut in 1978 as Minnie in *La Fanciulla del West,* returning there as Cio-Cio San, Odabella in *Attila,* and Maddalena in *Andrea Chenier.* On Feb. 4, 1985, she made her Metropolitan Opera debut in N.Y. as Musetta. She sang for the first time at Milan's La Scala in 1986 as the Dyer's Wife in *Die Frau ohne Schatten;* thereafter sang with major opera houses on both sides of the Atlantic. In 1993 she elctrified audiences with her debut at the London Promenade Concerts in a concert performance as Elektra with Andrew Davis conducting the BBC Sym. Orch. Among her many admired roles are Mozart's Countess, Fiordiligi, Aida, Desdemona, Leonora, Tosca, Octavian, the Marschallin, Salome, and Shostakovich's Katerina.

Zsolt, Nándor, Hungarian violinist, conductor, and composer; b. Esztergom, May 12, 1887; d. Budapest, June 24, 1936. He studied violin with Hubay and composition with Koessler at the Budapest Academy of Music. In 1908–09 he was concertmaster of the Queen's Hall Orch. in London, and also was active as a chamber music player until being interned as an enemy alien in 1914; returned to Budapest in 1919 as prof. of violin at the Academy of Music; in 1930 he founded the Budapest Chamber Orch.; from 1934 he was conductor of the Debrecen Phil. He wrote a Sym. (1918), a Violin Concerto (1906), a Piano Quintet (1908), various pieces for violin and piano, and songs.

Zucca, Mana. See **Mana-Zucca.**

Zuckerkandl, Victor, Austrian musicologist and aesthetician; b. Vienna, July 2, 1896; d. Locarno, April 25, 1965. He studied at the Univ. of Vienna (Ph.D., 1927). He conducted in Vienna and in other cities; also was a music critic for Berlin newspapers (1927–33) and taught theory and appreciation courses in Vienna (1934–38). He went to the U.S. to teach at Wellesley College (1940–42); during World War II, he worked as a machinist in a Boston defense plant (1942–44). He then taught theory at the New School for Social Research in N.Y. (1946–48). A grant from the American Philosophical Soc. enabled him to develop a course for non-musicians on the nature and significance of tonal music; after he joined the faculty of St. John's College in 1948, this course was adopted as a general requirement. He retired to Ascona in 1964, lecturing at the Jung Inst. and the Eranos Conference in Zürich before his death. His books represent a synthesis of theory (mostly following Schenker's analytic theories; music cognition; and intellectual metaphysics); they include *Sound and Symbol: Music and the External World* (1956), *The Sense of Music* (1959), and *Man the Musician* (1973).

Zuckert, Leon, Ukrainian-born Canadian violinist, violist, conductor, and composer; b. Poltava, May 4, 1904; d. Toronto, May 29, 1992. He studied violin with Boris Brodsky in Poltava (1916–18). Following sojourns in Poland and Argentina, he settled in Canada in 1929. IN 1937 he took a conducting course with Reginald Stewart at the Toronto Cons. of Music. He was active as a performer, composer, and arranger for Canadian radio programs. He also played in various orchs., including the Winnipeg Sym. Orch. (1932–34), the Toronto Sym. Orch. (1951–56; 1961–63), and the Halifax Sym. Orch. (1963–65; 1967–69). His works generally followed in the tonal tradition. His wife was the poet Ella Bobrow, who collaborated with him on many songs.

WORKS: BALLET: *Preciosa y el Viento* (1986). **ORCH.:** *My Canadian Travels* (1938); 2 syms. (1949, 1962); *Quetico* (1957); *Divertimento Orientale* for Oboe and Strings (1965); *2 Moods in 1* for Strings (1967); *My Paintings* for Strings (1969); *Impressions of Tenerife* (1970); *Fantasia on Ukrainian Themes* (1973); *2 Spanish Meditations* (1974); Concerto for Bassoon and Strings (1976); *Elegía: Elegy* (1977); *A Homage* (1980); *Escenas Granadinas: Spanish Ballet Suite* (1980); *Symphonic Sketch* (1982); *Evening in a Russian Village* for Mandolin Orch. (1985). **CHAMBER:** *N'ila* for Violin or Cello and Piano or String Quartet (1916; rev. 1953); *Gypsy Memories* for Violin and Piano (1938); *2 Hebrew Pieces* for String Quartet (1947; rev. 1982); *Preludio en Modo Antiquo* for Brass (1964); String Quartet (1965); *Psychedelic Suite* for Brass Quintet (1968); *Little Spanish Dance* for Flute and Piano (1970); *Sonata Amorfa* for Violin and Piano (1970); *Elegiac Improvisation* for Flute and Piano (1972); *Sue Le Lac Baptiste, Ontario* for Saxophone and Piano (1972); *Short Suite* for Trumpet or Clarinet or Viola and Piano (1974); Suite for Bassoon (1975); Concerto for 2 Cellos and Piano (1979; also for Cello, Bassoon, and Piano); *Melancholic Piece* for Trombone or Bassoon or Cello and Piano (1980); *For Ofra: 2 Contrasting Moods* for Cello and Piano (1982); Sonata for Solo Viola (1984); piano pieces. **VOCAL:** *Prayer* for Voice and String Quartet (1960); *Dnieper* for Chorus and Orch. (1961); *Song in Brass* for Voice, Viola, Brass, Timpani, and Percussion (1964); *Quinteto de la Luna y del Mar y Oceánida* for Medium Voice, String Quartet, and Piano (1972); *In the Gleam of Northern Lights* for Chorus, Dancers, and Orch. (1974; also for Chorus, 2 Pianos, Strings, and Percussion); *Longing for Peace* for Baritone, Chorus or Men's Chorus, and Piano or Orch. (1978); *Sholem-yeh! Milhome-nein!* for Chorus and Piano (1985); other choruses and songs.

Zukerman, Eugenia (née **Rich**), American flutist; b. Cambridge, Mass., Sept. 25, 1944. She studied flute with Julius Baker at the Juilliard School of Music in N.Y. (1964–66). In 1970 she won the Young Concert Artists Audition, which resulted in her formal recital debut at Town Hall in N.Y. in 1971; subsequently appeared as a soloist with orchs., as a recitalist, and as a chamber music player. From 1968 to 1985 she was married to **Pinchas Zukerman**, with whom she often appeared in concerts. She contributed various articles on music to newspapers and journals and appeared as a commentator on music on television; authored a novel deceptively titled *Deceptive Cadence* (1980).

Zukerman, Pinchas, outstanding Israeli violinist, violist, and conductor; b. Tel Aviv, July 16, 1948. He began to study music with his father, taking up the violin at age 6; he then enrolled at the Tel Aviv Academy of Music, where he studied with Ilona Feher. With the encouragement of Isaac Stern and Pablo Casals, he became a scholarship student at the Juilliard School of Music in N.Y., where he studied with Ivan Galamian (1961–67). In 1967 he shared 1st prize in the Leventritt Competition in N.Y. with Kyung-Wha Chung, and then launched a brilliant career as a soloist with the major American and European orchs. He also appeared as both violinist and violist in recitals with Isaac Stern and Itzhak Perlman. He subsequently devoted part of his time to conducting, appearing as a guest conductor with the N.Y. Phil., Philadelphia Orch., Boston Sym. Orch., Los Angeles Phil., and many others. From 1980 to 1987 he was music director of the St. Paul (Minn.) Chamber Orch. He was principal guest conductor of the Dallas Sym. Orch. summer music festival (1990–92). In 1993 he became a teacher at the Manhattan School of Music in N.Y. During the 1994–95 season, he made a world tour as a conductor with the English Chamber Orch. He was married to **Eugenia Zukerman** from 1968 to 1985, then to the American actress Tuesday Weld. His performances as a violinist are distinguished by their innate emotional élan and modern virtuoso technique.

Zukofsky, Paul, remarkable American violinist, conductor, and teacher; b. N.Y., Oct. 22, 1943. He was born into an intellectual family. His father was the poet and writer Louis Zukofsky, who late in life penned the novel *Little* (1970), which relates the life of a violin prodigy. Paul Zukofsky began music lessons at the age of 3 and violin instruction at 4. He was 7 when he became a student of Galamian in N.Y. At 8, he made his debut as a soloist with the New Haven (Conn.) Sym. Orch. His recital debut at N.Y.'s Carnegie Hall came when he was 13. At 16, he entered the Juilliard School of Music in N.Y., where he earned his B.M. and M.S. (1964). In 1964–65 he was a Creative Assn. at the Center for Creative and Performing Arts at the State Univ. of N.Y. at Buffalo. He then taught at the New England Cons. of Music in Boston and at the Berkshire Music Center at Tanglewood. In 1969 he became a teacher at the State Univ. of N.Y. at Stony Brook. In 1983–84 he held a Guggenheim fellowship. In 1984 he became conductor of the Contemporary Chamber Ensemble at the Juilliard School. He also taught violin there. From 1987 to 1989 he was director of chamber music activities there. From 1989 to 1995 he served as director of the Arnold Schoenberg Institute at the Univ. of Southern Calif. in Los Angeles; then taught violin there. From his earliest years he was fascinated by ultramodern music and developed maximal celerity, dexterity, and alacrity in manipulating special techniques, in effect transforming the violin into a multimedia instrument beyond its normal capacities. As both a violinist and conductor, Zukofsky has been a determined proponent of contemporary music. His astounding repertoire includes works by Ives, Schnabel, Rudhyar, Schuman, Cage, Carter, Sessions, Feldman, Babbitt, Penderecki, Wuorinen, Glass, and a host of others.

Zupko, Ramon, American composer and teacher; b. Pittsburgh, Nov. 14, 1932. He was a student of Persichetti at the Juilliard School of Music in N.Y. (B.S., 1956; M.S., 1957). Following further studies with Schiske at the Vienna Academy of Music on a Fulbright fellowship (1958–59), he pursued training in electronic music at Columbia Univ. and with Koenig at the Univ. of Utrecht. He taught theory and was director of the electronic music studio at the Chicago Musical College of Roosevelt Univ. (1967–71). In 1971 he joined the faculty of Western Michigan Univ. in Kalamazoo, where he served as a prof. of composition and director of the electronic and computer music there. He received NEA grants (1978, 1980, 1985), a Koussevitzky Foundation Award (1981), a Guggenheim fellowship (1981–82), an American Academy and Inst. of Arts and Letters award (1982), and a Gilmore Foundation Commission (1990). In his music, Zupko has pursued his interest in contemporary compositional modes of expression while attempting to synthesize them with both music of the past and with non-Western traditions. His Violin Concerto (1962) won 1st prize in the 1965 City of Trieste International Composition Contest.

WORKS: DRAMATIC: *Proud Music of the Storm*, multimedia theater-dance piece (1975–76; Kalamazoo, Mich., Dec. 1976); *Rituals*, musical dance-theater piece (1981). **ORCH.:** *Prologue, Aria, and Dance* for Horn and Strings (1961); *Prelude and Bagatelle* for Strings (1961); *Variations* (1961); Violin Concerto (1962); *Translucents* for Strings (1967); *Tangents* for 18 Brass Instruments (1967); *Radiants* (1971); *Windsongs*, piano concerto (1979; Kalamazoo, Mich., Feb. 1980); *Life Dances* (Tanglewood, Aug. 1981); *Canti Terrae* (1982; N.Y., Feb. 1989); 2 syms.: No. 1, *Earth and Sky*, for Symphonic Band (Kalamazoo, Mich., Nov. 1984) and No. 2, *Blue Roots* (1986; Kalamazoo, Mich., March 1989); *Vox Naturae*, concerto for Brass Quintet and Orch. (1991–92; Kalamazoo, Mich., Nov. 1992). **CHAMBER:** Violin Sonata (1958); Trio for Piano, Violin, and Cello (1958); *Reflexions* for 8 Instruments (1964); *Emulations* for Piano and Tape (1969); *Trichromes* for Wind Ensemble and Tape (1973); *Masques* for Amplified Piano and Brass Quintet (1973); *Fixations* for Piano, Violin, Cello, and Tape (1974); *Fluxus I* for Tape (1977), *II* for Piano (1978), *III* for Amplified Violin, Percussion, and Tape (1978), *IV* for Guitar (1987), *V* for Clarinet and Tape (1987), *VI* for Trumpet and Tape (1988), *VII* for Trombone and Tape (1988), *VIII* for Alto Saxophone and Tape (1988), *IX* for Piano and Tape (1990), *X* for Horn and Tape (1993), *XI* for Flute and Tape (1994), and *XII* for Mallet Instruments and Tape (1994); *Nocturnes* for 2 Pianos (1977); *Fantasies* for Woodwind Quintet (1979); *Noosphere* for String Quartet (1980); *Te Deum Trilogy* for Organ (1984); *Solo Passages* for Horn, Flute, Harp, and String Trio (1985); *Pro and Contra Dances* for Brass Quintet (1986); *Chorale* for Brass Quintet (1989); *Folksody* for Piano Trio (1990); *Chaconne* for Piano (1995). **VOCAL:** *All the Pretty Horses* for Choruses and Chamber Orch. (1962); *This is the Garden* for Chorus, Solo Instruments, and Strings (1962); *La Guerre* for Soprano and Chamber Ensemble (1965); *Voices* for Soprano and Tape (1972); *Where the Mountain Crosses*, song cycle for Mezzo-soprano and Piano (1982).

Zweig, Fritz, Bohemian-born American conductor and teacher; b. Olmütz, Sept. 8, 1893; d. Los Angeles, Feb. 28, 1984. He received training in theory from Schoenberg in Vienna. After serving on the staff of the Mannheim National Theater (1912–14; 1919–21), he was assistant conductor at the Barmen-Elberfeld Opera (1921–23). In 1923 he went to Berlin as a conductor at the Volksoper, and then was a conductor at the Städtische Oper from 1927. When the Nazis came to power in 1933, Zweig was banned from the Städtische Oper. In 1934 he became a conductor at the German Theater in Prague. In 1938 he fled Prague in the face of the Nazi dismemberment of Czechoslovakia and lived in Paris. With the defeat of France by the Nazis in 1940, he once more fled and made his way to the U.S. He subsequently was active as a music teacher in Los Angeles. His most notable student was Lawrence Foster.

Zwilich, Ellen Taaffe, remarkable American composer; b. Miami, April 30, 1939. She learned to play the piano, trumpet, and violin. During her high school studies, she was active as a conductor, arranger, and composer with the band and orch. Following training in violin and composition at Florida State Univ. in Tallahassee (B.M., 1960; M.M., 1962), she settled in N.Y. and pursued studies in violin with Galamian. From 1965 to 1972 she was a violinist in the American Sym. Orch. She continued her training in composition at the Juilliard School with Carter and Sessions, taking the first doctorate in composition ever granted there to a woman in 1975. While still at Juilliard, her compositions began to attract notice. In 1974 she received the Elizabeth Sprague Coolidge Chamber Music Medal. In 1975 she was awarded the gold medal at the G.B. Viotti composition competition in Vercelli, Italy. She received grants from the Martha Baird Rockefeller Fund in 1977, 1979, and 1982. In 1980–81 she held a Guggenheim fellowship. In 1983 she became the first woman to win the Pulitzer Prize in Music for her 1st Sym. In 1984 she received an award from the American Academy and Inst. of Arts and Letters, and in 1992 she was elected to its membership. From 1995 to 1998 she held the 1st Composer's Chair at Carnegie Hall. In her music, Zwilich has succeeded in combining technical expertise with a distinct power of communication. Her idiomatic writing is ably complemented by a the poetic element found in her handling of melody, harmony, and counterpoint.

WORKS: BALLET: *Tanzspiel* (1987; N.Y., April 27, 1988). **ORCH.:** *Symposium* (1973; N.Y., Jan. 31, 1975); 3 syms.: No. 1, originally titled *3 Movements for Orchestra* (N.Y., May 5, 1982), No. 2, *Cello Symphony* (San Francisco, Nov. 13, 1985), and No. 3 (1992; N.Y., Feb. 25, 1993); *Prologue and Variations* for Strings (1983; Chattanooga, April 10, 1984); *Celebration* (Indianapolis, Oct. 12, 1984); *Concerto grosso* (1985; Washington, D.C., May 9, 1986); Piano Concerto (Detroit, June 26, 1986); *Images* for 2 Pianos and Orch. (1986; Washington, D.C., March 28, 1987); *Symbolon* (Leningrad, June 1, 1988); Trombone Concerto (1988; Chicago, Feb. 2, 1989); Flute Concerto (1989; Boston, April 26, 1990); Concerto for Bass Trombone, Strings, Timpani, and Cymbals (1989; Chicago, April 30, 1991); Oboe Concerto (1990; Cleveland, Jan. 17, 1991); Concerto for Violin, Cello, and Orch. (Louisville, Dec. 5, 1991); Bassoon Concerto (1992; Pittsburgh, May 13, 1993); Concerto for Horn and Strings (Rochester, N.Y., Aug. 1, 1993); *Fantasy* (1993; Long Beach, Calif., Jan. 14, 1994); Trumpet Concerto, *American* (San Diego, Sept. 24, 1994). **BAND:** *Ceremonies* (1988; Tallahassee, Fla., March 3, 1989). **CHAMBER:** *Sonata in 3 Movements* for Violin and Piano (1973–74); String Quartet (1974; Boston, Oct. 31, 1975); *Clarino Quartet* for 4 Trumpets or 4 Clarinets (1977); Chamber Sym. for Flute, Clarinet, Violin, Viola, Cello, and Piano (Boston, Nov. 30, 1979); String Trio (1982); *Divertimento* for Flute, Clarinet, Violin, and Cello (1983); *Fantasy* for Harpsichord (1983; N.Y., April 10, 1984); *Intrada* for Flute, Clarinet, Violin, Cello, and Piano (1983); Double Quartet for Strings (N.Y., Oct. 21, 1984); Concerto for Trumpet and 5 Players (1984; Pittsburgh, May 6, 1985); Trio for Piano, Violin, and Cello (1987); *Praeludium* for Organ (1987; Philadelphia, May 1, 1988); Quintet for Clarinet and String Quartet (1990). **VOCAL:** *Einsame Nacht*, song cycle for Baritone and Piano, after Hesse (1971); *Im Nebel* for Contralto and Piano, after Hesse (1972); *Trompeten* for Soprano and Piano, after Georg Trakl (1974); *Emlékezet* for Soprano and Piano, after Sandor Petofi (1978); *Passages* for Soprano, Flute, Clarinet, Violin, Viola, Cello, Piano, and Percussion (1981; Boston, Jan. 29, 1982; also for Soprano and Chamber Orch., 1982; St. Paul, Minn., Nov. 17, 1983); *Thanksgiving Song* for Chorus and Piano (1986); *Immigrant Voices* for Chorus, Brass, Timpani, and Strings (N.Y., June 10, 1991); *A Simple Magnificat* for Chorus and Organ (New Haven, Conn., Dec. 6, 1994).

Zykan, Otto M., Austrian composer; b. Vienna, April 29, 1935. He received training in piano and composition (with Schiske) at the Vienna Academy of Music. In 1965 he founded the "Salonkonzerte" in Vienna, and appeared as a pianist in many contemporary scores. He also worked in contemporary music theater circles. From 1975 he devoted most of his time to film projects, for which he composed, wrote screen plays, and directed.

WORKS: DRAMATIC: *Sings Nähmaschine ist die beste*, theater piece (1966); *Schön der Reihe nach*, ballet (1966); *Lehrstück am Beispiel Schönbergs*, music theater-action (1974); *Kunst kommt von Gönnen*, opera (1980); *Auszählreim*, opera (1986; rev. 1987); *Wahr ist, dass der Tiger frisst*, choral opera (1994); *Mesmer*, film music (1994). **ORCH.:** Piano Concerto (1958); *Kurze Anweisung* (1969); *Symphonie der heilen Welt*, scenic concerto (1977); *Ausgesucht Freundliches*, concerto for 2 Soloists, Chorus, and Orch. (1979); Cello Concerto (1982). **CHAMBER:** Cello Sonata (1958); 4 string quartets (1958, n.d., 1990, 1990); *Kryptomnemie* for Winds, Percussion, and Piano (1963); *6 Chansons, die keine sind* for Piano (1965); *Kammermusik* for 12 Instruments (1965); *4 Nachtstück* for Piano (1968); *Miles Smiles*, chamber music (1970); Trio for Solo Violin (1977). **VOCAL:** *Inscene* for 1 to 5 Voices (1967); *Rondo: Alles ist Musik was nicht Gymnastik ist* for Speaker and Tape (1971); *Die Orgel der Barbarei* for 4 Singers, Soloist, and Tuba (1984); *Engels Engel* for 3 Vocalists or Chorus and Tape (1988).

Zylis-Gara, Teresa, Polish soprano; b. Landvarov, Jan. 23, 1935. She was a student of Olga Ogina at the Łódź Academy of Music. After taking 1st prize in the Warsaw Competition in 1954, she sang on the radio and with the Phil. in Kraków. In 1956 she made her operatic debut as Halka in Katowice, and then sang in various Polish music centers. In 1960 she won 1st prize in the Munich Competition, which led to an engagement in Oberhausen. In 1962 she sang in Dortmund and in 1965 in Düsseldorf. In 1965 she made her debut at the Glyndebourne Festival as Octavian. She sang in Paris in 1966. In 1968 she appeared as Donna Elvira at the Salzburg Festival and made her Covent Garden debut in London as Violetta. On Dec. 17, 1968, she made her Metropolitan Opera debut in N.Y. as Donna Elvira, and continued on its roster until 1984. From 1972 she also sang at the Vienna State Opera. In 1973 she appeared in Barcelona. She sang Li at the Orange Festival in 1979. In 1988 she appeared as Desdemona at the Hamburg State Opera. Throughout the years, she also pursued an active concert career. Among her other operatic roles were Fiordiligi, Tatiana, Manon Lescaut, Elisabeth, Elsa, Anna Bolena, and the Marschallin.

Glossary

Abecedarianism. As the etymology of the word indicates, abecedarianism (A-B-C-D-arianism) is alphabetarian in its nature. But abecedarianism is not necessarily a pejorative term. It takes a highly trained intellect and technical skill to create a truly Abecedarian masterpiece, as demonstrated, for instance, in the self-inverted redundant prose of Gertrude Stein. Musical abecedarianism is far from tonal INFANTILOQUY. Stravinsky's *Piano Pieces for 5 Fingers*, Bartók's *Mikrokosmos*, and Casella's *Valse diatonique* from his *Pezzi infantili* are illustrations of sophisticated abecedarianism. Abecedarian effects are naturally produced by small children banging at random on the white keys of the piano keyboard at the level of their heads, often resulting in the unintentional formation of interesting pandiatonic patterns vivified by asymmetrical rhythms. The walk across the keys by Domenico Scarlatti's cat provided the inspiration for a fugue; the critics who described the music they did not like as puerile or cat music had an imperfect understanding of the constructivist potentialities of random tonal juxtaposition.

Ablation. Extreme luxuriance of decorative and ornamental elaborations in the post-Romantic period of modern music resulted, through surfeit, in a profound repugnance to such practices. An inevitable consequence was a drastic ablation of all non-essential thematic excrescences and protuberances from a finished composition. A process of subjective ablation impelled some modern composers to revise their early works and reduce their instrumental luxuriance to an economic functional organization. The most striking instance of such ablation is Stravinsky's reorchestration of the score of his ballet *The Firebird*, removing some supernumerary instruments, excising florid cadenzas, and, in effect, plucking the fiery bird of its iridescent plumage. Most audiences prefer the original luxuriant version to this later parsimonious arrangement.

Absolute Music. The term absolute music is applied to music that is free from programmatic designs, psychological affiliations, or illustrative associations; its Latin etymology connotes independence. In its function absolute music is parasynonymous with ABSTRACT MUSIC, but the two terms are differentiated in their temporal points of reference. Absolute Music is of ancient heritage, while ABSTRACT MUSIC is a relatively recent phenomenon, marked by structural athematism in an atonal context.

Abstract Music. Abstraction in music implies a separation of sonic structures from representational images, whether pictorial or psychological. Abstract music is the antonym of all musical styles that are concrete or naturalistic; abstract works are usually short, athematic, and rhythmically asymmetric. Intellectual fantasy, rather than sensual excitation, is the generating impulse of abstract music; its titles are derived from constructivistic and scientific concepts: Structures, Projections, Extensions, Frequencies, Sound. The German composer Boris Blacher developed a successful form of ABSTRACT OPERA in which concrete action takes place in a swarm of discrete sonic particles, disjected words in several languages, and isolated melodic fragments. ABSTRACT EXPRESSIONISM, a term applied to non-objective painting, is sometimes used to describe musical works of abstract quality with expressionistic connotations. A subsidiary genre of abstract music is ALEATORY MUSIC, in which the process of musical cerebration is replaced by a random interplay of sounds and rhythms.

Absurd Music. The vocable *surd*, cognate with *sourdine*, implies a muted sound; *Absurd* suggests a becalmed truth, but not necessarily nonsense. There are mathematical equations that seem to contradict common sense; in fact, square roots that cannot be resolved precisely are called irrational numbers, or by the now obsolete term surd, a cousin of absurd. The inner validity of absurd logic was enunciated by Tertullian when he said: "Credo quia absurdum est." Oxymoronic pairs, such as "passionate indifference" or "glacial fire," are intrinsically absurd, and yet peculiarly eloquent in their self-contradiction. Absurd music cultivates analogous incompatibilities. It is particularly effective in modern opera, where a scene of horror may be illustrated by a frivolous waltz, or a festive celebration by the somber strains of a funereal march. The modern techniques of POLYTONALITY and ATONALITY represent MUSIC OF THE ABSURD to the withered sensitivity of an old-fashioned ear.

Accompaniment. In modern music, accompaniment transcends its traditional ancillary function and becomes an integral part of the entire composition. The simplest form of modern accompaniment is that of POLYTONALITY, in which the melody is set in one key and the harmony in another. Rhythmically, the modern accompaniment rarely follows the inflections of the melody; deliberate oxymoronic usages are enhanced by translocated accents.

Acousma. An auricular disturbance induced in hostile audiences by ULTRA-MODERN MUSIC is known as acousma. Music critics, even those not suffering from professional indigestion, are chronically prone to acousma, and their discomfort is often reflected in their reviews.

Acoustics. By definition, acoustical phenomena are fundamental to all music. The overtone series, which is the generator of the basic major triad, is also the source of nominal dissonances. The TRITONE, deprecated as "diabolus in musica" by medieval scholiasts, is the foundation stone of ATONALITY, POLYTONALITY, and other modern techniques. Acoustically, it is the 45th overtone at the distance of 6 1/2 octaves from the fundamental note, with which it forms a concord. Scriabin, theorizing ex post facto, regarded his MYSTIC CHORD as a consonance, because its constituents approximate the high overtones. An interesting practical application of the acoustical properties of the overtone series is found in Ravel's *Boléro,* where at one point the melody is accompanied by a group of flutes and piccolos constituting the 6th, 8th, 10th, and 12th overtones, progressing in parallel formations. In the score Ravel marks the gradually decreasing dynamics of these high notes, corresponding to a natural tapering of the strength of overtones in higher elevations. This calculated enhancement of natural overtones affects the timbre of the solo instrument. If performed correctly with the dynamics scrupulously observed, the solo player will find to his dismay that his instrument has undergone a curious change in its tone color. With the aid of electronic means of tone production, this effect can be produced artificially, generating hybrid sonorities such as a half-bassoon and a half-trombone, or a timbre that is a third-oboe, a third-clarinet, and a third-violin.

Rhythms can be combined in special proportions with the overtone series. In 1932 Henry Cowell, in collaboration with Leon Theremin, constructed the Rhythmicon, an instrument which generates a series of rhythmic beats in an overtone series, the number of beats being proportional to the position of each overtone, so that the octave has two beats per time unit, the interval of the 12th, three beats, the major third over two octaves, five beats, etc. This arrangement makes it possible to devise polyrhythmic counterpoint of great variety and unique sonority. Acoustical innovations and improvements in the purity of intonation are not without musical perils, however. Perfect tuning in orchestral performance would generate differential tones and make a sonic jungle out of a classical symphony. The desire of modern architects to attain acoustical perfection often leads to orchestral pollution in the concert hall. Old-fashioned rococo architecture, with its ornate brocades and heavy curtains, contributed the necessary dampening of sounds and echoes that secured harmonious euphony. Modern acousticians eliminated the decorations, removed the tasselled seat covers and cushioned surfaces, replacing them by plywood and plastic, and added an array of mobiles suspended from the ceiling to eliminate microsonic impurities. But these elaborations resulted in some unwelcome side effects. Parasitical noises were neutralized, but a variety of unsuspected musical microorganisms, overtones and differential tones, rose from the instruments themselves, flooding the hall in a harmonious plasma that all but destroyed the natural equilibrium of tonal imperfections and mutual reverberations that were responsible for the rich resonance intuitively achieved by the musical architects of the past. The consequences of such modernization were painfully evident in the scientifically designed Philharmonic Hall at Lincoln Center in New York. The resulting acoustical anarchy was fortunately corrected by an ingenious rearrangement of the physical properties of the auditorium and the stage, so that the natural heterogeneity of sonic euphony was restored.

Action Music. The term Action Music is applied to compositions resulting from an impulsive melosomatic urge. Like IMPRESSIONISM, the term itself arose by analogy with painting. Action Art, such as was practiced by Jackson Pollock, implies a free wielding of the brush in which the unpremeditated splash of color becomes a creative enzyme for the next projection. In Action Music there is no calculated design; the initial reflex generates a successive series of secondary reflexes in a network of musico-neural synapses, resulting in the formation of dynamically propelled sounds.

Action Music is primarily a manifestation in MIXED MEDIA, or HAPPENINGS with audience participation, in which the spontaneous psychological and physiological excitations determine the course of events. Composers of Action Music usually provide a set of instructions, leaving specific decisions to the performers. Action Music is a mass phenomenon, one which transcends national boundaries and energies in similar forms in many lands, like self-flagellation of medieval penitents and tergiversations of the whirling dervishes. This ubiquity of incidence is paralleled by the SYNCRETISM of cultures in Action Music. Western practitioners of the genre tend to annex the contemplative philosophies of the East, while Oriental composers of Action Music adopt serialistic methods and mathematical parameters. In mass manifestations, Action Music often finds its audible expression in the ululations of pullulating populations.

Additive Composition. As the term implies, additive composition is effectuated by a series of successive additions to an initial thematic statement. The connection is mechanistic by definition, but if by chance, or subliminal design, a dominant melorhythmic figure emerges, a paradoxical rondo is the result. Additive composition is an essential technique of MINIMALISM.

Adjunction. Melodic, rhythmic, or harmonic adjunction is produced by a juxtaposition of compatible thematic particles. Such a method suggests a less mechanistic connection than in ADDITIVE COMPOSITION, and a possibility of a thematic unity is not excluded. The Belgian composer Désiré Pâque used the term *Adjonctian constante* to describe an episodic use of recurrent or non-recurrent motives.

Aerostatic Suspension. In Impressionistic scores, the shimmering interference of euphonious dissonances generates a sonic inversion which forces the lighter elements to ascend into the upper harmonic regions. At some point an equilibrium of overtones and differential tones is established. This euphony, with ethereal sonorities wafted by the winds of flutes, oboes, clarinets, and flageolet-like upper strings, suggests a physical convection which may be described as aerostatic suspension.

Agglutination. When successive melorhythmic particles are not unified by common tonality or melorhythmic similarity, the resulting type of composition may be described as agglutination, a gluing together. The method differs from ADDITIVE COMPOSITION in possessing a greater malleability in the process of coalescence. On the other hand, it lacks the inherent compatibility that is present in the method of ADJUNCTION.

Aleatory Music. The word aleatory is derived from the Latin "alea," that is, a die. (Julius Caesar exclaimed after crossing the Rubicon, "Alea jacta est.") Aleatory music in the literal sense is not a new invention. "Dice music" was a popular parlor game in the 18th century. A celebrated example is *Musikalisches Würfelspiel,* attributed to Mozart. In the second half of the 20th century, composers of the AVANT-GARDE introduced true aleatory methods. A pioneer work was *Music of Changes* by John Cage, derived from chance operations found in the ancient Chinese book of oracles known as the *I-Ching* in which random numbers are obtained by throwing coins or yarrow sticks. By drawing an arbitrary table of correspondences between numbers and musical parameters (pitch, note-values, rests) it is possible to derive a number of desirable melorhythmic curves. Human or animal phenomena may also serve as primary data. Configurations of fly specks on paper, pigeon droppings on a park bench, the design of crushed mosquitoes on wallpaper, the parabolic curve of an expectoration directed towards a spittoon, dissection of birds as practiced in ancient Rome, etc. are all excellent materials for aleatory music. At one HAPPENING in an American midwestern university, the anal discharge of a pig, administered a clyster, was used as an aleatory datum. Mauricio Kagel made use of partially exposed photographic film for aleatory composition. The composer-engineer Iannis Xenakis organizes aleatory music in STOCHASTIC terms, which possess the teleological quality absent in pure aleatory pursuits. Among affiliated subjects of aleatory music are PROBABILITY, INFORMATION THEORY, STOCHASTIC COMPOSITION, CYBERNETICS, EXPERIMENTAL MUSIC, COMPUTER MUSIC, and INDETERMINACY.

Algorithm. In mathematical usage, an algorithm is an operator devised for the solution of problems arising in the theory of numbers. Directions given in puzzle canons to indicate the time and the interval of entry are algorithms. The most ubiquitous algorithm in modern music is the TRITONE. It compasses a chord containing 11 different intervals, for the sum of the first 11 numbers equals 66, which corresponds in semitone units to 5 1/2 octaves, the tritone being half an octave. The TRITONE is also the operating algorithm in the problem of distributing 12 different notes of the chromatic scale into four mutually exclusive triads. Here the modus operandi is to build two major triads separated by a tritone, and two minor triads a whole tone higher whose tonics are also at a distance of a tritone (e.g., C major, F-sharp major, D minor, G-sharp minor). Magical properties emerge from such operations. It is remarkable, for instance, that four mutually exclusive triads can be arranged only by using a pair of major triads and a pair of minor triads, and that no other distribution is possible. But it is also possible to split the chromatic scale into a group of diminished, minor, major, and augmented triads, one of each, a symmetric and elegant solution, suggesting similarly elegant formulas in mathematics. Algorithmic composition is a virgin field for experimentation in modern techniques, enhanced in its potential through the application of computer technology.

Allusive Quotation. Folk songs, contrapuntal elaborations on a given *cantus firmus*, quotations from the doom-laden chant *Dies irae*, have been for centuries a favorite resource of allusive quotations. Richard Strauss inserted the theme of the funeral march from Beethoven's *Eroica* in the score of his *Metamorphosen*, a dirge on the death of Germany, written during the last weeks of World War II. Alban Berg quoted Bach's chorale *Es ist genug* at the conclusion of his Violin Concerto as a memorial for Manon Gropius, daughter of Mahler's widow by a second marriage, who died young. Quotations from a composer's own scores are also not rare; a notorious modern example is the egocentric series of quotations used by Strauss in the score of his tone poem *Ein Heldenleben*. An extraordinary assembly of assorted thematic memos, memories, and mementos is found in *Sinfonia* by Luciano Berio, in which he quotes metamorphosed fragments from works of Mahler, Debussy, Ravel, and others. The crowning achievement of allusive quotation, however, is found in John Cage's *Europeras 1 & 2* (1984–87), a chance-determined, musico-dramatic stage collage self-referentially comprised in its orchestral and vocal materials of excerpts from extant operas across historical time.

Alphabetical Monograms. The origin of musical notation is alphabetical or syllabic. The names of the notes of the initial hexachord of the major scale were taken by Guido d'Arezzo from the first syllables of a Latin hymn, and this syllabic nomenclature is still in use in the Latin countries and in Russia. In German, the musical notes are designated by letters from A to H; thanks to this alphabetic denomination, it is possible to contrive musical themes out of words and names comprising these letters, the most illustrious example being the theme B-A-C-H. That such an artificial method of thematic invention does not hamper a composer of genius is proved by Schumann's *Carnaval*, which is based on the spelling of the name of the town of Asch (in German nomenclature either A-flat, C, B or A, E-flat, C, B). Dmitri Shostakovich based the main themes of his Tenth Symphony and Eighth String Quartet on his alphabetical monogram, in German nomenclature, D.SCH. Mario Castelnuovo-Tedesco extended his system of alphabetical monograms to 25 letters of the Italian alphabet, arranging the notes chromatically and filling two full octaves from A to Z.

Ambulation. Ambulatory activities by performers during a concert in the process of playing is a particular case of SPATIAL DISTRIBUTION, in which the position of the players in physical space is treated as an independent parameter. Ambulation is also related to VECTORIALISM; in both, the direction of the source of sound depends on the placement, stationary or kinetic, of the performers. In an ambulatory composition, the players are usually instructed to make their entrances onto the stage while playing the initial bars upon their instruments which they carry with them. Some AVANT-GARDE composers even demanded the pushing of a grand piano onto the stage with one arm while performing a one-hand composition with the other. Rational ambulation is practiced in *Antiphones* for string quartet by the Soviet composer Sergei Slonimsky. In the opening of the work the cello player, originally seated in the middle of the last row of the concert hall, is instructed to walk with his instrument to the stage while playing passages in a non-tempered scale; the other players are engaged in walking movements one after another, in a manner of an ambulatory fugato.

Anagrams. By analogy with literal anagrams, in which words and sentences are derived from a given matrix (e.g., "Flit on, cheering angel" from Florence Nightingale), notes of a musical subject can be rearranged in order to generate plausible thematic variations. The 12 notes of the chromatic scale yield 479,001,600 possible permutations suitable for dodecaphonic usages. Polyanagrams, formed by linear (melodic), vertical (harmonic), and oblique (fugal) parameters, are comprised in the generic term COMBINATORIALITY, introduced by Milton Babbitt. Perhaps the most intricate polyanagram is *Anagrama* by the Argentine-born AVANT-GARDE composer Mauricio Kagel, scored for speaking chorus, 4 vocalists, and instruments, to a text derived from Dante's *Divina Commedia*, subject to a number of permutations forming plausible sentences in different languages.

Analphabetism. There is a marked difference between musical analphabetism and ABECEDARIANISM. While ABECEDARIANISM is the art of using artless formulas, analphabetism is the inability to use even a limited tonal vocabulary owing to a faulty technique of composition. The most obnoxious type of analphabetism is FRAUDULENT MODERNISM, mimicking advanced idioms and putting wrong notes in elementary harmonies. In its most innocent and disarming form, analphabetism approaches INFANTILOQUY. It is only when it raises its turgid tentacles above the level of harmless romantic indulgence that analphabetism becomes its literal self, i.e., illiteracy.

Anamnesis. A vivid memory of a psychologically important event that passes the mind simultaneously with another seemingly identical experience is popularly attributed to METEMPSYCHOSIS, a remembrance of a previous incarnation. Anamnesis is a similar explosion of memory, but it is devoid of any mystical notions. In music, an unexpected appearance of a thematic motive amid irrelevant melorhythmic events is anamnestic.

Anarchy and Autarchy. Innovating composers since the time of Wagner have been accused of promoting musical anarchy.

An educated French music critic wrote after attending the first performance of Debussy's *Pelléas et Mélisande*, "No, I will never have anything to do with these anarchists of music!" But when Schoenberg enunciated his method of composition with 12 tones related only to one another, the outcries against atonal anarchy changed to charges of aesthetic autarchy. To refute such accusations, Schoenberg wrote, in a letter from Hollywood dated 3 June 1937 and addressed to Nicolas Slonimsky: "What I did was neither revolution nor anarchy. I possessed from my very first start a thoroughly developed sense of form and a strong aversion for exaggeration. There is no falling into order, because there was never disorder. There is no falling at all, but on the contrary, there is an ascending to a higher and better order." Schoenberg's student, John Cage, held similar views but he was more responsive to his critics; in 1988 he delivered an hour-long mesostic poem entitled *Anarchy*, which features innumerable quotes from anarchists across time, including Emma Goldman and Bakunin.

Animal and Human Noises. The introduction of parts for animals into musical composition is an old and cherished fantasy. Imitations of bird songs have been part of music since the Middle Ages, of course, but an actual sound of a bird occurs for the first time in Ottorino Respighi's *Pines of Rome* which includes a phonograph recording of a Roman nightingale. When a dog incidentally barked during a recording of Walter Piston's ballet suite *The Incredible Flutist*, the conductor decided to keep it in the final recording. A part for cat's meow appears in the score of Nicolas Slonimsky's *Anatomy of Melancholy*, to be enacted by a real cat whose tail is pulled during the performance. Electronic transcriptions provide an opportunity to supply recorded or synthetic animal noises. The tape recording of the cetacean song of a humpback whale has been incorporated into the symphonic poem *And God Created Great Whales* by the American composer Alan Hovhaness. In John Cage's *Europeras 1 & 2* a mechanical mocking bird traverses the stage cawing out the names of famous opera composers across time ("Verdi! Verdi! Monteverdi!"). Human noises—whistling, shrieking, grunting—were cultivated by the Italian Futurists and further propagated by the cosmopolitan AVANT-GARDE.

Anti-Music. Anti-Music is a concept formulated by analogy with the hypothetical phenomenon of anti-matter, in which the electrical charges of subatomic particles are reversed, so that the physical encounter between matter and anti-matter would result in mutual annihilation. Anti-Music reverses the acoustical charges of consonances and dissonances. The valences in the series of overtones are similarly reversed, so that the diminishing intervals in the upper part of the harmonic series are regarded as increasingly euphonious concords, and those close to the fundamental tone as discords, requiring a resolution. A manual of Anti-Music is yet to be written. Triadic formations, tonal sequences, symmetric periods, and harmonious cadences would be ruled out in such a textbook. Anti-Music of this nature would then be taught in elementary schools along with the physical principles of anti-matter. But old music would not be entirely excluded. In special seminars, courses will be given in Anti-Anti-Music, in which consonances will regain their respected status, while dissonances will once more be relegated to a dependency. It is even possible that in the fantastic world of Anti-Music, tolerance will be granted to such teratological practices as those of Bach, Beethoven, Brahms, Debussy, and Schoenberg.

Anti-Opera. While ANTI-MUSIC is still in its embryonic stage, Anti-Opera flourishes on the contemporary scene. Its modest beginnings consisted in the reversal of the Aristotelian unity of place and action. In the world of Anti-Opera, it is not enough to use librettos that make no sense; this has long been achieved in classical Italian opera. What is required is deliberate violence wrought on logic, drama, and comedy. Withal, Anti-Opera must be utterly solemn. The vocal parts must be written in an anti-larynx idiom. After the completion of an Anti-Opera, the score must be fractured, splintered, fragmented, and then reassembled in a random montage, making sure that no inadvertent euphony or any non-Anti-Musical matter would result. Anti-Opera may include elements of the opera of the absurd, but there are differences. In the opera of the absurd, there is drama in the very absurdity of the libretto, while in Anti-Opera the dialogue is an *actas interruptus*, without any continuity. Anti-Opera belongs to the category of MIXED MEDIA, approaching in its total absence of cohesion the improvisatory qualities of a HAPPENING.

Aposiopesis. In oratorical practice, aposiopesis is a sudden interruption of a speech as if in a state of overwhelming emotion. A locus classicus is Neptune's exhortation to his disobedient winds, "Quos ego . . .," in Virgil's *Aeneid*. In music, aposiopesis is used to best effect in opera. In Neo-Classical works, a dramatic break in a cadence or a rhythmic elision of a beat is a counterpart of aposiopesis.

Asomatous Variations. Etymologically, the adjective asomatous signifies incorporeality, the lack of a *soma*, a material body. In composition, asomatous variations are metamorphoses of an absent theme. Often a theme is cumulative, building up part by part, a practice as frequent among classical composers as in ULTRA-MODERN MUSIC. In DODECAPHONIC MUSIC, the principal series is sometimes evolved by such a cumulative thematic accretion. Asomatous variations serve a descriptive purpose in Vincent d'Indy's *Istar Variations*. In this work, portraying the passage of the goddess Istar through seven gates, at each of which she deposits a part of her garments, the theme does not appear in its totality until the final gate is reached. Elgar's *Enigma Variations* are based on a clearly outlined subject, but Elgar repeatedly hinted that this visible theme is but a counterpoint to a prime motive, which remains asomatous. Composers of the AVANT-GARDE cultivate the art of asomatous variations with such determination that, in some ultra-modern works, an accidental repetition of a motive automatically marks the end of performance.

Asymmetry. Classical music is based on an orderly succession of symmetric periods and phrases; modern composers relish asymmetrical patterns. Often a simple, quasi-abecedarian tune is deliberately thrown out of symmetry by the addition or elision of a rhythmic unit, while the accompanying figure continues its preordained course. Compound meters are intrinsically asymmetric, as are the subdivisions of binary and ternary meters into unequal groups. Such subdivisions are typical of Serbian, Croatian, Bulgarian, Macedonian, and Romanian folk music. Béla Bartók made artistic use of such meters derived from the multi-ethnic folkways of his native Transylvania.

Athematic Composition. Athematic composition is the product of a deliberate effort to separate the melodic line into segregated groups of phrases and motives bearing no relation to one another. Athematic music does not adhere to any formal organization; a work without connected themes can therefore start and end at any point. Karlheinz Stockhausen arranges some of his works in segments which can be played in any order whatsoever, with the stipulation that when a performer, accidentally or intentionally, arrives at the same segment, it marks the ending. Athematic composition tends towards atonal designs, in which the principle of non-repetition of melodic material is paramount. An athematic work need not be incoherent or inchoate; successive melodic statements may be related by a preferential use of a certain interval or a certain rhythmic configuration. In this sense, it may be said that an athematic composition has either zero or an indefinitely large number of themes.

Atonality. Etymologically, atonality is a negative concept which connotes the absence of tonality. The term was first applied by hostile critics as a derisive description of a type of modern composition in which tonality was almost entirely disenfranchised and integral chromaticism served as the guiding principle of melodic writing. Atonal composers avoid the repetition of a particular tone in order to preclude the appearance of an adventitious tonic. By natural predisposition such melodies invited a dissonant harmonization. Under such circumstances the key signature becomes superfluous. The desire to obviate the tonic-dominant relationship in atonal writing has led to the replacement of the perfect fifth by the tritone and of the octave by a major seventh. One of the most frequently occurring chordal formations in atonal music is a contraction of the four-part major triad, with the octave reduced to a major seventh, the fifth to a tritone, and the major third to a sesquitone: from C–E–G–C to C–D-sharp–F-sharp–B. The same chord can be obtained by raising the lowest note a semitone leaving the upper three notes unaltered: from C–E–G–C to C-sharp–E–G–C. This chord may also be analyzed as a diminished-seventh chord with an unresolved appoggiatura. Consecutive blocks of such chords at a distance of a minor third are favorite devices of IMPRESSIONIST composers.

The gradual atrophy of tonality has resulted in the non-repetition of essential melodic notes, culminating in the organization of melodic writing making use of all 12 different tones. Tertian melodies and harmonies, affiliated with triadic structures, gave way to quartal and quintal progressions. Ascending or descending melodic fourths became the hallmark of atonal writing, gradually approaching the asymptote of integral dodecaphony in a cumulative PANDIATESSARON, an edifice of perfect fourths comprising all 12 tonics of the cycle of scales in the counterclockwise direction. Atonal structures guided by the principle of non-repetition are found in many works by 20th-century composers. An interesting example is an ornamental passage in Stravinsky's opera *Le Rossignol*, introducing the song of the Chinese nightingale. It traverses two ascending perfect fifths, a descending minor sixth, an ascending major seventh, an ascending minor third, a descending major third, and an ascending major seventh. Not a single note is repeated, and the characteristic atonal interval of a major seventh occurs twice.

Tonal scales and modes derive their individuality from asymmetry of the pattern of tones and semitones. Atonal progressions are formed by the division of the octave into equal parts: two tritones, or three major thirds, four minor thirds, six major seconds, or 12 semitones. An augmented triad consisting of two major thirds is regarded as a dissonance in traditional harmony. When in 1903 the Russian composer Vladimir Rebikov used an augmented triad as the concluding chord of his opera *The Christmas Tree*, his daring was decried by academic critics. The diminished-seventh chord, consisting of minor thirds, is also an atonal dissonance, requiring a resolution into a triad. An atonal scale of 8 notes, obtained by the interpolation of symmetrically placed major or minor seconds in the sesquitone scale, is a frequently used coloristic device. It is described in Russian music dictionaries as Rimsky-Korsakov's scale. The WHOLE-TONE SCALE, representing the division of the octave into six equal parts, is a progression of a distinctly atonal nature, for it lacks the tonic-dominant complex and the leading tone.

The musical notation of atonal music, which in the larval phase of chromatic harmony bristled with double-sharps and double-flats, has been functionally simplified. When the fiction of a phantom tonality could no longer be maintained, double-sharps, double-flats, and such vestigial tonal symbols as E-sharp, B-sharp, F-flat, and C-flat were replaced by their enharmonic equivalents.

The cradle of atonality is Central Europe, the birthplace of Freud's psychoanalysis, Kafka's existential angst, the asymmetrical imagery of Kandinsky, and the relativistic universe of Einstein. It seems fitting that these artistic and scientific developments occurred at about the same time. The controlled hesitancy, directed anxiety, and Hesychastic omphaloskepsis of the period could be musically expressed with congenial intimacy only by atonal constructions. The circumstance that the TRITONE, the "diabolus in musica" of the medieval theorists, became the cornerstone of atonality is a most significant reversal of musicosophical concepts of good and evil. It is also interesting to note that the tritone, being half an octave, is a neutral interval. On the psychological level this neuter quality suggests sexlessness. In his *Harmonielehre* Schoenberg remarks that "angels, our higher nature, are also sexless." In this assertion Schoenberg contradicts St. Thomas Aquinas who argued that angels must be of the masculine gender because Jacob wrestled with one and he would not have wrestled either with a woman or with a neuter hermaphrodite.

Atonal melodies cultivate wide intervallic leaps in order to avoid the monotony of consecutive small intervals. Although individual phrases in atonal music are usually short, the cumulative melodic curve appears long and sustained. Moreover, there is a singular sense of equilibrium inherent in a good atonal melody, in which the incidence of high notes is balanced by a countervailing group of low notes, with the solid central range representing a majority of essential notes. The computation of the relative frequency of individual notes in an atonal melody reveals the characteristics of the bell-shaped probability curve of Gauss. Since the duration of an individual note affects the general equilibrium of a melody, the sum of the products of duration in arbitrary units multiplied by the distance in semitones from the center of the melodic range must be zero, if the intervals below the central line are to be counted with a minus sign.

Several systems of atonal notation have been proposed in which accidentals are replaced by special symbols. Joseph Matthias Hauer suggested a multilineal staff. Jefim Golvscheff, a Russian who was active in Germany after World War I as composer and painter, and who eventually settled in Brazil, notated sharps with a cross inside a white circle and designated note values by stems. A similar notation was forwarded by the Russian composer Nicolas Obouhov. He gave a demonstration of his system of "Absolute Harmony" at a concert of his works in Petrograd on 3 February 1916.

Herbert Eimert gives the following description of the essence of atonality in his *Atonale Musiklehre* (1924): "Atonality, as the word itself implies, lacks modes, major and minor keys, and eliminates the entire harmonic apparatus of tonal music-cadences, leading tones, anticipations, resolutions, enharmonism, altered tones, etc.—as well as the concept of consonance and dissonance in their technical harmonic, but not psychological, aspects. The 12 mutually unrelated and independent tones of the tempered scale form the material of atonal music. The foundation of atonal material is therefore not a scale, or a progression of tones, but a group of tones, a complex, and specifically the only possible number of different tones, namely 12 tones." Hauer has this to say about atonality: "In atonal music there are no tonic, dominant, subdominant, degrees, resolutions, consonances, dissonances, but only the 12 intervals of equal temperament; its scales consist therefore of 12 tempered semitones. In an atonal melody all purely physical, sensual, as well as trivial and sentimental elements, are eliminated, and its law, its nomos, is only that the 12 tones of the tempered scale must be played again and again."

Schoenberg and Alban Berg deprecated the use of the term atonality. Berg concluded his talk on the subject, broadcast over the Vienna Radio on 8 June 1936, with these words: "Antichrist himself could not have thought up a more diabolical appellation than atonal!"

Aud Music. Optical art has given rise to a concentrated type of visual craft known as Op Art. By analogy, auditory art in its intense modern organization may be termed Aud Music. Op Art makes its impact felt by a direct assault on the visual nerve. Aud Music directs its onslaught against the auditory nerve. If *trompe l'oreille* in Op Art deceives the eye by rotating spirals, three-dimensional palimpsests, etc., the technique of *trompe l'oreille* in Aud Music confuses the ear by an unnerving succession of explosive musical fragments and sudden silences. Op Art and Aud Music freely combine in audio-visual syndromes. Fascinated by the optically concentric grooves of a phonograph disc, the painter Picabia called it Optophone.

To paraphrase Apollinaire, Aud Music explores "a rational

use of non-similitudinarianism." It makes music out of elements that are non-musical. Op Art tends to become music; modern artists often depict musical objects, such as a realistic metronome with an eye on the pendulum by Man Ray, which he entitled *Object of Destruction*, or a burning tuba by René Magritte. Aud Music makes use of sound-producing objects that are not musical instruments, as exemplified by the symphonic poem for 100 metronomes of György Ligeti. Other examples of Aud Music and Op Art acting in concert are Sculptures Sonores, sound-producing sculptures. Engineering applications of Aud Music are illustrated by the Rhythmicon, constructed by Theremin and Henry Cowell, and the Sonotron, an acoustical accelerator built by Iannis Xenakis on the model of the Cyclotron and designed to synthesize sonic particles into a sound mass.

Jean Cocteau spoke of "oreilles myopes," referring to those suffering from auditory astigmatism. White light, analyzed by the spectroscope into primary colors, has inspired Op Art, by analogy, a linear evolution of a sonic complex generates Aud Music.

Augenmusik. Music for the Eye is a term of opprobrium often applied to works that look orderly and plausible on paper but are unimpressive to the ear. Yet visual symmetry usually corresponds to a fine musical organization. Some composers of the AVANT-GARDE have adopted the patterns of augenmusik as points of departure for their musical inspiration. Anestis Logothetis, a Bulgarian-born Greek composer, exhibited his scores of augenmusik in Vienna, bearing characteristic geometric titles, such as *Cycloid, Culmination, Interpolation, Parallax, Concatenation.* Villa-Lobos experimented with MILLIMETRIZATION by transferring a chart, a curve, or a silhouette onto a piece of graph paper, with the ordinate corresponding to intervals in semitones and the abscissa to the duration of a note.

Auricular Stimuli. Some musical ears are so sensitive that they perceive sonic stimuli at the threshold of audibility; they are also capable of generating such impulses from within, while reading a musical score, providing a realistic illusion of audible sounds. The secret of the process of composition, particularly of IMPRESSIONISTIC music, may lie in this type of inner stimulation. Such auricular stimuli perhaps explain the enigmatic title of a piece by Ravel, *Sites auriculaires.* The phenomenon of inner auricular stimuli may well be measurable and ought to be investigated by otologists.

Autogenetic Composition. Autogenetic composition, especially in modern music, is the function of melodic invention that makes the development of the basic idea seem inevitable. Bach anticipated the process in his riddle canons; modern composers, proceeding from premises entirely different from those of Bach, apply the method in advanced techniques. Autogenetic composition is an intelligent evaluation of the potentialities of an original invention, and may be profitably explored by modern composers conversant with the expanding capabilities of computer technologies.

Automatic Composition. True automatic composition can become a reality only with a considerable advance of electronic technologies. A photoelectric cell may be used to trigger selected groups of notes and to imprint them on a rotating roll of paper. A coordinating device can be constructed to dictate rhythms. An automatic musical typewriter can recapitulate whole sections of a composition. Digital computers, too, can be put to the purpose. Automatic music should not be confused with automatic writing as employed by spiritualists. A British housewife appeared on television in the summer of 1969 and claimed that her diluted imitations of works by Schubert and Liszt were dictated to her by them, and that she wrote them down automatically. Her claims were never subjected to controlled examination, but if substantiated they would prove that a prolonged state of death fatally affects the ability to compose even among celebrated musicians.

Avant-Garde. The term avant-garde is the heir to a long series of terms descriptive of progressive music—MODERN, ULTRA-MODERN, NEW, Modernistic, Experimental, Empiric. The unfortunate derivation from the military vocabulary does not seem to dismay progressive composers who accept the term as an honorable profession of artistic faith. The paradox is complicated by the fact that many avant-garde composers move in the direction of nullification of music as a complex art, with absolute zero as prospective Doomsday, as music diminishes in bulk and mass. There is an advantage to this minimusification, since the diminution in sonic mass, motion, and duration leads to a corresponding increase in the sensitivity of perception. When a composer writes a work consisting of a sustained note continuing indefinitely, the listener learns to appreciate the slightest variations in dynamics and pitch. After this, even a simple succession of two different tones would appear diversified and attractive.

Bebop. Bebop, Rebop, or simply BOP, is one of the many onomatopoeic vocables descriptive of JAZZ techniques. The most striking characteristic of bebop is its maximal velocity, sometimes reaching 20 notes a second in clear articulation, with a strong off-beat stress. The invention of the term and the technique is generally attributed to the African-American JAZZ player Dizzy Gillespie. Bebop is marked by irregular syncopation, a widely ranging melody of quasi-atonal configurations, and, most importantly, by an accompaniment in rapidly changing modernistic harmonies, making use of unresolved dissonances and polytonal combinations. The verbalization of bebop can be traced to a counting jingle *Four or Five Times*, a disc issued by the Victor Company in 1928, in which the following line occurs: "Bebop one, bebop two, bebop three." BOP as a verb was used in the comic strips in the 1920s, meaning to hit or to clobber. An erudite discussion of BOP is found in an article by Peter Tamony in the Spring, 1959, issue of the San Francisco periodical *Jazz.*

Bitonality. As the term indicates, bitonality is the simultaneous use of two different keys. The most effective type of bitonality is the combination of two polarized major triads whose tonics lie on the diametrically opposite points in the cycle of scales and thus form the interval of a tritone. The sum of the absolute values of sharps or flats in the key signatures of such triads is always six (e.g., C major and F-sharp major, with zero sharps and six sharps respectively, or A-flat major and D major, with key signatures of 4 flats and 2 sharps). The most frequently employed type of bitonality is the complex of C major and F-sharp major triads, which forms the harmonic foundation of Stravinsky's *Pétrouchka*, and is often called the "Pétrouchka Chord." It is also known as the "Parisian Chord," on account of the vogue that it subsequently acquired among Paris composers. The chord is of a clearly pianistic origin, with the white keys of C major contrasted with the black keys of F-sharp major; indeed, Stravinsky had originally planned to use these bitonal materials in a *Konzertstück* for piano and orchestra, and this accounts for the important piano part in the score of *Pétrouchka.* Acoustically, the most advantageous position of these two chords is the spacing of one in open harmony, in root position in the low register, and of the other in close harmony in the first inversion of the triad (e.g., C, G, E, A-sharp, C-sharp, F-sharp). In this disposition, the outer voices, the middle voices, and the inner voices are all in the relationship of a tritone. It is important to note that the major hexachords based on such polarized scales aggregate to 12 different notes. bitonality of minor triads is encountered with far less frequency owing to poor acoustical balance of such combinations. In NEO-CLASSICAL music, a modal type of bitonality came into existence, as exemplified by such complexes as C major and D major, in the Lydian mode. Such cases of bitonality are also part of PANDIATONICISM. Another type of bitonality is a combination of two major or minor triads with a tone in common, for instance C major combined with E major or E-flat major, favored particularly by composers of ethnic associations, among them Ralph Vaughan Williams and Roy Harris. It is interesting that a decreasing progression of intervals, beginning with 9 semitones and ending with 3 semitones, will form a bitonal major chord consisting of triads in second inversions (e.g., G, E, C, G, C-sharp, F-sharp, A-sharp, C-sharp) and that an increasing progression from 3 semitones to 9 semitones will form a bitonal combination of two minor triads in root positions (e.g., D, F, A, D, G-sharp, D-sharp, B, G-sharp). All these types of bitonality pursue the aims of euphony, either by polarization or by Pandiatonic approximation. A very important non-euphonious type of bitonality is homonymous bitonality of major and minor triads in close harmony (e.g., C, E, G, C, E-flat, G), with a friction point at a semitone between the major and the minor third of the same triad. It was cultivated assiduously by Stravinsky from his earliest period. In its linear devolution, it offers a stimulating quasi-atonal melodic design.

In his variations on the tune of *America*, written in 1891, Charles Ives combines F major with A-flat major. In order to bring out the bitonal resonance, he marks one of the tonalities *pianississimo* and the other *fortissimo*.

Blues. The word "blue" is an old American colloquialism expressing melancholy. The blues, in plural, is an American ballad form, marked by leisurely syncopation, 4/4 time, in slow tempo. In its melancholy lilt, the blues forms the counterpart of the Elegy, the Bohemian Dumka, or the Brazilian Modinha. Its distinctive characteristic is the "blue note" of the flatted seventh in major keys, although the third is often flatted too. The sentiment of the blues reflects the long history of suffering of the Negro people in the South; some elements in the Negro spirituals and in Stephen Foster's songs are direct progenitors of the blues. The first composer of the blues in the modern sense was W. C. Handy; his songs *The Memphis Blues* (1911) and *The St Louis Blues* (1914) established the genre. On 17 May 1969 the United States Post Office issued a commemorative 6-cent stamp showing W. C. Handy playing the trumpet, with the legend "Father of the Blues." Ravel has a blues movement in his Violin Sonata. The most famous concert piece in the blues idiom is Gershwin's *Rhapsody in Blue*.

In its classic form, blues consists of a series of 12-bar strophes, with the following harmonic progression: 4 bars of tonic, 2 bars of subdominant, 2 bars of tonic, 1 bar of dominant, 1 bar of subdominant, and 2 bars of tonic; the plagal cadence is *de rigueur*. As in all JAZZ, there are infinite variations on this harmonic succession, with atonal protuberances in the melody and pandiatonic excrescences in the accompaniment.

Boogie-Woogie. Like most terms of JAZZ, Boogie-Woogie is an onomatopoeic alliterative word suggesting a certain type of rhythmic beat. Boogie-Woogie invaded the public arena at a concert of popular American music given in Carnegie Hall in New York on 23 December 1938. It is the only JAZZ form that has adopted an explicit classical model, of the type of passacaglia and chaconne, with the principal theme given in the bass and thus determining the harmonic scheme. The pattern of Boogie-Woogie is remarkably regular. It consists of a 12-bar period: 4 bars of tonic, 2 bars of subdominant, 2 bars of tonic, 2 bars of dominant, and, again, 2 bars of tonic. As in all JAZZ forms, the meter is in 4/4 time, but the rhythmic pattern is set in rapid motion, most often with dotted-eighth notes followed by sixteenth-notes. The bass is usually written in even eighth-notes, in broken octaves, and is sometimes described as a "walking bass." The persistent eighth-note rhythm is suggested by the title of an early Boogie-Woogie song, *Beat Me Daddy, Eight to the Bar*.

Bop. Bop is an apocope of BEBOP; possibly it preceded BEBOP, for the exclamatory flagellant expletive bop appears in American comic strips in the 1920s, invariably followed by an exclamation point.

Boustrophedon. Boustrophedon is an ancient system of writing and reading in alternate directions, one line from left to right, and the next from right to left. The Greek etymology of the word derives from oxen turning around as in plowing a field.

Ophthalmologists find the boustrophedonic alignment beneficial in relieving the strain of shifting of the eye from right to left at the end of a line. In modern times, books have been published in a boustrophedonic arrangement, but no attempt has been made to publish music according to similar principles. The retrograde form of a thematic series is, to all effects and purposes, boustrophedonic.

Bruitism. Bruitism is a genre of musical composition consisting of noises. The pioneer work of Bruitism was *L'arte dei rumori* by the Italian Futurist Luigi Russolo, published in 1916, in which he codified the noises of friction, attrition, sibilation, percussion, and concussion; he also constructed a battery of noise-making instruments, which he called "intonarumori," with which he gave concerts in Milan; concertgoers became so outraged that once he and his fellow noisemakers were physically attacked. Edgar Varèse elevated the inchoate Bruitistic scheme to a purely musical form in his epoch-making work *Ionization*.

Chirality. The etymology of chirality (from the Greek *cheir*, hand) connotes the symmetry of human hands. Lord Kelvin, who coined the term, proposed the following definition: "I call any geometrical figure, or a group of points, chiral, and say it has chirality if its image in a plane mirror, ideally realized, cannot be brought to coincide with itself." Since music evolves in time and not in space, a composition that possesses chirality must consist of two symmetrical halves, the first note or chord being identical with the last, the second with the penultimate, the third with the antepenultimate, etc. In other words, musical chirality is achieved by the technique of SPECULAR REFLECTION, or retrograde imitation. In spatial terms relating to musical performance, chirality exists between the first violin and second violin sections in an orchestra, if they are placed traditionally to the left and to the right of the conductor.

Chromatic Torsion. Chromatic melodies are most effective when they are involuted towards a central tone in a spiral. The effect of constant vectorial changes during which such a central tone is approached alternately from above and from below may be described as chromatic torsion. An interesting example is the theme of the Queen of Shemaha in Rimsky-Korsakov's opera *Le Coq d'Or*, in which chromatic torsion (and contortion) is effectively applied along the stems of diminished-seventh chord harmonies.

Circatonalitarianism. The employment, whether successive or quaquaversal, of all 12 minor and major modalities in a single composition may be called circatonalitarian, by analogy with the biological term Circadian. Circatonalitarian structures are present literally in POLYTETRACHORDS, which traverse 12 major or minor tetrachords.

Circuitry. Modern scores for MIXED MEDIA performances often have the appearance of blueprints for the electric circuits in scientific instruments and digital computers. An early example of musical circuitry is the part marked "Luce" in Scriabin's *Prometheus*, intended to fill the concert hall with changing colors corresponding to fluctuations in instrumental timbre. The detailed directions as to lighting given by Arnold Schoenberg in his monodrama *Erwartung* are in the same category. The Russian composer Nicolas Obouhov, who called himself "Nicolas l'Illuminé," designed an electronic instrument in the form of a cross, called *Croix Sonore*. In the circuitry of some ultramodern scores the SPATIAL DISTRIBUTION of instruments becomes a musical parameter. Elliott Carter, Lukas Foss, Krzysztof Penderecki, Jani Christou, Henry Brant, Sylvano Bussotti, Iannis Xenakis, John Cage, and others wrote works stipulating the position of each instrument in relation to the rest of the ensemble.

Collective Nouns. The following are suggestions for collective nouns to designate groups of musical instruments: a fluviality of flutes, an exhalation of piccolos, a conviviality of clarinets, a scabrosity of bassoons, a promiscuity of saxophones, an oriflamme of French horns, a plangency of oboes, an ambrosia of harps, a flourish of trumpets, a pomposity of trombones, a phlogiston of tubas, a circumspection of pianos, an enfilade of violins, a reticence of violas, an elegance of cellos, a teratology of double basses, a titillation of triangles, and the Brobdingnagian borborygmuses of bass drums.

Combinatoriality. In general topology the concept of combinatoriality applies to the functional congruence of geometrical figures of the same order of continuity. Thus a square can be brought into topological congruence with a circle because all the points of the former are in an enumerable correspondence of the other. On the other hand, the geometry of the figure 8 cannot be made congruent with a square or a circle without cutting it in two. The American composer and theorist Milton Babbitt extended the term combinatorialty to serial techniques. The parameter of continuity in dodecaphonic writing is the order of succession of the 12 thematic notes in their four forms, basic, retrograde, inversion, and inverted retrograde, all of which are combinatorially congruent. Furthermore, the tone-row can be functionally divided into two potentially congruent groups of six notes each, or three groups of four notes each, or four groups of three notes each, with each such group becoming a generating serial nucleus possessing a degree of subsidiary combinatoriality. Extending the concept of combinatoriality to other parameters of serial music, a state of total SERIALISM is attained, in which not only the actual notes of a series, but also meter, rhythm, intervallic configurations, dynamics, and instrumental timbres are organized in sets and subsets. The subsets in turn are organized as combinatorial derivations, possessing their own order of continuity and congruence. Of these, the most fruitful is the principle of rotation, in which each successive set is obtained by the transposition of the first note of the series to the end of a derived set. Thus the first set, 1,2,3, . . . 12, appears after rotation as subset 2,3,4,5, . . . 12,1, or as 3,4,5,6, . . . 12,1,2, etc. Inversion, retrograde, and inverted retrograde can be subjected to a similar type of rotation. The additive Fibonacci series, in which each number equals the sum of the two preceding numbers, as in 1,1,2,3,5,8,13,21 . . ., is another fertile resource for the formation of sets, subsets, and other derivations. The Fibonacci numbers can be used for building non-dodecaphonic tone-rows, in which case the numbers will indicate the distance from the central tone in semitones, modulo 12, so that 13 becomes functionally identical with 1, 21 with 9, etc. The numerical field of combinatoriality is circumscribed by 12 different notes. But experiments have been conducted, notably by Ernst Krenek, with artificial scales of 13 equal degrees, obtained with the aid of electronic instruments. Potential uses of combinatoriality operating with sets of more than 12 notes in an octave are limitless.

Commodious Nomenclature. The musical AVANT-GARDE does not oppose euphony on general principle. Harmonious progressions are tolerated in MODERN MUSIC. The compromise between the prospective music of the future and the modality of the past is often achieved by resorting to commodious nomenclature, as exemplified by the neologisms NEO-CLASSICAL, NEO-BAROQUE, NEO-ROMANTIC, and beyond that by the exotic terms VECTORIALISM, LIPOGRAMMATICISM, and SPATIAL SERIALISM. NEW MUSIC, MODERN MUSIC, Contemporary Music, etc., once progressive slogans, have long been overgrown with a fungus of obsolescence. FUTURISM itself, a rebellious cry of the dawn of the century, is now an academic object of historical study.

Computer Music. Digital machines of various kinds have been used by composers to calculate details of compositions, store information for subsequent use, and generate new and/or transform existing sound(s). Digital computers are also ideal purveyors of random numbers, which in turn can be converted into musical parameters. Such data may furnish the natural sources for ALEATORY MUSIC. Care should be taken, however, not to program computer music excessively, for such input would amount to the dictation of the programmer's own musical ideas, which are often lamentable.

Conjugated Counterpoint. By definition, counterpoint is a conjugation of two or several melodic parts, but too often in common practice contrapuntal techniques follow harmonic formulas, to the detriment of the interdependence of component voices. It is therefore useful to introduce the term conjugated counterpoint in its etymological sense of "opposite notes yoked together." The locus classicus of conjugated counterpoint is the second movement of Béla Bartók's *Concerto for Orchestra,* in which conjugated pairs of wind instruments are arrayed in succession and intussusception.

Contrapuntal Intussusception. In many modern scores contrapuntal groups are arranged in pairs, and each pair becomes an individual entity which is subsequently combined with another prefabricated pair, and yet another. When two such pairs are widely separated in their ranges, an opportunity is presented for an intussusception of a new pair, forming a structure of six contrapuntal voices in three subdivisions. Alexander Tcherepnin made systematic use of this technique in his method of INTERPOINT (Contrapunctus inter punctum).

Controlled Improvisation. An arrangement of available thematic elements, following a definite formal design and confined within a specified period of time, has been described as controlled improvisation. Accordingly, the performer selects attractive or significant motives and phrases of an otherwise non-integrated work, as though drawing pre-set lines from a printer's tray, resetting them at will, duplicated, fragmented, or upside-down. Karlheinz Stockhausen, Lukas Foss, Earle Brown, and others have availed themselves of this manner of composition.

Country Music. As it is practiced in the American South, country music is deeply imbued with sentimental balladry, with curiously oblique cadences that impart an archaic flavor to the melody. The syncopated beat, characteristic of RAGTIME and JAZZ, is practically absent in these songs, which tend to mosey along in an unfettered 4/4 time. Through the medium of radio and television, country music spread far and wide in the United States, occasionally coalescing with ROCK 'N' ROLL.

Cubism. The musical counterpart of Cubism in art is the erection of massive sonorous complexes moving *en bloc* at different speeds and angular motion. Such harmonic boulders produce the best effect in POLYTRIADIC STRUCTURES. Cubistic music must be static, with a low potential. There should be no intermediate melodic or harmonic shifts between Cubistic complexes, but tremolo effects within each unit may contribute to resonant power congruent with massive sonic structures.

Cybernetics. The word cybernetics is derived from the Greek root for governing. As defined by its originator Norbert Wiener, cybernetics is the exercise of human control over mechanical and electrical apparatus, especially in the field of communication. In music, cybernetical data are collected by various ALEATORY, intuitive, or other means; the resulting materials are translated into a system of musical parameters, and a viable outline is drawn. It is in the selection and the programming of cybernetical elements that a composer can assert his or her personality. In music, cybernetical serendipity plays a beneficial part. Novel ideas often suggest themselves during the process of mutation and permutation of thematic elements, contributing to the all-important problem of musical communication.

Cyrenaic Hedonism. Hedonistic traits in MODERN MUSIC developed as a natural psychological reaction to the cataclysm of World War I. Composers and the public sought relaxation in hedonistic dalliance, Cyrenaic in its complete orgiastic abandon, and Sybaritic in its quest for mindless comforts. The center of this cult of music for pleasure was France; it enjoyed a particular vogue between 1920 and 1935, when the slogan of NEW SIMPLICITY was launched as an antidote to post-Romantic solipsism. In form and content this new music cultivated the elegant conceits of the French rococo period, with an emphasis on Epicurean qualities designed to please the palate. Historically, it was the long-delayed fruition of the musical cuisine of Rossini, with occasional polyharmonies and asymmetric rhythms used for modern seasoning.

Dadaism. The word Dadaism was invented by Tristan Tzara on 8 February 1916 at a congenial gathering of friends in a Zurich café. According to one of the many versions, the word Dada owes its origin to French infantiloquy as a sort of dental lallation. Aesthetically, Dadaism was the product of the frustrations endured during the First World War. Its philosophy was entirely negative. Derived from the vociferously proclaimed detestation of all art, music, and poetry, Dadaism stood close to FUTURISM in its furious onslaught on all established values, but failed to offer a new art to replace the old. Despite its violently negative code, Dadaism prepared a well-manured ground for the flowering of such fertile stylistic vegetation as SURREALISM. Dadaism also cast its proleptic shadow on the AVANT-GARDE of the 1920s and on the improvisatory art of HAPPENINGS.

Decomposition and Reassembly. The technique of decomposition and reassembly is suggested by the title of a painting by the Futurist artist Umberto Boccioni, "Scomposizione," in which the normal head of a woman is fragmented and reassembled in a topologically non-congruent shape. The idea is applicable to MODERN MUSIC. A melody can be fractured and its elements redistributed in a different configuration. Variations, tonal and atonal, can be experimentally rearranged, melodically, harmonically, and rhythmically. Decomposition and reassembly may provide interesting and novel combinations of thematic materials and stimulate a disadvantaged composer to explore the laws of musical congruence far beyond his or her ordinary capabilities.

Demolition. Public demolition of musical instruments as part of new techniques of the American and British AVANT-GARDE came into vogue shortly after the conclusion of World War II, possibly as a sado-masochistic exercise of aggressive tendencies, frustrated by the unconditional surrender of the ex-enemies. Contests in the swiftness of destroying upright pianos have been held in clubs and colleges. According to the established rules of the game, a piano had to be reduced to comminuted fragments that could be passed through an aperture of specified dimensions (usually a circle 6 inches in diameter). In Stockholm, a young pianist concluded his recital by igniting a dynamite charge previously secreted inside the piano, blowing it up. An exploding splinter wounded him in the leg. The American AVANT-GARDE composer La Monte Young set a violin on fire at one of his exhibits.

Bakunin, the scientific anarchist, said, "Die Lust der Zerstörung ist eine schaffende Lust." This "creative impulse of destruction" has received its full vindication in the anti-piano activities of modern times.

Demotic Music. Demotic music is a generic category that comprises all genres of popular music—rural, urban, pop, country, folk, Western, jazz, tin-pan alley, commercial jingles. Modern applications of the sources of demotic music are obtained by diatonic translocation, atonal dismemberment, and rhythmic compression. Hexachordal diatonic melodies may be metamorphosed into complex melorhythmic progressions without losing their demotic morphology. ABECEDARIAN MUSIC for children is a fruitful source of such topological transformation, although not all simple music is necessarily demotic, unless the folk quality is expressed in a composed work with utmost fidelity. Some obscure composers have succeeded in producing tunes that seem to be authentically demotic. The universally popular tune, *Dark Eyes*, regarded by many as an autochthonous Russian Gypsy song, is actually a violin piece, entitled *Valse-hommage* composed by a German band leader active in Russia in the 1880s. The Neapolitan ballad *Funiculi-Funicula*, mistaken by many for a genuine folk tune, was written by an Italian vocal teacher resident in London.

Dialectics. Etymologically, dialectics is a discourse. Musical dialectics may be a useful term to describe a kind of meaningful antiphony, an orderly exchange of melodic statements, sufficiently divergent to imply the sense of a debate and yet unified by a general melodic, rhythmic, or harmonic idea. Music in a dialectical form ought to be by definition a succession of free associations, not too strict in grammar and syntax, replete with asymmetrical rhythms and unresolved dissonances. The term is large enough to cover many idioms and techniques, from NEO-CLASSICAL structures to SERIAL COMPOSITION.

Dilapidation of Tonality. The disappearance of explicit key signatures from the notation of modern composition was the first symptom of the dilapidation of tonality and deterioration of traditional harmony. The key signature has a reason for existence in NEO-CLASSICAL works in which the tonic-dominant relationship is still extant and triadic modulations strong. But the dormant chromaticism erupts all the more viciously against tonal restraints, and the key signature, if it is set down at all, exists only to be denied. The chromaticization of the modern idiom during the last decades of the 19th century resulted in an enormous proliferation of double-sharps and double-flats. As enharmonic modulation reared its multicolored head, the antinomy between the tonality symbolized by the key signature and the florid panchromatic display reached the point of arithmetical incompatibility. Seven notes of the diatonic scale represented by seven positions on the music staff and seven letters of the alphabet were to provide notation for the 12 different notes of the chromatic scale. Academic musicians, eager to reserve the fiction of eminent tonality, and being unable to find a common denominator between 7 and 12, erected a fantastic network of accidentals; triple sharps and triple flats pullulate in the *Canons and Fugues* of Wilhelm Middelschulte. A whole section, acoustically equivalent to C major, masquerades in intervallic enharmonies as B-sharp and D-double-flat major in the piano part of Ravel's *Trio.* Debussy was similarly involved in exotic structures of double-flats and double-sharps in a triadic passage of his *Feuilles mortes.*

Even in the 19th century, tonality was often nominal and the key signature an armature without a function. *Intermezzo No. 4*, op. 76, by Brahms is ostensibly in B-flat major, but the tonic triad is not reached until the final two bars. This type of tonal convention may be described as teleological tonality in which the tonic is the goal rather than the point of departure.

The language of ATONALITY arose from the products of the decay of tonal relationships. Genuinely atonal melodies lack the homing instinct; they meander and maunder without the beacon of a tonic in sight. The attraction of the tonic does not exist in atonal writing; the members of an atonal melody are weightless. This atonal assembly deprived of tonal gravity came to be organized by Arnold Schoenberg in a mutually gravitating dodecaphonic complex. Key signatures are obviously superfluous in atonal and dodecaphonic music, but not in POLYTONALITY where different key signatures are used simultaneously.

The supremacy of tonality demanded that each composition end in the same key, or in a related key, in which it began. How strong the prerequisite of this tonal uniformity was felt by composers of the 19th century is illustrated by a whimsical annotation of Richard Strauss in his song entitled *Wenn*, published in 1897. In the original version, the principal key is D-flat major, but the final seven bars and the concluding chord are in D major. Strauss supplied an alternative coda in which the transition was made back to the original key, with the following footnote: "Vocalists who may perform this song before the end of the 19th century are advised by the composer to transpose the last seven bars a semitone lower so as to arrive at the end of the song in the same key in which it began."

Dislocation of Melodic Lines. A special case of modern variation is a linear dislocation of a melodic line. A high note may be pulled upwards and a low note may be pulled downwards without disrupting the intervallic balance of the melody itself. Virtually any tonal melodic line can be topologically transformed into a dodecaphonic series, with ascending intervals retaining their upward direction and descending intervals conserving their downward motion. Stationary notes in the melody may be pulled upwards or downwards at will. Examples of intervallic and modulatory translocation can be found in NEOCLASSICAL compositions. Translocation is also an excellent resource of modern burlesque.

Displaced Tonality. A modernistic resource in tonal techniques which has been successfully applied by composers who are reluctant to abandon tonality altogether is a displacement of the tonic by an instant modulation a semitone higher or a semitone lower. Translocation by larger intervals is generally not effective. Major scales are more suitable for such translocation because of the greater intervallic strength within a major tetrachord, while minor tetrachords are often ambiguous. Transposition of the initial three notes of a major scale a semitone higher or lower forms a group of six different notes; a similar translocation in a minor key will entail a duplication of one member of the series. Examples of melodic translocation are found in many works of Prokofiev and Shostakovich.

Dissonant Counterpoint. The term dissonant counterpoint came into usage in the 1920s as a sort of apologetic declaration by proponents of ATONAL MUSIC. It emphasized the functional equality of dissonance and consonance in all types of contrapuntal techniques. In fugal writing, in particular, a strong tendency was evinced to use the tritone as the interval of entry, instead of the traditional perfect fifth of the tonic-dominant complex. Dissonant counterpoint does not exclude consonances but puts them on probation. However, the perfect octave, as a cadential interval, is generally shunned by the theoreticians of dissonant counterpoint, and is usually replaced by a major seventh.

Dodecaphonic Music. In historical perspective, dodecaphonic music is the product of a luxuriant development of chromatic melody and harmony. A conscious avoidance of all tonal centers led to the abolition of key signature and a decline of triadic harmony. The type of composition in which all tonal points of reference have been eliminated became known as ATONALITY. It was from this paludous atmosphere of inchoate ATONALITY that the positive and important technical idiom of dodecaphonic composition was gradually evolved and eventually formulated by Arnold Schoenberg as the "method of composing with 12 tones related only to one another." Schoenberg's first explicit use of his method occurs in his *Serenade*, op. 24, written in 1924. Five fundamental ideas underlie Schoenberg's method: (1) Dodecaphonic monothematism, in which the entire work is derived from a 12-tone row (*Tonreihe*) which comprises 12 different notes of the chromatic scale; (2) The tone-row is utilized in four conjugate forms: the original, retrograde, inversion, and retrograde inversion; (3) Although the order of the notes in the tone-row is rigidly observed, the individual members of the series can be placed in any octave position, a peculiar feature of dodecaphonic music which results in the wide distribution of the thematic ingredients over the entire vocal or instrumental range of a single part or over sections of different parts; (4) Since each of the 4 forms of the basic 12-tone series can be transposed to any starting point of the chromatic scale, the total of all available forms is 48; and (5) Melody, harmony, and counterpoint are functions of the tone-row, which may appear in all its avatars: horizontally as melody, vertically as harmony, and diagonally as canonic counterpoint. It may also be distributed partly in melodic progressions, partly in harmonic or contrapuntal structures, creating dodecaphonic MELOHARMONY or MELOCOUNTERPOINT. Because of the providential divisibility of the number 12, the 12-tone row can be arranged in 6 groups in 2-part counterpoint, 4 groups in 3-part counterpoint (or harmony), 3 groups in 4-part harmony or 2 groups in 6-part harmony.

In a communication to Nicolas Slonimsky in 1939, Ernst Krenek describes the relationship between ATONALITY and the method of composing with 12 tones as follows: "ATONALITY is a state of the musical material brought about through a general historical development. The 12-tone technique is a method of writing music within the realm of ATONALITY. The sense of key has been destroyed by ATONALITY. The method of composing with 12 tones was worked out in order to replace the old organization of the material by certain new devices."

Schoenberg was not alone in his dodecaphonic illumination. Several musicians, mostly in Austria and Germany, evolved similar systems of organizing the resources of the chromatic scale in a logical and self-contained system of composition. Jef Golyscheff, a Russian composer and painter who lived in Germany and eventually settled in Brazil, worked on the problem as early as 1914, and in 1924 published a collection which he called *12 Tondauer Musik*, making use of 12 different tones in thematic structures. At about the same time Nicolas Obouhov invented a system which he called "Absolute Harmony" and which involved the use of all 12 chromatic tones without doubling; he played his piano pieces written in this system at a concert in Petrograd on 3 February 1916.

Passages containing 12 different notes in succession, apart from the simple chromatic scale, are found even in classical works. There is a highly chromaticized passage in Mozart's *G Minor Symphony* derived from three mutually exclusive diminished-seventh chords, aggregating to 12 different notes. The main subject in the section "Of Science" in the score of *Also sprach Zarathustra* by Richard Strauss contains all 12 different notes of the chromatic scale, but they remain uninverted, untergiversated, and otherwise unmetamorphosed, and thus cannot be regarded as a sampler of dodecaphonic writing.

Liszt's *Faust Symphony* opens with a theme consisting of four successive augmented triads descending by semitones comprising all 12 different tones, but it cannot be meaningfully described as an anticipation of the dodecaphonic method. Charles Ives has a 12-tone series of different chromatic notes in his instrumental piece *Tone Road No. 3*, which he wrote in 1915. This intuitive invention is important not only as an illustration of his prophetic genius, but also as another indication that dodecaphonic ideas appeared in the minds of musicians working in different parts of the world, completely independent of each other.

Among scattered examples of 12-tone composition of the pre-dodecaphonic years is *L'adieu à la vie* for piano by Alfredo Casella, which ends on a chord of 12 different notes. An amusing example of dodecaphonic prevision is the *Hymn to Futurism* by César Cui, written in 1917, when the last surviving member of the Russian Mighty Five was 82 years old. Intended as a spoof, the piece contains a passage of three mutually exclusive diminished-seventh chords in arpeggio adding up to 12 different notes, and another passage comprising two mutually exclusive augmented triads with a complementary scale of whole tones passing through the unoccupied six spaces, forming another series of 12 different notes. The fact that Cui had two dodecaphonic series in his short composition demonstrates that even in a musical satire the thematic use of 12 different notes was a logical outcome of the process of tonal decay, serving as a fertilizer for the germination of dodecaphonic organisms.

Schoenberg was intensely conscious of the imperative need of asserting his priority in the invention of the method of composition with 12 tones. Among contenders for the honor was Fritz Klein, the author of an extremely ingenious composition for orchestra, *Die Maschine*, subtitled "eine extonale Selbstsatire," published in 1921 under the characteristic pseudonym "Heautontimorumenos" (i.e., Self-Tormentor). Klein took this pseudonym from the title of a play by Terence, which contains the famous aphorism: "Homo sum; humani nil a me alienum puto." Klein's score contains a remarkable array of inventions: a "Mutterakkord" containing 12 different notes and 11 different intervals, a "Pyramidakkord," patterns of rhythmically repeated

12 notes, etc., all presaging the future developments of integral serialism. When queried by Nicolas Slonimsky regarding Klein's role in the history of dodecaphonic composition, Schoenberg replied (in English): "Although I saw Klein's 12-tone compositions about 1919, 1920 or 1921, I am not an imitator of him. I wrote the melody for *Scherzo* composed of 12 tones in 1915. In the first edition of my *Harmonielehre* (1911), there is a description of the new harmonies and their application which has probably influenced all these men who now want to become my models."

A much more formidable challenge to Schoenberg's dodecaphonic priority was made by Joseph Matthias Hauer of Vienna, who had experimented with 12-tone composition independently from Schoenberg. But his method differed from Schoenberg's in essential aspects. He built 12-tone subjects from 6-tone "tropes," and allowed free permutation of each trope, a concept that was entirely alien to Schoenberg's fundamental doctrine of thematic ordering of the tone-row. Still, Schoenberg regarded Hauer's theories as sufficiently close to his own method to take notice of them. Schoenberg described the dodecaphonic situation in Vienna in a retrospective note published in the program book of a concert of his chamber music given in New York in 1950: "In 1921 I showed my former pupil Erwin Stein the means I had invented to provide profoundly for a musical organization granting logic, coherence and unity. I then asked him to keep this a secret and to consider it as my private method with which to do the best for my artistic purposes." (The arcane character of this report calls to mind a Latin cryptogram in which the astronomer Huygens encoded his discovery of the rings of Saturn to insure the priority of his observations.) "If I were to escape the danger of being his imitator," Schoenberg continued, "I had to unveil my secret. I called a meeting of friends and pupils, to which I also invited Hauer, and gave a lecture on my new method, illustrating it by examples of some finished compositions of mine. Everybody recognized that method was quite different from that of others." Hauer refused to surrender his own claims as the spiritual protagonist of 12-tone music. A man of an irrepressible polemical temper, he even had a rubber stamp made, which he used in his private correspondence, and which carried the following legend: "Josef Matthias Hauer, der geistiger Urhaber und trotz vielen schlechten Nachahmern immer noch der einziger Kenner und Könner der Zwölftonmusik."

Although Schoenberg's title to the formulation and practical application of the method of composing with 12 tones was finally recognized, in 1948 he came into an unexpected collision with a fictional claimant, Adrian Leverkühn, the hero of Thomas Mann's novel *Doktor Faustus*, described as the inventor of the 12-tone method of composition. In an indignant letter to the editors of the *Saturday Review of Literature* Schoenberg protested against this misappropriation of his invention. The idea that Leverkühn might be considered as a fictional portrait of Schoenberg himself infuriated him. "Leverkühn is depicted," Schoenberg wrote, "from beginning to end, as a lunatic. I am seventy-four and I am not yet insane, and I have never acquired the disease from which this insanity stems. I consider this an insult."

John Stuart Mill once expressed fears that musical invention might soon exhaust its resources, considering the limited number of melodies that could be derived from the eight degrees of the major or the minor scale. He reckoned without the eventual proliferation of chromatic melodies. There are 479,001,600 permutations of 12 units, and as many possible melodies consisting of 12 different notes each. In the dodecaphonic firmament, the melodic horizon is practically unlimited.

The properties of 12-tone composition are truly magical. A priori, it would seem impossible that the 12 notes of the chromatic scale could be arranged in four mutually exclusive triads, considering that its organization was the product of negation of tonality. Yet it has been found empirically that there are two basic solutions of this problem, each capable of three transpositions. But there is a limiting condition: two of these triads must be major and two minor. On the basis of C, these solutions are: (1) C major, D minor, F-sharp major, G-sharp minor; and 2) C major, B-flat major, G-sharp minor, F-sharp minor. The ever-present tritone is the interval between the tonics of each pair in the first solution, and between the tonics of the first and last triad in the second solution. It is also possible to distribute the 12 chromatic tones in a group containing a diminished triad, a minor triad, a major triad, and an augmented triad. Furthermore, it is possible to arrange four mutually exclusive triads in a continuous chain of major and minor thirds, forming a chord of the minor 23rd, e.g., F-sharp major, E major, D minor, C minor in an ascending series. This is the unique solution of this particular problem. The symmetry of these arrangements is extraordinary. These findings were first published in 1947 in Nicolas Slonimsky's *Thesaurus of Scales and Melodic Patterns*, and have been since verified by a digital computer without adding any new solutions.

Far from being sterile excogitations, the theory of mutually exclusive triads has had its practical application long before it was explicitly formulated. A passage including four mutually exclusive triads occurs in the concluding section of Debussy's *Prélude à l'Après-midi d'un Faune* (E major, C, minor, D major, B-flat minor, with the melody descending chromatically from G-sharp down to F).

The method of composing with 12 tones related only to one another did not remain a rigid dogma. Its greatest protagonists, besides Schoenberg himself, were his disciples Alban Berg and Anton von Webern. Somewhat frivolously, they have been described as the Vienna Trinity, with Schoenberg the Father, Berg the Son, and Webern the Holy Ghost. Both Berg and Webern introduced considerable innovations into the Schoenbergian practice. While Schoenberg studiously avoided triadic constructions, Berg used the conjunct series of alternating minor and major triads capped by three whole tones as the principal subject of his last work, the Violin Concerto (1935). Schoenberg practically excluded symmetric intervallic constructions and sequences, but Berg inserted, in his opera *Lulu*, a dodecaphonic episode built on two mutually exclusive whole-tone scales. Webern dissected the 12-tone series into autonomous sections of 6, 4, or 3 units in a group, and related them individually to one another by inversion, retrograde, and inverted retrograde. This fragmentation enabled him to make use of canonic imitation much more freely than would have been possible according to the strict Schoenbergian doctrine.

The commonly used term for dodecaphonic music in German is Zwölftonmusik. In American usage it was translated literally as 12-tone music, but English music theorists strenuously objected to this terminology, pointing out that a tone is an acoustical phenomenon and that dodecaphony deals with the arrangement of written notes, and that it should be consequently called 12-note music. In Italy the method became known as *Dodecafonia* or *Musica dodecafonica*. Incidentally, the term *Dodecafonia* was first used by the Italian music scholar Domenico Alaleona in his article "L'armonia modernissima" published in *Rivista Musicale* in 1911, but it was applied there in the sense of total chromaticism as an extension of Wagnerian harmony.

The proliferation of dodecaphony in Italy was as potent as it was unexpected, considering the differences between Germanic and Latin cultures, the one introspective and speculative, the other humanistic and practical. Luigi Dallapiccola was one of the earliest adepts, but he liberalized Schoenberg's method and admitted tonal elements. In his opera *Il Prigioniero*, written in 1944, he made use of four mutually exclusive triads.

The greatest conquest of Schoenberg's method was the totally unexpected conversion of Igor Stravinsky whose entire aesthetic code had seemed to stand in opposition to any predetermined scheme of composition; yet he adopted it when he was already in his seventies. Many other composers of world renown turned to dodecaphonic devices as a thematic expedient without full utilization of the four basic forms of the tone-row. Béla Bartók made use of a 12-tone melody in his Second

Violin Concerto, but he modified its structure by inner permutations within the second statement of the tone-row. Ernest Bloch, a composer for whom the constrictions of modern techniques had little attraction, made use of 12-tone subjects in his *Sinfonia Breve* and in his last String Quartets. English composers who have adopted the technique of 12-tone composition with various degrees of consistency are Michael Tippett, Lennox Berkeley, Benjamin Frankel, Humphrey Searle, and Richard Rodney Bennett. William Walton makes use of a 12-tone subject in the fugal finale of his Second Symphony. Benjamin Britten joined the dodecaphonic community by way of tonality. In his expressionist opera *The Turn of the Screw*, he adopts a motto of alternating perfect fifths and minor thirds (or their respective inversions), aggregating to a series of 12 different notes. The Spanish composer Roberto Gerhard, who settled in England, wrote in a fairly strict dodecaphonic idiom. In France the leader of the dodecaphonic school was René Leibowitz, who also wrote several books on the theory of 12-tone composition. Wladimir Vogel, a Russian-born composer of German parentage, making his home in Switzerland, adopted Schoenberg's method in almost all of his works. The Swiss composer Frank Martin extended the principles of dodecaphonic writing to include a number of tonal and modal ramifications.

In America Schoenberg's method found a fertile ground, not only among his students but also among composers who had pursued quite different roads. Roger Sessions, Virgil Thomson, and David Diamond followed Schoenberg's method with varying degrees of fidelity. Aaron Copland used the dodecaphonic technique in some of his chamber music works; in the orchestral compositions entitled *Connotations* commissioned for the opening concert of Lincoln Center in New York in 1962, he applied the totality of dodecaphony to characterize the modern era of music. Walter Piston interpolated a transitional 12-tone passage in his ballet suite *The Incredible Flutist.* He resisted integral dodecaphony until his septuagenarian calendae, when in his Eighth Symphony he adopted Schoenberg's method in all its orthodoxy. Leonard Bernstein inserted a 12-tone series in the score of his *Age of Anxiety* to express inner agitation and anguished expectancy of the music. Samuel Barber made an excursion into the dodecaphonic field in a movement of his Piano Sonata. Gian Carlo Menotti turned dodecaphony into parody in his opera *The Last Savage* to illustrate the decadence of modern civilization into which the hero was unexpectedly catapulted from his primitivistic habitat.

In Soviet Russia dodecaphony still remains officially unacceptable as a "formalistic" device. (In a speech delivered in Moscow on 8 March 1963, Nikita Khrushchev, then prime minister of the Soviet Union, observed: "They call it dodecaphony, but we call it cacophony.") Nevertheless, some blithe spirits of the young Soviet generation, among them Andrei Volkonsky, Valentin Silvestrov, and Sergei Slonimsky, have written and published works in the 12-tone idiom.

The following is a summation of theoretical postulates, subsidiary lemmata, and practical usages of dodecaphonic techniques:

(1) The generating dodecaphonic series must be constructed in such a way as to establish a strong mutual valence of the component members, relating them only to one another in accordance with Schoenberg's prescription, and avoiding any suggestion of chordal derivation, particularly that of a triad nature.

(2) Intervals most suitable for the construction of a viable series are those that carry no tonal affiliation, with particular reference for the major seventh, the minor ninth, and the tritone. Since the intervallic difference between the major seventh and the tritone is a perfect fourth and the difference between the minor ninth and the tritone is a perfect fifth, these differential intervals have acquired a peculiar structural importance in dodecaphonic music, provided they do not appear poised strategically in the potential relationship of the tonic and dominant, or tonic and subdominant. Melodic successions of perfect fourths or perfect fifths are favored since they tend towards atonal asymptotes. Historically, such quartal and quintal progressions led to the distinctive evolution of atonal patterns preceding the formation of strictly dodecaphonic conformations.

(3) Identical intervals between successive pairs of thematic tones are to be used with circumspection so as not to impair the individuality of members of the tone-row and prevent their degeneration and entropic coalescence into chromatic or diatonic scales or into easily decipherable chordal combinations.

(4) Although the original tone-row must be stated in full in the exposition, immediate repetition of a single tone in the series is not to be regarded as a disruptive factor, for such repetition may be simply a synonym for a rhythmic prolongation.

(5) Since the concept of tonality is irrelevant to dodecaphonic music, the key signature is automatically eliminated. For the same reason, chromatic alterations pertinent to tonal usages and modulation are reduced to their simplest enharmonic equivalents; double-sharps and double-flats are completely eliminated. Some dodecaphonic composers insist on prefixing every note with a sharp, flat, or natural, but this type of notation is visually distracting and wasteful.

(6) Functional and operative equivalence of melody, harmony, and counterpoint is of fundamental importance to the dodecaphonic techniques and constitutes its most innovative feature; thus the 12 tones of the series may be distributed either horizontally in melodic lines, vertically in harmonic columns, or diagonally in contrapuntal formations, becoming different dimensions of a unified dodecaphonic space.

(7) Triadic chordal formations are unacceptable in vertical constructions as well as in horizontal melodies. Major triads, particularly in root positions, are inadmissible; their inversions are to be avoided in conspicuous positions. Only slightly less objectionable are minor triads in root positions, but inversions of minor triads in an atonal context are often tolerated. Explicit dominant-seventh chords, implying as they do the presence of the leading tone, are incompatible with the atonal essence of dodecaphony. Similarly obnoxious are diminished-seventh chords because of their connotations as leading-tone harmonies and also because of their uniform intervallic structure.

(8) PANDIATONICISM and POLYTONALITY have no place in the dodecaphonic vocabulary on account of their tonal derivation. Generally speaking, acoustical euphony, inflated sonorities, and facile fluidity of harmonic progressions are contrary to dodecaphonic aesthetics; any external effects of a melodious or harmonious nature are in conflict with the austere spirit and philosophical severity of the serial designs.

(9) Although the fundamental series and its derivations are available in 12 transpositions, such exhaustive utilization of serial materials is rarely found in actual works. Paradoxically, the most favored transpositions, particularly in sections corresponding to recapitulation in classical forms, stand in a quartal-quintal relationship, demonstrating once more the strength of the classical legacy in dodecaphonic composition. One would expect frequent transpositions at a tritone, but such is not the case, because the tritone is apt to be of strategic use in the original series, and would duplicate itself in such a transposition.

(10) The formal structure of works written in the 12-tone idiom is remarkably conservative, following the classical models of variations, passacaglia, prelude, suite, or serenade. The most striking instance of this classical consciousness is the organization of Berg's expressionistic opera *Lulu*, a definitely serial work, which nevertheless contains individual sections bearing titles of Baroque forms. Variations are especially congenial to dodecaphonic organization, with the 12-tone row representing the theme and the retrograde, inversion, and inverted retrograde being the three basic variations.

(11) Large forms, such as sonatas and symphonies, are not suited to dodecaphonic treatment owing to the essentially tonal thematic relationship between the exposition, the development, and the recapitulation. For similar reasons, dodecaphonic treatment cannot be applied to fugal forms. Canonic imitation is possible when the 12-tone row is fragmented into subdivisions of 3, 4, or 6 notes each, as in some works by Anton von Webern, where such infradodecaphonic segments stand in a

structural symmetric relationship of inverted and retrograde correspondence to one another.

(12) Polymetric and polyrhythmic developments are rarely encountered in dodecaphonic compositions. Binary and ternary time signatures of the classical type are prevalent, while compound meters are rare. Triplets, quintuplets, and other groups of prime divisions of note values are virtually absent because of the difficulty of fitting such groups into the serial melodic-harmonic scheme. Certain rhythmic predilections may be noted, especially the "Schoenberg Sigh," consisting of a short note on the strong beat immediately followed by an unstressed long note.

(13) In orchestration, traditional scoring prevails. There is no inclination to introduce exotic or unusual instruments, the flexaton in the score of Schoenberg's *Variations for Orchestra* is an exception. Special percussion effects are alien to the spirit of dodecaphonic music. On the other hand, there is a great variety of sound-color (*Klangfarbe*), with a fine gradation of dynamic elements.

(14) Historically, aesthetically, and structurally, 12-tone music is an evolutionary product of the ultra-chromatic modalities of the post-Wagnerian school of composition. The algorithms of chromatic convergence and divergence in dodecaphonic harmony are common. An experimental proof of this evolutionary origin of dodecaphonic melody and harmony may be provided by a calculated cancellation of a minimal number of sharps or flats, never exceeding a shift of a semitone, with the resulting product being an essentially diatonic composition with functional chromatic passing notes. Conversely, a simple diatonic melody may be metamorphosed into a dodecaphonic series provided that invariance of the vectorial factor is observed, so that the directional intervallic design remains unaltered. Repeated notes in the original diatonic melody can be replaced by their immediate neighbors. Operating according to these procedures, the Viennese melody *Ach du lieber Augustin*, the initial refrain of which happens to contain 12 notes if the last repeated note is omitted, can be transmuted dodecaphonically according to the following formula, in which the capital letters represent the notes of the original tune, ascending intervals are designated by the plus sign, descending intervals by the minus sign, and the numbers are semitone units: G, A, G + 1, F + 1, E + 1, C + 2, C + 1, D + 2, G + 4, G + 3, E – 1, C. It is to be observed that in this case a conscious effort has been made to retain the first and last notes of the original melody, thus preserving an explicit dominant-tonic relationship.

(15) The hereditary characteristics of the dodecaphonic techniques strongly point to their ultimate classical origins. The very foundation of the thematic arrangements in inversions and retrograde forms is an old classical and even pre-classical method of varying a thematic subject. Furthermore, there seems to be a tendency in the works of Schoenberg, Berg, and Webern to extend the field of classical devices, particularly in the use of ostinati composed of a segment of the 12-tone row. Thus the tolerance of an immediate repetition of a thematic tone is extended to the repetition of a thematic fragment.

In view of the possibility of such dodecaphonic self-pollination, there is no reason to fear that dodecaphonic composition would degenerate into an endless permutation of the available 479,000,600 combinations resulting from the factorial algorithm (12!). The second and the third generations of composers of 12-tone music have devised other methods of serial construction, the most interesting of them being a sort of dodecaphonic amputation, which reduces the 12-tone row to a hendecaphonic or decaphonic group of thematic notes. An attractive resource is to leave the amputated member of the series completely out of the account until the very end of a composition, when it would suddenly appear like a *tonus ex machina* and, suspended in a protracted fermata, would assert itself as a triumphantly recessive prodigal tonic.

Duodrama. Duodrama is a modern type of dramatic presentation in which only two actors conduct a dialogue, usually reciting their reciprocal experiences retrospectively without coming to a dramatic clash. It lends itself naturally to chamber opera.

Electronic Music. Electronic music was revealed to the world on 5 August 1920 when the Russian engineer and cello player Leon Theremin gave a demonstration of his *Thereminovox* at the Moscow Technological Institute. The apparatus consisted of a set of cathode tubes, a vertical antenna, and a metal arc; the sound was produced heterodynamically by the movement of the right hand which changed the electric potential in the area, creating a differential tone which determined the height of pitch. The left hand manipulated the field in the vicinity of the metal arc, regulating the power and the timbre of the sound. In constructing this instrument Theremin seemed to carry out Lenin's dictum that "socialism is proletarian dictatorship plus electrification." Theremin's invention was followed by a number of electronic instruments, among which the most successful was *Les Ondes Martenot*, a keyboard instrument for which a number of modern French composers wrote special works. In Germany, Joerg Mager constructed an electronic instrument which he called *Sphärophon*, and later developed other models, *Partiturophon* and *Kaleidophon*. A more practical and a more successful electronic instrument was *Trautonium* manufactured by Friedrich Trautwein; Hindemith wrote some music for it. Oscar Sala introduced some innovations into the *Trautonium* in an electronic organ which he called *Mixtur-Trautonium*.

Unlimited musical horizons opened to electronic music with the introduction of synthesizers, capable of producing any frequency with the utmost precision and distributing the relative strength of the overtones so as to create any desired instrumental timbre. With the aid of synthesizers it becomes possible to construct scales of any number of equal degrees. Among the capacities of the modern synthesizer is the reproduction of a recorded composition at any speed without altering the pitch. No problem of articulation arises, for the generation of the sound is electronic, completely independent of all mechanical elements. In 1969 an American engineer, providentially named Moog, perfected a portable synthesizer which advanced the techniques of electronic music further. The *Moog*, as it came to be called, showed promise of becoming the household instrument of the second half of the 20th century.

Electronic music requires special notation. One of the earliest attempts at a practical system was made in 1937 by Percy Grainger in his *Free Music* for 4 electronic instruments constructed by Theremin, indicating pitch and dynamic intensities in a four-part score on graph paper.

Elegant Variation. In his *Modern English Usage*, Fowler describes frivolous verbal substitutions as elegant variations. The phrase is suitable, with the application of similar gentle scorn, to some musical procedures. Variations that vary for the sake of variance, with an objective of sophisticated elegance of expression, are as offensive in their tautological and often teratological variety as their counterparts in literary diction. Reger's *Variations on a Theme by Mozart* are typical examples of elegant variation, turgid in reference, redundant in treatment. On the other hand, Rachmaninoff's 18th variation in his *Rhapsody on a Theme of Paganini* is both elegant and varied, for it represents an exact inversion of the minor triadic theme, resulting in a completely transformed, yet morphologically congruent melody, in which the ascending minor triadic figure of the theme becomes a descending major triadic figure.

Enharmonic Ambivalence. The Janus-like nature of an enharmonic tone, performing two different functions at a modulatory junction, opens the portals of chromatic modulation and establishes a democratic omnivalence of the 12 different tones in dodecaphonic melody and harmony. In this view, chromatic harmony is a functional derivative of enharmonic ambivalence.

Entropy. The luxuriant development of chromatic harmony and the concomitant equalization of enharmonic pairs may be described as musical entropy, in which the component thematic particles become evenly distributed in melody and harmony. In physics, entropy signalizes the dissipation of KINETIC ENERGY, the neutralization of electric potentials, and an ultimate thermodynamic stability of inertial matter. The pessimistic cosmology that postulates the eventual end in a total passivity of the universe does not, however, constitute a categorical imperative for composers. Nothing prevents them from reversing the process of entropy and reinstating the primacy of selected modalities. Verdi said: "Torniamo all'antico: sarà un progresso."

Environment. The concept of musical environment embraces the totality of technical resources. Ideally, the function of a composer is to establish a favorable environment for these techniques, and apply powerful detergents to remove the accumulated tonal impurities. Particularly toxic is chromatic supererogation; conversely, a fine atonal work may suffer from excessive triadic infusion. The environment also includes the parameters of VECTORIALISM; spatial arrangement of instruments on the stage is clearly environmental in its function. In this larger sense, the function of environment comprises not only every technical aspect of musical composition but also the conditions of the performance itself. In a more literal sense, certain composers of the AVANT-GARDE have created works which, in whole or in part, are literal transliterations of geographical environments, frequently with an artful highlighting of indigenous sounds.

Ethnic Resources. National musical cultures have developed from two distinct resources: the ethnic legacy and universally adopted techniques of composition. When Villa-Lobos was asked "What is folklore?" he replied, "I am folklore!" By this declaration he meant to say that in his original melodic inventions he gave expression to the artistic consciousness of the Brazilian people. In his *Bachianas brasileiras*, Bachian counterpoint gives ancillary service to ethnic Brazilianism. Charles Ives created single-handedly a modern American idiom that employs ethnic resources in a perfect SYNCRETISM of substance and technique. In Russia, the primacy of ethnic resources is maintained partly by the national spirit of the people and partly by the ideological principles of SOCIALIST REALISM which prescribes the realistic style of music within the framework of national modalities.

Ethnic musical materials are not necessarily incompatible with modern techniques. Various transmutations have occurred in modern works. It is possible, for example, to arrange a popular tune dodecaphonically by applying various intervallic extensions and compressions, while retaining the vectorial parameters of the original melody. Perhaps the most congenial modern technique in making use of ethnic resources is PANDIATONICISM, in which the tonal functions are preserved and enhanced.

Etiology. The study of causation, or etiology, is of importance not only in medicine and physics, but also in the fine arts. Particularly informing is the etiology of ultra-modern music which is often likened by hostile observers to a symptom of mass dyscrasia. But to its adepts NEW MUSIC is the revelation of a superior psyche. Dostoyevsky, who suffered from epilepsy, advances the daring notion that during an epileptic *grand mal* the mind penetrates the ultimate mysteries of life and death. Similarly, the manifestations of the musical AVANT-GARDE, whether in the popular or technically complex field, are to their participants the proleptic vistas of the new universal art. Schoenberg, more than any other composer, endured endless abuse on the part of uncomprehending critics, but he never doubted the correctness of his chosen path. Edgar Varèse, who was similarly abused, wrote in a personal letter in 1931: "I know where I am going, and what will follow. My plan is clearly drawn, its development logical, its result assured." From the perspective of history, both Schoenberg and Varèse proved right. The etiology of their genius is a lesson for the future.

Euphony. Etymologically, euphony implies a happy sound, but it is not necessarily synonymous with consonant harmony. A succession of dissonances, if they follow a natural tonal sequence, may sound entirely euphonious to the ear, while a progression of disembodied open fifths or disemboweled multiple octaves, theoretically consonant, could register as uneuphonious and unsettling. Psychological apperception is the determining factor in this aural impression. Generally speaking, soft dissonances are tolerated better than loud consonances. Even more decisive is the factor of linear euphony. A single line of an atonal melody impresses an untutored ear as an unacceptable dissonance, even though no simultaneous complex of sounds is involved. If an atonal melody were to be performed at a very slow tempo with long silences between the individual notes, no linear disharmony could then result. But the faster the tempo, the more disruptive to the peace of mind does an atonal melody become. It should be remembered that the word *harmonia* meant a melody in ancient Greek music. A rapid succession of tones unconnected by a uniform tonality will appear as a meaningless jumble of notes to an inexperienced listener. On the other hand, a musician trained in the art of listening to serial music will accept atonal melodies as legitimate expressions of a musical sentiment. The linearity of melody depends exclusively on the instant dampening of a sound in the cochlea without a tinnitus, but the memory of the previous sound persists, much in the manner that the retina of the eye retains the static images of a cinematographic film. It would be interesting to speculate on the possible course of music as an art if the cochlea, too, possessed the ability to retain sounds for a fraction of a second. Suffice it to say that all music, vocal, instrumental, or percussive, would then become inherently polyphonic.

Evolution and Devolution. In a famous definition, Herbert Spencer describes the process of evolution as an integration of matter and concomitant dissipation of motion, during which matter passes from an indefinite, incoherent homogeneity to a definite, coherent heterogeneity. He specifically included music in this process, with reference to the increasing complexity resulting from rhythmic changes and modulatory progressions, its specialization, and its gradual differentiation from poetry, drama, and dance. In recent times, however, the evolutionary process has been reversed. Once more, as in antiquity, music has entered into an intimate association with the theater and dance in the modern genre of MIXED MEDIA. ALEATORY procedures have accentuated the devolution of music by increasing the element of homogeneity and the degree of randomness of distribution of constructive elements.

It may be argued that devolution was unavoidable since the integration of music in the Spencerian sense has achieved its maximum of coherence in such techniques as the dodecaphonic method, and that a recoil from the stone wall of determinism reversed the evolutionary process, resulting in an aesthetic passivity, in which kinetic energy is reduced to zero. In the practice of the AVANT-GARDE, the demobilization of technical resources has reached the point of melorhythmic asceticism, with only a few different notes being used in an entire work, as though emulating the legendary philosopher Cratylus who spent his declining years by moving the index finger of his right hand to and fro in front of his nose in the firm belief that this motion was the only demonstrable truth.

Experimental Music. All music is experimental; tradition is merely a congealed experiment. Chromatic harmony was experimental in Wagner's time, and its ultimate dodecaphonic development became the most important type of experimental music of the 20th century. But perhaps the most literally correct application of experimental music is represented by ALEATORY operations, in which the manipulator merely sets the scene of action and nature supplies an experimental answer. With every turn of the aesthetic wheel, experimental music was decried and deprecated by the adepts of the preceding prevalent style as repugnant to normal senses. In the second half of the 20th century, experimental music finally moved into its proper enclave, that of the laboratory, where composers and experimenters conducted their research with electronic instruments and digital computers. There is a danger, however, that an imaginative computer may be hampered in its inventive productions by the limitations of the musical engineer who would program the data so as to adapt them to a preordained order, and in so doing would convert the machine into a mere servant. In one of such man-made pseudo-computerized compositions, the ending consists of a protracted C major coda which no computer in its right mental circuit would possibly turn out on its own accord. The only valid programming of musical composition is that generated by a collection of random numbers ejaculated like so many embryonic sea-horses out of their male parent's pouch, to be translated into notes and rhythms according to a predetermined code.

Expressionism. Expressionism stands in a reciprocal relationship to IMPRESSIONISM, as its functional and psychological counterpart. IMPRESSIONISM derives its source of inspiration from external sources, whereas Expressionism conjures up its images in the inner world of the human psyche and exteriorizes its states as an intimate subjective report. IMPRESSIONISM tends to be pictorial and exotic; Expressionism is introspective and metaphysical. Impressionistic literature, art, and music are easily projected outside; Expressionism is an arcane medium, born in the deepest recesses of the psychic complex and cannot easily be translated into the common language of the arts. The receiver of colorful images of Impressionist art or music has the means of comparing the precise reality with the artist's impressions of it. No such scale of comparison is available to an outside recipient of Expressionist art, for it is a product of the artist's dream in which the dreamer experiences both shock and surprise as both the author and the victim of his own dreams. Because of this duality of the Expressionistic process, the art of Expressionism itself suffers from the trauma of illogic; it is characterized by the breakdown of illation and by the disruption of the consequential processes of psychic transmission. The unreality of Expressionist drama, poetry, painting, and music is the greatest obstacle for general comprehension. But once the curtain is removed and the secret images of a dreamer reach the observer in the form of poetry, art, or music, Expressionism becomes a universal medium of mass communication and the greatest multiplier of artistic emotion.

It is natural that because of the basic antinomy between the sources of IMPRESSIONISM and Expressionism, each should generate a distinctive musical language. IMPRESSIONISM thrives on equilibrated euphony of harmonious dissonances, while Expressionism prefers the harsh syntax of ATONALITY. The coloristic opulence of Impressionist music is obtained through the expansion of tonal materials into the spacious structures of resonant harmonies and exotic scales. Expressionism, on the other hand, communicates its deep-seated anxieties through chromatic congestion and atonal dispersion. IMPRESSIONISM builds its thematic contents on fluctuating modality, block harmonies, and parallel progressions of triadic formations. Expressionism rejects modality, tonality, and all diatonic textures. Its melodies are constructed parabolically, away from a putative tonic. In its evocation of the classical past, IMPRESSIONISM integrates the diatonic materials into the enhanced edifices of PANDIATONICISM. The harmonic idiom of Expressionism is formed by the superposition of fourths and fifths. Progressions of consecutive perfect fourths or fifths result in the formation of 12 different notes in a panchromatic complex, preparing the foundation of the method of composing with 12 tones related only to one another, as formulated by Arnold Schoenberg.

There are also profound differences in the historic, cultural, and geographic factors in the development of IMPRESSIONISM and Expressionism. IMPRESSIONISM is Gallic, Expressionism Germanic. The French syllabification of IMPRESSIONISTIC poetry is a paradigm of euphonious instrumentation, with the vowels acquiring specific weights and distinctive colors. The German texts of Expressionist songs offer no sonorous gratification of resonant vocables, but in their guttural strength seem to deepen the penetration of the philosophical and often mystical notions underlying the words.

Though IMPRESSIONISM in music is a close counterpart of pictorial art, no Impressionist composer of any stature has ever tried his hand at painting pictures. Expressionism is basically a psychic development with far less aesthetic contact with painting, and yet composers of the Expressionist school, notably Schoenberg and Alban Berg, possessed a striking talent for painting in the Expressionist style. Jef Golyscheff, the composer of early atonal music, emigrated to Brazil and became an Expressionist painter. Carl Ruggles, an American composer who developed a sui generis Expressionist style in an atonal idiom, abandoned composition entirely and devoted himself to abstract painting.

Fasciculation. In view of the vagueness of such terms as section, part, division, subdivision, period, phrase, etc., it might be useful to introduce into musical nomenclature the term fascicle to designate a self-sufficient fragment of a musical work. Particularly, it is useful in application to serial music. In dodecaphonic exposition, fascicle I, fascicle II, fascicle III, and fascicle IV would indicate the four forms of the basic tone-row. In NEO-CLASSICAL compositions fasciculation may easily replace the conventional Baroque designations of sequences, modulatory digressions, and the like. This type of nomenclature may also contribute to the analytical clarity of theoretical discussion.

Fetishes and Taboos. In the inexorable course of history and of the arts, fetishes of yesterday become taboos of tomorrow. The following modernistic fetishes of the recent musical past have become taboos:

(1) The diminished-seventh chord, once favored by Italian opera composers, the *Accorde di Stupefazione*, used to melodramatize the high points in operatic action. Verdi, who was responsible for some of the most effective applications of this "Chord of Stupefaction," often in parallel chromatic progressions, in his own operas, issued a stern warning to young composers not to abuse it. No self-respecting composer of today would resort to such unsophisticated practices, except for musical persiflage.

(2) Tonal sequences, particularly those rising or descending by degrees, known as Rosalias, after an old popular Italian ballad, "Rosalie, mia cara." Indeed, sequences of any kind have virtually disappeared from 20th-century music.

(3) The WHOLE-TONE SCALE, once a fetish of IMPRESSIONISM, has now sunk into noxious desuetude as a cinematic effect used to portray strutting Nazis, mad scientists, or schizoid females on the sound track.

(4) Parallel progressions of major-ninth chords and consecutive formations of second inversions of major triads at intervals of minor thirds, one of the most prized formulas of IMPRESSIONISM.

(5) The "Pétrouchka Chord," also known also as the "Parisian Chord," consisting of two major triads at the distance of a tritone. This early instance of BITONALITY, which became a fetish of modern French music in the second quarter of the 20th century, has been disenfranchised and relegated to the category of FRAUDULENT MODERNISM. There are even signs and tokens on the firmament that the sacrosanct fetish of the 20th century, the DODECAPHONIC method of composition, is on the point of deciduous decay, losing its dodecuple integrity and degenerating into the lipogrammatic hendecaphonic or decaphonic series.

Formalism. The term Formalism has acquired a specific pejorative meaning in Soviet aesthetics, as a method inimical to the essence of desirable art. The *Encyclopedic Music Dictionary*, published in Moscow in 1966, defines formalism as follows:

"Formalism represents an artificial separation of form from content, and the attribution to formal elements of self-sufficient primary values to the detriment of musical content. . . . In contemporary aesthetics, Formalism becomes a method of art hostile to realism and cultivated especially by the adepts of MODERNISM. Formalism is based on the theory of art for art's sake, counterposing the artist to society and art itself to life, seeking to create an artistic form detached from objective reality. The governing precepts of Formalism are the negation of ideological and realistic content of a work of art, a construction of arbitrary new forms, combined with the denial of national cultural heritage. In the final analysis, Formalism results in the abolition of artistic imagery and disintegration of formal coherence. In musical practice, Formalism rejects the ideational and emotional musical values and denies the capacity of a musical work to reflect reality. Proponents of Formalism attempt to justify their fallacious doctrine by pointing out the specific nature of music as an art lacking the external connection with the world of real objects, such as is present in painting or sculpture, and intrinsically incapable of conveying a concrete narrative characteristic of literature. The aesthetic teaching of Marxism refutes Formalism by a scientific approach to music as a special form of social ideology. The reactionary theories of Formalism are assiduously cultivated in books and articles by the apologists of musical MODERNISM. The struggle for the correct formulation of SOCIALIST REALISM leads to the removal of Formalism from its pedestal. One should not confuse Formalism, however, with genuine individual originality or with true innovation in the field of musical forms and in the inner substance of a composition, which constitute an unalienable part of authentic realistic art."

Formant. Formant is an acoustical term, indicating the relative strength of partial overtones that determines the timbre of a musical instrument. In ultra-modern nomenclature, a formant is the catalytic element that forms, deforms, and transforms a given timbre into another by means of electronic manipulation.

Fraudulent Modernism. Commercially successful composers of marketable semi-classical music, eager to gain aesthetic equality with their more sophisticated counterparts, like to inject dissonant notes into their ABECEDARIAN and often ANALPHABETIC productions; proudly, they exhibit pieces using 12 different notes in a more or less chromatic order to earn membership in socially distinguished DODECAPHONIC circles. A combination of emaciated melodies in a spurious atonal manner and dietetic harmonies heavily spiced with discordant irrelevancies is the essence of Fraudulent Modernism. Its adepts often parade in panel discussions, glibly bandying about mispronounced names of the latest celebrities of the AVANT-GARDE. Fraudulent Modernism fails because of the technical inadequacy of its practitioners and because of their naïve belief that wrong notes are the credentials of advanced sophistication.

Frugal Ankyloglossia. Art thrives on economy of means, but modernistic frugality must not be allowed to reach the point of tonal ankyloglossia. The criterion is a freedom of expression without cacuminal retroflection.

Furniture Music. In his sustained effort to reduce music to its most menial level, Erik Satie was prompted to inaugurate a demonstration of *Musique d' ameublement*, which he defined as "new music played during intermission at theatrical events or at a concert, designed to create a certain ambience." At an actual performance at the Paris Art Gallery, Satie placed his musicians in separate groups, and urged the public to treat them as functional objects, to speak loudly and not to listen with professional attention. The performers were free to play anything they wished regardless of the repertoire selected by their confreres.

Futurism. Futurism is a modern movement in the arts that emerged in Italy early in the 20th century, under the aegis of the Italian poet Marinetti. Its musical credo was formulated by Balilla Pratella in his *Manifesto of Futurist Musicians* issued in Milan on 11 October 1910 and supplemented by a *Technical Manifesto of Futurist Music* of 11 March 1911. On 11 March 1913 Luigi Russolo responded with his own *Futurist Manifesto*, significantly addressed to Pratella, the "grande musicista futurista." In these declarations the Italian Futurists proclaimed their complete disassociation from classical, romantic, and IMPRESSIONIST music and announced their aim to build an entirely new music inspired by the reality of life in the new century, with the machine as the source of inspiration. And since modern machines were most conspicuous by the noise they made, Pratella and Russolo created a new art of noises, *L'arte dei rumori*. Russolo designed special noise instruments and subdivided them into six categories, including shrieks, groans, clashes, explosions, etc. His instruments were rudimentary and crude, with amplification obtained by megaphones, but there is no denying that the Futurists provided a prophetic vision of the electronic future of fifty years later. It is interesting to note that most Futurist musicians and poets were also painters. Their pictures, notably those of Russolo, emphasized color rather than machine-like abstractions, and generally approximated the manner of Abstract EXPRESSIONISM. In the music by Pratella and others we find a profusion of modern devices of their Futurist day, with a foremost place given to the WHOLE-TONE SCALE. The Futurists gave monody preference over polyphony, and steady rhythm to asymmetry. The future of the Futurists appears passé, but they opened the gates to the experimenters of the actual chronological future, which none of them lived to witness.

Game Music. Games of musical compositions, in which cards, each containing a musical phrase, are put together according to special rules, are of considerable antiquity. One such game, *Musikalisches Würfelspiel*, was put on the market in London in 1806 and was announced as "Mozart's musical game, enclosed in an elegant box instructing in a system of easy composition by mechanical means of an unlimited number of waltzes, rondos, horn pipes, reels and minuets." The attribution to Mozart is spurious, but the game itself has a certain ingenuity. The players were to throw a pair of dice, and the number indicated the particular card containing a musical phrase. Since the sequence was arranged so that each card was interchangeable with other cards containing melodies in approximately the same range set in similar harmonies, there was obviously no danger of running into difficulties. A much more modern conceit was suggested by an English musician William Hayes in his book, *The Art of Composing Music by a Method Entirely New, Suited to the Meanest Capacity*, published in 1751, in which the author, with a rather crude satirical intent, explained the principle of the game: "Take a brush with stiff bristles (like a toothbrush), dip it into an inkwell, and, by scraping the bristles with the finger, spatter with one sweep a whole composition onto the staff paper. You have only to add stems, bar lines, slurs, etc., to make the opus ready for immediate performance. Whole and half-notes are entirely absent, but who cares for sustained tones anyway!" This is indeed a proleptic anticipation of methods of composition used by AVANT-GARDE composers 200 years after the publication of this lively manual.

An interesting modern game can be devised using several sets of dodecaphonic cards, each set containing all 12 notes of the chromatic scale. The deck is shuffled and distributed among players. One after another, the players put down duplicates in their hands and collect a missing note of the next dodecaphonic series from the cards put down by other players. The winner is the player who first assembles all 12 different notes.

The most ambitious musical game of the modern era is *Stratégie* by Iannis Xenakis, first performed at the Venice Festival on 23 April 1963. In it, two conductors lead two different orchestras in two uncoordinated works. At the end, the audience declares the winner, taking into consideration the excellence of each orchestral group, marking points on the scoreboard for most striking rhythms, best color effects, and finest instrumental solos.

Modern scores descriptive of games are numerous. Arthur Honegger wrote a symphonic movement *Rugby*, Arthur Bliss composed a ballet entitled *Checkmate*, Paul Reif selected *Philidor's Defense* as the title of a work for a chamber orchestra, inspired by a chess game played in 1858. Stravinsky portrayed a poker game in his *Jeu de Cartes*, a ballet in three "deals" in which the joker is defeated by a royal flush in hearts. A more abstract score by Stravinsky, *Agon*, also portrays a game. Debussy's ballet score *Jeux* depicts an allegorical game of tennis.

Gauche Dexterity. Satire and burlesque depend for their effect on a deliberate violation of traditional rules of melodic structure, rhythmic symmetry, and harmonic euphony. A sophisticated imitation of such semi-literate gaucherie often becomes an art in itself. Examples are many: Stravinsky reproduces the heterogeneous harmony of the barrel organ in *Pétrouchka*, and Darius Milhaud tonalizes the natural cacophony of a barroom in the score of *Le Boeuf sur le toit*. Erik Satie elevated the dexterity of his gaucherie into a high art of musical persiflage.

Gebrauchsmusik. The term Gebrauchsmusik, or Utilitarian Music, came into vogue shortly after the end of World War I; its earliest mention is found in the German magazine *Signale für die Musikalische Welt* of December 1918. Gebrauchsmusik promoted the utilization of new mechanical instruments, the radio, the phonograph, and music for the films. A variety of Gebrauchsmusik was GEMEINSCHAFTSMUSIK, Community Music, which cultivated choral singing. The term GEMEINSCHAFTSMUSIK was later changed to Sing- und Spielmusik, in the generic category of HAUSMUSIK. Probably the first work written specially for such groups by a modern composer was *Das neue Werk* by Paul Hindemith. Stylistically, Gebrauchsmusik developed a type of modern melody, rhythm, harmony, and orchestration making free use of utilitarian dissonance, polytonal combinations, and polymetric arrangements. An innovation in Gebrauchsmusik is spoken rhythmic song, a variant of SPRECHSTIMME. In opera, the librettos were usually satirical and political, with a radical bent, especially PROLETARIAN MUSIC. From Germany, operatic Gebrauchsmusik was transplanted to America, where economic impoverishment contributed to its popularity. Gebrauchsmusik had little success in Russia, France, or Italy, countries with a rich operatic culture and in which there was no necessity of reducing operatic productions to miniature dimensions. HAUSMUSIK, and Gebrauchsmusik in general, relied on the participation of its audience. Children's music is a natural product of Gebrauchsmusik. Hindemith wrote the first piece of Gebrauchsmusik designed specially for singing and acting by children, *Wir bauen eine Stadt*.

Gemeinschaftsmusik. Gemeinschaftsmusik is a term used by German composers to designate communal singing or playing; although of ancient origin, the practice was popularized as part of the program of HAUSMUSIK, in the generic category of GEBRAUCHSMUSIK.

Gestalt. Gestalt is a fashionable psychological term which, in an attractively misapprehended scientific German nomenclature, connotes an ensemble of apperceptions produced by a series of sensory stimuli. The word, which can be literally translated as form, figure, or appearance, indicates a psychological interaction between the physical nature of a given phenomenon and the inner interpretation of it by a receptive mind. The shape of a white vase against a uniformly black background may be perceived as two human figures facing each other if the symmetric sides of the vase are drawn to resemble silhouettes. In music, Gestalt is capable of many interpretations, of which the most literal is ENHARMONIC AMBIVALENCE, as for instance the perception of a triad as a dissonance in the context of alien harmonies. Thus, if a C major triad is sounded immediately after an unrelated dominant-seventh chord based on E-flat, the ear would demand its resolution into the dissonant syndrome of the preceding dominant-seventh chord. Generally speaking, Gestalt is apprehended as an entire ensemble of musical parameters, comprising form, proportional distribution of consonances and dissonances, diatonic or chromatic tropism, symmetry or asymmetry of melorhythmic figurations, etc.

Graphic Notation. Ever since 1000 A.D. when Guido d'Arezzo drew a line to mark the arbitrary height of pitch, musical notation has been geometric in its symbolism. The horizontal coordinate of the music staff still represents the temporal succession of melodic notes, and the vertical axis indicates the simultaneous use of two or more notes in a chord. Durations have, through centuries of evolution, been indicated by the color and shape of notes and stems to which they were attached. The composers of the AVANT-GARDE, eager to reestablish the mathematical correlation between the coordinates of the musical axes, have written scores in which the duration was indicated by proportional distance between the notes. Undoubtedly such geometrical precision contributes to the audio-visual clarity of notation, but it is impractical in actual usage. A passage in whole-notes or half-notes followed by a section in rapid rhythms would be more difficult to read than the imprecise notation inherited from the past. In orchestral scores, there is an increasing tendency to cut off the inactive instrumental parts in the middle of the page rather than to strew such vacuums with a rash of rests. A graphic system of tablature notation was launched in Holland under the name *Klavarskribo*, an Esperanto word meaning keyboard writing. It has been adopted in many schools in Holland.

New sounds demanded new notational symbols. Henry Cowell, who invented tone-clusters, notated them by drawing thick vertical lines attached to a stem. Similar notation was used for similar effects by the Russian composer Vladimir Rebikov. In his book *New Musical Resources*, Cowell tackled the problem of non-binary rhythmic division and outlined a plausible system that would satisfy this need by using square, triangular, and rhomboid shapes of notes. Alois Hába of Czechoslovakia, a pioneer in microtonal music, devised special notation for quarter-, third-, and sixth-tones.

As long as the elements of pitch, duration, intervallic extension, and polyphonic simultaneity remained in force, the musical staff could accommodate these elements more or less adequately. Then noises were introduced by the Italian Futurists into their works. In his compositions, the Futurist Luigi Russolo drew a network of curves, thick lines, and zigzags to represent each particular noise. But still the measure and the proportional lengths of duration retained their validity. The situation changed dramatically with the introduction of ALEATORY processes and the notion of indeterminacy of musical elements. The visual appearance of aleatory scores assumes the aspect of ideograms. John Cage, in particular, remodeled the old musical notation so as to give improvisatory latitude to the performer. The score of his *Variations I* suggests the track of cosmic rays in a cloud chamber. His *Cartridge Music* looks like an exploding supernova, and his *Fontana Mix* is a projection of irregular curves upon a strip of graph paper. His *Renga* is an orderly conglomeration of 361 fractured drawings from the notebooks on nature, freedom, and civil disobedience of Henry David Thoreau. The Polish AVANT-GARDE composer Krzysztof Penderecki uses various graphic symbols to designate such effects as the highest possible sound on a given instrument, free improvisation within a certain limited range of chromatic notes, or icositetraphonic tone-clusters.

In music for MIXED MEDIA, notation ceases to function per se, giving way to VERBALIZATION or pictorial representation of the actions or psychological factors involved. Indeed, the modern Greek composer Jani Christou introduces the Greek letter *psi* to indicate the psychology of the musical action, with geometric ideograms and masks symbolizing changing mental states ranging from complete passivity to panic. The score of Sylvano Bussotti's chamber mystery, *Passion According to Marquis de Sade*, looks like a Surrealistic painting with musical notes strewn across its path. The British AVANT-GARDE composer Cornelius Cardew draws black and white circles, triangles, and rectangles to indicate musical actions. Iannis Xenakis prefers to use numbers and letters indicating the specific tape recordings to be used in his musical structures. Some composers abandon the problem of notation entirely, recording their inspirations on tape.

The attractiveness of a visual pattern is a decisive factor. The American AVANT-GARDE composer Earle Brown draws linear abstractions of singular geometric excellence. Karlheinz Stockhausen often supplements his analytical charts by elucidatory (or tantalizingly obscurative) annotations.

The chess grandmaster Tarrasch said of a problematical chess move: "If it is ugly, it is bad." *Mutatis mutandis*, the same criterion applies to a composer's musical graph.

Gymnosophistical Homophony. The description Gymnosophist is applied to an Indian sect that flourished about 1,000 A. D. who preached abstinence from carnal delights, refused to wear clothes, and limited themselves to the simplest modes of communication. Etymologically, the word is derived from the Greek roots for "naked" and "wisdom." Archaizing usages and affectation of utmost simplicity in musical composition may well be called Gymnosophistical; naked fifths, in particular, when applied ostentatiously in modern works, creating the impression of luxurious abstemiousness, are Gymnosophistical. Erik Satie, in his sophisticated practice of Gymnosophistical harmonies in such works as *Gymnopédies*, provides a perfect example of the style, deliberately bleak in its renunciation of harmonious carnality and yet thoroughly modern in its invocation of secret rites and suggested aberrations. For different reasons, Stravinsky adopted Gymnosophistical modalities in his neo-Grecian works, as a reaction against the proliferation of colorful sonorities in instrumental music, including his own. Gymnosophistical homophony is a natural medium also for neo-ecclesiastical composition in quintal or quartal gemination.

Happenings. A happening is a colloquial gerund that has assumed a substantive value as a result of collective activities among American actors, painters, poets, and musicians in the 1950s. The word itself was first used in this sense in the 1959 issue of the *Anthologist*, a review published by Rutgers University. It featured an article by Allan Kaprow, teacher of art history at Rutgers, entitled *The Demiurge*, in which he announced his aim of creating an entirely new art. As an illustration he appended the outline of a script, with a caption, "Something to Take Place: A Happening." In a New York art gallery in October 1956, Kaprow and others staged a production under the name "18 Happenings in 6 parts." The audience was distributed in 14 groups seated in chairs at random, and its participation in the action was earnestly solicited. The spectacle was synaesthetic, with sound, multicolored lights, and peripheral tactile and olfactory impressions. There were also "visual poems," of the graffiti type, randomly lettered in crayon on walls and placards, with such communications as "My Toilet is Shared by the Man Next Door who is Italian." The musical part consisted of aleatory superfetations of loudspeaking musical and anti-musical sounds. Activities included various commonplace actions performed with the meaningful air of an artistic act. Kaprow made an ex post facto statement bemoaning his choice of the word "happening" as unfortunate, but conceded that it helped him to achieve an all-embracing inclusivity in describing the uninhibited exhibits of the AVANT-GARDE. In the meantime, "happening" entered the language, penetrating the common speech so deeply that everyday events are often described as happenings simply because they have taken place at all. The term became popular in Europe as Le Happening, El Happening, Il Happening, or Das Happening.

Hausmusik. After a long period of alienation from the masses, modern composers in Germany came to the conviction that music should cease to be a hermetic art for select audiences and should be returned to its source, the home. Hausmusik, as such "home music" became known, was a development parallel to GEBRAUCHSMUSIK. Dissonant harmony and asymmetric rhythms were not excluded, as long as the performance did not present technical difficulties. Usually Hausmusik was written for voices or SPRECHSTIMME, with piano accompaniment and obbligato parts for instruments easy to play, such as recorders, clarinets, and violins.

Hebetude and Lubricity. A recipe for a musical work providing sensory and intellectual gratification is a judicious mixture of dissonant hebetude and euphonious lubricity. As a product of intellectual elucubration, hebetudinous abstruseness results from indiscriminate use of dodecaphonic, hendecaphonic, pandiatonic, or polymodal combinatorialities. Modernistic lubricity, on the other hand, flows from an incontinent evacuation of artificially flavored euphonious fluids sublimated in a feculent plasma. Hebetudinous excogitations by Hesychastically-minded introverts occasionally reveal serendipitous technicalities of interest, as demonstrated by tonal inventions in *Die Maschine* by Fritz Klein, while lubriciously scabrous effluvia of an ABECEDARIAN composer are usually productive of homogeneous sonic matter of glutinous consistency, fetid, infertile, and degenerative.

Hendecaphonic Serialism. With the gradual relaxation of dodecaphonic strictures in the orthodox Schoenbergian doctrine, serial composers began to resort to a lipogrammatic device of omitting a member of a 12-tone subject, reducing the series to a hendecaphonic form, containing only 11 tones. The missing tone, conspicuous by its absence, may be introduced in the coda with a panache suggesting the apparition of an actual tonic.

Hirsute Chromaticism. A judicious mixture of chromatic and diatonic modes in a serial work is entirely valid as a mode, idiom, or style. What cannot be tolerated in a modern composition of any pretensions to self-consistency is the hairy growth of chromatics upon a diatonic or pandiatonic melodic and harmonic surface, with membranous pellicles obscuring the melorhythmic lines without protecting them. When instances of such hirsute chromaticism occur inadvertently, a depilatory agent should be applied in order to restore the basic musical design. At the same time, care should be taken not to fall into the extremes of unaesthetic alopecia.

Homeological Variations. Modern variations are often derived from a subject by topological extensions and compressions of the constituent intervals and rhythms, a process known as homeological. This term denotes the compatibility of geometric figures which can be topologically altered without disrupting the continuity of their perimeters. Thus, a triangle can be stretched or crumpled like rubber and brought into congruity with a square or a circle, but not with a torus which is morphologically non-congruent with triangles, squares, or circles. In modern music, a diatonic melody may be analogously compressed and extended by intervallic changes, but it cannot be converted into a pointillistic configuration or a hocketus, without violating topological laws.

Homonymity. In music, as in verbal communication, identical sounds often acquire different connotations according to the context. For example, *mental process* in anatomy refers not to the state of mind but to the bony promontory that forms the chin, the key word being derived from *mentum*, chin, not from *mens*, mind, while the word *process* comes from proceed in the sense of outgrowth. A C-major chord, if written with an F-flat instead of E, loses its white immaculacy and becomes a dissonant suspension over the A-flat major triad. Homonymity plays a particularly significant role in DODECAPHONIC MUSIC. A segment of a 12-tone series may prove to be homonymous with another form of the same series. This fragmentary replication is of great structural importance in the theory and practice of COMBINATORIALITY.

Hörspiel. In search of a term that would apply to a great variety of musical works, the practitioners of GEBRAUCHSMUSIK in

Germany selected the generic appellation Hörspiel. Literally, Hörspiel means a play for hearing: early on it usually appeared a short composition for a solo instrument, a small instrumental ensemble, or a choral group, and thus was related to the practice of HAUSMUSIK; toward the latter half of the century it became synonymous with diverse works composed for radio broadcast. In its idiom, a Hörspiel should not appear strange to untutored ears, but non-toxic dissonances should not be shunned.

Icositetraphony. As the etymology of the term indicates, icositetraphony deals with music using 24 equal intervals in an octave (*icosi* = 20; *tetra* = 4; *phone* = sound), i.e., in quartertones. A tone-row composed of 24 different notes in quartertones is an icositetraphonic series. In modern works icositetraphony usually occurs in conglomerates, as in the coda of Krzysztof Penderecki's *Threnody for the Victims of Hiroshima* and in Sergei Slonimsky's *Concerto Buffo.*

Illation. In logic and rhetoric, illation is a conclusion drawn from given premises. In music, illation represents a consistent development of thematic ideas, a logical progression from one idea to the next. Illation is particularly important in DODECAPHONIC structures, in which the basic series serves as a postulate from which all subsequent patterns are derived.

Imbricated Counterpoint. Canonic imitation in stretto formation may be described as imbricated counterpoint, because it follows the pattern of roof shingles or tiles, all of the same size and all partly covered by adjacent shingles.

Immaculacy. The irresistible attraction that C major exercises on many modern composers is a curious phenomenon. Scriabin ends his *Poème de l'Extase* with a protracted coda of immaculate C major in a veritable sunburst of white-hot flame on the waves of the luminiferous ether. C major was also the favorite key of Prokofiev, a composer whose aesthetic precepts were diametrically opposed to Scriabin's; to him C major was simply a pianistic convenience lying naturally under the fingers. Pianistically, C major is associated with whiteness, but on many old keyboard instruments the keys of diatonic C major were black. Also pianistic in origin is PANDIATONICISM; a great many pandiatonic constructions in piano works are examples of C major immaculacy. Even Schoenberg, for all of his anti-triadic teachings, succumbed to the temptation: his Piano Concerto ends on an enhanced C major chord.

Impressionism. The term Impressionism was first used in an article by Louis Leroy published in the Paris journal *Charivari* in its issue of 25 April 1874, to characterize the type of painting cultivated by French artists who exhibited at the Paris Salon des Refusés, with specific reference to *Sunrise* by Claude Monet, subtitled "an impression." This painting was Impressionistic in the sense that it brought out the subjective impact of the landscape on the artist, as it registered in his inner eye. Far from being offended by the irony implied in the word Impressionism, the French modernists of the time accepted it as an honorable title. It was not the first time in cultural and political history that a sobriquet intended as a pejorative appellation was elevated to the dignity of a dictionary definition. When the French aristocrats dismissed the Paris revolutionaries as sansculottes, because they did not wear the culottes, or knee breeches, the expression was adopted triumphantly by the populace. When the German Kaiser described the British expeditionary force in World War I as "a contemptible little army," the English gleefully accepted this depreciative nomination, turning its sharp point against the Germans themselves as their vaunted superiority began to crumble. A group of American realistic painters, active in the first decade of the 20th century, was described as the Ashcan School by reactionary critics, and it was under that name that the group had proudly entered the annals of American art. The term Baroque originally meant uncouth, ungainly, or bizarre, but it has risen in its semantical evolution to represent one of the noblest periods in the history of fine arts.

Only slightly less derisive than Impressionism was the term Symbolism, applied to modern French poets whose imagery dealt with symbols rather than with realities. The word Symbolism appeared for the first time in print in the Paris daily *Le Figaro* of 18 September 1886. As Impressionism in art, Symbolism was the product of a reaction against the hegemony of academic realism. The painter Courbet said, "Le réalisme c'est la négation de l'idéal." To poets and painters alike, music was the supreme medium of artistic expression. Paul Verlaine formulated this belief in the famous line, "De la musique avant toute chose." He insisted that words themselves should be selected for the quality of their sound: "Les mots seront choisis en tent que sonores." Gauguin declared that he sought to achieve a musical expression in his exotic paintings: "Je cherche plus la suggestion que la description, comme le fait la musique." Conversely, the spectrum of light appears as a determining factor of musical expression to composers of the Impressionist school. Debussy spoke of "lumière sonore," such as is produced by an analytical diffraction of tones. The constant interchange of auditory and visual aspects in music and in art is illustrated by the titles both of Impressionist paintings and musical compositions. Whistler gave musical captions to his painting-symphonies, *Nocturnes,* while titles of Debussy's works are often taken from painting, *Esquisses, Images.* Poets were apt to speak of music that can be seen and of paintings that can be heard. After hearing Debussy's *Prélude à l'Après-midi d'un Faune,* Stephane Mallarmé, whose poem inspired the work, inscribed the book to Debussy, with a quatrain, which equates word, light and sound in one sensation: "Sylvain d'haleine première/Si ta flûte a réussi/Ouïs toute la lumière/Qu'y soufflera Debussy!" In a modern tale of fantasy a scientist transplants the optical nerve to the ear and the auditory nerve to the eye, so that the human subjects on whom he performed this experiment heard colors and saw tones.

In *Les Fleurs du Mal,* Baudelaire said: "J'aime avec fureur les choses où le son se mêle à la lumière."

The interpenetrability of all senses, including the olfactory and the gustatory, was the dream of poets, artists, and musicians. Baudelaire wrote: "Les parfums, les couleurs et les sons se répondent." In his book *À rebours,* J. K. Huysmans conjures up an organ of liqueurs. As the organist pulls out the stops, each discharges a drop of wine accompanied by the sound of corresponding instrumental color. The clarinet gives the taste of curaçao sec; the oboe serves kummel; for the flute there is anisette; for the trombone gin and whiskey, while the tuba filters strong vodka.

The flight from nominalism among poets, painters, and musicians of France over 100 hundred years ago had a touch of mystical taboo which forbade the naming of the deity in primitive religions. Mallarmé wrote: "To name an object is to suppress three quarters of the enjoyment of a poem; to divine gradually, to suggest that is to dream." In order to be effective, art had to be a matrix of uncertainties. The French poet Charles Brugnot wrote the lines which Ravel selected as an epigraph for his piano suite *Gaspard de la nuit*: "Je croyais entendre/une vague harmonic enchanter mon sommeil/et près de moi s'épandre un murmure pareil/aux chants entrecoupés d'une voix triste et tendre."

Above all, Impressionism should not serve a utilitarian purpose or perform a function. Henri de Regnier spoke of "le plaisir délicieux et toujours nouveau d'une occupation inutile." Ravel put these words in the score of his *Valses nobles et sentimentales.*

If the aim of Impressionism is to suggest uncertain images, then such images must be clothed in uncertain sounds; in music such sounds are dissonances. The yearning desire for dissonant harmonies can be traced back to Horace's pithy oxymoron, "Concordia discors," and to Keats, who said that "discords make the sweetest airs." Verlaine was explicit when he spoke poetically of "accords harmonieusement dissonants." Dissonances are indeed harmonious in Impressionist music as discordant tones are suspended in airy equilibrium above the sustained basses that support columns of natural overtones.

Walter Pater said: "Impressionism is a vivid personal reflection of a fugitive effect." Spectral evanescence lies in the nature of Impressionist art and music. Sounds that suggest perfumes are ephemeral; they shimmer, they waver, they vanish. Impressionist melodies are transparencies of a magic lantern; the images succeed each other without organic cohesion. There is no thematic development; the progress of the music depends on contrasts of contiguous thematic statements and colorful juxtapositions of sound. Impressionism shuns the grandiosity of epic arts and the emotionalism of romance. No human passions invest the scores of Impressionist music, and the sonorities are never overwhelming. It is characteristic of Impressionist composers that in the selection of their subjects they favor the moon over the sun, the night over the day. Verlaine's poem *Clair de Lune* inspired Debussy's famous piano piece. Schoenberg, in his *Pierrot Lunaire*, a work that possesses distinct Impressionistic qualities, selected a group of poems focused on a moonstruck lover with the pale disk of the moon projected on the back of his garment.

A suggestion of sensuality is often more forceful than a realistic description of carnality. Whispered words are more enervating than raucous outcries. Distant rhythms of throbbing drums, brief effervescences of quickly extinguished melodic phrases, muted instrumental colors, all this suggests faint mementos of passionate events. Debussy's most dyspeptic critic Camille Bellaigue (who was Debussy's classmate at the Paris Conservatoire) grudgingly admitted that Debussy's music "fait peu de bruit," but, he added malevolently, it makes "un vilain petit bruit." John Ruskin exploded in righteous indignation against modern French music: "Musicians, like painters, are almost virulently determined in their efforts to abolish the laws of sincerity and purity, and to invent, each for his own glory, new modes of dissolute and lascivious sound." When Debussy's *Prélude a l'Aprés-midi d'un Faune* was first performed in Paris in 1894, a cautionary notice was inserted in the program: "The poem of Mallarmé, which inspired Debussy, is so sadistic that the management decided not to print it in the program book, because young girls attend these concerts." The great romanticist of French music Gounod, addressing students at the Paris Académie des Beaux Arts on 20 October 1883, warned them: "Do not be seduced by those hollow words, Realism, Idealism, Impressionism. They belong to the nihilist vocabulary, which now constitutes modern art."

Paul Verlaine described Impressionism in a line of singular intimacy as "la chanson grise o l'Iindécis au Précis se joint." And he summarized the aesthetic code of Symbolist poetry and Impressionist art in a challenging invitation, "Pas la Couleur, rien que la Nuance!" The formula fits the music of French Impressionism to perfection: in it the indecisiveness of the design is mitigated by the precision of execution. Bright colors are relinquished in favor of infinitesimally subtle nuances. Just as the eye is trained to differentiate between light and shadow in Impressionist art, so the ear is disciplined to discriminate between the measured quanta of sonic impulses in Impressionist music.

Impressionism is the differential calculus of music, in which the infinitesimal particles of coloristic sound are integrated into a potent musical factor. Debussy himself insisted that he was a realistic composer and he deprecated the term Impressionism. He wrote to his publisher Durand, in March 1908: "I am trying to create musical reality, the kind that some imbeciles call Impressionism, a term which I consider most unfitting."

Impressionism created its own tonal vocabulary and harmonic syntax. Its inspiration came from remote antiquity in time and far distances in space. When the Paris Exposition of 1889 presented Oriental dancers from Indochina with their strange bell-like musical instruments, Debussy and his friends found new resources in the polychromatic monody of the exotic modes from the East, free from contrapuntal and harmonic artificiality of Western music. At the same time manufactured products from Japan began to arrive at the Paris markets, wrapped in Japanese rice paper with the symbolic prints by unknown masters. It was this wrapping paper, rather than the goods it enveloped, that provided pictorial resources to many French painters. Debussy selected a Japanese drawing of a typhoon wave for the cover of his score of *La Mer*. James Gibbons Huneker was not far wrong in his horrified contemplation of Debussy as a revenant from the East. "If the western world ever adopted eastern tonalities," he wrote, "Claude Debussy would be the one composer who would manage its system. I see his curious asymmetrical face, the pointed fawn ears, the projecting cheekbones. The man is a wraith from the East. His music was heard long ago in the hill temples of Borneo; was made as a symphony to welcome the head-hunters with their ghastly spoils of war!"

The innovations introduced by Impressionist techniques are as significant in the negation of old formulas as in the affirmation of the novelties. They may be summarized in the following categories:

MELODY: (1) Extreme brevity of substantive thematic statements; (2) Cultivation of monothematism and the elimination of all auxiliary notes, ornaments, melodic excrescences, and rhythmic protuberances; (3) Introduction of simulacra of old Grecian and ecclesiastical modes calculated to evoke the spirit of serene antiquity in stately motion of rhythmic units; (4) Thematic employment of pentatonic scales to conjure up imitative sonorities and tintinnisonant Orientalistic effects; (5) Coloristic use of the WHOLE-TONE SCALE for exotic ambience; and (6) Rapid iteration of single notes to simulate the rhythms of primitive drums.

HARMONY: (1) Extension of tertian chord formations into chords of the eleventh, or raised eleventh, and chords of the thirteenth; (2) Modulatory schemes in root progressions of intervals derived from the equal division of the octave into 2, 3, 4, 6, and 12 parts in preference to the traditional modulations following the order of the cycle of fourths and fifths; (3) Motion by block harmonies without transitions; (4) Preferential use of plagal cadences either in triadic harmonies or extended chordal formations; (5) Quartal harmonies used as harmonic entities which move in parallel formations; (6) Modal harmonization in root positions of perfect triads within a given mode, with the intervallic relationships between the melody notes and the bass following the formula 8, 3, 5, 8, etc. when harmonizing an ascending scale or mode, and the reverse numerical progression 8, 5, 3, 8, etc. in harmonizing a descending scale or mode, excluding the incidence of the diminished fifth between the melody and the bass; the reverse numerical progression, 8, 5, 3, 8, 5, etc. for an ascending scale results in a common harmonization in tonic, dominant and subdominant triads in root position; the same common harmonization results when the formula 8, 3, 5, 8, 3, etc. is applied to the harmonization of a descending scale; this reciprocal relationship between a modal and a tonal harmonization is indeed magical in its precise numerical formula; (7) Intertonal harmonization in major triads, in which no more than two successive chords belong to any given tonality, with the melody moving in contrary motion to the bass; since only root positions of major triads are used, the intervals between the melody and the bass can be only a major third, a perfect fifth, and an octave. In harmonizing an ascending scale, whether diatonic, chromatic, or partly chromatic, the formula is limited to the numerical intervallic progression 3, 5, 8, 3, 5, etc., and the reverse in harmonizing a descending scale, i.e., 8, 5, 3, 8, 5, 3, etc. Cadential formulas of pre-Baroque music are often intertonal in their exclusive application of major triads in root positions. A remarkable instance of the literal application of the formula of intertonal harmonization is found in the scene of Gregory's prophetic vision in Mussorgsky's opera *Boris Godunov*, in which the ascending melodic progression, itself intertonal in its peculiar modality, B, C-sharp, E, F-sharp, G, is harmonized successively in the major triads in root positions, E major,

C-sharp major, A major, F-sharp major, E-flat major. Another instance of intertonal harmonization occurs in the second act of Puccini's opera *Tosca*, in which the motto of the Chief of Police, a descending WHOLE-TONE SCALE in the bass, is harmonized in ascending major triads in root positions, in contrary motion; the intervallic relationship between the melody and the bass follows the formula 8, 3, 5, 8, 3, 5, 8; (8) Parallel progressions of inversions of triads, particularly second inversions of major triads, with the root progression ascending or descending in minor thirds, so that the basses outline a diminished-seventh chord; (9) Parallel progressions of major ninth-chords, also with a bass moving by minor thirds; (10) Parallel progressions of inverted dominant-seventh chords, particularly 6/5/3 chords; (11) Free use of unattached and unresolved dissonant chords, particularly suspensions of major sevenths over diminished-seventh chords; and (12) Cadential formulas with the added major sixth over major triads in close harmony.

COUNTERPOINT: (1) A virtual abandonment of Baroque procedures, and abolition of tonal sequences and of strict canonic imitation; (2) Reduction of fugal processes to adumbrative thematic echoes, memos, and mementos; and (3) Cultivation of parallel motion of voices, particularly consecutive fourths and organum-like perfect fifths.

FORM: (1) Desuetude of sectional symphonies of the classical or romantic type, and their replacement by coloristic tone poems of a rhapsodic genre; (2) Virtual disappearance of thematic development with its function being taken over by dynamic elements; (3) Cessation in the practice of traditional variations, discontinuance of auxiliary embellishments, melodic and harmonic figurations whether above, below, or around the thematic notes, and the concomitant cultivation of instrumental variations in which the alteration of tone color becomes the means of variegation. A theme may be subjected to augmentation or diminution and in some cases to topological dislocations of the intervallic parameters. Thus the tonal theme of Debussy's *La Mer* is extended in the climax into a series of whole tones; (4) Homeological imitation of melorhythmic formulas of old dance forms, often with pandiatonic amplification of the harmony; and (5) A general tendency towards miniaturization of nominally classical forms, such as sonata or prelude.

INSTRUMENTATION: (1) Coloristic employment of unusual instrumental combinations; (2) Predilection for attenuated sonorities, with muted strings and muted brass, and considerable expansion of the role of woodwind instruments and of the decorative sonorities of the harp and the celesta; (3) Projection of evocative but brief solos, often in unusual registers; (4) The planting of deep pedal points over which the strings and the woodwinds are suspended in aerostatic equilibrium, often with a muted horn, trumpet, or trombone, penetrating the euphonious mist; (5) Careful cultivation of multiple divided strings; (6) Periodic sonic expansions and compressions, massive heavings, and sudden recessions; (7) Fluctuation of dynamic rhythms and constant oscillation of thematic particles; (8) Fragmentation of melodic patterns and pulverization of ingredients in tremolos; (9) Heterogeneous instrumental combinations tending to alter the natural tone color of an individual instrument; and (10) Frequent application of dynamic antiphony of homogeneous or heterogeneous instrumental groupings.

Inaudible Music. Since electronic instruments are capable of generating any frequency, it is possible to reproduce sounds below and above the audible range. The first work for infrasonic and ultrasonic wavelengths was the inaudible symphony entitled *Symphonie Humaine* by the French composer Michel Magne, conducted by him in Paris on 26 May 1955. Its movements were entitled "Epileptic Dance," "Thanatological Berceuse," and "Interior View of an Assassin." The inaudible version was unheard first, followed by a hearing of an audible transcription. The mystical Russian composer Nicolas Obouhov devised in 1918 an inaudible instrument which he named Ether, theoretically capable of producing infrasonic and ultrasonic sounds ranging from five octaves below the lowest audible tone to five octaves above the highest audible tone. But Obouhov's instrument was never constructed. AVANT-GARDE composers working in MIXED MEDIA often compose visual music, which can be seen but not heard. A poetic example is the act of releasing a jar full of butterflies "composed" by La Monte Young. Imagination plays a crucial part in the appreciation of inaudible music. An interviewer on a broadcast of the British Broadcasting Corporation was sent a defective copy of John Lennon and Yoko Ono's Wedding Album (Lennon was a member of the Liverpudlian vocal quartet known as The Beatles) in which two sides were blank except for an engineer's line-up tone. The broadcaster gave it a warmly favorable review, noting that the pitches differed only by microtones, and that "this oscillation produces an almost subliminal uneven beat which maintains interest on a more basic level," and further observing that the listener could improvise an Indian raga, plainsong, or Gaelic mouth music against the drone. John and his Japanese bride sent him a congratulatory telegram, announcing their intention to release the blank sides for their next album. "Heard melodies are sweet, but those unheard are sweeter."

Indeterminacy. In nuclear physics, the principle of indeterminacy states that it is inherently impossible to determine both the position and velocity of any subatomic particle beyond the liminal degree of accuracy. This notion has impressed some modern composers and moved them to apply the indeterminacy principle, with free modification, to composition with ALEATORY or STOCHASTIC elements. With reference to a composition, indeterminacy may denote a conventional score produced by chance; with reference to performance, indeterminacy may denote a score, conventionally notated or not, which leaves much to be determined by performers.

Induction and Deduction. In new music which flaunts its affinity with exact sciences and mathematical logic, the terms induction and deduction may be applied with some profit. In serial composition, in particular, the method allows completion of a series by the process of induction. The Bach theme, B-flat, A, C, B, for instance, can be an inductive clue to a 12-tone series, to be completed by using the intervallic content of the subject in transposition by inversion and retrograde. The process of deduction also possesses a certain validity in composition. With the aid of thematic induction and deduction, it is easy to construct logical sequences of tones. Suppose we have a dodecaphonic series designated by the first 12 integers, 1, 2, 3 . . . 12; in its second appearance it assumes the succession 2, 3, 4 . . . 12, 1. By inductive reasoning the third series should be 3, 4, 5, 6 . . . 12, 1, 2, etc. This type of DODECAPHONIC COMPOSITION is known as ROTATION. Conversely, it is possible to derive identical serial rows by deduction from the principle of rotation, while other morphological variants can be obtained by omitting parts of the series.

Inertial Guidance. Borrowed from navigation, the term inertial guidance denotes an automatic sequence which depends entirely on previously accumulated data. At its most elementary level, inertial guidance is a signal of repeat, as in the recapitulation section of sonata form. In the original manuscript of Schubert's *Unfinished Symphony*, the initial 64 bars of the first movement are repeated in the recapitulation, but rather than writing them out, Schubert simply marked them numerically, 1–64. A conversion formula could be devised to take care of inertial guidance for transpositions to another key, augmentations of a theme, diminutions, and even fugal stretti, with symbolical directions according to a set code. For instance, S(I)), where S stands for Subject and I denotes Tonic Harmony, would indicate that the second subject is to be transposed to the tonic from its original appearance in the dominant. In DODECAPHONIC techniques, a symbolic system for inertial guidance would save the drudgery of writing out the basic forms of the tone-row. It would be possible, for instance, to program the composition of a tone-row consisting of three groups of identical intervallic conformations, the first of which spells BACH. In order to complete the 12-tone series, BACH would have to be transposed 4 semitones higher and 4 semitones lower. The formula would then appear as follows: BACH, (BACH + 4), (BACH – 4). If the second or the third group is to be inverted or reversed, it can be indicated by the subscripts *i* and *r.* In addition to inertial guidance, a set of formulas can also be devised for a command guidance, which would interrupt the automatic processes of inertial guidance, and dictate a new set of directives. It must be kept in mind, however, that the formula must not be allowed to be more complex than ordinary notation.

Infantiloquy. Onomatopoeia, whether tonal or electronically produced, is the most effective means of instrumental infantiloquy. Borborygmic rumbles and oral ejaculations of sonic particles in an asymmetric pattern are infantiloquacious by nature, and they can be easily imitated by an instrumental ensemble. An infantiloquent modern piece may include fragments from nursery rhymes. An example of successful infantiloquy is Karlheinz Stockhausen's *Gesang der Jünglinge,* in which a child's voice is combined with electronic sounds.

Information Theory. In relevant application to modern music, information theory touches on the problems of GRAPHIC NOTATION, semantics of certain melorhythmic figures, dynamic levels of various parts of a musical work, instrumental color, etc. A composer must be able to convey a maximum amount of information with optimum efficiency. Composers of complicated music have without exception insisted that the knowledge of their modus operandi is unnecessary for the complete comprehension of the musical message. The quality of performance cannot elevate a poorly constructed musical composition to a higher degree of excellence; nor can an indifferent execution of a great masterpiece impair its inherent validity. Musical information can be conveyed with considerable impact by playing a four-hand arrangement of a Beethoven symphony, but would fail to register even in a virtuoso performance of a work lacking in power of communication.

Infra-Modern Music. If ULTRA-MODERN MUSIC transcends the outer limits of modernism, infra-modern music fails to reach even its lowest boundaries and dwells in the penumbra of pretentious self-inflation. Composers of infra-modern music make frequent incursions into the alluring land of dissonant harmonies, but they seldom succeed in manufacturing even a similitudinarian counterfeit. Their attempts to inject atonal or polytonal elements in the effete body of their productions remain as sterile as their imaginations are impotent.

Integration. Harmonic integration of a linear progression in dodecaphonic works is an essential factor in Arnold Schoenberg's method of composition with 12 tones related only to one another. Melody and harmony become two dimensions of dodecaphonic space, thus contributing to a higher unity of the compositional design. True, melody and harmony are intimately associated in classical music theory in conformity with the laws of chordal relationship, but the great difference between the two concepts lies in the fact that in classical harmony the chordal accompaniment performs the function of melodic tonality, while in serial music it is an integral part of the entire meloharmonic scheme.

Interpoint. Interpoint, or Punctus Inter Punctum, is a term devised by the Russian composer Alexander Tcherepnin to describe a special kind of contrapuntal technique, in which pairs of conjugated contrapuntal voices enter a vacancy between another pair of contrapuntal parts without overlapping. The resulting four-part counterpoint becomes in turn the intussusception between a still more dehiscent coupling. In order to achieve interpuntal polyphony, it is obviously necessary to plan in advance the upper and lower limits of the range of each air, recalling to mind Swift's verses: "So, naturalists observe, a flea/Hath smaller fleas that on him prey/And these have smaller still to bite 'em/And so proceed ad infinitum."

Intervallic Symbolism. Symbolic associations between intervals and ideas are rooted in scholastic theories. An anonymous medieval tract explains the acoustical perfection of the octave by the circumstance that "octavo die Abraha circumcisus erat." The tritone was "diabolus in musica." Bach had correlated certain intervals to specific subjects with considerable precision. Since words could not always be heard, an intervallic equation contributed to the clarity of the meaning. The ascent to heaven was depicted by a rising diatonic scale. Torment was expressed by involuted chromatic passages. The descent into hell was intervallically related to the falling diminished seventh. Essentially, Wagner's system of leading motives is a species of intervallic symbolism. Some modern composers have revived a medieval symbolism of intervals. In Luigi Nono's MIXED MEDIA spectacle, *Intolleranza 1960,* the characters are associated with specific intervals: the woman with minor seconds and their inversions, major sevenths; the refugee with the tritone and perfect fourths; and his friend with perfect fourths and major seconds. As in Bach's day, such associations help listeners follow the leading motives of the score.

Invariants. With the growing fascination shown by modern composers for the theory of sets, the term invariants has acquired a certain practical validity. Its relevance is obvious. The 12 tones of the dodecaphonic series are invariants within a certain set; the derivatives of the tone-row are variables. Number 4 is the invariant in a set of instruments of a string quartet. A flute part interchangeable with that of the piccolo is a variable. Besides the advantage of scientific jargon, the system of musical invariants clarifies some processes of serial composition. Particularly frequent is the use of the term for segments of different forms of a tone-row, for instance, the basic series and its retrograde, transposed, which happen to have several notes in common, by accident or structural serendipity.

Jazz. The word "jazz" appeared for the first time in print in the sports column in *The Bulletin* of San Francisco in its issue of 6 March 1913. Describing the arrival of a baseball team, the writer "Scoop" Gleeson reported: "Everybody has come back to the old town, full of the old 'jazz' and they promise to knock the fans off their feet with their playing." Gleeson then asks himself a rhetorical question: "What is this jazz? Why, it's a little of that 'old life,' the 'gin-i-leer,' the 'pep,' otherwise known as the enthusiasalum." Reminiscing about the occasion in an article published in the same San Francisco newspaper in its issue of 3 September 1938, "Scoop" Gleeson volunteered the information that the expression "jazz" had been picked up by the Sports editor during a crap game. According to Gleeson, it was first applied to music when a bandleader named Art Hickman launched his dance band, but there is no evidence of such use in any published source. The next verified appearance of the word jazz was in *Variety* of 27 October 1916 in a brief communication from Chicago, reporting a concert of jazz music, with the word spelled *jass.* Another item in *Variety* followed on 5 January 1917 with the word spelled *Jaz.* An engagement of the Dixie Jass Band of New Orleans in a Chicago cabaret was noted in *Variety* of 16 January 1917. A week later jazz reached New York, and it was spelled with two z's in a report in *Variety.* An item in the Victor Record Review of 7 March 1917 reads: "Spell it *Jass, Jas, Jab* or jazz—nothing can spoil a Jass band. . . . It has sufficient power and penetration to inject new life into a mummy, and will keep ordinary human dancers on their feet till breakfast time . . ." It was about the same time that the Victor Company issued the first recording bearing the word Jass-Dixieland Jass One-Step.

The determination to track the word jazz down to some kind of sexual meaning has been the motivation of many imaginative but unsupported etymologies. The word *Jasm* is found in an American novel published in 1860, and a claim has been made without support that its colloquial meaning was male sperm. Another equally unfounded guess was that the word came from the French slang expression current in New Orleans in the 19th century meaning to copulate.

Some have tried to trace the term to native African languages. However, considering the specific, clear, and plausible description of the word jazz as it appeared in print for the first time in 1913, there is no reason to doubt that it was a spontaneous colloquialism generated around San Francisco. The entire history of the word jazz is thoroughly covered in the pioneer article by Peter Tamony in an ephemeral periodical *Jazz*, a quarterly of American music, in its issue of October 1958. Analytically, jazz may be described as a modern development of the counterpoint of the fourth species. Its rhythmic formula is related to the medieval Hocketus, in which the singing line is freely transferred from one voice to another in syncopated singultation. (The word hocketus itself is an etymological cognate of hiccups.) Another historical antecedent of jazz is the Quodlibet, a freely improvised interlude within a definite metrical framework. As practiced by untutored performers, jazz produces the collective impact of glossolalia, tonolalia, or rhythmolalia.

The paradoxical nature of jazz is its combination of unlimited variety of rhythmic patterns with a metric and modal uniformity. Jazz melodies, almost without exception, are set in major keys, in 4/4 time. But the major tonality is modified by the use of "blue" notes, especially the lowered seventh in the melody but also occasionally the lowered third as well. Some theorists speculate that the systematic incidence of the "blue" seventh is an approximation of the seventh overtone, and is therefore a natural consonance. The lowered third, however, cannot be explained on acoustical grounds. It may well represent a true case of harmonic equivocation, in which the melodic minor third is projected on the major complex in some sort of polytriadic superfetation. It is significant that this major-minor SUPERFETATION is the constant resource of Stravinsky's tonal harmonies.

The basic characteristics of jazz are the symmetrical divisions of binary meters and the strong tonality in major keys. Within this framework, the melody, of a syncopated nature, often departs widely from its harmonic connotations.

Historically jazz evolved from RAGTIME, a syncopated type of American music that flourished in the last decade of the 19th century and during the first years of the 20th. A parallel development is BLUES, a distinctively American ballad form, suffused with nostalgia and redolent of the remembered sufferings of the Negro race, as expressed in Negro spirituals. Semantically, the term is connected with the colloquialism "to have the blues." The "blue note," that is the flatted seventh in a major key, remains a paramount feature in the BLUES. The acknowledged creator of the genre was W. C. Handy, whose song *The Memphis Blues* (1911) was the first of its type.

In the meantime, the temperature of jazz kept rising, and soon acquired the sobriquet hot jazz, as contrasted with the more leisurely type of sweet jazz. Hot jazz gave way to cool jazz, which was actually a hotter product, as though the hot water and cold water faucets became switched around in the process of transition.

A new era of jazz dawned in 1935 with a riotous explosion of SWING, which signalized a certain rhythmic manner of performance rather than a definable structural form.

Jazz, SWING, and other types of popular American music of the 1930s coalesced into a general category of JIVE, a generic form that describes the playing style in the 1940s. SWING and JIVE were largely improvisatory in nature; a novel way of organizing popular forms emerged in 1938 with BOOGIE-WOOGIE, based on an orderly harmonic progression in the bass, relating it to the classical formulas of the passacaglia and the chaconne.

A lateral form, BEBOP, Rebop, or simply BOP, appeared in the 1940s; in it the main emphasis was on the strong off-beat. With its raucous sound and crude assault on the musical sensorium, SWING had no room for such poetic refinements as the "blue notes" which vanished from the SWING horizon.

For more than half a century, jazz in its various forms was separated from folk music. Jazz was an urban product; folk or country music remained stagnant in its rural recesses. The instrumentation of jazz was based on the trumpet, the saxophone, the banjo, the piano, and the drums, with the clarinet emerging as its flamboyant chanticleer in SWING. Country music replaced the piano by the guitar and the trumpet by the rustic fiddle. When country music invaded the radio airwaves, the television channels, and the sound movies, it gradually developed into a horrendously successful creation, especially in its coalescence with ROCK 'N' ROLL. Marked by an unrelenting, unremitting beat, ROCK 'N' ROLL reduced the rhythmic wealth of early syncopated music to a two-dimensional construction of bland uniformity. Its cumulative impact is apt to be as powerful as the rhythmic tramp of a regiment of soldiers which can bring down a suspension bridge by generating pendulum-like vibrations of increasing amplitude.

Throughout the history of American popular music, systematic incursions were made into the stylistically distant territory of classical and romantic music, carrying away loot and booty from the uncopyrighted remains of Chopin, Tchaikovsky, and Rachmaninoff. Some products of these predatory forays, such as *Russian Rag* fashioned from Rachmaninoff's defenseless C-sharp minor *Prelude*, are not devoid of inventive cleverness. Indignant outcries arose from the classical-minded musicians against such barbarous borrowings, but the practice continued well into the late 20th century, and especially certain urban forms of POP MUSIC. A reconciliation between popular and serious music was effected with taste and vitality in a movement known as the THIRD STREAM, wherein jazz is introduced into serious music.

Jive. Jive is a collective noun that describes the action of JAZZ. A jive session is a display of coordinated glossolalia or tonolalia, spontaneous and self-conscious in their manifestation. A jam session is conducted in the language of jive. The semantic distinctions and confluences of these terms are illustrated by the jazzy glossolalia in a song recorded by Columbia in 1940: "Romp it, stomp it, ride it too. Jam it, Jump it, Jive it through."

Kaleidophonia. By analogy with kaleidoscopic images, the term kaleidophonia may be used to describe a musical composition derived from multiple mirror-like reflections of a central subject. By selecting a code of parameters determining intervals and durations, a kaleidophonic structure can be designed as a harmonic complex composed of contrapuntal lines in quaquaversal rhythmic dispersion. Joseph Schillinger published in 1940 a volume of musical patterns entitled *Kaleidophone*.

Kinetic Energy. When applied to music, kinetic energy during a given interval of time connects the velocity (number of notes per time unit), amplitude (degree of loudness in decibels), and the height of pitch expressed in semitones counting from the lowest note in the audible range. Kinetic energy is the product of all these parameters. From this it follows that the auditory impact is directly proportional to velocity, loudness, and frequency of vibrations per second. There is also a psychological factor that affects the subjective measurement of kinetic energy. The off-beat chord in Haydn's *Surprise Symphony*, though in itself possessing a modest impact, carries a relatively greater charge of psycho-kinetic energy because it is unexpected. Generally speaking, a greater impression is produced by detonations of sonic quanta in asymmetrical rhythms than much stronger discharges occurring at regular intervals of time. Kinetic energy also aptly describes the realization of POP MUSIC in the late 20th century into music videos, wherein purely musical materials become freely translated into associative bodily rhythms.

Kitsch. The German patois word kitsch denotes a pretentiously manufactured object, an unimaginative arrangement of artifacts, or a heterogeneous collection which is more tasteless than artless. Christmas cards with rhymed doggerel and tinctured flowers, religious gypsum figurines with a clock in the center of the torso, a motion picture representing muscular men lifting rubber weights, chrome gargoyles, dinner plates with reproductions of members of the presidential family, and all sorts of tinsel and fustian are examples of middle-class kitsch. In music, kitsch is represented by so-called semi-classical compositions made up of harmonic detritus and melodic debris from the mutilated remains of Rachmaninoff's *Second Piano Concerto*, or

Beethoven's *Moonlight Sonata*, or from a mixture of both. Kitsch products are usually given colorful titles such as "Purple Piano" or "Sentimental Violin," and favor for some unfathomable reason the keys of D-flat major or C minor. Kitsch is the degenerate descendant of the German Biedermeier movement. At the distance of a century, the Biedermeier products possess a certain charm of old-fashioned sentiment and the musical compositions of the period were invariably correct from the technical standpoint. Modern kitsch is usually devoid of the most elementary type of technical proficiency and appeals to the lowest classes of commercially conditioned eyes, noses, and ears.

Klangfarbe. In its present semantical usage, Klangfarbe is a special dimension of the musical sound. "It must be possible," Arnold Schoenberg states in his *Harmonielehre*, "to form a succession of Klangfarben possessing a mutual relationship of a logical type equivalent to that of the melody formed by a succession of different tones." This melody of tone colors is exemplified in Schoenberg's movement originally entitled "The Changing Chord" in his *Five Orchestral Pieces*. Anton von Webern developed the idea in the direction of serialism of Klangfarben, almost reaching the ultimate dodecaphonic order, in which the fundamental Klangfarbe series is formed by the successive sounding of 12 different notes by 12 different instruments.

Lehrstück. The problems of writing music in a modern idiom adaptable for educational purposes among workers and young people preoccupied a number of German composers in the 1920s. The idea of a Lehrstück for accompanied chorus with the liberal application of inflected voice, SPRECHSTIMME, arose in Germany about that time. Paul Hindemith, Ernst Toch, and Kurt Weill wrote several such works. Often the "teaching" element in a Lehrstück was political, as exemplified in the "instruction pieces" of Hanns Eisler.

Lipograms. An omission of an essential member of a melodic series, be it a simple diatonic tune or a dodecaphonic tone-row, a musical apocopation or an APOSIOPESIS, or any other similar rhetoric device that interrupts the normal progress of a musical sentence, may be described as a lipogram, a vocable derived from Greek nomenclature, that denotes a deficiency of a letter. A lipogram in a dodecaphonic series results in the formation of a Hendecaphonic row. When the last note of a series is omitted, a melodic apocope results; when an interruption occurs dramatically in the middle of a melorhythmic paragraph, the effect is similar to that of an APOSIOPESIS. Lipogrammatic techniques provide ample resources for novel melodic, rhythmic, harmonic, and instrumental patterns.

Machine Music. The modern machine became an object of artistic inspiration early in the 20th century. The Italian Futurists made a cult of automobiles and airplanes. George Antheil's *Ballet mécanique* shocked concert audiences by its BRUITISM. Max Brand produced the first machine opera in *Machinist Hopkins*. Honegger made a declaration of love for powerful American locomotives in his symphonic movement *Pacific 231*. Frederick S. Converse glorified the Ford car in his automobilistic musicorama *Flivver 10,000,000*. But locomotives, automobiles, and airplanes soon lost their glamour and became public nuisances; by mid-century the machine as an artistic object became obsolete. It is ironic that no composer was moved to extol in lofty tones the greatest machine adventure of all ages, the landing of a spacecraft on the moon.

Major-Minor Syndrome. It was a traditional convention in Baroque music to end a work in a minor key on a major triad; a major third that replaced a minor third in the final triad acquired the name *Tierce de Picardie*. The preference for the major third in final chords is explained by its privileged position as the fifth partial note of the harmonic series, whereas a minor third of the fundamental tone does not occur acoustically. In the practice of modern composers, a major third is often superimposed on a minor third. Scriabin employed such a major-minor syndrome in his last opus numbers, but he spread the harmony widely, so that the frictional dissonance of a semitone was minimized. It was Stravinsky who cultivated a true major-minor syndrome in placing both the minor and the major third within a triad. He made use of it as a motto in his early choral work *Zvezdoliky*. It occurs also in *Le Sacre du Printemps*. Most importantly, Stravinsky uses it as a melodic palimpsest, breaking up the combined chord, with both the major and the minor third assuming a thematic significance.

Meloharmony. In a triadically constructed melody, the harmonic arrangement is clearly outlined. In such instances, it is proper to speak of meloharmony as a two-dimensional entity. In DODECAPHONIC MUSIC, meloharmony acquires a particular significance, because the fundamental series can be distributed horizontally (melodically) and vertically (harmonically) and still preserve its continuity. It is also possible to speak of melocontrapuntal structures, arranged vertically, horizontally, or diagonally. A cognate term is MELORHYTHM, in which melody and rhythm are combined into a dual entity.

Melorhythm. The term Meloritmo, frequently used by Spanish and Latin American writers on music, and signifying a synthetic two-dimensional entity possessing both melodic and rhythmic attributes, is sufficiently useful to be adopted in other languages. It is also a convenient substitute for the definition of a musical phrase, which must necessarily have the dual melorhythmic consistency. In serial music, melorhythms may be regarded as the integrals of the melodic and rhythmic differential series.

Melosomatic Effect. The neologism melosomatic suggests an interaction between Melos and the physical Soma. It may be traumatic when loud music is played without relief. But a more insidious psychological lesion is produced by personal associations. In his short story, *The Black Monk*, Anton Chekhov, who was a professional physician, describes the deadly effect produced on a young intellectual by the playing of *Angel's Serenade* by Gaetano Braga, resulting in a fatal cerebral hemorrhage when the piece is played again after a long interval of time. Autosuggestion may have been responsible for the death of the Hungarian composer Rezsö Seress, author of the pessimistic popular song *Gloomy Sunday* (it was banned in various localities after numerous suicides were purportedly engendered by it). By a delayed reaction, forty years after writing this song, the composer himself jumped out of a window. The Russian pianist Alexander Kelberine took a lethal dose of barbiturates after his last concert on January 27, 1940 in Town Hall in New York, for which he had arranged a funeral program, consisting entirely of works in minor keys, the last number being Liszt's *Totentanz*. Sexual stimulation is highly melosomatic, as amply demonstrated by the reactions of the young to concerts of POP MUSIC, particularly ROCK 'N' ROLL. Tolstoy, who turned against sex after a lifetime of indulgence and sixteen illegitimate children, presented a philosophical study of musical sexuality in his novel *The Kreutzer Sonata*, wherein he tells how the last movement of Beethoven's work, with its propulsive syncopation, overwhelms the natural restraints of the performers, a middle-class married Russian woman pianist and a male violinist, hurling them into a frenzy of illicit passion. It may be questioned whether amateurs could ever master the technical difficulties of that diabolically intricate last movement, let alone create enough excitement to carry them away. (There is a famous painting illustrating the climactic scene of the novel, showing the mustachioed violinist implanting a passionate kiss on the lips of a lady pianist while holding both the violin and the bow in his left hand, suggesting that he had the presence of mind to switch the bow from the right hand to the left, but leaving it unexplained as to why he did not deposit the instrument on the lid of the piano in that crucial moment. The painting was widely used as an advertisement for a brand of perfume with a sexy name.)

Melosomatic associations were responsible for the extraordinary vogue of the piano piece *A Maiden's Prayer* by the Polish composeress Thekla Badarzewska, a wish-fulfilling favorite of several generations of unmarried females. In 1937 Stravinsky instituted in Paris a suit against Warner Brothers for their production of a film entitled *The Firebird,* in which a submissive young girl is so unnerved by the phonograph playing of the "Pagan Dance" from Stravinsky's *Firebird* that she wanders into the flat of a professional seducer, who had the piece played continually with malice aforethought, and yields to his infamous desires. The judge failed to appreciate Stravinsky's attitude, since the seductive power of music is supposed to be the composer's greatest pride, and adjudicated the case by granting Stravinsky a token sum of one French franc in compensation for the offense.

Metamusic. Metaphysical visions have obsessed composers through the ages. They dreamed of a metamusical symphony in which all mankind would participate as a responsive reverberating assembly of congenial souls. Shortly before he died, Scriabin wrote an outline of a metamusical *Mysterium* that would embrace all senses in a pantheistic mystical action. Much more earthbound, but musically fascinating, was the project of a *Universe Symphony* by Charles Ives, a work that he hoped to see performed by several orchestras stationed on hilltops overlooking a valley. The Russian mystical composer Nicolas Obouhov envisioned a metamusical union of all religions. He completed a major part of this work which bore the title *Le Livre de Vie,* the manuscript of which he kept on a self-made altar under an icon in a corner of his small room in Paris. Since this was to be the book of his own life, body and soul, he made all annotations in the original scores in his own blood. He tried to interest American music lovers in producing the work in a specially built temple in Hollywood, but died with his dream unfulfilled.

Composers of the AVANT-GARDE have at their disposal the means of producing metamusical scores with the aid of electronic synthesizers. They may even plan to hitch their metamusical chariot if not to the stars then at least to the planets. There is nothing mystical in the term metamusic. It simply means an art transcending traditional music, by analogy with Aristotle's metaphysics, which indicates the position of a chapter dealing with philosophy, directly after a discussion of physics in his *Organon.*

Metempsychosis. A recurrence of a theme in an altered melorhythmic shape, suggesting the effect of *déjà entendu* without literal resemblance, may be called musical metempsychosis. The *idée fixe* in the *Symphonie Fantastique* of Berlioz does not fall into this category because here it was deliberately implanted and reproduced in a clearly recognizable form. The discovery of melorhythmic revenants may give a clue to the composer's inner impulses, and it is particularly fruitful in serial compositions, where metempsychosis may appear subliminally, despite the composer's efforts to guard himself against unintentional thematic references.

Metric Modulation. In a general sense, metric modulation refers to a change of time signature. In special modern usage, proleptically applied by Charles Ives and systematically cultivated by Elliott Carter, metric modulation is a technique by which a rhythmic pattern is superposed on another, heterometrically, superseding it and becoming the basic meter. Usually, such time signatures are mutually prime, e.g., 4/4 and 3/8, and so have no common divisors. Thus the change of the basic meter decisively alters the numerical content of the beat, but the minimal denominator (1/8 when 4/4 changes to 3/8; 1/16 when, e.g., 5/8 changes to 7/16, etc.) remains constant in duration.

Microtonality. Intervals smaller than semitones were used in ancient Greece, but were abandoned in Western music with the establishment of the ecclesiastical modes. When greater sensitivity towards tonal elements developed in modern times, composers and theorists began investigating the acoustical, coloristic, and affective aspects of intervals smaller than a semitone, particularly quarter-tones. The Mexican composer Julián Carrillo experimented with microtonal intervals as early as 1895, when he published his *Sonido 13* (13th Sound); the title referred to the tonal resources beyond the 12 notes of the chromatic scale. Later he organized an international society for the exploration of microtonality under the grandiose name "Cruzada Intercontinental Sonido 13." He devised special instruments for performance of microtonal intervals and proposed a numerical notation of 96 divisions of the octave, which enabled him to designate precise intervallic values for l/2-, 1/4-, 1/6-, 1/8-, and 1/16-tones. As an exercise in microtonality he arranged Beethoven's Fifth Symphony in quarter-tones by dividing each interval into two, so that the octave became a tritone, and the entire range of the work shrank to about three octaves, like some monstrous simulacrum of a physical universe in which the sensorium of auditory frequencies undergoes an extraction of the square root.

The English musician John Foulds experimented with quarter-tones in 1898. He writes in his book *From Music Today* (1934): "In the year 1898 I had tentatively experimented in a string quartet with smaller divisions than usual of the intervals of our scale, quarter-tones. Having proved in performance their practicability and their capability of expressing certain psychological states in a manner incommunicable by any other means known to musicians, I definitely adopted them as an item in my composing technique. . . . Facetious friends may assert roundly that they have heard quarter-tones all their lives, from the fiddle strings and larynxes of their mutual friends, who produced them without any difficulty."

The most systematic investigation of the theory and practice of quarter-tones was undertaken by Alois Hába in Czechoslovakia. "As a boy of 12," he writes, "I played with my three older brothers in my father's village band. We were poor; there were ten children in the family, and I had to contribute to household expenses. When we played for village festivals it often happened that folk singers used intervals different from the tempered scale, and they were annoyed that we could not accompany them properly. This gave me the idea to practice at home playing nontempered scales on my violin in intervals smaller than a semitone. This was my first 'conservatory' for music in quarter-tones and in sixth-notes."

Probably the first entirely self-consistent work in quarter-tones was Hába's String Quartet of 1919. He also compiled the first manual containing detailed instructions on composing in quarter-, third-, and sixth-tones, which he published under the fitting title *Neue Harmonielehre* (1928). Under Hába's supervision the August Foerster piano manufacturing company of Czechoslovakia constructed the first model of a quarter-tone piano which was patented on 18 March 1924. At the same time Hába established the first seminars of microtonal music at the Prague Conservatory. He and his students published a number of works in quarter-tones, in Hába's special notation containing symbols for half a sharp, a sharp and a half, half a flat, and a flat and a half. A quarter-tone upright piano was constructed by Willi Möllendorf even before Foerster's, but it was only an ordinary piano tuned in quarter-tones and not a specially-built instrument. It is now placed in the Deutsches Museum in Munich as an historical relic. The same museum also possesses a quarter-tone Harmonium built by Foerster and a harmonium of 19 divisions of the octave designed by Melchior Sachs.

In 1917 the Russian composer Ivan Wyschnegradsky devised a system of quarter-tones with a motto, inspired by Heraclitus, "Everything flows." In 1924, then living in Paris, he formulated the concept of "pansonority," which in his nomenclature meant a discrete continuum of quarter-tones. To produce fairly accurate quarter-tones he used two pianos or two pairs of pianos tuned a quarter-tone apart. On 10 November 1945 he conducted in Paris an entire program of his works, including a symphonic poem for four pianos entitled *Cosmos.* In Russia itself quarter-tone music had a brief period of success in the early 1920s, cultivated by the Quarter-Tone Society of Leningrad, founded by Rimsky-Korsakov's grandson Georg.

Charles Ives, whose universal genius touched on many

aspects of modern composition, contributed some pieces written in quarter-tones. He tells us that he became aware of the new resources of microtonal music when his father, a band leader in the Union Army during the Civil War, experimented in tuning band instruments a quarter-tone apart.

Probably the earliest published composition containing quarter-tones was a group of two pieces for cello and piano by Richard H. Stein, composed in 1906, but quarter-tone passages in them were used only as occasional ultra-chromatic interludes. Ernest Bloch inserted quarter-tones in his first piano quintet mainly for their affective value as coloristic appoggiaturas.

American composers David Zeikel and William Harold Halberstadt investigated the potentialities of quarter-tones in the 1940s and wrote special works, mostly for the violin. For the sake of completeness it may be mentioned that Nicolas Slonimsky composed an overture for strings, trumpet, and percussion in the Phrygian mode using as his theme an extant version of an ancient Greek tune from the accompaniment to the tragedy *Orestes* produced in Athens in 400 B.C.; he conducted this arrangement at the Hollywood Bowl on 13 July 1933. In order to produce the needed two quarter-tones, the open strings of the violins, violas, and cellos were tuned a quarter-tone up, with the rest of the string instruments preserving the ordinary pitch.

The first quarter-tone piano manufactured in the United States was patented by Hans Barth on 21 July 1931. His instrument had two keyboards of 88 notes each. The upper keyboard was tuned at the regular international pitch and had the usual five black keys and seven white keys. The lower keyboard was tuned a quarter-tone down, and its keys were blue and red.

James Paul White, a Boston musician, constructed in 1883 a microtonal keyboard which he called Harmon, and used a notation in which deviations from regular pitch were indicated by plus and minus signs. He theorized that 612 equal divisions of an octave would provide the most practical approximation to pure intonation. His instrument is preserved at the New England Conservatory of Music.

Perhaps the most ambitious project in microtonal music has been undertaken by the American composer Harry Partch who devised a scale of 43 intervals in an octave, and constructed a number of special instruments for playing his microtonal works, among them a microtonal cello, a reed organ with 43 registrations, and a modern version of the Greek kithara. He expounded his findings in his 1949 book, *Genesis of a Music*.

Musicologists have made numerous attempts to reconcile the tempered scale with Pythagorean intonation. Perhaps the most complete research in this direction was done by Joseph Yasser in his book *A Theory of Evolving Tonality*, published in New York in 1932, in which he proposed a system of "supra-tonality," with accidentals designated by special symbols for supra-sharp, supra-flat, and supra-natural of the synthetic scale.

Quarter-tones were used by composers to suggest the Greek enharmonic mode through the centuries. Halévy incorporated a few quarter-tones in his symphonic poem *Promethée enchaîné*, and Berlioz wrote an interesting account of its first performance in *Revue et Gazette Musicale de Paris* of 25 March 1849: "The employment of quarter-tones in Halévy's work is episodic and very short, and produces a species of groaning sound in the strings, but its strangeness seems perfectly justified here and enhances considerably the wistful prosody of the music."

The Romanian composer Georges Enesco inserted a transitional passage in quarter-tones in his opera *Oedipe*, produced in Paris in 1936. In this case, too, the composer's intention was to evoke the effect of the ancient Greek enharmonic scale.

In actual performance on instruments manipulated by humans, quarter-tones and other microtonal divisions are only rough approximations of their true acoustical value. With the advent of electronic instruments, however, it became possible to reproduce microtonal intervals with absolute precision. But despite the extraordinary resources offered by electronic instruments, composers of the AVANT-GARDE, overall, have remained surprisingly indifferent. The Polish modernist Krzysztof Penderecki is an exception; he used quarter-tones in massive multi-octave tone-clusters, creating sonorous complexes in icositetraphonic harmony. La Monte Young and Terry Riley, two early proponents of musical MINIMALISM, experimented much with quarter-tones, influenced by non-Western practices.

A curious disquisition on quarter-tones and other fractional intervals as a logical extension of Chopin's sensitive use of chromatic harmony is contained in a pamphlet by Johanna Kinkel, *Acht Briefe an eine Freundin über Clavier-Unterricht*, published in Stuttgart in 1852: "As we wonder what it is that grips us and fills us with foreboding and delight in Chopin's music, we are apt to find a solution that might appear to many as pure fantasy, namely that Chopin's intention was to release upon us a cloud of quarter-tones, which now appear only as phantom doppelgänger in the shadowy realm within the intervals produced by enharmonic change. Once the quarter-tones are emancipated, an entirely new world of tones will open to us, but since we have been accustomed to the long established divisions into semitones, these new sounds will seem weird, suggesting a splash of discordant waves. Yet the children of the next generation, or the one after next, will suck in these strange sounds with mother's milk, and may find in them a more stimulating and doubly rich art. Chopin seems to push at these mysterious portals; his melodies stream in colliding currents through the semitones as if groping for finer and more spiritual nuances than those that were available for his purposes. And when this door is finally sprung open, we will stand a step nearer to the eternal domain of natural sounds. As it is, we can only give a weak imitation of the Aeolian harp, of the rustle of the forest, of the magical ripple of the waters, unable to render them in their true impressions, because our so-called scales made up of whole tones and semitones are too coarse and have too many gaps, while Nature possesses not only quarter-tones and eighth-tones but an infinite scale of split atoms of sound!"

Migratory Tonics. When tonalities are in a state of constant flux, the laws of probability will still lead to the accidental formation of tonal centers, notes that occur more frequently than others, much in the line of the well-known paradox that if only three dozen individuals are assembled at a party, the odds are even that two of them will have the same day and month for a birthday. Such statistically established keynotes in an otherwise free modulatory environment may be called migratory tonics, a term particularly suitable for works in which tonality is not renounced unequivocally.

Millimetrization. This is a term introduced by Villa-Lobos to describe the transfer of mathematical curves or outlines of photographs onto graph paper, precise to a millimeter. His best-known piece arranged according to millimetrization is *New York Skyline*.

Minimalism. Little is big and less is more, and either adage aptly applies to musical Minimalism, a 1960s reductionist compositional movement that produced a significant body of works notable for its maximal effect out of remarkably minimal means. The movement sprang up on the opposite coasts of the United States, San Francisco and New York especially, and, in its early years, was closely associated with the visual arts; indeed many early works were performed in alternative spaces, including galleries. The shared interest among its early proponents in radically reduced means led to a set of shared compositional tendencies: an unwavering pulse, established at the onset; highly repetitive melodies that function like motivic cells and sub-cells, slowly metamorphosing into other, closely-related motifs; in electronic works, the use of tape loops; incessant and complex rhythms, often with two or more patterns coexisting; subtle phase-shifting in both melodic and rhythmic treatment; single-movement forms, frequently quite simple and cyclic; and very little harmonic movement, resulting in Minimalism's characteristic stasis.

The concerns of Minimalist composers represented a clear

departure from the prevailing SERIALISM of their time and thus from the prevailing practices of the principal AVANT-GARDE. The aesthetic owes much to John Cage and other American experimental composers, however, but with one notable difference: the Minimalist composer's desire for strict control over both compositional processes and performance, thus minimizing the potentials of aleatoric and indeterminate processes. The main proponents of early Minimalism were La Monte Young, Terry Riley, Steve Reich, and Philip Glass, although each has expressed himself in other, more maximal ways, including MIXED MEDIA works; Minimalism has been used with great effect in the theater and in dance works. Minimalism is also referred to as process music; see MONOTHEMATICISM and ADDITIVE COMPOSITION.

Mixed Media. Musicians of the AVANT-GARDE increasingly labor towards the coordination and unification of modern musical productions with those of other arts— painting, sculpture, phonograph recording, theater, radio, television, electronics— activities that are often generalized under the category of mixed media. The practice represents in fact a return to the ancient ideal of unity of liberal arts, with music occupying the honorable position as *ancilla artis.* This tendency has generated a number of novel developments of catalytic artistic powers.

Mobile. In modern sculpture, a mobile is a delicately balanced construction of metal or wood, easily swayed by a gentle flow of air, and often associated with Calder's fanciful constructions. Modern composers have adopted this term to describe a similarly flexible melorhythmic structure, usually scored or a small number of instruments, and characterized by a fine intervallic equilibrium, most often maintained by serial arrangements. The American composer Earle Brown was particularly fascinated by the parallelism, which prompted him to develop the idea of graphic notation in 1952 and of open form in 1953.

Modern Music. In the card catalogue of the British Museum, works written after 1800 are included in a section marked modern music. In American usage, modern music is a colloquialism for dance tunes and popular songs. Medieval manuscripts dealing with music theory often open with the phrase, "Brevitate gaudent moderni." The moderns that relished brevity were, in the opinion of the anonymous authors of these treatises, the adherents to Ars Nova. In present usage, modern music refers to that written since 1900. Its variants are 20th-century music, NEW MUSIC, Music of Our Time, Music of Today, and Contemporary Music.

Modernistic Music. The flexion "istic" denotes a depreciation in the purity of the original product. Hellenistic art is inferior to that of the Golden Age of Greece; PRIMITIVISTIC paintings or compositions suggest a less virile version of the artistic qualities of primitive man; IMPRESSIONISTIC idioms are dissipated derivatives of IMPRESSIONISM. To describe a piece of music as modernistic has an aura of indulgent condescension, suggesting an adoption of models of modern music and a facile pastiche "à la manière de . . . ."

Monism. Monism is a philosophical doctrine postulating the existence of a basic element that is the prime constituent of all material objects. In music, monism denotes an analogous primacy of a concept or a function. The dodecaphonic series is a monistic factor which determines the development of an entire work. A set of variations is intrinsically monistic since it is derived from a primary source, but it is pluralistic if the variations are regarded as mutually independent entities.

Monodrama. Monodrama is a stage work in which only one actor, speaker, or singer acts, recites, or sings. Arnold Schoenberg introduced a type of singing recitation, SPRECHSTIMME, in which the actor enunciates his lines in an inflected manner following the melorhythmic design of the music, a technique that came to its full fruition in his *Pierrot Lunaire.* The classical example of a staged monodrama is his *Erwartung.* The Russian composer Vladimir Rebikov evolved a novel type of monodrama which he described as psychodrama; in it an actor recites his state of mind with a musical accompaniment. In Schoenberg's *Die glückliche Hand,* the central character sings and mimes the story, and a chorus comments on the action in SPRECHSTIMME.

Monothematism and Polythematism. "Brevitate gaudent moderni," medieval theorists said of the moderns of their own time. In the 20th century, this "joy of brevity" assumed the form of monothematism, in which a single subject governs the entire composition. Monothematism is basic to the structure of a theme with variations; but if variations depart too widely from the theme, the result may be polythematic. Rigid monothematism carries an intrinsic danger of monotony; rigid polythematism courts the opposite danger of discontinuity. In monothematism the single theme must recur a sufficient number of times to produce an impression of uniformity; in polythematic constructions, similarities among successive themes must be avoided. Monothematism is an essential feature of musical MINIMALISM.

Monte Carlo Method. Statistical laws govern games of chance as well as the parameters of ALEATORY MUSIC. The Monte Carlo method is the most convenient of all gambling devices for easy musical application. The numbers from 1 to 36 of roulette, of the type used in the casino of Monte Carlo, can be equalized to the 36 chromatic tones of three octaves and notated accordingly as the roulette ball finds its niche, with zero corresponding to the lowest note of an arbitrarily selected progression. Rhythmic figures can be derived from a similar process by equalizing the 36 numbers to 36 different note values; if a smaller number of different rhythms is needed, then a dozen or a half-dozen sets on the roulette table can be selected as primary units. In the Monte Carlo method the probability of occurrence of a certain number depends on the frequency of previous incidences; thus certain notes may accumulate greater statistical probability of incidence and determine the tonal tropism. Harmonization and contrapuntal lines can be obtained by combining the single melorhythmic lines determined by individual Monte Carlo runs. Normally, atonal melodies and dissonant harmonies would result, but a spontaneous appearance of a dodecaphonic series is as unlikely as picking 12 different cards from a pack at random.

Morphology. The emergence of a great variety of new forms of composition makes it difficult to classify them according to traditional categories. It may be desirable therefore to substitute the term morphology for the formal analysis, with the nomenclature of botany replacing that of traditional historic terminology. The geometrical rubrics of botanical classification would add imaginative metaphors suitable to modern musical usages. It would be possible, for instance, to speak of radial symmetry in Neo-Classical music, of a chromatic inflorescence in an atonal melody, or even of agamogenetic axes in dodecaphonic cross-pollination. The advantage of such botanical similes lies in the precision and specificity of the terms and in their easy applicability to intervallic structures.

Musique Concrète. Musique Concrète was discovered and named on 15 April 1948 in Paris by Pierre Schaeffer, a French radio engineer. Experimenting with the newly-invented magnetic tape, Schaeffer found that a heterogeneous collection of songs, noises, conversations, radio commercials, etc., recorded on tape, presented a realistic phonomontage which may serve for actual composition by superimposing fragments of tape recordings in a polyphony of random sounds, splicing the tape in various ways, running it at different speeds or backwards, etc. The raw materials of "concrete music" are susceptible to all kinds of treatment and are therefore capable of unlimited transformations. The technique of double and triple recording on the same length of tape makes it possible to create a polyphony of concrete music of great complexity. In fact it is possible to recompose a classical symphony from a recording of a single note, which can subsequently be changed in pitch and arranged in the requisite rhythmic order, superimposed on other tones derived from the original note, altered in tone color by additional electronic manipulation, until a whole work is reconstructed from these constituent tonal dynamic and instrumental elements.

The Polish composer Wlodzimierz Kotonski composed an *Étude concrète* for orchestra using as his material a single stroke of the cymbal electronically altered and transposed. The American experimenter Richard Maxfield collected 30 seconds of coughs at a modern ballet recital and expanded these bronchial sonorities into a five-minute orchestral work entitled *Cough Music.* A particularly elaborate concoction, effected by the provocative Canadian composer and sound engineer John Oswald, is the CD anthology, *Plunderphonic,* which derives entirely from electronically juxtaposed snippets from recorded performances by such well-known artists as James Brown, Lorin Maazel and the Cleveland Orchestra, Glenn Gould, and Michael Jackson.

Mutations. In search for synonyms or paronyms to replace the ambiguous nomenclature of academic musicology, some modern composers have begun using the scientific-sounding words VARIANTS or mutations for variations. Mutations may be beneficial, musically speaking, when the mutant genes add to the brilliance of thematic adornment, as in some variations in the diaphanous music of Ravel; or they may be detrimental to the bio-musical organism, as in the cluttered polyphony of Max Reger. Recessive mutations such as Stravinsky's neo-Baroque ornamentation, may become dominant characteristics, with uncertain benefits. In human terms, mutations are found in large musical families, in which the embryo develops fully conditioned by the genetic complex of his parents. A striking example is that of Siegfried Wagner, a musical mutant who fully absorbed the musical genes of his father but acquired mutations that made him sterile. Some mutations are products of defective genes of the theme itself, a condition that may lead to melodic dyscrasia, harmonic dyslogia, and contrapuntal dyskinesia. There is no relief in such cases but to destroy the theme in statu nascendi in order to eliminate mutagenic elements and build afresh an untainted homunculus.

Mystic Chord. In conformity with his mystical beliefs, Scriabin described the basic chord of his *Prometheus,* C, F-sharp, B-flat, E, A, D, as the mystic chord. Ex post facto, he regarded these components, seriatim, as 8th, 9th, 10th, 11th, 13th, and 14th overtones. Analytically, the mystic chord belongs to the category of the dominant-ninth in a major key with two suspensions, as is made clear by resolving its F-sharp to G and its A to B-flat.

Narcolepsy. Symphony concerts are notoriously conducive to narcolepsy, and their attendance is sometimes recommended by psychologists as an effective cure of insomnia. Statistical surveys indicate that the narcogenic factors are mainly the pendulum-like rhythmic beats in classical music, particularly when there is no change in dynamics. An unexpected *sforzando* will wake up even the most inveterate narcoleptic, as illustrated by the story of Haydn's *Surprise Symphony* with its famous chord in the slow movement that was supposed to arouse the somnolent London concert goers from their middle-aged slumber. On the other hand, modern works rarely put people to sleep because of the constant changes in rhythm and dynamics. Narcolepsy is also an inevitable outcome of lectures on musicology; according to observations conducted by a trained psychologist at a session of the International Musicological Congress in New York, a deep coma overtook practically the entire audience during the first twenty seconds of a reading from manuscript of a paper by an eminent Dutch musicologist. At the same occasion, attention was suddenly increased by the appearance on the podium of the inventor of a double-bass flute and an ultra-sonic piccolo. He could never succeed in blowing through the long tube of the big flute, which met with sympathy in the audience. The hyper-piccolo could not be heard by humans, but a terrier dog who strayed into the hall showed agitation at the ultra-sonics that canines can hear easily. Both the dog and the inventor were rewarded by hearty applause.

Naturalism. In musical usage, Naturalism appears as an extreme case of VERISMO. Naturalistic opera emphasizes the negative phenomena of life without the redeeming quality of romance. In Soviet parlance Naturalism acquired a pejorative meaning; the word was launched as a verbal missile in the attacks on Shostakovich's opera *Lady Macbeth of the District of Mzensk,* particularly with reference to the scene of adultery illustrated in an orchestral interlude by sliding trombones.

Negative Music. Negative Music is synonymous with ANTI-MUSIC, but there is a scintilla of difference between the two. ANTI-MUSIC stresses its opposition to any musical actions, whereas Negative Music operates on the supposition that there may exist negative frequencies as mathematical abstractions, related to audible music as a negative to the positive in photography. Negative Music would reverse dynamic values; a vocal text containing tender sentiments would be harmonized by loud dissonant noises; conversely, a symphonic poem on the subject of the nuclear war would be depicted by the minutest distillation of monodically concentrated tones. The field for experimentation in Negative Music is limitless, precisely because it is impossible to speculate about its nature.

Neo-Classicism. When the luxuriance of IMPRESSIONISM reached its point of saturation, it became clear to many composers that further amplification of coloristic devices was no longer stimulating or novel. The Weber-Fechner law postulates that the force of physical impact must be increased exponentially in order to produce an arithmetical increase in the sensory impression, so that a hundredfold magnification of sound is needed to provide a tenfold increase in the physiological effect. It was to be expected that composers and audiences alike would rebound from such sonic inundation. This reaction coincided with the economic collapse following World War I so that it became financially impossible to engage large orchestras or grandiose operatic companies. The cry went all over Europe, "Back to Bach!" To this was added the slogan of NEW SIMPLICITY. Since it was no longer feasible to move forward, musical tastes with the aid of intellectual rationalization made a 180-degree turn towards the past. But the past could not be recaptured in its literal form, and the new retrograde movement was launched under the name of Neo-Classicism. It was characterized by the following traits: (1) Rehabilitation of diatonicism as the dominant idiom, enhanced pandiatonic constructions, in which all seven degrees of the diatonic scale are functionally equal; (2) Elimination of all programmatic and romantic associations either in the titles or the tonal content of individual works; (3) A demonstrative revival of the Baroque forms of sonata, serenade, scherzo, passacaglia, toccata, and the florid type of variations; (4) Demotion of chromatic elements of the scale to their traditional role as passing notes. (5) Restrained use of massive sonorities and renunciation of all external and purely decorative effects, such as non-thematic melismas and non-essential harmonic figurations; (6) Cultivation of compact forms, such as symphonies and sonatas having a single movement and operas without a chorus and with a reduced orchestral contingent (usually containing 13 instruments), with an important piano part performing the function of the cembalo in Baroque music; (7) Reconstruction of old Baroque instruments, particularly the harpsichord, and their employment in modernized classical techniques; (8) Exploration of canonic and fugal writing without adherence to strict rules of classical polyphony; and (9) Radical curtailment of the development section in Baroque forms with a purely nominal recapitulation, and a concise coda free from redundant repetition of final tonic chords.

Neo-Medievalism. NEW-CLASSICISM resuscitated Baroque music in a new guise of pandiatonic harmonies and asymmetrical rhythms. Retreating still further into the past, some modern composers discovered a world of surprisingly modernistic devices such as hocketus, heterophony, and quodlibet, and the techniques of inversion and retrograde composition that are basic to SERIAL MUSIC. Modernization of these resources resulted in the stylized idiom of Neo-Medievalism, which adopted not only the old musical modalities, but the verbal usages of ecclesiastical Latin for texts. The most remarkable example of this trend is Stravinsky's oratorio *Oedipus Rex* with a specially written text in medieval Latin. Carl Orff produced a number of successful works in a Neo-Medieval style, notably *Carmina Burana*, to texts in Latin and German dialects. A significant trait of these works is their imaginative repetitive technique. The liberating power of literal repetition has a particular attraction for composers of the AVANT-GARDE who follow oriental religious practices, exemplified by the interminable turning of the Tibetan prayer wheel.

Neo-Modality. The system of modes, so potent for centuries, nearly lost all its binding power under the impact of ATONALITY and DODECAPHONY. Dormant strains have achieved a new Renaissance in the ethnically deep-rooted works of Béla Bartók. A surprising revival of modality was its adoption by the purveyors of ROCK 'N' ROLL. Roy Harris built a sui generis *ethos* of modes by assigning specific emotions to each, according to the intervallic magnitude of the opening tetrachord, ranging from the most spacious, Lydian mode, expressing optimism, to the least spacious, Locrian mode, expressing pessimism. Avenir H. Monfred developed a practical method of modern modal composition, diatonic Neo-Modality, in which a modal change is effected by altering the key signature. Thus the Dorian mode on D can be transformed, either during the process of composition or by spontaneous improvisation, into any other mode by adding sharps or flats to the key signature; it would be transmuted into D major by placing two sharps in the key signature, into the Phrygian mode by two flats, etc.

Neo-Mysticism. The words "Laus Deo" which Haydn used to append to every manuscript upon its completion were simply the expression of his piety and did not imply a claim of direct communication with the Deity. Mystical composers of the 20th century, on the other hand, believed that they were oracles of higher powers. Gustav Mahler thought he was possessed by Beelzebub. He scrawled appeals to Satan in the manuscript of his unfinished Tenth Symphony; he believed in the mystical magic of all of his music. But it was left to Scriabin to formalize his mystical consciousness in musical terms. His symphony *Prometheus* is based on a six-note chord which he called MYSTIC CHORD. Shortly before his death he sketched out the text for a *Mysterium*, which he envisioned as a synaesthetic action which would comprise all human senses as receiving organs. A large ensemble of bells was an instrumental feature of this eschatological creation, to be performed high over the Himalayan Mountains.

Neophobia. Musical neophobia is a neurotic fear of radical innovations. Professional music critics are particularly prone to suffer from it, a condition that they attempt to disguise as profound devotion to the immutable laws of music. Like mental patients, they regard themselves as the only rational human beings in a mad world. The more enlightened among them often correct their former misapprehensions. At the first American performance of *Don Juan* by Richard Strauss, Philip Hale described it as "a good deal of a bore." Eleven years later he called it a work of "fascinating, irresistible insolence and glowing passion." Heinrich Strobel, who became the great panjandrum of the AVANT-GARDE, contributed some choice invectives against the American moderns in his report of a concert in Berlin in 1932: "For two hours Nicolas Slonimsky bore down on the musicians of the Berlin Philharmonic, until finally they could no longer refrain from openly showing their disgust. For an hour and three quarters the public tolerated the noise, but by the cacophonous melee of *Arcana* by Varèse the audience lost their patience. A scandal broke loose. It was understandable. No ear can endure this sort of noise for any length of time. It has nothing to do with music. It does not shock and it does not amuse. It is simply senseless."

Neo-Primitivism. An art saturated with culture is invariably tempted to return to its simple origins, chronologically to the cave paintings of primitive man and to the haunting drum rhythms of Homo Protomusicus, and biologically to INFANTILOQUY. Supreme mastery of design is used by abstract expressionist painters to emulate pre-historic color drawings, and a sophisticated instrumental technique is utilized by modern composers for children's pieces in asymmetrical rhythms.

From these dual resources, intuitively developed by primitive man and by a human child, grew the language of Neo-Primitivism. Discarding the civilized garments of romantic images and Impressionistic colors, it seeks to attain the crude power of massively arrayed sonorities, asymmetrical rhythms and percussive instrumentation. In Neo-Primitivism, melodies are brief refrains, often limited to the range of a major tetrachord. Reiteration of single notes in unchanged speed is cultivated to the point of stupefaction. Vacuous progressions of naked fifths and fourths are used to form an impression of inarticulate eloquence. Heterophony, in which a mobile voice elaborates on the principal subject ignoring the niceties of counterpoint, is encountered in numerous scores of Neo-Primitivistic music, as a curious recessive characteristic.

Neo-Primitivism is almost invariably nationalistic in character. The greatest masterpiece of Neo-Primitivism, Stravinsky's *Le Sacre du Printemps*, bears the subtitle *Scenes of Pagan Russia*. Béla Bartók's music evokes the Neo-Primitivistic landscape of immemorial Pannonia. Villa-Lobos recreates the inchoate sound of the Brazilian jungle in his symphonies. Neo-Primitivism is nurtured on the essential character of the race, but the composer himself need not be an archeologist; he derives his inspiration from the art of his own time. The French painter Henri Rousseau copied the subjects and color patterns of his exotic paintings from illustrations in a French children's book. Paul Gauguin painted his Tahitian women from photographs, preferring them to living models. Nonetheless, both created a genuinely novel type of pictorial Neo-Primitivism. In music, however, Neo-Primitivistic representation cannot be effected without a complete mastery of modern techniques of composition. The theory that an analphabetic musician can write primitivistically authentic works by simply disregarding the civilized rules of harmony and counterpoint is false.

Neo-Romanticism. Neo-Romanticism represents a secondary phase of the modern stylistic upheaval, following the repudiation of programmatic music as a valid medium. The frustrations of World War I sharpened a general disenchantment among poets, artists, and musicians, but the purely negative intellectual movements, such as DADAISM, soon exhausted their shock power and gave way to a mitigated type of romantic music in the form of Neo-Romanticism. Coloristic elements, so ingratiatingly used in the symphonies of Sibelius, in the tone poems of Richard Strauss, and in the early ballet scores of Stravinsky, were applied with apprehensive circumspection by Neo-Romantic composers. Representational onomatopoeia and literal reproduction of natural sounds replaced the subjective effusions of modern pictorialism. Benjamin Britten's sea gulls in the interludes of his opera *Peter Grimes*, Olivier Messiaen's bird-songs in his score *Chronochromie*, and the phonograph record of the song of a real nightingale in Ottorino Respighi's *Pines of Rome* are modern instances of Neo-Romanticism.

New Music. Newness is a recurring motive in musical nomenclature. The emergence of rhythmic modalities in the 14th century became historically known as Ars Nova. The monadic type of composition used by the Florentine initiators of opera was published under the name *Nuove musiche*. In painting, *Art Nouveau* was the description given the French art that flourished in the 1890s. The term New Music became current about 1920; it denoted a type of modern music marked by a dissonant counterpoint, ATONALITY, and brevity of expression. Later, New Music became synonymous with ULTRA-MODERN MUSIC.

New Simplicity. During the NEO-CLASSICAL flowering of the 1920s, the slogan New Simplicity was raised among composers eager to divest themselves of an enforced sophistication of the period. In practice, New Simplicity meant a return to elementary and sometimes ABECEDARIAN melodic and harmonic practices, barely covered with a patina of NON-TOXIC DISSONANCES.

Non-Toxic Dissonances. Dissonances can be said to be non-toxic or non-corrosive if they are embanked within a tonal sequence, or if their cadential illation corresponds to traditional modalities. It is the harmonic context that determines the toxicity of a dissonance for an untutored ear. Among the most corrosive dissonances are atonal combinations in which intervals of a high degree of discordance, such as major sevenths, minor seconds, and the tritone, are combined with acoustically euphonious intervals of a perfect fifth and a perfect fourth. The absence of thirds, whether major or minor, is the distinctive feature of corrosive harmony, but toxic sonic effects result also from the simultaneous use of two homonymous major and minor triads on account of the interference between the major and minor thirds. Changes in bio-chemical balance and nervous reactions to the impact of toxic dissonances can be measured on a neurograph, providing a scientific clue to the apperception of modern music.

Numbers. The Latin word *Numeri* had a second meaning, music, for it was governed by the law of proportions between two different sounds. In Shakespearean English, numbers refer to musical composition. St. Augustine drew a distinction between *Numeri sonantes*, the actual musical tones that are perceived by the senses, and *Numeri recordabiles*, music that is remembered. In St. Augustine's concept, a melody was formed by a single sound instantaneously perceived and memorably associated with several preceding sounds. Long before St. Augustine, Aristoxenus likened the musical tones of a melody to letters in a language. So intimate was the connection felt between numbers and music that in medieval universities music was taught as part of the Quadrivium of exact sciences, along with arithmetic, geometry, and astronomy. This association with numbers was lost in classical and romantic music. Not until the 20th century did the numerical element in music regain its status. Mathematical parameters lie at the foundation of serial music. The calculus of sets is an important tool in rhythmic serialization. Some composers have applied the Fibonacci numbers, in which each term is the sum of its two predecessors, to metrical, rhythmic, and intervallic parameters. Simple arithmetical progressions also yield material for rhythmic arrangements. The application of numbers to composition is limitless; the difficulty is to select numerical sets that would provide material for purely musical structures.

Objets Trouvés. Ready-made objects are often incorporated by modern artists as part of a sculpture or a montage. Ultra-modern composers sometimes insert passages from works by other composers as a token of homage and partly as an experiment in construction. Such objets trouvés need not harmonize with their environment which may be completely alien to the nature of the implant. An early example is the sudden appearance of the tune *Ach du lieber Augustin* in Schoenberg's Second String Quartet.

Omnitonality. In search of terms signifying various degrees of modulatory freedom, modern musicologists have chanced upon omnitonality to indicate a totality of tonalities entailing frequent collisions of different keys. Omnitonality enjoyed a certain vogue as a compromise definition for modern techniques that retained the basic sense of tonality but expanded it to the entire cycle of major and minor scales. It is almost synonymous with PANTONALITY.

Open Form Composition. Works based on CONTROLLED IMPROVISATION, in which materials are selected from available resources, have a venerable ancestry; classical composers supplied alternative versions for transitions and endings as a matter of course. In its modern avatar, open form composition often delegates the ordering of component parts to the performer. Chronological priority in developing such techniques belongs to the American composer Earle Brown whose *Folio*, written in 1952, affords great latitude in the arranging of given materials. Karlheinz Stockhausen further developed this technique in his *Klavierstücke*, which consist of separate sections which can be performed in any order.

Organized Sound. Sound is an acoustical phenomenon, which by itself does not make music. Composition begins at the point when two sounds are connected in linear succession or vertical superposition. But the nature of these links is not circumscribed by any rules of melody and harmony. With the emancipation of dissonances in the 20th century, the vertical combinations became free from restraints imposed on them by tradition. Linear progressions, once bound within the framework of modes and scales, are developed in atonal designs. Arnold Schoenberg replaced diatonic melody and consonant harmony by the new dodecaphonic discipline. Edgar Varèse advanced the concept of organized sound as a complex of successive acoustical phenomena unrelated to one another except by considerations of sonic equilibrium. Dissonant combinations are preferred because they constitute a probabilistic majority and therefore are entitled to greater representation in organized sound. For the same statistical reasons, successions of melodic notes are apt to generate atonal configurations. The form of works written according to the doctrine of organized sound is athematic, and the rhythms are usually asymmetric. The valence between successive units, in melody, harmony, and rhythm, under such conditions, is an idempotent.

Palimpsest. In musical semantics, the term palimpsest may be used as a substitution for an intentionally erased composition. This erasure may be complete or partial, with some elements of the original idea left under the sonic surface. A now-classic example in the 20th century is John Cage's *Apartment House 1776*, constructed in one of its primary aspects of 18th-century tunes, marches, drum solos, and imitations transformed by replacing original notes (most suggesting cadence points) with other less determining notes from the same basic tonal set. The hidden design in such works may be discovered by intervallic analysis, comparable to the use of ultra-violet rays in detecting the old text in a parchment covered by a newer piece of writing.

Palindrome. Palindromic words and sentences do not change when they are read backwards. Max Reger, whose last name is itself a palindrome, replied wittily to an admirer who complained that he could see only his back while he conducted a concert: "I am no different front or back." Musical palindromes are synonymous with retrograde movements. In a palindromic section in Alban Berg's opera *Lulu*, the music revolves backwards to depict the story of Lulu's incarceration and escape. Samplers of palindromic canons are found in Nicolas Slonimsky's *Thesaurus of Scales and Melodic Patterns.*

Palingenesis. The meaning of the word palingenesis is rebirth, and it is parasynonymous with METEMPSYCHOSIS. In modern musical usage palingenesis corresponds to a reprise, with the important difference that the original material is not recapitulated literally but appears metempsychotically in a form as dissimilar from its progenitor as a reincarnated cat is from its former human avatar. Palingenesis is a particularly convenient term to designate an electronically altered sonic substance, or a topologically metamorphosed thematic idea.

Pandiatessaron. This is a vertical column consisting of perfect fourths (from *Diatessaron*, the interval of a fourth in ancient Greek music). The Pandiatessaron contains all 12 notes of the tempered scale and represents a dodecaphonic integration of quartal melodies.

Pandiatonicism. The term pandiatonicism was coined by Nicolas Slonimsky and was first used in the first edition of his book *Music Since 1900* published in 1937. It is a technique in which all seven degrees of the diatonic scale are used freely in democratic equality. The functional importance of the primary triads, however, remains undiminished in pandiatonic harmony. Pandiatonicism possesses both tonal and modal aspects, with the distinct preference for major keys. The earliest pandiatonic extension was the added major sixth over the tonic major triad. A cadential chord of the tonic major seventh is also of frequent occurrence. Independently from the development of pandiatonicism in serious music, American JAZZ players adopted it as a practical device. Concluding chords in piano improvisations in JAZZ are often pandiatonic, containing the tonic, dominant, mediant, submediant, and supersonic, with the triad in open harmony in the bass topped by a series of perfect fourths. In C major, such chords would be, from the bass up, C, G, E, A, D, G. It is significant that all the components of this pandiatonic complex are members of the natural harmonic series. With C as the fundamental generator, G is the third partial, E the fifth partial, D the 9th, B the 15th, and A the 27th. The perfect fourth is excluded both theoretically and practically, for it is not a member of the harmonic series, an interesting concordance of actual practice and acoustical considerations. With the dominant in the bass, a complete succession of fourths, one of them an augmented fourth, can be built: G, C, F, B, E, A, D, and G, producing a satisfying pandiatonic complex. When the subdominant is in the bass, the most euphonious result is obtained by a major triad in open harmony, F, C, A, in the low register, and E, B, D, G in the upper register. Polytriadic combinations are natural resources of pandiatonicism, with the dominant combined with the tonic, e.g., C, G, E, D, G, B, making allowance for a common tone; dominant over the subdominant, as in the complex, F, C, A, D, G, B, etc. True POLYTONALITY cannot be used in pandiatonicism, since all the notes are in the same mode. Pedal points are particularly congenial to the spirit of pandiatonicism, always following the natural spacing of the component notes, using large intervals in the bass register and smaller intervals in the treble. The aesthetic function of pandiatonicism is to enhance the resources of triadic harmony; that is the reason why the superposition of triads, including those in minor, are always productive of a resonant diatonic bitonality. Although pandiatonicism has evolved from tertian foundations, it lends itself to quartal and quintal constructions with satisfactory results. Pandiatonicism is a logical medium for the techniques of NEO-CLASSICISM. Many sonorous usages of pandiatonicism can be found in the works of Debussy, Ravel, Stravinsky, Casella, Malipiero, Vaughan Williams, Aaron Copland, and Roy Harris. The key of C major is particularly favored in piano music, thanks to the "white" quality of the keyboard. Indeed, pandiatonic piano music developed empirically from free improvisation on the white keys. Small children promenading their little fingers over the piano keyboard at the head level produce pandiatonic melodies and harmonies of excellent quality and quite at random.

Panpentatonicism. By analogy with PANDIATONICISM, which denotes a free use of the seven diatonic degrees, panpentatonicism grants a similar dispensation to the five notes of the pentatonic scale. Consecutive fourths and fifths are frequent contrapuntal resources. Since the leading tone is missing in the pentatonic scale, plagal cadences are the only available endings. Panpentatonic tone-clusters are more euphonious than pandiatonic ones; when projected against a perfect fifth in the bass, they create an attractive sonority of a modernistic panpentatonic chinoiserie.

Pantonality. The term pantonality denotes the use of all major and minor keys with complete freedom and without preference for any particular tonality. Pantonality is almost synonymous with OMNITONALITY, the only difference being that pantonality includes atonal melodic progressions and uninhibited dissonant textures, while OMNITONALITY tends to enhance the basic sense of tonality.

Parerga and Paralipomena. Like Schopenhauer, who published fragments of his philosophical writings under the high-sounding name "parerga and paralipomena," Richard Strauss gathered some residual materials from his *Symphonia domestica*, and incorporated them in a work commissioned by the amputated pianist Paul Wittgenstein, denominated *Parergon zur Symphonia domestica*, and scored for piano left-hand and orchestra. While such creative thrift is justified when Schopenhauer or Strauss practice it, collections and arrangements of *disjecta membra* put together by composers of lesser endowment, and particularly those whose technical progress was arrested at the ABECEDARIAN or ANALPHABETIC niveau, are clearly objectionable.

Permeability. Permeability is a factor that determines the degree of interpenetrability of thematic, non-thematic, and bruitistic elements, reinforcing the structure of a given tonal complex, and occasionally coming to a mutually annihilating collision, in which the resulting GESTALT becomes a terraced and tesselated ziggurat. The term permeability is also used to describe the process of mutual osmosis among parameters of ORGANIZED SOUND.

Pernicious Interference. The law of contrasts is basic to every piece of modern music, but supererogatory acervation and ornamental promiscuity of melodic and harmonic elements constitute pernicious interference. Taste and technical skill are the sole means to avoid this danger.

Planarianism. A musical composition that can be dissected into two or more parts with each growing out into a separate independent body may be called planarian, by analogy with the flatworm of that name that possesses a trifid intestine and is capable of regenerating each of its severed parts into new flatworms. The structure of a work in the style of planarianism may reach great complexity. Karlheinz Stockhausen has written autogenetic works that can be cut up, with each musical planarian becoming a self-sufficient sonic organism. This process of vermiculation and its concomitant divisibility has been further advanced by John Cage; at his hands, each musical platyhelminth becomes a unique and irreproducible species.

Plastic, Elastic, and Spastic Variations. Plasticity of texture is essential in modern variations, securing a malleability of tonal materials. Tonal elasticity adds intervallic flexibility to a plastic theme. A rhythmic effect can be achieved by spastic convulsions of the melodic line, producing implosions which impart a stimulating sense of disquiet to the music.

Pluralistic Structures. Pluralism is an epistemological concept connoting a multiplicity of causes and events. Developments of modern music support the pluralistic view in such styles as NEO-CLASSICAL, IMPRESSIONISTIC, or EXPRESSIONISTIC, in which the factors of melody, rhythm, and intervallic values are of different formulation. But the same type of structure becomes monistic if it is derived from a uniform set, as for instance in variations. Pluralism and monism are mutually specular, but they are reconciled in serial music. Analogies with the visible spectrum invite themselves. White light is monistic in its sensory perception, but pluralistic when it is analyzed into the prismatic constituents of the rainbow. WHITE SOUND is a monistic aggregation of sonic particles, which can be separated into a pluralistic collection of its tonal components.

Pointillism. In the nomenclature of modern art, Pointillism is a method of applying colored dots to the canvas, forming a cumulative design as in the celebrated pixilated creations of Georges Seurat. In modern music, the term is descriptive of atonal and athematic idioms, in which separate notes are distributed individually rather than as parts of an integral melorhythmic curve. The maximal dispersion of members of a dodecaphonic series in different octave positions is an example of serial Pointillism.

Political Symbolism. In the affective usages of the Renaissance, major keys symbolized joy and minor keys sadness. Such correspondence of emotional states and sounds has an acoustical foundation, for the major third is the fifth overtone of the fundamental tone, while the minor third is not a member of the harmonic series and produces interference. This natural preference for major keys as acoustically superior to minor tonalities was the subject of an interesting philosophical exposition of political symbolism given by Anatoly Lunacharsky, Soviet Commissar of Education in an introductory speech at a Moscow concert on 10 December 1919: "Major keys lift the sound; they raise it a semitone up, and its power grows. By analogy with laughter, with its exultant feeling of joy, major keys elevate the mood and cheer us up. Minor keys, on the other hand, droop, leading to a compromise, to a surrender of positions; the sound is lowered, and its power diminishes. Allow me, as an old Bolshevik, to put it this way: major tonality is Bolshevik music; but a minor key is a deeply rooted inner Menshevik. Cultural history chose to call major and minor two different species of modes in the world of sound. Bolsheviks and Mensheviks are the two parties which have not only determined the fate of Russia in the greatest years of her life, but became a world phenomenon, and brought out, along with reactionary and bourgeois slogans, the two most important banners around which all humanity gathers."

Pollution. Harmonic pollution is characterized by indiscriminate disposal of chromatic refuse in a diatonic landscape. The process is vividly illustrated by a fetid organ arrangement of Chopin's *Nocturne* in E-flat major, in which the initial ascending interval of a major sixth, from B-flat to G, is infested by noxious chromatic runs. A polluted version of Prokofiev's *Peter and the Wolf* has been published in America in the absence of a copyright agreement with the Soviet Union; it is characterized by vulgar insertion of auxiliary material in every available melodic or harmonic vacancy. Orchestral pollution manifests itself in a general sonic flatulence and an infarction of supernumerary thirds and sixths. The rhythmic line, too, is an easy victim of pollution. In the remarkable compound rhythmic design in Gershwin's song *I Got Rhythm*, the original asymmetric line is often grossly mutilated, reducing it to abecedarian syncopation. Erudite arrangements of works of Bach and other classics, made by musicians of intelligence and taste, cannot be cited as examples of musical pollution. Even hyperchromatic pullulation found in some transcriptions by Max Reger possesses validity, though they should be labelled "artificially flavored with chromatic additives." Some morphological transformations and homeological modifications are legitimate means of modernization. Examples of such artistic enhancement are *Symphonic Metamorphoses on Themes of Carl Maria von Weber* by Hindemith and the ballet *Le Baiser de la Fée* by Stravinsky, imaginatively deformed from themes of Tchaikovsky.

Polymetry. In a linear application, polymetry is a succession of changing meters; polyphonically, polymetry is the simultaneous use of several different meters. polymetry dates back to the Renaissance exemplified in the double time signature of Spanish dance music, 3/4 against 6/8. In operatic usage, polymetry is encountered in scenes descriptive of simultaneous uncoordinated action, known under the name imbroglio (literally, entanglement). The concluding section of Stravinsky's *Le Sacre du Printemps*, with its constantly changing time signatures, represents linear polymetry at its greatest complexity. (It is characteristic of changing fashions that in 1940 Stravinsky rearranged this section in more uniform time signatures.) The unequal division of binary and ternary meters, which is a species of linear polymetry, is found in Rimsky-Korsakov's opera *The Legend of the City of Kitezh*, in which the invading Mongols are characterized by the irregularly divided measures of 2/8 + 2/8 + 2/8 + 3/8 = 9/8 and 3/8 + 2/8 + 3/8 = 8/8. Linear polymetry of this type is also characteristic of Balkan popular dances. Modern composers, fascinated by purely numerical properties of fractions representing traditional time signatures, often follow a predetermined arithmetical formula to establish a desired metrical progression. Boris Blacher makes use of the series of numerators 1, 2, 3, 4, 5, 4, 3, 2, 1, in his orchestral *Ornaments*. Elliott Carter employs "metric modulation" by changing meter and tempo in polyphonic writing. The Welsh composer Daniel Jones has developed a system of complex time signatures based on repeated numerical patterns, some of them of extraordinary length, e.g., 32322322232232323323332332/4 and 9864323468/8, both used in his *Sonata for Three Kettledrums*. He also has elaborated the techniques of augmentation, diminution, and retrograde in changing time signatures, designated by such arithmetical ALGORITHMS as 6432/8 and 3464/8. The numerators in all these examples represent the succession of repeated or changing numbers of beats in a bar.

Perhaps the most remarkable instance of contrapuntal polymetry is found in the second movement of *Three Places in New England* by Charles Ives, illustrating the meeting of two marching bands, with similar marching tunes played simultaneously at different tempi, in the ratio 4/3, so that four bars of the faster march equal three bars of the slower tempo. In his original manuscript Ives coordinated these different tempi within the uniform measures in 4/4 time, marking cross-accents wherever they occurred. At the suggestion of Nicolas Slonimsky, Ives agreed to incorporate in the published score an alternative arrangement with non-coincidental barlines, in clear polymetric notation. In his performances of the work, Slonimsky conducted three bars in 4/4 time with his right hand and four bars in *alla breve* time with his left hand. In this polymetric coordination, the downbeat of the left hand coincides successively with the downbeat of the right hand, then with the fourth beat of the right hand, with the third beat, with the second beat, and again with the downbeat of the right hand. In the first bar the upbeat of the left hand falls between the second and the third beats of the right hand; in the next bar the upbeat of the left hand occurs between the downbeat and the second beat of the right hand, and so on. Those in the orchestra who had parts with the faster march were to follow the conductor's left hand and the rest his right hand. (A critic remarked that Slonimsky's performance was evangelical, for his right hand knew not what his left hand was doing.)

Polymodality. Polymodality is a special case of POLYTONALITY in which the principal melodic lines are modal rather than explicitly major or minor. Polymodal harmonies are disposed with the best effect by the use of a triple pedal point in open harmony in a minor key, suggesting Dorian, Phrygian, or Aeolian constructions.

Polyrhythmy. As the etymology of the word indicates, polyrhythmy is the simultaneous occurrence of several different rhythms. polyrhythmy differs from POLYMETRY in that the former indicates a combination of two rhythmic groups, usually consisting of mutually prime numbers of notes or irregular groups of non-coincident patterns, while the latter merely indicates the superposition, or a palimpsest, of two different meters usually having the same note values as their common denominator. If two measures of different time signatures are isochronous, then the effect is both polymetric and polyrhythmic. The problems of the polyrhythmic notation have been solved by composers of the AVANT-GARDE who prefer to indicate the duration of individual notes or rhythmic groups in seconds rather than note values. Another possible solution of polyrhythmic notation would be to introduce time signatures with denominators not limited to the powers of two. A time signature of 2/3 or 4/7 would replace triplets or septuplets in binary meters, but attempts to introduce such numerical innovations have been unsuccessful.

Polytetrachord. A term introduced by Nicolas Slonimsky in his *Thesaurus of Scales and Melodic Patterns*, polytetrachord is omnitonal. A major polytetrachord consists of 12 conjunct major tetrachords, traversing all 12 keys of the cycle of major scales. A minor polytetrachord consists of 12 keys of the cycle of minor scales. A partial use of the polytetrachord affords a rapid linear modulation into any major or minor key.

Polytonality. Polytonality is the simultaneous use of several keys. In actual practice, it is difficult to sustain the acoustical separation of more than two different keys, thus reducing polytonality to BITONALITY. Four mutually exclusive triads are workable in linear arpeggios (e.g., C major, F-sharp major, D minor, G-sharp minor, distributed in ascending quadritonal passages), but the same four keys in columnar superposition could be made effective only by careful differentiation of instrumental groups (e.g., C major in the strings, F-sharp major in muted horns, D minor in clarinets and oboes, and G-sharp minor in flutes and piccolos, with optional support of the strings by the bassoons and double-bassoons).

Simultaneous linear progressions of two or more different tonalities are in the category of polytonality. Bitonal scales with their tonics at a distance of major or minor thirds or sixths are entirely consonant, even though they run along different tonalities. But even scales in parallel major sevenths, if played at sufficiently large distances, become technically consonant. Theoretically, C major played in the lowest available register of the piano and B major scale at a distance of four, five, or six octaves, minus a semi-tone, will form consonant harmony, because B in relation to the low C at such distances constitutes the 15th, 30th, and 60th partial of the harmonic series. The coda of *Also sprach Zarathustra* of Richard Strauss contains a B major triad in the high treble with a double bass playing a low C, an instance often referred to as the first explicit use of polytonality. Actually, the members of the B major triad in the treble represent the 60th, 75th, and 90th partials of the harmonic series, generated by the low C, and are therefore consonant combinations. Genuine, acoustically pure polytonal combinations can be provided by playing the triads of D major, E major, G major, and others against C major in the deep bass without falling into dissonance. Beyond the audible range, even F-sharp major, the farthest key in the cycle of scales from C major, can be brought into the harmonic series. Most polytonal combinations, however, are not even theoretically consonant. An amusing example of polytonality is Mozart's *Ein musikalischer Spass*, where he makes the horns play in different keys from the rest of the orchestra. But Mozart's professed intention in this "musical joke" was to ridicule the ignorance of village musicians. He could not have anticipated the time when such musical jokes would become a new technique.

Polytriads. Polytriadic harmony may be regarded as a special case of POLYTONALITY, with mobile parts containing complete triads. If the triads move along a single scale or a mode, the resulting technique is POLYMODALITY. Homonymous triads, major and minor, encased within the compass of a perfect fifth (e.g., C, E-flat, E-natural, G), are often found in modern works. Such polytriads are *e duobus unum*, giving rise to modes possessing the characteristics of both major and minor keys.

Pop Music. The colloquial abbreviation of the term Popular Music into Pop Music corresponds to the depreciation and devaluation of materials and resources of the original product. Pop Music is a counterpart of Pop Art, with its appeal directed mainly towards the heterogeneous musical, unmusical, and anti-musical masses. Its effects are achieved by the application of raucous and blatant sounds amplified by electronics. Pop Music annexes numerous forms from the vast arsenal of sentimental ballads and country music and it manages to instill a tremendous amount of kinetic energy into its public manifestations. While Pop Music belongs in the category of DEMOTIC MUSIC, it tends to be more cosmopolitan in its appeal and capable of attracting miscellaneous groups of people without requiring special adaptation to the changing tastes of the audiences.

Pornographic Music. It was Eduard Hanslick who said that the last movement of Tchaikovsky's Violin Concerto suggested to him the hideous notion that music can actually stink to the ear. The literal depiction of an episode in *Symphonia Domestica* by Richard Strauss, which illustrates his retirement to the bed chamber with Frau Strauss, to the suggestive accompaniment of two conjugated trumpets, impressed some listeners at its first performance as indecent. In a symphonic interlude in Shostakovich's opera *Lady Macbeth of the District of Mzensk*, with the marital bed occupying the center of the stage, the trombone glissandi seem to give an onomatopoeic representation of sexual intercourse. Graphic notation also offers excellent opportunities for suggestive pictorial pornography. The tetraphallic score *Mooga Pook* by the American composer Charles Amirkhanian is a fine example.

Potential Techniques. The number of potential techniques of musical composition is unlimited, as is the number of mathematical sets or matrices. The best-known numerical set in music is the method of composition with 12 tones, or DODECAPHONIC MUSIC. But it is possible to devise a hendecaphonic method, or decaphonic method, generated respectively by eleven or ten tones in a series. Any technique of composition is valid provided it is self-consistent. It is entirely justified to postulate a system in which only dissonant intervals are used. It is also conceivable to devise a method of composing only with nominal consonances (such a system was applied by Nicolas Slonimsky in his piano suite *Studies in Black and White*, in which only consonant intervals are used in a scheme of mutually exclusive counterpoint of pandiatonic sets in the right hand played on the white keys and panpentatonic figurations in the left hand played on the black keys). Any number of deficient or lipogrammatic systems of composition can be constructed by stipulating the omission of a note or a group of notes. Some modern poets, especially those of the Oulipian persuasion, experimented with all manner of contrived literary systems to achieve a special effect. Georges Perec's novel, *La Disparition (A Void)*, was written without ever using that most frequent letter of the English alphabet, E, thus dispensing with the definite article, most personal pronouns, etc. (as one critic from *The New York Times Book Review* put it "That's right: no here, there, where, when; no yes, no love, no sex!"). The following techniques in music may be tabulated as possessing a workable rationale and some attractive coloristic features which might give them statistical chances of survival:

(1) Exclusive use of a limited number of notes in a scale, exemplified by the five-note scale, or pentatonic scale, and the whole-tone scale of six notes, the so-called Rimsky-Korsakov scale of alternating whole tones and semitones, a scale of nine notes consisting of three disjunct minor thirds with passing notes within the interval of each minor third, etc.

(2) Various lipogrammatic lipographic scales, including the hendecaphonic scale and decaphonic scale, often used by serial composers who do not wish to be restricted to the orthodox dodecaphonic method.

(3) Residual scales, in which the notes left over in a lipogrammatic composition are used as a matrix in a coda or a cadential codicil. In a hendecaphonic composition, such a codicil would contain a single note repeated in unison, in octave duplications, or in triplicate, quadruplicate, quintuplicate, sextuplicate, and septuplicate, using all available octave points. Residual scales are legitimate devices in the building of dodecaphonic series. Thus the seven notes of the C major scale joined by the five notes of the pentatonic scale of the black keys would form a 12-tone matrix. Such a complex may also be called a conjugated diatonic-pentatonic complex.

(4) Intervallic lipographs, in which certain intervals are deliberately avoided in a serial set. Thirds and sixths, being most intimately associated with classical harmony, may be peremptorily excluded in favor of the seconds and sevenths in order to secure a prevalence of dissonant intervals. Emphatic use of naked fourths and fifths, to the exclusion of all other

intervals, is a lipographic device to conjure up an archaic effect. A growing fashion in modern music is the selective assignment of a certain interval to a specific instrument. Béla Bartók made such a selective distribution of intervals in the second movement, "Game of the Couples," of his *Concerto for Orchestra*, in which five pairs of wind instruments are each given a distinct interval to cultivate. Several modern composers apply such intervallic lipographs to instruments in chamber music.

(5) Derivative sets, made available as functions of a certain melodic figure differentiated by a given intervallic modulus. Let us differentiate a descending whole-tone scale in the bass by an ascending set of the following intervals: octave, major tenth, perfect 12th, two octaves, etc. Its derivative function will be the ascending melodic line of the following intervals: whole tone, semitone, sesquitone, whole tone, etc. This is a very important progression governing the harmonization in major triads in root position in contrary motion, found in Liszt's symphonic poem *Divine Comedy* and in the second act of Puccini's opera *Tosca*, announcing the entrance of the Chief of Police. Let us now harmonize the ascending whole-tone scale in the melody using the same function, that is harmonization by major triads in root position in contrary motion following the intervallic distances between the melody and the bass at a perfect octave, a major tenth, a perfect 12th, a double octave, etc. The function in the bass will be a descending pattern of the following intervals: whole tone, semitone, sesquitone, whole tone, whole tone. This is the inversion of the melodic function obtained by differentiating by the same modulus the descending whole-tone scale in the bass. We find then that the whole-tone scale differentiated either in a descending bass or in an ascending melodic line will result in an identical function, inverted, and will thus constitute a reciprocal function, or an idempotent. Most interesting of all such reciprocal sets are those in which the principal equation is tonal and the derivative is atonal. A good example is an ascending diatonic scale in the melody arranged in two-part counterpoint with the stipulation that the derivative function should be a descending set seeking the nearest available nominal consonance. Under such conditions the differentiated ascending C major scale in the melody will result in a quasi-chromatic descending derivative set in the bass: C, B, A, A-flat, G, F-sharp, E, E-flat. But an ascending C major scale in the bass, under similar conditions, will produce a different descending derivative in the melody, C, B, G-sharp, F, E, C-sharp, B, A. The different results are explained by the fact that while a perfect fifth is a consonance, its inversion, a perfect fourth, is not. Using consonant intervals as the functional operator is of interest because of the possibility of arranging atonally shaped melodies in triadic harmonies. There is a fertile field for experimentation along these lines, for instance harmonizing the ascending chromatic scale in the melody using only members of a single major triad in the bass. (Beginning with C in the melody, it is possible to harmonize the ascending chromatic scale up to A by using only members of the F major triad in the bass, descending and ascending without producing any dissonant intervals, e.g., C, A, F, C, A, F, A, C, F, A.) Such exercises in consonant counterpoint provide unexpected illumination on the nature of diatonic and chromatic scales in their relationship to triadic tonality.

(6) Intervallic progressions using only consonant intervals with certain specifications can provide a fresh resource for new contrapuntal techniques. A very fertile set of conditions is this: select two consonant intervals and use them in an unbroken series of alternations, with this proviso, that one of the voices must move by degrees, that is a major or a minor second up or down, the other voice adjusting itself accordingly to form the next interval. Let us take the octave E–E and the fifth as the next interval. We now move the upper E to F; since the next interval must be a perfect fifth, the lower voice must move to B-flat. Now let us move the upper note back to E, and since the next interval is again an octave, then the lower voice must go down to E as well. It is now the turn of the lower voice to move up and down gradually. It moves up to F; since the next interval must be a perfect fifth, the upper voice must come down from E to C. The F in the lower voice now returns to E, and since the next interval must be an octave, then the upper voice ascends from C to E. Now the lower voice goes down to D; the next interval is a perfect fifth, so the upper voice comes down from E to A. Trying again, while observing the same conditions of gradual progression vs. free intervallic leaps, the upper voice may go a major second up to F-sharp; in this case the lower voice must respond by moving up to B, forming a perfect fifth with F-sharp; after a return to the octave on E, the upper voice may descend to D-sharp, which will be seconded by the lower voice going up to G-sharp. Then both voices return to their respective E's, and the lower voice will take over the role of the *cantus firmus*. It will move, as the upper voice did before, to F-sharp, forcing the upper voice to move to C-sharp, and after passing through the octave, will descend to D-sharp, necessitating the lowering of the upper voice to A-sharp. The final interval will again be the octave. What is remarkable in this little exercise is that every note of the chromatic scale will be covered, and nine minor triads will be outlined by their tonics and dominants. By adding the missing mediants for each one of these chords in different octaves, one would obtain a third voice of surprising melodiousness. The next experiment may be conducted with a dissonant interval alternating with a consonant interval and finally with two dissonant intervals. The addition of supplemental contrapuntal voices will supply a further resource.

(7) Homeological variations, obtained by extensions or compressions of thematic intervals, provide a novel method of structural variations. The simplest case is exemplified by a uniform duplication of all intervals. Such an operation would convert Bach's *Chromatic Fugue* into an Impressionistic piece of music, because all its semitones would be replaced by progressions of exotic-sounding whole-tone scales. If the intervals of the same fugue are halved, the outcome will be a complex of icositetraphonic harmony.

Prepared Piano. Prepared piano refers both to a modern instrument as well as an instrumental technique, one which alters the sound by placing various small objects, such as bolts, nuts, metal clips, coins, on the piano strings. The idea may be traced to the old schoolboy trick of putting a piece of paper on the piano strings to produce a tinkling, harpsichord-like sound. The first modern composer to experiment scientifically with such devices was Henry Cowell, who initiated the technique of playing directly on the piano strings, mostly glissando, and developed an extraordinary skill in stopping the strings so as to change their pitch, enabling him to play an ascending scale on the keyboard which, because of the alteration of the length of strings, resulted in a descending scale in actual sound. His disciple John Cage, whose earliest compositional tendencies were toward percussion music, explored further possibilities along these lines, giving the name to the altered instrument and writing numerous works for it, including his *Sonatas and Interludes* (1946–48), which quickly became a standard of the prepared piano repertory. Other later developments along the lines of the prepared piano are the bowed or string Piano; both, as their names suggest, introduce novel performance techniques, requiring their players to spend most or all of their time under the instrument's lid. Of particular beauty are the solo bowed piano works of the American composer Stephen Scott.

Prepense Music. This is music aforethought, the antonym of UNPREMEDITATED MUSIC.

Probability. The probability of incidence of certain intervals, notes, and rhythms in a given piece of music depends on its predetermined melorhythmic idiom. The probability of occurrence of an unresolved major seventh in a composition written before 1900 is virtually nil, while the probability of such incidence in DODECAPHONIC MUSIC is very high. Similarly, the probability of a concluding chord being a dissonance is zero for the 19th century, but it increases exponentially after 1900.

The commanding importance of the tritone in ATONAL and DODECAPHONIC MUSIC makes its appearance a probable event in compositions in which the key signature is absent. The probability of incidence of all 12 different notes and 12 different intervals in relation to the starting tone in a full chromatic scale is obviously 100%. Some problems of probability lead to paradoxical solutions. Here is an example: How many tone-rows of 12 different notes and 11 different intervals is it possible to build within the range of the octave that would form an increasing or a decreasing arithmetical progression if only the absolute value of each interval is taken into consideration irrespective of its direction, whether ascending or descending? The surprising answer is 2. Taking C as the point of departure, the rows will be: C, B, D-flat, B-flat, D, A, E-flat, A-flat, E, G, F, F-sharp, and its retrograde, each one changing intervallic direction in alternation, pendulum-like.

Progressive Jazz. In the first half of the century JAZZ was principally a spontaneous product of mass improvisation with untutored instrumentalists achieving fantastic virtuosity simply because they were not told by any teacher that the technical tricks they performed were unplayable. In 1950 a natural desire arose among the second generation of JAZZ players to acquire gloss, polish, and even theoretical knowledge. They studied with eminent European composers resident in the United States and they listened to records of modern music. They became conversant with such terms as ATONALITY and POLYTONALITY and even DODECAPHONY. They discarded the lowly banjo of the early JAZZ period as though ashamed to confess their plebeian social origin; they annexed a full complement of the Baroque ensemble in their orchestras. With full credentials, a movement was launched grandly described as progressive jazz. Technical resources kept pace with the dignity of the orchestral presentation. The WHOLE-TONE SCALE was rediscovered as an ultra-modern device and played in unison by the violins. Two different keys were used simultaneously in a daring display of POLYTONALITY. The square time was diversified occasionally by asymmetric rhythms; sometimes compound meters were inserted. But despite these adornments and borrowings from respectable sources, progressive jazz could never attain distinction and soon gave way to a more homely but less pretentious style of jazzification.

Prolepsis. Schlegel said: "Der Historiker ist ein rückwärts gekehrter Prophet." The notion that a historian might be a prophet of the past is most provocative. The modern cultivation of some of the recessive traits of the musical past represents such a prophecy turned backwards. Consecutive fifths were the rule before the advent of tertian counterpoint; they were strictly forbidden in classical music, but returned early in the 20th century in the guise of neo-archaic usages, and were further reinforced in the practice of consecutive triadic harmonies. The dissonant heterophony of ancient modalities was incorporated as a novelty in NEO-PRIMITIVISM. The "Wicked Bible" became a collector's item because of a negative particle inadvertently omitted from the commandment forbidding adultery. Erik Satie drew a table of anti-commandments in his *Catéchisme du Consevatoire* in which he ridiculed the elevation of once forbidden practices to the status of harmonic laws: "Avec grand soin tu violeras/ Des règles du vieux rudiment./ Quintes de suite tu feras/ Et octaves pareillement./ Au grand jamais ne résoudras/ De dissonance aucunement. / Aucun morceau ne finiras/ Jamais par accord consonnant." The exclusion of major triads in the Schoenbergian table of commandments is the most striking instance of prolepsis. Indeed, every determined violation of the academic rules becomes a case for prolepsis if such a violation becomes itself a rule.

Proletarian Music. The ideological upheaval that accompanied the Soviet revolution of 1917 posed an immediate problem of creating arts that would be consonant with the aims and ideals of socialist society. Since the political structure of the Soviet government was that of the dictatorship of the proletariat, it was imperative to postulate a special type of literature, drama, art, and music that would be proletarian in substance and therefore accessible to the popular masses. Some Soviet theoreticians proposed to wipe off the slate of the arts the entire cultural structure that preceded the revolution and to create a *tabula rasa* on which to build a new proletarian edifice. Among suggestions seriously offered by some musicians in the early days of the Soviet revolution was the confiscation of all musical instruments in order to abolish the tempered scale and to construct new instruments based on the acoustically pure intervals. A more appropriate suggestion was made to compose music which included sounds familiar to a proletarian worker. A symphony of the factory was actually staged in an experimental demonstration, with singers and players placed on rooftops. Shostakovich included a factory whistle in the score of his *May First Symphony.* Alexander Mossolov wrote a ballet called *Iron Foundry,* in which a large sheet of steel was shaken to imitate the sound of the forge. Unsuccessful attempts were made to proletarianize the librettos of old operas. In one production, Puccini's opera *Tosca* was advanced from the Napoleonic times to those of the Paris Commune. Tosca kills not the chief of the Roman police but the anti-Communard general Gallifet, disregarding the fact that the actual general Gallifet died in bed long after the fall of the Commune. Meyerbeer's opera *The Huguenots* was renamed *The Decembrists* and the action transferred to December 1825 to celebrate the rebellion of a group of progressive-minded aristocrats against the accession to the throne of the Czar Nicholas I. The notorious Russian Association of Proletarian Musicians (RAPM) was founded in 1924 to pass judgment on the fitness and unfitness of all music for proletarian consumption. It stipulated an arbitrary code of desirable musical attributes, among them unrelenting optimism, militant socialism, proletarian class consciousness, representational programmaticism, and the preferential use of major keys. Beethoven was commended by the RAPM for his rebellious spirit; among Russian composers Mussorgsky was singled out as a creator of realistic art. A difficult problem was posed by Tchaikovsky. His profound pessimism and fatalism, his reactionary political views, and, particularly, his homosexuality seemed an insurmountable barrier for the RAPM theoreticians to overcome. But Tchaikovsky was a favorite composer not only of the popular masses but also of the entire Presidium of the Soviet of People's Commissars. Even from the purely musical standpoint Tchaikovsky was theoretically unacceptable. His preference for minor keys and for melancholy moods in his operas and symphonies were the very antinomy of all that the new society of Soviet Russia stood for. In their attempt to rationalize the popularity of the *Pathétique Symphony,* the RAPM reached the acme of casuistry. In this work, so the argument went, Tchaikovsky delivered a magnificent funeral oration on the tomb of the bourgeoisie, and the superb artistic quality of this lamentation could not fail to please proletarian listeners. But soon the dialectical self-contradictions became evident even to the most obdurate members of the RAPM and factional strife pulled their ideology apart. There were also signs of repugnance against the vicious attacks led by the RAPM against the surviving composers of the pre-revolutionary times, greatly esteemed conservatory professors, and any others who dared to oppose its untenable ideology. The entire controversy was suddenly resolved when the Soviet government summarily disbanded the RAPM. As one composer expressed the nearly unanimous satisfaction at this action, "We could once again dare to write music in 3/4 time," alluding to the RAPM's ridiculous insistence that Proletarian Music ought to be written in march time.

The valid residue of Proletarian Music found its way to Germany and to America assuming special national idioms. Simplicity of form, utilization of popular dance rhythms, and, in theatrical music, a selection of subjects from revolutionary history or class warfare were the main characteristics of music for the proletariat. In America, proletarian opera flourished briefly in the 1930s with Marc Blitzstein as its chief proponent. In Germany, Kurt Weill, working in close collaboration with the dramatist Bertolt Brecht, created a type of music drama that in its social consciousness had a strong affinity with Proletarian Music. In Russia itself, after the disbandment of the RAPM, viable ideas of Proletarian Music were absorbed in the doctrine of SOCIALIST REALISM.

Prolixity. Brevity is not necessarily an ideal and prolixity not always a fault. In classical music, prolixity was ingrained in the forms of sonata and court dances, with the required repetitions of complete sections. Only the impatience of modern performers impels them to disregard such redundancies. "Brevitate gaudent moderni," to quote a recurring incipit of medieval musical treatises. Beethoven's *Eroica* concludes with the tonic chord repeated 28 times. By contrast, Prokofiev's March from *The Love for Three Oranges* ends abruptly on a single C major triad. The natural aversion of modern musicians to restatement and overstatement extends also to tonal sequences with their predictable turns. This homologophobia led finally to the collapse of the tonal system itself, and inspired Arnold Schoenberg to promulgate the principle of non-repetition of thematic notes and the formulation of his method of composition with twelve tones related only to one another.

Proportional Representation. Among thousands of conflicting musical theories, each claiming superiority over the others, no attempt has yet been made to conduct a statistical survey of the frequency of occurrence of every note of the scale in a given composition. Yet such a computation might well provide an illuminating insight into proportional representation of diatonic and chromatic notes, and the role of tonal centers. In serial composition, in particular, a statistical analysis can measure the strength of the gravitational force that attracts atonal and serial groups to a putative keynote. The duration of each note will have to be considered as a multiplying factor. Thus, if the least common denominator is an eighth-note, then a half-note would carry the same specific weight as four eighth-notes. It would also be possible to evaluate the relative hierarchy of the members of a tone-row. A serial composer may plan in advance a proportional representation of specific notes, intervals, and durations. If desired, an artificial tonic can be posited by assigning to it the greatest frequency of incidence. This technique is applicable to all serial sets, even those containing only three or four notes. Rhythmic sets can be similarly arranged according to a predetermined formula of proportional representation. The method is particularly fruitful in building melodies and rhythms of a primitivistic type, in which the repetition is of the essence.

Pseudo-Exoticism. To an imaginative composer, the attraction of exotic lands is in inverse ratio to available information about such lands and in direct ratio to the square of the distance from the non-beholder. "Turkish" music, which had nothing in common with real Turkish modalities, enjoyed a great vogue in the 18th century and was used as a pseudo-exotic resource by Mozart. When dancers from Indochina came to perform at the Paris Exposition of 1889, French musicians were fascinated by the unfamiliar sounds of resonant bells and muffled drums in the percussion groups that accompanied the dancers. The emergence of IMPRESSIONISM in France owes much to this dance music from the Orient as refracted through the "auricular sites" of a European. The legends of the East provided poetic materials for song texts and operatic librettos. These tenuous impressions were transmuted into a *musique nouvelle*, vibrant with voluptuous frissons. Oriental scales were represented in the works of Debussy, Ravel, and their imitators by the pentatonic scale, which could be conveniently played on the black keys of the piano keyboard. Great composers were able to create a new art derived, however inaccurately, from Oriental sonorities; in fact, several composers, natives of Asia, who studied music in Paris, began to mold their own authentic modes in the Impressionistic manner. When the novelty began to fade, the pentatonic scale, the tinkling bells, and other paraphernalia of Oriental music found their way into the commercial factories of vulgar musicians plying their trade with much profit in the semi-classical division of modern music, in Broadway shows, and on the soundtrack of exotic movie spectaculars. The proliferation of this pseudo-exoticism resulted in the contamination of the genuine product, so that Orientalistic music eventually disappeared from decent practice.

Pseudo-Music. Pseudo-Music differs from ANTI-MUSIC in that the latter is a rebellious inversion of all musical values, while Pseudo-Music is an imitative product of specious validity. Pseudo-Music of the modern type is manufactured by semi-professionals who possess a modicum of Abecedarian talent for sentimental melody and hymn-book harmony. Feminine Pseudo-Music, usually produced by women pianists and singing teachers, has some documentary value as an illustration of neo-Biedermeier culture. Some such pieces of salon music have achieved tremendous popularity, among them, the romances of Carrie Jacobs Bond, the pianistic trivialities of Cécile Chaminade, and, the greatest of them all, *Prière d'une vierge* by Thekla Badarzewska.

Punitive Music. Relentless playing of a trivial tune arranged in repellent harmonies may well be used, and possibly has been used, by dictatorial régimes to extract confessions from suspected music lovers. A similar practice is pursued in the form of a musical massage in democratic countries, by means of jukeboxes or other instruments of torture, in public restaurants, in jet planes waiting for a chance to make a scheduled departure, and in elevators, with the ultimate intention of weakening sales resistance to a commercial product among captive listeners. For entirely different purposes, Erik Satie, who detested audiences, directed to have his piano piece, pointedly titled *Vexations*, to be performed 840 times in succession. His punitive design, however, was circumvented by a group of sadomasochists who carried Satie's instructions to the letter and had, on 9–10 September 1963, arranged in New York 840 performances of Satie's piece, played without interruption by a relay of willing pianists who obtained thereby not only a measure of secret gratification but also a great deal of publicity.

Quaquaversal Dispersion. Macropolysyllables are not necessarily frivolous when they define a phenomenon in a memorable or picturesque phrase. Quaquaversal dispersion is a convenient macropolysyllable to describe a radial expansion of the central cumulus of sonic matter, similar to the process of gradual sliding of geological layers, to which the term quaquaversal (literally, turning in different directions) is applied in science.

Quarter-Tones. Quarter-tones are not modern inventions; they are found in the ancient Greek enharmonic scale. Many romantic composers of the 19th century thought of reviving quarter-tones as a unit of an icositetraphonic scale. George Ives, father of Charles Ives, who was an army band leader during the Civil War, experimented with tuning his instruments a quarter-tone apart. A systematic investigation of quarter-tones began about 1900; among its pioneers were the Mexican composer Julián Carrillo and Alois Hába of Czechoslovakia. Further details are found in the entry on MICROTONALITY.

Radial distribution. Radial distribution of a linear series is a maximum dispersion of the constituent tones, such as occurs in a technique commonly described by a term borrowed from art, POINTILLISM. The visual impression from an actual score is a picture of tonal particles appearing and disappearing in the outer registers of orchestral instruments, or extreme octaves on the piano keyboard. The geometry of this image is particularly striking in the appearance of the instrumental works by Anton von Webern.

Ragtime. Ragtime is the earliest manifestation of American syncopated music, which was soon to rise to glory in JAZZ. It was Ragtime, too, that gave prominence to the piano in popular music. Its rhythmic formula approximates that of the toccata, with rapid motion and cross-accents. Henry F. Gilbert and Charles Ives cultivated Ragtime rhythms early in the century.

Debussy made use of Ragtime rhythms in his "Golliwog's Cake Walk" in the piano suite *Children's Corner.* The proliferation of Ragtime must have been pervasive, considering the outcries of shock and indignation in the music periodicals in the dying days of the old century. An editorial writer fulminated in an article entitled "Degenerate Music," published in *The Musical Courier* of 13 September 1899: "A wave of vulgar, filthy, and suggestive music has inundated the land. The pabulum of theater and summer hotel orchestras is 'coon music.' Nothing but ragtime prevails, and the cake-walk with its obscene posturings, its lewd gestures. . . . One reads with amazement and disgust of the historical and aristocratic name joining in this sex dance. Our children, our young men and women, are continually exposed to the contiguity, to the monotonous attrition of this vulgarizing music. It is artistically and morally depressing, and should be suppressed by press and pulpit." In 1901 the American Federation of Musicians adopted a resolution that its members "shall henceforth make every effort to suppress and discourage the playing and publishing of such musical trash by substituting the works of recognized and competent composers, thereby teaching the general public to appreciate a wholesome, decent, and intellectual class of music." When the famous prima donna Nordica included a song by the American composer Ethelbert Nevin in her Chicago recital in 1901, the *Chicago Tribune* deplored her "sense of the fitness of things" in singing a "coon song" alongside a group of German lieder. The monthly *Journal of the International Music Society,* in its issue of June 1905, described Ragtime in the following words: "It suggests the gait of a hurried mule among anthills; there is a cross-rhythm, with a kind of halting contrapuntal ornamentation in the accompaniment which sometimes brings a stress onto the fourth beat of the bar. The phrases being no longer presented with regular and recurrent pulsations, give rise to a sense of disorder, which, combined with the emotional expression of the music, suggests an irresponsibility and a sense of careless jollity agreeable to the tired or vacuous brain."

As late as 1916, Ragtime was still a phenomenon to be abhorred, to judge by a letter to the editor from the writer Ivan Narodny published in the New York *Evening Sun*: "The rhythm of ragtime suggests the odor of the saloon, the smell of backyards and subways. Its style is decadent. It is music meant for the tired and materially bored minds. It is essentially obvious, vulgar, and yet shockingly strong for the reason that it ends fortissimo." But there were also some philosophically analytic voices in the press. Rupert Hughes wrote soberly in the *Musical Record* of Boston of 1 April 1899: "If ragtime were called *tempo di raga* or *rague-temps,* it might win honors more speedily. If the word could be allied to the harmonic rage of the East Indians, it would be more acceptable. The Negroes call their clog-dancing 'ragging' and the dance a 'rag.' There is a Spanish verb *raer* (to scrape), and a French naval term, *ragué* (scraped), both doubtless from the Latin *rado.* Ragtime will find its way gradually into the works of some great genius and will thereafter be canonized, and the day will come when the decadents of the next, the 20th century, will revolt against it and will call it 'a hidebound, sapless, scholastic form, dead as its contemporaries, canon and fugue.' Meanwhile, it is young and unhackneyed, and throbbing with life. And it is racial."

Realism. Generally speaking, the term Realism as applied to music describes a type of programmatic romanticism, which is intended to picture a landscape or represent a psychological state. Realism has acquired a special meaning in the nomenclature of Soviet music, usually appearing in the dual formula of SOCIALIST REALISM whose function is to give a realistic reflection of contemporary life from the standpoint of Socialist society. Soviet composers are constantly urged to cultivate musical Realism, to write music of concrete images rather than abstract formalism, to preserve the national tradition of each of the constituent members of the Soviet Union, using the melodic and harmonic language accessible to the masses and contributing to the realistic understanding of life itself.

Redundancy. In electronics guidance systems, redundancy is a safety factor in the proper functioning of the machine. If a part fails, its redundant replacement immediately goes into action; and if that one fails, still another part is activated to perform the same function. In music, redundancy is represented by an ostentatious repetition of a thematic motive. It has its application in serial complexes of intervallic, rhythmic, and coloristic parameters. By assigning a certain interval for a redundant use by an instrument, an associative equation is established, so that the interval becomes the identifying motto of the instrument itself. Some serial composers assign a single note to an instrument, so that the instrument and the note become inalienably bound. This evokes the memories and practices of serf orchestras in Tsarist Russia, consisting of wind instruments, of which each could produce but a single note, so that each serf playing that instrument often became known under the nickname of E-flat, F-sharp, etc. (When several serfs escaped from the estate of a music-loving Russian landlord, he put out an official notice asking the police to be on the lookout for the fugitives, giving their musical names as identification.)

Replication. In their search for effective and direct musical formulas, modern composers have increasingly turned back to the primitivistic pattern of simple repetition, a sort of bio-musical replication of a subject keeping its identity as unalterable as the design on an ancient Peruvian poncho. The most celebrated instance of such replication is Ravel's *Boléro* in which the variations are limited to changes from one instrumental color to another. A less literal type of replication is MONOTHEMATISM, of which Debussy's String Quartet is a perfect example. Still another variant is the thematic replication of a musical monogram, which spells out a name or a common word in letter-notes, usually in German notation. A modern example is the Eighth String Quartet of Shostakovich, which is built on his initials in German spelling, D.S.C.H., the letter S representing E-flat (Es). Shostakovich used the same personal monogram in his Tenth Symphony. Some members of the AVANT-GARDE, and especially those of the Minimalist persuasion, have carried the principle of replication to the ultimate limit of a single note recorded on tape without any change in dynamics and without a rhythmic interruption.

Rescue and Escape Terms. Many new musicological terms ambiguously descriptive of a modern style, idiom, or technique are rescue and escape terms, words and phrases used as nebulous definitions of uncertain musical events. The term OMNITONALITY belongs to this category; others may be found by industrious perusal of music magazines beginning in 1910.

Retardation. The device of retardation, melodic, harmonic, or contrapuntal, consists of holding over a certain note or a harmonic complex while other parts of the musical fabric are shifted. In modern music, retardation is not developed in accord with the moving elements but continues indefinitely in order to create a sustained discord. In pandiatonic techniques, this procedure results in a chain of superpositions of the principal triadic harmonies.

Rock 'n' Roll. American popular music has evolved from the dual resources of urban and rural folksongs. Urban popular music found its primary inspiration in the unique modalities of the Negro spirituals, with their lowered third and seventh, which constitute the foundation of the BLUES. RAGTIME, JAZZ, SWING, and such lateral developments as BEBOP and BOOGIE-WOOGIE all preserve the character of city music. Quite different was the type of popular music cultivated in the rural regions of the country, which represented mostly the tradition of European, and particularly English, folksongs. This country music was marked by a leisurely pace devoid of the nervous excitement and syncopated beat peculiar to the popular productions of city life. However, with the advent of the electronic age, the barriers between urban and rural music were brought down. In the ensuing implosion and fusion of both genres, a new art was born, which found its fullest expression in the phenomenon of rock 'n' roll.

The combination of the words "rock" and "roll" appears for the first time on a Columbia phonograph record issued in the early 1930s; the rhythm of this specimen was that of a barcarolle, and the words Rock and Roll obviously referred to the gentle swaying of a boat on the river. This rural serenade was gradually transformed into a much more aggressive type of popular music, rock 'n' roll, or simply rock. Its cradle was in the radio broadcasting studios of Tennessee in about 1950. In it, the weaker rhythms of country music overflowed the syncopation of classical JAZZ and reduced the aggressive asymmetry of the urban product to the monotony of an even beat in square time. In rock 'n' roll the pendulum-like rhythmic motion produces a tremendous accumulation of KINETIC ENERGY, leading to a state of catatonic stupefaction among the listeners and the players themselves. The effect of this constant rhythmic drive is similar to that of the sinusoid wave with a steadily increasing amplitude created by the march of a regiment of soldiers across a suspension bridge, which can break the strongest steel. Thanks to electronic amplification, rock 'n' roll became the loudest music ever heard. Otologists have warned that its addicts may lose the sensitivity to the higher harmonics of the human voice and become partially deaf. Ralph Nader, the American Cassandra of urban civilization, has cautioned the public against the danger of sonic pollution by rock 'n' roll in a letter addressed to a member of the Congress of the United States.

The protagonist of rock 'n' roll was Elvis Presley, who developed the pelvic technique of rhythmic swing. (He became known as Elvis the Pelvis.) Four Liverpudlians, who became celebrated under the cognomen The Beatles (a palimpsest of Beat and beetles), joined the rock 'n' roll movement but evolved a distinctive style of their own, with some characteristics of the English ballad.

The remarkable feature of rock 'n' roll is the revival of archaic modality with its characteristic plagal cadences, the Dorian mode being a favorite. In harmony, the submediant is lowered in major keys and becomes the minor third of the minor subdominant triad. Parallel triadic progressions, adopted by rock 'n' roll, also impart an archaic modal quality to the music. It may well be that the fusion of old modes and modern rhythms will create a new type of SYNCRETISM of musical folkways.

Time magazine commented on rock 'n' roll in its issue of 18 June 1956: "An unrelenting, socking syncopation that sounds like a bull whip; a choleric saxophone honking mating-call sounds; an electric guitar turned up so loud that its sound shatters and splits; a vocal group that shudders and exercises violently to the beat while roughly chanting either a near-nonsense phrase or a moronic lyric in hillbilly idiom."

The Canadian underground newspaper, grandly named *Logos*, gave in 1969 this description of rock 'n' roll as a social force: "Rock is mysticism, revolution, communion, salvation, poetry, catharsis, eroticism, satori, total communication, the most vibrant art form in the world today. Rock is a global link, as young people everywhere plug into it and add to the form. What this new music suggested was raising your level of consciousness away from the fragmented, intellectual, goal-oriented time and material world to a unified sensual direction in a timeless spiritual environment."

The greatest mass demonstration of rock 'n' roll, and perhaps the greatest manifestation of the attractive power of music in all history, was the Woodstock (New York) Festival in August 1969, when an enormous crowd of young people, estimated at a quarter of a million heads, congregated in a farmland to hear their favorite rock groups. The HAPPENING had a profound sociological significance as well: the audience, consisting of youthful non-conformists popularly known as hippies, seemed to be infused with the spirit of mutual accommodation, altruism, and love of peace. Rock 'n' roll music, at least on that occasion, proved that it has indeed the power to soothe a savage breast.

Rotation. In post-Schoenbergian developments of DODECAPHONIC MUSIC, the 12-tone series is often modified by rotation. As the term implies, the series is shifted a space, so that at its next occurrence, it begins with the second note, and ends with the first; in the subsequent incidence, it starts on the third note, and ends on the second, etc. rotation in its various further developments is a fertile device of dodecaphonic techniques.

Scales. The American pedagogue Percy Goetschius used to play the C major scale for his students and ask them a rhetorical question, "Who invented this scale?" and answer it himself, "God!" Then he would play the WHOLE-TONE SCALE and ask again, "Who invented this scale?" And he would announce disdainfully, "Monsieur Debussy!"

Debussy did not invent the WHOLE-TONE SCALE, but he made ample use of it. Other scales, built on quaquaversal intervallic progressions, engaged the attention of composers: the so-called Hungarian Gypsy scale, the pentatonic scale suitable for orientalistic melismas, and the scale of alternating whole tones and semitones, which is classified in Russian encyclopedias as Rimsky-Korsakov's Scale. The modern Dutch composer Willem Pijper made prolix use of it, and his disciples, believing that it was his own invention, called it Pijper's Scale. In fact, this scale, formed by the insertion of passing notes in the melodically spaced diminished seventh chord, was used by Liszt, Tchaikovsky, and many other composers. Scriabin derived a scale of six notes from his MYSTIC CHORD, composed of three whole tones, a minor third, a semitone, and a whole tone. Alexander Tcherepnin devised a scale of nine notes consisting of a whole tone, a semitone, a semitone, a whole tone, a semitone, a semitone, a whole tone, a semitone, and a semitone. The Spanish composer Oscar Esplá wrote music based on the scale of the following intervals: semitone, whole tone, semitone, semitone, semitone, whole tone, whole tone, and whole tone.

Verdi was impressed by an exotic scale which he found in an Italian music journal, where it was described as "Scala enigmatica." It consists of a semitone, a minor third, three consecutive whole tones, and two consecutive semitones. At the age of 85 Verdi wrote a choral piece based on this "enigmatic" scale.

Ferruccio Busoni experimented with possible scales of seven notes and stated that he had invented 113 different scales of various intervallic structures. The first theorist to examine and classify scales based on the symmetrical division of the octave was Alois Hába in his book *Neue Harmonielehre.* Joseph Schillinger undertook a thorough codification of all possible scales having any number of notes from two to twelve, working on the problem mathematically. In his *Thesaurus of Scales and Melodic Patterns*, Nicolas Slonimsky tabulated some two thousand scales within the multiple octave range, including such progressions as the polytetrachord, bitonal scales of eight notes, scales of three disjunct major or minor pentachords aggregating to two octaves, etc.

Progressions of large intervals, thirds, fourths or fifths, cannot be properly described as scales, without contradicting the etymology of the word derived from *scala*, a ladder. But helix-like constructions involving spiraling chromatics may well be called scales. Quarter-tone scales and other microtonal progressions also belong in this category.

Scotophilia. In biology, scotophilia denotes the receptive phase of circadian rhythm in which the chief activity is performed in the dark; vampire bats, usually nocturnal, are outstanding examples of scotophiliac animals. As applied to musical composition, scotophilia is the love of dark and somber sonorities marked by a statistically certifiable prevalence of low registers and slow tempi, as in the symphonies of Sibelius. Interestingly enough, AVANT-GARDE composers, whose chosen self-appellation connotes a rapid movement forward, betray a curious addiction to static, somber, and darksome moods and compositorial habits. Such composers may well be called scotophiliacs.

Secundal and Septimal Harmonies. A distinct shift in harmonic structures occurred early in the 20th century as the tertian harmonies of triadic derivation began to give way to the more acute progressions in secundal harmonies and their septimal inversions. Debussy wrote special studies in consecutive major seconds, treating them as concords requiring no resolution. Secundal harmonies are also represented in Impressionistic works in the form of consecutive last inversions of seventh chords. Septimal harmonies are the familiar devices in early JAZZ cadences, in which the seventh was the "blue note." Composers of the later generation used tonic major sevenths as cadential chords. Secundal and septimal harmonies are commonly used in PANDIATONIC structures.

Sensory Impact. The quantitative expansion of technical devices in modern music led to a corresponding sensory impact on the listeners, often reaching the threshold of physical pain. Incessant playing of modern dance music, electronically amplified beyond the endurance of an average person, may well produce a positive conditioned reflex among the young. Professional music critics have for a century complained about the loudness of modern music, beginning with that of Wagner, but in their case the sensory impact is measured not so much by the overwhelming volume of sound as by the unfamiliarity of the idiom. The epithets such as "barbaric" were applied with a fine impartiality to Wagner, Tchaikovsky, Berlioz, and Prokofiev, while Debussy, Strauss, and Mahler were often described as "cacophonous." It is the relative modernity that makes the sensory impact intolerable to a music critic. "This elaborate work is as difficult for popular comprehension as the name of the composer," wrote the Boston *Evening Transcript* in its review of Tchaikovsky's First Piano Concerto. An index of vituperative, pejorative, and deprecatory words and phrases, the Invecticon appended to Nicolas Slonimsky's *Lexicon of Musical Invective*, demonstrates the extraordinary consistency of the critical reaction to unfamiliar music. Even the gentle Chopin did not escape contumely; he was described in a daily London newspaper as a purveyor of "ranting hyperbole and excruciating cacophony."

Serendipity. Serendipity is a nonce word, coined by Horace Walpole in 1754, and derived from the Arabian tale of the princes of Serendip who made important discoveries and found fortune by opportune accident and sagacious surmise. In music, serendipity is almost equivalent to intuition or inspiration, but it is applicable particularly to the realization of melodic, harmonic, and intervallic relationships seemingly unconnected with the primary aim of a composer or theorist. Examples of serendipity are tabulated in the article on POTENTIAL TECHNIQUES.

Serialism. Serialism is a method of composition in which thematic units are arranged in an ordered set. Tonal serialism was promulgated by Arnold Schoenberg in 1924, as the culmination of a long period of experiments with atonal chromatic patterns; in retrospect, Schoenberg's method may be regarded as a special case of integral serialism, much as the special theory of relativity is a subset of general relativity. Schoenberg's method deals with the 12 different notes of the chromatic scale; integral serialism organizes different intervals, rhythmic values, dynamics, etc. in autonomous sets. Fritz Klein expanded the serial concept of dodecaphonic sets to different rhythmic and intervallic values. In his score, *Die Maschine*, published in 1921, he employs sets of 12 identical notes in irregular rhythms, "Pyramid Chords" consisting of intervals arranged in a decreasing arithmetical progression of semitones, and a harmonic complex consisting of 12 different notes and 11 different intervals, the "Mutterakkord". The mathematical term "set," for a tone-row, was introduced by the American composer Milton Babbitt in 1946. He experimented with techniques of tonal, rhythmic, and intervallic sets. George Perle proposed the term "set-complex" to designate 48 different forms generated by a fundamental dodecaphonic series. In all these sets the magic number 12 plays a preponderant role. In the general concept of serialism, sets may contain any number of pitches, in any scale, including non-tempered intervals.

A summary of serial parameters comprises the following:

(1) Twelve different pitches as developed by using the method of composition with 12 tones, including apocopated sets, hendecaphonic, decaphonic, enneaphonic, octophonic, heptaphonic, hexaphonic, pentaphonic, tetraphonic, triphonic, diphonic, monophonic, and zerophonic.

(2) Organization of melody containing 12 different intervals, from a semitone to the octave and the concomitant chords containing 12 different notes and 11 different intervals.

(3) Twelve different rhythmic values, which may contain a simple additive set of consecutive integers, a geometrical progression, a set of Fibonacci numbers, etc.

(4) Twelve different KLANGFARBEN, in which a melody consists of a succession of disparate notes played by 12 different instruments either in succession, in contrapuntal conjugation, or harmonic coagulation.

(5) Spatial serialism, in which 12 different instruments are placed in quaquaversal positions, with no instruments in close proximity.

(6) Vectorial serialism, in which the sound generators are distributed at 12 different points of the compass, according to 12 hour marks on the face of a clock, or else arranged spatially on the ceiling, on the floor, and in the corners of the auditorium.

(7) Dynamic serialism, with 12 different dynamic values ranging from *pianississississimo* to *fortississississimo*, including the intermediate shadings of *mezzo-piano* and *mezzo-forte*.

(8) Ambulatory serialism, in which 12 musicians make their entrances and exits one by one, in contrapuntal groups, in stretto, or in the fugue, the latter being understood in the literal sense of running.

(9) Expressionistic serialism, in which actors and singers assume definite facial expressions marking their psychological identity.

(10) Serialism of 12 different sound generators, including steamrollers, motor lawn mowers, steam pipes, radiators, ambulance sirens, etc.

(11) Serialism of 12 visually different mobiles, each producing a distinctive noise.

(12) Serialism of 12 teratological borborygmuses and sonic simulacra of venous physiological functions.

Sesquipedalian Macropolysyllabification. Quaquaversal lucubration about pervicacious torosity and diverticular prosiliency in diatonic formication and chromatic papulation, engendering carotic carmination and decubital nyctalopia, causing borborygmic susurration, teratological urticulation, macroptic dysmimia, bregmatic obstipation, crassamental quisquiliousness, hircinous olophonia, and unflexanimous luxation, often produce volmerine cacumination and mitotic ramuliferousness leading to operculate onagerosity and testaceous favillousness, as well as faucal obsonation, parallelepipedal psellismus, pigritudinous mysophia, cimicidal conspurcation, mollitious deglutition, and cephalotripsical stultitiousness, resulting despite Hesychastic omphaloskepsis, in epenetic opistography, boustrophedonic malacology, lampadodromic evagination, chartulary cadastration, merognostic heautotimerousness, favaginous moliminosity, fatiscent operosity, temulencious libration, and otological oscininity, aggravated by tardigrade inturgescence, nucamentacious oliguria, emunctory sternutation, veneficial pediculation, fremescent dyskinesia, hispidinous cynanthropy, torminal opitulation, crapulous vellication, hippuric rhinodynia, dyspneic nimiety, and favillous erethism, and culminating in opisthographic inconcinnity, scotophiliac lipothimia, banaustic rhinorrhea, dehiscent fasciculation, oncological vomiturition, nevoid paludality, exomphalic invultuation, mysophiliac excrementatiousness, flagitious dysphoria, lipogrammatic bradygraphy, orectic aprosexia, parataxic parorexia, lucubicidal notation, permutational paranomasia, rhoncial fremitus, specular subsaltation, crapulous crepitation, ithyphallic acervation, procephalic dyscrasia, volitional volitation, piscine dermatology, proleptic pistology, verrucous alopecia, hendecaphonic combinatoriality, microaerophilic pandiculation, and quasihemidemisemibreviate illation.

Sesquitone Scales. Sesquitone is an interval of three semitones. The sesquitone scale is a progression of minor thirds, or augmented seconds, depending on notation, and is identical with the arpeggiated diminished-seventh chord. Attractive ornamental effects can be obtained by infrapolation, interpolation, and ultrapolation, or a combination of these processes. An infra-inter-ultrapolation of the sesquitone scale produces a chromatically inflected melodic pattern of an Orientalistic type. The interpolation of a single note between the successive degrees of the sesquitone scale forms a scale of alternating whole tones and semitones, widely used by many composers, beginning with Liszt and Tchaikovsky. In Russian reference books it is described as Rimsky-Korsakov's Scale.

Silence. Poets often spoke of the eloquent and the harmonious quality of silence. The lines in Félicien David's *Symphonic Ode* are appropriate: "Ineffables accords de l'éternel silence! / Chaque grain de sable / a sa voix. / Dans l'éther onduleux / le concert se balance: / Je le sens, je le vois!" The longest silence explicitly written out is the five-bar rest in the score of *L'apprenti Sorcier* by Paul Dukas. György Ligeti composed a movement of a work consisting of a quarter-note rest. The most ambitious composition utilizing the effect of total silence is *4'33"* by John Cage, scored for any combination of instruments, all tacet, and subdivided into three movements during which no intentional sounds are produced. It was unheard for the first time at Woodstock, New York, on 29 August 1952, with David Tudor at the silent piano.

Singultation. The modern practice of onomatopoeic singultation is derived from the medieval hocketus in which the singing line is interrupted by a syncopated translocation of thematic components, producing hocketus or a singultus (both words mean hiccups). Brief detonations of kinetic energy in modern works are forms of singultation.

Socialist Realism. The Soviet Union is the first modern state that has attempted to regulate its art, literature, drama, and music according to explicitly defined ideological principles. Since the structure of the Soviet government was derived from the doctrine of the dictatorship of the proletariat, a Russian Association of Proletarian Musicians (RAPM) arrogated to itself the right to dictate the proper musical forms suitable for the consumption of proletarian masses. It was disbanded by the Soviet government in 1932 after its failure to help in the creative formulation of mass music became evident. With the rise of the national consciousness in the component republics of the Soviet Union, it was realized by Soviet authorities that proletarian internationalism was no longer sufficient to serve as an enduring ideology. Surviving masters of old Russian music had to be accepted as representatives of the Russian masses; their classical precursors were glorified as exponents of progressive ideals consonant with the new Socialist reality of the Soviet era. Soviet composers were urged to create an art national in form and Socialist in content, a method which eventually became known as Socialist Realism. Stylistically, Socialist Realism requires the retention of the tonal system of composition, broadly based on the folk modalities of Russian songs and the native chants of other republics of the Soviet Union. The doctrine of Socialist Realism concentrates on the national development of operas and secular oratorios, in which revolutionary ideals can be expressed verbally as well as musically. The Aristotelian formula of catharsis through pity and terror underlies the librettos of most Soviet operas and the scenarios of most Soviet ballets. Patriotic subjects are particularly recommended; they lend themselves readily to the triune formula which opens with a scene of happiness, goes through a period of sudden horror, and concludes in a victory over adverse circumstances. The so-called "Leningrad Symphony" of Shostakovich is a remarkable example of this Aristotelian construction, particularly so because it was written during continued retreats of the Soviet armies before the Nazis, and yet its finale predicts Victory. The classical tradition of the *Tierce de Picardie*, with its major cadence, suits perfectly the Soviet preference for major keys. Anatoly Lunacharsky, first Commissar of Education of Soviet Russia, explained the political advantage of major keys by comparing them with the convictions of the Bolshevik party, while minor keys were reflecting the introvert pessimism of the Mensheviks.

The doctrine of Socialist Realism does not preclude lyrical expression or individual allusions. Shostakovich uses the monogram D.S.C.H., corresponding, in German notation, to the notes D, E-flat, C, and B as the main subject of his Tenth Symphony. However, many among Soviet composers, even as eminent as Miaskovsky, were often criticized by the exponents of Socialist Realism for their musical morbidity, anxiety, and solipsistic introspection. In the domain of rhythm, marching time is a natural medium for the optimistic attributes of Socialist Realism, but it is reserved for its proper position in the finale of a symphony or the final chorus of an opera. In this respect, Socialist Realism merely continues the old tradition of Russian music. Even such melancholy composers as Tchaikovsky and Rachmaninoff excelled in triumphant march-time movements.

In authoritative Soviet declarations, Socialist Realism is opposed to FORMALISM, which is described as an artificial separation of form from content and the excessive cultivation of purely external technical devices, particularly ATONALITY, POLYTONALITY, and DODECAPHONY. The statutes of the Union of Soviet Composers provide a specific guidance to Soviet composers for their ideological concepts: "The greatest attention of Soviet composers must be given to the victorious progressive foundations of reality, to the heroic and luminous beauty that distinguishes the spiritual world of Soviet man, which must be incarnated in musical images full of life-asserting force. Socialist Realism demands an implacable opposition against anti-social modernistic movements, expressive of the decadence and corruption of contemporary bourgeois art, against genuflection and slavish obsequiousness before the culture of the bourgeoisie."

Sonic Exuviation. The effectiveness of a modernistic climax depends on an astute interplay of contrasts. One of the most effective dynamic devices is sonic exuviation, the shedding of old skin of instrumental sonority, a return to a state of primordial nakedness, and a new dressing-up of musical materials and a gradual building of another climax, a cut-off of sonic matter, leaving a soft exposed bodily shape. Such a dramatic exuviation occurs at the end of the last movement of *Three Places in New England* by Charles Ives, where a tremendously powerful heterogeneous complex of sound suddenly crumbles, and a residual gentle chord is heard in the quiet air.

Sonic Organization. Edgar Varèse defined music as ORGANIZED SOUND. It is logical to describe any musical composition, especially of the modern constructivist type, as a Sonic Organism which follows bio-musical laws. It is autogenetic, capable of natural replication induced by contrapuntal interpenetration of contrasting melorhythmic entities. Sonic organization presupposes an engineering plan, which takes into consideration an appropriate cross-pollination of musical themes.

Spatial Distribution. The placement of musicians on the stage, long a matter of tradition, has assumed an unexpected significance in modern times in the guise of musical vectorialism. Elliott Carter specifies the exact position of the players in his string quartets. Lukas Foss, in his *Elytres* for 12 instruments, places the musicians at maximum distances available on the stage. The use of directional loudspeakers in performances of ultra-modern works is an electronic counterpart of spatial distribution. In German broadcasting studios experiments have been made in distributing a 12-tone row in serial works among 12 electronic amplifiers placed in a clock-like circle, with each amplifier being assigned an individual note of the series. Empirical applications of the principle of SPATIAL DISTRIBUTION have been made by various composers early in the century, notably by Erik Satie in his *Musique d'ameublement,* and, nearer its end, by Henry Brant.

Spectrum. By analogy with the prismatic spectrum of primary colors, a totality of KLANGFARBEN can be described as a tonal spectrum. Before the era of ELECTRONIC MUSIC, the colors of the auditory spectrum were limited to the available instruments of actual manufacture. With the aid of electronic generators it became possible to build a spectrum possessing an infinite capacity of instrumental colors, and the style and idiom of an entire work can be programmed by the proportional strength of such instrumental colors. The metaphor of a musical spectrum is therefore justified by the actuality of its realization.

Specular Reflection. The mirror image in Baroque counterpoint is applied to mutually conjugated melodic inversions in which the ascending intervals are reflected by descending intervals, and vice versa. It is theoretically possible to construct an infinite specular reflection, in which the intervallic distance between the two mirrors recedes, so that intervals are inverted in the outer regions of the instrumental range, extending even into the inaudible spectrum of ultra-sonic and infra-sonic sounds. In some modern works written specially for dog audiences, ultra-sonics can achieve considerable effectiveness. Beyond the canine auditory range, a gap occurs until the frequency of light waves is reached. Mystically inclined composers may find pantheistic inspiration in these notions of passing from men through dogs to infinity.

Sprechstimme. Sprechstimme—literally a speech-voice—is a term popularized in its expressive use by Arnold Schoenberg in *Pierrot Lunaire* and later works. It is an inflected speech, notated on the regular music staff by special symbols indicating the approximate height of the note. The method was used systematically for the first time in 1897 in the operatic melodrama *Königskinder* by Engelbert Humperdinck.

Static Music. Although the general trend of music since 1900 has been towards greater complexity of texture and greater variety of dynamics, an opposite movement has manifested itself in some circles of the AVANT-GARDE, and especially the Minimalists, aimed at total tonal immobility and static means of expression. Static Music finds its logical culmination in works that are limited to a single note in unchanging dynamics, usually in pianissimo. The melosomatic impact of such a production may be considerable if the listener is forced to hear a single note played by an instrumentalist for a long time. The expectation of some change, constantly deceived, may cause an emotional perturbation of great psychological interest.

Stochastic Composition. The term stochastic was introduced into music by the Greek engineer and composer Iannis Xenakis, to designate an aleatory projection in which the sonic trajectory is circumscribed by the structural parameters of the initial thematic statement. (The word itself comes from the Greek root meaning "the aim of an arrow.") STOCHASTIC procedures are in actual practice equivalent to controlled improvisation.

Strategy and Tactics. Modern composers are forever seeking metaphors from other fields to enrich the rapidly obsolescent musical nomenclature derived from vague Italian words indicating form, speed, dynamic force, or expression. Among such new metaphors are strategy and tactics. The general scheme of a modern symphony or a sonata is strategical, while variations, cadenzas, and contrapuntal elaborations are tactical devices. Iannis Xenakis, the originator of the STOCHASTIC method of composition, extended the concept of strategy and tactics into an actual tournament between two orchestras and two conductors, exemplified in his antiphonal symphony entitled *Stratégie.* According to the composer's specifications, two orchestras perform simultaneously two different compositions, following an uncoordinated pair of conductors, and stopping at climactic points to survey the mutual gains and losses. At the end of the maneuver the audience votes to nominate the winner of this instrumental encounter.

Superfetation. When several viable musical ideas occur simultaneously and are contrapuntally conjugated without a preliminary statement, a melorhythmic superfetation is the result. The thematic embryos may then be separated to pursue their different courses; or else, the non-identical geminal subjects may remain unified like Siamese twins, treated collectively as bipartite entities which subsequently may enter into a secondary superfetation. Given a complete freedom of dissonant counterpoint, superfetation can be extended to thematic triplets, quadruplets, quintuplets, sextuplets, septuplets, octuplets, etc., interpenetrating and disengaging themselves in a multiplicity of instrumental or vocal lines.

Surrealism. The word Surrealism was coined in 1903 by the French poet Guillaume Apollinaire in his fantastic play *Les Mamelles de Tirésias,* in which he treated the problem of a transsexual transplantation of mammary glands, and which he subtitled "drame surréaliste." Surrealism became a fashionable movement when André Breton published a Surrealist manifesto in 1924. In it, he described Surrealism as "psychic automatism," anti-rationalistic in essence and completely spontaneous in its creative process. Fantasy and free association were the normative factors of Surrealistic literature and art. Apollinaire described Surrealism as the rational technique of the improbable. Jean Cocteau equated it with the essence of poetry; in his film *Le Sang da Poéte* he proposed to give a "realistic account of unreal phenomena." The famous French handbook, *Nouveau Petit Larousse,* defines Surrealism tersely as "tendance d'une école à négliger toute préoccupation logique." Surrealism is oxymoronic in essence, thriving on the incompatibility of the opposites, exemplified by such images as cold flame, thunderous silence, painstaking idleness, quiet desperation. Names of persons often have a Surrealistic ring. A Boston dentist, Dr. Toothacher, a Chicago gangster, Alturo Indelicato, and a Canadian insurance salesman, John Death, were living examples of Surrealism. The fur-lined cup and saucer, created by the 23-year-old artist Megret Oppenheim in 1936, is a typical Surrealistic artifact. Surrealistic incongruity was exemplified also in a piece called *Bagel Jewelry,* a composition by a New York artist, in which a real bagel was encased in a jewelry box, with a price tag of $100.

In a modern production of *Hamlet,* the king's line, "We shall call up our friends," acquired a Surrealistic twist because of a telephone receiver placed on the table. The Renaissance paintings representing Biblical scenes in which musicians perform on the lute and the theorbo, are both anachronistic and Surrealistic in their effect. Surrealism possesses an oneiristic quality, in which dreams become more real than life. The etymology of the word implies a higher degree of realism, penetrating into the subliminal human psyche.

Surrealist artists are fascinated by musical subjects. Salvador Dali humanized musical instruments. In one of his paintings, a faceless cellist plays on the spinal column of a human cello mounted on a pin. On its buttocks are the familiar resonators in the forms of symmetric gothic F's. (Life imitates art. At an AVANT-GARDE concert in New York a lady cellist performed a solo on the spine of a fellow musician, using a regular bow and applying occasional pizzicatti to his epidermis.) Another musical painting by Dali, bearing the Surrealistic title *Six Apparitions of Lenin on a Piano,* represents several heads of Lenin crowned with aureoles strewn across the keyboard. The Belgian Surrealist René Magritte painted a burning bass tuba. In the art work *Object for Destruction* by the American Surrealist Man Ray, a print of a human eye was attached to the pendulum of a metronome. Real metronomes are the instruments in the score by the Hungarian modernist György Ligeti, containing 100 metronomes all ticking at different speeds. In his vision of Socialist music of the future, the Soviet poet Vladimir

Mayakovsky conjured up a symphony with rain conduits for flutes. The American band leader Spike Jones introduced a latrinophone, a Surrealistic lyre made of a toilet seat strung with violin strings.

Apollinaire urged artists, poets, and musicians to cultivate "the insane verities of art." No one has followed his advice more ardently than Erik Satie. He incarnated the spirit of inversion. He entitled his utterly Surrealistic score *Parade* "ballet réaliste." Jean Cocteau wrote: "Satie's *Parade* removes the sauce. The result is a completely naked object which scandalizes by its very nakedness. In the theater everything must be false in order to appear true." Satie was very much in earnest when he wrote, "J'emmerde l'art c'est un métier de con." The titles of his piano pieces are typical of Surrealistic self-contradiction: *Crépuscule matinal de midi, Heures séculaires et instantanées, Tyrolienne turque, Sonatine bureaucratique, Fantaisie musculaire, Trois morceaux en forme de poire* (the last, printed under a cover representing a pear, was a defiant response to criticism that his music was formless).

Swing. Among the many ephemeral terms descriptive of varieties of JAZZ, Swing has gained a permanent historical position. It is not a new slang expression. The word Swing appears in the titles of old American dance tunes: *Society Swing* of 1908, *Foxtrot Swing* of 1923, *Charleston Swing* of 1925. In 1932 Duke Ellington wrote a song with the incipit, *It Don't Mean a Thing if It Ain't Got That Swing.* Swing achieved its first great boom in 1935, largely through the agency of the jazz clarinet player Benny Goodman, introduced to the public as the King of Swing. The American magazine *Downbeat* described Swing in its issue of January 1935 as "a musician's term for perfect rhythm." The November 1935 issue of the magazine carried a glossary of "Swing terms that cats use," in which Swing was defined as "laying it in the groove." This metaphor, borrowed from the phonograph industry, gave rise to the once popular adjective "groovy," in the sense of neat, perk, and pert.

Swing must have exercised a hypnotic effect on the youth of the 1930s. The *New York Times* of 30 May 1938 ran the banner headline, "Swing Band Puts 23,400 in Frenzy . . . Jitterbugs Cavort as 25 Orchestras Blare in Carnival." Self-appointed guardians of public morals lamented the new craze: "Pastor Scores Swing as Debasing Youth, Declares it Shows an Obvious Degeneracy in our Culture and Frothiness of Age," the *New York Times* headlined. Stravinsky, then a recent American citizen, endorsed Swing. *Time* magazine quoted him as saying in January, 1941: "I love swings. It is to the Harlem I go. It is so sympathetic to watch the Negro boys and girls dancing and to watch them eating the long, what is it you call them, frankfurters, no—hot dogs—in the long rolls. It is so sympathetic. I love all kinds of swings."

Symbolic Analysis. An overwhelming compulsion on the part of many modern composers to return the art of music to its source, mathematics, is behind many manifestations of the AVANT-GARDE. Yet no attempt has been made to apply symbolic logic to the stylistic and technical analysis of modern music. A simple statistical survey can determine the ratio between unresolved dissonances and consonant structures in modern works as compared to those of the past. Such an analysis would indicate in mathematical terms the process of the emancipation of dissonances. The next step would be to tabulate certain characteristics of a given modern school of composition and note their presence in another category, which would help to measure the extent of its influence. The whole-tone scale, for instance, was cultivated particularly by the French Impressionists, but it can be found in works of composers who do not subscribe to Impressionist aesthetics. Progressions of second inversions of major triads in parallel formation, moving by sesquitones, are typical of IMPRESSIONISM. But the same formations can be encountered in the music of non-Impressionists. Ravel concludes his String Quartet with such triadic progression, and so does Gustav Holst in his suite *The Planets,* but they are never found in the works of Hindemith, a paragon of Neo-Classicism, or in those of Prokofiev. The index of tonality is very strong, amidst dissonances, in Stravinsky, but is totally absent in Schoenberg. All these styles, idioms, and techniques can be designated by a system of symbols; intervals would be numbered in semitones; upward motion would he symbolized by the plus sign, and downward motion by the minus sign. In this scheme the whole-tone scale would be shown by the formula 6 (2), denoting six degrees of two semitones each, with a plus or minus sign indicating the direction of the movement. A bitonal chord such as formed by C major and F-sharp major, can be indicated by the symbol MT for major triad and the number 6 for the tritone. The synchronization of these triads can be indicated by brackets: (MT) (MT + 6). More importantly, symbolic formulas can describe a style. The music of Hindemith, which lacks the Impressionistic element entirely, can be formulated as 50% NC (for Neo-Classical) + 50% NR (Neo-Romantic), with dissonant content and strength of tonal centers indicated by additional symbols or subscripts. Stravinsky's early music could be circumscribed by symbols ED for Ethnic Dissonance. Dodecaphonic method could be indicated by the coefficient 12. Other symbols would denominate metric and rhythmic symmetry or asymmetry. In the symbolic analysis of an eclectic composer such as Delius, with basic romanticism modified by a considerable influx of Impressionistic harmonies and colors, the following formula would be satisfactory, with R for Romanticism, C for Classicism, E for Ethnic quality, and I for Impressionism: 40% R + 20% C + 30% E + 10% I. A table of styles, idioms, and techniques may be drawn in the manner of the periodical table of elements. Just as vacant spaces in Mendeleyev's schematic representation indicated unknown elements which were actually discovered at a later time, so new techniques of modern composition may well come into being by searching application of symbolic analysis.

Synaesthesia. Color associations with certain sounds or tonalities are common subjective phenomena. It is said that Newton chose to divide the visible spectrum into seven distinct colors by analogy with the seven degrees of the diatonic scale. Individual musicians differed greatly in associating a sound with a certain color. The most ambitious attempt to incorporate light into a musical composition was the inclusion of a projected color organ in Scriabin's score *Prometheus,* in which the changes of instrumental coloration were to be accompanied by changing lighting in the concert hall. The most common association between tonality and color is that of C major and whiteness. It is particularly strong for pianists for the obvious reason that the C major scale is played on white keys. However, Scriabin, who had a very strong feeling for color associations, correlated C major with red. By all conjecture F-sharp major should be associated with black, for it comprises all five different black keys of the piano keyboard, but Scriabin associated it with bright blue and Rimsky-Korsakov with dull green. Any attempt to objectivize color associations is doomed to failure if for no other reason than the arbitrary assignment of a certain frequency to a given note. The height of pitch rose nearly a semitone in the last century, so that the color of C would now be associated with C-sharp in relation to the old standards. Some composers dreamed of a total synaesthesia in which not only audio-visual but tactile, gustatory, and olfactory associations would be brought into a sensual synthesis. Baudelaire said: "Les parfums, les couleurs et les sons se répondent." J. K. Huysmans conjured up an organ of liqueurs. He describes it in Chapter IV of his book *À rebours*: "Interior symphonies were played as one drank a drop of this or that liqueur creating the sensations in the throat analogous to those that music pours into the ear. In this organ of liqueurs, Curaçao sec corresponded to the clarinet with its somewhat astringent but velvety sound; Kummel suggested the oboe with its nasal quality; menthe and anisette were like the flute, with its combination of sugar and pepper, petulance and sweetness; kirsch recalled the fury of the trumpet; gin and whiskey struck the palate with the strident explosions of cornets and trombones; vodka fulminated with deafening noise of tubas, while raki and mastic hurled thunderclaps of the cymbal and of the bass drum with full force." Huysmans continued by suggesting a string ensemble functioning in the mouth cavity, with the violin representing vodka, the viola tasting like rum, the cello caressing the gustatory rods with exotic liqueurs, and the double bass contributing its share of bitters.

Composers in MIXED MEDIA, anxious to embrace an entire universe of senses, are seeking ultimate synaesthesia by intuitive approximation, subjective objectivization, and mystical adumbrations. Arnold Schoenberg was extremely sensitive to the correspondences between light and sound. In the score of his monodrama *Die glückliche Hand* he indicates a "crescendo of illumination" with the dark violet light in one of the two grottos quickly turning to brownish red, blue green and then to orange yellow.

Synchrony. Metric or rhythmic synchrony is an inclusive term of which POLYMETRY and POLYRHYTHMY are specific instances. Synchronization demands absolutely precise simultaneity of sets of mutually primary numbers of notes within a given unit of time, e.g., 3:2, 5:3, 11:4, etc. Triplets and quintuplets are of course common in free cadenzas since Chopin's time. (There is a consistent use of 4 beats against 3 in Chopin's *Fantaisie-Impromptu.*) But arithmetical precision in synchronizing larger mutually primary numbers of notes cannot be obtained by a human performer no matter how skillful, or by several performers playing different rhythms at once. Such synchrony becomes feasible with the aid of electronic machines. In 1931, Henry Cowell, working in collaboration with the Russian electric engineer, Leon Theremin, constructed a device, in the form of concentric wheels, which he called Rhythmicon. By manipulating a rheostat with a rudimentary crank, the performer automatically produced precise synchronization of the harmonic series, the number of beats per time unit being equal to the position in the series, so that the fundamental tone had one beat per second, or any other time unit, the second partial note had 2 beats, the third, 3 beats, etc. up to 32 beats produced by the rim of the Rhythmicon. The result was an arithmetically accurate synchrony score of 32 different time pulses. Since only the mutually non-primary numbers of beats coincided in the process, the collateral effect of rotating the machine was the production of an eerie scale of upper overtones, slower in its initial notes, faster as the position of the overtone was higher. The speed of rotation of the Rhythmicon wheel could be regulated at will, so as to create any desired alteration in tempo or pitch. The initial chord of each main division contains, necessarily so, the entire spectrum of overtones, and their simultaneous impact is of tremendous power, a perfect concord of multitonal consistency in non-tempered intonation.

An entirely novel idea of producing synchrony with mathematical precision was initiated by Conlon Nancarrow, an expatriate American composer living in Mexico City. He worked with a player-piano roll, punching holes at distances proportional to the desired rhythms. He wrote a series of etudes and canons, which could be performed only on the player piano, and which achieved the synchronization of different tempi that could not be attained by living instrumentalists. In his works he was free to select numbers with a fairly low common denominator, in which case there were occasional coincidences between the constituent parts. But the majority of his chosen proportions of the pulse tempi are such that the common denominator was not attained until the end of the piece, if at all. He also wrote a composition in which the relationship of the tempi was 2 to 2, and since the latter is an irrational number (which Nancarrow approximated to 3 decimal points) the contrapuntal parts could, at least theoretically, never meet.

Syncretism. In history and theology, syncretism denotes the coalescence of incompatible elements or concepts. Etymologically, the word is derived from the union of ancient Greece with Crete. Syncretism is a useful term in music as well, applied to describe the affinity between autogenetic ethnic melodies and cultivated triadic harmonies. A typical example of syncretism is the arrangement of pentatonic tunes in tonal harmonies, often resulting in the alteration of the intervallic content, as for instance in *Londonderry Air*, a pentatonic melody which has been altered by its arranger by changing the opening interval of a minor third to a semitone in order to provide the leading tone and to convert the modality of the song into a familiar major key. In modern music, syncretism assumes a polytechnical character through the application of widely incompatible techniques in a single work. An example is Alban Berg's opera *Lulu*, a serial work, which contains also triadic progressions, as well as harmonic figurations and tonal sequences.

Synergy. Synergy is defined by the American architect and design scientist R. Buckminster Fuller, the discoverer of new principles of spherical stability in designing structures, as the "behavior of a whole system unpredicted by the behavior of any of its separate parts, or the subassemblies of its parts." Synergy in music is a technique whereby the last note of a segment of several thematic notes is the first note of the second segment. These segments can be separated, in which case the conjunctive note is repeated. The method is of considerable value in building serial chains, in which the concatenations of adjacent links may be freely dissolved. With this separation of links, the function of the connecting tone becomes ambiguous, serving as the imaginary tonic of the first segment or an imaginary dominant of the second segment. The specification "imaginary" is important because of the aesthetic differences created by such a split of the chain.

Temporal Parameters. The conjectural duration of a musical composition is a factor of importance per se, a temporal parameter which has a decisive bearing on the cohesion and relative stability of the constituent parts of the entire work. The 20th century cultivated a type of Brobdingnagian grandiosity which seemed to equate quantity with quality. Among relatively well-known symphonic works, the *Alpine* by Richard Strauss held the record for absolute length, but it was eclipsed by the *Gothic Symphony* of the English composer Havergal Brian, containing 529 pages of full score. The longest piano work of the century is *Opus Clavicembalisticum* by the English-born Parsi composer Kaikhosru Sorabji, which he played for the first and last time in Glasgow on 1 December 1930. The work consists of 12 movements in the form of a theme with 44 variations and a passacaglia with 81 variations. Characteristically, it is dedicated "to the everlasting glory of those few men blessed and sanctified in the curses and execrations of those many whose praise is eternal damnation."

While some composers kept expanding the duration of their individual works, their contemporaries followed the opposite trend towards extreme brevity of musical utterance. The pioneer of this modern concision was Anton von Webern; one of his pieces written in 1911 for several instruments lasts only 19 seconds. The Hungarian composer György Ligeti wrote a movement consisting of a single quarter-tone rest. The ultimate in both the infinitesimally small and unfathomably large musical forms was achieved by John Cage in his *0′00″*, a work "to be performed in any way by anyone," and first presented in this ambiguous form in Tokyo on 24 October 1962.

Teratological Borborygmus. Modern works of the first quarter of the 20th century systematically increased the amount of massive sonorities as though their intention was to produce an orological ACOUSMA, or some other tonitruant Brobdingnagian teratological borborygmus, a huge and monstrous intestinal rumbling issuing from the mouthpieces of brass instruments, shrill flageolets of the piccolos, and high harmonics in the strings. It was inevitable that a reaction against this loss of all moderation should have set in among composers of the AVANT-GARDE. This reaction was made necessary because of the catastrophe of World War I, when it was no longer feasible to place huge orchestral apparatus at the service of composers of macrosonic works. The era of teratological borborygmus seemed to end without a hope of recurrence, but the emergence of electrically amplified popular music of the ROCK 'N' ROLL type generated an electronic circus that promised to eclipse the deafening potentialities of the past.

Text-Sound Composition. Text-sound composition is a translation of *text-ljud kompositioner*, introduced by Swedish composers in 1967 to denote a new, tightly-organized linguistic art first produced at the Swedish avant-garde center known as Fylkingen. It is related to its forerunning sound poetry in its exclusive focus upon wordplay: common words, uncommon phrases, and vocables combine to form new, highly rhythmicized "languages," which in turn create new poetic and musical values; it is differentiated by its complexity, made possible through a consistent use of electronic means. In most text-sound compositions an underlying pulse is established, which becomes the propagating force of more complex rhythmic structures; studio techniques include reiterative loops, delayed playback, incorporation of extraneous noises, including feedback, and real-time improvisation. Works generally fall into four categories: (1) studio tape pieces, (2) live pieces for solo performer, multiple readers, or solo voice with tape, (3) pieces incorporating environmental recordings, and (4) performance pieces combining live performers, tape, and visual images. In the United States text-sound composition saw its greatest flowering in the San Francisco Bay Area, which, in the 1940s and 1950s, was a world center for literary experimentation with the Beat poets; in the 1960s, with the institution of the San Francisco Tape Music Center, it became a world center for tape music experimentation as well. Charles Amirkhanian, long-time radio broadcaster and pioneer practitioner, produced the first comprehensive American anthology, *10 + 2: 12 American Text-Sound Pieces* (1974). His own works, often MULTI-MEDIA in design and belying a subtle, irreverent humor, include *Dutiful Ducks* (1977), for live performer and tape, *Mahogany Ballpark* (1976), an environmental text-soundscape, and the gloriously illogical *She She and She* (1974), composed in celebration of the 100th anniversary of the birth of text-sound composition's unmotherly matriarch, Gertrude Stein.

Third Stream. Third Stream denominates a combined art of Popular Music and modern techniques of composition. The term itself was used first by Gunther Schuller at his lecture at the Berkshire Music Center in Tanglewood, given on 17 August 1957. If the first stream is classical, and the second stream is jazz, Third Stream is their Hegelian synthesis, which unites and reconciles the classical thesis with the popular antithesis. Instances of such synthetic usages are found in a number of modern works. The Third Stream flows in "Golliwog's Cake Walk" from Debussy's *Children's Corner*, where bits of syncopated RAGTIME animate the music. Gershwin's *Rhapsody in Blue* is the most important precursor of Third Stream. In constructive application of Third Stream, ultra-modern techniques, including serialistic procedures, can be amalgamated with popular rhythmic resources.

Tinnitus. A sustained pressure on the auditory nerve causes a condition known as tinnitus, a persistent tintinnabulation in the cochlea in the inner ear. Schumann experienced it during the final stages of his mental illness; he heard a relentless drone on high A-flat. Smetana suffered a similar aural disturbance, but the note he heard was a high E, and he too eventually went insane. He introduced this high E in the violin part at the end of his string quartet, significantly entitled *From My Life*.

Some clinically sane composers active in the last third of the 20th century, who never suffered from a pathologic tinnitus, experimentally created an artificial one. Morton Feldman wrote a violin part with an interminable F-sharp calculated to generate a psychic tinnitus in the outer and inner ears of performers and listeners alike. La Monte Young devised a tinnitus of a perfect fifth with a notation, "to be held for a long time." Other ways of affecting the listener are a tape recording of a dripping faucet, or a simulacrum of "white noise" prolonged without a prospect of ever ending. Physical action may be added to a tinnitus, such as measured drops of lukewarm water on the occipital bone of the head held down by clamps, a device helpful to keep in subjection a particularly recalcitrant listener to a piece of AVANT-GARDE music. This method was widely practiced to subdue difficult patients in 18th-century insane asylums.

Tonal Aura. Aura is a medical term used to describe a premonitive sensation before an epileptic seizure. Tonal aura is a useful metaphor for a coloristic hypertension created in modern technical innovations, such as playing below the bridge of stringed instruments, fluttertongue on the flute, glissando in the French horn, or a particularly unsettling borborygmus in the bass trombone. Arnold Schoenberg's score *Begleitungsmusik zu einer Lichtspielscene*, written for an unrealized abstract motion picture, contains striking instances of musical aura, beginning with the sections marked "Threatening Danger" and "Fear" and culminating in the finale, "Catastrophe."

Tonal Tropism. By computing the frequency of recurrence of each particular note in an atonal work and finding which of the 12 notes of the chromatic scale has a marked preponderance over the others, it may be asserted that such a frequently recurrent note represents a tonal focus, and that other members of an atonal melody have a tonal tropism towards such a putative tonic. Other aspects of tonal tropism are: the approach to the most frequently occurring tone by a semitone from below, suggesting a leading tone; a preferential placement of a note in the bass; an extended duration of a certain tone; its appearance at the end of a musical fascicle; and a simulated cadence or some other kind of privileged position at strategic points, at a strong beat of the measure, etc. In verbal description of a composition containing such features, the term tonal tropism may be used with justification.

Tone Clusters. The technique of tone clusters was demonstrated for the first time in public by Henry Cowell at the San Francisco Music Club on 12 March 1912, on the day after his fifteenth birthday. It consists of striking a pandiatonic complex of two octaves on white keys using one's forearm or a panpentatonic set of black keys, as well as groups of 3 or 4 notes struck with the fists or the elbow. Cowell notated tone clusters by a thick black line on a stem for rapid notes or a white-note rod attached to a stem for half-notes. By a remarkable coincidence, the Russian composer Vladimir Rebikov made use of the same device, with an identical notation, at about the same time, in a piano piece entitled *Hymn to Inca*. Still earlier, Charles Ives made use of tone clusters in his *Concord Sonata*, to be played with a wood plank to depress the keys. Béla Bartók used tone clusters to be played by the palm of the hand in his Second Piano Concerto, a device that he borrowed expressly from Cowell, by permission.

Tonolalia. Glossolalia is a preternaturally inspired manifestation of spontaneous and simultaneous multilingual intercourse. Tonolalia is an analogous verbal neologism, in that different instruments and voices disport themselves in a modernistic quodlibet. Particularly effective are antiphonal uses of tonolalia in which an improvised interlude is echoed by another instrument or a group of instruments.

Tonotripsical Impact. A cephalotripsical blow crushes the skull. A tonotripsical impact is produced by an implosion of sonic matter calculated to stun into submission and psychically incapacitate the listeners to an ultra-modern concert. At a HAPPENING in New York, the complete Sunday edition of the *New York Times* was thrown on the floor of a chamber music hall, and a power lawn mower was wheeled in and proceeded to chew up the newspaper with cephalotripsical effect. A literal example of tonocephalotripsical music is the *Concerto for the Hammer and the Skull*, by a French composer who performed it himself by striking different parts of the bones of his head producing different tones, and opening his mouth as a resonator.

Total Music. In ancient Greece, music was an inalienable part of drama and literature. In medieval universities, it formed a division of the quadrivium, which included also arithmetic, geometry, and astronomy. In modern times, music lost this intimate connection with sciences and liberal arts. It maintained its proud independence until the middle of the 20th century when the AVANT-GARDE brought music out of its isolation and into the condominium of MIXED MEDIA. The slogan of Total Music was launched, and the once exclusive art became at various HAPPENINGS an action to be performed on equal terms with conversation, consumption of food, sexual intercourse, and sleep. Performing musicians willingly surrendered even their physical separation from the audience, and invited the collaboration of the public on the stage. Formal attire that placed musicians on a higher plane was abandoned. Since nudity became admissible in the theater, musicians followed suit. A topless female violoncellist gained notoriety by exposing her upper half to sophisticated music lovers. Total Music, which embraces all aspects of human behavior, is a counterpart of the French "roman total," a fictional form which combines factual reportage with unbridled fantasy.

Translocations. By altering the intervallic structure of a given musical subject and by translocating its tonal constituents, it is possible to bring any melorhythmic figure into topological congruity with any other. The number of such changes, in which the intervallic unit is a semitone and the rhythmic unit is the smallest note value occurring in the subjects, will indicate the degree of affinity existing between such two subjects. In isometric melodies, the index of rhythmic exchangeability will obviously be zero, so that only the index of the necessary intervallic changes measured by the number of semitones need be considered. In isotonal pairs only the rhythmic changes remain to be computed. The smaller the number of alterations required to transform the melorhythmic outline of one subject into that of another, the greater is the intrinsic similarity between the two. A cursive statistical survey indicates that virtually all principal leading motives in Wagner's music dramas are closely related. Thus we find that it requires but a few changes of intervals and rhythms to transmute the motive of erotic love in *Tristan und Isolde* to that of faith in *Parsifal.* The main motives of most tone poems of Richard Strauss are also topologically similar, no matter what the programmatic design is. On the other hand, the index of interchangeability of dodecaphonic tone rows is extremely high, characteristic of the numerical diversity of dodecaphonic themes. This result should not be surprising, for the works of Wagner and Richard Strauss (to take only these two composers as examples) are based on triadic formations with auxiliary chromatic notes, whereas serial music does not depend on tonality and the intervallic structure in the serial idiom is free of all restrictions. A composer, writing in any modern style, whether serial or non-serial, is in a position of selecting any desired table of approximations of main subjects, in relation to intervallic, melodic, metric, and rhythmic parameters, planning in advance such incidental factors as repetition of thematic notes, lipogrammatic omissions, and thus achieving any degree of variety. ALEATORY methods can be limited in advance by numerical parameters, thus imparting to the music an individual physiognomy. Intuition, being an aleatory mental state, may also enter this preliminary outline of substantive parameters. Ernst Krenek has pointed out that the German word *Einfall,* inspiration, connotes in its etymology a falling in as though by chance. The word inspiration itself has ALEATORY connotations, which is drawing in of breath. Once such a tabulation is set up, the composer can proceed to operate the field of desirable translocations, the topology of form, the degree of thematic cohesion or dispersion, etc. Thus the techniques of translocation and its cognate, that of computation of similarities, possess practical validity from both the analytical and synthetical viewpoints. A study of translocations may eventually become an integral branch of musical didactics in perfecting the skill of manipulating and coordinating a multiplicity of technical factors.

Tritone. The medieval theorists described the tritone as "diabolus in musica" and ejected melodic progressions involving the tritone from the body of church music as the work of the devil, encompassing as it did the discordant interval of the augmented fourth unfit for a proper tetrachord. In German schools in Bach's time a music student who inadvertently made use of the augmented fourth was punished in class by a rattan blow on the knuckles of the hand.

The earliest suggestion that the use of the tritone may not be a *peccatum mortale* was made by Ramos de Pareja in *Musica Practica* published in 1482, but his leniency received little approbation. It was in the natural course of events that the stone rejected by the medieval builders should become the cornerstone of modern music, in all its principal aspects, POLYTONALITY, ATONALITY, DODECAPHONY. The importance of the tritone is derived from the very quality that disenfranchised it before, namely its incompatibility with the tonic-dominant complex. Two major triads at the distance of a tritone formed the bitonal "Parisian chord" so popular in the first quarter of the century; complementary hexachords in major keys with tonics distanced by a tritone redound to the formation of a symmetrical 12-tone row; a series of intervals diminishing by a semitone beginning with a major sixth and ending with its inversion, the minor third, forms a bitonal major chord with tonics at a tritone's distance; a chord containing all eleven different intervals is encompassed by five octaves and a tritone from the lowest to the highest note.

Ultra-Modern Music. In the early 1920s it became evident to composers using advanced techniques that the term MODERN MUSIC was no longer sufficiently strong to describe the new trends. In search of further emphasis, they chose the term ultra-modern music, that is, music beyond the limits of traditional modernism. In announcing the publication of *New Music Quarterly* magazine, Henry Cowell, its founder and editor, declared that only works in the ultra-modern idiom would be acceptable for publication. Some decades later, it was realized that ultra-modern music, too, began to show unmistakable signs of obsolescence. Still, certain attributes of ultra-modern music have retained their validity: dissonant counterpoint, atonal melodic designs, polymetric and polyrhythmic combinations, and novel instrumental sonorities.

Unpremeditated Music. Strictly speaking, no piece of music can be composed with an absolute lack of premeditation. Great improvisers of the past always had a proleptic image, in definite sounds, of what they were going to play. However, the composers of ALEATORY MUSIC in the second half of the 20th century have made serious attempts to create music without a shadow of melody aforethought, or harmony prepense. The absence of premeditation in such cases becomes as essential as in capital crime.

Unwasity. Unwasity is an etymological transliteration of the Russian word *nebylitsa,* a fairy tale. This English neoterism may be used as an imaginative figure to describe a modernistic fairy tale, or a palingenetic form so dissimilar from its original that it becomes a literal unwasity, something that never was.

Urbanism. Urbanism is the music of the modern city. It derives its inspiration from urban phenomena, governed by the cult of the machine, and comprising the art of the motion pictures, automobile traffic, and newspapers and magazines. Interurban machines (locomotives, airplanes) also enter the general concept of Urbanism. Among the most durable works of Urbanist music was Honegger's symphonic movement, *Pacific 231,* glorifying the locomotive. Luigi Russolo wrote a suite for noise instruments, subtitled "a demonstration of automobiles and airplanes," in 1913; it was the first work which contains a reference to airplanes in the title. The American composer Emerson Whithorne composed the earliest piece of airplane music for orchestra, entitled *The Aeroplane,* in 1926. Sports (prize fights, football, rugby) also attracted composers by their new Urbanistic romanticism. "Machine" music received its greatest expansion in the 1920s; its typical products were the opera *Jonny Spielt Auf* by Ernst Krenek, *Machinist Hopkins* by Max Brand, and *Lindbergh's Flight* by Kurt Weill. In Russia musical Urbanism coalesced with the development of PROLETARIAN MUSIC, in which the machine was the hero of the production; an example is *The Iron Foundry* by Alexander Mossolov. *Technical Symphony* by the Hungarian composer Eugen Zador and *Poderes de Caballo* by Carlos Chávez are examples of Urbanist symphonic and ballet music, respectively. Prokofiev's ballet *Le Pas d'acier*, representing life in a Soviet factory, is also Urbanist in its subject matter. The ostentatious realism of Urbanist music fell out of fashion after World War II, but as late as 1964 Aaron Copland wrote a symphonic suite, entitled *Music for a Great City*, descriptive of the sounds of New York City.

Vectorialism. The modern preoccupation with mathematical factors in music has resulted in the formation of novel concepts and techniques, among them vectorialism, which specifies the angular value of the vector-radius from the center of the concert hall to musical instruments or electronic transmitters, so that each ingredient of a melodic or harmonic pattern receives its identifying index. Vectorialism of sonic sources is an aspect of SPATIAL DISTRIBUTION.

Verbalization. Karlheinz Stockhausen was the first to introduce the concept of verbalization in lieu of musical notation. One of his pieces represents a parabolic curve with the following inscription: "Sound a note. Continue sounding it as long as you please. It is your prerogative." John Cage elevated verbalization to the degree of eloquent diction. Earle Brown and Morton Feldman are inventive verbalizationists. La Monte Young tells the player: "Push the piano to the wall. Push it through the wall. Keep pushing." Nam June Paik dictates: "Cut your left arm very slowly with a razor (more than 10 centimeters)." Philip Corner limits himself to a simple command: "One anti-personnel type CBU (Cluster Bomb Unit) will be thrown into the audience."

Verismo. The term Verismo became popular in the 1890s when it was used to describe the type of operatic naturalism exemplified by Mascagni's opera *Cavalleria Rusticana* and Leoncavallo's *Pagliacci*. The obvious etymological derivation of Verismo is from *vero*, true, with reference to the realistic quality of the libretto. Soon the vogue spread into France with the production of *Louise*, a "musical romance" by Gustave Charpentier. In Germany Verismo assumed satirical and sociological rather than naturalistic forms; in England, Benjamin Britten's *Peter Grimes* may be described as Veristic in its subject and execution. Verismo had no followers in Russia, where nationalistic themes preoccupied the interests of opera composers.

Vigesimosecular Music. A Latinized form of a common word often imparts precision lacking in its vernacular counterpart. The neologism vigesimosecular compounds the Latin ordinal numeral 20 with the word for century. By the very ponderosity of its SESQUIPEDALIAN MACROPOLYSYLLABIFICATION, the term evokes deep erudition and concentrated anfractuosity of elucubration. It is therefore reserved for advanced theories and practices of 20th-century music.

Wagneromorphism. An obsessive idolatry of Wagner, common among composers around the turn of the century, a mass genuflection and humicubation before the unquestionable genius of Wagner, produced the phenomenon of Wagneromorphism. It is characterized by a total absorption of all familiar traits of Wagner's melody and harmony, particularly chromatic suspensions, triadic fanfares, modulatory sequences, and dynamic explosions followed by protracted recessions. A related term, Wagneromanticism, might also be introduced as a telescoped word to describe a style of composition much in vogue late in the 19th century in which romantic program music is invested in Wagnerian harmonies.

White Sound. By analogy with the complementary colors of the visual spectrum, white sound can be described as a sonic continuum containing all available tones within a certain auditory range, or a complex consisting of prescribed intervals, a pandiatonic or panpentatonic TONE CLUSTER, a dodecaphonic or icositetraphonic cumulus, etc. white sound can be prismatically analyzed into a linear progression forming a scale of discrete tones.

Whole-Tone Scales. The whole-tone scale gained ephemeral popularity early in the 20th century as an exotic resource cultivated by the IMPRESSIONIST school of composers. If major tonality is masculine, and minor is feminine, then the whole-tone scale is of the neuter gender. It lacks modality; the intervallic progression in the whole-tone scale remains the same in melodic rotation. The perfect fifth and the perfect fourth, the cornerstones of tonality, are absent in the whole-tone scale; there is no dominant or subdominant, and no leading tone. Analytically, the whole-tone scale is atonal. It can also be regarded as the linear function of two mutually exclusive augmented triads. The TRITONE, the "diabolus in musica" of the medieval scholiasts, is fundamental to the whole-tone scale, which can be built as the intussusception of three mutually exclusive tritones at the distance of a whole-tone from one another. Because of this association, the whole-tone scale itself became a favorite device of early modernism to portray diabolical forces, menacing apparitions, and ineffable mysteries.

The earliest mention of an intentional employment of the whole-tone scale occurs in Mozart's comical divertimento *Die Dorfmusikanten*, subtitled "a musical joke." But Mozart used the whole-tone scale here not to illustrate a malevolent agency, but to ridicule the incompetence of village musicians and their inability to play in tune. The whole-tone scale came into its own as an ominous symbol in Glinka's opera *Ruslan and Ludmila*, in which it is used as a motto of the magician Chernomor. Rossini made use of the whole-tone scale in a song written in 1864 entitled *L'Amour à Pékin*, in which it was described as "gamme chinoise." The possible reason for this reference is that an ancient Chinese panpipe contains two mutually exclusive whole-tone scales in symmetrically disposed tubes. Liszt was fascinated with the whole-tone scale, and was greatly impressed by the *Fantastic Overture* which the Russian amateur composer Baron Vietinghoff-Scheel sent him, and in which whole-tone scales were profusely employed. In his comment on the work, Liszt described the effect as "terrifying to all long and protruding ears." Liszt himself made use of the whole-tone scale in his symphonic poem *Divina Commedia*, illustrating the Inferno; and he used it systematically in his posthumously published organ pieces.

The problem of harmonizing the whole-tone scale tonally was solved by Glinka in a sequence of modulations. Liszt harmonized a descending whole-tone scale which occurs in the bass, by a series of divergent major triads in root positions. It is doubtful whether Puccini was aware of Liszt's application of this harmony, but he used a precisely identical triadic harmonization of the descending whole-tone scale in his opera *Tosca*, as an introduction to the appearance of the sinister Roman Chief of Police.

The Russian composer Vladimir Rebikov was probably the first to have written an entire composition derived exclusively from the whole-tone scale and its concomitant series of augmented triads, in his *Les Démons s'amusent* for piano; its title suggests that Rebikov was fully aware of the demoniac association of the whole-tone scale. But it was Debussy who elevated the whole-tone scale from a mere exotic device to a poetic and expressive medium. Its Protean capacity for change and adaptability greatly attracted Debussy and his followers, as an alternative variation of a diatonic scale. A very interesting application of the whole-tone scale occurs in *La Mer*, the principal theme of the first movement is in the Aeolian mode; in the third movement it appears isorhythmically as a progression of whole-tones. The first and the last sections of his *Voiles* for piano consist of whole tones with the middle section providing a contrast in the pentatonic scale.

A whole catalogue can be compiled of incidental usages of the whole-tone scale. Even Tchaikovsky, not usually given to modern inventions, made use of the whole-tone scale in a modulatory sequence illustrating the appearance of the ghost of the old Countess in his opera *The Queen of Spades.* Rimsky-Korsakov filled the second act of his opera *Le Coq d'Or* with whole-tone scales and augmented triads to convey the impression of death and devastation of the battlefield. The entrance of Herod in *Salomé* of Richard Strauss is announced by a leading motive composed of whole-tones. Gustav Holst characterized Saturn in his symphonic suite *The Planets* by a series of whole-tone passages to evoke the mystery of Saturn's rings. Apart from astronomy, the whole-tone scale serves pure fantasy. In his symphonic fairy tale *Kikimora,* Liadov paints the mischievous sprite in whole-tones. Paul Dukas introduces the hapless amateur magician in his *L'Apprenti Sorcier* in a series of whole-tones. The English composer Edward Maryon assigns the whole-tone scale to the changelings in his opera *Werewolf,* reserving the diatonic scale for normal children. Another English composer, Havergal Brian, has a chorus singing in whole-tone scales in his opera *The Tigers,* to illustrate the aerial bombardment of London by the Zeppelins during World War I. There are bits of whole-tone figures in Gian Carlo Menotti's children's opera *Help, Help, the Globolinks!* to describe the creatures from outer space. The earthlings in the opera overcome the invading globolinks in victorious C major.

The symbolism of the whole-tone scale is strong in Soviet music. In the opera *Battleship Potemkin* by Oles Tchisko, the Tsarist officers proclaim their authority in whole-tones. In the *Anti-Fascist Symphony* by Boris Mokrousov, the Fascists march in whole-tone steps.

A remarkable demonstration of the perdurability of the whole-tone scale as a symbol of evil is provided by Stravinsky's *Elegy for J. F. K.,* which contains within a 12-tone row two intervallically congruous groups of whole tones, each embanked in a tritone, itself a symbol of deviltry.

With the gradual decline of pictorial and sensorial programmaticism in contemporary music, the whole-tone scale sank into innocuous desuetude. It found its temporary outlet and a stylistic rehabilitation in dodecaphonic usages in the form of two mutually exclusive hexachords. Eventually it joined the subculture of film music. Nazis advance on the screen to the sound of whole-tone scales in the trombones. Mad scientists hatch their murderous schemes to blow up the world in mighty progressions of whole-tones. Mentally disturbed maidens pluck whole-tone scales on the harp. When Jean Harlow, in her screen biography, climbs up the ladder in the studio before her final collapse, she is accompanied by delicate whole-tone pizzicatti. The whole-tone scale is also used, wittily so, in satirical comment on pompous personages in animated cartoons.

Zen. The philosophy of Zen is at once an infinitely complex and fantastically simple doctrine that accepts irrelevance of response as a legitimate and even elevating part of human discourse. This paradoxical liberating trait exercised a compelling attraction for composers of the AVANT-GARDE, most notably the American composer John Cage, eager to achieve a total freedom of self-expression combined with the precision of indeterminacy. The verbal and psychological techniques of Zen can be translated into music through a variety of means which may range from white noise of (theoretically) infinite duration to (theoretically) instantaneous silences. In the case of Cage, the translation was in an adaptation of certain practices of Zen (meditation, sitting cross-legged, study of the koans, etc.) to the compositional practices of music, and especially through his adaptation of the ancient Chinese book of coin oracles, the *I Ching,* to a chance methodology. In the field of MIXED MEDIA, in particular, Zen provides a rich vocabulary of gestures, facial expressions, inarticulate verbalization, ambulatory exercises, performance of physiological functions, etc. In the composition of instrumental music, Zen expands perception of the minutest quantities of sonic material and imparts eloquence to moments of total impassivity, in which the audible tones become interlopers between areas of inaudibility. Imagination and fantasy in the mind of a practitioner of Zen may subjectively become more expressive than the realization of the creative impulse in written musical symbols.